A COPTIC
DICTIONARY

A COPTIC DICTIONARY

COMPILED

WITH THE HELP OF MANY SCHOLARS

BY

W. E. CRUM

M.A., F.B.A., Hon. D. Litt., Hon. Ph.D., Berlin

OXFORD

AT THE CLARENDON PRESS

OXFORD

UNIVERSITY PRESS

Great Clarendon Street, Oxford OX2 6DP

Oxford University Press is a department of the University of Oxford.
It furthers the University's objective of excellence in research, scholarship,
and education by publishing worldwide in

Oxford New York

Athens Auckland Bangkok Bogotá Buenos Aires Calcutta
Cape Town Chennai Dar es Salaam Delhi Florence Hong Kong Istanbul
Karachi Kuala Lumpur Madrid Melbourne Mexico City Mumbai
Nairobi Paris São Paulo Singapore Taipei Tokyo Toronto Warsaw

with associated companies in Berlin Ibadan

Oxford is a registered trade mark of Oxford University Press
in the UK and in certain other countries

Published in the United States
by Oxford University Press Inc., New York

© Oxford University Press 1939

British Library Cataloguing in Publication Data

Data available

ISBN 0-19-864404-3

1 3 5 7 9 10 8 6 4 2

Printed in Great Britain
on acid-free paper by
Bookcraft Ltd, Midsomer Norton, Somerset

PREFACE

PREPARATIONS for systematic work with a view to a Coptic dictionary were begun by me some thirty years ago, but intervening undertakings delayed effective progress for some time. Meanwhile it was ascertained that the Clarendon Press would be not unwilling to consider, when the time came, a project of publication. But early in 1914 a definite proposal to publish, at their expense and with provision of funds for collaboration, photography &c., came from the Berlin Academy. This generous offer I owed to Professor Erman, who saw the need of a Coptic dictionary on a scale worthy of that of the hieroglyphic *Wörterbuch* and who issued a statement on the subject.[1] A scheme was drawn up and work begun[2] and if the outbreak of war had not put an end to all hopes of carrying through such projects, the book would have been completed long ere now. Yet it was found possible to retain the help of German collaborators, as well as of those in the allied countries, and a few years after the end of the war a collection of material had been amassed large enough to justify a renewal of negotiations with the Clarendon Press. These resulted in the arrangement whereby the dictionary is now published.

In 1921 the late Professor Spiegelberg produced his *Handwörterbuch*, which he modestly described as a revision of Peyron's *Lexicon* (1835), but which in reality is far more than that. Its most conspicuous novelty was the addition, in all cases where in the author's opinion justifiable, of the hieroglyphic or demotic etymology of the Coptic form. The absence of this important element from the present work some students may regret; it was only after much hesitation that I decided to omit it. I cannot claim an independent judgement as to the appositeness of a demotic etymology, while to reproduce these in hieroglyphic type—for a mere transcription satisfies no one—would greatly have increased costs and yet have added nothing of adequate importance to what Spiegelberg has already given us.[3]

What is here offered represents an entirely new and independent working over of the total available material. Our word-collecting has all been done directly, from the texts; all those in print have of course been utilized—often after collation with the originals; so too all unpublished manuscripts, ostraca and inscriptions, to which access could be obtained. The quantity of material used amounts, at a rough estimate, to some 240,000 slips.[4] It is hoped that these resources give a sufficient basis for a comprehensive view of the language, in all its dialects and in all aspects of its literature: biblical, patristic and mundane. The total of recorded independent words—ignoring the countless derived forms—is 3,308, whereof some 390 are still of unknown meaning. These are mostly ἅπαξ λεγόμενα and some are no doubt misread.

If I name here only the principal sources which have become available within recent decades, some notion will be possible of the extent to which materials have increased.

To begin with the largest and, in some ways, the most important of extant collections, there are the fifty-six volumes from the Fayyûm, bought in 1911 by Mr. Pierpont Morgan,

---

[1] In the *Sitzungsberichte* 1915, 127. I may perhaps add that, had I not accepted this proposal, the Academy was to have set about producing a Coptic dictionary of its own.

[2] The committee responsible to the Academy consisted of Professors Erman, Harnack, Ed. Meyer and Wilh. Schulze.

[3] Much etymological work was done by the late Professor Dévaud, but only some of it had been published in his *Études d'Étymologie Copte*, 1922 and in *Recueil* 39, when his untimely death occurred in 1929.

[4] The total of slips made far exceeded this, but much was discarded as superfluous.

a body of texts unparalleled for completeness, if not for variety.[1]   Next in size comes the
Paris collection: some twenty-five volumes of fragments, the greater part of which has not
yet attained to print.   Then there is a considerable number of leaves in the Borgian collection, which Zoega's Catalogue merely mentions, the Curzon manuscripts (now the property
of the British Museum), an interesting series in the Berlin Library and an important and
varied collection acquired for the University of Michigan.

So far I have named mostly Saʿîdic MSS., emanating in great part from the library of
Shenoute's monastery.   Turning now to Bohairic, there is the imposing series, brought long
since from Nitria to the Vatican, considerable parts of which are not yet in print—conspicuously the volume of Chrysostom, with its thirty-seven complete homilies—and there is
besides a large number of important texts, chiefly liturgical, scattered among all the libraries:
service books, hymn books and especially lectionaries, whence interesting variants of the
received biblical texts may be gathered.   The lectionaries were exploited by La Croze and,
thanks to Dr. Burmester, we shall before long have certain of them available.   Last, but by
no means least, among our Bohairic resources come the vocabularies.   The fourteenth-century
Scala of Abû 'l-Barakât (transcribed and interpreted by Kircher, but cited here from his MS.
and a collation of eleven others) of course surpasses the rest in importance; yet there is
plenty worth recording in the lesser glossaries also: many an Arabic translation or Greek
equivalent, to throw light upon rare or doubtful words.   It is true that these glossaries are
the product of a late age, owing their existence to the disuse that had by then fallen upon
the ancient language; but I have thought it better, here as elsewhere, to include too much,
rather than too little, and to record everything from these medieval sources that could be
claimed as ultimately Coptic.

As regards the lesser dialects, reference must first be made to the great increase in material
resulting from the discovery and gradual publication of the Manichaean papyri, acquired by
Mr. Chester Beatty and the Berlin Museum.   These we have been able to use, thanks to the
permission of their owners and to copies of the unpublished portions kindly sent by
Dr. Polotsky and Mr. Allberry.   But this advantage has been ours only since reaching the
letter ⲡ [2] and so many would have been the insertions in the *Additions*, had we attempted to
record all new words and forms under the previous letters, that it seemed preferable to ignore
them almost entirely and to refer students to the indexes of the eventual publications.   The
at present confused idioms included under the term Middle Egyptian, or, as in this book,
Fayyûmic, may later cn require special vocabularies, but most of its strange phenomena, so
far as yet observed, have found a place here.[3]

Finally there is a large body of non-literary texts, which to the earlier lexicographer were
entirely unknown.   In Peyron's day not a single Coptic 'document' was available; nothing
of the kind was heard of until the first batch of the Jême papyri began to attract the attention
of C. W. Goodwin, E. Revillout and M. Kabis, in the 'sixties and 'seventies of last century.
To-day conditions are far different; a great deal of material of this class is now in print:
ecclesiastical and monastic documents, legal deeds, correspondence—official, commercial and
purely private—tax receipts, accounts, lists; besides epigraphic texts: epitaphs, dedicatory
inscriptions and the like.   Further, magical texts of various kinds: prayers, incantations,
curses, charms, whence many a strange, forgotten word may be unearthed.   In some of these

---

[1] *V* Hyvernat's *Check List of Coptic MSS. in the
Pierpont Morgan Library*, New York, 1919.
[2] First citation on p. 267 *b*.
[3] By the kindness of the late Professor Carl
Schmidt and Fr. A. Kropp we have had the use
of the latter's copy of the ancient Fayyûmic text

of Eccl., Cant. and Lam. (*Cf.* W. Schubart &
C. Schmidt, Πράξεις Παύλου, 1936, p. 5 ff.).   Quotations hence have sometimes been distinguished
as 'Schmidt'; the papyrus has since become the
property of the Hamburg Staatsbibliothek.

groups there is still plenty of material awaiting publication; nevertheless I think it may be claimed that but little—so far as it has been acquired for public or private collections—has remained unutilized.

Something must be said as to the method followed in recording and illustrating words.

From considerations of space and cost everything is abbreviated down to the limits, it is hoped, of intelligibility. For the context of words illustrated an English summary has often appeared sufficient. The punctuation and spacing are meant to be taken seriously, the use of the semicolon in particular being intended to separate groups in meaning or usage. All references are to the most recent editions of published texts, even where (as in Amélineau's *Schenoudi*) the later does not positively improve upon the older print.[1] Bible verses are given *in the numeration of the published Coptic editions*, without regard either to that of the LXX or of the English version. Manuscripts are cited, where possible, by their Coptic pagination; but this rule has been occasionally transgressed, notably in the Vatican series, where the modern foliation is followed. Quotations are printed as they appear in the MSS., their orthography uncorrected, except where ambiguity demanded emendation. Irregular variants in word-form are enumerated at the outset of each paragraph; at first those most rarely occurring were occasionally omitted, later on all were recorded. In the following subdivisions the Sa'ĭdic form often does duty for the rest. The gender of a noun is not stated except where positive evidence (by article, pronoun or the like) is to be had from the text.

As the long work progressed its quality has, I hope, improved; but if it were to be done again, not a few alterations in method would be desirable. Where a word is rare, it would be made clear that the instances given are exhaustive.[2] There would be some indication of the *relative* amounts of material drawn upon for each dialect; our paragraphs are apt to be misleading as to that: *B* is for the most part less fully represented than *S*, owing to the far greater variety of sources available in the latter. Less ambiguous and contradictory indications of dialect ought to have been achieved; *Sᶠ* has often been attached to a form found in a text otherwise purely Sa'ĭdic, while *Sᵃ* is used to include, besides forms especially Theban, those of more northern and less certain origin. Again, *A²* has not been always confined to MSS. in that dialect for which the name 'Siutic' has been proposed.[3] *F* of course embraces several varieties of idiom: that of the Fayyûm and those adjoining it in the river valley, wherein divergence from Sa'ĭdic is often slight; indeed I fear that in not a few cases (conspicuously where hybrid texts such as Mor 30 are drawn upon) examples from one and the same MS. may be found assigned to *S*, *Sᶠ* and *F*.[4] The addition of the dialectal equivalent, in literary texts as well as biblical, is perhaps less valuable than at first appeared; divergence in detail between the bible versions—far more frequent than has usually been admitted— and still wider differences between the versions, even within a single dialect, of other texts, tend to lessen the significance of apparent equivalents. The decision to maintain the terms 'transitive' and 'intransitive' would perhaps not commend itself; they are used to distinguish between the direct relation of verb and object ('accusative', ⲛ-) and the indirect (ⲉ- and other prepositions), besides cases of the objectless verb.

Illustration must obviously be limited by our collections. A word or form may thus appear to be absent in one or other of the dialects which future additions to material will supply; another may recur later on, whereof at present only a single instance has been recorded.

---

[1] Change in ownership of a MS., or subsequent publication, has unfortunately resulted in some texts being quoted under two designations.

[2] The word 'rare', after a group of dialect letters, must be taken as relating only to the last of these.

[3] By Fr. Chaîne in *Les Dialectes Coptes Assioutiques A²*, 1934.

[4] The classification in my British Museum Catalogue is often unsatisfactory: many MSS. in the *Middle Egyptian* section are in reality Sa'ĭdic, a few purely Bohairic.

No chronological arrangement of the illustrative quotations would have been feasible; the very nature of Coptic literature and the conservative traditions of its copyists make it impossible to arrive at more than approximate estimates of the relative ages of the literary texts—or rather, manuscripts. All that seemed practicable was to begin illustration with biblical, *i.e.* presumably the earliest, examples and those whereof the Greek originals and dialectal parallels give the best guarantees of meaning, and to follow these by quotations from the old Gnostic books—the *Pistis*, the Bruce Papyrus and the Berlin Gnostic text[1]—and next from the one conspicuous native writer whom the literature can boast: Shenoute[2] (322–451). Published biblical quotations in the Sa'îdic dialect can generally be traced in A. Vaschalde's indispensable lists (*Revue Biblique* 1919–22). To what age the mass of liturgical and patristic writings, be they of Egyptian origin or translations from the Greek, belong—whether mainly post-Chalcedonian and but rarely earlier—it would be difficult to determine. Non-literary documents are, in the majority, to be assigned to the seventh and eighth centuries. Wherever traceable the Greek original or equivalent—for the correspondence between them is often of the vaguest—has been added to patristic instances, but space forbade giving the references for these; the reader is asked to credit us with having in no case assumed a merely suppositional correspondent. In the biblical examples of common words I do not pretend to record exhaustively the Greek equivalents: those which occur but once or twice may be found to be absent.

The book being a dictionary of the Coptic language, the countless Greek words, scattered through every class of text, cannot claim inclusion. A very few are given hospitality which seem, by formal modification or distortion, to have attained to naturalization.

All the articles were written by me and mine of course is the sole responsibility for them.

The list of *Additions and Corrections* has grown to a portentous length; the quantity of the latter, seeing that at least four pairs of eyes had combined to avoid them, is humiliating. I can but hope that the list will not go unregarded by users of the book.

I have to express my gratitude to many friends for contributing in many ways towards the progress of the book. Before the organization of the Berlin project, referred to above, I had not contemplated extensive collaboration; but from that date I set about enlisting the services of collaborators and was thus able greatly to add to the body of slip-material which had already accumulated. The entire Sa'îdic and Fayyûmic and almost all the Achmîmic material was produced by myself and two friends. To one of these, Sir Herbert Thompson, I am indebted for far more than the mere making of slips: for he accepted the burden of reading the entire manuscript and has given opinions on many demotic matters, besides undertaking the long labour of the Greek index. His never-failing help and criticism have been of inestimable value, pointing the way to many improvements and saving me from countless inaccuracies.

To the other I owe a debt for collaboration of every kind, through many years—help so extensive, so fundamental and so effective, that I should be quite unable rightly to express here how much I owe to it. But for it the work would not have been carried through.

Of the Bohairic material a large part was gathered by the following scholars: Dr. H. Demel, Prof. De Vis, Prof. Drioton, Prof. A. Grohmann, the Abbé Porcher, Dr. H. Wiesmann; while

---

[1] Described by Carl Schmidt in 1896 (Berlin *Sitzungsb.*), but still unpublished.

[2] I have included here, perhaps unjustifiably, the writings of his successor Besa. The recognition of Shenoute's work often depends solely upon the writer's style—a none too reliable guide.

I have throughout attributed the well-known text C 73 129-153 to him (as did Amélineau, but not Zoega). I feel tolerably sure that it ought not to have been so ascribed; other parts of this MS. (especially P 130[3] 59 ff) are clearly not by him. *Cf.* Leipoldt's discussion, *Schenute*, p. 11.

less extensive contributions were made by the Rev. D. P. Buckle, Sir Stephen Gaselee and Mr. E. S. S. Harding.

To Professor Hyvernat my especial thanks are due, for he entrusted me with photographs of the greater part of the Borgian collection[1] and moreover lent his own photographic copies of many of the Pierpont Morgan manuscripts, while from the Cambridge University Library I had the inestimable loan of other volumes of that series. I owe a like debt to Prof. Lefort, from whom I have constantly borrowed photographs from the all-embracing collection at Louvain. The University of Michigan (thanks in the first instance to the mediation of the late Professor F. W. Kelsey) generously provided me with photographs of the entire Coptic collection.[2] Columbia University did me a similar kindness at the suggestion of Prof. A. A. Schiller. For photographs of certain Vatican MSS. I have to thank Fr. Chaîne, others I was enabled to procure through the liberality of the Griffith Egyptological Fund at Oxford and the Hort Fund at Cambridge, while acquaintance with the Vatican collection was completed by the loan of Professor De Vis's copies. I have been further indebted to the Hort Fund, as also to the British Academy, for generous financial contributions. Copies of Berlin ostraca and of Vienna manuscripts were put at my disposal by the late Prof. Erman and Prof. Till respectively, those of manuscripts in Russia by the late O. von Lemm and Prof. P. Jernstedt. To Prof. Erman I owe photographs of the already mentioned Berlin Gnostic papyrus. A find of Theban ostraca was, with M. Lacau's leave, sent to me in Bath by Mr. Winlock, while of ostraca from the Chicago excavations I had the benefit of Prof. Till's copies. I have had the use of M. de Ricci's MSS. and copies, of those of certain Cairo (Jkôw) papyri by M. Lacau, some of those at Columbia University by Prof. Schiller and of M. Munier's copy of an important Shenoute codex in the French Institute, Cairo. After Prof. Dévaud's death I was given his invaluable collection of etymological slips. The late Prof. A. A. Bevan, Mr. R. Guest and Dr. G. Sobhy have answered many enquiries respecting obscure Arabic equivalents of Coptic words; the late Dr. J. K. Fotheringham gave me help on astronomical questions, the late Mr. R. McKenzie on many Greek points, while Sir D'Arcy Thompson has done the like where natural history was involved. For an Arabic cross-index to Kircher's *Scala* I have to thank Dr. O'Leary's kindness.

Sir Herbert Thompson's Greek index silently rectifies many inaccuracies to be met with in the book. For the English index I have to thank Mr. Charles Hart-Davis, by whom it was almost entirely compiled. For the Arabic index I am responsible.

From many others too I have had help, either in verifying readings or sending copies of distant MSS. or in giving information on special points. I name those not already referred to: Messrs. Böhlig, Ludlow Bull, Burmester, Chassinat, Černý, Delaporte, Drioton, Farina, W. H. P. Hatch, Hebbelynck, Hengstenberg, Holmyard, Keimer, Kuentz, Lantschoot, Meyerhof, A. Möhle, Munier, Carl Schmidt, Schubart, Simaika, Steindorff, Tisserant, Winstedt, Worrell, Yassa Abd el-Masih, Mrs. Charlotte Baynes, Dr. Dora Zunz. To all these and to others, if inadvertently passed over, I offer my hearty thanks. And I must express them also to the University Press: to the Delegates for sharing in the expense of publishing and to the compositors and readers for the admirable production of a complicated piece of printing.

W. E. C.

February, 1939.

---

[1] Those of the Shenoute MSS. were unfortunately not available.

[2] The vellum leaves Mich 550 were subsequently numbered Mich 158, an alteration which I overlooked. The Librarian has, however, kindly arranged to leave the number 550 unused.

LIST OF ABBREVIATIONS

A (with Sh prefixed) = E. Amélineau, *Œuvres de Schenoudi*, 1907 ff.
A = Achmîmic dialect; *A²* = Subachmîmic dialect.
Absal = *Kitâb al-Abṣâlmudîyah al-Muḳaddasah al-Sanawîyah* (*Theotokia*), Alexandria, 1908.
Abst = *Kitâb al-Abṣâliyât wal-Ṭaruḥât*, Old Cairo, 1913.
Ac = Acts of the Apostles.
acc = accusative.
adj = adjective.
Aeg = Lagarde, *Aegyptiaca*, 1883.
Aegyptus = (periodical), Milan, acc. to vols.
AIssa = Ahmed Issa, *Dict. des Noms des Plantes*, Cairo, 1930.
AJSL = *American Journ. of Semit. Languages*.
Alex = MSS. &c. in Graeco-Roman Museum, Alexandria.
Almk 1 = H. Almkvist, *Kleine Beitr. z. Lexikographie d. vulg. Arabischen*, 8th Or. Congr., 1891.
Almk 2 = continuation of above, ed. K. V. Zetterstéen, in *Le Monde Oriental*, 1925.
ALR = Accademia dei Lincei, *Rendiconti*.
Am = Amos.
AM = H. Hyvernat, *Actes des Martyrs*, 1886.
Ann = *Annales du Service des Antiquités*, Cairo.
Ap = Apocalypse.
AP = *Acta Pauli*, ed. C. Schmidt, 1904, acc. to *asterisked* pp. of book.
Ar, ar = Arabic.
art = article.
Asmus = H. Asmus, *Über Fragmente im mitteläg. Dialekt* (Dissert.), 1904, acc. to pp.
AZ = *Zeitschr. f. Aegyptische Sprache*, acc. to vols.

B = Bohairic dialect.
Bal = papyri from Balaizah, in Bodleian, in so far as not numbered in series "Bodl. Copt. (P)".
Balestri = *Sacr. Bibl. Fragm.* III, ed. I. Balestri, 1904.
Baouit = *Le Monastère de B.*, ed. J. Clédat, I & II (= MIF. xii), 1904 ff.
BAp = Budge, *Coptic Apocrypha*, 1913.
Bar = Baruch.
Berl.Or = MSS. in the Staats(*olim* Kgl.)bibliothek, Berlin (Crum's copies).
Berl. *Wörterb* = Erman & Grapow, *Wörterbuch d. Aeg. Sprache*, 1926-31.
Besa *v* Sh (Shenoute).
Bess = *Bessarione* (periodical), acc. to vols.
BG = Berlin Gnostic Papyrus 8502 (*cf.* Preuss. Akad., *Sitz.* xxxvi, 839), from photographs.
BHom = Budge, *Coptic Homilies*, 1910.
BIF = *Bulletin de l'Instit. français ... au Caire*.
BKU = Berliner *Kopt. Urkunden*, acc. to vol., no. and, in long texts, lines.
Blake = Epiphanius, *De XII Gemmis*, ed. R. P. Blake, Coptic fragts. by H. De Vis, 1934 (in Lake's *Studies & Documents*).
BM = British Museum, *Catalogue of Coptic MSS.*, 1905, acc. to numbers.
BMar = Budge, *Coptic Martyrdoms*, 1914.
BMEA = British Museum, Dept. of Egyptian & Assyr. Antiquities (papyri, ostraca, inscriptions).
BMis = Budge, *Miscellaneous Coptic Texts*, 1915.
Bodl = Coptic MSS. in Bodleian, as (P) a 1 *e*, where italic = folio.
Bor = Codex Borgianus (where not printed by Zoega).
BP = Papyri & ostraca in Staatsmuseum, Berlin.
Br = *Gnostische Schr. in Kopt. Sprache* (Pap. Bruce), ed. C. Schmidt, 1892.
BSG = Budge, *Martyrdom & Miracles of St. George*, 1888.
BSM = Budge, *St. Michael the Archangel*, 1894.

C = *Corpus Scriptorum Christian. Oriental.*, acc. to the "numéros d'ordre":
  T. 41 *Sinuthii Vita*, ed. J. Leipoldt, 1906.
    42, 73 *Sinuthii Opera*, do., 1908, 1913.
    43, 86 *Acta Martyrum*, edd. I. Balestri & H. Hyvernat, 1907, 1924.
    89, 99, 100 *S. Pachomii Vitae*, ed. L. Th. Lefort, 1925, 1933.
c = constructed with (of verbs).
CA = *Canons of Athanasius* ed. Riedel & Crum (Text & Transl. Soc.), 1904.
Cai = MSS. &c. in the Egyptian Museum, Cairo.
(Cai)CoptMus = MSS. &c. in Coptic Museum, Cairo.
CaiEuch = *Kitâb al-Khulâgy al-Muḳaddas* (*Euchologion*), Cairo, 1902.
CaiThe = (Theotokia) *v* Absal.
Cant = Song of Songs.
Cat = *Catenae in Evangelia*, ed. Lagarde, 1886.
caus = causative verb.
CCVaI = *Codices Coptici Vaticani* &c., T.I, edd. Hebbelynck & Lantschoot, Rome, 1937.
CDan = L. Clugnet, *Vie de l'Abbé Daniel*, wherein Guidi's Coptic text, acc. to pp. of this work.
Chaîne = M. Chaîne, *Eléments de gram. dialectale copte*, 1933.
Chr. = Chronicles.
cit = cited, quoted in following place.
Cl = C. Schmidt, *Der I. Clemensbrief*. 1908
— = F. Rösch, *Bruchstücke des I. Clem.* 1910 } acc. to chh. of Greek text.
ClPr = Woide's MSS. belonging to the Clarendon Press (Crum's copies & photographs).
CMSS = Crum, *Coptic MSS. from Fayyûm*, 1893, acc. to pp.
CO = Crum, *Coptic Ostraca*, 1902.
Col = Epistle to Colossians.
Cor = Epistles to Corinthians.
CR = *Comptes Rendus de l'Acad. des Inscr.*, Paris, acc. to year & page.

Dan = Daniel.
dem = demotic.
Deu = Deuteronomy.
DeV = H. De Vis, *Homélies Coptes* (= *Coptica* I, V), 1922, 1929 (DeV alone = vol. i).
Dif = *The Difnar*, ed. O'Leary, I, II, III, 1926-30.
diff = different reading, not useful for comparison.
DM = *Demotic Magical Papyrus*, ed. Griffith & Thompson, 1904 ff.
do = ditto, same as last word cited in this dialect.
Dozy = R. Dozy, *Supplém. aux dict. arabes*, 1881.

Eccl = Ecclesiastes.
EES = Egypt Exploration Soc. (*olim* Fund), MSS. &c. in their possession (Crum's copies).
El = *Die Apokalypse d. Elias*, ed. G. Steindorff, 1899.
EnPeterson = phot. of vellum leaves lent by Enoch P. (Univ. of Michigan). Originals not now traceable.
Ep = *Monastery of Epiphanius*, ed. Winlock, Crum & Evelyn White, 1926, acc. to numbers.
Eph = Epistle to Ephesians.
EpJer = Epistle of Jeremiah.
esp = especially.
Est = Esther.
EtLeem = *Études ... dédiées à C. Leemans*, 1885.
EW = *New Texts from the Monastery of St. Macarius*, ed. H. G. Evelyn White, 1926.
— = do., his copies of MSS from Nitria (in Coptic Museum, Cairo).

Ex = Exodus.
Ez = Ezekiel.

f = feminine.
F = Fayyûmic & related dialects; *F^b* do. with Bohairic tendency.
Faras = Griffith, *Oxford Excavations in Nubia*, in Liverpool *Annals of Archaeol. & Anthropol.* (1) xiii 17, (2) *ib.* 49, (3) xiv 57.
FR = Forbes Robinson, *Coptic Apocr. Gospels* (= *Texts & Studies* iv), 1896.

Gal = Epistle to Galatians.
Ge = Genesis.
gen = genitive.
GFr = Georgi, *Fragm. Evang. S. Iohannis*, 1789.
Gk = Greek.
Glos = Greek-Coptic Glossary, ed. Bell & Crum, in *Aegyptus* vi 179, acc. to lines.
GMir = Georgi, *Miracula S. Coluthi*, 1793.
GöttA = Göttinger *Abhandlungen*; GöttN = do. *Nachrichten*.
GPar = S. Gaselee. *Parerga Coptica*, 1912, 1914.
GriffStu = *Studies Presented to F. Ll. Griffith*, 1932.
Gu = I. Guidi, *Frammenti Copti* I–VII (from ALR 1887 ff.), acc. to continuous pagination.
GuDorm = I. Guidi, *Teste . . . sopra i Sette Dormienti* (Mem. Acad. Linc., 1884).

H = G. Horner's text of N.T., 1898–1924.
Hab = Habakkuk.
Hag = Haggai.
Hall = H. R. Hall, *Coptic & Greek Texts . . . Brit. Museum*, 1905, acc. to pp.
HCons = G. Horner, *Consecration of Church & Altar*, 1902.
He = Epistle to Hebrews.
HengB = W. Hengstenberg in *Beiträge z. Forschung . . .* Heft III, J. Rosenthal, München, 1914.
HL = E. Amélineau, *De Historia Lausiaca*, 1887; but *Hist Laus* = E. C. Butler's edition of Greek text (= *Texts & Studies* vi).
Hor = Griffith, *The Old Coptic Horoscope*, in AZ 38 76 ff., acc. to pp. of publication.
Hos = Hosea.
HSt = G. Horner, *Statutes of the Apostles*, 1904; *v* also Stat.
HT = Sir Herbert Thompson's Sa'idic MSS. (now in Cambridge Univ. Library), acc. to letters (*B–Z*) which distinguish them; or other references to him.

IF = Institut français, Cairo, MS. of Shenoute's Epistles (H. Munier's copy).
IgR = Ignazio Rossi, *Etymologiae Aegyptiacae*, 1808.
ImpRussArS = Imperial Russian Archaeolog. Soc. xviii, 1907 (Turaief).
inf = *infra*.
interj = interjection.
interrog = interrogative.
intr = intransitive (*i.e.* verb without immediate object, or one constructed with prep. e-).
Is = Isaiah.

J = Crum & Steindorff, *Kopt. Rechtsurkunden . . . aus Djême*, acc. to no. & line; JLeip = two such papyri in Leipzig University, Aegyptologisches Institut (*cf* below).
Ja = Epistle of James.
JA = *Journal Asiatique*, acc. to year, vol. & page.
J&C = H. I. Bell, *Jews & Christians*, 1924, acc. to pp.
JAOS = *Journ. of American Orient. Soc.*
Jer = Jeremiah.
Jern = P. Jernstedt, *Kopt. Papyri d. Asiat. Mus.* (Soc. Egyptol. Univ. Leningrad, no. 6, 1930), acc. to numbers.
JKP = H. Junker, *Koptische Poesie*, 1908, 1911 (from *Oriens Christianus*.)
Jo = John.
Jon = Jonah.
Jos = Joshua.

JSch = A. A. Schiller, *Ten Coptic Legal Texts*, New York, 1932 (includes JLeip, *v* above), acc. to numbers & lines.
Jth = Judith.
JTS = *Journal of Theological Studies*.
Jud = Judges.

K = A. Kircher, the *Scalæ* in *Lingua Aegyptiaca Restituta*, variants from Loret in *Ann.* I and other MSS.
Kam = *Kambysesroman* in BKU I, no. 31, acc. to pp. in lower margins & line.
Kandil = ⲡϫⲱⲙ ⲛⲧⲉ ⲡⲓⲱϩⲥ ⲉⲥⲑ (*Kitâb al-Mashah, ay al-Ḳandîl*), ed. C. Labîb, Cairo, AM. 1625, *v* TRit 144 ff.
Kg = 1, 2 Samuel, & 1, 2 Kings.
KKS = O. von Lemm, *Kleine Kopt. Studien*, acc. to continuous pagination.
Kr = J. Krall, *Kopt. Texte* (Rainer *Corpus* II), acc. to numbers.
Kropp = A. Kropp, *Ausgewählte Kopt. Zaubertexte*, 1930–31, numbered by letters A, B &c.

l = *legendum*.
Lab = C. Labîb, Coptic-Arabic Dictionary (ⲡⲓⲗⲉϩⲓⲕⲟⲛ ⲛⲧⲁⲥⲡⲓ ⲛⲧⲉ ⲡⲓⲣⲉⲙⲛⲭⲏⲙⲓ *Kâmûs al-Luġah al-Ḳibṭîyah al-Maṣrîyah*), Cairo, AM. 1611 ff.
Lacau = fragments of Jo & Ap *F*, copied by P. Lacau (*v Bull. Corr. Hellén.* xxv 400).
Lacr = M. V. La Croze, *Lexicon Aegyptiaco-Latinum*, 1775.
Lag = P. de Lagarde, his editions of Coptic texts.
Lakân = *Kitâb al-Lakân*, Cairo, 1921.
LAl = Lemm, *Der Alexanderroman*.
Lam = Lamentations.
Lammayer = *Die sogen. Gnomen d. Concils v. Nicaea* (Dissert.), Beirut, 1912.
Lant. = A. van Lantschoot, *Recueil de Colophons . . . sahidiques*, 1929, acc. to numbers; also copies by.
LAp = Lemm, *Apokryphe Apostelacten*.
LBib = Lemm, *Sahidische Bibelfragmente* I, II, III.
LCypr = Lemm. *Cyprian v. Antiochien*.
LDi = Lemm, *Eine dem Dionysios Areopag. zugeschr. Schrift*.
Lect = Lectionary.
Leip = Leipzig University, Tischendorf's Bohairic MSS. (Crum's copies).
LeipBer = *Berichte* d. phil.-histor. Klasse d. kgl. säch. Gesellsch. d. Wissensch.
Lev = Leviticus.
Leyd = *Manuscrits coptes du Musée . . . à Leide*, 1897, acc. to pages.
LeydAC = *Antiquités Coptes* (Catal. du Musée), 1900, acc. to pp.
LIb = Lemm, *Iberica*.
lit = literally.
LMär = Lemm, *Bruchstücke Kopt. Märtyrerakten*.
LMis = Lemm, *Koptische Miscellen*, acc. to continuous pagination.
Löw = Im. Löw, *Aramäische Pflanzennamen*, 1881, acc. to pp.
LöwF = *Flora der Juden*, 1926 ff.
Lu = Luke.

m = masculine.
Mac = Maccabees.
Mal = Malachi.
Mallon = A. Mallon, *Grammaire copte*², 1907.
Mani 1 = copies of Chester Beatty's unpublished Manichaean papyri by H. J. Polotsky & H. Thompson.
Mani 2 = copies of sim. papyri at Berlin by Polotsky.
ManiH = *Manichäische Homelien*, ed. Polotsky, 1934.
ManiK = *Kephalaia*, edd. Polotsky & A. Böhlig, 1934 ff.
ManiP = *A Manichaean Psalm-book*, Pt. ii, ed. C. R. C. Allberry, 1938.
MartIgn = Lightfoot, *Ignatius*¹, ii 1 865 ff.
MélOr = *Mélanges de la Faculté Orientale*, Université de Beyrouth.
MG = *Annales du Musée Guimet*, Paris.
Mic = Micah.

Mich 550, a series of vellum leaves at Michigan University, independently numbered thus (but *cf* note in Preface).

MIE = *Mémoires de l'Instit. Égyptien*, Cairo.

MIF = *Mémoires . . . de l'Instit. franç. d'Archéol. orient. au Caire.*

Ming = J. A. Mingarelli, *Aegyptiorum Codd. Reliquiae*, 1785.

Miss = *Mémoires . . . de la Mission archéol. franç. au Caire.*

Mk = Mark.

MMA = MSS. & ostraca in the Metropolitan Museum of Art, New York.

Montp = Bohairic *Scala* in library of Faculté de Médecine, Montpellier (H. Munier's copy).

Mor = MSS. belonging to Mr. J. Pierpont Morgan, New York, as reproduced & numbered in 56 vols. of photographs, acc. to nos. & pp. of these volumes (not identical with those of *Check List*, 1919).

MR = *Mittheilungen a. d. Papyrussamml. Erzh. Rainer.*

Mt = Matthew.

Mun = *Manuscrits coptes*, par H. Munier (Catal. Gén. Musée du Caire, 1916), acc. to pages.

Mus = *Le Muséon* (periodical), acc. to vols.

My = *Le Mystère des Lettres grecques*, ed. A. Hebbelynck (from *Muséon*, 1900, 1901).

N&E = *Notices et Extraits des MSS. de la Bibliothèque Nationale*, Paris.

Nah = Nahum.

ⲡ̄ⲉ̄ = ⲛⲟⲩⲧⲉ.

nn = noun.

Nu = Numbers.

O = Old Coptic idiom (AZ 21 93 ff., 38 76 ff.)

Ob = Obadiah.

obj = object.

O'LearyH = De Lacy O'Leary : *Fragmentary Coptic Hymns*, 1924.

———The = De Lacy O'Leary : *The Coptic Theotokia*, 1923.

OLZ = *Orientalistische Litteraturzeitung.*

om = omits, omitted.

opp = as opposed to, contrasted with.

Ora = *Orientalia* (periodical), Rome.

OratCyp = *Oratio Cypriani* in *Veröffentl. a. d. badischen Papyrussamml.*, Heft 5, 1934, p. 305 ff.

OrChr = *Oriens Christianus* (periodical).

Osir = M. A. Murray, *The Osireion*, 1904.

Ostr = ostracon.

Ostr.Chicago = Till's copies of ostraca from Chicago Expedition, 1931.

P = MSS. in the Bibliothèque Nationale, Paris (Crum's copies).

PAl = Papyri in Museum at Alexandria, ed. de Ricci & Winstedt in *Sphinx* x, also Crum's copies.

PAmh = *The Amherst Papyri*, ed. Grenfell & Hunt, 1901.

paral = parallel word or phrase.

PasH = Paschal Hymns : *Kitâb Ṭaruḥât al-Baskhah al-Muḳaddasah*, Old Cairo, 1914.

PasLect = ⲡⲓϫⲱⲙ ⲛ̄ⲧⲉ ⲡⲓⲡⲁⲥⲭⲁ ⲉⲑ̄ⲃ̄, Cairo, 1921 (*cf* PO xxiv).

pass = *passim.*

PBad = *Veröffentl. a. d. badischen Papyrussamml.*, Heft 5.

P. Beatty = Papyri in collection of Mr. Chester Beatty, London (Crum's copies).

PBu = Coptic legal papyrus *olim penes* Sir E. A. W. Budge (Crum's copy), now at Columbia University.

p c = conjunctive participle.

PCai = *Papyrus grecs d'époque byzantine*, ed. J. Maspero (Catal. Gén. Musée du Caire, 1911 ff.).

PChass = Two medical papyri *penes* E. Chassinat.

Pcod = *Papyruscodex saec. vi–vii . . . Cheltenham*, ed. Crum, 1915, acc to pp. of printed book.

PcodF = fayyûmic text of same, ed. W. Erichsen (Danish Acad., 1932).

PcodMor = Mr. Pierpont Morgan's papyrus volume of Psalms &c. (H. Thompson's copy).

PCol = Papyri at Columbia University, New York (A. Schiller's copies).

Pet = Epistles of Peter.

Pey = A. Peyron, *Lexicon Linguae Copticae*, 1835.

PG = Migne's *Patrologia*, Series Graeca.

PGen = magical papyrus in University Library, Geneva (photograph).

PGM = *Papyri Graecae Magicae*, ed. K. Preisendanz I, II, 1928, 1931.

PGol = Papyri formerly in W. Golenischeff's collection, from photographs sent by O. von Lemm.

Phil = Epistle to Philippians.

PJkôw = Papyri (6th c.) thence, Cairo Mus. (Lacau's copies).

pl = plural.

PLich = Papyri belonging to N. P. Lichatschev (P. Jernstedt's copies).

PLond = *Greek Papyri in British Museum*, ed. Kenyon & Bell, acc. to pp.

PMéd = *Un Papyrus Médical Copte*, ed. E. Chassinat (= MIF. 32), 1921, acc. to pp.

PMich = Papyri at Michigan University, with year of acquisition where no. not ascertained.

PMon = *Byzantinische Papyri . . . zu München*, ed. Heisenberg & Wenger, 1914, acc. to pp.

PNolot = rest of papyrus ed. V. Loret, *Rec* 16 103 (Kuentz's copy).

PO = *Patrologia Orientalis.*

poss = possessive pronoun.

POxy = *Oxyrhynchus Papyri*, ed. Grenfell & Hunt.

PRain = Papyri in the Rainer Collection (Staatsbibl.), Vienna (Till's copies), more often as Vi.

pref = prefix.

Preisigke = F. Preisigke, *Namenbuch*, 1922.

prep = preposition.

pres = present tense, thus : 1 pres, 2 pres.

Pro = Proverbs.

prob = probably.

pron = pronoun.

PS = *Pistis Sophia*, ed. C. Schmidt (= *Coptica* II), 1925.

Ps = Psalms, acc. to the LXX numeration.

PSBA = *Proceedings of Soc. of Biblical Archaeology.*

PStras = Papyri in University Library, Strassburg (Crum's copies, 1912).

PVi = Papyri in Staatsbibliothek, Vienna (Till's copies).

qual = qualitative of verb ; also indicated by †.

R = *I Papiri Copti . . . di Torino*, ed. F. Rossi, acc. to volume, fascicule & page.

RAC = E. Revillout, *Actes et Contrats . . . de Boulaq et du Louvre*, 1876.

RAl = F. Rossi, *Alcuni MSS. Copti . . . di Torino* (= Memorie . . . Torino, ser. ii, tom. xliii), acc. to pp. of separate publication.

RChamp = *Recueil d'Études . . . J. F. Champollion*, 1922.

RE = *Revue Égyptologique.*

Rec = *Recueil de Travaux &c.*

refl = reflexive use.

rel = relative.

Rendiconti, *v* ALR.

Ricci = MSS. & copies belonging to Seymour de Ricci (Crum's copies).

RNC = F. Rossi, *Un Nuovo Cod. Copto* (Memorie Accad. Lincei, 1893), acc. to pp. of separate publication.

Ro = Epistle to Romans.

ROC = *Revue de l'Orient Chrétien*, acc. to vol.

Rösch = F. Rösch, *Vorbemerkungen zu e. Gramm. d. achmîmischen Mundart*, 1909, acc. to pp.

Ru = Ruth.

Ryl = *Catal. of Coptic MSS. in John Rylands Library*, 1909, acc. to numbers ; RylSuppl = MSS. acquired since publication of catalogue (*cf* Ryl *Bull.* 5).

S = Saʿidic dialect ; Sᵃ Saʿidic with Achmîmic tendency (mostly Theban), Sᶠ with Fayyûmic tendency.

Sa = Wisdom of Solomon.
Salib = *Kitâb aṣ-Ṣalîb*, Cairo, 1921.
Saq = Coptic texts ed. by H. Thompson in Quibell's *Excavations at Saqqara*, 1909, 1912.
Sdff = G. Steindorff, *Koptische Grammatik²*, acc. to §§, or information from him.
s f = *sub fine*.
sg = singular.
Sh = works of Shenoute (& of his disciple Besa). Prefixed to all quotations from their writings (doubtfully to Mor 54).
SHel = G. P. G. Sobhy, *Le Martyre de St. Hélias*, Cairo, 1919.
Si = Ecclesiasticus, acc. to Lagarde's numeration.
sim = similar in use or in meaning to the last quoted instance.
Sitz = *Sitzungsberichte*.
Sobhy = information supplied by Dr. G. P. G. Sobhy, Cairo.
Spg = W. Spiegelberg, *Koptisches Handwörterbuch*, 1921.
Sph = *Sphinx* (periodical).
ST = Crum, *Short Texts from Coptic Ostraca & Papyri*, 1921.
Stat = G. Horner, *Statutes of the Apostles*; also HSt.
Stegemann = *Kopt. Zaubertexte*, ed. V. Stegemann (Sitz. d. Heidelb. Akad., 1934).
Stern = L. Stern, *Koptische Grammatik*, acc. to §§.
Su = Susanna.
suff = suffix.
Synax = *Synaxarium Alexandrinum*, ed. J. Forget (*CSCO.*), 1905, 1912.

Tatt = H. Tattam, *Lexicon Aegyptiaco-Latinum*, 1835.
TDi = Tuki, *Diurnum Alexandrinum*, 1750.
TEuch = do., *Pontificale et Euchologium*, 1761.
Thes = Epistles to Thessalonians.
Ti = Epistle to Titus.
Till = W. Till, *Achmîmisch-Kopt. Grammatik*, 1928, acc. to §§.
— Bau = *Eine Kopt. Bauernpraktik* (Mitt. d. deut. Inst. Kairo, vi, 1936).
— Oster = *Osterbrief u. Predigt in achm. Dialekt*, Vienna, 1931 (at first as Vi 10157).
Tim = Epistles to Timothy.
Tob = Tobit.
Tor = *Coptic Ostraca*, ed. H. Thompson in *Theban Ostraca ... Toronto* (University of Toronto Studies), 1913, acc. to numbers.
tr = transitive.
Tri = Lemm, *Das Triadon*, 1903, acc. to stanzas.

TRit = Tuki, *Rituale*, 1763.
TSBA = Transactions of the Soc. of Bibl. Archaeology.
TstAb = I. Guidi, *Testo copto del Testam. di Abramo &c.* (= ALR, 1900).
TT = Crum, *Theolog. Texts from Coptic Papyri*, 1913.
TThe = Tuki, *Theotokia*, 1764.
TU = Gebhardt, Harnack & C. Schmidt, *Texte u. Untersuchungen* (Bd. 43 *Gespräche Jesu*).
Tuki = Tuki, *Rudimenta Linguae Coptae*, 1778.
TurM = B. Turaief, *Materiali &c.* (*v* AZ 40 150, *Orient. Bibliographie* xv, no. 111 *a*), acc. to numbers.
TurO = do., *Koptskia Ostraka ... Golenishtshef* (= Bull. Acad. Imp. x, no. 5, 1899), acc. to numbers.
Turin ostr = ostraca in Museo Archeol., Turin (Crum's copies).

V = *vide*.
Va = MSS. in Vatican Library, acc. to photographs or to copies by H. De Vis.
var = variant, in same dialect.
vb = verb.
Vi = Vienna, MSS. & ostraca in the Staats(*olim* Hof) bibliothek.

Wess = C. Wessely, *Studien z. Paläographie &c.*, acc. to vol. & page.
WHatch = a *B* MS *penes* the Rev. W. Hatch, Cambridge, Mass.
Win = ostraca from Winlock's excavations 1927-8, in Cairo Museum.
Wor = W. H. Worrell, *Coptic MSS. in Freer Collection* (University of Michigan Studies), 1923.
WS = Crum & Bell, *Coptic Texts from Wadi Sarga* (= Coptica III), 1922, acc. to pp.
WTh = E. O. Winstedt, *Coptic Texts on St. Theodore* (Text & Transl. Soc.), 1910.
WZKM = *Wiener Zeitsch. f. d. Kunde d. Morgenlandes*.

Z = G. Zoega, *Catalogus Codd. Copticorum &c.* 1810, acc. to pp.
Zech = Zechariah.
Zeph = Zephaniah.
ZNTW = *Zeitsch. f. d. Neutestamentl. Wissenschaft*.

† = (after verbal forms) qualitative.
( ) = Coptic letter inserted by editor, except in headings, where they indicate variants or hypothetical forms.
? = perhaps, possibly.

ADDITIONS AND CORRECTIONS

a, b refer to columns 1 & 2.

1 *a* 11 up, add ⲁⲁ- *S*: Mor 50 62, HT*W* 79 ⲛⲁⲁ-ⲛϣⲁⲩ.

1 *b* 21 up, add ⲁⲓⲉⲩ† *A* oftenest.

—— 13 up, read μεγαλύνεσθαι.

—— 7 up, read πληθύνεσθαι.

2 *a* 13, add Miss 4 205 *B* ⲧⲁⲓⲛⲓϣϯ ⲉⲧⲟⲓ (delete ⲛⲧⲟⲓ) ⲛⲧⲁⲓⲙⲁⲓⲏ.

—— 18 up. *Cf* ManiP 201 29 ⲁⲃⲏ.

—— 15 up, add ostr Chicago 855 ⲟⲩⲁⲃⲉ among metal utensils.

2 *b* after 21, add

ⲁⲃⲉⲛ *v* ⲟⲃⲛ.

3 *a* 12, MG 25 370 thing seen *in* glass (Polotsky).

—— 18 up, for *B* read *BF*.

—— 15 up, for *S* read *SF*.

—— 11 & 7 up, read ἐγκαινίζειν.

3 *b* 7, add BMOr 6201 B 66 ⲁⲕϭⲱⲡ ⲧⲁ. ⲛⲡⲓⲧⲁⲗⲁⲓⲡⲱⲣⲟⲥ, *ib*]ⲗⲁⲕⲟⲟⲧⲉ ⲡⲏⲣⲡ ϩⲓⲧⲉⲩⲁ., Turin ostr (Farina 651) ⲧⲁ. ⲙⲡⲡⲁⲣⲅⲟⲁⲟⲥ, *ib* (426) ⲧⲃⲃⲟ ⲧⲁ. ⲉⲃⲟⲗ; pl Bodl(P) d 203 *S* ye wrote ⲉⲧⲃⲉⲛⲁⲕⲟⲟⲩⲉ.

5 *b* 26, add Griff Stu 163 *F* ⲑⲁⲗⲉⲕ ⲃ̄ ⲙⲡⲡⲟⲩⲛ.

6 *a* 20 up, add ShViK 9223 67 = C 73 161 ⲟⲗⲙⲉϥ ⲉⲅⲟⲩⲛ ⲉⲡⲉϥⲁⲗⲟⲙ.

6 *b* 12, Gk of Nu 24 ἐκμυελίζειν, of Ps 65 μυελοῦσθαι.

—— 17, for *ib* read MG 17.

7 *a* 13, πανούκλας = ? groin (cf βουβών), so *groin of direction*, whereon archer rests bow in *aiming* (Chaîne).

—— 28, add Ora 4 23 ⲉⲃⲣⲓ ⲁⲁⲙ.

—— *ult*, add ManiP 18 *A*² ⲡⲓⲁⲙⲏ.

7 *b* 16, add ⲁⲙⲉⲓ *A* TillOster 24.

—— after 17 up, add

ⲁⲙⲟⲕ, -ⲅ *S*, liquid measure: Ora 4 24.

8 *a* 7 up, after He 12 2 add ὑπομένειν.

8 *b* after 2, add

—— ⲉⲃⲟⲗ, *endure*: Orat Manas 5 ⲁϥⲁ. ⲉⲃ. ⲁⲛ ἀνυπόστατος.

—— 18 up, pl *S* add ⲁⲙⲣⲏⲅⲉ Landesbibl Munich Kopt 21 (Reich's copy).

9 *a* 13, read جِّ.

9 *a* after 22 up, add

ⲁⲙⲱⲓ *B* nn f, *rope*: P 54 171 †ⲁ. حَبْل.

—— 8 up, read δικαιοῦσθαι.

9 *b* 29, read γίνεσθαι.

10 *b* after 6, add ϭⲓⲛⲁⲧⲁⲙⲁⲅⲧⲉ *S*: Mor 53 60.

11 *a* 5, ⲁⲛⲁⲓ might be differently treated, AZ 47 141 ff. *V* ⲁⲛⲓⲧ† below.

12 *a* after 15 up, add

ⲁⲛⲓⲧ *SA*² qual of ⲁⲛⲁⲓ: CO 282 *S* ⲕ]ⲁⲛ ⲉⲛⲁⲛⲓⲧ ⲕⲁⲛ ⲉⲛϩ[ⲟⲟⲩ ?, ⲁⲛⲓⲧ *A*² Mani *pass*.

—— after 5 up, add

ⲁⲛⲧⲉⲗⲉⲥ *B* nn f, *assembly, festival*: Va 57 70 πανήγυρις; MG 25 376 begged to be taken ⲉϯⲁ. to see what befell there = BMOr 5652 95 عيد = ROC ·8 289 ܠܡܐܙܠ ܠܚܙܘ. Coptic?

12 *b* 9 up, add Ora 4 25 ⲕⲗⲁⲍⲟⲥ ⲡⲁⲛⲓϣ ⲙⲡⲣⲏ.

14 *a* 10, *v* ⲥⲟⲛ, a measure.

—— 28, read ϣⲁⲗⲭ.

—— after 30, add

ⲁⲡⲁⲓ *B* nn as pl: Is 41 7. *V* ⲗⲁⲧⲃⲥ.

—— 31, for 19 read 21.

—— after 18 up, add

ⲁⲡⲟⲩ, ⲁⲡⲟⲩϩ *S* nn m, title or epithet heading oil accounts: BMOr 6201 B 201 ⲡⲁⲡⲟⲩϩ ⲉⲃⲣⲟⲉⲓⲥ ⲉⲛϣⲟⲛⲧⲉ, *ib* 197 ⲡⲁⲡⲟⲩ ⲥⲛⲁⲩ ⲉⲩⲕⲏ ⲛ[, *ib* 239 ⲡⲁⲡⲟⲩ ⲛⲙⲁⲛϩⲉⲣⲙⲏⲛ.

14 *b* 11, for 458 read 58.

—— after 18, add

ⲁⲡⲉⲓⲧ *S*, a metal object: BP 69109.

—— 19, add ManiP 142 ⲉⲡⲁⲧ.

—— 16 up, read ⲕⲁ ⲟⲉⲓⲕ.

15 *a* 12, add prob Ep 543, TurM 13.

16 *a* 20 up, translates τόσῳ *by so much* (Griffith).

16 *b* 19 up, for ⲉⲣϣⲟ(ⲩϩ.), read ⲧⲁⲣϣⲟ.

18 *a* 13. *Cf* Kropp 2 240, A Delatte *Textes grecs* 1927, 553.

18 *b* 16 up, for do read ἄβατος.

19 *a* 7. *Cf* Ryl 349 7 ⲛⲁⲧⲡⲉⲩϩⲟⲕϩⲕ.

—— 28, read πολύς.

19 *b* 3, for *B* read *BF*.

—— 7, after *A*² add *F* (Polotsky).

—— 19 up, ω *S* often AZ 23 104 ff.

—— 24 up. *Cf n-iw* (ⲡⲏⲩ) (Griffith).

20 *b* 14, more prob pl of αὐλαία.

22 *a* 6 up, for 237 read 236.

23 *b* 26, for *Stories* read DM (Edgerton).

—— 9 up, Cl 4 add πρός, *cf* p 685 *a* 30.

24 *a* 15, occurs in Eccl 7 12.

25 *a* 13, ⲁϩⲱⲙ is in Pro 23 5, 24 22 ἀετός.

—— after 17 up, add

ⲁϩⲁⲛ S conj: ST 240 10, *cf* ⲁϧⲁⲛ, ⲁϧⲛ *A²* Mani K 6, 142 &c., P 133.

—— 12 up. *Cf* ? places ⲧⲙⲟⲩⲛⲁϧⲓ (BM 1171), Θμοιναχῆ (PHib 1 8), Ψιναχις (PFior 3 364).

25 *b* 16 up, for ⲟⲩⲟⲥⲉ read ⲟⲩⲁⲥⲉ.

—— 6 up. *Cf* also AZ 55 89.

26 *a* 18, add EW 170 *B* ⲁⲥⲡⲉⲛⲥⲉⲧⲁⲗⲟⲓ.

—— 23 up, prob *l* ⲁϧⲁⲩ, pl of ⲁϧⲱ (KKS 179) & add ⲁϧⲣⲁⲩⲓ *F* Lam 4 3 δράκων.

—— 6 up, delete *B* & add ⲁⲥⲟⲗ✝ *B*.

—— *ult, l* ⲁⲥⲟⲗ✝ (*cf* JEA 8 117). Yet ⲁⲥⲟⲗ *calf* (*v* Rec 19 100) was formerly known: *Actes 5ᵉ Cong. Papyrol.* 1938 79, glossary 3d cent. ʙ ᴄ μόσχος· αγολ.

26 *b* 19, add Cai 67324 ⲁⲥⲁⲛ in list of σκευῆ.

28 *a* 2, as measure CO 139.

28 *b* 8 up, after 1st *S* add ἀναπηδύειν (HT).

29 *a* 28, read Τβῆκις (Griffith).

—— 32, read ⲃⲁⲕ- *S*.

29 *b* 2, read PS.

30 *a* 16 up, add ⲃ. ⲟⲩⲕⲟⲧ. *V* ⲕⲱⲧⲉ (ⲕⲟⲧ).

31 *a* upper margin, read ⲃⲏⲕⲉ.

32 *a* 3, read Eccl 11 9 (*F* ⲓⲱⲣϩ ⲛⲛⲃⲉⲗ) ὅρασις ὀφ., Pro 27 20 (*A* ϩⲁⲣⲃⲉⲗ) στηρ. ὀφ.

33 *a* 15, read ϧⲱ, 32 read ϧⲁ.

—— 16, read Mic 4 13 *S* (ShA 1 385) *AB* (Grossouw).

33 *b* 20, not Sh, but Chrysostom (PG 63 206 om).

—— 10 up, read ϩⲏⲧ.

34 *b* 4 up, read (ⲙⲙⲁⲩ).

35 *b* 4 up, read 88.

36 *b* 18, read ἀσυνάκτους.

37 *b* 10, add ShIF 151 ⲃ. ⲉϩⲣⲁⲓ ⲛⲥⲁⲡⲡⲟⲩⲛⲉ.

38 *a* 1. *Cf bkr·t* throne (Dévaud). But ⲃⲗⲕⲉ *A²* Mani *pass* confirms meaning as given.

38 *b* 17, add TEuch 1 124 ⲃⲁⲗⲛϩⲙⲱⲟⲩ.

—— 19 up, after *S* add κίβδηλος (HT).

39 *b* 5, read Deu 28 48 *S* (*B* ϩⲕⲟ).

40 *a* 5 up, m in Ps 91 13 *B* (Griffith).

—— 22 up, *v* p 755 *a penult* ϧⲁⲧⲃⲁⲓⲛⲉ.

—— 14 up. *Cf* ? BMOr 6201 A 111 *S* bring 400 ⲛⲟϭ ⲛⲃⲱⲛⲓ (or ? ⲃⲱⲛ✝)...ⲉⲛⲁⲡⲟⲩ ⲡⲗⲉⲩⲕⲟⲛ.

41 *b* 21 up, for 14 read 15.

42 *a* 19, for 23 read 47.

—— 29, for ϫⲁϫ read ⲃⲏⲡⲉ 1ᵒ.

42 *a* 8 up, read ROC 18.

43 *a* 2, *v* rather ϧⲃⲟⲣⲃⲣ.

—— 4 up, read ShBM.

43 *b* 20, delete In...(Preisigke). *V* Spg *DemStud* 1 55*, 403 (Spiegelberg).

—— 18 up, add & ? ⲃⲗϣⲁⲧⲉ among implements, BMOr 6201 A 90.

44 *a* 16 up, add vb: P 54 174 ⲉⲩⲃⲁⲣϣⲓ ‏يقلف‎.

44 *b* 10, add & ⲙⲃⲣⲉϧ *cart.*

—— 8 up, add ManiK 33 *A²* ⲃⲁⲥⲡϭ.

45 *a* 7, read ἠμφιεσμένος.

—— 10, ⲃⲁⲥⲧϧⲟ paral ϣⲓⲡⲉ, ⲡⲟ(ⲟ)ⲛⲉ, ⲧⲁⲕⲟ, ϣⲱϥ, ⲙⲉⲧϫⲁϫⲉ, *v* p 648 *b infra.*

—— 25, read ϧⲁⲧⲃⲏⲡⲉ.

—— 27, ⲃ. ϧⲁⲧⲉ *v* ⲙⲉⲗϧⲉ.

—— 14 up, add Cai 67324 *vo* ϣⲟⲩϣⲧ ⲛⲃ.

—— after 4 up, add

ⲃⲓⲧ *F* nn m, *edge, side* ? of pot: OratCyp 123 drop ⲉⲥⲁϣⲓ ⲉⲛⲃ. ⲡⲟⲩⲕⲉⲧⲟⲩⲥ (*cf* Is 40 15), PBad 5 402 write names ⲉⲛⲃ. ⲟⲩⲥⲁⲗⲉϧⲧ.

45 *b* after 4, add

ⲃⲱⲧ-, ⲃⲟⲧ⸗ *v* ⲟⲩⲱⲧⲉ.

46 *a* 7 up, gloss ⲃⲱⲱ =? ⲟⲩⲱⲧϧ *smelting.*

46 *b* 1, ⲃⲁⲑⲟ in ViK 954 (Till).

47 *a* 6 up, in Synax 2 105 = ‏ضبع‎ *hyena.*

47 *b* 21, read ‏سذاب‎ ‏ري‎.

48 *a* 1, read ⲟⲩⲱϧⲉ.

—— 10, prob from PascLect ⲟⲩⲁϧⲃⲉϧ (Cai), ⲟⲩⲃⲁϧⲃⲉϧ (Gött) (Dévaud).

—— 21, read ⲟⲩⲟϧⲛ-.

48 *b* 6, read ⲟⲩⲁⲥⲉ.

—— 9, after ϧⲁⲥⲓⲉ add ναυάγειν.

49 *b* after 14, add

ϭⲱ *v* ϭⲛⲟⲛ (ϭⲟⲛ).

52 *b* 18, add Mor 30 27 *F* ⲙⲛⲧⲉⲃⲃⲉ of blind woman.

53 *a* 5 up, read βρῶσις.

53 *b* 19. Ostr *penes* Crum ⲃⲣⲏⲉⲓⲛⲉ, paral κόκκος.

54 *a* 19-21, delete all & *v* ⲧⲟⲩⲟ (ⲧⲉⲃⲟ).

55 *b* after 5 add

ⲉⲗⲟⲓϧ *S*: Ora 4 21, paral ⲉⲙⲉ. *Cf* DM 1 17 n *mrḥ*, Πελαίας (Polotsky).

—— *ult,* add

ⲉⲙⲙⲁⲙⲉⲓ *S v* ⲙⲉ *truth* (ⲛⲁⲙⲉ).

ⲉⲙⲙⲟⲛ *v* ⲙⲙⲟⲛ *verily.*

56 b 1, from *imskaw* (*Kémi* 2 6).

—— 10 up, rather vb than nn (Griffith).

—— 18 up, for whence ? read P 70 268.

57 a 15. *Cf* also ⲥⲣⲡϩ.

57 a 23, Va 61 97 = 2 Tim 4 10.

57 b 12 up, add Ryl 268 ⲛϭⲓⲥⲉ ⲉⲣⲉⲓ ⲉϫⲱϥ ; not in J&C 95 18, where *l* ⲉ(ⲧ)ⲣ-.

—— after 3 up, add

ⲉⲣⲓ B: Lev 22 7 Lag ἄρτος, substantiated (?) by K 331 περι لبب.

58 a 6 =? ἐρέβινθος (Jernstedt).

—— 15 up, read προεπαγγέλλειν.

58 b 17 up, add Ora 4 21 ⲣ ⲉ. ⲛϩⲱⲣ (Horus).

60 a 8, add ⲉⲥⲓⲧ F LAp 530 &c.

62 a 5, add TillBau 129 ⲧⲁⲗⲟ ⲟⲩⲁⲧⲁϩ ⲉⲡⲛⲁⲧ.

—— 6 up, for *SF* read *SAA²F*.

62 b 6 up, for ⲉⲟⲩⲓⲛ &c read ⲟⲩⲓⲛ, *v* ⲟⲩⲉⲓⲛ.

63 b 11, add ⲛⲉϣⲱ pl PMéd 105 ? *scrofula* (Chassinat otherwise).

—— 15, add ϣⲡⲉ A Louvain C 128 (Lefort).

64 b 11, delete ?.

65 b 12, ⲉϭⲁⲁϣ also F, Jer 26 9 (Mus 49 173).

66 b 27. *V* also ⲛⲏⲃ.

—— 11 up. *V* ? PGM 1 60 667 ⲛⲓ ⲉⲣⲓⲛⲕ. *Cf* 665 ⲁⲡⲟⲕ ⲱϩ.

67 a 21, for *F* read *S*.

67 b 17 up, ⲛϭⲓ *F* add (Mor 30 53).

68 a 8 up, add ⲑⲟⲃϣ†, ⲑⲟⲡϣ†.

68 b 9, delete *fix &*.

—— 20, = P 54 143 ⲑⲁⲗⲓⲗⲁϩⲓ.

69 a 6, read El.

—— 7 up, for ⲧⲱⲣϣ read ⲧⲣⲟϣ.

69 b 15 up, ' ex Scala ', this is P 54 168. For ⲁϥⲑ. *v* ⲛⲟⲩϥⲧ.

70 b 16, *B* also f, DeV 2 5.

—— 19, ⲉⲓ ⲛⲛ prob also Lu 11 33 (Lefort).

73 a 5 up, read ⲡⲉⲭⲁⲓⲱⲥ.

—— 4 up, as *Sᵃ* place-name BMOr 9533 *vo* ⲡⲉⲓⲁⲉ.

74 a 2, for *raise* read *open* (*v* ⲧⲟⲩⲛⲟ & AZ 47 146).

—— 10 up, add Blake 302 amethyst ⲉⲧⲉⲓ· ⲙⲡⲛⲱⲛⲉ called &c.

74 b c, add JKP 2 20 *S* ⲓⲉ ⲥⲁⲃⲁ *Oh*, (*queen of*) *Sheba*.

75 a 26, add ⲉⲓⲉ- *Sf* P 130⁴ 90 ⲉⲓⲉ ⲧⲟⲟⲧϥ ⲛⲥⲱϥ.

—— 14 up, add P 129¹² 16 ⲡⲉⲓⲱ ⲙⲡⲉⲩϩⲟ.

76 a 9, read ⲧⲱⲟⲩ.

77 b 24, add ⲣⲙⲓⲟⲙ ? *man of wine-press* (Drioton): WS *lc*, MIF 59 60 n.

78 a 18, add ⲉⲓⲙⲉ ⲉⲣⲁⲧ⸗ *S*: ViK (Sh ?) 9317 ⲛⲧⲁϣⲓⲛⲉ ⲛⲥⲁⲉⲓ. ⲉⲣⲁⲧϥ ⲙⲛϩⲱⲃ.

78 b *ult*, add ⲛ ⲧⲟⲟⲧ ⲛ- KKS 302 ⲁ[ⲩ ?]ⲛ ⲧⲟⲟⲧⲟⲩ ⲛϣⲙⲟⲩⲛ ⲛⲟⲩⲱⲛ ϩⲙⲡⲉⲩⲁϩⲉ.

81 a 24. *Cf* ShViK 934 222 ⲧⲓⲛⲉ ⲙⲡⲉⲕⲱⲧ.

82 a 12 up, add ϫⲓ(ⲟ)ⲟⲣⲉ A² vb & nn, Mani *pass*.

83 a 7, ⲉⲉ⸗ also *A* (Gunn).

83 b 16 up, read 24 90.

84 a 3 up, add Cai 67324 *vo* in list of σκευῆ ⲟⲩⲉⲓⲣⲏ ⲟⲩⲉⲓⲉⲓ (*one*), therefore f.

84 b 12 up, add DeV 2 10 B ⲓⲟⲣϩ⸗.

85 a 19 up, add name Νεφεριηρι (PGM 1 114).

85 b 5 up, add ShA 2 113.

86 a 24, add *S* Ora 4 22 ⲉⲕⲛⲏⲧ ⲉⲕⲛⲥ.

87 b 12 up, for *full of*, prob read *smeared with*.

88 a 6, var ⲉⲩⲉⲛⲉⲡⲓⲧⲛ (Lefort Mus 42 123).

—— 10, add TillOster 30 *A* ⲉⲓⲱⲱ.

—— 18 up, add Vi ostr 740 ϣⲛⲧⲁⲉⲥⲉ ⲛⲡⲁⲁⲩ.

—— 12 up, var *Mart. d. heil. Viktor* ed. (not publ.) Lemm 27 ⲙⲛⲧⲁϥⲧⲉ ⲛⲁⲧⲁⲓⲟⲩ.

88 b 1, add BKU 1 26 (8117) *F* child ⲉⲁ[ϥⲉⲣ ⲓ]ϣ ⲉⲧⲟⲩϣⲛ ϩⲁⲣⲁϥ.

89 a 18, add BP 8098 *S* *my father dead* ⲁⲧⲉⲕⲕⲗⲏⲥⲓⲁ ⲉⲓ. ϩⲓⲱⲱⲧ.

—— 15 up, add *cf* Stegemann 64 ⲟⲩⲛϣⲧⲉ opp ⲟⲩϩⲁⲣⲁϣ.

89 b 4, for *ib* read 58.

—— 5 = λωποδυσία (Euseb iii 23 9).

90 a 19, f numeral ⲕ✝ *B* MG 25 196.

92 a 6 up. *Cf* ⲕⲱ 98 b *infra* (HT).

92 b 12 up, after *A* add *B* (C 86 91), & add ⲕⲁⲓ *F* (Baouit 107, 108).

94 a 1. read ⲕⲁⲓⲟⲩⲁⲉⲓϣ ϣⲏⲙ.

—— 5 up, for 27 read 17.

94 b 9, ⲕⲉ-, add *Sf* Mor 55 67 ⲕⲉ ⲧⲟⲟⲧϥ ⲉⲃⲟⲗ *et saepe*.

98 b 15 up, add ⲣⲟⲟⲩϣ, ⲥⲛⲧⲉ.

99 a 18 up, *v* also ⲣⲟ *strand*.

99 b 11, read ⲕⲉⲗ.

100 a after 4 up, add

ⲕⲃⲃⲉ *v* ⲕⲱⲃ *s f*.

100 b after 7, add

ⲕⲱⲃϩ *S* vb tr, *bind* (?): Mor 31 202 (Abimelech & Jeremiah) ⲁϥⲕ. ⲛⲡⲉⲧⲟⲉⲓⲥ ⲛⲡⲉⲛⲟⲩϩ.

—— 16 up, prob also Jer 50 12 *S* ed. Maspero.

101 b after 2, add

ⲕⲱⲕ, ϫⲱⲕ, ⲕⲟⲕ (Ann 27 63), ⲕⲟⲭ (Ora 4 23,

Kropp D 97), ϫⲱⲱϫ (Kropp K 15) *S*, rubric in magical texts.

—— 5, ϫⲱⲱϫ *v* Sethe, *Amun u. die 8 Götter* 65.

—— 24, read ϣⲗⲟⲡⲗⲡ.

102 *a* 9 prob not error; *cf* PGM 1 22 2 κοκκούφατ also called γυπαλέκτωρ (Keimer).

—— after 12, add

ⲕⲟⲩⲕⲥ *S* nn f, *tip of nose*: P 46 245 ⲧⲕ. طرف الانف (*cf* ϣⲁ *nose*).

—— 14 up. *Cf* כליב (Calice).

—— after 15 up, add

ⲕⲗⲁ   *v* ⲕⲣⲟ.

103 *b* 22, read C 41 10.

—— 20 up, add ⲕⲉⲗⲗⲓ *O* κλεῖστρον POslo 312.

—— 12 up, ⲕⲉⲗⲓ *knee* prob not same as ⲕⲗⲗⲉ *bolt* (Sdff).

104 *a* 19, ϩⲁⲙⲕ. = ϩⲁⲙⲕⲗⲗⲉ, not ϩⲁⲙⲕⲉⲗⲡⲕⲉϩ.

107 *b* 2, add ⲕⲁⲗⲉϫ† *S*(*S*ᵃ) BKU 1 1 *ro*.

—— 24 up, read ⲉϥϭ.†

108 *a* 4, add Pcod *F* 29 ⲕⲉⲗϫⲓ.

108 *b penult*, add ViK 9584, cit Cant 2 17 ⲡⲧⲡϩⲁⲓⲃⲉⲥ ⲕⲓⲧⲟⲩ (*bis*) κινεῖσθαι. *Cf* HT's text.

111 *a* 20, after ⲛⲟⲩ) add ἐν τῷ, after 11 ἡνίκα ἄν.

111 *b* after 8 up, add

ⲕⲁⲛⲕⲗⲱ   *v* ϭⲓⲛϭⲗⲱ.

—— 6 up, for ٔ *v* Dozy, ? = ⲧⲕⲟⲩ(ⲡ)ϫⲟⲩ *p* 113 *a*.

112 *b* 8 up, *v* also ⲥⲉⲧⲛ.

113 *a* 14, read *computruerit*.

—— 16 up, add ⲕⲓⲗϫⲟⲩ *F* BP 8095 twice in list of εἴδη.

113 *b* 22, for 535 read 536.

—— 26, *v* ϭⲟⲡ 2°.

115 *a* 9 up, for ⲉⲁⲧ read ⲙⲟⲩ ⲡⲥⲱⲣⲙ.

118 *a* 19 up, delete *ib* to ϭⲱⲛϭ & *v* ϭⲱⲣϥ.

119 *b* 18, add ⲕⲉⲛⲥⲓ *F* Mor 30 50.

120 *a* 5, ϫⲱⲣⲓⲥ &c, add BM 1165 *S* ⲛⲁⲧⲕ.

—— 5 up, for ⲑⲱⲙⲥ read ϫⲱⲗ.

121 *a* 21 up, add ⲕⲛⲥⲉ in ostr *penes* Crum.

121 *b* 13, add ViK 9624 170 *S* on those that pray ⲉⲣⲉⲡⲉⲩϭⲓϫ ⲕⲉⲥⲕⲟⲥⲧ ⲉⲡⲉⲥⲛⲧ ⲡⲙⲙⲁⲩ.

—— 22, for 9 read 19.

122 *b* 3 up, for *A* read A.

127 *b* 10, read 172 4 17.

128 *a* 12 up, Lu 19 43 περι-, not μεταβάλ.

129 *b* 4, for ⲱϭ, read ⲥⲱⲕ.

—— 18 up, is qual of ⲕⲏⲡⲉ (Dévaud).

130 *b* after 22, add place-name ⲧⲁⲡⲕⲉϣ (var -ⲕⲁϣ PLond 4 598).

130 *b* 22 up, add Ostr *penes* Crum ⲧⲕⲓϧⲉ ⲛϫⲁⲣⲧⲏⲥ.

131 *a* 5. *Cf* Persian *gaoša-bâra*, Bartholomä *Altiran. Wbuch* (Jernstedt).

—— 14 up, ⲕⲁϧⲓ Ps 39 8 = κεφαλίς, this word ?

132 *a* 2, add ? Ez 23 42 ⲕⲉϧⲱⲣ(ⲓ) (*S* ρ ⲧⲱⲣⲉ) ἀνακρούεσθαι.

132 *a* 20, add ⲕⲁⲁϥ *F* BKU 1 26 (8116 *b*) 38.

133 *b* after 1, add

ⲕⲓϧⲉ   *v* ⲕⲏϣⲉ.

135 *b* 12 up, add Ryl 106 4 ⲁⲗⲟϥ ⲉⲡⲕⲱϧⲧ.

137 *a* 2, add θηλυμανής.

137 *b* 10 up, var شر.

—— 14, read قماري.

138 *a* 11 up, pl ? ⲗⲟⲟⲕ *S* Ora 4 27.

140 *a* 20, var ViK 9067 ⲧⲉⲧⲡⲗⲓⲕⲧϥ ⲙⲡⲉⲧⲡϧⲛⲧ *bring a veil upon*.

140 *b* 10 up, add ShViK 934 222 ⲡⲣⲉϥϧⲣⲱⲃ ⲉⲡϧⲟⲙⲛⲧ ⲁⲩⲱ ⲡⲗ., *ib* ⲣⲉϥⲥⲁⲛ ⲗ.

141 *a* 14 up, read ϩⲁⲗⲟⲗⲓ.

—— 26, add EpJer 16 *S*(Mus 50 230) ϣⲟⲉⲓϣ ⲉϣⲁϥⲗⲁⲁⲗⲉ ⲉⲣⲟⲟⲩ (*BF* Gk om).

141 *b* 17, for 27 read 17 & add νεότης.

—— 22 up, delete ⲉⲃⲟⲗ.

142 *a* 4 up, P 54 145 عشب, which suits βοτάνη.

—— 15 up, *l* prob ⲙⲡⲉⲣⲥⲉ ⲙⲡ[. *Cf* ⲡⲉⲣⲥⲉ خوخ *peach* Tri 498, K 177 &c. (*V* LöwF 3 347).

142 *b* 12, add Mani 1 *A*² ⲙⲟⲟⲗⲉ.

143 *a* 2. *Cf* ϭⲗⲟⲙⲗⲙ.

144 *b* 19, read ϧⲙ.

145 *a* 17 up, read 23 1†.

—— 10 up, add Kr 129 *F* ⲗⲱⲥ ⲉϧⲟⲩⲛ (*sic* prob, Till).

148 *a* 14 up. *Cf* name (gen) Πλεσωνου RevEpigr 1913 146.

—— after 4 up, add

ⲗⲁϣⲉⲉⲣ: BMOr 6201 B 244 *S* ⲁⲡⲁⲱⲛⲉ ⲡⲗ.

—— after 17, add

ⲗⲟⲩⲏ ⲍ *S* (?) vb tr, PMéd 211.

—— 17 up. On etymology *v Acta Or.* 16 93, citing Sethe *Von Zahlen* 42.

148 *b* 19, read ⲉⲥⲗ.† ⲉϧⲉ.

149 *b* after 20, add

ⲗⲉϧⲗⲏⲙ *B*   *v* ⲗⲉⲗⲏⲙ, ϧⲗⲱⲙ.

150 *a* after 16, add

ⲗⲁϧⲙⲓ *B* C 86 162 prob Coptic, *renegade* ? *V* Amélineau & Casanova.

—— 16 up, add MIF 59 195 *S* ⲡⲣⲉϥϣⲱ ⲙⲡⲗⲉϧ., Ora 4 22 *S* ϧⲛⲧϥ ⲙⲡⲉⲩⲧⲟⲟⲩⲉ ⲉϥⲧⲏϭ ⲡⲗⲁϧ. ⲡⲕⲉⲙ (var *ib* ⲛⲗⲁⲥ ⲡⲕⲁⲙ).

150 *a* after 12 up, add

ⲗⲉϩϯ *F* *v* ⲣⲁϩⲧⲉ.

—— 12 up, ⲗⲁϩⲱⲝ EW 238 line 1 = لِ[ج]اِ *filth*.

151 *b* 16, *S* also BHom 85 (Polotsky).

—— 21 up, for ϯ ⲟⲩⲱ read om.

152 *b* after 16 up, add

ⲗⲱϭⲉ, -ⲕⲉ *S*, among utensils : Ostr 3042 Univ Col Lond. *Cf* λώκιον (Preisigke *Wbuch*).

155 *b* 19, for 621 1° read 622.

155 *b* 24.   Phrases with ⲉϣⲱⲡⲉ do not belong here (Jernstedt in *Soc Egypt Univ Leningrad* 6 29, 30).

156 *a* 1, delete *A*.

157 *b* 13, in Mk 15 39 -ⲙⲉⲉⲓ.

159 *a* 4. ManiP 57 &c shows Zoega's ⲙⲡⲉⲓⲟⲕ right.

160 *b* *ult*, add

ⲙⲟⲩⲓ *S*, metal utensil : OstrChicago 855 ⲟⲩⲙ. ⲛⲃⲁⲣⲱⲧ, BP 69109 metal objects ⲙⲟⲩⲓ.

161 *a* 14, read *wroth*.

161 *b* after 27, add

ⲙⲟⲕⲉ† *S* : Ora 4 27 ⲡⲉϩ ⲡⲥⲓⲙ ⲉϥⲙ.; meaning obscure.

163 *b* 7, read *A*²*B*(*SA* diff).

—— 13 up, pl ⲙⲕⲉⲩϩ *F* Jer 22 23 (MR 1934 23).

165 *b* 16, read ἔνεδρον.

166 *a* 14, add ManiK 33, 114 *A*² ⲙⲗⲁϩ.

—— 11 up, add Griff Stu 163 *F* ⲙⲁⲗⲁϩ.

166 *b* 11, add Mor 51 35 *S* ⲙⲟⲩⲗⲁϩⲝ opp ϭⲣⲟⲙⲡⲉ.

—— 15 up, read ϩ.

171 *a* 10, add Ps 80 3 *B* ⲉϩⲟⲟⲩ ⲙⲙ. (*S* ϩ. ⲉⲧⲟⲩⲟⲡϩ ⲉⲃⲟⲗ) εὔσημος.

173 *b* 11, ⲙⲁⲡⲏⲩ is properly sg, *cf* *mniw-iꜣwt* (Černý in *Miscel Vatic* 1939) & ⲙⲉⲡⲏⲩ *A*² ManiH (p 22*).

176 *a* 11 up, read (*S* ϣⲓ, *F* ⲁⲓⲡⲓ).

176 *b* 19, ⲙⲡⲟⲧ properly a dual (Sdff 146).

178 *a* 8, *until* is ⲉⲙⲡⲉ-, not ⲙⲡⲉ- (Polotsky).

182 *a* 6, for ? read 5 21.

183 *b* *ult.* As name Πμέρεζ (Preisigke).

184 *a* 11 up, read 215.

184 *b* 4 up, add ⲙⲁⲥⲓ† *F*(*v* ϣⲁⲣⲱⲧ).

186 *a* 6, read ϣⲟϣ.

186 *b* 17, add Ora 4 20 *S* ⲧⲙⲁⲥⲓⲟ.

187 *a* 11 up, on ⲙⲉⲥⲧⲉ &c, GöttGA '06 588.

187 *b* 19, add ⲙⲉⲥⲉϩ *F* Ora 4 203.

—— 13 up, add f *B* ⲓϯ (Lu 15 8 var).

188 *a* 5, add Dioscorides, μιθ = σέλινον κηπαῖον.

189 *a* 2 up, add Col 2 19 *B*(*S* ⲧⲣⲁ) ἁφή. (*cf* ⲙⲟⲩⲧ).

190 *a* 20 up, add ⲁⲙⲁⲧⲉ *S*ᵃ Miss 1 387.

193 *b* 13, the two are distinct, *v* Spiegelberg *Orakel-glossar* p 60 (HT).

—— 16 ⲙⲁⲧⲉⲙ Is 30 24 θρῖναξ Sym (Möhle).

195 *a* 5 up. In Si ⲙ. is qual, not nn.

—— 3 up, ⲙⲁϩⲉ is *ell*, but transl doubtful.

195 *b* 4 up, ⲙⲁⲧⲛⲉ prob = BM 310 67 *S* ⲙⲙⲱⲧⲛ (*v* OLZ '31 842).

198 *a* 18 up, for ⲟⲟⲉ read ⲟⲩⲱⲧⲣ.

199 *a* 15 up, read ϫⲁⲣⲱⲧⲉⲛ.

203 *a* after 22 up, add c ϩⲓⲣⲡ- *S*: Mor 51 38 ⲙ. ϩⲛ ϩⲉⲛϣⲃⲟⲧ...ϩ. ⲡⲣⲟ *strike upon*.

203 *a* 7 up, delete this.

206 *a* 12 up, add ManiP 46 &c *A*² physician opens ⲡⲉϥⲙ. *drug-box*.

206 *b* 22 up, also prob TillBau 124.

208 *a* 8, read ⲙⲁϣⲉ.

—— 16 up, read ⲙⲁⲣⲟⲩⲁⲗ *S*, -ⲃⲁⲗ *B*.

—— 13 up, in Mor 48 ⲙⲉϩⲟⲩⲁⲗ.

209 *a* 22, delete As nn to ⲡⲉ. *Cf* 211 *b*.

210 *b* 11, read *A* 2 279.

211 *a* 13, add PBad 5 376 *S* ⲙⲟⲣⲟⲩ ⲙⲙⲁϩⲕⲱⲕ.

211 *b* 7 up, add ⲙⲉϩⲧⲉ *A*² ManiK 91.

212 *a* 11, add ⲙ. ⲛϭⲣⲟϭ, *v* ϭⲣⲟⲟϭ s f.

213 *a* 22 up.   Primary meaning *chisel* (Gardiner, *cf* PSBA 21 270).

213 *b* 10, add BP 6910 9 ⲙⲓⲝⲗ (*ter*).

215 *a* 15 up, to 216 *b* 23.

The treatment of ⲛ- needs entire revision (Sdff, Gardiner).

218 *b* 19 up, read ⲉϩⲟⲧⲉ- only (Polotsky).

219 *a* 18, add ⲛⲉⲉ *A*² ManiK 111.

219 *b* 7, after ⲛⲁⲩ† *S* add *F* Lam 1 2.

224 *a* after 13, add

ⲛⲁⲕⲟⲧ *S* nn m, part of lamp, *v* ϩⲱⲧ(ⲉ)ⲡ qual TurM 18, & ϩⲏⲃⲥ s f.

226 *b* 19, read ⲥⲟⲉⲣⲧⲉⲣ.

227 *a* 9, ⲛⲁⲡⲉ-, add *F* Pcod 39 (*cf* OLZ '33 418). ⲛⲁⲡⲉ- *S* rare.

227 *b* 13 up, add Cant 5 16 *F* ⲛⲏⲓⲓ (*S* ϩⲉⲗϭⲉ) γλυκασμός.

229 *a* 11.   *Cf* ⲛⲟⲩⲥⲓ magical name PGM 1 198, 2 123.

229 *b* 20, add ⲛⲟⲩⲧ f *A*² ManiK 114, *receptacle*.

—— *ult.* *Cf* Gardiner JEA 14 86 ff.

230 *b* 22, add ⲛⲧⲱⲣⲉ *A*² ManiP 209 & *cf* PGM 2 25 μασυ ⲛⲧⲟⲣⲓ (or ? ϩⲧⲱⲣⲉ).

232 *a* 17, ⲛⲧⲱⲟϣⲡ occurs Job 7 13, *ib* 31 8, ViSitz 172 4 19, P 131⁴ 104, BM 343.

233 *a* 12 up, read ⲥⲙⲉϩ.

235 *a* 8, read ноγ- (Sdff).

236 *a* after 4, add

    наϫ BM 1020, prob read нат.

—— 18 up. *Cf* اخيِّ *fever* (Worrell).

238 *a* 3 up. *Cf* Va 68 178 реч† ϩап пшате (*sic*).

238 *b* ult, add ShViK 934 222 ϩно пн.

239 *b* 16, in Gött ar 114 133 نام فيه قليلا.

—— 18, read ϩεм-, ϩамн.; 19 read пιϩ.; 20 read نفس, not منِّ.

—— 26, add ? печер- *B* Pro 6 3 (*SA* тωбс παρο-ξύνειν).

239 *b* 27, начр- in п. тωρε Sa 14 18 *S*(*sic l* Polotsky, var мнтречр т.) φιλοτιμία. *Cf* ManiK 132.

240 *b* 3, read ورم.

—— 5, add ? Ora 4 20 for teeth-cutting † сϩбннтε пмоγλαϩ епечнутε.

241 *a* 5 up, read *sewing*.

241 *b* 20 up, add наϩ- *S*, *v* шλαϩ (шλϩч). наϩ⸱ & наγϩ⸱ distinct vbs : *cast off* & *turn* (AZ 73 137).

242 *b* penult, cf Φερετνοῦις POxy 937.

—— 5 up, read (наϩпϩ) (Sdff).

244 *b* 4 up, for ϩенϩωп read пеϩнωϩ (Lagarde).

246 *b* 20, should be о ппϩот, *cf* JEA 18 194 (Polotsky).

—— after 10 up, add

    наϩтε *S* among metal (?) implements : Pap *penes* BHStricker.

249 *a* 26, for ϩεмсι read рωтеб.

—— 17 up, add Ora 4 25 *S* ноγϫт, *ib* 27 ноϫт⸱.

249 *b* 15 up, пεϫпεϫ а- *A²* ManiK 220 *take disgust at* or sim.

—— 9 up, *l* ноγшс.

250 *a* 16, add MR 5 54 *F* оγнат пеϩι *long life*.

254 *a* 7, for ωтϩ read оγωтϩ.

—— 31, add name папобϩε Bodl ostr 428, Πανόβε ? (Preisigke).

254 *b* 13 up, read

    оειλε (misprinted after 1st proof).

255 *a* 5 up, ϫαϫομн *S* ViK 4734 (*ter*) cannot be this word.

257 *a* 12 up, for ωтϩ read оγωтϩ.

257 *b* *after* 15 up, add

    ошмεч *v* шϫм.

258 *b* 11, read Ps.

260 *b* 21, for -тε- read -тε.

261 *a* after 6, add

    пак *S*, *air hole* : MS Cai Copt Mus поγοεπ... ετπτ[пε мп]пак = C 89 133 *B* ϫαθноγ = Va Ar 172 منور 77.

261 *a* after 28, add

    пкпιϭε *S* nn f, meaning unknown : Ostr *penes* Crum among edibles соε мп.

—— after 29, add

    паλε *S* nn f, measure of shadow on sundial : MIE 3 580 ff †ε мп., сεптε εмп., оγпεшп., оγп. поγωт. *Cf* таϭсε.

—— 15 up, add паλαλωωт † *A²* ManiH 4.

261 *b* 18 up, read كُ (Polotsky).

262 *b* 27, add пλаϫ *Sf* Mor 32 41.

262 *b* 10 up, for п. read ф.

264 *a* 20, read μεθιστ.

—— 17 up, read ٱلاذ (Polotsky).

267 *a* 8. Delete this. пара prob = ٮٯٮ.

271 *b* 23, read 14†.

272 *b* 14 up, add Hos 13 15 *A* διαστέλλειν (Grossouw).

273 *b* 6, add f *B* ə† C 43 80.

—— 8 up, for *long-footed* read *with well-covered foot* (Polotsky).

276 *b* after 21 add

    патсε *v* паϭсε.

—— 3 up, Hos 13 12 in BM 729 27 фωпϩ (Burmester).

279 *a* 11, add P 129¹⁴ 84 *S* church птаγпошпеч ерос ῇ ἐχειρ.

279 *b* 12 up, not Sh, but Chrysostom (PG 63 206 ἐπιμαίνεσθαι for both).

282 *b* 2, for *SF* read *Sf*.

283 *b* 18 up, add HM 2 17 оγп. мпетра = Miss 4 730 паϩч *q v* (281 *a*).

285 *a* 16 & 10 up, пεϫа-, пετϫач *O* better.

—— 14 up, add пεϫετнутп P 131⁴ 126.

285 *b* 24, read اُ (Polotsky).

—— 6 up, поϭε sim in 3 Kg 21 25 (Mus 50 200), where = ? κατ᾽ εὐθύ.

286 *b* 21, add паϭλε *A²* ManiK 57 мп. ппшнп.

287 *b* 2, Gk is περὶ τῶν λαληθέντων, Ryl *Gk & Lat Papyri* 3 21 6.

—— 19, after рн add φῶς.

291 *b* 16, delete (?). *V* Pro 4 20.

292 *a* 9 up, read ачракч (Grossouw).

293 *a* 22 up, read

    рекрιкε (CSchmidt).

295 *a* 13 up, мптрωмε *funeral* ? (Gunn).

299 *a* 9 up, add сγрω *S* J 108 11.

301 *b* 4, after *S* 1° add & PBad 5 376.

301 b 15 up, ϣⲣⲱⲓⲥ for ⲟⲩϣⲏ ⲛⲣⲟⲉⲓⲥ (Jernstedt).

303 a 23, MS has ⲥⲁⲣⲁⲧϥ.

—— 23 up, add Mic 5 5 A ἐπιβαίνειν (Grossouw).

304 b 17, delete ⲣⲁⲧⲉ, var ⲣⲁⲥⲧⲉ (ViK 9543).

306 a 1. Cf Griffith's suggestion AZ 46 133 n.

309 a 24, delete ⲣⲁϣⲓ† B.

—— 26, read ἀρκεῖν (CSchmidt).

310 a 8 up, read ⲕⲁϩ ϩⲟⲩⲣ. (P 8) & P 91 A² tree ⲉⲧϩⲟⲩ ⲣⲉϣⲣⲉϣ.

310 b 20 up, ϩ. m in Mt 16 2 (Sdff).

311 a 25 up, add ⲣⲁϩⲧ- Mor 29 31 Sſ.

314 a 3, Mani in P 196 bis.

314 b 26. Similar phrases, Raccolta…GLumbroso 283, Kr 228 3.

315 b 24, read ὀφθ. (Allberry).

—— 20 up, after F v Till HM 1 39.

316 a 17, بزّار is grain-dealer (Kazimirski).

—— 16 up, read ⲥⲉ, not ⲥⲉ- (HT).

318 a 21, after nn add m.   ⲥⲱ = θρύον ROC 37 57.

318 b 5 up, read Ps 50 ὁλοκαύτωμα.

319 a 21, read 8 228².

319 b 2 up, add Lev 18 3 B(Va, S ϩⲃⲏⲩⲉ) ἐπιτήδευμα, confused ? with ἀπαιδευσία.

321 a 22 up, read κωμῳδεῖν.

—— 11 up, for λαγνεία read κῶμος.

321 b 28, for 218 read 2 118.

323 a 4, read ⲥⲉⲃⲑⲁⲓⲟⲩ.

—— 20 up, after ⲥⲁⲃⲧⲉ add Sᵃ RE 10 34.

—— 19 up, after SB add F Jer 26 9 (Mus 49 173).

323 b ult, read προσδοκᾶν.

325 a 25 for A read SA.

—— 6 up, read ἀντλεῖν; b 19 up do.

325 b 17, draw & gather prob not same word. (Polotsky).

328 b 8, for 32 read 3 2.

329 b 19, add Ostr penes Crum S ⲁⲓⲥⲕⲩⲣⲕⲣ ϩⲁⲡⲁⲣⲟϣ.

—— 23, add ViK 9330 S ⲛⲧⲡⲥⲕⲣⲕⲣ ϩⲛⲉⲡⲓⲑⲩⲙⲓⲁ ⲛⲓⲙ.

330 a 17, for 107 read 171.

—— 12 up, delete ⲥⲟⲗϩ B & in next line Job 21 &c & for tr read intr.

330 b penult, delete -ⲉⲛ (Polotsky).

332 a 13 up, for ⲥⲗⲥⲟⲗϩ read ⲥⲗⲥⲱⲗϩ (TillOster 17).

333 a 19 up, for another explanation v AZ 43 88.

335 a 25, for 28 read 23.

336 b 15, add ? ⲥⲁⲙⲑⲉ, v ⲗⲁϫⲛⲉ.

337 a 11, add ⲁⲛⲥⲉⲙⲙⲓ F Mk 10 4 (Mor 21 141).

—— 13, add † ⲁ. F: Mt 13 30 (SB ϫⲱ) εἰπεῖν; 1 Cor 7 10 (S = Gk, B ϩⲟⲛϩⲉⲛ) παραγγέλλειν.

339 a 3, add repose, tranquillity: K 94 B ⲛⲓⲥ, هدو, اطمان, a hymn (Burmester) †ⲥ. ⲙⲛⲁⲛⲁⲧⲓⲁ زنزله.

339 b 1, add ⲥⲁⲙⲓⲧ F: Eccl 2 6 (S = Gk) κολυμβήθρα & BM 1203 S ⲧⲥⲁⲙⲛⲏⲧ.

340 a 14 up, read † ϩⲧⲏϩ.

340 b 18 up, add Ostr penes Crum ⲥ ⲉⲙⲡⲧⲉ(ⲛ)ⲡⲉⲣⲥⲟⲥ ⲉⲓ ⲁⲡⲛϩⲏⲧ ⲉⲙⲡⲧϥⲥ. ⲉⲣⲟⲓ ⲛⲧⲉⲣⲉⲛϣⲁϫⲉ ϣⲱⲡⲉ.

345 b 15, read Zech 9 8.

346 b after 10, add

ⲥⲱⲛⲧ   v ⲥⲱⲙⲧ.

—— 11 add F Jer 26 27 (Mus 49 174).

—— 6 up, examples with ⲛⲟϭ should be under b (Polotsky).

348 a 19, read -ⲟⲩϥ Sᵃ Sſ.

349 a 14 up, ⲥⲡ- is constr of ⲥⲟⲛ; ⲧ- properly for (ḥ꜀)t, not f art, v AZ 51 138.

350 b 28, prob means at a given moment (Polotsky).

352 a 6, add ⲣ ⲥⲁⲥ. S OraChrPeriod 4 49.

353 a 19, ⲥⲡⲁⲧⲟⲩ A² f ManiP 220 (ter).

353 b 18 up, for ⲧⲱⲛ ⲉϩ. ⲉϫ. read ⲃⲱⲧⲥ ⲉ-.

355 a 1. Cf Mor 33 (A III) fol 14 Meletians whom Egyptians call ⲛⲥⲁⲣⲁⲕⲱⲧⲉ (Hyvernat). Cf ManiP, Introd xxi.

356 b 8. Cf name Πσαρσωρτωϩ (v ⲧⲱϩ chaff).

358 b 6, for ⲥⲟϭⲓ prob read ϭⲓⲥⲓ (so 1 var).

—— 11, add F ⲟⲩⲕⲁⲣⲁⲕⲁⲗⲓ ⲛⲥⲁⲥⲓ ViK 76.

359 a 21 up, ⲥⲁⲁⲧⲉ C 99 10, l ? ⲣ ⲥⲁⲁⲧⲉ.

363 a 19, read Peterson.

—— 20, read ⲙⲡⲉⲥ.

—— 11 up, read μηρυκισμόν.

363 b 19 up, add ⲥⲧⲃⲉⲓϩ F(Cant 9 17).

—— 17 up, Jer 31 7 is for ⲥⲉⲃⲑⲁⲓⲟⲩ, v ⲥⲟⲃⲧ (Calice).

364 a 14, c. ⲉⲧⲁⲥⲡⲉ understand, as occasionally in Egyptian (Gunn).

—— 17 up, add B C 86 305 ⲛⲁⲓ ⲉⲧⲁϥⲥⲟⲟⲙⲟⲩ ϩⲁⲣⲟϥ.

366 b 11, read ϣⲕⲗⲕⲉⲗ.

369 a 19 up, ⲥⲁⲩⲃⲟⲩ also Mk 4 28 (Mus 49 189).

370 a 2, add ⲥⲓⲛⲟⲩⲱⲛ F Lam 4 8.

371 a 14, add ViK 9622 157 capable ⲉⲥ. ⲙⲡⲉⲓⲛⲟϭ ⲡⲗⲁⲟⲥ ⲉⲧⲥⲟⲣⲙ.

371 b 10 up, for ϩⲓ† read ϩⲓⲟⲩⲓ.

374 b 13, delete ⲥⲁⲓϣ A².

—— 14 up, add Lam 5 13 S ⲥⲁϣ ⲛϣⲉ ξύλον stocks (B ϣⲉ only).

375 a 25, add ShMing 89 ϣⲁⲅⲭⲉⲩ ϩⲉⲡⲥⲛϣⲉ (l prob ⲭⲏⲩ ⲛⲥ.).

377 b 17, ⲥⲁϩⲧ⳽ (cf also ⲥⲓϩⲉ).

379 b 13 up, ⲥⲁϩⲧ⳽ (cf also ⲥⲱϣⲧ).

380 a 17, add ⲥⲁϩⲏⲅⲧ† ShViK 9066.

381 b 17, add ⲥϩⲏⲅⲧ† S 4 Kg 19 19 (Polotsky).

384 a 27, add ⲥⲁⲥ̄ⲟ B Va 61 210 ⲛⲓⲥ. mixing their colours ζωγράφος (v CCVa 1 429).

—— 15 up, 9525 (12) is now 9536.

384 b 9. In Va 58 c. πομφόλυξ.

384 b after 16, add

ⲥⲭⲏⲗ S nn (?), meaning?: RE 10 34 (collated) ⲙⲡⲟⲩϣⲱⲗⲥ̄ ⲟⲩϩⲙⲟⲩ ⲉⲣⲟⲥ ⲟⲩⲇⲉ ⲥ. ⲉⲩⲣⲟ.

—— 17. Two words here confused: *sink & press down* (Kuentz). As nn prob BP 10587 S ⲟⲩⲥⲱϩⲙ ⲡϩⲏⲧ ⲙⲡⲟⲩϣⲧⲟⲣⲧⲣ.

385 a 4 up, not Sh, but Chrysostom (PG 63 206 om).

385 b 15 up, add ⲗ]ⲉⲃⲥⲉ(ϩ)ⲡⲓ F προστάσσων Is 55 4 (*Chester Beatty Bibl. Pap.* VI, p xii).

386 b 5, for ϣⲱϣ read ϩⲓⲟⲅⲓ ⲉⲃⲟⲗ.

—— 23 up, after 4 Kg 2 8 add εἰλεῖν.

—— 11 up, add P 54 154 B among weapons ϩⲁⲛⲥⲁϩⲥⲁϩ عيدان.

387 a 2, add Ryl 382 S ϣⲭⲁⲧ.

387 b 14 up, read S(var ⲣⲉϥϭ.)A(CSchmidt).

391 a 3, read ἐνδοξότ.

392 b 9, ⲧⲁ- also BM 583 13 F ⲛⲃ̄ⲧⲁ ⲡⲉⲕⲁⲡⲁⲉⲓⲕ ⲛⲏⲡ.

393 b 8 up, read πολιορκεῖν.

395 b 23, read παρεμβάλλειν.

396 a 11 up, add My 121 S ⲑ representing dry land ⲡⲉⲧⲟ ϣⲟⲩⲱⲩ, surrounded by ⲟⲕⲓⲁⲛⲟⲥ.

396 b 11 up, also A² ManiK 221.

397 a 16, ⲧⲁⲓⲃⲉ, -ⲃⲓ from ḏbꜣ·t; ⲧⲏ(ⲏ)ⲃⲉ, ⲑⲏⲃⲓ from ṯb·t (Sdff).

397 b 1, for ⲧⲁⲅⲟ read ⲧⲟⲅⲟ.

—— 21, in recipes ⲧ.? pustules or sim, cf K 77 ⲛⲓⲧⲉⲃ املة (v Dozy 2 726). R 2 1 71 ⲧ.=articulations of spine.

400 a 8 up, add Am 7 13 A(Grossouw).

401 b 7 up, for *from* read *form*.

402 a 8, var *Mart.d.heil.Viktor*, ed. Lemm 7 ⲧⲃ̄ⲧ.

—— 15, add ⲧⲁⲃϩ- F Jo 16 26 (Mus 49 192), Mani P 44.

411 a 23, var ViK 9223 68 ϭⲗⲟⲙ.

—— 26, read ⲉϫⲛ.

—— 21 up, read *Amenemope*.

411 b 23. Cf? ⲉⲗⲟⲯ (D'Arcy Thompson).

414 a 25, for ὁρᾶν read δεικνύναι (Grossouw), B diff.

417 b 17, for (Jo) read (JoMa).

419 b 2, add ⲟⲩ PBaden 5 402, 406.

—— 6, ⲧⲡⲏⲟⲟⲩⲥ⳽ also BM 1139.

421 a 18 up, add Mor 32 46 Sᶠ ⲁⲓⲧⲟⲛϩ (l ⲧⲱ.) ⲛⲛⲁϩⲓⲥⲉ ⲧⲏⲣⲟⲩ am relieved, refreshed.

422 a 21, is a place-name (*Gnomon* 9 341).

425 a 2, as hand in ⲛⲁϥⲣⲧ. Sa 14 18 S(sic l), Mani K 132, 210 A².

427 a 27 up, for *upper arm* read *assistance*.

431 b 16, ⲧⲣⲟⲡⲣⲛ vb tr, Ostr *penes* Crum ϣⲗⲟⲡ ⲛϩⲣⲉ ...ⲡⲣⲱⲙⲉ ⲧⲣⲟⲡ[ⲣⲛ] ⲙⲙⲟϥ.

—— 12 up, read ⲉⲣ ϩⲟϯ.

—— 9 up, before Sh add εὐλαβεῖσθαι.

432 b 28, add ? شرش red & green ribbon (HAWinkler *Bauern* 85).

—— 20 up, read ϩⲓϫⲛ-.

436 b ult, read ϣⲗⲁϩ.

439 b 5, read ثياب.

—— 18 up, read προσδεῖσθαι.

440 a 10, read Mani 1.

—— 7 up, for ⲥⲁⲣⲁⲑ. read ϩⲣⲟⲩⲣ vb.

440 b 8, read ϫⲡⲧ.

444 b 1, 2, delete & v ϫⲟⲉⲓⲧ vb.

—— 4, for Jos read Jo.

450 a 5 on Mic 5 1 v OLZ '37 162.

—— 20, read 386.

458 b 2, add PBad 5 401, 410 F ⲑⲗⲁ ⲉⲃⲁⲗ among evils invoked, paral ϣⲁⲣⲃⲁ.

459 a 17 up, Zedekiah at mill, v DeV 2 91 n.

461 a 19 up, add ⲧⲩⲣⲕⲟ S Si 39 36 (collated).

461 b 2, for *repress* read prob *make heavy* (Ora 4 417).

—— 6, for ⲧ, ⲁ. read ⲧⲁ.,

—— 30, read (ⲉ)ⲡⲕⲉⲉⲥ (Polotsky).

462 b 15 up, for ϫⲣⲟ read ⲱⲣϫ.

463 a 8, read Ac 27 41 SB ἐρ.

464 a 7 up. Prob = preceding word: *tare*. Cf? ⲛⲧⲏϭ & F ϯϫⲓ Cant 4 13, 7 13.

465 b in upper margin read ⲧϭⲁ(ⲉ)ⲓⲟ.

466 a 19 up, prob caus of ⲧⲱⲱϭⲉ, v p 752 a.

467 a 17, ϩⲉ=ﻻ in Ar, v Mt 27 41 S Balestri (Polotsky).

468 b 5 up, read 'uncertain'.

470 a 8 up, read ϫⲉⲡⲉϥⲁⲟⲩⲁⲧ.

—— 2 up, F also ⲟⲩⲉ⳽: Cant 2 11 ⲛⲁⲟⲩⲉϥ ἑαυτῷ, ib 4 6 ⲛⲁⲟⲩⲉⲓ ἐμαυτῷ (Kropp).

470 b 12 up, add tr (?): Jon 4 8 B(SA diff) ἀπολέγειν.

472 b 13 up, or l ϫι ογαιϣ ʌ-. V ManiP 9 n, ib K 107, 203 (Allberry).

—— 11 up, add ⲛⲟⲩⲁⲓ A² ManiP 152.

473 a 18, read advb.

474 b after 28, add ⲙⲛⲧⲣⲟⲅⲟ S Deu 1 12 ἀντιλογία prob = ⲣ ⲟⲩⲱ, cf Mor 31 198 when ye repent ϣⲁⲓ† ⲉⲣⲟⲩⲱ ⲉⲁⲣⲱⲧⲛ, saying &c.

476 a ult, read ⲁⲓⲃⲉ, often in ManiP. Cf Berl Wörterb 1 6 ib Brandstempel (HT).

480 a 16, delete comma before ⲡⲱⲛⲉ.

483 b after 8, add

ⲟⲩⲱⲛ in ϣϭⲉ (v ϭⲱϣ 1°) ⲡⲟⲩⲱⲛ ⲙⲡⲉϥⲁⲛ†- ⲥⲧⲟⲙⲁⲭⲟⲥ Mor 32 23 (var R 1 5 49 ⲡⲉϥⲕⲉⲉⲥ ⲉⲁⲙ- ⲡⲉϥⲥⲧⲱⲙⲁⲭⲟⲥ), meaning ?

484 a penult, for S² read S¹.

485 a 10.up, read ϫⲓⲛ- A.

488 b 18, delete O. It applies to preceding §, which should join this.

490 a 4, is f in ManiP 21, 151.

491 a after 16 up, add

(ⲟⲩⲁⲣⲟⲩⲣ), ⲟⲩⲣⲟⲩⲱⲣ⳿ v ⲉⲃⲟⲣⲃⲣ.

491 b 9, for that read thou.

493 a 5 up, add ⲃⲱⲧ B in ϣⲁⲣⲃⲱⲧ.

497 b 19, after comma add sim Leyd 402 inf.

498 a 23 up, delete ⲉⲧⲁⲉ A² which = ⲁⲑⲁⲉ B (v p 532 b, Polotsky).

499 a 5, read ⲡⲟⲩⲱ ⲁⲃ. (now ManiK 54).

501 b 3 up, ⲟⲩⲱϣ ? Thursday, cf TillBau 121, Orat Cyp 264 (Polotsky).

504 b ult, in Va 58 = συντρίβειν (PG 89 1088).

508 b, in upper margin read ⲟⲩⲓⲉⲉ.

509 b 6 up, add ⲟⲩ. ⲉⲉⲟⲩⲛ ⲉ-: ShP 130⁴ 99 ⲉϥϣⲁⲛ- ⲟⲩ. ⲉⲉ. ⲉⲛϣⲱⲛⲉ if he have another attack of sickness.

511 b 8, var Mart.d.heil.Viktor ed. Lemm 29 † ⲑⲏⲡ ⲉϫⲛ̅ⲧⲉϥⲁⲡⲉ.

—— 12, also S ⲟⲩϫⲁⲓⲧⲉ BG 69.

513 a 3 up, add S ⲉⲉⲣⲁⲓ, v ϭⲣⲓⲙ.

513 b 14 up, Gk misunderstood: hand is robber's, not John's & ⲟⲩⲉϫⲟⲩⲱϫⲥ = ἀποκρύπτων or ? (PG 89 1109 inf) ἐκράτει.

520, 521 in upper margins read ⲱⲗ.

521 b 10 up, better as P 43 126 ‎اِجِل.

522 a 22 up, read ἀνάτασις.

522 b 23 up, add prob B ⲉⲱⲗⲉⲙ TstAb 242.

523 a 2, add F Ps 34 25 (Mus 49 180).

529 a 13 up, delete '9th letter of alphabet'.

529 b 24 up, read Am.

531 a 15, read ⲥⲁϫⲓ.

531 b 14 up, read ‎عِذ.

—— 6 up, delete ⲉϭ.

532 a 22, not Sh, but Chrysostom (PG 63 206 σκια- τροφία).

532 b 25, add Pachomiana Latina 157 (cf Mus 40 38) books to be returned at even ⲛϥ[ⲱ]ⲧⲉ ⲉⲣⲱⲟⲩ fasten doors of cupboard.

—— 13 up, add ViK 240 S ⲧⲁⲗⲟ ⲟⲩⲁⲧⲁⲉ ⲉⲡⲛⲁⲧ (l ⲟⲩⲟⲩⲁⲧⲉⲉ Till).

535 b 5. In Va 58 ʌ. = σπινθήρ (PG 55 559).

—— 18, for ⲉⲱⲣ read ⲥⲱⲉⲣ.

536 b 2 up, add ⲉⲣⲓ† F EpJer 9 (Polotsky).

538 a 21, read συνεπιτιθέναι ἐπί (Grossouw).

539 a 21, after SB add F(Mus 49 189) ⲡⲉϥⲟⲩⲁⲉⲥ.

—— 12 up, ⲱϫ here idle, slothful.

540 b 28, ⲃⲉϭⲧϥ from *ⲃⲓϭⲉ = B ⲃⲓϫⲓ (Polotsky).

541 b 21 up, semicolon after (ⲉ)ⲃⲁⲗ (omitted after proof).

—— 19 up, add MIF 9 26 S ⲡⲉϣⲧⲉⲡⲕⲁⲉ ⲉϣϭⲓ ⲉⲁ-.

543 b ult, ϣⲉ should ? be ϣⲉⲡⲓ, as in ib 4.

546 a 11. Possible pl ϣⲉⲉⲩ q v.

551 a after 4 up, add

ϣⲛⲓⲃⲓ B v ϣⲛ̅ⲅⲉ.

554 b 8 up, delete nn.

555 a 6, for as nn read prob vb.

—— 8. V also ϣⲱⲣⲃ.

—— 14. As name ? Σαθουλ (Ryl 255).

—— 25. Cf ? DM 1 25 pyšteh 'y (gloss ϣⲧⲉⲩ ⲛⲓ).

556 b 6 up, read 76.

557 b 10 up, add ⲉⲱⲗ S BMar 160.

558 a 22 up. Cf p 697 a, Z 233.

564 a after 7, in place-name ⲡⲉⲣⲡϣⲙ (BM 585).

565 a 8, delete ⲣ.

567 a 13. Cf AM 313.

568 b 19, add ϣⲟⲟⲡⲉ.

571 b 9 up. For meaning v ManiP 216 n.

579 a ult, read ⲟⲩⲧⲱ[ⲅ] ⲛⲛ- (Polotsky).

585 a 5 up, ϣⲉⲣⲥ., ϣⲉⲗⲥ. should stand after ϣⲣ- ⲉⲟⲟⲩⲧ ib b 4 (Polotsky).

586 b 1, S not ⲧⲏⲩ but [..]ⲣⲟⲟⲃ, prob related to ϣⲁⲣⲃⲁ.

589 b after 15, add

ϣⲉⲉⲥ, ϣⲏⲥ v ϫⲏⲏⲥ.

591 a 28, ϣⲧⲃ̅ⲟ not thus; cf 595 b 16 (Polotsky).

592 b 13, for ? ϫⲱⲗⲉ.

594 b after 16 up, add

ϣⲧⲉ v ϣⲓⲕⲉ.

595 b 16, v also 591 a 28.

599 a 10. *Cf* rather ḫtj (Kuentz).

— 13, read نچت (Kuentz. MS has 'ܙ).

601 a 18, for ⲙⲛϣⲉⲩ *v* ⲙⲉϣⲉ p 201 b. ManiP 210 also ⲙⲛϣⲉⲩ ⲣⲱ ⲛⲧⲁⲩ ⲛⲁⲧϭⲉⲃⲁⲟⲙⲁⲥ, *ib* 135 ⲙⲛϣⲉⲩ ⲅⲁⲣ ⲁⲧⲅⲁⲧⲉ.

605 b 4 up, read بحيرة.

607 b in upper margin read ϣϣⲉ.

611 a after 6, add ϣⲃⲱⲱⲥ *SA*'nn, meaning as ϣϥⲱ: EpApp 1 21, ManiK 153.

612 a 1, Mk 15 46 *F*(Mus 51 233) ⲉⲁϥϣⲉϥϣⲱϥ(ϥ) (*S* ϣⲱⲧϣⲧ, *B* ϣⲏⲕ) λατομεῖν.

612 a 8, read ⲉϥⲥⲗⲉϭ-.

615 b 12, after ⲥⲁ. *A²* add *F* & before *B* ⲥⲟⲝⲛⲓ (AZ 61 110 n).

— 31, after *F* add ⲥⲁ.

623 b 17. *Cf* above 595 b 16.

625 b 2, add ϥⲧⲉⲩ ⲉⲡⲟⲟⲩ Ac 10 30 (Polotsky).

631 a 16, = ϩⲁⲣⲡⲥ 703 b (Kuentz).

637 a 18 up, for 223 read 233.

647 a 7, here ? belongs MG 25 118 n *B* ⲙⲛϥ ⲛϩⲟ ⲛϫⲱⲙ *page of book*.

— 19 up, add ShC 73 99 *S* ⲉⲓⲣⲉ ⲙⲛϩⲟ ⲙⲡⲣⲱⲙⲉ.

650 b 2, *B* pl of ϩⲟⲓ ? in C 41 42 ⲑⲙⲟⲩⲓ ⲙⲡⲁⲡⲉϩⲛⲟⲩ = Miss 4 395 جزيرة السوّاق (ⲉϩⲏⲩ is *S* pl of ⲉϩⲉ).

654 b ult, add Va 58 153 *B* ⲙⲉⲧⲣⲉϥⲉⲣ ϩⲉⲃⲃⲱⲛ κακουργία.

661 a 8, Delete this ; ⲉⲥϩⲁⲕ = اسق *pound* (Chassinat).

662 b 6 up, *cf* ? hk3·t (Berl *Wörterb* 3 174 Kuentz).

670 b 21, add ⲗⲉⲙⲗⲉⲙ *B* Ps 54 163.

671 a 18, θαλαμηγός has Gk etymol & is phonetically difficult to equate with ϩⲁⲗⲙⲏϩⲉ (Kuentz).

672 b 13 up, add Ostr *penes* B. Groterjahn ⲛϩⲁⲗⲁϩⲱⲙ ⲉⲛⲧⲁⲕⲧⲁⲁϥ ⲡⲁⲓ ⲁⲃⲓⲕⲧⲱⲣ ϥⲓⲧϥ (Till).

674 a 18, with ϩⲁⲙ *cf* ϩⲁⲛ- 1° (Polotsky).

675 b 12, FR 96 should stand under ⲛⲧⲉ- (Polotsky).

684 b 1 ff. *Cf* Polotsky's review of Part V in JEA 25.

703 b 4 up, = ⲋⲟⲣⲡⲥ (Kuentz).

704 b 9, or *twist*, *cf* ϩⲣⲱⲧ (Kuentz).

708 b 15, read نخير.

711 a 24, read (κακό)μοχθος (Polotsky).

721 b 9, ⲣⲉϥⲣ ϩ. *coward* in BKU 1 31 5 (AZ 74 61).

723 a 11 up, Pap *penes* Maggs Bros. 1937, letter to ⲡⲉϥϫⲥ ⲡⲉⲓⲱⲧ ⲁⲡⲁ ϩⲏⲣⲁⲕⲗⲉⲓⲁⲏ ⲁⲩⲱ ⲡⲉϥⲣⲙⲣⲟ, so not related to *horse*.

724 b 25, add Mus 51 52 ⲟⲩϭⲟⲥⲙ ⲉϥⲣ ⲧⲙⲧⲱⲙ.

725 a 22 up, read συναρμόζειν.

— 8 up, read ἀνταλλάσσειν.

731 a 2 up, ϩⲟⲟⲩ qual of *ϩⲟⲩⲁⲓ (AZ 74 69).

732 b 4 up, here belongs ϩⲟⲩ ⲣⲉϣⲣⲉϣ p 310 a 8 up (Allberry).

740 b 20 up, read (?) ذڡم.

741 a 10, *serpent-charmer* confirmed by Synax 1 425 ساحر حاوى.

743 a 20 up, ϩⲡⲁⲥⲡϭ *A²* ManiK 209, so ϫⲁⲡϫⲡ prob not same.

755 b after 14, add ϫⲟⲥ *B* nn m, *saying*: Cat 55 ⲛⲓϫ. ϫⲉⲉⲩϯ ϩⲁⲛ (Mt 19 28), *ib* 155 ⲛⲓϫ. ϫⲉϥⲟⲟⲩ ⲛⲉⲙⲣⲁⲥϯ (Lu 13 32).

780 b 4 up, صير still name of a fish species at Luxor (HAWinkler).

787 b 18, read ⲡⲉⲧⲉⲡⲟⲥ.

ⲁ

ⲁ first letter of alphabet, called ⲁⲗⲫⲁ *S* (PS 353, Br 124, Leyd 458, P 131ᵇ 77, My 38) & *B* (Ap 1 8, K 1, Stern p 418), الف. As numeral = *one BF*, rarely *S* (Br 127) except in semi-Gk documents. Represents vowels unwritten in earlier hierogl., but sometimes visible in the half-consonants of later & of dem. Dialectal equivalents: **a.** *S* ⲁ = elsewhere (*AF*) ⲉ, ⲏ, as ⲁⲗ, ⲁⲅⲁⲡ, ⲃⲁⲣⲥⲉ, ⲙⲁ, ⲙⲁⲁⲃ, ⲛⲁⲣⲟⲩ, ⲣⲙⲙⲁⲟ, ⲟⲩⲁⲣⲉ, ⲣⲧⲁⲓ. **b.** *S* ⲁ = elsewhere ⲟ (*AB*), as ⲁⲛⲣ, ⲕⲁⲉ, ⲥⲛⲁⲩ. **c.** ⲁ elsewhere (mostly *B*) = *S* ⲉ, as ⲉⲃⲟⲧ, ⲉⲗⲟⲟⲗⲉ, ⲉⲅⲱ, ⲕⲉⲗⲉⲡⲕⲉⲅ, ⲙⲉⲣ-, ⲣⲉⲙⲛⲓϧⲉ, (or *A*) as ⲃⲉⲡⲓⲡⲉ, ⲉ-, ⲉⲣⲏⲩ, ⲉⲡⲉϩ. **d.** ⲁ elsewhere (*AF*) = *S* ⲟ, as ⲁⲗⲟⲩ, ⲉⲓⲟⲟⲣ, ⲕⲟⲉⲓⲣ, ⲗⲟ, ⲙⲁϣⲟ, ⲟⲉⲓⲙⲉ, ⲟⲟⲧⲉ, ⲣⲟⲟⲗⲉ & in causatives, as ⲧⲁⲗⲟ, ⲑⲃⲃⲓⲟ. **e.** *S* final ⲁ = *B* ⲁⲓ, as ⲛⲁ, ⲟⲩⲁ, ϣⲁ. **f.** *B* adds prosthetic ⲁ- in ⲁⲙⲟⲛⲓ, ⲁⲡⲁⲓⲱ, ⲁⲟⲩⲱ *await*, ⲁⲟⲩⲱⲛ, ⲁⲟⲩⲏⲣ, ⲁⲭⲟ, ⲁⲭⲡ, ⲁⲥ̌ⲟ, *F* in ⲁⲛⲟⲩϩ, *S*(?) in ⲁⲧⲟ. On changes from & to ⲁ in *AA*² *v* Rösch 35, El 27, AP *Einl* 14; in *S*ᵃ *v* Ep 1 236; in *F v* Asmus 16. Before final ϩ *SF* in 3-rad. words ⲁ sometimes replaces ě, as ⲉⲓⲱⲣⲁϩ, ⲥⲱⲟⲩⲁϩ (*cf* JKP 2 46 48 ⲥⲱⲟⲩϩⲁ), ⲱⲛⲁϩ.

ⲁ- *SABF* verbal prefix derived from ⲉⲓⲣⲉ, characterizes (*a*) perf, (*b*) pluperf, (*c*) aorist tenses, as (*a*) ⲁⲧⲉⲩϭⲟⲙ ⲱϫⲛ, ⲁⲕⲥⲱⲧⲉ ⲙⲡⲉⲕⲗⲁⲟⲥ, ⲡⲁⲓϭⲉ ⲛⲧⲁⲩϣⲱⲡⲉ, (*b*) ⲛⲉⲁⲩϣⲧⲟⲣⲧⲣⲡⲉ, (*c*) ϣⲁⲣⲉⲟⲩⲉⲓⲱⲧ ϣⲡϣⲏⲣⲉ, ϣⲁⲥⲣ ϣⲡⲏⲣⲉ.

ⲁ- *SABFO* (also ⲉ- *O*) imperat prefix of vbs ⲗⲟ, ⲛⲁⲩ, ⲟⲩⲱⲙ (*B* only, Ez 12 18, BSM 44), ⲟⲩⲱⲛ, ⲟⲩⲱϩ (*S* in ⲁⲟⲩⲱ, ⲁⲩⲱ *and*), ⲭⲱ; *v* Sethe *Verbum* 2 507, Spg *Dem Gram* 214, Sdff 331 (ⲁⲭⲱⲣⲙ is 2 sg f pf); also prefixed to special imperat forms: ⲁⲗⲓⲟⲅⲓ, ⲁⲙⲟⲩ &c, ⲁⲛⲓ &c, ⲁⲣⲓ, ⲁⲩ, ⲁⲅⲉⲓⲥ.

ⲁ- *A* prep *v* ⲉ-.

ⲁ- *SABF* (*B* rare, *A* El 44), ⲁⲩ- *B*, adv of indefiniteness, *about*; often with ⲛ- (rare ⲛⲛ-) prefixed; *v* AZ 51 122. **a.** of distance, mostly ⲛⲁ-, ⲛⲁⲩ-: Ge 21 16 *SB* ⲛⲁⲩ-, Jon 3 3 *B* ⲛⲁⲩ- (*SA* ⲉⲥⲛⲁⲣ) ὡσεί, Mt 14 24 *B* ⲛⲁⲩ- (*S* ⲛ-), Jo 21 8 *S* ⲛⲁ- (*B* ⲛⲁⲩ-), El 44 *A* ⲛⲁⲧⲉⲓⲟⲩⲉ ⲛⲥⲧⲁⲁ., N & E 39 339 *B* near village ⲁⲩⲧⲟ̄ϯ ⲙⲙⲅⲗⲗⲓⲟⲛ, MG 25 347 *B* distant from cell ⲉⲛⲁ̄ⲫⲟⲅⲱϣ ⲙⲓⲃ̄ ⲙⲙⲓⲗ., BM 524 *F* let them not dwell ⲛⲁϣⲏⲧ ⲙⲙⲓⲗ. ⲉⲡⲕⲱⲧⲓ, BMis 448 *S* when was distant ⲛⲁϣⲟⲙⲛⲧ ⲙⲙⲓⲗ. **b.** of height, depth: Nu 11 31 *S* ⲛⲡⲁ- (*B* ⲛⲁⲩ-) ὡσεί,

cf BAp 88, ShC 42 200 *S* down into earth ⲛⲁⲡϣⲱⲕⲉ ⲛⲟⲩϣⲛⲓ, SHel 55 *S* palace ⲉϥⲛⲁⲉⲣ ⲁϣⲉ ⲙⲙⲁⲣⲉ ⲛϫⲓⲥⲉ, AM 56 *B* plunged in river ⲛⲁⲩ̄ϯ ⲙⲙⲁϩⲓ, Mor 24 25 *F* pits dug ⲉⲛⲁⲡ̄ ⲙⲙⲉϩⲓ (*S* ⲛϣϥⲉ ⲛ-). **c.** of weight: Mk 6 37 *S* ⲛⲁ- (*B* Gk om), ShC 73 145 *S* ⲉⲛϣⲁⲩ ⲛⲁϯⲟⲩ ⲛⲃ̄ⲓⲣ (var ⲛ-), TstAb 168 *B* tears exceeded smiles ⲛⲁⲅⲓⲁ̄ ⲛⲕⲱⲃ ⲛⲥⲟⲡ. **d.** of number, mostly ⲁ-, ⲁⲩ-: Ex 32 28 *S* (*B* om) ⲁ- εἰς, Jos 7 4 *S* ὡσεί, 1 Kg 22 2 *S* ⲁ- ὡς, Ac 4 4 *S* ⲁϯⲟⲩ ⲛϣⲟ (var ⲛⲉ̄, *B* om) ὡσεί, Va 77 177 *B* ϩⲁⲡⲁⲑⲃⲁⲡⲉ ⲧⲟⲩⲛⲡⲓ (Gk om). **e.** of time: Dan 1 12 *B* (*S* Gk om), Ac 19 34 *S* ⲛⲁ- (var ⲛⲛⲁ-), *B* ⲛⲁⲩ- ὡς ἐπί acc, Mk 5 25 *S* ⲛⲁ- (*B* Gk om), Lu 8 42 *S* ⲁ- (*B* om) ὡς, Ro 4 19 *S* ⲁ- (*B* ⲛⲁⲩ, varr ⲁⲩ-, ⲁ-) ποῦ, MG 17 316 *S* ⲛⲉϥϩⲁⲭⲟⲩⲱⲧⲉ ⲛⲣⲟⲙⲡⲉ (*B ib* 5 om) περί acc, Est 4 11, Mk 9 21 *S* ⲉⲓⲥ ⲁ- (*B* Gk om), BAp 78 *S* ⲉⲓⲥ ⲁⲟⲩⲏⲣ ⲛⲛⲁⲩ, 1 Thes 2 17 *S* ⲛⲁ-, *F* ⲁ- (*B* Gk om), PSBA 10 398 *B* ⲛⲁⲡϣⲁⲩ ⲛⲟⲩⲟⲩⲛⲟϥ, *cf* Va 63 7 *B* loaves ⲛⲁⲡϣⲁⲩ ⲛϫ̄ⲱ ⲥ̌ⲁⲣⲱⲟⲩ (*S* BMis 374 ⲛⲁⲡϣⲓ).

ⲁ- in ⲁⲧⲟⲟⲧ⸗, ⲁⲡⲁⲧⲟⲟⲧ⸗ *v* ⲧⲱⲣⲉ (ⲧⲟⲟⲧ⸗).

ⲁ- in ⲁⲧⲱϥ *v* ⲡⲱ⸗ (ⲧⲱ⸗).

ⲁⲉⲓⲉ *A* *v* ϩⲁⲉⲓⲟ.

ⲁⲓⲁⲓ (ⲁⲁⲓ J 89 & 96) *SB*, ⲁⲓⲉⲩⲉ (Ex 2 10), ⲁⲉⲓⲉⲩⲧⲉ *A*, ⲁⲓⲉⲓ (Mor 38 103) *F*, ⲟⲓ *SBO*†, ⲁⲉⲓ *AO*†, vb **I.** intr, *increase in size, advance in age*: Ge 1 28 *SAB*, 35 11 *SB*, Jer 3 16 *SB*, Ac 7 17 *BF* (paral ⲁϣⲁⲓ), Mt 6 28 *B*, 13 30 *SBF*, *ib* 32 *BF* (*S* p ⲛⲟϭ), Jo 3 30 *B* (*S* ⲭⲓⲥⲉ) αὐξάνειν, Lammayer 37 *S* God's spirit ⲧⲣⲉⲩⲁ.= R 1 2 36 ⲁⲩⲝⲁⲛⲉ ⲙⲙⲟⲟⲩ, ROC 17 401 *B* ⲉⲁϥⲟⲣⲉⲡⲉⲡⲁⲣⲉⲧⲏ ... ⲁ. συναυξάν.; Ps 19 6 *SB*, 91 6 *S* (*B* ⲉⲣ ⲛⲓϣϯ), Pro 8 16 *SA* (*B* do), Ez 16 7 *SB* (paral ⲁϣⲁⲓ) μεγαλύνεσθαι; Ge 18 11 *S* (var ⲁⲗⲉ ⲉϩⲣⲁⲓ) *B*, Jos 13 1, 23 1 *S* (var do) *B*, Jth 16 23 *S*, 2 Mac 6 18 *A*, Lu 1 7 *SB* προβαίνειν; Is 44 14 *S* (*B* ϣⲓⲁⲓ) μηκύνειν, Ex 2 10 *A*, ROC 17 401 *B* ἀδρύνεσθαι, Job 14 8 *B* (*S* p ϩⲗⲗⲟ) γηράσκειν, BMar 159 *S* ⲡⲉⲛⲧⲁϥⲁ. ϩⲛⲑⲏⲗⲓⲕⲓⲁ πρεσβύτης εἶναι, Ge 7 17 *S* (*B* ⲛⲏⲟⲩ ⲛⲁϣⲁⲓ) πληθύναι, Ex 10 1 *SB* (? *l* ἐπλήσθη, *cf* 11 9), C 86 189 *B* ⲛⲛⲁϩϯ ⲉϥⲏⲟⲩ ⲛⲛⲁ.(*sic*), Abst 263 *B* of crops, Wess 18 54 *S* of hair. **II.** tr Deu 6 3 *B* (PSBA 25 101, var ⲁϣⲁⲓ) πληθ. Qual *great, goodly, honoured*: Jos 4 4 *SB*, 1 Kg 22 14 *S*, 2 Kg 23 19 *S*, Nah 3 10 *A* (*B* ⲧⲁⲓⲏⲟⲩⲧ),

ἔνδοξος, Jud 5 29 S (Masp.) ἄρχων, 2 Kg 1 23 S
ⲉⲅⲟⲓ ϩⲙⲡⲉⲅⲱⲡϩ (Mor, cf Masp), Cl 60 4 A ⲡⲕⲣⲉⲡ
ⲉⲧⲁⲉⲓ (so BM 205 S) πανάρετος (var ἔνδοξος) ; ShP
130⁴ 157 S ⲡⲉⲥⲭⲛⲙⲁ ⲉⲧⲟⲓ ⲉⲧϩⲁⲉⲟⲟⲩϥ, 2 Kg 1 19
(Mor, cf Masp) S ⲡⲉⲧⲱⲉⲓ ⲛⲧⲟⲟⲧⲕ τὰ ὕψη σου ; ShC
73 27 S ⲡϣⲏⲣⲉ ⲉⲧⲟⲓ ⲛⲧⲟⲟⲧⲥ, ShBM Or 8800 3 S
ⲡⲉⲧϥⲟⲉⲓ ⲛⲧⲟⲟⲧⲟⲩ (sic l R 2 8), Hor 79 O ⲁϥⲁⲉⲓ
ⲡⲧⲱⲧⲕ, AZ 21 94 O Michael ⲉⲧⲟⲓ ⲛⲧⲉⲙⲡⲡⲉ, Ryl
94 (33 f 2) S some ⲉⲅⲟⲓ ⲛⲧⲟⲟⲧⲧⲏⲩⲧⲛ like right
hand (cf Sa 12 7, Jth 15 11 ⲉⲧⲧⲁⲉⲓⲏⲩ ⲛⲧⲟⲟⲧ⸗, also
Ps 138 17 S where ⲁ. = B ⲧⲁⲓⲟ), Bor 284 2 S
ⲡⲉⲓⲛⲟϭ ⲡⲛⲓ ⲉⲧⲡⲉⲥⲱϥ ⲁⲩⲱ ⲉⲧⲟⲓ, AM 15 B ⲉⲅⲟⲓ ⲛⲟⲓ
ⲡϭⲁⲥⲓϩⲏⲧ, EW 4 B God made man ⲉⲅⲟⲓ ⲉⲛⲁϥϣⲱϥ.

—— SB nn m, increase, growth : Eph 4 16, Col
2 19 B αὔξησις, My 32 S ⲡⲁ. ⲡⲧⲅⲩⲗⲓⲕⲓⲁ, Va 61
118 B ⲡⲁ. ⲡⲡⲓⲟⲩⲧⲁϩ ; with ϯ B : Eph 4 15, Va 57
21, ib 134 αὐξάνειν, Va 58 29 ⲉⲣⲉϥϯ ϯ ⲁ. ⲡⲡⲓϣ-
ϣⲏⲛ, C 89 35 ⲡⲁϥϯ ⲉⲡⲁ. ϩⲉⲛⲡⲓⲥⲃⲱⲟⲩⲓ (? l ⲁⲡⲁⲓ,
cf ib infra) ; with ϭⲓ B : Va 57 175 ⲉⲅⲟⲓ ⲁ. ⲟⲩⲟϩ
ⲉⲅⲟⲓ ⲙⲃⲉⲣⲓ ἀκμάζειν, ib 98 ἀνθεῖν.

ⲭⲓⲛⲁ. B nn m f, increase : Va 57 99 ⲡⲓⲭ. ⲡⲧⲉ
ⲡⲟⲩⲕⲁⲣⲡⲟⲥ, Va 58 10 ϣⲁⲧⲉϥⲭ. ϩⲉⲛϯⲅⲩⲗⲓⲕⲓⲁ ;
ⲭⲓⲛϯ ⲁ. B : Va 57 79 ⲡⲭ. ⲡϯⲕⲁⲕⲓⲁ.

ⲁⲉⲓⲏⲥ, ⲁⲏⲥ, ⲁⲉⲏⲥ (C 42 98) S Sh only, ⲁⲉⲓⲉⲓⲥ,
ⲁⲉⲓⲥ, ⲁⲓⲉⲓ (Cl) A, nn f, greatness, size, quality : C
73 23 ⲡⲉⲓⲉⲟⲟⲩ ⲡⲧⲉⲓⲁ. (var ⲙⲡⲉ), C 42 37 ⲟⲩϭⲙⲟⲣ
ⲡⲁϣ ⲡⲁ. (paral ϭⲟⲧ), BMOr 8664 7 ⲡⲁϣ ⲡⲁ. ⲡⲉ
ⲡⲉⲯⲩⲭⲏ of virgins ?, Cl 45 7 A τοσοῦτο.
V also o great.

ⲁⲉⲓⲟ B v ϩⲁⲉⲓⲟ.

ⲁⲃ v ⲁϥ flesh & ⲁϥ fly.

ⲁⲃⲉ A, ⲁⲃⲓ F v ⲉⲓⲃⲉ.

ⲁⲃⲉ S v ⲱϥⲉ.

ⲁⲃⲉ S nn f, meaning unknown : ST 389 they
imprisoned me in village, ⲉⲓⲥ ⲡⲡⲟⲩ(ⲧⲉ) ⲙⲡⲡⲉⲧⲛ-
ⲧⲉⲡϣⲗⲏⲗ ⲁⲩϯ ⲑⲉ ⲡⲁⲓ ⲁⲓⲡⲟⲩϩ ⲧⲁⲃⲉ ⲁⲓⲃⲱⲕ ⲡⲁⲓ and
am come to you. L ? ⲁⲃⲱ or ⲧⲁⲃⲉⲡⲡⲏⲥⲉ or ⲧⲁ-ⲃⲉ.

ⲁⲃⲱ SBF, ⲁⲃⲟⲩ A, pl ⲁⲃⲟⲟⲩⲉ S (R 1 2 13, Mor
52 25), sg as pl (Eccl 7 27) S nn f, drag net for
fish or animals : Eccl 7 27 S, Hab 1 16 AB, Is 19
8 SB, Mt 13 47 SF σαγήνη شبكة ; opp ϣⲡⲉ : Hab
lc, Gu 98 S ϣⲡⲏ ϩⲓⲁ., BAp 40 S ⲁⲓⲥⲟⲕⲟⲩ ⲡⲡⲁϣⲡⲏ
ⲉⲧⲁ., Mich '22 (sermon) S ⲉⲣⲉⲧⲁ. ⲡⲟⲣϣ ⲉⲃⲟⲗ
ⲉⲅⲣⲱϯ ⲙⲡⲉϣⲡⲏ, Cai 42573 1 ⲡⲟⲩⲭ ⲡⲟⲩⲁ. ⲉⲑⲁⲗⲁⲥⲥⲁ ⲏ ⲟⲩϣⲡⲏ ⲉⲑⲁⲡ ⲧⲃⲧ, BMis 478 S whilst
drawing ϣⲡⲏ, boy fell into water ⲁϥⲃⲱⲕ ⲉϩⲣⲁⲓ
ⲉⲧⲁ. & I could not draw up ϣⲡⲏ, ShA 2 164 S
fisher ⲡⲁⲡⲉⲭ ⲧⲁ. ⲉⲡⲙⲟⲟⲩ, PSBA 33 115 S heaven
& earth shall tremble like ⲡⲟⲩϩ ⲡⲁ., Tri 713 S for
bird-catching, MG 25 319 B net of saint's prayers
hath gathered us here, Mor 54 41 S ⲣⲉϥⲛⲉϩ ⲁ.

ⲉⲑⲁⲗⲁⲥⲥⲁ. A pun upon ⲁ. & name ⲡⲁⲃⲱ Baouit
1 115.

ⲁⲃⲱ S, pl. ⲁⲃⲁⲧⲉ, nn f قلة. So AZ 24 88
(Bsciai). Cannot be traced. Cf KKS 54. But
MS seems to read ⲃⲱ, v ϥⲟ.

ⲁⲃⲱⲕ SBF, seldom ⲁⲃⲟⲕ SB, ⲉⲃⲱⲕ DM, f
ⲁⲃⲟⲕⲉ S (Ryl 63 1), ⲁⲃⲱⲕⲓ B (BSM 119, Cat 147), pl
ⲁⲃⲟⲟⲕⲉ S, ⲁⲃⲁⲕⲉ A (Pro 24 52, Zeph 2 14), ⲁⲃⲱⲕⲓ
B (Va 57 271), ⲁⲃⲁⲁⲕⲓ F (Is 34 11), sg often as pl,
nn m, crow, raven : Lev 11 14 SB, Job 38 41 SB
κόραξ ; Jer 3 2, Ep Jer 54 B κορώνη ; Miss 8 237
S ⲟⲩⲁ. ⲉϥⲕⲏⲙ, MG 25 8 B ⲟⲩⲁ. ⲡⲭⲁⲙⲉ, LCyp
3 S ⲧⲁⲥⲡⲉ ⲡⲡⲁⲃⲟⲟⲕⲉ, BM 527 F ⲥⲡⲁϥ ⲡⲁ. ; ⲃⲁⲗ
ⲡⲁ. κύαμος ἑλληνική Z 629 S, PMéd 267 S, CR
'87 376 S, WS 52 S (all medic), Bal S in list of
herbs, cf DM 5 24 bel n ⲉⲃⲱⲕ ; Ps 146 9 SB
ⲙⲁⲥ ⲡⲁ.

As name : Bodl(P) g 14 S ⲁⲡⲁ (ⲁ)ⲃⲱⲕ, ’Αβόκ,
’Αβῶκ (Preisigke).

ⲁⲃⲁⲗ A v ⲃⲱⲗ (ⲉⲃⲟⲗ).

ⲁⲃⲁⲡ v ⲁⲅⲁⲡ.

ⲁⲃⲏⲡ v ⲁⲅⲉⲓⲡ.

ⲁⲃⲓⲡ O nn pl, meaning unknown : AZ 21 105
ⲡⲉⲣⲥⲉ ⲡϣⲟⲓ ⲛⲥⲁⲧϣⲁⲡϣⲓ…ⲡⲉⲣⲥⲓ ⲡⲑⲱⲩⲑ ⲛⲥⲁⲡⲁⲃⲓⲡ
(cf ib 38 92).

ⲁⲃⲏⲣ B v ⲟⲩⲏⲣ.

ⲁⲃⲣⲉⲙ B nn, only 1 Chr 16 3 (Lag, HCons)
ⲟⲩⲱⲓⲕ ⲡⲁ. ἄρτος ἀρτοκοπικός torta panis ; cf ⲁⲙⲣⲉ
(Spg). But ? l ⲱⲓⲕ (ⲡ)ⲡⲁⲃⲣⲉ ⲙⲫⲣⲱⲙⲓ ; v HCons
176 (cf ⲡⲁⲡⲣⲉ).

ⲁⲃⲉⲣⲏⲭ S nn m, a stone, only Mor 52 13,
where jewels likened to 12 apostles ; λιγύριον
a water-hued stone resembling ⲁ., which is ⲟⲩⲱⲡⲉ
ⲉϥϩⲟⲕⲣ, not soluble like salt. ? = Pers فيروز tur-
quoise, ابريز ὄβρυζον not likely. Cf K 203 (for
ⲃⲁⲣⲁⲗⲓⲟⲛ 1° l ⲗⲓⲕⲓⲣⲓⲟⲛ), Ludolf Comment. 210
(both confused lists).

ⲁⲃⲥⲱⲡ (Pey), ⲁⲩⲥⲟⲡ (K) B nn m, wild mint :
K 195 نعناع جبلي.

ⲁⲃⲁⲧ F, ⲁⲃⲟⲧ B v ⲉⲃⲟⲧ.

ⲁⲃⲏⲧ v ⲁⲅⲏⲧ.

ⲁⲃⲓⲧ B nn (?), Monday (?) : BM 872, 886,
heading of Monday's Theotokia, ⲑ. ⲡⲧⲉ ⲫⲟⲟⲩ ⲡⲁ.
يوم الاثنين, P 44 186 ⲫⲟⲩ ⲡⲁ. do. Elsewhere Monday B ⲡⲓⲉϩⲟⲟⲩ ⲙⲙⲁϩⲃ̄ O'LearyTh 22, or ⲡⲉϩ.
ⲙⲡⲃ̄ Absal 159 ; S P 44 21 (from Theot.) ⲡⲣⲁⲥⲧⲉ
ⲃ̄ Cf ⲁⲩⲏⲧ sub fin.

ⲁⲃⲏϣ *S* nn or adj, meaning unknown, epithet of certain edibles : Ep 533 ⲧⲏⲃⲧ ⲡⲁ., BP 5181 ⲥⲟⲩⲟ ⲡⲁ.

ⲁⲃϩⲉ *A*, ⲁⲃϩ, ⲁⲃⲁϩ *F* v ⲟⲃϩⲉ.

ⲁⲃⲁϭⲏⲉⲓⲛ (*PS*), ϩⲁⲃ- (Ap 4), ⲁⲃⲓϭⲉⲓⲛ, ⲁⲃⲁⲕⲏⲓⲛⲉ, ⲁϥⲉϭⲉⲉⲛⲉ (Mor 31 211), ⲁⲃⲓϭⲉⲉⲓⲛⲉ *S*, ⲁⲃⲁⲭⲏⲛⲓ, ⲁⲃⲁⲭⲓⲛⲓ, ⲃⲁⲭⲓⲛⲓ, ⲃⲁⲭⲏⲛⲓ, ⲃⲁⲭⲏⲛⲓ *B*, ⲁⲃⲓϭⲉⲛⲓ *F* (many varr *SB*), sg as pl Mor 47 178, C 43 128, nn m f (C 86 356, 359), *glass*, cf Pers اَبْكِينَه (Tattam) : Job 28 17 *B*, Ap 21 18 *SB*, ὕαλος, Ap 4 6 *SB* ὑάλινος, P 44 61 *S* زجاج. Objects of glass : εἶδος MG 25 370 *B*, PMéd 219, 230 *S*; σκεῦος Mor 19 91 *S*, *ib* 48 56 *S* = C 43 128 *B*, MG 25 255 *B* (chalices in poor churches, *cf* PO 5 62, Ryl *Bulletin* 11 293); ποτήριον BM 1008 *S*; ⲙⲟⲕⲓ MG 25 191 *B*; ⲡⲟⲛⲕⲩ Mor 31 211 *S*; ϭⲁⲗⲗⲁϭⲧ Kropp *F*; ϩⲁⲃⲥ cover, lid BKU 1 26 18 *F*; ⲕⲁⲩⲧⲏⲣ, ⲕⲁⲧⲏⲗ قدير Bodl(P) a 1 f, a 3 22 (*cf* a 2 60); sapphire-hued from Alexandria Mor 47 178 *S*, pure (καθαρός) violet-hued (ⲓⲱⲓⲁⲥ ? ἰόεις) Z 611 *S*, white Syrian ⲡⲁϣ-(ϣ)ⲉⲙⲓ (الشامى) ⲡⲁⲗⲁⲩ Bodl(P) a 2 38.

ⲥⲁⲡⲁⲃⲁϭⲏⲉⲓⲛ, -ⲭⲏⲓⲛⲓ *SB* nn m, *glass-blower* or *seller* : C 41 67, K 128 *B* زجّاج; Mor 50 45 *S*, CO 162 *S*. ⲃⲁⲭ(var ⲣ)ⲏⲓⲡⲓⲧⲏⲥ زجّاج K 111 *B*.

In place-name : PSBA 29 301 Monastery of ⲡⲓⲁⲛ (? ⲡⲓⲥⲁⲡ)ⲁⲃⲁⲭⲱⲡⲓ دير الزجاج, W. of Alexandria.

ⲁⲑⲏⲣ *B* v ϩⲁⲧⲏⲣ.

ⲁⲑⲱⲣ *B* v ϩⲁⲧⲱⲣ.

ⲁⲑⲣⲉⲩ *B* v ϩⲁⲧⲣⲉ.

ⲁⲑⲁϩ *B* v ⲱⲧϩ.

ⲁⲕ v ⲱⲕ.

ⲁⲉⲓⲕ *AF* v ⲟⲉⲓⲕ.

ⲁⲉⲓⲕ *SA²*, ⲁⲓⲕ *B* nn m, *consecration* of church, altar, house &c : Nu 7 10 *B* (*S* ⲭⲓⲁ.), 2 Chr 7 9 *B*, Dan 3 3 *B*, Ps 29 1 *B* (*S* ⲭⲓ ⲁ.) ἐγκαινισμός ; Dan 3 2 *B*, Jo 10 22 *B* (*S* ⲭⲓ ⲁ.) ἐγκαίνια, MG 25 112, 113, 387 *B* bishops & clergy gathered for ceremony, EW 127 *B* lections for ⲡⲓⲁ. of a σκηνή *ie* its anniversary, Miss 4 685 *S*, Pcod 6 *S*.

ⲉⲣ ⲁ. *B*, consecrate : 3 Kg 8 63, 2 Chr 7 5 ἐγκαινεῖν, P arab 203 150 *B* of patriarch ⲛⲧⲉϥⲓⲣⲓ ⲙⲡⲁ. ⲡⲣⲁⲛⲏⲓ ⲙⲃⲉⲣⲓ كرس.

ⲭⲓ, ϭⲓ ⲁ. *SB*, consecrate : He 9 18 *S* (*B* ⲧⲟⲩⲃⲟ), Deu 20 5 *B* (*S* ⲭⲓ ⲁ. ⲉⲃⲟⲗ) ἐγκαινεῖν.

—— *SA²B* nn m, *consecration*, cf above, ⲁ. nn : Mor 22 40 *S* ⲡⲭⲓ ⲁ. (ⲟⲉⲓⲕ) ⲙⲡⲉϥⲧⲟⲡⲟⲥ = *B* ⲡⲓⲁ-ⲅⲓⲁⲥⲙⲟⲥ, Mich 550 41 *S* saint urged to perform ⲭⲓ ⲁ. of new church acc to canons, BMis 526 *S*, cf *ib* ϩⲁⲧⲓⲁϫⲉ used of same ceremony ; but *ib* 225 *S* ⲭⲓ ⲁ. & ϩⲁⲧ. seem distinct, cf also Miss 4 631 *S*.

Prob = نكريز by bishops at new or restored church (PO 16 749, Synax 1 156, 269, 2 171, Abû Ṣâliḥ 30 b, 45 b, 47 b), which = ⲭⲓⲛⲉⲣⲁⲅⲓⲁⲍⲓⲛ HCons 1, TEuch 1 463; C 86 257 *B* ⲡⲓⲉϩⲟⲟⲩ ⲛⲧⲉ ⲡⲉⲕϭⲓ.

ⲁ., Tri 141 *S* = تجديد *renovation*.

ⲁⲕⲉ *A* v ⲟⲕⲉ.

ⲁⲕⲏ *S* nn, meaning unknown : WS 140 ⲡϭⲁⲙⲁ. *V* ϩⲁⲙ.

ⲁⲕⲱ, ⲁⲧⲱ, ⲧⲱ *SB* nn f, *thing destroyed, carrion, filth, destruction* : Lev 5 22 *B* (*S* ⲡⲕⲁ) ⲁ. ⲉⲥ-ⲧⲟⲣⲉⲙ *res perdita*, Pro 1 26 *B* (var ⲧⲁⲕⲟ) Jer 12 11 *B* (*S* ⲧⲁⲕⲟ), *ib* 18 17 *B* (*S* do), 2 Pet 2 1 *B* (*S* do) ἀπώλεια ; ShP 130⁵ 17 *S* ⲛϥⲣ ⲧⲏⲓⲛ ⲁⲛ ⲙⲡⲁⲣⲥ ⲛ ⲡⲁ., P 131⁵ 76 *S* ⲟⲩⲁ. ⲉⲥⲡⲏϫ ⲉⲃⲟⲗ, Mor 50 57 *S* demoniac ate excrement ϩⲓⲁⲧⲱ ⲛⲓⲙ, Mor 51 22 *S* wine spoilt...ⲉⲧⲟ ⲛⲧⲱ ϩⲓϩⲛⲁⲭ ; Lev 5 2, 7 24 *S* (*B* diff) θηριάλωτος, ShWess 9 86 *S* sim. *Cf* ⲧⲁⲕⲟ.

ⲁⲕⲗⲏ, ⲕⲁⲗⲏ *B* nn f, *weasel* : K 173 عرسة = γαλῆ ; *cf* PMéd 245. *V* ⲕⲗⲏ.

ⲁⲕⲗⲏ, ⲁⲕⲗⲓ, ⲁⲗⲕⲏ (P 55 11, Montp 167), ⲕⲁⲗⲏ (Lab) *B* nn f, among vessels : K 150 لقتية (so mostly), قنية (Montp), *l* ? لقنية (λεκάνιον) ; *cf* ? *ib* 151 ⲕⲗⲏ زير.

ⲁⲕⲟⲩⲗⲁⲩϫⲉ *S* nn f, a vessel, receptacle ? : Mor 51 42 no herbs in garden, ⲟⲩϫⲉ ϣⲗϭⲟⲙ ϩⲛⲧⲁ.

ⲁⲕⲉⲥ *S* v ⲁⲥϭ.

ⲁⲕⲏⲥ *SB*, ⲁⲕⲉⲥ (Tri 592, P 44 115), ⲁⲕⲓⲥ (P 43 116) *S* nn m, *girdle, breeches* : Ge 3 7 *B* περίζωμα, *cit* ShA 2 47 ⲡⲉⲣⲓϩⲱⲙⲁ, as elsewhere in *S* (Ru 3 15, Pro 29 42, Jer 13 11, BMar 219, last 2 *B* also); Ez 44 18 *SB* περισκελής, *cit* CA 91 *S*, Tri *lc S*, both اسافيط, *l* ? اساديط (περισ. not understood in Ex 39 28 where Va 1 تلاسم, Lev 6 3, 16 4 where merely ϩⲃⲟⲥ, in Ex 34 29 سروالة) ; C 43 110 *B* hermit's *girdle* for liturgical use. *Cf* ? ϭⲟⲩⲛⲁⲃⲥ.

ⲁⲕⲧ, ⲁⲕⲏⲧ *S* vb tr, in late alchem. texts, *cause to solidify, congeal*, assuming = عقد (IV اعقد) : Ryl 106 12 pound & cast mixture (of drugs) into pot with oil, ⲁⲕⲏⲧ ⲉⲙⲟⲟⲩ ϩⲓϫⲱⲡⲥⲁϩⲧⲉ, AZ 23 111 of metal ⲁⲕⲏⲧ ⲉⲙⲱϥ ϩⲙⲡⲕⲟⲩⲧ ⲉⲧ⳨ⲏⲛ, Bodl(P) a 1 *b* of metals ⲁⲕⲏⲧ ⲙⲙⲟⲟⲩ ϩⲛⲟⲩⲕⲱϩⲧ ⲉϥⲕⲉⲣⲁ (κεραν-νύναι), Bodl *ib* ⲉⲕϣⲁⲛϭⲟⲗϥ ⲉⲃⲟⲗ...ⲛⲧⲁⲕⲧ ⲙⲙⲟϥ ϣⲁϥⲣⲱϣⲉ.

ⲁⲗ *S*, *deaf*, sg & pl, always = *B* ⲕⲟⲩⲣ, as nn : Ex 4 11, Ps 37 13, Is 29 18, Mt 11 5 κωφός ; as adj : Lev 19 14, Ps 57 4, R 2 62 ; ⲣ ⲁ. *be deaf* : Aeg 232 ⲡⲉⲧⲟ ⲛⲁ., BM 216 1 ⲉⲩϣⲁⲛⲣ ⲁ. ; ⲉⲓⲣⲉ ⲛⲁ. *make deaf* : Miss 4 689.

ⲁⲗ *SBA*, ⲉⲗ *F* nn m. ⲁ. *pebble* : Ex 4 25 *B*, Lam 3 16 *B* (*S* ⲁ. ⲛⲱⲛⲉ), Apoc 2 17 *B* (*S* = Gk)

ψῆφος, K 205 *B* حصا, P 44 61 *S* ⲱⲡⲉ ⲡⲁ. = ἀκρότομος حجر الاصم, Mor 23 35 *S* pits full of ⲁ. ⲡⲕⲱⲣⲧ,
BMis 539 *S* ⲁⲗⲱⲗⲉ ⲡⲱⲡⲉ prob belongs here,
though Lat & Syr § 32 suggest ἀνέμη in original
(*cf* ⲁⲗⲟⲩ *s f*).   **b.** *hail stone*: Ex 9 18 *B*, Ps
148 8 *B* (*S* = Gk), Is 32 19 *B* (*F* ⲉⲗ ⲉⲙⲡⲏ, *S* =
Gk), Hag 2 17 *B* (*SA* ⲁ. ⲙⲡⲉ), Ap 16 21 *B* (*S* do)
χάλαζα; ⲁ. ⲙⲡⲉ Jos 10 11 *S*, Ps 77 47 *SB*, Sa 16
16 *S* χάλαζα.   **c.** *testicle*: Lev 21 20 *B* (in MIE
2 366 ⲃⲁⲗ, *S* ϫⲟⲉⲓⲧ), *ib* 22 24 *B* (*S* om).   **d.** *spot,
patch on skin, eruption*: Lev 13 38 *B* (*S* ⲧⲟ) αὔγασμα
بهق (but Wilkins ⲓⲁⲗ, *cf* Gk); prob also in ⲁⲗⲟⲩ-
ⲃⲉⲣ (-ⲃⲁⲣ Wilkins) *B white* shining *spot*.   **e.** *seed,
pip of fruit* ?: PMéd 153 *S* ϯⲉ ⲡⲁⲗ [ⲛϭⲓ]ⲗⲓⲗⲓϭ
هليلج (*cf* P 44 83 ⲁⲗⲟⲟⲗⲉⲕⲁ هليلج).

ⲁⲗ *S* (P 44 88 ⲟⲗⲉ = 43 70 ⲱⲗⲉ) nn, meaning
unknown, always with vb ⲁϣ-, *cry*: P 43 47 ⲡⲁ.
κραυγή جلبة = 44 74 ⲡⲁϣⲕⲁⲕ, P 43 79 ⲡⲛⲟϭ ⲡⲁ.
ⲉⲧⲥⲏⲕ تغويت *long-drawn cry* (*cf* AZ 24 89), P 131¹
58 ⲟⲩϩⲣⲟⲟⲩ ⲡⲁ., Mor 36 34 sim, Mor 41 227 ⲡⲁ.
ⲙⲡⲛⲏⲛϣⲉ, Mor 48 64 sim = C 43 132 *B* ⲡⲁⲓⲙⲏⲛϣ
ⲉⲧⲱϣ ⲉⲃⲟⲗ.   Prob = ⲁϣϩⲏⲗ *A²* (*v* ϩⲏⲗ).

ⲁⲗⲉ *S*, ⲁⲗⲏⲓ *B*, ⲁⲗⲏ *F*, ⲁⲗⲟⲩ *S* (*v* **II.** below),
ⲁⲗⲏⲩ† *S*, imper ⲁⲗⲓ⳹ *B* (Ac 21 36), ⲁⲗⲱⲧⲡ *S*
(BMar 190), vb.   **I.** intr, *mount, go up, go on
board*: Jo 21 11 *S* (*B* ⲓ ⲉⲡϣⲱⲓ), Ac 8 31 *SB*, Ex
15 19 *F* ⲁⲗⲏ (? *l* ⲧⲁⲗⲏ, *v* ⲧⲁⲗⲟ) ἀναβαίνειν; Jer
26 4 *B*, 4 Kg 4 24 *B* ἐπιβαίνειν; LAA 570 *F* ἀνέρχεσθαι, RNC 27 *S* persuading him ⲉⲧⲣⲉϥⲁ. ⲛⲙⲙⲁⲩ
ἀποπλεῖν μετά; Mor 31 88 *S* ⲁϥⲁ. ⲁϥⲉⲓ ⲉⲡⲧⲟⲟⲩ,
AZ 21 144 *S* ⲡⲧⲉⲣⲟⲩⲁ. ⲁⲩⲣ ϩⲱⲧ, BM 1131 *S*
ϣⲁⲡⲧⲉϥⲁ. ⲡϭⲕⲱ ϩⲏⲧ, Mor 19 6 *S* ⲁ. ⲙⲡⲡⲁⲣⲭⲓ-
ⲉⲡⲓⲥⲕ. (*B* ⲧⲁⲗⲟⲕ ⲡⲉⲙ-), *ib* 87 *S* the apostle ⲧⲁⲗⲏⲩ
ⲡⲙⲏⲧⲓ = Mor 18 80 ⲁ. ⲡⲙ-;   *c* ⲉ-: Ex 15 1
F, Ps 67 19 *S* (*B* ϣⲉ ⲡⲁϥ), Jon 1 3 *B* (*S* ⲧⲁⲗⲟ),
Mt 14 32 *SBF* ἀναβαίνειν; Mk 5 18, 6 45 *S* (var
ⲧⲁⲗⲟ) *B*, Lu 5 3 (*B* ⲱⲗⲓ) ἐμβαίν.; Ge 24 61 *B*,
Nu 22 22 *B* (*S* ⲧⲁⲗⲟ), Sa 14 4 *S* ἐπιβαίν.; Mk 11
7 *S* (*B* ϩⲉⲙⲥⲓ ϩⲓϫⲉⲡ-), Ap 19 19 *S* (*B* do) καθίζειν ἐπί, 2 Kg 13 29 *S* ἐπικαθ. ἐπί, RNC 41 *S*
ⲡⲧⲉⲣⲟⲩⲁ. ⲉⲡϫⲟⲓ ἀνέρχ. ἐν, BMar 111 *S* ⲁⲩϣⲓⲡⲉ
ⲛⲥⲁⲁ. ⲉⲡϫⲟⲓ εἰσέρχ. εἰς, Ac 27 17 *S* (*B* ⲱⲗⲓ) αἴρειν
prob erroneous, BKU 1 186 *S* ⲁⲩⲡⲡⲁ ⲡⲕⲱϩ ⲁ.
ⲉⲣⲟϥ, C 86 274 *B* ϣⲁϥⲁ. ⲉⲡϣⲱⲓ to heaven, Mor
42 52 *S* ⲉϥⲁⲗⲏⲩ ⲉⲡⲉϥⲟⲥ (var ⲧⲁⲗⲏⲩ), JKP 2 18 *S*
tree ⲉⲣⲉⲟⲩⲕⲁⲣⲡⲟⲥ ⲁⲗⲏⲩ ⲉⲣⲟϥ AZ 33 56 *S* bird
ⲉϥⲁⲗⲏⲩ ⲉⲡϣⲏⲛ.   **II.** tr *S*, rare, late (? incorrect
for ⲧⲁⲗⲟ, but *cf* DM 25 11 gloss ⲁⲗⲟ): JKP 2
66 ⲁⲩⲁⲗⲟⲓ ⲉⲧⲉⲥⲕⲁⲫⲏ, *ib* 146 ⲁⲓⲁⲗⲟ ⲙⲡⲉⲥϥⲟⲥ Ryl
106 4 &c ⲁⲗⲟⲩ ⲉⲡⲕⲱϩⲧ, BM 1088 ⲡⲉϥⲉⲓⲱ ⲡⲧⲁϥⲁ-
ⲗⲟⲟⲩ.

—— ⲉϩⲣⲁⲓ *S*, ⲉϩⲣⲏⲓ *B*, *mount up, ascend* in
years: Ge 18 11 (*B* ⲁⲓⲁⲓ), Jos 23 1 (*B* do) προβαίνειν, ShC 42 99 sim, C 43 42 *B* ⲁⲩⲁ. ⲉⲣ. to
feast as guests. This & following (ⲉⲭⲡ-, ⲉⲣ.
ⲉⲭⲡ-) sometimes confused with or equiv to ⲱⲗ:
Bor 290 195 *S* ⲁⲕⲁⲗⲉⲕ ⲉⲣ. ⲉⲭⲙⲡⲉⲃⲗⲟϭ = Ge 49
4 ⲟⲗⲕ (both = ἀνέβης & *B* ϣⲉ ⲉⲡϣⲱⲓ), Mor 19
53 *S* ⲁ. ⲉⲣ. ⲉⲭⲙⲡⲗⲁ ⲡⲛⲕⲟⲧⲕ = *ib* 46 & Wess 18
62 ⲟⲗⲟⲩ ⲉⲭ.; *cf* ? Lu 14 10 *S*, R 1 1 76 *S*.

—— ⲉϩⲣⲁⲓ ⲉ- *S*, *mount, climb up*: Is 37 24
(*B* ϣⲉ ⲉⲡϣⲱⲓ), Cant 7 8 ἀναβαίνειν, BM 256 ⲁ. ⲉⲣ.
ⲉⲡⲭⲓⲥⲉ ⲡⲧⲁⲣⲉⲧⲓ.

—— ⲉⲭⲡ- *SBF*, *ascend, go up*: Si 50 11 *S* ἐν
ἀναβάσει, Is 35 9 *SF* ἀναβαίν. εἰς, *ib* 22 6 *SB* ἀναβάτης (doubtful), Ps 67 5 *B* (*S* ⲁ. ⲉϩⲣⲁⲓ ⲉⲭ.), Pro
21 22 *S*, Si 46 15 *S*, Ez 10 18 *B* ἐπιβαίν. ἐπί, Lev
18 23 *B* (*S* diff) βιβασθῆναι ὑπό, Job 40 15 *S* (*B*
ϣⲉ ⲉⲭ.) ἐπέρχεσθαι, Mor 19 21 *S* (var ⲉϩⲣⲁⲓ ⲉⲭ.,
B ⲉϩⲣⲏⲓ ⲉⲭ.), Tri 270 *S* ⲁⲩⲁ. ⲉⲭⲙⲡⲉⲣⲧⲟ, BSM
108 *B* not again shall such thoughts ⲁ. ⲉⲭⲉⲡⲡⲁϩⲛⲧ.

—— ⲉϩⲣ. ⲉⲭⲡ-, as last: Mt 5 1 *S* (*B* ϣⲉ
ⲉⲡϣⲱⲓ ⲉⲭ.), Lu 24 38 *S* (*B* ⲡⲛⲟⲩ ⲉⲭ.), BMar 110
S ἀναβαίν. ἐν, εἰς, 1 Cor 2 9 *S* (*B* ϣⲉ ⲉϩⲣⲏⲓ ⲉⲭ.)
ἀναβ. ἐπί, Is 14 14 *S* (*B* ϣⲉ ⲉⲡϣⲱⲓ ⲉ-) ἀναβ.
ἐπάνω; Ps 17 10 *S* (*B* ⲱⲗⲓ ⲉⲭ.), Jer 22 4 *B* (*S*
ⲧⲁⲗⲟ ⲉⲭ.), Mt 21 5 *S* (*B* ⲧⲁⲗⲟ ⲉ-) ἐπιβαίν. ἐπί of
riding upon; Mt 21 7 *S* (*B* ϩⲉⲙⲥⲓ ⲥⲁⲡϣⲱⲓ ⲡ-) ἐπι-
καθίζ. ἐπάνω; Aeg 275 *S* ⲁ. ⲉⲣ. ⲉⲭⲡⲟⲩⲙⲁ ⲉϥϫⲟⲥⲉ
ἀνέρχ. ἐπί, C 43 63 *B* ⲁ. ⲉϩⲣ. ⲉⲭⲉⲡⲣⲁⲡⲉⲭⲛⲟⲩ,
ShC 42 159 *S* hill tops that waters cannot ⲁ. ⲉⲣ.
ⲉⲭⲱⲟⲩ.

—— ϩⲓϫⲡ- *S*, *be raised upon*: Miss 8 255 ⲡⲉⲣⲉ-
ⲡⲉϥϭⲓϫ ⲁⲗⲏⲩ ϩⲓϫⲡⲧⲉϥⲁⲡⲉ.

—— ⲉϩⲣ. ϩⲓϫⲡ- *S*, *mount up upon*: ROC 1913
174 ⲁ. ⲉϩⲣ. ϩⲓϫⲙⲡϣⲏⲛ τρέχειν ἀνὼ εἰς.

—— ⲉϩⲣⲏⲓ ⲉⲭⲡ- *B*, *descend upon* (unless *l*
ⲉϩⲣⲏⲓ): C 41 66 ⲁⲟⲩⲁⲃⲱⲕ ⲁ. ⲉϩ. ⲉⲭⲉⲡϯⲭⲟⲓ.

ⲣⲉϥⲁ. *SBF* nn, *mounted man, rider*: Is 36 8 *SF*
(*B* ϭⲁⲥⲓϩⲑⲟ), *ib* 30 16 *B* (*S* = Gk) ἀναβάτης.

ϭⲓⲡⲁ. *S* nn f, *ascent, mounting up*: Gu 105 ⲧⲉⲕϭ.
ⲉⲡⲉⲥϥⲟⲥ.

ⲙⲁ ⲡⲁ. *B*, *sitting place* when mounted: Cat 102
ass's colt ⲟⲩⲙ. ⲡⲧⲉ ⲡⲭ̅ⲥ̅.

ⲁⲗⲉ *S* nn f, a utensil of bronze: St 125 ⲥⲡⲧⲉ
ⲡⲡⲁⲗⲉ ⲡⲣⲟⲙⲛⲧ (? *l* ⲡⲁⲗⲉ).   Prob = ⲁⲣⲏ, *v* Ep
449 n.

ⲁⲗⲓ *B* nn m, *fenugreek (trigonella)*: K 193, 260
حلبة or فول.   *Cf* ? ⲧⲓⲗⲓ.

ⲁⲗⲓ *F*   *v* ⲉⲓⲣⲉ.

ⲁⲗⲓ- *B*   *v* ⲱⲗ.

ⲁⲓⲗⲉ *A*, ⲁⲓⲗ *F*   *v* ⲟⲉⲓⲗⲉ.

ⲁⲗⲟⲩ S (rare) BF, ⲁⲗⲁⲩ AB (from S, C 89
83, cf MG 17 448), ⲁⲉⲓⲗⲟⲩ F (Lab, ?ⲗⲉⲓⲗⲟⲩ),
pl. ⲁⲗⲱⲟⲩⲓ B, ⲁⲗⲁⲩⲓ F nn m & f (S only as name).
a. *youth, maiden*: Job 1 15 B, Ac 3 13 B (S ϣⲏⲣⲉ),
ROC 17 407 B παῖς; Ex 21 22 B (S ϣ.̇), Is 11 6
B ⲕⲟⲩϫⲓ ⲛⲁ. (S ⲕⲟⲩⲓ ⲛϣ.), ib 11 8 B do, C 89 74
(S ϣ. ϣⲏⲙ), Jo 4 49 BF (S ϣ., opp νεανίσκος)
παιδίον; Su 45 B, Joel 3 3 B (S ϣ. ϣⲏⲙ) παιδάριον; Is 65 20 B, EW 149 B νέος; Ps 151 1 B
(S ⲥⲟⲃⲕ), Is 40 30 B (S ϣ. ϣⲏⲙ), Ac 5 6 B (S
ⲟⲣϣⲓⲣⲉ) νεώτερος, cf ib 10; He 5 13 B (S ⲕⲟⲩⲓ),
Ps 16 14 BF (Mor 33 2, S ϣ.) ⲕⲟⲩϫⲓ ⲛⲁ., Ez 9 6
B do νήπιος; Ez 44 9 B υἱός; Ac 7 19 B (S ϣ.)
ⲕⲟⲩϫⲓ ⲛⲁ. βρέφος, Mt 9 25 B f (S ϣⲉⲉⲣⲉ ϣⲏⲙ)
κοράσιον; PS 3 S ⲛⲁ. ⲙⲛⲁ., BKU 1 1 S ⲛⲁ. ⲛⲧⲉ
ⲧⲁ., BG 21 S ⲟⲩⲁ... ⲉⲡⲉⲓⲡⲉ ⲉⲅⲟⲗⲗⲟ, AM 287
B ⲟⲩⲁ. ⲙⲃⲉⲣⲓ, TEuch 1 327 B ⲡⲉⲕⲙⲟⲛⲟⲅⲉⲛⲏⲥ
ⲛⲁ.; Ex 2 3 B a babe, MIE 2 398 B ⲕⲟⲩϫⲓ ⲛⲁ.
of 16 years (S ϣ. ϣⲏⲙ), C 86 73 B do of 25 years,
C 41 39 B ⲁ. ⲛ̄ ⲙⲙⲟⲛⲁⲭⲟⲥ. **b.** *servant*, παῖς,
οἰκέτης, mostly B: Ge 14 15 B, Ex 21 2, Lev 25
55 B (S ϩⲙϩⲁⲗ), Jo 4 51 F (SA² ϩ., B ⲃⲱⲕ), Ac 12
13 B (S ϣ. ϣⲏⲙ) παιδίσκη, Va 61 102 B ⲁⲗⲱⲟⲩⲓ
opp ϣⲏⲣⲓ, BSM 71 sim, ShP 130¹ 133 S ⲡⲉⲛⲣⲙ-
ϩⲁⲗⲡⲉ ⲛ ⲡⲉⲛⲁ. ϣⲏⲙⲡⲉ, Z 317 S he followeth
me ⲛⲑⲉ ⲛⲟⲩⲁ. (B ⲟⲩⲁⲡⲉⲙⲓ) ὡς ἄνεμι (v LMis
130 551, cf ⲁⲗ pebble).

ⲙⲛⲧⲁ., ⲙⲉⲧⲁ. BF nn f, *time of youth, youthful-
ness*: Ge 8 21 B (S ⲙⲛⲧⲕⲟⲩⲓ), 1 Kg 17 33 B
(S do), Ps 42 4 B (S ⲙⲛⲧϣ. ϣⲏⲙ), Pro 24 54 B
(S ⲙⲛⲧⲃⲣⲣⲉ) νεότης; Hos 2 15 A (B ⲙⲉⲧⲕⲟⲩϫⲓ)
νηπιότης, Mor 30 10 F (S ⲙⲛⲧⲃⲣⲣⲉ).

ⲙⲉⲧⲣⲉϥϧⲁⲧⲉⲃ ⲁ. B nn f, *child-slaying*: EW 46
sorcery, fornication & ⲙ.

ⲉⲣ ⲁ. B, *be young*: Ps 36 25 (S ⲣ ⲕⲟⲩⲓ) νεώτερος
γίνεσθαι, Gal 4 3 (S do) νήπιος εἶναι, Va 57 193
old men once ⲁⲩⲟⲓ ⲛⲁ. νέοι ἐγένοντο.

In names ⲡⲁⲗⲟⲩ AZ 16 12, -ⲗⲁⲩ Mich wooden
tablet, ⲧⲁⲗⲟⲩ S f, Wess 18 11, Ryl 63, ib 262 -ⲗⲁⲩ,
Miss 1 399 ⲧⲁⲗⲟⲩ ϣⲏⲙ; cf Preisigke 407, 408.

Cf ⲗⲓⲗⲟⲩ, with which there is ? confusion of
forms.

ⲁⲗⲱ, ⲁⲗⲟⲩ (ⲁⲣⲟⲩ) S, ⲉⲗⲟⲩ (Zach 2 8), ⲁⲗⲟⲩ
A, ⲁⲗⲗⲟⲩ B, pl ⲁⲗⲟⲟⲩⲉ, ⲁⲗⲁⲩⲉ, ⲁⲣⲟⲟⲩⲉ S, &
sg as pl SAB, nn f, *pupil* (? daughter, maiden,
v below) *of eye*: Deu 32 10 B (S ⲕⲉⲕⲉ, which =
βρέφος Klio 13 31), Ps 16 8 B (S do), Pro 20 10 A
(S do), ib 7 2 AB, R 2 2 21 S κόρη, K 75 B ﺣﺪﻗﺔ;
Gal 4 15 S (B ⲃⲁⲗ) ὀφθαλμός, Lam 2 18 B θυγάτηρ (var κόρη) ὀφθ., Mor 48 94 S ⲧⲁⲁ. ⲡⲟⲩⲛⲁⲙ =
C 43 146 B, BMar 40 S ⲧⲉϥⲁ. ⲥⲛⲧⲉ, C 43 218 B
ⲛⲓⲁ. ⲛⲧⲉ ⲡⲉϥⲃⲁⲗ, Mor 43 226 S of Lazarus ⲁⲩⲱⲙⲥ
ⲉⲡⲉⲥⲛⲧ ⲛϭⲓ ⲛⲁ. ⲛⲛⲉϥⲃⲁⲗ, LCyp 8 S (ⲁⲣⲟⲟⲩⲉ)
sim, R 1 5 51 S ⲧⲉϥⲁⲣⲟⲩ fell to ground, Mor
41 342 sim, BIF 14 113 S Christ replaces martyr's ⲁⲣⲟⲟⲩⲉ, Miss 4 651 S λεύκωμα in ⲛⲉⲥⲁⲗⲟⲟⲩⲉ, BM 180 376 S beryl glitters like snake's
ⲁⲗⲁⲩⲉ.

ⲁⲗⲱ, ⲉⲗⲱ S, ⲁⲗⲟⲩ A, pl ⲁⲗⲟⲟⲩⲉ, ⲉⲗⲟⲟⲩⲉ
S nn, *snare, trap*: Mor 18 152 S better to choose
death ϩⲓⲧⲟⲩⲁ., Mor 44 32 S ⲉⲕⲛⲁⲟϭⲧⲕ ϩⲛⲟⲩⲁ.,
Pro 6 5 A (SB ϩⲁϭⲉ, -ϫⲓ), 1 Cor 7 35 S ⲉⲗⲱ
(Mor, B do) βρόχος, ShR 2 448 S birds ⲉⲁⲩϫⲱⲗⲉϫ
ⲡⲣⲉⲛⲁⲗⲱⲟⲩ (?), ShC 73 6 S ⲛⲉⲥⲁⲗⲟⲟⲩⲉ ⲙⲛⲡⲉ(ⲥ)-
ϣⲛⲏⲟⲩ, ShZ 595 sim, ShP 130⁵ 65 ⲡⲉⲧⲥⲱⲗⲡ ⲛⲟⲩⲁ.,
Bor 248 61 S lest he die ϩⲛⲧⲉϥϩⲁϭⲉ ⲙⲛⲧⲉϥⲉⲗⲱ,
Aeg 26 S attached to ⲛⲉⲗⲟⲟⲩⲉ ⲛⲛⲉϥⲃⲁⲗ (B ⲕⲟⲩϩⲓ
error), cf BHom 6 S cares of life & ⲛⲉϥⲁⲗⲟⲟⲩⲉ
βρόχους.

ⲁⲗⲁⲃⲗⲉⲡ B v ⲗⲁⲡⲗⲉⲡ.

ⲁⲗⲟⲩⲃⲉϩ B v ⲁⲗ pebble, & ϭⲁⲗⲟⲩⲃⲓϩ.

ⲁⲗⲁⲕ SB v ϩⲁⲗⲁⲕ.

ⲁⲗⲟⲕ B, once S (P 44 110 = 43 105), nn m,
corner, angle: 3 Kg 3 20 S (lc) ἀγκάλη, Va 57 213
ϫⲉⲛⲟⲩⲕⲟⲡⲓⲁ ⲛⲧⲉ ⲟⲩⲁ. ἐν γωνίᾳ, Va 61 93 ⲉϥⲉⲛⲕⲟⲧ ϫⲉⲛⲡⲁ. ⲛⲧⲉ ⲡⲉϥⲛⲓ, MG 25 312 (S ⲕⲗϫⲉ)
southern a. of marsh, C 86 247 oath by sun, moon
ⲛⲉⲙⲡⲁ. ⲡⲧⲉ ⲫⲛⲟⲩⲛ.
Cf ⲁⲗⲟϭ, ⲱⲗⲕ (ⲉⲗⲕⲥ).

ⲁⲗⲕⲉ, ⲁⲗⲕⲏ (Cai 8530 ⲉⲣⲕⲉ, CO 303 ⲣⲕⲉ)
SB nn m (Cai 8399), *last day of month* (BM
920 207, Samannûdi's *Scala*, تدل على رأس الشهر
(ورأس الهلال), without art: BM 298 S ⲉⲧⲕⲩⲣⲓⲁⲕⲏ
ϫⲱⲛϥ ⲁ. ⲙⲡⲁⲣⲙⲟⲩⲧⲉ, Ryl 53 S heading in di-
rectory ⲁ. ⲛⲑⲟⲟⲩⲧ, Mor 52 52 S ⲉⲣⲧⲟⲟⲩⲧⲉ ⲛⲁ.
ⲙⲡⲁⲣⲙⲟⲩⲧⲉ; with ϩⲛ-, ϫⲉⲛ-: GöttN '01 329 S
ϩⲛⲁ. ⲙⲡⲉⲃⲟⲧ, EW 217, AM 179 B sim; with ⲛ-:
BIF 14 182 S ⲛϭⲙⲟⲩ ⲛⲁ. ⲙⲡⲁϣⲟⲛⲥ, Saq 234
S ⲉⲛⲧⲁⲃⲙⲧⲟⲛ ⲙⲟϩ ⲛⲁ. ⲡⲁϣⲟⲛⲥ, ib 287 ⲛⲁ. ⲗ̄
ⲧⲱⲃⲉ, C 86 167 B he entered Cairo ⲛⲁ. ⲙⲫⲁⲣ-
ⲙⲟⲩⲑⲓ.

ⲁⲗⲓⲕⲓ F v ⲁⲣⲓⲕⲉ.

ⲁⲗⲕⲟⲩ B nn f, *flask*: K 149, P 55 10, ϯⲁ.
قارورة (φλασκίον), but K 263 ⲛⲓⲁ. (var ⲉⲗⲕⲟⲩ).
Prob confused with ⲛⲓⲁ. (ⲉⲗⲕⲱ) *sycamore fruit*.
Cf ⲃⲁⲗⲕⲟⲩ.

ⲁⲗⲕⲟⲩ B *sycamore fruit* v ⲉⲗⲕⲱ.

ⲁⲗⲓⲕⲧ S nn m, *meaning unknown*: CO 477 in
list of metal objects ⲥⲛⲱ ⲛ̄ⲁ. But in Ep 495
l ϯ ⲛⲁ. ⲉⲣⲟϥ & cf DM 13 15 n 'lykt f, a metal
object.

ⲁⲗⲓⲗ *SB*, ⲁⲗⲓⲗⲓ *B* nn m, *field mouse*: Lev 11
30 μυγαλῆ = Va 1 خلد *mole* (but P 44 55 خلدة
ἐχῖνος). As name ? = ᾿Αλέλε (Preisigke).

ⲁⲗⲱⲗ *S* vb intr, meaning unknown, ? *be impatient, desire eagerly*: P 129¹⁶ 9 martyr to judge,
Settle our affair speedily, ϫⲉⲧⲛⲁ. ⲙⲙⲁⲧⲉ (*l* ⲉⲙ-)
ⲉⲧⲣⲛⲃⲱⲕ ⲉⲣⲁⲧϥ ⲙⲡⲉⲭ̄ⲥ̄, ib 10 sim (an incorrect
MS.). ⲧⲏ(ⲛ)ⲁ-ⲗⲱⲗ not prob.

ⲁⲗⲟⲩⲗⲁ *S*, ⲁⲗⲓⲗⲁⲓ *A* nn, an insect: Nah 3
17 ἀττέλαβος *S* (P 44 116 = 43 119, *B* = Gk) هزج،
word variously explained. BM 729 93 translates
قمل *louse*.

ⲁⲗⲗⲁ *v* ⲗⲁ.

ⲁⲗⲗⲟⲩ *v* ⲁⲗⲱ.

ⲁⲗⲁⲁⲗⲓ *F*, ⲁⲗⲟⲗⲓ *B* *v* ⲉⲗⲟⲟⲗⲉ.

ⲁⲗⲱⲗⲉ *S* *v* ⲁⲗ *pebble*.

ⲁⲗⲗⲱⲏ *SSʲ*, ⲁⲗⲗⲟⲏ *SB* nn m, fabulous
eastern bird, strongly scented: AZ 33 54 *Sʲ*, K 169
B سندال *salamander* (= BM Or 8775 74 وجى ‘
المرّ), LMis 81 360 *B*; or animal (ζῷον): Mor 25
18 = JTS 4 394 *S* = AZ 12 125 *B* (Va 61 100).
Cf PMéd 63 & Lab 23 *inf*. Doubtless mere mis-
use of plant-name ⲁⲗⲗⲱⲏ, ⲁⲗⲗⲱⲓ ἀλόη (Cant 4 14,
Jo 19 39, Gu 33, WTh 152).

ⲁⲗⲗⲱⲕⲓ, -ⲱⲕⲏ, -ⲟⲕⲓ *B* nn m, a plant: K
178, 271 موز (banana) which = ⲡ̄ⲧⲉⲕⲓⲡⲟⲛ (? ἰνδικός)
P 44 81, var قسطالى موز 43 55. Possibly *l* ⲡⲁⲗ-
ⲗⲱⲕⲓ, cf P 55 6 ⲙⲡⲓⲟⲗⲗⲟⲕⲓ. Coptic? ᾿Αγάλλοχον
seems unsuitable.

ⲁⲗⲟⲙ *S* nn m, *bosom*: Ps 128 7 (Budge &
Mich, *B* ⲕⲉⲛϥ) κόλπος, ShP 130² 56 cursed whoso
runneth to neighbour ⲉⲧⲣⲉϥⲕⲧⲉ ⲡⲉϥⲁ. ⲉⲃⲟⲗ [ⲉ]ⲣⲟϥ
ⲛϥϯⲡⲓ [ⲉⲣ]ⲟⲩϥ ϩⲛⲟⲩⲡⲁⲑⲟⲥ ⲡⲉⲡⲓⲟⲩⲙⲓⲁ.

ⲁⲗⲱⲙ *B* *v* ϩⲁⲗⲱⲙ.

ⲁⲗⲁⲥⲱϯ *B* nn pl, *army*: BM 920 265 scala
ⲡⲁ. عسكر. Coptic ?

ⲁⲗⲱⲧ *SF* nn f. **a.** *compulsory service, forced
labour*, paral ⲕⲃⲁ ἀγγαρεία q *v*: BMis 207 *S* of
Jews in Egypt ⲙⲁⲣⲟⲩⲣ ⲕⲃⲁ ϩⲓⲁ. ⲧⲏⲣⲟⲩ, var Mor
16 50 ⲛⲉⲕⲃⲁ ⲙⲡⲛⲁ. of all the land, TurM 6 *S*
nothing beyond due tax shall be demanded ⲛⲁⲧ-
ⲣⲟⲕⲧⲱⲛ (ὄγδοον, cf Ryl 124 I) ⲡⲁⲧⲁ. ⲡⲁⲧⲗⲁⲁⲩ
ⲛⲃⲁⲣⲟⲥ, Kr 145 *S* no services beyond those stipu-
lated ⲡⲁⲧⲁ. ⲡⲁⲧⲣⲟⲩⲁ/ ⲡⲁⲧⲛⲉⲉϥ, BM 589 *F* ⲉⲕⲕⲱ
(ⲙ)ⲙⲁⲓ ⲉⲃⲁⲗ ϩⲛⲧⲁ., Ryl 253 *S* as item in expenses
ϩⲁⲧⲁ. **b.** *a turn, course* of service: 4 Kg 12 9 *S*
ⲉⲧⲣⲉⲡⲟⲩⲁ ⲡⲟⲩⲁ ⲙⲙⲟⲟⲩ ⲣ ⲁ. in Lord's house
(Gk om, or Brooke suggests = ? Lucian's εἰσπο-
ρευομένων ἀνδρῶν), ShMiss 4 283 *S* 2 men at door

ⲟⲩⲁⲗⲱⲧ ⲉⲟⲩⲁ...ⲡⲧⲉⲓϩⲉ ⲉⲩⲡⲁⲣ ⲁ. ⲡϭⲓ ⲡⲉⲧⲥⲟⲃⲧⲉ
ϩⲓⲡⲙⲁ ⲡⲟⲩⲱⲙ, Ep 1 p 7 *S* graffiti ⲁⲓⲣ ⲟⲩⲁ.
ⲙⲡⲓⲙⲁ, BMar 180 *S* advice to novice to choose a
pious teacher, ⲙⲡⲣⲕⲁⲁϥ ⲉⲃⲟⲗ ϩⲛⲧⲕⲁ. ⲛⲧⲃⲱⲕ
ϣⲁⲕⲉⲟⲩⲁ (cf Esaias Scet. ed Jerusalem 17, though
this phrase om). **c.** a certain number, quantity
(cf ? brace, pair): ST 378 *S* for 2 years past hath
he caught doves, the 1st year ⲁϥϭⲱⲡ ϩⲓ̈ ⲡⲁ., the
2nd ⲡⲓ̈ ⲡⲁ., RE 9 136 *S* they sent by night ⲁⲩ-
ϩⲁⲣⲡⲁϫⲉ ⲙⲯⲓⲧⲉ ⲡⲁ. ⲡ[ⲧ]ⲃⲏⲏ (*sic l*).

ⲁⲗⲧⲕⲁⲥ *S*, ⲁⲧⲕⲁⲥ *B* nn m, mostly as pl, *marrow*: Ge 45 18 *B* sg, Nu 24 8 *S* (*B* ⲱⲧ), Ps 65 15
B ⲱⲧ ⲡⲁ. (*S* diff), Job 21 24 *S* pl *B* sg, ib 33 24
SB, He 4 12 *SB* μυελός; Ryl 94 103 *S* cold pierced
ϣⲁⲛⲉⲩⲁ., Leyd 401 *S* seal of baptism reaches ϩⲛⲡⲁ.
ⲙⲡⲥⲱⲙⲁ, TT 150 *S* = C 89 77 *B*, with false etymol,
ib 444 عظم بغير عظم *boneless place*, BHom 123 *S* ⲁⲗⲕⲥ
sic, *l* ⲁⲗⲧⲕⲁⲥ, P 44 68 *S* = ἐνκρόταφος شبكة الدماغ
(? error), PMéd 238 *S* calf's marrow in a plaster.

ⲁⲗⲟⲩ *S*, ⲁⲗⲉⲩ, ⲁⲗⲏⲩ *SF* adj, *white*: P 44 66
= 43 35 λευκόν, λεύκωσις; of metals: AZ 23 103
S ⲃⲁⲣⲟⲑ (opp ⲧⲟⲣϣ), 112 ⲕⲁⲥⲓⲧⲏⲣⲉ, 115 ⲧⲁϭⲧ (opp
ⲕⲁⲙⲏ), BM 1135 *S* ⲟⲃⲉⲛ; glass: Bodl(P) a 2 38
S (*v* ⲁⲃⲁϭⲛⲉⲓⲛ); gum: PMéd 157 *S*; pepper: *ib*
154; beans: WS 124, Ryl 347 *S*; olives: Bodl(P)
b 9 *S*; wine: BKU 1 8 34 *S*, CMSS 30 *F* (cf οἶνος
ἄσπρος); wool: Ryl 107, PMéd 244 *S*; clothing:
Bodl(P) a 1 pass; sheep: MR 2 46 *S* (opp ⲕⲁⲙⲉ);
swan: P 44 56 ⲧϫⲓⲕⲡⲁⲥ (cygnus) ⲟⲩϩⲁⲗⲏⲧ ⲡ(ⲁ)-
ⲗⲁⲩⲡⲉ (*sic l*) طائر ابيض; doubtful BM 527 19 *F*.
In name prob: Κακαλαῦ, -εῦ (Preisigke); in
place-name ? PLond 4 232 Πια(ϩ) Αλαυ.

ⲁⲗⲏⲟⲩ *F* *v* ⲁⲣⲏⲩ & ⲉⲣⲏⲩ.

ⲁⲗⲓⲟⲩⲓ *B* *v* ⲱⲗ.

ⲁⲗⲱⲟⲅⲉ *S*, ⲁⲗⲱⲟⲩ, ⲁⲗⲱⲟⲅⲓ (*v* Stern 210) *B*
nn pl, *bunch* of grapes (Kabis), P 46 152 *S*, K 177
B شماريخ *stalks* with bunch (Löw 119 n); قلب النخل
pith of (palm) stem (Lab). Cf ϩⲡⲁⲩ *B* & ? ⲗⲟⲟⲩ *S*
bunch.

ⲁⲗϣⲱⲟⲩ *B* *v* ⲉⲗⲟⲟⲗⲉ.

ⲁⲗⲉϩ *F* *v* ϩⲁⲣⲉϩ.

ⲁⲗⲟϫ *B* *v* ⲁⲗⲟϭ.

ⲁⲗⲟϫ⳿ *F* *v* ⲁⲣⲏϫ⳿.

ⲁⲗⲓϫⲓ *B* nn m, *fuller's earth*: K 205 طفل, *v*
AZ 12 125, Dozy 2 47.

ⲁⲗⲭⲁⲓ *B* nn pl, *large fish*: BM Or 8775 136
ⲡⲓⲁ. حيتان elsewhere = κῆτος: Ge 1 21, Mt
12 40, P 44 54, K 170).

ⲁⲗⲟϭ *S* (rare), ⲁⲗⲟⲭ *B*, pl ? ⲁⲗⲱⲝ *B* nn m (f BM Or 8775 129, Ap 19 16 var), *cf* ⲁⲗⲟⲕ, ⲱⲗⲕ (ⲉⲗⲕⲥ), **a.** *thigh*: Ge 32 25, 47 29 *B* (opp ϯⲡⲓ), Deu 28 57 *B*, Ps 44 4 *B*, Ez 7 17 *B*, Ap 19 16 *B* (all *S* = Gk) μηρός (which once, Cant 7 2 *S*=ⲕⲉⲣⲧⲉ); Va 59 19 *B* ⲁⲅϭⲱϣ ⲛⲡⲁϥⲁⲧ ⲡⲉⲙⲡⲁⲁ. = GMir 263 *S* ⲙⲉⲗⲟⲥ (μηρός), C 43 167 *B* sim, *ib* 8 *B* ϩⲓⲟⲩⲓ ⲛⲧⲉⲕϭⲓϫ ⲉϩⲟⲩⲛ ϩⲉⲡⲡⲉⲕⲁ. (or ? under **d**), AM 286 *B* πρόσταγμα given to messenger, ⲁⲩⲧⲱϩ ⲙⲡⲉϥⲁ. = Mor 48 46 *S* ⲉϥⲧⲟⲟϩⲉ ⲉⲡⲉϥ ⲙⲉⲣⲟⲥ (μηρός), Va 61 25 *B* he smote him ⲉϫⲉⲛⲡⲉϥⲁ. the place called his ⲁⲗⲁⲕⲥⲱⲟⲩⲧⲉⲛ μηρόν...λεγομένης πανούκλας (though παν. = *panicula* tumour, Du Cange), Rec 39 96 *S* magician splits bull & weighs ⲡⲁ. ⲥⲛⲁⲩ (μέρος ? was read μηρός, *cf* C 86 210, 7), RAl 129 *S* ⲡⲉϥⲁ. ⲥⲛⲁⲩ doubtful. **b.** *knees*, pl: Ge 30 3, 48 12 *B* (*S* ⲡⲁⲧ), 4 Kg 4 20 *B* γόνατα, Va 57 198 *B* Joseph ϩⲁⲧⲉⲛⲡⲉⲡⲁ. ⲛⲑⲁⲓ Potiphar's wife, *ib* sim ⲕⲉⲗⲓ. **c.** *arms*, pl: Pro 5 20 *B* (*S* ϭⲃⲟⲓ) ἀγκάλαι, *cf* ⲁⲗⲟⲕ. **d.** *shoulders*, pl: C 43 221 *B* arms cut off ⲓⲥϫⲉⲛⲡⲉϥⲁ. ⲉⲃⲟⲗ, Va 59 10 *B* that his arms ϫϥⲟⲓ be cut off ⲛⲥⲉϥⲁϩⲟⲩ ϣⲁⲉϩⲟⲩⲛ ⲉⲡⲉϥⲁ. In Mk 14 65 *B* ϭⲓ ⲁ. (*S* ϯ ⲁⲁⲥ) ῥαπίσμασι λαμβάνειν ? diff word, or ? *cf* Mt 26 67 *S* var ⲕⲗⲭ (ⲕⲗⲭⲉ) for ⲕⲗⲯ.

ⲁⲁⲙ *S* nn, a drug prescribed, with jujube, euphorbium & myrrh, for an intestinal malady: PMéd 316. *Cf* ⲉⲙ (Chassinat).

ⲁⲙⲁ *v* ⲁⲡⲁ.

ⲁⲙⲉ *S*, ⲁⲙⲏ *F* (sg rare), pl ⲁⲙⲏⲩ, ⲁⲙⲏⲅⲉ *S*, ⲁⲙⲏⲟⲩ *Sf* (P Beatty) *B*, ⲁⲙⲁⲅⲉⲓ *F* nn m, *herd* (*pastor*) of cattle or sheep: J 80 60 *S* ⲁⲡⲟⲕ ⲙⲛⲁⲡⲁ ...ⲡⲁ., CMSS 63 *F* Abraham ⲡⲁ., Mus 40 38 *S* none shall enter fold save ⲛⲁⲙⲏⲩ *armentariis et bubulcis*, P Beatty *S* list of cultivators ⲟⲩⲟⲉⲓⲉ and herdsmen ⲁⲙⲏ, MG 25 236 *B* the ⲁⲙⲏⲟⲩ bring their ⲉϩⲱⲟⲩ, Ryl 158, 160 *S* lessee to water land with own beasts ⲙⲛ ⲛⲁⲧⲣⲟⲫⲟⲟⲩⲉ ⲙⲛⲛⲁ ⲃⲉⲕⲉ ⲁⲙⲏⲩ, CMSS *lc F* ⲛⲉⲁⲙⲁⲅⲉⲓ.

In place-names: ⲡⲟⲩⲱϩ ⲛⲁⲙⲏⲩ Mor 48 105 = ⲡⲡⲓⲁⲙⲏⲟⲩ C 43 149, village N. of Ahnâs on W. bank, *cf* ابوامى near Beni Suêf (WS 152 n); & ⲧⲁⲡⲁⲙⲏⲩ BM 1036, 1077; also Mor 37 93 *S*. ⲡⲁⲙⲏⲅⲉ = τὰ βουκόλια PG 26 913 (*v* Quatremère *Mém* 1 224).

ⲁⲙⲉ *B* *v* ⲉⲙⲉ.

ⲁⲙⲉ *A* *v* ⲟⲙⲉ.

ⲁⲉⲓⲙⲉ *A* *v* ⲟⲓⲙⲉ.

ⲁⲙⲏ *S* nn m, *wasp*: Ex 23 28, Deu 7 20, Jos 24 12 σφηκιά زنبور, Sa 12 8 σφήξ, ? = corresponding pl *B* (ⲁϥ) ⲙⲃⲓⲟⲩ; *cf* also ϩⲁⲃⲟⲩⲉⲓ (ⲁⲃⲟⲩⲉⲓ). *Cf* Stern 221.

ⲁⲙⲏ *v* ⲁⲙⲟⲩ.

ⲁⲙⲟⲓ *B* *v* ϩⲁⲙⲟⲓ.

ⲁⲙⲟⲩ *SAA²BFO*, ⲉⲙⲟⲩ *O*, 2d sg m, used as imper of ⲉⲓ *come*, often where several are addressed: Ge 31 44 *SB*, 1 Kg 16 1 *B*, Ap 21 9 *SB* δεῦρο; Pro 1 11 *SAB*, Mt 14 29 *SBF* ἐλθέ, Mt 5 24 *B*, Ap. 22 17 *SB* ἐλθών, Jo 11 34 *SAA²*, Ap 6 1, 22 17 *SB* ἔρχου; 4 Kg 4 25 *B* ἄγε; **a.** ⲉ-: Ac 16 9 *SB* διαβὰς εἰς, BM 590(2) *B*, ⲁ. ⲉϩⲏⲧ; ⲁ. ⲉⲃⲟⲗ: Jo 11 43 *SA²B* δεῦρο ἔξω; ⲁ. ⲉϩⲣⲁⲓ: Jud 1 3 *S*, Ap 4 1 *S* (*B* ⲁ. ⲉⲡϣⲱⲓ) ἀνάβα, ἀνάβηθι; ⲁ. ⲉⲡⲉⲥⲏⲧ: Mt 27 40 *SB*, Jo 4 49 *S* (*A²* ⲁϩⲣⲏⲓ, *B* ⲉϩⲣⲏⲓ) κατάβηθι; ⲁ. ⲉϩⲟⲩⲛ, ⲉϩ-: Jer 18 2 *B* κατάβ. εἰς, AZ 21 98 *O* ⲉⲙⲟⲩ ⲡⲁⲓ ⲉϩⲟⲩⲛ (*ib* 99 ⲁⲙⲟⲩ), Ep. 213 *S*.

ⲁⲙⲏ *SA²BF* 2d sg f: Ge 19 32 *SB*, Jud 9 10 *S*, Jo 4 16 *BF*, KKS 24 *S*, R 1 5 35 *S*, AP 16 *A²*, Hall 36 *S* ⲁⲙⲉ ⲁϩⲟⲩⲛ, C 43 118 *B* ⲁ. ⲉⲃⲟⲗ.

a ⲁⲙⲏⲛⲓ, *b* ⲁⲙⲏⲉⲓⲧⲛ, *c* ⲁⲙⲱⲓⲛⲉ *S*, *d* ⲁⲙⲏⲉⲓⲛⲉ *A*, *e* ⲁⲙⲏ(ⲛ)ⲧⲛ *A²*, *f* ⲁⲙⲱⲓⲛⲓ *BF*, *g* ⲁⲙⲟⲓⲛⲓ, *h* ⲁⲙⲱⲛⲓ, *i* ⲁⲙⲱⲧⲛ, ⲁⲙⲱⲓⲧⲛ *F*, 2d pl of above: *a* Is 27 11, 56 9, 10 (var ⲁⲙⲏⲓⲧⲛ), Jer 26 9 *B* ⲁⲙⲱⲓⲛⲓ, Mt 25 34 (BHom 39, 63, 78 = H ⲁⲙⲏⲓⲧⲛ), BHom 130 δεῦτε, but *ib* 11, 13, 37, Br 112 Copt implies 1st pl, though Gk 2d (*v* KKS 1*.5*); *b* = *f* Ps 45 8, Jer 11 19, Mt 11 28; *c* only MIF 9 60 (= Stern 385) ⲁ. ⲧⲁⲅⲅⲉⲗⲓⲕⲏ ⲧⲏⲣⲥ (var ⲁⲙⲏⲉⲓⲧⲛ); *d* Ex 1 10, Pro 9 5, Hos 6 1, Jon 1 7, Mic 4 2; *e* Jo 4 29, AP 9; *f* mostly = *b*, Ps 99 2 = *S* ⲃⲱⲕ ⲉϩⲟⲩⲛ, Ps 33 6 = *S* ϯ ⲟⲩⲟⲓ, C 43 247 ⲁ. ϫⲱⲕ ⲉⲃⲟⲗ ⲙⲡⲉⲧⲉⲛⲡⲣⲱⲃ, AM 6 ⲁ. ⲛⲧⲉⲛϣⲉ ⲡⲁⲛ, Mor 24 8 *F*; *g* Jo 4 29; *h* Mor 30 31, 40; *i* Pcod Mor 49, 52.

ⲁⲙⲟⲩ *cat* *v* ⲉⲙⲟⲩ.

ⲁⲙⲏ *F* *v* ⲁⲙⲣⲉ.

ⲁⲙⲁⲗⲏⲝ *B* **a.** vb intr, *embrace*: *c* ⲉ-, Ge 29 13 (*S* ϩⲱⲗϭ), 48 10 (*S* ϩⲱⲡ ⲉϩⲟⲩⲛ) περιλαμβάνειν, Va 57 189 ⲁⲥⲁ. ⲉⲛⲉⲥⲕⲉⲗⲓ ἅπτεσθαι, WTh 40 ⲉϥⲁ. ⲉⲡⲉϥⲓⲱⲧ; *c* ⲉϩⲟⲩⲛ ⲉ-, TstAb 229 ⲁϥⲁ. ⲉϩ. ⲉⲡⲉϥⲓⲱⲧ. **b,** more often as nn with ⲉⲣ-: Pro 4 8 περιλαμβ., ROC 17 405 ⲉⲥⲉⲣⲁ. ⲉⲣⲟϥ ἀγκάλαις ἐμπλέκεσθαι; TstAb *lc* ⲁϥⲉⲣ ⲁ. ⲉϩ. ⲉⲓⲁⲕⲱⲃ, MG 25 384 ⲉϥⲉⲣ ⲁ. ⲉϫⲉⲛⲡⲟⲩⲗⲩⲙϣⲁⲡⲟⲛ.

ϫⲓⲛⲉⲣ ⲁ. *B* nn m, *act of embracing*: Va 62 271 they spread hands ⲉⲡϫ. ⲉϩⲟⲩⲛ ⲉⲣⲱⲟⲩ. *Cf* ⲙⲟⲩⲗϫ.

ⲁⲙⲓⲛ *B* nn m, *pot* of soapstone: K 129 ⲡⲓⲁ. برام (*v* Dozy 1 77, Almk 2 52).

ⲁⲙⲛⲁ *B* nn m, among herbs & perfumes: K 189 ⲡⲓⲁ. ؟ (on plant *manna* *v* Encycl. Bibl. s v, ii). In Lu 19 μνᾶ is ⲙⲛⲁ, ⲉⲙⲛⲁ *SB*, sg & pl, امناء منا.

ⲁⲙⲟⲛⲓ B, vb **I.** intr, mostly = *SA* ⲁⲙⲁϩⲧⲉ (here abbrev -ⲧⲉ), *F* ⲁⲙⲉϧⲓ, *prevail, be in possession, be strong*: Pro 12 24, Jer 20 7 κρατεῖν, Jon 2 7 (*S* -ⲧⲉ); 1 Cor 7 30 (*S* -ⲧⲉ, *F* -ϧⲓ) κατέχειν; Miss 4 203 Synod of Chalcedon, lo, 31 years ⲓⲥϫⲉⲛⲉⲧⲁⲥⲁ.; c ⲉ-, *v* below ⲁ. ⲛⲉⲙ-. **II.** tr, *seize, possess, detain*: Jer 47 1 λαμβάνειν; Ps 106 17, Is 67 7 (both *S* ϣⲱⲡ ⲉ-) ἀντιλ. (*cf* ⲁ. ⲛⲧⲉⲛ-); AM 279 ἀπολ.; ROC 17 409 ⲁⲡⲓⲱⲧ ⲁ. ⲙⲡⲉϥϣⲏⲣⲓ διαλ.; Ex 4 4 (*A* -ⲧⲉ), Jer 30 24, Zech 14 13 (*A* ? -ⲧⲉ), Mt 14 31 (*S* -ⲧⲉ), 1 Tim 6 12 (*S* ϭⲱⲗϫ) ἐπιλ.; Dan 12 21, Ac 1 16 (*S* ϭⲱⲡⲉ) συλλ.; Ps 16 12 (*S* ⲉⲓⲱⲣⲙ ⲛⲥⲁ-, *F* ⲁⲙⲉϧⲓ) ὑπολ.; 4 Kg 4 8, Ps 72 23 (*S* -ⲧⲉ), Pro 14 8, Dan 5 12, Mt 14 3 (*S* -ⲧⲉ, *F* -ϧⲓ), Ac 2 24 (var ⲁⲙⲁϧⲓ, *S* -ⲧⲉ) κρατεῖν; 1 Cor 9 25 (var ⲁ. ⲛⲧⲉⲛ-, *S* = Gk) ἐγκρ.; Jer 47 10, Nah 3 14 (*A* ⲱϧⲉ ⲁⲣⲉⲧ ⲁϫⲛ-) κατακρ.; Job 2 3 (*S* ⲉϥϭⲏⲛ-), Pro 1 21 (*S* ϭⲱⲗϫ) ἔχειν; Jer 51 10 (*S* -ⲧⲉ), Is 56 2 (*S* ϭⲱⲗϫ) ἀντέχ.; ROC 17 400 ἐπέχ. *hold out, toward* (breast to babe); Ps 68 37, Jer 27 16 (both *S* -ⲧⲉ), Ps 138 10 (*S* ϣⲱϫⲡ), Va 63 81 my tongue a reed ⲉϥⲁ. ⲙⲙⲟϥ ⲛϫⲉ ⲡⲓⲡⲛ̄ⲁ̄ κατέχ.; Ps 21 13, 114 3 (*S* -ⲧⲉ) περιέχ.; Pro 5 20 (*S* diff), Lu 22 63, Phil 1 23 (both *S* -ⲧⲉ) συνέχ.; Ps 2 12 (*S* ϭⲱⲗϫ) δράσσεσθαι; Ez 31 15 ἐφιστάναι; Lu 24 29 (*S* -ⲧⲉ) παραβιάζεσθαι; C 89 65 (*S* -ⲧⲉ) ⲁ. ⲙⲙⲟϥ ϣⲁϯ κωλύειν; Ps 17 5 (*S* -ⲧⲉ) προφθάνειν (*cf* Ps 114 3); Miss 4 202 darkness ⲁ. ⲡϯⲟⲓⲕⲟⲩⲙⲉⲛⲏ. Va 61 13 ⲟⲩⲛⲏⲥⲧⲓⲁ…ⲡⲉⲧⲉⲛⲁ. ⲙⲙⲟⲥ *ib* 16 ⲉⲩⲁ. ⲙⲙⲟϥ ϩⲉⲛⲟⲩϧⲟϯ, MG 25 58 woman ⲉⲁϧⲁ. ⲙⲙⲟⲥ ϧⲓⲧⲉⲛⲟⲩϫⲟⲙ (*cf* below, ⲉϫⲉⲛ-), Cat 31 ⲁϥⲁ. ⲙⲙⲟϥ ⲡⲧⲉϥϫⲓϫ, WTh 48 ⲁϥⲁ. ⲙⲙⲟϥ ⲛⲥⲁⲡⲓϧⲱ of his head, BSM 77 ⲁⲡⲁ. ⲙⲙⲱⲟⲩ ⲉⲣ ⲡⲗⲟⲅⲕⲟϫⲓ *arrest* for debt, sim Va 58 65 lest God ⲉⲣ ⲡⲕⲉⲁ. ⲙⲙⲟⲕ ⲉⲡⲁⲥⲛⲟϥ (*cf* -ⲧⲉ tr), C 86 309 ⲁⲣⲉϣⲁⲛⲧϥⲉ ⲁ. ⲡⲡⲉⲥⲙⲟⲩ ⲡⲣⲱⲟⲩ (*cf* ⲧⲁϧⲛⲟ συνέχ. Ge 8 2 &c).

—— ⲉϫⲉⲛ-, same meanings; MG 25 307 (*S* -ⲧⲉ) a fever ⲁϥⲁ. ⲉϫⲱϥ (*cf* above), CaiEuch 585 every soul ⲉⲧⲟⲩⲁ. ⲉϫⲱⲟⲩ περιέχ. (in durance).

—— ⲛⲉⲙ-, *support, help*: Va 68 41 Noah in evil world, ⲛⲓⲙⲡⲉ ⲉⲑⲛⲁⲁ. ⲛⲉⲙⲁϥ ?, *cf ib* 36 Eve Adam's helpmeet ϫⲉⲉⲥⲛⲁⲁ. ⲉⲣⲟϥ in his labours.

—— ⲛⲧⲉⲛ-, **a.** *hold, be in possession of*: 1 Tim 6 2 (*S* ϭⲱⲗϫ) ἀντιλαμβάνειν (*v* above). **b.** *endure, wait for*: Job 6 11 (*S* = Gk), Ps 36 34, Jer 14 19, Mt 10 22, He 12 2 (*S* all = Gk), MG 25 173 Our Lord ⲛⲁⲁ. ⲛⲧⲟⲧϥ ⲉⲣⲱⲟⲩ, C 43 203 ⲉϥⲁ. ⲛⲧⲟⲧϥ in orthodoxy. **c.** *restrain self*: Ge 43 31 ἐγκρατεύεσθαι, Va 64 160 ⲁ. ⲛⲧⲟⲧⲕ ⲥⲁⲃⲟⲗ ⲙⲡⲓⲟⲩⲱⲙ.

—— ϧⲓϫⲉⲛ-, *overcome*: C 43 38 fear ⲁ. ϧⲓϫⲱϥ.

ⲁⲧϣⲁ. ⲛⲧⲉⲛ- adj, *unrestrained, uncontrollable*:

Va 64 156 wrath ⲛⲁⲧⲁϣⲁ. ⲛⲧⲟⲧϥ ὀξυθυμία, Va 58 110 they bore a mighty name ⲛⲁⲧϣⲁ. ⲛⲧⲟⲧϥ.

ⲙⲉⲧⲁⲧϣⲁ. ⲛⲧⲉⲛ- nn f, *uncontrolledness, intemperance*: Va 58 72 of youth, 109 of drunkenness, *ib* 192 (*S* ⲙⲛⲧⲁⲧⲁⲙⲁϩⲧⲉ) ἀκολασία.

ⲁⲙⲟⲛⲓ nn m, *handle*: K 126 قبض (*cf* under ⲁⲙⲁϩⲧⲉ I).

ⲁ. ⲛⲧⲉⲛ- nn m, *endurance, patience*: Ps 61 6, 2 Cor 1 6, Ap 2 2 (all *S* = Gk) ὑπομονή, AM 221 ⲉⲧⲁⲓⲉⲣ ⲡⲕⲉⲁ. ⲛⲧⲟⲧ ⲉⲡⲁⲓϧⲓⲥⲓ, *ib* 212 sim.

ⲙⲉⲧⲣⲉϥⲁ. ⲛⲧⲉⲛ- nn f, *endurance*: He 12 3 (*S* Gk diff).

ϫⲓⲛⲁ. nn m, *arrest, restraint*: Cat 111 give us sign ⲉⲡϫ. ⲙⲙⲟϥ (*v* Mk 14 44), Va 57 277 ⲡⲓϫ. ⲉϫⲉⲛϯⲡⲉϫⲓ κρατεῖν τοῦ.

ⲁⲙⲟⲛⲓ B *v* ⲙⲟⲟⲛⲉ.

ⲁⲙⲱⲓⲛⲉ S, ⲁⲙⲏⲉⲓⲛⲉ A *v* ⲁⲙⲟⲩ.

ⲁⲙⲛ̄ⲧⲉ SA, ⲉⲙⲛ̄ⲧⲉ AA² (Cl, AP), ⲁⲙⲉⲛϯ BF nn m (Job 15 16, Ps 48 15, Hos 13 14 *A*, Is 5 14, 14 9), *hades*, lit the *western* place (*v* ⲉⲙⲛ̄ⲧ), treated as name without art.: Deu 32 22, 1 Kg 2 6, Job 7 9 *SB*, Eccl 9 10 *S* & bible pass ᾅδης مست ?; 2 Kg 22 6 *S* θάνατος, Ez 31 14 *B* βόθρος, Job 40 15 *S* τάρταρος, *cf* Z 233 *S*, AM 40 *B*, C 43 229 *B* ⲧⲁⲣⲧⲁⲣⲟⲥ ⲛⲁⲙⲛⲧⲉ, Pro 15 11 *S* ⲁ. ⲙⲛⲡⲟⲩⲛ, Mor 41 193 *S* ⲁ. = BIF 22 106 *F* ⲛⲟⲩⲛ. In Job 15 16 *S* (*B* = Gk), Jer 15 7 *B* erroneous ?; BHom 116 *S* ⲡⲙⲁ ⲉⲧⲟⲩⲙⲟⲩⲧⲉ ⲉⲣⲟϥ ϫⲉⲁ.

ⲁⲙⲡⲏⲣϣ S *v* ⲡⲏⲣϣ.

ⲁⲙⲉⲣ O (DM) *v* ⲙⲏⲣ.

ⲁⲙⲏⲣ B *v* ϧⲁⲙⲏⲣ.

ⲁⲙⲣⲉ SB, ⲁⲙⲣⲏ S, ⲛⲙⲣⲏ (? ⲉⲙ-) Sᵃ (Hall 47), ⲁⲙⲗⲏ F, pl ⲁⲙⲣⲏⲟⲩ S, ⲁⲙⲣⲏⲟⲩ B & sg as pl, nn m, *baker*: Ge 40 1 *SB* (ἀρχι)σιτοποιός, *ib* 17 *B* (*S* ⲙⲛⲧⲁ.) σιτοπ.; BMis 1194 *S* an ἐργάτης ⲟⲩⲁ. ϩⲛⲧⲩⲧⲉⲭⲛⲏ, Miss 4 637 *S* ⲛⲁ. (sg, *B* ⲁⲙⲣⲏⲟⲩ) ⲉⲧⲧⲱϣ ⲛⲟⲉⲓⲕ, Ep 296 *S* ⲟⲩⲁ. ⲉⲧⲥⲟⲟⲩⲛ ⲛⲧⲱⲕ, BMis 376 *S* (*F* ⲁⲙⲗⲏ) he bought corn & gave it to the ⲁ., ShC 73 146-7 *S* ⲁ. in charge of bakery; his oven: MG 25 222 *B* ⲡⲓϧⲣⲱⲡ ⲛⲧⲉ ⲡⲓⲁ., C 41 20 *B* sim = *S* ⲧⲣⲓⲣ (*cf* Lev 26 26), EW 82 *B* ⲙⲁ ⲛⲁ. *bakery* (so prob *l* Va 58 66 *B* he that baked ϩⲉⲛⲡⲓⲁ.), Cai 8010 2 *S* (Severus) heretics who ask, Did ϩⲉⲛⲁⲙⲣⲏⲩ follow the Lord to bake for him ?, ST 363 *S* letter from a baker. On bakers & baking *v* Ep 1 162. *Cf* ⲁϩⲣⲉⲙ.

ⲙⲛⲧ-, ⲙⲉⲧⲁ. *SB* nn f, *art, process of baking*: Ge 40 17 *S* (BIF 12 294) ἔργον σιτοποιοῦ, C 89 82 *B* ⲡⲓⲙⲁ ⲛⲟⲩⲱϣⲙ ⲡⲉⲙⲡⲓⲕⲉⲙⲉⲧⲁ. (*sic* MS), Miss 4 583 *S*.

In name, Παμλῆ (Preisigke). In place-name, ⲡⲥⲉⲛⲧⲓⲟⲡ ⲛⲧⲉ ⲡⲓⲁⲙⲣⲏⲧ S WTh 186 (cf سنديون in markaz Fuwah).

ⲁⲙⲣⲉ B nn f, meaning doubtful: BM 920 265, Ryl 453 336 مقشّ cleansed, winnowed corn (cf K 233 ⲉϥⲕⲏⲕ مقشّ), but ? l مقشّ kneaded flour (قشد = عجن Sobhy).

ⲁⲙⲛⲏⲣⲓ B v ⲉⲙⲛⲣⲉ.

ⲁⲙⲣⲏϩⲉ SA, ⲁⲙⲣⲉϩⲉ S, ⲁⲙⲣⲉϩⲓ F, (ⲉ)ⲙⲣⲉϩⲓ, ⲙⲃⲣⲉϩⲓ, ⲏⲃⲣⲉϩⲓ, ⲉⲣⲡⲣⲉϩⲓ (C 86 286) B, nn m (P 44 66, Mor 24 25), bitumen, asphalt, opp ⲗⲁⲙϫⲁⲡⲧ pitch: Ge 11 3 B, 14 10 B, Ex 2 3 AB ἄσφαλτος زفت; Ge 6 14 SB † ⲁ. ἀσφαλτοῦν, cf Wess 18 80 S ⲱⲥϭ ⲙⲙⲟⲥ ⲛⲁ.; Dan 12 27 (Bel) B στέαρ (? error); in martyrs' tortures ⲁ. & ⲗⲁⲙϫ. often named together: C 43 120, 234, C 86 286 R = BSG 185 S, BIF 14 116 S, in Arabic زفت وقطران; sometimes ⲁⲥⲫⲁⲗⲧⲟⲛ for ⲁ.: C 43 70 B, Ann 1917 152 S (cf where ⲁⲥⲫ. alone: C 43 80, C 86 221, AM 310); Bor 264 ult S firewood smeared with wax & ⲁ., Mor 24 25 F pits filled with ⲓⲉⲃⲓ ⲛⲟⲏ ⲛⲟⲩⲁ. ⲉϥⲗⲁϫ, FR 24 S chambers filled with ⲁ., PS 380 S seas of ⲁ., Mor 41 164 S black river ⲉϥⲗⲟⲙⲥ ⲛⲑⲉ ⲛⲟⲩⲑⲏⲡ ⲙⲡⲟⲩⲁ.

ⲁⲙⲓⲥⲓ B v ⲉⲙⲓⲥⲉ.

ⲁⲙⲧⲱϩ v ⲧⲱϩ.

ⲁⲙⲁⲓⲟⲩ B v ⲉⲓⲟⲙ.

ⲁⲙⲛⲏϣ B v ⲉⲙⲛϣ.

ⲁⲙϣⲉ B v ϩⲁⲙϣⲉ.

ⲁⲙϩⲓ AB, ⲁⲙⲉϩⲓ F v ⲁⲙⲁϩⲧⲉ.

ⲁⲙϩⲁⲧ S v ⲟⲙⲉ.

ⲁⲙⲁϩⲧⲉ, ⲁⲙⲁϩⲉ SA, ⲁⲙⲁϩⲓ BA, ⲉⲙⲁϩⲧⲉ A², ⲁⲙⲉϩⲓ, ⲉⲙⲉϩⲓ, ⲙⲉϩⲓ F (on final -ⲧⲉ v Rösch 119) vb I. intr, prevail, rule, be in possession, valid, also lay hold on, so restrain (in Copt intr), often = B ⲁⲙⲟⲛⲓ: Job 9 19 SB, Pro 12 24 A (B ⲁⲙⲟⲛⲓ), Ez 21 11 SB, Lu 1 80 B (S ϭⲙ ϭⲟⲙ) κρατεῖν; Ex 6 1 B (A diff), Deu 7 21 B (S ⲧⲁϫⲣⲏⲩ), Job 26 2 S, Ps 46 10 B (S ϫⲱⲱⲣⲉ) κραταιὸς εἶναι, Ps 15 6 SB κράτιστος; Ge 7 18 B (S ϭⲙ ϭⲟⲙ), Lam 2 22 SB ἐπικρ.; Mic 1 9 B (SA ⲁ. ⲉϫⲛ-) κατακρ.; Is 5 29 S (B ⲧⲁϫⲣⲏⲟⲩⲧ) ἐπιλαμβάνειν; 1 Cor 15 2 SF (B ⲁⲙⲟⲛⲓ) κατέχειν; Job 34 14 S (B ⲁⲙⲟⲛⲓ) συνέχ.; Ge 38 26 B δικαιοῦσθαι; Ac 28 13 B (S diff) ἐπιγίνεσθαι; Zech 14 13 SA (B ⲙⲟⲩⲗϫ) συμπλέκεσθαι, Bor 253 162 S of famine ⲡⲧⲉⲣⲉϥ ⲁ. ⲡⲣⲟϫⲟ κατεπείγειν; R 1 4 63 S ⲁⲡⲡⲣⲟ ⲁ. in his kingdom (cf as tr C 86 214 B), Va 68 180 B ⲉⲕⲁ. ⲉⲕⲉⲛⲏϣ ⲉⲕⲟⲓ ⲛⲟⲩⲣⲟ, PLond 4 483 S ⲡϫⲓⲥⲟⲟⲩⲉ ⲉⲧⲁ., Ep 200 S if invaders ⲁ. there will be great distress, BHom 60 S ⲕⲁ. ⲙⲡⲣⲣ ϫⲓⲛϭⲟⲛⲥ, Mor

16 49 S ⲁⲧⲉⲓⲥⲅⲡⲏⲑⲓⲁ ⲁ. in Jerusalem, PS 302 S how long each mystery ⲛⲁⲁ., 327 sim, Mor 22 56 S of saint's fame ⲉⲁⲡⲉϥⲣ ⲡⲙⲉⲉⲩⲉ ⲁ., Va 58 111 B so long as darkness ⲁ., BIF 13 111 S (B ⲁⲙⲟⲛⲓ) both feet broken, skin alone ⲉⲧⲁ. (hold good), BMis 452 sim, ShMun 96 S ⲁ. ϩⲛⲛⲉⲧⲉⲛⲟⲩⲕⲡⲉ (continue in thy charity & love), R 1 3 21 S the νομός ⲛⲧⲁϥⲁ. ⲛϩⲏⲧϥ (administer, cf R 2 4 86), Bor 260 101 S recruit tested till it appear ϫⲉⲉϥⲛⲁⲁ. or no, J 75 53 S of διαθήκη ⲉⲧⲣⲉⲥϭⲙ ϭⲟⲙ ⲛⲥⲁ.; Ge 48 4 S ⲙⲁ ⲛⲁ. (B ⲁ. nn), Lev 25 33 S (B do), Ez 48 20 B κατάσχεσις; ShC 73 16 S of sword-hilt ⲧⲉⲥⲧⲱⲣⲉ ⲛ ⲡⲉⲥⲙⲁ ⲛⲁ. (cf ⲁⲙⲟⲛⲓ nn).

Rarely c ⲉ-: J 106 129 S (cf ib 42 17, 65 53), PLond 5 132 S.

II. tr, grasp, embrace, possess, restrict, detain: Ge 8 9 S (var ϣⲱⲡ, B diff), Job 16 13 S (B ⲁⲙⲟⲛⲓ), Mk 12 3 S (B ϭⲓ) λαμβάνειν; Is 51 18 B (S ϣⲱⲡ), Ez 20 6 SB ἀντιλ.; Job 38 13 S (B diff), Ps 34 2 S (B ϭⲓ), Pro 4 13 A (B ⲁⲙⲟⲛⲓ), Lu 20 26 B (S ϭⲱⲡⲉ), He 2 16 SF ἐπιλ.; Aeg 275 S ye mothers ⲁ. ⲡⲛⲉⲧⲛϣⲏⲣⲉ προσλ. ضمّ; Jer 43 26 B, Ac 1 16 B (var ⲁⲙⲟⲛⲓ, S ϭⲱⲡⲉ) συλλ.; Ge 21 18 S (B ⲁⲙⲟⲛⲓ), Ruth 3 15 S, Pro 16 32 S, Is 32 17 SBF κρατεῖν, in Gospels κρ. always (exc Mk 14 1 S) S ⲁ. = B ⲁⲙⲟⲛⲓ (but Jo 20 23 S = B ⲧⲁϩⲛⲟ), RNC 30 S place ⲉⲧⲟⲩⲁ. ⲙⲙⲟϥ (prisoner) ⲛϩⲏⲧϥ κρ., Si 27 30 S ἐγκρατὴς εἶναι; Ac 27 16 SB περικρατὴς γένεσθαι, Jer 27 15 B (S ⲁ. ⲉϫⲛ-) κατακρ.; Am 4 7 S (B ⲧⲁϩⲛⲟ) ἀνέχειν; Jer 2 8 B ἀντέχ.; Jth 4 7 S διακατέχ.; Jer 6 11 S (C 42 196, B ⲧⲁϩⲛⲟ) ἐπέχ.; Ps 68 36 S (B ⲁⲙⲟⲛⲓ), Jud 13 15 S, Lu 4 42 S (B do), ib 8 15 S (B do), Aeg 274 S deacons ⲁ. the Gospels κατέχ., ib 258 sim, Job 31 11 S (B do) ⲉⲙⲉⲅⲉϣⲁ. ⲙⲙⲟϥ ἀκατάσχετος, Ps 16 9 SBF, Si 51 8 S περιέχ., EW 149 B ⲉⲧⲁ. ⲡⲧⲥⲩⲥⲧⲁⲥⲓⲥ ⲙⲡⲧⲏⲣϥ περιεκτικός; Job 38 2 S (B ⲁⲙⲟⲛⲓ), Jer 2 13 SB, BMar 157 S ⲥⲉⲁ. ⲙⲙⲟⲓ ⲛϭⲓ ⲡⲉⲥⲛⲁⲩ συνέχ.; Si 26 7 S, 1 Cor 3 19 B (S ϭⲱⲡⲉ) δράσσεσθαι, Aeg 241 S ἡνιοχεῖν; Si 8 22 S στέγειν; Si 4 27 S (B do) βιάζειν, BMis 367 S sim; Lu 24 29 S (B·do) παραβιάζ.; ShA 2 313 S ⲟⲩ ⲡⲉⲧⲕⲱⲗⲅⲉ ⲛ ⲡⲓⲙ ⲡⲉⲧⲁ. ⲙⲙⲟⲛ ⲉⲧⲣⲉⲛ-; Sa 7 22 S do ἀκώλυτος, cf Va 57 71 B ⲟⲩⲁⲧϣⲁ. ⲡⲓⲣⲓⲧⲏⲥ; AP 7 A² what passion ⲡⲉⲧⲁ. ⲙⲙⲟ?; Jo 8 20 A² (S ϭⲱⲡⲉ, B ⲁⲙⲟⲛⲓ) πιάζειν; Ge. 39 12 S (B ⲙⲟⲩⲗϫ) ἐπισπᾶν; detain: ShC 42 182 S impossible ⲉⲧⲣⲉⲛⲁ. ⲛⲁⲛ the day, when hours complete; R 1 3 61 S Baptist in womb to Elizabeth, Let me out ⲙⲡⲣⲁ. ⲙⲙⲟⲓ, BHom 138 S ⲡⲥⲁⲉⲓⲛ ⲁ. ⲛⲧⲟⲟⲧϥ; retain by heart: CO 30, ib Ad 7 S ordinand will learn & repeat gospel ⲛⲧⲁⲁ. ⲙⲙⲟϥ, BM 186 S sim; ShC 73 37 S ⲉⲧⲉⲧⲛⲁ. ⲙⲙⲱⲧⲛ in heat of baths, Ryl 62

2 *S* ⲉⲧⲙⲧⲣⲉϭⲁ. ⲙⲙⲟⲟⲩ in worldly cares; *hold liable for* (? lit. *arrest*), often ⲙⲁⲣⲉ, ⲙⲉⲣⲓ: Miss 4 734 *S* thy monastery ⲥⲉⲡⲁⲁ. ⲙⲙⲟⲕ ⲉⲣⲟϥ, SHel 49 *S* ⲙⲏ ⲉⲣⲉⲡⲣⲣⲟ ⲁ. ⲙⲙⲟⲕ ⲉⲣⲏⲭⲣⲓⲙⲁ, BM 481 *S* ⲁϥⲁ. ⲙⲙⲟⲓ ⲉⲧⲃⲉⲡⲉϥ ⲭⲣⲉⲱⲥ (? *sic, cf* ST 233), BM 1158 *S* ⲥⲟϭⲁ. ⲙⲙⲟⲓ ⲉⲕⲁⲓϣⲟⲙⲛⲧ ⲛϩⲟⲗⲟⲕ/, CO 180 *S* send the money ⲙⲡⲁⲉϭⲁ. ⲙⲙⲟϥ ϩⲁⲣⲁⲟϥ, TurM 6 *S* ⲛⲡⲉⲡⲁ. ⲡⲁⲟⲕ ⲗⲁⲩ beyond..., Ryl 127, 324, ST 431 *S*, Kr 147 *F* sim, MR 5 50 *F* ⲉϥⲙⲉⲣⲓ ⲙⲁⲛ ϫⲉⲓⲟⲩⲉϣ half a *solidus*.

—— ⲉϫⲛ-, or ⲉϩⲣⲁⲓ ⲉϫⲛ-, *rule, have power over*: Ez 12 13 *B* (*S* ϣⲱⲡ) συλλαμβάνεσθαι; 2 Kg 3 6 *S*, Pro 17 2 *S*, Dan 4 33 *B*, Cai Euch 486 *B* ⲛⲏ ⲉⲧⲟϭⲁ. ⲉⲭⲱⲟⲩ ϩⲓⲧⲉⲡⲁⲙⲉⲡϯ, Mor 17 45 *S* ⲉϥⲁ. ⲉⲣ. ⲉϫⲛⲡⲣⲱϣⲉ ⲉⲡⲉⲡⲕⲁ, *cf* BMar 93 *S* ⲁ. ⲉϫⲛ- κρατεῖν; Jth 7 12 *S* ἐπικρ.; Mic 1 9 *SA* κατακρ.; Aeg 245 *S* ἐπέχειν; Ex 32 13 *S* (*B* ⲁⲙⲟⲛⲓ ⲛ-) κατέχ.; Ps 68 15 *S* (*B* diff), Pro 11 26 *B* (*S* diff) συνέχ.; Aeg. 28 *S* ⲉⲓⲁ. ⲉϫⲛⲡⲉϥⲥⲙⲁⲩ, Bor 240 60 *S* how shall falsehood ⲁ. ⲉϫⲛⲧⲙⲉ?, ShA 1 115 *S* ⲉⲓⲛⲁⲁ. ⲛⲧⲁⲙⲡⲧⲁⲏⲧ ⲏ ⲉϫⲛ- do, ShC 42 39 *S* with my foot ⲁⲓⲁ. ⲉϫⲛⲧⲉϥⲙⲉⲥⲧⲟϩⲧ, WTh 68 *B* spear pierced dragon ⲡⲁⲣⲉⲡⲓⲁⲧⲓⲟⲥ ⲁ. ⲉⲭⲱϣⲡⲉ with all his might, BAp 123 *S* ⲁ. ⲉϫⲛ- what I have bidden thee (*B* ⲁⲣⲉϩ ⲉ-), ShC 73 198 *S* he in authority over the waters ⲁ. ⲉⲭⲱⲟⲩ (*detain, hold back*).

—— ⲙⲛ-, ⲛⲉⲙ-, *hold with, support*: Dan 10 21 *B* (*S* ⲁϩⲉ ⲣⲁⲧ ⲙⲛ- BMis 178) ἀντέχεσθαι, BM 581 *F* I trust ϫⲉϣⲁⲗⲉⲡⲛ̄ⲧ ⲙⲉⲣⲓ ⲛⲉⲙⲉⲛ this year, CMSS 37 *F* I rejoice ⲧⲁⲛⲟⲥ̄ⲧ ⲙⲉⲣⲓ ⲛⲉⲙⲉⲕ.

ⲛⲥⲁ-, *hold, abide by*: Mor 55 51 *S* ⲙⲡⲣⲁ. ⲛⲥⲁⲡⲉⲥϩⲁⲓ, but seek the spirit.

—— ϩⲓϫⲛ-, *possess, master*: BM 216 79 *S* sickness ⲁ. ϩⲓϫⲛⲡⲥⲱⲙⲁ, J 65 13 *S* ⲡⲉⲧⲁ. ϩⲓϫⲛⲡⲕⲁϩ; *hold back, detain*: Pro 11 26 *B* (*SA* ⲱⲧⲡ ⲉϩⲟⲩⲛ) συνέχειν, sim Va 61 92 *B* (*S* ⲁ. ⲉϩⲣⲁⲓ ⲉϫⲛ- P 131³ 82).

—— *SBF* nn m, *power, possession*: Ge 49 24 *B* (*S* ϭⲟⲙ), Ps 75 4 *B* (*S* ⲧⲁϫⲣⲟ), Is 40 26 *SB*, He 2 14 *SBF* κράτος; Ps 22 5 *SB* κράτιστος, *ib* 45 4 *B* (*S* ϭⲟⲙ) κραταιότης; Ps 59 9 *B* (*S* ⲧⲁϫⲣⲟ) κραταίωσις; Ge 47 11 *B*, Ps 2 8 *SB*, Ac 7 45 *SB* κατάσχεσις (*cf* above ⲙⲁ ⲛⲁ.); Sa 12 17 *S*, Ap 5 12 *SB* ἰσχύς; Ps 107 9 *B* (*S* ϣⲱⲡ ⲉ-) ἀντίληψις; Va 57 256 *B* ϯ ⲁ. ἀκμάζοντα ἔχειν; C 43 35 *B* every province ⲉⲧϩⲁⲡⲉⲛⲁ., BMis 257 *S* ⲛⲁ. of Romans, Mun 51 *S* ⲡⲉⲕⲁ. as title (κράτος), C 43 71 *B* thine the glory ⲡⲉⲕⲛⲓⲁ. for ever, Miss 4 621 *S* ⲛⲁ. ⲙⲡⲉⲕⲗⲁⲥ.

ⲁⲧⲁ. *SAB* adj, *unrestrained, uncontrollable*: Pro 20 1 *A*, 21 11 *S* ἀκόλαστος, Si 16 7 *S* ἀπειθής, 2 Tim 3 3 *S* (*B* ⲁⲧϣ ⲁⲙⲟⲛⲓ ⲛⲧⲉⲛ-), R 1 4 55 *S* ἀκρατής, PSBA 10 401 *B* ἀκατάσχετος, Br 227 *S* ⲡⲣⲱⲙⲉ ⲛⲁⲧⲁ. ⲙⲙⲟϥ, Z 579 *S* ϩⲉⲛⲁⲧⲁ. ⲡⲉ ϩⲉⲛⲑⲏ.

ⲙⲛⲧ-, ⲙⲉⲧⲁⲧⲁ. *SB* nn f, *uncontrolledness, incontinence*: 1 Cor 7 5 *SF*(?) (*B* ⲁⲧⲟⲱⲧ) ἀκρασία, BHom 48 *S*, R 2 2 23 *S*, Va 58 192 *B* ἀκολασία, ShRE 11 18 *S* ⲡⲉⲩⲗⲓⲃⲉ ⲛϩⲏⲧ ⲙⲛⲧⲉⲅⲙ., ShR 2 3 67 *S* lewd songs, dances & ϩⲱⲃ ⲛⲓⲙ ⲙⲙ.

ⲣⲉϥⲁ. *S* nn, *self-controlled person*: Si 26 15 ἐγκρατής.

ϭⲛⲁ. *S* nn f, *control, restraint*: Br 248 ⲧϭ. ⲙⲙⲟⲟⲩⲡⲉ ⲡⲉⲧϥϫⲧ ⲉϩⲟⲩⲛ ⲉⲡⲗⲟⲟⲥ, Bor 240 53 ⲧϭ. ⲉϫⲉⲛⲑⲏ (*cf* ϫⲛⲁⲙⲟⲛⲓ).

ⲁⲛ- *SB*, nn m, lit *great-one* (ⲟ) of (AZ 42 56, 51 124) in ⲁⲛϫⲱϫ (*v* ϫⲱϫ), before certain numerals & ? other words: Ex 18 21 *SB* ⲁⲛ (var ⲁⲙ) ⲙⲏⲧ δεκάδαρχος, *ib*, Deu 1 15 *SB* ⲁⲛϣⲟ χιλίαρχος.

ⲙⲛⲧⲁⲛϣⲟ *S* nn f, χιλιαρχία Nu 31 48 (*B* ⲙⲉⲧ ⲭⲓⲗⲓⲁⲣⲭⲟⲥ).

ⲁⲛ- *SB*, pl ⲁⲛⲁⲛ-, prefix in collective numerals: Ryl 72 352 *S* ⲡⲁⲛϣⲟ ⲡⲁⲛϣⲉ, Jud 7 11 *S* ⲁⲛⲧⲁⲓⲟⲩ πεντήκοντα, Ps 90 7, Mic 5 2, Ap 5 11 *B* (*SA* ϣⲟ, ϩⲟ) χιλιάς, 1 Kg 18 7 *B* ⲁⲛⲁⲛⲑⲃⲁ (*S* ⲡⲉⲧⲃⲁ) μυριάς, Ex 34 22 *B* ⲁⲛⲍ̄ (var ⲁⲛⲁⲛ-) ἑβδομάς, Deu 16 16 *SB* sim, *ib* 1 11 *S* ⲁⲛϣⲟ ⲡⲕⲱⲃ (*B* ϣⲟ ⲡⲕ.) χιλιοπλασίως.

ⲁⲛ *SB*, ⲉⲛ *AF*, neg particle, following subj & predic, the clause mostly beginning with ⲛ- (Stern 386–393, Sdff 457–463, *cf* Spg *Dem Gr* 472); used **a.** in nominal clauses: Job 22 2 *S* ⲙⲏ ⲙⲡϫⲟⲉⲓⲥ ⲁⲛ (var ⲙⲏ ⲛϫ.), Sa 4 8 *S* ⲡⲟⲩⲁϣⲏ ⲁⲛ ⲡⲣⲟⲙⲡⲉⲧⲉ. **b.** verbal clauses: 1 pres, Ps 38 6 *S* ⲛⲧⲣ ⲭⲣⲓⲁ ⲁⲛ = *B* om ⲛ-; 2 pres, Ps 43 6 *S* ⲡⲉⲓⲕⲱ ⲁⲛ ⲡⲛ̄ⲧⲏⲓ = *B* ⲟⲩ ϯⲛⲁ-ⲁⲛ; 1 fut, Ap 7 16 *S* ⲡⲥⲉⲡⲁϩⲕⲟ ⲁⲛ = *B* ⲛⲛⲟⲩ-; 2 fut, Ps 61 1 *SB* ⲙⲏ ⲉⲣⲉⲧⲁⲯⲩⲭⲏ ⲛⲁϩⲩⲡⲟⲧⲁⲥⲥⲉ ⲁⲛ; 2 perf, Sa 12 13 *S* ⲡⲧⲁⲕⲕⲣⲓⲛⲉ ⲙⲙⲟⲟⲩ ⲁⲛ; impf, PS 25 *S* ⲡⲉⲩⲛⲁⲩ ⲁⲛ ⲉⲗⲁⲁⲩ; aor (rare), Sa 16 7 *S* ⲉϣⲁϥⲡⲟϩⲣⲙ ⲁⲛ; aor preter, Va 58 192 *B* ⲛⲉϣⲁⲡⲓ ⲁⲛ ⲉⲃⲟⲩⲛ. **c.** relative clauses: Ps 114 14 *SB* ⲡⲉⲧⲙⲟⲟⲩⲧ ⲁⲛ ⲡⲉⲧⲁⲥⲙⲟⲩ ⲉⲣⲟⲕ, Ap 13 8 *S* ⲡⲉⲧⲉⲙⲡⲉϥⲣⲁⲛ ⲥⲏϩ ⲁⲛ = *B* om ⲁⲛ. **d.** addition to neg pref ⲙⲡⲉ-: Esth 4 2 *S* ⲙⲡⲉⲥⲧⲟ ⲡⲁϥ ⲁⲛⲡⲉ, ShA 1 114 *S* ⲙⲡⲓⲉⲓⲙⲉ ⲁⲡⲟⲕ ⲁⲛ; ⲙⲡⲣ- (*v* AZ 55 75): Ryl 110 *S* ⲛⲡⲉⲣⲥⲉ ⲙⲟⲟⲩ ⲁⲛ, C 86 79 *B* ⲙⲡⲉⲣϯ ⲁⲥⲟ ⲉⲣⲟⲓ ⲁⲛ (var om), *ib* 351 *B* ⲙⲡⲉⲣⲭⲁϥ ⲉⲃⲟⲗ ⲁⲛ; ⲙⲙⲟⲛ (AZ *lc*): ShA 1 365 *S* ⲙⲛⲧⲉⲧⲛⲥⲟⲟⲩⲛ ⲙⲙⲟϥ ⲁⲛ, C 89 45 *B* ⲙⲙⲟⲛ ϩⲗⲓ ⲛϩⲱⲃ ⲛⲁϩⲱⲡ ⲉⲣⲟⲕ ⲁⲛ = *S* ⲙⲉⲣⲉⲗⲁⲁⲩ ...ϩⲱⲡ. **e.** prepos clauses: Aeg 259 *S* ϩⲛⲟⲩϯ ⲧⲱⲛ ⲁⲛ, Wess 11 169 *S* wherefore art come to be monk? ϫⲉⲕⲁⲥ ⲁⲛ ⲉⲕⲡⲁⲧⲱⲟϩⲛ ϩⲁⲛⲟⲃⲗⲓⲯⲓⲥ οὐχὶ ἵνα; Jo 12 6, 2 Thes 3 9 *S* ⲉⲃⲟⲗ ⲁⲛ ϫⲉ- οὐχ ὅτι.

ⲁⲛ *B* interrog *v* ⲉⲡⲉ.

ⲁⲛ- *S v* ⲁⲛⲟⲕ.

ⲁⲛ *AF* *v* ⲟⲛ.

ⲁⲛ- *B* *v* ϩⲁⲡ-.

ⲁⲛ *S* in ⲥϯⲁⲛ *v* ⲁⲡⲁⲓ.

ⲁⲡⲁ- *O* *v* ⲏⲡ *ape.*

ⲁⲡⲁⲓ *SB*, ⲁⲡⲉⲓ *A* (Pro 19 18) vb intr, *be pleas-ing, pleasant, grow better* (very seldom = ⲉϩⲛⲁⲥ *be willing* θέλειν): Pro 24 14 *S* (var ⲣ ⲁⲡⲁⲓ) καλὸς εἶναι, ib 19 18 *A* εὔελπις εἶναι, Jer 42 15 *S* βελτίων ποιεῖσθαι, BHom 18 *S* after Lent ⲛⲧⲁⲕⲁ. ϩⲓⲟⲩ β. γενέσθαι, P 131² 147 *S* sinner is able ⲉⲡⲱⲱⲡⲉ ⲁⲩⲱ ⲉⲁ., MG 25 213 *B* a good word ϣⲁϥⲟⲣⲟϥⲁ. καλὸν ποιεῖν those that are bad.

—— *SB* nn m, *beauty*: Ps 44 3 *S* (*B* ⲥⲁⲓ) κάλλος, ib 77 61 *B*, Sa 13 5 *S*, Si 6 15 *S* καλλονή; Ps 48 2 *S* (*B* ⲙⲉⲧⲥⲁⲓⲉ) εὐπρέπεια, Va 63 95 *B* that corrupt may ϣⲓⲃϯ ⲉⲡⲁ. τὸ βέλτιον; Br 238 *S* ⲡⲉϥⲥⲁ ⲙⲡⲉϥⲁ.; 1 Kg 2 26 *S* ⲉⲓ ⲉⲡⲁ. μεγαλυνό-μενος, 2 Kg 5 10 *S* sim, ib 3 1 *S* (Bor 163 102) ⲙⲟⲟϣⲉ ⲉⲡⲁ. (var ⲡⲏⲩ ⲉⲧⲁϫⲣⲟ) κρατεῖσθαι; Miss 4 743 *S* ⲉϥϯ ⲉⲡⲁ. ⲉⲡⲁⲡⲟⲩϥ, FR 14 *S* ⲡⲉⲥϯ ⲉⲡⲁ. in fear of Lord, Mor 22 101 *S* ⲉⲩϯ ⲉⲡⲁ. = *B* ⲙⲡⲥⲁⲓ, cf Mor 31 16 *S* ϯ ⲙⲡⲁ., BMis 177 *S* = BSM 87 *B* sim.

ⲣ ⲁ. *S* be pleasing: Ge 17 1 *S* (C 73 23, R 2 1 20) εὐαρεστεῖν, Pro 24 14 *S* καλὸς εἶναι.

ⲣ ⲁⲡⲁ *S* (once) *B* (always ⲣ, not ⲉⲣ) vb **a.** intr, *be pleased*: Saq 366 *S* I beheld heavens ⲉⲩⲣ ⲁ., earth rejoicing. **b.** tr, *please*: AM 27 ⲉϣⲱⲡ ⲡⲓⲣⲱⲃ ⲣ ⲁ. ⲙⲙⲟⲕ, C 86 308 sim, Va 68 38 ϥⲣ ⲁ. ⲡⲡⲉⲥϩⲁⲗ, BSM 84 ⲁϥⲣ ⲁ. ⲙⲡⲓⲁⲣⲭⲏⲉⲡ., Cai Euch 390 every thought ⲉⲧⲉⲛⲉϥⲣ ⲁ. ⲁⲛ ⲛⲧⲉⲕⲙⲉⲧⲁⲅⲁⲑⲟⲥ.

ⲣ ⲁⲡⲉ *B* (? st const of last): Ge 3 6 ϥⲣ ⲁ. ⲡⲓⲃⲁⲗ (varr ⲁⲡⲉ ⲛ̄ⲡⲓ-, ⲁⲛ ⲛ̄ⲡⲓ-) ἀρεστὸς εἶναι, cf Va 68 38 ⲣ ⲁ. ⲡⲉⲥⲃ., 1 Kg 24 5 ⲣ ⲁ. ⲡⲡⲉⲕⲃ. (*S* diff) ἀγαθός, Ge 41 37 ⲣ ⲁ. ⲫⲁⲣⲁⲱ ἀρέσκειν ἐναντίον, Jer 18 12 ⲉⲑⲣ ⲁ. ⲡⲉⲛϩⲏⲧ, cf 16 12 ⲣ ⲁⲡⲁϥ ⲙⲡⲉⲧⲉⲡⲣ., Va 61 211 ⲁⲕⲣ ⲁ. ⲡⲟ̄ⲥ̄.

ⲣ ⲁⲡⲥ *SB*, ⲉⲡⲥ *A*; suffixes: *S* ⲁⲡⲁⲓ, -ⲁⲕ, -ⲉ (Ge 16 6), -ⲁϥ, -ⲁⲥ, -ⲁⲛ, -ⲏⲧⲛ, -ⲁⲩ; *AA²* ⲉⲡⲉⲕ, -ⲉϥ; *B* ⲁⲡⲏⲓ, -ⲁⲕ, -ⲉ, -ⲁϥ, -ⲁⲥ, -ⲁⲛ, -ⲱⲧⲉⲛ, -ⲱⲟⲩ; *F* ⲁⲡⲏϥ (Ro 12 1), -ⲏⲛ (Mor 30 3). With nominal obj these pronom forms are used in addition: Jos 9 31 *S* ⲛⲑⲉ ⲉⲧⲣ ⲁⲡⲏⲧⲛ, but Ac 6 5 *S* the word ⲣ ⲁⲡⲁϥ ⲙⲡⲙⲏⲏϣⲉ, Cl 64 4 *A* ⲧⲁⲣ ⲉⲛⲉϥ ⲙⲡⲉϥⲣⲉⲛ. Commonest modes of employing this word. (1) nominal: Ge 34 18 *SB* ἀρέσκειν, He 11 5 *SB* εὐαρεστεῖν, Jth 12 14 *S* ἀρεστὸς εἶναι, Ro 12 1 *SBF* εὐάρεστος, Job 1 21 *SB* δοκεῖν, Miss 8 40 *S* ⲡⲉⲧⲣ ⲁⲡⲁϥ ⲙⲡⲡⲟⲙⲟⲥ τὸ δοκοῦν τοῖς κανόσι. (2) pro-nominal: 2 Kg 18 4 *S* ἀρ., Ps 25 3 *SB* εὐαρ., Jo 8 29 *SB* ἀρεστός, Lu 1 3 *B* (*S* ⲣ ϩⲛⲁ-) δοκ., Aeg 231 *S* τὸ δοκ., Hos 9 4 *A* (*B* ϯ ⲟⲩⲛⲟϥ) ἡδύνειν.

(3) impersonal: Aeg 244 *S* ⲁⲥⲣ ⲁⲡⲁⲩ ⲉⲧⲣⲉ-, BMis 159 *S* ⲁⲥⲣ ⲁⲡⲁⲓ to go over to thy religion (var ⲛⲧⲁⲓⲣ ϩⲛⲁⲓ ⲉ-), J 1 69 *S* price ⲁⲥⲣ ⲁⲡⲁⲛ ⲛⲡⲙⲉⲣⲟⲥ ⲥⲛⲁⲩ, Miss 4 121 *B* ⲁⲥⲣ ⲁⲡⲁϥ to revile king.

ⲣ ⲁⲡⲁϥ *B* nn m, *that which pleases*: Col 1 10, Va 59 159 ⲡⲓⲣ ⲁ. ⲙⲉϥϯ ἀρεσκεία.

ⲙⲉⲧⲣ ⲁⲡⲁϥ *B* nn f, *act of pleasing*: Va 64 155 ϯⲙ. ⲡⲣⲱⲙⲓ ἀνθρωπαρέσκου πρόθεσις, Va 58 72 ⲟⲩⲙ. ⲡⲡⲓⲁⲣϫⲱⲡ.

ⲣⲉϥⲣ ⲁⲡⲁⲥ *B* nn, *one who pleases*: Ps 52 6 ⲛⲓⲣ. ⲁⲡⲁϥ ⲡⲣⲱⲙⲓ, Eph 6 6 ⲣ. ⲁⲛⲱⲟⲩ ⲛⲡⲓⲣⲱⲙⲓ ἀνθρωπ-άρεσκος.

ⲙⲉⲧⲣⲉϥⲣ ⲁⲡⲁⲥ *B* nn f, *act of pleasing*: Cat 12 ⲙ. ⲁⲛⲱⲟⲩ ⲛⲡⲓⲣⲱⲙⲓ.

ϭⲓⲛ-, ϫⲓⲛⲣ ⲁⲡⲁϥ *SB* nn f m, meaning as last: Mus 40 257, Bor 240 59 *S*, Cat 78, C 89 175 *B*.

ⲁⲛ, ⲉⲓⲁⲁⲛ *S*, ⲉⲡⲉⲓ *A*, ⲓⲛⲓ *B* adj (?), *pleasant*, always with ⲥⲧⲟⲓ (ⲥϯ-), so *perfume*: Cant 5 13 *S* ⲥϯⲁⲛ (var ⲥϯⲛⲟⲩϥⲉ) μυρεψικά; Zech 9 17 *A* wine ⲡⲉⲧⲉ ⲡⲥϯⲉⲡⲉⲓ (*B* ⲥⲟⲟⲓ ⲡⲟⲩϫⲓ) εὐωδιάζειν; ShA 1 128 *S* ⲉϥϣⲉϣ ⲥϯⲁⲛ ⲉⲃⲟⲗ, 129 ⲡⲉⲥϯⲛⲟⲩϥⲉ ⲛ ⲡⲉⲥⲧⲁⲛ, Bor 242 158 = BMOr 8811 222 *S*, per-fumed raiment ⲉϥϣⲉϣ ⲥϯⲉⲓⲁⲁⲛ ⲉⲃⲟⲗ, paral 223 ϣⲉϣ ⲥϯⲃⲱⲟⲛ ⲉ.; EW 218 *B* rubric ⲡⲓⲥⲟⲉⲓⲛⲓ. (*AB* forms forbid ⲓⲁⲛ = ἴον, as in P 44 66, K 179)

ⲁⲛⲓ- *SB* *v* ⲉⲓⲛⲉ *bring*.

ⲁⲛⲁⲓⲱ *B* *v* ⲡⲁⲉⲓⲱ.

ⲁⲛⲅ- *v* ⲁⲡⲟⲕ.

ⲁⲛⲍⲏⲃⲉ *v* ⲁⲛⲥⲛⲃⲉ.

ⲁⲛⲑⲱⲡ *B* *v* ϩⲁⲙⲛⲧⲱⲡ.

ⲁⲛⲑⲏⲣ *B* *v* ϩⲁⲧⲏⲣ.

ⲁⲛⲑⲟⲩⲥ *B* nn m (but DM 13 24 ϩⲁⲛⲧⲟⲩⲥ f), a species of *lizard*: Lev 11 30 (*S* ϩⲁⲕⲗϥ), Pro 24 63 (*S* do) καλαβώτης, MIE 2 378 could be swal-lowed by a child, K 172, all = حرذون, P 55 18 var اغز; Bodl 325 154 ’حر = ⲡⲓϩⲉⲡϫⲉⲡ. As name: BM 1252 ϩⲁⲛⲧⲟⲩⲥ.

ⲁⲛⲁⲕ *S* nn m, meaning unknown: J 5 R 18 account of expenses, ϩⲁⲡⲙⲉⲥⲧⲟⲩ ⲙⲡⲁⲡⲁⲕ (? abbre-viated).

ⲁⲛⲟⲕ *SBO*, ⲁⲛⲁⲕ *AF* personal pron, 1 sg m f; **a.** independent forms, other persons: 2 sg m ⲛⲧⲟⲕ *S*, ⲛⲑⲟⲕ *B*, ⲛⲧⲁⲕ *AF*; 2 sg f ⲛⲧⲟ *SA*, ⲛⲑⲟ *B*, ⲛⲧⲁ *F* (Jo 4 10); 3 sg m ⲛⲧⲟϥ *S*, ⲛⲧⲁϥ *AF*, ⲛⲑⲟϥ *B* (*v* also ⲛⲧⲟϥ below); 3 sg f ⲛⲧⲟⲥ *S*, ⲛⲑⲟⲥ *B*, ⲛⲧⲁⲥ *AF* (Mt 14 8); 1 pl m f ⲁⲛⲟⲛ *SB*, ⲁⲛⲁⲛ *AF*; 2 pl m f ⲛⲧⲱⲧⲛ *S*, ⲛⲧⲱⲧⲛⲉ *A*, ⲛⲑⲱⲧⲉⲛ *B*, ⲛⲧⲁⲧⲉⲛ *F* (Ro 11 30); 3 pl m f ⲛⲧⲟⲟⲩ *S*, ⲛⲧⲁⲩ *AF* (Ac 7 25), ⲛⲑⲱⲟⲩ *B*. **b.** construct forms: 1 sg ⲁⲛⲅ- (*O* ⲁⲛⲕ-); 2 sg ⲛⲧⲕ-, ⲛⲧⲉ-; 3 sg ⲛⲧϥ- (2 Cor 10 7 *S*, all MSS); 1 pl ⲁⲛⲛ- (2 Cor 2 15 *S*), ⲁⲛ- (Job 4 19, PS 352 *S*); 2 pl ⲛⲧⲉⲧⲛ-. *Cf* Stern 254, 304.

ⲁⲛⲕⲟⲕⲓ, -ⲕⲟⲕⲓ, ⲉⲛⲕⲟⲕⲓ B nn m, *third* (ring) *finger* : K 77 ⲡⲓⲁ. (*sic*) بنصر (= παράμεσος P 43 40).

ⲁⲛⲓⲕⲁⲙ *SB* nn m, kind of *vitriol* : PMéd 131, 187 *S*, BMOr 8775 136 *B* زاج, K 205 *B* قلقند χάλκανθον, which is Pliny's *atramentum sutorium* (μελαντηρία), v PMéd 127. If so, ⲕⲁⲙ = ? *black.*

ⲁⲡⲟⲙ *B* nn m, *skin* : Ex 28 42 χρώς (var σῶμα), ib 34 29 (*S* ⲥⲁⲣⲝ) χρῶμα (var χρώς).

ⲁⲡⲁⲗⲏⲓ *B* v ⲱⲡⲉ.

ⲁⲡⲉⲙⲣⲱ *B* v ⲙⲣⲱ.

ⲁⲛⲁⲛ- *B* v ⲁⲛ- prefix.

ⲁⲛⲓⲛⲉ *S*, ⲁⲛⲓⲛⲓ *O* v ⲉⲓⲛⲉ *bring.*

ⲁⲛⲟⲛⲓ *B* vb intr, *live luxuriously, wantonly* : Ja 5 5 ⲁⲣⲉⲧⲉⲛⲁ. (var ⲉⲣ ⲥⲡⲁⲍⲁⲗⲁⲛ DeV 166) σπαταλᾶν, which = ϫⲉⲣϫⲉⲣ 1 Tim 5 6 *B* (*S* always = Gk). ⲛⲟⲛⲓ *B*, *q v*, can hardly be compared.

ⲁⲛⲛⲟϣⲉⲣ *B* nn m, *wild endive, chicory* : K 196 هندبا بري, BMOr 8775 133 = ⲥⲁⲣⲓⲥ (σέρις) سريس.

ⲁⲛⲁⲡⲁⲓ *B* nn f, *hen* : K 168, where = ⲉⲣϣⲱ.

ⲁⲛⲁⲡⲁⲓ *B*, *valley* v ⲉⲓⲁ.

ⲁⲛⲣⲟ *B* v ⲣⲟ (ϩⲁⲛⲣⲟ).

ⲁⲛⲥⲏⲃⲉ, -ⲍⲏⲃⲉ, -ⲥⲏⲃ, -ⲍⲏⲃ, -ⲥⲏⲃⲓ, -ⲥⲏⲃⲉⲛ, -ⲍⲏⲃⲛ (Mor 31 244, ib 48 35) *S*, ⲁⲛⲍⲏⲃ *B*, ⲁⲡⲥⲩⲃⲉ, -ⲍⲉⲃⲉ *F* (cf Ryl Dem 3 337, Rec 18 63), nn f, *school* : BIF 14 170 *S* ⲧⲁ. ⲡⲧⲉⲓⲡⲟⲗⲓⲥ, BM 528 *F* ⲧⲁ. ⲡⲗⲟⲅⲟⲥ sch. of *reckoning* (arithm), BMar 220 *S* sent to ⲧⲁ. ⲉⲧⲣⲉⲩⲡⲁⲓⲍⲉⲩⲉ ⲙⲙⲟⲛ, Miss 4 743 *S* at ⲧⲁ. ϩⲁⲣⲁⲧϥ ⲡⲟⲩⲥⲁϩ to be taught Scriptures, C 89 33 *B* sent to ϯⲁ. to learn to write, Z 549 *S* ⲥⲁϩ ⲛⲁ. = *ib* ⲥⲁϩ ⲡⲡⲟⲗⲓⲕⲟⲥ of town.

ⲁⲛⲥⲁⲙⲉ v ⲥⲓⲙⲉ.

ⲁⲛⲧⲟⲗⲓ *B* nn m, *a fish-eating bird* : K 169 نورس. Cf Damîrî 2 10 نورس = زمّج (Bevan), latter a species of eagle (osprey) which in P 44 55 = ⲕⲟⲣⲟⲫⲁⲍⲟⲥ (P 43 22 ⲕⲟⲣⲁ-), ? l κόραφος.

ⲁⲛⲧⲏⲗⲙ, -ⲧⲉⲗⲙ *S* (-ⲗⲟⲙ Lev 5 8 HT) nn m, *skull* : Jud 9 53 κρανίον, *cit* P 44 108 دماغ (which = ἐγκέφαλος, μῆνιγξ, but *ib* 94 ⲁⲅⲣⲓⲟⲅⲉ ⲉⲭⲡⲁ.), Lev 5 8 as gloss on σφόνδυλος (*B* ⲙⲟϯ), P 129²⁰ 131 apostle James thrown from roof, ⲁⲅⲟⲩⲱϭⲡ ⲙⲡⲉϥⲁ. Exact meaning doubtful.

ⲁⲛⲧⲱⲣⲓ *B* nn m, *one of mature age* : K 72 كهل, followed by ϫⲉⲗⲗⲟ شيخ; cf P 44 68 *S* γηραλέος = ϭϩⲏⲡ ⲉϩⲟⲩⲛ ⲉⲣ ϩⲗⲗⲟ كهل, followed by γέρων شيخ. Lab has ⲁⲧⲁ. & ⲁⲡⲁ. قاصر, *minor, under age* (whence ?).

ⲁⲛⲧⲱⲧⲉⲣ *B* v ⲧⲱⲣⲧⲣ.

ⲁⲛⲧⲱⲟⲩ *B* v ⲧⲟⲟⲩ.

ⲁⲛⲧⲁϣ *S*, ⲁⲡⲑⲁϣ *B* nn m, *sneeze* : Job 41 9 *SB* πταρμός; v Rec 39 158.

ⲁⲛⲟⲩⲓ *B* v ⲉⲓⲛⲉ *bring.*

ⲁⲛⲟⲩⲣϣⲉ v ⲟⲩⲣϣⲉ.

ⲁⲛⲁϣ *SB*, ⲁⲡⲁϩ *A*, ⲁⲡⲉϣ, -ⲛϣ *F*, pl ⲁⲡⲁⲩϣ *SB*, ⲁⲛⲏⲩϣ *F* (Mt 14 9) & sg as pl, nn m, *oath* : Ex 22 11 *SB*, Pro 29 24 *SA*, Mk 6 26 *SB*, He 6 16 *SBF* ὅρκος; Lev 5 1 *SB* ὁρκισμός; Ez 17 18 *B* ὁρκωμόσια; Ac 23 13 *SB* συνωμόσια; Ez 17 16 *B* ἀρά; Ac 23 14 *SB* ἀνάθεμα. Verbs with ⲁ. as object : ⲁ. ⲉⲓⲣⲉ, Jos 9 21 *S* (cf ib 24), Ps 14 4 *B* (*S* ⲱⲣⲕ), ShC 42 17 *S* ⲙⲡⲛⲥⲁⲧⲣⲉⲩⲣ ⲁ. ⲛⲁⲕ, ShC 42 139 *S* ⲉⲓⲣ ⲁ. ⲉⲣⲱⲧⲛ, ShC 73 79 *S* ⲡⲉⲧⲛⲁⲣ ⲁ. ⲉⲣⲟⲓ (adjure), WTh 137 *S* ⲁϥⲣ ⲁ. ⲉⲛⲉⲧⲟⲩⲁⲁⲃ, ShC 42 16 *S* let them swear ⲙⲡⲣⲁⲛ ⲙⲡⲡⲉ, C 43 245 *B* swear to me ⲙⲡⲉⲕⲡⲧ, Am 6 8 *A* ⲁⲡ͞ϫ͞ⲥ ⲣ ⲁ. ⲙⲙⲁϥ καθ' ἑαυτοῦ; c ⲉϩⲣⲉⲛ-, Ja 5 12 *B* (*S* ⲱⲣⲕ), ST 115 *S* ⲁⲛⲣ ⲁ. ϫⲉⲙⲡⲛⲥⲱⲟⲩϩ ⲡⲓⲙⲛⲧⲛ, Eccl 8 2 *S* ⲟⲩϣⲁϫⲉ ⲡⲣ ⲁ. **b.** ⲥⲙⲛⲉ, ⲥⲉⲙⲛⲓ, Jer 11 5 *B*, Ac 23 13 *S* (var ⲉⲓⲣⲉ). **c.** ⲱⲣⲕ, Lu 1 73 *SB*, Ac 2 30 *SB*, AZ 33 133 *S* ⲉⲓⲱ. ⲁ. ⲉϫⲱⲕ ⲙⲡⲛⲟϭ ⲡⲧⲏⲃⲉ (adjure), CO 116 *S*, ST 399 *S*, Am 8 14 *A* sim, c dat ⲛⲥⲁ- CO 131 *S*. **d.** ⲧⲁⲣⲕⲟ c double accus, Nu 5 21 *SB*, Ac 23 14 *B* (*S* ⲱⲣⲕ), BAp 118 *S* if thou desirest ⲉⲧⲁⲣⲕⲟⲥ ⲙⲡⲁ., BMar 185 *S* ⲁϥⲧⲁⲣⲕⲟϥ ⲡϩⲉⲛⲛⲟϭ ⲡⲁ. ἀνακρίνειν, J 66 18 *S* ϯⲧ. ⲡⲣⲱⲙⲉ ⲡⲓⲁ ⲡⲡⲁ., J 76 48 *S* ⲡⲡⲉⲩⲉϣⲧ. ⲡⲉⲩⲉⲣⲏⲧ ⲡⲁ. **e.** ϯ, Mt 5 33 *SB*, Va 64 160 *B* ⲡⲓⲁ. ⲉⲧⲁⲩⲧⲏⲓϥ. *Ask on oath* : Hall 82 *S* ⲡⲧϫⲡⲟⲩϥ ⲉⲡⲁ. whether this is it, PLond 5 132 *S* ⲉⲁⲩⲁⲓⲧⲉⲓ ⲙⲙⲟⲓ ϩⲡⲟⲩⲁ., cf BM 919 *B* ⲉⲧⲁⲥⲁⲙⲟⲛⲓ ⲙⲙⲟϥ ⲉⲡⲓⲁ. *Be liable to oath* : J 113 18 *S* ⲙⲁⲣⲉϥϣⲱⲡⲓ ϩⲁⲡⲓⲁ. (cf ἔνοχος τῷ ὅρκ., PLond 5 24, PMon 24), J 44 140 *S* ϯϩⲡⲡⲉⲓⲁ. ⲧⲁⲯⲩⲭⲏ ⲡϩⲏⲧϥ.

ⲣ ⲁ. *A* as nn m, Zech 8 17 ὅρκος.

ⲙⲉⲧⲣⲉϥϯ ⲁ. *B* nn f, *a swearing* : Cat 11 ⲡⲓⲭⲓⲛⲱⲣⲕ ⲕⲁⲧⲁ ϩⲗⲓ ⲙⲙⲉⲧⲣⲉϥϯ ⲁ.

ⲁⲛⲁϣ *S* nn, name of a plant (?) : PMéd 242 ⲁ. ⲡⲡⲣⲏ ⲉⲧⲣⲱϫ in recipe with burnt papyrus & λίβανον. Cf ϣⲏⲛ ⲙⲡⲣⲏ ἀρτεμισία (Chassinat).

ⲁⲛϣⲓⲣⲓ, -ϭⲓⲣⲓ *B* nn m, species of *bean, phaseolus* : K 194 ماش (sim كسنة orobus Lab).

ⲁⲛϣⲧⲏⲩ v ⲧⲏⲩ.

ⲁⲛϣⲉⲩⲗⲉ *S* nn, an animal, whose blood used in recipe for binding (impeding ⲙⲟⲩⲣ) bridegroom : Cai 42573 1 (post-Muslim) ϭⲁⲡ ⲃ̄ ⲡⲁ. ⲙⲡⲡⲉϥⲥⲛⲟϥ ⲟ(ⲡ)ⲟⲟⲩ ϩⲓⲙⲟⲟⲩ. Cf ? ἔγχελυς انكليس.

ⲁⲛⲁϩ *A* v ⲁⲛⲁϣ.

ⲁⲛⲁϧ S nn, an ornament (?) woven upon clothes &c, ? the *crux ansata* (hierogl ʿnḫ): Ryl 244 list of clothing, ⲟⲩϣⲧⲛ...ⲉⲥϣⲟⲡⲧ ⲛⲁ., ⲟⲩϩⲃⲟⲥ do, ⲟⲩϩⲃⲟⲥ ⲛⲁ. ⲡⲁⲅⲉⲓⲁϥⲁⲛ, ib 254 in account of expenses ϧⲁⲛⲁ. for the 2 ⲥⲧⲣⲱⲙⲁⲧⲁ.

ⲁⲛϧ S, ⲟⲛϧ SB nn m, *yard, court*: BMOr 8775 87 B ⲁⲩⲗⲏ جٮ, MG 25 236 B he sat ϩⲉⲛⲡⲓⲟ. ⲁⲩⲗⲏ (cf ib 99), HL 113 B an o. wherein ascete spent day, Va 61 18 B stylite had 2 o. μάνδραι, inner ⲉⲧⲥⲁϫⲟⲩⲛ with door, outer with pillars.   S in documents only: J 24 48, 25 11, 47 23 ⲁ. below house, CO 145 A ⲁ. outside house door, J 27 39 ⲁ. with door, ib 26 loom in ⲁ., COAd 4 palms in ⲁ., J 24 65, 41 24, 47 60 house & ⲁ., J 28 6 ⲁ. & tower, J 68 50 whether in house, ⲁ. or workshop, ST 48 ⲁ. as dowry, J 3 19, 26 ⲕⲁϧ = ib 45 51 ⲁ., J 1 50 χώρημα = ib 81 ⲁ.   Cf αὐλή in PMon nos 13, 15, 16.

ⲁⲛⲟⲩϧ, ⲁⲛⲛⲟⲩϧ F v ⲛⲟⲩϧ.

ⲁⲛⲏϧⲉ A v ⲉⲛⲉϧ.

ⲁⲛⲁϧⲱⲣ B v ⲁϧⲟ.

ⲁⲛϫⲓⲣ v ϫⲓⲣ.

ⲁⲛϫⲱϫ v ϫⲱϫ.

ⲁⲛϭⲓⲣⲓ B v ⲁⲛϣⲓⲣⲓ.

ⲁⲡⲁ SBF nn m, title of reverence, corresponding to ἀββᾶς (as in Apophthegmata, BM 216 S, 915 B) & mostly in B to ⲁⲃⲃⲁ; in Arabic to اب (constantly with certain names: Hôr: PO 3 370, ib 10 255 &c, Kâu: PO 11 736, 10 264), while ⲁⲃⲃⲁ commonly = انبا (for pronunc. of this cf Leyd 428 ⲁⲛⲃⲁ, C 89 43 ⲁⲙⲡⲁ, EW 237, 242, 245 ⲁⲙⲡⲁ, ⲉⲁⲙⲡⲁ, ⲉⲛⲡⲁ), both eventually represented by ابو, بو (often in Synax), which in later S = ⲁⲛⲟⲩ: J 91 21, BM 535, 545, 602, while ⲁ. ⲁⲡⲧⲉⲗⲗ(ⲁ) BM 1231, ⲁ. ⲁⲙⲣⲟⲩ Bodl(P) d 20 is for ابو. By crasis: ⲁⲡⲁⲅⲁⲑⲉ (AM 31), ⲁⲡⲁⲡⲟⲗⲓ, ⲁⲡⲁⲣⲓ, ⲁⲡⲁⲙⲟⲩⲛ, ⲁⲡⲁⲛⲟⲩϧ; or by elision: ⲡⲁⲕⲓⲣⲉ, ⲡⲁⲙⲟⲩⲛ; further ⲁⲡⲁⲧⲏⲣ, rarely (Leyd 212 S, BMis 14 S) = ⲁⲡⲁ ⲡⲁⲧⲏⲣ. With names of certain martyrs ⲁ. coalesces: ⲁ. ϩⲓⲕⲧⲱⲣ, ⲁ. ϩⲓⲟⲥ, ⲁ. ⲙⲏⲛⲁ, ⲁ. ⲕⲗⲁⲩⲧⲉ, ⲁ. ⲕⲩⲣⲟⲥ (cf ST 319 S ⲁⲃⲃⲁ ⲕⲩⲣⲓ); cf also ⲁⲃⲃⲁ ⲁ. ⲉⲡⲓⲙⲁ Mor 45 56 S. Both ⲁ. & ⲁⲃⲃⲁ often applied to one person in same B MS: HL 92, 94, 103 B Pamô, Va 62 147, 149 John of Siût, Miss 4 119, 158 Macarius of Tkôw, AM 225, 233 Macrobius, EW 139 Samuel (cf Ep 144 n); or in different MSS: Miss 4 5, 110, MIE 2 373, DeV 76 Shenoute, C 86 73 n Isaac.   ⲁ. in B Acta not confined to S saints: Sarapion, Til, Anoub in C 43 are all from Delta; but never used in B of

archbishops, bishops: Athanasius, Dioscorus, Benjamin &c always ⲁⲃⲃⲁ, which also in S is more ceremonious.   Applied to biblical persons (cf PG 65 116 ἀββᾶ 'Ιακώβ): ST 162 S, RE 14 30 S prophets, BM 309 S apostle Peter, BM 1117 S angels; to non-clerical martyrs: Justus, Isidore, Victor, Claudius. ⲁ. alone, without name, reserved for certain venerated persons: Pachôm esp (v TT 187 n) Mor 51 33 S ϧⲁⲙⲡⲉϥⲟⲉⲓϣ ⲛⲁ., ib 37 ⲡⲉⲛⲧⲟⲗⲏ ⲧⲏⲣⲟⲩ ⲛⲁ. Often forms names borne by laymen: MR 5 31 ⲁ. ⲙⲁⲣⲕⲟⲥ, PLond 4 511 ⲁ. ⲉⲡⲓⲙⲁⲭⲟⲥ pagarchs, MR 2 65 ⲁ. ⲍⲁⲭⲁⲣⲓⲁⲥ chartulary; cf PLond 4 541, Wess 8 287.

The corresponding f ⲁⲙⲁ represents ἀμμά: R 1 5 32 S, Saq 12, 27, 306 &c S, Cai 8095 S, Ryl 124, 404 S.

ⲡⲁⲡⲁ, often in colophons & late documents, with art ⲡⲡⲁⲡⲁ, is παπᾶς *priest*.

ⲁⲡⲉ SAA², ⲁⲫⲉ B, ⲁⲡⲏ F, pl ⲁⲡⲏⲩⲉ SA, ⲁⲫⲏⲟⲩⲓ B, ⲁⲡⲏⲟⲩ F nn f (m v below), *head* **a.** of a living being: Ge 3 15 SB, Ex 39 2 S (CA 111), Job 1 20 SB, Mk 15 17 F (SB ϫⲱ-), Jo 19 30 SA² (B do) κεφαλή; Ge 49 26 S (B ϫⲱ-) Pro 1 9 SA (B ϫⲱ-) κορυφή; PS 115 S ⲟⲩⲕⲗⲟⲙ ⲉⲧⲉⲥⲁ., AM 209 B ⲉⲩⲟⲓ ⲛ︦ⲭ︦ ⲛⲁ. *individuals*; pl: Ps 65 12 SB, Am 2 7 AB, Ap 4 4 SB.   **b.** metaphor: Nu 6 9 SB, Ps 17 43 S (B ϫⲱϫ), 1 Cor 11 3 SB κεφ., Ex 19 20 B, Nu 23 28 S (var ϫⲱ-) B κορ., Ps 117 22 S, Mt 21 42 S, 1 Pet 2 7 S (all B ϫⲱϫ) κεφ. γωνίας, RE 9 146 S I swore ⲛⲧⲁ[ⲡ]ⲉ of 4 Gospels, C 43 47 B sitting ⲉϫⲉⲛⲧⲁ. ⲙⲡⲓⲧⲱⲧⲉⲣ (cf Ge 28 12), ShP 131⁶ 37 S they eat ⲛϧⲉⲛⲁ. ⲡⲁⲥⲡⲁⲣϫ (ἀσπάραγος), P 44 71 = 43 41 S ⲁ. ⲙⲡⲥⲏⲧ φάλλος راس الذكر, ب, ShA 1 156 S ⲛⲁ. ⲛⲡϧⲟⲉⲓⲧⲉ *top, upper part* of garment.   **c.** as title, *magistrate, chief*: Jud 11 11 S, Aeg 219 S κεφ., Si 30 28 S μεγιστᾶνες, ClPr 56 3 S imperial letter to ⲡⲛⲟϭ ⲛⲁ. ⲉⲧϣⲟⲟⲡ ⲕⲁⲧⲁ ⲙⲁ, Mor 56 24 S he was ⲁ. & αἴτιος of destruction, CDan 92 B, Va 58 147 B ⲁ. ⲛⲥⲟⲛ, MG 25 360 B of reapers; village headman, κεφαλαιωτής, πρωτοκωμήτης (v Wess 19 47, CO 308 n), here m: BM 1079 S πρωτοκ., BMOr 6201 A S Peter ⲛⲁ. ⲛⲡⲁⲉⲡⲟⲓⲕⲓⲟⲛ, Ryl 173 S ⲛⲁ. ⲛⲡⲉⲛⲧⲓⲙⲉ, CO 342 S ⲛⲁ. ⲙⲛ(ⲡ)ⲛⲟϭ ⲡⲣⲱⲙⲉ of Jême, Mor 48 105 S = C 43 151 B ⲡⲉⲧⲟ ⲛⲁ. ⲉⲧⲕⲉⲙⲏⲡ, TurM 6 S village κοινότης represented by ⲁ. & βοηθός, AZ 60 107, 109 S ⲁ. headman of trade-guild, J 42 17, 57 16 S ⲁ. ⲛϩⲟⲩϧⲣⲓⲧ ἀρχιφύλαξ; sometimes with f art: Kr 34 S ⲧⲁ. ϩⲓⲕ[ⲧⲱⲣ, Baouit 1 42 S ⲧⲁ. ⲫⲟⲓⲃⲁⲙⲱⲛ, Raccolta G. Lumbroso 283 S ⲧⲁ. ⲁⲙⲙⲱⲛⲉ ⲁϥⲉⲓ, but Osir 40 (11, 12) ⲧⲁ. ⲛⲡⲏⲛⲏⲧ woman in charge of loom; head of religious community (cf ϫⲱϫ ⲛⲁϩⲏⲧ): Z 302 S =

ἀρχιμανδρίτης, BMis 150 S ⲟⲩⲁ. ⲛⲥⲟⲟⲩϩⲥ father of monastery, Mor 51 40, C 89 202 B, Mich 550 40 S, ST 435 S sim, ShC 73 112 S ⲛⲁ. ⲛⲡⲉⲓⲥⲩⲛⲁⲅⲱⲅⲏ, JA '75 5 246 S ⲛⲁ. = μείζονες.   **d.** *capital* of money (κεφάλαιον): BSM 46 B (S ⲕⲉⲫ.) ⲧⲁ. ⲙⲡⲉⲧⲉⲛⲭⲣⲏⲙⲁ; *poll tax* (as in dem): BMis 244 S; *total*: BMis 392 S making 300 *solidi* ⲛⲁ., BM 605 S ⲧⲉⲙⲙⲉϩ ⲧⲁ. of our ἐμβολή, ST 418 S what thou gavest ϩⲁⲧⲉⲕⲁ., Mor 30 39 F ⲁⲕϭⲓ ⲟⲩⲁ. ⲛⲧⲱϩⲓ.

ⲙⲛⲧⲁ. S nn f, *headship*: Bor 248 48, paral ⲙⲛⲧⲉⲓⲱⲧ.

ⲁⲧⲁ. SB adj, *headless*: Mor 22 110 S = BSM 98 B ⲡⲥⲱⲙⲁ ⲛⲁⲧⲁ., PO 11 370 B heresy of ⲡⲓⲁⲧⲁ. (ἀκέφαλοι).

ⲙⲉⲧⲁⲧⲁ. B nn f, *headlessness*: MG 25 108 of army without leader.

ⲣ ⲁ. SB, *be at head of*, *lead*: Deu 28 44 S (B ϣⲱⲡⲓ ⲛⲁ.) κεφ. εἶναι, 1 Kg 22 2 S, Si 44 5 S ἡγούμενος εἶναι, Br 47 S ⲉϥⲟ ⲛⲁ. ⲉⲣⲟⲟⲩ, BAp 45 S I will increase thy planting & Holy Sp. shall ⲣ ⲁ. ⲉⲣⲟϥ, BMis 396 S after parents' death ⲁⲧⲉⲧⲛⲣ ⲁ. ⲉⲧⲉⲟⲩⲥⲓⲁ = BSM 47 B ⲉⲣ ⲕⲗⲏⲣⲟⲡⲟⲙⲓⲛ ⲛ-, Pcod 21 S we have prayed God ⲉⲧⲣⲉϥⲣ ⲁ. ⲉⲡⲉⲛⲗⲁⲥ.

ⲃⲁϣ ⲁ.   *v* ⲃⲱϣ *s f.*

ⲕⲱϣ ⲛⲁ.   *v* ⲕⲱϣ.

ϣⲁⲗϫⲓ ⲁ.   *v* ϣⲱⲗϭ.

ϭⲓ ⲁ. S, ⲱⲗⲓ ⲁ. B   *v* ϭⲓ, ⲱⲗ.

ⲁⲓⲡⲉ S*A, ⲁⲓⲡⲓ F   *v* ⲟⲓⲡⲉ.

ⲁⲡⲉⲓ S nn.m, a purple *dye-stuff*: BKU 1 19 recipe, Bind some of ⲛⲁ. ⲉⲧⲥⲁⲕⲓ (pounded) upon object in dye-pot, *ib* pound ⲁ. well & put in water. *Cf* Erman-Lange *Pap. Lansing* 53 *ipɜ*.

ⲁⲡⲁⲗⲁϥ F nn, meaning unknown: BM 524 incantations to protect woman about to bear child, Cast forth (remove) from her … & every demon ⲙⲛⲁ. ⲛⲓⲃⲓ & every vampire &c. *Cf* ? (ⲁ)ⲗⲁⲡⲗⲉⲡ B.

ⲁⲡⲣⲏⲧⲉ SA nn f (C 73 110, Pcod 49), *space of time*, long or short (mostly latter): BHom 41 S ϩⲛⲟⲩⲕⲟⲩⲓ ⲛⲁ. ἐν μιᾷ ὥρᾳ, *ib* 12 ϩⲛⲕⲟⲩⲓ ⲛⲁ. ἐν ἀκαριαίῳ, Pro 6 10 SA ⲛⲟⲩⲁ. (B ϩⲛⲟⲩⲕⲟⲩϫⲓ) ὀλίγον, μικρόν, *ib* 24 48 S sim, Mor 16 97 S ⲙⲛⲛⲥⲁⲟⲩⲁ. (var ⲟⲩⲕⲟⲩⲓ), BAp 117 S he cast himself at his feet ϩⲛⲟⲩⲛⲟϭ ⲛⲁ., BMis 480 S ⲁⲩⲣ ⲟⲩⲛⲟϭ ⲛⲁ. knocking at door, Miss 4 531 S he used to arise & pray ⲕⲁⲧⲁ ⲁ. = B ⲕⲁⲧⲁ ⲕⲟⲩϫⲓ ⲕⲁⲧ' ὀλίγον (*cf* ⲕⲟⲩⲓ advb g) ShC 73 110 S workers may rest ⲛⲥⲉⲙⲧⲟⲛ ⲙⲙⲁⲩ ⲛⲁ., ShRE 10 159 S he would not bear pain ⲡⲣⲟⲥ ⲟⲩⲁ., BerlOr 1607 3 ⲉⲩϣⲁⲛⲣ ⲟⲩⲁ. ⲛⲣⲓⲙⲉ, Pcod 49 S ϣⲁⲧⲉⲓⲁ.

ⲁⲡⲥ S nn f (m ShAm 1 253 *sic* MS), *number*: Job 38 21 (B ⲏⲡⲓ) ἀριθμός, Ge 30 29 ὅσος (B diff), 1 Cor 11 25 ⲧⲁ. ⲛⲥⲟⲡ (B ⲥⲟⲡ ⲛⲓⲃⲉⲛ), Ap 11 6 ὁσάκις, Ac 27 20 ⲟⲩⲁ. ⲛⲣⲟⲟⲩ (B ⲙⲛⲏϣ) πλείων, Mor 18 111 ⲉⲓⲧⲉ ϩⲱⲃ ⲉϥⲟ ⲛⲟⲡⲥ (*sic*) ⲛⲥⲙⲟⲧ πολύτροπος, R 1 1 26 ⲟⲩⲁ. ⲛⲣⲱⲙⲉ πολύς, Pcod Mor 25 Sᶠ ⲧⲁ. ⲛⲥⲟⲩⲁ (in arithm. problem), ShA 1 253 I am servant ⲙⲡⲁ. ⲛⲭⲟⲉⲓⲥ.

ⲏⲡⲥ, ⲉⲡⲥ SB, identical with ⲁⲡⲥ: ShC 73 198 S, BM 1160 S ⲛⲟⲩⲏ. ⲛⲥⲟⲡ, JTS 5 562 S ϣⲁⲟⲩⲉ. ⲉⲛⲥⲟⲡ, Ep 458 S ⲉⲓⲥ ⲟⲩⲉ. ⲛⲣⲟⲙⲡⲉ, C 41 22 B ⲟⲩⲏ. of money, PO 14 341 B he did obeisance ϩⲉⲛⲣⲁⲡⲏ. ⲛϣⲟ, BMOr 9525 (3) S ⲛⲛⲟⲩⲃ…ⲛ†ⲥⲟⲟⲩⲛ ⲁⲛ ⲛⲧⲉⲩⲏ.

V also ⲱⲡ (ⲏⲡⲉ).

ⲁⲡⲁⲥ SB, -ⲉⲥ F   *v* ⲁⲥ.

ⲁⲡⲟⲩⲥ B nn m, *bald* from ring-worm: K 72 اقرع (between اصلع & ابلج, so ἄπους unlikely).

ⲁⲡⲟⲧ S, ⲁⲫⲟⲧ B, ⲁⲡⲁⲧ F (CMSS 78), pl ⲁⲡⲏⲧ S, ⲁⲫⲏⲧ B (Lab, whence?), or ? ⲁⲡⲱⲧ (*v* place-name, below), ? ⲁⲡⲟⲟⲩⲧⲉ S (Ryl 222), nn m, *cup*: Ps 10 6 B (S ϫⲱ), Is 51 17 SB, Jer 48 5 SB, Pro 23 31 S, Mt 26 27 S (var ϫⲱ) B, CaiEuch 642 B sacramental *chalice* ποτήριον; for water: Mt 10 42 B (S ϫⲱ); wine: Ps 368 S, AM 82 B; poison: AM 60 B; of glass: MG 25 255 B (*cf* C 43 128), CO 459 S cups in metal 'crown' (chandelier?); Va 58 66 B ⲛⲓⲁ. ⲉⲧⲭⲟⲣϫ chalice ready filled (*cf* BKU 1 8 31 S ⲛⲡϭⲱⲣϭ ⲛⲧⲉ ⲛⲁ.), Glos 357 S ⲛⲟϭ ⲛⲁ. θηρίκλειον, 360 do σωρότερο[ς].

ⲥⲁⲛⲁⲡⲟⲧ S nn m, *cup-maker* or seller: Ryl 369, Saq 207.

In place-name ⲙⲁⲛⲕⲁⲡⲱⲧ, now منقباض, P 43 51 S, translated موضع الكاسات (ⲙⲁ ⲛⲕⲁ ⲁⲡⲱⲧ pl, *cf* ⲙⲁ ⲛⲕⲁ ⲣⲉⲓⲕ R 1 3 74, BMis 387).

ⲁⲡϭⲗⲁ A   *v* ϭⲗⲁ.

ⲁⲣⲁ S nn m, *title*, prob financial or legal, only in Theban documents: CO 165, Tor 30, RE 14 24 (69), ALR 15 475, Ep 189; pl CO 93, 209, BKU 1 260, Ep 281. Context never instructive.

ⲁⲣⲁ S nn f, *chain*?: P 131³ 47 (Epiphan. *De Gemm.*) ⲧⲥⲛⲧⲉ ⲛⲁ. ⲛⲡⲛⲟⲩⲃ *catenulae* on either side of high-priest's neck, *cf* Ex 36 24 (39 16) δακτύλιον = B ϣⲟⲩⲣ, AZ 60 107 ⲛⲉϩⲙⲉⲩ ⲛⲁ. ? *chain-smiths*. *V* next word.

ⲁⲣⲁ B nn m, *door-ring*: K 157 زرفين in parts of house, between ⲭⲗⲓⲧⲟⲥ (χλίδων) & ⲕⲉⲗⲗⲓ, while in Montp 164, P 55 9 (various tools) ⲁ. is between ⲧⲣⲁⲭⲟⲥ (τροχός *compass*) & ⲉⲙⲥⲟϩⲓ (*cf* K 132). But زرفين may be *capital* of pillar (Dozy).

ⲁⲣⲉ, ⲁⲗⲉ (ST 125) *S* nn m, *pail, bucket*: Glos
192 209 ἔκχυσις, ὑδροδοχεῖον, Ep 449; BM 480
ⲟⲩⲁⲣⲉⲓ ⲛ̄ⲣⲟⲙⲡⲧ, TurM 18, ST 439 both sim ⲁⲣⲏ
(no gender).

ⲁⲣⲉ *S* nn, a plant: P 43 56 ⲥⲱ̅ⲃⲉ ⲛⲁ. ورق السدر
but = 44 81 ⲥ̅. ⲡ̄ⲕⲏ̄ⲛⲁⲣⲏ παλαίουρος *zizyphus,*
jujube tree; so for ⲁⲣⲉ prob *l* (ⲕⲏⲡ)ⲁⲣⲏ κινάρα,
though this = artichoke. *Cf* K 177 *B* ⲕⲉⲛⲛⲁⲣⲓ
نبق (= سدر). Yet παλαίουρος = ῥάμνος, which =
عوسج = ⲁⲣⲟⲟⲩⲉ, *q v. Cf* ⳝⲣⲱⲟⲩⲛⲓ.

ⲁⲣⲓ- *v* ⲉⲓⲣⲉ.

ⲁⲣⲟ *S* nn f, an object made of lead, used in
weighing (?) tow: Ryl 211 (leaden vessels are ὑδρία,
πίθος, σκεῦος; *v* ⲧⲁⲣⲧ & Reil *Beiträge* 71).

ⲁⲣⲟ *B* nn, *cyperus*: K 188 ﺳﻌﺪ, used as fodder
(Lab).

ⲁⲣⲱ *SF* *v* ⲟⲩⲣⲱ.

ⲁⲣⲏⲃ̄, ⲉⲣⲏⲃ̄, ⲣⲏⲃ̄ *SBF* nn m, **a.** *pledge*: Ge
38 17 *B*, 2 Cor 1 22 *SBF*, Eph 1 14 *SB* (*F* ⲉⲗⲗⲏⲧ), BAp 52 *S* = Wess 15 132 *S* (var BM 295
ⲉⲣⲏⲧ) ἀρραβών; TRit 244 *B* bride ⲁⲥⳝⲓ ⲁ. ⲉⲟⲩⲣⲁⲓ
ⲙ̄ⲃⲟⲏⲑⲉⲓⲁ ἁρμόζεται ἀνδρί, BHom 30 *S* ⲛⲁ. of
celestial rest: Mor 25 14 *S* the rich fool (Lu 12
18) ϣⲁⲣⲉⲡⲙⲟⲩ ⳁ ⲁ. ⲉⲭⲱϥ (var P 131³ 85 ⲣ ⲭ̅ⲥ̅
ⲉⲭⲱⲟⲩ, *B* Va 61 90 = *S*). **b.** *deposit of money*:
PSBA 34 174 *S* bridegroom paid bride's father 20
solidi ⲛⲁ., ShMiss 4 277 *S* forbids to take or give
ⲁ., New York Hist Soc ostr *S* ⲉⲥ ⲛⲁ. ⲁⲓⲧⲛ̄ⲛⲟⲟⲩϥ
for work to be done, BM 538 *S* ⳁ ⲛⲁ. ⲛ̄ⲡⲉⲉⲣⲅⲁⲧⲏⲥ,
ib 1090 *S* ⲡⲉⲧⲁⲓⲧⲁⲁϥ ⲛ̄ⲁⲓⲁⲡⲟⲙⲏ ϩⲁⲡⲉⲣⲏⲃ̄, *ib* 1067
S ⲟⲩⲉⲓⲣⲏⲃ̄ ⲛ̄ⲛⲓⲱϩⲉ, Kr 95 *S* δημόσιον of ⲡⲣⲏⲃ̄
ⲛ̄ⲡⲉⲓⲱϩⲉ, Ryl 158 *S* (*bis*) ⲧϣⲟⲙⲧⲉⲣⲏⲃ̄ ⲛ̄ⲡⲥⲉⲧⲓⲱϩⲉ
(for these *cf* Mitteis *Grundz*. 184).

ⲁⲣⲃ̄ⲟⲧ, ⲁⲣⲃ̄ⲱⲧ *B* *v* ϩⲣⲃ̄ⲱⲧ.

ⲁⲣⲓⲕⲉ *SA*, ⲁⲣⲓⲕⲓ *B*, ⲁⲗⲓⲕⲓ *F* nn m, *blame,*
fault: Ac 25 16 *B* (*S* ⲕⲁⲧⲏⲅⲟⲣⲓⲁ), BM 172 1 *S*
ἔγκλημα; Job 33 23 *SB*, μέμψις; c ⲉ- of person
blamed: Sa 13 6 *S* (Gk do), JA '75 5 237 *S* ἐγκαλεῖν; MG 25 27 *B* ⲡ̄ⲧⲉϥⲧⲁⲗⲉ ⲡⲉϫⲁ. ⲉⲣⲟϥ σφάλμα;
LMis 81 363 *S* ⲡⲉⲧⲉⲟⲩⲛ̄ⲧϥ ⲟⲩⲁ. ⲉⲡⲉϥⲥⲟⲛ, *cf* Mt
5 23 *S*); Aeg 276 *S* ⲕⲁ ⲁ. ⲉⲣⲟⲩⲛ ⲉ- κατά τινος (*cf*
Lev 19 18 *B* ⲥ ⲛ̄ⲧⲉⲛ-), ⲥ ⲙ̄ⲛ-, ⲟⲩⲧⲉ-, ⲟⲩⲧⲉ & ⲛⲉⲙ-:
Col 3 13 *SB* μομφή, (*cf* Miss 4 187 *B*), Mk 11 25 *S*
(*B* om) τι κατά; Leyd 431 *S* ⲉⲣⲉⲟⲩⲁ. ⲡⲧⲁϥ ⲙⲉ(ⲛ)-
ⲡⲉϥⲥⲟⲛ; c ⳝⲓ ⲉ-: Ge 17 1 *B* ἄμεμπτος; Ep 256 *S*
ⲙ̄ⲡⲉϥⲕⲱ ⲁ. ϩⲓⲱϥ.

ⲁⲧⲁ., -ⲕⲓ *SB* adj, *blameless*: AZ 30 41 = Ryl
267 *S* ⲡ̄ⲗⲁⲟⲥ ⲉⲧⲟ ⲛⲁ., Job 1 1 *B*, Phil 2 15 *B*,
(*S* ⲁⲧⲛⲟⲃⲉ), He 8 7 *B* (*S* ⲁⳝⲛⲁ.) ἄμεμπτος; Col
1 22 *B* (*S* diff) ἀνέγκλητος, *cf* Ti 2 8 *S* ⲁⳝⲛⲁ.

ἀκατάγνωστος, HL 99 *B* ⲛ̄ϯⲛⲁϣⲉⲣ ⲁⲧⲁ. ⲁⲛ; Miss
4 203 *B* before the βῆμα ⳅⲉⲛⲟⲩⲙⲉⲧⲁ.

ⳝⲛ, ϫⲉⲙ ⲁ. *SAB* vb, *blame, find fault*: c ⲉ- Job
33 10 *SB* μέμψιν εὑρίσκειν, Si 41 7 *S*, Gu 33 *S*
μέμφεσθαι; Ex 22 9 *B*, Ac 23 28 *B* (*S* = Gk)
ἐγκαλεῖν; Pro 18 22 *A* αἰτιᾶσθαι, *ib* 28 11 *SA*, Gal
2 11 *S* (*B* = Gk) καταγινώσκειν; ShC 73 64 *S*
ⲉϥⳝⲛ ⲁ. ⲉⲣⲟⲩⲛ ⲉⲣⲟⲛ. *B* nn m, *fault-finding*:
Cat 207, Va 59 156 good is thy ϫⲉⲙ ⲁ. ⲉⲣⲟⲛ.

ⲣⲉϥⳝⲛ ⲁ. *S* nn, *fault-finder*: Jude 16 (*B* ⲣⲉϥϥⲓ
ⲁ.) μεμψίμοιρος.

ⲙⲛⲧⲣⲉϥⳝⲛ ⲁ. *S* nn f, *fault-finding, criticism*:
ShC 42 119 ⲙ. ⲉⲣⲟⲩⲛ ⲉⲡⲉⲧⳁ ⲥⲃⲱ.

—— *SF* vb tr, *blame*: BMar 13 *S* Romanus
hath condemned his son & ⲁϥⲁ. ⲙ̄ⲡⲣⲣⲟ ⲙ̄ⲛⲡⲉϥⲛ̄ⲉ,
CMSS 23 *F* ⲙ̄ⲛⲉⲣⲁ. ⲙⲁⲛ. Both ? erroneous.

ⲁⲣⲓⲙ *SB* (BM 1247 228), ⲁⲣⲁⲣⲓⲙ *B* nn, an
edible plant, *saltwort*: Job 30 4 *bis* ἅλιμον (*v* Encycl.
Bibl. 2911). Prob = the Gk (*cf* Löw 37). In BM
459 = J 5 R different word.

ⲁⲣⲓ- *A* *v* ⲣⲟ (ⲉⲣⲓ-).

ⲁⲣⲓⲣⲉ *S* *v* ⲉⲓⲣⲉ.

ⲁⲣⲱⲥ *F* nn f, obscure word: BM 684 account
begins ⲡ̄ⲗⲟⲅ(ⲟⲥ) ⲛ̄ⲁⲣⲱⲥ ⲧⲁⲓⲧⲉⲓⲧⲥ (ⲉ)ⲃⲟⲗ ϩⲉⲡⲁⲗ-
ⳝⲟⲩ[. Prob *l.* ⲛ(ⲧ)ⲁⲣⲱⲥ.

ⲁⲣⲱⳁ *F* *v* ⲉⲣⲱⲧⲉ.

ⲁⲣⲧⲟⲃ̄ *S* *v* ⲣⲧⲟⲃ̄.

ⲁⲣⲟⲩ *S* *v* ⲁⲗⲱ *pupil of eye*.

ⲁⲣⲏⲩ, ϩⲁⲣⲏⲩ (*cf* ? ϩⲁⲣⲁ *B* = ἄρα) *S*, ⲉⲣⲏⲩ
Sᵃ, ⲁⲣⲏⲟⲩ *B*, ⲁⲗⲏⲟⲩ *F* (Gal 6 14), ⲁⲣⲉⲟⲩ *O* (Hor
79, 84) adv, *perhaps, if*, or merely interrog (*cf*
nonne); *S* not bibl (mostly ⲙⲏⲡⲟⲧⲉ): Jer 20 10 *B*
εἰ; Nu 22 11 *B* (*S* ⲭⲉ-), *ib* 23 27 *B* (*S* ⲉϣϫⲉ),
Ac 8 22 *B* (*S* ⲉϣⲱⲡⲉ) εἰ ἄρα; Jer 28 8 *B*, Ac 27
12 *B* εἰ πῶς; Jer 33 3 *B* (*S* ⲙⲉϣⲁⲕ), MG 25 11
B ἴσως; Ez 2 5 *B* ἐὰν ἄρα; Si 19 13 *B* (Va 57
182, *S* ⲭⲉⲙⲉϣⲁϥ) μήποτε; Lu 13 9 *B* (*S* ⲉϣⲱⲡⲉ)
κἄν; LCyp 30 *S* τάχα. Used with following
tenses: **a.** 1 pres, BMis 353 *S* (*B* ⲙⲏ) ⲁ. ⲧⲉⲧⲛ̄-
ⲣⲁϣⲉ, WTh 38 *B* ⲁ. ⲕ̄ⲥⲱⲟⲩⲛ. **b.** 2 pres, Gu
Dorm 5 *S* ⲁ. ⲉⲕⲟⲩⲱϣ ⲉⲥⲱⲃⲉ ⲛ̄ⲥⲱⲛ, BAp 80 *S* ϩⲁ.
ⲉⲕϣⲱⲡⲉ, BMis 269 *S* ϩⲁ. ⲉⲩϫⲓ ⳝⲟⲗ, C 86 282 *B*
ⲁ. ⲁϥϩⲟⲡⲛ ⲙ̄ⲙⲟϥ. **c.** 1 perf, Va 61 23 *B* ⲁ. ⲁⲥⳁ
ⲙⲁⳁ ⲉⲣⲟⲟⲩ ⲛ̄ϫⲉ ⲟⲩϣⲟⲙ (*cf* TU 32(4) 40), AM
184 *B* ⲁ. ⲛⲓⲡ̄ⲡⲁ̄ ⲁϥⲟⲩⲱⲛϩ ⲙ̄ⲫⲁⲓ ⲛⲁϥ. **d.** 2 perf,
WTh 139 *S* ⲁ. ⲡ̄ⲧⲁⲩⲕⲁⲁϥ ⲉⲡⲉⲥⲏⲧ whilst alive,
Miss 4 574 *S* ⲁ. ⲉⲡⲧⲁⲛ̄ⲭⲉ ⳝⲱⲡⲧ ⲉⲣⲟⲛ, BMis 236 *S*
ϩⲁ. ⲧⲁⲭⲁ, EW 176 *B* ⲁ. ⲉⲧⲁⲡⲁⲓ...ⲉⲣ ⲙⲁⳝⲓⲁ. **e.**
1 perf neg, Va 62 177 *B* ⲕⲁⲧⲁⲣⲟⲓ ⲁ. ⲙ̄ⲡⲉⲕⳁ ϩⲗⲓ.
f. 1 fut (oftenest), Mor 56 22 *S* ϩⲁ. ⲅⲁⲣ the Lord

will visit them, BMar 69 *S* ϩⲁ. ⲕⲛⲁⲧⲱⲟⲅⲡ ⲛⲧⲛⲃⲱⲕ,
Miss 8 255 *S* sim, Mor 43 291 *S* ⲁ. ⲥⲉⲡⲁⲙⲉⲧⲁⲡⲟⲓ
= R 1 ι 75 ⲙⲉⲱⲁⲕ, Ep 169 *Sᵃ* ⲉⲣⲉⲟⲩ ⲛ̄ⲡⲉ̄ ⲡⲁϫⲓ
ⲙⲁⲉⲓⲧ, CO 372, 385, ST 306 sim, AM 141 *B* I am
weary of long-suffering ϫⲉⲁ. ⲧⲉⲧⲉⲛⲡⲁⲉⲣ ⲑⲩⲥⲓⲁ.
g. 2 fut, Aeg 19 *SB* ⲁ. ⲉϥⲛⲁⲙⲟⲩ. **h.** 3 fut,
Ep 196 *S* ⲁ. (ⲉ)ⲕⲁⲩⲡⲱⲗⲕ, ST 287 *Sᵃ* ⲁ. ⲥⲁⲏⲣ
ⲟⲩⲛⲁⲉⲓⲛ. **i.** impf fut, ShC 42 118 *S* ⲁ. ⲛⲉⲣⲉ-
ⲡⲝ̄ⲥ̄ ⲛⲁⲡⲁⲩ, Leip Ber '02 144 *S* ⲁ. ⲉⲛⲉϥⲛⲁⲁⲓⲥⲱⲁⲛⲉ
(? due to interrog τάχα, Epiph Ancorat. § 105).
j. aor, Ryl 290 *S* ⲁ. ϣⲁⲛⲉⲣ ⲡⲉⲗⲓⲡϣⲁ, Va 57 186
B ⲁ. ⲧⲁⲭⲁ ϣⲁⲅⲁⲣⲉϩ ⲉⲣⲱⲟⲩ ἄν ἀκούσωσιν. **k.**
subj, PS 267 *S* ⲁ. ⲣⲱ ⲛⲧⲉⲛⲧ ϩⲏⲩ, C 41 14 *B* ⲁ.
ⲡⲧⲉϥⲛⲁⲓ ⲙⲉϥⲧ ⲧⲁϩⲟⲓ, Va 57 2 *B* ⲁ. ⲧⲁⲭⲁ ⲛⲧⲟⲩⲅⲁ-
ⲥⲓⲁⲓ, Rec 6 173 *B* I entered ϫⲉⲁ. ⲛⲧⲁⲛⲡⲁⲩ. **l.**
rel, BMis 438 *S* ϩⲁ. ⲡϫⲁⲓⲙⲱⲛ ⲡⲉⲧⲡⲓⲣⲁⲍⲉ ⲙⲙⲟⲛ.
m. partic, BMis 258 *S* ⲁ. ⲉⲡⲉⲣⲏⲧ ⲡⲓⲑⲉ ⲁⲡ, MG 25
309 *B* ⲁ. ⲡⲁⲛⲧⲱⲥ ⲉϥϫⲉⲛⲡⲓⲙⲁ. **n.** nominal or
impersonal, AM 25 *B* ⲁ. ⲟⲩⲟⲛ ⲟⲩⲭⲣⲟϥ ϫⲏ in his
heart, RE 9 137 *S* ⲁ. ⲡⲁⲛⲧⲱⲥ ⲟⲩⲛ ⲟⲩⲁⲓⲟⲓⲕⲏⲥⲓⲥ
ⲡⲁϣⲱⲡⲉ, P 131⁵ 17 *S* ⲁ. ϩⲉⲛⲁⲅⲩⲥⲧⲏⲣⲓⲟⲛⲡⲉ ⲡⲁⲓ.

ⲉⲃⲏⲗ ⲁ. *B, except, S* mostly ⲉⲓⲙⲏⲧⲓ: Dan 2 11
ἀλλ᾽ ἤ, Jo 10 10, 2 Cor 12 5 (var om ⲁ.), Gal 6 14
(*F* ⲉⲙⲉϣⲏⲓⲉ ⲁ.) εἰ μή, MG 25 237 where didst
find this hide ⲉ. ⲁ. ϫⲉⲁⲣⲉⲟⲩⲟⲙ ⲟⲩⲉⲥⲱⲟⲩ?
ⲙⲉⲱⲁⲕ ⲁ. *S, lest perhaps:* BMis 571 I fear ⲙ.
ⲁ. ⲧⲓⲙⲡϣⲁ ⲁⲡ, Miss 4 641 ⲁ. ⲙ. ⲡϥϣⲓⲡⲉ ⲛϩⲏⲧϥ.

ⲁⲣⲏⲟⲩ *B* v ⲉⲣⲏⲩ.

ⲁⲣⲉⲓⲟⲩⲉ *A*, ⲁⲣⲱⲟⲩⲓ *B* v ⲣⲟⲟⲩⲉ.

ⲁⲣⲓⲟⲩⲓ *B* v ⲉⲓⲣⲉ.

ⲁⲣⲟⲟⲩ *S* nn (?): Si 11 13 (Lag, HT) one there
is laboureth, being at pains & in haste ⲁⲩⲱ ⲉϥⲣ
ⲥⲣⲱϥ ⲡⲁⲣⲟⲟⲩ προγο καὶ τόσῳ μᾶλλον ὑστερεῖται
tanto magis non abundabit. Inexplicable at present.

ⲁⲣⲟⲟⲩⲉ, ⲁⲣⲱⲟⲩ (BMis 201, Mor 15 29 om)
S, ⲁⲣⲁⲩ *A* nn, with sg art Tri 423, elsewhere pl
art, *burr, thistle:* Ge 3 18 *S* (*B* ⲥⲟⲩⲅⲣⲓ ⟨ar⟩), Pro
22 5 *SA*, Hos 10 8 *SA* (*B* = Gk), He 6 8 *S* (*BF*
ⲥⲟⲩⲅⲣⲓ), Mt 7 16 *S* (*B* ⲥⲉⲣⲟϫⲓ ⟨ar⟩) τρίβολος (but
'ⲥ K 176 = ῥάμνος), Tri 423 *S* ⟨ar⟩, ib 440 var
⟨ar⟩, BM 201 *S* ⲡϣⲟⲛⲧⲉ ⲙⲡⲛⲁ. ⲙⲡⲛⲥⲟⲩⲅⲣⲉ. *Cf*
ⲁⲡⲉ a plant.

ⲥⲣⲁⲣⲟⲟⲩⲉ (ⲥⲟⲩⲣⲉ+ⲁ.) *S* nn, with pl art, *briar*(?),
ShA 2 321 *S* he that pusheth through ϩⲉⲛⲥⲣⲁ.,
paral ⲥⲟⲩⲣⲉ: Jud 8 7 in P 44 108 = 43 98 ⟨ar⟩
⟨ar⟩ as gloss on ⲁⲃⲁⲣⲕⲏⲛⲓⲙ (βαρακηνείμ) ⟨ar⟩; but
lc HT has ⲁⲣⲟⲟⲩⲉ. For βαρακηνείμ *cf* ? K 176
ⲃⲁⲣⲓⲕⲁⲕⲓⲛⲁ ⟨ar⟩; hawthorn.

ⲁⲣⲟϣ *S*, ϩⲣⲟϣ *B* (Stern 101) vb intr, *become
cold:* Sa 16 18 ἡμεροῦσθαι, Mt 24 12 (var ⲱϣⲃ, *B*
ϩⲣⲟϣ) ψύχειν, Z 347 *S* ⲙⲛ ⲁⲣⲟϣ...ⲟⲩⲇⲉ ⲙⲛ

ⲣⲱⲕϩ (*B* MG 25 220 ϩⲣⲟϣ) ῥιγοῦν. For other
verbal forms v ⲱⲣϣ.
—— *SB* (ⲉ)ⲣⲁϣ *A*, ⲁⲣⲁϣ *F* nn m, *cold:* Ge 8 22
SB ψῦχος, Deu 28 22 *SB* ῥῖγος, Am 4 9 *B* (*S* =
Gk) ἴκτερος, though Va 57 165 (*v* below) ἴκ. distinct; K 59 *B* ⟨ar⟩; as malady opp ϩⲙⲟⲙ: ShZ
593 *S*, C 43 85 *B* every sickness whether ⲟⲩϩⲙⲟⲙ
ⲓⲧⲉ ⲟⲩⲁ., ib 240, C 86 326 *B*, BM 524 *F*, Ryl
105 *S*, amulet *penes* Ricci *S* (ⲁⲣⲟⲟⲩϣ) all sim;
paral ϫⲁϥ HengB 10; BM 1223 *A* ⲟ]ⲩⲣⲁϣ
ⲙⲡⲟⲩⲛⲟⲩⲅⲥ (*sic l*) ⲛⲣⲏⲧ; Va 68 41 *B* those over-
taken by ⲟⲩⲁ. shall be anointed, HL 110 *B* ⲟⲩ-
ⲭⲟⲥⲉⲙ ⲛϩⲙⲟⲙ ⲡⲁ. περίστασις πυρετοῦ, Va 57
165 *B* ⲛⲓϩⲙⲟⲙ ⲡⲁ. φλογώδης; cold atmosphere:
PS 317 *S* ϫⲁϥ, ϣⲟⲉⲓϣ, ⲁ., Pcod 17 *S* ⲡⲁ. ⲙⲛⲡ-
ⲕⲁⲩⲙⲁ, BHom 121 *S*, BAp 136 *S* sim.

ⲁⲣⲉϣⲁⲛ- *B* v ⲉⲣϣⲁⲛ-.

ⲁⲣϣⲓⲛ *SBF*(CMSS 78), ⲉⲣϣⲓⲛ, ⲉⲣϣⲁⲡ *Sᵃ*
(ST 120) nn m, *lentil:* Ge 25 29 (P 44 103) *S* (*B*
diff), ib 25 34 *B*, 2 Kg 17 28 *S*, Ez 4 9 *SB*, Z 293
S prepare us a little ⲁ., C 89 117 *B* fields sown
with ⲁ. φακός ⟨ar⟩; Va 61 18 *B* ⲟⲩⲁ. ⲉϥϣⲟⲣⲡ
ⲙⲙⲟⲟⲩ φακῆ βρεκτή; Mor 37 86 *S* Jacob's pottage of ⲁ. ⲉϥⲕⲏⲙ, Ryl 352 *S* measured by ⲣⲧⲟⲃ,
ST 219 *S* by ⲁⲓⲡⲉ, Hall 131 *S* by ⲙⲁϫⲉ & ϩⲱ,
Bodl(P) d 20 *S* ⲡⲁ. ϩⲙⲡⲓⲕⲁⲣⲡⲟⲥ ⲡⲁⲓ, Kr 9 *S*
? ⲡⲁ., ib 247 *S* ⲁ. ϥⲛⲟⲣϫ (*cf* Lev 2 14 *B*), Bodl(P)
d 47 ⲁ. ⲉϥⲥⲟⲣϣ; on these v Ep 1 146 n.

ⲁⲣϣⲁⲛ *S* nn, a skin disease, *lentigo* (cf φακός spot,
freckle): Lev 22 22 (*B* ⲑⲟⲩ ⲑⲟⲩ) μυρμηκοῦν, ib P
44 106 ⟨ar⟩, var (P 129¹ 65) ⲟ ⲡⲥⲁϫⲓϥ; Tri 494
old woman ⲉⲧⲟ ⲛⲁ. ⟨ar⟩ (? nasal polypus).

ⲁⲣϣⲏⲧ, ⲉⲣϣⲏⲧ *B*, Job 19 3 ἐπικεῖσθαι. V
ⲉⲣϣⲟ(ⲧϩ.).

ⲁⲣⲉϩ *B*, ⲁⲣⲏⲣⲧⲉ *A* v ϩⲁⲣⲉϩ.

ⲁⲣⲏϫ, -ⲏⲏϫ (Job 38 16, BM 1001 1) *SA*,
ⲁⲩⲣⲏϫ *B*, ⲁⲗⲟϫ *F* (Mt 24 31, Mk 13 27) nn,
limit, end, always with suff of thing limited (3 pl
S -ⲟⲩ, Job 34 24, Is 42 11, 2 Pet 2 4 &c). **a.**
Deu 30 13 *S* (*B* ⲙⲏⲣ) ⲁⲣⲏϫⲥ ⲛⲑⲁⲗⲁⲥⲥⲁ, Jer 22
20 *B* ⲁⲩⲣⲏϫϥ ⲙⲫⲓⲟⲙ πέραν; Ps 7 7 *B* (*S* ϩⲁⲏ),
47 10 *SB*, 97 3 *B* (*S* ⲕⲣⲟ), 144 3 *B* (*S* ϣⲓ) πέρας;
Job 11 7 *SB*, Ps 138 9 *S* (*B* ϩⲁⲉ), Is 49 6 *S* (*B* do),
Jer 6 22 *B* ἔσχατον; Deu 33 17 *SB*, Pro 8 26 *SA*
(*B* ⲗⲁⲕϩ), Is 41 5 *S* (*B* ⲉⲁⲧ), Mk 13 27 *B* (*S* ϫⲱ)
ἄκρος; PS 117 *S* ϫⲓⲛⲁ. ⲙⲡⲕⲁϩ ϣⲁⲁ. **b.** approximate: Job 13 27 *S* ῥίζα, 38 16 *S* ἴχνος, Is 24
16 *SB* πτέρυξ, Zech 9 10 *SA* διεκβολή, Mic 4 3 *SA*
μακράν. **c.** negative: Si 30 15 *S* ἀμέτρητος:
Bar 3 17 *B* οὐ τέλος; 1 Tim 1 4 *B* (*S* ϩⲁⲉ) ἀπέραντος; Ps 123 5 *B* (*S* diff) ⲁⲧϣ ⲉⲛ ⲁ. ἀνυπόστατος
Va 57 41 *B* sim.

ⲁⲧⲁⲣⲏⲭ̅, -ⲁⲩⲣⲏⲭ̅ *SB* negative adj, *limitless, boundless*: Job 5 9 *S* (*B* ⲁⲧϭⲟⲧϭⲉⲧ) ἀνεξιχνίαστος, *cf* Eph 3 8 *B*; 2 Pet 2 4 *S* (*B* Gk diff); BMis 416 *S* of sea, BG 81 *S* of light.

ⲁⲥ *SF*, ⲁⲁⲥ *S*, ⲉⲥ *AF*, ⲁⲡⲁⲥ *SB*, ⲁⲡⲉⲥ *F* adj, *old*: **a.** Lev 25 22 *SB*, Jos 9 10 *S*, Jer 45 11 *B*, Mt 9 17 *SB*, Ro 6 6 *SB* παλαιός; Is 65 22 *SB* ⲉⲓⲣⲉ ⲡⲁ., He 8 13 *SBF* sim παλαιοῦν; Si 9 12 *S* (only) ἀρχαῖος; CaiEuch 460 *B* ⲙⲉⲧⲭⲁⲝⲓ ⲡⲁ. χρόνιος; AM 252 *B* ϯⲅⲣⲁⲫⲏ ⲡⲁ. Old Test, MG 25 47 *B* sim, BSM 76 *B* of overdue tax, DeV 101 *B* ⲡⲁⲓⲁ. ⲡⲕⲟⲗⲟⲃⲓⲟⲛ (*cf* Lu 5 36 *B* ⲁ. = *S* ⲡⲗϭⲉ, *v* below), PMéd 294 *S* wound, *ib* 225 ῥεῦμα, Z 629 *S* vinegar, WS 126 *S* beans. **b.** ⲁⲡⲁⲥ *S*: Dan 7 9, PMéd 185 wine (*cf ib* 56 ⲁⲥ), *ib* 277 vinegar, Z 630 vine leaves, BM 1045 reeds, Bodl(P) a 2 ⲱⲡⲉ ⲛ ⲃⲏⲗϫⲉ ⲡⲁ., Ryl 189 ⲡⲟϭⲉ ⲡϭⲟⲓ ⲡⲁ., J 90 7, 98 7 oblate to serve like ϭⲁⲅⲟⲛ ⲡⲁ.; ⲁⲡⲉⲥ *F*: CMSS 61 parchment books, BM 691 sim (*cf* Rec 11 138). **c.** without ⲡ- *S*: ShA 1 194, Z 630, CO 235 ⲏⲣⲡ ⲁⲥ, Kr 234 opp ⲉⲓⲙⲣⲓⲥ, WS 87, 188 ⲉⲣⲡ, ⲣⲡ ⲁⲥ, BM 473 ⲏⲣⲡ ⲡⲉⲣⲡ ⲁⲥ. **d.** ⲛⲛ: Cant 7 13 *S*, Dan 7 9 *SB*, Mt 13 52 *SBF* παλαιός.

ⲁⲧⲁⲡⲁⲥ *F* privative adj, *not old*: BM 527 in recipe (doubtful).

ⲙⲛⲧⲁⲥ *S*, -ⲉⲥ *A*, ⲙⲉⲧⲁⲡⲁⲥ *B* nn f, *oldness*: Nah 1 15 *AB* παλαίωσις; Ro 7 6 *SB* παλαιότης; Bor 226 173 *S* ⲧⲙ. ⲡⲧⲕⲁⲕⲓⲁ, HL 112 *B* ⲡⲉϥⲙ. (*sic*) *old age*.

ⲣ ⲁⲥ *S*, ⲉⲣ ⲁⲡⲁⲥ *B*, ⲉⲗ ⲉⲥ, -ⲁⲥ *F*, *become old*: Job 9 5 *B* (*S* ϭⲓⲧⲉ), Lam 3 4 *B* sim, Ps 6 8 *B* (*S* ⲱⲥⲕ), Is 51 6 *B* (*S* ⲣ ⲡⲗϭⲉ, *cf* Lu 5 36), He 1 11 *BF* (*S* ⲇⲟ) παλαιοῦσθαι, *ib* 8 13 *SBF* ⲣ ⲁⲥ, ⲣ ϩⲗⲗⲟ ⲡⲁⲗ., γηράσκειν; Is 51 8 *B* (*S* ⲣ ⲡⲗϭⲉ) βεβρῶσθαι.

ϫⲓⲡⲉⲣ ⲁ. *B* nn f, *a growing old*: Va 58 140 ϯϫ. in all sins.

ⲁⲁⲥ, ⲁⲥ *S*, ⲉⲉⲥ *A²* (? Jo 19 3) *F*, ⲉⲥ *F*, nn (Pey f, *whence* ?), *blow with hand*, mostly on face: Is 50 6 *S*; with ϯ Mk 14 65 *S* (*B* ⲁⲗⲱϫ), Jo 19 3 *S* (*B* ⲕⲟⲩⲣ), R 1 1 61 *S* ⲁⲁⲥ, *ib* 73 ⲁⲥ (opp ⲕⲗⲯ) ῥάπισμα; Mt 26 67 *S* (*B* ϩⲓⲟⲩⲓ ⲉ-), Mor 17 35 *S* (*B* ⲕⲟⲩⲣ) ῥαπίζειν, Glos 280 *S* ἀλάφη; Pcod 44 *S* ⲁⲩϯ ⲁ. ⲡⲁϥ, BIF 22 107 *SF*, Wess 15 23 = Louvre 10032 *S* ⲉⲁϥϯ ⲡⲁⲓ ⲡⲟⲩⲕⲟⲩⲓ ⲡⲁ. ἠρέμα κοσσίσας, ShP 130¹ 139 *S* a blow ϩⲁⲙⲡⲣⲟ...ⲛ ⲉϩⲣⲁⲓ ⲉϫⲡⲧⲉⲥⲁⲡⲉ, BIF 13 111 *S* blow ϩⲓⲧⲉϥⲟⲩⲟϭⲉ; with ⲣⲱⲧ: Jo 18 22 *S* (*A²B* ⲕⲟⲩⲣ) ῥάπισμα, R 1 5 28 *S* ⲁϥⲣⲁϩⲧϥ... ⲡⲟⲩⲛⲟϭ ⲡⲁ.; other vbs: R 1 1 68 *S* ⲁⲩϩⲓⲟⲩⲉ ⲡⲣⲉⲡⲁ. ⲉϩⲟⲩⲛ ϩⲡ-, Turin Atti 30 806 *S* unworthy ⲡⲟⲩⲉⲙ ⲟⲩⲁ. for Christ's name.

ϣⲥ ⲡⲁⲥ *S*, ⲡⲉⲉⲥ *F* (Mor 30 38), meaning sim:

Wess 18 124 *S* I cannot strike with ⲟⲩϣ. or with ⲟⲩϭⲉⲣⲱϭ, Mor 31 58 *S* ϯ ⲡⲟⲩⲗⲏⲛϣⲉ ⲡϣ.

ⲁⲉⲓⲏⲥ *S* *v* ⲁⲓⲁⲓ.

ⲁⲥⲁⲓ *SF*, ⲉⲥⲓⲉⲉⲓ *A*, ⲁⲥⲓⲁⲓ *B*, ⲁⲥⲱⲟⲩ† *SF* (ⲁⲥⲟ-ⲟⲩⲧ? PS 219, ⲁⲥⲱⲟⲩ *ib*), ⲁⲥⲉⲓⲱⲟⲩ† *S* (Tor 27), ⲉⲥⲓⲱⲟⲩ† *A*, ⲁⲥⲓⲱⲟⲩ† (ⲥⲁⲓⲱⲟⲩ 2 Kg 1 23, Cat 53 &c) *BO* (AZ 21 100) vb, **I.** intr, **A** *be light, relieved*. **a.** Jo 4 52 *B* (*S* ⲙⲧⲟⲛ) κομφότ. ἔχειν, Ac 27 38 *SB* κουφίζειν, BSM 13 *B* of floods ⲉⲁϩⲁ., BM 1104 *S* of health, Tell us ϫⲉⲁⲧⲡⲉⲁ. **b.** with dependent prep: ⲥ ⲉ-, Jon 1 5 *SA* (*B* ⲉⲃⲟⲗ ϩⲁ-) κουφίζεσθαι ἀπό, C 86 337 *B* ⲁⲡⲉϥϣⲱⲙⲁ ⲁ. ⲉⲣⲟϥ; ⲥ ⲉⲃⲟⲗ ϩⲁ-, Ex 18 22 *B* (*S* ϯ ⲙⲧⲟⲛ) κουφ. ἀπό, C 86 280 *B* may these pains ⲁ. ⲉⲃⲟⲗ ϩⲁⲣⲟⲓ = BSG 179 *S* ϯ ⲙⲧⲟⲛ ⲡⲁⲓ ⲉⲃ. ϩⲡ- κουφ. ἐκ; ⲥ ⲉⲃⲟⲗ ϩⲡ-, Mor 37 49 *S* ⲁϩⲁ. ⲉⲃ. ϩⲡⲧⲙⲟⲕϩⲥ κουφ. τῶν, C 89 50 *B* (*S* = Gk) ⲁϩⲁ. ⲉⲃ. ϫⲉⲛⲡϣⲱⲡⲓ κουφ. τῆς; ⲥ ϫⲉⲡ-, TstAb 175 *B* ⲁⲡⲁⲡⲓϥⲓ ⲁ. ⲡϫⲏⲧ; ⲥ ⲉϫⲡ-, ⲉϩⲣⲁⲓ ⲉϫⲡ-; ⲥ ϩⲓϫⲡ-, BMar 92 *S* disease ⲁⲕⲧⲣⲉϥⲁ. ϩⲓϫⲱⲓ; Va 57 2 *B* my tears ⲡⲧⲟⲩⲁ. ⲉϫⲱⲓ, P 129¹⁶ 77 *S* (prayer of 40 Martyrs) Let bitter air ⲁ. ⲉϩⲟⲩⲡ .ⲉϫⲱⲡ. **c.** qual: Sa 5 11 *S*, Is 19 1 *SB* κοῦφος R 1 4 59 *S* benefits against which ⲡⲃⲁⲥⲁⲛⲟⲥ ⲁ. ἐπικουφ.; Ex 18 26 *B* (*S* ⲥⲟⲃⲕ), Job 24 18 *B*, Mt 11 30 *SB* ἐλαφρός; Sa 7 22 *S* λεπτός; Si 30 8 *S* προαλής; Pro 13 3 *B*, 2 Tim 3 4 *SB* προπετής; Pro 7 11 *SA* ἀνεπτερωμένος; BM 187 1 *S* of air, R 2 1 66 *S* of diet, ClPr 47 2 *S* of women opp ⲟⲣϫ, Va 61 103 *B* empty ship ⲉϥⲁ. ⲡⲁⲟⲩⲛ, Tor 27 *S* of empty sacks, ShC 42 149 *S* of words opp ϩⲟⲣϣ, Miss 4 568 *S* he answered ⲉϥⲁ. *thoughtlessly* = MG 17 298 ϩⲛⲟⲩⲙⲛⲧⲃⲁⲗ ϩⲏⲧ. **B** *be swift*: **a.** PS 39 *S* their pace ⲁⲓⲧⲣⲉⲥⲁ. **b.** qual, 2 Kg 1 23 *SB*, *ib* 2 18 *S*, Is 18 2 *SB*, *ib* 30 16 *SBF*, Lam 4 19 *SB* κοῦφος; Job 9 25 *SB*, Hab 1 6 *SAB* ἐλαφρός; Am 2 15 *SB* ὀξύς; DeV 178 *B* ⲑⲏ ⲉⲧⲁ. ϫⲉⲡⲧⲉⲥϫⲓⲡϭⲟϫⲓ, BKU 1 31³ *S* horses ⲉⲩⲁⲥ[ⲱⲟⲩ.

II. tr, *lighten*: MG 25 317 *B* ⲉⲁϥⲁ. ⲙⲡⲉϥⲥⲕⲁⲫⲟⲥ ⲥⲁⲡϣⲱⲓ ⲡⲧⲉⲡⲉⲣⲅⲓⲁ of powers of darkness.

—— *SB* nn m, **a.** *lightness, alleviation*: Si 31 1 *S* ἀναπτεροῦν; 2 Cor 4 17 *B* (*S* ⲥⲃⲟⲕ) ἐλαφρόν; Va 57 30 *B* ⲟⲩⲁ. ⲡⲉⲙⲟⲩⲕⲟⲩϥⲓⲙⲟⲥ ⲡⲧⲉ ϯⲧⲉⲫⲱ, Va 61 10 *B* ⲡϩⲣⲟϣ opp ⲡⲓⲁ., P 131² 153 *S* ⲟⲩ-ⲙⲧⲟⲛ...ⲙⲡⲟⲩⲁ. from trials. **b.** qual, *hastiness*: JEA 13 24 *S* Athanasius on intrusive ordinations ⲡⲉⲓⲁⲥⲱⲟⲩ ⲡⲧⲉⲙⲓⲛⲉ. **c.** adv, ϩⲡⲟⲩⲁ., *lightly*: Is 5 26 *B* (*S*†) κούφως, Ac 19 36 *SB* προπετές, 2 Cor 1 17 *SB* τῇ ἐλαφρίᾳ χρᾶσθαι, Miss 4 549 *S* sim, RNC 56 *S* he bore tortures ϩⲡⲟⲩⲁ., Bor 248 47 *S* I departed ϩⲡⲟⲩⲥϩⲁⲣⲧ ⲙⲡⲟⲩⲁ., Mor 28 249 *S* child learnt ϩⲡⲟⲩⲁ. in short time, BMis 246 *S* ϩⲡⲟⲩⲁ. var ϩⲡⲟⲩϭⲉⲡⲏ.

ⲉⲥⲓⲉ *B* 2 Tim 3 2 (ⲏ & Götting lectionaries, *S*

ⲃⲁⲃⲉⲣⲱⲙⲉ) ἀλαζών خفيف (& in *ib* 3 4), ? confused
with ⲉⲥⲓⲉ, *v* ⲣⲁⲥⲓⲉ. Elsewhere ἀλαζών, ἀλαζονεία
never thus. AZ 21 104 *O* ⲟⲩⲡⲱⲕⲉ ⲡⲉ. (same ?).

ⲁⲥⲉ *A*, ⲁⲥⲓ *F* *v* ⲟⲥⲉ.

ⲁⲥⲟ, ϯ *B* *v* ⲥⲟ, ϯ.

ⲁⲥⲕ *S* nn, meaning unknown : CO 482 sowing
contract]ⲙⲡⲛⲭⲁⲉⲓ ⲁⲥⲕ (*sic*) ⲙⲡⲡⲣⲟⲅⲣⲓⲧ. Prob
compound with ⲭⲁⲓ- (ⲭⲓ).

ⲁⲥⲕ *S* (reading practically certain) nn m : J 85
46 on whoso ventures to sue (ⲉⲓ ⲉⲃⲟⲗ ⲉ-) monastery shall come curse of Deu (28 15) & ⲡⲁⲥⲕ of
holy Zacharias shall destroy his belongings (*cf*
? Zech 5 3, 4).

ⲁⲥⲓⲕ *S*, ⲥⲓⲕ *SB* nn m, a periodic malady, *fever,*
? *ague* : Ryl 104 *S* recipe for shivering & ⲡⲁ.
ⲙⲡⲛⲭⲟⲧϣⲟⲙⲧⲉ the 23(-day fever ?), BM 260 1 *S*
I remembered dread Judgement ⲁⲡⲁⲥⲱⲙⲁ ⲧⲏⲣϥ
ⲧⲁϧⲉ ⲥⲓⲕ, Ryl 105 *S* ⲁ. named with ⲁⲣⲟϣ, ϧⲙⲟⲙ,
Amulet *penes* Ricci *S* do, AM 313 *B* ⲥ. with ϧⲣⲟϣ,
ϭⲛⲙ, PMéd 240 *S* a plaster good for ⲡⲁ. or gout
(ποδάγρα, which P 44 79 = ⲟⲩⲁⲙⲟⲙⲉ).

ⲁⲥⲕⲉ *S* *v* ⲱⲥⲕ.

ⲁⲥⲟⲩⲗⲓ *B* nn pl, *butterflies* : K 173 فراش.

ⲁⲥⲡⲉ *S*, ⲉⲥⲡⲉ *A*, ⲁⲥⲡⲓ *B* nn f, *language, speech* :
Ps 80 5 *S* (*B* ⲗⲁⲥ), Is 19 18 *SB*, Ez 3 6 *S* paral
ϭⲓⲛϣⲁⲭⲉ & ϧⲣⲟⲟⲩ, Mk 16 17 *S* (*B* ⲁ. ⲛⲗ.),
1 Cor 14 39 *S* (*BF* ⲗ.) γλῶσσα ; Ps 18 3 *SA*
(Cl 27 7, *B* ⲥⲁⲭⲓ), Mt 26 73 *S* (*B* ⲭⲓⲛⲥⲁⲭⲓ)
λαλιά ; Ac 1 19 *SB* διάλεκτος ; Est 1 22 *S* λέξις ;
El 56 *A* ⲉϥⲥⲛϧ ϧⲛⲧⲁⲉ., AM 190 *B* ⲉⲧⲁⲩⲥⲁⲭⲓ ⲛⲛⲓⲁ.
ⲧⲏⲣⲟⲩ, AZ 21 145 *S* ⲁϥⲡⲉⲉⲡⲉ ⲧⲉϭⲁ., R 1 3 67 *S*
ⲧⲁ. of Egyptians, ShA 1 254 *S*, J 12 53 *S* sim, P
44 64 *S* ⲕⲉⲁ. = ἀλληγορία, Ep 1 19 = AZ 23 100
S ⲁ. in pl ? *words.*

ⲁ. ⲛⲗⲁⲥ : Dan 7 14 *SB*, Mk 16 17 *B* (*v* above),
1 Cor 14 26 *B* (*S* ⲁ.) γλῶσσα ; ⲉ. ⲡϣⲉⲭⲉ El 56 *A*.

ⲣⲉⲙⲛⲧⲁ. *eloquent man* ? TRit 499 *B*, paral ⲣⲉⲙⲛ-
ⲥⲱⲟⲩⲛ.

ⲁⲥⲏⲣ *S* nn m, *belonging(s), chattel(s)* : Deu 20 14
ἀποσκευή (elsewhere = ⲥⲟⲃⲧⲉ), CO 243 his λῶδιξ
is mislaid, ϣⲁⲣϯ ⲡⲁ. ⲛⲁϥ that he may cover himself, ST 339 ⲛⲥⲉϥⲓ ⲛⲡⲉⲛⲁ. ⲛⲭⲓⲟⲩⲉ & leave us to
die.

ⲁⲥⲟⲩ *S*, ⲉⲥⲟⲩ *A* (Cl 55 2), nn f, *a. price, value* :
Lev 27 2 (*B* = Gk), Ps 48 8 (*B* ⲥⲟⲩⲉⲛ), Ac 4 34
(*B* = Gk), 1 Cor 6 20 (*BF* = Gk) τιμή ; Ex 21 21,
35 (*B* ϧⲁⲧ) ἀργύριον ; Deu 23 18 (*B* ϣⲉⲃⲓⲱ) ἀλ-
λαγμα ; ⲁⲭⲛⲁ. : Job 31 39, Ps 43 12 (both *B* ⲛ-
ⲭⲓⲛⲭⲏ) ἄνευ τ. ; ShZ 501 poor find not wherewith ⲉⲧⲟⲟⲩ ⲛⲧⲉⲓⲛⲟϭ ⲡⲁ., Bor 255 252 he was sold
ϧⲁⲟⲩⲕⲟⲩⲓ ⲡⲁ. **b.** ϯ ⲁ., *pay* : BHom 2 ⲁϥϯ

ⲙⲡⲉϥⲥⲛⲟϥ ⲡⲁ. ϧⲁⲣⲟ ἀγοράζειν, BM 223 1 ϣⲁϥϯ
ⲛⲧⲉϭⲁ. ⲛⲧⲉϥϣⲃⲉⲓⲱ, Mich 550 30 for water ⲙⲉϥ-
ϯ ⲁ. **c.** ⲣ ⲁ., *set value on* : ShA 1 249 ⲧⲁ.
ⲛⲧⲁⲅⲁⲁⲥ ϧⲁⲣⲟⲟⲩ.

ⲁⲥⲟⲩⲓ *B* nn f, *purse, wallet* : Job 14 17, Lu 10 4
(both *S* ⲧⲱⲙⲗⲉ) βαλάντιον ; Deu 25 13, Pro 1 14,
Is 46 6 (all *S* ⲧⲱⲙⲗⲉ), Mic 6 11 (*sic l*) μάρσιππος,
-πιον ; Pro 7 20 ἔνδεσμος ; Hag 1 6 δεσμός ; C 41
15 hung from neck = همیان, PO 14 346 put money
into ϯⲁ. ⲡⲧⲉ ϯⲑⲓⲁⲕⲟⲛⲓⲁ.

ⲁⲥⲫⲟⲩⲓ *B* nn, *first year* of reign (*cf* Sethe
Untersuch. 3 95) : Dan 1 21 ϣⲁⲁ. ⲡⲧⲉ ⲕⲩⲣⲟⲥ = *S*
ϣⲁϧⲣⲁⲓ ⲉⲧⲥⲡⲉⲛ (*l* ⲧⲥⲡ) ⲟⲩⲉⲓ ἕως ἔτους ἑνός. *Cf*
ⲥⲡ.

ⲁⲥⲁϥ *B* nn, a plant explained as *bark, rind* of
caper-root (*cf* καππαρόριζον) : K 191 وهو قشر
الاصل (but Ann 1 60 الاصطل), or its *pith, marrow*
(Lab). Prob *l* الاصف (Löw 262, *cf* Dozy *s v*, though
Schweinfurth *Arab Pflanz* 68 لصاف), which = the
Coptic. On كبر in Egypt *v* Almk 1 385.

ⲁⲥⲟⲩⲡⲉⲣ *B* nn (m Lab, f only BM 926) a plant
explained as *bitter nut* : K 187 جوزة المر. Ἀψαφέρ
heracleum spondylium (Langkavel) seems unsuitable.
Coptic ?

ⲁⲥϧ, ⲁⲥϧϥ *A*, ⲁⲥϧ, ⲁⲥϧϥ *S* *v* ⲱⲣϧ.

ⲁⲥϭ *S* nn m, ST 125 in list of metal objects,
? = ⲁⲕⲉⲥ in sim list AZ 16 17 *ult* (*l* ⲟⲩⲁⲕⲉⲥ). In
Bor 170 90 ⲟⲩⲁ. ⲉⲧⲉⲟⲩⲧⲱⲣⲉⲧⲉ = PG 26 916 δίκελλα, so prob ἀκίς (Pey 249).

ⲁⲧ- *SABF*, ⲁⲑ- *B* before liquids, ⲁⲧⲉ- *S* (Sa 11
18, J 80 4, though elsewhere ⲁⲧ- in this formula ;
for ⲁⲧⲉ- Sa 7 22, Eph 3 10, BHom 98 *v* ⲁⲧⲟ),
privative prefix forming adj, often = Gk ἀ-, ἀν- ;
a. with vb : Ge 1 2 *B* ⲟⲩⲁⲑⲛⲁⲩ ⲉⲣⲟϥ ἀόρατος,
Ps 62 1 *SB* ⲁⲧⲙⲟⲟϣⲉ ἄβατος, Ps 99 5 *SB* ⲁⲧⲥⲉⲓ
ἄπληστος, Am 5 24 *B* ⲁⲧⲉⲣ ⲭⲓⲛⲓⲟⲣ do, Mk 7 2 *B*
ⲁⲧⲓⲁ ⲧⲟⲧ- ἄνιπτος ; BG 24 *S* ⲡⲓⲁⲧⲭⲱ ⲙⲡⲉϥⲣⲁⲛ,
R 1 2 65 *S* ⲟⲩⲁⲧⲥⲟⲧⲡ var ⲛⲟⲩⲥⲱⲛⲧ ⲁⲛ, AM 239 *B*
ⲉⲧⲟⲓ...ⲛⲁⲧϣⲟⲡ ⲉⲣⲱⲟⲩ ⲛⲛⲓϧⲱⲣⲉⲁ, BKU 1 21 33 *F*
cover it ⲛⲁⲧⲕⲁ ⲣⲱⲙⲉ ⲉⲡⲉⲩ ⲉⲣⲁϥ, J 23 19 *S* naught
remaineth ⲛⲁⲧⲧⲁⲁϥ ⲉⲃⲟⲗ ⲡⲁⲕ, ST 341 *S* ⲙⲡⲣⲕⲱ
ⲛⲁⲧⲣ ⲡⲉϧⲱⲃ, BM 583 *F* that he give us bread
ⲛⲁⲧⲧⲉⲡⲗⲟⲩ, Vizant Vremen 14 185 *B* ϯⲁⲧⲥⲟⲩⲉⲛ
ϧⲱⲟⲩⲧ ⲙⲡⲁⲣⲑⲉⲛⲟⲥ. **b.** with nn : Ex 12 8 *S*
(*B* ⲁⲧϣⲉⲙⲏⲣ) ⲁⲑⲁⲃ (ⲁⲧϧ,), ἄζυμος, ⲁϧⲣⲏⲓ *SAB*
(ⲁⲧϭ. BM 1223 *A*, Ge 11 30, Lu 1 7 *B*) στεῖρα,
Job 24 6 *B* (*S* ⲉⲭⲛ- for ⲁⲭⲛ-) ⲁⲑⲃⲉⲭⲉ ἀμισθί, Kr
141 *S* sim, Cai 8510 *S* epitaph ⲁⲧⲙⲟⲩ ἀθάνατος,
Ps 9 28 *SB* ⲁⲧⲛⲟⲃⲉ ἀθῷος, Sa 7 23 *S* ⲁⲧⲣⲟⲟⲩϣ
ἀμέριμνος, Mic 1 8 *B* ⲁⲧⲱⲟⲩⲅⲓ ἀνυπόδητος Mt 25
30 *SB* ⲁⲧϣⲁⲩ ἀχρεῖος, BKU 1 313 *S* perform the

liturgy ⲡⲁⲧⲉⲩⲁⲅⲅⲉⲗⲓⲟⲛ, Miss 4 116 *B* gate opened ⲡⲁⲧϣⲟⲩⲧ, BKU 1 1 vo *S* he slew it ⲡⲁⲧϭⲟⲣⲧⲉ, MR 5 47 *S* ⲡⲁⲧϩⲱⲃ unemployed, C 86 12 *B* lifted up ⲡⲁⲧⲕⲁϩⲓ off ground, PMéd 297 *S* pig's fat ⲡⲁⲧⲅⲙⲟⲩ, Ann 23 221 *S* of lion ⲁϥⲣ ⲡⲣⲓⲟⲟⲩⲉ ⲡⲁⲧⲣⲱⲙⲉ, Ryl 130 *S*, PLond 4 451 *S* ⲡⲁⲧⲗⲟⲧⲟⲥ ⲡⲁⲧⲥⲧⲁⲩⲣⲟⲥ &c formula in deeds of surety; peculiar: MR 5 42 *Sᶠ* I have written to thee ⲡⲁⲧⲡⲉⲕϭⲓⲟⲩⲥ (ϫⲟⲉⲓⲥ).

ⲙⲛⲧⲁⲧ-, ⲙⲉⲧⲁⲧ- forming nn f. **a.** with vb: Lev 12 3 *SB* ⲙⲛⲧⲁⲧⲥⲃⲃⲉ ἀκροβυστία, Sa 6 19 *S* ⲙⲛⲧⲁⲧⲧⲁⲕⲟ ἀφθαρσία, Va 57 129 *B* ⲙⲉⲧⲁⲧⲥⲉⲣ ⲙⲉⲗⲓ(ⲛ) ⲡⲱϣ. **b.** with nn: Ps 34 12 *SB* ⲙⲛⲧⲁⲧϣⲏⲣⲉ ἀτεκνία, ClPr 41 3 *S* ⲙⲛⲧⲁⲧⲣⲟⲩ ⲙⲡⲉ, PLond 4 520 *S*]ϫⲓ ⲡⲁⲛⲙⲟⲥⲓⲟⲛ ⲡⲁⲧⲡⲥⲩⲙ(ⲙ)ⲁⲭⲟⲥ.

ⲁⲧ- *S* *v* ⲉⲓⲱⲧ *father*.

ⲁⲉⲧ *F* *v* ⲉⲁⲧ.

ⲁⲧⲉ *A* *v* ⲟⲟⲧⲉ.

ⲁⲧⲟ *S*, ⲁⲧⲁ *SF*, ⲑⲟ *B*, ⲁⲧⲉ- *SF*(EpJer 12, Mt 13 58) nn m (*BF*), *multitude*, **a.** rarely alone: BG 46 *S* ⲡⲁϧⲟ ⲡⲁⲧⲥⲟⲟⲩⲛ ⲡⲟⲩⲁ., *ib* 110 ⲁⲩⲁ. ⲟⲩⲟⲡϩⲟⲩ ⲉⲃⲟⲗ, Miss 8 187 *S* ⲡⲡⲉⲓϫⲉ ⲟⲩⲁ. ⲡⲁⲕ ⲉⲧⲃⲉⲡⲁⲓ, Is 30 17 *F* (*S* ϩⲁϩ, *B* ⲙⲏϣ), Mk 14 56 *F* (*SB* do) ⲟⲩⲁ. πολλοί, Mor 30 9 *F* (*S* ϩⲁϩ) he persuaded not ⲛⲟⲩⲁ. **b.** adjectival constr or with ⲛ-, *many, various*, oftenest with *S* ⲥⲙⲟⲧ, *B* ⲣⲏϯ: Ps 21 16 *SB*, *ib* 13 *B* (*S* ⲙⲛⲏϣⲉ), Jo 3 23 *F* (*S* ϩⲁϩ, *B* ⲙⲏϣ), Ro 4 17 *F* (*S* do) πολλός; Sa 7 22 *S* ⲏⲧ ⲁⲧⲟ ⲡ[ⲥⲙⲟⲧ = Lag ⲁⲧⲉⲥⲙⲟⲧ, CaiEuch 651 *B* ⲡⲟⲩϧⲟ ⲡⲣⲏϯ πολυμερής, He 1 1 *BF* (*S* ϩⲁϩ) πολυμερῶς; BHom 135 *S* creatures made ⲛⲟⲩⲁ. ⲡⲥⲙⲟⲧ ποικίλος; Ex 27 16 *B* ⲡⲓϩⲟ ⲡⲣⲏϯ ποικιλία; Ps 44 14 *B* (*S* ⲡⲁⲅⲉⲓⲛ ⲁⲅⲁⲡ) πεποικιλμένος; Ez 16 13 *B* (*S* do), Ja 1 2 *B* (*S* ϣⲟⲃⲉ) ποικίλος; Ez 23 15 *B* (*S* ⲡⲁⲅ. ⲁⲅ.) ποικίλμα; Eph 3 10 *S* ⲡⲁⲧⲉⲥⲙⲟⲧ (*B* ⲑⲟ ⲡⲣⲏϯ) πολυποίκιλος; EpJer 12 *F* ⲡⲟⲩⲁⲧⲉϣⲁⲓϣ πλείων; P 44 30 *S* ⲧⲉϥⲥⲟⲫⲓⲁ ⲡⲁⲧ(*sic*)ⲥⲙⲟⲧ, sim BHom 102 *S*, Mor 30 9 *F* ⲟⲩⲁ. ⲡⲁϫⲓⲱⲙⲁ, Mor 39 6 *S* ⲡⲟⲩⲁ. ⲡⲥⲟⲡ (var ⲛϩⲁϩ ⲡⲥⲟⲡ), Ryl 238 *S* ⲟⲩⲕⲁⲙⲡⲁⲡⲟⲥ ⲡⲁⲧⲉϣⲏⲧⲉ (or ? = ⲁⲧ-, *q v*); approx, loose transl: Ez 38 4 *B* ϩⲱⲥ ⲡⲟⲩϧⲟ ⲡⲣⲏϯ θώραξ, *ib* 44 18 *B* ⲭⲗⲟⲙ do κίδαρις λινῆ, 1 Pet 4 3 *B* (*S* om) ϩⲁⲛϩⲟ ⲙⲃⲟϯ ἀθέμιτος.

ⲁⲧⲱϣ in ⲣ ⲁⲧⲱϣ *S* *v* ⲡⲱϣ (ⲧⲱϣ).

ⲁⲧⲃⲉⲥ *S* *v* ⲁϭⲃⲉⲥ.

ⲁⲧⲕⲁⲥ *v* ⲁⲗⲕⲁⲥ.

ⲁⲧⲛ- *A* *v* ⲧⲱⲣⲉ (ⲉⲧⲛ-).

ⲁⲧⲡⲱ *F* *v* ⲱⲧⲡ (ⲉⲧⲡⲱ).

ⲁⲧⲟⲟⲧϥ, ⲣ *S*, ⲁⲩⲧⲟⲧϥ, ⲉⲣ *B* *v* ⲧⲱⲣⲉ (ⲧⲟⲟⲧ).

ⲁⲑⲁⲃ *S* *v* ⲑⲁⲃ (ⲧϩⲁⲃ).

ⲁⲧϭⲛⲉ- *B* *v* ⲁϫⲛ-.

ⲁⲩ, ⲁⲩⲉ, ⲁⲩⲉⲓⲥ *S*, ⲁⲩⲉⲓ *SA²*, ⲁⲩⲉⲉⲓ *A*, ⲁⲩⲉⲓⲥ *A²*, ⲁⲩⲓⲥ *B*, ⲁⲟⲩⲉⲓ *F* (?? CMSS 51), imperat particle (*v* above ⲁ- imperat, also Rec 26 37, AZ 47 6), oftenest with f (neut) -ⲥ; **I.** *give, bring hither!* **a.** intr: 1 Kg 13 9 *S* προσαγάγετε; Mic 7 3 *A* (Gk *SB* diff), Jo 4 7 *SA²* (*B* ⲙⲟⲓ) δός; BMar 181 *S* if thou lack aught (at table), say not ⲁⲩⲉⲓⲥ. **b.** tr, all forms used as constr, except Mor 19 59 *S* ⲁⲩⲉ ⲡⲡⲉⲭⲁⲣⲧⲏⲥ = Mor 18 51 ⲙⲁ ⲡⲁⲓ ⲙ-, (or ? *l* ⲁⲩⲉⲛ as from ⲁⲩ + ⲉⲓⲛⲉ): Ru 3 15 *S*, Jo 20 27 *SA²* ⲁⲩ (varr BAp 44 *S* ⲁⲩⲉⲓ, Mor 34 60 ⲁⲩⲉ = *B* ⲙⲁ) φέρε; 1 Kg 14 18 *S* ⲁⲩⲉⲓⲥ (var ⲁⲩⲉ), Lu 9 41 *S* (*B* ⲁⲡⲓ) προσάγαγε; 2 Kg 14 7 *S* δός; Mt 18 28 *S* (*B* ⲙⲁ), Lu 16 2 *S* (*B* do) ἀπόδος, BMis 379 *S* ⲁⲩⲉⲓⲥ ⲧϯⲙⲏ; sometimes with (2d) obj suff: Mt 17 17 *S* ⲁⲩⲉⲓⲥϥ (*B* ⲁⲡⲓⲧϥ), *ib* 14 18 *S* ⲁⲩⲉⲓⲥⲟⲩ (var ⲁⲡⲓⲥⲟⲩ, *B* ⲁⲡⲓⲧⲟⲩ) φέρετε, Hall 117 *S* ⲡⲕⲟⲩⲥⲛⲁⲩ ⲙⲡⲣⲟⲗⲟⲕ/ ⲁⲩⲥⲟⲩ (prob *sic*). **II.** *come!* (not = δεῦρο ⲁⲙⲟⲩ) not bibl; ⲁⲩⲉⲓⲥ mostly c subjunct, often + ⲧⲉⲛⲟⲩ, ⲟⲡ ⲧ., ⲟⲩⲛ: BHom 47 *S* ⲁ. ϭⲉ ⲧⲉⲛⲟⲩ ϩⲱⲱⲛ (ⲛ)ⲧⲛ-, Va 57 125 *B* ⲁ. ⲟⲩⲛ ϯⲛⲟⲩ ⲉⲑⲣⲉⲛ- φέρε; BHom 94 *S* ⲁ. ⲛⲧⲛⲭⲛⲟⲩ ἐρωτήσωμεν, C 43 46 *B* ⲁ. oh beloved, ⲛⲧⲉⲛϫⲱ, BM 274 *S* ⲁ. ⲟⲩⲛ ϩⲱⲥ ⲡⲧⲁⲧⲟⲗⲙⲁ ⲉⲧⲣⲉⲛ-.

ⲁⲩ- *B* *v* ⲁ- *about*.

ⲁⲩ *Sᵃ* *v* ⲟ *great*.

ⲁⲁⲩ *F* *v* ⲉⲓⲱ *ass*.

ⲁⲓⲟⲩ *B* nn (?), meaning unknown, with ⲉⲣ prob *go, travel* or sim: C 86 164 he arose ⲁϥⲉⲣ ⲁ. ϣⲁⲭⲏⲙⲓ.

ⲁⲩⲱ *SA²F*, ⲁⲟⲩ *Sᵃ* (ST 357) *A*, ⲁⲩⲟⲩ (*ib* 225), ⲁⲩ (Br 256 6, Ryl 243, BP 9420) *S*, (BKU 1 26 30) *F*, ⲱ (Sph 10 4 xiii) *F*, ⲟⲩⲟϩ *B*; properly imperat of ⲟⲩⲱϩ (cf ⲁⲟⲩⲱ J&C 98 *Sᶠ*, BM 1239, 1241 *F*, ⲁⲟⲩⲟⲩ ZNTW 1925 88), *v* AZ 26 94, *ib* 52 114, Spg Dem Gram 55, conjunction, *and* (Stern 592). *Cf* paral use of *F* ⲁⲣⲁ.

I. joins phrases (often in *B* between verbal clauses where *S* omits): Ge 18 14 *SB*, 1 Kg 8 12 *S*, Mt 18 18 *SB*, Ap 6 15 *S* (*B* ⲡⲉⲙ-) καί, C 43 89 *B* ⲡⲏ ⲉⲧϭⲏ...ⲟⲩ. ⲉⲧⲟⲡⲥ ϭⲉⲛⲡⲟⲣⲛⲓⲁ, Br 45 *S* ⲡⲧⲡⲧⲁⲕⲟ ⲁ. ⲡⲧⲛⲥⲱⲣⲙ, AP 27 *A²* ⲉϥⲙⲁⲕϩ ⲡⲣⲏⲧ ⲁ. ⲉϥⲣⲱϣⲉ ⲁϩⲟⲩⲛ, PS 247 *S* ϣⲡ ϩⲧⲏⲕ...ⲁ. ⲡⲧϭⲱⲗ, ShC 42 225 *S* ⲟⲩⲛ ⲟⲩⲛⲟϭ ⲡⲥⲟⲉⲓⲧ ⲁ. ⲁⲩⲅⲣⲁⲓ ⲡⲁⲓ ...ϫⲉ-, Leyd 450 *S* ⲡⲁⲓ ⲧⲏⲣⲟⲩ ⲡⲉⲣⲁⲡ ⲁ. ⲟⲩⲟⲛ ⲡⲓⲙ ⲉⲧⲉⲟⲩⲛⲧⲁⲩ ⲙⲙⲁⲩ, J 75 64 *S* tower that they built ⲁ. ⲉⲁⲓⲣ ϩⲩⲡⲟⲩⲣⲅⲉⲓ ⲉⲣⲟϥ ϩⲱⲱⲧ, CO 58 *S* endeavour to teach them ⲁ. ⲉⲓⲥ ⲡⲟⲩⲣⲟⲟⲩϣ ⲧⲏⲣϥ ϩⲓϫⲱⲕ, J 106 70 *S* ⲡⲣⲱⲧⲟⲡ ⲙⲉⲛ ϫⲉ-...ⲁ. ϫⲉϣⲁⲣⲉ-, Phil 1 18 *B* ϯⲣⲁϣⲓ ⲁⲗⲗⲁ ⲟⲩ. ϯⲡⲁⲣⲁϣⲓ ⲟⲡ (*SF* ⲁ. ⲟⲡ) ἀλλὰ καί, PS 201 *S* ⲟⲩ ⲙⲟⲛⲟⲛ...ⲁⲗⲗⲁ ⲁ.

II. introduces narrative or statement (mostly bibl): Ge 1 3 *B*, 8 1 *SB*, Nu 10 1 *SB*, Is 12 4 *SB* καί; *S* often om: Ge 18 22, 22 1, Lu 14 22 (all = *B* ⲟⲩ.); Mor 51 28 *S* wife said ⲁ. ⲁϣⲡⲉ ⲡⲛⲟⲃⲉ ⲛⲧⲁⲓⲁⲁϥ, sim ShC 73 98 *S* ⲁ. ⲣⲙⲡⲏⲓ ⲛⲓⲙ ⲉϥⲛⲁϣⲱⲡⲉ, ShC 42 117 *S* I will dwell apart repenting ⲁ. ⲛⲧⲱⲧⲛ ϩⲉⲛⲕⲁⲧⲁⲣⲱⲧⲛ.

III. introducing apodosis, *B* (imitating otiose initial καί in LXX): Ex 13 5 ⲟⲩ. ⲉⲥⲉϣⲱⲡⲓ…ⲟⲩ. ⲉⲕⲉⲓⲣⲓ καί, *ib* 18 14 ⲉⲧⲁϥⲛⲁⲩ ⲍⲉ…ⲟⲩ. ⲡⲉϫⲁϥ (*S* Gk om), Nu 21 8 (do), Deu 28 58-59 (*S* ⲁ.) καί; C 86 240 ⲟⲩ. ⲉϣⲱⲡ…ⲟⲩ. ⲙⲁⲣⲉⲡⲓⲕⲣⲓⲍ ⲱϣ ⲉⲃⲟⲗ, DeV 146 ϩⲟⲥⲟⲛ ⲡⲥⲱⲟⲩⲛ ⲍⲉ-…ⲟⲩ. ⲙⲁⲣⲉⲛ-, Miss 4 193 ϫⲉⲛⲡⲭⲓⲛⲑⲣⲉϥⲥⲱⲧⲙ ⲍⲉ-…ⲟⲩ. ⲁϥⲧⲱⲡⲥ, *ib* 156 notaries hid their pens, ⲟⲩⲛⲟⲧ. ⲍⲉ…ⲟⲩ. ⲁϥϯ ⲙⲫⲱϣ ⲛⲁϥ; perhaps *S* Jos 6 25 ⲁ. ⲉⲃⲟⲗ ϫⲉ- (Gk om).

IV. joins nns or adjs: Ps 67 5 *SB*, Sa 14 26 *S* καί, ShC 42 122 *S* ⲡⲁⲓ ⲁ. ⲡⲉⲧⲙⲙⲁⲩ, C 89 113 *B* ⲙⲙⲁⲓⲡⲟⲩϯ ⲟⲩ. ⲡⲁⲥⲕⲏⲧⲏⲥ, RE 9 136 *S* ⲧⲉⲧⲛⲁⲥⲓⲟⲥⲩⲛⲏ ⲛⲭ̅ⲥ̅ ⲡⲉⲓⲱⲧ ⲁ. ⲉⲧⲟⲩⲁⲁⲃ, J 74 91 *S* ⲧϭⲟⲙ ⲁ. ⲧϭⲓϫ ⲙⲡⲁⲣⲭⲱⲛ. **a.** *S* often = *B* ⲡⲉⲙ-: Ps 30 3, Ac 12 17 καί. **b.** or *S* varies with ⲙⲛ-: Jos 17 3, Ap 5 12, 13 καί, Aeg 239 John ⲙⲛ- Matthew ⲙⲛ- Peter ⲁ. Judas, Mor 51 27 *S* ⲙⲡⲛⲉⲥⲣⲱⲙⲉ ⲏ ⲡⲉⲥⲣⲉⲙⲣⲁϣⲏ ⲁ. ⲡⲉϥ(*sic*)ϩⲙϩⲁⲗ, J&C 92 ϯϣⲓⲛⲉ ⲉ…ⲁ. ⲡⲉⲥⲛⲟⲩ, ϯϣⲓⲛⲉ ⲉ… ⲙⲡⲧⲉϥⲙⲁⲁⲩ, RE 9 156 lemons ⲙⲛⲟⲩⲑⲉⲣⲙⲁⲛ ⲁ. ⲟⲩϣⲛⲏⲛ ⲡⲗⲁⲭⲁⲛⲟⲡ, J 92 6 martyr('s monastery) ⲙⲛⲡϥⲉⲥⲱⲙⲉⲛⲟⲥ ⲁ. ⲡⲉϥⲡⲣⲱⲉⲓⲥⲧⲟⲥ. **c.** *S* + ⲙⲛ- (archaic?): PS 11 worldly troubles ⲁ. ⲙⲛⲡⲉⲛⲕⲓⲛⲇⲩⲛⲟⲥ ⲁ. ⲙⲛⲡⲉⲅⲁⲓⲱⲧⲙⲟⲥ, *ib* 138 ⲡⲓⲣⲁ ⲡⲣⲟϥ ⲁ. ⲙⲛⲡⲓⲣⲁ ⲡⲥⲓⲧ, BG 83 ⲡⲧⲟϥ ⲟⲩⲁⲁϥ ⲁ. ⲙⲛⲡⲉⲧⲉⲣⲛⲁϥ, J 69 15 ϩⲙⲙⲡⲧⲣⲉ…ⲁ. ⲙⲛⲟⲩⲣⲉϥⲥϩⲁⲓ (*cf* Byzantine καὶ σύν, καὶ μετά, PMon 18). **d.** *S* + ϩⲓ- (rare): Br 109 ϣⲁⲗ ⲁ. ϩⲓⲗⲓⲃⲁⲛⲟⲥ.

V. for δέ: Ge 21 16 *SB*, Pro 3 16 *S* (*B* = Gk); or varies with δέ: Miss 4 18 *B* ⲟⲩ. ⲁⲡⲓ ϣⲁⲣⲟϥ = *ib* 636 *S* ⲁⲡⲉⲓ ⲍⲉ, *ib* 525 *S* ⲁ. ⲁⲥϣⲱⲡⲉ = C 89 44 *B* ⲁⲥϣⲱⲡⲓ ⲍⲉ.

VI. + ⲟⲛ (ⲟⲩⲁⲛ *A*, Cl 2 2, 17 5 &c, TU 43 11, also ⲁⲟⲩ ⲁⲛ), *moreover, further*: 2 Chr 6 33 *B* καί, Eccl 6 3 *S* καίγε, Ez 4 4 *B* (*cf S* ⲁⲡⲟⲕ ϩⲱ), *ib* 5 4 *SB* καὶ ἔτι, *ib* 28 12, 37 24 *B* (*S* om ⲟⲛ) καί, Lu 14 22 *S* (*B* ⲟⲩ. ⲉⲧⲓ) καὶ ἔτι, Jo 6 11 *SA*² (*B* ⲡⲁⲓⲣⲏϯ ⲟⲛ) ὁμοίως καί, Ac 26 6 *S* (*B* ⲟⲩ.) καί, R 1 5 37 *S* thou hast not had pity on monks ⲁ. ⲙⲙⲟⲛⲁⲭⲏ…ⲁ. ⲟⲛ ⲙⲡⲉⲕⲛⲁ ϩⲁⲣⲟⲟⲩ, Miss 4 522 *S* = C 89 42 *B* I brought it for my soul's good ⲁ. ⲟⲛ because ye are godly men, AM 12 *B* ⲉϥⲥⲱⲟⲩⲛ… ⲟⲩ. ⲟⲛ ⲉϥⲉⲙⲓ, CO 36 *S* we go surety for him, his κρῖμα is on us ⲁ. ⲟⲛ ⲧⲛⲥⲧⲟⲓⲭⲉ ⲉⲡⲓϫⲁⲉ.

VII. in addition to subjunct (Stern 447): Ep

Jer 43 *B* (*F* Gk om), Lu 12 43 *B* (Cat 150, *S* Gk om), BG 67 *S* ϣⲁϥⲥⲱⲕ ⲙⲙⲟⲥ…ⲁ. ⲛⲥⲡⲗⲁⲛⲁ, Leyd 442 *S* ⲟⲩⲟⲛ ⲛⲓⲙ ⲉⲧⲛⲁϫⲓⲧⲉ ⲁ. ⲛⲥⲉⲟⲩϫⲥ, Aeg 39 *B* all adorn streets ⲟⲩ. ⲛⲧⲉⲡⲓⲕⲉⲡⲉϥ ⲥⲟⲗⲥⲉⲗ ⲛⲛⲟⲩⲉⲭⲛⲟⲩ, CO 29 *S* we are ready to observe ⲁ. ⲛⲧⲛⲥⲱⲧⲙ…ⲁ. ⲛⲧⲛϩⲩⲡⲟⲧⲁⲥⲥⲉ.

ⲗⲟⲩⲱ *B* vb   *v* ⲟⲩⲱ *cease*.

ⲗⲟⲩⲱ *B* nn   *v* ⲉⲅⲱ.

ⲗⲟⲩϩⲏⲧ *B*   *v* ⲁϩⲏⲧ.

ⲁⲩⲗⲏⲟⲩ *B* nn pl, part of monk's dress: K 120 شقف (شقّة in list of monk's garments MG 17 510, being neither cloak, hood nor leather apron), so ? *bands* or *strips* of stuff (*v* Dozy). Coptic? (identical with pl of αὐλή).

ⲁⲩⲁⲛ *SF*, ⲁⲩⲁⲁⲛ, ⲁⲅⲉⲓⲛ *S*, ⲉⲟⲩⲉⲛ *A*, ⲁⲟⲩⲏⲛ *F*, ⲁⲟⲩⲁⲛ, ⲁⲃⲁⲛ *B* & other forms, nn m **I.** *colour*: Ex 4 7 *B*, Sá 13 14 *S* χρόα (sim BMis 237 *S*), Lev 13 14, 15 *SB* χρώς, 4 Kg 5 10 *S* (Gk om), Sa 15 4 *S* χρῶμα, Ge 30 42 *S* ⲟ ⲡⲁ. ἐπίσημος, Lev 19 19 *S* ⲡⲁ. ⲥⲛⲁⲩ (*B* Gk om), Jer 13 23 *S* ⲡⲁ. ⲙⲡⲉϥⲥⲱⲙⲁ (*B* ϣⲁⲣ) δέρμα, Miss 4 143 *B* leprosy healed ⲁϥϣⲱⲡⲓ ϫⲉⲙⲡⲁ. ⲙⲡⲉϥⲥⲱⲙⲁ ⲧⲏⲣϥ (sim MG 25 362 *B*) Mich 550 29 *S* hyacinth stone ⲙⲡⲁ. ⲙⲡⲥⲱⲙⲁ of men, Mor 25 93 *S* garments ⲡⲁϣⲏ ⲡⲁ., AZ 23 109 *S* melt 2 metals ϣⲁⲛⲧⲟⲩⲉⲣ ⲟⲩⲁ. ⲉⲛⲟⲩⲱⲧ. Colours named: of honey Ryl 244 *S* ⲁ. ⲡⲉⲃⲓⲱ (*cf* μελίχρους); of grapes Mor 44 40 *S* ⲁ. ⲡⲉⲗⲟⲟⲗⲉ; of wine P 44 66 *S* ⲁ. ⲙⲡⲏⲣⲡ (*cf* οἰνόχροος); of leek Ge 2 12 *SB* ⲁ. ⲡⲛⲥⲉ πράσινος, Cant 5 14 *S* (Gk om), BMis 275, 538 *S*; of sea BM 180 375 *S* ⲁ. ⲛⲑⲁⲗⲁⲥⲥⲁ (*cf* θαλασσόχροος); of ashes Ge 30 39 *SB* ⲁ. ⲛⲕⲣⲙⲉⲥ σποδοειδής; of lily R 2 2 22 *S* ⲁ. ⲛⲕⲣⲓⲛⲟⲛ κρινόχροος; of fire Nah 2 3 *A* ⲉ. ⲡⲕⲱϩⲧ coccinus, Ap 9 17 *S* ⲁ. ⲡⲕ.= *B* ⲛⲭⲣⲱⲙ πύρινος, *ib* 6 4, 12 3 *B* ⲁ. ⲛⲭⲣⲱⲙ = *S* ⲧⲣⲉϣⲣⲱϣ, sim BAp 271 *S*, Mor 30 47 *F*; of gold JKP 2 50 *S*, Mun 123 *S* ⲁ. ⲙⲡⲛⲟⲩⲃ (*cf* χρυσόχροος); of sky Mor 25 92 *S* clothes of ⲁ. ⲙⲡⲉ, Mich 550 29 *S* chrysolite is ⲡⲁ. ⲙⲡⲉ, sim BMis 570 (*cf* Ex 24 10 *B*); of mouse Zech 6 3 *AB* ⲉ. ⲙⲡⲓⲛ, ⲁ. ⲙⲫⲓⲛ ψαρός; of blood LCyp 7 *S* ⲁ. ⲙⲡⲉⲥⲛⲟϥ αἱματώδης, Z 629 *S*, Va 62 171 *B*; of wool R 1 2 43 *S* ⲁ. ⲙⲡⲥⲟⲣⲧ; of *stibium* Ryl 243 (*cf* 244 18) *S* ⲁ. ⲉⲥⲧⲏⲙ; of corn Mor 44 26 *S* ⲁ. ⲡⲥⲟⲅⲟ (*cf* σιτόχροος); of woman's bath Cai 42573 *S* ⲁ. ⲡⲥⲓⲟⲟⲩⲛ ⲛⲥϩⲓⲙⲉ (or *l*? ⲥⲓⲟⲩ ⲛⲥϩ. of female star); of lead P 44 66 *S* ⲁ. ⲙⲡⲧⲁⲥⲧ μολυβδώδης; of rose P 44 66 *S* ⲁ. ⲙⲡⲟⲩⲉⲣⲧ (*cf* Mor 30 10 *F* like rose ⲣⲙⲡⲉϭ.); grey Ge 30 32 &c *S* φαιός (*B* twice ⲁⲟⲩⲓ ⲁⲟⲩⲁⲛ); of lentils ? Ryl 244 *S* ⲁ. ⲉϥⲁϭⲓⲛⲁ (? φάκινος); of snow BAp 14 *S* ⲙ[ⲡⲉ]-

ⲭⲓⲱⲛ (cf χιονώδης); of a poison plant ⲁ. ⲛⲭⲗⲟ
Lev 21 20 B (v KKS 49); green My 46 S ⲁ.
ⲛⲭⲗⲟⲣⲟⲛ; of silver P 44 66 S ⲁ. ⲛϩⲁⲧ ἀσημό-
χροος; of coal Ge 2 12 B ⲁ. ⲛⲭⲉⲃⲥ ὁ ἄνθραξ, Va
67 80 B ⲛⲗⲁϩ ⲛⲁ. ⲛⲭ.; of apple Ryl 244 S ⲁ.
(ⲉ)ⲭⲱⲡⲉϣ; of purple R 2 2 21 S ⲁ. ⲛⲭⲏⲥⲉ πορφυρίζων, Mich 550 29 S topaz is ⲛⲁ. ⲛⲭ. ⲙⲛⲛⲁ.
ⲙⲛⲛⲟⲩⲃ, Va 66 297 B ϩⲁⲡⲁ. ⲉⲩⲛⲏⲭ.

II. metaphor, *appearance*: Lam 4 8 B, Lu 9
29 B (S ⲉⲓⲛⲉ) εἶδος, Dan 3 19 B ὄψις, ib 5 9 B
μορφή, Lu 22 44 B, R 2 1 10 S hath my face
changed ϩⲁⲙⲡⲁ. ⲛⲧⲡⲁⲣⲑⲉⲛⲓⲁ?, Mor 43 160 S ⲡⲉϥⲁ.
(var ϩⲟ) changeth not, Mun 158 S ⲉⲕⲱ ⲙⲡⲉⲩⲁ.

ⲥⲉⲕ ⲁ. S vb intr, to *tend towards a colour*: Lev
13 24 ⲉϥⲥ ⲁ. ⲉϥⲟⲩⲟⲃϣ (B om) ἔκλευκος, ib 2 14
ⲡⲉⲕⲥⲣⲱⲟϣ...ⲉⲁⲩⲥ. ⲁ. (B ⲉⲩⲫⲟⲣⲁ ⲉⲩⲛⲏⲭ Va 1)
πεφρυγμένα χίδρα (which in 23 14 = ⲉϥⲟⲩⲟϣⲙ).
Cf ⲥⲱⲕ Ge 30 37 S, Z 609, BM 180 375.

ⲁⲩⲁⲡ ⲁ., ⲁⲩⲉⲓⲛ ⲁ., ⲁⲩⲉⲓ ⲁ., ⲁⲩⲉⲓⲛ ⲁⲩⲉⲓⲛ S,
ⲉⲟⲩⲉⲡ ⲉ. A, ⲁⲟⲩⲓ ⲁ., ⲁⲃⲓ ⲁ. B, distributively
variety of colours: Ge 30 37 B (S ⲧⲟ ⲧⲟ), 30 40
SB, 30 39 S (B ⲑⲟⲓ ⲑⲟⲓ), 37 3 B (=S BMar 130),
Ez 16 10, 18 S (B ⲑⲟ ⲛⲣⲏϯ), ib 13 S as nn ϩⲉⲛⲁ.
(B ⲇⲟ), Zech 1 8 AB ποικίλος; Ps 44 9 S (B ⲑⲟ
ⲛⲣⲏϯ) ποικίλλεσθαι; Jud 5 30 S, Si 43 27 S, Ez
27 7 S (B ⲇⲟ) ποικιλία; Jer 13 23 B (S ⲧⲟⲉ), Ez 23
15 S (B ⲇⲟ) ποίκιλμα; Ge 30 33, 35 B (S ⲁ.) φαιός,
ib 32 B (S ⲥⲟⲩⲥⲓⲟⲩ) διάραντος, 2 Kg 6 14 B (S diff)
ἔξαλλος; EW 118 B ⲡⲱⲛⲓ ⲛⲁⲟⲩⲏⲛ ⲁⲃⲁⲛ, BSM 113
B ⲫⲁϩⲣⲓ ⲛⲁ., ShA 2 156 S ⲙⲙⲓⲛⲉ ⲙⲓⲛⲉ ϩⲓⲁ., sim
BMis 227 (of giraffe), Tri 660 S ϩⲟⲓⲧⲉ ⲛⲁ. موشّاة.

ⲁⲟⲩⲓⲛ B nn m, *jaundice*: K 160 يرقان, cf ib 206
(among colours) اصفر.
As name: Αὐᾶν (Preisigke).
Place-names compounded? with ⲁ., v Ryl p. 80 n.

ⲁⲩⲉⲓⲛ, ⲁⲩⲁⲛ (Pcod 41, Tri 428 &c) S, ⲁⲟⲩⲓⲛ,
ⲁⲃⲏⲛ, ⲁⲃⲓⲛ B nn m, a. ship's *cargo, load*: Ac 27
10 SB, BMar 189 S ⲧⲁⲗⲉ ⲛⲁ. ⲉⲡϫⲟⲓ, Va 57 122,
175 φόρτιον; Ac 21 3 B (S diff) γόμος; Va 57 176
B ⲛⲓⲁ. ⲛⲧⲉ ⲡⲓⲕⲁⲣⲡⲟⲥ φορά (v WS 25), BHom 14 S
after wreck they lose ⲡⲉⲩⲁ., P 130⁴ 89 S ship
loaded παρὰ ⲡⲉϥⲁ., Va 61 104 B ship ⲉϥⲁⲥⲓⲱⲟⲩ
ⲛⲁ....ⲉϥⲟⲧⲡ ⲛⲁ., cf R 1 4 45 S ⲉϥⲟⲧⲡ ϩⲙⲡⲉϥⲁ.,
Pcod 41 S whoso setteth God ⲛⲁⲡⲉ ⲉⲡⲉϥⲁ.; BM
1111 S she hath sent me ⲟⲩϣⲏⲙ ⲛⲁ., Kr 245 S
in list of expenses ϩⲁⲁ. (though meaning uncertain
in last two). *Cf* ⲉⲓⲟⲡⲉ (ⲉⲓⲉⲡϣⲱⲧ). **b.** metaphor: Va 57 4 B branches bent down ⲛⲉⲙⲡⲟⲩⲁ.,
Mor 22 66 S burdened ϩⲙⲡⲁ. of sin, R 1 2 54 S
with ⲛⲁ. of devil.

ⲁⲧⲁ. B, *without cargo*: MG 25 343 ship ⲛⲁⲧⲁ.

ⲁⲟⲩⲱⲛ B v ⲟⲩⲱⲛ.

ⲁⲩⲏⲣ, ⲁⲟⲩⲏⲣ B v ⲟⲩⲏⲣ.

ⲁⲩⲣⲏⲭⲋ B v ⲁⲣⲏⲭⲋ.

ⲁⲩⲉⲓⲥ S, ⲁⲩⲓⲥ B v ⲁⲩ *give*.

ⲁⲩⲏⲧ S, ⲁⲃⲏⲧ, ⲁⲟⲩⲏⲧ, ⲁⲟⲩⲃⲏⲧ B nn m, a. *collection, company* of persons: Mk 6 39 S (B = Gk)
συμπόσιον contubernium حزب, ib 40 (B ⲙⲁ) πρασιά
ﺍﺑﺎ; Miss 4 241 S celestial throngs ⲉⲩⲟ ⲛⲁ. ⲁ. ⲉⲭⲉⲛ-
ⲡⲉⲩⲉⲅⲣⲏⲩ, Mor 47 80 S ⲛⲁ. ⲁ. like waves. **b.** monastic *congregation*, monastery: HL 114 B Evagrius
wrote of monks ⲛⲁ. & of those in desert cells, Va
61 9 B those in ⲛⲓⲁ. (μοναστήριον) & deserts, ib 16
he quitted ⲙⲟⲛⲁⲥⲧⲏⲣⲓⲟⲛ..., having quitted ⲛⲓⲁ.,
MG 25 219 B κοινόβιον, ib 242 μονή, Va 58 65 B
went to be monk in ⲟⲩⲁ. (var with ⲙⲟⲛⲁⲥⲧ.), MG
25 241 B Tabennesi ⲟⲩⲁ. in south, EW 105 B
monast. τῶν πατέρων called ⲟⲩⲁ. outside Alexandria, BMar 207 S ϩⲛⲟⲩⲥⲟⲟⲩϩⲥ ⲙⲙⲟⲛⲁⲭⲟⲥ ⲛⲁ.
(Mor 48 8 om ⲛⲁ.) = B (Rec 6 170) ⲋⲉⲛⲟⲩⲁ. ἐν
ἀβαγῆ μοναστ. (?= this word), ib ⲛⲁ. ⲙⲙⲟⲛⲁⲭⲟⲥ
(var ⲧⲙⲏⲧⲉ ⲛⲛⲉⲥⲛⲏⲩ, B om), ib 210 ⲟⲩⲥⲟⲟⲩϩⲥ
ⲙⲙⲟⲛⲁⲭⲟⲥ = B ⲟⲩⲁ. ⲙⲙⲟⲛ.; MG 25 241 B
ⲫⲓⲱⲧ ⲙⲡⲓⲁ. ἀρχιμανδρίτης, ib 243 ϫⲱϫ ⲛⲁ. ἡγούμενος; ST 181 Sᵃ]ⲃⲱⲕ ⲁⲡⲁ., BM ostr 44720 S
promise to repay, ⲛⲧⲁⲧⲁⲁⲩ ⲛⲁⲕ ϩⲙⲡⲁ. (meaning
uncertain in last two; for last cf ?B ⲁⲃⲓⲧ).

In name? Πανεῖτ, -ουεῖτις (Preisigke).

Place-name Bâwît باويط, ابويط (no Coptic extant),
W. of Derût, prob = ⲡⲁⲩⲏⲧ, owing to Apollo's
great monastery there (v Miss 4 321, AZ 40 60).
Cf ?another village E. of Fayyûm, ابويط بويط, prob
= ⲡⲟⲩⲁⲓⲧ BM 580, 591 &c and ⲡⲟⲩⲟⲉⲓⲧ=ⲫⲟⲩⲱⲓⲧ
Mor 48 105 = C 43 150.

ⲁⲉⲓⲉⲩⲧⲉ A v ⲁⲓⲁⲓ.

ⲁⲩϫⲁⲗ B v ϩⲁⲩϭⲁⲗ.

ⲁⲩϫⲱⲗ B v ϭⲱⲱⲗⲉ *swathe*.

ⲁⲩⲥⲉ A adv as adj, *all together*: Ja 3 1 πολλοί,
Cl 2 1, 16 6 (= Is 53 6 S ⲧⲏⲣⲛ), 46 9 πάντες, TU
43 12 ϩⲓ[ⲱⲱⲧⲛ]ⲉ ⲁ. ⲡⲉⲧⲣ ⲡⲓⲥⲧⲉⲩⲉ. *Cf* ?El 74
ⲁⲩⲕⲛⲛⲉⲓ ?*all these*.

ⲁⲫⲉ B v ⲁⲡⲉ.

ⲁⲫⲟⲧ B v ⲁⲡⲟⲧ.

ⲁⲫⲱϥ B, pl ⲁⲫⲟϥⲓ, ⲁⲫⲟⲡⲓ nn, *giant*: Ge 10
8, Nu 13 34, Ps 18 6, Is 49 24 (S all = Gk), Ps 32
16 (S ϫⲱⲱⲣⲉ) γίγας, BSM 14 Jacob was ⲛϫⲱⲣⲓ
ⲋⲉⲛϥϯ ⲟⲩⲟϩ ⲛⲁ. ⲋⲉⲛⲡⲓⲣⲱⲙⲓ; pl form: Ge 6 4,
14 5, Bar 3 23 (26).

ⲁⲭⲓ B v ⲁϩⲣ.

ⲁⲭⲱ B v ϩⲁⲕⲟ.

ⲁϣ *SB*, ⲉϧ *A*, ⲉϣ *A²F* **I.** interrog pron, *who, what?*, m f, sg pl, var with ⲛⲓⲙ, ⲟⲩ: Deu 5 26 *S* ⲁϣ...ⲏ ⲛⲓⲙ τίς...τίς (*B* ⲛⲓⲙ...ⲛⲓⲙ), ι Kg 26 18 *S* ⲁϣ...ⲏ ⲟⲩ τί...τί, 2 Cor 6 14 *SB* ⲁϣ ... ⲟⲩ τίς... τίς, Job 6 11 *SB*, Mk 4 41 *S* (*B* ⲛⲓⲙ) τίς; Is 1 5 *SF* τί, Si 9 14 *S* (var ⲟⲩ) τί, Mt 23 17 *S* (var & *B* ⲛⲓⲙ) τίς (var τί), Mk 2 9 (*B* ⲟⲩ), Phil 1 22 *S* (*B* do) τί; Jth 5 3 *S* τίνες; Aeg 288 *S* ⲁϣ ⲍⲉ ⲡⲉⲣϧⲏⲅⲉ (var ⲁϣ ⲡⲉⲧⲛⲁϣⲱⲡⲉ), Pcod 7 *S* ⲁϣ ⲍⲉⲡⲉ ⲡⲁⲓ; Job 28 12 *SB*, Is 66 1 *SB*, Mt 19 18 *SB*, Lu 24 19 *S* (*B* ⲟⲩ), BHom 56 *S* ⲟⲩⲁϣ ⲙⲙⲓⲛⲉ ⲡϣⲏⲛ, Va 57 19 *B* ⲁϣ ⲟⲩⲡⲉ ⲫⲁⲓ *ποῖος*; Ps 118 82 *S* ⲉⲛⲁϣ ⲛ̄ⲟⲩⲟⲉⲓϣ (*B* ⲡⲉⲛⲁⲩ) Pro 6 9 *A* (*S* ⲧⲛⲁⲩ, var ShMIF 23 163 =*A*), Jo 6 25 *S* (*B* ⲡⲉⲛⲁⲩ) πότε; Mt 8 27 *SB*, Lu 1 29 *SB* ⲟⲩⲁϣ ⲙⲙⲓⲛⲉ (ⲣⲏϯ) ποταπός; 2 Kg 2 1 *S* ποῦ; Deu 12 30 *SB* ⲁϣ ⲛ̄ⲥⲙⲟⲧ (ⲣⲏϯ), Ps 10 1 *S* (*B* = Gk) πῶς; ShA 1 226 *S* ⲛ̄ⲓⲙⲡⲉ ⲡⲛⲟϭ ⲁⲅⲱ ⲁϣⲡⲉ ⲡⲕⲟⲩⲓ, ShC 73 194 *S* ⲁϣ ⲛ̄ⲭⲱⲣⲙ ⲏ ⲟⲩ ⲙⲡⲗⲁⲛⲏ, Mor 40 30 *S* ⲁϣⲡⲉ (var ⲛⲓⲙ) ⲡⲉⲕⲣⲁⲛ, Miss 8 258 *S* ⲉⲓⲡⲁⲧⲁⲅⲉ ⲁϣ...ⲡⲧⲁⲕⲁ ⲁϣ; ? as nn, Ep 434 *S* write me ⲭⲉⲟⲩ (ⲡ)ⲧⲉⲟⲩⲁϣ ϣⲱⲡⲉ (or *l* ⲟⲩ ⲁϣϣⲱⲡⲉ, *v* ⲁϧ-).

II. indef pron, *a certain, whatever*: Mor 23 42 *S* wicked souls ⲛⲟⲭⲟⲩ ⲉⲁϣ ⲛ̄ⲕⲟⲗⲁⲥⲓⲥ, Z 346 *S* ϩⲛⲁϣ ⲛ̄ϯⲙⲉ ἤδε, C 86 173 *B* I will make thee governor ⲉⲭⲉⲛⲁϣ ⲛ̄ⲟⲟϣ (*sic l*) ⲉⲧⲉⲕⲟⲩⲁϣϥ, *ib* 206 *B* we saw ⲛⲛⲁϣ ⲡⲣⲏϯ ⲡⲉⲛⲁϣ ⲛ̄ⲥⲙⲟⲧ *thus & thus*, R 2 1 47 *S* ⲧⲏⲛⲁⲣ ⲁϣ ⲙ̄ⲡⲁϣ ⲛ̄ⲣⲱⲃ, Mor 37 99 *S* wearing clothes ⲛⲁϣ ⲙⲙⲓⲛⲉ, ShC 73 210 *S* ⲁⲩⲭⲟⲟⲩⲧ ⲛⲁϣ ⲛ̄ⲣⲱⲃ.

III. indef interrog particle: Ge 26 9 *B* ἆρα γε, ROC 25 244 *B* ⲁϣ ⲁϥϯ ⲕⲏⲡ ⲉⲧⲁⲙⲉ-, MG 25 244 *B* ⲁϣ ⲛ̄ⲉⲟⲕⲡⲉ ⲥⲩ ⲉⲓ̂, *ib* 308 *B* ⲁϣ ⲉϥⲥⲟⲙⲥ ⲉⲡⲭⲱⲣⲟⲥ ⲡⲡⲛⲉⲑⲟⲩⲁⲃ (*S* ⲁⲗⲗⲁ, *l* ? ⲁⲣⲁ), C 43 228 *B* ⲁϣ ⲡⲓⲁⲗⲟⲩⲡⲉ *where?*

ⲁϣ *SO* nn m, *furnace, oven*: smith's Si 34 29 (31 26), 38 33, κάμινος; for warmth P 129¹² 6 (Reg. Pachom.) ⲡⲡⲉⲗⲁⲁⲩ ⲭⲉⲣⲉ ⲁϣ ϩⲛⲡⲉⲅⲏⲓ *focum facere*; for cooking ShC 73 137 when cooking in ⲭⲗⲱϥ or ⲧⲣⲓⲡ firewood to be spared, only ϣⲟⲙⲧ ⲉⲡⲛϣⲉ ⲉⲡⲁϣ (*cf ib* ⲡⲥⲉⲧⲙⲛⲉⲭ ϩⲁϩ ⲛ̄ϣⲉ ⲉϩⲟⲩⲛ ⲉⲡⲕⲱϩⲧ), ST 236 = Tor 36 ϣⲉ ⲙ̄ⲡⲁϣ; PMéd 208 ashes from before ⲟⲩϩⲣⲱ ⲛⲁϣ (ϩⲣⲱ & ⲁϣ both = κάμινος), Ep 546 a bronze ⲁϣ (but *v* n), AZ 21 100 *O* ⲁϣ ⲛ̄ⲥⲁⲧⲓ. Dem ꜥḫ is both portable censer (Griffith *Stories* 128, 134) & large furnace (Ryl Dem 3 91, 237). In name? Ταπάϣ (Preisigke).

ⲁϣ *S* nn, meaning unknown: Mor 51 34 ⲁⲡⲛⲉⲭ ϣⲧⲉ ⲉϩⲣⲁⲓ ⲛ̄ϣⲉ ⲡⲉⲗⲛⲥⲉ ⲁⲡⲛⲉⲭ ⲗⲁⲅⲟ ⲉϩⲣⲁⲓ ⲡⲕⲟⲩⲕⲉ ⲡⲉⲗⲭⲱⲗ ⲁⲡⲛⲉⲭ ⲁϣ ⲉⲡⲉⲕⲣⲟ ⲛ̄ϣⲉ ⲛ̄ϣⲉ ⲙⲁⲣ (so made of wood).

ⲁϣ- *Sᵃ*   *v* ⲁϧ-.

ⲁϣ- *SA*   *v* ⲱϣ.

ⲁϣⲁⲓ *SB*, ⲁϣⲉⲓ *A*, ⲁϣⲉⲉⲓ *A²F*, ⲁϣⲛⲉⲓ *O* (Hor 82), ⲁϣⲉⲉⲓⲧⲉ *A* (TU 43 8), ⲟϣ⁺*SB*, ⲁϣ⁺*AF*, p c (?) ⲁϣ- in ⲁϣⲓⲣⲓ (*v* ⲉⲓⲣⲉ) vb intr, **a.** *become many, multiply*: Ge 3 16 *S* (*B* ⲧⲁϣⲟ), 7 17 *B* ⲡⲓⲙⲙⲟⲟⲩ... ⲡⲁϣⲛⲏⲟⲩ ⲛⲁ., 48 16 *SB*, Lev 25 16 *B* opp ⲥⲃⲟⲕ, Ps 3 1 *SB*, Is 14 2 *SB* πληθύνειν, -εσθαι; often paral ⲁⲓⲁⲓ (*q v*): Ge 1 28 *SA* (ⲁϣⲉⲓⲧⲉ) *B*, 35 11 *SB*, Lev 26 9 *B* (*S* ⲧⲁϣⲟ), Jer 23 3 *SB*; Ps 49 19 *B* (*S* do), Ro 5 20 *SB*, ι Thes 3 12 *B* (*S* ⲣ ϩⲟⲩⲟ) πλεονάζειν; Ge 30 30 *S* (*B* ⲁⲓⲁⲓ) αὐξάνεσθαι, Ex 23 29 *SB*, Jos 10 11 *S*, Job 14 21 *SB* πολλοὶ γίνεσθαι; Ro 5 15 *S* (*B* ⲉⲣ ϩⲟⲩⲟ), 2 Cor 9 8 *B* (*S* ⲧⲁϣⲟ) περισσεύειν; Ez 9 9 *B*, Zech 12 11 *SAB* μεγαλύνεσθαι; Ps 91 5 *S* (*B* ϣⲱⲕ), Nah 2 9 *A* (*B* ϩⲣⲟϣ) βαρύνεσθαι; R 2 2 23 *S* ⲡⲧⲉⲣⲉⲡⲉⲭⲣⲟ ⲡⲟⲥ ⲁ. μηκύνειν, MG 25 300 *B* (*S* ⲣ ⲛⲟϭ) ⲡⲓⲥⲁⲭⲓ ⲛⲁⲁ. ⲉⲡⲓϩⲟⲩⲟ, Miss 4 100 *B* where sin ⲁ. ⲙⲙⲟϥ (reflex) ϫⲉⲛⲡⲓⲕⲟⲥⲙⲟⲥ; ⲥ ⲛ-: Ps 64 14 *B* (*S* ⲧⲁϣⲟ) ⲁ. ⲛ̄ⲥⲟⲩⲟ, Va 68 40 *B* ⲁⲡⲓⲕⲟⲥⲙⲟⲥ ⲁ. ⲛ̄ⲣⲱⲙⲓ, PO 14 354 *B* ⲁ ⲅⲁ. ⲙⲡⲉⲡⲓⲱⲧ & *consecrated him* (sic, ? *l* ⲁ ⲙⲟⲛⲓ). **b.** qual, *many*: Ge 15 1 *S* (*B* ⲉⲣ ⲡⲓϣϯ), Deu 7 17 *B* (*S* ⲛⲁϣⲉ), Job 3 15 *SB*, Ez 33 24 *SB*, 47 7 *B* (*S* ⲛⲁϣⲉ), Lu 6 17 *S* (var ⲛⲁϣⲉ) *B* πολύς, πλείων εἶναι; Job 2 13 *S* (*B* ϩⲣⲟϣ) μέγας; Ps 71 7 *S* (*B* nn), Is 51 10 *SB* πλῆθος; ι Tim 5 23 *SB* πυκνός; Job 38 25 *SB*, Pro 28 3 *S* λάβρος; Hos 10 1 *SA* (*B* nn) εὐθηνῶν; R 1 2 56 *S* I smote them ϩⲛⲟⲩⲙⲟⲩ ⲉϥⲟ., Va 63 81 *B* ⲉϥⲟ. ϫⲉⲛⲡⲓⲥⲁⲭⲓ like torrent, Va 65 21 *B* ⲫⲁⲛⲓⲁϩⲟⲣ ⲉⲧⲟ.; ⲥ ⲛ-: ι Kg 2 5 *SB*, Pro 14 29 *SA* πολύς; Lev 11 42 *SB* πολυπληθής; Aeg 236 *S* ⲉⲧⲟ. ⲛ̄ⲥⲃⲱ πολυμαθής; CaiEuch 534 *B* ⲟ. ⲙ̄ⲃⲁⲗ πολυόμματος; Ge 27 23 *B* δασύς; Jer 17 8 *S* (BMOr 8810 521) ἀλσώδης; BAp 168 *S* ⲉⲣⲉⲡⲉϥⲥⲱⲙⲁ ⲟ. ⲛ̄ϣⲱⲡⲉ.

—— *SB*, ⲁϣⲉⲓ *AF*, ⲁϣⲛⲓ *F*, ⲁϣⲉⲓⲧⲉ *A* (Hos 8 12), nn m, *multitude, amount*: Ge 32 12 *SB*, Ps 48 6 *SB*, Si 36 11 *S*, Is 31 4 *SBF*, Jo 21 6 *B* (*S* ⲁϣⲛⲓ) πλῆθος; Ex 15 16 *BF* μέγεθος; Hag 2 17 *A* (*S* do) Vulg *acervus*; 2 Cor 12 7 *B* (*S* ⲙⲛ̄ⲧⲛⲟϭ) ὑπερβολή; BHom 46 *S* ⲡⲁ. ⲛ̄ⲡⲉⲭⲣⲏⲙⲁ ὄγκος; Va 61 13 *B* ⲡⲁ. ⲙ̄ⲡⲓⲥⲑⲟⲓⲃⲱⲛ, sim ShA 1 247 *S*, TstAb 246 *B* ⲡⲁ. of old age.

ⲙⲉⲧⲁ. *B* nn f, *number, multitude*: Ez 27 33 (*S* ⲁϣⲛⲓ) πλῆθος.

ⲣⲉϥⲁ. *SB* nn, *multiplier*: Si 23 11 *SB* ⲣ. ⲛ̄ϣⲱⲣⲕ πολύορκος.

ⲉⲣ ⲁ. *B*, *multiply*: Si 22 12 ⲙ̄ⲡⲉⲣⲉⲣ ⲁ. ⲛ̄ⲥⲁϫⲓ (*S* ⲧⲁϣⲟ).

ⲁϣⲛ *SA²*(AP 19), ⲁϣⲉ *B* (Ez 28 19 *bis*), ⲁϣⲛⲓ *F* (Ex 15 16) nn f, *multitude*: Deu 1 10 *S* (*B* ⲁϣⲁⲓ), Jo 21 6 *S* (*B* do), Ac 28 3 *S* (*B* ⲙⲏϣ) πλῆθος; Deu 25 15 *S* (*B* do) πολυ(ήμερος); Ps 20 4 *S*

μακρότης; Sa 4 8 S ἀριθμός; Ez 28 19 B (S ογοπ
пıм) πᾶς; Sa 6 2 S ὄχλος; Mt 15 33 S (B нпı)
τοσοῦτος; BHom 17 S πόσος; BM 255 3 S птє-
роүсшк ммшaχє єγа., Pcod 16 S repaid пoγa.
пкwd, Z 630 S oγa. ппєр, ShC 42 104 S oγa.
пoγϩор (cf Ps 21 16 aтo), ShC 73 20 S wounds
пoγa. ммıпє, BMar 92 S ϩєпa. ппрп.

V пашє, ташo.

ашє S, ашı B v єıшє.

ашb F vb intr, c єca-, meaning unknown:
BM 587 (3 or 4 times) a. єcaпcaн.

ашєbєп B nn m, enchanter (аш- prob = ш rḫ):
Deu 18 11 (var χє мтaγ q v, S рєϥмoγтє) ἐπαείδων ἐπαοιδήν, K 114 عرّاف; Z 128 = Va 59 156
aχω ммaтoc, рєϥєр ϩıк, па., шєп ϩıп, Va ib
121 sim, but here пıашєγbєп (v ?ашєγ below).
Cf Spg 300.

ашкaк SF v шкaк.

ашaλ, ашwλє S v aλ (last).

ашıλı F v єıрє (ашıрı).

ашмı B v wшм.

ашıп псоoı B v ϩaϭıп.

ашıрa B nn f, chameleon: K 172 حربا (var
حرباية). Cf Murray Engl. Nub. Dict. 15. (χαμαιλέων Lev 11 30, Zeph 2 14 is untranslated.)

ашıрı B v єıрє.

ашєıтє, -єєıтє A v ашaı.

аштaп SB v тaп.

ашєγ B nn pl, astrologers: Is 47 13 (S рєϥкa
oγпoγ птпє) ἀστρολόγοι. V ашєbєп.

ашϭнλ A v ϭнλ.

ашϭaп SA, -шкaп B v шϭaп.

aϥ SB, aaϥ (PMéd 157 &c, BAp 87), ab SF,
єϥ A, aϥγ (?PMéd 183, Chassinat), aϥ- S (aϥрıр
Is 65 4, Mor 51 19), pl aϥoγı, aboγı SBF, aϥoγı
B & sg as pl, nn m (Ez 4 14, PMéd) flesh, human
or animal: Ge 9 4 SB, 3 Kg 17 6 B, Job 10 11
SB ϩєпaϥ, Si 36 27 S do, Hos 8 13 A do, Ro 14
21 SB κρέας; pl form :Deu 14 8 B, Jer 37 16 B
κρέας; Ge 40 19 B (S = Gk), Lev 4 11 B (S do),
Ps 26 2 B (S do) σάρξ, Mor 24 8 F we filled place
of rib па., C 43 232 B пєϥкac пємпєϥa., Tri 395
S п(a)a. ϩрє for ravens; a. ппплaχє gums PMéd
290 S; a. пϩoγo excrescent flesh ib 157; Ps 16
14, Is 65 4, Z 270 swine's flesh, Mor 25 13 S rich
man's food wbт, папoı, a. пррıр; Ps 49 13 bull's
flesh; ST 46 sheep's; Ez 39 20 horse's.

caпaϥ SB nn, meat dealer, seller: Kr 158 S, K
131 B لقّام.

шaтaϥ S nn m, butcher: J 2 25, MMA 24 6 5.

єр aϥ S nn m: Lev 13 18 (Ciasca; Masp &
Mor om) gloss on caрχ пϩєλкoc (but ?l cрaϥ).

єр aϥ B, become flesh (of consecrated bread):
C 43 194.

oγєм aϥ SB, eat flesh: Lev 7 9 S, Is 22 13 SB,
1 Cor 8 13 SB.

шєп aϥ S, buy flesh: Pro 23 20 S (= Z 639,
Mor 43 136).

aϥ, aaϥ, ab SB, єϥ Sa (Ps 104 31 Rahlfs) A
nn m, f (K 173), fly, or ?insect, since flying sometimes added: ShC 42 47 S = Eccl 10 1 μυῖα, sim
Mor 31 93 S, also MG 25 210 B ϩaпa. єγϩaλaı,
Bor 252 129 S birds & ϩaпa. єγϩнλ мпрєпшoλ-
мєc; Is 7 18 B μυῖα; ShZ 600 S every beast
шaϩрaı єпa.; K 173 B (= Loret) ذبابة.

—пєbıw SAB, honey fly, bee: Ps 117 12 SB,
Pro 6 8 SAB, Is 7 18 B μέλισσα, MIF 9 86 S like
a. пє. ϩєпoγмoγλϩ, Jud 14 8 S cooϩc па. пє.
συναγωγὴ μελισ., P 44 56 S a. пє. ϩooγт نحل بري.

—пoγϩор SB, dog fly: Ex 8 17 B, Ps 77 45
SB, P 44 57 S κυνόμυια; Sa 16 9 S μυῖα, ShC 42
47 S flies commonly called a. пo.

—пкaλλaıпє S (καλάινος, cf Griffith Stories
175), Kropp K.

—пϩooγт S, wild fly (bee): R 1 3 74 that
gathers honey.

aϥ мbıoγ v aмн wasp.

aϥλєєλє SB v ϩaϥλєєλє.

aϥoγı S, aboγı B v aϥ flesh.

aϥχıр B nn m, greedy of shameful gain: 1 Tim
3 8 (S маıϩнγ пшλoϥ) αἰσχροκερδής; Va 61 20
єтoı пϭєппє oγoϩ па., K 89 بخيل (var وضيع).

мєтa. B nn f, greed of shameful gain: 1 Pet 5
2 (S мптмаıϩ. пш.) αἰσχροκερδῶς.

аϩoγп A v ϩoγп.

аϩрнı A v ϩраı.

аϩтп- A prep, against, in opposition to: Cl 4
12 (var oγb]є), 51 3 aγр cтacıaζє. аϩтпшoγcнc.

аϭı, aχı B v aϩр.

аϭo?, aϩa? F v aϩрo?.

аϭwм B v aϩoм.

аϭωрı, aϭωıрı (Ps 55 18, Bodl 325 154),
aϭoрı (K 173) B nn m, asp: llc ثعبان, MG 25
238 oγa. (Hist Laus 18 ἀσπίς) dwelt among reeds,
ib пєoγрєϥϭwтєbпє. In name (?)папaχωрє.

ⲁϧ-, ⲁϣ- *SᵃA* (not *A²*), qual of ⲟⲩⲱϧ as verbal particle in rel perf clause, in both numbers & persons (AZ 52 112): Ex 4 11 *A* ⲡⲉⲧⲁϧϥ (*S* ⲡⲉⲛⲧⲁϥ-), Pro 12 2 *A* ⲡⲉⲧⲁϧϭⲓⲛⲉ (*S* do), Jo 11 45 *A* ⲉⲧⲁϩⲉⲓ (*A²* ⲛⲧⲁⲩ-, *S* ⲉⲛⲧⲁⲩ-), El 102 *A* ⲡⲉⲧⲁϧⲣ, ST 60 *Sᵃ* ⲡⲕⲁϧ ⲉⲧⲁϣⲉⲓ ⲉϫⲱⲓ, *ib* 308 *Sᵃ* ⲡⲧⲟⲕ (ⲉ)ⲧⲁϣⲃⲓ, ST 191 *Sᵃ* ⲑⲉⲕⲗⲁ (ⲉ)ⲧⲁϣⲧⲁⲁⲥ ⲡⲁⲓ, J 68 27 *Sᵃ* ⲡⲉⲓⲣⲟⲙⲡⲉ ⲡⲧⲁϣⲡⲁⲣⲁⲅⲉ. Sometimes ⲉⲧ- omitted: Ep 544 *Sᵃ* he said ⲕⲁⲑⲁⲣⲱⲛ ⲁϧⲧⲡⲟⲟⲩⲧ, *ib* ⲡⲁⲉⲓⲱⲧ ⲁϣⲧⲡⲡⲟⲟⲩⲧ. *V* Ep *lc* n.

ⲁϧ *S* interj   *v* ⲱϧ.

ⲁⲁϧ *F*   *v* ⲟⲟϧ.

ⲁϧⲁ *F* nn   *v* ⲁϧⲟ.

ⲁϧⲁ, ⲁϧ, ϧⲁ *F* conjunct, *and*, not in literary texts: ALR '06 473 ⲡⲉⲕⲕⲗⲏⲥⲓⲁ ⲁ. ⲡⲉⲙⲟⲡⲁⲥⲧⲏⲣⲓⲟⲛ, Kr 17 ⲃⲓⲕⲧⲱⲣ ⲁ. ⲡⲁⲡⲁ ⲙⲏⲛⲁ, BM 580 21 pray that God guide me again ⲁ. ⲡⲉⲗⲕⲉ ⲗⲁⲁⲩ ϧⲓⲧⲉⲯⲩⲭⲏ, *ib* 664 ⲁⲙⲟⲩ ⲉϧⲟⲩⲛ ⲁϧ ⲉϣⲧ[, *ib* 626 (otherwise *B*) I greet my children ϧⲁ ⲡⲉⲛϣⲏⲣⲉ ⲧⲁϧⲣⲓ, AZ 23 28 ϫⲓⲧⲟⲩ ϧⲁ ⲛϣϫⲓⲧⲟⲩ; ⲁ. & ⲁⲩⲱ in same text: CMSS 28 ⲁ. ⲙⲡⲉⲣⲕⲁⲧⲉⲭⲉ...ⲁⲩⲱ ⲙⲡⲉⲣϭⲱ, BM 582 (2) I greet lord brother ⲁⲩⲱ ⲧⲓϣⲓⲛⲓ ⲉⲡⲁⲓⲱⲧ...ⲁ. ⲡⲁⲡⲁ ⲭⲁⲏⲗ...ⲁⲩⲱ ⲡⲉⲥⲡⲉⲟⲩ ϣⲓⲛⲓ ⲉⲣⲁⲕ, *ib* 592 I greet &c...ⲁⲩⲱ ⲙⲉⲡⲉⲥⲁⲡⲁⲓ... ⲁ. ϧⲉⲓ ⲡⲓⲣⲱⲙⲓ...ⲁ. ϯⲡⲓⲥⲧⲉⲩ ⲡϭ̄ⲥ̄...ⲁ. ϯϣⲓⲛⲓ ⲣⲁⲕ.

ⲁϧⲁ *B*, ⲁϧⲉ *SA*, ⲁϧⲏ *BF*   *v* ⲉϧⲉ *yea*.

ⲁϧⲉ *SA* *stand, need*   *v* ⲱϧⲉ.

ⲁϧⲉ *SA*, ⲁϧⲓ *B*, ⲉϧⲓ *F* nn m, *length, limit of life*: Job 7 1 *S* (*B* ⲱⲛϧ̄), 10 5 *S* (*B* ϫⲓⲡⲱⲛϧ̄), Pro 3 2 *SB*, Sa 2 4 *S*, Si 34 4 *S* βίος; Ge 7 11 *S*, Ps 30 10 *S*, Pro 4 13 *S*, Si 48 27 *S*, He 2 15 *SF* (*B* all ⲱⲛϧ̄) ζωή; Is 65 20 *S* (*B* ⲥⲛⲟⲩ) χρόνος; Job 32 10 *S* ⲛⲟϭ ⲛⲁ. πολυχρόνιος, Si 30 22 *S* μακροημέρευσις, Is 53 10 *S* μακρόβιος; Job 14 1 *SB* ⲕⲟⲩⲓ ⲛⲁ., Cl 30 5 *A* ⲁ. ϧⲏⲙ = *S* ϣⲁⲣⲁ. ὀλιγόβιος; ShA 1 44 *S* slain ϧⲁⲑⲏ ⲙⲡⲉϥⲁ., TstAb 177 *B* any may die ϩⲁϫⲉⲛⲡⲉϥⲁ., ShC 42 43 *S* ⲡⲉϥⲁ. ⲡⲉ his fated term of life, Mor 25 31 *S* lest ⲡⲉⲕⲁ. ⲧⲁϩⲟⲕ unlooked-for, Miss 4 791 *S* ⲁⲡⲉⲧⲛⲁ. ϧⲱⲛ ⲉϧⲟⲩⲛ = *B ib* 115 ⲁⲡⲉⲧⲉⲛⲁ. ⲕⲏⲛ, P 129¹⁶ 16 *S* ⲡⲉⲭⲣⲟⲛⲟⲥ ⲙⲡⲟⲩⲁ. for thee to die, BM 661 *F* God give thee ⲟⲩⲛⲁϭ ⲡⲉ., sim BAp 126 *S*.

ⲣ ⲁ. *S*, ⲉⲣ ⲁϧⲓ *B*, ⲉⲗ ⲉϧⲓ *F*, *pass life*: Pro 9 6 *S* (*B* ⲡⲉⲃⲁ.) ζῆν, EpJer 46 *F* πολυχρ. γίνεσθαι, 1 Tim 2 2 *S* (*B* ⲱⲛϧ̄) βίος, BHom 10 *S* ζωή; Miss 4 110 *B* ⲉⲕⲛⲁⲉⲣ ⲁ. ⲟⲛ ⲙⲉⲡⲉⲡⲥⲁⲡⲁⲓⲛⲓϣϯ ⲡⲁ. ?, *ib* 643 *S* ⲛⲧⲁ[ⲩⲣ] ⲁ. ⲉⲡⲕⲁⲓⲣⲟⲥ ⲙⲡⲉⲓⲱⲧ, Pcod 22 *S* ⲛⲧⲁϥⲣ ⲡⲉϥⲁ. (var ⲟⲩⲟⲉⲓϣ) ⲧⲏⲣϥ.

ⲡⲉⲃⲁ. *B* nn, *long-lived*, only with ⲁ. ⲙⲉⲧ-: Bar 3 14 μακροβίωσις, Ps 90 16 (*S* ⲙⲏⲛϣⲉ ⲛϩⲟⲟⲩ) μακρότης ἡμερ., Pro 3 2 (*S* ⲛⲟϭ ⲛⲁ.) μῆκος

βίου.   **ⲃ.** ⲉⲣ ⲛ.: Ex 20 12 (*S* ⲣ ⲛⲟϭ ⲛⲟⲩⲟⲉⲓϣ) μακροχρον. γίνεσθαι, Deu 6 2 (*S* ⲉⲓⲣⲉ ⲛⲟⲩⲙⲏ. ⲛⲣ.) μακροημερεύειν, Ps 11 8 (*S* ⲧⲁϣⲟ, *cf* Ps 137 3) πολυωρεῖν.

ϣⲁⲣⲁ. *SA* nn, *short-lived*: Job 14 1 (*B* ⲕⲟⲩϫⲓ ⲛⲁ.), Sa 3 16 ἀτέλεστος, Pro 10 6 *SA*, Is 65 20 *S* ἄωρος (*B* diff).

ⲙⲛⲧ-, ⲙⲉⲧϣⲁⲣⲁ. *SB* nn f, *short life*: R 1 2 46 *S* opp ⲣ ϧⲗⲗⲟ, BMis 180 *S* he died in a ⲙ., TSBA 9 368 *B*.

ⲣ, ⲉⲣ ϣⲁⲣⲁ. *SB*, *be short-lived*: Pro 13 2 *S*, Sa 14 15 *S* ἄωρος, sim R 2 1 39 *S*, BIF 15 234 *S*, Va 58 127 *B* reap me not ⲉⲓⲟⲓ ⲛϣ.

ϫⲉⲙ ⲁ. *B*, have (*find*) *long life*: TEuch 2 500 of babe ⲙⲁⲣⲉϥϫ. لِيطَل.

ⲁϧⲏ *F*   *v* ⲉⲣⲉ ox.

ⲁϧⲓ *F*   *v* ⲟϧⲉ.

ⲁϧⲟ *SB*, ⲁϧⲟⲩ (? J 66, *v* below) *S*, ⲉϧⲟ (-ⲱ Hos 13 15) *A*, ⲁϧⲁ *F*, ⲁϧⲟⲣ *B*, pl ⲁϧⲱⲱⲣ *S*, ⲉϧⲱⲣ *A*, ⲁϧⲱⲣ *B*, ⲁϧⲱⲱⲣ *F* & sg as pl, nn m, **a.** *treasure*: Sa 7 14 *S*, Si 29 14 *S*, Mt 6 19 *S* (*BF* pl), 13 44 *SBF*, 2 Cor 4 7 *SB* θησαυρός.   **b.** *treasury, store house*: Deu 28 12 *SB*, Dan 1 2 *B*, Hos 13 15 *A* (*B* Gk om, Vulg thesaurus) θησ.; Ge 41 56 *B* σιτοβολῶν; ShC 42 17 *S* ⲧⲱⲃⲉ...ⲉⲣϧⲟⲩⲁ., Miss 4 636 *S* we opened ⲛⲁ. ⲛⲛⲟⲉⲓⲕ,...ⲡⲣⲟ ⲛⲛⲁ., Mor 19 48 = 18 40 *S* ⲟⲩⲁ. full of corn, PLond 4 499 *S* ⲛⲁϧⲱ state granaries at Babylon (Fustât)=ὅρριον, BMis 386 *S* = BSM 41 *B* when door opened ⲁ. found full of wine, J 66 30 *S* among testatrix's bequests ϧⲟⲓ, ⲛⲏⲙⲟⲥⲓⲟⲛ ⲙⲡⲉϥⲁϧⲟⲩ ⲙⲡⲉϥⲥⲙⲟⲩ = 76 27 (duplicate, same scribe) ⲛϧⲟⲓ ⲙⲡ-[ⲛⲉϥ]ⲁ. ⲧⲏⲣⲟⲩ (or ? = ⲓⲁϧⲟⲩ);   pl form: **a.** Ge 43 23 *SB*, Pro 3 14 *SAB*, Is 2 7 *SB*, *ib* 30 6 *F* (*SB* ⲙⲛⲧⲣⲙⲙⲁⲟ); **b.** Deu 32 34 *SB*, 4 Kg 12 18 *S*, Ps 134 7 *SB*, Is 39 2 *SB*, Ez 28 13 *SB*.

ⲁⲛⲁϧⲱⲣ *B* nn pl, *storehouses*: C 89 118 straw stored in ⲛⲉⲛⲁ. (Gk Ar om).

ⲁϧⲟ *B* (? *l* ⲟⲩⲁϧⲟ) nn, *dwelling, abode*: K 152 دَار مَنْزِل (*cf* Pey 16 & 160).

ⲁϧⲕⲱ *S* nn, meaning unknown: CO 466 & duplic ostr Univ Coll London, in list of *varia*, ⲭⲗⲁⲙⲉⲥ, ⲟⲩⲁϧⲕⲱ, ⲙⲉⲗⲁⲛ (or ? *l* ⲟⲩⲁϧⲕⲱ, but art ⲟⲩ- often in this list).

ⲁϧⲟⲙ *SB*, ⲉϧⲟⲙ *O* (AZ 21 100) ⲉϧⲁⲙ *AA²*, ⲁϧⲁⲙ *A²F* nn m, only with ⲁϣ- *SF* (*B* only Ez 5 15), ⲱϣ- *A* = ϥⲓ- *B*, forming vb intr, *sigh, groan*, ⲉ- (ἐπί dat) Job 31 38, ⲉϫⲛ-, ⲉϧⲣⲁⲓ ⲉϫⲛ- (do) Job 18 20, Ez 9 4, Nah 3 7 (acc); Job 9 27 *S* ⲁϣⲁ. (*B* ϥⲓ ⲁ.), Sa 5 3 *S*, Is 30 15 *SBF*, Nah 3 7 *AB*, Ro 8 23 *SB*, BHom 3 *S* στενάζειν; Lam 1 5 *B*,

Mk 8 12 *SB* ἀναστεν.; Ex 2 23 *SB*, Jer 38 19 *B*,
Ez 21 6 *SB* κατ αστεν.; Jer 15 5 *SB* δειλιᾶν (?error);
Ez 28 19 *B*, Va 58 178 *B* ⲉϥϥⲓ ⲁ. ⲓⲉ ⲉϥⲟⲕⲉⲙ
στυγνάζειν, AP 37 *A²* ⲁϥⲁϣ ⲉ. ⲁϩⲣⲏⲉⲓ ⲟⲩϭⲉⲡⲭⲁⲉⲓⲥ.

—— with ⲁϣ-, ϥⲓ- nn m, *groan, yawn, roar*:
Ge 3 16 *SB*, Job 3 24 *SB*, Ps 30 10 *SB*, Ac 7 34
SB στεναγμός, Pro 19 12 *SA* βρυγμός (*cf* BM 286
ⲡⲧⲉⲣⲉϥⲁϣ ⲁ. ⲛϭⲓ ⲡⲙⲛⲏϣⲉ); Mor 53 56 *S* ⲡⲁϣ
ⲁ. ⲛⲛⲉⲥⲣⲙⲉⲓⲟⲟⲩⲉ, DeV 100 *B* ⲁϥϥⲓ ⲛⲟⲩⲛⲓϣϯ ⲛϭⲓ
ⲁ., Bor 235 117 *S* ⲉⲣϣⲁⲡⲟⲩⲁϣ ⲁ. ⲉⲓ ⲉⲣⲱⲕ χάσμη.

ⲁϩⲱⲙ, ⲁϩⲱⲙⲉ (Job 9, Pro 23, Is 40), ⲁϩⲱⲱⲙⲉ
(Lev 11) *S*, ⲁϩⲱⲙ *A*, ⲁϧⲱⲙ *B*, pl (?)ⲡⲁϩⲱⲙⲉⲓ *S*
(Mor 32 5, picture of 2 birds) nn m, *eagle* (originally = ἱέραξ *falcon*, AZ 58 150, also 53 86; *cf* Z
599 among Egyptian idols, ⲡⲁⲉⲧⲟⲥ in whom ye
trust): Ex 19 4 *B*, Deu 14 12 *B*, Ob 1 4 *B*, Mic
1 16 *B*, Hab 1 8 *B*, Lu 17 37 *B*, Ap 4 7 *B* (*SA* =
Gk in all) ἀετός, which Lev 11 13 *S* glossed ⲉⲧⲉⲡⲁ.
ⲡⲉ; Job 5 7 *B* (*S* ⲛⲟⲩⲣⲉ) γύψ. Always transl نسر
vulture, exc P 44 55 = 43 22 عقاب, where ἱέραξ,
ἀετός نسر. Copts ? uncertain as to meaning of
ἀετός (*cf* LMis 81 365), BP 11965 4 *S* ⲡⲉⲗⲉⲧⲟⲥ
ⲙⲛⲛⲉϩⲁⲗⲁⲧⲉ; MG 25 63 transl *birds* طيور (Götting
Ar 114 10), but mostly not translated.

In name ⲡⲁϩⲱⲙ, -ⲙⲉ (*v* TT 100 n = dem AZ
26 67, Taf 2) *S*, ⲡⲁϩⲱⲙ *B*, ⲡⲁϩⲱⲙⲓ *F*, Παχούμιος
& varr; Παχομ- in compounds: Π. βῆκις, Π. ταῶς;
also ⲡⲁϩⲱⲙⲟ, -ⲙⲱ, -ⲙⲁ PSBA 21 247, Cai 8190 *S*
ⲧⲁϩⲱⲙ, WS 198 *S* ?ⲧⲁϩⲟⲙⲱ. *Cf* C 89 217 *B*
ⲡⲓⲁⲅⲓⲟⲥ ⲡⲁϩⲱⲙ ⲡⲓⲛⲓϣϯ ⲡⲁ. (? ref Ez 17 3). In
place-names: PLond 4 175 ⲡⲙⲟⲩ ⲛⲡⲁ., J&C 92
ⲧⲙⲟⲩ ⲛⲡⲁ.

ⲁϩⲙⲓ *S* *v* ϩⲙⲓ.

ⲁϩⲣ, ⲁϩⲣⲉ *S*, ⲁϭⲓ, ⲁϫⲓ *B* nn m, *marsh herbage,
sedge*: Ge 41 2 *B* ⲁϭⲓ(var ⲁϫⲓ) ἄχει (var ἕλος), ib
18 *S* ⲁϩⲣⲉ = *B* ⲁϫⲓ مرج, Is 19 7 ⲁϩⲣ ⲉⲧⲟⲩⲉⲧⲟⲩⲱⲧ
= *B* ⲁϭⲓ نبات, Si 40 16 *S* ⲁϩⲣⲉ ⲉⲧ- (var ⲁϩⲣ ⲉⲧ-)
ἄχει. In Job 8 11 same Heb אחו = βούτομον.
Cf ⲕⲉϭⲏⲡ.

ⲁϩⲱⲱⲣ *S*, ⲁϩⲱⲣ *B* *v* ⲁϩⲟ.

ⲁϩⲣⲉ, ⲁϩⲣⲏ *Sᵃ* (Ep 296) *v* ⲉⲓ ⲉϩⲣⲁⲓ.

ⲁϩⲣⲏⲓ, ⲁϩⲣⲏⲓ *A* *v* ϩⲣⲁⲓ.

ⲁϩⲣⲟ⸗ *SO*(AZ 21 100), ⲁϩⲣⲁ⸗ *A²*, ⲁϧⲟ⸗ *B*,
ⲁϩⲁ⸗ *F*, interrog pron with suff, referring to subject of phrase, *what, why?* always = Gk τί, ἵνα
τί. **a.** with following vb: Ge 40 7 *S* (*B* ⲉⲑⲃⲉⲟⲩ),
Job 3 11 *B* (*S* ⲉⲧⲃⲉⲟⲩ), Ps 51 1 *S* (*B* do), Jo 4 27
SA² (*B* do), BHom 84 *S* ⲁϩⲣⲟⲟⲩ ⲡⲉⲕⲙⲁⲑⲏⲧⲏⲥ &c
= Mt 15 2 ⲉⲧⲃⲉⲟⲩ, Ac 1 11 *SB*, FR 68 *S* ⲁϩⲣⲱⲧⲛ
ⲧⲉⲧⲛⲣⲓⲙⲉ (var Wess 15 124 ⲉⲧⲃⲉⲟⲩ), ShC 73 42 *S*

ⲁϩⲣⲟϥ ⲡⲧⲟϥ ⲏ ⲉⲧⲃⲉⲟⲩ ⲛϥⲛⲁϥⲓ ⲣⲟⲟⲩϣ ⲁⲛ; Ps 113
5 *S* (*B* ⲟⲩ ⲡⲉⲧϣⲟⲟⲡ), Is 45 10 *S* (*B* ⲟⲩ ⲡⲉⲧ-),
Ro 6 15 *S* (*B* ⲟⲩ ⲡⲧⲉ-); Jos 15 18 *S* τί σοι, Tob
3 15 *S* τί μοι; BHom 19 *S* ⲁϩⲣⲟⲓ ⲉⲓϣⲁϫⲉ τί
λέγω, EW 68 *B* ⲁϧⲟⲓ ⲁⲓⲥⲁϫⲓ ⲉⲛⲁⲡⲓⲕⲁϩⲓ = BSM
7 ⲟⲩⲡⲉ ⲡⲁⲭϥⲟ ⲁⲓⲥ. Pcod 14 *S* ⲁϩⲣⲟⲕ ⲉⲕⲕⲛⲟⲩ
ⲙⲙⲟⲓ. **b.** without vb: Mt 27 4 *B* (*S* ⲙⲛⲧⲛ
ϩⲱⲃ); MG 25 361 *B* ⲁϧⲟⲕ ϩⲱⲕ *what aileth thee?*,
BM 220 1 *S* ⲁϩⲣⲟϥ ⲡⲱⲣⲉ ϩⲱⲱϥ, PSBA 30 234 *S*
ⲁϩⲣⲁϭⲥⲉ ⲁϩⲣⲁϧⲁⲙ *what of A.?* Phil 1 18 *B* ⲁϧⲟϥ-
ϫⲉ, ⲁϩⲁϥϩⲏ *F*, τί γάρ. **c.** with following ⲙⲛ-,
ⲛⲉⲙ-: BM 343 *S* ⲁϩⲣⲟϥ ⲣⲱ ⲡⲁϩⲱⲙ ⲙⲡⲟⲟⲩ ⲙⲛϯ-
ϭⲓⲛϣⲁϫⲉ ⲉⲧⲡⲁϣⲧ, 3 Kg 17 18 *B* ⲁϧⲟⲕ ⲛⲉⲙⲏⲓ ϩⲱⲕ
τί ἐμοὶ καὶ σοί, sim Mt 8 29 *B* (*S* ⲉⲕⲟⲩⲉϣ ⲟⲩ
ⲙⲛ-), Jo 2 4 *BF*(Lacau, *S* diff) ⲁⲣⲁ ⲛⲉⲙⲏⲓ, Z 290
S ⲁϩⲣⲟⲓ ⲁⲡⲟⲕ ⲙⲛⲡⲣⲱⲙⲉ τί θέλω ἐγὼ μετά, C 86
76 *B* ⲁϧⲟⲕ ⲛⲑⲟⲕ ⲛⲉⲙⲡⲁⲓⲣⲁⲛ ϫⲉⲧⲃ, ShC 73 156
S ⲁϩⲣⲟⲓ ⲙⲛ(ⲡ)ⲣⲱⲙⲉ ϫⲉⲉⲩⲟⲩⲱⲙ ⲡⲁϣ ⲡⲣⲉ.

Without suffix *B* (*v* Stern 236 *s f*): Nu 22 9
(Va Lag) ⲁϧⲟ ⲡⲁⲓⲣⲱⲙⲓ ⲁⲩⲓ τί, MG 25 250 would
ye know ϫⲉⲁϧⲟ ϯⲥⲙⲁⲩⲗⲓ ⲙⲡⲉⲥϫⲉⲙϫⲟⲙ.

. ⲁϩⲣⲛ- *A* *v* ϩⲟ (ⲉϩⲣⲛ-).

ⲁϩⲥⲏⲧⲁⲛ *S*. In Ryl 229, 5 times, following
proper names, *eg* ⲕⲟⲩⲗⲟⲉ ⲅⲉⲱⲣⲅ ⲁ. ϭⲁⲙⲉ (though
might be otherwise divided). Inexplicable at present.

ⲁϩⲉⲥⲁⲩ *A* *v* ⲟϩⲉ.

ⲁϩⲁⲧⲱⲧϥ (*l* ? ⲧⲟⲟⲧϥ) *S* nn f, meaning unknown: CO 472 in list of towels & cloths, ⲥⲁⲃⲁ-
ⲕⲁⲧⲉ (σαβακάθιον), ⲙⲁⲣⲭⲱⲝⲉ, ⲥⲡⲧⲉ ⲡⲁ., ⲥⲡⲧⲱⲡⲉ
(σινδόνη), so ? *hand-towel*.

ⲁϩⲏⲩ *v* ⲕⲱⲕ.

ⲁϩⲟⲩⲛ *A* *v* ϩⲟⲩⲛ.

ⲁϫⲉ, ⲁⲁϫⲉ (or ? ⲟⲩⲁϫⲉ, *cf* ⲟⲩⲟϭⲉ) *S* nn, *blow*:
Ex 21 18 ϩⲛⲟⲩⲁⲁ. (*B* ⲉⲣⲃⲟⲧ) πυγμή, Aeg 228
ⲡⲉⲙⲟⲩ ϩⲛⲟⲩⲁ. ⲡⲟⲩⲱⲧ κροῦσμα, HT R 2 ⲁϥⲣⲁϩⲧϥ
...ⲛⲟⲩⲏϣ ⲛⲟⲩⲁ. (*cf* ϣⲉ ⲛⲁⲁⲥ), R 1 5 28 ⲁϥϩⲉϥ
ⲟⲩⲁⲁ. ⲉⲣⲟⲩⲛ ϩⲙⲡⲉϥⲣⲟ (لطم PO 3 418), Mor 41
258 he struck him ⲛⲟⲩⲙⲏⲛϣⲉ ⲛⲡⲟⲩⲁ.

ⲁϫⲓ- *SA*, ⲁϫⲉ- *B* *v* ϫⲱ *say*.

ⲁϫⲱ, ⲁϫⲟ, ⲁϫⲟⲩ, ⲉϫⲱ, ⲉϫⲟⲩ *B* nn f (Ac, PO
11), *viper*: Is 34 11 (*F* ϩⲃⲱ), Zeph 2 14 (*A* ϩⲃⲟⲩ)
ἐχῖνος (sic), Mt 3 7, ib 23 33, Ac 28 3 (all *S* ϩⲃⲱ)
ἔχιδνα, PO 11 330, K 172 افعى. *Cf* Rec 39 159.

ⲁϫⲱ *B* *crook-backed* *v* ϫⲟ κυρτός.

ⲁϫⲱ *S* *v* ⲉϫⲱ.

ⲁϫⲟⲗϯ *B* *v* ⲁϭⲟⲗⲧⲉ.

ⲁϫⲛ- *SA*, ⲉϫⲛ- *S*, ⲁⲧϭⲛⲉ-, ⲁϭⲛⲉ- *B*, ⲁϫⲉⲛ-
(ⲁⲧϫⲉⲛ- BerlP 5569) *F*, ⲁϫⲛⲧ⸗, ⲉϫⲛⲧ⸗ (on ⲉϫⲱ⸗ *v*

below), ⲁⲧϭⲛⲟⲩⲋ, ⲁⲭⲉⲛⲧ⳿ prep, *without*: Ge 41 44 *SB* (cf Wor 323 *F* ⲁϫⲛⲧ), 1 Kg 6 7 *S* Job 24 7 *S* (*B* ⲛⲁⲧ-), Ps 9 26 *S* (*B* ⲛⲟⲩⲉϣⲉⲛ-), 43 12 *S* (*B* ⲛⲭⲓⲛⲭⲛ), 57 4 *S* (*B* ⲭⲱⲣⲓⲥ), Si 38 41 *S*, Mt 10 29 *SB* ἄνευ; Mt 13 34 *S* (*B* = Gk), Ro 3 21 *SB*, He 4 15 *B* (*S* ϣⲁⲧⲛ-), Ja 2 20 *S* (*B*=Gk) χωρίς; Is 45 21 *S* (*B* ⲉⲃⲏⲗ ⲉ-) παρέκ; Mt 5 32 *S* (*B* ⲛⲟⲩⲉϣⲉⲛ-) παρεκτός; Lu 22 35 *SB* ἄτερ; Job 24 6 *S* (*B* ⲛⲁⲧ-) ἀ-μισθί, Pro 21 26 *SA* ἀ-φειδῶς Sa 7 4 *S* ἀ-φόβως, 19 6 *S* ἀ-βλαβής, Ez 7 22 *SB* ἀ-φυλάκτως, Ac 24 16 *S* (*B* ⲛⲁⲧ-) ἀ-πρόσκοπος, Va 66 295 *B* ⲁⲧⲛⲉⲣⲓⲙⲓ ἀ-δακρυτί; BM 253 2 *S* ⲉⲭⲛϣⲓⲡⲉ...ⲉ. ⲥⲱϣ, Mor 18 39 *S* ye have held service (συνάγειν) alone ⲁⲭⲛⲧ, BMar 6 *S* ⲉϥⲁⲡⲁⲭⲱⲣⲉⲓ ⲁ. ⲛⲉϥⲉⲓⲟⲧⲉ *apart from*, C 43 178 *B* that I may endure this fire ⲁ. ϩⲓⲧⲧ ⲉⲃⲟⲩⲛ ⲉⲛⲁⲓⲟⲣⲅⲁⲛⲟⲛ (instrument of torture), AM 58 *B* they beat him ⲁ. ϯⲁⲥⲟ, J 3 11 *S* ⲁ. ⲗⲁⲁⲩ ⲛⲕⲣⲟⲅϥ (var 9 29 ⲙⲛⲃⲟⲗ ⲛ-); verbal: Ep 141 *S* ⲁⲭⲛⲧⲣⲁⲧⲟϣϥ; ShC 42 34 *S* ⲧⲡⲓⲥⲧⲓⲥ, man cannot know God ⲉϫⲱⲥ *without it*, ib 42 impossible any should die ⲉϫⲱϥ *without Him*, ShC 73 113 ⲙⲡⲉϥϣⲱϥ...ⲛⲧⲉϥⲁⲡⲉ ⲉϫⲱⲓ (cf ib 171). On these 3 last cf Spg 13, 33 (but ? confusion with ⲉϫⲛ- *upon*. In Aeg 219 *S* ⲉϫⲛⲧϥ is from ⲉ. *without*, though = περιττόν).

ⲁϫⲛ- *AO* v ϫⲱ *head* (ⲉϫⲛ-).

ⲁϫⲛ- *B* v ϫⲛ-.

ⲁϫⲁⲩ *Sf* nn pl, meaning unknown: JKP 2 30 Solomon the just judge ⲉⲣⲉⲛⲓⲁ. ϩⲉⲛⲉⲃⲏⲓ...ⲉⲣⲉⲛ-ϫⲉⲙⲱⲛⲓⲱⲛ ϩⲉⲙⲡⲉⲃⲉⲓ. (?? for ⲁⲧϣⲁⲩ).

ⲁϫⲉⲩ *A* v ϣⲁⲩ *use*.

ⲁϭⲟ *B* ϫⲟ *armpit*.

ⲁϭⲃⲉⲥ, ⲁⲧⲃⲉⲥ *S* nn f (R, Ryl), *moisture*: Jer 17 8 (C 42 175, BMOr 8810 521, BAp 99, Hall 29, P 44 113, all ⲁⲧ.), Lu 8 6 (ⲁⲧ., ⲁϭ., *B* ϭⲛⲟⲛ) ἰκμάς; Job 14 9 ὀσμὴ ὕδατος; Ryl 94 109 (AZ 25 65) body crackles in flames ϩⲁⲧⲁϭ. ⲛⲧⲥⲁⲣⲝ, R 1 2 11 ⲛⲃⲁⲣⲟⲥ ⲛⲧⲁϭ. in cellar, P 131⁴ 99 heaven withstands sun's heat ⲉⲧⲃⲉ ⲧⲁϭ. of water above it, P 131⁵ 32 trees in desert with no ⲁⲧ. beneath them, ShA 1 449 tree's root ϩⲛⲟⲩⲕⲟⲩⲓ ⲛⲁⲧ., Mor 41 165 in hell great ⲁϭ. & cold. *Cf* ⲱϭⲃ, also LAl 52 n.

ⲙⲛⲧⲁⲧ. nn f: R 1 5 15, prob *l* -ⲁⲧⲥⲉⲓ as JA '75 5 ²⁴⁴.

ⲁϭⲟⲗⲧⲉ, ⲁⲕⲟⲗⲧⲉ (Tor 36) *SB*, ⲁϭⲁⲗⲧⲉ *S/A*, ⲁϫⲟⲗϯ *B* (C 89 only) nn f, *wagon, cart* (cf עֲגָלָה): Nu 7 3 *S* (*B* ⲙⲛⲫⲣⲉϩⲓ عجلة), 1 Kg 6 7 *S*, Si 36 5 *S*, Is 25 10 *S* (*B* ⲙⲛⲫⲣ.), 41 15 *S* (*B* do), Am 2 13 *SA* (*B* do), Jth 15 11 *S* ἅμαξα (ἅρμα never transl *S*, rarely *B*), C 89 56 *B* among agricult properties

ⲁϭ. عجلات, CO 138 *S* ⲧⲁⲕⲁⲗⲧⲉ ⲡⲣⲏⲃⲃⲉ (sic); ShC 42 83 women & children fleeing on beasts & ϩⲛⲡⲉϭⲁ., ib 87 ϩⲓⲛⲁ., Wess 11 153 ϩⲓⲧⲉϥⲁ., BM 348 *S* frozen lake bore ⲁ. ⲛⲃⲁⲓⲟⲩⲧⲁϩ, C 89 28 *B* (ⲁϫ. & ⲁϭ.) whereon corpse carried, bier نعش (cf PLond 5 103 *inf*), Tor 36 = ST 236 *S* loaded with firewood, BM 1152 *S* with earth, ST 37 *S* in sowing contract, obscure (seed-corn & cart in common ?), C 89 181 *B* at launch of boat monks quarrel ⲉⲩϯ ⲧⲱⲛ ⲛⲉⲙⲣⲁⲡⲁϫ. (? = ϫⲟⲣϯ); Is 28 27 *S* (*B* = Gk) ⲡⲕⲟⲧ...ⲛⲧⲁ. τρόχος ἁμ., Miss 8 227 *S* tortures ⲉⲧϩⲏⲣ more than wheels of ⲁ., Hall 108 *S* ⲧⲏⲛⲉ (q v) ⲛⲡⲉⲣⲧⲟⲛ (? ὄργανον) ⲉⲧⲛⲧⲟⲟⲧⲛ ⲉⲧⲉⲧⲁ. ⲧⲉ, ib ⲧⲧⲱⲣⲉ ⲛⲧⲁ., Glos 206 *S* sim = ἄξων, Mus 40 39 *S* ⲙⲣⲏϭ ⲡⲁ. *temo plaustri*; in astronomy, P 44 122 *S* ⲧⲁ. ⲙⲡⲉⲥⲣ ⲃⲟⲗ ⲙⲡⲉⲥⲧⲱϣ دورة الفلك لم تخرج عن (Bodl 325 96 دور الفلك = ⲡⲓⲕⲩⲕⲗⲟⲥ).

ⲁϭⲓⲛ ⲡⲥⲱⲟⲩ *B* v ϩⲁϭⲓⲛ.

ⲁϭⲟⲛ, ⲁϭⲁⲛ (AZ) *S* nn, a vessel or tank of metal: AZ 16 17 ⲟⲩⲁ. ⲛⲣⲟⲙⲡⲓⲧ; or of wood: PLond 4 517 ⲟⲩⲁ. ⲛϣⲉ[; Mor 25 14 ⲟⲩⲡ ⲟⲩⲟⲡ ⲉⲁϥϣⲓⲕⲉ ⲛⲣⲉⲛ-ⲛⲟϭ ⲛⲁ. & planted vineyards = *B* (Va 61 96) ⲉϥϣⲱⲕ ⲛⲣⲁⲡⲗⲁⲕⲕⲟⲥ (ref to Lu 12 18). For ? ⲗⲁⲕⲟⲛ (but v Ep 283 n).

ⲁϭⲛⲉ- *B* v ⲁϫⲛ-.

ⲁϭⲛⲓ *B* nn m (2 Chr Lag H), f (Deu), *blemish, stain*: Lev 24 19 (*S* = Gk), Deu 19 21 (*S* om), Dan 1 4 (*S* ϫⲃⲓⲛ) μῶμος; Job 14 4 (*S* ⲧⲱⲗⲙ) ῥύπος; Eph 5 27 (*S* ϫⲱⲣⲙ) σπίλος; 2 Chr 6 29 μαλακία; C 86 301 ϩⲗⲓ ⲡⲁ. ⲡⲧⲉ ⲡϫⲉⲙⲱⲛ κνίσα (?); MIE 2 365 virgin ⲉⲣⲉⲙⲙⲟⲛ ⲁ. ⲛϩⲏⲧⲥ, C 86 222 martyr emerges from cauldron ⲙⲙⲟⲛ ϩⲗⲓ ⲡⲁ. ⲛϩⲏⲧϥ.

ⲁⲧⲁ. privative adj, *stainless*: Ps 63 5 (*S* ⲉⲧⲟⲩⲁⲁⲃ), CaiEuch 331 hands ⲛⲁⲧⲁ. ⲟⲩⲟϩ ⲛⲁⲧⲑⲱⲗⲉⲃ ἄμωμος; ib 640 ἄχραντος; AM 270 ⲥⲛⲟϥ ⲛⲁⲧⲁ.

ⲙⲉⲧⲁⲧⲁ. nn f, *stainlessness*: Ps 14 2 (*S* ⲉⲧⲟⲩⲁⲁⲃ).

ⲉⲣ ⲁ., *be stained*: Cat 125 ⲛⲏ ⲉⲧⲟⲓ ⲛⲁ. ⲟⲩⲟϩ ⲉⲧⲑⲟⲗⲉⲃ.

ⲉⲣ ⲁⲧⲁ., *be stainless*: Ps 17 24 (*S* ϣⲱⲡⲉ...ⲟⲩⲁⲁⲃ), Col 1 22 (*S* ⲁⲧⲧⲱⲗⲙ) ἄμωμος.

ϩⲓ ⲁ., *cast a stain* c ⲛⲥⲁ-: Pro 9 7 (*S* diff) μω-μᾶσθαι, Ja 3 6 (*S* ϫⲱⲣⲙ) σπιλοῦν; c ⲉ-: Miss 4 137 ⲙⲡⲉⲣϩⲓ ⲁϭⲛⲓ (*l* ⲁϭ.) ⲉⲡⲙⲁ where God is (=*S* MR 4 73 ϫⲱⲣⲙ, sic *l*).

ⲁϭⲡⲥ (ⲟⲩⲁϭⲡⲥ) *S* v ⲟⲩⲱϭⲡ.

ⲁϭⲣⲏⲛ *SBA*, ⲁⲧϭⲣⲏⲛ (ⲁⲧ- ? privat) *AB* nn f (1 Kg 2 5, Is 54 1), *barren female*: Ge 11 30 *SB*, Ex 23 26 *S* (ⲁⲧϣⲏⲣⲉ ⲟⲩⲇⲉ ⲁ.) *B*, Is 54 1 *SA* (El 80) *B*, Lu 1 7 *SB*, pl ib 23 29 στεῖρα; Bor 226 158 *S* soul ⲟⲩⲁ. ϩⲛⲡⲁⲣⲉⲧⲏ; Pcod 30 *S* He made

Abimelech's house ⲛⲁ., BM 1223 *A* ⲁⲕⲁⲉⲥ ⲛⲁ.;
of *sterile male*: J 76 50 *S* ⲟⲩⲁ. ⲡⲓⲣⲟⲟⲩⲧ (*l* ⲛϥ.).

ⲙⲛⲧⲁ. *S* nn f, *barrenness*: Deu 7 14 (*B* ⲁ.) στεῖρα.

ⲣ ⲁ. *SA*, *be barren*: Si 42 13 *S* στειροῦσθαι.

ⲁϭⲟⲧⲉ *S* nn f, *meaning unknown*: Ryl 234 in

account with dates & Muslim names, 4 times, *e g* ⲡⲉⲡⲥⲓⲧⲉ ⲛⲁ., ⲟⲩⲙⲛⲧⲉ ⲛⲁ. Before or after ⲁ. always ⲥⲁⲧⲁⲕⲉ.

ⲁϭⲟⲟⲩⲣ (? or ⲁϭⲟⲟⲩⲣⲉ) *S* nn m, *meaning unknown*: WS 96 let one go north ⲛⲃⲙⲟⲩⲧⲛ (? ⲙⲟⲩⲧⲉ ⲛ-) ⲡⲉⲓⲁ.

ⲃ

ⲃ, second letter of alphabet, called ⲃⲏⲧⲁ *S* (My 61), ⲃⲓⲇⲁ *B* ويضا (K 1, Stern p 418). As numeral *BF*, rarely *S* (Br), = *two*, f ⲃ︤ⲧ = ⲥⲛⲟⲩⲧ. Derived mostly from hierogl. *b*, as ⲁⲃⲱ, ⲃⲁⲕⲓ, ⲃⲗⲃⲓⲗⲉ, ⲉⲓⲃ, ⲕⲃⲁ, ⲗⲁⲃⲟⲓ, ⲙⲃⲱ (Ombos), ⲓⲛⲃⲓ, ⲟⲩⲣⲉ, ⲥⲃⲱ, ⲧⲱⲱⲃⲉ, ⲟⲩⲱⲧⲃ, ⲣⲏⲃⲉ, ϭⲱⲃ; rarely from *p*, as ⲉⲃⲣⲁ, ⲥⲟⲃⲧⲉ, ⲱⲃⲧ. Dialectal equivalents: **a.** *S* ⲃ = *B* ⲡ, as ⲙⲁⲁⲃ, ⲥⲓⲃ, ⲧⲟⲃϥ, ϣⲱⲃ, ϣⲱⲣⲃ, also *B* ⲃ = *F* ⲡ in ⲃⲓⲛⲁϫ & ⲡⲓⲛⲉϭ. **b.** *S* ⲡ = *B* ⲃ, as ⲡⲡ(ⲛ)ⲏ, ⲡⲉⲡⲓⲡⲉ, ⲙⲡⲟ, ⲙⲡⲁⲓ, ⲧⲟⲡ. **c.** *S* ⲃ = *B* ϥ, ⲫ, as ⲥⲃⲏⲧⲉ, ϣⲏⲣ, ϭⲃⲟⲓ, converse in ⲟⲩϥ. **d.** *S* ⲃ = *BF* ⲙ, as ⲣⲓⲡⲛⲃ, ⲥⲁⲧⲃⲉ, ϭⲉⲣⲱⲃ, ϫⲉⲙϣⲁⲓ & ϫⲉⲃ-ϣⲁⲓ both *B*, ϫⲗⲱⲃ & ϫⲗⲱⲙ both *S*, *cf* also ⲣⲁ-ⲃⲓⲟⲩⲓ & ⲁⲙⲏ, ⲧⲥⲁⲃⲟ & ⲧⲥⲁⲙⲟ (PLond 4 519), converse in ⲡⲓⲙ, ⲧⲱⲗⲙ. **e.** *S* ⲃ = *B* ⲛ, as ⲥⲟⲧⲃⲉϥ. **f.** *S* ⲃ = *B* ⲟⲩ in ⲃⲟⲓⲛⲉ, converse in ϣⲟⲩⲉ. Occasional, irregular variants: **g.** replaces ϥ, ⲫ, as ⲃ-, ⲉⲃ-, ⲃⲓ, ⲃⲟⲣⲉ (φορεῖν Z 632), ⲃⲱⲧⲉ, ⲃⲧⲟⲟⲩ, ⲛⲟⲃⲣⲉ, ⲗⲉⲃ- (*F*), ⲥⲡⲟⲃ, ⲧⲏⲣⲃ, ϣⲃⲉ, ϣⲡⲃⲉ. **h.** replaced by ϥ, ⲫ, as ⲉϥⲓⲱ, ⲉϥⲣⲏϭⲉ (Jer 10 13), ⲧⲁϥⲣⲓⲏⲗ (RAl 129), ⲁϥⲃⲁⲕⲟⲩⲙ (ClPr 25 2), ⲧⲉϥⲃⲏⲩ (*ib*), ⲣⲏϥⲉ (Mor 31 174), ⲃⲏϥ (ShA 2 252), ϥⲓⲣ (WS 153), ϥⲣⲉϥⲟⲥ (Mor 34 16) ⲫⲣⲟⲛ-ⲧⲓϫⲉ P 44 91, ϥⲣⲟⲩⲭⲟⲥ (Ps 104 34), ⲙⲉϥⲣⲱⲛ μέμβρανον (BM 704), these 2 changes oftenest in *F*. **i.** replaces ⲛ rarely, as ⲉⲃⲉⲑⲉⲙⲓ (JKP 2 46), ⲗⲉⲃⲧⲟⲛ (Lu 12 59 *B*); converse often in *B*, as ⲉⲣⲧⲟⲛ, ⲁⲣⲏⲡ (Va 66 304), ⲛⲟⲩⲡ (Cat 158), ⲟⲛϣ- (Va 62 278) ⲡⲉϩ- (Job 9 27), ϣⲱⲡⲧ (Job 12 20), ⲣⲟⲡⲥ- (*ib* 21 26), also *S*: ⲉⲙⲡⲟⲗⲏ (Kr 200), ⲡⲗⲁⲡ-ⲧⲉⲓ (BMis 531, *cf* C 89 13 *B* ⲙⲛⲡⲗⲁⲡⲧⲓⲛ). **j.** replaces ⲟⲩ, as ⲁⲃⲏⲧ, ⲃⲟⲥⲣ, ⲃⲉⲥⲱⲡ, ⲃⲱϭⲙ, ⲣⲁ-ⲃⲛⲟⲩⲧ, ϣⲃⲱⲃ, ϣⲁⲣⲃⲱⲧ & *v* in Gk diphthongs, as ⲉⲃⲥⲉⲃⲏⲥ (BMis 428), ⲑⲁⲃⲙⲁϫⲉ (*ib* 276), ⲭⲗⲓⲃⲁϫⲉ (χλευάζειν *ib* 270), ⲥⲕⲏⲃⲩ (σκεύη CO 172), ⲧⲩⲃⲗⲉⲣⲁ (δεύτερα J 12 70); lost in ⲉⲣⲏϥⲟⲥ. (βρέφος AZ 52 126). **k.** replaced by ⲟⲩ, as ⲑⲟⲩⲁⲓ, ⲟⲩⲛⲏⲃ (ⲃⲏⲃ BAp 79), ⲁⲅⲁⲕⲟⲩⲙ (BMis 305), ⲉⲩⲉⲓⲏⲛ (J 73 3), ⲉⲣⲧⲁⲩ (BMis 494), ⲥⲧⲁⲩⲗⲟⲛ (BAp 110). **l.** where Arabic transcribed, ⲃ represents ﺏ: ⲁⲃⲟⲩ- (oftener ⲁⲡⲟⲩ-), ⲁⲃⲁ-, ⲑⲉⲃⲓⲧ, ⲧⲁⲃⲃⲁⲣ; or ﻦ: ⲃⲁⲣⲁϭ, ⲃⲁϯⲙⲁ (BM 586), *cf* AZ 23 118; or ﻮ: ⲁⲕⲃⲉ أقوي, ⲃⲉϫⲓⲁ وردبعة, ⲧⲁⲩⲃⲁⲣ دوّار, ⲃⲉ- (all EW 234 ff); or is represented by ﺏ: شبرا برابارة (ϫⲉⲃⲣⲟ); or ﻒ: منفلوط فرجوط اصفون ادفون (ⲡⲁⲙⲉⲃⲟ), or ﻮ: بمفوا واطس (ⲃⲁⲧⲟⲥ), وبما (ⲃⲏⲥⲁ); واحس (Bacchus), sometimes strengthened by ⲡ: ⲉⲃⲡⲛⲉ ابن (Kr 11 *F*). **m.** In Latin words (through Gk) ⲃ represents *v*: ⲃⲉⲣⲉⲧⲁⲣⲓⲟⲥ, ⲃⲉⲥⲧⲓⲧⲱⲣ (BM 1146), ⲃⲏⲗ-ⲗⲟⲛ (BSM 66), ⲫⲗⲁⲃⲓⲁⲛⲟⲥ. **n.** ⲃ doubled in old *S* MSS, = ⲛⲃ: ⲃⲃⲁⲗ, ⲃⲃⲟⲗ, ⲃⲃⲟⲧⲉ, *cf* also ⲃⲃⲣⲏϭⲉ (Ps 96 4, Apoc 11 19), ⲙⲏⲃⲃⲉ Memphis (LCyp), *cf* ⲛⲃⲃⲣⲟⲩⲭⲟⲥ (Joel 1 4 *A*). It is omitted in ⲟⲩⲉ = ⲟⲩⲃⲉ (PS, BKU 1 23). **o.** inserted between ⲙ & ⲣ: ⲁⲙⲃⲣⲉ, ⲁⲙⲃⲣⲟⲥ ('Amrû, *cf* BM 1090 ⲁⲃⲣⲟⲥ), ⲉⲙⲃⲣⲱ, ⲉⲙⲃⲣⲉⲣⲓ, ⲙⲃⲣⲓⲥ, separates syllables: ⲡⲣⲟⲃⲁⲥⲧⲓⲟⲛ (BMar 82, ⲡⲁⲟⲩⲃⲏ (Ναυή C 89 83); *cf* ⲑⲃⲃⲓⲟ *S* for ⲑⲃⲓⲟ (Lam 3 16 in P 130⁴ 148), ⲃⲓⲃⲣⲟⲥ, ⲃⲓϥⲣⲟⲥ Βῆρρος Verus (BAp 54, Mis 69).

ⲃⲁ, ⲃⲁⲉ (ShR 2 3 47, Mun 110), ⲃⲁⲉⲓ (J 111 8), ⲃⲟⲓ (PMéd 320) *S*, ⲃⲁⲉ *AA²*, ⲃⲁⲓ *B*, ⲃⲉⲓ, ⲃⲉⲉⲓ (BM 528), ⲃⲁⲉⲓ (BKU 1 21) *F* nn m, once f (K 141) = βάϊον, جربدة سعف (K 263, Dif 1 34, *cf* Rec 16 97), *branch of date-palm*: Jo 12 13 *SAA²B* βάϊον, C 41 19 *B* ⲃ. ⲛⲃⲉⲛⲓ, Gu 65, FR 74 *S* sim, N&E 39 340 *B* ⲣⲁⲛⲃⲁⲓⲃⲏⲧ in their hands; opp ⲃⲉⲛⲓ MG 25 87 *B*; as victor's crown 1 Cor 9 24 *B* (*S* ⲕⲗⲟⲙ) βραβεῖον; for decorating houses, streets: Aeg 39 *B* ⲣⲁⲛⲃ. ⲛⲃⲛⲧ, ShR 2 3 47 *S* rich pagan ⲡⲉⲧⲟⲩϫ[ⲉ]ⲃ. ⲉⲃⲟⲗ ⲙⲡⲉϥⲏⲓ; as staff: C 41 42 *B* he struck earth with ⲕⲟⲩϫⲓ ⲛⲃ. ⲉⲧϫⲉⲛⲧⲉϥϫⲓⲝ, Va 59 158 *B* ϣⲃⲱⲧ ⲛⲃ. βάϊνη ῥάβδος (var βάϊον) carried by Macarius, AM 190 *B*, MG 25 335 *B*, EW 159 *B* sim, PMéd 320 *S* stir mixture with ⲟⲩⲃ. ⲉϥⲗⲏⲕ, *cf* AZ 23 106 *S* ⲣⲉⲣⲃ[ⲟⲟ]ϭⲉ; as scourge: BMar 14 *S* soldiers ⲙⲉϩ ⲡⲉⲩϭⲓϫ ⲛⲃ. & beat him, Mor 41 338 *S* ⲁⲩⲧⲣⲟⲩⲥⲱⲗⲡ ⲛϩⲟⲩⲱⲧ ⲛⲃ. ϩⲓⲡⲉϥⲥⲱⲙⲁ, EW 88 *B* ⲁⲩⲕⲱϣ ⲛⲣ̄ ⲙⲃ. ⲉⲧⲗⲏⲕ ⲉϫⲱϥ; as measure

of length : BM 528 F (cf قصب), PLich fields measured by ⲛⲃ. ⲛⲡⲙⲟⲛⲁⲥⲧⲏⲣⲓⲟⲛ ; as door screen :
Z 352 S ⲟⲩⲣⲟ ⲛⲃ. ; as roofing : MG 25 87 B
ⲃⲉⲡⲓ, ⲃ. & ⲕⲁϣ for covering monks' caves ; for
making baskets : Z 344 S = MG 25 209 B ϩⲉⲛⲃ.
from ἕλος.

V ⲃⲛⲛⲉ, ⲃⲏⲧ, ⲕⲁⲃⲁⲓ, ϣⲉ blow.

ⲃⲁ S nn f, ? threshing-floor : SHel 86 husbandman with fan ⲛϥϫⲟⲕⲙⲁⲍⲉ ⲡⲧⲉϥⲃⲁ, lest he find
no meal therein, but merely ⲕⲟⲩⲕⲉ (cf Mt 3 12).
J 57 8 ⲧⲃⲁⲉ (? place) might contain this.

ⲃⲁ SA in ϣⲁⲣⲃⲁ q v.

ⲃⲁ- SB in names of metals : v ⲃⲉⲛⲓⲡⲉ (ⲃⲁ-),
ⲃⲁⲣⲱⲧ, ⲃⲁⲥⲡϭ.

ⲃⲁⲉ A, ⲃⲁⲓ B v ⲃⲁ.

ⲃⲁⲓ, ⲃⲉⲓ sky in ⲡⲣⲟⲩⲃⲃⲁⲓ q v.

ⲃⲁⲓ- v ϥⲓ, also ⲕⲁϩ, ⲙⲟⲟⲩ, ϭⲓϫ.

ⲃⲁⲓ, ϥⲁⲓ SB, ⲃⲁⲩ B (Deu 14 17 in Va 1) nn m,
a. night raven : Lev 11 17 S, Deu 14 17 S, 1 Kg
26 20 S, Ps 101 6 S νυκτικόραξ (untranslated ShC
42 51). In Lev, Ps = B ⲙⲟⲩⲗⲁⲝ, in Deu these
distinct, former = ساف . b. screech-owl : P 44
56 S βοῦβος (bubo) بوم (v ⲃⲟⲙ), P 43 23 S هام =
ام قويق with gloss در soul, بعجة bogey (cf ? below
ⲃⲁⲓ spirit & ⲉⲗϭⲱⲃ), K 169 = ⲕⲁⲕⲕⲁⲙⲁⲩ (κικ-
καβαῦ IgR 77). For قويق ام v also ⲕⲟⲩⲕ nn f.
Perhaps in name ⲡⲃⲁⲉⲓ Christian. Vostok 1 48.

ⲃⲁⲓ O nn, ⲛⲉⲃ ⲃⲁⲓ, lord of spirit(s), DM 28 1,
gloss. βαί = ψυχή, acc. to Horapollo 1 vii. Cf ?
above, ⲃⲁⲓ owl as soul, also in gnostic name ⲃⲁⲓ
ⲛϫⲭⲱⲱϫ spirit of darkness (Erman Aegypt. Relig.²
250) & in βαινεφώθ Glos 405 (v ⲉϥⲱⲧ), cf AZ
62 35.

ⲃⲏ SB nn f, grave : Mt 23 29 B (many varr. ⲃⲏⲃ,
q v, prob error, so too Nah 2 12 B = S ⲙϩⲁⲁⲩ
μνημεῖον). Is dug Tob 8 9 (10) S, is filled in ib 18,
Leip 24 31 B, all man's glory ϧⲉϧ ϣⲁϯⲃⲏ, ShA 1
65 S, shall we purify selves of all evil in ⲃⲏ, or at
God's judgement seat ?

ⲃⲓ v ϥⲓ,

ⲃⲟ v ϥⲟ.

ⲃⲟⲓ v ⲃⲁ palm branch.

ⲃⲟⲓ (ϣⲁⲧⲃⲟⲓ) v ϥⲱ.

ⲃⲱ hair v ϥⲱ.

ⲃⲱ SA²BF, ⲃⲟⲩ A nn f, tree where its fruit
specified, opp ϣⲏⲛ (eg Ps 104 33) tree in general.
V ⲉⲗⲟⲟⲗⲉ, ⲕⲛⲧⲉ, ⲥⲧⲟⲓ, ⲧⲱⲣⲉ. ϫⲛⲡⲉϩ, ϫⲟⲉⲓⲧ,

ϭⲗⲟϭ ; ShP 130² 27 ⲃ. ⲛⲟⲩⲟⲟⲧⲉ. Properly wood,
plantation of trees, v Berl. Wörterb 1 416.

ⲃⲏⲃ SABF(Bal), ⲃⲏⲃⲉ (? pl only R 1 2 72) nn m
(ⲃⲏⲃⲉ in place-name J 118 4 S is f.), cave, hole,
den, nest of animals : Ps 103 22 S μάνδρα, Jer 12
9 S σπήλαιον, Nah 2 12 AB νοσσία, Mt 8 20 SB
φωλεός, MG 25 271 B (ib = ⲙⲟϩ), ShA 1 39 S ;
birds : AZ 33 54 F (swallow's, used in medicine
PMéd 305) ; insects : (ant's Bor 233 231, wild bee's ?
ShP 130² 25, v ⲃⲟⲗⲃⲗ) ; demons : ShA 1 433 S ;
thieves : Jer 7 11 B, Mk 11 17 B σπήλαιον ; fugitives : 1 Kg 24 4 B, Heb 11 38 B (S ⲉⲓⲁ) σπ. ;
hermits : BAp 79 S, RChamp 371 S, MIE 2 344
B, Z 342 S, Miss 4 651 S, J 75 16 S, cf Ep 1 226 ;
cleft in rock : Jer 13 4 B τρυμαλία. Confused with
ⲃⲏ, Nah 2 12 B, Mt 23 29 B.

ⲃⲏⲃ S nn f, meaning unknown : Ep 543 in list
of σκεύη (vessels &c), Ryl 240 ?

ⲃⲁⲁⲃⲉ SA, ⲃⲁⲃⲱ- (Bor 265 86 ⲛϣⲁⲕⲃⲁⲃⲱ
ⲡⲣⲉϥⲣ ⲛⲟⲃⲉ, BM 180 ⲙⲡⲉϥⲃ. ⲡϣⲁϫⲉ), ⲃⲁⲃⲱⲟⲩⲥ,
ⲃⲁⲃⲟⲧ† & ⲃⲁⲃⲱⲧ†, p c ⲃⲁⲃⲉ- (ⲃ. ⲣⲱⲙⲉ) vb I. intr,
be insipid : of salt, Mt 5 13 S (B ⲗⲱϧ) μωραίνειν ;
of food, Miss 4 284 S ; of wine, Mich '21 S recipe
ⲏⲣⲡ ⲉϥⲃⲁⲃⲱ ⲡⲟⲩϣⲏⲙ ; be foolish : of words, PSBA
32 251 S ; of conduct, Bor 258 41 S ⲡⲉⲧⲃⲁⲃⲱ
ϩⲛⲧⲁⲛⲟⲙⲓⲁ, paral ib ⲡⲧⲁⲕⲛⲟⲥ ϩⲙⲡⲛⲟⲃⲉ. II. tr,
regard as foolish, despise : Gal 4 14 S (B diff)
ἐκπτύειν, BMar 199 S ϣⲁⲣⲃⲁⲃⲱⲟⲧ because I am
wretched ὑπερηφανεῖν, TU 43 17 A ⲥⲉⲛⲁϩⲱⲡⲉ ⲉϥ-
ⲃⲁⲃⲉ ⲛⲙⲁⲩ, BAp 166 S ⲁⲕⲥⲱϣⲧ ⲁⲕⲃⲁⲃⲱⲟⲧ,
BMis 3 S, Mus 40 274 S sim, Mor 43 274 S if
rich man bequeath naught, he is despised ⲛⲥⲉ-
ⲃⲁⲃⲱⲟⲩϥ ϩⲙⲡⲉϥⲥⲙⲟⲩ.

—— + ⲣⲱⲙⲉ nn, boaster : Pro 21 24 SA, Ro 1
30 S (B ϩⲓ ⲡϧⲟ), 2 Tim 3 2 S (B ⲉⲥⲓⲉ) ἀλαζών ;
ShC 42 84 S, ShZ 476 S.

ⲙⲛⲧⲃ. ⲣⲱⲙⲉ SA nn f, boastfulness : Sa 5 8 S,
Cl 13 1 A ἀλαζονεία, ShBMOr 8800 5 S = R 2 3
10 ⲡⲉⲧⲕⲁⲧⲁⲫⲣⲟⲛⲉⲓ...ϩⲟⲩⲙ. ⲙⲛⲧⲣⲉϥⲃ. AZ 12
128 S (prob ⲃ. ⲣⲱⲙⲉ).

ⲃⲉⲉⲃⲉ, ⲃⲉⲃⲉ S, ⲃⲉⲃⲉ A (Pro 18 4), ⲃⲉⲃⲓ B
(R 2 1 12 S ⲃⲉⲃⲟⲩ sic, but is this word intended ?)
vb I. intr a. ⲃ. ⲉϩⲣⲁⲓ, bubble, well up : of a spring
Pro 18 4 S, FR 26 S, of evil passions R 2 2 32 S
= BHom 48 ⲃ. ⲉⲧⲡⲉ. b. ⲃ. ⲉⲡϣⲱⲓ of soil freshly
thrown up EW 37 B (but cf BAp 58), of tumours,
worms Va 57 177 B ⲉⲩⲃ. ⲉⲡϣⲱⲓ...ⲛϫⲉ ϩⲁⲡⲙⲟⲩⲙⲓ
ⲡϭⲉⲡⲧ βρύειν.

II. tr pour forth, bring forth, rain down : Si 10
13 S ἐξομβρεῖν, ib 18 28 S ἀνομβρεῖν Ps 44 2 B
(S ⲧⲁϩⲟ ⲉⲃⲟⲗ), ib 143 14 B (S ⲡⲱⲛ ⲉⲃ.) ἐξερεύγειν,

Ps 104 30 B (S ⲧⲁⲅⲟ ⲉⲃ., ⲉϩⲣⲁⲓ), Ja 3 11 B (S ⲧⲁⲅⲟ ⲉϩ.) βρύειν, MG 25 367 B ⲉϥⲃ. ⲙ̄ⲡⲥⲁϫⲓ ⲙ̄ⲡⲓⲣⲙⲟⲧ. With nn: ⲙⲟⲩ ⲛⲃ. S ⲙⲱⲟⲩ ⲙⲃ. B Ps 77 44 ὄμβρημα.

ⲣⲉϥⲃ. B, *bringer forth*: Va 60 123 ⲟⲩⲣ. ⲡⲧⲉ ϯⲙⲉⲑⲙⲏⲓ.

ⲙⲉⲧⲣⲉϥⲃ. nn f, *outpouring*: of a spring Va 58 III ⲟⲩⲙ. ⲉϩⲣⲏⲓ ⲛ̄ⲟⲩⲙⲱⲟⲩ.

ϫⲓⲛⲃ. B nn m, *pronouncing* of a name: MG 25 160.

ⲃⲏⲃⲉ, ⲧ- nn f, in Theban place-name J 118 4 S, *cf* Ep 1 122.

ⲃⲟⲩⲃⲟⲩ (Mor 42 54 ⲃⲟⲩⲃⲉ) S vb intr, *shine, glitter*: of σπινθήρ Br 238, of ἀκτίς BAp 80, of person FR 14 S, of face JA '05 1 416 ⲉⲣⲉⲡⲉⲩϩⲟ ⲃ. ⲉⲩⲟ ⲛ̄ⲗⲁⲙⲡⲣⲟⲛ, P 131¹ 32 (*cf* PG 61 763) ⲉⲣⲉⲡⲉⲃⲏⲧ (of Cross) ⲃ. ⲉϩⲟⲩⲉ ⲉⲛⲟⲩⲟⲉⲓⲛ, Bor 289 57, J 106 42 the monastery ⲉⲧⲃ. ϩⲛ̄ⲡⲉϥⲁⲕⲧⲓⲛ; less clearly PS 171, Br 50, 139.

—— nn, Br 227, of sun R 1 3 64, of stars Wess 18 85.

ⲃⲱⲱⲃⲉ, ⲃⲟⲟⲃⲉ *v* ⲃⲱⲱⲡ.

ⲃⲁⲃⲟⲧ *v* ⲃⲁⲁⲃⲉ.

ⲃⲁⲕ-, in ⲃⲁⲕⲙⲁⲧⲟⲩ, ⲃⲁⲕⲱⲡⲉ *v* ⲃⲱⲕ vb; in ⲃⲁⲕϣⲁⲣ *v* ⲃⲱⲕⲉ.

ⲃⲏⲕ S nn f, as boundary of land: J 5 31, *ib* R 2 ⲡⲣⲏⲥ ⲧⲃ.; or ? f name (occupant of adjoining land), *cf* Ⲧⲃⲉ̄ⲕⲓⲥ (ⲧⲃⲏϭ).

ⲃⲏⲕ (?) S nn m, in list of utensils, tools &c: Ep 547 ⲗⲓⲧⲣⲁ ⲛ̄ⲃ. ⲉϥϩⲟⲥⲉ.

ⲃⲱⲕ, ⲃⲁⲕ, ⲃⲏⲕ† SAA²B (B only C 86 115, 120 ff ϥⲱⲕ, ϥⲏⲕ) F (BM 1241), p c ⲃⲁⲕ-. All refs are S except where marked. In B generally = ϣⲉ, in F ⲡⲱⲧ. vb **I.** intr **a.** literal, *go, depart*: Eccl 5 14, Lu 4 30 πορεύεσθαι; Sa 4 20, Tob 10 1 ἔρχεσθαι; Ge 29 7, Mt 20 5 ἀπέρχ.; Ge 22 5 διέρχ.; Mk 10 52, Jo 14 28 SA² ὑπάγειν; Ps 54 15, Ac 8 15 καταβαίνειν; Pro 8 20† ἀναστρέφεσθαι; Ex 4 18 βαδίζειν; Mt 2 13 ἀναχωρεῖν; Si 48 22 ἀπαίρειν; Ge 12 19 ἀποτρέχειν; BG 135, ShC 73 26, 47; of a ship: Z 232, Pcod 17; c ethic dat: BHom 93, Ryl 158, Ep 182, 281, CO 107; merely approximate: Mk 11 23, Ac 27 32, Gal 2 13, or additional: Jos 2 5, 1 Kg 19 5, *ib* 20 22, Eccl 9 3, Mk 5 13. **b.** metaphor: for *die* Job 14 10, Mk 4 38, Pcod 20, 30, J 106 62, *cf* Pro 10 7 A 24 20 A σβέννυσθαι (both S ϫⲉⲛⲁ), Mic 4 9 A ἀπολλύεσθαι. **c.** *be about to*: P 129¹⁷ 81 = Mor 17 21 ⲉϥⲃⲏⲕ ⲉϩⲉ ⲉϩⲣⲁⲓ μέλλειν, Mor 28 146 ⲁⲓⲃ. ϫⲉⲉⲓⲛⲁⲧⲛ̄ⲛⲟⲟⲩ ⲡⲥⲱ, *cf* Ge 15 17. **d.** quasi-

auxil: ShZ 592 18, ShA 2 146, Pcod 21. **e.** c cognate obj.: Ps 8, 286. **f.** with nn: Cai 8013 ⲡⲙⲁ ⲛⲃ. ⲙ̄ⲡⲁⲓⲉⲧⲟⲥ (*cf* Pro 24 54), BM 253 1 at Judgement ⲉⲙ̄ⲡ ⲙⲁ ⲛⲃ., Miss 4 777, BMis 148 ϩⲓⲏ ⲛⲃ., Tor 29 ⲕⲁⲙⲏⲗⲉ ⲛⲃ.

V also ⲙⲧⲱ, ϩⲁⲥⲓⲉ.

With following preposition:

—— ⲉ-, *go, depart to* (not of persons): Gk mostly as above, but Ge 7 15 εἰσέρχ., Aeg 211 εἰσιέναι; *reach*: Is 24 22 γίνεσθαι ἐπί acc., PS 243, BMis 161; *befit, suit*: PMéd 103, CO 459.

—— ⲉⲣⲛ-, *go to* (of places): Ac 12 12 ἔρχ. ἐπί; Z 231.

—— ⲉⲣⲁⲧ-, *go to, visit, frequent* (of persons): Mk 14 10 ἀπέρχ. πρός; Hos 5 13 SA πορεύ. πρός; PS 178, BIF 13 119 (=B MG 25 313 ϩⲓ ⲕⲟⲧ), J 70 23.

—— ⲉϫⲛ-, *go upon*: 1 Kg 1 11, Jer 3 16 ἀναβαίν.; Deu 33 36 ἐπιβαίν.; BMis 175.

—— ⲛ̄ⲧⲛ-, *go from*, quit: Ac 16 19, ἐξέρχ.; BHom 5 ἐάν τι ἀπολέσωμεν; Miss 4 817, BIF 14 171, Mor 19 14 of eyesight ⲡⲁⲟⲩⲟⲉⲓⲛ ⲛⲁⲃ. ⲛ̄ⲧⲟⲟⲧ (var Mor 18 7 ⲡⲱⲧ, B ϩⲱⲗ).

—— ⲛ̄ⲡⲁϩⲣⲛ-, *go to* (of persons): Ge 15 15 ἀπέρχ. πρός; Ac 28 26 πορεύ. πρός.

—— ϣⲁ-, *go to* (of persons): Ex 3 11, Mt 26 14 πορεύ. πρός; Ge 32 6 ἔρχ. πρός; Jo 6 68, Ap 19 9 ἀπέρχ. πρός; Lu 2 15 διέρχ. ἕως; Nu 21 7 παραγίν. πρός; Pcod 46 (sexual, *cf* ⲃ. ⲉϩⲟⲩⲛ).

—— ϩⲁϫⲛ- A, *go toward*: El 86.

—— ϩⲁ-, *go (from) under*: 2 Cor 11 25 ναυάγειν.

—— ϩⲓ- **a.** *go upon* (a road): Ps 80 13 πορεύ. dat; Pro 1 15 πορεύ. ἐν; Jos 23 14 ἀποτρέχ. acc; J 65 51. **b.** *undergo, incur*: Mor 28 269 king to martyr ϩⲉⲛⲛⲟϭ ⲛ̄ⲧⲓⲙⲱⲣⲓⲁ ⲛ̄ⲃⲱⲕ ϩⲓⲱⲟⲩ.

—— ϩⲓⲧⲛ-, *go through, traverse*: Sa 5 7 διοδεύειν (*cf* ⲃ. ⲉⲃⲟⲗ ϩⲛ-); *quit*: BAp 81, J 67 24, CO 324.

—— ϩⲁϩⲧⲛ-, *go, appear before*: J 30 6.

—— ϩⲓϫⲛ-, *go from off*: Nu 12 10 ἀφιστάναι ἀπό (var ⲥⲟⲟϩⲉ ⲉⲃⲟⲗ ϩⲓϫⲛ-).

With following adverb:

—— ⲉⲃⲟⲗ, *go forth*: Deu 20 1, Lu 14 18 ἐξέρχ.; Ru 2 2 Mt 22 9 πορεύ.; Mk 1 5 ἐκπορ.; Ex 21 5, Su 7 ἀποτρέχ.; ShC 42 226, BHom 112, CA 111. As nn m: Sa 3 3, f *ib* 7 6 ϭⲓⲛⲃ. ⲉⲃ.

—— ⲉⲃⲟⲗ ϩⲛ-, *go through*: Mt 4 24 ἀπέρχ. εἰς, Lu 8 39 ἀπέρχ. κατά; 1 Kg 9 4 διέρχ.; Sa 11 2 διοδεύειν; Mk 9 30 παραπορεύ.; ShC 73 46, MG 17 331. *Cf* B ϩⲓⲧⲉⲛ-. Here ϩⲛ- often = ⲉⲃ. ϩⲛ-: Mt 19 15, Mk 7 19, Ac 18 7, ShC 73 46 ⲉⲧⲣⲉⲩⲃ. ⲉⲃ. (ⲉⲃ.) ⲡⲣⲏⲧⲉ. *V* Stern 532, 556 *s f*.

—— ⲉⲃⲟⲗ ϩⲓⲧⲛ-, *quit*, = last: Lu 1 38 ἀπέρχ.

ἀπό; Ac 1 21 ἐξέρχ. ἐπί; Z 306 ἀφιστ. ἀπό; Br 258, ShC 73 35, BMar 32.

—— ⲉⲡⲁϩⲟⲩ, *go behind*: Mt 16 23 ὑπάγειν ὀπίσω; *recede*: Jo 6 66 ἀπέρχ. εἰς τὰ ὀπ. *Cf B* ϩⲓⲡⲁϩⲟⲩ.

—— ⲉⲡⲉⲥⲏⲧ, *go down*: Ez 32 21, Ac 10 20 καταβαίν.; BHom 129, BMis 270.

—— ⲉⲑⲏ, *go forward*: Mk 13 45 προέρχ.

—— ⲉϩⲟⲩⲛ, *go in, enter*, Pro 10 2, Mt 23 14 εἰσέρχ.; *sexually* Ge 16 2, Mt 1 18 do; Mt 15 17, Lu 18 24 εἰσπορεύ.; Pro 25 17 εἰσάγειν πόδα; Mt 26 18 ὑπάγειν εἰς; Nu 18 22 προσέρχ. εἰς; BG 69, PS 106, Leyd 444, MR 5 45, BAp 98, J 75 17. With nn: ⲙⲁ ⲛⲃ. ⲉϩⲟⲩⲛ, Ps 18 6 κατάντημα; Pro 8 3 εἴσοδος (*cf* ϭⲓⲛ ⲛⲃ. ⲉϩⲟⲩⲛ). ϭⲓⲛⲃ. ⲉϩⲟⲩⲛ nn f, *entry*: LMär 19.

—— ⲉϩⲣⲁⲓ a. *go up*: Nu 13 18, Eccl 3 21, Ac 10 9 ἀναβαίν.; Jos 15 6 προσαναβ.; R 1 1 44 ἀναλαμβάνειν; Lu 24 51 ἀναφέρεσθαι; BHom 30 ἀνέρχ.; Ac 1 10 πορεύ. εἰς. nn f ϭⲓⲛⲃ. ⲉϩⲣⲁⲓ BMis 65. b. *go down*, less often: Cant 5 1, Ez 32 18, Ac 8 38 καταβαίν.; Ps 104 23 εἰσέρχ.; 1 Tim 1 6 ἐκτρέπειν; Aeg 256. c. *go*: Ge 12 5, Jud 16 1, Ps 106 7 πορεύ. εἰς; Lev 25 10, Mt 28 10 ἀπέρχ. εἰς; Mk 5 19, Jo 7 3 ὑπάγειν εἰς; Jer 50 7 εἰσέρχ. εἰς; Mt 2 14 ἀναχωρεῖν εἰς; Lu 13 22 πορεύ. εἰς; J 106 207 (*cf* 91 28). With nn: ⲙⲁ ⲛⲃ. ⲉϩⲣⲁⲓ, Am 9 6 *SA* ἀνάβασις; JTS 4 396 = Va 61 116 B ⲙⲱⲓⲧ ⲛϣⲉ ⲉⲡϣⲱⲓ; ϩⲓⲏ ⲛⲃ. ⲉϩⲣⲁⲓ Jos 15 3 προσανάβασις, BHom 9 ἄνοδος; BMis 85.

—— ⲉϩⲣⲁⲓ ⲉϫⲛ-, *go up upon, along*: Jos 17 7 πορεύ. ἐπί acc.

—— ϩⲓⲡⲁϩⲟⲩ, *go behind*: Jos 12 19 ἀπέρχ. ὀπίσω. *Cf* ⲃ. ⲉⲡⲁϩⲟⲩ.

II. tr. rare but in Theban documents, *put into, add to, send*: Ep 89 176 366, CO 74 287 461, ST 116 354, BKU 1 125, J 24 161, *ib* 105 31; reflex COAd 2, Hall 79. ⲃ. ⲡⲥⲕⲩⲗⲙⲟⲥ, *be at the trouble*: Ep 301 n. ⲃ. ⲉϩⲟⲩⲛ: CO 354 ⲁⲡⲃⲁⲕⲏ ⲉϩ. ⲉⲙⲁ ⲛ-, Ep 1 162.

Not Theban: Osir pl 37 (ostr), Ryl 381 (?).

V also ⲗⲉⲥⲉ, ⲙⲁⲧⲟⲩ, ⲧⲃⲕⲟ, ⲱⲡⲉ.

ⲃⲱⲕ *BF*(only MR 5 33) nn m, f ⲃⲱⲕⲓ, pl ⲉⲃⲓⲁⲓⲕ, sg as pl *B*, *servant, slave*, mostly = *S* ϩⲙϩⲁⲗ, opp ⲣⲉⲙϩⲉ ἐλεύθερος: Is 14 2, Mt 10 24, Eph 6 8, Gal 3 28 δοῦλος, Ex 21 7, Is 56 6 δούλη; Pro 13 13, Is 36 9 οἰκέτης, Lev 19 20 οἰκέτις; Ge 12 16, Is 24 2, Jer 41 9 παῖς, Ge 16 1, Ps 85 16 παιδίσκη; AM 1 ⲃⲱⲕⲓ ⲛϭⲣⲓⲙⲓ; Nu 11 11 θεράπων, Pro 31 15 θεράπαινα; pl Is 42 19, Ez 38 17 δοῦλοι, Lev 25 55, 1 Pet 2 18 οἰκέται, BSM 103, TstAb 163 ⲉⲃ. ⲛϭⲣⲓⲙⲓ; sg. as pl. Is 14 2, Ac 2 18, Cat 48.

ⲉⲣ ⲃ., *serve, labour*: Ge 14 4 (*S* ⲣ ϩⲙϩ.), Bar 1 12, Ro 7 6, Gal 4 25 δουλεύειν; Jer 41 14, Ez 48

18 ἐργάζεσθαι; ⲓⲣⲓ ⲙⲃ., *enslave*: Jer 15 14 (*S* ⲧⲟⲟⲧⲉ ⲛϩ.), 2 Cor 11 20 καταδουλοῦν, 1 Cor 9 27 δουλαγωγεῖν, 1 Cor 7 23 δοῦλ. γίνεσθαι.

With nn: ⲁⲗⲟⲩ ⲙⲃ. Ge 9 25 (*S* ϩⲓϩⲁⲗ), οἰκέτης, Va 57 198 παῖς, Ac 12 13 παιδίσκη; pl Va 57 227 ⲁⲗⲱⲟⲩⲓ ⲛⲃⲓⲁⲓⲕ.

ⲙⲉⲧⲃ. nn f, *servitude*: Ps 103 14, Rom 8 15 (*S* ⲙⲛⲧϩⲙϩⲁⲗ), Is 14 3 δουλεία, Va 57 16 ἀνδράποδον; ⲙⲉⲧⲃⲁⲗ ⲙⲃ. nn f, *eye-service*: Eph 6 6, Col 3 22 ὀφθαλμοδουλεία. *Cf* ⲉⲓⲁ eye.

In name: Τβοκενοῦφις (Preisigke).

ⲃⲉⲕ. For this supposed form *v* ⲥⲧⲉⲃⲁⲉⲓϩ.

ⲃⲁⲕⲓ *B* nn f (*S* ? ⲃⲁⲕⲉ *v* below), *city, town*, as Constantinople Va 64 172, Alexandria Miss 4 160, Antioch AM 325, Jerusalem Ez 33 21, and nome-capitals: Shmoun AM 92, Siut C 41 25, Athribis *ib* 43 210, Pshati AM 328. Always = πόλις: Ge 4 17, Jer 4 5, 2 Cor 11 32. ⲧⲙⲏⲧ ⲙⲃ. Mt 4 25 Decapolis, ⲇⲓⲟⲥ ⲧⲃ. Ez 30 16 Diospolis. Var ⲧⲙⲓ C 41 38, Aeg 6 = *S* ⲧⲙⲉ; opp ⲧⲙⲓ (κώμη) Mt 9 35, Rec 7 129, C 43 63, Va 62 275.

ϣⲁⲧⲃ., *citizen*: C 41 25.

ⲣⲉⲙⲛⲃ., πολίτης: Ge 23 11, Jer 38 34, Ac 21 39, Va 66 293 ⲉⲛⲏⲡ ⲉⲧϥⲉ ⲕⲁⲧⲁ ⲡⲉⲡⲣ. ⲉⲣ ⲣⲉⲙⲛⲃ., *be citizen* C 43 66.

ⲙⲉⲧⲣⲉⲙⲛⲃ. nn f, πολίτευμα: Phil 3 20. For these nouns *S* mostly = Gk.

In place-name ? *S* ⲧⲃⲁⲕⲉ, BM 1194, Kr 182, Ryl 155.

ⲃⲉⲕⲉ *SAA²* nn m, pl ⲃⲉⲕⲏⲅⲉ, ⲃⲉⲕⲉ(ⲉ)ⲅⲉ *S* (Ez 27 15, ShP 130² 6), ⲃⲉⲕⲛⲟⲩⲅⲉ *A* (Hag 1 6); ⲃⲉⲭⲉ *B*, pl ⲃⲉⲭⲛⲟⲩⲓ; ⲃⲉⲕⲏ *F*, pl ⲃⲉⲕⲁⲅⲉ (JEA 11 244), ⲃⲉⲕⲁⲅⲓ; ⲃⲓⲕⲉ *O* (Hor 80), *wage*: Nu 18 31, Ps 126 3, Is 40 10, Lu 6 23 all *SB* μισθός, Deu 23 18 *SB*, Mic 1 7 *SAB* μίσθωμα; pl: Ez 16 32 *S*, R 1 4 70 *S*, Mic 1 7 *AB*, Hag 1 6 *B*, for *F v* below; sg as pl (*B* only): Ez 16 32, *ib* 27 15, Hos 2 12.

ⲧ ⲃ., ⲧ ⲙⲛⲃ. *SB*, *pay wage, reward*: Ge 30 16 *B* μισθοῦσθαι, Sa 10 17 *S*, Ap 11 18 *SB* μ. διδόναι, BHom 15 82 *S*, BMis 211 *S*, WTh 15 *B*. ⲧⲁⲓⲃ., *wage-giver, hirer*: He 11 6 *S* (var ⲣⲉϥⲧ ⲃ.) μισθαποδότης, Aeg 243 *S*, Bor 253 146 *S* ⲡⲧ. ⲙⲛⲃⲁⲧⲱⲡ. ⲣⲉϥⲧ ⲃ., *same*: LMis 109 *S*, WTh 134 *S*, He 11 6 *B* (*cf S*).

ϫⲓ ⲃ., ϫⲓ ⲙⲛⲃ. *S*, ϭⲓ ⲃ. *B*, *receive wage*: Mt 6 2 *SB* μ. ἀπέχειν, Ez 16 32 *SB*, 1 Cor 3 8 *SB* μ. λαμβάνειν, BMis 530 *S*, AZ 21 147 *S*. ϫⲓ, ϭⲓ ⲉⲃ. *take at a wage, hire*: Is 46 6 *B* μισθοῦσθαι (*S* ⲑⲛⲟ), BerlOr 1607 2 *S* (Acta Andr.) ⲛⲧⲁⲓ ϫⲓⲧⲟⲩ (*l* -ϥ) ⲉⲛⲉϧⲃ. μεμίσθωμαι αὐτούς. ϫⲁⲓⲃ. *SA*, *wage-taker, hireling*: Lev 19 13 *S*, Is 21 16 *S*, Mal 3 5 *SA* (all *B* ⲣⲉⲙⲃ.) μισθωτός, Si 37 15 *S* μίσθιος, ST 364 *S*, COAd 42 *S*, Hor 80 *O*.

ⲥⲱⲣⲙ ⲙⲡⲃ., *lose reward*: Mt 10 42 S (B ⲧⲁⲕⲟ).
ⲥⲙⲛ ⲃ., *fix wage*: ShC 73 72 S.
ⲣⲙⲃ., ⲣⲙⲙⲃ. S, ⲣⲉⲙⲃ. B, ⲗⲉⲃⲉⲕⲏ F, pl ⲗⲉ-
ⲃⲉⲕⲁⲅⲓ (Kr 140, BM 1228, AZ 23 32), *wage-man*,
hireling: Deu 15 18 SB, Jer 26 21 B, Mal 3 5 B
(A ϫⲁⲓⲃ.) μισθωτός.
ⲁⲧⲃ. BF, *wageless*: Job 24 6 ἀμισθί, TRit 426 B,
Kr 141 F, Mor 27 44 F I shall not be ⲛⲁⲧⲃ. (S
ⲉⲭⲛⲃ.)
ϣⲉⲃⲓⲱ ⲃ. B nn m, *recompense*: Ro 1 27, 2 Cor
6 13 μισθαποδοσία; *cf* S ϣⲃⲃⲉⲓⲱ ⲛⲃ., ⲙⲛⲃ.
V also ⲁⲙⲉ, ⲙⲟⲟⲛⲉ, ⲛⲟⲩⲧ, ⲣⲣⲟ, ⲣⲟⲉⲓⲥ, ⲟⲩⲟⲉⲓⲉ,
ϧⲟⲓ.

ⲃⲏⲕⲉ S nn, meaning doubtful, prob = last:
Hall 117 in list of σκεύη, ⲟⲩϫⲓⲥⲧⲉ(*sic*)ⲛⲃ.

ⲃⲏⲕⲉ S nn m, *woof* (B ϣⲉ) κρόκη, opp ϣⲧⲓⲧ
στήμων: Lev 13 49 (ﻟﺤﻤﺔ), ShEp 56, Z 581.

ⲃⲓⲕⲓ, B nn, among horse furniture K 136, where
half the MSS ﺣﺰﺍﻡ *strap*, *girth*, other half ﺧﺰﺍﻡ *nose-
ring*; prob former.

ⲃⲟⲕⲓ B nn, verbally in ⲙ(ⲉⲙ)ⲃ., ⲉⲣ ⲃ. (S ⲱⲱ),
I. intr, **a.** *conceive*: ⲙⲃ. Ge 38 25 (var ⲉⲣ ⲃ.),
Is 40 11, 1 Thes 5 3, Ap 12 2, Va 61 23 ⲟⲩϣⲟϣ...
ⲛⲁⲥⲙⲃ. ⲡⲉ, sim RAl 94 ἐν γαστρὶ ἔχειν; ⲉⲣ ⲃ. 4 Kg
4 17, Is 7 14 ἐν γ. λαμβάνειν (cf Mt 1 23), Ge 16 4,
Hos 1 3, Lu 1 24 συλλαμβ., JA '87 1 146 ϣⲁⲥⲉⲣ ⲃ.
ϣⲁⲥϯ ⲛⲁⲕⲣⲓ ⲁⲥⲙⲓⲥⲓ ⲙϥⲙⲟⲩ. **b.** *conceive by*:
ⲙⲃ. ⲉⲃⲟⲗ ϧⲉⲛ- Ge 38 24, Mt 1 18 ἐν γ. ἔχειν ἐκ;
ⲉⲣ ⲃ. ⲉⲃⲟⲗ ϧⲉⲛ- Ge 38 18 ἐν γ. λαμβ. ἐκ.
II. tr, *conceive a child*: Cat 107 13 ϥⲁⲓ ⲉⲧⲉⲣ-
ⲡⲓⲁⲅⲓⲟⲥ ⲙⲃ. ⲙⲙⲟϥ (cf Is 26 18), C 86 230; ⲉⲣ ⲃ.
Ge 25 23 ἐν γ. εἶναι, Nu 11 12 ἐν γ. λαμβ., 4 Kg 4
16 περιλαμβ., Ps 7 15 συλλαμβ., Va 61 109 ⲉⲧⲁⲩⲉⲣ
ⲃ. ⲙⲙⲟⲓ...ⲙⲟ̄ ⲡⲁⲃⲟⲧ.
ⲙⲃ., nn m, *conception*: K 103, pl Hos 9 11 σύλληψις; f *pregnant* (*woman*) K 271 ﺣﺒﻠﻰ.
ϫⲓⲛⲉⲣ ⲃ. nn m f, *conception*: Cat 115 ⲛϫ. ⲛⲧⲉ
ⲡⲉⲡⲟ̄ⲥ̄, ROC 17 400 ⲡⲁⲓ ⲉϣⲁⲣⲉϫ. ϣⲱⲡⲓ ⲉⲃⲟⲗ
ⲛϧⲏⲧⲟⲩ σύλληψις.

ⲃⲱⲕⲉ S, p c ⲃⲁⲕ- SB vb tr, *tan*: ShA 2 349
(P 129¹² 3 *sic* MS) in list of artificers ϧⲉⲛⲣⲉϥⲣ
ϧⲱⲃ ⲉϣⲁⲣ ϣⲁⲧⲛⲃ. ⲙⲙⲁⲧⲉ (ϣⲁⲧⲛ- with vb only
Si 22 24, ShR 2 3 47), Jud 16 7 cords of sinew
ⲉⲙⲡⲟⲩⲃⲟⲕⲟⲩ ξηραίνεσθαι siccus (fieri). ⲃⲁⲕϣⲁⲁⲣ βυρσεύς, v ϣⲁⲁⲣ skin.

ⲃⲁⲕⲃⲉⲕ F v ⲟⲅⲟⲃⲟⲩⲉϥ.

ⲃⲓⲕϫⲓ, ⲃⲅⲕϫⲓ, ⲃⲓϫⲕⲓ, ⲃⲅⲕⲕⲓ B nn, a plant
or fruit: K 176 ﺳﻌﺪ = ﺣﺐ ﺍﻟﻌﺰﻳﺮ (b. Baitâr) *cyperus esculentus*; v AZ 12 128, Sph 6 107, Lab 1
90 (sweet edible plant, growing in clay soil). *Cf*
? βήχιον coltsfoot (not βικίον vicia = κύαμος).

ⲃⲉⲕⲏⲉ S P 44 56, ⲃⲁⲕⲏⲛ BM 491 nn f (with
art ⲉⲧ-, ⲧ- respectively) = σίλφη a beetle, ﻋﺮﺱ
weasel. The incongruity of these is observed AZ
24 90. For ﻋﺮﺱ K 173 has ⲁⲕⲗⲏ (ⲕⲁⲗⲏ) γαλῆ,
whence these are ? distorted forms.

ⲃⲁⲗ AF v ⲃⲟⲗ.

ⲃⲁⲗ (in ⲙⲁϧ.) v ⲙⲁϧ *nest*.

ⲃⲁⲗ SB, ⲃⲉⲗ AA²F, DM *bel* nn m, *eye*: Job
16 20 SB, Ps 53 7 SB, ib 33 16 SA(Cl 22 6) B, Pro
4 25 SAB, Is 30 20 SBF, Lam 2 18 B, ὀφθαλμός;
Sa 11 19 S, Mk 8 23 SB ὄμμα; ⲉⲓⲁⲧ Ge 18 2 S not
true var, cf Ps 53 7, 91 11 S ⲁⲛⲁⲃ. ⲙⲉϧ ⲉⲓⲁⲧϥ,
ib 90 8 B ϯ ⲛⲓⲁⲧⲕ ⲛⲡⲉⲕⲃ.
ⲕⲉⲕⲉ ⲛⲃ. Ps 16 8 S (B ⲁⲗⲟⲩ ⲛⲃ.) κόρη ὀφθ., which
Glos 25 S = ϫⲡⲣⲱⲙⲉ ⲛⲛⲃ.; ⲃ. ⲛⲡⲉϧ S (l ⲛⲉⲛϧ)
ﺍﻟﻌﻴﻦ ﺍﻟﺴﻔﻼ *lower eye*(*lid*?) Scala frag EW 1921.
ⲃ. ⲉⲧⲕⲏⲕ PMéd 61 S, *peeled*, *skinned eyes* (disease),
cf ⲕⲁⲕ ⲃ. πτίλος Lev 21 20 B & ? PLond 4 217 name
Πκακουϧάλ; ⲃ. ⲉⲧⲱ (l ⲟ) ⲛⲥⲓⲟⲩ PMéd 64 S *star-
eyed* (disease); ⲃ. ⲉⲧⲱ ⲛⲕⲁⲕⲉ ib 89 S *darkened,
obscured eye* (disease), cf Ps 68 23, Lam 5 17 B;
ϣⲟⲩⲃ. charm in Cambridge Univ Libr (Taylor-
Schechter) B *streaming eye* (disease), cf ϣⲟⲩⲙⲏ;
ϣⲧⲉⲙⲃⲉⲗ BM 524 F *closing of eye* (blindness?),
cf Is 33 15 F; other diseases v PMéd 331; *eyes
dazzled* by light ⲛⲉⲁⲡⲉⲩⲃ. ϧⲧⲟⲙⲧⲙ PS 5, 8 S, cf
Ge 48 10 S.
ⲃ. ⲃⲱⲛ, *evil eye* Va 61 93 B ⲁⲕⲟⲩⲱⲙ ϧⲉⲛⲟⲩⲃ.
ⲃ. ⲛⲥⲁⲙⲡⲉⲧϩⲱⲟⲩ.
ⲙⲉⲧⲃ. ⲙⲃⲱⲕ ὀφθαλμοδουλεία Eph 6 6 B, Col 3
22 B = S ⲙⲛⲧⲉⲓⲁ ⲛϭⲁⲟⲡ, cf Ps 122 2.
ⲃ. ⲛⲁⲃⲱⲕ κύαμος ἑλληνικός PMéd 267 S, Z 629
S, WS 52 S, cf DM 5 24 ⲃⲉⲗ ⲛ ⲉⲃⲱⲕ.
ⲃ. ⲛⲉⲙⲟⲩ S, *cat's eye* αἰλούρου ὀφθ., CR '87 376.
ⲃ. ⲛⲃⲛⲛⲉ S *date's eye*, i e ? date stone, P 43 233
(ϯ)ⲅⲁⲣⲧⲟⲡ· ⲛⲃ. ⲛⲃⲃⲏⲛⲛⲉ ﻋﻴﻮﻥ ﺍﻗﻤﺎﻉ ﺍﻟﺒﻠﺢ (though ﻗﻤﻊ
is said to be the outer casing of a fruit). In P 44
80 ⲧⲏⲅⲁⲣⲧⲁ = ﻋﻨﺐ, in Nu 6 4 B = ﺯﺑﻴﺐ.
ⲣⲓⲕⲉ ⲙⲃ. ῥιπὴ ὀφθ. 1 Cor 15 52 SB, Miss 4 711
S, BMis 532 S, Va 69 124 B divinity of Only begotten not divided from humanity ⲛⲟⲩⲣ. ⲛⲃ.
ϭⲱⲣⲙ ⲛⲃ. νεῦμα ὀφθ. Is 3 16 B = S ⲕⲓⲙ ⲛⲃ.
ⲥⲁⲓⲏ ⲛⲃ. S = B ⲥⲁⲓⲉ ⲃ. μετὰ κάλλους ὀφθ. 1 Kg
16 12, εὐόμματος Mélanges Ch. Moeller 3 S, Miss
4 738 S, C 43 63 B.
ϯ ϣⲟⲩ ⲛⲃ. μακαρίζειν Ge 30 13 B, Job 29 11 B
(cf ϣⲟⲩ ⲛⲓⲁⲧϥ).
ϥⲁⲓ ⲃ. ⲉⲡϣⲱⲓ B αἴρειν ὀφθ. Is 60 4, Zech 1 18,
Lu 6 20 (all = S ϥⲓ ⲉⲓⲁⲧϥ ⲉϧⲣⲁⲓ).
ϧⲓ ⲛⲟⲩⲃ., *cast a glance* (from window) MG 25
128 B.

ⲧⲁⲥⲃ. *S* BAp 160, *cf* ⲙⲡⲧⲧⲁⲥⲃ. ⲙⲉⲧⲉⲱⲣⲓⲥⲙⲟⲥ ὀφθ. Si 23 5 *S* = *ib* 26 9 ⲙⲡⲧⲭⲁⲥⲓⲃ.

ⲭⲁⲣⲃ. στηρίζων ὀφθ. Eccl 11 9 *S*, Mor 37 78 *S* ἀναιδέστερος, BMis 521 *S*.

ⲁⲧⲃ. ἀναιδής Is 56 11 *S* (in Pro 25 23 *S*, Si 23 6 *S* = ⲁⲧϣⲓⲡⲉ *A*), ShZ 476 *S*. ⲙⲛⲧⲁⲧⲃ. Pro 21 29 *S* (var ⲙⲛⲧⲁⲧϣⲓⲡⲉ, Gk adv), ShWess 18 142 *S*, ShMun 165 *S*.

ⲉⲧⲙⲉϩ ⲙⲃ. πολυόμματος CaiEuch 317 *B* = ⲉⲧⲟ ⲛⲣⲁϩ ⲛⲃ. P 129²⁰ 127 *S*.

ⲛⲃ. ϩⲓⲃ. ὀφθ. κατ' ὀφθ. Nu 14 14 *S* (ⲃ. ⲟⲩⲃⲉⲃ. *B*).

In place-name τόπος Πταρϣⲃάλ (Preisigke).

ⲃⲓⲗ *F* v ⲃⲓⲣ.

ⲃⲱⲗ, ⲃⲉⲗ-, ⲃⲟⲗ⸗ (ⲃⲁⲗ⸗), ⲃⲏⲗ†, ᵖᶜ ⲃⲁⲗ- *SAA²BFO*(AZ 21 100) **a.** *loosen, untie,* mostly tr. ; of chains, cords &c : Job 39 5 *S* (*B* ϯ ⲟⲩⲱ), Mt 21 2 *SB* λύειν, Va 59 161 *B* ⲁϥⲃ. ⲛⲛⲓⲥⲛⲁϩ ⲉⲃⲟⲗ ϩⲁⲣⲟϥ ; Ep 277 *S* ⲃ. ϩⲛ-; refl. BMar 11 *S* ⲁϥⲃⲟⲗϥ ⲙⲡⲉϥⲙⲟⲅⲥ ; of sandals : Ac 7 33 *SB* λύ., Is 20 2 *B* (*S* ⲃ. ⲉⲃⲟⲗ) ὑπολύ.; of knots : Is 58 6 *S* (*B* ⲃ. ⲉⲃⲟⲗ) διαλύ.; of seal : RNC 22 *S*. **b.** *melt* : Si 3 15 *S* (Gk om), AM 195 *B* coins. **c.** *unstring* sinews : Deu 21 4 *S* (*B* ϫⲱϫⲓ), Jos 11 6 *S* νευροκόπτειν, R 2 2 24 *S* of Potiphar's wife ⲛⲥⲃⲗ ⲛⲕⲱⲃ ⲙⲡⲭⲱⲣⲉ ἐκνευρίζειν. **d.** *interpret, explain* scriptures, dreams &c : Mk 4 34 *SB* ἐπιλύειν, Lu 24 27 *SB*, 1 Cor 14 5 *S* διερμηνεύειν, R 1 1 10 μεθερμ., Ge 41 8 *S*, Jud 14 12 *S* ἀπαγγέλλειν, R 2 2 29 *S* σαφηνίζειν, Mt 13 36 *SBF* διασαφην., Mt 15 15 *S* (*B* ⲃ. ⲉⲃⲟⲗ) φράζειν, Ac 17 3 *S* (*B* ⲟⲩⲱⲛϩ ⲉⲃⲟⲗ) διανοίγειν, Br 46 *S*, Miss 8 167 *S* (*cf* BMis 461), BMOr 8811 243 *S* wise understand our words ⲛⲥⲉⲣ ⲭⲣⲉⲓⲁ ⲁⲛ ⲛⲃⲟⲗⲟⲩ ⲉⲣⲟⲟⲩ, ShC 73 184 *S* ⲡϣⲁⲛⲃⲗ ⲡⲁⲓ ⲉϫⲛⲧⲥⲩⲛⲁⲅⲱⲅⲏ (*in regard to the congreg.,* cf MG 25 140 *B* ⲉⲣⲉⲡⲉⲥⲃⲱⲗ ⲡⲛⲟⲩ ⲉϫⲉⲛⲟⲩ. **e.** *be softened, persuaded* : Pro 6 35 *S* (*B* ⲡⲟⲩϯ ⲉⲃⲟⲗ) διαλύειν. **f.** *weaken, make faint* : Jer 12 5 *S* (*B* ϯ ⲟⲩⲱ) ἐκλύ., ShZ 502 *S* ⲧⲉⲧⲛϭⲟⲙ ...ϥⲃ. ⲙⲙⲟⲥ ⲏ ⲉϥⲟⲩⲱϣϥ ⲙⲙⲟⲥ, O'LearyH 14 *B* ⲙⲡⲉⲣϣⲱⲡⲓ ⲡⲣⲏⲧ ⲉϥⲃⲏⲗ. **g.** *nullify* order, deed Z 260 *S*, J 109 12 ; magic : C 86 210 *B* ⲁⲡⲟⲕ ⲉⲑⲛⲁⲃ. ⲛⲡⲉϥⲙⲁⲅⲓⲁ Mor 53 27 *S*, a blessing ⲉⲃⲗ ⲡⲉⲓⲥⲙⲟⲩ (*B* ⲃ. ⲉⲃⲟⲗ). **h.** *dissolve, destroy* : BSM 117 *B* (*S* ⲁⲛϩⲁⲗⲓⲥⲕⲉ) of Job destroying his body by worms, R 1 5 51 *S* ⲁⲡⲥⲁⲓⲉ ⲛⲃⲱ ⲛⲧⲉϥⲁⲡⲉ ⲃ. (*cf* BMar 78 ⲃ. ⲉϩⲣⲁⲓ). **i.** *be immaterial* (?): BM 847 21 *B* of Christ ⲁϥⲉⲣⲫⲟⲣⲓⲛ ⲡⲟⲩⲥⲁⲣⲝ ⲉϥⲃⲏⲗ ⲫⲏ ⲉⲧⲟⲓ ⲡⲁⲧϣⲧⲁϩⲟϥ. **j.** *pay* (*cf* λύειν): Ge 4 24 *B* (*cf* ⲃ. ⲙⲛ- *F*) ἐκδικεῖν, but Kr 7 ⲁⲕⲃⲟⲗⲉⲛ *remit.* **k.** obscure: ShP 130¹ 37 *S* none shall attempt to see another's nakedness ⲉⲓⲧⲉ

ⲉϩⲣⲁⲓ ϩⲓϫⲡⲟⲩϫⲟⲉ ⲉⲓⲧⲉ ... ⲉⲩⲃⲱⲗ ⲡⲟⲩⲙⲟⲟⲩ ⲏ ⲙⲟⲟϣⲉ ϩⲛⲟⲩⲟⲙⲉ, Ep 554 *S* a book ⲉⲧⲃⲏⲗ ? *unbound* or ? *translated.*

—— *SB* nn m, **a.** *solution, interpretation* : Eccl 7 30 *S*, Sap 8 8 *S* λύσις, 2 Pet 1 20 *SB* ἐπίλυσις, Si 42 22 *S* ἑρμηνεία, Gal 4 24 *S* ἀλληγορούμενος, Ge 40 8 *SB* διασάφησις, Dan 2 16 *B* σύγκρισις, 1 Cor 12 10 *B* διάκρ., R 1 1 15 *S* ⲟⲩⲡⲉ ⲡⲃ. ⲡⲱⲥⲁⲡⲁ τί ἑρμηνεύεται, PS 122 *S* ⲡⲁⲓⲡⲉ ⲡϣⲁϫⲉ ⲙⲡⲡⲉⲩⲃ., MG 17 296 *S* = 41 *B*, *ib* 4 *B* γνῶσις, BAp 89 *S* ϩⲉⲛⲃ. ⲙⲡⲡⲉⲩⲙⲁⲧⲓⲕⲟⲛ, as liturg rubric Leyd 138, 142, 261 *S*. **b.** *loosening, weakness* : ShA 1 432 *S* horse falls to ground ϩⲓⲧⲙⲡⲃ. ⲙⲡⲉϥⲡⲁⲧ ϩⲓⲑⲏ (var MIF 23 122 ⲃ. ⲉⲃⲟⲗ), opp ⲡⲕⲱ ⲙⲡⲉϥⲟⲩⲉⲣⲓⲧⲉ ⲉⲡⲁϩⲟⲩ.

ⲃⲁⲗ (*sic*) *A* nn, only Nah 2 10 : ⲧⲃ. ⲡⲉⲧ (*B* ⲃⲱⲗ ⲉⲃⲟⲗ ⲡⲧⲉ ϩⲁⲡϥⲁⲧ) ὑπόλυσις. Initial ⲧ- obscure, ? causative.

—— ⲙⲛ- *SF*, *agree, come to terms with* (cf ⲃ. ⲉⲃⲟⲗ εὐνοεῖν): ShA 1 96 *S* ⲙⲡⲟⲩⲃ. ⲡⲙⲙⲁⲡ ⲁⲗⲗⲁ ⲥⲉⲣ ⲡⲕⲉⲟ ⲛϫⲁϫⲉ, BMis 311 *S* creditor to debtor ⲛⲧⲡⲗⲏⲣⲟⲫⲟⲣⲉⲓ ⲙⲙⲟⲓ ⲁⲩⲱ ⲧⲓⲡⲁⲃ. ⲡⲙⲙⲁⲕ, Mor 28 241 *S* sim, Kr 129, 131, 140 *F* rent of land ⲡⲧⲁⲓⲃⲁⲗⲉⲃ ⲡⲉⲙⲉⲕ, BMis 7 *S* disputants come to king ⲉⲧⲣⲉϥⲃⲟⲗⲟⲩ ⲙⲡⲡⲉϥⲉⲣⲏⲩ, Bor 241 211 *S* ⲡϥⲃ. ⲡϣⲟⲣⲡ ⲙⲡⲡⲉⲧⲣⲓⲧⲟⲩⲱϥ ϩⲛⲁⲣⲓⲕⲉ ⲡⲓⲙ, TT 28 n *S* I resolved ⲉⲧⲁⲧⲣⲁⲃ. ⲡⲙⲙⲁϥ, opp ⲙⲟⲩⲣ ⲙⲛ-.

—— ⲉⲃⲟⲗ *SAA²BF*, intr & tr, meanings often = ⲃⲱⲗ, with which it varies. **a.** *loosen* chains, cords &c : Is 5 27 *S*, Ps 145 7 *SB*, Dan 3 25 (92) *B*, Jo 1 27 *B*, BMis 237 *S* λύειν, C 43 113 *B* ⲁⲩⲃ. ⲉ. ⲡϫⲉ ⲡⲓⲃⲉⲡⲓⲡⲓ, *untie* basket : BIF 14 164 *S*, *break* seal : Ap 5 2 *S* λύ. **b.** *unclose* womb Jth 9 2 *S* λύ., virginity R 2 4 58 *S* ⲙⲡⲉⲧⲟⲩⲡⲁⲣⲑⲉⲛⲓⲁ ⲃ. ⲉ. **c.** *unfold* book : RNC 41 *S* ἀναπτύσσειν (cf Lu 4 17), MR 4 71 *S* = Mor 18 61 ⲟⲩⲡⲉ ⲡⲉⲓⲭⲁⲣⲧⲏⲥ ⲉϥⲃ. ⲙⲙⲟϥ ⲉ., Imp Russ Ar *S* 18 029 *A* ⲡⲉⲧⲛⲁⲃ. ⲁⲃⲁⲗ ⲙⲡⲓⲭⲁⲣⲧⲏⲥ, El 52 *A*. **d.** *be melted,* of the elements : 2 Pet 3 12 *SB* τήκειν, ice : Job 6 17 *SB* τήκ., wax : Ps 57 9, 96 5 *SB* τήκ., lead : AM 230 *B*, bricks : Is 24 23 *SB*, Mich 550 39 *S* Pachôm prayed so fervently ϩⲱⲥⲧⲉ ⲧⲧⲱⲃⲉ ⲉⲧϩⲁⲣⲁⲧϥ ... ⲃ. ⲉ., manna : Ex 16 21 *SB*, Mor 22 49 *S* hell fire ⲛⲁⲃⲟⲗⲡ ⲉ. **e.** in alchemy : Bodl(P) a 1 *S* ⲕⲁⲁⲩ ϣⲁⲡⲧⲟⲩⲃ. ⲉ. ⲧⲉⲩⲣ ⲙⲟⲟⲩ, PMéd 237 *S* ⲃⲟⲗⲟⲩ ⲉ. ⲙⲡⲡⲉⲩⲉⲣⲏⲩ. **f.** *release, terminate,* of fast : Mor 28 221 *S* of untimely fast-breaking, LCyp 27 *S* ἀπονηστεύειν, GöttN '01 329 *S*, BAp 106 *S*, R 1 3 44 *S*, BMis 543 *S*, Hall 54 *S* opp ⲙⲟⲩⲣ ⲉⲣⲟⲩϩ ἄρχεσθαι, v CO 99 n ; of divine service (? cf nn **a.**): CO 94 *S*; of thirst : PS 131 *S*. **g.** *be dispersed, scattered,* of dust : Va 62 181 *B* ⲡⲥⲉⲣⲉⲓ ⲡⲥⲉⲃ. ⲉ. ⲙⲫⲣⲏϯ ⲡⲟⲩϣⲟⲓϣ, of

corpse : Ming 341 = BMar 205 *S*, of smoke : Sa 5 15 *S* διαχεῖσθαι.   **h.** *dissolve, nullify* drugs, magic : C 43 139 *B* ⲃ. ⲉ. ⲛⲛⲓⲫⲁⲣⲙⲁⲅⲓⲁ, Leyd 441 *S* ⲉⲧⲣⲉⲥⲃ. ⲉ. ⲡⲉⲡⲉⲣⲅⲓⲁ ⲛⲓⲙ, Va 57 165 *B* gluttony ⲉⲧϯ ⲟⲩⲃⲉⲧⲧⲉⲭⲛⲏ … ⲛⲧⲉ ⲡⲓⲥⲛⲏⲩ ⲉⲥ (*l* ⲉϥ)ⲃ. ⲉ. ⲡⲛⲟⲩϥⲁⳝⲣⲓ ὑπερβαίνειν, MIF 23 16 *S*, AZ 33 132 *S*, R 1 5 30 *S*, BSM 110 *B*.   **i.** *be loose, flowing*, of hair : Aeg 255 *S*, JA '75 5 259 (var om ⲉ.) *S*, R 2 1 65 *S*, beard P 131⁴ 130.   **j.** *be loose*, of sand mixed with stones or clay : Tri 679 *S*.   **k.** *relax, annul* laws : Mt 5 17 *S* καταλύειν, Jo 7 23 *SB* λύ., legal deeds : Gal 3 17 *B* (*S* ⲧⲥⲧⲟ ⲉⲃ.) ἀκυροῦν Wess 18 63 *S*, J 67 117 *S*, CO 229 *S*, BSM 46 *B* (*S* ⲥⲱⲧⲉ) redeem pledge.   **l.** *absolve* sins : Job 42 9 *S* (*B* ⲕⲱ ⲉⲃ.) λύ., cf Mt 16 19 &c.   **m.** *destroy* : Nah 1 6 *SB* τήκ., Mic 4 13 *B* (ShA 1 385, *A* ⲣⲱϩ) κατατήκ., Eph 2 14 *SB* λύ., Is 38 12 *B* (*S* ϯⲟⲩⲱ), Gal 2 18 *B* (*S* ϣⲟⲣϣⲣ) καταλύ.   **n.** *resolve* difficulties, *come to terms* : Mt 5 25 *S* (var ⲟⲩⲱϣⲙⲉ, *B* ⲕⲁϯ) εὐνοεῖν, Ac 19 39 *SB* ἐπιλύ. (cf ⲃ. ⲙⲛ-).   **o.** *pay* penalty : Ge 4 15 *B* παραλύ.   **p.** *go to pieces, perish* : Jos 2 9 *S* τήκ., Jon 1 4 *B* (*S* ⲧⲁⲕⲟ) συντρίβεσθαι, Ac 27 41 *SB* λύ., PS 361 *S*, BM 185 i *S* the soul ⲉⲧⲉⲙⲉⲥⲃ. ⲉ. ⲟⲩⲇⲉ ⲙⲉⲥⲱⲕⲡ, C 43 2 *B*.   **q.** *slacken, grow weak, faint* : Deu 32 24 *B* τήκ., Mt 15 32 *B*, He 12 3 *B* ἐκλύ. (these 3 = *S* ⲥⲱϣⲙ), Jer 20 9 *B*, He 12 12 *S* (cf *B*) παριέναι, Jer 45 4 *B*, Ez 7 17 *SB* ἐκλύ., RNC 56 *S* at Christ's appearance the executioner's hands ⲃ. ⲉ., R 2 4 63 *S* ⲁⲣⲃ. ⲉ. ϩⲓⲧⲙⲡⲕⲱϩ, Leyd 298 *S* ϩⲁⲑⲟⲧⲉ, BMis 396 *S* ⲁⲛⲃ. ⲉ. ⲉⲭⲛⲛⲉⲕϣⲁϫⲉ (BSM 47 *B* ⲕⲁ ⲧⲟⲧⲉⲛ ⲉ. ⲉⲑⲃⲉ-).   **r.** *be wearied* : Ge 19 11 *B* (*S* ⲕⲁ ⲧⲟⲟⲧ⳽ ⲉ.) παραλύ.   **s.** *be loosened, paralysed* : Is 35 3 *SF* (*B* ϣⲱⲗ ⲉ.), Ez 21 7 *SB* παραλύ., BHom 140 *S* (opp ⲣⲱⲕ) Gu 73 *S* limbs suddenly paralysed, BM 242 *S* martyr's body after tortures ⲃ. ⲉ. ⲛⲥⲁⲥⲁ ⲛⲓⲙ διαλύ.   **t.** *be released, die* : Phil 1 23 *B* ἀναλύ. (cf ἀναλύ. in PG 65 216 D), Bor 248 62 *S* ⲁϥⲃ. ⲉ. ⲁϥϣⲱⲡⲉ ⲙⲡⲉⲭ̄ⲥ̄, C 43 2 *B* ⲟⲩⲟⲩⲣⲟ ⲉϣⲁϥⲃ. ⲉ.   **u.** *upset, unhinge* morally : R 2 2 25 *S* ⲙⲏⲡⲟⲧⲉ ⲛⲥⲟϭⲛ…ⲃ. ⲉ. ⲙⲡϣⲏⲣⲉ ϣⲏⲙ χαυνοῦν, Va 57 163 *B* souls ⲛⲯⲩⲭⲣⲟⲛ ⲟⲩⲟϩ ⲉⲅⲃⲏⲗ ⲉ. χαῦνος.   **v.** *be dissolute, loose* in conduct, doctrine : Pro 3 21 *S* παραρρεῖν, ROC 20 51 *S* ⲡⲉϩⲓⲟⲙⲉ ⲉⲧⲃⲏⲗ ⲉ. ⲙⲛⲛϣⲁϫⲉ ⲛⲅⲃⲱ, Ryl 62 1 *S* gluttony is for him that ⲃⲏⲗ ⲉ. ⲁⲩⲱ ⲉϥⲟ ⲛⲁⲙⲉⲗⲏⲥ, MG 25 358 *B* worldly songs ⲉⲅⲃ. ⲉ., LCyp 26 *S* ⲱϣⲕ ⲉⲧⲃⲏⲗ ⲉ. (var ⲉⲅⲃⲏⲗ) λύ., R 1 5 14 *S* ⲟⲩⲥⲭⲏⲙⲁ ⲉϥⲧⲁⲕⲏⲩ ⲙⲡⲟⲩⲥⲙⲟⲧ ⲉϥⲃ. ⲉ., BMar 181 *S* ⲙⲡⲣⲛⲕⲟⲧⲕ ⲉⲕⲃ. ⲉ.   **w.** reflexive : 1 Cor 7 27 *BF* λύ., BMis 237 *S* ⲁϥⲃⲟⲗϥ ⲉ. ⲛⲧⲉϥϩⲓⲙⲉ, AM 236 *B*.   **x.** *approximate* : Si 38 33 *S* ⲡⲏ

γνύναι, Jer 22 19 *S* (Bor 277 2) συμψᾶσθαι, 2 Tim 3 6 *S* σωρεύεσθαι.

—— ⲉⲃⲟⲗ nn m, **a.** *loosening, slackening, solution* : of the Fast (end of Lent) Leyd 200 *S* ⲧⲕⲩⲣⲓⲁⲕⲏ ⲡⲧⲁⲡⲁⲥⲧⲁⲥⲓⲥ ⲙⲛⲃ. ⲉ., BHom 90 *S* ⲧⲕⲩⲣ. ⲙⲛⲃ. ⲉ. τὸ ἅγιον πάσχα, Mor 51 36 *S* ⲛⲃ. ⲉ. ⲙⲛⲡⲁⲥⲭⲁ, C 89 205 *B* ⲡⲓⲃ. ⲉ. ⲛⲧⲉ ⲡⲓⲡⲁⲥⲭⲁ τῷ σαββάτῳ ὀψέ نهار السبت, Leyd 141 *S* ⲡⲥⲁⲃ. ⲙⲛⲃ. ⲉ., BAp 79 *S* = MIE 2 352 *B* the 3d day of feast of ⲃ. ⲉ., opp ⲙⲟⲩⲣ ⲉⲣⲟⲩⲛ, v CO 99 n.   **b.** *release, pardon* : CaiEuch 515 *B* prayer for exiles.   **c.** *annulling* of magic, demons : TRit 14 *B* blessing of oil.   **d.** *weakening, feebleness* : Is 21 3 *B* (*S* ⲥⲱϣⲙ, cf **q.** above), Jer 29 3 *S* (prob) *B* ἔκλυσις, K 159 *B* انحلال collapse.   **e.** *laxity, dissoluteness, unrestraint* : BMar 161 *S* ⲟⲩⲉⲡⲓⲥⲧⲏⲙⲏ ⲙⲡⲟⲟⲩ… ⲣⲁⲥⲧⲉ ϩⲛⲟⲩⲃ. ⲉ. ἀλαζὼν καὶ ὑπερήφανος, Ryl 62 3 *S* ⲧⲁⲙⲉⲗⲓⲁ ⲙⲡⲛⲃ. ⲉ. ἔκλυσις, P 131⁶ 125 *S* women walking ϩⲛⲟⲩⲃ. ⲉ. beguiling onlookers, Aeg 259 *S* of greedy eating, ShLeyd 304 *S* ⲧϭⲓⲛⲥⲡⲁⲧⲁⲗⲁ ⲙⲡⲡⲉⲓⲃ. ⲉ., BMar 168 *S* ⲡⲃ. ⲉ. ⲉⲡⲉⲣⲟⲩⲟ ϩⲛⲟⲩⲣⲓⲛⲃ χαυνότης.   **f.** *dissolution* = death : 2 Tim 4 6 *SB* ἀνάλυσις, FR 32 *S*.   **g.** *destruction* of the world : PS 208, 260 *S*.

—— ⲉⲃⲟⲗ ⲛⲉⲙ- *B*, *be open, free with* : Va 69 109 of drunkard ϣⲁⲣⲉⲡⲉϥϩⲏⲧ ⲃ. ⲉ. ⲛⲉⲙⲡⲉϥⲥⲟⲛ and he hides nothing from him.

—— ⲉϩⲣⲁⲓ *S*, *become loose, detached* : BMar 78 of dying man's hair ⲁⲛϥⲱ ⲃ. ⲉϩⲣⲁⲓ.

ⲁⲧⲃ. *B*, *indissoluble, unending* : He 7 16 (*S* diff) ἀκατάλυτος, TEuch 1 303 Trinity ⲛⲁⲧϣⲃⲟⲗⲥ; *ib* 315 ⲙⲉⲧⲁⲧⲃ. nn : Christ begotten ϫⲉⲛⲟⲩⲙⲉⲧⲁⲧⲃⲟⲗϥ.

—— ⲉⲃⲟⲗ *SB* same : BMis 241 *S* of chains, *ib* 98 *S* ⲛⲣⲣⲟ ⲛⲁⲧⲃ. ⲉ. ϣⲁⲉⲛⲉϩ, BMar 35 *S*, ShHT *B* 67 *S* ⲛⲧⲩⲡⲟⲥ ⲉⲧⲟⲩⲛⲁⲧⲟⲩϣⲟⲩ ⲉⲧⲣⲉⲅϣⲱⲡⲉ ⲛⲁⲧⲃ. ⲉ.

ⲣⲉϥⲃ. *S* nn, *solver, interpreter* : 1 Cor 14 28 (*B* = Gk) διερμηνευτής, Aeg 282 ⲣⲉϥⲃ. ⲙⲡⲕⲓⲙ ⲡⲁⲙⲉⲗⲟⲥ ⲡⲁⲗⲙⲱⲛ ἑρμηνεύς (var TU 26 1 *b* 42 ⲡⲉⲧⲙⲟⲩⲣ ⲙⲡⲕ.), Bor 280 55 Joseph ⲣⲉϥⲃⲉⲗ ⲣⲁⲥⲟⲩ.

ϫⲓⲛⲃ. *B* nn f, *interpretation* : Va 63 92 ⲧϫⲓⲛⲃ. ⲙϥⲏ ⲉⲧⲥⲁϫⲓ ἑρμηνεία; ϫⲓⲛⲃ. ⲉⲃⲟⲗ m, *loosening, freeing* : Ps 101 21 λύειν (cf *S*).

ⲃⲁⲗϩⲏⲧ v ϥⲏⲧ.

ⲃⲟⲗ *SB*, ⲃⲁⲗ *AF* nn m, *the outside*. As nn only *S* : Mt 23 27 ⲡⲉⲩⲃ. = ἔξωθεν, ShC 73 110 ⲉϣⲱⲡⲉ ⲡⲃ. ⲟ ⲡⲕⲁⲅⲙⲁ outer (air), MG 17 297 ⲁϥⲉⲓ ϣⲁⲡⲃ. ⲙⲡⲣⲟ (var Miss 4 567 ϣⲁⲡⲣⲟ), Ep 575 recipe for liver ⲡⲧⲉⲡⲉϥⲃ. ⲕⲏϥ, 1 Thes 4 12 ⲛⲁⲡⲃ. οἱ ἔξω, Mk 7 15 ἔξωθεν, ShC 42 226 opp ⲛⲁⲡϩⲟⲩⲛ BMis 136.

As prep *SA* (Jo 18 16 *A²* ⲙⲡⲁⲗ) with art ⲡⲃ., often ⲙⲡⲃ. In Sh (C 73 5, P 130⁴ 115, Mun 176,

Wess 9 112), Br 276 &c written ⲃⲗ; ShClPr 22
357 ⲃⲏⲗ, MIF 23 52 ⲃⲗ = ShA 1 398 ⲃⲟⲗ, also
Pro 26 17 *A* = *S* ⲃⲟⲗ.

I. of place, *outside*: **a.** rest, mostly = *B* ⲥⲁⲃⲟⲗ,
Job 2 8 *S*, Ex 33 7 *S*, Jth 13 3, Lu 13 33, Aeg 219
ⲡⲃ. ⲙⲡⲉϥⲧⲟϣ ἔξω; Ex 26 35, Ps 151 1, Jer 40 10,
Ez 40 5 ἔξωθεν; Ac 14 13, πρό (*B* ⲥⲁϫⲉⲛ-), R 1 3
51 she wrote ⲙⲡⲉⲥⲃ. *on its outside* (of coffin), Bor
233 243 ⲟⲩⲥⲟⲛ ⲉϥⲙⲡⲉϥⲃ. *absent*, BIF 14 103 he
hid himself ⲙⲡⲃ. ⲙⲡϩⲟ of Diocletian, J 2 26, 3 30
ⲡⲃ. ⲙⲙⲟϥ *beyond*, 1 Kg 22 17 πρός acc (var ἐπί
dat) *round about*, ib 4 20, Est 4 5, Zech 4 14 (var
ⲙⲡⲃ., *B* ⲙⲡⲉⲙⲑⲟ) παριστάναι dat, Miss 8 237
ⲉⲣⲉⲡϩⲏⲕⲉ…ⲙⲡⲉⲕⲃ.…ⲉⲩϭⲓⲣⲙⲡⲉⲕⲣⲟ. **b.** motion,
outwards, mostly = *B* ⲥⲁⲃ.: Lev 6 11, Jth 14 2,
Sa 1 8 (*B* ⲉⲃ.) παροδεύειν, Mt 21 39 (var ⲙⲡⲃ.),
Ac 14 19 ἔξω, ib 21 5 ϣⲁⲡⲃ. (*B* ϣⲁⲥⲁⲃ.) ἕως ἔξω,
BAp 54 πρό, Is 57 9 (*B* ⲥⲁⲙⲡⲓⲛ) ὑπέρ acc, ShC 73
70 those that bring food ⲡⲃ. ⲙⲡⲙⲁ ⲛⲟⲩⲱⲙ (var
ϩⲓⲃ., cf ib 104), R 1 4 36 ⲉⲁⲛⲁⲭⲱⲣⲉⲓ ⲙⲡⲃ. ⲛⲓⲉ-
ⲥⲛⲏⲩ. **c.** metaphor, *outside, independent of, beyond*: 1 Cor 6 18 (*B* ⲥⲁⲃ.), ib 15 27 (*B* ϣⲁⲧⲉⲛ-)
ἐκτός, Gal 1 8 (*B* ⲥⲁⲃ.), Aeg 247 παρά acc, Si 49 5
παρέξ, Aeg 288 δίχα, Sa 2 9 ἄμοιρος, Jos 22 29,
Eccl 7 30 πλήν; *free from*: Miss 8 75 ⲡⲃ. ⲡⲁⲣⲓⲕⲉ
ⲛⲓⲙ, Bor 166 6 Lord keep us ⲡⲃ. ⲛⲡϩⲁⲓⲣⲉⲧⲓⲕⲟⲥ,
J 9 29 I write to thee ⲙⲡⲃ. ⲛⲕⲣⲟϥ (vars ϩⲓⲃ., ⲁϫⲛ-,
ⲭⲱⲣⲓⲥ); *contrary to*: Bor 236 3 He shall not die
ⲙⲡⲃ. ⲙⲡⲉϥⲟⲩⲱϣ, J 67 19 ShC 73 119 cursed he
that eateth ⲡⲃ. ⲙⲡⲕⲱⲧ, Miss 8 27 teaching ⲡⲃ.
ⲛⲧⲡⲓⲥⲧⲓⲥ. The usage of PS (prob archaic) omits
ⲙ-: 205, 298, 334 inf.

II. of time (rare), *out of, beyond*: Eccl 7 18,
ShC 42 43 (ⲡⲃ., var ⲙⲡⲃ.), Mor 41 169 none should
die ⲡⲃ. ⲙⲡⲉϥⲁϩⲉ.

ⲉⲃⲏⲗ *v* ⲡⲥⲁⲃⲏⲗ.

ⲉⲃⲟⲗ *SB*, ⲁⲃⲁⲗ *AA*[2], ⲉⲃⲁⲗ *F*, commonest post-
posit adv, *out, forth, outward*, adding this sense
to many vbs, *e g* coming, going, bringing, loosing,
throwing, opening, sprouting, pouring, crying;
though elsewhere primary sense scarcely modified.
Gk vbs thus translated are often compounds of
ἐκ- (as ⲉⲓ, ⲉⲓⲛⲉ, ⲙⲟⲟϣⲉ, ⲡⲱⲣϣ, ⲡⲱⲣⲧ, ⲣⲓⲕⲉ, ⲧⲁϭⲟ,
ⲟⲩⲱⲧ, ϥⲓ), or of ἀπο- (as ⲁⲣⲉ, ⲕⲧⲟ, ⲥⲟⲟϩⲉ *remove*,
ⲡⲱⲣϫ, ⲧⲥⲧⲟ, ϩⲉ, ϫⲟⲟⲩ), or with many both of these
are found (as ⲛⲟⲩϫⲉ, ⲥⲟⲟⲩⲧⲛ, ⲧⲛⲛⲟⲟⲩ, ϭⲱⲧⲉ,
ϣⲱⲱⲧ, ϫⲓ). Besides vbs admitting idea of direction *outward*, ⲉⲃ. is less explicably added to others,
where however motion *outward* (sometimes as endurance, thoroughness) may ? be implicit, (as ⲃⲱϣ,
ⲉⲓⲱ, ⲕⲱ, ⲙⲟⲩⲛ, ⲡⲟⲩϣⲡ, ⲥⲟⲗⲥⲉⲗ *B*, ⲥⲱⲧϥ, ⲧⲱⲟⲩⲛ,
ⲱⲃϣ, ⲱⲡϣ, ϭⲱⲣ, ϩⲱⲃⲥ, ϩⲱⲱⲕⲉ, ϫⲱⲕ, ϫⲱⲗ,
ϭⲱⲗ). Its use figurative elsewhere & less ob-

vious, as with ⲟⲱⲃϣ, ⲙⲟⲕⲙⲉⲕ, ⲙⲉⲉⲩⲉ, ⲡⲁⲩ, ⲧⲟⲩⲡ
ⲉⲓⲁⲧⲌ, ⲱⲡ. Dif (a late text) adds ⲉⲃ. abnormally,
eg 1 57 nuns ⲟⲩⲟϩ ⲉⲃ. ⲛϩⲏⲧϥ, 70 ⲉⲣ ⲫⲟⲣⲡ ⲉⲃ.,
84 ⲡⲁⲩⲧⲁⲭⲣⲏⲟⲩⲧ ⲉⲃ., 87 ⲁⲩⲁϣⲁⲓ ⲉⲃ., 94 ⲑⲁⲣϭ
ⲉⲃ. ⲛⲟⲩⲣⲟ. Cf also Mor 40 28 *S* ⲙⲡⲁⲧⲙⲟⲩ ⲉⲃ.
ⲛϣⲁⲉⲛⲉϩ (as if ⲛⲃⲟⲗ *q v*). After Gk vbs rare:
Lev 19 23 *S*, PS 44, 253-4 *S*.

Opp ⲉϩⲟⲩⲛ: Ps 143 14 *S* ϩⲓⲛ ⲛⲃⲱⲕ ⲉϩ. ⲉⲃ.
διέξοδος, PS 10 *S* the mysteries ϫⲓⲛϩⲟⲩⲛ ⲉⲃ.,
J 186 33 *S* ⲙⲟⲟϣⲉ ⲉϩ. ⲉⲃ.; often with ref to *coming forth* from distant, inner, desert, or its monasteries, to river valley, *v* Ep 1 183.

Added after ⲙⲛⲛⲥⲁ-, *after, beyond, henceforth*:
Aeg 286 *S* bishops are heads of church ⲙⲛⲛⲥⲁⲡⲡⲉ ⲉⲃ., BMis 417 *S* Oh my lord ⲙⲛⲛⲥⲁⲡⲡⲉ ⲉⲃ.,
C 89 110 *B* ⲙⲉⲛⲉⲡⲥⲱⲕ ⲉⲃ. ⲁⲡⲟⲕⲛⲉ; or after
ϫⲓⲛ- *S*, ⲓⲥϫⲉⲛ- *B*: Ep 192 *S* I have trusted in thy
fatherhood ϫⲓⲛⲡⲡⲉ ⲉⲃ., CA 98 *S* ϫⲓⲛⲡϣⲱⲙ ⲉⲃ.,
RE 9 137 *S* ⲛⲧⲉⲩⲛⲉⲗⲑⲉ ⲛⲓⲙⲁⲛ ϫⲓⲛⲡⲟⲟⲩ ⲉⲃ.,
C 43 221 *B* martyr's arms severed ⲓⲥϫⲉⲛⲡⲉϥⲁⲗⲱϫ
ⲉⲃ., ShP 130[1] 14 *S* ϫⲓⲛⲡⲟⲟⲩ ⲉϩⲣⲁⲓ ⲏ ⲉⲃ.; or
after nn: Ez 47 3 *B* (Mich Pasch Lect) ⲟⲩⲙⲱⲟⲩ
ⲛⲧⲉ ⲡⲓⲕⲉⲗⲓ ⲉⲃ., ⲁⲧⲟ ⲉⲃ. *SBA*, ⲙⲱⲓⲧ ⲉⲃ. *B*, ϩⲟⲧ ⲉⲃ.
S q v; otherwise rarely: PS 1, 205, 221 *S* the 24th
mystery ⲉⲃ. (*cf* ? ⲉⲧϩⲓⲛⲥⲁⲃⲃⲟⲗ 205), Ez 36 18 *S*
(prob error, Gk *B* om), Lev 13 45 *S* ἀκάλυπτος
(? vb omitted).

In nominal clause with prep: 1 Cor 2 12 *S*
ⲡ(ⲉ)ⲃ. ⲛ- τό ἐκ, CaiEuch 327 *B* ⲡⲓⲉⲃ. ⲙⲡϣⲱ-
ἡ ἄνωθεν, ShA 1 289 *S* ⲛⲉⲃ. ⲙⲙⲟⲟⲩ *kinsfolk*, Mk
14 69 *S* ⲟⲩⲉⲃ. ⲛ- ἐκ, Pro 4 23 *SA* (*cf B*), Jud 5
14 *S*, Hos 5 1 *A*, ShC 42 119 *S* ⲛϫⲁⲥⲓϩⲏⲧ ⲛⲉⲃ.
ϩⲛⲟⲩ†ⲧⲱⲛ, ib 122 words ⲛⲉⲃ. ϩⲛⲛⲉⲧⲣⲁⲫⲏ, Ex 4
20 *A* ⲛⲁⲃ. ϩⲓⲧⲟⲟⲧϥ ⲙ- παρά gen, Ps 11 5 *S* ϩⲉⲛⲉⲃ.
ϩⲓⲧⲛ- (*B* ϩⲁⲛⲉⲃ. ⲛ-); with interrog ⲧⲱⲛ *S*, ⲑⲱⲛ *B*:
Ge 29 4 *SB* πόθεν, Mk 6 2 *S* τίς, AM 251 *B*.

ⲉⲃⲟⲗ ϫⲉ- *SB*, ⲁⲃⲁⲗ ϫⲉ- *A*, ⲉⲃⲁⲗ ϫⲉ- *F* (BM
1221) conj, *because, for*, mostly *S*: Jud 17 13 *S*,
Ps 118 45 *S* (*B* ϫⲉ-), Sa 15 11 *S*, Jer 6 9 *B*, Mic
7 18 *SAB*, Mt 20 7 *S* (var ⲉⲧⲃⲉϫⲉ-, *B* ϫⲉ-), Z 296 *S*
ὅτι; Nu 12 11 *S* (*B* ϫⲉⲟⲩⲏⲓ), Est 4 8 *S*, Ez 7 4 *SB*,
Phil 2 26 *SB* διότι; Nu 25 13 *S* (*B* ϫⲉ-), 2 Kg 3
30 *S*, Job 36 15 *S*, (*B* do), Ez 15 8 *SB* ἀνθ᾽ ὧν;
Ex 2 3 *A* (*B* diff), Job 13 15 *S* (*B* ⲉⲡⲉⲓⲇⲏ), He 5
2 *S* (*B* ϫⲉ-) ἐπεί, Mt 21 46 *S* (*B* ϫⲉ-) ἐπειδή; Ge
39 23 *S* (*B* do), Ez 33 28 *SB*, Ac 12 20 *S* (var ⲉⲧ-
ⲃⲉϫⲉ- = *B*) διὰ τό; Is 50 2 *S* (*B* do) ἀπὸ τοῦ; ShA 1
468 *S* ⲉ. ϫⲉϥⲉⲣⲟⲟⲩ ⲣⲱ ⲙⲙⲓⲛⲉ, PS 201 *S* ⲉ. ⲡⲁϫⲟⲉⲓⲥ
ϫⲉ-, El 132 *S* ⲉ. ϫⲉⲙⲛ ϭⲟⲙ ⲙⲙⲟⲕ = ib 98 *A*.

V also ⲉ- (**I.** ⲉ), ⲙⲁⲩ (ⲉⲙⲁⲩ), ⲡ-, ⲣⲟ (ϩⲓⲣⲛ-),
ⲥⲁ-, ⲧⲁⲓ, ⲧⲱⲛ, ⲧⲱⲣⲉ (ⲉⲧⲛ-, ⲛⲧⲛ-, ϩⲓⲧⲛ-), ⲟⲩⲧⲉ-,
ϭⲁ-, ϩⲁ-, ϩⲓ-, ϩⲛ-, ϩⲟⲧⲉ (ⲉⲣⲟⲧⲉ), ϫⲱ (ⲉϫⲛ-, ϩⲓϫⲛ-).

ⲛⲃⲟⲗ *S*, ⲙⲃⲟⲗ *B* (never so *S*).

I. adj, *outer, on outside, outwards*: Lev 18 9 *S* ⲟⲩⲭⲡⲟ ⲛⲃ. opp ⲛϩⲟⲩⲛ (*B* here as adv), BAp 120 *S*, C 41 23 *B* ⲧⲉⲭⲱⲣⲁ ⲛⲃ., J 35 33 *S* ⲡⲣⲟ ⲛⲃ.

II. adv, **a.** *outside, without*: Jo 18 16 (*A²* ⲙⲡⲁⲗ *B* ⲥⲁⲃ.) ἔξω, J 93 36 *S* in monastery or ⲛⲃ. ϩⲓⲕⲏⲙⲉ, CA 96 ⲡⲡⲉϥⲥⲱ ⲛⲃ. at 6th hour, BKU 1 31 vii, Mor 18 47 *S* ⲁⲣⲉ ⲛⲃ. ⲉ- = *ib* 19 55 ⲁⲡⲧⲓⲗⲉⲩⲉⲓ (*cf* ⲁⲣⲉ ⲉⲃ.), ShBMOr 8810 369 *S* ⲉⲩⲡⲁⲥⲱⲧⲙ ⲉⲡⲉⲧⲛϣⲁϫⲉ ⲛⲃ. ⲉⲙⲡⲕⲟⲥⲙⲟⲥ, LMis 196 *S* lo, many days ϯⲉⲛⲃ. seeking a servant, Aeg 3 *B* Joseph ⲡⲁϭⲙⲛⲃ.ⲡⲉ at work, BMis 95 *S*, Z 354 *S*, MG 25 164 *B* ⲁⲩϭⲉⲙ ⲡⲓⲥⲕⲉⲩⲟⲥ ⲙⲃ. *absent*; ⲛⲁⲩ ⲙⲃ. frequent *B* (*S* ⲛⲁⲩ ⲉⲃ.) βλέπειν, ἀναβλ. prob belongs here; PS 84 *S* ϫⲓⲛⲡⲃ. ϣⲁⲟⲩⲛ (incorrect *ib* 9, 207, 328 ϫⲓⲛⲃ.); *ib* 33 320 ⲛⲃ. ⲧⲁⲓ *hence*, Br 47 *S* ⲉⲧⲛⲃ. ⲧⲁⲓ, *cf* Deu 9 12 *B* ⲉⲃ. ⲧⲁⲓ ἐντεῦθεν. **b.** *spread abroad, famed*: Va 61 29 *B* robber chief ⲉⲣⲉⲡⲉϥⲣⲁⲛ ⲙⲃ. ὀνομαστός, Z 334 *S* anchorite ὄνομα ἔχοντα μεγάλου ἀναχ., ? Is 38 16 *S* ⲟⲩⲱⲛⲉ...ⲛⲕⲟⲟⲩ ⲛⲃ. (Gk om, *cf* Eph 2 20). **c.** *merely = extant, in existence*: of darkness Jo 20 1 *SB*, of cold *ib* 18 18 *S* εἶναι, of light Ac 27 20 *S* ἐπιφαίνειν, of famine C 89 125 *B*, of wind (ceasing) Mk 6 51 *S* ⲗⲟ ⲛⲃ. κοπάζειν, of time Ge 29 7 *S*, of persecution Aeg 279 *S* ⲡⲁⲓⲱⲧⲙⲟⲥ ⲉⲧⲛⲃ. ὄντος, Va 62 290 *B* ⲟⲩⲟⲛ ⲕⲉⲃⲟⲧ ⲃ̄ ⲙⲃ. ἔτι, RE 4 28 *S* epitaph ⲙⲡⲁⲧⲙⲟⲩ ⲛⲃ. In BIF 14 133 *S* ⲁϥⲣⲟⲕ ⲉⲣⲉⲡⲉⲕϩⲏⲧ ⲛⲃ. (var LMär 30 ⲟⲕⲙ) ? = ἐξιστάναι.

ⲛⲃⲗ- *S*, ⲙⲡⲃⲗ- *A* prep, *beyond, except*, mostly = *B* ⲉⲃⲏⲗ ⲉ-: Nu 5 20, 28 31 *S* πλήν (*B* ⲭⲱⲣⲓⲥ, ⲥⲁⲃ. ⲙ-), *ib* 16 49 *S* χωρίς, Is 43 11 *S*, Hos 13 4 *A* παρέξ; yet sometimes c gen ⲛ-: ⲛⲃⲗ ⲛ- Ge 46 26 *S*, Nu 6 21 *S*, Ps 17 31 *S*, Lu 24 21 *S* (var ⲛⲃ.), Br 87 *S* (not *ib* 53), Tri 498 *S*; sometimes ⲛⲃⲗⲗ: Ps 17 31 *S* (var), Jth 8 25 *S*; with suff: ⲛⲃⲗⲗⲁ⸗ (2 sg f ⲛ ⲃⲗⲗⲁ Mor 41 100), Ex 20 3 *S*, Deu 32 39 *S*, Sa 12 13 *S*, Pro 7 1 *A*, Hos 13 4 *A*, ⲙⲡⲃⲗⲗⲉ⸗, Joel 2 27 *A* ⲙⲃⲗⲗⲉ⸗.

ⲡⲥⲁⲃⲏⲗ (once ⲥⲁⲃ. BHom 30) *SF*, ⲥⲁⲃⲗⲗ *A* (El 88), ⲉⲃⲏⲗ *BF* (not so *S* Deu 32 20), but ⲉⲃⲏⲗ mostly = *S* ⲉⲓⲙⲏⲧⲓ, ⲛⲥⲁ-, *outside of, except*: **I.** prep with following ⲉ- (rare *S*), Ps 105 23 *SB*, Mt 14 17 *BF* (*S* ⲛⲥⲁ-), Ro 13 1 *B* (*S* ⲉⲓⲙⲏⲧⲓ), MG 25 209 *B* εἰ μή, Ge 14 24 *B*, 1 Kg 2 2 *B*, Is 45 21 *B* (*S* ⲛⲃⲗⲗ-), Si 7 28 *S* *nisi per illos*, Ac 27 22 *B* (*S* ⲉⲓⲙⲏⲧⲓ) πλήν, Ge 21 26 *B* ἀλλά, Ps 132 1 *B* (*S* ⲛⲥⲁ-) ἀλλ' ἤ, CaiEuch 582 *B* ⲡⲕⲉⲟⲩⲁⲓ ⲁⲛ ⲉⲃ. ⲉⲣⲟⲕ ἔκτος, Is 43 11 *B* (*S* ⲛⲃⲗⲗ-) παρέξ, MIE 2 404 *B* come not hither ⲉⲃ. ⲉⲡⲥⲁⲃⲃⲁⲧⲟⲛ, C 89 135 *B* this word shall not be for edification ⲉⲃ. ⲉⲟⲩϣⲟⲣϣⲉⲣ (*S* ⲉⲓⲙⲏⲧⲉⲓ ⲛϥϣⲣϣⲱⲣϥ).

II. conj, **a.** with following prep ⲉ-: C 86 298 *B* ⲉⲃ. ⲉϯⲛⲟⲩ οὐδέποτε; or ⲛ-: Deu 32 27 *S* (*B* ⲉⲃ. ⲉⲟⲃⲉ-); or ⲉⲧⲃⲉ-: BAp 110 *S* ⲛⲥⲁⲃ. ⲉⲧⲃⲉⲧⲙⲡⲁⲛⲧ, BMar 27 *S* sim; ϫⲉⲛ- Mt 12 24 *B* (*S* ⲉⲓⲙⲏⲧⲓ) εἰ μή; or ⲙⲛⲛⲥⲁ-: MG 25 234 *B* εἰ μή μετά. **b.** with adv: ⲁⲣⲏⲟⲩ (*B* only) Dan 2 11 ἀλλ' ἤ, 1 Cor 7 5 *B* εἰ μήτι ἄν, 2 Cor 13 5 *B* (*S* ⲉⲓⲙⲏⲧⲓ ϫⲉⲙⲉϣⲁⲕ) εἰ μήτι; ⲛϣⲟⲣⲡ EW 147 *B* ⲉⲃ. ⲛϣ. ⲉⲁⲟⲩⲛⲓ ⲟⲩⲱⲛϩ ⲉⲣⲟϥ πρίν, BHom 7 *S* ⲛⲥⲁⲃ. ⲛϣ. ⲛϥϫⲟ. **c.** with vb (subjunct): Ex 33 15 *B*, Mt 5 13 *B* (*S* ⲛⲥⲁ-) εἰ μή, Rec 6 181 *B* ⲉⲃ. ⲛⲧⲉⲡⲥⲱⲟⲩⲧⲉⲛ ⲉⲃⲟⲗ ⲡⲉⲙⲡⲉⲡⲉⲣⲛⲟⲩ (*S* ϣⲁⲡⲧⲛ-), Mor 37 37 *S* ⲙⲉϥⲕⲧⲟϥ...ⲛⲥⲁⲃ. ⲛϥⲛⲁⲩ ⲉⲡⲣⲱⲙⲉ εἰ μή.

ⲛⲥⲁⲃⲏⲗ ϫⲉ- *SF*, ⲉⲃⲏⲗ ϫⲉ- *B* with vb, introduces condit: Ge 31 42 *SB*, Ps 93 17 *SB*, Is 1 9 *SBF* εἰ μή, Job 6 5 *SB* ἀλλ' ἤ, ShC 42 118 *S* ⲛⲥⲁⲃ. ϫⲉⲧⲛϣⲓⲛⲉ, BAp 92 *S* ⲛⲥⲁⲃ. ϫⲉⲛⲡⲉⲓⲣ ⲁⲧⲥⲱⲧⲙ *except I had been heedless*, C 43 164 *B* ⲉⲃ. ϫⲉϯⲙⲉⲓ ⲙⲙⲟⲕ; vb rarely unexpressed: Aeg 17 *S* ⲛⲥⲁⲃ. ϫⲉⲛⲧⲟⲕⲡⲉ ⲡⲁⲉⲓⲱⲧ (*B* ⲉⲃ. ϫⲉ-).

With ⲛⲥⲁⲃⲏⲗ, ⲉⲃⲏⲗ *cf* ⲃⲏⲗ† under ⲃⲱⲗ.

ⲥⲁⲃⲟⲗ, ⲥⲁⲡⲃⲟⲗ (ⲥⲁⲃⲃⲟⲗ), ⲛⲥⲁⲃⲟⲗ, ⲛⲥⲁⲡⲃⲟⲗ *SBO*, ⲥⲁⲡⲃⲗ *AF*. Where *S* ⲛⲥⲁⲃ., *B* mostly ⲥⲁⲃ. **I.** prep, c ⲛ-, rarely ⲉ-, *outside of, beyond, away from*: often with vbs of distance or motion from, as ⲟⲩⲉ: Ps 9 21, Jer 2 5 *SB* μακρόθεν ἀφιστάναι, Pro 4 24 *SB* (*A* ϩⲓⲥⲁⲃ.) μακρὰν ἀπῶσαι, Ps 70 12 *SB*, Is 29 13 *S* (var ⲉⲃ.); ϣⲱⲡⲉ: PSBA 20 102 *O* σωβι σαβολ απο; ⲡⲱⲧ: Ja 4 7 *SB* ἀπό, Aeg 254, 269 *S*, LMärt 5 *S* (all ⲛⲥⲁⲃ.); ⲡⲟⲩϫⲉ: 2 Kg 13 9 *S* ἀπὸ ἐπάνωθεν, Mt 5 29 *S* (varr ⲛⲥⲁⲃ., ⲉⲥⲁⲃ., *B* ⲉⲃ. ϩⲁ-) ἀπό; ⲥⲓⲧⲉ: ShMich 550 13 *S* ⲡⲧⲁϥⲥ. ⲙⲡⲉⲩϩⲏⲧ ⲛⲥⲁⲃ. ⲙⲡⲝ̅ⲥ̅ (*cf* WTh 189 *S* ⲛⲥⲁⲃ., LMärt 38 *S* ϩⲁⲃ. & *v* below ϩⲁⲃⲟⲗ); ⲡⲗⲁⲡⲁ: Deu 13 5 *S* (var ⲉⲃ. ϩⲛ-), Ryl 89 *S*; ⲁⲡⲁⲭⲱⲣⲉⲓ: Wess 15 119 *S*, Leyd 445 *S*, Miss 4 182 *B*; ⲕⲧⲟ: Ps 21 24 *SB*, Pro 24 18 *S*, Is 1 15 *F* (both var ⲉⲃ.) ἀπό; with other vbs, as ⲉⲓⲣⲉ: Lev 8 33 *B* ἀπό, 1 Thes 4 6 *B* (both *S* ⲛⲃ.) ὑπερ-, TstAb 177 *B* ⲉⲣ ⲥⲁⲃ. ⲙⲫⲣⲟ, Mor 39 39 *F* ⲉⲣⲥⲁⲃ. ⲛⲧⲡⲟⲗⲓⲥ (*B* ⲟϩⲓ ⲥⲁⲃ. ⲛ-, where *cf* AM 125) BG 127 *S* ⲣ ⲁⲧⲟⲩⲱⲛϩ ⲛⲥⲁⲃ. ⲙⲙⲟⲟⲩ; ⲣⲓⲕⲉ: Ps 138 19 *SB* ἀπό, ShC 73 152 *S*, C 41 66 *B*, MG 25 4 *B* ἐκκλίνειν gen; ⲫⲱⲣϫ: Ac 1 4 *B* ἀπό; ⲱⲥⲕ: Va 62 277 *B* ⲛϯⲛⲁⲱ. ⲁⲛ ⲥⲁⲃ. ⲙⲙⲟⲕ (*cf* PS 33 ⲛⲃ., Miss 4 696 ⲙⲛⲃ.). Further: Is 42 2 *B* (*S* ϩⲓⲃ.), MG 25 6 *B*, C 86 278 *B* ἔξω, Ge 7 16 *SB*, Jer 21 4 *B*, Ez 40 5 *B* ἔξωθεν; Dan 11 4 *B*, 1 Cor 14 5 *B*, *ib* 15 2 *B* (both *S* ϩⲓⲃ.) ἐκτός, Est C 14 *S*, Job 42 8 *S* εἰ μή; MG 25 13 *B* ἄνευ, Ac 18 12 *B*, 1 Cor 3 11 *B* (*S* = Gk) παρά; Lev 23 38 *B*, Si 22 24 *A* (both *S* ϣⲁⲧⲛ-) πλήν, also El 8 8 *A* ⲥⲁⲃⲗⲗ ⲉⲧⲟⲩⲡⲥ ⲣⲙⲉϥⲙⲁⲩⲧ, Eph 2 12 *B* (*S* ⲁϫⲛ-) χωρίς, BMis 557 *S* tongues ⲉⲩⲥⲁⲃ. ⲛⲧⲉⲩⲧⲁⲡⲣⲟ, PS 358 *S* ⲉⲡϣⲁⲁⲧ ⲥⲁⲃ. ⲙⲙⲟⲕ, Va 64 162 *B* ⲉⲣⲉⲧⲉϥⲥⲁⲣⲝ ⲭⲏ ⲥⲁⲃ.

ⲡϣⲱⲡⲓ, PLond 4 523 *S* not to take aught ⲥⲁⲃ. ⲡⲡⲉϩⲙⲟⲥⲓⲟⲛ, AZ 23 150 *S* ϩⲱⲃ ⲛⲓⲙ ⲉⲧⲡⲥⲁⲃ. ⲙⲙⲟϥ (var ⲉⲣⲟϥ) his *existing* responsibilities, PLond 4 483 *S* whether akin to us or ⲉⲩⲥⲁⲃ. ⲙⲙⲟⲛ, BMis 62 *S* not divided ⲥⲁⲃ. ⲉⲡⲉⲛⲧⲁϥϫⲡⲟϥ, MR 5 28 *S* Lord keep thee ⲥⲁⲃ. ⲉⲡⲉⲑⲟⲟⲩ ⲛⲓⲙ.

II. adv, *outside, without*: 3 Kg 8 8 *B*, Is 42 2 *B* ἔξω, Ez 7 15, ib 46 2 *B*, 2 Cor 7 5 *B* (all *S* ϩⲓⲃ.) ἔξωθεν, BMis 359 *S* ⲧⲟⲩϫⲉⲧⲏⲅⲧⲛ ⲛⲥⲁⲃ. (var om.), Gu 64 *S* ⲡⲉϥⲕⲏⲡⲉ ⲛⲥⲁⲃ., of excommunication C 41 36 *B* ⲕϫⲏ ⲥⲁⲃ., Miss 4 97 *B* sim (*S* ⲕⲁⲑⲉⲣⲟⲩ), MIE 2 393 *B* ⲧϫⲱⲣⲁ ⲉⲧⲥⲁⲃ. (*S* ⲛⲃ.), AM 252 *B* ⲥⲟⲫⲓⲁ ⲉⲧⲥⲁⲃ. worldly wisdom, HL 81 *B* ϫⲓⲡⲥⲱⲧⲙ ⲉⲧⲥⲁⲃ. φήμη.

ϣⲁⲃⲟⲗ, ⲡϣⲁⲃⲟⲗ *SB* (*B* mostly ϣⲁⲉⲃ., rarely *S*, Z 268), ϣⲁⲃⲁⲗ *F*. **I.** prep (*S* only, rare), *to the outside of, out of*: BM 379 *S* they escorted us ϣⲁⲃ. ⲙⲡⲣⲟ, Z 335 *S* they reached ϣⲁⲃ. ⲡⲟⲗⲉⲓⲧ.

II. adv, *outwards*: PS 9 *S* ϫⲓⲛⲡⲣⲟⲩⲡ ϣⲁⲃ. *henceforth*: ShA 1 247 *S* some wine is good ϫⲉⲓⲡⲧⲉϥⲁⲣ-ϫⲏ ϣⲁⲃ.; *to the end, for ever*: Deu 31 30 *B* (*S* ϣⲁⲡⲉⲥϫⲱⲕ, cf Hab 3 13 *SA* διάψαλμα), Job 20 28 *SB*, Ps 15 11 *SB*, Mt 10 22 *SB*, Lu 18 5 *SB* εἰς τέλος, Sa 19 1 *S*, He 3 14 *SB*, Aeg 290 *S* μέχρι τέλ., Dan 6 26 *B*, 1 Cor 1 8 *SB* ἕως τέλ., Ap 2 26 *SB* ἄχρι τέλ., 2 Kg 2 26 *S* εἰς νῖκος (cf Am 8 7 *SB* ⲉⲅⲭⲣⲟ); also ἕως συντελείας, ἕως αἰῶνος, (He 13 8 *S*, cf C 42 93), ἐνδελεχῶς, διὰ παντός, εἰς τὸ διηνεκές, ἐπέκεινα, ἕως σφόδρα (Ps 118 43 *B* + ⲉⲙⲁ-ϣⲱ), Mor 48 12 *S* ϫⲓⲛⲧⲉⲡⲟⲩ ϣⲁⲃ. (var BMar 209 ϣⲁⲉⲡⲉϩ); *finally*: Ge 46 4 *S* (P 131⁵ 30, *B* ϣⲁ-ⲇⲁⲉ) εἰς τέλ., Ep 87 *S* a contract ⲉϥϯ ϣⲁⲃ. ⲡⲟⲩⲡⲟ-ⲅⲣⲁⲫⲏ of scribe (cf elsewhere ⲙⲡⲓⲥⲱⲥ); *utterly*: Nu 17 13 *S*, Ps 9 7 *B* (*S* ⲉⲡⲧⲏⲣϥ), Si 10 14 *S* εἰς τέλ., ShBor 246 82 *S* of Naaman ⲡⲟⲉ ⲉⲡⲧⲁϥ-ⲧⲏⲃⲃⲟ ϣⲁⲃ., PS 49 *S*; *at all*: AZ 23 39 *F* lo, 15 years hath he paid no tax ⲡϣⲁⲃ. With J 122 37 *S* cf ? CO 144 *S* & with this ? ST 109 *S* ϣⲁⲉⲡⲉϩ.

III. nn m, *the uttermost*, only J 50 70, ib 75 57 *S* ⲡⲥⲉϩⲣⲁ ⲙⲙⲟⲛ ⲙⲡϣⲁⲃ.

ϩⲁⲃⲟⲗ *S*, ϩⲁⲃⲁⲗ *F*, not in bibl or early *S*, where = ⲉⲃ. ⲛ-, ⲉⲃ. ϩⲛ. **I.** prep c ⲛ-, *from, away from*: Ps 33 13 *S* (Mor 54 63, var ⲉⲃ. ϩⲛ-, *B* ⲉⲃ. ϩⲁ-) ἀπό, Is 30 11 *F* (*S* ⲉⲃ. ⲛ-), Lam 5 10 *F*, Ap 6 16 *F* (*S* ⲙⲡⲉⲙⲧⲟ ⲉⲃ. ⲛ-), Mt 6 13 *F*, ZNTW 24 84 *F* ἀπό, RChamp 543 *F* ⲃⲓ ⲙⲉⲅ ⲡⲉⲣⲙⲁⲙ ϩⲁⲃ. ⲙⲁⲥ; Mk 16 3 *F* (*S* ⲉⲃ. ϩⲓⲣⲛ-) ἐκ, P 129¹⁸ 114 *S* ⲧⲁⲥⲱⲧⲉ ϩⲁⲃ. ⲡⲡⲁⲡⲟⲃⲉ κἀμὲ ἐλευθεροῦσιν ἐκ (cf Ps 129 8 *S* ⲉⲃ. ϩⲛ-) Mor 17 85 *S* Cynops ⲗⲟ ϩⲁⲃ. ⲡⲟⲩⲟⲡ ⲛⲓⲙ ἐξ ὀφθαλ. ἐγένετο, Mor 54 125 *S* bodies pure ϩⲁⲃ. ⲡⲭⲱⲣⲙ ⲛⲓⲙ, LMärt 38 *S* ⲥⲱⲣⲙ ⲡⲉⲩϩⲏⲧ ϩⲁⲃ. ⲙⲡⲡⲉ (v above, ⲥⲁⲃⲟⲗ), Mor 27 30 *S* ⲁϥⲡⲱⲧ ϩⲁⲃ. ⲡⲧⲉϩⲓⲏ (var BMis 380 he drew aside ⲛⲃ. ⲡⲧⲉϩⲓⲏ), Lam-

mayer 51 *S* of one ⲉϥⲡⲏⲧ ϩⲁⲃ. ⲙⲡⲥⲱⲙⲁ ⲙⲡⲉⲭ̅ⲥ̅ (= R 1 2 47 ⲕⲧⲟ ⲉⲃ. ⲙ-), Bor 253 152 *S* Potiphar's wife ϯⲡⲁⲁⲡⲟⲗⲁⲅⲉ ⲙⲙⲟⲓ...ϩⲁⲃ. ⲙⲡⲥⲁ ⲡⲓⲱⲥⲏⲫ τοῦ κάλλους, Mor 30 15 *F* martyr condemned ⲡⲥⲉϫⲁ-ⲗⲉⲕϥ ⲉⲡⲭⲓⲥⲉ ϩⲁⲃ. ⲙⲡⲕⲉⲣⲓ (*S* ⲟⲩⲧⲉⲡⲉ ⲙⲡⲡⲕⲁϩ), BM 598 *F* ⲡⲉⲗⲕⲁⲧⲉϫⲓ ⲙⲁⲃ ϩⲁⲃ. ⲙⲁⲓ; c ϩⲁ-, *from*: Z 292 *S* ϩⲁⲃ. ϩⲁⲡϫⲓϩⲣⲁϥ ἀπό.

II. adv (*F* only, rare): BM 587 1 ϣⲁⲗⲉⲕⲉⲣⲱⲃ ϣⲱⲡⲓ ϩⲁⲃ. (ⲡ)ⲧⲉⲡⲉⲧⲉⲡⲉⲣⲏⲧ ⲧⲱⲧ, CMSS 20 ⲧⲁⲗⲉⲅⲓ ϩⲁⲃ., BM 589 obscure.

ϩⲓⲃⲟⲗ *S*, ϩⲓⲃⲁⲗ *AF*. **I.** prep, **a.** *outside*: R 1 5 16 *S* let them pray ϩⲓⲃ. ⲙⲡⲕⲁⲧⲁⲡⲉⲧⲁⲥⲙⲁ (var ⲛⲃ. ⲛ-), Br 267 *S* he made thereof an ἔνδυμα ϩⲓⲃ. ⲙⲡⲣⲱⲙⲉ, J 70 13 *S* ϩⲓⲃ. ⲡⲗⲁⲁⲩ ⲡⲕⲣⲟϥ (cf ib 9 29 ⲙⲡⲃ. ⲡⲕⲣⲟϥ, v ⲃⲟⲗ I. c); of excommunication: Sh(?)P 130⁵ 72 whoso curseth his fellow ϥϩⲓⲃ. ⲡⲧⲉⲕⲕⲗ. ⲙⲡⲉⲭ̅ⲥ̅, RNC 34 *S* ⲁϥⲕⲁⲁⲩ ϩⲓⲃ. ⲡⲙⲁⲩⲥ-ⲧⲏⲣⲓⲟⲛ ἀσύνακτους καὶ ἀκοινωνήτους, ST 366 *S* ⲧⲉⲧⲣⲓⲃ. ⲡⲙⲏⲥⲧⲏⲣⲓⲟⲛ, CO 287 *S* ϯⲡⲁⲃⲱⲕ ϩⲓⲃ. ⲡⲡϣⲁ (v also **II. a**). **b.** *beyond, excepting*: Ep 140 *S* what is ϩⲓⲃ. ⲡⲧⲉⲩⲅⲣⲁⲫⲏ. **c.** *before, in presence of* (judicial): CO 481 *S* thus he spake ϩⲓⲃ. ⲙⲙⲟⲓ, Ep 143 *S* ⲁⲕⲣⲟⲙⲟⲗⲟⲅⲉⲓ ϩⲉⲃ. ⲙ-.

II. adv, **a.** *on the outside, from without*, mostly = *B* ⲥⲁⲃ.: Lev 17 4 *S* (*B* ⲥⲁⲃ.), Deu 25 5 *S*, Pro 7 12 *SA*, Mk 3 31 *S* ἔξω, Jud 12 9 *S*, Ez 7 15 *S*, Mt 23 28 *S*, Z 303 *S* ϩⲡϣⲁⲭⲉ ϩⲓⲃ. ἔξωθεν, 1 Cor 14 5 *S*, ib 15 2 *SF* ἐκτός (which in Copt ends the phrase), Aeg 217 *S* χωρίς, Aeg 235, 236 *S* apocrypha ϩⲓⲃ. *outside* the canon, Z 587 *S* ⲥⲉϩⲩⲡⲟ-ⲕⲣⲓⲛⲉ ϩⲓⲃ. thinking themselves virgins, ShC 73 122 *S* ϩⲉⲡⲕⲁⲧⲁⲥⲁⲣϫ ⲡⲧⲁϥ ϩⲓⲃ., Ep 461 *S* ⲱϣ ϩⲓⲃ. = verte; *from without*: ShC 42 123 *S* all that come ϩⲓⲃ., ShC 73 72 *S* if books be brought us ϩⲓⲃ., ShA 2 240 *S* as one that looketh ϩⲓⲃ. ⲉⲣⲟⲩⲛ ⲉⲩⲏⲓ; of excommunication: Aeg 218 *S* ⲕⲁ...ϩⲓⲃ. ἀφωρισ-μένος γίνεσθαι (v ⲕⲱ), CA 88 *S* he shall pass a year ϩⲓⲃ. (v also **I. a**). **b.** *to the outside, to the end, forth*: JTS 4 389 *S* at communion ⲁⲧⲉϫⲣⲓⲁ ϣⲱⲡⲉ ⲉⲧⲣⲉⲡⲉⲓⲡⲉ ⲛⲣⲉⲡⲕⲉⲟⲉⲓⲕ ϩⲓⲃ., Bor 260 100 *S* Christ tempted until it should be manifest ϫⲉⲉϥⲡⲁⲁⲙⲁϩⲧⲉ ϩⲓⲃ. or should succumb (cf ϣⲁⲃ.).

III. adj (rel), *outer, outward*: 2 Kg 13 18 *S* ⲡⲣⲟⲓⲧⲉ ⲉⲧϩⲓⲃ. ἐπενδύται, Mt 22 13 *S* (*B* ⲥⲁⲃ.) ἐξώτερος, 2 Cor 4 16 *S* (*B* ⲥⲁⲃ.) ὁ ἔξω, Mor 37 107 *S* ⲡⲧⲟⲟⲩ ⲉⲧϩⲓⲃ. do, CA 108 *S* ⲧⲉϫⲟⲩⲥⲓⲁ ⲉⲧϩⲓⲃ. *the civil power*, Miss 8 156 *S* ⲡⲥⲟⲫⲟⲥ ⲉⲧϩⲓⲃ., Mor 36 60 *S* ⲡⲉⲭⲱⲙⲗⲉ ⲉⲧϩⲓⲃ. of gentiles, Z 317 *S* ⲧⲉⲣⲛⲙⲟⲥ ⲉⲧϩⲓⲃ. ἡ παρακάτω ἐρ. (but = *B* MG 25 125 ⲉⲧⲥⲁϫⲟⲩⲡ ⲙⲙⲟϥ).

ⲣ ⲃⲟⲗ or ⲣ ⲡⲃⲟⲗ (rare ⲣ ⲡⲃⲗ) *S*, ⲣ ⲃⲁⲗ *AA²*, ⲉⲣ ⲉⲃⲟⲗ *B*, ⲉⲗ ⲃⲁⲗ *F*, *become loosened, become free*, hence *avoid, escape*. **I.** intr: Is 66 7 *SB*, Si

6 36 *S*, He 2 3 *SBF* ἐκφεύγειν, Pro 6 5 *SA* (*B* ⲛⲟϩⲉⲙ) σώζειν, PS 257 *S* ⲧⲁⲣⲉⲧⲛⲣ ⲃ. (paral ⲛⲟⲩϩⲙ), ShC 42 39 *S* he strove with me ⲉϥⲟⲩⲱϣ ⲉⲣ ⲃ. (var ⲉⲃⲱⲕ); with poss: Deu 15 16 *S* (*B* ⲉⲃ. ϩⲁ-) ἐξέρχεσθαι ἀπό, Si 14 14 *S* παρέρχ. acc, BHom 20 *S* ⲉϥϣⲁⲛⲣ ⲡⲉⲛⲃ. ἀπεῖναι, PS 117 *S* ϯⲛⲁⲣ ⲡⲉϥⲃ. ⲁⲛ.

II. with obj: **a.** c ⲉ- Deu 2 36 *S* (*B* ⲫⲱⲧ ⲛⲧⲉⲛ-) διαφεύγειν, Job 5 15 *S* (*B* ϧⲉⲛ-) ἐξέρχ. ἐκ, Pro 10 19 *SB* ἐκφεύγ. ἐκ, Ro 2 3 *S* (*B* ⲫⲱⲧ ⲛⲧⲉⲛ-) ἐκφεύγ. acc, Mt 23 33 *S* (*B* ⲫⲱⲧ ⲉⲃ. ϧⲉⲛ-) φεύγ. ἀπό, R 2 1 64 *S* ⲉⲁⲩⲣ ⲃ. ⲉⲛⲉⲧⲕⲁⲥ, BM 215 1 *S* ⲛⲥⲉⲣ ⲃ. ⲉⲣ ⲁⲥⲉⲃⲏⲥ, MIE 2 420 *B* ⲉⲧⲛⲁⲉⲣ ⲉⲃ. ⲉⲧⲉⲙϫⲉⲙ ϯⲡⲓ, ShC 73 158 *S* ⲉⲩϣⲁⲛⲣ ⲡⲃ. ⲉⲧⲥⲟⲟⲩϩⲥ. **b.** c ⲛ- (mostly = *B* ⲉⲣ ⲥⲁⲃ.) Lev 8 33 *S* ἐξέρχ. ἀπό, Mk 11 19 *S* ἐκπορεύεσθαι ἔξω, Sa 6 25 *S* παροδεύειν, 1 Thes 4 6 *S* ὑπερβαίνειν, Deu 4 9 *S* (*B* ⲉⲃ. ϧⲉⲛ-) ἀφιστάναι ἀπό, Va 67 31 *B* dying man ⲉϥⲟⲩⲱϣ ⲉⲉⲣ ⲉⲃ. ⲙⲫⲙⲟⲩ, P 131[2] 104 *S* ⲉⲧⲙⲣ ⲡⲃⲗ ⲛⲧⲙⲉ, ShP 130[4] 104 *S* none doth ⲣ ⲡⲃⲗ ⲛⲛⲉⲛⲧⲁⲡϫⲟⲉⲓⲥ ϩⲱⲛ ⲙⲙⲟⲟⲩ, Cl 20 6 *A* ⲙⲁⲥⲣ ⲡⲃⲗ ⲡⲡⲕⲗ παρεκβαίνειν. **c.** c ⲛⲧⲛ- El 58 *A* ⲁⲕⲣ ⲁⲃ. ⲛⲧⲟⲟⲧϥ, R 1 5 30 *S* the cup ⲣ ⲃ. ⲛⲧⲟⲟⲧϥ and broke (*cf* C 43 13 *B*), Va 59 35 *B* stone ⲉⲣ ⲉⲃ. ϧⲉⲛⲛⲉⲛϫⲓϫ. **d.** c ϩⲁ- (*B* only) AM 48 ⲛⲧⲉⲕⲉⲣ ⲉⲃ. ϩⲁⲛⲃⲁⲥⲁⲛⲟⲥ (mostly in this phrase c ⲉ-: C 43 16, AM 211). **e.** c ϩⲛ-, ϧⲉⲛ- BIF 13 113 *S* animal running ⲁϥⲣ ⲃ. ϩⲛⲟⲩϣⲓⲕ (*cf* ? C 86 31 *B* javelin ⲉⲣ ⲉⲃ. ϧⲉⲛⲡⲓⲁⲏⲣ fell *from*), Tob 9 4 *S* ἐξέρχ. ἀπό Pro 11 8 *B* (*S* ⲉⲓ ⲉⲃ. ϩⲁ-) ἐκδύειν.

III. approxim transl: Ex 21 19 *S*, Job 12 6 *S* ἀθῷος εἶναι, *ib* 14 4 *S* καθαρὸς εἶναι, Si 20 28 *S* (Miss 8 151) ἐξιλάσκεσθαι, HSt 469 *S* (var ⲛⲟⲩϩⲙ) περιγίνεσθαι gen, 1 Thes 2 17 *SF* ἀπορφανίζεσθαι ἀπό. In Pro 16 29 *S* ἀποπειρᾶσθαι obscure (?misunderstood).

ⲕⲁ ⲃⲟⲗ *S*, -ⲃⲁⲗ *A* (mostly = *B* ϣⲓϯ) vb **I.** intr *cast forth*, so *vomit*: Is 19 14 *S* ἐμεῖν, Pro 25 16 *S* ἐξεμ., Si 34 23 *S* *evomere*, ShRE 11 18 *S* of taking sacrament repeatedly ϣⲁⲛⲧⲟⲩⲕ. **II.** tr: Pro 23 8 *SA* ἐξεμ., Ap 3 16 *S* ἐμ., PMéd 319 *S* let him drink it, ϥⲛⲁⲕ. ⲛⲛϩⲓⲕ, ShR 2 3 47 *S* ⲡⲉⲧⲉϩⲛⲁϥ ⲉⲕⲁ ⲃ....ⲛⲛⲉⲛⲧⲁϥⲟⲩⲟⲙⲟⲩ, ShA 2 338 *S* of maneaters ϩⲁⲛⲥ ⲉⲧⲣⲉⲩⲕ. ⲙⲙⲟⲟⲩ.

—— nn, *vomit*: Pro 26 11 *S* (*B* 2 Pet 2 21 ϣⲓϯ) ἔμετος, BMOr 8811 243 *S* ⲧⲉⲓⲁϣⲏ ⲛⲕ....ⲛⲧⲁⲕⲛⲟϫⲟⲩ ⲉϩⲣⲁⲓ, ShC 42 81 *S* ⲡⲉⲕϣⲁϫⲉ ⲛⲕ.

ⲃⲗⲁ *B* nn, among musical instruments, K 139 جنك، مُطَيل; the 1st of these a kind of harp, the 2nd a small bell (*v* مطل Dozy). But ⲃ. prob error for ⲛⲁⲃⲗⲁ (νάβλα), which in P 44 58 طبول (*l* طبور).

ⲃⲟⲗⲃⲗ, ⲃⲗⲃⲱⲗ⸗, p c ⲃⲁⲗⲃⲗ- *S* (esp Sh, not bibl), *cf* ⲫⲟⲣⲡⲉⲣ *B*. vb **I.** intr (passive), **a.** *be undermined*, c ϩⲛ-, ⲛⲥⲁ-, ⲉ-: R 1 4 44 floods threaten ϫⲉⲛⲉⲧⲡⲟⲗⲓⲥ ⲃ....ϫⲓⲛⲛⲉⲥⲛⲧⲉ *subverti*. **b.** *burrow, delve*: ShAZ 13 111 (= P 130[2] 99) canal bank wherein an animal *burrows* ⲃ. ϩⲣⲁⲓ ⲛϩⲏⲧⲥ (*cf* ⲃ. ⲉⲃⲟⲗ), ShP 130[2] 25 soft trees ⲉϣⲁⲣⲉⲡⲓⲁϥ ⲡⲁⲅⲣⲓⲟⲛ ...ⲃ. ⲁⲩⲱ ⲛϥϣⲟϥϣϥ[...]ⲛⲉϥⲃⲏⲃ [ϩⲣⲁⲓ ⲛ]ϩⲏⲧⲟⲩ, ShA 2 71 seeking things stolen ⲉⲧⲉⲧⲛⲃ. ϩⲛⲛⲏⲉⲓ, *ib* 111 they spared not ⲉⲃ. ⲉⲡⲕⲁϩ & to shed blood thereon, ShC 42 186 ⲃ. ⲛⲥⲁⲧⲕⲁⲕⲓⲁ hidden in heart, ShA 1 281 sim, AZ 60 108 guild (κοινότης) of ϩⲙⲉⲩ ⲛⲃ. *diggers*? **c.** *wallow*: ShC 73 45 ⲛⲣⲓⲣ ⲉⲧⲃ. ϩⲛⲁⲕⲁⲑⲁⲣⲥⲓⲁ ⲛⲓⲙ.

II. tr, *dig up, out*: ShC 42 81 thou art weed fit to be cut & ⲉⲃ. ⲛⲧⲉⲕⲛⲟⲩⲛⲉ, ShLouvre R 117 (SN 105) wrath like one that cuts & ⲉϥⲃ. ⲛⲧⲛⲟⲩⲛⲉ ⲛⲟⲩϣⲏⲛ, Mor 30 31 *S[f]* to one unearthing bones ⲁⲕⲃⲉⲗⲃⲱⲗ ⲛⲕⲱⲱⲥ, Mor 50 63 bidden exhume corpse, he prays for miracle ⲙⲡⲁⲧⲁⲃⲉⲗⲃⲱⲗϥ; forming nn: BMis 151 wizards, sorcerers, ⲛⲃⲁⲗⲃⲗ ⲕⲱⲱⲥ (*cf* τυμβωρύχος Const Ap 2 52 1), Mor 28 179, *ib* 25 81 ⲣⲉϥⲃⲟⲗ. ⲕⲱⲱⲥ among criminals (*cf* ⲫⲟⲣⲡⲉⲣ), ShA 1 245 ⲃ. ⲛⲛⲉⲧϩⲉⲓϩⲟⲩⲛ ⲙⲙⲟⲕ ⲉⲃⲟⲗ ⲛϩⲏⲧⲕ.

—— ⲉⲃⲟⲗ **I.** intr, *be overturned*: Miss 8 196 when ploughed, earth ⲃ. ⲉⲃ.; *be hollowed, perforated*: ShC 73 90 holes in dyke ⲁⲩⲃ. ⲉⲃ. (var ⲃⲟⲣⲃⲣ) ⲁⲩⲱ ⲁⲩⲟⲩⲱϣⲥ ⲉⲃ. **II.** tr, *undo, take to pieces*: BAp 124 his pillow when dying ⲁϥⲧⲣⲉⲩⲃⲗⲃⲱⲗϥ ⲉⲃ. & gave in alms (*cf* ⲃⲟⲣⲃⲣ ⲉⲃ. *unweave* opp ⲥⲱϩⲉ); *undo, divest*: Mor 25 124 ⲛⲥⲉⲃⲗⲃⲱⲗⲛ ⲉⲃ. ⲛⲧⲉⲥⲧⲟⲗⲏ that clotheth us.

ⲃⲗⲃⲓⲗⲉ *SA[2]* nn f, **a.** a single *grain*: of corn = *B* ⲡⲁⲫⲣⲓ, Jo 12 24 *SA[2]*, 1 Cor 15 37 *S* κόκκος, ShZ 490 *S* many the ⲃ. that wind lays in chaff, BMis 555 *S* Job's sores like ⲃ. ⲛⲥⲟⲩⲟ; of mustard, Mt 13 31 &c *S* κόκκος; of a drug, ShC 73 89 *S* none may appropriate even a ⲃ. ⲛⲡⲁϩⲣⲉ; pebble, Leyd 272 *S* scattered stones ⲉⲧⲟ ⲛⲃ.; sand, Si 18 8 *S* ψῆφος. **b.** a single fruit: a grape in a bunch (ⲥⲙⲁϩ), Lev 19 10 *S*, Is 65 8 *S* ῥώξ (often cited: ShA 2 10, HT Y[b] 2, P 131[4] 126, TT 41, Miss 4 732, Mor 51 8), BMis 562 *S* (Gk Tischend. 51, Lat James 23 give no help); a date in a bunch, BAp 142 *S*, on a stalk (branch ϩⲙⲥ) *ib*.

ⲃⲉⲗⲑⲱⲛ *B* nn, *lion*: K 164 سبع ضرغام. Coptic?

ⲃⲱⲗⲕ *A*, ⲃⲱⲣⲕ *F*, ?ⲃⲱⲛⲕ *S* (BM 1103 16), **I.** vb intr, *be wrath*: El 92 *A* (*S* ϭⲱⲛⲧ), Mor 54 56 *S[f]* ⲡⲛⲉⲕⲃ., TU 43 11 (?) *A* c ⲁ-. **II.** nn., *wrath*: Is 5 25 *F*, Ro 2 8 *F* (*B* ⲙⲃⲟⲛ, *S*=Gk in both) ὀργή.

ⲃⲗⲕⲉ *A* nn f, *wrath* (?) : El 100 ⲥⲉϥⲉⲓⲧⲟⲩ ϩⲓⲧϩⲓ ⲛⲧϥⲃ.

ⲃⲁⲗⲕⲟⲩ *B* nn f, *bottle* for water : BMOr 8775 123 ϯⲃ. جرّ (gender not elsewhere, unless the vessel K 149 ϯⲁⲗⲕⲟⲩ be thus emended) ; of portable size : HL 104 visitor brought own bread ⲛⲉⲙⲕⲉⲃ. ⲙⲙⲟⲟⲩ, MG 25 248 (*cf* HLButler 2 55) water gushed from every (bodily) opening as from ϩⲁⲛⲟⲩⲱⲧⲉⲛ ⲙⲃ. IgR 32 suggests = βαύκαλις (? قلة), water-cooler, *cf* place last quoted.

ⲃⲗⲗⲉ *SAA²*, ⲃⲉⲗⲗⲉ *B*, ⲃⲉⲗⲗⲏ *F*, f ⲃⲗⲗⲏ *S* (ShC 42 210, ShZ 425), ⲃⲉⲗⲗⲏ *B* (CDan 94), pl ⲃⲗⲗⲉⲉⲩ *SA²*, -ⲉⲅⲉ *S*, ⲃⲗⲗⲉⲉⲅⲉ, -ⲉⲟⲩⲉ *A*, ⲃⲉⲗⲗⲉⲩ (-ⲏⲩ BSM 27) *B*, ⲃⲉⲗⲗⲏⲟⲩ *F*, sg as pl (*S*, not *B*) : Job 29 15, Ps 145 8, Is 29 18, Mt 23 24, **a.** nn, *blind person*, always τυφλός : Ex 4 11 *SB*, Is 59 10 *SB*, Zeph 1 17 *SAB*, Mk 8 23 *SB*, PS 279 *S*, El 60, 88 *A*, Aeg 43 *B*, Is 35 5 *SBF* ; BKU 1 23 *F* ⲡⲓⲕⲟⲩⲗ ⲙⲉⲡⲓⲃⲗⲏⲟⲩ, ⲃ. ⲙⲙⲓⲥⲉ one *born* blind, Mor 31 132 *S* ⲟⲩⲃ. (ⲙ)ⲙⲓⲥⲉ, AM 215 *B* ⲉⲡⲁϥⲟⲓ ⲙⲃ. ⲙⲙⲓⲥⲓ ; ⲡⲃ. ⲛⲧⲥⲟⲟⲅⲣⲉ Z 629 *S*, PMéd 240, 277 *S* white (*blind* part) of egg (in ophthalm recipes, prescribed by Diosc 2 50, Galen-Kühn 12 350, but Chassinat, 240, prefers yolk) ; in man's name J 27 27 *S* ⲓⲁⲕⲱⲃ ⲃ. **b.** adj, Mt 15 14 *SB*, Ap 3 17 *SB*, AM 120 *B*, EpJer 36 *F*, J 1 62, 6 18 *S* ⲡϩⲓⲣ ⲃ. (*cf* ῥύμη τυφλή PLond 3 235, PMon 11 31).

ⲙⲛⲧⲃⲗⲗⲉ *SA*, ⲙⲉⲧⲃ. *B* nn f, *blindness* : Lev 22 22 *S*, Zech 11 17 *AB*, BG 104 *S*, MIE 2 384 *B* ⲡⲓⲥϫⲛⲙⲁ ⲛϯⲙⲉⲧⲃ. (*S* ⲛⲛⲃ.), AZ 34 86 *S* bring upon them ⲟⲩⲙ. ⲡⲡⲉⲩⲃⲁⲗ ⲥⲡⲁⲩ.

ⲣ ⲃ., **a.** be, become blind : Is 42 19 *B* τυφλοῦσθαι, *ib* 56 10 *SB* ἐκτυφλ., Jo 9 2 *SA²B*, Ac 13 11 *SB*, τυφλ. εἶναι, γίνεσθαι, Is 44 18 *S* ἀπαμαυροῦν (*cf B*) ; c ⲛ- AM 188 *B* ⲉϥⲟⲓ ⲙⲃ. ⲡⲟⲩⲃⲁⲗ, Va 61 26 *B* sim. **b.** *make blind* : Jer 52 11 *B* ἐκτυφλ. ; c ⲉ- BMis 209, 312 *S* ⲁϥⲣ ⲃ. ⲉⲡⲉϥⲃⲁⲗ ; elsewhere expressed by ⲧⲱⲙ, eg Ex 23 8 *SB*, Jo 12 40 *SA²B*.

ⲃⲗⲁⲗⲉ *A* v ⲟⲩⲱⲱⲗⲉ.

ⲃⲁⲗⲙⲟⲩ (?) *F* nn, meaning obscure, CO 507, as pl ⲛⲉⲃⲁⲗⲙⲟⲩ ⲧⲏⲣⲟⲩ ; but ? l ⲛⲉⲃ-ⲁⲗⲙⲟⲩ.

ⲃⲁⲗⲙⲃⲉϩ *B* v ⲁⲗ *pebble* & ϭⲁⲗⲟⲩⲃⲓϩ.

ⲃⲁⲗⲟⲧ *S*, ⲃⲁⲗⲁⲧ *A* (Cl 17 1) *F* (Mor 48 34) nn f, **a.** *skin garment* : P 43 75 *S* سطمي فروة, ضأن, of sheep, opp goatskin, Bal *S* ⲃ. ⲡⲉⲥⲟⲟⲩ ⲛϣⲁⲣ ⲛⲃⲁⲙⲡⲉ, BM 1206 *S* of ass ; He 11 37 *SA* (*B*= Gk) μηλωτή, Mor 37 142 *S* Antony's apron μηλ., *ib* 141 ϣⲧⲏⲛ ⲛϣⲁⲣ μηλ., BMar 219 *S* ϩⲉⲛⲃ. ⲡⲉⲥⲟⲟⲩ as περιζώματα (var P 129¹³ 16 ⲃ. ⲛϣⲁⲣ ⲡⲉⲥⲟⲟⲩ

= *B* ⲙⲉⲗⲱⲧⲏ ⲛϣⲁⲣ), 3 Kg 19 13, 4 Kg 2 8 *S* μηλ. not translated. **b.** *skin bag*, containing sleeping mat : Z 352 *S* opp ⲥⲟⲟⲕ WS 74 ; used as pillow : Z 351 *S*, *cf* Bodl(P) f 19 *S* ⲟⲩϣⲟⲧ ⲛⲃ., Bodl(P) e 33 ⲟⲩⲃ. ⲡⲉⲧⲕⲟⲧⲕ ; obscure : CO 346, Ep 368 (*v* n).

In place-name : ⲙⲁⲛⲃⲁⲗⲟⲧ Manfalût, etymol (P 43 51) prob = *place of fleeces* فراء (فروو), not فرا *mule*, though neighbouring village البغلة, Ibn Dukmâk 5 22, recalls latter). Possibly ⲃ. & μηλωτή same word.

ⲃⲓⲗⲧⲓ *S* nn f, *thighs & hips*, *rump*, *anus* (?) : P 43 41 قطنة, مقعدة, ثقبة (*sic*, *cf* AZ 24 89), named between ⲉϩⲣⲁ and ⲙⲉϣⲕⲟⲗ (P 44 71 om).

ⲃⲉⲗϩⲱⲗ *B* v ⲃⲉⲣϩⲱⲗ.

ⲃⲗⲙⲓⲟⲩ (ShMIF 23 84), pl ⲃⲗⲙⲟⲟⲩⲉ (BM 280) *S*, ⲃⲁⲗⲙⲱⲟⲩ (P 203 153 Abû'l-Barakât), ⲃⲁⲗⲡⲉⲙⲱⲟⲩ̈ⲓ (C 41 43) *B* ; sg only MIF *l c*, whence Βλέμυς, pl Βλέμυες, barbarian people, dwelling in Christian period on E of Nile, S of Philae (*v* Sethe in Pauly-Wissowa 3 566) ; named with Nuba : MIF *l c*, Miss 4 642, with Saracens : BM *l c* (*cf* PCai 1 147) ; identified later with Begâ بجه : Miss 4 396 (but *v* Stern AZ 19 74). Abû'l-Barakât *l c* equates with بلاد علي, properly much farther S. Through their land Gihon flows : P 131¹ 62 (*v* ⲉⲓⲟⲟⲣ) ; their language : BMis 475 ; some among Shenoute's monks : MIF *l c*. Other forms : Mor 47 141 ⲃⲉⲗⲉϩⲙⲟⲩ, Miss 4 642 ⲃⲗⲉϩⲙⲟⲩ (*sic*), P 131¹ 88 (Epiphan De Gem) ⲃⲉⲗⲉϩⲙⲟⲟⲩⲉ, BMis *l c* ⲃⲗⲉϩⲙⲟⲟⲩⲉ, ⲃⲉⲗϩⲙⲟⲟⲩⲉ, HT Y^b ⲃⲗϩⲙⲁⲅⲉ.

ⲃⲗϫⲉ *SA*, ⲃⲗⲗϫⲉ *S*, ⲃⲉⲗϫ *B*, ⲃⲏⲗϫⲉ (-ϫⲓ) *F* nn f & m, *earthenware*, *pottery* : P 44 23 شقفة, خزف ; opp ⲟⲙⲉ clay : Sa 15 7-9 *S*, ShBor 246 115 *S* potter's vessels ⲉϩⲉⲛⲟⲙⲉⲛⲉ ϩⲓⲃ. **a.** f : *S* ShBM 206 85 false virginity ⲧⲃ. ⲥⲟⲧⲡ ⲉⲣⲟⲥ (this cited Miss 4 699) ; often = document written on sherd (ostracon) : CO 48, 165, Hall 52, Tor 12, Ep 302, WS 91, PLond 4 490. **b.** m (rare) : Dan 2 41, 45 *B* ὄστρακον, LCyp 7 *S* ⲉϥⲟ ⲙⲡⲉⲥⲙⲟⲧ ⲙⲡⲃ. compounded with iron, MR 4 129 *S* in glossary ⲟⲥⲧⲣⲁⲕⲱⲡ· ⲡⲃ. **c.** no gender : Job 2 8 *SB*, Ps 21 16 *SB*, Pro 26 23 *SA*, Si 22 7 *SB*, BM 216 109 *S* ὄστρ. **d.** pl : Va 57 47 *B* ⲉⲥⲣⲱⲟⲩ ⲛⲣⲟⲩϩ ⲉⲛⲓⲃ. ὄστρ., Va 69 117 *B* idols ⲛⲓϣⲉ ⲛⲉⲙⲛⲓⲃ., JTS 10 52 *B* broken like ϩⲁⲛⲃ. **e.** utensils of ⲃ. (*v* Reil Beiträge 43) : ἄγγος, ἀγγεῖον Nu 5 17 *SB*, Is 30 14 *SBF*, Jer 39 14 *SB*, LAl 17 *S* ; βῖκος Jer 19 1 *SB*, θύσκη CO 217 *S*, εἶδος J 36 26 *S*, κάδος C 89 74 = MG 17 328 *SB*, ⲉⲙⲣⲱϣⲉ Bodl(P) b 6 *S* (*v* Ep 549 n), σκεῦος Lev 6 28 *SB*, Ez 4 9 *B*, 2 Cor 4 7 *B*, ShC 73 72 *S*, ὕλη (chattels) J 68 51 *S*

(opp wood), ϩⲛⲁⲁⲩ Wess 18 20 S, Tri 303 S; ingredient in alchemy: AZ 23 114 S ⲃ. ⲉⲡⲁⲧⲟϣⲙ (cf Z 628 ⲑⲏⲡ ⲡⲁⲧⲱϣⲙ, AM 154 ⲕⲟⲡⲓⲁ ⲡⲁⲧ.) ? unslaked potsherd (dust, or ? here = shells ὄστρακα, whence ἄσβεστος, Dioscorides 2 4), Bodl(P) a 2 ⲃ. ⲡⲁⲡⲁⲥ, PMéd 298 ⲃ. ⲛⲧⲣⲓⲣ (cf ὄστρ. κριβάνων, v Chassinat's n). Written ⲃⲗⲗⲭⲉ S: Lev 11 33 var, Job 2 8 var, Ps 21 16 var, ShA 2 152, CO 217, BKU 1 67, Ep 232.

ⲡ ⲃ., *be made of pottery*: Jud 1 35 S, Dan 2 41 B. In place-name: ⲡⲥⲓⲛⲃⲗⲭⲉ Mor 18 73, BerlOr 1607 6 (v Z 237) S, ⲡⲥⲩⲙⲃⲉⲗⲉⲭ Miss 4 145 B, اسنفلجة Va ar 172 102, = Ὀστράκινη الشقف كوم, in nome of Achmîm, whither Nestorius banished (v KKS 6).

ⲃⲟⲗ S nn m, *owl*: Lev 11 17 νυκτικόραξ هام, only P 44 105 = 43 90 (after ⲅⲗⲁⲩⲕⲟⲛ, ⲗⲁⲣⲟⲥ) = Ciasca, Maspero, Mor. ⲃⲁⲓ q v (? merely بوم).

ⲃⲁⲁⲙⲡⲉ, ⲃⲁⲙⲡⲉ SA, ⲃⲁⲉⲙⲡⲓ B, ⲃⲁⲙⲡⲓ, ⲃⲁⲡⲓ F (AZ 23 41), beempe DM, ⲃⲁⲁⲙⲡ- S (Lev 4 23), ⲃⲁⲡ- F? (AZ lc) nn, *goat*: Ge 15 9 SB, Lev 3 12 SB, Dan 8 21 SB αἴξ; Ex 12 5 SB, Ez 45 23 B, Mt 25 32 SB ἔριφος; Pro 24 66 SA τράγος (this elsewhere = ϭⲓⲉ); ⲃⲁⲁⲙⲡⲣⲟⲟⲩⲧ S, ⲃ. ⲡⲣⲟⲟⲩⲧ B he-goat: Ez 43 25 B ἔριφος, Lev 4 23 SB χίμαρος; ⲃ. ⲛⲥϩⲓⲙⲉ she-goat: ib 28 SB χίμαιρα (✝ⲃ. Lev 4 29 B Lag, not in Va 1 or BM 712); ⲙⲁⲥ ⲙⲃ. kid: Is 11 6 SB, AM 6 4 AB, Lu 15 29 SB ἔριφος, Deu 14 4 S (B ⲃⲁⲣⲏⲓⲧ) χίμαρος, P 44 55 S جدي, K 166 B جدي عنز. Cf ⲃⲁⲣⲏⲓⲧ. On possible etymol v AŽ 51 126. ϣⲁⲣ ⲛⲃ. goatskin: He 11 37 SB αἴγειον δέρμα, Ep 380 S used for book-binding, ? BM 1160 (ϭⲁⲣ). ϥⲱ ⲛⲃ. goat's hair: Z 618 S, Miss 4 743 S; ⲭⲁⲕ ⲛⲃ. same P 131¹ 59. ⲙⲁⲛⲉⲃ. SA, ⲙⲁⲛⲓⲃ. B goatherd: Am 7 14 SAB αἰπόλος, C 86 97, 138 B of Diocletian (cf τραγωνάριος, l δραγ-, JTS 10 463). ϣⲁⲥⲃ. F goatherd: CMSS 77. In names: Πανβαάμπε, Σενβαμπουῆρις, Τβαάμπε (Preisigke).

ⲃⲱⲱⲛ, ⲃⲱⲱⲃⲉ (var ? ⲃⲱⲱⲃⲉ, v below) S, ⲃⲟⲩⲟⲛⲉ (ⲃⲱⲱⲡⲉ Am 8 11) A, ⲃⲱⲡ BO (Hor 78), ⲃⲱⲱⲛ F I. adj, *bad*: Va 61 93 B ⲃⲁⲗ ⲃ. (S ⲃⲁⲗ ⲙⲡⲟⲛⲏⲣⲟⲥ), Job 2 8 B ⲙⲟⲟⲩ ⲃ. (S ⲉⲓⲁⲃⲉ) ἰχώρ, MG 25 190 B (cf 189), Job 7 5 B, Va 67 74 B ⲙⲟⲩ ⲃ., BMar 39, 61 S, Wess 18 68 S, Va 61 14 B ⲙⲟⲩ ⲛⲃ. (cf ShA 1 257 S ⲙⲟⲟⲩ ⲉⲑⲟⲟⲩ); ShA 1 128 S, AZ 21 151 S, Pcod 18 S, Mor 24 31 Sᶠ ⲥϯⲃ., Aeg 30 B, BSM 110 B ⲥⲟⲟⲓ ⲃ. (Ez 36 17 S ⲥϯⲃ. = ? ἄφεδρος which elsewhere = ϣⲣⲱ); 2 Kg 13 16 (P 43 103, var ⲥϯ ⲛⲃ.) S ⲥⲟⲩⲃ. (var ⲡⲉⲑⲟⲟⲩ) κακία, Tri 508 S ϩⲃⲏⲩⲉ ⲛⲥⲟⲩⲃ. القبيح (lit evil

star, v AZ 38 77); Pro 11 22 B ⲥⲃⲱ ⲃ. (var ⲃⲟⲡⲓ) κακόφρων; Va 58 109 B ⲑⲏⲟⲩ ⲃ.; MG 25 239 B ⲫⲩⲥⲓⲥ ⲃ.; Pro 24 35 S ⲡϣⲣⲃ. (var P 44 117 ϣⲏⲣⲉ ⲃ.), A ⲡϣⲏⲣⲃⲟⲩⲟⲛⲉ, K 234 B ϣⲉⲛⲃⲟⲡ شر; Deu 28 48 SB, Si 18 24 S, Mk 13 8 SB, El 102 A ϩⲉⲃ. ϩ. λιμός opp ϩⲉⲡⲟⲩϭⲉ; MG 25 122 B ϩⲏⲧ ⲃ.; Ps 21 17 B ⲭⲁⲭⲃ. (S ⲡⲟⲡⲏⲣⲟⲥ, cf ? κακὴ κεφαλή) πονηρευόμενος, Dif 1 46 synod of Chalcedon ⲡⲧⲁⲧⲃ. (sic); BM 1113 S ϭⲁⲅⲟⲡ ⲃ., ShC 73 46 S ⲡϭⲁⲅⲟⲡ ⲃⲱⲱⲃⲉ ⲛ ⲡϭ. ⲃ. (as if these equivalents), ShBMOr 8664 2 S ⲉⲓⲉⲣ ⲃⲟⲟⲃⲉ (v below).

II. **ⲃⲟⲟⲡⲉ** SA, ⲃⲟⲡⲓ B, ⲃⲱⲡⲉ O, ⲃⲁⲁⲡⲉ Sᶠ, ⲃⲁⲡⲓ F nn f, *evil, misfortune*: a. BMOr 8811 237 slanderer, eager to hear ⲧⲃ. ⲙⲡⲉⲧϩⲓⲧⲟⲩⲱϥ, P 44 75 S ⲧⲃ. ضر (or ? l ⲉⲧⲃ.). b. with rel pref: Pro 22 8 S ⲡⲉⲧⲃ. (A ⲡⲉⲧⲣ ⲃ. κακά, Bor 260 104 S ⲧⲉⲥⲃⲱ ⲉⲧⲃ.; Pro 12 4 S ⲉⲥⲃ. (A ⲉⲥⲣ ⲃ.), ib 19 27 S (BMOr 8810 376) ⲉⲩⲃ.; ShBor 204 247 S ϩⲉⲛϣⲁⲭⲉ ⲉⲩⲃ. c. with ⲉⲓⲣⲉ (prob more correct form of last), *be evil, hurtful*, c ⲛ- opp ⲣ ⲡⲟⲩϥⲣⲉ: Pro 10 26 SA (B ⲧⲁⲕⲟ), 1 Tim 6 9 S, Va 64 160 B ⲛⲓⲡⲛⲁ ⲉⲧⲉⲣ ⲃ. ⲛⲁⲛ βλαβερός, Mk 16 18 S, BHom 133 S gold ⲉⲧⲉⲙⲁⲣⲉⲧⲉϩⲣⲙ ⲣ ⲃ. ⲛⲁϥ, Wess 18 91 S βλάπτειν, ShC 73 72 S some words ⲉⲩⲣ ⲃ. others ⲉⲩⲣ ⲡⲟⲩϥⲣⲉ, ShC 42 195 S, Va 68 49 B ⲙⲡⲉϥϩⲓⲟⲙ ⲑⲣⲉⲡⲉϥⲉⲛϣⲁϣⲓ ⲉⲣ ⲃ. ⲛⲛⲓⲁⲣⲱⲟⲩ, ROC 20 50 S ϩⲉⲛⲟⲩⲉⲗⲗⲉ ⲉⲩⲟⲩⲉⲣ ⲃ. (l ⲉⲩⲉⲣ).

ⲙⲛⲧⲃ. O nn, *misfortune* (?): Hor 79, 82.

ⲙⲛⲧⲣⲉϥⲣ ⲃ. S nn f, *evil doing*: Bor 226 170 ⲡⲭⲓ ϭⲟⲗ ⲉⲡⲉⲕⲥⲟⲡ ⲧⲙ. ⲧⲉ.

ⲉⲓⲉⲣ ⲃ. SA (var ⲃⲟⲟⲡ Deu 28 54, 56 S, HT K 1 S), ⲓⲉⲣⲃ. BF (BM 524) nn (for ⲉⲓⲉⲣ v ⲉⲓⲁ eye), I. f, *evil eye*: Aeg 282 S (prob = περικαθαίρων), KKS 300 S mothers asperge children saying We cast forth ϯⲣⲃ.; Mor 18 111 S maladies caused by old women ⲉⲧⲃⲉⲟⲩⲉⲣ(sic) ⲃ.; pl AM 313 B.

II. m, a. nn, *envious, niggardly person*: Si 18 17 S (var ⲉⲣ ⲃ.), ib 37 13 βάσκανος. b. as adj: Pro 23 6, 28 22 SA, ShBMOr 8664 2 S ⲧⲉⲥϩⲓⲙⲉ ⲡⲉⲓⲉⲣ ⲃⲟⲟⲃⲉ (v above).

ⲙⲛⲧⲉⲓⲉⲣ ⲃ. S nn f, *envy, greed*: Sa 4 12 βασκανία, ShA 1 448, ib 2 144, PO 2 156 of Judas's wife, Bor 226 180 table spread, but ⲧⲙ. ⲙⲛⲧⲙⲛⲧⲥⲕⲛⲟⲫⲟⲥ (? σκνιφότης) ⲧⲁⲕⲟ ⲡⲣⲱϣ ⲛⲧⲟⲟⲧⲛ.

ⲣ ⲉⲓⲉⲣ ⲃ. S *be envious*, c ⲉ-: Deu 28 54, 56 (B ⲉⲣ ⲃⲁⲥⲕ.) βασκάνειν, Si 14 5 πονηρός; c ⲉⲭⲛ-: ib 14 10 φθονερὸς ἐπί.

ⲣⲉϥⲉⲓⲉⲣ ⲃ. S nn, *one who casts an evil eye, enchanter*: Aeg 242 ⲣⲉϥⲣ ⲡⲁϩⲣⲉ ⲟⲩⲭⲉ ⲣ. ? περικαθαίρων, R 2 1 91 ⲣⲉϥⲙⲟⲩⲧⲉ ϩⲓⲣ.; Deu 18 10 ⲣⲉϥⲉϣ ⲉⲓⲉⲣ ⲃ. (? no Gk, ϩⲱⲡⲡ here = περικαθ.), ShHT K 1 ⲣⲉϥⲭⲓ ⲙⲁⲉⲓⲛ, ⲣⲉϥⲉϣ ⲉⲓⲉⲣ ⲃ., ⲣⲉϥⲙⲟⲩⲧⲉ (here ⲉϣ- prob from ⲱϣ).

ⲙⲛⲧⲣⲉϥⲉⲓⲉⲣ ⲃ. nn f, *greed, concupiscence*: Aeg 13 *S* my eyes have loved ⲧⲙ.

ϫⲓ ⲉⲓⲉⲣ ⲃ., *take, receive evil eye*, in 4 Kg 16 3 *S* seems = Vulg *consecrare* (no Gk), but KKS 295 *S* Manasse brought children through fire ⲉϥϫⲓ ⲉⲓⲉⲣ ⲃ. & *ib* 298 ⲉⲩϫⲓ. ⲛⲛⲉϥϣⲏⲣⲉ refer to 4 Kg 21 6 κληδονίζειν, οἰωνίζειν. *Envy* in Mor 54 27 *S* of devil ϫⲓ ⲉⲣ ⲃ. ⲉⲡⲉⲡⲟⲩϫⲁⲓ.

In place-name (?) Πιαρ βωῶν PLond 4 596.

On corresponding hierogl. term *v* AZ 59 154 (but for ⲥⲧⲓⲗⲃⲟⲛⲉ there *l* ⲥⲓⲗⲃⲟⲛⲉ Silvanus).

ⲃⲏⲛⲉ (Is 38 14, Jer 8 7), ⲃⲏⲛⲛⲉ (Mor 51 33) *S*, ⲃⲏⲛⲓ, ⲃⲉⲛⲓ (Is *l c*) *B*, ⲃⲏⲛⲓ (EpJer 21) *F*, nn m (only BMOr 8771 85 *B*), f (Va 57 23 *B*, BMOr 8781 47 *B*), *swallow* χελιδών سنونة, سنونو P 44 113 *S*, K 169, *B*; Tri 492, P 43 24 *S* ⲃⲉⲛⲉⲃⲉⲛⲉ.

ϭⲁϫ ⲙⲃ. *S*, lit *swallow-sparrow*, cf ϭⲁϫ ⲙⲃⲓⲣⲓ K 169, AZ 14 118 *B* (in both = سنونة); its nest PMéd 305 & its dung ⲣⲁⲥ *ib* 319 in recipes.

As name: ⲧⲃⲏⲛⲉ J 23 22, Βῆννε (Preisigke, or ? = ⲃⲏⲛⲉ).

ⲃⲏⲛⲉ (Hall 108), ⲃⲓⲛⲉ (Glos 391) *S* nn f, *a part of a cart*: Hall ⲧⲃ. ⲛⲡⲉⲣⲅⲟⲛ (? ⲟⲣⲅⲟⲛ) ⲉⲧⲓⲧⲟⲟⲧⲛ ⲉⲧⲉⲧⲁϭⲟⲗⲧⲉⲧⲉ, ? = ⲧⲧⲱⲣⲉ of cart, named afterwards; in Glos among (or ? following) agricultural implements, context obscure.

ⲃⲓⲛⲓ (var ⲃⲓⲛⲓ) *B* nn f, *crucible* K 128 بوتقة, among goldsmith's utensils.

ⲃⲟⲓⲛⲉ *S*, ⲟⲩⲱⲓⲛⲓ *B* nn, *harp* (meaning assured by determin. of hierogl *bnt*); *S* only 2 Kg 6 5 νάβλα (P 44 109 = طنبور kind of mandoline, Lane); *B* in Ge 31 27 κιθάρα, Ap 18 22 (*sic*, for κιθαρῳδός as *S*), *ib* 7 9 φοῖνιξ (error for ⲃⲉⲛⲓ; in Va 1 Ge 31 27 & some MSS Ap ⲟⲩⲱⲓⲛⲓ, mistaken for *light*).

ⲉⲣ ⲟⲩ. *B* Is 23 16 κιθαρίζειν (*S* = Gk).

ⲣⲉϥⲉⲣ ⲟⲩ. *B* Apoc 14 2 κιθαρῳδός (*S* = Gk).

ⲃⲱⲛⲉ *S* nn m, meaning unknown, presumably an edible: only CO 282 ⲁⲓϫⲓ ⲧⲕⲁ(ⲗⲁ)ϩⲧ ⲛⲃ., ST 282 ⲛⲟⲉⲓⲕ ⲙⲡⲕⲟⲩⲓ ⲛⲃ., PMich '21 recipe for extracting thorns ⲑⲛⲟ ⲟⲩⲃ. ϩⲓⲉⲃⲓⲱ.

ⲃⲁⲛⲏ *S* nn, bird named in magical text with hawk & pelican (?): BKU 1 1 ro 23. Spg gives an etymology.

ⲃⲱⲛⲕ *S* *v* ⲃⲱⲗⲕ.

ⲃⲏⲛⲉ *SAA*[2], ⲃⲉⲛⲓ *B*, ⲃⲏⲛⲓ, ⲃⲏⲛⲛⲓ *F*, ⲃⲛ- *S* nn f, **I.** *date palm-tree*: P 44 81 *S*, K 174 *B* نخلة, Cant 7 8 *S*, Joel 1 12 *AB* φοῖνιξ, BMOr 8811 242 *S* ⲉⲕϣⲁⲛⲭⲟ ⲡϫⲉⲃⲉⲗ ⲛⲧⲃ. ⲉϩⲣⲁⲓ ⲉⲡⲕⲁϩ, Tri 612 *S* ⲧⲃ. ⲉⲧⲧⲛⲅ ϩⲙⲡⲉⲕⲛⲓ, J 110 4 *S* ⲟⲩⲃ....ⲉⲥϭⲓⲙⲙⲉⲣⲟⲥ ⲙⲡⲕⲁϩ &c; as pl: Lev 23 40 *SB*, Ez 41 25 *SB*,

Jo 12 13 *SA*[2]*B* φοῖ.; BMar 208 *S*, BAp 144 *S*, COAd 4 *S*, PLond 4 516 *S*, Kr 3 *F*, AZ 23 39 *F*; m only Ps 91 13 *B*, BM 528 (p 260) *F*; opp ϣⲏⲛ: ShC 73 ix, *ib* 98 *S*, yet Is 1 18 *A* (Cl 8 4) ϣⲛⲃ. prob *palm-tree* and J 65 58 *S* ϣⲏⲛ(ⲡ)ⲃ. ⲕⲟⲩⲕ ? = κουκιοφόρον. **II.** *its fruit, dates*: Gu 48 *S* ⲁϥⲁⲗⲉ ⲉⲧⲃ. ⲁϥⲙⲉϩ ⲧⲟⲟⲧϥ ⲛⲃ.; mostly as pl: CO 213, 372, ST 329, Ep 174, 309, 520 *S*, BM 615 *F*; m (rare): ShC 73 136 *S*, PMéd 185 *S*, ? WS 118 *S*, ? BM 1087 *S*; dates sometimes merely *fruit of* ⲃ.: EW 160 *B* ⲟⲩⲧⲁϩ, C 41 19 *B* ⲕⲁⲣⲡⲟⲥ (*cf* Ar ثمر); dates measured in κεντηνάρια Ryl 217, ⲣⲧⲟⲃ ST 319, 438, Hall 111, ⲟⲓⲡⲉ Bodl(P) d 27, PAl 1, ⲙⲁⲁϫⲉ ST 123, WS 106, ⲕⲁⲗⲟⲩⲥ ST 329, ⲃⲉⲥⲉ CO 213, ⲕⲉⲗⲱⲗ PAl 1, ϭⲟⲟⲩⲡⲉ ST 319, ⲑⲁⲗⲓⲥ BM 637; date season (καιρός) Wess 18 5 *S*.

ⲃⲡⲣⲁⲩⲛⲉ, *virgin palm*: KroppK *S* girdle of ⲃⲉⲧ ⲛⲃⲏⲣ., *ib* to ensure conception woman shall eat ϩⲉⲛⲃⲏⲛⲉ ⲡⲣⲁⲩⲛⲉ.

ⲃ. ⲉϥⲗⲏⲕ *S*, *fresh dates*: Wess 18 5.

ⲃⲛϣⲟⲟⲩⲉ *S*, *dried dates*: WS 118 (*cf* ? PLond 4 517 ⲃⲉⲛⲉϣⲏⲩ).

ⲃ. ⲉϥⲧⲁϩ *S*, *pounded dates*: PMéd 185 cf φοίνικες πατητοί (cf ⲧⲱϭⲥ P 131[6] 37, Hall 81).

ⲃ. ⲛⲡⲁⲣⲉⲟⲛ (παλαιόν Chassinat) *S*: PMéd 111.

ⲃⲁ *S*, ⲃⲁⲓ *B* ⲛⲃ., *palm-branch*, *v* ⲃⲁ; *cf* also ⲃⲏⲧ.

ⲃⲁⲗ ⲛⲃ. *S*, *date stone*, *v* ⲃⲁⲗ.

ⲉⲃⲓⲱ ⲛⲃ. *S*, *honey of dates*: PMéd 307, P 43 241 عسل الثمر.

ⲕⲁϥ *S*, ⲭⲁϥ *B* ⲛⲃ., *stem, trunk of palm*: Ex 15 27 *SB*, Nu 33 9 *SB*, Job 29 18 *B* (*S* ϣⲗϩ), Si 50 12 *S* στέλεχος.

ⲗⲟⲟⲩ *S*, ⲗⲁⲩ *B* ⲛⲃ., *cluster of dates*: Lev 23 40 *S* (var ⲃⲏⲧ ϩⲁⲧ ⲃ.) κάλλυνθρον, BMar 208 *S* (var ⲕⲗⲁⲇⲟⲥ, *B* ⲥⲡⲁⲑⲓ), BAp 142 *S*, P 44 96 *S*, K 177 *B* عراجين.

ⲙⲟ ⲛⲃ. (*l* ⲙⲟⲩ), *date water*: ShC 73 136 *S*.

ⲥⲁⲛⲃ., *date seller*: BM 1095 *S*, ST 329 *S*.

ⲥⲣⲃ. *S*, ⲥⲉⲣⲃ. *B*, *palm-thorn*: Nu 33 55 *S* (var ⲥⲟⲩⲣⲉ) *B*, 2 Cor 12 7 *B* (*S* ⲥⲟⲩⲣⲉ) σκόλοψ, BMar 39 *S* = AM 62 *B*.

ⲧⲁϭ ⲛⲃ., *cake of dates*: 1 Kg 25 18 *S* παλάθη.

ϣⲡⲃ., ϣⲉⲃ., ϣⲏⲃ. (Hall 117), ϣⲟⲩⲃ. (P 44 66), ⲥⲟⲩⲡⲃ. (J 111 9) *S*, ϣⲉⲡⲃ., ϣⲉⲃ. (AM 166) *B*, *palm-fibre*, σεβέννιον ليف, growing round base of branch; gathered by monks: ShC 73 54 *S*; used for rope: AM 166 *B*, Va 61 12 *B*, Hall 117 *S*, C 43 79 *B* ϣⲭⲱⲧ ⲛϣⲉⲃ.; for clothing: MG 25 14 *B*, Mor 32 6 *S*, raiment of ϣ. abandoned by luxurious monks: Wess 11 165, ShP 131[6] 37 *S*; darning-needles (ἀκίς) of it: P 132[1] 16 *S*; seller of it: ⲥⲁⲛϣⲃ.WS 96 *S*.

ϣⲁⲧⲓⲗⲁ ⲛⲡⲩⲃ̅. basket (?) *of palm-fibre*: ST 118 *S*.
Cf شيبانة towing-rope BIF 20 70.

On names of palm tree and its parts *v* Rec
16 95.

ⲃⲉⲛⲛⲏ *B portal v* ⲡⲡⲛⲏ.

ⲃⲉⲛⲓⲡⲉ (PS 212, PLond 4 515, Ann 22 270) *S*,
(AZ 21 100)*O*, ⲡⲉⲛⲓⲡⲉ (PS 101, 108 & *pass*, Kropp*B*),
ⲃⲓⲛⲓⲃⲉ (BKU 1 1 ro, 21 ro), ⲡⲓⲛⲓⲡⲓ (Ryl 365, J 113
6, ST 30), ⲃⲁⲛⲓⲡⲉ (Hall 82, 131, TurM 18, ST
294, 437), ⲡⲁⲡⲓⲛ (*sic* PMich '21) *S*, ⲃⲁⲛⲓⲡⲉ *A*,
ⲃⲉⲛⲓⲡⲓ *BFO*, ⲡⲉⲛⲓⲡⲉ, ⲃⲓⲛⲓⲡⲓ *F* (ⲃⲁ-, ⲃⲉ- ? *metal*,
as in ⲃⲁⲣⲱⲧ, ⲃⲁⲥⲡⲉϭ, *v* AZ 53, 51) nn m, *iron*
I. as metal: Job 28 2 *SB*, 41 18 *SB*, Is 60 17 *SB*,
Ez 27 19 *SB* σίδηρος, PS 212 *S*; Job 6 12, 20 24 &c
S χάλκεος (mostly = *B* ϧⲟⲙⲛⲧ); opp ϧⲟⲙⲛⲧ: Ge
4 22 *SB*, Lev 26 19 *SB*, BG 74 ϧⲟⲙⲛⲧ ⲙⲛⲡⲛ.;
opp ⲗⲁⲓⲛ: BM 174 1, PS *lc*; opp ⲃⲁⲣⲱⲧ: J 38
23, 68 30 *S*.
II. a. as chains, fetters: Ps 106 10 *SB* σίδ.,
Mor 53 28 *S* = TstAb 32 *B* ⲡⲡⲉⲡⲓ. ϫⲓ ⲙⲡⲉϥⲥⲱⲙⲁ
BIF 15 242 *S* ⲉⲕⲙⲏⲣ ϧⲁⲡⲛ., C 43 211 *B* ⲉϥⲧⲁϫ-
ⲣⲏⲟⲩⲧ ⲛⲃ̅., P 129¹⁶ 10 *S* ⲉϥⲙⲏⲣ ⲉⲡⲛ. ⲙⲡⲛⲉⲩⲉⲣⲏⲩ,
BMar 21 *S* ⲁϥⲭⲣⲭⲱⲗϥ ⲧⲏⲣϥ ⲙⲛ. from head to
feet, PGol 17 *S* ⲟⲩⲡⲛ. on Martyria's right hand
and her father's left, RNC 83 *S* ϧⲉⲡⲛ. ⲡⲣⲟⲙⲛⲧ
bronze chains, *cf* ? Ryl 102 *S* ⲡ. ⲛϣⲉ ⲡⲕⲁϣⲟϣ.
b. as sword: Job 5 20, 15 22 *SB* as Gk; surgi-
cal: Z 278 *S*, Va 63 102 *B* cauterizing iron, Va
57 226 *B* woodman's, Cat 112 *B* razor, Si 48 21 *S*,
Is 44 12 *B*, WS 122 *S*, AM 273 *B*, AZ 21 100 *O*
iron tool; here ? Ryl 365 *S* ⲡϭⲏⲙⲁ ⲙⲡ., WS 122 *S*
ⲟⲩⲛⲟϭ ⲙⲡ. **c.** in magic: Ryl 102 *S* ⲡ. ⲡⲣⲱⲟⲩⲧ, ⲡ. ⲛⲥϧⲓⲙⲉ *male, female iron*.
III. adj, with names of weapons, tools, utensils,
eg ⲥⲕⲉⲩⲟⲥ AZ 21 156 *S*, ⲥⲟⲧⲃⲉϥ 3 Kg 6 7 (BHom
106) *S*, ϧⲛⲁⲁⲩ Nu 35 16 *SB*, BM 1064 *S* and
often, mostly = σιδηροῦς (*v* Reil *Beiträge* 64).
ϯ ⲡ., *put irons upon*: Aeg 39 *B* ⲉⲣⲉⲡⲓⲃ̅. ⲧⲟⲓ ⲉⲡⲟⲩ-
ϫⲓϫ, ShC 73 200 *S* they decided ⲉϯ ⲡ. ⲉⲣⲟϥ,
DeV 88 *B* ⲁⲛϯ ⲃ̅. ⲉⲣⲱⲟⲩ, C 86 106 *B* prisoner ⲉϥ-
ⲧⲟⲓ ⲛⲃ̅.
ϫⲓ ⲡ., *wear, be in irons*: Mor 17 98 *S* ⲉⲩϫⲓ ⲡ.
σιδηρωμένους, Ep 219 *S* ϣⲁⲧⲛⲁⲩ ⲉⲓϫⲓ ⲡ, PRain
4716 *S* admonitions end with ⲡⲡⲉⲣϫⲓ ⲡ. ⲉϥϧⲣⲟⲟⲩ.
As name, ⲃⲉⲛⲓⲡⲉ, ⲃⲁⲛⲓⲡⲉ, ⲃⲉⲛⲓⲡⲓ, transl حديد,
a saint in Diptychs (CaiEuch 360, Renaudot *Lit* 1
18), Synax (3d Baremhât), Hymns (Ryl 423);
Βενῖπις, Βανῖ-; *cf* Σίδηρος (Preisigke).

ⲃⲛⲧ *v* ⲃⲟⲛⲧⲉ & ϭⲡⲧ.

ⲃⲟⲛⲧⲉ, ⲃⲁⲛⲧⲉ *S*, ⲃⲁⲛⲧⲉ *A*, ⲃⲟⲛϯ *B*, ⲃⲁⲛϯ *F*,
ⲃⲛⲧ- *S*, ϭⲡⲧ- *A*, ϭⲉⲛⲧ- *B* nn f, **a.** *gourd, cucumber*: P 44 82 = 43 58 *S* ⲧⲃ̅., ⲧϯϭⲉ σικύδιον, σικυή-

λατον (-ρατον) مقثا, C 41 69 ⲕⲁⲥ ⲛⲃ̅.=Miss 4 434
ⲛⲃ̅., CR '87 377 *S* recipe ϭⲱⲃⲉ ⲛⲃ̅., Cai 42573
1 *S* title of recipe ⲟⲩⲧⲁⲕⲟ ⲃ̅. ? a gourd-pest. In
simile Is 1 8 *SBF*, EpJer 69 *BF* ⲃ̅. or ⲙⲁ ⲛϧⲁⲣⲉϧ
(ⲁⲣⲉϧ, ⲁⲗⲉϧ) ⲛⲃ̅. = σικυήρατον; sim Mic 3 12
SA ⲃ̅. (*B* ϫⲓⲝⲓ) ὀπωροφυλάκιον. **b.** *gourd-garden* (?): Ryl 215 *S* gourd-seller sells half his ⲃ̅.,
P 46 150 *S* among names of house & its belongings, ⲧⲃ̅. مقثاة.

ⲥⲁⲃⲃ̅. *S* nn m, *gourd-seller*: Ryl 215.

ϭⲗⲟϧ ⲙⲃ̅., *gourd*: AM 47 *B* = Jon 4 6 *SA*,
Tri 304 *S* ⲃⲛⲧ ⲛⲉϭⲗⲟϭ κολοκύντη.

In place-names ⲡϣⲁⲧⲃⲁⲛⲧⲉ Ep 519 *S* (*cf* CO
314 *S* ⲁⲩϣⲱⲧ (?) ⲃ̅.) & ? ⲧⲉⲗⲃⲟⲛⲧ Θελβῶνθις Kr
133 (*cf* EW 100), P 44 82 ⲙⲛⲁⲓⲧⲏ = 43 57 ⲙⲛⲓⲧⲉ
(i e bête) بادنجان . مقثا, ? miswritten for ⲃⲟⲛⲧⲉ.

ⲃⲟⲛⲧⲉ (?) *A* nn f, *meaning unknown*: BM
1224 12, imprecation on ⲟⲩⲁⲡ ⲛⲓⲙ ⲉⲧⲧⲁⲩ(ⲁ) ⲙⲡⲁ-
ⲣⲉⲛ ⲁⲧⲃ̅. ⲙⲡⲛⲉⲧⲥⲁϧⲟⲩ ⲙⲙⲁⲓ.

ⲃⲁⲓⲉⲛϧ *S* *v* ⲥⲧⲉⲃⲁⲉⲓϧ.

ⲃⲁⲛϧⲟ *S* nn m, *meaning unknown*: BM 1113
letter upbraiding dilatory messenger, entrusted
with bringing 100 *solidi*, ⲡⲛⲉⲕϫⲓ ⲡⲟϭ ⲡⲕⲁⲓϥⲁⲗⲁⲓⲟⲛ
ⲁⲕⲁϣⲧⲕ ϧⲓⲡⲉⲓⲃ̅. ⲡⲣⲟⲗⲟⲕ/...ⲧⲁⲣⲉⲡⲡⲉ ⲛⲃⲉⲣⲃ. ⲉⲣⲟⲕ
and thy family. Prob opp large sum (κεφάλ.), so
implying smallness, poverty.

ⲃⲓⲛⲁϫ *B*, ⲡⲓⲛⲉϭ *F* (Mt 14) nn m, *dish*, is Gk
πίναξ: Mt 14 8, Mk 6 25, Lu 11 39 (all *S* ⲡⲓⲛⲁϧ);
Ex 25 29 τρύβλιον (var πίναξ & *ib* 37 16) جام,
Mt 26 23 τρύβλ. (*S* ϫⲏ, *cf* Si 34 14), TEuch 2
44 = ϫⲓⲥⲕⲟⲥ (*cf* BM 340) صينية, C 89 13 = MG
17 352, K 150 صحن, صفحة, *ib* 252 قصعة, P 55 11
جفنة, TEuch 2 494 ⲧⲁⲕⲟⲗⲟⲅⲓⲁ ⲙⲡⲓⲃ̅. طشت
(*cf* BM 920 n). In P 44 11, 54, 66 πίναξ = طبق;
سكرجة; MG 25 257, PO 11 373 dishes for food.

ⲃⲉⲛϫⲓ *B* nn f, *elephant's trunk*: K 164 زلومة
الفيل.

ⲃⲁⲣ *S* nn, *meaning unknown*: Ep 332 enquiring as to ⲥⲙⲥⲙ sesame, ϫⲉⲉϥⲟⲩ ⲛⲃ̅. ⲙⲡⲉϥϣⲁϧ[.
? *l* ⲃⲣⲁ (*v* ⲉⲃⲣⲁ).

ⲃⲏⲣ *F* *v* ⲟⲩⲏⲣ.

ⲃⲓⲣ *SA²B*, ⲃⲏⲗ *Sf* (Glos 114), ⲃⲓⲗ, ϧⲓⲗ *F* nn m
(f P 44 128, Glos *lc*); ⲃⲓⲣⲉ (CO 335, Ep 547,
BAp 107), ⲃⲁⲓⲣⲉ *S* (ST 349, Bodl(P) b 9), ⲃⲁⲓⲣⲓ *B*
(HL 97, *ib* ⲃⲓⲣ, MG 25 373, K 151) f; pl ⲃⲣⲛⲟⲩⲉ *S*
قفافة P 44 128 (only), ⲃⲣⲛⲟⲩⲓ *B* Mallon 143, Lab
(whence?), *basket* of palm-leaf (*v* Ep 1 155, also
67, 72): C 89 10 = MG 17 350 قفة, P 44, K *ut
sup*; Mt 15 37, Mk 8 8 *SB* (*cf* Lu 9 17 ⲕⲟⲧ *SB*)
σπυρίς; Jo 6 13 *A²* (SB ⲕⲟⲧ) κόφινος; Glos *lc* S

γυργαθός; Miss 4 636 *S*, CO 352 *S* for bread (*cf* WS 153 n), BAp 107 *S* for cheese, CO 465 *S* for wool, *ib* 335 *S* for fuel, LAA 543 *F* = P 129¹⁸ 103 *S* = EW 38 *B*, O'LearyH 3, Ryl 319 *S* for straw, BAp 54 *S* ⲕⲟ́ⲫ., ShC 73 152 *S* for earth, C 89 10 *B* = Miss 4 537 *S* σπυρίδιον for sand; Z 296, 300 *S*, MG 25 204 *B* σπυρίδ., Z 338 *S* = MG 25 209 *B*, *ib* 70, 200 *B*, HL *lc B* made by hermits; in Ac 9 25 *SB* σπυρίς holds a man. ⲃⲓⲣ, ⲃⲓⲣⲉ confused ? with βήριν = πήριον (πήρα), eg CDan 34.

ⲃ̄ⲣⲉ *A*, **ⲃ̄ⲣⲉⲉⲓ** *F* v ⲉⲃ̄ⲣⲁ.

ⲃ̄ⲁⲁⲣⲉ *S* nn, ? *boat, barge*: PMich '24 letter instructing pagarch as to dyke (?) repairs, naming ⲡⲉⲓⲡⲁⲓⲱ ⲙ̄ⲡⲉⲩⲥⲟⲧⲁⲣ̄ϭ (? *cf* ⲥⲧⲉⲃ̄ⲁⲓϭ) ⲙ̄ⲡⲉⲩⲃ̄ⲁⲁⲣⲉ. Cf ? βᾶρις an Egyptian boat.

ⲃ̄ⲁⲓⲣⲉ, ⲃ̄ⲓⲣⲉ *S*, ⲃ̄ⲁⲓⲣⲓ *B* v ⲃ̄ⲓⲣ.

ⲃ̄ⲉⲣⲱ *S* nn f, *whirlpool*: ShP 131⁴ 92 ⲧⲃ̄. ⲙ̄ⲙⲟⲟⲩ ⲉⲧⲃ̄ⲣ̄ⲃ̄ⲣ ⲁⲩⲱ ⲉⲧⲕⲱⲧⲉ wherein foolish drift hither & thither, Mor 32 23 boiling cauldron threw up ⲟⲩⲛⲟϭ ⲛ̄ⲃ̄. ⲙ̄ⲙⲟⲟⲩ, Job 28 10 δίνη (gloss ἶλιγξ, κοίλωμα), Ps 68 15 (*B* ⲥⲁⲣⲁⲑⲟⲩ) καταιγίς, which elsewhere = ⲣⲁⲧⲏⲩ.

ⲣ ⲃ̄., *be as a whirlpool*: ClPr 54 5 of lake dried up ⲧⲉⲧⲟ ⲛ̄ⲃ̄. ⲙ̄ⲡⲉⲩⲟⲉⲓϣ ὅσον βύθιον.

ⲃ̄ⲓⲣⲓ ϭⲁϫ ⲙ- v ϫⲁϫ.

ⲃ̄ⲟⲩⲣⲉ *S* vb intr, BKU 1 22 charm for insomnia, begins ⲁϥⲃ̄. ⲁϥⲃ̄., ? = ⲁϥⲡⲱⲣⲉ *q v*.

ⲃ̄ⲱⲣⲉ *S* (only P 46 237 ⲛ̄ⲃ̄., unless BM 1127 6 ⲃ̄ⲟⲣⲉ), ϥⲟⲣⲓ, ⲫⲟⲣⲓ *B* K 170, 172 nn m, a fish, *mugil cephalus* بوري (v MIF 51 66, 93).

ⲃ̄ⲱⲱⲣⲉ, ⲃ̄ⲉⲉⲣⲉ-, ⲃ̄ⲟⲟⲣ⸗, ⲃ̄ⲟⲟⲣⲉ† *S* vb **I.** intr (rare), *be excrescent, imposing, overbearing*: ShBMOr 8800 4 = R 2 3 9 rich man before tribunal lies, ⲛϥ̄ⲃ̄., swears falsely, bribes.

II. tr, *push, drive*: ShA 1 48 ⲉⲩⲥⲱⲕ ⲙ̄ⲙⲟϥ... ⲣⲉⲡⲕⲟⲟⲩⲉ ⲃ̄. ⲙ̄ⲙⲟϥ ⲡⲥⲱⲟⲩ (sim Ryl 70 246, Mor 36 34, C 73 10), *ib* 450 ⲁϥⲃ̄. ⲙ̄ⲙⲟϥ...ⲁϥⲧⲟϭⲛ̄ϥ (these vbs often paral), P 131³ 83 rich ⲉⲩⲃ̄. ⲛ̄ⲛⲏⲕⲉ ⲡⲥⲁⲃⲟⲗ ⲙ̄ⲙⲟⲟⲩ (*B* ⲥⲓϥ ⲉⲓϥⲟⲅⲉⲓ) ShP 130² 95 ⲁϥⲁⲣⲭⲉⲓ ⲛ̄ⲃ̄. ⲙ̄ⲡⲙⲏⲏϣⲉ forcing them to work, GuDorm 6 ⲡⲉⲩⲃ̄. ⲙ̄ⲙⲟϥ ⲣ̄ⲡⲟⲅⲁⲡⲉⲓⲗⲏ, Mor 56 37 sim, P 131³ 31 beasts feeding ϣⲁⲩⲃ̄. ⲡⲡⲉⲩⲉⲣⲏⲩ; *repel* ⲥ ⲡⲥⲁ-: Ps 117 10 ἀμύνεσθαι, ROC 13 171 ὠθεῖν, Mor 36 34 walk not overbearingly ⲉⲧⲉⲧⲛ̄ⲃ̄. ⲡⲥⲁⲡⲉⲧⲛ̄ⲉⲣⲏⲩ, Ryl 94 98 martyrs repelling their dissuaders, PCod 18; *defend*: Is 59 16 ἀμύν.; *prevail over, defeat*: 2 Kg 24 4 ὑπερισχύειν πρός, Col 2 18 (*B* ϭⲣⲟ ⲉ-) καταβραβεύεσθαι, Miss 4 537 of sleep ⲉϥⲃ̄. ⲙ̄ⲙⲟⲟⲩ (*B* ⳾ϫⲓⲥⲓ) βαρεῖν; *repress, expel* (?): ShMiss 4 285 rulers of these τόποι ⲛⲥⲉⲃ̄.

ⲁⲛ ⲙ̄ⲡⲥⲟⲟⲩⲧⲛ̄, Ep 238 ⲙ̄ⲡⲣ̄ⲙⲉⲉⲩⲉ (*sic*) ϫⲉⲛⲧⲁⲩⲃ̄. ⲙ̄ⲙⲟⲓ, P 131² 105 pray to Word that He ⲃ̄. human thoughts from mind; ⲥ ⲉⲃⲟⲗ ⲛ-: ShBMOr 8810 380 ⲉⲣⲃ̄. ⲙ̄ⲡⲛⲁ ⲙ̄ⲡⲛⲉ̄ ⲉⲃ̄. ⲙ̄ⲙⲟ, ShA 1 69, Mun 177; ⲥ ⲉⲃⲟⲗ ϩⲓϫⲛ-: Wess 18 106 ἀποτρίβεσθαι.

—— ⲉⲃⲟⲗ **I.** intr, *protrude, be swollen*: of pregnant womb, FR 18 ⲉⲣⲉϩⲏⲧⲥ̄ ⲃ̄ⲟⲟⲣⲉ ⲉⲃ̄., sim R 2 1 7, *ib* 10, BMis 89, 108 (= Mor 33 70 ⲉⲓ ⲉⲃ̄.), Bor 258 6 ⲉⲥⲃ̄. ⲉⲃ̄. ϩⲓⲧⲙ̄ⲡⲉϩⲣⲟϣ ⲙ̄ⲡϣⲏⲣⲉ ϣⲏⲙ, Ryl 73 ⲁⲡⲟ]ⲧⲧⲟⲥ ⲡⲣⲏ[ⲧⲥ ⲃ̄ⲱ]ⲱⲣⲉ ⲉⲃ̄. (*cf* KKS 281); of overflowing waters, Cant 5 12 (misapplied Miss 4 230). **II.** tr, *repel*: Ez 34 21 (*B* ⲃ̄ⲟⲣⲃ̄ⲉⲣ) διωθεῖν, GFr 434 ἐκβάλλειν, BMis 357 (var ⲃ̄.). —— nn m., *protuberance*: BMis 135 ⲡⲃ̄. ⲉⲃ̄. ⲡⲧⲉⲥⲕⲁⲗⲁϩⲏ.

ⲃ̄ⲣⲃ̄ⲉ (*sic* MS) *S* nn, vessel or receptacle, holding a medicinal mixture: Z 629 (or ? *l* ⲉⲩⲗⲁⲁⲩ ⲛ̄ⲃ̄ⲣⲣⲉ).

ⲃ̄ⲣⲃ̄ⲣ *S*, ⲃ̄ⲉⲣⲃ̄ⲉⲣ *SᶠB* vb intr, *boil*: Job 32 19 *B*, Ez 24 5 *S* (*B* ⳽ⲙⲟⲙ), Ac 18 25 *S* (*B* ⲇⲟ), Ap 3 15 *B* (*S* ϧⲙⲟⲙ) ζεῖν, Job 41 22 *SB*, ROC 17 403 *B* ἀναζεῖν, Ge 49 4 *SB* ἐκχεῖν. **a.** of water: PS 258, 374 *S*, ShA 1 246 *S* ⲉⲧⲃ̄. ⲉⲧⲛⲟⲉ (*l* ⲛⲟⲉ) ⲡⲟⲩⲙⲟⲟⲩ over fire, Tri 355 *S* ϩⲉⲡⲟⲑⲉ ⲙ̄ⲙⲟⲟⲩ ⲉⲩⲃ̄.; of oil: BMar 27 *S*, AM 62 *B*; of fat: C 43 167 *B*; of pitch: C 43 120, *ib* 86 219 *B*; of sulphur: C 43 151 *B*; of lead: BSG 182 *S*, AM 231 *B*; of chemical compounds: AZ 23 113, 114 *S*. **b.** or of vessels holding liquid: LCyp 29 *S*, C 43 113 *B* = Mor 39 41 *Sᶠ*, AM 236, C 41 77 *B*. **c.** metaph: Ez 47 9 *B* (BM 1247 154) ἐκχεῖν, Ro 12 11 *SF* (ⲃ̄ⲁⲣⲃ̄ⲉⲣ, *B* ϧⲙⲟⲙ) ζεῖν, PS 71 *S*, ShA 1 398 *S* ⲁⲡϫⲓⲛϭⲟⲛⲥ ⲃ̄. the earth is filled with iniquity, Br 88 *S* ⲁⲓⲃ̄. ⲁⲓⲡⲱⲡⲉ ϩⲣⲁⲓ ⲡⲣⲏⲧ̄ϥ, Va 64 174 *B* ⳾ⲙⲉⲧⲁⲗⲟⲩ ⲉⲥⲃ̄., BMar 115 *S* remembrance ⲃ̄. ⲡⲣⲏⲧ̄ϥ ἀνανεῖσθαι.

—— ⲉⲃⲟⲗ tr, *cause to boil, pour forth*: MG 25 248 *B* all his members ⲃ̄. ⲙ̄ⲱⲟⲩ ⲉⲃ̄. (HL ἐνήνοχε).

—— ⲉϩⲣⲁⲓ **I.** tr, *cast up*: BIF 14 164 *S* sea ⲃ̄. ⲉϩ. ⲡⲡⲉⲥϭⲟⲉⲓⲙ, BHom 110 *S* fountains ⲃ̄. ⲉϩ. ⲡⲟⲩⲙⲟⲟⲩ. **II.** intr, *boil up, over*: GPar 2 6 *S* horn of oil ⲃ̄. ⲉϩ. ⲉϫⲛ̄ⲡⲁⲅⲉⲓⲁ, BMis 538 *S* pit ⲉϥⲃ̄. ⲉϩ. like cauldron, *cf* AM 323 *B* ⲃ̄. ⲉⲡϣⲱⲓ.

—— nn m, *boiling* heat: Mor 17 28 *S* βρασμός *eruption*, Va 67 3 *B* chill of poverty & ⲡⲓⲃ̄. ⲉⲧⲟⲓ ⲛⲑⲉⲣⲙⲟⲥ of wealth, C 86 286 *B* ⲃ̄. & ϣⲁϩ of boiling cauldron. Adj: ShC 42 50 *S* plague ⲛ̄ϫⲡⲟⲩϥ ⲛ̄ⲃ̄.

ⲃ̄ⲉⲣⲃ̄ⲓⲣ *B* nn f, *missile*: Jer 27 9 (*S* ⲥⲟⲧⲉ) βολίς, BMOr 8771 55 ⳾ⲃ̄. کسي, but this in K 116 = μάχαιρα.

ⲃⲟⲣⲃⲣ *v* ϩⲟⲣⲃⲣ.

ⲃⲟⲣⲃⲣ ⲉⲃⲟⲗ *unloose v* ⲃⲟⲗⲃⲗ.

ⲃⲱⲣⲕ *F v* ⲃⲱⲗⲕ.

ⲃⲁⲣⲙⲉⲥⲓ *F* nn, meaning unknown: CMSS 64 in account of payments, ⲉⲃ. Almost all entries relate to persons, rarely to places; only one other, ⲛⲙⲁ ⲛⲙⲟⲩⲉⲓ, has preceding prep ⲉ-. Possibly contains ⲙⲉⲥⲓ.

ⲃⲁⲣⲛⲉϩ *F* nn, *linseed*? (ⲃⲣⲁ + ⲛⲉϩ): AZ 23 39 in account ⲟⲩⲱⲡⲓ (? measure) ⲛⲃ., ⲡⲁϫⲓ (? *S* ⲡⲟϭⲉ) ⲥⲛⲏⲧⲓ ⲛⲃ., ⲍ̅ ⲡⲭⲡⲉϩ (? *S* ϫⲁⲡⲉ) ⲛⲃ. Occurs also PMich 1553. *Cf* Wess 18 93 *S* corn, grape-seed ⲙⲡⲡⲃⲣⲁⲡⲉϩ. *S* ⲡⲁⲣⲡⲉϩ (BP 3267 = ⲡⲣⲡⲉϩ) not same; *v* ⲛⲉϩ.

ⲃⲣⲣⲉ *SAA*[2] (ⲃⲏⲣⲉ *S* often in documents: BM 1045, Kr 59, Ryl 207), ⲃⲉⲣⲓ, ⲃⲉⲣⲉⲓ *BF*.   **I.** adj, *new, young*: Ps 32 2 *SB*, Is 8 1 *SB*, Mt 9 17 *SB*, Ap 2 17 *SB*, AP 7 *A*[2] ⲟⲩϣⲉϫⲉ ⲛⲃ. καινός; Ps 68 31 *SB*, Zech 9 9 *SAB*, Lu 5 17 *SB* νέος; Job 14 9 *SB*, Ps 127 3, Is 5 7 *SB*, 1 Tim 3 6 *SB* νεό-φυτος, TT 110 *S*, C 89 22 *B* ⲧⲱϭⲉ ⲛⲃ. neophyte, ROC 13 171 *S* ⲁⲛⲛⲟⲩⲣⲱⲙⲉ…ⲛⲃ. ἀρχάριος, Aeg 251 *S* ⲡⲣⲱⲙⲉ ⲛⲃ., Miss 4 524 *S* ⲣⲙⲛⲃ. (*B* ⲧⲱϫⲓ ⲛⲃ.); Sa 16 3 *S*, Ac 17 18 *S* (*B* ϣⲉⲙⲙⲟ) ξένος; Ez 11 19 *SB* ἕτερος; Ps 80 9 *SB*, He 10 20 *B* πρόσφατος; BHom 98 *S* ϯⲟⲩⲱ ⲛⲃ., PSBA 10 395 *B* ⲟⲩⲁⲗⲟⲩ ⲛⲃ. ⲉⲙⲁϣⲱ; of fresh crops: corn BM 1031 *S*, Kr 59 *S*, lentils WS 143 *S*, wine CO 235 *S*; in calendar: Hall 120 *S* ⲥⲟⲩⲁ ⲛⲧⲣⲟⲙⲡⲉ ⲛⲃ. (*v* ⲥⲏⲩ), C 43 122 *B* 1st of Pharmouthi introducing ϯⲧⲣⲟⲙⲡⲓ ⲛⲃ., BSM 5 *B* do (*S* ⲥⲟⲩⲁ ⲛⲃ.), Kr 1 *S* ⲡⲥⲟⲩⲁ ⲛⲃ., BMis 57 *S* ⲡⲉⲃⲟⲧ ⲛⲃ. Parmoute (*cf ib* 145); ClPr 25 2, Mor 34 53 *S*, BM 777 *B* ⲧⲕⲩ-ⲣⲓⲁⲕⲏ ⲛⲃ. (*Domin. in Albis*); rarely before nn: Va 67 167 *B* ⲛⲓⲃ. ⲍⲁⲅⲓⲁ.

II. as nn, *new thing*: Eccl 1 10 *S*, Is 42 9 *SB*, Hos 10 12 *A* (Gk om, *novalis*), He 8 12 *SBF* καινόν, -νά; opp ⲁⲥ, ⲁⲡⲁⲥ: Cant 7 13 *S*, Mt 13 52 *SB*, 2 Cor 5 17 *SB*, BM 691 *F*; *young person*: BHom 122 *S* ⲃ. ϧⲓⲛⲟϭ ⲡⲣⲱⲙⲉ, C 86 104 *B* ⲟⲩⲃ. ⲡⲉ ϫⲉⲡⲡⲉϩⲣⲟ.

ⲙⲛⲧ-, ⲙⲉⲧⲃ. nn f, *newness, youth*: 3 Kg 8 53 *B*, Ro 6 4 *SB* καινότης, Ro 12 2 *SBF* (var *F* ⲙⲉⲧⲙⲟⲩⲓ) ἀνακαίνωσις, Pro 24 54 *S* (var ⲙⲛⲧⲕⲟⲩⲓ), Sa 2 6 *S*, ROC 17 400 *B*, BM 174 1 *S* νεότης, CaiEuch 654 *B* ἐπανανέωσις, Miss 8 99 *S* ⲛⲉⲱⲧⲉ-ⲣⲓⲥⲙός of doctrines, R 1 5 27 *S* of one 20 years old, Cat 49 *B* second age of man ⲉⲧⲉⲧⲙ. ⲧⲉ, ShC 73 50 *S* opp ⲙⲛⲧⲛⲟϭ ⲡⲣⲱⲙⲉ, BM 230 2 *S* opp (ⲙⲛⲧ)ϣⲏⲣⲉ ϣⲏⲙ & ⲙⲛⲧⲗⲗⲟ, BSG 183 *S* ⲡⲥⲁ ⲛⲧⲉϥⲙ., sim often of youthful martyrs. *Cf* ⲙⲛⲧ-ⲁⲗⲟⲩ.

ⲛⲃⲣⲣⲉ *S*, ⲙⲃⲉⲣⲓ *B* adv, **a.** *newly, recently*: Ez 11 3 *B* προσφάτως, Miss 4 583 *S* he had come ⲛⲃ. ὡς νεόφυτον, sim ShC 42 16, *ib* 73 46 *S* (var ⲛ-ϣⲟⲣⲡ), Leyd 365 *S*, Cat 182 *B*, Aeg 251 *S* (vb mostly ⲉⲓ ⲉϩⲟⲩⲛ), ShC 42 21 *S* ⲛⲧⲁⲓⲥⲟⲅⲱⲡⲉ ⲁⲛ ⲛⲃ. ⲁⲗⲗⲁ ϯⲥⲟⲟⲩⲛ ⲙⲙⲟ ϫⲓⲛⲛϣⲟⲣⲡ, PSBA 10 396 *B* ⲉⲧⲁϥⲓ ⲙⲃ. from Phrygia.   **b.** *afresh*: MIF 23 210 *S* this book ⲛⲧⲁⲛⲥⲁϩϥ ⲛⲃ., Alex stele 274 *S* ruined τόπος ⲁⲅⲕⲟⲧϥ ⲙⲃ., BMis 526 *S* ⲛⲃ. sim.

ⲉⲓⲣⲉ, ⲓⲣⲓ ⲛⲃ., **I.** tr, *make new, renew*: Job 10 17 *SB* ἐπανακαινίζειν, Ps 103 30 *SB* ἀνακαιν., Sa 7 27 *S*, καιν., Ap 21 5 *SB* καινὰ ποιεῖν, Job 33 24 *S* ἀνανεοῦσθαι.   **II.** intr p ⲃ., *become new*: Ps 50 11 *S* (*B* tr) ἐγκαιν., *ib* 38 2 *SB*, Lam 5 21 *B*, Zeph 3 17 *A* (*B* tr), 2 Cor 4 16 *SB* ἀνακαιν.; Wess 15 137 *S* of dogmas ἀναζωπυρεῖσθαι, ShBIF 23 146 *S* tree put forth roots ⲁϥⲉⲓ ⲛⲣ ⲃ., TstAb 166 *B* sun strengthening me ⲛⲧⲁⲉⲣ ⲃ. ⲛⲕⲉⲥⲟⲡ.

In name: Τχεντβῆρις (Preisigke).   In place-name: WS 207 ⲡⲓϩⲛⲃⲣⲣⲉ, Σενβέρρις, Miss 4 751 a meadow ⲡⲕⲁϩ ⲛⲃ., Ep 1 115n a monastery ⲑⲉ-ⲛⲉⲉⲧⲉ ⲛⲃ.

ⲃⲉⲣⲥⲓ *B* nn m, *orach* (*atriplex*) قطف, سرمق K 195 (in P 44 82 قطف χρυσολάχανον). *Cf* ⲃⲉⲣⲥⲓϯ. ⲃⲉⲣ- ? = (ⲉ)ⲃⲣⲉ as in ⲃⲣⲉϣⲏⲩ.

ⲃⲉⲣⲥⲙ *S* nn, among names of victuals: Bodl(P) b 7 ϭⲟⲩϭ, ϩⲟⲩⲅ, ⲃ., ⲟⲩⲣⲱ (this MS *ca* AD 730). *Cf* رسيم *clover*; *cf* also ⲃⲁⲣ or ? (ⲉ)ⲃⲣⲉ as in ⲃⲣⲉϣⲏⲩ.

ⲃⲉⲣⲥⲓϯ *B* nn m, *basket* holding bread: AM 178 ⲁϥϫⲓⲙⲓ ⲙⲡⲓⲃ. full of bread = مقطف PO 17 645 (but var قطف, *cf* ⲃⲉⲣⲥⲓ), Bodl 325 154 مقطف (which K 151, 261 = ϭⲛⲟⲩϥ). *Cf* ? ⲃⲓⲣ.

ⲃⲁⲣⲏⲓⲧ (varr K ⲃⲁⲣⲁⲏⲓⲧ, ⲃⲁⲣⲏⲟⲩⲧ) *B*, ⲃⲁⲣⲓⲧ *F* (AZ 23 41) nn m, *he-goat*, جدي, تيس: Ge 31 10, Ps 49 13, He 9 12 (all *S* ϭⲓⲉ), Dan 8 8 τράγος; Lev 4 23, Nu 7 16, *ib* 28 30, Ps 65 15 (all *S* ϭⲓⲉ) χίμαρος; Deu 14 4 (*S* ⲙⲁⲥⲉ) χίμ.; Lev 1 10 (*S* ϩⲟⲟⲩⲧ) ἄρσεν, as if of sheep or goats. *Cf* ⲃⲁⲁⲙⲡⲉ, ⲃⲟⲉⲓⲧ.

ⲃⲁⲣⲱⲧ, ⲃⲁⲣⲟⲧ *SABF* (ⲃⲁⲗⲱⲧ *S* Ryl 240) nn m, pl ? ⲃⲁⲣⲁⲧⲉ *S* (ST 122), *brass, bronze*: P 44 61 *S* نحاس, P 55 8 *B* ⲃ. & ϩⲟⲙⲧ both نحاس; 4 kinds: AZ 23 103 *S* ⲃ. ⲡⲁⲗⲁϫ, *ib* 116 ⲉⲧⲧⲟⲣϣ, ⲁⲗⲁⲥⲃⲁⲣ, الأصفر, ⲁⲗⲕⲟⲡⲣⲟⲥⲓ (cinnabar); no Gk equiv (*eg* Nu 21 22 *S*). In enumerations of property seems = χάλκωμα of sim Gk deeds (PLond 1 233, PMon 69); ShBIF 23 163 *S* seeking lead he found silver, going after ⲃ. he found gold, so ? a yellow metal (brass; *cf* ? ὀριχάλκιον opp χάλκωμα PCai 1 26 &

orichalcum Ap 1 15). But many utensils of ⲃ. show it to be prob *bronze*, eg CMSS 76 F ⲕⲁⲕⲉⲗⲓ (καγκέλλιον), PLond 4 517 S ⲕⲟⲩϫⲟⲩ for oil, J 66 40, ST 439 S ⲗⲁⲕⲁⲡⲏ, Ryl 240 S ⳓⲉⲥⲧⲏⲥ, *ib* ⲡⲁⲡⲁⲗⲏⲛ (πανάριον), CO 459 S ⲧⲩⲗⲱⲧⲣⲓⲡⲟⲥ (? τυροτρίπτης), C 86 191 B ⲭⲁⲗⲕⲓⲟⲛ, Ryl 241, 243 S ϧⲏⲃⲥ, *ib* 238 S ⳓⲣⲟⲟⲩⲡⲉ. In BM 1206 S ⲟⲩⲃ. ⲡⲉⲓⲱ prob an implement of ⲃ. (*cf* ⲃⲉⲡⲓⲡⲉ).

ϧⲟⲙⲡⲧ ⲛⲃ., ϧⲟⲙⲡⲧ ⲃ. S, ϧⲁⲙⲧ ⲃ. A (El 50), ϧⲟⲙⲧ ⲃ. B, a composite metal: Ez 40 3 S (B ϧⲟⲙ. ⲉϥⲫⲟⲥⲓ) χαλκὸς στίλβων (but this in Dan 10 6 S ϧⲟⲙ. ⲉϥⲧⲁⲁⲧⲉ, *cf* Ez 1 7 S), Ap 1 15, 2 18 S (B= Gk) χαλκολίβανον, sim Mor 25 219 S, BSM 128 B; also BIF 14 167 S idols ⲛϧ. ⲃ., Va 62 152 B time and moisture had made golden idol like ϧ. ⲛⲃ., Mor 41 19 S κάγκελος of ϧ. ⲃ. (B ϧⲟⲙⲧ) surrounds miraculous pillar, Mor 46 16 S χάλκιον of ϧ. ⲃ.; Ryl 153 S ϧ. ⲛⲃⲁⲣⲱϧ (gloss ⲃⲁⲗⲟⲧ) l ? ⲃⲁⲣⲱⲧ. *Cf* ⲧⲃⲥ̄ϯ: (Tatt) used in several of above bibl places. In name Πβαρωτ (? as title, Preisigke).

ⲃⲉⲣⲧ   *v* ⲟⲩⲣⲧ.

ⲃⲁⲣⲁⲧⲉ   *v* ⲃⲁⲣⲱⲧ.

ⲃⲁⲣⲟϣ S nn m, meaning unknown, prob designates a trade or office: Kr 149 ⲕⲟⲥⲙⲁ ⲛⲃ. Prob not = ⲃⲁⲣⲱϧ.

ⲃⲉⲣϣⲟ B nn m, meaning uncertain: C 86 287 when cauldron, wherein are martyr's limbs & filled with ⲗⲁⲙϧⲁⲡⲧ, ⲙⲃⲣⲉϧ &c, had boiled high, they brought ⲡⲓⲛⲉⳝⲓ of cauldron to king, saying ⲁϥⲟⲩⲱ ⲁϥⲙⲟⲩⲛⲕ ⲛϫⲉ ⲡⲓⲃ. ⲉⲧⲉⲙⲙⲁⲩ = S (BSG 185, but by later hand) ⲡⲓⲧⲁⲗⲁⲓⲡⲱⲣⲟⲥ, but ar (*ib* 217) = زفت; *pitch*.

ⲃⲁⲣϣⲓⲛ B nn: K 112 ⲫⲏ ⲉⲧⲉⲣ ⲃ. قلفاط (καλαφάτης, P 43 37 = ναυπηγός), therefore ⲃ. ? *caulker, caulker's material*, or *act of caulking*.

ⲃⲣⲉϣⲏⲩ (PSBA 28 57, Wess 9 38, ⲃⲉⲣⲉ- P 44 66, 43 233), ⲃⲣϣⲏⲩ S, ⲃⲉⲣϣⲏⲟⲩ B nn m, *coriander seed* κόριον: Ex 16 14 SB, Nu 11 17 SB, P 44 66, 82 S, K 196 B كزبرة (so Va 1 *ll cc*), P 43 233 S ⲅⲟⲣⲓⲟⲩ· ⲃ. حب الرشاد . Prob = (ⲉ)ⲃⲣⲉ + *ϣⲏⲩ (*v* ϣⲱⲏⲟⲩ).

ⲃⲁⲣⲱϧ S nn m, pl ⲃⲁⲣⲁϧⲉ, ⲃⲁⲣⲁⲁϧ (?), a transport animal, not ass, ? *camel, cf* برق: CO 379 ⲛⲧⲉⲧⲛⲧⲁⲙⲓⲟ ⲛⲃ., BM 1171 do thou saddle 2 horses ⲙⲛ̄ⲡⲁⲛⲃ. for these men going south, BM 529 let him mount the ass...or one of ⲛⲉⲃ., BP 7893 in account ⳍ ⲛⲫⲱⲣⲁ ⲛⲃⲁⲣⲁⲁϧⲓ (or ? -ⲁⲁϧ); in ShZ 501 ⲡⲉⲩⲃⲁⲣⲁϧⲉ obscure. In place-name (prob = this word): PMich 3586b ⲡⲉⲣⲱⲙⲡⲓⲗⲁ ⲛⲃ.

ⲃⲁⲣⲱϧ S, ⲃⲁⲣⲟϧ B nn m, *fodderer* or sim: Saq 13, 227, 350 S among monastic officials, K 115 B علاف.

ⲃⲁⲣⲱϧ (ST 161), ⲃⲁⲣⲉϧ (CO 340), ⲃⲁⲣⲏϧ (ST 125) S nn; 3d of these is in list of metal utensils, 1st in list of vessels & contains 4 χοίνικες, 2d is pl.

ⲃⲁⲣⲁϧ F nn: BM 587, 706, uncertain to which of above words these belong.

ⲃⲁⲣⲁϧⲉ   *v* ⲃⲁⲣⲱϧ *animal*.

ⲃⲣⲉϧⲓ B   *v* ⲁⲙⲣⲏϧⲉ.

ⲃⲉⲣϫⲱⲟⲩ   *v* ⲙⲁⲣⲟⲩϭⲉ.

ⲃⲱⲣϭ S vb intr: Ez 13 11 (B ϧⲉⲓ) ῥήγνυσθαι. Prob not = ⲃⲱⲗⲕ, ⲃⲱⲣⲕ; *cf* ? ⲡⲱⲣⲕ, ⲫⲱⲣϫ.

ⲃⲣⲏϭⲉ   *v* ⲉⲃⲣⲏϭⲉ.

ⲃⲣϭⲟⲟⲩⲧ (Is 66 20), ⲃⲉⲣⲉϭⲱⲟⲩⲧ (P 44 20) S, ⲃⲉⲣⲉϭⲱⲟⲩⲧⲥ B nn f (B, for S *v* place-name), *chariot, cf* מרכבה: Ge 41 43, 46 29, Ex 14 6, Is 2 7 B (S = Gk) ἅρμα; TstAb 256 B ⲃ. opp ϧⲁⲣⲙⲁ, Ex 14 17, 18 B they alternate (Va 1 مركب for both). In place-name ⲃⲉⲣϭⲟⲟⲩⲧ فرجوط P 43 51 S, ⲧⲃⲉⲣϭⲱⲧ Miss 4 743 S *Farshût* this word ? preserved.

ⲃⲁⲥ S nn, named among utensils of bronze (ϧⲟⲙⲡⲧ): BP 9421 ⲟⲩⲃ. ⲛⲣ ⲛⲉϧ, so used in oil making (*v* ⲛⲉϧ). BM 1103 9 ⲡⲓⲃⲁⲥ ? same.

ⲃⲏⲥⲉ S nn f, *pail, well-bucket*: BAp 88 (=دلو) ⲧⲃ. needed to fill ⲕⲉⲗⲱⲗ (جرّة), Ep 551 large and small ⲃ., CO 213, ST 257 holds dates, COAd 56, ST 320 grapes; also ST 161, WZKM 26 339. Prob = βῆσις (Reil *Beiträge* 65, *cf* Ep *lc* n).

ⲃⲓⲥⲓ B   *v* ⲟⲩⲉⲓⲥⲉ.

ⲃⲉⲥⲛⲏⲧ, ⲃⲉⲥⲡⲁⲧ S, ⲃⲉⲥⲡⲏⲧ, ⲃⲁⲥⲡⲏⲧ B nn m, pl ⲃⲉⲥⲡⲁⲧⲉ (AZ 60 111), *smith*: Ge 4 22 working copper & iron, Job 32 19, Is 41 7, 2 Tim 4 14 B (all S ϧⲁⲙⲕⲗⲉ) χαλκεύς; P 44 67 S = ϧⲁⲙⲕ. σιδηρουργός حدّاد, sim K 110 B; his anvil MG 25 142 B, C 86 45 B, his tools J 38 23 S ⲡⲥⲧⲉⲃⲁⲉⲓϧ (*sic*) ⲛⲃ., paid for repairing cart Hall 108 S; also C 86 212 B, J 68 41, Ep 561, 681, Alex 178, 297 S. ⲙⲛⲧⲃⲉⲥⲛⲏⲧ (*sic* l) S nn f, *smith's craft*: My 107.

ⲃⲁⲥⲛϭ (Si 47 23), ⲃⲁⲥⲉⲛϭ (Mor 44 12), ⲃⲁⲥⲛⲏϭ (P 44 67), ⲃⲁⲥϭ (Nu 31 22), ⲃⲁⲥⲓϭ (Mor 23 30) S, ⲃⲁⲥⲓⲛϭ (Zech 4 10) A nn m, *tin* κασσίτερος, κασσιτέρινος قصدير = B ⲑⲣⲁⲡ Nu, Zech. ⲃⲁ- as in ⲃⲁⲛⲓⲡⲉ, ⲃⲁⲣⲱⲧ; *v* AZ 53 51.

ⲃⲁⲥⲟⲩⲣ B nn m, *antimony* اثمد K 204, among minerals, next to ⲥⲧⲏⲙ *q v.* ⲃⲁ- ? as in ⲃⲁⲛⲓⲡⲉ, ⲃⲁⲣⲱⲧ, ⲃⲁⲥⲛϭ.

ⲃⲟⲥⲉⲣ *B*   *v* ⲟⲩⲟⲥⲣ.

(ⲃⲱⲥⲧ), ⲃⲁⲥⲧ- *B* (?), ⲃⲟⲥⲧ† *S*, p c *S* ⲃⲁⲥⲧ- vb intr, *be dry, parched*: R 1 3 76 of Baptist ⲉⲣⲉⲧⲉϥⲥⲁⲣⲝ ϣⲟⲃⲉ ⲉⲥⲃⲟⲥⲧ ⲉⲙⲁⲧⲉ ⲉⲧⲃⲉⲡⲉϩ (cf Ps 108 24, opp λιπαίνειν Ps 22 5), Bor 252 187 wearing filthy garments ⲉⲣⲉⲧⲉϥϩⲁⲡⲉ ⲃⲟⲥⲧ (= Bor 311 102 ϭⲟⲥⲧ), ῥακία ἠμφιέσμενος ῥυπῶν αὐχμῶν (PG 63 133), PSBA 27 167 in preparing papyrus, if thou see it [ⲉⲥ]ⲃⲟⲥⲧ ⲉⲕⲡⲁⲗⲉⲁⲡ[ⲧⲏ]ⲣⲓⲉ ⲙⲙⲟⲥ, Cai 42573 1 title of recipe ⲟⲩⲃⲁⲥⲧϩⲟ (ⲉ)ⲧⲁⲁⲥ ⲉⲅⲥϭⲓⲙⲉ obscure; K 367 *B* ⲁⲕⲃⲁⲥⲧⲉⲡ صفته (? not this word).

ⲃⲏⲧ *SBF* nn m (P 44 134 *S*, K 138 *B*), f (ShC 42 110, BIF 14 166 *S*, neither quite certain), **I.** *palm-leaf* سعف (عزج), خوصة (MG 17 350 = *ib* 14); PO 2 176 *S* ϩⲉⲛⲃ. ϩⲁⲙⲡⲓⲃⲁ, Z 297 *S*, Wess 11 169 *S*, MG 25 119, 206 *B* θαλλία for weaving ⲛⲏⲃⲧⲉ (σειρά), whence baskets made by hermits; BP 954 *S* ⲃ. ϩⲁⲃⲓⲣ; also θαλλός MG 25 243 *B*, HL 95 *B*, or βάιον Va 62 287 *B* (only, though Z 344 = MG 25 209 σειρά = ⲃⲁ, ⲃⲁⲓ & MG 25 227 ⲃ. & ⲃⲁⲓ vary). Before weaving ⲃ. soaked: MG 25 243 *B*, Wess *lc S*; to pluck, gather ⲃ.: ShC 73 54 *S* ⲣⲱⲱⲗⲉ, MG 25 97, 134 *B* ⲓⲛⲓ ⲉⲃⲟⲗ; Cai 42573 1 *S* ⲃ. ⲡⲥⲟⲅϭ ⲙⲁⲣⲏⲥ (*v* ⲃⲏⲡⲉ & ⲕⲟⲩⲕ); Lev 23 40 *S* ⲃ. ϩⲁⲧ ⲛⲃⲏⲡⲉ (var ⲗⲟⲟⲩ ⲛⲃⲏⲡⲉ) κάλλυνθρα φοιν., whence BM 1008 54 *S* ⲃ. ϩⲁⲧ of gold hung upon tabernacle. In ROC '13 174 ⲃ. ϩⲁⲧⲉ = λευκάς which here = Syr per'a, Lat germen (cf LMis 88); ⲃ. ⲛⲃⲛⲣⲟⲟⲩⲡⲉ KroppJ, *ib* K *S* in magic; ϣⲟⲗ (ϣⲁⲗ) ⲛⲃ. Miss 4 766, Wess 11 170 *S* δεσμός, Bodl(P) e 37 *S* ⲙⲟⲩⲣ ⲛⲃ.; BKU 1 151 *S* ⲃⲁ ⲛⲃ. for making ⲡⲟⲩϩ; as garment: Mor 48 30 *S* = Rec 6 183 *B*; ϩⲁⲛⲃⲁⲓ ⲃ. carried in procession: N&E 39 340 *B*; as decoration Aeg 39 *B*; ⲃⲁⲓⲃ. ⲉⲩⲣⲱⲟⲩⲧ FR 110 *B*, Aeg 54 *B* ⲃⲁⲓⲃ. ⲉⲧϥⲟⲣⲓ ⲉⲃⲟⲗ used at burial; obscure: Bodl(P) e 47 *S* letter ⲉϣⲱⲡⲉ ⲡⲟⲩⲥⲁⲕ ⲃ. ⲁⲛ ⲡⲉⲧϣϣⲉ ⲉⲣⲟⲓ ⲁⲛⲟⲕ ⲉⲧⲣⲁⲡⲟⲩϫⲉ ⲉⲃⲟⲗ ⲉϩⲟⲩⲉⲣⲟⲕ, R 1 4 21 *S* ⲁⲡⲟⲧ ⲛⲃ. (? *sic*) *fictilis*, BM 1127 *S* ⲡⲉⲓⲃⲉⲧⲕⲁⲧ; ⲃ. ? leafed twig of other trees: Baouit 130 *S* ⲃ. ⲛⲡⲁⲙ.

II. *SB*, ⲃ. ⲥⲡⲓⲣ *S* f, *rib* (from resemblance of ribs on spine to fronds on stem): Ge 2 22 *S* (*B* ⲃ. only) πλευρά, Tri 466 *S*, P 44 70 *S* ضلع, BAp 68, BMar 236, BM 335 *S*.

ⲡⲓⲕⲁⲥ ⲃ. Va 62 174 *B* (var Va 69 ⲡⲓⲕⲁⲥ) broken by a fall; also ⲃ. alone thus: Mor 48 83 *S* martyr pierced ϣⲁⲛⲧⲟⲩϫⲱⲧⲣ ⲛⲡⲉⲃ. ⲛⲡⲉϥⲥⲡⲓⲣⲟⲟⲩ.

ⲃⲟⲉⲓⲧ *S*, ⲃⲁⲓⲧ *Sᵃ* nn m f, *ox or cow*: R 1 4 57 among Egypt's gods ⲟⲩⲃ. ⲙⲡⲟⲩⲟⲥⲓⲉ (*B* ⲙⲁⲥⲓ, ⲃⲁⲣⲏⲧ) βοῦς, τράγος, Glos 65 *Sᵃ* ταῦρος · ⲃⲁⲓⲧ, μόσχος · ⲙⲉⲥⲉ, βοῦς · ⲉⲣⲉ, ST 437 among animals

sold ⲧⲃ. opp ⲧⲉϩⲉ, ST 185 ⲁⲡⲉⲡⲕⲟⲩⲓ ⲙⲃ. ⲙⲟⲩ. Cf ? ⲃⲁⲣⲏⲓⲧ, or ? βοΐδιον.

As name (?): ⲡⲃⲟⲉⲓⲧ J 67 76 *S*, Παβόειτ (Preisigke).

ⲃⲏⲧⲉ *S* nn f in Nu 16 38 = λεπίς, so *scale-like plate* of metal (*B* ⲕⲏⲕⲥ, cf also ϣⲛϥⲉ); Hall 48 ⲡⲡⲓⲛⲁϩ ⲛⲃ., CO 459 in list of metal implements ⲥⲛⲧⲉ ⲛⲃ. ⲛϩⲱⲕ ϣⲧⲉ (last word ambiguous), *ib* 472 *Sᵃ* in list of *varia* ⲟⲩϭⲛⲧ (? = ⲥⲁⲧ) ⲛⲃⲉⲧⲏ, Cai 42573 2 medical mixture ⲟⲗϥ ϩⲓⲟⲩⲃⲉⲧⲉ & pour into cloth.

ⲃⲓϯ *B*   *v* ⲟⲩⲉⲓⲧⲉ.

ⲃⲱⲧⲉ *SA* (& ϥⲱϭⲉ Mic 3 9), ⲃⲟϯ *B* (Ez 13 19, 23 38 only), ⲃⲉⲧ-, ⲃⲟⲧ- (Job 30 10 ⲃⲟⲟⲧ-), ⲃⲏⲧ†, all forms often with ϥ for ⲃ, vb tr, **a.** *pollute, befoul*: Lev 11 43 (*B* ⲥⲱϥ), *ib* 21 7 (*B* do), Ps 88 39 (*B* do), Ez 23 38 *SB*, 1 Tim 1 9 (*B* ⲥⲁϥ ϩⲏⲧ) βεβηλοῦν. **b.** *hate, abominate*: Lev 11 13 (*B* ⲱⲣⲉⲃ), *ib* 26 11 (*B* ϭⲓ ⲃⲟϯ), Ps 5 6, Pro 28 9 *SA*, Hos 9 10 *A*, Am 6 8 *A*, Ro 2 22 (*B* ⲥⲱϥ) βδελύσσειν; Ap 18 2 (*B* ⲙⲟⲥϯ) μισεῖν; Gal 1 8 ἀνάθεμα εἶναι (cf ⲉⲓⲣⲉ ⲛⲃⲟⲧⲉ); Lev 18 25 (*B* ϩⲣⲟϣ) προσοχθεῖν; with ϫⲁϩⲙ, ⲁⲕⲁⲑⲁⲣⲧⲟⲛ: ShA 2 65, Mor 17 54, 25 130; P 131 105 ⲉⲥⲃⲏⲧ like saltless food, GöttN '98 176 voices empty ⲁⲩⲱ ⲉⲩⲃⲏⲧ.

ⲃⲟⲧⲉ (Deu 13 15 var ⲃⲱⲧⲉ) *S*, ⲃⲁⲧⲉ *AA²*, ⲃⲟϯ *B*, ⲃⲁϯ *F* nn f (rarely m Lev 7 11, 11 10 *S*), *hateful thing, abomination*: Ge 46 34 *S* (*B* ⲱⲣⲉⲃ), Ex 8 22 *B*, Lev 7 11 *S* (*B* ⲥⲱϥ), Ps 87 8 *S*, Pro 6 16 *A*, Is 1 13 *F*, Zech 9 7 *A*, Mt 24 15 *S* βδέλυγμα, Sa 12 4 *S* ἔχθιστος; Deu 13 15 *S*, Jos 7 12 *S* ἀνάθεμα, Ap 22 3 *S* (*B* ⲥⲱϥ) κατανάθεμα; as adj: BHom 60 *S* ⲡⲣⲟⲥⲫⲟⲣⲁ ⲛⲃ., AM 139 *B* ⲓⲱⲱⲗⲟⲡ ⲙⲃ., C 89 112 *B* ⲛⲏⲣⲡ ⲙⲃ.

ⲉⲓⲣⲉ ⲛⲃ. *S*, *make abominable*, also *anathematize*: Nu 21 3 (var ⲉⲓⲣⲉ ⲛⲁⲡⲁⲑ.), Jud 21 11 ἀναθεματίζειν, Jos 6 18 ἀναθ. ποιεῖν, CA 89 sim; as nn, *filth* Mor 50 57 *S* ⲡⲉⲅⲁⲕⲁⲑⲁⲣⲥⲓⲁ ⲙⲡⲛⲉⲅⲉⲓ. ⲛⲃ.

ⲣ ⲃ., ⲟ ⲛⲃ. *S*, ⲟⲓ ⲙⲃ. *B*, *become, be hateful*: Lev 5 2 *S* (*B* ⲱⲣⲉⲃ) βδέλυγμα, Ps 52 1 *S* (*B* ⲥⲱϥ) βδελύσσεσθαι, BHom 36 *S* ϩⲏⲛϫⲉ ⲉⲧⲟ ⲛϭⲟⲧⲉ ⲉⲡⲉⲭ̄ⲥ̄ ⲱⲛ ἀπαγόρευσε, AM 202 *B* idols ⲉⲧⲟⲓ ⲙⲃ. ⲛⲁⲣⲣⲉϥⲉⲣϯ.

ϫⲓ ⲃ. *SA*, ϭⲓ ⲃ. *B*, *loathe, abominate*, c *SA* ⲉ-, *B* ⲛ-: JA '75 5 247 ⲛⲧϫⲓ ⲃ. ⲁⲛ ⲉⲗⲁⲁⲩ, Ex 1 12 *A* (*B* ⲟⲓ ⲙⲃ.), Deu 7 26 *B*, Ps 106 18 *B* (both *S* ⲃⲱⲧⲉ) βδελύσ., Mich 550 46 *S* he had place cleansed ϩⲱⲥ ⲉϥϫⲓ ⲃ. ⲉⲣⲟⲕ O king, PO 11 372 *B*, WTh 62 *B*, DeV 174 *B*, JTS 4 392 *S*.

ⲗⲁⲃⲟϯ *B*, so Lab as = لوطي *sodomite*; cf Aeg 281 *S* ⲉⲓⲣⲉ ⲛⲧⲃ., var ⲥⲟϫⲟⲙⲓⲧⲏⲥ.

ⲃⲱⲧⲉ *S*, ⲃⲱϯ, ⲃⲟϯ *B* nn m, *durah*, a cereal: Ex

9 32 *B* ὄλυρα ﺯ (var Va 1 حَمُّص), Ez 4 9 *SB* ὄλυρα (BMOr 1326 3 = ? شونان), 3 Kg 19 6 *S* ὀλυρίτης, Ann 1 62 *B* الدرا حِمَّص; but Tri 493, P 44 114 = 43 115 *S* ⲃ. دخن *millet*.

ⲃⲱⲧⲉ　*v* ϥⲱⲧⲉ *wipe out*.

ⲃⲱⲧⲉ　*v* ϥⲱⲧⲉ *sweat*.

ⲃⲉⲧⲃⲉⲧ *B* nn f, among vegetables : BM 926 لسَّ *common pea* : (P 43 58 لسَّ = ἄρακος, which P 44 83 = ἐρέβινθος, κύαμος, ⲁⲣⲱ; K 193 لسِّ = ϯⲗⲁⲕⲟⲡⲑⲉ).

(ⲃⲱⲧⲉ), ⲃⲟⲧⲥⲍ *S* vb **I**. tr, *draw up, set out, assess*(?) in certain fiscal documents : PLond 4 472 we assent to this διασταλμός respecting 5⅙ solidi ⲛⲧⲁⲡ̄ⲃⲟⲧⲥⲟⲩ; elsewhere ⲃ. ⲉⲃⲟⲗ : *ib* 466 ⲃ. ⲉⲃ. as nn : *ib* 475, 480 we assent to this ⲃ. ⲉⲃ. ⲛⲍⲉⲡⲟⲛ, *cf ib* 472, 473 we assent to this διασταλμός ϩⲁⲡⲉⲍⲉⲡⲟⲛ; thus ⲃ. ⲉⲃ. prob = διαστέλλειν (*v* PLond 5 83). *Ib* 473 inf var *l* ⲥⲱⲣ (not ⲃⲱⲣ) ⲉⲃⲟⲗ *assessment* (*cf* ⲥⲱⲣ, ⲥ. ⲉⲃⲟⲗ παρατάσσεσθαι).

B vb **II**. intr, *be drawn up* for battle, *fight* : Nu 31 7, Ps 26 3 (*S* ⲥⲱⲣ) παρατάσσεσθαι ἐπί, Is 2 4 (*S* ⲙⲓϣⲉ), Jer 28 30 πολεμεῖν, Va 57 78 ⲉⲧⲃ. ϫⲉⲛⲡⲓⲡⲟⲗⲉⲙⲟⲥ; c ⲉ- : Job 11 19 (*S* ϯ ⲟⲩⲃⲉ-), Ps 34 1 (*S* ⲙⲓϣⲉ) πολεμ., Ex 1 10 ἐκπολεμ., Deu 1 30 (*S* ⲙⲓϣⲉ) συνεκπολεμ., Is 9 21 (*S diff*) πολιορκεῖν; c ⲟⲩⲃⲉ- : Jer 21 5, Ap 12 7 (*S* ⲙⲓϣⲉ), Va 57 215 πολεμ., *ib* 173 ⲉⲕⲃ. ⲟⲩⲃⲉⲡⲓⲣⲁⲙⲁⲟⲓ ϫⲉⲛⲡⲉⲕⲥⲟⲑⲛⲉϥ ὁπλίζεσθαι; c ⲡⲉⲙ- (*against*) : 1 Kg 17 32, Ap 17 14 (*S* ⲙⲓϣⲉ ⲙⲛ-) πολεμ. μετά gen.

―― *B* nn m, battle *array*, *war* : 1 Kg 17 20 παράταξις, Nu 10 9, Is 22 2 (*S* = Gk) πόλεμος, Va 57 36 ⲡⲁⲓⲡⲟⲗⲉⲙⲟⲥ πόλ....ⲡⲁⲓⲃ. μάχη; pl Ps 45 10, Mt 24 6 πόλ. (both *S* = Gk). ⲁⲧⲃ., *impugnable* : TRit 35 faith unconquerable & ⲛⲁⲧⲃ.

ⲣⲉϥⲃ. nn, *warrior* : Joel 2 7 πολεμιστής, Va 57 174 πολέμιος, *ib* 88 ⲣⲉϥⲃ. ⲉϥϯ.

ⲉⲣ ⲃ., *array against, make war with* c ⲡⲉⲙ- : Ge 14 2, Ap 11 7 (*S* ⲙⲓϣⲉ) πόλεμ. ποιεῖν.

ⲃⲉⲧⲥ nn, *war* : ⲣⲱⲙⲓ ⲛⲃ. 1 Kg 17 33, Jer 52 7 (*S* ⲣⲱⲙⲉ ⲡⲣⲉϥⲙⲓϣⲉ) πολεμιστής; ⲣⲉⲙⲃ. Stern 182 (whence ?).

ⲃⲏⲧⲥⲛ (*l* ⲃⲉⲧⲥⲉ) nn f, *female warrior* : Is 27 4 (*S* ⲧⲉⲓⲣⲉϥⲙⲓϣⲉ) πολέμια.

ⲃⲟⲓⲟⲑ (glossed ⲃⲱⲱ) *O* nn, meaning unknown : AZ 21 100 (*cf* 38 90) ⲉ(ⲣ)ⲟⲙ ⲛⲓⲃⲓ ⲉⲗ(ⲣ)ⲱⲃ ⲛⲓⲃⲓ ⲃ. ⲛⲓⲃⲓ ⲉⲧⲕⲙⲁⲁⲓⲧⲟⲩ.

ⲃⲁⲑⲱ *S* nn f, prob a garment or napkin : BP 4977 in list of clothes, between ⲙⲁⲛⲧⲏⲗⲓ and ⲕⲟⲩⲗⲓϭⲧ (ⲕⲗⲁϭⲧ), Hall 117 ⲃ. wherein salt is wrapped, CO 465 pl among garments, EES ostr

unpubl ⲥⲛⲧⲉ ⲛⲃ. If for ⲣⲱ *l* ⲣⲟ, might = *face towel* (*cf* ⲃⲁⲧ ϭⲓⲝ, *v* ϥⲱⲧⲉ *wipe*); ⲟⲩⲁⲧⲣ ⲱ less likely.

ⲃⲓⲟⲩ in ⲁϥ ⲙⲃⲓⲟⲩ. *V* ⲁⲙⲏ, ⲣⲁⲃⲓⲟⲩⲓ.

ⲃⲟⲟⲩ, ⲃⲁⲩ *S*, ⲃⲱⲟⲩ *B* nn m, in name of Pbow, Pachôm's monastery at ٮﺎٯ, and in other place-names (*v* Ep 1 120). Meaning unknown. *Cf* next word.

ⲃⲟⲟⲩ in ϭⲉⲗⲃⲟⲟⲩ *q v*. Mor 51 33 shows ? a play upon this and preceding place-name.

ⲃⲏⲏϣ (Wess 18 44), ⲃⲉⲉϣ *S*, ⲃⲉϣ, ⲃⲏϣ *B* nn (? pl form, Stern 224), *unripe fruit* of fig tree : Cant 2 13 *S*, Ap 6 13 *B* (*S diff*) ὄλυνθος, Bor 248 52 *S*; more generally P 131¹ 32 *S* after winter fair trees ⲡⲟⲩϫⲉ ⲉⲃⲟⲗ ⲛⲛⲃ. ἀνθοκόμα πρέμνα.

ⲃⲱϣ *SABF* (ⲃⲱⲭ *B* MIE 2 410, ⲃⲟϭⲍ He 13 5 *S* var), ⲃⲉϣ- *S*, ⲃⲁϣ- *BF*, ⲃⲟⲩϣⲍ, ⲃⲁϣⲍ *S*, ⲃⲁϣⲍ *BF*, ⲃⲏϣⲧ *SB*, p c ⲃⲁϣ-(?) *S* vb, **I**. intr, *be loosened, undone* : BHom 123 *S* limbs ⲛⲧⲁⲩⲃ. after death, *ib* 47 *S*, BMis 455 *S* bonds ⲁⲩⲃ., Mor 41 117 *S* sick man's pains ⲁⲩⲃ. BHom 47 *S* she suffered not senses ⲉⲧⲣⲉⲩⲃ. ἁπλῶς φέρεσθαι; ⲃⲏϣ, *be naked* : Ge 3 7 *B*, Job 1 21 *B* (*S* ⲕⲱⲕ ⲁⲣⲏⲩ), Am 2 16 *SB*, Mt 25 36 *B* (*S* ⲕ. ⲁⲣ.), MG 25 219 *B* γυμνός (εἶναι) BSM 90 *B* ⲉⲣⲉⲡⲓϧⲏⲕⲓ ⲃ., EW 160 *B* how can I sit ⲉⲓⲃ. ?

II. tr (obj sometimes unexpressed) **a.** *strip, divest* c acc & ⲛ- : Ge 37 23 *B*, Lev 6 4 *B* (*S* ⲕⲱⲕ ⲁⲣⲏⲩ), 1 Kg 31 8 *S*, Ez 16 39 *B*, 2 Cor 5 4 *B* (*S* do) ἐκδύειν, Col 2 15 *B* (*S* do) ἀπεκδυ., Va 63 100 *B* ϣⲁϥⲃⲁϣϥ ⲛⲡⲓϧⲱⲥ ἀποδυ., Ex 33 5 *B* (*S* ϥⲓ ϩⲓ-) ἀφαιρεῖν, Ge 38 19 *B* περιαιρ., Ge 24 32 *B* ἀποσάττειν, Jer 7 29 *B* κείρειν (? *l* ϣⲱⲃ). **b.** *flay* : BMar 41 *S* ⲉⲕϣⲁⲛϥⲱϣⲧ ⲙⲡⲉⲓϣⲁⲣ, MG 25 362 *B* sim; *lay bare, unsheath* : Hab 1 17 *B* (Gk diff = *A*), C 43 224 *B* he caused soldiers ⲃ. ⲛⲛⲓⲥⲏϥⲓ, RAl 132 *S* ⲉⲣⲉⲧⲉϥⲥⲏⲃⲉ ⲃⲏϣ ⲡⲧⲟⲟⲧϥ, Mor 40 26 *S* ⲁϥⲃⲉϣ ⲡ̄ⲙⲉⲣⲉϩ ⲣⲛⲧⲉϥ(serpent's)ⲁⲡⲉ = *B* (C 43 55) ϥⲉⲭ; *despoil* (thieves, with ϣⲱⲗ ShMIF 23 20, 165) : Hos 7 1 *B* (*cf A*) ἐκδύειν, Miss 4 765 *S* ⲁⲡⲉⲥⲟⲟⲛⲉ ⲃⲁϣⲧ, Va 61 28 *B* ⲉϥϭⲓⲟⲩⲓ ⲉϥⲃ. ⲉϥⲃⲱⲧⲉⲃ. **c.** *metaphor* : BAp 68 *S* ⲛⲧⲁⲡ̄ⲡⲉ ⲃⲉϣ ⲁⲍⲁⲙ ⲛⲧⲁⲓⲕⲁⲓⲟⲥⲩⲛⲏ, Bor 265 89 *S* to Judas ⲙⲡⲓⲃⲁϣⲕ of thy apostolate, Mor 27 14 *Sf* ⲁϥⲃⲁϣⲕ ⲡⲧⲉϥⲥⲁⲙ, Cat 78 *B* ⲡⲧⲉϥⲃⲁϣⲧⲉⲛ of the old man. **d.** *loosen, unfasten* : Hab 3 14 *A* (*B* ⲟⲩⲱⲛ) διανοίγειν, P 132¹ 5 *S* chests which Theodosius ⲃⲟⲩⲟⲩ ⲣⲛⲧⲉⲥϥⲣⲁⲅⲓⲥ ⲙⲡⲉϥϩⲟⲩⲣ, Mun 46 *S* ⲁⲩⲃⲁϣ ⲡⲉⲭⲁⲙⲟⲥ ⲣⲛⲣⲱϥ, BMis 45 *S* martyr in chains ⲃ. ⲛⲁⲓ ⲡⲟⲩⲕⲟⲩⲓ that I may pray, ShA 1 40 *S* of snake ⲙⲡϥⲃⲉϣ ⲣⲱϥ ⲙⲙⲟⲟⲩ ⲛ ⲡϩⲏⲧⲟⲩ. **e.** *release,*

give leave: Job 7 19 *SB* προιέναι, Sa 16 24 *S*, Ps 38 13 *S* (*B* ⲭⲱ), Si 30 34 *S* ⲃⲉϣ ⲧⲟⲟⲧ, Jer 27 7 *B* (*S* ⲕⲱ) ἀνιέναι, Is 52 2 *B* (*S* ⲃⲱⲗ ⲉⲃⲟⲗ) ἐκλύεσθαι, P 129²⁰ 121 *S* in prayer ⲁⲣⲓ ⲡⲉⲩⲙⲉⲉⲩⲉ…ⲛⲧⲃ. ⲛⲁⲩ, PSBA 19 213 *S* sim, Bor 240 94 *S* we must watch that we permit not soul ⲟⲩⲇⲉ ⲡⲛⲉⲡⲃ. ⲡⲁⲥ ⲉⲧⲣⲉⲥⲣⲓⲕⲉ.   **f.** *forsake*: Is 2 6 (*B* ⲭⲱ ⲛⲥⲁ-), He 13 5 *S* (*B* ⲥⲱⲭⲡ) ἀνιέναι.

—— *B* nn m, *nakedness*: Ge 9 22 γύμνωσις, Deu 28 48, Ro 8 35, Ap 3 18 (all *S* ⲕⲱⲕ ⲁϩⲏⲩ) γυμνότης; Ex 22 27 ἀσχημοσύνη, MG 25 139 in cold, in ⲃ., in suffering, *ib* 376 she covered ⲡⲉⲥⲃⲱϣ.

ⲣⲉϥⲃ. *S* nn, *despoiler, robber*: ShA 1 238 ⲛⲣⲉϥϫⲓⲟⲩⲉ ⲛ ⲛⲣⲉϥⲃ., Tatt 408.

ⲣⲉϥⲃⲏϣϣ *B* nn, *naked person*: CaiEuch 361, Z 657n Barsôma العريان (Tatt 54 ⲛⲓⲃⲉϣ ? error).

ⲃⲉϣϣⲱⲓ *B* nn pl *lit, the secret parts uncovered* مكشوف السوٱ : BM 920 266 (*cf* K 78).

—— ⲉⲃⲟⲗ *SBF* vb **I.** intr, *be naked, revealed*: He 4 13 (*S* ϭⲱⲗⲡ ⲉⲃ.), HL 116, Ge 9 21 *B* (*S* ⲕ. ⲁϩ.) γυμνοῦσθαι, Cat 28 *B* all things ⲥⲉⲛⲁⲃ. ⲉⲃ., BP 4935 *S* letter asking for clothes ⲙⲡⲣⲕⲁⲓ ⲉⲓⲃⲉϣ (*sic*) ⲉⲃ. in midst of men. **II.** tr, **a.** *uncover, lay bare*: Ex 20 26, Deu 27 20 (both *S* ϭⲱⲗⲡ ⲉⲃ.), Su 32 *B* ἀποκαλύπτειν, Is 47 2 *B* (*S* ϭ. ⲉⲃ.) ἀνακαλύπ. **b.** *divest of*: Rec 6 183 *B* ⲁⲓⲃⲁϣⲧ ⲉⲃ. ⲙⲡⲁⲗⲉⲃⲓⲧⲟⲛ (*S* ⲕ. ⲁϩ.), TEuch 2 174 *B* ⲃ. ⲛⲧⲟⲩⲙⲉⲧⲥⲁⲥⲓϩⲏⲧ ⲉⲃ. **c.** *set free* (? of debt): Ryl 370 *S*.; obscure: BM 660 *F*, 1152 *S*.

—— ⲉⲃⲟⲗ *B* nn m, *nakedness*: Va 57 244 ⲫⲃ. ⲉⲃ. ⲙⲡⲟⲩⲥⲱⲙⲁ γυμνός, MG 25 376 ashamed ⲉⲑⲃⲉⲡⲟⲩⲃ. ⲉⲃ.

ϫⲓⲛ ⲃ. ⲉⲃⲟⲗ *B* nn m, *laying bare, display*: Va 57 126 ⲡϫ. ⲉⲃ. of wounds to physician δεικνύναι.

ⲃⲁϣ ⲁⲡⲏ (? *l* ⲁⲡⲉ) *S*, *? bareheaded*: BM 1142 letter, I went to the amîr ⲁⲓϭⲉⲛ ⲟⲩⲣⲱⲙⲉ ⲛⲃ. ⲁ.

ⲃⲁϣ ⲁϩⲏⲩ, ⲡⲕⲁϩ ⲛ-, among localities S. of Egypt in P 43 51 *S* ارض العريان (though MS has عريان?), named between بلاق الجنادل (Philae) and ارض التاكة(?). *Cf* ? ⲕⲏⲕ ⲁϩⲏⲩ. *V* KKS 69 70, LMis 379.

ⲃⲱϣ *B* v ⲟⲩⲱϣ *cleft*.

ⲃⲁϣⲓ *B* nn m, *meaning unknown*: C 86 178 after martyr's crucifixion there remained on cross naught save ⲛⲓⲃ. ϭⲓϫⲉⲛⲡⲓϣⲉ (? corrupt, *cf* ⲁϣⲓ *hanging, hung*).

ⲃⲟⲓϣⲓ *B* nn f, a desert animal: MG 25 134, ⲟⲩⲃ. ⲉⲥϣⲁⲧ ⲃⲟⲓ (ⲃⲟⲓ = *hair* or *canal* & ϣⲁⲧ = *cut* or *lack*, so ? *mangy*). *Cf* Ethiop *be'ezâ* kind of antelope (Tatt, Ludolf), or *b'aše* Sudanese jackal (Z f Assyr 31 28, Murray *Engl Nub Dict* 21).

ⲃⲟϣⲃⲉϣ *B* v ⲟⲩⲟϣⲟⲩⲉϣ.

ⲃⲁϣⲟⲣ *SB*, ⲃⲁϣⲁⲣ *S* (CO 469) *F*, ⲃⲁϣⲁⲁⲣ (Mich 550 25) *S*, ⲃⲁϣⲟⲟⲣⲉ (Mor 34 25), ⲃⲁϣⲟⲣⲉ (Mor 33 55) *S*, ⲃⲁϣⲁⲁⲣⲉ (? f form Mor 18 29) *Sᶠ*, pl ⲃⲁϣⲟⲟⲣ (Lu 9 58, Ryl 68) *S*, nn f (except P 44 54 m), *fox*: ShHT D 59 *S*, Mor 18 29, 19 38 *S* = Miss 4 122 *B*, Mich 550 25 *S*, CO 469 *S*; in bible ἀλώπηξ: Jud 1 35 *S*, Ps 62 10 *SB*, Lam 5 18 *SBF*, Mt 8 20 *SB*; K 164 *B* ⲃⲁⲣⲥⲁⲣⲓⲟⲥ (βάσσαρος) ثعلب.

ⲃⲁϣⲟⲩⲣ *SAB* nn f (m Is 10 15 in P 104 146, P 44 59), *saw*, *cf* משור منشار: 2 Kg 12 31 *S*, Is *lc* *SB* πρίων, He 11 37 *B* sawn with ⲟⲃ. πρίζεσθαι: Am 1 3 *SAB* of iron, BMar 42, Bor 267 104 *S* Isaiah sawn with wooden saw, AM 309 *B* with olive-wood saw; C 86 221 *B* ⲛⲁϧⲣⲓ ⲛⲧⲃ.; *ib* 271 *B* ϧⲁⲛⲃ. ⲉⲩⲙⲟⲥⲕ; BMis 285 *S* ⲧⲣⲟⲭⲟⲥ ⲛⲃ. circular saw, C 43 47 *B* sim; opp ⲗⲉⲡⲟⲏⲡ: ShZ 637 *S* ⲃ. ⲉⲧⲃⲉϣⲱⲱⲧ ⲗ. ⲉⲧⲃⲉⲟⲩⲉⲓⲥⲉ; var ⲗⲉⲡⲟⲏⲡ: BMis 352 *S* ⲗ. = BSM 17 *B* ⲃ.; P 44 59 *S* both = منشار. In lists of implements: CO 468, PLond 4 517 *S* ⲟⲩⲕⲟⲩⲓ ⲛⲃ. *Cf* Murray *Engl Nub Dict* 21.

ⲣⲁ ⲛⲃ. (ⲗⲁ BMis 557) *S*, ⲣⲟ ⲙⲃ. *B* *saw-edged* (KKS 134): Is 41 15 *SB* πριστηροειδής, sim ShA 1 385 *S* = Leyd 157, AM 43 *B* μάγγανον ⲉϥⲟⲓ ⲡⲣⲟ ⲙⲃ., C 43 218 *B* ἀστήριον ⲡⲣⲱϥ ⲛⲃ., BMis 557 *S* ϩⲉⲛⲕⲟⲣⲁϩ ⲉⲩⲟ ⲡⲗⲁ ⲛⲃ.

ⲃⲁϣⲟⲩϣ *SB*, *bašouš* DM, *cf* Syr *bašâšâ* and *bašušâ* (Lag *Gesam. Abh.* 173) nn m., *rue*: Lu 11 42 *SB* πήγανον, P 44 82 = 43 57 *S*, K 195 ·*B* سذاب; PMéd 102 n *S*; Z 629, PMéd 279 *S* ⲃ. ⲉϥⲗⲏⲕ, *ib* 139 ⲃ. ⲉϥϣⲟⲟⲩⲉ, P 43 245 *S* ⲡⲁϣⲟⲩϣ (ⲡ)ⲧⲟⲟⲩ بري سذاب, *cf* PMéd 292 ⲃ. ⲡⲁⲧⲣⲓⲟⲡ.

ⲃⲟϥ v ⲟⲩⲟϥ.

ⲃⲁϧ, ϧⲁϧ *S* nn m, *penis*(?): P 44 71 ⲃⲟⲩⲃⲟⲡ (βουβών) ⲡϥⲁϧ أبلغ (which in P 43 41 ἀκροβυστία), CR '87 376 (P 132⁵ 1) recipe for painful breasts, ϣⲁϥϣⲁⲩ ⲟⲡ ⲡ(ⲛ)ⲭⲟⲓⲧ ⲙⲡⲛⲃⲁϧ ⲉⲧⲙⲟⲕϩ. *V* ⲙⲙⲁϧ (*cf* Rec 18 179).

ⲃⲱⲱϧ, ⲃⲟϧ *B* nn, an idol at Alexandria destroyed by Michael on 12th Hathor, *temp.* Eumenius: Mor 25 23 *S* name of idol ⲃⲱⲱϧ, Va 58 28 *B* ⲁϥϭⲟⲙϭⲉⲙ ⲛⲃⲟϧ ⲡⲓⲇⲱⲗⲟⲛ in city Rakoti.

(ⲃⲱϧ), ⲃⲉϧ- (ⲡⲉϧ- Job 9 27), ⲃⲏϧ† *S* vb tr, *bend the head* (ϫⲱϩ): Job *lc* (*B* ⲕⲱⲗϫ, cit ShC 42 183, ShA 2 223, Z 511 n, LMis 17), Si 19 22 συγκύπτειν, *ib* 12 10 ⲃⲏϧ συγκεκυφώς; confused ? with ⲡⲱϧⲧ Lu 24 5. *V* LMis *lc*, Rec 30 143. Possibly = ⲟⲩⲉϧ- (ⲟⲩⲱϧ).

ⲃⲉϧⲓ *B* nn m, *file*: K 125 مبرد (which also = ⲙⲁϩⲥⲟⲗ), BMOr 8775 119, P 54 119, حديد.

ⲃⲟϭⲓ (? *l* ⲟⲩⲟϧⲓ) *B* nn m, *dyke, trench*: K 152 خندق (for which *cf* ϣⲁⲧⲥ).

ⲃⲟϭⲓ *B* v ⲟⲩⲟϭⲉ.

ⲃⲟⲩϭⲉ *S*, ⲃⲱϭⲉ *SA*, ⲃⲟⲩϭⲓ *B* nn m, *eyelid* : Job 16 16 *SB*, Ps 10 4 *SB*, Pro 4 25 *SAB*, Si 26 9 *S* βλέφαρον, Glos 24 *S* also ὑποβλέφ., C 86 44 *B* ϣⲁⲣⲉⲡⲓⲃ. ⲗⲧⲟⲡ ⲗⲗⲟϥ ⲉⲭⲉⲡⲡⲓⲃⲁⲗ. ⲣ ⲃ., ⲟ ⲛⲃ. *S*, *grow*, *develop* (abnormally ?) *eyelids* : PMéd 219 ⲛⲃⲁⲗ...ⲛⲥⲉⲣ ⲃ., *ib* 299 ⲉⲣⲉⲡⲉϥⲃⲁⲗ ⲱ ⲛⲃ. ; *cf ib* 226 ⲣⲱⲧ ⲃ.

ⲃⲉϩⲃⲉϩ *B* nn m, *howling*, *barking* : so Lab (whence ?). *Cf* ⲟⲩⲁϩⲃⲉϥ Spg 305, Lange *Amenope* 129.

ⲃⲉⲣⲱⲗ *S*, ⲃⲉⲗⲣⲱⲗ (var ⲃⲉⲣⲣⲱⲗ) *B*, ⲃⲟⲩⲣⲱⲗ *F* nn f (*S*), kind of *date-palm*, casting its fruit : Miss 4 695 = Z 531 *S* ; but K 177 *B* = بلح بسر *unripe date* ; AZ 23 39 *F* artabae of ⲃ. & ϫⲁⲓⲧ (sic l), ; O'LearyTh 14 *B* ⲡⲉⲧⲉⲛⲛⲟⲃⲓ ⲟⲓ ⲡⲟⲩϭⲉⲗⲣⲱⲗ ⲉϥ-ⲑⲣⲉϣⲣⲱϣ الصبغ الاحمر, where ⲃ. = φοῖνιξ (φοινικοῦς Is 1 18). *Cf* DM Indices p. 109.

ⲃⲱⲣⲉⲗ v ⲟⲩⲱϭⲗ.

ⲃⲁⲣⲉⲓ *B* v ⲟⲩⲁϭⲙⲉ.

(ⲃⲱⲣⲛ), ⲟⲩⲱⲣⲛ *B*, ⲃⲉⲣⲛ-, ⲃⲁⲣⲛ† *S*, ⲃⲁⲣⲛⲉ† *A* (Zach 1 8) vb tr, *cover with roof, awning* : Nu 7 3 *S* λαμπηνικός (var κατασκεπαστός), Ps 103 3 *S* (*B* ⲟⲩⲟϭⲛ)στεγάζειν, Ps 117 27 *S* (*B* ϧⲉⲣ, l ? ϥⲉⲣⲛ) πυκάζειν.

ⲃⲱⲣⲛ, ⲃⲁⲣⲛ *S* nn m, *canopy, awning* : Nu 4 13 (*B* = Gk) καλύπτηρα, Is 4 6 (*B* = Gk) σκέπη, Bor 260 9 goat-skins whereof ⲛⲃ. covering σκηνή (cf δέρρις Ex 26 7), JTS 5 559 ⲛⲃ. for 2 σκηναί in church of White Monastery, sim *ib* 561.

ⲃⲁⲣϭⲉ *SA*, ⲃⲁⲣϭⲓ *B*, ⲃⲉⲣϭⲓ *F* nn f, *heifer* : Ge 15 9 *SB*, Jud 14 18 *S*, 1 Kg 16 2 *S* (*B* ⲗⲁⲥⲓ), Ps 67 31 *SB*, Is 5 18 *SBF*, Hos 4 16 *AB*, He 9 13 *SB*, δάμαλις عجلة (μόσχος always = ⲗⲁⲥⲉ). In name ⲡϣⲓⲛⲧⲃⲁⲣϭⲉ (Miss 4 743), ϣⲡⲧⲃⲁⲣ(ⲥ)ⲉ TurO 20 *S*, a Pachomian abbot.

ⲃⲏϫ *B* v ⲃⲏϭ.

ⲃⲓϫ *B* nn m, *bones* used as dice, among utensils of gamester, gambler مقامر, K 138 فصّ (next to ⲑⲓⲃⲥ كعب). In place-name (?) : ST 319 ⲡⲗⲁ ⲛⲃ. *Cf* ? فصّ mosaic *tessera*, Abû Ṣâlih 50 b n., Fleischer *De Gloss.* 105.

ⲃⲁⲭⲓ *B* v ⲟⲩⲟϭⲉ.

ⲃⲉϫⲓ *B* v ⲃⲏϭ.

ⲃⲓϫⲓ *B* vb intr, *be wrecked*, of ship : 2 Cor 11 25 (*S* ⲃⲱⲕ ϧⲁ-), 1 Tim 1 19 (*S* ϣⲉ ⲛϭⲁⲥⲓⲉ), MG 25 19, Va 68 164.

—— nn m, *bending, twisting* : K 268, 335 ⲛⲃ. كسر تعويج. ⲉϥϫⲓ *B* nn, *wrinkle* : HL 90 ⲉⲣⲉⲡⲟⲩⲣⲟ ⲟⲓ ⲡⲉ. ϫⲉⲛϯⲙⲉⲧϫⲉⲗⲗⲟ ῥυτίς.

ⲃⲟⲭⲃⲉⲭ *B* v ⲟⲩⲟϭⲟⲩⲉϭ.

ⲃⲁⲭⲏⲓⲛⲓ *B* v ⲁⲃⲁϭⲛⲉⲓⲛ.

ⲃⲁⲭⲣⲱⲟⲩ *B* v ⲟⲩⲟϭⲉ.

ⲃⲏϭ, ⲃⲉϭ, ⲃϭ *S*, ⲃⲏϫ, ⲃⲉϫⲓ *B*, ⲃⲏϭ, ⲃⲓϭ *F*, *big* DM, cf Βαιήθ (Rec 22 162) nn m, *falcon* : Lev 11 16 *S* (*B* om), Deu 14 16 *SB* صقر (? or رمّ), Job 39 26 *B* (*S* om) ἱέραξ, Tri 638 *S* باشق, P 44 55 = 43 22 *S* ⲉϩⲏⲛⲧⲉⲣⲓⲛ (*accipiter*)باشق, K 167 *B* ⲃⲏϫ صقر, ⲃⲉϫⲓ جرادي ; also BM 1008 *S* invocation ⲡⲁϯ-ⲙⲟⲣⲫⲏ ⲛⲃϭ, Mor 52 52 *S* idol Serapis ⲡⲣⲁⲛⲁⲃⲏϭ (? ϩⲟ ⲛⲃ.), BMis 244 *S* Julian sacrificed ⲟⲩⲃ. to gods, *ib* 445 ⲃ. sacred bird at Philae, LAA 534 *SF* ⲃ. worshipped, PMich 599 *S* fried egg of ⲃ. in recipe. In Arabic : Amélineau *Contes* 2 8, cf C 38 (Pereira) 178.

ϣⲗⲱⲙⲃⲏϫ *B* nn m : Lev 11 17 καταρράκτης (*S* = Gk).

In many names : Βῆκις, Πβῆκις, Τβῆκις, Ταχομτβῆκις, Ὀρβῆκ &c (Preisigke).

ⲃⲱϭⲉ, ⲃⲟϭ v ϥⲱϭⲉ.

ⲃⲉϭⲏⲛ (Job 8 11), ⲃⲉⲭⲏⲛ (*ib* 40 16) *B* nn, a *rush* βούτομος = *S* ⲧⲣⲃⲛⲉⲓⲛ. *Cf* ⲁϩⲣ.

Ꞓ

Ꞓ third letter of alphabet, called ⲅⲁⲙⲙⲁ (K 1, My 60, BMis 8), جمّة, جامة, كمّة, (P 43 233), غمّة (P 44 137) ; as numeral = *three*, B, f ⲅ̄. In Coptic words rare (esp in early texts), not in *B* & only as equivalent in *S* of other letters. **a.** for ⲕ after ⲛ : ⲁⲛⲅ- (v ⲁⲛⲟⲕ), ⲉⲛⲅ, ⲛⲅ- (verbal pref 2 sg m) *S*, ⲙⲟⲩⲛⲅ *SA* (Hos 11 2) *O* (AZ 21 100), ⲡⲱⲛⲅ *S*

(-ⲛⲕ *BF*), ⲥⲱⲛⲅ *S*, ⲥⲟⲩⲱⲛⲅ (suff 2 sg) *S* (-ⲛⲕ *A* Hos 8 2), ⲧⲏⲧⲱⲛⲅ (do Z 286) *S*. To mark its sonant pronunciation ⲛ is prefixed in ⲛⲅⲁⲣ (archaic), as in dem (*e gg* DM *Indices* 117, 118, 123, 134) ; cf ⲛϫⲉ. **b.** for ⲕ elsewhere : ⲁⲅⲱ *S*, ⲅⲗⲁϥ *F* (2 Cor 12 16), ⲅⲓⲙ *S* (Miss 4 766), ⲅⲣⲟⲃ *S* (1 Kg 29 4), ⲅⲱⲥ *S* town Kôs (COAd 35), ⲛⲁⲁⲅⲉ *S*

(Wess 18 25), ⲅⲁⲧⲟ S (P 44 78); & in foreign words: ⲁⲧⲣⲱⲁⲧⲏⲥ, ⲅⲁⲧⲉⲗⲟⲥ (κάγκελ.), ⲅⲉⲗⲉⲅⲉ, ⲡ̅ⲅⲣⲁⲧⲏⲥ (C 89 106), ⲉⲡⲓ̅ⲅⲓ (ἐποίκιον), ⲕⲁⲅⲓⲁ, ⲕⲉⲡⲛⲉⲱⲥ (γενναῖος), ⲗⲟⲧⲉⲅ̅ⲅ (ST 315), ⲙⲁⲗⲁⲅⲟⲥ, ⲡⲉⲛⲁⲅⲓⲥ (πινακίς), ⲧⲁⲅⲁⲓⲕⲟⲥ, ⲣⲩⲡⲁⲅⲓⲥⲧⲁ (ὑποκεῖσθαι). **c.** replaced by ⲕ (S): ⲁⲕⲱⲣⲁ, ⲁⲡⲁⲕⲟⲕⲏ, ⲁⲡⲕⲏⲡ (ἀγγεῖον KroppK), ⲉⲓⲡⲧⲁⲕⲓ (ἐντάγιον), ⲕⲉⲣⲉⲡⲡⲁ, ⲕⲓⲱⲣⲕⲓⲟⲥ, ⲕⲡⲱⲗⲏ, ⲙⲁⲕⲉⲅⲉ, ⲡⲏⲣⲕⲟⲥ, ⲥⲡⲗⲁⲕⲓⲟⲛ (WTh 64), ⲥⲩⲕⲉⲗⲓⲟⲛ (σιγίλ.). **d.** for ϭ (S): -ⲅⲏ (J 69 29), ⲅⲁⲗⲡ (CO 251), ⲅⲁⲥ (Ep 532), ⲅⲓⲡⲏ (ϭⲉⲡⲏ), ⲅⲣⲟⲙⲡⲉ (TurM 22), ⲕⲗⲟⲅⲉ *ladder* (Ep 222), ⲛⲅⲉ (BM 545), ⲡⲟⲗⲅ (Ep 261), ⲥⲓⲅⲏ (CO 434). **e.** replaced by ϭ (S): ⲛϭ- (RE 9 164, Ep 144); ⲡⲱⲡϭ (RE 9 166), & in Gk ⲁϭⲱⲡ, ϭⲡⲟⲗⲏ (Ep 145), ⲕⲉⲣⲉϭⲙⲁ, ϭⲉⲉⲓⲥⲉⲓ (CO 71), ⲙⲡⲧⲉϭⲉ (μέντοιγε), ⲡϭⲉⲏⲧⲏⲥ (ἐγγυητής), ⲥⲉϭⲏ (ζυγή ST 378 *sic* !), ⲥⲓⲡⲁⲣⲡⲁϭⲏ. **f.** replaced by ⲝ: ⲁⲡⲁⲗⲗⲁⲝⲓⲛ B (var -ⲅⲓⲛ, Va 57 64, 65),

ⲁⲡⲧⲓⲗⲉⲝⲉ S (? CO 171), ⲝⲉⲥⲉⲙ B (Ge 47 27, Va 1 ⲅⲉⲥⲉⲙ), ⲝⲓⲥⲙⲓⲥ B (var ⲅⲓⲥ-); or for ⲝ: ⲅⲁⲕ̅ⲱⲡ B (Dif 1 46). Cf under ⲕ (ⲝ for ⲕ). **g.** = Ar غ: ⲅⲟⲣⲡⲉ غربة, ⲙⲉⲅⲁⲣⲉ مغارة, ⲥⲁⲅⲁⲣ صغار, ϣⲟⲅⲗ شغل (all EW 243 ff), ⲙⲁⲣⲁⲅⲉ مراغة (Sph 6 103), ϯⲙⲁⲅ دماغ (PMéd 212), ⲅⲁⲍⲟⲩⲁⲛ غزوان (Bodl(P) c 10); less often = ج: ⲁⲃ̅ⲅⲉⲗⲅⲁⲃⲃⲁⲣ جبّار (MR 1 65). Cf on transcription in late periods PMéd 26 ff. **h.** inserted between vowels (S): ⲓⲉⲅⲟⲩⲗ = Ἰεούλ (Ge 36 18), Παγεῦς = Παιηοῦς ⲡⲁⲉⲓⲛⲟⲩ (J&C), ⲡⲁⲅⲟⲓⲉ gen ⲡⲁⲅⲱⲧⲟⲥ (Gött Abh '17 77, 78); or omitted: ⲁⲭⲟⲩⲥ = Ἀγχοῦς (1 Kg 29 2); or become = i: ⲁⲓⲱⲛ (= ἀγών Ep 1 151), ϥⲣⲁⲡⲓⲉ (= ϥⲣⲁⲡⲅⲉ CO 394).

ⲅⲁⲍⲅⲁⲍ, ⲅⲁⲍⲅⲓⲍ S nn, a tree: P 44 66 = 43 33 عنّاب, which *ib* & K 179 B = ζίζυφα *jujube*. Coptic ?

ⲇ

ⲇ, fourth letter of the alphabet, called ⲁⲗⲇⲁ (Stern p 418), ⲇⲁⲗⲇⲁ (K 1, My 55), دالة (*sic*), دلد (P 43 234). As numeral *BF*, rarely *S* (Br 91, 131) = *four*, B f often without -ϯ (Ge 2 10, 47 24, Ac 10 11, 21 9, Aeg 235). **a.** in Coptic words rare & only as equiv of other letters (S): ⲥⲁⲓⲱⲣⲉ (CO 139), ⲇⲉ (*ib* 174), ⲇⲓ = ϯ vb (BKU 1 21 pass, LAl pass), ⲇⲓ- = ⲧⲉⲓ- pron J 69 41, ⲇⲓ- = ϯ- pref 1 sg (JKP 2 70, CO 195), ⲇⲓⲙⲉ (Bodl(P) e 70), ⲇⲓⲡⲉ (Nu 11 8), ⲇⲏⲣ⸗ (Aeg 287n, J 69 21). Common in foreign words; **b.** for ⲧ: ⲁⲡⲇⲁⲗⲓⲅⲉ (BMis 135), ⲁⲥⲕⲏⲇⲏⲥ (Ep 205), ⲃⲁⲡⲇⲓⲥⲙⲁ (Wess 2 96), ⲕⲁⲇⲏⲅⲟⲣⲟⲥ (BMis 325), ⲕⲓⲃⲟⲩⲇⲟⲥ (LDi ˙277), ⲙⲉⲇⲣⲓⲧⲏⲥ (BSM 41), ⲡⲉⲇⲁⲗⲟⲛ (*ib* 99), ⲇⲉⲭⲡⲏ (C 73 177), ⲇⲣⲁⲡⲏⲅⲍⲁ (BMis 7), ⲇⲟⲩⲃⲓⲧ, ⲧⲟⲩⲃⲓⲇ (Τωβείτ), ⲣⲩⲡⲟⲇⲁⲍⲉ (Wess 11 110), ⲭⲁⲣⲇⲏⲥ (C 86 129). **c.** replaced by ⲧ: ⲁⲧⲁⲙⲁⲥ (BMis 271), ⲉⲓⲡⲧⲏⲙⲁ (ἔνδυμα DeV 46), ⲇⲓⲁⲧⲉⲭⲉ (Wess 15 28), ⲧⲟⲗⲟⲥ (C 89 198), ⲕⲁⲧⲟⲩⲥ (*ib* 74), ⲕⲛⲧⲏⲡⲟⲥ

(Bodl(P) ė 27), ⲡⲉⲧⲏⲥ (C 86 148), ⲡⲣⲉⲇⲁ (*praeda* Miss 4 112), ⲥⲕⲁⲡⲇⲁⲗⲟⲛ (BMis 160), ⲣⲩⲙⲡⲟⲧⲟⲥ (*ib* 301); both: ⲕⲁⲑⲉⲇⲣⲁ (C 43 47), ⲧⲇⲣⲁⲙⲁ (R 2 1 58). **d.** for ⲑ (B): ⲁⲡⲇⲁⲣⲁⲍ (Ex 39 11 Lag), ⲁϥⲇⲁⲣⲧⲟⲥ BMEA 10587, ⲇⲣⲟⲡⲓⲍⲓⲛ (AM 280), ⲥⲩⲡⲇⲣⲟⲡⲟⲥ (Va 67 72), ⲕⲟⲗⲩⲙⲃⲏⲇⲣⲁ (BM 848, BSM 85). **e.** replaced by (ⲑ B): ⲑⲉⲥⲡⲟⲇⲏⲥ (BM 848), ⲑⲉⲟⲡⲏⲥⲓⲟⲥ (Dionysius C 89 43), ⲑⲣⲓⲙⲟⲥ (δρυμός K 174), ⲟⲣⲑⲓⲡⲟⲛ (DeV 94, C 89 16), ⲥⲩⲛⲏⲑⲏⲥⲓⲥ (συνείδ. Va 61 9), ⲥⲧⲁⲑⲓⲟⲛ (C 86 97). **f.** for ⲥ, ⲍ: ⲕⲁⲗⲁⲡⲇⲁⲓⲟⲥ (Ep 135), ⲥⲩⲙⲡⲟⲇⲓⲟⲛ (EW 47, CO 86), ⲧⲱⲡⲁⲇⲓⲟⲛ (Z 610, LAl 3). **g.** transcribed into Ar ⲇ becomes د: دسقورس, اندراوس, ناودورس; where Ar is transcribed ⲇ represents د, ذ: ⲇⲉⲇⲁⲗⲉⲑ دخلت, دخلت, ⲕⲁⲇⲓⲥ قديس, ⲣⲁⲇ ⲇⲉ عاد ذه, ⲓⲇⲉ اذا, ⲇⲉϩⲉⲡ ذهب (all EW 234 ff), ⲁⲃⲇ- (& ⲁⲡⲇ-) عبد in names, ⲉⲙⲭⲉⲇ امجد (BM 726), ⲓⲉⲍⲓⲇ يزيد, ⲣⲁⲥⲇⲓⲇ رشيد (Kr), though د may also = ⲧ (AZ 23 117-119, BIF 5 92 ff).

ⲉ

ⲉ, fifth letter of alphabet, called ⲉⲓ S (My 62, 63), ⲉⲓ, ⲉⲓⲉ B (K 1, Stern p 418), اية, ايبة (P 43 238, 44 133). As numeral m & f = *five BF*, rarely S (Br 130). Represents vowels unwritten in earlier hierogl, though visible in certain half-consonants in later periods. Dialectal equivalents: **a.** S ⲉ =

A ⲁ rare, as ⲉ- prep, ⲉⲛⲉϩ; converse often *A*, as ⲁⲣⲟⲙ, ⲕⲁⲕⲉ, ⲥⲁϥ, ⲧⲥⲁⲃⲟ; *F*, as ⲃⲁⲗ, ⲙⲁⲁϫⲉ, ⲣⲁⲗⲁⲧⲉ & in Gk as ⲗⲓⲧⲣⲉ (BM 530), ⲡⲁⲣⲉ- (*ib* 610), ⲥⲁⲣⲉ (Sarah *ib* 580). **b.** S ⲉ = F ⲏ, as ⲁⲡⲉ, ⲃⲗϫⲉ, ⲥⲉⲉⲡⲉ, ϣⲉ. **c.** S -ⲉ final = BF -ⲓ, as ⲙⲉⲉⲩⲉ, ⲣⲱⲙⲉ, ⲥⲣⲓⲙⲉ, ⲙⲁⲕⲁⲣⲉ (Μακάριος),

ϫⲓⲥⲉ; or = *B* ⲉⲓ, as ⲣⲡⲉ, ϧⲉ *fall*. In Gk words:
d. ⲉ for ⲁ rarely, as ⲉⲡⲉⲧⲉ (Wor 178, J pass);
converse ⲁⲣⲧⲁⲧⲏⲥ (Kr 245). **e.** for ⲁⲓ (oftenest,
esp *B*), as ⲁⲣⲭⲉⲟⲥ, ⲧⲉⲡⲏ (καινή), ⲉⲑⲏⲣ, ⲭⲉⲣⲉ, or
in passive vb, as ⲁⲥⲡⲁⲍⲉⲥⲑⲉ; converse ⲁⲓⲡⲉⲡⲟⲥ
(ἔπαι.), ⲡⲁⲓⲇⲉⲥ (πέδας). **f.** for ⲏ, as ⲕⲟⲙⲉⲥ,
ⲥⲕⲉⲅⲉ, ⲧⲉⲙⲉⲅⲉ (δημ. BMis 219), ⲅⲩⲡⲉⲣⲉⲧⲏⲥ; converse ⲁⲓⲣⲏⲥⲓⲥ, ⲑⲏⲥⲡⲉⲥⲓⲟⲥ (LDi 275). **g.** for ⲉⲓ,
ⲓ, as ⲁⲡⲟⲇⲉϫⲓⲥ, ⲧⲉⲧⲓⲡⲁ, ⲉⲡⲱⲭⲗⲉ; converse ⲁⲡ-
ⲁⲓⲗⲓⲧⲉ, ⲡⲓⲥⲧⲁⲣⲙⲁ (ἐπίσταλμα PLond 4 481). **h.**
for ⲩ, as ⲉⲥⲉⲭⲁⲍⲉ (ἡσυχ.), ⲕⲉⲕⲗⲟⲥ, ⲥⲉⲕⲉ (ζυγή
J 16 23); converse ⲁⲣⲁⲡⲩⲅⲁ, ⲅⲣⲏⲙⲟⲥ. **i.** for
ⲉⲩ, as ⲗⲉⲕⲟⲫⲟⲣⲉⲓ, ⲥⲕⲉⲟⲥ. **j.** for ⲟⲓ, as ⲧⲉⲡⲉⲧⲟ
ⲉⲡⲉⲧⲉ (ἐποίκιον J 81 3), ⲙⲉⲡⲧⲉⲧⲉ (μέντοιγε Kr 157),
ⲥⲧⲉⲭⲉ. Prosthetically, before ⲙ, ⲡ, ⲗ, ⲣ, sometimes ⲡ, ⲧ (Pcod xi), ⲃ (*S* ? archaic), ⲉ is represented by line over following consonant, as ⲙ̄ⲙⲁⲩ,
ⲛ̄ⲧⲟⲡ, ⲛ̄ϭⲓ, ⲗ̄ⲗⲏⲃ, ⲣ̄ⲣⲟ, ⲃ̄ⲃⲁⲗ; *cf sim* ⲛ̄ⲕⲁⲕⲓⲡ,
ⲛ̄ⲕⲗⲏⲥⲓⲁ, ⲙ̄ⲡⲟⲣⲓⲁ, ⲣ̄ⲣⲁⲥⲓⲁ; elsewhere before 2
consonants, mostly *B*, as ⲉⲙϩⲣⲱ (Ez 36 17), ⲉϧⲕⲟ
(C 86 238), ⲉϧⲗⲓ (Mus 34 208), ⲉϧⲣⲟϣ (TstAb
246); *S* as ⲉⲡⲣⲱ (Ryl 94 101), ⲉϣⲧⲉⲕⲟ (Miss 4
619), ⲉϧⲓⲉⲓⲃ (1 Kg 7 9), ⲉϧⲓⲱⲱϫ (Mor 20 42, *ib* 54
56 &c); *sim* ⲉⲃⲗⲁⲡⲧⲓⲡ (Va 57 12, *cf* C 89 13 *inf*),
ⲉⲃⲣⲁⲃⲓⲟⲡ (MG 25 319), ⲉϧⲣⲉϫⲓⲕⲟⲥ (αἱρετ. EW
173). Also represented by superline if toneless
between consonants *S*, as ⲥⲱⲣⲙ̄, but *B* ⲥⲱⲣⲉⲙ;
in good *SB* MSS also before suffix, ⲥⲟⲣⲙ̄ϥ.
Wrongly between consonants, as ⲏⲣⲉⲡ (often
ⲏⲣⲏⲡ), ⲡⲉⲥⲁⲧⲉ (ψⲁⲧⲉ), ⲥⲁⲣⲉϩ (KKS 183), ⲥⲉⲗⲉ-
ⲡⲓⲡ (σπλήν), ⲭⲉⲣⲱⲡⲱⲥ (? χρόνος PLond 4 524),
ϣⲉⲣⲉⲡ (Kr 7), ϧⲉⲡⲉⲟⲩ (*ib* 225). In late, esp *F*
texts ⲉ- often for ⲛ̄-, as ⲡⲣⲁⲡ ⲉⲡⲡⲉ, ⲙⲉⲡⲉⲥⲡⲉⲩ,
ϩⲉⲡⲉⲃⲏⲓ; rare in early: PS 55 *S* ⲉⲡⲡⲉ, 200 ⲉϥⲃⲁⲉ.

ⲉ- *SBF*, **ⲁ-** *AA²O*, with suff ⲉⲣⲟϫ (ⲉⲣⲱϫ 2 pl)
SB, ⲁⲣⲁϫ *AO*, ⲉⲗⲁϫ *F*, prep (hierogl *r*), simple or
compound with nn: ⲉⲃⲟⲗ, ⲉⲙⲁⲩ, ⲉⲣⲏ-, ⲉⲣⲁⲧϫ,
ⲉⲧⲃⲉ-, ⲉⲧⲟⲟⲧϫ, ⲉϧⲟⲩⲡ, ⲉϧⲣⲁⲓ, ⲉϧⲣⲡ-, ⲉϧⲟⲩⲟ, ⲉϫⲓⲡ-;
or with art & nn: ⲉⲡⲕⲱⲧⲉ, ⲉⲡⲉⲥⲏⲧ, ⲉⲡⲧⲏⲣϥ, ⲉⲡⲟⲩⲉ,
ⲉⲡϣⲱⲓ, ⲉⲡϧⲁⲉ, ⲉⲡϫⲓⲥⲉ, ⲉⲑⲏ; also in verbal pref
3 fut ⲉϥⲉ- *SB*, ⲉϥⲁ- *A*. Often strengthened by
preceding ⲉⲃⲟⲗ, ⲉϧⲟⲩⲡ, ⲉϧⲣⲏⲓ, ⲉϧⲣⲁⲓ, with hardly
changed meaning. Used for many purposes, chief
of which are here illustrated:

I. a. dative, *to, for, according to, as regards*:
Lu 5 29 *SB* made feast ⲉⲣⲟϥ αὐτῷ, Ps 96 4 *SB*
give light ⲉⲧⲟⲓⲕⲟⲩⲙ. τῇ, BMis 33 *S* king ⲉⲧⲉⲓⲡⲟⲗⲓⲥ, Job 27 17 *S* ⲣ ϫⲟⲉⲓⲥ ⲉⲡⲉϥⲭⲣⲏⲙⲁ τά, Mt 8 4
SB show self ⲉⲡⲟⲩⲏⲏⲃ τῷ, Ez 15 5 *B* useful ⲉϧⲗⲓ
ⲡϧⲱⲃ εἰς, Lu 23 12 *SB* friends ⲉⲡⲉⲩⲉⲣⲏⲩ μετά,
C 43 186 *B* love ⲉϧⲟⲩⲡ ⲉⲣⲟϥ, Ps 48 20 *SB* likened
ⲉⲡⲧⲃⲡⲟⲟⲩⲉ τοῖς, 2 Kg 9 13 *S* lame ⲉⲡⲉϥⲟⲩⲉⲣⲏⲧⲉ
τοῖς, Ps 68 3 *SB* a stranger ⲉⲡⲁⲥⲡⲏⲩ τοῖς, CO 135

S ἀνάθεμα ⲉⲡⲉⲓⲱⲧ, Is 19 9 *SB* working ⲉⲡⲙⲁϧⲉ,
BMis 236 *S* of one mind ⲉϧⲟⲩⲡ ⲉⲡⲡⲉ, Jud 7 12 *S*
there was no number ⲉⲣⲟⲟⲩ (= countless) ταῖς,
AM 251 *B* call him ⲉϥⲣⲁⲡ of apostle, Ac 2 38 *SB*
baptism ⲉⲡⲣⲁⲡ ἐν τῷ, Ez 16 11 *SB* bracelets ⲉⲡⲟⲩ-
ϭⲓϫ περί, Kr 5, Ryl 129 *S* set crosses ⲉⲣⲟⲥ (deed),
Jos 8 29 *S* he hung ⲉⲡϣⲉ ἐπί, J 65 61 *S* peg ⲉⲧ-
ⲧⲟϫ ⲉ(ⲧ)ϫⲟⲉ, 2 Kg 8 2 *S* he cast them ⲉⲡⲕⲁϩ ἐπί,
R 1 5 52 *S* he lay ⲉⲩⲡⲟⲓ (var ϧⲓ-), Mt 18 20 *S*
gathered together ⲉⲣⲟϥ (sc ⲡⲙⲁ), CO 96 *S* perform
liturgy ⲉⲡⲧⲟⲡⲟⲥ, Ap 22 18 *S* written ⲉⲡⲉⲓϫⲱⲙⲉ
(*B* ϧⲓ-) ἐν, Si 2 3 *SB* cleave ⲉⲣⲟϥ αὐτῷ, AM 268
B entrusted ⲉⲣⲟϥ, *ib* 299 *B* set (as guard) ⲉⲣⲟϥ,
Ro 4 10 *S* stand ⲉⲡⲉⲏⲙⲁ (*B* ⲡⲁϧⲣⲉⲡ-) τῷ, Ps 104
23 *S* sojourn ⲉⲡⲕⲁϩ (*B* ϫⲉⲡ-) ἐν, PS 15 *S* saying
these words ⲉⲡⲉϥⲙⲁⲑⲏⲧⲏⲥ (cf *ib* ⲡⲡⲉϥⲙ.) *ib* 31 *S*
shall not speak truth ⲉⲣⲟⲟⲩ, Mk 5 41 *S* ⲉⲓϫⲉⲣⲟ
(*B* ϫⲉ ⲉⲣⲟ) σοί λέγω, Jo 13 18 *sim*, Lu 7 14 diff
(*v* TT 65 n), P 132¹ 3 *S* ⲉⲓϣⲁϫⲉ ⲉⲣⲟⲕ, Ps 136 3
SB sing a song ⲉⲣⲟⲡ ἡμῖν, *ib* 29 8 *S* cry ⲉϧⲣⲁⲓ
ⲉⲡϫⲥ̄ (*B* ⲟⲩⲃⲉ-), CO 139 *S* at 6 acres ⲉϥⲟⲗⲟⲕ/,
Kr 11 *sim*, J 7 50 *S* price ⲡⲧⲁⲩϭⲡⲧⲙⲙⲁⲍⲉ ⲡⲁⲡϥ
ⲉⲣⲟⲥ, Mt 27 9 *sim*, BMar 5 *S* price fixed ⲉϣⲏⲧ
ⲡⲕⲉⲡⲁϫⲉⲡⲁⲣⲓⲟⲛ. **b.** purpose, *for, in order to*:
(*a*) + nn, 1 Kg 16 2 *B* (*S* ⲛ̄-) am come ⲉⲡϫⲓⲛϣⲱⲧ,
Job 5 7 *S* born ⲉⲡϧⲓⲥⲉ (*B* diff) κόπῳ, Ps 2 8 *SB*
give ⲉⲧⲉⲕⲕⲗⲏⲣⲟⲡⲟⲙⲓⲁ acc, Mk 16 18 *B* ⲉⲡϫⲁⲓ
ⲉϥⲙⲟⲩ θανάσιμον, Eph 1 5 *SB* set apart ⲉⲩⲙⲓⲧ-
ϣⲏⲣⲉ εἰς, BMis 303 *S* speak ⲉⲡϧⲏⲩ ⲡⲡⲉⲧⲛ̄ψⲩⲭⲏ;
(*b*) following ϣⲱⲡⲉ, Ps 108 7 *SB* ϣ. ⲉⲩⲡⲟⲃⲉ εἰς,
Jer 38 9 *B* ϣ. ⲉⲩⲓⲱⲧ εἰς, PS 50 *S* ϣ. ⲉⲩⲥⲟⲣϫⲉⲥ;
(*c*) + vb, Nu 11 13 *SB* where shall I find ⲉϯ
δοῦναι, Jud 19 25 *S* wish ⲉⲥⲱⲧⲙ, Job 1 15 *S* come
ⲉⲧⲁⲙⲟ τοῦ, Ep 162 *S* ordained ⲉϣⲱⲡⲉ; or with
ⲧⲣⲉ- (*v* ⲧⲣⲟ), C 43 8 *B* prepared ⲉⲑⲣⲓⲙⲟⲩ, Mt 27
31 *B* led away ⲉⲑⲣⲟⲩⲁϣϥ εἰς, Jer 34 10 *B* ⲉⲡϫⲓⲡ-
ⲑⲣⲉⲧⲉⲛⲟⲩⲉⲓ ⲉⲃⲟⲗ πρός, Ro 1 11 *B* ⲉⲡϫⲓⲡⲧⲁⲭⲣⲉ-
ⲑⲏⲡⲟⲩ (*S* ⲉ-), PS 10 *S* ⲉⲧⲣⲁϣⲁϫⲉ. Here ? belongs
ⲉ- after ⲉⲓⲙⲏⲧⲓ, ⲉⲙⲉϣⲏⲓⲉ, ⲉⲃⲏⲗ (Stern 587):
ShC 42 144 *S* what my sin ⲉⲓⲙ. ⲉⲧⲣⲁⲕⲟⲗⲁⲍⲉ
ⲙⲙⲱⲧⲛ?, Cl 50 2 *A* who ⲉⲓⲙ. ⲁⲡⲉⲧⲉⲡⲡⲉ ⲡⲁⲧⲟⲩⲙ-
ⲡϣⲁ?, PS 99 *S* none knew ⲉⲓⲙ. ⲉⲡⲓϣⲟⲣⲡ ⲙⲙⲩⲥⲧⲏⲣⲓⲟⲛ, MG 25 130 *B* none to hear ⲓⲙ. ⲉⲡϣⲁⲛⲉ-
ⲙⲁϭⲧ. **c.** *about, because of*: Ac 28 6 *B* saying
ⲉⲣⲟϥ ϫⲉⲟⲩⲡⲟⲩϯ ⲡⲉ acc, PS 93 *S* asking me ⲉⲙⲙⲩⲥⲧⲏⲣⲓⲟⲛ, *ib* 80 teach them ⲉⲡⲉϥⲥⲟⲟⲩⲛ, Jo 6 71
B (*S* ⲉⲧⲃⲉ-) said ⲉⲓⲟⲩⲇⲁⲥ acc, Cat 31 *B* ⲉϥϫⲉⲣⲟϥ
said *of* him, ShC 42 224 *S* silent ⲉⲡⲁⲓ (*ib* paral
ϧⲡⲡⲁⲓ), Miss 4 736 *S* lay down ⲉⲡϣⲱⲡⲉ, Rec 11
134 *S* sermon ⲉⲁⲡⲁ ϣⲉⲡⲟⲩⲧⲉ (paral ⲉⲧⲃⲉ-), BMis
1, 321 *sim*, J 70 54 *S* he shall pay ⲉⲡⲗⲟⲅⲟⲥ ⲙ̄ⲡ-
ⲡⲣⲟⲥⲧⲓⲙⲟⲛ, *ib* 41 96 *S* ⲉⲩⲱⲣϫ ⲡⲁⲕ (Kr 7, Ryl 182
paral ⲉⲧⲃⲉ-). **d.** *from, by means of*: Mt 4 4 *SB*

live ⲉⲡⲟⲉⲓⲕ ἐπί, BMar 30 *S* trade ⲛⲧⲁⲱⲡ ⲉⲣⲟⲥ, C 41 71 *B* take loaves & live ⲉⲣⲱⲟⲩ. **e.** direction *towards, to*: Ge 3 16 *S* ⲕⲧⲟ ⲉⲡⲟⲩⲅⲁⲓ, BM 175 *S* place ⲉⲧⲛⲛⲁⲃⲱⲕ ⲉⲣⲟϥ, PS 11 *S* ⲉⲓⲏⲩ ⲉⲡⲕⲟⲥⲙⲟⲥ, AM 306 *B* ⲁⲓⲓ ⲉⲣⲟⲕ (paral C 43 117 *B* ϩⲁⲣⲟⲕ), BMis 261 *S* ⲁϥⲙⲟⲟϣⲉ ⲉⲣⲟϥ, C 43 68 *B* place ⲉⲧⲛⲁϣⲉ ⲡⲏⲓ ⲉⲣⲟϥ, Ps 56 1 *SB* ⲡⲱⲧ...ⲉⲡⲉⲙⲣⲗⲁⲁⲩ εἰς, PS 21 *S* ⲡⲱⲣ ⲉⲧⲡⲩⲗⲏ, AM 330 *B* places ⲉⲧⲉⲕⲡⲁϩⲱⲗ ⲉⲣⲱⲟⲩ, Is 24 18 *SB* ϩⲉ ⲉⲡⲉϩⲓⲉⲓⲧ εἰς, ib 9 20 *SB* ϥⲛⲁⲣⲁⲕⲧϥ ⲉⲟⲩⲛⲁⲙ εἰς, Ps 44 15 *SB* bring ⲉⲡⲉⲣⲡⲉ εἰς, PS 56 *S* ⲛⲧⲭⲓⲧ ⲉⲡⲭⲓⲥⲉ, C 43 133 *B* every place ⲉⲧⲟⲩⲛⲁⲟⲗⲧ ⲉⲣⲟϥ, Mt 15 24 *S* ⲙⲡⲟⲩⲧⲛⲛⲟⲟⲩⲧ ⲉⲗⲁⲁⲩ (*B* ϩⲁ-), Lu 16 27 *S* ⲉⲕⲉⲭⲟⲟⲩϥ ⲉⲡⲏⲓ, *ib B* ⲟⲩⲟⲣⲡϥ, Ac 21 18 *S* ⲡⲉⲩⲥⲟⲟⲩ ⲉⲣⲟϥⲡⲉ, C 43 20 *B* ⲁⲩⲑⲱⲟⲩϯ ⲉⲣⲟϥ, MG 25 14 *B* ⲁϥⲧⲁⲥⲑⲟϥ ⲉⲧⲉϥⲙⲟⲛⲏ, Ps 104 29 *S* ⲁϥⲕⲧⲟ ... ⲉⲩⲥⲛⲟϥ, C 41 30 *B* ⲁϥⲥⲱⲟⲩⲧⲉⲛ ⲙⲙⲟⲟⲩ ⲉⲡⲁⲓⲱⲧ (var ⲙⲡ.), Miss 4 700 *S* ⲡⲱⲣⲧ ⲛⲛⲉⲅⲁⲕⲁⲑⲁⲣⲥⲓⲁ ⲉϩⲣⲁⲓ ⲉⲣⲟⲟⲩ, Jer 31 11 *B* ⲭⲱϣ...ⲉⲩⲙⲟⲕⲓ; Ge 31 4 *S* (*B* ⲉ-) he called Leah ⲉⲃⲟⲗ ⲉⲧⲥⲱϣⲉ εἰς, J 45 31 *S* ⲛⲧⲉⲕⲟⲧⲣ (ⲥⲱⲧⲣ) ⲡⲣⲟ...ⲉⲃⲟⲗ ⲉⲡⲓⲣ, 2 Kg 2 30 *S* ⲁϥⲕⲧⲟϥ ⲉⲃⲟⲗ ⲉⲁϩⲓⲡⲏⲣ ἀπὸ ὀπίσω τοῦ. **f.** (*a*) in hostile sense, *against*: Ps 3 8 *SB* ⲣ ⲭⲁϫⲉ ⲉ- μοι, Hor 79 O ⲣ ⲭⲁϫⲉ ⲁⲣⲁⲥ, Is 50 8 *S* ⲁϩⲉ ⲣⲁⲧ ⲉ- (*B* ⲟⲩⲃⲉ-) μοι, Job 30 5 *S* ⲧⲱⲟⲩⲛ ⲉ- (*B* ⲉϫⲉⲛ-) μοι, ROC 20 50 *S* ϫⲉⲣ ϭⲟⲣⲧⲉ ⲉ-, PS 33 *S* ϭⲱⲡⲧ ⲉ-, Hos 7 13 *S* ϣⲁϫⲉ ⲉ- (*AB* ⲛⲥⲁ-) κατά, Ap 2 20 *S* ⲟⲩⲛⲧⲁⲓ ⲉⲣⲟⲕ (*B* ϩⲁ-) κατά, BMis 109 *S* ϫⲓ ⲟⲩⲁ ⲉ-, Va 61 30 *B* ⲉⲣ ⲥⲕⲁⲛⲇⲁⲗⲓⲍⲉⲥⲑⲉ ⲉⲃⲟⲗ ⲉ-, Su 41 *B* ϯ ϩⲁⲡ ⲉ- acc, R 1 1 38 *S* ⲣ ϩⲱⲃ ⲉ- κατά, PS 104 *S* ⲣ ⲕⲣⲟϥ ⲉ-, R 1 3 42 *S* ϫⲓ ϣⲟⲭⲛⲉ ⲉ-, Joel 3 4 *SAB* ⲙⲉⲉⲩⲉ ⲉⲛⲕⲁⲕⲓⲁ ⲉ- ἐπί, Ps 37 20 *S* ϯ ϣⲧⲟⲩⲛⲧ ⲉ- (var ⲛ-, *B* ϩⲁ-) acc, Mt 26 62 *S* ⲣ ⲙⲛⲧⲣⲉ ⲉ- (*B* ϧⲁ-), Ep 84 *S* ⲡ ⲙⲁⲣⲧⲩⲣⲟⲥ ⲉ-, J pass *S* ⲉⲓ ⲉⲃⲟⲗ ⲉ- (ἐπέρχεσθαι, ἐνάγειν), C 43 107 *B* ⲱⲡ ⲉ-, RE 9 141 *S* ϩⲉ ⲉⲣⲱⲃ ⲉ-, 1 Kg 29 8 *S* ⲣ ⲛⲟⲃⲉ ⲉ- (var ⲛ-), MG 25 120 *B* ⲙⲙⲟⲛ ϣϭⲟⲙ ⲙⲙⲟⲓ ⲉ-, R 1 4 72 *S* ⲕⲱ ⲉⲃⲟⲗ ⲉ- let loose *against*, 2 Kg 13 17 *S* ϣⲧⲁⲙ ⲉ-, Si 12 10 *S* ϯ ϩⲏⲧ ⲉ- ἀπό, J 76 76 *S* ϥⲓ ⲛⲭⲓⲟⲩⲉ ⲉ-; (*b*) or indicating *debt, responsibility*: Deu 24 11 *S* ⲉⲧⲉⲟⲩⲛⲧⲁⲕ ⲉⲣⲟϥ (*B* ⲉⲧⲉⲡⲉⲛⲭⲁⲓ ⲉ-) οὗ τὸ δάνειόν σου, Mt 18 24 *SB* ⲉⲣⲉϩⲁϩ ⲛϭⲓⲛϭⲱⲣ ⲉⲣⲟϥ ὀφειλέτης μυρίων ταλ., Lu 17 10 *SB* ⲡⲉⲧⲉⲣⲟⲛ ὃ ὠφείλομεν, Ro 13 7 *SB* ⲡⲉⲧⲉⲣⲱⲧⲛ τὰς ὀφειλάς, ShMiss 4 278 *S* ⲡⲁⲛⲟⲩⲥ ⲉⲟⲩⲛⲧⲁⲛ ⲉⲣⲱⲙⲉ ⲡⲣⲟϭⲟ ⲉⲟⲩⲛⲧⲁⲩ ⲉⲣⲟⲛ, MG 25 254 *B* ⲙⲏ ⲟⲩⲟⲛ ϩⲗⲓ ⲛⲧⲁⲕ ⲉⲣⲟⲓ μή τί σοι χρεωστῶ, Va 68 168 *B* ϩⲱⲥ ⲉⲟⲩⲟⲛ ⲉⲣⲟⲓ ὑπεύθυνος, Ge 26 11 *B* ⲉϥⲣⲁⲟⲩⲛⲟⲩⲧ ⲉϥⲙⲟⲟⲩ, Ex 22 3 *S* ⲉϥϭⲏⲡ ⲉⲡⲙⲟⲩ ἔνοχος; Kr 237, Ryl 287, BM 1103 *S* ϭⲱⲡⲉ ⲉ- prob in this sense; Jer 2 18 *S* ⲟⲩ ⲉⲣⲟⲕⲧⲉ τί σοι, BMis 36 *S* ⲟⲩ ⲉⲣⲟⲓ ⲁⲡⲟⲕⲡⲉ ⲕⲱⲗⲅ, PBu 102 *S* ⲛⲓⲙ ⲟⲩⲛⲡⲉ ⲓⲱⲁⲛⲛⲏⲥ ⲉⲣⲟⲛ; (*c*) impersonal: Gal 5 3 *SB* ⲥⲉⲣⲟϥ ὀφειλέτης ἐστί,

Miss 4 830 *S* ⲥⲉⲣⲟⲛ ⲉⲡⲓⲥⲧⲉⲩⲉ, ShA 2 60 *S* ϩⲉⲛⲣⲃⲏⲛⲅⲉ...ⲥⲉⲉⲣⲟϥ ⲉⲗⲁⲩ (so often, *l* ⲥⲉⲣ-). **g.** ethic dative (*dat commodi*, cf ⲛ- prep): 2 Kg 2 18 *S* ⲡⲉⲣⲉⲣⲁⲧⲥ ⲁⲥⲱⲟⲩ ⲉⲣⲟϥ τοῖς ποσίν, Si 2 2 *SB* ϭⲁⲓ ⲉⲣⲟⲕ κρατέρησον, Job 21 3 *S* ϭⲉⲓ ⲉⲣⲱⲧ βαστάσατέ (με), Mt 7 15 *SB* take heed ⲉⲣⲱⲧⲛ προσέχετε, Mor 40 42 *S*, Miss 4 10 *B* ⲁⲓⲛⲁⲩ ⲉⲣⲟⲓ, ib 149 *B* ⲕⲏⲛ ⲉⲣⲟⲕ ⲉⲕⲭⲱ ⲛⲛⲁⲓ, BAp 172 *S* ϩⲙⲟⲟⲥ ⲉⲣⲟⲕ (cf Mk 14 32 *S* ϩ. ⲛⲏⲧⲛ), C 89 123 *B* ⲛⲁⲣⲉⲧⲁⲁϥⲉ ⲙⲟⲕⲣ ⲉⲣⲟⲓⲡⲉ, Miss 4 568 *S* ⲡⲥⲉⲥϭⲣⲁϩⲧ ⲉⲣⲟⲟⲩ, Va 61 105 *B* God hath made thy body ⲉϥⲟⲩⲟⲝ ⲉⲣⲟⲕ, El 98 *A* ⲛϩⲁⲧ ⲁ- = *ib* 134 *S* ⲡⲱϣⲥ ⲉ- (cf Stern 506 end). **h.** distance of time, past or fut: Ge 31 2 *S* ϣⲙⲧ ⲉⲡⲟⲟⲩ PMich 3571 *S* ϣⲏⲙⲧ ⲉⲧⲣⲟⲙⲡⲉ, *until* BMis 216 *S* six generations ⲉⲡⲓⲣⲱⲃ *since*, ib 248 *S* = Z 264 ϩⲁⲑⲏ ⲛϣⲟⲙⲛⲧ ⲛⲣⲟⲟⲩ ⲉⲡⲙⲟⲩ *until* = before (= PO 1 420 قبل), Wess 18 11 *S* ϩⲁⲑⲏ ⲛⲡⲧⲟ ⲛⲣⲉⲃϩ. ⲉⲡⲣⲟⲩⲙⲓⲥⲉ, Ps 95 2 *S* ϩⲛⲟⲩϩⲣⲟⲟⲩ ⲉⲩⲣⲟⲟⲩ ἡμέραν ἐξ ἡμ., BM 998 *S* each ⲉⲡⲉϥⲛⲁⲩ, J 121 5 *S* no claim against thee until Koiahk ⲉⲕⲉⲣⲟⲙⲡⲉ, ShC 73 58 *S* shall be taken from him ⲉⲣⲟϥϩⲉ. **i.** distance of place, separation, freedom from: Mt 10 35 *SB* ⲡⲱⲣϫ ⲉ- κατά, C 43 225 *B* ⲟⲩⲛⲟⲩ ⲉ-, ib 86 330 sim (oftener ⲛ-), R 1 2 64 *S* ϣⲙⲙⲟ ⲉ-, Jer 21 7 *S* ϣⲟⲭⲛ ⲉ- (*B* ⲉⲃⲟⲗ ϩⲁ-) ἀπό, Ps 130 2 *S* ⲱⲙⲝ ⲉ- ἐπί, Ge 18 17 *S* ϩⲱⲡ ⲉ- (*B* do) ἀπό, Job 5 20 *S* ⲡⲟⲩϩⲙ ⲉ- (*B* ⲛⲧⲉⲛ-) ἐκ, Ps 90 3 *S* ⲧⲟⲩϫⲟ ⲉ- (*B* ⲉⲃⲟⲗ ϩⲁ-) ἐκ, ib 120 7 *S* ϩⲁⲣⲉϩ ⲉ- (*B* do) ἀπό, ib 118 134 *S* ⲥⲱⲧⲉ ⲉ- (*B* do) ἀπό, Mt 23 33 *S* ⲣ ⲃⲟⲗ ⲉ- (*B* ⲉⲃⲟⲗ ϧⲉⲛ-), 2 Kg 3 28 *S* ⲟⲩⲁⲁⲃ ⲉ- ἀπό, Si 26 22 *S* ⲧⲏⲗⲟ ⲉ- ἀπό, Gal 4 1 *S* ϣⲓⲃⲉ ⲉ- gen. **j.** distributive: BM 258 *S* two robes ⲉⲡⲟⲩⲁ, BMis 375 *S* sim, *ib* 168 *S* they shall demand 100 *solidi* ⲉⲡⲟⲩⲁ, BAp 65 *S* ten thousand ⲉⲧⲗⲉⲩⲉⲱⲛ, J 13 22 *S* half to Patermouthius, half ⲉⲣⲟⲛ, BMis 570 *S* so & so long ⲉⲧϫⲟ *on each side* (*lit.* wall). **k.** comparison: Jo 4 12 *SAB* ⲛⲁⲁ- ⲉ-, Ps 71 16 *S* ϫⲓⲥⲉ ⲉ- (*B* ⲉϩⲟⲧⲉ-), PS 8 *S* ⲟⲩⲟⲧⲃ ⲉ-, Aeg 40 *B* ⲛⲉⲥⲉ- ⲉ-, Si 17 26 *S* ⲟ ⲛⲟⲩⲟⲉⲓⲛ ⲉ-, Ps 18 10 *S* ϩⲟⲗϭ ⲉ- (= *B* ⲉϩⲟⲧⲉ-), Nu 4 19 *S* ⲛϣⲟⲣⲡ ⲉ-, Job 20 10 *S* ⲑⲃⲃⲓⲏⲩ ⲉ-, ShLeyd 184 *S* ⲙⲏ ⲟⲩⲛ ϭⲉⲣⲣⲟ ⲉⲡⲭ̅ⲥ̅ ⲓ̅ⲥ̅, 1 Cor 13 13 *S* ⲡⲛⲟϭ ⲉ- τούτων, *cf* with ⲉⲥⲛⲧ, Miss 4 724 *S* ⲡⲁⲓ ⲙⲡⲉⲥ. ⲉⲣⲟϥ; with ϩⲟⲩⲟ: Mt 12 7 *S* mercy ⲛϩ. ⲉⲑⲩⲥⲓⲁ, BHom 52 *S* overwhelming ⲛϩ. ⲉⲩⲭⲓⲙⲱⲛ, Nu 14 12 *S* (*B* ⲉϩⲟⲧⲉ-) great ⲛϩ. ⲉⲡⲏ μᾶλλον ἤ, Si 24 21 *S* sweet ⲛϩ. ⲉⲡⲉⲃⲓⲱ ὑπέρ, 1 Cor 15 6 *SF* ⲛϩ. ⲉϥⲟⲩ ⲛϣⲉ (*B* ⲥⲁⲡϣⲱⲓ ⲛ-), BMis 371 *S* better die ⲛϩ. ⲉⲣⲟⲥ ⲛⲧⲏⲣ ⲡⲱϩϣ, Va 66 300 *B* loved holiness ⲛϩ. ⲉϭⲓ ⲛⲧⲁⲡⲟⲗⲁⲩⲥⲓⲥ. **l.** elliptic: C 86 278 *B* ⲡⲓⲥⲧⲁⲩⲣⲟⲥ ⲉⲣⲟⲕ = BSG 177 *S* ϯⲱⲣⲕ ⲉⲣⲟⲕ ⲙⲡⲉⲥⲧ. (cf τὸν σταυρὸν σοί), Va 62 295 *B* ⲡⲓϣⲗⲏⲗ ⲛⲧⲉⲡⲓⲇⲓⲕⲉⲟⲥ

ερок, Miss 4 759 *S* калwс ерак *welcome, cf* ? Miss 4 672 *S* w ḟιа ерок, AM 312 *B* λιϣι ерwτεп, MG 25 68 *B* crying ероϥ ероϥ (*cf* PG 65 257 λάβετε αὐτόν), J 4 49 *S* ϫιπτεпоу ϫε ерок пток... екпλει (often so in J, elliptic ?, *cf* PMon 4 24 &c πρὸς τῷ σὲ...ἀπεντεῦθεν), paral ϱwστε ерок J 11 38 &c (*cf* PLond 5 198 ὥστε σε), prob sim J 19 103, 106 137, επι τw ероι, paral ерwтп (for 78 60 *v* 7 53), J 68 65 пϣорп ерок екпаϥ; perhaps elliptic Mk 9 23 *S* (*B* diff) ϫεεϫооc, BM 267 *S* пϭε εϫооc, Wess 9 148 *S* εϫооc, BMis' 225 *S* cϫεϫоп εϫооc, PO 11 322 *B* sim.   **m.** in adverbial expressions: time, Ps 118 148 *S* εϱτооуε, Si 36 18 *S* епϱαε, ShC 73 60 *S* εϣωрп BMar 30 *S* епооу (*cf B* λιϥооу); direction, Ge 32 17 *SB* ετwп, Ps 39 14 *SB* епаϱоу, Ps 121 4 *S* εμαу (*B* λιμαу), J 1 62 *S* ернс; degree, manner, BMar 208 *S* επτнрϥ, PS 7 *S* εμаϣо, Ps 46 9 *S* εμатε, AM 1 *B* епιϱоϭо, Pro 23 29 *S* επϫιпϫн.

II. indicating direct obj, **a.** with many vbs of sensual perception, mental action (though many of these also use п-): *think*, Ac 28 22 *SB*, J 65 20 *S* μεεуε ε-; *see*, Ro 1 11 *SB* пау ε-; *hear*, Deu 5 1 *SB* сwτμ ε-; *smell*, Lev 26 31 *SB* ϣwλμ ε-; *feel*, Ge 27 22 *B* ϫомϫεμ ε-; *touch*, Ps 143 4 *S* ϫwϱ ε- (*B* ϭι пεμ-), Hor 84 *O*; *know*, C 89 30 *B* εμι ε- (= MG 17 297 *S* сооуп п-); *forget*, Is 40 26 *S* (*B* diff) wḟϣ ε-; *fear*, Ps 90 5 *S* ϱ ϱотε ε- (*B* εβολ ϱα-); *entreat*, PS 100 *S* кwрϣ ε-; *greet*, Ro 16 3 *SB* ϣпε ε-; *call*, Jo 15 15 *SA²B* моутε ε; *await*, Ac 1 4 *S* ϭw ε- (*B* wϱι п-); *find*, Lu 13 7 *S* ϱε ε- (but *B* ϫιμι п-); *bless*, Ps 21 26 *SB* сμоу ε-; *trust in*, Sa 6 24 *S* паϱτε ε-; sim with many Gk vbs.   **b.** with various vbs (classed as intr), as *meet*, Ps 151 6 *S* тwμпт ε- (*B* εϱреп-); *surround*, Is 9 18 *S* кwтε ε-; *set up*, Zech 4 7 *S* (*B* diff) сооϥε ε-; *strike*, Jo 18 23 *SA²B* ϱιоуε ε-, ShC 42 50 *S* ϣаар ε-; *conquer*, Ap 12 11 *SB* ϫро ε-; *keep*, Ge 3 24 *S* ϱареϱ ε- (*B* п-).

III. co-ordinating a 2d vb: Job 34 19 *S* ϱμптреуϫι ϣак εβολ ауw ετεḟϱ рwμε =*B* псетwḟϱ, Va 57 175 *B* пιϫιпḟωт пϱнτ пεμεсwτεμ, Aeg 242 *S* μпртсаḟо ерооу н εсwτμ ерооу.

No account is here taken of ε- erroneously (phonetically) for prep п-, esp in later *S* and in *F* texts.

ε- *SABF* verbal prefix, from hierogl *iw*, before nominal subj ере- (*A* ε-), еλε- *F*, characterizes (*a*) 2 pres (*B* а-), (*b*) 2 fut (*B* а-), (*c*) 3 fut, as (*a*) еуμεεуε еϱепкроϥ, ерепϣоϣт птоот, (*b*) еретеуто паϣwпε ϱптλιμпн, аιеι епаḟωк, (*c*) ϫекаc еуееιμε, аϥμερε псаϱоу еϥеει паϥ; or precedes other auxiliaries, either in subordinate or co-ordi-

nate clause: еаϥ-, еϣаϥ-, епеϥ-, ептаϥ-; or neg, емпеϥ-, емпатϥ-, емеϥ-; or in nominal clause: епеϥраппе пμоу, еукрмεспе пεϥϱнт, ереϱепḟϱ ϱппеуϭιϫ, пεусμоупε ϱптеутапро еусаϱоу ϱμпеуϱнт. In condit clause ε- sometimes = *if*, *when*, Sdff 481, Ep 1 p 251. As relat: оуϱооу еаϥпараϭε, таψуϫн ептаксотс.

е† *A*   *v* еιре.

еw *SB*   *v* еιw ass.

еḟн *S*, еḟι *AB*, еḟеι *A* (? = ϱнḟе *S*, ϱеḟι *B*, *v* LAl 111 n) nn, *darkness*; only with р, ер: Eccl 12 2 *S* σκοτίζειν (*ib* 3 cit ShC 42 211 р какε), Ez 32 7 *B*, Joel 2 10 *A* (*S* р ϱнḟе, *B* ер ϫакι), *ib* 3 15 *A* (*SB* р какε) συσκοτίζειν, R 1 4 66 *S* φθίνειν = AM 126 *B* (*l* еḟι, *cf* р ϱнḟе ἀσθενεῖν 2 Kg 3 1 *S*), Mor 44 50 *S* ϣареpри р какε птепооу р е., BMar 160 *S* апрн р е. а
уw аϥр какε σκοτίζειν.

μετεḟн *B* nn f: Ac 3 10 (var тwμт, *S* аупwϣс) ἔκστασις (? confused with σκότωσις, *cf* Ge 15 12).

еḟιw *SBF*, еḟιоу *A* (ḟḟιоу Pro 6 8 &c), еḟιе- *S* nn m, *honey*: Nu 11 8 *SB*, Ps 18 11 *SB*, Pro 5 3 *SAB*, Mt 3 4 *B* (*S* еḟιеϱооут), Ap 10 10 *SBF* μέλι; LAp 336 *S* е. па[тик]оп = Ἀττικὸν μ. used to preserve corpse (*cf* BKU 1 8 33, Cai 42573 е. патактоп,) Aeg 257 *S*, BM 1007 *S* liturgical use, Br 112 *S* myrrh & incense & оуε.; RE 9 160 *S*, Ryl 106 *S*, CO 487 *S*, WS 52 *S*, Z 628, 639 *S* medicinally; Ep 184 *S* as gift to ascete, ShA 1 200 *S* μαρτύρια are become μа пϯ е. εβολ, BM 1088 *S* еϥеιw пμε (*cf* етсwтп Ez 27 17 *SB* μ. πρῶτον, *cf* Leont Neap Gelzer 23), PMéd 267 *S* е. патμооу, *ib* 294 е. еϥпосе; Ryl 355, Ep 535 *S* кап епе., WS 121 *S* кеλλаре ппе., BM 1126 *S* λакоп ппе. sealed, PMich 4567 оуλаϱн пе.

е. **μμε**, *pure honey*: KroppE *S* е. μ. патμооу паткwϥт.

еḟιеϱооут *S*, *wild honey*: Mk 1 6 (*B* еḟιw) μέλι, BAp 136 ϱепеḟιw ϱооут.

μапе.: Job 20 17 *SB* νομὴ μέλιτος.

сапе. *S*, *honey dealer* ST 272, Ep 561. As name: Ψανεβιῶ (Preisigke).

еḟιт *S*, еḟеιт *S*ᶠ, *honey dealer*: PMich 2066, Sph 10 2, pl *ib* еḟеιетι (*sic l*). *Cf* AZ 45 106. As name ? Ἐβῆτις (Preisigke).

V also аϭап, аϥ *fly*, ḟπе, еιwте, поуϱе *sycamore*, ϯλιεϥ, таϭ, ϣнр, ϭλап.

еḟо, еḟw *SAB*   *v* μпо.

еḟιаιк *B*   *v* ḟωк *servant*.

еḟоλ *SB*, еḟаλ *F*   *v* ḟωλ.

ⲉⲃⲗⲉⲅⲉ *S* nn: P 44 71 (43 41 om) = ⲁⲣⲟⲥⲉⲓ (? δρόσος) عرق (*vein & sweat*). For ? ⲫⲗⲉⲃⲉ φλέβιον.

ⲉⲃⲉⲛ *B* v ⲁϣⲉⲃⲉⲛ.

ⲉⲃⲓⲏⲛ *SABF*, ϩⲉⲃⲓⲏⲛ *A* (Cl 15 6) nn m f, **a.** *a poor, wretched person* (cf אביון): Ps 36 14 *S* (*B* ϫⲱⲃ) πένης, so in Ps often with paral ϩⲏⲕⲉ *SB* πτωχός, Ez 16 49 *SB* sim, ib 18 12, 22 29 *B* do πένης; or *S* ⲉ. = *B* ϩⲏⲕⲓ: Ps 9 18, 71 4 πένης; Sa 3 11, 13 10 *S* ταλαίπωρος, ib 15 13 *S*, Is 6 5 *S* τάλας; BHom 7 *S* he reckoneth neglectful ϫⲉⲟⲩⲉ. ⲡⲉ ταλανίζειν; ib 139 *S* ⲧⲉⲓⲉ., Z 296 *S* ⲧⲉ. ἄθλια; Hos 7 13 *B* (*SA* diff), Nah 3 7 *A* (*B* ⲧⲁⲗⲉⲡ.) δείλαιος; 1 Cor 15 19 *SF* (*B* diff) ἐλεεινός; ShRE 11 18 *S* leading astray ϩⲁϩ ⲡⲉ. ⲡⲁⲧⲥⲟⲟⲩⲛ, BMis 349 *S* ⲁⲓϣⲱⲡⲉ ⲡⲉ. ⲡⲧⲁⲗⲁⲓⲡ., BM 264 *S* reader addressed as ⲡⲉ., ib 490 *S* term of humility ⲡⲉⲓⲉⲗⲁⲭ. ⲁⲩⲱ ⲡⲓⲉ., ShC 42 13 *S* ⲧⲉⲕϭⲓⲛϭⲣⲁⲓ ϣⲁⲡⲁⲉ., CO 302 *S* ⲡⲓⲉⲃⲃⲓⲏⲛ Apa Dius (the writer). **b.** as adj, *miserable, wretched*: Ez 5 15 *SB* δειλαιστός; Ap 3 17 *S* (*B* ϫⲱⲃ) ἐλεεινός; J 73 3 *S*, Va 62 277 *B*, BHom 72 *S* ⲧⲉⲡⲯⲩⲭⲏ ⲡⲉ., cf C 43 248 *B* ⲡⲉϥⲉ. ⲡ̅ⲯ., Bess 7 65 *S* he died ϩⲛⲟⲩⲙⲟⲩ ⲡⲉ., Ep 438 *S* ⲡⲉⲧⲛⲥⲟⲡ ⲡⲉ., ST 396 *S* ϩⲏⲕⲉ ⲡⲉ., BM 225 1 *S* ye are come ϣⲁⲡⲉⲛⲉ. ⲡⲣⲱⲙⲉ, ShBM 200 n *S* ⲙ̅ⲡⲥⲁⲧⲣⲉⲡⲁⲉ. ⲡⲣⲱⲙⲉ ⲉⲓ ⲉϩⲟⲩⲛ, Mun 150 *S* sim (the patriarch).

ⲙⲡⲧⲉ. *SA*, ⲙⲉⲧⲉ. *BF* nn f, *misery*: Hos 7 13 *SA* (*B* ⲉ.) δείλαιος; ROC 18 36 *B* ϫⲉⲛⲟⲩⲙ. ἐλεεινῶς; ShA 1 104 *S* ⲧⲁⲙ. ⲛ ⲡⲁⲉ., ShMIF 23 162 *S* have pity on ⲧⲉⲛⲙ., Ep 175 *S*, MR 5 33 *F* sim, Hall 4 *S* grief ⲉϫⲛⲧⲙ. of my youth, Miss 4 170 *B* corpse in tomb ϫⲉⲛⲟⲩⲡⲓϣ̅ϯ ⲙⲙ.

ⲣ ⲉ. *S*, *be miserable, feeble*: PS 358 *S* ⲉⲡⲟ ⲡⲉ. ⲉⲛϣⲁⲁⲧ, ShWess 9 86 *S* demon...ⲉⲁϥⲣ ⲉ. ϩⲓⲱⲱϥ *impotent* against (righteous), Wess 11 155 *S* mourners beat faces ϩⲱⲥ ϫⲉⲁⲩⲣ ⲉ. (cf C 89 209), AM 126 *B* l ⲉⲣ ⲉⲃⲏ (v ⲉⲃⲏ).

ⲉⲃⲣⲁ, ⲃⲣⲁ, ⲃⲣⲉ-, ⲃⲣⲓ- *S*, ⲃⲣⲉ *S* (ostr EES Antinoe) *A*, ⲃⲣⲁⲓ, ⲙⲃⲣⲁⲓ, ⲉϥⲣⲁⲓ (P 55 8), ⲉⲙⲣⲁⲓ *B*, ⲃⲣⲉⲉⲓ *F*, pl ⲉⲃⲣⲏⲅⲉ, ⲃⲣⲏⲅⲉ, ⲃⲣⲏⲛⲅⲉ (Mor 50 8) *S*, nn m, *seed* (sometimes *meal*) **a.** of cereals: K 193 *B* قمح يوسف (*triticum vulg. jos.*), P 44 91 *S* pl حبوب; Ge 25 30 *B* ? πυρός (for πυρρός), Ps 125 5 *S* (*B* ϫⲣⲟϫ), Dan 1 16 *S* (*B* do) σπέρμα, Cl 24 4 *A* σπόρος, Glos 397 *S* σπερμοβολία, Mor 37 9 *S* ὄσπριον, Lev 25 37 *S* (*B* ϫⲣⲉ), Deu 23 19 *S* (*B* do), Hab 3 17 *A* (*B* do) βρῶμα, R 1 5 12 *S* γέννημα (γέν-); ShMun 156 *S*, Kr 11 *F* opp ⲥⲟⲩⲟ, BP 5567 *F* sacks of ⲥⲟⲩⲟ & ϩⲉⲣⲉⲓ (sic), Va 63 7 *B* ⲡⲓⲉ. for προσφορά (= BSM 33, BMis 375 ⲥⲟⲩⲟ), Va 69 115 *B* no bread to eat but ⲡⲓϣⲟ (? ϣⲱ) ⲉⲑⲛⲏⲟⲩ

ⲉⲃⲟⲗ ϫⲉⲛⲡⲓⲉ., ShA 2 29 *S* cold withered grain ⲉⲙⲡⲁⲧⲟⲩϭⲉⲡ ⲉ., KKS 667 *S* fields bring forth ⲡⲉⲃⲣⲁ ⲛⲧⲉⲡⲟⲩⲟⲉⲓⲛ ϫⲟⲟⲩ, BMis 532 *S* ⲡⲉϥⲉⲃⲣⲁ, Miss 4 699 *S* ϩⲙⲥ...ⲉⲩⲙⲉϩ ⲡⲉ., ShBerlOr 1611(5) 40 *S* high price for ⲟⲩϣⲱϫⲧ ⲡⲉ., CO 230 *S* ⲟⲩⲕⲁⲙⲟⲩⲗ ⲛⲃⲣⲁ, Kr 11 *F* ⲉⲗⲧⲁⲃ ⲃ̅., ShMiss 4 278 *S* common things such as ⲉ. ⲏ ⲥⲟⲣⲧ. **b.** of other plants (always without gen ⲛ-): flax, PMéd 111 *S*; lettuce, ib 235; oil (? olives), Wess 18 93 *S*; purslane, P 43 34 *S*; endive (σέρις), ib; cucumber, ib; onion, Ryl 106, ST 316 *S*; weeds generally, ShA 1 244 (= P 130³, 83) *S* ⲡⲧⲛϭ ⲉⲡⲁϣⲉ ⲡⲉϥⲉ. ⲉⲑⲟⲟⲩ. *V* also ⲃⲉⲣⲥⲓ, ⲃⲉⲣⲥⲓⲙ, ⲃⲣⲉϣⲏⲛ.

· ⲉⲃⲣⲁ (often ⲉⲃⲣⲓ, ⲃⲣⲓ, ⲉⲃⲣⲉ Ryl 352) ⲥⲱϣⲉ *S*, nn f (on gender, Sethe *Dem Urk* 216), *seed-corn* (dem Tor Dem 57), v CO 219 n : ST 37 thou shalt sow field ⲙⲛⲡⲉⲕⲉ. ⲥ., CO 482, BKU 1 48 sim; BM 1166 ⲧⲉϥⲃⲣⲁ ⲥ. as barley seed.

ⲉⲃⲣⲓⲉⲓⲛ *S* nn, material for or quality (? colour) of garments: P 131⁶ 37 *S* (v Ryl 213 n) luxurious monks discard *lebiton* and wear ϣⲧⲏⲛ ⲡⲕⲟⲣⲁϭⲉⲡ · (? καρακάλλιον) ϩⲓⲙⲟⲗⲟϫⲣⲉ (? μολόχινος) ϩⲓⲉ. ⲉⲩⲧⲟϭⲥ ϩⲓⲧⲙⲡⲣⲁⲣⲧ.

ⲉⲃⲣⲏϭⲉ, ⲃⲣⲏϭⲉ (Ps 96 4, 143 6, Ap 4 5), ⲉϥⲣⲏϭⲉ, ⲃⲣⲏϭⲉ, ⲧⲉⲣⲃⲏϭ &c *S*, ⲉⲃⲣⲏϭⲉ, ϩⲃⲣⲏϭⲉ *A* (Nah 2 4), ⲉⲃⲣⲏϫ (mostly ⲥⲉⲧ ⲉ. m) *B*, ⲉϥⲣⲏϫ, ⲧⲉⲣⲃⲏϭ *F* nn f (Mt 24 27, Lu 17 24 *S*, Hab 3 11 *A*), *lightning* (cf ברק): Deu 32 41 *S* ⲟⲩⲃ. (var ⲟⲩⲉⲃ.), Ps 76 18 *S*, Jer 10 13 *S*, Dan 10 6 *S* ⲟⲩⲉ., Ap 4 5 *S* ϩⲉⲛⲃⲃ., Dan 3 73 *F* (CMSS 15), Mt 28 3 *F* ⲧⲣⲃⲏϭ (also LAp 532 *F*, PO 2 180, Gu 22 *S*) all = *B* ⲥⲉⲧ ⲉ. ἀστραπή. With ϯ-: Ez 1 4 *SB* ἐξαστράπτων; with ϩⲓ- ⲉⲃⲟⲗ: Ps 143 6 *B* (*S* ϩⲱⲟⲩ ⲛ-) ἀστράπτειν, C 89 163 *B* ⲡⲓⲡⲓϣϯ ⲡⲟⲩⲱⲓⲛⲓ ⲉⲧϩⲓ ⲉ. ⲉⲃ.; with ⲛⲉϫ- ⲉⲃⲟⲗ : P 131² 88 *S* smaragd ⲉϥⲛⲏϫ(sic) ⲉ. ⲉⲃ.

ⲉⲃⲟⲟⲥ (?) *S* nn pl, *base, socket* of pillar: Ex 26 25 (P 44 104) ⲙⲛⲡⲉⲥⲡⲉⲥⲉⲃⲟⲟⲥ (sic, var 43 88 ⲙⲛⲡⲉⲥⲉⲃⲱⲥ) دعائمها (var والدعائم) βάσεις, as in ib 26 19 &c *B* (Va) ⲃⲁⲥⲓⲥ قاعدة. Prob corruption of Gk, as other *S* MSS have here ⲃⲁⲥⲓⲥ.

ⲉⲃⲓⲧ *S* v ⲉⲃⲓⲱ.

ⲉⲃⲓⲧ *F* v ⲱϥⲧ (ⲉⲓϥⲧ).

ⲉⲃⲟⲧ *S*, ⲉⲃⲁⲧ *AA*², ⲁⲃⲟⲧ *B*, ⲉⲃⲁⲧ, ⲁⲃⲁⲧ *F*, pl ⲉⲃⲁⲧⲉ (Job 39 2, Gal 4 10 sic), ⲉⲃⲁⲧⲉ (NTest Balestri lx) *S*, ⲉⲃⲏⲧ (Nu 28 14), ⲁⲃⲏⲧ (Gal 4 10) *B*, ⲁⲃⲁⲧⲓ *F* (PStras 334) & sg as pl, nn m, *month*: Ez 46 1 *S* ⲡⲉ., ib 29 17 *B* ⲡⲓϣⲟⲣⲡ ⲛⲁ., Ge 8 13 *S* do = *B* ⲡⲓⲁ. ⲛϩⲟⲩⲓⲧ μήν; PS 4 *S* ⲡⲉ. ⲛⲧⲱⲃⲉ, Kr 25 *F* ⲡⲁ. ⲛϩⲁⲑⲟⲗ; when named mostly without ⲛ-: BAp 75 *S* ⲡⲉ. ⲉⲡⲓⲫ, C 43 122 *B* ⲡⲓⲁ. ⲫⲁⲣⲙ.; C 43 135

B ⲡⲉⲥⲁ. ⲙⲙⲓⲥⲓ, Nu 3 15 S ⲡⲉⲧⲣⲡⲟⲩⲉ. μηνιαῖος; Nu 11 20 SB, Dan 6 7 S ⲟⲩⲉ. ⲛϩⲟⲟⲩ ἡμερῶν λ, AZ 21 146 S, J 96 50 S, AM 30 B sim; BMis 368 S = BSM 28 B ⲕⲁⲧⲁ ⲉ., AM 141 B sim, Ap 22 2 S ϩⲣⲉⲃⲟⲧ=B ⲥⲁⲣⲁⲃⲟⲧ. Coptic (S) months: ⲑⲟⲟⲩⲧ, ⲡⲁⲱⲡⲉ, ϩⲁⲑⲱⲣ, ⲕⲓⲁϩⲕ, ⲧⲱⲃⲉ, ⲙϣⲓⲣ, ⲡⲁⲣⲙϩⲁⲧⲡ, ⲡⲁⲣⲙⲟⲩⲧⲉ, ⲡⲁϣⲟⲛⲥ, ⲡⲁⲱⲡⲉ, ⲉⲡⲏⲡ, ⲙⲉⲥⲱⲣⲏ. ⲕⲟⲩϫⲓ ⲛⲁ. B, *little month*, 5 intercalary days after Mesorê: EW 219. *Cf* K 63 (*sic*) ⲡⲓⲉ̄ ⲡⲧⲉ ⲡⲓⲧⲉⲩⲧⲉⲣⲟⲛ خمس النسي. S uses ἐπαγόμεναι (ἡμέραι): BMis 526, Ryl 131, BM 462, PSBA 29 192. ⲉ. ⲛⲃⲣⲣⲉ S, *new month*: In BMis 57 145, Z 607, R 2 4 31, Miss 4 406 (*cf* BM 349) Parmoute (on 7th of which Annunciation & Incarnation in S calendar); but PO 5 108 *new month* is Tout (*cf* ⲥⲟⲩⲁ ⲛⲃⲣⲣⲉ BMis 322). In Ex 23 15 &c S ⲉ. ⲛⲃⲣⲣⲉ (B ⲛⲧⲉ ⲛⲓⲃ.) = μὴν τῶν νέων.

ⲉⲃⲧⲟⲧϥ *v* ϥⲧⲱⲧϥ.

ⲉⲃⲁⲩ A nn f, meaning unknown: El 80 boys will be seized ⲥⲉⲧⲉⲟⲩⲉ ⲁⲧⲉ. ⲁϯⲕ ⲥⲁⲧⲉ. *Cf* ⲁⲃⲱ & KKS 54. Or? *l* ⲧⲥⲉⲃⲁⲩ.

ⲉⲃϣⲉ (ⲃϣⲉ) S, ⲉⲃϣⲓ B *v* ⲱⲃϣ.

ⲉⲃⲟⲩϩⲓ B *v* ϩⲟϥ.

ⲉⲑⲃⲉ- B *v* ⲉⲧⲃⲉ-.

ⲉⲑⲱϣ B *v* ⲉϭⲱϣ.

ⲉⲕⲓⲃⲉ, ⲕⲓⲃⲉ, ⲕⲓⲉⲃⲉ (R 2 1 10, 39, 71, 2 4 94 all same MS) S, ⲕⲉⲓⲃⲉ, ⲕⲓⲃⲉ A, ⲕⲓϥⲓ (K 77) B, ⲉⲕⲓⲃⲓ F nn f, *breast*: Ge 49 25 S (B ⲙⲛⲟⲧ), Cant 8 8 S, Is 32 12 SF (B do), Ap 1 13 S (B do) μαστός, R 2 1 10 S ⲛⲧⲁⲡⲁⲕ. ϩⲉ, ShMIF 23 144 S ⲛⲁⲉ., ⲛⲕ., ⲛⲓⲕ., ⲧⲉⲓⲉ., 148 ⲧⲟⲩⲉ., ϩⲉ., ⲡⲉⲥⲕⲉⲛ., Glos 40 S ⲛⲕ. μαστοί, *ib* 42 ⲛⲁⲕⲣⲟⲛ ⲡⲧⲕ. θρόμβος, K 77 B ⲡⲓⲉⲙⲛⲟⲧ ثدي, but ϯⲕ. حلمة *nipple*, Wess 9 52 S mud reached ϣⲁⲡⲉ. ⲙⲡⲣⲱⲙⲉ (*v* LMis 225 & *cf* Ap *ut sup*), P 129^{15} 23 silver ⲉ. as thank-offering.

ⲡⲉⲣⲕⲓⲃⲉ S nn f (Nu 6 20 Mor), m (*ib* Masp), *breast* (B ⲙⲉⲥⲧⲛϩⲏⲧ) στηθύνιον, which elsewhere in S = Gk; R 2 1 71 ϩⲉⲡⲛ. rounded like φιάλαι.

ϯ ⲉ. SA, *give breast, suckle*: Ex 2 9 A, Nu 11 12 S (B ⲟⲩⲉⲙ ϭⲓ) θηλάζειν, BMis 108 S ⲉⲥϯ ⲉ. ⲙⲡϣⲏⲣⲉ, El 80 A every woman ⲉⲧϯ ⲕ.

ϫⲓ ⲉ. SAF, *take breast, be suckled*: Deu 32 25 S (B ϭⲓ ⲙⲡⲟⲩⲧ), Ps 8 3 S (B ⲟⲩⲉⲙ ϭⲓ), Joel 2 16 A (B do) θηλάζειν; Is 66 11 S (B ϭⲓ ⲙⲡⲟⲧ) ἐκθηλ.; BIF 22 107 F ⲡⲉⲧϫⲓ ⲉ. ⲛⲧⲉ ⲧⲉϥⲙⲉⲟⲩ.

ⲉⲕⲗⲟⲗⲓ B *v* ⲕⲉⲗⲱⲗ.

ⲉⲕⲣⲟϫ, ⲉⲕⲕⲣⲟϫ, ⲉⲕⲗⲟϫ S *v* ⲕⲣⲟϫ.

ⲉⲕⲟⲧ S nn, ? = ⲕⲟⲧ *visit*: WS 89 Papnoute is sick & the *papa* ϣⲁϥⲉⲣ ⲟⲩⲕⲟⲧⲓ ⲡⲉ.

ⲉⲕⲱⲧ SB *v* ⲕⲱⲧ.

ⲉⲕⲧⲉ, ⲉⲓⲕⲧⲉ S nn f, meaning unknown: Hall 103 asks for cooking fat (ⲥⲕⲉⲡⲉⲛⲓⲥⲉ) to put upon (into?) ⲧⲉ. ⲙⲡⲛⲓ, *ib* 115 ϩⲉⲡⲓ. among metal objects between ⲙⲟⲩⲣⲟⲩⲑⲏⲕⲉ (μυροθήκιον) & ϫⲟⲩⲣ, J 76 40 among woman's clothes &c (*ib* 66 38 om).

ⲉⲗ F *hail* v ⲁⲗ.

ⲉⲗⲉ- F *v* ⲉ- vbal prefix.

ⲉⲗⲱ S *v* ⲁⲗⲱ *snare*.

ⲉⲗⲃⲓϫⲓ B nn m, meaning?: K 137 نفف (*quid?*) among implements of irrigation, = ناعور central post of *sâkiyah* (Sobhy), its circulating cable (Lab).

ⲉⲗⲕⲟⲩ F *v* ϩⲗⲕⲟⲩ.

ⲉⲗⲕⲱ (Sh), ⲉⲗⲕⲟ S, ⲗⲕⲟⲩ A, ⲉⲗⲕⲟ, ⲉⲗⲕⲟⲩ, ⲁⲗⲕⲟⲩ B nn m, *fruit of sycamore*: Am 7 14 AB (S ⲕⲛⲧⲉ sic l) συκάμινον *ficus sycom.*, K 178, 263 B جميز (*cf* ⲛⲟⲩϫⲉ), ShC 42 48 S insects born ϩⲛⲛⲉ. In PMéd 233, 295, 315 S recipes contain ⲉ. ⲛⲡⲁⲙ, ? same (L Keimer *Acta Or* 6 288, tamarisk gall).

ⲉⲗⲕⲉⲙⲏ B nn, meaning unknown: Job 26 14 (S om) ⲟⲩⲉ. ⲛⲧⲉ ⲟⲩⲥⲁϫⲓ ἰκμὰς λόγου. Elsewhere ἰκ. = B ϭⲛⲟⲛ, S ⲁⲧⲃⲉⲥ. ? *l* ⲗⲁⲕⲙⲏ.

ⲉⲗⲕⲥ B *v* ⲱⲗⲕ.

ⲉⲗⲉⲗ B *v* ⲉⲓⲉⲗⲉⲗ.

ⲉⲗⲓⲗⲉ S ? interj: BP 8503 saying ⲉ. ⲙⲡⲟⲩϫⲁⲓ of Satan.

ⲉⲗⲟⲟⲗⲉ S, ⲉⲗⲁⲁⲗⲉ A, ⲉⲗⲁⲗⲉ A², ⲁⲗⲟⲗⲓ B, ⲁⲗⲁⲁⲗⲓ, ⲁⲗⲁⲗⲓ, ⲉⲗⲁⲁⲗⲓ, ⲓⲗⲁⲗⲓ (AZ 33 56) F, ⲉⲗⲉⲗ-, ⲗⲉⲗ-, ⲗⲉⲉⲗ-, ⲗⲓⲗ- S, ⲉⲗⲁⲗ- A, ⲁⲗ-, ⲉⲗ-, ⲗⲉⲗⲉ- B nn m (but *v* below **III** & Glos 220), sg as pl, **I.** grape: Ge 40 11 SB, Is 5 2 SB, Mt 7 16 SB, Ap 14 18 SB σταφυλή; single gr: Lev 19 10, Is 65 8 S ⲃⲗⲃⲓⲗⲉ ⲡⲉ. = B ⲛⲁϥⲣⲓ ⲛⲁ. ῥώξ; bunch of gr: Ge 40 10 SB, Nu 13 24 SB, Ap 14 18 SB ⲥⲙⲁϩ ⲡⲉ. βότρυς σταφ. or ἀμπέλου; unripe, sour gr: Job 15 33 S, Pro 10 26 SA, Is 18 5 S, Jer 38 29 S ⲉⲗⲉⲗϩⲙϫ (all B ϣⲉⲗϣⲏ-ⲗⲓ) ὄμφαξ; fresh gr: Nu 6 3 S ⲉ. ⲛϣⲟⲩⲉⲓ (B ⲁ. ⲛⲣⲏⲛ ⲡⲗⲱⲕ) σταφ. πρόσφατος; mellow, purple gr: Ge 40 10 SB πέπειρος, Si 51 17 S ⲟⲩⲉ. ⲉⲁϥⲡⲱϩ, sim Am 9 13 SA, Cl 23 4 A περκά-ζειν; dried gr, raisins: Nu 6 3 S ⲉ. ⲉϥϣⲟⲩ-ⲱⲟⲩ (var ⲉⲗⲉⲗϣⲟⲟⲩⲉ, B ⲁⲗϣⲱⲟⲩ), 1 Kg 25 18 S ⲉⲗⲉⲗϣⲟⲩⲱⲟⲩ, Hos 3 1 A ⲉⲗⲁⲗϣⲟⲩⲱⲟⲩ (B ⲉⲗϣⲱⲟⲩ), P 43 54 S ⲗⲉⲗϣⲟⲟⲩⲉ σταφίς, ST 118 S ϣⲟⲙⲧⲉ ⲛⲟⲓⲡⲉ ⲛⲗⲓⲗϣⲟⲟⲩ, P 44 62 S, K 176 B زبيب; rasins stoned: Z 630 χωρὶς ⲡⲉⲩⲕⲁⲥ; grape-stone, pip: Nu 6 4 S ⲕⲁⲥ ⲡⲉ. γίγαρτον; other sorts: PMéd 247, P 43 235 S ⲉ. ⲡⲟⲩⲱⲛϣ عنب الذئب *nightshade* (Dozy 2 179, Löw

296, PMéd 255); KroppE *S* ε. ⲡⲟⲅⲱⲃϣ as ? equiv of ⲏⲣⲡ ⲡⲗⲉⲅⲕⲟⲡ; PMéd 318 *S* ελολογοϣε, prob = λιλοοϣε *q v*; عنب البري P 43 59 *S* λεελϩⲟⲟⲅⲧ = 44 83 (*l* λελ-) as = θρίδαξ, σμυρνοσέλινον &c. *V* also ⲁⲅⲁⲡ.

II. *vine*: **a.** ⲁⲗⲟⲗⲓ *B* (elliptic), Nu 6 4, Is 7 23, 16 8, Ap 14 18 (all *S* ϩⲱ ⲡⲉ.) ἄμπελος. **b.** ϩⲱ ⲡⲉ. *SA*, ⲡⲁ. *BF*: Ge 49 11 *SB*, Ps 77 47 *SB*, 104 33 *SB*, Ez 19 10 *SB*, Joel 2 22 *AB*, Mt 26 29 *SB* ἄμπελος. *vineyard*: ⲙⲁ ⲡⲉ. *SA*, ⲡⲁ. *BF*, Ge 9 20 *S*, Pro 9 12 *S*, Is 1 8 *SF*, Am 9 14 *SA*, Mt 20 1 *S* (all *B* ⲓⲁϩⲁ.), Job 24 6 *SB*, Mic 1 6 *S* (*AB* ⲙⲁ ⲡⲭⲟ ⲡⲉ.), Jos 24 13 *S* ⲉⲓⲉϩⲉ. ἀμπελών, Va 69 103 *B* ⲓⲟϩⲓ ⲡⲁ., 1 Cor 9 7 *F* ⲓⲉϩⲗⲁⲁⲗⲓ; *vinedresser*: ⲟⲩⲱⲓ ⲡⲁ. *B*, Is 61 5, Lu 13 7 (*S* ⲥⲙⲉ), Jer 52 16 *B* ⲟⲩⲓⲏ ⲡⲁ. ἀμπελουργός; *vine-wood* as fuel: ϣⲉ ⲡⲉ. *S*, ⲡⲁ. *B*: P 44 80 *S* = κληματίς, حطب الكرم, Dan 3 46 *B* (*S* ? ⲥⲗⲱ) κλημ. زرجون, whence AM 311, C 43 70 &c *B*.; *magical use*: PGen, Br 114 *S*; C 86 220 *B* ⲕⲁϣ ⲡⲁ. with which martyr's body pierced.

III. ⲉⲗⲉⲗⲕⲙⲙⲉ *S*, λελεχⲙⲏⲓ *B*, λεⲕⲙⲏⲓ *F* nn m (Z 639), *bruise*, dark coloured like grapes: Ge 4 23 *SB*, Ex 21 25 *SB*, Ps 37 6 *B* (*S* ⲥⲁϣ), Is 1 6 *S* (opp ⲥⲁϣ) *BF* μώλωψ; Pro 20 30 *S* ὑπώπιον, *ib* 23 29 *S* ⲟ ⲡⲉ. πελιός, πελιδνός, MG 25 88 *B* smote him so that body was ⲙⲫⲣⲏϯ ⲛϩⲁⲡⲗ., *ib* 42 *B* muddy swine ⲥⲉⲛⲁⲓⲕ ⲡⲗ. *blacken*.

ⲉⲗⲟⲟⲗⲉ *S* nn f, *tonsil*: P 44 69 = 43 39 ⲧⲉ. ⲙⲡⲣⲱϣ · παρίσθμιον عنب الفم.

ⲉⲗⲟⲟⲗⲉ *S* nn f, *pupil* of eye: PMich 1926 glossary, ὄμμα · ⲡⲃⲁⲗ κόρε (*sic*) · ⲧⲉ. Prob error for ⲁⲗⲟⲟⲩⲉ (*v* ⲁⲗⲱ *pupil*).

In names: ⲡⲁⲗⲟⲗⲓ ST 129, ⲡⲁⲧⲗⲟⲗⲉ C 89 96 (*sic l*), ⲡⲁⲧⲗⲱⲗⲉ J 96 93, Πατελλολί *Acta SS Maii* 3 64*, BKU 1 36, ⲡⲁⲧⲉⲗⲗⲟⲗⲩ Cai 8412, ⲡⲁⲧⲣⲱⲣⲓⲟⲥ *ib* 8413, Παλῶλις, Πελόολε &c (Preisigke); ⲧⲁⲗⲟⲗⲉ BP 975, ⲧⲉⲗⲗⲱⲗⲉ J 74 73, ⲧⲉⲣⲉⲣϣⲟⲩ PMich 4279.

In place-names: ⲡⲓϩⲁⲣⲁⲗⲟⲗⲓ Miss 4 386 n, ⲡⲙⲁ ⲡⲧⲉⲗⲱⲟⲗⲉ RNC 90, τόπ(ος) Τελοολε Bal, ⲧϩⲱ ⲡⲁⲗⲁⲁⲗⲓ Kr 10, ϣⲉⲡⲁⲗⲟⲗⲉⲧ (*sic* MS) C 41 8 = شنلاله Miss 4 301 (*v* Synax Forget 2 208, n 11), *cf* Ψινελοολε &c (Preisigke).

Cf also λοοⲩ.

ⲉⲗⲗⲏⲧ *F v* ⲉⲣⲏⲧ.

ⲉⲗⲁⲙⲉ *S* nn, *measure or quantity*, applied to papyrus & ? loaves: ST 270 ⲉⲕⲛⲁϫⲓ ⲕⲉⲉ. ⲡⲭⲁⲣⲧⲏⲥ ⲛⲁⲓ, *ib* 277 ⲛ]ⲧϥϯ ⲟⲩⲉ. ⲡⲭⲁⲣ[ⲧⲏⲥ, COAd 55 ⲛⲧⲛ (ⲛ)ⲉ. ⲛⲕⲁⲕⲉ(ⲥⲁⲁϭⲉ). *Cf* Ep 1 187.

ⲉⲗⲉⲛ- *F v* ⲣⲟ (ⲉⲣⲛ-).

ⲉⲗⲡⲏⲏⲓ *F v* ⲣⲡⲉ.

ⲉⲗⲧⲁⲃ *F v* ⲣⲧⲟⲃ.

ⲉⲗⲧⲟϥ *B v* ⲧⲁϥ.

ⲉⲗⲟⲟⲩⲉ *S v* ⲁⲗⲱ *snare*.

ⲉⲗϣⲁⲛ- *F v* ⲉⲣϣⲁⲛ-

ⲉⲗϣⲱⲟⲩ *B v* ⲉⲗⲟⲟⲗⲉ.

ⲉⲗϩⲱⲃ *BO v* ⲗϩⲱⲃ.

ⲉⲗϩⲉⲗ, ⲣⲉϥ- *Sf v* ϩⲁⲗ.

ⲉⲗϩⲏⲙ *S*, -ϩⲉⲙ *B v* ⲗϩⲏⲙ.

ⲉⲗϩⲏⲥ *B v* ⲗϩⲏⲥ.

ⲉⲗϫⲱⲃ *B v* ⲉⲗϭⲱⲃ.

ⲉⲗϭⲟⲓ *S v* ⲉⲣϭⲟⲓ.

ⲉⲗϭⲱⲃ *S*, ⲉⲗϫⲱⲃ *B* nn m, *heron*: Lev 11 19 *SB*, Deu 14 15 *B* (*S* om), Ps 103 17 *SB* ἐρωδιός, all = بلشوم (*i e* ⲡⲉⲗϫⲱⲃ), var بلشون, K 293 *B* بلشوم = هان, var Bodl 325 10 هام with mistaken gloss الهامة هي البومة (*cf* ⲃⲁⲓ); Zech 5 9 *B* (*SA* = Gk) ἔποψ, though Heb same as in Lev, Deu, Ps.

ⲉⲙⲉ *SA*, ⲁⲙⲉ, ⲁⲙⲏ *B* nn f, *hoe* for digging: MG 25 12 *B* δίκελλα opp ⲙⲁⲛϭⲁⲗⲉ (μάκελλα shovel), K 124 *B* مسحاه (*cf* MG 17 438, TT 144 n); *plough* drawn by oxen: ShZ 471 *S* he followed beasts, his hand ⲧⲁⲗⲏⲩ ⲉⲭⲡⲟⲩⲉ., ShA 2 24 *S* (*cf* Lu 9 62) place hand on ⲟⲩϩⲃⲃⲉ ⲛ ⲟⲩⲉ. (as synon), PRain 4741 *S* ⲕⲁϣ ⲡⲉ. handle (?) of plough, Mic 4 3 *A* ⲉ. ⲡⲥⲕⲉⲓ (*S* ⲥⲓⲡⲉ ⲡⲥ., *B* ϩⲉⲃⲓ) ἄροτρον, but Is 2 4 ⲁⲣ. = *SB* ϩⲃⲃⲉ, Joel 3 10 ⲁⲣ. *SA* ⲥⲓⲡⲉ ⲡⲥ., *B* ϩⲉⲃⲓ, Glos 386 *S* ⲁⲣ.ⲧⲉⲙ[ⲏ]. *Cf* Rec 39 156. But ? *cf* Gk ἄμη (*v* Reil *Beitr* 64).

ⲉⲙⲏ *S* nn f: Si 38 35 ⲉⲧⲥⲁⲡⲟ ⲡⲧⲉⲅⲉ. κοσμῆσαι ἐπὶ συντελείας. Prob *l* ⲧⲉⲩϩⲁⲛ (as in 22 8, 43 7).

ⲉⲙⲓ *BO v* ⲉⲓⲙⲉ.

ⲉⲙⲟⲩ *SBF*, ⲁⲙⲟⲩ *S* (PS 355), pl ⲉⲙⲟⲟⲩⲉ *S*, ⲉⲙⲱⲟⲩⲓ (*sic* ? *l*) *B*, nn f (dem m f), *cat*: EpJer 21 *B* (sg as pl) *F* αἴλουρος (but P 44 55 ⲁⲓⲗ. = نمس ichneumon, *cf* ϣⲁⲑⲟⲩⲗ), PS 318, 355 *S* an ἄρχων with ⲟⲩϩⲟ ⲡⲉ., BG 62 *S* ⲉⲗⲱⲉⲓⲙ ϥⲟ ⲛⲡⲉ.; ShA 2 251 *S* ⲧⲉ. with scratching claws, *ib* 1 268 ⲧⲉ. worshipped, ShMich 550 13 *S* ⲛⲉⲙⲟⲟⲩⲉ among hierogl signs; CR '87 376 *S* βοτάνη named ⲃⲁⲗ ⲡⲉ., *cf* عين القط = بابونج *camomile* (*v* ⲃⲁⲗ).

In names ? Πεμοῦς, Τεμοῦς (Preisigke).

ⲉⲙⲟⲩ *O v* ⲁⲙⲟⲩ.

ⲉⲙⲃⲣⲓⲥ *B v* ⲙⲣⲓⲥ.

ⲉⲙⲙⲉ *O* nn m, *shrew mouse*: DM 11 15 n, *v* Spg *Demotica* 1 11. *Cf* ⲁⲗⲓⲗ.

ⲉⲙⲛⲧ S (ⲉⲓⲙⲛⲧ, ⲉⲙⲛⲧⲉ often J, ⲉⲙⲛⲧⲉ AZ 33
132) AF, ⲉⲙⲉⲛⲧ B nn m, *the west*: Ge 13 14 SB,
Nu 34 4 S (B ⲥⲁⲡⲉ.), Jos 18 13 S ⲡⲉⲥⲉ., Ps 77 26
S ⲟⲩⲉ. (B ⲛⲓⲉ.), Ac 27 12 S (B ⲡⲓⲥⲁ ⲡⲉ.) λίψ; Ps
74 6 S (B ⲡⲓⲙⲁ ⲛϣⲟⲣⲡ), Mt 8 11 S (B ⲇⲟ), Lu
12 54 S (B ⲥⲁⲡⲉ.), Ap 21 13 SB δυσμαί (this
mostly SAB ⲙⲁ ⲛϩ. pl); Si 48 9 S λαῖλαψ west
wind?; Nu 2 10 S ϩⲓⲡⲥⲁ ⲉ. (var ⲛⲉ., B ⲥⲁⲡⲉ.), Jos 18
13 S ϩⲩⲙⲡⲥⲁ ⲙⲡⲉ. πρὸς λίβα, Jos 15 7 S ⲉⲧⲥⲁ ⲉ. (var
ⲉⲧⲥⲁⲡⲉ.) κατὰ λίβα; 3 Kg 22 19 S ϩⲓⲥⲁⲡⲉ. (?) ἐξ
εὐωνύμων, Br 117 S ⲥⲉⲡⲁⲡⲱⲧ ⲉⲡⲉ. ⲉⲣⲃⲟⲩⲣ (cf 104),
BM 594(2) S ϩⲓⲭⲟⲡⲡⲉ. on right, AM 200 B church
ⲥⲁϩⲛⲧ ⲡⲉ. on north-west, C 43 225 B they turned
ⲉϩⲏⲧ ϫⲉⲛⲫⲓⲁⲣⲟ ⲡⲉ., BM 346 1 S to moor ⲉⲡⲉⲕⲣⲟ
ⲙⲡⲉ.   As adj (rare): PLond 4 435, 499 S ⲛⲕⲟⲓⲉ
ⲡⲉ. (cf ib 497 ⲛⲡⲉ.).

ⲉⲙⲛⲧⲉ A *v* ⲁⲙⲛⲧⲉ.

ⲉⲙⲣⲁⲓ B *v* ⲉⲃⲣⲁ.

ⲉⲙⲏⲣⲉ S, ⲁⲙⲏⲓⲣⲓ B, ﺍﺑﻣﻴﺮﻯ, nn f, *inundation*,
high water: Job 40 18 S (B ⲡⲓϣϯ ⲙⲙⲟⲟⲩ, cf ShA
1 395), Lu 6 48 S (B ⲙⲟⲩ ⲛⲣⲱⲟⲩ ⲉⲩⲟϣ) πλήμμυρα, K 214 253 B ϯⲁ. ﻧﻴﻞ, Glos 436 S πλήμ.
ⲧⲁⲡⲁⲃⲁⲥⲓⲥ ⲧⲉ., Mor 37 105 S *river (canal)* Lycus
at time of ⲧⲉ. πλήμ. τ. ὑδάτων, ShRE 10 161 S
ⲡⲙⲟⲟⲩ ⲡⲧⲉ. *a wonder throughout Egypt*, ShBM
194 3 S *water of* ⲧⲉ. ϩⲛⲧⲉϥϭⲓⲛⲉⲓ ⲙⲛⲧⲉϥϭⲓⲛⲃⲱⲕ,
Mor 51 37 S *summer, winter* & ⲛⲥⲉⲉⲡⲉ ⲡⲛⲉⲣⲟⲟⲩ
ⲡⲉ., *Nov Test* Balestri xx, BM 81 S *as rubric*
ⲧⲉ. (cf Leyd 153 inf, Wess 18 5).   In place-
name?: ϯⲁⲙⲏⲓⲣⲓ ﺩﻣﻴﺮﻯ (Amélineau *Géog* 118).

ⲉⲙⲓⲥⲉ S, ⲁⲙⲓⲥⲓ B, *emis* DM, nn m, *dill, anise*:
Mt 23 23 SB ἄνηθον, P 44 82 S *do* ﺷﺒﺖ, ib 66
στύψιν (στῦψις), K 195 B ﻧﻌﻨﺎﻉ (error, cf 198 ⲁⲡⲓϫⲟⲡ
ﺷﺒﺖ), Mor 51 34 S *ship's mast of* ϣⲉ ⲡⲉⲙⲓⲥⲉ,
DM 3 23 *wood of* ⲉ. *as fuel or incense* (cf ἀνηθό-
ξυλον Langkavel 39).

ⲉⲙⲁⲧⲉ *v* ⲙⲁⲧⲉ.

ⲉⲙⲧⲁⲛ F *v* ⲙⲧⲟⲛ.

ⲉⲙⲛϣ S, ⲁⲙⲛϣ B nn m, *anvil*: Job 41 15
SB, Si 38 32 S ἄκμων, P 44 67 = 43 36 S σίδηρος
ﺳﻨﺪﺍﻝ; MG 25 142 B *smith's* ⲁ., C 86 45 B, Va
62 182 B *sim*, Mor 41 180 S *golden calf molten
without* ⲉ. ϩⲓϩⲁⲑⲏⲣ, Pcod 39 S ⲡⲉ. ⲡⲧⲙⲡⲧⲁϣⲁⲣⲧⲉ,
Cai ostr 46304 119 S *in list* ⲉⲙⲉⲓϣ (not certain).

ⲉⲙⲁϣⲟ S, ⲉⲙⲁϣⲱ B, *v* ⲙⲁϣⲟ.

ⲉⲙⲉϣⲏⲓⲉ, -ⲏⲓ F (? *l* ⲉⲙⲉϣⲏ ⲓⲉ, *v* ⲙⲉϣⲉ) conj,
except: Jo 3 5 ⲉⲙⲉϣⲏⲓ ⲡⲥⲉϫⲡⲉ = SA² ⲉⲩⲧⲙ-,
B ⲁⲩϣⲧⲉⲙ- ἐὰν μή, ib 13 ⲉ. ⲉⲡⲉⲧⲁϥⲓ ⲉⲃⲁⲗ ϩⲣⲧⲡⲏ
= SA² ⲉⲓⲙⲏⲧⲓ, B ⲉⲃⲏⲗ ⲉ- εἰ μή, Gal 6 14 (Mich)
ⲉ. ⲁⲗⲏⲟⲩ = S ⲉⲓⲙⲏⲧⲓ, B ⲉⲃⲏⲗ ⲁⲣⲏⲟⲩ εἰ μή.

ⲉⲙⲉϣⲅⲉ S nn, *a Nile fish*: Glos 411 ἀβραμίς.
Cf ⲕⲟⲩⲗⲁϫⲓ.

ⲉⲙⲉϩⲓ F, ⲉⲙⲁϩⲧⲉ A *v* ⲁⲙⲁϩⲧⲉ.

ⲉⲛ B *ape* *v* ⲏⲡ.

ⲉⲛ AF neg *v* ⲁⲛ.

ⲉⲛ- B *v* ⲉⲓⲛⲉ *bring*.

ⲉⲛⲁ A *v* ⲁⲡⲁⲓ.

ⲉⲛⲉ, ⲛⲉ SA, ⲉⲛ S (Ac 10 18), ⲁⲛ B interrog
particle, precedes subj: Ge 43 7 SB, Ex 2 14 S
(var ⲉⲓⲉ, B om), Jud 20 28 S, Is 44 8 SB Ez 37 3
S (B ϩⲁⲣⲁ), Hag 2 13 SA (B ⲙⲏ), Zech 11 13
SAB, Mk 10 2 SB, Ac 1 6 S (B ⲓⲉ), ib 17 11 B
(var ⲙⲏ, S om) εἰ; Ps 29 10 B ⲙⲏ ϥⲛⲁ-...ⲓⲉ ⲁⲛ
ⲉϥⲉ- (S ⲙⲏ...ⲙⲏ) μή...ῇ, Jer 8 4 B (S Gk om),
Mt 13 28 B (S Gk om), Lu 14 3 S (B Gk om); El
102 A ⲉ. ⲁⲧⲉⲧⲛⲥⲱⲧⲙⲉ, TU 43 24 A, Pcod 6 S
ⲁⲣⲁ ⲉ. ⲥⲉⲡⲁϫⲓⲧⲟⲩ, AM 148 B ⲡⲧⲉⲡⲡⲁⲩ ϫⲉⲁⲡ
ⲥⲉⲱⲡϣ, MG 25 353 B ⲁⲛ ⲡⲉⲕⲣⲏⲧ ⲟⲏⲧ ⲛⲑⲟⲩ ⲁⲛ,
AM 229 B ⲁⲛ ⲛⲥⲟⲕⲡⲉ ⲙⲁⲕⲣⲟⲃⲓ.

ⲉⲛⲉ-, ⲉⲛ(ⲉ)- SABF vbal pref of unfulfilled condition: Lev 10 19 S (B ⲓⲥϫⲉⲛ), Job 4 12 SB, ib
6 2 S (B ⲉϣⲱⲡ), Ps 50 16 SB, Is 48 18 SB, Mk
13 20 SB, Jo 4 10 SB (ⲉⲛ) F εἰ; BHom 118 S
ⲉⲡⲉⲣⲉⲧⲉⲯⲩⲭⲏ ⲙⲏⲣ ⲁⲛ...ⲡⲉ ⲡⲉⲥⲛⲁⲣ ϩⲙⲙⲉ ⲙⲡⲉⲥ-
ⲥⲱⲙⲁⲡⲉ, PS 78 S ⲉⲡⲉⲥⲉⲛⲁⲡⲧⲥ ⲉϩⲣⲁⲓ; after S
ⲛⲁⲡⲟⲩⲥ, SB ϩⲁⲙⲟⲓ: Job 14 13, Mt 26 24, Ap 3 15
(B impf), ShRE 11 18 S ϩⲁⲙⲟⲓ ⲉⲡⲉⲣⲉⲟⲩⲥⲩⲛⲣⲟϫⲟⲥ
...ⲛⲁⲧⲁϣⲉ ⲡⲁⲓ, ShA 2 46 S ϩ. ⲉⲡⲉⲡⲉ ⲛⲡⲟⲩⲃ ϣⲱⲡⲉ
ⲁⲩⲱ ⲡⲉⲩⲛⲁϯ ⲡⲁⲓⲕⲁⲓⲟⲥ ⲉⲃⲟⲗ ⲁⲛ ϩⲁⲟⲩϩⲁⲧ.

ⲉⲛⲉ- S *stone* *v* ⲱⲛⲉ.

ⲉⲛⲅ, ⲉⲛⲟⲩⲛⲅ S, ⲉⲛⲟⲩⲕ B (Rec 7 25 whence?)
nn, *a plant*: Is 55 13 S (B = Gk) ⲉⲡⲙⲁ ⲡⲟⲩⲉⲛⲅ
(Ciasca), ⲡⲟⲩⲉⲡⲟⲩⲛⲅ (Mus 14 198, Mor) κόνυζα
fleabane (BM 726 81, K 197 ﺳﻮﻛﺮﺍﻥ *hyoscyamus*),
P 44 83 = 43 59 S ⲟⲣⲓⲕⲁⲡⲟⲩ (ὀρίγανον) · ⲡⲟⲩⲛⲕ
ﻣﻌﺘﺮ, ﻛﺮﺍﻭﻳﺎ (*l* ﻛﺮﻭﻳﺎ) *thyme* or *cumin*.   Cf hierogl *ink*,
also *innk*, & DM *inq* (v PDém Lille 1 65).

ⲉⲛⲕⲟⲕⲓ *v* ⲁⲡⲕⲟⲕⲓ.

ⲉⲛⲓⲙ (?) SA² nn (?), *lot*: Ps 21 18 S ⲁⲩⲉⲡⲓⲙ
(*l* ⲉⲡ ⲉ.) ⲉⲧⲁϩⲃⲥⲱ = B ϩⲓ ⲱⲡ κλῆρον βάλλειν ἐπί, Jo
19 24 S ⲙⲁⲣⲡⲉ. (var ⲉⲡⲓ, ⲉⲓⲙⲉ, *l* ⲉⲛ ⲉ.) ⲉⲣⲟⲥ, A²
ⲙⲁⲣⲡⲟⲩ[ⲁϩ sic ⲉ]ⲛⲓⲙ ⲁⲣⲁⲥ = B ϩⲓ ⲱⲡ λαγχάνειν
περί; R 1 3 46 S ⲁⲩⲧⲣⲉⲅⲉ. ⲙⲛⲛⲉⲩⲉⲣⲏⲩ.

ⲉⲛⲟⲩⲟⲓ B *v* ⲟⲩⲟⲓ *way*.

ⲉⲛϣⲁϣⲓ B *v* ⲥⲓϣⲉ.

ⲉⲛϩ, ⲛϩ SA nn, *eyebrow*: R 2 2 22 S ⲛⲉϭⲉ. of
equal thickness ὀφρύες, (cf Ryl 402), ib 2 1 71 S
ϩⲉⲡⲉ. ⲉⲩⲕⲏⲙ, El 120 S = 90 A ⲡϥϩⲡϩ reached to

ears, *Mél Ch Moeller* 3 S ⲉⲣⲉⲡⲉϥⲛ. ⲥⲛⲕ συνόφρυες, BHom 135 S ⲃⲟⲩϥⲉ, ⲃⲁⲗ, ⲛϩ, P 44 121 S ⲛⲉϥⲉ. صدرۃ، جنيبة (both erroneous). *V* ? ⲃⲁⲗ ⲛⲡⲉϩ (ⲃⲁⲗ).

ⲁⲭⲛϩ, ⲉⲁⲭⲛϩ S (Ryl 402), ⲁⲉⲭⲉⲛϩ, ⲁⲁⲛⲭⲉⲛϩ (AZ 14 84, BM 924) *B* nn m (P 44 68), same meaning: Lev 14 9 SB ὀφρύες, PMich '26 glos S ὀφρύων · ⲛⲁ., ἐπισκήνιον · do, Mor 43 253 S women's πάλλια come down ⲉⲭⲛⲡⲉⲩⲁ. (*cf* BMis 77, Aeg 253), Mor 33 11 = 34 6 S ⲁⲡⲉⲥϯ...ⲟⲩⲕⲣⲟⲕⲟⲥ ⲉⲡⲉⲥⲁ. (var BMis 77 ⲟⲩⲟⲓⲥⲉ = ⲟⲩⲟⲥⲉ); P 131⁶ 125 S ϣⲁⲩⲕⲉⲁⲉⲧ ⲡⲉⲩⲁ. ⲉϩⲣⲁⲓ ⲡⲥⲉⲕⲓⲁ ⲡⲛⲉⲩⲃⲟⲩϩⲉ, Mor 37 165 S ⲉⲣⲉϩⲛⲁ. ⲟ ⲛⲁⲩ (sc eyes) ⲡⲛⲉⲓⲉⲛⲥⲁ.

Cf ? ⲡⲟϩ *B* eyelid.

ⲉⲛϩ, ⲃⲁⲓ- S *v* ⲥⲧⲉⲃⲁⲉⲓϩ.

ⲉⲛⲉϩ SBF, ⲉⲛⲉϩⲉ (J 79 7), ⲉⲛⲏϩⲉ (Ep 98, CO 314) S, ⲁⲛⲏϩⲉ AA² nn m, **I. a.** eternity: sg, Ex 14 13 B, Is 14 20 B (S diff); pl, Ps 54 19 SB, Si 24 10 B (S ⲡⲉ.), Ap 11 15 S (B sg) αἰών. **b.** age, period of time: Mt 12 32, 13 22 B (S = Gk), 2 Cor 4 4 B (S do), He 6 5 B (S do) αἰ.; Mus 34 193 B ⲡⲭⲱⲕ ⲁⲡⲁⲓⲉ. ϥⲁⲓ, PO 11 310 B sim, Va 61 97 B ⲡⲁⲓⲉ. ⲡⲧⲉ ϯⲡⲟⲩ, MIE 2 422 B ⲡⲓⲉ. ⲧⲏⲣⲟⲩ.

With ϣⲁ-: sg, Job 33 12 SB, Is 48 12 S, Bar 4 10 B; pl, Job 3 18 SB, 2 Cor 4 18 SB αἰώνιος; ShMIF 23 97 S ⲉⲁⲩϯ ⲟⲥⲉ ⲡⲛϣⲁⲉ., Pcod 17 S who prefers not ϩⲉⲛϣⲁⲉ. to these?

II. adj, eternal: Ge 17 8 B, Is 45 17 B (S ϣⲁⲉ.), Mt 25 46 B (S ⲡϣⲁⲉ.) αἰώνιος, MG 25 350 B ⲉⲅⲉⲣϥⲁⲉⲅⲓ ⲡⲉ. With ⲡϣⲁ-: Job 21 11 S (B ⲡⲉ.), Ps 104 10 S (B do), Mt 19 29 S (var ϣⲁ-, B do) αἰώνιος; Sa 7 26 S (B do) ἀείδιος; Is 53 10 (Cl 16 11) A μακρόβιος; PS 64 S ⲟⲩ(ⲟⲩ)ⲟⲉⲓⲛ ⲡϣⲁⲉ.; with ϣⲁ-: Job 10 21 SB, Ez 16 60 B (S ⲡϣⲁ-) αἰώνιος; B 261 S ⲡⲱⲛϩ ϣⲁⲉ., C 43 78 B sim; BG 32 S ⲡⲓϣⲁⲉ. ⲁⲡⲁⲣⲑⲉⲛⲓⲕⲟⲛ, EW 225 B ⲡⲓϣⲁⲉ. ⲡⲟⲩⲣⲟ (S om, Gu 37).

III. adv, for ever, eternally, ever: **a.** in interrog clause, 1 Cor 9 7 SB, He 1 5 S (B ⲛⲉⲛⲁⲩ) ποτέ; BM 175 1 S ⲡⲓⲁ ⲉ. ...ⲡⲉⲡⲧⲁϥⲉⲓ, BG 26 S ⲡⲓⲁⲁ ⲡⲉⲧⲛⲁⲡⲟⲉⲓ ⲁⲁⲟϥ ⲉ., J 11 46 S ⲡⲉⲡⲧⲁⲉⲓ ⲉⲃⲟⲗ ⲉⲣⲟⲕ ⲉ. **b.** with neg vb, Sa 15 17 S, Mt 7 23 SB, Lu 15 29 SB, Jo 13 8 SA² (B ϣⲁⲉ.), (οὐδέ)ποτε; BM 355 3 S like one ⲁⲡϥϣⲱⲡⲉ ⲉ. With ϣⲁ-, ⲛϣⲁ-: Ps 5 11 SB, 14 5 SB, Si 7 37 S ϣⲁⲉ. (var ⲛϣⲁⲉ.), Is 30 8 sim εἰς τὸν αἰ., τοὺς αἰ., Ap 20 10 S ϣⲁⲉ. ⲡⲉ. = B ϣⲁⲉ. ⲡⲧⲉ ⲡⲓⲉ. εἰς τοὺς αἰ. τῶν αἰ., Br 247 S ⲉⲡⲉϥⲕⲓⲁ (l ⲡⲡⲉϥ-) ⲡϣⲁⲉ., C 43 7 B ϣⲁⲉ. ⲡⲧⲉ ⲡⲓⲉ. ⲁⲩⲱ ϣⲁⲉ. ⲡⲉ. ϣⲁⲡⲓⲉ.: Jer 29 14 S (B ϣⲁⲉ.), Dan 3 52 SB εἰς τοὺς αἰ., Cl 58 2 A ϣⲁⲡⲓⲁⲛⲏϥⲉ

ⲡⲁ. εἰς τοὺς αἰ. τῶν αἰ. ϣⲁⲉ. ⲡⲟⲩⲟⲉⲓϣ: Is 9 7 S (B ϣⲁⲡⲥⲛⲟⲩ ⲡⲧⲉ ⲡⲉ.) εἰς τὸν αἰῶνα χρ., Mor 41 181 S go to hell ϣⲁⲉ. ⲡⲟⲩ., J 3 23 S ϣⲁⲉ. ⲡⲟⲩ. ⲡⲓⲁ. *Cf* ⲃⲱⲗ (ϣⲁⲃⲟⲗ). With ⲭⲓⲡ-, ⲓⲥⲭⲉⲡ-: Ge 6 4 B ⲓⲥⲭⲉⲡⲡⲉ., Ps 24 6 B do = S ⲭⲓⲡⲉ., Si 39 27 S, Eph 3 9 S ⲭⲓⲡⲉ. = B ⲓⲥⲭⲉⲡⲡⲓⲉ. ἀπ᾽ αἰ., ἀπὸ τοῦ αἰ., ShA 2 341 S ⲭⲓⲡⲉ. ⲁⲡⲟⲩⲭⲟⲟⲥ ⲭⲉ- was it *ever* said that...?, My 21 S hidden ⲭⲓⲡⲉⲡⲉ. As nn: Pro 8 21 SA ⲡⲭⲓⲡⲉ. = B ⲡⲁⲓ ⲓⲥⲭⲉⲡⲡⲉ. τὰ ἐξ αἰ., P 129²⁰ 132 S those recently dead & ⲡⲁⲡⲭⲓⲡⲉ.

ⲁⲡⲧϣⲁⲉ. S nn f, eternity: BG 25 ⲡⲣⲉϥϯ ⲡⲧⲁ., Mun 121 remaining as He was ϩⲛⲧⲉϥⲁ.

ⲉⲡ- S *v* ⲉⲓⲟⲡⲉ.

ⲉⲡⲱ S nn f, part of fastening of door: TT 101 door with ϣⲟϣⲧ, ⲕⲗⲉ, ⲁⲟⲭⲗⲟⲥ & ⲉ., BM 259 door with neither ⲉ. nor ⲁⲟⲩⲭⲗⲟⲥ, Ryl 252 in builder's account ⲧⲉ. ⲡⲡⲣⲟ ⲡϥⲓⲣ, MMA 14 1 59 ostr]. ϭⲛ ⲧⲉⲡⲱ. *Cf* Dévaud *Études* 1922 57.

ⲉⲡⲏⲡ SB nn, name of 11th month, Gk ᾽Επείφ, ᾽Επίφι, to which Copt varr often approximate: ⲉⲡⲉⲓⲡ, ⲉⲡⲓⲫ, ⲉⲡⲉⲓⲫ, ⲉⲡⲉⲓϥⲓ &c; Ar ابيب. In literary texts mostly ⲉⲡⲏⲡ: S, ShC 73 198, R 1 4 75, Miss 4 240, 682; B, AM 135, C 43 120, 200, MIE 2 333; or ⲉⲡⲏⲫ S: BAp 75, BMis 574, Mich 550 41, Aeg 11, Miss 8 37.

ⲉⲡⲣⲁ S nn, pl only, vanities, often = B ⲉϥⲗⲏⲟⲩ: Is 59 4 (B ⲁⲉⲧⲉϥ.) μάταια, ShC 73 206 ϩⲉⲡⲉ. ⲡⲉ ⲡⲉⲓϣⲁⲭⲉ, ib 93 ⲉⲧⲭⲱ ⲡⲣⲉⲡⲉ. Adj, vain: Ti 1 10 (B ⲁⲉⲧⲉϥ.) ⲣⲉϥⲭⲓ ϣⲁⲭⲉ ⲡⲉ. ματαιολόγος, ShBMOr 8800 202 ⲟⲩⲁⲡⲧⲣⲁⲁⲁⲟ ⲡϣⲁⲭⲉ ⲡⲉ., Z 601 ϣⲁⲅⲉⲓ ⲉⲭⲡⲟⲩⲧⲉⲗⲟⲥ ⲡⲉ. Adv, in vain: Pro 1 17 = B ⲭⲉⲡⲟⲩⲁⲉⲧⲟⲭⲓ ἀδίκως, Vulg frustra, BM 979 ⲣⲱⲁⲉ ⲡⲓⲁ ϣⲧⲣⲧⲱⲣ ⲉⲡⲭⲓⲛⲭⲏ ⲁⲩⲱ ⲉ. ⲁⲡⲧⲉ. nn f, vanity: Ps 23 4 (B ⲁⲉⲧⲉϥ.) μάταιον, Ps 61 9 (B do) ματαιότης, Miss 8 34 ⲡⲉϥϣⲟⲩⲉⲓⲧ ⲁⲡ...ⲡϥϣⲟⲟⲡ ⲁⲡ ϩⲛⲟⲩⲁ. εἰκαῖα...μάταιος, P 44 97 ⲕⲁⲕⲟⲡⲟⲓⲁ ⲁⲉⲁ. ترصيف الكذب (?) Z 601 empty words striking ear ϩⲛⲟⲩⲁ.

ⲉⲣ- SA² archaic rel pref with past tenses, where rel is subj of clause (*v* GöttN '19 151): PS 304 S ⲣⲱⲁⲉ ⲡⲓⲁ ⲉⲣϭⲓ ⲁⲩⲥⲧⲏⲣⲓⲟⲛ, ib 294 ⲧⲉⲯⲩⲭⲏ ⲉⲣϭⲓ ⲁⲩⲥ., ib 298 ⲡⲉϥⲯⲩⲭⲟⲟⲩⲉ ⲉⲣϭⲓ ⲁⲩⲥ., ib 314 ⲡⲉⲣⲥⲟⲡ ⲧⲁⲁⲡⲡⲏ; Jo 5 36 A² ⲡⲉⲓⲱⲧ ⲡⲉⲣⲧⲉⲅⲁⲉⲓ = S ⲡⲉⲡⲧⲁⲩ-, B ⲡⲉⲧⲁⲩ-, ib 17 8 A² ⲡⲧⲁⲕ ⲉⲣⲧⲡⲡⲁⲟⲩⲧ = S ⲡⲉⲡⲧⲁⲕ-, B ⲡⲉⲧⲁⲕ-, ib 19 21 A² ⲡⲉⲧⲁⲁⲉⲩ ⲡⲉⲣⲭⲟⲟⲥ = S ⲡⲉⲡⲧⲁϥ-, B ⲡⲉⲑⲟⲩ ⲁϥ- (*v* HT *Gosp of Jo* xix).

ⲉⲣⲉ- SB *v* ⲉ- vbal prefix.

ⲉⲣⲓ- A *v* ⲉⲓⲣⲉ.

ⲉⲣⲟ S *v* ⲣⲣⲟ.

ернⲃ   *v* арнⲃ.

ерⲃι *B v* рⲃе.

ерⲃηⲍ *S v* ерⲃιcι.

ерⲃιⲛ *B* nn m, *papyrus*: K 198 пιе. برّدي. *Cf* احذا‎ (Tatt, *v* Lag *Mitth* 2 65) & трⲃнеⲓⲛ.

ерⲃⲓⲛⲥ *S* nn, *?* = last: Ryl 291 among vegetables ογⲙⲁⲓре пе. In name ⲧⲥⲁерⲃⲏⲛⲓⲥ m (*sic*) (Hall 113).

ерⲃⲱⲥ *B* nn m, *rope* of single ply: K 138 سيل.

ерⲃιⲥι *B* nn m, *hemp*: K 122 قنّب. *Cf ?* Saq 367 *S* ерⲃⲏⲍ. In P 43 56 بزر قنب is erroneously пепарⲓⲥ = 44 81 пеϥарⲓⲥ. Possibly *l* eⲃр- (*v* eⲃрⲁ).

ерⲃⲓⲧ *B* nn m, *camel's saddle* or *pack*: K 137 رحل.

ерⲃⲧ *S v* рⲃⲧ.

ерⲙⲁⲛ *B v* ⲑⲣⲙⲁⲛ.

ерп- *S*, ереп- *B v* ро (ерп-).

ерпⲱ *SF v* рпⲱ.

ерⲣⲁ *F v* ⲩⲣо.

ерcⲱ *BF v* рcⲱ.

ерⲧ *S* nn, Bodl(P) b 7, twice in list of farm produce: арⲁⲧⲉ, ерⲧ, оеⲓк, ⲙⲟⲩϥ, ⲥⲓⲙⲉⲛⲡ, папоⲓ, cоⲩо &c. Prob not = ογерⲧ &, as папоⲓ is there, not = ерⲝ *B*.

ерⲏⲧ *SA²B*, ⲣⲏⲧ *SB*, еⲣⲣⲏⲧ *SF*, ⲣⲣⲏⲧ *SF*, еⲗⲗⲏⲧ *F*, **I** vb mostly tr, *vow, promise, devote*, c ⲛ- of thing vowed & ⲛ- (rarely е-) to whom: Ge 28 20 *S* (*B* ⲧⲱⲃ̅), Jud 11 30 *S* (*B* ⲱϣ), Eccl 5 3 *S* εὔξασθαι; Sa 17 8 *S*, AP 8 *A²* ὑπισχνεῖσθαι; Est 4 7 *S*, Si 20 22 *S*, Mk 14 11 *S* (*B* om), Ro 1 2 *S* (*B* ⲱϣ), ἐπαγγέλλεσθαι; Lev 27 15, 26 *S*, 2 Kg 8 11 *S* (е. glossing ⲧⲏⲃⲟ), Pro 20 25 *S* ἁγιάζειν; PS 204 *S* ⲣ̄ⲛⲟⲩⲉ. аке. паⲓ, BHom 15 *S* ⲛⲧⲁⲅⲉ. паⲕ ⲡⲟⲩⲙⲛⲧⲉⲣⲟ, Bor 241 209 *S* пепⲧⲁⲅⲉ. ⲙⲙⲟⲟⲩ to virginity, BAp 170 *S* ⲁⲡⲉ. ⲙⲡⲡⲉ̅ ⲡⲟⲩⲙ̅ⲛⲧⲙⲟⲛⲁⲭⲟⲥ, Mor 27 44 *F* ⲡⲧⲁⲓⲣⲣⲏⲧ ⲙⲙⲁⲩ, Gu 89 *S* еϥерⲣⲏⲧ паⲩ ⲛ-, J 78 19 *S* аⲓе. ⲙⲙⲟϥ еⲣⲟⲩⲛ епⲧⲟпⲟⲥ Hall 86 *S* ⲧⲙ̄ⲛ̄ⲧⲛⲁ ⲛⲧⲁⲕе. ⲙⲙⲟⲥ ⲛⲡⲣⲏⲕе;   vbal obj: Pcod 3 *S* аⲅе. паϥ еⲝⲓⲧϥ, BMis 313 *S* аⲓе. еⲝⲱ ерⲱⲧⲛ ⲛ-, Mor 41 13 *S* ⲁⲟⲩⲁ е. етреϥ- = Va 59 38 *B* ϯ ⲣⲏⲧ ероϥ еⲑⲣеϥ-.

obj not expressed: Ps 75 11 *S* (*B* ⲧⲱⲃ̅), Pro 20 25 *S*, Si 18 22 εὔξασθαι; LMis 36 198 *S* great sin it is е. ⲛⲧⲁⲙⲉⲗⲉⲓ, WTh 43 *B* ⲁⲡⲉⲭ̅ⲥ̅ ⲕⲏⲡ ерⲏⲧ паⲩ (var *ib* 156 ер еⲣⲣⲏⲧ), BMar 53 *S* аⲅе. еⲩⲝⲱ

ⲙⲙⲟⲥ, J 114 5 *S* апе...епⲙⲟпаⲥⲧ. ⲍⲉ-, Ricci L 260 *F* еϥеⲗⲗⲏⲧ ⲛⲏⲡ.

II. *SBF* nn m, pl ерⲁⲧе *S* (Pro 7 14, 19 10), & sg as pl, *vow, promise*: Lev 22 23 *S* (*B* = Gk), Ps 55 13 *S* (*B* do), Nah 1 15 *S* (*A* ϣпⲱⲡ, *B* = Gk), Ac 18 18 *S* (*B* do) εὐχή; Am 9 6 *S* (*AB* do), Lu 24 49 *S* (*B* ⲱϣ), Ac 7 17 *SF* (*B* = Gk), 2 Cor 1 20 *SF* (*B* ⲱϣ) ἐπαγγελία; Lev 27 28 *S* (*B* om) ἀναθεῖναι; 1 Kg 6 15 *S* θέμα; Sa 12 21 *S* ὑπόσχεσις; BM 185 1 *S* I cannot ⲝⲓ ϭⲟⲗ епⲁе., J 89 42 *S* пеⲧⲛⲁⲕⲱⲗⲩ ⲙпе. ⲙ̅пⲭⲟеⲓⲥ, CA 101 *S* е. ⲛⲓⲙ of bronze or gold, Mor 51 25 *S* пе. (wine) ⲡⲧⲁⲩⲧⲁⲁϥ еⲩоⲩⲛ епⲧопоⲥ, BMis 431 colophon паⲓпе пе. аⲩⲱ пⲁⲱⲣⲟⲡ of NN, R 2 4 63 *S* sim., BMis 54 *S* аⲩϯ пⲡеⲅе. еⲡⲟⲩⲛⲏⲃ, Va 59 46 *B* пеаϥϯ ⲣⲏⲧпе еⲑⲣеϥⲑⲁⲙⲓⲟϥ; J 99 13 *S* like every one еϥⲱ пе. еⲩⲟⲩⲛ еⲙⲙⲟⲛⲁⲥⲧ. *V* also арⲏⲃ.

As name: перⲏⲧ BM 1075, Baouit 111, 113, CO 101 n, Περίτ, Πελῆτ (Preisigke), терⲓⲧ Ep 270, ST 48.

ерⲱⲧе *SA*, ерⲱϯ *BF*, арⲱⲧе *S̅ʲ* (Mor 31 255), арⲱϯ *F* (Mor 27 17, 30 29) nn m (oftener) & f, in Deu 14 21 *B* f, *S* m & f, 1 Kg 28 24 *S* sim, *milk*: Ge 18 8 *SB*, Lev 20 24 *SB*, Job 29 6 *S* m, Pro 24 68 *SA*, Si 39 33 *S* m, Is 7 22 *SB* m, *ib* 28 9 *SB* f, *ib* 60 16 *SB* m, Lam 4 7 *SB* m, Am 6 4 *AB*, 1 Cor 3 2 *F* (Mor 38 104) f ар., *ib* 9 7 *SB* m γάλα; ShMIF 23 144 *S* m (*cf* He 5 13); in recipes: woman's, PMéd 148, 207, 301 *S*, cow's *ib* 233, sheep's Deu 32 14, goat's BMis 178, ass's PMéd 207, camel's *ib* 166, of sycamore *ib* 145, PMich 593 ⲟⲩерⲱⲧ ⲛⲟⲩϭⲉ (or *? l* еⲩⲉ), of figs TurM 9 *S*, of lettuce *ib* 70, pure milk Ryl 106 18 *S* е. ⲛаⲗⲭаⲗеⲥ (الخالص), sweet milk AZ 23 103 *S* е. еϥⲥⲟⲗⲉϭ.

ⲣ̄ е. *S*, *make, give forth milk*: CR '87 376 recipe for breasts етреⲩⲣ е.; *cf* Is 7 22 *S* ⲉ̄ⲣ е. ποιεῖν γ.

ϯ е. *SB*, *give milk, suckle*: C 41 69 *B* of camel аⲥϯ е. ⲛаϥ, Wess 15 152 *S* sim of women.

ϭⲓ е. *B*, *get milk, suck*: Aeg 12 breasts еⲧаϭⲓ е. ⲛⲃⲏⲧⲟⲩ = *S* ⲧⲥ̄ⲡⲕⲟ.

оⲩⲙ е. *SB*, *feeding on milk*: Si 46 22 *S* (оⲩаⲙ-) γαλαθηνός, Z 273 *S* пⲥⲁⲛϣ ⲙⲡⲟⲩⲙ е. γαλακτοτροφία, Mor 18 140 *S* babes еⲧⲟⲩⲙ е. γαλουχεῖν, CDan 98 *B* sim.

ⲱⲗⲝ еⲃⲟⲗ ⲣ̄пⲧе. *S*, *wean*: BMis 55, *cf* Ps 130 2 *B* ⲧⲟϯоⲩ пⲧе.

ⲣⲁⲡⲉ. (ⲧе.) *SB*, of animal still *sucking*: Ge 18 7 *S* gloss on еϥϭⲏⲡ, 1 Kg 7 9 γαλαθηνός, *ib* 28 24 νομάς (Ex 23 19, 34 26 *S l ?* ⲣⲛⲧе., *cf* Deu 14 21).

ерⲧⲱ *B v* ⲣⲧⲱ.

ерⲧⲱ *B* Ge 3 18, *l* ⲣⲱⲓ, *q v*.

ерⲧоп *B v* ⲣⲧоⲃ.

ернү *SAA²*, ерноү *AB*, арноү *B*, алноү,
арнү *F* nn m f, mostly with poss pref & agreeing
in gender & mostly number with subj of clause,
fellow, companion, hence expressing reciprocity:
each other, together, mutually &c: MG 25 15 *B*
ϣареоүаі ϫфо мфмоү пемпωнϩ ебол ϩітеп-
пıа. (*sic* MS, print om) ἐκ τοῦ πλησίον (PG 65 77),
ib 356 *B* ϭι пемпіарноү; Jud 6 29 *S*, 1 Kg 14
20 *S*, Ac 7 27 *F* (*S* ϩітоүωϥ, *B* ϣфнр), MG 25 7
B πλησίον; Nu 2 2 *B* (*S* diff) ἐχόμενος αὐτοῦ;
EpJer 48 *BF*, Mk 3 24 *S* (*B* diff); Lu 23 12 *SB*,
ἑαυτοῦ; Deu 19 17 *S* (*B* оүтшоү); Sa 14 24 *S*
(var ϩітоүω-), Su 13 *SB*, Mt 11 16 *B* (*S* ϣфнр)
ἕτερος; Pro 22 2 *AB*, Sa 18 23 *S*, Is 34 15 *SBF*,
Dan 7 3 *B*, Am 4 3 *SB*, Ac 7 26 *SBF*, Ro 12 5
SBF, MG 25 8 *B* ἀλλήλων; Deu 12 15 *S* (*B* еү-
соп), Jos 11 5 *S*, Ps 61 9 *S* (*B* diff), Jer 4 25 *S*
(ἐπτοεῖτο mistaken, *cf B*), Nah 1 9 *A* (*S* ϩіоүсоп,
B еүс., *cf* Aeg 215), Ac 2 1 *S* (*B* ϩіоүма) ἐπὶ τὸ
αὐτό; Jos 10 42 *S* εἰς ἅπαξ; vbs with συν-: Ge
14 3 *S*, 2 Kg 2 25 *S*, Job 1 4 *SB*, 14 12 *S*, Ps 84
10 *SB*, Is 34 15 *B*, Ez 33 31 *SB*, Su 39 *B*, Mt 1
18 *SB*, 22 34 *S*, Ro 1 12 *SB*; v further Jud 20 1
S, Sa 18 9 *S*, Ez 16 16 *SB*, 37 7 *SB*, Su 52 *B*,
Joel 3 11 *SA*. HL 122 *B* піϩоүіт ... аϥсек
пеϫа., MG 25 376 *B* асϯ ϩап етесе., R 1 30 *S*
аϥеіпе мпмнпϣе...епеϫе., BSM 78 *B* watchman
еϥкшϯ пемпеϫе. (BMis 168 diff), Mor 55 65 *S*
Trinity есϣнϣ мппесе., C 43 27 *B* clapped his
hands епеϫе., ShP 130⁵ 15 *S* grain mixed with
straw еүпωрϫ ебол ппеϫе., C 43 13 *B* tortured
body ϩі арϫн мфωрϫ епеϫа., BIF 14 156 *S*
lamed foot астшϭе епесе., BMar 209 *S* after
incision аϥтшϭе мппıа...еϫппϭе., Kr 218 *F* contract петеі ебол епепа. shall pay fine, PS 130 *S*
аүр ϩоте ехппеϭе., *ib* 20 sim, J 66 37 *S* my
belongings shall my daughters ϭітоү мппеϭе.,
C 86 330 *B* паүϣıпе пемпоүе. ϫе-, BMis 63 *S*
brothers мппеϭе., *cf* ST 46 *S* пспнү ппеϭе., Br
89 *S* асмооϣе ебол псапесе., *ib* 51 sim, BHom
112 *S* things continue еүмооϣе псапеүе. *of themselves*, unaided, PS 280 *S* all cried out ϩıпеүе., *ib*
7 *S* перепоүоеіп тнрϥ ϩıпеϭе. пе, *ib* 22 *S* gates
аүоүωп ϩıпеүе., AZ 23 108 *S* in recipe таϭϥ
ϩапеϭе. *mix* (*all*) *together*.

ероүот *B* v оүрот.

ерфеі *B* v рпе.

ерϣ *B* v ерϫ.

ераϣ *A* v арοϣ.

ерϣап-, ереϣап- (archaic, Deu 12 20 Budge,
Sa 16 14, PS 169), ерϣа- (Rahlfs *Psalt* 36), еϣа-

(Ep 1 249) *S*, аϣа- *A* (Rösch 162, Till 221), аре-
ϣап- *B*, алеϣап- (Is 30 26, EpJer 32), ерϣап *F*,
condit vbal pref formed of 2 pres + ϣап, ϣа *if*,
mostly = ἐάν: *S* еıϣапоүωϣ = *B* аıϣап-, *S* еϥ-
ϣапϣωпе, *S* ететпϣапсωтм (Ps 94 7) = *F* ате-
тепϣап- (EpJer 5) = *B* аретепϣап- (*cf S* ер-
ϣапететпкеттнүтп Ps 89 17); with nom subj:
S ерϣаппеϥϭωпт моүϩ = *B* ареϣап-, also *S*
ерϣапте- J 4 64, 65 73, CO 140.

ерϣωп *BF* v рϣωп.

ерϣıϣ *B* nn m, *chick-pea*: K 193 حمص; in
P 54 134, Bodl 325 152 реϥϣıϣ & in *S* glos P 46
159.

ерϣıϣı *B* I. vb (rare), tr & intr *have power, authority*: C 86 84 my body ке. ммоϥ, AM 95 пϑок
ете. Lu 22 25 пн ете. еϫωoү (var v below). II.
nn m, *power, authority*: Ps 135 8, Si 24 11, Dan 7
14, Mt 7 29, Ac 9 14, Ro 9 21, Jude 25 (all *S* =
Gk) ἐξουσία; Lu 22 25 (var oı пе.), 1 Cor 6 12,
7 4 ἐξουσιάζειν (all *SF* о пϫоеıс); Mt 20 25 (*S*
о птеүϩ.) κατεξουσιάζ., AM 243 пе. мфмоү ϫн
птотк, Cat 174 оүебол ϩеппе. пırωмнс, MG
25 276 мпоүϫе оүсаϫı ϩепоүе., but were humble; with ϩа- *under authority*: Job 12 5 (*S* om),
Is 3 6 (*S* ϩа-), *ib* 58 3 (*S* diff) ὑπό, Mt 8 9 (*S* =
Gk) ὑπὸ ἐξ., Va 57 187 servants еүϫн ϩаоүе.
ὑπ' ἐξ.

ϯ е., *give authority*: Bel 26, Mt 10 1 (*S* = Gk),
Ac 8 9 (*S* do), MG 25 304 (*S* оүеϩсаϩпе) Christ
gave пеϭе. пωoү.

ϭі е., *receive authority*: Ac 26 10 (*S* = Gk),
1 Cor 9 12 (*S* do), PO 11 355 етаϥϭі мпıе.
ϩıтепϥϯ.

ерϭот *B* v рωϭт.

ернϩ, ернϩте *A* v ϩареϩ.

ерϫ *B*, нрϫ *S*(only PMéd) nn m & f, *small
bird, chicken*: Lev 14 4, 6 *B* (*S* папоі) f ὀρνίθιον
عصفور, *ib* 14 49, 50, 51 *B* (no *S*) m ὀρ. طائر, K 168 *B*
ерϣ دجاج, PMéd 177 *S* among diet for sick оүнрϫ
(*cf* 179 *jucella e pingium gallinarum* Oribasius), Va
57 267 *B* піорпıϑос етепı(*sic*)е. пе ὄρνις.

ерϫω *B* nn f, ? *a larger bird* (v o *great*): K 168
دجاجة, which also = апапаı.

ерϭоі, елϭоі *S* nn m, meaning uncertain:
PMéd 283 in recipe for eye disease сıϣе пер.
(*chicken's gall, cf* ерϫ, Chassinat), Mor 44 33
suicide of Judas's wife foretold спар пϣoү пклω
етепел. пе псωϣт етесоүωϩе (so ? name here
of disease). In name: BM 1077 Φανερϭοι (про
пе.). *Cf* ? place-name пелϭоеı (= دلجاي) RNC
87. V клο.

ес *AF old* v ас.

еес *A*, ес *F blow* v аас.

ес *SᵃA* interj v еіс.

есіе *BO* v асаі *sf* & ѕасіе.

есіееі *A* v асаі.

есны *B* v ωск (аскє).

еспе *A* v аспе.

есит *SAA²BF* nn m, sg as pl (ShA 2 74 *S*),
I. nn, *ground*, so *bottom, lowest part* (v KKS 161,
AZ 38 145): Ps 43 25 *SB* γῆ, ShA 2 253 *S* animals
hiding ѕмпщω н ѕмпе., *ib* 74 *S* єѱолщл препе.
ѕппкопрia, ShC 73 152 *S* reeds to be plucked
only пе. прнтс нтбо, FR 20 *S* birds flew out ѕмпе.
ппехалхіон, Z 291 *S* пщik пте пе., *ib* 337 *S*
water reached ankles пе. ѕе петтахриупе τὸ δὲ
λοιπόν (so ? *l* псеепе), BMar 241 *S* pillars all of fire
хіпте епе., Mor 31 211 *S* Jeremiah's pit ерепе.
ѕмоч ѕну like bottle, PS 5 *S* хіппе. ѕмпкаѕ;
PS 44 *S* петщооп епече., *ib* 170 птопос етм-
поуесит, *ib* 205 птахіс етпече. opp етпечсаѕре,
ib 242 ѕмустиріоп пім етпеуе.

II. as adv with preceding prep + art, mostly =
verbal κατα- (-άγειν, -αιρεῖν, -βαίνειν, -βάλλειν &c)
or κάτω & sim.   епесит, *to the ground, downward*, **a.** absolutely: with vbs, Ge 15 11 *SB*, Si
1 30 *B*, Is 26 5 *SBF*, Ez 32 30 *B* (*S* еѕраі), Am 9
2 *SB* (*A* аѕрнi), Mt 15 36 *S* (*B* еѕрнi), Lu 9 37
S (*B* do), Ac 10 21 *S* (var еѕр.) *B*; for κάτω, Jos
2 11 *S*, Is 51 6 *SB*, Mt 27 51 *SB*, Lu 4 9 *SB*;
κατωτέρω, Mt 2 16 *S* (*B* сапе.); PS 41 *S* аѕре
епе., BMis 538 *S* pit ечщωкѕ епе., ShRyl 70 252
S еаѕнту епе. ѕмпесѕос, C 89 151 *B* I drank ебол
хєпфіом епе. **b.** with following prep & obj:
PS 12 *S* аіѕωщт епе. епкосмос, Mor 41 181 *S*
earth opened епе. еппоуп, AP 19 *A²* аспахтс апе.
ахпмма, BMis 79 *S* еі епе. ѕмптωртр *down* the
stair, CaiEuch 496 *B* хіпі епе. ѕіхеппкаѕі, Ann
27 64 *S* ѕмоу епе. епеіаωт, Mt 11 23 *S* (*B* еѕр.)
бωк епе. щаѕмпте.

ѕмпесит *S*, almost as adj, *at the bottom, below*,
a. absolutely: Ex 20 4 (*B* епе.), Si 51 7, Ac 2 19
(*B* епе.) κάτω, BHom 53 прωме етѕмпе. οἱ κάτω
ἄνθρ. opp петпtпе; Ps 85 13 (*B* етсапе.) κατώτατος, Ez 41 20 пма ѕмпе. = *B* етсапе. ἔδαφος,
PS 91 пкаке ѕмпе., BG 52 ѕммерос ѕмпе. of ὕλη,
Mor 28 233 ттахіс ѕмпе., cf 231 етѕріпе. **b.**
with following п-: Z 316 ѕмпе. ѕмоч παρακάτω,
BAp 150 Daniel ечѕмпе. ѕмпщнi, BMar 37 martyr
prayed ѕмпе. птетрір, J 12 7 witnesses ппе. ппеі-
епграфоп (cf ѕапе.); Ez 43 14 *B* фоуωп ѕмпе.
prob from *S*.

сапесит, (*on*) *lower side, below*, **a.** absolutely:
Cat 162 *B* писапе. іе пщωк, opp писапщωі, P 44
69 *S* ѕупωтлωтнс (ὑπογλωττίς) сапіт(*sic*)ѕмплас;
Is 14 9 *B*, Ez 42 6 *B* (*S* ппса ѕмпе.), Mt 2 16 *B*
(*S* епе.), Eph 4 9 *B* (*S* do), Va 57 38 *B* ісхепсапе.
епщωі κάτωθεν, C 86 272 *B* еппп епп етсапе.
Cf below p песит. **b.** with following п-: Ge
6 17 *B* (*S* псапе.), Ps 13 37 *B* (*S* ѕарат-), Ob 7 *B*
(*A* ѕарет-) ὑποκάτω; 3 Kg 8 6 *B*, Ac 2 5 *B* (*S*
етѕапе.), 1 Cor 15 25 *BF* (*S* ѕа-) ὑπό; MIE 2
415 *B* earth opened сапе. ппечбаланх, PLond
4 435 *S* we will set out names сапе. пти...ѕомо-
лоуіа;   or псапе.: BMis 510 *S* abyss псапе.
ѕмпкаѕ, *ib* 392 *S* пс. ѕммооу тироу, Kr 3 *F* subscribe псапе. еткатаурафи, *ib* 121 sim.   **c.**
псапе. as nn: Ge 6 17 *S* (*B* сапе.), Job 9 6 *B*;
better пса ѕмпе. Ez 42 5 *S* = *B* сапе., Z 341 *S*
пса ѕмпе. of Egypt κάτω μέρη.

щапесит, *as far as, down to the ground*: Deu 32
22 *S* (*S* щаеѕр.) ἕως κάτω, HSt 465 *S* thou shalt
be pure щапе. ппекоуеріте (Lag ща-), CA 91 *S*
sim.

ѕапесит, *below ground, under*, **a.** absolutely:
Deu 28 13 *S* (*B* сапе.), Ez 40 10 *S* (*B* do) ὑποκάτω. **b.** with following п-: Ex 20 4 *S* (*B* diff),
Jth 6 11 *S*, Ap 6 9 *S* (*B* сапе.) ὑποκ., Jos 12 3 *S*
ὑπό, Ps 62 9 *S* (*B* етсапе.) τὰ κατώτερα, PS 374 *S*
water ечѕапе. птесфаіра, ShA 2 83 *S* hide them
ѕапе. ѕмпкаѕ, Mor 43 283 *S* ѕапе. ппечоуеріте
(var ѕа-), J 108 14 *S* for whom I shall sign ѕапесит ппіхωріастікоп (*cf* ѕмпе.).

ѕіпесит **a.** *on, to the ground*, absolutely: Si 11
6 *S*, Mk 8 6 *S* (var ѕіхмпкаѕ = *B*), *ib* 9 20 *S*
(*B* ехеппікаѕі) ἐπὶ τ. γῆς; Ps 7 6 *B* (*S* = Gk)
εἰς χοῦν, Jud 4 22 *S* ἐρριμένος, BHom 39 *S* тѕмп-
пкотк ѕіпе. χαμευνία; 2 Kg 15 30 *S* ерератѕ
ѕіпе., Mic 1 8 *SA* (*B* патеωоуі) ἀνυπόδετος, *ib* 7
17 *SA* σύροντες γῆν, cf BHom 122 *S* babe crawls
ѕіпе. (cf *ib* ѕмпкаѕ), Va 59 161 *B* firewood found
ѕіпе., BMOr 6203 *S* thou shalt have lordship
ѕіѕраі ѕіпе. **b.** *from off ground*: 1 Kg 28 23 *S*,
Jth 10 2 *S* ἀπό.

ѕппесит *A*, *at bottom*: El 58 ѕпппе. паѕмпте.

хіппесит *S*, *from the ground, from below*: Ez
41 7 (*B* ісхепепе.) ἐκ τ. κάτωθεν, Br 118 тетп-
бωщт етпе хіппе., BG 49 аѕархесѳаі хіппе.,
PS 225 пщорп...хіппе. reckoning *from below* (cf
ib хіппхісе).

р песит *S*, *go, be below*: Deu 28 43 (var р сапе.,
B епе.) καταβαίνειν κάτω, PS 332 when sun р пе.
ѕмпкосмос;   ер сапе. *B*: C 43 175 nails driven
in щатоуер сапе. ѕмпечсоі, C 86 106 my honour
паер сапе. поуоп пібеп.

есте *SA* *v* еιс.

есооγ *S*, есаγ *SªAA²F*, есωоγ *B* nn m, есω *S* f (MR), mostly as pl (*v* AZ 47 17), *sheep*: Ge 12 16 *SB*, Job 1 3 *SB*, Ps 8 8 *SB*, Jer 27 17 *BF*, Joel 1 18 *AB*, Jo 10 3 *SAB* πρόβατον; Lev 4 32 *SB* е. нсζιме πρ. θῆλυ, Hall 121 *S*, *cf* MR 2 46 *S* in list е. παλαγ, есω нсζιме (*bis*); ST 46 *S* аϥ пе., *ib* 117, CO 459 *S* ϣар пе., Bal *S* ϩалот пе. (? of sheep's wool), BMis 412 *S* ζвсω пе. (? *l* есооγ), PMéd 308 *S* in recipe копрос пе., Z 628 *S* sim тап пе.

маπесооγ, -есωоγ, mostly *B* nn m, *shepherd* (*v* мооне): Ge 4 2 *B*, Nu 27 17 *B*, Job 1 16 *B*, Jer 12 10 *B*, Lu 2 8 *B* (all *S* ϣωс) ποιμήν; MIE 2 360 *B* м. = *S* ϣωс, BMis 378 *S* м. (var Mor 27 29 ϣωс ем.), *ib* later ϣωс = BSM 35 *B* м.; Ge 46 34 *S* ϣωс мм., R 1 5 25 *S* sim.

оρе песооγ, *sheepfold* or *flock* *v* оρе.

As name: песооγ J 8 30, BM 1033, 1075, Osir pl 37, песаγ Kr 164, Πεσόου, Πεσάν (Preisigke).

есоγ *A* *v* асоγ.

ет- *SABF*, еθ- *B* (before liquids & half-vowels), also ете-, rel pref. *V* Stern 400 ff, Sdff 511 ff, Mallon 378 ff, Till 235.

еат *B*, ает *F* nn m, **a.** *end, farthest part*: pl *B*, 1 Kg 2 10 (var ιат, *S* diff), Is 41 5 (*S* арнϫϛ) ἄκρος, Ps 58 14, 66 8 (*S* кρωоγ), Dan 4 8, Mt 12 42 = Lu 11 31 (*S* арнϫϛ) πέρας, К 59 اقاصي, 439 قطار, اقاص; Cat 40 proclaimed пπе. мπказι, MG 25 58 sim, Va 67 73 gathered from пе. пπказι. **b.** *opposite side*: sg *F*, Mt 14 34 аγϫιааλ еπа. = *S* ϫιоор, *B* еρ ϫ. емнр διαπερᾶν, *ib* 22]еπа[ет = *S* еπекρо, *B* емнр, Jo 18 1 еπает мπеχιмарос = *SA²* еπек., *B* do πέραν.

еет† *S* *v* ωϣ.

еетϛ *A* *v* еıρе.

е† *B* *v* мамет, оγамет.

етве- *SAA²F*, пϭтве- (PMich 602), пϣе- (PLond 4) *S*, еθве- *B*, етвннтϛ *S*, етвнтϛ *AF*, еθвнтϛ *B* prep, *because of, concerning*, *cf* тωве vb: Ge 7 7 *SB*, Job 36 18 *SB*, Hos 2 6 *AB*, Mt 13 13 *SBF*, R 1 2 62 *S*, Cl 3 4 *A* διά acc; Deu 32 47 *SB*, Ps 30 3 *SB*, Mk 8 35 *SBF* ἕνεκα; Ge 29 20 *SB*, Job 1 5 *S* (*B* ζа-), Is 23 5 *SB*, Jo 2 25 *SA²* (*B* do), Cl 17 3 *A*, P 129¹⁴ 61 *S* title е. пπταγαпιλе ерооγ περί gen, Z 263 *S* sim, also Ep 525, ST 438 *S*; Ps 106 34 *S* (*B* евол ζеп-), 118 53 *S* (*B* евол ζа-) ἀπό; Ps 68 6 *S* (*B* еζρнı еϫп-), Si 40 12 *S* (var е-) ἐπί dat, acc; Ps 104 14 *S* (*B* do), Ro 15 9 *B* (*S* ζа-) ὑπέρ gen; He 1 7 *BF* (*S* паζρн-), *ib* 8 *B* (*SF* do)

πρός acc; PS 126 *S* voice еπтаπρωме кıм етвн-(н)тс, *ib* 37 *S* service еπтаγтаρмет етвннтс, PLond 4 500 *S* е. петпеωρϫ *for your assurance*, TT 32 *S* clothing е. теπρω, Miss 4 521 *S* sad е. пеθρωζ = C 89 41 *B* е. †метζнкı, DeV 65 *B* bread eaten е. тϫом мπıсωла, ShA 1 301 *S* ζеπρωме е. сеζρ, Mor 43 74 *S* = R 2 4 17 аγеı е. паγ ероϥ, PMich 593 *S* е. етρеγтоγп еıатк.

ет-, еθвеϫе-, conj, *because*: Nu 12 11 *S* (var евол ϫе-, *B* ϫеоγнı), Deu 31 17 *SB*, Jon 1 12 *S* (*B* do), 1 Cor 15 9 *B* (*SF* ϫе-) διότι; Is 30 12 *SF* (*B* ϫе-), Su 11 *B* (*S* ϫе-), Mt 20 7 *S* (var евол ϫе-, *B* ϫе) ὅτι; Ex 16 8 *B* (*S* ϭар), Ac 27 4 *SB*, He 10 2 *B* (*S* евол ϫе-), Cl 4 12 *A* διὰ τό; Lu 18 1 *S* (*B* еπхıпте-) πρός τό; Lev 26 43 *S* (*B* птϣевıω ϫе-), Ez 5 11 *SB*, Lu 1 20 *S* (*B* ефма ϫе-) ἀνθ' ὧν; Sa 18 12 *S*, Mt 18 32 *S* (*B* евол ϫе-) ἐπεί; Pcod 43 *S* аγаπоρеı ... е. ϫемπетпıстıс χорнгеı паγ, C 89 44 *B* е. ϫеπаϥемпе = Miss 4 524 *S* евол ϫе-, MG 25 304 *B* = MIF 13 113 *S* do, PLond 4 464 *S* we agree to fine пτϣеϫеапоп апсотпоγ, *ib* 436 sim, J 10 45 *S* ye shall possess ground е. ϫеатеϥтıмн еı етоотн. *V* also вωλ (псавнλ II a).

етвепаı *S*, -пеı *AF*, еθвефаı *B* conj, *wherefore*: Ge 47 22 *B*, Job 20 21 *SB*, Is 30 18 *SBF*, Ap 12 12 *SB* διὰ τοῦτο; Cl 7 2 *A* διό; Sa 12 23 *S* ὅθεν; PS 11 *S* е. паı ρω аıхоос, ShC 42 74 *S* е. паı пкаıросπе етρе-, AP 26 *A²* еϥмоγ е. пееı. *Cf* also HL 116 *B* е. паıρωϣ гар аϥϭнтоγ.

етвеоγ *v* оγ interrog.

етн- *S*, етеп- *B* *v* тωρе (тоот-).

етнıζ *A* nn m, *ashes*: Ge 18 27 (Cl 17 2, *SB* крмес, кермı) σποδός, Cl 25 4 (no Gk) of phœnix аϥϣаζρογ аоγ ϥр е. еаϥтеко авал ζмπетнıζ.

етпω *S*, етпоγ *A*, етфω *B* *v* ωтп.

етте *S* nn, *meaning unknown*: Ryl 243 in list of varia оγе. worth 8 *solidi*. *Cf* PLond 4 508 in sim list, basket (саρо *v* Ep 531) есмнζ петтеı. Ar اِتِّ, *set of towels*, unlikely.

етоγн- *S* *v* тоγω-.

етнϣı *B* nn f, *rust* (blight), *mildew*: Deu 28 42 (*S* пıрϣ) مرصور (Va 1 marg طواط), for which *cf* ζλωм, 3 Kg 8 37, Ps 77 46 (*S* кооlϥ) تفل, Hos 5 7 (*A* пıрϣ), Joel 1 4, 2 25 (*S* пıрϣ, *A* ζζтωρϣ) ἐρυσίβη, Am 4 9 κάμπη. Ar understands it as an insect pest.

етнϣı, етеϣı *B* nn m, *crane* (*v* AZ 6 55):

K 168 ﺟﺲ, with gloss BM 924 35 ﺷﺮﺏ, while ⲧⲓϭⲓ (*q v*) is ﺷﺮﻭﺏ. If related to ⲧⲣⲟⲩ &c, may be *flamingo* (Sethe).

ⲉⲧⲁϧ *A*   *v* ⲟⲩⲧⲁϧ.

ⲉⲧⲟϧ, ⲉⲧⲁϧ *S* nn m, a garment or certain length of stuff : CO 466 in list ⲉ. ⲡⲕⲁⲧⲓⲧⲱⲡⲉ (var ⲉ. ⲕⲁϯⲧⲱⲡⲉ), Ep 564 two ⲉ. make one veil ϣⲟⲣⲧ, *Rev Ég Anc* 1 15 letter ⲡⲧⲟⲩⲱϫⲉ ⲡⲉ. ⲡⲁⲓ. *Cf* ⲱⲧⲉ.

ⲉⲩ *A*   *v* ⲟⲩ interrog.

ⲉⲟⲟⲩ *SO*(AZ 21 94), ⲉⲁⲩ *AA²F*, ⲱⲟⲩ *BO* (*l c* 104) nn m, *honour, glory*: Ex 33 5 *S* pl (*B diff*), Deu 5 24 *SB*, Job 19 9 *SB*, Sa 7 25 *SB*, Is 53 2 *SA* (Cl) *B*, Mt 6 13 *SBF* δόξα; Is 46 13 *SB* δόξασμα; *ib* 64 3 *B* ⲡⲓⲣⲉⲛⲟⲩⲓ ⲡⲧⲉ ⲡⲱ. (*S* ⲡⲉⲧⲣⲁⲉ.) τὰ ἔνδοξα, Eph 5 27 *B* (*S* ⲧⲁⲉⲓⲏⲩ) ϫⲉⲡⲟⲩⲱ. ἔνδοξος; Dan 3 26 *B* ⲙⲉϧ ⲡⲱ. δεδοξασμένος; MG 25 251 *B* ⲡⲓⲱ. ⲉⲧϣⲟⲩⲓⲧ κενοδοξία, Aeg 242 *S* ⲙⲁⲓⲉ. ⲉϥϣⲟⲩⲉⲓⲧ, Gal 5 26 *B* ⲙⲉⲧⲙⲁⲓⲱ. ⲉϥϣⲟⲩ. κενόδοξος, ShA 1 248 *S* sim; Sa 8 18 *S* εὔκλεια; TstAb 158 *B* ϫⲉⲡⲟⲩⲱ. ⲡⲉⲙⲟⲩⲧⲁⲓⲟ, MR 5 45 *S* ⲡⲉ. ⲉⲡⲡⲉ ϣⲏⲡ...ⲉⲓⲡⲁϧ[ⲙ, C 43 7 *B* ⲡⲓⲱ. ⲡⲁⲕ my lord, AZ 21 104 *O* ⲡⲕⲗⲟⲙ ⲡⲱ. ⲡⲡⲣⲏ. As complimentary periphrasis: BM 1109 *S* I venerate ⲡⲉ. ⲡⲧⲉⲧⲛⲙⲛⲧ͞ⲭ͞ⲥ, MR 5 31 *S* sim, ST 197 *S* I salute ⲡⲉⲕⲉ. ⲉⲧⲥⲙⲁⲙⲁⲁⲧ.

ϧⲁⲉ. *SF, honourable, glorious*, **a.** with rel ⲉⲧ-, Nu 23 21, Job 34 24, Is 23 9 (*B all* ⲧⲁⲓⲏⲟⲩⲧ) ἔνδοξος, Wess 15 156 ἐνδοξότατος; Si 48 6 δεδοξασμένος.   **b.** adjectival, Deu 26 19 ⲉⲕⲣⲁⲉ. δοξαστός, Jth 16 21 ⲉⲕⲣⲁⲉ., Is 32 2 *SF* sim ἔνδ., J 4 71 any authority ⲉϥϫⲟⲥⲉ ⲉϥϧⲁⲉ., R 1 3 35 they beheld her ⲉⲣⲉⲡⲉⲥϧⲟ ϧⲁⲉ., *cf* Ex 34 30 *S*.

ϯ ⲉⲟⲟⲩ *S*, ⲱⲟⲩ *B, give glory, glorify*: 2 Kg 10 3 *S*, Ps 29 15 *SB*, Is 4 2 *SB*, Jo 17 5 *SA²B*, He 5 5 *SBF* δοξάζειν; Jos 7 19 *S*, 1 Chr 16 28 *B*, Jer 13 16 *SB*, Ap 11 13 *SB* δόξαν δοῦναι;   as nn : 1 Cor 10 31 *B* ⲡϯ ⲱ. (*S* ⲟⲩⲉ.) δόξα; Sa 10 20 *S* αἰνεῖν; Ps 30 21 *S* (*B* ⲉⲣ ϣⲫⲏⲣⲓ); Ac 10 46 *S* (*B* ϭⲓⲥⲓ) μεγαλύνειν; BSM 130 *B* crying out ⲉⲩϯ ⲱ. ⲙⲫϯ, BAp 110 *S* ⲁⲓϯ ⲉ. ⲉϫⲡⲡⲉⲡⲧⲁⲩϣⲱⲡⲉ, R 1 3 51 *S* sim.

ⲙⲛⲧⲣⲉϥϯ ⲉ. *S*, ⲙⲉⲧⲣⲉϥϯ ⲱ. *B* nn f, *glorification*: P 44 90 *S* εὐδοξία, Va 58 19 *B* ϧⲁⲡⲉⲩϥⲛⲏⲓⲁ ⲓⲉ ϧⲁⲡⲓⲁ.

ϫⲓⲛϯ ⲱ. *B* nn m, *act of glorifying*: Miss 4 217 if Christ accept ⲡⲉⲧⲉⲡϫ. ⲡⲁϥ.

ϫⲓ ⲉ. *SF*, ϭⲓ ⲱ. *B, be glorified*: Deu 33 16 *SB*, Jth 12 13 *S*, Ps 36 20 *SB*, Is 33 10 *SBF*, 1 Cor 12 26 *SB*, CaiEuch 6 56 *B* δοξάζεσθαι; Sa 8 10 *S* δό. ἔχειν; Jo 5 41 *SA²B* δό. λαμβάνειν; BHom 11 *S* τιμᾶσθαι; R 1 3 26 *S* ⲁϥϫⲓ ⲉ. ⲛϭⲓ ⲡⲣⲁⲡ, Mor 25 206 *S* God ⲉϥⲟⲩⲱϣ ⲉϫⲓ ⲉ. ϧⲙⲡⲉϥⲡⲉⲧⲟⲩⲁⲁⲃ,

TU 43 9 *A* ⲁϥⲡⲁϫⲓ ⲉ. ⲡⲧⲉⲧⲏⲡⲉ, C 43 96 *B* ⲡⲧⲉⲡϭⲓ ⲡⲟⲩⲱ. ⲉⲃⲟⲗ ϧⲓⲧⲟⲧⲟⲩ.

ⲉⲟⲟⲩ, ⲉⲟⲟⲩⲉ *S*   *v* ⲉⲓⲱ ass.

ⲉⲩⲱ, ⲉⲟⲩⲱ *S*, ⲟⲩⲱ *SB*(Ez 18), ⲁⲟⲩⲱ *B*, ⲁⲩⲱ (Mor 42 24), ⲉⲓⲟⲩ *F* (? Kr 36) nn f (Deu 24 10, Job 22 6, BHom 62), pl ⲉⲩⲟⲟⲩⲉ, ⲉⲟⲩⲁⲟⲩⲉ (Hall 115), ⲉⲩⲁⲩⲉ (Louvre R 1780) *S, pledge, surety*: Ex 22 26 *SB*, Ez 33 15 *SB* ἐνεχύρασμα; Ez 18 7 &c *B* ⲟⲩⲱ -ασμός; Deu 24 10 *SB* ἐνέχυρον (*cf* CA 110, CO 270); Is 28 15, 30 1 *S* (*B = Gk*) συνθήκη; Is 58 6 *S* (*B diff*) συνάλλαγμα; Is 18 2 *S* ⲟⲩⲱ, Va 68 175 *B* thy cross ϫⲏ ⲡⲧⲟⲧⲉⲡ ⲡⲁ. ὅμηρος; 1 Kg 22 2 *S* (? *l* ϫⲓ ⲟⲩⲱ); Is 50 1 *SB* (Lacr, Tatt diff) ὑπόχρεως.

ϯ ⲡⲉⲩⲱ *S*, ⲡⲁ. *B, give as pledge*: Deu 24 6 *S* (*B* ⲱⲗⲓ) ἐνεχυράζειν; Mor 25 8 *S* ⲉⲕⲡⲁϯ ⲟⲩ ⲡⲁⲓ ⲡⲉ. = Va 61 91 *B* ⲟⲩⲟⲡ ⲁ. ⲡⲧⲟⲧⲕ, BSM 45 *B* corn ⲉⲧⲁⲣⲉⲧⲉⲡⲧⲛⲏϧ ⲙⲡⲓⲣϧⲱⲥ ⲡⲁ. ⲉϫⲱϥ, ShLMis 414 *S* they gave themselves ⲡⲉ. ⲡⲡϫⲁⲡⲓⲥⲧⲏⲥ, C 86 53 *B* prince given ⲡⲁ. to Roman kings. ST 435 *S* things ⲡⲧⲁⲓϯⲟⲩ ⲡⲁⲕ ⲡⲡⲉ., Sph 10 155 *S* ⲡⲧⲣⲓⲙⲡⲥⲓⲟⲡ ⲙⲡⲉⲓϯ ⲉ. ϧⲁⲣⲟϥ, Pcod 35 *S* ⲡⲧⲁϥϯ ⲡⲡⲕⲉⲓⲙⲓⲗⲓⲟⲡ ⲡⲉ.

ⲟⲩⲱϧ ⲡⲉⲩⲱ *S, deposit as pledge*: Mor 23 50 in need of bread ⲁϥⲟⲩⲉϧ ⲡⲉϥⲉⲛⲉⲭⲏⲣⲱⲡ ⲡⲉ. ϧⲁⲣⲧⲏϥ (baker), Mor 55 4 needy buyer ⲡϥⲟⲩⲱϧ ⲡⲟⲩⲉ(ⲩ)ⲱ ϣⲁⲡⲧⲟⲩⲧⲁⲡⲣⲟⲩⲧϥ, J 18 40 thou mayest sell or give them ⲡⲕⲟⲩⲁϧⲟⲩ ⲡⲉⲃⲱ, Pcod 36 ⲁϥⲟⲩⲁϧⲟⲩ (var ⲧⲁⲁⲩ) ⲡⲉ., PBu 227 regarding a ὑποθήκη ϫⲉⲡⲏ ⲟⲩⲏϧ ⲡⲉ. ⲡⲧⲟⲟⲧϥ (mortgagee), Ann 22 270 *S* ⲁⲓⲟⲩⲱϧ ⲟⲩϧⲣⲁⲧⲏⲣ ϧⲁⲣⲧⲏⲕ ⲡⲉⲟⲩ(ⲱ).

ⲕⲱ ⲡⲉⲩⲱ *S*, ⲭⲱ ⲡⲁ. *B*, meaning as last: C 86 327 *B* ⲭⲁ ⲁ. ⲉϧⲣⲏⲓ ⲡⲉⲙⲛⲓ ϣⲁⲧ ⲡⲗⲟⲅⲕⲟϫⲓ, MMA 24 6 5 *S* solidi ⲡⲧⲁⲡⲕⲁⲁⲩ ⲡⲉ., ST 92 *S* ⲉⲓϭⲱ(ⲕⲱ) ⲡⲡⲓⲉⲩⲟⲟⲩⲉ ⲡⲧⲱⲧⲧⲉⲩⲧⲛ (pl also CO 454); Mk 14 71 *S* (var ⲁⲣⲡⲁ *sic*, *B = Gk*) ἀναθεματίζειν, *cf* Mt 26 74 (var Mor 42 24 ⲕⲉ ⲁⲩⲱ).

ϫⲓ ⲡⲉⲩⲱ *S*, ϭⲓ ⲡⲁ. *B, take as pledge*: Ex 22 26 *SB*, Deu 24 6 *SB*, Job 22 6 *S* (*B* ⲱⲗⲓ, *cf* 34 31), *ib* 24 3 *SB*, Ez 18 16 *B* ἐνεχυράζειν; sim ϥⲓ ⲉ.: Mor 25 118 *S* ⲡⲛϥⲓ ⲡⲧⲉ. of widow for debt. As nn: Is 58 6 *S* (*B diff*).

ⲉⲟⲩⲱ (?) *O* nn (?), in ⲉⲟⲩⲱⲧϥ ⲟⲩϭⲓⲣⲉ *hail*(?) Osiris!   *V* AZ 21 94, 22 84, 38 86, DM Index no 36.

ⲉⲟⲩⲉⲡ *A*   *v* ⲁⲅⲁⲡ.

ⲉⲟⲩⲓⲛ, ⲉⲩⲓⲡ *S* nn m, meaning unknown: BMEA 10577 about repair of 2 ⲥⲁⲙⲡⲧ ⲙⲡ(ⲡ)ⲉⲩ-ⲉⲉⲩⲓⲡ, *ib* ⲡⲉⲟⲩⲓⲡ ⲥⲡⲁⲩ ⲉⲧⲓ ⲙⲟⲟⲩ ⲉϧⲟⲩⲡ ⲉⲣⲟⲟⲩ (*sc* the ⲥⲁⲙⲡⲧ).

ⲉⲩⲛⲓ *B* nn f, *nether millstone*: Deu 24 6 (*S* ⲡⲉϣⲁⲩⲡⲟⲩⲧ ϧⲓⲱⲱϥ) ἐπιμύλιον; hence *mill*: Nu

11 8 (S ⲙⲏⲭⲁⲡⲏ, var ⲙⲁ ⲡⲡⲟⲩⲧ), Mt 24 41 (S ⲙⲏⲭ.) μύλος. Cf? εὐνή, KKS 34 n.

εϥⲗⲏⲟⲩ, ϥⲗⲏⲟⲩ (Jer 23 16, Ez 13 19) B nn, sg & pl, a. vanity, emptiness: Ps 5 10 (S ϣⲟⲩⲉⲓⲧ), 61 10 (S ⲡⲟⲩϫ), Is 30 7 (S ⲡⲉⲧϣⲟⲩ.), ib 15 (S ϫⲓⲡϫⲏ), 1 Cor 15 17 (SF ϣⲟⲩ.) μάταιος ; Ps 38 6 (S do) ματαιότης ; Va 57 134 ϩⲁⲡⲉ.ⲡⲉ ⲡⲉⲙϩⲁⲡⲡⲉⲧϣⲟⲩⲓⲧ εἰκῆ καὶ μάτην ; MIE 2 403 ⲟⲩⲉ.ⲡⲉ ⲡⲁⲓⲕⲟⲥⲙⲟⲥ.   b. adj, vain, empty : Ex 23 1 (S ϣⲟⲩ.), Jer 10 15 (S do), Mic 1 14 (SA do) μάταιος ; Miss 4 205 misled by ⲟⲩⲟⲩⲏⲃ ⲡⲉ.   c. advb, vainly, in vain : Ps 38 7, Is 41 29; Mt 15 9 μάτην ; Ps 126 1, Jer 8 8 εἰς μάτην (all S ⲉⲡϫⲓⲡϫⲏ) ; MG 25 212 ⲡⲉⲕⲉⲙⲓ ⲁⲛ ϫⲉⲉⲕϭⲟⲥⲓ ⲉ. (sic MS) εἰς κενόν ; Cat 9 ϩⲓⲕⲏ (εἰκῆ) ⲅⲁⲣⲡⲉ ⲉ. (cf Mt 5 22).

ⲙⲉⲧⲉϥⲗⲏⲟⲩ nn f, vanity, emptiness : Ex 20 7, Lev 17 7, Is 30 15, Jon 2 9 μάταιος ; Ps 4 3, Ro 8 20 (all S ⲡⲉⲧϣⲟⲩⲉⲓⲧ), Ps 61 10 (S ⲙⲡⲧⲉⲡⲣⲁ) ματαιότης ; Job 30 16, Ps 88 48 (S ⲉⲡϫⲓⲡϫⲏ) ματαίως ; Ps 23 4 ϫⲉⲡⲟⲩⲙ. = S ⲉϫⲡⲟⲩⲙⲡⲧⲉⲡⲣⲁⲉⲡⲓ ματαίῳ ; C 43 222 whoso sweareth falsely ⲓⲉ (ⲛ)ⲧⲉϥⲓⲣⲓ ⲡⲟⲩⲙ.

ⲉⲣ εϥ., act vainly, be vain, empty : Jer 28 17, Ro 1 21 (S ⲣ ⲡⲉⲧϣⲟⲩⲉⲓⲧ) ματαιοῦν.

εϥⲱⲧ, ⲁϥⲱⲧ B nn m or f, a kind of crocodile (?) : K 171 f زرن (cf Dozy 1 144), but BMOr 8775 136 m تمساح. V AZ 62 35, where ε. connected with Glos 405 Βαινεϥώθ ·ⲙⲥⲁϩ ; also Chron Pasch PG 92 385, where εϥώθ = κροκόδειλοι. In Job 20 18 (Lag) زرن (cf AZ 30 25) occurs for στρίφνος. ʿAbd al-Latif (DeSacy 147) has زرن = لجاﺓ, while in K 171 latter = ὄστρεον.

ⲉϣ SB cry v ⲱϣ.

ⲉϣ SF be able v ϣ vb.

ⲉϣ AF interrog v ⲁϣ.

ⲉϣⲟ, ϣⲟ B, ϣⲁ F nn m, bran : EpJer 43 B burning incense ⲉⲃⲟⲗ ϫⲉⲛⲡⲓⲉϣⲟ (BMOr 1319 14 pri man ϣⲟ) = F ⲱⲣⲉⲃ ⲡⲡⲓϣⲁ (? l ⲡⲓⲉϣⲁ) πίτυρον, Vulg ossa olivarum (πιτυρίς) ; K 260 ⲡⲓϣⲟ (var ϭⲱ) نخال. Confused ? with ⲉϣⲱ(ⲟ) sow ; cf πίτυρον a skin eruption.

ⲉϣⲟⲩ B v ⲉϫⲱ.

ⲉϣⲱ SBF, ⲉϣⲟ (PMéd), ϣⲟⲩ S, ⲉϩⲟⲩ A, ⲉϣⲁⲩ B (K), ⲉϣⲟⲩ SF, ϣⲁ- A, pl ⲉϣⲁⲩ SB, ϣⲁⲩ S, ⲉϣⲉⲩ F nn f (once B m), sow ; ϣⲉ S m (only Ps 16) : sg, Pro 11 22 SAB, Is 65 4, 66 3 B (S ⲡⲓⲣ) ὗς, ὕειος, Tri 263 S ⲧⲉ. خنزير, K 165 B ⲡⲓⲉϣⲁⲩ خنزير ; ShA 2 62 S ⲡⲉⲩϩⲟⲣ ⲛ ⲧⲉ., KroppB 35 S as bitch waiting for dog or ⲟⲩϣⲟⲩ ϩⲁⲟⲩⲕⲁⲡⲣ(ⲟ)ⲥ ;   pl, Mt 7 6 SB, ib 8 31 SB (but 30 ⲡⲓⲣ SB), Mk 5 12 S (B

ⲡⲓⲣ) χοῖρος ; BMis 209 S water ⲛϣⲁⲣⲉⲛϣ. ⲥⲓ ⲉⲃⲟⲗ ⲙⲙⲟϥ, Mor 34 41 S ἀγοραῖοι who ϯ ⲉⲃⲟⲗ (ⲡ)ⲡⲉⲛ-ϣⲁⲩ, Z 610 S ϭⲓⲛⲗⲓⲃⲉ (ⲡ)ⲡⲉⲉ., C 43 115 B ⲡⲓⲟⲩ-ϩⲱⲣ ⲡⲉⲙⲡⲓⲉ., BM 1252 F ⲡⲗⲟ(ⲅⲟⲥ) [ⲡⲡⲉ]ϣⲉⲩ, BMEA 10576 F ⲡⲓⲉϣⲉⲩ.   Wild swine : Louvre ostr Edfu '28 S ⲉϣⲟⲩ ϩⲟⲟⲩⲧ, El 42 A ϣⲁⲣⲉⲩⲧ (KKS 37).   Swine's flesh : Ps 16 14 S ⲁϥ ⲡϣⲉ (sic all MSS) = F ⲡⲉϣⲟⲩ (Mor 33 2) = B ⲡⲣⲓⲣ ὗς, Is 65 4, 66 17 B ⲁϥ ⲡⲉϣⲱ = S ⲡⲣⲓⲣ ὕειος ; swine's fat : PMéd 297 S ⲕⲛⲡⲉ ⲡⲉϣⲟ.   Scrofula(? χοιράς) : PMéd 316 S ⲡϣⲉⲡⲉϣⲁⲩ.

ⲉϣⲡⲉ A² v ⲉϣϫⲉ.

ⲉϣⲱⲡⲉ SA, ⲉϣⲱⲡ B, ⲉϣⲱⲡⲓ F conj v ϣⲱⲡⲉ.

ⲉϣⲱⲧ SABF v ϣⲱⲧ.

ⲉϣϫⲉ, ⲉϣϫⲡⲉ SF, ⲉⲓϩϫⲉᵃ, ϩϫⲉᵇ, ⲉⲓϩⲡⲉᶜ, ϩⲡⲉᵈ A (v AZ 63 144), ⲉϣⲡⲉ A², ⲓⲥϫⲉ, ⲓⲥϫⲉⲕ B conj, a. if : Ge 13 16 SAᵈ (varᶜ) B, Nu 23 27 S (var ⲉϣⲱⲡⲉ, B ⲁⲣⲏⲟⲩ), Jos 17 15 S, Jud 11 36 SB, Job 31 5 B (S ⲉⲓⲉ), Ps 21 9 SAᵈB (cf Mt 27 43), ib 130 2 B (S ⲉϣⲱⲡⲉ), Pro 11 31 SAᵈB, Is 47 ·12 B (S ϫⲉ-), Jer 13 23 SB, Zech 11 12 SAᶜB, Mt 6 23 S (B ⲉϣⲱⲡ), Lu 11 8 S (B ⲕⲁⲡ), Jo 3 12 SA²BF, ib 10 35 SAᶜB, Ac 25 20 B (S ⲉⲡⲉ-), 1 Cor 15 2 SBF, Cl 27 7 Aᶜ εἰ ; Mk 14 29 S (B ⲕⲁⲡ), Gal 3 4 SB, He 6 9 SBF, R 1 4 55 S εἰ καί, ib 1 4 54 ⲕⲁⲡ ⲉ., ib 2 2 29 S, LCyp 17 S sim εἰ καί ; Ez 3 11 B, 1 Tim 3 15 B (B ⲉϣⲱⲡ), MG 25 217, 220 B ἐάν (rare) ; ShRE 10 160 S ⲉ. ⲉϣⲱⲡⲉ ⲁⲡ-ⲧⲟⲩⲅⲁⲃⲉ, ShR 2 3 14 S ⲉ. ⲡⲡⲟⲃⲉ ϩⲟⲗϭ...ⲁⲗⲗⲁ ⲡⲕⲱⲣⲧ ⲥⲁϣⲉ, Miss 8 216 S ⲕⲁⲡ ⲉ. ⲁⲩⲥϩⲁⲓⲥⲟⲩ ⲡⲁⲕ ⲁⲗⲗⲁ ϯⲡⲁ-, AM 21 B ⲓ. ⲡⲁⲓⲣⲏϯ ⲉⲧϣⲟⲡ ⲓⲉ ⲙⲁⲣⲉⲡ- ; Pcod 26 S ⲉ. ⲥⲉ (var ⲉⲣⲉ) ⲉⲓⲉ ⲧⲁⲙⲟⲓ, AM 306 B ⲓ. ⲥⲉ ⲓⲉ ⲙⲟϣⲓ ⲡⲥⲱⲓ, BMis 160 S, ShA 2 285 S sim, ib 284 S ⲉ. (ⲉ)ⲣⲉ ⲉⲓⲉ ⲉⲧⲃⲉⲟⲩ ⲙⲡⲉⲧⲛ-.   b. as if, as it were : Pro 17 28 SAᵇ, ib 27 14 S (var ϫⲉ-) Aᵇ, He 12 11 S (B om) δοκεῖν, Hag 2 3 SAᵃ (B ⲙϥⲣⲏϯ) καθώς ; Ac 16 9 S (B om) ὡσεί ; ib 17 22 S (B ϫⲉ-), Ap 9 7 S (B ⲉⲟⲩⲟⲡ) ὡς ; Job 6 3 SB ὡς ἔοικεν ; Bor 170 91 S ⲡⲟⲉ ⲉ. ⲡⲧⲁⲅⲉⲣ ϩⲟⲧⲉ ὥσπερ, Z 263 S re-joiced ⲡⲟⲉ ⲉ. ⲡⲧⲁϥⲡⲁⲩ ⲉⲣⲟⲟⲩ (var BMis 246 ϩⲱⲥ ϫⲉ-) ; CaiEuch 465 B send us not to judgement ⲓ. ⲧⲉⲡⲧⲟⲩⲃⲏⲟⲩⲧ ⲁⲡ ὑπὲρ μή ; Bor 267 47 S stood up ⲉ. ⲙⲡⲉⲛⲉϥⲟⲩⲉⲣⲏⲧⲉ ϣⲱⲡⲉ ⲉⲡⲧⲏⲣϥ, Miss 4 587 S saw a man ⲉ. ⲡⲉⲡⲉⲓⲱⲧ ⲡⲁⲱⲗⲡⲉ, El 52 Aᶜ recorded as sin ⲉ. ⲙⲡⲓϣⲉ ⲁϥⲡ ⲡϣⲡⲉ of sick ; B here uses ⲓⲥϫⲉⲕ : Ge 37 9 ὥσπερ ; ib 40 16 (S ⲉ.) οἴεσθαι, Rec 6 184 fresh loaves ⲓ. ⲉⲧⲁϥϭⲉⲡⲟⲩ from oven = S ϩⲱⲥ ϫⲉⲡⲧⲁⲩ-, MG 25 302 ⲙϥⲣⲏϯ ⲓ. = S ϩⲱⲥ ⲉ., EW 55 vision ⲓ. ⲉⲓⲡⲁⲩ ⲉⲡⲁϣⲏⲣⲓ, Va 57 254 ⲙϥⲣⲏϯ ϩⲱⲥ ⲓ. ⲉⲩϭⲉⲡⲟⲩⲙⲟⲟⲩ ὥσπερ, C 43 173 martyr healed ϩⲱⲥ ⲓ. ⲙⲡⲉϥϣⲉⲡ ϩⲗⲓ ⲡϭⲓⲥⲓ, Rec 7 91 I was wroth ⲓ. ⲡⲁⲓⲟⲩⲱϣ ⲉⲓ ⲉⲃⲟⲗ.

c. exclamatory, *how, quam !* (*B* here ιϲϫεκ): Ge 28 17 *SB*, Ps 30 20 *B* (*S* ϫε-), ib 83 1 *S* (*B* = Gk), Si 20 1, ib 32 22 *S*, Jer 38 20 *B* (Gk om), Bar 3 22 *B*, Ro 10 15 *S*, ib 11 33 *F* (var = *S* ⲛⲑⲉ, *B* = Gk) ὡς, BIF 13 115 *S* light the lamp, е. ⲛⲁⲛⲟⲩ ⲡⲟⲩⲟⲉⲓⲛ.   d. *to be sure, indeed,* or as interrog : R 1 4 32 *S* е. ⲡⲉⲓⲛⲁⲉⲓ ⲡⲓⲙⲉⲛⲉ *vellem,* ib 1 5 27 *S* why wast thou brought ? е. ϯⲥⲟⲟⲩⲛ ⲁⲛ, ShBor 246 38 *S* е. ⲑⲉ ⲙⲡⲁⲥⲉⲃⲏⲥ ⲑⲉ ⲙⲡⲉⲩⲥⲉⲃⲏⲥ, KKS 234 *S* е. ⲟⲩⲡⲉⲛⲉ ⲓ̄ⲥ̄, TU 43 23 *A*[b] ⲉ̣. ⲥⲉⲣⲉϣⲉ ⲉⲛ ⲛⲛⲉⲧⲁⲩⲛⲕⲁⲧⲉ *surely they rejoice not over them that slept?* (*cf* AZ 57 138, 63 145), BG 17 *S* not thus did Saviour speak, е. ⲡⲓⲥⲃⲟⲟⲩⲉ ⲅⲁⲣ ⲉ̣(ⲉ)ⲡⲕⲉⲙⲉⲉⲩⲉⲛⲉ, Mor 32 9 *S* how fair a youth, е. ⲟⲩϣⲏⲣⲉ ⲙⲡⲗⲟⲅⲥⲓⲟⲥⲡⲉ, ? sim Mt 25 26 *SB* (Gk om).   е. introducing apodosis, *then :* Mor 38 84 *S* ⲉⲡⲉⲙⲡⲉⲕⲭⲟⲟⲥ...ⲭⲉϣⲱ ⲛⲁⲕ ϣⲁⲡⲟⲟⲩ е. ⲁⲓⲃⲱⲕ ⲡⲭⲓⲛⲥⲁ̣ϥ, BM 217 5 *S* ⲉⲡⲉⲙⲡⲉϥⲧⲁⲙⲓⲟⲕ е. ⲙⲡⲉϥϣⲱⲡⲉ ⲣⲱ ⲛϭⲓ ⲡⲉⲕⲣ ⲡⲙⲉⲉⲩⲉ ; *S* oftener ⲉϣⲡⲉ (*cf* ⲉⲓⲥⲡⲉ *s v* ⲉⲓⲥ): Ge 43 10 *S* (*B* ⲡⲉⲓⲥⲟⲡⲉⲓ) ἤδη ἄν, Is 1 9 *SF* (var ⲉϣⲭⲉ, *B* do) ἄν; Mt 11 21 = Lu 10 13 *S* (*B* do) πάλαι, Gal 4 15 *S* (*B*, Gk om), ShRE 10 162 *S* if He had not come, е. ⲁⲥϣⲱⲡⲉ ⲛϭⲓ ⲑⲁⲛ, ShA 2 341 *S* they swore not to..., ⲉⲙⲙⲟⲛ е. ⲁⲩ̣ⲟⲡⲟⲩⲡⲉ ϩⲱⲥ ϩⲁⲓⲣⲉⲧⲓⲕⲟⲥ, MR 4 72 *S* if thy mother had not sought refuge..., е. ⲁⲡⲏⲡⲧ ⲁⲡⲣⲁⲗⲓⲥⲕⲉ ⲙⲡⲉⲥⲥⲱⲙⲁ = Miss 4 137 *B* ⲙⲙⲟⲛ ⲡⲁⲣⲉ-.

ЄϤ *A*   *v* ⲁϥ *flesh, & fly.*

ЄϤⲢⲀⲤⲞⲨ (*sic,* not ⲉⲛ-) *B nn m,* a plant, ? *abrotonum, artemisia* : K 197 قيصوم (*v* Löw 79). *Abrot.* in P 44 83 = *S varia,* Ar هندبا & سذاب. Pey 46 е. *S* = سيكران (*l* زيكران), erroneously as in P 44 where 65 ′j = κώνειον, 83 = σμιχαραν (? σάκχαρον).

ЄϤⲢⲎϪ *F*   *v* ⲉⲃⲣⲏϫⲉ.

ЄϤϪⲒ *B*   *v* ⲃⲓϫⲓ.

ЄϨ *A* interrog   *v* ⲁϣ.

ЄϨⲞⲨ *A*   *v* ⲉϣⲱ.

ЄϨⲞⲨⲚ *B*   *v* ϩⲟⲩⲛ.

ЄϨⲰⲠЄ *A*   *v* ϣⲱⲡⲉ.

ЄϬⲢⲎⲒ *B*   *v* ϩⲣⲁⲓ.

ЄϨЄ *SBA,* ⲁϨⲏ (BIF 14 116, Mor 38 63) *F,* pl ⲉϩⲟⲟⲩ, ⲉϩⲏⲩ *S,* ⲉϩⲉⲩ *SAB,* ⲉϩⲁⲩ *A*², ⲉϩⲱⲟⲩ, ⲉϩⲉⲟⲩ *B,* ⲁϩⲁⲩ, ⲏⲣⲁⲟⲩ (*l* ⲉϩ-) *F nn m* (rare) & *f,* *ox & cow:* sg, Ge 41 20 f *SB,* 1 Kg 6 10 f *S,* Job 21 10 f *SB,* Pro 14 4 f *AB,* Is 1 3 f *SBF,* Hab 3 17 *AB,* Lu 13 15 f *B* (*S* ⲙⲁⲥⲉ), 1 Cor 9 9 m *B* (*S* do) βοῦς ; pl, Ge 13 5 *SB,* Ex 29 1 *SB,* Ps 65 15 *B* (*S* do), Is 30 24 *F* ⲁϩⲁⲩ, Joel 1 18 *A,* Jo 2 14 *SA*²*B* βόες ; Jer 27 11 *B* (*S* ⲕⲟⲩⲓ ⲙⲙⲁⲥⲉ), MG 25 205 *B,* Glos 69 *S* βοίδιον ; Lev 22 19 *SB,* 1 Kg

8 16 *S,* Eccl 2 7 *S,* Ez 46 6 *SB* βουκόλιον ; K 165 زاف (var Ann 1 50 ندابﻟ *i e* زاف ; by error) ; PMéd 215 *S* е. ⲡⲕⲁⲙⲉ (*sic l*), BM 528 *F* ⲡⲉϩⲟⲟⲩ (as sg) ⲡⲧⲁⲩ, ST 437 *S* ⲧⲉ. ϩⲗⲗⲟⲩ ; Job 1 3 *S,* Is 5 10 *S,* Lu 14 19 *S* ⲥⲟⲉⲓϣ ⲡⲉ. = *B* ϩⲉⲃⲉ ⲡⲉ. ζεύγη βοῶν ; 2 Kg 12 2 *S,* Is 17 2, 65 10 *B,* Am 6 4 *B* ⲟϩⲉ (ⲟϩⲓ) ⲡⲉ. βουκόλιον ; BSG 183 *S* е. ⲡⲣⲟⲙⲡⲧ = C 86 283 *B* ⲙⲁⲥⲓ ⲛϩ. brazen cow as torture, TT 76 *S,* Mun 38 *S* sim.

V also ⲃⲟⲉⲓⲧ.

ЄϨЄ, (ⲉ)ϩⲉ, ⲁϩⲉ, ⲁϩⲁ(Ryl 284) *S,* ⲁϩⲉ (? TU 43 5), ⲁϩⲟ (ib 6) *A,* ⲁϩⲁ, ⲁϩⲏ *B,* ⲁϩⲏ *F* particle, *yea* a. answers question affirmatively (Gk often om): 2 Kg 12 19 *S* is child dead ? е. (τέθνηκε), ib 20 17 *S* art thou Joab ? е. (ἐγώ), Miss 4 764 = Z 368 *S* art thou Ezekiel ? ⲉϩⲉⲟⲩ(*sic*), Dan 3 91 *B* did we not cast ? a. (ἀληθῶς), Mt 13 51 *SBF* have ye known ? a. (ναί), Ro 3 9 *SB* is He not ? a. (ναί), Miss 4 104 *B* is this the garment ? a. ⲑⲁⲓⲧⲉ, Gu 24 *S* shalt Thou be crucified again ? е. (ναί), BMar 208 *S* didst thou (ἆρα) at first suffer ? a., MG 25 247 *B* knowest thou (ἆρα) why ? a. (ναί), BSG 194 *SB* are gods then (οὔκουν) demons ? е.= ib 28 *B* a.,MG 25 176 *B* so (οὔκουν) he that works gets wage ? a., Aeg 274 *S* ⲉϥϣⲁⲛⲭⲟⲟⲥ ϫⲉⲉ. ἐπινευσάντων ;   b. varies with ⲥⲉ : Mt 5 37, Ja 5 12 *B* a. = *S* ⲡⲥⲉ, Pcod 26 *S* ⲉϣϫⲉ е. (var ⲥⲉ), BMis 347 *S* ⲥⲉ ϯⲣⲁϣⲉ = BSM 13 *B* a., ib 381 *S* ⲥⲉ ⲧⲱⲡⲟⲩ = ib 37 *B* a.;   c. sometimes ⲥⲉ more emphatic, or contradictory (PS 234 5, Z 309 32, C 41 23, MG 25 280) ; a. sim : Mor 44 34 *S* ⲁⲣⲁ ⲙⲡⲣⲱⲙⲉ ϩⲓⲡⲓⲙⲏⲛϣⲉ ⲡⲥⲁⲡⲁⲓ ϩⲉ ⲡⲉϫⲁϥ, Bor 263 27 *S* it may be said He came not for us all, we say ϫⲉⲁ., DeV 72 *B* sim, Ryl 284 *S* [I said] we gave no promise, they said to me ⲁϩϩⲁ ⲁⲕⲧⲓ ; MIE 2 409 *B* wast never granted rest ? a. I was ;   d. answers μή: Miss 8 147 *S* ⲙⲏ ⲁⲕⲥⲟⲩⲱⲡⲧ ? a., RNC 51 *S* ⲙⲏ ⲡⲁⲓ ⲁⲡⲡⲉ ⲡⲉⲕⲥⲃⲟⲩ⳿ ? a., BSM 13 *B* ⲙⲏ ⲕⲣⲁϣⲓ ? a. = BMis 347 *S* ⲁⲣⲁ... ⲥⲉ ;   e. with condit ⲉϣϫⲉ, ⲉϣⲱⲡⲉ &c, *if so, if indeed :* 1 Kg 25 8 *S* ⲉϣⲱⲡⲉ е. (Gk om), 2 Kg 18 23 *S* ⲉⲓ(ⲉ) е. (Gk om), 1 Cor 5 10 *S* (*B* ⲙⲙⲟⲛ) ἐπεί... ἆρα, ? Ex 2 14 *A* ⲉⲓⲁϩⲉ (*S* ⲉⲡⲉ) εἰ οὕτως, C 43 117 *B* ⲭⲟⲩⲟϣ ⲉⲓⲙⲓ ϫⲉⲁ., Mor 41 75 sim, RNC 74 *S* ⲉϣⲱⲡⲉ ϫⲉ е. ⲁⲕⲟⲩⲱ ⲉⲕⲉⲓⲙⲉ, ShA 2 284 *S* ⲉϣϫⲉ е. ⲉⲓⲉ ⲉⲧⲃⲉⲟⲩ, C 73 86 *S* sim, ShBM 209 4 *S* they loved us not, ⲉⲛⲉⲉ. ϫⲉⲛⲉ they would have stayed, R 2 1 9 *S* sim, Dif 1 85 *B* ⲓⲥϫⲉ a. ⲡⲉ ⲡⲉⲕⲥⲁϩⲓ (*cf* PO 3 443) ;   f. *verily, well then, indeed :* Ge 42 21 *B,* Mt 5 37 *B* (*S* ⲡⲥⲉ *ut sup*), CaiEuch 453 *B* a. ⲡⲟ̄ⲥ̄ repel me not ναί, Job 19 4 *S* a. ⲡⲧⲟⲟⲩⲛ (*B* ϫⲁⲥ ϫⲉ-) ναὶ δή ; Mor 22 118 *S* (*B* BSM 107 om) е. ⲙⲁⲧⲁⲙⲟⲓ ϩⲱ ⲉⲡⲉⲓⲣⲱⲙⲉ, Mor 19 97 = 18 94 *S* (*B* om) ⲙⲡⲓⲉⲣ ⲡⲟⲃⲉ ϣⲁⲧⲉⲡⲟⲩ a. ; Ps 34 21 *S*

(*B* ⲕⲁⲗⲱⲥ) εὖγε.   **g.** introduces question : Job 17 2 *S* (? *B* ⲟⲩⲟϩ) καί, Ez 27 32 *B* (*S* om) καί, Mor 44 36 *S* ⲉ. ⲡⲧⲟⲕⲡⲉ ⲡϣⲏⲣⲉ ⲙⲡⲛⲡⲉ, PS 381 *S* ⲁⲣⲁ (ⲁ)ϧⲏ ⲟⲩϧⲱⲃ ⲉϣϣⲉⲡⲉ ⲭⲛⲙⲙⲟⲡ, RNC 73 *S* ⲁ. ⳅⲉ ⲁⲕⲣ ϧⲟⲧⲉ, C 86 303 *B* (*S* BSG 197 om) ⲁ. ⲡⲑⲟⲕⲡⲉ ⲫϯ, Mor 37 206 *S* ⲉ. ⲡⲟⲩⲱϣ ⲙⲡⲡⲉⲡⲉ.

ⲉϧⲏ *SA²*, ⲉϧⲓⲉⲓ, ⲉϧⲓ *A*   *v* ϧⲏ *front*.

ⲉϧⲓ *F*   *v* ⲁϧⲉ *length of life & need*.

ⲉϧⲟ *A* particle with neg vb : Am 6 6 (*B* ϧⲗⲓ) ⲉⲙⲡⲟⲩⲙⲕⲁϩ ⲡϩⲏⲧ ⲡⲉϧⲟ οὐδέν.

ⲉϧⲟ *A* a treasure   *v* ⲁϧⲟ.

ⲉϧⲗⲏⲓ *F*   *v* ϧⲣⲁⲓ.

ⲉϧⲗⲉⲛ- *F*   *v* ϧⲟ(ⲉϧⲣⲡ-).

ⲉϧⲁⲙ *A*, ⲉϧⲟⲙ *O*   *v* ⲁϧⲟⲙ.

ⲉϧⲛ- *S*   *v* ϧⲛ- prep.

ⲉϧⲟⲩⲛ *SF*   *v* ϧⲟⲩⲛ.

ⲉϧⲛⲉ-, ⲉϧⲛⲁⲍ *SABF*   *v* ϧⲛⲉ.

ⲉϧⲱⲣ *A*   *v* ⲁϧⲟ.

ⲉϧⲣⲁⲓ *S*, ⲉϧⲣⲏⲓ *B*   *v* ϧⲣⲁⲓ.

ⲉϧⲣⲛ- *S*, ⲉϧⲣⲉⲛ- *B*   *v* ϧⲟ.

ⲉϧⲧⲁ *F*   *v* ϧⲧⲟ.

ⲉϧⲟⲟⲩ *B*   *v* ϧⲟⲟⲩ *day*.

ⲉϫⲱ, ⲁϫⲱ *S*, ⲉϭⲟⲩ, ⲉϣⲟⲩ *B* nn f, *tongs, pincers* : Ex 37 17 *B*, Nu 4 9 *SB*, 2 Chr 4 21 *B*, Is 6 6 *SB* λαβίς ; K 125 *B* كلبتين (which P 44 67 is ⲉⲣⲥⲉⲧⲏⲣ = ἀρυστήρ) ; Mor 53 40 *S* iron ⲉ. 3 ells long, Z 506 *S* ⲉ. for extracting thorns, PMéd 272 *S* how to extract tooth without ⲉ. ϧⲓⲡⲉⲡⲡⲉ, C 86 271 *B* ⲉ. ⲛϭⲟϫ ϣⲁⲗ (= ϣⲟⲗ). *V* Dévaud *Études* 1922 43.

ⲉϫⲱ *B*   *v* ⲁϫⲱ *viper*.

ⲉϫⲛ- *S*, ⲉϫⲉⲛ- *BF*   *v* ϫⲱ *head*.

ⲉϫⲛ- *S* without   *v* ⲁϫⲛ-.

ⲉϫⲱⲣϩ *BF*   *v* ϭⲱⲣϩ.

ⲉϫⲏⲩ *S*, ⲉϫⲛⲟⲩ *B*   *v* ϫⲟⲓ.

ⲉϭⲟⲩ *B*   *v* ⲉϫⲱ.

ⲉϭⲗⲁϭ *A*   *v* ϭⲗⲟϭ *gourd*.

ⲉϭⲉⲛ- *S*   *v* ϫⲓⲛ-.

ⲉϭⲉⲛ *O*   *v* ϫⲱ *head* (ⲉϫⲛ-).

ⲉϭⲱϣ *SA*, ⲉϭⲱϣ *B* nn m, f ⲉϭⲟⲟϣⲉ (PS 362), ⲉϭⲟϣⲉ (ⲉⲕ- Cai 8504) *S*, ⲉϭⲟϣⲓ (Nu 12 1) *B*, pl ⲉϭⲟⲟϣ, ⲉϭⲟⲟϣⲉ, ⲉϭⲱϣⲉ, ⲉϭⲁⲁϣ (P 131³ 64) *S*, ⲉϭⲁⲁϣⲉ, ⲉϭⲁϣⲉ *A*, ⲉⲟⲁⲅⲱ *B* (cf כוש Χούς Cush), *an Ethiopian*, i e of tribes S of 1st Cataract (cf AZ 40 129 ε. & 132 Beja), confusion as to their *habitat v* PSBA 32 28 : sg, Jer 13 23 *SB*, *ib* 45 7 *B*, Ac 8 27 *SB* ; pl Ge 2 13 *SB*, Ps 67 32 *SB*, Ez 29 10 *SB*, Nah 3 9 *AB*, Zeph 3 10 *AB* Αἰθίοψ ; P 131¹ 62 *S* Gihon flows from ⲧⲉϫⲱⲣⲁ ⲡⲡⲉϭⲟⲟϣⲉ, thence to ⲕⲟⲩⲓ ⲡⲭⲱⲣⲁ ⲡⲡⲉ. ⲙⲡⲡⲟⲩⲃⲁ, Blemmyes, Axumites &c, JKP 2 20 *S* ⲓⲉⲥⲁⲃⲁ queen of ⲡⲉϭ. (3 Kg 10). Miss 4 647, 766 *S* devil as ⲟⲩⲛⲟϭ ⲡⲉ., BSM 110 *B* sim, ShC 42 68 *S* Egyptians fleeing ϧⲛⲧⲟⲩ ⲛⲡⲉ., C 43 121 *B* ⲡⲓⲗⲁⲕϩ (Philæ) ϫⲁⲧⲉ(ⲛ)ⲛⲓⲉ. (cf *ib* 200 12), AM 23 *B* Philæ ⲛⲧⲉ ⲛⲓⲉ., *ib* 284 sim, C 43 90 *B* from Libya ϣⲁⲉϭⲟⲩⲛ ⲉⲛⲓⲉ., KKS 579 *S* ϣⲁϧⲣⲁⲓ ⲉⲡⲕⲁϩ ⲛⲡⲉ., PMéd 145 *S* in recipe ⲡⲁϧⲣⲉ ⲛⲉ. (what ?).

As name : ⲡⲉϭⲱϣ (Πεκῶς, Πεκῦσις, كوش), ⲡⲓⲉⲟⲱϣ (AM 156, C 89 23), ⲧⲉϭⲱϣⲉ (Τεκῶς, Τεκῦσις).

ⳅ

ⳅ, 6th letter of alphabet, called *S* ⳅⲏⲧⲁ (My 64), *B* ⳅⲓⲧⲁ, ⳅⲁⲧⲁ (K 1, Stern p. 418), زاد, زيد (P 43 238). As numeral ⳅ m & f = *seven* (ⲋ̄ = *six*) *BF*, rarely *S* (Br 84, KroppE, AZ 40 19).   **a.** very rare in Copt words, mostly replacing ⲥ : *SB* ⲁⲛⳅⲏⲃⲉ *q v*, *S* ⲉⳅⲏⲧ (AZ 23 111, 113), ⲉⲣⲃⲏⳅ *q v*, ⲙⲁⳅⲉ (2 Kg 6 13, ShA 1 240), ⲙⲁⲃⲧⲁⳅⲉ (J 23 45), ⳅⲱⲧⲙ (RAl 126), ⳅⲁⲭⲟ (BM 1135).   **b.** in Gk sim : ⲁⳅⲉⲃⲏⲥ (Mor 20 33), ⲃⲁⳅⲁⲛⲟⲥ (BMar 23, DeV 123), ⲉⳅⲩⲭⲁⳅⲉ (BMis 489), ϯⳅⲧⲁⲥⲉ διστά- ζειν (Z 269), ⳅⲱⲙⲁⲧⲓⳅⲉ (J 74 111) ; converse oftener : ⲁⲕⲣⲓⲃⲁⲥⲉ (PS 308), ⲁⲥⲡⲁⲥⲓ (BM 586, 592), ⲗⲱⲣⲣⲓⲥⲉ (J 106 151) ⲥⲩⲧⲏ (BM 1103), ⲟⲛⲟⲙⲁⲥⲉ (P 131¹ 81), ⳅⲏⲡⲥⲕⲧⲉⲓ συνζητεῖν (ShC 42 30).   **c.** ⳅ or ⲥⳅ for ⲥⲥ : ⲁⲗⲉⳅⲉ ἀλλασσείν (J 7 22 &c), ⲉⲗⲓⲥⳅⲉⲟⲥ (Z 324), ⲕⲩⲣⲓⳅⲓⲛ κηρύσσειν (Dif 1 99) cf ⲕⲩⲣⲓⲥⳅⲉ (BMis 259), ⲡⲗⲁⳅⲓⲛ (DeV 13) cf ⲡⲗⲁⲥⳅⲉ (P 131⁶ 25), ⲡⲁⲧⲁⳅⲉ (BM 307) cf ⲡⲁⲧⲁⲥⳅⲉ (Mor 27 16), ϧⲩⲡⲟⲧⲁⳅⲉⲥⲟⲉ (Cat 128) cf ϧⲏⲡⲱⲧⲁⲥⳅⲉ (JKP 2 46) ; rarely converse : ⲗⲁⲥⲥⲁⲣⲟⲥ (CO 437), ⲧⲣⲁⲡⲓⲥ- ⲥⲁ (Mòr 27 10), ⲥⲡⲟⲩⲧⲁⲥⲥⲉ (ST 250).   **d.** ⳅⳅ for ⳅ : ⲟⲛⲟⲙⲁⳅⳅⲉ (Br 91).   **e.** In ⲁⲛⳅⲏⲛⲱⲛ (C 86 122), which prob = Ἀντινοέων(πόλις), ⳅ for ⲧ, or ? influenced by Ar انصنا.   On possible phonetic value of ⲛⳅ- (ⲉⲛⳅ-) *v* Berl Sitzb '12 1044.   In transcripts of Ar ⳅ = ج or ب (EW 234 ff), some- times ⲋ (PMéd 29 ff).

ⳅⲁⳅ *B* nn, *asphodel* : K 183 اشراس (Löw 290). Coptic ?.

ⳅⲉⲛⳅⲉⲛ *B* nn m, *lizard, chameleon* : Bodl 325 154 حرذون (not جر), which K 172, P 55 18 = ⲁⲛ- ⲑⲟⲩⲥ *q v*. Coptic ?

H

ϩ, seventh letter of alphabet, called ϩⲏⲧⲁ S (My 64), ⲏⲧⲁ (Leyd 434), ⲏⲓⲧⲁ (K 1), ϩⲁⲧⲉ B (Stern p 418), اطه, اطيه (latter especially B according to P 43 239). As numeral m & f = *eight* BF(Ac 9 33), rarely S (Br 132). Represents vowels unwritten in earlier hierogl, though visible in certain half-consonants in later periods. **a.** dialectal interchange is irregular: final S ⲉ often = F ⲏ, otherwise ⲏ for ⲉ mostly mere inaccuracy, often in F documents, as Kr 228. **b.** in Gk words ⲏ for ⲉ rarely, as ⲗⲏⲧⲟⲥ, ⲥⲉⲡⲧⲏⲗⲉⲅⲏ (J 92 21), ⲧⲣⲏⲫⲁ (τρέφειν DeV 56); converse ⲁⲓⲥⲑⲉⲥⲓⲥ, ⲉⲥⲩⲭⲓⲁ, ⲥⲕⲉⲅⲉ. **c.** for ⲓ, as ⲁⲕⲣⲏⲃⲓⲁ, ⲕⲣⲏⲧⲏⲥ, ⲡⲟⲗⲏⲧⲓⲁ; converse ⲁⲑⲗⲓⲧⲏⲥ, ⲉⲧⲓⲗⲁ (αἴτημα), ⲡⲓⲥⲏ. **d.** for ⲩ, as ⲉⲡⲑⲏⲙⲁ, ⲙⲏⲥⲧⲏⲣⲓⲟⲛ; converse (oftenest) ⲁⲡⲟⲑⲩⲕⲏ, ⲕⲩⲣⲓⲍ, ⲙⲩⲡⲉⲅⲉ (PS 222), ⲥⲡⲩⲗⲁⲓⲟⲛ, ⲯⲏⲭⲩ (R 1 2 44). **e.** for ⲟⲓ, as ⲉⲡⲏⲧⲓⲟⲡ, ⲥⲧⲏⲭⲉⲓ; converse ⲕⲁⲧⲟⲓⲅⲱⲣⲉⲓ, ⲟⲓⲣⲡ (BM 1063). Esne-Edfû MSS S often double ⲏ, as ⲏⲏⲡ, ⲙⲏⲏⲧⲉ, ⲟⲩⲏⲏⲃ, ϭⲣⲏⲏⲡⲉ (all in BAp).

ⲏⲓ *SABFO*, ⲏⲉⲓ *SAA²*, (for ⲉ-, ⲓ- ? *v* AZ 25 115 n, *ib* 27 108), pl ⲏⲟⲩ *ABF* (*S* J 12 22 prob for ⲏⲓ) & sg as pl, nn m, **a.** *house*: Deu 5 6 *SB*, Pro 1 13 *SAB*, Is 31 2 *SBF*, Jo 2 16 *SA²B* οἶκος; Job 4 19 *SB*, Ps 48 12 *S B* οἰκία; Sa 13 15 *S* οἴκημα; Ps 108 10 *S* (*B* ⲙⲁ ⲛϣⲱⲡⲓ) οἰκόπεδον; Sa 17 4 *S* μυχός; *ib* 17 2 *S* ὄροφος; Job 11 14 *B* (*S* ⲙⲁ ⲛⲟⲩⲱϩ) δίαιτα; C 89 71 *B* (*S* ⲙⲁ ⲛϣⲱⲡⲉ) σκηνή; Jer 39 2, 8, *ib* 44 21 *B* αὐλή; BSM 39 *B*, AP 19 *A²*, AZ 21 100 *O* ⲁⲡⲏⲓ ⲡⲗⲟⲥ ⲡⲏⲓ ⲡⲏⲓⲙ, J 58 9 *S* ⲡⲁⲏⲓ ⲛⲃⲣⲣⲉ; ⲏⲟⲩ Nu 24 5 *B*, Deu 5 30 *B* (*S* ⲙⲁ ⲛϣⲱⲡⲉ), Ez 16 41 *B*, Nah 2 6 *A* (*B* diff), Mk 12 40 *F* (*B* ⲏⲓ), Va 57 247 *B*; part of house ⲙⲉⲣⲟⲥ ⲛⲡⲏⲓ sold or inherited: J 35, 74, BM 1017, CO 132, 145, quarter of house: J 13, 20, half: J 21, 44, Ryl 171. **b.** *household, family*: Ge 7 1 *B* (*S* ⲛⲁⲡⲉⲕⲏⲓ), Nu 1 4 *SB*, Ps 114 6 (113 17) *SB* οἶκος; Jo 4 53 *SA²B* οἰκία; C 43 21 *B* ⲉⲕⲉⲥⲙⲟⲩ ⲉⲣⲟϥ ⲡⲉⲙⲡⲉϥⲏⲓ ⲧⲏⲣϥ, CO 265 *S* ⲡⲉⲕⲏⲓ ⲧⲏⲣϥ men & beasts. ⲏⲟⲩ Ex 6 14 *B*, *ib* 12 3 *B*, Nu 26 2 *B*. With poss art & pron: Lu 9 61 *S* ⲛⲁⲡⲁⲏⲓ (= *B* ⲡⲏ ⲉⲧϩⲉⲛⲡⲁⲏⲓ) οἶκος; Mk 6 4 *S* ⲡⲁⲡⲉϥⲏⲓ (*B* ⲡⲉϥⲏⲓ) οἰκία; CA 105 *S* sim, C 89 61 *B* ⲛⲧⲁϫⲉⲙ ⲡϣⲓⲛⲓ ⲛⲁⲡⲁⲏⲓ = Miss 4 546 *S* ⲛⲁⲣⲱⲙⲉ.

ⲙⲉⲥϩⲛ-, ϩⲉⲛⲏⲓ *SB* nn, *born in the house*: Ge 15 2 *SB*, Jer 2 14 *B* οἰκογενής; Mor 43 258 *S* ⲧⲏⲡⲉ ⲛⲡⲉϥⲙⲉⲥϩⲛⲏⲓ ⲧⲏⲣⲟⲩ...ⲣ ϣⲟ.

ⲣⲙ-, ⲣⲙⲛⲏⲓ *SABF*, ⲣⲙⲛⲏⲓ *S* (ShC 73 160 as var), ⲣⲉⲙϩⲉⲛⲏⲓ *B* nn m & f, **a.** *member of household, domestic, kinsman*: Lev 18 17 *B* ⲣⲉⲙϩⲉⲛⲏⲓ (*S* ⲣⲱⲙⲉ), Is 31 9 *SBF*, Am 6 10 *AB*, Eph 2 19 *SB* οἰκεῖος; Mt 10 25, *ib* 36 *SB* οἰκιακός; Jer 3 4 *B* οἶκος; BHom 51 *S* ⲡⲉⲥⲣⲙⲣⲁϫⲓ ⲙⲡⲡⲉⲥⲣ. οἰκέτης; Nu 9 14 *B* (*S* diff) αὐτόχθων; TRit 498 *B* those she hath left behind ⲛⲉⲙⲛⲉⲥⲣ., J 5 46 & *pass* *S* ⲟⲩⲇⲉ ϣⲙⲙⲟ ⲟⲩⲇⲉ ⲣ. **f** ShC 73 xii *S* of Virgin ⲧⲣ. ⲛⲡⲁⲅⲅⲉⲗⲟⲥ. **b.** *monastic superintendent, warden* (Ladeuze *Pachôme* 287, dem in Rec 28 196): Miss 4 533 *S* ⲁϥⲧⲱϣ ⲡϩⲣⲉⲡⲣ. ⲙⲡⲙⲙⲉϩⲥⲛⲁⲩ = C 89 51 *B*, C 89 26 *B* the work that ⲡⲓⲣ. bade them οἰκιακός وكيل البيت, C 41 54 *B* our father assembled ⲛⲓⲡⲓϣϯ ⲛϣⲏⲣⲓ ⲛⲉⲙⲡⲓⲣ., ShC 73 44 *S* all employed shall be under ⲧⲉⲍⲟⲩⲥⲓⲁ ⲛⲡⲉⲩⲣ., *ib* 159 ⲡⲣ. var ⲡⲣⲱⲙⲉ ⲙⲡⲏⲓ, Mun 76 *S* ⲡⲣⲱⲙⲉ ⲙⲡⲏⲓ *praepositus domus*, cf *ib* ⲡⲉⲧϩⲣⲙⲏⲓ, Mor 51 38 *S* Victor ⲡⲣ. of the shoemakers (ⲕⲁⲥⲉ), Wess 18 46 *S* ⲟⲩⲡⲟϭ ⲛⲣ.ⲡⲉ & all archimandrites, Mor 51 34 sim. **f** Miss 1 383 *S* = Osir 41 among nuns.

ⲙⲉⲧⲣⲉⲙϩⲉⲛⲏⲓ *B* nn f, *kinship*: Lev 20 19 (*S* ⲥⲩⲅⲅⲉⲛⲓⲁ) οἰκειότης.

ⲣ ⲣⲙⲛⲏⲓ, ⲟ ⲡⲣ. *S*, *be akin*: Lev 18 6 (*B* diff) gloss ⲉⲧⲉⲥⲩⲅⲅⲉⲛⲏⲥ ⲛⲧⲁϥⲡⲉ οἰκεῖος; BMar 108 ⲉϣⲁⲩⲣ ⲣ. ⲛⲁϥ οἰκειοῦν.

ϫⲙⲡⲏⲓ *A* nn, *roof*: Zeph 1 5 δῶμα.

ⲏⲓ *SB* nn m, *pair, couple* (*v* AZ 37 27): Lev 5 11 *B* (*S* ⲥⲡⲁⲩ) ζεῦγος, cf Lu 2 24 ⲥⲟⲉⲓϣ, ϣⲱⲓϣ; HL 119 *B* angel brought ⲟⲩⲏⲓ ⲛⲱⲓⲕ...ⲁϥⲭⲁϥ ⲉϩⲣⲏⲓ, cf 120 he found ⲛ̄ ⲛⲱⲓⲕ, Ryl 159 *S* ⲧⲁⲓⲟⲩ ⲡⲏⲓ ⲛϭⲁⲗϭⲉ in rent, cf Wess 20 116, PG 65 368 ψωμίων ζεύγη, ST 43 *S* ϩⲙⲏ ⲡⲏⲓ ⲛⲕⲁϣⲉ in wages, Kr 242 *S*]ⲡⲏⲓ [ⲛϩⲁ]ⲗⲱⲙ.

ⲏⲓ *O* interjection, DM 7 24, 16 9.

ⲏⲗⲗⲉ *S* nn f, a measure: ST 235 in list, ⲡⲱϩ ⲟⲩⲏⲛⲣ ϣⲁϥⲣ ϫⲟⲩⲱⲧⲉ ⲡ̇ⲏ. ϩⲓⲧⲙⲡⲥⲉⲕⲏ (ζυγόν).

ⲏⲗⲡ *F* *v* ⲏⲣⲡ.

ⲏⲛ *S*, ⲉⲛ *B*, *en*, *een* DM 3 28, ⲁⲡⲁ *O* nn m, *ape*: P 46 158 *S*, K 165 *B* قرد; AZ 21 101 *O* ⲡⲁⲓⲟⲩⲧ ⲡⲁⲡⲁ ⲑⲟⲟⲩⲧ *ape Thoth*.

ⲏⲡⲉ *SA*, ⲏⲡⲓ *BF* *v* ⲱⲡ.

ⲏⲡⲥ *SB* *v* ⲁⲡⲥ.

ⲏⲣⲡ *SAA²BF*, ⲏⲗⲡ *F*, *erp* DM, ⲉⲣⲡ-, ⲣⲡ- *S* nn m (f twice, Ep 1 250), sg as pl, *wine*: Ge 9 21

SB, Ps 59 5 SB, Pro 3 10 SAB, Is 5 11 SBF, Ob 16 SAB, Ap 19 15 SB, MG 25 206 B ⲉⲑⲃⲉⲟⲩⲉⲙⲧⲟⲡ ⲡⲁⲅϯ ⲏ. ⲡⲁϣⲡⲉ οἶνος; P 44 66 S, MG 25 254 B = Gött Ar 114 107 نبيذ, K 131 B خمر = ⲁⲡⲁⲣⲭⲏ; EW 44 B ⲡⲧⲁⲓⲣⲓ ⲡⲟⲩϣⲟⲡⲥ ⲉⲣⲟⲕ ϭⲉⲡⲟⲩⲏ. ⲉϥⲟϣ, C 43 27 B ⲡⲏ ⲉⲧⲟⲩⲡⲟϥ ϭⲉⲡⲡⲏ., Hall 91 S ⲁⲡⲕⲣⲙⲟⲅⲟⲉⲓⲉ ϥⲓ ⲡⲁⲏ., Ep 531 S ⲁⲩⲥ(ϩ)ⲓⲙⲉ ⲕⲉⲗⲱ ϧⲉⲡⲉⲣⲡ [ⲉⲣⲟ]ⲓ, Ryl 359 S ⲡⲉⲏ. ⲉⲧϩⲛⲡⲕⲉⲗⲗⲁⲣ[ⲓⲛ, BM 1130 S ⲉⲧⲣⲉⲕϫⲱⲗϩ ⲡⲏ. ⲉⲃⲟⲗ ⲛⲧϯ ⲡⲡⲉⲓⲣⲱⲙⲉ, BP 4949 S the camels are come, ⲧⲁⲗⲟ ⲛⲓⲣⲡ ⲡⲁⲩ, Bess 7 66 S ⲡⲉⲧⲛⲁϭⲱⲗⲡ ⲡⲟⲩⲏ. ϩⲙⲡⲉⲕⲣⲁⲛ, Mor 51 24 S ⲁⲩϭⲱⲗⲡ ⲡⲥⲁⲡⲉⲗⲁⲕⲟⲛ ⲡⲏ. & found them good, 1 Kg 1 14 S ⲡⲉϩ ⲡⲟⲩⲏ. ⲉⲃⲟⲗ ⲙⲙⲟ περιαιρεῖν, Z 285 S after supper [ⲛⲧ]ⲉⲣⲉⲡⲣⲣⲟ ⲡⲉϩ ⲡⲏ., ShA 1 280 S ⲡⲉⲛⲧⲁⲩⲡⲉϩ ⲡⲉⲩⲏ. ⲏ ⲡⲉⲧⲙⲡⲟⲩϯϩⲉ ⲣⲱ, Mor 32 14 = P 129¹⁶ 50 S although hast had no wine ⲉⲓⲥ ⲡⲉⲕϩⲟ ⲧⲣⲉϣⲣⲱϣ ⲙⲡⲁⲧⲉⲕⲡⲉϩ ⲡⲏ. **a.** old wine (cf παλαιός), ⲏ. ⲁⲥ, ⲉⲣⲡⲁⲥ, ShA 1 194 S, Ryl 158 S, Kr 234 S opp ⲙⲣⲓⲥ, BM 473 S, WS 87 n S, CO 235 S opp ⲃⲣⲣⲉ, BM 588 S ⲏ. ⲙⲡⲁⲗⲉⲟⲛ. **b.** white, BKU 1 8 34 F ⲁⲗⲉⲩ, BM 697 F ⲁⲥⲡⲣⲟⲛ. **c.** perfumed, spiced, ShR 2 3 47 S ⲉⲧⲙⲟⲭϭ ⲉ[ⲡⲉⲥ]ϯ ⲣϩⲏⲡⲉ, Va 69 107 B ⲉⲧⲟⲓ ⲡⲥⲑⲟⲓ ⲡⲟⲩϥⲓ, ib 61 95 sim = Mor 25 13 S ⲛⲕⲟⲡⲧⲓⲧⲟⲛ (κονδῖτον). **d.** fine, choice (cf εὐάρεστος, κάλλιστος), BSM 27 B ⲉϥⲥⲟⲧⲛ, BMar 94 S, BM 1129 S ϩⲓⲛⲥⲁⲉ ⲡⲏ., ib 613 S ⲉⲥⲁⲓⲉ, CMSS 30 F sim. **e.** sweet, Wess 18 14 S a Sunday in Mesorê called ⲉϫⲙⲡⲏ. ⲉⲧϩⲟⲗϭ. **f.** new, must (v ⲙⲣⲓⲥ), BM 1042 S ⲙⲟⲩⲥⲟ(ⲟⲛ); cf **a.** **g.** from wine harvest, Kr 152, 153 S ⲛⲧⲱⲱⲗⲉ, cf WS 132. **h.** as προσφορά, BSM 26 B, BMar 92 S, J 70 44 S, Bodl(P) d 32 S, cf CA 143 S = Mor 54 91. **i.** spoilt, putrid, Miss 4 644 S ⲡⲏ. ⲛⲣⲉⲙⲁϫ ϩⲓⲗⲱⲙⲥ = C 41 42 B, but = Miss 4 395 عصير, ShA 2 131 S rich impose on poor ⲡⲏ. ⲉⲧⲗⲟⲙⲥ ⲁⲩⲱ ⲉⲧⲟ ⲛϭⲡⲧ, ShC 42 84, 91, 92 S, ShR 2 3 34, ShEp 56 S sim. **j.** in recipes, PMéd 335, Z 627, 630. **k.** whence brought: Fayyûm, CO 500-505, ST 135, 440; Tiloj, Ep 1 162; native & foreign, ShR 2 3 47 S ⲡⲕⲛⲙⲉ ⲙⲛ...ϩⲛⲡⲉⲭⲱⲣⲁ ⲉⲧⲟⲩⲏⲩ. **l.** wine vessels: ἀγγεῖον CO 213, ST 46, BKU 1 63; ⲁⲡⲟⲧ PS 368, Z 291, AM 82; διπλῆ BM 613, CO 234, Ep 101, AZ 23 68; διδιπλᾶ BKU 1 94, COAd 17; κάδος Ryl 206, BM 691, Kr 154; κοῦρ(ι) CMSS 20, cf 75, ST 440, BM 1234; κοῦφον Pcod 27, Ryl 210; λακοⲛ

(? λάκκος, v WS 23) Mor 51 24, Bal account λ. ⲉϥϩⲙⲟⲥ (? lager), λ. ⲙⲡⲓⲥ (? boiled); λακοⲟⲧⲉ Kr 152 (= κνίδιον), BM 473, 1064, WS 134, Mor 46 24; λαϩⲛ (λάη, v WS lc) Ryl 158, MR 5 34; σκεῦος BM 549, Ryl 360, CO 501; φορος, φορης (? φορά, v WS lc); ϣⲟϣⲟⲩ Jer 42 5 SB κεράμιον, BMis 387, CO 160, WS 119; ϩⲛⲁⲩ PS 370 = 369 ἀγγεῖον, CO 104, ϩⲛⲉⲩ BM 706, CMSS 51; ϩⲟⲧⲥ CO 348, Ryl 347, WS 88 198 (v ib 26); ϫⲡⲟϭ CO 160, ST 132, Ep 90; ⲟⲩⲥⲟⲉⲓϣ ⲡⲏ. pair (? of jars) PRain 4723 S.

ⲥⲁⲩ ⲏⲣⲡ SB, **ⲥⲉ ⲏ.**, **ⲣⲉϥⲥⲉ ⲏ.** S, wine-drinker: Pro 23 21 SB (DeV 75, Gk diff), Mt 11 19 SB οἰνοπότης, Si 34 35 S ⲙⲁ ⲡⲥⲉ ⲏ. συμπόσιον οἴνου.

ⲣ ⲏⲣⲡ, become wine: Jo 4 46 SBF.

ⲥⲁ ⲏⲏ. SF, wine-dealer: Ryl 255 S, BM 681, Kr 25 F.

ϫⲁ ⲏ. S, title: BMOr 6201 A 178. As name, Πῆρπ Ryl 196.

ⲏⲧ S nn m, meaning unknown: ST 357 ⲁⲩⲃⲱⲕ ϩⲁⲧⲛⲧⲓⲙⲟⲓ (?? Timotheus) ⲁϥⲛⲟϫⲧ ⲁⲃⲟⲗ ⲛϩⲟⲩⲛ ⲛⲡⲏⲧ (not ⲏⲓ). ? l ⲛⲡⲡⲏⲧ.

ⲏⲟⲩ v ⲏⲓ.

ⲏⲟⲩ O nn pl, meaning uncertain: AZ 21 100 that she put what is in her hand into mine, in her mouth into mine, in her belly into mine, ⲡⲉⲧⲉⲛ-(ⲛ)ⲉⲥⲏ. ⲛⲥⲓⲙⲉ ⲉⲛⲁⲏ. ⲛϩⲟⲟⲩⲛⲧ, ? limbs as pl of ⲏⲓ (Erman), genital members?

ⲏϭⲉ S, **ⲏϫⲓ** B, **ⲏϭⲓ** (?) F nn m, leek: Nu 11 5 SB πράσον; P 44 82 S, K 196 B كرّاث; TT 155 S ⲉϥⲟⲩⲉⲙ ⲅⲁϩ ⲡⲏ. = C 89 84 B, Tri 422 S do ϥ, Cai 42573 2 S in recipe ϭⲣⲟϭ ⲡⲏ., PMéd 56 S, Ryl 106 67 (sic l) S ⲙⲟⲟⲩ ⲡⲏ., PMéd 267 S ⲏ. ⲉϥϣⲟⲟⲩⲉ; leek-coloured: Ge 2 12 SB πράσινος (cf PSBA 32 28), Cant 5 14 S ⲡⲁⲅⲁⲡ ⲡⲏ. glossing ⲥⲁⲡⲡⲓⲣⲟⲛ, cf P 44 61 do زمرد = 43 31 زمرد الذبابي (sic l Guest, citing Qalqashandî 1913 2 104), Mor 47 141 S ⲟⲩⲡⲟⲣⲫⲩⲣⲁ ⲡⲁⲩ. ⲡⲏ., BMis 275 S stones ⲡⲁⲩ. ⲉⲡⲓϭⲉ decorating εἰκών, Mor 28 141 S ⲟⲩⲥⲕⲉⲩⲏ ⲡⲁⲩ. ⲡⲏ. (? glass) full of oil, BMis 538 S hell's flames ⲙⲡⲁⲩ. ⲙⲡⲏ., AZ 23 41 F list of clothes ⲟⲩⲁⲗϫⲁⲥ (أخضر Stern) ⲡⲡⲉⲛⲏⲥⲓ (or l ⲡⲁⲥⲉⲛⲏⲥⲓ), K 206 B ⲡⲏⲛⲏϫⲓ (sic) الأخضر, which also = ⲟⲩⲉⲧⲟⲩⲱⲧ. **ⲥⲁ ⲛⲏϭⲉ** S, leek-seller: COAd 49 send them ⲉⲙⲁ ⲡⲡⲥⲁ ⲡⲛⲏϭⲉ, Ep 566 ϣⲁ ⲡⲛⲏⲕ (sic).

Θ

For initial ⲑ- S v under ⲧⲣ-.

ⲑ eighth letter of alphabet, called ⲑⲏⲧⲁ S (BMis 8, My 66), ⲑⲓⲧⲁ, ⲑⲉⲑⲉ B (K 1, Stern p 418) تيتة (P 43 239, 44 137). As numeral m & f ⲑ̅ (BSM 31) = *nine* BF, rarely S (Br 128). Used sometimes in SA for ⲧ + ⳉ, as ⲙⲉⲥⲟⲛⲧ, ⲑⲙ̅ⲕⲟ (B ⲧⲣⲉⲙⲕⲟ), ⲟⲩⲟⲑⲉ; converse (archaic?, rare) ⲕⲁⲧⲣⲓⲥⲧⲁ (Cl 4 10, 42 4), ⲧⲣⲉⲥⲁⲩⲣⲱⲥ (PcodMor 14); in B regularly for S ⲧ (1) before liquids, as ⲑⲟⲗⲱⲙ, ⲑⲙⲁⲩ, ⲣⲟⲑⲃⲉϥ; (2) before tone vowel, as ⲑⲱⲕⲉⲙ, ⲑⲓϭⲓ, ⲟⲩⲉⲥⲑⲱⲡ; (3) beginning a syllable, after consonant, as ⲉⲙⲑⲟ, ⲥⲉⲃⲑⲁⲓⲟⲩ. **a.** in Gk words replaces or replaced by ⳉ (*q v*); **b.** or ⲧ, as ⲁⲕⲁⲧⲁⲣⲑⲟⲛ (Cat 47, 91), ⲁⲧⲣⲟϥⲃⲟⲣⲟⲥ (ἀθλ. Leyd 437), ⲃⲁⲣⲱⲑ (AZ 23 103 ff), ⲓⲱⲑ (RAl 130 &c), ⲟⲥⲉⲣⲟⲗⲟⲅⲟⲥ (EW 175), ⲡⲣⲟⲥⲑⲓⲙⲱⲛ (PLond 4 438 &c), ⲧⲣⲓⲥⲕⲓⲁ (Cat 141), ⲥⲡⲁⲑ̅ (C 41 19), ⲑⲣⲓⲧⲟⲛ (BSM 45); **c.** or rarely ϥ, as ⲑⲗⲟⲡⲟⲡⲟⲥ (ϥⲓⲗⲟ. BMis 259, 279), ⲑⲉⲃⲣⲱⲡⲓⲁ (J 70 30). In Ar transcripts represents ت, ث, as ⳉⲓⲡⲣⲓⲉ كربت (PMéd 230) ⲥⲁⲩⲑ صوت, ⲑⲁⳉⳉ تحت, ⲉⲑⲡⲉⲡ اثنان; or ط, as ⲑⲁⲗⲁⳉ طلم, ⲓⲉⲑⲓⲣⲟⲩ بطيرا (all from EW 234 ff).

ⲑⲟ B *multitude* v ⲁⲧⲟ.

ⲑⲟ B *earth* v ⲧⲟ.

ⲑⲟⲓ B v ⲧⲟ, ⲧⲟⲉ *spot*.

ⲑⲃⲁ B v ⲧⲃⲁ.

ⲑⲃⲁⲓ, ⲑⲟⲩⲁⲓ B v ⲧⲟⲩⲁ.

ⲑⲏⲃⲓ B v ⲧⲁⲓⲃⲉ.

ⲑⲱⲃⲓ B nn (?), meaning unknown: Pro 24 29 (Lect Instit Cath Paris) ⲛⲧⲉⲣ ⲣⲉϥϭⲓ ⳉⲟⲗ ⲡⲉϥⲑ. (gloss?).

ⲑⲉⲃⲓⲟ B v ⲑⲃⲃⲓⲟ (ⲧⲣⲃⲃⲓⲟ).

ⲑⲃⲁⲗ, ⲑⲃⲏⲗ B v ⲧⲃⲏⲗ.

ⲑⲓⲃⲥ B v ϯⲃⲥ.

ⲑⲟⲃⲧⲉⲃ B v ⲧⲟⲃⲧⲃ.

ⲑⲱⲃϣ, ⲑⲱϣⲡ B vb intr, *be astonished, stare with astonishment*: Bess 7 16 when woman with ointment entered (Mt 26) ⲡⲁⲣⲉⲟⲩⲟⲛ ⲛⲓⲃⲉⲛ ... ⲑⲟⲃϣⲡⲡⲉ (*sic*), C 43 206 ⲁϥⲑⲱϣⲡ...ⲉϧⲟⲩⲛ ⲉϧⲣⲉⲡⲓⲕⲟⲩϫⲓ ⲛⲁⲗⲟⲩ.

—— ⲉⲃⲟⲗ, same meaning: C 43 238 ⲁϥⲟⲣⲓ ⲉϥⲑⲟⲃϣ ⲉⲃ. *a long while.* *Cf* C 86 141 he spent long time ⲉϥⲑⲟⲃϣ ⲉⲃ.

ⲑⲱⲃϣ nn m, *influence* (astrological): K 49 ⲥⲧⲉⲣέⲱⲙⲁ ⲛⲉⲙⲡⲉϥⲡⲩⲣⲅⲟⲥ (برج signs of Zodiac) ⲛⲉⲙⲡⲉϥⲑ. تاثير, *ib* 54 among astron. terms ⲡⲓⲑ. do. *Cf* ⲑⲱⲣϣ & ⲧⲱⲃⲥ.

ⲑⲓⲕ B v ⲧⲓⲕ.

ⲑⲟⲕ B v ⲧⲟⲕ.

ⲑⲟⲕ, ⲑⲟⲕ B nn m, *mast of ship*: K 133, P 55 13 ماري, which P 44 54 S = ϣⲧⲉ. *Cf* ? ⲑⲟⲕ *fix*.

ⲑⲱⲕ B v ⲧⲱⲕ *fix & kindle*.

ⲑⲱⲕⲉⲙ B v ⲧⲱⲕⲙ.

ⲑⲱⲕⲥ, ⲑⲟⲩϫ B v ⲧⲱⲕⲥ.

ⲑⲟⲕⲧⲉⲕ B v ⳉⲟⲕⳉⲕ.

ⲑⲁⲗ B v ⲧⲁⲗ.

ⲑⲗⲏ B v ⲧⲗⲏ.

ⲑⲱⲗⲉⲃ B v ⲧⲱⲗⲙ.

ⲑⲉⲗⲏⲗ B v ⲧⲉⲗⲏⲗ.

ⲑⲗⲏⲗⲓ B v ⲧⲗⲏ.

ⲑⲗⲟⲙ B v ⲧⲗⲟⲙ.

ⲑⲱⲗⲥ B v ⲧⲱⲗⲥ.

ⲑⲁⲗⲓϭⲓ B nn m, a fruit-tree: BMOr 8775 133 مخيط (Dozy 2 572. Löw 68 = سبستان which K 178 = ⲥⲓⲥⲁⲙⲏⲡ ⲥⲏⲥⲁⲙⲟⲛ, *ib* 192 = ⲙⲓⳉⲁⲡⲁⲣⲧⲟⲩ ⲙⲩⳅⲁⲛⲁⲣⲟⲥ ?).

ⲑⲟⲙ B v ⲧⲟⲙ.

ⲑⲱⲙ B v ⲧⲱⲙ *shut & sharpen*.

ⲑⲙⲏ B v ⲧⲙⲏ.

ⲑⲙⲏⲓ B v ⲙⲉ *truth*.

ⲑⲟⲩⲙⲉ B nn, zodiacal sign *Virgo*: K 50 ⲡⲁⲣⲑⲉⲛⲟ(ⲥ)ⲡⲉ سنبلة, ⲑⲟⲩⲙⲉ do.

ⲑⲙⲁⲓⲟ B v ⲧⲙⲁⲉⲓⲟ.

ⲑⲁⲙⲓⲟ B v ⲧⲁⲙⲓⲟ.

ⲑⲉⲙⲙⲓⲟ B v ⲧⲓⲙⲟ.

ⲑⲙⲓⲥ B, ⲑⲉⲙⲓⲥ F nn pl, *dust*, ? l ἀτμίς: Is 5 24 F (*sic* l, S ϣⲟⲉⲓϣ, B ⲣⲏⲓⲥⲓ) χνοῦς (var χοῦς), C 86 290 ⲁⲩϥⲓ ⲛⲡⲓⲑ. ⲉⲃⲟⲗ ϧⲉⲛⲡⲓⲕⲁⲥ in tomb = χοῦς. (v *ib* 371, 380 n on meanings of ϣⲱⲓϣ). *Cf* ⲙⲓⲥ.

ⲑⲱⲙⲥ B v ⲧⲱⲙⲥ.

ⲑⲙⲉⲥⲓⲟ B v ⲙⲉⲥⲓⲟ.

ⲑⲟⲙⲧⲉⲙ B v ⳉⲧⲟⲙⲧⲙ.

ⲐⲎⲚ (ϩⲏⲡ Z 630) *SABF* nn m (Bor 241 55, AM 218), *sulphur*, ? is Gk θεῖον: Deu 29 23 *SB*, Ps 10 6 *SB*, Is 30 33 *SBF*, Ap 19 20 *SB* θεῖον, P 44 66 *S* ⲑⲉⲓⲟⲛ· ⲡⲉⲧⲟⲏⲛ كربيت; Dan 3 46 *B* (*S* ⲙⲁⲣⲉ, cf Tri 526) νάφθα; often with ⲗⲁⲙⲭⲁⲧⲡ: PS 259 *S*, EL 46 *A*, BMar 23 *S*, AM 218 *B*, CO 43 167 *B*; or ⲁⲥⲫⲁⲗⲧⲟⲡ: *ib* 70, 72 *B*; or ⲥⲓϥⲓ: AM 34 *B*; ⲑ. ⲡⲁⲧⲱϣⲙ *S*, *unslaked sulphur*: Z 628, *ib* 630 ϩⲏⲡ ⲉⲙⲡⲁⲧⲟⲩⲁϣⲙⲉϥ (cf ⲕⲟⲡⲓⲁ ⲡⲁⲧⲱ.); ⲑ. ⲉϥⲟⲩⲱⲧ *S*, *fresh sulphur*: PMéd 278, cf ⲑ. ⲁⲡⲉⲣⲟⲡ (ἄπυρον) *ib* 139 ff & DM vo 9 6.

ⲐⲰⲚ *B* v ⲧⲱⲛ.

ⲐⲎⲚⲒ, ⲑⲉⲡⲓ (Cat 89) *B* vb intr, *sprout, grow*: Mk 4 27 (*S* ϯ ⲟⲩⲱ) βλαστάνειν. ? = εὐθηνεῖν (IgR.)

ⲐⲀⲚⲚⲞ *B* vb tr, *accomplish, perform*: PO 11 349 ⲉⲟⲩⲱϣ ⲉⲑ. ⲟⲩⲣⲱⲃ ⲡⲁⲣⲁ ⲡⲓⲕⲁⲡⲱⲛ *viz* in consecrating archbishop. *Cf* ? ⲧⲁⲡⲟ.

ⲐⲞⲠⲦⲉⲚ *B* v ⲧⲟⲡⲧⲛ.

ⲐⲰⲚϢ ⲉⲃⲟⲗ *B* v ⲑⲱϩϣ.

ⲐⲀⲠⲉⲚ *B* v ⲧⲁⲡⲛ.

ⲐⲢⲉ *B* nn v ⲧⲣⲉ.

ⲐⲢⲞ *B* v ⲧⲣⲟ.

ⲐⲰⲢⲒ *B* v ⲧⲱⲣⲉ *willow*.

ⲐⲢⲎⲂ *B* v ⲧⲏⲣ.

ⲐⲢⲒⲘ *B* nn m, *quicksilver*: K 203 زيبق. In P 44 65 quicks. is (ϩⲩ)ⲁⲣⲁⲣⲅⲩⲣⲟⲡ · ⲍⲁⲏⲡⲁⲕⲟⲡ (*l* ⲍⲁⲏ.).

ⲐⲀⲢⲘⲒ *B* nn f, *leathern shield, cuirass*: K 116 درقة (*sic*), طارقة. ⲑ. prob miswritten for one of these.

ⲐⲢⲀⲚ *B*, ⲧⲣⲉⲛ DM nn m, *tin*: Nu 31 22, Zech 4 10 both (*S* ⲃⲁⲥⲛϭ), Ez 22 18 κασσίτερος, -τέρινος; K 203 قصدير.

ⲐⲰⲢⲠ *B* v ⲧⲱⲣⲡ *sew*.

ⲐⲢⲀⲠⲤ *B* v ⲧⲱⲣⲡ *sew*.

ⲐⲢⲒⲢ *B* v ⲧⲣⲓⲣ.

ⲐⲈⲢϢ, ⲑⲏⲣϣ (once) *B* nn m, *linseed*: K 194, 266 بزرالكتان. *Cf S* ⲃⲁⲣⲡⲉϩ, ⲉϥⲣⲁ ⲙⲁⲣⲉ.

ⲐⲢⲞϢ vb, ⲑⲱⲣϣ nn *B* v ⲧⲱⲣϣ.

ⲐⲰⲢϢ *B* vb intr, *stare in astonishment* (?): C 86 334 wild beasts stood by terrified asses ⲉⲩⲑ. (var ⲑⲟⲣϣ) ⲉϩⲣⲏⲓ ⲉϫⲱⲟⲩ = دهش. *Cf* ? ⲑⲱϩϣ.

ⲐⲢⲞϢⲢⲈϢ *B* v ⲧⲣⲟϣⲣⲉϣ.

ⲐⲞⲨⲢⲀϪⲒ *B* nn m = θωράκιον: K 120 تراج, part of monastic costume. *V* Ep 1 150 n.

ⲐⲞⲨⲤ *B* nn m, *point of beard*: MG 25 254 hair grew on lips ⲡⲉⲙⲡⲓⲑ. ⲛⲧⲉ ⲧⲉϥⲙⲟⲣⲧ εἰς τὸ ἄκρον τοῦ πώγωνος, C 43 196 beard ⲟⲓ ⲡⲑ. ⲉⲡⲉⲥⲏⲧ (of Theodore Stratelates, as in Hyvernat *Alb* xvi).

ⲐⲰⲦ *B* v ⲧⲱⲧ *persuade, mix & scrape*.

ⲐⲰϯ *B* v ⲧⲱⲧⲉ.

ⲐⲎⲞⲨ *B* v ⲧⲏⲩ.

ⲐⲞⲨⲀⲒ, ⲑⲃⲁⲓ *B* v ⲧⲟⲩⲁ.

ⲐⲞⲨⲰ⳿ *B* v ⲧⲟⲩⲱ⳿.

ⲐⲰⲞⲨⲒ *B* v ⲧⲟⲟⲩⲉ.

ⲐⲞⲨⲐⲞⲨ *B* vb intr, *to have the skin disease lentigo*: Lev 22 22 ⲉϥⲑ. (*S* ⲁⲣϣⲁⲛ *q v* (ⲁⲣϣⲓⲛ)). Prob ⲑⲟⲩ ⲑⲟⲩ, cf ⲧⲟ ⲧⲟ (ⲧⲟⲉ) *spotted*.

ⲐⲞⲨⲈⲖⲞ, ⲧⲟⲩⲗⲟ *B* vb caus, *overflow, submerge*: Job 14 19 (no *S*) ⲑ. κατακλύζειν, where TRit 321 (= Va 46 51) has ⲑⲱⲟⲩⲉⲗ, Va 57 225 ⲡⲓⲙⲟⲩ ⲡⲣⲱⲟⲩ ϣⲁϥⲧ. ἐπικλύζειν. *Cf* ⲟⲩⲱⲗⲉ.

ⲐⲒⲞⲨⲎⲞⲨⲦ *B* v ⲟⲩⲱ *cease* (ϯ ⲑ. ⲉⲃⲟⲗ).

ⲐⲞⲨⲰⲦ, ⲑⲟⲩⲟϯ *B* v ⲧⲟⲩⲱⲧ.

ⲐⲰⲞⲨϯ *B* v ⲧⲟⲟⲩⲧⲉ.

ⲐⲰϢ, ⲑⲟⲩϣ *B* v ⲧⲱϣ.

ⲐⲈϢⲈ *B* v ⲧⲉϣⲉ.

ⲐⲰϢⲠ *B* v ⲧⲱϩϣ.

ⲐⲀϤ *B* nn v ⲧⲁϥ.

ⲐⲀϤ⳿ *B* vb tr, meaning unknown (cf Stern 343): C 86 18 = ROC 9 328 = AZ 13 56 martyr in fiery pit, by Christ's power ⲁⲩⲑⲁϥ ⲁⲩⲟϥⲟϩ ⲙⲙⲟϥ before king. Ethiop ROC 11 349 21 om incident.

ⲐⲒϤⲒ *B* nn m, *swelling, tumour*: K 158 ورم. AZ 13 56 'ex Scala' vb intr, ⲁϥ. انتفخ *swell*.

ⲐⲞϤⲦⲈϤ *B* vb tr, *let fall* drop by drop (rain): MG 25 258 sky began ⲉⲑ. ⲛϩⲁⲛⲧⲉⲗⲧⲓⲗⲓ = Gött Ar 114 108 نقط.

ⲐⲰϦ *B* v ⲧⲱϩ vb.

ⲐⲒϦⲒ *B* v ϯϩⲉ.

ⲐⲞϦⲦⲈϦ *B* v ⲧⲁϦⲧϩ.

ⲐⲞϦ *B* v ⲧⲱϩ vb, ⲧⲱϩ *chaff*.

ⲐⲞϦ *B* vb intr, *become bad*: Cat 72 Judas ⲁϥⲑ. ⲛϩⲟⲩⲟ in his iniquity, *ib* 189 sim, Va 57 189 ⲉϥⲑⲏⲟⲩ ⲡⲑ. ⲛϩⲟⲩⲟ ⲟⲩⲟϩ ⲉϥϣⲱⲡ ⲙⲙⲟⲥ, *ib* 262 ϣⲁϥⲑ. ⲛϩⲟⲩⲟ ἀνευλαβέστερος γενόμενος. *Cf* Mk 5 26 *B* ⲧϩⲟ & v ⲧϩⲟ *S*.

ⲐⲰϦⲘ *B* v ⲧⲱϩⲙ.

ⲐⲰϦⲤ *B* v ⲧⲱϩⲥ.

ЄI, I

ı or єι, ninth letter of alphabet, called ιωτα (Leyd 434, Tri 483, My 66), ιοτα (Stern p. 418), ιαγⲇⲁ (K 1), ⲓⲃⲩ (P 44 129, Tri lc), ⲓⲱⲩ (Stern lc). As numeral m & f = ten BF, rarely S except in semi-Gk documents. On relation to hierogl half-consonants & vowels v Sethe *Verbum* 1 90-108. In S (mostly archaic) AF єι after vowel often for ı, as ⲁєι-, ⲉⲣⲟєι, ⲛєι, ⲕⲟγєι; similarly ⲉєι- for єι; converse (S archaic) as ⲣⲟⲓ̈ⲥ, ⲥⲁⲓ̈ⲛ, ⲟγⲓ̈. Dialectal equivalents: **a.** S єι = BF ı, as ⲉιⲱⲧ, ⲟⲉⲓⲕ, ⲣⲟⲉⲓⲙ, ⲟγⲉⲓⲡⲉ. **b.** BF -ı = S -ⲉ, as ⲏⲡⲉ, ⲙⲁⲧⲉ, ⲙⲉⲉγⲉ, ⲱⲏⲣⲉ, ⲥ̄ⲟⲟγⲡⲉ & names as ⲁⲡⲧⲱⲡⲉ, ⲕγⲣⲉ, ⲯⲱⲧⲉ. **c.** BF -ı = S om, as ⲉⲙⲣⲁⲓ, ⲓⲱⲓ, ⲕⲁⲣⲓ, ⲙⲉⲓ, ⲡⲉⲉⲓ, ⲟγⲱⲡⲓ; also B ı- = S om, as ⲓⲟⲣ, besides erroneous ı-, as ⲓⲟⲣⲓ B & names as ⲓⲉⲛⲱⲭ, ⲓⲉⲥⲁⲕ, ⲓⲉⲣⲏⲡⲡⲁⲓⲟⲥ (v Ep 1 238). **d.** A ⲉⲓⲉ, ⲓⲉ = S -ⲉ, as ⲕⲡⲡⲓⲉ, ⲡⲣⲣⲓⲉ, ⲟγⲉⲓⲉ, ⲣⲉⲓⲉ; also erroneous S, as ⲣⲓⲏ for ⲣⲉ (Mt 19 8 S, Ep 382) or ⲣⲏ. (Job 31 15 Miss 4 631) **e.** A єι = S ⲏ, as ⲣⲏ, ⲥⲙⲏ, ⲟγⲏⲏⲃ, ⲣⲁⲏ. **f.** in Gk words: ı for єι, in infin S (archaic) A for -ⲉⲓ̂ⲛ, ⲁⲓⲧⲓ, ⲑⲉⲱⲣⲓ, B (always) ⲁⲁⲓⲧⲓⲍ, ⲫⲟⲣⲓⲛ; ⲁⲡⲟⲇⲓⲍⲓⲥ, ⲧⲉⲗⲓⲟⲥ, ⲭⲣⲓⲁ; converse S ⲉⲡⲉⲓⲃⲟγⲗⲏ, ⲟⲣⲇⲉⲓⲛⲟⲛ. **g.** ı, єι for ⲏ, as ⲁⲥⲕⲓⲧⲏⲥ, ⲗⲓⲥⲧⲏⲥ, ⲡⲓⲧⲏ; converse ⲁⲕⲣⲏⲃⲱⲥ, ⲓⲣⲏⲡⲏ. **h.** ı for γ, as ⲗⲓⲡⲏ, ⲕγⲡⲁⲓⲡⲟⲥ; converse ⲁⲣⲅⲟⲙⲟⲥ, ⲏⲗγⲕⲓⲁ. **i.** ı for ⲟⲓ, as ⲗⲓⲡⲟⲛ, ⲡⲣⲟⲡⲓⲁ; converse ⲕⲟⲓⲃⲟγⲧⲟⲥ, ⲟⲓⲣⲏⲡⲏ (BMis 250). For irregular uses SSᵃ of ı, єι v Ep 1 239.

єι SAA²F, ı BFA², (ⲉιγ 5 times in letter PMich 4558 S), ⲡⲏγ, ⲡⲛⲟγ used as its qual, ⲁⲙⲟγ as imperat, qq v, vb intr, *come, go*: Ge 27 35 SB, 2 Kg 11 10 S, Job 1 15 SB, PS 104 31 SB, Is 50 2 SB, Mt 6 10 SBF, Jo 4 7 SA²BF, ib 10 10 SAA²B ἔρχεσθαι, Sa 1 5 SB ἐπέρχ., Mt 4 11 SB προσέρχ.; Ps 101 13 SB, Is 35 4 B (SF ⲡⲏγ), Ap 2 25 SB ἥκειν; Am 9 10 S (AB ⲱⲱⲡⲓ) γίνεσθαι, cf Mk 14 31 S (var ⲱⲱⲡⲉ, B ⲫⲟⲣ) δεῖν, Ex 2 17 S (B ı ⲉⲣⲣⲏⲓ), Ac 23 16 B (S om) παραγίν.; Jud 4 8 S πορεύειν; PS 98 S ⲁⲓⲉⲓ ⲉⲃⲟⲏⲑⲓ ⲉⲣⲟⲥ, Br 239 S ⲁⲡⲟγⲟⲉⲓⲛ ⲉⲓ ⲛⲁγ, C 41 51 B ⲁϥⲟⲣⲉⲡⲓⲙⲱⲟγ ı (inundation), AM 32 B ⲕⲁⲗⲱⲥ ⲁⲕⲓ (cf ⲉⲓ ⲉⲣⲟγⲛ), PMéd 272 S tooth ⲧ(ⲣ)ⲉⲥⲉⲓ without forceps, ShMiss 4 822 S of clothes fitting ⲙⲡⲉⲛⲕⲉⲣⲟⲓⲧⲉ ⲉⲧⲙⲁγ ⲉⲓ.

As auxil. or subsidiary, *be about to* (cf ⲛⲟγ) SA²BF: **a.** +2 or 3 fut, Ac 16 27 S (B om) μέλλειν, Si 4 33 S, Jo 16 21 SA²(B ⲛⲟγι); PS 167 S ⲁⲓⲉⲓ ⲉⲓⲡⲁⲃⲱⲕ, Mor 31 56 S sun ⲉϥⲱⲁⲡⲉⲓ ⲉϥⲡⲁⲣⲱⲧⲛ,

AM 56 B ⲉⲧⲁⲓⲓ ⲍⲉ ⲉⲓⲡⲁⲙⲟγ, Z 326 S ⲛⲧⲉⲣⲉϥⲉⲓ ⲉϥ-ⲡⲁⲙⲟγ ⲟⲧⲉ ἦλθε κοιμηθῆναι (often 2 fut thus without єι, Ge 43 25 S, Job 26 2 SB, Lu 21 7 SB), PLond 5 132 S ⲁⲡⲉⲡⲉⲓⲱⲧ ⲉⲓ ⲉⲃⲁⲙⲟγ; **b.** + ⲍⲉ- & 2 fut, BMis 257 S ⲁϥⲉⲓ ⲍⲉⲉϥⲡⲁϥⲟⲥ̄ϥ ⲉⲃⲟⲗ, C 41 39 B ⲁϥⲓ ⲍⲉⲉϥⲡⲁⲁⲙⲟⲡⲓ ⲛⲧⲉϥϫⲓⲍ, Bodl(P) d 21 S ⲁⲡⲓ ⲍⲉⲡⲁⲉⲓ ⲉⲣⲏⲥ; **c.** + 2 pres = *whilst*, Ac 5 15 S ⲉⲣⲉⲡⲉⲧⲣⲟⲥ ⲉⲓ ⲉϥⲡⲏγ ἐρχόμενος, PS 13 S ⲉⲣ-ⲱⲁⲡⲡⲉⲭ̄ⲥ̄ ⲉⲓ ⲉϥⲡⲏγ, C 41 28 B ⲁⲓⲓ ⲉⲓⲙⲟⲱⲓ; **d.** + prep ⲉ- & vb, R 1 3 80 S ⲁⲡⲉⲓ ⲉⲙⲟγⲟγⲧ ⲙⲡⲉⲡ-ⲱⲏⲣⲉ, BMis 261 S ⲁϥⲉⲓ ⲉⲡⲁⲣⲁⲧⲉ, BMOr 9525 8 S ⲙ̄ⲡⲡⲁγ ⲡⲧⲁⲓⲉⲓ ⲉϥ ⲡⲁϥ (ⲡ)ⲧⲭⲉⲓⲣⲟⲧⲟⲡⲓⲁ; **e.** + ⲡ & vb (cf B ⲡⲛⲟγ ⲡ-) *grow gradually*, Mk 5 26 S ⲡⲧⲁⲥⲉⲓ ⲛⲉⲟ (var ⲉ-) εἰς χρεῖον ἔρχ., ShMIF 23 146 S of tree ⲁⲥⲉⲓ ⲛⲣ ⲣⲗⲗⲱ.

ϭⲓⲡⲉⲓ SF n̄n f, ϫⲓⲡⲓ B nn m: 2 Thes 2 8 B (S = Gk) παρουσία, BMis 142 S ⲧϭ. ⲱⲁⲣⲟⲡ of Saviour, BSM 27 B ⲡⲍ. ⲡⲡⲉⲧⲉⲛⲥⲁⲗⲁⲅⲍ to our house.

єι S nn, *coming, advent*: ShZ 595 ⲣⲡⲟγⲉⲓ ⲕⲡⲏγ.
A. with following preposition.

єι ⲉ- SAA²BF, *come to*, seldom of persons (cf єι ⲱⲁ-): 1 Kg 24 4 B, Job 3 9 SB, Mk 11 27 SB ἔρχεσθαι εἰς, Lu 19 5 ἔρχ. ἐπί; Is 35 10 SBF ἥκειν εἰς; Lu 22 33 S (B ⲱⲉ) πορεύεσθαι εἰς; Jo 7 8 SA² ἀναβαίνειν εἰς, MG 25 233 B ⲡⲧⲉⲟγⲙⲉγⲓ ı ⲉⲣⲟⲕ ἀναβ. σοί; C 86 166 B ⲁⲡⲉϥⲣ̄ⲛⲧ ı ⲉⲣⲟϥ, BMis 267 S sim, J 80 19 S often ⲁϥⲉⲓ ⲉⲡⲁⲙⲟγ.

—— ⲉⲣⲛ- S, *come to, arrive at*: Nu 20 6 S (B ⲉⲣⲣⲉⲛ-) ἔρχ. ἐπί, Jud 11 12 S ἔρχ. πρός; 1 Kg 7 10 S προσάγειν ἐπί; Ac 10 17 S ἐφιστάναι ἐπί; PS 20 S ⲁⲓⲉⲓ ⲉⲣⲏⲧⲡγⲗⲏ.

—— ⲉⲣⲁⲧ- S, *come to* superior or dignitary: Mk 5 15 S (B ⲣⲁ-, cf Lu 8 35 S ⲱⲁ-), Lu 18 16 S (B do, cf Mk 10 14 S ⲱⲁ-) ἔρχ. πρός; Nu 21 7 S (var ⲱⲁ-, B ⲣⲁ-) παραγίνεσθαι πρός; Miss 8 221 S people shall ⲉⲓ ⲉⲣⲁⲧϥ ⲙⲡⲉⲕⲧⲟⲡⲟⲥ, C 86 316 B sim.

—— ⲉⲧⲛ- (ⲉⲧⲟⲟⲧⲋ) SBF, *come into the hand of*, power of: Si 8 1 S, Lu 10 36 SB ἐμπίπτειν εἰς, Mor 41 4 S a book ⲉⲓ ⲉⲧⲟⲟⲧⲛ = B Va 59 31, DeV 162 B sword slaying ⲡⲏ ⲉⲑⲡⲁⲓ ⲉⲧⲟⲧⲥ, J 97 48 S any authority ⲉⲣⲉⲡⲉⲓⲱⲣⲉⲁⲥⲧⲓⲕⲟⲡ ⲡⲁⲉⲓ ⲉⲧⲟⲟⲧϥ, CO 405 S a *solidus* ⲁϥⲉⲓ ⲉⲧⲟⲧ (tax receipt), Kr 45 F ⲧⲉϥⲧⲓⲙⲏⲏ ⲉⲥⲓ ⲧⲁⲧ.

—— ⲉⲣⲣⲉⲛ- B (S rare), *come against, to meet*: 1 Kg 20 1 S ἔρχ. ἐνώπιον; Ez 42 14 B (S ⲉ-) Gk diff; Ac 17 5 B (S ⲉⲣⲛ-) ἐφιστάναι dat.

—— ⲉϫⲛ- SABF, *come upon, arrive at, be applicable to*: Ge 46 1 B, Deu 30 1 B (S ⲉⲣⲣⲁⲓ ⲉϫ.),

Mk 11 13 *SB*, Jo 19 33 *S* (*B* ϧⲁ-) ⲉⲣⲭ. ἐπί, Pro 1
27 *AB* (*S* ⲧⲁϩⲟ) ⲉⲣⲭ. dat, Lu 10 33 *S* (*B* ⲉϧⲣⲏⲓ
ⲉⲝ.) ⲉⲣⲭ. κατά, Z 343 *S* ⲁⲡⲉⲓ ⲉⲭⲡⲟⲩⲥⲡⲏⲗⲁⲓⲟⲛ
κατά; Mt 15 29 *S* (*B* ⲉⲥⲕⲉⲡ-) ⲉⲣⲭ. παρά, Job 3 5
SB ⲉⲡⲉⲣⲭ. ἐπί; Is 32 19 *SBF* ἥκειν ἐπί; Jon 1 7
S (*B* ⲉⲓ), Ac 1 26 *SB* πίπτειν ἐπί; Lu 22 40 *S*
(*B* ϧⲉⲓ) γίνεσθ. ἐπί; ROC 17 408 *B* καταλαμβ.;
2 Pet 2 22 *B* (*S* ⲉϩⲣⲁⲓ ⲉⲝ.) συμβαίν. ἐπί; CA 88 *S*
if cleric repent ⲉϥⲉⲉⲓ ⲉⲭⲡⲉϥⲧⲁϫⲓⲥ *come (again)
into*, MG 25 345 *B* through abstinence ⲁϥⲓ ⲉⲭⲉⲛ-
ⲟⲩⲙⲉⲧⲣⲉⲙⲣⲉ, Mor 53 75 *S* friend ⲡⲉⲛⲧⲁϥⲉⲓ
ⲉϫⲱⲓ (cf Lu 11 5 *S* ϣⲁⲣⲟⲓ), BSM 35 *B* sim (=
BMis 378 *S* ϣⲁ-), Ryl 53 n *S* this hymn ⲉⲓ ⲉⲭⲙ-
ⲡⲁⲣⲭⲁⲅⲅⲉⲗⲟⲥ on, Leyd 196 *S* sim, J 3 19 *S*
lands ⲡⲧⲁϥⲉⲓ ⲉϫⲱⲛ ϩⲁⲡⲉⲡⲉⲓⲟⲧⲉ, CO 145 *S* sim.

—— ⲛ- *SB*, *come to*, of persons (cf ⲉⲓ ϣⲁ-, ⲉⲓ
ⲉ-): Job 3 24 *S* ἥκειν dat, Ro 3 8 *B* (*S* ⲧⲁϩⲟ) ⲉⲣⲭ.,
Z 572 *S* ⲁⲓⲉⲓ ⲡⲏⲧⲛ ϩⲛⲡⲁⲟⲩϩⲣⲏⲧⲉ, BM 175 231 *S*
ⲛⲧⲁⲓⲉⲓ ⲅⲁⲣ ⲡⲏⲧⲛ ϩⲁⲣⲟϥ.

—— ⲛⲥⲁ- *SBF*, *come after, to fetch*: KKS 428
S ⲛⲧⲁⲕⲉⲓ...ⲛⲥⲁⲟⲩ, BAp 93 *S* ⲁϥⲉⲓ ⲛⲥⲱⲛ, C 43 22
B angels ⲉⲧⲁϥⲓ ⲛⲥⲁⲧⲯⲩⲭⲏ, BM 585 *F* ⲡⲉϣϩⲏⲛⲓ
...ⲁⲃⲓ ⲛⲥⲱⲟⲩ.

—— (ⲡ)ⲛⲁϩⲣⲛ- *SB*, *come before, into presence of*
superior: Ac 24 19 *B* (*S* diff) παρεῖναι ἐπί gen.,
PS 68 *S* my hymn ⲙⲁⲣⲉϥⲉⲓ ⲛⲛⲁϩⲣⲁⲕ.

ι ⲟⲩⲃⲉ- *B*, *come against*, oppose: Is 50 8 *B* (*S*
ⲁϩⲉⲣⲁⲧϥ ⲉ-) ἀνθιστάναι.

—— ϣⲁ- *SA²BF*, *come to, approach*, mostly
persons (cf ⲉⲓ ⲉ- & ⲉⲓ ⲛ-): Ge 18 21 *S* (*B* ϩⲁ-),
Nu 22 16 *S* (*B* do), Mt 14 28 *S* (*B* do) ⲉⲣⲭ. πρός,
Est 4 2 *S* ϣⲁϩⲣⲁⲓ ⲉ- ⲉⲣⲭ. ἕως; Lu 7 4 *S* (*B* do)
παραγίν. πρός; PS 22 *S* ⲁⲓⲉⲓ ϣⲁⲧⲡⲩⲗⲏ, C 41 23
B ⲁϥⲓ ϣⲁⲡⲉⲡⲓⲱⲧ (cf ib 25 ⲉⲧⲁϥⲓ ϩⲁⲣⲟⲛ).

ι ϩⲁ- *B*, *come to, approach*, mostly persons: Lev
13 16 (*S* ⲉⲣⲁⲧϥ ⲛ-), Ez 33 31 (*S* ϣⲁ-), Ro 1 10
(*S* do) ⲉⲣⲭ. πρός; 1 Kg 17 40 (*S* ⲙⲟⲟϣⲉ ⲉϩⲟⲩⲛ ⲉ-)
προσέρχ. πρός; AM 35 ⲁϥⲓ ϩⲁⲣⲟⲓ ⲁϥⲧⲁⲗϭⲟⲓ.

—— ϩⲁ(ϩ)ⲧⲛ-, ϩⲁⲧⲉⲛ- *SB*, *come up to, near to*:
Ge 34 20 *SB*, Mk 7 31 *S* (*B* ⲉ- as var εἰς) ⲉⲣⲭ.
πρός, Mor 37 52 *S* ⲁϥⲉⲓ ϩ. ⲡⲣⲟ προσέρχ. ἐγγὺς τῆς,
Mor 17 45 *S* ⲁϥⲉⲓ ϩ. ⲡⲭⲟⲓ ἀνέρχ. ἐν τῷ, Z 282 *S*
ⲁϥⲉⲓ ϩ. ⲡⲙⲟⲛⲁⲥⲧⲏⲣⲓⲟⲛ, MIE 2 416 *B* prepare
ⲛⲧⲉⲕⲓ ϩⲁⲧⲟⲧⲉⲛ, C 43 61 *B* ⲁϥⲓ ϩ. ⲡⲓϣⲃⲉ.

—— ϩⲓϫⲉⲛ- *B*, *come up to, upon*: BSM 35 (=
BMis 378 *S* ⲉϫⲛ-) ⲁϥⲓ ϩ. ⲟⲩⲙⲁⲡⲉⲥⲟⲟⲩ, ib 33 (=
ib 375 *S* ⲉ-) ⲫⲏ ⲉⲧⲁϥⲓ ϩ. ⲡⲁϩⲏⲧ, C 43 228 ⲉⲧⲁϥⲓ ϩ.
ⲡⲓⲃⲏⲙⲁ.

B. with following adverb.

—— ⲉⲃⲟⲗ *SABF*, *come, go forth, be displayed*:
Ge 8 7 *SB*, Ps 145 4 *SB*, Ez 5 4 *SB*, Mt 13 49 *BF*,
Cl 24 5 *A* ἐξέρχ., Ps 72 7 *S* (*B.*ⲥⲓⲛⲓ) διέρχ.; Pro
24 64 *S* διαβαίν.; Mk 14 41 *S* (*B* om) ἀπέχειν;

1 Kg 13 21 *S* ἕτοιμος (εἶναι); MG 25 243 *B* ἐξιέναι;
BSM 42 *B* ⲁϥⲓ ⲉⲃ. ⲙⲡⲉⲙⲑⲟ ⲡⲡⲓⲥⲡⲛⲟⲩ, MG 17
323 *S* wait ϣⲁ(ⲡⲧⲉ)ⲡⲉⲡⲉⲓⲱⲧ ⲉⲓ ⲉⲃ., Z 283 *S* begged
him ⲉⲧⲣⲉϥⲉⲓ ⲉⲃ. ⲡⲙⲙⲁⲩ *set forth*, C 86 210 *B*
halves weighed ⲁⲩⲓ ⲉⲃ. ⲉⲩϣⲏϣ ⲡⲉⲙⲡⲟⲩⲅⲉⲣⲛⲟⲩ,
MIE 2 373 *B* ⲁⲧⲉⲕⲁⲡⲟⲫⲁⲥⲓⲥ ⲓ ⲉⲃ., AZ 23 32 *F*
ⲁⲡⲉⲩ ⲉⲡⲉⲧⲁⲃⲓ ⲃⲁⲗ for Sarapion's son respecting
the δημόσιον, ST 351 *S* ⲁⲓⲟⲩⲱϣ ⲉⲧⲣⲁⲉⲓ ⲉⲃ. ⲛⲕⲏⲧⲕ
(*out from* desert to river valley, v Ep 1 183), BSM
114 *B* ⲉⲧⲁⲡⲓⲟⲩⲱⲓⲛⲓ ⲓ ⲉⲃ., ShA 2 28 *S* ⲁⲡⲕⲁϩ ⲧⲏⲣϥ
ⲉⲓ ⲉⲃ. ϩⲁⲛⲟⲃⲉ, Hall 71 *S* ⲁⲡⲣⲱⲃ ⲉⲓ ⲉⲃ. respecting
the book, ShZ 472 *S* sim.   merely *come, go*:
Mt 14 25 *SB*, Mk 5 14 *SB*, Ro 7 9 *SB* ἔρχ.; Ge
12 4 *S* (*B* ϣⲉ ⲛⲁϥ) πορεύεσθαι.

—— ⲉⲃⲟⲗ ⲉ- *SABF*, *come forth to* places, things:
2 Kg 18 6 *S*, Ps 72 7 *S*, ib 103 23 *SB*, Mt 26 71
SB ἐξέρχ. εἰς, ἐπί; Mk 10 17 *S* ἐκπορεύ. εἰς; PS
121 *S* ϣⲁⲛⲧⲉⲓ ⲛⲏⲧⲛ ⲉⲃ. ⲉⲧⲥⲱϣⲉ; MG 17 319 *S*
= ib 93 *B* carrying loads ϣⲁⲛⲧⲟⲩⲉⲓ ⲉⲃ. (from
marsh) ⲉⲡⲭⲟⲓ;   merely *come to*: Jo 20 1 *S* (*B*
ⲓ ⲉ-) ἔρχ. εἰς;   *sue, proceed against* in *SF* legal
texts (cf ἐνάγειν, ἐπέρχ.): J 1 94 *S* ⲡⲉⲧⲛⲁⲉⲓ ⲉⲃ.
ⲉⲣⲟⲕ, Ep 88 *S* if I venture ⲛⲧⲁⲉⲓ ⲉⲃ. ⲉⲣⲟⲕ ϩⲁⲗⲁⲁⲩ
ⲙⲡⲣⲁⲅⲙⲁ, Ryl 385 *S* ⲁⲓⲥⲁⲕ ⲉⲓ ⲉⲃ. ⲡⲉⲙⲁⲓ ⲉⲩⲧⲣⲓ-
ⲙⲏⲥⲡ, Kr 218 *F* ⲡⲉϣⲧⲉⲡⲓ ⲃⲁⲗ ⲉⲡⲉⲡⲁⲗⲛⲟⲩ.

—— ⲉⲃⲟⲗ ϩⲛ-, ϩⲉⲛ- *SABF*, *come forth from*:
Is 23 10 *SB* ⲉⲣⲭ. ἐκ, Ge 9 18 *SB*, Job 3 11 *SB*,
Ap 9 3 *SB* ἐξέρχ. ἐκ, Mt 12 43 *SB*, Lu 17 29 *SB*
ἐξέρχ. ἀπό; Deu 33 2 *SB*, Ro 11 26 *B* ἥκειν ἐκ;
Jud 1 24 *S*, Ap 19 21 *SB* ἐκπορεύ. ἐκ; Mt 2 1 *S*
παραγίν. ἀπό, Jud 6 21 *S* ἀναβαίν. ἐκ, Lu 9 54 *SB*
καταβαίν. ἀπό; Br 81 *S* ⲛⲧⲁⲓⲉⲓ ⲉⲃ. ϩⲙⲡⲟⲅⲟⲉⲓⲛ,
PS 239 *S* ϣⲁⲕⲉⲓ ⲉⲃ. ϩⲛⲡⲉⲕⲥⲱⲙⲁ, Cl 10 2 *A* ⲁϥⲉⲓ
ⲁⲃ. ϩⲙⲡϥⲕⲁϩ, P 129[19] 30 *S* ⲁⲡⲉϥϫⲟⲩⲣ ⲉⲓ ⲉⲃ. ϩⲙ-
ⲡⲉϥⲧⲛⲏⲃⲉ.   In these cases either 2d ⲉⲃⲟⲗ is
? understood (Stern pp 353, 371 *inf*, cf Nu 33 38
SB, Lu 2 1 *B*) or prep may be ⲉⲃ. ϩⲛ- & ⲉⲃⲟⲗ not
here adv. (cf Mt 3 13 *SB*).

—— ⲉⲃⲟⲗ ϩⲓⲧⲛ- *SB*, *come through, forth from*,
quit: Job 1 12 *SB* ἐξέρχ. παρά, Jo 16 28 *S* (*B* ⲉⲃ.
ϩⲉⲛ-) ἐξέρχ. ἐκ (var παρά); Nu 20 18 *S* (*B* ⲥⲓⲛⲓ
ⲉⲃ. ϩⲓ.), Ps 65 12 *S* (*B* do), Sa 19 8 *S* διέρχ. διά,
Job 9 11 *S* (*B* ⲥⲓⲛⲓ) παρέρχ.; Mk 2 23 *S* (*B* ⲙⲟϣⲓ
ⲉⲃ. ϩⲓ.) διαπορεύ. διά, CDan 95 *B* ⲁϥⲓ ⲉⲃ. ϩⲓⲧⲉⲛⲡⲓ-
ⲥⲡⲛⲟⲩ, ShC 42 185 *S* ϩⲙⲡⲧⲣⲉⲡϩⲗⲟ ⲉⲓ ⲉⲃ. ϩⲓⲧⲉ-
ⲧⲏⲩⲧⲛ, CO 128 *S* ⲕⲁⲧⲁ ⲑⲉ ⲛⲧⲁⲓⲉⲓ ⲉⲃ. ϩⲓⲧⲱⲧⲥ
ⲛⲧⲉⲧⲛⲁⲅⲁⲡⲏ.   Sometimes ⲉⲃ. ϩⲉⲛ- like ⲉⲃ.
ϩⲓⲧⲛ-, *pass through*: Va 69 112 *B* ⲁϥⲓ ⲉⲃ. ϩⲉⲛⲑ-
ⲙⲏϯ of fire, PO 11 357 *B* when patriarch ⲓ ⲉⲃ.
ϩⲉⲛⲭⲏⲙⲓ, cf Lu 4 30 *S* διέρχ. διά.

ⲉⲓ ⲉⲃ. with various preps: ⲉϩⲣⲉⲛ- *B*, Deu 28 25
(*S* ϣⲁ-) πρός, Ac 28 15 εἰς ἀπάντησιν, Va 57 178 ⲁⲥⲓ
ⲉⲃ. ⲉϩⲣⲁⲓ συνήντησέ μοι;   ⲉϫⲛ- *SB*, Ps 18 4 *S*

(*B* ⲣⲓⲭⲉⲡ-) *εἰς*, BMar 5 *S* ⲛϭⲉⲓ ⲉⲃ. ⲉⲭⲁⲡⲣⲟ ; ⲡ- *SB*, Mk 5 30 *SB* ἐκ, BMis 271 *S* at spear thrust bowels ⲉⲓ ⲉⲃ. ⲙⲙⲟϥ ; ⲣⲁ- *SB*, Pro 11 8 *S* (*B* ⲥⲉⲡ-) ἐκ, 1 Cor 10 13 *S* (*B* ⲥⲉⲡ-) Gk diff, CA 112 *S* ⲁϭⲉⲓ ⲉⲃ. ⲣⲁⲡⲣⲟ ⲡ- (4 Kg 5 27 ἐκ) ; ⲣⲓ- *SB*, Jer 19 14 *B*, Mk 1 42 *SB* ἀπό, BMis 450 *S* ⲁϭⲉⲓ ⲉⲃ. ⲣⲓⲡⲧⲟⲟϥ ; ⲣⲏⲧ⳽ *S*, Jud 4 17 *S* εἰς συνάντησιν, Ps 94 2 *S* προφθάνειν, Jo 11 20 *S* (*B* ⲉⲣⲣⲉⲡ-) ὑπαντᾶν, Miss 4 567 *S* ⲁϭⲉⲓ ⲉⲃ. ⲣⲏⲧⲟϥ ϣⲁⲡⲣⲟ, BMis 361 *S* let widows ⲉⲓ ⲉⲃ. ⲣⲏⲧⲕ rejoicing = BSM 23 *B* ⲓ ⲉⲃ. ⲥⲁⲧⲟⲧⲕ ; ⲣⲓⲑⲏ *S*, Ps 67 7 *S* (*B* ⲙⲡⲉ-ⲙⲑⲟ) ἐνώπιον, Mk 2 12 *S* (*B* ⲇⲟ) ἔμπροσθεν.

ⲉⲓ ⲉⲃ. nn m, ⲥⲓⲛ- *S* f, ⲭⲓⲛⲓ ⲉⲃ. *B* m, *coming forth, departure from* : Ex 19 1 *S* (*B* ⲭⲓⲛⲓ ⲉⲃ.), Ps 104 38 *S* (*B* ⲇⲟ), Si 38 25 *S* ἔξοδος, Jos 15 4 *S* διέξοδ. ; Ez 47 11 *B* διεκβολή ; PS 16 *S* ⲡⲉⲓ ⲉⲃ. ⲧⲏⲣϥ ⲙⲡⲡⲱⲗ ⲉⲣⲣⲁⲓ ; ⲥⲓⲛⲉⲓ ⲉⲃ. : Ps 120 8 *S* (*B* ⲙⲱⲓⲧ ⲉⲃ.) ἔξοδ., TstAb 4 *B* ⲡⲭⲓⲛⲓ ⲉⲃ. ⲥⲉⲡⲥⲱⲙⲁ ; ShA 1 241 *S* ⲙⲁ ⲡⲉⲓ ⲉⲃ. of torrent.

—— ⲉⲡⲉⲥⲏⲧ *SABF*, *come down* : Ge 15 11 *SB*, Ps 106 26 *S*, Is 32 19 *SBF*, Mic 1 3 *S* (*A* ⲁϧⲣⲏⲓ, *B* ⲉⲥⲣ.), Jo 4 47 *S* (*A*² ⲁϧⲣ., *B* ⲉⲥⲣ.) καταβαίν. ; Lu 4 31 *S* (*B* ⲉⲥⲣ.), Gu 71 *S* κατέρχ. ; Z 261 *S* death of Arius ⲡⲉϥⲙⲁⲣⲧ...ⲁϭⲉⲓ ⲉⲡ., Bor 143 27 *S* pitch ⲉⲓ ⲉⲡ. ⲣⲓⲡⲉϥⲥⲱⲙⲁ *flowed down* like water. nn m, *descent* : CaiEuch 496 *B* ⲡⲉⲕⲭⲓⲛⲓ ⲉⲡ. συγκατάβασις.

—— ⲉⲡϣⲱⲓ *B*, *come, go up* : Ex 19 12, Is 11 1 (*S* ⲉⲣⲣⲁⲓ), Mt 3 16 (*S* ⲇⲟ), Jo 21 11 (*S* ⲁⲗⲉ), ἀναβαίν., AM 277 ⲁϥⲓ ⲉⲡ. ⲉⲭⲱⲟⲩ εἰσῆλθεν καὶ ἔστη ἐπάνω αὐτ., Va 62 284 ⲁⲓⲓ ⲉⲡ. from childhood (*cf* ⲉⲓ ⲉⲣⲣⲁⲓ).

—— ⲉⲡⲁϩⲟⲩ, ⲛⲥⲁⲡ. *S*, ⲣⲓⲫⲁϩⲟⲩ *B*, *come after, go back* : Mt 16 24 *S* (*B* ⲙⲟϣⲓ ⲡⲥⲁ-) ὀπίσω ἔρχ. ; Mk 5 27 *S* (*B* ⲣⲓⲫ.) ὄπισθεν ; Jo 18 6 *S* ⲛⲥⲁⲡ. (*B* ⲫⲱⲧ ⲉⲫ.) ἀπέρχ. εἰς τὰ ὀπ. ; Pro 10 30 *S* (*A* ϯ ⲁⲡ., *B* diff), Mun 89 *S* avoid rich ⲭⲉⲛⲡⲉⲧⲉⲕⲙⲡⲧⲉⲛⲕⲉ ⲱⲭⲉⲛ ⲡⲥⲱⲱⲧ ⲡⲧⲉⲓ ⲉⲡ., BMis 369 *S* ⲙⲡⲟⲅⲉⲓ ⲉⲡ. ⲛⲗⲁⲁⲩ = BSM 29 *B* ⲭⲱⲭⲓ (*cf* ὑστερεῖν).

—— ⲉⲑⲏ(ⲧⲣⲏ) *SB*, *come forward, progress* : 2 Tim 3 13 *B* (*S* = Gk) προκόπτειν, MG 25 4 *B* ⲉⲧⲁϥⲓ ⲉ. ⲡⲕⲉⲕⲟⲩⲭⲓ προβαίν., C 86 337 *B* sim, PS 32 *S* ⲁⲫⲓⲗⲓⲡⲡⲟⲥ ⲉⲓ ⲉ. ⲁϥⲡⲁⲣⲧϥ, BMis 451 *S* ⲡⲧⲉⲣϥ-ⲉⲓ ⲉ. ⲉⲭⲛⲧⲗⲉⲭⲓⲥ, ST 98 *S* guarantee to fugitive ⲉⲡϣⲁⲡⲉⲓ ⲉ. ⲟⲛ we will observe the right by thee (*cf* MMA 23 3 717A ⲡⲧⲁⲡⲱⲡⲣ ⲉⲑⲏ). nn m, *advancement* : 1 Tim 4 15 *B* (*S* = Gk) προκοπή, TEuch 1 6 *B* ⲧⲉⲕⲡⲣⲟⲕⲟⲡⲏ ⲡⲉⲙⲡⲉⲕⲓ ⲉ.

—— ⲉϩⲟⲩⲛ, ⲉⲥ. *SABF*, *come in, enter* : Ex 21 3 *SB*, Job 14 3 *SB*, Ps 117 2 *S* (*B* ϣⲉ ⲉⲥ.), Lu 14 23 *SB* εἰσέρχ., Ps 78 1 *SB*, Sa 2 24 *S*, Jo 3 5 *SA*²*BF*, MG 25 11 *B* εἰσέρχ. εἰς, Nu 18 4 *S* (*B* ⲓ

ⲣⲁ-), Mt 26 60 *S* (*B* ⲓ), Aeg 233 *S* προσέρχ., Ro 5 20 *SB* παρεισέρχ. ; 1 Kg 16 6 *SB* εἰσιέναι ; MIE 2 376 *B* they called him ⲁϥⲓ ⲉⲥ., El 42 *A* give them power ⲁⲧⲟⲅⲉⲓ ⲁϩ. ⲁⲣⲁⲉⲓ, ShClPr 22 357 *S* after my humility had ⲉⲓ ⲉϩ. ⲉⲡⲉⲓⲃⲓⲟⲥ as monk, C 89 164 *B* στρατηλάτης ϭⲡⲁⲓ ⲉⲥ. ⲉϥⲙⲟⲡⲏ (*in* from valley to desert), Miss 4 530 *S* at even ⲁϧⲉⲓ ⲉϩ. to monastery, OLZ 6 69 *S* ⲡⲧⲁⲉⲓ ⲉϩ. (to monast.) ⲡⲧⲁ-ⲡⲣⲟⲥⲕⲩⲡⲉⲓ (*cf* ⲉⲓ ⲉⲃⲟⲗ sim), BMis 373 *S* ⲕⲁⲗⲱⲥ ⲁⲕⲉⲓ ⲡⲁⲓ ⲉϩⲟⲩⲛ = *ib* ⲕⲁⲗⲱⲥ ⲏⲗⲑⲉⲥ (= BSM 32 *B* misunderstood, *cf* ⲉⲓ *init*), ShC 42 195 *S* ⲁⲧⲉ-ⲡⲗⲏⲛⲕⲏ ⲉⲓ ⲉϩ. ϣⲏⲙ ϣⲏⲙ, ShA 2 234 *S* sim malady ⲉⲓ ⲉϩ. ⲏ ⲙⲟⲅⲥ ⲉϩⲣⲁⲓ, J 67 50 *S* if legacy ⲉⲓ ⲉϩ. ⲉⲭⲱⲟⲩ from mother, J 68 43 *S* ⲡⲉⲧⲉϣⲁϭⲉⲓ ⲉϩ. ⲉⲭⲱⲡ from handicraft, CO 217 *S* sim, J 1 79 *S* sale contract ⲉⲕⲡⲁⲉⲓ ⲉϩ. ⲡⲧⲁⲙⲁⲣⲧⲉ &c (*cf* PMon 98 εἰσελθεῖν), J 71 41 *S* sim of legatee ⲉⲕⲡⲁⲉⲓ ⲉϩ. & be master of, J 70 55 *S* ⲛϭⲉⲓ ⲉϩ. ⲛϭⲣⲱⲡ ⲉⲧⲉⲓⲁ-ⲑⲏⲕⲏ, CO 168 *S* sim. nn m, *coming in, entry* : Ac 13 24 *S* (*B* ⲙⲱⲓⲧ ⲉⲥ.) εἴσοδος, BHom 38 *S* day of ⲡⲉϭⲉⲓ ⲉϩ., Bodl(P) e 36 title of account ⲡⲙⲉϧ-ⲩⲧⲟⲟⲩ ⲡⲕⲟⲡⲧⲁⲕⲉ ⲙⲡⲉⲓ ⲉϩ. *income* ; ⲙⲁ ⲡⲉⲓ ⲉϩ. : Pro 8 34 *S* (*B* ⲙⲱⲓⲧ ⲉⲥ.) εἴσοδ., Z 281 *S* ⲙⲙⲁ ⲡⲉⲓ ⲉϩ. ⲉⲧⲡⲟⲗⲓⲥ ; ⲥⲓⲛⲉⲓ ⲉϩ. : Miss 4 656 *S*.

—— ⲉϩⲣⲁⲓ *SABF*, *come up* (in *B* MSS ⲉϩ. often for ⲉⲥ.) : Ex 19 24 *S* (*B* ⲉⲡϣⲱⲓ), *cf* 25 ⲉⲓ ⲉⲡⲉⲥⲏⲧ, Is 34 3 *SF* (*B* ⲇⲟ), Mt 13 7 *S* (*B* ⲥⲁⲡϣⲱⲓ), Ac 7 23 *F* (*S* ⲁⲗⲉ ⲉϩ., *B* ⲓ ⲉⲭⲉⲡ-) ἀναβαίν., Lu 12 54 *S* (*B* ⲓ ⲉⲃⲟⲗ) ἀνατέλλειν ; Sa 2 1 *S* ἀναλύειν ; BMar 221 *S* ⲡⲧⲉⲣⲉⲡⲟⲩⲟⲉⲓⲛ ⲉⲓ ⲉϩ., Miss 4 730 *S* fallen down ⲙⲡⲉϥⲱϣⲉⲓ ⲉϩ., Ryl 94 104 *S* ⲛϭⲉⲓ ⲉϩ. ⲣⲏⲧⲗⲓ-ⲙⲏⲏ ; *grow up* : Miss 8 260 *S* ⲡⲧⲁⲅⲉⲓ ⲉϩ. in same school, Kr 228 *S* she is as thy daughter ⲡⲧⲁⲥⲓ ⲉϩ. ⲣⲓⲡⲏⲕⲏⲓ, J 75 29 *S* elders ⲉⲛⲧⲁⲡⲉⲓ ⲉϩ. ϩⲁⲣⲁⲧⲟⲩ ; *come upon* in addition : Ep 296 *S*, Hall 69 *S* the *x* day ⲛⲛϯ ⲁϧⲣⲏ, ⲛⲛⲡⲧⲉⲓ ⲁϩⲣⲉ *of those added*, the 5 epagomenal days at year's end (*cf* ⲉⲃⲟⲧ). Often merely *come* : Ge 35 27 *S* (*B* ⲓ ⲣⲁ-), 1 Kg 16 4 *SB*, Job 3 4 *S* (*B* ⲓ ⲉⲭⲉⲡ-), Mk 10 1 *S* (*B* ⲓ ⲉ-), Jo 3 19 *F* (*SA*²*B* ⲉⲓ ⲉ-) ἔρχ., Jos 15 10 *S* παρέρχ. ; Jud 16 2 *S* ἥκειν ; Nu 20 5 *S* (*B* om) παραγίν. ; PS 179 *S* ⲁⲥⲉⲓ ⲉϩ. ⲉⲧⲙⲏⲧⲉ, Va 59 48 *B* let us return ⲡⲧⲉⲛⲓ ⲉϩ. ⲉⲭⲉⲛⲣⲁⲡϩⲛⲟⲩⲓ meet for repentance, C 41 40 *B* ⲉⲁϥⲓ ⲉϩ. ⲥⲉⲡⲡⲓⲡⲗⲁⲧⲓⲁ, Miss 4 716 *S* she remained thus ϣⲁⲡⲧⲉⲥⲉⲓ ⲉϩ. ⲉⲡⲭⲱⲕ of 10 months, Mun 48 *S* this hour ⲡⲧⲁⲓⲉⲓ ⲉϩ. ⲉⲣⲟ[ⲥ]. ⲉⲓ ⲉϩ. ⲉⲭⲛ- *SBF* (where ⲉϩ. strengthens ⲉⲭⲛ-), *come upon, up upon, reach* : Job 38 16 *S* (*B* ⲓ ⲉϩ. ϣⲁ-), Ps 43 17 *SB*, Ac 7 11 *SB* (*B* var ⲉⲭⲉⲡ-) ἔρχ. ἐπί, Lev 16 9 *SB*, Sa 12 28 *S* ἔπερχ. ἐπί ; Eccl 10 4 *S*, Jer 27 3 *BF*, Ap 20 9 *S* (*B* ⲉⲡϣⲱⲓ ⲉⲭ.) ἀναβαίν. ἐπί ; Ac 4 1 *S* (*B* ⲧⲱⲟⲩⲛⲟⲩ ⲉϩ. ⲉⲭ.) ἐφιστάναι dat (*contra ib* 18 12).

-— ⲉϩⲣⲁⲓ, ⲉϩⲣ. *SABF*, *come down, descend*: Deu 32 2 *SB*, Jud 5 14 *S*, Jer 31 15 *B*, Mt 14 29 *BF* (*S* ⲉⲡⲉⲥⲏⲧ, *cf* Lu 5 2 ἀποβαίν.), Mk 5 2 ἐξέρχ.), Lu 6 17 *B* (*S* do), Ap 12 12 *S* (*B* ⲉⲡⲉⲥⲏⲧ) καταβαίν. ; Ez 38 8 *B* ἥκειν ; Ex 1 1 *B* εἰσπορεύ., *cf* Ge 12 11 *B* εἰσέρχ., Ac 1 8 *SB* ἐπέρχ. ; Ep 185 *S* ⲁϥⲉⲓ ⲉϩ. ⲉⲧⲙⲡⲧⲏⲛⲕⲉ, AM 32 *B* ϣⲁⲡⲧⲉⲕⲓ ⲉϩ. ⲉⲡⲁⲡⲛϣϯ ⲡ̄ⲑⲉⲃⲓⲟ, ShMich 550 16 *S* ⲉⲓ ⲉϩ....ⲧⲁⲗⲟ ⲉϩ., var C 73 156 ⲉⲓ ⲉⲡⲉⲥⲏⲧ...ⲉⲓ ⲉϩ., Cat 190 *B* ⲁϧⲓ ⲉϩ. ⲡⲉⲙⲱⲟⲩ in lowly words (*cf ib* 191 he said this in συγκατάβασις).　　nn *SB*, *coming down, descent*: Si 43 18 *S* κατάβασις ; Jos 8 24 *S* ϧⲏ ⲡⲉⲓ ⲉϩ. κατάβ. ; BIF 13 111 *S* ⲙⲁ ⲡⲉⲓ ⲉϩ. ⲙ̄ⲡϩⲉⲗⲗⲟⲥ = MG 25 301 *B* ⲡⲓ ⲉⲡⲉⲥⲏⲧ ⲉϩ. ; C 86 41 *B* ϯϫⲓⲡⲓ ⲉϩ. ϩⲉⲛⲧⲟⲅⲁⲣⲭⲏ συγκατάβ. (*cf* TT 108).　　ⲉⲓ ⲉϩ. ⲉϫⲛ- *SB*, *come (down) upon, befall*: Ps 54 5 *SB*, Si 47 34 *S* ἔρχ. ἐπί, Sa 16 4 *S* ἐπέρχ., *ib* 11 23 *S* κατέρχ. ἐπί ; Ps 77 31 *SB*, Jer 51 21 *S* (= *B* ⲓ ⲉϫⲉⲡ-) ἀναβαίν. ἐπί, Job 2 10 *S* (*B* ϣⲱⲡⲓ acc) συμβαίν. ; PS 123 *S* spirit ⲉⲛⲧⲁϥⲉⲓ ⲉϩ. ⲉϫⲱⲕ, C 41 18 *B* ⲁϥⲓ ⲉϩ. ⲉϫ. ϯϣⲱϯ, C 86 357 *B* arrow from sky ⲓ ⲉϩ. ⲉϫ. ⲧⲉϥⲁⲫⲉ, Ryl 62 II *S* ⲉⲁⲡⲉⲓ ⲉϩ. ⲉϫⲙ- ⲡⲉⲓⲣⲟⲟⲩ.　Here also often = *come to*.

Varies with ⲃⲱⲕ, **a.** in *S*: Nu 21 7, Jud 14 1, *cf* 5, 1 Kg 29 6, Mt 21 10, Lu 7 17, Leyd 443 ϧⲏ ⲡⲓ ⲉⲣⲟⲩⲡ, *cf* 444 ϧⲏ ⲡⲃ̄. ⲉϩ. ; **b.** between *S* & *B*: Nu 20 15, Ps 65 13, 104 23, Su 7, Lu 14 1, Ac 10 24.　Mostly ⲉⲓ *come*, ⲃⲱⲕ *S* (ϣⲉ, ⲙⲟϣⲓ *B*) *go* (oftenest with ⲉⲃⲟⲗ): Ex 21 3 *S*, Deu 31 2 *S*, Job 1 21 *S*, Eccl 1 4, 5 14 *S*, Mk 6 10 *S*, Jo 10 9 *SBA²*, PS 36 *S*, Cl 12 4 *A* (*cf* Jos 2 5), JKP 2 36 *S*.　Less often *S* ⲉⲓ varies with *B* ϣⲉ + ethic dat: Ge 12 4, Ps 68 1, Mt 9 26, Ac 1 13, Ap 9 2.

ⲉⲓⲁ, ⲓⲁ *S*, ⲉⲓⲁⲉⲓⲉ, ⲓⲁⲓⲉ *A*, ⲓⲁ *B* (only K), ⲓⲉⲉⲓ *F* nn m, sg as pl, *valley, ravine*: Ge 14 3 *S*, Deu 4 46 *S*, Ps 103 10 *S*, Pro 24 52 *SA*, Is 30 28 *SF*, Zech 14 5 *A* φάραγξ (all *B* ϩⲉⲗⲗⲟⲧ) ; Nu 14 25 *S*, Jud 1 19 *S*, Mic 1 4 *SA* κοίλη ; He 11 38 *S* (*B* ⲃⲏⲃ) σπήλαιον ; 1 Kg 17 3 *S* αὐλών gloss ⲉⲧⲉⲡⲓⲁⲡⲉ ; K 214 *B* ⲡⲓⲁ ⲡⲁⲡⲁⲓ (*sic l*, *cf* Deu 3 29 *S* ⲡⲁⲡⲏ), PSBA 29 301 *B* ? ⲡⲓⲁ ⲡⲁⲃⲁϫⲱⲡⲓ (*v* ⲁⲃⲁϭⲏⲓⲡ), P 44 54 *S* ⲡⲓⲁ ﺍﻟﻮﺍﺩﻱ, *cf ib* ⲙⲟⲩ ⲡⲥⲱⲣⲙ do ; ShMich 550 15 *S* ⲡⲉⲕⲣⲱⲟⲩ ⲡ̄ⲧⲟⲓⲕⲟⲩⲙⲉⲛⲏ ⲙ̄ⲡⲡⲉⲓⲁ ⲙ̄ⲡⲕⲁϩ, Mor 37 137 *S* ⲡⲉⲙⲟⲩ ⲡⲥⲱⲣⲙ ⲁⲩⲥⲱⲕ ϩ̄ⲡⲡⲉⲅⲉⲓⲁ, Z 264 *S* ⲡⲉⲓⲁ filled with monasteries, P 131² 89 *S* ⲡⲉⲓⲁ ⲉⲧϣⲟⲕϩ ⲉⲡⲉϩⲟⲩⲟ *convallis profundissima*, Mor 25 18 *S* hunters in ⲡⲉⲣⲅⲗⲟⲥ (ἕλος) ⲙ̄ⲡⲡⲉⲓⲁ, Mor 24 10 *F* (*S* ⲓⲁ) ⲡⲓ. ⲙ̄ⲡⲭⲁⲱⲥ.

In ? place-names : ⲡⲉⲓⲁ near Syene BMis 472, Πίⲁ POxy 1899, ⲡⲓⲁⲙⲟⲩⲡ (? = ⲡⲓⲁ ⲁⲙⲟⲩⲡ, or ⲡⲓⲁϩ) in Nitria N&E 39 8 *B* cave (σπήλ.) near tower (πύργος) called that of Piamoun (*cf* He 11 38

above & EW 122 the rock of ⲡ.).　Also ? in ﺑﻴﻬﻤﻮ Biahmû (? ⲡⲓⲁ ϩⲙⲟⲩ).　In Greek texts Πια- often = ⲡⲓⲁϩ- (ⲉⲓⲱϩⲉ).

ⲉⲓⲁ-, ⲓⲁ- *v* ⲉⲓⲱ ass.

ⲉⲓⲁ (only Eph, Col, *v* Stern p 94 *inf*) *S*, ⲉⲓⲉⲣ- *S*, ⲓⲉⲣ- *BF* (*v* ⲃⲱⲱⲡ), ⲉⲓⲁⲧⲥ, ⲉⲓⲁⲁⲧⲥ *S*, ⲉⲓⲉⲧⲥ *A*, ⲓⲁⲧⲥ *B*, ⲓⲏⲧⲥ *F*, ⲓⲉⲧⲥ *O*, *iet* DM nn, *eye & its sight*: Eph 6 6, Col 3 22 *S* ⲙ̄ⲡⲧⲉⲓⲁ (var ⲓⲁ) ⲡ̄ϭⲁⲟⲡ = *B* ⲙⲉⲧⲃⲁⲗ ⲙⲃⲱⲕ ὀφθαλμοδουλεία, ? Job 4 16 *S* ⲡⲉϫⲟ ⲉⲓⲁⲧⲉ = *B* ϧⲟⲣⲧϥ ⲁⲩⲣⲁ ; Independently: Ge 29 17 *B* (*S* diff), Lam 2 4 *S* (C 73 77), Tob 11 13 *S* ὀφθαλμός, Mk 8 25 *S* (Gk om), AZ 21 100 *O* ⲉⲓⲁⲧⲥ ⲭⲁ ⲉⲙⲣⲏ, *ib* ⲡⲉⲣⲙⲟⲟⲩ ⲡⲓⲉⲧⲉ (2 sg f).

With various tr vbs, obj suff & farther obj (mostly dat): ⲕⲱ *v* below ϩⲁ- ; ⲕⲧⲉ ⲉⲓ. *S*, *look round*, lit *turn eye*: Jud 20 42 ἐπιβλέπειν, Mk 10 23 (*B* ϫⲟⲩϣⲧ) ⲁϥⲕ. ⲉⲓⲁⲧϥ ⲉⲃⲟⲗ ⲉϫⲱⲡ (var P 129¹³ 25 ⲁϥⲙⲉⲣ ⲉⲓ. ⲡⲟⲩⲁ ⲡⲟⲩⲏⲧⲓ) περιβλέπ.　ⲙⲉⲗⲭ ⲓ. *B*, *look upon*, c ⲛ- : Ps 21 18 (*S* ϯ ϩⲏⲧ) κατανοεῖν.　ⲙⲟⲩϩ ⲡ- (rare), ⲙⲉϩ- *S*, ⲙⲁϩ- *A* ⲉⲓ., *look intently*, lit *fill eye*, c ⲡ- &c : Ps 34 21 *S* (*B* ⲡⲁⲩ) ὁρᾶν, *ib* 91 11 *S* (*B* ⲡⲁⲩ), *ib* 111 8 *S* (*B* ϫⲟⲩϣⲧ ⲉϫⲉⲡ-), Mic 7 10 *SA* (*B* do) ἐφορ. ; Si 37 11 (ⲙⲟⲩϩ) *S* ὑποβλέπ. ; Ps 90 8 *S* (*B* ϯ ⲡⲓⲁⲧⲥ) κατανοεῖν ; ShBMOr 8800 56 *S* fire & darkness ⲡⲉⲧⲛⲁⲙ. ⲉⲓⲁⲧⲟⲩ ⲙⲙⲱⲧⲛ, Mor 43 52 *S* ⲙ. ⲉⲓⲁⲧⲉ (f) ⲡⲡⲁϭⲓⲝ (*cf* Lu 24 39), Miss 4 610 *S* ⲁϥⲙ. ⲙⲙⲟϥ ⲕⲁⲗⲱⲥ ⲁϥⲥⲟⲩⲱⲡϥ, Gu 105 *S* sim. *Cf* ⲙⲟⲩϩ *look at*.　ⲥⲙⲡ ⲉⲓ. *SA*, *fix eyes*, c ⲉϫⲡ- : Pro 23 5 ἐφιστάναι πρός.　ϯ ⲡⲓ. *B*, *see, observe*, c ⲛ-, ⲡⲥⲁ- : Ge 42 9, Ex 33 8 (*S* ⲡⲁⲩ), Ps 141 5 (*S* ϭⲱϣⲧ), Is 57 1 (*S* ϯ ϩⲏⲧ), Hab 3 2 (*SA* ⲥⲟⲟⲩⲡ), Ro 4 19 (*S* ⲡⲁⲩ, *F* ⲡⲉⲩ) κατανοεῖν ; Lev 14 36, Job 35 5 (*S* ϯ ϩⲏⲧ) καταμανθάνειν ; Mt 6 26 (*S* ϭⲱϣⲧ) ; Su 16, Lu 6 7, MG 25 233 ⲉϥϯ ⲡⲓⲁⲧϥ ⲙ̄ⲡⲙⲱⲓⲧ & saw παρατηρεῖν, EW 37 ⲉⲁⲕⲟⲣⲉⲥϯ ⲡⲡⲓⲁⲧⲉ ⲙⲫⲏ ⲉⲧⲙⲙⲁⲩ = BAp 55 *S* ⲧⲥⲁⲃⲉ ⲉⲓ. ⲉⲃⲟⲗ ; once *S*: Ryl 324 ⲧⲓ ⲉⲓⲁⲧⲕ ⲉⲡⲉⲧⲉϣⲁⲕϣⲁⲧϥ ⲉⲙⲟϥ.　As nn m : Ge 3 6.　ⲧⲥⲁⲃⲟ ⲡ- (rare), ⲧⲥⲁⲃⲉ-, ⲧⲥⲃⲃⲉ- (Ac 8 31, 10 22) *S*, ⲧⲥⲉⲃⲉ- *A*, ⲥⲉⲃ- *SF* ⲉⲓ. ⲉⲃⲟⲗ, *instruct, inform*, lit *teach eye*: ShC 42 163 *S* ⲡⲉⲧ(ⲧ)ⲥⲁⲃⲟ ⲡⲉⲓⲁⲧⲟⲩ ⲉⲃ. ϩⲓⲧⲙⲡⲡ̄, CO 386 *S* ⲉⲕ-ⲡⲧⲥⲁⲃⲟ ⲉⲓⲁⲧ ⲉⲃ. if thou wishest &c ; Is 40 13, 14 *S* (*B* ⲧⲥⲁⲃⲟ), Miss 4 530 *S* = C 89 49 *B* ⲧⲟⲩⲡ ⲓⲁⲧϥ ⲉⲃ. συμβιβάζειν, *cf* Ro 11 34 *SF*, Ac 8 31 *S* (*B* ϭⲓ ⲙⲱⲓⲧ), *ib* 10 22 *S* (*B* ⲧⲁⲙⲟ) χρηματίζειν, R 1 1 43 *S* διδάσκειν, ShC 42 142 *S* ⲡⲧⲥⲁⲃⲉ ⲉⲓⲁⲧ ⲉⲃ. how I have injured thee, TU 43 19 *A* ⲁⲕⲧⲥⲉⲃⲉ ⲉⲓⲉⲧⲛⲉ ⲁⲃ., Mor 41 2 *S* ⲁϥϣⲣⲡ ⲥⲉⲃ ⲓⲁⲧⲛⲉ ⲉⲃ. = Va 59 30 *B* ⲧⲥⲁⲃⲟ, Mor 31 120 *S* ⲉⲕⲉⲥⲉⲃ ⲉⲓⲁⲧϥ ⲉⲃ....ϩⲡⲡⲉⲧⲅⲣⲁⲫⲏ, BMEA 10585 *F* ⲥⲉⲃ ⲓⲏⲧ ⲉⲃ. ⲉⲡⲁⲉ ⲉⲕⲟⲩⲉϣ ⲧⲁⲡⲱⲧ ⲉⲗⲁⲃ.　ⲧⲟⲩⲡ-, ⲧⲟⲩⲡⲉ-, ⲧⲟⲩⲡⲟ-

S, τογπογ- *SA*, τογπ- *BF* ει. εⲃⲟⲗ same meaning, lit *raise eye*, c dat or e- final : Jud 13 8 *S* συμβιβ., var φωτίζειν, Miss 4 522 *S* = C 89 42 *B* συμβιβ., Mt 14 8 *S* (*B* ⲧⲥⲁⲃⲟ) προβιβ. ; Ez 3 18 ff *B* διαστέλλειν ; He 11 7 *S* (*B* ⲧⲁⲙⲟ) χρηματίζ. ; 1 Kg 28 15 *S* γνωρίζειν ; Jos 4 7 *S* (*B* ⲉⲣ ογω) δηλοῦν ; Zech 10 8 *A* (*B* ϯ ⲗⲏⲓⲓⲓⲓ) σημαίνειν ; BG 61 *S* ⲁⲥⲧογⲡογ ⲉⲓⲁⲧϥ ⲉⲃ. ⲉογⲱⲙ, Mor 30 10 *F* ⲧογⲡ ⲓⲏⲧ = BMis 236 *S* ⲧⲥⲁⲃⲉ ⲉⲓ., Pcod 27 *S* resurrection ⲉⲡⲧⲁⲕⲧογⲡⲉ ⲉⲓⲁⲁⲧ ⲉⲃ. ⲙⲙⲟⲥ (var ⲧογⲡογ ⲓⲁⲧ), HT X 1 *S* God ⲧογⲡ ⲉⲓⲁⲧογ of saints ⲡⲛⲉⲧⲛⲁ-ϣⲱⲡⲉ.   ωογ ⲡⲓⲁⲧ⸗ *B* v ωογ.   ϥⲓ ⲉⲓⲁⲧ⸗ &c ⲉϩⲣⲁⲓ *SA*, *raise eye* : Jud 19 17 *S*, 1 Kg 6 13 *S*, Is 60 4 (*B* ϥⲁⲓ ⲃⲁⲗ), Zech 1 18 *SA* (*B* do), Lu 6 20 *S* (*B* do) ὀφθ. αἴρειν, ἐπαίρ. ; Ge 31 12 *S* (var ϥⲓ ⲡⲓⲁⲧⲕ = *B* ϫογϣⲧ ⲛⲡⲉⲕⲃⲁⲗ), Deu 4 19 *S* (*B* ϫ. ⲉϩⲣ. ⲉ-), Is 8 22 *S* (*B* ⲥⲟⲙⲥ), Mk 6 41 *S* (*B* ϫ.) ἀναβλέπ. τοῖς ὀφθ., ib 9 8 *S* (*B* do) περιβλέπ. ; El 80 *A* ⲁⲥⲡⲁϥⲓ (ⲓ)ⲉⲉⲧⲥ ⲁⲧⲡⲉ.   ϩⲁⲉⲓⲁⲧ⸗ *S*, *before eye* : Mor 17 44 such peril that we kept death ϩⲁⲉⲓⲁⲧογ ⲛⲡⲉⲛⲃⲁⲗ πρὸ ὀφθ., J 70 6 ⲡⲣⲱⲃ ϩⲁⲉⲓⲁⲧ ⲉⲧⲣⲁⲣ ⲡⲕⲟⲧ ; so ⲕⲱ ϩ., *intend to do* : Ps 118 30 (*B* ⲥⲱⲧⲡ) αἱρετίζειν, Ac 26 9 (*B* ⲙⲉϥⲓ + ⲉ- ethic) δοκεῖν refl, Ro 1 13 (*B* ⲥⲟⲃϯ refl) προτίθεσθαι.

ⲛⲁⲓⲁⲧ⸗ *SB*, ⲛⲉⲉⲓⲉⲧ⸗ *AA²*, ⲛⲓⲁⲧ⸗ *B*, ⲛⲁⲓⲏⲧ⸗ *F*, *blessed art, is* &c, lit *great thy, his eye* (ⲛⲁ- = ⲛⲁⲁ-Spg) ; in *B* (bibl) mostly = ωογ ⲡⲓⲁⲧ⸗ (v ωογ) : Job 5 17 *S*, Ps 2 12 *S*, Pro 3 13 *SA*, Mt 5 3 *S*, Jo 13 17 *SA²* (all *B* ωογ ⲡⲓⲁⲧ⸗) μακάριος ; but cf Cat 150 *B* he shall be ϫⲉⲟγογ ⲛⲛⲁⲓⲁⲧϥ (*l* ⲛⲓⲁⲧϥ), Job 11 3 *S* (*B* ⲥⲙⲁⲣⲱογⲧ) εὐλογημένος ; Ps 40 3 *B* (*S* = Gk) ⲁⲓϥ ⲛⲛⲁⲓⲁⲧϥ μακαρίζειν ; AM 266 *B* ⲡⲉⲛⲛⲁ(ⲓ)ⲁⲧϥ ⲡⲓⲱⲧ ἅγιε πάπα, Leyd 467 *S* ⲛⲁⲓⲁⲧⲥ ⲛⲧⲉⲕⲡⲟⲗⲓⲥ, Mor 24 9 *F* ⲛⲁⲓⲏⲧⲉⲡ.   adj *B* : Ti 2 13 (*S* = Gk) μακάριος. FR 118 ϯⲛⲁⲓⲁⲧⲥ ⲙⲡⲁⲣⲑⲉ-ⲛⲟⲥ, TEuch 1 316 ⲡⲛⲓⲁⲧϥ ⲛⲱⲛⲃ.

ⲙⲛⲧ-, ⲙⲉⲧⲛⲁⲓⲁⲧ⸗ *SB* nn f, *blessedness* : BG 24 *S* ⲟγⲙⲛⲧⲧⲉⲗⲓⲟⲥ.ⲟγⲙ., HL 73 *B* μακαρισμός, Va 68 166 *B* μακαριότης.

BM 1091 *S* in account ⲡⲣⲱⲙⲉ ⲡⲉⲓⲁⲧ (ⲥⲓⲁⲧ improb) ?? *overseer, watchman*.

V also ⲃⲱⲱⲡ.

ⲉⲓⲁⲓⲱ† *S* vb intr, meaning unknown (? corrupt), as epithet of species of jacinth (Epiphan *De Gem*) : P 131² 89 ϩⲣⲱϫⲓⲉⲱⲥ...ⲁⲡⲁⲧⲓⲃⲱⲥ ⲁγⲱ ⲟγⲉⲡ ⲕⲉⲟγⲁ ⲉϥⲉⲓⲁⲓⲱ ⲉγⲙⲟγⲧⲉ ⲉⲣⲟϥ ϫⲉϫⲁγⲡⲓⲉⲱⲥ. Seems to = *like to colour of water* in Georgian version (R P Blake), so ?? *l* ⲉϥⲉⲓ(ⲏ) ⲁγⲱ.

ⲉⲓⲉ, ⲉⲉⲓⲉ (Sa, PS), ⲉⲓ *S*, ⲉⲓⲁ *A*, ⲓⲉ *BF* particle, **a.** introducing apodosis (often in condit clause) *then* (ergo, igitur, profecto) : Sa 5 6 *S*, Mt 12 28 *S* (*B* = Gk), Lu 11 48 *S* (*B* do), Gal 5 11 *S* (*B* do) ἄρα ;

Ge 13 16 *SA* (Cl, *B* do), Ex 21 3 *S* (*B* om), Jer 13 23 *SB*, ib 38 36 *B*, Lu 11 34 *S* (*B* om) καί ; Ro 6 5 *S* (*B* = Gk) ἀλλά ;   without Gk : Ge 43 4 *S* (*B* om), Jud 6 37 *S* (var om), Sa 13 9 *S*, Mt 8 31 *S* (*B* om), ib 27 42 *S* (*B* om), Ro 7 20 *SB*, He 10 18 *SBF* ; PS 218 *S* if knowledge of all these be in this mystery ⲉⲓⲉ ⲡⲓⲙⲡⲉ ⲡⲣⲱⲙⲉ that can know ?, Stat 468 *S* ⲉϥⲧⲙⲟγⲱϣ ⲉⲓⲉ ⲙⲁⲣⲟγⲛⲟϫϥ ⲉⲃⲟⲗ, Va 61 115 *B* if he be archangel ⲓⲉ ⲛⲑⲟⲟϥⲡⲉ ⲡⲓⲛⲓϣϯ = JTS 4 395 *S* ⲟγⲕⲟγⲛ ⲡⲧⲟⲡⲉ, AM 140 *B* when we have told thee ⲓⲉ ⲧⲉⲛⲡⲁϯ ϣⲓⲡⲓ ⲛⲁⲕ, J 89 40 *S* whoso shall hinder...ⲉⲓⲉ ⲡⲉⲧⲙⲙⲁγ ⲡⲁⲥⲱⲕ ⲉϩⲣⲁⲓ ϩⲁⲡⲉⲕⲣⲓⲙⲁ, Cat 206 *B* ⲕⲁⲧⲁ ⲡⲁⲓⲭⲉ ⲟγⲡ ⲙⲡⲁⲓⲣⲏϯ ⲓⲉ ⲥϣⲉ ⲉⲣⲟⲛ &c., Ryl 320 *S* if he would remit tax ⲉⲓ ⲥϩⲁⲓ ⲡⲁⲓ ⲉⲃⲟⲗ, ST 225 *S* if thou wouldst come ⲉⲓ ⲁⲙⲟγ.   **b.** *unless, without* : Bor 265 91 *S* I will not believe Christ risen ⲉⲓⲉ ⲙⲡⲓⲛⲁγ ⲉⲣⲟϥ, Mor 39 35 *S* I will not release thee ⲉⲓⲉ ⲙⲡⲉⲕⲧⲁⲙⲁⲓ ϫⲉ- (var 40 25 om, cf Ge 32 26), Mor 31 57 *S* sim ⲉⲓⲉ ⲡⲡⲉⲕⲟγⲱϣⲧ = BM 917 *B* ϣⲁⲧⲉⲕⲟγⲱϣⲧ, Mor 53 89 *S* no sinner could approach altar ⲉⲓⲉ ⲙⲡⲟγ-ⲉⲓⲙⲉ ⲉⲣⲟϥ, BM 599 *F* ⲁϩⲁ ⲓⲉ ⲡⲁⲓ(ⲁⲕⲱⲛ) ⲡⲱⲧ ⲉⲡⲙⲉ...(?).   **c.** interj strengthening next word, *well then, surely* : 2 Kg 18 23 *S* what if I run ? Answer ⲉⲓⲉ (ⲉ)ϩⲉ ⲡⲱⲧ, ? Ex 2 14 *A* (*S* ⲉⲡⲉ) ⲉⲓⲁ ϩⲉ εἰ οὕτως, Sa 13 3 *S* let them know that lord of these ⲉⲉⲓⲉ ⲡⲉⲥⲱϥ ⲉⲣⲟⲟγ, ib 13 4 sim, Mt 12 12 *B* (*S* om), Mk 7 9 *S* (*B* om) ⲉⲓⲉ ⲕⲁⲗⲱⲥ, cf Leyd 153 *S* (rubric) if priest wish to...ⲉⲓⲉ ⲕⲁⲗⲱⲥ ϥⲛⲁⲁⲁⲥ, PS 321 *S* ⲡⲉ-ϫⲁⲥ ϫⲉⲉⲓⲉ ⲟγⲟⲓ ⲛⲡⲉⲯγⲭⲟⲟγⲉ, cf 322 ϫⲉⲟγⲟⲓ ⲛⲓⲣ-ⲉϥⲣ ⲛⲟⲃⲉ, Wess 18 85 *S* ⲱ ⲉⲓⲉ ⲡⲉⲓⲛⲟϭ ⲛⲉⲃⲃⲓⲟ, PS 201 *S* ⲉⲧⲃⲉⲡⲁⲓϫⲉ ⲉⲓⲉ ⲙⲛ ⲑⲉ ⲛϣⲁϫⲉ, PS 218 *S* ⲡⲉⲓ-ϣⲁϫⲉ...ⲉⲓⲉ ⲙⲡⲁⲧⲕϭⲱⲛ ⲉⲣⲟγⲡ to fulfil it, BG 18 *S* ⲡⲁⲡⲧⲱⲥ ⲉⲓⲉ ⲡⲥⲱⲧⲏⲣ ⲥⲟⲟγⲛ ⲙⲙⲟⲥ, BKU 1 1 5 *S* Horus wept saying ϫⲉⲉⲓ(ⲉ) ϫⲓ ⲛ̄ⲥⲉ ⲧⲁⲙⲁⲁγ ⲉⲣⲟⲓ.   **d.** interrog or condit : Ex 2 14 *S* (var ⲉⲡⲉ-, *B* om), Lam 2 20 *B* (*S* ⲉⲡⲉ-), Ac 1 6 *B* (*S* ⲉⲡⲉ-) εἰ, BM 344 *S* ⲉⲓⲉ ⲡⲉⲧⲡⲉⲓⲱⲧ ⲡⲧⲟϥ ϣⲟⲟⲡ...ⲉⲓⲉ ϥⲟⲛϩ (cf Ge 43 7 *S* ⲉⲡⲉ (ⲉ)ⲧⲉⲓ εἰ), Ps 57 11 *S* (*B* ϩⲁⲣⲁ) εἰ ἄρα, Mt 19 25 *S* (*B* = Gk) ἄρα, ib 17 26 *S* (*B* do) ἄραγε, 2 Kg 2 20 *S*, Job 31 5 *S* (*B* ⲓⲥϫⲉ), ib 6 4 *S* (*B* ⲉϣⲱⲡ), Ps 93 9 *S*, Lu 24 32 *S* (*B* ⲗⲏ), Ja 2 4 *SA* (*B* do) ; MG 25 232 *B* ⲓⲉ ⲙⲙⲟⲛ ϩⲗⲓ ⲡϣⲫⲏⲣ ⲡⲧⲁⲕ ⲙⲙⲁγ ⲁⲛ, BMis 351 *S* ⲉⲓⲉ ⲡⲧⲣⲁϣⲉ ⲁⲛ (var ⲁⲣⲁ, BSM 16 *B* ⲗⲏ), AM 130 *B* ⲓⲉ ⲭⲛⲁγ ⲛⲑⲟⲕ ⲁⲛ, BG 18 *S* ⲉⲓⲉ ⲉⲕⲗⲙⲉⲉγⲉ ⲉⲟγ, PS 264 *S* ⲉⲓⲉ (ⲉ)ϣⲱⲡⲉ ⲟγⲣⲱⲙⲉ ⲡⲣⲉϥⲣ ⲛⲟⲃⲉ...must we forgive him ?, ShC 73 28 *S* ⲉⲓⲉ ⲉⲣϣⲁⲛ ϩⲟⲓⲛⲉ ... ⲁⲡⲟⲧⲁⲥⲥⲉ... ⲉϥⲡⲁϣⲱⲡⲉ ⲉγⲧⲥⲁⲓⲏγ ⲡⲟγⲏⲣ, Mor 19 11 *S* (var om) prove them ϫⲉⲉⲓⲉ ⲥⲉⲡⲁⲙⲓϣⲉ ⲕⲁⲗⲱⲥ = Miss 4 99 *B* ϫⲉⲁⲛ ⲥⲉⲡⲁ-, P 129¹⁴ 124 *S* Shenoute forbidden to embark says ⲉⲓⲉ ⲙⲙⲟⲛ, God's will be done = Miss 4 13 *B* ⲓⲥϫⲉ ⲙⲙⲟⲛ. Pcod 11 *S* ⲉⲓⲉ

ⲉⲩⲧⲁⲙⲕⲁⲁϥ ⲉⲃⲟⲗⲣⲉ prob here. *V* also ⲉⲙⲉϣ-
ⲛⲓⲉ. **e.** *S BF* conj, *or, whether…or* : Lev 1 14 *B*,
4 Kg 4 13 *B*, Ps 132 1 *B*, Is 7 11 *B*, Mt 7 9 *B*
(all *S* = Gk) ἤ ; 2 Chr 6 28 *B* (Gk om) ; 1 Chr 29
14 *B*, Ps 72 11 *B* (*S* ⲁⲩⲱ ⲝⲉ-), Is 30 14 *BF* (*S* =
Gk), EpJer 9 *B* (*F* ⲙⲏ-), MG 25 11 *B* ⲡⲱⲥ ⲁⲕⲭⲁⲧ
…ⲓⲉ ⲉⲟⲃⲉⲟⲩ &c καί ; Z 347 *S* they asked how is
world (compounded) ⲉⲓⲉ ⲡⲁⲓⲟⲟⲩ…ⲏ ⲡⲕⲟⲥⲙ. ⲥⲏⲩ
= MG 25 219 *B* ⲝⲉⲁⲡ ⲡⲁⲓⲱⲟⲩ…ⲁⲛ ⲡϭⲉⲡⲟⲩϥⲓ
ⲙⲡⲕⲟⲥⲙ. καὶ εἰ ἔρχεται…καὶ εἰ ἔχει, Miss 8 31 *S*
that none go elsewhere ⲉⲓⲉ ⲛⲧⲟϥ ⲡϥⲉⲓ…ⲏ ⲛϥⲟⲩⲱϣ
ⲉⲕⲧⲟϥ μήτι μήν…ἤ, CA 104 *S* archpriest ⲉⲓⲉ ⲡⲉⲧ-
ⲙⲙⲡⲥⲱϥ, GuDorm 6 *S* his brethren ⲉⲓⲉ ⲡⲉϥⲥⲩⲅ-
ⲅⲉⲛⲏⲥ, PMéd 130 *S* ten days ⲉⲓⲉ ⲡⲉϩⲟⲩⲟ ⲉⲡⲁⲓ,
ST 266 *S* ϩⲉⲛⲕⲟⲩⲓ ϭⲁⲗⲁϩⲧ ⲉⲓⲉ ⲛⲟϭ, *ib* 241 *S*
ⲉϥⲧⲁⲁⲥ ⲛⲁⲕ ⲉⲓⲉ ⲕⲁⲗⲱⲥ (*cf* c above) ⲉϥⲧⲁⲓⲧⲁⲁⲥ,
J 99 15 *S* if they would remain within ⲏ (*l* ⲉⲓⲉ)
ⲕⲁⲗⲱⲥ if they wish to dwell without, BMis 567 *S*
These are Zacharias & John. I said unto angel ⲝⲉⲉⲓⲉ
ⲡⲉⲓⲕⲉⲟⲩⲁ (? interrog here), AM 221 *B* ⲁⲡⲁⲩ ⲝⲉ-
ϭⲟⲛⲥ…ⲓⲉ ⲁϥⲙⲟⲩⲛⲕ, C 43 230 *B* whence art thou
ⲓⲉ ⲡⲓⲙⲡⲉ ⲡⲉⲕⲣⲁⲛ, BM 585 *F* ⲓⲉ ⲡⲕⲓ ⲓⲉ ⲡⲕⲟⲩⲁⲧⲓ.

ⲉⲓⲉ† *A* *v* ⲉⲓⲣⲉ.

ⲉⲓⲏ *S* *v* ⲉⲓⲱ wash.

ⲉⲓⲱ *SA*, ⲉⲓⲟⲩⲉ *S* (BMEA 10587) *A²*, ⲓⲱⲓ, ⲓⲱ
(only Ez 40 38) *B*, ⲓⲱⲱⲓ *F*, ⲉⲓⲁ- *SAA²*, ⲓⲁ- *SB*,
ⲉⲓⲁⲁϥ *SA*, ⲓⲁϥ *B*, ⲓⲉⲉϥ *F*, ⲉⲓⲏⲧ *S*, ⲓⲱⲟⲩ† *B* vb **I.**
intr (rare), *wash* : Bor 283 75 *S* nun's feet ⲉⲩⲉⲓⲏ
ⲕⲁⲕⲱⲥ (*cf* ShC 73 118 *inf*), Kr 6 *S* 23 litres of wool
ⲉⲩⲉⲓⲏ ⲛⲡⲁⲧϭⲱⲃⲉ (*sic* MS), Job 14 18 *B* ⲉϥⲓⲱⲟⲩ (? *l*
ϩⲓⲱⲟⲩⲧ, or Copt read νίπτον), Ryl 368 *S* ⲁⲡⲟⲕ ⲟⲩⲣⲱⲙⲉ ⲙⲉⲓⲱ ⲛⲥⲱⲓ (meaning ?), Tri 319 *S* cannot
cleanse sins ⲁⲩⲱ ⲙⲉⲥⲉⲓⲁ (*sic* for rhyme). ⲁⲑⲓⲱⲟⲩ *B* *unwashed* : Zech 3 4 (*SA* ⲗⲁⲁⲙ), Ja 2 2
(*S* do) ῥυπαρός. ⲉⲓⲱ ⲉⲃⲟⲗ : ShA 2 119 *S* ⲙⲡⲉ-
ⲡⲉⲥⲡⲱⲱϣ ⲉⲧⲣⲏⲧⲟⲩ (clothes) ⲉⲓⲱ ⲉⲃ., *ib* 1 103 *S*
ⲙⲡⲁϯⲉⲓⲱ ⲣⲱ ⲉⲃ. ϩⲙⲡⲥⲁⲣⲟⲩ, ShR 2 3 81 *S* ϣⲁⲡ-
ⲧⲉⲧⲙⲗⲁⲧⲟⲩ ⲉⲓⲱ ⲉⲃ., Ep 351 *S* flax ⲉϥⲉⲓⲏ ⲉⲃ.

ⲉⲓⲱ *S* nn m, *washing* (?) : Mor 51 36 among
Pachomian monks ⲡⲉⲓⲡⲁⲥ ⲧⲁⲣⲓⲭⲓⲟⲛ ⲛⲡⲣⲁⲙⲡⲓⲱ
ⲡⲉⲓⲡⲁⲥ ⲁⲣϣⲓⲛ (ⲛ)ⲡⲉⲣⲁⲧⲣⲁⲡⲓⲥⲁ (τράπεζα).

II. tr : Ge 18 4 *B* (*B* ⲓ. ⲉⲃⲟⲗ), Ps 25 6 *S* (*B* do),
Mt 6 17 *SF* (*B* do), Jo 13 12 *SA²B* (*B* var ⲓ. ⲉⲃ.),
Aeg 282 *S* (var ⲉ. ⲉⲃ.), R 1 5 11 *S* νίπτειν, Pro 24
55 *SA* (*B* ⲓ. ⲉⲃ.), Mt 27 24 *S* (*B* do) ἀπονίπ. ; Nu
19 21 *S* (var ⲣⲱϩⲉ = *B* ⲣⲱϭⲓ), Ps 50 7 *A* (Cl, *S*
ⲝⲱⲕⲙ, *B* ⲣⲱϭⲓ), Lu 5 2 *S* (*B* do) πλύνειν, Jer 4
14 *B*, Ez 16 9 *SB* ἀποπλύν. ; CA 104 *S* ⲙⲁⲣⲉϥⲉⲓⲱ
ⲡⲡⲉⲩⲟⲩⲉⲣⲏⲧⲉ (var ⲉⲓⲁ ⲡⲉⲩ.), Aeg 254 *S* ⲉⲧⲣⲉⲩ-
ⲝⲱⲕⲙ…ⲡⲥⲉⲉⲓⲁⲁⲩ (reflex), Ep 314 *S* ⲡⲥⲟⲩⲟ…
ⲉⲩⲡⲁⲉⲓⲁⲁⲩ, ST 439 *S* ⲟⲩⲛⲏⲯⲓⲥ (νίψις) ⲡⲉⲓⲁ ϭⲓⲝ,
Nu 7 13 *S* (*B* = Gk) ϩⲡⲁⲩ ⲡⲉⲓⲁ ⲧⲟⲟⲧⲟⲩ τρύβλιον,

Z 335 *S* ⲗⲁⲕⲁⲡⲏ ⲡⲉⲓⲁ ⲡⲡⲟⲩⲉⲣⲏⲧⲉ νιπτήρ ; Mk
7 2 *B* (*S* diff) ⲁⲧⲓⲁ ⲧⲟⲟⲧ- ἄνιπτος.

ⲉⲓⲱ ⲉⲃⲟⲗ *SABF* tr, same meaning : 2 Kg 11 8 *S*,
Ps 57 11 *B* (*S* ⲉⲓⲱ), Mt 6 17 *B* (*S* do), Va 57 48 *B*
ⲉϣⲧⲉⲙⲓⲁ ⲡⲉϥϩⲁⲗⲁϩ ⲉⲃ. νίπτειν ; Lev 8 21 *SB*,
Ez 40 38 *SB* πλύνειν, BHom 3 *S* ⲉⲓⲱ ⲉⲃ. ⲙⲡⲧⲱⲗⲙ
ἀποπλύν., CaiEuch 452 *B* sim ; Lev 22 6 *S* (*B*
ⲝⲱⲕⲉⲙ) λούειν, Ac 22 16 *S* (*B* do) ἀπολού. ; 1 Kg
20 26 *S* καθαρίζεσθαι ; C 43 246 *B* ⲁϥⲓ. ⲡⲡⲉϥϭⲓⲝ
ⲉⲃ., Va 69 122 *B* ⲡⲧⲉⲕⲓⲁϥ ⲉⲃ. ϩⲉⲡⲡⲁⲓⲱⲟⲩ, Bodl(P)
a 1 *b* *S* ⲉⲓⲱ ⲡⲉⲕⲁⲡⲁⲧ ⲉⲃ. 7 times, ShC 42 129 *S*
ⲉⲙⲡⲟⲩⲉⲓⲱ ⲉⲃ. ⲙⲡⲉⲩϩⲏⲧ ⲉⲃ. ϩⲛⲧⲕⲁⲕⲓⲁ, BM 226 1
S ϣⲁⲩⲉⲓⲱ ⲉⲃ. (ⲉⲃ.) ⲙⲙⲟⲟⲩ ⲡ[ϩ]ⲱⲃ ⲛⲓⲙ ⲙⲡⲧ-
ⲡⲟⲩⲝ, ShC 73 37 *S* ⲡⲙⲁ ⲡⲉⲓⲱ ⲉⲃ. of sins.

ⲉⲓⲱ ⲉⲃⲟⲗ *SB* nn m, *washing* : Wess 18 84 *S*
water used ϩⲛⲟⲩⲥⲱⲱϣⲉϣ ⲏ ϩⲛⲟⲩⲉⲓⲱ ⲉⲃ., TEuch
1 667 *B* ⲟⲩⲓ. ⲉⲃ. of sins.

ⲣⲉϥⲉⲓⲱ ⲉⲃ. *S* nn m, *washer* in baths : P 44 86 =
43 66 р. · πλύτης غلّا (which 67 = τρίβεϛ), *ib* 62
غسال.

ⲉⲓⲁ ⲧⲟⲟⲧϥ ⲛⲥⲁ- *SAB*, *despair of, renounce* : Si 22
22 *SA*, BMar 112 *S* ⲁⲡⲉϥⲉⲓⲱⲧ ⲉⲓⲁ ⲧⲟⲟⲧϥ ⲡⲥⲱϥ
ἀπελπίζειν, BHom 12 *S* let us not ⲉⲓⲁ ⲧⲟⲟⲧⲛ ⲡⲥⲱⲛ
ἀπογινώσκειν, MélOr 6 508 *B* ⲙⲡⲉⲣⲓⲁ ⲧⲟⲧⲕ ⲛⲥⲁ-
ⲡⲉⲕⲟⲩⲝⲁⲓ ; BMar 169 *S* ⲟⲩⲙⲛⲧⲉⲓⲁ ⲧⲟⲟⲧⲕ
ⲡⲥⲱⲕ ⲙⲙⲓⲛ ⲙⲙⲟⲕ ἀγνωσία (? ἀπογν.), BMis 83 *S*
sim ; Va 58 108 *B* ⲟⲩⲝⲓⲛⲓⲁ ⲧⲟⲧⲟⲩ ⲡⲥⲁⲡⲟⲩⲟⲩ-
ⲝⲁⲓ. *V* in **I.** Ryl 368.

ⲉⲓⲱ *SA²*, ⲉⲉⲓⲱ (Ep 373), ⲉⲓⲟⲩ (Cai 42573), ⲉⲟⲩ
(Glos, Hall 73) *S*, ⲓⲟⲩ *A*, ⲓⲱ *SBF*, [ⲓ]ⲁⲱ (Mt 21
2 Mich), ⲉⲱ *SB*, ⲉ̄ (DM), ⲉⲓⲁ-, ⲓⲁ- *S*, ⲉⲓⲁ- *AF*,
ⲓⲁ- *B*, pl ⲉⲟⲟⲩ, ⲉⲱⲟⲩ (Tri 665 اتال), ⲉⲓⲱⲟⲩⲉ f (P
44 129 اتال), ⲉⲟⲟⲟⲩⲉ (rare) *S*, ⲉⲁⲩⲉ (Zech 14 15) *A*,
ⲉⲉⲩ, ⲉϩⲉⲩ *B* (these vary : Ge 32 5, Nu 31 28 &c),
ⲁⲁⲩ (Is 30 6) *F*, & sg as pl, nn m & f, *ass* : Ge 22
3 *SB* f, Ex 21 33 *SB*, Pro 26 3 *SA*, Is 32 20 *SBF*
Mt 21 2 f *SBF* ὄνος (which sometimes = *S* ⲧⲃⲛⲏ :
Ge 43 18, Jud 19 19, 1 Kg 10 2) ; Ex 34 20 *B*
(*S* ϭⲁⲓ ⲡⲁⲣⲃ), Job 24 3 *SB*, Zech 9 9 *B* (*SA* ϭⲁⲓ ⲡ.),
2 Pet 2 16 *B* (*S* diff) ὑποζύγιον ; BM 603 *F*]ⲡⲓⲱ
ⲡⲗⲏⲣϣ light (bay) coloured, Cai 42573 1 *S* ⲓⲱ ⲕⲁⲙ,
BG 41 *S* gnostic figure ⲫⲟ ⲡⲉⲓⲱ, P 131³ 31 *S*
mules born of horses & ⲡⲉⲟⲟⲩⲉ, Pcod 15 *S* archbishop ⲧⲁⲗⲏⲩ ⲉⲡⲉϥⲉⲓⲱ, OLZ 6 69 *S* ⲙⲡⲉⲓⲟⲡ
ⲉⲓⲱ that I might come, Miss 4 752 *S* ⲁϥϩⲱⲕ ⲡⲧⲉϥ-
ⲉⲓⲱ, ShMing 322 *S* monks ⲉⲩϩⲏⲕ ⲛⲑⲉ ⲡⲡⲓⲉⲓⲱ,
BM 1152 *S* ⲧⲁⲣⲟⲧⲉⲣ ⲡⲓⲱ, Ep 542 *S* ⲥⲡⲁⲩ ⲡⲓⲟ ⲡⲕⲗⲱ
ass-loads (transport-asses *v* Ep 1 165), BMis 485 *S*
ass working in ⲡⲟⲩⲉⲓⲧ, Bodl(P) b 8 *S* ⲧⲉⲓⲱ ⲙⲡⲡⲉⲥ-
ϣⲏⲣⲉ cost 1 *solidus*, BM 1068 *S* 3 asses cost 10
sol. ; in recipes : AZ 23 109 ff *S* ⲥⲟⲧ ⲡⲉⲓⲱ, ⲥⲟⲧ
ⲉⲓⲱ with which vessel covered (*cf* DM 3 27 *hs n* ⲉ̄),
Cai 42573 1 *S* sweat of black ass, *ib* 2 of wild ass,

PMéd 207 *S* ass's milk for eyes, *ib* 302 *S* ass's hoof for same, Z 628 *S* ram's horn & ass's skin; P 43 248 *S* ⲥⲓⲕ(ⲅ)ⲁⲓⲟⲡ· ⲕⲉⲑⲉ ⲡⲓⲱ قثا الحمار (Löw 331).

ⲉⲓⲁ, ⲓⲁ ⲡⲧⲟⲟⲩ *SABF*, *desert*, *wild ass*: Job 39 5 *B* (*S* ⲉⲓⲁ ⲡⲣⲟⲟⲩⲧ), Ps 79 14 *B* (*S* do), Is 32 14 *SBF* ὄν. ἄγριος; Job 11 12 *SB* ὄν. ἐρημίτης; Hos 8 9 *A* (*B* om) *onager*; BAp 172 *S* devil bound like ⲉⲓⲁ ⲡⲧ., Mor 40 27 *S* snorting like ⲓⲁ ⲡⲧ.

ⲉⲓⲁⲅⲟⲟⲩⲧ *S*, *wild ass* = ⲓⲁ ⲡⲧⲟⲟⲩ *B*; Cai 42573 2 ⲉⲓⲟⲩ ⲅⲁⲟⲩⲧ.

ⲉⲓⲁ (ⲡ)ⲥϩⲓⲙⲉ *SB* (only Job 1 14), *she ass*: Jud 5 10, Job 1 14, *ib* 42 12 (*B* ⲉⲓⲱ ⲙⲙⲉⲥⲓⲱϯ) ὄν. θήλεια.

ⲙⲉⲥⲓⲱ *F*, *young ass*: BM 1252 among animals ⲟⲩⲙ., ⲕⲉⲙ.

ⲉⲓⲱ *S* nn, name of small animal ShA 1 254 (= Z 436), explained as kind of worm ⲥⲙⲟⲧ ⲛϥⲛⲧ. *Cf* AZ 24 97. Pl of this? BMis 538 *S* pit filled with worms ϥⲛⲧ, another with ⲉⲓⲟⲟⲩⲉ (but *v* ⲉⲓⲟⲩⲉ.)

ⲉⲓⲱ *S* peg *v* ⲡⲁⲉⲓⲱ.

ⲉⲓⲃ, ⲉⲓⲉⲓⲃ, ⲉⲓⲉⲃ &c *S*, ⲉⲓⲃ, ⲓⲉⲓⲃ *A*, ⲓⲉⲃ, ⲓⲏⲃ *B*, ⲓϥ *F*, pl ⲉⲓⲉⲃⲏ *S*, ⲓⲉⲉⲃⲉ *A* & sg as pl, nn m, *hoof*: Deu 14 6 *SB*, Ps 68 32 *SAB*, Ez 26 11 *B*, Mic 3 11 *SAB* ὁπλή; Lev 11 3 *SB* ὀνυχιστήρ; PMéd 302 *S* in recipe ⲉⲓϥ of ass.   *claw*: Ez 17 3 *B* (*v* PSBA 22 75 n), Dan 7 19 *B*, Job 28 16 *B* (as jewel) ὄνυξ, MG 25 13 *B* lions dig ϭⲉⲛⲛⲟⲩⲓ., ShWess 9 139 *S* fox's as amulet, ShA 2 251 *S* cat's, BSM 119 *B* raven's, BKU 1 26(4) 17 *F* ⲡⲓϥ ⲉⲡⲉⲧ ⲛⲟⲩⲡⲁⲙ of cock, R 1 4 57 *S* martyr scraped with iron ⲉⲓⲉⲓⲃ, C 43 167 *B* sim.   *sting*: Hos 13 14 *A*, 1 Cor 15 55 *S*, Ap 9 10 *S* (all *B* ⲥⲟⲩⲣⲓ) κέντρον.   *nail*: Deu 28 35 *S* (*B* ⲥⲛⲃⲓ), 2 Kg 14 25 *S* ἴχνος, ? Ap 4 8 *SB* (no Gk, but in Gwynn's Syriac ܪܝܫܐ *talon*). Deu 21 12 *SB*, 2 Kg 19 24 *S* pare (ⲉⲓⲡⲉ, ⲱⲗⲓ) nails περιονυχίζειν, ὀνυχίζ., TU 24 5 *S* paralysed ϫⲓⲛ- ⲡⲉⲥⲉⲓⲃ ϣⲁⲧⲉⲥⲁⲡⲉ, MIF 9 93 *S* ⲡⲡⲉⲡⲉⲕⲉⲓⲃ ϭⲱⲗ, C 89 130 *B* ⲛⲓⲓ. of foot, El 94 *A*, AM 235 *B* of hands torn out, Z 611 *S* onyx glistens like ⲛⲉⲉⲓⲃ ⲛⲡⲣⲱⲙⲉ ⲡⲁⲥⲧⲓⲟⲥ; K 292 *B* ⲡⲛⲉⲃ (*l* أظافير) ⲛⲓⲃⲉⲛ, or ? = *tresses*, *v* ⲉⲓⲟⲡⲉ). Sa 13 13 *S* ὄζος; Gu 38 *S* (Epiphan *De Gem*, on Ex 30 34 ὄνυχα) ⲡⲉⲓⲃ ⲟⲩⲥⲟϭⲛⲡⲉ ⲛϣⲁⲩⲧⲁⲙⲓⲟϥ.

ⲓⲉⲃ-, ⲓⲏⲃ- *B* *v* ⲉⲓⲟⲡⲉ.

ⲉⲓⲃⲉ *SAA²*, ⲓⲃⲓ *BF*, ⲟⲃⲉ† *S*, ⲁⲃⲉ† *AA²*, ⲟⲃⲓ† *B*, ⲁⲃⲓ† *F* vb intr, *thirst*, without object: Jud 15 18 *S*, Pro 25 21 *SA*, Is 32 2 *SBF*, *ib* 41 18 *SB* (var ShMIF 23 141 *S* ⲟ ⲛⲟⲃⲉ), Jo 4 13 *SA²BF* διψᾶν; Ps 142 6 *S* (*B* ⲁⲑⲙⲟⲩ) ἄνυδρος, Nah 1 10 *SA* (*B* ϣⲟⲩⲱⲟⲩ) sim.   ⲥ ⲛ-: Ex 17 3 *SB*, Job 22 7 *SB*, Ps 41 2 *S* ⲛ-, *B* ⲉϩⲣⲏⲓ ϩⲁ-, Si 24 22 *S*, Mt 5 6 *SB* διψᾶν; ShC 73 211 *S* ⲉϥⲟⲃⲉ ⲙⲡⲙⲟⲟⲩ, Mus 34 210 *B* ⲁϥⲓ. ⲙⲙⲟⲩ.

—— nn m *SABF*, *thirst*: Ex 17 3 *SB*, Is 5 13 *SBF*, Hos 2 3 *SA* δίψος, Deu 8 15 *SB*, Is 41 17 *SB* δίψα; PS 132 *S* ⲁⲡⲉⲅⲓ. ⲃⲱⲗ ⲉⲃⲟⲗ, Pcod 48 *S* throat ϫⲁϫⲉ ϩⲁⲡⲉⲓ., J 65 24 *S* water ⲉⲱϣⲙ ⲡⲉⲅⲉⲓ. ⲙⲁ ⲡⲉⲓ.: Pro 9 12 *SAB* διψώδης, ⲕⲁϩ ⲡⲉⲓ. Is 35 7 *SF* (*B* ⲉⲧⲟⲃⲓ).

ϭⲓⲡⲉⲓ. *S* nn f, *thirst*: P 129¹⁴ 53 ϭⲓⲡϩⲕⲟ, ϭ., ϭⲓⲡⲱⲃϣ (*cf* Ep Append 1 105).

ⲉⲓⲁⲃⲉ, ⲉⲓⲁⲁⲃⲉ, ⲓⲁⲁⲃⲉ, ⲓⲁⲓⲃⲉ (MIF 9 93, Mor 43 226 &c) *S*, ⲓⲁⲃⲓ *B*, ⲓⲉⲃⲓ *F* nn f, **a.** *matter* from sores, wounds, *pus*: Job 2 8 *S* (*B* ⲙⲱⲟⲩ ⲃⲱⲛ) ἰχώρ, P 44 90 *S* صديد, C 41 24 *B* stinking like ⲟⲅⲓ. ⲡⲣⲉϥⲙⲱⲟⲩⲧ الموات *ω*, Va 66 311 *B* ϯⲓ. flowing from body ἰχώρ, MIF 9 93 *S* ⲧⲓ. of tomb shall not destroy thy body, Aeg 30 *B* sim, EW 175 *B* ⲙⲱⲟⲩ ⲛⲓ. upon thieves' crosses, BMar 38 *S*, KKS 45 *S*, SHel 41 *S*, AM 60 *B* ⲉⲓ. of corpse as ingredient in mixed poison, Mor 24 25 *F* pits full of ⲓⲉⲃⲓ ⲛⲟⲉ ⲛⲟⲩⲁⲙⲣⲉϩⲓ ⲉϥⲗⲁϫ = Mor 23 35 *S* ⲓⲁⲓⲃⲉ, Sh BM 285 = R 2 3 17 *S* ⲡϣⲱⲡⲉ ⲛϯ. ⲉⲧⲥⲱⲕ ⲉⲃⲟⲗ ⲛϩⲏⲧϥ.   **b.** *sickness*, *malady*, *B* only: Ex 23 25, Is 38 9, Mt 9 35 (all *S* ⲗⲟϫⲗⲉϫ) μαλακία; 3 Kg 17 17, Ps 40 4 (*S* ϣⲱⲡⲉ) ἀρρωστία; Jo 11 4 (*SA²* do) ἀσθένεια; Mt 8 17 (*S* ⲗⲟϫ.) νόσος, HL 110 ⲡⲓϣϯ ⲛⲓ. νόσος μακρός, TEuch 1 337 ϣⲱⲛⲓ ⲛⲓⲙ ⲛⲓⲃⲉⲛ.

ⲉⲓⲉⲃⲧ, ⲉⲉⲓⲃⲧ (oldest MSS), ⲉⲓⲃⲧ (PS), ⲉⲓⲏⲃⲧ, ⲓⲏⲕⲧ (BKU 1 8), ⲉⲉⲃⲧ, ⲉⲉⲓⲃⲧⲉ, ⲉⲓⲉⲃⲧⲉ, ⲉⲉϥⲧⲉ, ⲛⲉⲓⲏ ⲃⲉⲓⲧⲏ (Hall 97) &c (esp in J) *S*, ⲉⲓⲃⲧ *A*, ⲉⲓⲃⲧⲉ *A²*, ⲉⲓⲉⲃⲧ, ⲓⲉⲃⲧ *B*, ⲓⲏⲕⲧ, ⲁⲓⲏⲃⲧ *F* nn m, rarely without art except as adj, *the east* (but this in OTest *S* often, in NTest always ⲙⲁ ⲛϣⲁ or ⲙⲡⲉⲓⲣⲉ, except Ap 21 13; in Ps *B* always ⲙⲁ ⲛϣⲁⲓ): Ge 13 14 *SAB*, 2 Chr 4 4 *B*, Ps 67 34 *S*, Sa 16 28, Bar 4 36 *B* ἀνατολή; PS 353 *S* faces ⲕⲏⲧ ⲉⲡ., AM 323 *B* ϭⲏⲧ ⲓⲉ ⲣⲏⲥ ⲓⲉ ⲡⲉⲓ.   ⲥⲁⲡⲉⲓ., *on east side*: Ge 13 11 *B* (*S* ⲙⲁ ⲛϣⲁ), Mt 2 1 *B* (*S* do) ἀπὸ ἀν., 3 Kg 17 3 *B*, Ez 40 6 *S* ⲛⲥⲁ ⲙⲡⲉⲓ. = *B* ⲡⲓⲥⲁ ⲛⲧⲉ ⲡ., Ge 12 8 *B* ⲥⲁⲡⲉⲓ. ⲙⲃⲉⲑⲏⲗ κατὰ ἀν., Jer 32 26 *B*, Ez 20 47 *SB* ἀπηλιώτης; TT 148 *S* ⲧϫⲟ ⲉⲧⲥⲁⲉⲓ., Va 69 111 *B* palace built ⲥⲁⲡ. ⲉⲣⲏⲥ ⲛϯⲃⲁⲕⲓ, N&E 39 345 *B* palace ⲥⲁⲣⲏⲥ ⲡⲉ. of church.   As adj: PS 214 *S* ⲧⲏⲩ ⲡⲉⲓ., BM 1008 *S* ⲯⲁ ⲉⲓ., AM 328 *B* ⲭⲣⲟ ⲡⲉⲓ.

In place-name Οὐρειηβτ POxy 922.

ⲉⲓⲃⲧ *S* nail *v* ⲱϥⲧ (ⲉⲓϥⲧ).

ⲉⲓⲕⲧⲉ *S* *v* ⲉⲕⲧⲉ.

ⲉⲓⲁⲗ, ⲓⲁⲗ (Br 229), ⲓⲏⲗ (Mor 31 184) *S*, ⲉⲓⲉⲗ *A*, ⲓⲁⲗ *B* nn f, *mirror*, reflecting water: Sa 7 26 *SB*, Si 12 10 *S*, 1 Cor 13 12 *SB*, Ja 1 23 *SB* ἔσοπτρον, Ex 38 8 (26) *B* κάτοπτρον, 2 Cor 3 18

SB κατοπτρίζεσθαι; K 360 *B* مرآ; Job 41 22 *S* ἐξάλειπτρον (? mistaken for ἔσοπτρον, *B* diff), Br 229 *S* ϯαλ μπτηρϥ (*v* KKS 220), BMis 542 *S* αιπαυ εγει. ϩραι ϩιμπϣικ, *cf vidi alium senem deorsum in fovea*; ShA 2 240 *S* that he may see ⲛⲑⲉ ⲉⲃⲟⲗ ϩⲓⲧⲛⲟⲩⲉⲓ., Va 57 1 *B* parables ϩⲱⲥ ⲉⲃⲟⲗ ϩⲓⲧⲉⲛⲟⲩⲓ., MG 25 109 *B* looking to him as to ⲟⲩⲉⲓ., Va 58 15 *B* Christ shines ϩⲓⲧⲉⲛϯ. ⲡⲁⲧⲟⲱⲗⲉⲃ of incarnation, Miss 4 767 *S* looking ⲉⲩⲉⲓ. ϩⲛⲟⲩϣⲟⲩϣⲧ (? glazed window), Ryl 369 *S* potter (ⲥⲁ ⲛⲁⲡⲟⲧ) to make ιαλ, ST 117 *S* 3 ⲕⲉⲗⲗⲁⲣⲓⲁ of ει. (? glass), AP 11 *A²* ειελ of silver ἔσοπ., Mich 550 29 *S* jacynth ⲥϯⲉⲗⲗⲉ gleams like ⲧⲉⲓ. ⲡⲟⲩⲙⲟⲟⲩ ⲉϥⲥⲟⲧϥ, Mor 31 184 *S* ⲧⲏⲗ of Joseph's divining φιάλη (Gen 44 5), Z 610, 611 *S* jewel ⲉϥⲧⲉⲕ ει. ⲉⲃⲟⲗ (as if ιⲉⲗⲗⲉ). *Cf* ιⲉⲗⲗⲉ.

ιααλ *F v* ειⲟⲟⲣ.

ειⲟⲩⲗ *SABF*, ⲉⲉιⲟⲩⲗ *SA*, ⲉⲓⲉⲟⲩⲗ *S* (Job 39 1) *F*, ιⲟⲩⲗ *S*, ⲉⲟⲩⲗ (C 86 117) *B* nn m & f, *cf* איל ایل (*v* OLZ 4 223), *hart, hind*: Deu 12 15 *SB*, Ps 17 34 *SB*, Pro 7 23 *SAB*, Is 34 15 *SBF* ἔλαφος; f in Job 39 1, Jer 14 5 ἐλ.; BMar 104 *S* ⲁⲅⲉⲗⲏ ⲛⲉⲓ., Cant 8 14 *S* ⲙⲁⲥ ⲛⲉⲓ. νεβρὸς τ. ἐλ.; BM 527 *Sᶠ* put drugs ⲉϩⲟⲩⲛ (ⲉ)ⲟⲩⲙⲟⲩⲥ ⲛⲉⲓ. thong of doe skin, PMéd 54 *S* ⲧⲁⲡ ⲛⲉⲓ. *hartshorn*, KroppK 52 *S* sim.

ιⲉⲗⲗⲉ *S*, ιⲉⲗⲗⲓ, ιⲏⲗⲗⲓ *F* nn, *brightness, light* (*cf* ειⲁⲗ): with ⲥιⲧⲉ, ⲥιϯ, EpJer 23 *F* (*B* ϯ ⲙⲟⲩⲉ), Mk 9 3 *F* (*S* ⲧⲟⲩⲟ, ⲙⲟⲩϩ, *B* ϥιⲣι) στίλβειν; EpJer 66 *F* (*B* ⲉⲣ ⲟⲩⲱιⲛι) λάμπειν; Mich 550 29 *S v* ειⲁⲗ.

ειⲉⲗⲉⲗ, ⲉⲓⲉⲗⲉιⲉⲗ(Mor) *S*, ιⲉⲗⲉⲗ, ⲉⲗⲉⲗ *B* vb intr, *shine, glitter*: Ez 21 28 *B* (Mich Paschal Lect 246) ⲡⲧⲉιⲉⲗⲏⲗ (var ϥιⲣι) στίλ., Z 332 *S* ⲡⲉⲩⲟⲩⲟⲓ ει. ⲉⲃⲟⲗ φωτὸς ἀποστίλ., Mor 37 159 *S* spiritual body ει. ⲉⲃⲟⲗ like pure mirror. As nn m, *brightness*: Ez 21 15 *B* (*ut sup*) ⲟⲩⲓ. (var vb, *S* ⲧⲁⲁⲧⲉ) στίλβωσις, Va 57 228 *B* ⲧⲁⲗιⲙⲯιⲥ (ἄλειψις) ⲛⲉⲙⲛⲓⲉ. of his garments (Gk PG 62 484 om), N&E 39 340 *B* lamps ⲉⲩϩι (ι)ⲉ. ⲉⲃⲟⲗ, P 54 119 = BMOr 8775 119 *B* ⲉϥϩι (ι)ⲉ. مصقول; Va 57 90 *B* ⲡιϩι (ι)ⲉ. gloss on στίλβωσις.

ιⲗι *F v* ειⲣⲉ.

ειⲟⲙ, ιⲟⲙ *S*, ⲉιⲁⲙ, ιⲁⲙ *A*, ιⲟⲙ *B*, pl ⲁⲙⲁιⲟⲩ *B* & sg as pl, nn m, *cf* ים, *sea B* (*S* only PMéd): Ge 1 26, Ez 27 26, Hos 4 3, Mt 14 25, He 11 29 (all *SAF* = Gk) θάλασσα; Ex 10 19 *B*, Ps 105 7 (*S* = Gk) ϥι. ⲛϣⲁⲣι, Ex 23 31 *B*, Deu 1 1 *B* (*S* = Gk) ϥι. ⲛϩⲁϥ, ἐρυθρά θ., K 214 ϥι. ⲡⲭⲁⲕι رِجْل الظلمات Atlantic; ⲥⲁϥι., ⲥⲁ ⲡⲧⲉ ϥι.: Nu 35 5, Ez 48 23 πρὸς θ.; ϩⲓⲥⲕⲉⲛϥι.: Mt 4 13, ϩιⲭⲉⲛϥι. Ez 25 9 παραθαλάσσιος; PMéd 159 *S* ⲗⲁⲥ ⲛⲉⲓ., *cf*

السمك cuttle-fish bone.   pl form: Ge 1 21, Ps 8 9, Is 11 9 θάλ.; Ex 20 4 (*S* ⲙⲟⲟⲩ), Ez 32 14 (*S* ⲙⲟⲩⲛⲉιⲟⲟⲩⲉ) ὕδατα; Ja 3 7 (*S* diff) ἐνάλιοι; K 3 ⲛιⲁ. ينابيع.   metaph, **a.** *trench, conduit B*: 3 Kg 18 35 (in TSBA 9 363), 2 Chr 4 2 θάλ.

wine press SAB: Pro 3 10 *SA* (*B* diff), Joel 2 24 *SA* (*B* ϩⲣⲱⲧ) ληνός; Is 5 2 *S* (*B* do) προλήνιον; ib 16 10 *S* (*B* do), Hag 2 16 *SAB*, Mk 12 1 *S* (*B* do) ὑπολ.; Ann 19 232 *S* ⲧⲉϩⲣⲱⲧ in midst whereof ⲛⲉι. shall be dug = C 86 112 (*cf* 107) *B*, BMis 207 *S* ει. opp ϩⲣⲱⲧ, CA 106 *S* ἀπαρχή of [ⲭⲱⲱ]ⲗⲉ & of ει. (*cf* Ex 22 29 ϩⲣⲱⲧ), ib 107 *S* ⲛⲉι. ⲣ ϩⲟⲩⲉ ⲡⲱⲡ ⲉⲃⲟⲗ ϩⲁⲛⲏⲣⲡ, C 89 195 *B* grapes to be trodden in ⲛⲓι., Ryl 159 *S* all ἀνάλωμα (of wine) ⲧⲛⲧⲁⲁϥ ϩⲩⲡι., BM 1036 *S* wine drawn ϩιⲭⲛⲡⲉⲕι., ib 1039 *S* ⲛϣⲓ ⲛⲡι. ⲛϭⲟⲟⲙ of NN;   Mor 23 35 *S* field ⲛⲉⲥⲟ ⲡι. ι. ϩιϣιⲕ ϣⲓⲕ *troughs, holes*.

In name Saq 218, 324 *S* ⲡⲁιⲟⲙ (Παιόμ, Παιάμ).

As place-name: Mor 37 54 *S* ⲡιⲟⲙ τοῦ Ἀρσενοείτου διώρυγμα, Mor 41 223 *S* Arsinoe ⲉⲧⲉⲧⲛⲟⲗιⲥ ⲙⲛⲓⲟⲙⲧⲉ, P 44 79 *S* ⲡιⲟⲙ · ⲁⲣⲥⲉⲛⲉⲱ الفيوم, K 210 *B* ⲫιⲟⲙ do, Kr 22, BM 706 *F* ⲡιⲁⲙ Crocodilopolis-Arsinoe-Medînet el-Fayyûm.   Doubtful if ιⲟⲙ alone = this, *v* WS 75 n.   Also in ⲯⲁⲣιⲟⲙ AM 153.

ειⲙⲉ, ⲉιⲙⲙⲉ (C 42 110) *S*, ⲙⲙⲉ *AA²*, ⲉⲙι *B*, ⲉιⲙι, ιⲙι *F*, ⲉⲙι, ⲙⲙι *O* vb intr, *know, understand*, **a.** *without obj*: Ge 18 21 *SB*, Jos 22 22 *S* (*cf* ib ⲥⲟⲟⲩⲛ), Is 5 19 *BF* (*S* co.), ib 48 8 *SB* (*cf* ib co.), Dan 9 25 *SB* (*cf* ib ⲛⲟⲓ, ⲕⲁϯ), Mk 15 45 *SB*, Jo 10 38 *SA²B* (*cf* ib co.), 1 Cor 13 9 *B* (*S* co.) γινώσκειν, Job 24 13 *SB*, Mk 6 33 *S* (*B* ⲥⲱ.), 2 Cor 1 13 *B* (*S* co.) ἐπιγν.; Ge 28 16 *B* (*S* co.), Pro 23 35 *S* (var co.), Is 26 11 *SB*, BHom 94 *S* εἰδέναι, Jos 1 7 *S*, Ac 12 12 *S* (*B* ⲛⲁⲩ) συνειδέναι Deu 29 9 *S*, Ps 93 7 *S*, Lu 8 10 *S* (all *B* ⲕⲁϯ) συνιέναι (mostly *S* ⲛⲟⲉι); Ex 2 4 *AB*, Sa 16 26 *S*, Mt 11 29 *SB* μανθάνειν; EpJer 23 *BF* αἰσθάνεσθαι; Si 11 8 *S*, Jer 10 21 *B* νοεῖν; PS 40 *S* how hath Lord transported us ⲉⲙⲡⲛⲉι. *whilst we knew not*?, Miss 4 727 *S* he spake in riddles, but ϣⲁⲩⲉι. ⲡⲧⲉⲩⲛⲟⲩ.   **b.** + ⲭⲉ- ὅτι, with above Gk vbs: Ex 18 11 *SB*; Si 9 18 *S*; Ps 33 8 *S* (*B* ⲛⲁⲩ); Mt 16 12 *S* (*B* ⲕⲁⲧ); Ac 23 27 *SB* & with others; He 11 8 *B* (*S* co.) ἐπίστασθαι; Sa 9 13 *S* ἐνθυμεῖσθαι; Ac 23 34 *SB* πυνθάνεσθαι; PS 1 *S* ⲙⲡⲉⲙⲙⲁⲑⲏⲧⲏⲥ ει. ⲁⲩⲱ ⲙⲡⲟⲩⲡⲟι ⲭⲉ-, C 89 72 *B* ⲉϥⲉ. ⲭⲉϥϭⲟⲥι = MG 17 325 *S* ⲉϥⲥⲟ., AM 12 *B* ⲉϥⲥⲱⲟⲩⲡ ⲭⲉ-...ⲟⲩⲟϩ ⲉϥⲉ. ⲭⲉ-, ShZ 475 *S* ⲙⲡⲟⲩⲉι. ⲏ ⲡⲥⲉⲥⲟ. ⲁⲛ ⲭⲉ-, C 86 16 *B* ϯⲉ. ⲭⲉⲉⲧⲁⲕⲥⲟⲩⲉⲛ ⲡⲉⲕιⲱⲧ, BKU 1 68 *S* when tasted ⲉιⲉι. ⲭⲉⲟⲩⲏⲣⲡⲡⲉ, PLond 4 522 *S* ει. [ⲭ]ⲉⲕⲣ ⲟⲩ, *Ancient Eg.* '27 97 *S* be so good ⲛⲧⲉι. ⲭⲉ- *ascertain*.   **c.** *with ethic dat*: R 1 138 *S* ει. ⲛⲁⲕ ⲭⲉ-,

PO 11 333 *B* ⲁⲣⲓ ⲉ. ⲡⲁⲕ ⲭⲉ-, Miss 8 39 *S*, C 41
32 *B* sim, RE 9 136 *S* ⲉⲓ. ⲡⲏⲧⲛ ⲣ̄ⲟⲩⲱⲣⲝ ⲭⲉ-,
Ep 404 *S* sim, C 86 325 *B* ⲁⲓⲉ. ⲉⲣⲟⲓ ⲉⲧⲁⲓⲁⲥⲓⲁⲓ
ϩⲉⲛⲡⲁⲥⲱⲙⲁ.   **d.** direct obj, as if constr (rare,
? incorrect): Is 8 9 *SB* ⲉⲓ. ⲡⲣⲉⲑⲛⲟⲥ, Dan 1 4 *S*
ⲉⲅⲉⲓ. ⲥⲟⲫⲓⲁ ⲛⲓⲙ, AZ 21 104 *O* ⲉⲓⲉⲙⲙⲓ ⲡⲉⲧⲉⲛ-
ⲡⲉⲥⲣ̄ⲏⲧ, *cf ib* 106 ⲉⲙⲓ ⲉⲡⲉⲧ-.   **e.** obj with ⲉ-,
Gk vbs as above : Deu 29 9 *S*, Jud 16 9 *S*, Job 21
14 *S*, Ps 39 9 *SB*, Is 63 16 *SB*, Jer 20 11 *B*, Lu
24 45 *S* (*B* ⲕⲁϯ), 1 Cor 14 35 *BF* (*S* ⲥⲟ.) ; Br 25
6 *S* ⲁⲅⲥⲟⲩⲛ ⲡ̄ⲡ̄ⲉ̄ ⲁⲅⲉⲓ. ⲉⲡⲙⲩⲥⲧⲏⲣⲓⲟⲛ, ShP 130[5]
16 *S* ⲡⲟⲉⲓ ⲙ̄ⲡⲉⲛϣⲓⲡⲉ ⲉⲓ. ⲉⲡⲉⲛⲥⲱϣ, PGol 47 *A*
none ⲙⲙⲉ ⲁⲧⲉⲅⲁⲣⲭⲏ, MIE 2 383 *B* I thought
not ⲭⲉⲡⲓϩⲉⲗⲗⲟ ⲛⲁⲉ. ⲉⲡⲁⲣⲱϩ, CA 99 *S* bishop
cannot ⲉⲓ. ⲉⲣⲟϥ, but God ⲡⲉⲧⲥⲟⲟⲩⲛ, C 86 356 *B*
splinter pierced head, but ⲙ̄ⲡⲉϥⲉ. ⲉⲣⲟⲥ, Ep 151 *S*
have received letters ⲁⲓⲉⲓ. ⲉⲣⲟⲟⲩ ; with ethic dat :
BMis 316 *S* ⲉⲓ. ⲡⲁⲕ ⲉⲡⲁⲓ ⲭⲉ-.   **f.** with ⲉⲧⲃⲉ- :
Jer 47 14 *B* ⲟⲧⲓ, Lu 2 17 *B* (*S* ⲉ-), Jo 7 17 *S*
(*B* ⲥⲱ.), Ac 24 8 *S* (*B* diff) ⲡⲉⲣⲓ.   **g.** with ⲛ- *B*
(rare) : Pro 1 2 (*SA* ⲉ-, ⲁ-), Sa 2 19 (*S* ⲇⲟ), but
ib ⲉⲙⲓ ⲉ- ; BSM 58 ⲛϯⲉ. ⲛ̄ⲡⲛⲏⲃⲓ ⲁⲛ = BMis 416 *S*
ϯⲛⲟⲉⲓ ⲁⲛ ⲛⲛ.

ⲉⲙⲓ, ⲓⲙⲓ *BF* nn m, *knowledge* : Ge 2 17 (*S* diff)
ⲅⲓⲛⲱⲥⲕⲉⲓⲛ, 1 Kg 2 3, Ps 72 11, Dan 1 4 (all *S*
ⲥⲟⲟⲩⲛ), Ro 11 33 (*SF* do) ⲅⲛⲱⲥⲓⲥ, Eph 4 13 (*SF*
do) ⲉⲡⲓⲅⲛ., Ro 1 19 (*S* do) ⲅⲛⲱⲥⲧⲟⲛ ; Is 29 14
(*S* ⲙⲛⲧⲥⲁⲃⲉ), 1 Cor 1 19 (*S* do), ZNTW 19 90 *F*
ⲥⲩⲛⲉⲥⲓⲥ ; Dan 1 17 (*S* ⲙⲛⲧⲣⲙⲛϩⲏⲧ) ⲫⲣⲟⲛⲏⲥⲓⲥ ; 1 Jo
5 20 (*S* do) ⲇⲓⲁⲛⲟⲓⲁ ; EpJer 41 *BF* ⲁⲓⲥⲑⲏⲥⲓⲥ ; *B* as
imperat with ⲁⲣⲓ (ⲓⲣⲓ) : Job 19 3, Ps 4 4, Jer 15 15,
BSM 28.   Adj : AM 259 *B* ⲟⲩⲥⲁⲭⲓ ⲡⲉ.

ⲁⲧⲉⲓⲙⲉ *S*, -ⲉⲙⲓ *B*, -ⲓⲙⲓ *F*, *ignorant, innocent* :
Ge 20 4 *B* (*S* ⲁⲧⲥⲟ.) ⲁⲅⲛⲟⲉⲓⲛ, Pro 25 3 *S* ⲁⲛⲉⲝⲉ-
ⲗⲉⲅⲕⲧⲟⲥ ; Ps 48 12 *SB* ⲁⲛⲟⲏⲧⲟⲥ ; Nu 14 23 *B* (*S*
ⲃⲁⲗϩⲏⲧ) ⲁⲡⲉⲓⲣⲟⲥ, C 86 3ⲟ3 *B* ⲁⲛⲁⲓⲥⲑⲏⲧⲟⲥ ; ShC 42
49 *S* beasts ⲛⲁⲧⲉⲓ., BM 527 *F* potion ⲧⲥⲁ[ⲥ] ⲛⲁⲧⲓⲙⲓ
(she) being *unaware*.   ⲣ̄ ⲁⲧⲉⲓⲙⲉ, ⲟ ⲛⲁⲧ. &c *SB*,
be ignorant, unconscious : Nu 12 11 *B* (*S* ⲁⲧⲥⲟ.),
Ro 11 25 *BF* (BM 506, var MR 2 70, *S* ⲉⲓⲙⲉ)
ⲁⲅⲛⲟⲉⲓⲛ, Cat 99 *B* ⲟⲓ ⲛⲁⲧ. opp ⲟⲓ ⲛⲥⲟⲫⲟⲥ, Mor 17
58 *S* ⲁⲡⲉⲣ ⲁⲧ. ⲉⲣⲟⲛ ⲉⲡⲉϥϭⲃⲏⲅⲉ ⲏⲅⲛⲟⲏⲥⲁⲙⲉⲛ ⲧⲁ
ⲕⲁⲧ' ⲁⲩⲧⲟⲛ, BMis 271 *S* he lay ⲉϥⲟ ⲛⲁⲧ., C 86 324
B sim.   ⲙⲛⲧⲁⲧ. *S* (rare), ⲙⲉⲧⲁⲧ. *B* nn f, *ignorance, innocence* : Ge 43 12 *B* ⲁⲅⲛⲟⲏⲙⲁ, Lev 5 18 *B*,
Ps 24 7 *B*, Eph 4 18 *B* (all *S* ⲙⲛⲧⲁⲧⲥⲟ.) ⲁⲅⲛⲟⲓⲁ ;
Job 1 22 *B* (*S* ⲙⲛⲧⲁⲑⲏⲧ) ⲁⲫⲣⲟⲥⲩⲛⲏ ; FR 20 *S*
Virgin bore son ϩⲛⲟⲩⲙⲛⲧⲁⲧ. ⲉⲣⲟⲥ, *cf* Miss 4 227
B ϩⲉⲛⲟⲩⲙⲉⲧⲁⲧϣⲉ. ⲉⲣⲟϥ, C 43 105 *B* cease from
ⲡⲉⲥϣⲟⲣⲡ ⲙⲙⲉⲧⲁⲧⲉ.

ⲣⲉϥⲉⲙⲓ *B* nn m, *one that knows* : Va 63 26 ϩⲏⲧ
ⲡⲣ. = BMis 417 *S* ⲣⲉϥⲛⲟⲓ, PasH 94 Moses ⲁϥⲧⲁⲙⲉ
ⲡⲣ. God, K 83 عالم.

ϭⲓⲛⲉⲓⲙⲉ *S* nn f, *knowledge* : BM 189 1 ⲧϭ̄. ⲉⲡ-
ⲡⲉⲧⲛⲁⲡⲟⲅϥ ⲧⲟ ⲉⲓⲇⲉⲛⲁⲓ.

ⲛⲁϣⲧⲉⲓⲙⲉ, -ⲉⲓⲙⲙⲉ, ⲛⲁϣϯⲙⲙⲉ, ⲛⲁϣⲧⲙⲙⲉ,
-ⲙⲉ *S*, ⲛⲁϣⲧⲙⲙⲉ *A* adj, *presumptuous, impudent,
obdurate*, cf Rec 31 159 : Pro 9 13 *SA* (*B* ϭⲁⲥⲓϩⲏⲧ),
ib 13 17 *S* (*B* ⲛⲁϣⲧ), Si 22 5 *S* ⲑⲣⲁⲥⲩⲥ, Pro 21 24 *S*
(-ⲉⲓⲙⲙⲉ, var -ⲙⲙⲉ) ⲑⲣ. ⲕⲁⲓ ⲁⲩⲑⲁⲇⲏⲥ ; RNC 26
audax ; Si 26 10 *S* ⲁⲇⲓⲁⲧⲣⲉⲡⲧⲟⲥ ; (ⲑⲣ. in Nu 13 29
= ⲛⲁϣⲧϩⲏⲧ *S*, ⲛⲁϣⲧ *B*, in Pro 18 6, Sa 11 18 =
ⲛⲁϣⲧ *S*, in Pro 28 26 ⲑⲣ. ⲕⲁⲣⲇⲓⲁ = ⲙⲛⲧⲛ. ϩⲏⲧ *S*) ;
in Sh often paral with other adj : A 2 304 ⲛⲁϣⲧ
ϩⲏⲧ ⲛ. ⲉⲓⲙⲉ, C 42 121 ⲛ. ⲙⲁⲕϩ ⲛ. ⲓⲙⲙⲉ, *ib* 172
ⲛ. ⲉⲓⲙⲉ ⲭⲁⲥⲓϩⲏⲧ, C 73 115 ⲛ. ⲉⲓⲙⲉ ⲟⲩⲁϩⲓϩⲏⲧ ;
C 42 129, 134 ⲛ. ⲙⲙⲉ (var -ⲉⲓⲙⲉ) ;   JTS 10
398 *S* wives ⲟ ⲛⲁⲧⲥⲱⲧⲙ ⲛⲛ. ⲙⲉ ; as nn, ShC 42
20 *S* murmurs, strifes, ⲛ. ⲙⲙⲉ.   ⲙⲛⲧⲛ. ⲙⲙⲉ,
-ⲙⲉ (not -ⲉⲓⲙⲉ) *S* nn f, *presumption, stubbornness* :
Is 24 8 *S* (*B* = Gk) ⲁⲩⲑⲁⲇⲉⲓⲁ ; Deu 31 27 *S* (Mor,
= *B* ⲙⲉⲧⲣⲉϥϯ ϣⲟⲛⲏⲛ) ⲉⲣⲉⲑⲓⲥⲙⲟⲥ ; R 1 1 74 *S*
ⲙⲛⲧⲛ. ⲙⲛⲧⲟⲩⲁϩⲓϩⲏⲧ ⲙⲛⲧⲁⲅⲑⲁⲑⲏⲥ, ShBMOr 8810
377 *S* ⲡⲉⲡⲧⲱⲙ ⲡϩⲏⲧ ⲙⲛⲧⲉⲡⲙⲛⲧⲛ., BAp 8 *S*
among vices.

ⲉⲓⲟⲙⲙⲉ *S*   v ⲟⲓⲙⲉ.

ⲉⲓⲡⲉ *SA*, ⲓⲡⲉ *AA*[2], ⲓⲡⲓ *BF*, ⲡⲓ *F* ; ⲡ-(ⲙ-) *SAA*[2],
ⲉⲡ- *SBF* ; ⲛⲧ⸗ *SAA*[2], ⲉⲡ⸗ *B*, ⲉⲡⲧ⸗, ⲓⲛⲧ⸗, ⲡⲓⲧ⸗ *F* ;
imperat ⲁⲡⲉⲓⲡⲉ, -ⲓⲡⲉ *S*, ⲁⲡⲓⲟⲩⲓ *B* (Mk 12 15 *SB*),
ⲁⲡⲓ- *S* (Jos 2 3) *B* (rare BM 590(2)) *F* (*ib* 597),
ⲉⲡⲓ- *O* (AZ 21 94, cf ⲉⲡⲁ- PSBA 19 185), ⲁⲡⲓ⸗
S, ⲁⲡⲓⲧ⸗ *B* (2 Tim 4 13) *F* (BM 528), ⲁⲡⲓ⸗ *A*
(Pro 6 22), ⲉⲡⲓ⸗ *A*[2] (AP 28), ⲁⲡⲉⲛⲧ⸗ *F* (Mt 14 18),
vb tr, *bring, bear* : Is 42 16 *SB*, Mt 21 7 *SB* ⲁⲅⲉⲓⲛ,
Ps 7 11 *S* ⲉⲡⲁⲅ., Ps 77 26 *SB* ⲁⲡⲁⲅ., Job 8 10 *SB*
ⲉⲝⲁⲅ. ; Is 17 13 *B* (*S* ϥⲓ), Jo 2 8 *SB* ⲫⲉⲣⲉⲓⲛ, Ro 3
5 *SB* ⲉⲡⲓⲫ., Mk 8 23 *SB* ⲉⲕⲫ. ; Lev 22 18 *SB*
ⲡⲣⲟⲥⲫ., Is 28 2 *SB* ⲕⲁⲧⲁⲫ., Jude 12 *B* ⲡⲁⲣⲁⲫ. ;
Job 30 24 *S* ⲡ ⲡⲙⲟⲩ (*B* ϩⲱⲧⲉⲃ) ⲭⲉⲓⲣⲟⲩⲥⲑⲁⲓ ; Deu
21 12 *S* (*B* ⲱⲗⲓ) ⲡⲉⲣⲓⲟⲛⲩⲭⲓⲍⲉⲓⲛ, Mor 48 79 *S* =
C 43 139 *B* sim ; Ez 17 23 *B* ⲡⲟⲓⲉⲓⲛ ; Va 57 251 *B*
voice ⲉⲧⲟⲩⲓ. ⲙⲙⲟⲥ ⲁⲫⲓⲉⲛⲁⲓ ; CA 104 *S* some corn
left ⲛⲥⲉⲛⲧⲉ ϩⲛⲡⲉⲩϭⲓⲝ, AZ 21 142 *S* ⲟⲩ ⲡⲉⲧⲛⲁ-
ⲉⲛⲧϥ ⲡⲙⲙⲁⲓ?, PLond 4 438 *S* ⲉⲡ ⲁⲡⲟⲇⲉⲓⲝⲓⲥ
produce receipt, BMOr 6948 1 *F* ⲁⲕⲟⲥⲙⲁ ⲡⲓⲧⲟⲩ,
PcodMor 22 *F* (arithm) ⲁⲡⲓⲧⲟⲩ ⲉⲓⲥ ⲱⲕⲧⲟⲩ (ⲉⲓⲥ
ⲟⲕⲧⲱ) *reduce* to (cf ⲉⲓⲡⲉ ⲉⲃⲟⲗ).   ⲡ ⲣⲁⲧ⸗ (ⲁⲛ)-
ⲉⲝⲓⲭⲛⲓⲁⲥⲧⲟⲥ, v ⲣⲁⲧ⸗ ; ⲡ ⲧⲟⲟⲧ⸗ v ⲉⲓⲡⲉ ⲉ- & ⲉⲭⲛ- ;
ⲉⲡ ⲁⲣⲏⲭ⸗ (ⲁⲛ)ⲩⲡⲟⲥⲧⲁⲧⲟⲥ, v ⲁⲣⲏⲭ⸗.
    With following preposition.

ⲉⲓⲡⲉ ⲉ- *SABF*, *bring to, for* : Ge 48 9 *S* (*B* ϩⲁ-),
Mt 14 18 *SF*, Lu 4 9 *S* (*B* ⲉϩⲣⲏⲓ ⲉ-) ⲁⲅ., ⲡⲣⲟⲥⲁⲅ.
dat, ⲉⲓⲥ, ⲉⲡⲓ ; AM 51 *B* ⲁⲅⲉⲛϥ ⲉⲏⲣⲥ, El 104 *A*
ⲁⲛⲕⲟⲩⲁⲓϣ ⲓ. ⲁⲣⲁⲕ thou shalt die, Ep 84 *S* ⲡ ⲙⲁⲣⲧⲩⲣⲟⲥ ⲉ- against.   ⲡ ⲧⲟⲟⲧ⸗ ⲉ- *S* : Jos 10 6 ⲉⲕⲗⲩⲉⲓⲛ
retrahere, 1 Kg 23 13 ⲁⲛⲓⲉⲛⲁⲓ, Si 4 33 (*B* ⲥⲱⲕ) sim.

—— ⲉⲣⲁⲧ⸗ *SB, bring to, before*: Ge 2 9 *S* (*B* ⲟⲩⲁ-), Mk 11 7 *S* (*B* do) ἄγ., φέρ. πρός; C 43 40 *B* ⲁϥⲉⲛϥ ⲉⲣⲁⲧϥ ⲛⲑⲉⲟⲇⲱⲣⲟⲥ.

—— ⲉϫⲛ- *SBF*, a. *bring upon*: Ge 6 17 *SB*, Ps 42 3 *SB*, Is 31 2 *SF* (*B* ⲉϩⲣⲏⲓ ⲉϫ.) ἄγ., ἐπάγ. εἰς, ἐπί, C 86 276 *B* ⲁⲅⲉⲛϥ ⲉϫⲉⲛⲡⲓⲃⲏⲙⲁ ἐπί (*cf* below ϩⲓϫⲛ-); Ps 80 14 *S* (*B* ⲉϩⲣ. ⲉϫ.) ἐπιβάλλειν ἐπί; Ez 23 49 *B* (*S* ⲉϩⲣ. ⲉϫ.) διδόναι ἐπί; Jud 16 3 *S*, 1 Kg 24 11 *B*, Jer 42 17 *SB* φέρ., ἀναφ., ἐπιφ. ἐπί; Ez 34 23 *B* (*S* ⲉⲓ. ⲉⲃⲟⲗ ⲉϫ.) ἀνιστάναι ἐπί; Sa 16 18 *S* ἀποστέλ. ἐπί; Nu 23 14 *B* (*S* ⲧⲁⲗⲟ) ἀναβιβάζειν ἐπί; Gk om: Ex 29 36 *B* (*cf* 14), Ez 29 3 *SB*; PS 11 *S persecutions* ⲉⲧⲟⲩⲛⲁⲡ-ⲧⲟⲩ ⲉϫⲱⲧⲛ, AM 235 *B* sim, ShA 2 157 *S* ⲙⲡⲣⲉⲓ. ⲡⲧⲉⲕⲁⲙⲉⲗⲉⲓⲁ ⲉϫⲛ- *thy guide toward light*, J 67 57 *S* ⲙⲡⲉⲥⲛ ⲗⲁⲁⲩ ⲉⲣⲟⲩⲛ ⲉϫⲱⲓ *contributed.* **b.** *liken to, compare with* (also ⲉϩⲣⲁⲓ, ⲉϩⲣⲏ ⲉϫ.): ShMIF 23 186 *S* ⲉⲓⲛⲁⲧⲛⲧⲛ ⲡⲉⲩⲧⲛⲧⲛ ⲉⲟⲩ ⲛ ⲉⲓⲛⲁⲡ-ⲧⲟⲩ ⲉϫⲛ̄ⲛⲓⲙ?, Leyd 287 *S* ⲙⲁⲣⲡⲉⲓ. *sycamore* ⲉϫⲛⲡⲓϣⲉ of Cross, BM 908 *B* ark ⲁⲅⲓ. ⲙⲙⲟⲥ ⲉϩⲣⲏⲓ ⲉϫⲉⲛ- Mary (*cf* in Cat 210 *B* ass's colt ⲉⲩⲙⲉⲅⲓ ⲉⲣⲟϥ ⲉϩ. ⲉϫⲉⲛ- *the people, ib* 226 ⲉⲕⲡⲁⲉⲣ ⲛⲟⲏⲙ ⲛⲧⲁϥⲉ ⲉϩ. ⲉϫⲉⲛ- *Godhead*). **c.** *lay hands on* (ⲧⲟⲟⲧ⸗, ϭⲓϫ), *seize*: 2 Kg 1 14 *S* ἐπιφέρ. χεῖρα, Jth 11 12 *S*, Mk 14 46 *S* (*B* ϫⲓϫ) ἐπιβάλ., Miss 8 92 *S* ⲁϥⲛ ⲧⲟⲟⲧϥ ⲉϫⲛⲧⲉϥⲙⲁⲁⲩ…ⲉⲛⲟⲩⲥⲛⲃⲉ ἐπανατείνειν dat; ShMIF 23 19 *S* ⲛ ⲧⲉⲩϭⲓϫ ⲉϫⲱϥ *set hand to* (slaying) *him* (*cf* ⲉⲓ. ⲉϩⲣⲁⲓ).

—— ⲛ- *SA²BF, bring to, of persons*: Is 48 21 *SB*, Si 46 5 *S*, Su 56 *B*, Mt 21 2 *SBF*, ἄγ., ἐπ-, προσ-; Ge 4 3 *SB*, Job 7 13 *S* (*B* diff), Sa 10 14 *S*, Mt 4 24 *SB* φέρ., ἀναφ., προσφ.; MG 25 240 *B* ⲁⲅⲉⲛ ⲟⲩⲡⲁⲣⲑⲉⲛⲟⲥ ⲛⲁϥ κομίζειν, Gu 46 *S* ϯⲛⲁⲉⲛ ⲡⲁⲙⲟⲩ ⲡⲁⲓ ⲙⲁⲅⲁⲁⲧ, MG 25 361 *B when reaping* ⲙⲡⲁϥⲉⲛ ⲡⲉϥⲥⲟⲓ ⲛⲁϥ *so as to rest*, MR 5 37 *F* ϣⲁⲃⲛⲓ ⲛⲁⲥⲟⲉⲓ ⲛⲉⲕ, *ib* 2 60 sim, *ib* 5 54 *F* ⲉϥⲉⲛⲓ-ⲧⲟⲩ ⲛⲉⲕ.

—— ⲛⲥⲁ- *S, bring against, accuse of*: Z 268 ⲁϥⲉⲓ. ⲡⲟⲩⲥⲱϣ … ⲛⲥⲁⲡⲁⲓ, BM 1079 ⲉⲕϣⲁⲡⲉⲛⲧⲥ ⲛⲥⲱⲛ ϫⲉ-, PRain 4738 *God give me not* ⲉⲡⲉⲓⲛ ⲥⲱⲃⲉ ⲛⲥⲁⲣⲱⲙⲉ. *Cf* ⲉⲓ. ⲉⲃⲟⲗ.

—— ⲛⲁϩⲣⲛ- *SB, bring before*: Ez 16 21 *SB* ἀποτροπιάζειν; Mor 31 111 *S* ⲛϥⲉⲛ ⲡⲣⲱⲃ ⲛⲁϩⲣⲁϥ, J 42 8 *S*, BMis 143 *S* sim.

—— ϣⲁ- *SB, bring to*: Mk 2 3 *S* (*B* ⲛ-) φέρ. πρός, Lu 10 15 *S* pass (*B* diff) καταβιβάζ., BSM 71 *B* ⲉⲧⲁⲩⲉⲛⲟⲩ ϣⲁⲣⲟϥ.

—— ϩⲁ- *B, bring to, of persons*: Ge 2 19 *S* ⲉⲣⲁⲧ⸗) ἄγ. πρός, Is 30 6 (*SF* do) φέρ. πρός, C 43 136 ⲁⲛ. ϩⲁⲣⲟⲥ ⲡⲟⲩⲙⲛϣ ⲛⲥⲛⲏⲓ.

—— ϩⲓϫⲛ- *SB, bring, carry upon*: Lu 5 18 *SB* φέρ. ἐπί; Ez 37 14 *B* τιθέναι ἐπί; C 86 247 *B* ϯ.

ⲡⲡⲓⲣⲓⲙⲓⲁ ϩ. ⲡⲓⲣⲱⲙⲓ, C 43 214 *B* ⲁⲅⲉⲛϥ ϩ. ⲡⲓ-ⲃⲏⲙⲁ (*cf* above ⲉϫⲛ-).

With following adverb.

—— ⲉⲃⲟⲗ *SAA²BF, bring, put out, publish*: Nu 5 15 *B* (*S* ϫⲓ), Lu 23 32 *S* (*B* om ⲉⲃ.) ἄγ., Ge 1 20 *B* (*S* ⲧⲁⲅⲟ ⲉⲃ.), Job 12 22 *SB* ἐξάγ., Pro 4 27 *A* (*B* diff) προάγ.; Ge 14 18 *SB*, Ac 5 6 *B* (*S* ϫⲓ) ἐκφέρ., Lu 6 45 *S* (*B* ⲧⲁⲅⲟ ⲉⲃ.) προφέρ., ClPr 30 5 *S* ⲥⲉⲉⲓ. ⲉⲃ. ⲡⲛⲉⲩϣⲁϫⲉ *in agreement* προσφέρ.; AP 11 *A²* ⲁⲥⲛ ⲡⲕⲗⲉⲗ ⲁⲃ. περιαιρεῖν; Jer 24 10 *B* (*S* ϫⲟⲟⲩ) ἀποστέλ.; Deu 17 14 *S* (*B* ϫⲱ) καθιστάναι; Cl 17 3 *A* (*cf* Job 1 1) ἀπέχειν; Va 58 180 *B* fasting vain ⲁⲕϣⲁⲡⲉⲛⲥ ⲉⲃ. before men, Lu 7 12 *S* (*B* ⲱⲗⲓ) ἐκκομίζειν; Bor 241 210 *S* ⲉⲅⲛ ϫⲱ ⲉⲃ. ⲉⲡⲡⲉ, AM 286 *B* edict ⲁϥⲟⲣⲟⲅⲉⲛϥ ⲉⲃ. in all Egypt, ST 96 *S* ⲉⲅϣⲁⲡⲛ ⲁⲥⲫⲁⲗⲉⲥ ⲉⲃ. ⲉⲣⲟ, ShA 1 98 *S* errors ⲉⲛⲧⲁⲛⲛⲓⲧⲟⲩ ⲉⲃ. ⲛⲥⲱⲟⲩ (*cf* above ⲛⲥⲁ-), Ryl 226 *S* tax-money ⲡⲉⲛⲧⲁⲩⲛⲧⲟⲩ ⲉⲃ., Ep 353 *S* bundles of flax ⲁⲓⲛⲧⲟⲩ ⲉⲃ. *finished* (weaving) them, Ryl 277 *S* fugitives *extradited*, *cf* MG 17 316 *S* = *ib* 6 *B* recruits *carried off*, RE 9 ·143(8) *S* steward *dismissed*, BM 528 16 *F* (arithm.) [ⲡⲉⲧϣ]ⲁϥⲓ ⲁⲛⲓⲧⲟⲩ ⲉⲃ. ⲛⲓⲥ(ⲉⲓⲥ) ρ *reduce them to* (?), *ib* 18 ⲁⲛⲓⲧⲟⲩ ⲉⲃ. ϩⲓϫⲉⲛ(ⲛ)ⲉⲛⲟⲩⲃ (*cf* above ⲉⲓ. alone), Mor 28 51 *S* (on Ap 11 12) ϣⲁⲅⲉⲓ. ⲉⲃ. ⲙⲡⲉⲅⲁⲣⲓⲱⲙⲟⲥ ⲡⲣⲟⲥ *the 2 years & 3 weeks*, Bor 295 108 *S* ⲙⲁⲣⲉϥⲉⲓ. ⲉⲃ. *take off* sandals, BMar 181 *S* sim, C 43 151 *B* ⲁϥⲟⲣⲟⲅⲓ. ⲉⲃ. *teeth*, ShZ 506 *S* pincers to ⲛ ⲥⲟⲩⲣⲉ ⲉⲃ., C 89 106 *B* sim, ST 109 *S* ⲛϥⲉⲛ ⲧⲉⲩϫⲟⲓ ⲉⲃ. *produce, extend*. ⲉⲓ. ⲉⲃ. ⲉϫⲛ-, *bring out upon, for*: Deu 17 15 *S* καθιστ. ἐπί, HL 102 *B* he *introduced* a custom ⲉϫⲉⲛⲛⲓ-ⲥⲛⲟⲩ, Wess 11 158 *S* brought a good father ⲉⲃ. ⲉϫⲱⲟⲩ as abbot = C 86 57 *B* ⲓ. ⲉⲃ. ⲉⲓ. ⲉⲃ. (ⲉⲃ.) ϩⲛ-, *bring out from*: Ex 3 10 *S* (*B* ⲓ ⲉⲃ. ⲉⲃ. ϫⲉⲛ-), Ps 30 4 *SB* ἐξάγ. ἐκ; PS 156 *S* ⲉⲓⲧ ⲉⲃ. ϩⲙⲡⲉⲭⲁⲟⲥ (*cf* ⲉⲓ. ⲉϩⲣⲁⲓ), ShA 1 17 *S* ⲉϣϫⲉ ⲧⲉⲧⲛⲁⲛⲧ ⲉⲃ. ϩⲙⲡⲉⲓⲙⲁ, Miss 4 138 *B* iron taken ⲉⲃ. ϫⲉⲛⲡⲓⲭⲣⲱⲙ.

—— ⲉⲡⲉⲥⲏⲧ *SBF, bring down*: 2 Kg 17 23 *B*, Ps 77 16 *S* (*B* ⲉⲭⲣⲏⲓ), Is 26 5 *SBF*, Ro 10 6 *SB* κατάγ.; Dan 5 20 *B* καταφέρ.; Mk 15 36 *S* (*B* ⲉⲭⲣ.) καθαιρεῖν; PO 11 356 *B* eyes ⲓ. ⲉⲡ. ⲡⲁⲛⲉⲣ-ⲙⲓⲱⲟⲩⲓ, C 43 41 *B* ⲁϥⲉⲛ ϫⲱϥ ⲉⲡ. = Mor 39 16 *F* ⲕⲉ ϫ., Mor 18 14 *S* women ⲉⲛ ϩⲓⲧⲟⲩ ⲉⲡ. (abortion) = Miss 4 109 *B* ⲉⲭⲣ., *ib* 717 *S* sim.

—— ⲉⲡϣⲱⲓ *B, bring, raise up*: 2 Kg 6 15, Ez 19 4 (*S* ⲉⲓ. ⲉϩⲣ.) ἀνάγ.; Lev 31 14, He 7 27 (*S* ⲧⲁⲗⲟ ⲉϩⲣ.) ἀναφέρ.; Ex 17 3 (*S* ⲉⲓ.) ἀναβιβάζ., AM 117 ⲁϥⲓ. ⲉⲡ. ⲛϯⲡⲣⲟⲥⲫⲟⲣⲁ, C 86 90 nurse ⲁⲥⲉⲛⲟⲩ ⲉⲡ. *Cf* ⲉⲓⲛⲉ ⲉϩⲣⲁⲓ.

—— ⲉⲡⲁϩⲟⲩ, ϩⲓⲛ. *SB, bring back*: AM 53 *B*

bade ⲓ. ⲡⲛⲉϥϫⲓϫ ϧⲓⲛ. ⲙⲙⲟϥ, BMar 183 *S* of faith ⲙⲡⲣⲕⲁⲁⲩ (ⲉ)ⲛⲧⲕ ⲉⲛ. ⲛⲣⲏⲧⲥ.

—— ⲉⲧⲙⲏⲧⲉ *SB, bring into midst, recall*: ShZ 592 *S* ⲁⲛⲛ ⲡⲉϥⲣ ⲡⲙⲉⲉⲩⲉ ⲉⲧⲙ., Miss 8 9 *S* he began ⲉⲉⲓ. ⲉⲧⲙ. ⲛⲑⲓⲥⲧⲟⲣⲓⲁ, Va 69 104 *B* ⲉϥⲓ. ⲉⲑⲙ. Saviour's sufferings.

—— ⲉⲑⲏ *S*, ϧⲓⲧⲉⲛ *B, bring forward*: Z 298 *S* seek not to ⲉⲓ. ⲙⲡⲉⲕϣⲁϫⲉ ⲉⲑⲏ *verbum tuum potentiam habere*, BMis 439 *S* sim, AM 294 *B* ⲁⲩⲉⲛϥ ϧⲓⲧⲉⲛ ⲙⲙⲟϥ.

—— ⲉϧⲟⲩⲛ, *SA²BFO, bring, put in*: Ge 8 9 *B* (*S* diff), Deu 8 6 *B* (var ϭⲓ), Ps 44 16 *B* (*S* om ⲉϧ.), Ac 6 12 *B* (*S* ϫⲓ) ἄγ., εἰσάγ., Aeg 276 *S* ⲉⲓ. ⲛⲛ-ⲍⲱⲡⲟⲛ ⲉϧ. προσάγ. dat; 2 Kg 6 17 *B* (*S* om ⲉϧ.), Jer 17 24 *SB*, Mt 6 13 *BF* (*S* ϫⲓ), Jo 18 29 *SA²* (*B* ⲓ. ϧⲁ-) φέρ., εἰσφ., Wess 15 135 *S* letter ⲙⲁⲣⲟⲩ-ⲉⲛⲧⲥ ⲉϧ. ⲉⲧⲡⲓⲥⲧⲓⲥ *insert* ἐμφ., Nu 3 4 *SB*, Lu 23 14 *S* (var, *B* om ⲉϧ.), Leyd 130 *S* priests that ⲉⲓ. ⲉϧ. (sacrament), P 129¹⁷ 77 *S* ⲕⲉⲓ. ⲉϧ. these words ⲕⲁⲧⲁⲣⲟⲕ προσφ.; BHom 47 *S* gold ⲛⲧⲁϥⲏⲧϥ ⲉϧ., AM 271 *B* schisms ⲉⲧⲁϥⲉⲛⲟⲩ ⲉϧ. to church βάλλειν; AZ 21 94 (*v* 38 88) *O* ⲉⲛⲓ ⲙⲓⲭⲁⲏⲗ ⲡⲁⲓ ⲉϧ., ShWess 9 133 *S* Origen ventured ⲉⲉⲓ. ⲉϧ. Stoicism into dogmas, PMéd 166 *S* mixture ⲛⲧⲉⲓ. ⲙⲙⲟⲥ ⲉϧ. to camel's milk, BSG 180 *S* bade angel ⲉⲓ. ⲛⲁⲙⲙⲉⲗⲟⲥ ⲉϧ. ⲉⲡⲉⲅⲉⲣⲏⲩ, C 43 122 *B* ⲛⲥⲉⲉⲛⲟⲩ ⲉϧ. to Rakoti, CO 94 *S* forgive me ⲛⲧⲛⲧ ⲉϧ. ⲉⲡϣⲁⲉ, *ib* 40, Ep 238 sim.   nn m *SB, reception, receipt*: MG 17 313 *S* bodily wants, their ⲉⲓ. ⲉϧ. opp ϫⲟ ⲉⲃⲟⲗ, Ro 11 15 *B* (*S* ϣⲱⲡ ⲉϧ.) πρόσλημψις. ⲣⲉϥⲛ-ⲉϧ. *S, bringer in*: Lev 19 31 (*B* diff) ⲣ. ⲕⲱⲱⲥ ⲉϧ. ἐγγαστρίμυθος, BMis 151 ⲣ. ⲣⲱⲙⲉ ⲉϧ. *raiser* of (dead) men.

—— ⲉϩⲣⲁⲓ *SAA²BF, bring up* (often *B* ⲉⲡϣⲱⲓ): Ez 40 2 *S* (*B* ⲉⲡϣⲱⲓ), Ac 11 26 *B* (*S* ϫⲓ), 1 Cor 12 2 *SB* ἄγ., 1 Kg 2 6 *S* (*B* do), Ps 29 3 *S* (*B* do), ἀνάγ. (oftenest), Zech 4 12 *SA* (*B* do) ἐπανάγ., Ac 9 8 *B* (*S* ϫⲓ ⲉϧⲟⲩⲛ) εἰσάγ.; Nu 9 13 *B* (*S* om ⲉϧ.), Deu 26 2 *S* (*B* ϭⲓ), 1 Kg 17 54 *S* (*B* ϫⲓ), 2 Kg 6 17 *B* (*S* ⲧⲁⲗⲟ ⲉϧ.), Is 57 6 *B* (*S* do) φέρ., ἀναφ., προσφ.; Jer 51 18 *B* (*S* do) θυμιᾶν; Lu 14 5 *S* (*B* ⲉⲡϣⲱⲓ) ἀνασπᾶν; Pro 20 5 *S* ἐξαντλᾶν; PS 78 *S* ⲥⲉⲛⲁⲓⲧⲥ ⲉϧ. from chaos (*cf* ⲉⲓ. ⲉⲃⲟⲗ), KroppK 52 *S* treasure (χρῆμα) ⲉⲛⲧϥ ⲉϧ. *unearth*(?), C 86 209 *B* for the dead ⲁⲩⲓ. ⲉϧ. ⲉϫⲱϥ liturgy = Miss 4 560 *S* ⲧⲁⲗⲟ ⲉϧ., BMis 244 *S* Julian ⲁⲩⲉⲓ. ⲙⲙⲟϥ ⲉϧ. as pagan, BMis 492 *S* if God ⲉⲓ. ⲉϧ. Nile inundation.   ⲉⲓ. ⲉϧ. ⲉϫⲛ- (often = ⲉⲓ. ⲉϫⲛ-): Ex 22 13 *SB*, Si 48 2 *S*, Ac 5 28 *SB* ἄγ., ἐπάγ. ἐπί; Jer 30 5 *SB*, Jude 9 *SB* φέρ., ἐπιφ.; Jo 7 30 *SA²B* ἐπιβάλ. (*cf* ⲉⲓ. ⲉϫⲛ-), Ac 9 29 *BF* (*S* ϧⲓ ⲧⲟⲟⲧⲥ) ἐπιχειροῦν; Mor 37 123 *S* Vulcan's lameness ⲉⲧⲉⲧⲛⲉⲓ. ⲙⲙⲟⲥ ⲉϧ. ⲉϫⲙⲡⲕⲁϩ ἀλληγορεῖν

εἰς (*cf* ⲉⲓ. ⲉϫⲛ-), PS 69 *S* ⲁⲕⲉⲓ. ⲙⲡⲉⲕⲧⲱϣ ⲉϧ. ⲉϫⲱⲓ.

—— ⲉϧⲣⲁⲓ, ⲉϧⲣⲏⲓ *SAB, bring down*: Ps 21 16 *B* (*S* ϫⲓ), Joel 3 2 *SB* (*A* ϫⲓ), Ac 9 30 *S* (*B* om ⲉϧ.) κατάγ.; Zech 11 2 *A* (*B* ⲕⲱⲣϫ) κατασπᾶν; ShA 2 146 *S* strong cities ⲕⲛⲁⲛⲧⲟⲩ ⲉϧ., ShCai 8007 *S* destroying (houses) ⲛϥⲉⲓ. ⲉϧ. ⲛⲛⲉⲩⲥⲛⲧⲉ.   ⲉⲓ. ⲉϧ., ⲉϧ. ⲉϫⲛ- Ez 23 46 *SB* ἄγ. ἐπί; TU 43 17 *A* ⲁϥⲉⲓ. ⲛⲧⲟⲟⲧϥ ⲁϩⲣⲏⲓ ⲁϫⲱϥ (Ethiop *stretched forth*), Z 264 *S* sim (var BMis 248 ⲁⲙⲁⲣⲧⲉ), C 43 167 *B* troubles ⲉⲧⲁⲅⲉⲡⲟⲩ ⲉϧ. ⲉϫⲱⲟⲩ.   ⲉϧ. here often for ⲉϧⲣⲏⲓ.

ϫⲓⲛⲓⲛⲓ, -ⲉⲛⲥ *B* nn m f, *bringing*: Dan 9 24 τὸ ἄγειν, Va 62 176 filled basket ⲉⲛϫⲓⲛⲉⲛϥ, Va 58 18 didst grant us ⲧϫⲓⲛⲉⲛⲧⲉⲛ ϧⲁⲣⲟⲕ;   ⲡϫ. ⲉⲃⲟⲗ: Bar 2 26 τὸ ἐξενεχθῆναι; ⲡϫ. ⲉϧⲟⲩⲛ: Ro 5 2 προσαγωγή; ⲡϫ. ⲉϧⲣⲏⲓ ⲉϫⲛ-: Ez 38 17 τὸ ἄγ. ἐπί; *ib* 43 18 (HCons 303) ἀναφέρειν.

ⲉⲓⲛⲉ *SA*, ⲓⲛⲓ *BF*, ⲉⲓⲛⲓ *F*, ⲟⲛⲓ⁺ *B* vb tr, *resemble, be like*, ⲉ ⲛ-, ⲙⲙⲟ-: Ge 34 15 *SB*, Ps 39 6 *SB*, EpJer 38 *BF*, Mt 7 24 *S* (*B* ⲑⲟⲛⲧⲉⲛ), *ib* 13 24 *BF* (*S* ⲧⲟⲛⲧⲛ), Ac 14 11 *S* (*B* ⲉⲣ ⲙⲫⲣⲏϯ) ὁμοιοῦν, EpJer 4 *BF* (*S* ϫⲓ ⲙⲡⲥⲙⲟⲧ) ἀφομ., Ex 15 11 *BF*, Job 37 23 *S* (*B* ⲑⲟⲛ.), Ps 49 21 *B* (*S* ϣⲱⲡⲉ ⲛⲧⲣⲉ), Pro 27 19 *SA*, Dan 7 5 *B* (*S* ⲟ ⲛⲑⲉ), Jo 9 9 *SA²B* ὅμοιος, ὅμ. γίνεσθαι + dat, where *B* ⲟⲛⲓ mostly = *S* ⲉⲓⲛⲉ, as Ap 11 1 *B* ⲉϥⲟ. ⲡⲟⲩϣⲃⲱⲧ, *S* ⲉϥⲉⲓ. ⲡⲟⲩ-ϭⲉⲣⲱⲃ; He 13 7 *B* (*S* ⲧⲟⲛ.) μιμεῖσθαι, Eph 5 1 *B*, 1 Thes 1 6 *BF* (*S* do) μιμητὴς γίν.; Sa 19 20 *S* (κρυσταλλο)ειδής, *cf* Nu 11 7 *S* (*B* ⲥⲙⲟⲧ); Job 1 8 *B* (*S* ⲧⲟⲛ.), 11 6 *S* (*B* diff) κατά acc., MG 25 4 *B* ⲉϥⲟⲛⲓ ⲙⲙⲟϥ κ. τ. ἡλικίαν αὐτοῦ; Si 49 17 *S*, Ap 9 7 *B* (*S* ⲟ ⲛⲑⲉ) ὡς; PS 121 *S* we found thee ⲉⲕⲉⲓ. ⲙⲙⲟϥ, Va 58 18 *B* thy son ⲉϥⲟⲛⲓ ⲙⲙⲟⲕ, Miss 8 229 *S* ⲉⲣⲉⲡⲛ̄ ⲉⲓ. ⲡⲟⲩⲛⲟⲩⲃ or silver, R 1 2 42 *S* He found none ⲡⲉⲧⲉⲓ. ⲙⲙⲁⲣⲓⲁ (var ⲧⲟⲛ.), AM 140 *B* ⲉⲣⲉⲧⲉⲛⲟⲛⲓ ⲛⲛⲉⲧⲉⲛⲉⲣⲏⲟⲩ.

—— *SABF* nn m, *likeness, aspect*: Deu 4 15 *S* (*B* ⲥⲙⲟⲧ), Ps 105 20 *SB*, Ez 1 5 *SB*, Phil 2 7 *B* (*S* ⲥⲙ.) ὁμοίωμα, Ge 1 26 *SB*, Ps 57 5 *B* (*S* ⲛⲑⲉ), Ja 3 9 *SA* (*B* diff) ὁμοίωσις, Ge 1 11 *B* ὁμοιότης; Ez 40 3 *SB*, Ap 4 4 *SB* ὅρασις; Ex 24 10 *S* (*B* ⲁⲅⲁⲡ), Is 53 2 *S* (*B* ⲥⲙ.) εἶδος; He 9 23 *F* (*SB* do) ὑπόδειγμα; Is 1 9 *F* (*SB* vb) ὡς, Ez 40 22 *SB* καθώς; ShBM 205 *S* ⲡⲉⲓ. ⲛⲛⲉϥϣⲁϫⲉ calling me father, yet obeying not, ShWess 9 159 *S* ⲡⲉⲓ. (? ἴσον) of magistrate's προστάγματα, C 43 7 *B* ⲁⲛⲟⲕ ⲟⲩϩⲟ ⲛⲟⲩϧⲟⲣ ϧⲉⲛⲡⲁⲓ., CDan 84 *B* ⲟⲩⲥⲁⲗⲉⲥⲡⲉ ϧⲉⲛⲡⲉϥⲓ. προσποιούμενος ἑαυτὸν σαλόν, C 86 198 *B* fair ⲙⲫⲣⲏϯ ⲛⲡⲓ. ⲛⲛⲓⲟϥ, P 131³ 81 *S* each healed ⲕⲁⲧⲁ ⲡⲉⲓ. ⲙⲡⲉϥϣⲱⲡⲉ = Va 61 90 *B* ⲙⲁⲓⲏ.   PS 12 *S* ⲁⲓⲣ ⲡⲓ. ⲛⲧⲁⲃⲣⲓⲏⲗ & they knew me not.   ShA 2 22 *S* demons ϫⲓ ⲉⲓ. ⲛⲣⲱⲙⲉ,

Pcod 23 *S* God ϫι πει. of man. ϫ̄πτρεϥει. *S* nn f, *resemblance*: ClPr 30 10 τϫ. ππεϥερηγ ὁμοιότης.

ειπε *SA* nn m (Ps, Is), *chain*: Ps 67 6 *S* το ϫπει. (*B* πεϫεc) πεπεδημένος; *ib* 104 18 *S* (*B* = Gk), Lu 8 29 *S* (*B* ϧαλγcιc) πέδη; *ib* 149 8 *S* (*B* do), Is 45 14 *S* (*B* do), Nah 3 10 *A* (*B* πεϫ. πϫιϫ) χειροπέδη; Sa 17 2 *S* πεδήτης; Mk 5 3 *S* (*B* = Gk) ἄλυσις; Eccl 12 6 *S* σχοινίον; Miss 4 659 *S* put on him ϧρηπεϫηc ϫ̄πρπει.

ειπε, ιπε *S*, ιπι *B* nn f, **a.** *thumb*: Glos 299 *S* τιπε ἀντίχειρ, P 44 70 = 43 40 *S* τει. πτϭιϫ ἀντ., *ib* ππιοϭ πτηηϧε ἀντ. اباب., K 77 *B* pl ابهام; Z 549 *S* πεϥει. cπτε, *ib* 550 thumbs broken, hence named παπιπε πτϩογοϫπογ, C 86 38 *B* τεϥι. cut off, ShBerlOr 1613 2 *S* extracting thorn ϧϫπεπτηηϧε ϫ̄πτεπει., PMéd 292 *S* sim tooth & C 41 18 *B* stone. **b.** *great toe*: P 44 71 *S* τει. πογερητε ἀντίπους ابهام الرجل, C 41 43 *B* tongue bound εϥι. πτε τεϥϭαλοϫ.

ειπε *S*, ιπι *B* nn f, *carpenter's axe, adze*: Is 44 12 *SB* σκέπαρνον, ShZ 637 *S* branches cut with κελεϧιπ or ει. (opp πεπκα πcλοϭλεϭ), Ryl 239 *S* ει. πραϫ̄ϣε (*cf ib* κελ. πεκωτ), Ep 547 *S* ει πραϫ̄, CO 468 *S* in list of tools. *V* Rec 39 165.

ιωπαϫ *F* *v* ογπαϫ.

ιπτωκ, π- *v* τωκ *kindle*.

ειοπε, ιοπε *S*, ειαπε *S*ᵃ(Ep 406), ιαπε *A*, ιοπη, ιοπι, ιεϧ, ιηϧ *B*, ειαπε (Hor 77), ιαπι, ιοπι *O*, ειεπ- *SAO*, ιεπ- *BF*, ιεϕ-, ιεϧ- *B* nn f, *craft, art, occupation*: Lev 13 51 *SB*, Ps 103 23 *B* (*S* = Gk), Si 38 37 *S*, Jon 1 8 *SAB* ἐργασία, *cf* Ac 19 25 *S* (*B* diff) ετρ ϧωϧ ετει. ἐργάτης; P 44 67 *S* πι. πτεχπη, Mor 17 15 *S* τέχνη, C 89 26 *B* monks work upon πιι. πεϫπιϣοϫ τεχ., ψίαθοι; Ac 18 3 *S* τεϥει. τωογτε ὁμότεχνος; Gu 68 *S* = EW 32 *B* ογει. εcϧροογ κακοτεχνία, P 129¹⁷ 79 *S* what is thy ει. ἐπιτήδευμα?, C 43 2 *B* sim, ShA 1 155 *S* πτεχ̄πιτηc πει. ϫεcϣϣε, ST 41 *S* τι. ρϫογα (*cf* below, ιεπ ογοειε), Aeg 252 *S* πει. ϫ̄πεπιcτϫ̄ϫ (*sic l*), P 131⁴ 137 *S* physician's ει. is ϯ παϧρε, JTS 9 379 *S* oh idol priests απετπει. ογωcϥ, EES ostr unpubl (*v* ϧλϧω) in list ογι. πcϧριϫε ? *ornament* (*cf* K 122 *B* as rubric to list of metal ornaments πιιεϧ الحلي), R 1 2 38 *S* adorn thyself ϧπτει. ππογϭιϫ; Jer 4 3 *B* ιεϧ ϫ̄ϧερι νέωμα (? confused with νῆμα, *v* below).

ειεπ-, ιεϧ- (or with π-) + name of craft, its material or product: ειεπcα, Cant 4 9 *S* ἔνθεμα; *ib* 5 14 *S* τορευτός; Jud 8 26 *S* περίθεμα, *cf* ShZ 638 *S* gloss on περίθ.; Hos 2 13 *A* (*B* diff) καθόρ-

μιον; 2 Kg 13 19 *S* καρπωτός (*cf* 18), Ez 41 25 *SB* (*sic l*) γλυφή, *ib* 26 *S* = *B* cα, *cf* ShP 130² 104 *S* εϥϫοκϫκ εϥϯ ει. εροογ & *ib* 130² 88 sim εcϯ cα εροc, Louvre 10022 *S* πι. τηρογ whence crown woven. ι. παϫ̄ϣε, Ex 31 5 *B* ἔργον τεκτ. ι. πcωϭι, *ib* 38 23 *B* ὑφαντός, ι. πϣωρπ, *ib* ῥαφιδευτός, *cf* ShP 130⁵ 19 *S* garment εϥο πει. ρ ϧωϧ with needle. ει. ϣπτε, P 44 112 *S* (gloss on 2 Chr 3 5 χαλαστά) ابرة, Tri 533 *S* needle πει. ϣοπτε. ι. πϧωλκ, 1 Pet 3 3 *B* ἐμπλοκή. ι. πϣπε K 156 *B* شبال. ει. ϣε, Lev 26 30 *S* (*B* ι. πϣε), EpJer 38 *F* ιεπϣη ξύλινος, Hag 1 4 *A* (*B* Gk diff). ι. πωπι, Ex 31 5 *B* λιθουργικός (*cf* 28 11). ι. προϫτ, 2 Chr 4 9 *B* κατακεχαλκ. χαλκῷ. ει. πογϧ, Is 2 20 *B* (*S* ππ.) χρυσοῦς, Est 5 1 *S*, Ps 44 9 *S* διάχρυσος, EpJer 7 *BF* περίχρ., Ap 17 4 *B* (*S* ϭοολε ππ.) κεχρυσμ.; Va 62 279 *B* ϧαπι. ππ. on hands & feet, Mor 28 89 *S* κοποπιοπ (κολόβιον) πι. π., *cf* 69 same εϥcαρτ ππ., BMis 174 *S* ϫαππα πι. π. = Mor 26 33 *S*, BSM 83 *B* πϣεπc. ι. πϧατ, Ps 104 37 *B* (*S* ϧ.), Ex 27 11 *B*, Ps 67 14 *B* (*S* πϧ.) περιηργυρωμ., EpJer 7 *F* ι. ϧετ περιάργυρος, Jer 10 4 *S* (*B* εϥϥοτϧ) ἀργ. τορευτόν. ει. επε ϫϫε, Si 50 9 *S* κεκοσμ. παντὶ λίθῳ. ει. ϫηϭε *S*, ϭηϫι *B*, Jud 8 26 *S* πορφύρεος, Is 3 21 *B* (*S* diff) περιπόρφ. ει. cοογϧε, P 44 104 *S* اسيور (but *cf* Ex 25 33 σφαιρωτήρ). ει. κοιρια, *ib* *S* اتوب (*lc* καρνίσκος). ει. ϧρηρε, *ib* 106 *S* (Nu 8 4 κρίνον), *cf* 2 Chr 4 5 *B* ι. πϣωϣεπ. ιηπ ϧϧαι, *script* PS 16 *S*. ει. ογοειε, ιεϕογωι **a.** *tillage, tilled land* (*cf* Ryl Dem 3 296 *inf*): Ge 26 14 *B*, Pro 6 7 *B* (*S* cωϣε, *A* κ̄αειε), 1 Cor 3 9 *BF* (*S* ϫα πογ.) γεώργιον, ShC 73 151 *S* πτωϣ πϯ. ογ., Ep 62 *S* keeping ἐντολαί which is τει. ογ. in Paradise. **b.** *produce of tillage*: COAd 38 *S* πτρηϫ(ιcιοπ) πεπαειε, BP 5183 *S* αγϣωc ογωϫ ϧπεπογ. **c.** ρ ει. ογ., *till*: He 6 7 *B* (*S* ρ ϧωϧ), Mor 37 95 *S* γεωργεῖν, Va 58 114 *B* ερ ι. ογ. επιποϧι, Ep 85 *S* will sow fields πτηααγ πει. ογ. ει., ι. ϣωτ **a.** *trade*, also *merchandise*: Deu 33 19 *SB*, Ez 27 13 *SB*, Nah 3 16 *AB* ἐμπορία; Hor 80 *O* αϥαπωρϫ ϣπογει., AZ 21 141 *S* going to sea πcαογκογι πει. ϣ., BSM 58 *B* frail my ship, modest τα ι. ϣ. = BMis 416 *S* αγειπ, BKU 1 22 *S* ε[ι]ϫοογκ επαϧωϧ κπαρ ταει. ϣ. (*sic l*) *business, affair* (*cf* DM 2 9). **b.** ρ ει. ϣ. *S*, ερ ι. ϣ. *B* *trade* (vb): Ge 34 10 *B* (*S* ϫι ϯ), Pro 3 14 *B* (*S* ρ ϧωϧ), Hos 12 1 *B* (*A* ρ εϣωτ) ἐμπορεύεσθαι; 2 Cor 2 17 *B* (*S* ρ εϣωτ) καπηλεύειν; Lu 19 13 *B* (*S* ρ ϧωϧ) πραγματεύεσθαι; BMis 207 *S*, AM 136 *B*. **c.** ϫετιεϧ ϣ. *B* nn f, *trading, merchandise*: MG 25 318 ϭϫ. πτεϥπιϣϯ ϫ̄πρακτικη (costly) *wares* of his eminent conduct,

BSM 2 I have naught ϫⲉⲛⲧⲁⲙ. = BMis 323 *S* ⲡⲁⲁⲡⲟⲑⲏⲕⲏ (ἀποθ. thus ? PSBA 19 221).

ϩⲁⲣⲉⲓⲟⲡⲉ *S*, *of variegated work*: Ex 26 31 (*B* = Gk) ⲉϥⲟ ⲛⲣ. χερουβείμ *pulchra varietate*; BHom 94 veil ⲛⲣ. ποικίλος.

ⲣ ⲉⲓⲟⲡⲉ *S*, ⲉⲣ ⲓⲉⲃ, ⲓⲏⲃ(ϩⲓⲏⲃ) *B*, *spin*: Mt 6 28 *SB*, Lu 12 27 *B* (*S* ⲱⲧⲣ), Ex 35 25 *B* νήθειν, cf Ryl 238 (p 114 n) *S* women shall ⲱⲣ ⲛⲥⲉⲣ ⲉⲓ. & learn ⲡⲥⲱⲣⲉ, Ex 26 36, 36 35 *B* νενησμένος مفتول opp ⲡⲥⲁϯ κεκλωσμ. لزيق, though *ib* 26 31 *B* (*S* ⲥⲏⲧ), *ib* 25 4 (var ⲙⲟⲛⲕ) διπλοῦς (var διπ. διανενησμ.)

ⲣⲉϥⲣ ⲉⲓ. *S* (*B* rare) nn, *craftsman*: 4 Kg 12 11 *S* τέκτων, Si 9 22 *S* τεχνίτης, ShA 1 107 *S* gloss on ποικιλτής (cf Ex 26 36), Va 63 86 *B* ἐπ' ἐργαστηρίου paral ἀγοραῖος, Mor 22 35 *S* paral παγανός, Ep 380 *S* skins for bookbinding from ρ.   ⲙⲛⲧⲣⲉϥⲣ ⲉⲓ. *S* nn f, *craft, art*: Deu 27 15 (*B* diff) τεχνίτης; LCyp 4 ϩⲱⲃ ⲛⲓⲙ ⲙⲙ. ἔντεχνος.

ⲉⲓⲟⲡⲉ *S* nn f, a measure (or vessel) of oil: ShC 42 71 where it holds 5 ἀρτάβαι, Ep 539 1st ⲉⲓ. holds 47 ξέσται, 2d holds 50 ξ.

ⲉⲓⲉⲣ- in ⲉⲓⲉⲣ ⲃⲟⲟⲛⲉ *v* ⲃⲱⲱⲛ & ⲉⲓⲁ *eye.*

ⲉⲓⲟⲟⲣ, ⲉⲓⲟⲟⲣⲉ(BAp, *cf* place-names) *S*, ⲓⲟⲟⲣⲉ, ⲓⲱⲱⲣⲉ *A*, ⲓⲟⲣ *B*, ⲓⲁⲁⲣ, ⲓⲁⲁⲗ *F*, nn m, *cf* יאר, *canal*: Is 19 6 *SB*, Jer 38 9 *B*, Ex 7 19 *B* ⲓ. ⲡϣⲓⲕ διῶρυξ; opp ⲉⲓⲉⲣⲟ ποταμός: Si 24 30 *S*, Is 33 21 *SBF* διῶρ., ShZ 593 *S*; El 130 *S* running ⲉⲭⲛⲡⲉⲓ. saying Ferry us to desert = *ib* 94 *A* ⲡⲭⲓⲱⲣⲉ, C 89 97 *B* ϩⲁⲡⲓⲁⲣⲱⲟⲩ, ϩⲁⲡⲓⲟⲣ, ϩⲁⲡϣⲓⲕ, ShZ 461 *S* ⲟⲩⲉⲓ. ⲉϥⲥⲱⲕ ? as if = ⲟⲩϩⲟ, BAp 35 *S* fiery river was as ⲟⲩⲕⲟϯ ⲡⲉⲓ. ⲙⲙⲟⲟⲩ, BM 1073 *S* inherited lands include ⲡⲉⲅⲉⲓ. ⲉϥϩⲁϫⲱⲟⲩ, Hall 57 *S* in boundaries ⲡⲓⲱⲣ ⲡⲁⲥ (*sic l*), CO 308 *S* (ⲓⲟⲣ), Kr 127 sim, BKU 1 315 *S* litigation ⲉ]ⲧⲃⲉⲡϩⲱⲃ ⲛⲡⲓⲱⲣ, *cf* Ep 85.

ϫⲁⲓⲟⲣ *B* nn m, *canal* (? *river*) *bank*: BSM 38 go to ⲡⲓϫ. (*sic l*) & say to fishermen = BMis 382 *S* ⲉⲓⲉⲣⲟ = BSM 145 زرع (landing-place, K 134 = ⲁⲡⲉⲓⲣⲱ).

ϫⲓⲟⲟⲣ (ϫⲓⲉⲓⲟⲟⲣ) *S*, ϫⲓⲟⲟⲣⲉ & ⲣ ϫ. *A*, ⲉⲣ ϫⲓ ⲡⲓⲟⲣ (rarely ϭⲓ) *B*, ϫⲓⲁⲁⲣ (Mor 24), -ⲓⲁⲁⲗ (Mt 14 34) *F* vb, *ferry over, ford river, cross sea or land,* **a.** *intr*: Deu 3 25 *SB*, Jos 4 8 *SB* διαβαίνειν; Sa 19 5 *S*, R 1 1 47 *S* περᾶν, Mt 9 1 *S* (*B* ⲓ ⲉⲙⲏⲣ), Lu 16 26 *S* (*B* ⲥⲓⲛⲓ) διαπερᾶν; Sa 14 5 *S* διέρχεσθαι; Gu 58 *S* man ⲉⲧϫ. ⲉϩⲟⲩⲛ to city, MG 25 191 *B* make prayer that we ⲉⲣ ϫ., AM 93 *B* ⲁϥⲉⲣϭⲓ. ⲁϥⲓ ⲉⲣⲏⲥ. **b.** *tr*: c ⲛ- of person, thing carried, ⲛ- or ⲉ- of place crossed: Ge 31 21 *SB* ⲙⲡⲓ., *ib* 32 10 *S* ⲉ-= *B* ⲛ-, Nu 32 5 *SB* ⲙⲙⲟⲛ ⲉ-, *ib* 29 *B* ⲙⲡⲓⲟⲣϫⲁⲡⲏⲥ = *S* ⲉⲡ., Jos 7 7 *S* ⲁϥϫ. ⲙⲡⲉⲓ-

ⲗⲁⲟⲥ ⲙⲡⲓⲱⲣϫ., Pro 9 18 *SA* ⲡⲟⲩⲙⲟⲟⲩ = *B* ⲥⲓⲛⲓ διαβαίν.; Deu 30 13 *SB*, Is 23 2 *S* ⲛⲑⲁⲗ. = *B* ⲉϥⲓⲟⲙ διαπερ.; Ez 47 5 *SB* διέρχ., BMar 112 *S* could not ϫ. ⲙⲡⲉϥϣⲏⲣⲉ ⲥⲛⲁⲩ διελθ. βαστάζων, BSM 2 *B* ship ϫ. ϫⲉⲛϥⲓⲟⲙ = BMis 323 *S* ⲡⲗⲉⲁ; Nu 34 4 *S* (*B* ⲥⲓⲛⲓ) παρέρχ. land, not water; Mor 25 143 *S* Nile so low that men can ϫ. ⲙⲙⲟϥ ⲡⲡⲉϩⲟⲩⲅⲉⲣⲛⲧⲉ, 4 Kg 2 14 *S* sim, P 131[1] 62 *S* Gihon comes from Ethiopia ⲉϥϫ. (? *traverses, reaches*) ⲉⲧⲕⲟⲩⲓ ⲡⲭⲱⲣⲁ ⲡⲡⲉϣⲟⲟⲩϣⲉ &c, thence to sea.   ϫ. ⲉⲃⲟⲗ: Nu 11 31 *S* (var, *B* om ⲉⲃ.), Mk 5 21 *S* (*B* ⲓ ⲉⲙⲏⲣ).   ⲁⲧϫⲓⲟⲟⲣ *S*, ⲁⲧⲉⲣ ϫ. *B* adj, *not to be crossed*: Am 5 24 *B* ἄβατος, Br 229 *S* epithet of the Father (?), *inaccessible*; ⲁⲧϣⲉⲣ ϫ. *B* Dif 2 58.

ϭⲓⲛϫⲓⲟⲟⲣ *S* nn f, *crossing, transit*: BMis 532 ⲧⲉⲕϭ. ⲛⲑⲁⲗⲁⲥⲥⲁ.

ϫⲓⲟⲟⲣ *S*, ϫⲓⲱⲣⲉ *A*, ϫⲓⲡⲓⲟⲣ *B* nn m, **a.** *place of ferry, ford*: K 404 *B* = BMOr 920 265 ϭⲓⲟⲣ عبر, معديّة; mostly ⲙⲁ ⲛϫ.: Ge 32 22 *S* (*B* ϫⲓⲛⲥⲓⲛⲓ), Jos 2 7 *S*, Jer 28 32 *B* διάβασις; Is 37 25 *S* (*B* ϫⲓⲁⲃⲑⲟⲣⲁ) γέφυρα; El 54 *A* shalt cross at ⲡⲙⲁ ⲛϫ., BAp 121 *S* sim., ST 88 *S* ? place-name. **b.** *ferry-boat*: BAp 140 *S* ⲡϫ. which is golden σκάφος, Mor 32 8 *S* at river ⲁϥⲁⲗⲉ ⲉⲡϫ., *ib* sprang out of ⲡϫ., MG 25 193 *B* sim, C 89 115 *B* he awaited ⲡⲓϫ. πορθμεῖον, *ib* 119 *B* ⲁϥⲙⲟⲛⲓ ⲡϫⲉ ⲡⲓϭ. معديّة, El 94 *A* they will flee ϩⲓϫⲛⲡϫⲓⲱⲣⲉ, Bodl(P) d 32 *S* account ϩⲁⲑⲏⲙⲉ ⲡⲡⲉϫ.   **c.** *ferryman*: BMOr 9270 *S* Paul ⲡϫ., cf Gu 57 *S* ⲟⲩⲣⲉϥϫ.; PMich 3595 *S* ⲡⲡⲉⲃ ϫ.; MG 25 178 *B* at river he saw ⲡⲓⲡⲉϥϭⲓⲟⲣ.

In place-names: ϩⲁⲙⲉⲓⲟⲟⲣ, ϩⲁⲡⲉⲡⲓⲟⲟⲣ *S* Ep 1 124, ⲕⲁϩⲓⲟⲣ *B* C 89 200, ⲕⲁϩⲓⲟⲣⲉ *S* Ep 1 119.

ⲉⲓⲉⲣⲟ, ⲓⲉⲣⲟ (Sa, PS) *S*, ⲓⲉⲣⲟ *A*, ⲓⲁⲣⲟ *B*, ⲓⲉⲣⲁ *F*, pl ⲉⲓⲉⲣⲱⲟⲩ, ⲓⲉⲣ- *S*, ⲓⲉⲣⲱⲟⲩ *AA[2]*, ⲓⲁⲣⲱⲟⲅⲉ *A* (Nah), ⲓⲁⲣⲱⲟⲩ *B*, ⲓⲉⲣⲱⲟⲩ (Is), ⲓⲉⲣⲣⲱⲟⲩ (Mor 24) *F* nn m, *river*, lit *great canal, stream* (ⲉⲓⲟⲟⲣ + ⲟ, cf Hist. Laus. ii 29 διῶρυξ τοῦ μεγάλου Νείλου), **a.** Nile & branches (cf ⲉⲓⲟⲟⲣ): Ge 41 1 *B*, Ex 2 3 *B*, Sa 19 10 *S*, Ez 29 3 *SB* ποταμός; BSM 113 *B* Michael intercedes for waters of ⲫⲓ. ⲡⲭⲏⲙⲓ, P 129[20] 124 *S* prayer for waters of ⲡⲉⲓ. in season, CaiEuch 263, 589 *B* sim, BMis 493 *S* prayed God ⲡⲁⲧⲣⲉⲡⲉⲓ. ⲙⲟⲩϩ ⲙⲙⲟⲟⲩ, C 86 6 *B* temple ϩⲓⲭⲉⲛⲫⲓ., BMis 476 *S* Nubians drink ϩⲙⲡⲉⲓ., AM 325 *B* ⲁⲩⲥⲱⲕ ⲡⲉⲙⲁϥ ϫⲉⲛⲫⲓ. to Rakoti.   **b.** other rivers: Euphrates, Ex 23 31 *SB*, Ap 9 14 *SB*; Tigris, Dan 10 4 *SB*; Jordan, Jos 4 7 *SB*, Mt 3 6 *SB*; Danube, BMis 13 *S*.   **c.** general & figur: Ps 104 41 *SB*, Pro 9 18 *SAB*, Ap 12 15 *SB*; opp ⲉⲓⲟⲟⲣ: Si 24 32 *S*, Is 33 21 *SBF*, ShZ 593 *S*, C 89 97 *B*; PS 258 *S* ⲡⲓ. ⲡⲕⲱϩⲧ, MG 25 226 *B* ⲡⲭⲣⲱⲙ; Mor 22 57 *S* ⲡⲉⲧⲣ ϩⲱⲧ ϩⲛⲡⲉⲓ., C 86 104

B sim, AM 286 *B* letters brought south ⲥⲉⲛϥⲓ., WTh 43 *B* ϩⲓϫⲉⲛⲡⲉⲛⲥϥⲟⲧⲟⲩ ⲙϥⲓ. = *ib S* ϩⲓⲭⲙⲡⲓ., AM 75 *B* town at ⲡⲓⲗⲁⲕⲣ ⲛⲧⲉ ϥⲓ.

ⲉⲓⲣⲉ *SAA²O,* ⲓⲣⲉ *A²,* ⲓⲣⲓ *B,* ⲓⲗⲓ *F,* ⲣⲁ, ⲗⲁ *BF* (*v* below); ⲣ- *SAA²O,* ⲉⲣ- *SBO,* ⲉⲗ- *F*; ⲁⲁ⸗, ⲉⲓⲁⲧ⸗ *S*(MMA 23 3 709), ⲉⲉⲧ⸗ *AA²* (Cl 53 3, Jo 8 38), ⲉⲉⲓⲧ⸗ *A²* (AP 28), ⲉⲉ⸗, ⲁⲉ⸗ (BM 1223) *A²,* ⲁⲓ⸗ *B,* ⲉⲓ⸗, ⲉⲓⲧ⸗ *F,* ⲁⲓⲧ⸗ *O* (AZ 21 100); ⲟ† *SA²F,* ⲉ, ⲉⲓⲉ† *A,* ⲟⲉⲓ† *A²* (AP), ⲟⲓ† *BF,* ⲁⲓ, ⲉⲓ (Wor 325), ⲉ† *F*(BM 582, MR 5 52); *imperat* ⲁⲣⲓⲣⲉ *S*(Jer 22 3), ⲁⲣⲓⲟⲩⲓ *B* (Is 56 1), ⲁⲣⲓ- *SAB* (Ps 2 11, Zeph 2 3 & *cf* ⲉⲓⲙⲉ), ⲉⲣⲓ- *AA²* (Cl 8 4, AP 41), ⲁⲗⲓ- (Ro 11 20), ⲁⲗⲉ- (CMSS 20) *F,* ⲁⲣⲓ⸗ *SA²* (Mt 7 12, with -ⲥ as neut: Miss 8 179 ⲁⲣⲓⲥ ⲉⲧⲃⲉⲡⲏⲉ̄), ⲁⲣⲓⲧ⸗ *B* (Phil 4 9), ⲁⲗⲓⲧ⸗ *F,* vb **I.** intr *SABF.* **a.** *act*: Ps 36 5 *SB,* Dan 9 19 *SB* ποιεῖν; Pro 14 17 *A* (*B* ⲉⲣ ϩⲱⲃ) πράσσειν; Ge 16 6 *SB,* 2 Cor 13 10 *B* (*S* = Gk) χρᾶσθαι; CA 109 *S* those baptized ⲉⲙⲡⲁⲧⲟⲩⲉⲓ. *performed* (functions). **b.** *become, befall*: Nu 5 8 *S* (*B* ⲩⲱⲡⲓ), Is 11 16 *B* (*S* diff), Mk 12 7 *SB* εἶναι; Nu 1 45 *S* (*B* ⲩ.), Su 64 *B,* Mt 23 15 *S* (*B* do) γίνεσθαι, ShBor 246 76 *S* their heart ⲣ ⲣⲏⲧ ⲛ̄ⲗⲁⲓⲙⲱⲛ, Va 57 42 *B* ⲙⲡⲉⲛⲉⲣ ⲡⲕⲉⲓⲣⲓ ⲩⲁⲡⲩⲓ of servants, PS 132 *S* ⲁⲥⲣ ⲟⲩⲛⲟϭ ⲛ̄ⲉⲣⲟ. **c.** as substitute for a preceding vb, *do* (*so*): Job 42 18 *S,* Si 34 11 *S,* El 104 *A* who sinned in heaven & ⲡⲉⲧⲁϥⲉⲓ. on earth, Va 68 44 *B* haply they might repent ⲙⲡⲟⲩⲓ., Mor 43 79 *S* call them not Jews ϫⲉⲁⲩⲗⲟ ⲉⲟ̄ⲓ (sic, *l* ⲟ), ShMIF 23 71 *S* if I sin ⲏ ⲉⲓⲩⲁⲛⲧⲁⲙⲉⲓ., Mor 51 36 *S* we lacked pottage ⲁⲛⲉⲓ. ⲉⲧⲉⲣⲱⲧⲉ, BMar 13 *S* thou art estranged from us & ⲁⲛⲟⲛ ⲡⲧⲏⲉⲓ. ⲉⲣⲟⲕ. **d.** c dat, Ge 50 12 *SB,* Lu 6 27 *SB* ποιεῖν, PS 13 *S* ⲁⲩⲉ. ⲛⲁϥ as they pleased.

II. tr, **a.** *make, do*: Nu 6 17 *SB,* PS 14 5 *SB,* Is 30 1 *SBF,* Mt 12 33 *SBF* ποιεῖν; Ps 43 1 *SB,* Jo 3 21 *SBF* ἐργάζεσθαι (oftener ⲣ ϩⲱⲃ); 2 Cor 3 12 *B* (*S* = Gk) χρᾶσθαι; PS 48 *S* ⲁⲓⲣ ⲡⲁⲓ in innocence, Va 61 107 *B* lions ⲉⲣ ⲛⲟⲩⲕⲁⲥ in pieces, BMar 136 *S* ⲉⲓⲙⲁⲣ ⲡⲥⲱⲙⲁ … ⲛⲁϣ ⲛⲣⲉ how to *treat,* J 67 94 *S* I saw my father ⲉⲁϥⲣ ⲧⲉϥⲥⲱⲛⲉ *treat* thus; Va 57 *B* uses ⲉⲣ-+suff (*v* AZ 12 157): 35 ⲑⲏ ⲉⲧⲁⲡⲉⲣⲥ ἣν ἐποιησάμεθα, 182 ⲙⲡⲉϥⲉⲣϥ οὐκ ἐποίησεν (= Si 19 13); also *B* ⲉⲣ ⲛ-: Rec 6 179 ⲧⲉⲧⲉⲛⲉⲣ ⲡⲭⲣⲓⲁ ⲛ̄ⲡⲁⲓ = BMar 214 *S* ⲣ ⲭ., DeV 29 ⲙⲡⲉⲥⲉⲣ ⲡⲭ. ϫⲉ-; PS 71 *S* all Jesus said & ⲛⲉⲧϥⲉⲓ. ⲙⲙⲟⲟⲩ, AM 256 *B* ⲁⲓⲓ. ⲛϩⲁⲛⲕⲟⲩϫⲓ ⲙ̄ⲯⲁⲗⲙⲟⲥ, AZ 21 143 *S* sailors leaped ashore ϫⲉⲉⲩⲛⲁⲉⲓ. ⲛ̄ⲧⲉⲭⲣⲓⲁ of body. **b.** *make, bear fruit*: Ge 1 11 *B,* Mt 13 26 *SF* (*B* ϯ) ποι. **c.** *pass* time, Jos 11 18 *S,* Ja 4 13 *SB* ποι.; Gk diff or om: Lev 12 4 *SB,* Job 29 18 *S,* Lu 6 12 *S,* Jo 2 20 *SB,* Tit 3 12 *SB*; ShBor 246 50 *S* ⲕⲁⲡ

ⲁϥⲣ ϣⲉ ⲡⲣⲟⲙⲡⲉ, R 1 2 57 *S* ϣⲁϥⲣ ⲟⲩⲕⲁⲓⲣⲟⲥ, Aeg 285 *S* commemorative days ⲉⲧⲩϣⲉ ⲉⲁⲁⲩ for dead, BM 217 1 *S* ⲉⲥϣⲁⲡⲉⲣ ⲡⲉϩⲟⲟⲩ weaving. **d.** *make* total, *amount to*: Job I 3 *S* (*B* ⲟⲩⲟⲛ), Lu 8 42 *S,* Ap 5 11 *S* εἶναι; Gk often om: Dan 3 1 *B,* Ac 27 37 *SB*; Va 69 111 *B* palace ⲉϥⲓ. ⲛ̄ϥ ⲙⲙⲁϩⲓ in height, My 153 *S* 4 & 2 ϣⲁⲩⲉⲣ ⲥⲟⲟⲩ, Mor 48 31 *S* ⲉⲓ̈ⲟ ⲡϣⲟⲙⲧ, TT 188 *S* house ϥⲉⲓ. ⲡⲟⲩϩⲣ ⲡⲟⲩϩⲁⲙⲉ, CO Ad 36 *S* account ⲥⲁⲃⲁⲛⲉ ζ(ύγη) δ ⲉⲓⲣⲉ νο(μίσμα) κγ, Hall 108 *S* sim. **e.** *make* price, *value* at: PRain 4721 *S* ⲁⲩⲣ ⲡⲉⲩⲥⲟⲉⲓϣ ⲛⲉⲣⲉ ⲡⲩⲙⲟⲩⲡ ⲡⲣⲟⲗⲟⲕ/; *cf* ⲣ ϣⲁⲁⲣ. **f.** as vb of direction: Lam 1 9 *B* ⲉⲣ ⲥⲁϩⲣⲏ καταβαίνειν, Wor 294 *S* he came forth ⲛϥⲣ ⲥⲁⲡⲃⲟⲗ of city, PRain 4726 *S* ⲁⲩⲉⲣ ⲡⲣⲏⲥ ⲙⲡⲓⲟⲣ, C 41 9 *B* ⲁϥⲉⲣ ϩⲓⲫⲁϩⲟⲩ ⲙⲙⲟϥ.

III. With prepositions: ⲉ-, *befall, be incumbent on*: Job 6 20 *S* (*B* ϣⲱⲡⲓ ⲛ̄-) ὀφείλειν, ShA 1 127 *S* curse ⲣ ⲉⲣⲟϥ ⲙⲡⲁⲓ ⲉⲧⲭⲱ &c; *do on behalf of, make into*: Deu 9 14 *S* (var ⲛ-, *B* ⲛ̄-) *A* (Cl 53 3) ποι.; Ep 351 *S* ⲉⲕⲉⲓ. ⲉⲣⲟⲉⲓ, I will…, BM 1160 *S* ⲙⲁϥⲉⲓ. ⲉⲣⲟⲓ except a half-carat, J 68 7 *S* ⲧϣⲉⲗⲏⲧ ⲛ̄ⲧⲁⲓⲁⲁⲥ ⲉⲣⲟϥ. other preps: ⲉϫⲛ-, Lu 2 27 *B* ποι. περί, J 76 45 *S* sickness ⲛ̄ⲧⲁⲡⲏⲉ̄ ⲁⲁϥ ⲉϫⲱⲓ, BMOr 9525 8 vo *S* of linen weaving ⲥⲉⲣ ⲉϫⲱⲟⲩ *be at work upon*; ⲙⲛ-, ⲛⲉⲙ-, Ps 147 9 *B* (*S* ⲛ-) ποι. dat, PS 103 *S* ⲁⲕⲉⲓ. ⲛ̄ⲙⲙⲁⲓ, BMar 188 *S* what thou wouldst ϯⲛⲁⲁϥ ⲛ̄ⲙ̄ⲙⲁⲕ, CO 196 *S* ⲛ̄ⲧⲉⲡⲏⲉ̄ ⲣ ⲡⲉϥⲛⲁ ⲛⲙⲙⲁⲓ; ϩⲁ-, BMis 77 *S* ⲁⲩⲉⲓ. ϩⲁⲣⲟⲥ ϩⲓⲛⲁⲓ *did regarding her* thus, ST 310 *S* if thou wilt ⲉⲓ. ϩⲁⲣⲟⲓ *oblige me*; ϩⲁⲭⲛ-, Ps 17 18 *S* (*B* ⲉⲣ ϣⲟⲣⲡ) προφθάνειν, JA '05 1 430 *S* ⲁⲥⲉⲣ ϩⲁⲭⲱⲟⲩ ⲁⲥⲡⲁⲣⲧⲥ; ϩⲓϫⲛ-, Deu 28 43 *S* ἀναβαίν. ἐπί, PS 44 *S* she wished to ascend ⲛ̄ⲥⲣ ϩⲓϫⲱⲟⲩ.

ⲣⲁ, ⲗⲁ *BF* tr = ⲓⲣⲓ esp in rel clauses, not with fut: var ⲓⲣⲓ, Ac 19 10, Ro 12 20, Ja 2 8, *cf* Jo 5 19 ⲣⲁ…ⲓⲣⲓ; further Ge 39 22 (*S* ⲉⲓⲣⲉ), Ez 12 11 (*S* do) Jo 10 25 (*SAA²* do), ZNTW 19 90 *F* ⲛ̄ⲧⲉⲓϩⲏ ⲁⲛ ⲡⲁⲩⲣⲁ ⲙⲁⲥ ποιεῖν, Ro 7 15 (*S* do), Eph 6 21 *F* ⲡⲉϥⲗⲁ ⲙⲙⲁϥ πράσσειν, *ib* 5 12 (*S* do) γίνεσθαι; Cat 9 they say words & ⲥⲉⲣⲁ ⲙⲙⲱⲟⲩ ⲁⲛ, MG 25 119 ⲡⲉⲧⲉⲕⲓⲣⲓ ⲙⲙⲟϥ ϯⲣⲁ ⲙⲙⲟϥ ϩⲱ.

ⲣ-, ⲉⲣ- &c, or ⲟ, ⲟⲓ &c combined with nn, adj *SABO,* as ⲣ ⲁⲛⲁ ἀρέσκειν, ⲣ ⲁⲡⲁⲧⲟⲟⲧ⸗ σπουδάζειν, ⲣ ⲁⲧϣⲁⲩ ἀχρειοῦν, ⲉⲣ ⲃⲱⲕ δουλεύειν, ⲣ ⲃⲟⲗ, ⲉⲃⲟⲗ φεύγειν, ⲣ ⲕⲣⲟϥ δολοῦν, ⲣ ⲙⲕⲁϩ ⲡϩⲏⲧ λυπεῖσθαι, ⲟ ⲙⲙⲁⲧⲟⲓ στρατεύειν, ⲣ ⲛⲟϥⲣⲉ συμφέρειν, ⲣ ⲡⲁϩⲣⲉ θεραπεύειν, ⲉⲣ ⲟⲩⲣⲟ, ⲟ ⲛ̄ⲣⲣⲟ βασιλεύειν, ⲣ ⲥⲟϭ μωραίνειν, ⲣ ⲟⲩ πῶς εἶναι, ποιεῖν, ⲣ ⲟⲩⲱ ἀποκρίνεσθαι, ⲣ ⲟⲩⲟⲉⲓⲛ λάμπειν, ⲣ ϣⲡⲏⲣⲉ θαυμάζειν, ⲣ ϣⲁⲩ εὔχρηστος εἶναι, ⲣ ϩⲁⲉ ὑστερεῖν, ⲣ ϩⲱⲃ ἐργάζεσθαι, ⲣ ϩⲁϩ ⲛ̄ϣⲁϫⲉ βαττολόγειν, ⲟ ⲛ̄ϫⲟⲉⲓⲥ κυριεύειν, ⲣ ϭⲱⲃ δειλιᾶν; also forming nn: ⲣ ⲛⲉϩ, ⲉⲣ

λωκ (v ⲛⲉϧ, ⲗⲱⲕ);   or with art, as ⲣ ⲡⲙⲉⲉⲩⲉ μιμνήσκειν, ⲣ ⲡⲱⲃϣ ἐπιλανθάνειν, ⲣ ⲡⲡⲉⲧⲛⲁⲛⲟⲩϥ εὐεργετεῖν, ⲣ ⲑⲉ ὅμοιος γίνεσθαι (cf ⲑⲉ ⲉⲧⲉⲕⲟ ⲙⲙⲟⲥ, ⲉϥⲟ ⲡⲁϣ ⲡⲣⲉ, v ϧⲉ).   With Gk vb SSᵃ, only in early MSS : Ps 24 13 (Rahlfs), TU 24 9, Ryl 274, 312 (cf 272), J&C 95, J 75 66 (in Tri 637, 468 prob B influence); A, as ⲣ ⲁⲓⲧⲓ, ⲣ ⲉⲗⲡⲓⲍⲉ, ⲣ ⲡⲗⲁⲡⲁ; A², as ⲣ ⲃⲁⲡⲧⲓⲍⲉ, ⲣ ⲡⲁⲣⲁⲇⲓⲇⲟⲩ; B always, as ⲉⲣ ⲁⲇⲓⲕⲓⲛ, ⲉⲣ ⲥⲧⲁⲩⲣⲟⲩⲛ, ⲉⲣ ⲭⲁⲣⲓⲍⲉⲥⲑⲉ; F sometimes, as ⲉⲗ ⲉⲧⲓⲛ, ⲉⲗ ⲡⲓⲥⲧⲉⲩⲓⲛ.   With Gk nn, as ⲣ ⲙⲉⲗⲟⲥ μελίζειν, ⲣ ⲡⲁⲡⲓⲥⲧⲟⲥ ἅπ. κρίνεσθαι, ⲣ ⲕⲁⲩⲙⲁ καυματίζειν, ⲣ ⲣⲉⲡⲧⲉⲭⲛⲏ τεχνᾶσθαι.

ⲣ ⲡⲕⲉ- SB, where ⲕⲉ- = very, even, etiam, ipse : Cant 5 7 S, Si 36 1 S, 1 Cor 5 11 S, Eph 5 12 SB, PS 303 S sins forgiven ⲙⲉⲩⲣ ⲡⲕⲉⲱⲡ ⲣⲱ ⲉⲣⲟⲟⲩ, Va 57 133 B ⲫⲁⲓ ⲉⲧⲁϥⲉⲣ ⲡⲕⲉⲁⲓϥ καὶ...ἐποίησε. V ⲕⲉ-.

ⲣⲉϥⲉⲓⲣⲉ, -ⲓⲣⲓ SB nn, maker, doer : Ja 4 11 SB ποιητὴς νόμου; Z 315 S ⲣ. ⲙⲙⲁⲉⲓⲛ σημειοφόρος, Va 58 20 B drug ⲡⲣ. ⲙϥⲙⲟⲩ.   ⲣⲉϥⲣ-, -ⲉⲣ-, ⲗⲉϥⲉⲗ- SBF, meaning sim, as ⲣ. ⲉⲓⲟⲡⲉ τεχνίτης, ⲣ. ⲡⲟⲃⲉ ἁμαρτωλός, ⲣ. ⲟⲩⲟⲉⲓⲛ φωστήρ, ⲣ. ⲣⲁⲧ ἀργυροκόπος, ⲣ. ϭⲟⲧⲉ εὐσεβής.   ⲙⲛⲧⲣⲉϥⲣ-, ⲙⲉⲧ- SB nn f, doing, making : ⲙ. ϩⲁⲗ ἀπάτη, ⲙ. ⲫⲁⲃⲣⲓ.

ⲣⲙⲛⲉⲓⲣⲉ S nn, worker : ShC 73 101 opp ⲣⲙⲡⲟⲩⲉⲣϩⲱⲃⲛⲉ.

ⲉⲓⲣⲉ S nn m, doing : Mor 37 81 = BM 251 ⲡⲉⲓ. ⲡⲣⲉⲡⲙⲁⲉⲓⲛ τὸ ποι. σημεῖα; or with suff : Gal 3 10 B ⲡⲁⲓⲧⲟⲩ (S ⲉⲁⲁⲩ) τὸ ποι.   ⲭⲓⲡⲓⲣⲓ B nn m, meaning sim : Lev 4 27 (S ⲉⲓ. vb) τὸ ποι.

ⲁϣⲓⲣⲓ B, -ⲓⲗⲓ F (p c of ⲁϣⲁⲓ + ⲓⲣⲓ Sethe) nn, diligent person (lit doing much) : Pro 10 4, 11 16, 13 4 B (S ϫⲱⲱⲣⲉ) ἀνδρεῖος; MIE 2 359 B ⲉϥⲟⲓ ⲡⲥⲡⲟⲩⲇⲉⲟⲥ ⲛⲁ., Cat 93 B ⲙⲁⲣⲉⲛⲉⲣ ⲁ. ⲉⲣⲟⲛ ere we be called from world, MG 25 353 B sim.   ⲙⲉⲧⲁ. nn f, activity, diligence : EpJer 58 F (B ϫⲟⲙ) ἀνδρεία, Va 61 20 B incited slothful ⲉⲇⲟⲩⲛ ⲉϥⲙ.

ⲧⲁϣⲉ ⲉⲓⲣⲉ, ⲓⲣⲓ SB vb, do more, increase doing : Ps 65 9 S (B ⲁϣⲁⲓ ϩⲉⲛ-) ⲁⲕⲧ. ⲁⲁϥ ⲡⲣⲙⲙⲁⲟ πληθύνειν; Ps 125 2 SB ⲧ. ⲉⲓ. ⲙⲛ- μεγαλύνειν τοῦ ποιῆσαι, Bor 240 61 S ⲉϥⲉⲣ ϩⲟⲩⲉ ⲧ. ⲉⲓ. ⲛⲙⲙⲁⲩ requiting their inhumanity.

ⲉⲓⲣⲉ, ⲉⲉⲓⲣⲉ, ⲉⲓⲉⲓⲣⲉ S nn, meaning uncertain : CO 218, 221, 299 in furniture (ὕλη) of camel ⲙⲁⲛⲧⲁⲕⲏ (μανδάκη ‎ strap, girth) ⲡⲕⲗⲁⲗ, ⲙⲁⲡ. ⲡⲉⲓ., Glos 190 parts of well ὑδροκόμος ⲟⲅⲉⲓ. ⲡϣⲏⲓ, ST 401 instructions for weaving (?) ⲡⲧⲟⲩⲱϩ ⲟⲩⲉⲓ. ⲉϧⲟⲩⲛ ⲉ[, ? Ep 246 send thy ϧⲱⲃ ⲡⲉⲓ., ST 122 ⲡⲥⲁ ⲡⲉⲉⲓ. These ? not all same word.

ⲉⲓⲱⲣⲙ, ⲓⲱⲣⲙ S, ⲓⲱⲣⲉⲙ BF, ⲉⲓⲟⲣⲙ† S, ⲉⲓⲁⲣⲙ† A²F, ⲓⲟⲣⲉⲙ† B vb intr, stare, be astonished,

dumbfounded; 1 Kg 16 4 S (B ⲉⲣ ϣⲫⲏⲣⲓ), ib 21 1 S ἐξιστάναι; EpJer 40 F (B ⲱⲡϣ sic l) ἐνεός; Ez 3 15 B μετέωρος; AP 7 A² ἔκπληκτος; TThe 228 B ⲁⲡⲁϧⲏⲧ ⲓ. ⲇⲉⲟⲩϩⲟϥ ⲟ̄ϣ, PS 92 S I was grieved ⲉⲓⲓ., ShA 2 299 S sitting ⲉⲛⲉⲓⲟ. ⲏ ⲉⲛⲟⲡϣ ⲉⲃⲟⲗ, BIF 14 146 S sim, MG 25 153 B why thine eyes ⲓⲟ. ⲇⲉⲛⲣⲁⲡⲉⲣⲙⲙⲟⲩⲓ?, Mor 39 13 F when shot ⲁⲡⲉⲣⲧⲁ ⲓⲱ. & fell = C 43 39 B ⲉⲣ ⲥⲕⲟⲧⲟⲥ.

With following preposition a. ⲉ- SA² : Job 15 12 S (B ϫⲟⲩϣⲧ) ἐπιφέρειν; Ps 24 15 S (B ⲇⲟ) Gk om, Pro 4 25 S (BMOr 8810 472, = B sic l, as in Lect Inst Cath Paris, v below) νεύειν; AP 7 A² ⲉⲥⲉⲓⲁ. [ⲁ]ⲡⲉⲉⲓ ἀτενίζειν; Z 571 S ⲙⲡⲣⲉⲓⲱ. this way & that προέχειν; R 2 2 41 S ⲉⲕⲉⲓⲟ. ϩⲙⲡⲉⲕⲣⲏⲧ ⲉⲧⲉⲥϩⲓⲙⲉ. b. ⲡⲥⲁ- SA²BF, stare after : 1 Kg 14 13 S, Ja 2 3 F (SB ϭⲱϣⲧ, ⲝ.) ἐπιβλέπειν, Si 42 15 S ἐμβλέπ.; Ac 1 10 SB, ib 3 12 S (B ⲥⲟⲙⲥ) ⲁⲧⲉⲛⲓⲍ.; ib 28 6 S (B ⲇⲟ) προσδοκεῖν; Ps 16 12 S (B ⲁⲙⲟⲛⲓ, F ⲁⲙⲉϩⲓ) ὑπολαμβ.; C 43 111 B his eyes ⲓⲟ. ⲡⲥⲱϥ.

With following adverb a. ⲉⲃⲟⲗ SB, wonder, expect, or like ⲉⲓⲱⲣⲙ : PS 26 S ⲁⲥⲉⲓⲱ. ⲉⲃ. ϩⲙⲡⲁ-ⲏⲣ for an hour, ShBMOr 8800 1 S ⲁϧⲣⲟⲕ ⲕⲉⲓⲱ. ⲉⲃ. ϩⲙⲡⲉⲕⲃⲁⲗ, ShMich 550 15 = ShA 2 251 S ⲉⲩⲉⲓⲟ. ⲉⲃ. ⲁⲛ ϫⲉ- when he shall knock ? BM 175 229 S ϣⲁⲧⲉⲧⲛⲉⲓⲱ. ⲉⲃ. ϫⲉⲙⲡⲉⲧⲛⲛⲁⲩ ⲉⲣⲟⲟⲩ, DeV 97 B ⲁϥⲓⲱ.(? sic l) ⲉⲃ...being in ecstasy (cf Miss 4 814 S ⲥⲟⲣⲙ, but = Wess 15 3 ⲉⲓⲟⲣⲙ, cf BMar 10 S ⲉⲓⲟ. ⲉⲃ. = RAl 108 B ⲥⲟⲣⲙ ⲉⲃ.), PMich 593 S charm for one ⲉϥⲉⲓⲟⲣⲙ ⲉⲃ. dazed, deranged. b. ⲉϩⲟⲩⲛ, ⲉⲇ., look intently : Lu 22 56 S (B ⲥⲟⲙⲥ), Ac 23 1 S (B ⲇⲟ) ἀτενίζειν; ib 2 12 B (S ⲁⲡⲟⲣⲉⲓ) διαπορεῖν, BSG 181 S ⲁϥⲉⲓⲱ. ⲉⲣ. ⲉϩⲣⲁϥ (= ib 12 B ⲥⲟⲙⲥ ⲉⲃ.). c. ⲉϩⲣⲁⲓ, ⲉϩⲣⲏⲓ, meaning same : Ac 7 55 S (B ⲥⲟⲙⲥ ⲉⲣ.) ⲁⲧⲉⲛ.; ROC 18 36 B ⲉϥⲓⲟ. ⲉⲣ. ϩⲁⲣⲟϥ ἀναβλέπ.

—— B nn, look : Pro 4 25 (lect Inst Cath Paris) ⲡⲧⲉⲡⲉⲕⲃⲁⲗ ϩⲓ ⲉⲓⲱⲣⲉⲙ ⲡⲥⲁ- (but prob l ⲡⲉⲕⲃⲟⲩϩⲓ).

ⲉⲓⲱⲣϩ, ⲉⲓⲱⲣⲁϩ S, ⲓⲱⲣϩ SBF, ⲓⲱϩ F (BMEA 10585), ⲉⲓⲉⲣϩ-, ⲓⲁⲣϩ- SF, ⲓⲁϩ- F, ⲉⲓⲟⲣϩ⸗ ⲓⲟⲣϩ⸗ S, ⲓⲁϩ⸗ F vb I. intr, see, perceive : Ge 48 10 S (var ⲛⲁⲩ ⲉⲃⲟⲗ, B ⲛⲁⲩ ⲙⲃ.), Eccl 12 3 S, Mk 8 18 S (B ⲇⲟ) βλέπειν; Nu 24 3 S (B ⲛⲁⲩ), Deu 4 28 S (B ⲇⲟ) ὁρᾶν; Mor 37 120 S divine nature ⲉⲧⲉⲓ. νοερός, PMéd 293 S if recipe be applied to eyes, ϥⲛⲁⲉⲓ.   opp ⲛⲁⲩ : Is 6 9 S (B ⲡ....ⲡ.) ὁρ., Mk 8 25 S (B ⲡ. bis, F ⲓ. bis) διαβλ., ShA 2 240 S ⲉⲧⲣⲉϥⲉⲓ. ⲁⲩⲱ ⲡϥⲛ. kingdom of heaven, Mor 41 28 S blind's eyes ⲉⲓ. ⲁϥⲛ. ⲉⲃⲟⲗ = Va 59 47 B ⲟⲩⲱⲛ.

II. tr : 1 Kg 26 12 S, Job 20 9 B βλ.; Deu 28 68 S (B ⲛⲁⲩ), Mk 6 50 S (B ⲇⲟ), Z 291 S ⲁⲕⲉⲓⲉⲣϩ

ⲡⲁⲓ ὁρᾶν; BHom 139 *S* every place sun ει. ⲙⲙⲟϥ
ἐφορ.; 1 Jo 1 1 *S* (*B* ⲥⲟⲙⲥ) θεᾶσθαι; Ac 27 39 *S*
(*B* ϯ ⲡⲣⲏⲧ) κατανοεῖν; 2 Cor 3 18 *S* (*B* ϫⲟⲩϣⲧ)
κατοπτρίζεσθαι; P 131ᶜ 101 *S* ει. ϧⲁⲙⲡⲉⲡ̄ⲡ̄ opp
ⲡⲁⲩ ⲡⲟⲛⲧⲱⲥ, BMis 417 *S* who can know ⲛ ⲡϭⲓ.
ⲙ̄ⲡⲭⲱⲕ of thine honour? = Va 63 26 *B* (BSM 59
diff); BM 586 *F* I wish ειⲁϧ ⲡⲉⲕϧⲁ, *ib* come ⲧⲉⲛ-
ιⲁϧⲕ, *ib* 630 *F* lo 2 years ⲙ̄ⲡⲓⲁϧⲕ, PMich 777 *F*
thou didst lend to me ⲛⲧⲁⲕⲓⲁϧ ⲡⲁϣⲕⲁⲕ (ⲛ)ⲡⲁ-
ϧⲗⲁⲧⲓ.   ειⲱⲣϧ ⲛⲥⲁ- *S*, look after, toward: BG
85 ⲉϥⲉι. ⲡⲥⲁⲥⲁ ⲡⲓⲙ ⲉϥⲛⲁⲩ ⲉⲣⲟϥ, JKP 2 82 hearest
wind ⲉⲙⲡⲉⲕ ιⲱⲣϧ ⲉⲥⲱϥ.

—— *SB* nn m, *sight, vision*: Eccl 5 10 *S* τὸ
ὁρᾶν, K 75 *B* نظر; C 89 75 *B* ⲡⲉϫι. ⲉⲧⲏⲛⲕ ⲉⲃⲟⲗ
prophetic *vision*, Pcod 9 *S* is ⲡει. bishop's chief
ἀρετή? ⲡⲡⲁⲩ ⲉⲃⲟⲗ profiteth him less than alms
giving, BAp 56 *S* ⲡϭⲱϣⲧ ⲛ ⲡει. (var Gu 45 ει.
ⲡⲥⲁ-) *sight* of women, Mich 550 25c pure shall receive νόημα in spirit & ⲡϣⲟⲣⲡ ⲡει. in soul. BMEA
10585 *F* ⲧⲁⲙⲁⲛ ⲉⲡⲉⲕιⲱϧ ⲉⲃⲁⲗ ϧⲉⲡⲉⲓⲕⲉϧⲱⲃ ϧⲓ-
ⲧⲉⲛ(ⲡ)ⲉⲓⲥϧⲉι *view, opinion*.

ⲣ̄ ⲉⲓⲁϧ (*sic* MS) *S* nn, *likeness*: Tob 7 2 ⲡⲉⲓϣⲏⲣⲉ
ϣⲏⲙ ϯ ⲣ. ⲉⲧⲱⲃⲓⲧ ὅμοιος τῷ *T*.

ⲙⲉⲧιⲟⲣϧ *B* nn f, *sagacity*: K 57 فراسة.

ⲣⲉϥⲉⲓⲱⲣϧ *S* nn, *one that sees*: Bor 252 188 soul's
eye becomes ἥμερος & ⲣⲉϥⲉι.; Mor 37 89 *S* ⲧⲙⲛⲧ-
ⲣⲉϥⲉι. ⲡⲧⲉϥψⲩⲭⲏ τὸ νοερόν *libertas*.

ϭⲓⲛ-, ϫⲓⲛⲉⲓⲱⲣϧ *SB* nn f, *vision, power to see*:
Mor 37 108 *S* saints' ϭ. ⲉⲑⲏⲡ beholding all world,
Bor 252 176 *S* ⲑⲟⲣⲁⲥⲓⲥ ⲛ ⲧϭ., Cat 81 *B* raising
thoughts ϫⲉⲛⲟⲩⲝ. ⲉⲥⲧⲟⲩⲃⲏⲟⲩⲧ.

ⲉⲓⲉⲣϧⲉ *S* nn f, *ray of light, sight* of eye: Mor 37
165 ⲉⲣⲉ ϯ ⲣϧⲉ ϧⲛ ⲧⲕⲉⲕⲉ as wick in lamp, GMir 19
blind cured ⲁⲙ̄ⲛⲁⲩ ⲉⲃⲟⲗ ⲛⲟⲩⲕⲟⲩⲓ ⲡει., ShA 2 138
houses underground have not ⲟⲩⲉι. ϣⲏⲙ ⲛⲟⲩⲟⲉⲓⲛ.

ⲉⲓⲥ, ⲉⲥ *SSᵃAAᵃ*, ιⲥ *B*, interj. **a.** *behold, lo, here
is*, used properly before nn: Ge 12 19 *B*, Ex 4 14
A ⲉⲥ...ⲉⲥⲧⲉ = *S* ⲉⲓⲥ...ⲉⲓⲥϧⲏⲧⲉ, *B* ιⲥ...ϧⲏⲡⲡⲉ, Deu
3 11 *S* (*B* ϧⲏⲡⲡⲉ ιⲥ), Jer 9 25 *SB*, Mt 3 17 *B* (*S*
ⲉⲓⲥ ϧⲏⲧⲉ ⲉⲓⲥ), *ib* 12 49, Lu 7 37 *S* (var ⲉⲓⲥ ϧ. ⲉⲓⲥ,
B ϧⲏⲡⲡⲉ ιⲥ), Mk 13 21 *SB* ⲉⲓⲥ (*F* ϧⲉⲓ)...ⲉⲓⲥ ϧ.,
He 8 8 *B* (*S* ⲉⲓⲥ ϧ., *F* ϧⲉⲓⲧⲉⲥ) ἰδού; BHom 52 *S*
ⲉⲓⲥ ⲡϧⲙϧⲁⲗ...ⲁⲩⲡⲱⲧ, BM 341 *S* monk nudged
boy saying ⲉⲓⲥ ⲡⲉⲕⲉⲓⲱⲧ, MG 17 323 *S* introducing
letter-bearer ⲉⲓⲥ ⲡⲉⲓϧⲗⲗⲟ ⲛⲧⲁⲓⲧⲛ̄ⲛⲟⲟⲩϥ, Cat 161
B heaven ιⲥ ⲡϭⲓⲥⲛ̄ ⲫⲁⲓ, hell ιⲥ ⲫⲁⲓ ⲡϣⲱⲕ (*cf
ib* in paral ⲉⲧⲉⲑⲁⲓⲧⲉ), DeV 182 *B* Hezekiah righteous, ιⲥ ⲙⲁⲛⲁⲥⲥⲏ was he not sinner? (as if = ιⲉ,
cf PS 294 14 with 293 6, 376 12 with 375 2), CO
107 *S* ⲉⲓⲥ ⲡⲗⲟⲩⲟⲥ ⲙ̄ⲡⲡ̄ⲉ̄ ⲡⲧⲟⲟⲧⲕ (*v* Ep 96 n), *ib*
409 *S* tax receipt ⲉⲓⲥ ⲟⲩϧⲟⲗⲟⲕ/ ⲁϥⲉι ⲉⲧⲟⲟⲧ, PLond
4 454 *S* sim receipt of fugitives, Ep 295 *S* letter
begins ⲉⲓⲥ ⲉⲧⲃⲉ ⲡϣⲏⲣⲉ ⲙ̄ⲡⲡ̄ⲉ̄ ⲡⲧϫⲁⲟⲩ;   ⲉⲓⲥ ϯⲙⲉ-

ⲧⲁⲡⲟⲓⲁ in letters or colophons = *I beg*: Ryl 290 *S*
ⲉⲓⲥ ϯⲙ...(ⲡ)ⲧⲉⲕⲉⲓ, BM 545 *B* ιⲥ ϯⲙ. ⲧⲉⲧⲉⲡⲉⲣ
ⲡⲁⲙⲉⲣⲓ, BMis 524 *S* ⲉⲓⲥ ⲧⲁⲙ. ⲡⲧⲉⲛⲧⲧ̄ϥ, Z 104 *B*,
BM 489 *S*; Miss 8 88 *S* ⲉⲓⲥ this is 3d time synod
calleth thee, AM 25 *B* ιⲥ many times have I sent,
C 43 174 *B* ιⲥ ⲟⲩⲏⲣ ⲙⲃⲁⲥⲁⲡⲟⲥ have I brought
on thee. *Cf* following.   **b.** *since, ago*: Deu 8 4 *S*
(*B* ϧⲏⲡⲡⲉ, var ιⲥ), Lu 15 29 *SB*, Z 347 *S* = MG
25 219 *B* we came hither ⲉⲓⲥ ϧⲙⲉ ⲡⲣⲟⲙⲡⲉ ἰδού;
Mt 15 32 *SB* (*cf* Mk 8 2) ἤδη; Ac 24 10 *SB* ἐκ,
Aeg 278 *S* husband dead ⲉⲓⲥ ⲟⲩⲛⲟϭ ⲛⲟⲩⲟⲉⲓϣ ἐκ
πολλοῦ; Ro 15 23 *SB* ἀπό; *B* Gk om: Ge 31 41 *S*,
2 Kg 17 20 *S*, Zech 1 12 *SA*, Ac 20 31 *S*; GuDorm
5 *S* he died ⲉⲓⲥ ϧⲁϧ ⲡⲣⲟⲙⲡⲉ, Va 67 88 *B* pillars
stand ϧⲱⲥ ϫⲉⲓⲥ ⲟⲩⲙⲏⲏϣ ⲛⲥⲛⲟⲩ, ShC 73 172 *S* ϯ-
ⲙⲟⲕⲙⲉⲕ ⲙⲙⲟⲓ ⲉⲓⲥ ϧⲉⲛⲣⲟⲙⲡⲉ, MG 25 355 *B* ⲉⲧⲓ
ιⲥ ⲕⲭⲏ ϧⲱⲛ ϫⲉⲛϯⲥⲁⲣⲝ, Va 62 130 *B* ιⲥ ⲡⲉⲕⲥⲟⲛ
ⲟⲛϧ *whilst* (*l* ? ιⲥϫⲉⲛ-).

—— ϧⲏⲏⲧⲉ, ϧⲏⲧⲉ *SAᵃ*, ϧⲏⲛⲡⲉ *S* (rare),——ϧⲏⲡⲡⲉ or ϧⲏⲡⲡⲉ ιⲥ *B*, meaning as ⲉⲓⲥ, properly before
pron, vb (exc Mt 7 4 *S*, ST 335 *S*, *v* 1 Kg 3 9
Maspero): Ge 18 9 *SB*, Ps 7 14 *S* (*B* ϧ. ιⲥ), *ib*
26 6 *S* (*B* ϧ., so mostly in Pss), Is 33 7 *S* (*B* ϧ.,
F ϧⲉⲓⲧⲉⲥ), Mt 9 10 *S* (*B* ιⲥ) *ib* 21 5 *S* (var better
om ϧ., *B* do), Lu 17 21 *B* ϧ. ⲅⲁⲣ ιⲥ (*S* ⲉⲓⲥ), Jo 4
35 *SAᵃ* (*B* ϧ., *F* ϧⲉⲓⲧⲉ), He 2 13 *S* (*BF* do) ἰδού;
rarely = ἴδε: Mt 25 25, 26 65 *S*, ἴδετε: Jos 23 4 *B*;
Br 92 *S* ⲉⲓⲥ ϧ. ⲁⲓϫⲱ ⲉⲣⲱⲧⲛ, PS 20 *S* ⲉⲓⲥ ϧ. ϭⲉ
ⲁϥϫⲱⲕ ⲉⲃⲟⲗ, AM 221 *B* ιⲥ ϧ. ϫⲡⲁϯ ⲟⲥⲓ to thy
soul, BM 1128 *S* ⲉⲥ ϧⲏⲧⲁⲓ ⲁⲓⲉⲣ ϧⲱⲃ ⲉⲡⲗⲁⲥ.   ⲉⲓⲥ
ϧⲏⲏⲡⲉ *S*: Ap 5 5, 22 12 (var -ⲧⲉ, *B* ϧⲏⲡⲡⲉ), ShZ
590, Ep 492 ⲉⲥ ϧⲏⲡⲉ ⲁϥⲉι.   ⲉⲓⲥ ϧ. ⲉⲓⲥ *SB*, before nn (exc Jud 6 15 *S*, Jer 22 17 *B*): Ge 29 2 *S*
(var ⲉⲓⲥ ϧ., *B* ϧ. ιⲥ), Job 1 14 *S* (*B* ιⲥ, oftenest),
Lu 7 37 *S* ⲉⲓⲥ ϧ. ϫⲉ ⲉⲓⲥ (var ⲉⲓⲥ, *B* ϧ. ιⲥ) ἰδού;
Ryl 284 *S* ⲉⲓⲥ ϧ. ⲉⲓⲥ ⲡⲗⲟⲩⲟⲥ I have sent you, C 43
44 *B* ιⲥ ϧ. ιⲥ Satan appeared.   ⲉⲓⲥ ϧⲏⲏⲡⲉ *S* before pl nn or pron: Eccl 2 11 ἰδού; ShC 42 89 ⲉⲓⲥ
ϧ. ⲧⲏⲣⲟⲩ we observe them, ShA 1 291 rest of words
ⲉⲓⲥ ϧ. ⲥⲉϧⲏⲡⲉ ⲭⲁⲣⲧⲏⲥ.

ⲉⲓⲥⲧⲉ *SA*(PVi 10157 vo), ⲉⲥⲧⲉ *A* for ⲉⲓⲥ ϧⲏⲏⲧⲉ:
Hab 1 6 *SA* (*B* ϧⲏⲡⲡⲉ), Zech 4 2 *A* ⲉⲥⲧⲉ = ⲉⲓⲥ =
S ⲉⲓⲥ, *B* ϧ. ιⲥ ἰδού; ST 394 *S* ⲉⲓ. ⲧⲉⲧⲛ̄ⲣⲓⲃⲟⲗ,
ib 247 *S* ⲉⲓⲥⲧⲁⲓ ⲁⲓⲁⲃⲱⲕ ⲉⲣⲏⲥ, *ib* 411 *S* ⲉⲥ ϫⲏ ⲁⲡ-
ⲡⲟⲗⲕ ⲉⲃⲟⲗ.   For ⲉϧⲟⲩⲟ ⲉⲓⲥⲧⲉ *S v* ϧⲟⲩⲟ.   ⲉⲓⲥⲡⲉ *SA* for ⲉⲓⲥ ϧⲏⲏⲡⲉ: Zech 14 1 *A* (*S* ⲉⲓⲥ ϧⲏⲏⲧⲉ,
B ϧⲏⲡⲡⲉ) ἰδού, ShA 1 95 *S* if they were elsewhere
they would strangle them ⲛ ⲡⲉⲉⲓⲥⲡⲉ ⲁⲩⲕⲟⲛⲥⲟⲩⲡⲉ,
ib 107 sim (but here ? = ⲉϣϫⲡⲉ *q v*).

ϧⲏⲡⲡⲉ *B* alone = ⲉⲓⲥ ϧⲏⲏⲧⲉ *S* (*q v*) before pron,
vb: Lev 13 5, Ps 38 6, Ez 13 12, 2 Cor 6 9 ἰδού;
mostly = ⲉⲓⲥ *S* before nn: Is 32 1 (= *F* ϧⲉⲓ), Ez
34 3, Ac 10 17 ἰδού; CDan 87 (Gk om) ϧ. ⲁϥⲟⲩ-

ⲱⲛϩ ⲉⲣⲟⲓ, *ib* 90 (Gk do) ϩ. ϭⲟⲓ ⲡⲉⲡⲁⲣⲭⲟⲥ; Miss 4 95 ϩ. ⲁⲡⲟⲕ for thou calledst me; MIE 2 336 ⲓⲥ ⲡⲓⲱⲟⲅⲓ ⲧⲟⲓ ⲉⲡⲁϭⲁⲗⲁⲅϫ ϩ. ⲁⲅⲣⲱⲕϩ. ϩ. ⲓⲥ *B* ἰδού, before nn = *S* ⲉⲓⲥ, before pron, vb, mostly = ⲉⲓⲥ ϩⲏⲏⲧⲉ, *q v.*

ϩⲉⲥ, ϩⲏⲥ *S*, ϩⲉⲓⲥ *F* sim: BM 458 ϩⲉⲥ ⲟⲩⲕⲣⲁⲙⲙⲁ ⲁϥⲉⲓ ⲉⲧⲟⲟⲧ, Bal]ⲡⲉⲧϩⲣⲁⲓ ⲁⲡⲗⲱ ϫⲉⲣⲉⲥ[, Sph 10 4 ϩⲉⲓⲥ ⲁⲡⲥⲥϩⲉⲓ ⲡⲏⲕ, Bodl(P) d 31 ϩⲏⲥ ⲙⲉϫⲟⲙⲧⲉ ⲟⲩϭⲟⲥ [ⲡ-. *Cf* ? AZ 21 100 *O* ϩⲉⲥ ϩⲁⲃϥⲉⲡⲥ.

ϩⲉⲓ *F*, use as ⲉⲓⲥ **a**: Is 30 27 (*S* ⲉⲓⲥ, *B* ϩⲏⲡⲡⲉ), Mk 13 21 (Mor 21, *SB* ⲉⲓⲥ) ἰδού; Mor 24 32 (*S* ⲉⲓⲥ) ϩ. Michael is come; BM 585 ϩ. ⲑⲁⲡⲁⲏⲗ ϩⲁⲧⲏⲡ; as **b**: Mor 24 17 (*S* do) ϩ. ⲝ̄ ⲡⲗⲁⲙⲡⲓ, Mor 27 31 archôn that passed thee ϩ. ⲟⲩⲕⲟⲅⲓ; Mor 30 39 ⲉⲓⲥ ϩⲉⲓ God seeth thee. ϩⲉⲓⲧⲉ *F*, use as ⲉⲓⲥ ϩⲏⲏⲧⲉ: Jer 27 18 (*B* ϩⲏⲡⲡⲉ), Jo 4 35 (*S* ⲉⲓⲥ ϩ., *B* ϩ.), He 2 13 (*SB* do) ἰδού.

ϩⲉⲓⲧ, ϩⲉⲧ, ϩⲧ *F*, as last: AZ 23 35 ϩ. ⲁⲅⲓ(ⲉ)ⲧⲁⲁⲧ, Kr 21 ϩⲧ ⲁⲓⲭⲣⲓⲁ, *ib* 146 ϩ. ⲁⲓⲡⲓⲟⲓ, BM 589 ϩ. ⲙⲡⲉⲕⲓ.

ϩⲉⲓⲧⲉⲥ *F*, as last: Is 33 7, 35 4, He 8 8 ἰδού; LAp 520 (*S* ⲉⲓⲥ) ϩ. ⲁϥⲟⲩⲱⲡⲁϩ ⲉⲗⲁⲩ.

Also in ⲓⲥ ⲑⲛⲉⲓⲡⲉ (*v* ⲡⲉⲓ), ⲓⲥϫⲉⲡ- (*v* ϫⲓⲡ-), ? ⲓⲥϫⲉⲕ (*v* ⲉϣϫⲉ).

ⲓⲱⲥ *BF*, ⲓⲏⲥ⁺ (oftenest, as if ⲓⲱⲥ) *B*, ⲉⲓⲉⲥ⁺ *F* vb **I.** intr, *hasten, be urgent*: Is 21 3⁺ (*S* ϭⲉⲡⲏ), 2 Cor 8 22⁺ (*S* = Gk), 1 Thes 2 17⁺ (*S* ϭ.), Job 4 5⁺ (*S* ϣⲧⲟⲣⲧⲣ), Dan 11 44⁺ (*S* ϣ. nn) σπουδάζειν; Ex 34 8⁺ (*S* ϭ.), Ac 22 18⁺ (var ⲓⲱⲥ, *S* do) σπεύδειν, Ex 10 16⁺ κατασπεύ.; Is 59 7⁺ ταχινός, Zeph 1 14⁺ (*S* ⲉⲓ ⲡⲧⲉⲅⲡⲟⲩ) ταχύς, Ja 1 19⁺ (*S* ϭ.) ταχύς, MG 25 10 ⲡⲁϭⲏⲥ ⲉϥⲙⲟϣⲓⲡⲉ ταχύνειν; Ps 13 3⁺ (*S* ϭ.), Ro 3 15⁺ (*S* do) ὀξύς; C 86 71 ⲁϭⲓⲏⲥ...ⲉϣⲧⲉⲙⲟⲣⲉⲡ-, ROC 17 405 ⲁϭⲓⲏⲥ ⲉϩⲉⲡ ⲡⲓⲣⲱⲃ ἐπιτηδεύειν; Bess 7 7 let me go, for ϯⲓⲏⲥ, Va 58 115 ⲙⲁⲣⲉⲡⲓⲱⲥ ⲉϥⲱⲧ ⲉⲃⲟⲗ, *ib* 156 ϣⲁϥⲓⲱⲥ ⲉⲕⲟⲃⲟⲩ (*sic l*), Miss 4 120 ϣⲁⲓⲏⲥ ⲉⲉⲣⲫⲟⲣⲓⲛ, C 89 214 ⲁϥⲓⲱⲥ ⲁϥⲥϩⲁⲓ, C 43 107 ⲡⲁⲓ ⲉⲧⲓⲏⲥ ⲉⲟⲩⲕⲁⲕⲓⲁ, BM 636 *F* ⲉⲓⲉⲥ ⲉⲧⲃⲏⲧ & sell them, BM 527 *Sf* recipe ⲓⲱⲥ ⲁⲁϥ ⲡⲁⲕ ⲉϣⲱⲡⲓ. With preposition: ⲛⲥⲁ-, Job 23 16 (*S* ϣⲧⲟⲣⲧⲣ) σπουδ.; Ge 19 15⁺ (*S* do) ἐπισπουδ.; Is 16 5⁺ (*S* ϭ.) σπεύδ.; Bel 30⁺ ἐπείγειν; AM 244 ⲡⲁⲓⲱⲥ ⲡⲥⲱϥ. ϩⲁⲧϩⲏ ⲛ-: Job 23 15⁺ κατασπουδ. ἀπό. With adverb: ROC 17 401 ⲉϥⲓⲏⲥ ⲉϩⲟⲩⲛ ⲉⲡⲓⲙⲁⲑⲏⲙⲁ.

II. refl, meaning same, **a.** ⲉ ⲛ-, ⲙⲙⲟ-: Job 23 14⁺ (*S* ⲡⲱⲧ), He 4 11 (*S* ϭ.) σπουδ.; Ge 18 6⁺ (*S* do), Jer 4 6 σπεύδ.; AM 118 ϯⲓⲏⲥ ⲙⲙⲟⲓ to quit flesh, Miss 4 208 ϯⲡⲁⲓⲱⲥ ⲙⲙⲟⲓ ⲉϯ, C 89 146 ⲓⲱⲥ ⲙⲙⲟⲕ, *ib* 85 ⲓⲏⲥ ⲙⲙⲟⲕ, Va 63 15 ⲁⲅⲓⲱⲥ ⲙⲙⲱⲟⲩ = BSM 42 ϫⲱⲗⲉⲙ = BMis 389 *S* ϭ. **b.** ⲉ ⲡⲧⲉⲛ-: Ge 44 11⁺, 2 Tim 4 9⁺ (var ⲓⲱⲥ ⲙⲙⲟϥ, *S* ⲣ ⲁⲡⲁⲧⲟⲟⲧϥ) σπουδ.; Ex 9 19⁺ κατασπεύδ.; Cat 139 ⲙⲡⲉⲣⲓⲏⲥ ⲡⲧⲉⲛⲑⲏⲛⲟⲩ ⲉⲓ.

ⲣⲉϥⲓⲏⲥ nn m, *one that hastens*: Is 14 4 (*S* ⲡⲉⲧ ϣⲧⲟⲣⲧⲣ) ἐπισπουδαστής.

ⲓⲱⲥ, ⲓⲏⲥ nn m, *speed, diligence*: Ex 12 11 (*S* = Gk), Deu 16 3⁺ (var ⲓⲱⲥ, *S* ϣⲧⲟⲣⲧⲣ), Lam 4 6⁺, Zeph 1 18 (*SA* ϣ.), Lu 1 39⁺ (*S* ϭⲉⲡⲏ) σπουδή, K 99 ⲡⲓⲱⲥ ⲓ̅ⲥ̅ϩⲙ. As adv (oftenest), ϩⲉⲛⲟⲩⲓⲱⲥ: PS 147 4⁺ (*S* ϭ.), Nah 1 14 ταχύς, ταχύ; Is 8 1 (*S* do) ὀξύς; C 86 65 bade set a table ϩ. εὐθέως, Va 61 21 δρομαίως, C 89 51 ⲁϥⲟⲅⲱⲣⲡ ϩ. = Miss 4 533 *S* ⲁⲩⲥⲡⲟⲩⲇⲁⲍⲉ ⲁⲩϫⲟⲟⲩ, C 43 30 ran to him ϩⲉⲛⲟⲩⲓⲏⲥ.

ⲉⲓⲥⲡⲉ *SA v* ⲉⲓⲥ.

ⲉⲓⲥⲧⲉ *S*, ⲓⲥⲧⲉ *F v* ϩⲟⲩⲟ.

ⲓⲥϫⲉ, ⲓⲥϫⲉⲕ *B v* ⲉϣϫⲉ.

ⲓⲥϫⲉⲛ- *B v* ϫⲓⲛ-.

ⲉⲓⲁⲧ⸗ *v* ⲉⲓⲁ *eye*.

ⲉⲓⲱⲧ *SAA²*, ⲓⲱⲧ *SBF*, ⲓⲟⲩⲧ *O* (AZ 21 100), pl ⲉⲓⲟⲧⲉ *S*, ⲉⲓⲁⲧⲉ, ⲉⲓⲁϯ *AA²*, ⲓⲟϯ *B*, ⲉⲓⲁϯ *F*, ⲓⲁⲧⲉ DM, ⲉⲓⲧ- &c *S*, nn m, *father* πατήρ, γονεύς (Pro 29 15 *S*), pass. Pl, πατέρες, γονεῖς: *S* Ps 44 16, Mk 13 12; *A* 2 Mac 6 1, Am 2 4; *A²* Jo 6 31, AP 24; *B* Ex 20 5, Su 30; *F* Ro 11 28, He 1 1; Mor 43 259 *S* ⲉⲓ. ⲡϩⲟⲟⲩⲧ, ⲉⲓ. ⲡⲥϩⲓⲙⲉ. ⲉⲓⲧ- &c, mostly with ⲡⲁ- *S* (*v* Ep 1 248) *F*: CO 336 ⲡⲁⲉⲓⲧ ⲓⲁⲕⲱⲃ, ST 260 ⲡ. ⲡⲁⲣⲁⲙ, P 131¹ 40; Baouit 1 126 ⲡⲉⲓⲧ- (*bis*); J 67 130, CO 184, 447 ⲡⲁⲓⲧ-; Ep 395, BM 646 *F* ⲡⲁⲧ- (= ⲡⲁⲉⲧ-, but *cf* DM 8 2 ⲡⲓⲁⲧ-). *V* proper name below.

Title of abbot, head of congregation: TT 146 *S* become ⲉⲓ. ⲉⲧⲥⲟⲟⲩϩ, BMis 150 *S* ⲁⲡⲉ ⲡⲥⲟⲟⲩϩ ⲉⲧⲉⲡⲓ. of monastery, C 89 52 *B* ⲉϫⲉⲛⲟⲩⲑⲱⲟⲩⲧⲥ, Pcod 12 *S* ⲡⲧⲕⲟⲓⲛⲱⲛⲓⲁ (esp of Pachomians: BM 299, BAp 101, 127, C 73 148), Miss 4 698 *S* archimandrite & ⲉⲓ. ⲡⲧⲕⲟⲓⲛ., *ib* 526 *S* ⲡⲑⲉⲡⲉⲉⲧⲉ πατήρ, MG 25 241 *B* ⲙⲡⲓⲁⲃⲏⲧ ἀρχιμανδ., DeV 91 *B* ⲙⲡⲓⲧⲟⲡⲟⲥ, (*cf* GMir 26 *S* ⲡⲡⲁⲧⲏⲣ ⲙⲡⲉⲓⲧⲟⲡ.), RAC 100 *S*, Baouit 1 79, 96 *S* ⲡⲡⲧⲟⲟⲩ, Ryl 294 *S* ⲡⲧⲡⲉⲧⲣⲁ (*v* WS p 6), Bodl(P) d 17 *S* greet *x* & *y* ⲙⲡⲡⲉⲡⲉⲓ. & all God's people (*cf* Saq 192), ShC 73 58 *S* ⲡⲉⲓ. inferior of ⲡϩⲗⲗⲟ, *cf* ShC 42 157 *S* ⲡⲉⲓ. ⲉⲧϩⲣⲏⲓ ⲉⲧⲉⲡⲣⲙⲛⲏⲏⲓ. Other monastic officials: Saq 2 *B* ⲡⲓ. (ⲙ)ⲡⲙⲁ (ⲛ)ⲡⲉⲧϣⲱⲡⲓ, *ib* 69 *S* sim, *ib* 192 *S* ⲙⲡⲙⲁ ⲡⲟⲩⲱⲙ, *ib* 241 *S* (ⲙ)ⲡⲙⲁ ⲡϩⲣⲧ, Baouit 1 105 *S* ⲡⲓ. ⲛⲧⲣⲓ, BM 1130 n *S* ⲛⲧⲣⲓ (ⲛ)ⲡⲉⲕⲟⲩⲓ. Clerics, monks, reverend persons: Leyd 131 *S* patriarch or bishop, CaiEuch 345 *B*, ShC 42 13 *S*, CO 29 *S* sim, RE 9 136 *S* priest, C 89 71 *B* ⲡⲁϭⲥ̄ ⲡⲓ. Pachom, Z 317 *S* = MG 25 233 *B* ⲡⲁⲉⲓ. ἀββᾶ Macarius, Miss 4 638 *S* ⲡⲉⲡⲉⲓ. ⲉⲧⲟⲩⲁⲁⲃ = C 41 35 *B* (om ⲉⲧ.) Shenoute. Anchorites: Ep 110 *S* beloved holy & God-loving fathers,

ib 261 *S* lords fathers, CO 280 *S*, Ep 162 *S* ⲣⲁⲅⲓⲟ-
ⲥⲩⲛⲏ ⲡⲉⲓ. (*v* CO Index 117), EW 99 *B* martyrs in
prison.   ⲛⲁⲉⲓ. as title (*cf* ⲡⲁⲥⲟⲛ): PO 14 335 *B*
ⲡⲉⲡⲓⲱⲧ...ⲡⲁⲓ. Teroti, *ib* 354 sim; ⲡⲉⲡⲉⲓ. sim: WS
174 *S*, *ib* 83 ⲡⲉⲕⲉⲡⲉⲡⲉⲓ. Apa Paul, *cf* Ep 360 *S*
hinder him not, ⲝⲉⲡⲉⲡⲉⲓ. ⲡⲉ, C 89 20 *B* I have
called thee brother, henceforth (in admiration) ⲡⲁⲓ.,
PO 11 366 *B* I deemed John great, now I know
ⲝⲉⲡⲟⲟⲕ ⲫⲓ. of him.   Biblical persons: Mor 3
134 *S* Isaiah, BMis 352 *S*, ShC 42 197 *S*, Ep 376
S Jeremiah, *ib* 379 Daniel, Bor 143 23 *S* Raphael,
Gu 17 *S*, EW 43 *B* Peter, Ryl 67 n *S* apostles;
angels, patriarchs, apostles often on stelae: Saq 15,
27, 52, 80, 211, WS 59, 61.   Patron saints:
Miss 8 262 *S* I am Victor ⲡⲉⲓ. ⲙⲡⲉⲓⲧⲟⲡⲟⲥ, Ryl 50
S Theodore do, C 43 194 *B* Theodore ⲫⲓ. ⲙⲡⲁⲓ-
ⲙⲁⲣⲧⲩⲣⲓⲟⲛ, BMar 68 *S* sim.   *Father & son or
brother* used of same person: Va 61 21 *B* my son
ⲟⲩⲟⲅ ⲡⲁⲓ., Mor 48 100 *S* ⲙⲉⲣⲓⲧ ⲛⲥⲟⲛ ⲁⲩⲱ ⲡⲉⲓ.,
Bodl(P) c 15 *S* ⲧⲉⲧⲛⲡⲁⲛⲁⲧⲥⲓⲟⲛ ⲡⲉⲓ. & brother &
lord, Sph 10 3 *S* mother to son (bishop), My dear
lord ⲡⲓⲱⲧ ⲁⲩⲱ ⲡϣⲏⲣⲉ.

ⲁⲧⲉⲓ. *S*, ⲁⲧⲓ. *BF, fatherless*: He 7 3 *SB* ἀπάτωρ;
BMar 32 *S* ⲁⲓⲣ ⲁⲧⲉⲓ. ⲅⲓⲙⲁⲁⲩ.

ⲣ ⲉⲓ. *S*, ⲉⲣ ⲓ. *B, be father*: Ep Append I *a S*
ⲙⲉⲣⲉⲡϣⲏⲣⲉ ⲣ ⲉⲓ., MG 25 312, N&E 39 332 *B* he
who ⲉⲣ ⲓ. in Shiêt; Ryl 83 *S* Son ⲙⲡⲉϥⲛⲱⲡⲉ
ⲉⲧⲥⲓⲏⲣ ⲉⲓ.

ⲙⲛⲧⲉⲓⲱⲧ *S*, ⲙⲉⲧⲓ. *B* nn f, **a.** (bible) *family*: Nu
17 17(2) *B* (*S* = Gk, *cf ib* 1 20, 2 2 &c), Est 9 27
S, Is 8 21 *SB*, Eph 3 15 *SB* πατριά.   **b.** *fatherhood*: BM 217 3 *S* we confess Father ⲅⲓⲧⲁⲁⲍⲓⲥ
ⲛⲧⲙ. opp ⲙⲛⲧϣⲏⲣⲉ, Va 59 166 *B* ⲉⲧⲁϥⲥⲓ ⲛⲧϯⲙ.
of desert (monasteries), CO 178 *S* ⲧⲁⲣⲉⲧⲉⲕⲙ. ⲉⲓⲙⲉ
ⲝⲉ-, ShA 1 461 *S* ungrateful toward ⲧⲙ. (spiritual)
ancestry, Leyd 410 *S* sim (*cf* LMis 33).

ϣⲡⲉⲓⲱⲧ *S*, ϣⲉⲡⲓ. *B, relative on father's side*: Ge
20 12 *SB*, Deu 13 6 *SB* ἐκ πατρός, Lev 18 11 *SB*
ὁμοπάτριος, C 41 11 *B* his sister ⲛϣ. ⲅⲓⲙⲁⲩ.

ⲡⲉⲓ. ⲙⲡⲉⲓⲱⲧ *S*, *grandfather*: Si prol, P 43 42
πάππος.   In name: ⲡⲁⲉⲓⲧⲱ J 58 11 *S*, ?ⲡⲁⲉⲓⲧ (son of)
ⲙⲁⲣⲓⲅⲁⲙ ostr Ashmolean Mus 534.

ⲉⲓⲱⲧ *SA²*, ⲉⲓⲟⲩⲧ *S* (BAp 130), ⲓⲱⲧ *SABF* nn m,
barley: Ge 26 12 (Z 583) *SB*, Ruth 1 22 *S*, 2 Kg
14 30 *S*, Hag 2 17 *SBA* κριθή, Jo 6 9 *SA²B* κρί-
θινος; P 44 83 *S*, K 193 *B* شعير;   sifted: Is 30 24
SBF, BM 689 *F* men who ⲕⲁⲑⲁⲣⲉ ⲛⲡⲉⲓ.;   barley
meal: PMéd 318 *S*;   supplies of fodder: CO
222 *S* ⲡⲝⲓⲧⲱⲅ, ⲛⲝⲓⲉⲓ., *cf* Ryl 346;   for cattle:
BM 602 *F*, pigs: WS 98 *S*, dogs: BM 1166 *S*,
CMSS 78 *F*;   measures: PLond 4 499 *S*, BM

1161 *S*, ST 191 *S* ⲉⲣⲧⲟⲃ, Ryl 388 *S*, Kr 157 *S*
ⲟⲓⲡⲉ, Ep 176 *S* ⲙⲁϫⲉ;   as rent: COAd 15 *S*;
as wage: Kr 152 *S*, WS 132 *S*.

   In place-name: Ryl 158 *S* ⲡⲁⲟⲩⲁⲛ ⲡⲓⲱⲧ.

ⲉⲓⲱⲧⲉ *SA*, ⲓⲱϯ *BF* nn f, sg as pl, *dew*: Ex 16
13 *SB*, Pro 3 20 *AB*, Hos 13 3 *AB* δρόσος; Jud 6
38 *S* ⲙⲟⲟⲩ ⲡⲉⲓ. δρ., Sa 11 23 *S* ⲧⲗϯⲗⲉ ⲡⲉⲓ. ῥανίς
δρ.; Job 2 9 *SB* αἴθριος; C 43 229 *B* ⲟⲩⲓ. ⲉϥⲕⲏⲃ,
Bor 143 27 *S* made furnace like ⲟⲩⲧⲏⲩ ⲡⲉⲓ. ⲉϥⲥⲱⲕ
at dawn, BSM 19 *B* sim, *cf* Mor 24 25 *F* ⲁⲅⲛⲁⲥ
ⲡⲓⲱϯ ⲥⲱⲕ, BM 174 1 *S* ⲡⲓϣⲉ ⲡⲉⲓ. ἔνδροσος, KKS
667 *S* ⲧⲡⲉ ϯ ⲡⲛⲉⲥⲉⲓ., BM 511(2) *F* ⲉⲧϣⲟⲩⲁ ⲓ. ⲉⲅⲣⲁⲓ upon earth, J 65 24 *S* ⲟⲩⲉⲓ. ⲙⲙⲟⲟⲩ to slake
them, BKU 1 26 *Sᶠ* recipe ⲕⲱ ⲙⲁⲥ ⲅⲓⲧⲓ.;   honey
as dew: ShC 42 46 *S* bee gathers ⲟⲩⲉⲓ. that cometh
from heaven, Z 617 *S* ϯ. ⲙⲡⲉⲃⲓⲱ sweet while yet
in ἀήρ, ere it descends on grass that bee may work
it (ἐπεξεργάζ.);   manna as dew: Wess 9 51 =
Mor 31 210 *S*.

ⲙⲉⲧϣⲁⲣ ⲓⲱϯ *B* nn f, *poverty of dew*: Va 57 79
ⲅⲁⲛⲙ. & fruitlessness.

ⲉⲓⲧⲛ, ⲓⲧⲛⲉ *S*(ST 350, J 4 32), ⲧⲛⲏ *S* (J 108),
ⲓⲧⲛ *SA²*, ⲓⲧⲉⲛ *SBF* (ⲅⲓⲧⲉⲛ *B* AM 317), nn m,
ground, earth, dust, rubbish: 1 Kg 4 11 *S*, Job 2
12 *S* (*B* ⲕⲁⲅⲓ), Ez 27 30 *S* (*B* ϣⲱⲓϣ), Mic 1 10 *S*
(*A* ⲕⲣⲙⲉⲥ, *B* ⲕⲁⲅⲓ) γῆ; Ps 82 11 *SB* κόπρος;
Est C 13 *S*, Si 27 4 *S*, Is 5 25 *S* (var + ⲙⲡⲕⲁⲅ)
B (Lacr, Tatt = Gk) *F*, Lam 4 5 *S* (*B* = Gk) κοπρία;
Is 46 1 *S* (? κοπριῶν for κοπιῶντι); Jos 7 6 *S*, Ap
18 19 *S* (*B* ⲕⲁⲅⲓ) χοῦς; Is 25 2 *B* (*S* ⲕⲁⲅ) χῶμα;
AP 37 *A²* fell on his knees ⲙⲡⲓⲧⲛ, Mor 31 238 *S*
each put ⲉⲓ. on head and threw ϣⲟⲉⲓϣ into air,
Mor 51 33 *S* ⲁⲛϣⲉϣ ⲉⲓ. ⲙⲡⲧⲏⲩ, MG 25 303 *B*
face ⲙⲉⲅ ⲓⲛⲓ. because of ⲕⲁⲅⲓ he had carried, R 1
3 34 *S* whoso ⲡⲁⲛⲉϫ ⲉⲓ. (*sic l*) ⲙⲡⲉϥⲏⲓ ⲉⲃⲟⲗ, *cf*
BMis 218 *S* (same story) ⲉⲓ. ⲛⲓⲙ ⲉϣⲁⲩⲡⲟⲛⲧⲟⲩ
ⲉⲃⲟⲗ, Ryl 252 *S* builder's account ⲅⲁⲛⲉⲓ. ⲛⲧⲁⲓ-
ⲡⲟⲛⲕⲟⲩ ⲉⲃ., BM 1152 *S* we load ⲡⲓ. ⲅⲓⲧⲁⲥⲟⲗⲧⲉ,
C 86 149 *B* ⲡⲛⲓ. ⲛⲧⲉ ⲡⲓϣⲱⲓϣ as dragon moved, *ib*
214 *B* pit ⲁⲩϣⲟⲣϥ ⲛⲓ., RicciL 260 *F* ⲁϥⲙⲉⲅ ⲧⲁⲧϥ
ⲛⲛⲓ., BHom 122 *S* crawling babe's mouth full
of ⲝⲓⲅ ⲅⲓⲉⲓ., Mor 25 93 *S* beggar ⲉϥⲗⲁⲗⲱⲟⲩ
ⲡⲉⲓ.   *Ground as bottom, lower part*, *S* (*v* PSBA
21 249 & *cf* ⲉⲥⲛⲧ): TU 24 5 ⲁⲡⲉⲓ ⲉⲡⲓ., ? AP 20 *A²*
ⲉⲁϥⲥⲉⲕ ⲧⲟⲟⲧϥ ⲁⲡⲓ., Ep 327 ⲉⲓ ⲉⲡⲉⲓ. ? of *fall* in
money's value, J 108 10 its south side ϣⲁϥⲃⲱⲕ
ⲉⲣⲏⲥ ⲁⲡⲧⲛ ⲉⲅⲣⲁⲓ ⲉⲧⲅⲓⲛ, ST 442 instructions for
a craft (? weaving) ⲣⲱⲃ ⲙⲡⲓ. ⲥⲉ(= ⲛⲥⲁ)ⲧⲡⲉ, ShA
1 107 of rent veil ⲧⲡⲉ ⲙⲙⲟϥ ⲛ ⲡⲓ. ⲙⲙⲟϥ, BKU
1 94, Ep 400 sim opp ⲧⲡⲉ, J 25 11 house ⲉⲧⲡⲉⲓ.
ⲙⲡⲏⲓ, *ib* 21 opp ⲙⲡⲅⲣⲁⲓ, J 42 22, CO 151 ⲧⲉⲍⲉⲁⲣⲁ
ⲧⲁⲡⲉⲓ., JLeip 2 ⲡⲧⲱⲣⲧ ⲙⲡⲁⲡⲁⲡⲓ. ⲙⲡⲏⲓ; of wit-

nesses subscribing (*cf* ἑξῆς): J 9 23 ⲉⲧⲛⲁⲙⲁⲣⲧⲩ-ⲣⲓ�ze ϩⲁⲣⲟⲓ ⲙⲡⲓ. (*cf* 82 5 ϩⲁⲡⲉⲓⲥⲏⲧ, but this always +gen), Ep 87 ⲉⲧⲛⲁⲥϩⲁⲓ ϩⲁⲣⲟⲓ ⲙⲡⲓ.

ⲉⲡⲓⲧⲛ *S* as nn: AZ 52 121 demons appeared ϩⲛⲟⲩⲉ. ⲣⲁⲙⲡⲧⲁⲫⲟⲥ, Mich 550 39 he descended ⲉⲟⲩⲁ ⲡⲡⲉ. ⲣⲁⲙⲡⲧⲙⲉ εἰς κατάγειον = MG 17 361 موضع سفلى (both instances from same MS). Possible compounds of ⲉⲓⲧⲛ *v* AZ 53 132.

ⲉⲓⲧⲟⲩⲛ- *F v* ⲧⲟⲩⲱ∠.

ⲉⲓⲁⲁⲩ *S*, ⲉⲓⲱ, ⲓⲱ *S* (ostraca), ⲓⲁⲩ *B'* nn m, *linen*: Lev 6 10 *SB*, Deu 22 11 *S*(Mor)*B*, Pro 31 13 *S* (var ⲙⲁϩⲉ) *B*, Ez 44 18 *S* (*B* diff) λίνον, λινοῦς, MG 25 231 *B* ⲥⲧⲓⲭⲁⲣⲓⲟⲛ ⲛⲓ. = Z 316 *S* ϩⲃⲟⲥ λινοῦς; Ac 10 11 *B* ϩⲃⲱⲥ ⲛⲓ. (*S* om), Aeg 230 *S* ὀθόνη, Jo 19 40 *B* ϣⲉⲛⲧⲱ ⲛⲓ. (*S* ϩⲃⲱⲱⲥ, as Lu 24 12) ὀθόνιον; Lev 13 47 *B* (*S* = Gk, var λίνον) στιππύινος; K 244 *B* كتان (but 122 ʹ*S* ⲥⲉⲡⲡⲓ), P 46 151 *S* do (but 165 ʹ*S* ⲥⲓⲡⲡⲉ), BMOr 9525(8) vo *S* shows ⲉⲓ. woven from ⲥⲓⲡⲡⲟⲛ (στιπ.), *cf* Ep 1 156, Tri 589 *S* sim كتان, HL 97 *B* corpse in ϩⲁⲡϩⲃⲱⲥ ⲛⲓ., ShBerlOr 1611 5 *S* among articles sold ⲉⲓ., ⲭⲟⲕ, ⲡⲟⲩϩ; Ep 351 *S* ⲭⲟⲟⲩ ⲟⲩⲓ. for weaving shrouds, *ib* 372 ϥⲧⲁⲟⲩ ⲛⲉⲓ. Other garments: Miss 4 225 *B* ϩⲉⲃⲥⲱ, AM 267 *B* ⲕⲟⲗⲟⲃⲓ, Va 63 10 *B* ⲡⲁⲛⲡⲓⲛ, P 132¹ 17 *S* ⲙⲟⲭϩ. As name of garment: BMOr 8810 390 *S* ye (nuns) steal even ⲡⲕⲉⲉⲓ. ⲉⲧⲉⲧⲛϥⲓ ⲙⲙⲟⲟⲩ; bleached: Ep 353 *S*, Hall 115 *S* ⲉⲓⲱ ⲉⲩ(ⲟⲩ)ⲟⲃϣ ⲙⲡⲛⲉⲛⲧⲁⲕⲭⲁⲕⲟⲩ; measured by λίτραι: Ep 350 *S*, BMOr 9525(8) vo *S*, ⲙⲟⲩⲣ bundle *ib*. 'Wood' of ⲉⲓ. (? stalks of flax) Ep 360 *S*.

ⲡⲉⲓⲁⲁⲩ, **ⲡⲓⲁⲁⲩ** *S* for ⲉⲓ.: Deu 22 11 (Budge, *v* above), Z 581 (= Lev 13 48), Mor 18 123, Ep 351, or **ⲡⲁⲁⲩ**: Ep 569, Aegyptus 3 282.

ⲉⲓⲟⲅⲉ, **ⲉⲓⲟⲟⲅⲉ** *S* nn pl, *waters*(?): Br 92 ⲕⲁⲧⲁⲡⲉⲧⲁⲥⲙⲁ ⲉⲧⲥⲛⲕ ⲉⲣ̅ⲡⲉⲓⲉⲓⲟⲅⲉ when drawn back, allow to ⲭⲓⲟⲟⲣ (*v* at ⲉⲓⲟⲟⲣ), BMis 538 in hell pits full of pitch, fire & one ⲉϥⲙⲉϩ ⲡⲉⲓⲟⲟⲅⲉ ⲉϥϩⲁⲣⲟⲧⲉ. *V* ⲙⲟⲟⲩ (ⲙⲟⲟⲩ ⲡⲉⲓⲟⲟⲅⲉ), but also ⲉⲓⲱ nn.

ⲉⲓⲁⲟⲩⲃⲁ (*sic*) *S* nn, meaning unknown: BMar 21 they gave martyr ⲙⲙⲛⲧⲁϥⲧⲉ ⲡⲉⲓ. ϩⲛϩⲉⲛⲙⲟⲭⲕⲥ *blows*(?) with belts.

ⲉⲓⲟⲟⲩⲛ, **ⲓⲟⲟⲩⲛ** nn m, **ⲓⲟⲟⲩⲡⲉ** *S* nn f, a title, meaning unknown: Ryl 280 ⲡⲥⲁϩ Victor ⲛⲓ., Kr 94 sim, *ib* 78 Pous ⲡⲉⲓ., WS 116 women's names ⲧⲣⲏⲛⲏ ϯⲓ., but PMich 526 ⲧϣⲉ ⲛⲡⲓⲧⲉⲓⲟⲟⲩⲛ, Ryl 226 men that have not paid κλάσμα ϩⲛⲡⲉⲓ. (? = from among those entitled ⲉⲓ.). ⲥⲓⲟⲟⲩⲛ title (*q v*), prob different.

ⲓϣ *SBF* nn f, *urine*: Is 36 12 *F* (*S* ⲗⲏ ⲙⲟⲟⲩ, *B* ⲙⲱⲟⲩ) οὖρον, Bodl(P) a 2 44 *S* recipe ⲟⲩϣⲓ ⲛⲓϣ

ⲉϥⲡⲟⲥⲉ, Ryl 106 56 *S* (doubtful if in this); ⲡⲣⲉⲙⲓⲥⲓ *B*: 1 Kg 24 4 ⲉⲣ ⲧⲉϥⲓ. ⲛϭ. (var ⲓϣⲉ ⲛ̄-) παρασκευάζειν (euphemism).

ⲉⲓϣⲉ *SA²*, **ⲉⲓϩⲉ** *A*, **ⲓϣⲓ** *BF*, **ⲁϣⲧ-**, **ⲉϣⲧ-** *S*, **ⲉϩⲧ-** *A*, **ⲉϣ-** *B*, **ⲁϣⲧ∠** *S*, **ⲉϣⲧ∠** *A²F*, **ⲁϣ∠** *BF*, **ⲁϣⲉ**† *S*, **ⲁϩⲉ**† *A*, **ⲁϣⲓ**† *B*, **ⲉϣⲓ** (Mor 30), **ⲉϣⲉ**† (?) *F* vb **I.** tr, *hang, suspend*: Ps 136 2 *SB*, Ez 27 10 *SB*, Jth 14 11 *S*, 2 Mac 6 10 *A*, C 86 273 *B* Apollo ⲉⲧⲁϥⲉϣ ⲧⲫⲉ κρεμαννύναι, Cl 12 7 *A* Rahab ⲡⲁⲉⲓ. ⲡⲟⲩⲕⲟⲕⲕⲟⲥ ἔκκρ.; Mt 20 19 *B*, Mk 15 14 *BF*, Gal 5 24 *B* (*S* = Gk, as mostly in this sense) σταυροῦν, He 6 6 *SB* ἀνασταυ.; Ac 2 23 *SB* προσπηγνύναι; C 86 296 *B* ⲁϥⲟⲣⲟⲅⲁϣϥ, BM 527 *F* recipe ⲁϣⲟⲩ ϩⲓⲡⲕⲱⲣⲧ, Br 44 *S* blessed he ⲛⲧⲁϥⲁϣⲧ ⲡⲕⲟⲥⲙⲟⲥ (*cf* Gal 6 14), Bor 267 42 *S* wood ⲛⲧⲁⲩⲁϣⲧ Jesus thereon, Va 67 85 *B* God ⲉⲧⲁϥⲓ. ⲛⲁϥⲃⲁⲕⲟⲩ & bore him to Babylon, BMis 305 *S* sim, Va 67 86 *B* ⲁⲩⲓ. ⲡⲟⲩⲥⲙⲏ crying *Kyrie eleison* (? l ⲥⲓⲥⲓ). **A.** With preposition: **a.** ⲉ-, *hang upon, to*: 2 Kg 4 12 *S* (var ⲉⲭⲛ-), Ac 10 39 *S* (*B* ⲉⲭⲉⲛ-) κρ. ἐπί, R 1 1 53 *S* κρ. ἐκ, Mt 18 6 *B* (*S* diff) κρ. περί, ShRyl 70 241 *S* ⲉⲩⲛⲁⲁϣⲧϥ ⲉⲩϣⲉ; **b.** ⲉⲭⲛ-, *hang upon*: Jos 8 29 *S* κρ. ἐπί, BHom 125*S* ⲁⲩⲁϣⲧϥ ⲉⲭⲛ- cross; **c.** ⲛⲥⲁ-, *hang from*: MG 25 343 *B* by virtues ⲁϥⲉϣ ϣⲓⲛⲧ ⲧⲏⲣϥ ⲛⲥⲁⲡⲉϥⲧⲏⲃ κρ. ἐν, BMis 57 *S* angel ⲁϣⲧⲩ ⲛⲥⲁⲡⲛⲃⲱ of head, C 86 133 *B* ⲁϥⲁϣⲩ ⲛⲥⲁⲡⲉϥϩⲉⲣⲟⲟ *suspended* him from horse; **d.** ϩⲛ-, Mor 40 18 *S* ⲁⲟⲩⲁ...ⲁϣⲧ ϩⲁⲡⲛⲃⲱ = C 43 48 *B* ⲥⲁⲡⲓϣⲱⲓ; **e.** ϩⲓⲭⲛ-, Ps 136 2 *B*, Jth 14 1 *S* κρ. ἐπί, C 86 213 *B* ⲁϣⲕ ϩ. ⲟⲩϣⲉ. **B.** With adverb: **a.** ⲉⲡϣⲱⲓ *B*, *hang up*: Aeg 39 ⲛⲥⲉⲓ. ⲛϩⲁⲛⲃⲏⲗⲗⲟⲛ ⲉⲡ., CDan 90 ⲉⲫⲟⲩⲁϣⲧ ⲉⲡ. ὄπισθάγκωνα; **b.** ⲉϩⲣⲁⲓ, -ⲛⲓ, meaning same: Lam 5 12 *SB* κρ., Z 310 *S* if he ⲁϣⲧⲩ ⲉϩ. ⲛⲥⲁⲡⲉϥϭⲃϣⲁ κρ. ἀπό, C 43 212 *B* ⲛⲥⲉⲁϣϥ ⲉϩ. ⲥⲁⲭⲱϥ, Ep 177 *S* ⲉⲁⲩⲁϣⲧⲛ ⲉϩ. ⲛⲥⲁⲡⲁϩⲟⲩ (*cf* above CDan), BKU 1 21 (*bis*) *Sª* object to be dyed ⲛⲕⲓⲧⲩ ⲉϩ. ⲛⲧⲉϣⲧ ⲉϩ. to dry. As nn: WTh 135 *S* ⲡⲉⲕⲉⲓ. ⲉϩ. ⲉⲡⲉϣⲟⲩⲉ.

II. intr (rarely not qual), *be hung, depend*: Deu 28 66† *SB*, Lu 23 39† *S*, Z 317 *S* from every hole ⲡⲉⲣⲉⲟⲩϩⲛⲁⲁⲩ ⲁ., Lu 19 48 *S* (*l* ⲁϣⲉ), κρεμαννύναι; Ep 358 *S* (ⲡ)ⲡⲣⲁ. ⲡⲟⲩϣ ⲛⲭ[ⲟⲟⲩ *wait* (? for ⲁϩⲉ). **A.** With preposition: **a.** ⲉ-, Deu 21 23† *SB*, Cant 4 4† *S* κρ. ἐπί, Hos 11 7† *A* (*B* ⲁ. ⲉⲃⲟⲗ ϧⲉⲛ-) ἐπικρ. ἐκ, MG 25 231 *B* ⲁ. ⲉⲣⲟϥ = above Z 317, Mk 9 42† *SB* περικεῖσθαι περί, Miss 4 3, 634 *SB* ⲉⲓⲁ. ⲉⲡⲡⲉ = *ib* 305 انظر الى, CA 107 *S* grapes ⲁ. ⲉⲡⲃⲱ, Wess 18 65 *S* shalt stay ⲉⲕⲁ. ⲉⲡⲁⲏⲣ, ShZ 637 *S* ornaments of ships ⲉⲧⲁ. ⲉⲣⲟⲟⲩ, BIF 14 132 *S* ⲉⲕⲁ. ⲉⲡⲉⲓⲡⲉ ⲡⲁⲧϭⲟⲙ *rely on*; **b.** ⲉⲭⲉⲛ- *B*, *hang over, threaten*: Va 58 120 pestilence ϥⲁ. ⲉⲭⲱⲛ; **c.** ⲛ-, Is 22 24† *S* (*B* ⲛⲥⲁ-) ἐπικρ., ShBerlOr 1611

5 *S* εϥⲁ. ⲙⲙⲟϥ *pendent from* body like disabled
limb, R 1 2 12 *S* ⲉⲣⲉⲡⲉⲡⲣⲏⲧ ⲁ. ⲙⲡⲏⲡⲉ, BHom 125
S heaven & hell ⲉⲅⲁ. ⲙⲡⲉϥϣⲁϫⲉ; **d.** ⲛⲥⲁ-, Ac
28 4† *SB* ⲕⲣ. ἐκ, Lu 19 48† *B* (*S* diff) ἐκκρ. gen,
AM 228 *B* ⲛⲁⲅⲁ. ⲛⲉⲱϥ *attached to him*, RNC 71
S whole city ⲁ. ⲛⲥⲁⲥⲛⲁⲟⲡⲏ of his voice, LCyp 7
S ⲉⲅⲁ. ⲛⲥⲁϫⲱⲟⲩ; **e.** ⲟⲩⲧⲉ-, 2 Kg 18 9† *S* ⲕⲣ.
ἀνάμεσον; **f.** ϣⲁ-, MG 25 119 *B* thy good deeds
ⲛⲁⲓ. ϣⲁ- ends of earth, C 86 304 *B* I fly ⲉⲓⲁ. ϣⲁ-
ⲡⲓⲥⲧⲉⲣⲉⲱⲙⲁ; **g.** ϩⲛ-, ϩⲉⲛ-, Ge 44 30† *B* ἐκκρ. ἐκ,
Jth 8 24† *S* sim, Mt 22 40† *S* (*B* e-) ⲕⲣ. ἐν, Ac 27
40† *S* ἐὰν εἰς, BSM 129 *B* picture ⲉⲥⲁ. ϩⲉⲛⲡⲓⲁⲏⲣ,
Pcod 13 *S* ⲉⲡⲁ. ⲡⲣⲏⲧⲕ *depend on*, BMis 140 *S*
babe walking ⲉϥⲁ. ϩⲛⲡⲉⲣⲟⲓⲧⲉ of mother (var P
131¹ 65 ⲁ. ⲉ-), Mor 31 25 *S* σπήλαιον ⲉϥⲁ. ϩⲓⲛ-
ⲡⲧⲟⲟⲩ; **h.** ⲉⲃⲟⲗ ϩⲓⲧⲛ-, Ps 37 13† *S* (*B*, Gk om),
BHom 88 *S* all ⲁ. ⲉⲃⲟⲗ ϩⲓⲧⲟⲟⲧϥ (God); **i.** ϩⲓϫⲛ-,
My 24 *S* earth ⲁ. ϩ. ⲡⲙⲟⲟⲩ. **B.** With adverb:
a. ⲉⲃⲟⲗ, *hang out, overhang*: Job 39 28† *B* ἐπ᾽ἐξοχῇ,
Ac 27 40† *S* (var, *B* diff) ἐὰν εἰς, BHom 15 *S* road
has ⲙⲁ ⲙⲡⲉⲧⲣⲁ & ⲙⲁ ⲉϥⲁ. ⲉⲃⲟⲗ κρημνός, MG 25
371 *B* stones rough & ⲉⲅⲁ. ⲉⲃ., Mor 30 31 *F* rider
falling from mule ⲉϥⲉϣⲓ ⲉⲃ. between heaven &
earth (cf BMis 257), KroppB *S* may she pass 40
days ⲉⲥⲁ. ⲉⲃ. ⲛⲥⲱⲓ like bitch after dog, Ep 333 *S*,
ST 260 *S* sim?; **b.** ⲉⲡϣⲱⲓ *B*, *be hung up*: C 43
165 whilst saint ⲁ. ⲉⲡ. (but mostly tr); **c.** ⲉϩⲣⲁⲓ,
-ⲛⲓ, meaning same: Wess 18 65 *S* ⲉⲕⲛⲁϣⲱⲡⲉ
ⲉⲕⲁ..., forthwith ⲁϥⲉⲓϣⲉ ⲉϩ. in air, 2 Chr 3 5 *B*
ⲡⲏ ⲉⲧⲁ. ⲉϩ. χαλαστά, Ming 341 *S* cloak ⲉϥⲁ. ⲉϩ.,
C 86 217 *B* martyr ⲁ. ⲉϩ. on tree (*ib* a. ⲉⲡϣⲱⲓ),
BMis 265 *S* ⲉϥⲁ. ⲉϩ. ⲛⲥⲁϫⲱϥ, Va 58 108 *B* His
wrath ⲁ. ⲉϩ. ⲉϫⲱⲛ to smite us, BKU 1 22 *S* Isis
& Nephthys ⲉⲧⲁ. ⲉϩ. twixt heaven & earth.

ϫⲓⲛⲓϣⲓ *B* nn m, *hanging, crucifixion*: TDi 219
Mary to Jesus ⲉⲓⲛⲁⲩ ⲉⲡⲉⲕ.

ιϣⲧ *S* nn, meaning unknown: KroppK 24 recipe
ⲉⲓⲃⲉⲟⲩϣⲡ ιϣⲧ a malady. *V* ϣⲱⲡⲉ (ϣⲡ-).

ⲉⲓϣⲟⲩⲉⲓ, ⲉϣⲟⲩⲉⲓ *S* vb, prob Ar شوى (imperat
اشوِ), *roast, dry* by heating: AZ 23 107 recipe ⲧⲁⲁϥ
ⲉⲩⲧⲟ[ⲉⲓⲥ] ⲉϣ. ⲙⲙⲟϥ ϩⲓⲡⲕⲟϩ[ⲧ], 115 sim, 106
ϣⲟⲩⲉⲓ, Bodl(P) a 2 26 ⲉⲓϣ. ⲙⲙⲟϥ ϩⲓⲟⲩⲁⲗⲕⲟⲩⲥ
(الكور). Often in these MSS.

ιϣϫⲉⲛ *B* *v* ⲉϣϫⲉ.

ⲉⲓϥⲧ *v* ⲱϥⲧ.

ⲉⲓϩⲉ *A* *v* ⲉⲓϣⲉ.

ⲉⲓϩⲡⲉ, ⲉⲓϩϫⲉ *A* *v* ⲉϣϫⲉ.

ιϩ *B* nn m, *demon*: Ps 90 6 (*S* = Gk), 105 37
(*S* diff), Mt 17 18 (*S* = Gk) δαιμόνιον; *ib* 8 31
(*S* ⲣⲉϥϣⲁⲁⲣ) δαίμων; *ib* 8 28 (*S* do) δαιμονίζε-
σθαι, not in other gospels; TRit 95 ⲟⲩⲛⲧⲁ ⲛιϩ of

those under earth ڃ, Ac 17 22 (*S* diff) ⲣⲉϥϣⲁⲙ-
ϣⲉ ⲛιϩ δεισιδαίμων, cf Ap 21 8 εἰδωλολάτρης; Dif
1 6 worship of idols & of ⲛιϩ شياطين; Va 57 210
ϥⲁⲣⲡⲉⲣ ⲛιϩ τυμβώρυχος (cf ⲃⲟⲗⲃⲗ), *ib* 144 de-
praved by robberies & ϩⲁⲛⲙⲉⲧϥ. ⲛιϩ.

ⲉⲓⲁϩ *S*, ⲓⲁϩ, ⲓⲱϩ *F* *v* ⲉⲓⲱⲣϩ.

ⲓⲟϩ *B* *v* ⲟⲟϩ.

ⲉⲓⲱϩⲉ, ⲓⲱϩⲉ *SA*, ⲓⲟϩⲓ *BF*, ⲓⲱϩⲓ *F*, ⲉⲓⲉϩ-, ⲉⲓⲱϩ-
S (rare), ⲓⲁϩ- *B* (ⲓⲁ- in Gk), ⲓⲉϩ- *F*, pl ⲉⲓⲁϩⲟⲩ,
ⲉⲓⲁϩⲟⲩⲉ (once) *S*, sg as pl, nn m, *field*: Ex 20 17
B (*S* ⲥⲱϣⲉ), Ruth 2 8 *S* (cf 2 2 ⲥⲱϣⲉ), Is 36 2 *B*
(*SF* do), Mic 2 4 *B* (*S* do, *A* ⲕⲁⲓⲉ), Mt 13 31 *BF*
(*S* do) ἀγρός; Pro 24 45 *SA*, *ib* 31 16 *B* (*S* do),
Jer 28 23 *SB* γεώργιον; Mt 26 36 *B* (*SF* ⲥⲱⲙ),
Jo 4 5 *BF* (*S* do), Ac 1 18 *B* (*S* do) χωρίον; Br 45
S, ShMIF 23 99 *S* opp ϭⲱⲙ, C 86 234 *B* opp ⲙⲁ
ⲛⲁⲗⲟⲗⲓ, Miss 4 679 *S* crops stolen from ⲉⲓ., Ryl
385 *S* (ⲛ)ⲟⲩⲥⲕⲁⲉⲓ ⲛⲓ., ShC 73 152 *S* ⲉⲅⲧⲱϭⲉ
ⲙⲡⲉⲓ., C 89 117 *B* we will till ϯⲕⲟⲓ...ⲉⲟϩⲉⲡϯ ⲙⲙⲟⲩ
ⲙⲡⲓⲓ., *ib* ⲛⲧⲉⲡϭⲟ ⲙⲡⲓⲓ....ⲉⲧⲁ ⲅ ⲕⲏⲛ ⲉⲅϭⲟ ⲡⲧⲟⲩⲕⲟⲓ,
.BM 849 41 *B* prayer at sowing ⲟⲩ ⲓ. بستان, ST 37
S land to be sown as ⲉⲓ. ⲙⲡⲁϣⲉ, BP 11349 *S* sim,
Kr 137 *F* ⲧⲉⲡϫⲁ ⲟⲩⲡⲱⲥⲟⲡ (πόσον) (ⲡ)ⲓ., C 43 122
B ⲡⲓⲫⲟⲣⲟⲥ ⲡⲧⲉ ⲡⲟⲩⲓ., WS 198 *S* δημόσιον on ⲉⲓ.,
Ryl 158 *S*, Kr 95 *S* ⲡⲣⲏⲃ ⲛⲡⲉⲓ., BM 1013, 1061
S ⲧⲓⲥⲧⲱⲧⲉ ⲡⲉⲓ., RE 14 23 *S* ϩⲙⲉⲍⲉ ⲛϫⲉⲥⲉ ⲛⲡⲉⲓ.,
BKU 1 48 *S* ⲡⲉⲕⲙⲉⲣⲟⲥ ⲡⲉⲓ., cf WS 135 *S* ⲧⲟ ⲛⲓ.,
Miss 8 248 *S* martyr's body ⲡⲉⲛⲧⲁϥⲁⲁϥ ⲛⲓ. ⲛⲕⲁⲑⲁⲣ-
ⲟⲥ.   Plural: *S* CO 169 rent of ⲛⲉⲓⲁϩⲟⲩⲉ, J 38
24 ϩ(ⲉ)ⲛⲉⲓ., ST 108 (ⲛ)ⲉⲓ. ϩⲱⲣⲉ, ST 396 ⲛⲉϥⲉⲓ.,
BMostr 44717 we lease to you...ⲡⲉⲓ. ⲛⲁⲓ ⲉⲧϩⲓⲃⲟⲗ.

Compounds: Jos 24 13 *S* ⲉⲓⲉϩ ⲉⲗⲟⲟⲗⲉ, Ex 23
11, Ps 106 37 *B* ⲓⲁϩ ⲁⲗⲟⲗⲓ (*S* ⲙⲁ ⲛⲉⲗ.), 1 Cor
9 7 *BF* (*F* var & *S* do) ἀμπελών, C 86 95 *B* ⲓⲟϩ
ⲁⲗ.; Deu 6 11 *B* ⲓⲁϩ ϫⲱⲓⲧ (*S* ⲙⲁ ⲛϫ.), Jer 5 17
B ἐλαιών; *ib* *B* ⲓⲁϩ ⲡⲕⲉⲡⲧⲉ συκῶν; Deu 23 25 *B*
ⲓⲁϩ ⲥⲟⲩⲟ (*S* ⲉⲓ. alone) ἄμητος; Cat 34 *B* (on Mt
12 1) ⲓⲁϩ ϩⲉⲗⲥ; Deu 7 5 *S* ⲉⲓⲉϩ ϣⲏⲛ (var ⲙⲁ
ⲛϣ., *B* ϣ. alone) ἄλσος, *ib* 19 5 *B* ⲓⲁϩ ϣⲏⲡ (*S* ⲙⲁ
ⲛϣ.), Ps 131 6 *B* (*S* ⲥⲱϣⲉ ⲛⲛϣ.) δρυμός; J 1 50,
68 49 *S* ⲓⲱϩ ⲃⲉⲣⲃⲱⲣⲉⲧ (*v* ϩⲟⲣⲃⲣ), BMOr 6201 *B*
136 ⲓⲱϩ ⲕⲁⲙ.

ⲥⲧⲉⲓⲱϩⲉ, ⲥⲧⲱϩⲉ *S* (J 57 8, ST 437), ⲥⲉⲑⲓⲟϩⲓ *B*
(rare) ⲥⲉⲧ-, ⲥⲓⲧⲓ. *F* nn f, a measure of tilled land:
Ge 21 33 *SB*, 1 Kg 22 6 *S* ἄρουρα; P 44 23 *S*
فدان; *ib* 63 ζευγάριν; K 253 *B* فدّ.; BMis 219 *S*
rubbish mound ⲉⲧⲉⲓⲣⲉ ⲛⲭⲟⲩⲱⲧⲉ ⲡⲥ. ⲉⲥⲕⲱⲧⲉ, CO
139 *S* 6 c. (or their crop?) sold for 1 *solidus*,
CMSS 55 *F* 1 c. for 5½ *sol.* (?), Kr 72 *F* 1 c. for
⅓ *sol.* (?).   ShMIF 23 99 *S* ⲟⲩⲥ. ⲛⲕⲁϩ, COAd
20 *S*, ST 216 *S*, BM 1027 *S* sim, ST 216 *S* ⲥⲧⲉⲓⲱϩⲉ ⲕⲁϩ, BM 1073 *S* -ⲓⲁϩ ⲕ., Ryl 158 *S* c. ⲛϣⲁϥ

ϩⲓⲕⲁϩ, ST 422 *S* c. ⲙⲁϩⲉ, Kr 92 *S* -ⲓⲁϩ ⲙ., J 43
21 *S* -ⲓⲱϩ ⲕⲉⲗⲙ(ϭⲗⲙ), Kr 72 *F* -ⲓⲁϩ ⲥⲓ (?), BMOr
6201 *B* 19 -ⲓⲁϩ ϩⲣⲉ, Ryl 158 *S* -ⲓⲁϩ ϩⲟⲩⲱⲣ, *ib*
-ⲓⲁϩ ϭⲱⲙ, BMar 5 *S* c. ⲛϭⲱⲙ.

ϣⲓ ⲉⲓⲱϩⲉ *S*, ϣⲓ ι. *A*, ϣⲓ ι. *F* vb, *measure field*,
whence ⲡⲟⲩϣ ⲛϣ. a measure of length: Is 34 11
SF ⲡⲟⲩϩ ⲛϣ. (*B* ⲡⲟϩ ⲛⲣⲱϣ) σπαρτίον γεωμετρίας
Zech 2 1 *A* (*B* do) σχοινίον γεωμ., ShC 73 62 *S*
brethren when walking to keep a ⲛ. ⲛϣ. between
them; ShR 2 3 34 *S* ⲥⲁϩ, ⲡⲣⲟⲡⲟⲛⲧⲏⲥ, ⲣⲉϥϣⲓ ⲉⲓ.

ⲗⲉϩⲓⲱϩⲉ *S* nn, meaning unknown: PMich 4557
letter, ⲡⲁⲗⲁ (ⲛ?)ⲡⲉⲗ. ⲧⲏⲣⲟⲩ ⲡⲕⲏⲙⲉ.

ⲡⲉϩ ⲓⲟϩⲓ *B* v ⲛⲏⲃ.

In many place-names (mostly in Gk texts): CO
36 ⲧⲕⲱⲙⲏ ⲙⲡⲉⲓ., *ib* 227 ⲡⲓ. ⲙⲃⲣⲣⲉ (*cf* PLond 4

596 Πιαϩ νβρρε), PLond *lc* Πιωϩε ⲕⲟⲩⲓ, Π. ⲡⲛⲁⲙ,
Ep 1 120 ⲡⲓⲱϩ; PLich ⲡⲓⲱϩ ⲡⲉⲙⲟⲡ, Miss 4 386n
ⲡⲓⲓⲁϩ ⲁⲗⲟⲗⲓ, PLond *lc* Πιαϩ ⲕⲁⲙ, Π. ⲙⲏⲗϩ, Π.
ⲛⲧⲟⲟⲩ, PCai 2 213 Πιαϩ ⲥⲉ & Πια ⲥⲉ, *ib* 3 206 Πια
Διοσκόρου; as pl: PLond 4 594 Νιαϩ ⲉⲥⲟⲟⲩ, Νεια
τζην.

ⲓⲟϩⲓ *B* often wrongly for ⲟϩⲓ *fold*: 1 Kg 17 34
ἀγέλη, Ez 34 14 μάνδρα, Zeph 2 6 ποίμνιον, AM 115
ⲓⲟϩⲓ ⲛⲉⲥⲟⲟⲩ.

ⲓⲟϩⲓ *B* ? for ϩⲟⲓ *S water-wheel*: C 89 23 who will
yoke beast ⲉⲟⲩⲓⲟϩⲓ? = MG 17 370 ساقية.

ⲉⲓϭⲣⲓ *S* vb tr, meaning unknown: Bodl(P) a 2
32 alchem recipe begins ⲕⲟⲩⲱϣ ⲡⲛⲟⲩⲃ ⲉⲓϭⲣⲓ ⲙ-
ⲙⲟⲩ ϩⲓⲡⲁⲧⲓⲣⲓⲥⲭ, ends ϣⲁϥⲉⲓ. ϩⲓⲡⲁⲧⲓⲣⲓⲥⲛ ⲉϥϩⲛⲙ. Prob Arabic.

Ⲕ

ⲕ, tenth letter of alphabet, called ⲕⲁⲡⲡⲁ *S* (My
65), ⲕⲁⲡⲡⲁ, ⲕⲁⲡⲁ *B* (K 1, Stern p 418), كاف (P 44
137, 43 240, Stern *lc*); *cf* Preisigke W.buch 1 723
κάκ. As numeral *BF*, rarely *S* = *twenty* (ϫⲟⲩⲱⲧ).
Derived from hierogl. ḳ, as ⲉⲛⲕⲟⲧ, ⲟⲉⲓⲕ, ⲙⲟⲩⲕⲓ; or
k, as ⲁⲛⲟⲕ, ⲕⲉ-, ⲣⲱⲕϩ; rarely g, as ⲕⲉϩⲧ (Koptos),
ⲕⲁϣ. **a** *SAF* ⲕ replaced in *B* by ⲭ before ϩ,
ⲗ, ⲙ, ⲛ, ⲣ, ⲓ, ⲟⲩ & tone-vowel, as ⲭⲗⲁⲗ, ⲭⲛⲁⲩ,
ⲁⲭⲱ, ⲥⲭⲁⲓ. **b** replaces ⲧ, as ⲁⲕⲱⲛ (BHom 50),
ⲕⲣⲁⲫⲏ (*ib* 42), ⲡⲉⲗⲁⲕⲟⲥ (MG 25 19); converse, as
ⲁⲧⲟⲗⲟⲅⲟⲑⲓⲁ (*ib* 113 var), ⲧⲉⲣⲓⲥⲙⲁ (CO 18), ⲧⲗⲁϥ
F (2 Cor 12 16), ⲡⲉⲕ-(ⲛⲧ-) LAl 6; both: ⲛⲧⲕⲁ (BG
101, CO 196), Z 330 ⲛⲧⲕⲣⲁⲧⲥ. **c** replaces ϭ,
as ⲉⲕⲟⲟϣ (Ps 73 14 var), ⲕⲓⲏ *SF* (Is 1 11), ⲕⲁⲧϩ *A*
(Hag 1 6), ⲕⲁⲗⲱⲟⲩ (J 76 3), ⲕⲱϣⲧ (Lu 1 48 var);
converse (oftenest), as ⲍⲟϭⲙⲁϩⲉ (Sa 3 6), ϭⲉ-
(Br 44), ϭⲓⲧⲁⲣⲓⲥ (Ex 29 9), ⲉⲩⲕⲁϩⲉⲓ (PS 359),
ϭⲗⲝⲉ (BMis 93), ⲧⲁϭⲟ (El 142), ⲛϭⲃⲱⲕ...ⲛϭⲭⲛ-
ⲟⲩϥ (Ep 336); both: ⲧⲁⲗϭⲕⲁ (BM 524 *sf*), ⲕϭⲟⲗ
(ST 280). **d** replaces ⲭ (rare), as ⲑⲉⲕⲛⲏ (τέχνη
Va 66 305), ⲕⲗⲁⲙⲓⲥ (C 89 95), ⲕⲣⲓⲁ (CO 245),
ⲥⲧⲟⲓⲕⲉⲓ (ST 318); converse, as ⲥⲭⲉⲩⲉ (Ep 258),
ⲭⲁⲥⲧⲣⲟⲛ (Hall 106); also ⲙⲉⲭϩ (AZ 21 9 *O*, Hos
10 11 *A*), ⲙⲟⲭϩ (Si 30 35, *cf ib* 25 16), ϣⲓⲭϩ
(Mic 7 19 *A*); both: ⲧⲕⲭⲣⲓⲁ (Ep 217). **e** replaced by ⲧ (rare, mostly ϭ), as ϣⲓⲧⲉ *dig* (Zech
3 9 *A*), ϩⲁⲡⲟⲣⲧ (P 44 103 *S*), ⲁⲓⲧⲟⲕⲧ *l* ⲁⲓ-
ⲕⲟⲧⲧ (KroppB 9); converse: ⲉⲗⲓⲥⲁⲃⲉⲕ (Ep 1
243). **f** ⲕⲥ for ⲍ, as ⲕⲥⲟⲩⲣ (CO 342), ϩⲉⲕⲥⲓⲥ
(C 89 135), ⲉⲕⲥⲟⲩⲥⲓⲁ (BKU 1 26 (3)); converse:
ⲉⲗⲍ (Ac 26 26 *B*), ⲗⲟⲩⲍ; both: ⲥⲁⲣⲉⲕⲍ (Baouit

57), ⲑⲟⲕϩⲟⲩ, ⲗⲟⲕϩⲟⲩ (C 86 219, 220). **g** where
Ar transcribed ⲕ = ق, as ⲕⲁⲗ قال, ⲣⲁⲕⲁⲍ رقد, ϩⲁⲕⲕⲁ
حقا; rarely ⲭ: ⲭⲁⲗⲁ قلعة (C 86 168), or ك
(final, otherwise ⲭ, which rarely as init, ⲉⲗⲭⲉ-
ⲙⲉⲗ الكامل *ib* 163), as ⲗⲁⲕ لك, ⲓⲉⲍⲛⲓⲕ يديك (all
EW 234 ff); converse: قوص ⲕⲱⲥ, قاو ⲧⲕⲱⲟⲩ,
ⲡⲓⲗⲁⲕ; or ك, as ⲑⲉⲟⲧⲟⲕⲓⲁ تداكية, ⲥⲕⲏⲡⲛ اسكنا.

ⲕⲁ-, ⲕⲁⲁϥ *v* ⲕⲱ.

ⲕⲁⲉ, ⲕⲁⲓⲉ *v* ⲕⲟⲓⲉ.

ⲕⲁⲓ *v* ϭⲁⲓ.

ⲕⲉ *SAA²BFO*, ϭⲉ *S*, ⲕⲏ, ϭⲏ *F*, ⲕⲁⲓ- *A²*, ⲕⲟⲩ- *S*,
pl forms *v* below, & sg as pl, nn m & f, *another*,
I substant (always ϭⲉ): 1 Kg 21 9 *S* f (var ⲕⲛⲧⲉ
Mor), Ac 15 20 *S* (*B* om), Gal 1 19 *S* (*B* do), R 2
2 28 *S* dove mates not ⲙⲛϭⲉ, Mor 17 85 *S* ⲙⲛϭⲉ
ⲛⲉⲗⲗⲁⲕ ἕτερος, *cf* Br 44 *S* ⲙⲛϭⲉ ⲛⲉⲗⲗⲁⲥ; Mk
12 32 *S* (*B* do), 1 Thes 2 6 *SF* (*B* ϩⲁⲛⲕⲉⲭ.), Aeg
240 *S* ⲙⲡⲉⲣⲁⲁϥ ⲛϭⲉ (*cf ib* ⲡⲕⲉⲟⲩⲁ) ἄλλος. No
Gk: 1 Kg 21 1 *S*, Is 45 6 *S* (*B* ⲕⲉ-); ShBMOr
8810 458 *S* ⲟⲩⲧⲉ ⲛⲧⲟⲕ ⲟⲩⲧⲉ ϭⲉ, Mun 147 *S* ϩⲓⲧⲟⲟⲧϥ ⲏ ϩⲓⲧⲛϭⲉ. With demonst, *this other*:
Lev 11 7 *S*, Eccl 1 17 *S*, Lu 3 20 *S* (*B* ⲭⲉⲧ), He 6
3 *S* (*B* ⲫⲁⲓ, *F* ⲡⲉⲓⲕⲉⲟⲩⲉⲓ) οὗτος; Ps 37 10 *S* (*B* om)
καὶ αὐτό; ShClPr 44 1 *S* ⲡⲁⲓ ⲁⲩⲱ ⲡⲓⲕⲉ (*cf ib* ⲡⲁⲓ
...ⲛⲓⲕⲟⲟⲩⲉ).
II ⲕⲉ- adj, a *other, different*: Ge 26 21 *SB*.
Is 30 10 *SBF*, Ro 7 3 *SB*, ZNTW 24 90 *F money*
ⲓⲉ ⲕⲉⲛⲡⲕⲉⲓ; as pl: Deu 5 7 *SB*, Sa 19 3 *S*, Lu 3
18 *S* (*B* ⲕⲉⲭ.), Ac 2 4 *SB* ἕτ.; Lev 6 13 *SB*,

Is 43 10 *SB*, Mt 4 21 *SB*, Jo 18 15 *SB* (*A²* ⲡⲕⲉ-), as pl: Sa 14 23 *S*, Mk 7 4 *S* ἄλ.; Job 40 3 *S* (BAp 79) ἄλλως; Mk 1 38 *SB* ⲕⲉⲙⲁ ἀλλαχοῦ, Lev 18 19 *S* (*B* diff) ⲕⲉⲥⲁ χωρισμός; Ge 2 9 *B*, Job 14 7 *S*, Ps 59 tit *S*, Ac 18 18 *SB* ἔτι, Ps 88 *S* (*B* ⲛⲉⲙ-) ἔτι δὲ καί, Ap 10 7 *S* (*B* om) ⲙⲡⲕⲉⲟⲩⲕⲉⲧⲓ. No Gk: 4 Kg 2 14 *S*, Sa 11 19 *S*, Is 21 16 *SB*; ⲕⲉⲭⲉⲙ *B* 2 Cor 12 19 (*S* ⲙⲉϣⲁⲕ, *F* ⲡⲁⲛⲧⲱⲥ πάλαι var πάλιν *olim*) prob contains this word, *cf* Spg 270; PS 118 *S* ⲁⲕⲉϭⲟⲙ ⲉⲓ ⲉⲃⲟⲗ ⲛϩⲏⲧ, BMis 369 *S* = Va 63 4 *B* this troubleth me ⲉⲓⲥ ⲕⲉⲣⲟⲟⲩ ⲥⲛⲁⲩ = BSM 29 *B* ⲓⲥϫⲉⲛϭⲁⲧϩⲛ ⲡⲥⲁϥ, C 89 6 *B* shall befall thee ⲙⲉⲛⲉⲛⲥⲁⲕⲉⲥⲛⲟⲩ μετὰ ταῦτα, TU 43 6 *A* ⲙⲡⲛⲥⲉⲕⲉⲟⲩⲏⲣ ⲡⲣⲁⲙⲡⲉ, 1 Kg 25 6 *S* (Gk diff) ⲉⲡⲟⲟⲩ ⲛⲧⲕⲉⲣⲟⲙⲡⲉ *next year*, Mor 40 22 *S* ϩⲛⲧⲕⲉⲟⲩϣⲏ ⲉⲧⲓⲛⲏⲩ (var *ib* 41 137 om), J 121 5 *S* I have no cause with thee before 27th Koiahk ⲉⲕⲉⲣⲟⲙⲡⲉ, CO 221 *S* sim, *ib* 252 *S* ⲙⲡⲕⲉⲥⲁϥ, Ep 169 *S* ⲛⲡⲕⲟⲩⲥⲛϥ *already yesterday*. **b** with ⲥⲟⲡ: Jud 16 18 *S* ἄπαξ, Ge 18 32 *B* ⲙⲡⲁⲓⲕⲉⲥ. (*S* ⲕⲉⲥ.) Hag 2 6 *SAB* ἔτι ἄπαξ, Ps 103 30 *SB* ἀνα-, Jer 3 1 *B* ἀνα- ἔτι, Jo 3 3 *SB* ἄνωθεν; PS 242 *S* as I have already told you ⲛⲕⲉⲥ., *ib* 276 ⲁⲓⲭⲟⲟϥ ⲉⲣⲱⲧⲛ ⲛⲕⲉⲥ. but will tell you again, ShC 73 82 *S* sim, Mt 19 28 *S* (*B* diff) ⲡⲉϫⲡⲟ ⲛⲕⲉⲥ. παλιγγενεσία, Gu 68 *S* not to dwell in this city ⲛⲕⲉⲥ. τοῦ λοιποῦ, BMis 153 *S* there is no repentance for them ⲛⲕⲉⲥ., BM 580 21 *F* pray God may guide me ⲕⲉⲥ., Kandil 46 *B* ϣⲧⲉⲙ-…ⲛⲕⲉⲥ. μηκέτι; BMis 323 *S* = BSM 6 *B*, BMar 38 *S* sim. *V* also ⲕⲟⲩ below. **c** ⲕⲉ…ⲕⲉ *B*, *any other*: Ja 5 12 ⲕⲉⲁⲛⲁϣ (*bis*) = *S* ⲗⲁⲁⲩ ⲛⲁ. ἄλλος τις, Cat 220 food or drink ⲓⲉ ⲕⲉϩⲱⲃ (*bis*) of this sort, Va 57 265 such are qualities of bishop ⲕⲉϩⲱⲃ (*bis*) ϫⲉ ⲟⲩⲇⲉ ϩⲟⲗⲱⲥ περαιτέρω δὲ μηδέν, C 43 112 hegemôn ⲙⲡⲉϥϫⲁ ⲕⲉϩⲱⲃ (*bis*) ⲛⲁϥ but that of the martyr. **d** ⲕⲟⲩ- *S* = ⲕⲉ- (mostly *Sᵃ*, Theban), oftenest with number or measure: RE 9 141 *S* ⲕⲟⲩ(ⲟⲩ)ⲉⲓⲉ (*sc* ⲕⲁⲉ), ST 325 ⲕⲟⲩϧⲟⲩⲱⲧⲉ, CO 186 -ϯⲟⲩ, ST 327 -ϯⲡⲗⲉ, *ib* 389 -ⲍⲩⲧⲏ, Ep 349, 534 -ϭⲓⲝ; or with ⲥⲟⲡ (*cf* above): Tor 31, BKU 1 100, CO 229; *v* Ep 1 247 *inf*; also Ann 18 284 ⲕⲟⲩⲕⲁⲗⲁϩⲧ. **e** with number: Sa 7 5 *S*, Mt 12 45 *SB* ἔτ., *ib* 25 16 *SB* ἄλ., Deu 19 9 *SB*, Is 7 8 *SB* ἔτι; ⲕⲉⲟⲩⲁ, -ⲟⲩⲉⲓ, *another*: Job 30 24 *SB*, Is 42 8 *SB*, Lu 9 29 *S* ἔτ.; Ex 8 10 *B*, Jo 5 7 *SA²B* ἄλ.; Joel 2 27 *SA* (*B* -ⲭⲉ), Lu 18 22 *SB* ἔτι; Mt 22 5 *S* ϩⲟⲓⲛⲉ (*B* ⲟⲩⲁⲓ) ⲙⲉⲛ…ⲕⲉⲟⲩⲁ ϫⲉ ὁ μέν…ὁ δέ, *cf* MG 25 243 *B* ϩⲁⲡⲟⲩⲟⲡ ⲙⲉⲛ…ϩⲁⲛⲕⲉⲟⲩⲟⲡ; ClPr 30 15 *S* ⲕⲉⲟⲩⲁⲡⲉ ⲡⲁⲛⲣ ⲕ. ⲡⲉ ⲡⲧⲛⲩ, AZ 21 106 *O* ⲉⲥⲛⲕⲱⲱⲧ ⲙⲉⲛⲕⲉⲟⲩⲉ. **f** with def art, *the other*: 3 Kg 22 20 *S* ⲡⲁⲓ…ⲡⲉⲓⲕⲉⲟⲩⲁ ⲟⲩⲧⲟⲥ…ⲟⲩⲧⲟⲥ, Eccl 4 8 *S* δεύτερος, Mt 6 24 *S* (*B* ⲭⲉⲧ) ἔτ., Lu•

20 11 *S* (*B* do) ἐκεῖνος; ShC 73 59 *S* ⲧⲉⲩⲕⲉⲟⲩⲉⲓ *neighbour*. **g** with adj, esp ⲕⲉⲕⲟⲩⲓ, ⲕⲟⲩϫⲓ: Ex 17 4 *SB*, Job 2 9 *SB*, Jo 13 33 *SA²B* ἔτι μικρόν; Mk 14 70 *S* μετὰ μικ., TstAb 232 *B* keep pure ⲧⲉⲕⲕⲉⲕ. ⲛⲥⲁⲣⲝ, MR 5 33 *F* ⲡⲉⲡⲕⲉⲕⲟⲩϭⲓ ⲛⲁ ⲡⲕⲁϩⲟⲩ on earth, ShC 73 81 *S* ⲏ ⲕⲉⲕ. ⲁⲡⲡⲉ that we should tap with feet & clap hands; adverbial: BMis 540 *S* ⲁⲓⲛⲁⲩ ⲉⲕⲉⲥⲁ ⲛⲕⲉⲕ. *non longe*, MG 25 4 *B* having gone forward ⲛⲕⲉⲕ.; or ⲕⲉϣⲏⲙ: Pro 5 14 *SA* (*B* ⲕⲉⲕ.), Mk 8 7 *S* (*B* do); ⲕⲉⲗⲁⲁⲩ: Pcod 33 *S* ⲉⲧⲃⲉϭⲉⲗ. ⲛϥⲱϩ, J 3 35 *S* there remains not ⲕⲉⲗ. ⲛϩⲁⲓⲕⲁⲓⲟⲛ.

III Pl: **a** ϩⲉⲛⲕⲟⲟⲩⲉ *S* = ϩⲁⲛⲕⲉⲭⲱⲟⲩⲛⲓ *B* Job 18 19, Mt 15 30 (*B* diff) ἔτ.; Pro 5 9, Is 49 12, Jo 7 12 ἄλ.; ⲛⲕ. *S* = ⲡⲓⲕⲉⲭ. *B* Job 31 8 ἄλ., Mt 20 4 ἐκεῖνος; ⲡⲉⲓⲕ. *S* = ⲡⲁⲓ, ⲡⲏ *B* Nu 18 3, Ps 19 7, Ro 5 14 οὗτος, ὁ δέ, καὶ ὁ, ShC 73 10 *S* ⲡⲁⲓ ⲏ ⲡⲉⲓⲕ., Br 239 *S* ϩⲟⲉⲓⲙⲉ ⲙⲉⲛ…ϩⲉⲛⲕ.; ⲕⲛⲉⲅⲉ *S* Jer 12 6, ⲕⲛⲏⲅⲉ Ep 314; ⲕⲁⲅⲉ *A²* Jo 4 38, 17 20; ⲕⲁⲅⲉⲓ *F* Mor 30 33; ⲕⲉⲩ- *S* Deu (Budge) 13 13, 28 64 &c (var & *B* ⲕⲉ-), but *cf ib* 5 7, 13 2 ⲕⲉ-. **b** ⲕⲉⲕⲟⲟⲩⲉ *S* Bor 263 14 ϯⲛⲟϭ ⲛϩⲣⲟⲧⲉ…ⲙⲛⲛⲕⲉⲕ., BIF 13 114 ⲡⲉⲓⲕⲉⲕ. *those there*, ST 172 ⲕⲉⲟⲩⲁ…ⲛ̄ⲕⲟⲱⲟⲩⲉ; ⲕⲉⲕⲉⲟⲩⲉ, -ⲉⲩⲉ *A* Pro 5 9, Hag 2 2, Zach 11 9, ⲕⲉⲕⲁⲅⲉ *A²* AP 28, *ib* 40; ⲕⲉⲕⲁⲅⲓ *F* Mk 15 31, Ro 11 23, 1 Cor 15 6 (Mor 38 3), ⲕⲉⲕⲁⲩⲓⲉ Mor 15 6, ⲕⲉⲕⲁⲩⲛⲓ Jo 4 38, AZ 23 42, ⲕⲁⲩⲡⲉ Baouit 1 138.

IV ⲕⲉ- with def art **a** may = *also*, *even*: Deu 1 28 *SB*, Job 12 6 *S* (*B* diff), Lu 14 26 *SB*, Ac 12 3 *SB* καί (oftenest), Mt 13 12 *S* (*B* ⲫⲏ, *F* ⲡⲏ) καί ὁ, Jud 3 22 *S*, 4 Kg 13 6 *S* καί γε, Job 1 16 *S* (*B* om) ὁμοίως, *ib* 1 4 *SB* ἄμα καί, Sa 19 14 *S* ἤ, BHom 24 *S* ἀλλα ⲡⲕⲉⲇⲁⲓⲙⲱⲛ αὐτός ὁ, Aeg 274 *S* ⲡⲕⲉⲉⲡⲓⲥⲕⲟⲡⲟⲥ λοιπός. No Gk: Ge 31 30 *S* (*B* om), Deu 4 7 *S* (*B* do), Jos 2 1 *S*, Lu 23 15 *SB*, Jo 9 3 *S*; PS 123 *S* came forward ⲛϭⲓ ⲧⲕⲉⲙⲁⲣⲓⲁ, CA 89 *S* not Peter only ⲁⲗⲗⲁ ⲡⲕⲉⲛⲁⲩⲗⲟⲥ, C 86 219 *B* ϫⲉⲛ̄ⲓⲕⲉϣⲉ ⲉⲧϣⲟⲩⲟⲩ thou showest thy power, AP 23 *A²* before God & also (ἄμα δέ) before ⲡⲕⲉⲣⲱⲙⲉ. Here prob belong ShBor 246 61 *S* ⲙⲡⲟⲩⲕⲁ ⲕⲉⲥⲃⲱ ϫⲉⲙⲡⲟⲩⲭⲟⲟⲩ ⲛⲁϥ *even teaching have they not omitted, that hath not been told them*, *ib* sim ⲙⲡⲟⲩⲕⲁ ⲕⲉⲧⲱϣⲉ ⲙⲡⲟⲩⲕⲁ ⲕⲉⲧⲥⲟ, ShA.1 53 *S* thy mother is deranged & ⲕⲉϩⲗⲟⲥⲧⲛ ⲏ ⲕⲉ ϩⲃⲥ hath covered her eyes. **b** advb: Mk 7 4 *S* (*B* diff, Gk om) ⲡⲁⲧⲕⲉⲉⲃⲟⲗ ϩⲓⲧⲁϩⲟⲣⲁ, Va 57 12 *B* ⲡⲕⲉϯ ⲛⲟⲩ ⲟⲛ καὶ νῦν. **c** with pron & sg m art *B*: Va 57 100 ⲡⲕⲉⲁⲛⲟⲕ ϩⲱ κἀγώ, C 89 184 ⲡⲕⲉⲁⲛⲟⲛ ϩⲱⲛ hath God saved, Cat 31 prophets ⲛⲉⲙⲡⲕⲉⲛⲑⲟⲟⲩ Baptist, Va 57 40 ⲡⲓⲕⲉⲛⲑⲱⲧⲉⲛ. **ρ** ⲡⲕⲉ-, *be, do also*: Job 13 15 *B* (*S* diff), Ps 68 29 *S* (*B* = Gk), Si 22 22 *S* (HT), Ac 23 3 *B*, Eph 5 12 *SB*,

Va 63 80 *B* not ashamed ⲁⲗⲗⲁ ⲁⲓⲡⲁⲉⲣ ⲡⲕⲉϣⲟⲩ-
ϣⲟⲩ ⲙⲙⲟⲓ ⲛϩⲟⲩ *καί*; ShC 73 6 *S* hard to escape
sin ⲥⲣ ⲡⲕⲉⲙⲟⲕϩ ⲇⲉ ⲟⲛ ⲡⲣⲟⲅⲟ to escape God's
wrath, Ep 141 *S* not only] did he not consent...
ⲁⲗⲗⲁ ⲕⲁⲓ ⲁϥⲣ ⲡⲕⲉⲟⲩⲉⲛϩ ⲉⲃⲟⲗ great impudence.
With these *cf* Jud 11 17 *S* ⲙⲡⲉⲕⲉⲣ ϩⲛⲁϥ *καὶ οὐκ*,
Va 57 126 *B* ⲉⲣⲉⲧⲉⲛⲕⲉⲟⲓ ⲛϣⲣⲱⲓⲥ *καὶ μετὰ ἀγρυ-
πνίας*, *ib* 233 *B* what excuse wilt find ⲉⲧⲉⲙⲡⲉⲕⲕⲉⲁⲣ-
ⲉϩ ⲉⲡⲓϣⲓ, PS 294 *S* she will find that soul hath
sinned & ⲉⲙⲡⲥⲕⲉϩⲉ ⲉⲙⲙⲩⲥⲧⲏⲣⲓⲟⲛ ⲛⲙⲙⲁⲥ.

ⵡ ⲕⲉⲧ *S*, ϫⲉⲧ *B*, ⲕⲏⲧ *F*, f ⲕⲉⲧⲉ, ⲕⲏⲧⲉ *S*, ϫⲉϯ
B nn m f (*v* AZ 40 93), *another*, **a** without art :
Mt 13 23 *S* ⲟⲩⲁ...ⲕ. ὁ δέ = *B* ⲟⲩⲁⲓ...ⲟⲩⲁⲓ, 1 Cor
12 8 *S* sim = *B* ⲟⲩⲁⲓ...ⲕⲉⲟⲩⲁⲓ ἄλλος, Aeg 269 *S*
ⁱthou hast received this ⲕ. ⲇⲉ ⲡⲕⲉⲟⲩⲁ, ShCO 13 *S*
ⲕⲉⲟⲩⲁ...ⲕ. ⲇⲉ, ST 262 *S* if mercifully they require
not of us ϭⲉⲧ *further* tax. **b** with art or demonst,
the, this other : Ge 29 33 *B* (*S* ⲕⲉⲟⲩⲁ), 1 Kg 16 9
B, Job 31 28 *S* (varr ⲕⲏⲧ BM 252 1, ⲕⲉ BMOr
4717 frag uncatal) *B*, Eccl 3 19 *S*, Mor 17 66 *S*
report saith ⲟⲩⲛ ϭⲟⲙ ⲙⲙⲟϥ ⲉⲣ ⲡⲉⲓⲕ. καὶ οὗτος ;
Su 56 *B*, Mt 6 24 *B* (*S* ⲕⲉⲟⲩⲁ), MG 25 219 *B*
ὁ ἕτ. ; *ib* 208 *B* ὁ ἄλ. ; Ac 5 37 *B* (*S* ⲛⲧⲟϥ ϩⲱⲱϥ),
Mk 12 4 *S* (var & *B* ⲡⲕⲉⲟⲩⲁ) ἐκεῖν., BHom 43 *S*
ⲡⲉⲓⲕ...ⲡⲉⲓⲕⲉⲟⲩⲁ ἐκεῖν. ...ἄλ.; Is 23 13 *B* (*S* ⲡⲉⲓⲕⲉ-)
αὕτη ; Ap 17 10 *B* (*S* ⲕⲉⲟⲩⲁ) ὁ εἷς ; Aeg 287 *S*
ⲡⲁⲓ...ⲡⲉⲓⲕ. (var ⲡⲁⲓ ϩⲱⲱϥ) ὁ δέ ; Mk 17 59 *F* ϩⲉⲙ-
ⲡⲉⲓⲕⲏⲧ (*SB* diff) οὕτως ; C 43 161 *B* as Daniel
slew dragon so may I ⲙⲡⲁⲓϫ., BMar 133 *S* one
monk only visited me & ⲙⲡⲉⲡⲉⲓⲕ. ⲛⲁⲩ ⲉⲣⲟⲓ, Bor
265 92 *S* none greater than Baptist, yet ⲡⲉⲓⲕ.
ⲙⲡⲉⲓⲉⲣⲏⲧ ⲛⲁϥ to judge world, ROC 9 321 *B* ⲡⲁⲓ-
ⲕⲉⲭ. *this other* good deed. **Fem** : 1 Kg 21 9 *S*
ⲕⲏⲧⲉ (var ϭⲉ) ἕτ., Mt 5 39 *S* ⲕⲉⲧⲉ (Mor, CO 17) *B*
ἄλ., Ge 26 21 *B* (*S* ⲕⲉⲟⲩⲉⲓ) ἑκ., Cat 61 *B* ⲑⲁⲓ.
ϯϫ., Aeg 273 *S* ⲧⲟⲩⲉⲓ...ⲧⲕⲉⲧⲉ (var ⲧⲕⲉⲧ ⲇⲉ),
BMOr 8811 239 *S* ⲡⲁⲓ ⲁⲩⲱ ⲧⲉⲓⲕⲉⲧ, Aeg 283 *S*
ⲧⲕⲉⲟⲩⲉⲓ (var ⲧⲕⲉⲧ) ; as pl ? ST 171 *S* ⲧⲉⲥϭⲓⲙⲉ
ⲙⲛ ⲡⲕⲉⲧⲉ, Kr 225 *F* ⲙⲉ(ⲛ)ⲡⲉⲕⲉⲧⲏ. **Adv**, *again* :
Ep 327 *S* value of coin ⲙⲡⲁⲧϥⲉⲓ ⲉⲡⲉⲓⲧⲛ ⲛϭⲉⲧ.

ⲕⲏ *B* nn f, meaning unknown, ? *river-bank* :
MG 25 192 water beast bore us across river &
ⲉⲧⲁⲛϣⲱϫⲓ ⲉϥⲕⲏ, EW 135(E iii)same. Might be f
(?) of ⲕⲉ *other* (side).

ⲕⲏⲏ *BF* *v* ϭⲓⲉ.

ⲕⲟ *O* nn m, ? *bull* (*cf* names Πικῶς, ϩⲁⲣⲕⲟ,
Κοπρής HT) : AZ 21 105 ⲛⲉϭⲓ ⲛϥⲏⲧ ⲛⲡⲓⲕⲟ, paral
ⲡⲉϭⲓ ⲛϥⲏⲧ ⲛⲟⲩⲥⲓⲣⲓ.

ⲕⲟ *S* nn m, meaning unknown : CO 355 ⲛⲧϯ
ⲡⲕⲟ to this messenger ; ? same Hall 86 ⲥⲛⲁⲩ ⲡⲕⲟ
(or ? ⲕⲁ).

ⲕⲟ *S* nn f, meaning unknown or ? = ⲕⲟⲓⲉ : Ryl
162 boundaries of plough land]ⲉⲓⲛϩⲧ ⲡⲟⲩⲱⲧ ϩⲓϫⲛ-
ⲧⲕⲟ ⲛⲡⲥⲁ ⲛ[.   Possibly CO 79 9 ⲧⲕⲱ.   *Cf* ? Kr 1
12 *S* ϣⲁⲧⲉⲅⲕⲱ (ⲉ)ϩⲟⲩⲛ (*v* ⲕⲱ vb).

ⲕⲟⲓⲉ *S*, ⲕⲁⲉ *S^a*, ⲕⲁⲓⲉ, ⲕⲁⲉⲓⲉ *SA*, ⲕⲟⲓ *S* (PMich
4557) *B* nn f, oftenest *B*, *field* (high lying, *v* hierogl
determ) as tillage or pasture : Ge 2 5 *B*, *ib* 25 9 *B*
(TstAb 254, var ⲓⲟϩⲓ, *S* ⲥⲱϣⲉ), Nu 20 17 *B* (*S* do),
cf 22 ⲓⲟϩⲓ (*S* do), Job 5 25 *AB* (*S* do), Ps 102 15,
103 11 *S* (ShZ 599, var c.) *B*, Pro 24 42 *A* (*S* c.),
Is 33 12 *B* (*SF* do), EW 28 *B* ⲟⲩⲕ. named Mar-
mareôn ἀγρός ; Ex 1 14 *A* (*B* ⲙⲉϣϣⲟϯ), Ps 8 8 *B*
(*S* c.), Pro 27 25 *A* (*S* do), Ez 29 5 *B* (*S* do), Joel
2 22 *A* (*S* c., *B* ⲙ.) πέδιον, *v* below, place-names ;
Ge 9 2 *B* (*S* ⲕⲁϩ), Dan 1 12 *B* (*S* do) γῆ ; Pro 9
12 *A* (*S* c., *B* ⲓⲉϥⲟⲩⲱⲓ) γεώργιον ; K 128 *B* غِي,
لَيْف ; C 86 223 *B* ⲡⲧⲉϥⲥϫⲁⲓ ϩⲉⲛⲧⲕ., C 43 125 *B*
ⲉⲟⲩ(ⲟⲩ)ⲱϣⲡⲉ ϩⲉⲛⲧⲕ., MG 25 362 *B* going forth
ϩⲉⲛⲧⲕ. at summer harvest, Miss 4 171 *B* his ⲕ.
ⲙⲉⲣ ⲛⲕⲁⲣⲡⲟⲥ, ShC 42 87 *S* ⲕ. ⲉϥⲣⲏⲧ, Va 69 104
B ⲛⲓϩⲉⲗⲉ ⲛⲧⲉ ⲧⲕ., BSM 88 *B* sim ϫⲣⲱϫ ; C 89
117 *B* ϭⲟ ⲙⲡⲉⲛⲓⲟϩⲓ...ⲱⲥϩ ⲛⲧⲉⲕ., Ep 300 *S* corn
sown ⲉⲧⲕⲁⲉ, MIE 2 383 *B* pasturing sheep ϩⲉⲛⲛⲓ-
ϣⲟⲛϯ ϩⲉⲛⲧⲕ., C 41 8 *B* sim, BM 1144 *S* tax
(δημόσ.) on 7 ⲕ., ShC 73 18 *S* ⲕⲱⲗⲏ, ⲕ. (var c.),
ⲧⲟⲟⲩ, ⲧⲟϣ, ⲭⲱⲣⲁ, J 18 29, 68 49 *S* opp ϯⲙⲉ.

ⲙⲁ ⲛⲕ. *B*, *plain* : Lu 6 17 (*S* ⲙⲁ ⲉϥⲟⲩⲟϣⲥ)
τόπος πεδινός.   ⲣⲉⲙⲛⲕ. *B*, *husbandman* : Ge 16
12 *B* ἄγροικος, PMich 4557 *S* ⲡⲣⲙⲛⲧⲕⲟⲓ ; ⲣⲱⲙ- :
PLond 4 463 *S* ⲡⲣⲱⲙⲧⲉⲛⲕ., *ib* 494 ⲡⲣⲱⲙⲛⲓⲕ.
ⲡⲟⲩⲱⲧ.   ⲟⲩⲟⲓ ⲛⲕ. *B* : Jer 52 16 ⲟⲩⲓⲏ ⲛⲕ. γεωργός, Va 57 225 *B* sim.   In place-names : PLond
4 435 *S* ⲧϫⲟⲙⲧⲉ ⲛⲕⲟⲓⲉ = γ̄ πεδιάδες, *ib* 492 ⲧⲧⲓⲉ
ⲛⲕ. = ε̄ πεδ. (at Jkôw), RE 9 141 *S* ⲧⲕⲁⲉ ⲡⲕⲱⲥ,
Bodl(P) c 14 ⲧⲕⲟⲓ ⲛⲧⲙⲟⲩⲙⲏⲣ.

ⲕⲟⲩ *S* nn as pl, meaning unknown : PMich
597 = 602 recipe for ⲟⲩⲁ ⲉϥⲕⲱⲗϩ, pound together
ϩⲉⲛⲕ. ⲛⲧⲉ ⲣⲁⲕⲟⲧⲉ (var -ⲱⲧⲉ), pine cones (στρόβιλος)
& pepper. So ? fruit or plant from Alexandria.
Cf ⲉⲗⲕⲟⲩ (ⲉⲗⲕⲱ).

ⲕⲟⲩⲓ *SAFO*, ⲕⲟⲩⲉⲓ *A²*, ⲕⲟⲩϫⲓ *B*, ⲕⲟⲩϭⲓ *F*
(MR 5 33), ⲕⲟⲩ- *SF*, ⲕⲁ-, ⲕⲟ- *F* (*v* below) **ⵏ** nn
m f, *small person or thing, young person* : Ge 42 32
B, Job 3 19 *SB* Ps 151 1 *SB*, Jon 3 5 *SAB*, Mt
13 32 *SBF*, Z 345 *S* = MG 25 209 *B* μικρός,
-ότερος ; Nu 35 8 *B* (*S* ⲥⲟⲃⲕ), Ro 9 12 *SB* ἐλάσσων ;
Sa 6 7 *S*, Mt 25 45 *SB*, 1 Cor 15 9 *BF* (*S* = Gk)
ἐλάχιστος ; Nu 11 32 *SB*, Ps 36 16 *SB*, Lu 13
23 *SB* ὀλίγος ; Jo 6 7 *S* (*BA²* ϣⲏⲙ), He 13 22 *SB*
βραχύς ; Ge 29 16 *SB*, Job 32 7 *SB*, Ez 16 61 *SB*
νεώτερος ; Jos 6 21 *S* νεανίσκος ; Ps 18 7 *S* (*B* ⲕ.
ⲛⲁⲗⲟⲩ), Pro 1 32 *S* (*A* ⲗⲓⲗⲟⲩ, *B* ⲁⲗ.), Gal 4 1 *S*

(B ⲕ. ⲡⲁⲗ.) νήπιος; AZ 21 99 O παῖς, Z 318 S, Bor 239 57 S ⲟⲩⲕ. ⲡⲧⲁⲕ παιδίον; ShC 73 111 S have eaten ⲟⲩⲕ., MIE 2 351 B ϯⲕ. ϩⲉⲡⲡⲉϥⲡⲟⲗⲓⲧⲉⲓⲁ *least*, TT 31 S didst suckle him ϩⲱⲥ ⲕ., CO 384 S ⲡⲓⲕ. as letter-bearer, Aeg 255 S baptize first ⲡⲕ., then ⲛⲛⲟϭ ⲡⲣⲱⲙⲉ, Ryl 349 S all our house ϫⲓⲛⲉⲡⲕ. ϣⲁⲡⲛⲟϭ, AM 202 B every man ⲓⲧⲉ ⲕ. ⲓⲧⲉ ⲡⲓϣϯ; *few, small* number: Ap 2 14 S (B diff) ὀλ., BSM 51 B good deeds ⲓⲧⲉ ⲕ. ⲓⲧⲉ ⲟⲩⲙⲏϣ, Mor 44 8 S book ⲁⲓⲱϣ ϩⲓⲱⲱϥ ⲡϩⲛⲕ., C 43 182 B ϧⲁϩⲛⲕ. of the miracles. Comparative ⲥ ⲉ-: 1 Kg 16 11 S (B diff) ⲡⲕ. ⲉⲡⲁⲓ, Mt 11 11 SB μικ., Jud 1 13 S νεώτερος. Iterated: Is 13 14 F (S ϣⲏⲙ ϣⲏⲙ) λεπτός, Va 61 107 B lions ⲉⲣ ⲡⲟⲩⲕⲁⲥ ⲡⲕ. ⲕ. (*cf* Dan 6 24 λεπτύνειν).

II adj, *small*, **A** before nn: Is 30 14 SBF, Mk 15 40 S (B nn), Z 344 S = MG 25 210 B ⲕ. ⲛϭⲓⲛⲟⲩⲱⲙ μικ., Ge 1 16 B ἐλάσσ., 1 Cor 6 2 SB ἐλάχ.; Ge 29 20 SB, Ez 5 3 SB ὀλ., Mt 16 8 SB ὀλιγό-(πιστος); Ex 18 22 SB, Sa 16 27 S βρα.; for Gk dimin: Is 11 6 B (S om) μοσχάριον, Jer 27 11 S (B om) βοίδιον, C 89 57 B πλοιάριον. Often as dimin or in humility (*cf* also **B**): BMOr 6954 (53) S Apa Matthew ⲡⲕ. ⲙⲙⲟⲛⲁⲭⲟⲥ ⲡⲧⲉⲗⲓⲟⲥ, BM 291 S Elisha ⲡⲉⲩⲕ. ⲙⲙⲁⲑⲏⲧⲏⲥ, Miss 8 15 S ⲡⲉⲩⲕ. ⲡⲥⲛⲁⲩ ⲡϩⲙϩⲁⲗ (*sic* MS), Va 62 143 B ⲉⲓⲡⲣⲓ ⲡⲧⲁⲕ. ⲡⲥⲩⲛⲁϩⲓⲥ, BMOr 6201 A 120 S ⲡⲓⲕ. ⲣⲱⲙⲉ ⲡⲟⲩⲡⲛⲉ, Va 59 31 B assigned a ⲕ. ⲙⲙⲁ ⲡⲉⲗⲧⲟⲡ where we found ⲕ. ⲡⲉⲕⲕⲗⲏⲥⲓⲁ with ⲕ. ⲡⲃⲓⲃⲗⲓⲟⲑⲏⲕⲏ, MG 25 414 S ⲁⲅⲭⲓ ⲡⲧⲉⲩⲕ. ⲡⲭⲣⲓⲁ (*ie* their food), Z 328 S ϩⲛⲕ. ⲡϣⲏⲙ ⲡⲧⲉ ⲡϯⲙⲉ, Wess 11 164 S sent to fetch ϩⲉⲡⲕ. ⲡϣⲏⲙ ⲡⲭⲣⲉⲓⲁ, MIE 2 401 B ϯⲕ. ⲡⲧⲣⲟⲫⲏ, ⲡⲓⲕ. ⲙⲙⲟⲟⲩ, *cf* Ge 43 4 B (S Gk om), Ep 245 S I send thee ⲡⲉⲓⲕ. ⲡⲥⲙⲟⲩ, CO 252 S I learn that ⲁⲕⲣ ⲟⲩⲕ. ⲛϣⲱ[ⲛⲉ, Z 231 S if thou wouldst do ϩⲉⲡⲕ. ⲡⲧⲁⲗϭⲟ. *Few*: Mt 15 34 B (S ϣⲏⲙ) ὀλ., Miss 4 231 S planted ϩⲉⲡⲕ. ⲡϣⲏⲡ, Mor 31 53 S naught except ϩⲉⲡⲕ. ⲛⲃⲛⲛⲉ ⲙⲙⲁⲧⲉ, BSM 74 B ⲉⲧⲁϩⲁⲡⲕ. ⲡⲣⲟⲟⲩ ϣⲱⲡⲓ; with ⲕⲉ- (*qv*): Dan 7 8 SB ἕτερος μικ., Ap 6 11 SB ἔτι μικ., *ib* 12 12 SB ὀλ., TstAb 232 B keep pure ⲧⲉⲕⲕⲉⲕ. ⲡⲥⲁⲣⲝ, AM 260 B devil raised ⲕⲉⲕ. ⲡϣⲟⲣⲧⲉⲣ. *Young, younger*: Ge 49 22 S (B ϩⲉⲣⲓ) Ez 16 46 SB νεώτερος; 1 Cor 3 1 B ⲕ. ⲡⲁⲗⲟⲩⲅⲓ (S ⲕ.) νήπιος; Jos 6 26 S ἐλάχ.; BMis 166 S = BSM 75 B ⲡⲉⲓⲕ. ⲡⲥⲟⲛ *younger* brother. Without ⲛ-: J 85 23 S ⲕ. ϣⲏⲣⲉ (*ib* 26 ⲕ. ⲡϣ.), PLond 4 508 S ⲕⲁⲙⲓⲥⲏ ⲕ. ϣ., Ryl 244 S garment ⲉϥϫⲓ ⲕ. ϣⲱⲡⲧ, CMSS 70 S^f ⲕ. ⲙⲁⲡⲡⲁ (or ? = ⲙⲙ-).

B after nn (B only WTh 1, where forms S): 1 Kg 17 28 S (B ⲕ. ⲛ-); Cant 2 15 (ShA 1 293) S μικ.; Deu 26 5 S (var, B ⲕ. ⲛ-) βραχύς; Ge 43 3 S (B do) ⲡⲉⲧⲡⲥⲛ ⲕ., Bor 304 58 S ⲥⲟⲡ ⲕ.,

Nu 14 23 S ϣⲏⲣⲉ ⲕ. (var ϣ. ϣⲏⲙ, B ⲕ. ⲡⲁⲗ.) νεώτ.; Ps 115 6 S (B do), Lam 2 20 S (B do) νήπ.; Jud 13 8 S, Mt 14 21 F (S ϣ. ϣⲏⲙ, B ⲁⲗ.) παιδίον; ShA 2 280 S ⲗⲉϥⲗⲓϥⲉ ⲕ. of wage, *ib* 1 80 S ⲡⲁϣϩⲏⲗ ⲕ., ShLeyd 345 S παράπτωμα ⲕ. After names: WS 168 S ⲓⲱⲁⲛⲛⲏⲥ ⲕ. (*cf ib* 1. ⲡⲟϭ), Rec 13 65 S ⲥⲁⲙⲟⲩⲏⲗ ⲕ., *ib* 11 147 S ⲁⲃⲣⲁϩⲁⲙ ⲕ., PLond 4 592 Βησκοΰι (*cf ib* Βησσῆμ); rarely before: J&C 92 S ⲡⲕ. ⲡⲁⲉⲓⲛⲟⲩ.

Construct *SF* (always + ⲛ-), **ⲁ** ⲕⲟⲩ-: P 131⁵ 69 S ⲟⲩⲕⲟⲩⲡϣⲗⲏⲗ ⲡⲉⲧⲓⲧⲁϥ ⲙⲓⲕ. ἐξομολόγησις, BMar 62 S ⲟⲩⲕⲟⲩⲙⲙⲉⲣⲟⲥ, *ib* 79 ⲟⲩⲕⲟⲩⲡϣⲁϫⲉ, PStras 226 S ⲧⲕⲟⲩⲡ(ⲛ)ⲛⲏⲥⲧⲓⲁ, Kr 3 F ⲛⲉⲛⲁϭ ⲡⲧⲉⲭⲛⲓⲧⲓⲥ, ⲡⲉⲕⲟⲩⲛⲧⲉⲭ., MR 5 49 F ⲁⲓⲉⲗ ⲕⲟⲩⲛⲯⲓⲭⲏ *impatient* (*cf* ⲕ. ⲡϩⲏⲧ), PMich 577 F ⲡⲉⲓⲕⲟⲩⲡϣⲏⲣⲓ ⲡⲧⲛⲕ, CMSS 50 F ⲧⲉⲥⲕⲟⲩⲡϣⲏⲛⲗⲓ, BM 1240 F sailor of [ⲡ]ⲉⲓⲕⲟⲩⲛϫⲁⲓ ⲡⲧⲛⲓ, BM 659 F ⲕⲟⲩⲓⲱⲧ (? *l* ⲕⲟⲩⲛⲓⲱⲧ), CMSS 68 F name ⲧⲕⲟⲩⲛⲉⲣⲱ. **ⲃ** ⲕⲁ- *S^fF*: AZ 23 28 F ⲡⲉⲓⲕⲁⲛϣⲏⲛⲗⲓ ⲡⲧⲉⲓ, *ib* 38 ⲡⲉⲓⲕⲁⲡⲗⲱⲙⲓ ⲡⲧⲛⲉⲓ, CMSS 33 S^f ⲕⲁⲛⲁⲣⲓ for cattle, *cf ib* ⲕⲟⲛⲥⲁⲃⲧⲓ, *ib* 37 ⲁⲕⲁⲗⲉ ⲡⲉⲕⲁⲡⲁⲗⲁⲗⲓ, CO 504 F sim., BM 582(2) F ⲟⲩⲕⲁⲡⲉⲣⲧⲁϩ ⲡⲥⲟⲩⲁ, BM 596 F ϩⲉⲡⲕⲉⲕⲁⲡϩⲏⲧ; reduplicated in CMSS 61 F ⲡⲉⲕⲁⲡⲕⲟⲩⲓ ⲡⲭⲱⲱⲙⲓ, *cf* BMOr 6948 (1) F ⲡⲉⲕⲁⲡϫⲱⲙⲉ, BM 548 S^f ⲡⲕⲁⲡⲕⲟⲩⲓ ⲉⲧϩⲓⲱⲧⲏⲛⲟⲩ, *ib* 599 sim.

ⲕ. ⲡϩⲏⲧ *SBF, faint-hearted, impatient person*: Is 35 4 F (S ϩ. ϣⲏⲙ, B om) ὀλιγόψυχος, *cf* Pro 14 29 SA ϩ. ϣⲏⲙ, ClPr 29 245 S ⲟⲩⲕ. ⲡϩ. ⲡⲉϣⲁϥⲣ ϩⲁⲣϣ ϩⲏⲧ, AM 288 B ϩⲱⲛϫ ⲉⲡⲓⲕ. ⲡϩ. ⲣ ⲕ. ⲛϩ. Ps 76 4 B (S ϩ ϩ. ϣⲏⲙ), Hab 2 13 B, CaiEuch 632 B ὀλιγοψυχεῖν; Pro 3 11 SB (A ϩ. ϩⲏⲙ), He 12 5 SB ὀλιγωρεῖν, MG 25 349 B ⲟⲓ ⲡⲓⲕ. ⲡϩ. ⲉⲭⲉⲡ- ὀλιγωρ. ἐπάνω; Va 66 307 B ⲟⲓ ⲡⲓⲕ. ⲡϩ. ἀθυμεῖν, Sh(?)Bor 247 102 S ⲡⲉⲧⲟ ⲡⲓⲕ. ⲡϩ. ⲉⲭⲙⲡⲁⲓⲱⲡϩ ⲡⲁⲓ. ⲙⲛⲧⲕ. ⲛϩ., *discouragement*: Ex 6 9 B, Ps 54 8 B (S ⲙⲛⲧϩ. ϣⲏⲙ) ὀλιγοψυχία, Pcod 46 S did thus from ⲟⲩⲙ. ⲛϩ.

III advb, **ⲁ** ⲛⲟⲩⲕ., *a little*: Is 26 20 SB, 2 Cor 11 1 SB μικρόν; Job 10 20 SB, Pro 6 10 B (SA ⲁⲡⲣⲓⲧⲉ), Zech 1 15 B (S ϩⲛⲟⲩⲕ., A ϩⲛⲟⲩϩⲛⲙ), MG 25 212 B ὀλίγον; Ps 8 6 SB, Ac 5 34 SB βραχύ; PS 9 S distant ⲛⲟⲩⲕ., *cf ib* ⲛⲟⲩϣⲏⲙ, El 120 S ⲟⲩⲡⲉⲗⲏⲕ ⲛⲟⲩⲕ. = *ib* 90 A ⲛⲟⲩϩ., C 43 239 B ⲥⲁϩⲛⲧ ⲙⲙⲟⲥ ⲛⲟⲩⲕ., BMis 168 S ϭⲱ ⲉⲣⲟⲓ ⲛⲟⲩⲕ. = BSM 77 B; without ⲛ-: 1 Pet 5 10 S (B ⲛⲟⲩⲕ.) ὀλίγον; *somewhat, rather*: Mor 37 259 S I will cease (discourse) for I see ϫⲉⲁϥⲟⲩⲱϣⲥ ⲛⲟⲩⲕ., Miss 4 679 S braggart & rough of speech ⲛⲟⲩⲕ., HL 91 B (Gk om) those in deserts ⲓⲧⲉ ⲡⲉⲧϩⲉⲛⲧ ⲉⲡⲓⲣⲱⲙⲓ ⲛⲟⲩⲕ., Ep 540 S cakes (?) ⲉⲩⲛⲟϥⲣⲉ ⲛⲟⲩⲕ. (obscure); **ⲃ** ⲡⲕⲉⲕ., ⲕⲉⲕ., *yet a little*: Ex 17 4 SB, Job 36 2 S (B ⲛⲟⲩⲕ.), Jo 13

33 *SB* (*A²* каιογλειϣ) ἔτι μικρόν; Ps 36 10 *SB*, MG 25 4 *B* ὀλίγον; Ac 27 28 *S* (*B* diff) βραχύ; BSG 177 *S* ετι кεκ. πτλλοκιλλλჳε ллоч, BMOr 6954 (43) *S* кεκ. πε & thou shalt receive the crown from Christ, AM 233 *B* sim.   **с ллпιсλογκ.,** -кεκ., *after a little:* Mk 14 70 *S* ль. ογκ. (*B* ль. кεκ.) μετὰ μικ.; Jth 13 9 *S* ль. ογκ., Sa 15 8 *S* ль. кεκ. μετ' ὀλ., Lu 22 58 *S* ль. ογκ. (*B* ль. кεκ.) μετὰ βραχύ.   **d ϩα-, ϩα-, ϩιϑн πογκ.,** *a little before :* Sa 15 8 *S* πρὸ μικ., Mic 2 9 *A* (*SB* Gk om, *cf* Vulg) ϩιτεϥι πογκ.; BMar 90 *S* grape that was sour ϩλϑн πογκ. will become sweet, BSM 105 *B* didst thou not say ϩλτϩн πογκ. ჯε-? *Cf ib* 101 ϩλჯεнογκ.   **e ϣλτπογκ.,** -кεκ., *S* mostly πλρλ, *almost :* Ps 93 17 *B* (*S* πλρλ ογκ.), R 1 4 38 *S* a year ϣ. ογκ. *plus minus*, AM 301 *B* ϣ. кεκ. they will stone us, ShBor 246 77 *S* πλρλ кεκ. πε πчϣшпε ϩιπτλко, Z 611 *S* onyx εчτϥшϥшϣ πλρλ ογκ.   **f προс ογκ.,** *for a little :* Sa 16 6 *S* π. ὀλ., 2 Cor 7 8 *B* (*S* π. ογнογ) π. ὥραν.   **g клтл к.,** *occasionally :* BIF 13 119 *S* = MG 25 315 *B* going there кλ. к., C 89 9 *B* regular prayers besides those ετεϣλπλιτογ кλ. к. (*v* Ep 1 169 n), C 43 132 *B* what is sign thou makest кλ. к.? (*cf* λπϥнτε), Wess 15 146 *S* demon attacked him кλ. к.   **h коүі коүі, пк. к.,** *little by little :* BMar 117 *S* began to recognize him к. к. μετὰ μικ., MG 25 61 *B* gave away possessions пк. к. (*var* клтл к.), J 91 13 *S* convalescent λчϣшк εϩн к. к., Va 62 289 *B* пк. пк. λчεпε εβολ ϩεππιллоγ;   клтл к. к.: Ex 23 30 *B* (*S* ϣнль ϣнль) к. мικ., BMis 239 *S* that he be burnt клтл к. к.

p к. *SBF, be small, few:* Ps 106 38 *B* (*S* тсβко), Dan 3 37 *B* (*S* сϭок) σμικρύνειν; Lev 26 22 *B* (*S* do) ὀλιγοστὸν ποιεῖν; Is 21 17 *B* (*S* do) ὀλίγος εἶναι; Ps 104 12 *B* (*S* do) βραχύς; Jer 51 18 *B* (*S* do) ἐλαττοῦν; Mk 9 35 *S* (*B* ϩλε) ἔσχατος; PO 11 377 *B* when bishops εϥ к., BMar 78 *S* when death near tongue ϥ к. ϥнτεκϣογшβε, TstAb 175 *B* sim, AM 177 *B* Simeon οι пк. ϩεпϥллн, Mor 22 10 *S* inundation has ϥ к. because of our sins, Z 284 *S* λчϥ кεκ. ллλγ *passed short time*.   *Be young :* Ps 36 25 *S* (*B* λλογ), Si 51 15 *S* νεώτερος; 1 Cor 13 11 *S* (*B* do) νήπιος.

ллнт-, ллεтк. nn f, *smallness, youth :* Bar 2 31 *B* μικρός; Va 57 179 *B* σμικρότης; 1 Cor 4 3 *B* (*S* = Gk) ἐλάχ.; Ge 6 5 *S* (*B* om), Job 13 26 *S* (*B* ллεтλλογ), Ez 23 3 *B* (*S* ллптϣεερε ϣнль) νεότης; Pro 2 27 *S* (*A* ллнтλιλογ, *B* ллεтλλ.), Ez 16 22 *SB* νηπιότης; Ge 46 34 *S* (*B* ллεтλλ.) παῖς; Mor 25 29 *S* many die in ль., others in τεγллнтϩρρε *infancy*, BMis 489 *S* have dwelt with wife since тлль., AM 83 *B* пснογ πτλль.

In many names (*cf Μικρός*), *eg* коүі, Ἀπκοῦις, Ἑλκοῦις (*cf* Ἑλλῶς), Μεεγκοῦι, Πακοῦι, ткоүі, Τακοῦις, Τκοιкοῦις, Τσανκοῦι (Preisigke), Κουειαλῶ Wess 20 133, тк. πλλλ[γ] PMich 1545, Κουισόν, Κουισνόβ BM 1075, also ? Πκοῦτσε (Preis.), πλκοүϥε (J 28 51).   In place-names : тк. πεϥшт Miss 4 759, BM 1146, пк. λγсιль(λ·ჯιс ?) Ryl 138.

кѡ *SA²F,* коү *AA²F,* кѡε *A²*(AP), ϫѡ *B,* кλ- *SAA²F,* ϫλ- *B,* кε-, *F,* клл· *SAA²,* ϫλ· *B,* кεε·, кε·, кн† *SF,* кει† *A,* клλт† *A²,* ϫн† *B,* vb. tr, *a place, appoint, set down, make:* Ge 2 15 *SB,* *ib* 32 12 *SB,* Lev 26 19 *B* (*S* τρεϣшπε), Jud 1 18 *S* (var ποιεῖν), Job 17 6 *SB,* Ps 16 11 *S* (*BF* сεллι), Ps 17 32 *SB,* *ib* 109 1 *SBF,* Si 36 9 *S,* Is 13 9 *SB,* *ib* 26 1 *SBF,* Hos 13 1 *AB,* Mt 14 3 *SBF,* Jo 10 15 *SAA²B* τιθέναι; compds of τιθ. sim: ἀπο- Jos 4 8 *SB,* δια- Ge 9 17 *S* (*B* сεллι), ἐπι- Lev 8 15 *S* (*B* тλλο), Mic 7 16 *SAB,* παρα- Ge 30 38 *SB,* MG 25 210 *B,* περι- Job 31 36 *S* (*B* ✝), προ- Ps 85 14 *SB,* Ro 3 25 *SB,* ὑπο- CaiEuch 487 *B* submit (*cf* Is 50 6); Ge 3 24 *SB,* Job 30 22 *S* (*B* ѳшϣ), Jer 19 8 *B* τάσσειν; Deu 4 19 *S* (*B* ✝) ἀπονέμειν; Jth 14 2 *S,* Ez 30 12 *SB,* Lu 14 9 *SB* διδόναι; Job 14 3 *S* (*B* ѳре-), Is 8 2 *B* (*S* ειϥε), Lu 16 9 *S* (*B* ѳλллιο), Aeg 232 *S* кλ ϩоειπε as heirs ποιεῖν; Ez 17 8 *B* φέρειν; Jth 1 3 *S,* AP 15 *A²* λсклλϥ εчϩλλпϣ ἱστάναι, Is 1 26 *B* (*S* сллπε) ἐφιστ., Deu 17 14 *B* (*S* ειπε εβολ), Jer 6 17 *B,* He 8 3 *B* (*S* = Gk) καθιστ.; PS 69 *S* λγκλλτ ϩρεπкλκε, R 1 2 54 *S* let each кλ πпλ ϩллπεчϩнт, Br 132 *S* кѡ πτειψнфос in your hands (*ib* paral λллϩτε), Z 352 *S* he gave away the good shirt λчкλ тετϥроογ, Faras 3 pl 68 16 *S* sim, BAp 156 *S* кλ πεкϩнт ллок *take heed*(?), ShR 2 3 4 *S,* CO 227 *S* sim, BMis 451 *S* λчклλс ϩллπεчϩнт ετль-, DeV 83 *B* ϣλπϫλс ϩεππεϥϩнт εѳреп-, BHom 66 *S* that angel may кλ тεчϥρн ϣλλροн, ShC 73 58 *S* none may кλ ѳ`оειк πтоотϥ, Mor 20 5 *S* creation of 4 Beasts пкεоγλ λчклλϥ плετоς, CA 90 *S* wife пϥкλ ϣнρε пллλс, Ryl 100 *S* sim ?, *cf* Ge 30 3 *S,* Si 16 4 *S,* BHom 118 *S* λчклλс εροс that she should not help, BMar 164 *S* кλ тετϥβϥсш εспριшоγ, BMis 192 *S* God λкκѡ ллос (sea) εγсιϣε, Pcod 45 *S* λчкλ тεчϥγсιс of iron to overcome stone, AP 23 *A²* λчкѡε ллλϥ at door, Va 63 94 *B* λιϫѡ пплι *I have related this* (not in PG 64 29), PO 11 359 *B* old man ϫѡ ллпεϥршoγϣ εϥ✝, Mor 40 39 *S* πεчкѡ ллооγ псελскει = MG 25 265 *B* ѳρо.   **b** *esteem:* Job 32 3 *S* τιθ., *ib* 30 19 *S* (*B* ιρι ллϥρн✝), 1 Thes 5 13 *SB* ἡγεῖσθαι, BIF 13 102 *S* ετρεчкλ sons of church honourable.   **с** *with dat, have, get, keep:* Est 3

11 S, Sa 7 10 S, Mt 12 11 S (B ⲟⲩⲟⲡⲧ⸗), Mk 4 40 S (B ϣⲱⲡⲓ), Ro 14 22 S (B ϫⲁⲥ ϩⲉⲛ-), 1 Cor 7 2 BF (S ϫⲓ) ἔχειν; Deu 32 6 S (B ϫⲫⲟ), 2 Kg 12 3 S, Si 24 6 SB, Mt 10 9 B (S ϫⲡⲟ) κτᾶσθαι; Mt 18 12 S (B ϣⲱⲡⲓ) γίνεσθαι; ShA 2 101 S ⲉϥϣⲁⲛⲕⲱ ⲛⲁϥ ⲡⲟⲩⲙⲛⲧϣⲃⲏⲣ, ShC 73 63 S let none ⲕⲁⲁϥ ⲛⲁⲩ ⲙⲡⲁⲑⲟⲥ ⲉⲧⲣⲉⲩ-, MG 25 255 B chalice of glass, for they could not ϫⲁ ϩⲁⲧ ⲡⲱⲟⲩ, BM 580 F ⲕⲉ ⲑⲁⲧⲓ ⲡⲡⲟⲩⲧⲓ ⲡⲉ, Z 579 S monk may not ⲕⲁ ⲗⲁⲁⲩ ⲛⲁϥ ϩⲁⲣⲟϥ, Hall 109 S hast power to sell camel or ⲉⲕⲁⲁϥ ⲛⲁⲕ. **d** *preserve,* in greetings in letters (late): BM 1132 S Lord ⲕⲁⲧⲏⲩⲧⲛ (ⲡ)ⲁⲓ unto my last breath, Ryl 337 S ⲉⲣⲉⲡⲟⲥ ⲕⲁⲁⲩ ⲛⲏ (*sc* her family), Kr 227 F Lord ⲕⲉⲉⲩ ⲉ(ⲡϥ)ⲃⲓ ⲡⲡⲉϥⲥⲙⲟⲩ ϩⲓϫⲱⲛ, MR 5 28 S I greet thee ⲉⲣⲉⲡⲟⲥ ⲕⲁⲁⲕ, BM 582 (1) F parenthetic ⲗⲓⲡⲟⲛ, ⲉⲗⲉⲡⲛ̄ⲧ̄ ⲕⲉⲕ, ϥⲉⲓ ⲕⲥⲁⲟⲩⲡ ϫⲉ-. **e** *permit, set free:* Ex 32 10 SB, Job 7 19 S (B ⲭⲱ ⲉⲃⲟⲗ), Mt 24 43 SB, Ac 23 32 B (S ⲧⲣⲉ-) ἐᾶν; Lev 16 10 S (B + ⲉⲃⲟⲗ), Ps 38 13 B (S ⲃⲱϣ) ἀνιέναι, Job 39 5 S (B do) ἀφιέναι; *ib* 32 14 SB, Lu 9 59 S (B ⲟⲩⲁϩⲥⲁϩⲛⲓ), Ac 21 39 S (B do), Mor 37 67 S ⲡⲥⲉⲕⲱ ⲙⲙⲟⲛ ⲁⲛ ⲉⲡⲕⲟⲧⲕ ἐπιτρέπειν; Ps 54 22 S (B ϯ) διδόναι; PS 325 S ⲙⲉⲥⲕⲁⲁϥ ⲉⲕⲟⲗⲁⲍⲉ ⲙⲙⲟⲥ, Br 44 S blessed whoso ⲙⲡⲉϥⲕⲁ ⲡⲕⲟⲥⲙⲟⲥ ⲉⲁϣⲧϥ, ShMIF 23 32 S ⲁϥⲕⲁⲁϥ ⲉϥⲟⲛϩ, TU 43 9 A ⲁⲕϣⲁⲕⲁⲁⲡⲉ, C 43 10 B ⲁⲕϣⲁⲡϫⲁ ⲡⲁⲓⲙⲁⲧⲟⲥ here, all will believe on him, MG 25 362 B ⲭⲱ ⲡⲏⲓ ⲡⲧⲁⲓ ⲉⲃⲟⲗ, TT 122 S ⲕⲁⲁⲩ ⲙⲁⲣϥⲣⲓⲙⲉ, PMéd 219 S ⲙⲡⲣⲕⲁϥ ⲉⲧⲁϩⲟ ⲡⲉⲛⲓⲝ, BMis 270 S ⲁϥⲕⲁ ⲡⲧⲃⲛⲏ ⲉϫⲙⲡϣⲏⲣⲉ ϣⲏⲙ *let loose,* *ib* 261 S sim. **f** qual, *be loose, limp, unrestrained, permitted:* Si 2 13 S παρειμένος, Is 5 24 B + dat (S ⲥⲱⲕ), *ib* 35 3 F (S ⲥⲏϭ, B ϯ ⲟⲩⲱ ⲉⲃⲟⲗ) ἄνειμ., Ac 26 1 S (B diff) ἐπιτρέπεσθαι, Mor 18 117 S heart ⲉϥⲕⲏ χαῦνος. **g** as imperat, *admit, concede, suppose that:* Nu 16 3 B (S om) ⲭⲁⲥ ⲡⲱⲧⲉⲛ ϫⲉ- ἐχέτω ὑμῖν, Job 19 5 S (B diff) ⲕⲁⲁⲥ ϫⲉ- ἔα (*cf ib* 4 B ⲭⲁⲥ), C 89 116 B ⲭⲁⲥ that none can work for him = MG 17 580 ﻭﺍﻥ ﻛﺎﻥ, C 86 246 B ⲭⲁⲥ ϫⲉ- thou hast chosen darkness, yet why &c?, MIE 2 363 B ⲭⲁⲥ ϫⲉ- thou wilt not do liturgy, ⲕⲁⲛ &c, ﺍﻥ ﻛﻨﺖ ﻻ. Diff in Mt 3 15, Lu 13 8, Jo 12 7 B. **h** *bequeath:* Ps 16 14 SB, Eccl 2 18 S, Jo 14 27 SA²B ἀφιέναι: Sa 2 9 S, Mk 12 19 S (B ⲥⲱϫⲡ) καταλείπεσθαι, Bor 235* 131 S ⲡⲉⲧⲉⲕⲡⲁⲕⲁⲁⲩ *ἃ* καταλιμπάνεις, J 3 48 S property ⲉⲕⲁⲁⲩ ⲡⲡⲉⲕϣⲏⲣⲉ. **i** *quit, abandon, fail:* Is 32 14 S (B ⲭⲱ ⲡⲥⲁ-), Jer 12 7 B (S ⲕⲱ ⲡⲥⲁ-), Mt 13 36 S (BF + ⲉⲃⲟⲗ), Jo 4 28 SA²B (F + ⲉϩⲣⲏⲓ) ἀφιέναι; Ac 7 39 B (S + ⲡⲥⲁ-), Ro 13 12 S (B do) ἀπωθεῖν; Is 58 11 S (B ⲙⲟⲩⲛⲕ) ἐκλείπειν; Lu 23 46 S (B ϯ) ⲕⲁ ⲡⲧⲏⲩ ἐκπνεῖν; ClPr 54 6 S ⲕⲁ ⲡϣⲁϫⲉ σιγᾶν; R 2 2 30 S ⲕⲁ ⲡϣⲁϫⲉ ⲉⲕⲉϩⲟⲟⲩ *postpone,* ShC 73 159 S none shall go forward ⲉⲕⲁ ⲡⲉϥⲉⲣⲏⲩ, MG 25 60 B blind man ⲉⲁϥⲭⲁ ⲟⲩⲱⲓⲛⲓ = GöttAr 114 9 ﻋﺪﻡ ﻧﻮﺭ ﺑﺼﺮﻩ. **j** *leave, omit* (also + ⲉⲃⲟⲗ) Mt 24 40 SB ἀφιέναι, Lu 15 29 S παρέρχεσθαι, ShR 2 3 46 S can not decide ϥⲛⲁⲟⲩⲉⲙ ⲟⲩ ⲉⲕⲁ ⲟⲩ, Va 62 178 B ⲡⲧⲁⲱⲗⲓ ⲡⲟⲩⲕⲟⲩϫⲓ ⲡⲧⲁⲭⲁ ⲟⲩⲕⲟⲩϫⲓ, Mor 51 36 S ragged garment ⲉⲛⲛⲁⲡⲓ ⲧⲟⲉⲓⲥ ⲉⲧⲱⲛ ⲛⲧⲉⲛⲕⲁ ⲧⲱⲛ, PLond 4 473 S ⲡⲡⲓⲕⲁ ⲟⲩⲣⲱⲙⲉ ⲡⲟⲩⲱⲧ *unregistered* (varr + ⲉⲃⲟⲗ, ⲉⲡⲁϩⲟⲩ, *cf* BM 1079 *sf*). **k** qual + prep or advb, *be, exist, lie:* Ge 43 5 B (S om vb), Ex 20 21 B (S do), Ez 11 23 B (S ϣⲟⲟⲡ), Mt 13 56 B (S do, F ϩⲁⲧⲉⲛ-), Ro 3 18 B (S om), MG 25 6 B ϯⲭⲏ ⲙⲙⲁⲩⲁⲧ εἶναι; B *ib* 240 ⲉⲛϫⲏ ⲙⲙⲁⲩ παρεῖ.; Jer 24 1 B, Lu 2 34 SB, Phil 1 16 B (S + ⲉϩⲣⲁⲓ), 1 Thes 3 3 SBF κεῖσθαι, Lu 19 20 SB ἀπόκει., Ro 7 18 SB παράκει., Jude 7 B (S + ⲉϩⲣⲁⲓ) πρόκει.; Jer 2 31 B, Hos 10 4 SA ⲕⲏ ⲉⲡϣⲱ χερσοῦσθαι, χέρσος (*cf* B ⲕⲁⲡϣⲱ), BIF 13 101 S city's harbour ⲕⲏ ⲉⲣⲏⲧⲉⲥⲙⲛⲧⲉ, Pcod 10 S what thou askest ⲕⲏ ⲉⲣⲏϣⲱⲙⲧⲉ ⲡⲉⲩⲡⲟⲑⲉⲥⲓⲥ, J 75 73 S whose bodies ⲕⲏ ⲉⲣⲏⲡⲧⲟⲡⲟⲥ, DeV 123 B Herod ⲉϥⲭⲏ in these torments, PO 11 339 B ⲉϥϫⲏ ⲛⲁⲑⲟⲩⲱⲙ, TstAb 179 B ⲉϥϫⲏ ⸢ϩⲉⲛⲡⲣⲟ ⲡⲣⲟⲙⲡⲓ⸣. **l** in later SF letters *go to, reach,* lit *enter* (*cf* ⲕⲱ ⲉϩⲟⲩⲛ *bring into port*), qual *be in:* Cai 8074 S I learnt that ⲑⲉⲟⲇⲟⲥⲓ ⲕⲱ ϩⲏⲧ, BM 1131 S ⲙⲡⲓϣ ⲕⲱ ⲉⲡⲁⲛⲓ, *ib* 1174 S I sent him ⲧⲁⲣϥⲕⲱ ⲣⲏⲥ, *ib* 665 F ϣⲁⲡⲧⲁⲕⲟⲩ (ⲧ)ⲡⲱⲗⲓⲥ, *ib* 1115 S ⲁⲓⲉⲓ ϩⲣⲁⲓ ⲧⲁⲕⲱ ⲁⲡⲧⲓⲡⲟⲟⲩ; *ib* 1153 S ⲁⲓⲉⲓ ⲉⲓⲕⲏ ⲉϩⲏⲧ, Ryl 374 S ⲉⲩⲕⲏ ⲉⲣⲏⲥ ⲉⲣⲏⲥ, BM 1112 S I forgot to tell thee ⲉⲕⲕⲏ ⲣⲏⲥ, BMOr 6201 A 176 S account ϩⲁⲣⲱⲧⲛ ⲉⲧⲡⲉⲕⲏ ϩⲧ ⲙⲡⲓⲡⲣⲓⲧⲟⲣⲉ (qual shows this not for ϭⲱ). **?** belongs here. Rev Ég Anc 2 85 S graffito ⲡⲁϩⲙ ⲁϥⲕⲱ ⲡⲉⲓⲙⲁ. **m** auxil (causative) use: Deu 8 3 S (B ⲑⲣⲉ-) ⲁϥⲕⲁⲁⲕ ⲉⲕⲣⲟⲕⲣ ⲗⲓⲙⲁⲅⲭⲟⲛⲉⲓ, Eccl 4 8 S ⲕⲁ ⲯⲩⲭⲏ ⲉⲥϣⲁⲁⲧ στερίσκειν, Mt 23 5 S (B do) ⲕⲱ ⲡⲡⲉⲩⲧⲱⲧⲉ ⲛⲁⲁⲩ μεγαλύνειν, Mk 6 31 S (B diff) ⲕⲁⲁⲩ ⲉⲥⲣϥⲉ εὐκαιρεῖν, Jud 11 19 S = Gk optat.; supplem to Gk: Mk 3 9 S, Ac 27 30 S, Ap 9 6 S; TstAb 173 B God & Enoch as scribe ⲁϥⲭⲁϥ ⲉϥⲥϧⲁⲓ.

ⲙⲁ ⲡⲕⲁ-, ϫⲁ-, *place for putting:* Ez 4 2 B (S ⲙⲁ ⲡⲛⲉϫ-) βελοστάσις, Va 57 185 B -ⲡⲓϭⲁⲗⲁⲩϫ ἴχνος, BMis 387 S -ⲟⲉⲓⲕ (var ⲛϯ-), C 41 61 B sim.

ϭⲓⲛⲕⲱ, ϫⲓⲛϫⲱ nn m B, f S, *placing, laying down:* My 30 S stars ⲧϭⲓⲛⲕⲁⲁⲩ in firmament, ROC '05 70 B at tonsure ⲡⲓϫ. ⲙⲡⲓⲫⲱⲓ.

—— nn m SB, *loosening, slackness:* ShA 1 431 S horse may stumble through ⲕⲱ of hind or ⲃⲱⲗ of forefeet; as name of malady: K 159 B ﺍﺳﺘﺮﺧﺎ; *depository* of flour: Montp 207 B (ﻛﻨﻮﺯ؟) ﻭﻫﻮ ﻣﻮﺿﻊ ﺍﻟﺪﻗﻴﻖ.

With following preposition :

ⲕⲱ ⲉ- *SABF, rely upon*: with ϩⲏⲧ, Deu 32 37 *B*
(*S* ⲡⲁϩⲧⲉ), Ps 2 12 *SB*, Is 36 5 *SBF* πέποιθα;
ShC 73 213 *S* heart ⲕⲏ ⲉⲡⲉⲡⲟⲩϫⲁⲓ, R 1 5 28 *S*,
WTh 163 *B* sim ; *appoint, doom* with ⲧⲁⲕⲟ : Jer
9 11 *SB*, Mic 1 7 *SAB* τιθ. εἰς ἀφανισμόν.

—— ⲉϫⲛ- *SB, put, lay upon*: Ps 88 20 *SB*, Is
42 25 *B* (*S* ϩⲛ-), 2 Cor 3 13 *B* (*S* ⲉϩⲣⲁⲓ ⲉϫⲛ-)
τιθ. ἐπί, 2 Chr 3 16 *B*, MG 25 248 *B* ἐπιτιθ. ἐπί,
Jer 1 10 *B* (*S* = Gk) καθιστ., Ez 24 7 *B* (*S* ϩⲓϫⲛ-)
τάσσειν ἐπί ; Ge 34 19 *S* (*B* ϯ ⲙⲁϯ ⲉϫⲉⲛ-) ἐγκεῖσθαι dat, Z 299 *S* he would not ⲕⲁ ⲡⲉϥϣⲁϫⲉ ⲉϫⲛ
ⲡϣⲁϫⲉ of another διδόναι ἐπάνω, Va 58 67 *B*
ⲁⲥⲭⲱ ⲛ̄ⲧⲉⲡⲓⲑⲩⲙⲓⲁ ⲉϫⲱⲥ ⲉϩⲟⲩⲛ ⲉⲣⲟϥ.

—— ⲛⲥⲁ- *SAA²BF, put, leave behind, renounce*:
Is 2 6 *B* (*S* ϩⲱⲱϣ) ἀνιέναι, ib 32 14 *BF* (*S* om ⲛⲥⲁ-),
Mt 19 27 *SB*, Jo 16 28 *SA²B*, CDan 89 *B* ⲭⲁ
ⲛⲁⲓⲥⲁϫⲓ ⲛⲥⲱ (f) ἀφιέναι ; Is 55 7 *SB* ἀπολείπειν, Ge
2 24 *SB*, Mt 21 17 *S* (*B* om ⲛⲥⲁ-) καταλ., Deu 12
19 *SB*, Ps 9 10 *SB*, Pro 4 6 *SAB*, Mk 15 34 *SBF*
ἐγκαταλ. ; Ps 93 14 *S* (*B* ϩⲓⲟⲩⲓ ⲛⲥⲁ-), Ez 16 45 *SB*,
Ac 7 39 *S* (*B* om ⲛⲥⲁ-) ἀπωθεῖν ; Job 8 10 &c *SB*
ἀποποιεῖν ; ib 6 14 *SB*, 2 Cor 4 2 *SB* ἀπειπεῖν ;
Is 24 5 *SB*, Lu 15 29 *S* (*B* ⲉⲣ ⲥⲁⲃⲟⲗ) παρέρχεσθαι ;
Ps 49 20 *S* (*B* ⲭⲱ dat) τιθ. κατά does not belong
here ; PS 110 *S* ⲁⲓⲕⲱ ⲛⲥⲱⲓ places on high, AM
40 *B* ⲁϥⲭⲁ ⲫϯ ⲛⲥⲱϥ, R 2 1 67 *S* iron ⲕⲱ ⲛⲥⲱϥ
ⲙ̄ⲡⲉϥϣⲓⲃⲉ by whetstone, *ib* 71 sim, CO 303 *S* land
contract ⲉⲧⲁⲓⲥ̄[ⲱ] ⲉⲣⲟϥ ⲉⲛⲥⲱ *neglect*. As nn
m, *leaving behind*: Jer 2 19 *B* ⲡⲓϫⲁⲧ ⲛⲥⲱⲕ τὸ
καταλείπειν, Ep 74 *S* ⲛ̄ⲧⲟⲩ ⲛⲥⲙⲟⲧ ⲙ̄ⲡⲕⲱ ⲛⲥⲱϥ
renunciation.

—— ⲛⲧⲛ- *SAB, put, keep in hand, have, entrust
to, esteem* (Stern 535) : Ge 38 23 *B*, Lu 14 18 *SB*,
Ro 1 28 *B* (*S* ⲕⲱ dat) ἔχειν ; Job 13 24 *B* (*S* ⲕⲱ
ⲟⲩⲃⲉ-), He 10 29 *B* (*S* ⲱⲡ) ἡγεῖσθαι ; Am 6 5 *A*
(*B* ⲱⲡ) λογίζειν ; P 129¹⁴ 97 *S* purple dyers ⲉϥⲕⲱ
ⲙ̄ⲙⲟⲟⲩ ⲛ̄ⲧⲟⲟⲧϥ (= Euseb *HE* vii 32 3), CO 341 *S*
please to ⲕⲱ ⲧⲉⲓⲑⲗ̄ⲃⲉ ⲛ̄ⲧⲟⲟⲧⲕ till I come, MIE 2
418 *B* ⲙⲡⲓⲭⲁ ϩⲗⲓ...ⲛⲧⲟⲧ ⲉⲡⲉϩ *set aside* for self,
CO 29 *S* ordinands to learn gospel ⲛⲧⲓⲕⲁⲁϥ
ⲛⲧⲟⲟⲧⲛ & say by heart. Qual *be for someone* :
Su 59 *B*, Mt 21 46 *B* (*S* om vb), Ap 1 18 *B* (*S*
ϣⲟⲟⲡ) ἔχειν, PO 11 337 *B* ⲡⲁϥⲭⲏ ⲛⲧⲟⲧⲟⲩ as
angel, Z 307 *S* sim.

—— ϩⲁ-, ϩⲁ- *SA²B, place under, on behalf of,
renounce for* : Mk 4 21 *SB*, Jo 15 13 *SA²* (*B* ⲉϫⲉⲛ-)
τιθ. ὑπό, ὑπέρ ; Ro 1 13 *S* ⲕⲱ ϩⲁⲉⲓⲁⲧ⳿ (*B* ⲥⲟⲃϯ)
προτιθ. ; Gu 98 *S* ⲕⲁ ⲡⲁⲙⲩⲥⲧⲏⲣⲓⲟⲛ ϩⲁⲡⲉⲧⲛⲙⲁ-
ⲁϫⲉ, AM 126 *B* ⲁⲥⲭⲱ ϩⲁⲣⲟϥ ⲛⲟⲩϩⲟⲣⲟⲡⲟⲥ, BMar
175 *S* earth shall tremble ⲛ̄ϥⲕⲱ ϩⲁⲣⲱⲟⲩ (*l* -ⲟⲟⲩ)
give way under. Qual *be under* : 1 Cor 10 1 *B*

(*S* ϣⲟⲟⲡ) εἶναι ὑπό ; Mt 3 10 *B* (*S* ϩⲁⲧⲛ-) κεῖσθαι
πρός ; EpApp 1 107 *S* flesh ⲉⲧⲕⲏ ϩⲁⲡⲙⲟⲩ.

—— ϩⲁⲣⲛ-, ϩⲁⲣⲉⲛ- *SAB, place before* (of food):
Ge 18 8 *SB*, Pro 23 1 *SA*, Mt 6 41 *S* (*B* ⲛⲁϩⲣⲉⲛ-)
παρατιθ. dat or ἐνώπιον ; Jth 12 1 *S* καταστρωννύναι ; BAp 135 *S* feast ⲕⲏ ϩⲁⲣⲱⲛ.

—— ϩⲁⲣⲁⲧ⸗, ϩ. *SB, place at feet of, before* :
Jth 6 13 *S* ῥίπτειν ὑπό, Ac 4 35 *SB* τιθ. παρὰ πόδας ;
C 43 9 *B* ⲁⲩⲭⲁⲩ ϩⲁⲣⲁⲧϥ of governor, Aeg 45 *B*
ⲛⲁⲡⲭⲏ ϩⲁⲣⲁⲧϥ̄ⲡⲉ like workmen.

—— ϩⲁⲣⲧⲛ-, ϩⲁⲧⲉⲛ- *SABF, place before, commit to* : 1 Kg 17 20 *B* ἀφιέναι dat ; Pro 2 18 *SAB*
τιθ. παρά, Bel 1 *B* προστιθ. πρός, Ac 25 14 *B* (*S*
diff) ἀνατιθ. dat, 1 Cor 10 27 *B* (*S* ϩⲁ-) παρατιθ.
dat ; JKP 2 36 *S* my riches ⲕⲁⲁⲩ ϩⲁⲣⲧⲏⲕ, Ryl 72
353 *S* Joseph sought midwife ⲉⲧⲣⲉϥⲕⲁⲁⲥ ϩⲁⲣⲧⲏⲥ,
AM 275 *B* ϯⲭⲱ ϩⲁⲧⲟⲧⲕ my flock, CMSS 41 *F*
ⲧⲟⲩⲕⲉⲉⲩ ϩⲁⲑⲏⲅ (*l* ϩⲁⲣⲧⲏⲅ). Qual *be beside,
with* : 1 Chr 29 12 *B* παρά, Dan 10 4 *B* (*S* om vb
ϩⲁⲧⲛ-) εἶναι, MIE 2 353 *B* ⲛⲁϥⲭⲏ ϩⲁⲧⲟⲧϥ̄ⲡⲉ was
visiting him.

—— ϩⲓϫⲛ- *SB, place, let loose upon* : Ps 20 4 *B*
(*S* ⲉϫⲛ-), Is 42 4 *SAB*, Mk 10 16 *S* (*B* ⲉϫ.) τιθ.
ἐπί, Lev 2 1 *S* (*B* ⲉϩⲣⲏⲓ ⲉϫ.) ἐπιτιθ. ἐπί, Deu 17
15 *SB* καθιστάναι ἐπί, Is 9 4 *B* (*S* om vb) κεῖσθαι
ἐπί, 1 Cor 9 16 *B* (*S* diff) ἐπικεῖ. dat ; 2 Kg 7 11
S τάσσειν ἐπί ; AM 105 *B* let them ⲭⲱ ⲙⲡⲉⲥⲥⲱⲙⲁ ϩ. ⲡⲓⲕⲁϩⲓ, Mor 18 54 *S* in battle champion
ⲕⲁⲁϥ ϩ. ⲡⲣⲣⲟ = Miss 4 130 *B* ϭⲟϫⲓ ⲉϩⲟⲩⲛ ⲉ-,
P 129¹⁹ 30 *S* my debts ⲛ̄ⲧⲕⲁⲁⲩ ϩⲓϫⲱⲓ yet a year.
Qual *be set over, be upon* (mostly *B*) : Ge 6 17 *B*
(*S* diff), Dan 8 2 *B* εἶναι ἐπί ; Nu 10 14 *B*, Ps 132
2 *B*, Ez 1 5 *B* (var ϣⲟⲡ ϩⲉⲛ-), Ac 12 20 *B* (*S* Gk
om vb) ; PS 358 *S* ⲉⲩⲕⲏ ϩ. ϩⲉⲛⲛⲟϭ ⲛⲕⲟⲗⲁⲥⲓⲥ,
EW 32 *B* ⲫⲏ ⲉⲧⲭⲏ ϩⲓϫⲱⲓ, Va 59 35 *B* horns ⲭⲏ
ϩ. ⲧⲉϥⲁⲫⲉ.

With following adverb :

—— ⲉⲃⲟⲗ *SAA²BF* (meanings often as ⲕⲱ)
a tr, *release, loosen, dismiss* : Nu 20 29 *SB*, Mk 15
6 *SB*, He 13 23 *B* (*S* diff), Z 321 *S* ⲁⲩⲕⲱ ⲉⲃ.
ⲛ̄ⲧⲉⲕⲕⲗⲏⲥⲓⲁ ἀπολύειν ; Ge 32 26 *S* (*B* ⲟⲩⲱⲣⲡ)
Jer 41 14 *SB* ἀποστέλλειν, Ex 4 21 *AB*, 1 Kg 19
17 *S* ἐξαποστ. ; Job 7 19 *B* (*S* om ⲉⲃ.), Ac 27 32 *S*
(*B* om ⲉⲃ.) ἐᾶν ; Va 66 298 *B* hair ⲭⲏ ⲉⲃ. ἄνετος ;
PS 340 *S* ⲉⲥϣⲁⲛⲃⲱⲕ ⲕⲁⲁⲥ ⲉⲃ. ⲉⲉⲓ, ST 171 *S*
ⲧⲁⲕⲁⲁϥ ⲉⲃ. (ⲛ)ⲧⲉϥⲃⲱⲕ ⲛⲁϥ, Mus 40 40 *S* let none
ⲕⲁ ϫⲟⲓ ⲉⲃ. ϩⲓⲧⲉⲙⲣⲱ solvere (*funiculum*), ShC 73
174 *S* sim, P 131² 92 *S* ⲙⲉⲥⲕⲁ ⲗⲁⲁⲩ ⲉⲃ. ⲙⲙⲁ
ⲙ̄ⲡⲉⲥⲥⲱⲙⲁ suffered not to be uncovered, Va 58 18
B ⲭⲁⲧ ⲉⲃ. ϩⲁⲫⲛⲁⲣⲃⲉϥ, BSM 127 *B* her slaves
ⲁⲥⲭⲁⲩ ⲉⲃ. ; *free from care* : Mor 25 32 *S* ⲡⲧⲉⲣⲉϥⲕⲁ
ⲡⲉϥϩⲏⲧ ⲉⲃ. saying Lord delayeth, ROC 25 259
B until now ⲙⲡⲁϯϣ ⲕⲁ ⲡⲁϩⲏⲧ ⲉⲃ., C 86 347 *B*

ⲁⲩⳉⲁ ⲡⲟⲩⳉⲏⲧ ⲉⲃ. ⲛⲉⲙⲁϥ for they suspected not, Pcod 11 *S* ⲉⲓⲉ ⲉⲩⲧⲁⲕⲁⲁϥ ⲉⲃ. then they *expel, dismiss* him not? (*cf* ⲕⲱ ⲣⲓⲃⲟⲗ); of liturgy (ἀπολύειν): ShC 73 132 *S* ⲉⲩϣⲁⲡⲕⲁ ⲡⲥⲱⲟⲩⳉ ⲉⲃ., CA 97 *S* ⲙⲡⲁⲧⲟⲩⲕⲁ ⲡⲗⲁⲟⲥ ⲉⲃ., MG 25 244 *B* ⲙⲉⲛⲉⲡⲥⲁⲑⲣⲟⲩⳉⲁ ⲡⲓϣⲗⲏⲗ ⲉⲃ., & in rubrics: Leyd 145 *S* ⲕⲁ ⲡϣⲁ ⲉⲃ. ⳉⲡⲡⲉⲧⲟⲩⲁⲁⲃ, Wess 18 3, 5 sim; *let loose against* c ⲉ- (*cf* ⲕⲱ ⲉ): PS 315 *S* ⲙⲡⲁϯⲕⲱ ⲉⲃ. ⲙⲡⲕⲱⳉⲧ ⲉⲡⲕⲟⲥⲙⲟⲥ, C 43 106 *B* he bade ⳉⲱ ⲉⲃ. ⲉⲣⲟϥ ⲡⲟⲩⲗⲟⳉⲓ, R 1 4 72 *S* sim; AM 237 *B* ⳉⲱ ⲉⲃⲟⲗ ⲉⳉⲉⲛ- sim; *dispatch, send out*: Mor 41 332 *S* ⲁϥⲕⲁ...ⲥⲟⳉⲟ ⲉⲃ. ⲉϣⲓⲛⲧ = Synax 1 390 وصل الى; *remit, forgive* with dat of person: Ex 32 32 *SB*, Ps 31 1 *SB*, Mt 18 21 *SB* ἀφιέναι; Ge 18 24 *SB*, Is 2 9 *SB* ἀνι.; Lu 7 42 *SB*, 2 Cor 12 13 *SBF* χαρίζειν; Ps 24 11 *SB*, Is 54 10 *B* (*S* ⲟⲩϫⲁⲓ) ἱλάσκεσθαι; MG 25 220 *B* συγχωρεῖν; ShC 42 151 *S* ⲉⲩⲕⲱ ⲉⲃ. ⳉⲡⲡⲉⲧⲣⲓⲧⲟⲩⲱⳉ, El 72 *A* ⳉⲁⲣⲉⲥⲕⲁ ⲡⲁⲃⲉ ⲁⲃ., J 36 42 *S* ⲁⲡⲕⲱ ⲡⲁⲡⲁϣ ⲉⲃ. ⲡⲏⲧⲡ, C 86 193 *B* taxes ⲉⲧⲁⲩ ⳉ ⲁⲩ ⲡ ⲁⲩ ⲉⲃ., HT Z 3 *S* praying ⲉϥⲉⲕⲁⲁϥ ⲡⲁⲩ ⲉⲃ. yet a while, PJkôw *S* ⲁⲓⲕⲁ ⲫⲟϥ(ⲡⲣⲱⳉ) ⲡⲁⲡⲟⲗⲗⲱ ⲉⲃ. ⲡⲁⲕ, Mor 50 33 *S* ⲧⲉⲕⲕⲏ ⲛⲉ. ⳉⲁⲡⲡⲉⲕϣⲱⲡⲉ; Job 42 9 *B* ⲉⲟⲃⲉ- (*S* ⲃⲱⲗ ⲉⲃ.) λύειν; *quit, abandon*, qual *be empty*: Jos 8 17 *S*, Is 17 2 *S* (*B* ⲥⲱⳉⲡ), Mk 14 52 *S* (*B* do) καταλείπειν, Is 1 8 *S* (*B* do), Jer 28 9 *S* (*B* om ⲉⲃ.) ἐγκαταλ.; 1 Kg 20 25 *S* vacuus; EpJer 30 *F* (*B* ⲥⲱⲣⲡ ⲉⲃ.) ἀκάλυπτος εἶναι; PS 139 *S* were afraid ⲁⲩⲕⲱ ⲉⲃ. ⲡⲧⲡⲓⲥⲧⲓⲥ, ShC 73 147 *S* ⲡⲥⲉⲕⲁⲁⲥ (neut) ⲉⲃ. ⲡⲟⲩⲕⲟⳉⲓ ⲉⲧⲣⲉⲩⲙⲉⲗⲉⲧⲁ, AM 328 *B* wind ⳉⲁⲩ ⲉⲃ., MR 5 47 *F* ϫⲓⲡⲧⲁⲓⲕⲉⲉⲛ ⲉⲃ., LMärt 13 *S* thenceforth king ⲕⲁⲁϥ ⲉⲃ., ShC 42 86 *S* fields sown or ⲉⲧⲕⲏ ⲉⲃ., C 43 34 *B* throne ⳉⲏ ⲉⲃ. without king; *omit* (*cf* ⲕⲱ j): R 1 5 35 *S* to martyr ⲕⲁ ⲡⲉⲓϣⲁϫⲉ ⲉⲃ. & sacrifice, BMOr 8802 5 *S* am tempted to praise words ⲡⲧⲁⲕⲁ ⲡⲣⲃⲏⳉⲉ ⲉⲃ., Cat 46 *B* ⲁϥⳉⲁ ⲡⲓⲣⲟⲟⲩ ⲉⲃ., Va 58 28 *B* rubric ⳉⲁ ⲫⲁⲓ ⲉⲃ., read it not; *refl, desist from*: Ex 32 12 *B* ⳉⲁⲕ ⲉⲃ. ϭⲉⲡⲡϫⲱⲡⲧ (lectionaries Va 34 49 &c = Va 1, Lag ⲧⲁⲣⲡⲟ, *S* ⲗⲟ), Ac 13 10 *B* ⳉⲱ ⲡⲧⲟⲧ⸗ ⲉⲃ. (*S* do) παύειν, *cf* Miss 4 134n ⳉⲁⲕ ⲉⲃ., C 89 60n ⳉⲁ only (opp apparently ⲥⲱⲕ) sim meaning also? Ann 27 63, 64 ⳉⲱⲕ, ⲕⲱⲕ; *cf* rubric Leyd 151 *S*; *publish*: C 89 5 *B* ⲁϥⳉⲁ ⲡⲓⲡⲣⲟⲥⲧⲁⲅⲙⲁ ⲉⲃ., at end of legal texts (*cf* ἐκδιδόναι), J 35 79 *S* ⲁⲡⲕⲁⲁⲥ (sc διάλυσις) ⲉⲃ.   ⲕ. ⲉⲃ. ⲡⲥⲁ- *S*, *release to*: Si 30 8 ⲉⲁⲩⲕⲁ ⳉⲏⲣ ⲉⲃ. ⲡⲥⲱϥ ἀνειμένος (*cf*? ⲕⲁ ⳉⲱ ⲉⲃ. Mal 4 2, Ac 27 40 &c), Lu 6 29 *S* (*B* diff).

b intr, *become loose, dissolved*: 2 Kg 4 1 *S* ἐκλύεσθαι, PS 36 *S* caused their cycles to ⲕⲱ ⲉⲃ., TT 77 *S* tortures caused crown of head to ⲕⲱ ⲉⲃ.; Ac 21 2 &c *S* (*B* ϫⲱⲟⲩⲡ ⲉⲃ.) ἀνάγεσθαι, RNC 27

S ἀποπλεῖν *be loosed* from port, put to sea; *be at ease*: BSM 99 *B* consent so that my heart ⲡⲁⳉⲱ ⲉⲃ. = Mor 22 111 *S* ⲧⲁϫⲣⲟ, AM 83 *B* sim; *be left desolate*: Is 23 15 *S* (*B* ⲥⲱⳉⲡ) καταλείπεσθαι, Jer 9 10 *S* (*B* ⲙⲟⲩⲡⲕ) ἐκλείπ., Ryl 72 357 *S* mother's bosom ⲕⲱ ⲉⲃ. childless; *forgive*: Is 46 4 *SB* ἀνιέναι, CaiEuch 524 *B* ἀφι., Dan 9 19 *B* (*S* + dat) ἱλάσκεσθαι, 3 Kg 8 30 *B* ἵλεως εἶναι, Hab 1 11 *SAB* ἐξιλάσκ., Lev 25 9 *S* (*B* ⲡⲛ) ἱλασμός, Si 5 5 *S* ἐξιλ.; Lu 6 37 *SB* ἀπολύειν. Qual *be, exist* (rare): BHom 70 *S* let us repent ⳉⲟⲥⲟⲡ ⲧⲡⲕⲏ ⲉⲃ., PCol 2 *F* ⲉⲓⲁⲩ ϫ(ⲉ)ⲁⲕⲗ ⲟⲩⲡ ⲉⲥⲁⲓⲛ ⲙⲁⲛ ⲁⲗⲉⲡⲁⲣⲏⲧ ⲕⲉ ⲃⲁⲗ ⳉⲁⲣⲁⲕ ⳉⲉⲣⲟⲃ ⲡⲓⲙ.

—— ⲉⲃ. *SAB* nn m, *freedom, remission*: Ex 23 11 *B* (*S* vb), Is 61 1 *SB* ἄφεσις; Eccl 8 8 *S* ἀποστολή; BHom 21 *S* συγγνώμη; *forgiveness*: Mk 3 29 *SB*, He 9 22 *SBF* ἄφ.; Nu 5 8 *SB*, Am 8 14 *B* (*SA* diff) ἱλασμός, Si 32 3 *S*, Ez 7 24 *SB* ἐξιλ.; TU 43 20 *A*. Also ⲡⲕⲁ ⲡⲟⲃⲉ ⲉⲃⲟⲗ: Br 126 *S*.

ⲁⲧⳉⲱ ⲉⲃ. *B* adj, *without forgiveness*: Is 13 9 (*S* Gk om).

. ⲙⲁ ⲡⲕⲱ ⲉⲃ. *S*, *place of forgiveness, mercy-seat*: Ex 25 17 (P 44 104, *B* = Gk) ἱλαστήριον.

ⲣⲉϥⲕⲱ ⲉⲃ. *SB*, *forgiver*: Ps 98 8 *B* (*S* vb) εὐίλατος, Jer apocr (Z 216) *S* (*B* vb), TstAb 233 *B* thou art ⲡⲓⲣ.

ⲙⲡⲧ-, ⲙⲉⲧⲣⲉϥⲕⲱ, ⳉⲱ ⲉⲃ. *SB, forgiveness*: ShC 73 132 *S*, Cat 185 *B*.

ϭⲓⲛ-, ϫⲓⲡⲕⲱ ⲉⲃ. nn m f *B*, f *S, forgiveness*: P 44 63 *S* ἱλασμός, Dan 9 24 *B* m (*S* vb) ἐξιλάσκεσθαι, Va 58 18 *B* I beg of thee ϯϫⲓⲡϫⲁⲧ ⲉⲃ.

—— ⲉⲡⲉⲥⲏⲧ *SB, put, let down*: Ge 24 46 *B* καθαιρεῖν, Ex 17 11 *S* (*B* ⳉ. ⲉⳉⲣⲏⲓ) καθιέναι; Ac 27 17 *B* (*S* ⲡⲟⲩⲣⲉ) χαλᾶν; Is 46 7 *B* (*S* ⲕ. ⲉⳉⲣⲁⲓ) τιθέναι; Va 63 100 *B* ⲡⲧⲉϥⳉⲁ ⲡⲉϥϣⲟⲩ ⲉⲡ. ἀφιέναι; PS 71 *S* ⲁϥⳉⲁ ⲡⲭⲱⲱⲙⲉ ⲉⲡ., BMis 341 *S* head ⲡⲧⲁⲕⲕⲁⲁⲥ ⲉⲡ. in worship, BMar 23 *S* bade ⲕⲁⲁϥ ⲉⲡ. from rack, AM 136 *B* sim & often in martyrdoms, P 131⁴ 103 *S* God ⲕⲱ ⲉⲡ. ⲙⲡⲉϥϣⲱⲡⲧ.

—— ⲉⳉⲟⲩ, ⲉϥ. *SAB, leave behind, over*: Lev 7 5 *S* (*B* ⲥⲱⳉⲡ), Ruth 2 14 *S* καταλείπ.; Zeph 3 3 *A* (*B* do) ὑπολείπ.; Ap 11 2 *S* (*B* ⳉⲓⲟⲩⲓ ⲉⲃ.) ἐκβάλλειν ἔξω; BMar 212 *S* I thought ⲉⲧⲣⲁⲕⲁⲁⲧ ⲉⲡ. ὑποστρέφειν, AM 261 *B* ⲉⲁⲡⳉⲁ ⲟⲩⲙⲏϣ ⲉϥ. of what we might have said, BM 1079 *S* ⲡⲡⲕⲁ ⲣⲱⲙⲉ ⲉⲡ. unregistered (*cf* ⲕⲱ j).

—— ⲉⳉⲟⲩⲡ, ⲉϫ. *SBF, put in, admit*: Deu 32 24 *S* (*B* ⲟⲩⲱⲣⲡ) ἀποστέλλειν εἰς, Si 51 30 *S* ὑποτιθ. ὑπό, ViSitz 172 4 18 *S* ἔργον ἔχειν κατά, Aeg 220 *S* ⲡⲥⲉⲧⲙⲕⲁⲁϥ ⲉⳉ. δέχεσθαι; DeV 77 *B* they begged me ⲉⲟⲣⲓⳉⲁϥ ⲉϫ. = P 129¹⁴ 122 *S* ⳉⲓⳉⲟⲩⲡ, BM 601 *F* ⲧⲁⲗⲉⲃⲕⲉⲉⲃ ⲉⳉ. to monastery; *bring into port* a ship (*cf* ? ⲕⲱ I): BIF 13 101 *S* king

ordained ⲉⲧⲣⲉⲩⲕⲁⲁⲩ ⲉϩ., Mor 50 47 *S* ⲁⲩⲕⲱ
ⲡϫⲟⲓ ⲉϩ. ⲁⲩⲙⲟⲟⲡⲉ ⲉⲡⲉⲕⲣⲟ, Kr 228 2 *S* God
guided us ⲁⲛⲧⲉ (*sic, l* ⲕⲏ) ⲉϩ. ⲉⲃⲁⲃⲓⲗⲟⲛ; Aeg 276
S ⲕⲁ ⲁⲣⲓⲕⲉ ⲉϩ. ⲉ- *bring upon*;   as nn f BM 1131
22 *S* day of ⲧⲉⲡⲕⲱ (? *sic l*) ϩⲟⲩⲛ ⲉⲡⲏⲓ, Kr 1 12 *S*
ⲧⲉⲩⲕⲱ ϩⲟⲩⲛ (context obscure), *cf* Ryl 162 ⲧⲕⲟ;

ⲋⲓⲛⲕⲱ ⲉϩ. *S* nn f, *entrance* of house : BM 1023
roof & court & ⲧⲋ., Ryl 158 ⲧⲋ. ⲙⲛⲧⲋⲓⲛⲉⲓ ⲉⲃⲟⲗ
(εἴσοδος Wess 20 218), PStras 220 sim.

—— ⲉϩⲣⲁⲓ, ⲁϩ., ⲉⲋ. *SAA²BF, put, lay down,
aside*, literal & metaph (*S* ⲉϩ. *up* hardly ever here,
v ⲋⲓⲛⲕⲱ ⲉϩ. *s f* & ⲕⲱ ⲉϩ. ⲉϫⲛ-) : Deu 14 27 *S* (*B*
om ⲉⲋ.), Is 46 7 *S* (*B* ⲭ. ⲉⲡⲉⲥⲛⲧ), Jer 13 16 *B*
(*S* om ⲉϩ.), Mk 4 30 *S* (*B* om ⲉⲋ.), Jo 13 4 *SB*,
1 Cor 3 10 *SB* τιθ., Miss 8 33 *S* ⲕⲱ ⲉϩ. dogmas
ἐκτιθ., Z 278 *S* opinions ⲁⲩⲕⲁⲁⲩ ⲉϩ. in books
ἐντιθ., Lev 16 23 *S* (*B* om ⲉⲋ.), Va 57 25 *B* ⲙⲁ-
ⲣⲉⲛⲭⲱ ⲉⲋ. extravagance, Mor 37 136 *S* who came
(for comfort) that did not ⲕⲱ ⲉϩ. ⲙⲡⲛⲃⲉ ἀποτιθ. ?,
Ge 43 31 *B*, Pro 6 8 *SA*, Mt 13 24 *SF* (*B* ⲭ.
ⲋⲁⲧⲉⲛ-) παρατιθ.; Ex 17 11 *B* (*S* ⲕⲱ ⲉⲡⲉⲥⲛⲧ), Ac
9 25 *B* (*S* ⲭⲁⲗⲁ) καθιέναι, Pro 24 67 *SA* προιέναι;
Is 33 23 *BF* (*S* diff) χαλᾶν; El 128, 92 *SA* ⲧⲛ-
ⲛⲁⲕⲱ ⲉϩ. bodily flesh, RNC 76 *S* bade ⲕⲱ ⲉϩ.
martyr from tree, AM 62 *B* ⲁϥⲭⲱ ⲡⲟⲩⲥⲉⲛϯ ⲉⲋ.,
ShLeyd 310 *S* misers ⲉⲩⲕⲁ ⲡⲟⲩϩ ⲉϩ., BKU
1 68 vo *S* ? sim;   *lay down, publish* (law, deed) :
Aeg 239 *S* canons ⲛⲧⲁⲩⲕⲁⲁⲩ ⲉϩ., LIb 4 *B* ⲁϥⲭⲱ
ⲉⲋ. edict, J 67 118 *S* oath ⲛⲧⲁⲛⲕⲁⲁϥ ⲉϩ., BMis
246 *S* ⲁϥⲕⲁ ⲟⲩⲱϣ ⲡⲁⲩ ⲉϩ. *allowed them leisure*;
expose, set forth : AM 261 *B* ⲁⲛⲭⲱ ⲡⲱⲧⲉⲛ ⲉⲋ.
ⲡⲛⲁⲓⲕⲟⲩϫⲓ, Miss 4 743 *S* ⲉⲛⲛⲁⲕⲱ ⲡⲏⲧⲛ ⲉϩ.
ⲙⲡϣⲁϫⲉ, Bor 305 97 *S* Paul (Phil 2 5) ⲕⲱ ⲉϩ.
ϫⲉⲡⲉⲭ̅ⲥ̅ *useth* (name) ' Christ ' to avoid misunderstanding;   *leave behind* : BMis 273 *S* daughter
ⲛⲧⲁϥⲕⲁⲁⲥ ⲉϩ. orphan;   *lay down, abandon* :
TstAb 158 *B* ⲁϥⲭⲁ ⲥⲱⲙⲁ ⲉⲋ., in epitaphs Hall
9 *S*, Ann 23 56 *F*.   Qual *be laid down, exist* :
Lu 12 19 *S* (*B* om ⲉⲋ.), Jo 19 29 *SA²B*, Ap 4 2 *S*
(*B* om vb) κεῖσθαι, Ge 49 10 *S* (BHom 139, *B* om
ⲉⲋ.), 2 Tim 4 8 *S* (*B* do) ἀποκεῖ., Nu 4 7 *SB*,
CaiEuch 340 *B* gifts ⲉⲧⲭⲏ ⲉⲋ. προκεῖ.; Jos 4 9
SB, Ez 24 6 *B* (*S* om vb), BHom 16 *S* in scriptures
remedies ⲕⲏ ⲛⲁⲛ ⲉϩ. εἶναι; 3 Kg 19 6 *S* (no Gk);
C 89 183 *B* according to canons ⲉⲧⲭⲏ ⲉⲋ., ClPr
40 1 *S* text of my discourse ⲉⲧⲕⲏ ⲡⲁⲓ ⲉϩ. (*cf* τὸ
προκείμενον), J 1 35 *S* no compulsion ⲕⲏ ⲡⲁⲛ ⲉϩ.
(*cf* ἐπικείμενος PMon 123), J 39 12 *S*, this time
ⲉⲧⲕⲏ ⲉϩ., ib 65 53 *S* ⲧⲟⲡⲟⲥ...ⲉⲧⲕⲏ ⲉϩ. ϩⲓⲡⲧⲟⲟⲩ,
Z 280 *S* left not empty one of seats ⲉⲧⲕⲏ ⲉϩ.,
ShMIF 23 82 *S* ⲉⲥⲕⲏ ⲡⲁⲛ ⲉϩ. that we should
repent, Aeg 7 *B* ⲙⲫⲣⲏϯ ⲉⲧⲥⲭⲏ ⲉⲋ. for all.

—— ⲉϩ. nn m, *laying down, provision* : Pro 6 8

SA (*B* ⲑⲱⲟⲩϯ) παράθεσις, BAp 124 *S* ⲡⲉϥⲕⲁ
ⲥⲱⲙⲁ ⲉϩ., JBMOr 9525 1 *S* to observe every
ⲙⲉⲣⲟⲥ, ⲕⲉⲫⲁⲗⲁⲓⲟⲛ & ⲕⲱ ⲉϩ. (*cf* θέμα J 75 58),
Br 100 *S* the ⲕⲱ ⲉϩ. of a δύναμις *form, constitution*,
Mor 30 40 *F* ⲡⲕⲱ ⲉϩⲗ. ⲙⲡⲁⲧⲟⲡⲟⲥ (*cf* BMis 264
inf) *foundation-tracing*.

ⲋⲓⲛⲕⲱ, ϫⲓⲛⲭⲱ ⲉϩ., ⲉⲋ., nn f *S*, m *B, laying
down, what is laid down, nature, fashion* : Am 66 *B*
day of thy ϫⲓⲛⲕⲁ ⲥⲱⲙⲁ ⲉⲋ., Mor 17 24 *S* he
taught him ⲧⲉϥϭ. οὐσία, Br 84 *S* ⲧϭ. ⲙⲡⲉⲓⲑⲛⲥⲁⲩ-
ⲣⲟⲥ (*cf ib* ⲋⲓⲛⲥⲱⲣ ⲉⲃⲟⲗ), My 45 *S* sim, PStras
220 *S* (*v* ⲋⲓⲛⲕⲱ ⲉϩⲟⲩⲛ) ϭ. ⲉϩ. ⲙⲛⲧⲋⲓⲛⲉⲓ ⲉⲡⲉⲥⲛⲧ
ascent & *descent* (ἄνοδος PLond 5 193), BMOr
6201 A 35 *S* sim.

—— ⲉϩ., *go up S* (rare) : BMOr 6201 ⲡⲧⲱⲣⲧⲣ
ⲡⲕⲟⲩ (ⲉ)ϩ. ⲉⲧⲭⲉⲡⲉⲡⲱⲣ (*cf* above ⲕⲱ 1).

ⲉϩ. ⲉϫⲛ- *S*, where = *B* ⲉϩⲣⲏⲓ (rare) *lay, raise up
upon* : Ez 4 4 *SB* τιθ.; *B* alone : Deu 1 13 (*S*
= Gk), Ps 108 6 (*S* do), Ac 7 10 (*S* do) καθιστ.;
elsewhere *S* ⲕⲱ ⲉϩ. ⲉϫⲛ- prob *down*, as ⲕⲱ ⲉϩ. :
Nu 11 11 (*B* ⲧⲁⲗⲟ ⲉ-), Mt 12 18 (*B* ⲭⲱ ϩⲓϫⲉⲛ-),
BMis 432 ⲁⲓⲕⲱ ⲡⲧⲁⲉⲓⲣⲏⲛⲏ ⲉϩ. ⲉϫⲱⲟⲩ.

—— ⲥⲁⲃⲟⲗ mostly *B, put outside, exclude* : C 43
160 ⲁⲩⲭⲁϥ ⲥ. ⲡⲧⲡⲟⲗⲓⲥ, EW 55 Christ to Virgin
ⲛⲧϥⲡⲁⲭⲁϯ ⲥ. ⲙⲙⲟⲓ ⲁⲛ, WS 98 *S* bids *set apart* pigs
for fattening.   Qual : Eph 2 12 (*S* ϣⲟⲟⲡ ⲁϫⲛ-)
εἶναι χωρίς, MIE 2 411.if thou reveal this ⲕⲭⲏ ⲥ.

—— ϩⲓⲃⲟⲗ *S*, as last, *excommunicate* : Aeg 228
transgressing laymen ⲙⲁⲣⲟⲩⲕⲁⲁⲩ ϩ. ἀφορίζειν (*cf*
καθαιρεῖν depose cleric), ib 279 deacon may ⲕⲁ
ⲡⲉⲩⲡⲟϫⲓⲁⲕ. ϩ. ἀφορ., CA 88 cleric visiting wizards ⲉⲩⲉⲕⲁⲁⲩ ϩ., Z 308 when archbp heard ⲁⲩⲕⲁⲁⲩ ϩ. χωρίζειν, Bodl (P) 9 34 ⲧⲉⲧⲛⲕⲏ ϩ. from
mysteries; *lay out, distribute* : Mor 46 51 at time
when husbandman ⲕⲁ ⲟⲉⲓⲕ ϩ. for his labourers.

V also ⲕⲱ with following : ⲃⲟⲗ (ⲕⲁ ⲃⲟⲗ), ⲉⲩⲱ,
ⲉⲓⲁ (ⲉⲓⲁⲧ⸗), ⲙⲁ, ⲙⲟⲛⲧⲉ, ⲙⲁⲁϫⲉ, ⲡⲟⲃⲉ, ⲟⲉⲓⲕ, ⲡⲁⲧ,
ⲣⲟ, ⲣⲁⲧ⸗, ⲥⲟⲧⲉ, ⲧⲱⲣⲉ (ⲧⲟⲟⲧ⸗), ⲧⲏⲩ, ⲟⲩⲡⲟⲩ, ϩⲟ
(ϩⲣⲁ⸗), ϩⲏⲧ, ϫⲱ⸗, ϭⲟⲙ, ϭⲓϫ & in ϫⲉⲕⲁⲥ.

ⲕⲱ *S* nn, as pl, meaning unknown, paral *idols* :
ShZ 599 wood, stone & other things made into
ϩⲉⲛⲉⲓⲍⲱⲗⲟⲛ ⲁⲩⲱ ϩⲉⲛⲕⲱ. Cf ? dem *kꜣ, shrine* ναός
(AZ 56 17n).

ⲕⲱⲓ *B* nn m, *elbow* : K 77 ⲉⲣⲥ̄, between ⲕⲁⲗⲁⲛ-
ⲕⲁϩ & ϫϥⲟⲓ (? is the Ar word).

ⲕⲱⲃ *SABF* (often ⲕⲱⲡ *B*), ⲕⲃ-, ⲕⲉⲃ- *S*, ⲕⲟⲃ⸗
SB, ⲕⲏⲃ† *SABF*, vb **I** intr, *be doubled* : 4 Kg 2 9
(PMich 607) *S* διπλοῦς γίνεσθαι, Miss 4 110 *B*
work with his talent ϣⲁⲧⲉϥⲕ. (*cf* Mt 25 27); Mor
40 40 *S* his spirit ⲕ. ⲉϫⲱⲟⲩ = MG 25 270 *B*
ⲉϩⲣⲏⲓ ⲉϫ., BMar 85 *S* his troubles ⲕ. ⲉϫⲱϥ; P 131ˢ
56 *S* joy ⲕ. ⲡⲁⲩ, PO 14 348 *B* fruits ⲕⲱⲡ ⲡⲁⲕ,

ST 242 *S* ⲙ]ⲡⲣ ⲕⲱⲃ ϩⲁⲣⲟϥ obscure. **II** tr, *make double*: Ap 18 6 *B* (*S* ⲧⲱⲱⲃⲉ) διπλοῦν, Deu 21 17 *S* (*B* ⳁ ⲛⲁⲓⲡⲗ.), Job 42 10 *B* (*S* ⳁ) διπλᾶ διδόναι; ShR 2 3 51 *S* usury ⲉⲧⲕ. ⲙⲙⲟⲟⲩ ⲉⲣⲟⲟⲩ, AM 133 *B* ⲕⲱⲃ ⲡⲁϥ ⲙⲡⲉϥⲃⲉⲭⲉ, Va 66 291 *B* ⲁϥⲕⲟⲡⲟⲩ ⲛⲝ ⲛⲕⲱⲃ, PSBA 26 177 *S* stars ⲕⲧⲟⲟⲩ ⲁⲩⲕⲉϥ ⲡⲉⲩϩⲣⲟⲙⲟⲥ, HL 81 *B* walked 30 days ⲡⲁⲗⲓⲛ ⲟⲛ ⲁⲓⲕⲟⲡⲟⲩ καὶ δίς, CO 42 *S* if I accept not verdict ⳁⲛⲁⲕⲱⲃ ⲡⲟⲥⲉ ⲛⲧⲁⲓⳁ, *cf* Ep 183, ST 242 *S*]ⲛⲧⲕⲟⲃⲟⲩ ⲛⲡⲧⲟϭⲟⲩ obscure; *double back, fold, close*: Lu 4 20 *S* (*B* ⲕⲱⲗ) πτύσσειν; ShIF 91 *S* soft bandages ϥⲛⲁⲕⲟⲃⲟⲩ ⲉϩⲣⲁⲓ ⲉⲡⲉⲕϭⲓⳍ. Qual as adj: Ex 16 22 *SB*, *ib* 22 4 *B* (*S* ⲛⲥⲉⲡ ⲥⲛⲁⲩ), 1 Tim 5 17 *SB*, BHom 37 *S* all our limbs ⲉⲩⲕ. διπλοῦς, Mt 23 15 *SB* διπλότερος; Si 12 5 *S* διπλάσιος; Ge 43 12 *SB*, Jer 17 18 *B* δισσός; Lev 27 3 *B* (*S* diff) ⲥⲁⲧⲉⲣⲓ ⲉⲩⲕ. δίδραχμα; BG 41 *S* other names given them ⲉⲩⲕ., BMis 150 *S* ⲟⲩⲟⲓ ϩⲛ(ⲟⲩ)-ⲟⲩⲟⲓ ⲉϥⲕ., Z 232 sim; ShMIF 23 82 *S* judgement ⲉⲥⲕ. ⲉⲣⲟⲛ, Mus 35 23 *B* Baptist ⲡⲣⲟϩⲣⲟⲙⲟⲥ ⲉⲧⲕ. ⲛⲡⲉⲧⲟⲛϩ & dead.

—— *SABF* nn m, *double, return, repetition*: Zech 9 12 *SA* (*B* ⲕⲏⲃ) διπλοῦς; Lu 6 34 *S* (*B* ϣⲉⲃⲓⲱ) ἴσος, Aeg 230 *S* ⲡⲉϥⲕ. ⲛⳑⲟⲩ ⲛⲥⲟⲡ ἐπίπεμπτον, ST 242 *S*]ⲉⲧⲕⲏⲃ ⲉⲡⲕ. ⲛⳑⲉ, BMis 396 *S* repaid ⲙⲡⲡⲉⲩⲕ. (var Bor 155 ϥⲧⲟⲟⲩ ⲡⲕ.) = Va 63 18 *B* ⲙⲛⲥⲓ, ShC 42 150 *S* we love them as they us, ⲙⲙⲓⲛⲧⲕ. ⲡⲣⲟϥⲟ ⲉⲡⲁⲓ who say we hate them, whereas they hate us. Gk -πλάσιος, -ως: JA '75 5 245 *S* ⲡⲕ. δι-, Si 43 4 *S* ⲛϣⲙⲧ ⲕ. τρι-, Ps 11 7 *B* (*S* ⲥⲟⲡ), Pro 6 31 *AB* ἑπτα-, Mk 10 30 *S* (*B* ⲥⲟⲡ) ἑκατοντα-; Deu 4 1 *B* ⲛⲧⲉⲧⲉⲛⲁϣⲁⲓ ⲡⲕ. πολυπλασιάζειν (? error); ⲕ. + ⲥⲟⲡ: 2 Kg 12 6 *S*, Is 30 26 *F* (*SB* om c.), Dan 1 20 *B*, PS 21 *S* ⲛϩⲙⲉ ⲯⲓⲧ ⲡⲕ. ⲛⲥⲟⲡ.

ⲕⲏⲃⲉ *S* nn, *fold, crease* in skin: Job 41 4 (*B* ⲥⲛⲁⲩϩ) πτύξις, BMOr 8800 203 (Theophil Alex) that I may unfold ⲡⲕ. ⲙⲡϩⲱⲕ compagem loricæ (cf Job) of thoughts of this crafty one (Origen), P 44 121 ⲛⲓⲕ. in his neck & brows طيات.

ⲕⲟⲟⲃⲉϥ, ⲕⲱⲃⲉϥ *S* nn m, *doubling*: P 44 87 ضاعفة = 43 68 مضاعفة.

ⲕⲱⲃ *B* nn m, *leaven*: Mk 8 15 (var ϣⲉⲙⲏⲣ, *S* ⲑⲁⲃ) ζύμη, Va 69 122 ϣⲉⲙⲏⲣ ⲉⲧⲉⲡⲓⲕ. ⲡⲉ, K 14 خمير. ⲁⲧⲕ. adj, *without leaven*: Lev 23 6 (*S* ⲁⲑⲁⲃ), cf *ib* ⲁⲧϣⲉⲙⲏⲣ, Cat 171 (Lu 22) ⲁⲧⲕ., var ⲁⲧϣ. ἄζυμος.

ⲕⲁⲃⲁⲓ *B* nn as pl, cages, baskets (?) of *wickerwork*: Montp 169 among tools ⲛⲓⲕ. اقفاص, between ⲕⲁⲙ & ϫⲁⲛⲓϫⲓ. Prob from ⲃⲁ (ⲃⲁⲓ) qv.

ⲕⲁⲃⲁⲓⲧⲏⲥ *maker* of such work (ⲕⲁⲃⲁⲓ + -ⲧⲏⲥ, Stern 169): K 113 قفاص.

ⲕⲏⲃⲓ, ⲕⲁⲃⲓ *B* nn f, *jar, pitcher*: MG 25 231 ⲕⲏ. ληκύθιον carrying γεύματα = Z 317 *S* ϩⲛⲁⲁϥ; K 150, P 55 11 ⲕⲁ. مسرجة lamp (cf K *ib* ϩⲏⲃⲥ, λυχνία). *Cf* Murray *Engl Nub Dict* 65 gubē, kebē.

ⲕⲏⲃⲓ, ⲕⲉⲃⲓ *B* nn m (Tatt Lab), *honey cake*: P 54 118 قرص العسل, K 200 pl اقراص الشهد.

ⲕⲓⲃⲉ *SA* v ⲉⲕⲓⲃⲉ.

ⲕⲓⲃⲓⲩ *S* nn as pl, among fish: P 46 237 قيل, between ⲥⲓⲗⲟⲩⲣⲟⲥ & ⲃⲱⲣⲉ (ϥⲟⲣⲓ). Error? for ⲕⲏⲗ, or ? for its pl.

ⲕⲱⲱⲃⲉ, ⲕⲱⲱϭⲉ, ⲕⲉⲉⲃⲉ-, ⲕⲁⲁⲃⲉ-, ⲕⲟⲟⲃⲉⳍ *S* vb tr, *compel, seize by force*: Mt 5 41 (*B* ϭⲓ ⲡⲭⲃⲁ), *ib* 27 32 (*B* do), Mk 15 21 (*BF* do) ἀγγαρεύειν سخر; Sh(?)Mor 54 132 ⲙⲡⲉⲣⲕⲁⲁⲃⲉ ⲡⲉⲧⲟⲓⲧⲟⲩⲱⲕ, BMOr 8810 489 (Besa) ⲡⲡⲉⲩⲕⲉϥⲉ ⲣⲱⲙⲉ to virtue, Mor 31 110 ⲁⲩⲕ. camels to carry corn, Miss 4 563 on reaching Antinoe ⲁⲩⲕ. ⲙⲡⲉⲩϫⲟⲓ, *ib* 566 opp ⲕⲁⲁϥ ⲉⲃⲟⲗ, BMis 464 sim. Intr ? BAp 40 harbour with demons ⲉⲩⲕ. ⲛϩⲏⲧⲥ, I drew them into the net (? a diff vb).

I ⲕⲃⲁ *S*, ⲭⲃⲁ *B* nn, *compulsion, forced labour*: Cat 175 *B* (on Lu 23 26) ⲁϥⲟⲗϥ ⲛⲭ., BIF 13 111 *S* ϥⲓ ⲡⲡⲉϥϭⲁⲙⲟⲩⲗ ⲡⲕ. = MG 25 300 *B*, ShC 42 84 *S* ye oppress them with ⲡⲉⲧⲛⲕ., ST 101 *Sᵃ* ϩⲁϥⲁⲩ ⲉⲓϫⲉ ϩⲁⲕ. ⲣ ⲕ. *S*, *do forced labour*: ShC 42 83 poor ⲣ ⲕ. for rich in building for them, ShRyl 68 260, oppressors complain that poor induced ⲉⲧⲙⲉⲣ ⲕ., BMis 207 Jews in Egypt ⲙⲁⲣⲟⲩⲣ ⲕ. ϩⲓⲁⲗⲱⲧ. ϭⲓⲛⲣ ⲕ. *S*, *doing of forced labour*: ShR 2 3 34 hard toil ϣⲁⲣⲁⲓ ⲉⲧϭ. ϭⲓ ⲡⲭ. *B*, *compel*: Mt 5 41, 27 32 (*S* ⲕⲱⲱⲃⲉ) ἀγγαρεύειν.

II ⲕⲃⲁ *SAF* (*B* ⲙⲡϣⲓϣ, once ⲕ.) nn m, *vengeance* (? not connected with preceding): Nu 31 2 *S* (*B* diff), Si 32 19 *S*, Mic 7 4 *S* (*A* ϫⲓ ⲕ.) ἐκδίκησις; Ps 34 23 *S* δίκη. ⲉⲓⲣⲉ, ⲣ ⲕ., *do vengeance*: Deu 32 43 *S*, Ps 9 4 *S* δίκην ποι., Ro 12 19 *S* ἐκδικεῖν, P 131² 117 *S* drinking before Fast is like ⲡⲉⲧⲧⲱⲱⲃⲉ ⲙⲡⲛⲟⲙⲟⲑⲉⲧⲏⲥ ⲉⲕⲉⲓⲣⲉ ⲙⲡⲉ(ⲕ)ⲕ. = Va 58 192 *B* ⲓⲣⲓ ⲙⲡⲉⲕⲕⲁⲡ. ὡς ἀμυνόμενος…ὡς κατασοφιζόμενος; *do vengeance for* c ⲛ-: 2 Kg 9 7 *S*, Ps 98 8 *S* ἐκδικ.; Ac 7 24 *S* (*B* ⲓⲣⲓ ⲡⲟⲩϭⲓ ⲙⲡⲙ.) ⲉⲕⲇ. ⲡⲟⲓ.; Joel 3 21 *S* (*B* ϭⲓ ⲙⲡⲙ.) ἐκζητεῖν: c ⲙⲡ-: Jth 2 1 *S* ἐκδικ.; MG 17 304 *S* Lord ⲣ ⲡⲁⲕ. ⲡⲓⲙⲁⲕ.; c ϩⲡ-: Ex 12 12 *S* (*B* do ⲛϩⲣⲏⲓ ϧⲉⲛ-) ⲉⲕⲇ. ποι. ⲉⲛ. ⳁ ⲕ., *avenge*: Si 30 6 *S* ⲟⲩⲧⲁⲓⲕ. ἔκδικος, opp ⲧⲁⲓⲭⲁⲣⲓⲥ. ϫⲓ ⲕ., *take vengeance*: Ex 21 20 *S*, Aeg 215 *S*; c ⲛ-: Lev 19 18 *S*, 1 Kg 3 13 *S* ἐκδικ., Aeg 288 *S* ϫⲓ ⲕ. ⲙⲙⲟϥ ⲉϫⲛⲡⲡⲁⲣⲁⲛⲟⲙⲓⲁ δίκας εἰσπράσσειν ἐπί; BM 228 2 *S* ⳁⲛⲁϫⲓ

ⲕ. ⲙⲙⲟⲟⲩ ϩⲁⲡⲉⲅⲡⲟⲃⲉ, R 2 1 41 S ϫⲓ ⲙⲡⲉⲕ.
ⲙⲙⲡⲧⲁⲧⲥⲱⲧⲙ ⲡⲓⲙ, Mor 25 187 S ⲉⲕⲡⲁϫⲓ ⲕ.
ⲙⲙⲟϥ ⲛⲥⲁⲟϥ ?, C 43 222 B ⲧⲉⲡⲡⲁϣⲓ ϫⲃⲁ ⲙⲙⲟϥ;
c ϩⲛ-: Si 5 3 S, 2 Mac 6 15 A ἐκδικ. ϫⲓ ⲕ.
nn m, *retribution, compensation*: Ge 4 15 S ἐκδικού-
μενος, Deu 32 35 S, Mic 7 4 A (ⳃ ⲕ.) ἐκδίκησις,
Jer 27 18 S (ShA 2 345) ἐκδικεῖν ἐπί, Sa 11 21 S
δίκη, PS 50 S bring upon them ⲡⲉⲅⲝ.; ⲉⲓⲣⲉ ⲙⲡϫ.:
Nu 33 4 S ἐκδ. ποι.; PLich A ⲁⲕⲁⲉⲓⲣⲉ (ⲙ)ⲡϫ.
ⲡⲉⲛⲱϫ; ϫⲓ ⲙⲡϫ.: Ap 6 9 S; ⲣⲉϥϫ.: Ps 8
3 S ἐκδικητής.

ⲕⲃⲁ *compulsion & vengeance* v ⲕⲱⲱⲃⲉ.

ⲕⲃⲟ (v Sethe *Verbum* 2 625 & p 461, but cf
ⲧⲕⲃⲟ below), ⲕⲃⲁ S, ⲕⲃⲁⲃ S^aF, ϫⲃⲟⲃ B, ⲕⲃⲉ- S,
ⲕⲏⲃ† SAB, ⲕⲏⲡ† B vb I intr, *be, become cool*: Ps
38 14 B (S ⲙⲧⲟⲛ) ἀναψύχειν, Z 320 S having drunk
ϣⲁⲅⲕ. from poison καταψύχειν, ShIF 104 S
ⲉϥϣⲁⲛⲕ. ϩⲓⲧⲟⲩϫⲁϥ, CO 94 S^a if God ordain
ⲛⲧⲁⲕⲃⲁⲃ from sickness, ShMIF 23 185 S why
hath not heart ⲕ. ⲉⲃⲟⲗ ϩⲙⲡⲣⲱϫⲉ?, DeV 102 B
water that tongue may ϫ. ⲡⲟⲩⲕⲟⲩϫⲓ, AZ 23 113
S molten metals ⲕⲁⲁⲩ ⲛⲥⲉⲕ.   Qual, *cool*: Pro
25 25 SA ψυχρός; Dan 3 50 B διασυρίζειν; BM
320 S ⲟⲩⲁⲏⲣ ⲉϥⲕ. (*sic* MS) εὔδιος (Mor 37 76 om),
ShMiss 4 283 S water ⲉⲥⲕ., opp ⲉⲥϩⲙⲙ.
II tr, *make cool*: Ge 18 4 B (S ⲙⲧⲟⲛ), Lu 16
24 SB καταψύχειν; ShC 73 23 S we like ⲉⲕⲃⲉ
ⲡⲉⲛⲡⲗⲁⲥ.   Cf ⲧⲕⲃⲟ.
—— SBF nn m, *coolness*: 1 Kg 20 5 S δείλη,
Lev 6 13 S (B ϩⲁⲛⲁⲣⲟⲩϩⲓ) δειλινός; Ac 3 19 B
(S ⲙⲧⲟⲛ) ἀνάψυξις; ShBM 263 2 S ⲕ. & ⲭⲁϥ,
PS 348 S opp ⲕⲁⲩⲙⲁ, ϩⲙⲟⲙ, ShRE 10 161 S
opp ϩⲙⲙⲉ, MG 25 63 B paral ⲙⲧⲟⲛ, Mor 23 35
S great ⲕ. came upon them = ib 24 25 F ⲁⲡⲉⲕⲃⲁⲃ
ⲧⲁϩⲁⲩ, Tri 147 S برد.   As adj: ShC 42 195
S ⲡⲡⲁϩⲣⲉ ⲡⲕ. ⲛ ⲉⲧⲕⲏⲃ, Va 61 94 B ⲡⲓϣⲓ ⲡϫ.
† ⲕ., ϫ., *make cool*: Lu 16 24 B (S ⲕ.) καταψύχειν; Jud 3 20 S θερινός; ShR 2 3 43 S dwellings
ⲉⲩ† ⲕ. in summer, TstAb 224 B ⲫⲁϩⲣⲓ ⲉⲧ† ϫ.,
Z 637 S sim.; Va 58 13 B ⲫⲣⲉϥ† ϫ. ⲛⲛⲏ ⲉⲧⲣⲟⲕϩ.
ϫⲓ ⲕ., ϭⲓ ϫ., *get cooling, refreshment*: MG 25
362 B came from reaping ⲉϩⲣⲟⲩϭⲓ ϫ., Am 3 15
S (B om) house ⲉⲧϫⲓ ⲕ. ⲙⲡϣⲱⲙ θερινός, DeV
156 B sim.
ⲕⲃⲱⲟⲩ B nn (?), *coolness*: Jer 22 14 high places
ⲉⲩⲡⲉϣⲡ ⲕ. ῥιπιστός. V Spg *Kopt Etym* no 5.
ⲧⲕⲃⲟ B vb tr, *make cool*: Jer 6 7 ψύχειν (so
ⲕⲃⲟ S ? for ⲧⲕⲃⲟ, cf ⲕⲧⲟ, ⲥⲧⲟ).

ⲕⲱⲃϩ, ⲕⲟⲟⲃϩ S, ⲕⲟⲃϩ B nn, *sinew, cord*: Jud
16 7 S νεῦρον; P 44 71 π(τ)έρνα, χόρδη عصب =
43 42 زر; Sa 19 17 S ⲟⲩⲗⲗⲉ ⲛⲕ. (Gk diff) melody
on *strings* (cf ⲟⲩⲗⲗⲉ ⲛⲭⲱ), ShA 1 40 S ⲙⲙⲟⲩⲧ

ⲡⲡⲉⲅⲙⲏⲣⲟⲥ (*sic* l) ϣⲁϩⲣⲁⲓ ⲉⲡⲉⲅⲕ., BMis 241 =
298 S a 4-ply whip ⲡⲕ. = Mor 30 16 F ⲉⲥⲁⲓ ⲛⲧ
ⲡⲣⲁ = Va 866 τετράπλοκον, cf Mun 35 sim (ⲧⲁⲩⲗⲉ
i e ταυρέα).   ⲃⲗ ⲕ., *cut sinews*: Ge 49 6 SB,
Deu 21 4 S (B ϫⲱϫⲓ), Jos 11 6 S (var ⲕⲟⲟ.) νευροκοπεῖν; Tob 2 4 S στραγγαλοῦν; ⲣⲉϥϣⲉⲧ ⲕ.
hamstringer P 44 94 S العصب قطاعين.   Cf ⲕⲱⲣϥ.

ⲕⲁⲕ SF, ϫⲁⲕ B nn as pl, *part of bird*: Mor 38
62 S ἀλέκτωρ killed, ⲁⲓⲕⲁⲑⲁⲣⲓϩⲉ ⲡⲡⲉϥⲕ. & put it
into cooking pot, BKU 1 26 (2) F recipe begins
ⲡⲉⲕ. ⲉⲡⲓϩⲁⲗⲉⲧ if burnt.   Montp 128 B ⲡⲓϫ. رش
= K 170 ⲕⲁⲕⲟⲓ.   Same word?

ⲕⲁⲕ in compounds   v ⲕⲱⲕ.

ⲕⲟⲩⲕ S nn as pl, *rind* (?): Ryl 106 5 in preparation of bdellium ⲥⲁⲧ ⲡⲉϥⲕ. ⲉⲃⲟⲗ.   Or ? l ⲕⲟⲩⲕⲉ
q v.

ⲕⲟⲩⲕ S nn f, *a bird* (?): P 46 146 ⲧⲕ. قيوق ام
(l قويق) after bird names, between ⲙⲉⲣⲉ & ⲧⲉⲡϩ.
Cf قوق *small owl* (Dozy), v also ϫⲁⲕⲕⲁⲙⲁⲩ &
ⲃⲁⲓ *night raven*.

ⲕⲟⲩⲕ, ϭⲟⲩϭ S nn (?), as epithet of ϣⲏ ⲛⲃⲛⲛⲉ:
J 65 58 among properties of monastery, κώμη,
χωρίον, ϣⲏ ⲛⲃ. ⲕ., well, field or meadow; Cai
42573 1 recipe ⲃⲛⲧ ⲛϭ. ⲙⲁⲣⲏⲥ.   *Cf* dem *bne
kwk* PHauswaldt, DM Index 905 b, κουκιοφόρον
(δένδρον) dûm palm.

ⲕⲱⲕ SAA²BF, ϫⲱⲕ B (K 231), ⲕⲉⲕ- SBF,
ⲕⲟⲕ⸗ SB, ⲕⲁⲕ⸗ S, ⲕⲁⲁⲕ⸗ SA, ⲕⲉⲕ⸗ F, ⲕⲏⲕ† SBF,
ⲕⲁ(ⲁ)ⲕ† A, ⲣ ⲥ ⲕⲁⲕ- SABF, vb I tr, *peel, strip off,
divest*: Ge 30 37 SB λεπίζειν; 4 Kg 6 6 S ἀποκνίζειν; Sa 13 11 S περιξύειν; Joel 1 7 S (C 42 196)
A (B = Gk) λευκαίνειν; Nu 12 10 B ⲕ. ⲛⲥⲉⲣⲧ
λεπρᾶν, Mk 14 3 F ⲡⲛ ⲉⲧⲕⲏⲕ (l ⲕⲉⲕ) ⲥⲁⲃϩ λεπρός;
K 231 B قشر; MG 25 155 B shepherd treats
mangy sheep ϣⲁⲧⲉϥⲕ. ⲡⲓⲡⲭⲉⲣϫⲓ (cf ⲕ. ⲉⲃⲟⲗ),
Ryl 160 S of a crop (? flax, cf Is 19) ⲧⲁϩⲟⲟⲗⲉϥ
ⲧⲁⲥⲟⲙⲉϥ ⲧⲁⲕⲟⲕⲕϥ.
II intr S, *peel off, become bare*: Mor 18 70
leprosy ⲕ. ⲛⲟⲉ ⲛⲟⲩϣⲉⲗⲃⲉ, var ib 19 78 ϭⲱⲗ,
P 129^16 2 ⲁⲧⲉϥϥⲁⲡⲉ ⲕ. not a hair remaining.
—— SAB nn m, *bareness, nakedness*: Ge 9 22
S (B ⲃⲱϣ) γύμνωσις; Lev 13 24 B (S ϫⲟⲩϥ)
κατάκαυμα; Deu 24 8 B ⲕ. ⲛⲥⲉⲣⲧ ἀφὴ τῆς λέπρας,
El 120 S ⲟⲩⲕ. ⲛⲥⲱϩϥ = ib 90 A ⲕⲟⲕ.   As adj:
Is 19 9 SB ⲙⲁϩⲉ ⲛⲕ. σχιστός *split, carded*.
—— ⲉⲃⲟⲗ SB, meaning as ⲕⲱⲕ tr: MG 25
246 B head ⲕⲏⲕ ⲉⲃ. βιβρώσκειν; Sh(?)Mor 54 98
S^f Jacob ⲕ. ⲛⲡⲃⲁⲣⲱⲙ ⲉⲃ. (Ge 30 37), BM 290 2 S
ⲁϥⲕ. ⲉⲃ. some of painting with his nail, MG 25 126
B rolling stone will ⲕ. ⲛⲧⲉϥϭⲉⲣϫⲓ ⲉⲃ.

—— ⲁϧⲏⲅ SAA²F, ⲁϧⲛⲟⲩ AF, ⲉϧⲏⲅ S, but S mostly as ⲕⲱ (ⲕⲁⲁⲍ) ⲕⲁϧⲏⲅ (v KKS 67) a tr, *strip, make naked*, c ⲛ̄- of thing discarded: Lev 6 4 S (B ⲃ̄ⲱϣ), Job 11 15 S (B do), Is 32 11 S ⲕⲁⲁⲍ & ⲕⲏ = F ⲕⲉⲕⲍ & ⲕⲏⲕ (B diff), Lu 10 30 S (B ⲃ̄ⲱϣ) ἐκδύειν; EstC 13 S, Zech 3 4 S ⲕⲁⲁⲍ = A ⲕⲁⲁⲕⲍ (B ⲱⲗⲓ ⲉⲃⲟⲗ ϩⲓ-), 1 Kg 17 39 S (B do) ἀφαιρεῖν, Deu 21 13 S (B do) περιαιρ.; AP (Berl Sitzb '09 218) A² ⲕⲁ]ⲕⲥ a., BG 69 S ⲙ̄ⲡⲛ̄ⲥⲁⲡⲧⲣⲉⲥⲕⲁⲕⲥ a., PVi A ⲉⲧⲁϥⲕⲁⲁⲕϥ a. ⲛ̄ⲡϧⲁⲣⲙⲁ, BMEA 10587 S ⲁⲓ]ⲕⲁⲁⲕϥ a. ⲛ̄ⲡⲉϥϧⲟⲓⲧⲉ, Mor 41 144 S ⲕⲁⲧⲏⲅⲧⲛ̄ ⲕⲁ. = ib 39 38 F ⲕⲉⲕⲧⲏⲅⲧⲛ̄ a. = C 86 57 B ⲃ̄ⲁϣⲟⲏⲡⲟⲩ, BMis 236 S ⲁϥⲕⲁⲁϥ ⲕⲁ. of old man = Mor 30 10 F ⲕⲉⲕϥ a., Mor 18 14 S ⲉⲅⲕⲱ ⲙⲙⲟⲟⲩ ⲕⲁ., var ib 19 23 S ⲕⲱⲕ ⲙ̄. a., Leyd 395 S tree ⲙⲉⲥⲕⲱⲕ a. (or ⲕⲱ ⲕⲁ. as throughout) ⲛ̄ⲡⲉⲥϭⲱⲃⲉ, Pcod 45 S sim.   Qual: Ge 3 10 S (B ⲃ̄ⲏϣ), Pro 23 31 SA, Mk 14 52 SF (B do) γυμνὸς εἶναι, BHom 93 S God ⲕⲏⲕ a. ⲛ̄ⲧⲥⲁⲣⲝ, BM 181 1 S ⲥⲉⲕⲏⲕ a. ⲛ̄ⲧⲕⲁⲕⲓⲁ γυμνοῦν; Hos 2 3 A (B do) ⲕⲁⲕ a. ἐκδύ.; TU 43 17 A ⲉⲅⲕⲁⲁⲕ a., ShC 42 114 S ⲡⲉⲧⲕⲏⲕ ⲉϧⲏⲅ. b intr S, *be naked*: Ge 9 21 (B ⲃ̄ⲱϣ ⲉⲃⲟⲗ) γυμνοῦν, Z 284 Noah ⲁϥⲕⲱⲕ ⲉϧⲏⲅ.

—— ⲁϧⲏⲅ S nn m, *nakedness*: Deu 28 48 (B ⲃ̄ⲱϣ), Ro 8 35 (B do) γυμνότης, JTS 10 400 how fair is she ⲉⲁⲛⲉⲥⲕ. a.

P c in compounds: ⲕⲁⲕⲃⲁⲗ B, *with bare eye* (lids) Lev 21 20 (S diff, v ⲗⲉⲯ) πτίλος (?), cf PMéd 56 S ⲛ̄ⲃⲁⲗ ⲉⲧⲕⲏⲕ & names ⲕⲁⲕⲃⲁⲗ Dict Arch Chrét 1 1570 = ? Πκακουϧαλ, Κακτζακ (? *hairless* Preisigke), Win 5 ⲡⲕⲁⲕϧⲟ (m); (Κακό is f); ⲕⲁⲕⲥⲏⲃⲓ F, *bare-shinned*, PStras 555 Chael ⲛ̄ⲕ. c., cf PMéd 292 S ⲉⲣⲉⲡⲉϥⲥ. ⲕⲏⲕ; ⲕⲟⲕϣⲁⲣ DeV 2 202; ⲕⲁⲕⲥⲉϧⲧ B, *leprous* Mt 26 6 = F ⲉⲧⲕⲏⲕ ⲙ̄ⲡⲥⲁⲃⲉ = S ⲡⲉⲧⲥⲟⲃ̄ϩ λέπρος; ⲕⲁⲕϧⲣⲁϥ B *bare-faced*: Miss 4 159 (cf AZ 13 57) = Mor 18 100 S ϭⲁⲗⲡ ϩ., var ib 19 101 S φⲁⲗⲁⲕⲣⲟⲥ, cf ⲛ̄ⲕⲁⲕϧⲟ above.

ⲕⲟⲩⲕⲉ S, ⲕⲟⲩⲕⲓ B nn f, *rind, skin* (DM crocodile's egg skin): Cant 4 3 S λέπυρον, Sa 13 11 S φλοιός, P 44 81 = 43 56 S δερμοϧάς (sic l?) ⲛ̄ⲕ. ⲛ̄ⲡⲉⲣⲙⲁⲛ تشر الرمان; sim in recipes Z 628 S, PMéd 321 S; Z 629 S ⲕ. ⲛ̄ⲗⲓⲃⲁⲛⲟⲥ; Mor 51 34 S ⲕ. ⲛ̄ⲉⲙ̄ϫⲱⲗ; SHel 86 S no meal in granary, but only ⲟⲩⲥⲙⲟⲧ ⲛ̄ⲕ. *chaff*(?); ShC 73 145 S ⲕ. *crusts* reserved for sick, BMOr 6201 A 180 S account ϧⲁⲕ. (or ? diff word), Mor 48 81 S tortured ϣⲁⲡⲧⲉⲛⲉⲕ. ⲙ̄ⲡⲉϥⲥⲱⲙⲁ ϭⲱⲗ = C 43 140 B ϣⲁⲣ, BMar 23 S sim, ib 44 ⲁⲧⲉϥⲁⲡⲉ ⲉⲓ(ϣⲉ?) ⲛ̄ⲥⲁⲧⲕ.; K 246 B διπλοῖς ⲟⲩⲥⲧⲟⲗⲏ ⲉⲥⲟⲓ ⲛ̄ⲕ. ⲥⲡⲟⲅⲧ̄ مضربة قشر اثنين with double *lining*.   V ⲕⲟⲩⲕ.

ⲕⲏⲕⲥ, ⲕⲉⲕⲥ B nn f, *what is peeled off, strip, scale*: Ge 30 37 (S ⲧⲟ) λέπισμα; Nu 17 3 (S ⲃⲏⲧⲉ), Ac 9 18 (S ϧⲃⲥ) λεπίς; K 262 ⲕⲉ. قشر, ib ⲕⲏ. تفريق (l تصفيف) *clap* Lab); MG 25 397, C 86 295 *scales* from eyes like ϣⲛⲓϥⲓ.

ⲕⲁⲕⲉ S *cake*   v ϭⲁⲁϭⲉ.

ⲕⲁⲕⲉ S, ⲕⲉⲕⲉ AA², ⲕⲉⲕⲉⲓ (Ge 1 18) A, ⲭⲁⲕⲓ B, ⲭⲱⲱⲭ O (v ⲃⲁⲓ O) nn m, *darkness*: Deu 5 22 SB, Job 15 30 SB, Jo 3 19 SA²B (F ⲕⲉⲙⲧⲥ) σκότος, Mic 3 6 SAB, Mt 10 27 SB σκοτία, Ps 87 6 S (B ⲙⲁ ⲛ̄ⲭ.) σκοτεινός; He 12 18 SB, 2 Pet 2 17 SB ζόφος; PS 49 S ⲛ̄ⲕ. ⲛ̄ⲧⲉ ⲡⲉⲭⲁⲟⲥ, AM 300 B ⲟⲩⲭ. *covered the soldiers*.   As adj: Ge 15 12 SB, Ps 142 3 SB, Is 45 3 SB σκοτεινός, Pro 2 13 SA (B ⲛ̄ⲧⲉ ⲛ̄ⲭ.) σκότος nn; Sa 17 15 S ἀσίδηρος; PS 113 S ϩⲗⲟⲥⲧⲛ̄ ⲛ̄ⲕ., ib 187 S *count world* ϩⲱⲥ ⲕ. ⲛ̄ⲕ., C 43 32 B *cast into* ⲟⲩⲙⲁ ⲛ̄ⲭ. ⲣ̄ ⲕ. S, ⲉⲣ ⲭ. B *be, become dark*: Job 3 9 SB, Ps 68 23 S (B ⲉⲣ ⲭⲣⲉⲙⲧⲥ), Mt 24 29 B (S ϣⲱⲡⲉ ⲛ̄ⲕ.), Ro 1 21 SB σκοτοῦν, Mt 6 23 SB σκοτει. εἶναι; Miss 8 178 S ⲁⲡⲉⲕϧⲏⲧ ⲣ̄ ⲕ. ⲉⲣⲟⲕ, Va 58 191 B ⲟⲓ ⲛ̄ⲭ. *in his thoughts*, BM 342 S demon ⲁϥⲣ̄ ⲕ. *became invisible*, PMéd 89 S remedy for eyes ⲉⲧⲱ ⲛ̄ⲕ.   V ⲉⲃⲏ.

ⲕⲁⲕⲉ S *pupil* of eye   v ⲕⲉⲕⲉ b.

ⲕⲁⲕⲟ S nn, prob is κόκκος: Ez 16 11 (B ⲕⲟⲕⲕⲟⲥ, Gk diff, v Pey 364), ShA 2 64 ϧⲱⲥ ⲛ̄ⲕ., Louvre 10022 ϣⲗⲟⲡⲗⲉⲡ ⲛ̄ⲕ., JTS 8 242 ⲱⲛⲉ ⲛ̄ⲧⲁⲧⲟ.   Elsewhere κόκκος (κόκκινος) is ⲕⲟⲕⲕⲟⲥ.

ⲕⲁⲕⲟⲓ, -ⲱⲓ B nn m, *mucus of nose*: K 160 مخاط.

ⲕⲉⲕⲉ S a nn m, *child*: Deu 28 57 ⲛ̄ⲕ. (Mor ⲡⲕⲉⲕⲉⲧ, B ϣⲏⲣⲓ) τέκνον, Z 617 *swathed like* ⲛⲉⲓⲕ. ⲛ̄ⲁⲡⲟⲛⲧⲟⲥ, Klio 13 31 (triling glos) *infantes · τὰ βρέφη·* ⲛ̄ⲕ. b ⲕⲉⲕⲉ, ⲕⲁⲕⲉ, ⲕⲁⲁⲕⲉ nn m & f, *pupil* (lit *maiden*) of eye: no gender, Deu 32 10 (B ⲁⲗⲟⲩ), Pro 20 20 (A ⲁⲗⲟⲩ) κόρη, Journ Soc Or Research '28 27 *guard him like* ⲟⲩⲕⲉⲕⲉ ⲃⲁⲗ (sic bis); f, Zech 2 8 (BHom 28, AB do) ⲕ., P 44 69 حدقة, Mor 37 165 *sight in* ⲧⲕ. *as wick in lamp*; m, Aeg 242 ⲕ., Tri 288.   For name ⲕⲁⲕⲃⲁⲗ v ⲕⲱⲕ (p c).

ⲕⲟⲩⲕⲉ S, ⲕⲟⲩⲕⲓ B   v ⲕⲱⲕ.

ⲕⲁⲕⲟⲓ B   v ⲕⲁⲕⲧⲉ.

ⲕⲁⲕⲕⲁⲙⲁⲩ B   v ⲭⲁⲕⲕⲁⲙⲁⲩ.

ⲕⲟⲩⲕⲗⲉ S, ⲕⲟⲩⲕⲗⲓ Sᶠ, ⲕⲟⲩⲕⲗⲁ F, ⲕⲟⲩⲗⲗⲁ (? ⲕⲟⲩⲕⲟⲩⲗⲗⲁ) B nn f, *hood, cowl* of monks, whence ? κουκούλλιον (in CO 395 S ⲕⲟⲩⲕⲗⲓⲛ, K 120 B ⲕⲟⲩⲕⲗⲓⲟⲛ غفار, opp ⲕⲗⲁϥⲧ): RE 9 164 S *tailoress sends 2 ⲕ. to bishop*, BAp 125 S *levitum, schema*, ⲕ. & *girdle as grave-clothes* = MIE 2 418 B ⲕⲟⲩⲗⲗⲁ = P arab 4785 210 قلسـ, P 44 91

S Ar do., Mor 31 15 S⸗ ⲕⲟⲩⲕⲗⲓ, BM 699, AZ 23 41 F, C 86 177 B ⲕⲟⲕⲉⲗ. Cf كاكزلي Almk 1 320.

ⲕⲟⲩⲕⲙⲙ S, ⲕⲟⲩⲕⲉⲙ F v ⲕⲙⲕⲙ.

ⲕⲟⲩⲕⲟⲩⲙⲁⲩ S nn, pan : Ep 549 list of metal vessels. Cf κούκουμα cucuma.

ⲕⲁⲕⲟⲩⲡⲁⲧ S⸗, ⲕⲟⲩⲕⲟⲩⲫⲁⲧ B, ⲕⲟⲩⲕ[ⲟⲩ]ⲡⲉⲧ F, koukoupet DM, κουκούφα (cf דוכיפת), nn m f, hoopoe : K 168 B هدهد (1 var عنقا, cf P 44 56 = γύψ by error), BKU 1 26 (1) F to obtain a certain stone by help of ⲧⲕ., Cai 42573 2 S⸗ blood of ⲕ., DM 10 31 sim. V Rec 18 131. Cf ⲕⲁⲣⲁⲡⲏⲡ.

ⲕⲏⲕⲥ B v ⲕⲱⲕ s f.

ⲕⲁⲕⲧⲉ (P 44, so Pey, but not found), ⲕⲁⲧⲕⲉ S (Z 630 ? same), ⲕⲁⲕⲟⲓ, -ⲧⲓ, ⲭⲁⲕⲟⲓ B nn f, louse : K 173 B ⳨ⲕ. قمل, BMOr 8775 113 B φθεῖρες ⲡⲕ. قمل, Z l c S ⲥⲱⲙⲁ ϩⲱⲕⲉ ⲉϥⲱ ⲡⲕ. ⲥⲉⲕ ⲭ. B: Jer 50 12 (S diff) φθειρίζειν.

ⲕⲗ A v ⲕⲗⲗⲉ.

ⲕⲁⲗ B v ⲕⲗⲗⲉ.

ⲕⲉⲗ, ⲕⲏⲗ B nn m & sg as pl, a fish (of species شال Sobhy): K 171 قيل.

ⲕⲉⲗ DM V 30 4 nn, unidentified animal.

ⲕⲏⲗ S nn as pl, iron object in list of metal varia : PLond 4 515 ⲡⲉⲥϫⲉⲣⲓⲧ ⲙⲡⲡⲉⲥⲧⲃⲛⲧ ⲙⲡⲛⲉⲥⲕⲏⲗ ⲛⲃⲉⲛⲓⲡⲉ. ? = ⲕⲗⲗⲉ.

ⲕⲱⲗ S nn, meaning uncertain (joint Chassinat): PMéd 204 among maladies ⲡⲡⲗⲩⲧⲛ ⲙⲛⲕ. ⲛⲡⲁⲧ ⲉⲧⲥⲱⲟⲩϩ ⲉϩⲟⲩⲛ, BM 525 S⸗ charm against ⲛⲕ. ⲛⲥⲛⲟⲟⲩϥ and pains in bones. Same ?

ⲕⲱⲗ vb v ⲥⲱⲗ.

ⲕⲗⲁ (ⲕⲉⲗⲁ) F v ⲥⲁⲗⲟ.

ⲕⲗⲉ, ⲕⲉⲗⲏ S, ⲕⲗⲏ, ⲭⲗⲏ B, ⲕⲉⲗⲉ F nn m, vessel for liquids : Kr 242 S ⲕⲗⲉ ⲛⲛⲁⲩ of honey, BKU 1 133 S ⲧϥⲉ ⲡⲕⲉⲗⲏ of oil, CMSS 78 F ⲕ. & ⲁⲡⲁⲧ, K 151 B زير (v Fleischer De Glos 20, Almk 2 49). Cf ⲁⲕⲗⲏ.

ⲕⲗⲉ S nn m, meaning unknown : WS 93 ... ϩⲱⲕ ⲉ[?]ⲉⲡⲉⲓⲕ. ⲡⲃ[.

ⲕⲗⲏ S nn f, cat : P 43 60 ⲙⲁϫⲉ ⲕ. ودن القطّ cat's ear, a plant, cf ὑποχοιρίς (in P 44 83 ورق السدر by error, v ⲁⲡⲉ). Cf DM V 7 1 msz n qlet. ⲕⲁⲗⲏ (ⲁⲕⲗⲏ q v) SB weasel : Lev 11 29 SB ابن عرس, K 173 B عرس ? same. As name ⲧⲕⲁⲗⲉ ST 152. Cf γαλῆ (as in Lev l c).

ⲕⲗⲓ S v ⲕⲣⲓ.

ⲕⲗⲟ SA DM, ⲭⲗⲟ B, ⲕⲗⲁ F nn m, vegetable (?) poison used for arrows : BMis 284 S ⲥⲟⲧⲉ ⲡⲕ. wherewith to wound, R 1 3 58 S sim, AZ 24 90 (sic, not ⲭⲗⲟ) B ⲥⲟⲫⲛⲉϥ ⲛⲭ., El 80 A ⲡⲕ. ⲡⲡⲥⲁⲧⲉ ; used by magicians : BMar 37 = KKS 45 S ⲡⲁϥⲣⲉ ⲡⲕ. opp ⲙⲁⲧⲟⲩ ⲛϩⲟϥ snake poison, AM 60 B sim, but PSBA 33 116 S ⲕ. ⲛϩⲁⲣⲁⲕⲱⲡ (prob improperly) ; produces cold numbness (? aconite) : PSBA l c cold shall encompass & penetrate as ⲕ. ⲡⲁⲣ., Mor 50 49 S ⲉⲓϩⲣⲡⲱϩϥ ⲙⲡⲉⲕ. of Hell, Mor 23 35 S pits full of ⲱϭϩ ⲛⲟⲉ ⲙⲡⲉⲕ. = ib 24 25 F full of snakes ϩⲓϫⲉⲃ ⲡⲕⲗⲁ ; DM 24 27 sym n ⲕⲗⲟ as if plant-name, cf Lev 21 20 B eyes colour of ⲭ. = S with ϩⲁⲧⲁⲓⲗⲉ in eyes ἔφηλος (var λεύκωμα vid). V KKS 43 ff, LMis 373.

ⲕⲗⲱ S nn, ? same as ⲕⲗⲟ : Mor 44 33 death of Judas's wife foretold, ⲥⲛⲁⲣ ⲡϣⲟⲩ ⲡⲕ. ⲉⲧⲉⲡⲉⲗϭⲟⲓⲛⲉ ⲡⲥⲱⲟⲧ ⲉⲧⲉⲥϣⲟⲩⲱⲃⲉ. V ⲉⲣϭⲟⲓ.

ⲕⲗⲟ A hole v ϣⲕⲟⲗ.

ⲕⲗⲱ S v ϭⲗⲱ.

ⲕⲁⲗⲉ S nn m, meaning unknown : Ann 18 285 burn wood so as to leave no ash ⲛⲧϥ ⲡⲕ. ⲉϫⲱϥ.

ⲕⲁⲗⲏ B v ⲕⲗⲏ.

ⲕⲉⲗⲓ BO v ⲕⲗⲗⲉ.

ⲕⲉⲗⲟⲩ B vb tr, meaning uncertain : C 43 212 whilst sailing southward hegemôn spent day eating & drinking ⲁⲩⲕ. ⲙⲡⲓⲗⲁⲃⲟ = P ar 4893 118 ... اقام يأكل ويشرب والقلع مرضي the sail being slack, so ? to loosen, slacken. Cf ⲗⲁⲧⲟ (ⲗ. ⲡϭⲱⲃ).

ⲕⲱⲗⲉ S nn v ϭⲱⲗⲉ.

ⲕⲱⲱⲗⲉ ⲉⲃⲟⲗ S vb intr, meaning uncertain, ? return, so collapse (opp swell, protrude) : ShBerlOr 1613 1 = P 130[4] 121 if Mary conceived Christ ⲉⲓⲉ ⲟⲩⲕⲟⲩⲡ ⲁϩⲏⲧⲥ ⲙⲟⲟϣⲉ ⲉⲃⲟ ⲛ ⲕ. ⲉⲃ. ? = ϭⲱⲱⲗⲉ ⲉⲃ. C 73 152.

ⲕⲉⲗⲉⲃⲓⲛ SBF, ⲕⲉⲗⲁ-, ⲕⲁⲗⲁ- (ST 125) S, nn m, axe, pickaxe : 3 Kg 6 7 S (BHom 111), EpJer 14 BF, Ez 9 2 S (P 130[2] 86) B, MG 25 208 B πέλεκυς, πέλυξ ; Deu 19 5 SB, Is 10 15 SB, Mt 3 10 SB ἀξίνη ; Ps 73 6 SB ἀξ. & πέλ. ; ShZ 637 S branches cut with ⲕ. or (ⲉ)ⲓⲛⲉ, Ryl 239 S mason's ⲕ., carpenter's ⲉⲓⲛⲉ, Bodl(P) f 24 S ⲕ. ⲛϭⲓⲝ, WS 122 S sim, Mor 36 78 S rock that no mason (λατόμος) may cut with ⲕ., C 43 78 B bade hack them with ϩⲁⲛⲕ. Prob is πέλεκυς IgR 84, Spg, but cf AZ 62 55.

As name : Κελεβῖν (Preisigke).

ⲕⲉⲗⲕⲁ B nn m as pl, lump, pustule : Ex 9 9 ⲕ. ⲉⲩϫⲏϥ φλυκτίς ἀναζέουσα جدري منتفخ, K 159

ⲡⲓⲅⲉⲗⲗⲁ (*l* ⲅⲉⲗⲕⲁ) جدري ورشكين, MG 25 394 ⲑⲁⲡⲕ. ⲡϫⲱϥ causing blindness = Gött ar 114 143 مرض جدري, Va 58 77 ⲕ. ⲡϫⲟϥⲟ destroyed eyes. جدري also = ⲗⲉⲯ *q v.*

ⲕⲁⲗⲟⲩⲕⲓ *B nn m, young camel or ox:* K 165 بقر (*l* بكر, var بكر تعود, as all MSS, cf AZ 13 57). Or *?l* ⲕⲁⲙⲟⲩⲗⲓ. *V* Byzant Z 30 323.

ⲕⲉⲗⲕⲉⲃ *S nn (?), on oval figure beside drawings of 2 animals, at end of Kropp K ϧⲏⲧ ⲙⲡⲓⲛ (ⲡ)ⲕ., so *?* epithet of ⲡⲓⲛ *mouse.*

(ⲕⲟⲗⲕⲗ), ⲕⲉⲗⲕⲱⲗ† *S vb, be round, curved (?):* R 2 1 71 *S* among man's bodily beauties ϧⲉⲡⲡⲁⲧ ⲉⲩⲱⲗⲕ ⲉⲩⲥⲟⲩⲧⲱⲛ ⲉⲩⲕⲗⲕⲱⲗ knees drawn in, straight & *rounded.* In place-name (?): POxy 997 Τακολκεῖλις. *Cf* ϭⲱⲗ (ⲕⲱⲗ).

ⲕⲁⲗⲕⲓⲗ (CO 454, ST 125 &c), -ⲕⲉⲗ (Louvre R 93 vo), ⲕⲉⲗⲕⲓⲗ (CO 466), ϭⲉⲗϭⲓⲗ (Ryl 94, TT 77), ⲕⲉⲗⲕⲉⲗ (BerlP 11965 1), ϭⲉⲓⲗϭⲉⲓⲗ (PLond 4 516) *S nn m, wheel, cf* גלגל, גליל, גלגל, γελγέλ (PO 16 856): Ostr N. de G. Davies ⲕ. ⲡⲣⲟⲙⲡⲧ, CO 466 ⲕ. ⲡⲡⲉⲧ, PLond ϭ. ⲡⲟⲃⲉⲗⲟⲥ, Ryl ϭ. ⲙⲡⲣⲟⲓ, BerlP ⲧⲣⲟⲭⲟⲥ which Adonai Messias named ⲕ., Louvre]ϧⲁⲙ ⲡⲕ. *wheelwright.* Also ϭⲁⲗⲓⲗ: as torture, Gu 61 = عجل, BIF 15 253 sim, *ib* 14 112 ϭ. ⲙⲡⲉⲡⲓⲡⲉ, Mor 46 17 ϭ. ⲡⲣⲁⲙϣⲉ, P 43 27 دولاب, AZ 23 116 in alchem recipe; or ϭⲗⲓⲗ: BSG 179 = *B* ⲧⲣⲟⲭⲟⲥ.

ⲕⲟⲕⲉⲗ *B nn, meaning unknown:* Va 57 226 dry places & land ⲡⲁⲧⲕ. ⲟⲩⲟϩ ⲡⲁⲧⲣⲗⲓ ⲛϭⲟⲡ ἔνθα νοτὶς οὐκ ἔστιν. *Cf* AZ 13 57, also *?* قلقيل clay, mud (Dozy, Spiro).

ⲕⲉⲗⲕⲟⲩⲗⲉ, -ⲱⲗⲉ *S nn as pl, meaning prob as* ⲕⲉⲗⲕⲁ: EW frag of *scala* (Nitria) ⲡⲕⲉⲗⲕⲟⲗⲓ جدري between ψώρα ἀγρία & μονόφθαλμος, Z 633 physician operates not with ξύριον or φάρμακον until all ⲡⲕ. have appeared on sick man's body, Bodl(P) a 2 7 in recipes for gilding (?), knead with water ⲁⲁϥ ⲡⲕⲉⲗⲕⲱⲗⲉ, Ryl 106 67 (*sic l*) sim, Bodl *lc* 11 knead with alkaline water, ⲉⲃⲱ (*l* ⲉϥⲟ) ⲡⲕ., WS 94 ⲕⲉⲗⲕⲟⲗⲉ ⲡⲕⲁⲡ ⲡⲁⲃⲱ *ball* of net-string (or *?* hair, *v* ⲕⲁⲡ). As name (m): Κελκουλέ POxy 1911.

ⲕⲗⲁⲕⲗⲉⲕ *S nn, astragalus,* the plant or its gum: P 43 34 كثيرا بيضا (*v* Löw 50). *Cf* K 182 ⲧⲣⲁⲕⲁⲡⲟⲑⲉ كثيرا.

ⲕⲗⲁⲗ, ⲕⲗⲏⲗ *S,* ⲕⲗⲉⲗ *SAA²F,* ⲭⲗⲁⲗ *B nn m, chain esp on neck:* Ge 41 42 *SB,* Pro 1 9 *SAB,* Hab 2 6 *AB* κλοιός; Nu 31 50 *S* (*B =* Gk), 2 Kg 1 10 *S,* Jth 10 4 *S* χλίδων; AP 11 *A²* ψέλλιον (var κλάλιον); dog's chain: Pro 7 22 *SA* δεσμός; Mor

31 203 *S* ⲟⲩϩⲁⲣ ⲉⲅⲉⲓⲛⲉ ⲙⲙⲟϥ ⲉⲡⲉⲕ., BMis 15 *S* captive ⲉϥⲥⲙⲟⲛⲧ ⲉⲡⲉϥⲕ. like dog; camel's: CO 218 *S* ⲙⲁⲛⲧⲁⲕⲏ (μανδάκη) ⲡⲕ.; BKU 1 21 vo *F* in dying recipe ⲕ. of nitre, BMEA 10391 *S* recipe ⲕ. ⲛⲣⲉⲙⲟⲩ, burnt & pounded, ShP 131⁴ 111 *S* weaving tools ϩⲛⲗⲁⲩ ⲡⲕⲱⲗϩ...ⲕ. ⲡϫⲟⲗⲕⲟⲩ, ST 54 *S* ⲕ. as ἐνέχυρον. *Cf* ⲕⲗⲁⲗⲓⲟⲛ. As name: Πεκλῆλ POxy 1917.

ⲕⲁⲗⲉⲗⲉ (Miss 4 632, BAp 123), -ⲉⲉⲗⲉ (P 43 246), -ⲏⲗⲉ (TurO 15 *sic*), -ⲏⲗⲁ (BKU 1 73), ⲕⲉⲗⲉⲉⲗⲉ (BMis 455, Mor 51 34, 37) *S,* ⲕⲉⲗⲉⲗⲓ (only C 41 10) *B nn f, sonorous wooden board (or pl),* struck to assemble congregation: BAp ⲡⲧⲣ ⲧⲕ. hourly that brethren may pray = MIE 2 417 *B* ϣⲉ ⲛⲉⲱⲟⲩϥ = P ar 4785 207 خدمة الناقوس, BMis ⲕⲱⲗϩ ⲡⲕ. that congreg assemble to church, Miss 4 man shall arise ⲉϥⲕⲱⲗϩ ⲡⲧⲕ. ⲉⲭⲁⲡϣⲱⲡⲉ = Va ar 172 105 ناقوس, P 43 ⲣⲉϥⲕⲱⲗϩ ⲡⲡⲕ. الـ ضارب الناقوس, BKU as punishment ⲧⲛⲥⲱϣⲧ ⲡϣⲁ ⲙⲡⲧⲕ. ⲡⲁⲡⲁ ⲁⲡⲁⲡⲓⲁⲥ, Mor 51 37 among weapons of war ϧⲉⲡⲕ. ⲡϣⲉ ⲡⲣⲁⲕⲟⲧⲉ, *ib* 34 parable of ships ⲁⲙⲡⲟⲩⲕⲟⲡⲟⲛ ⲙⲟⲟⲛⲉ ⲁⲡⲁⲕⲏ ⲡⲕ. ⲉⲣ ⲣⲱⲧ, C 41 he took a small ⲕ. & began to smite demon = Miss 4 308 فاس (*l* ناقوس, *Rev Sémit* 8 156 سهولة *staff*). *Cf* *?* Z 506 ⲕⲁⲗⲗⲏⲣⲉ. *V* ZDMG 68 183. TurO 15 ⲉϣⲱⲡⲉ ⲟⲩⲡ ⲕⲁⲗⲏⲗⲉ ⲙⲙⲁⲩ ⲧⲛⲟⲟⲩ ⲟⲩϣⲟⲡ ⲡⲁⲡ (*sic l*) prob diff word (*?* for ⲕⲁⲡⲑⲏⲗⲉ κανθήλιον *lc bis*). Coptic?

In names Καλεέλε, Πατκ. also Παπκ. (Preisigke) & in place-name, ⲡⲁⲡⲕⲁⲗⲏⲗⲉ, -ⲗⲁ CO 127, Ep 2 144ⁿ.

ⲕⲗⲗⲉ *S,* ⲕⲗ *S* (C 73 72) *A,* ⲕⲉⲗⲓ *BO,* ⲕⲁⲗ *B* (Lev 6 3, 16 4) ⲕⲏⲗⲗⲓ, ⲕⲩⲗⲓ *F,* ⲕⲉⲗ- *SB,* ⲕⲁⲗ- *B nn m* (Ez 47 *B bis*), *f, mostly as pl,* **a** *bolt:* Job 38 10 *SB,* Cant 5 6 *S,* EpJer 17 *BF,* Cl 20 6 *A* sea exceeds not appointed ⲕⲗ, κλεῖθρον; El 44 *A* ϩⲉⲡⲕⲗ, opp ⲙⲟⲭⲗⲟⲥ, TT 101 *S* door has ϣⲟϣⲧ, ⲕ., ⲙⲟⲭⲗⲟⲥ, ⲉⲡⲱ, ShR 2 3 85 *S* sim, Mor 51 38 *S* in parable ⲡⲡⲁⲧ & ⲧⲕ. interpreted as patience & silence. **b** *knee, mostly B:* Deu 28 35 *B* (*S* ⲡⲁⲧ), Ps 108 24 *B* (*S* do), Ac 7 60 *B* (*S* do), MG 25 11 *B,* Va 57 194 *B* ⲡⲓⲕ. ⲡⲧⲉ ⲡⲉⲕϭⲁⲗⲁⲩϫ γόνυ, K 78 *B* †ⲕ. ركبة; Va 58 75 *B* he set babe on his ⲕ., *ib* 57 198 *B* ⲉⲥⲁⲙⲟⲛⲓ ⲙⲙⲟϥ ⲉⲭⲉⲡⲡⲉⲥⲕ., *ib* sim ⲁⲗⲱϫ, Mor 25 11 *S* Lazarus walked on ⲕ. & elbows, for had not hands or feet = Va 61 94 *B,* *ib* 62 186 *B* grieving with face on ⲡⲉϥⲕ., El 110 *S* ⲡⲁϭⲗⲗⲉ ⲡⲥⲉⲃⲱⲗ ⲉⲃⲟⲗ, AM 84 *B* ϩⲁⲡⲕⲉⲗϫ ⲕ. without number (*v* ⲕⲱⲗϫ). **c** *other joints:* Ez 47 3 *B* (BMAd 5997 154 = *S,* Or 1326 فخذين) μηρός, Zech 11 16 *AB,* Z 337 *S* ⲕ. ⲡⲣⲁⲧ ἀστράγαλος;

Job 31 22 *B* (*S* = Gk) κλείς; Dan 10 6 *B* (*S* ⲟⲅⲉ-
ⲣⲏⲧⲉ) σκέλος; C 86 46 *B* they cut off ϯⲕ. ⲛⲧⲉ
ⲧⲉϥϥⲁⲧ = GMir 257 *S* ⲧⲥⲟⲟⲗⲉⲥ ⲛⲧⲟⲅⲉⲣⲏⲧⲉ, ShA
2 87 *S* mud reached to *ankles* ⲛⲕ. or knees ⲛⲡⲁⲧ,
Z 261 *S* slew them so that blood reached ⲕ. of
soldiers = PO 1 414 كب, Wess 18 60 *S* sim, AZ
21 106 *O* her 365 ⲕⲉⲗⲓ (*sic l*, *cf* BKU 1 1 vo 5).
d *limb, trunk B*: Lev 26 30, Nu 14 29, Is 66 24 (*S*
all ϣⲁⲅ) κῶλον.

ⲕⲉⲗⲉⲛⲕⲉⲣ (ⲕ. ⲛⲕⲉⲣ) *S*, ⲕⲁⲗⲁⲛⲕⲉⲣ, -ⲕⲁⲣ *BF* (*v*
place-name) nn m, *elbow* (*v* ⲕⲉⲣ): Job 31 22 *SB*,
Ez 13 18 *SB* ἀγκών, P 43 39 *S*, K 77 *B* مرفق,
P 44 69 *S* = καρπός ἀγκ. عضد, ShC 73 162 *S*
clothes covered arms ϣⲁⲣⲟⲩⲛ ⲉⲡⲉⲛⲕ., Gu 61 *S*
ⲁⲛⲉⲅϭⲓⲝ ⲥⲱⲗⲡ ⲉⲃⲟⲗ ϣⲁⲡⲉⲛⲕ. As place-name
in Fayyûm: Kr 10 &c, BIF 15 258, *cf* χω(ρίον)
Ἀγκών. ⲕⲉⲗⲟⲅⲟⲛⲭϥ *B* nn, *jawbone*: Va 57
271 Samson drank from ⲟⲩⲕ. σιαγών. *Cf* ⲟⲩⲟϭⲉ
(ⲟⲩⲟϫⲓ). ⲣⲁⲙⲕ. *SA²BF*, *bolt-smith, smith*: Ge
4 22 *S*, Job 32 19 *S*, Is 41 7 *S*, 2 Tim 4 14 *S*
(*B* all ⲃⲉⲥⲡⲏⲧ *q* v), AP 4 *A²* χαλκεύς, K 110 *B* حداد;
ShZ 505 *S* ⲣⲁⲙϣⲉ & ⲣ., C 73 72 *S* sim, Ep 49 *S*
ⲟⲩⲧⲉⲭⲛⲏ ⲛⲣ., Pcod 39 *S* ⲣ. testing iron, CMSS
63 *F*.

ⲕⲉⲗⲱⲗ, ⲕⲟⲅⲗⲱⲗ *SB*, ⲕⲟⲗⲟⲗ *S* (J 106), ⲕⲉ-
ⲗⲟⲗ *B* (Bodl g 1) nn m, ⲕⲉⲗⲟⲗⲓ, ⲉⲕⲗⲟⲗⲓ *B* f, pl
? ⲕⲉⲗⲟⲟⲗⲉ *S* (Bodl(P) b 6), *pitcher, jar*: for water,
Z 316, 319 *S*, MG 25 210 *B* βαυκάλιον, C 41 22 *B*
= Miss 4 355 كوز, K 150 *B* f do, MIE 2 390 *B* =
P ar 4785 150 قسط, *cf* Spg 301; Ryl 238, 242 *S*
of bronze; for dates, Sph 10 4 *S*; for fruit ⲉⲓ-
ⲡⲱⲣⲁ (ὀπώρα), BM 1166 *S*, ST 184 *S* obscure.
? Hollow place, ? cellar: PBu 4, 67 (ⲕⲉⲗ-, ⲕⲟⲅⲗ-)
S house consists of ⲣⲓ, ⲥⲩⲙⲡⲟⲥⲓⲟⲛ, ⲕⲟⲓⲧⲱⲛ, ⲕ., *cf*
? J 48 2 ⲡⲏⲓ ⲛⲕ. As name: Κελῶλ, Κελούλις (Prei-
sigke), ⲕⲟⲅⲗⲟⲩⲭ CO 65. As place-name: J 106
18 ⲛⲕ. ⲙⲡⲧⲟⲟⲩ ⲡⲭⲏⲙⲉ = MMA 24 2 6 ⲛⲕ. of Apa
Paul, which *ib* 24 2 4 (= JEA 12 266) is Καύκοις
(*cf* καῦκος, -η, also καυκάλιον as var of βαυκάλιον),
also J 20 49 &c ⲡⲉⲓⲣ ⲛⲕ. (*v* Ep 1 112); also
PLond 4 374 Παροβ Κελῶλ.

ⲭⲗⲟⲗ *B* nn m, prob same: K 150, P 55 11
شربة، ابريق.

ⲕⲉⲗⲱⲗ (or ? ⲁⲕⲉⲗⲱⲗ) *B* nn as pl, *curling hair*:
BMOr 8775 119, P 54 119 ⲛⲁⲕ. شعر مجعد.

ⲕⲗⲱⲓⲗⲓ *B* nn f, *caul, secundina*: K 103 مشيمة
(*sic l*).

ⲕⲗⲟⲟⲗⲉ *SA*, ⲕⲗⲁⲗⲉ *F* nn f, *cloud*, always =
B ϭⲏⲡⲓ: Nu 9 15 *S*, Ps 67 35 *SF*, Nah 1 3 *SA*,
Lu 9 34 *S* νεφέλη; Job 30 15 *S*, Pro 3 20 *SA*, Sa 5
22 *S* νέφος; PS 114 *S* ⲟⲩⲕ. ⲡⲕⲣⲙⲧⲥ, TT 26 *S*
Virgin ⲧⲉⲕ. ⲉⲧⲁⲥⲱⲟⲩ.

ⲕⲗⲟⲟⲗⲉ *S* nn f, meaning unknown, among
agricultural (?) tools: BKU 1 94 ⲧⲟⲩⲁϩⲣⲉ, ⲧⲙⲁⲡⲕⲉ,
ⲧⲣⲉⲗⲙⲓⲥ, ⲧⲉⲕ. (*sic l*, not as AZ 23 75).

ⲕⲗⲗⲁⲙⲉ *A* *v* ⲕⲗⲟⲟⲗⲉ.

ⲕⲉⲗⲗⲟⲝ *B* nn as pl, a *puppy, whelp*: BMOr
8771 82 ⲕⲁⲗ. (as var of ⲕⲁⲗⲟⲅⲕⲓ), *ib* Or 8781
ⲟⲩϩⲱⲣ followed by ⲡⲓⲕⲉⲗ. (جرو) اجراء. *Cf*
قلوص. **b** *buffalo*: BM 920 266, Ryl 453 337
جاموس. Diff words? As name: ⲕⲉⲗⲗⲟⲩⲭ,
ⲕⲗⲟⲩⲭ, f ⲕⲟⲩⲗⲱⲭⲉ, كلوج = Κολλοῦθος, *v* Ep 2 532
n, RylDem 3 259 n & Spg *Aeg u Gr Eigennamen*
18*, where hierogl & dem show it prob an animal
name. *V* Byzant Z 30 323.

ⲕⲉⲗⲙ *S* *v* ϭⲗⲙ.

ⲕⲱⲗⲉⲙ *F*, ⲭⲱⲗⲉⲙ *B*, ⲕⲗⲁⲙ (Pro 1 16), ϭⲗⲁⲙ
AA², ⲭⲟⲗⲉⲙ† *B* vb **a** intr, *hasten*: Ge 45 13 *B*,
Ps 30 3 *B* (*S* ϭⲉⲡⲏ) ταχύνειν; Pro 6 18 *A* (*S* ϭ.,
B ⲓⲏⲥ) σπεύδειν; 1 Thes 2 17 *F* (*SB* do) σπουδάζειν; Ryl 446 *B* ⲡⲉⲧⲉⲥⲭ. ⲉϩⲟⲟⲃⲉϥ κατεπείγειν;
C 43 30 *B* ⲭ. ⲁⲛⲓⲟⲅⲓ, *ib* 43 *B* ⲁϥⲭ. ⲁϥⲉⲣ ⲡⲣⲟⲥⲕⲩ-
ⲛⲓⲛ = Mor 39 11 *S* ⲁϥϭ., Va 57 199 *B* melt frost of
wrath ⲉⲧⲧⲉⲙⲥⲱⲙ ⲟⲩⲟϩ ⲉⲧⲭ†.; **b** tr (refl): Lu
19 6 *B* (*S* ϭ.) σπεύδ., C 89 19 *B* ⲭ. ⲙⲙⲟⲕ ⲁⲙⲟⲩ.

—— *AA²BF* nn m, *haste*: K 99 *B* ⲡⲓⲭ. عرس,
elsewhere only as adv *in haste*: Ps 77 33 *B* (*S* ϭ.)
μετὰ σπουδῆς; Joel 3 4 *A* (*B* ⲓⲱⲥ) ὀξέως; Jo 11 29
A² (*S* do, *B* ⲛⲭ.) ταχύ; MIE 2 368 *B* shall befall
thee ϭⲉⲛⲟⲩⲭ., LAp 536 *F* ⲁⲩⲡⲟⲧ ϩⲛⲟⲩⲕ. As adj:
Pro 14 17 *B* ⲣⲉϥϫⲱⲛⲧ ⲛⲭ. (*S* ϭ. vb) ὀξύθυμος.
ⲣⲉϥⲭ. *B*, *hasty man*: Si 4 29 ταχύς.

ⲛⲕ. *F*, ⲛⲭ. *B*, ⲛϭ. *A* adv, *in haste, quickly, soon*:
Ex 32 7 *B* (*S* ϩⲛⲟⲩϭⲉⲡⲏ), Is 5 19 *B* (*S* ϭ. vb),
Mt 28 7 *B* (*S* ϩⲛⲟⲩϭ.), Ac 22 18 *B* (var + ⲓⲏⲥ,
S ϭ. vb), He 13 19 *B* (*S* ϩⲛⲟⲩϭ.), Cl 23 5 *A* ταχύ,
τὸ τάχος &c; Mt 13 21 *F* (*S* ⲡⲧⲉⲩⲛⲟⲩ, *B* ⲥⲁⲧⲟⲧϥ)
εὐθύς; Ez 7 11 *B* (*S* ϩⲛⲟⲩϭ.) μετὰ σπουδῆς; C 86
270 *B* ⲁⲙⲱⲓⲛⲓ ⲛⲭ., PO 11 322 *B* all this shall befall ⲛⲭ.

ⲕⲱⲗⲙ *S*, ⲕⲱⲗⲙⲉ *A*, ⲭⲱⲗⲉⲙ *B* nn m, *corner
of eye*: Tob 11 11 *S* κανθός, P 44 69 *S* καν. = 43
38 *B* ⲭ. مأق; Zech 14 12 *SA* ὀπή; PMéd 294 *S*
ⲡⲕⲱⲣⲙ ⲉⲧϩⲱⲣ. *Cf* ⲕⲟⲉⲓⲣ.

ⲕⲗⲟⲙ *SO*, ⲕⲗⲁⲙ *Sª AA²F*, ⲭⲗⲟⲙ *B*, pl
ⲕⲗⲟⲟⲙ *S* (? El 132), ⲕⲗⲟⲟⲗⲉ *A* (2 Mac 6 7, El 96)
nn m, *crown, wreath*: Ps 64 11 *SB* (as in prayers:
Hall 138, CaiEuch 593), Pro 1 9 *SAB*, Mk 15 17
SBF, Jo 19 2 *SA²B*, AP 15 *A²* στέφανος, Ex 30 3
B ⲭ. ⲙⲙⲟⲛⲛⲉⲡ στεφάνη στρεπτή; Ac 14 13 *SB*
στέμμα; 1 Cor 9 24 *S* (*B* ⲃⲁⲓ) βραβεῖον; Ez 44 18
SB κίδαρις; AZ 21 104 *O* ⲡⲕ. ⲡⲱⲟⲩ ⲡⲡⲣⲏ, C 43

233 *B* snake bidden be a ⳉ. on judge's shoulders (*cf* ⲕⲟⲩⲗⲱⲗ vb sim), KroppJ ⲕ. ⲡⲁⲣⲧⲉⲙⲉⲥⲓⲁⲥ, Sa 2 8 *S*, RAl 125 *S* ⲕ. ⲡⲟⲩⲉⲣⲧ, GPar 2 4 *S* prayer of ⲡⲉⲕ. at wedding = TRit 274 *B* (*cf* Lane *Mod Eg* 1836 2 333), *cf* PMéd 287 *S* ⲕ. ⲛϣⲉⲗⲗⲉⲧ a plant, CO 459 *S* ⲕ. ⲛⲃⲁⲣⲱⲧ fitted with 6 cups (? chandelier, *v* Ep 550n), BMis 270 *S* wood of ἀψίς miraculously blossoms, Jew asks who has put these leaves ⲉⲡⲉⲕ., BKU 1 94 *S*ᵃ ? agricultural implement ; *cf* BMOr 6201 *A* 90 *S* ⲕ. ⲡⲁⲍⲟⲡ (ἄξων).

ⲉⲓⲣⲉ ⲡⲕ. *S*, ⲓⲣⲓ ⲛⳉ. *B*, *make a crown, circle* : Ps 8 6 *S* (*B* ✝ ⳉ.) στεφανοῦν, Br 227 *S* ⲡⲉⲧⲉⲣⲉⲡⲁⲓⲱⲙ ⲟ ⲡⲟⲩⲕ. ⲉⲭⲱϥ, Aeg 55 *B* we all ⲟⲓ ⲡⲟⲩⳉ. ⲉⲣⲟϥ, EW 118 *B* sim of trees.

✝ ⲕ. *SF*, ⳉ. *B*, *crown, set a crown* upon, c ⲉϫⲛ-, ϧⲓϫⲛ- : Ps 102 4 *SB*, He 2 7 *BF* (*S* = Gk), CaiEuch 473 *B* στεφανοῦν ; CA 110 *S* ✝ ⲕ. ⲉⲭⲱϥ as virgin, AM 165 *B* ⲉϥ✝ ⳉ. ϧⲓϫⲉⲛⲡⲓⲙⲁⲣⲧⲩⲣⲟⲥ. ϫⲓⲛ✝ ⳉ. *B* nn f, *crowning* of bridal pair : K 219 تكليل.

ϫⲓ ⲕ. *SO*, ϭⲓ ⳉ. *B*, *receive, bear crown* : 2 Tim 2 5 *SB*, Bor 253 168 *S* ⲡⲉⲧⲛⲏϣ ⲉϫⲓ ⲕ. στεφανοῦν ; Hor 82 *O* ϫⲓ ⲕⲗⲙ (sic) ⲙⲡ(ⲗ ⲡ)ⲟⲩⲅ, Z 282 *S* our fathers ⲛⲧⲁⲩϫⲓ ⲕ. *martyred*, AZ 21 157 *S* sim, WTh 152 *S* receive (bridal) crown (*cf* LMis 357). ⲣⲉϥϫⲓ ⲕ. *SB*, *crown bearer* : TEuch 1 675 *B* Stephen ⲡⲓⲣ., BSM 132 *B* Chrysostom ; of emperor : Miss 8 29 *S* τροπαιοῦχος. ⲣⲉϥⲭⲣⲟ ⲕ. *S*, *victoriously crowned* : J 98 4, 102 4 Phoebammon, *cf* νικηφόρος, στεφανοφ. &c ib 13 6, 15 32. ϭⲁⲓⲕ. *S*, *crown bearer* : P 129¹⁶ 26 martyr ⲡϭ. ⲙⲡⲉⲭ̄ⲥ̄. In place-name : Ταπεκλάμ POxy 1916. *V* also ⳉⲗⲟⲙⲗⲉⲙ vb, *crown*.

ⲕⲗⲱⲙ *F v* ⲕⲣⲱⲙ.

ⲕⲗⲁⲙⲉ *A v* ⲕⲗⲟⲟⲙⲉ.

ⲕⲗⲙⲁ *S v* ϭⲗⲙⲁⲓ.

ⲕⲗⲙⲉ *S* nn f, *pad, poultice* of wool, *cf* qlmet DM V 6 7 : PMéd 124 (5 times) soaked in drugs & applied to painful womb or as suppository, ShP 131⁶ 37 luxurious monks wear ϧⲉⲛⲡⲣⲏϣ ⲉⲩⲟ ⲡⲕ. *padded* cloaks.

ⲕⲗⲟⲟⲙⲉ *S*, ⲕⲗⲁⲙⲉ (Pro ? *l* ⲕⲗⲁⲁⲙⲉ), ⲕⲗⲁⲙⲉ *A* nn f, *weal* : Pro 9 7 *A* (*S* ⲉⲗⲉⲗⲕⲛⲙⲉ, *B* ⲁϭⲛⲓ) μωμᾶσθαι, ib 20 24 *A* (*S* do) ὑπώπιον ; Is 53 5 (Cl 16 5) *A* (*S* ⲥⲁϣ, *B* ⲗⲉⲗⲉⲭⲏⲙⲓ) μώλωψ ; ShA 1 49 *S* heart ⲟ ⲡⲕ. from tortures, ShIF 92 *S* neither ⲕ. nor ⲉⲗⲉⲗⲕⲛⲙⲉ found on his body. ? pl of ⲕⲗⲙⲉ.

ⲕⲗⲉⲙⲗⲉⲙ *F v* ⲕⲣⲙⲣⲙ.

ⲕⲁⲗⲁⲙⲉϥⲟ *B* nn f (2 Kg 6 3), pl -ϥⲱⲟⲩ (Ps

148 9) & sg as pl, *hill*, often paral ⲧⲱⲟⲩ : Nu 23 9 (*S* = Gk), Ps 64 13 (*S* ⲥⲓⲃⲧ), Is 2 14 (*S* do), Jer 13 27 (*S* ⲧⲁⲗ) βουνός ; Ez 18 11 &c ὄρος ; Ge 49 26 (*S* ⲕⲣⲟ *collis*), Bar 5 7 θίς ; Is 40 12 (*S* do *collis*) νάπη ; Ez 34 13 φάραγξ. (Job 38 22 *l* ⲁⲗ ⲙϥⲉ χάλαζα.)

ⲕⲉⲗⲉⲛⲕⲉϧ *S*, ⲕⲁⲗⲁⲡⲕⲉϧ *B v* ⲕⲗⲗⲉ.

ⲕⲗⲁⲛⲧⲁ, -ⲍⲁ *S* nn f, apparently gloss on λοβός in Lev 3 4, 4 9 &c ⲡⲗ. ⲏ ⲧⲉⲕ. ⲉⲧϧⲓⲭⲡⲡϧⲩⲡⲁⲣ, cited P 44 105 حجاب المقدم على الاحشاء = 43 89 , so *screen*, membrane (unless confused with τὸ κατακαλύπτον ἐπὶ τῆς κοιλίας 9 19 *alibi*).

ⲕⲱⲗⲡ, ⲕⲉⲗⲡ-, ⲕⲟⲗⲡⸯ, ⲕⲟⲗⲡ† (Ge 30 33), p c ⲕⲁⲗⲡ- *B* vb tr, *steal, rob* : Ge 31 19 (*S* ϧⲱϥⲧ), Ob 5 (*A* ϭⲓ), Mt 6 19 (*S* ϫⲓⲟⳉⲉ) κλέπτειν ; EpJer 17 (*F* ϥⲓ ⲛⳉⲓⲟⲩⲓ), 2 Cor 11 8 (*S* = Gk) συλᾶν, Va 63 80 care ⲉⲧⲕ. ⲛϥⲧⲛ̄ϣⲱⲗⲙ ἀποσυλ., Col 2 8 (*S* ϣⲱⲗ) συλαγώγειν, Ac 19 37 ⲕⲁⲗⲡⲉⲣϥⲉⲓ (*S* ϣⲗ ⲣⲡⲉ) ἱερόσυλος ; MG 25 164 ⲁϥⲕ. ⲣⲁⲛⲕⲟⲩϫⲓ ⲛⲥⲕⲉⲩⲟⲥ, ib 330 ⲡⲓⲙⲉⲩⲓ...ⲉⲧⲕ. ⲙⲙⲟⲩⲅ, C 41 15 thieves had ⲕ. ⲡⲟⲩⲛⲓϣ✝ ⲡⲣⲱⲙ, EW 191 houses ⲡⲥⲉⲕ. ⲙⲙⲱⲟⲩ, C 86 330 not again will I ⲕ. ⲡⲥⲁ ϧⲗⲓ ⲡⲣⲱⲙⲓ, AM 248 ϫⲉⲛⲡϫⲓⲛⲟⲣⲉⲕⲕⲟⲗⲡⲥ ⲡⲧⲟ-ⲧⲟⲩ. As nn, *theft, thing stolen* : MG 25 164 knew not ϫⲉⲣⲁⲛⲕ. ⲡⲉ. As adv, *thievishly* : Leip 24 36 (*v* EW 176) took gold vessel ⲡⲕ. ⲉⲡⲉϥⲓⲟ✝ *unbeknown to*. ϫⲓⲛⲕ. nn m, *robbing* : Cat 178 breaking in ⲉⲡⳉ. ⲙⲡⲓⲑⲛⲥⲁⲩⲣⲟⲥ. ⲁⲧⲕ. adj, *unstolen, inviolate* : TRit 37 that they keep seal (of baptism) ⲡⲁⲧⲕ. ἄθραυστος, Va 57 125 prayer is ⲟⲩⳉⲱⲣⲓⲟⲛ ⲡⲁⲧⲕ. ἄσυλος.

ⲕⲟⲗⲡⲥ *SB* nn f, *theft* : P 129¹⁵ 23 *S* ⲉⲡⲟⲩⲁⲁⲃ ⲉⲧⲕ., C 43 184 *B* sim. In Ez 43 13 *B* (HCons 301) ⲕ. is for κόλπωμα.

ⲕⲁⲗⲁⲡⲏⲓ *B* nn as pl, *quail* : K 168 سمان .

ⲕⲁⲗⲱⲡⲟⲩ, -ⲟⲡⲟⲩ, ϭⲁⲗⲟⲡⲟⲩ *S*, ϭⲁⲗⲁⲡ *F* nn m f, *small dog, lapdog* (?) : ShP 130⁵ 34 *S* ⲡⲉⲩϧⲟⲟⲣ ⲛ ⲡⲕ. of rich covered with ϧⲉⲛⲡⲣⲏϣ, ShR 2 3 50 *S* ⲛϭ. ⲡϫⲉϧⲏⲡⲓ lie on rich man's couch (*cf* ib 47 ⲟⲩϧⲟⲟⲣ ⲡⲧⲉϫ. ie ἐκ τῆς ξένης, ἀπὸ ξ.), BIF 14 159 *S* ⲟⲩⲕ. ⲡⲟⲩϧⲟⲣ...ⲧⲕⲟⲩⲓ ⲡⲕ., Mor 51 39 *S* in parable ⲁϥⲕⲁ ⲡⲕ. ⲉⲃⲟⲗ interpreted as ⲡⲗⲓϣⲉ, AZ 23 41 *F* list of animals (goats, rams) ⲡⲉϭ. *Cf* محد كلب .
As name : Καλόπου, -ώπου (Preisigke).

ⲕⲗⲯ *SA* nn, *blow* : ⲣ ⲕ., ShC 73 184 *S* ⲛⲕ. ⲉⲡⲧⲁⲅⲁⲁⲩ ⲡⲁⲩ. ✝ ⲕ. ⲉϫⲛ-, Mt 26 67 *S* (*B* ⲕⲟⲩⲣ), Mk 14 65 *S* (*B* ⲕⲉϧ) κολαφίζειν ; Am 2 7 *SA* (*B* do) κονδυλίζειν ; ShBM 212 *S* ⲉϥⲛⲁ✝ ⲕ. ⲉϫⲛⲡⲥⲁ-ⲧⲁⲡⲁⲥ, R 1 1 73 *S* opp ⲁⲁⲥ. ϣⲥ ⲡⲕ., Mor 43 145 *S*. *Cf* ? κόλαφος.

κολπϲ *v* κωλπ.

κλογϲⲙⲉ *S* nn m, meaning unknown: J 68
41 testatrix has paid son's δημόσιον & hired smith
for him ⲉⲡⲉⲕ., BM 1090 ⲡⲕ. (*bis*) in account.
Coptic?, or ? κλῶσμα, κροῦσμα.

ⲕⲁⲗⲧ- *B* vb p c (?), *be hairless* on front of head:
BM 920 266 ⲕ. ϫⲱϥ الرأس اجلح (but K 72 has
ϲⲁⲗⲱϲ *ie* σαλός for اجلح). *Cf* ϭⲁⲗ- in ϭⲁⲗⲟⲩϩⲓϩ.

ⲕⲟⲗⲧⲁϭ *B* nn m, *colocasia*, water plant: Bodl
325 151 (= Tatt 838) قلقاس (which in K 197 is
ⲕⲟⲣⲕⲁϲⲓ). Prob *l* ⲕⲟⲗⲧⲁϲ.

ⲕⲉⲗⲟⲩⲟⲛϫϥ *B* *v* ⲕⲗⲗⲉ & ⲟⲩⲟϭⲉ.

ⲕⲉⲗⲫⲁϫ *B* nn, *truffle*: BMOr 8775 123 عرد,
P 54 127 عدد (*l* غرد Löw 303).

ⲕⲉⲗϣⲱⲧ (P 44 83), ⲕⲉⲧϣⲱⲗ (P 43 59) *S* nn,
a plant (?): P 44 ⲁⲣⲓⲱⲛ ⲕ. (no Ar) = 43 ⲁⲣⲓⲱⲛ
غبيرة service-tree (*sorbus*), ⲕ. زريقا a herb (Lab),
or food of milk & oil (Bsciai AZ 24 91, Lane).

ⲕⲁⲗⲁϣⲓϣⲧⲉ (CO 149, 150), ⲕⲁⲗⲁϣⲓⲧ (J 42
21) *S* nn f, part of a house, on its roof: CO the
ⲕ. ⲉⲧϭⲓⲡⲁⲏⲣ to be held in common, J share of house
to include ἐξέδρα up to air (roof) & ⲡⲧⲉⲧⲕ. ⲧⲱⲙ *to
be closed* or *shut off*. PMich 4240 letter]ⲧⲁⲕⲏ
ⲡⲧⲁⲕⲁⲗⲁϣⲓϣ prob same. *Cf ?* ⲕⲁⲗϫⲧⲟⲣⲧ (under
ⲕⲱⲗϫ).

ⲕⲗⲁϥ *F* *v* ⲕⲣⲟϥ.

ⲕⲉⲗϥⲓ *B* nn as pl, *eyelid*: BMOr 8775 119 =
P 54 119 (where next to ⲙⲉⲭⲉⲛϩ) اجفان.

ⲕⲗⲁϥⲧ *SB*, ⲕⲗⲉϥⲧ (P 130² 131), ⲕⲗⲏⲧ (Mich
550 39) *S*, ϫⲗⲁϥⲧ *B* nn f, *hood, cowl* mostly of
monks: Dan 3 21 *S* (*B* diff) τιάρα; K 120 *B*
قلنسوة, P 55 14 do (next ⲕⲟⲗⲗⲁ also = 'ϫ. On
'ϫ *v* Almk 1 322. In P 44 91 = ⲕⲟⲩⲕⲗⲉ, in K 120
opp to it, in P 43 240 = καμελαύκιον. *V* also CO
248 n). Monk at consecration endued with ⲕ.
(κουκούλιον): TEuch 1 171 *B*, Bodl Marsh 32 90
B called ⲕ. of humility (*cf ib* 152 at consecr of
bishop ⲕⲟⲩⲗⲗⲁ 'ϫ), ROC '02 139 *S* sim; part of
monk's dress: Z 351 *S* ⲟⲩⲕ. ⲛϭⲁϭⲓⲧⲱⲛ *hood* of
cloak, MG 25 40 *B* ⲕⲟⲗⲟϥⲓ, ⲙⲁⲣϭⲡⲁϩ, ϫ., R 1 4
50 *S* ϣⲧⲏⲡ, ⲕ. (*cuculla*), ⲡⲁⲗⲗⲓⲛ, MIE 2 345 *B*
covered head with ⲧⲉϥϫ. = P ar 4785 127 'ϫ;
ornamented with crosses: CDan 93 *B* ⲟⲩⲕ. ⲉⲧⲙⲉϩ
ⲡⲥⲧⲁⲩⲣⲟⲥ, MG 25 268 *B* = Mor 40 42 *S* sim,
Sh(Besa) Z 504 *S* cursed whoso stealeth ϩⲟⲉⲓⲧⲉ,
ⲡⲣⲏϣ, ⲕ.; youth's cap: BMis 16 *S* ⲧⲉⲕ. ⲡⲧⲉϥ-
ⲙⲡⲧⲕⲟⲩⲓ; glowing iron cap as torture: BIF 14
III *S* ⲟⲩⲕ. ⲙⲡⲉⲡⲓⲡⲉ (*cf* κασσίς TT 77 n).   BP

4977 *S* in list of clothes ⲕⲟⲩⲗⲓϭⲧ, ? same (or =
ⲕⲟⲩⲓ ⲗⲉⲃⲓⲧⲱⲛ).

ⲕⲱⲗϩ *SAA²B*, ⲕⲗϩ- *S*, ⲕⲟⲗϩ⳿ *S*, ⲕⲁⲗϩ⳿ *AA²*,
ⲕⲟⲗϩ† *S* (AZ 23 108) *B* (Ez 25 6) vb I intr, *strike,
knock*: Mt 7 7 *B* (*S* ⲧⲱϩⲙ), Ap 3 20 *B* (*S* do),
MG 25 7 *B* κρούειν; Am 6 5 *B* (*A* ⲣ ⲧⲱⲣⲉ) ἐπικροτεῖν; Is 41 7 (*S* ⲡⲱⲝϭ) ἐλαύνειν; to summon
congregation: Z 311 *S* ⲕ. ⲙⲁⲣⲟⲩⲥⲱⲟⲩϩ κρού.,
Miss 8 207 *S* ⲡⲧⲕ. ⲧⲛⲓϣⲗⲏⲗ, ShC 73 60 *S*, DeV
85 *B* sim, ShZ 507 *S* if they need aught ⲉⲩⲡⲁⲕ.,
C 41 62 *B* ⲁⲩⲕ. that each should go to work
(*v* also II); process in mat weaving: MG 17 328
S = *ib* 103 *B* not to press reeds too closely so that
mat may ⲕ. ⲕⲁⲗⲱⲥ = *ib* 441 انسفق (= Va ar 172
45 حتى تعمل للحصر انفرد الى ناحية), ShP 131⁴ III
S in parable of loom ⲡϩⲛⲁⲁⲩ ⲡⲕ. are adversaries
of doctrine; AZ 23 108 *S* put mixture into ⲟⲩⲧⲟⲉⲓⲥ ⲉⲥⲕⲟⲗϩ & this into water, sim Bodl(P) a 1 *a*
ⲧⲟⲉⲓⲥ ⲉⲥⲕⲁⲣⲉϩ; in disease, *throb, ache* (?): PMich
597 *S* recipe for one ⲉϥⲕ. ⲡⲛⲁⲩ ⲡⲓⲙ, Wor 273
S dying man ⲥⲱⲙⲁ ⲧⲏⲣϥ ϭⲱⲗϩ = Mor 16 102
l ⲕⲱ(ⲗϩ), Mich 550 39 *S* lying sick his head ⲕ.
ⲉⲣⲟϥ so that he asked for pillow, Ep 575 *S* in liver
disease ⲉⲣⲉⲡⲣⲱⲙⲉ ⲕ. ϫⲉⲛⲉϥ(*l*? ⲡⲡⲉϥ)ⲱⲃϣ; *cf* as
nn: c e-: Jth 14 14 *S*, C 89 22 *B*, Va 57 129 *B*,
Mor 17 87 *S* ⲉⲓⲕ. ⲉⲡⲣⲟ (var BM 294 ⲧⲱⲣⲙ) κρούειν: BSM 39 *B* sim = BMis 384 *S* ⲧⲱϩⲙ, Miss
4 763 *S* my father ⲕ. ⲉⲡⲱⲡⲉ thrice, Va 58 70 *B* ⲁⲥⲕ.
ⲉⲣⲟⲓ ⲡϫⲉ ϯⲥⲩⲛⲏⲑⲓⲁ;   c e- of purpose (*v* prep
e- I b): ShC 73 144 *S* ⲉⲩϣⲁⲡⲕ. ⲉⲡⲟⲩⲱⲙ, C 41
44 *B* ⲉⲧⲁⲩⲕ. ⲉϥⲥⲩⲡⲁϫⲓⲥ.

II tr *SAA²B*, *strike, clap*: Ps 46 2 *B* (*S* ϫⲁⲕ),
Lam 2 15 *B*, Nah 3 19 *B* (*A* ⲣ ⲧⲱⲣⲉ) κροτεῖν, Nu
24 10 *B* (*S* ⲣⲱϥⲧ) συγκρότ.; Jud 16 13, 14 *S* ἐγ-
κρούειν dat, κατακρ. ἐν *hammer in, fix*; Ez 22 13 *B*
(*S* ϩⲁⲣϩϩ) πατάσσειν; Mk 12 4 *S* (*B* ϥⲱⲗϩ)
κεφαλιοῦν; Lu 20 12 *S* (*B* do) τραυματίζειν; Jo 11
8 *A²* (*SB* ϩⲓⲟⲩⲉ, *A* ϯⲕⲉ) + ⲱⲡⲉ, sim Cl 5 6 *A* (var
ⲧⲱⲕ) λιθάζειν; Mt 7 25 *B* (*S* ϩⲓ. ⲉϩⲟⲩⲛ, *cf* Lu 6
48) προσπίπτειν dat; Ez 26 4 *B* καταβάλλειν; Ryl
95 *S* with stones ⲁⲩⲕ. ⲙⲡⲣⲟ = MG 25 100 *B* ⲕⲱϣ
ⲛⲥⲁ-, BMis 455 *S* ⲕ. ⲡⲡⲕⲉⲗⲉⲉⲗⲉ as summons to
church (*cf* I), P 68 1 *S* archdeacon to ⲕ. ⲙⲡⲥⲁⲗⲡⲓⲝ
الكلم بيديه ضرب بالناقوس, *ib* ⲡⲉϥⲕ. ⲡⲡⲉϥϭⲓϫ
1607 2 42 *S* ⲡⲉϣⲁϥⲕ. ⲉⲣⲟⲟⲩ ⲙⲡⲉϣϣⲁⲣ which he
wore. C 43 28 *B* blinded ⲉⲩⲕ. ⲡⲧⲟⲩⲁϥⲉ ⲉϩⲟⲩⲛ
ϫⲉⲛϯϫⲟⲓ (*sic l*), MG 25 235 *B* sim; Mor 19 84 *S*
ⲁⲓⲕ. ⲡⲡⲁϭⲓϫ ⲉϫⲛⲡⲉϥⲉⲣⲏⲩ = *ib* 18 76 ⲣⲱϩⲧ.

With following preposition.

—— ⲉϫⲉⲛ- *B*, *strike upon*: Ez 29 7 (*S* ϫⲁⲕ)
κροτεῖν ἐπί (*cf* ⲕ. ϫⲉⲛ-).

—— ⲛ- (dat) *SB*, *knock for* someone : Z 323 *S* at door ⲁϥⲕ. ⲛⲁϥ, AM 85 *B* sim ⲉⲡⲓⲣⲟ.

—— ϫⲉⲛ- *B*, *strike upon, in*: 2 Kg 6 14 (*S* ⲣ ⲧⲱⲣⲉ) ἀνακρού. ἐν, Ez 21 12 (*S* ϫⲁⲕ) κροτ. ἐπί, Lu 18 13 (*S* ϩⲓⲟⲩⲉ ⲉⲣ. ⲉ-) τύπτειν, MG 25 308 ⲉϫⲕ. ϫⲉⲛⲧⲉϥⲙⲉⲥⲧⲉⲛϩⲏⲧ = BIF 13 116 *S* ⲕ. ⲉ-, MIE 2 350 *B* sim.

—— ϩⲓⲣⲉⲛ- *B*, *knock upon, at*: Ac 12 13 (*S* ⲧⲱϩⲙ ⲉⲣⲛ-) κρου. acc.

With following adverb.

—— ⲉⲃⲟⲗ *B*, *knock outwards* from within : AM 272 ϯⲛⲁⲕ. ⲉⲃ. ⲥⲁⲃⲟⲗ ἔσωθεν.

—— ⲉϧⲟⲩⲛ, ⲉϩ. *SB*, *knock inwards* from without : MG 25 99 *B* beggars at door ⲁⲩⲕ. ⲉϩ., Rec 6 183 *B*, Cat 154 *B* sim ; BMar 129 *S* ⲁϥⲕ. ⲉⲣ. ⲉⲡⲣⲟ, C 89 8 *B* sim ἔκρουσεν τ. θύραν ; Lu 6 48 *B* (*S* ϩⲓⲟⲩⲉ ⲉⲣ. ϩⲛ-) ⲕ. ⲉϩ. ⲛⲥⲁ- προσρηγνύναι dat, MG 25 236 *B* sim, Job 40 18 *B* ⲕ. ⲉϩ. ϫⲉⲛ- προσκρού. εἰς ; Mor 48 6 *S* ⲁⲓⲕ. ⲉⲣ. ϩⲙⲡⲣⲟ (var BMar 206 ⲧⲱⲣⲙ ⲉⲣ. ⲉ-).

—— *SB* nn m, *blow, knock*: C 41 49 *B* brother appointed for ⲡⲓⲙⲁ ⲛⲕ. (cf Miss 4 408), MG 25 237 *B* when heard ⲡⲓⲕ. ⲛⲧⲉ ⲡⲓⲣⲟ ; disease (*v* I): BKU 1 25 *S* recipe ⲉⲧⲃⲉⲡⲕ., Ryl 106 1 *S* ⲡⲉⲡⲁⲓⲣⲉ ϩⲉⲛⲕ., *ib* 15 another, PMich 595 recipe, May ⲡⲓⲕ. of heart & liver be stilled (καταστέλλειν). ⲉⲣ ⲕ. *B* : 2 Kg 6 16 (*S* ⲣ ⲧⲱⲣⲉ) ἀνακρου.

ⲕⲗϩⲉ *S* nn f, *blow*: ShP 130² 104 brittle objects ⲥⲉⲛⲁϥⲓ ⲁⲛ ϩⲁⲧⲕ. ⲡⲓⲥⲟⲧⲃⲉϥ.

ⲕⲁⲗⲁϧⲏ *SF* nn f, *womb*, prob ⲕⲁⲗⲁ + ϧⲏ (*belly*) q v (rarely bibl) : Nu 5 22 *S* (*B* ⲛⲉϫⲓ), Ps 16 14 *F* (Mor 33 2, *S* ϧⲏ, *B* ⲡ.) γαστήρ ; Nu 5 27 *S* (*B* do) Mt 15 17 *F* (*SB* do) κοιλία ; PS 12 *S* Elizabeth's ⲕ., Pcod 44 *S* Word entered Virgin's ⲕ. (var ϧⲏ), Mor 24 34 *F* (*S* ϧⲏ) ⲧⲕ. ⲛⲧⲉϩⲙⲉⲟⲩ, Mor 40 49 *S* ⲁⲑⲏ ⲉⲧⲣⲉⲡⲧⲉⲥⲕ. ⲉⲓ ⲉⲡⲉⲥⲏⲧ = Gött ar 114 189 البشيمة مع امعاها = PO 5 763 (cf ⲙⲁⲁⲩ caul), AZ 52 126 *S* ⲉⲓⲣⲏⲧⲟⲩⲕ....ⲁⲓⲕⲓⲙ ϩⲏⲧⲟⲩⲙⲛⲧⲣⲁ, cf MIF 9 26 *S* Mary bare me ϩⲉⲛⲧⲉⲥⲙ. ⲉⲡⲉⲓⲣⲉⲧⲉⲥⲕ., BHom 122 *S* babe lying in blood of ⲧⲕ. Rarely *belly* : BerlOr 1611 6 *S* snake in man's ⲕ., Mor 51 27 *S* man bidden anoint his ⲕ. with milk, P 131⁶ 16 *S* Jonah in whale's ⲕ., LMär 40 *S* sim. RChamp 539 *A* ϭⲁⲗⲁⲧϣⲉ same ?

In place-names ? ⲧⲕⲁⲗⲁϩⲓⲧⲏⲥ Amélineau *Géogr* 573, [ⲧ]ⲕⲁⲗⲁϩⲛⲧⲉ[ⲥ] RNC 87 = خلاخس Synax 1 416 (cf Baouit 2 83 ⲧϩⲁⲗⲁϩⲛⲧⲥⲉ[), ? ⲕⲁⲗⲁϩⲁ Kr 11.

ⲕⲁⲗⲁϩⲧ *v* ϭⲁⲗⲁϩⲧ.

ⲕⲟⲩⲗϩⲟⲧ, ⲕⲟⲗϩⲟⲧ, ⲕⲟⲗϩⲧ *B* nn m, *a fish, clarias anguillaris* (MIF 51 133) : K 170 قرموط.

ⲕⲱⲗϫ *SB*, ϭⲱⲗϫ *SAA²* ⲕⲗϫ- *S*, ⲕⲉⲗϫ- *B*, ϭⲗϫ- *SA²*, ⲕⲟⲗϫ⸗ *SB*, ⲕⲟⲗϫ, ϭⲟ.† *SB*, ⲣ ⲥ ⲕⲁⲗϫ- *S* vb I intr, *bend, be bent*: Ps 9 31 *B* (*S* ⲡⲱⲣⲧ) κύπτειν ; Job 9 13 *B* (*S* tr) κάμπτειν, Ps 37 7 *B* (*S* ⲱⲗⲕ) κατακάμπ., *ib* 68 24 *SB*, Ro 11 10 *B* (*S* do) συγκάμπ. ; Mic 2 3 *A* (*SB* ⲛⲛⲉ-...ⲥⲟⲩⲧⲱⲛ) οὐ μὴ ὀρθός ; Mor 48 72 *S* maimed woman ⲁⲥⲕ. ϩⲙⲡⲉⲥⲥⲱⲙⲁ ⲧⲏⲣϥ, cf Lu 13 11 *B*. With ⲡⲁⲧ, ⲕⲉⲗⲓ : Is 45 24 *SB*, Phil 2 10 *SB* κάμπ.

II tr, *bend, twist*: 2 Kg 22 40 *S*, Si 7 24 *S* κάμπ., Ps 68 10 *SB* συγκάμπ. ; Bar 2 23 *B*, Leyd 132 *S* κλίνειν, Deu 24 17 *B* (Va, var ⲣⲓⲕⲓ) ἐκκλίν. ; Pro 26 15 *SA* κρύπτειν, *ib* 19 21 *AS* ἐγκρύπ. ; *ib* 24 48 *SA* ἐναγκαλίζειν ; Lev 25 46 *S* + ⲙⲁⲕϩ (*B* ⲧⲣⲉⲙⲕⲟ) κατατείνειν ; Ps 74 9 *S* (*B* ϫⲟⲙϫⲉⲙ) συγκλᾶν. Qual : Deu 32 5 *B* (*S* ϭⲟⲟϭ), Pro 2 15 *B* (*S* ϭⲟⲟⲙⲉ, *A* ϭⲁⲩϭ), Lu 3 5 *B* (*S* do) σκολιός ; Ps 77 57 *B* (*S* do) στρεβλός ; *ib* 100 3 *B* (*S* do) σκαμβός ; Hos 7 16 *B* (*S* do) ἐντείνειν ; BM 185 1 *S* ⲉⲡⲉϥ ϭⲟⲗϫ ⲁⲛ ⲛⲗⲁⲁⲩ was not *deflected*, MG 25 177 *B* carpenter makes ⲛⲏ ⲉⲧⲕⲟⲗϫ ⲉⲩⲥⲟⲩⲧⲱⲛ, C 89 92 *B* ⲉϥⲕⲟⲗϫ like hook, Cat 30 *B* thoughts ⲉⲧⲕⲟⲗϫ. Refl : FR 22 *S* ⲁⲛⲥⲓⲧⲛⲟⲛ ⲕⲟⲗϫⲟⲩ (cf R 1 1 15), *v* ClPr below. With ⲡⲁⲧ, ⲕⲉⲗⲓ, ⲁⲡⲉ &c : Dan 6 10 *SB*, Ro 11 4 *SB*, Cl 57 1 *A* κάμπ. ; Mk 15 19 *S* (*B* diff), Ac 7 60 *S* (*B* do) τιθέναι ; Mor 37 98 *S* κλίνειν ; TSBA 9 364 *B* ⲁϥⲕⲉⲗϫ ⲕⲉⲗⲓ before Lord, ClPr 25 1 *S* ⲁϥⲕⲟⲗϫϥ ⲉϫⲛⲛⲉϥⲡⲁⲧ, ShC 73 130 *S* ⲉⲩⲕⲱⲗϩ ⲉϭⲗϫ ⲡⲁⲧ, Miss 4 186 *B* ⲁⲡⲕ. ⲡⲛⲉⲡⲁⲫϩⲟⲩⲓ ⲡⲁϥ, BАp 147 *S* ⲟⲩⲙⲁⲕϩ ⲉϥϭϯ. As nn : Z 345 *S* he made 3 ⲕⲗϫ ⲡⲁⲧ, Miss 4 613 *S* ⲡⲉⲧϣⲟⲟⲡ ϩⲛⲟⲩⲕⲗϫ ⲡ. & prayer, Bor 100 215 *S* title of prayer ⲕⲗϫ ⲁⲡⲉ ⲛⲣⲁⲛ. ϫⲓⲛⲕⲉⲗϫ ⲕⲉⲗⲓ *B*: Va 57 213 κάμπ. τὰ γόνατα.

With following preposition : 1 Kg 18 9 *S* his heart ⲕ. ⲉⲣⲟϥ ⲉϩⲁϩⲉⲓⲁ (var ⲕ. ⲛⲥⲁ-, *B* ϫⲟⲩϣⲧ ⲛⲥⲁ-) ὑποβλέπειν. With following adverb : ⲉⲡⲉⲥⲏⲧ, Is 2 9 *B* (*S* ⲡⲱⲣⲧ) κύπτ. ; BHom 20 *S* hearts ⲕⲟⲗϫ ⲉⲡ. κλίν. χαμαί. ⲉϧⲟⲩⲛ, Vat 57 163 *B* vain aims ⲉⲩⲕⲟⲗϫ ⲉϩ. *are opposed to* zeal & amendment. ⲉϩⲣⲏⲓ, Is 51 23 *B* κύπτ., Job 9 27 *B* (*S* ⲃⲱϩ) συγκύπτ. ; DeV 187 *B* (Orat Manas 10) κατακάμπ.

—— *SB* nn m, *bent state, perversion, depression*: ShBMOr 8810 448 *S* friendless are in ⲟⲩⲕ. ⲙⲛⲟⲩⲙⲕⲁϩ, EW 125 = ROC 25 248 *B* ⲟⲩⲡⲉ ⲡⲓⲡⲉⲧϩⲱⲟⲩ ⲓⲉ ⲡⲓⲕ. in our faith ? BHom 75 *S* no tears without ⲕ. ⲛϩⲏⲧ *conversion*.

ⲕⲁⲗⲁϫⲧⲱⲣⲧ, ⲕⲁⲗϫⲧⲟⲣⲧ *S* nn f, *part of house*: TurM 16 assigning shares of house, His is the water-trough (?) in court & his ⲧⲕ. ⲉⲧϩⲁⲡⲧⲱⲣⲧ (*ie* in angle below staircase, cf ? ὑποπέσσιον, but *v* PLond 5 170. Klunzinger *Bilder* 42, Fig 4 *x* may

be compared), J 24 160 half тк. in exchange for ½
of house. As ? place-name: Τκαλειτῶρε (Preisigke). *Cf* каладщите.

кλεε *SA* nn f (m Z 492 = ShA 2 63, ̄error),
angle, corner: Pro 7 8 *SA* (*B* ελκε), Mt 6 5 *S*
(*BF* λακϩ) γωνία; Nu 34 3 *S* (*B* сϥιρ), Ps 127 3 *S*
(*B* do) κλίτος; P 131³ 83 *S* Lazarus hid self in к.
= Va 61 94 *B* ελκс, TU 24 1 3 *S* she lies мписа
пϯк., BIF 13 118 *S* southern к. of ἕλος = MG 25
312 *B* аλοк, ShA 2 138 *S* к., ϧιρ, ταµιоп, *ib* 63,
64, Mun 113 sim.   метк. *B* nn f, *crookedness*:
Pro 10 8 (*SA* diff) σκολιάζειν.

As place-name in Scete: P 68 1 *S* rubric, They
shall assemble at тк. мпсаϧ تل المعلمين.

кλιϫι (so all MSS) *B* nn m, part of a bird:
K 170 (*l* ? زنيف) زنق projecting or pendant crop,
Sobhy).

коуλαϫι *B* nn as pl, a fish ἀβραμίς: K 171
ابرميص (*v* AZ 6 84). *Cf* емеϣϣе.

каµ *SB*, ? ϭεµ *Sᵃ* (Ep 334), кнµ *Sᶠ* (Miss 4
782 *sic* MS, Mor 31 103) nn m, *reed, rush* (*v* Löw
166): MG 17 318 *S* = *ib* 92 *B* θροῖον = *ib* 412
حلف, Miss 4 530 *S* = C 89 49 *B* sim, P 44 83 θρύον,
ξυλεφεс (? ξυλήφιον) حلفا, 43 60 غاسول, K 138 *B* حلفا
used by ropemaker, ShP 131⁶ 37 *S* пк. ппоуϩ
formerly sufficed monks for mat, BM 343 2 *S* we
go еϥι к. еταλο таµн, BKU 1 8 35 *S* таµн пк.,
Z 307 *S* прнϣ пк. ψίαθος, MG 25 239 *B* λас пк.
splinter of reed, P 132¹ 16 *S* λас пк. darning
needle, var Mor 31 209 ϫωϫ пкнµ; MG 17 328
S кап пк. λῶμα; AM 102 *B* as hafts for spikes;
AZ 52 120 *S* к. moistened for mat (сω) making =
Va ar 172 15 (MG 17 362 *inf* diff), C 89 10 *B*
ϧωрп п[ϧαп]к.;   reaping rushes: ShC 73 54, 159
S, C 89 22 *B*; C 43 226 *B* martyr's bodies thrown
into пк. (*cf* Synax 1 144 6), Mor 50 6 *S* bones
hidden in пєрωт пк., MG 25 238 *B* asp lies there,
BM 1073 *S* land cleared of к. (*cf* Waszinski *Boden-*
pacht 69).   J (*penes* Crum) *S* John пϣλ(к) к.,
reed-weaver.   поупє пк. *S* nn f, lit *root of reed*,
a plant: P 44 83 μελεντήριον اصل للحلفا = 43 60 سمار
(*juncus*). But ? *l* μελαν- & connect with каµе
black.   In place-names (?) Πκαμ, Πιαϧ καμ &
κημ (PLond 4), Πανκαμ (PCai 67138).

каλµ *S v* ϭωµ.

кеµ *F v* кµоµ (каµе).

кιµ *SABF*, кєµт-, кєµтϫ *S* (*v* II), p c кµ-
SA (*v* кµто), vb I intr, *move, be moved*: Job 13 25
SB, Is 33 20 *SBF*, Ac 17 28 *SB* κινεῖν, Ep 592
B 14 ἀκίνητος; Ps 12 5 *SB*, Pro 3 26 *SAB*, Jth 12
16 *S*, Nah 1 5 *S* (*A* пαειπε, *B* моπµεп), Ac 4
31 *SB* σαλεύειν; Pro 24 56 *SA*, Is 13 13 *S* (*B*

µоп.) σείειν; Lev 26 36 *S* (*B* diff) φέρειν; Sa 5
2 *B* (*S* ϣτорτр) ταράσσειν; Job 6 7 *B* (*l* ? кнп,
S diff), Ac 5 42 *S* (*B* χω птотϩ еϧоλ) παύειν
(*cf* below к. ϧп-); Nah 1 4 *S* (*A* ωϫпе, *B* моупк)
ἐκλείπειν; PS 126 *S* voice whereat прωµе к., AM
144 *B* птепкαϧι к. thrice, J 106 143 *S* property
петк., петк. ап κινητά, ἀκίνητα.

With following preposition.

—— **е-** *SB*: BAp 59 *S* heavens к. епеιса мп-
паι.

—— **ϧп-, ϩεп-** *SAB*: Dan 3 79 *B* κιν. ἐν, Lu
1 41 *SB* σκιρτᾶν ἐν, Br 226 *S* city етоук. прнтс;
Pro 17 13 *SA* κιν. ἐκ, TT 188 *S* перетµптатсооуп
пак. ап ϧпеспну *depart from* (*cf* above παύειν);
sim еϧоλ ϧп-: Ap 6 14 *SB* κιν. ἐκ.

—— **еϫп-** *S*: PS 24 аук. еϫппеϥерну.

—— **пса-** *B*: BSM 130 pillar мпаϥк. псаϧλι
пса.

—— **ϧιϫп-** *SB*: Ge 7 21 *SB* κιν. ἐπί.

With obj c **е-** *SB*, *move, touch, make sign to*:
Is 22 25 *SB*, Mt 23 4 *SB*, Miss 8 57 *S* еук.
еϧепθορύϧос κινεῖν, Aeg 287 *S* not dare ек. еλααу
παρακιν.; Ps 35 11 *SB*, Si 28 15 *S*, Mt 11 7 *SB*,
Z 339 *S* skull аϥк. ероϥ птеϥϧрϧωт σαλεύειν; Hag
2 6 *SA* (*B* моп.) σείειν, Gu 71 *S* катасе., Ps 28
8 *S* (*B* к. п-) συνσεί.; MG 25 210 *B* апппϣϯ к.
епιкоуϫι = Z 345 *S* тϧс νύσσειν, R 1 1 51 *S* аук.
епιкоλnµoc to speak διανεύειν dat; PS 88 *S* spirit
did к. ероι, BM 217 2 *S* wrath к. еоуα мµооу,
Z 287 *S* аук. епϫнтµλα, C 43 112 *B* аϥкιµ ероϥ
мµαуату, Va 63 13 *B* мперк. ероϥ ап till I come
(var ϧоϥ, *S* ϫωр), FR 124 *B* аϥк. етеϥкуθαρα
(*cf* BSM 16 к. п-), BMOr 8802 5 *S* птерепк.
еϧαϧ пϣαϫе, Br 52 *S* аϥтреоукιµ птаϥ к. еппе,
J 19 61 *S* whoso shall к. ерωтп ϧαпнι (*cf* κινεῖν
катά), *ib* 75 44 *S* property петк. ерооу мµιп
мµооу αὐτοκίνητα, *cf* *ib* 106 143 *S* петеϣаук.
ероϥ, Wess 15 10 *S* our father к. епеспну ϫεϭопϥ
= Miss 4 117 *B* ϭωреµ.   With 2nd prep: ShA
2 251 *S* ϧωϧ пιµ етеϥпак. ерос (soul) ерооу
етресаау, P 129¹³ 10 *S* what ἐπιβουλή will devil
not к. ероϧп епϫικαιос? Miss 8 15 *S* аук. епе-
пισκοπос еϧоλ ϧптеєπαρχια, Mun 30 *S* not
decreed етреϥк. ероι мпµα, Faras 3 pl 69 17 *S*
мпеϥк. етеоугрнте ϧιϫωс *from off it.*

II tr *SBF*, *move*: Sa 5 11 *S*, Jer 14 10 *SB*, Mk
15 29 *SBF* κινεῖν; Ps 108 25 *SB*, He 12 26 *SB*
σαλεύειν; Jo 5 4 *B* (*S* om) ταράσσειν; MG 25 12
B σείειν; BAp 102 *S* thy mind к. ппонµα of
Scripture; refl: HT X 1 *S* so soon as barbarians
к. µµооу *began to move.*

Constr & pronom: 2 Kg 24 1 *S* оуорύн...ас-
кεµт ϫαγεια ἐπισείειν; 1 Kg 4 5 *S* пкаϧ аϥкеµтϥ

(refl) ἠχεῖν; P 131ᵇ 125 S women ϣⲁⲩⲕⲉⲙⲉⲧ ⲡⲉⲩⲙⲉⲭⲡⲣ ⲉϩⲣⲁⲓ ⲡⲥⲉⲕⲙ ⲛⲛⲉⲩⲃⲟⲩⲣⲉ ensnaring beholders.

With following preposition.

—— ⲉ- S (hostile): Ac 12 17 (B ⳝⲱⲣⲉⲙ) ⲕⲁⲧⲁⲥⲉⲓ. dat, SHel 63 beasts attacked him ⲉⲩⲕ. ⲡⲡⲉⲩⲥⲁⲧⲉ ⲉⲣⲟϥ, PS 93 ⲡⲁⲓ ⲉⲧⲕ. ⲛⲛⲉⲩⲃⲁⲗ ⲉⲣⲟⲩⲡ ⲉⲣⲟⲓ.

—— ⲉⲃⲟⲗ ϩⲛ- SB: Ge 11 2 B ⲕⲓⲛ. ἀπό, Ap 6 14 SB ⲕⲓⲛ. ἐκ; Is 28 7 S (B ⲥⲱⲣⲉⲙ ⲋⲉⲡ-) ⲥⲉⲓ. ἀπό.

—— ⲉⲭⲛ- SB: Job 16 4 SB ⲕⲓⲛ. κατά, Lam 2 15 SB ⲕⲓⲛ. ἐπί; ⲉϩⲣⲁⲓ ⲉⲭⲛ-: Is 37 22 SB ⲕⲓⲛ. ἐπί.

With following adverb.

BM 184 1 S ϩⲙⲡⲧⲣⲉⲡⲣ ϩⲟⲩⲟ ⲕ. ⲡⲧⲟⲣⲅⲛ ⲙⲡⲛ̄ⲉ̄ ⲉϩⲣⲁⲓ, MG 25 237 B ⲕ. ⲡⲧⲉⲥⲁϥⲉ ⲉϩⲣⲏⲓ ⲡⲉⲙⲉⲡϣⲱⲓ, cf JTS 10 394 S ⲕ. ⲡⲧⲉϥⲁⲡⲉ ⲡⲥⲁⲡⲉⲥⲏⲧ.

—— nn m SB, movement: Job 16 5 SB, Ps 43 14 SB, ClPr 30 14 S κίνησις, BMar 115 S ⲡⲕ. ⲛⲧⲉⲩⳝⲓⲛⲙⲟⲟϣⲉ τρόπος τ. κινήσεως; Ps 54 23 B (S vb), Si 40 6 S, Lu 21 25 S (B ⲙⲟⲛⲙⲉⲛ) σάλος; Is 29 6 S (B do) σεισμός; ib 3 16 S (B ⳝⲱⲣⲉⲙ) νεῦμα, Aeg 282 S ⲡⲕ. ⲛⲛⲙⲉⲗⲟⲥ παλμός; Mun 110 S ⲟⲩⲕ. ϩⲓⲧⲡⲡⲧⲏⲩ, Va 61 102 B show assent ϩⲓⲧⲉⲡⲕⲓⲛ. ⲡⲧⲉⲧⲉⲛⲁⲫⲉ.

ⲁⲧⲕ. SB adj, immovable: 1 Cor 15 58 B (S ⲡⲱⲱⲡⲉ ⲁⲛ) ἀμετακίνητός, Z 278 S faith ἀπαρακόμιστος, ROC 17 408 ἀκλινής, Miss 8 117 S, J 65 14 S testament ⲛⲁⲧⲕ. ἀσάλευτος, ib 86 6 sim ⲛⲁⲧⲕ. ⲉⲣⲟϥ, PO 11 336 B remained ⲉϥⲟⲓ ⲛⲁⲧⲕ.

ⳝⲓⲛ-, ϫⲓⲛⲕ. SB nn, f m, movement: Ps 37 17 B (S vb) σαλεύειν, Va 68 39 B passions & ϯϫ. ⲛⲧⲉ ϯⲥⲁⲣⲝ, ib 57 33 B much ϫ. σάλος, PO 4 580 S dog's pleasure shown by ⲧⳝ. ⲉⲣⲟϥ of tail, K 241 B ⲯⲁⲗⲙⲟⲥ explained as ⲡⲓϫ. ⲙⲙⲟⲩⲥⲓⲕⲟⲛ ⲧⲣⲃⲓⲟ.

ⲕⲙⲧⲟ SA, ⲕⲉⲙⲧⲟ B (only Tuki) nn m, always = B ⲙⲟⲛⲙⲉⲛ, moving of the earth (ⲧⲟ q v), earthquake: Job 41 20.S, Is 15 5 S, Mt 27 54 S σεισμός, 3 Kg 19 11 SB (Tuki 288), Si 22 17 SA ⲥⲩⲥⲥⲉⲓ.; Zech 9 14 A σάλος; Pcod 11 S He raised ⲡⲕ. on those in ship (cf Jon 1 4 SB great wind), BMar 175 S winds ⲉⲩⲙⲉϩ ⲡⲕ. Cf AZ 38 93 ⲕⲟⲙ ⲫⲧⲟ, ⲕⲟⲙ ⲛⲟⲩⲛ, PGM 60 O ⲕⲙⲡⲧⲟ (? ἐννοσίγαιος).

ⲕⲱⲙ S nn m, part of a farm cart, exact meaning uncertain: PCai 3 74 σὺν ἀλύσεσι, ἄξονι καὶ ξυλινοβαστάκιῳ ἤτοι ⲡⲕⲱⲙ.

ⲕⲁⲙⲉ SA, ⲕⲉⲙⲓ F v ⲕⲙⲟⲙ.

ⲕⲏⲙⲉ SA, ⲕⲏⲙⲓ F Egypt v ⲕⲙⲟⲙ.

ⲕⲏⲙⲉ S, ⲕⲟⲙⲓ B gum v ⲕⲟⲙⲙⲉ.

ⲕⲙⲉ (ⲕⲛⲏⲙⲉ) S v ⲕⲙⲟⲙ.

ⲕⲙⲕⲙ, ⲕⲟⲩⲅⲕⲙ (Ge 31 27), ⲕⲟⲩⲕⲙ S, ⲕⲉⲙⲕⲉⲙ B, ⲕⲟⲩⲕⲉⲙ F vb intr, a strike, beat a musical instrument: FR 120 B David ⲉϥⲕ. ⲉⲧⲉϥⲕⲩⲑⲁⲣⲁ

(cf ib 124 ⲕⲙ ⲉⲧⲉϥⲕⲓⲑ.), Dif 1 52 B sim ⲕ. ⲋⲉⲛⲧⲉⲕⲕⲓⲑ. ⲋⲣⲃ. Cf ⲕⲙ thus used: R 1 2 13 S, BSM 16 B &c. b make a repeated sound, as of bird's voice: Mich 550 24 S ⲉⲩⲕ. ϩⲛⲧⲉⲅⲁⲥⲡⲉ (var TT 18 ϫⲙ]ϫⲙ). nn m, drum: P 44 58 S ⲙⲋⲣ, Ge 31 27 SB, Ex 15 20 S (Mor 22 102) B, 2 Kg 6 5 SB (P 44 109 ⲧⲃⲗ), Ps 80 3 B (ⲛⲋ), Is 5 12 SBF τύμπανον; He 11 35 B (S om) beaten like ⲕ. τυμπανίζειν; BAp 23 S angel Kadiel with his ⲕ., Va 67 70 B ⲕⲓⲑ. & ⲕ., ShZ 639 S psaltery, flutes & ⲕ., BMis 13 S ϩⲉⲛⲙⲟⲩⲙⲕⲟⲩⲙ (sic) & flutes. ⲣⲉϥⲕ., var ⲣⲉϥⲉⲣ ⲕ. B nn, drummer: Ps 67 26 (S ⲣⲉϥϫⲛⲭⲛ) τυμπανίστρια. In ⲣⲙⲕⲙⲕⲙ Glos 204 S τύμπανον ? cart-wheel (ⲣⲙ- here obscure). Cf ⳝⲛⳝⲛ (ⳝⲙⳝⲙ).

ⲕⲙⲟⲙ S, ⲕⲙⲁⲙ F, ⲭⲙⲟⲙ B, ⲕⲏⲙⲧ SAF, ⲭⲏⲙⲧ B vb intr, be, become black: EpJer 20 BF μελανοῦσθαι, Mt 5 36 S (B adj) μέλανα ποιεῖν, Ap 6 12 SB μ. γίνεσθαι; Job 30 30 S (B ⲭⲁⲕⲓ) σκοτοῦν; Lam 5 10 S (B diff) πελιοῦσθαι; BHom 31 S ⲁⲩⲕ. through time γρυλλοειδής, BIF 14 175 S ⲁⲡⲣⲏ ⲕ., BMOr 8800 1 S dying man's tongue ⲁϥⲕ. Qual: Lev 13 37 S (B adj), Cant 5 11 S, Z 320 S μέλας, Cl 8 3 A μελανώτερος, BMis 542 S sim; Mor 17 59 S ⲉⲣⲉⲡⲉϥϩⲟ ⲕ. μελαίνειν; Lev 13 56 S (var better ⲕⲣⲙⲣⲱⲙ, B ϩⲗⲟⲗ) ἀμαυρὸς εἶναι; C 89 92 B evil soul ⲉⲥⲭ. ⲉⲥⲟⲓ ⲛⲭⲁⲙⲉ = Va 172 54 ⲋⲱⲋⲁ ⲋⲃⲋⲏⲉ, Mor 24 11 F ⲁϥⲕ. like sackcloth, Mor 38 67 S wine ⲉϥⲕ. like ink, Mor 37 86 S Jacob's pottage of ⲁⲣϣⲓⲛ ⲉϥⲕ., PMéd 177 S ⲥⲁϣ ⲉϥⲕ. ⲕⲙⲟⲙ nn m, blackness: ShC 42 127 S gold ⲁⲩⲕⲣⲟⲙⲣⲙ ϩⲣⲟⲩⲕ. ⲉⲡⲁϣϣⲱϥ (cf Lam 4 1), ShMIF 23 185 S ⲡⲓⲕ. ⲡϣⲱϩⲣ from feverish vices, Louvre 10010 S face ⲣ ⲡⲉⲕ. ⲡⲟⲩⳝⲁⲗⲁϩⲧ.

ⲕⲁⲙⲉ SA, -ⲏ S (m & f), ⲕⲉⲙⲉ (Cai 42573 2, var ⲕⲁ-), ⲕⲙⲙⲉ, ⲕⲁⲙ S, ⲭⲁⲙⲉ, -ⲏ, ⲭⲉⲙⲓ B, ⲕⲉⲙⲓ, ⲕⲉⲙ (Lam 5) F, pl ⲕⲁⲙⲁⲅⲉ S, ⲭⲁⲙⲉⲩ B adj, black: Lev 13 37 B (S vbᵗ), Zech 6 2 AB, Ap 6 5 SB, Z 335 S ϩⲛⲣⲧⲟ ⲡⲕ. μέλας; AM 215 B dog, MIE 2 408 B horse, BM 529 S foal, PS 318 S bull, MR 2 46 S sheep, TT 74 S, AM 187 B snake, Tri 435 S raven, Mor 40 41 S = MG 25 268 B ϩⲃⲥⲱ, CDan 93 B ⲃⲁⲗⲗⲓⲛ (πάλλιον), O'LearyTh 46 B ϣⲁⲣ; rarely without ⲛ-: Cai 42573 1 Sᶠ ⲓⲱ ⲕⲁⲙ (sic), ib ⲉⲥⲁ⳿ⲅ -ⲙⲉ CO 467 S ⲟⲩϣⲃⲱⲧ -ⲙⲏ, BMOr 9525(11) S ϩⲟⲓⲧⲉ -ⲙⲏ (cf ⲟⲩ ⲱⲃϣ), ? ⲁⲡⲓⲕⲁⲙ q v (& add Ann 18 285 S ⲁⲡⲕⲉⲙ); so with some names: PO 14 321 B ⲓⲱⲁⲡⲡⲏⲥ ⲭ. (also ⲡⲓⲭ. CaiTh 291, cf Moses ⲡⲓⲭ. MG 25 262); preceding nn (?): BMEA 10391 S magic ⲁⲓⲕⲓⲛⲉ ⲡⲟⲩⲥⲁⲉⲓⲛ ⲡⲧⲱⲣϣ ⲡⲕⲁⲙⲃⲁⲗ ruddy & black-eyed.

—— *SBF* nn m f, *black* person or thing : Cant 1 4 *S*, Mor 37 42 *S* thou art ογκ. in thy heart μέλας, MG 25 129 *B* пекϫαμεγ *black* hair opp пексϫιμ (*cf* Z 654 n), K 206 *B* among colours πιϫ. اسود, AZ 23 107 *S* пк. resulting from alchemical process, Lant 51n *S* from Christ till пекамαγει came to Egypt, that wore пекαμη (*i e* Abbâsids), *cf* ? BP 9544 *F* пекαμη псιρι (? Bousiris), *ib* Abd alla пк. ; сϯκεμε, -κιμε, κημμε, ϭμε (P 43) *S*, стγϫεμι *B* nn m, *black cumin*: Is 28 25, 27 *SB* μελάνθιον *nigella sativa*, P 43 58 *S* شونيز وهو, الكمون الاسود (*cf* Chassinat PMéd 200, Löw 366).

p, ер к. *SBF*, *be black*: Lam 5 17 *F* (*SB* κακε) ελ κεμ σκοτοῦν, Cat 147 *B* colour of body ϭωϫ, πτεϥερ ϫ., BM 527 *F* eyes εγω пкεμι, Bor 241 217 *S* (on Cant 1 4) птαςр к. from asceticism, ShMIF 23 152 *S* тετο пкαμη асογⲃαϣ.

In many names, *eg* καμε, Πκαμέ, Τκαμέ, Ἑρκᾶμ, Πκῆμις & in place-names, папкαμη, Τβενκῆμ (?) *Journ Philol* 32 273.

V also αпικαμ, ελελκημε (ελοολε).

κμε *S* nn f, *darkness*: ShC 73 180 in тк. of night ظلام الليل opp погоеин of day. Prob *l* κμη μe *q v*.

κμηе *SA*, ϫ нмι *B*, кнмι *F* nn m, rarely f (*v* below), *the black land, Egypt,* (*cf* χημία, Plutarch): bible pass Αἴγυπτος ;   as m : Ps 134 9 *SB*, Jer 26 20 *B*, Ac 7 11 *SB*, El 84 *A*, PS 27 *S*, C 43 63 *B*, BKU 1 31⁹ *S* ;   as f : Ez 29 2 *B* (*S* m), Mor 50 61 *S* к.... пеϩ птαγταрϭес αμαϥ is Christ's blood птαϥϭοι λε ерос, wherefore martyrs μεριτε, P 131⁸ 147 *S* named к. ετⲃеϫескнμ;   opp desert : BM 320 *S*, PO 11 340 *B*, J 65 44 *S* ;   opp Shiêt : MG 25 77, 200, 400, BM 915 18 *B* ;   opp Lower Egypt : Miss 4 666–8 *S* (?), but also to Thebaid : C 89 1 *B*, or μαрнс (рнс) : C 43 90, AM 263 *B* ;   was north of Thebes : CO 385 *S* еϩн[т] ек. ;   opp Rakote (Alexandria) : C 43 137, CDan 86 *B*, Mor 48 51, 103 *S* ;   к. later = Babylon (Fustât) : BM 346 *S*, *ib* 580 25 *F*, Ryl 461 *B* (18th cent). Same word ? in place-name пελϫнμι بلكيم EW 94.   *V* A J Butler *Babylon of Egypt* 15 ff.

рμпк., -ϫ. *SABF, Egyptian* (*cf* AZ 43 158 ἑρμοχύμιος): Ex 2 12 *SAB*, Is 30 7 *SBF*, Ac 7 22 *SBF* Αἰγύπτιος ; BMis 408 *S* = BSM 55 *B* тр. Potiphar's wife, J MMA 24 2 3 пеιεттрαφοп пр., BIF 13 102 *S* ϭепос пр. μптрμпк., -ϫ., *Egyptian nationality, speech* (*cf* αспе пк.): PSBA 10 195 *S* she learnt тм., MG 17 302 *S*=*ib* 258 *B* interpreters between Greek & μ., MG 25 238 *B* ϯсμη αμμ., J 75 48 *S* αспе μμ., *cf ib* 106 21 пαιπтιακη.

ϫнμι *B* nn f, ? *brazier, hearth*: C 41 54 in

winter they sat ⲋатенϯϫ. = Miss 4 420 قلابة (*l* ? مقلابة).

кинме *S* nn, *darkness* (*cf* DM 10 19 *kmeme*): Sh(Besa)BMOr 8810 425 dark minds ето пρⲃα & false knowledge ето пк., P 131⁸ 147 before Mark's coming Egypt named]ϫекнме н ετⲃеϫескнμ н ϫеογκ.те (*cf* TT 68 n).

коммε (PMéd 157, Cai 42573 1), комн (P 44 66), коми (P 43 33), кμμе (PMéd 173), кнмμе (*ib* 131, Bodl(P) a 2 28), кнме (Ryl 106 8) *S*, комн (K 187), коми (C 89 173) *B* nn m (Ryl), *gum*, dem *qme, qmϡ, κόμμι*: P 43, 44, K صمغ ; PMéd 157 к. пαλεγ, C 89, Ryl from tree ϣопте, Bodl water of к. пϣαпте, DM 5 4 sim (*cf* ὑδροκόμμιον), Cai in recipe, water of corpse & пк. п птαфос.

кαμпι *B* nn f, among birds : K 168 صرصور, which P 44 57 = ϩλομ (λεϩλεμ) σκνίψ. Acc to AZ 6 56 'ه is *sparrow* or *finch*, but usually is *cricket* (Lab also *cockroach*). Cf ? κάμπη *caterpillar*, though this also = коомϥ & етнϣι *q v*.

кαμте *S* nn f, *vessel containing oil* : CO 213 αϭпеп перп, ϯк. ппеϩ.

кμто *SA*, кемто *B*   *v* κιμ.

кемтс *F*   *v* κωрμ *smoke* (кρμтс).

коммϣ, кμϣ-, комϣϡ *S* vb I intr, *sneer*: ShZ 597 сепαϫоос εγк. ϩιтписαⲃεεγ ϫе-, ShA 1 152 paral сωⲃе, елк ϣα, к,; Mor 41 13 began to murmur & to к.   **II** tr, *mock*: Job 22 19, Ps 2 4, Pro 11 12 (*A* ωλк ϣе), Gal 6 7 (all *B* елк ϣαι) μυκτηρίζειν ; Z 305 monk & demons αϥкоммογ εὐτελίζειν ; ShIF 226 птαпепϫоειс кμϣ ϩнрω ϩнс (Lu 13 32).

—— пса-, *mock, contemn*: Pro 12 8 (*A* ω. ϣе), Lu 16 14 (*B* елк.) μυκτ., Aeg 270 (var к. п-) ἐκμυκτ. ; 2 Kg 6 16 (*B* ϣωϣ) ἐξουδενοῦν, BMis 539 ϣαγк. псαпεγερнγ *innuunt sibi*, ShA 1 378 Gentiles εγк. αγω εγсωⲃе псапμγстнριοп.

—— nn m, *mockery, contempt*: Ps 34 16 (*B* елк.) μυκτηρισμός ; Z 298 огпе пк. ἐξουδένωσις (in bible сωϣϥ), Sh(Besa)Bor 205 367 they will say ϩпогϫпιо μпогк., ShC 73 35 ϩпогк. μпогсωϣϥ, ShRE 10 164 огпоϭпеϭ μпогк.

μптреϥк. nn f, *mockery, contempt*: ShBMOr 8810 380 тогμ. εϫппетпειоте, ShC 73 115 μ. & μптреϥϯ погϭс μпϣαϫе μппē.

коомϥ, комϥ (P 44, BM 491) *S* nn m, *blight*: Ps 77 46 (*B* етнϣι) ἐρυσίβη قبل ; Joel 1 4 (Mor 22 9, *A* = Gk, *B* ϫепт), *ib* 2 25 (*AB* = Gk) κάμπη ; P 44 57 قبل *louse*. Cf етнϣι, кαμпι.

ⲕⲁⲛ- *F* *v* ⲕⲟⲩⲓ B ⲃ.

ⲕⲉⲛⲥ *B* *v* ⲕⲟⲩⲡⲥ.

ⲕⲏⲛ *B* vb **I** intr, *cease, fail*: Job 18 2 (*S* ⲕⲁ
ⲣⲱⲥ), Is 16 10 (*S* ⲱϫⲛ), *ib* 24 13 (*S* ⲟⲩⲉⲓⲛⲉ), *ib*
57 10 (*S* ⲕⲁ ⲧⲟⲟⲧⲥ ⲉⲃⲟⲗ), Jer 51 10 (*S* ⲗⲟ) παύειν,
Ex 31 17 (*S* ⲙⲧⲟⲛ, *cf* 34 33 ⲟⲩⲱ), Dan 9 27 καταπαύ.; Mk 4 39 (*S* ⲅⲣⲟⲕ) κοπάζειν; Job 31 26 (*S*
ⲣⲱⲧⲡ) ἐκλείπειν; Jos 3 13 (*S* ⲱϣⲙ) ἱστάναι; Mt
11 1 (*S* ⲟⲩⲱ) τελεῖν, Ge 17 22 συντελ.; Mt 5 28
(*S* ⲇⲟ) ἤδη; Gk om: Mt 6 2 (*S* ⲇⲟ), Lu 6 24 (*cf*
below c ⲉ-); C 89 4 persecution ⲉⲧⲁϥⲕ. = MG 17
316 *S* do, Rec 7 92 ϣⲁϥⲕ. ⲛ̄ϫⲉ ⲡⲟⲩϩⲏⲧ through
avarice, MIE 2 384 ⲉⲧⲁϥⲕ. ⲉϥϫⲱ ⲙⲡⲁⲓⲥⲁϫⲓ = BAp
108 *S* do, C 41 50 ⲙⲡⲁⲓⲕ. ⲉⲓⲡⲉⲙⲱⲧⲉⲛ. *Suffice,
be enough* impersonal (*S* ⲅⲱ): Ge 30 15 ⲕ. ⲁⲛ ϫⲉ-,
ib 33·15 sim ἱκανός; with ⲉ-: Deu 3 26 ἱκανοῦν;
Mt 6 34 ἀρκετός, 2 Cor 12 9 ἀρκεῖν, PSBA 10 402
ⲕ. ⲉⲣⲱⲧⲉⲛ ⲡⲉⲙⲏⲓ ἀφέτέ με.

With following preposition.   ⲉ- verbal, *complete, do already*: Ez 3 27 (*S* ⲡⲟⲩ), *ib* 35 11, Va
57 20 ⲛⲏ ⲉⲧⲁϥⲕ. ⲉⲭⲟⲧⲟⲩ ἤδη, Cat 1 ⲉⲧⲁⲓⲕ. ⲉⲉⲣ.
ϣⲟⲣⲡ ⲛϫⲟⲥ, Aeg 36 gladly had they ⲕ. ⲉⲙⲟⲩ,
BSM 31 sim, C 89 130 ⲁⲡ ⲡⲭⲥ̄ ⲕ. (ⲉ)ⲉⲣⲏⲧ (*cf* below
c ⲛ- verbal).   ⲉ- refl (ethic dat, *v* ⲉ- prep g):
Is 1 16 (DeV 137) ⲕ. ⲉⲣⲱⲧⲉⲛ ϩⲉⲛ- (*S* ⲗⲟ) παύειν
ἀπό, MG 25 260 ⲧⲛⲁⲕ. ⲉⲣⲟⲓ ϣⲁⲙⲡⲁⲓ, Va 61 20
he taught greedy ⲡⲥⲉⲕ. ⲉⲣⲱⲟⲩ ⲉⲅⲣⲱⲗⲉⲙ.   ⲛ-
ethic dat: C 86 179 ⲕⲏⲛ ⲡⲁⲕ.   ⲛ-, *from*: C 43
29 ⲛⲧⲉϥⲕ. ⲙⲡⲁⲙⲑⲟ.   ⲛ- verbal: BSM 38 ⲁⲡⲉⲕⲛ-
ⲣⲱⲃ ⲕ. ⲛ̄ϫⲱⲕ = BMis 383 *S* ⲣ ϣⲁⲩ, Cat 42 after
we had ⲕ. ⲛ̄ϫⲱ ⲙⲡⲥⲁϫⲓ.   ⲛⲉⲙ-, *finish with*:
C 43 141 ⲧⲛⲁⲕ. ⲁⲛ ⲡⲉⲙⲁϥ.   ⲛⲧⲉⲛ-, *as regards,
from*: MIE 2 398 water ⲕ. ⲛⲧⲟⲧⲛ = BAp 97 *S*
ⲱϫⲛ ⲛⲧⲛ-, Bess 7 ('03) 9 why do I delay ⲛⲧⲉⲛ-
ⲡⲓⲥⲛⲟⲩ ⲕ. ⲛⲧⲟⲧ ? ⲡⲁϩⲣⲉⲛ-, *from*: Aeg 29 all
pains ⲕ. ⲡⲁϩⲣⲁϥ.   ϩⲉⲛ-, *from*: Job 6 26 (*S* diff)
παύειν dat, 3 Jo 10 (*S* ⲅⲱ) ἀρκεῖν ἐπί, C 43 214
ⲉⲧⲁϥⲕ. ϩⲉⲛⲟⲩⲁⲣⲓⲥⲧⲟⲛ, Va 61 96 fish die ⲁⲩϣⲁⲡⲕ.
ϩⲉⲛⲡⲓⲙⲱⲟⲩ = P 131³ 85 *S* ⲗⲟ.   ⲉⲃⲟⲗ ϩⲉⲛ-,
from, away from: Ez 14 6 ἀποστρέφειν ἀπό, Joel 1
13 (*SA* ⲱϫⲛ) ἀπέχειν, Cat 17 ⲁⲛⲡⲁⲕ. ⲉⲃⲟⲗ ϩⲉⲛ-
ⲡⲁⲓⲃⲓⲥⲓ.   ϩⲁⲧⲉⲛ-, *from*: C 41 19 Christ ⲡⲉⲧⲁϥⲕ.
ϩⲁⲧⲟⲧ ⲧⲛⲟⲩ, C 43 195 sim.   ⲉⲃⲟⲗ ϩⲁ-, *from*:
Jer 38 16 διαλείπειν ἀπό, C 89 130 ⲙⲡⲉϥⲕ. ⲉⲃ.
ϩⲁⲧⲉϥⲙⲉⲧⲁⲑⲛⲁϩⲧ.

With following adverb.   ⲉⲃⲟⲗ (late ?): TEuch
1 306 bishop prays during *Credo* ϣⲁⲛⲧⲉϥⲕ. ⲉⲃ.,
PasH 27 ⲙⲉⲛⲉⲡⲥⲁⲉⲧⲁϥⲕ. ⲉⲃ.   ⲙⲙⲁⲩ: Rec 7
92 ϣⲁϥⲕ. ⲛ̄ϫⲉ ⲡⲟⲩϩⲣⲧ ⲙⲙⲁⲩ.

II tr, *finish*: C 89 74 ⲉⲧⲁϥⲕ. ⲛ̄ⲑⲟⲙⲛ = MG 17
328 *S* ⲟⲩⲱ ⲛ-, *ib* 75 when he had ⲕ. ⲁⲡⲉϥϩⲱⲃ
ⲛϫⲓϫ, C 41 47 when brother had ⲕ. ⲁⲡⲓ̄ⲃ̄ Minor

Prophets, C 43 245 ⲕ. ⲙⲙⲟⲕ ⲥⲁⲃⲟⲗ ⲙⲙⲟⲓ.   Or
? intr: *cease from* ⲛ- (*cf* ⲗⲟ ⲛ-).

ⲁⲧⲕ. adj, *unending*: BSM 52 ⲙⲉⲧⲟⲩⲣⲟ ⲡⲁ., AM
81 ⲡⲓϣⲧ ⲛⲥⲛⲟⲩ ⲡⲁ.   ⲙⲉⲧⲁⲧⲕ. nn f, *unending-
ness*: 2 Pet 2 14 ἀκατάπαυστος.

ⲕⲟⲛ (*sic* MS) *S* nn, meaning unknown: ShR 2
3 44 sweet smelling plants strewn in pagan temple
ⲟⲩⲣⲧ, ϣⲗϩ ⲙⲡⲉⲛⲕ. ϩⲓⲉⲣⲡⲱ ⲡ̄ϣⲱⲃⲉ ⲡⲉⲗⲟⲟⲗⲉ, so
? part of vine.

ⲕⲟⲩⲛⲥ *SF*, ⲕⲟⲩⲟⲩⲛⲥ *SA²*, ⲕⲟⲩⲟⲡⲥ (BMar 151),
ⲕⲟⲩⲱⲡⲥ (BMis 449) *S*, ⲕⲟⲟⲡⲥ, ⲕⲟⲡⲥ *A*, ⲕⲉⲡⲥ *S*
(Tri 729) *B* (ⲕⲟⲩⲛⲥ Ez 23 20) nn, only with suffix
(3 sg *SF* rarely ⲕⲟⲩⲛⲧϥ Deu 25 11 Mor, Lu 16 22
var, PMéd 267, Ann 23 55, Lant 50 ; pl *S* ⲕⲟⲩⲛⲧⲟⲩ,
ⲕⲟⲩⲟⲩⲛⲧⲟⲩ Pro 16 33, Is 65 7, var both ⲕⲟⲩⲟⲩ-
ⲡⲟⲩ), *bosom*: Ge 16 5 *B* (*S* diff), Ex 4 6 *A* (*B*
ⲑⲟⲩⲱⲥ), Job 19 27 *SB*, Ps 128 7 *B* (*S* ⲁⲗⲟⲙ), Pro
24 27 *SA*, Hos 8 1 *B* (*A* ⲧⲁⲡ), Jo 13 23 *SA²B* κόλπος; Pro 24 48 *SA* στῆθος (*cf* 6 10 ⲙⲉⲥⲧϩⲏⲧ), PS
96 *S* prayer shall return ⲉⲕⲟⲩⲟⲩⲛⲧ, C 86 295 *B*
laid child ϫⲉⲛⲕⲉⲛⲥ ⲙⲡⲓⲱⲙⲓ, Mor 25 11 *S*
ϩⲛⲕⲟⲩⲛϥ of Abraham (var P 131³ 83 ⲧⲟⲡ), Mor 33
113 *S* ⲕⲟⲩⲛⲥ of Mary (var BMis 58 ϩⲁⲙⲏⲣ).   As
genital parts: Deu 23 1 *B* (*S* Gk om) الحبلي, *ib* 25
11 *S* (*B* ⲁⲑⲣⲉⲩ) δίδυμοι, Ez 23 20 *SB* αἰδοῖα.   ⲕⲟⲩⲛϥ *S*, ⲕⲉⲛϥ *B* nn m & f, sg & pl: BMOr 8811 238
S ϩⲛⲕⲟⲩⲛϥ ⲡⲧⲉⲥϩⲓⲙⲉ, Ez 23 20 *B* ⲛⲏ ⲉⲧⲉⲟⲩⲟⲩ
ⲡⲕⲟⲩⲛϥ, BSM xi *B* ⲕⲉⲛϥ ⲛⲛⲉⲡⲓⲟⲧ, CaiEuch 362
B sim ; PMéd 267 *S* ⲟⲩⲕⲟⲩⲛⲧϥ ⲡⲟⲩⲣⲱⲙⲉ ⲉϥϣⲱⲡⲉ ⲉⲣⲟϥ, *ib* ⲟⲩⲕⲟⲩⲛⲧϥ ⲡⲟⲩⲁ.   In place-name
? ⲧⲡⲉⲧⲣⲁ ⲡⲕⲟⲩⲡⲡⲉϫⲓ MG 25 292 *B* = ⲕⲟⲡⲡⲉϫⲓ
BIF 13 = لكم الجوف Gött ar 114 200 (so ⲕⲟⲩ =
ⲕⲟⲩⲓ improb).

ⲕⲟⲩⲛ- *SF* *v* ⲕⲟⲩⲓ **B a.**

ⲕⲉⲛⲓ *B* *v* ⲕⲛⲡⲉ.

ⲕⲉⲉⲛⲓ *F* *v* ⲡⲕⲁ.

ⲕⲏⲛⲉ *S* *v* ⲕⲏⲡⲉ nn.

ⲕⲛⲉⲓⲉ *A* *v* ⲕⲏⲡⲉ.

ⲕⲛⲟ *A* *v* ⲕⲡⲁⲁⲩ *sheaf*.

ⲕⲓⲛⲃⲏⲗ *S* *v* ϭⲓⲟⲩⲏⲗ.

ⲕⲛⲓⲕⲓϫⲓ *B* nn f, *vessel or measure for liquids*:
Ez 46 14 εἷν (*cf* same phrase Nu 15 6 &c), K 149,
P 55 11 (among vessels ماعون) دكجة. *Cf* ? ⲕⲟⲩ-
ⲡⲭⲟⲩ, κνίδιον.

ⲕⲏⲛⲉ *S*, ⲕⲛⲉⲓⲉ, ⲕⲛⲡⲓⲉ *A*, ⲕⲉⲡⲓ *B*, ⲕⲏⲛⲡⲓ *F*,
ⲕⲡⲓⲱⲩ† *A*, ⲕⲉⲡⲓⲟⲩⲧ† *B*, vb intr, *be fat, sweet*:
Ps 64 13 *B* (*S* ⲟⲩⲣⲟⲧ), Is 58 11 *SB* πιαίνειν, Ge
49 20† *B* (*S* ⲕⲓⲱⲟⲩ), Ps 21 13† *B* (*S* ⲥⲁⲛⲁϣⲧ),

Mic 6 7† *AB* πίων; Deu 32 15 *SB* λιπαίνειν; Ps
54 21 *S* (*B* ϭⲟⲡ) ἀπαλύνειν; Pro 24 13 *SA* γλυκαίνεσθαι, Va 57 199 *B* heart ⲉⲧⲁϭⲕ. ⲟⲩⲟϩ ⲁϥϭⲟⲡ
καταψύχειν; C 89 77 *B* oil ⲉⲧⲕ.† = TT 151 *S*
ⲕⲓⲱⲟⲩ, BMis 243 *S* perfumes ⲉⲩϭⲛⲡⲉ, MélOr 6
499 *B* ϥⲁϩⲣⲓ ⲉⲧⲕ.†, Cat 176 *B* regenerated heart
pure & ⲉϥⲕ.†, Abst 147 *B* voices ⲉⲩⲕ.†, Aeg 15 *S*
his name ⲕ. ⲁⲩⲱ ⲉϥⲕⲓⲱⲟⲩ.

—— *SBF* nn m, *fatness, sweetness*: Jud 9 9 *S*,
Job 36 17 *B*, Ro 11 17 *SBF* πιότης; Ap 18 14 *B*
(*S* diff) λιπαρός; Deu 32 14 *S* (*B* Gk om, cf Ps 80
16), P 44 70 *S* μελιλίπος دسم, Bodl 325 151 *B*
دسم الشيرج grease from sesame oil, *ib* 155 *B* ϩⲣⲏⲣⲓ
ⲡⲧⲉ ⲡⲓⲕ. رائحة المسك (? *l* سلي melted butter, *cf* K 200
سم, though there ? *l* ϭⲉⲗⲓ), C 43 167 *B* paral ⲱⲧ,
PMéd 237 *S* ⲕ. of calf, *ib* 216 of goose, *ib* 261 of
swine, sim DeV 88, AM 310, BIF 14 116 (or
LMär 4 ⲕ. alone) in tortures; BMis 178 *S* ⲡⲟⲩⲣⲟⲧ
ⲙⲡⲕ. (cf Ps 64 13) & sweetness of olive, BM 293
S locusts & wild honey ⲉⲩⲏⲏⲩ ⲉⲡⲉⲥⲛⲧ ϩⲁⲙⲡⲕ.
ⲙⲡϯⲧⲉ, BAp 31 *S* ⲕ. ⲛⲥϯⲛⲟⲩϥⲉ ascended from
sacrifice (MIF 9 65 om).
ⲣ ⲕ. *S*, *be fat*: Mor 18 116 ⲉϥⲥⲁⲡⲁϣⲧ ⲉϥⲟ ⲡⲕ.
εὔτροφος εὔσαρκος (LCyp 8 diff).
ϯ ⲕ. *SB*, *make fat, salve, anoint*: Ps 140 5 *B*
(*S* ⲧⲱϩⲥ), Pro 5 3 *B* (*SA* ϯ ϩⲗⲟϭ), Si 32 5 *S* λιπαίν.;
ib 26 13 *S*, HL 84 *B* πιαίν.; R 2 61 *S* thy voice ϯ
ⲕ. ⲡⲛⲁⲕⲉⲉⲥ, C 43 72 *B* honey in throat ϯ ⲕ. ⲡⲏⲓ;
BMis 533 *S* ⲣⲉϥϯ ⲕ. ⲡⲛⲉⲯⲩⲭⲏ opp ⲣⲉϥϯ ϩⲟⲧⲉ.

ⲕⲛⲛⲉ (or *l* ⲕⲏⲡⲉ) *S* nn f, *meaning unknown*:
Ep 543 in list of vessels (σκεύη) ⲥⲛⲁⲩ ⲛⲕⲏⲡⲛ
(ἀγγεῖον), ⲥⲛⲧⲉ ⲡⲕ., ⲥⲛⲧⲉ ⲡⲃⲏⲃ.

ⲕⲱⲛⲥ *SAF*, ⲕⲱⲱⲛⲥ *SA²*, ϫⲱⲛⲥ (only C 86) *B*,
ⲕⲉⲡⲥ-, ⲕⲟⲛⲥⲋ, ⲕⲟⲟⲛⲥⲋ *S*, ⲕⲁⲡⲥⲋ *AF*, ⲕⲁⲁⲡⲥⲋ *A²*,
ⲕⲟⲡⲥ† *S* vb **I** tr, *pierce, slay*: Ge 22 10 *S* (*B* ϩⲟⲗ-
ϩⲉⲗ), Ex 12 6 *S* (*B* ϣⲱⲧ), Pro 9 2 *SA* (*B* ϩⲟⲗ.),
1 Jo 3 12 *S* (*B* ϩⲱⲧⲉⲃ) σφάζειν, Zech 11 5 *A* (*B*
ϩⲟⲗ.), Lu 19 27 *S* (*B* do) κατασφ.; Nu 22 29 *S*
(*B* do), Is 14 19 †*S* (*B* do), Jo 19 37 *S* (*A²B* ⲧⲱⲕⲥ,
ⲑⲱ-) ἐκκεντεῖν, Nu 25 8 *S* (*B* ϩⲟⲗ.), Ez 21 11 *S*
(*B* ϩⲱⲧ.) ἀποκεν.; Job 30 14 *S* (*B* ϩⲓⲟⲩⲓ ⲉϩⲟⲩⲛ)
κατακοντίζειν; Deu 33 17 *S* (*B* ϯ ϣⲉ ⲛϥⲁⲧ), Ps
43 5 *S* (*B* ϩⲟⲗ.) κερατίζειν; Deu 1 44 *S* (*B* ϫⲱⲧϩ),
Pro 7 26 *SA* (*B* ⲱϫϩ) τιτρώσκειν; Is 66 3 *S* (*B*
ϣⲱⲧ), Lu 15 23 *S* (*B* do) θύειν; Jo 19 34 *SA²*
(*B* ⲑⲱⲕⲥ) νύσσειν; 2 Kg 4 7 *S* τύπτειν, Miss 8 44
S of conscience ἐπιπλήσσειν; ShC 42 180 *S* ⲙⲁⲣⲡⲕ.
ⲙⲡⲉⲡϩⲏⲧ with fear of God, ShZ 601 *S* ⲡⲉⲓⲭⲟⲟⲕⲉϥ
ⲉⲩⲕ. souls, C 86 136 *B* men are not beasts ⲉϫ.
ⲙⲙⲟⲟⲩ, Aeg 264 *S* ⲛⲧⲁⲩⲕⲉⲡⲥ Christ in side with
spear, P 131³ 45 *S* ϣⲁⲩⲕⲟⲡⲥⲟⲩ ⲉⲡⲉⲩⲙⲁⲕⲉ like
doves, Gu 14 *S* ⲁϥⲕ. apostle ⲉϫⲛⲡⲉϥϭⲗⲟⲟⲧⲉ,

Mor 27 17 *F* ⲉϥⲛⲁⲕⲁⲡⲥⲧ. ⲙⲁ ⲡⲕ.: Pro 7 22
SA (*B* om), Ac 8 32 *S* (*B* ⲉⲡϩⲟⲗ.) σφαγή. Infin
+m art & suff as nn: Job 27 14 *S* ⲉⲡⲕⲟⲡⲥⲟⲩ (*B*
do), Is 34 2 *SF* (*B* do) εἰς σφαγήν, Hos 9 13 *A* (*B*
do) εἰς ἀποκέντησιν.

II intr: Jer 27 11 *S* (*B* ϩⲟⲗ.) κερατίζειν: Ez
21 10 *S* (*B* do) σφάζειν; Mor 30 37 *F* bull ⲡⲉⲧⲕ.
= BMis 262 *S* ⲡⲉⲧϯ ⲟⲩⲃⲉ, ShA 1 259 *S* ϩⲛⲁⲩ ⲡⲕ.

—— nn m, *slaughter*: Job 21 20 *S* (*B* ϩⲟⲗ.),
Is 34 6 *SF* (*B* do), Ja 5 5 (*B* do) σφαγή; R 2 1
65 *S* ⲡⲕ. of Innocents, Wess 15 9 *S* celebrate
ⲡⲉⲡⲕ.

ⲣⲉϥ-, ⲗⲉϥⲕ. *SF*, *slayer*: Ex 21 29 *S* (*B* ⲣⲉϥϩⲟⲗ.)
κερατιστής; Mor 30 37 *SF* sim, ClPr 47 3 *S* father
ⲉϥⲟ ⲛⲣ.

ⲕⲱⲛⲥ, ⲕⲟⲟⲛⲥ *prepare for burial, corpse* *v* ⲕⲱⲟⲥ.

ⲕⲛⲟⲥ, ⲕⲛⲟⲟⲥ, ⲕⲛⲱⲱⲥ (BMar) *S*, ϫⲱⲛⲥ *B*, ⲕⲟⲡⲥ†
(R) *S*, ϫⲱⲡⲥ† *B* vb **I** intr, *stink, be putrid*: Ex 8
10 *B*, Jo 11 39 *B* (*SA²* ⲣ ⲥⲧⲟⲓ) ὄζειν, Ex 16 24 *SB*,
C 89 53 *B* ἐπόζ., Ps 37 5 *SB* προσόζ.; BMar 197
S body ⲁϥⲕ., Mor 22 101 *S* flesh ϣⲁⲩⲕ. ⲛⲥⲉ-
ⲧⲁⲕⲟ = BSM 95 *B* ϫ., C 41 24 *B* ⲉϥϫ.† like ⲓⲁⲃⲓ
of corpse, R 2 1 76 *S* superstitious parents wash
children in ⲙⲙⲟⲟⲩ ⲉⲧⲕ.†, Bor 258 41 *S* paral
ⲃⲁⲁⲃⲉ. **II** tr, *make to stink, defile*: Va 61 26 *B*
why ⲕϫ. ⲡⲛⲉⲕϫⲓϫ by carrying worm ? ἀφανίζειν. As nn m, *stink*: ShA 1 247 *S* ⲡⲁϣⲁⲓ
ⲙⲡⲉⲕ., Pcod 26 *S* (var) neither death nor ⲕ., Va
57 247 *B* ϫ. & ⲥⲱⲟⲓ ⲃⲱⲛ of dirty cauldron.

ⲕⲛⲧⲉ *SA*, ⲕⲉⲡⲧⲉ *B*, ⲕⲉⲡⲧⲓ *F* nn m (PMich 601
S charm ⲡⲓⲕ. ⲉⲧⲣⲛⲧⲁϣⲓⲝ bis, Montp 174 *B* ⲡⲓⲕ.,
cf dem qnte), fig: Nu 13 24 *SB*, Is 38 21 *SB*, Mt 7
16 *SB* σῦκον; Miss 4 725 *S* ϫⲉⲙⲡⲉϩ, ⲕ. ϩⲩⲡⲱⲣⲁ
(ὀπώρα) ⲛⲓⲙ, Z 628 *S* leaves of ⲕ. ⲡⲣⲟⲟⲩⲧ in
recipe, PMich 593 *S* poultice of ⲕ., PMéd 111 *S*
ⲙⲟⲟⲩ ⲡⲕ., TurM 9 *S* ⲉⲣⲱⲧⲉ ⲡⲕ., C 89 13 *B* ϩⲁⲡⲕ.
ⲉⲩⲡⲁϣⲧ يابس, P 44 82 *S* ⲕ. ⲉⲧⲕⲟⲧϥ ⲁⲥⲕⲁⲧⲓⲁ
(? ἰσχάδες) الجموع, C 89 74 *B* eaten after fast;
Mun 130 *S*, BMar 219 *S* = Rec 6 185 *B* ⲕ. as figtree. ⲃⲱ ⲡⲕ., *figtree*: Ge 3 7 *B*, Pro 27 18 *SA*,
Is 34 4 *SBF*, Mt 24 32 *SBF* συκῆ; Lu 19 4 *S*
(*B* = Gk) συκομορέα. ⲓⲁϩ ⲡⲕ., *fig-garden*: Deu
8 8 *B* (P 104, *S* ⲃⲱ ⲡⲕ.) συκῆ, Jer 5 17 *B* συκῶν.

ⲕⲛⲁⲁⲩ *S*, ⲕⲛⲟ *A*, ϫⲛⲁⲩ *B*, ⲕⲛⲉⲩ *F* nn m,
sheaf: Ge 41 47 *SB*, Lev 23 11 *SB*, Hos 8 4 *AB*
δράγμα; Job 24 19 *B* (*S* ϭⲗⲱ) ἀγκαλίς; Tri 321
S, K 128 *B* حزمة, ShR 2 3 56 *S* ⲡⲉⲕ. ⲉⲧⲟⲩⲏⲣ ⲡⲥⲁ-
ⲡⲉⲧⲱⲣⲥ, AM 183 *B* ⲟⲩϫ. ⲛⲓⲱⲧ gleaned after
reapers, PCol 2 *F* about harvest ϭⲁⲡ ⲡⲉⲕ. ⲉⲧⲁⲟⲩⲁⲩ
(ⲉ)ⲡⲁⲛⲓ.

ⲕⲛⲁⲁⲩ S nn m, meaning unknown (? trade or office) : PMich 3553 in list *bis* ⲙ]ⲏⲛⲁ ⲡⲉⲕ.

ⲕⲉⲛⲉϥⲓⲧⲉⲛ B nn, kind of loaf or cake, as sg : 3 Kg 17 3 ; as pl : Ge 18 6 (S = Gk) فرني = K 374, Ex 12 39 غيف, Nu 11 8 (S = Gk) ἐγκρυφίας (which Ez 4 12 SB = Gk, Hos 7 8 A = Gk, B ⲟⲩⲱϣⲉⲙ ⲉϥϩⲏⲡ). ⲕⲉⲡⲉϥⲓⲧⲏⲥ, *baker* : K 132 فرّان (v Stern 169). *Cf* AZ 53 132.

ⲕⲟⲛϥ S nn m, a title or epithet : Saq 251 ⲓⲱ-ϩⲁⲛⲛⲏⲥ ⲡⲕ.

ⲕⲁⲛⲟⲩϥⲓ B nn m, a fish, *barbus bynni* : K 170 بنّي.

ⲕⲛⲭ (*sic* MS, ? *l* ⲕⲛⲟⲥ) S nn, a disease : R 1 4 39 ⲁϥⲣ ⲕ. ⲁϥⲣ ϫⲟⲟⲗⲉⲥ ⲧⲏⲣϥ *computuerit morbo regio* διαρρεύσας ὅλος (P. Kerameus Ἀνάλ. Ἱεροσ. 5 126).

ⲕⲛϩⲉ S, **ⲕⲉϩⲡⲓ** B (only K, v AZ 24 91) nn f, *porch, shrine* (?) : 1 Kg 5 4 ἐμπρόσθιος, *ib* πρόθυρον = P 44 109 حانوت, *ib* 60 = 43 29 ⲕ. ⲧⲁϩⲓⲣ دفير, خزانة, Am 8 3 (gloss, B Gk om), FR 72 ⲕ. in temple within Holy of Holies, BMis 104 Zacharias slain in ⲡⲧⲁϩⲓⲣ ⲡⲧⲕ. of sanctuary (Mor 33 63 om), P 129¹⁴ 127 cudgels fetched from ⲧⲕ. ⲙⲡⲉⲑⲩⲥⲓⲁⲥ-ⲧⲏⲣⲓⲟⲛ, Ryl 94 ⲧⲕ. ⲙⲡⲥⲓⲕⲛⲟⲛ (σίγνον) where soldiers take oath, K 157 B معتبة (threshold, between ⲗⲁϫ-ⲗⲉϫ & ⲟϩⲁⲓ); *side, angle*(?) : 3 Kg 6 13 ὠμία حانوت (P 44 111).

ⲕⲛϩⲏⲣ, ⲕⲓⲛϩⲏⲣ, ⲧⲓⲛϩⲏⲣ, ⲧⲓⲛϩⲏⲗ (BMOr 6201 B 13) S nn, a plant : BM 1114, Kr 245 ; Ryl 291, BM *lc* ϣⲱⲗϩ ⲛⲕ.; *ib* 1197, Ryl 196 ⲥⲁ ⲛⲕ. seller of it. *Cf* ? κινάρα كنجر *artichoke* (but P 44 81 ⲕⲛⲛⲁⲣⲓ سدر, نبق, PMéd 316 ⲕⲉⲡⲡⲁⲣⲉ, K 177 ⲕⲉⲡⲡⲁⲣⲓ نبق). V ⲗⲓⲗⲟⲟⲣⲉ.

ⲕⲟⲩⲛϫⲟⲩ, ⲕⲟⲛ-, ⲕⲟⲩϫⲟⲩ (oftenest) &c S nn f, a vessel : BKU 1 66 ϯⲕⲟⲛ., Ep 548 ⲥⲛⲧⲉ ⲛⲕⲟⲩⲛ., ST 125 ⲥⲟⲟⲩⲉ ⲛⲕⲟⲩⲛ., J 70 40 ⲕⲟⲩⲛ., Ryl 262 ⲕⲟⲩ., Cai ostr 47400 ⲧⲕⲟⲩ., BMEA 44808 ϭⲛϫⲟⲩ ; of bronze : PMich 3559 ⲛⲟϭ ⲛⲕⲟⲩ. ⲡⲣⲟⲙⲡⲧ ; of copper : PLond 4 517 ⲕⲟⲩ. ⲛϩⲁⲣⲱⲧ ; of pottery containing money : BMOr 9525 (1) ; worth 1 *tremis* : Ep 545 ; for oil : PMich 523 ⲕⲟⲩ. ⲛⲥⲡⲁϩⲣⲉ (? σπάθιον) ⲛⲧⲓ ⲛⲉϩ, PStras 41 sim, Preisigke *Sammelb* 1 1160 κόντσου f large & small. *Cf* ? ⲕⲛⲓⲕⲓϫⲓ, κόνδυ.

ⲕⲱⲛϭ S *v* ϭⲱⲛⲧ.

ⲕⲁⲡ SB nn m, *string* of harp &c : Ps 32 2 SB, Nah 3 8 B (SA = Gk) χορδή, Ps 143 9 SB δεκαχ.; *thread, string, strand* : Eccl 4 12 S (TurM 1, var & B Miss 4 120 ⲣⲟ) σπαρτίον ; Nu 15 38 S ⲕⲁⲡ

ⲉϥⲥⲟⲧⲉ (P 44 107, var ⲧⲱⲧⲉ, B diff) κλῶσμα ; R 1 4 23 S ⲕ. ⲡϩⲱⲥ *licium*, ShMIF 23 30 S snake's tongue like ⲕ. ⲛⲡⲟⲩϩ ⲉϥϣⲟⲓ, ShMiss 4 280 S ⲕ. ϣⲏⲙ ⲛⲡⲟⲩϩ spun by heedless during σύναξις, MG 17 328 S ⲕ. ⲛⲕⲁⲙ (*ib* 103 B & 441 Ar om ⲕⲁⲙ) in mat-weaving λῶμα, K 123 B carpenter's *measuring cord*, *ib* 124 B ⲙⲁϣ(ⲓ) ⲡⲧⲉ ⲡⲓⲕ. *plumb line*, BP 9543 S ⲙⲡⲧⲉ ⲡⲗⲓⲧⲣⲁ ⲡⲕ. (? same). single *hair* : Mt 5 36 B (S ϥⲱ ⲡⲟⲩⲱⲧ) μία θρίξ, P 131⁴ 106 S bind not virtue ϩⲓⲧⲛⲟⲩⲕ. ⲡⲟⲩⲱⲧ ⲛϩⲱ, Mor 34 7 S ⲕ. ⲛϩⲱ of his head = BMis 78 ⲛϥⲥⲕⲓⲙ, WS 94 S ⲕⲉⲗⲕⲟⲗⲉ ⲡⲕ. ⲡⲁϩⲱ (prob = ϩⲱ), Dif 1 68 B not one ⲕ. ϫⲉⲛⲛⲟⲩⲥⲱⲙⲁ burnt شـ. *letter* of alphabet (ref to *linear* form) : BMis 8 S ⲡⲉⲓⲕ. ⲥⲛⲁⲩ ⲛⲥⲣⲁⲓ *viz* ⲑ & ⲧ, Leyd 434 S in name ⲓⲱⲁⲛⲛⲏⲥ are 7 ⲕ. ⲉⲥϩⲁⲓ. P 44 55 = 43 22 S μαλ(λ)ός · ⲕ. جلـ sheep's wool cloak ? (same ?). ⲥⲁ ⲡⲕ. B, *rope-maker, seller* (?) : N&E 39 343 ϩⲁⲡⲕ. from Fayyûm.

ⲕⲁⲡ S nn m, receptacle or measure for corn : AZ 30 39 (? paral Ryl 267 ⲉⲣⲧⲟϥ) ; for honey : Ryl 355, Ep 535 ϭⲁⲡ ; obscure : BM 1135 ; put mixture in ⲧⲟⲉⲓⲥ ⲉⲥⲕⲁⲣⲉϩ (ⲕⲟⲗϩ) ⲙⲁⲣⲥ ⲉⲩⲕ. Bodl(P) a 1 a (*cf* ? BKU 1 21 ro 13 ⲧⲁⲡ).

ⲕⲁⲡ S nn f, a cutting tool : CO 468 list ϩⲁϣⲟⲩⲣ, ⲉⲓⲡⲉ, ⲧⲕ. ⲡϣⲱⲗϭ.

ⲕⲏⲡ S nn, a measure, less than ⲥⲟⲉⲓϣ : ST 442 below table of figures (instructions for weaving ?) ⲧⲁⲓⲟⲩ ⲥⲡⲟⲟⲩⲅⲉ ⲛⲥⲁⲉⲓϣ ⲡⲁⲣⲁ ⲟⲩⲕ.

ⲕⲱⲡ S (rare) F, ϫⲱⲡ, ϫⲉⲡ-, ϫⲟⲡ⸗ B, ⲕⲁⲡ⸗ F, ⲕⲏⲡ† S, ϫⲏⲡ† B, vb **I** intr, *hide, be hidden* : Is 32 2 B (SF ϩⲱⲡ), Jer 29 10 B (S do), Mt 5 14 B (S do) κρύπτειν ; Job 13 8 B (S do) ὑποστέλλειν ; Aeg 24 B sought ⲙⲱⲓⲧ ⲉϫ. = S ⲙⲁ ⲛϩⲟⲡⲉ, ShC 42 201 S whither goest ⲉⲕ. ⲏ ⲉⲣⲁϩⲟⲡⲉ ⲧⲱⲛ ? RChamp 372-3 S if he decide ⲉⲕⲱⲡ. With following preposition : Va 61 205 B where is sheep ? ⲙⲡⲉⲣϫ. ⲉⲣⲟⲓ, PO 11 383 B ⲡⲧⲉⲕϣⲧⲉⲙϫ. ⲉⲣⲟⲓ in what I ask thee ; Ge 4 14 B ⲉⲃⲟⲗ ϩⲁ- ⲕⲣ. ἀπό ; Jer 4 29 B ϫⲉⲡ- = S ϩⲟⲡⲟⲩ ϩⲛ-, *ib* 23 34 B ϫ. ϫⲉⲡⲟⲩⲙⲁ ⲉϥϩⲏⲡ ⲕⲣ. ἐν κρυφαίοις.

II tr, *hide* : Ex 2 3 B, Ps 63 6 B (S ϩⲱⲡ), Mt 25 18 B (S ⲧⲱⲙⲥ) ⲕⲣ., Is 2 18 B (S ϩ.) κατακρ., EpJer 48 F (B intr) συναποκρ. ; Ps 31 5 B (S ϩ.) καλύπτειν, Ge 38 15 B κατακαλ. ; Ex 2 2 B σκεπά-ζειν ; Ps 118 110, 139 6 B ? *l* ϫⲱ τιθέναι (S ⲕⲱ, but *cf ib* 63 6) ; C 43 241 B ⲁⲩϫⲟⲡϥ till persecution ended, AM 272 B ⲉϥϫ. ⲙⲡⲓϫⲣⲟϥ. With 2d prep : e-, Job 13 24 B (S ϩ.) ⲕⲣ. ἀπό, Jer 18 20 B (S do) ⲕⲣ. dat, MG 25 244 B ἀποκρ. ; HL 111 B ⲙⲡⲉⲣϫ. ⲙⲡⲉⲕⲙⲉⲩⲓ ⲉⲣⲟⲓ. ⲉⲃⲟⲗ ϩⲁ-, Ps 54 13

B (S ϩ- ⲉ-) ⲕⲣ. ἀπό. ϩⲁ-, Ge 35 4 B (S ϩ. ϩⲁ-) κατακρ. ὑπό. ϩⲉⲛ-, Pro 7 1 B (SA ϩ. ϩⲁⲣⲧⲛ-) ⲕⲣ. παρά, Ac 7 24 F (SB om) ⲕⲣ. ἐν, Am 9 3 B (S ϩ. ϩⲛ-, A ϩ. ϩⲓϫⲛ-) ἐγκατακρ. εἰς, cf Cat 108 B ϣⲁⲛϫⲟⲡϥ ⲡⲧⲉϥϫⲗⲁⲙⲅ. ϩⲁⲣⲁⲧ⸗, Cat 123 B ⲁⲥϫⲟⲡⲉ ϩⲁⲣⲁⲧⲟⲩ of hills. ϩⲁⲧⲉⲛ-, Jer 13 5 B ⲕⲣ. ἐν, C 41 9 B ⲁϥϫⲟⲡϥ ϩⲁⲧⲉⲛ†ⲡⲟⲩϩⲓ. ϩⲁ- ϫⲉⲛ-, Va 61 94 B ⲡⲧⲉϥϫⲟⲡϥ ϩⲁϫⲱϥ ⲙⲡⲓⲣⲁⲙⲁⲟ = P 131³ 83 S ϩⲟⲡϥ ϩⲁϩⲣⲟ ⲛ-.

Qual : 1 Kg 23 19 S, Ez 12 6 B (S ϩ.), Sus 16 SB κρύπτεσθαι; ShA 1 12 = BM 992 S ⲉⲅⲕ. ⲁⲡ ⲉⲡⲉϥⲉⲅⲉⲣⲏⲅ, C 89 30 B place where ⲉⲡⲁϥϫ. ⲙⲙⲟϥ = MG 17 296 S ϩ. ⲡϩⲏⲧϥ, Bor 263 13 S Christ walked publicly lest ⲡⲛⲉⲩ ⲑⲉ ϫⲉⲉϥⲕ., C 86 321 B she buried †ⲕⲟⲗⲗⲁⲑⲓ ⲉⲥϫ.

—— SB nn m, hiding, concealment : BSM 18 B ⲉⲡϫⲏ ϩⲉⲡ...ⲡⲓϫ. = BMis 354 S ⲉⲡϩⲏⲡ. ϫⲓ ⲕ. ⲕ., take hiding, steal away : 2 Kg 19 3 S δια- κλέπτεσθαι (var ὑποστέλ.), Tri 503 S sim نقل روبدا روبدا. ⲙⲁ ⲡϫ. B, hiding place : Mt 21 13 (S = Gk) σπήλαιον, Va 57 249 sim καταγώγιον, C 86 178 ⲙⲡⲉⲛϫⲉⲙ ⲙ. ⲡⲁⲡ. ϩⲉⲛⲟⲩϫ. B, secretly (cf below ⲡϫ.) : Jo 7 10 (SA² ϩⲓⲟⲩϣⲱⲡ) ἐν κρυπτῷ; C 43 42 sent gifts ϩⲉⲛⲟⲩϫ.

ⲡϫ. B adv, secretly (cf above ϩⲉⲛⲟⲩϫ.) : Hab 3 14 (A ⲡϩⲱⲡ), Jo 11 28 (SA² ⲡϫⲓⲟⲩⲉ) λάθρᾳ, C 89 61 he went ⲡϫ. ⲉⲡⲓⲥⲟⲡ λ. ἐκείνου, 1 Kg 24 5 λαθραίως; Deu 28 57 (S ⲡϩ.), Eph 5 12 (S ⲡϫ.) κρυφῇ, Jer 44 17 κρυφαίως; AM 11 to enter town ⲡϫ.

ⲕⲁⲡⲁⲓ, ϭⲁⲡⲉⲓ(?) S, ⲕⲁⳓⲁⲓ B nn, partridge : K 168 B قطا (which P 44 56 = φασιανόν). S only as name : BM 448, MR 5 36, Ryl 132, & in BG 42 ⲫⲟ ⲡϭⲁⲡⲉⲓ (if same).

ⲕⲏⲡⲉ, ϭⲏ-, ϭⲉⲡⲏ (BMis 234) S, ϫⲏⲡⲓ B nn f, vaulted place, cellar, canopy, whence ? κύπη (γύπη) : P 44 22 S قبّة (which P 55 7 = σκηνή, κόγχη), Ge 8 13 SB στέγη var κάλυμμα, Is 40 22 S (B = Gk) καμάρα, cf ShA 1 404 S ⲟⲩⲥⲕⲏⲡⲏ ⲏ ⲟⲩϭⲏⲡⲉ & AM 126 B, PSBA 10 403 B flame rose & became as ⲟⲩϫ. καμάρα, Mor 37 121 S ⲧⲕ. ⲡⲧⲡⲉ ἁψίς; BMOr 6203 B S ⲙⲁ ⲡϣⲱⲡⲉ sold with ⲡⲉϥⲕ. & ⲡⲉϥⲁⲡⲁⲣⲟⲡ (antrum). palate of mouth : MR 4 128 S οὐρανίσκος · ⲧⲕ. ⲡⲣⲱⲕ, P 44 69 S, Bodl 325 156 B سفق الفم. ϭⲓⲃⲉ S pl : Glos 387 εἰλή- ματα, same ?

ⲕⲟⲩⲡⲣ S, ⲕⲟⲩⲡⲣⲉ A, ⲕⲟⲩⲡⲉⲣ, ϫⲟⲩⲡⲉⲣ B, ⲕⲟⲩⲡⲉⲣ F, DM V 8 5 qupre nn m, a plant Lawsonia inermis, is κύπρος כפר = henna : P 44 23 S حنّا, ib 81 = 43 56 S ⲕ. · ⲕⲉⲡⲣⲓⲥ حنّا, K 179, 405 B ϫ. do, Cant 4 13 S κύπρος, ib 7 12 S κυπρισμός; ib 1 14 ⲥⲙⲁϩ ⲡⲕ. βότρυς τῆς κ., Mor 23 11 S ⲥⲙⲁϩ

ⲡⲕ. ⲡⲥ†ⲛⲟⲩϥⲉ = ib 24 7 F, Bodl g 1 (hymns) B ⲟⲩⲕⲉⲗⲟⲗ ⲉϥⲧⲁⲟⲩⲉ ⲕ. ⲉⲃⲟⲗ. Blossom of vine ἄνθος (cf κύπρις) : Cl 23 4 A ϭⲱⲃⲉ, ⲕ., ⲉⲗⲁⲗϩⲙⲝ. Cf LMis 292, Löw 212. Two words ? here confused. As name f Kr 125 S ⲕⲟⲩⲡⲉⲣ.

(ⲕⲱⲡϣ), ⲕⲟⲡϣ† B vb intr, prob bow down : Va 57 215 proud man, even should he see king ⲉϥⲕⲟⲡϣ ⲡⲁϥ ὑποκύπτειν & doing him obeisance προσκυνεῖν, will not be content.

ⲕⲁⲡϣⲁ S, ϫⲁⲡϣⲟ B nn m, immature thorns on palm leaves (Schweinfurth Ar Pfl 228) : Tri 426 S who lay upon ⲡⲕ. & trod the ⲥⲟⲩⲡⲉ سلا, K 396 B do. Cf ϣⲡⲁ which also = سلا. V next word.

ⲕⲁⲡϣⲱ, -ϣⲟ B nn, sandy (waste) land : Is 5 6 B ϣⲟⲡⲧⲉ shall grow there like ⲟⲩⲕ. ὡς εἰς χέρσον, but S ϣⲡⲁ (cf ⲕⲁⲡϣⲁ), Vulg vepres et spinae, C 89 145, field ⲉϥⲟⲓ ⲡϫⲉⲣⲥⲟⲥ ⲉϥⲟⲓ ⲡⲕ. ⲉϥⲣⲏⲧ ⲡⲥⲟⲩⲣⲓ = Va ar 172 83 cleanse field والشوك خرسا من السلا والشوك (MG 17 515 om سلا). This and foregoing word prob confused. V ⲕⲱ k (ⲕⲏ ⲉⲡϣⲱ) & Spg Kopt Etym no 22.

ⲕⲁⲡⲁϫ[S nn m : Ostr penes GJéquier ⲧ]ⲛⲟⲟⲩ ⲡⲕⲁⲡⲁϫ[, or l ⲡⲕⲁⲡ ⲁϫ[. Cf ? name Καπόοϫε (Preisigke).

ⲕⲁⲡⲓϫⲉ S v ϭⲁⲡⲓϫⲉ.

ⲕⲁⲣ⸗ F v ⲕⲱⲱⲣⲉ.

ⲕⲉⲣ B nn m, haunch, thigh : K 78 زرّك.

ⲕⲟⲩⲣ SBF, ⲕⲟⲩⲗ F, ⲕⲁⲩⲣⲓ B f (Ps 57) nn, deaf person : Ex 4 11 B ابكم, Lev 19 14 B اخرس, Ps 37 14 B اصم, Is 35 5 BF, Hab 2 18 B (A ⲉⲙⲁⲅ- ⲥⲱⲧⲙⲉ), Mt 11 5 B اصم (S all ⲁⲗ) κωφός; Mk 7 32 B ⲕ. ⲡⲉⲃⲟ اصم اخرس (S ⲁⲗ ⲡⲁⲡⲟ) ⲕⲱ., Mor 31 72 S, AM 162 B sim, BIF 14 114 S he made ⲡⲕ. to hear, WS 158 S Enoch ⲡⲕ. (? name), BKU 1 23 F ⲡⲓⲕⲟⲩⲗ ⲙⲉⲡ(ⲡ)ⲓⲃⲗⲏⲟⲩ. Adj, deaf : Ps 57 4 B (S ⲁⲗ) κωφός; AM 120 B ⲡⲓϩⲱⲗⲟⲡ ⲡⲕ., MG 25 91 B ⲟⲩⲉⲃⲟ ⲡⲕ., BP 8503 S ⲫⲁⲡⲕ. (ⲡⲣⲟ ⲡ-) demon (?). ⲉⲣ ⲕ. B, become deaf : Ps 38 10 (S ⲣ ⲙⲡⲟ), Mic 7 16 (SA ϩⲱϫⲡ, -ⲧ) κωφοῦν, Is 44 11 (S ⲙⲉⲅⲥⲱⲧⲙ) κωφός (εἶναι). ⲙⲉⲧⲕ. B nn f, deafness : K 159 طراش. As name, Πκοῦρ (Preisigke).

ⲕⲟⲩⲣ A²B nn, blow (prob deafening blow) : with †, Is 50 6 B (S ⲁⲁⲥ), Jo 18 22 B (S do) ῥάπισμα; Mt 5 39 B (S ⲣⲱϩⲧ), Va 57 261 B ⲁⲩ† ⲕ. ⲛⲏⲓ ῥαπίζειν; Mt 26 67 B (S ⲕⲗⲯ) κολαφίζειν; MG 25 300 B ⲁϥ† ⲡⲟⲩⲕ. ϩⲉⲡⲧⲉϥⲟⲩⲟϫⲓ = BIF 13 111 S ϣⲉ ⲡⲁⲁⲥ; with ϣⲱϣⲉ, Jo 18 22 A². ϣⲉ ⲡⲕ. B same meaning : CaiEuch 487

thou gavest cheeks ⲉϧⲁⲛϣ. ῥάπ., EW 29 = Wess 15 130 S ϣⲥ ⲡⲁⲁⲥ, C 41 40 ⲁϥϯ ⲡⲟⲩϣ. ⲉϩⲟⲩⲛ ⲥ̄ⲉⲛⲡ̄ⲣⲟ = Miss 4 642 S ϣⲥ ⲡⲁⲁⲥ.

коүр SA, ϭⲟⲣ S (? same) nn m, *pivot, hinge* of door : Pro 26 14 A (S ⲙⲉϣϯⲃⲥ) στρόφιγξ, CO 233 S ⲥⲡⲁⲩ ⲛⲕ. ⲡⲣⲱ (*sic l*) for door of θυσιαστή- ριον, Bodl(P) f 78 S c]ⲡⲁⲩ ⲛϭ. ⲛ̄ϣⲉ. *Cf* dem *gwre* Griffith *Stories* 156 14 & ? قور كور. *V* Ep 1 60.

кωр, ϭⲱⲣ SF nn, *measure or quantity of money, less than carat* : ST 40 S 10 carats ⲡⲁⲣⲁ ϥⲧⲟⲩϣⲉ ⲛⲕ., CO 456 S ϭ. with κεράτια, Ep 535 S 24 carats & ϣⲉ ⲛϭ., *ib* 349 S ⲟⲩⲱⲣ(ⲣ) ϣⲏⲧ ⲛⲕ. ⲡⲁⲥ, *paral* ϣⲏ (ϣⲉ) a small coin (*v ib* 168 n), *ib* 534 S (money ?). In Kr 30 F ⲏⲗⲡ ⲕⲁⲧⲁ ⲡⲉ̄ ⲕ. ? = коүрι κοῦρι, wine measure : CMSS 20, 68, 75, ST 440 F. *Cf* короү & WS 23.

кра F *v* кро.

крι, ⲕⲗⲓ S nn m, *substance whence a perfumed & medicinal oil* : PMéd 244 with rose oil, P 129¹⁴ 125 of oil exuded by frescoes at approach of archbp Benjamin ⲁⲩⲧⲁⲩⲁ ⲉⲃⲟⲗ ⲡⲟⲩⲛⲉϩ ⲛ̄ⲕⲣⲓ ⲁⲩⲱϣ ⲉⲃⲟⲗ &c., CO 362 if thou desirest incense ⲥⲧⲟⲓ for τόπος lo a man hath brought a little ⲕ. ⲉⲛⲁⲡⲟⲩϩ.

кро SAA², ⲭⲣⲟ B, ⲕⲣⲁ F, ⲕⲗⲁ S, *pl* ⲕⲣⲱⲟⲩ SA nn m, *shore, further side, limit*, **a** of sea, river : Deu 30 13 S (B ⲉⲓⲙⲏⲣ), Is 9 1 S (B do), Mt 4 25 S (B do) πέραν, Zeph 3 10 pl A (B do) πέρας ; Is 18 1 S (B ⲥⲁⲙⲉⲛⲣⲏ) ἐπέκεινα ; Si 24 15 S, Mt 13 48 BF (S diff), Ac 27 39 B (S ⲙⲁ ⲙⲙⲟⲟⲛⲉ) αἰγιαλός ; Job 6 3 S (B om) παραλία ; Jos 7 7 S παρά acc ; Mk 6 53 S (B ⲉⲙⲏⲣ), Lu 5 3 SB γῆ ; ShC 73 172 S ϫⲓⲡⲡⲓⲕ. ϣⲁⲡⲉⲓⲕ. of sea, JTS 8 243 S sim, AZ 21 143 S sailors leaped ⲉⲡⲉⲕ., BMis 416 S = BSM 58 B = Mor 27 43 F bring ship to ⲕ., AM 328 B ⲡⲓⲭ. ⲡⲉⲓⲉⲃⲧ, C 43 67 B ship distant a little ⲉⲃⲟⲗ ⲙⲡⲓⲭ. ; opp sea : Sa 19 18 S, Ap 10 8 S (B ⲕⲁϩⲓ) γῆ. **b** of territory : Nu 21 11 S (B ⲉⲓⲙ.), Jud 11 29 S πέραν, Ps 18 4 pl S (B ⲁⲩⲣⲏϫ⳽), *ib* 66 6 pl S (B ⲉⲁⲧ) πέρας, Ez 47 8 S (gloss, B ⲙⲏⲣ) Galilee ⲉⲧⲉⲡⲉⲥⲣⲁⲛ ⲟⲛⲡⲉ ⲡⲉⲕ. **c** *valley, hill* S, all pl : Nu 24 6 (B ϭⲓⲥⲓ), Is 40 12 (B ⲕⲁⲗⲁⲙϥⲟ), Ez 6 3 (B ⲉⲁⲧ) νάπη ; Ge 49 26 (B ⲕⲁⲗ.) θίς, Job 15 7 (B ⲧⲱⲟⲩ) θ.var βουνός.
  In place-names : Πεκρο (PLond 5 221), Πκρω Κοητος (PLeip no 2), ⲡⲕⲣⲟ ⲛⲧⲟⲟⲩ, var ⲡⲕⲗⲁ ⲛ. (PLond 4 471 n) = Ἐποίκιον Βουνῶν = شبرا بنان (CHBecker P Schott-Reinh 1 109).

кроү S nn, *meaning unknown* : CO 192 list of varia : ⲟⲩⲕ. ⲛ̄ⲣ̄ⲛⲁⲁⲩ ⲛ̄ⲣⲟⲙⲡⲧ[.

каιре S, ⲕⲁⲣⲓ B nn f, *gullet, belly* : P 44 69 =

43 38 S ⲡⲁⲣⲩϫ (φάρυγξ) حلق, BSM 44 B take out ⲧⲉϥⲕ. (of fish wherein money found) = *ib* 149 مصران = *K. al-Taʿāza al-Rūḥīyah* (1902) 76 بلعوم = Va 63 10 B ⲧⲉϥⲟⲩⲉⲙⲥ̄ⲃⲣⲉ = BMis 391 S, Mor 27 35 S ⲕⲟⲓⲗⲓⲁ, AM 190 B snake she had swallowed 1 ⲉⲡϣⲱⲓ ⲥ̄ⲉⲛⲧⲉⲥⲕ. (*cf* Hyvernat *Alb* xliii).   **каρι** F m, ? same word : BM 527 recipe for one ⲉⲗⲉ- ⲡⲉϥⲕ. ϯ ⲥⲡⲁϥ.

коρι B nn, *skylight, trap-door* : K 153 روزنة.

коүрι F *v* кωр.

короү B, ⲕⲁⲣⲟⲩ F nn m, *a coin, prob less than carat* : BM 528 F arithm problems relating to corn measures *eg* no 55 ⲓⲱⲧ ⲍ ϩⲁⲟⲩⲕ. (also in 48, 56, 64) ; BM 590 B bring ⲥⲡⲁⲩ ⲛⲕ. *Cf* кωр.

кωоре S, ⲕⲉⲉⲣⲉ-, ⲕⲉⲣⲉ- S, ⲕⲁⲣⲉ- F, ⲕⲟⲟⲣⲉ⳽, ⲕⲟⲟⲣ⳽ (once) S, ⲕⲁⲁⲣⲉ⳽ Sᶠ, ⲕⲁⲣ⳽ F vb I tr, *cut down* trees, crops : Deu 19 5 (B ⲕⲱⲣϫ) κόπτειν, *ib* ⲕⲉⲣⲉ ϣⲉ (B diff), Zech 12 11 (A ϣⲟⲩⲧ, B ⲕ.), Mt 3 10 (B ⲕ.) ἐκκόπ. ; 4 Kg 6 4 τέμνειν ; Sa 13 11 (var ϣⲱⲱⲧ) ἐκπρίειν ; P 129¹⁴ 133 ⲥⲡⲁⲕ. ⲙⲡⲙⲁ ⲡⲉⲗⲟ- ⲟⲗⲉ, Miss 8 188 Sᶠ ϥⲛⲁⲕⲁⲁⲣⲉⲕ with axe, CMSS 63 F husbandmen ⲉⲩⲕⲁⲣⲉ ⲥⲓⲙ, AZ 23 39 F sycamores & palms ⲡⲧⲁⲃⲕⲁⲣⲟⲩ, Ryl 340 S ⲕ. ⲕⲁϣ.   **II** intr S, *be cut down* : JKP 2 20 tree ϣⲁϥⲕ. opp ϯ ⲟⲩⲱ. As nn m S : Zech 12 11 (A ϣⲟⲅⲟⲩⲧ, B ⲡⲉϩⲡ⳽) κοπετός (confusion with κόπτειν, κοπή), Saq 134 ⲡⲕⲟⲟⲣⲉ title (same ?).   ⲣⲉϥⲕ. S nn. *tree-cutter* : Sa 13 11 ⲣⲉϥⲕ. ⲛ̄ⲙⲙⲁ ⲡϣⲏⲛ ὑλο- τόμος, P 131⁴ 135 ⲣⲉϥⲕⲉⲉⲣⲉ ϣⲏⲛ.

коρⲃⲓ B *v* ⲭⲣⲟⲃⲓ.

коркр S *v* ⲥⲕⲟⲣⲕⲣ.

коρϫ S, ⲕⲟⲣⲕⲥ B nn, *an iron instrument, prob* = κόραξ (P 44 59 S ⲡⲕⲟⲣⲁϫ مرزاب *clubs*) : C 43 147 B martyr's tortures ⲛⲓⲕ. ⲉⲣⲉⲡⲓⲁⲧⲓⲟⲥ ⲙⲏⲣ ⲛ̄ϧⲏⲧⲟⲩ, *ib* ϩⲁⲛⲕ. ⲛⲃⲉⲛⲓⲡⲓ ⲥⲁϧⲟⲩⲛ ⲙⲡⲓϩ̄ⲗⲟϫ = Mor 48 98 S. *Cf* K 124 B ⲕⲉⲣⲁϫ معول.

кραⲙ, ⲕⲣⲟⲙ, ⲕⲣⲱⲙ B nn m, *wild safflower* : K 193 قرطم بري, or *wild parsley* : *ib* 195 كرفس بري (*cf* ⲗⲁⲧ). But ? = κράμβη كرنب. *Cf* ? Ep 566 S ⲕⲣⲁⲙⲉ. Not قرم (Löw 202, Schweinf *Ar Pfl* 110, 129).

кршм S (archaic), ⲭⲣⲱⲙ B, ⲕⲗⲱⲙ F nn m (f Va 69 113 B), *fire* : Ge 19 24 B (S ⲕⲱⲣⲧ), Deu 9 15 B (S ⲥⲁⲧⲉ), Jos 2 24 S, Is 30 14 B (SF ⲕⲱ.), Mt 3 10 B (S ⲥⲁ.) πῦρ ; Ez 23 37 B (S do) ἔμ- πυρος ; *ib* 24 10 B (S ⲕⲱ.) ἄνθραξ ; Lam 4 19 B ⲁϩⲙⲟϩ ⲛ̄ⲭ. (S vb only) ἐξάπτειν ; Mt 13 30 BF burn them in ⲡⲓⲭ., ⲡⲉⲕ. (S vb only) κατακαίειν ; Br 102 S baptism ⲙⲡⲉⲕ., PS 378 S ⲕ. ⲡⲕⲁⲕⲉ paral

кⲱⲣⲧ ⲙⲡⲟⲡⲏⲣⲟⲡ, BM 1008 *S* кⲱⲣⲧ ϧⲓк. ⲡⲁⲧⲱϣⲙ, Mor 46 5 *S* = BMOr 7561 46 *S* ⲡⲉк. ⲉⲧⲉⲛⲙ ⲡⲁⲣⲁ ⲡкⲱⲣⲧ, BerlSitzb '25 314 *S* ⲡⲉк. ϧⲛⲟⲩⲣⲟⲟⲩⲉ = El 66 *A* кⲱ. (*cf* Sa 3 7 *S* ϯ̇к), AZ 23 114 *S* put mixture in ⲡк. ⲉϥϧⲏⲙ, BSM 32 *B* ⲭ. devours my inwards = BMis 374 кⲱ., RAl 101 *B* irons ⲉⲩⲙⲉϧ ⲡⲭ. *red hot.* As adj *SBF, of fire, fiery:* Is 5 24 *BF* (*S* кⲱⲣⲧ), Ro 12 20 *B* (*S* do), He 1 7 *B* (*SF* ⲥⲁⲧⲉ) πυρός, Lev 14 37 *B* (*S* ⲙⲣⲟϣ) πυρρίζειν, C 89 13 *B* πυρκαιά; 2 Thes 1 8 *B* (*S* do) φλόξ, Ge 3 24 *B* (*S* ⲥⲁ.) φλόγινος; PS 257 *S* ⲉⲓⲉⲣⲟ ⲡк., *cf* 256 ⲉⲓ. ⲡкⲱⲣⲧ, BSM 132 *B* worshipping ⲡϣⲁϧ ⲡⲭ., Mor 24 18 *F* ϣⲉⲣ ⲡк.

ⲉⲣ ⲭ. *B, be on fire, burn:* C 43 229 whole body ⲉⲣ ⲭ., Rec 6 181 ⲁϥⲉⲣ ⲭ. ⲧⲏⲣϥ = BMar 216 *S* ⲣ ⲑⲉ ⲡⲟⲩкⲱⲣⲧ, CaiEuch 464 ⲉкⲟⲓ ⲡⲭ. ⲉϥⲟⲩⲱⲙ.

ϯ ⲭ. *B, put fire (to), set alight:* AM 308 ⲁⲩϯ ⲭ. ϧⲓⲭⲉⲡ- martyrs in pits.

ϧⲓ ⲭ. *B, as last e* ⲉ-: Ps 25 2 (*S* ⲡⲓⲥⲉ), 104 19 (*S* do) πυροῦν, TSBA 9 360 ⲁϥϧⲓ ⲭ. ⲉϧⲁⲡⲙⲛϣ (*cf* 3 Kg 18 10 ἐμπιμπράναι); Va 57 254 ϧⲓ ⲭ. ⲉⲣⲟⲡ ⲡⲥⲉⲣⲟкⲣⲉⲡ κατακαίειν. C 43 25 martyr seated ⲡⲥⲉϧⲓ ⲭ. ϧⲁⲣⲟϥ, *ib* 100 sim ⲥⲁⲡⲉⲥⲏⲧ ⲙⲙⲟϥ. ϧⲓ ⲭ. ⲉⲃⲟⲗ, *throw out fire, shine:* ROC 25 259 of saint's corpse.

ϭⲓ ⲭ. *B, take fire:* 1 Cor 7 9 (*SF* ⲣⲱкϩ) πυροῦσθαι.

кⲱⲣⲙ κανθός   *v* кⲱⲗⲙ.

кⲱⲣⲙ *S nn m, smoke:* ShA 1 253 evil smell of ⲡкⲁⲡⲡⲟⲥ ⲛ ⲡк. of fuel opp кⲁⲡ. of incense. *Cf* кⲣⲟⲙⲣⲙ.

кⲣⲙⲉ *S,* кⲉⲣⲙⲓ *B*   *v* кⲣⲙⲉⲥ.

кⲣⲙⲣⲙ *SA*[2], ⲭⲣⲉⲙⲣⲉⲙ *B,* кⲗⲉⲙⲗⲉⲙ *F* vb I intr, *murmur, be vexed:* Jud 1 14 *S*, Ps 58 16 *SB*, Is 29 24 *SBF*, Jo 6 61 *SA*[2]*B* γογγύζειν, Lu 19 7 *S* (*B* ⲉⲣ ⲭ.) διαγογ.; Mt 21 15, 26 28 *B* (*S* = Gk) ἀγανακτεῖν.

With following preposition.

ⲉ- direct obj: Nu 11 1 *S* (var & *B* ⲛ-) γογ., Si 34 27 *S* διαγ. dat. ⲉ-, *against:* Ex 17 3 *S* (*B* ⲡⲥⲁ-) γ. πρός, Nu 14 2 *S* (*B* ⲉⲭⲉⲛ-) διαγ. ἐπί; ShR 2 3 59 *S* it befits thee not ⲉк. ⲏ ⲉкⲱϣ ⲉⲡⲣⲙⲙⲁⲟ; ⲉϧⲟⲩⲛ ⲉ-: Nu 17 5 *S* (var ⲉϩⲣⲁⲓ ⲉⲭⲛ-, *B* ⲉⲭⲉⲛ-) γ. ἐπί, Lu 5 30 *S* (*B* ⲟⲩⲃⲉ-) γ. πρός, Mt 20 11 *S* (*B* ⲡⲥⲁ-) γ. κατά. ⲉⲧⲃⲉ-, *concerning:* Lam 3 39 *B*, Jo 6 41 *SA*[2]*B* γ. περί, AM 281 *B* ⲁⲡⲓⲗⲁⲟⲥ ⲭ. ⲉⲑⲃⲉⲫⲁⲓ. ⲉⲭⲛ-, *against:* Ex 16 2 *B* (*S* ⲉϩⲣⲁⲓ ⲉⲭⲛ-), Jos 9 24 *S* διαγ. ἐπί, Miss 4 570 *S* ⲁⲩк. ⲉⲭⲡⲟⲉ ⲉⲧⲩⲧⲁⲉⲓⲟ ⲡⲡⲉⲥⲡⲏⲩ. ⲡⲥⲁ-, *against:* Nu 14 36 *B* (*S* ⲉ-) διαγ. κατά, Va 57 192 *B* ⲙⲡⲉϥⲭ.

ⲡⲥⲱк ἀγανακ.; Pcod 10 *S* many will к. ⲡⲥⲁⲡⲉⲡⲧⲁⲩⲧⲁⲡⲣⲟⲩⲧϥ. ϩⲁ- *B, against:* Ex 16 7 (*S* ⲉ-) διαγ. κατά.

II tr (rare): Jo 7 32 *SA*[2]*B* ⲉϧк. ⲡⲡⲁⲓ ⲉⲧⲉⲃⲏⲛⲧϥ ⲅⲟⲩ. ταῦτα.

—— nn m, *murmuring, complaint:* Ex 16 7 *SB*, Sa 1 11 *S*, Ac 6 1 *SB* γογγυσμός; MG 25 128 *B* ϣⲁⲧϣⲱⲡⲓ ϧⲉⲛⲟⲩⲭ. As adj: Is 58 9 *SB* γογγυσμός. ⲁⲧⲭ. *B, without complaint:* 1 Pet 4 9 (*S* ⲁⲭⲛк.) ἄνευ γ. ⲣⲉϥⲭ. *S,* -ⲭ. *B, murmurer:* Aeg 242 *S* γόγγυσος, Jude 16 *SB* (var ⲣⲉϥⲉⲣ ⲭ.) γογγυστής.

кⲣⲟⲙⲣⲙ *S,* кⲣⲁⲙⲣⲙ *A,* кⲣⲓⲣⲱⲙ† *S,* ⲭⲣⲉⲙⲣⲱⲙ† *B* vb intr, *be dark:* of hair, scar, Lev 13 4 *S* (*B* ϧⲗⲟⲗ), *ib* 56 *S* (var кⲏⲙ, *B* do) ἀμαυρός, Lam 4 1 *S* (C 42 127, *B* do) ἀμαυροῦν; *ib* 4 8 *S* (*B* ⲭⲁкⲓ) σκοτίζειν; Zeph 1 15 *SA* (*B* ⲡⲁⲑⲡⲁⲩ ⲉⲫⲟⲣⲱⲓⲡⲓ) ·ἀωρία; Va 57 244 *B* evil woman devoured by ⲡⲡⲁ ⲡⲭⲣⲱⲙ...ⲉⲥⲭ.† ⲧⲏⲣⲥ ἀτερπής; ShC 73 49 *S* souls ⲡⲁк. like coal, P 131[8] 147 *S* Mark brought light ϧⲛⲧⲉⲡⲭⲱⲣⲁ ⲉⲧк.†, Cat 141 *B* Adam from paradise to this world ⲉⲧⲭ.†, Mor 52 18 *S* stone ⲉϧк.† ⲡⲁⲅⲁⲡ ⲡкⲉⲣⲙⲉⲥ, BMOr 7561 48 *S* smoke ⲉϧк.† As nn m *S, darkness:* Deu 28 28 (*B* ⲙⲉⲧⲁⲧⲛⲁⲩ ⲙⲃⲟⲗ) ἀορασία, BHom 72 ⲡⲉк. ⲡⲧⲉⲩϧⲓкⲱⲡ.

кⲣⲙⲧⲥ *SA,* кⲣⲙⲡⲧⲥ (BG) *S,* ⲭⲣⲉⲙⲧⲥ *B* (*cf* ⲭⲣⲉⲙⲥ) nn m (f BG *S,* Ps 17 *B*), *smoke, mist:* Ps 17 9 *B* (*S* = Gk), *ib* 67 3 *B* (var f, *S* do), Is 34 10 *B* (*SF* do), EpJer 20 *B* (*F* кⲱⲣⲧ), Ap 8 4 *B* (*S* do) καπνός; Lev 16 13 *B* (*S* do), Ez 8 11 *B*, Ac 2 19 *B* (*S* ⲗϧⲱⲃ) ἀτμίς; Miss 4 96 *B* demons dispersed like ⲟⲩⲭ. *obscurity, darkness:* Joel 2 2 *SA* (*B* ⲡⲓϭⲓ) ὀμίχλη; Is 59 9 *S* (*B* ⲙⲉⲧⲁⲧⲟⲩⲱⲓⲡⲓ, *cf* Zeph 1 15) ἀωρία; BG 62 *S* ⲧк. ⲡкⲁкⲉ, ShA 2 284 *S* ϭⲟⲥⲙ, к. *rust:* Ez 24 11 *B* (*S* ϣⲛⲉⲉ) ἰός, but *ib* 24 6, 12 ἰός = ⲭⲉⲃⲥ. *fire:* C 86 283 *B* ϭⲉⲣⲉ ⲟⲩⲡⲓϣϯ ⲡⲭ. As adj *SB, dark:* Va 58 188 *B* ⲡⲓⲉⲗⲣⲱⲃ ⲡⲭ. of food αἰθαλώδης, Z 330 *S* ⲛⲓ ⲡкⲁкⲉ ⲁⲩⲱ ⲡк. ζοφερὸς λίαν, PS 114 *S* ⲟⲩⲅкⲗⲟⲟⲗⲉ ⲡк., ShMIF 23 34 *S* ϧⲟⲓⲧⲉ ⲡк. ϧⲓⲣⲧⲟⲙⲧⲙ. ⲣ к. *S,* ⲉⲣ ⲭ. *B* be smoky, dark: Ge 15 17 *B* (*S* ϯ кⲁⲡⲡⲟⲥ), Is 7 4 *B* (*S* do), *ib* 42 3 *B* (*S* ϧⲧⲟⲙⲧⲙ) καπνίζειν; Ps 68 24 *B* (*S* ⲣ кⲁкⲉ), *ib* 138 12 *B* (*S* ϧⲱⲡ), Ro 11 10 *B* (*S* ⲣ кⲁ.) σκοτίζειν; Mt 12 20 *B* (*S* ϧⲧ.) τύφεσθαι; Bor 254 176 *S* demons ⲟ ⲡкⲁкⲉ ϧⲓк., C 43 201 *B* town ⲉⲣ ⲭ. through smoke. ϣⲉϣ ⲭ. *B, scatter smoke:* Ps 103 32, 143 5 (*S* both ϯ кⲁⲡ.) καπνίζειν.

ⲭⲣⲉⲙⲥ[1], ⲭⲉⲙⲥ[2], ⲭⲉⲙⲧⲥ[3] *B,* кⲉⲙⲧⲥ[4], кⲏⲙⲉⲧⲥ[5] *F* nn f, *darkness:* Is 5 20 *F*[1] (*SB* кⲁкⲉ), Jo 3 19 *F*[4] (*SA*[2]*B* do), 2 Pet 2 17 *B*[1] (*S* diff), Jude 13 *B*[1]

(var², S diff) σκότος, Jo 1 5 F⁴ (SB κα.), ib 6 17 B² (S do), ib 20 1 B² (var¹, S do), Lu 11 36 B² (S do) σκοτεινός; Va 58 155 B one accuses neighbour ϫεαϥωλι ⲡⲡⲓⲑⲛⲟⲩ ⲡⲧⲉ ⲡⲉϥⲏⲓ ⲓⲉ ϫⲉⲁϥⲁⲓϥ ⲡⲭ.²   ⲉⲣ, ⲉⲗ ⲭ., ⲕ.⁴ BF, MG 25 239 B caves ⲉⲧⲟⲓ ⲡⲭ.² σκοτία, BMEA 10576.

κρμεϲ SA, κερμε (Ann 19 77 sic?) S, κρμε A, κερμι B, κυρμι F nn m & f, ash, soot, dust, cf? قرماص (not قرموس): Ge 18 27 SB (A ⲉⲧⲛⲓϩ), Lev 1 16 S m B f, Si 40 4 S m, Is 58 5 SB, Jon 3 6 SAB, He 9 13 SF m B σποδός, Lev 4 12 S m B f (var m) σποδία, Ge 30 39 SB ⲁⲅⲁⲡ ⲡⲕ. σποδοειδής; Deu 28 24 B (S ⲕⲁϩ), Mor 56 12 S ⲡⲕ. ϩⲓϫⲡⲡⲉⲅⲁⲡⲏⲅⲉ χοῦς; Mic 1 10 A (S ⲉⲓⲧⲛ, B ⲕⲁϩⲓ) γῆ; Bel 14 B, Va 57 206 B τέφρα; Ex 9 8 B αἰθάλη; Mor 17 59 S ἀσβόλη; Miss 4 637 S = C 41 20 B ⲡⲕ. of ovens, Ann 19 77 S ⲟⲩⲕ. ϩⲛⲧϣⲛⲟⲩⲉ, R 1 2 39 S ⲡⲕ. ⲙⲡⲣⲏⲃϲ as eye-paint, PMéd 284 S ⲕ. ⲡⲭⲁⲣⲧⲏϲ in recipe, BMis 488 S ⲟⲩⲕⲟⲩⲓ ⲡⲕ. from before door, ib 481 paral ⲕⲁϩ, Cai 42573 2 S in recipe ⲕ. ⲡⲧⲁϥⲡⲁⲧ (sic) ⲡⲟⲩⲡⲁⲙ, KroppK 62 S sim ⲡⲕ. ⲡⲧⲉϥⲁⲡⲉ, Miss 4 699 S empty corn ears ϣⲁⲩϣⲟⲩⲉ ⲕ. ⲉⲃⲟⲗ, Gu 61 S of bodies burnt ⲧⲉⲅⲕ., C 86 232 B, RAl 102 B sim ⲧⲉϥⲕ., ib ⲡⲓⲕ., AM 103 B ⲡⲓⲕ. of martyr, Ryl 433 B ⲁⲡⲟⲕ ⲡⲓⲕ. Nicodemus.

ⲣ κ. SB, become ashes, dust: Ez 28 18 SB ϭⲡ. διδόναι; Va 57 242 B ⲡⲧⲟⲅⲉⲣ κ. τεφροῦν; 2 Chr 4 16 B ⲡⲏ ⲉϣⲁⲅⲉⲣ κ. ⲉⲃⲟⲗ ⲙⲙⲱⲟⲩ τοὺς ποδιστῆρας (reading? ϭⲡⲟⲇ-); ShBor 246 60 S if his deeds (ϩⲱⲃ) become as κ., man ⲡⲁⲣ ϩⲟⲩⲉ ⲣ κ., C 86 52 B to be burnt ϣⲁⲧⲟⲩⲉⲣ κ.;   ⲣ ⲁⲧⲕ. S, make (leave) no ash: Ann 18 285 burn wood ϣⲁⲡⲧⲉϥⲉⲣ ⲁ.

κρμⲧϲ v κⲣⲟⲙⲣⲙ.

κⲁⲣⲡⲉ F v ϭⲣⲱⲡ.

κⲣⲁⲡⲉⲛ S, κⲁⲣⲁⲡⲏⲡ, -ⲓⲛ B nn m (Ann 1 52), hoopoe: P 43 23 S, K 169 B هدهد. Cf ⲡⲉⲧⲉⲡⲏⲡ & κⲁⲕⲟⲩⲡⲁⲧ. Formed? from ἔποψ (ἔποπα).

κⲣⲟⲩⲣ SF O (PGM 60) DM, ⲭⲣⲟⲩⲣ B nn m, frog: Ex 7 27 B, Ps 77 45 SB, Ap 16 13 SB βάτραχος; P 44 57 S β βατ. ضفدع; ShC 42 49 S who asketh ⲡⲉⲕ. whether (river's) water will rise.   ⲙⲁⲥ ⲡⲕ. S, young frog: P 44 57 فرخ ضفدع = BM 491 ⲅⲣⲟⲩⲡⲟⲥ (γέρυνος). As name: Κροῦρ, Κροῦρις (Preisigke). Same? κⲁⲣⲟⲩⲣ CO 132 (sic l), ϭⲁⲣⲟⲩⲣ Mor 51 33 Καροῦρ, ? Κιαροῦλ (Preis.). But cf κⲁⲣⲟⲩⲣ = κολοβός Epist Ammon § 17 (Acta SS, Maii 3 69*); PMich 4552 they run after thee ⲥⲟⲩⲙⲟⲩⲧⲏ (ⲡ)ⲥⲱⲕ ϫⲛⲃⲁⲡⲛ κⲁⲣⲟⲩⲣ.

κⲣⲟⲩⲣ S nn, meaning unknown, among articles pledged Win 67 ϣⲟⲙ]ⲛⲧ ⲡⲕ. ⲁⲩⲱ ⲟⲩⲗⲁⲃⲁⲣⲓⲥ...κⲁⲗⲁϩⲧ.

κⲁⲣⲁⲣⲉ S nn m, meaning unknown: ST 183]ⲙⲡⲧⲟⲅⲁ ⲡⲃⲏ[...] ⲙⲡⲡⲕⲁⲣⲁⲣⲉ[. Cf? K 127 B ⲡⲓⲕⲁⲣⲓⲣⲁ خطاف حديد. Or? Arabic, as amîr is named (but κⲁⲣⲁⲣⲉ BM 530 18 is f, cf κⲁⲣⲟⲟⲣⲉ AZ 23 111, Ryl 106 59).

κⲣⲏⲣⲉ S nn f, meaning unknown: PRain 4741 in list of utensils κ. ⲥⲡⲉ (so cannot be ⲧⲭⲣⲏⲣⲉ = ὑποπέσσιον PLond 5 170, PMon 131).

κⲉⲣϲ, ⲭⲉⲣϲ B nn m, a fish, synodontis schal: K 171 شال.

κⲁⲣⲟⲩⲥ SB nn (adj), curled (?) of hair: AM 136 B ⲟⲩⲙⲏⲣϣⲡⲉ ⲡⲁϥⲉ ⲡⲕ. = PO 17 637 اشقر اجعد (but K 206 B ⲡⲓⲕ. اشقر), C 43 196 B hair ⲟⲓ ⲙⲙⲏⲣϣ ⲡⲕ., Mor 44 27 S of Christ's varying appearance, hair ⲟⲗⲙ ⲉϥⲕⲏⲙ opp ⲉϥⲟ ⲡⲕ., Mor 42 21 = 43 21 S sim ⲟⲩϭⲟⲡ ⲡⲕ. ⲟⲩϭⲟⲡ ⲉⲣⲉⲡⲉϥϥⲱ ϣⲟⲓ, BSG 187 S = Wess 15 145 S ⲟⲩⲣⲱⲙⲉ ⲡⲟⲩⲱⲃϣ ⲡⲕ.   As name: ⲡκⲁⲣⲟⲩⲥ BM 1240 S, Πκαροῦς (Preisigke).

κⲉⲣⲥⲟ S nn m, pylon, gate: 3 Kg 6 13 (P 44 110–11) ⲡⲕ. ϫⲉ ⲉⲧⲥⲁⲥⲡⲓⲣ (43 106 ⲧⲉ ⲧⲥⲁ-) ⲙⲡⲉⲥⲛⲧ ὁ πυλὼν τ. πλευρᾶς τ. ὑποκάτωθεν. In ib 6 7 = ⲉⲑⲣⲓⲟⲛ (αἰλάμ), in K 216 = ⲉⲗⲁⲙ. Or? l κⲉⲥⲣⲟ.

κⲁⲣⲁⲉⲓⲧ S v ⲣⲟ (κⲁ ⲣⲱ).

κⲉⲣⲏⲧ Sᶠ nn, part of swine or name of a medicament: PMéd 289 2 drams of κ. ⲡⲗⲓⲗ(ⲣⲓⲣ) in recipe.

κⲟⲣⲧⲉⲛ, var ⲭⲟⲣ- B nn m, house-leek: K 198 حيّ العالم (ἀείζωον).

κⲱⲣϣ SAB (Si 12 17) F, ϭⲱⲣϣ, κⲉⲣϣ-, κⲟⲣϣⲍ S vb I intr, request, persuade, cajole: Si 12 17 SB (sic l) γλυκαίνειν, R 1 1 28 S ⲉⲓⲕ. ⲉⲧⲣⲁⲧⲁⲅⲟ ⲡⲟⲩϣⲁϫⲉ ἀξιοῦν; Pro 26 25 SA Gk diff; Pcod 5 S of Hezekiah ⲡⲧⲁϥϭ. & 15 years were added, Mor 25 12 S ⲡⲉϫⲁϥ ⲉϥⲕ. ϫⲉ- = Va 61 94 B ϩⲱⲡⲍ, BMEA 10582 S ϩⲟⲛⲉⲓ ⲉⲓⲕ. ϫⲟⲟⲩ ⲧⲁⲡⲟⲕⲣⲓⲥⲓⲥ, BMOr 6201 A 165 S ⲧⲓⲕ. ⲡⲧⲉⲡⲙⲁ ⲉⲙⲡϣⲁ ⲡⲧⲉⲕⲡⲁⲣϩⲏⲥⲓⲁ, Ryl 200 S ⲁⲓⲕ. ⲁⲕϯ.

c e- direct obj: Job 19 17 S (B ⲧⲱⲃϩ) ἱκετεύειν; ib (B ϯϩⲟ), Sa 14 17 S, R 2 2 23 S of Potiphar's wife κολακεύειν; GFr 434 S tell me ϯκ. ⲉⲣⲟⲕ, R 1 1 55 S ⲁⲩⲕ. ⲉⲁⲡⲡⲁⲥ, Z 354 S ⲡⲧⲕ. ⲉⲣⲟⲟⲩ to pray παρακαλεῖν; AP 4 A² ⲉⲕⲗⲓⲡⲁⲣⲉⲓⲛ; PS 93 S ⲡⲉⲩⲕ. ⲉⲣⲟⲓⲛⲉ with sweet words, Aeg 21 S ⲉϥⲕ. ⲉⲣⲟⲓ ϫⲉ- = ib B ϯϩⲟ, ShBor 247 99 S ϥⲉ ⲉⲧⲟⲩⲕ. ⲉⲡⲣⲉϥϯ

ⲣⲁⲡ so that they may do evil, BM 1031 *S* scribe of deed ⲡⲧⲁⲩⲕ. ⲉⲣⲟⲓ ⲁⲓⲥⲣⲁⲓ (*cf* below).   ⲥ ⲉⲭⲛ-, *on behalf of*: Bor 254 179 *S* ⲙⲡⲟⲩⲉⲩ ϭⲙϭⲟⲙ ⲉⲕ. ⲉⲭⲱⲓ, Mor 25 151 *S* at Last Day who will ⲉⲩ ⲕ. ⲉⲭⲱϥ?

II tr *S*, meaning same: R 2 2 27 dost think ⲧⲉⲡⲁϣ ⲕⲟⲣϣⲧ with promises? θωπεύειν, Z 337 ⲉⲡϣⲁⲡⲕⲟⲣϣϥ on his behalf παρακαλεῖν, Mor 37 11 ⲁϥⲕⲉⲣϣ ⲡⲡⲣⲟⲉⲥⲧⲱⲥ saying (*cf* JKP 2 32), Pcod 18 thou shouldst give ⲕⲁⲡ ⲉϥϣⲁⲡⲧⲙϭⲟⲣϣⲕ, Kr 59 corn ⲡⲧⲁⲓⲕⲟⲣϣⲕ thou hast given me, Ryl 280 ⲧⲓⲕ. ⲡⲡⲁⲭⲥ̄, BM 1035 scribe ⲁϥⲕⲟⲣϣⲧ ⲁⲓⲥⲣⲁⲓ, Ryl 147, 159 sim.

—— *S* nn, *entreaty, persuasion*: He 5 7 (*B* ϯⲣⲟ) ἱκετηρία, TT 99 their deeds & ⲡⲕ. ⲡⲧⲉⲩⲧⲁⲡⲣⲟ, Miss 4 692 his words were ⲣⲛⲟⲩⲕ., never saw we him angry, KKS 581 devil spoke ⲣⲛⲟⲩⲕ., BP 11349 ⲙⲟⲛⲓⲥ ⲣⲓⲧⲛⲣⲁⲣ ⲡⲕ.   As adj: Job 40 22 (*B* ⲧⲱⲃⲣ) ἱκ., 1 Thes 2 5 *SF* (*B* ⲥⲟⲡⲥⲉⲡ) κολακεία; ShC 73 167 ⲣⲣⲃ ⲡⲕ. (var ⲣⲉⲩⲕ.) ⲡⲣ̄ⲩⲡⲟⲕⲣⲓⲧⲏⲥ, Mor 23 68 ⲟⲩⲗⲁⲥ ⲡⲕ.

ⲣⲉⲩⲕ. *S, flatterer*: P 131⁶ 58 Meletians ⲡⲣ. ⲁⲩⲱ ⲙⲡⲁⲣⲁⲥⲓⲧⲟⲥ.   ⲙⲛⲧⲣⲉⲩⲕ., *flattery*: PS 209.

ϭⲓⲛⲕ. *S* nn f, *flattery, cajolery*: R 2 2 24 of Potiphar's wife κολακεία.

ⲕⲟⲣϣϥ *S*, ⲕⲁⲣ- *A* nn m, *flatterer*: Pro 26 22 κέρκωψ ﺟﻞ.

ⲕⲱⲣϥ *SB*, ϭⲱⲣⲃ *S* (*S* rare), ⲕⲉⲣϥ-, ⲕⲟⲣϥ⸗ *B*, ⲕⲟⲣϥ† *SB*, vb **I** tr, *bring to naught, cancel, destroy*: Lu 13 7 *B* (*S* ⲟⲩⲱⲥϥ), Ro 3 3 *B* (*S* = Gk), He 2 14 *B* (*SF* ⲟⲩ.) καταργεῖν; Mt 15 6 *B* (*S* ⲧⲥⲧⲟ ⲉⲃⲟⲗ); Va 66 309 *B* ⲉⲟⲣⲉⲡⲕ. ⲙⲡⲣⲱⲃ ⲙⲉϥϯ λύειν; Va 57 124 *B* ἐκεχειρίαν ἔχειν; CaiEuch 393 *B* ἄπρακτος; Ez 29 7 *B* (same?, *S* ⲣⲱⲣϥ, *cf* ⲕⲱⲣⲭ) συγκλᾶν *dissolvere*; ib 17 4 *S* (P 43 115, *B* ⲱⲗⲓ) ἀποκνίζειν (same?, *cf* ϭⲱⲡϭ), P 129¹⁶ 85 *S* ⲡⲡⲉⲛⲕ. ⲡⲧⲉⲡⲣⲟⲥⲫⲟⲣⲁ = C 86 347 *B*, EW 82 *B* cannot ⲕ. ⲡⲧⲕⲉⲗⲉⲅⲥⲓⲥ of king, P 131⁵ 51 *S* at Resurrection ⲁϥⲟⲩⲱⲥϥ ⲙⲡⲥⲁⲃⲃⲁⲧⲟⲛ ⲁϥⲕ. death, Va 61 119 *B* that God may ⲕ. ⲙⲡⲁⲓⲕⲉⲟⲅⲁⲓ (idolatry) = Mor 25 24 *S* ⲕⲁⲧⲁⲣⲅⲉⲓ, AM 112 *B* I will ⲕ. your heresy, ShA 2 105 *S* ⲙⲡⲉⲧⲛϭ. ⲙⲡⲉϥⲉⲓⲃ (of hell or disease?), Tri 338 *S* ⲁⲕⲕ. ⲡⲛⲉϥⲡⲁϣ, Aeg 39 *B* craftsmen ⲕ. ⲡⲛⲟⲩⲉⲣⲅⲁⲥⲧⲏⲣⲓⲟⲛ & make holiday (*cf* **II**), BSM 4 *B* officer whom king ⲛⲁⲕⲟⲣϥϥ when he will.

II intr, *be idle, deficient*: Mt 20 3 *B* (*S* ⲟⲩⲱⲥϥ) ἀργὸς ἱστάναι, 2 Pet 2 3 *B* (*S* diff), EW 155 *B* so that chosen vessel ⲟⲣⲓ ⲉⲩⲕ.† ἀργεῖν, Ro 6 6 *B* (*S* = Gk), 1 Cor 2 6 *B* (*S* ⲟⲩ.) καταργεῖν; Zeph 2 7 *B* (*SA* ϯ ⲟⲩⲱ) καταλύειν; Va 58 186 *B* food ⲉⲟⲃⲁⲕ. φθείρεσθαι; Mor 43 42 *S* at festival ⲉⲡⲉⲅⲕ. ⲧⲏⲣⲟⲩ ⲡⲉ = ib 42 39 *S* ⲟⲩ., BSM 9 *B* = BMis 326 *S* ⲟⲩ. sim, MG 25 309 *B* pleasures ⲉⲟⲛⲁⲕ. = BIF

13 117 *S* ⲧⲁⲕⲟ, Va 63 7 *B* lest our ⲑⲩⲥⲓⲁ ⲕ. = BMis 374 *S* ⲭⲉⲡⲁ, PasH 124 *B* their lamps ⲕ. (*cf* Mt 25 8), AM 75 *B* idolatry ⲕ. ⲉⲃⲟⲗ ϩⲉⲛⲡⲕⲁⲣⲓ.   With following preposition.

ⲉ- *B*, Va 58 17 ⲉⲁϥⲕ. ⲉⲟⲩⲟⲛ ⲡⲧⲁϥ ⲙⲙⲁⲩ ⲙⲡⲓⲁⲙⲁⲣⲓ, C 89 38 men are found ⲉⲩⲕ. ⲉⲣⲱⲟⲩ (sic, prob *l* ⲕⲱⲣϣ).   ⲡⲧⲉⲡ-, BIF 13 103 *S* cannot ⲕ. ⲡⲧⲉⲕⲕⲉⲗⲉⲅⲥⲓⲥ ⲡⲧⲟⲟⲧⲛ, Va 63 5 *B* lest our ⲑⲩⲥⲓⲁ ⲕ. ⲡⲧⲟⲧⲉⲛ = BMis 370 *S* ⲟⲩⲱⲥϥ tr.   ϩⲁ- *B*, Miss 4 209 shall be condemned ⲉⲡⲕ.†...ϩⲁϯⲙⲉⲧⲟⲩⲏⲃ; ⲉⲃⲟⲗ ϩⲁ- *B*, Ro 7 2 (*S* ⲃⲱⲗ ⲉⲃ. ϩⲛ-), Gal 5 4 (*S* ⲟⲩ. ⲉⲃ. ϩⲓⲧⲛ-) καταργεῖσθαι ἀπό, C 86 45 why stand ye ⲉⲧⲉⲧⲛⲕ.† ⲉⲃ. ϩⲁϥⲉⲣⲅⲁⲥⲓⲁ, Cat 47 so as to ⲕ. ⲉⲃⲟⲗ ϩⲁϯⲙⲉⲧⲣⲱⲙⲓ this devilish habit.

—— *B* nn m, *ceasing, idleness*: Ex 21 19 (*S* ⲟⲩⲁⲥϥⲉ), Is 1 13 (*S* ⲟⲩⲱⲥϥ) ἀργία, Va 57 37 ⲡⲕ. of the law παύεσθαι, AM 276 martyr's blood ⲟⲩⲕ. ⲡⲧⲉ ⲡⲓⲁⲓⲱⲣⲙⲟⲥ σφραγίς, C 89 49 ⲡⲕ. ⲡⲡⲓⲉⲡⲧⲟⲗⲏ = Miss 4 530 *S* ⲟⲩⲱⲥϥ (sic *l*), Va 57 31 lest we ϣⲱⲡⲓ ⲛⲕ. & become ⲁⲣⲅⲟⲥ.

ⲁⲧⲕ. *B*, *unceasing*: BSM 10 ϣⲁⲓ ⲛⲁⲧⲕ. = BMis 327 *S* ⲁⲧⲱⲭⲛ.

ⲕⲣⲟϥ *S*, ⲕⲣⲁϥ *AF*, ⲭⲣⲟϥ *B*, ⲕⲗⲁϥ *F* nn m, *guile, ambush*: Ge 34 13 *SB*, Job 13 16 *SB*, Pro 10 10 *SAB*, Mk 14 1 *SBF* δόλος, Nu 25 18 *S* (*B* ⲙⲉⲧⲍⲟⲗⲓⲟⲥ) δολιότης, *ib* 35 20 *S* (*B* ⲭⲟⲣⲭⲥ), Ob 7 *A* (*B* do) Ac 23 16 *S* (*B* do) ἔνεδρον, 1 Kg 15 5 *S* ⲥⲙⲛ ⲕ. ἐνεδρεύειν, BMis 14 *S* sim; PS 88 *S* ⲡⲉⲧⲟⲩⲉϣ ⲟⲙⲕⲧ ϩⲛⲟⲩⲕ., ShC 73 48 *S* who cometh upon him ϩⲛⲟⲩⲕ., Miss 4 138 *B* Flavian's creed ⲟⲩⲭ. ⲡⲉ, P 129¹⁴ 72 *S* ⲟⲩⲕ. ⲡⲉⲧϣⲟⲟⲡ O bishop (*cf* ⲙⲛⲧⲕ.).   *guileful person*: Pro 12 24 *SA* (*B* ⲣⲉⲩⲉⲣ ⲭ.) δόλιος; Job 9 23 *S* (*B* ⲥⲁ ⲙⲡⲉⲧⲣⲱⲟⲩ) φαῦλος; ShBor 246 88 *S* ϩⲉⲛⲕ. ⲡⲉ ⲡϩⲁⲓⲣⲉⲧⲓⲕⲟⲥ, BHom 500 *S* ⲡⲧⲟ ⲟⲩⲕ.

—— as adj, *guileful, false*: Ps 11 2 *SB*, Pro 13 9 *SAB*, 2 Cor 11 13 *SB* δόλιος; Am 8 5 *S* (*B* ϭⲓⲛ ⲭⲟⲛⲥ) ἄδικος *dolosus*; ShRyl 67 398 *S* ⲱ ⲡⲥⲟⲡ ⲡⲕ., Mor 50 28 *S* phantasm of ship ⲙⲡⲣⲡⲡⲉⲉⲃ ⲡⲕ.

ⲁⲧⲕ. *S*, ⲁⲧⲭ. *B*, *guileless*: 1 Pet 2 2 *B* (*S* ⲉⲧⲉⲙⲛ ⲕ. ϩⲛ-) ἄδολος, FR 146 *S* = Aeg 5 *B* Joseph ⲛⲁ.   ⲙⲉⲧⲁⲧⲭ. *B*, *guilelessness*: Aeg 22 of Virgin ϩⲉⲛ-ⲟⲩⲙ.

ⲙⲛⲧⲕ. *S*, *guile*: Ps 72 18 (*B* ⲙⲉⲧⲍⲟⲗⲟⲥ) δολιότης, Mk 7 22 (*B* do) δόλος; Jos 9 10 πανουργία; Bor 253 164 ⲡⲉϥⲙ. μεθοδεία, 4 Kg 11 14 ⲟⲩⲙ. σύνδεσμος.

ⲣ ⲕ. *SA*, ⲉⲣ ⲭ. *B*, *be guileful, lie in wait*: Ps 14 3 *SB*, Ro 3 13 *SB* δολιοῦν, δολοῦν, Dan 11 23 *B* δόλον ποιεῖν; Jud 9 32 *S* ἐνεδρεύειν; Mor 25 35 *S* worldlings ⲣ ⲕ. ϩⲁⲡⲱⲛϩ ⲡⲛⲣⲓⲕⲉ.   With following prep: ⲉ-, Nu 25 18 *S* (*B* om) δολιοῦν; Deu 19 11 *S* (*B* ϭⲓ ⲭ.), 2 Kg 3 27 *S* ἐνεδρεύειν, Ac 25

3 *SB* ἐνέδραν ποιεῖν; 1 Kg 22 8 *S* συγκεῖσθαι ἐπί; Ac 20 3 *S* ἐπιβουλὴ γίνεσθαι; PS 104 *S* ⲁⲩⲣ ⲕ. ⲉⲣⲟⲓ, C 86 116 *B* devil ⲉⲣ ⲭ. ⲉⲣⲟϥ to mislead him, Mor 25 176 *S* wife ⲉⲥⲟ ⲡⲕ. ⲉⲡⲉⲥϩⲁⲓ.   ⲉⲣⲡ-, Jud 9 34 *S* ἐνέδρ. ἐπί.   ⲛ-, 2 Cor 4 2 *S* ⲣ ⲕ. ⲙ̅ⲡϣⲁϫⲉ (*B* ϩⲉⲡⲡⲓⲥ.) δολοῦν acc.   ⲣⲉϥⲣ ⲕ. *S*, ⲉⲣ ⲭ. *B*, *deceiver, traitor*: Ps 108 2 *B* (*S* ⲕ. ⲛⲛ), Pro 12 24 *B* (*SA* ⲇⲟ) δόλιος; CaiEuch 464 *B* ⲡⲣⲟⲇⲟⲧⲏⲥ ⲡⲣ. δολερός; Job 19 12 *S* (*B* ⲣⲉϥϧⲱⲣⲝ), Lu 20 20 *B* (*S* ⲣⲉϥⲥⲱⲣⲥ) ἐγκάθετος; Job 25 3 *B* (*S* ⲥⲟⲟⲡⲉ) πειρατής.   ⲥⲁ ⲡⲕ. *S*, ⲭ. *B*, *maker of guile, deceiver*: BM 251 *S* (*Vita Anton*), let us despise this c. πανοῦργος, Mor 22 122 *S* = BSM 111 *B* save me from this c. (devil), BMar 235 *S* sim, C 86 95 *B* of Joab.   ϫⲓ ⲕ. *S*, ϭⲓ ⲭ., ⲛⲭ. *B*, *use guile, lie in wait*: Deu 19 11 *B* (*S* ⲣ ⲕ.), Jud 9 25 *S*, Lu 11 54 *B* (*S* ⲥⲱⲣⲥ) ἐνεδρ.; Est 3 15 *S* (reading? ἐγκαθίζοντο); Jer 18 18 *S* (*B* ϣⲁⲣⲓ) πατάσσειν (reading? ἀπατᾶν); Cat 200 *B* ⲁϥⲑⲣⲉϥϭⲓ ⲙ̅ⲡⲉϥⲥⲟⲛ ⲛⲭ. (Ge 4 8), PS 101 *S* ⲁⲅⲟⲩⲱϣ ⲉϫⲓⲧ ⲡⲕ.   ϭⲁⲩⲭ. *B*, *deceiver*: Va 62 269 of Herod, Cat 125 of devil.   ϫⲓⲛⲭ. *B*, *snares*: Va 57 173 ϩⲁⲛⲑⲃⲁ ⲛϭⲓⲛⲭ. (*sic* MS) ϩⲉⲙⲙⲁⲓ ⲡⲓⲃⲉⲛ.

ⲕⲁⲣⲉϩ *S* v ⲕⲱⲗϩ I.

ⲕⲉⲣϩ *S* nn, *meaning unknown*, connected? with loom: Univ College London ostr ⲕⲉⲗⲕⲓⲗ: ⲡⲡⲉⲧ ⲛⲛⲟⲩⲱⲭⲉ ⲕ., var CO 466 om ⲛⲛⲟⲩ. ⲕ.

ⲕⲣⲁϩ *O* vb or nn?, *meaning unknown*: Hor 77, 78 ⲛ̅ⲡϥ̅ⲕⲣⲁϩ ⲧⲟⲩⲱⲧ.

ⲕⲣⲟϩ *S* nn m, *meaning unknown*: COAd 54 give him the rope...ϣⲁⲛⲧⲁⲉⲓ...ⲛⲧⲁⲃⲓ ⲡⲕⲟⲩⲕ.

ⲕⲱⲣϩ *S* v ⲥⲱⲣϩ.

ⲕⲉⲣϩⲉ *B* (*S* only Saq) nn m, *bald person* (*cf* קֵרֵחַ IgR): Lev 13 40 (*S* ⲟⲩⲥ) φαλακρός; Miss 4 119 ⲟⲩⲕ. ⲡⲉ ⲡⲕⲁⲕϩⲣⲁϥ (but *cf* ⲗⲁ-), Saq 158 *S* Mena (?) ⲡⲕ.   ⲙⲉⲧⲕ. nn f, *baldness*: Lev 13 42 (*S* ⲙⲛ̅ⲧⲟⲩⲥ), Deu 14 1 (*S* om), Is 15 2 (*S* ϩⲱⲱⲕⲉ nn), Am 8 10 (*S* ⲇⲟ vb) φαλάκρωμα. *Cf* ϭⲁⲗⲟ̄ϥⲓϩ.   As name: Saq 361.

ⲕⲱⲣϫ, ⲕⲉⲣϫ-, ⲕⲟⲣϫ⸗, ⲣⲥ ⲕⲁⲣϫ- *B* vb **I** tr, *cut down, break off*: Deu 19 5 (*S* ⲕⲱⲱⲣⲉ), Is 14 8 (*S* ϣⲱⲱⲧ), Mt 21 8 (*S* ⲇⲟ) κόπτειν, Ps 73 5 (*S* ⲇⲟ), Mt 7 19 (*S* ⲕⲱⲱⲣⲉ) ἐκκόπ.; Mt 15 13 (*S* ⲡⲱⲣⲕ) ἐκριζεῖν; Lev 1 17 (*S* ϩⲱⲣⲃ) ἐκκλᾶν, Va 57 264 of firewood διακλᾶν; Ez 34 12 ἀπελαύνειν (var συνάγειν); C 86 82 smitten on mouth ϣⲁⲧⲟⲩⲕ. ⲡⲉϥⲛⲁϫϩⲓ, C 41 57 of idols ⲁⲩⲕⲟⲣϫⲟⲩ, *ib* 271 if obdurate ϯⲛⲁⲕ. ⲛ̅ⲡⲟⲅⲁϥⲛⲟⲩⲓ, Va 58 192 after drink head is heavy ⲉⲕⲕⲉⲣϫ ⲕⲁⲥ ⲉⲕⲫⲉⲣϫ ⲣⲟ = P

131² 117 *S* ⲟⲩⲉϭⲡ ⲕⲉⲉⲥ (*cf*? ὀστεοκόπος), C 86 271 among tortures ϩⲁⲛⲕⲉⲣϫ ⲕⲁⲥ (*l* prob as adj ⲛ̅ⲕⲉⲣϫ).   ⲕⲁⲣⲭϣⲁⲓ, *broken-nosed*: BM 920 266, Ryl 453 337 كسر الانف (*cf* Dozy 1 41 كسر انف, *mortify*).   **II** intr, *be in a broken state*: Ro 11 17, 19 (*SF* ϣⲱⲱⲧ tr) ἐκκλᾶσθαι.   As nn m: Jer 11 16 περιτομή.

ⲕⲣⲟⲩϫ, ⲕⲣⲟϫ & varr *S* nn, *a baked or fried cake*: Hos 3 1 (P 44 116 = 43 118) ϩⲉⲛⲕⲣⲟⲩϫ (*A* ⲣⲁⲭⲏ *ie* ⲣⲁⲭⲏ, *B* ϥⲓⲥⲓ) πέμματα خشكنانك, خشتنانك (Dozy 1 373); P 44 89 ⲡⲉⲕⲣⲟⲩϫ كماج; 2 Kg 6 19 Ciasca ⲟⲩⲱⲡ (*l* ⲟⲩⲟⲩⲱⲡ) ⲡⲉⲕⲣⲟϫ, varr Mor ⲟⲩⲉⲕⲣⲟϫ, P 44 110 ⲟⲩⲟⲩⲕⲕⲣⲟϫ عَجّ, 43 103 ⲟⲩⲉⲕⲗⲟϫ لقمة عَجّ ἐσχαρίτης.   Same? as قرص.

ⲕⲁⲥ *F* nn, *cry, roaring* (?): EpJer 31 ϣⲁⲩϯ ⲕⲁⲥ (*B* ϩⲉⲙϩⲉⲙ) ὠρύεσθαι. Pey 424 compares ⲕⲁⲥⲕⲉ.

ⲕⲁⲥ *SB*, ⲕⲉⲉⲥ *SA*, ⲕⲏⲥ, ⲕⲓⲥ *S*, ⲕⲏⲏⲥ, ⲕⲉⲥ *S^f F*, pl ⲕⲁⲁⲥ, ⲕⲁⲉⲥⲉ (WS) *S*, ⲕⲉⲉⲥ *SA*, ⲕⲏⲏⲥ *F* & sg as pl, nn m, *bone*: sg, Ps 138 15 *SB*, Jo 19 36 *SB*; pl, Jos 24 32 *S*, Ps 52 5 *S* (var ⲕⲁⲉⲥⲉ WS 30) *B*, Pro 3 8 *SAB*, Jer 27 17 *S* (ShA 2 343) *BF* ὀστέον; Job 7 5 *B* (*S* = Gk), MG 25 205 *B* σῶμα; PS 158 *S* ϩⲉⲛⲕ. ⲉⲩⲙⲟⲟⲩⲧ, C 43 130 *B* ⲡⲉϥⲙⲁϩⲧ, ⲡⲉϥⲕ., ShP 130² 95 *S* weight broke ⲡⲕ. ⲛ̅ⲧⲉⲩϫⲓⲥⲉ (*cf* Job 40 13 *S*), Gu 38 *S* (Epiphan *De Gem*) ⲕ. *shell* of κόχλος covers it, Va 58 121 *B* when idling ⲧⲉⲛⲫⲟⲗϫ ⲣⲟ ⲧⲉⲡⲉⲗϫ (? ⲕⲉⲣϫ *q v*) ⲕ., Mor 30 40 *F* ⲡⲕⲉⲥ ⲉⲡⲉⲕⲥⲁⲓ.   In alchem recipes: Bodl(P) a 1 *e* = *ib* a 3 37 *S* white garment to be dyed ϯ ⲕⲏⲥ ⲡⲣⲱⲙⲉ ⲉϫⲱϥ...ⲛⲧϯ ⲡⲕⲏⲥ ⲉϩⲟⲩⲛ ⲉⲣⲟϥ, Cai 42573 2 *Sf* with dust (or scurf) ⲍ̄ ⲛⲕⲓⲥ of (ϩⲛ-) black dog & same of black horse.   ⲕ. ⲡⲕⲱⲱⲥ *S* Mt 23 27 (*B* ⲕ. ⲛ̅ⲣⲉϥⲙⲟⲩⲟⲩⲧ) ὀσ. νεκρῶν, ShC 42 17, ShA 1 215 sim (var ⲕⲉⲉⲥ *ib* 212, 219).   ⲕⲉⲉⲥ as sg: Ge 2 23 *S* (var ⲕⲁⲥ BG 60, ⲕⲓⲥ AZ 55 70) *A* (Cl 6 3), Nu 9 12 *S*, BHom 119 *S* ⲟⲩⲕ. ⲉⲧⲣⲉⲩⲧⲟⲥⲥϥ ⲉⲡⲉϥⲥⲱⲙⲁ, *cf* 120 ⲡⲕⲁⲥ *bis*, R 1 3 48 *S* ⲡⲕ. ⲡⲣⲱⲙⲉ in tomb, Mor 24 8 *F* ⲟⲩⲕⲛⲏⲥ.   ⲕⲁⲁⲥ pl *S*: Ps 42 2 (Rahlfs), Si 26 13, 38 33, 46 18.

ⲕⲉⲣϫ ⲕⲁⲥ *B* v ⲕⲱⲣϫ.

ⲙⲁⲣ-, ⲙⲉⲣⲕ. *S*, ⲙⲉⲣ-, ⲙⲟⲣⲕ. *B*, ⲙⲁⲣⲕ. *F* nn m, *bone-setter*: P 44 67 = 43 36 *S* جَبّر opp ⲥⲁⲉⲓⲛ ἰατρός, Miss 8 259 *S* ⲥⲁⲉⲓⲛ ϩⲓⲙ., Va 62 174 = 69 91 *B* ⲟⲩⲙ. ⲟⲩⲟϩ ⲛⲥⲛⲏⲛⲓ heals broken leg, Mor 41 10 *S* ⲙ. = Va 59 36 *B* ⲣⲉϥⲙⲟⲣⲕ., BKU 1 26 (8117) 8 *F* ⲉⲩϭⲁϯ ⲙⲁⲣⲕⲉⲥ ⲉⲡⲉϥⲧⲉϩⲉⲛ ⲡⲟⲩⲛⲁⲙ (could be read otherwise?).

ⲣ, ⲉⲣ ⲕ. *SB*, *become bony* through sickness: Miss 4 532 = C 89 50 *B* whole body ⲣ ⲕ.

ⲕⲁⲥⲃⲏⲧ *B* nn, *rib-bones*: Va 62 174 ⲕ. of his body broken, AM 235 martyr scraped till ⲡⲉϥⲕ. laid bare.

ⲕⲁⲥⲣⲟ *B* nn f, *jaw-bone*: RAl 99 Samson's ⲕ. ⲡⲓⲱ (*cf* ⲙⲉⲣⲟⲩⲟϭⲉ), K 76 ϯⲕ. اَضْرَاس.

ⲕⲁⲥ *SB*, *stone, pip* of fruit: grapes, Nu 6 4 *S* (*B* = Gk) γίγαρτον, Ryl 106 45 *S* of ⲥⲓⲡⲓⲡ (زبيب), Z 630 *S* raisins ⲭⲱⲣⲓⲥ ⲡⲉⲩⲕ.; gourd, C 41 69 *B* ⲕ. ⲡϫⲟⲡϯ (*q v*), RAl 87 *B* Jonah comforted by ⲡⲓⲕ. ⲡⲉϭⲗⲟϫ (DeV 195 diff).

ⲕⲁⲥ *SB*, **ⲕⲉⲥ** *F* nn m, *carat*, a coin: CDan 87 *B* labourer's daily wage ⲟⲩⲕ. = *ib* 32 κεράτιον = PO 16 365 قيراط ذهب, Kr 222 *F* ⲕⲉⲥ ⲥⲛⲟⲟⲩ transcribed *ι̅β̅* (of solidus), so 1 ⲕ. = 1/24 *i e* 1 κεράτιον, Cat 158 *B* (on Lu 15 8) drachma is woman's working tool ⲉⲣⲉⲟⲩⲟⲡ ⲓ̅ⲏ̅ ⲡⲓⲕ. ⲡⲡⲟⲩⲃ (money) ⲛϩⲏⲧⲥ, ST 118 *S varia* priced in ϩⲟⲗⲟⲕ/, ⲧⲣⲓⲙⲏⲥⲓⲟⲛ or ⲕ., Baouit 1 9 *S* ⲕ. ⲡⲣⲟⲙⲉⲧ ⲡⲁⲣⲁ ⲧⲓⲟⲩ ⲡⲫⲟⲗⲟⲥ (φόλλις), Bal *S* receipt ⲉⲓⲥ ⲕ. ⲥⲡⲁⲩ ⲁⲅⲉⲓ ⲉⲧⲟⲟⲧ, PLond 4 45 *S* sim ⲟⲩⲧⲣⲓⲙⲏⲥⲓⲛ ⲙⲡⲥⲡⲁⲩ ⲡⲕ., BMOr 6201 B 57 *S* ⲟⲩⲕ. ⲟⲩϭⲟⲥ, BM 556 *F* ⲓ̅ⲁ̅ ⲡⲓⲕ. ⲟⲩϭⲁⲥ, Baouit 1 130 *S* payments of ⲟⲩⲕ. & ⲡⲁϣⲕ., BM 690 *F* sums in ⲧⲉⲣⲣⲁⲙ & ⲕ., Kr 236 *F* ⲡⲉⲕ....ⲙⲡⲡⲉⲧⲉⲣⲣⲁⲙ, ShZ 506 *S* ⲟⲩⲕ. as small coin; also in arithm problems BM 528 *F* nos 13, 19, 25, 34, 63. As weight: WS 113 *S* ϩⲙⲏ ⲡⲕ. ⲡϫⲓⲣ. ⲕⲁⲥ sometimes for ϭⲟⲥ *q v*.

ⲕⲁⲥ *S*, **ⲕⲁⲁⲥ** *A*, **ⲕⲉⲥ**, **ⲕⲉⲉⲥ** *F* *v* ϫⲉⲕⲁⲥ.

ⲕⲉⲥ *S* vb *v* ϭⲱⲥ.

ⲕⲟⲉⲓⲥ, **ⲕⲁⲉⲓⲥ** *S* nn m, κόις, vessel for liquids: wine, Vienna ostr 156 ⲟⲩⲕ. ⲡⲏⲣ[ⲡ, PMich 602 in wine-account ⲕ. ⲱ; vinegar, CO 217 ⲕⲁ. ϣⲏⲙ ⲡϩⲙϫ; or solids: ST 117 ⲥⲡⲁⲩ ⲡⲕ. ⲡϭⲟⲩϫ. Glos 237 ἡμικάδια· ϣⲕⲁⲓⲥ (? ⲡⲁϣⲕ.). Its maker: Kr 223 (ⲉ)ⲕⲟⲧ ⲡⲕⲁⲧⲕ. translated κερμ[=(κεραμεύς), *ib* 182 ⲉⲕⲟⲧⲉ ⲡⲕⲁⲧⲕ. transl πλοκουφ/ (as if ⲕ. = κοῦφον). Same ? ⲕⲟⲓⲥⲉ *S* f: BM 1103 holding κολοκάσιον.

ⲕⲱⲱⲥ, **ⲕⲱⲡⲥ**, **ⲕⲱⲱⲥⲉ** *S*, **ⲕⲱⲥ** *B*, **ⲕⲱⲱⲥⲓ** *F* (Mor 30 14), **ⲕⲉⲥ-** *B*, **ⲕⲟⲟⲥ⸗**, **ⲕⲟⲟⲡⲥ⸗**, **ⲕⲟⲟⲥⲉ⸗** *S*, **ⲕⲁⲥ⸗** *S* (BM 445) *A* (? El 34), **ⲕⲟⲥ⸗** *B*, **ⲕⲏⲥ** &c †*SB* (*v* below) vb tr, *dress, prepare corpse for burial, bury*: Ge 50 26 *B* (*S* ⲧⲱⲙⲥ), Deu 21 23 *B* (*S* do), Ps 78 3 *B* (*S* do), Jer 22 19 *S* (Bor 277 215) *B*, Lu 9 60 *B* (*S* ⲧⲱ.) θάπτειν, Col 2 12 *B* (*S* do) συνθάπ.; Ge 50 2 *B* ⲕⲉⲥ-, Jo 19 40 *SB*, HL 97 *B* ⲁⲥⲕⲟⲥϥ in woollen raiment (*cf* below PSBA), C 89 28 *B* they sing ϣⲁⲡⲧⲟⲩⲕⲟⲥⲥ, then carry her to burial ἐνταφιάζειν; Lu 23 53 *S* (var ϭⲗⲟⲙⲗⲙ, *B* ⲕⲟⲩⲗⲱⲗ) ἐντυλίττειν; Ez 29 5 *B* περιστέλλειν, Ac 5 6 *S* (*B* ⲑⲱⲙⲥ) συστ.; BAp 125 *S* = MIE 2 418 *B* ⲡⲧⲉⲡⲕⲟⲥⲧ ⲡⲧⲉⲛⲧⲟⲙⲥⲧ = Par 4785 210 كفنوني وادفنوني, BSM 78 *B* ⲁⲛⲕⲟⲥϥ = BMis 168 *S* ⲁⲩϯ ⲕⲁⲓⲥⲉ ⲉⲣⲟϥ, ShBM 204 1 *S* he laid corpse ϩⲓϫⲙⲡⲙⲁ ⲡⲕⲟⲧⲕ ⲡⲡⲉⲧⲛⲁⲕⲟⲟⲥϥ, FR 40 *S* = BMis 70 *S* ⲱⲗ, Mor 28

270 *S* mother shall ⲱⲗ ⲙⲡⲉⲕⲥⲱⲙⲁ ⲡⲥⲕ. ⲙⲙⲟϥ & lay it on a ship, C 41 60 *B* ⲁⲩⲕⲟⲥϥ ⲁⲩⲟⲗϥ ⲉⲃⲟⲗ ⲁⲩⲑⲟⲙⲥϥ, R 1 3 51 *S* ⲁⲥⲕⲟⲟⲥϥ ⲕⲁⲗⲱⲥ & laid him in ⲧⲏⲏⲃⲉ, AM 76 *B* ⲁϥⲕⲟⲥϥ ϫⲉⲛⲟⲩⲕⲁⲓⲥⲓ, N&E 39 348 *B* ⲁⲩⲕⲟⲥⲟⲩ in ϣⲉⲡⲧⲟ & ⲥⲑⲟⲓⲛⲟⲩϥⲓ, LMis 464 *S* sim, C 43 87 *B* ⲟⲩϣⲟⲏⲛ...ⲕ. ⲙⲡⲥⲱⲙⲁ ⲙⲙⲟⲥ (*cf* AM 330), PSBA 29 193 *S* sim ϩⲣⲏϩⲣⲟⲓⲧⲉ ⲡⲥⲟⲣⲧ (*cf* above HL), Mus 34 204 *B* ⲡⲓⲣⲃⲱⲥ ⲉⲧⲁⲕⲕⲟⲥⲟⲩ ⲉⲣⲟϥ, Rec 6 169 *B* ⲧⲁⲥⲧⲟⲗⲏ ⲁⲓⲕⲟⲥⲥ ⲉⲡⲉϥⲥⲱⲙⲁ = BMar 206 *S* ⲥⲟⲩⲗⲱⲗ. Forms ⲕⲱⲡⲥ, ⲕⲟⲡⲥ &c *SF*: Mor M 663 A 145 *S* ⲁⲩⲕ. ⲙⲡⲉϥⲥⲱⲙⲁ, Mor 41 9 *S* ⲉⲩⲕⲟⲟⲡⲥ ⲙⲡⲥⲱⲙⲁ, Mor 31 132 *S* wished to kiss him ⲙⲡⲁⲧⲟⲩⲕⲟⲡⲥϥ (var Wess 15 4 ⲕⲟⲟⲥϥ), Mk 14 8 *S* ⲉⲡⲕⲟⲟⲡⲥⲧ, 1 Cor 15 4 *F* (Mor 38 3) ⲁⲩⲕⲁⲁⲡⲥϥ (var Z 155 ⲧⲁⲗⲙⲉⲥϥ). ⲕⲱⲱⲥⲉ *S*: Z 328 ⲉⲩⲡⲁⲕ. ⲛⲙⲙⲁⲥ ⲙⲡⲕⲉⲁ(ⲛ)ⲣ κηδεύειν, Louvre 10024 ⲁⲩⲕ. ⲙⲡⲉϥⲥⲱⲙⲁ, Mor 16 55 ⲉⲧⲣⲉⲩⲕⲟⲟⲥⲉⲕ. Qual *SB*: MIE 2 403 *B* clothes ⲉⲧⲉϥⲕⲏⲥ ⲡϩⲏⲧⲟⲩ, *ib* ⲉⲣⲉⲡⲉϥⲧⲏⲃ ⲕⲏⲥ ⲡⲟⲩⲁⲓ ⲟⲩⲁⲓ, P 129^16 38 *S* lo corpse (σκήνωμα) is in bishop's house ⲉϥⲕⲏⲥ (Mor 39 19, 40 14 om, *cf* C 43 43 *inf*), Aeg 57 *B* ϩⲁⲛⲣⲃⲱⲥ...ⲉⲧⲕⲏⲥ ⲉⲣⲟϥ, Gu 51 *S* ⲙⲁⲣⲟⲩⲃⲟⲗϥ ⲉⲃⲟⲗ ⲉϥⲕⲱⲱⲥ, Mor 43 229 *S* ⲡⲓⲙ ⲡⲉⲛⲧⲁϥⲧⲱⲟⲩⲛ ϩⲁⲣⲟϥ ⲉϥⲕⲁⲁⲥ ?, Mor 41 128 *S* ⲉϥⲕⲟⲟⲥⲉ ⲡⲡⲟⲩⲕⲁⲓⲥⲉ.

—— **ⲉ-** (? prolonged process): Mor 51 25 *S* vowed ⲉⲕ. ⲉⲡⲥⲱⲙⲁ ⲡⲡⲉⲧⲟⲩⲁⲁⲃ, TstAb 255 *B* he bade ϫⲉⲕ. ⲙⲡⲁⲓⲱⲧ...they spent 40 days ⲉⲩⲕ. ⲉⲡⲓⲏⲗ̅, MG 25 405 *B* ⲉⲧⲓ..ⲉⲩⲕ. ⲉⲣⲟϥ.

—— nn m f(once), *a B*, *burial, funeral*: Ge 50 3 (*S* ⲕⲁⲓⲥⲉ), Deu 21 23 (*S* ⲧⲱⲙⲥ), Jer 22 19 (*S* ⲕⲁ.) ταφή; Jo 12 7 (SAA² do) ἐνταφιασμός; Va 69 119 ⲁⲩⲕⲟⲥϥ ϫⲉⲛⲟⲩⲕ. ⲙⲙⲉⲧⲟⲩⲣⲟ, CaiThe 403 Jonah 3 days in whale ⲕⲁⲧⲁ ⲡⲓⲕ. of Saviour. *b S*, *corpse*: Lev 21 5 (*B* ⲣⲉϥⲙⲱⲟⲩⲧ), Ps 30 12 (*B* do), EpJer 31 (P 44 114, *F* ⲗⲉϥⲙⲁⲟⲩⲧ, *B* diff) Mt 23 27 (*B* ⲣⲉϥⲙ.) νεκρός; LeipBer '02 151 Antinous ⲉⲩⲕ. ⲡⲉ κεκηδευμένος; PS 158 didst bring them out from midst of ⲡⲕ., Miss 4 768 cave ⲉⲥⲙⲏϩ ⲡⲕⲟⲟⲡⲥ, Cai 42573 1 ⲡⲙⲟⲟⲩ ⲡⲕ. in recipe, KroppK 41 ⲟⲩϩⲙⲟⲩ ⲡⲕ. f, ST 399 *S* ⲧⲉⲕ. ⲧⲁⲓ. MIE 2 402 *B* ϩⲁⲡⲙⲗⲏϣ ⲡⲕ. ⲡⲧⲉ ϩⲁⲡⲥⲱⲙⲁ (? for ⲕⲁⲥ).

ⲃⲁⲗⲃⲗ ⲕ. *S*, *dig up corpses*: *v* ⲃⲟⲗⲃⲗ **II**.

ⲣⲉϥⲛ ⲕ. ⲉⲣⲟⲩⲛ *S*, *invoker, producer of dead*: Lev 19 31 (*B* ⲣⲉϥⲙⲟⲩϯ ϫⲉⲛⲑⲛⲉϫⲓ), 1 Kg 28 3 ἐγγαστρίμυθος, BHom 138 ⲥϩⲓⲙⲉ ⲡⲣ. μαγγανεύτρια.

ⲣ ⲕ. *SF*, *be corpse, be dead*: BMis 240 *S* yesterday ⲁϥⲣ ⲕ., to-day ϥⲟⲩⲟϫ, Mor 17 23 *S* where Dioscorides lay ⲁϥⲣ ⲕ. νεκρὸν κείμενον, Mor 30 14 *F* wast carried forth ⲉⲕⲱ ⲡⲕ., PBu 246 *S* ⲉⲩⲉⲓⲣⲉ ⲙⲡⲡⲣⲟⲥⲱⲡⲟⲛ ⲡⲟⲩϭⲣⲓⲙⲉ ⲁⲥⲣ ⲕ.

ⲣⲉϥⲕ. *B*, *embalmer*: Ge 50 2 ἐνταφιαστής, Aeg 32, TstAb 255.

ϫⲓⲛⲕ. *B* nn m f, *burial*: Aeg 32 ϯϫ. of Jews, AM 223 ⲟⲩⲕⲁⲓⲥⲓ ⲉⲡϫ. of my body; Mt 26 12 ⲡϫⲓⲛⲕⲟⲥⲧ (*S* ⲡⲕⲟⲟⲥⲧ) τὸ ἐνταφιάσαι με.

ⲕⲁⲓⲥⲉ, ⲕⲉⲓⲥⲉ (CO 352), ⲕⲉⲥⲉ (Is 53 9) *S*, ⲕⲉⲉⲥⲉ *AA²*, ⲕⲁⲓⲥⲓ *B*, ⲕⲏⲓⲥⲓ, ⲕⲉⲛⲥⲓ *F*, ⲕⲁⲛⲥⲉ *O* nn f, *a preparation for burial, embalming*: Ge 50 3 *S* (*B* ⲕⲱⲥ), Job 17 1 *B* (*S* diff), Is 57 2 *SB* ταφή, Va 66 313 *B* Joseph's ⲙⲉϫⲁⲅ τάφος, Nicodemus's ⲕ. ταφή (cf Jo 19 39), Jo 12 7 *SAA²* (*B* ⲕⲱⲥ) ἐνταφιασμός, J 74 23 *S* bequests for προσφορά & ⲕ. (cf ib 106 101 ⲡⲣⲱⲃⲉ ⲙⲡⲁⲥⲱⲙⲁ & PLond 1 234, 5 120 περιστολή), CO 352 *S* sim; Deu 34 6 *SB* (var ⲕⲱⲥ) ταφή *place of burial*(?); Z 328 *S* ⲁⲩϯ ⲡⲟⲩⲛⲟϭ ⲡⲕ. ⲉⲣⲟⲥ κηδεία; AZ 21 94 *O* Osiris ⲡⲛⲏⲃ ⲛ̇ⲧⲕ. (cf DM 21 2). **b** *grave-clothes, shroud*: Mor 22 24 *S* ⲁϥϯ ⲉⲣⲟϥ ⲛⲟⲩⲕ. & laid him in tomb, Mor 43 229 *S* Lazarus came forth ⲉⲣⲉⲧⲕ. ϭⲟⲟⲗⲉ ⲉⲡⲉϥⲥⲱⲙⲁ, BMar 43 *S* I have brought ⲕ. & ⲧⲏⲃⲉ lest I be buried in ⲟⲩⲕ. ⲛϣⲙⲙⲟ, DeV 105 *B* I caused bring ⲟⲩⲕ. ⲉⲓⲟⲩⲱϣ ⲉⲕⲟⲥϥ, MIE 2 418 *B* spend a *solidus* ⲛⲕ. ⲉⲡⲁⲥⲱⲙⲁ = BAp 125 *S* ⲣ̇ⲃⲟⲟⲥ, C 86 145 *B* shrouded in ⲟⲩⲕ. ⲛⲟⲗⲟⲥⲩⲣⲓⲕⲟⲛ, P 43 244 *S* ⲟⲑⲟⲛⲓⲁ (*sic l*) ⲛ̇ⲕ. الاكفان. **c** *corpse*: MIF 9 43 *S* death talked with ⲧⲕ. of Jesus in tomb, AZ 21 143 *S* weeping for ⲧⲕ. ⲉⲧⲕⲏ ⲉϩⲣⲁⲓ, Mor 30 50 *F* ⲡⲉⲕ. (? ⲕⲉⲉⲥ) of martyr = BMis 274 *S* ⲥⲱⲙⲁ. ⲥⲙⲟⲧ ⲛ̇ⲧⲕ., *effigy, imitation of body*: 1 Kg 19 13 *S* κενοτάφιον statua, Mor 40 13 *S* ⲡⲉⲥ. ⲛ̇ⲧⲕ., var *ib* 39 18 ⲡⲉⲥⲕⲏⲛⲡⲱⲙⲁ ⲙⲡⲉϥⲥⲱⲙⲁ = C 43 43 *B* ⲡⲓⲥ. ⲛ̇ⲧⲉ ⲧⲉϥⲕ.

ⲕⲁⲥⲉ, ⲕⲉⲥⲉ, ⲕⲏⲥⲉ *S* nn m, *shoemaker*: Mor 52 38 Mark on arrival at Alexandria ⲁϥϭⲓⲛⲉ ⲛⲟⲩⲕ. seated at work, *ib* 39 Anianus ⲡⲕ. (cf PO 1 142), AZ 60 109 ⲧⲕⲟⲓⲡⲱⲧⲏⲥ ⲛ(ⲡ)ⲛⲥⲕⲉⲧⲉⲱⲥ (σκυτεύς) corresponds *ib* to ⲡⲕⲉⲥⲉ, Mor 51 38 ⲡⲣⲉⲙⲏⲛⲏ ⲛ̇ⲧⲕ. at Pboou, *ib* 40 he swears by the kingdom he rules ⲉⲧⲉⲧⲕⲁⲃⲁⲡⲱⲧⲉ (?? κάμπανος) ⲙ̇ⲡⲕⲟⲣⲙⲟⲥ (κορμός) ⲛⲛⲕ. (HistLaus 2 96 σκυτοτομεῖον among Tabennesiote trades), Mor 43 140 heretics Antonius ⲡ̇ⲕ. & Severus, ShC 73 59 among abusive names ⲕ., ⲣⲁⲕ (cf AZ *ut sup*), Osir pl 37, Hall 18 among trade-names ⲕⲏⲥⲉ, Saq 89, LeydAC 14, WS 59, PLond 4 511, Bodl(P) d 22 in lists, epitaphs. In place-name ? ⲡⲙⲁ ⲛ̇ⲕ. PMich 3557.

ⲕⲓⲥⲉ *S* nn f, *an eruptive disease*: P 43 51 (44 om) ⲧⲕ. ⲛ̇ⲕⲏⲛ (*sic*) الحبّة التي لا تعرف *boils of unknown kind*.

ⲕⲱⲱⲥⲉ *S*, ⲕⲱⲱⲥⲓ *F* v ⲕⲱⲥ.

ⲕⲁⲥⲕⲥ *S*, ⲕⲉⲥⲕⲥ *A*, ϫⲁⲥⲕⲉⲥ *B*, ⲕⲉⲥⲕⲉⲥ *F* vb intr, *whisper*: 2 Kg 12 19 *S*, Aeg 275 *S* ψιθυρίζειν, R 2 4 82 *S* ϣⲁϫⲉ ⲉⲩⲕ. ἐν ψιθυρισμῷ, LAl 6 *S* ⲡⲉⲕ-

ⲭⲁϥ ⲡⲁϥ ⲉϫⲕ. With following preposition: Ps 40 7 *S* ⲕ. ⲉ- (*B* ϫ. ϩⲁ-) ψιθ. κατά, Z 291 *S* serpent ⲕ. ⲉⲉϩⲣⲁ ψιθ. acc, BAp 158 *S* devil ⲕ. ⲉⲣⲟⲕ, Bor 248 55 *S* when saying Psalms ⲛⲉⲕ. ϣⲁⲡⲣⲁ ⲙⲙⲁⲧⲉ ⲙⲟⲟⲓⲥ ⲉⲧⲣⲉⲡⲥⲱⲧⲙ ⲉⲡⲉⲡⲉⲣⲏⲩ.

—— *SABF* nn m, *whispering*: Eccl 10 11 *S*, 2 Cor 12 20 *SBF*, Cl 30 3 *A* ψιθυρισμός, Sh 42 128 *S* demons ⲉⲧϣⲁϫⲉ ϩⲛⲟⲩⲕ. As adj: Aeg 13 *S* ⲡϣⲁϫⲉ ⲛ̇ⲕ.

ⲣⲉϥⲕ. *S*, ⲣⲉϥϫ. *B*, *whisperer*: Si 5 16, 28 14 *S* ψίθυρος, Ro 1 30 *SB* ψιθυριστής, Aeg 248 *S*.
Cf ⲕⲁⲥ *F*.

ⲕⲟⲥⲕⲥ ⲉⲃⲟⲗ *S*, -ⲕⲉⲥ ⲉⲃ. *B*, ⲕⲉⲥⲕⲱⲥⲥⲍ *SB* vb tr a *bend, entwine* (refl): Jud 5 27 *S* συγκάμπτειν (var κατακυλίνδειν), ShC 73 49 *S* neck & arms where snake ⲕⲉⲥⲕⲱⲥϥ ⲉⲃ. ϩⲓϫⲱϥ, ShA 1 40 sim. **b** *stretch out, extend*: Bor 235 117 *S* ⲙⲡⲣⲕ. ⲡⲉⲕⲥⲱⲙⲁ ⲉⲃ. in sight of men ἐκτείνειν, FR 70 *S* she laid herself on shroud ⲁⲥⲕⲉⲥⲕⲱⲥ (*l* ⲕⲉⲥⲕⲱⲥⲥ) ⲉⲃ. ⲙⲁⲅⲁⲁⲥ, MG 25 99 *B* ⲁϥⲕⲉⲥⲕⲱⲥϥ ⲉⲃ. as if to sleep, *ib* 405 *B* cripple at saint's tomb ⲁⲩⲕⲉⲥⲕⲱⲥϥ ⲉⲃ. ⲉⲭⲉⲛϯⲧⲁⲓⲃⲓ (ROC 9 45 ـاسمـ *laid him*).

ϩⲟⲡ *S* nn: BodlCopt inscr 427 ⲟⲩⲥⲧⲓⲱⲣⲉ (ⲙ)- ⲙⲁⲉ ⲙ̇ⲡⲟⲩϩⲟⲡ. Prob = ϣⲟⲡ παλαιστή.

ϩⲟⲩⲣ, ⲕⲥⲟⲩⲣ (CO 342), ϭⲥⲟⲩⲣ (PMich 4567) *S*, ϣϩⲟⲩⲣ *B* nn m, *a finger-ring*: Ge 38 18 *B*, Nu 31 50 *SB*, Lu 15 22 *SB* δακτύλιος, Ja 2 2 *SB* χρυσοδακ.; ShMIF 23 149 *S* ⲟⲩϩ. ϩⲛⲛⲉϥⲧⲏⲏⲃⲉ, BMis 41 *S* sim, BKU 1 32⁹ ⲉⲩϫⲓ ϩ. ⲉⲡⲉϥⲧⲏⲏⲃⲉ, BMar 18 *S* ⲁϥⲛⲟⲩϭⲉ ⲙ̇ⲡⲉϥϩ. ⲉⲧⲙ̇ⲡⲉϥⲧ.; esp. for sealing: Est 3 10 *S*, Dan 6 17 *B*, Cl 43 2 *A* δακ., Ez 28 12 *B* (*S* ⲥⲫⲣⲁⲅⲓⲥ), ἀποσφράγισμα, Tri 269 *S* خاتم; Va 69 116 *B* treasury whereon ⲡⲁⲓϣ., Leip 24 36 *B* he sealed box ⲙ̇ⲡⲉϥϣ. ⲁϥϯ ⲙ̇ⲡⲉϥϣ. ⲉⲡⲉϥⲧⲏⲏⲃ, Ryl 319 *S* ⲁⲓ̈ϩⲟⲩⲗⲗⲓⲍⲉ ⲡⲡⲉⲓⲥⲓⲧⲉⲗⲗⲓⲛ ⲛ̇ⲡⲁϩ., *ib* 154, BM 352 *S* sim, AM 11 *B* letter ⲁϥⲧⲟⲃⲥ ϩⲉⲛⲡⲉϥϣ. **b** as key (cf δακτυλοκλείδιον, Pomialowski *Zhitie Prepod Paisie* 1900 72): R 1 5 42 *S* golden ϩ. ⲉϥⲟ ⲛ̇ϣⲟϣⲧ...ⲉϣⲁϥⲟⲩⲱⲡ ⲡ̇ⲕⲁⲯⲁ, BKU 1 299 *S* I send 2 ϣⲟⲩϣⲧ (*l* ϣⲟϣⲧ) that thou mayest ϯ ϩ. ⲉⲣⲟⲟⲩ, *ib* ⲡⲛⲉϩ. ⲟⲩⲏⲡ ⲉⲣⲟⲥ except its own, CO 459 *S* ϩ. ⲉⲩϣⲟⲟϣⲉ *beaten, wrought* (iron) *keys*, v Ep 397 n. **c** other rings: Ex 25 12, 37 3 *B* δακ., WS 94 *S* of a balance ⲙⲁϣⲉ. ⲥⲁ ⲡⲉϩⲟⲩⲣ *S* nn, *key-maker*: BMOr 6201 A 180 ϩⲁⲡⲥⲁ ⲛⲉϩ., PStras 46 letter begins ⲡ]ⲥⲁ ⲛⲉϩ. ⲡⲣⲱⲙⲉ ϣⲙⲟⲩⲡ, BP 9517 *S* ⲯⲁ ⲡⲉϩⲟⲩⲗ.

ⲕⲁⲥⲣⲟ *B* v ⲕⲁⲥ.

ⲕⲁⲥⲓⲥⲉ *S* nn f, *meaning unknown*, prob a metal utensil or tool: ST 125 list of metal objects, Ep 553 sim ⲥⲛⲧⲉ ⲛ̇ⲕ. Coptic? (cf κασσίδιον).

ⲕⲁⲧ *SAF* v ⲕⲱⲧⲉ (ⲕⲟⲧ, *wheel, basket*).

ⲕⲁⲧ- *S* v ⲕⲱⲧ & ⲕⲟⲉⲓⲥ.

ⲕⲁⲧ- *B* v ⲕⲁϯ.

ⲕⲁⲁⲧ *A* v ⲕⲱ.

ⲕⲉⲧ *S*, ⲕⲏⲧ *F* v ⲕⲉ.

ⲕⲏⲧ† *S* v ⲕⲱⲧ, ⲕⲱⲧⲉ.

ⲕⲟⲧ, *wheel, basket, circular motion (visit)* v ⲕⲱⲧⲉ.

ⲕⲟⲧ *S, potter* v ⲕⲱⲧ (ⲉⲕⲱⲧ).

ⲕⲱⲧ *SABF*, ⲕⲉⲧ- *SB*, ⲕⲁⲧ- *F*, ⲕⲟⲧ⸗ *SB*, ⲕⲁⲧ⸗ *AF*, ⲕⲏⲧ† *SB*, ⲣⲥ ⲕⲁⲧ- *S* vb tr & intr, **A** *build*, form **I** tr: Ge 2 22 *SB* (*cf* KKS 216 n), Nu 13 23 *SB*, Ps 95 tit *SB*, Pro 9 1 *SAB*, Zech 8 9 *A* (*B* ⲥ ⲉ-), Mk 14 58 *SBF* οἰκοδομεῖν, Jer 24 6 *SB*, Lam 3 9 *SB* ἀνοικ.; Br 114 *S* ⲁϥⲧⲣⲉϭⲕ. ⲡⲟⲩϣⲟⲩⲣⲏ, Miss 4 526 *S* ⲉϭⲕ. ⲡⲟⲩⲙⲁ in wall = C 89 45 *B* ⲕ. ⲉⲟⲩⲙⲁ, Va 62 170 *B* began to ⲕ. ⲙⲡⲧⲟⲡⲟⲥ, (*cf ib* having begun ⲡⲏⲕ. ⲉⲡⲧⲟⲡⲟⲥ), Va 62 180 *B* bricks ⲛⲧⲁⲕⲟⲧⲟⲩ ⲉⲡⲉⲕⲉⲣⲫⲉⲓ, Mor 30 43 *F* shrine ϣⲁⲡⲧⲟⲩⲕⲁⲧϥ, Miss 4 235 *S* on whose foundation ⲧⲛⲕ. ⲙⲙⲟⲛ, PS 156 *S* ⲁⲕⲕⲉⲧ ⲧⲉⲕⲙⲛⲧⲣⲙⲙⲁⲟ thereon (*l* ⲙⲛⲧⲣⲣⲟ, *cf* Odes of Solom 22 12), *ib* 342 *S* ⲉϭⲕ. ⲡⲛⲉⲩⲙⲉⲗⲟⲥ in likeness of body, Mor 24 8 *F* Eve's creation ⲁⲡⲕ. ⲛⲧϥⲃⲏⲧⲥⲡⲓⲗ…ⲡⲟⲩϭⲣⲓⲙ; of potter: *S*, Glos 234 κεραμοπλάστης · ⲕⲁⲧϣⲟϣⲟⲩ, BMOr 8903 ⲡⲉⲕⲁⲧⲉⲓ ⲕⲁⲧϣⲁϣⲟⲩ, Kr 223 ⲡ(ⲉ)ⲕⲟⲧ ⲛⲕⲁⲧⲕⲟⲉⲓⲥ, *ib* 182 sim, BM 1083 sim ⲕⲁⲧⲕⲟⲩϥⲟⲡ, ST 124 *S*]ⲟⲙⲉ ⲡⲕⲱⲧ (*v* Dévaud *Études* '22 8). Qual: Lu 4 29 *S* (*B* diff), BHom 11 *S* temple ⲉⲧⲕ. ⲉⲃⲟⲗ ϩⲓⲣⲉⲛⲱⲡⲉ οἰκοδ.; Ap 21 18 *S* (*B* diff, Gk om); Deu 9 1 *S* (but var ⲕⲧⲏⲩ = *B*) τειχήρης, BMis 564 *S* city ⲉⲥⲕ. ⲡⲓⲟⲩⲃ, EW 118 *B* house ⲡⲁϥⲕⲏⲧⲡⲉ like church, ShMIF 23 192 *S* ⲡⲉϥⲙⲁ ⲉⲧⲕ. ⲉⲧⲙⲉϩ ⲙⲙⲟⲟⲩ, *pools, baths*, TSBA 9 364 *B* stones ⲉⲧⲕⲏⲧ ⲉⲡⲓⲙⲁ ⲛⲉⲣ ϣⲱⲟⲩϣⲓ. **II** intr: Job 12 14 *SB*, Ps 117 22 *S* (*B* nn), Is 44 28 *SB*, Ro 15 20 *SB* οἰκοδομεῖν, Jer 1 10 *SB* ἀνοικ., 1 Cor 3 10 *SB* ἐποικ.; ⲥ ⲉ- (rare): BMEA 10460 *S* ⲉϭⲕ. ⲉⲧⲭⲟ; ⲥ ⲉϫⲛ-: J 35 48 *S* ⲉⲣⲟⲩϣ ⲉⲕ. ⲉϫⲡⲧⲏⲣⲉ.

B metaph, **I** tr, *edify, encourage* spiritually: 1 Thes 5 11 *SB* (*cf* 4 18 *B*), οἰκ., Jude 20 *SB* ἐποικ.; Aeg 266 *S* sacraments ⲥⲉⲡⲁⲕⲉⲧⲧⲏⲩⲧⲛ, BM 355 3 *S* a word ⲉϥⲡⲁⲕⲉⲧ ⲡⲣⲱⲙⲉ ⲁⲡ, PSBA 32 198 *S* ⲉϭⲕ. his people in God's law. **II** intr, *be edified*: 1 Cor 8 10 *SBF*, *ib* 14 7 *S* (*B*†), Ac 9 31 *B* (*S* tr) οἰκ., Mor 56 53 *S* ⲉⲡⲕ. ⲡⲧⲁⲙⲡⲧⲡⲉ (ⲡ- = ϩⲛ-) ⲉⲃⲟⲗ ϩⲓⲧⲟⲟⲧϥ.

—— ⲉⲃⲟⲗ *B*, *build*: TEuch 1 638 = HCons 321 house which Holy Spirit ⲕⲟⲧϥ ⲉⲃ. As nn: Ez 42 5 ⲡⲕ. (*sic l*) ⲉⲃ. *aedificium*.

—— *SBF* nn m **I a**, *act of building*: 1 Chr 28 2 *B* οἰκοδομεῖν, Si 40 21 *S*, Mk 13 1 *SB*, 2 Cor 13 10 *SBF* οἰκοδομή; BSM 84 *B* they finished ⲡⲓⲕ. in 6 days, BMis 224 *S* all materials for ⲡⲕ., Va 67 75 *B* ⲁⲡⲕ. ⲙⲡⲓⲱⲛⲓ rose to 12 ells, Mor 55 61 *S* ⲡⲉⲕⲕⲗⲏⲥⲓⲁ ⲡⲕ. ⲡⲧⲱⲃⲉ ϩⲓⲱⲡⲉ. **b** *thing built*: Si 22 17 *S*, Mt 24 1 *SB* οἰκοδομή, Ez 40 5 *SB* aedificium; ShA 2 148 *S* inscription ⲉⲧⲥϩ ⲉⲡⲉϥⲕ. ⲁⲩⲱ ⲡⲉϥϣⲉ, GFr 310 *S* Adam ⲟⲩⲡⲗⲁⲥⲙⲁ Eve ⲟⲩⲕ., AM 242 *B* fell down from ⲡⲓⲕ., BMis 246 *S* ⲡⲕ. ⲡⲧⲁⲩⲕⲟ ⲧⲟⲩ destroyed. *Cf* ⲕⲱⲧⲉ nn **c**. **II a** *SB*, *edification*, spiritual: Ro 14 19 *SB*, 2 Cor 12 19 *SBF*, Bor 226 161 *S* ⲡⲕ. ⲡⲡⲁⲣⲉⲧⲏ οἰκοδομή; Miss 4 617 *S* a word ⲉⲙⲡ ⲕ. ⲡⲣⲏⲧϥ. **b** *rule for edification*: C 89 27 *B* he wrote ⲡⲓⲕ. of brethren in book, *ib* 189 *B* ⲡⲓⲕ. ⲡⲉⲙⲡⲓⲕⲁⲡⲱⲛ of Pachôm, MIE 2 354 *B* ⲡⲕ. ⲉⲧⲁⲕϯ = BAp 80 *S* ⲧⲉⲡⲧⲟⲗⲏ, Mor 51 37 *S* ⲡⲉⲛⲧⲟⲗⲏ…ⲙⲡⲡⲉⲕ., Va 59 121 *B* ⲟⲩⲥⲁⲕ ⲡⲉⲙⲟⲩⲕ. of humility, Sh 73 58 *S* ⲡⲕ. ⲉⲧⲕⲏ ⲉϩⲣⲁⲓ, *ib* paral ⲡⲧⲱϣ. 2 Tim 4 7 *S* (*cit* Mor 28 188), *B* (*cit* C 41 76) ⲕ. by error for ⲡⲱⲧ.

ⲙⲁ ⲡⲕ. *SF*, *building place, builder's workshop*: FR 148 *S* ⲡⲉⲙ. where Joseph worked = *ib* 229 οἰκοδομαί, BMis 270 *S* stones & bricks lying ϩⲛⲡⲙ., BM 1230 *F* ⲡⲉⲣⲕⲁⲧⲉⲥ ⲉⲡⲙ.

ⲙⲉⲧⲕ. *B* nn f, *building*: TEuch 1 464 = HCons 4 hast granted us ⲟⲩⲥⲟⲫⲓⲁ ⲡⲧⲉ ⲟⲩⲙ. that we may escape cold & heat.

ⲣⲉϥⲕ. *S* nn m, *builder*: Is 58 12 (*B* ⲉⲕⲱⲧ) οἰκοδόμος; ShC 73 74, Miss 4 704 ⲉⲕⲱⲧ ⲡⲣⲉϥⲕⲉⲧ ⲛⲓ.

ϯ ⲕ. *SB*, *edify*: MG 25 244 *B* ⲁⲕϯ ⲕ. ⲡⲁⲛ οἰκοδομεῖν, Ming 171 ⲉϥϯ ⲕ. ⲡⲁⲛ ⲉϩⲟⲩⲛ ⲉⲡⲉⲕⲃⲓⲟⲥ (but prob *l* as var MG 17 299 ⲕⲱϩ), Mor 41 322 *S* ⲡⲟⲩϭⲱⲃ ⲁⲡ ⲉϥϯ ⲕ. ⲙⲡⲉⲡⲃⲓⲟⲥ.

ϫⲓ ⲕ. *S*, ϭⲓ ⲕ. *B*, *receive edification*: 1 Cor 14 5 *B* (*S* ϫⲓ ⲡⲟⲩⲕ.) οἰκοδ. λαμβάνειν, Z 300 *S* they departed ⲉⲁⲩϫⲓ ⲕ. ϩⲙⲡⲉⲑⲃⲓⲟ (*v* above Mor 56) οἰκοδομηθέντες εἰς, ROC '13 172 *S* ⲁⲩϫⲓ ⲕ. ὠφελεῖσθαι, Cat 89 *B* ⲡⲥⲉϭⲓ ⲕ. ⲉⲃⲟⲗ ⲙⲙⲟϥ.

ϭⲓⲛ- *S* (once), ϫⲓⲛⲕ. *B* nn m, *building*, process, act of: 1 Chr 29 16·*B*, Dan 9 25 *B* (*S* ⲕⲱⲧ) οἰκοδομεῖσθαι, JTS 5 561 *S* he provided for ⲡϭⲓⲛⲕ. of the 2 tabernacles (prob *l* ⲧϭⲓⲛ-).

ⲉⲕⲱⲧ *SBF*, pl ⲉⲕⲟⲧⲉ, ⲉⲕⲁⲧⲉ, ⲉⲕⲁⲧⲟⲩ (J 3 41) *S*, ⲉⲕⲟ ϯ *B* & sg as pl, nn m, *a builder, mason*: 4 Kg 12 11, Is 58 12 *B* (*S* ⲣⲉϥⲕ.) οἰκοδόμος, Ps 117 22 *B* (*S* ⲡⲉⲧⲕ.), Mt 21 42 *B* (*S* do) οἰκοδομῶν; Miss 4 637 *S* ⲡⲉⲣⲕⲁⲧⲛⲥ, ⲡⲉ., Va 62 179 *B* sim, Miss 4 755 *S* ⲉⲣⲧ., ⲉ., ⲗⲁϫⲟⲥ, Va 62 175 *B* ϥⲙⲁ ⲡⲡⲓⲧⲉⲭⲡⲓⲧⲏⲥ…ϥⲙⲁ ⲡⲡⲓⲉ., Miss 4 704 *S* ⲉ. ⲡⲣⲉϥⲕⲉⲧ ⲛⲓ, BMOr 6201 *A* 41 *S* ⲡⲉⲕ. ⲡⲕⲁⲧ ⲛⲓ, Ryl 252 *S* cell (σπήλαιον) ⲡⲧⲁⲡⲉ. ⲥⲙⲛⲧϥ, CMSS 33 *F* ⲉ. to build cattle-shed ⲁϥⲓ, Miss 8 258 *S* ⲉ. building

wall, Va 62 170 B digging foundations ; as expert or referee at house valuations : J 7 29 S δοκιμασία of ε. & other ἔμπειροι, ib 42 12 ε. & others fix price (cf on paral τέκτων Steinwenter in Wess 19 21 & PLond 5 127 ἔμπειροι οἰκοδόμοι). **b** *potter* S : Glos 233 κεραμεύς · ε., Kr 223 ⲡ(ⲉ)ⲕⲟⲧ ⲛⲕⲁⲧ ⲕⲟⲉⲓⲥ = κερ(α)μ[εύς], ib 182 sim ⲡⲉⲕⲟⲧⲉ, BM 1083 ⲡⲉⲕⲟⲧⲉ ⲛⲕⲁⲧ ⲕⲟⲩϥⲟⲛ PRain 4746 ε. ϣⲟϣⲟⲩ, AZ 60 107 guild of ⲡⲉⲕⲁⲧⲉⲓ ⲕⲁⲧ ϣⲁϣⲟⲩ (cf ib 109 that of ⲡⲉⲕⲁⲧⲉ ⲕⲁⲧ[ⲛⲓ.)

ⲥⲉⲕⲱⲧ, ⲥⲓ-, pl v place-name, S nn f, *potter's place, workshop* : Is 30 14 ϩⲛⲗⲁⲩ ⲛⲃⲗϫⲉ ⲛⲥⲓ. (var ⲥⲉ-, B ⲙⲁ ⲡⲕⲉⲣⲁⲙⲉⲩⲥ, F ⲡⲕⲉⲣⲁⲙⲉⲩⲥ) κεράμιον, BM 695 S⸍ ⲡⲉⲕⲟⲩϥⲱⲛ ⲉⲡⲧⲱⲕ ⲙⲙⲁⲩ ϩⲉⲡⲧⲥ., CO 306 shares in a c. Cf WS 144 n, Dévaud lc. In place-name : ⲡⲓⲥⲉⲕⲁⲧⲉ = Κεράμιον (PLond 4 588).

ⲕⲁⲧⲁⲓ S nn, *locust* : P 44 56 ⲕⲁⲧⲩⲟⲡ · ⲕ. جراد = ⲁⲕⲣⲓⲥ · ϣϫⲉ. Coptic ?

ⲕⲁⲧⲉ O v ⲡⲕⲟⲧⲕ.

ⲕⲁϯ B ⲣ ⲥ ⲕⲁⲧ- vb **I** intr, *know, understand* : 1 Kg 2 10 (paral ⲥⲟⲩⲛ, S ⲉⲓⲙⲉ), Ps 100 2 (S do), Is 6 10 (S ⲛⲟⲉⲓ), Mt 13 13 (S do) συνιέναι ; Is 44 18 (S = Gk), He 11 3 (S do) νοεῖν, Is 41 20 (S ⲗⲟⲕⲙⲉⲕ) ἔννο.; ib 44 18 (S ⲣ ⲣⲙⲛϩⲏⲧ) φρονεῖν, 2 Cor 5 13 (S ⲥⲁⲛ ϩⲏⲧ) σωφρον.; Ez 26 15 σείσθαι (taking S ⲛⲟⲉⲓⲛ for ⲛⲟⲉⲓ) ; Miss 4 99 whoso readeth ⲙⲁⲣⲉϥⲕ. With ϫⲉ- : Ac 7 25 συνι. ὅτι, MG 25 13 ⲛⲟ. ὅτι, C 41 77 ⲁϥⲕ. in heart ϫⲉϥⲁⲓⲡⲉ NN, Va 57 106 ⲡⲧⲉⲛⲕ. ϫⲉⲉⲧⲁⲥⲙⲓⲥⲓ ⲛⲟⲡⲁⲩ συλλαμβάνειν. With ⲉ- : Deu 29 9 (S ⲉⲓ. ⲉ-), Ps 5 2 (S ϯ ϩⲏⲧ ⲉ-), Dan 8 23 (S ⲉⲓ. ⲉ-) συνι. ; Pro 1 6 (SA = Gk), Ro 1 20 (S do), C 89 171 ⲙⲁⲣⲉⲡⲕ. ⲉⲡⲁⲓⲕⲉⲣⲱⲃ ⲛⲟ., Mt 5 25 (S ⲟⲩⲱⲱⲙⲉ ⲉ-) ⲉⲩⲛⲟ., Ex 31 3 διανο., Ps 118 15 (S ⲙⲟⲩϣⲧ) κατανο. ; Lev 26 41 (S ⲉⲓ. ⲉ-) εὐδοκεῖν ; Lu 9 45 (S do) αἰσθάνεσθαι ; HL 105 ⲁϥⲟⲣⲓⲕ. ⲉϯⲅⲣⲁⲫⲏ, Cat 208 Martha & Mary ⲉϣⲁⲡⲕ. ⲉⲣⲱⲟⲩ ⲉϩⲣⲏⲓ ⲉϫⲉⲛ- Old & New Test., CaiEuch 464 power ⲛⲁⲧϣⲕ. ⲉⲣⲟⲥ. With ⲉϫⲉⲛ- : Ps 40 2 (S ϯ ϩⲏⲧ ⲉ-), Dan 11 37 (S ⲛⲟⲓ ⲉϩⲣⲁⲓ ⲉϫⲛ-) συνι. ἐπί.

II tr (obj with ⲛ-, prob erroneous) : C 86 351 ⲙⲡⲓⲕ. ⲙⲡⲓϩⲟⲣⲁⲙⲁ (var ⲉ-).

—— nn m, *knowledge, understanding* : Deu 4 6 (S ⲙⲛⲧⲣⲙⲛϩⲏⲧ), Is 56 11 (S ⲙⲛⲧⲥⲁⲃⲉ), Ob 7 (A ⲙⲛⲧⲣ.), Eph 3 4 (S ⲙⲛⲧⲥ.) σύνεσις ; Ex 28 3 αἴσθησις ; Bar 3 28 φρόνησις ; Pro 4 1 (SA ⲙⲉⲉⲩⲉ) ἔννοια ; Ro 12 2 (S diff) νοῦς ; Eph 6 4 (S ⲧⲥⲁⲃⲟ) νουθεσία ; AM 70 blindness of my ⲕ., PO 11 375 ⲡⲓϣϯ ⲛⲕ. of his answers to king.

ⲁⲧⲕ. nn, *ignorant person* : Ps 118 158 (S ⲁⲧϩⲏⲧ), Mt 15 16 (S do) ἀσύνετος ; Ps 48 11 (paral ⲁⲧϩⲏⲧ, S ⲁⲧⲥⲃⲱ), Hos 7 11 (A ⲁⲑ.) ἄνους ; adj, *ignorant* :

Ro 10 19 (S ⲁⲑ.) ἀσύν. ; HL 116 ⲧⲉϥⲃⲛⲏ ⲡⲁ. ἄλογος ; C 43 139 ⲡⲓⲁⲧϩⲏⲧ ⲡⲁ. ⲉⲣ ⲁⲧⲕ., *be ignorant* : Job 13 2 (S ⲁⲑ.), Ro 1 31 (S do) ἀσύν. ⲙⲉⲧⲁⲧⲕ., *ignorance* : Mk 7 22 (S ⲙⲛⲧⲁⲑ.) ἀφροσύνη, Va 57 178 ⲟⲩⲃⲁⲓⲛ ⲙⲙ. ἄνοια, ib 33 ⲙ. of youth τὸ ἀνόητον.

ⲣⲙⲛⲕ., *man of understanding* : Cat 99 ⲣ., ⲕⲁⲧϩⲏⲧ, ⲥⲩⲛⲉⲍⲟⲥ (l -ⲧⲟⲥ), TThe 228 Basil ⲛⲓⲣ.

ⲣⲉϥⲕ., same meaning : Is 5 21 (Lacr, var ⲕⲁⲧϩⲏⲧ, S ⲣⲙⲛϩⲏⲧ, F ⲥⲁⲃⲏ) ἐπιστήμων, Hos 4 14 (A ⲉⲧⲉⲟⲩⲥⲁⲩⲛⲉ ϩⲟⲏⲧϥ) συνίων.

ϯ ⲕ., *instruct* : Ps 118 27 (S ⲧⲁⲙⲟ) συνετίζειν, Dan 11 33 συνιέναι εἰς ; C 43 199 ⲧⲉϥϯ ⲡⲓⲕ. ⲡⲟⲟⲩ (sic) ϭⲉⲛϯⲙⲉⲧⲥⲁⲃⲉ.

ϫⲉⲙ ⲕ., *find understanding* : 1 Pet 4 7 (S ϭⲛ ϩⲏⲧ) σωφρονίζειν, Va 58 118 God encourageth them ⲁⲩϣⲁⲛϫ. ⲕ.

ϫⲓⲛⲕ. nn f, *understanding* : Dan 9 13 (S ⲉⲓⲙⲉ vb) συνιέναι, Va 58 109 scriptures searched ϭⲉⲛⲟⲩϫ. ⲉⲥϣⲟⲙ, HL 75 sim.

ⲕⲁⲧϩⲏⲧ, *knowledgeable, wise person* : Deu 1 13 (S ⲣⲙⲛϩ.), Jer 29 7 (S ⲥⲁⲃⲉ), Lu 10 21 (S do) συνετός ; Dan 12 10 νοήμων ; Is 5 21 v ⲣⲉϥⲕ. ; adj, *knowledgeable* : Ac 13 7 (S ⲣⲙⲛϩ.) συν., BSM 20 ⲱ ⲛⲓⲗⲉⲙⲣⲁϯ ⲡⲕ. = BMis 357 S ⲙⲁⲓⲥⲃⲱ. ⲉⲣ ⲕⲁⲧϩ., *be wise* : Ex 31 6 συν. ⲙⲉⲧⲕⲁⲧϩ., *understanding* : ROC 17 408 τὸ συνετόν, AM 210 ⲙⲉⲧⲥⲁⲃⲉ, ⲙⲉⲧⲕ.

ⲕⲁⲧⲟ S, ⲕⲁⲧⲱ, ⲕⲁⲧⲟⲁ (K all MSS) B nn f, *boat, skiff* (if ⲕⲁⲧ + ⲟ, ⲕⲁⲧⲱ would be correct) : Ac 27 30 S (B = Gk) σκάφη ; K 133 B ⲡⲓⲕ. مركب opp ϫⲟⲓ سفينة, ib ϯⲕ. معدية, قرقورة (κέρκουρος corn ship), ST 330 S ⲙⲁⲣⲉⲧⲉⲕⲕ. ⲡⲟϩⲟⲩ (? oil cargo) ⲉⲗⲏⲣ, PRain 4736 S load the wine ⲉϩⲟⲩⲛ ϩⲛⲧⲕ., BM 1097 S ⲧⲕ. ⲛⲧⲁϭⲃⲓ Apa Shenoute, ib 1237 B ⲁⲓⲧⲁⲗⲱⲓ ϯⲕ. ⲁⲓⲣⲱⲗ ⲉϫⲛⲧ (l ϩⲏⲧ).; ib 1110 S letters brought by ⲡⲓⲛⲏⲃ ⲉⲧⲕ. ; P 44 54 S ⲧⲃⲟⲩⲗⲓⲥ (βολίς) · ⲧⲕ. مقياس (intruded from Ac 27).

ⲕⲉⲧⲉ S vb tr, meaning unknown : Z 613 (sic MS, often incorrect) of wrecked ship miraculously retrieved ⲁⲡⲙⲟⲟⲩ ⲕ. ⲙⲡϫⲟⲓ & cargo & it came floating into port. (? for ⲕⲱⲧⲉ **II** a).

ⲕⲓⲧⲉ S, ⲕⲓϯ B nn f, *double drachma = ½ stater* : Ge 20 14 B 1000 ⲕ. (S 500 ⲥⲁⲧⲉⲉⲣⲉ), Ex 21 32 B 30 ⲕ. (S 15 ⲥ.), Nu 3 47 SB δίδραχμον ; Lu 10 35 S (B = Gk) δηνάριον ; K 68 B ϯⲕ. درهم, CA 111 S ⲧⲕ. ⲉⲧⲉⲧⲛⲁϣⲉ ⲛⲥⲁⲧⲉⲉⲣⲉ ; as tribute : Mt 17 24 SB ϫⲓ, ϭⲓ ⲕ. δίδρ. λαμβάνειν, Dif 1 38 B ⲁϥϣⲓ (? ϭⲓ) ⲕ. ⲉⲟⲃⲏⲧϥ الجالية, cf K 146 B ϯϭⲓ ⲕ. جالية, Mor 44 11 S tax gatherer to Jesus ⲁⲅⲉⲓⲥ ⲧⲉⲕⲕ. ⲉⲕⲁⲏⲕ ⲉϩⲟⲩⲛ ⲉⲧⲡⲟⲗⲓⲥ ; as weight : Cat 48 B ϯⲕ. ⲡⲓⲧⲉⲣⲉⲍⲡⲉ ⲡⲧⲉ ϯⲟⲡⲕⲓⲁ, K 145 B ϯⲕ. نصف اوقية or 20 folles. Cf AZ 54 120, 58 154.

ⲥⲓⲕ- S, ϫⲉⲥⲕ. B f, *half a* ⲕ. = 1 *drachma* : Lu 15
8 SB δραχμή, Cat 158 v ⲕⲁⲥ *carat*, 1 Kg 9 8 S
ⲥⲓⲥⲕ. ⲡⲥⲁⲧⲉⲉⲣⲉ τέταρτον σίκλου, P 44 58 S ⲧⲥ̄.
μιλιαρήσιον مرد .

ⲕⲓⲧⲉ S nn f, *sleep* : only BKU 1 22 charm ⲉⲕⲁⲡ
ⲧⲕ. ⲉⲭⲱϥ ⲙⲡϥⲓⲛⲏⲃ̄. *Cf* AZ 33 50, also ? ⲕⲁⲧⲉ O.

ⲕⲓⲧⲉ S nn, *meaning unknown* : BKU 1 123…
ⲙⲛⲟⲩ[? ⲡ]ⲗⲁⲯⲁⲡⲉ ⲡⲛⲕⲓⲧⲉ ? *by weight, v above.*

ⲕⲓϯ (1 var ⲕⲟϯ), ⲣⲉϥ- B nn, *player, gambler* :
K 138 مقامر (Lab also معلم , كاتب *scribe, whence ?*).

ⲕⲱⲧⲉ SAA²O(AZ 21 100), ⲕⲱϯ BF, ⲕⲟϯ O, ⲕⲉⲧ-
SB, ⲕⲁⲧ- F, ⲕⲟⲧ⸱ SB, ⲕⲁⲧ⸱ AA²F, ⲕⲏⲧ† S vb **I** intr,
a turn, go round : Deu 32 10 SB, Ps 26 6 SB, Cant
3 2 S κυκλοῦν ; ShC 73 92 S ⲉⲅⲕ. ⲡⲏⲓ ⲉⲏⲓ, RNC
52 S ⲉϥⲕ. ⲉϥⲑⲉⲣⲁⲡⲉⲅⲉ, MIF 9 84 S mountain ⲕ.
like wheel, C 89 135 B though dead ⲡⲟⲩⲡⲡⲁ ⲕ.
on among men, BMis 168 S watchman ⲉϥⲕ. ⲡⲧ-
ⲉⲅⲩⲏ = BSM 78 B, HCons 389 B bishop ⲉϥⲕ.
ⲡⲃ̄ⲛⲧⲉ (sc ⲥⲕⲏⲡⲏ) ⲧⲏⲣϥ, Ryl 150 S ⲡⲕ. ϩⲓⲡⲡ[*we
visiting* (? *monastery*) ; Sa 13 2 S ⲉⲧⲕ. κύκλος, Ex
19 12 B (S nn) ⲉϥⲕ., Nu 3 37 S ⲉⲧⲕ., B ⲉϥⲕ., Jer
52 4 B ⲉϥⲕ. κύκλῳ, or *ib* 27 29 do κυκλόθεν (these
often as adv without concord in gender) ; C 89 76
B ϩⲁⲡⲏⲓ ϩⲓⲭⲉⲛⲡⲓⲭⲗⲟⲙ…ⲉϥⲕ. (*cf* TT 148), AM
322 B ϯⲃⲁⲕⲓ ⲧⲏⲣⲥ ⲉϥⲕ., J 4 36 S ⲡⲣⲟⲥ ⲡⲉϥⲧⲟϣ
ⲉⲅⲕ., BMis 564 S each wall 100 furlongs ⲉⲅⲕ. *in
circuitu* ; Ge 3 24 S (B ⲫⲱⲛϩ), Si 36 5 S, MG 25
232 B στρέφεσθαι, Nu 36 7 S (B ⲧⲁⲥⲑⲟ) περιστ. ;
Mt 4 23 B (S ⲉⲓ ⲉⲃⲟⲗ ϩⲛ-) περιάγειν ; Ac 8 40 B
(S ⲙⲟⲟϣⲉ) διέρχεσθαι ; Miss 8 38 S ⲉⲅⲕ. ϩⲛⲧⲡⲟ-
ⲗⲓⲥ· περιέναι κατά ; Pro 7 12 SA (B ⲗⲉⲗⲉ) ῥέμβεσθαι. **b** *go round* with waterwheel, *water* (*cf*
κυκλεύειν) : PMich 1298 S (ⲉ)ⲃⲁⲕ. ⲡⲏⲧⲡ as he
undertook, *ib* beast ⲉⲕ. ϩⲙⲡⲁϩⲟⲓ. Obj with ⲉ-:
ShA 2 130 S men yoked ⲉⲧⲣⲉⲅⲕ. ⲉ̄ⲣⲉⲛⲥ̄ⲱⲙ ⲉⲧⲥⲟⲟⲩ,
PMich *l c* ⲡⲉϩⲣⲏⲅ…ϯⲡⲁⲕ. ⲉⲣⲟⲟⲩ ⲧⲁⲧⲥⲟⲟⲩ, BP
11349 S his beasts in field ⲉⲧⲕ. ⲉⲣⲟϥ, Ryl 158 S
ⲧⲁⲕ. ⲉⲣⲟⲟⲩ with my beasts, *ib* 159 S ⲧⲁⲕ. ⲉⲣⲟⲟⲩ
ⲡⲙⲟⲩ ⲡⲙⲡⲏⲧⲓ, *ib* 341, Kr 112 sim, BMOr 6201
A 90 S ⲡⲁⲣϥ (*l* ⲡⲁⲣϩ) ⲡⲕ. opp ⲡ. ⲡⲥⲕⲁⲓ ; seldom
with ⲡ-: ShC 42 82 = MIF 23 44 S compelling
poor ⲉⲧⲣⲉⲅⲕ. ⲙⲙⲟⲟⲩ (*sc* ⲥⲟⲟⲙ) ; with ϩⲁ-:
CMSS 48 B]ⲁⲡⲁⲧⲧⲉ ⲕ. ϩⲁⲧⲕⲁϣ. As nn m *v*
below (nn **b**). **c** *form circle* : PMich 554 snake
ⲉⲣⲉⲡⲉϥ ⲥⲁⲧ ⲕ. coming to its mouth ; *return* : Ryl
413 F leave not fields fallow ϣ]ⲁⲧⲉⲡⲙⲁⲟⲩ ⲕ, PGM
60 O ⲕⲟϯ as rubric. **d** *wander, stray* : Job 38 41
S (B ⲥⲱⲣⲉⲙ), Si 51 15 S πλανᾶν, *ib* 13 7 S ἀποπλ. ;
ShC 73 98 S ⲡⲱⲧ ⲉϩⲟⲩⲛ ⲉⲃⲟⲗ ⲡⲑⲉ ⲙⲡⲉⲧⲕ. **e**
go about seeking, *seek* : Ps 9 34 B (S ϣⲓⲛⲉ), Is 40
20 B (S do), 1 Cor 4 2 B (S do), MG 25 13 B

ⲉⲅⲕ. ϫⲉⲡⲧⲉϥⲥⲙⲟⲩ ⲉⲣⲱⲟⲩ ζητεῖν, Deu 17 9 B (S
ϩⲟⲧϩⲧ) ἐκζητ., Lu 24 15 B (S = Gk) συζητ. (*cf* ⲕ.
ⲙⲡ-) ; Deu 23 20 S (B ϣⲱⲡ) ἐκτοκεῖν (*cf* ⲕⲧⲟ) ;
Miss 4 197 B ⲕ. ϫⲉⲁϫⲭⲏ ⲡⲱⲱⲡ, Wess 18 61 S
women ⲕ. ϫⲉⲉⲩⲡⲁⲥⲟⲩⲡ ⲡⲉⲩϩⲁⲓ, CA 108 S ⲟⲩⲁ
ⲉϫⲕ. ϩⲓⲣⲉⲡⲭⲱⲙⲙⲉ of magic, *ib* 102 S suffer not
clerics ⲉⲕ. ϩⲛⲗⲁⲁⲩ ⲙⲙⲛⲧⲉϣⲱⲧ.

────── ⲉ- (obj), *surround* : Nu 34 5 S (B ⲕ. no obj),
Ps 21 16 SB, Hos 11 12 AB, Jo 10 24 SA² (B
ⲧⲁⲕⲧⲟ) κυκλοῦν ; Ge 19 4 SB, Ps 16 11 SB, Lu 19
43 SB περικυ. ; Ps 127 3 B (S ⲕ. nn), Is 9 18 B
(S do), Ez 40 5 SB κύκλῳ, Ap 4 3 SB κυκλόθεν ;
Ps 31 7 SB περιέχειν ; Ez 47 2 B (var ⲧⲁⲥⲑⲟ
ⲃⲁⲧⲉⲡ-, S ⲕⲧⲟ), Mt 23 15 B (S ⲙⲟⲩϣⲧ) περιάγειν ;
Jos 6 11 S, 1 Tim 5 13 SB περιέρχεσθαι ; Lev 6 3
(10) B (S ⲗⲱϫⲕ) περιτιθέναι, Jud 1 27 S περίοικος ;
Mt 8 18 B (S ⲕ. nn) περί acc ; Jer 29 18 SB πάροικος ; 1 Kg 31 2 S συνάπτειν ; Ez 1 13 B (HCons
281, var ⲙⲙⲟ-) συστρέφεσθαι ; Job 17 7 S (B ⲃⲱⲧⲥ),
Is 37 8 S (B ϯ ⲟⲩⲃⲉ-) πολιορκεῖν ; PS 5 S power
came to him & ⲁⲥⲕ. ⲉⲣⲟϥ ⲧⲏⲣϥ, Br 60 S ⲉⲣⲉⲟⲩⲉⲓ
ⲕ. ⲉⲟⲩⲉⲓ (*cf* 58 ⲉⲣⲉⲟⲩⲉⲓ ⲙⲡⲃⲟⲗ ⲡⲟⲩⲉⲓ), Va 62 136
B beard ⲕ. ⲉⲡⲉϥϩⲟ, BMar 78 S sweat ⲕ. ⲉⲧⲕ-
ⲧⲉⲣⲡⲉ ; *seek, visit* : Jer 33 21 B, Ac 13 7 B (*cf*
8 ⲕ. ⲡⲥⲁ-, S ϣⲓⲛⲉ) ζητεῖν ; Bor 226 163 S ⲉⲕϣⲁⲡⲕ.
ⲉⲡⲉⲧⲧⲁⲉⲓⲏⲩ of world περιτρέχειν εἰς : BSM 34 B
ⲁⲥⲕ. ⲉⲣⲟϥ = BMis 376 S ϯ ⲡⲉⲥⲟⲩⲟⲓ ⲉ-, El 54 A
ⲉⲙⲡⲓⲕ. ⲁⲡϣⲏⲣⲉ ⲙⲡⲓⲏⲗ, MG 17 306 S ⲡϫⲕ. ⲉⲡⲏⲓ
= *ib* 243 B, JTS 8 242 S ⲁⲡⲕ. ⲉⲧⲙⲉϫϣⲱⲙⲧⲉ ⲙⲡⲉ
ⲧⲏⲣⲥ, C 86 104 B ⲁϥⲕ. ⲉϥⲱⲧ, KroppE S prayer
for eloquence ⲟⲩⲗⲁⲥ ⲉϥⲕ. ⲉⲟⲣⲧⲁⲡⲟⲡ ⲡⲓⲙ ϩⲛⲟⲩ-
ⲗⲁⲗⲓⲁ ⲡⲡⲓϣⲉ (meaning ?), Leyd 274 S ⲁⲕⲓⲣⲉⲡⲥⲱϩⲉ
ⲕⲱⲧⲉ (*sic*) ⲉⲡⲣⲓⲙⲉ *turn to.*

Qual S (archaic), *turned* : PS 353 ⲉⲣⲉϩⲣⲁⲩ ⲕⲏⲧ
ⲉⲡⲉⲓⲃⲧ, KroppA ⲉⲣⲉⲡⲉⲥϩⲟ ⲕ. ⲉϩⲟⲩⲛ ⲉϫⲡⲥⲁϣϥⲉ
ⲡⲟⲩⲥⲉ.

Iteration SB : *continue to turn, seek*, CDan 86 B
ϣⲁⲑⲡⲁⲩ ⲡⲕ. ⲕ. ? γυρεύειν, Z 270 S ⲁϥⲗⲟ ⲙ(ⲉ)ⲡ
ⲉϥⲕ. ⲕ., C 43 128 B ⲉϣⲁⲓⲕ. ⲕ. ⲕⲁⲧⲁ ϯⲙⲓ, Va 58
193 B ⲉⲣⲉⲙⲁⲓ ⲡⲓⲃⲉⲛ ⲕ. ⲕ. before thee.

II tr, *a turn*, often of face : Ps 12 2 S (B ⲫⲱⲛϩ),
Is 54 8 S (B ⲧⲁⲥⲑⲟ), He 12 25 B (S ⲕⲧⲟ) ἀποστρέφ. ;
PS 63 S ⲙⲡⲣⲕ. ⲡⲧⲉⲕⲣⲓⲕⲱⲡ ⲡⲥⲁⲃⲟⲗ ⲙⲙⲟⲓ, MG
25 309 B ⲁⲩⲕⲉⲧ ⲡⲟⲩϩⲟ ⲉⲣⲟⲓ = BIF 13 117 S
ⲕⲧⲟ ; further : BKU 1 1 S ⲁϥⲕⲉⲧ ⲡⲉϥⲃⲁⲗ ⲉϫⲟⲥ,
MR 5 34 F ⲕⲁⲧ ⲡⲉⲕⲡⲉⲓ ϩⲓϫⲱⲡ, BMar 80 S ⲁⲩⲕ.
ⲙⲡⲉⲩⲥⲟⲓ ⲉⲣⲟϥ, J 71 55 S ⲉⲓⲕ. (? ⲡ)ⲛⲁⲟⲩⲉⲣⲏⲧⲉ,
paral *ib* 66 66 ⲙⲟⲟϣⲉ ϩⲛⲡⲁ-, Va 68 46 B sailors
ⲕ. ⲙ̄ⲡϥⲓⲣⲉ with hands (*cf* ⲕⲧⲟ **II**). **b** *surround* :
Ps 47 12 S (B ⲕ. ⲉ-) κυκλοῦν, 1 Chr 28 12 B, Ez
41 7 B (S ⲕ. ⲉ-) κύκλῳ ; TstAb 176 B come & see
ϥⲁⲓ ⲉⲧⲕ. ⲙⲡⲁⲙⲁ ⲡⲉⲡⲕⲟⲧ. *Cf also* **I** **b** ⲕⲱⲧⲉ ⲉ-.

Refl (oftenest) with suff or ⲙⲙⲟ⸗, *turn self, return, repeat*: Ex 4 17 *A* (*S* ⲕⲧⲟ, *B* om), Job 41 16 *S* (*B* ⲫⲱⲛⲣ), Pro 12 7 *SB* (*A* ⲕⲧⲟ), Jo 12 40 *SA²B*, ZNTW 24 86 *F* στρέφεσθαι; Ge 8 9 *S* (*B* ⲧⲁⲥⲑⲟ), Deu 24 19 *SB*, Jer 26 16 *B* (*S* ⲕⲧⲟ), Ac 15 16 *S* (var ⲕⲧⲟ, *B* ⲧⲁⲥ.) ἀναστ., Job 16 22 *S* (*B* do) ἐπαναστ., Ex 4 21 *A* (*B* do), Ps 9 17 *SF* (*B* do), Is 30 11 *F* (*S* ⲕⲧⲟ, *B* do), Ac 3 26 *S* (var ⲕⲧⲟ, *B* ⲣⲉⲛ-) ἀποστ., Nu 14 25 *B* (*S* ⲕⲧⲟ), 3 Kg 8 48 *B* (*S* do), Ps 58 6 *S* (var ⲕⲧⲟ) *B*, *ib* 77 41 *B* (*S* do), Is 31 6 *SBF*, Hos 7 16 *F* (JEA 11 245, *SA* ⲕⲧⲟ, *B* ⲧⲁⲥ.), Mk 5 30 *S* (var ⲕⲧⲟ, *B* ⲫⲱⲛⲣ) ἐπιστ., Joel 2 31 *S* (*A* ⲕⲧⲟ, *B* ⲟⲩⲱⲧⲉⲃ), Ja 4 9 *SB* μεταστ., Nu 36 7 *S* (*B* ⲧⲁⲥ.) περιστ., Ez 1 13 *B*, Mt 17 22 *B* (*S* ⲕⲧⲟ), Ac 28 3 *B* (*S* om) συστ., Ge 43 10 *SB*, Lu 9 10 *S* (*B* ⲧⲁⲥ.), Gal 1 17 *B* (*S* ⲕⲧⲟ) ὑποστ.; Job 10 8 *SB*, Is 60 5 *S* (*B* ⲟⲩⲱⲧⲉⲃ), Ac 28 6 *S* (*B* do) μεταβάλλειν; Jer 15 5 *B* (*S* do), Mt 2 12 *SB*, He 11 15 *S* (*B* ⲧⲁⲥ.) ἀνακάμπτειν; Pro 7 20 *S* (*A* ⲕⲧⲟ, *B* do), Si 27 9 *S* ἐπανάγειν; Eccl 1 6 *S* κυκλοῦν (cf ib ⲕⲧⲟ), Pro 20 28 *S* (var & *A* ⲕⲧⲟ) περικυκ.; Jer 2 36 *S* (ShIF 293) δευτεροῦν; PS 85 *S* ⲁⲅⲕⲟⲧⲟⲩ ⲁⲅⲣⲱⲭ ⲙⲙⲟⲥ, *ib* 353 ⲉϥⲕ. ⲙⲙⲟϥ to 4 corners, BG 20 *S* ⲁ]ⲓⲕⲟⲧ(ⲧ) ⲉⲃⲟⲗ from temple, Aeg 49 *B* grief ⲕⲟⲧϥ ⲛⲁⲡ ⲉⲅ-ⲣⲁϣⲓ, ShA 1 84 *S* our blood ⲛⲁⲕ. ⲙⲙⲟϥ & come upon us, El 78 *A* ϥⲛⲁⲕⲁⲧϥ ⲁⲃⲁⲗ from city = *ib* 118 *S* ⲕⲧⲟ, AP 3 *A²* ⲛϥⲡⲁⲕⲁⲧϥ ⲉⲡ ϣⲁⲣⲁⲅ, BSM 34 *B* ⲁϥⲕⲟⲧϥ ⲉⲡⲉϥⲏⲓ = BMis 376 *S* ⲕⲧⲟ, Mun 61 *S* ⲁⲅⲕⲟⲧⲟⲩ ⲉⲡⲙⲁ…ⲁϥⲕⲧⲟ[ϥ to Theodore. With neg, *not repeat, not do again* (*B* bibl only Ez 16 41, 35 9): Lev 27 20 *S*, Zeph 3 15 *A*, Wess 11 170 *S* οὐκέτι, Job 7 9 *S* (var ⲧⲥⲧⲟ, *B* ⲧⲁⲥ.), Is 32 5 *SF* οὐκέτι μή, Mk 9 25 *S*, Jo 5 14 *SA²* (all *B* neg + ϫⲉ), Z 354 *S* μηκέτι; 2 Kg 20 10 *S* οὐ δευτεροῦν; C 89 19 *B* ⲛⲧⲉⲕϣⲧⲉⲙⲕⲟⲧⲕ ⲉⲓ, Aeg 23 *S* ⲙⲡⲉⲕⲕⲟⲧⲡ ⲉⲡⲁⲩ ⲉⲣⲟⲥ, DeV 79 *B* ⲙⲡⲟⲩⲕⲟⲧⲟⲩ ϫⲉ ⲉⲡⲁⲩ. ⲙⲛⲧ-ⲣⲉϥⲕⲁⲧ⸗ *A* nn f refl, *good conduct*: Pro 14 35 (*S* ⲕⲧⲟ) εὐστροφία.

With following prepositions.

—— ⲉϫⲛ-, ⲉϫⲉⲛ-, *turn upon, go round, among*: Pro 26 14 *SA* στρέφεσθαι; Is 28 27 *B* (*S* ⲕ. ϩⲓϫⲛ-) περιάγειν; Ez 5 7 *B* (*S* ⲕ. ⲉ-) κύκλῳ gen; Tri 715 *S* على لباط; MIE 2 389 *B* ⲁϥⲓ ⲉϫⲕ. ⲉϫⲉⲛⲡⲓⲉⲕⲕⲗⲏⲥⲓⲁ = BAp 112 *S* ⲙⲟⲩϣⲧ, P 68 47 *S* rubric ⲕ. ⲉϫⲛⲧⲉⲕⲕⲗⲏⲥⲓⲁ ⲡⲥⲁⲛⲃⲟⲗ & say, DeV 38 *B* Herodias to daughter ⲕ. ⲉϫⲱⲟⲩ dancing & singing.

—— ⲙⲛ-, ⲛⲉⲙ-, a *go round with, turn hither & thither*: Ex 13 8 *B* κυκλοῦν acc; Eccl 7 8 *S* περιφέρειν *conturbare*, Ac 13 49 *B* (*S* diff) διαφέρεσθαι; AM 2 10 *AB* περιάγ. acc; MG 25 23 *B* περιπομπεύειν; Va 68 46 *B* sailors ⲉⲅⲕ. ⲛⲉⲙⲡⲓϫⲟⲓ ϣⲁ-ⲧⲟⲩⲥⲉⲡ ⲛⲓⲱⲙⲓ, PS 284 *S* ⲉⲅⲕ. ⲙⲛⲧⲉⲯⲩⲭⲏ in all places: ShA 1 217 *S* sacrament ⲉⲅⲕ. ⲛⲙⲙⲁϥ

ⲣⲡⲡⲏⲓ, BG 69 *S* ⲛⲥⲉⲕ. ⲛⲙⲙⲁⲩ ϣⲁⲡⲧⲟⲩⲡⲟϭⲙ ⲙⲙⲟⲟⲩ, C 43 5 *B* bade ⲕ ⲛⲉⲙⲧⲉⲣⲉ ϩⲉⲛⲣⲁⲙⲙⲁⲟ-ⲧⲁⲡⲟⲛ, sim Mu 38 *S* ⲕ. ⲛⲧⲉⲣⲉ, BSG 183 *S* (cf ⲕ. ⲉϩⲟⲩⲛ), CO 15 *S* ⲉⲧⲁⲕ. ⲙⲡⲣⲱⲙⲉ ⲉϥϩⲟⲟⲩ *consort with*. ♭ *inquire of, dispute with B*: Mk 8 11, 9 14, Ac 6 9 (all *S* ϯⲧⲱⲛ) συζητεῖν dat or πρός.

—— ⲛⲥⲁ-, *go round seeking, seek*: Ge 43 30 *B*, 1 Kg 19 2 *S* (var ϣⲓⲛⲉ), Ps 39 15 *B* (*S* do), Hos 5 15 *SAB*, Mt 13 45 *BF* (*S* ϣ.), Mk 14 55 *S* (var ϣ.) *BF*, Jo 7 1 *B* (*SA²* do) ζητεῖν, Ex 18 15 *B* (*S* do), Is 31 1 *B* (*SF* do), He 11 6 *B* (*S* do) ἐκζ., Is 62 12 *B* (*S* do), Phil 4 17 *B* (*S* do), ἐπιζ.; Job 30 4 *S* (*B* ⲕ. ⲉ-) περικυκ.; Deu 12 30 *SB* ἐπακολουθεῖν; Dan 2 10 *B* ἐπερωτᾶν; Ps 39 15 (*S* ⲟⲩⲱϣ), MG 25 119 = 206 *B*, Va 59 159 *B* ⲛⲁⲅⲕ. ⲛⲥⲁⲉⲡ ⲡⲟⲩϫⲓϫ ⲉϩⲣⲏⲓ ⲉϫⲱϥ θέλειν; ShC 73 125 *S* ⲛϥⲕ. ⲛⲥⲁⲑⲉ ⲡⲉⲓ ⲉⲃⲟⲗ, BSM 33 *B* ϥϯ ⲕ. ⲛⲥⲁⲣⲗⲓ ⲡⲧⲟⲧⲉⲛ = BMis 375 *S* ϫⲡⲟⲩ, LMis 196 *S* ⲉⲓⲕ. ⲛⲥⲁⲟⲩϩⲙϩⲁⲗ (var ϣ.). ⲣⲉϥⲕ. ⲛⲥⲁ- *S, seeker*: Ro 1 30 (*B* ⲣⲉϥϫⲓⲙⲓ) ἐφευρετής, Mor 43 218 Christ's feet ϩⲉⲛⲣⲉϥⲕ. ⲛⲉ ⲛⲥⲁ- *erring sheep*. ϫⲓⲛⲕ. ⲛⲥⲁ- *B, search after*: BSM 56 ϫⲕ. ⲛⲥⲁⲡⲓⲡⲁⲓ, C 43 45 *B* ϫⲕ. ⲛⲥⲁⲡⲓⲭⲣⲓⲥⲧⲓⲁⲛⲟⲥ = Mor 39 21 *S* ϣ.

—— ⲛⲧⲉⲛ- *B, seek, beg from*: Is 8 19 *B* (*S* ϣ.) ἐκζ. acc, BSM 8 *B* Michael & God ⲉϥⲕ. ⲛⲧⲟⲧⲩ ⲉϫⲉⲛⲛⲉⲛⲟⲥ of men.

—— ⲥⲁⲃⲟⲗ ⲛ- *B, turn about, circumvent*: AM 280 ⲉⲧⲁⲕ. ⲥ. ⲙⲡⲓⲫⲁⲣⲟⲥ κατακάμπτειν.

With following adverbs.

—— ⲉⲃⲟⲗ a intr, *wander out, round, return*: My 97 *S* circle ⲉⲧⲕ. ⲉⲃ. ⲡⲧⲉ ⲉⲓ (ἰῶτα) ⲙⲡⲉⲛⲑⲁ &c (cf ⲕ. ⲉϩⲟⲩⲛ), AM 7 *B* troops ⲕ. ⲉⲃ. ⲥⲁⲫⲁϩⲟⲩ ⲙⲙⲱⲟⲩ *outflank*, ShC 73 196 *S* table of devils ⲡⲁϣⲉ ⲡⲉⲧⲕ. ⲉⲃ. ⲉⲣⲟⲥ المأمون حولها, Rec 6 65 *S* undertaking (ⲛ)ⲡⲓϣ ⲕ. ⲉⲃ. ⲉⲣⲟⲕ ⲡϣⲁⲉⲡⲉ ? *circumvent*, ShC 73 66 *S* commemorative services ⲛⲧⲉⲧ-ⲛⲥⲩⲛⲁⲅⲉ ϩⲁⲧⲛⲧⲏⲩⲧⲛ ⲛⲟⲩⲥⲟⲡ ϣⲁⲡⲧⲛⲕ. ⲉⲃ. ⲉⲛⲥⲟⲡ, Va 68 48 *B* ⲡⲧⲉⲛⲕ. ⲉⲃ. ϩⲉⲛⲓ ⲉⲛⲓ; *reach out, attain to*: ShHT H 4 *S* shepherd abandons not feeble sheep because ⲙⲡⲟⲩⲕ. ⲉⲃ. ⲙⲡⲓϣⲓ ⲡⲟⲩⲱⲧ of stronger. ♭ tr, *turn away*: TU 43 11 *A* ⲙⲡⲕ. ⲡⲡⲉⲧⲛⲣⲟ ⲁⲃ. ⲙⲡⲗⲁⲟⲥⲉ, C 89 33 *B* ⲁϥⲕⲉⲧ ϩⲣⲁϥ ⲉⲃ. ♭ refl, same meaning: Ps 73 21 *S* (*B* ⲧⲁⲥⲑⲟ), Ez 21 5 *B* (*S* ⲕ. ⲉ-) ἀποστρέφ.; Lu 8 13 *S* (*B* diff) ἀφιστάναι; Si 18 5 *S* παύειν; C 89 167 *B* waited ϣⲁⲛⲧⲉϥⲕⲟⲧϥ ⲉⲃ. ϣⲁⲣⲟϥ, BM 1103 18 *S* obscure.

—— ⲉⲡⲁϩⲟⲩ a tr, *turn back*: Mor 48 109 *S* ⲁϥⲕⲁⲧ ⲡⲉϥⲣⲟ ⲉⲡ. ⲙⲙⲟϥ = C 43 152 *B* ⲫⲱⲛⲣ. ♭ refl: Ps 113 4 *SB*, Jo 20 14 *SA²* (*B* ⲫⲱ.) στρέφ., Ps 69 2 *SB*, Is 45 23 *S* (*B* ⲧⲁⲥ.) ἀποστ., Ez 1 9 *S* (*B* do), Mt 24 18 *SB* ἐπιστ., Jud 3 19 *S* ὑποστ., BMar 53 *S* ⲁⲅⲕⲟⲧⲟⲩ ⲉⲡ. ϩⲙⲡⲉϩⲣⲏⲧ, AZ 13 59 *S* voice ⲛⲁⲧⲕⲟⲧⲥ ⲉⲡ.

—— ⲉϧⲟⲩⲛ, ⲉϧ. **a** intr, *turn, bend inwards*: Br 53 *S* heads on this side & that ⲉⲅⲕ. ⲉϧ. ⲉⲣⲟⲟⲩ, WTh 136 *S* devil chained ⲉϧⲕ. ⲉϧ. as beast beneath yoke, Wess 9 52 *S* Jeremiah's λάκκος ⲉϧⲕ. ⲉϧ. *was circular*, Mor 55 58 *S* heaven consists of ascending stairs ⲉⲅⲕ. ⲉϧ., My 89 *S* circle ⲉⲧⲕ. ⲉϧ. on top of letter ρ (*cf* ⲕ. ⲉⲃⲟⲗ), BSG 14 *B* machine attached to brazen bull ⲡⲧⲟⲩⲕ. ⲉϧ. so as to crush body, *cf ib* 183 *S* & ⲕ. ⲙⲡ- above.   ⲕ. ⲉϧ. ⲉⲃⲟⲗ, *go in & out*: Z 577 *S* restless ascetes ⲉⲧⲕ. ⲉϧ. ⲉⲃ., ShC 73 81 *S* ⲕ. ⲉϧ. ⲉⲃ. ⲉⲡⲭⲓⲛϫⲏ. As nn: Bor 283 75 *S* ϧⲉⲡⲕ. ⲉϧ. ⲉⲃ. in monastery.   **b** tr, *turn, bring round*: Z 282 *S* Lord will ⲕⲟⲧⲟⲩ ⲉϧ. ⲉⲧⲉϥϧⲟⲧⲉ, Mor 31 33 *S* ⲛϧⲕⲉⲧⲧⲏⲅⲧⲡ ⲉϧ. ⲉⲡⲉⲡⲧⲟⲡⲟⲥ (*v* ⲕⲧⲟ ⲉϧ.)   **c** refl, *return*: Jer 8 4 *S* (*B* ⲧⲁⲥ.) ἀναστ. (var ἐπιστ.), Pro 23 5 *S* (*A* ⲕⲧⲟ ⲁϧ.) ὑποστ., Mor 37 95 *S* ἐγγίζειν; BMis 469 *S* ⲁϥⲕⲟⲧϥ ⲉϧ. to his dwelling.

—— ⲉϧⲣⲁⲓ, -ⲏⲓ **a** intr, *turn, go round*: Is 23 16 *B* (*S* diff) ῥεμβεύειν; Bor 240 78 *S* cattle at mill ⲉⲅⲕ. ⲉϧ., *ib* ⲉⲅⲕ. ⲉϧ. like turning of mill. As nn m: ShC 42 210 *S* ⲡⲉⲥⲕ. ⲉϧ. as one that grinds mill.   **b** refl, *return*: Ac 13 46 *S* (var ⲕⲧⲟ, *B* ⲉ-) στρέφ., Ge 3 19 *S* (*B* ⲧⲁⲥ.) ἀποστ., Ex 16 10 *S* (*B* ⲕ. ⲉ-) ἐπιστ., Est 6 12 *S*, Ac 1 12 *S* (*B* ⲇⲟ) ὑποστ.; Mt 21 18 *S* (*B* ⲧⲁⲥ.) ἐπανάγειν; BMis 64 *S* Elizabeth ⲕⲟⲧⲥ ⲉϧ. ⲉⲇⲱⲣⲓⲡⲏ ⲡⲧⲉⲥϧⲉ.

—— ϧⲓⲃⲟⲗ *SA*, *go about outside*: Pro 7 12 (*B* ⲗⲉⲗⲉ ⲉⲃ.) ῥεμβεσθαι ἔξω.

—— nn m, **a** *turning round, circuit, surroundings*: Deu 34 3 *S* (*B* = Gk) περίχωρα, Is 40 22 *SB* γυρός, 2 Kg 5 7 *S* περιοχή, Mt 9 16 *S* (*B* ⲙⲟϧ) πλήρωμα, BKU 1 1 vo *S* ⲡⲉⲕ. ⲡⲧⲉϥϧⲉⲗⲡⲉ were painful, *cf* AZ 21 100 *O* ⲡⲕⲁⲧⲁⲕⲟⲓⲧⲓ (glossed ⲕⲱⲧⲉ) ⲡⲟⲉⲗⲡⲓ, Br 227 *S* ⲡⲕ. ⲙⲡⲉϥϧⲣⲟⲧⲉ ⲧⲙⲡⲧⲁⲧⲥⲟⲩⲱⲛⲥ paral ⲡⲱⲣϧ ⲉϧⲟⲩⲛ, Mu 34 *S* voice filled ⲡⲕ. ⲧⲏⲣϥ of ⲧⲟⲡⲟⲥ, P 44 71 *S* ⲡⲕ. ⲙⲡⲣⲏⲧ · περικάρδιον, PMich 593 *S* sleep-charm ⲡⲧⲭⲱⲕⲙⲉ ⲙⲡⲕ. ⲙⲡⲉϥⲙⲁ ⲛⲡⲕⲟⲧⲕ with water, RChamp 372 *S* the caves ⲙⲡⲕ. ⲉⲧⲙⲙⲁⲩ, Va 61 112 *B* dead bones assembled ⲡⲥⲉϭⲓ ⲙⲡⲟⲩⲕ. as at first, C 86 117 *B* appeared like ⲡⲕ. (circle?) of sun when rising (*cf* ⲕⲟⲧⲉ **a**, PVi), ST 37 *S* ⲡⲣⲙⲡⲕ. of city Ermont (or ? as place-name), Mor 16 67 *S* convent ⲙⲡⲕ. of Askalon.   **b** *turning* of water-wheel (*v* vb **I b**): GöttAbh '17 78 *S* ⲉⲩϣⲁⲡⲕⲁ ⲡⲕ. ⲉⲃⲟⲗ hired wheel-pots shall be returned.   ⲙⲁ ⲡⲕ., *turning-place*, water-wheel, *saqiyah*: Ryl 158 *S* ϣⲏⲓ with 2 ⲙⲁ ⲡⲕ., *ib* ⲡⲙⲁ ⲡⲕ. ⲙⲡⲧⲣⲥⲱ (*cf* κυκλευτήριον, βοοστάσιον).   **c** *seeking, inquiry*: 2 Tim 2 23 *B* (*S* ϣⲓⲛⲉ), MG 25 1 *B* ζήτησις.   **d** ? confused with ⲕⲱⲧ, *building*: *cf* Ez 41 2 (*bis*), 42 1 *S* ⲕⲱⲧⲉ with *ib* 41 13, 15, 42 10 ⲕⲱⲧ all = *B* ⲕⲱϯ τὸ διορίζον *aedificium*; Ap 21

18 *B* (*S* ⲉϥⲕⲏⲧ) ἐνδώμησις, Va 57 233 *B* married ⲕⲁⲧⲁ ⲡⲁⲡⲕ. ⲙⲡⲓⲧⲁⲗⲟⲥ *rule, ordinance* (*cf* ⲕⲱⲧ nn **II b**).   **e** adverbial ⲙⲡⲕ., *round about*: Ex 16 13 *SB*, Lev 25 44 *S* (*B* vb) Is 6 2 *SB*, Mk 6 6 *SB* κύκλῳ, Ps 88 7 *S* (*B* ⲇⲟ) περικύκλῳ, Si 47 17 *S*, Is 30 32 *SBF*, Ap 4 8 *S* (*B* ⲇⲟ) κυκλόθεν, Jos 4 3 *B* ϫⲉⲡⲡⲉⲧⲉⲡⲙⲁ ⲡϣⲱⲡⲓ ⲙⲡⲕ. (*S* om ⲙⲡⲕ.) οὗ ἐὰν παρεμβάλητε;   without ⲡ(ⲙ)-, Job 41 5 *S* (*B* vb), Ps 77 28 *SB* κύκλῳ, Jer 17 26 *B* κυκλόθεν, Mk 3 8 *S* (*B* diff) περί.   **f** as prep, *about, concerning*: Is 29 3 *B* (*S* om), Dan 3 48 *B* (*S* ⲣⲙⲡⲕ.), Ac 22 6 (var ⲉⲡⲕ., *S* ⲙⲡⲛⲟⲩ), 1 Tim 6 4 *B* (*S* diff), Bor 305 98 *S* heresies ⲙⲡⲕ. ⲡⲡⲉϥⲫⲩⲥⲓⲥ of Lord περί; Va 57 33 *B* ⲡⲓⲙⲕⲁϧ ⲉⲧⲉⲙⲡⲕ. ⲡϯⲁⲣⲉⲧⲏ τοὺς τῆς ἀ. πόνους, *ib* 50 *B* said it ⲙⲡⲕ. ⲡϯⲙⲉⲧⲁⲥⲑⲉⲏⲛⲥ of woman (*v* Mt 26 11) πρὸς τὴν ἀ., MG 17 321 *S* = *ib* 95 *B* ϯⲙⲡⲕ. ⲡⲟⲩⲣⲱⲙⲉ πρὸς ἄνθρ. εἰμί, P 131¹ 32 *S* flying ⲙⲡⲕ. ⲙⲡⲁⲏⲣ ἀνὰ τὸν αἰθέρα; ϧⲙⲡⲕ.: Nah 3 8 *A* (*B* vb) κύκλῳ;   ϧⲙ-, ϫⲉⲡⲡⲕ.: Nu 1 50 *S* (*B* ϧⲓ ⲕⲟⲧ), Ez 5 12 *SB* κύκλῳ, Deu 6 14 *S* (*B* vb) περικ., Ps 30 13 *SB*, Ez 23 22 *B* (*S* ⲙ-) κυκλόθεν; Mk 9 14 *S* (*B* ⲙ-) περί; BAp 173 *S* will reprove thee ϧⲁⲙⲡⲕ. ⲡⲧⲉⲡⲧⲟⲗⲏ; ⲉⲡⲕ.: Jos 6 20 *S*, Is 60 4 *B* (*S* ϧⲙ-) κύκλῳ; FR 76 *S* we encircled him ⲉⲡⲕ., BSM 127 *B* ⲕⲱϯ ⲉⲣⲟϥ ⲓⲉ ⲡⲥⲉⲓ ⲉⲡⲉϥⲕ.

ϭⲓⲡ-, ϫⲓⲡⲕ. nn f *S*, m f *B*, *turning round, cycle*: Job 37 12 *B* κύκλωμα, PS 38 *S* ⲧⲉⲩϭ. ⲏ ⲧⲉⲩϭⲓⲡ-ϭⲱϣⲧ, Va 57 112 *B* ⲡϫ. of year;   *enquiry*: 1 Tim 1 4 *B* (*S* ϣⲓⲛⲉ) ζήτησις; OriensChr NS 3 36 *B* ⲧϫ. (*sic l*) ⲑⲁⲓ ⲉⲧⲉⲣⲉϥϯ ⲙⲉⲓ ⲙⲙⲟⲥ;   + refl suff: ShC 73 14 *S* sword's ϭⲓⲡⲕⲟⲧⲉ to sheath, *cf ib* ϭⲓⲡⲕⲧⲟⲥ, P 131¹ 1 *S* to renegade ⲙⲏ ⲉⲕⲡⲟⲉⲓ ⲡⲧϭⲓⲡⲕⲟⲧⲕ?

ⲕⲟⲧ *SB*, ⲕⲁⲧ *Sa* nn m, *circular motion, turn, visit*: Jos 6 16 *S* περίοδος; ShA 1 427 *S* ϧⲛⲟⲩⲣⲟⲙⲡⲉ ⲡⲟⲩⲱⲧ, ϧⲛⲟⲩⲕ. ⲡⲟⲩⲱⲧ, BKU 1 296 *Sa* delay not to send ⲙⲡⲓⲕⲉⲕⲁⲧ, PMich 1526 *B* ϯⲡⲛⲟⲩ ⲉⲣⲏⲥ ⲡ-ⲡⲟⲩⲕ., Mich 166 *S* (Paul of Tamah) sage will bring upon wicked ⲡⲡⲟⲩⲕ. ⲙⲡⲉⲑⲟⲟⲩ.   ⲃⲱⲕ ⲟⲩⲕ. *SSa*, *pay visit, go turn*: Louvre SN 114 ⲡⲧϭ. ⲟⲩⲕⲁⲧ ϧⲏ(*l* ϧⲓ)ⲡⲭⲟⲉⲓ ⲉⲧⲡⲟⲗ[ⲓⲥ, *ib* ϧⲁⲡⲕⲁⲧ ⲡⲧⲁⲕⲃⲁⲕϥ, Ep 84 contract with camel-herd, If I send thee to one & he pay not freight I will suffer thee to ⲃ. ⲡⲉⲕⲕ. ϧⲱⲱⲕ ⲡⲣⲟⲥ ⲧⲁⲡⲁⲗⲟⲩⲓⲁ ⲙⲡⲕ. ⲉⲧⲙⲙⲁⲩ, J 76 19 quit this world ⲛⲧⲁⲃ. ⲡⲕ. that everyone oweth.   ⲣ ⲕ. *S*, sim: BMar 88 the righteous ⲡⲧⲁⲡⲉϥⲕ. ⲡⲧⲁϥⲁⲁϥ ⲉⲡⲕⲟⲥⲙⲟⲥ ϣⲱⲡⲉ ⲡⲁϥ ⲉϧⲣⲏⲓ, J 70 6 I am about to ⲣ ⲡⲕ. (as J 76 above), Ryl 365 ⲁⲓⲣ ⲕ. ⲥⲡⲁϥ ⲉⲣⲟϥ & I found &c, WS 89 ⲉⲕⲟⲧ (? same).   ϯ ⲕ. *S*, sim: ShC 42 30 if I be right-thinking, good is ⲡⲕ. ⲡⲧⲁⲧⲉⲧⲡⲧⲁⲁϥ ϣⲁⲣⲟⲡ, TT 188 ⲁϥϯ ⲕⲉⲕ. & came up to him, *cf ib* ⲁϥⲕⲟⲧⲩ & came up, Ep 300 ⲁⲓϯ ⲟⲩⲙⲏⲏϣⲉ ⲡⲕ. ⲉⲣⲟⲟⲩ saying Write.   ⲕⲱⲱⲃⲉ ⲡⲟⲩⲕ. *S, compel*

(to go) a turn: Mt 5 41 (B = Gk) μίλιον. ϧⲓ ⲕ.,
ⲟⲩⲕ. S (once) B, lit *throw a turn*, so *make a move,
pay visit*: BM 915 17 ⲁϥϧⲓ ⲟⲩⲕ. ⲉⲁⲡⲁ ⲛⲁⳕⲱⲙ
παραλαμβ. πρός, ROC 25 248 why ⲙⲡⲉⲕϧⲓ ⲕ. ⲉⲣⲟⲡ
παραβάλλειν dat; HL 91 consort with holy men
ⲉⲕϧⲓ ⲕ. ⲉⲣⲱⲟⲩ μεταδιώκειν gen, BM 1102 S ⲁⲕⲣ. ⲧⲉ
ⲡϧⲓ ⲟⲩⲕ. ϣⲁⲣⲟⲡ, PO 14 345 angels shall ϧⲓ ⲕ. ⲉⲡⲉⲕ-
ⲙⲟⲛⲁⲥⲧⲏⲣⲓⲟⲛ. *encompass, encamp*: Ge 33 18
(S ⲟⲩⲉϩ ⲛⲁϥ), Nu 2 3 (S ϧⲙⲟⲟⲥ), ib 31 19 (S
ϣⲱⲡⲉ), Ps 33 8 (S ⲕⲱⲧⲉ ⲉ-) παρεμβάλ. (? as if παραβάλ.); Ex 2 4 (A ⲥⲱⲡⲧ) κατασκοπεύειν; ϧⲓ ⲕ.
ⲉⲃⲟⲗ B, *pay visit*: MG 25 364 ⲁϥϣⲁⲛϧⲓ ⲕ. ⲉⲃ.
ⲉⲡⲓⳕⲉⲗⲗⲟⲓ. ϫⲓⲛϧⲓ ⲕ. B nn m, *visit*: MG
25 286 (S ⲥⲕⲩⲗⲙⲟⲥ), Nu 1 51 (S diff) παρεμβάλ.

ⲕⲟⲧ SB, ⲕⲁⲧ SSᵃA nn m, *wheel*: Pro 20 26 SA,
Si 36 5 S, Is 28 27 S (B = Gk) τροχός (τρ. mostly
untranslated SB: Ps 76 18, Eccl 12 6, Ja 3 6 &c);
Ryl 94 S ⲕ. & ⲧⲣ. alternate, P 131⁶ 31 S ϧⲉⲛⲕⲟⲧⲉ
ⲛⲁⳕⲟⲗⲧⲉ (prob l ⲕⲟⲧ ⲉⲛ-, cf Is 41 15 S ϧⲉⲛⲕⲟⲧ ⲛ-,
Miss 8 227 S ⲛⲕⲟⲧ ⲛⲛ-), WTh 199 S ⲕ. ⲛⲥⲓⲕⲉ,
BIF 14 163 S (or ⲕ. alone 165), EW 84 B sim,
CA 110 S ⲛⲕ. ⲙⲡⲧⲁⲗⲏⲭⲁⲛⲏ, J 113 4 S ⲕⲁⲧ ϧⲛⲙ
(ϣⲏⲙ) among parts of water-wheel, BKU 1 94 Sᵃ
ⲛⲕⲁⲧ ⲛⲧⲡⲉ, ⲡⲕ. ⲙⲡⲓⲧⲛⲉ (? wheel or basket), Ryl
244 S as embroidered ornament (v n) ⲟⲩϣⲧ(ⲛ)ⲡ
ⲉⲥϫⲓ ⲕ., ib ⲉⲥϣⲟⲡⲧ ⲉⲥⲡⲁⲑⲏ ϧⲓⲛ. ⲙⲁ ⲡⲕⲟⲧ (so
Revillout, or l ⲕⲓⲧ) related to water-wheel (ϧⲁⲓ):
J 67 82 S.

ⲕⲟⲧ SB, ⲕⲁⲧ SBF nn m, *basket*: holding bread,
Mt 14 20 SBF, Jo 6 13 SB (A² ϩⲓⲣ) κόφινος, BMis
57 S Habakkuk ⲡⲱϣ ⲛⲣⲡⲟⲉⲓⲕ ⲉⲩⲕ. (Bel 33 σκάφη);
fruit, Deu 26 2 S (B = Gk, but ref in Rec 7 91 =
Ryl 424 ⲕⲱⲧ) κάρταλλος, Jer 24 2 SB κάλαθος;
meat, Jud 6 19 S κόφ. (var κανοῦν); pickled fish
(ταρίχιον), CO 465 S paral ϩⲓⲣ; earth (?) Ps 80 6 SB
κόφ.; bricks, BM 1089 S; bartered or sold among
monks: ShBerlOr 1611 5 S ⲡⲟⲩϧ, ⲕ., ϫⲱⲱⲙⲉ,
ShC 73 43 S sim., Mor 53 71 S as vinedresser ϫⲱ
ⲱⲗⲉ ⲉⲡⲉϥⲕ. ⲕⲁⲧ ⲕⲟⲩⲓ, *small basket*: RE 9 176
S, Win 29 S ⲕⲁⲧ ϣⲏⲙ. *nest?*: Cat 147 B insects sent to young ravens ϧⲓϫⲉⲛⲡⲟⲩⲕ. (cf Lauchert
Physiologus 142).

ⲕⲟⲧ B nn: BSM 67 I will give ⲛⲱⲧⲉⲛ ⲕⲟⲧ (sic
MS) ⲡⲟⲗⲓⲥⲙⲁ دينار = BMis 159 ϫⲓ ⲛⲧⲟⲟⲧ ⲛⲡⲟⲙ.
ⲥⲛⲁⲩ (Mor 26 10, 22 17 sim), ? l ⲡⲟⲩⲛⲡⲟⲗⲓⲥⲙⲁ.

ⲕⲟⲧⲉ SB, ⲕⲁⲧⲉ A nn f, *a going round, turning,
circuit*: Eccl 1 6 S κύκλος; Deu 33 14 S (B ϫⲓⲛ-
ⳙⲓⲃⳓ), Jer 30 10 S τροπή; Sa 8 8 S στροφή, Si 43
17 S συστρ.; Va 58 193 B who hath brought us
ⲉⲧⲁⲓⲕ. ⲛⲧⲉ ⲡⲁⲓⲥⲛⲟⲩ περίοδος: PVi 10157 A ⲉⲛ[ⲣ]
ϧⲁⲉ ⲇⲉ ⲡϧⲣⲏⲓ [ϧⲡⲧ]ⲕ ⲙⲡⲣⲓ, ShC 73 175 S ⲛⲕ.
ⲛⲧⲉϧⲓⲛ المسالك, ShC 42 212 S ⲟⲩϧⲓⲛ...ⲉⲡⲁϣⲉ
ⲛⲕⲟⲧⲥ ⲛ ⲙⲙⲟⲉⲓⲧ ⲙⲡⲉⲥⲥⲱⲣⲙ, P 129¹⁶ 19 S sailing

on Nile ⲁϥⲉⲓ ⲉⲩⲕ. ⲛⲧⲉ ⲡⲓⲉⲣⲟ, BMis 465 S ship
wafted ϧⲛⲕ. ⲛⲓⲙ, Bor 240 78 S vagrants going
round like ⲧⲕ. ⲛⲡⲧⲁⲗⲉⲭⲁⲛⲏ. b *twist, knot*: Is
58 6 SB στραγγαλιά; ShC 73 93 S jar ⲉⲩⲕⲧⲟ ⲉⲣⲟϥ
ⲛϧⲁϥ ⲛⲕⲟⲧⲉ, C 89 132 B window with ϧⲁⲡⲡⲓϣⳓ
ⲛⲕ., Va ar 172 76 مطالبن, MG 17 499 حبل (sic (?) l)
lest light penetrate. c *crookedness, guile*: EstE
13 S μέθοδος, Eph 4 14 SB μεθοδεία; Pro 2 15 SA
(B ⲕⲟⲗϫ) καμπύλη; ib 8 8 B (v ϫⲓ ⲕ.) στραγγα-
λιώδης; Si 1 6 SB πανούργευμα; ViSitz 172 17 S
ἐνέδρα; Miss 8 98 S ἀμφίβολος; BMOr 8802 4
(1st text) S beguiled them ϧⲛϧⲉⲛⲕ., Tri 668 S
ⲛⲉⲩⲙⲟⲕⲙⲉⲕ ⲙⲛⲛⲉⲩⲕ., AM 217 B ϥⲁϯⲕ. ⲉⲧϧⲱⲟⲩ.

ⲉⲓⲣⲉ, ⲣ ⲕ. SB, *make a turn, plan, circumvent*:
LCyp 26 S ⲉⲅⲉⲓⲣⲉ ⲛⲣⲉⲡⲕ. to overcome τροποῦν,
BMar 109 S striving ⲉⲣ ⲕ. ⲛⲓⲙ ἐπίνοια, P 44 73 S
ⲙⲉⲭⲁⲛⲁⲧⲁⲓ (μηχανητής) دبر حيل ·ⲁϥⲣ ⲕ., Miss 4
171 B ϣⲁϥⲉⲣ ⲕ. ⲛⲓⲃⲉⲛ to destroy him, ShA 1 306
S ⲉⲩϣⲁⲛⲣ ϧⲁⲣ ⲛⲕ. ϣⲁⲡⲧⲟⲩⲃⲱⲕ ⲉϧⲣⲁⲓ.

ϯ ⲕ. S, *make a turn, go about*: Ex 32 27 (B
ⲧⲁⲥⲑⲟ) ἀνακάμπτειν; BMis 154 devil ⲉϥϯ ⲕ. roaring like lion, Mor 46 26 S martyr dragged ⲁϥϯ
ⲥⲁϣϥ ⲛⲕ. ⲙⲙⲟϥ (sic l, cf ⲕⲟⲧⲥⲓ) in town.

ϫⲓ ⲕ. SA, *take turn, be crooked*: Pro 8 8 SA (B ⲕ.,
not ϫⲓ), P 131³ 36 S all his paths ϫⲏⲩ ⲛⲕ., BMOr
8802 6 S will speak truth ⲛϥϫⲁϫⲓ ⲕ. ⲁⲛ, R 1 5 47
S martyr on horse ⲁϥⲧⲣⲉⲩϫⲓ ϣⲟⲙⲧ[ⲉ] ⲛⲕ. ϧⲛ
ⲡⲁⲗⲁⲧⲓⲟⲛ (cf ⲕⲟⲧⲥⲓ), ShA 1 106 S he on right of
altar cometh ϧⲙⲡⲣⲉϥϫⲓ ⲟⲩⲕ. ⲛϧⲏⲧϥ & standeth
on left.

ⲥⲁ ⲛⲕ., *man of turns, guileful person*: Job 5 13
SB πολύπλοκος (var -τροπος), P 44 73 S ⲥ. ⲉⲑⲟⲟⲩ ·
ⲕⲁⲕⲟⲙⲏⲭⲁⲛⲟⲛ, Z 571 S devil is ⲟⲩⲥ. ⲙⲛⲧ-,
ⲙⲉⲧⲥⲁ ⲛⲕ., *crookedness, dishonesty*: Ps 63 3 B (S
ⲥⲟⲟⲩϧⲥ cf multitudo) συστροφή, ib 124 5 S (B ⳓⲣⲟⲡ)
στραγγαλιά, JA '75 5 237 S wise ϧⲛⲡⲉⲩⲙ. (var
ⲡⲉⲩⲕ.) πανουργία, CA 99 S sim (cf 1 Cor 3 19),
Jth 11 8 S πανούργευμα, EW 150 B ⲙⲟⲕⲙⲉⲕ ⲙⲙ.
περίνοια τεχνική, C 43 218 B evil eye ⲉⲧⲥⲟⲙ ⳓⲉ-
ⲛⲟⲩⲙ., ShMiss 4 284 S whoso washeth self ϧⲛⲟⲩ-
ⲃⲱⲗ ⲉⲃⲟⲗ ⲙⲡⲟⲩⲙ.

ⲕⲟⲧⲥⲓ B nn f, *circuit?*: AM 322 lion pursued
him ϣⲁⲧⲉϥⳓⲓ ⲡⲟⲩⲕ. ⲙⲙⲟϥ ⲉϥϯⲃⲁⲕⲓ ⲧⲏⲣⲥ ⲉϥⲕⲱϯ
(cf ϯ ⲕⲟⲧⲥ), C 43 226 martyrs judged ⳓⲉⲛϯⲕ.
bay (?) of Touphôt on river bank.

ⲕⲱⲧϥ S nn, *circumference*: Lepsius Denkm 6
102 measurements of garments ⲙⲛⲧ ⲛⲧⲛⲃⲉ ⲛⲕ.
Cf Ep 1 9.

ⲕⲧⲟ (for ⲧⲕⲧⲟ JTS 10 400 S, caus of ⲕⲱⲧⲉ, cf B
ⲧⲁⲕⲧⲟ) SAA²B (rare), ⲕⲧⲁ F, ⲕⲧⲉ- SAA²B (Jer 52
4), ⲕⲧⲟⲍ S, ⲕⲧⲁⲍ AA², ⲕⲧⲏⲩ† SA, ⲕⲧⲟⲉⲓⲧ, -ⲁⲉⲓⲧ† S
(ShA 1 465, 129), ⲕⲧⲏⲟⲩⲧ† B caus vb I intr, *turn,
surround*: Ps 79 3 S (B ⲧⲁⲥⲑⲟ), Cant 6 12 S, Is

57 9 S (B ⲧⲁⲥ. ⲉⲃⲟⲗ) ἀποστρέφεσθαι ; Cant 4 8 S
διέρχεσθαι.   With ⲉ- : Jer 2 21 S (ShIF 253,
B ⲕⲱϯ) στρέφεσθαι, Ge 3 16 S (B diff) ἀποστροφή ;
Pro 20 28 S (var ⲕⲱⲧⲉ) περικυκλοῦν ; Is 31 9 F
(S diff, B ⲧⲁⲕⲧⲟ) περιλαμβάνειν.   With advb. :
ⲉⲃⲟⲗ, turn away, Ps 88 43 S (B ⲧⲁⲥ.), Jer 15 6 S
(B do), Ez 21 30 S (C 73 12, B ⲕⲱϯ ⲉⲃ.) ἀπο-
στρέφ.   ⲉⲡⲁϩⲟⲩ, turn back, ShBMOr 8810 483
S to nun ⲙⲡⲱⲣϭⲉ ⲉⲕ. ⲉⲡ.   ⲉϧⲟⲩⲛ, surround,
R 1 3 6 S antelopes ⲡⲉϣⲁⲅⲕ. ⲡⲉ ⲉⲣ. ⲉⲣⲟϥ.

Qual, be turned, be around (of wall) : Lev 25 29
S (B ⲧⲁⲕⲧⲟ), Hos 8 14 A (B do) τειχίζεσθαι, Is 26
1 S (B diff) περίτειχος, Jer 4 5 B τειχήρης ; Ps 59
9 S (B diff) περιοχή ; Mor 37 131 S ⲉⲅⲕ. ⲉⲣⲟⲥ
κύκλῳ ; Ap 4 4 B (S ϭⲱⲱⲗⲉ) περιβάλλεσθαι ; ShC
42 38 S to strangle him ⲟⲙⲡⲉⲣⲛⲁⲁⲩ ⲉⲧⲕ. ⲉⲡⲉϥ-
ⲙⲁⲕⲟ, ShA 1 465 S tree watered from springs
ⲉⲧⲕ̄ⲧⲟⲉⲓⲧ ⲉⲣⲟϥ, BMis 70 S face ⲕ. ⲉⲡⲥⲁ ⲛⲧⲁⲛⲁⲧⲟ-
ⲗⲏ, Mor 44 43 S sim ⲉⲕ̄ⲙⲡⲣⲏ, ShA 1 40 S
serpent ⲉϥⲕ. ⲉϧⲟⲩⲛ ⲉⲣⲟⲟⲩ from breast to feet.

II tr, make to turn, return, go round, also (as
ⲕⲱⲧⲉ) surround : Ps 40 3 S (B ⲧⲁⲥⲑⲟ), Is 38 8 S (B
ⲫⲱⲛϧ), Mt 27 3 S (B ⲧⲁⲥ.) στρέφειν, Nu 14 25 S
(B ⲕⲱϯ), Ps 13 7 S (B ⲧⲁⲥ.), Si 18 12 S, Mal 3
10 A (B do) ἐπιστ., Ge 43 12 S (B do), Ru 1 21 S
Jer 14 3 S (B do), Mt 5 42 S (B do) ἀποστ., Su 9
S (B ⲫⲱ.) διαστ. ; Hos 2 3 A (B ⲧⲁⲥ.) ἀποκαθιστάναι ; Job 1 6 S (B diff) περιέρχ. ; Si 43 13 S
γυροῦν ; R 2 2 23 S ⲉⲥⲕ. ⲡⲡⲉⲥⲃⲁⲗ ϧⲡⲟⲩⲥⲧⲛⲙ
ὑπογράφειν ; PS 132 S ⲁⲅⲕ. ⲛⲣⲉⲡⲥⲡⲟⲧⲟⲩ ⲉⲁⲩϣⲟ-
ⲟⲩⲉ ⲟⲙⲱϥ sedaverunt), R 1 4 42 S ⲁϥⲕⲧⲉ ⲧⲟⲓⲕⲟⲩⲙⲉⲛⲏ seeking him, BMar 91 S ⲁⲓⲕⲧⲉ ⲡ̄ϣⲓⲉⲓ (l ϭⲓⲉ)
ⲛ̄ⲡⲁⲗⲁⲥ (cf ⲕⲱⲧⲉ II a).   ⲕⲧⲉ ⲉⲓⲁⲧ⸗, turn eye,
v ⲉⲓⲁ eye.   ⲕⲧⲉ ⲧⲟⲟⲧ⸗, turn, lay hand : 2 Kg 8 3 S
ἐφιστάναι ; Mk 9 36 S (B ⲁⲙⲟⲛⲓ) ἐναγκαλίζειν, AP
25 A² ⲁϥⲕⲧⲉ ⲧⲟⲟⲧϥ ⲁⲛⲅⲙⲫⲁ.   ⲕⲧⲉ ⲙⲛⲥⲉ, require
interest : Deu 23 19 S (B ϣⲱⲡ) ἐκτοκεῖν.   With
acc & dat ⲉ- : Ps 1138 S (B ⲫⲱ.), Ap 11 6 S (B do)
στρέφ., 2 Kg 3 12 S ἐπιστ., Ge 28 21 S (B ⲧⲁⲥ.),
Job 10 9 S (B do) ἀποστ., Deu 23 5 S (B ⲫⲱ.),
Ps 77 44 S (B do) μεταστ. ; Is 29 3 S (B ⲧⲁⲕⲧⲟ)
βάλλειν, Lu 19 43 S (B ⲧⲁⲕⲧⲟ), BHom 33 S ⲕ̄ⲧⲉ
ⲧⲉϥ̄ⲯⲩⲭⲏ ⲉⲅⲣⲁϣⲉ μεταβάλ., Pro 28 4 S περιβάλ. ;
Is 37 33 S (B do) κυκλοῦν ; Mt 21 33 S (B do)
περιτιθέναι ; EpJer 17 F (B ⲧⲁⲭⲣⲟ) περιφράσσειν ;
Lu 5 4 S (B ⲉⲓ ⲉⲃⲟⲗ) ἐπανάγειν ; Zech 9 12 SA
(B Gk diff) converti ; PS 163 S ⲁϥⲕⲧⲉ ⲡⲁⲕⲁⲕⲉ ⲉⲩ-
ⲟⲉⲓⲛ, ShA 2 108 S self-slayers ⲁⲧⲉⲧⲛⲕ. ⲉⲣⲱⲧⲛ ⲛ-
ⲡⲉⲧⲛϭⲓⲝ, R 1 4 17 S ⲁϥⲕ. ⲉⲣⲟϥ ⲛⲛⲉϥϭⲓⲝ amplexus
eum, ShC 73 93 S vessel ⲉⲅⲙⲟⲣϧ...ⲉⲅⲕ. ⲉⲣⲟϥ ⲛϩⲁϥ
ⲡⲕⲟⲧⲥ, BMis 395 S ⲛⲡⲣ...ⲕ. ⲉⲣⲟⲛ ⲛⲣⲉⲛϣⲁϫⲉ
beyond our capacity = BSM 46 B ⲛⲡⲉⲣⲭⲱ ⲛⲣⲁⲛ-
ⲥⲁϫⲓ.   With vbal ⲉ- : 1 Kg 10 9 S ⲕ. ⲧⲉϥⲛⲁϩⲃ̄

ⲉⲗⲟⲟϣⲉ, Ac 7 42 S ⲕⲧⲟⲟⲩ...ⲉⲧⲣⲉⲩ- (B ⲕⲱϯ ⲉ-)
ἐπιστ. + infin.
   With following prepositions.
—— ⲉϫⲛ- S, turn upon, toward : Lev 19 9
(Maspero, as gloss on ϫⲱⲕ ⲉⲃⲟⲗ συντελεῖν), Miss
4 711 demons ⲙⲟⲛⲉ ⲡ̄ⲕⲧⲉ ⲡⲉϩⲣⲟ ⲉϫⲱⲟⲩ, Z 272
ⲙⲁⲣⲓⲕⲧⲟⲛ ⲉϫⲛ̄ⲡⲉⲧⲕⲏ ⲛⲁⲛ ⲉϩⲣⲁⲓ ; ⲉϩⲣⲁⲓ ⲉϫ.,
Deu 28 60 (B ⲧⲁⲥ.), Jth 7 30 ἐπιστ. ἐπί.
—— ϣⲁ- S, turn, bring to : BMar 89 ⲁⲓⲕⲧⲉ ⲛ̄ⲡⲁⲗⲁⲥ
ϣⲁⲣⲱⲧⲛ & said these few words, Miss 8 73 ⲛ̄ⲧⲕ.
ⲛ̄ⲛⲉⲧⲁⲓϫⲟⲟⲩⲥⲟⲩ ϩⲓⲧⲟⲟⲧⲕ ϣⲁⲣⲟⲓ ἄγαγε ἐνταῦθα.
   With following adverbs.
—— ⲉⲃⲟⲗ SA, turn away : Ps 29 7 S (B ⲫⲱ.
ⲥⲁⲃ.), Is 58 13 S (B ⲧⲁⲥ.), Mic 2 4 S (A ⲗⲁϭⲉ, B
do) ἀποστ., Is 49 6 S (B do) ἐπιστ., Pro 10 9 SA
(B ⲕⲱⲗϫ) διαστ. ; ib 21 14 SA ἀνατρέπειν, Si 20
28 S ἀποτ. ;   turn toward (?) : ShA 2 315 ϩⲙ̄ⲡⲥⲟⲡ
ⲉⲧⲛ̄ⲕⲧⲏⲩ ⲉⲃ. ⲉⲡⲉⲧⲥⲟⲛϩ ⲉϧⲟⲩⲛ, ShP 130² 56 v ⲁ-
ⲗⲟⲙ.   ⲉⲃ. ⲛ- : Deu 31 17 (B ⲫⲱ. ⲥⲁⲃ. ⲛ-), Is
12 1 (B ⲧⲁⲥ. ⲉⲃ. ϩⲁ-), Mic 3 4 SA (B do) ἀποστ.
ἀπό ; R 1 4 53 ⲁⲓⲕⲧⲉ ⲧⲉⲩⲣⲓⲁ ⲉⲃ. ⲛ- gentile worship
μεταβάλ. ἀπό.   ⲉⲃ. ϩⲛ- : Job 33 17 (B do) ἀποστ.
ἀπό, Ac 13 8 (B ⲫⲱ. ⲉⲃ. ϫⲉⲛ-) διαστ. ἀπό.
—— ⲉⲡⲁϩⲟⲩ S, turn back, return : Deu 17 16
(B ⲧⲁⲥ. ⲉϩⲣⲏⲓ), Ps 43 10 (B ⲧⲁⲥ. ⲉⲫ.) ἀποστ., Jud
18 23 ἐπιστ. ; ShMIF 23 135 rather than ⲕⲧⲉ ⲡⲉϥϣⲁϫⲉ ⲉⲡ., Wess 15 9 ⲙ̄ⲡⲁⲧⲛⲕ. ⲙ̄ⲡⲉⲛϩⲟ ⲉⲡ. =
Miss 4 116 B ⲕⲱϯ.
—— ⲉϧⲟⲩⲛ S, turn inward, toward : BM 151
prayer ⲡⲉⲛⲧⲁⲅⲕⲧⲟⲟⲩ ⲉⲃ. ⲛ̄ⲕⲧⲟⲟⲩ ⲉϧ. ; mostly
with dat ⲉ- : Jud 5 29 ἀποστ. dat ; Jer 23 3 (B ⲱⲗⲓ
ⲉϧ.) καθιστάναι εἰς ; Sh 73 63 ⲛ̄ⲧⲉⲛⲕⲧⲉⲛⲏⲛⲉ ⲉϧ.
to your τόποι (var -ⲕⲉⲧⲧⲏⲩⲧⲛ).   As nn : Br 247
ⲡⲉⲩⲕ. ⲉϧ. again.
—— ⲉϩⲣⲁⲓ S, return : Ge 28 15 (B ⲧⲁⲥ. ⲉ-),
Deu 28 68 (B ⲧⲁⲥ. ⲉⲃ̄. ⲉ-) ἀποστ. εἰς.
—— ⲛ̄ⲥⲁⲃⲟⲗ ⲛ-, turn away from : Ps 50 9 S
(B ⲧⲁⲥ. ⲥⲁⲃ.), Is 1 15 F (S ⲕ̄. ⲉⲃ̄., B ⲫⲱ. ⲥⲁⲃ.)
ἀποστ.
Refl, with suff or ⲙ̄ⲙⲟ⸗ (rare), turn self, return,
bring round : Ex 4 17 S (A ⲕⲱⲧⲉ), Jud 7 13 S
(ⲙ̄ⲙⲟ⸗), Lu 7 44 S (var ⲕⲱⲧⲉ, B ⲫⲱ.) στρέφ., Ge
22 5 S (B ⲧⲁⲥ.), 2 Kg 2 30 S, Pro 26 11 SA ἀναστ.
ἐπί, ib ἐπέρχ. ἐπί, Ge 31 55 (var ⲕⲱⲧⲉ = B), Ex 4
18 SA (B ⲧⲁⲥ.), Ps 84 3 S (B do), Jer 4 28 S (B do),
R 1 4 60 S ⲛⲉⲧⲕ. ⲙ̄ⲙⲟⲟⲩ from demons ἀποστ.,
Eccl 12 3 S διαστ., Nu 16 50 S (B ⲕⲱϯ), Jos 19
27 S, Si 17 24 S (ⲙ̄ⲙⲟ⸗), Mk 5 30 S (var ⲕⲱⲧⲉ,
B ⲫⲱ.) ἐπιστ., Dan 10 8 S (B ⲧⲁⲥ.) μεταστ., Ge
14 17 S (B do), Lu 2 39 S (var ⲕⲱⲧⲉ = B) ὑποστ. ;
Job 11 19 S (B ⲕⲱϯ), Hab 1 11 SA (B ⲟⲩⲱⲧⲉⲃ)
μεταβάλ. ; Jer 15 5 S (B ⲕⲱϯ) ἀνακάμπτειν ; Jos
6 11 S ἀπέρχ. ; Lu 10 35 S (B ⲧⲁⲥ.) ἐπανέρχ., Jos

18 17 S (3 pl as passive) παρέρχ.; Bor 164 104 S
ϥⲛⲁⲕⲟⲧϥ from his opinions μεθιστάναι gen; Nu 30
6 S (B ⲣⲓⲕⲓ) ἀνανεύειν; Hos 9 16 A (B -ⲭⲉ) οὐκέτι
μή (cf ⲕⲱⲧⲉ refl sf), BHom 14 S ϣⲁⲕⲧⲟⲟⲩ ⲉ- to
their trading πάλιν ἐμπορευσάμενοι; R 1 2 71 S
magician ⲉϥϣⲁⲡⲕⲧⲟϥ, J 86 30 S ⲁⲓⲟⲅⲉⲣⲙ ⲕⲧⲟⲓ &
entreated, RE 9 146 S gavest me command ⲉⲧⲙ-
ⲧⲣⲁⲕⲧⲟⲓ ⲉⲁⲡⲁⲓⲧⲁ ⲉⲣⲟⲥ, Mor 37 138 S ⲛⲧⲛⲛⲁⲕⲧⲟⲛ
ⲁⲛ ⲉⲡⲁⲩ.

—— nn m, *turning, return, what surrounds*: Pro
1 3 SA (B ⲫⲱ.), Si 39 3 S sim στροφή, Is 1 27 S (B
ⲭⲓⲛⲧⲁⲥ.), Mic 2 12 A(S ⲕⲧⲏ *sic* MS, B ⲧⲁⲥ.) ἀποστ.,
Si 18 20 S ἐπιστ.; Sa 2 5 S ἀναποδισμός; Job 38
33 S (B ⲭⲓⲛϣⲓⲃ†) τροπή; ib 38 31 S (var ⲭⲟⲗⲭⲗ,
B = Gk) φραγμός; Mor 52 32 S ⲡⲉⲕ. of heathen,
Miss 4 597 S ⲧⲙⲣⲣⲉ ⲙⲡⲉⲕ. granted us (this community) by Lord, Br 45 (= 40) S what I say unto
you ⲙⲡⲉⲕ. ⲙⲡⲁϣⲁⲭⲉ *metaphor, trope* (?). ⲕ.
ⲉⲃⲟⲗ S, Ez 16 53 (B ⲧⲁⲥ. ⲉⲃ.) ἀποστροφή. ⲕ.
ⲉⲡⲁϩⲟⲩ S, J 97 62 good faith ⲉⲙⲛ ⲕ. ⲉⲡ. therein.

ⲁⲧⲕ. S adj, *irrevocable*: J 90 17 ⲟⲩⲗⲟⲅⲓⲥⲙⲟⲥ
ⲛⲁⲧⲕⲧⲟϥ.

ⲙⲛⲧⲣⲉϥⲕ. S, *v* ⲕⲱⲧⲉ refl sf.

ϭⲓⲛⲕ. S, *turning, return, repentance*: BMis 528
ⲧϭ. of sinners, P 131⁶ 52 to Virgin ⲧⲟⲩϭⲓⲛⲙⲟⲟϣⲉ
filled with all κατάστασις, ⲧⲟⲩϭⲓⲛⲕ. perfect in
beauty, Bor 295 103 ⲧϭⲓⲛⲕⲧⲟⲛ ⲉϩⲟⲩⲛ ⲉⲡⲡⲉⲑⲟⲟⲩ.

ⲕⲁⲧⲕⲉ S *v* ⲕⲁⲕⲧⲉ.

ⲕⲁⲧⲟⲩⲗⲓ B nn m, *mallow*: K 196 خبّيز.
Coptic?

ⲕⲁⲧⲙⲓⲥ (1 var ⲕⲁⲧⲙⲓⲁⲥ) B nn m, *Egyptian
mulberry*: K 178 ⲡⲓⲕ. توت مصري (but *cf* توتيا =
καδμεία calamine). Coptic?

ⲕⲧⲏⲣ S nn m, *calf*: Ex 29 1 (B ⲙⲁⲥⲓ), Lev 9
2 ⲙⲁⲥⲉ ⲡⲕ. (B do), μοσχάριον, 1 Kg 28 24 δάμαλις;
P 44 55 = 43 22 ⲙⲟⲥⲭⲟⲛ · ⲕ. عجل; 1 Kg 14 32
τέκνον βοῶν; BAp 112 ⲡⲕⲟⲩⲓ ⲡⲕ. As name:
ⲡⲉⲕⲧⲏⲣ Ann 14 124 (cf Μόσχος), CO 168 ⲕⲁⲧⲏⲣ
(same?).

ⲕⲧⲁⲣϣⲛⲟⲩⲧ B *v* ⲧⲁⲣϣⲟ.

ⲕⲟⲧⲥ SB, ⲕⲁⲧⲥ A *v* ⲕⲱⲧⲉ.

ⲕⲟⲧⲥⲓ B *v* ⲕⲱⲧⲉ.

ⲕⲧⲟⲩ S nn, *young plant, sprout* (?): P 44 66
نشأ, but prob for 43 33 ⲕⲁⲧⲟⲩⲛ قلب نشأ *young
saxifrage*. Coptic?

(ⲕⲱⲧϣ), ⲕⲁⲧϣ⳥ S vb tr, *meaning unknown*:
BKU 1 27 recipe for ἀκακία (*v* K 186) ⲛⲧⲕⲁⲧϣϥ
ⲛⲧⲱϥ ⲡⲉϥ[...& add water thereto ⲛⲧⲕⲁⲧϣϥ ⲛⲧⲁϥϥ
& set it in the sun. (? *l* ⲛⲧⲁϣⲧϥ).

ⲕⲉⲧϣⲱⲗ S *v* ⲕⲉⲗϣⲱⲧ.

ⲕⲱⲧϥ SAF, ⲕⲉⲧϥ- S, ⲕⲁⲧϥ- Sf, ⲕⲟⲧϥ⳥ S,
ⲕⲁⲧⲃ⳥ F, ⲕⲟⲧϥ† S vb, cf ꜣꜱⲩ (IgR) I tr, *gather
corn, fruit, wood &c*: Lev 19 9 S (B ⲱⲥϭ), Nu
11 8 S (var ⲥⲱⲟⲩϩ ⲉⲣⲟⲩⲛ, B ⲥⲱⲕⲓ), Mt 13 28 F
(S ⲥⲱ. ⲉϩ., B do), ib 13 48 SF (B do), Mor 37 195
S ⲉϥⲕⲉϥⲧ (*sic*, var Z 337 ⲥⲉⲗ) ϣⲉ συλλέγειν, 1 Kg
20 38 S, Miss 4 552 S = C 89 74 B do ἀναλέγειν;
Ru 2 7 S, Mic 7 1 SA συνάγειν; Deu 24 20 S ⲕ.
ⲙⲁ ⲛⲭⲟⲉⲓⲧ (B ⲥⲉⲕ ⲭ.) ἐλαιολογεῖν; Glos 226 Sf
[ⲡⲉⲧ]ⲕⲁⲧϥ ϭⲱⲃⲉ φυλλολόγος *leaf-gatherer*; ShC 73
98 S ⲕ. opp ϭⲱⲗ, ib 42 196 paral ⲭⲱⲱⲗⲉ, Mor
23 39 S robes ⲉⲣⲉⲙⲓⲭⲁⲏⲗ ⲕ. ⲙⲡⲉⲕⲁⲣⲡⲟⲥ ⲉⲣⲟⲟⲩ
= ib 24 28 F ⲕⲱⲃⲧ. II intr: ShC 42 29 ⲉⲓⲕ.
ⲭⲗⲗⲉ ⲭⲗⲗⲉ; ⲕ. ⲉⲃⲟⲗ, PLond 4 438 S sailors
ⲉⲩⲕⲟⲧϥ ⲉⲃ. ⲉⲡⲗⲟⲅⲟⲥ ⲛⲡⲕⲟⲩⲣⲥⲟⲛ *collected*; ⲕ.
ⲛⲥⲁ-, EpJer 19 F (B ⲗⲱⲭⲣ) ἐκλείχεσθαι (reading?
ἐκλέγ.).

ⲕⲱⲧϥ S nn *v* ⲕⲱⲧⲉ.

ⲕⲁⲧⲁϩ S nn m, *meaning unknown*: ST 298
ⲛⲣⲁⲗⲁϩⲱⲙ ⲉⲧⲛⲧⲡⲉ ⲙⲡⲕ. ⲛⲛϣⲁϣⲟⲧ ⲛⲧⲙⲁⲭⲁⲁⲧ.
But the words might be otherwise divided.

ⲕⲁⲩ SAF *v* ⲕⲟⲟⲩ.

ⲕⲉⲟⲩⲟⲩ B nn, *crude wax*: K 187 خام شمع
(which P 55 7 B = ⲙⲟⲩⲗϩ). Misread? for ⲕⲏ-
ⲣⲟⲛ.

ⲕⲏⲩ† S vb, *meaning unknown*: Br 90 (lost fol)
Father's great name ⲉⲧϣⲟⲟⲡ ⲭⲓⲛⲛϣⲟⲣⲡ ⲛ ⲉⲧⲕⲏⲩ
ⲉⲣⲟϥ. Improb for ϭⲏⲩ; ? *l* ⲕⲧⲏⲩ (ⲕⲧⲟ) or ⲛⲏⲩ.

ⲕⲓⲅⲏ(*sic*)B nn or adj, *meaning unknown*: N&E
39 341 possessed man, hung up in church, cried out
ⲉϥⲟⲓ ⲛⲕⲓⲅ̅ⲏ̅ saying &c.

ⲕⲓⲱⲟⲩ SF, ⲕⲓⲛⲟⲩⲧ F (Ps 16) vb (qual), *be fat,
soft*: of beasts, land, old age &c: Ge 49 20 S, Nu
13 21 S opp ⲭⲁⲭⲱ, Ps 91 14 S, Is 30 23(2) SF, Mic
6 7 S (A ⲕⲏⲓⲱⲟⲩ, all B ⲕⲉⲡⲓⲱⲟⲩⲧ) πίων, Ps 19 3
S (B do) πιαίνειν; ib 65 15 S (B ⲱⲧ) μυελοῦσθαι,
ib 16 10 F (Mor 32 2, S ⲱⲧ, B ⲭⲏⲡ); Is 30 23
(1) S (B ⲕⲉⲡ.) λιπαρός; Z 278 S remedies ⲉⲩⲕ.
ἤπιος, BMar 159 S his body polished, his fingers
ⲉⲩⲕ. τρυφερός; ShA 1 258 S fruit ⲉϥⲕ. opp ⲉϥⲡⲁϣⲧ, TT 151 S oil ⲉϥⲕ. = MG 17 444 دسم دهن,
ShIF 91 S of φασκία ⲉⲧⲕ., BM 337 S when they
see field ⲉⲥⲕ., P 129¹⁴ 115 S magnet causes iron to
become ⲉϥⲕ., Z 602 S soul's power grows not ⲉⲥⲧⲕ.
ⲁⲩⲱ ⲉⲥⲕ. through flesh eating, Aeg 15 S Jesus whose
name ⲕⲛⲡⲉ ⲁⲩⲱ ⲉϥⲕ. = ib B ⲕⲉⲡ., Mor 17 69 S
taught him with words ⲉⲩⲕ. P 44 82 S after
ⲕⲩⲡⲉⲣⲏⲥ & ⲕⲩⲡⲉⲣⲱⲛ سعد (*sic*), ⲕⲉⲃⲟⲡ · ⲕ., *l*? ⲕⲉⲃⲱ
ⲡⲕ., but cf etymol Spg 47. *Cf* Rec 39 158 n.

ⲕⲟⲟⲩ, ⲕⲱⲟⲩ (BAp) *S*, ⲕⲁⲩ *SAF* nn m, *length of time*, often with ⲛⲟϭ: 1 Kg 20 41 *S* (var ⲛⲁⲩ) συντέλεια, *ib* 25 6 *S* (var om) ⲉⲕⲉⲕ. ⲁⲡ (*l* ⲟⲡ) εἰς ὥρας *multis annis*; Ac 28 6 *S* (*B* om) ἐπὶ πολύ; Hos 7 4 *A* (*B* Gk diff) *paululum*; PS 230 *S* ⲙⲡⲕ. *whilst man shoots arrow*, ShC 73 51 *S* ⲡⲁⲕ. (no art, *cf* BM below) ⲛ ⲡϣⲁⲩ of 3 hours, BAp 98 *S* after he had ⲣ ⲟⲩⲛⲟϭ ⲡⲕ. ⲙⲡⲟⲩⲉ = MIE 2 399 *B* ⲟⲩⲡⲓϣϯ ⲡⲡⲁⲩ, *ib* 80 *S* tarried at door ⲉⲓⲥ ⲟⲩⲛⲟϭ ⲡⲕ. 355 *B* om, Mor 30 27 *F* they wept ⲡⲟⲩⲛⲟϭ ⲡⲕ. = *ib* 29 23 *S* ⲡⲁⲩ., BM 1131 *S* ⲉⲥ ⲕ. ⲙⲉⲓⲧⲛⲟⲟⲩ.

ⲕⲟⲟⲩⲉ, ⲕⲛⲉⲅⲉ, ⲕⲛⲉⲅⲉ *S*, ⲕⲁⲅⲉ *A²*, ⲕⲁⲅⲉⲓ, ⲕⲁⲩ-ⲏⲓ *F* *v* ⲕⲉ **III.**

ⲕⲟⲩⲗⲱⲗ, -ⲱⲗⲍ, -ⲱⲗ† *B* vb tr, *wrap, wind*: Job 38 9, Lu 2 7 (*S* ϭⲱⲱⲗⲉ) σπαργανοῦν; Mt 27 59 (*S* ⲕⲱⲱⲥ), Jo 20 7 (*S* ϭⲗⲟⲙⲗⲙ) ἐντυλίσσειν; Ez 17 7, MG 25 12 περιπλέκειν; Ez 2 10 (*S* ⲥⲁⲣϭⲋ) ἀνειλεῖν, Mk 15 46 (*S* ϭⲗ.) ἐνειλεῖν; Jo 19 40 (*S* ⲙⲟⲩⲣ) δέειν; TEuch 2 48 ⲣⲃⲱⲥ ⲉⲧⲟⲩⲛⲁⲕⲟⲩⲗⲱⲗⲟⲩ ⲉⲡⲓⲅⲙⲯⲁⲡⲟⲡ لفّ, Dif 1 65 wool ⲁⲥⲕⲟⲩⲗⲟⲗϥ ϩⲉⲡⲉϥⲥⲱⲙⲁ على لفّ; AM 38 ⲁϥⲕⲟⲩⲗⲱⲗⲥ ⲛⲣⲁⲛⲙⲁⲡⲡⲁ, TstAb 179, C 86 257 sim ϩⲉⲛⲣⲁⲡ-, C 43 234 snake ⲉⲧⲕ†. ⲉⲡⲉϥⲙⲟⲩⲧ, *ib* 80 ⲉⲣⲉⲡⲓⲧⲉⲃⲓ ⲕ†. ⲉⲣⲟϥ.

ⲕⲁϥⲁⲓ *B* nn as pl, *Egyptian partridge*: K 168 ⲡⲓⲕ. قطا (which P 44 56 *S* = φασιανόν). *V* AZ 30 26.

ⲕⲟⲩϥⲁⲧ *B* nn as pl, *carpet, mattress* (?): K 126 among weaver's tools (? & products) ⲡⲓⲕ. زرابي. Coptic?

ⲕⲁϥⲁϫⲓ (var ϫⲁ-) *B* nn m, *part of date-palm*: K 138 ⲡⲓⲕ. ورق الليف *lit leaf of fibre*, but *ib* 177 كرناف, *stump of branch*. *V* AZ 13 82. *Cf* ⲗⲉⲡⲁϣⲓ. As name ? Καπόοϫⲉ (Preisigke).

ⲕⲁϣ *SB*, ⲕⲉϣ *AF*, ⲕⲉϣ- *B* nn m f (rare *v s f*), *reed*: Job 40 16 *SB*, Ps 67 31 *B* (*S* ⲙⲁ ⲡⲕ.), Is 35 7 *SBF*, Mt 11 7 *SB* κάλαμος; Is 1 31 *S* (*B* ⲣⲱⲟⲅⲓ) καλάμη; as stalk: ShIF 188 *S* ⲟⲕⲩ. ⲙⲙⲁϭⲉ; as measure (5 cubits, BMOr 8781 *B* قصبة خمسة ادرع), Ez 40 3 *SB*, Ap 11 1 *SBF*, BMis 570 *S* each side of paradise measures 240,400 ⲡⲓⲕ.; as pen: Ps 44 2 *SB*, 3 Jo 13 *SB* κάλ., ShP 130³ 15 those that take ϩⲉⲛⲗⲁⲕⲙⲉ ⲡⲕ. that they may write, TT 9 *S* lay ⲕ. in καλαμάριον, AM 310 *B* ⲡⲓⲕ. ⲡⲉⲙⲡⲓⲙⲉⲗⲁ, Miss 4 188 *B* I took ⲕ. & subscribed, K 125 *B* ⲕ. ⲙⲉϥⲱⲓ قلم الشعر; as shin-bone: LMis 467 *S* break ⲕ. ⲡⲣⲁⲧⲟⲩ, *cf* 468 ⲥⲛϭⲉ ⲛⲣ.; as staff to lean on: ClPr 29 244 *S* walking ⲉϥⲧⲁϫⲣⲏⲩ ⲉϫⲛⲟⲩⲕ., Va 62 187 *B* ⲕ. in his hand ⲉϥⲟⲩⲏϩ (*sic l*) ⲉϫⲱϥ; as plough-pole:

Glos 390 *S* ἱστοβοεύς· ⲡⲕ. ⲙⲛⲧ..[; as stem (of candelabra): Nu 8 4 *B* (*S* = Gk) καυλός; as spike (? metal): C 86 278 *B* wheel with nails & ϩⲁⲡⲕ. ⲉⲩⲑⲟⲩⲍ τρυπανίσκος, *ib* 220 sim; as paling: Si 22 19 *S*, Is 29 3 *B* (*S* ϣⲱⲗϩ) χάραξ, or plantation: P 44 80 *S* ⲡⲕ. · ⲫⲟⲓⲧⲉⲅⲙⲁ قصب; large quantity: Ryl 355 *S* 40,000 reeds. in bundles: BM 1045 *S* ⲙⲁⲁⲣ ⲡⲕ. ⲡⲏⲏⲣⲉ...ⲡⲁⲥ, C 86 220 *B* ⲙⲏⲣⲓ ⲡⲕ.; as adj: Is 36 6 *SBF*, Ez 29 6 *SB* καλάμινος.

ⲙⲁ ⲡⲕ. *SA*, *bed, plantation of reeds*: Nah 1 10 *SA* (*B* ⲣⲱⲟⲅⲓ) καλάμη, P 131¹ 32 *S* ⲟⲩⲙ. ⲉϥⲟⲩⲉⲧⲟⲩⲱⲧ πόα, Ps 67 31 *S* sim (*B* ⲕ.).

ⲕⲱⲱⲣⲉ ⲕ. *S*, *pluck, gather reeds*: Ryl 340.

ϯ ⲉⲡⲕ. *S*, *hedge with reeds*: Is 5 2 (*B* ⲧⲁϩⲟ ⲉⲡⲕ.) χαρακοῦν, PS 121 ϯ ⲙⲡⲙⲁ ⲡⲉⲗⲟⲟⲗⲉ ⲉⲡⲕ., BMOr 6201 A 38 vinedresser's contract] ⲧⲁⲧⲁⲁⲩ ⲉⲡⲕ. ⲧⲁϣⲁϣⲟⲩ ⲉⲡⲕⲁ[ϩ ? ⲧⲁ]ϫⲟⲗϩⲟⲩ.

——— nn f *SB*, *reed-bed, plantation* (*cf* καλαμεία): Ryl 158 *S* ⲡⲉϩⲏⲡⲉ [ⲙⲡ]ⲧⲕ., ⲡⲉϩⲟⲟ[ⲙ ⲙⲡ]ⲧⲕ., *ib* 159, BMOr 6201 A 55 *S* ut sup ⲧⲕ. ⲧⲏⲣⲥ, CMSS 48 *B* must needs ⲕⲱϯ ϩⲁⲧⲕ.

ⲕⲱϣ *B* *v* ⲕⲱϣⲉ.

ⲕⲁϣⲉ *S* nn m, among metal utensils: ST 125 ⲥⲛⲁⲩ ⲡⲕ. ⲥⲟⲟⲩⲉ ⲡⲕⲟⲩⲛⲭⲟⲩ.

ⲕⲁϣⲱ *S*, -ⲟⲩ *B* nn as pl, among fish: P 46 237 *S* ⲡϫⲓⲣ, ⲡⲕ. قشوات, ⲡⲓϫⲏⲗ, Bodl 325 159 *B* ⲡⲕ. قشوة. Ar not found. *Cf* MIF 51 33.

ⲕⲏϣⲉ (?) *S* nn as pl, meaning unknown: Tor 42 ⲧⲁⲧⲓ ⲟⲩⲃⲗⲭⲉ ⲙⲡⲛⲕ. *Cf* ? CO 100 ⲕⲓϩⲉ (*bis*). But the words might be otherwise divided.

ⲕⲱⲱϣⲉ *S* (rare), ⲕⲱϣ *B*, ⲕⲱϣⲓ *F* (?), ⲕⲁϣ- (Ge 19), ⲕⲁϣⲍ *B*, ⲕⲟⲟϣⲉ† *S* vb **I** intr, *break, be broken*: Ex 22 10 *B* (*S* ⲧⲁⲕⲟ), Va 57 193 *B* ⲡⲧⲉⲡⲉϥϩⲏⲧ ⲕ. συντρίβειν; Jer 31 25 *B* καταγνύναι; *ib* 27 23 *B* κλᾶν; Ac 1 18 *B* (*S* ⲡⲱϣ) λακεῖν; Mk 15 19 *F* ? ⲕⲱϣⲓ (*SB* ϩⲓⲟⲩⲉ) τύπτειν; LCyp 8 *S* body ⲉϥⲕⲟⲟϣⲉ ⲉϥⲟⲩⲟϣϥ (Gk diff = Mor 18 116), C 43 140 *B* rack ⲕ. ϩⲉⲡⲧⲉϥⲙⲏϯ = Mor 48 81 *S* ⲟⲩⲱϣⲡ, MG 25 255 *B* noise of cup ϫⲉⲁϥⲕ. ⲡⲧⲟⲧϥ, PO 11 351 *B* lamp ⲕ. ⲉϫⲱϥ *upon his head*. ⲕ. ⲡⲥⲁ- *B*, *strike upon* (?): MG 25 100 took stones ⲁⲩⲕ. ⲡⲥⲁⲡⲓⲣⲟ (*cf* ϩⲓⲟⲩⲉ ⲡⲥⲁ-).

II tr, *break, split*: Ge 19 9 *B* (*S* ⲟⲩⲱϣϥ), Is 42 3 *B* (*S* ϩⲱⲣⲃ, *cf* Mt 12 20), *ib* 59 5 *B* (*S* ⲟⲩⲱϣⲡ), Ez 26 2 *B* (? refl, *l* ⲕⲟϣⲥ), Jo 19 36 *B* (*SA²* ⲟⲩⲱϣϥ) συντρ.; Mt 12 20 *B* (*S* ⲟⲩⲱϣⲡ), Jo 19 31 *B* (*S* do) καταγνύναι; Is 45 2 *B* (*S* ϩⲱⲣⲃ) συγκλᾶν; Sh(?)Mor 54 26 *S* ⲡⲧⲕ. ⲡⲥⲟⲧⲉ ⲡⲙ of evil one (*cf* Eph 6 16 ⲱϣⲙ), C 86 115 *B* ⲁϥⲕⲁϣϥ in pieces, C 43 227 *B* ⲁⲥⲕⲁϣⲟⲩ ϩⲓϫⲉⲡⲧⲟⲩⲁϥⲉ.

—— *B* nn, *a breaking* : Joel 1 7 (*S* ⲟⲩⲱϣϥ *C* 42 196, *A* ⲟⲩⲱϭⲡ vb) συγκλασμός ; a malady : C 43 85 if he hath fever, chill or ⲉϥϭⲓϯ ⲓⲧⲉ ⲟⲩⲕ. ⲛⲁϥⲉ or if distressed &c.

ⲕⲁϣⲁⲃⲉⲗ *SA* nn m, *earring* : Pro 11 22, 25 12 *A* (*S* ⲥⲁⲝⲉ, *B* ⲗⲉⲟⲛ), Hos 2 13 *A* (*B* do) ἐνώτιον ; ShA 2 64 *S* ⲡⲕ. in their ears, *ib* 329 *S* maiden ⲉⲙⲉⲩϯ ⲕ. ⲉⲣⲟⲥ ⲉⲥϣⲟⲟⲡ ϩⲓⲡⲧⲟⲉⲓⲥ.

ⲕⲁϣⲟⲩⲗⲓ *B* nn m, *desert fruit* : K 176 ثمر الواحي (Kabis AZ 13 83, Lab *desert dates*).

ⲕⲁϣⲙⲟⲩ, -ⲙⲁⲩ *S* nn, meaning unknown : CO 466 list of *varia* = Univ Coll Lond ostr duplicate.

ⲕⲟⲩϣⲧ (above ⲧ a letter, *sic* MS) *S* nn, plant or mineral : Br 114 laid on altar with vine-twigs, juniper, malabathrum, ἀμίαντος, agate, incense (?? *cf* ⲕⲉⲗϣⲱⲧ).

ⲕⲁϣⲟϣ *S* nn, tree or plant : Ryl 102 charm for painful eyes, Male iron, female iron, ⲡⲉⲡⲓⲡⲉ ⲛϣⲉ ⲡⲕ. named on Ezekiel's mount (? Ez 17 22 κέδρος), whereof lance made to pierce Jesus' side. *Cf* ? كشوش *cuscuta* Löw 230.

ⲕⲁϥ *S*, ϫⲁϥ *B* nn m, *trunk* of tree : Ex 15 27 *SB* (Va 1 اصل), Nu 33 9 *S* (var ⲥⲟⲓ) *B* (Va 1 نخلة), Job 14 9 *S* (*B* ϯ ⲟⲩⲱ), *ib* 29 18 *B* (*S* ϣⲁⲗ) στέλεχος ; Ge 40 10 *B* (Va 1 قصب, *S* ⲧⲁⲣ) πυθμήν ; P 55 10 *S*, BM 900 267 *B* ' أ.

ⲕⲱϣ *SF* vb tr, *roll up* (? = ⲕⲱⲃ) : He 1 12 *F* (*S* ⲥⲁⲣϭⲣ, *B* ⲕⲱⲗ) ἑλίσσειν. As nn (?) : Bodl(P) a 3 38 *S* (*ib* a 1 *e* om) garment to be dyed ϯ ⲕⲏⲥ ⲡⲣⲱⲙⲉ ⲉϫⲱϥ ⲙⲡⲕⲟϥϥ.

ⲕⲓϭⲓ *B* *v* ⲉⲕⲓⲃⲉ.

ⲕⲱⲱϣⲉ *S* *v* ⲕⲱⲱⲃⲉ.

ⲕⲁϥⲕⲁϥ *S* *v* ϭⲁⲃϭⲁⲃ.

ⲕⲁϩ *SAA²*, ⲕⲁϩⲓ *B*, ⲕⲉϩⲓ *F* nn m (f *v* below), a *earth*, *soil* : Ex 20 24 *SB*, Nu 5 17 *SB*, Job 42 6 *SB*, Mt 13 5 *SB* γῆ ; Lev 14 41 *S* (*B* ⲣⲏⲓⲥⲓ), 4 Kg 13 7 *S*, Ps 102 14 *SB*, Zeph 1 17 *SAB* χοῦς ; Jth 5 18 *S*, Ps 118 25 *SB* ἔδαφος ; Job 17 16 *SB* χῶμα ; Ge 11 3 *B* πηλός, Job 13 12 *S* (*B* ⲉⲣ ⲕ.) πήλινος ; *ib* 1 20 *S* (*B* ⲉⲥⲏⲧ), Jo 9 6 *SA²* (*B* do) χαμαί ; Mor 16 49 *S* (var BMis 206 ⲉⲓⲧⲛ) ⲙⲁⲣⲉⲛⲣⲟⲥϥ ⲡⲕ., MG 25 303 *B* opp ⲓⲧⲉⲛ, J 9 47 *S* ϫⲓⲡⲛⲕ. ϣⲁⲣⲁⲧⲏⲩ, paral *ib* 4 53 ⲥⲡⲧⲉ (*cf* PLond 5 170 ἔδαφος), BMis 481 *S* took ⲕ. from door = *ib* 488 ⲕⲣⲙⲉⲥ, Va 57 84 *B* ⲥⲕⲉⲩⲟⲥ ⲡⲕ. unbaked *clay*, C 41 53 *B* ϯ ⲕ. ⲉϥⲭⲏⲣⲓ ⲙⲫⲟⲣϣ ⲱⲓⲕ = Miss 4 413 طين, Bodl(P) a 1 *a S* recipe ⲧⲁⲥ ⲉⲧⲕ. ⲉϥⲗⲏⲕ, FR

104 *B* house ⲡⲕ. ⲛⲉⲙⲧⲱⲃⲓ, BSM 57 *B* we are ⲕ., ⲱⲗⲓ, ⲕⲉⲣⲙⲓ. b *earth* (opp sea, heaven), *land*, *country* : Deu 16 3 *SB*, Ps 9 36 *SB*, *ib* 41 6 *SB*, Pro 2 21 *SAB*, Is 30 23 *SBF*, Mt 24 35 *SB*, 1 Cor 8 5 *SB*, He 11 29 *SB*, Ap 7 3 *SB*, Cl 12 2 *A* all γῆ, Ps 48 11 *SB* γαῖα, Sa 15 13 *S*, ROC 17 405 *B* ⲉⲧϥⲱ ⲡⲕ. γεώδης, 1 Cor 15 40 *B* ⲡⲁⲡⲕ. (*S* ⲡⲉⲧⲣⲓⲭⲙⲡⲕ.), 2 Cor 5 1 *B* ⲉⲧⲣⲓⲭⲙⲡⲕ. (*S* ⲙⲡⲕ.) ἐπίγειος ; Job 2 2 &c *S* ἡ ὑπ' οὐρανόν ; El 100 *A* ⲡⲕ. ⲛⲁϣⲉⲟⲩⲉ, PS 109 *S* be his memory expelled ⲉⲃⲟⲗ ϩⲙⲡⲕ., Mun 53 *S* each went ⲉⲡⲉϥⲕ., BMis 367 *S* ⲡⲕ. ⲛⲕⲏⲙⲉ, R 1 3 29 *S* ⲡⲕ. ⲛⲡⲉϩⲣⲱⲙⲁⲓⲟⲥ, J 3 21 *S* ⲡⲕ. ⲉⲧⲙⲙⲁⲩ named ⲡⲕ. ⲛⲧⲣⲁⲙⲡⲉ (κράμβη ?). c measures of land *S* : ⲡⲟⲩϩ(ⲛⲱϩ) ⲡⲕ., J 107 12 ; ⲥⲧⲱⲣⲉ ⲡⲕ., *ib* 57 8, Kr 132, Ep 85 ; ⲣⲉⲣⲙⲏ ⲡⲕ., ST 41 ; ⲙⲉⲣⲟⲥ ⲡⲕ., J 110 11, COAd 3 ; also ⲙⲁ ⲡⲕ., ShA 1 244 *piece of land*.

—— *SB* f in certain place-names, *district*, *province* : PLond 4 505 *S* ⲧⲕ. ⲕⲱⲟⲩ, WS 65 *S* ⲧⲕ. ⲧⲓⲛ, J 99 4, Miss 4 535 *S* ⲧⲕ. ϣⲙⲓⲛ = C 89 95 *B*. *Cf* AZ 51 70.

ⲁⲧⲕ. *B* adj, *without ground*, off the ground : ROC '04 323 ⲁϥⲁϣϥ ⲉⲡϣⲱⲓ ⲛⲁ.

ⲣ, ⲉⲣ ⲕ. *SB*, *become earth*, *dust* : Tob 3 6 *S* γίνεσθαι γῆ ; Mor 28 188 *S* body ⲣ ⲕ. in tomb, BMar 206 *S* κολόβιον when touched ⲣ ⲕ. = Rec 6 169 *B* ⲉⲣ ⲕ. in my hand.

ⲣⲙⲕ., ⲣⲙⲡⲕ. *S*, ⲣⲉⲙⲡⲕ. *B*, *man of earth*, earth-born : Sa 7 1 *S* γηγενής ; Va 66 293 *B* ἐπίγειος ; 1 Cor 15 47 *B* (*S* diff) χοϊκός (*cf* Glos 64 *S* ⲡⲉⲃⲟⲗ ϩⲓⲡⲕ.) ; PS 124 *S* Maria ϯⲣ., Va 58 13 *B* ⲣⲉⲙⲡⲕⲉ opp ⲣ., Br 47 *S* ⲡⲟⲩⲥ ⲡⲣ., Mor 41 57 = P 131⁵ 77 *S* Christ born ⲭⲱⲣⲓⲥ ⲉⲓⲱⲧ ⲡⲣ. ; ⲣⲙⲡⲕ., ? place-name : BMEA 44721 *S* ⲁⲛⲟⲕ...ⲡⲣ. ⲉϥⲥⲣⲁⲓ ⲛ- (*v* Ep 1 118). ⲣⲱⲙⲉ ⲙⲡⲕ. *S*, *native of the soil* : Nu 9 14 (var ⲙⲡⲙⲁ ⲡⲧⲉ ⲡⲕ., *B* ⲣⲉⲙⲛⲓ ⲡⲧⲉ), Jos 9 6 αὐτόχθων.

ⲟⲩⲁⲙⲕ. *S* nn f, *earth-eater*, a corroding process or agent : JTS 5 559 of dilapidated buildings ϩⲙⲡⲧⲣⲉⲧⲟⲩ. ⲟⲩⲱⲙ ⲛⲛⲓⲙⲁ ⲙⲡ[ⲛⲥⲱⲥ] ⲁⲩϩⲉ ⲁⲡⲙⲁ ϭⲱⲗⲡ ⲉⲃⲟⲗ.

ⲃⲁⲓⲕ. *S* nn, *earth-carrier*, utensil or tool : Bodl(P) e 54 list ⲟⲩⲃ. ⲙⲛ[?]ⲛⲣⲱⲕ ⲙⲡⲥⲡⲁⲉ ⲡϫⲱⲧ.

As name (if this word) : PLond 4 426 Κάϩ = *ib* 278 Καά (same man). In place-names : C 89 200 ⲕⲁϩⲓⲟⲣ = كاهيور (Amélineau *Géog* 205, *cf* Ep 1 206 n), Miss 4 751 monastery named ⲡⲕ. ⲛⲃⲣⲣⲉ.

ⲕⲁϩ *Sᶠ* *v* ⲕⲟⲟϩ.

ⲕⲉϩ, ⲕⲁϩ (Am) *B* nn, *arm* (?), with ϯ, so *smite* : Mk 14 65 (*S* ⲕⲗϣ), 1 Cor 4 11 (*S* do), 1 Pet 2 20 (*S* ϩⲓⲟⲩⲉ) κολαφίζειν ; Am 2 7 (*SA* ⲕⲗϣ) κονδυλίζειν ; Job 31 10 (*S* = Gk) ταπεινοῦσθαι.   ϣⲉ

ⲡⲕ., *blow, buffet* : Zeph 2 8 (*SA* diff) κονδυλισμός, Mal 3 5 ϯ ϣⲉ ⲡⲕ. (*A* ϯ ⲁϫⲡ-) κονδυλίζειν. *V* ⲕⲗⲗⲉ (ⲕⲉⲗⲉⲡⲕⲉϩ).

ⲕⲟⲉⲓϩ, ⲕⲁⲓϩ *S*, ⲕⲁⲉⲓϩ *A²*, ⲕⲱⲓϩ *B* nn m, a *sheath* : 1 Kg 17 51 *S*, Jer 29 6 *SB*, Ez 21 3 *SB* (var ⲑⲏⲕⲓ) κολεός; Jo 18 11 *SA²*(*B*=Gk)θήκη; AP 22 *A²* sword into ⲡⲉⲥⲕ., C 89 187 *B* sword ϩⲉⲛⲡⲉⲥⲕ., Mor 18 53 *S* ⲧϭⲟⲣⲧⲉ from its ⲕ.   **b** *cover, case* containing book : ShP 130⁴ 157 *S* among tools &c ⲟⲩⲕ. ⲛ̄ϫⲱⲱⲙⲉ, JTS 5 564 *S* in book-list, gospels ⲛ̄ⲡⲁⲧⲕ. *without cover*, RE 9 158 *S* ⲉⲧⲉ]ⲥⲁϣϥ ⲡⲕ.ⲡⲉ namely (books named).   **c** *brickmaker's mould, form* (?) : Mor 38 86 *S* brickmaker puts brick in his basket (ϭⲓⲣ) with ⲡⲉϥⲕ. ⲙ̄ⲡⲁⲡⲉ ⲧⲱϩⲉ.   **d** *inner corner of eye* : P 46 245 *S* (scala) ⲣⲓⲙⲉ, ⲕⲁⲓϩ ميق (*l* ⲙⲁϧ), ϩⲟ (*cf* ⲕⲱⲗⲙ); *socket* (?) : Mor 41 170 *S* martyr seizes bull's horns until each ϩⲉ ⲉϩⲣⲁⲓ ϩⲙⲡⲉϥⲕ. & its ἐγκέφαλος rent in twain. *Cf* ⲕⲟⲓϩⲓ.

ⲕⲟⲟϩ *SA*, ⲕⲱϩ *S*, ⲕⲟϩ *A* (Pro 1 21) *B*, ⲕⲁϩ *Sᶠ* (Mor 17), ⲭⲟϩ *B* nn m f (rare, *v* **d**), a *angle, corner* : Ex 26 24 *S*, 4 Kg 14 13 *S*, Job 1 19 *S*, Ps 117 22 *S*, Ap 7 1 *S* (all *B* ⲗⲁⲕϩ) γωνία, Job 38 6 *S* (*B* do) γωνιαῖος, Is 28 16 *S* ⲕ. ⲛ̄ⲃⲟⲗ *B* (var ϫⲱϫ ⲛⲗ.), 1 Pet 2 6 *S* (*B* do) ἀκρογωνιαῖος; ShA 2 149 *S* ϩⲉⲛⲕ. ⲛ̄ϭⲉⲡⲛⲓ ⲏ ϩⲉⲛϫⲟ, ShIF 152 *S* scratching sores ϩⲣⲁⲓ ϩⲛϩⲉⲛⲕ. ⲛ̄ϫⲟ, BMis 208 *S* cross on pillars ⲙ̄ⲡⲕ. ⲛ̄ⲛⲏⲓ, Ryl 165 *S* on east of ⲡⲕ. ⲙ̄ⲡⲉⲛⲏⲓ, P 129¹⁸ 115 *S* laid selves below shady ⲕ. ⲙ̄ⲡⲉⲧⲣⲁ, BIF 13 112 *S* ⲡⲕ. ⲙ̄ⲡⲉϥⲡⲱⲣⲕ = MG 25 303 *B* ⲗⲁⲕϩ.   ϥⲧⲟⲟⲩ ⲡⲕ., *four-cornered* : Ge 6 14 *S* (*B* = Gk) τετράγωνος; J 21 39 *S* house ⲡⲣⲟⲥ ⲡⲉϥ. ⲡⲕ. ⲉⲧⲕⲱⲧⲉ ⲉⲣⲟϥ;   **b** *point, top* : Ge 28 18 *S* (*B*ⲗ.), Pro 1 21 *SA* (*B* do) ἄκρον; adj : Deu 8 15 *B* (*S* ⲡⲉⲧⲣⲁ ⲉⲥⲛⲁϣⲧ), Job 40 15 *S* (*B* ϭⲓⲥⲓ) ἀκρότομος; Deu 34 1 *S* (*B* ⲁϥⲉ), Mic 4 1 *SA* (*B* ϭ.) κορυφή; Jud 9 36 *S* κεφαλή; Ez 41 22 *S* (*B* ⲗ.) κέρας; Jos 18 19 *S* λοφιά, Lu 4 29 *S* (*B* ϭ.) ὀφρύς; Mor 17 43 *Sᶠ* ⲡⲕⲁϩ *prow of ship* ἐξοχή; Mor 40 44 *S* = MG 25 270 *B* there was ⲟⲩⲕ. ⲡⲧⲟⲟⲩ in road, BMar 210 *S* = Rec 6 174 *B* I mounted upon ⲟⲩⲕ. ⲡⲧⲟⲟⲩ.   **c** *fragment, piece* : BMis 193 *S* 2 small ⲕ. ⲛ̄ϣⲉ for making cross, Aegyptus 3 280 *S* ⲁⲓⲧⲁϩⲟ ⲟⲩⲕ. (ⲛ)ⲙⲁ & built thereon house, Ryl 357 *S* 2 ⲕ. ⲙ̄ⲙⲁ, BKU 1 135 *S* ⲕ. ⲡⲉⲓⲱϩⲉ, Miss 4 749 *S* ⲕⲟⲩⲓ ⲡⲕ. ⲡⲟⲉⲓⲕ, BMOr 9525(1) *S* ⲕ. ⲡⲭⲁⲣⲧⲓⲛ, BM 1135 *S* ⲕ. ⲛ̄ⲟⲃⲛ, Bodl(P) a 2 25 half a ⲕ. ⲡⲁⲗⲣⲱϩⲁⲙ (الرخام), PRain 4725 *S* I send ⲕⲟⲩⲓ ⲡⲕ. ϩⲛⲟⲟⲓⲧⲉ of Apa Severus, PBu 96 *S* ⲡⲉⲓⲕ. ⲛ̄ϣⲁϫⲉ.   **d** *rarely* f : Ps 113 8 *B* ἡ ἀκρότομος (sc πέτρα), BM 479 *S* ⲃⲧⲟ ⲡⲕ. ⲉⲥⲟⲓ (*l* ⲛⲥⲟⲓ), PBu 94 *S* ⲧⲙⲟⲣⲡ ⲡⲕ. ⲛ̄ⲥⲭⲓⲧⲁⲣⲓⲛ (σχεδάριον), Mor 56 60 *S* mount of ⲧⲕ. = P ar

4888 153 جمبل ادكوهي . As name : *Κόοϩ* (Preisigke); place-name : CO 57 ⲡⲕⲱϩ (*v* Ep 1 118).

ⲕⲟⲩϩ *S* nn, *meaning unknown* : BP 10589 ye know ϫⲉϩⲉⲡⲟⲭⲗⲏⲣⲟⲥⲡⲉ ⲡⲕ. ⲙⲡⲉⲛⲏⲉⲓ ⲡⲁⲣⲁ ⲣⲱⲙⲉ ⲛⲓⲙ. Or *l* ? ⲕⲟⲩ ϩⲙ-.

ⲕⲱϩ *SAA²F*, ⲭⲟϩ *B*, ⲕⲏϩ† *S* vb intr, *be envious, zealous, emulate* : 3 Kg 19 10 *S*, Si 45 36 *S*, Ac 17 5 *SB*, 1 Cor 13 4 *SB*, BM 247 4 *S* if another be preferred ⲙⲉϥⲕ. ζηλοῦν; ShC 73 23 *S* ⲧⲡⲕ.† ⲧⲏⲙⲟⲥⲧⲉ, J 96 29 *S* our child being sick ⲉⲡⲕ. beholding others hale.   Obj with ⲉ- : Ge 30 1 *SB*, Nu 11 29 *S* (*B* dat), Ps 72 3 *S* (ἐπί, *B* ⲉϩⲣⲏⲓ ⲉϫⲉⲛ-), Si 51 20, Is 11 11 *B* (*S* ϯ ⲕ.), Zech 1 14 *SAB*, 1 Cor 14 39 *SBF*, BHom 57 *S* ⲕ. ⲉⲡⲉⲥⲙⲟⲧ ⲡⲧⲁⲓ ζηλ., Si 26 6 *S* ἀντίζηλος, Ps 36 1 *SB* παραζηλοῦν; BMar 157 *S* enemies ⲕ. ⲉⲣⲟⲟⲩ μιμητὴς γίνεσθαι; Z 284 *S* Saul ⲁϥⲕ. ⲉϩⲁⲅⲉⲓⲁ, AM 21 *B* ⲁⲩⲭ. ⲉϩⲟⲩⲛ ⲉϯⲙⲉⲧⲙⲁⲣⲧⲩⲣⲟⲥ, Aeg 260 *S* ⲉⲣⲉⲡϩⲉⲑⲛⲟⲥ ⲕ.† ⲉⲣⲟⲛ, C 89 18 *B* strove ⲉⲭ. ⲉⲣⲟϥ in all things, ShA 2 17 *S* ⲉϥⲕ.† ⲉⲧⲣⲉⲡⲉϥϩⲛⲓ ϣⲱⲡⲉ ⲉϥⲟⲩⲁⲁⲃ, ShIF 238 *S* ⲡⲥⲱⲟⲩϩ ⲉϩⲟⲩⲛ...ⲉϯⲕ.† ⲉⲧⲣⲉϥϫⲱⲕ ⲉⲃⲟⲗ ⲕⲁⲗⲱⲥ.   With ⲉϫⲡ- : Ro 10 19 *SB* ϯⲛⲁⲕ. ⲛⲏⲧⲛ ⲉϫⲡ- παραζηλ. ἐπί, *v* Ps 72 3 above.

ⲣⲉϥⲕ., ⲭ. *SAB*, *zealous person, rival, imitator* : Ex 34 14 *B* (*S* ⲕ.), Nah 1 2 *SAB*, Lu 6 15 *B* (*S* = Gk), Gal 1 14 *SB* ζηλωτής; Nu 5 14 *S* (*B* ⲭ.) ζήλωσις; ShWess 9 134 *S* Origen ⲉⲁϥⲣ ⲣ. ⲉⲧⲁⲅⲟ ⲛ̄ⲡϣⲁϫⲉ ⲛ̄ⲡⲓⲟⲩⲁⲓ, ShHT *B* 67 *S* become ⲣ. ⲁⲩⲱ ⲛ̄ⲕⲟⲓⲛⲱⲛⲟⲥ of heresy, ROC 20 45 *S* ⲣ. ⲉⲧⲁⲛⲁⲥⲧⲣⲟⲫⲏ of righteous.

—— *SAA²BF* nn m, *envy, zeal* : Job 5 2 *SB*, Pro 6 34 *SAB*, Jo 2 17 *SA²BF*, 2 Cor 12 20 *SBF* ζῆλος, Nu 5 15 *SB*, BM 174 1 *S* ⲙⲉⲥⲃⲱⲗ ⲉⲃⲟⲗ ϩⲛⲟⲩⲕ. ζηλοτυπία; PS 81 *S* hated me ϩⲛⲟⲩⲕ., AM 132 *B* ⲡⲁⲓⲭ. ⲡⲟⲩⲱⲧ *this same zealous* (service), DeV 2 160 *B* great ⲡⲁⲭ. toward you, saints.

ϯ ⲕ., ⲭ. *SB*, *cause envy, make zealous* : Nu 11 29 *B* (*S* ⲕ. ⲉ-), Is 11 11 *S* (*B* ⲟⲣⲉ ⲭ.), 2 Cor 11 2 *SB* ζηλοῦν, Ps 77 58 *SB*, Ro 10 19 *SB* παραζηλ.; Bar 4 7 *B* παροξύνειν, He 10 24 *B* (*S* = Gk) παροξυσμός; EpJer 43 *B* (*F* ϯ ϣⲱϣ) ὀνειδείζειν (*cf* ϩⲓ ⲭ.); 2 Cor 9 2 *B* (*S* ⲧⲱⲃⲥ) ἐρεθίζειν; MG 17 299 *S* ⲉϥϯ ⲕ. ⲛⲁⲡ ⲉϩⲟⲩⲛ ⲉⲡⲉⲕⲃⲓⲟⲥ (var Ming 171 ⲕⲱⲧ, prob error), PO 11 355 *B* sim.

ϩⲓ ⲭ. *B*, *upbraid* : Mt 11 20 (*S* ⲛⲟϭⲛⲉϭ) ὀνειδείζειν.

ⲕⲟⲓϩⲉ *S* nn f, *rival woman* : Si 37 12, Lev 18 18 ⲟ ⲛⲕ. (*B* ⲉⲥⲟⲑⲏⲥ ϩⲉⲡⲟ ⲣⲭⲟϩ) ἀντίζηλος.

ⲭⲟⲣⲭⲉϩ *B*, ⲭⲉⲣⲭⲟϩ† (AZ 14 18) vb tr, *make zealous* : Dif 1 84 ⲡⲉϥⲭ. ⲡⲛⲉϥϣⲏⲣⲓ toward virtue كست.

(ⲕⲱϩ) *SB*, ⲕⲉϩ- *S*, ⲕⲁϩⲋ *SB*, ⲕⲏϩ† *S*, ⲕⲉϩ† *B* vb
I tr, *make level, smooth, tame*: PS 158 *S* ⲁⲧⲉⲕϭⲓⳉ
ⲕⲉϩ ⲧⲉϩⲓⲏ (= Od Solom 22 7 ـهـل), Va 58 188 *B*
road ⲉⲧⲁⲛⲕⲁϩⳗ ⲛⲁⲛ to God's service, Va 68 170 *B*
calf ⲉⲧⲉⲙⲡⲟⲩⲕⲁϩⳗ ἀδάμαστος; Mus 40 37 (Reg
Pachom) *S* ⲡⲛⲉⳓⲓ ⲉⲓⳓⲟⲥ ⲉⲕⲁϩⳗ without leave
(Gk *ib* 37 19, Lat *ib* 40 49 ? mistransl of ἐπικενῶσαι,
aemulari). ⲕ. ⲉⲃⲟⲗ: Études Leemans 89 *S* =
Mor 47 141 *S* art thou come ⲉⲕⲉϩ ⲉϩⲧⲟ ⲉⲃ. *to tame
horses* (v KKS 538, Rec 37 21; P ar 4793 46 om,
v Amélineau *Contes* 2 50. **II** intr (qual) ⲥ ⲉ-,
be familiar, accustomed: BIF 13 107 *S* ⲡⲥⲉⲕ. ⲁⲛ
ⲉⲡⲉⲓⲣⲓⲥⲉ = MG 25 291 *B*, *ib* 236 *B* they went to
pool ⲉⲡⲁⲩⲕ. ⲉⲣⲟϥ, ROC 25 240 *B* disciple ⲛⲁϥⲕ.
ⲉⲣⲟϥⲡⲉ ⲉⲙⲁϣⲱ, K 233 *B* ⲉϥⲕ. مستأنس.

ⲕⲁϩⲥ *B* nn f, *custom*: Bel 14, Lu 2 42 (*S* ⲥⲱⲡⲧ),
He 10 25 (*S* do), C 86 298 ⲟⲩⲕ. ⲁⲛⲧⲉ of Galileans
ἔθος; Nu 24 1 (*S* do), Mt 27 15 (*S* ⲡⲉϣⲁⲣⲉ- + vb)
εἰωθώς; 1 Cor 8 7 (*S* ⲧⲱⲛ) συνηθεία; Ac 26 5 (*S*
= Gk) αἵρεσις; HL 103 ⲁϥⲓⲛⲓ ⲛⲟⲩⲕ. ⲉⲃⲟⲗ ⲉϫⲉⲛ⳿
ⲛⲓⲥⲛⲏⲟⲩ, Miss 4 200 physicians ⲧⲟⲩⲕ.ⲧⲉ to cut
off diseased limbs. ⲉⲣ ⲕ., *become custom*: MG
25 56 ⲁⲥⲉⲣ ⲕ. ⲡⲱⲟⲩ ⲉⲙⲟⲩϯ, HL 103 ⲁϥⲁⲓ ⲉⲣ ⲕ.
ⲡⲱⲟⲩ.

ⲕⲁϩⲕ *SABF*, ⲕⲉⲣⲕⲉϩ- *S*, ⲕⲉⲣⲕⲱϩⳗ *SF*, ⲕⲉⲣ-
ⲕⲱϩ† *S*, ⲕⲁⲣⲕⲁϩⲧ† *A*, ⳝⲉⲣⳝⲟⲟⲣⲧ† *B* vb tr, **a** *hew
out, smooth*: Ex 34 1 *S* (*B* diff), Deu 3 27 *S* (*B*
ϥⲱⲧϩ), Ez 40 42 *S* (*B* ϣⲟⲕϣⲉⲕ), Lu 23 53 *S* (*B*
ϣⲱⲕⲓ) λαξεύειν; Is 51 1 *S* (*B* ϥ.), Mt 27 60 *S*
(*B* ϣⲱⲕⲓ) λατομεῖν, 4 Kg 12 12 *S* λατομητός, Nu
21 18 *S* (*B* ϥ.) ἐκλατομεῖν; Pro 15 19 *SA*, Mor
37 50 *S* ⲟⲩϩⲓⲛ...ⲉⲥⲕ.† τρίβεσθαι; BM 920 266 =
Ryl 453 337 *B* ⲉⲧⳝ.† الطرقة; ShC 42 191 *S*
paths ⲉⲛⲧⲁⲩⲕⲉⲣⲕⲱϩⲟⲩ to walk therein, ShR 2 3
13 *S* path ⲕ.† ⲁⲩⲱ [ⲛ]ⲟⲩⲅⲉⲥⲧⲱⲛ (Mt 7 13), BMis
204 *S* ⲙⲁⲣϥⲕ. ⲙⲡⲧⲁⲫⲟⲥ, BM 1109 *S* ⲁϥϭⲛ ⲧⲉⲙ⳿
ϩⲁⲣⲧ ⲙⲡⲕⲟⲧ ⲁⲥⲟⲩⲟⲙⲉϥ ϣⲁϥ[ⲣ ⳝ]ⲉⲣⲓⲁ ⲡⲕⲉⲣⲕⲱϩⲥ,
Dif 2 22 *B* Antony ⲉⲧⲁⲕ. ⲛⲁⲛ ⲙⲡⲓⲙⲱⲓⲧ. ⲃ
make smooth, cause to heal up, of wound: PMéd 103
S lay it upon wound ϣⲁⲥⲕⲉⲣⲕⲱⲥ, *ib* 174 ϣⲁϥ⳿
ⲕⲉⲣⲕⲱϩⲟⲩ & dries them up; also intr: PMich
593 *S* wounds ⲉⲧⲉϣⲁⲩⲱⲥⲕ ⲉⲕ.

ⲣⲉϥⲕⲉⲣⲕ- *S*, *hewer of stone*: BMis 204 ⲣⲱⲙⲉ
ⲛⲗⲁⲧⲟⲗⲟⲥ ⲛⲣ. ⲱⲛⲉ.

ⲕⲁϩⲕ, ⲕⲉⲣⲕ- *S*, ⲕⲁϩⲕⲉ-, ⲕⲉⲣⲕⲉ- *B* vb **a** tr, meanings same: Deu 10 1 *S* (*B* ϥⲱⲧϩ), Is 9 10 *S* (*B* do)
λαξεύειν; *ib* 22 16 *S* (*B* do) λατομεῖν. **b** intr, *be
healed*: Lev 13 18 *B* (*S* ⲗⲧⲟⲛ) ὑγιάζειν; PMéd
219 *S* ⲛⲃⲁⲗ ⲉⲧⲕⲏⲕ ϣⲁⲩⲧⲣⲉⲩⲕ. & grow eyelashes,
ib 294 *S* causing wounds ⲉⲧⲣⲉⲗⲟ ⲛⲥⲉⲕ., *ib* 240
sim. As nn *B*: CDan 88 ⲡⲓⲕⲉⲣⲕⲉ ⲱⲡⲓ λατόμος. ⲣⲉϥⲕⲉⲣⲕ-: Si 45 18 *S* λιθουργός, CDan
87 *B* ⲣⲉϥⲕⲁϩⲕⲉ ⲱⲡⲓ.

ⲕⲁϩⲣ *B*, ⲕⲉⲣⲓ *F* v ⲕⲁϩ.

ⲕⲟⲓϩⲉ *S* v ⲕⲱϩ be envious.

ⲕⲟⲓϩⲓ *B* nn m, ? same as ⲕⲟⲉⲓϩ: K 74 فرق ونجي
الغلاف, but most MSS ⲙⲟⲓϩⲓ & عرق; AZ 13 83
مرفق *elbow*.

ⲕⲱϩⲃ *Sf* nn(?), meaning unknown: BM 678 in
account ⲙⲁ ⲛϭⲁⲗ ϩⲣⲏ, ⲙⲁ ⲛⲕ., ⲙⲁ ⲛⲕⲱⲧ (? *l* ⲕⲟⲧ).
Since camels are mentioned ? *l* ⲕⲱⲃϩ. (ⲙⲁ = ϩⲁⲡⲙⲁ,
ϩⲁⲙⲁ).

ⲕⲁϩⲕ v ⲕⲱϩ *make level*.

ⲕⲟⲓⲁϩⲕ, ⲕⲓⲁϩⲕ, ⳝⲟⲓⲁϩⲕ (oftenest), ⳝⲓⲁϩⲕ,
ⳝⲟⲓⲁⲕ, ⳝⲟⲓⲁ ⳝ, ⳝⲁⲓⲁⲕ (Ann 8 91), ⳝⲟⲓⲁⲕϥ
(Wor 124) *S*, ⲕⲁⲓⲁⲕ *A* (Rec 11 149), ⳝⲟⲓⲁⲕ *B*,
ⲕⲓⲁ ⳝ (BM 671), ⳝⲓⲁⲕ (Kr 72) *F* nn, name of 4th
month, Gk Χοιάκ, Ar كيهك. *Cf* AZ 52 112.

ⲕⲁϩⲕ v ⲕⲱϩ *make level*.

ⲕⲟϩⲗⲉϥ *B* v ϩⲟⲕⲗⲉϥ.

ⲕⲱϩⲙⲉ *S* nn (?), meaning unknown: Ryl 243
list of clothing (ⲟⲩ)ⲁⲗⲕⲁⲡⲁ ⲛⲕ., so a quality of
veil (القناع) or its use.

ⲕⲉⲣⲛⲓ *B* v ⲕⲛⲣⲉ.

ⲕⲁϩⲥ v ⲕⲱϩ *make level*.

ⲕⲁϩⲧ *S* nn f, prob *l* ⲕⲁⲗⲁϩⲧ. *V* ϩⲱⲡⲉ.

ⲕⲱϩⲧ *SAA²F* nn m, *fire*: Lev 21 9 *S*, Job 1
16 *S*, Ps 96 3 *S*, Pro 6 27 *SA*, Is 30 14 *SF*, Joel
2 3 *S* (*A* ⲥⲉⲧⲉ), Mic 1 7 *A* (*S* ⲥⲁⲧⲉ), Mt 3 12 *S*
(var ⲥ.), Jo 15 6 *SA²*, Ja 3 5 *SA* (all *B* ⳝⲣⲱⲙ)
πῦρ; Ap 8 10 *S* (*B* do) λαμπάς; Is 1 31 *S* ⲧⲓⲕ. ⲛⲕ.
(*B* do) σπινθήρ; Ob 18 *S* ϣⲁϩ ⲛⲕ. (*B* ϣⲁϩ) φλόξ;
Mk 14 54 *S* = Lu 22 56 *S*, Ac 16 29 *S* (all *B*
ⲟⲩⲱⲓⲛⲓ) φῶς; PS 77 *S* ⲛⲕ. ⲛⲥⲁⲃⲉ across which
the perfect pass, ShC 73 137 *S* let not over much
wood be cast ⲉϩⲟⲩⲛ ⲉⲡⲕ., Pcod 6 *S* angels are ϩⲉⲛⲕ.
(*cf* He 1 7), AZ 23 105 *S* recipe ⲧⲁⲗⲟⲟⲩ ⲉⲡⲕ.,
BM 527 *F* sim ⲁϣⲟⲩ ϩⲓⲡⲕ., Leyd 168 *S* = P 129²⁰
159 *S* rubric ⲛϣⲁ ⲙⲡⲕ. on 20th Hathor. Adj:
Ap 9 17 *S* (*B* ⳝ.) πύρινος, Sa 11 19 *S* ⲛϭⲉ ⲛⲕ.
πυροπνόος, Job 41 20 *S* (*B* ϣⲁϩ ⲛⳝ.) πυροφόρος,
BM 184 1 *S* ⲥⲟⲃⲧ ⲛⲕ., Mor 23 35 *S* pits full of
ⲁⲗ ⲛⲕ.

ϯ ⲣ ⲕ. *S*, *be of fire*: PS 46 half ⲟ ⲛⲕ. other half
ⲟ ⲛⲕⲁⲕⲉ, Mich 550 29 ⲉϣⲁϥⲣ ⲕ. ⲧⲏⲣϥ ⲛϥⲉⲣ ⲟⲩⲟ⳿
ⲉⲓⲛ, PMéd 149 eyes ⲉⲧⲱ ⲛⲕ.

† ⲕ. or ⲛⲕ. *S*, *put fire, set on fire*: Jos 8 19
ἐμπιπράναι, 2 Kg 14 30 ἐμπυρίζειν; Mor 16 68
ⲧⲉⲓⲡⲟⲗⲓⲥ ⲁⲩϯ ⲕ. ⲉⲣⲟⲥ = BMis 216 ⲣⲱⲕϩ.

ϫⲓ ⲕ. *S*, *take, undergo fire*: Ep 574 in recipe sulphur ⲉⲁϥϫⲓ ⲕ. *Cf* ϭⲓ ⲭⲣⲱⲙ.

As name (nickname?): BMis 461 Apa Aphou ⲡⲕ. (same saint in an Abydos graffito).

ⲕⲉϩⲧⲉ *S* nn f sg & pl (prob dual), *loin, hip*: Cant 7 2 μηρός; Si 47 24 λαγών; Ez 44 18 (CA 91) ὀσφύς; Br 269 ⲧⲕ. ⲥⲛⲧⲉ, R 2 1 71 among beauties of body ϩⲉⲛⲕ. ⲉⲩⲙⲉϩ, PSBA 26 178 Jesus's birth ⲙⲛϥϯ...[ⲛ]ⲟⲩⲧⲕⲁⲥ ⲛⲛⲟⲩⲕ., Z 629 recipe for ⲡⲉⲧϩⲱϩ ϩⲓϫⲉⲛⲧⲉⲩⲕ. = PMéd 314 ⲛⲉⲩⲕ.

ⲕⲁϫ *S* nn m sg & pl, meaning unknown, relates to agriculture: Bodl(P) b 9 account ϩⲁⲧⲧⲓⲙⲏ ⲛⲟⲩⲕ., Ann 22 272 we authorize thee ⲧⲁⲣⲕϫⲟ ⲛⲕ. ⲕⲁⲕⲉ ϩⲙⲡϫⲟ ⲉϩⲣⲁⲓ (καταсπορά) ⲛⲧⲉⲣⲟⲙⲡⲉ, Hall 41 ⲛϭⲱⲙ ⲛⲕ. ⲉⲥ [ⲁⲡⲛⲟⲩⲧⲉ] ⲥⲟⲃⲧⲉ ⲁⲛϫⲟⲗⲉϥ, J 122 37 shares of land include ⲕ. ⲙⲙⲁⲁϫⲉ (?), CO 198 ⲛⲕ. (context uncertain), ST 371 ⲛⲉⲓⲕ. (do).

ⲕⲱϫ *S* *v* ϭⲱϫ.

ⲕⲁϫⲓ *B* nn m, *pitcher, bucket*: K 246 ⲁⲛⲑⲗⲏⲙⲁ (ἄντλημα) ⲡⲓⲕ. ⲙⲙⲁϩ ⲙⲱⲟⲩ دلو, *ib* 248 ⲕⲣⲁⲧⲏⲣ ⲡⲓⲕ. ⲡⲉ ⲓⲉ ⲡⲓⲥⲓⲧⲗⲁ باطية, سطل. ? *l* ⲕⲁⲇⲓ κάδος (*cf* Jo 4 11 *S*).

ⲕⲟⲩϫⲓ *B* *v* ⲕⲟⲩⲓ.

ⲕϫⲁ *S* nn m, meaning unknown: ST 149 title in list of names ⲡⲁⲙⲙ ⲡⲕ.

ⲕⲁϫⲓϥ *v* ϭⲁϫⲓϥ.

ⲕⲁϫϩⲉ *S* nn, meaning unknown: Hall 57 boundaries ⲡϣⲟⲛⲧⲉ ⲛⲕ. ⲙⲛⲛⲓⲱϩ ⲗⲁⲕⲱⲛ.

ⲕⲟⲩϫⲟⲩ *v* ⲕⲟⲩⲛϫⲟⲩ.

ⲕⲉϫⲉⲙ *B* *v* ⲕⲉ **II a**.

ⲕⲟⲩϭⲓ *F* *v* ⲕⲟⲩⲓ.

ⲗ

ⲗ eleventh letter of alphabet, called ⲗⲁⲩⲇⲁ (*i e* λάβδα, K 1, P 43 242 لودا), ⲗⲁⲩⲗⲁ (My 66, 117, Stern p 7, though these ? mere confusion of ⲇ & ⲗ), ⲗⲟⲗⲉ (Stern p 418) لولا; *cf* Preisigke *W.buch* 1 723 λάλ. As numeral *BF*, rarely *S*, ⲗ = *thirty* (ⲙⲁⲁⲃ). Derived from hierogl *l-r*, sign or signs representing both sounds & parent of both in Coptic (Stern 33, Sdff 11, 12, Till 35) as ⲁⲗⲕⲉ, ⲉⲓⲟⲩⲗ, ⲕⲗⲟⲙ, ⲗⲟⲕ, ⲥⲟⲗ, ⲟⲩⲱⲱⲗⲉ, ϣⲗϩ nn, ϭⲱⲗϫ; rarely from *m*, as ⲗⲉ-ⲙⲏⲏϣⲉ, ⲗⲁ-ϣⲁⲛⲉ (or ? here from *r*); or *n*, as ⲗⲁⲥ, ⲙⲟⲩⲗϩ, ⲧⲗⲟⲙ (var ⲧⲛⲟⲙ). Dialectal equivalents: **a** ⲗ = ⲣ, esp *F* (purest *F* texts show this oftenest, Asmus 7 ff), as ⲁⲗⲏⲟⲩ (ⲉⲣⲏⲩ), ⲃⲓⲗ, ⲉⲗⲧⲁⲃ, ⲏⲗⲡ, ⲗⲁⲕⲁⲧⲓ (ⲣⲁⲕⲟⲧⲉ Kr 22), ⲗⲓⲗ, ⲡⲁⲡⲁⲗⲉ (πανάριον BM 707), ⲧⲣⲓⲗ (*ib* 1221), ⲟⲩⲉⲛⲁϥⲉⲗ (CMSS 68), ⲱⲗ (Hôr), ϣⲏⲗⲓ, ϩⲁⲑⲟⲗ; also *S*, as ⲃⲉⲗⲉⲧⲁⲣⲓⲟⲥ (*veredarius* Miss 4 638, BMis 147), ⲉⲗⲩⲑⲣⲁ (BMis 498), ⲕⲗⲩⲥⲧⲁⲗⲟⲥ (Ps 148 8), ⳍⲟⲩⲗ (BP 9517), ⲗⲟⲙⲡⲉ (& ⲣⲟⲙⲡⲉ, BM 1119), ⲗⲟϩⲧⲉ (PLond 4 516), ϭⲟⲗⲧⲉ (*ib* 508), ⲡⲗⲟⲟⲥ (πρός *ib* 454). **b** replaced by ⲣ *S*, as ⲁⲅⲉⲣⲁⲣⲭⲏⲥ (BMis 530), ⲃⲱⲣ (PLond 4 473), ⲉⲃⲟⲩⲣ (ⲉⲃⲟⲗ BM 1119), ⲉⲡⲓⲥⲧⲟⲣⲏ (*ib* 1120), ⲉⲣⲉⲡⲟⲛ (λοιπόν *ib* 1103), ⲏⲣ (ⲏⲗ אל Leyd 456), ⲕⲁⲣⲱⲥ (BM 1120), ⲣⲕⲉ (ⲁⲗⲕⲉ CO 303), ⲣⲉⳍⲁⲣ (Λάζαρος R 1 1 20), ⲧⲁⲣⲟ (PLond 4 473); both: ⲉⲣⲗⲉⲅⲓⲛ (ἐλέγχειν AM 127); ⲗ & ⲣ vary also in ⲣⲙⲁⲛ *S* = ⲗⲉϩⲙⲉⲛ *A*, ϩⲉⲣϣⲓⲣⲉ *S* = ϩⲉⲗϣⲏⲣⲓ *B*. **c** ⲗ = ⲛ *F* (rarely): ⲃⲉⲗⲓⲁⲙⲓⲛ (BMEA 10585), ⲟⲩⲉⲗ ⲗⲁⲁⲩ (Mor 30 35); also in ϭⲣⲙⲡϣⲁⲛ *S*, ϭⲣⲟⲙⲡϣⲁⲗ *B*; ⲛ assimilated to following ⲗ *S* (archaic, *cf* ⲣ), as ⲗⲗⲁⲟⲥ, ⲗⲗⲁⲙⲡⲁⲥ. **d** in transcriptions of Ar ⲗ represents ل, as ⲉⲗϫⲉⲃⲉⲗ الجبل, ⲕⲁⲗ قال, ⲭⲉⲗⲉⲙ كلام (EW 234 ff); or where Ar transcribed, as ⲧⲁⲗⲕ طلق, ⲙⲁϩⲗⲟⲩⲗ محلول (AZ 23 118 ff), ⲗⲟⲩⲗⲟⲩ لولو (PMéd 150); sometimes ⲗ = ر (PMéd), as ⲁⲥϥⲁⲗ اصفر, ⲕⲁⲗⲁⲛⲃⲟⲩⲗ قرنفل, ⲙⲟⲩⲗ مر.

ⲗⲁ *SAB*, ⲗⲉ *F* nn m, *envy, slander*: Ro 1 29 *S* (*B* = Gk), 1 Pet 2 1 *S* (*B* do) φθόνος; Ps 118 134 *S* (*B* ⲙⲉⲑⲛⲟⲩϫ), Am 2 8 *F* (JEA 11 246, *S* ⲙⲛⲧⲗⲁ, *A* ⲙⲛⲧⲁⲛϭⲗⲁ) συκοφαντία; Job 18 14 *S* (*B* = Gk) αἰτία *interitus*; P 44 73 = 43 46 *S* ⲙⲩⲥⲧⲟⲩⲥ (? μῖσος) · ⲡⲗⲁ بغى; PS 256 *S* renounce ⲡⲗⲁ ⲛⲛⲟⲩϫ, Mor 52 32 *S* devil's wiles ϩⲉⲛⲗⲁ ⲛⲛⲟⲩϫ, ShA 1 396 *S* ⲕⲁⲧⲁⲗⲁⲗⲓⲁ, ϭⲟⲗ, ⲗⲁ, Bodl(P) b 5 *S* God knoweth (ⲙ)ⲡⲉⲕⲉⲣ ⲛⲟⲃⲉ ϩⲛⲛⲗⲁ ⲛⲧⲁⲩⲛⲟϫϥ ⲛⲥⲱⲕ.

ⲙⲛⲧⲗⲁ *S* nn f, *slander*: Eccl 7 8 (*F* ⲙⲛⲧⲛⲟⲩϫ) συκοφαντία; Deu 17 8 (*B* ϭⲟϩ) ἀφή.

ϩⲓ ⲗⲁ *SA* (ϩⲟⲩ-) *B* vb intr, *slander*: Si 51 6 *S* διαβολή; Br 102 *S* ⲛϥⲧⲙϩ. ⲛⲛⲟⲩϫ paral ⲕⲁⲧⲁⲗⲁⲗⲉⲓ. c ⲉ-: Ge 43 18 *S* (*B* ϭⲓ ⲛϫⲟⲛⲥ), Lev 19 11 *S* (*B* do), Pro 14 31 *SA*, Lu 3 14 *S* (*B* do), Z 296 *S* = MG 25 204 *B* συκοφαντεῖν; Mor 17 21 *S* καταψεύδεσθαι; Sa 10 14 *S* μωμᾶσθαι; ShBMOr 8800 202 *S* Origen ϩ. ⲉⲡⲉⲭ̅ⲥ̅, BMis 166 *S* theft ⲉⲧⲟⲩϩ. ⲉⲣⲟⲓ ⲉⲧⲃⲏⲏⲧⲥ = BSM 75 *B* ϫⲉⲙ ⲗⲱⲓϫⲓ, C 89 80 *B* ⲫⲏ ⲉⲧⲁⲩϩ. ⲛⲛⲟⲩϫ ⲉⲣⲟϥ, BMis 395 *S*

ⲙⲡⲣϩ. ⲉⲣⲟⲛ with thy words = Va 63 17 B ϧⲓ ϧⲉⲗⲓ.

ϧⲓ ⲗⲁ S nn m, meaning same: Si 26 5 καταψευσμός, BAp 119 ⲡϧ. ⲛⲡⲟⲩⲭ, R 2 4 88 ⲟⲩϩ. ⲡⲗⲁⲥ.

ϧⲓ ⲁⲗⲗⲁ B, var of ϧⲓ ⲗⲁ: MG 25 71 ⲉⲧⲁϥϧⲓ ⲗⲁ ⲛⲡⲟⲩⲭ ⲉⲣⲟⲕ var ϧⲓ ⲁⲗⲗⲁ.   As nn: MIE 2 367 vices ⲡⲓϧ. ⲡⲓⲑⲓϭⲓ, K 238 ⲡⲓϧ. كثر الكلام (though this ib 94 = ⲗⲁⲥⲁⲭⲓ φλυαρός, cf AZ 12 125.   In BMar 108 sup S ϧⲓ ⲁⲗⲗⲁ cannot be same.

ⲣⲉϥϧⲓ ⲗⲁ S, slanderer: Ps 71 4 (B ⲥⲁ ⲙⲙⲉⲑⲛⲟⲩⲭ) συκοφάντης; ShP 130³ 9 ⲣⲉϥϧ. ⲉⲧⲙⲉ.

ⲙⲛⲧⲣⲉϥϧⲓ ⲗⲁ S nn f, slander, calumny: Miss 8 141, BHom 51 συκοφαντία, ib 26 λοιδορία, ShLeyd 355 Jesus bore ⲙ. ϧⲓⲧⲡⲟⲩⲥⲩⲕⲟⲫⲁⲡⲧⲏⲥ.

ⲗⲁⲃⲗⲁ S adj, eager for slander: ShA 2 309 ⲉⲣⲃⲏⲗ ⲉⲃⲟⲗ ϧⲓⲡⲟⲩⲙⲛⲧⲗ.

ⲗⲁ- S (rare) B vb (? p c) + nn forming adj, possessing, endued with (Sethe Verbum 1 231 s f): C 43 207 ⲉⲕⲟⲓ ⲡⲗⲁⲥⲁⲭⲓ loquacious, but BM 920 267, ib Or 8775 113 ⲟⲩⲗⲁ ⲡⲥ. كثر الكلام (cf ϧⲓ ⲁⲗⲗⲁ above), so ? = ⲗⲁⲃ- (ⲗⲓⲃⲉ) q v (cf ⲗⲁ nn); MG 25 232 ⲟⲩⲗⲁⲟⲩⲁⲓ ⲡϣⲫⲏⲣ single = Z 317 S ⲟⲩⲥⲟⲛ ⲡⲟⲩⲱⲧ ἕνα μοναχόν, HL 110 ⲟⲩⲗ. ⲡⲉϩⲟⲟⲩ μιᾶς ἡμέρας, MIE 2 418 ⲟⲩⲗⲁϭⲓ (sic) ⲡⲟⲗⲟⲕⲟⲭⲓ = BAp 125 S ⲟⲩϩⲟⲗⲟⲕ/ ⲡⲟⲩⲱⲧ; Mor 37 112 S ⲟⲩⲗⲁϣⲓⲏ μακρός, Mor 40 5 S recruits ⲡⲗⲁϣⲓⲏ = C 43 36 B ⲉⲅϭⲟⲥⲓ; Miss 4 159 Elisha ⲟⲩⲗⲁϥⲱⲓ hairy (prob error, cf ib 119 = ⲟⲩⲕⲉⲣϧⲉ); Lev 23 40 trees ⲗⲁϫⲱⲃⲓ (S ⲟⲩ ⲡϣⲱⲃⲉ) δασύς; Deu 12 2 ⲗⲁⲭⲁⲗ (var ⲟϣ ⲡⲭ., S ⲟ ⲡϧⲁⲓⲃⲉⲥ) δασύς; ⲗⲁⲃⲟϯ v ⲃⲱⲧⲉ vb s f.   In names: ⲗⲁϧⲛⲟⲩ BM 1252, Λαϧῆ, Λαήου (Preisigke), ⲗⲁϭⲱⲃⲉ PAntinoe EES unpubl.   ⲗⲁⲙⲁⲣⲧ, -ⲝⲏⲧϥ v ⲗⲓⲃⲉ.

ⲗⲁ F vb   v ⲗⲟ.

ⲗⲁ F   v ⲉⲓⲣⲉ(ⲣⲁ).

ⲗⲁ F nn   v ⲣⲟ mouth.

ⲗⲁ-, ⲗⲉ- F   v ⲣⲁ- part.

ⲗⲓ ⲉⲃⲟⲗ S vb tr, meaning unknown, relates to melting of metals: AZ 23 111 various metals ⲗⲓ ⲙⲙⲟⲟⲩ ⲉⲃ. ⲡⲁⲥⲧⲟⲩ ϧⲓⲙⲟⲟⲩ, ib 112 ⲗⲓⲓ(sic)ⲙⲙⲟⲟⲩ ⲉⲃ. a black liquid will issue therefrom, ib melt them in earthen crucible (ⲕⲁⲣⲟⲟⲣⲉ بوطة) ⲡⲧⲗⲓ ⲙⲙⲟⲟⲩ ⲉⲃ.   BSM 113 B ⲗⲓ ⲙⲙⲉⲣⲟⲥ ⲙⲉⲣⲟⲥ, prob l ⲁⲓⲥ = Mor 22 124 S ⲁⲁⲥ ⲡⲗⲁⲕⲙ ⲗⲁⲕⲙ.

ⲗⲓ F   v ⲣⲓ.

ⲗⲟ SA², ⲗⲁ SF, imperat ⲁⲗⲟⲕ (ⲁⲗⲁⲕ CA 88), ⲁⲗⲟ f (R 1 5 37), ⲁⲗⲱⲧⲛ SA² vb **I** intr. cf Rec 25 148, **a** cease, stop: Job 14 13 S (B ϭⲓⲛⲓ), Is 10 25 S (B ⲗⲱⲝⲓ), ib 33 8 S (B ⲕⲏⲛ, F ⲟⲩⲱ), Lu 8 24 S (B ϧⲉⲣⲓ) παύειν; Si 39 13 S, Is 33 14 SF (B prob do) ἀφιστάναι; Mt 14 32 F (S ϭⲱ, B do) κοπάζειν. **b** cease, be ended, healed, of sickness: Deu 32 33 S (B ⲧⲁⲗϭⲟ) ἀνίατος; Ac 19 12 S (B ϣⲉ ⲉⲃⲟⲗ ϧⲓ-) ἀπαλλάσσειν; Deu 28 35 S (B ⲗⲱⲝⲓ), Jer 15 18 S (B ⲟⲩϫⲁⲓ), Mt 8 13 S (B do), He 12 13 S (B ⲗⲱⲝⲓ) ἰᾶσθαι; Job 24 23 S (B do) ὑγιάζειν; Mk 3 5 S (B ⲟⲩ.), ib 8 25 F (S diff, B do) ἀποκαθιστάναι; ib 6 56 S (B do) σώζεσθαι; Jo 5 10 S (B tr ⲉⲣ ⲫⲁϩⲣⲓ) θεραπεύεσθαι: BM 355 2 S ⲡⲉⲓⲡⲁⲣ ⲡⲁⲣⲣⲉ ⲉⲣⲟⲕⲡⲉ ϣⲁⲡⲧⲕⲗⲟ, Mor 30 14 F I think not that ⲁⲕⲗⲁ ⲭⲱⲣⲓⲥ ⲙⲁⲅⲓⲁ, Ryl 106 14 S ⲉⲕⲁⲗⲱ ⲉⲕⲟⲩⲱⲙ whilst eating, Miss 4 705 S ⲡⲧⲉⲣⲟⲩⲗⲟ ⲛϭⲓ ⲡⲉϥⲡⲗⲏⲅⲏ, PMéd most recipes end ϣⲁϥ-, ϣⲁⲩⲗⲟ sc affected parts. Cf ⲗⲟ ⲙⲙⲁⲩ. **c** followed by coordinated vb (2 pres, Sdff 325), cease to do, be: Job 37 19 S (B ⲕⲏⲛ), Is 38 20 S (B ⲗⲱⲝⲓ), Ac 13 10 S (B ⲭⲱ ⲡⲧⲟⲧ⸗ ⲉⲃⲟⲗ) παύειν; Ge 29 35 S (B ⲟϧⲓ), Jos 3 13 S (B ⲕⲏⲛ), Ru 2 7 S ἱστάναι, Is 59 13 S (B ϧⲉⲛ⸗ ⲉⲃⲟⲗ) ἀφιστ.; Pro 3 27 S (A ⲟⲩⲁϩⲣⲉ, B ⲧⲁϧⲛⲟ) ἀπέχεσθαι, Ge 8 2 S (B do) συνέχ. ἀπό; Lu 7 45 S (B ⲭⲁ ⲧⲟⲧ⸗ ⲉⲃⲟⲗ) διαλείπειν; PS 175 S ⲡⲧⲉⲧⲏⲗⲟ ⲉⲧⲉⲧⲡⲛⲏⲧ ⲡⲥⲱⲓ, Br 247 S ⲁϥⲗⲟ ⲉϥⲕⲓⲙ, ShA 2 159 S ⲁⲗⲟⲕ ⲉⲕⲙⲟⲥⲧⲉ, ib 276 I will weep ϣⲁⲡϯⲗⲟ ⲉⲓⲉϣ ϭⲙϭⲟⲙ, BSG 187 S ⲁⲓⲗⲟ ⲉⲓⲡⲁⲩ ⲉⲣⲟϥ = Wess 15 146 S ⲙⲡⲉⲓⲡⲁⲩ ⲉⲣⲟϥ ⲡⲕⲉⲥⲟⲡ.   Translates Gk neg: 1 Kg 28 20 S ⲁϥⲗⲟ ⲉϥϭⲙϭⲟⲙ οὐκ ...ἔτι, ib 30 4 S sim, Jth 10 10 S, Jo 6 66 SA² (B ⲡ-...ⲁⲡ ϫⲉ) οὐκέτι, Ac 19 27 S ⲥⲉⲛⲁⲗⲟ ⲉⲧⲱⲡ (B do) εἰς οὐδὲν λογισθῆναι, cf sim P 129¹⁶ 18 S pagans complain that saints ⲗⲟ ⲉⲅⲕⲁ ⲣⲱⲙⲉ ⲉⲉⲓ ⲉⲡⲣⲡⲉ; conversely with neg: Ac 12 16 S ⲙⲡϥⲗⲟ ⲉϥⲧⲱϧⲙ (B ⲙⲟⲩⲛ) ἐπιμένειν; GMir 18 S do not thus lest ⲡⲥⲉⲧⲙⲗⲟ ⲉⲅⲥⲱⲃⲉ ⲡⲥⲱ(ϥ).

II tr (refl ?): Mor 28 194 S petitions king ⲛϥⲗⲟ ⲙⲙⲟⲩ ϧⲓⲧⲁⲣⲭⲏ withdraw self from (or ? = ⲗⲟ ⲙⲙⲁⲩ).

With following prepositions.

—— ⲉ- S (rare), cease from, leave: Mt 13 30 (B diff, cf ϧⲁ-) ἀφιέναι, ShIF 260 ⲁⲗⲱⲧⲛ ⲉⲣⲟⲥ ⲡⲁⲥ (ethic dat).

—— ⲛ- S, cease, recede from: Ps 108 23 (B ϥⲱϯ ⲉⲃⲟⲗ) ἀνταναιρεῖσθαι; Lu 13 31 (B ϧⲱⲗ) πορεύεσθαι; 2 Thes 2 7 (B ⲗⲱⲝⲓ); Z 319 I wish not ⲉⲗⲟ ⲙⲡⲉⲓⲙⲁ ἐξέρχεσθαι ἔνθεν; BM 174 1 cook's knife ⲁⲥⲗⲟ ⲡⲧⲙⲛⲧⲉ παύεσθαι; R 1 1 31 (Gk diff) ⲧⲁⲗⲟϭⲉ ⲛⲓⲥ (would ye) that I release (desist from) Jesus?, Mor 48 61 S ⲡⲧⲉⲣⲉⲡⲉϥϩⲏⲧ ⲗⲟ ⲙⲙⲟϥ fainted, LMär 25 S sim (l ⲙⲙⲟϥ), Ryl 99 S ⲉⲁⲡⲉϥϩⲏⲧ ⲁⲗⲁⲥⲥⲉ ⲁϥⲗⲟ ⲙⲙⲟϥ (cf PO 2 251). V ⲗⲟ ⲙⲙⲁⲩ.

—— ⲟⲩⲃⲉ- S, cease from opposing: BHom 92 caused war to ⲗⲟ ⲟⲩⲃⲏϥ ἀπαλλάσσειν.

—— ογτε- *S, cease from among*: Eph 5 14 (*B* ογι ερατ⸗ εϧολ ϧεn-) ἀνιστάναι ἐκ.

—— ϧα- *SA²* (Jo), *cease from, leave, allow*: 2 Kg 16 10, Mt 13 30 (var ShA 2 14 ε-, *BF* ϧω, κω), Jo 12 7 *SA²* (*B* δο) ἀφιέναι, Ex 23 11 (*B* ϯ ⲗιτοn n-) ἀνιέναι; 1 Kg 18 13 ἀφιστάναι tr; Ex 16 23 (*B* cωϧn) Is 10 14 (*B* δο)καταλείπεσθαι, Si 17 21 ἀπολείπειν; Jud 9 21, 1 Kg 6 20 ἀπό (no vb); PS 167 ειπαϧωκ nταλο ϧαροc, ShC 42 160 their teachers did λο ϧαρоογ (cf ib 161 καας πϲωογ), BMis 134 Mary at Gabriel's appearance αϲλο ϧαπετϧαπεϲϧιϫ αϲϲπογⲁⲁⲍε ϧαπετϧαπεϲϧαλ, Mor 43 155 grave-clothes αϥλο ϧαρоογ nϧογn επταφοc.

—— ϧαϧολ *S*, -ϧαλ n- *F*, *depart from*: Mor 17 85 *S* Cynops λο ϧ. nογоⲓ nⲓⲙ ἐξ ὀφθαλ. ἐγένετο; BMEA 10585 *F* ϥαϧ nταⲓⲗⲁ ϧ. (ⲗ)ⲙⲁⲕ.

—— ϧⲓ- *S, cease, depart from*: Lev 13 58 (*B* om), 1 Kg 6 3 ἀφιστ. ἀπό; *ib* 1 14 πορεύ. ἐκ; Mk 7 30 (var ει εϧολ ϧⲓ-, *B* ϣε εϧ. ϧⲓ-) ἐξέρχεσθαι; HSahid III 382 πεnταϧλο ϧⲓⲛϥϲωⲛϧ (cf ϧⲓ-), Bodl(P) a 1 c wash it till acid taste λω ϧⲓⲱϥ.

—— ϧⲛ- *S, cease from, quit*: Ex 32 12 (*B* ταϧⲛо n-), Nu 25 8 (*B* λωϫι), Is 1 16 (*B* ταλϭо εϧ. ϧⲉⲛ-, *F* ϥⲓ εϧ. ϧⲛ-), 1 Pet 4 1 (*B* ταλ. εϧ. ϧⲁ-) παύειν ἀπό or gen; Sa 12 2 ἀπαλλάσσ. gen; 4 Kg 23 26 (R 2 1 38) ἀποστρέφ. ἀπό; 2 Kg 12 10 (var ⲣ ϧολ n-) ἀφιστ. ἐκ; PS 304 ⲁⲩλо ϧⲛⲧⲉⲩⲡⲓⲥⲧⲓⲥ (cf 306 nⲧⲉⲩⲡ.), R 1 5 37 ⲁⲗо ϧⲛⲧⲟⲩⲙⲁⲧⲓⲁ, CO 97 ϣⲁⲛⲧⲩⲗⲟ ϧⲛⲡⲉϥϣⲱⲡⲉ, P 131⁶ 31 they arise nⲥⲉⲗо ϧⲛⲡⲉⲩⲙⲁ ⲛϣⲱⲡⲉ; εϧολ ϧⲛ-, n-: Mk 5 29 (*B* ογⲭⲁⲓ εϧ. ϧⲁ-) ἰᾶσθαι ἀπό; CA 93 (Hermas *Sim* 1 4) ἐκχωρεῖν ἐκ; BHom 19 ⲁⲕⲗⲟ εϧ. nⲧⲙⲧⲣⲉϥϣⲱⲥ (*l* ϲⲱϣ).

—— ϧⲣⲁⲓ (? εϧⲣⲁⲓ) *S*, *obscure*: Ep 218 ⲙⲡⲣⲕⲱ nϣⲟⲩⲗⲟ ϧⲣⲁⲓ ϧⲛⲟⲩϭⲉⲡⲉ.

—— ϧⲓⲣⲛ- *S, depart from above, upon*: 2 Kg 20 21 ἀπέρχ. ἀπάνωθεν.

—— ϧⲓϫⲛ- *S, cease from*: Nu 17 10 ⲡⲧⲉⲡⲉⲩⲕⲣⲙⲣⲙ λο ϧⲓϫⲱⲓ (var εϧⲉⲗⲟ ϧⲉⲡⲡⲉⲩⲕ. εϧⲟⲩⲛ ⲉⲣⲟⲓ, *B* λωϫⲓ) παύειν ἀπό; 1 Kg 6 3 ἀφιστ. ἀπό; Leyd 279 caused rain to λο ϧⲓϫⲛⲡⲏⲓ. *V* also λο ⲗⲙⲁⲩ.

With following adverbs.

—— αϧⲁλ *A²*, *cease* from sickness, *be healed*: AP 20 αϥⲗⲟ αϧ. ϧⲛⲧⲟⲩⲅⲡⲟⲩ; *desist*: Jo 6 66 prob (*S* λο, *B* n-...αn ϫⲉ) οὐκέτι.

—— ⲗⲙⲁⲩ *S, cease thence, cease* (as if λο alone, *v* ⲗⲙⲁⲩ b): Lev 14 3 (*B* ταλϭⲟ) ἰᾶσθαι; 2 Kg 13 9 ἐξάγειν tr; Lev 19 32 ⲧⲱⲟⲩⲛ ⲉⲗⲟ ⲗ. (*B* ⲧⲱⲛ ϧⲁϧⲉⲛ-) ἐξανιστάναι; ShA 2 5 ⲁⲗⲱⲧⲛ ⲗ. ⲧⲁⲭⲩ, Miss 4 713 whose hearts λо ⲗ. nⲥⲉⲗⲓϧⲉ (var *ib* ⲡⲱϣⲥ ⲉⲣⲟⲟⲩ, *v* above λο n-). λο ⲗ. ϧⲓϫⲛ-: ShC 73 196 such as will not rise (from table) nⲥⲉⲗⲟ

—— ⲗ. ϧⲓϫⲱⲥ يفارقونها لا, PSBA 30 237 pray that this trouble λο ⲗ. ϧⲓϫⲱⲡ.

—— nⲃⲟⲗ *S, cease*: Mk 6 51 (*B* ϧⲉⲣⲓ) κοπάζειν. *V* ϧⲱⲗ (nⲃⲟⲗ **II**).

λο *S* nn f, PMéd 176 *v* ⲣⲟ.

λⲱ *F* *v* ⲣⲱ.

λⲉϧ- *F* *v* ⲣⲱⲙⲉ (ⲣⲉϥ-).

λⲁϧⲟⲓ *SB*, λⲁϧⲁⲓ *S* (Job) *A* nn f, *a lioness*, cf לביא لبؤة: Job 4 10 *S* (*B* ⲗⲓⲏ) λέαινα, Glos 84 *S* λέαινη (*sic*) · λ., P 44 54 *S* λεαιπα · ταⲣⲍ · ⲧλ. لبؤة, K 164 *B* ϯλ., (ⲧ)αⲣⲉⲍ, ⲗⲓⲉ all = لبؤة, BIF 14 162 *S* ψⲓⲥ ⲙⲙⲟⲅⲓ, ψⲓϲⲉ nλ., ϲαⲩϣⲉ ⲡαⲣⲍ (ἄρκος, *v* KKS 60 ff), BM 286 *S* ⲗⲟⲅⲓ, λ., αⲣⲍ, SHel 26 *S* ⲟⲩⲗ. εⲥⲙⲁⲥⲉ (*sic l*), C 43 30 *B* sim, JKP 2 92 *S* ⲟⲩⲗ. εϣⲁⲩϭⲓ ⲡⲡⲉⲥϣⲏⲣⲓ, DeV 29 *B* Herodias ϯλ., El 48 *A* hair like that of nⲓλ. **b** *she-bear*: 1 Kg 17 34, 37 *B* lion & ϯλ. (*S* αⲣⲍ), Is 11 7 *B* (*S* do), Lam 3 10 *B* (*S* do) f, Dan 7 5 *B* (*ib* 4 λέαινα = ⲗⲟⲅⲓ), Ap 13 2 *B* (*S* do), Va 58 169 *B* ϯλ. ἄρκος; m only P 129¹⁸ 165 *S* (text = BM 286 as above) nⲧⲟⲩ nλ. As name m f: Λαβάϊς, Λαβόϊς, Ὀϲλαβάει (Preisigke). *Cf* Spg *Mythus* p 190.

λⲁϧⲱ *S*, λⲁϧⲟ *B* *v* λⲁⲅⲟ.

λⲁϧⲱ *B* *v* λⲉϧⲁⲡ.

λⲓϧⲉ *SAA²* DM (V 32 9), λⲓϧⲓ *B*, λⲉϧⲧ⸗, λⲟϧⲉ† *S*, λⲟϧⲓ† *B*, λⲁϧⲉ† *A²*, p c λⲁϧ-, λⲁ- *SB* vb **I** intr, *be mad*: Jer 36 26† *B*, Jo 10 20† *SA²B*, 1 Cor 14 23† *SB* μαίνεσθαι, Sa 5 4† *B* (*S* λ. nn) μανία, Aeg 282 *S* εϥⲗⲟⲩϧⲉ εϥⲑⲉⲱⲣⲉⲓ in theatre θεατρομανία; 1 Kg 21 15† *S* (cf 14 ⲡⲱϣⲥ ⲡϧⲏⲧ), 4 Kg 9 11 *S* (? *l* λⲟϧⲉ) ἐπίληπτος; ShA 2 330 *S* ⲧⲉⲧλ.† like pagans, AM 261 *B* Arius ϥⲁⲓ εⲑλ.†, *ib* 271 *B* Origen ϥⲏ εⲧαϥλ., ClPr 38 *S* ⲗⲉⲣⲉⲗⲁⲁⲩ λ. ⲡϥϫⲟⲟⲥ *none is so mad as to say*, DeV 2 76 *B* drunkards do ϧⲁⲡϧⲛⲟⲅⲓ εⲅλ.†, Miss 4 199 *B* ⲟⲩⲥⲙⲏ εⲥλ.†

—— *SAB* nn m, *madness*: Ps 39 5 *B* (*S* = Gk), Sa 5 4 (*B* vb†), Hos 9 7 *AB*, HL 76 *B* εⲥϣⲱⲡⲓ ϧⲉⲛⲟⲩλ. μανία, Ac 26 11 *B* (*S* ϭⲱⲡⲧ) ἐμμαίνειν, Mor 17 26 *S* nλ. of idols εἰδωλομανία, BHom 13 *S* εϥⲣⲟⲕϧ ϧⲛⲟⲩλ. μανικός...ἐρᾷ; Deu 28 28 *B* (*S* ⲟⲛϣⲥ) παραπληξία amentia; Va 63 97 *B* εⲩϣⲟⲡ ϧⲉⲛⲟⲩλ. ἐκβακχευόμενος; BMar 167 *S* nλ. nϧⲏ γαστριμαργία, *ib* 169 λ. nⲣⲏ; ShWess 9 145 *S* λ. ϧⲓⲡⲱⲱϫⲉ of heretics, *ib* 134 nλ. ⲗⲡⲓⲁⲑⲏⲧ Origen, AM 229 *B* ⲟⲩⲥⲡⲟⲩϧⲁⲛ ⲡⲉⲗⲟⲅλ. of devil.

With following preposition.

—— εϧⲟⲩⲛ, εϧ. ε- *SB*, *be mad toward, concerning*: Ryl 94 100 *S* ⲡⲉⲧλ.† εϧ. εⲑⲩλⲏ of this life, AM 237 *B* αϥλ. εϧ. εϥⲏ εⲑⲟⲩⲁϧ, Va 58 184 *B* gluttony causing to λ. εϧ. ε- idolatry.

—— ⲉϫⲉⲛ- *B*, *be mad after*: Jer 5 8 ⲉⲩⲗ.† ⲉϫⲉⲛⲡⲓϧⲓⲟⲙⲓ (*S* ⲗⲁⲃⲥϧⲓⲙⲉ *q v, cf* DeVis 142).

—— ⲛⲉⲙ- *B*, *meaning same*: AM 270 ⲉⲧⲗ.† ⲛⲉⲙⲡⲓⲙⲉⲧϣⲁⲙϣⲉ ⲓⲍⲱⲗⲟⲛ εἰς.

—— ⲛⲥⲁ- *SB*, *meaning same*: ShLeyd 303 *S* ⲛⲉⲧⲡⲟϣⲥ ⲁⲩⲱ ⲉⲧⲗ.† ⲛⲥⲁⲡϩⲟⲟⲩⲧ, ShP 130⁴ 117 *S* ⲉⲩⲗ.† ⲛⲥⲁⲱϣ *apocryphal books*, MIE 2 365 *B* ⲉⲃⲗ.† ⲛⲥⲁⲡⲁⲓⲣⲁⲡ ϫⲉⲟⲩⲛⲃ.

—— ⲛⲧⲛ- *S*, *be mad through, made mad by*: PMich 601 ⲉⲥⲁⲣ (ⲑⲉ) ⲡⲟⲩϭⲧⲱⲣⲉ [ⲉⲥ]ⲗ.† ⲡⲧⲟⲟⲧϥ ⲡⲟⲩⲧⲱ (*l* ϧⲧⲟ).

—— ϩⲁ- *S*, *meaning same*: Sa 14 28 ⲥⲉⲗ.† ϧⲁⲡⲧϩⲣⲉ (Gk diff); ⲉⲃⲟⲗ ϩⲁ- Jer 32 16(2) *B* ἐκμαίνειν ἀπὸ προσώπου.

—— ϩⲛ-, ϫⲉⲛ- *SB*, *meaning same*: ShC 73 194 *S drunk &* ⲉⲧⲗ.† ϧⲛⲛⲟⲃⲉ بَتّل, DeV 2 207 *B* ⲉⲩⲗ.† ϫⲉⲛⲡⲓⲟⲓϯⲓ, BM 332 *S Nestorius* ⲡⲉϥⲗ.† ϧⲛⲧⲙⲛⲧⲛⲟⲩϫ.

—— ϩⲓⲧⲛ- *S*, *meaning same*: Cai 8010 1 ϧⲙⲡⲧⲣⲉⲩⲗ. ϩⲓⲧⲁⲡⲧϩⲣⲉ.

II tr *S* (*rare*), *make mad*: Ac 26 24 *S* ⲗⲉⲃⲧⲕ (*B intr*) εἰς μανίαν περιτρέπει; PS 280 ⲁⲕⲗⲃⲧⲛ ⲉⲃⲟⲗ ⲡⲙⲙⲛⲧⲛⲟϭ *which Thou tellest us.* In Ez 39 23 (ShA 1 233) *l* ⲛⲉⲧ(ⲟ)ⲗⲉⲓⲃⲉ ἐχθρός (*cf* Sa 5 4 HT ⲉⲩⲟⲗⲓⲃⲉ).

ⲣⲉϥⲗ. *B* nn, *madman*: K 89 مجنون.

ϭⲓⲛⲗ. *S* nn f, *madness*: Z 160 ὑδρομανία ⲉⲧⲉⲛϭ. (ⲡ)ⲡⲉⲉϣⲁⲩ.

ⲗⲁⲃⲗⲁ *S*   *v* ⲗⲁ *envy*.

ⲗⲁⲃ-, ⲗⲁⲙⲁϧⲧ *S*, ⲗⲁⲙⲁϧⲧ *B* adj, *belly-mad, gluttonous*: Wess 18 75 *S* ⲙⲡⲉⲣϣⲱⲡⲉ ⲛ̄ⲗⲁⲙ. γαστρίμαργος; Mun 83 *S* ⲡⲉ]ϩⲟⲩⲟ ⲗⲁⲙ[ⲁϧⲧ. *Oftenest* ⲙⲛⲧ-, ⲙⲉⲧⲗ. *SB* nn f, *gluttony*: R 2 1 46 *S among sins*, Leyd 453 *S*, BMis 154 *S sim*, Va 58 189 *B through overeating* ϣⲁⲣⲉϯⲙ. ⲓ ⲉⲃⲟⲩⲛ. ⲗⲁⲙⲁϫⲓⲧⲏⲥ (-ϩⲓⲧⲏⲥ *once*) *B, glutton* (*cf* Stern 169): K 115 بطون (*sic*). *Cf* ⲗⲁⲃϧⲏ.

ⲗⲁⲃⲥϧⲓⲙⲉ *S*, ⲗⲁϥⲥϧⲓⲙⲓ *B* adj, *woman-mad, lecherous*: Jer 5 8 *S* (*B vb†*) θηλυμανής, *cf* MG 25 172 *B* ϩⲱⲟⲣ ⲛⲗ.

ⲗⲁⲃϧⲏ, ⲗⲁϧⲉ *S*, ⲗⲁⲃϩⲏⲧϥ *B* nn, *belly-mad, greedy person* (*cf* ⲗⲁⲃⲙⲁϧⲧ): CO 469 *S dog is* ⲟⲩⲗⲁϧⲉ, K 89 *B* ⲡⲓⲗ. بطين. ⲙⲛⲧ-, ⲙⲉⲧⲗ. nn f, *greed, hunger*: Mor 38 62 *S* ⲁⲧⲙ. ⲁⲡⲁⲧⲕⲁϫⲉ ⲙⲙⲟⲓ, *ib* 19 91 *S* (var *ib* 18 86 -ϩⲏⲧ) = Miss 4 153 *B*, Faras 3 67 6 *S* ⲙ. *as cause of* πορνεία, DeV 2 161 *B* ϯⲙ. ⲡⲧⲉ ϯⲛⲉϫⲓ. ⲣ ⲗ. *S*, ⲟⲓ ⲛⲗ. *B, be hungry, greedy*: Aeg 261 *S* ⲉϥϣⲁⲛⲣ ⲗ. *before end of fast*, DeV 2 76 *B all that* ⲟⲓ ⲛⲗ. *& are drunken. V* ⲗⲟⲃⲗⲉⲃ, ⲗⲏⲃⲧⲉ.

ⲗⲃⲉⲓ *A*   *v* ⲙⲡⲁⲓ.

ⲗⲟⲃⲉ *S*   *v* ⲗⲟⲟϭⲉ.

ⲗⲟⲩⲃⲟⲓⲉ *S* nn as pl, *kind of Nile ship*: PLond 4 506]ⲛⲉⲗ. ⲉⲩⲥⲙⲓ[ⲛⲉ (?). *Cf ib* 6 λουφοιων (pl), *ib* 313 λουφιων; RE 9 154 12 ⲡⲗⲟⲩ[ⲃⲟⲓⲉ (?).

ⲗⲉⲃⲉⲕⲏ *F*   *v* ⲃⲉⲕⲉ.

ⲗⲟⲃⲗⲉⲃ *B* vb intr, *feel violent love, only as nn* ⲙⲉⲧⲣⲉϥⲗⲱⲃⲗⲉⲃ: K 98 شغف. *Cf* ⲗⲓⲃⲉ.

ⲗⲉⲃⲁⲛ *SB*, ⲗⲁⲃⲱ *B* nn m, *ship's hauling-cable* (*v* BIF 20 70 *on* لبان): MG 25 160 *B* ⲥⲉⲛϩ ⲛⲗ. ⲉϯⲁⲡⲁⲓⲱ, WS 96 *S paral* ⲧⲙⲁϣⲣⲧ *needed by sailors of* λίβυρνον-*ship*; K 134 *B* ⲡⲓⲗⲁⲃⲱⲓ (var -ⲃⲟⲛ) لبان, *ib* 270 ⲗⲁⲃⲱ المركب ١ (? *confusion with* ⲗⲁⲃⲱ, *v* ⲗⲁⲩⲟ).

ⲗⲁⲃⲁⲥ, -ⲟⲥ *B* nn, *aloe-wood*: K 192 ⲡⲓϣⲉ ⲛⲗ. عود القماري (*v* Dozy 2 404). Prob for (ἀ)λόῆς.

ⲗⲁⲃⲏⲥ *S*   *v* ⲗⲉⲓϥⲓ.

ⲗⲓⲃⲟⲥ, -ⲱⲥ *B* nn m, *colic*: K 159 ⲡⲓⲗ. مغس (*l* مغص). ? *l* (ⲕⲱ)ⲗⲓⲕⲟⲥ.

ⲗⲏⲃⲧⲉ *S* vb intr, *meaning unknown*: P 131⁵ 27 *shameful before God's* βῆμα ⲉⲣⲉⲧⲉϥⲯⲩⲭⲏ ⲗ. ϧⲛⲡⲁⲑⲟⲥ ⲉⲧⲣⲟⲟⲩ. ? *l* ⲗⲏⲃⲧⲥ (ⲗⲓⲃⲉ).

ⲗⲉⲃϣ nn *B*   *v* ⲗⲱⲃϣ vb.

ⲗⲱⲃϣ *S(BF)*, ⲗⲟⲃϣ̇ *B*, ⲗⲟⲃϣ† *SB*, ⲗⲟⲡϣ† *B*, ⲗⲁⲃⲉϣ† *SᶠF* vb **I** intr, *be hot, glow*: Ps 118 140† *S* (*B* ϥⲓⲥⲓ), BMis 241 *S* ⲟⲩⲡⲉⲛⲓⲡⲉ ⲉϥⲗ.† πυροῦσθαι; ShC 73 198 *S iron in fire* ⲛⲥⲉⲛⲓϣⲉ ⲛⲉⲱϥ ⲛⲉϥⲗ., Miss 8 251 *S if dog show teeth* ϣⲁⲛⲗ. ϩⲙⲡⲉⲛⲗⲟⲅⲓⲥⲙⲟⲥ *& courage* (lit *mind*) *weakens*, C 86 296 *B martyr's ribs* ⲗ. ϧⲓⲧⲉⲛ- *great fire*, P 129¹⁴ 127 *S Macedonius* ⲣ ⲑⲉ ϫⲉⲛⲧⲁϥⲗ. ϩⲙⲡⲕⲱϩⲧ, BMar 23 *S iron bed* ⲗ.† ϩⲁⲣⲟϥ, LAl 2 *S he is come at once* ⲉⲣⲉⲡⲉϥϩⲏⲧ ⲗ.† ⲉⲣⲟϥ, Ep 114 *S* ⲙⲡⲣⲗ. ⲉⲡⲉⲕ[ⲥⲟⲡ; *often in martyrdoms* ⲗ.† ⲡⲕⲱϩⲧ *S*, ⲡⲭⲣⲱⲙ *B, glowing with fire, red hot*: BMar 23 *S* ϩⲉⲛϣⲗⲓϭ...ⲉⲩⲗ.† ⲡⲕ., BIF 14 111 *S*, C 86 131 *B*, AM 53 *B sim*; Mor 24 24 *F hill of iron* ⲉϥⲗ.† ⲡⲕ. = *ib* 23 34 *S* ⲗ.† ϩⲛⲟⲩⲕ.; *or* ϧⲙⲡⲕ., ϫ.: BIF 15 239 *S*, MG 25 351 *B*, Mor 19 72 *S* = Miss 4 138 *B* ϥⲟⲥⲓ.

II tr *SB*(*rare*), *burn, heat*: R 1 4 59 *S light torch* ⲛⲧⲉⲧⲛⲗ. ⲙⲡⲉϥⲥⲡⲓⲣⲟⲟⲩⲉ φλέγειν, MG 25 145 *B gold* ⲁⲩϣⲁⲛⲗⲟⲃϣ *in fire*, AM 102 *B nails* ⲛⲥⲉⲗⲟⲃϣⲟⲩ ⲡⲭⲣⲱⲙ.

—— *SB* nn m, *glow*: Va 57 41 *B* ⲛⲗ. ⲙⲡⲓⲭⲣⲱⲙ φλογώδης; *fervour*: Ryl 94 106 *S* ⲛⲗ. *of soul toward God, cf ib* ϫⲡⲟⲩϥ.

ⲗⲉⲃϣ, ⲗⲉⲡϣ *B* nn m, *heating material, fuel, also twigs, brushwood*: Job 30 7 (*S* ⲛⲧⲏϭ), Is 40 24 (*S* ϭⲗⲙ), Jer 13 24 (*S do*), Hos 10 7 (*A* ϭⲗⲃⲉ), Ac 28 3 (*S do*), MG 25 205 ⲡⲓϣⲉ ⲉⲧϥⲱⲛϩ ⲡⲡⲓⲗ.

L

ϫⲉⲛⲡⲓⲭⲣⲱⲙ, PSBA 10 402 as fuel ϩⲁⲛϣⲉ ⲡⲉⲗ-
ⲟⲩⲗⲁⲛϣ ⲛⲗ. φρύγανον; Phil 3 8 (S ⲗⲁⲁⲩ) σκύβαλον,
AM 208 sim; K 260 قش, ib 406 حشيش; ROC 25
255 ⲣⲟⲕϩ, ⲗ.

ⲗⲱⲃϣ SB nn m, **a crown, coping, battlement**
of roof: Deu 22 8 SB στεφάνη (Va 1 حظير); Lu 5
19 B (S = Gk) κέραμος; Tri 715 S women walking on ⲛⲗ. of castrum شراريف, K 152, 261 B ⲛⲓⲗ.
'ش., P 44 95 = 43 82 S foundation of πλήρωσις
whereof Father is ⲗ. شرفها; P 43 25 S علو, سقف,
cf ⲙⲉⲗⲱⲧ سقف (opp ϫⲉⲡⲉⲡⲱⲣ سطح), TEuch 1 672
B Paul ⲫⲗ. of church حصن (but var HCons 393 فخر),
K 260 B ⲛⲓⲗ. اساسات (error); ShC 42 215 S ⲛⲗ.
ⲉⲧϭⲉ through tempests, ShBMOr 8664 1 S she with-
draws her face ϩⲁⲛϣⲟⲩϣⲧ ⲛ ⲛⲗ. of house, Miss
4 716 S look forth from church's ⲗ., BMis 177 S
ⲗ. set on new church in 8 months = BSM 86 B,
cf C 86 89 B I built chapel ⲁⲓϯ ⲙⲡⲉϥⲥⲧⲉⲫⲁⲛⲟⲩ,
Mor 28 218 S man falls from roof because ⲛⲉⲙⲛ
ⲗ. ϩⲁⲡⲉϫⲏⲓ, P 129¹⁶ 58 S prays ⲡⲧⲉⲧⲉⲓⲡⲩⲗⲏ ⲱⲁⲥ
ⲉⲡⲉⲥⲛⲧ ϣⲁⲡⲉⲥⲗ., ib 129¹⁴ ¹²³ S humility ⲛⲗ. &
ⲡⲭⲱⲕ of virtues, MG 25 42 B Athanasius ⲛⲗ. &
butress of faith's κρηπίς. **b** B **crown, consumma-
tion**, title of final stanza (or longer section) in certain
hymns(1) in Theotokia of week-days: CaiThe 168–
257 (TThe mostly om) called تفسير interpretation
(cf K 261), except TThe 277 لبش; or (2) in hymn-
books: PsH 21, 26, 29, 68 مرد refrain (بحري 'م &
قبلي 'م sung by opposite choirs).

—— S vb tr (rare), **set crown upon, adorn** (cf
لبش make stockade, bulwark of reeds Spiro): Mor
31 255 arise Jerusalem ⲛⲧⲉⲗ. ⲡⲡⲟⲩⲅⲩⲗⲗⲉ (πύλη),
ib ⲁⲅⲗ. ⲡⲡⲉⲡⲩⲗⲏ...ϩⲁⲭⲱϭ (cf Amélineau Contes
2 147), P 130⁵ 121 ϣⲁⲅⲗ. ⲙⲡⲉϥⲏⲓ ⲛϩⲉⲛⲃⲁ, BIF
14 102 king bade ⲛⲥⲉⲗ. ⲙⲡⲉⲣⲡⲉ.

ⲗⲉⲃⲓⲱϩⲉ S v ⲉⲓⲱϩⲉ.

ⲗⲓⲕ SB nn m, **pot, jar**: AZ 23 113 S metals
melted in ⲟⲩⲗ., K 150, AZ 13 84, P 55 11 B ⲛⲓⲗ.
كوز, زير. Prob not = ابريق. Cf ? ⲗⲟⲕ.

ⲗⲟⲕ SB, ⲗⲟϭ S, ⲗⲁⲕ SF nn m, **bowl, cup**, cf لب:
as measure for oil, Lev 14 10 &c SB κοτύλη (cf var
λόγγη) sextarius, K 148 B قسط (ξέστης), CO 217, 352
S, PMéd 238 S (cf ib 50), BM 606 F, PMich 3593 F;
wine, Wess 3 1160 ⲗⲁⲕ; water, ShC 73 210 S drink
not 2 ⲗ. one after the other; honey, BKU 1 259 S;
made of bronze ⲃⲁⲣⲱⲧ, CO 459 S, Tor 29 S, Ryl
243 S ⲕⲟⲩⲓ ⲗⲟⲕ ⲃ̄. ϭⲓⲥⲗⲁⲕ F, **half a ⲗ.** (cf ἡμι-
κοτύλη): CMSS 76. ϣⲡⲗⲁⲕ S, -ⲗⲟⲕ B, **measure
containing a ⲗ.**: Ep 293 S, Ex 37 16 B, Nu 4 7 B
(S ⲟⲩⲟⲧϩ) κύαθος, so less than ⲗ. (? l ⲡϣⲗ., cf

ϭⲓⲥⲗ.), also ϣⲗⲟⲕ, -ⲱⲕ B Ex 25 29, Jer 52
19. Ryl 106 3 S put dried ⲗⲓⲗⲟⲟϩⲉ ⲉⲡⲗⲱⲕ
until it soften (same? or v ⲗⲱⲕ vb).

ⲗⲟⲩⲕ B nn m, **cheek** or **corner of mouth**: K 76
الشدق (sic, ı var صدغ). Cf لوق which ? misled K's
interpreter to qui os habet contortum. P 44 69 =
43 39 شدق = ⲥⲧⲟⲓⲭⲟⲥ (quid?) between γνάθος &
τράχηλος.

ⲗⲱⲕ, ⲗⲏⲕ† SB, ⲗⲏⲏⲕ† F (Mor 30 44) vb intr, **be
soft, fresh**: Ge 18 7† S(var ϭⲏⲡ, B ϫⲏⲡ), Is 47 1 B ⲗ.†,
ϫⲏⲡ (S ϭ., ⲗ.), Mk 13 28 S = Mt 24 32† S(BF ϭⲛⲟⲡ)
ἀπαλός, Ez 17 4† B ἁπαλότης; Jud 16 7† S, Lu 23
31† B (S ⲟⲩⲱⲧ), Va 57 41 B ⲉⲅⲗⲏ ⲉϥ(sic)ⲗ.† ὑγρός;
Nu 6 3 B (S ϣⲟⲩⲉⲓ) πρόσφατος; Deu 28 54 B ϫⲏⲡ,
ⲗ.† (S ϭⲏⲡ, ⲥⲗⲉϭⲗⲱϭ, ? confusion) ἀπ., τρυφερός;
Job 7 5 B (S diff) τήκειν; C 89 58 B ⲡⲓⲱⲕ ⲗ.† καλός
= MG 17 576 لين, C 89 86 B pray until loaves ⲗ. =
Miss 4 547 S ⲧ[ⲥⲟ?]; P 43 51 S ψορα(sic l)ⲉⲥⲗⲁⲕ(l
ⲗⲏⲕ) opp ψ. ⲉⲥⲕⲉⲥ جرب اللين, K 73 B ⲫⲏ ⲉⲧⲗ.†
سمين, جسيم; ShP 131¹ 89 S ⲙⲟⲩⲓⲥ ⲁⲡⲉⲓⲗⲱⲱⲙⲉ...ⲛ-
ⲧⲁⲩⲟⲩⲙⲟⲧ ϩⲓⲱⲱⲛ ⲗ. ⲣⲱ; Va 61 201 B child's limbs
ⲉⲥⲗ.†, BMar 47 S after rain ϣⲁⲣⲉⲛⲥⲱϣⲉ ⲗ., ShC 73
137 S grain in oven ⲉⲅⲉⲗ. ϩⲛⲟⲩⲙⲟⲧⲛⲉⲥ, Wess 18 5
S(rubric)day when ⲃⲛⲛⲉ ⲉϥⲗ.† given to community,
PMéd 279 S ⲃⲁϣⲟⲩϣ ⲉϥⲗ.† opp ib 278 ⲃ̄. ⲉϥϣⲟⲟ-
ⲟⲩⲉ, ib 271 sim, BMis 269 SF print ⲉϥⲗ.†, PSBA 32
286 S martyr in cell filled with ass's dung ⲉⲧⲗ.†, AM
230 B ϩⲁⲛϣⲱⲧ ⲉⲅⲗ.† (cf ϣⲁⲣⲟⲩⲱⲧ), AZ 23 106 S
ⲟⲩϩⲉⲣⲃ̄(ⲟⲟ)ϣⲉ ⲉⲧⲗ.†, EW 88 B ϩⲁⲛⲃ̄ⲁⲓ ⲉⲧⲗ.†, J 117
5 S ⲟⲩⲧⲉⲣϭⲁⲙ ⲛⲥⲟⲅⲟ ⲛⲗ. As nn m B: P 54
116 ⲛⲗ. حبوب **fresh grain**. ⲙⲉⲧⲗⲏⲕ B nn, **softness, freshness**: K 58 رطوبة. ⲉⲣ ⲗ. S nn m, **making soft, softening**: PMéd 103 ⲛⲡⲗⲁⲥⲧⲣⲟⲛ ⲛⲡⲉⲣⲗ.

ⲗⲟⲕⲗⲕ S, ⲗⲁϭⲗⲉϭ Sᶠ (Mor 54), ⲗⲉⲕⲗⲱⲕ⸗ S,
ⲗⲉⲕⲗⲱⲕ† SB vb **I** intr, **become soft**: BM 1149 S
ⲉⲣϣⲁⲛⲡⲁⲛⲣ ⲗ., ALR '93 519 S same spirit was rigid
(στύφειν) in Paul & ⲉϥⲗ.† in Barnabas (var P 131⁵
114 ⲗⲟⲕⲗⲉⲕ), PSBA 32 29 S one sort of stone ⲉⲥϫⲁ-
ϫⲱ another ⲉⲥⲗ.†, PChas 1 S ⲟⲩⲅⲁⲧ ⲉϥⲧⲏⲥ...ⲛϥⲗ.,
BMar 161 S = Ming 345 ⲗⲓⲃⲓⲧⲟⲛ ⲛ ⲟⲩϭⲟⲟⲩⲡⲉ opp
ϣⲧⲏⲛ ⲉⲥⲗ.†, MG 25 314 B ⲡⲓϫⲓⲛⲟⲩⲱⲙ ⲉⲧⲗ.†,
TurM 9 S 2 measures of dung ⲉⲅⲗ.† (cf ⲗⲱⲕ),
BMOr 8775 111 B ⲫⲏ ⲉⲧⲗ.† · ⲧⲣⲉⲫⲉⲟⲥ (τρυφερός),
الشيء السمين, cf ⲫⲏ ⲉⲧⲗⲏⲕ. **II** tr S (rare), **soften,
smooth** (?cf ⲥⲗⲟϭⲗϭ): ShP 130⁵ 72 women adorned
in church ϣⲁⲅⲗ. ⲙⲡⲃ̄ⲱ ⲡⲧⲉⲅⲁⲡⲉ, Sh(?)Mor 54 138
why score ye cheeks & ⲉⲧⲉⲧⲛⲗ. hair ?, Bodl(P) a 3
69 recipe ⲟⲩⲡⲁϩⲣⲉ...(ⲛ)ⲧⲉⲕⲗⲉⲕⲗⲱⲕϥ ⲕⲁⲗⲱⲥ. Cf
ⲗⲱϫ (ⲗⲟϫⲗϫ). As nn m SB, **softness**: Job 33 25
B ϯ ⲗ. ἀπαλύνειν (S ⲧⲣⲉ- ϭⲛⲟⲡ), Z 609 S sardius

stone ✝ ⲗ. to tumours μαλακτικός, HL 112 B ⲁⲥⲕⲏⲥⲓⲥ devoid of ⲗ., Mor 37 79 S bodies like jars ⲉⲩ-
ϣⲟⲩϣⲟⲩ ⲉⲃⲟⲗ ϧⲏⲗ. ⲛⲓⲙ ⲛⲧⲉ ⲟⲩⲍⲟⲡⲛ, ib 244 S
ⲡⲗ. ⲙⲡⲛⲉϧ ; Montp 121 B ⲗⲉⲕⲗⲱⲕ طرب, between
ⲭⲃⲟⲃ & ⲙⲉⲧⲧⲱⲥⲓ, cf ⲙⲉⲧⲗⲏⲕ.   P 43 234 S ⲁⲗⲁ-
ⲕⲁⲕⲁⲡⲟⲏⲥ (τραγάκανθα)· ⲡⲗⲟⲕⲗⲉⲕ كثيرا (astragalus), حريرة, ib 34 ⲕⲗⲁⲕⲗⲉⲕ بيض 'S (ⲗ. erroneously
here from confusion with ⲁⲗⲁⲕ-, ⲧⲣⲁⲅ-).

Ⲗⲁⲕⲗⲁⲕ S nn, kind of sweet paste or jelly :
P 43 64 خبيصة which in 44 61 is ⲙⲉⲗⲓⲕⲓⲁ = 43 241
ⲙⲉⲗⲕⲁ, v AZ 24 92, Almk 1 404 ; ib 407 on حريرة
(v above).

Ⲗⲕⲉ S   v ⲱⲗⲕ.

Ⲗⲓⲕⲓ F   v ⲣⲓⲕⲉ.

Ⲗⲕⲟⲩ A   v ⲉⲗⲕⲱ.

Ⲗⲁⲕⲗⲁⲕ nn, ⲗⲟⲕⲗⲕ vb   v ⲗⲟⲕ.

Ⲗⲟⲩⲕⲗⲁⲕ B adj, bad, wicked : BMOr 8771
131 scala شرير, ردي .

Ⲗⲁⲕⲙ, ⲗⲁⲕⲙⲉ S, ⲗⲉⲕⲙⲏ Sᶠ (Cai 67324), ⲗⲉⲕⲙⲉ AA², ⲗⲁⲕⲙⲏ, -ϫⲙⲏ B (both only Ps 147),
ⲗⲉⲕⲙⲓ, ⲗⲉⲭⲙⲓ (Mor 30) F nn f, once m, cf لقمة,
piece, fragment : Jud 9 53 S, Ez 13 19 S (P 129¹³
52 Paul of Tamah), Mt 14 20 SF, Jo 6 12 SA²
(all B ⲗⲁⲕϩ) κλάσμα ; Ps 147 6 B (S = Gk), Ru 2
14 S (var -ⲙⲉ ShP 131ᶜ 37) ψωμός ; BM 180 375
S beryl contains ϧⲉⲛⲗ. ⲛⲁⲃⲉⲓⲥⲉⲓⲛⲉ κέγχρος ; ShC
42 114 S ⲗ. ⲡⲱⲛⲉ & ⲗⲉⲯⲉ ⲡϧⲁⲧ, Ryl 365 S ⲧⲓⲗ.
ⲛϣⲉ, ShA 2 19 S ϭⲉⲗ ϧⲉⲛⲗ. (var -ⲙⲉ) ⲛϣⲉ (cf
Nu 15 33), ib 1 220 S ⲗ. ⲛⲕⲉⲉⲥ paral ⲕⲉⲉⲥ ⲛⲕⲱⲥ,
KroppK 42 S recipe ⲟⲩⲗⲁϭⲙ ⲛⲕⲟⲥ (? l ⲕⲉⲥ) ⲛⲕⲟⲥ,
Mor 52 53 S Mark's martyrdom ⲁⲛⲗ. ⲛⲧⲉϥⲁⲡⲉ
ⲛⲟⲩϧⲉ ⲉⲃⲟⲗ, Mor 30 32 F ⲛⲉⲗ. of broken idol =
BMis 258 S ⲙⲡⲛϣⲉ ⲛϣⲉ, Miss 8 252 S ⲟⲩⲗ.
ⲛⲣⲃⲟⲟⲥ, Mor 46 22 S, Wess 15 2 S sim as potent
relics, ShP 130³ 15 S ϧⲉⲛⲗⲁⲕⲙⲉ ⲛⲕⲁϣ for writing,
Mor 31 112 S bread spent all but ϧⲛⲕⲟⲩⲓ ⲛⲗⲁⲕ-
ⲙⲉ ⲙⲡⲛⲕⲟⲩⲓ ⲛⲥⲣⲉϥⲣⲓⲃⲉ, Cai 67324 vo Sᶠ ⲃⲓⲣ
ⲛⲗ., ϣⲁⲉⲓⲥ ⲛⲗ., ⲗ. ⲛⲥⲓⲥⲙⲛ ⲥⲛⲉⲩ.   Distributive
SA : ⲗⲁⲕⲙ ⲗⲁⲕⲙ : ShA 1 108 S clothes cut into
ⲡⲟϭⲉ ⲡⲟϭⲉ ⲛ ⲗ. ⲗ., P 129¹⁶ 84 S they tore his
shroud [ⲛ]ⲗ. ⲗ.   ⲣ ⲗ. ⲗ., break, tear in pieces :
Lev 2 6 S (B ⲓⲣⲓ ⲛⲗⲁⲕϩ) κλάσμα ; Mic 1 7 A (S
ⲣ ϣⲏⲙ ϣⲏⲙ, B ϫⲟⲙϫⲉⲙ) κατακόπτειν, Mor 22
124 S ⲧⲁⲁⲥ ⲛⲗ. ⲗ. = BSM 113 B ⲙⲉⲣⲟⲥ ⲙⲉⲣⲟⲥ,
R 1 5 30 S ⲁϥⲣ ⲡⲉⲓϫⲱⲗⲟⲡ ⲛⲗ. ⲗ., Gu 10 S they
fell ⲁⲩⲣ ⲗ. ⲗ.

Ⲗⲟⲕⲙ S nn m, meaning unknown : Bodl(P) f
78 among furniture or utensils ϣⲟ]ⲙⲛⲧ ⲉⲡⲗ. ⲁⲩⲱ
ϣ[ⲟ]ⲙ[ⲛⲧ ? ⲟⲩⲡⲟ]ϭ ⲛⲥⲕⲁⲗⲁ ⲉⲥⲱ ⲙⲙⲛ[ⲧ- ? ⲥ]ⲡⲁⲩ
ⲛϭⲟⲣ ⲛϣⲉ ⲡⲁⲧⲁⲣⲙ[.

(Ⲗⲱⲕⲉⲙ), ⲗⲟⲕⲉⲙ✝ B vb intr, be moist, sodden :
Va 57 41 (AZ 13 84) of fire-wood ⲉⲥⲗⲏⲕ (sic l)
ⲟⲩⲟϩ ⲉⲥⲗ.✝ διάβροχος, ib ⲉⲡⲓⲟⲩⲙⲓⲁ ⲉⲧⲗ.✝ ⲟⲩⲟϩ
ⲉⲧⲟⲟⲗⲉⲃ Gk (PG 57 29) diff.

Ⲗⲁⲕⲁⲙⲟⲩ B nn, colocynth : K 198 ⲟⲩⲗ. حنظل.
Prob distortion of κολοκύνθη.

Ⲗⲉⲕⲏⲁⲙ F   v ⲉⲗⲟⲟⲗⲉ (ⲉⲗⲉⲗⲕⲏⲙⲉ).

Ⲗⲁⲕⲏⲧ, ⲗⲁϭⲛⲧ S, ⲗⲁⲕⲉⲛⲧ B nn f S, m B (Ez
4, K), frying-pan, cauldron : Lev 2 5 SB, 2 Kg 6
19 SB, Ez 4 3 SB, LCyp 29 S ⲧⲗ. ⲉⲧⲃⲉⲣⲃⲉⲣ τήγανον, P 44 59 = 43 26 S طاجن, K 129 B sim, Jer 36
22 B ⲓⲣⲓ ⲛⲗ. ἀποτηγανίζειν ; often in tortures : Gu
62 S iron ⲗ. into which bodies cast seems = ib
ⲑⲉⲑⲣⲓⲁ (ὑδρία), Mor 18 192 S ⲗ. 3 ells deep (ϣⲓⲏ),
R 1 5 36 S ⲗ. of iron, C 43 175 B sim opp ⲭⲁⲗⲕⲓⲟⲛ,
SHel 32 S ⲗ. of boiling oil, RNC 56 S ⲗ. of molten
lead ;   among household utensils S : AZ 16 17,
Ep 553, CO 192, 459, ST 125, PLond 4 517 ⲟⲩⲗ.
ⲛⲧⲓ [ⲟ]ⲗⲃⲉ (ⲟⲣⲃⲉ, cf 2 Kg above).

Ⲗⲓϫ B   v ⲗⲓⲕⲧ.

Ⲗⲩϫ (? for ⲗⲓⲕⲥ) S nn, crested lark or hoopoe :
P 43 23 قنبرة, but P 44 56 ϩⲓⲡⲟⲥ · ⲗ. · ⲉⲡⲟⲯ · ⲧⲩⲯ
هدهد.   Coptic ?

Ⲗⲱⲕⲥ, -ϭⲥ, ⲗⲱϧ S, ⲗⲟⲩϫ SB, ⲗϫ- S, ⲗⲟⲕⲥ✝
S, ⲗⲟϫ✝ B, ⲗⲁⲕⲥ✝ F, ⲗⲟϫ✝ B vb I tr, bite, pierce,
stab : Nu 21 6 S (B ϭⲓ ⲗⲁⲡⲥⲓ), Eccl 10 8 S, Mic
3 5 S (A ⲡⲱⲥϧ, B do), Am 9 3 S (A do, B ϫⲱⲕϧ),
Gal 5 15 S (B ϭⲓ ⲗ.), C 89 124 B δάκνειν, Sa 16
9 S δῆγμα, Si 12 14 SB (ὀφιό)δηκτος ; ROC 25
241 B diseased so that no spot found on body ⲉⲗ.
ⲙⲡⲉⲕⲧⲏⲃ ⲉⲣⲟϥ πηγνύναι ; BMis 168 S cerastes
ⲗⲟⲕⲥϥ, ib 191 S if snake ⲗϫ ⲟⲩⲁ, BKU 1 26(4) F
ⲡⲱⲡⲓ ⲉⲧⲁⲡⲟⲩϧⲁⲣ ⲗⲁⲕⲥϥ, BMis 557 S scorpions
ⲗⲱⲥⲥ ⲛⲡⲉϥⲯⲩⲭⲟⲟⲩⲉ, MG 25 239 B one whom
splinter of reed ⲗⲟϫϥ, C 86 177 B ⲛⲁⲩⲗ. ⲙⲡⲉϥⲥⲱⲙⲁ with spears, Va 57 226 B thistle ⲉⲥϫⲱⲕϧ
ⲟⲩⲟϩ ⲉⲥⲗ. them that grasp it, EW 5 B cross ⲁⲩⲗⲟϫϥ ἑρρη in rock, C 43 131 B long nails ⲁϥⲟⲣⲟⲩ-
ⲗⲟⲕⲥⲟⲩ ⲉⲡⲉⲥⲛⲧ ϫⲉⲡⲡⲉϥϫⲫⲟⲧ.
II intr SB : Deu 8 15 S (B ϭⲓ ⲗⲁⲡⲥⲓ), Eccl 10
11 S (l ⲗⲱ-), Va 66 302 B snake ⲉⲧⲗ. ϩⲓⲛⲓⲙⲱⲓⲧ
δάκ., Ryl 104 S (ⲛ)ⲡⲉⲗⲁⲁⲩ ⲉϫⲁⲧⲃⲉ ⲉϣ ⲗⲟⲕⲥ, Miss
4 99 B ⲟⲩⲧⲟⲙⲟⲥ ⲛϫⲱⲙ ⲗ.✝ ϫⲉⲡⲣⲱϥ = Mor 19
11 S ⲧⲟⲕⲥ.

ⲗ. ⲛⲥⲁ- S, bite, snap at : Mor 37 97 hyena
threatening him ⲉⲥⲗ. ⲛⲥⲱϥ δάκ.

ⲣⲉϥⲗ. S, biter : ShC 42 131, BHom 110 snake
ⲡⲣ.   ϣⲥ ⲛⲗ. S, piercing blow, stab : ShZ 601
ⲡⲉϣ. ⲛⲧⲉ ⲡⲛⲟⲃⲉ.

—— nn *SB*, *bite* : JA '75 5 230 *S* ⲟⲩⲗ. ⲛ̄ϫⲁⲧϥⲉ, PMéd 293 *S* ⲡⲣⲱϩ (= ⲗⲱⲕⲥ) ⲡⲟⲩϧⲟⲣ, R 2 4 88 *S* ⲟⲩⲗ. ⲙ̄ⲡⲟⲩⲕⲁⲧⲏⲅⲟⲣⲓⲁ *backbiting*, OrChrNS 3 54 *B* ϭⲣⲟⲡ, ⲗ., ⲥⲕⲁⲛⲇⲁⲗⲟⲛ.

ϣⲉ ⲛ̄ⲗ. *B*, *piercing wood*, *splinter* : Va 61 27 small ϣ. in his eye ξύλον = *ib* 28 ⲡⲓϣⲉ.

This vb ? confused with ⲧⲱⲕⲥ *S*, ⲑⲟⲩϩ *B* : *cf* above C 43 131 with BMis 3 nails ⲛ̄ⲧⲁⲩⲧⲟⲕⲥⲟⲩ ⲉⲡⲉϥⲥⲱⲙⲁ, *cf* EW 5 with BMis 202 cross ⲧⲟϩ ⲉⲡ̄ⲕⲁϩ, Va 57 226 with *ib* words ⲉⲩⲟ. ⲟⲩⲟϩ ⲉⲩⲧⲱ ⲕⲏ like thorns, *cf* C 86 220 split reeds ⲁⲩⲗⲟϩⲟⲩ ⲉϩⲟⲩⲛ in martyr's shoulders with *ib* 221 reeds ⲑⲟϩ in body, *cf* above C 86 177 with *ib* 43 197 ⲁϥⲑ. ⲛ̄ⲧⲁϥⲉ with spear. ROC 25 above sim.

ⲗⲁⲍⲉ (or ⲗⲁϩ) *S* nn as pl, ? *clouts* : Z 351 diseased feet wrapped in ϩⲉⲛⲗ. ⲛ̄ⲧⲟⲉⲓⲥ.

ⲗⲁⲕⲥⲓ *B* nn, *skip, bound* : Va 61 29 mare ⲉⲡⲁⲥϭⲓ ⲗⲁⲡⲥⲓ ⲟⲩⲟϩ ⲉⲥϯ ⲗ. σκιρτᾶν. IgR 337 compares λάξ.

ⲗⲓⲕⲧ (once) or ? ⲗⲓⲕⲧⲏ, ⲗⲓⲕⲧⲉ *S*, ⲗⲓϩ *B* nn m, *veil, covering* : ShEp 56 *S* ⲙ̄ⲡⲁⲧⲥⲱⲧⲙ ⲧⲉⲧⲛ̄ⲗⲓⲕⲧ (*l* ? ⲧⲉⲧⲟ ⲛ̄ⲗ. or vb) ⲙ̄ⲡⲉⲧⲛ̄ϩⲏⲧ ; Ps 17 11 *S* ⲁϥⲕⲱ ⲛ̄ⲟⲩⲕⲁⲕⲉ ⲛ̄ⲗⲓⲕⲧϥ (*B* ⲡⲗⲓϩ ⲡⲁϥ) ἀποκρυφὴ αὐτοῦ, PS 332 *S* darkness ϭⲱ ⲛ̄ⲗⲓⲕⲧϥ ⲙ̄ⲡⲣⲏ, ShC 42 31 *S* clouds ⲉⲧⲛ̄ⲗⲓⲕⲧϥ of sun, ShMiss 4 281 *S* if there be darkness ⲛ̄ⲗⲓⲕⲧⲕ (*sic* ?) ϩⲙ̄ⲡⲉⲕϩⲏⲧ, P 44 96 *S* ⲁϥⲣ ⲗⲓⲕⲧϥ ⲙ̄ⲡⲥⲱⲙⲁ ‎حجاب‎, Va 57 5 *B* (on Lu 12 20) he chose ⲛ̄ⲗ. ⲛ̄ⲧⲉ ⲡⲓⲉϫⲱⲣϩ, *ib* 200 *B* ⲟⲓ ⲛ̄ϩⲗⲟⲗ ⲟⲩⲟϩ ⲛ̄ⲗ. ⲉⲡⲓⲟⲩⲱⲓⲛⲓ, P 44 60 *S* = 43 29 church furniture ⲛ̄ⲗⲓⲕⲧϥ · ⲡⲕⲁⲧⲁⲡⲉⲧⲁⲥⲙⲁ ‎حجاب‎. As vb *S* : *ib* 121 ϣⲁⲣⲉⲡⲙⲁ ⲗⲉⲕ.ϥ ‎يحتجب المكان‎.

ⲗⲁⲕⲟⲟⲧⲉ, ⲗⲁⲕⲟⲧⲉ, ⲗⲁⲁⲕⲟⲧⲉ *S* nn f, *a liquid measure*, mostly of wine = κνίδιον : BM 1064 ⲙⲁⲃⲧⲁⲥⲉ ⲛ̄ⲗ. of wine = *ib* οἶνο(υ) κν(ί)δ(ια) λϛ, Kr 152 ϫⲟⲩⲧⲁϥⲧⲉ ⲛ̄ⲗⲁⲁⲕⲟⲧⲉ (*sic l*) of wine = *ib* οι, κυδ κδ, PMich 4567 ⲟⲩⲗ. ⲛ̄ⲡⲣⲟⲡⲱⲙⲁ (*v* POxy 2047), Baouit 1 162 ⲕⲟⲩⲓ ⲗ., *ib* 8 ⲗ. ⲫⲁⲓ ϣⲱⲙ opp ⲕⲟⲩⲓ ⲗⲁϩⲏ, Saq 226 ⲗⲁⲕ(ⲟⲟⲧⲉ) opp ⲛⲟϭ ⲛ̄ⲗⲁϩⲏ. On capacities of ⲗ. & ⲗⲁϩⲏ *v* WS 23.

ⲗⲉⲕⲱⲧⲥⲓ *F* *v* ⲗⲟⲩⲕⲟϫⲓ.

ⲗⲱⲕϣ, ⲗⲟⲕϣ† *S*, ⲣ c ⲗⲁⲕϣ- (?) vb intr, *be weak* : Hermas Sim 2 5 (P 131⁵ 69) rich man's prayer ϥⲗ.† βληχρός, ShC 42 215 of new house ϩⲉⲛⲥⲁ ⲉⲩⲗ. within & without, Mor 37 159 bodies soft & ⲉⲧⲗ.† ϩⲛ̄ⲧⲉⲧⲣⲩⲫⲏ ; ShC 73 59 among abusive names ⲗⲁⲕϣ ϣⲁ (or ? = ⲗⲁⲕ ϣⲁ). As nn, *weakness* : BAp 112 thou hast taught him ϩⲛ̄ⲟⲩⲗ. as is written of Eli, ROC 20 49, Pcod 20 sim of Eli.

ⲗⲁⲕϣⲁ *S* *v* ⲱⲗⲕ.

ⲗⲁⲕϩ *S* (not bibl) *B*, ⲗⲉⲕϩ *S f F* nn m (f once *v* below), *corner, extremity, top* : Ge 28 18 *B* (*S* ⲕⲟⲟϩ), Ex 34 2 *B* (*S* ⲁⲡⲉ), Deu 4 32 *B* (*S* ⲁⲣⲏϫⲉ), Pro 8 26 *B* (*SA* do), Is 28 4 *B* (*S* ϩⲧⲏⲉ), Mic 5 4 *B* (*A* ⲁⲣ.) ἄκρος ; Ex 26 17 *B* ἀγκωνίσκος ; *ib* 26 23 *B*, Job 1 19 *B* (*S* ⲕⲟ.), Zeph 1 16 *B* (*S* ⲧⲟⲟⲩ, *A* ⲧⲁϣ), *cf* *ib* 3 6, Mt 6 5 *BF* (*S* ⲕⲗⲁⲭⲉ) γωνία ; Ez 41 26 *B* (*S* ⲕⲟ.) ὀρόφωμα ; *ib* 46 22 *B* κλίτος *angulus* ; *ib* 41 22 *B* (*S* do) κέρας *ang.*, *ib* 46 21 *B* μέρος *ang.* ; Ex 25 26 *B* πούς ; Is 11 12 *B* (*S* ⲥⲁ) πτέρυξ ; Deu 22 12 *B* (*S* do) κράσπεδον ; P 55 7 *B* parts of church ⲛ̄ⲗ. ‎زوايا‎, ‎اركان‎. *Piece, fragment* : Lev 2 6 *B* (*S* ⲗⲁⲕⲙ), Mt 14 20 *B* (*SF* ⲗⲁⲕⲙ) κλάσμα ; TSBA 9 358 *B* (*cf* 3 Kg 17 11 ψωμός) ; Lev 7 2 *B* (Lag) ⲗ. error, var Va 1 ⲗⲁ-ⲕⲁⲡ(ⲟⲛ). PS 353 *S* ⲡⲉϥⲧⲉⲩⲗ. of world, MIF 9 55 *S* to Peter ⲉⲕⲉϣⲱⲡⲉ ϩⲙ̄ⲡⲗⲁⲭ of my kingdom, My 66 *S* τρίγωνον which is the 3 ⲗ., AM 75 *B* village ϧⲓϫⲉⲛⲡⲓⲗ. ⲛ̄ⲧⲉ ⲫⲓⲁⲣⲟ *bend*, MG 25 303 *B* ⲡⲓⲗ. ⲛ̄ⲧⲉ ⲡⲓⲫⲟⲣⲕ that he wore = BIF 13 112 *S* ⲕⲟⲟϩ. Builder's *square* : K 124 *B* ϯⲗ. ‎زاوية‎.

ϫⲁϫ ⲗ. *B* adj, *hard-cornered*, of stone : Deu 8 15 (Lect P 104 93, Lag ⲕⲟϩ ⲡϣⲟⲧ, *S* ⲡⲉⲧⲣⲁ ⲉⲥⲡⲁϣⲧ), Job 28 9 ἀκρότομος. *Cf* Jos 5 2 *S* ⲉⲥϩⲟϭⲉ ⲉⲥⲧⲛⲁ.

ϫⲱϫ ⲛ̄ⲗ. *B* nn, *chief corner* (*stone*) : Ps 117 22, Mt 21 42 (*S* ⲁⲡⲉ ⲛ̄ⲕⲟ.) κεφαλὴ γωνίας ; Is 28 16 (*S* ⲕⲟ. ⲛ̄ⲃⲟⲗ), Eph 2 20 (*S* ⲱⲡⲉ ⲛ̄ⲕⲟ.) ἀκρογωνιαῖος.

Place-name ⲡⲓⲗⲁⲕϩ *B Philae* does not contain this word : etymol *Pꜣ-iw-rk*. In *S* is ⲡⲓⲗⲁⲕ.

ⲗⲱⲕϩ *F* *v* ⲣⲱⲕϩ.

ⲗⲟⲩⲕⲟϫⲓ *B* nn m (MG 25 138, Miss 4 183), f (AM 112, 137, BM 1227), ⲗⲟⲕⲟϫⲓ (C 86 173), ⲟⲗⲟⲕⲟϫⲓ f (MIE 2 418) ; ⲗⲉⲕⲱⲧⲥⲓ *F* (CMSS 30), ⲗⲟⲩⲕⲱϭⲉ (BM 530), ⲟⲩⲗⲟⲩⲕⲱⲧⲥⲓ (Kr 53), ⲟⲗⲟⲕⲟⲧⲥⲓ f (Kr 22) = ϩⲟⲗⲟⲕⲟⲧⲧⲓⲛⲟⲥ &c *S* m, ϩⲟⲗⲟⲕⲱⲧⲥⲓ &c f = ὁλοκόττινος = νόμισμα *solidus*. *V* Kr p 30, MR 2 47.

ⲗⲁⲗ *S* nn (?), meaning unknown : ShA 2 349 (*sic* P 129¹² 3) among trades, weavers, clothiers, ⲣⲉϥⲧⲁⲙⲓⲉ ϫⲱ ⲛ̄ⲗ. *makers of cups* (?) of... ? Same ? in place-name ⲡⲗⲁⲗ ⲛ̄ϩⲟⲓⲣⲉ WS 120 *S*. *Cf* also ? name Πλάλ PLond 4 425.

ⲗⲁⲗ in ⲗⲁϩⲣⲟ *B* *v* ϩⲟ(ϩⲁϩⲣⲟ).

ⲗⲏⲗ *B* nn m, *necklace* : K 123 ⲡⲓⲗ. ‎كلبند‎ (*l* ‎كلوبند‎). *V* RylDem 3 269.

ⲗⲓⲗ *F* *v* ⲡⲓⲣ.

ⲗⲓⲗ *SB* *v* ϫⲁϫ *sparrow*.

ⲗⲟⲗ *B* nn m, *bed, bench*: MG 25 99 ⲡⲁϥⲣⲓ
ⲙⲙⲟϥ ⲉⲡⲗ. (*sic* all MSS), *ib* 100 ⲁϥϩⲟⲣⲓ ⲉϥϩⲓ ⲙⲙⲟϥ
ⲉⲡⲗ. as if asleep, Va 57 176 ⲛⲧⲉϥϩⲓⲧϥ ⲉⲡⲗ. (Gk diff).

ⲗⲁⲗⲉ, ⲗⲟⲟⲗⲉ *S*, ⲗⲁⲗⲱ, -ⲟ *B*, ⲗⲁⲗⲱ- *SB*,
ⲗⲁⲗⲉ- *B*, ⲗⲁⲗⲱⲱⲟⲩ, -ⲗⲱ⳿ *SB*, ⲗⲉⲗⲱⲱⲟⲩ⳿ *SⱮ* (BIF
14 127), ⲗⲁⲗⲱⲟⲩ†, -ⲗⲱ†, -ⲗⲏⲅ†, ⲗⲟⲟⲗⲉ† *S*,
ⲗⲁⲗⲏⲟⲩⲧ† *B* vb **I** tr, *smear, paint, overlay* c ⲛ-
(ⲙⲙⲟ⳿), ϩⲉⲛ- of stuff used, acc of obj smeared,
ⲉ- of further obj: Is 38 21 *S* ⲛⲡⲗⲁⲗⲱⲟⲕ ⲙⲙⲟϥ
(*B* ⲙⲛⲓϥ ⲉⲣⲟⲕ) καταπλάσσειν; 1 Chr 29 4 *B* (HCons
194) silver ⲉⲗⲁⲗⲱϥ ⲉⲡⲓϫⲟⲓ ἐξαλείφεσθαι; Jer 22
14† *B* χρίεσθαι; Ex 29 12 *B* ⲗⲁⲗⲉ ⲡⲉⲛⲧⲁⲡ (var
-ⲗⲱ), Jo 9 6 *B* clay ⲗⲁⲗⲱϥ ⲉⲡⲉⲛⲃⲁⲗ (*S* ϫⲱϩ, *A²*
ⲥⲱⲗϭ) ἐπιτιθέναι; Ex 12 22 *B* ⲗⲁⲗⲉ ⲡⲉⲧⲉⲛϩⲟⲟⲩⲁⲓ
ⲕⲁⲑⲓⲍⲉⲓⲛ; 2 Chr 3 7 *B* ⲗ. ⲛ̄ⲛⲟⲩⲃ χρυσοῦν, Ex
26 29 *B*, 2 Chr 3 5 *B* καταχρυ., Is 40 19 *SB* περι-
χρυ.; Bor 143 25 *S* brought pitch ⲛⲥⲉⲗⲁⲗⲱ
ⲡⲉϥⲥⲱⲙⲁ, AM 319 *B* sim, Ann 19 77 *S* ⲁϥⲗⲁⲗⲱ
ⲡⲣⲟ of idol, AM 300 *B* blood ⲁⲩⲗⲁⲗⲱϥ ⲉⲡⲓ-
ⲣⲉϥⲙⲱⲟⲩⲧ; Ps 67 13 *S* ⲉⲩⲗⲁⲗⲱ (var BMis 434
-ⲗⲱⲟⲩ, *B* ⲱϣⲭ) ⲛϩⲁⲧ περιαργυροῦσθαι; ShA 2 87
S swine ⲉⲩⲗⲁⲗⲱ in mud, P 132¹ 17 *S* head ⲗⲁⲗⲱ
ⲛⲓⲧⲛ, Mor 25 93 *S* ⲗⲁⲗⲱⲟⲩ ⲛⲉⲓⲧⲛ, Bodl(P) a 1 *a*
vessel ⲉϥⲗⲁⲗⲏⲩ ⲡⲕⲁϩ ⲡⲥⲟⲫⲟⲥ, PasH 213 *B* ⲉϥ-
ⲗⲁⲗⲏⲟⲩⲧ ϩⲉⲛⲡⲓⲥⲛⲟϥ.
  II intr c ⲉ-: 2 Chr 9 18 *S* (P 44 112) ⲉⲩⲗⲟⲟⲗⲉ
ἐνδεῖσθαι; Z 627 *S* itching feet ⲛⲧⲗⲟⲟⲗⲉ ⲉⲣⲟⲟⲩ,
ib 628 ⲗⲟⲟⲗⲉ ⲉⲣⲟⲥ ϩⲓⲛⲉϩ, PMéd 193 *S* eyes ⲗⲁⲗⲉ
ⲉⲣⲟⲟⲩ, *ib* 265, 305 sim.   *Cf* ⲗⲉⲉⲗⲓ.
  In place-name (?) Πελαλωου PFior 1 150.

ⲗⲁⲁⲗⲉ *S* vb intr, of putrified food producing
worms: ShP 130² 128 manna ⲛⲧⲁϥⲗ. ⲛⲃⲛⲧ ⲁϥ-
ⲗⲱⲙⲉⲥ (*cf* Ex 16 20 ⲣ ϥⲛⲧ), *ib* unsalted meat
ⲉϣⲁⲩⲧⲁⲕⲟ ⲁⲩⲱ ⲡⲥⲉⲉⲣ ⲡⲕⲉⲗ. ⲛⲃⲛⲧ.

ⲗⲁⲗⲟ, ⲗⲁⲗⲱ *B* *v* ⲗⲁⲗⲉ.

ⲗⲉⲗⲉ *B* vb intr, *wander about*: Va 68 172 (AZ
13 84) †ⲗ. ⲉⲓⲙⲟϣⲓ περιέρχεσθαι, P 54 116 scala
ⲉⲩⲗ. (*l* ⲉϥⲗ.) بطيش (*cf* ϩⲁⲗⲟⲗⲉ).   ⲗ. ⲉⲃⲟⲗ,
wander forth, about: Job 2 9 (*S* ⲛⲏⲩ ⲉⲃ.) περιέρχ.;
Pro 7 12 (*SA* ⲕⲱⲧⲉ ϩⲓⲃ.); Va 57 126 mind ⲗ. ⲉⲃ.
ϩⲉⲛⲡⲓϭⲓ ϩⲣⲁϥ ἔξω ῥέμβεσθαι; CDan 84 ⲡⲉϥⲗ. ⲉⲃ.
as if mind were absent περιάγειν; MG 25 180
thoughts ⲗ. ⲉⲃ. ⲟⲩⲟϩ ⲉⲩⲥⲏⲣ ⲉⲃ., *ib* 170 let not
monk ⲗ. ⲉⲃ. ϩⲉⲛⲡⲓⲙⲉⲧⲉϥⲗⲏⲟⲩ.   ⲙⲉⲧⲣⲉϥⲗ. ⲉⲃ.
nn f, *wandering about*: Cat 189 †ⲙ. ϩⲉⲛⲛⲁ ⲉⲙⲁ.

ⲗⲉⲉⲗⲉ *S*, ⲗⲉⲗⲓ *B* in ϩⲁϥⲗ. *q v.*

ⲗⲉⲉⲗⲓ *S* vb intr, meaning unknown: P 129¹⁸
174 martyrs dragged through town until blood ⲗ.
ⲉⲡⲉⲡⲗⲁⲧⲓⲁ, RylSuppl 34 until my blood ⲗ. ⲉⲡⲉ-
ⲛⲡⲗⲁ†ⲁ. *Cf* ⲗⲱⲕⲣ, ⲱϣⲭ, ϩⲱⲣⲡ in sim phrases.
Related ? to ⲗⲁⲗⲉ, ⲗⲟⲟⲗⲉ.

ⲗⲉⲉⲓⲗⲉ† (Maspero), ⲗⲉⲉⲗⲉ† (HT), *S* vb intr,
be pointed, high (?): Cant 4 13 ⲡϣⲏⲛ ⲉⲧⲗ. ἀκρόδρυα (which *ib* 5 1, 7 13 is merely ϣⲏⲛ).   *Cf*
? מגדים.   *V* ϩⲗⲟⲓⲗⲉ.

ⲗⲉⲗⲟⲩ *S*, ⲗⲉⲓⲗⲟⲩ, ⲗⲓⲗⲟⲩ *A*, pl ⲗⲉⲗⲁⲅⲉ
(Ep 359), ⲗⲁⲅⲉ (BKU 1 266, Hall 27, ST 359),
ⲗⲟⲟⲅⲉ (? ST 381), ⲗⲁⲁⲩ (*ib* 376) *S*, ⲗⲓⲗⲁⲅⲉ (Pro
1 32, Cl 16 3) *A* nn m f, mostly with ϣⲏⲙ, *youth,
maiden*: Ex 2 8 *A* f (*B* ⲁⲗⲟⲩ) παιδίον; Pro 1 32 *A*
(*S* ⲕⲟⲩⲓ, *B* do) νήπιος; Cl 1 3 *A* νέος; Sh(Besa)
Z 511 *S* ⲟⲩⲗ. ⲉⲥϩⲓⲙⲉ, ShC 73 98 *S* ⲗ. ϣ. shall
not be set to gather dates (var ϣⲏⲣⲉ ϣ.), Ep 431
S ⲛ̄ⲗ. ϣ. (or ? name), Tor 34 *S* ⲛ̄ⲗ(ⲉⲗ)ⲟⲩ ϣ.,
BP 903 *S* ⲛⲧⲱ ⲟⲩⲗ. ϣ., Ep 452 *S* ⲉⲧⲃⲉⲧⲗ. ϣ.,
Hall 27 *S* greeteth…& ⲛⲉⲗ. ϣ. by name, ST 376
S ⲛⲉⲗ. ϣ. ⲁⲩϩⲕⲟ.   ⲙⲛⲧⲗ. (om ϣⲏⲙ) *A* nn f,
youth, childhood: Pro 2 27 (*S* ⲙⲛⲧⲕⲟⲩⲓ, *B* ⲙⲉⲧⲁ-
ⲗⲟⲩ), Hos 2 15 (*sic* Till, *v* ⲁⲗⲟⲩ, *B* ⲙⲉⲧⲕⲟⲩϫⲓ)
νηπιότης, El 52 ϫⲛⲧⲁⲙ.
  In many names: ⲗⲉⲗⲟⲩ, ⲗⲓⲗⲟⲩ (BM, CO),
Λελοῦς, Λιλ-, Πλελοῦς, Πλιλ-, Ἀρλιλοῦς &c (Preisigke), also ? ⲗⲓⲗⲁⲙⲙⲱⲛ (Saq 150), ⲗⲓⲗⲁⲙⲟⲩ
(BM 1235).   In BMOr 6201 A 22 ⲡⲥⲁϩ ⲗⲓⲗⲟⲩ is
ⲗⲟⲩⲗⲟⲩ in *ib* 66, ⲗⲟⲩⲗⲏ *ib* 103, so *cf* ⲧⲗⲟⲩⲗⲉ
(graffito Nagâdah EW), Τλοῦλλα.

ⲗⲟⲩⲗⲁⲓ *S*, ⲗⲓⲗⲱⲓ *A*, ⲗⲏⲗⲟⲩⲓ *B* (always with
ⲉϣ, ϣ) nn m, *shout*: Ps 26 6 *B* (*S* ⲥⲙⲟⲩ), *ib* 43
12 *S* (*B* diff, reading ἄλλαγμα), *ib* 88 16 *SB*, Jer
20 16 *B* ἀλαλαγμός; 2 Kg 6 15 *S* (*B* ϩⲣⲱⲟⲩ)
κραυγή; Zeph 1 10 *B* (*A* ⲣⲓⲙⲉ ⲉⲃⲟⲗ) ὀλολυγμός;
ShR 2 4 54 *S* day of ⲁϣⲕⲁⲕ ϩⲓ ⲗ., BAp 135 *S*
ϩⲁϩ ⲛⲗ. of distress, Aeg 39 *B* hearkening to ⲡⲓⲉϣ
ⲗ. ⲉⲧⲛⲟⲧⲉⲙ, Va 57 208 *B* story (διήγησις) full of
ⲉϣϣⲗ. (*sic*) ⲛⲧⲉ ϩⲁⲡⲉⲣⲙⲱⲟⲩⲓ, Mor 23 80 *S* those
that respond ⲛⲥⲁⲡⲗ. ⲉⲧⲙⲙⲁⲩ (sc Trisagion).
  ⲱϣ *SA*, ⲉϣ-, ϣ- ⲗ. *SB*, *shout aloud*: 1 Kg 17 52 *B*
(*S* ⲡⲉϫ ⲗ.), Ps 94 1 *B* (*S* † ⲗ.), Jer 29 2 *B* (*S* ⲁϣⲕⲁⲕ),
Mk 5 38 *B* (*S* ⲟⲩⲛ ⲣⲟ ⲉⲃⲟⲗ), 1 Cor 13 1 *B* (*S* ⲱϣ
ⲉⲃ.) ἀλαλάζειν; Joel 1 11 *A* θρηνεῖν; Ez 21 12 *B*
(*S* ⲡⲉϫ ⲗ. ⲉⲃ.) ὀλολύζειν; El 128 *S* ⲥⲉⲡⲁⲱϣ ⲗ.
ⲉⲧⲡⲉ, Tri 327 *S* †ⲛⲁⲱϣ ⲗ. ϩⲁⲡⲁⲓ أتيها.   ⲉϣ ⲗ.
ⲉⲃⲟⲗ *SB*, meaning same: 1 Kg 17 20 *B* (*S* ⲧⲱⲕ
ⲗ. ⲉⲃ.), Ps 80 1 *B*, *ib* 97 4, 6 *B* (*S* † ⲗ.) ἀλαλ.;
Is 13 6 *B* (*S* do) ὀλολ.; FR 32 *S* ⲉⲡⲉⲩⲉϣ ⲗ. ⲉⲃ.
= BMis 66 *S* ⲁⲩϭ̄ⲙ̄ⲡⲉⲩⲉ, BMis 477 *S* ⲁϥⲉϣ ⲗ.
ⲉⲃ. ϩⲁⲡⲣⲁϣⲉ.   ⲉϣ ⲗ. ⲛⲥⲁ- *S*, *cry against*: JTS 9
379 meeting apostles ⲛⲥⲉϣ ⲗ. ⲛⲥⲱⲟⲩ as if in war.
  ⲡⲉϫ ⲗ. ⲉⲃⲟⲗ *S*, *utter shout*: Jos 6 20 ἀλαλ.;
Hos 7 14 (*A* †ⲕ ⲗ. ⲁⲃ., *B* ⲉϣ ⲗ.) ὀλολ.
  ⲧⲱⲕ ⲗ. ⲉⲃⲟⲗ *S*, †ⲕ ⲗ. ⲁⲃ. *A*, meaning same:
1 Kg 17, Hos 7 *ut sup*.

† ⲗ. S, *give shout*: Jth 14 9, Ps 80 1 (*B* ⲉⲱ ⲗ. ⲉⲃ.) ἀλαλ.; Is 13 6 (*B* ⲇⲟ) ὀλολ.; Mus 42 266 cymbal ⲉϥϯ ⲗ. ⲛⲛⲁϧⲣⲏⲡⲉⲧⲟⲩⲉⲡⲉⲣⲅⲉⲓ ⲙⲙⲟⲟⲩ.

ⲗⲱⲓⲗⲓ *B* *v* ϧⲗⲟⲓⲗⲉ.

ⲗⲏⲏⲃ, ⲉⲗ-, ⲗⲗⲏⲏⲃ (ShA 1 198) S nn, *jesting, buffoonery*: Eph 5 4 (*B* = Gk) εὐτραπελία (cit ShWess 18 138, Leyd 404), BAp 164 ⲡⲉⲗ. ⲡⲭⲓ ϧⲣⲁϥ ⲉⲑⲟⲟⲩ, ShP 130² 104 ⲥⲱⲃⲉ, ⲗ., ⲗⲩⲡⲏ, Sh(?)A 2 262 ⲛϭⲉⲓⲣⲉ ⲛⲣⲉⲡⲉⲗ., P 44 122 ز̇ه. As adj: BAp 151 make not merry ϧⲛⲗⲁⲁⲩ ⲛϣⲁϫⲉ ⲡⲉⲗ., PBu 114 ⲛⲉϥϣⲁϫⲉ ⲛⲗ. that [? stink] like woman's ⲧⲟⲉⲓⲥ ⲛⲡⲣⲱ, BHom 19 ϣⲭⲗⲏϥ. *Cf* Dévaud *Études* '22 47.

ⲗⲁⲗⲟⲩⲕⲏⲛ, -ⲕⲏⲡ *B* nn, *betelnut* (or *cedar*?): K 180 تنبل, Löw 58 ε. *Cf* P 43 34 ⲕⲟⲡⲧⲟⲥⲟⲕⲁⲗⲉ (*cf* κένδρος, κέδρος) · ورق, تنبل. Coptic?

ⲗⲉⲗⲏⲙ, ⲗⲉⲣⲗⲏⲙ *B* *v* ϧⲗⲱⲙ.

ⲗⲁⲗⲉⲉⲧ *S*ᶠ nn m, *meaning unknown*: CMSS 75 account ⲁⲣ ᶿⲁ ⲗⲁⲗⲉⲉⲧ, *ib* ⲧⲁⲕⲏ ⲉⲡⲗⲁⲗⲉ[ⲉⲧ.

ⲗⲏⲗⲟⲩⲓ *B* *v* ⲗⲟⲩⲗⲁⲓ.

ⲗⲉⲗⲉⲭⲏⲙ *B* *v* ⲉⲗⲟⲟⲗⲉ.

ⲗⲉⲗϣⲟⲟⲩⲉ, ⲗⲓⲗϣⲟⲟⲩ *S* *v* ⲉⲗⲟⲟⲗⲉ.

ⲗⲓⲗⲟⲟⲣⲉ, ⲗⲉⲗⲱⲣⲉ, ⲉⲗⲟⲟⲣⲉ, ⲗⲟⲣⲉ *S* nn f, *bdellium*: P 44 81 ⲧⲗⲓⲗ. ⲙⲩⲅⲁⲣⲉⲗ (*quid* ?) مقلة (مقل), P 43 241 ⲉⲗ. ⲙⲉⲭⲁⲣⲓⲥ ⲙⲓⲭⲗⲁⲧⲟⲥ مثلة (*l* مقلة) مقل is *hyphæna theb.*, dûm palm), EW scala (Nitria) list of trees ⲧⲗ. مقل, R 1 5 48 martyr bound ⲉ[ⲟⲩ]ϣⲗⲗⲟⲣⲉ (*sic* MS = ? ϣⲡⲗⲟⲣⲉ) & there burnt (In Mor 32 50 this is thorny ⲕⲛⲡⲁⲣⲓⲟⲛ (κόναρος) = Synax 1 327 سدر, *cf* P 44 81 ⲕⲛⲡⲁⲣⲓ, K 177 ⲕⲉⲡⲡⲁⲣⲓ); *v* ⲕⲛϧⲏⲣ. Elsewhere ? diff word: as sg, BMOr 6201 A 149 ⲉⲓⲥ ⲧⲉⲓⲃⲧⲟ ⲛⲗⲓⲗⲱⲣⲉ[, *ib* B 15 sim, *ib* A 9 ⲱ(*l* ⲟⲩ)ⲗⲓⲗ., Ryl 106 2 recipe ⲟⲩⲣⲁ ϥⲧⲟⲟⲩ ⲛⲗⲓⲗ. ϣⲟⲟⲩⲉ, BM 477 ⲟⲩⲗⲉⲗ. ⲛⲡⲉⲣⲥⲉⲙ (? ⲃⲉⲣⲥⲓⲙ); as pl, BM 1114 ⲡⲉⲣⲓⲗⲱⲣⲉ ⲡⲉⲗⲟⲗⲉ, PMich 4550 co ⲗⲉⲗⲱⲣⲉ ⲡⲉⲗⲟⲗⲉ (*cf* ? ⲉⲗⲉⲗⲟⲩⲟⲣⲉ, *v* ⲉⲗⲟⲟⲗⲉ).

As place-name: PLond 4 205 Τλειλόορει, 201 Τριλόορε, 202 Τλιλόολε (all same).

ⲗⲁⲙ *B* nn m, *meaning unknown*: Va 61 100 fabulous animal ⲁⲗⲗⲱⲏ (*q v*) whose food ⲡⲓⲗ. ⲛⲥⲟⲓ ⲛⲟⲩϥⲓ...nothing but ⲛϣⲉ ⲛⲥⲟⲓ ⲛⲗ.= Mor 25 18 S ⲃⲱⲝⲁⲡⲏ (βοτάνη) ⲡⲓⲙ ⲛⲥϯ ⲛⲟⲩϥⲉ & JTS 4 394 S, which both om ⲛϣⲉ ⲛ-, so ⲗ. may ? = ϣⲉ *wood, stalk*. K 197 ⲡⲓⲗ. عشار (عشر) *calotropis procera* (Schweinfurth *Ar Pflanz* 10, 109) scarcely same. *Cf* ⲗⲁⲙⲣⲏⲧ.

ⲗⲉⲙ- *F* *v* ⲣⲱⲙⲉ (ⲣⲙ-).

ⲗⲟⲙ *S* nn, *meaning unknown*: BM 1203]ϧⲓⲗ. ⲁⲩⲱ ⲛⲡ[. *Cf* ? Kr 196 *S*]ⲗⲁⲙ.

ⲗⲟⲙ, ⲗⲱⲙ, ⲗⲱⲙⲓ (3 Kg), ⲗⲱⲓⲙⲓ (Stern 133) *B* nn m, *morsel, bit*: 3 Kg 17 11 (var Cai Copt Mus 1051 ⲗⲟⲙ), Jo 13 26 (*SA²* ⲟⲉⲓⲕ) ψωμός, -μίον, K 261 om ⲡⲓⲗ. لقمة, though all MSS have it. Bodl 325 54 scala, Ar note : this Coptic word, translated bread (خبز), recurs not in this form (صيغة) in church books save here & it is said those of Saʿîd that speak Coptic call *bread* in their idiom (طانة) ⲡⲓⲗⲱⲙ.

ⲗⲱⲙ in ⲡϣⲗⲱⲙ *S* *v* ⲗⲱⲣⲉ.

ⲗⲟⲟⲙⲉ, ⲗⲟⲩⲙⲉ (R), ⲙⲟⲟⲗⲉ *S*, ⲗⲁⲁⲙⲓ *S*ᶠ nn m f, *bait*: R 2 2 31 S ⲛⲗ. ⲛⲧⲁⲡⲁⲧⲏ (var BHom 48 ⲙⲙ.) ἁπαλοῖς δελέασμασι, BAp 170 S riches ⲉⲧⲟ ⲙⲙ. ⲛⲧⲟⲓⲙⲉ, BMOr 6201 A 125 S ⲟⲩϥⲓⲗ. (*l* ϥⲓⲣ) ⲛⲗ. ⲡ[, *ib* ⲉⲣⲉⲥⲁϣⲥ̄ ⲛⲛⲟϭ ⲛⲗ. ϧⲓⲱⲱϥ (unless these = *bread*, *v* last word, Bodl 325), BM 529 *S*ᶠ ⲕ̄ⲃ̄ ⲛⲗ. ⲛⲧⲃⲧ, *ib* ⲧⲉⲓⲥⲩⲡⲧ[ⲉ ⲛⲗ]ⲁⲁⲙⲓ ⲉⲧⲟⲩⲱⲧ *fresh bait*, Kr 245 S among expenses ϧⲁⲗ. ⲙⲟⲟⲗϥ S nn m, ? same : P 131⁴ 101 devil ⲕⲏⲣⲁ (κεραννύειν) ⲙⲡⲙ. ⲛⲧⲉϥⲕⲁⲕⲓⲁ ϧⲛⲟⲩⲉⲃⲓⲱ.

ⲗⲱⲱⲙⲉ, ⲗⲱⲟⲙ, ⲗⲱⲙ *S*, ⲗⲱⲙ *B*, ⲗⲟⲟⲙⲉ†, ⲗⲟⲙⲉ† (ShA 2 157), ⲗⲁⲁⲙⲉ† *SS*ᶠ*A*, ⲗⲁⲁⲙ† *S*, ⲗⲁⲙ† *B* vb intr, a *wither, fade*: Jos 9 11 S ⲗⲁⲁⲙ παλαιοῦσθαι; Job 24 24 *B* (*S* ϧⲱϭⲃ), Ja 1 11 *B* (*S* ⲇⲟ) μαραίνειν; Ez 21 7 *B* (*S* ⲇⲟ) ἐκψύχειν; Va 57 170 *B* flowers ⲁⲩⲗ., BMis 2 *S* ⲙⲉⲣⲉⲡⲉⲥϣⲏⲛ ⲗⲱⲱⲙ, *ib* 90 S womb ⲡⲧⲁⲥⲗⲱⲱⲙ & dried up, Aeg 31 *B* ⲛⲡⲉⲡⲓϣⲱ...ⲗ. b *be filthy* (mostly qual): Zech 3 3 *S* ⲗⲁⲁⲙ *A* (*B* ⲁⲑⲓⲱⲟⲩ), Ja 2 2 *S* ⲗⲁⲁⲙ (*B* ⲇⲟ) ῥυπαρός, Wess 18 74 *S* ⲙⲡⲉⲣⲕⲁ ⲡⲉⲕⲥⲱⲙⲁ ⲉϥⲗⲁⲁⲙ ἐν ῥυπαρίᾳ; BMis 542 *S* raiment ⲉⲩⲗⲁⲁⲙ μέλας; FR 14 *S* ⲙⲡⲉⲧⲉⲥϣⲧⲏⲛ ⲗⲱⲱⲙⲉ ⲉⲛⲉϧ, ShA 2 87 *S* streets ⲉⲩⲗⲟⲟⲙⲉ with mud, ShR 2 3 69 *S* ⲉϥⲗⲁⲁⲙⲉ with filth of sins, Mor 27 21 *S*ᶠ ϧⲁⲓϥ ⲉⲧⲗⲁⲁⲙⲉ = BMis 360 *S* ⲗⲁⲁⲙ, Mor 19 35 *S* sim ⲉⲧⲗⲁⲁⲙ = *ib* 18 26 ⲗⲁⲁⲙ = Miss 4 119 *B* ⲗ.†, Mich 550 39 *S* ⲉⲣϣⲁⲛⲧϭⲁϭⲓⲧⲱⲛ ⲗⲱⲙⲉ they washed it.

ⲁⲧⲗ. *SB* adj, *unfading*: Tri 514 *S* fruit ϧⲛⲟⲩⲙⲛⲧⲁⲧⲥⲣⲟϥⲣⲉϥ ⲙⲡⲟⲩⲙⲛⲧⲁⲧⲗⲱⲙ غير ذبول، C 43 220 *B* crown ⲛⲁⲧⲗ., Bor 109 282 *S* Christ's ⲥⲛⲟϥ ⲛⲁⲧⲗ.

ⲗⲱⲱⲙⲉ, ⲗⲱⲱⲙ(Mor) *S*, ⲗⲱⲙ(K), ⲗⲟⲙ *B* nn m, *filth, witheredness*: Mor 17 123 *S* ⲛⲗ. of soul ῥύπος; ShP 131⁴ 89 *S* ⲙⲟⲟⲓⲥ ⲁⲡⲉⲓⲗ. ⲛⲧⲁⲟⲩⲙⲟⲧ ϧⲓⲱⲱⲛ ⲗⲱⲕ ⲣⲱ, ShMIF 23 195 *S* ⲉⲓⲁⲁϥ ⲉⲃⲟⲗ ϧⲙⲡⲉⲥⲗ. (*l* ⲡⲉϥ-), P 131⁴ 104 *S* ashamed ⲉⲧⲃⲉⲡⲗ. ⲙⲡⲁϧⲟ, EW 12 *B* (Descensus in Infern.) ⲁϥϣⲓⲟⲩⲓ ⲉⲃⲟⲗ ⲙⲡⲗⲟⲙ ⲙϥⲙⲟⲩ, K 261 *B* ذبول (*manuring* of land, or ? *l* ذبول *fading*).

ⲗⲱⲙⲓ *F* *v* ⲣⲱⲙⲉ.

(ⲗⲟⲙⲗⲙ *S*), ⲗⲉⲙⲗⲱⲙ† *SF* vb intr, meaning unknown: PMéd 162 *S* ⲟⲩⲥⲟⲗ ⲉⲡⲕⲁⲑⲓⲥⲙⲁ ⲉϥⲗ.† suppository for anus that is…(Chassinat: *putrified*, cf ⲗⲱⲱⲙⲉ), Ryl 106 23 *S* recipe ⲧⲉϥⲥⲟ ⲡⲭⲉ[. ⲡ]ⲉⲣⲱⲧⲉ ⲉⲡⲁⲧⲥⲁⲣⲧⲉ ⲣⲓⲭⲱⲥ ⲗⲉⲙⲗⲱⲙ ⲉⲉⲩⲁ… (obscure), BMEA 10585 *F* letter ϩⲉⲓ ⲧⲓⲱϩ (*l* ϯⲟⲩⲱϩ) ϥⲱⲃ ⲉⲃⲗⲉⲙⲗⲱⲙ.

ⲗⲟⲙⲗⲙ, ⲗⲉⲙⲗⲏⲙ *v* ϭⲗⲟⲙⲗⲙ.

ⲗⲉⲙⲙⲉⲁ, ⲗⲉⲙⲉⲁ *F* *v* ⲣⲱⲙⲉ (ⲣⲙⲙⲁⲟ).

ⲗⲓⲙⲏⲛ, ⲗⲓⲙⲛ (BMis 271) *SB* nn m (not bibl) *portrait, image*, painted (ζωγράφειν, ⲥϩⲁⲓ) or engraved (sculptured ϥⲱⲧⲣ), corresponds to no Gk word, nor confused with λιμήν, but? Coptic: BMis 1191 *S* saint's gold ⲗ. set up (πηγνύναι) before sanctuary, *ib* 271 I will make thy ⲗ. with mine lying at thy feet, P 129¹⁴ 125 *S* ϩⲛⲗ. ⲙⲙⲟⲡⲟⲭⲟⲥ (painted) on wall, KKS 89 *S* εἰκών whereon ⲗ. painted (var ⲭⲁⲣⲁⲕⲧⲏⲣ), BSM 98 *B* ζωγράφος to carve (ϥ.) ⲗ. on piece of wood, C 43 186 *B* ⲗ. depicted on wall, P 43 28 *S* ⲗ. · صورة = ⲥⲟⲅⲣⲁϥⲓⲁ, ϩⲓⲕⲱⲡ قرن, K 216 *B* sim.

ⲗⲁⲙⲡⲓ *F* *v* ⲣⲟⲙⲡⲉ.

ⲗⲁⲙⲣⲏⲧ *B* nn, a herb: P 54 127 حشيش (*i e* unidentified by author). Cf ? ⲗⲁⲙ (ⲗⲁⲙ + ⲣⲱⲧ).

ⲗⲉⲙⲁⲥ *S* nn m, meaning unknown: BM 1165 letter naming ⲡⲥϩⲁⲩ (*sic*) ⲁⲑⲁⲡⲁⲥⲉ ⲛⲗ.

ⲗⲱⲙⲥ, ⲗⲁⲙⲉⲥ (Bodl) *S*, ⲗⲟⲙⲥ† *SB*, ⲗⲁⲙⲥ† *F* (Lant 11 D) vb intr (not bibl), *be foul, stink*: ShA 1 261 *S* unsalted meat ϣⲁϥⲗ., *ib* 2 158 *S* carrion ⲉϥⲗ.†, Bor 145 8 *S* ⲉⲓⲁⲃⲉ…ⲉϥⲗ.†, DeV 2 98 *B* spring of water ⲉⲑⲗ.†, ShZ 501 *S* wine ⲉⲧⲗ.† ⲁⲩⲱ ⲉⲧⲟ ⲛϭⲡⲧ, CA 107 *S* that wine turn not to vinegar ⲛϥⲧⲙⲗ., Mich 550 40 *S* mouths ⲗ. ϩⲁⲡⲉⲣⲕⲟ, DeV 2 235 *B* air ⲗ.† ⲉⲑⲃⲉⲡⲓⲥⲟⲩⲃⲱⲛ.

—— *S* nn m f (once), *foulness, putrescence*: ShA 1 253 fish if die ⲭⲱⲣⲓⲥ ⲗ. are eaten, ShR 2 3 84 waters of sea & ⲡⲉⲥⲗⲱⲙⲥ (*sic l*?), Mor 22 88 ⲡⲗ. ⲛϯⲁⲁⲃⲉ of corpse, BHom 87 salt cannot ϫⲱⲕⲣ ⲛⲡⲗ. of Judas, BMar 95 crop ⲁⲓⲧⲣⲉϥⲣ ϭⲟⲛ (= ϭⲛⲟⲛ) ϩⲓⲗ., Miss 4 643 wine ϣⲁⲩⲉⲣ ϩⲉⲙϫ ϩⲓⲗ. (*cf* C 41 42 *B*), PMich 4237 sorts of wine ϥⲓⲭ, ⲡϭⲱⲛ, ⲡⲗ., Kr 29 wine contract ⲉⲕϣⲁⲛϭⲛ ϩⲙϫ ⲏ ⲗ. ϩⲓⲱⲟⲩ, Tor 7, ST 89, Ryl 206, PMich 4241 sim (*cf* Wess 20 104 ὀζόμενος), Bodl(P) a 1 e garment ⲓⲁϥ ⲉⲃⲟⲗ ϩⲛⲧⲗⲁⲙⲉⲥ ⲉⲧⲣⲓⲱϥ. Adj: ShEp 56 ⲡⲉⲧⲛⲏⲣⲡ ⲛⲗ.

ⲗⲁⲙⲧⲓ *F* nn f, meaning unknown: BM 580 11 to woman ⲉⲣⲓ ⲉⲕⲛⲙⲓ ⲉⲛ ⲉⲧⲉⲓⲗ., *ib* 15 ⲧⲣⲁⲙⲧⲓ, PMich 1193 vo ϭⲣⲉⲓ ⲛⲁⲓ ⲧⲓⲗ., *ib* ⲧⲁⲙⲁⲓ ϫⲉϩⲛⲡⲧⲁⲡϫⲁⲧ ⲧⲁⲗⲁ ⲧⲓⲗ. ⲁⲃⲥⲉⲧ ⲡⲉⲃⲁⲧⲉϥ ⲉⲃⲁⲗ. Prob not = ⲗⲁⲙⲡⲓ (ⲣⲟⲙⲡⲉ).

ⲗⲁⲙϣⲟⲩ *B* nn (?), meaning unknown: P 54 117 scala ذلك خلاف *contrary to, beyond this* (? refers to preceding word). Cf name or place Πλαμόου (Preisigke).

ⲗⲉⲙⲛⲏϣⲉ *S* nn m, *warrior, champion*: 1 Kg 17 51 (P 44 109 رئيس حربهم, *B* ⲣⲉⲙⲛϫⲟⲙ) δυνατός, Job 15 24 (*B* = Gk) στρατηγός. V PSBA 21 271, RylDem 3 234 n (citing λεμεῖσα), Spg *Demotica* 1 6. *V* ⲙⲛⲏϣⲉ & for ⲗⲉ- also ⲗⲁϣⲁⲡⲉ.

ⲗⲉⲙϩⲏ *F* *v* ⲣⲙϩⲉ.

ⲗⲁⲙϫⲁⲧⲡ *S* (oftenest) *B*, ⲗⲁϫ. (BMis 538), -ϫⲁⲧ (Bor 143 25) *S*, -ϫⲁⲡⲧ *SB* (oftenest), -ϫⲁⲡ *S*, -ϫⲉⲡ (PMéd), -ϫⲉⲧ (CO) *S*, -ϫⲉⲉⲧⲡ (El 46) *A*, -ϫⲉⲧⲡ *SF*, -ϫⲉⲡⲧ *F* nn m, *tar, pitch*, cf זפת (IgR): Si 13 1 *SB*, Is 34 9 *SBF*, Dan 3 46 *SB*, Bel 26 *B*, Glos 231 *S* πίσσα, Ex 2 3 *B* ⲉⲙⲃⲣⲉϩⲓ ϩⲓⲗ. (*A* ⲁⲙⲣⲏϥⲉ only) ἀσφαλτόπισσα, Glos 235 *S* ⲗ. ⲉⲃⲟⲩⲱⲧ ὑγρόπισσα. As pl: CO 510 *S* ⲛⲉⲗ. ⲛⲡⲧⲟⲡⲟⲥ, BMOr 6201 A 176 *S* in account ϩⲁⲛⲗ. ⲗ. ⲛϫⲩⲣⲟⲛ (π. ξηρά) PMéd 271 *S*, opp ⲗ. ⲉϥϣⲟⲡ (π. ὑγρά) Z 628 *S*. Often with ⲁⲙⲣⲏϥⲉ *q v*, or ⲁⲙ. & ⲁⲥϥⲁⲗⲧⲟⲛ Bor 264 40 *S*, or ⲑⲏⲛ *q v*. PS 257 *S* that ye be saved from raiment ⲛⲗ. ϩⲓⲕⲱϩⲧ of the cynocephalus, *ib* 259 the sea of ⲗ. of Ialdabaoth. Pots coated with ⲗ.: Pcod 27 *S*, cf BM 531 *S*. ⲥⲁ ⲛⲗ. *F*, *pitch-dealer*: AZ 23 28.

ⲗⲁⲓⲛ, ⲗⲁⲉⲓⲛ, ⲗⲉⲉⲓⲛ (BAp), ⲗⲁⲓⲏⲛ (BM, *cf* name) *S* nn m, *steel*: Si 34 29 στόμωμα, BM 174 1 fasting hardeneth body like ⲟⲩⲗ. ⲏ ⲟⲩⲡⲉⲡⲓⲡⲉ οἰονεὶ βαφὴ σιδήρου…στομώσασα; PS 212 gold, silver, bronze, ⲡⲃⲉⲛⲓⲡⲉ ⲙⲛⲡⲗ., PMich 1190 magic ⲡⲣⲁⲧ ϫⲉⲉⲕⲉ ⲙⲟⲟⲩⲧϥ ⲛⲗ. ϫⲉ(ⲉ)ⲕⲉⲟⲅⲟⲗⲡϥ ⲡⲉⲡⲓⲛⲉ (ϫⲉ)ⲉⲕⲉ ⲃⲟⲗⲉⲃ ⲉⲃⲟⲗ, MIF 9 43 chain of iron & ⲗ. (BAp 6 om), BAp 162 if stone strike ⲡⲗ. fire is kindled, Ryl 239 ⲟⲩⲗ. ⲛⲥϩ ⲕⲱϩⲧ, *ib* 242 ⲗ. ⲥⲡⲁⲩ. ⲗⲁⲉⲓⲛⲉ &c, *steel-smith* (?), Spg & Preisigke *Inschr… Gebel Silsile* 16; *cf* name.

As name: ⲡⲗⲏⲉⲓⲛ, ⲡⲗⲏⲓⲡⲉ (Hall 32), ⲡⲗⲁⲉⲓⲛⲉ (CO 140), Πλῆνις &c (Preisigke), Πλεεῖν POxy 1910.

ⲗⲉⲛ *F* *v* ⲣⲁⲛ.

ⲗⲉⲟⲛ *S* (Jud) *B*, ⲗⲉⲟⲥ *B* nn, *earring, bracelet* (once): Ge 35 4 (*cf S* ϭⲁϫⲉ CA 89), Ex 32 2 (*S* do), Jud 8 24 *S* (+ϭ. as gloss), Is 3 20 (*S* ϭ.), Hos 2 13 (*A* ⲕⲁϣⲁⲃⲉⲗ), Ez 16 12 ⲗⲉⲟⲥ (? transposed, *S* do) ἐνώτιον; K 122 ⲗⲉⲟⲥ القرط في الأذن; Va 62 282 *B* ψέλιον & ⲗ. on feet & hands. ? from (ποδοψέλ)λιον, cf P 44 86 ⲡⲟⲇⲟⲧⲓⲉⲗⲉⲟⲛ خلخال.

ⲗⲉⲛⲧⲏⲛ, -ⲑⲏⲛ, ⲗⲁⲡⲑⲏⲛ (BMis 352), ⲗⲁⲡⲑⲉⲛ (*ib* 554) *S* nn m, *saw*: P 44 59 = 43 27 ⲡⲗ.,

ⲛⲃ̅ⲁϣⲟⲩⲣ both منشار, ShZ 637 carpenter has ⲃⲁϣ. to cut or ⲗ. to saw, cf Z tab VII (same MS) word ⲗ. above drawing of a saw, BMis 352 Isaiah sawn with ⲗ. ⲛϣⲉ = Mor 27 19 ⲃ̅. ⲛϣⲏ = BSM 17 B ⲃⲁϣ., MR 4 132 word-list (mostly Gk) ⲗⲏⲡⲧⲏⲡ (but = λέντιον Krall). Coptic?

ⲗⲉⲛϫⲓ (var ⲗⲓⲛ-) B nn m, *coat of mail, cuirass*: K 117 ⲡⲓⲗ. كازغند (l كَزاغَند). Cf? Ryl 139 S ⲗⲏⲛⲧⲥⲉ (? λέντιον) among dowry. C 86 177 B among clothing ⲧⲉϥⲗⲉⲛⲧⲓ is f, so not same.

ⲗⲁⲡⲗⲉⲡ, ⲁⲗⲁⲡⲗⲉⲡ B v ϩⲗⲟⲡⲗⲡ.

ⲗⲁⲡⲏⲓ F nn m, meaning unknown: BM 599 9 ⲟⲩⲡⲁⲣϣ ⲉⲡϯ ⲡⲉⲓ ⲧⲁⲥⲉⲧ ϩⲁⲗⲁⲓ ϩⲓⲡⲗ., ? again *ib* 14.

ⲗⲁⲡⲥ F nn, also as indef pron, rare except in literary texts = S ⲗⲁⲁⲩ, B ϩⲗⲓ, *anyone, -thing, someone, -thing*, but oftenest with neg vb or particle: **a** positive, Jo 4 33 (Z, JTS 1, SBA² ⲟⲩⲁ) τις. **b** neg, Mt 13 34 (S ⲗⲁⲁⲩ, B om), 1 Cor 2 15 (Mor 38 104, S do, B ϩⲗⲓ), Gal 6 17 (Mich 550 9, SB do) οὐδείς, μηδείς. **c** ⲛ-, EpJer 68 (B diff) οὐδείς, Mor 24 14 ⲙⲉⲡⲧⲏ ⲙⲓⲭⲁⲏⲗ ϩⲁⲗ. ⲡϩⲱⲃ ⲡⲥⲁ-, BMEA 10585 letter ⲙⲉ(ⲡ) ⲗ. ⲉϩⲱⲃ ϣⲁⲡⲕⲉⲗⲉⲩⲉⲓ ⲡⲉⲓ (but I will do it).

ⲗⲁⲡϯ used as ⲗⲁⲡⲥ, sometimes both in one text (Mk in ÉtLeem, Jo in JTS), originally ? l ⲗⲁⲡⲯ: Mk 16 8 (S ⲗⲁⲁⲩ, B ϩⲗⲓ), Jo 3 27 (SB do), *ib* 4 27 (SB do), ZNTW 24 86 ⲙⲡⲉⲣⲧⲉϥϫⲓ ⲗ. οὐδείς, μηδείς; Worr 323 ⲁϫⲉⲡⲧ (sic) ⲙⲡⲉⲗ. ϣⲱⲡ[ⲓ] (cf Jo 1 3), BIF 22 106 ⲙⲡⲉⲗϣⲁⲡⲡ ⲗ. ⲉⲡⲉϩⲟⲩ = Mor 41 192 S ⲗⲁⲁⲩ. **c** ⲛ-, Mor 30 14 ⲙⲡⲗ. ⲙⲡⲱⲗϩ in thy body = BMis 240 S do, cf Mor *l c* ⲗⲁⲁⲩ ⲡⲧⲁⲕⲟ.
As nn, Mor 30 16 ⲁϥⲁⲡϥ ⲉⲩⲗ. = BMis 242 S do. V ⲗⲁⲁⲩ, ϩⲗⲓ.

ⲗⲉⲯ (Lev), ⲗⲓⲯ (Tri) S nn m, *one having an eye-disease*: Lev 21 20 ⲉϥⲟ ⲡⲗ. (B ? ⲟⲓ ⲡⲕⲁⲕ ⲃⲁⲗ, v KKS 50, PMéd 217) ἔφηλος (or ? πτίλος *ll c*) = P 44 106 مجدم, cf ? Vulg *lippus*; Tri 531 ⲡⲗ. جدري. ⲗⲉⲯⲉ as disease of eyelids: PMéd 216 recipe for growth of lashes when lids o ⲡⲗ. ⲗ. ? *cracked, broken*. Cf ⲗⲉⲯⲉ below.

ⲗⲱⲡⲥ S vb tr, meaning unknown: ShC 73 169 cursed he that shall ⲗ. ⲙⲡⲉⲧϩⲓⲧⲟⲩⲱϥ ϩⲛⲟⲩⲕⲣⲟϥ. Related ? to next.

ⲗⲁⲡⲥⲓ B vb tr, *bite, seize*: MG 25 134 animal ⲁⲥⲗ. ⲡⲧⲁϣⲟⲛⲡ, *ib* 239 asp ⲁϥⲗ. ⲙⲡⲓϭⲉⲗⲗⲟ ϩⲉⲡⲧⲉϥϥⲁⲧ. As nn + ϭⲓ, meaning same: Deu 8 15 (S ⲗⲱⲕⲥ), Mic 3 5 (S do, A ⲡⲱⲥ), Va 61 29 mare ϭⲓ ⲗ. & ϯ ⲗⲁⲕⲥⲓ δάκνειν; **c** ⲉ-: Nu 21 8

(S ⲗⲟⲩϫ ⲛ-), Gal 5 15 (S-do); ⲥⲛ-: Hab 2 7 (A ⲡⲱϩⲥ *sic l*), Aeg 17 snake ϭⲓ ⲗ. ⲙⲡⲓⲁⲗⲟⲩ; ⲥ ⲡⲥⲁ-: Nu 21 9 (S ⲟⲩⲱⲙ); ⲥ ϩⲓ-: Ge 49 17 all Gk δάκ.

ⲗⲉⲯⲉ, ⲗⲉⲡⲥⲉ, ⲗⲓⲯⲉ S, ⲗⲁⲡⲥⲓ B nn m, *fragment, small portion*: ShC 42 114 S idols are ⲗⲁⲕⲙ ⲡⲱⲛⲉ & ⲗⲉ. ⲡϩⲁⲧ ϩⲓⲛⲟⲩⲃ, ShC 73 173 S ⲡⲗⲉ. ⲛⲏⲣⲡ, ShZ 507 S eating or drinking ⲡⲗⲉ. ⲛⲭⲣⲉⲓⲁ, CO 211 S ⲟⲩⲗⲓ. ⲛⲥⲕⲉⲡⲓⲛ[ⲓⲥ]ⲉ, Ep 356 S pray for me ⲡⲧⲁⲱⲗ ⲡⲉⲓⲗⲓ. ⲡⲉⲡⲟⲩⲁⲉ (sic l, v ⲉⲓⲟⲡⲉ), *ib* 360 ϣⲱⲧ ⲟⲩⲗⲓ. ⲛϣⲏ, MG 25 255 B cup fell & ⲁϥⲉⲣ ⲟⲩⲙⲏϣ ⲛⲗ. = GöttAr 114 108 قطعا تكسر. Prob related to ⲗⲉⲯ.

ⲗⲁⲡⲧ B v ⲗⲁⲧⲡ.

ⲗⲁⲡϯ F v ⲗⲁⲡⲥ.

ⲗⲉⲡⲁϣⲓ B nn as pl, *trunks of trees*: BMOr 8775 132 ⲛⲓⲗ. كرناف (K 177 om). Cf ⲕⲁϥⲁϫⲓ.

ⲗⲁⲥ SBO, ⲗⲉⲥ AF nn m, *a tongue*: Ex 11 7 B, Job 6 30 SB, Is 32 4 SBF, Lu 1 64 SB γλῶσσα; Ex 4 10 A ϯϩⲣⲁϣ ϩⲙⲡⲁⲗ. (S ⲗ. ⲛϣⲏⲣⲉ, B ⲥⲁⲓⲱⲟⲩ ⲁⲛ) βραδύγλωσσος, cf AZ 21 100 O ⲉϥⲟⲣϣ ⲛⲡⲉⲃⲗⲁ[ⲥ; PS 94 S ⲡⲁⲗ. ⲡⲁⲅⲙⲡⲉⲣⲉ ⲉⲣⲟⲕ, ShP 130¹ 139 S ⲡⲉⲥⲗ. ⲡⲣⲉϫⲉ ⲛⲟϭ ⲛϣⲁϫⲉ, RO 14 369 B forgive ⲡⲁϣⲱϥⲧ ⲡⲗ., KroppB S magic ⲛⲧⲁϩⲉ ⲣⲁⲧⲕ ⲡⲡⲉⲕ ⲥⲁϣϥ ⲛⲗ. ⲉⲃⲟⲗ. **b** *language*: Ge 10 5 B, Ac 2 4 B (S ⲁⲥⲡⲉ), 1 Cor 12 10 B (S do) γλ.; *ib* 14 10 B (var & S ⲥⲙⲏ) φωνή; ⲁⲥⲡⲉ, -ⲡⲓ ⲛⲗ. SB γλ., v ⲁⲥⲡⲉ. ⲕⲉ ⲗ. B, *other tongue, foreign-tongued*: 1 Cor 14 21 (S ⲕⲉ ⲁⲥ.) ἑτερόγλωσσος; Bar 4 5 ⲕⲉⲁⲥ. ⲡⲗ. ἀλλόγλ. **c** ⲗⲁⲥ ⲥⲛⲁⲩ SAB, *two tongues, double-tongued*: Pro 11 13 SAB, Si 28 14 S δίγλωσσος; TstAb 253 B slanderers & ⲛⲓⲗ. ⲃ̅; ⲙⲛⲧⲗ. ⲥⲛⲁⲩ S nn f, *double-tonguedness, duplicity*: Bor 226 158 διγλωσσία; ⲣ ⲗ. ⲥⲛⲁⲩ S, *be double-tongued*: Aeg 240 ⲡⲡⲉⲕⲣ ⲗ. ⲥ. **d** *tongue-shaped objects*: ⲗ. ⲡⲉⲓⲟⲙ S, *sea-tongue, cuttle-fish bone*, v ⲉⲓⲟⲙ; ⲗ. ⲡⲕⲁⲙ SB, *splinter, needle of reed*, v ⲕⲁⲙ; ⲗ. ⲡⲛⲟⲩⲃ S, *tongue, wedge of gold*: Jos 7 21 S γλ. χρυσῆ, P 129¹⁴ 127 S ⲛⲗ. ⲛⲡ. & rings of gold torn from rich; ⲗ. ⲛϣⲓⲣⲉ S, *uvula* (cf above Ex 4 10): Glos 151 κιονίς· ⲡⲗ. ⲛϣ.; ⲗ. ⲡⲙⲥⲁϩ S, *crocodile's tongue*, plant (? κροκοδείλιον): P 44 83 ⲕⲟⲣⲕⲟϫⲓⲗⲟⲩⲃⲟⲧ(ⲁⲡⲏ) لسان التمساح = 43 59 التّ ⲗ. حشيش; ⲗ. ⲡⲟⲩϩⲟⲟⲣ S, *hound's tongue*, plant (κυνόγλωσσον): P 44 *l c* الكلب 'ا; PMéd 134 S ⲟⲃⲉⲛ ⲛⲗ. ? *schistous alum* (Chassinat). ⲫⲁⲡⲓⲗⲁⲥ B nn m, *the tongued*, among weaver's tools: K 126 ملسن. ϫⲁϫ, ϫⲟϫ ⲗ. B nn as pl, *tongue-cutting*, epithet of ⲥⲛⲏⲓ: C 86 191, 271. ϭⲁϫⲉ ⲗ. S, *with cut tongue*: Lev 22 22 (JTS 7 72 *sic l*, var Mor ϭⲁⲡⲁϩ, B ⲉⲣⲉⲡⲉϥ ⲗ. ϣⲁⲧ) γλωσσότμητος. SF, *stammering*: Is 35 6 (B ⲗ.

...ⲡⲧⲉ ⲡⲓⲉⲃⲟ) μογιλάλος, cf ? Va 61 5 B ⲟⲩⲥⲁϫⲓ ⲉϥⲟⲓ ⲙⲡⲓⲥⲙⲟⲧ ⲛⲡⲓϫⲁϧⲉⲃ ⲗ., or for ⲗ. ⲉⲧϧⲟϫⲉⲃ as Is 29 24 B, though this = SF ⲉⲧⳓⲟⲟϫⲉ.

As title: Ann 8 79 S ⲁⲛⲇⲣⲉⲁⲥ ⲡⲗ., cf ? ostr unpubl ⲁⲡⲁ ⲇⲁⲅⲉⲓⲁ ⲡⲗⲁⲥ (sic).

ⲗⲁⲥ S, ⲗⲉⲥ F (once) nn m, *flax, tow*: Jud 15 14, 16 9 στύππιον, Lev 13 47 gloss on ⲥⲓⲡⲡⲟⲛ (B ιⲁⲩ) στιππύινος, Si 21 10 στυππεῖον; Ez 40 3 ⲛⲟⲩⲅ ⲛⲗ. (B diff) σπαρτίον *funiculus lineus*; P 131⁴ 107 Samson brake ⲛⲛⲟⲩⲅ ⲛⲗ. (v Jud 15 14), BMOr 6201 A 104 supply of 6 κεντηνάρια of ⲗ. ⲉⲩϧⲏⲕ *beaten flax*, Ryl 211 ϩⲙⲉ [ⲛⲗⲓ]ⲧⲣⲁ ⲛⲗ. ⲛⲣⲱⲕⲉ, PRain 4714 ⲡϣⲏⲙ ⲛⲗ. ⲛⲣⲱⲕ, Kr 5 δεσμοί 55 of ⲗ. cost 1 *solidus*, BMOr 6201 A 72 (v Ryl 160 n) I owe thee 16 ⲙⲁⲣ ⲉⲗ....ⲛⲁⲩ ⲛⲓⲙ ⲉⲣⲉⲡⲉⲕⲙⲁⲣⲉ ⲡⲁⲉⲓ ⲉⲃⲟⲗ ⲧⲛⲉⲓ ⲧⲓⲣϩⲟⲟⲗⲟⲩ ⲛⲁⲕ, BM 1128 ⲁⲓⲣ ϩⲱⲃ ⲉⲡⲗ. ϣⲁⲕϧⲉ ⲙⲏⲧ ⲛⲕⲛⲏⲧⲉⲡⲁⲣⲓⲟⲛ ⲛⲥⲓⲡⲡⲱⲛ (στύππιον) ⲁⲓⲛⲏⲧⲟⲩ ⲉⲃⲟⲗ (so c. is product of ⲗ.), TurM 3 ⲛⲧⲁⲭⲟⲟⲩ ⲛⲗ...ⲛ̄ⳓⲣⲓⲥⲧⲟⲩ, WS 93 ϣⲟⲙⲛⲧ ⲛⲗ. ⲛⲥⲓⲛⲟⲩ *flax for making tow* (?, *cf* Lev 13 above), PMich 1193 ro 7 *F* ⲧⲉⲃϧⲏ (= ⲛⲧϧⲣⲉ) ⲛⲉⲗⲥⲓⲡⲡ ⲗⲉⲥ ⲕⲁⲗⲱⲥ, vo 23 ⲉⲡⲡⲉⲕϣⲉⲡ ⲕⲁⲗⲱⲥ ⲁⲗⲥⲓⲡⲡⲓ ⲗⲉⲥ (with Ar art), also ? BM 580 17 *F*. *Cf* ⲙⲁϩⲉ *flax*.

ⲗⲁⲉⲓⲥ F v ⲣⲟⲉⲓⲥ.

ⲗⲏⲥ SB nn m, meaning uncertain, *? jaw*: MG 25 239 B seized serpent's lips ⲁϥⲫⲟⲣϫϥ ϧⲉⲛⲧⲉϥ ⲙⲏϯ ϣⲁⲡⲉϥⲗ. ⲁϥⲁⲓϥ ⲛ̄ⲃ, BIF 13 114 S seized ⲛⲗ. ⲃ̄ of serpent swallowed by other & drew it forth (though ? *l* ⲗⲏⲥⲃ, as numeral ⲃ̄ unlikely in S).

ⲗⲱⲱⲥ SS'F, ⲗⲱⲥ SB, ⲗⲟⲩⲥⲉ(?)A, ⲗⲉⲥ- S, ⲗⲁⲥ/ B, ⲗⲁⲁⲥ, -ⲥⲉ† S, ⲗⲁⲥ† B vb **a** intr, *be bruised, crushed*: Lev 22 24† SB, Deu 23 1 B (S ⲥⲟϩϧ) θλαδίας, Mt 21 44 S (B refl) συνθλᾶσθαι, Is 63 3 B ⲗ. ⲉϫⲉⲛ- (S ⲗⲱϧϧ) καταθλᾶν. **b** tr, *bruise, crush*: Ps 73 14 S/ (PcodMor, S ⲗⲱϧ, ⲗⲱϫϧ) B συντρίβειν; Hab 3 13 A (S ⲛⲟⲩϫⲉ ⲉϫⲛ-, B ϩⲓⲟⲩⲓ ⲉϫⲉⲛ-) *percutere*; ShA 1 394 S ⲗⲉⲥ ⲟⲩⲏⲡⲧ with his foot, K 472 B ⲉϥⲉⲗⲁⲥϥ [Arabic]; PasH 35 B shall fall on them ϥⲛⲁⲗⲁⲥⲟⲩ ⲉϩⲣⲏⲓ.
ⲙⲛⲧⲁⲧⲗ. S nn f, quality of *not being crushed*: Mor 37 165 of Antony ⲧⲉϥⲙ. ϩⲛⲛⲁϩⲓⲱⲧⲥⲙⲟⲥ.

ⲗⲱⲱⲥ S nn m, fruit of *sycamore-fig*: Aeg 261 among fruits not to be blessed ⲛⲗ. [Arabic] (PO 8 612 = HSt 104, Lat Hauler 115 om). *Cf* ⲉⲗⲕⲱ, ⲛⲟⲩϩⲣⲉ.

ⲗⲉⲥⲉ S nn, meaning unknown: Ryl 381 ⲁϥⲃⲁⲕ ⲗ. (ⲙ)ⲙⲟϥ ⲁϥⲙⲟⲩⲣ ⲛⲧ[. Or ? ⲃⲁⲕⲗⲉⲥⲉ = *μαγκλ(αβ)ίζειν.

ⲗⲉⲥⲓ F nn, meaning unknown: CMSS 78

account ⲛ̄ ⲕⲟⲗⲗⲁⲑⲓ ⲛⲗ. (κόλλαθον is dry or liquid measure, WS 22).

ⲗⲟⲩⲥⲉ A v ⲗⲱⲱⲥ vb.

ⲗⲱⲥⲕ S vb intr, *putrify*(?) or sim: ShA 1 67 (= Z 396 sic) filthy is dog returning to vomit (pl) ⲙⲡⲁⲧⲟⲩⲱⲥⲕ, more filthy if ⲙⲛⲡⲥⲁⲧⲣⲉⲩⲗ. ⲛⲥⲉⲕⲛⲟⲥ ⲛⲥⲉⲣ ϭⲛⲧ. ⲱⲥⲕ would suit, but v Z.

ⲗⲉⲥϯ F v ⲣⲁⲥⲧⲉ.

ⲗⲁⲧ, ⲗⲉⲧ S nn, *parsley*: P 44 83 ϩⲃⲉⲣⲡⲁ(σμύρνα)ⲥⲉⲗⲓⲛⲟⲩ ⲁⲅⲣⲓⲟⲩ · ⲑⲁⲣⲙⲁⲛ ⲑⲉⲇⲣⲁϧ (θρίδαξ) · ⲗⲉⲧ ϩⲟⲟⲩⲧ [Arabic]; but (1) P 43 59 here ⲗⲉⲉⲗ (l ⲉⲗⲉⲗ) ϩⲟⲟⲩⲧ [Arabic], (2) [Arabic] ⳓ = ⲕⲣⲁⲙ & ⲙⲓⲧ qq v; BP 11349 crops of field ϣⲟⲙⲧⲉ ⲛⲥⲁⲙⲛⲧ ⲛⲥⲓⲙ ⲛⲗⲁⲧ ⲛⲟⲩⲧϥ.

ⲗⲉⲧ F v ⲣⲁⲧ.

ⲗⲟⲩⲧ (sic) S nn, meaning unknown: CO 292 letter from clerics about one who had said ⲁⲩⲙⲓⲥⲉ ⲛⲟⲩⲗ. ⲛⲁⲡⲥⲟⲛ (ⲛⲁ- dat).

ⲗⲱⲧ F v ⲣⲱⲧ.

ⲗⲱⲧⲉ, ⲗⲱⲱⲧⲉ S vb intr, *be hard, callous*, of skin: Deu 8 4 (Mor, Bodl(P) d 53) feet ⲙⲡⲟⲩⲗ. ⲉⲣⲟⲕ (B ⲉⲣ ϣⲁϣ) τυλοῦν; *be wounded*: P 44 121 = 43 129 hands ⲁⲩⲗ. & poured forth blood [Arabic]. As nn, ? *hardness* of skin: PMéd 314 recipe useful for ⲛⲗ. & itchings in loins; but *cf* Z 629 where paral ⲡⲉⲕⲟⲗⲟⲧⲏ (? καλλωσόν, whence ? ⲗⲱⲧⲉ Chassinat), or *l* ⲡⲉⲕⲉ-.

ⲗⲱⲧⲉⲃ F v ⲣⲱⲧⲃ.

ⲗⲁⲧⲃⲥ, -ⲃⲉⲥ S nn f, *patch, joining material*: Is 41 7 (B ⲡⲁⲡⲁⲓ) σύμβλημα; ϩⲓ ⲗ. ⲉ-, *put patch upon*: Jos 9 11 καταπελματοῦσθαι or ἐπίβλημα ἔχειν which in P 44 108 ⲗⲁⲧⲃⲉ = 43 97 ⲗⲁⲧⲃ [Arabic].

ⲗⲁⲧⲡ S, ⲗⲁⲡⲧ, ⲗⲉⲃⲧ B nn m, *turnip*: BMOr 8775 133 B ⲛⲓⲗⲉ. [Arabic], Bodl 325 151 B (Tatt 841) ⲛⲓⲗⲁ. [Arabic]. P 44 82 S ⲛⲗⲁⲧⲡ (*l* ⲛⲗ., or ? *l* ϣⲁⲗⲧⲙ = ϣⲗⲧⲙ) · ⲥⲓⲛⲁⲡⲓ [Arabic]. *Cf ib* = 43 57 ⲅⲟⲅⲅⲏⲗⲓⲟⲩ (γογγυλίς) [Arabic], no Coptic; K 196 sim; Bodl(P) b 6 S ⲟⲩⲁⲅⲕⲏⲛ (ἀγγεῖον) ⲛⲗ. same?

ⲗⲟⲧϫ S vb intr, meaning unknown: PLond 4 518 account ⲉⲣⲉⲗⲉⲁⲥ (ⲡⲉ)ⲫⲩⲗⲁϧ ⲗ. ⲉⲣⲟⲓ. ? for ⲗⲱϫⲧ (v ⲗⲱϧⲕ).

ⲗⲁⲩ F v ⲗⲟⲟⲩ.

ⲗⲁⲁⲩ, ⲗⲁⲩ SS/ nn, a textile material, or ? indicates use of a garment: PMich 3552 ⲟⲩⲗⲱⲧⲏϧ

(λῶδιξ) ⲡⲗⲉⲅⲕ(ⲟⲥ) ⲡⲗ., J 66 41 = 76 44 ⲗⲟⲧⲍ ⲡⲗ., Ep 545, 546, ST 110 (prob) sim, P 131⁶ 37 (MS of C 73 209) luxurious monks wear ⲥⲟⲩⲛⲁⲥϭ ⲡⲗ. ⲙⲡⲣⲉⲡⲗⲱⲧⲍ, ST 125 ⲗⲟⲧⲓⲍ ⲡⲗⲁⲅⲉ ⲡⲭⲏⲕⲉ (? *l* ⲗⲁⲅ ⲉⲡ-), cf BP 4977 list ⲗ. ⲡⲭⲉⲕⲉ as if ⲗ. a kind of garment, cf Ep 351, BM 699 *Sf* ⲡⲁⲣⲉⲕ ⲡⲗ., but *contra* ST 199 ⲟⲩⲃⲓⲣ ⲡⲗ. basket (full) of ⲗ. *Cf* ⲣⲱⲧ *wool*.

ⲖⲀⲀⲨ *SF,* ⲗⲁⲁⲅⲉ, ⲗⲁⲅⲉ, ⲗⲁⲟⲅⲉ *SAA²,* ⲗⲁⲟⲩ, ⲗⲁⲅⲉⲓ, -ⲓ *F* nn used as pron, mostly = *'B* ϩⲗⲓ, sometimes *F* ⲗⲁⲡⲥ, ⲗⲁⲡϯ.

I positive, *anyone, -thing, something,* **a** without art : Jo 9 32 *SA²* (var ⲟⲩⲟⲛ. *B* ⲟⲩⲁⲓ), Ac 24 19 *S* (*B* ⲟⲩϩⲱⲃ), 1 Cor 8 2 *SF* (*B* ϩⲗⲓ), Z 334 *S* ⲉⲣϣⲁⲛⲗ. ϣⲱⲡⲉ ⲙⲙⲟϥ *τις, τι*; PS 281 *S* hide naught ⲉⲗ., BM 229 *S* ⲟⲩⲛ ⲗ. ⲡⲁϣ ⲁⲙⲁϩⲧⲉ ⲡⲧⲟⲣⲅⲛ?, Miss 4 637 *S* ⲉⲓⲛⲁϭⲛ ⲗ. ⲧⲱⲛ?, BMis 260 *S* = Mor 30 35 *F* ⲟⲩⲛ ⲗ. ⲛⲧⲟⲟⲧ, ST 228 *S* when abroad thou wilt need ϩⲁϩ ⲡⲗ. (cf Cl 52 1 *A* ϩⲗⲉⲓ ⲡⲗ.), PBu 127 *S* if one die ⲉⲟⲩⲛⲧⲁϥ ⲡⲣⲱϣⲉ ⲡⲗ., J 68 84 *S* sim. **b** with art or poss pron : Ge 14 23 *S* (*B* ϩ.) Gk om., Ac 3 5 *S* (*B* ⲡϫⲁⲓ) *τι*; ShC 73 86 *S* constrain him ⲉⲟⲩⲉⲙ ⲟⲩⲗ., Mich 550 39 *S* ⲕⲁ ⲟⲩⲗ. ϩⲁϫⲱⲓ as pillow, Mor 25 11 *S* if thou needest ⲟⲩⲗ. (var P 131 83² ⲉⲓⲁⲟⲥ, Va 61 93 *B* ⲡϫ.), ST 261 *S* ask him ⲛϥϯ ⲟⲩⲗ. ⲛⲁⲡ, PBu 122 *S* sought to take ⲟⲩⲗ. ⲉⲡⲱϣ ⲁⲡⲡⲉ, Bor 263 21 *S* if we labour ⲛⲧⲛϫⲡⲟ ⲡⲟⲩⲗ., BM 253 2 *S* know we not ϫⲉⲟⲩⲗ.ⲡⲉ ⲉϩⲁⲣⲉϩ ⲉⲡⲉⲛⲥⲱⲙⲁ ⲉϥⲟⲩⲁⲁⲃ *something* (important), RNC 50 *S* ⲟⲩⲗ. ϣⲏⲙ remaineth, CO 256 *S* ⲟⲩⲕⲟⲩⲓ ⲡⲗ. to poor, Z 353 *S* sim; *ib* 629 *S* cast mixture ⲉⲩⲗ. ⲛⲃⲣⲃⲉ (*q v*), Ryl 243 *S* ⲟⲩⲗ. ⲛϯ ⲥⲧⲟⲓ ⲉϩⲣⲁⲓ, ShA 2 63 *S* ⲡⲥⲉⲕⲁ ϩⲉⲡⲗ. ⲉⲡⲁϩⲟⲩ, BMEA 10503 *S* ϩⲛⲗ. ⲛⲧⲁⲅⲉⲓ ⲉⲃⲟⲗ ϩⲛⲡⲁⲟⲩⲅⲉⲣⲏⲧⲉ; BM 1131 *S* send ⲡⲉⲗ. ⲛⲁⲓ, Raccolta ...*Lumbroso* 283 *S* ϣⲓⲛⲉ ⲛⲥⲁⲡⲓⲗ. that I sent thee, Ryl 243 *ut sup* ⲡⲗ. ⲛⲃⲁⲣⲱⲧ. Doubtful are Ep 351 *S* ⲧⲓⲡⲁⲥⲉⲡⲱ (ⲧⲥⲁⲡⲟ) ⲡⲉⲗ., Hall 36 *S* ⲉ]ⲣⲁϭⲛ ⲡⲉⲗ. ⲛⲥⲱϣ ⲙⲡⲧⲉⲙⲛⲥⲉ (*sic l*), Vi ostr unpubl *S* ⲁⲓϣⲓⲛⲉ ⲛⲥⲁⲡⲗ. ⲙⲡⲁⲉⲓⲱⲧ ⲡⲥⲱⲕ, Tor 1 *S* loan repaid ⲁⲓⲁⲡⲟⲧⲁⲥⲥⲉ ⲡⲛⲕⲁⲇⲟⲥ ⲡⲁⲕ ϣⲁⲡⲉⲕⲗ. ϫⲉⲓⲭⲣⲉⲓⲱⲥⲧⲁ ⲡⲁⲕ, MR 5 45 *S* have received 3 *solidi* ϩⲁⲡⲉⲕⲗ., PAntinoe(*penes* EES)*S*(ⲉ)ⲕⲁϭⲡ ⲡⲉⲕⲗⲁⲟⲩ (ⲉ)ⲕⲁϯ ⲟⲟⲥⲉ ⲁⲡ, ST 199 *S* ⲛ ⲛⲥⲟⲩⲱⲣ(ϩ) ⲡⲛⲓ ⲉⲃⲟⲗ ⲡⲁϥ ⲛ ⲡⲥⲧⲓ ⲡⲉϥⲗ. ⲡⲁϥ (or ? *v* ⲗ. textile). **c** ⲕⲉⲗ., *any other* : BHom 28 *S* anger or ⲕⲉⲗ. ⲙⲡⲁⲑⲟⲥ *ἄλλος τις*; Aeg 232 *S* ⲛ ⲕⲉⲗ. ⲡⲉⲧⲩⲅⲅⲉⲛⲏⲥ *ἕτερος*; ShA 1 141 *S* ⲡⲁⲧϫⲓⲁⲕⲟⲡⲓⲁ ⲛ ϭⲉⲗ. ⲡⲣⲱⲙⲉ, Pcod 36 *S* ⲉⲧⲃⲉⲕⲉⲗ. ⲡⲭⲣⲉⲓⲁ. **d** ⲗ. ⲡⲓⲙ, ⲡⲓⲃⲉⲛ, *every ...on, -thing* : BM 217 3 *S* ⲗ. ⲡ. ⲉⲧⲣⲓⲭⲙⲡⲕⲁϩ whether man or beast, BMar 219 *S* God who named ⲗ. ⲡ. = Mor 48 32 ⲉⲡⲕⲁ ⲡ. = Rec 6 185

B ⲟⲩⲟⲛ ⲛⲓⲃⲉⲛ, J 73 14 *S* ⲗ. ⲡ. ⲉϥϩⲣⲁ, Kr 116 *Fᵇ* ⲗ. ⲡⲓϥⲉⲛ that king ordain (*ὁρίζειν*), BMar 243 *S* ⲗ. ⲡⲣⲱⲙⲉ ⲡ., J 53 5 *S* ⲗ. ⲡⲁⲥⲫⲁⲗⲉⲓⲁ ⲡ. **e** adj +ⲡ-, *any, every, some* : Deu 5 8 *S* (*B* ⲡⲕ ⲧⲏⲣⲟⲩ) *πᾶς*; Aeg 209 *S* ⲗ. ⲛ̄ⲣⲡⲗⲁⲁⲩ *τις*; *B* Gk often om : Lev 7 17, Deu 28 51, Ps 13 2, Eccl 4 8, Ap 7 1; Br 100 *S* ⲗ. ⲡⲣⲱⲙⲉ ⲉϥϩⲡⲗ. ⲙⲡⲓⲥⲧⲓⲥ, ShC 73 148 *S* ⲗ. ⲛϭⲓⲛⲟⲩⲱⲙ ⲉϥϣⲟⲃⲉ, BM 708 *F* iron articles ⲟⲩⲗ. ⲡⲉⲃⲓⲧ (ⲉⲓϥⲧ), BMis 534 *S* ⲟⲩⲁⲁⲃ ⲉⲗ. ⲡⲭⲱⲣⲙ, PMich 1828 *S* ⲕⲛⲟⲣⲙ ⲉⲗ. ⲡⲡⲉⲑⲟⲟⲩ, ROC 20 49 *S* let not women stare ⲉⲙⲡϩⲟ ⲡⲗ. ⲡⲣⲟⲟⲩⲧ, Ep 247 *S* ye have not spoken with me ⲡⲟⲉ ⲡⲗ. ⲛⲥⲟⲡ, CMSS 45 *F* ⲗ. ⲛⲛⲁⲡⲟⲕⲣⲓⲥⲓⲥ that thou biddest I will perform, Mor 55 71 *S* ϣⲁⲣⲉⲗ. ⲛⲡⲟⲃⲉ ...ⲉⲓⲱ ⲉⲃⲟⲗ, PRain 4711 *S* if I have ⲗ. ⲛⲡⲁⲣⲟⲩⲥⲓⲁ (*παρρησία*) with you, J 106 163 *S* ⲗ. ⲛⲟⲩⲟⲡ. Adj also **II d** & **IV**. **f** partitive : 1 Kg 12 3 *S* ⲗ. ⲙⲙⲱⲧⲛ *τις*, Hag 2 13 *SA* (*B* om) ⲗ. ⲛⲛⲁⲓ *πᾶς*; BMar 73 *S* ⲗ. ⲙⲙⲟⲛ.

II with Coptic neg (oftenest), **a** no art, (not) *any*: Ge 31 44 *S* (*B* ϩⲗⲓ), Nu 16 15 *S.*(*B* ⲟⲩⲁⲓ), Pro 8 8 *SA* (*B* ϩ.), Mt 10 26 *S* (*B* om), Jo 3 27 *S* (*B* ϩ., *F* ⲗⲁⲡϯ), AP (BerlSitz '09 217) *A²* *οὐδείς*; Ex 16 29 *S* (*B* ϩ.), Ps 55 6 *S* (*B* do), Mk 8 30 *S* (*B* do, *F* ⲗⲁⲡⲥ), Ro 12 17 *SF* (*B* do) *μηδείς*; Mt 12 19 *S* (*B* ⲟⲩⲁⲓ), Lu 8 17 *S* (*B* om), Ac 10 47 *S* (*B* ϩ.), Mor 37 74 *S* let not ⲗ. ϯ ϩⲧⲏϥ ⲉⲥⲱⲧⲙ *τις, τι*; AP 10 *A²* ⲛϥⲣ ⲭⲣⲓⲁ ⲉⲛ ⲡⲗ. *ἀπροσδεής*; Gk om : 4 Kg 9 10 *S*, Si 33 9 (36 12) *S*, Is 5 14 *S* (*BF* diff), Mic 4 4 *SA* (*B* om), Mt 14 17 *S* (*BF* om); BMar 111 *S* he departed ⲉⲙⲛ ⲗ. ⲥⲟⲟⲩⲛ *λεληθότως*; BG 44 *S* ⲁϫⲛⲧ ⲙⲛ ⲗ., PS 19 *S* ⲉⲙⲡⲉⲗ. ⲉⲓⲙⲉ, Br 257 *S* ⲛⲛⲉⲗ. ⲕⲱⲗⲅ ⲙⲙⲟϥ, PS 16 *S* ϯⲛⲁϩⲉⲛ ⲗ. ⲉⲣⲱⲧⲛ ⲁⲛ, CA 93 *S* ⲛⲧⲟⲩⲉϣ ⲗ. ⲁⲛ, Kr 140 *F* (ⲛ)ⲡⲉⲡⲉⲗ. ϫⲁⲉ[ⲓⲥ ⲉ]ⲉⲙⲉⲣⲓ (ⲙ)ⲙⲁⲕ ⲉⲗ. ⲡⲣⲟⲩⲡ (ⲉ)ⲗⲁⲃ. **b** with art : Am 3 4 *S* (*B* ϩ. om art) *τι*, Ryl 106 14 *S* eat it ⲙⲡⲁⲧⲉⲕⲟⲩⲱⲙ ⲟⲩⲗ. **c** ⲕⲉⲗ. (not) *any other* : Gal 5 10 *S* (*B* ϩⲱⲃ) *οὐδ.*; Sa 14 21 *S* name not given to ϭⲉⲗ. *ἀκοινώνητος*, ShBor 246 24 *S* ⲡⲕⲉⲗ. ⲁⲡⲡⲉ ⲡⲥⲁ-, CO 306 *S* ⲡⲡⲉⲉⲓϣ ϫⲡⲟⲩⲕ ⲉⲕⲉⲗ. ⲛϭⲡⲗⲁⲁⲩ, ST 41 *S* sim. **d** adj +ⲡ-, (not) *any one, -thing* : Deu 24 5 *S* (*B* ϩ.), Sa 7 5 *S*, Mk 6 5 *S* (*B* ⲟⲩⲁⲓ) *οὐδ.*; Job 12 6 *SB*, Ac 8 24 *S* (*B* ϩ.) *μηδ.*; Lev 23 3 *S*, Ps 142 2 *S*, Ap 22 3 *S* (all *B* ⲛⲓⲃⲉⲛ) *πᾶς*; Lu 11 36 *S* (*B* om), Aeg 270 *S* that not ⲗ. ⲡⲣⲱⲙⲉ be faithless *τις*; Gk om : Lev 26 7 *S* (*B* om), Jud 16 11 *S*; PS 277 *S* ⲡⲡⲉϥϣⲛ ⲗ. ⲛϭⲓⲥⲉ, BM 217 *S* let us not have ⲗ. ⲙⲛⲡⲧϣⲃⲏⲣ with them. Adj also **I e** & **IV**. **e** partitive; Jos 2 11 *S*, Job 2 13 *S* (*B* ⲟⲩⲟⲛ), Lu 1 61 *S* (*B* ϩ.), Ac 27 34 *S* (*B* ⲟⲩⲁⲓ) *οὐδ.*; BAp 144 *S* let not ⲗ. ⲙⲙⲟⲛ ⲕⲁ ⲧⲟⲟⲧϥ ⲉⲃⲟⲗ.

ⲁⲧⲗ. *SF* adj, *without, lacking any* : Lu 22 35 (*B*

diff) ϣⲱⲡⲉ ⲛⲁⲧⲗ. τινος ὑστερεῖν ; BMis 259 he arose
ⲛⲁⲧⲗ. ⲛⲧⲁⲕⲟ in his body ; J 51 10 ⲛⲁⲧⲗ. ⲛⲕ-
ⲗⲟⲙⲗⲙ (l ϭⲗ-), Kr 11 F ⲛⲁⲧⲗ. ⲡⲁⲙⲫⲓⲃⲟⲗⲓⲁ,
BM 1226 F sim (cf PLond 5 131 δίχα πάσης ἀμφ.),
CO 153, ST 97, J 64 16 ⲛⲁⲧⲗ. ⲡϣⲁϫⲉ ; ⲡⲟⲩⲉϣ
ⲡⲗ. S, meaning same : Ps 80 14 (B ϩⲉⲛϩⲗⲓ) ἐν
τῷ μηδενί ; ST 172 (ⲡ)ⲡⲓⲕⲁⲁϥ ⲉⲃⲟⲗ ⲡⲟⲩ. ⲡⲗ.

III negative, *no one, nothing* : Nu 20 19 S, Job
21 34 S, Sa 7 8 S, Is 40 23 S, 2 Cor 12 11 SF
(all B ϩⲗⲓ) οὐδέν, Aeg 214 S count the punishment
ⲉⲅⲗ. παρ᾽ οὐδέν ; Si 11 28 S κοῦφος ; Phil 3 8 S
(B ⲗⲉⲁϣ) σκύβαλον ; PS 87 S ⲁⲡⲧ ⲟⲩⲗ. ⲛⲡⲁϩⲣⲁⲕ,
Mor 37 97 S what wilt thou of him ? ⲟⲩⲗ. ⲧⲁⲣⲡⲉ,
ShIF 308 S ⲗ. ⲡⲉ ϩⲱⲃ ⲛⲧⲉⲓⲣⲉ, ShA 1 13 S in God's
hands all things ⲛⲟⲉ ⲡⲡⲉⲓⲗ., Pey *Gram* 167 S tortures ϩⲛⲗ. ⲡⲉ, AP 23 A² riches ϩⲛⲗ. ⲡⲉ, Mich 550
39 S with whom spakest thou ? ⲙⲡⲗ., ShP 131⁴ 140
S not distant ϣⲁⲟⲩⲉⲗⲁⲭⲓⲥⲧⲟⲛ ⲡⲗ., also ? PBu 208
S ⲡϥⲉⲙⲫⲁⲛⲓⲍⲉ ⲡⲟⲩⲗⲉϩ (? λέξις) ⲡⲗ. *of no value*,
which not even a simpleton would heed.

IV adj following nn SA², *any* : Job 11 14 (B ϩⲗⲓ
ⲡ-) τις ; Jos 5 1 ⲙⲟⲕⲙⲕ ⲗ. οὐδείς, BM 174 1 ⲙⲛ
ⲁⲡⲟⲫⲁⲥⲓⲥ ⲗ. οὐδαμοῦ ; or no Gk : Jud 16 17, 1 Kg
11 11 ⲥⲡⲁⲩ ⲗ. ⲡϩⲏⲧⲟⲩ, Ac 15 9 (B ϩ.) ⲡⲱⲣϫ ⲗ.,
Ro 3 10 (B om), AP 37 A² ⲙⲡⲉⲡ[ⲉⲧⲉ]ⲡⲁⲡⲟⲩϥ ⲗ.
ϣ[ⲱ]ⲡⲉ, Miss 8 7 ⲡϥⲧⲁϥ ⲣⲟⲟⲩϣ ⲗ. ϩⲁⲣⲟⲛ, Ostr
penes G. Jéquier ⲙⲡⲧⲉ ⲣⲱⲙⲉ ⲗ. ⲡⲣⲟⲩⲡ ⲙⲙⲁⲩ.

V ⲗ., ⲡⲗ. advb SAF, (not) *at all* : Deu 28 56
(B om) οὐχί ; Ru 2 7 μικρόν ; Si 9 10 τὸ σύνολον ;
Ac 4 18 (B ⲉⲡⲧⲏⲣϥ) τὸ καθόλου ; Mt 5 34 (B = Gk)
ὅλως ; Jos 22 28 πότε, Mk 2 25 (B ⲉⲡⲉϩ) οὐδέποτε ;
Job 1 22 (B ϩ. ⲛ-), Zech 11 5 A (B ⲛϩ.) Mt 27 12
(B do) οὐδέν ; Tob 6 15 ⲙⲡⲣⲣ ϩⲟⲧⲉ ⲗ. μηδ. λό-
γον ἔχε, Pro 24 23 SA, Phil 1 28 SF (B ϩⲉⲛϩ.),
Ap 2 10 (B om) μηδέν ; Z 295 they hurt him not
ⲗ. ; ShC 42 137 ⲉⲙⲡⲓϫⲓⲧⲟⲩ ⲛϭⲟⲡⲥ ⲗ., ShHT D
59 ⲙⲡϥⲁϩⲉ ⲣⲁⲧϥ ⲗ. ⲟⲩⲃⲉ- (var ShA 2 246 ⲡⲗ.),
Bor 283 131 Godhead not divided ⲗ. ⲉⲡⲥⲱⲙⲁ,
PSBA 25 274 answered him not ⲗ., Mor 31 22 sim
ⲡⲗ., R 1 1 21 ⲡⲧⲉⲧⲛⲁⲧⲁⲩⲉ ⲧⲙⲉ ⲗ. ⲁⲡ.

Concord : ⲗ. is m, *v* above **Ⲁ ⲃ**, also with vb,
as Sa 2 5 ⲡⲡⲉⲗ. ⲕⲟⲧϥ, R 2 1 74 ⲙⲡⲗ. ⲉϥⲉⲓⲣⲉ ; or
f, as Ap 22 3 ⲗ. ⲁⲃⲃⲟⲧⲉ, Miss 4 554 ⲗ. ⲡⲥϩⲓⲙⲉ,
BMis 260 ⲗ. ⲙⲙⲛⲧⲥⲟⲡ ; sg as above, or pl, as
Lu 1 61 (B ϩ.), ShC 73 168 ⲡⲡⲉⲗ. ⲡⲣⲱⲙⲉ ⲉⲩⲛ-
ⲕⲟⲧⲕ, J 28 34 ⲗ. ⲡⲣⲱⲃ ⲉⲩϫⲓ ⲉϩⲟⲩⲛ, PLond 4 483
sim.

ⲙⲡⲧⲗ. S nn f, *nothingness, insignificance* : Ryl
292 ⲡⲕⲧⲙϭⲱϣⲧ ⲉⲧⲁⲙⲡ(ⲧ)ⲗ.

Place-name ⲙⲁⲙⲡⲗⲁⲩ (P 43 51, Amélineau *Géogr*
239) was thus understood, as translated موضع الاشيا

ⲖⲎⲞⲨ B nn m, *meaning unknown* : P 54 117

---

words relating to war, arms ⲡⲗ. شدة, BMOr 8775
118 do شدد (l ? شدّة).

ⲖⲞⲞⲨ, ⲗⲟⲟⲩⲉ S, ⲗⲱⲟⲩ SB, ⲗⲁⲁⲩ, ⲗⲁⲩ S,
ⲗⲁⲩ BF, nn m, a *curl* of hair : Jud 16 13 S σειρά
var βό(σ)τρυχος, JA '75 5 259 = R 1 2 37 S woman
wearing ϩⲉⲛⲗ. (var ⲗⲁⲩ) on head, BM 293 S ⲛⲉⲗ.
ⲛⲃⲱ of head & beard, JTS 10 397 S ⲙⲡⲉⲥϯ ⲡϩⲉⲛ-
ⲗⲟⲟⲩⲉ on her head ; cf R 1 3 81 S ⲡⲉⲗⲟⲟⲗⲉ of
(Salome's) head dropped upon cheeks as eggs fallen
from nest (as if ⲉⲗ. = *cluster of curls* βότρυς, ? confused with ⲗ.). *ring, link* in chain : MG 25 143
B ⲗ. of gold, silver, iron composing chain.   **b**
fringe (tasselled ?) : Ex 28 33 B λῶμα, Deu 22 12 S
(B ϣⲱⲧϯ) στρεπτός ; Ps 44 13 S (B ϣⲧⲁϯ) κροσ-
σωτός ; Is 3 16 S (Mor 43 251, elsewhere ϣⲧⲏⲛ)
χιτών ; Mt 14 36 F (S ⲧⲟⲡ, B do) κράσπεδον ;
ShIF 67 S ϩⲉⲡⲧⲱⲧⲉ ⲛ ϩⲉⲡⲗⲁⲁⲩ ϩⲛⲡⲧⲟⲡ (on
Nu 15 38), Mor *lc* 252 ⲛⲟϭ ⲡⲧⲱⲧⲉ ⲡⲗ. on heads,
ib who putteth ϩⲉⲡⲗ. on head round about face,
Ryl 244 S list of clothing ⲟⲩⲗ. ⲡⲡⲁⲙⲓⲉⲛⲏⲛ (?)
of goat's hair (αἴγειον).   ⲟⲓ ⲡⲗ. B, *be fringed* :
Ex 28 4 κοσυμβωτός.   **c** *bunch, cluster* of dates :
Lev 23 40 S ⲗ. ⲡⲃⲏⲡⲉ (var ⲃⲏⲧ ϩⲁⲧ) gloss on
κάλλυνθρον, P 44 96 S, K 177 B عرجون (but *v*
ⲁⲗⲱⲟⲩⲉ), BMar 208 S twelve ⲗ. ⲡⲃⲏⲡⲉ yearly =
Mor 48 10 ⲕⲗⲁϫⲟⲥ ⲡⲃ̅. = Rec 6 171 B ⲥⲡⲁⲑⲓ,
BMis 562 S 10,000 dates on each ⲗⲱⲟⲩ, BAp 142
S how many ⲗⲱⲟⲩ to each palm, how many dates
(ⲃⲗⲃⲓⲗⲉ) to each tree or (ⲛ) each ⲗ. ?, Mor 37 151
S palm called ⲡⲕⲓⲛⲟⲛ bearing 1 ⲗ. at a time.   In
Aeg 26 S ⲗⲟⲟⲩⲉ (B ⲃⲟⲩϩⲓ) prob = ⲁⲗⲟⲟⲩⲉ, *v* ⲁⲗⲱ
pupil.

ⲖⲰⲞⲨ S as interj (?) of emphasis or asservera-
tion : BMOr 8810 366 Besa to nuns, Ye run upon
walls & to gate crying ϫⲉⲗ. ⲗ., we will not abide
in this iniquitous convent, *ib* 381 crying ϫⲉⲗ. ⲗ.,
I will depart to where my children are, I will not
submit to reproof.

ⲖⲀⲞⲨⲀⲒ, ⲗⲁⲅⲓ B   *v* ⲗⲁ-.

ⲖⲀⲨⲈ SA, ⲗⲁⲅⲉⲓ F   *v* ⲗⲁⲁⲩ *any one.*

ⲖⲀⲞⲨⲎ F   *v* ⲣⲁⲟⲩⲏ.

ⲖⲀⲞⲨⲒ F   *v* ⲣⲟⲟⲩⲉ.

ⲖⲀⲄⲞ, ⲗⲁⲃⲱ S, ⲗⲁⲟⲅⲟ, ⲗⲁⲃⲟ B nn m f, a
ship's *sail* : Is 33 23 S (B ϣⲟⲉ ⲡϩⲁⲉ, F ϣⲧⲕ),
BM 216 80 S sailors ⲡⲱⲣϣ ⲉⲃⲟⲗ ⲡⲧⲉⲩⲗ., Va 57
122 B sim ⲡⲟⲩⲗ. ἱστίον, Tatt 178 B sim f ; PSBA
10 403 B ⲟⲩⲗ. ⲡϫⲟⲓ ὀθόνη ; K 133 B ⲡⲓⲗ., *ib* 270
ⲡⲓⲗⲁⲃⲱⲓ (*sic*) قلع ; ClPr 25 2 S they spread ⲡⲉⲩⲗ.,
Rec 7 90 B sim, C 43 212 B ⲁⲩⲕⲉⲗⲟⲩ ⲙⲡⲓⲗ.,
R 2 1 55 S ⲧⲉⲕⲗ. filled with wind, Mor 48 104 S

ⲁⲩⲡⲟⲅϭⲉ ⲙⲡⲗ. & sailed south (C 43 212 B om), BMar 26 S sim (-ⲃⲱ), Mor 28 139 S sailing north ⲁⲩⲡⲉϩ ⲧⲗ. ⲉϧⲏⲧ for south wind blew, C 43 213 B wind ⲡⲓϧⲓ ⲉⲡⲓⲗ., P 131² 157 S if wind blow upon ⲟⲩⲗ. ⲡⲥϩⲱⲃ ⲙⲉϥⲉϣ ϭⲙ ϭⲟⲙ ⲡϫⲉⲕ ⲧⲉϥⲉⲡⲉⲣⲅⲓⲁ ⲉⲃⲟⲗ ⲡϧⲏⲧⲥ, Bor 143 40 = Mor 28 141 S ⲉⲣⲉⲧⲗ. ⲥⲱⲕ ⲙⲡⲭⲟⲓ, BIF 13 101 S saints' names written on ⲡⲗ. = MG 25 281 B sim written on ⲡⲉⲥϫⲟⲗⲁⲕⲉⲓ (σκολάκιν PG 65 324) ⲉⲧⲧⲟ ⲉⲧⲗ., ib 282 B, BMis 12 (-ⲃⲱ), Mor 37 191 S sim. ᵇ awning, curtain S: Nu 3 26 (B = Gk), ib 4 26 (B ⲡⲟϧ) ἱστίον; Miss 4 236 tabernacle of skins & ϧⲉⲛϣⲟⲣⲧ ⲡⲗ. (v Ex 40 19); Is 30 17 (BF ⲙⲏⲓⲛⲓ) σημαία ensign, flag. Obscure: ST 240 S letter demanding half solidus-worth of ⲗⲁⲅⲱ.

ϭⲓⲥ ⲗ. S nn f, half-sail, foresail: Ac 27 40 (B = Gk) ἀρτέμων.

ⲗⲟⲟⲅⲧ S v ϧⲁⲧⲗⲟⲟⲅⲧ.

ⲗⲟⲅⲗⲱⲟⲩ B v ϧⲗⲟⲅⲗⲱⲟⲩ.

ⲗⲁⲅⲏⲓ F v ⲣⲟⲟⲩⲡⲉ.

ⲗⲁⲟⲩϣ F v ⲣⲟⲟⲩϣ.

ⲗⲉϣ† S vb intr, meaning unknown: PRain 4794 ⲙⲓⲉϣ ϭⲱ ϧⲓ ..... ⲧⲁⲕⲁ ⲡⲁϧⲱⲃ ⲃⲗⲉϣ (? l ⲗⲏϣ).

ⲗⲏϣ F in ⲗⲉⲙⲗⲏϣ v ⲣⲁϣ (ⲣⲙⲣⲁϣ).

ⲗⲁϣⲓⲉ S nn as pl: P 44 88 منافقين hypocrites (between ⲅⲁⲥⲧⲣⲓⲙⲩⲑⲟⲥ & ⲫⲟⲛⲉⲩⲥ), but = 43 70 طويل القامة tall, glossed شبح هائل monstrous form. Error for ⲗⲁϣⲓⲏ (v ⲗⲁ-) or ? -ϣⲓⲃⲉ.

ⲗⲉϣⲓ F v ⲣⲁϣⲉ.

ⲗⲱϣⲓ F ⲣⲱϣⲉ.

ⲗⲁϣⲁⲛⲉ, pl ⲗⲁϣⲛⲏⲩ, -ⲛⲏⲟⲩ, -ⲛⲓⲩ, -ⲛⲓⲟⲩ, -ⲁⲛⲓⲟⲩ (J 38 9) or ⲗⲁϣ/ϣ/ (BMOr 9525(1)) S nn m, village magistrate or official; cf λασάνι Lepsius Denkm 6 gr 349. Doubtful if = λεσῶνις a priestly title: v RylDem 3 219, Steinwenter in Wess 19 38, 52. Equivalent μειζότερος (PLond 4 435, 436) or πρωτοκωμήτης (J 105 25, 45) or ? more general title: J 68 20 ⲁⲣⲭⲱⲛ ⲡⲓⲙ ϧⲓⲉⲡⲓⲥⲕⲟⲡⲟⲥ ϧⲓⲇⲓⲕⲁⲥⲧⲏⲥ ϧⲓⲗⲁⲁⲅⲉ ⲡⲗ., J 66 61 fine paid to ⲁⲣⲭⲱⲛ or ⲗ., BM lc ⲗ. (pl) of that year, ST 352 three ⲗ. of village; ⲁⲡⲟⲗ. ex-lashane: J 35 101, 65 95. On functions &c v Steinwenter lc, Ep 1 176. Cf ⲗⲉⲙⲏⲛϣⲉ.

ⲗⲱϣϫ, ⲗⲉϣϫ- B vb intr, be troublesome, oppressive: MG 25 182 tarry not in friend's house ⲙⲏⲡⲱⲥ ⲡⲧⲉⲕϣⲩⲧⲉⲙⲗ. tr, molest, oppress: Lu 3 14 (S ⲧⲧⲉ ⲟⲥⲉ) διασείειν. Cf ⲗⲟϭ.

ⲗⲁϥ B adj (?), pleasant: P 54 117 مستلذ (l ذ) = BMOr 8775 118 ⲗⲁⲱϥ. Cf ? ⲗⲓⲃⲉ (ⲗⲁⲃ-).

ⲗⲏϥ S v ⲗⲗⲏⲃ.

ⲗⲱϥ, ⲗⲟϥ† B vb intr, be insipid (opp be salt): Mt 5 13, Lu 14 34 (S ⲃⲁⲁⲃⲉ) μωραίνειν; MG 25 264 souls ⲉⲧⲁⲩⲗ. in iniquity = Mor 40 37 S ⲛⲧⲁⲩ-ⲃⲁⲁⲃⲉ, C 89 53 we are come to salt you ⲭⲉⲧⲉⲧⲉⲡⲗ.†, Cat 99 wisdom salts ⲡⲓϧⲏⲧ ⲉⲧⲗ.† As nn: Cat 7 ⲡⲗ. ⲡⲉⲙⲡⲛϫⲱⲛⲥ of passions.

ⲗⲉⲓϥⲓ B, cf S Gk ⲗⲁⲃⲏⲥ, nn m, fish cyprinus niloticus: Glos 419 S ⲡⲗⲁ. · ἀλάβης, K 170 ⲡⲓⲗ. ليس; Bodl 325 156 ⲡⲓⲗ. ⲱ, (error, cf ⲥⲗⲓϥⲓ ⲱ,); ib 159, P 55 17 ⲡⲓⲗ. بلطي (error, v ⲣⲁⲙⲉ); BM 1114 S ? ⲡⲗⲁⲃⲉⲥ ⲥⲡⲁⲩ. Its gall in recipes: PMéd 236, Cai 42573 1 S. V JEA 14 23.

(ⲗⲱⲱϭⲉ), ⲗⲟⲟϭⲉ†, ⲗⲟⲟⲃⲉ†, ⲗⲟⲃⲉ†, S vb intr, be prone to fall, decadent: Sa 4 4†, ib 9 14† ἐπισφαλὴς (γίνεσθαι), BM 982 none builds house ϧⲛⲟⲩⲡⲟⲗⲓⲥ ⲉⲥⲗ.† μελλούση καταπίπτειν; ShP 130³ 7 ⲁⲥⲕⲟⲥ ⲉϥⲗ.† ⲏ ⲉϥⲥⲙⲟⲛⲧ ⲁⲛ not fit to hold wine. ShBMOr 8800 201 Origen's notions ⲉⲧⲗ.† (or ? = ⲗⲟⲃⲉ).

ⲗⲟϥⲗϥ, -ⲗⲉϥ, ⲗⲟⲃⲗⲉϥ, ⲗⲟϥⲗⲃ S, ⲗⲟϥⲗⲉϥ B, ⲗⲉϥⲗⲱϥ⸗ SB, ⲗⲉϥⲗⲱϥ† SB, ⲗⲉϥⲗⲟϥⲧ†(Sh) S, -ⲗⲱϥⲧ† B vb I intr, mortify, become rotten, perish: Job 33 21 SB, ib 19 20 S (B ⲉⲣ ϧⲟⲗⲓ), Ps 37 5 S (B ⲇⲟ) σήπειν; Ps 33 21 B (S ⲟⲩⲱϣϥ) συντρίβεσθαι; Va 66 292 B through sickness ⲉⲁⲡⲟⲩⲥⲁⲣⳉ ⲗ. βιβρώσκειν; Va 57 210 B ⲉⲣⲉⲡⲟⲩⲥⲱⲙⲁ ⲗ.† ἀνάπηρος; P 129¹⁴ 97 S sim λωβᾶσθαι, ShMun 112 S diseased parts [ⲥⲉ]ⲡⲁⲣ ϥⲏⲧ [ⲏ] ⲥⲉⲡⲁⲗ., LDi 278 S limbs dissolved ⲁⲩⲗ. ⲉⲡⲉⲥⲛⲧ ⲉⲧⲕⲁⲗⲟϧⲛ (meaning ?), BHom 119 S nose ⲁϥⲗ. lips ⲁⲩⲥⲣⲟϥⲣⲉϥ, P 131³ 84 S Ninive's tongue ⲗ.† ϧⲓⲧⲙⲡⲕⲱϧⲧ = Va 61 94 B ⲣⲉⲕⲣⲱⲕ (cf Lu 16 24), R 2 1 68 S worm-eaten wood perisheth ⲛϥⲗ. II tr, make rotten, destroy: Job 16 8 S (B ⲉⲣ ϧⲟⲗⲓ) σεσηπότα ποιεῖν, ShP 130⁴ 140 S Christ's limbs ⲉⲧⲡⲗ. ⲙⲙⲟⲟⲩ, ShC 42 110 S pulling twig to pieces ⲛϥⲗⲉϥⲗⲱϧⲥ ⲉϧⲣⲁⲓ ⲉⲡⲕⲁϧ, Miss 4 137 B worms would have ⲗ. ⲙⲡⲉⲥⲥⲱⲙⲁ = MR 4 72 S ⲁⲛϧⲁⲗⲓⲥⲕⲉ, Worr 263 S heat will ⲗ. thy body.

—— S nn, corruption: Si 19 3 σήπη.

—— ⲉⲃⲟⲗ SB I intr, meaning as ⲗ.: EpJer 72 B (F ⲉⲗ ϧⲁⲁⲗⲓ), BMar 175 S flesh ⲛⲧⲁⲩⲗ. ⲉⲃ., C 86 302 B withered trees ⲉⲧⲁⲩⲗ. ⲉⲃ. σήπειν; LDi 298 S if foot not cut off body ⲛⲁⲗ. ⲉⲃ. putrifieri; ShP 130² 130 S wood ⲉⲧⲗⲉϥⲗⲟϥⲧ ⲉⲃ., Aeg 30 B shroud shall not ⲗ. ⲉⲃ. ϫⲉⲡⲓⲕⲁϧⲓ, DeV 123 B of Herod ⲉⲁⲡⲉϥⲥⲙⲟⲧ ⲡϧⲱⲟⲩⲧ ⲗ. ⲉⲃ., Mor 18 114 S spirit ⲉϥⲗ.† ⲉⲃ. like flame (LCyp 7 om, meaning?). II tr (rare), destroy: ShP 130⁵ 43 S

demons ⲉⲁⳟⲗ. ⲉϩ. ⲡⲓⲙⲉⲗⲟⲥ, ShIF 226 S sim, Va 58 129 B ⲁϥⲁⲓⲧ ⲛϣⲟⲗⲣⲥ ⲁϥⲗⲉϭⲗⲱϭⲧ ⲉϩ.

ⲗⲉϥⲗⲓϥⲉ S, -ϭⲓ B nn f, *what drops off*, fragment, crumb : Mt 15 27 B (S ⲥⲣⲉϥⲣⲓϥⲉ), Lu 16 21 B (var ⲡⲏ ⲉϣⲁⳓⲣⲉⲓ ⲉⲃⲟⲗ = S) ψιχίον ; ShA 1 217 S ⲟⳟⲗ. or grain of mustard-seed, *ib* 2 280 S ⲧⲁⲗ. ⲕⲟⳓⲓ ⲡϩⲉⲕⲉ, ShP 130⁶ 101 S ⲟⳟⲗ. ⲙⲙⲛⲧϣⲁⲛϩⲧⲏϥ, ShBMOr 8810 454 S long they fasted, but we are not like them ϧⲏⲧⲉⲡⲗ. ⲡⲉⲗⲁⳓⲓⲥⲧⲟⲛ.

ⲗⲁϭⲉⲙ *B* nn m, *trunk, branch, stalk, tube* : Ge 8 11 (S ? ϣⲉ, var om) κάρφος ; *ib* 41 5 πυθμήν ; *ib* 49 9 (S ϯⲟⳟⲱ) βλαστός ; *ib* 21 (S ϣⲁⳟ) στέλεχος ; Ex 38 14 (37 18) καυλός ; *ib* 16 (12) (S = Gk, A ϧⲗⲁⲡ) κλάδος ; Zech 4 2 (S ⲭⲟⲗ(ϧ)ⲥ, A do) ἐπαρυστρίς ; MG 25 83 shall become as ⲟⳟⲗ. ⲉϥϩⲛⲟⳟ whose fruit sweet = GöttAr 114 19 غصنا .

ⲗⲱϭⲉⲙ B ⲗⲱϧⲙ.

ⲗⲁϩⲏⲧϥ B, ⲗⲁϧⲉ S *v* ⲗⲓⲃⲉ.

ⲗⲁϧ F nn m, meaning unknown : AZ 23 39 list of varia ϣⲁⲙⲧ ⲡⲗ. ⲡⲏⲓ.

ⲗⲉϧ S nn m, *care, anxiety* : Job 11 18 ⲗⲉϧ, ⲣⲟⲟⳟϣ (but P 44 117 = 43 121 ⲣ., ⲗ., B ⲣⲟϯ) μέριμνα ; BMar 77 what are ⲡⲉⲓⲗ. ⲙⲡⲉⲓⲣⲟⲟⳟϣ ?, Mor 41 39 martyr to judge ⲙⲡⲁⲗ. ϭⲉ ϧⲁⲣⲟⲛ ⲁⲡⲡⲉ, Ryl 358 ⲉϣⲁⲕⲥϧⲁⲓ ⲡⲁⲓ ϧⲁⲟⳟϧⲱⲃ ⲡⲉⲕⲗ. ϧⲓⲭⲱⲓ I will make thy care mine, P 131⁶ 18 ⲡⲧⲉⲡⲡⲓⲥⲧⲟⲥ ϥⲓ ⲗ. (ⲉ)ⲉⲓⲱ ⲉⲃⲟⲗ his sins ⲛϥϥⲓ ⲡⲣⲟⲟⳟϣ ⲉⲡⲉⲓⲣⲁ his soul. As vb intr ?, *take thought, be concerned* : PRain 4737 about repayment to woman ⲉϣⲁⲥⲙⲛϣⲁ ⲛϫⲓ ⲟⳟⲙⲉ[ⲣⲟⲥ] ϧⲙⲡⲁⲕⲧⲟⲡ ⲙⲙⲉⲥⲗⲏϥ.

ⲗⲱϧ F vb intr, meaning unknown : CMSS 30.

ⲗⲁϧⲏ S (λάη WS 24) nn f, *liquid measure* = κνίδιον, *v* Kr 234 ⲡⲗ. ⲡⲉⲙⲣⲓⲥ = *ib* μούσθ(ον) κν(ι)δ(ια) ; mostly of wine : Saq 226 wine account ⲡⲟϭ ⲡⲗ., Ryl 158, Bodl(P) g 33, WS 132, MR 5 34 ⲗ. of wine ; of olive (oil) : *ib* 32 opp ξέστης of fine oil (ⲡⲉϧ ⲗⲏ), BM 1088 sim ; of milk : PRain 4710 ; of honey : PMich 4567 ; of pickle (ⲭⲓⲣ) : WS 85 where 5 ξέσται = 1 ⲗ., BMOr 6201 A 165 wine priced 25 ⲗ. to solidus & 2 ⲗ. to ὀγγία ; ⲡⲟϭ ⲡⲗ. : Saq *lc* opp ⲗⲁⲕ(ⲟⲟⲧⲉ), WS 91 ; ⲕⲟⳟⲓ ⲡⲗ. : *ib* 137, BM 1166, *ib* 1129 ⲣⲁϧⲏ opp ⲕⲟⲗⲗⲁⲑⲟⲡ, Baouit 1 8. On capacity *v* WS 23 (Ryl 159 ⲗ. seems = Wess 20 218 ἀγγεῖον μέγα). As name ? ⲗⲁϧⲏ BM 1075 (or *l* ⲗⲁϧⲏⳟ, *cf* ⲗⲁϧⲛⲟⳟ, Λαήου).

ⲗⲟⲓϧⲉ, ⲗⲩϧⲣⲉ (? BKU 1 22) S, ⲗⲱⲓϧⲓ B nn a mostly m, *mud, filth* : Is 14 23 SB ⲗ. ⲡⲟⲙⲉ πηλοῦ βάραθρον ; Jer 45 6 B, 2 Pet 2 21 SB, BHom 17 S, Z 325 S ⲉⲁⲥⲥⲗⲁⲁⲧⲉ ⲉ…ⲡⲗ., MG 25 18 B ⲗⲱϧⲓ (*sic* & *ib* 119, 177, all one scribe) βόρβορος ; CaiEuch

466 B ⲫⲗ. of sin τρύγος ἁμαρτ. ; ShC 42 106 S Jeremiah's ϣⲏⲓ ⲡⲗ., ShMun 141 S ⲟⳟⲗ. … ⲉⲁϥⲥⲱⲣⲡ ⲉⲣⲣⲁⲓ ⲉⲣⲟϥ, ROC 19 76 S pour not ointment ⲉϫⲛⲟⳟⲗ. ⲡⲥϯ ⲃ̅ⲱⲱⲡ, Bor 145 8 man ⲉϥⲧⲟⲗⲙ ⲡⲗ.   **b** f S : Ps 39 2, 68 2 (both B ⲣⳟⲗⲏ for ἰλύς) ; BM 267 ⲧⲗ. ⲙⲡϣⲏⲓ.   Adj SB : BMar 162 S ⲟⳟⲟⲙⲉ ⲡⲗ. βόρβ. ; ShA 1 439 S, LCyp 7 S, Va 61 99 B sim (*cf* above ⲗ. ⲡⲟⲙⲉ).

ⲗⲟⳟϧⲓ F *v* ⲣⲟⳟϧⲉ.

ⲗⲣⲱⲃ SA, ⲗⲣⲱⲱϥ S, ⲁⲗⲣⲱⲃ S⁥, ⲉⲗⲣⲱⲃ BO, -ϧⲱⲡ B nn m, *steam, vapour* : Si 22 27 SA, *ib* 24 17 S, Joel 2 30 SA (B om), Ac 2 19 S (B ⲭⲣⲉⲙⲧⲥ), Ja 4 14 S (B ϣⲱⲓϣ) ἀτμίς ; Joel 2 6 B (A ⲭⲟⳟϧ) Nah 2 10 B (A om) προσκαῦμα ; Va 58 188 B ⲡⲓⲉⲗ. of food ἀναθυμίασις ; AZ 21 100 O of fire ⲉϧⲟⲙ ⲡⲓϩⲓ ⲉⲗ. ⲡⲓϩⲓ, PS 382 S ⲡⲉⲗ. ⲙⲡϣⲁⲣ, ShBIF 23 22 S ⲗ. & ⲕⲁⲡⲡⲟⲥ, C 41 25 B ⲉⲗ. ⲡⲧⲉ ⲟⳟⲕⲁⲡⲡⲟⲥ, LCyp 29 S ⲡⲉⲗⲣⲱⲱϥ of boiling cauldron, Miss 4 762 S⁥ warmth of ⲡⲁⲗ. ⲉⲧϧⲛⲧⲉⳟⲧⲁⲡⲣⲟ (*cf* R 1 3 6 ⲡⲓϥⲉ).

(ⲗⲁϧⲗϧ), ⲗⲉϧⲗⲱϧ† S vb intr, *be tall, high* : P 44 88 ϥⲗ.† = طويل طوال = τραγορ̇ιος, 43 70 ⲟⳟⲗⲁⲣⲟⲣⲓⲟⲥ (quid ? *cf* K 196 طوال ⲭⲁⳟⲗⲏ, prob confusion), BMis 569 ⲟⳟⲙⲏⲛϣⲉ ⲡϣⲏⲡ ⲉϥⲗ.† ⲗ.† ⲉⲃⲟⲗ, meaning same : Mor 40 6 ⲉϥⲗ.† ⲉⲃⲟⲗ among them = Mor 39 8, 41 120 ⲉϥⲣⲟⲟⳟⲧ ⲉϧⲟⳟⲉ ⲉⲣⲟⲟⳟ = C 43 36 B ⲉϥⲟⳟⲟⲧ ⲉⲣⲱⲟⳟ, R 1 4 36 place ⲉⲧⲗ.† ⲉϩ. …ϧⲡⲡϣⲏⲡ.   ⲗⲁϧⲗⲉϧ nn m, *height, pride* : Mus 40 46 (*cf* Mun 188) not caught by ⲡⲗ. [ⲡ]ⲡⲉϥⲃⲁⲗ concupiscentiae ocul. (*cf* Si 23 5 μετεωρισμὸς ὀφθ.)

ⲗⲉϧⲗⲱϧⲉ S nn as pl, meaning unknown : Ryl 94 (33 3) martyr bound upon τροχός like waterwheel ⲉⲣⲉⲡⲗ. ⲛⲧⲟⳟⲉⲓⲣⲉ ⲁϣⲉ ⲉⲣⲟϥ (ⲗ. ?? water-pots ; ⲟⳟⲉⲓⲣⲉ obscure).

ⲗⲱϧⲙ S, ⲗⲱϭⲉⲙ B, ⲗⲉϧⲙ- S, ⲗⲟϧⲙⳇ, ⲗⲁϧⲙⳇ S, ⲗⲉϧⲙⳇ F, ⲗⲁϧⲉⲙ†, ⲗⲟϧⲙ† S, ⲗⲁϭⲉⲙ† B vb a intr, *be boiling, boiled* : BKU 1 21 10 Sᵃ dyeing recipe ϣⲁⲕϧⲓ (*l* ϯ) ⲟⳟⲕⲟⳟⲓ ⲡⲓⲱⲧ ⲙⲡⲡⲥⲁⲣⲧ ϣⲁⲡⲧⲟⳟⲗ., *ib* 1 9 S heat it ϣⲁⲡ]ⲧϥⲗ., Bodl(P) a 2 63 S a measure of ⲁⲥⲱϥⲣⲁ (? الصفر) ⲉϥⲗⲁ.†, PMéd 301 S ⲙⲟⲟⳟ ⲡϣⲱⲃⲉ ⲉϥⲗⲟ.†, C 41 73 B ⲟⳟⲕⲟⳟϫⲓ ⲡⲟⳟⲟϯ ⲉϥⲗ.† = Miss 4 469 سلى مسلوق.   **b** tr, *boil* : ShC 73 136 ⲉⲧⲙⲗⲉϧⲙ ⲑⲁⲣⲙⲟⳟⲥ over much, Z 630 S ⲡⲉⲗ. ⲡⲟⳟⲁⲣϣⲓⲛ, Cai 42573 2 S ingredients ⲗⲁϧⲙⲟⳟ ⲡⲥⲁⲓⲛ PMéd 318 S raisins &c ⲗⲟϧⲙⲟⳟ ⲧⲥⲟϥ ⲡⲉⳟⲙⲟⲟⳟ, BKU 1 26 (4) F ⲗⲉϧⲙⲉϥ ϧⲓⲙⲁⳟ ϣⲁ ⲧⲉϥⲗ., CR '87 376 S leeks ⲗⲁϧⲙⲟⳟ ϧⲓⲁⲡⲕⲣⲁⲧⲟⲛ (ἄκρατον).   **c** as nn m : K 264 B ⲡⲓⲗ. سليق, C 41 *lc* ⲡⲓⲕⲟⳟϫⲓ ⲡⲗ. ; with ⲡⲉϣ, ⲫⲁϣ, *half-boiled* : Is 51 20 S (ShA 1 466 = Z 477 ⲗⲱⲙ) B ἡμίεφθος, 1 Kg 2 15 S ἐφθός.

ⲗⲁϩⲙⲉⲥ *S* nn, *boiled food* (?): ShMich 550 18 food of sick ⲟⲩⲗ. ⲏ ⲟⲩⲁⲑⲁⲣⲁⲥ (ἀθήρα), ShC 73 212 ⲁⲣϣⲓⲛ, ⲗ., ⲟⲩⲟⲟⲧⲉ.

ⲗϩⲙⲉ, ⲗϩⲙ (Mor 41), ⲉⲗϩⲙ, ⲣϩⲙⲙ (Mus 41 231) *S*, -ϩⲉⲙ *B* vb intr, *roar*, esp of lions: Ps 21 13, 103 21 *S* (*B* ϩⲉⲙϩⲉⲙ), ι Pet 5 8 *S* (*B* do), Z 342 *S* lion ⲁϥⲉⲗ. ὠρύεσθαι; Am 3 4 *B* (*S* ⲱϣ ⲉⲃⲟⲗ) ἐρεύγεσθαι; Ap 10 3 *S* (*B* do) μυκᾶσθαι; Sa 11 19 (var ⲗϩⲏⲥ ⲓⲉ ⲝⲗϩⲏⲥ) φυσᾶν; ShA 1 279 *S* ⲙⲡⲉⲕⲉⲗ. ⲉⲝⲓⲡ- ⲡϩⲏⲕⲉ like lion, Mor 41 105 *S* ⲁⲥⲗ. like wild asses. ⲝⲓⲡⲉⲗ. *B* nn f, *roaring*: Ryl 453 336, BM 920 265 ﺯﺋﺮ. As nn m *S*: Ez 19 7 (*B* ϩ.) ὠρυῶμα.

ⲗⲁϩⲙⲉ, -ϩⲙ *S* nn f, *kneading-trough* (?): ShC 73 146 ⲡⲉⲧⲟⲩⲱϣⲙ ϩⲡⲡⲗ., ib ⲧⲉϥⲗ. wherein he kneads, BM 1103 10, 24 obscure, BP 5131 list ⲕⲟⲩⲓ ⲡⲧⲉⲣⲙⲉ, ⲟⲩⲗ. *V* AZ 62 44.

ⲗⲉϩⲙⲟⲩ *S* nn (?), meaning unknown, descriptive of a field: Win 8 sowing contract ⲡⲓⲱϩ ⲗ. ⲡⲟϭ, ⲡⲗ. ϣⲏⲙ, Turin ostr 5944 have received [price] ϩⲁⲡⲉⲓⲁϩ ⲗ. Contains ? ϩⲙⲟⲩ.

ⲗⲉϩⲙⲉⲛ *A* *v* ϩⲣⲙⲁⲛ.

ⲗⲁϩⲙⲉⲥ *S* *v* ⲗⲱϩⲙ.

ⲗⲁϩⲙⲉϥ, -ⲙⲉϥ *S*, ⲗⲉϩⲙⲉϥ, -ⲙⲉⲃ *F* nn m f (?), meaning unknown, ? relates to pecuniary matters (hire, wage): Tebtunis church fresco of hell (phot ASHunt for Univ California) *F* serpents attacking man's mouth & penis ⲡⲉⲧⲡⲱⲣⲡⲉⲅⲉ ⲙⲉⲛ(ⲡ)ⲉⲥϩⲓⲙⲉ ⲡⲗⲉϩⲙⲉϥ, serpents devouring woman's breasts ⲧⲉⲥϩⲓⲙⲉ ⲡⲧⲁⲥϥ ⲧⲉⲥⲕⲓⲃⲉ ⲡ(?)ⲡⲗ., Kr 45 *F* ⲁⲓⲥⲓⲧ ⲧⲗ. ⲡⲡⲉⲡⲧⲓⲙⲓ[, BP 9544 *F*]ⲉⲗ. ⲙⲡϣⲏⲡⲥⲓⲣⲓ, ib ⲗ. ⲡⲧⲙⲡⲓⲁⲃⲉⲥϥ (l ? ⲧⲙⲟⲩⲅⲟⲩⲃ.), BM 1117 *S* ⲡⲗⲁϩⲙⲉϥ (context obscure), Bodl(P) d 22 *S* ⲁⲡ[ⲁ ⲓⲱ]ⲁⲡⲏ[ⲥ] ⲡⲁⲗ. (*sic*, l ? ⲡⲗ.). All same ?

ⲗϩⲏⲥ, ⲉⲗϩⲏⲥ *SB* *v* ⲝⲗϩⲏⲥ.

ⲗⲉϩⲧ, ⲗⲉϩⲧⲉ *F* *v* ⲣⲱϩⲉ (ⲣⲁϩⲧ).

ⲗⲱϩⲧ *F* *v* ⲣⲱϩⲧ.

ⲗⲁϩⲱⲝ *B* nn as pl, meaning unknown: MG 25 142 babe all filthy, but nurse not repelled by stink & ⲡⲓⲗ. *V* ? ⲗⲁ-.

ⲗⲟⲩⲝ *S* nn as pl, secretion in corner of eye: P 46 237 ⲡⲗ. ﺭﻣﺎﺹ, between ⲧⲁⲗⲟⲩ & ⲡⲡⲱⲣⲧ (P 44 69 ', ⲗⲓⲙⲡⲁ, K 75 ', ⲗⲏⲙⲟⲥ, prob = λήμη).

ⲗⲱⲝ *SAB*, ⲗⲉⲝ- *SB*, ⲗⲟⲝⲋ *SB*, ⲗⲟⲝⲧ *S*, ⲗⲁⲝⲧ *S/F* (*cf* ⲗⲱⲝⲕ, ⲗⲱⲝϩ) vb, **a** intr *be sticky, adhesive*: Mor 23 35 *S/* ⲡⲓⲁⲃⲉ ⲉϥⲗ.ⲧ ⲡⲑⲉ ⲡⲟⲩⲙⲛⲧⲣⲁ, ib 24 25 *F* ⲟⲩⲁⲙⲣⲉϩⲓ ⲉϥⲗ.ⲧ, Wess 9 52 *S* sim, Mor 31 240 *S* ⲁⲡϣⲟⲉⲓϣ ⲗ. ⲉⲡⲉϥⲥⲱⲙⲁ, ib 31 72 *S* fingers ⲗ. ⲉϩⲟⲩⲛ ⲡⲡⲉⲩⲉⲣⲏⲩ;   tr *SB*, *stick, cleave to*:

Ez 29 4 *S* (var ⲗⲱⲝϭ) *B* προσκολλᾶν;   refl *B*: Va 57 176 ϯⲙⲉⲧϩⲏⲕⲓ ⲥⲡⲁⲗⲟⲝⲥ ⲡⲧⲟⲧⲕ ἐπέρχεσθαι. **b** tr *SAB*, *lick*: Ps 71 9 *B* (var & *S* ⲗⲱⲝϩ), Mic 7 17 *A* (*SB* ⲗⲱⲝϩ) λείχειν; P 130³ 59 *S* hungry at mills ⲉⲩⲗⲉⲝ ⲛⲟⲉⲓⲧ with tongues.   **c** tr *SF*, *crush, bruise*: 2 Kg 22 39 *S* θλᾶν; Ps 73 14 *S* (var ⲗⲱⲝϩ, *B* ⲗⲱⲥ) συντρίβειν; nn *F*, *straits*: 2 Cor 12 10 (*S* ⲗⲱⲝϩ, *B* ϩⲟⲝⲣⲉⲝ ⲉϩⲣⲏⲓ) στενοχωρία.

ⲗⲟⲝⲗⲝ *S*, ⲗⲁⲝⲗⲝ *A* vb tr, *rub, crush, oppress*: Nu 22 25 *S* (*B* ϩⲟⲝⲣⲉⲝ) ἀποθλίβειν, Mic 7 2 *A* (*SB* do) ἐκθλ.; Mor 41 235 *S* martyr & wounded boy ⲁϥⲥϥⲣⲁⲅⲓⲍⲉ ⲙⲙⲟⲩ ⲁϥⲗⲉⲝⲗⲱⲝ ⲡⲉϥⲥⲱⲙⲁ & flesh came together. As nn *A*: Mic *lc*.

ⲗⲁⲝⲓ *B* nn m, *latrine* of ship: K 134 ﻣﻨﺪﺍﺱ (Dozy, Almk 2 30).

ⲗⲁⲝⲓ *B* *importunity* *v* ⲗⲟϭ.

ⲗⲓⲝⲓ *B* nn, *bowl, dish*: K 151 ﻃﺎﺱ.

ⲗⲱⲝⲓ *B* *v* ⲗⲁϭⲉ.

(ⲗⲱⲝⲓ) *B*, *lie hid* *v* ⲗⲱϭⲉ.

ⲗⲱⲓⲝⲓ *B* *v* ⲗⲟⲓϭⲉ.

ⲗⲱⲝⲕ, -ⲝϭ, -ⲝⲧ, ⲗⲟⲝⲕ, ⲗⲟⲝϭ, ⲗⲟⲝⲧ, ⲗⲟϭⲕ (? same PMich 3546), ⲗⲟⲝⲧ† *S* (*cf* ⲗⲱⲝ, ⲗⲱⲝϩ) vb **a** intr, *be sticky, adhesive*: Deu 13 17 ⲗⲱⲝϭ (*B* ⲧⲱⲙⲓ) προσκολλᾶν, PS 232 your thrones shall be ⲉⲩⲗ.† ⲉⲡⲱⲓ *be close, joined to*, ShC 73 147 let no flour ⲉϥⲗ.† ⲉⲡⲥⲱⲙⲁ ⲡⲧⲗⲁϩⲙⲉ, BHom 123 hair ⲉⲡ- ⲧⲁϥⲗⲱϭ (*sic*) at death, P 129¹⁴ 92 dream-tellers ⲉⲩⲗ.† ⲉⲡⲁⲓⲙⲱⲛ παρέδροις τισὶ δαίμοσι (*v* PSBA 24 75), Z 321 angel ⲉⲧⲗ.† ⲉⲣⲟϥ παρεπόμενος, PMich 601 charm to compel woman ⲡⲧⲉⲡⲉϥⲧⲟ ⲕⲟⲟϩ (ⲡ)- ⲡⲉϩⲛⲓ(l ⲡⲉⲥ-) ⲗⲱⲝⲕ ⲡⲕⲱⲣⲧ ⲁⲣⲟⲥ, BMis 141 (Virgin *loq*) Gabriel entered my womb ⲉⲡⲉϥⲗ.† ⲉⲣⲟⲓⲡⲉ, Ann 23 220 hands ⲗⲱⲝⲧ ⲉϩⲟⲩⲛ ⲉⲧⲕⲁⲓⲥⲉ. tr *stick, join to*: Lev 6 3 (10) *S* (*B* ⲕⲱϯ ⲉ-) περιτίθεσθαι, Ez 29 4 *S* (var & *B* ⲗⲱⲝ) προσκολ.; Jth 10 17 *S* -ⲝⲧ παραζευγνύναι; ShIF 162 *S* ⲁⲕⲁⲑⲁⲣⲥⲓⲁ...ⲁⲧⲉⲧⲡⲗⲟ- ⲝⲧⲉ ⲉϩⲟⲩⲛ ⲉⲡⲕⲁⲧⲁⲡⲉⲧⲁⲥⲙⲁ, GMir 182 *S* martyr dragged over stones till blood ⲗⲱⲝⲕ ⲡϩⲛ[.   **b** *lick*: Miss 4 730 ⲁⲥⲗⲱⲝⲧ ⲉⲡⲟⲩϭⲉⲣⲓⲧⲉ of our father, P 129¹⁶ 2 ⲁⲥⲗⲱⲝⲧ ⲙⲙⲟϥ ⲙⲡⲉⲥⲗⲁⲥ, CO 41 undertaking to sleep in church & to ⲗⲱⲝⲕ ⲡⲉϥϩⲏⲃⲥ *feed, tend* (?) lamp.

ⲗⲁⲝⲕⲉ *S* nn (?), meaning unknown: PStras 409 vo ⲉⲓⲉ (*i e* ⲉⲓⲟ) ⲡⲁⲥⲟⲛ ⲏⲡⲕ ⲙⲟⲡ [ⲙⲓ]ϣ ⲉⲓ ⲉϩⲟⲩⲛ ϩⲓⲡⲙⲟⲟⲩ ⲙⲡⲗ. ⲁⲗⲗⲁ ⲉⲝⲱⲡⲕⲓⲥⲁⲙⲟⲉ. *Cf* ? ⲗⲁⲝⲧⲉ.

ⲗⲁⲝⲗⲉⲝ *B* *girder* *v* ⲗⲟϭⲗⲉϭ.

ⲗⲟⲝⲗⲝ, ⲗⲟϭⲗⲉⲝ *S*, ⲗⲟⲝⲗⲉⲝ *B*, ⲗⲉⲝⲗⲱⲝϭ, ⲗⲉϭⲗⲱϭ *S*, ⲗⲉⲝⲗⲱⲝⲧ, ⲗⲉϭⲗⲱϭⲧ *S* vb **a** intr, *languish, be sickly*: Job 24 23 *S* (*B* ϣⲱⲡⲓ), Is 38 1 *S*

(B do), ib 53 5 B (O'LearyTh 55, Tatt prob ϣⲱⲡⲓ, S tr), Dan 8 27 S (B do) μαλακίζειν; Pcod 18 S righteous ⲉⲅϣⲁⲡⲗ., P 129¹⁶ 11 S ⲁϥϣⲱⲡⲉ ⲁϥⲗ. & about to die.   Qual : 1 Cor 11 30 S (var ⲗⲉϭⲗⲱϭ, B ⲙⲟⲕϩ) ἄρρωστος; ShC 73 212 S ⲉϥⲙⲟⲕϩ ⲉϥⲗ., R 1 4 27 S ⲉⲅⲗ. ϩⲛϥⲉⲛϣⲱⲛⲉ. ⲃ tr, make sick : Is 53 5 S (v above, var ⲗⲉϭⲗⲱϭϥ) μαλακ.

——, ⲗⲟϭⲗⲉϭ, ⲗⲟϭⲗⲉϫ S, ⲗⲁϫⲗⲉϫ A²B, ⲗⲁϭ-ⲗⲉϭ, -ⲗⲁϭ F nn, sickness : Deu 7 15 B ⲗ. & ϣⲱⲡⲓ (S ϣ. & ⲗ.), Is 53 3 S (B ϣ.), Mt 9 35 S (B ⲓⲁϧⲓ) μαλακία; ShRE 11 18 S ⲟⲩϣ. ⲙⲡϩⲉⲛⲗⲟϭⲗⲉϫ, AP 22 A² shall turn strength ⲁⲅⲗ., BM 511 (2) F healing ϣ. & ⲗ., LAp 514 F cured...ϩⲛⲗⲁϭⲗⲁϭ, K 485 B ⲗ. تواضع humility.   As adj S : J 76 45 ⲡⲁϣⲱⲡⲉ (l ϣ.) ⲡⲗⲁϫⲗⲉϭ (l -ⲗⲉϫ).

ⲗⲟϫⲗϫ S, ⲗⲁϫⲗϫ A rub   v ⲗⲱϫ.

ⲗⲁϫⲁⲛ B nn m, moisture : Jer 31 18 ὑγρασία.

ⲗⲱϫⲧ S   v ⲗⲱϫⲕ.

ⲗⲁϫⲧⲉ S nn, mud, dirt (?) : R 1 4 26 gold was as ⲟⲩⲗ. ϩⲁⲣⲱⲟⲩ aurum pro luto. Cf ? ⲗⲁϫⲕⲉ.

ⲗⲱϫϩ SAA²B, ⲗⲉϫϩ- SB, ⲗⲟϫϩ⳽ SB, ⲗⲟϫϩ† S, ⲗⲁϫϩ† A (cf ⲗⲱϫ) vb ⲁ intr, be crushed, effaced : Is 28 14 S (B ϩⲟϫϩⲉϫ) θλίβεσθαι, TU 43 11 A path narrow & ⲉⲧⲗ.†, Tri 483 S ⲡⲡⲉⲅⲣⲉ ⲉⲃⲟⲗ ⲟⲩϫⲉ ⲡⲡⲉⲅⲗ. ⲓ⳽.   tr crush : Ps 17 38 S (B ϩⲟϫ.), Is 29 2 S (B do) ἐκθλίβειν, Nu 22 25 S c ⲉϩⲟⲩⲡ ⲉ- (B do) προσθλ.; Si 30 12 S θλᾶν, Ps 41 10 S (B ⲟⲅⲟⲭⲟⲩⲉϫ) Is 63 3 S (B ⲗⲱⲥ) καταθλᾶν, Ps 109 5 S (B ϫⲟⲙϫⲉⲙ) συνθλᾶν; Ps 73 14 S (var ⲗⲱϫ, B ⲗⲱⲥ) συντρίβειν.   As nn m, anguish, oppression : Is 30 6 S (B ϩⲟϫ., F ϩⲁⲙϫ), Ro 8 35 S (B ⲧⲁⲧϩⲟ), 2 Cor 12 10 S (B ϩⲟϫ., F ⲗⲱϫ) στενοχωρία; Ps 106 39 S (B do) θλῖψις; 2 Cor 2 4 S (B ⲙⲕⲁϩ) συνοχή.   ⲃ intr S, be sticky, adhesive : Mor 48 84 S lips ⲁⲩⲗ. = C 43 141 B ϫⲱⲗϫ ⲉⲡⲟⲩⲉⲣ-ⲏⲟⲩ.   ⳽ tr SA²B, lick : Ps 71 9 SB (var ⲗⲱϫ), Is 49 23 SB, Mic 7 17 SB (A ⲗⲱϫ), Z 295 S crocodiles ⲗ. ⲙⲡⲉϥⲥⲱⲙⲁ, MG 25 13 B λείχειν, Nu 22 4 SB, EpJer 19 B (F ⲕⲱⲧϥ ⲡⲥⲁ-) ἐκλ., Lu 16 21 SB ἐπιλ., AP 15 A² περιλ.; Ps 67 24 S (B Gk om); Aeg 262 S spill nought from chalice lest ⲛⲛⲁ ⲛⲁⲗ-ⲗⲟⲧⲣⲓⲟⲛ ⲗⲟϫϩⲟⲩ, P 131⁶ 24 S I entreat you & ϯⲗ. ⲙⲛϣⲟⲉⲓϣ of your feet, Ep 164 S sim, C 43 30 B ⲉⲥⲗ. ⲙⲙⲟⲩ ⲙⲡⲉⲥⲗⲁⲥ, MG 25 132 B what mother gives babe ⲉⲟⲣⲉϥⲗ. ⲙⲙⲟⲩ.   As nn m S : Tri 521 ⲡⲗ. of blood on door-posts رشاش (cf ? ⲡⲟⲩϫⲕ, ⲡⲟⲩϫϭ, though Ex 12 7 S has ⲱϭϭ).

ⲗⲱϫϭ   v ⲗⲱϫⲕ.

ⲗⲟϭ, ⲗⲁϭ S, ⲗⲁϫⲓ B nn, impudent, persistent person, cf لج , ⲁ with p, ⲉⲡ, importune : Mor 19 45 S

ⲁϩⲣⲱⲧⲛ ⲧⲉⲧⲛⲟ ⲛⲗ. in prayers ? = Miss 4 129 B ⲟⲓ ⲡⲟⲩⲗⲏϣϣ ⲛⲥⲁϫⲓ; c ⲉ- ShP 130¹ 15 S saying They compelled me or ϫⲉⲁⲩⲣ ⲗ. ⲉⲣⲟⲓ, Mor 19 80 Sᶠ I invited him ⲁⲉⲓⲣ ⲗⲉϭ (sic) ⲉⲣⲟϥ ⲉⲡⲉϩⲟⲩⲟ, ib 18 71 ⲡⲧⲉⲣⲉⲡⲉⲣ ⲗⲟϭ ⲉⲣⲟϥ = Miss 4 144 B ϩⲣⲓ ⲛϯϩⲣⲟ, SHel 5 S ⲙⲡⲉⲣⲉⲣ ⲗ. ⲉⲣⲟⲓ for I will not worship, MIE 2 345 B sick women ⲉⲧⲁⲩⲉⲣ ⲗ. ⲉⲣⲟϥ = Par 4785 124 لجوا عليه.

ⲗⲁⲡⲧⲗ. S, ⲙⲉⲧⲗ. B nn f, impudence, persistence : Lu 11 8 SB ἀναίδεια, P 44 88 S ⲉⲡⲟⲭⲗⲉⲓ · ⲧⲙ., ShWess 9 131 S Origen spake ⲟⲩⲁϣⲏ ⲛϣⲁϫⲉ ⲙⲙ., Cat 164 B on Lu 18 3 ⲉⲥϯⲣⲟ ϫⲉⲡⲟⲩⲙ., MG 25 161 B of beggar ⲧⲉϥⲙ. ⲉϫⲟⲩⲡ ⲉⲡⲓⲁⲣⲭⲱⲛ, Tri 450 S ⲧⲙ. لجاجة.   Cf ⲗⲱϣϫ.

ⲗⲟϭ bowl   v ⲗⲟⲕ.

ⲗⲁϭⲉ S(PS only) AA², ⲗⲱϫⲓ B, ⲗϭ- A, ⲗⲁϭ- A², ⲗⲁϭ⳽ AA², ⲗⲟϫ⳽ B vb intr, though mostly refl, ⲁ cease : Ge 11 8 B, Nu 25 8 B(S ⲗⲟ), Pro 24 24 A Is 1 16 A (Cl, var & B ⲧⲁⲗϭⲟ), ib 10 25 B, Ac 21 32 B, 1 Cor 13 8 B (all S do) παύεσθαι, Lam 5 14 B (S do), Hos 7 4 A(B diff) καταπαύ.; Jon 1 11 A (S do, B ϩⲣⲟⲩϩⲣ) κοπάζειν; Ge 18 11 B (S diff) ἐκλείπειν, Jer 51 18 B (S ⲗⲟ) διαλείπ.; ib 7 10 ἀπέ-χεσθαι; Zeph 1 6 A (B ⲣⲓⲕⲓ ⲉⲃⲟⲗ ϩⲁ-) ἐκκλίνειν; Mic 2 4 A (S ⲕⲧⲟ⳽ ⲉϧ., B ⲧⲁⲥϧⲟ) ἀποστρέφειν; 2 Thes 2 7 B (S ⲗⲟ) Gk diff; Cat 108 B ⲉⲑⲣⲟⲩⲕⲏⲡ ⲉⲣⲱⲟⲩ...ⲡⲧⲟⲩⲗⲟϫⲟⲩ ⲉⲅⲉⲣ ⲉⲧⲓⲡ, C 86 76 B ⲁϥⲗⲟϫϥ ⲉϥϫⲁϫⲓ, Mus 34 191 B Jews' Pascha ⲛⲧⲉϥⲗⲟϫϥ ⲙⲙⲁⲩ, Saviour's begins, AM 230 B bade ⲉⲑⲣⲟⲩⲗⲟϫⲟⲩ ⲉϣⲧⲉⲙϭⲓⲟⲅⲓ ⲉⲣⲟϥ.   ⲃ cease, recover from sickness B : Lev 13 37 (S ϯ ⲟⲩⲱ), Job 24 23 (S ⲗⲟ) ὑγιάζειν; Deu 28 27 (S ⲗⲧⲟⲡ), Jer 28 9, Lu 17 15 (S ⲧⲏⲃⲟ), He 12 13 (S ⲗⲟ) ἰᾶσθαι; AM 311 ϣⲁⲧⲉϥⲗⲟϫϥ ϫⲉⲡⲡⲉϥⲉⲣϩⲟⲧ, MIE 2 391 boy ⲗⲟϫϥ ⲉⲃⲟⲗ ϧⲉⲛ- malady; Lev 13 24 ⲉⲧⲁϥⲗⲱϫⲓ ⲉϧ. ⲙ-(S ⲗⲧⲟⲡ) ὑγ.   ⳽ c ⲉ- SA², cause to cease, remove : Jo 11 39 A² (S ϥⲓ, B ϣⲱⲡ) αἴρειν, PS 106 S ⲡⲥⲉⲗⲁϭⲉ ⲉⲡⲉⲅⲣⲁⲛ from 13th aeon.   ⲇ tr A², make to cease, cure : Jo 4 47 (SF ⲧⲁⲗϭⲟ, B ⲧⲟⲩϫⲟ) ἰᾶσθαι.   V ⲧⲁⲗϭⲟ.

ⲗⲁϭⲟⲩ B nn as pl, meaning unknown : C 86 191(=AZ 13 86) among implements of torture ϩⲁⲛ-ⲧⲣⲟⲭⲟⲥ ⲡⲉⲙϩⲁⲛⲗ. of iron, ib 212 ϩⲁⲛⲗ. & ϩⲁⲛ-ⲱⲧⲉⲛ of iron set upright on torture wheel.

ⲗⲟⲓϭⲉ S, ⲗⲁⲉⲓϭⲉ AA², ⲗⲱⲓϫⲓ B, ⲗⲁⲓϭⲓ F nn f, cause, excuse : Pro 18 1 SA, Dan 6 4 SB, Mk 12 40 SBF, Jo 15 22 SA²B, Phil 1 18 SBF, Bor 170 91 S ⲉⲧⲃⲉⲧⲗ. ⲙⲡⲙⲟⲟⲩ, BMar 109 S soldiers sent ⲛⲧⲗ. ⲛϣⲱⲣϫ ⲉⲛϫⲱⲟⲡ πρόφασις; Pro 28 17 SA(var ⲡⲟϭ, misread for ⲗ.), Sa 18 18 S, Jo 19 6 SA²(B=Gk), Ac 22 24 SB, AP 15 A² ⲧⲗ. ⲉⲡⲧⲁⲩⲥⲁϩⲥ ⲛⲥⲱⲥ αἰτία,

He 5 8 B (S = Gk) αἴτιος, Ac 25 7 B (S ⲁⲓⲧⲓⲁ) αἰ-
τίωμα; Ez 5 7 SB, Ro 7 8 B (S = Gk) ἀφορμή;
BHom 24 S is for us ⲡⲗ. πρόξενος; ib 27 S ⲁϣⲧⲉ
ⲧⲗ. λόγος; BMar 172 S I hungered ⲛⲧⲕⲗ. διά σε;
Ac 4 21 B (S diff) Gk om; PS 29 S ⲥⲉⲛⲁⲉⲓⲣⲉ ⲡⲟⲩⲗ.
ⲣ̄ⲛⲡⲉⲧⲥⲟⲟⲩⲛ the mysteries, ShC 42 130 S have
separated from us ⲟ̄ⲣⲉⲡⲗ. ⲙ̄ⲙⲧⲣⲉϥⲟ̄ⲡ ⲁⲣⲓⲕⲉ,
ShA 2 157 S blackening eyes ⲟ̄ⲛⲧⲗ. ⲙ̄ⲡ̄ϣⲱⲡⲉ, P
129¹⁴ 135 S art thou physician? ⲉⲓⲥ ⲧⲗ. to display
thy skill, C 43 117 B ⲉⲧⲁⲧⲁⲓⲗ. ϣⲱⲡⲓ ⲛⲁⲛ thìs *opportunity*, Mor 41 198 S all that supplicate martyr
whether ⲟ̄ⲛⲟⲩⲗ. ⲡⲣⲱⲧⲃ̄ ⲏ ⲭⲓⲟⲅⲉ, BIF 14 122 S he
departed ⲛⲧⲗ. ⲡⲣⲉⲡⲕⲉⲙⲁⲣⲧⲩⲣⲟⲥ, BMar 237 S they
cast me out ⲡⲧⲉⲅⲗ. *on their account*, BIF 13 104 S
Jacob went to Egypt ⲟ̄ⲓⲧⲡⲧⲗ. of famine = MG 25
286 B ⲡⲱⲗ., AM 280 B ⳨ⲗ. ⲭⲉ…ⲑⲁⲓⲧⲉ the *reason*
was the following, ib 81 B I weep ⲡⲧⲉⲕⲗ.   As
adj: Hos 10 4 SAB ϣⲁⲭⲉ ⲡⲗ. πρόφασις, Deu 22
13 SB προφασιστικός.

ⲁⲧⲗ. *SB* adj, *without cause*: 1 Tim 3 2 B (S ⲉⲙ-
ⲡⲟⲩⲧⲁⲣⲟϥ ⲟ̄ⲛⲗⲁⲁⲩ ⲡⲱⲃ) ἀνεπίλημπτος; Tit 1 7
B (S ⲉⲧⲙ̄ⲧⲣⲉⲩⲟ̄ⲡ ⲣⲱⲃ ⲉⲣⲟⲩⲛ ⲉ-) ἀνέγκλητος; Ro
1 20 B (S Gr om); Mor 17 119 S ⲡⲁⲓ ⲉⲧⲟ ⲛⲁ. ἀναίτιος; ib 18 14 S = ib 19 22 ⲛⲧⲣ ⲁ. ⲉⲡⲉⲩⲥⲡⲟⲩ =
Miss 4 108 B ⲉⲣ ⲁⲗⲗⲟⲧⲣⲓⲟⲛ ⲉ-, BMar 8 S Pilate
washed hands ⲁϥⲁⲁϥ ⲡⲁ., C 89 196 B ⲉϥⲟⲓ ⲛⲁ.
ⲉⲃⲟⲗ ϩⲁⲣⲱⲟⲩ. *Cf* Ac 10 29 S ⲡⲟⲩⲉϣ ⲡⲗ. (B ⲉⲣ
ⲁⲛⲧⲓⲗⲉⲅⲓⲛ) ἀναντιρρήτως.

ⲕⲉ ⲗ. *F*, *give occasion, excuse*: Kr 3 ⲡⲡⲉⲗⲕⲉ ⲗ.
ⲕⲁⲧⲁ ⲧⲉⲕⲯⲩⲭⲏ.

⳨ ⲗ. *SB*, meaning same: Pro 9 9 B (SA = Gk,
but Miss 4 700 S = B), 2 Cor 5 12 B (S = Gk)
ἀφορ.; PSBA 10 395 B judge & martyr ⲉϥ⳨ ⲗ.
ⲛⲁϥ by reason of his youth προβαλλόμενος; MG
25 260 B ⲡⲧⲁϣⲧⲉⲙ⳨ ϩⲗⲓ ⲡⲗ. to mine eyes, RE 14
26 S repay what is his & ⲡⲡⲣⲧⲓ ⲗ. ⲡⲁϥ for complaint.

ϭⲛ, ⲭⲉⲙ ⲗ. *SAB, find occasion, excuse*: Ps 140 4
SB, Pro 22 13 SA (var ϭⲉⲡ), Z 317 S ⲁϥϭⲛ ⲗ.
= MG 25 233 B ⳨ ⲙⲁ ⲡ- προφασίζειν, Dan 6 5 B
(S ϭⲉ ⲗ.) προφ. εὑρίσκειν, Ac 27 30 S (var ϭⲉⲡ, B
ϭⲉⲡⲟⲩⲗ.) προφάσει ὡς; Ac 13 28 SB αἰτ. εὑρ.;
2 Cor 11 12 B (S = Gk) ἀφορ. no vb; Jo 8 6 B
(SA² om) ἔχειν κατηγορεῖν; BHom 21 S ϣⲁⲕϭⲛ ⲗ.

on account of feebleness προβάλλειν, ShC 42 27 S
sim, BAp 112 S = MIE 2 388 B suffer him not
ⲉϭⲡ ⲗ. ⲉⲣⲟⲕ at Christ's βῆμα, BSM 75 B things
stolen ⲉⲧⲟⲩⲭⲉⲙ ⲗ. ⲉⲣⲟⲛ ⲉⲑⲃⲏⲧⲥ = BMis 166 S ϩⲓ
ⲗⲁ ⲉ-, BSM 46 B ⳨ⲛⲁⲭⲉⲙ ⲗ. ⲉⲭⲱⲧⲉⲡ ϭⲁⲧⲟⲧϥ =
BMis 395 S ⲁⲡⲟⲗⲟⲅⲓⲍⲉ ϩⲁ-, MG 25 266 B ⲙⲁⲣⲉⲡ-
ⲭⲉⲙ ⲗ. ⲙ̄ⲡⲉⲡⲓⲱⲧ & say to him. *V* also ϭⲛ ⲗ.

ϭⲛ ⲗ. *S, seize occasion, excuse*: Pro 22 13 (var &
A ϭⲛ), BM 216 79 if fasting ⲙ̄ⲡⲣ̄ⲟ̄. ⲟ̄ⲣⲉⲛⲉϣⲱⲡⲉ
προφασίζειν, ShC 72 103 close not door lest late
comers ϭ. ⲗ. ⲉⲧⲃⲉⲡⲣⲟ, Mor 40 39 ⲙⲁⲣⲉⲛϭ. ⲗ. ⲭⲉ
= MG 25 266 B ⲭⲉⲙ, JTS 4 389 ⲥⲉϭ. ⲗ. ⲉⲣⲟⲛ *seize
chance* (to speak) *against us*, Mor 33 88 ϭ. ⲗ. ϩⲓⲧⲛ̄
= BMis 117 ϭⲛ ⲗ. ⲡ- *makest excuse* of thy hardness
of heart.

ⲗⲱϭⲉ, ⲗⲉϭ-, ⲗⲟϭ⸗ *S*, ⲗⲟⲭ⸗ *B* (once), ⲗⲏϭ†,
ⲗⲏⲭ† *S* vb a intr (qual), *lie hid*: 1 Kg 10 22, ib 14
22 (var ⲡⲏⲭ or *l* ⲗ.), 4 Kg 6 9 κρύπτεσθαι, Jos 7
21 ⲥⲉⲗ. ⲉⲅⲣⲏⲡ ἐγκρύπ.; 1 Kg 26 1 ⲗⲏⲭ σκεπάζεσθαι, BHom 138 he that fighteth with her ⲗ. ϩⲓϩⲟⲩⲛ ⲙⲙⲟⲥ, R 1 2 19 ⲉⲓⲗ. ϩⲛϩⲁϩ ⲛⲧⲟⲡⲟⲥ during
persecution, BM 1119 23 ⲉⲥ ⲡⲙⲁ ⲣⲟϭⲉ (*l* ⲗ.) ϣⲁⲧⲉⲛⲟⲩ (belongs? here). b tr, *hide, pilfer*: Jos
7 1 (HT, P 44 108 خبأ) νοσφίζεσθαι (*q v* in Ac 5
2, Tit 2 10), Z 352 ⲁⲡⲉⲣⲗⲗⲟ ⲗⲏϭ (*l* ⲗⲉϭ) ⲡⲥⲟⲡ,
Bor 241 217 they that shout or laugh or ⲉⲅⲗ. ⲙ̄-
ⲡⲉⲧⲙ̄ⲡⲉⲩϭⲟⲩⲛ;   refl: 1 Kg 14 11 κρύπ., AM
272 B ⲁϥⲗⲟⲭϥ ὑποστέλλεσθαι (PO 1 395 سكّ or
? = ⲗⲱⲭⲓ). As nn: 2 Kg 17 9 hiding in hills or
ⲙⲁ ⲡⲗ. τόπος, PRain 4741 ⲟⲩⲡⲣⲏϣ ⲡⲗ. (? same).

ⲗⲁϭⲗⲉϭ *Sᶠ* *v* ⲗⲱⲕ (ⲗⲟⲕⲗⲕ).

ⲗⲟϭⲗⲉϭ *S*, ⲗⲁϭⲗϭ *A*, ⲗⲁⲭⲗⲉⲭ *B* nn m f (?),
girder, joint, frame: Si 22 17 *SAB* ἱμάντωσις, P 44
119 *S* نطاق, K 157 B ⲡⲓⲗ. (⳨ⲗ. once) قائمة, نطاق
(AZ 13 85, Lab *s v* distinguish *B* m & f, though K
does not).

ⲗⲟϭⲗⲉϭ *S sickness v* ⲗⲟⲭⲗⲭ.

ⲗⲁϭⲡⲁⲟⲩ *F v* ⲭⲡⲟⲟⲩ.

ⲗⲱϭⲥ *S v* ⲗⲱⲕⲥ.

ⲗⲱϭⲭ *S v* ⲗⲱⲭⲕ.

ⲙ

ⲙ, twelfth letter of the alphabet, called ⲙⲏ (P
131³ 77, *cf* BM 219, TT 13), ⲙⲉ (My 34) *S*, ⲙⲓ *B*
(K 1, Stern p 418), ⳨ (P 43 242, 44 133). As
numeral *BF*, rarely *S* = *forty* (ϩⲙⲉ). Derived from
hierogl *m*, as ⲁⲙⲟⲩ, ⲕⲏⲙⲉ, ⲡⲟⲩⲣⲙ, ϣⲙⲟⲩⲛ, ϭⲱⲙ;

or *b*, as ⲙⲁ, ⲙⲙⲁϩ, ⲙ̄ⲡⲉ-, ⲑⲙⲟⲅⲓ; or (rarely) *n*, as
ⲉⲙⲃⲱ *Ombos*, ⲣⲟⲙⲡⲉ. ⲁ varies with ⲃ, as ⲡⲓⲙ ⲡⲓⲃⲉⲛ, ⲥⲁⲧⲃⲉ ⲥⲁⲑⲙⲓ, ⲟⲩⲁϩⲃⲉϥ ⲟⲩⲁϩⲙⲉϥ, ⲭⲉⲃⲡⲟⲩⲧⲉ
ⲭⲉⲙⲡⲟⲩ⳨ *Samanûd*, ϭⲗⲙ ϭⲗⲃⲉ, ϭⲃ̄ϣⲁ ⲭⲉⲙϣⲁⲓ;
or replaced by it, as ⲙⲉⲃⲣⲁⲡⲟⲛ (BMis 513), converse

ⲙⲱⲁⲙ (Mic 6 5 *A*), ⲧⲥⲁⲙⲁⲩ (Kr 3 *F*).   **b** varies with ⲗ in ⲙⲡⲁⲓ *S* ⲗⲃⲉⲓ *A*; with ⲛ, as ⲋⲓⲡⲉ ⲭⲓⲙⲓ; with ⲡ (rare) as ⲙⲉⲭⲉ ⲡⲉⲭⲉ (Ep 1 243); with ⲟⲩ, as ⲕⲟⲩⲕⲙ ⲕⲓⲕⲙ, ⲟⲩⲁⲙⲉϥ ⲙⲁⲙ-, ⲥⲁⲗⲟⲩϩⲓⲣ ϩⲁⲗⲓⲃⲉⲣ.   **c** ⲙ̄ = ⁿ*m*, as ⲙ̄ⲧⲟ, ⲙ̄ⲡⲟⲣⲓⲁ, ⲭⲱⲕⲙ̄ & replaces ⲛ before initial ⲙ, ⲡ (ⲫ, ⲯ), as ϩⲁⲡ ⲙⲙⲉ, ⲡⲟⲥ ⲙⲡⲟⲗⲓⲥ, ⲉⲭⲙⲡⲕⲁϩ, ⲙϥⲩⲭⲏ, though not in old *S* texts, as ⲋⲏⲡⲧⲁⲕⲟ, ⲡⲁϩⲣⲏⲡⲣⲟ.   **d** rarely doubled, *v* Ep 1 246, JKP 1 90, KKS 84.   **e** omitted, as *F* ⲡⲓ- for ⲙⲡⲓ- (BM 595), ⲡⲉⲗ- for ⲙⲡⲉⲗ- (*ib* 580), *cf* ⲉⲡⲉⲣ- (P 129¹⁷ 5), ⲗⲉⲃⲉⲕⲏ (ⲣⲙⲃⲉⲕⲉ Kr 140); further ⲉ̂ⲣⲉϩⲓ for ⲙⲉ̂ⲣⲉϩⲓ, ⲭⲉⲡⲉⲣ for ⲭⲙⲡⲉⲣ.   ⲙ has disappeared in ⲣⲉϥ-, but *cf* *A*² ⲣⲙⲉϥ-.   **f** where Arabic transcribed ⲙ = ﻣ, as ⲁⲙⲓⲣ أمير, ⲉⲙⲭⲉⲁ اﺟﻞ, ⲉⲓⲓⲉⲙ ايام, ϩⲁⲙⲉⲗ ﻋﻞ.

ⲙⲁ *SAA²B*, **ⲙⲁⲓ** *B* (only with ⲛⲓⲃⲉⲛ, *v* below), **ⲙⲉ** (ⲙⲁ before gen ⲛ-) *F*, **ⲙⲟⲩ** *B* (C 43 192) *F* (Is 33 14 *sic*) nn m, *place*, **a** in general: Ge 28 11 *SB*, Job 28 20 *S* (*B* ⲙⲱⲓⲧ), Pro 4 15 *SAB*, Ac 27 29 *SB* τόπος; PS 132 *S* flood not restrained by ϩⲉⲛⲙⲁ ⲉⲅⲕⲏⲧ (*cf* Od Solom 6 9), J 1 63 *S* ⲡⲙⲁ ⲉⲧⲉⲣⲉⲡⲣⲟ... ⲟⲩⲏⲓ ⲉⲣⲟϥ, BSM 132 *B* ⲡⲓⲙⲁ ⲉⲑⲙⲟⲕϩ of his head, PMéd 292 *S* ⲡⲙⲁ ⲡⲧⲛⲟⲩⲛⲉ ⲙⲡϣⲟⲗ, ⲕⲟⲟⲥ ⲙⲙⲁ *S* (*v* ⲕⲟⲟⲥ *c*), Wess 18 5 *S* ⲡⲙⲁ ⲙⲡⲉⲭⲣⲏⲙⲁ *sc* certain place in a homily.   **b** ⲡⲉⲓⲙⲁ, *this world*: ShA 1 88 *S* opp ⲡⲉϩⲟⲟⲩ ⲙⲡⲣⲁⲡ, CaiEuch 381 *B* sojourners ⲙⲡⲁⲓⲙⲁ, BHom 38 *S* opp ⲡⲕⲉⲙⲁ, Va 57 10 *B* life of ⲡⲁⲓⲙⲁ ἐπίκηρος.   **c** *dwelling-place* (*cf* ⲙⲁ ⲛϣⲱⲡⲉ): Wess 18 39 *S* ⲁⲅⲕⲧⲟⲟⲩ ⲉⲡⲉⲩⲙⲁ, AP 16 *A*² ⲕⲁⲁⲥ ⲡⲉ ⲁⲡⲁⲙⲁ τόπ.; Deu 16 7 *S* (*B* ⲏⲓ), Jo 7 53 *B* (*SA*² om) οἶκος; PO 14 357 *B* came to ⲫⲙⲁ ⲙⲡⲓⲙⲁⲑⲏⲧⲏⲥ, MG 25 268 *B* ⲁⲩⲧⲁⲙⲙⲱⲟⲩ ⲉⲡⲉϥⲙⲁ, PLond 4 462 *S* authorized to stay ϩⲙⲡⲉϥⲙⲁ.   **d** *chamber*, monk's *cell*: 4 Kg 4 10 *B* τόπ.; Tob 2 5 *S*, Ez 16 24 *SB* οἴκημα; BMar 197 *S* make for me καλύβη & small ⲙⲁ, Miss 4 554 = Wess 11 162 *S* ⲙⲁ built in church whither he retired, ShCai 8007 *S* ⲡⲙⲁ ϣⲏⲙ that ye have built me.   **e** *temple, shrine, monastery*: Deu 12 2 *SB* τόπ., C 89 6 *B* ⲫⲙⲁ of Serapis, *ib* 30 *B* ⲡⲓⲙⲁ of Tabennêsi, AM 280 *B* ⲫⲙⲁ of St Mark τὰ τοῦ ἁγ. M., CO 32 *S* deacon of ⲙⲁ of St George, *ib* 105, 290, 485 sim, ShA 1 215 *S* ⲡⲙⲁ ⲡⲙⲙⲁⲣⲧⲩⲣⲟⲥ, *ib* 216 *S* ϩⲉⲛⲙⲁ for martyrs' bones, Mor 50 63 *S* lay my body in church till thou build me ⲟⲩⲕⲟⲩⲓ ⲙⲙⲁ, C 86 317 *B* ⲡⲓⲙⲁ ⲉⲧⲁⲩⲕⲟⲧϥ for martyr, Z 513 *S* ⲡⲉⲓⲙⲁ *sc* ? monastery, Miss 4 694 *S* greetings to ⲡⲙⲁ ⲧⲏⲣϥ.   **f** *part, district*: Jos 18 16 *S*, Jer 30 32 *B*, Ac 19 1 *SB*, Mor 37 75 *S* ⲡⲙⲁ ⲡⲡⲉϣⲟⲟϣ μέρος.   **g** *part, duty*: Ac 1 25 *SB* τόπ., ShC 73 134 *S* ⲉⲡⲉⲩⲙⲁⲡⲉ ⲡⲣ ⲕⲟⲙⲉⲥ, WTh 190 *S* ⲡⲉⲕⲙⲁⲡⲉ to take kingship, BMar 18 *S* said no word, for ⲙⲡⲉϥⲙⲁ ⲁⲡⲡⲉ.

ⲣⲉⲙⲫⲙⲁ *B*, *man of the place, native*: BM 834 36 in prayer ⲡⲓϣⲉⲙⲙⲟ ⲡⲉⲙⲡⲓⲣ.

ⲙⲁ ⲛ-, I *place of*, auxiliary in translating single Gk word, as ⲙⲁ ⲡⲁⲙⲁϩⲧⲉ κατάσχεσις, ⲡⲁⲣⲉ ⲣⲁⲧⲥⲧⲁⲥⲓⲥ, ⲛⲃⲱⲕ ⲉϩⲟⲩⲡ εἴσοδος, ⲡⲭⲁ ⲡⲓϭⲁⲗⲁⲭ ὑποπόδιον, ⲡⲕⲁⲕⲉ μυχός, ⲙⲙⲟⲟⲡⲉ αἰγιαλός, ⲡⲕⲱⲧⲉ κυκλευτήριον, ⲡⲕⲟⲧⲕ θάλαμος, κοίτη, ⲡⲁⲧⲟⲡ κατάπαυσις, ⲙⲙⲟⲟϣⲉ τρίβος, ⲡⲁⲧⲗⲟϣⲓ ἄβατον, ⲡⲡⲉⲭ ⲥⲟⲧⲉ βελόστασις, ⲡⲛⲟⲭ⸱ ⲡϣⲟⲣⲡ πρωτοκλισία, ⲡⲧⲡⲉ φάτνωμα, ⲙⲡⲱⲧ καταφυγή, ⲣⲙⲁⲡ ῥοῶν, ⲡⲣⲁⲉⲓⲥ, ⲡⲁⲣⲉϩ προφυλακή, ⲡⲥⲱ πότος, ⲡⲥⲟⲟⲡⲉ, ⲡⲥ̂ⲱⲡⲧ πειρατήριον, ⲡⲥⲱⲡ δεσμωτήριον, ⲡⲥⲱⲧⲙ ἀκρόαμα, ⲡϯⲙⲟⲟⲩ ἄφεσις, ⲡⲭⲓ ⲙⲁⲩ ὑδραγωγός, ⲡϯ ϩⲁⲡ κριτήριον, ⲡⲟⲩⲟⲉⲓⲉ γεώργιον, ⲡⲟⲩⲱⲧⲉ χωνευτήριον, ⲡⲟⲩⲱϣⲉⲙ ἀρτοκοπεῖον, ⲡⲱⲡⲉ λιθώδης, ⲡⲱϣ ἀνάγνωσμα, ⲙⲡⲉⲓⲣⲉ ἀνατολή, ⲡϣⲉ ⲉⲡϣⲱⲓ κλιμακτήρ, ⲡϣⲉⲗⲉⲉⲧ παστός, ⲡϣⲏⲛ δρυμός, ⲡϣⲓⲡⲉ μαντεῖον, ⲡϣⲱⲡⲉ οἰκητήριον, ⲡⲥⲁⲭⲓ μῦθος, ⲡⲡⲉϩⲓⲟⲙⲉ γυναικῶν, ⲡⲣⲁⲧⲉ διέξοδος, ⲡⲭⲉⲗⲭⲉⲗ ψυγμός, ⲡⲭⲟⲉⲓⲧ ἐλαιῶν, ⲡⲥϭ ⲥⲃⲱ παλαίστρα, ⲡⲥⲱⲣϭ ἐνέδρα.   Also with Gk words, as ⲙⲁ ⲡⲉⲓⲍⲱⲗⲟⲡ εἰδωλεῖον, ⲙⲡⲉⲧⲣⲁ πετρώδης, ⲡⲧⲉⲗⲱⲡⲏⲥ τελώνιον, ⲡⲭⲱⲣⲁ (Ac 27 12 *B* χῶρος misunderstood), BMis 13 *S* ⲡⲑⲉⲱⲣⲉⲓ (? θεώριον).   Further: Cat 102 *B* colt ⲟⲩⲙⲁ ⲡⲁⲗⲏⲓ for Christ (Mt 21 7), PMich 3583 *S* ⲡⲁⲙⲣⲉ, R 1 3 74 *S* ⲡⲕⲁ ⲟⲉⲓⲕ, ShA 1 244 *S* ⲡⲕⲕⲁϩ *piece* of ground, C 41 49 *B* ⲡⲕⲱⲗϩ of *striking* (gong), MIE 2 345 *B* ⲙⲙⲟϣⲓ *path*, ShA 1 393 *S* ⲙⲡⲱⲧ *race-course*, Saq 241 *S* ⲡⲣⲁϩⲧ, ST 329 *S* ⲡⲥⲁ ⲡⲃⲉⲛⲉ *date-sellers' place* (*shop*), ShIF 267 *S* ⲡⲥⲱϣⲉ (*cf* Job 24 5 ⲥⲱϣⲉ), BMis 245 *S* ⲡⲱⲧⲡ ⲉϩⲟⲩⲡ, P 131¹ 73 *S* ⲡϣⲁⲭⲉ *subject* for talk, Va 58 159 *B* be charitable ere cometh ⲡⲙⲁ ⲙϭⲓ ⲱⲡ, Miss 4 778 *S* ⲡ(ⲉ)ϩⲙⲟⲩ *salt-pit*, Rec 6 174 *B* ⲡϩⲱⲟⲩⲧ *virilia*, ShC 42 202 *S* ⲡⲭⲟ *fragment of wall*.   Sim with rel: Jud 9 46 *S* ⲙⲁ ⲉⲧⲟⲣⲭ ὀχύρωμα, Nu 35 3 *S* ⲉⲧⲡⲟⲣⲭ ⲉⲃⲟⲗ ἀφόρισμα, Ps 131 8 *SB* ⲉⲧⲟⲩⲁⲁⲃ ἁγίασμα, Cant 7 8 *S* ⲉⲧⲭⲟⲥⲉ ὕψος, Ez 41 20 *SB* ⲉⲧⲥⲁⲡⲉⲥⲏⲧ ἔδαφος, Mt 12 1 *S* ⲉⲧⲏⲩ σπόριμον, Ps 105 14 *S* ⲉⲙⲡ ⲙⲟⲟⲩ ⲡϩⲏⲧϥ (*B* ⲡⲁⲑⲙⲱⲟⲩ) ἄνυδρος, Z 261 *S* ⲉⲧⲉϣϣⲉ *latrine* (ἀναγκαῖον P 78 12).

II In prepositional phrases. ⲉⲡⲙⲁ ⲛ-, ⲡⲙⲁ ⲛ- *SB*, ⲉⲡⲙⲉ ⲛ- *F* merely indicating place *where*, direction *to*: Ru 2 9 *S* ⲉⲡⲙⲁ ⲡⲡⲉⲥⲕⲉⲩⲏ εἰς τὰ σκ., AM 281 *B* ⲉⲫⲙⲁ ⲙⲡⲓⲑⲣⲟⲛⲟⲥ ἔγγιστα τοῦ θ., MG 25 17 *B* went ⲉⲫⲙⲁ ⲡⲁⲃⲃⲁ ⲁⲡⲧⲟⲡⲓ πρός, BSM 85 *B* gather ⲉⲫⲙⲁ ⲛϯⲗⲩⲙⲡⲏ = BMis 175 *S* ⲉⲭⲛⲧⲗ., ShC 73 54 *S* shall not take (them) ⲉⲡⲙⲁ ⲙⲡⲣⲟ, Mor 48 68 *S* soldiers sought ⲡⲙⲁ ⲡϩⲁⲣⲙⲉⲛⲓⲟⲥ = C 43 134 *B* sought Armenius, LMär 32 *S* led us to ⲡⲙⲁ ⲙⲡⲣⲣⲟ, Mor 30 41 *F* ⲉⲡⲙⲁ(ⲉ) ⲡⲡⲉⲡⲓⲥⲕⲟⲡⲟⲥ = BMis 265 *S* ⲉⲣⲁⲧϥ ⲙ-, C 43 246 *B* go to ⲫⲙⲁ ⲙⲡⲓⲉⲣⲫⲉⲓ, *ib* 213 *B* went to ⲫⲙⲁ ⲙⲡⲓⲧⲉⲧⲣⲁⲡⲩⲗⲱⲛ,

RNC 82 *S* bring him to ⲡⲙⲁ ⲛⲧϣⲛⲅⲉ. ⲉⲙⲁ ⲛ-, ⲙⲁ ⲛ-, ⲙⲁ *S* of motion *to* (not literary): Ep 181 ye go ⲉⲙⲁ ⲙⲡⲗⲁϣⲁⲡⲉ, COAd 49 send camel ⲉⲙⲁ ⲛⲡⲥⲁ ⲡⲏϩⲉ, Ep 96 ⲡⲥⲟⲩϣⲉ ⲉⲣⲟⲩⲛ ⲙⲁ ⲛⲡⲁⲡⲁⲥ, CO 462 ⲡⲉⲛⲧⲁⲓⲃⲁⲕⲟⲩ ⲙⲁ ⲡⲕⲩⲣⲓⲁⲕⲟⲥ, Cai ostr 47400 ⲁⲥⲃⲱⲕ ⲙⲁ ⲡⲕⲩⲣⲓⲥ ⲁⲍⲁⲣⲓⲁⲥ. Indefinitely, *anywhere*: P 129¹⁵ 24 shalt find them all ⲙⲡⲉⲗⲁⲁⲩ ⲃⲱⲕ ⲉⲙⲁ ⲡⲣⲏⲧⲟⲩ, CO 30 ⲡⲡⲉⲓⲃⲱⲕ ⲉⲙⲁ without leave = *ib* 34 ⲉⲙⲁ ⲉϥⲟⲩⲏⲩ, *ib* 29 ⲉⲡϣⲙⲙⲟ, RE 9 141 come forth ⲛϥⲃⲱⲕ ⲉⲙⲁ, *cf* C 89 165 *B* as if to go ⲉⲟⲩⲙⲁ, AM 184 *B* went not ⲉⲣⲗⲓ ⲙⲙⲁ (4 Kg 5 25). ⲙⲁ ⲛ- *S*, *at the place of, dwelling of, at*: ST 41 ⲡⲕⲁϩ ⲉⲧⲣⲓⲃⲟⲗ ⲙⲁ ⲡⲧⲉϩⲓⲏ, *ib* 411 we came to terms ⲙⲁ ⲙⲡⲉⲧⲣⲟⲥ, Ep 88 sim, RE 9 167 thou saidest ⲙⲁ ⲡⲡⲁⲡⲁⲥ ⲝⲉ-, J 51 4 outer wall ⲙⲁ ⲡⲧⲭⲱⲧⲉ. ⲉⲡⲙⲁ ⲛ- *SF*, *as regards, about*: WS 85 ⲉⲡⲙⲁ ⲙⲡⲣⲱⲃ ⲙⲡⲉϣⲡⲉ (*cf*? *ib* 91 ⲙⲡⲙⲁ), Kr 136 *F* ⲉⲡⲙⲉ (ⲉ-)ⲡⲓⲱⲣⲓ; or ⲉⲧⲃⲉⲙⲁ ⲛ-: ST 195 go to Apa Dios ⲉⲧ. ⲡⲣⲱⲃ ⲡⲡⲉⲧⲣⲟⲥ, *ib* 287 have mercy with me ⲉⲧ. ⲡⲁⲥⲫⲁⲗⲉⲥ, CO 174, Hall 53, Ep 338 sim; or ⲙⲁ ⲛ-: BKU 1 264 ⲙⲁ ⲡⲣⲱⲃ ⲙⲡⲱⲡⲉ, Hall 93 begged me write ⲙⲁ ⲡⲧⲉϥϣⲉⲉⲣⲉ that is with you, CO 196 please to go ⲙⲁ ⲡⲕⲟⲅⲓ ⲡⲟⲉⲓⲕ (*sic l*). ⲉⲡⲙⲁ ⲛ-, *SB in place of*: Ge 31 41 *S* (*B* ⲉⲑⲃⲉ-), Ex 21 23 *S* do (*B* ϣⲁ-), Is 3 24 *S* do (*B* ⲡⲧϣⲉⲃⲓⲱ ⲛ-), Eph 5 31 *S* (var & *B* ⲉⲧⲃⲉ-), Ja 4 15 *SB* ἀντί; Ps 116 3 *S* (*B* do) περί; here? belongs Pro 7 23 *S* ⲡⲙⲁ ⲙⲡⲉϥⲧⲏⲩⲡⲉ (*A* ⲡⲧⲉϥψⲩ.) περὶ ψυχῆς τρέχει; PS 105 *S* ⲁⲅⲙⲉⲥⲧⲱⲓ...ⲉⲡⲙⲁ ⲡⲥⲉⲙⲉⲣⲓⲧ, FR 30 *S* will send Spirit ⲉⲡⲁⲙⲁ = BMis 66 *S* ⲡⲧⲁϣⲃⲃⲓⲟ, RNC 70 *S* ⲡⲧⲟⲩⲥⲓⲁⲍⲉ ⲉⲡⲁⲙⲁ, Bor 260 106 *S* ⲉⲡⲙⲁ ⲉⲧⲣⲉϥⲟⲩⲱϣⲃ *instead of answering* in wrath, C 86 306 *B* ⲉϥⲙⲁ ⲉⲧⲉⲕⲟⲩⲱϣⲧ gods, thou hast..., ShA 2 279 *S* ⲉⲡⲙⲁ ⲡⲧⲉⲧⲛϣⲱⲡⲉ ⲡⲁⲡ ⲡⲟⲩⲥⲟⲗⲥⲗ. ⲉϥⲙⲁ *B, because*: Ge 19 8 (*S* ⲝⲉ-), Nu 14 43 (*S* ⲉⲃⲟⲗ ⲝⲉ-), Am 2 6 (*A* ⲝⲉ- prob) οὗ ἕνεκεν; Lu 1 20 (*S* ⲉⲧⲃⲉⲝⲉ-) ἀνθ' ὧν; MG 25 204 I know ⲉϥⲙⲁ ⲝⲉ- ὅτι.

ⲉⲩⲙⲁ *B*, ⲉⲩⲙⲁ ⲡⲟⲩⲱⲧ *S*, *to, in one place, together*: Ps 47 4, Jer 3 18, Su 14, 1 Cor 14 23 all *SB* ἐπὶ τὸ αὐτό. *Cf* ϩⲓⲟⲩⲙⲁ.

ⲕⲁⲧⲁ ⲙⲁ *SB*, *in different, several places*: Mt 24 7 *SB* κ. τόπ., Lu 9 14 *B* (*S* diff) ὡσεί, Miss 8 76 *S* bishops ⲕ. ⲙⲁ ἀπανταχοῦ, BerlOr 1607 3 92 *S* seek ⲕ. ⲙⲁ till ye find, C 43 157 *B* enquiring ⲕ. ⲙⲁ, J 93 16 *S* traversed northern nomes ⲕ. ⲙⲁ *from place to place*, AM 135 *B* ⲡⲓⲉⲣⲫⲏⲟⲩⲓ ⲡⲕ. ⲙⲁ. ⲙⲁ ⲙⲁ sim, Mk 6 40 *B* (*S* ⲁⲅⲏⲧ) πρασιά.

ϣⲁⲡⲉⲓⲙⲁ *SAB*, *up to here, so far*: Job 38 11 *SA* (Cl, *B* ϣⲁⲙⲡⲁⲓ) μέχρι τούτου, Lu 23 5 *B* (*S* ϣⲁⲣⲁⲓ ⲉⲡ.) ἕως ὧδε (*cf* Dan 7 27 *B* ϣⲁⲙⲡⲁⲓ ἕως ὥ.), Aeg 271 *S* these we have said ϣⲁⲡ. ἐπὶ τοσοῦτον, Va 57 9 *B* ⲉⲁⲥⲟϩⲓ ⲉⲣⲁⲧⲥ ϣⲁⲡ. ⲡⲭⲉ ϯⲁⲡⲧⲓⲑⲉⲥⲓⲥ πρὸς ταύτην, BG 17 *S* having said this Mariham was silent

ⲣⲱⲥⲧⲉ ⲡⲧⲁⲡⲥⲱⲣ ϣⲁⲭⲉ ⲡⲙⲁⲥ ϣⲁⲡ., Miss 4 752 *S* ⲙⲁⲣⲡϩⲱ ⲉⲣⲟⲛ ϣⲁⲡ., MG 25 261 *B* sim, BMis 73 *S* ⲙⲁⲣⲉⲡϯ ⲡⲟⲩⲭⲱⲕ ⲉⲡϣⲁⲭⲉ ϣⲁⲡ., Mor 18 18 *S Confessio Cypr.* ends ⲡⲁⲓ ϣⲁⲡ., Wess 18 87 *S* = Miss 4 100 *B* ϣⲁⲡ. ⲡⲉ ⲡⲥⲱⲗⲡ ⲉⲃⲟⲗ, C 43 47 *B* sim; 1 Kg 7 12 *S* ϣⲁⲣⲁⲓ ⲉⲡ. ἕως ἐνταῦθα.

ϩⲁⲡⲙⲁ *SF* (not literary), *as to the matter of, as regards*: J 8 2 *S* ϩⲁⲡ. ⲙⲡⲙⲉⲣⲟⲥ ⲡⲁⲡϩ, ST 284 *S* ϩⲁⲡ. ⲡⲡⲗⲁⲕⲟⲛ ⲡⲥⲟⲩⲱ deposited with thee, Louvre ostr 8260 *S* ϩⲁⲡ. ⲡⲡⲏⲉⲣ &c, send & fetch them, BP 3248 *F* ϩⲉⲡⲙⲉ ⲡⲁⲕⲁⲡⲏⲓ; or ϩⲁⲙⲁ: Hall 80 *S* ϩⲁ. ⲧⲁⲡⲟⲕⲣⲓⲥⲓⲥ thou knowest of, CO 456 *S* account ϩⲁ. ⲡⲗⲟⲅⲟⲥ ⲡⲣⲟⲙⲡⲧ, *ib* 119 *S* he besought me ϩⲁ. ⲡⲁⲑⲁⲛⲁⲥⲓⲟⲥ.

ϩⲓⲟⲩⲙⲁ *B*, *to, in one place*: Ex 26 9, Ac 2 44 (*S* ϩⲓⲟⲩⲥⲟⲡ), 1 Cor 11 20 (*S* diff) ἐπὶ τὸ αὐτό; Is 11 7 (*S* ϩⲓⲟⲩⲥⲟⲡ) ἅμα; MG 25 8 stretching forth hands ϩ. ἀμφότεροι.

ⲙⲁ ⲛⲓⲙ *S*, ⲙⲁⲓ ⲛⲓⲃⲉⲛ *B*, *every place, everywhere*: Sa 18 16 *S*, CaiEuch 651 *B* τὰ πάντα, Ez 7 14 *SB* τὰ σύμπαντα; Ps 32 8 *S* (*B* = Gk) οἰκουμένη; Sa 2 9 *S* πανταχῇ, Is 24 11 *SB*, Lu 9 6 *SB*, Aeg 247 *S* πανταχοῦ; BHom 4 *S* καθόλου; Ez 16 33 *S* ϩⲛ-*B* ⲉ- κυκλόθεν. ⲙⲁⲓ ⲛⲓⲃⲉⲛ mostly as pl: ⲙ. ⲛ. ⲉⲧⲉⲕⲡⲁϣⲉ ⲡⲁⲕ ⲉⲣⲱⲟⲩ; sometimes as sg: C 43 134 ⲙ. ⲛ. ⲉⲧⲟⲩⲡⲁⲟⲗⲕ ⲉⲣⲟϥ, BSM 103 ⲙ. ⲛ. ⲉⲧⲉⲙⲙⲟⲛ ϩⲱⲟⲩⲧ ⲡϩⲏⲧϥ, C 86 350 ⲙ. ⲛ. ⲉⲧⲉⲕⲟⲩⲁϣϥ.

ⲡⲙⲁ ⲉⲧⲙⲙⲁⲩ *SB, that place, there*: Ge 35 7 *SB*, Ez 40 3 *SB*, Mt 2 13 *S* (*B* ⲙⲙⲁⲩ) ἐκεῖ; Ez 5 3 ⲉⲃⲟⲗ ϩⲓⲡⲙⲁ ⲉⲧ. *SB*, Hos 2 15 *AB* ἐκεῖθεν, Ac 21 3 *B* ⲡⲡⲓⲙⲁ ⲉⲧ. (*S* ⲙⲙⲁⲩ) ἐκεῖσε.

III translating Gk advb or prep. Jer 3 2 *B* ϩⲉⲡⲁϣ ⲙⲙⲁ, Mt 8 20 *SB* ⲙⲡⲧϥ ⲙⲁ, Lu 12 17 *SB* sim, He 2 6 *SBF* ⲡⲟⲩⲙⲁ ποῦ, Ru 1 16 *S*, Mt 26 57 *SB*, Ap 2 13 *SB*, ⲙⲁ + rel ὅπου; Ps 13 5 *SB*, Ac 1 13 *SB*, Ro 4 15 *SB* ⲙⲁ + rel οὗ, Jer 7 12 *B*, Ez 6 9 *SB* ⲙⲁ + rel...ⲙⲙⲟ⸗, ⲉⲣⲟ⸗, ⲡⲣⲏⲧ⸗ οὗ...ἐκεῖ, Tob 13 5 *S*, 2 Cor 16 6 *SB* οὗ ἐάν; Sa 15 8 *S* sim ἐξ ἧς; Jer 39 3 *B* sim ἐν ᾗ; CaiEuch 363 *B* ⲡⲓⲙⲁ ⲉⲧⲁϥⲫⲱⲧ ⲉⲃⲟⲗ ⲡϩⲏⲧϥ ἔνθα; 1 Kg 23 3 *S* ϩⲁⲡ., Ps 72 10 *SB*, BHom 10 *S* ⲡⲉⲓⲙⲁ, ἐνταῦθα; Jer 2 37 *B* ⲉⲃⲟⲗ ϩⲁⲡⲉⲓⲙⲁ, Jo 2 16 *SA²* ⲉⲃ. ϩⲁⲡ. (*B* ⲧⲁⲓ), Va 57 131 *B* ⲓⲥⲭⲉⲡ. ἐντεῦθεν, BHom 40 *S* ⲭⲓⲡⲙⲡ. ἀπεντεῦθεν, PS 126 *S* write these names, that sons of God may appear ⲭⲓⲡⲙⲡ.; Job 10 21 *SB*, Ez 29 14 *B* (*S* ⲡⲕⲁϩ) ὅθεν; Aeg 216 *S* ϩⲛ-ⲗⲁⲁⲩ ⲙⲙⲁ οὐδαμοῦ; Mk 1 38 *SB*, MG 25 208 *B* ⲕⲉⲙⲁ ἀλλαχοῦ, ShBor 246 76 *S* they say ⲟⲩⲙⲁ ⲙⲉⲛ ⲝⲉ-...ⲕⲉⲙⲁ ⲍⲉ ⲝⲉ- (ⲟⲓ ⲡⲕⲉⲙⲁ *v* **IV**); Jud 7 21 *S* ⲙⲡⲉϥⲙⲁ ἐφ' ἑαυτῷ, Cant 2 11 *A* (PVi 10157) rain hath departed ⲁⲡⲉϥⲙⲁ ἑαυτῷ; Ge 19 12 *SB*, Is 22 16 *SB* ⲙⲡⲉⲓⲙⲁ, Zech 7 3 *A* ⲁⲡⲓⲙⲁ (*B* ⲉⲙⲡⲁⲓ), Mt 14 8 *SF* (*B* om) ⲙⲡⲉⲓⲙⲁ ὧδε, 2 Kg 20

16 ⲉⲡⲉⲓⲙⲁ ἕως ὧδε;   Mt 26 36 *S* ⲉⲡⲉⲓⲙⲁ (*B* ϣⲁⲛⲡⲁⲓ) ἐκεῖ, Ex 24 14 *SB*, Mt *lc SBF* ⲙⲡⲉⲓⲙⲁ αὐτοῦ.

With vbal pref : Job 1 7 *SB* ϯⲙⲡⲉⲓⲙⲁ, Jth 9 6 *S* ⲧⲙ., Sa 4 2 *S* ⲉⲥⲙ., Ac 10 33 *B* (*S* om) παρεῖναι ; Ge 22 11 *S* ϯⲙ. (*B* ϩⲏⲡⲡⲉ ⲁⲛⲟⲕ) ἰδοὺ ἐγώ, 1 Kg 9 12 *S* ϭⲙ. ἐστί.

IV With vbs. ⲕⲁ, ⲭⲁ ⲙⲁ *SB*, allow place, give opportunity : Eccl 10 4 *S* τόπ. ἀφιέναι, Si 16 15 *S* τόπ. ποιεῖν ; ShR 2 3 32 *S* ⲙⲡⲕⲕⲁ ⲙⲁ ⲛⲁϥ to stay in his house, MG 25 142 *B* Lord hath ⲭⲁ ⲙⲁ ⲛⲁⲛ to repent, R 1 2 58 *S* ⲕⲁ ⲙⲁ ⲛⲁϥ that he may sit, C 86 36 *B* ⲭⲁ ⲙⲁ ⲛⲏⲓ ⲛⲟⲩⲕⲟⲩϫⲓ that I may give thanks, SHel 86 *S* woe unto him ⲉⲧⲛⲁⲕⲁ ⲙⲁ to Satan.   ⲕⲁ ⲡⲙⲁ, ⲭⲁ ⲡⲙⲁ *SB*, meaning same : Ac 26 1 *S* (*B* diff) ⲡ. ⲕⲏ ⲛⲁⲕ ἐπιτρέπεταί σοι, Ro 12 19 *S* (*B* ϯ ⲙⲁ) τόπ. διδόναι, ClPr 54 4 *S* ⲁϥⲕⲁ ⲡ. ⲛⲧⲉϥϭⲓⲥⲉ παραδιδ. dat, PS 377 *S* ⲕⲁ ⲡ. ⲛⲡⲉⲧⲛ̄- ⲥⲛⲏⲩ to enquire, C 86 107 *B* ⲭⲁ ⲡ. ⲙϥϯ & He will not forsake us, Miss 8 51 *S* ⲉⲁϥⲕⲁ ⲡ. ⲛⲁⲩ ⲉⲕⲣⲓⲛⲉ, KKS 427 *S* servants before her ⲉⲧⲣⲉⲛⲕⲁ ⲡ. ⲛⲁⲥ, Mor 16 86 *S* ⲙⲁⲣⲉⲛⲕⲁ ⲡ. ⲛⲧⲗⲓⲧⲟⲩⲣⲅⲓⲁ of baptism = BMis 226 *S* ϯ ⲙⲡⲛⲟⲩϭⲓ to baptistry.

ⲣ ⲡⲙⲁ, ⲉⲣ ⲫⲙⲁ *SB*, take place of, succeed : Est 10 3 *S* διαδέχεσθαι, Si 46 1 *S* διάδοχος (γίνεσθαι), GFr 434 *S* voice ⲉⲣ ⲡ. ⲛⲧϭⲓϫ καθάπερ, Wess 18 87 *S* = Miss 4 100 *B* ⲁⲣⲓ ⲡ. ⲛⲛⲁⲓ who have fled, Mor 18 80 *S* ⲁⲣⲓ ⲡ. ⲙⲡⲉⲕⲉⲓⲱⲧ = *ib* 19 87 *S* ϣⲱⲡⲉ ⲉⲡⲙⲁ ⲛ- = Miss 4 150 *B* ϣⲱⲡⲓ ⲉⲕⲙⲏⲛ ⲉ- stay with, TstAb 172 *B* dwell with me ⲛⲧⲉⲕⲉⲣ ⲫ. ⲙⲡⲁϩⲁⲓ.

ⲟⲓ ⲛⲕⲉⲙⲁ *B*, be elsewhere, separated, unclean (of menstruation) : Lev 15 33 (*S* ⲟ ⲛⲡⲓⲣⲱ), *ib* 20 18 (*S* ⲟ ⲛⲕⲉⲥⲁ), Is 64 6 (*S* ⲓⲣⲱ), EpJer 28 (*F* ⲁⲓ ⲛϣⲗⲱ), Ez 36 17 (Mich Paschal Lect 237, Tatt ⲟⲓ ⲛϣ., *S* diff) ἀποκαθημένη.

ϯ ⲙⲁ *SABF*, give place permit : Sa 12 10 *SA* (Cl), Si 38 12 *S*, Eph 4 27 *SB*, Mor 18 157 *S* ig- norance ϯ ⲙⲁ ⲛⲁⲕ ⲛⲟⲩⲁⲡⲟⲗⲟⲅⲓⲁ τόπ. διδόναι ; 1 Tim 2 12 *S* (*B* ⲟⲩⲉϩⲥⲁϩⲛⲉ), ZNTW 24 84 *F* ⲙⲁ ⲙⲉ (ⲛ)ⲛⲉⲡⲣⲟⲫⲏⲧⲏⲥ, BM 320 152 *S* they begged ⲉⲧⲣⲉϥϯ ⲙⲁ ⲛⲁⲩ ἐπιτρέπειν, Mor 37 114 *S* ϣⲁϥϯ ⲡⲙⲁ ⲛⲁϥ to pray before him παραχωρεῖν ; Lam 3 8 neg *S* (*B* ϣⲧⲁⲙ ⲡⲣⲱⲥ) ἀποφράσσειν ; MG 25 233 *B* ⲁϥϯ ⲙⲁ ⲛⲁϥ ⲉⲥⲁϫⲓ προφασίζεσθαι ; ShRE 11 16 ⲧⲛⲛⲁϯ ⲙⲁ ⲙⲡⲛϫⲁϫⲉ ⲉⲣⲟⲩⲛ ⲉⲣⲟⲛ, Va 57 146 *B* fishermen & fish ⲉϣⲁⲩϯ ⲙⲁ ⲛⲁϥ *play him* little by little.   ⲣⲉϥϯ ⲙⲁ : Mor 40 5 *S* wizards ⲛⲣ. ⲡ- ⲧⲟⲟⲧⲟⲩ = C 43 36 *B* (? *F*) ⲣⲉϥϯ ⲙⲉ ⲛⲧⲁⲧⲟⲩ, Mor 39 7 *S* ⲣⲉϥϯ ⲙⲁ ⲧⲱⲛ, *ib* 41 119 om.   ϯ ⲙⲁ *S* often *l* ⲧⲓⲙⲁ (τιμᾶν) : Lev 19 32, R 2 3 50, BMis 333.

ϫⲓ ⲙⲁ *S*, take, usurp place : PS 58 we cannot suffer woman ⲉⲥϫⲓ ⲙⲁ ⲛⲧⲟⲟⲧⲛ, BMar 180 if thou

---

go to monastery ⲉϫⲓ ⲙⲁ ⲙⲡⲏⲧϥ *to settle there* (cf ? Esaias Scet 17 παραβάλλειν τοῖς ἀδελφοῖς).

ⲧⲉϣ ⲙⲁ, ⲣⲉϥ- *S*, one set over a place, house-guard : Tit 2 5 (*B* ⲣⲉϥⲥⲉⲣⲡⲉ ⲡⲟⲩⲏⲓ) οἰκουρός.

ϭⲙ, ϫⲉⲙ ⲙⲁ *SB*, find place, opportunity : Ap 12 8 *S* (*B* ⲭⲁ ⲙⲁ) τόπ. εὑρεσθαι ; Ac 25 16 *B* (*S* ϭⲛ ⲑⲉ) τόπ. λαμβάνειν ; ShC 73 6 *S* if sin ϭⲛ ⲙⲁ ϩⲙ- ϩⲉⲡⲣⲱⲙⲉ, ShA 2 293 *S* ⲉⲛⲛⲁϭⲓⲛⲉ ⲛⲟⲩⲙⲁ to re- pent, Cat 103 *B* so as to ϫⲉⲙ ⲙⲁ ⲡⲉⲣ ⲕⲁⲧⲏⲅⲟⲣⲓⲛ ⲉⲣⲟϥ (on Mk 12 13).

In place-names often : ⲙⲁ ⲛⲃⲁⲗⲟⲧ(P43 51), ⲡⲙⲁ ⲛⲡϣⲟⲉⲓⲭ(Ryl 132), ⲡ. ⲛⲥⲁⲃⲏⲥ(PLond 4 512), also prob in ⲙⲁⲣⲏⲥ (*v* ⲣⲏⲥ) ; mostly with man's name : ⲡ. ⲛⲥⲉⲣϭⲉ (Ryl 177), ⲡ. ⲛϩⲱⲣ (BMOr 6201 B 150), ⲡ. ⲡⲁⲣⲥⲉⲡⲏ (Kr 108).

ⲙⲁ *Sᵃ v* ⲙⲙⲛ neg vb, *sf*.

ⲙⲁ-, ⲙⲁⲋ *SF*, ⲙⲉⲋ *S* (?) vbal pref, *if, when* : BM 493 *F* ⲙⲁⲩϣⲁϣⲕ ⲡⲉⲗϭⲱ(ⲡ)ⲧ ⲙⲁⲩⲧⲁⲉⲓⲁⲕ ⲡⲉⲗϫⲓⲥⲓ ⲡϩⲏⲧ, *ib* 621 *F* ⲙⲁⲕϫⲓ ⲡⲁⲥϭⲉⲓ = *ib* 621 *F* ⲡϣⲁⲕϫⲓ, *ib* 591 *F* ⲙⲁⲕ(ⲉⲣ) ⲭⲉⲣⲓⲁ ⲙⲁϥ ϣⲁⲓⲟⲩⲁⲧⲛϥ ⲛⲉⲕ, *ib* ⲙⲁⲕⲟⲩⲁⲧⲉ ⲡⲉϭⲁⲙⲟⲩⲗ send (also) 2 jars, ⲃKU 1 26 (1) 17 *F* ⲙⲁⲕⲟⲩⲱϣ ⲉⲡⲁⲩ, BM 528 *F* ⲙⲁⲩ- ⲧⲁⲙⲁⲕ ϫⲉ- (introducing arithm problems), *ib* 536 *Sf* ⲙⲁ ⲡⲭⲟⲉⲓⲥ ⲟⲩⲱϣ ;   with ⲉϣⲱⲡⲉ : J 97 48 *S* official (ἐξουσία) adjured as to confirming deed ⲉϣ. ⲙⲁϥⲧⲁϩⲟϥ ⲉⲣⲁⲧϥ God will bless him (cf var 104 43), JKP 2 38 *S* ⲉϣ. ⲙⲉⲕⲉⲓ ⲉⲃⲟⲗ (ⲛ)ⲧⲁⲡⲁⲩ ⲉⲡⲉⲕϩⲟ.   *Cf mj* Erman *Grᵗ* 541, BM 528 n. *V* Crum AZ 65.

ⲙⲁ- *SAA²BF* imperat of ϯ *give, q v,* & of causatives formed with ⲧ- (ϯ) : Ps 79 19 *S* ⲙⲁⲕⲧⲟⲛ *B* ⲙⲁⲧⲁⲥⲑⲟⲛ, Ex 20 12 *SB* ⲙⲁⲧⲁⲓⲉ-, Ge 48 18 *S* ⲙⲁⲧⲁⲗⲟ (var & *B* ⲕⲱ), *ib* 6 14 ⲙⲁⲧⲁⲙⲓⲟ, AP 8 *A²* ⲙⲁⲧⲁⲙⲁⲉⲓ, Ge 43 8 *S* ⲙⲁⲧⲛⲛⲟⲟⲩ (*B* ⲟⲩⲱⲣⲡ), J&C 98 *A²* sim, Mt 8 25 *S* ⲙⲁⲧⲁⲛϩⲟⲛ (*B* ⲛⲁϩⲙⲉⲛ), Ex 1 22 *A* ⲙⲁⲧⲁⲛϩⲉⲩ, *B* ⲙⲁⲧⲁⲡϧⲱⲟⲩ, Ps 78 11 *S* ⲙⲁⲧⲟⲩϫⲟ (*B* ⲙⲁⲧϧⲟ), Jo 9 23 *SA²* ⲙⲁϫⲡⲟϥ (*B* ϣⲉⲛϥ), Ac 10 5 *S* ⲙⲁϫⲟⲟⲩ (*B* ⲟⲩⲱⲣⲡ) ;   also of *B* ϣⲉ (with ethic dat) : Ge 12 19 ⲙⲁϣⲉ ⲛⲁⲕ, Jer 19 1, Mt 27 65 (all *S* ⲃⲱⲕ) & ϣⲟⲗⲙ (*v* ϣⲧⲁⲙ). *Cf* DM 1 11, 18 ⲙⲁ ⲱⲃⲛ.   *V* ⲙⲁⲣⲉ- optat pref.

ⲙⲁ- *SᵃA* = ⲙⲉⲣⲉ- pref neg aor, *q v.*

ⲙⲁⲉⲓⲉ *A² v* ⲙⲉ *love.*

ⲙⲁⲓ, ⲙⲁⲓⲉ *F* vb, meaning unknown : BM 645 (ⲉ)ϣⲟⲡ ⲙⲉⲡⲧⲉⲉϣ ⲧⲁⲗⲁⲩ (*sc* ⲧⲁⲣⲓⲭⲓ) ϣⲁⲙ. ⲙⲉ- ⲡⲉⲧⲉⲛ ϣⲁⲧⲉϣⲁ[ⲣⲡ, Kr 65]ⲡⲁⲕⲛⲓⲧⲉⲡⲱⲥ ⲉⲗⲁⲟⲩ ⲥⲉⲙⲁⲓⲉ ⲉⲙⲉⲣⲓⲥⲙⲱⲥ ⲧⲁⲧⲁⲗⲉⲟⲩ[(*ib* 64 om).   Prob for ⲁⲙⲁϩⲓ (*v* ⲁⲙⲁϩⲧⲉ).

ⲙⲁⲓ *F v* ⲙⲟⲩⲓ *new.*

ⲙⲁⲓ- *v* ⲙⲉ *love.*

ⲙⲁⲓ *B*, ⲙⲁⲓⲟ *AB* *v* ⲧⲙⲁⲉⲓⲟ.

ⲙⲁⲓⲏ, ⲙⲁⲏ (Cat, Va 61) *B* nn f, *size, age, kind*: 1 Kg 16 7 (*S* ϣⲓⲏ), Ez 19 11 (*S* do), HL 107 μέγεθος; Job 29 18 (*S* ϭⲟⲧ), Mt 6 27 (*S* do), Jo 9 21 (*SA²* ⲧⲉ), Eph 4 13 (*S* ϭⲟⲧ), C 89 35 became comforter of many ⲡⲁⲣⲁ ⲧⲉϥⲙ. ἡλικία, Col 2 1 (*S* do) ἡλίκος, Dan 1 10 συνήλικος, Gal 1 14 (*S* do) συνηλικιώτης, OrChrNS 3 40 who had passed ⳾ⲙ. παρῆλιξ, Zech 2 2 (*A* ⲟⲩⲏⲣ), Gal 6 11 (*S* do) πηλίκος, Ja 3 4 (*S* do) τηλικοῦτος; Mt 8 10 (*S* do), He 1 4 (*S* om), ib 12 1 (*S* ⲙⲛⲓϣⲉ), Va 57 124 τοσοῦτος; 1 Jo 3 1 (*S* ϭⲟⲧ) ποταπός; Va 58 168 ⲧⲁⲙ. ⲭⲉⲟⲩⲕⲟⲩϫⲓⲧⲉ εἶδος; Ez 17 3 ἔκτασις; Da 4 17 (*S* ⲡⲱⲭϣ) κύτος *aspectus*; MG 25 13 ⲑⲙ. ⲡⲟⲩⲣⲱⲙⲓ διάστημα; Ps 88 48 (*S* = Gk) ὑπόστασις; Dan 1 15 ϣⲫⲏⲣ ⲙⲙ. (*S* Gk om); MG 25 243 when he heard ⲉⲑⲙ. ⲛⲡⲉϥⲡⲟⲗⲓⲧⲓⲁ τὰ περὶ τῆς αὐτοῦ π.; Va 57 59 r̄ ⲙⲙⲁⲣⲓ ϫⲉⲡⲧⲉϥⲙ., C 86 317 foundations traced ⲕⲁⲧⲁ ⲑⲙ. of τόπος حد, Cat 15 ⲙ., ⲣⲩⲗⲓⲕⲓⲁ, ⲡⲣⲟⲕⲟⲡⲏ, RAl 88 ⲉϥⲭⲏ ϫⲉⲡⲑⲙ. ⲡⲧⲉϥⲙⲉⲧⲁⲗⲟⲩ, DeV 167 ⲡⲟⲩⲏⲣⲉⲧⲏⲥ ⲡⲧⲁⲙⲙ. *the many servants*, ib 191 ⲫⲁⲓ ⲡⲧⲁⲙⲙ. (sic) *aforesaid* (cf *S* ⲙⲛⲡⲉ), C 89 76 great figure ⲛⲟⲙ. ⲡⲟⲩⲛⲓϣϯ ⲛⲧⲣⲁⲡⲉⲍⲁ (cf TT 148 *S* ⲛⲟⲉ), Va 61 206 Abraham seizing Isaac's hair ⲁϥⲕⲱⲗⲭ ⲛⲧⲉϥⲙⲁⲏ ⲥⲁⲫⲁϩⲟⲩ ⲙⲙⲟϥ but his face was full of gladness.

ϭⲓ ⲙ., *grow in size, increase*: MG 25 345 προκόπτειν, ib 25 if one love Christ soul ϭⲓ ⲙ. & beareth fruit, ib 118 ⲉⲧⲁϥϭⲓ ⲙ. ϫⲉⲛϯ ⲁⲣⲉⲧⲏ.

ⲙⲉ, ⲙⲉⲓ(Sa 8 7 Lag) *S*, ⲙⲁⲉⲓ *A*, ⲙⲁⲉⲓⲉ *A²*, ⲙⲉⲓ, ⲙⲛⲏ *B*, ⲙⲛⲓ, ⲙⲓ *F*, ⲙⲉⲣⲉ- *S*, ⲙⲣⲣⲉ- *AA²*, ⲙⲉⲡⲣⲉ, *B*, ⲙⲉⲣⲓ-, ⲙⲉⲗⲗⲓ- *F*, ⲙⲉⲣⲓⲧ⳾ *SA²*, ⲙⲣⲣⲓⲧ⳾ *AA²*, ⲙⲉⲡⲣⲓⲧ⳾ *B*, p c ⲙⲁⲓ- *SBF*, ⲙⲁⲉⲓ- *SA* vb tr, *love*: Ge 24 67 *B* (*S* ⲟⲩⲱϣ), Job 19 19 *SB*, Ps 115 1 *S* (*B* ⲉⲣ ⲁⲅⲁⲡⲁⲛ), Hos 11 1 *AB*, Jo 3 16 *SA²BF* ἀγαπᾶν; Ge 29 11 *B* (*S* ⲟⲩ.), Pro 15 12 *SA*, Mt 6 5 *SBF* φιλεῖν, CaiEuch 392 *B* ⲉⲑⲙ. ⲛϯⲙⲉⲧⲁⲅⲁⲑⲟⲥ φιλάγαθος; Pro 4 6 *SAB* ἐρᾶν, Jer 4 30 *SB* ἐραστής; Sa 6 22 *S* ἥδεσθαι; Pro 7 15 *B* (*SA* ⲟⲩ.), Sa 15 5 *S* ποθεῖν, Jer 13 14 *B* (*S* ⲟⲩ.), Phil 1 8 *B* (*SF* do) ἐπιπο.; PS 105 *S* ⲁⲅⲙⲉⲥⲧⲱ ϫⲉⲁⲙⲉⲣⲓⲧⲕ, KroppB *S* charm ⲁⲓⲟⲩⲱϣ ⲉⲙⲉⲣⲉ ⲡⲓⲙ ⲧⲩⲡⲓⲙ, C 41 13 *B* ⲡⲏ ⲉⲑⲟⲩⲱϣ ⲉⲙⲉⲡⲣⲉ ⲡⲓⲱⲛϩ, Miss 8 190 *S* ⲛⲧⲁⲕⲙⲉⲣⲉ ⲧⲉⲓⲁⲣⲭⲏ *didst desire*, AP 4 *A²* ⲡⲉϫⲙ. ⲙⲙⲁⲩ, AZ 33 56 *F* ⲉϥⲙⲓ ⲙⲙⲁⲥ.   With infin vb: Mor 37 133 *S* ⲡⲉϥⲙⲉⲣⲉ ϭⲱ ϩⲓⲡⲧⲟⲟⲩ ἀγαπᾶν, PS 101 *S* ⲁⲓⲙⲉⲣⲉ ⲉⲓ ⲉⲡⲉⲥⲛⲧ, ShIF 156 *S* ⲛⲧⲁⲥⲙⲉⲣⲉ ⲕⲧⲟⲥ ⲉⲡⲁϩⲟⲩ, R 1 2 38 *S* ⲙⲡⲣ ⲙⲉⲣⲉ ⲕⲟⲥⲙⲉⲓ ⲙⲙⲟ. With art as nn: Ro 13 8 *S* ⲡⲙⲉⲣⲉ ⲡⲉⲧⲡⲉⲣⲏⲩ (*B* ⲉⲙⲉⲡⲣⲉ) τὸ ἀγαπᾶν; Bor 226 170 *S* ⲡⲙⲉⲣⲉ ⲡⲉⲓⲃⲓⲟⲥ. ϣⲟⲩⲙⲉⲣⲓⲧ, -ⲙⲉⲡⲣⲓⲧ *SB*, *worthy of love*: Ps 83 1 *B* (*S* ⲙⲉⲣⲓⲧ) ἀγαπητός; Est D 5 *S*, Si 4 6 *S* προσ-

φιλής; BMOr 7561 85 *S* sacred calf named ⲡϣⲟⲩⲟⲩⲁϣϥ & ϣⲟⲩⲙⲉⲣⲓⲧϥ, AM 111 *B* ⲡⲓϣⲟⲩⲙⲉⲡⲣⲓⲧϥ ⲡⲧⲉ ⲓ̄ⲥ̄, ib 12 *B* ⲡⲉⲡϣⲟⲩⲙⲉⲡⲣⲓⲧⲟⲩ ⲡⲉⲡⲛⲟⲩ.

ⲙⲁⲓ-, *loving*, often = φιλο-: Sa 7 22 *S* ⲙ. ⲁⲅⲁⲑⲟⲛ φιλάγ.; ib 15 5 *S* ⲙ. ⲡⲉⲑⲟⲟⲩ κακῶν ἐραστής; Phil 2 3 *B* (*S* diff) ⲙ. ⲱⲟⲩ ϥϣⲟϭⲓⲧ κενοδοξία; Pro 17 19 *SA* ⲙ. ⲡⲟⲃⲉ φιλαμαρτήμων; CaiEuch 395 *B* ⲙ. ⲣⲱⲙⲓ φιλάνθρωπος; Si prol *S* ⲙ. ⲥⲃⲱ φιλομαθῶν; Tit 2 4 *SB* ⲙ. ⲡⲉⲩϩⲁⲓ φίλανδρος; Aeg 247 *S* ⲙ. ϫⲁϫⲉ φιλεχθρῶν; ⲙ. ⲡⲉ̄ θεόφιλος, -έστατος (Miss 8 32, 77, 140, but 2 Tim 3 4 *B* φιλόθεος); MG 25 212 *B* ⲙ. ϫⲁⲥϥ καματηρός; ShP 78 50 *S* ⲙ. ϫⲱⲙ ⲡⲣⲟϭⲟ ⲉⲙⲉⲣⲉ ⲡⲧⲃ̄ⲃⲟ, ShG 73 43 *S* ⲙ. ⲧⲁⲉⲓⲟϥ ⲉⲃⲟⲗ ϩⲓⲧⲙⲡⲣⲱⲙⲉ, JKP 2 106 *S* ⲙ. ⲡⲉⲩⲙⲧⲟⲛ, ClPr 40 2 *S* ⲟⲩⲙ. ⲡⲉⲧⲣⲁⲫⲏⲡⲉ, P 131² 12 *S* ⲡⲉⲟⲩⲙ. ⲱϣⲡⲉ.   ⲙⲛⲧ-, ⲙⲉⲧⲙⲁⲓ-, *love of*: Ac 28 2 *SB* ⲙ. ⲣⲱⲙⲉ φιλανθρωπία, Pro 1 7 *SA* (*B* ⲙⲉⲧⲉⲅⲥⲉⲃⲏⲥ) ⲙ. ⲡⲉ̄ εὐσέβεια εἰς θ̄ν, Ro 12 13 *SBF* ⲙ. ϣⲙⲙⲟ φιλοξενία, R 1 1 46 *S* ⲙ. ⲧⲟ ⲡⲣⲟϭⲟ πλεονεξία, Va 57 19 *B* ⲙ. ϩⲁⲧ φιλαργυρία.   ⲣ, ⲉⲣ ⲙⲁⲓ-, *be lover of*: Br 102 *S* ⲛϥⲧⲙⲣ ⲙⲁⲓϩⲁⲧ, ROC 20 49 *S* ⲉⲧⲉⲣϥ ⲙⲁⲓⲡⲉϩⲛⲓ, TstAb 259 *B* ⲉⲣ ⲙⲁⲓⲡⲟⲅⲉⲣⲛⲟⲩ, JA '75 5 246 *S* ⲉⲕⲟ ⲙⲙⲁⲓϩⲏⲕⲉ.

ⲣⲉϥⲙⲉⲓ *B*, *loving, benevolent*: Ryl 433(2) ⲁⲙⲱⲓⲛⲓ ⲛⲓⲣ.

ⲙⲉ *S*, ⲙⲉⲓ *B* nn m, *love*: 2 Kg 13 15 *S* ἀγάπη, ib 1 26 *S* (*B* = Gk), Ps 108 5 *SB* ἀγάπησις; Pro 7 18 *B* (*SA* ⲙⲛⲧϣⲃⲏⲣ) φιλία; ib *SB* ἔρως; Ro 15 23 *B* (*S* ⲟⲩⲟⲩϣ) ἐπιποθία, 2 Cor 7 7 *S*(*B* ⲙ. ⲛϩⲏⲧ) ἐπιπόθησις; ROC 17 403 *B* στοργή; PS 215 *S* ⲡⲙⲟⲥⲧⲉ ...ⲡⲙⲉ, BMar 6 *S* ⲟⲩⲙⲉ ⲛϭⲣⲙⲉ, DeV 117 *B* to kiss parents ϫⲉⲛⲟⲩⲙ., C 43 53 *B* ⲡⲙ. ⲛϩⲏⲧ of his son.   ϯ ⲙⲉⲓ *B*, *make love*: Va 61 97 harlot eats with one ⲉⲥϯ ⲙ. ⲡⲉⲙⲕⲉⲟⲩⲁⲓ.

ⲙⲉⲣⲓⲧ *SA²*, ⲙⲉⲡⲣⲓⲧ, ⲙⲣⲣⲉⲓⲧ *AA²*, ⲙⲉⲛⲣⲓⲧ *B*, ⲙⲉⲡⲣⲓⲧ, ⲙⲉⲗⲓⲧ, ⲙⲉⲗⲗⲓⲧ (Mk 9 7) *F*, pl ⲙⲉⲣⲁⲧⲉ *S*, ⲙⲣⲣⲉⲧⲉ, ⲙⲉⲣⲉⲧⲉ *A*, ⲙⲉⲡⲣⲁϯ *B*, ⲙⲉⲣⲣⲉⲧⲉ, ⲙⲉⲣⲉⲧⲉ, -ϯ, ⲙⲉⲗⲉϯ (2 Cor 12 19) *F* & sg as pl (not *B*) adj, *beloved*: Ge 22 2 *SB*, Ps 59 5 *SB*, Zech 13 6 *SAB*, Ro 11 28 *SBF* ἀγαπητός, Deu 33 5 *SB*, Ps 28 6 *SB*, Hos 8 12 *AB*, Ap 20 9 *SB*(sic l) ἠγαπημένος; Jer 4 30 *S* (*B* vb), Ez 16 36 *SB*, Hos 2 12 *F* ⲙⲉⲣⲣⲉⲧⲉ (JEA 11 244, *A* ⲙⲣⲣ-) ἐραστής; PS 75 *S* hail Philip ⲡⲙ., J 67 39 *S* son ⲡⲧⲁⲓⲟⲩⲁϣϥ ⲡⲁⲙ., BSM 2 *B* ⲡⲁⲙⲉⲡⲣⲁϯ ⲡⲉⲙⲡⲁϣⲏⲣⲓ ⲙⲙⲉⲡⲣⲓⲧ, PVi 10157 *A* ⲥⲛⲏⲩ ⲙⲉⲣⲉⲧⲉ, Bor 166 8 *S* ⲧⲁⲓ ⲉⲧⲟ ⲙⲙ. ⲡⲁⲕ.

ⲙⲉ *SO*, ⲙⲉⲉ (Jo 6 55, PS 125, ST 174) *S*, ⲙⲛⲉ *SAA²*, ⲙⲓⲉ *A*, ⲙⲛⲓ, ⲙⲉⲓ *B*, ⲙⲉⲓ, ⲙⲉⲉⲓ, ⲙⲛⲓ *F* nn f (ⲡⲙⲉ once, cf ⲫⲙⲏⲓ below), *truth, justice*, also *true person*: Ge 32 10 *S*, Ps 24 5 *S*, ib 109 7 *S* (all *B* ⲙⲉⲑⲙ.), ib 50 6 *SA* (Cl) *B*, Ro 2 8 *SB* ἀλήθεια, Job 17 10 *S* (*B* ⲙⲉⲑⲙ.), Sa 2 17 *S* (*B* do), Mt 22

16 S (B ѳм.), Jo 3 33 SF (B do) ἀληθής, Deu 32 4
S (B do), Ps 18 9 S (B adj), Jo 7 28 SA² (B ѳм.),
Ap 19 11 S (B do) ἀληθινός, Gal 4 16 B ταмо
еѳм. (S ϫε тме) ἀληθεύειν; Eccl 7 16 F (S = Gk)
δίκαιος, Pro 2 8 SA (B ѳм.) δικαίωμα, Ro 3 8 S
(B diff) ἔνδικος; Ap 21 5 S(B меѳм.) πιστός; PS
122 S тме ϩωωϲτε тϭoм that dwelleth in me, BG
32 S тмне ετιϩητᴴ, ib 83 S none can find тме,
ShA 2 111 S ϩεппе аппе what they say, ST 198
S мп λaaϒ мме therein, AZ 30 42 S тмете таι
ϫε-, ib 21 145 S пептагмееϒе ероϥ оϒмепе, AM
126 B this word оϒмнι аппе, Mus 41 232 S птко-
оϒмε, BM 524(7) F properties of angels соϒрιнλ
τι оϒωϣ, ϩρατоϒнλ τι мнι, апапанλ τι еаоϒ,
Z 234 S bird named тмε, cf ib пϩaλнт пϫικαιос.   Ap 19 11 S пмε (but var мме, B пιѳм.)
ἀληθινός.

м. adj SAA²B, truthful, righteous: Job 4 12 S
(B diff), Ps 18 10 SB, Ap 3 14 S (B = Gk) ἀληθινός, Dan 3 28 SB, Cl 60 2 A ἀλήθεια, Pro 1 3 SA
(B ταфм.), Sa 12 27 S ἀληθής; Job 31 6 S(B ѳм.),
Ps 7 11 SB, Phil 1 7 B (SF = Gk) δίκαιος; AP 42
A² service of God мм., ShC 73 22 S eat & drink
ϩιпϣι мме, AM 314 B wrote it ϫεппеϥϭιϲι мм.
(cf Pro 3 9).   real, genuine (cf πιστικός): PMéd
130 S of recipe апϩннтс мме, Job 31 24 S епе
мме (B епаϣε соϒеп·) πολυτελής; Ps 18 10 S
ωпе мме (B do), ib 20 4 S do (B таιноϒт), Ap 18
16 S епе м.(B епаϣе с.) τίμιος, Sa 7 9 S ωпе
м. ἀτίμητος; Mt 13 45 S епе м. B апамнι (F
= Gk) μαργαρίτης; Z 626 S пеϩ мме, C 43 234
B п. ммнι, ShC 42 71 S п. мε, PMéd S pass,
AZ 23 103, 116, Cai 42573 2 S sim (cf DM 5 5,
6 2 &c); PMéd 269 S, BM 1088 S, Ryl 106 45 S
(v n) еϥιω(еѣ.) мме; GMir 185 S соϩп мме (v
Ps 132 2); JA '05 3 413 S ϫнϭε мме (cf Sophocles
s v ἀληθινός, Preisigke ἀληθινοπόρφυρος).

мпт-, меѳм. SBF nn f, truth, righteousness: Ps
11 1 SB, Jer 14 13 B (S мε), Dan 9 13 B (S do),
2 Cor 13 8 B (S do) ἀλήθεια, Is 43 9 B (S do) ἀληθής, Jos 2 12 S, Dan 3 27 B(S do) ἀληθινός, CaiEuch
324 B ϫоϒаѣ ϫεпоϒ. ἀληθῶς; Ge 15 6 B, Is 5
16 BF, Ez 33 13 B, Phil 1 11 B (all S = Gk) δικαιο-
σύνη, Ex 21 1 B, Ez 5 6 B (S = Gk) δικαίωμα, Job 34 10 SB, Pro 11 16 SAB, Is 5
23 B (SF = Gk) δίκαιος, 1 Thes 2 10 SB ϩпоϒм.
δικαίως; Sa 6 11 S ὅσιος; BHom 9 S ρ ϩιϩaλ
ϩпоϒм. γνησίαν δουλίαν; PS 152 S еιϲмϭoм ϩп-
текм., ShA 2 174 S апм. еѣок еѣoλ ϩιρωп, C
41 29 B all he saith ϣaϒϣωпι мм.; Ge 20 16 B
ер м. (S ϫι мε) ἀληθεύειν. реϥϫε м. B, truth-
teller: Ro 3 4 (S мε). V below ϫε мε.

пaмε S, -мιε A advb, truly: Ge 18 13 S (varr

еιε (а)ρа & епе-, B ϩaρа тафм.), Ex 33 16 S (B
птaфм.), Mt 14 33 S(B тафм., F емамеι) ἀληθῶς
Nu 24 3(var ϩпоϒмε, B ϫепоϒмеѳм.) ἀληθινῶς,
Job 19 4 S (B тафм.), Ps 57 1 S (B do), Ac 4 27 S
(B ϫепоϒмеѳм.), Cl 23 5 A ἐπ' ἀληθείας; Nu 22
37 S (B = Gk), 1 Tim 5 3 S (B do) ὄντως; Wess
11 168 S п. еιс ϣϫε пρoмпе ϫιп- φύσει; Br 237
S пaι...етϣooп оптως п., ShC 42 58 S (on Jo 4
35) мн аρа еϥϣaϫε егϫωρa п. in fact, literally?,
BMis 363 S Well said (п)пιстос п. (var ϩпоϒмε)
= BSM 24 B ϫепоϒмеѳм., Pcod 46 S епеп. п-
тaϥр паι.   мамне A² = п. S, тафм. B: Jo 4
42, 6 14, 8 31.   емамеι F sim: Mt 14 33, Mk 15
39.   On etymol v AZ 64 63, also Spg DemGr 117.

ϩпоϒмε SO meaning as last: Jos 2 4 (v Gk var),
Lu 9 27 (B тафм.) ἀληθῶς, Tob 14 6 ἀληθινῶς,
Job 9 2(B do), Mk 12 32(B ϫепоϒмеѳм.) ἐπ' ἀλ.;
PS 49 ϲωτм ероι ϩ., PGM 60 O, BG 123 ϩппоϒ-
мме, BMis 394 in oath ϩ. итε пⲡⲉ & weal of king
= BSM 46 B тафм. ϣε пωнϭ &c; in honorific
titles, CO 279 пρωмε етϥoρeι мпеⲭⲥ̄ ϩ., Ep 133,
163 sim, ib 354 реϥмϣϣе пⲡⲉ̄ ϩ.

рммε, -мιε SA, true, honest person: Job 1 1
SA (Cl, B ѳмнι) ἀληθινός, 2 Cor 6 8 S (B do)
ἀληθής; ShA 1 65 пιстос п р., Bor 248 54 S оϒ-
ρωмε пр. to carry letters, Tri 300 S prob l рмϭε.

р мε S, be true, be verified: Deu 19 15 S (B оϩι
ерaт·, cf Mt 18 16) ἱστάναι; ShIF 201 S ye have
not purified yourselves unto him мпетιр тмε пaϥ
мпетιϲωτм пaϥ, Z 267 S аϥер пϣaϫе мпϲωτнр
мме, paral ib ер пεϣaϫε...пϭoλ.   ер ѳ., оι пѳ.
B: Is 54 17 (S = Gk), Ro 3 26 (var пмнι, S do)
δίκ. εἶναι; Eph 4 15 (S ϫε мε) ἀληθεύειν.

ϫε SA², ϫι мε S, speak truth: Ge 20 16 S (B ер
меѳм.), Eph 4 15 S (B ιρι пѳм.) ἀληθεύειν, Is 43
9 S (B ϫω пϫапмеѳм.) ἀληθῆ εἰπεῖν, Jo 19 35 SA²
(B ϫε меѳм.) ἀλ. λέγειν; PS 31 S пϲепаϫе тмε
ероoϒ ап, Bor 154 114 S if thou wouldst етρaϫe
оϒкоϒι мме.   реϥϫε мε, truth-teller: MIF 9
15 S thou art оϒр. пϩoϒo епаι.   Cf мптмε.

таϒе мε S, tell truth: RE 14 26 I swear ϫεει-
таϒo мε, ST 300 аϥтаϒo ϩεпмε, ib 280 Sa еιϫε
кϭoλ ап еιтеоϒ(е) мε.

ѳмнι (м. + ? art) B nn m, true, righteous person
or thing: Ps 144 17 оϒ ѳ. пе пⲟⲥ̄ (S = Gk), Su 3
ϩапѳ.(S do) δίκαιος; Job 1 1 (S рммε) ἀληθινός,
2 Cor 6 8 (S do), Phil 4 8 (S ϩωѣ мме) ἀληθής,
Aeg 3 Joseph пеоϒо. пе; Ge 18 23 пιѳ. (S рмм.),
Ps 33 18 пιѳ. (S do) δίκ., C 43 232 пιѳ. апа ап-
оϒѣ;   as adj: Lev 19 36 (S do), Is 57 1 (S do)
δίκ., 1 Thes 1 9 (S мε) ἀληθινός; C 86 297 пι-
пaιатϥ пѳ. = BSG 190 S пϫικαιос, HL 104 оϒ-
ϩωѣ пѳ. δίκαιον.

ⲧⲁⲫⲙⲏⲓ *B* nn m, *truth*: Lu 16 11 (*S* diff), Jo 4 37 (*SA²* ⲙⲉ), He 9 24 (*SF* do) ἀληθινός; adj, *true*: Is 65 16 (*S* ⲙⲉ), Jo 1 9 (*S* do) ἀληθινός; 1 Tim 6 19 (*S* do) ὄντως; Va 61 8 ⲡⲓⲫⲓⲗⲟⲥⲟⲫⲟⲥ ⲛ̄ⲧ. As adv, *truly, indeed*: 3 Kg 8 27, Ps 57 2 (*S* ⲛⲁⲙⲉ), Mt 26 73 (*S* do) ἀληθῶς, Dan 2 8 ἐπ᾽ ἀληθείας; MG 25 71 ⲧ. ⳨ⲓⲡϣⲁ ⲙⲫⲙⲟⲩ (var ⲥⲉ), BSM 43 ⲧ. ⲧⲉⲡⲣⲁϣⲓ = BMis 390 *S* ⲁⲗⲏⲑⲱⲥ; or ⲛ̄ⲧⲁⲫ.: Ex 33 16 (*S* do), MG 25 14 ἀληθῶς.

ⲙⲏⲧ *S*(archaic)*O* adj, *true, real*, in magic (*cf* DM 8 9, 18 12): AZ 21 94 *O* (*cf ib* 38 89) ⲡⲁⲣⲉⲛ ⲙⲙ., KroppK 15 *S* ⲡⲣⲁⲛ ⲙⲙ. of God, BP 10587 *S* thine only son whose ⲣⲁⲛ ⲙⲙ. is Sêth, AZ 33 133 *S* seven ⲣ. ⲙⲙ., Leyd 459 *S* great name & ⲣ. ⲙⲙ., BKU 1 1 vo 3 *S* ⲡⲣⲉⲙ (ⲙ)ⲏⲧ of Isis. *Cf* αὐθεντικὸν ὄνομα PLond 1 121. In Ryl 72 352 *S* (? a play upon this & ⲙⲏⲧ *ten*) word ⲁⲭⲁⲧⲏⲥ = 1110, whereof 1000 refers to Father, 100 to Son, 10 to H. Ghost, thus ϣⲉⲡⲉ ⲓ̄ⲥ̄ ϣⲉⲡⲉ ⲙⲏⲧ ⲙⲙⲏⲧ ⲉⲧⲉⲡⲁⲓⲡⲉ ⲓ̄ⲥ̄ ⲙⲏⲧⲡⲉ ⲓ̄ⲥ̄.

ⲙⲉ *S* bird name *v* ⲙⲉ *truth*.

ⲙⲉⲓ, ⲙⲏⲓ *F* *v* ⲙⲉ *love*.

ⲙⲉⲉⲓ *F* *v* ⲙⲉ *truth*.

ⲙⲏ *SBF*, ⲙⲓ *S* (*B* in ⲡⲁⲗⲙⲓ *q v*) nn f, *urine* (*v* Berlin *Wörterb* 2 53, DM Index no 341): ROC 25 273 *B* ⲛ̄ⲧⲉϥⲥⲱ ⲛ̄ⲧⲉϥⲙⲏ (var *ib* 255 ⲙⲏ ⲙⲙⲱⲟⲩ) οὖρον; Mor 16 55 *S* drank ⲧⲙⲏ of horses = BMis 209 *S* ⲙⲏ ⲙⲙⲱⲟⲩ, Mor 46 29 *S* ϣⲟϣⲟⲩ ⲙⲙⲏ poured over martyr. In recipes: Cai 42573 1 *S* ⲧⲙⲏ of woman, PMéd 299 *S* ⲛⲁⲫⲑⲁⲣⲧⲟⲥ, *ib* 289 *S* ⲙⲛⲙⲏ ⲛ̄ⲕⲟⲩⲓ ϣⲏⲣⲉ (*v* note), *ib* 296 *S* ⲛⲟⲓⲛϭⲗⲟⲩ (*cf* Rec 16 94), BKU 1 21 vo *Sⁱ* ⲧⲙⲏ ⲛ̄ⲡⲫⲁⲥⲙ, Z 630 *S* sim & *v* below. ⲙⲏ ⲙⲙⲱⲟⲩ, ⲙⲓ ⲙⲙⲓ. *S*, ⲙⲏ ⲙⲙⲱⲟⲩ *B*, ⲙⲉⲙⲏ *F*, meaning same: Is 36 12 *S* (*B* ⲙⲱⲟⲩ, *F* ⲓϣ) οὖρον, MR 4 128 *S* glossary ⲟⲩⲣⲓⲁⲡ (? οὐρίδιον) · ⲧⲙⲏ ⲡⲡⲟⲩ (? ⲙⲙⲟ-ⲟⲩ); ShC 42 79 *S* ⲡⲉⲕⲙ. ⲉⲧⲟⲣⲏⲣⲉⲡϣⲟϣⲟⲩ like wine, Leip 27 1 *B* Victor's prophecy ⲡⲁⲓⲱⲧ ⲡⲁⲉⲣ ⲭⲁϥⲭⲁϥ (sic) ⲙⲏ ⲙⲱⲟⲩ ϥ(ⲡ)ⲁⲙⲟⲩ (*cf* BMar below); recipes: AZ 23 108 *S* ⲙⲓ ⲙⲙ. (sic), *ib* 109 *S* fill jar with ⲙⲓ ⲙ. or vinegar.

ⲕⲟⲩⲓ ⲙⲏ *S*, meaning same ?: RE 9 160 *S* I learn you are troubled ⲟⲛⲧⲉⲧⲛ. ⲙⲏ. *Cf* ⲣ ⲡⲟϭ ⲙⲙⲏ below.

ⲙⲏ ⲟⲉⲓⲕ *S*, ⲙⲏ ⲡⲁⲓⲕ *F* nn f, lit *urine of bread* (food), *excrement*: Is 30 22 *S* (*B* ϩⲱⲓⲣⲓ, *F* ⲙⲉⲙⲏ, *cf* PMéd above), *ib* 36 12 *SF* (*B* ϩⲉⲗⲥⲓ), Ez 4 12 *S* (var ⲟⲉⲓⲕ alone, *B* ϩⲁⲗⲙⲓ) κόπρος.

ⲣ, ⲉⲣ, ⲉⲗ ⲙⲏ *SBF*, **a** *make water*: 1 Kg 25 34 *S*, 4 Kg 9 8 *S* οὐρεῖν; P 43 234 *S* ⲙⲟⲩⲕϩ ⲡⲉⲣ ⲙⲏ · ⲁⲅⲥⲥⲱⲣⲓⲁⲥ (δυσουρία); عمار البول ; ShC 73 124 *S* if one]ⲣ ⲙⲏ into βαυκάλιον, Ep 176 *S* ⲁⲓⲣ ⲧⲁⲙⲏ ϩⲁⲣⲟⲓ (*v* note ὕδωρ ποιῆσαι), Miss 4 700 *S* foul like

pot wherein ϣⲁⲩⲣ ⲙⲏ, PMéd 134 *S* ⲟⲩⲁ ⲉϥⲣ ⲙⲏ ⲛⲥⲡⲟϥ. *Cf* ⲫⲉⲡ ⲙⲱⲟⲩ ⲉⲃⲟⲗ. **b** *evacuate dung*: Tob 2 10 *S* ἀφοδεύειν, *cf* Mor 22 128 *S* = BSM 117 *B* sim, EpJer 21 *F* (? error, *B* ⲟⲩⲟϩ, *v* KKS 151) ἐφίπτασθαι.

⳨ ⲙⲉ *S* nn m, *penis* (?): Cai 42573 1.

ⲙⲁ ⲡⲣ ⲙⲏ *SB*, **a** *anus*: Mt 15 17 *S* (*B* ⲙⲁ ⲡ-ϩⲣⲉⲙⲥⲓ *latrine*, *F* = Gk), Mk 7 19 *S* do (*B* do) ἀφ-εδρών, 1 Kg 5 12 *S* ἕδρα (= *ib* 3 ⲙⲁ ⲡⲣⲙⲟⲟⲥ), P 129¹⁴ 127 *S* ⲧⲁⲅⲉ ⲥⲛⲟϥ ⲉⲡⲉⲥⲏⲧ ϩⲛ̄ⲡⲉⲩⲙⲁ ⲡⲣⲙⲙⲉ ⲛ(ϩ)ⲡⲁϩⲟⲩ, LCyp 3 *S* blood issuing ⲉⲃⲟⲗ ϩⲛⲙⲙ., DeV 123 *B* worms plagued Herod's ⲙ., Mor 31 123 *S* (on 1 Tim 5 23) ⲁⲡⲉⲭⲙ. ϩⲱⲕ ϩⲓⲣⲟⲩⲡ ⲙⲙⲟϥ after fasting, Mor 50 47 *S* will ye that I sit ⲧⲁⲡⲁ-ⲣⲁⲥⲕⲉⲅⲁⲍⲉ ⲙⲙⲟⲓ ϩⲓⲡⲁⲙ.?, R 2 1 71 *S* among beauties of human body ϩⲉⲡⲁⲙ. ⲉⲩϩⲏⲡ *buttocks*, PMéd 304 *S* ⲡⲙⲁ ⲡⲣ ⲡⲟϭ ⲙⲙⲏ (*cf* ⲕⲟⲩⲓ ⲙⲏ above). **b** *place of evacuation, latrine*: R 1 3 25 *S* pagan altars ⲁⲁⲩ ⲙⲙ., P 131⁶ 83 *S* food & ⲡⲉ-ⲧⲉϣⲁⲅⲉⲓ ⲉⲃⲟⲗ ⲛⲥⲉⲃⲱⲕ ⲉⲡⲙ., TurM 9 *S* recipe ⲕⲟⲡⲣⲟⲥ ⲉⲩⲗⲉⲕⲗⲱⲕ ϩⲛⲟⲩⲙ. *Cf* MG 25 156 *B* ⲙⲁ ⲡⲣⲉⲙⲥⲓ. ⲣ ϣⲟⲩ ⲙⲏ *S*, to have (abnormal) *flow of urine*, or ? *diarrhoea, dysentery*: BMar 17 Victor's prophecy ⲡⲁⲉⲓⲱⲧ ⲡⲁⲣ ϣ. ϥⲙⲟⲩ (*cf* Leip 27 above), PMéd 173 recipe for ⲡϣⲱ (? ϣⲟⲅⲟ) ⲡⲙⲏ (or, as Chassinat, *gravel*). *V* LMis 326, Rec 39 166.

Cf ⲙⲟⲟⲩ.

ⲙⲏⲓ *S* nn, meaning unknown, an implement of brass: PLond 4 515 ⲟⲩⲙ. ⲡⲃⲁⲣⲱⲧ. ⲉⲙⲉ, ⲁⲙⲏ un-likely.

ⲙⲏⲓ *B* *v* ⲙⲉ *truth*.

ⲙⲏⲓ *BO* imperat *v* ⳨ *give*.

ⲙⲓⲉ *A* *v* ⲙⲉ *truth*.

ⲙⲓⲏ *B* *v* ⲙⲟⲩⲓ *lion*.

ⲙⲓⲟⲩ, with suff ⲙⲓⲟⲕ *SB*, -ⲁⲕ *SⁱF*, f ⲙⲓⲱ *S*, pl ⲙⲓⲱⲧⲛ *S*, -ⲁⲧⲛ *Sⁱ*, -ⲱⲧⲉⲛ *B*, ⲙⲓⲟⲟⲩ *S*, -ⲱⲟⲩ *B* vb (*v* Tri below), *be hale*, often implying gratitude: MG 25 231 *B* Macarius to demon ⲙⲓⲱⲟⲩⲡⲉ *are they well?* σωθείης (? reading -θεῖεν). Reply ⲁϥⲟⲩⲱⲡ ⲙⲓⲱⲟⲩⲡⲉ ποῦ ἔνι μοι σωθῆναι? = Z 317 *S* (reply only) ⲁϣⲡⲉ ⲡⲁⲙⲓⲟⲕ? MG 25 350 *B* never said he to him ⲙⲓⲟⲕ *thanks*, for his nature (ἕξις) was harder than most, yet dying he said thrice ⲙⲓⲟⲕ σωθείης (*cf* PG 65 296 γ), *ib* 212 *B* sim σωθ., P 44 121 = 43 129 *S* ⲙⲓⲱⲧⲛ ⲧⲱⲛⲟⲩ *much thanks to you*, for ye have taught me قد احسنتم; ShC 42 25 *S* ⲙⲓⲱⲧⲛ ⲧⲏⲣⲧⲛ we give God much thanks, P 129¹⁸ 106 *S* come & I will feast thee. ⲙⲓⲟⲕ ⲧⲟⲛⲟⲩ *much thanks* = EW 44 *B* = Ar (ASLewis 60) الله يحسن لك الجزا, RAl 103 *B* to those offering him food ⲙⲓⲱⲧⲉⲡ ⲧⲏⲣⲟⲩ, LAp 572 *F* ⲙⲓⲁⲕ ⲧⲱ[ⲛⲁ] sim, AM 110 *B* sim, AZ 21

150 S ⲙⲱⲕ ⲧⲟⲡⲟⲩ ⲡⲉⲕϩⲙⲟⲧ ϣⲏⲡ, BIF 15 251 Sᶠ ⲙⲓⲁⲕ ⲧ. O Arian, for thou hast [. As greeting, *hail!*: BMar 116 S friend ⲙⲓⲟⲕ χαίροις, ShZ 427 n S ye say χαῖρε ⲏ ϫⲉⲗⲙⲉⲓⲟⲕ (*sic ? l*), ib 22 S ⲙⲓⲱⲕ ⲧ. O Victor, ShIF 211 S think not that I blame them that have said this to us ⲛⲡⲉⲡⲡⲉ̄ ϫⲟⲟϥ ⲙⲓⲟⲟⲩ ⲧ., R 1 2 22 S ⲙⲓⲱⲧⲛ O athletes of Christ, PO 2 177 Sᶠ ⲙⲓⲁⲧⲛ ⲛⲧⲱⲧⲛ, depart ye, DeV 2 87 B Christ to Three Children ⲙⲓⲱⲧⲉⲛ honoured servants, PO 14 357 B ⲙⲓⲟⲕ ⲧ. O obedient servant, Wess 18 37 S ⲙⲓⲟⲧⲛ my brethren, they replied ⲙⲓⲟⲕ ⲧ., Mor 31 252 S ⲙⲛⲁⲧⲉⲧⲛ ⲧ. God hath given you rest.

neg: BMis 557 S ⲙⲓⲱ ⲁⲛ ⲱ ⲧⲉⲯⲩⲭⲏ οὐαί σοι, MG 25 254 B Macarius upbraiding his body ⲙⲓⲟⲕ ⲁⲛ (Gk om)=GöttAr 114 107 ما افلت قط . Refl once: Tri 261 S ⲁⲧⲉⲧⲛⲙⲓⲱⲧⲛ ⲧ. wherefore I praise you. *V Rec* 27 155, 28 210.

ⲙⲟ, ⲙⲱ, ⲙⲙⲟ S, **ⲙⲁ** Sᵃ (BMis 376), **ⲙⲟ** B, f **ⲙⲉ** B, pl **ⲙⲙⲏⲉⲓⲧⲛ** S, **ⲙⲱⲓⲛⲓ** B imperat particle, *take !*, a c e-: Lu 16 6 sg B(S ϫⲓ), HL 97 B to woman ⲙⲉ ⲉⲧⲁⲓϩⲁⲓⲣⲓ δέχεσθαι; Lu 22 17 pl B(varr ⲙⲟⲡⲓ, ⲙⲱⲡⲓ, S ϫⲓ, ϭⲓ) λαμβάνειν; P 132¹ 59 S ⲙⲙⲟ ⲉⲡⲉⲓϣⲁⲁⲣ, C 43 82 B ⲙⲟ ⲉⲡⲁⲓϥⲁϩⲣⲓ, *ib* 195 B said to priest ⲙⲟ ⲉⲡⲁⲓⲙⲩⲥⲧⲏⲣⲓⲟⲛ...ⲁϥϭⲓ ⲙⲡⲓⲙⲩⲥⲧ., EW 80 B ⲙⲟ ⲉⲡⲁⲓⲁⲗⲟⲅ. ♭ ϭ ⲡ-: P 132¹ 26 S ⲙⲟ ⲛⲛⲉⲓϩⲱⲣⲟⲡ, C 41 69 B ⲙⲟ ⲛⲛⲁⲓⲕⲟⲩϫⲓ ⲛⲕⲁⲥ. c without prep: RNC 89 S ⲙⲙⲟ ⲡⲉⲕϩⲱⲕ, *Festschr Ebers* 37 S sim (var BMar 4 ϫⲓ), PS 290 S giveth them ἀντίμιμον...saith to them ⲙⲙⲏⲉⲓⲧⲛ ⲡⲉⲧⲛⲡⲁⲛⲧⲓⲙ., BMis 376 S ⲙⲁ ⲧⲁϣⲧⲏⲛ (var ϫⲓ) = BSM 61 B ϭⲓ, O'LearyH 2 B ⲙⲟ ⲫⲏ ⲉⲧⲉⲡⲱⲕ. d without obj: BMar 29 S handing him paper, ⲙⲱ thou knowest handwriting, *ib* 37 offering poison, ⲙⲟ ⲛⲅ-ⲟⲩⲟⲙⲟϥ, *ib* 38 ⲙⲟ ⲙⲡⲉⲓⲕⲉ ⲥⲟⲡ.

ⲙⲟ A v **ⲙⲁⲩ** there & **ⲙⲁⲁⲩ.**

ⲙⲟⲓ B imperat v **ϯ** *give.*

ⲙⲟⲩ SAA²BFO, **ⲙⲟⲟⲩⲧ**† S, **ⲙⲁⲩⲧ**† Sᵃ A, **ⲙⲁ-ⲟⲩⲧ**† A²F, **ⲙⲱⲟⲩⲧ**† B vb intr, *die* (euphemisms ⲙ-ⲧⲟⲛ, ⲛⲕⲟⲧⲕ often in place of ⲙⲟⲩ): Ge 50 15 SB, Sa 18 18 S, Mt 2 20 SB θνήσκειν, Ex 16 3 SB, Job 14 14 SB, Ez 33 9 SB, Jo 4 47 SBF, 1 Cor 9 15 SBF ἀποθν., Lev 22 8 S (B†), Ez 4 14 SB θνησιμαῖος, Is 51 12 SB, Ro 6 12 SB θνητός; Ge 30 1 SB, Job 12 2 SB, Ac 2 29 SB τελευτᾶν; Pro 9 18 SA (B ⲧⲁⲕⲟ) ὀλλύναι, Jon 1 6 SA (B do), AP 10 A² ἀπολ.; Ro 4 19 B (S diff) νεκροῦν; Sa 4 16, 15 9 S κάμνειν; AZ 38 84 O ⲛⲡⲉϥⲙ., Pcod 24 S ϣⲁϥⲙ. (var ⲣ ⲡⲉⲕⲣⲟⲥ), C 86 338 B better ⲛⲧⲉϥⲙ. ⲉϩⲟⲧⲉ ⲉⲱⲛϩ, BSM 31 B ⲁⲛⲕⲏⲛ ⲉⲙ. ⲉⲙⲁϣⲱ, J 100 21 S all that saw him said ϣⲁϥⲙ. In recipes: AZ 23 107 S ⲡⲁⲥⲥⲓⲛⲁⲕ (الزيبق) ϩⲓⲧϥ ϣⲁⲡⲧⲉⲙ. ⲕⲁⲗⲱⲥ *rub till it solidify* (cf ما Holmyard), *ib* 110, 113 sim.

Qual, *dead*: Ro 7 8 SB, Eph 2 5 SB, Ap 3 1 SB νεκρός; Lu 7 12 S(B ⲙⲟⲩ) θν., 1 Cor 15 31 BF (S ⲙⲟⲩ) ἀποθν.; BSM 98 B ϭⲙ. ϩⲁⲣⲓϩⲁⲣⲟϥ, J 67 91 S be thou alive or ⲉⲕⲙ., Ep 344 S ⲉϥⲙⲁⲩⲧ from hunger; or with rel: Ps 114 14 S (B ⲣⲉϥⲙ.), Sa 15 17 S, Is 37 36 SB, Mt 14 2 SBF, Cl 24 1 A, AP 18 A² ⲛⲉⲕ., Lev 11 8 S ⲡⲉⲧⲙ. ⲡⲣⲏⲧⲟⲩ (var ⲙ. ⲛⲧⲁⲩ, B ⲛⲧⲱⲟⲩ) θνησιμαίων αὐτῶν; PS 158 S ϩⲉⲛⲕⲁⲥ ⲉⲩⲙ., ST 399 Sᵃ sim, El 100 A birds shall fall ⲉⲩⲙ., C 86 273 B thy gods ⲉⲟⲙ.

With following preposition. **ⲉⲧⲃⲉ-**, *because of*: Is 50 2 SB ἐν; Ro 8 10 SB δία. **ⲉϫⲛ-**, *for, because of*: PO 11 320 B ⲉϫⲉⲛⲫⲣⲁⲛ of Lord, Miss 4 745 S sim, C 86 74 B sim (var ϩⲓϫⲉⲛ-). **ⲛ-**, *from, by means of*: Jer 16 4 B ἐν (cf ϩⲛ-). **ⲛⲧⲛ-**, *meaning as last*: BMis 320 S ⲛⲧⲟⲟⲧϥ ⲙⲡⲉⲑⲏⲣⲓⲟⲛ; oftener refers to those bereft: 2 Kg 14 2 S ⲟⲩⲁ ⲛⲧⲁϥ. ⲛⲧⲟⲟⲧⲥ (Gk om), Z 341 S on road child ⲙ. ⲛⲧⲟⲟⲧⲥ συνέβη ἀποθανεῖν, Miss 4 548 S = C 89 87 B sim, Hall 4 S whoso weepeth ⲉϫⲛⲛⲉⲛⲧⲁⲩⲙ. ⲛ-ⲧⲟⲟⲧⲟⲩ, ShC 42 214 S ⲡⲉⲧⲙ. ⲛⲧⲟⲟⲧⲩ (var ⲛⲧⲁϥ, cf Qual below). **ϩⲁ-** S, **ϩⲁ-** A, *from, because of*: Jud 15 18 S ἐν (var dat), Lu 15 17 S(B ϩⲉⲛ-) dat, El 84 A ⲛⲡⲟⲩⲙ. ϩⲁⲡⲗⲓⲙⲏⲛ. **ⲉⲃⲟⲗ ϩⲁ-** B, *from*: MG 25 36 wouldst ⲙ. ⲉⲃ. ϩⲁⲡⲓⲕⲟⲥⲙⲟⲥ. **ϩⲛ-** S, **ϩⲉⲛ-** B, *by means of*: Jer 11 21 SB, Ez 7 15 SB, Ap 11 13 SB ἐν; ib 9 18 SB ἐκ; Z 264 S death ⲛ-ⲧⲁⲩⲙ. ⲡⲣⲏⲧϥ (var BMis 247 ⲙⲙⲟϥ as if vb tr); **ⲉⲃⲟⲗ ϩⲛ-** SB, Ap 8 11 ἐκ. **ϩⲓⲧⲛ-** SB, *through, by*: Job 21 25 SB ὑπό, PS 277 S lest man ⲙ. ϩⲓⲧ-ⲛⲙⲟⲩ ⲉⲧⲏⲡ ⲉⲣⲟϥ.

ⲙⲟⲩ SAA²BFO nn m, *death*: Ge 21 16 SB, Job 3 5 SB, Sa 2 20 SB, Ez 33 11 SA (Cl) B, Jo 8 51 SA²B, ShR 2 3 17 = BM 285 III a θάνατος; Deu 31 29 SB, Sa 5 4 SB τελευτή; Lam 4 9 B (S diff) τραυματίας; 2 Cor 4 10 SB νέκρωσις; AZ 38 79 O ⲙ. ⲡⲣⲱⲙⲉ, ShC 42 49 S ϩⲙⲡⲉϩⲟⲟⲩ ⲙⲡⲉⲩⲙ. they shall be feeble, Va 59 45 B he sought to ⲉⲡ ϥⲙ. ⲛⲁϥ *kill self*, Ryl 321 S ⲁⲩϯ ⲁⲡⲁⲅⲕⲏ ⲉⲣⲟⲓ ϣⲁϩⲣⲁⲓ ⲉⲡⲙ., ST 177 S ⲉϥⲥⲛⲕ ⲉⲡⲙ. *drawing toward death.*

As *plague, pestilence* SB: Jer 14 15 S ⲙ. ⲛ ⲡϣⲱ-ⲡⲉ(B ⲙ. ⲡⲣⲉϣϣ.) θαν. νοσερός, CaiEuch 518 B λοι-μός; R 1 2 56 S I smote your children ϩⲛⲟⲩⲙ. ⲉϥⲟϣ, Ep 131 S troubles now abroad ⲙⲛⲡⲙ. ⲉⲧⲣⲓ-ϫⲱⲛ, TurMat 12 S ⲡⲉⲓⲙ. ⲉⲧⲛⲣ ⲉⲃⲟⲗ ⲙⲡⲡⲉⲓϣⲱⲡⲉ, DeV 122 B wiped out ϫⲉⲛⲟⲩϣⲱⲧⲉⲃ ⲡⲉⲙⲟⲩⲙ.

—— adj SB, *deadly*: Sa 1 14 S ὄλεθρος; Lu 23 22 S (B nn) θάνατος, Mor 17 120 S ⲑⲏⲣⲓⲟⲛ ⲙⲙ., var GMir 119 S ⲑ. ⲡⲣⲉϥⲙⲟⲟⲩⲧ θανατικός; ShC 73 134 S ϣⲱⲛⲉ ⲙⲙ., Miss 4 178 B sim, BMis 213 S having found no ϩⲁⲡ ⲙⲙ. against him; *dead*: ShA 2 158 S ϩⲉⲛⲁϥ ⲙⲙ.

ⲣⲉϥⲙⲟⲩ SB, **ⲗⲉⲃⲙ.** F adj, *dead, mortal*: Sa 15

17 *S* θνητός, KKS 26 *S* begat children ⲛⲣ., Mus 34 189 *B* life came to ⲛⲓⲣ., Aeg 20 *B* ⲥⲁⲣⲝ ⲛⲣ., R 1 3 73 *S* mortals girt with ⲙⲟⲭ ⲛⲣ., opp ⲣⲉϥⲙⲟⲟⲩⲧ (*v* below), Win 6 *S* bequest by ⲛⲣ. *deceased*. ⲙⲛⲧ-, ⲙⲉⲧⲣ., *mortality*: Mor 23 16 *S* = *ib* 24 11 *F* thou hast chosen ⲙ., Ep 62 *S* ϯ ϩⲓⲱⲟⲩ ⲛⲧⲙ. (Ge 3 21), TEuch 1 200 *B*.

ⲣⲉϥⲙⲟⲟⲩⲧ *S*, -ⲙⲁⲩⲧ *AA²*, -ⲙⲱⲟⲩⲧ *B*, ⲗⲉ̄-, ⲗⲉϥⲙⲁⲟⲩⲧ *F*, ⲣⲙⲉϥⲙ. *A* (El), *dead person, thing*: Lev 21 5 *B* (*S* ⲕⲱⲱⲥ), Is 5 13 *SBF*, Ac 4 2 *B* (var ⲡⲏ ⲉⲑⲙ. = *S*) ⲛⲉⲕ.; Jer 41 20 *SB* θνησιμ.; Ez 35 8 *B* τραυματίας; AP 56 *A²* ⲧⲟⲩⲛⲁⲥ ⲣ., R 1 3 72 *S* ⲡϣⲁⲁⲣ ⲟⲩⲣ. ⲡⲉ, Mus 34 188 *B* God went to ⲛⲓⲣ., Life to ⲛⲣⲉϥⲙⲟⲩ. *Deadly thing*: Bor 253 165 *S* caused wine ϣⲱⲡⲉ ⲛⲣ. νοσηρός. ⲙⲉⲧⲣⲉϥⲙ. *B*, *deadness*: Ro 4 19 *B* (*S* ⲙⲟⲩ) νέκρωσις; Cat 126 ⲧⲙ. of idolatry. ⲉⲣ ⲣⲉϥⲙ. *B*, *become dead*: MG 25 126 ⲁⲣⲓ ⲣ. νεκρὸς γίνεσθαι; Va 66 295 part of body ⲉⲣ ⲣ.

ϭⲓⲛ-, ϫⲓⲛⲙ. *SB*, *manner of dying, death*: Va 57 215 *B* ϩⲁⲛϫ. ⲛⲉⲙⲣⲁⲛⲍⲱⲧⲉⲃ θάνατος, ShBor 247 127 *S* ⲧϭ. ⲉⲧⲛⲁⲛⲟⲩⲥ, Cat 223 *B* Eli's sons died in ⲟⲩϫ. ⲉⲥϩⲱⲟⲩ.

ⲣⲉϥϫⲓⲣⲓ ⲙϥⲙⲟⲩ *B*, *deadly*: DeV 2 24 drug ⲛⲣ. ⲡⲁϣ-, ⲡⲉϣⲙⲟⲩ *S*, ϥⲁϣⲙ. *B*, *half-dead*: Sa 18 18 *S* ἡμίθνητος, Lu 10 30 *SB*, MG 25 212 *B* ἡμιθανής; ShA 1 402 *S* ⲁⲅⲁⲁⲩ ⲙⲡϣⲙ., BMis 239 *S*, C 43 224 *B* sim.

ⲁⲧ-, ⲁⲑⲙⲟⲩ *SA²* (AP 51)*BF* adj, *deathless*: Sa 1 15 *S*, BMar 171 *S* ⲡⲗⲟⲩⲟⲥ ⲛⲁ., CaiEuch 462 *B* ⲧⲉⲕϫⲱⲣⲉⲁ ⲛⲁ., BKU 1 181 *F* ⲛⲕⲉⲗ ⲁ. ἀθάνατος, BM 299 *S* Athanasius ⲉⲧⲉⲛⲁ. ⲡⲉ, BG 82 *S* ⲟⲩⲁ. in midst of mortal men; on epitaphs: Cai 8631 *S* ⲙⲛ ⲁ. ϩⲓϫⲛⲡⲕⲁϩ οὐδεὶς ἀθ. ⲙⲛⲧ-, ⲙⲉⲧⲁ., *deathlessness, immortality*: 1 Cor 15 53 *SBF*, 1 Tim 6 16 *SB* ἀθανασία; BAp 36 *S* ⲡⲧⲟⲡⲟⲥ ⲛⲧⲙ.

ⲙⲟⲩ *v* ⲙⲟⲟⲩ.

ⲙⲟⲩⲉ, ⲙⲱⲟⲩⲓ *B* nn m, *light, brightness*: Ez 1 13, Hos 7 6 (*A* ϣⲁϥ), Hab 3 11 (*SA* ⲟⲩⲟⲉⲓⲛ) φέγγος; He 1 3 (*SF* do) ἀπαύγασμα; Ps 17 13 (Lacr ⲙⲱⲟⲩⲓ, *S* do) τηλαύγησις; Bar 4 2 λάμψις; MG 25 186 when we saw ⲡⲓⲙ. ⲉⲧϭⲉⲡⲉϥϩⲣⲟ, C 86 192 sun's ⲙ. & ⲁⲕⲧⲓⲛ.

ϯ ⲙ., *shine, be bright*: Lev 13 28 (*S* ⲧⲟ ⲡⲟⲩⲱⲃϣ) αὐγάζειν, ib 13 25 (*S* ⲣ ⲙⲁⲉⲓⲛ) τὸ αὐγάζον, Job 37 22 (*S* diff) χρυσαυγεῖν; MG 25 11 ἀστράπτειν, Ez 1 7 (*S* ⲧⲁⲁⲧⲉ) ἐξαστρ., Va 68 173 returned prodigal ⲁⲕⲑⲣⲉϥϯ ⲙ. ϫⲉⲡⲉⲕϣⲟⲩϭⲣ περιαστρ.; EpJer 23 (*F* ⲥϯⲉⲗⲗⲓ), Ez 40 3 (HCons 288, Tatt *S* diff), Nah 3 3 (*A* ⲧⲁⲕⲙⲉ, *l*? ⲧⲁⲁⲧⲉ) στίλβειν; Ex 30 34 διαφανής: C 89 158 ⲟⲩⲡⲟⲣⲫⲩⲣⲁ ⲉⲥϯ ⲙ. like lightning = MG 17 332 *S* ϯ ϣⲁ, PO 14 322 ϯ ⲙ. ⲛⲟⲩⲱⲓⲛⲓ like sun's rays, Va 61 27 pearl ⲉϥϯ ⲙ. ⲛⲟⲩⲱⲓⲛⲓ,

Va 58 152 ϥϯ ⲙ. ⲉⲡϣⲱⲓ like flame.   As nn: Lev 13 26 (*S* ⲙⲁⲉⲓⲛ ⲉⲧⲡⲟⲟⲣⲉ) τὸ αὐγάζον.

ϫⲓⲛϯ ⲙ. nn m, *shining, brightness*: Va 57 112 ⲟⲩϫ. ⲉϥⲉⲣ ⲟⲩⲱⲓⲛⲓ.

ⲙⲟⲩⲉ, ⲙⲟⲩⲉⲓ, ⲙⲟⲩ *S*, ⲙⲟⲩⲓ *SB* nn f sg & pl, *island*, mostly in Nile: Is 20 6 *S* ⲙⲟⲩ (*B* = Gk, *cf* 23 2, 6 where *S* = Gk), ib 42 15 *S* do (*B* do), Miss 4 530 *S* (var 808 ⲙⲟⲟⲩⲉⲓ) reaping reeds ϩⲓ ⲟⲩⲙ. = *ib* 67 *B* ⲟⲩⲙⲁ, Z 299 *S* ⲧⲙⲟⲩ ⲙⲡⲉⲕⲗⲟⲅⲥⲙⲁ νῆσος; Miss 4 643 *S* = *ib* 46 *B* = *ib* 394 جزٮ, ib 238 *S*, BMar 26 *S* ⲙⲟⲩⲉⲓ, BP 11932 *S* ⲛⲧⲉⲙⲟⲥⲓⲟⲛ ⲛⲡⲉⲙⲟⲩⲉ, BMar 249 *S* ⲡⲟⲩⲟⲉⲓ ⲙⲙⲟⲩⲓ = BAp 175 ⲛ. ⲙⲙⲟⲩⲓⲉ (*cf*? ⲟⲩⲟⲉⲓ ⲛⲕⲟⲓ, ⲛⲣⲟⲓ).

In place-names (but *cf*? ⲙⲟⲩⲓ ram): ⲙⲟⲩⲉⲓ (Kr p 26), ⲧⲙⲟⲟⲩⲉ (Ep 1 122), ⲧⲙⲟⲩ (Kr 246), ⲧⲙⲟⲩⲟⲩ (? Lant 27), ⲑⲙⲟⲩⲓ (C 86 219, BM 1227), Θμοι (Kr 4), ⲧⲙⲟⲩⲉⲓ (*sic l*) ⲙⲡⲉⲓⲥⲉⲛⲁⲓ (J 97 95), ⲧⲙⲟⲩⲓ ⲡϣⲁϯ (C 43 91), ⲧⲙⲟⲩⲓ ⲡⲡⲥⲁϫⲟ (CO 227), ⲧⲙⲟⲩⲓ ⲟⲩⲃⲉⲥⲧⲓ (BM 529), ⲧⲙⲟⲩ ⲡⲥⲓⲙ (WS 167), Θμονύχθη (PLond 5 36) or Μουνάχθη (ib 4 pass), Μουνπτόου (PCai 67022), Τμονπιτέβ (ib 3 17, *cf* DemRyl 3 159 n), Θμοιενψῶβθις (POxy 1659), Θμουνπαμοῦν (PFiorent 3 377), ⲧⲁⲡⲉⲙⲟⲟⲩⲉ (Baouit 121).

ⲙⲟⲩⲓ, ⲙⲟⲅⲟⲩⲓ (Lam, Gal) *F* adj, *new*: Mt 13 52 (*SB* ⲃⲉⲣⲣⲉ), Gal 6 15 (*SB* do), Mor 30 10 (= BMis 237 *S* do, *cf* Eph 4 24) καινός; Ro 12 2 ⲙⲉⲧⲙⲟⲩⲓ (var & *SB* ⲙⲉⲧⲃⲉⲣⲣⲉ) ἀνακαίνωσις; Lam 5 21 ⲉⲗ ⲙ. (*SB* ⲣ ⲃ.) ἀνακαινίζειν; CMSS 64 *Sᶠ* account ⲉⲡⲙⲁ ⲙⲟⲩⲉⲓ (often), though this might be ⲙ. *island*.   Here ? belongs PMich 1291 *F* ϩⲁⲓ[ϫⲓ] ϣⲓⲡⲉ ϩⲓⲧⲛⲟⲩⲕⲟⲩⲓ ⲛⲁⲗⲟⲩ ⲛⲉⲟⲩⲙⲁⲓⲛⲉ ⲛⲉⲟⲩϭⲉⲣϣⲓⲣⲉⲡⲉ.

ⲙⲟⲩⲓ *SAA²BFO*, -ⲉⲓ *SA*, pl ⲙⲱⲟⲩⲓ *B* Stern 214 (*sic* MS, ? error), nn m f, *lion*: Deu 33 20 *SB*, Job 4 10 *SB*, Pro 19 9 *SA*, Jer 27 17 *SBF*, Ap 4 7 *SB* λέων; PGM 60 *O* ⲥⲉⲣⲱⲧ ⲛⲙ. (*v* DM 1 12 n), El 76 *A* ⲟⲩⲙ. ⲉϥϩⲣⲉⲣⲙⲉ, 1 Kg 17 34 *B* ⲙ. & ⲗⲁⲃⲟⲓ (*q v*), AP (BerlSitz '09 218) *A²* ⲙ. & ⲁⲣϩ, BM 528 *F* picture of ⲥⲛⲉⲩ ⲙⲙⲉⲩⲓ (*sic*), Mor 40 30 = 41 145 *S* Leontius says ⲙ. is my name which interpreted is ⲡⲕⲱⲣⲧ =. C 43 59 *B* ⲭⲣⲱⲙ (refers ? to zodiacal sign *Leo*).   *lioness*: AP 15 *A²* Thecla bound upon ⲟⲩⲙ. ⲛⲥϩⲓⲙⲉ...ⲧⲙ. λέαινα, EW 97 *B* ⲟⲩⲙ. ⲛⲥϩⲓⲙⲓ ...ϯⲙ.

ⲙⲟⲩⲓϩ, ⲙⲓⲏ, ⲙⲩⲏ, ⲙⲓⲉ *B* f, *lioness*: Job 4 10 ⲙⲓⲏ (*S* ⲗⲁⲃⲟⲓ), Dan 7 4 ⲙⲩⲏ (*S* do) λέαινα; C 43 106 ϯⲙⲟⲩⲓⲏ, K 164 ϯⲗⲁⲃⲟⲓ, ϯⲙⲓⲉ, ϯⲧⲁⲣⲉϩ all لبؤة.

ⲙⲁⲥ, ⲙⲉⲥ ⲙ. *SBF*, *young of lion, whelp*: Ge 49 9 *SB*, Is 30 6 *SBF* σκύμνος λέοντος, Ps 103 21 *SB*, Ez 19 2 *SB* σκύμνος.

As name: ⲙⲟⲩ TT 75 (*v* n), Μοῦι, Πμοῦι, Φμοῦις, Ἁρπμοῦις, Μεσμοῦις, Χεσφμόις (Preisigke, but ? *v* next word).

ⲙⲟⲩⲓ *B* nn m, *ram*: only in place-name ⲑⲙⲟⲩⲓ Θμοῦις نمي (Spg 299, Quatremère *Mém* 1 131).

ⲙⲁⲁⲃ *SA²*, ⲙⲁⲁⲃⲉ, ⲙⲁⲃⲉ *A*, ⲙⲁⲡ *B* (but mostly ⲗ̄), ⲙⲏⲃ *F*, f ⲙⲁⲁⲃⲉ *S*, ⲙⲁⲁⲃ-, ⲙⲁⲃ- *SA²*, ⲙⲁⲡ- *B*, numeral *thirty*: Deu 34 8 *S* ⲙ. ⲡⲣⲟⲟⲩ, 2 Chr 4 2 *B* ⲙⲁⲡ ⲙⲙⲁⲣⲓ, Zech 11 12 *A* ⲙⲁⲃⲉ ⲛϩⲉⲧ, Kr 131 *F* ⲙⲏⲃ(ⲉ)ϩⲉⲧ; Ge 11 12 *S* ϣⲉ ⲙⲁⲁⲃⲉ ⲛⲣⲟⲙⲡⲉ, Br 236 *S* ⲙⲁⲁⲃⲉ ⲛϩⲛⲁⲗⲓⲥ; PS 94 *S* ⲡⲙⲉϩⲙⲁⲃ-ⲧⲁϥⲧⲉ ⲙⲯⲁⲗⲙⲟⲥ, Br 234 *S* ⲙⲁⲁⲃⲧⲁⲥⲉ… ⲡⲉⲓⲱⲧ, 2 Chr 3 15 *B* ⲙⲁⲡϯⲟⲩ ⲙⲙⲁⲣⲓ, Jo 5 5 *A²* ⲙⲁⲃ-ϣⲙⲏⲛ ⲛⲣⲟⲙⲡⲉ, PLond 4 497 *S* ⲧⲁⲓⲟⲩⲙⲁⲃ.

ⲙⲃⲁⲓ *B v* ⲙⲡⲁⲓ.

ⲙⲃⲟⲛ, ⲉⲙⲃⲟⲛ *B* (*S* once P 44 64) vb intr, *be wrath*: c ⲉ-: Deu 1 37, 2 Kg 6 7 (both *S* ϭⲱⲛⲧ) θυμοῦν; Mk 14 5 (*S* do) ἐμβριμᾶσθαι; Ge 27 42 (*S* ⲡⲟⲩϭⲥ), Is 66 14 (*S* do), Nah 1 4 (*SA* ⲉⲡⲓⲧⲙⲁ) ἀπειλεῖν; Ge 27 41 (*S* ϭ.) ἐγκοτεῖν, Ps 54 4 (*S* ⲛ.) ἐν ὀργῇ ἐγκ.; Miss 4 143 ⲙⲡⲉⲣⲙ. ⲉⲣⲟⲓ; c ⲉⲝⲉⲛ-: Dan 11 30 θυμ.; ⲉϩⲣⲏⲓ ⲉⲝ.: Is 47 6 (*S* ⲛ.) παροξύνειν; Cat 86 ⲙ. ⲉϩ. ⲉⲝ. ⲡⲓⲱⲙ ⲛϩⲏⲧ; no obj: Mt 2 16 (*S* ϭ.) θυμ., Ge 6 7 (*S* do) ἐνθυμ.; Nu 14 11 (*S* ϯ ϭ.) παροξ.; Lam 1 5 πικραίνεσθαι; Ps 102 9 (*S* ⲛ.) ὀργίζεσθαι; AM 281 ἀγανακτεῖν; PO 11 308 ⲁϥⲙ. ϫⲉⲡⲟⲩⲛⲓϣϯ ⲛϩⲱⲡⲧ. ⲣⲉϥⲙ., *wrathful person*: Pro 24 72 (CaiCoptMus, *SA* ⲣⲉϥϭ.) θυμώδης.

—— nn m, *wrath*: Ge 49 6, Ps 9 35, Is 30 27 (*F* ϭⲱⲛⲧ), Hab 3 12 (*A* ϭ.), Ro 2 8 (*F* ⲃⲱⲣⲕ, all *S* ϭ.) θυμός; Nu 14 34, Is 5 25 (*F* ⲃⲱ.), Mk 3 5 (all *S* = Gk), Ps 36 8, Lam 2 22 (*S* ϭ.) ὀργή; ib 2 6 ἐμβρίμημα; Eph 4 27 (*S* ⲡⲟⲩϭⲥ) παροργισμός; Pro 13 8 (*SA* = Gk) ἀπειλή; Hos 5 10 (*A* ϭⲁⲙ) ὅρμημα ira; C 43 232 snakes filled with ⲕⲁⲕⲓⲁ ⲡⲉⲙ-ⲛⲃⲟⲛ (*sic*), Va 57 175 ⲡⲉⲙ. of lions & ⲟⲙⲁⲛⲓⲁ of leopards.

ϯ ⲙ., *make angry*: Deu 32 16 c dat (*S* ϯ ϭ.), Ez 12 25 (*S* do) παραπικραίνειν; ib 20 27 c dat (*S* do) παροργίζειν. ⲣⲉϥϯ ⲙ., *causer of wrath*: Ez 3 26 (*S* ⲣⲉϥϯ ϭ.) παραπικραίνων.

ⲙⲃⲣⲁⲓ *B v* ⲉⲃⲣⲁ.

ⲙⲃⲣⲉϩⲓ, ⲉⲙⲃ., ⲃⲣⲉϩⲓ, ⲉⲃⲣ. *B* nn m f, *cart*: Ge 45 19, 46 5 ⲡⲓⲙ., Nu 7 7 ⲡⲓⲙ. (*S* ⲁϭⲟⲗⲧⲉ), 2 Kg 6 3 ⲡⲓⲙ. (*S* do), Is 25 10 (*S* do) roller-cart for threshing, Am 2 13 f (*SA* do) ἅμαξα; K 318 نورج, بكر, عجل, P 55 12 among wooden implements ϯⲙ. ذ', 'ع.

ⲙⲃⲣⲉϩⲓ *B bitumen v* ⲁⲙⲣⲏϩⲉ.

ⲙⲁⲍⲉ *S* nn as pl, 1 Kg 6 15 (Ciasca) ⲡⲉⲣⲏⲧ ⲙⲡⲛⲙ. τὸ θέμα ἐργὰβ μετ' αὐτῆς, but prob corruption of var (Mor) ⲡⲉⲣⲏⲧ ⲉⲧⲛⲙⲙⲁⲥ. In *ib* 20 19 ἐργάβ not translated.

ⲙⲉⲑ- *B* ⲙⲏⲧ-.

ⲙⲉⲑⲟ *B v* ⲙⲧⲟ.

ⲙⲉⲑⲁⲓⲟ, ⲙⲉⲧⲁⲓⲱ (Pey) *B* nn, *carthamus, safflower*: K 189 عصف (which P 44 65 = ανθοκνηκον). *V* Rec 16 5.

ⲙⲟⲩⲑⲟⲩⲙ *B v* ⲙⲟⲟⲩ (ⲙⲟⲩⲃⲱⲱⲡ).

ⲙⲟⲑⲛⲉⲥ *B v* ⲙⲧⲟⲛ.

ⲙⲉⲑⲣⲉ *B v* ⲙⲛⲧⲣⲉ.

ⲙⲁⲑⲟⲩⲓ *B v* ⲙⲁⲧⲟⲩ.

ⲙⲟⲩⲕ *S*, ⲙⲟⲟⲩⲕ *F v* ⲙⲟⲩⲛⲕ *cease*.

ⲙⲓⲕⲉ, -ⲕⲓ *SF* vb a intr, *rest*: BMar 219 *S* ⲛⲧⲉⲣⲉⲓⲙ. ⲁⲩⲱ ⲡⲧⲁⲙⲧⲟⲛ = Rec 6 185 *B* diff, Mor 51 15 *S* king to martyr ⲁⲣⲁ ⲁⲕⲙ. ⲡⲟⲩⲕⲟⲩⲓ ϩⲧⲁⲣⲭⲏ ⲛⲛⲃⲁⲥⲁⲛⲟⲥ ?, BP 3248 *F* sale of house ⲁⲓⲙ. ⲡⲉⲙⲉⲕ ⲁⲕⲥⲗⲱⲗⲉϥ (*sic*) ⲁⲓⲧⲉⲓⲃ ⲡⲉⲕ (obscure), AZ 23 104 *S* in alchem process ϣⲁⲣⲉⲡⲉⲧⲧⲟⲣϣ ⲙ. ⲛⲃⲟⲗ *remain unaffected* (?). b tr (refl), *rest oneself*: Mor 48 94 *S* sat down ϫⲉⲉϥⲙⲁⲙ. ⲙⲙⲟϥ = C 43 146 *B* ⲙⲧⲟⲛ ⲙⲟϥ, P 132¹ 41 *S* sim = DeV 2 141 *B* do, Mor 31 228 *S* ⲧⲁϭⲱⲣⲕ ⲧⲁⲙ. ⲙⲙⲟⲓ ⲡⲟⲩⲕⲟⲩⲓ, KKS 584 *S* ⲁⲓⲙ. ⲙⲙⲟⲓ ⲡⲟⲩⲕⲟⲩⲓ ⲁⲩⲱ ⲡⲧⲉⲣⲉⲓⲙⲧⲟⲛ ⲙⲙⲟⲓ, P 44 89 *S* ⲉⲩⲙ. ⲙⲙⲟⲟⲩ ليستريحوا. c nn m *S*, *rest*: ShR 2 3 69 body sleek from much food, drink & ⲡⲙ.; *fallowness* (cf ἀνάπαυσις): Kr 92 [I will sow] ⲟⲩⲥⲉⲓⲁϩ ⲙⲁⲣⲉ ⲡⲁⲕ ⲙⲙ., *ib* 91 payment for [ⲡ]ⲙⲓⲕⲉ (? *sic l*) ⲡⲥⲉⲧⲓⲁϩ. ϯ ⲙ., *give rest*: Mor 31 228 he lay down ⲁⲡⲕⲁϩ ϯ ⲙ. ⲡⲁϥ, *ib* 213 sim.

ⲙⲟⲛⲕⲓ *B* nn m, *jar, vessel, quiver*, container generally: Deu 23 25 (*S* ϩⲛⲁⲁⲩ), Am 8 1 (*SA* do) ἄγγος, Ge 42 25 a (var ⲥⲟⲕ), Lev 14 5 (*S* = Gk), Is 30 14 (*S* ϩ., *F* = Gk), Mt 25 4 (*S* ϩ.) ἀγγεῖον; Jer 19 1 (*S* = Gk) βῖκος; Mt 26 7 (*SF* = Gk) ἀλάβαστρον; Pro 9 2 (var & *A* = Gk, *S* ϩ.) κρατήρ; Va 61 24 drank from ⲡⲓⲙ. ⲙⲙⲟⲟⲩ λαγήνιον (var κάλπιον); ib 220 Samuel's oil horn (1 Kg 16 ⲧⲁⲡ); Ex 25 29 ⲙ. ⲡⲟⲩ-ⲱⲧⲉⲛ ⲉⲃⲟⲗ σπόνδιον; Ge 42 25 b σάκκος; ib 27 3, Ps 10 2 (*S* ϩ. ⲡϯ ⲥⲟⲧⲉ), Is 49 2 (*S* ϩ. ⲡⲕⲁ ⲥ.) φαρέτρα; Ex 16 23, 32 (*S* om) ἀποθήκη; Lev 15 12 σκεῦος, cf C 89 136 ⲡⲓⲙ. at banquet = ib ⲡⲓⲥⲕⲉⲩⲟⲥ = Bor 296 148 *S* ⲁⲩⲕⲏⲛ (ἀγγ.); HCons 451 ⲡⲓⲙ. ⲛⲧⲉ ⲡⲓⲙⲩⲧⲣⲟⲛ وعاء, K 147 وعاء, اناء, ماعون; Rec 6 180 ⲟⲩⲙ. of water = BMar 215 *S* ϩⲛⲁⲩ, MIE 2 398 sim = BAp 97 *S* ⲡⲕⲁ, C 41 77 ⲡⲁⲓⲙ., ib later ⲡⲓ-ⲗⲁⲕⲟⲛ, MG 25 191 ⲙ. of glass, C 86 283 ⲙ. shaped like iron tube (χώνη).

ⲙⲟⲩⲕⲓ *B* nn f, *ladder*: Ge 28 12 (*S* ⲧⲗⲟⲟϭⲉ *sic*) κλίμαξ; K 253 ϯⲙ. سلم; CaiThe 255 Virgin compared to Jacob's ⲙ., C 86 330 ⲁⲡⲓⲟⲩⲓ ⲡⲟⲩⲙ. that

we take him down, *ib* 92 dragon that is below ⲧⲙ.
= WTh 136 *S* ⲋⲗⲟⲟⲥⲉ, *cf* C 43 50 *B* ⲧⲱⲧⲉⲣ, PO
14 364 set ϩⲁⲡⲙ. against wall.

ⲙⲟⲕⲙⲉⲕ *SB*, ⲙⲁⲕⲙⲉⲕ *Sᶠ* (Mor cod 663 A)*F*,
ⲙⲁⲕⲙⲕ *A*, ⲙⲉⲕⲙⲉⲕ- *B* (2 pl), ⲙⲉⲕⲙⲟⲩⲕⲍ *SB* vb
I intr, *think, ponder*: Is 10 7 *SB*, *ib* 44 19 *B* (*S*
ⲙⲉⲉⲩⲉ), MG 25 11 *B* ⲛⲉϥⲙ. ϫⲉ- λογίζεσθαι, Ps
118 58 *B* (*S* do), Mt 16 7 *B* (*S* do) διαλογ.; Si 14
21 *S* νοεῖσθαι, Ge 8 21 *B* (*S* diff) διανο.; *ib* 6 6 *B*
(*S* diff) ἐνθυμεῖσθαι; ShC 73 80 *S* ⲡⲉⲧⲛⲁⲙ. ϫⲉⲧⲛ
ϣⲁⲁⲧ, Va 62 170 *B* ⲉⲧⲓ ϫⲉ ⲉϥⲙ. in his heart.
с ⲉ- *SB*: Ps 35 5 *B* (*S* ⲙⲉⲉⲩⲉ), Is 53 4 *B* (*S* ⲱⲡ),
Jer 33 3 *SB* λογ., Ps 76 6 *B* (*S* ⲙⲉ.) διαλογ., Is 43
18 *B* (*S* ⲣ ⲡⲙⲉ.) συλλογ.; Jer 7 31 *B* διανο.; Mt 1
20 *B* (*S* ⲙⲉ.) ἐνθυμ.; PS 96 *S* ϣⲁϫⲙ. ⲉⲅⲟⲣϩⲏ,
DeV 2 49 *B* God to Jonah ⲕⲙ. ⲉⲣⲟⲓ ϫⲉ- wherefore I had been patient. **с ⲉⲅⲟⲡ ⲉ-** *S*: Nah 1 9
v C 42 41) *A* (*B* ⲙⲉⲅⲓ ⲉϫⲉⲡ-) λογ. ἐπί. **с ⲉⲑⲃⲉ-**
B: EW 147 ⲉϥⲙ....ⲉⲑⲃⲉⲡⲓⲥⲁϫⲓ σκοπεῖσθαι περί.
With vbal **ⲉ-** *SB*: Jer 18 8 *B* ⲉⲧⲁⲓⲙ. ⲉⲁⲓⲧⲟⲩ, *ib* 33
3 *S* ⲛⲧⲁⲓⲙ. ⲉⲧⲣⲁⲁⲩ λογ. τοῦ ποιῆσαι, C 86 202 *B*
ⲉⲧⲓ ⲉϥⲙ. ⲉⲓⲣⲓ ⲙⲡⲓϩⲟⲡ.

II tr, *meditate, intend*: Jer 29 20 *B* (*S* ⲙⲉ. ⲉ-)
λογ., Ps 34 20 *B* (*S* do) διαλογ.; Jth 9 5 *S* ἐννοεῖ-
σθαι; C 86 195 *B* ⲉⲧⲓ ⲉϥⲙ. ⲡⲛⲁⲓ.
Refl (oftenest), *consider* **a** with suff: Va 57 219
B ⲙⲉⲕⲙⲟⲩⲕ(ⲕ) ⲉⲡⲓⲭⲣⲱⲙ, ClPr 54 4 *S* Solomon
judging ⲉⲁϥⲙⲉⲕⲙⲟⲩⲕϥ ϫⲉ- λογ., He 12 3 *B* ⲙⲉⲕ-
ⲙⲉⲕⲉⲛⲏⲡⲟⲩ (*S* ϯ ϩⲏⲧ) ἀναλογ., Mk 11 31 *S* (*B* ⲙ.
ⲡⲉⲙ-) διαλογ.; Ge 8 21 *S* (Ryl 70 254, *B* ⲙ.), Ps
72 8 *S* (*B* ⲙⲉⲅⲓ), Si 21 18 *S* διανο., Dan 9 23 *S* (*B*
ⲉⲣ ⲛⲟⲓⲛ) ἐννο.; Deu 32 29 *S* (*B* ⲉⲣ ⲥⲁⲃⲉ) φρονεῖν,
Sa 8 17 *S* φροντίζειν; PS 115 *S* ⲁⲩⲙⲉⲕⲙⲟⲩⲕⲟⲩ
ⲉⲩϣⲟⲭⲡⲉ (*cf* Ps 20 11 *S* ⲙⲉⲉⲩⲉ), ShC 42 165 *S*
ⲛⲑⲉ ⲛⲧⲁϥⲙⲉⲕⲙⲟⲩⲕϥ...ⲉⲧⲣⲉϥϩⲣⲟϣ ⲉϩⲣⲁⲓ, Mor 39
41 *S* ⲁⲩⲙⲉⲕⲙⲟⲩⲕⲟⲩ = *ib* 40 31 *S* ⲥⲕⲩⲡⲉⲓ (σκέπτεσθαι) ⲙⲙⲟⲟⲩ, BIF 13 105 *S* ⲁⲥⲙⲉⲕⲙⲟⲩⲕⲥ ϫⲉ
= MG 25 288 *B* ⲁⲥⲙⲟⲕⲙⲉⲕ. **b** with ⲙⲙⲟ:
Lu 1 29 *S* (*B* ⲙ.) διαλογ., MG 25 12 *B* ⲉϥⲙ. ⲙ
ⲙⲟϥ ϫⲉ- διαλογ. ἐν ἑαυτῷ; Ac 10 19 *S* (*B* ⲥⲟϭⲛⲓ)
διενθυμ.; Dan 10 9 *B* (*S* ⲗⲩⲡⲉⲓ) κατανύσσεσθαι;
BMar 105 *S* ⲉϥⲙ. ⲙⲙⲟϥ as to how *considerans*;
Lu 15 17 *S* (*B* ϩⲏⲧ ⲓ ⲉ-) εἰς ἑαυτὸν ἔρχ.; ShC 42
117 *S* ⲧⲉⲧⲛⲙ. ⲙⲙⲱⲧⲛ ⲧⲱⲡⲟⲩ ϩⲙⲡϣⲁϫⲉ ⲉⲧⲥⲏϩ,
MG 17 322 *S* ⲉϥⲙ. ⲙⲙⲟϥ ⲉⲡⲁⲓ = C 89 69 *B* sim
ϫⲉⲛⲡⲁⲓ, Va 63 12 *B* ⲁϥⲙ. ⲙⲙⲟϥ ϫⲉⲛⲡⲉϥϩⲏⲧ ϫⲉ-
= BSM 38 *B* ⲙⲉⲅⲓ, BIF 13 108 *S* ⲁⲡⲙ. ⲙⲙⲟⲛ
ⲉⲧⲃⲉ- = MG 25 293 *B* ⲙ. ⲉⲃⲟⲗ ⲉⲑⲃⲉ-, P 129¹⁵ 23
S whilst he ⲙ. ⲙⲙⲟϥ ⲉⲃⲁⲥⲁⲡⲓϫⲉ ⲙⲙⲟⲟⲩ.

—— *SAB* nn m, *thought*: Jth 8 14 *S*, Ps 32 10
B (*S* ⲙⲉⲉⲩⲉ), Jer 18 18 *S* (*B* ⲥⲟϭⲛⲓ) λογισμός, Ps
93 11 *SB*, Is 59 7 *SB*, Mk 7 21 *S* (var ⲙⲉ.) *B*, Ja
2 4 *SA* (*B* ⲙⲉ.), Cl 21 3 *A* ⲡⲙⲉⲩⲉ ⲙⲡⲛⲙ. διαλο-

γισμός; Jer 7 24 *B* ἐνθύμημα, Ac 17 29 *SB*, He 4
12 *B* (*S* ⲙⲉ.) ἐνθύμησις; Si 35 18 *S*, Ez 14 3 *B*
διανόημα, Nu 15 39 *S* (*B* ⲙⲉ.), Va 57 45 *B* ⲟⲩⲙⲉⲅⲓ
ⲡⲥⲁⲧⲁⲡⲓⲕⲟⲛ ⲡⲁⲓⲙ. διάνοια; Jos 5 1 *S* φρόνησις;
2 Kg 14 13 *S* ⲁⲕⲙⲉⲉⲅⲉ ⲉⲩⲙ. ⲡϯⲙⲡⲉ ⲉⲗⲟⲅⲓⲥⲱ
ⲧⲟⲓⲟⲩⲧⲟ; BHom 51 *S* no such ⲙ. ϭⲙ ϭⲟⲙ ⲉⲧⲉⲓⲥ
ϭⲓⲙⲉ ⲛⲣⲁⲕ, BMis 384 *S* archangel knew ⲛϥⲙ. (var
ⲙⲉ.) = BSM 39 *B*.
—— **ⲉⲃⲟⲗ** *SB*, *reflect, ponder*: ShZ 478 *S* ⲉⲕⲙ.
ⲉⲃ. ⲉⲣⲉⲡⲙⲛⲧϣⲟⲩϣⲟ, C 86 319 *B* ⲉⲕⲙ. ⲉⲃ. ⲉⲑⲃⲉⲡⲓ-
ⲧⲟⲡⲟⲥ, Rec 6 183 *B* ⲉⲓⲙ. ⲉⲃ. ϫⲉⲟⲩ ϩⲁⲣⲁ, MG 25
293 as above. As nn *S*: Mor 43 48 ⲡⲙ. ⲉⲃ.
ϫⲉⲡⲓⲙ ⲁⲣⲁ = *ib* 42 48 *S* ⲡⲙ.
ⲁⲧⲙ. *S* adj, *unthinkable, inconceivable*: Br 229
Father ⲡⲁⲧⲛⲟⲓ ⲙⲙⲟϥ ⲛⲁ. ⲉⲣⲟϥ;   **ⲁⲧϣⲙ.** *B*:
CaiEuch 557 Holy Spirit ⲛⲁ. ⲉⲣⲟϥ.
ϭⲓⲛ-, ϫⲓⲛⲙ. *SB*, *thought, imagination*: BM 151
134 *S* above all power of words & ϭ. ⲛⲓⲙ ⲛⲧⲉ ⲟⲩ
ⲣⲱⲙⲉ = CaiEuch 301 *B* φαντασία, Cai 8080 *S* lest
we proclaim 2 natures (φύσις) after ⲧϭ. ⲛⲧⲙⲛⲧⲟⲩⲁ.

ⲙⲟⲩⲕⲛⲁⲓⲉ *S* nn, *white cock*: P 43 24 دجاج
ابيض (*cf* Pey 93).   *Cf* ܡܘܩܡܩ (Brockelmann *Lex¹*
192), misread ? as ܡܘܡܩ.

ⲙⲁⲕⲣⲟ *B* nn m, *trough, mortar* among household vessels (ماعون): K 149 هاون, جرن .   *Cf* ⲙⲏ-
ⲣⲁⲡ, ⲙⲭⲁⲣⲧ.

ⲙⲁⲕⲁⲥ *S* nn f, *beard*: P 46 245 among parts
of body ⲧⲙ. لحية, after ⲡⲣⲱϥ.   *Cf* ? μουστάκας.

ⲙⲓⲁⲕⲏⲥ *B* nn as pl, *shells, pearl-shells*: K 171
صدف.   Coptic ? (*cf* ⲙⲁⲓⲁⲕⲏ Is 3 18 *B* μανιάκης).

ⲙⲁⲕⲟⲧ, -ⲕⲱⲧ *S*, -ⲕⲁⲧ *SA*, -ⲧⲁⲧ *S* (ShA 1),
-ⲧⲁϫ (2 Kg 5) nn m f, *javelin, dirk*: Mic 5 6 *A*
(*B* ⲧⲁϥⲣⲟ *i e* τάφρος, or ? *cf* חתם) *lancea*; 2 Kg 5 8
S παραξιφίς; TT 143 *S* ⲁⲩϥⲓ ⲡⲟⲩⲙ. = PO 4 462
ξίφος, MG 17 439 حربة, Mor 47 141 *S* guards had
ϩⲉⲡⲙⲁⲕⲁⲁⲧ (? pl) like Blemmyes = P ar 4793 45
حراب, Miss 4 237 *S* ⲥⲟⲧⲉ ϩⲓⲙ. = *ib* 397 both نشاب,
ShP 130⁵ 55 *S* ⲑⲟⲧⲉ ⲙⲡⲙ. ⲙⲛⲡⲥⲟⲧⲉ, ShA 1 234 *S*
barbarians ϣⲁⲁⲧⲟⲩ (? = ϣⲁⲥⲟⲩ, *cf* ShC 42 69)
ϩⲛⲧⲙ.; P 44 116 (Mic 5 6 v above) = 43 119 *S*
طياش وهو كرباج.   *V* KKS 404 for this word ? in Gk.

ⲙⲁⲕϩ, ⲙⲁⲭ (Deu 9 13), ⲙⲟⲕϩ *S*, ⲙⲉⲕϩ, ⲙⲉⲭϩ
A, ⲙⲉⲣⲭ *O* nn m, *neck* of man or beast: Ge 33 4
S (*B* ⲛⲁϩⲃⲓ), Jud 5 30 pl *S*, Job 41 13 *S* (*B* do),
Pro 1 9 *SA* (*B* ⲙⲟⲧ), Ez 16 11 *S* (*B* ⲙⲟⲩⲧ), Mt 18
6 *S* (*B* ⲋⲏ), Ac 15 10 *S* (*B* ⲙⲟ ϯ) τράχηλος; Ps 128
4 *S* (*B* do) αὐχήν; Lev 25 43 *S* ⲕⲉⲗⲭ ⲙ. (*B* diff)
κατατείνειν; AZ 21 98 *O* ⲡⲁⲡⲙ. ⲡϣⲉ, Mor 48 66
S collar on ⲡⲉϥⲙ. = C 43 133 *B* ⲙⲟⲩⲧ, *ib* 68 *S* =
ib 134 *B* ⲙⲟϯ, Mor 31 57 *S* ⲁϥϩⲉⲓ ⲙⲡⲉϥⲙ. ⲛⲧⲟⲟⲧϥ

ⲙⲡⲃⲁⲣⲃⲁⲣⲟⲥ = BM 917 *B* ⲡⲉϥⲙⲟⲩⲧ, R 2 1 71 *S* body's beauties ⲟⲩⲙ. ⲉϥⲥⲟⲩⲧⲱⲛ ϩⲓⲧⲡⲉ, Miss 4 546 *S* ⲉⲕⲛⲁϯ ⲡⲉⲕⲙ. ϩⲁⲡⲉⲓⲥⲟⲛ *submit self to* = C 89 62 *B* ⲡⲁⲣϩⲓ = MG 17 410 توافق في كل شي = Va 172 38 وابدل نفسك عن

ⲡⲁϣⲧ ⲙ. *S*, ⲡⲁϩⲧ ⲙ. *A, stiff-necked person*: Ex 33 5 *S* (*B* ⲡ. ⲡⲁⲣϩⲓ), Pro 29 1 *SA*, Ac 7 51 *S* (*B* do) σκληροτράχηλος; ShMun 95 *S* flee from ⲛⲓⲙ. ⲙ. As adj: R 1 1 38 *S* ϣⲁϫⲉ ⲛⲓⲙ. ⲙ. ὑπερήφανος. ⲙⲛⲧⲡ. ⲙ. *SA* nn f, *stiff-neckedness*: Cl 30 8 *A* αὐθάδεια, ShMIF 23 52 *S* among vices, BHom 111 *S* ⲧⲙ. of Pharaoh. ⲣ ⲡ. ⲙ. *S, be stiff-necked*: Bor 206 575 ⲙⲡⲣⲕⲉⲧⲧⲏⲩⲧⲛ ⲉⲣ ⲛ. ⲙ. *V* also ⲛⲟⲩϭⲉ vb.

ⲙⲟⲩⲕⲣ *SAF* (BMEA 10576), ⲙⲉⲕⲣ-, ⲙⲟⲕⲣ⸗ *S*, ⲙⲁⲕⲣ⸗, ⲙⲁⲭⲣ⸗ (Cl) *A* vb **I** tr, *afflict, oppress* (cf ⲙⲕⲁⲣ): Job 5 18 *SA* (Cl, *B* ϯ ⲙⲕⲁⲣ) ἀλγεῖν ποιεῖν, Pro 14 23 *SA* ⲙⲉϥⲙⲟⲕⲣϥ (*B* do) ἀνάλγητος, Eph 4 19 *S* (*B* ⲉⲣ ⲁⲧⲙ.) ἀπαλγεῖν; Lu 16 25 *S* (*B* ϫⲏ ϩⲉⲛⲟⲩⲙ.) ὀδύνειν, Ex 1 14 *A* (*B* ⲧⲣⲉⲙⲕⲟ) κατοδ.; Ge 16 6 *S* (*B* do), Job 30 11 *S* (*B* ϯ ⲙ.), Is 53 7 *A* (Cl, *SB* ⲑⲙⲕⲟ) κακοῦν, BMar 114 *S* ⲙⲡⲉⲣⲙ. ⲡⲉⲕϩⲏⲧ ἐγκακεῖν; Si 11 13 *S* πονεῖν, Ac 7 24 *S* (*B* ⲧⲣ.) καταπον.; Mt 14 24 *S* (*B* ϯ ⲟⲩϩⲉ-), 2 Pet 2 8 *S* (*B* ϯ ⲙ.) βασανίζειν; Deu 23 16 *S* (*B* ϩⲟⲭⲣⲉϩ) θλίβειν; Aeg 246 *S* ⲡⲥⲉⲙ. ⲁⲛ ⲙⲡⲣⲏⲕⲉ καταδυναστεύ.; Mic 4 6 *SA* (*B* Gk diff) *affligere*; Lam 3 53 *S* (ShA 2 95, *B* ϩⲱⲧⲉⲃ) θανατοῦν; Miss 8 249 *S* ⲉⲩⲙ. ⲙⲙⲁϥ ϩⲓⲧⲛⲡⲁⲅⲣⲁⲡⲟⲥ. Refl: Nu 14 44 *S* (*B* ⲉⲣ ϭⲓ ⲛϫⲟⲛⲥ) διαβιάζεσθαι; Eccl 2 21 *S* μοχθεῖν; Si 14 14 *S* ἀφυστερεῖν; ROC '13 175 *S* ⲉϥⲙ. ⲙⲙⲟϥ πονικὸς (ὤν); Z 310 *S* ⲉⲩⲙ. ⲙⲙⲟⲟⲩ κοπιᾶν; ShA 2 279 *S* ⲙⲡⲟⲅⲟⲩϣϣ ⲉⲙⲟⲕϩⲟⲩ *humble selves*, Mor 25 76 *S* ⲁⲧⲉⲧⲛⲙⲉⲕⲣⲧⲏⲩⲧⲛ ⲛⲣⲓⲥⲉ ⲛⲙⲙⲁⲓ *take trouble, be longsuffering*, Lant 5 26 *S* sim (cf ib 7 ϥⲓ ϩⲁⲣ).

II intr (rare), *labour, find difficult*: Mor 17 13 *S* gladly thou eatest ⲉⲣ ϩⲱⲃ ϫⲉ ϣⲁⲕⲙ. = EW 29 *B* ⲉⲣ ϭⲉⲡⲛⲉ σιαίνειν, BG 74 *S* ⲛⲧⲁϥⲙ. ⲛⲙⲙⲁⲩ ϩⲙ ⲡⲕⲁⲕⲉ, P 43 234 *S* ⲡⲉⲧⲙ. ⲛⲉⲣ ⲙⲛ (v ⲙⲏ).

ⲙⲕⲁⲣ *SAB* DM, ⲉⲙ., *B*, ⲙⲕⲉⲣ, ⲉⲙ. *F*, ⲙⲟⲕⲣ⸸ *SB*, ⲙⲟⲭⲣ⸸ *S* (BG 139), ⲙⲁⲕⲣ⸸ *AF*, ⲙⲁⲭⲣ⸸ *A*, ⲙⲁⲭ⸸ *AA²* vb intr (for tr v ⲙⲟⲩⲕⲣ), *be painful, difficult, be grieved*; Job 14 22 *S* (*B* ϭⲓ ⲙ.), Ps 68 30⸸ *B* (*S* ⲣ ⲙ.⸸) ἀλγεῖν, Jer 10 19⸸ *B* ἀλγηρός; Lam 1 22⸸ *B*, Mt 26 22⸸ *B* (*F* ⲙ.⸸ ⲛϩⲏⲧ, *S* = Gk), 2 Cor 2 4 *B* (*S* do) λυπεῖσθαι; Ac 26 14⸸ *S* (*B* ϩⲱⲃ ⲉϥⲡⲁϣⲧ) σκληρός; Si 3 21⸸ *S*, Miss 8 43 *S* ⲟⲩϣⲁⲭⲉ ⲉϥⲙ.⸸ χαλεπός; 2 Kg 13 2 *S difficilis esse*; Is 53 4⸸ *S* (*A* Cl ⲙ.⸸ ⲛϩⲏⲧ, *B* ⲉⲣ ⲙ. ⲛϩ.), Lu 16 24⸸ *SB* ὀδυνᾶσθαι, Jer 14 17⸸ *SB* ὀδυνηρός; Job 2 13⸸ *B* (*S* ⲡⲁϣⲧ) δεινὸς εἶναι; Mt 14 35⸸ *SF* (*B* ⲧⲣⲉⲙⲕⲛⲟⲩⲧ), Lu 5 31⸸ *SB* (opp ⲧⲏⲕ) κακῶς ἔχειν, Ps 37 8 *S* (*B* ϭⲓ ϩⲓⲥⲉ) κακοῦσθαι, He 13 3⸸ *SB* κακου-

χεῖσθαι; Si 38 16⸸ *S*, Ac 28 5 *S* (*B* ⲡⲉϩⲟⲟⲩ ϣⲱⲡⲓ), Va 61 301 *B* ⲡⲏ ⲉⲧⲙ.⸸ πάσχειν; Pro 23 35 *SA*, Si 13 6 *S*, Jer 28 29 *B* πονεῖν; Ge 48 1⸸ *S* (*B* ϣⲑⲟⲣⲧⲉⲣ), 1 Kg 19 14⸸ *S*, Lu 6 18⸸ *S* (*B* ⲧⲣⲉⲙ.) ἐνοχλεῖσθαι; Aeg 247 *S* ⲡⲉⲧⲙ.⸸ θλίβεσθαι; Lev 25 25⸸ *S* (*B* ⲉⲣ ϩⲏⲕⲓ) πένεσθαι, Ps 11 6⸸ *B* (*S* ⲉⲃⲓⲏⲛ) πένης; Jo 11 33 *B* (*SAA²* diff) ἐμβριμᾶσθαι; Ps 108 16⸸ *B* (*S* ⲙ.⸸ ⲛϩⲏⲧ) vulneratus, Su 10⸸ *S* (*B* ⲙⲉⲅⲓ) vulneratus, Ac 2 37 *SB* κατανύσσειν; AM 268 *B* τήκειν; BMar 192 *S* ⲡⲁϩⲧ ⲙ.⸸ *toward monkhood* πολὺς πόθος (? πά-) μοι ἐστί; Ps 60 2 *S* (*B* ⲉⲣ ⲙ.) ἀκηδιᾶν; PS 321 *S* ⲛⲕⲟⲗⲁⲥⲓⲥ...ⲡⲁϣⲧ? ⲥⲉⲙ.⸸ παρὰ ⲛⲕⲟⲗ. ⲧⲏⲣⲟⲩ, Br 257 *S* a place ⲉϥϩⲛⲟⲩ ⲁϩⲱ ⲙ.⸸, AM 187 *B* ⲁⲥⲙ. ⲉⲙⲁϣⲱ *was in great pain*, MG 25 239 *B* when trodden on ⲁⲛⲓⲁⲥⲱⲣⲓ ⲙ., Mun 344 *S* martyr tortured but ⲙⲡⲉϥⲙ. ϩⲁⲡⲉⲓⲕⲉⲧ, Ep 201 *S* pray for my son ϫⲉⲙ.⸸ ⲧⲟⲛⲡⲉ, C 89 122 *B* sitting ϩⲉⲛⲟⲩⲙⲁ ⲉϥⲙ.⸸ *uncomfortable place*, Miss 4 535 *S* I have heard ⲛⲟⲉ ⲉⲧⲕⲙ.⸸ ⲙⲙⲟⲥ.

Qual ⲥ ⲛ-, ⲉ-, ⲉⲧⲣⲉ- often = δυσ-, *difficult, hard to*: Pro 23 5 *SA*, Mt 23 4 *S* -βάστακτος, BMar 105 *S* -βατος, Aeg 282 *S* -ἔκνιπτος, He 5 11 *SB* -ερμήνευτος, Jer 29 8 *SB* -κολος, 2 Pet 3 16 *SB* -νοητος (cf P 44 119 *S* ⲗⲉⲝⲓⲥ ⲉⲩⲙ.⸸ ⲛⲡⲟⲉⲓ ⲙⲙⲟⲟⲩ), 2 Mac 6 3 *A* -χερής, Is 3 10 *S* -χρηστος (*B* ⲁⲧϣⲁⲩ). Sim ShC 73 6 *S* ⲥⲙ.⸸ ⲉⲧⲣⲉⲩⲣ ⲃⲟⲗ ⲡⲣⲏⲧⲟⲩ, ShC 42 41 *S* enquiring about ⲡⲉⲧⲙ.⸸ ⲛⲁⲩ ⲉⲉⲓⲙⲉ ⲉⲣⲟⲟⲩ, C 89 144 *B* ⲥⲙ.⸸ ⲡⲱϣ ⲉϥⲣⲟⲅⲟⲩϫⲁⲓ, ShC 42 210 *S* his eyes ⲙ.⸸ ⲛⲛⲁⲩ ⲉⲣⲟⲟⲩ *sad to behold* (or ? *hard to see*), ALR '93 524 *S* ⲡⲗⲏⲥⲏ...ⲉⲥⲙ.⸸ ⲛⲛⲁⲩ ⲉⲣⲟⲥ, ShMun 112 *S* disease ⲉϥⲣ ⲛⲕⲉⲙ.⸸ ⲛⲛⲁⲩ ⲉⲣⲟϥ.

ⲥ ⲉ- of painful part: Jer 4 19 *B* ⲧⲁⲡⲉϫⲓ ϯⲙ.⸸ ⲉⲣⲟⲥ κοιλίαν μου ἀλγῶ, Lam 4 6 *S* (*B* ϭⲓ ⲙ.) ἐπόνεσαν χεῖρας; PS 374 *S* shall spend time ⲉⲩⲙⲁϥⲙ. ⲉⲡⲉϥϩⲏⲧ, Phil 2 26 *S* & Su 10 *S*, Ac 2 37 *S* sim;   or as *dat commodi*: MG 25 12 *B* his heart ⲙ. ⲉⲣⲟϥ, ἐλυπεῖτο, BMar 157 *S* my soul ⲙ.⸸ ⲉⲣⲟⲓ ἀλγεῖ.

ⲥ ⲛⲛ-: Mich 550 45 *S* disputing ϩⲱⲥⲧⲉ ⲉⲧⲣⲉⲩⲙ. ⲙⲡⲛⲉϥⲉⲣⲏⲩ, ShA 1 69 *S* ⲉⲣⲉⲙ.⸸ ⲛⲟⲩ ⲛⲙⲙⲁⲥ *what is thy grievance with her?*

—— *SAA²BF*, pl ⲛⲕⲟⲟⲣ *SAA²*, ⲛⲕⲁⲩϩ *B* & sg as pl, nn m, *pain, difficulty, grief*: Ps 68 29 *S* (*B* vb), Lam 1 18 *B* ἄλγος, Ps 37 17 *SB* ἀλγηδών; Ps 12 3 *B* (*S* ⲗⲩⲡⲏ), Sa 4 19 *S* ὀδύνη; Nu 11 15 *S* (var & *B* ⲑⲙⲕⲟ), Is 53 4 *A* (Cl, *S* ⲙⲟⲕⲣⲥ, *B* do), Ac 7 34 *S* (*B* do) κάκωσις; Ro 8 18 *B* (*S* ϩⲓⲥⲉ), Cl 2 1 *A* ⲙⲕⲟⲟϩ, 2 Cor 1 7 *S* ⲛⲕⲟⲟⲣ, Col 1 24 *S* do *B* πάθημα; Job 2 9 *B* (*S* ϩⲓ.), Is 1 5 *B* (*S* ⲧⲕⲁⲥ), Ap 16 10 *SB* πόνος, Va 61 15 *B* ϩⲓⲥⲓ, ⲙ. μόχθος, πόν.; Ez 23 29 *B* (*S* ⲙⲟⲕⲣⲥ), 1 Thes 2 9 *SBF* μόχ.; Ge 31 42 *B* (*S* ϩⲓ.) κόπος; Ro 2 9 *BF* (*S* ⲗⲱϫϩ), 2 Cor 6 4 *B* (*S* do) στενοχωρία; Ac 27 10, 21 *S* (*B* ϣⲱϣ) ὕβρις; Sa 6 13 *S* ⲁⲝⲛⲙ. εὐχερῶς; ib 19

6 *S* do ἀβλαβής; BMar 202 *S* ϧⲓⲧⲙⲡⲁϣⲁⲓ ⲙⲡⲉⲥⲙ.
much grief, BSM 53 *B* feeble ⲉⲑⲃⲉⲟⲩⲙ. ⲡⲥⲱⲙⲁ,
AP 20 *A²* lest he be in ϧⲉⲡⲙⲕⲟⲟϩ (*cf ib* 42 ϧⲉⲡ
ⲙⲕⲁϩ), C 89 72 *B* their life ⲟⲩⲙ. ⲡⲱⲟⲩ = MG 17
326 *S* ⲥⲙⲟⲕϩ ⲡⲁⲩ to live.

ⲁⲧⲙ. *B* adj, *without pain*, with ⲉⲣ: Eph 4 19 (*S*
ⲙⲡⲟⲩⲉϣ ⲙⲟⲕϩⲟⲩ) ἀπαλγεῖν, CaiEuch 548 ⲉϥⲟⲓ ⲛⲁ.
as God ἀπαθής, FR 90, DeV 2 118 sim.

ⲣ ⲙ. *SB*, *be pained, grieved*: Is 19 10 *B* (*S* ⲙ.
ⲉⲡⲣⲏⲧ) πονεῖν; Mt 14 9 *F* (*S* = Gk, *B* ⲙ.) λυπεῖσθαι, Is 51 19 *B* (*S* do) συνλ.; Ps 60 2 *B* (*S* ⲙ.)
ἀκηδιᾶν; Va 58 178 *B* ⲉϥϩⲟⲥⲓ ⲡϧⲏⲧ ⲓⲉ ⲉϥⲟⲓ ⲡⲉⲙ.;
be difficult: ShC 73 6 *S* ⲥⲣ ⲡⲕⲙ....ⲉⲧⲣⲉⲩ-.

† ⲙ. *AA²B* (once *S* Ac 15), *give pain* & vaguely
related meanings: Ex 22 21 *B* (*S* ⲙⲟⲩⲕϩ), Ps 43 3
B (*S* ⲑⲙⲕⲟ), Zeph 1 12 *B* (*A* ⲑⲙ.), Ac 18 10 (*S*
ⲣ ⲡⲉⲑⲟⲟⲩ) κακοῦν; Ez 16 43 *B* (*S* = Gk), 2 Cor 7 8 *B*
(*S* do) λυπ.; He 12 15 *B* (*S* ⲙⲟⲕϩⲥ), AP 7 *A²* ἐνοχλ.;
ROC 17 402 *B* ⲉϥⲡⲁ†. ⲡⲛⲓⲥⲡⲗⲁⲅⲭⲛⲟⲛ πλήσσειν;
ib 408 *B* tears do not †. ⲡⲁϥ καταπνίγειν; Ac 15
24 *S* (*B* ϣⲧⲟⲣϧ) ἀνασκευάζειν; *ib* 22 24 (*S* ϧⲓⲟⲅⲉ)
ἀνετάζειν; Job 33 19 *B* ⲛⲁⲣⲕⲁⲛ; *ib* 27 2 (BM 1247)
πικραίνειν; *ib* 31 16 *B* (*S* ϣⲧⲟⲣⲧⲣ) ἐκτήκειν; El 72
A whoso neglecteth fasts ⲁϥ†. ⲡⲧⲉϥⲯⲩⲭⲏ *hath
hurt*, C 89 125 *B* ⲉϥ†. ⲡⲁϥ with fastings, *ib* 86 111
B ⲁⲕϣⲁⲡ†. ⲙⲡⲁⲡⲡⲁ I will send thee to war, Va
58 187 *B* ⲙⲁ ⲙ. ⲡⲁⲕ ⲉⲑⲣⲉⲕⲉⲣ ⲉⲃⲟⲗ.

ϣⲡ, ϣⲉⲡ ⲙ. *SB*, *receive pain, suffer*: Mt 17 12 *B*
(*S* ϣⲡ ϧⲓⲥⲉ), Ac 1 3 *B* (*S* ⲙⲟⲩ), 1 Pet 5 10 *B* (var
ϭⲓ, *S* ϣⲡ ϩ.) πάσχειν, He 10 34 *B* (*S* do) συμπάσ.;
1 Kg 14 15 *S* πονεῖν, Eccl 10 9 *S* (*F* ⲙ.) διαπον.;
R 1 2 66 *S* Christ ⲁϥϣ., DeV 2 106 *B* Godhead ϣ.
together with manhood, TRit 448 *B* ⲁⲅⲉⲣ ϣⲫⲏⲣ
ⲡϣ. *fellow mourners* (*cf* 469 ϣⲫⲏⲣ ⲡϭⲓ ⲙ.); Miss
4 205 *B* ⲙⲉⲧϣⲫⲏⲣ ⲡⲣⲉϥϣ.

ϭⲓ, ϫⲓ ⲙ. *BF*, *meaning same*: Ac 9 16 *B* (*S* ϣⲡ
ϩ.), 1 Cor 12 26 *B* (*S* ϣⲱⲡⲉ) πάσχ., CaiEuch 548
B ⲁϥϭ. ϫⲉⲡⲉϥⲟⲩⲱϣ ⲡ. ἑκουσίως; Dan 10 12 *B*,
He 11 37 *B* (*S* ⲙ.†) κακοῦν; Lam 4 6 *B* (*S* diff), Lu
13 2 *B* (*S* ϣⲡ ϩ.) πονεῖν; Mt 14 24 *F* (*S* ⲙⲟⲩⲕϩ, *B*
† ⲟⲩⲃⲉ-), MG 25 204 *B* = Z 296 *S* ϧⲓⲥⲉ βασανίζειν;
C 89 120 *B* eyes ϭⲓ ⲙ. from weeping βλάπτειν;
Aeg 47 *B* Lord ⲙⲡⲁⲧⲉϥϭ., JKP 2 144 *F* (Pilate's
wife) ⲁⲓϫⲓ ⲉⲙⲕⲉϩ, HL 112 *B* ⲉⲁϥϭ. ϫⲉⲡⲉϥⲙⲓⲁ
ⲡϥⲉⲡ ⲙⲙⲟⲩ. As nn, *pain, suffering B*: Miss 4
219 ⲡⲓϭ. & miracles πάθος, BM 849 31 deliver them
(travellers) from ϭ. ⲡⲓⲃⲉⲡ. ⲣⲉϥϭⲓ ⲙ. *B*, *sufferer,
apt to suffer*: Ac 26 23 (var ⲣⲉϥϣⲉⲡ ⲙ., *S* diff)
παθητός, Va 57 197 ϣⲫⲏⲣ ⲡⲣ. συμπαθ.

ⲙ. ⲡϧⲏⲧ *S* (oftener than ⲙ.) *AA²BF*, *be pained,
troubled at heart*: 2 Kg 1 26† *SB* ἀλγεῖν; Est 2 21
S, Mk 10 22 *S* (*B* ⲡⲉϥϩ. ⲙ.), *ib* 14 19 *S* (*B* ⲉⲣ ⲙ.
ⲡϧ.) λυπεῖσθαι, Ps 41 6 *B* (*S* ⲗⲩⲡⲉⲓ) περίλυπος εἶναι;

Pro 29 21 *SA*, Is 21 10 *SB*, Lu 2 48 *S* (*B* ⲉⲣ ⲙ.
ⲡϧ.) ὀδύνειν, Si 30 10 *S* συνοδ.; Am 6 6 *A* (*B* ⲙ.†,
v below) πάσχ.; Ac 4 2 *S* (*B* diff) διαπονεῖσθαι; Jo
11 33 *A²* (*S* ⲟⲟⲧ, *A* ϣⲧⲃ̄ⲟ, *B* diff) ἐμβριμᾶσθαι; Ge 34
7 *S* (*B* ⲡⲟⲩϧ. ⲙ.), Ps 34 15 *S* (*B* ⲉⲣ ⲙ. ⲡϧ.), Is 6 5
S (*B* ⲧⲱⲙⲧ) κατανύσσειν; Ps 101 tit *S* (*B* ⲉⲣ ⲙ. ⲡϧ.),
Bar 3 1 *B* ἀκηδιᾶν; Is 13 8 *S* (*B* ⲉⲣ ϧⲏⲃⲓ) ὠδίνειν
stupere; C 86 111 *B* ⲉϥⲙ.† ⲡϧ. ⲥⲁⲡⲓⲥⲁ ⲃ̄ *in difficulty on both sides*, Mor 24 22 *F* ⲁⲩϣⲱⲡⲓ ⲉⲩⲙ.† ⲡϧ.,
BKU 1 22 *S* Isis & Nephthys ⲉⲧⲙⲟⲟⲩⲕϩ (= ⲙⲟⲕϩ)
ⲡϧ. ⲉⲧⲗⲩⲡⲏ (= -ⲉⲓ) ⲡϧ., BM 253 57 *S* ⲡⲉⲧⲙ.† ⲡϧ.
ⲓⲏⲧⲡ ye have let their souls be estranged from you,
C 89 43 *B* ⲉⲟϥⲓ ⲙ. ⲡϧ. ⲉⲧⲯⲩⲭⲏ ⲡⲟⲩⲣⲱⲙⲓ = Miss
4 523 *S* ⲗⲩⲡⲉⲓ βλάπτειν; Ep 507 *S* ⲁⲕⲙ. ⲡϧ. ⲉⲭⲙ-
ⲡⲣⲱⲃ, Mun 46 *S* ⲡⲉⲧⲙ.† ⲡϧⲏⲧ ϩⲁⲣⲁⲩ.

ⲙ. ⲡϧ. *SAA²BF* nn m, *pain, grief*: Ge 3 16 *B*
(*S* = Gk), *ib* 17 *SB*, Is 1 5 (*SF* do), 2 Cor 2 1 *B*
(*S* do) λύπη; Deu 28 60 *SB*, Job 3 7 *B* (*S* ⲙⲟⲕϩⲥ),
Is 38 15 *B* (*S* ϣⲥ ⲡϧⲏⲧ), Hos 5 13 *AB* (*S* ⲙ.) ὀδύνη;
Is 65 14 *B* (*S* do) πόνος, AP 16 *A²* ϩⲓⲟⲩⲙ. ⲡϧ. ἐμ-
πόνως; Ps 118 28 *SB*, Is 61 3 *SB* ἀκηδία; Ps 59
3 *S* (*B* ⲧⲱⲙⲧ) κατάνυξις; *ib* 118 85 *S* (*B* ⲙⲟϭⲏ ⲡ-
ⲥⲁϫⲓ, *cf ib* 54 3) ἀδολεσχία; *ib* 118 53 *SB* ἀθυμία;
FR 86 *S* why are ye in ⲡⲉⲓⲡⲟϭ ⲙ. ⲡϧ. (var ⲱⲕⲙ.)?,
BSM 12 *B* Eve's ⲙ. ⲡϧ. for Abel = BMis 345 *S*
ⲗⲩⲡⲏ, TT 75 *S* ⲡⲉⲙ. ⲡϧ. ⲙⲙⲁⲓ more than one
in exile. As adj: ShZ 472 *S* ⲡⲣⲱⲃ ⲡⲙ. ⲡϧ.

ⲙⲉⲧⲁⲧⲙ. ⲡϧ. *B* nn f, *without grief*: HL 75 ἀλυπία.

ⲉⲣ ⲙ. ⲡϧ. *B*, *be grieved*: Ps 54 3, Is 15 2, 2 Cor
7 9 (all *S* = Gk), Jon 4 9 (*SA* ⲙ. ⲡϧ.) λύπ.; Am 6
6 (Va 66 306, Tatt ⲙ.†, *A* ⲙ. ⲡϧ.) πάσχ.; Ps 4 5
(*S* ⲙ. ⲡϧ.) κατανύσ.; Ez 9 4 κατοδυνᾶν; C 89 189
those that ⲟⲓ ⲡⲙ. ⲡϧ. he encouraged.

† ⲙ. ⲡϧ. *SB*, *grieve, vex*: Ge 4 5 *B* (*A* Cl ⲣ ⲗⲩⲡⲉⲓ), Jer 15 18 *SB*, Eph 4 30 *B* (*S* = Gk) λύπ.; Is
40 29 *B* (*S* † ⲗⲩⲡⲏ) ὀδύνειν; Pro 14 23 *B* ⲉⲧ† ⲙ.
ⲡϧ. ⲁⲛ (*SA* ⲙ. neg) ἀνάλγητος; LMär 30 *S* hath
king † ⲟⲩⲙ. ⲡϧ. ⲡⲁⲕ? (var BIF 14 133 ⲗⲩⲡⲉⲓ),
MIE 2 357 *B* †ⲡⲁ† ⲙ. ⲡϧ. ⲡⲁⲕ ⲁⲛ = BAp 81 *S*
ⲗⲩⲡⲉⲓ.

ϭⲓ ⲙ. ⲡϧ. *B*, *be pained, troubled*: Lam 1 13 ὀδύνειν; Ps 118 158 (*S* ⲃⲱⲗ ⲉⲃⲟⲗ) ἐκτήκειν (*cf* Job 31
16 *B*). *Cf* ⲙⲟⲩⲕϩ.

ⲙⲟⲕϩⲥ, ⲙⲟⲭⲥ (Si) *S*, ⲙⲁⲕϩⲥ *Sf* (Ryl 94) *A* nn
f, *pain, grief*: Eccl 1 18 *S* ἄλγημα; Job 3 20 *S* (*B*
ⲙⲕⲁϩ), Ps 114 3 *S* (*B* ⲙ. ⲡϧⲏⲧ) ὀδύνη; Deu 16 3
S (*B* ⲧⲣⲉⲙⲕⲟ), Is 53 4 *S* (*B* ⲙ.) κάκωσις, 2 Kg 24
16 *S* ⲧⲉⲓⲕⲁⲕⲓⲁ ⲏ ⲧⲉⲓⲙ. as gloss; Job 2 9 *S* (*B* ⲙ.
ⲡϧⲏⲧ), Ez 23 29 *S* (*B* ⲙ.) μόχθος; 2 Cor 1 5 *S* (*B*
do) πάθημα; Hab 1 3 *SA* (*B* do) πόνος; Si 23 13
S (*B* ⲧϧ.) ἐπαγωγή; 2 Kg 22 5 *S* συντριμμός (*cf* Ps
17 4 ⲡⲁⲁⲕⲉ); Pro 19 26 *SA* τιμωρία; PS 279 *S* ⲙ.
ⲡⲓⲙ. & every sickness, ShR 2 3 77 *S* ⲙⲡⲕϫⲓ ⲗⲁⲁⲩ

ⲙ̄. in thy body, EpApp 1 20 S Christ risen divested self of ⲛⲓϭⲓⲥⲉ…ⲙ̄ⲛⲧⲁⲙ̄., BHom 66 S ⲉⲛϣⲁⲛⲧⲁⲁⲛ ⲉⲧⲙ̄. in fasts.

ⲙⲁⲗ ⸗ F v ⲙⲟⲩⲣ.

ⲙⲁⲗⲉ-, ⲙⲉⲗⲉ- F v ⲙⲁⲣⲉ-.

ⲙⲉⲗⲉ S nn m, meaning unknown: Saq 161 Mena son of Theodosius ⲡⲙ̄.

ⲙⲟⲟⲗⲉ S v ⲗⲟⲟⲙⲉ nn.

ⲙⲟⲩⲗⲕ B vb intr, meaning uncertain: P 54 127 ϣⲁⲩⲙ̄. تمتغص (cf? تمغص have colic), BMOr 8775 123 do تمشص.

ⲙⲁⲗⲓⲗ, ⲙⲁⲗⲗⲓⲛ S v ⲙⲁⲛⲓⲛ.

ⲙⲉⲗⲗⲓ F v ⲙⲣⲣⲉ.

ⲙⲟⲩⲗⲱⲗ F nn, meaning unknown, part of plough: BM 708 among iron objects ⲙ̄. ⲛ̄ϩⲃ̄ⲃⲓ. Coptic?

ⲙⲓⲟⲗⲱⲛ, -ⲟⲛ, ⲙⲛⲟⲗⲟⲛ B nn, bitumen extracted from embalmed corpses: K 183 مومیا. V Rec 16 161 (from mnnn, Loret).

ⲙⲁⲗⲧ F v ⲙⲟⲣⲧ.

ⲙⲁⲗⲁⲧ F nn, meaning unknown: PMich 1193 vo]ⲉⲛⲧⲉⲛⲱⲧ (ⲧ)ⲁϣⲁⲡ ⲙ̄. ϩⲓⲡⲟⲩⲱϣ (ⲡ)ⲡⲟⲩⲧⲓ, ib ⲁⲡⲕⲉⲣⲓ ⲧⲏⲣⲉϥ ⲉⲗ ϩⲱⲃ ϩⲓⲙⲁⲗⲁⲧ [.

ⲙⲉⲗⲓⲧ F v ⲙⲉ love.

ⲙⲁⲗⲗⲱⲧ, ⲙⲉⲗ. S nn f, Ryl 244 = μηλωτή or ⲃⲁⲗⲟⲧ (μηλωτή Rec 6 185 = ⲃⲁⲗⲟⲧ BMar 219).

ⲙⲉⲗⲱⲧ SAB, pl ⲙⲉⲗⲁⲧⲉ S (Am) & sg as pl, nn f (once m), ceiling, canopy: Am 8 3 S ⲙ̄ⲙ̄. ⲡ̄ⲕⲏⲣⲉ gloss on ⲙⲉϣϯⲃⲥ φάτνωμα (B Gk om), Zeph 2 14 A (B ⲥⲉⲛϯ) φάτ. limen; Mor 37 49 S ⲧⲙ̄. of cave, ib 65 reaching up to ⲧⲙ̄., ClPr 30 12 S ⲧⲙ̄. divides upper from lower story στέγη; Tri 720 S ⲛⲙ̄. (sic) of various woods سقف, P 44 58 S ⲙ̄ⲙ̄. · ⲡⲟⲩⲉⲣⲥⲟⲓ سقوف = 43 25 sg, K 216 B parts of church ϯⲙ̄. خيمة, قبة, P 55 7 B ϯⲙ̄. جملون; ShA 1 404 S ⲧⲙ̄. ⲉⲧⲕⲏ ⲉⲝⲁⲡⲛⲓ, R 1 3 32 S chamber has gold & silver ϩⲛⲡⲉϥⲉⲭⲏ ⲙ̄ⲡⲉϥⲙ̄., Mor 43 147 S Christ crucified not beneath ⲟⲩⲙ̄. ⲡⲧⲁⲣⲉϥϭⲛ ⲟⲩⲕⲃⲁ but in full heat, ShMIF 23 192 S rich man's belongings ⲛⲉϥⲙ̄. awnings (?). Cf ⲗⲱⲃϣ crown.

ⲙⲉⲗϭ B v ⲉⲓⲁ eye.

ⲙⲟⲗⲟⲭ B nn, planet Mars: K 49 مريخ (? = Ar), ib 528 ⲙⲉⲗⲟⲭ. Cf DM 23 29 Mlḫ a certain star.

ⲙⲟⲟⲗϥ S v ⲗⲟⲟⲙⲉ nn.

ⲙⲗⲁϩϥ A v ⲙⲗⲁϩ.

ⲙⲗⲁϩ, ⲉⲙ. B, ⲙⲗⲉϩ F vb intr, fight, quarrel: Lev 24 10 B (S ⲙⲓϣⲉ), Ac 7 26 BF (S do), ROC 25 272 B ⲁⲅⲉⲙ. ⲛⲉⲙⲡⲓⲣⲱⲙⲓ μάχεσθαι, Ac 23 9 B (S do) διαμάχ., 2 Tim 2 14 B ⲙ. ϩⲉⲛⲡⲥⲁϫⲓ (S ϯⲧⲱⲛ), AM 280 B λογομαχεῖν; Ez 32 27 B rel (S ⲙⲓ.) πολεμικός, C 89 2 B ⲁⲅⲙ. ⲛⲉⲙⲁϥ…ϫⲉ- = MG 17 340 ⲙⲉ تخاصم λυπεῖσθαι περί; C 41 9 B mother ⲉⲙ. ⲛⲉⲙⲛⲓⲙⲁⲛⲉⲥⲱⲟⲩ saying &c = Miss 4 634 S ⲙⲓ.

ⲙⲗⲁϩ S, ⲙⲗⲁϩϥ A, ⲙⲗⲁϩ B, ⲙⲗⲉϩ F, pl ⲙ̄ⲗⲟⲟϩ S & sg as pl, nn m, battle, battle-array, quarrel: Nu 31 27 S (B ⲃⲱⲧⲥ), Is 22 6 S (B ϯ), Zech 14 3 A (S ⲙⲓ., B ⲡⲟⲗⲉⲙⲟⲥ) παράταξις; Tit 3 9 B (S do) μάχη, 1 Tim 6 4 B (S ϯⲧⲱⲛ) λογομαχία, Is 16 4 S (B ⲡⲏ ⲉⲧϯ ⲉϩⲣⲏⲓ ⲉϫⲉⲛ-) συμμαχία; Jth 6 6 S στρατιά; Jos 8 19 S ⲡⲉⲙⲗⲟⲟϩ ἔνεδρα; Job 15 24 S (B diff) ϧⲁⲑⲏ ⲡⲟⲩⲙ̄. πρωτοστράτης; 1 Kg 13 17 S ἀρχή; ib 17 1 S as gloss on ⲡⲁⲣⲉⲙⲃⲟⲗⲏ (cf Ps 26 3 S); Cl 55 4 A συγκλεισμός siege; ShMIF 23 18 S smote enemy ϩⲛⲟⲩⲙ̄., P 131⁵ 33 S ⲁϥⲕⲁⲧⲁⲗⲩ ⲙ̄ⲡⲉⲙ. that serpent had cast amid them, BKU 1 31 (12) S collect ⲙ̄ⲗⲟⲟⲩ troops & arms, Va 59 165 B ⲃⲱⲧⲥ & ⲙ̄., BMis 15 S betwixt ⲡⲙ̄. of Persians & that of Romans, Bor 226 159 S mourning healeth ⲡⲉⲙ. ⲛⲡⲭⲁϫⲉ vulnus.

ⲥⲱⲣ, ⲥⲣ ⲙ. ⲉⲃⲟⲗ SAF, set battle in array: Ex 17 9 S (B ϯ ⲡⲉⲙ-), Nu 21 23 S (B ϯ ⲟⲩⲃⲉ-), 2 Kg 10 8 S ⲥ. ⲙ. ⲉⲃ. ⲉⲡⲡⲟⲗⲉⲙⲟⲥ, Ps 139 2 S (B ⲥⲟⲃϯ ⲛ̄ⲣⲁⲛⲃⲱⲧⲥ), Is 36 5 SF ⲙ. ⲥⲱⲣ ⲉⲃ. (B ⲡⲟⲗ. ϣⲱⲡⲓ), Jer 27 14 S (B ϭⲱⲕ ⲉϩⲣⲏⲓ ⲉϫⲉⲛ-), Joel 2 5 SA (B ⲑⲱⲟⲩϯ ⲉⲡⲡⲟⲗ.) παρατάσσεσθαι; 1 Kg 14 23 S ⲙ. ⲥⲏⲣ ⲉⲃ. διασπείρεσθαι; ShRE 10 163 S ⲛⲉⲧⲥ. ⲙ. ⲉⲃ. ⲟⲩⲃⲏⲩ; rarely without ⲉⲃ.: Nu 1 45 (var c. ⲙ. ⲉⲃ.) S, Ps 26 3 S παρατάσ. ϭⲓⲛⲥ. ⲙ. ⲉⲃ. S nn f, fighting: Leyd 342 20 (sic l).

ⲉⲣ ⲙ. ⲉϫⲉⲛ- B, fight for, on behalf of: Ez 27 27 (S. ⲙⲓ.) πολεμιστής.

ⲣⲉϥⲙ. B, fighter: 1 Tim 3 3 (S ⲣⲉϥⲙⲓ.) (ἄ)μαχος.

ϫⲓ ⲙ. S, fight: P 131¹ 42 angel ⲉⲧϫⲓ ⲙ. fighting for his Lord. ⲣⲉϥϫⲓ ⲙ. S, fighter: Leyd 436 ⲡⲱⲗⲉⲙⲁⲣⲭⲏⲥ ⲉⲧⲛ̄ⲁⲓⲡⲉ ⲡⲣ., BMis 34 ⲙⲁⲧⲟⲓ ϩⲓⲣ.

ⲙⲟⲩⲗϩ, ⲙⲟⲩⲗϩⲧ B v ⲙⲟⲩⲗϩ be hooked into.

ⲙⲗϩ S, ⲙⲉⲗϩ SB v ⲙⲟⲩⲗϩ make salt.

ⲙⲟⲩⲗⲁϩ S nn as pl: Mor 51 35 (bis) ⲙ̄ⲙ̄. ⲛ̄ⲛⲓⲁⲥⲡⲟⲣⲕ, but ? cf ib ⲛ̄ⲣⲁⲙⲟⲩⲗⲁϩⲭ ⲙⲓⲥⲉ ⲛ̄ⲣⲏⲧⲟⲩ, so = ⲙⲟⲩⲗⲁ μούλα (as R 1 3 49, BMis 223 &c), or ⲙⲟⲩⲗⲁⲝ B q v.

ⲙⲟⲩⲗϩ SABF, ⲙⲉⲗϩ- S (Tri), ⲙⲟⲗϩ⸗ SB, ⲙⲁⲗϩ⸗ Sᶠ (Mt 5 13), ⲙⲟⲗϩ† SB, ⲙⲁⲗϩ† SᵃA vb tr, make salt, cf מלח: Lev 2 13 B (S ϫⲱⲕⲣ), Ez 16 4 SB, Mt 5 13 SB ἁλίζειν, Ge 14 3† B (S nn) ἁλυκός,

Jer 17 6† *B* (*S* nn, *v* ShC 73 186), Va 57 276 *B* пкарі
...палмнрос еум.† ἁλμυρός; Ja 3 11† *SAB* пікрос; EpJer 27 *BF* ταριχεύειν; Tri 425 *S* гмоу
...етрегм. песшар لمح; ShC 73 173 *S* cheese
еум.†, *ib* egg есм.†, *ib* 85 herbs sim, Sh(Besa)Z
513 *S* pigeon (?) егоүшт н еум.†, Mor 38 98 *S*
killed swine агмолгоү, C 89 52 *B* olives молгоу
пгмоу, Va 57 211 *B* drug еум.† іе ефепшаүі,
CO 210 *Sᵃ* мхшл етм.†, ShC 42 141 *S* land етм.†
агш етхахш, Bodl(P) a 2 57 *S* recipe Wash it till
it cease еумолаг.   As nn *S*: ShIF 100 еум.†
пое мпм. мпкаг етм.†   In place-name: PCai
67140 Піа Μουλ.

млг *S*, мелг *SB*, мнрг *S* (PMéd 166) nn, *salt*:
Jud 9 45 *S* агкаас пкаг мм. ἔσπειρεν αὐτὴν ἅλας,
Ez 47 11 *B* sim, Ps 106 34 *S* (*B* гмоу) ἁλμη, ShC
73 186 *S* fruitful land птаγаач мм. ملح, ShMIF
23 142 *S* sim, Z 304 *S* our land оүкаг (*sic l*) мм.
ἁλμυρός (*v* KKS 244), Ge 14 3 *S* іа мм., Nu 34
3 *S* (var гмоу) θαλασσα мм. (both *B* етм.†), Ja
3 12 *S* (*l* ппеш м., *B* петм.†), ἁλυκός.   In place-
name: PLond 4 182 Піаг Мηλг (*cf* 162 Піа Мελ).

мелге *S* nn f, *saltness*: Mor 16 22 sea abandons
not тесм. = BMis 192 ceaseth not есм.†, Mor 53
52 land птаγер м. opp fruitful land.   *V* штемелг.

моүлг *SAB*, -лаг, -рг (PMéd) *S*, pl ? моле
B nn m, a *wax*: Ps 57 9 *SB*, Si 24 21 *S*, Mic 1 4
SAB κηρός; AM 310 *B*, C 43 59 *B* boiling wax
&c as torture; in recipes: AZ 23 106 *S* gold heated
till it ер ѳе [поүм]оүлег, Z 628 *S*, PMéd *pass S*;
BMEA 44748 *S* send оүгха мм., BM 1090 *S*
price of пем.;   *candle*: TEuch 2 34 *B* procession
with gongs пемпимолг شموع, C 86 178 *B* гапмолг пемгаплампас.   **b** *honey comb*: 1 Kg
14 27 *S*, Ps 18 10 *S* (*B* пнні), *ib* 117 12 *SB*, Ez
20 6 *SB* κηρίον, Lu 24 42 *B* м. пеѣіш (*S* мелікнріс Z 633, P 131¹ 66, 131³ 1) ἀπὸ μελισσίου κηρίου;
MIF 9 86 *S* bee in a м.

моүлг *S*, мол *B* (*sic* MS), моле *S*, моле
B, молг† *S* vb **a** intr, *be hooked into, twisted into,
attached to*: P 131³ 47 *S* (*cf* Ex 28 8) chains holding breastplate еүм.† пгшс of gold & hyacinth,
Mor 19 63 *S* spear м.† пгнтч = Miss 4 131 *B* ϯ
мaϯ епечсфір, MG 25 373 *B* пачм. пешпе пхе
оүѣ(е)лле whom she led.   м. егоүп *S* meaning same: Ex 25 32 (P 44 104 = 43 88) петм.†
ег. ерос гп (var е-) піепкоіріа (*B* оі мпісмот п-)
ب خصص ἐκτετυπωμένος, GMir 182 chain м.† егоүп
гппечѣс.   **b** tr, *involve, enmesh*: Job 10 11 *SB*
ἐνείρειν, cit C 43 26 *B*, Va 66 295 *B*; TEuch 2 409

B hast captured devil акмолгч ѕептекскккіпн
(σαγήνη) ἀγκιστρεύειν.

моүлг, -ѕт *B* nn as pl, *joints*: K 74 (1 var мо.)
مفاصل, BMOr 8775 137, Ryl 453 336, BM 920 265
-ѕт أوصال.

мелге *S* nn f, meaning uncertain, part (? central hole) of mill-stone: BIF 14 166 (*ie* Mor 45 95)
he took small ѣнт гаат[е] (*sic*) ачтаас егоүп гптм.
мпкот псіке & (thereby) hurled it far off.

мелге *S* saltness   *v* моүлг.

моүлах *B* (*cf* DM 10 31) nn m, *night raven*:
Lev 11 16 صدا, Deu 14 17 بوم, Ps 101 6 (all *S* ѣаі)
νυκτικόραξ; K 168 пім. بوم, Montp 127 صدا, بوم
وهو الكركو.

моүлх, молх, моле, молх† *B* vb **a** intr,
enwrap, embrace: Ps 118 61 (*S* длоүлм), Nah 1
10† (*SA* do) περιπλέκειν; Va 68 175 м. еѣнтү of
thy brother περιπτύσσειν; TRit 264 thy servants
(bridal couple) етагм. ѕептаіоүпоү ѳаі اقترن; Dif 2 44 lips мо. е- those of Saviour التصق; C 43
186 ечмо. ерос embracing her.   м. егоүп,
meaning same: MG 25 7 агм. еѕ. епоүгрноү
περιπτύσ.   **b** tr: Pro 6 10 (*SA* diff) ἐναγκαλίζειν;
Va 68 167 ачм. ппечхіх патшлеѣ е[роч?] περιλαμβ. χερσί, C 86 326 took hands ачмолхоү ечмоүт of lame man.   Refl: Ge 39 12 (*S* амагте)
ἐπισπᾶν; Ac 20 10 (*S* гшлѕ) συμπεριλαμβ.   As
nn m, *embrace*: K 261 пімолх تعانق.   *Cf* амалнх.

моүлѕ *S*, моүлх *B* nn m, *branch*: Ps 79
12 *B* (*S* ϯ оүш) παραφυάς; K 261 *S* пім. غصن,
فرخ; Sh(?)Mor 54 69 *S* true vine птштпе пем.
(*cf* Jo 15 5).

мамe *F*   *v* ма (ϯ ма).

маммнe *A*²   *v* мe truth (наме *s f*).

мme *A*, ммі *O*   *v* еіме.

мемн *F*   *v* мн.

мопe *S*   *v* оүамопe.

моүмe, -мі *SB*   *v* мооү.

ммо *S*   *v* мо imperat.

ммо *A*   *v* маү.

ммо́   *v* п- gen particle.

ммп-, мп- *SAA*², ммоп *B*, ммп-, мe- *F*, with
prep пте (мп-пте =) мпте́, мпт- *SAA*²*F*, мапмтн- *S*, мпта- *S*, ммопт́, ммопта́ (rare) *B*, емпемпмтн- *F* vb, **I** *not to be* (paral throughout оүоп,

be), а οὐκ εἶναι without other vb: Ps 13 5 *SB*, *ib* 134 17 *SB*, Is 59 16 *SB*, Mk 12 32 *SB*; οὐκ alone: Ja 1 17 *SAB*; Br 276 *S* ⲙⲛ ⲗⲁⲁⲩ ⲛⲧⲟⲡⲟⲥ beyond this, PS 131 *S* ⲉⲧⲉⲙⲛ ⲟⲩⲟⲉⲓⲛ ⲛⲣⲏⲧⲥ, BHom 11 *S* ⲙⲛ ⲑⲉ ⲛⲣ ⲅⲁⲗ, C 43 228 *B* ⲙⲙⲟⲛ ⲣⲏⲟⲩ ⲛϧⲏⲧϥ, BM 586 *F* ⲙⲉ ⲗⲱⲁⲓ ⲛⲧⲏⲓ, Mor 24 26 *F* ⲙⲉ ⲱϣⲁⲙ ⲛⲧⲉⲡⲓⲕⲟⲗⲁⲥⲓⲥ ⲃⲱⲗ ⲉⲃⲁⲗ, ST 335 *S* ⲙⲁⲛ (*sic*) ⲣⲱⲙⲉ ⲅⲏⲡⲉⲓⲙⲉ(ϯⲙⲉ), Cai 86 30 *B* epitaph ⲙⲛ ⲁⲧⲙⲟⲩ ⲅⲓⲭⲛⲡⲕⲁϩ; with particip е-: Ps 31 2 *S* (*B* ⲙ.), Cant 6 7 *S*; PS 25 *S* ⲉⲙⲛ ⲡϣⲉ ⲛⲣⲏⲧⲟⲩ, Hos 7 11 *A* ⲉⲙⲛ ⲙⲛⲧⲥⲁⲃⲉ ⲙⲙⲁⲥ, TU 43 11 *A* ⲉⲙⲛ ϭⲁⲙ ⲛⲛⲁⲕ; of past, ⲡⲉ-: Nu 3 4 *S* (*B* ⲛⲉⲙⲙⲟⲛⲧⲉ), Jud 17 6 *S*, Ps 43 12 *S* (*B* ⲙ.), Dan 8 27 *B* (*S* ⲙ.); El 34 *A* ⲛⲉⲙⲛ ⲗⲁⲟⲩⲉ before my eyes, C 43 186 *B* ⲛⲉⲙ. ϩⲓ ⲛⲉⲙⲁⲥⲡⲉ, Ep 459 *S* ⲛⲉⲙⲙⲁⲛ ⲁⲣⲉⲓϭⲉ ⲉⲣⲟⲕⲡⲉ.   Negating another Copt vb: Deu 10 9 *S* (*B* ⲙ. alone), 1 Kg 2 2 *SB*, Job 1 8 *SB*, Pro 14 5 *SA* (*B* ⲙⲡⲁⲣⲉ-), Mt 13 57 *SBF*, Ap 10 6 *S* (*B* ⲛⲡⲉ-); TU 43 19 *A* ⲙⲛ ⲗⲁⲁⲅⲉ ϣⲡⲉ ⲣⲏⲧⲕ, PS 4 *S* ⲙⲛ ⲗⲁⲁⲩ ϣⲟⲟⲡ ⲙⲫⲟⲅⲏ, AM 84 *B* ⲙ. ⲛⲏⲓ ⲧⲟⲓ ⲉⲣⲱⲟⲩ, C 43 191 *B* ⲙ. ⲙⲉⲧⲁⲡⲟⲓⲁ ⲡⲁϣⲱⲡⲓ ⲡⲁϥ; of past, ⲡⲉ-: PS 39 *S* ⲛⲉⲙⲛ ⲗⲁⲁⲩ ⲙⲯⲩⲭⲏ ⲉϣ ⲟⲩⲭⲁⲓ (*cf* Mk 13 20).   Sometimes +ⲁⲛ *BF*: Is 45 18, Jer 16 19; C 43 225 ⲙ. ⲣⲱⲙⲓ ⲛⲧⲏⲓ ⲁⲛ, AM 307 ⲙ. ϭⲓϭⲓ ⲙⲙⲁⲩ ⲁⲛ, C 86 148 ⲙ. ⲟⲩⲡⲁⲛⲧ ϭⲉⲛⲧⲁⲓⲡⲟⲗⲓⲥ ⲁⲛ, Brussels Musée Cinqu E 6346 *F* letter ⲙⲉ(ⲛ) ⲗⲁⲩ ⲅⲓⲭⲱⲓ ⲉⲛ.

b οὐκ with other Gk or Ar vb: Deu 34 6 *S* (ⲙⲛ, var ⲙⲙⲛ) *B* οὐκ οἶδα; Job 6 7 *SB*, Is 29 11 *SB* οὐ δύνασθαι; *ib* 13 16 *B* (*S* ⲛ-...ⲁⲛ) οὐ λογίζεσθαι; Ps 37 15 *SB*, EpJer 72 *BF* (ⲉⲙⲙⲛⲧⲏⲅ), Mt 13 21 *SF* (*B* ⲙⲙⲟⲛⲧⲉ); of past Jo 15 22 *SA²* (*B* ⲛⲉⲙⲙⲟⲛⲧⲉ) οὐκ ἔχειν;   BM 1247 169 *B* rubric ⲙ. ϥⲓ ⲉⲩⲁⲅⲅⲉⲗⲓⲟⲛ لا تقبل Ỳ, Mich Pasc Lect 216 *B* sim ⲙ. ⲱϣ ⲛⲕⲁⲑⲟⲗⲓⲕⲟⲛ لا يقرا Ỳ; with particip е-: Ps 37 14 *S*, Mk 4 17 *S* (both *B* ⲙ.).

c μή: Ps 49 22 *B* (*S* ⲛϥⲧⲙϣⲱⲡⲉ), Is 6 11 *SB*, Lu 8 6 *S* (*B* ⲙⲙⲟⲛⲧⲉ); with particip е-: Ps 7 2 *S*, Mk 8 1 *S* (both *B* ⲙ.), Ro 5 13 *S* (ⲉⲙⲛ, var ⲉⲙⲙⲛ) *B* (ⲙ., var ⲉⲙ.).

d οὐ μή: Sa 3 1 *S*, Jer 30 23 *B*.

e οὐδείς, -έν, mostly ⲙ. +ⲗⲁⲁⲩ, ϩⲓ: Sa 1 8 *SB*, Is 57 1 *SB*, Mk 7 15 *S* (ⲙⲛ, var ⲙⲙⲛ) *B*, Ap 2 17 *S* (*B* ⲙⲡⲉ-), Cl 21 3 *A* ⲙⲛ ⲗ. ϩⲏⲡ ⲁⲣⲁϥ, Va 57 8 *B* ⲙ. ϩⲓ ⲉϥⲟⲓ ⲛⲁⲧⲥⲱⲧⲉⲙ; of past Jer 4 23 *B* (*S* ⲙⲛ).

f Gk privatives (*S* mostly ⲉⲙⲛ): Lev 23 18 *S* (*B* ⲁⲧ-) ἄμωμος, Ez 20 35 *B* (*S* ⲉⲙⲛⲧⲉ-) ἔρημος τῶν, Ps 62 1 *S* (*B* ⲁⲧ-) ἄνυδρος, Mt 12 5 *S* (ⲙⲙⲛ) *B* ἀναίτιος, Ac 16 37 *S* (*B* diff) ἀκατάκριτος.

With ⲙⲙⲟ⳽ of person or thing *not having* (mostly +ϭⲟⲙ, ϣϫⲟⲙ): Ps 52 6 *B* ⲡⲓⲙⲁ ⲉⲧⲉⲙ. ϩⲟϯ ⲙⲙⲟϥ (var ⲛϧⲏⲧⲣ, *S* ⲛ.) οὗ οὐκ ἦν, Is 45 9 *B* ⲙ. ϫⲓⲭ ⲙⲙⲟⲕ (*S* ⲙⲛⲧⲕ ⲧⲟⲟⲧⲕ ⲙⲙⲁⲩ) οὐδὲ ἔχεις;

EpJer 7 *BF* ⲙ. ϣϫⲟⲙ ⲙⲙⲱⲟⲩ οὐ δύνανται, *ib* 63 *B* do (*F* ⲙⲉⲩⲉϣ); PSBA 10 195 *S* ⲉⲙⲛ ⲙⲟⲣⲧ ⲙⲙⲟⲥ (Hilaria), AM 156 *B* ⲙ. ϩⲗⲓ ⲛⲧⲁⲕⲟ ϣⲟⲡ ⲙⲙⲱⲟⲩ, J 74 38 *S* ⲉⲙⲛ ϫⲓ ⲛϭⲟⲛⲥ ϣⲟⲟⲡ ⲙⲙⲟⲓ.

II ⲙⲛⲧⲉ- *SAA²F*, ⲙⲙⲟⲛⲧⲉ- *B* (often +ⲙⲙⲁⲩ), *not to have*: Hos 3 4 *A* +ⲙⲙⲟ(*B* ⲙⲙⲟⲛ) οὐκ εἶναι; Pro 6 7 *SA* (*B* +ⲙⲙⲁⲩ) μὴ ὑπάρχειν dat; Sa 8 16 *S* +ⲙⲙⲁⲩ, Jo 4 44 *SA²* (*B* ⲙⲙⲟⲛ), Ap 20 6 *S* (*B* ⲛⲡⲉ-), Va 57 15 *B* ⲙⲙⲟⲛⲧⲉ ⲟⲩⲁⲓ ⲉⲭⲟⲥ οὐκ ἔχ.; PS 269 *S* ⲙⲛⲧⲉ ⲗⲁⲁⲩ ⲙⲙⲩⲥⲧⲏⲣⲓⲟⲛ ⲕⲱ ⲡⲁϥ ⲉⲃⲟⲗ, ShA 2 338 *S* ⲙⲛⲧⲉ ⲡⲛⲁⲭⲣⲉ ⲕⲉⲣⲱⲃ ⲛⲥⲁⲟⲩⲱⲙ, BMOr 6943 12 *S* ⲙⲁⲛⲧⲉ ⲡⲁⲧⲉⲣⲙⲟⲩⲧⲉ ⲛⲣⲏⲧⲟⲩ *hath not (share) therein*.   With suff: Lev 25 31 *S* (*B* ⲙⲙⲟⲛ), 4 Kg 4 14 *B* +ⲙⲙⲁⲩ, Job 29 12 *S* (*B* do), Ps 54 19 *S* (*B* ϣⲟⲡ ⲁⲛ dat), *ib* 118 165 *S* (*B* ⲙⲙⲟⲛ ...ϣⲟⲡ dat), Jer 29 12 *B* (*S* ⲙⲡⲉ-...ⲁⲛ), Lu 9 13 *S* (*B* ⲙⲙⲟⲛ...ⲛⲧⲟⲧⲉ) οὐκ εἶναι dat or gen; Job 4 11 *SB* +ⲙⲙⲁⲩ, Sa 3 18 *S* do, Mt 22 24 *SB* do, Jo 4 17 *SA²BF* do, 1 Jo 1 8 *B* do (*S* ⲙⲙⲛ...ⲉⲣⲟϥ) οὐκ ἔχ.; Ps 71 12 *SB* οὐκ ὑπάρχ., Lam 5 3 *BF* +ⲙⲙⲁⲩ μὴ ὑπ.; Ps 87 4 *S* ⲙⲛⲧϥ ⲃⲟⲏⲑⲟⲥ (*B* ⲁⲧ-) ἀβοήθητος, Is 29 19 *SB* ⲙⲛⲧⲟⲩ ϩⲉⲗⲡⲓⲥ ἀπηλπισμένος; PS 275 *S* ⲙⲛⲧⲟⲩ ⲕⲱ ⲉⲃⲟⲗ, *ib* 268 *S* ⲙⲛⲡⲓⲟⲩ ⲥⲧⲟ ⲛⲧⲉϥⲯⲩⲭⲏ, TU 43 18 *A* ⲙⲛⲧⲉϥ ⲁⲡⲟⲗⲟⲅⲁ ⲛⲙⲟ, C 43 108 *B* ⲡⲓⲉⲡⲉϩ ⲉⲧⲉⲙⲙⲟⲛⲧⲟⲩ ϫⲱⲕ, Mor 24 24 *F* ⲡⲉⲧⲉⲗⲉⲡⲧⲏⲩ ⲃⲟⲏⲑⲓⲁ ⲙⲙⲉⲩ, Ep 176 *S* ⲙⲁⲛⲧⲏⲓ ⲣⲱⲙⲉ, J 56 11 *S* ⲙⲁⲛⲧⲏⲕ ⲗⲁⲁⲩ ⲛϩⲱⲃ;   with following vb (rare): ShA 1 365 *S* ⲙⲛⲧⲉⲧⲛⲥⲟⲟⲩⲛ ⲙⲙⲟϥ ⲁⲛ (for ⲁⲛ *cf* **I** a s f).   Forms ⲙⲛⲧⲁ⳽ *S*, ⲙⲙⲟⲛⲧⲁ⳽ *B*: Pro 22 27 *S* (*A* diff) ⲉⲙⲛⲧⲁⲕ ⲉⲧⲁⲁⲩ, ShC 42 91 *S* ⲙⲛⲧⲁϥ ⲉⲥⲉⲓ, Sa 9 6 *S* ⲉⲙⲛⲧⲁϥ ⲙⲙⲁⲩ ⲛⲧⲉⲕⲥⲟⲫⲓⲁ, Is 28 2 *B* ⲙⲙⲟⲛⲧⲁϥ ⲥⲕⲉⲡⲏ ⲙⲙⲁⲩ (*S* ⲉⲙⲛ), 2 Cor 6 10 *S* ⲉⲙⲛⲧⲁⲛ ⲗⲁⲁⲩ (*B* ⲙⲙⲟⲛⲧⲉⲛ), Ja 2 14 *S* ⲉⲙⲙⲛⲧⲁϥ ⲙⲙⲁⲩ, *A* ⲉⲙⲡⲉ[ϥ (*B* ⲙⲙⲟⲛ ⲡⲧⲁϥ *v* below); BAp 166 *S* ⲙⲛⲧⲁⲓ ⲛⲙⲙⲁⲕ, BHom 63 *S* ϯ ⲛⲡⲉⲧⲉⲙⲛⲧⲁϥ;   for these *B* sometimes ⲙⲙⲟⲛ ⲛⲧⲉ: Lu 8 18 ⲫⲏ ⲉⲧⲉⲙ. ⲛⲧⲁϥ, MG 25 205 ⲙ. ϩⲱⲃ ⲛⲧⲁϥ, AM 79 ⲙ. ⲓⲱⲧ ⲛⲧⲁⲛ ⲙⲙⲁⲩ.   ⲙⲛⲧⲁ⳽ varies with ⲙⲛⲧ⳽ *S*: Mt 14 17, *ib* 27 4 ⲙⲛⲧⲓ var ⲙⲛⲧⲁⲛ, CA 92 ⲙⲛⲧϥ ϭⲣⲓⲙⲉ var ⲙⲛⲧⲁϥ c., BMis 310 ⲙⲛⲧⲕ ⲗⲁⲁⲩ *ib* ⲙⲛⲧⲁⲕ ⲗ., ShA 2 271 ⲉⲙⲛ ϯ ⲗⲁⲁⲩ ⲛϩⲱⲃ ⲛⲁⲙⲛⲧⲓ, *cf* CO 44, TurO 5 ⲙⲛⲧⲁⲓ ⲗ. ⲛϩ. (*B* C 43 105 ⲙⲙⲟⲛϯ ϩ. ⲛⲉⲙ-).

Double suff *S* (as with ⲟⲩⲟⲛ *qv*): Mt 18 25 ⲉⲙⲛⲧⲁϥⲥⲟⲩ (*B* ⲙⲙⲟⲛⲧⲉϥ) μὴ ἔχοντος; ShA 1 365 ye cannot speak truth ϫⲉⲙⲛⲧⲏⲧⲛ ⲙⲙⲁⲩ, ShC 42 90 ⲕⲁⲛ ⲉⲩⲛⲧⲁⲩ ⲡⲕⲟⲥⲙⲟⲥ ⲧⲏⲣϥ ⲙⲛⲧⲁⲩϥ ⲅⲁⲣ; with intervening ⲥ (Sdff 370, Till 144 B 3): 2 Cor 8 12 ⲡⲉⲧⲉⲙⲛⲧⲁϥⲥϥ (*B* ⲡⲉⲧⲉⲛⲧⲁϥ ⲁⲛ) ὃ οὐκ ἔχει.

As condit in subord clause, *that not, lest* (not literary): ST 243 fail not to come ⲙⲛⲧⲣ ϫⲟⲗⲏ ⲉⲣⲱⲧⲛ, BP 4993 send...ⲙⲛⲧⲉ ⲡⲁⲉⲓⲱⲧ ⲉⲓ & find fault, *ib* 12495 delay not to agree with him ⲙⲛⲧϥ-

ⲥⲧⲟϥ, Hall 79 ask him not ⲙⲡⲧⲩⲕⲱ ⲡⲧⲟⲡⲟⲥ ⲉⲃⲟⲗ, J 76 76 ⲉϣⲱⲡⲉ ⲙⲡⲧⲉ ⲡϣⲏⲣⲉ ⲙⲡⲁⲥⲟⲡ ϭⲛ ϫⲁⲣⲧⲏⲥ (cf 66 76), CO 335 ⲙⲏⲡⲱⲥ ⲙⲡⲧⲛϭⲛ, Hall 74 ⲙⲏⲡⲟⲧⲉ ⲙⲡⲧⲉⲡⲡⲱⲗⲕ ⲉⲃⲟⲗ ; *if not, unless:* COAd 52 S^a ⲙⲡⲧⲉⲧⲉⲣⲟⲓ *if ye meet me not* I will report you, Rec 6 70 S if I deceive thee ⲙⲡⲧⲁⲃⲓⲧⲥ ⲛⲁⲕ (&) *bring her not to thee.* V Ep 1 251.

ⲙⲁ S^a for ? ⲙⲛ-: Ep 459 12 ⲙⲁ ⲡⲟⲃⲉ ⲉⲣⲟⲟⲩⲡⲉ, *ib* 19 ⲙⲁ ϭⲟⲙ (ⲙ)ⲙⲟⲓ, ST 227 ⲙⲙⲁ ⲧⲁϭⲟⲙ ⲁⲛ, *ib* 300 ⲙⲁ ϭⲟⲗ ϣⲁⲡⲉⲙⲁ; for other doubtful instances v Ep 1 249.

III ⲙⲙⲟⲛ, ⲉⲙ. *SB,* ⲙⲟⲛ *S,* ⲙⲙⲁⲛ, ⲙⲁⲛ *AA^{2}F* as particle, *no,* answering question: Ge 18 15 *SB,* Hag 2 13 *SAB,* Mt 5 37 *SB,* 2 Cor 1 19 *SBF* οὐ, οὐχί, Jud 4 20 *S,* Lu 22 58 *S* (*B* ⲁⲡⲟⲕ ⲁⲛⲡⲉ), Jo 18 17 *SA^{2}B* οὐκ εἰμί, Mk 14 29 *S* (*B* ⲁⲡⲟⲕ ⲁⲛ) οὐκ ἐγώ, BMar 117 *S* ⲁϥⲁⲣⲡⲁ ϫⲉⲙ. οὐκ εἰμὶ ἐγώ; as nn m: 2 Cor 1 17 *SB* ⲡⲉⲙ. τὸ οὔ, *ib* 18 ⲟⲩⲙ. οὔ; Job 13 3, 17 10 &c *SB, ib* 2 5, 5 8 *S* (*B* ⲡⲁⲓ ⲣⲏϯ ⲁⲛ) οὐ μήν; ShA 1 418 *S* unclean food, ⲁⲣⲁ ⲡⲣⲓⲣⲡⲉ ? ⲡⲉϫⲁⲓ ϫⲉⲙ., C 86 318 *B* knowest thou me not ? ⲙ., AZ 52 120 *S* = C 89 19 *B* thinkest thou beasts are lords over selves ? ⲙ., Va 63 6 *B* ⲙ. ⲧⲁⲥⲱⲡⲓ = BMis 373 *S* ⲙⲡⲱⲣ, but = BSM 31 *B* ϫⲉⲟⲩⲏⲓ, C 43 113 *B* ⲙ. ⲡⲡⲉⲥϣⲱⲡⲓ, Ep 222 *S* send & fetch bed ⲉϣⲱⲡⲉ ⲕⲟⲩⲁϣⲥ ⲙ. *if thou wilt (not), do not (do so).*

——, *if not, else:* Bel 29 *B,* Jo 14 2 *SA^{2}B* εἰ δὲ μή, 1 Cor 15 2 *F* (*S* ⲉϣϫⲉ, *B* = Gk) εἰ μή; Ro 3 6 *SB,* 1 Cor 15 29 *S* (var & *BF* ⲉⲙ.), *ib* 7 14 *B* (*SF* ⲉϣϫⲉ ⲙⲡⲉ), He 9 26 *S* (*BF* ⲉⲙ.) ἐπεί; PS 39 *S* I have shortened time ⲉⲙ. ⲛⲉⲙⲛ ⲗⲁⲁⲩ ⲙⲯⲩⲭⲏ ⲉϣ ⲟⲩϫⲁⲓⲡⲉ (cf Mk 13 20), *ib* 24 *S* world cannot bear light ⲉⲙ. ⲡⲕⲟⲥⲙⲟⲥ ⲛⲁⲃⲱⲗ ⲉⲃⲟⲗ, Miss 4 136 *B* blaspheme not ⲙ. ϯⲛⲁϫⲱ ⲛϯⲡⲟⲗⲓⲥ under interdict = MR 4 71 *S* ⲟⲛⲧⲱⲥ; BM 344 *S* ⲟⲩⲥⲓⲁϩⲉ ⲙ. ϯⲡⲁⲧⲣⲉⲩⲡⲱⲣⲕ your tongues, Bor 241 148 *S* Adam repented ⲙ. ⲡⲉϥⲛⲁϣⲱⲡⲉ ϩⲛ ⲛⲓⲕⲟⲗⲁⲥⲓⲥ, FPetrie frag Athribis '08 *F* ϯ ⲧⲱϣ ⲉⲧϩⲁⲁⲓ ⲙⲁⲛ ⲡϣⲁⲥϩⲉⲉⲓ, FR 106 *B* except Thou hadst risen ⲙ. ⲡⲁⲅⲛⲁⲙⲟⲩ ⲧⲏⲣⲟⲩⲡⲉ, J 97 10 *S* except we had besought the holy place ⲙ. ⲁϥⲁⲡϩⲁⲗⲓⲥⲕⲉ ; Miss 8 235 *S* except doors had been shut ⲉⲡⲉⲙ. ϣⲁⲣⲉⲙⲙⲛⲓϣϫⲉ ⲟⲩⲟϩⲡⲟⲩ, BMis 480 *S* mother invoked thee at his birth ⲉⲡⲉⲙ. ⲡⲉ both had died, ShA 2 341 *S* they swore to desist ⲉⲙ. ⲉϣϫⲡⲉ ⲁⲩⲟⲡⲟⲩⲡⲉ as heretics, MIF 9 51 *S* except I had found Peter ⲙ. ⲉϣϫⲉ ⲁⲓⲕⲁ ⲧⲟⲟⲧ ⲉⲃⲟⲗ, Gu 87 *S* bring thy son ⲉⲡⲓ (ἐπεί) ⲙ. ⲧⲛⲛⲁϫⲓⲧⲕ to governor; ⲉϣⲱⲡⲉ, ⲉϣⲱⲡ ⲙ. *SB, if not, else:* Ge 30 1 *S* (*B* om ⲉϣ.), Nu 20 18 *S* (*B* do), Jer 11 21 *S* (*B* do), Job 24 25 *S* (*B* ⲓⲥϫⲉ ⲙ.), Lu 10 6 *SB,* Ap 2 16 *S* (var ⲙⲙⲛ, *B* ⲟⲩⲟϩ ⲙ.) εἰ δὲ μή, AM 94 *B* if bribed he admitteth them, ⲉϣ. ⲙ.

ϣⲁϥϩⲓⲧⲟⲩ ⲉⲃⲟⲗ ; ⲉϣϫⲉ, ⲓⲥϫⲉ ⲙ. *SB,* meaning same: Jo 14 11 *S* (*B* om ⲉϣ.) εἰ δὲ μή, C 43 15 *B* this is but magic, ⲓ. ⲙ. ⲙⲁⲣⲉⲡϣⲉⲡϥ ⲉϩⲁⲡⲙⲏⲓⲡⲓ, AM 254 *B* if ye have aught to say..., ⲓ. ϫⲉ ⲙ. be silent, BAp 82 *S* ye know that..., ⲉ. ⲙ. ⲥⲱⲧⲙ ⲉⲡⲉⲅⲣⲁⲫⲏ (cf R 1 1 73 *S* wouldst thou know, ϫⲉ(ⲛ) ⲙⲟⲛ ⲁⲡⲟⲕ ϯⲛⲁⲧⲁⲙⲟⲕ).

—— *SB, or, S* mostly ⲏ ⲙ.: Ex 21 33 *S* ⲏ ⲙ. (*B* ⲓⲉ), Zech 11 12 *S* do (*B* ⲓⲉ ⲙ., *A* ⲏ), Ac 24 20 *S* do (*B* ⲙ.), Aeg 284 *S* each may pray alone ⲏ ⲙ. ⲉⲅⲉⲙⲙⲁⲩ two or three (var TU 26 *ib* 49 ⲉϣⲱⲡⲉ ϫⲉ), Ps 14 1 *B* (*S* ⲏ), 1 Cor 7 11 *B* (*S* do, *F* ⲓⲉ), ClPr 54 36 *S* ⲙ. ⲉⲧⲉⲧⲛⲣⲭⲣⲱϫ ϩⲁⲑⲁⲓⲃⲉⲥ ⲛⲧⲡⲉ = EW 153 *B* ϣⲁⲡ ⲙ. ἤ; Job 6 6 *S* do (*B* ⲓⲉ) εἰ δὲ καί; PS 241 *S* ⲉⲁϥⲱⲥⲕ ⲏ ⲙ. ⲡⲧⲟϥ ⲙⲡϥⲱⲥⲕ, *ib* 70 *S* ⲏ ⲙ. ⲡⲧⲟϥ ⲉⲅⲡⲁϫⲱ ⲙⲡⲉⲕⲣⲁⲛ (paral Ps 87 12 ⲙⲏ ⲉⲅⲛⲁ-), ShA 2 327 *S* have I not admonished ⲏ ⲙ. ⲡⲥⲉⲥⲟⲟⲩⲛ ⲁⲛ ⲛϭⲓ ⲡϩⲗⲗⲟ ? Here ? belongs J 66 48 *S* males shall inherit of males ⲉⲙⲛ (cf Ap 2 16 above) ⲉϣⲱⲡⲉ it be daughter, sister shall inherit, *ib* 76 76 sim.

ϫⲛ, ϫⲓⲛ ⲙ. *SF,* ϣⲁⲡ ⲙ. *B, or not, or else, rather:* Nu 11 23 *SB,* Mk 12 14 *SB,* Lu 20 22 *B* (*S* ϫⲛ ⲟⲩⲕ), *ib* 14 3 *BF* (*S* do), Aeg 243 *S* shall it befall ϫ. ⲙ. ἤ οὔ, 1 Cor 9 6 *SF* (*B* om ⲙ.) ἤ; Br 241 *S* from out the indivisible ϫ. ⲙ., ShRE 11 18 *S* not such as observe canons are misled ϫ. ⲙ. ⲡⲧⲟⲟⲩ through whom speak demons, EW 153 *B* ϣ. ⲙ. ⲉⲣⲉⲧⲉⲡⲭⲣⲱϫ (v above), Mor 56 40 *S* is Decius king to-day ϫ. ⲙ. ⲕⲉⲟⲩⲁⲡⲉ ?, C 43 238 *B* whether yet alive ϣ. ⲙ. ⲁϥⲕⲏⲛ ⲉⲃⲱⲗ ⲉⲃⲟⲗ, SHel 75 *S* shall I tell of tyrant's wrath ϫⲉⲙ. martyr's patience ? BM 331 45 = Mor 18 143 *S* strangers I slew ϫ. ⲙ. ⲡⲉϫⲓⲱⲧⲙⲟⲥ ⲛⲉⲡⲧⲁⲓⲉⲛⲧⲟⲩ.

ⲙⲙⲓⲛ *SAA^{2}BF,* ⲙⲙⲓⲛⲉ *SBF,* ⲙⲙⲓⲛⲟⲩ *S* particle + ⲙⲙⲟ≠, ⲙⲙⲁ≠ emphasizing a preceding pron, mostly poss, *own, proper, self* (Stern 298 3, Till 153 f): Is 14 18 *B* (*S* om), Ez 13 3 *SB,* Mt 13 57 *SF* (*B* om), BHom 4 *S* them that love ⲡⲉⲩ ϫⲟⲉⲓⲥ ⲙ. ⲙⲙⲟⲟⲩ αὐτοῦ, -ῶν, Deu 24 16 *S* (*B* om), Pro 20 2 *SA,* Is 5 21 *F* (*SB* ⲙⲁⲩⲁⲁ≠), Lu 12 57 *S* (*B* do), Cl 55 1 *A* ⲡⲟⲩⲥⲛⲁϥ ⲙ. ⲙⲙⲁⲩ, CaiEuch 486 *B* ⲁⲕϣⲟⲩⲱⲕ ⲉⲃⲟⲗ ⲙ. ⲙⲙⲟⲕ ἑαυτοῦ, -ῶν, Ge 22 16 *S* (*B* om), Ps 41 7 *B* (*S* ⲡⲣⲏⲧ≠), ROC 17 404 *B* ⲡⲁϫⲓϫ ⲙ. ⲙⲙⲟⲓ ἐμαυτοῦ, Ex 32 13 *SB* σεαυτοῦ, Jo 5 30 *SA^2* (*B* om) ἐμός, BHom 24 *S* ⲛⲉⲡⲗⲟⲅⲓⲥⲙⲟⲥ ⲙ. ⲙⲙⲟⲛ ἡμέτερος, CaiEuch 498 *B* ⲧⲉⲕⲥⲙ ⲙ. ⲙⲙⲟⲕ σός; Job 24 12 *S* (*B* om), Pro 11 24 *SA* (*B* do), Lu 10 34 *S* (*B* ⲡⲉⲧⲉⲫⲱ≠ ⲛ-), Ac 1 25 *S* (*B* do), 1 Cor 6 18 *B* (*S* ⲙⲁⲩⲁⲁ≠), Cl 46 7 *A* ⲡⲉⲡⲥⲱⲙⲁ ⲙ. ⲙⲙⲁⲛ ἴδιος; Br 97 *S* ⲁⲕⲧⲁϩⲟⲥ ⲉⲣⲁⲧⲥ ⲉⲥⲕⲱⲧⲉ ⲉⲣⲟⲕ ⲙ. ⲙⲙⲟⲕ, PS 268 *S* ⲥⲟⲟϩⲉ ⲙⲙⲟⲕ

ⲟⲩⲧⲱⲕ ⲛⲙⲙⲁϥ ⲙ. ⲙⲙⲟⲕ, R 1 2 36 S neglecteth
his ⲟⲩⲁⲓ ⲙ. ⲙⲙⲟϥ (var Lammayer 38 ⲙⲁⲅⲁⲁϥ),
PS 320 S bringeth back his tail ⲉϩⲟⲩⲛ ⲉⲣⲱϥ ⲙ. ⲙ-
ⲙⲟϥ, ShA 2 67 S ⲉⲡⲥⲱϣ ⲙⲙⲟⲛ ⲙⲁⲅⲁⲁⲛ ⲉⲡⲥⲱϣ
ⲙⲙⲟⲛ ⲙ. ⲙⲙⲟⲛ, C 43 4 B ⲧϭⲣⲕ ⲙⲙⲟⲓ ⲙ. ⲙⲙⲟⲓ,
ib 13 B fell ⲉⲭⲉⲛⲧⲉϥⲁϥⲉ ⲙ. ⲙⲙⲟϥ, Aeg 30 B ⲡⲁ-
ⲧⲏⲃ ⲙ. ⲙⲙⲟⲓ, Miss 8 33 S ⲛⲉϥⲉⲡⲓⲥⲧⲟⲗⲏ ⲙ. ⲙⲙⲟϥ,
MR 5 117 F ⲧⲁϭⲓⲝ ⲙⲓⲛ ⲙⲁⲓ = Leyd 468 S. ⲙ.
ⲙⲓⲛⲉ var of ⲙⲙⲓⲛ: Job 7 10 S, Mt 19 12 S, Jo 7
18 S, ROC 20 417 S, Ryl 62 S pass, ShRE 11 18
S ⲡⲉⲩϩⲏⲧ ⲙⲙⲓⲛⲉ ⲙⲙⲟⲟⲩ, BMis 19 S ⲛⲉϥϭⲓⲝ ⲙ-
ⲙⲓⲛⲉ ⲙⲙⲟϥ, J 1 24 S ⲧⲉⲡⲓⲛⲧⲉⲥⲓⲥ ⲧⲱⲛ ⲙⲙⲓⲛⲉ ⲙ-
ⲙⲟⲛ, AZ 23 35 F ⲡⲁⲟⲩⲱϣ ⲙⲓⲛⲉ ⲙⲁⲓ, Mor 30 22
F ⲡⲉϥⲥⲛⲁϥ ⲙⲙⲓⲛⲉ ⲙⲙⲁϥ, Ryl 436 B]ⲁⲥⲑⲉⲛⲏⲥ
ⲙⲙⲓⲛⲉ ⲙⲙⲟϥ, RAl 93 B ⲁⲓⲧⲏⲓⲧ ⲙⲙⲓⲛⲓ ⲙⲟⲓ;
ⲙⲙⲓⲛⲟⲩ sim S: ShA 1 233, 239, 271 (same MS,
where also ⲙⲙⲓⲛ), P 129¹⁴ 89 shall eat ⲛⲉⲩⲥⲁⲣⲝ
ⲙⲙⲓⲛⲟⲩ ⲙⲙⲟⲟⲩ, Bor 263 24 gave self for thee
ⲙⲙⲓⲛⲟⲩ ⲙⲙⲟⲕ, FR 70 ⲛⲉϥϭⲓⲝ ⲙⲙⲓⲛⲟⲩⲉ (sic)
ⲙⲙⲟϥ (or ? ⲉⲙⲙⲟϥ).

ⲙⲙⲟⲛ SAB, ⲙⲙⲁⲛ, ⲙⲁⲛ F, verily, for (v FR
203 n, AZ 44 134): Ge 42 16 B ἦ μήν; Deu 23 21
S (B 3 fut) καί; 1 Cor 2 16 BF ⲉⲙ. (S = Gk) γάρ;
Wess 18 91 S ⲙ. ⲁⲛⲧ ⲛⲓⲙ that I should escape?,
RNC 43 S ⲙ. ⲉⲕϣⲁⲛϣⲓⲃⲉ ⲙⲡⲁϣⲁϫⲉ thou shalt
perish ἐπεί, Mor 27 31 F get me fish ⲙ. ϯⲟⲩⲁⲙ
ⲉⲥⲟⲟⲩ ⲉⲛ = BMis 382 S ⲉⲡⲉⲓ = BSM 38 B ⲟⲩⲉⲓ
(l ⲟⲩⲏⲓ); Mic 2 4 A ⲙⲙⲟⲛ (? sic) ⲡⲉⲧⲛⲕⲁⲓⲉ ⲁⲅⲣⲓ-
ⲧⲟⲩ (SB Gk om), Ja 1 22 B (SA Gk om); AM 194
B bring him to me ⲙ. ⲁⲓϯ ⲗⲟⲅⲟⲥ ⲙⲡⲉϥⲓⲱⲧ, KKS
483 S slay me not ⲙ. ⲛⲧⲁⲕⲉⲣ ⲡⲙⲉⲉⲩⲉ surely thou
hast mind of, Cai 42573 1 S charm for preserving
(?) fishing-net ends ⲙⲟⲛ ⲙⲉⲥϯ ⲙⲟⲟⲩ, PMéd 158
S after recipe ⲙⲟⲛ ⲡⲁⲡⲟⲩϥ ⲕⲁⲗⲱⲥ, BKU 1 26 34
F sim ⲙⲁⲛ ⲟⲩⲭⲁⲣⲓⲥⲡⲓ, C 41 9 B take child away
ⲙ. ⲛⲧⲉⲙⲡϣⲁ ⲙⲙⲟϥ ⲁⲛ, Ep 370 S fetch my shoe
ⲙ. ⲁⲓⲣ ⲡⲉϥⲱⲃϣ ⲛⲥⲁϥ, AZ 23 38 F be kind to my
men ⲙⲁⲛ ϣⲁⲧⲛⲉϭⲓ ⲭⲉⲃⲓⲱ (ⲧϫⲉⲃ.) of the good ye
do, WS 90 S send us camels ⲉⲙ. ϣⲁⲡⲉⲓ ⲉϩⲣⲁⲓ,
CMSS 32 F ⲙⲁ(ⲛ) ⲧⲁⲭⲣⲓⲁ ⲗⲁⲩ.

ⲙⲁⲙⲣⲉϩ B nn as pl, name of 20th lunar
station, meaning unknown: K 52 ⲛⲓⲙ. النعائم (the
ostriches, though this can have other meanings).
Or ? ⲙⲁ ⲙⲣⲉϩ.

ⲙⲁⲙⲉϯ B v ⲟⲩⲁⲙⲉϯ.

ⲙⲙⲁⲅⲁⲧⲝ B v ⲙⲁⲅⲁⲝ.

ⲙⲟⲩⲗⲉϣ S nn, permission (?): BAp 80 is this
rule that thou shouldst enter ⲁⲭⲛⲙ. ? = MIE 2
355 B ⲥⲟϭⲛⲓ (cf ib 383 c. = S ⲥⲃⲱ) = P ar 4785
112 ٮربست .

ⲙⲙⲁϩ- v ⲙⲁϩ-.

ⲙⲁⲛ B in ⲡⲁϥⲙⲁⲛ, -ⲑⲙⲁⲛ, -ⲧⲙⲁⲛ pron, a
certain person or thing: Mt 26 18 (varr ⲫⲙⲁⲛ,
ⲡⲁⲑ., S ⲛⲓⲙ), HL 109 ⲡⲁⲫ. ⲡⲣⲱⲙⲓ, MG 25 71 =
ib 205 ⲡⲁϥ. ⲛϩⲉⲗϣⲓⲣⲓ (var ⲡⲁⲧ.) = Z 296 S ⲙⲉϣⲉ
ⲛⲓⲙ, MG 25 216 ⲡⲁϥ. ⲉⲧⲁⲕⲭⲁ ϯⲡⲁⲣⲁⲑⲏⲕⲏ…
ⲛⲑⲱⲛ? = Z 339 S do, Va 57 258 ⲡⲁⲑ. ϭⲭⲉⲙ ϫⲟⲙ,
ib 264 ⲡⲁⲑ. ⲟⲩⲉⲩⲗⲁⲃⲏⲥⲡⲉ ὁ δεῖνα; ib 234 ⲡⲁⲧ.
ⲧⲉϥⲫⲩⲥⲓⲥ ⲛⲁⲡⲉⲥ ⲡⲁⲡⲓⲙ ⲧⲉϥ. ⲧⲁⲕⲛⲟⲩⲧ, C 86 154
go into ⲡⲁⲧ. ⲛϫⲓⲣ; f Va 57 227 ϩⲁⲣⲁ ⲁⲥⲡⲁⲩ
ⲉⲣⲟⲓ ⲛϫⲉ ⲧⲁⲑⲙⲁⲛ ἡ δεῖνα?

ⲙⲁⲛ, ⲙⲁⲡⲉ v ⲙⲟⲟⲛⲉ.

ⲙⲁⲁⲛ F v ⲙⲁⲡⲕ.

ⲙⲛ- SAA²F, ⲛⲛ- S (archaic, Budge BiblTexts,
BerlPsalt, BM 142 mostly, ib 932), ⲙⲉⲛ- O, ⲙⲉ- F,
ⲛⲉⲙ- BFO, ⲛⲙⲙⲁⲍ S, ⲛⲉⲙⲉⲍ Sᵃ (Ryl 396) AA²F,
ⲛⲙⲙⲉⲍ, ⲛⲁⲉ Sᵃ (Ryl 269) A², ⲛⲉⲙⲁⲍ B, ⲙⲉⲡⲉ F
I prep, with: Ge 6 18 SB, Job 12 2 SB, Pro 1 11
SAB, Ap 3 20 SB μετά; Ps 54 18 SB, Sa 14 10 S,
Ac 2 14 SB σύν; Lev 21 16 SB, Job 29 24 SB,
Ps 104 42 SB, He 11 18 SB πρός; Ps 77 60 SB,
ib 130 1 S (B ϩⲉⲛ-), Pro 1 14 SA (B diff) ἐν; Jud
19 24 S, Job 16 13 S (B ϩⲉⲛ-), Ro 9 1 SB, MG 25
233 B ϩⲁⲡⲕⲉⲙⲉⲩⲓ ⲉⲩϯ ⲛⲉⲙⲁϥ, AP 7 A² ⲛϣⲉϫⲉ
ⲛⲙⲙⲉⲥ Gk dat; Jos 9 2 S Gk acc; Jo 8 49 SA²B
ⲟⲩⲟⲛ ⲙⲛ- ἔχειν (cf Mt 11 18 S ϩⲓ-); or where Gk
vb compound: Job 31 17 S ϯ ⲙⲛ- μεταδιδόναι,
Ps 82 8 SB ϭⲓ ⲙⲛ- συμπαραγίνεσθαι, Sa 6 25 S
ⲃⲱⲕ ⲙⲛ- συνοδεύειν; PS 184 S wonders ⲉⲛⲧⲁⲓⲁⲁⲩ ⲛⲙⲙⲁⲥ, ib 5 S, ⲛⲉϥϣⲏϣ ⲙⲡⲡⲉϥⲉⲣⲏⲩ,
ShBM 209 39 S God shall judge ⲉⲣⲱⲧⲛ ⲛⲙⲙⲁⲛ,
El 74 A angels ⲣ ⲡⲉⲓⲑⲉ ⲛⲉⲙⲉϥ ⲉⲛ = ib 114 S ⲉⲣⲟϥ,
AZ 21 100 O ⲉⲥⲉⲡⲕⲁⲧⲕⲉ ⲙⲉⲛ (altered to ⲛⲉⲙ) ⲟⲩⲥⲓⲣⲓ, ib 106 ⲉⲥⲡⲕⲱⲱⲧ ⲙⲉⲛⲕⲉⲟⲩⲉ, ShBIF 23 63 S
ⲡⲟⲩⲛ ⲛⲙⲙⲁϥ ours & his, Va 62 280 B they suffice
ⲙⲙⲟⲓ ⲛⲉⲙⲁⲕ, BM 464 S I would then ⲛⲧⲟϥ ⲛⲙⲙⲁⲕ ⲛⲧⲉⲧⲛⲱϣⲥ (l ⲟϣⲥ), BKU 1 318 S that there
be peace ϩⲛⲧⲉⲧⲛⲙⲛⲧⲉ ⲛⲙⲙⲁⲩ ϩⲓⲟⲩⲥⲟⲡ, C 43 141
B ϯⲛⲁⲕⲏⲛ ⲁⲛ ⲛⲉⲙⲁϥ until &c, AZ 23 38 F ⲉⲗ
ⲡⲉⲧⲛⲁⲡⲟⲩⲃ ⲙⲉⲛⲉⲓⲕⲁⲡⲗⲱⲙⲓ, Kr 129 F ⲁⲡⲁϩⲏⲧ
ⲧⲱⲧ ⲛⲉⲙⲉⲕ, BM 582 (1) F ⲉⲛⲧⲁⲣⲓⲛ (θαρρεῖν) ⲉⲛ-
ⲛⲟⲩⲧⲓ ⲙⲉⲛⲉⲕ, ib 631 F ⲛⲧⲁⲓⲧⲛⲁⲅⲧⲃ ⲙⲉⲛⲏⲃ.

Vbal pref + ⲙⲛ-, no vb SB: Ps 90 15 S (B ⲭⲏ
ⲛⲉⲙ-), Is 43 2 S(B do), Mk 1 13 S(B do) εἶναι μετά,
1 Cor 5 3 B(S ϩⲁⲧⲛ-) παρεῖναι, Pro 8 27 SAB συμπα-
ρεῖναι; AM 246 B ⲉϥⲛⲉⲙϣⲟⲩ ⲛϫⲉ ⲉⲩⲭⲁⲣⲓⲥⲧⲟⲥ.

Rel pref + ⲙⲛ- SB: Sa 11 9 S τότε quæ tunc fuit
(or l-ⲙⲙⲁⲩ); Is 33 8 S (B diff) πρός; Mt 12 30 B
(S ϣⲱⲡⲉ ⲙⲛ-), Ap 17 14 S (B diff) μετά; PS 52 S
thy spirit ⲉⲧⲛⲙⲙⲁⲓ, ShC 73 160 S he that governeth
ⲙⲡⲡⲉⲧⲛⲙⲙⲁϥ (var ⲡⲉⲧⲛϣ ⲛⲙ.), AM 275 B ⲁⲛⲟⲕ
ⲡⲉⲗⲡⲏ ⲉⲑⲃⲉⲗⲏⲓ, P 131³ 83 S sick of ⲡϣⲱⲡⲉ
ⲉⲧⲛⲙⲙⲁϥ = Va 61 93 B ⲉⲧⲭⲏ ϩⲓϫⲱϥ; Nn

N

or pronn+ⲙⲛ- *SBF*: Ps 49 10 *S* (*B* ϫⲏ ⲡⲉⲙ-),
Is 8 8 *SB* μετά; Mk 3 22 *S* (*B* ⲉⲑⲡⲉⲙ-) ἔχειν;
MG 25 240 *B* men ⲉⲣⲉⲡⲓⲏϯ ⲡⲉⲙⲱⲟⲩ δαιμονῶν;
PS 16 *S* ⲁⲡⲟⲛ ⲍⲉ ⲧⲏⲣⲡ ⲡⲙⲙⲁⲕ, TSBA 9 359 *B*
ⲧⲱⲟⲩⲛ ⲁⲡⲟⲕ ⲡⲉⲙⲁⲕ & let us divide, BMEA
10585 *F* wherever ⲡⲛⲟⲩϯ ⲙⲉⲡⲉⲕ *God & thou*
shall call me, AM 305 *B* 𝕏 ⲡⲣⲱⲙⲓ ⲡⲉⲙⲁϥⲡⲉ.

II *SAA²BF* conjunct, *and* (rarely written *s*,
ST 202, 203), **a** joining nns (pronns), *cf* ⲁⲩⲱ **IV**:
Ge 10 16 *SB*, Deu 9 26 *S* (var ⲁⲩⲱ) *B*, Pro 29 31
SA (var ϩⲓ-), Ps 44 8 *SB*, *ib* 106 3 *S* ⲙⲛ-...ⲁⲩⲱ
...ⲙⲛ- (*B* all ⲡⲉⲙ-), Is 60 5 *S* sim (*B* do), Ac 2
9–11 *S* sim (*B* do), Ap 21 8 *S* sim (var & *B* do)
καί;   Gk om: Job 18 14 *S*, Ps 8 9 *SB*, Mic 5
14 *A* (*B* ⲟⲩⲟϩ), Ro 1 29 *B* (*S* ϩⲓ-), Ap 11 3 *SB* (in
numeral), Va 57 15 *B* (often when 2 words used
for 1 Gk) ⲟⲩⲁⲥⲓ ⲡⲉⲙⲟⲩⲕⲟⲩϥⲓⲥⲙⲟⲥ κοῦφον; Sa
18 11 *S* ἅμα; Ps 67 7 *S* (*B* ⲡⲁⲓⲣⲏϯ) ὁμοίως; Sa
18 17 *S* δέ, Ap 7 16 *S* (*B* = Gk) οὐδέ; *ib* 7 3 *SB*
μήτε; Br 122 *S* ϩⲉⲙϣⲉ... ⲙⲡⲟⲩⲁⲣⲕⲉϥⲉⲓⲥ ⲙⲡⲟ-
ⲟⲩ..., *cf ib* 109 sim ϩⲓ-... ϩⲓ-..., PS 107 *S* ⲉⲡⲓⲥⲁ
ⲙⲡⲡⲁⲓ, *ib* 102 *S* ⲡⲙⲉϩⲧⲁⲓⲟⲩ ⲙⲡⲟⲅⲁ, Baouit 1 138
F Martha ⲙⲛ Hanna ⲙⲛ Apa Georgius, C 86 214
B thy mercy ⲉϩⲣⲏⲓ ⲉϫⲱⲛ ⲡⲉⲙⲁⲡⲟⲕ thy servant.
b begins phrase *B*: Mt 2 6 (*S* om), Gal 1 9 (*S*
do), Ac 2 26 (*S* do), C 86 286 ⲡⲉⲙⲡⲓⲕⲉϣⲉ ⲉⲧϣⲟⲩⲱⲟⲩ *even in dry sticks* (*S* BSG 184 om) καί,
TRit 151 ϩⲓⲛⲁ (ἵνα) ⲡⲉⲙⲍⲉⲛⲫⲁⲓ Thy name may
be glorified.   **c** emphasizes foregoing statement *B*: Ex 8 28 Pharaoh hardened hearts ⲡⲉⲙ-
ⲉⲭⲉⲡⲡⲁⲓⲥⲛⲟⲩ ⲟⲛ, Va 57 46 thou seest His body,
yea more ϫⲉⲡⲉⲙⲉⲕⲉⲣ ⲡⲕⲉⲥⲱⲧⲉⲙ His voice καί,
MG 25 101 hast overcome us ⲡⲉⲙϩⲉⲛⲡⲁⲓⲕⲉⲥⲟⲡ,
Cat 77 silent ϩⲱⲥⲧⲉ ⲡⲉⲙⲡⲑⲟϥ ϩⲱϥ governor marvelled.   **d** joins vbal clauses *B*: Deu 6 7 (*S* ⲁⲩⲱ
...ⲡⲙ-...ⲁⲩⲱ ⲡⲙ-), 2 Chr 7 13 ⲁⲓϣⲁⲡⲣⲟⲩϩⲉⲛ...
ⲡⲉⲙⲁⲓϣⲁⲡⲟⲩⲱⲣⲡ, Ps 105 27 (*S* diff) ⲉⲡϫⲓⲡⲣⲁϫ-
ⲧⲟⲩ...ⲡⲉⲙⲉⲣⲱϫⲧ, Va 57 174 ⲉⲑⲣⲉϥϫⲟⲟϥⲉϥ...ⲡⲉⲙ-
ⲉⲑⲣⲉϥⲟⲗⲥ (? *l* -ϥ) ⲉⲡϣⲓⲕ, Ps 78 6 (*S* ⲁⲩⲱ) ϫⲱϣ
ⲙⲡⲉⲕϫⲱⲡⲧ ⲉϫⲉⲡ-...ⲡⲉⲙⲉⲭⲉⲡ-..., 3 Kg 8 46 ⲉϥ-
ⲟⲩⲛⲟⲩ ⲓⲉ ⲡⲉⲙⲉϥϫⲉⲡⲧ (var HCons 258 om ⲓⲉ), Ac
9 28 *B* ⲉϥⲛⲁ ⲉϧⲟⲩⲛ ⲡⲉⲙⲉⲃⲟⲗ καί; C 89 89 em-
powered ⲉϫⲱⲡⲧ ⲉϧⲟⲩⲛ ⲡⲉⲗⲟⲅⲉⲓ ⲉⲃⲟⲗ;   advbial:
Ps 124 2 (*S* om) ⲓⲥϫⲉⲡϯⲡⲟⲩ ⲡⲉⲙϣⲁⲉⲣ, *ib* 15 7
(*S* do) ⲉϯ ϫⲉ ⲡⲉⲙϣⲁ- καί, Va 57 46 ⲡⲁⲓⲣⲏϯ ϫⲉ
ϩⲱϥ ⲡⲉⲙⲡⲕⲉϯⲡⲟⲩ ⲟⲛ.

ⲁⲩⲱ ⲙⲛ- *S*, ⲟⲩⲟϩ ⲡⲉⲙ- *B* (once), *v* ⲁⲩⲱ **IV** c,
meaning same or *and also*: Ge 12 20 (*B* ⲡⲉⲙ-),
Deu 6 7 ⲁⲩⲱ...ⲡⲙ-...ⲁⲩⲱ ⲡⲙ- (*B* all ⲡⲉⲙ-, *ib* 11
19 sim ⲙⲛ- for ⲁⲩⲱ ⲙⲛ-), 1 Kg 14 47 ⲙⲛ-...ⲁⲩⲱ
...ⲁⲩⲱ ⲙⲛ-...ⲙⲛ-...ⲁⲩⲱ ⲙⲛ- καί, C 89 176 *B*
always ⲟⲩⲟϩ ⲡⲉⲙϣⲁⲉⲣ (*cf* Mt 28 20); Br 112 had
received baptism ⲁⲩⲱ ⲙⲡⲧⲉⲥϥⲣⲁⲅⲓⲥ, PS 2, 18, 71,

188 & *pass*, Miss 8 193 hostile to citizens ⲁⲩⲱ ⲙⲛ-
ⲡⲉϥⲉⲓⲱⲧ, PLond 4 435 Jkôw ⲙⲙⲡⲉⲥⲉⲡⲟⲓⲕⲓⲟⲛ ⲁⲩⲱ
ⲙⲛⲡⲉⲥⲡⲉϫⲓⲁⲥ (*cf ib* 465 sim ⲁⲩⲱ om), J 69 15
ϩ(ⲉ)ⲡⲙⲡⲧⲣⲉ...ⲁⲩⲱ ⲙⲡⲟⲩⲣⲉϥⲥϫⲁⲓ.

ⲁⲗⲗⲁ ⲡⲉⲙ- *B*, *but also*: Ex 10 25, Deu 1 28,
Jo 17 20, Ac 26 29, Ro 8 23 (all *S* ⲁⲗⲗⲁ), 1 Jo 5
7 (*S* ⲙⲛ-), CaiEuch 581 peace from heaven ⲁ. ⲡⲉⲙ-
ϯⲕⲉϩⲓⲣⲏⲛⲏ of this life, Va 57 45 not only raiment
ⲁ. ⲡⲉⲙⲡⲉϥⲕⲉⲥⲱⲙⲁ ἀλλὰ καί; Va 59 166 not only
monks of Shiêt ⲁ. ⲡⲉⲙⲡⲧⲉ ϫⲏⲙⲓ ⲧⲏⲣϥ, Cat 44 ⲟⲩ
ⲙⲟⲛⲟⲛ...ⲁ. ⲟⲛ ⲡⲉⲙⲡⲑⲟϥ ⲧⲏⲣϥ.

ⲁϩⲣⲟⲥ ⲙⲛ- *v* ⲁϩⲣⲟⲥ c.

ⲱ ⲡⲉⲙ- *B* exclamatory, *O !* or *and O !*: Va 58
169 ⲱ ⲡⲉⲙⲡⲁⲓⲥⲙⲟⲩ...ⲱ ⲡⲉⲙⲫⲟⲩⲱⲡϩ ⲉⲃⲟⲗ ⲛ-
ⲧⲁⲓⲁⲣⲉⲧⲏ ⲱ̆...ⲱ̆..., MG 25 263 ⲱ ⲡⲉⲙⲡⲁⲓⲧⲱⲟⲩ
ⲉⲑⲟⲩⲁⲃ = Mor 40 37 *S* ⲱ ⲡⲧⲟⲟⲩ, C 41 66 ⲱ ⲡⲉⲙ-
ϯⲙⲉⲧⲁⲧϩⲏⲧ يا لهذا الجهل, Miss 4 169 ⲱ ⲡⲉⲙⲡⲁⲓϩⲟ
ⲙⲙⲟⲩⲓ ⲡⲉⲙⲡⲁⲓϩⲟ ⲛϩⲣⲁⲕⲱⲡ ⲡⲉⲙⲡⲁⲓ- &c, AM 246
ⲱ ⲡⲉⲙⲡⲁϣⲁⲓ...ⲡⲉⲙⲡⲓϣⲫⲏⲣⲓ ⲡⲉⲙⲡⲓⲧⲁⲗϭⲟ, Cat
185 ⲱ ϫⲉⲟⲩⲛ ⲡⲉⲙⲡⲁϣⲁⲓ of the goodness;   not
sim are DeV 2 191 ⲱ ϩⲓⲁ ⲡⲉⲙⲱⲧⲉⲛ, MG 25 69 ⲱ
ϩⲓⲁ ⲡⲉⲙⲡⲁⲓϫⲓⲕⲁⲥⲓⲙⲟⲛ (*cf* often ⲱ ϩⲓⲁ ⲡⲧⲟⲧⲥ).
Here ? belongs C 86 177 muezzin's call ⲫϯ ⲡⲉⲙ-
ⲡⲓⲡⲓϣϯⲡⲉ (الله اكبر) on which *v* Lane *Lexicon* 2587).
V also ca *side* (ⲙⲡⲡⲥⲁ-).

ⲙⲡⲛ- *A* pref neg imperat (vetitive), *v* Till 118 a:
Ps 50 11 ⲙⲡⲛϥⲓⲧϥ (Cl, *SB* ⲙⲡⲣ-), Pro 1 8 ⲙⲡⲕⲟⲩ
(*SB* do), *ib* 3 5 ⲙⲡⲭⲓⲥⲉ (*SB* do), Mic 7 5 ⲙⲡⲛ-
ⲡⲣⲟⲩⲧⲧⲏⲡⲉ...ⲙⲡⲣⲕⲁ ϩⲧⲏⲡⲉ (*SB* both do) μή;
with causat ⲧⲉ- : Pro 2 16 ⲙⲡⲧⲉⲟⲩϣⲁϫⲡⲉ...ⲧⲉϩⲁⲕ
(*S* ⲙⲡⲣⲧⲣⲉ-, *B* ⲙⲡⲉⲛⲟⲣⲉ-), Jon 1 14 ⲙⲡⲣϣⲱⲡⲧ...
ⲙⲡⲧⲛⲙⲟⲩ (*SB* do), El 72 ⲙⲡⲧⲟⲩⲣ ⲡⲗⲁⲛⲁ = Berl
Sitz '25 315 *S* ⲙⲡⲣⲧⲣⲉⲩ-.   *Sᵃ* ?: CO 152 ⲙⲙⲉⲡ-
ϭⲱ, TurMat 37 ⲙⲡⲗⲩⲡⲏ.   *V* Ep 1 249.

ⲙⲛ- vb *v* ⲙⲓⲛ-.

ⲙⲁⲉⲓⲛ *SA²*, ⲙⲉⲉⲓⲡⲉ, ⲙⲉⲓⲛⲉ *A*, ⲙⲏⲓⲛⲓ *B*, ⲙⲏ-
ⲉⲓⲛ, ⲙⲏⲓⲛ *F* nn m, *sign, mark*: Ge 9 12 *SB*, 1 Kg
10 9 *S*, Is 33 23 *SBF*, Jo 11 47 *SB* (*A* = Gk), 2
Cor 12 12 *SBF*, Aeg 267 *S*, Z 338 *S* ⲙⲙ. *features*,
BM 247 5 *S* ⲟⲩⲙ. ⲡⲧⲉⲣⲅⲁⲥⲓⲁ of this world σημεῖον,
Is 30 17 *BF* (*S* ⲗⲁⲩⲟ) σημαία, Lev 13 6 *SB* σημασία,
Ps 59 4 *SB*, Cl 11 2 *A* σημείωσις, Is 5 26 *SB*, AM
272 *B* ⲁⲅⲉⲙⲓ...ⲉⲡⲓⲙ. *signal* σύσσημον, Ac 28 11 *SB*
παράσημον; 1 Chr 16 12 *B*, Ez 12 11 *SB*, Joel 2
30 *SAB* τέρας; Sa 5 11 *S*, Ac 1 3 *SB* τεκμήριον;
Gal 6 17 *S* (*BF* ϣⲱⲗϩ) στίγμα; Deu 33 8 *S* (*B*
ⲡⲏ ⲉⲑⲟⲩⲟⲛϩ ⲉⲃⲟⲗ) δῆλος; Sa·19 8 *S* θαυμαστός;
Lev 13 23 *S* (*B* diff) τηλαύγημα; BMar 105 *S* ⲙ.
ⲛⲥⲫⲟⲥ τύπος; often with ϣⲫⲏⲣⲉ, *wonder* (τέρας or
σημεῖον): Ex 7 3 *AB*, Ps 104 27 *SB*, Mt 24 24 *SB*,
Ac 2 19 *SB*; PS 126 *S* write names ϩⲛⲟⲩⲙ. *in*

cypher, ShA 1 66 *S* self-maimed as ⲙⲡⲁⲣⲁⲇⲓⲅⲙⲁ ⲛ ⲙⲙ. to passers-by, R 1 2 58 *S* ⲛⲙ. of repentance is tears, El 90 *A* Antichrist's transformations ϥⲛⲁϣⲃⲧϥ ϩⲙⲙ. ⲡⲓⲙ, Mor 33 70 *S* ⲙⲙ. of women with child ⲁⲩϣⲱⲡⲉ ϩⲓϫⲱⲓ, DeV 2 190 *B* ⲡⲓⲙ. ⲛⲧⲉ ⲡⲓϫⲓⲛⲉⲣ ⲃⲟⲕⲓ, Wess 15 150 *S* ⲡⲉⲓⲙ. ⲛⲡⲱⲗϩ ⲛⲥⲏⲃⲉ on forehead, Mor 24 11 *F* ⲟⲩⲙ. on foreheads, Z 611 *S* in onyx ϩⲛⲙ. ⲛⲕⲣⲟⲕⲟⲥ, AZ 21 153 *S* pillar ⲉⲣⲉⲟⲩⲙ. ⲛϩⲱⲅⲣⲁⲫⲓⲁ ⲥⲏϩ ⲉⲣⲟⲥ, AM 14 *B* ⲡⲓⲙ. ⲛⲧⲉ ⲡⲓϭⲣⲟ *standard* (?).

ⲁⲧⲙ. *B* adj, *without mark*: Ge 30 42 (*S* ⲟⲩⲱⲃϣ) ἄσημος.

ⲣ, ⲉⲣ ⲙ. *SB*, *be marked*, *remarkable*: Lev 13 25 *S* ⲙⲁ ⲉⲧⲟ ⲙⲙ. (*B* ϯ ⲙⲟⲩⲉ) τὸ αὐγάζον, Ps 4 7 *B* (*S* ⲟⲩⲱⲛϩ ⲉⲃⲟⲗ) σημειοῦσθαι; *indicate*: BM 219 *S* letters of Virgin's name ⲥⲉⲣ ⲙ. ⲉⲛϯⲟⲩ books of Moses. ⲣⲉϥⲉⲓⲣⲉ ⲙⲛⲙ. *S*, *wonder-doer*: Z 315 σημειοφόρος.

ϯ ⲙ. *SAB*, *give sign*, *signify*, c ⲉ- of what is indicated: Pro 6 13 *SA* (*B* = Gk), Ac 11 28 *B* (*S* = Gk) σημαίνειν, Job 14 17 *SB*, ClPr 54 45 *S* river's name ϯ ⲙ. ⲉⲡⲉϥϣⲟⲧ of its torrent ἐπισημ., Ro 16 7 *S* (*B* ⲥⲟⲩⲏⲛ) ἐπίσημος εἶναι, 2 Thes 3 14 *SB* σημειοῦσθαι, Lev 25 10 *B* (*S* diff) σημασία εἶναι; RNC 36 *S* Jezebel ⲥⲉϯ ⲙ. ⲉⲣⲟⲥ unto this day, LeipBer '02 147 *S* ⲥⲉϯ ⲙ. ⲉⲣⲟϥ with finger δακτυλοδεικνύναι, EW 150 *B* place ⲉⲧⲁⲡⲓⲟⲩⲏⲃ ϯ ⲙ. ⲉⲣⲟϥ ὑποδεικν.; Mor 30 40 *F* I will cause thy head & backbone to ϯ ⲙⲏⲓ(ⲛ) ⲉⲡⲕⲱ ⲉϩⲗⲏⲓ ⲙⲡⲁⲧⲟⲡⲟⲥ = BMis 264 *S* ϯ ⲡϣⲱⲗϩ, MS Inst franç Epiph *De Gemm* amethyst ϣⲣⲡ ϯ ⲙ. ⲉⲩⲭⲓⲙⲱⲛ, TstAb 242 *B* ⲉϥϯ ⲙ. ⲉⲣⲟϥ by winking; c ⲛ- of person to whom indicated: Zech 10 8 *B* (*A* ⲧⲟⲩⲛⲟⲩ ⲓⲉⲧ⸗) σημαίνειν, C 89 206 *B* dead man ϯ ⲙ. ⲛⲕⲉⲟⲩⲁⲓ about to die σημεῖον εἶναι, BMar 117 *S* ⲛⲧⲉⲣⲟⲩϯ ⲛⲙ. ⲛⲁϥ ⲙⲡⲥⲁϣ ἐπιδεικν. τὸ σύσσημον; Br 258 *S* ⲛⲧⲟⲕ ⲡⲉⲧϯ ⲙ. ⲉⲣⲟⲟⲩ ⲛⲁⲛ, WTh 45 *S* ϣⲁϥϯ ⲙ. ⲛⲁⲩ...ⲉⲙⲓϣⲉ, Va 67 81′*B* place ⲉⲧⲁⲥϯ ⲙ. ⲛⲏⲓ ⲉⲣⲟϥ, Bor 254 171 *S* ⲁϥϯ ⲙ. ⲙⲡⲣⲣⲟ ϫⲉⲡⲁⲓ ⲡⲁϣⲱⲡⲉ. ⲣⲉϥϯ ⲙ. *S*, *one who points out*, *gives augury*: Mor 50 10 (angel) Azael ⲡⲣ. ϩⲛⲛⲥⲓⲟⲩ. ⲙⲛⲧⲣⲉϥϯ ⲙ. *S*, *making of signs*: Sh(Besa)Bor 206 571 ϩⲉⲛⲙ. with feet (Pro 6 13).

ϫⲓ, ϭⲓ ⲙ. *SB*, *take sign*, *augury*: Ge 30 27 *S* (*B* ϭⲓ ϣⲏⲙ), Lev 19 26 *S* (*B* ⲉⲣ ⲣⲉϥϭⲓ ϣ.), Deu 18 10 (*B* ϭⲓ ϣ., var ϫⲉ ⲙⲧⲁⲩ) οἰωνίζειν; Sa 16 6 *S* σύμβουλον ἔχειν; Ez 21 21 *B* ϭⲓ ⲛⲟⲩⲙ. ϧⲉⲛⲛⲓϩⲏⲡⲁⲣ ἡπατοσκοπεῖσθαι; C 41 66 *B* many ϭⲓ ⲙ. ϧⲉⲛⲧⲥⲙⲏ of birds. As nn: 1 Kg 15 23 *S* οἰώνισμα; Si 31 5 *S* μαντεία. ⲣⲉϥϫⲓ, ϭⲓ ⲙ. *SAB*, *augur*, *diviner*: Zach 3 8 *SA* (*B* ⲣⲉϥϯ ϩⲟϩ⸗ ⲛϩⲁⲛϣⲫⲏⲣⲓ) τερατο κόπος, Aeg 242 *S* οἰωνοσκόπος; ShHTK 1 *S* ⲣⲉϥϫⲓ ϣⲏⲙ ϩⲓⲣ., Mor 29 13 *S* ⲡⲉⲣⲉϥⲙⲟⲩⲧⲉ ⲙⲛⲡⲣ., DeV 164 *B* ⲛⲓⲣ. ϧⲉⲛⲛⲓⲥⲓⲟⲩ. ⲙⲛⲧⲣⲉϥϫⲓ ⲙ. *S*, *augury*, *divination*: Nu 24 1 (*B* ϭⲓ ϣⲏⲙ) οἰωνός, Jer 14 14 *S* (*B* do) οἰώνισμα; Is 2 6 (*B* do) κληδονισμός.

ⲙⲟⲩⲛ *SAA*^{2}*BF*, ⲙⲟⲩⲛⲉ *SO*, ⲙⲟⲩⲛⲓ *B* (BM 626), ⲙⲏⲛ† (oftenest) *SABF*, ⲙⲏⲛⲉ† *S* vb intr, *remain*, *continue*: Ryl 62 6 *S* vices ⲛⲥⲉⲙ. ⲛϩⲏⲧⲟⲩ, BSM 30 *B* lest ⲡⲁⲓϩⲟϫϩⲉϫ ⲙ. ⲉϫⲱⲛ, Hor 78 *O* ⲁⲥⲙⲟⲩⲛⲉ ϧⲛⲟⲩⲛϥⲣⲉⲧⲉ, BM 626 *B* (*v* ⲁϩⲁ) ⲙ. ⲛⲏⲓ ϯⲛⲟⲩ, BG 93 *S* ⲉⲩⲙ.† ⲉⲩⲣⲁϣⲉ (101 ⲉⲩⲙ.† ⲉⲃⲟⲗ ⲉⲩⲣ.), Ps 76 13† *B* (*S* diff) ἀδολεσχεῖν (*cf* below nn); Pro 12 11† *B* (*SA* diff) διατρίβειν; Ac 12 16† *B* (*S* ⲙⲏϥⲗⲟ), 1 Tim 4 16† *B* (*S* ϭⲱ) ἐπιμένειν; Ac 18 5† *B* (*S* ⲙ.† ⲉⲃⲟⲗ) συνέχεσθαι; C 86 282 *B* ⲉϥⲙ.† ⲉϥⲥⲟⲙⲥ ἀτενίζειν, BSM 23 *B* ϥⲙ.† ϥϯ ϩⲟ = BMis 363 *S* ϭⲱ. Qual adverbial, *constantly*, *continuously* *B* (*S* PS, *cf* ⲙ. ⲉⲃⲟⲗ): Ex 29 38, Dan 6 20 ἐνδελεχῶς; 4 Kg 4 9 διὰ παντός (*cf* Ez 46 15); PS 320 *S* ⲛⲥⲉϭⲱ ϩⲙⲡⲉⲩⲛⲟⲃⲉ ⲉϥⲙ., MG 25 205 fire devoureth it ⲉϥⲙ. δι' ὅλου; *ib* 76 ϯⲛⲁϫⲉⲙ ⲡⲉⲕϣⲓⲛⲓ ⲉⲓⲙ., BSM 28 ̅ⲅ ⲛⲣⲟⲙⲡⲓ ⲉⲩⲙ. = BMis 368 *S* ⲛⲥⲁⲡⲉⲩⲉⲣⲏⲩ; ⲉϥⲙ. not in concord with subj: MG 25 215 ⲉⲥⲣⲓⲙⲓ ⲉϥⲙ., *ib* wherefore ⲧⲉⲣⲓⲙⲓ ⲉϥⲙ. πάντοτε?, C 89 135 ⲛⲓⲡⲟⲗⲓⲧⲓⲁ ⲉⲧⲟⲩⲓⲣⲓ ⲙⲙⲱⲟⲩ ⲉϥⲙ.

—— ⲉ- *B*, *remain by*, *wait upon*, *continue in*: He 11 27 (*S* ϭⲱ) καρτερεῖν, PSBA 10 397 ⲡⲁϥⲙ.† ⲉⲡⲓϣⲗⲏⲗ διακαρτ., Mk 3 9, Ac 10 7, Col 4 2 (all *S* = Gk), AM 277 ⲙ. ⲉⲣⲟⲓ προσκαρτ.? Is 30 18 (*S* ϭⲱ) ἐμμένειν; 1 Cor 9 13† *BF* (*S* ϥⲣϥⲉ) παρεδρεύειν; HL 107 woman ϣⲱⲡⲓ ⲉⲥⲙ.† ⲉⲣⲟϥ ἐπικεῖσθαι; Miss 4 150 ϣⲱⲡⲓ ⲉⲕⲙ.† ⲉⲡⲉⲕⲓⲱⲧ = Mor 19 87 *S* ϣⲱⲡⲉ ⲉⲡⲙⲁ ⲙ-, BSM 27 ⲉⲩⲙ.† ⲉⲡⲁⲓϩⲱⲃ = BMis 367 *S* ⲉⲩⲙ.† ⲉⲃⲟⲗ, TstAb 259 prayer & fasts ⲛⲧⲉⲧⲉⲛⲙ. ⲉⲣⲱⲟⲩ, MG 25 351 ⲉϥⲙ.† ⲉϥϯ in prayers.

—— *SB* nn m, *perseverance*, *continuance*: Ps 118 85 *B* (*S* diff) ἀδολεσχία, Eph 6 18 *B* (*S* ϥⲣϥⲉ) καρτέρησις, Gu 78 *S* ⲟⲩⲙ. ϣⲁⲉⲛⲉϩ, MG 25 125 *B* ⲡⲓⲙ. ⲉϥϯ is man's rest. As adj *B*: Ex 29 38 ⲟⲩϭⲗⲓⲗ ⲙⲙ. ἐνδελεχισμός.

ϫⲓⲛⲙ. *B* nn m f, meaning same: MG 25 18 ⲡⲓϫ. ⲉϥϯ φυλακή (PG 65 77), *cf ib* 38 ⲡⲓⲙ., PO 14 349 ⲧⲉⲕϫ., Va 61 8 ⲡⲓϫ. ⲉϯⲡⲣⲟⲥⲉⲩⲭⲏ.

—— ⲉⲃⲟⲗ *SAA*^{2}*BF*, meaning as ⲙⲟⲩⲛ: Eccl 7 16† *S*, Jo 6 27 *SA*^{2} (*B* ϣⲱⲡⲓ) μένειν, 2 Pet 3 4† *S* (*B* do) διαμέν., Nu 23 19 *S* (*B* ⲟϩⲓ), Si 28 6 *S* ἐμμέν., Lev 13 52† *S* (*B* do), Si 30 17† *S* ἔμμονος, Ge 49 26† *S* (*B* ⲙⲁ ⲙⲙⲟⲛⲓ) μόνιμος, Ps 60 7 *S* (*B* ϣⲱⲡⲓ), *ib* 101 27 *B* (*S* ϣⲱⲡⲉ), Aeg 226 *S*, Z 347 *S* = MG 25 219 *B* ⲟϩⲓ ἐπιμέν., Pro 12 7 *SA* (*B* ϣⲱⲡⲓ ⲉⲩⲥⲙⲟⲛⲧ), Phil 1 25 *SF* (*B* ϣⲱⲡⲓ), Z 290 *S*

ⲉⲣϣⲁⲡⲟⲩⲁ ⲙ. ⲉⲃ. ϩⲛⲡⲁⲓ παραμέν., Job 15 31 S
(B ⲥⲙⲟⲡⲧ) ὑπομέν., Ex 18 18 B (S ⲉⲩϣ ϭⲓ) (ἀν)ὑπο-
μόνητος ; Si 41 6 S ἐνδελεχίζειν ; Ac 18 5† S (B om
ⲉⲃ.) συνέχεσθαι ; ib 27 33 S (B ⲥⲟⲙⲥ ⲉⲃ.) προσδοκεῖν ; Lu 23 23 S (B ⲟⲩⲁϩ ⲧⲟⲧ⸗) ἐπικεῖσθαι ; Cl 20
10 A ⲡⲏϭⲛ ⲉⲧⲙ.† ⲉⲃ. ἀέναος, Dan 7 14† S αἰώνιος ;
Miss 4 660 S ⲡⲧⲉⲣⲉϥⲙ. ⲉⲃ. praying, DeV 2 112 B
answered thus so that they should not ⲙ. ⲉⲃ. ⲉⲩ-
ⲋⲟⲧⲋⲉⲧ ⲡⲧⲟⲩ, R 2 1 48 S ⲉϥϣⲁⲛⲥⲱ ⲉϥⲙ.† ⲉⲃ. in
fornication, JTS 8 244 S, Z 263 S sim, BMar 133
S ⲑⲉ ⲉⲧⲙ.† ⲉⲃ. ⲉϥⲏⲩⲅ ϣⲁⲣⲟⲓ, P 130⁴ 84 S ϯⲛⲁ-
ⲙⲟⲩⲛⲉ ⲉⲃ. knocking, P 129²⁰ 122 S all creation
ⲙⲟⲩⲛⲉ ⲉⲃ. in thankfulness, ib ⲟⲩⲣⲓⲙⲉ ⲉϥⲙⲏⲛⲉ
ⲉⲃ., BM 267 S ⲥⲉⲙⲏⲛⲉ ⲉⲃ. in Christ's help, MMA
23 3 702 S ⲡ]ⲣⲱⲃ ⲅⲁⲣ ⲙⲟⲩⲛⲉ ⲉⲃ.　Adverbial
(as ⲙ.†): PS 374 S ϣⲁϥⲙⲕⲁϩ ⲉⲡⲉϥϩⲣⲏⲧ ⲉϥⲙ.† ⲉⲃ.,
ib 38 S ⲉⲣⲉⲡⲉⲩⲧⲟⲡⲟⲥ ⲱⲥⲕ ⲉⲅⲙ.† ⲉⲃ., Br 92 S take
heed ⲙⲡⲣϫⲟⲟⲩ ⲉⲧⲉⲧⲛⲙ.† ⲉⲃ., DeV 2 138 B I arose
ⲁⲓⲙⲟϣⲓ ⲉⲓⲙ.† ⲉⲃ. persevered in walking.

——— ⲉⲃⲟⲗ nn m SB, continuance, perseverance :
Job 25 3 B (S diff) παρέλκυσις ; Jth 4 14 S ἐνδελεχισμός ; J 76 10 S oath by ⲡⲧⲁϩⲣⲟ ⲁⲩⲱ ⲡⲙ. ⲉⲃ.
of rulers (νίκη καὶ διαμονή, cf GFr 359).　Adverbial (oftenest) ϩⲛ-, ϫⲉⲛⲟⲩⲙ. ⲉⲃ., continually :
Nu 28 3 SB ἐνδελεχῶς ; BM 247 S taking thought
for soul ϩ. ἀδιαλείπτως ; ib 181 S beseech Him ϩ.,
CaiEuch 317 B ⲉⲣ ϩⲩⲙⲛⲟⲥ ϩ. διὰ παντός ; BMis
494 S Nile continues ⲉϥⲙⲟⲩϩ ϩ., AM 269 B this
care was upon me ϩ., BM 1132 S letter begins
ϯϣⲓⲛⲉ ϩ. ⲡⲥⲁⲡⲟⲩϫⲁⲓ.

ⲙⲁⲁⲛⲉ A, ⲙⲁⲁⲡⲓ F, ⲙⲁⲡⲟⲩ- S　v ⲙⲟⲟⲛⲉ.

ⲙⲉⲛⲉ- S　v ⲙⲟⲟⲛⲉ.

ⲙⲉⲉⲓⲛⲉ A, ⲙⲏⲓⲛⲓ B　v ⲙⲁⲉⲓⲏ.

ⲙⲏⲛⲉ, ⲙⲏⲏⲡⲉ SA, ⲙⲏⲓⲛⲓ BF, ⲙⲉⲡⲓ F (BKU),
always ⲙⲙⲏⲛⲉ &c, advb, daily, every day : Jer 44
21 B τῆς ἡμέρας, Ac 5 42 SB πᾶσαν ἡμ., Jud 17
10 S εἰς ἡμ., Nu 7 11 SB, Pro 8 21 SAB, Su 8 SB,
Mk 14 49 SBF, 1 Cor 15 31 SBF καθ᾽ ἡμ., Est 3
4 S, Job 1 4 SB, Ps 41 10 SB καθ᾽ ἑκάστην ἡμ.,
Job 7 1 SB ϫⲁⲓⲃⲉⲕⲉ, ⲣⲉⲙⲃ. ⲙⲙ. αὐθημερινός ; El
62 A ϩⲛⲟⲩϩⲟⲩⲛⲟϭⲉ ⲙⲙ., Aeg 262 S let them
meet ⲙⲙ., AM 312 B ⲙⲙⲟⲡ ⲁⲩⲱⲡ ⲙⲙ. ⲁⲡ, CO
32 S ⲛⲧⲁⲣ ϣⲉ ⲛⲥⲟⲡ ⲛϣⲗⲏⲗ ⲙⲙ., BKU 1 26
(8116) F ϣⲁⲛϯ ⲛⲥⲁⲡ ⲉⲙⲉⲡⲓ.　Iterated, ⲙⲙ.
ⲙⲙ. or ⲙⲙ. ⲙⲏⲛⲉ, meaning same : Lev 23 37 B
(S ⲙⲙ.+ ϫⲓⲡⲣⲟⲟⲩ ⲉⲣⲟⲟⲩ) καθ᾽ ἡμ. εἰς ἡμ., Ps 144
1 SB καθ᾽ ἑκάστην ἡμ.; ShA 2 278 S ⲡⲉϩⲟⲟⲩ ⲡⲉϩⲟⲟⲩ ⲁⲩⲱ ⲙⲙ. ⲙⲙ. (sic MS), ShC 42 77 S by day,
by night ⲙⲙ. ⲙⲙ., PMéd 230 S ⲉⲕⲥⲱⲙ ⲡⲥⲱϥ ⲙⲙ.
ⲙⲙ. (cf 155, 222 sim ⲙⲙ.).

ⲙⲓⲛⲉ SAA², ⲙⲉⲓⲛⲉ SA, ⲙⲓⲛⲓ B (rare) F nn f,

a sort, quality, manner : Ge 39 11 S, Job 8 19 S,
Pro 6 14 SA, Jo 4 23 SA², 2 Cor 12 2 S (all B ⲣⲏϯ),
Si 20 14 S (var ϧⲉ), Cl 46 1 A, Aeg 274 S ⲟⲩϯⲙ.
ⲡⲉ τοιοῦτος ; BHom 26 S ⲟⲩⲧⲣⲩϭⲫⲛ ⲡⲧⲉⲓⲙ. τοσοῦτος ; R 1 4 54 S I know not ϫⲉⲟⲩ ⲙⲙ. ⲡⲉ ὅστις ;
3 Kg 3 12 S ὡς, Mk 2 12 S (B ⲇⲟ) οὕτως ; Is 56
11 S (B ⲥⲙⲟⲧ) τὸ ἑαυτοῦ ; BM 320 S ⲧⲙ. ⲙⲡⲁⲛⲣ
κατάστασις ; Si 38 17 S κρίσις, Job 37 16 S (B ϫⲓⲛ-
ⲟⲩⲱϯ ⲉⲃⲟⲗ) διάκρισις ; 1 Cor 14 10 S (B ϣⲗⲟⲗ)
γένος ; Ro 11 24 SF (B = Gk) φύσις ; 3 Kg 3 13 S,
4 Kg 9 11 S Gk om ; ShA 2 152 S ⲧⲙ. of gold &
silver, BHom 137 S ⲧⲙ. of sickness, BMOr 8811
211 S ⲱ ⲟⲩⲙ. ⲡϣⲧⲟⲣⲧⲣ ⲡⲁϣ ⲡⲣⲉ, HCons 2 B ⲍ̄
ⲙⲙ. ⲡⲁϣⲓⲛ, BAp 69 S Solomon learned ⲧⲙ. ⲙⲡ-
ⲡⲁϩⲣⲉ sorts of drugs, cf Mor 22 124 S painted with
ϩⲉⲡⲙ. ⲙⲡⲁϩⲣⲉ divers colours, Bor 294 119 S slay
us ϩⲛⲡⲉⲓⲙ. ⲡϩⲱⲧⲃ, PSBA 32 29 S beryl (πράσινος)
has 8 ⲙ., Va 61 201 B Sarah to Abraham, Whither
wilt take my son ? ⲙⲙⲟⲛ ⲙ. ϩⲓⲱⲧϥ, he is small
ⲋⲉⲛⲡⲉϥⲁϭⲟⲩⲓ, ShA 1 246 S new wine is changed
ⲉⲟⲩⲁϣⲏ ⲙⲙ. both good & bad, Bor 240 53 S ⲟⲩⲛ
ϩⲉⲡⲙ. ⲡⲣⲱⲙⲉ strong in body, MIE 2 374 B ⲟⲩⲟⲛ
ϩⲁⲡⲙ. ⲡⲣⲱⲙⲉ without discernment, ShBMOr 8800
51 S not seemly to say to ⲧⲉⲕⲙ. ⲡⲣ. ϫⲉ- one of thy
dignity, ShMIF 23 98 S poverty is boast ⲡⲧⲉⲡⲙ.
ⲡⲣ., ShMiss 1 402 S ⲱ ⲧⲉⲓⲙ. ⲡⲣ. ⲡⲁϩⲏⲧ, C 89 145
B each one ⲡⲛⲁⲧⲁⲙ. ⲡⲣ., ShMIF 23 33 S ⲡⲧⲕ
ⲟⲩⲧⲓⲙ., P 131¹ 7 S ⲉϥϣⲁⲛⲧⲓϣⲱⲡⲉ ⲡⲟⲩⲧⲉⲓⲙ.　b
pl : ShC 42 94 S ⲡⲉⲓⲙ. ⲡⲣ. ⲡⲁⲣⲅⲟⲥ, ShClPr 24
353 S ⲱ ⲡⲓⲙ. ⲡⲥⲟⲛ ⲁⲩⲱ ⲡⲥⲱⲡⲉ, ShRE 10 159 =
BM 253 58 S ⲡⲁⲡⲓⲙ. ⲡⲣ. ⲉⲧⲙⲙⲁⲩⲡⲉ.　c κατὰ
ⲙ.: ShBor 246 40 S ⲕ. ⲡⲉⲩⲅⲣⲁⲡ ⲁⲩⲱ ⲕ. ⲧⲉⲩⲙ.,
Leyd 324 S ⲡⲕⲟⲩⲓ ⲕ. ⲧⲉϥⲙ. ⲡⲛⲟϭ ⲕ. ⲧⲉϥⲙⲛⲧⲛⲟϭ,
P 131³ 43 S Enôs means God ⲕ. ⲟⲩⲙ. ⲡϭⲓⲛϣⲁϫⲉ
ⲡⲣⲉⲃⲣⲁⲓⲟⲥ.　d ⲕⲉⲙ.: ShR 2 3 22 S ⲙⲡⲧⲛⲟⲉⲓⲕ
...ϩⲉⲛⲕⲉⲙ. ⲡⲭⲱⲣⲓ, Mor 31 86 S corn & ϩⲛⲕⲉⲙ.
ⲡϭⲣⲟⲟϭ (var Miss 4 777 ⲕⲉϭ.).　e ⲙ. ⲡⲙ., ⲡⲓⲃⲉⲛ : PS 334 S like unto it ⲙⲙ. ⲡ. (cf 333 sim
ϩⲛⲡⲥⲙⲟⲧ ⲡ.), ShMIF 23 35 S ⲙ. ⲡ. ⲡⲣⲱⲃ ⲡⲁⲧⲁⲑⲟⲡ,
C 86 285 B pieces of wood ⲙⲙ. ⲡ. (BSG 184 =
Mun 38 S om), BMis 387 S ϩⲟⲓⲧⲉ ⲙⲙ. ⲡ. ⲉⲧⲧⲁⲓⲏⲩ
= BM 305 S ⲙⲙ. ⲙ. ⲡ. = BSM 41 B ⲥⲙⲟⲧ ⲡ.
f iterated, of divers sorts, colours : PS 5 S light was
ⲙⲙ. ⲙ., ib 335 S ⲟⲩⲧⲉ ⲧⲙ. ⲧⲙ. of soul ?, ShMIF
23 183 S ⲡⲕⲟⲗⲁⲥⲓⲥ ⲙⲙ. ⲙ., ShC 73 56 S ⲕⲁⲧⲁ
ⲧⲙ. ⲧⲙ. of sickness, BMis 227 S giraffe ⲟ ⲡⲙ. ⲙ.
= Mor 16 87 ⲧⲟ ⲧⲟ, Va 66 297 B dyed garments
ⲉⲅⲟⲓ ⲙⲙ. ⲙ., ShIF 139 S Joseph's coat ⲉⲥⲟ ⲙⲙ.
ⲙ. (Ge 37 3 ποικίλος).　Cf ⲁϭⲁⲡ s f.

ⲁϣ ⲙⲙ. SA, of what sort : Mt 8 27 S (B ⲣⲏϯ),
Mk 13 1 S ϭⲟⲧ...ⲙ. (B ⲇⲟ ⲇⲟ) ποταπός ; BHom 56
S ⲟⲩⲁϣ ⲙⲙ. ⲡϣⲏⲛ ποῖος (Su 54 τί) ; Is 40 18 S
(B ⲥⲙⲟⲧ) τί ὁμοίωμα ; Cant 5 9 S τί ; TU 43 6 A

Thou wilt come in power ⲛⲉϩ ⲙ̅ⲙ., PS 233 S world existeth ⲡⲁϣ ⲙ̅ⲙ., BIF 13 101 S ϩ(ⲉ)ⲡⲁϣ ⲙ̅ⲙ. ⲡⲉ ϩⲙ̅ⲡⲉⲩⲥⲙⲟⲧ = MG 25 284 B ⲣⲏϯ, Hall 4 S ⲱ ⲭⲉⲟⲩⲁϣ ⲙ̅ⲙ. ⲡⲉ ⲡⲉⲓⲡⲱⲣⲝ. R 1 4 54 S I know not ⲭⲉⲟⲩⲟⲩ ⲙ̅ⲙ. ⲡⲉ.

ⲛ̅ⲧⲉⲓⲙ., *of this sort* (1) = *aforesaid*: PS 334 S ⲡⲉⲯⲩⲭⲏ ⲛ̅ⲧ., ShC 73 23 S ⲡⲉⲓⲉⲟⲟⲩ ⲛ̅ⲧ. (var ⲁⲉⲓⲏⲥ), BAp 93 S ⲧⲉⲓⲧⲁⲝⲓⲥ ⲛ̅ⲧ., TU 43 21 A dost promise us ⲛ̅ⲡⲉⲓ ⲛ̅ϯ., Miss 8 32 S when synod had received ⲧⲉⲓⲥⲁⲕⲣⲁ ⲛ̅ⲧ., J 89 42 S if boy ⲛ̅ⲧ. shall wish &c., *ib* 12 29 S price ⲛ̅ⲧ. ⲁⲥⲉⲓ ⲁⲧⲟⲧ, Kr 3 F ⲛ̅ϭⲓ ⲡⲉⲓⲕⲁⲧⲁⲅⲣⲁⲫⲓ ⲛ̅ⲧ.; KKS 634 S iniquities done ϩⲙ̅ⲡⲉⲓⲉⲣⲡⲉ ⲛ̅ⲧ. *Cf* ⲙⲁⲓⲏ. (2) = *as follows*: BG 56 S that tree ⲟⲩⲧ. ⲡⲉ, RNC 32 S wrote a rescript ⲛ̅ⲧ. τοιοῦτος, Z 320 S related a thing ⲛ̅ⲧ., BMOr 6954 60 S addressed us ϩⲛ̅ϩⲉⲛϣⲁϫⲉ ⲛ̅ⲧ., PLond 5 132 S ⲉⲩϯⲙ. ⲡⲉ ⲡⲉⲩⲣⲱⲃ. BM 247 11 S ϩⲉⲛⲉⲧⲉⲓⲙ. ⲡⲉⲛⲧⲁϫⲟⲟⲥ, SHel 68 S do, *ib* 73 ⲛ̅ⲧⲕ ⲟⲩⲉⲧⲉⲓⲙ. (*l* ? ⲛ̅ⲧⲉⲓⲙ., but *cf* **a** *sf*).

ϭⲙ̅ⲙ. S, *quality*: Br 255 ⲙ̅ⲙⲟⲣⲫⲏ ⲁⲩⲱ ⲛ̅ϭⲓⲙ̅ⲙ. (*sic l*) ⲁⲩⲱ ⲡ̅ϫⲓⲁⲫⲟⲣⲁ.

ⲙⲟⲟⲛⲉ S, ⲙⲁⲁⲛⲉ, ⲙⲁⲛⲉ SᵃA, ⲙⲟⲛⲓ, ⲁⲙⲟⲛⲓ (oftener) B, ⲙⲁⲁⲛⲓ F, ⲙⲉⲛⲉ- S (Is 14 30), ⲙⲁⲛⲟⲩⲍ, -ⲟⲩⲟⲩⲍ SB (Ez 34), ⲙⲉⲡⲛⲏⲧⲍ B (Ps 79), p c ⲙⲁⲛⲉ- &c, v below, vb **I**, *pasture*, *feed*, intr **a** flocks as subj: Job 1 14 SB, Is 30 23 SBF, Mt 8 30 B (S tr) βόσκεσθαι, Is 11 6 SB ⲥⲩⲙⲃ.; Cant 4 5 S, Jer 27 19 S (ShA 2 344) B νέμεσθαι; ShC 42 219 S flocks ⲉⲧⲙ̅. ϩⲛ̅ⲡⲉⲓⲉⲛⲧⲏϭ, FR 14 S ⲉⲥⲙ̅. like doves, C 43 64 B ⲛ̅ⲧⲁⲱⲗⲓ ⲛ̅ⲛⲓϭⲁⲙⲟⲩⲗ ⲉϣⲱⲡ ⲛ̅ⲥⲉⲙ̅., PLich sale of 3 ⲥⲓⲧⲓⲱϭⲉ ϩⲉⲣⲉ & 25 ⲥⲓⲧⲓⲱϭⲉ ⲙⲟⲛⲉ = χόρτ(ου) ἄρου(ραι) γ̅ϛ̅, ⲕⲁⲧⲁⲙᵉ ⲕⲉ. **b** herdsman as subj: 1 Kg 16 11 SB, Pro 22 11 SA, Lu 17 7 SB ποιμαίνειν; Ge 29 7 SB, *ib* 37 16 S (Bor 243 157) B βόσκειν; AM 178 B send him to meadow ⲉⲙ̅.

Tr **a** *feed*, *tend cattle*: Ex 2 16 SAB, Ps 22 1 SB, Mic 7 14 SAB, 1 Cor 9 7 SBF, Ap 7 17 SB (var ⲙⲟϣⲓ ⲛⲉⲙ-, *cf* Ez 19 7 B) ποιμαίν.; Hos 4 16 AB νέμ.; Ge 29 6 S (B om), Is 5 17 SBF, Lu 15 15 SB, MG 25 205 B ⲡⲁⲓⲙ. ⲡⲉⲣⲁϩⲉⲣⲱⲟⲩ βόσκ.; Deu 32 12 S (B ⲙ̅ⲛⲓ), Is 11 6 S (B do) ἄγειν; Tri 697 S sheep ⲛ̅ⲧⲁϥⲙⲁⲛⲏⲩ (= ⲙⲁⲛⲟⲩⲟⲩ) رعى; Bodl(P) b 9 S payment ϩⲁⲡⲃⲉⲕⲉ ⲙ̅. ⲡⲉⲥⲟⲟⲩ, ShA 1 218 S herbs ⲉⲧⲟⲩⲙ̅. ⲙ̅ⲙⲟⲟⲩ (sheep) ⲡ̅ⲣⲏⲧⲟⲩ. **b** *feed on*, *devour*: Sa 19 9 S, Ez 34 18 B (ⲙⲁⲛⲟⲩⲍ) νέμ., Ps 79 14 S (ⲙⲁⲛⲟⲩⲟⲩⲍ) B (ⲙⲉⲡⲛⲏⲧⲍ, Stern 346 ⲙⲟⲛⲏⲧⲍ) κατανέμ.; ShA 2 338 S ⲧⲙ̅ⲕⲁⲁⲩ ⲉⲙ̅. ⲙ̅ⲙⲟⲟⲩ…ⲛⲁⲕⲟⲧⲟⲩ ⲁⲛ ⲉⲙⲁⲛⲟⲩⲟⲩ, ShP 130⁵ 19 S ⲁⲩⲟⲟⲗⲉ ⲙⲁⲛⲟⲩϥ, ShP 131⁴ 88 S ⲡⲉϥⲙⲁⲛⲟⲩⲥ (soul) like wild ass.

ⲙⲁ ⲙ̅ⲙ. SAA²BF, *place of pasture*: Is 32 14 SBF βόσκημα; Si 13 21 S, Jer 23 3 SB, Zeph 2

6 SAB, Jo 10 9 SA²B, 2 Tim 2 17 B (S ⲣ ⲟⲩⲙ̅ ⲟⲙⲉ), Job 20 17 SB ⲙⲁ (*l* ? ⲙ̅ⲁ ⲙ̅ⲙ.) νομή; Ez 34 13 B κατοικία; Mich 550 24 = TT 19 S cattle ⲥⲕⲓⲣⲧⲁ ϩⲛ̅ⲙ̅ⲙ., Va 57 213 B that Antichrist find not ⲟⲩⲙ̅. χώρα.

ⲣⲉϥⲙ̅. SB, *one who pastures*: Job 1 3 SB (*cf* 42 12 B), *ib* 20 17 B (S diff) νομάς; BMar 139 S shepherd ⲡⲣ̅. ⲕⲁⲗⲱⲥ. ⲙ̅ⲛⲧⲣⲉϥⲙ̅. S, *part*, *function of shepherd*: Bor 100 102 S ⲟⲩϣⲁϫⲉ ⲙ̅ⲙ. bringing sheep into fold.

ⲙⲁⲛⲉ SAF, ⲙⲁⲛⲓ B (Am), ⲙⲁⲛ- SB, pl ⲙⲁⲛⲏⲩ S, ⲙⲁⲛⲏⲟⲩ, ⲙⲉⲛⲉⲩ (AM 181) B & sg as pl, nn m (p c of vb), *herdsman*, *pastor*: shepherd, cowherd Ge 4 2 B ⲙⲁⲛⲉⲥⲱⲟⲩ ⲡⲧⲉ ϩⲁⲡⲉⲥⲱⲟⲩ (S ϣⲱⲥ ⲛ̅ⲡⲉⲥⲟⲟⲩ) ποιμὴν προβάτων, *ib* 46 34 B do (S ϣ. ⲙ̅ⲙ.) Gk do, *ib* 13 7 B ⲙⲁⲛⲉⲥⲱⲟⲩ ⲡⲧⲉ ⲡⲓⲧⲉⲃⲛⲱⲟⲩⲓ (S ϣ.) π. κτηνῶν, Jer 40 12 SB, Jo 10 14 B (SAA² ϣ.) π., BMis 378 S = BSM 35 B ⲟⲩⲙⲁⲛⲉⲥ., MIE 2 360 B do = BAp 89 S ϣ., CMSS 72 F ⲙⲁⲛⲉⲙⲁⲥⲓ, Va 57 60 B ⲟⲛⲟⲗⲁⲧⲏⲥ (*l* ⲟⲛⲏⲗ.) ⲙ̅ⲙⲁⲛⲧⲉⲃⲛⲏ; *goatherd* Am 7 14 SAB (ⲙⲁⲛⲓ ⲛ̅ⲃⲁⲉⲙⲡⲓ) αἰπόλος, TT 74 S, C 86 97 B; *swineherd* ShC 73 147 S, BMis 33 S ⲙⲁⲛⲉⲣⲓⲣ; *camelherd* MG 25 215 B καμηλίτης, J 66 82 S, WS 91 S ⲙⲁⲛϭⲁⲙⲟⲩⲗ; *whoremonger* Va 57 250 B devil ⲡⲓⲙⲁⲛⲡⲟⲣⲛⲏ πορνοβοσκός. Pl form: 3 Kg 22 17 S, Ez 34 5 S (B om), Mich 550 24 S ⲙ̅ⲙ. ⲙ̅ⲛ̅ϩⲟⲩⲕⲟⲗⲟⲥ, AM 178 B they got them ⲡ̅ϫⲁⲡⲙ̅. ⲁϩⲁⲙⲟⲛⲓ ⲛ̅ⲛⲓⲧⲉⲃⲛⲱⲟⲩⲓ (*cf ib* 181). As name: Μανεσοῦς (Preisigke).

II SA²BF ⲁⲙⲟⲛⲓ B, ⲙⲉⲛⲉ-, ⲙⲁⲛⲉ-, ⲙⲁⲛⲟⲩ-, ⲙⲁⲛⲟⲟⲩⲧ† S vb **a** intr, *be made fast, so come to land, into port* (of ship): Mk 6 53 SB προσορμίζεσθαι; BM 346 S sailed after him & found him ⲉϥⲙ̅., wind not suffering him ⲉⲥϭⲏⲣ, BSM 88 B ships ⲓⲧⲉ ⲉⲩϣⲏⲣ ⲓⲧⲉ ⲉⲩⲙ̅., LAp 566 F sitting in ship ⲉⲃⲙ̅., Z 230 S ⲛ̅ⲧⲉⲩⲛⲟⲩ ⲛ̅ⲧⲁⲡⲡⲉⲉϥ ⲙ̅., TT 40 S when they reach shore ⲛ̅ⲧⲉⲡϫⲟⲓ ⲙ̅., Va 57 175 B ⲟⲩⲗⲏⲙⲏⲛ (λιμήν), ⲙ̅ⲙ., PRain 4712 S load (cargo) speedily ⲉⲓⲥ ⲡⲉⲭⲏⲩ ⲙⲁⲛⲟⲟⲩⲧ. **c** *e- of place of landing*: Jo 6 21 SA² (B ⲓ ⲉ-) γίνεσθαι ἐπί gen, Ac 27 40 B (var ⲁⲙⲁϩⲓ ⲛ̅-, S diff) κατέχειν εἰς, *ib* 28 12 SB (var ⲛ̅-) κατάγεσθαι εἰς; ShC 73 174 S ⲡⲛⲁⲩ ⲙ̅ⲙ. ⲉⲧⲉⲙⲣⲱ, MG 25 192 B ⲁⲡⲓⲉⲛⲣⲓⲟⲛ ⲙ̅. ⲉⲡⲓⲭⲣⲟ, BIF 15 248 S went toward town ⲁϥⲙⲁⲛⲉ ⲉⲣⲟⲥ, AM 67 B ship ⲙ̅. ⲉⲡⲓϩⲟⲣⲙⲉⲥ (ὅρμος), CDan 86 B ⲙⲁⲣⲉⲛⲙ̅. ⲙ̅ⲡⲁⲓ (*l* ? ⲉⲙⲡⲁⲓ). **c** ⲛ̅- dat: Aeg 266 S ⲙ̅ⲡϣⲁ ⲙ̅ⲙ. ⲙ̅ⲡⲗⲓⲙⲏⲛ, *cf* Ac 27 above. **c** ϩⲁ-: Lu 5 2 SB ἱστάναι παρά acc; **c** ϩⲓ-: Miss 4 238 S ⲁⲩⲙ̅. ϩⲓⲟⲩⲙⲟⲩⲉ till evening; sim **c** ϣⲉⲛ-: C 43 149 B ⲉⲩⲙ̅. ϣⲉⲛⲡⲙⲁ ⲉⲧⲉⲙⲙⲁⲩ 3 days, BSM 134 B sim. **b** tr, *bring to land, into port*: Lu 5 11 S ⲙⲁⲛⲉ- (B ⲥⲱⲕ) κατάγειν; Ac 27 41 S do (B ϩⲉⲣϣ) ἐπικέλλειν; Miss 4 566 S ⲁⲩⲙⲁ-

ⲡⲉ ⲡϫⲟⲓ ⲉⲡⲉⲕⲣⲟ ὁρμᾶν; BMar 26 S sim ⲁⲩⲙⲉⲡⲉ-,
C 89 215 B ⲉⲧⲁϥⲙ. ⲙⲡⲉϥϫⲟⲓ ⲉⲡⲗⲓⲙⲏⲛ = MG 17
311 S ⲁⲡⲁⲛⲧⲁ ⲉⲡⲗ., Bor 256 152 S archangel ⲙⲁⲡⲟⲩ ⲡⲉⲕϫⲟⲓ...ⲉⲡⲉϥⲗⲓⲙⲏⲛ, Mor 41 108 S ⲉⲧⲣⲟⲩ-
ⲙⲁⲡⲟⲩ ⲡϫⲟⲓ ⲉⲡⲉⲕⲣⲟ.

ⲙ. ⲉϩⲟⲩⲛ, ⲉϩ. SB vb **a** intr, *come in to shore, lie
in port* (cf ⲕⲱ ⲉϩ.): BIF 13 101 S = MG 25 282
B ships ⲉⲧⲙ. ⲉϩ., Mor 50 45 S ⲙⲁⲣⲉⲡⲙ. ⲉϩ. (cf
ib ⲙⲁⲣⲉⲡⲕⲁ ⲡϫⲟⲓ ⲉϩ.), C 86 122 B passed 2 days
ⲉⲩⲙ. ⲉϩ., AM 63 B wind fell & ⲁϥⲁⲙ. ⲉϩ. **c** e-
as above: RNC 88 S king ⲙ. ⲉϩ. ⲉⲡⲕⲁⲥⲧⲣⲟⲛ, MG
25 421 S till ship ⲙ. ⲉϩ. ⲉⲣⲁⲕⲟⲧⲉ (cf ib ⲡⲧⲉⲣⲟⲩⲙ.
ⲉϩ.), C 43 213 B ⲉⲧⲁⲩⲁⲙ. ⲉϩ. ⲉϥⲃⲁⲕⲓ. **b** tr,
bring into shore, port: P 129¹⁶ 19 S ⲁⲩⲙⲁⲡⲉ ⲡϫⲟⲓ
ⲉϩ., Va 57 122 B ⲁⲡⲙ. ⲙⲡϫⲟⲓ ⲉϩ. ⲉⲡⲓⲗⲓⲙⲏⲛ.

ⲙⲁ ⲙⲙ. SB, *harbour*: Ge 49 13 S (B ⲉⲙⲃⲣⲱ)
ὅρμος, Ps 45 4 S (error, B ⲟⲩⲟⲓ) ὅρμημα; ib 106
30 SB λιμήν; Ac 27 39 S (B ⳧ⲣⲟ) αἰγιαλός, P 129¹⁴
72 S (v PSBA 24 80) to take no dues ϩⲓⲙⲙ. ⲧⲏⲣⲟⲩ; ⲙⲱⲓⲧ ⲙⲙ. B DeV 2 151. The place-name
ⲧⲙⲟⲟⲛⲉ (P 44 79) = ⲧⲙⲱⲛⲏ (P 43 52) المينة (sic
both), ⲑⲙⲟⲛⲏ (K 209) امينة cannot be connected
with this word. Prob = μονή *station* (as elsewhere:
Amélineau *Géogr.* 258, 261).

ⲙⲟⲟⲛⲉ S, ⲙⲁⲁⲛⲉ A, ⲙⲟⲛⲓ B, ⲙⲁⲁⲛⲓ F nn f,
nurse: Ge 35 8 S (B ⲙⲁⲩ ⲙⲙ.), 1 Thes 2 7 SBF
τροφός; Nu 11 12 SB, 2 Kg 4 4 S τιθηνός; BHom
99 S caused flames to become ⲟⲩⲙ. for 3 Children
ⲙⲁⲗⲱⲃ, BMis 9 S ϩⲙⲙ....ⲉⲧⲣⲉⲩϭⲗⲟⲟⲗⲉ ⲙⲙⲟⲟⲩ, MG 25 61 B cherishing soul ⲙⲫⲣⲏϯ ⲛⲟⲩⲙ.,
C 86 90 B they honour ⲧⲟⲩⲙ. ϫⲉⲁⲥⲉⲛⲟⲩ ⲉⲡϣⲱⲓ,
Wess 18 25 S babe's ⲙ. ⲁⲥⲥⲁⲡⲟⲩϣϥ. As adj,
foster-mother &c: Ge 1c B ⲙⲁⲩ ⲙⲙ., Is 49 23 S
ⲥϩⲓⲙⲉ ⲙⲙ. (B ⲣⲉϥϣⲁⲛϣ) τροφός, Ex 2 7 A ⲥϩ.
ⲙⲙ. (B ⲥϩ. ⲡⲣⲉϥϣ.) τροφεύειν, Ac 13 1 S (B ϣ-
ⲫⲏⲣ ⲛϣ.) σύντροφος; DeV 2 70 B Daniel & ⲧⲉϥⲙⲁⲩ ⲙⲙ. brought to Babylon.

ⲙⲟⲩⲛⲉ (? ⲉⲙⲟⲩⲛⲉ) S nn, meaning unknown:
WS 48 homily on Ex 12 7 ⲡⲟⲩϫϭ[ⲣⲟ] ⲙⲡⲉⲧⲟⲩⲁ
ⲡⲣⲣⲟ with ⲉⲙⲟⲩⲛⲉ as marginal gloss on ⲧⲟⲩⲁ φλία.
Pl of this ? BMEA 10577 S letter about repairing
stone water-conduits & ⲡⲉⲙⲟⲩⲛⲟⲟⲩⲉ ⲉⲧϣⲉⲣϣⲱⲣ
for which bricks needed.

ⲙⲟⲩⲛⲉ (? ⲙⲟⲩⲛ, ? ⲙⲟⲩ) S nn, meaning unknown: Mor 44 39 Jesus's appearance (μορφή) ⲉϥⲟ
ⲛⲙⲟⲩⲛⲉⲥⲟⲩⲟ. Cf ib 26 ⲁⲩⲁⲛ ⲛⲥⲟⲩⲟ & Mor 42·
21 = 43 21 sim, so ? *colour* (ⲁⲩⲁⲛ misread).

ⲙⲟⲩⲛⲉ S, ⲙⲟⲩⲛⲓ B *remain v* ⲙⲟⲩⲛ.

ⲙⲡⲁⲓ B advb, *here, hence, hither* (? for ⲉⲙⲡⲁⲓ):
Ge 45 5, Mt 14 18 (SF ⲉⲡⲉⲓⲙⲁ), CDan 86 ⲙⲁⲣ-
ⲉⲛⲙⲟⲛⲓ (ship) ⲙ. ὧδε; Ex 13 3, Va 57 199 your

departure ⲙ. ἐντεῦθεν; C 86 289 bring them ⲙ.
ἐνταῦθα; Mus 35 28 I hear feet ⲉⲩⲛⲏⲟⲩ ⲙ., MG
25 95 since we came ⲙ. (var ⲉⲡⲁⲓⲙⲁ), C 43 28 ⲡⲁⲩ-
ⲕⲱϯ ⲙⲡⲏ ⲡⲉⲙⲙ. *hither & thither.* ⲉⲙⲡⲁⲓ,
hither: Ge 15 14 (S ⲉⲡⲉⲓⲙⲁ), Is 57 3 (S do), Mt
17 17 (cf Lu 9 41 ⲙ., S do), MG 25 205 I fled &
came ⲉⲙ. ὧδε; Va 57 193 ⲉⲩⲛⲏⲟⲩ ⲉϩⲟⲩⲛ ⲉⲙ.
ἐνταῦθα, Ac 19 37 (S do) ἐνθάδε; C 43 137 bring
thy sister ⲉⲙ. (Mor 48 76 S do); Ex 2 12 ⲉⲙ.
ⲡⲉⲙⲙ. (A ⲁⲡⲓⲥⲁ ⲙⲡⲉⲓ) ὧδε κ. ὧδε, Va 61 218
ⲉϥⲕⲱϯ ⲉⲙⲡⲏ ⲡⲉⲙⲙ. (sic) περιέρχεσθαι, C 43 87
looked ⲉⲙⲡⲏ ⲡⲉⲙⲉⲙ. ⲥⲁⲙⲡⲁⲓ, *on this side*: 1
Kg 23 26 (S ϩⲓⲡⲓⲥⲁ) ἐκ τούτου; Dan 12 5 ἐντεῦθεν; repeated: Ex 17 12 (S ϩⲓⲡⲓⲥⲁ...ϩⲓⲡⲁⲓ), Nu 11
31 (S ⲉⲡⲉⲓⲥⲁ...ⲉⲡⲁⲓ), Jo 19 18 (SA² ⲛⲥⲁⲡⲉⲓⲥⲁ...
ⲛⲥⲁⲡⲁⲓ) ἐντεῦθεν...ἐντ., Ez 40 10 (var & S ⲛⲥⲁⲡⲁⲓ
...ⲛⲥⲁⲡⲁⲓ) ἔνθεν...ἔνθ., C 86 171 soldiers ⲥⲁ(ⲙ)ⲡⲁⲓ
ⲡⲉⲙⲥ. ⲙⲙⲟϥ. ϣⲁⲙⲡⲁⲓ, *to here, so far*: Ge 22
5 (S om), Dan 7 27, AM 268 ϣ. ⲡⲉ ⲡⲓⲥⲁϫⲓ ἕως
ὧδε; Job 38 11 (S ϣⲁⲡⲉⲓⲙⲁ) μέχρι τούτου; C 86
329 ⲁⲙⲟⲩ ϣ. ϩⲁⲙⲡⲁⲓ, *here*: Mk 6 3 (S ⲙⲡⲉⲓⲙⲁ) ὧδε; Va 68 176 ⲡⲓⲥⲏⲡⲓ ϩ. for believers παρεῖναι; Ge 45 8 ϩ. ⲙⲫⲁⲣⲁⲱ Gk om, Va 61 209 hast
brought me the boy ⲉⲡϣⲱⲓ ϩ. *V AZ* 50 102.
Cf ⲙⲡⲏ.

ⲙⲡⲏ B advb, *there, thither*; ⲉⲙⲡⲏ with ⲉⲙⲡⲁⲓ
(ⲙⲡⲁⲓ): MG 25 293 looking ⲉⲙ. ⲡⲉⲙⲙⲡⲁⲓ = BIF
13 108 S ⲉⲡⲓⲥⲁ ⲙⲡⲡⲁⲓ, BSM 112 (ⲉ)ⲛϭⲏⲗ ⲉⲙⲡⲏ
ⲡⲉⲙ(ⲙ)ⲡⲁⲓ. ⲥⲁⲙⲡⲏ, *beyond*: Nu 32 19 (S ⲙⲡ-
ⲛⲥⲁ-), Am 5 27, Mic 4 5 (SA diff) ἐπέκεινα; Is 57
9 (S ⲛⲃⲟⲗ ⲡ-) ὑπέρ; Va 57 207 shalt have requital
for them ⲥ. ἐκεῖ, ib 69 ⲛⲁⲡⲁⲓⲙⲁ...ⲛⲁⲥ. ϩⲁⲙⲡⲏ,
there: Ja 2 3 (S ⲙⲡⲉⲓⲙⲁ) ἐκεῖ; Cat 135 who would
save soul ϩ. will humble it ⲙⲡⲁⲓⲙⲁ, TRit 396 ⲁ-
ⲡⲟⲛ ϩ. ποσ̄ اينا كم short is our time on earth.

ⲙⲁⲛⲑⲱⲣⲡ B *v* ⲧⲱⲣⲡ *sew*.

ⲙⲁⲛⲕ, ⲙⲁⲛⲅ F vb†, distinct ? from following,
meaning unknown: Mor 27 33 ⲁⲙⲟⲓ ⲉⲡⲉⲁⲙⲙ. ⲡⲉ
ⲛⲑⲉ ⲛϣⲟⲣⲡ = BMis 386 S ϩⲁⲙⲟⲓ (ⲉ)ⲛⲉⲡⲉϩⲟⲟⲩ
ⲙⲡⲁϩⲟⲩⲛⲉ ⲉⲣⲉⲧⲛϩⲓⲛ ⲧⲏϣⲛⲉ (ib var ϩ. ⲉⲡⲟⲩⲛ ⲑⲉ
ⲙⲡⲁϩⲟⲩⲛⲉ) = Va 63 13 B ⲁⲙⲟⲓ ⲉⲣⲉⲧⲉⲛⲡⲉ ⲥⲙⲟⲛⲧ
ⲙⲫⲣⲏϯ ⲡϣⲟⲣⲡ = BSM 40 B ⳧ⲁ ϣⲉⲛ ⲙⲫⲟⲟⲩ.
Here ? belong following: BM 580 19 F ϩⲉⲓ ⲧⲓⲙ.
ⲡⲉⲣⲙⲁⲧ ⲉⲡϫⲁⲓ[ⲥ ϣⲏⲡ ?], ib 585 12 F about price
(?) of sheep ϭⲁⲡ ⲡⲉⲧⲙ. ϩⲓⲗⲉⲩ, Kr 22 F ⲉⲃⲙⲁⲁⲛⲕ
as epithet of ⲏⲣⲉⲡ.

ⲙⲟⲩⲛⲕ SBF, ⲙⲟⲩⲛⲅ S, ⲙⲟⲛⲕ B, ⲙⲟⲩⲅ O,
ⲙⲉⲛⲕ- SB (Jer 10 16), ⲙⲟⲛⲕ SB, ⲙⲟⲛⲅ S,
ⲙⲁⲛⲕ A, ⲙⲟⲛⲕⲧ S, -ⲕⲧ B, ⲣ ⲥ ⲙⲁⲛⲕ- B vb tr,
make, form: Ex 26 31 S (B ⲑⲁⲙⲓⲟ), 1 Kg 8 12 S,
Is 29 16 B (S ⲧⲁⲙⲓⲟ) ποιεῖν; Ge 2 7 B, Ps 93 9 B
(S = Gk), Is 29 16 S (B = Gk). Hab 1 12 B (A =

Gk), Ro 9 20 B (S do) πλάσσειν; Sa 14 2 S, EpJer 9
F (B ⲑⲁ.), He 11 7 B (S ⲧⲁ.) κατασκευάζειν; Sa 13
13 S γλύφειν, Ez 41 19 SB διαγλ.; Hos 13 2 A (B
ⲑⲁ.) συντελεῖν; ShZ 637 S ⲉⲙⲁϥⲙ. ⲁⲡ ⲙⲡⲡⲉⲡⲓⲡⲉ
with water but with fire, ShIF 148 S clay ⲡⲉⲡⲧⲁⲅ-
ⲙⲟⲡⲕ̄ϥ ⲡⲟⲩⲃⲏⲃ whereof (snake's) hole formed, ShZ
599 S who wrought at (idol) Isis ϣⲁⲡⲧϥⲙⲟⲡⲥ̄ⲥ,
ShA 1 300 S who build & ⲉⲧⲙ. ϣⲉ, ShC 42 82 S
new boats ⲡⲧⲁⲧⲉⲧⲙⲟⲡⲕⲟⲩ, Mor 37 151 S papyrus
ϣⲁⲩⲙⲟⲡⲥ̄ϥ in Egypt alone, AZ 21 100 O ⲙⲟⲩⲧ ⲡⲉ
ⲡⲟⲩⲃⲧ.   c e- B: Jer l 5 ⲙⲡⲁϥⲙ. ⲉⲣⲟⲕ (S=Gk)
πλάσ. acc.

Qual, be made, formed, worked: Jer 19 1 SB πλάσ-
σεσθαι, EpJer 45 B (F nn) κατασκευάζεσθαι; Nu
31 51 S (B ⲉⲣ ⲣⲱⲃ̄) ⲉⲣⲅάζεσθαι, Ez 27 19 SB ἐργάζεσθαι; ib
41 20 S (B om) διαλύφεσθαι; Jer 10 4 B (l ⲟⲩⲣⲁⲧ
ⲉϥⲙ.†) προσβλητός; Ex 28 8 B διανήθεσθαι; ShIF
184 S material whence ⲧⲉⲥⲕⲏⲛⲏ ⲙ. ⲉⲃⲟⲗ ⲡⲣⲏⲧϥ.

ⲙⲁⲡⲕ- B pc, maker: Ac 19 24 ⲙ. ⲣⲁⲧ (S ⲣⲉϥⲣⲣⲁⲧ)
ἀργυροκόπος; Va 57 47 church ⲟⲩⲙ. ⲣⲁⲙⲡⲟⲩⲃ
ⲁⲓⲡⲡⲉ…ⲟⲩⲙ. ⲉⲣ ϣⲁⲓ χρυσοχοεῖον…πανήγυρις.

ⲣⲉϥⲙⲉⲡⲕ- B, meaning same: Jer 6 29 ⲣ. ⲣⲁⲧ
ἀργυροκόπος.

—— SB nn m, thing made, formation, fashion:
Lev 8 8 S (B ⲑⲁⲙⲓⲟ) ποίησις, Is 29 16 B (S ⲡⲗⲁⲥ-
ⲙⲁ) ποίημα; ib 45 9 B (S=Gk), Ro 9 20 B (S do)
πλάσμα; Nu 8 4 S (B ⲥⲟⲃϯ) κατασκευή, EpJer 45
F (B vb) κατασκεύασμα, Sa 14 12 εὔρεσις; Deu 31
11 S ⲡⲙ. ⲡⲧⲉⲥⲕⲏⲛⲏ σκηνοπηγία; Bor 260 121 S
weapon of evil is terrible ⲭⲓⲡⲡⲉϥⲙ. Auxil to another nn (cf ⲉⲓⲟⲡⲉ): Deu 27 15 B ⲙ. ⲙϥⲱⲧⲣ, ⲙ.
ⲡⲟⲩⲅⲱⲧⲣ γλυπτόν, χωνευτόν, 1 Kg 5 10 S ⲙ. ⲙⲡⲁ
ⲡⲣⲙⲟⲟⲥ ἕδρα, 4 Kg 1 2 S (P 44 111) ⲙ. ⲡϣⲡⲉ
δικτυωτός, 2 Kg 13 18 S ⲙ. ⲡϣⲡⲥ (var ϣⲏⲡ) καρπωτός. ⲙ. ⲛϭⲓⲝ, ⲡϫⲓⲝ SABF, things hand-made:
Lev 26 30 SB, Is 31 7 SBF, Mk 14 58 SB χειρο-
ποίητος; Ps 77 58 S, Is 44 17 S, Hos 11 2 A (all
B ⲫⲱⲧⲣ) γλυπτός; BMar 28 S ⲣⲉⲡⲙ. ⲡϭ., AM 154
B idols ⲙⲙ. ⲡϫ. ⲁⲧⲙ. ⲡϭ., ⲁⲑⲙ. ⲡϫ. SB adj,
not hand-made: 2 Cor 5 1 SB ἀχειροποίητος.

ⲙⲟⲡⲕⲥ B nn as pl, place for making?, mould?,
crucible?: MG 25 333 ⲉϥⲁⲥϥ ⲉⲡⲡⲉⲡⲙ. ⲡϯⲁⲣⲉⲧⲓ
= ROC '17 362 [Syriac] .

ⲙⲟⲩⲛⲕ B, ⲙⲟⲩⲕ S (PS), ⲙⲟⲟⲩⲕ F (Lam) vb
I intr, cease, be lacking, perish: Ge 11 6, ib 25
8 (S ⲕⲁ ⲧⲟⲟⲧⲥ ⲉⲃⲟⲗ), Jos 4 7 (S ⲱϫⲡ), Ps 106 5
(S do, but PS 179 ⲙⲟⲅⲕ), ib 118 123 (S ⲥⲱϣⲙ),
Is 58 11 (S ⲕⲱ), ib 60 20 (S ϭⲱϫⲃ), Jer 9 10 (S ⲕⲱ
ⲉⲃⲟⲗ), Lam 4 22 BF (ⲙⲟⲟⲩⲕ), Hos 4 3 (SA ⲱ.),
He 11 32 (S ⲕⲱ) ἐκλείπειν, Jer 14 17 (S ⲱ.) διαλείπ.;
Is 1 28 (S ϭⲱⲧⲉ ⲉⲃⲟⲗ) συντελεῖσθαι; ib 32 10 (S
ⲟⲩⲱ) συντελ., Gal 5 15 (S ⲱ.) ἀναλίσκειν, Nu 14 35 (S do)
ἐξαναλ., Jer 3 24 καταναλ., ROC 17 400 whilst youth

ⲙ. ⲡⲧⲟⲧϥ ⲩⲡⲁⲛⲁⲗ.; Ge 7 21 (S ⲙⲟⲅ), Nu 23 10 (S
do) ἀποθνῄσκειν; Job 5 5 (S do) ἐκσιφωνίζειν; ib
14 11 (S do) σπανίζειν; Lam 3 49 καταπίνεσθαι;
ib 5 14 (S ⲗⲟ) καταπαύειν; Ez 7 26 (S ⲥⲱⲣⲙ) ἀπόλλυσθαι; Jo 2 3 (S ϣⲱⲱⲧ) ὑστερεῖν; EW 110 tortured till flesh ⲙ. ⲣⲓⲧⲉⲡⲡⲓⲭⲣⲱⲙ, Va 58 186 animal
ἀμίαντος ⲙⲡⲁϥⲙ. in fire, AM 208 our swords ⲙ.
from numbers slain;   c e-: MG 25 281 time
ⲡⲁⲙ. ⲉⲣⲟⲓ ⲉⲓⲥⲁϫⲓ = BIF 13 100 S ⲡⲁⲕⲁⲁⲧ (v ⲕⲱ i),
C 41 13 his flesh ⲙ. ⲉⲣⲟϥ ⲉⲙⲁϣⲱ.

II tr, cause to cease, destroy: Ge 41 30, Ez 19
12 (S ⲱϫⲛ), Joel 2 3 (SA ⲟⲩⲱⲙ), ROC 25 273 (cf
255) ϣⲁϥⲙⲟⲡⲕⲟⲩ as if by fire ἀναλίσκειν, Ex 32 12
(S ϭⲱⲧⲉ ⲉⲃⲟⲗ), EpJer 62 (F ⲧⲁⲕⲁ) ἐξαναλ., Deu
7 22 (S do), Jer 27 6 (S ⲧⲁⲕⲟ) καταναλ.; Job 30
23 (S ⲟⲩⲱϣϥ), Ez 43 8 ἐκτρίβειν; Ps 118 87 (S ϥ.
ⲉⲃ.), Jer 5 3 (S ⲱ.), Joel 2 8 (A ⲱ.) συντελ.; Lam
3 11 (S ⲣⲱⲣⲧ) καταπαύ., EpJer 30 (F diff) διαφθείρ.;
Va 66 294 ⲉⲧⲁⲩⲙ. ⲙⲡⲟⲩⲥⲱⲙⲁ in sickness δαπανᾶν,
ib 58 167 envy ϣⲁϥⲙ. ⲙⲡⲓⲣⲉϥϫⲟⲣ διατήκειν; C
41 52 ⲉϥⲙ. ⲡⲉϥⲉⲣⲟⲟⲩ in vanities, AM 141 ϯⲡⲁⲙ.
ⲡⲡⲉⲧⲡⲥⲱⲙⲁ little by little.

—— nn m, ceasing, absence, destruction: C 89
139 relief would be for righteous ⲉⲡϥⲙ. ⲡⲡⲁⲓ (sc
evil-doers) = MG 17 509 [Arabic] = Va ar 172 80 [Arabic],
MG 25 354 ⲁⲧϭⲡⲉⲙ. ἀδιαλείπτως.

—— ⲉⲃⲟⲗ a intr, meaning as ⲙ.: Jer 43 23, ib
51 18 (S ⲱϫⲡ) ἐκλείπ.; ib 14 15 (S do) συντελ.;
Job 31 26 B (S ⲥⲃⲟⲕ) φθίνειν; AM 268 ⲡⲁⲣⲉⲡⲁⲣⲏⲧ
ⲙⲟⲡⲕ ⲉⲃ. ⲡⲣⲏⲓ ⲡϫⲏⲧ τήκειν; C 86 239 ⲁⲓⲙ. ⲉⲃ.
ⲣⲓⲧⲉⲡⲡⲓⲃⲁⲥⲁⲡⲟⲥ.   b tr, meaning as ⲙ.: Lev 26
44 (S ϥ. ⲉⲃ.), Deu 5 25 (S do), Jer 25 37 ἐξαναλ.;
Ez 22 15 (S ⲡⲟⲩϫⲉ ⲉⲃ.) διασπείρειν.   As nn m,
destruction: Deu 28 20 (S ϥ. ⲉⲃ.) ἀνάλωσις.

—— ⲉϩⲟⲩⲛ, perish (?): MG 25 105 eyes began
to ⲉⲣ ⲣⲗⲟⲗ ⲉⲁⲩⲙ. ⲉϩ. through much ἄσκησις (var
Va 59 ϭⲱⲗⲕ ⲉϩ.)

ⲁⲑ-, ⲁⲧⲙ. adj, unceasing, imperishable: Lu 12 33
(S ⲁⲧⲱϫⲡ) ἀνέκλειπτος, CaiEuch 477 crying with
mouths ⲡⲁ. ἀκαταπαύστος, Aeg 62 prayers ⲡⲁ.
ⲙⲉⲧⲁⲑⲙ., always adverbial ⲉⲛⲟⲩⲙ., unceasingly:
1 Thes 1 2 (SF ⲁⲭⲛⲱϫⲡ) ἀδιαλείπτως; MG 25 310
= BIF 13 117 S ⲣⲛⲟⲩⲙⲡⲧⲁⲧⲕⲁ ⲧⲟⲟⲧⲕ ⲉⲃ.

ⲙⲁⲛⲕⲉ S nn f, meaning unknown, among articles of ? iron: BKU 1 94 = AZ 23 75 ⲧⲟⲩⲁⲣⲣⲉ,
ⲧⲙ., ⲧϥⲉⲗⲙⲓⲥ.

ⲙⲏⲕⲉ, ⲙⲛϭⲏ S nn f, meaning unknown (? place-
name): CO 307 about sowing 3d part ⲣⲓⲧⲙ. ⲛ-
ⲡⲭⲟⲥ (= ϣⲱⲥ, cf BKU 1 48), ib 53 priest bidden
go ⲉϩⲟⲩⲛ ⲉⲧⲙ. & there do liturgy, Hall 80 ⲧⲙⲛϭⲏ
obscure; cf ST 273 place ⲧⲙⲛϭ ⲡⲁϫⲏⲙⲉ. V Ep
1 119.

ⲙⲁⲛⲕⲟⲩ *B* nn f, meaning uncertain: BM 920
265, Ryl 453 336 among *varia* ⲧⲉϥⲙ. ᷐ᴧ᷐ *his wea-*
pon or ? *his excrement.*

ⲙⲟⲩⲛⲕⲟⲩⲙ *S* v ⲕⲙⲕⲙ.

ⲙⲟⲛⲕⲥ *B* v ⲙⲟⲩⲛⲕ *make.*

ⲙⲁⲛⲙⲟⲛ *B* nn m, *orange*: Montp 174 ⲡⲓⲙ.,
K 178 ⲡⲓⲙ. نارنج.

ⲙⲟⲛⲙⲉⲛ *B* vb a intr, *shake, be shaken*: Ps 67 9
(*S* ⲛⲟⲉⲓⲛ), Pro 24 56 (Lect Copt Mus Cai, *SA* ⲕⲓⲙ),
Is 33 20 (*SF* ⲕⲓⲙ), Hab 3 14 (*A* ⲡⲁⲓⲛⲉ), Mt 27 51
(*S* ⲛⲟ.) σείειν; MG 25 258 earth ⲡⲁⲥⲱϫⲉⲙ ⲡⲧⲉϥⲙ.
from much rain, C 41 38 at his coming all town
ⲙ. = Miss 4 635 *S* ⲛⲟ.   b tr, *shake*: Job 9 6 (*S*
ⲛⲟ.), Is 10 14 (*S* ⲇⲟ) σεί., Ps 28 8 (*S* ⲕⲓⲙ) συσσεί.
As nn m (Cat 22), *shaking, earthquake, tempest*: Job
41 20 (*S* ⲕⲓⲧⲟ), Jer 29 3 (*S* ⲛⲟ.), Mt 8 24 (*S* ⲕⲙ.)
σεισμός, Jer 23 19 συνσεισ.; C 86 206 great ⲙ. shaking town, MG 25 186 ⲟⲩⲙ. ⲡⲧⲉ ⲣⲁⲑⲛⲟⲩ, DeV 2
41 great ⲙ. ϫⲉⲛϥⲓⲟⲙ.

ⲙⲟⲛⲙⲉⲛ *B*(vb tr ?) adj, *twisted*: Ex 25 25 ⲅⲟⲧⲡ
ⲙⲙ., ib 30 3 ϫⲗⲟⲙ ⲙⲙ. στρεπτός مقلوب.

ⲙⲁⲛⲓⲛ, ⲙⲁⲗⲗⲓⲛ, ⲙⲁⲗⲓⲗ *S* nn, *band, cord* (?):
BMar 42 martyr bound to 2 palms ⲛⲥⲉϯ ⲙⲁⲛ. ⲛⲁⲩ
ϣⲁⲛⲧⲉⲣⲉⲧⲟⲩ (*l* ⲣⲧⲏⲩ) ⲧⲱⲣⲕ ⲉⲡⲉⲅⲉⲣⲏⲩ, var Cod
Tischendorf 2 33 (Jernstedt) ⲙ]ⲁⲗⲗⲓⲛ, *cf* P 78 52
bound to 2 palms ⲛⲥⲉϯ ϫⲗⲁⲕ ⲛⲁⲩ hauling them
till brought together, sim P 129¹⁶ 69 tips (ⲣⲏⲧ) of 2
palms bound together ⲁⲩϯ ⲙⲁⲗⲓⲗ ⲛⲁⲩ ϣⲁⲛⲧⲟⲩ-
ϫⲱⲗⲕ. (Not impossibly ϫⲗⲁⲕ, ⲙⲁⲗⲓⲗ same word
misread.) *Cf* Berl *Wörterb* 2 47 m῾nn.

ⲙⲉⲛⲛⲥⲁ- *S*, ⲙⲉⲡⲉⲛⲥⲁ- *B* v ⲥⲁ *side*.

ⲙⲉⲡⲣⲓⲧ *B* v ⲙⲉ *love*.

ⲙⲛⲧ *S* (not literary), ⲙⲉⲛⲧ *B*, μέντ nn m, a
measure of grain &c, less than ⲣⲧⲟⲃ: Mt 5 15, Mk
4 21 *B* (gloss ⲱⲓⲡⲓ, *S* ϣⲓ), ROC 25 273 *B* ⲅ̄ ⲙⲛⲧ.
of bread, MG 25 252 *B* ⲙ. ⲁ̄ of sand μόδιος; Ge
18 6 *B* (*S* ϣⲓ), Deu 25 14 *B* (*S* ⲟⲓⲡⲉ), Is 5 10 *B*
(*SF* ⲇⲟ) μέτρον; Hall 130 *S* 23 ⲡⲁⲣⲧⲟⲃ ⲙⲡⲟⲩⲙ.,
ib 111 *S* ⲟⲩⲙ. ⲉⲡⲉⲣⲧⲟⲃ, ST 87 *S* sim, ib 38 *S* ⲟⲩⲙ.
ⲡⲁⲡⲁⲣⲭⲏ as scribe's fee, WS 116 *S* ⲟⲩⲡϣ ⲙⲛⲧ (*l*
ⲙⲛⲧ), Ryl 165 *S* ⲟⲩⲡϣⲏ ⲙⲉⲛⲧ of corn (*l* ⲡⲉϣ ⲙⲛⲧ).
On its capacity *v* PLond 5 160.

ⲙⲛⲧ-, *SAA²*, ⲙⲉⲧ- *BF*, ⲙⲉⲑ- *B*, ⲙⲉⲛⲧ- *O* pref
to nn or adj forming abstracts (constr of ⲙⲟⲩⲧⲉ):
ⲙⲛⲧⲉⲓⲱⲧ *fatherhood*, ⲙⲛⲧⲣⲣⲟ *kingdom*, ⲙⲛⲧⲕⲟⲙⲉⲥ
rank of κόμης (BMar 14), ⲙⲉⲧⲉϥⲗⲏⲟⲩ *vanity*,
ⲙⲛⲧⲁⲅⲁⲑⲟⲥ *goodness*, ⲙⲛⲧⲁⲉⲧⲟⲥ *likeness to eagle*
(BM 250 31), ⲙⲉⲧⲥⲩⲣⲟⲥ *Syriac (language)*, ⲙⲛⲧ-

ⲟⲩⲉⲉⲓⲛⲓⲛ *Greek (do)*, ⲙⲛⲧⲡⲉⲧϣⲟⲩⲉⲓⲧ *emptiness*,
ⲙⲉⲧⲁⲑⲙⲟⲩ *deathlessness*, ⲙⲛⲧⲁⲧⲥⲣⲟϥⲣⲉϥ *unfading-*
ness, ⲙⲉⲧⲁⲧϣⲓⲗⲓ *childlessness*;   or with compounds: ⲙⲛⲧⲙⲁⲓⲧⲟ ⲛⲣⲟⲩⲟ *love of larger part,*
greed, ⲙⲉⲧⲣⲏⲧ ⲡⲱⲛⲓ *stony-heartedness* (Cat 176),
ⲙⲉⲧⲣⲉϥⲉⲣ ⲫⲁϧⲣⲓ ⲛϭⲓⲕ *making of magic potions*
(Gal 5 20), ⲙⲛⲧⲣⲉϥⲧⲁⲧⲉ ⲥⲛⲁⲩ ⲛϣⲏⲣⲉ *professing*
(*belief in*) 2 Sons (Miss 8 96), ⲙⲛⲧⲙⲁⲓ ⲡⲉⲩⲙⲧⲟⲛ
loving their ease, slothfulness (ShC 73 29); rarely
with vb: ⲙⲉⲧⲓⲟⲣϩ *insight*, ⲙⲉⲧⲗⲏⲕ *softness*, ⲙⲛⲧ-
ⲥⲱⲧⲡ *election, choice*, ⲙⲉⲛⲧⲱⲟⲩ *conception* (?) *O*
(AZ 21 100), ⲙⲉⲧⲟⲓ ⲛⲛⲓϣϯ *being great* (Va 66 288);
or advb: ⲙⲛⲧϣⲁⲉⲛⲉϩ *eternity* (Mun 121).   As pl:
ⲙⲛⲧⲣⲣⲱⲟⲩ Is 37 16 *S*, Mt 48 5 *SB*, ϩⲁⲛⲙⲉⲧ-
ⲙⲉⲑⲣⲉϥ Ps 26 12 *B*. Doubled *S*(? error): Bor 305
98 division of natures according to ⲧⲙⲛⲧⲙⲛⲧⲛⲟ̄ⲧ̄ⲉ̄
ⲙⲛⲧⲙⲛⲧⲙⲛⲧⲣⲱⲙⲉ θεότης ἀνθρωπότης, *ib* 97 sim.

ⲙⲛⲧ- *SA* v ⲙⲏⲧ *ten*.

ⲙⲛⲟⲧ *B*, pl ⲙⲛⲟϯ, ⲉⲙ- & sg as pl, nn m,
breast: Is 28 9 (*S* ⲉⲕⲓⲃⲉ) μαστός; ROC 17 400
θηλή; K 77 ثدى, Aeg 40 ⲡⲉⲙ. ⲃ̄;   pl: Ge 49 25
(*S* ⲇⲟ), Lam 4 3 (*S* ⲇⲟ), Hos 9 14 (*A* ⲕⲓⲃⲉ), Ap 1
13 (sic *l*, *S* ⲇⲟ) μαστός; MG 25 57 nourished from
ⲡⲉⲕⲙⲛⲟⲧ, DeV 116 sucking from ⲡⲉⲡⲙⲛⲟϯ.   ϭⲓ
ⲙ., *suck the breast*: Ge 32 15 (*S* ⲧⲥⲛⲕⲟ), Deu 32
13 (*S* ⲟⲩⲱⲙ), Is 66 11 (*S* ϫⲓ ⲉⲕ.) θηλάζειν.

ⲙⲛⲟⲩⲧ *SA²BF*, ⲉⲙⲛⲟⲩⲧ *BF*, ⲙⲛⲟⲧ *B*, f ⲙ-
ⲛⲟⲧⲉ, ⲙⲛⲟⲟⲧⲉ *S*, ⲙⲛⲉⲟⲩⲧⲉ *A²*, ⲉⲙⲛⲟⲧⲉ *B* & m as
f, nn, *porter, doorkeeper*: Mk 13 34 *SBF*, Jo 10 3
SA²B θυρωρός; 1 Chr 15 23 *B*, Job 38 17 *SB*, AP
11 *A²* πυλωρός; Ge 39 21 *B* (*S* diff) ἀρχιδεσμοφύ-
λαξ; BHom 142 *S* ⲙⲛ ⲙ. ⲕⲱⲗⲩ ⲙⲙⲟⲕ from entering διάκονος; C 89 41 *B* ⲡⲓⲙ. ⲡⲧⲉ ⲡⲓⲣⲟ (*ib* 42
ϥⲁⲡⲓⲣⲟ) = Miss 4 522 *S* ⲡⲉⲧⲇⲓⲁⲕⲟⲡⲉⲓ ⲉⲡⲙⲁ ⲙⲡⲣⲟ
= MG 17 554 خادم (*cf* TEuch 1 366 وهو للخادم,
الامنوت), HCons 469 = TEuch 2 128 *B* after bishop rest of
ⲡⲓⲙ. خادم shall strike gong; ShLeyd 370 *S* none
but ϩⲓⲣⲁⲗ ϩⲓⲙ., BMis 265 *S* = Mor 30 41 *F* =
Mor 29 35 *S* ϩⲙϩ., AM 94 *B*, DeV 2 248 *B* (=
Mor 41 3 *S* ⲑⲩⲣⲱⲣⲟⲥ) ⲙ. of monastery (*cf* Synax
2 274), CDan 93 *B*, C 43 118 *B* ϯⲙⲛⲟⲩⲧ of nunnery, C 43 38 *B* of palace = Mor 39 10 *S* ⲡⲣⲟⲧⲟ-
ⲡⲁⲗⲗⲁϯⲟⲡ (*cf* ⲡⲁⲗⲗⲁⲧⲓⲟⲛ LMär 39 27);   among
minor clerical orders: Aeg 47 *B*, CA 89 *S*, Ann 19
240 *S*, P 129²⁰ 121 *S* (*cf* Gk in Leyd 135), Wess 18
32 *S*, EW 46 *B*, CA 97 *S* ⲡⲉⲙ. keeping church doors
during service (= *ib* Ar 32 19 امنوتين).   *Porteress*
(f forms): 2 Kg 4 6 *S*, Jo 18 17 *SA²B* (this in PO
2 174 *S* ⲧⲉⲙⲡⲟⲩⲧ) θυρωρός; R 1 3 54 *S* ⲑⲙϩⲁⲗ
ⲙⲛⲟⲧⲉ, Tri 381 *S* do بواب.

ⲙⲟⲩⲛⲧⲉ *A* v ⲙⲟⲩⲧⲉ.

ⲙⲛⲧⲣⲉ *SAA²*, ⲙⲉⲑⲣⲉ *B*, ⲙⲉⲧⲣⲏ *SF*, pl ⲙⲛⲧ-
ⲣⲉⲉⲩ *S*, ⲙⲉⲑⲣⲉⲩ *B* & sg as pl, nn m, *witness, testi-*
mony: Ex 23 1 *SB*, Nu 35 30 *SB* pl, Ps 26 12 *S*
(*B* ⲙⲉⲧⲙ.), Jer 39 10 *S* pl *B* sg, Mt 18 16 *SB*, Ac
22 20 *S* (*B* = Gk), 2 Cor 13 1 *SBF* μάρτυς, Nu 18
31 *S* (*B* ⲙⲉⲧⲙ.), Job 15 34 *S* (*B* do), Ps 79 tit *S*
(*B* do), Is 55 4 *SB*, 1 Tim 2 6 *SB* μαρτύριον; Hos
11 12 *A* (*B* Gk diff) *testis*; R 1 5 17 *S* lest we be
verbose ⲙⲡⲉⲛⲛ ⲙ. ⲏ ⲙⲁⲣⲧⲩⲣⲓⲁ ⲉⲧⲓⲛⲧⲉ, MIE 2
378 *B* ⲡⲁⲙ. ⲡⲉ ⲡϭ̄ⲥ ϫⲉ-, Tor 8 *S* I have signed for
ⲛⲓⲙⲛⲧⲣⲉⲉⲩ, DeV 2 274 *B* if thou find ⲙ. ⲉϩⲣⲏⲓ
ⲉϫⲱⲓ = Mun 68 *S* ϭⲓⲛⲉ ⲙⲡ[ⲙⲛⲧ]ⲣⲏ ⲉⲣⲟⲓ, J 1 21
S confirm it ϧⲓⲧⲛϧⲉⲙⲙ. ⲡⲁⲍⲓⲟⲡⲓⲥⲧⲟⲥ, Hall 108 *S*
payments in kind ⲟⲩⲁⲓⲡⲉ ⲙⲡⲃⲉⲥⲡⲏⲧ, ⲟⲩⲁⲓⲡⲉ ϩⲁⲙ.,
ⲟⲩⲙⲛⲧ ⲛϥⲁⲙ (carpenter).

ⲙⲛⲧ- *SAA²*, ⲙⲉⲧⲙ. *BF* nn f, *testimony*: 2 Chr
5 5 *B*, Ps 121 4 *B*, Mic 7 18 *SA* (*B* diff), Mk 1 44
SB μαρτύριον, Ps 18 8 *SB*, Mk 14 59 *SBF*, Jo 3
11 *SA²B*, Ap 11 7 *SB* μαρτυρία; ShA 2 323 *S* what
they said ⲉⲩⲙ. ⲉⲣⲟⲟⲩ ⲏ ⲡⲁⲩ (*cf* ⲉ below).   As
pl (pl form *B*): Deu 4 45, Ps 77 56.

ⲣ, ⲉⲣ ⲙ. *SAA²BF*, *testify, bear witness*, **a** no obj:
Jo 12 17 *SAA²B*, 2 Cor 8 3 *SB* μαρτυρεῖν, Jer 6 10
B, Ac 2 40 *S* (*B* + dat) διαμαρτύρεσθαι, Is 44 8 *B*
(*S* nn) μάρτυς εἶναι; AP 27 *A²* ⲉⲁϥⲣ ⲙ. all the
night long, ShA 2 275 *S* ⲉⲛϫⲟⲉⲓⲥ ⲡⲉⲧⲟ ⲙⲙ., AM
210 *B* grey hairs ⲉⲣ ⲙ. that thou art wise, J 3 72
S ϯⲱ ⲙⲙ., AZ 23 37 *F* ϯⲁⲓ ⲙⲏⲧⲣⲏ, PMich 1843
S ϯⲉⲣ ⲙ.   **b** *testify of, concerning* c ⲛ-: Lam
2 13 *SB*, Su 41 (BHom 54) *B*, Jo 3 11 *SBF* μαρτυρεῖν, Deu 32 46 *SB*, Ez 20 4 *SB*, διαμαρτ., Sa
10 7 *S* ἐπὶ μαρτύριον καθιστάναι; PS 72 *S* ⲛⲧⲁⲣ
ⲙ. ⲛⲉⲣⲱϧ ⲛⲓⲙ, ShC 73 80 *S* ⲡⲉⲧⲟ ⲙⲙ. ⲙⲙⲟϥ, C
89 101 *B* what hast seen ⲁⲣⲓ ⲙ. ⲙⲙⲱⲟⲩ to brethren,
Aeg 268 *S* ⲉϥⲣ ⲙ. ⲙⲡⲁⲓ, Miss 4 176 *B* ϯⲟⲓ ⲙⲙ.
ⲛⲛⲁⲓⲥⲁϫⲓ.   **c** *testify to* c ⲛ- dat: Jth 7 28 *S*,
Gal 4 15 *SB*, Ap 22 16 *SB* μαρτυρεῖν, Ex 21 29 *SB*, Zech
3 6 *SAB*, Ac 2 40 *B* (*S* no obj) διαμαρτ., Is 43 12
B (*S* nn), Ac 2 32 *SB* μάρτυς(εἶναι); AZ 21 157 *S*
eye witnesses ⲣ ⲙ. ⲛⲁⲡ.   **d** c ⲉ-, *against, in respect*
of, for: Deu 5 20 *SB*, Aeg 231 *S* μαρτυρεῖν κατά,
Mt 23 31 *S* (*B* ϫⲁ-) ⲙⲁⲣⲧ. dat, Job 15 6 *S* (*B* do),
Pro 25 18 *SA*, Mt 26 62 *S* (*B* do) καταμαρτ. gen,
Ja 5 3 *S* (BAp 171, *B* dat) εἰς μαρτύριον εἶναι; PS
283 *S* ⲉⲩⲉⲣ ⲙ. ⲉⲣⲟⲥ in all sins she doeth, ShA 1
103 *S* each ⲟ ⲙⲙ. ⲉⲣⲟϥ ⲏ ⲡⲁϥ ⲙⲙⲓⲛ ⲙⲙⲟϥ, FR
22 *S* idols to ⲣ ⲙ. ⲉⲡⲉⲛⲧⲁⲩⲧⲁⲙⲓⲟⲟⲩ;   *for*: Ro 9 1
B (*S* om) συμμαρτ. dat; C 43 68 *B* ϧⲉⲣ ⲙ. ⲉⲣⲟⲓ
ⲛϫⲉ ⲡϭ̄ⲥ that I have done you no ill, BAp 107 *S*
Lord ⲟ ⲙⲙ. ⲉⲧⲁⲯⲩⲭⲏ ϫⲉ-, J 113 13 *Sᵃ* Father
Son & HGhost ⲱ ⲙⲙ. ⲁⲡⲓϣⲁϫⲉ, AZ 23 35 *F* ⲡⲓ-
ⲗⲟⲙⲓ...ⲉ ⲙⲙⲉⲧⲣⲏ (ⲉ)ⲗⲁⲓ.   **e** c ϩⲁ-, ϩⲁ, ϫⲁ-
SAB, *on behalf of*: Ac 6 3 *SB*, He 7 17 *SBF*, Cl

18 1 *A* μαρτ., Ac 1 22 *B* (*S* ϣⲱⲡⲉ ⲙⲙ. ⲛ-) μάρτυς
γίνεσθαι gen, C 86 186 *B* Baptist ⲉⲣⲉⲡϭ̄ⲥ ⲉⲣ ⲙ.
ϧⲁⲣⲟϥ, PS 72 *S* words ⲛⲧⲉⲡⲣ ⲙ. ϧⲁⲣⲟⲟⲩ; *against*:
Jo 18 23 *SA²* (*B* ⲛ-) ⲙⲁⲣⲧ. περί, Su 21 *B* (*S* ⲉ-), Mt
27 13 *B* (*S* do) καταμαρτ. gen, 1 Cor 15 15 *BF* (*S*
do) (ψευδο)μάρτυς gen; DeV 2 275 *B* archangel
will not ⲉⲣ ⲙ. ϧⲁⲣⲟϥ = Mun 69 *S* ⲉ-.   **f** c ⲉⲧ-
ⲃⲉ- *SB*, *concerning*: MG 25 204 *B* ϕⲏ ⲉⲧⲉⲕⲉⲣ ⲙ.
ⲉⲑⲃⲏⲧϥ = Z 296 *S* ϩⲁ- μαρτυρεῖν ace, BHom 34 *S*
scripture ⲣ ⲙ. ⲉⲧⲃⲉⲓⲟⲩⲍⲁⲥ.   **g** c ⲉϫⲛ-, ⲁϫⲛ-
SAB, as last: He 11 4 *SB* (ⲉϩⲣⲏⲓ ⲉϫ.) μαρτ. ἐπί,
TU 43 1 *A* Lord [ⲉⲧⲁⲩⲣ] ⲙ. ⲁϫⲱϥ.   **h** c ⲙⲛ-,
ⲛⲉⲙ- *SB*, *to, for*: Lu 4 22 *S* (*B* ⲛ-) ⲙⲁⲣⲧ. dat, Va
59 164 *B* Lord ϧⲉⲣ ⲙ. ⲡⲉⲙⲏⲓ ϫⲉ-.

† ⲙ. *S*, *take to witness*: Miss 8 86 ⲁⲛϯ ⲙ. ⲙ-
ⲙⲟⲩ ⲙⲡⲙⲙⲁⲧⲟⲓ διαμαρτ. αὐτὸν κ. τοὺς στρατ. ;

† ⲙⲉⲧⲙ. *B*, *bear witness*: AM 264 martyrs in
persecution † ⲛ̄ⲧ̄ⲙ. ϧⲁⲑⲙⲉⲧⲟⲩⲣⲟ, C 43 89 ⲛⲧⲁⲩϯ
ⲛ̄ⲧ̄ⲙ. ϧⲁⲧⲁⲡⲁⲥⲧⲁⲥⲓⲥ.

ⲙⲟⲛⲱⲟⲩⲓ *B*, pl of ⲙⲟⲛⲏ (μονή): C 89 24,
MG 25 29, 311.

ⲙⲟⲩⲛⲟⲟⲩⲉ *S* *v* ⲙⲟⲩⲛⲉ (ⲉⲙⲟⲩⲛⲉ) nn.

ⲙⲉⲛϣⲟϯ *B* *v* ⲙⲉⲛϣϣⲱⲧ.

ⲙⲉⲛ̄ⲏ, -ϧⲉ, -ϧⲏϧ *B* nn with ⲥⲁ- forming prep,
after: Ge 31 36 -ϧⲛⲓ (*S* ⲛⲥⲁ-), ib 32 18 -ϧⲛⲏ (*S* do),
ib 44 4 -ϧⲉ ⲛ-, Lev 17 7 -ϧⲏⲟⲩ (*S* do), Nu 15 39
(*S* ϧⲓⲡⲁϩⲟⲩ ⲛ-), 3 Kg 17 10 -ϧⲏⲥ, Ps 62 9 -ϧⲏⲕ (*S*
diff), Jer 16 11 -ϧⲉ ⲛ- (var ⲥⲁϕⲁϩⲟⲩ, *S* ϧⲓⲡ.), Jo
12 19 -ϧⲏϥ (*SAA²* ϧⲓⲡ.) ὀπίσω, 1 Kg 24 2 -ϧⲏ ⲛ-,
Mt 15 23 (*S* do) ὄπισθεν, Ge 37 17 κατόπισθεν, Ex
26 23 -ϧⲏⲥ ἐκ τ., ὀπισθίων; Deu 15 20 -ϧⲏ ⲛ- (var
ϧⲁⲧϧⲏ ⲛ-, *S* ϫⲓⲛ-) ἐξ; Miss 4 135 he sat down
ⲥⲁⲙⲉⲛⲣⲉ (ⲛ)ⲡⲓⲉⲡⲓⲥⲕⲟⲡⲟⲥ = MR 4 68 *S* ⲙⲛⲛⲉⲡ.
ⲛⲥⲁⲟⲩⲥⲁ, Va 61 202 put thy hands ⲥⲁⲙⲉⲛϧⲏⲕ, AM
270 drew the people ⲥⲁⲙⲉⲛϧⲏϥ.

ⲙⲁⲛϭⲁⲗⲉ *SB*, -ⲗⲏ *S* (Ryl), -ϫⲁⲗⲉ *S* (BM)
nn m = μάκελλα مِعْزَق : **a** *B* *pick, hoe*: C 86 13
earth ⲉⲩϭⲓⲟⲩⲓ ⲛϧⲏⲧϥ ⲙⲡⲓⲙ., MG 25 12 ⲟⲩⲁⲙⲉ
(ἅμη) ⲛⲉⲙⲟⲩ ⲙ. that I may dig πέλεκυς, DeV 2 44
tearing out roots ϧⲓⲧⲉⲛϥⲙ., P 55 10 ⲡⲓⲙ. مِجْرَفة (*cf*
K 127 ⲁⲥⲟⲉⲣⲓⲱⲛ مِجْرَفة, *cf* Ryl 94 n).   **b** *winnow-*
ing fan: Am 9 9 *B* (*SA* ϧⲁ) λικμός;   the following doubtful: PLond 4 517 *S* ⲧⲓⲉ (? f) ⲛ[ⲙ]ⲁⲛ-
ϭⲁⲗⲉ, Bodl(P) f 33 *S* ⲕⲟⲩⲓ (ⲙ)ⲙ., Ryl 238 *S* list
of *varia* ⲟⲩⲙ., BMOr 6201 B 44 *S* ⲛ]ⲉⲕⲙ. ⲡⲧⲁⲕ-
ⲧⲥⲁϩⲟⲓ ⲉⲣⲟⲟⲩ.

ⲙⲁⲡ *B* *v* ⲙⲁⲁⲃ.

ⲙⲡⲁⲓ *S*, ⲗϩⲉⲓ *A* (*sic*?), ⲙⲃⲁⲓ *B* nn m, *spindle*:
Pro 31 19 *SAB* ἄτρακτος. But P 44 92 *S* ⲡⲥⲟⲣⲧ
ⲙⲛⲡⲉⲙ. والكتان = ? Pro 31 13 (*SA* ⲙⲁϧⲉ, *B*

ιαⲩ λίνον) or ? confused with 31 19, *cf* Tri 481 *S*
ⲥⲟⲩⲍⲁⲣⲓⲟⲛ ⲙ̄ⲡⲉⲗⲡⲁ (for sake of rhyme) كلاس, *so*
linen.

ⲙ̄ⲡⲉ-, ⲙ̄ⲡ⸗ *SAA²BF* **I** pref neg 1 perf, as *S*
ⲙ̄ⲡⲉⲙⲙⲁϫⲉ ⲥⲱⲧⲙ̄, ⲙ̄ⲡⲉϥϫⲟⲟⲥ, ⲙ̄ⲡⲉⲣ ⲙ̄ⲡϣⲁ,
ⲙ̄ⲡⲟⲩϭⲛ ⲡⲉϫⲙⲁ, *A* ⲙ̄ⲡⲓⲧⲉⲃⲁⲕ, ⲙ̄ⲡⲟⲩⲙⲣⲣⲓⲧⲥ, *B*
ⲙ̄ⲡⲉⲧⲉⲡⲁⲓⲧⲟⲩ, ⲙ̄ⲡⲟⲩⲙⲁⲥϥ, *F* ⲙ̄ⲡⲉⲟⲩⲉⲉⲓ ϣⲓⲛⲓ, ⲙ̄-
ⲡⲉⲥϣⲱⲡⲓ. Where action uncompleted, *until S =*
ⲉⲱⲥ ἄⲛ: Job 27 5 (*B* ϣⲁⲧⲉ-), Si 23 20, Mt 10 23
(*B* ⲇⲟ), Lu 21 32 (*B* ⲇⲟ), Ep 359 ⲙ̄ⲡⲣϣⲱ ⲙ̄ⲡⲉⲕ-
ϫⲟⲟⲩ. With ⲁⲛ *SF*: Est 4 2 *S* ⲙ̄ⲡⲉⲥⲧⲟ ⲛⲁϥ
ⲁⲛⲡⲉ, ShA 1 114 *S* ⲙ̄ⲡⲉⲓⲙⲉ ⲁⲛⲟⲕ ⲁⲛ, Kr 38 *F*
ⲙ̄ⲡⲉⲃⲱⲛⲧⲃ ⲉⲛ. With ⲡⲉ- neg pluperf *S* (rare):
PS 6 ⲛⲉⲙⲡⲟⲩⲕⲁ ⲧⲟⲟⲧⲟⲩ ⲉⲃⲟⲗⲡⲉ, *ib* 113 ⲛⲉⲙⲡⲟⲩ-
ϣϭⲓⲧϥ.

ⲙ̄ⲡⲉ *S*, ⲙ̄ⲫⲏ *B*, ⲙ̄ⲡⲏ *F* **II** particle **a** of denial
after question as to past event: Nu 22 30 *SB*, MG
25 214 *B*, *ib* 247 *B*, Va 57 128 *B* was he torpid (in
prayer)? ⲙ. ⲟⲩ, ⲟⲩⲭⲓ́, ROC 17 405 *B* did Abraham...?
ⲙ. ⲙⲉ ⲅⲉⲡⲉⲧⲟ (ⲙὴ γένοιτο) ⲟⲩ ⲙέν ⲟⲩ̂ν, Lu 22 35 *SB*
ⲟⲩ̓ⲇέⲛ; BMis 552 *S* knowest thou them not? I said
ⲙ., Mor 31 186 *S* she denied ϫⲉⲙ. ⲙ̄ⲡⲉⲓϫⲓⲟⲅⲉ,
MG 25 63 *B* didst see anyone? ⲙ. ϩⲟⲗⲱⲥ, RNC
76 *S* see if he be dead, ⲙ. ϭⲟⲛϩ, BMar 85 *S* wast
glad? ⲙ. ⲙ̄ⲡⲉⲕⲉⲩⲫⲣⲁⲛⲉ, Job 19 4 *S* ⲡⲉⲅⲧⲓ ⲁⲛⲡⲉ
(? *l* ⲁⲛⲡⲉ), ⲟⲩ̓ⲕ ⲉ̓ⲡⲓ̀ ⲕⲁⲓⲣⲟⲩ̂. **b** after ϫⲛ-, ϣⲁⲛ-,
or: Ge 24 21 *B*, CA 99 *S* whether he hath spent
them well ϫⲛⲙ., BAp 68 *S* was Eve created together
with Adam ϫⲛⲙ.?, C 43 171 *B* is thy mind made
up to sacrifice ϣⲁⲛⲙ.?, Win 4 *S* send us the decision ϫⲉⲁϩⲉ ϫⲛⲙ.; or with ⲓⲉ *F*: Sph 10 4 ⲟⲩⲁⲧⲉ
ⲛⲥϥⲉⲓ ⲡⲏⲛ ϫⲁϥⲁϭⲓ (*sic*) [ⲛ]ⲏⲕ ⲓⲉ ⲙ̄ⲡⲏ; or ⲉⲛⲉ *S*:
ShIF 237 ⲁⲧⲉⲧⲛ̄ϫⲱⲡⲧ ⲉⲕⲁ ⲡⲙⲁ ⲙ̄ⲡⲧⲁⲕⲟ ⲉⲉⲓ ⲉϩⲟⲩⲛ
ⲉⲣⲟⲛ ⲉⲛⲉⲙ. or (*was this*) *not so?* **c** with ⲉϣⲱⲡⲉ,
ⲉϣⲱⲡ *SB*, *if not*: Mor 31 41 *S* if I come...ⲉϣ. ⲙ.,
ib 41 345 *S* hast come to senses? ⲉϣ. ⲙ. ⲧⲁⲡⲁⲓ-
ⲍⲉⲅⲉ ⲙ̄ⲙⲟⲕ ⲕⲁⲕⲱⲥ, Miss 4 167 *B* ⲓⲉ ⲉϣ. ⲙ. ⲓⲉ
ⲥⲉⲡⲁⲛⲁⲓ ⲛⲁⲕ ⲁⲛ, Bodl(P) a 2 52 *S* recipe, it will
harden in 7 days ⲉϣ. ⲡⲡⲉ ⲕⲁϥ ⲡⲕⲉ ⲍ̄; or ⲉϣϫⲉ *SF*,
ⲓⲥϫⲉ *B*: 1 Cor 7 14 *SF* (*B* ⲙⲙⲟⲛ) ⲉ̓ⲡⲉⲓ́, MG 25 42
B if hast received spirit, go, ⲓⲥ. ⲙ. ϯⲟⲩⲱϣ ⲁⲛ.

ⲙ̄ⲡⲟ, ⲉⲙⲡⲟ *S*, ⲉⲃⲱ *SA*, ⲉⲃⲟⲟ *A*, ⲉⲃⲟ *A²* (?) *B*,
f ϩⲙ̄ⲡⲱ *S*, pl ⲉⲃⲟⲟⲅⲉ *Sᵃ* (El), ⲉⲃⲱⲟⲩ *B* (Mt 15) &
sg as pl, nn, *dumb person*: Sa 10 21 *S*, Mt 12 22
SB, *ib* 15 31 *SB*, Lu 11 14 *S* (*B* ⲕⲟⲩⲣ) ⲕⲱⲫόⲥ (but
cf PS below), Ex 4 11 *S* ⲙ. ⲁⲗ, *A* ⲉ. ⲥⲱϩ, *B* ⲉ.
ⲕⲟⲩⲣ ⲇⲩⲥⲕⲱ. ⲕⲱ.; Ps 37 13 *S* (*B* ⲁⲧⲥⲁϫⲓ), Mt 9
17 *S* (*B* ⲇⲟ) ἄⲗⲁⲗⲟⲥ, Is 35 6 *B* (*SF* ⲥⲁϫⲉ ⲗⲁⲥ), Mk
7 32 *S* ⲁⲗ ⲡⲓⲙ., *B* ⲕⲟⲩⲣ ⲡⲉ. ⲙⲟⲅⲓⲗⲁⲗⲟⲥ; Z 327 *S*
ἄⲫⲱⲛⲟⲥ; PS 279 *S* ⲡⲉⲙ. ⲙ̄ⲡⲡⲕⲱⲫⲟⲥ, Miss 4 689
S ⲁⲗ ⲙ., MG 25 91 *B* ⲉ. ⲡⲕⲟⲩⲣ, AM 167 *B* ⲕⲟⲩⲣ
ⲡⲉ. f, ST 149 *S* Sara ⲧⲏⲙ̄ⲡⲱ, El 118 *Sᵃ* = *ib* 88

A will make ⲛⲉ. ϣⲉϫⲉ. ⲙ̄ⲡⲧⲙ., ⲙⲉⲧⲉ. *SB* nn f,
dumbness: Leyd 449 *S* ϩⲉⲡⲙ. ⲁⲩⲱ ⲡⲁⲗ ⲙ̄ⲡⲣⲉⲛ-
ⲙ̄ⲡⲧⲁⲧϣⲁϫⲉ, BMis 88 *S* ⲧⲙ. of Zacharias (Lu 1
20), Aeg 20 *S* could not speak for ⲧⲙ. of death had
overcome him, AM 298 *B* magistrate condemned
to ⲙ. so that cannot speak. ⲣ ⲙ., ⲉⲣ ⲉ. *SB*, *be-*
come, be dumb: Ps 38 2 *S* (*B* ⲉⲣ ⲕⲟⲩⲣ) ⲕⲱⲫᾶⲥⲑⲁⲓ,
Lu 1 22 *SB* ⲕⲱ. ⲇⲓⲁⲙⲉ́ⲛⲉⲓⲛ, Ez 3 26 *S* (*B l* ⲉⲣ ⲉⲙⲡⲟ)
ⲁ̓ⲡⲟⲕⲱ.; Ps 30 18 *S*, (*A* (Cl) ϩⲱⲡⲉ ⲡⲉ., *B* ⲉⲣ ⲁⲧⲥⲁϫⲓ) ἄⲗ. γίνεⲥⲑⲁⲓ, Miss 4 530 *S* ⲟ ⲡⲙ. ϩⲙ̄ⲡϭⲟⲗ
= C 89 48 *B* ⲙόγγⲟⲥ ⲉ⸗ⲛⲁⲓ, Va 61 19 *B* ⲡⲉⲧⲟⲓ ⲡⲉ.
in their tongues, BIF 14 121 *S* sim, AP 30 *A²*
ⲉϥⲟⲉⲓ ⲡⲉⲃ[ⲟ ?. As name: ⲡⲉⲃⲱ J 15 42, Πⲉⲃⲟⲩ̂,
Πⲉⲃⲱ̂, -ⲱ̂ⲥ, Τⲉⲃⲟⲩ̂, -ⲱ̂ⲥ (Preisigke, *cf* Πⲕⲟⲩ̂ⲣ).

ⲙ̄ⲡⲱⲣ *SAA²*, ⲙⲫⲱⲣ *B* deprecatory interj, *do*
(*it*) *not !, by no means !, nay !*, often precedes its
construct ⲙ̄ⲡⲣ- (*v* below): Ge 18 25 *B* (*S* om),
Jth 8 14 *S*, Ez 4 14 *SB*, Ac 10 14 *SB* ⲙⲏⲇⲁⲙⲱ̂ⲥ,
Jud 19 23 *S*, 2 Kg 13 12 *S*, Ps 113 9 *SB*, Ap 22
9 *SB*, Z 322 *S* ⲙ. ϭⲉ ⲙ̄ⲡⲣⲧⲣⲉⲡⲉⲓⲁ ⲧⲟⲟⲧⲛ, Va 57
110 *B* ⲙ. ✝✝ ϩⲟ ⲉⲣⲱⲧⲉⲛ ⲙ̄ⲡⲉⲛⲑⲣⲉⲛ- ⲙⲏ́, Ru 1 13
S ⲙⲏ̀ ⲇⲏ́; PS 328 *S* ⲙ. ⲡϫⲟⲉⲓⲥ ⲙ̄ⲡⲣⲕⲁⲁϥ ⲛⲥⲱⲕ,
BMar 216 *S* = Rec 6 182 *B* ⲙ. it is not given to thee
to &c, LMär 39 *S* go ye & take his head, ⲙ. ⲁⲗⲗⲁ
ⲕⲉⲗⲉⲅⲉ ⲉⲧⲣⲉⲩ-, Miss 4 638 *S* ⲙ. ⲡⲁϣⲏⲣⲉ, ⲃⲱⲕ =
C 41 34 *B* ⲙⲙⲟⲛ; with following ⲉ- (*cf* AZ 56 99),
ShP 131⁴ 156 *S* ⲙ. ⲧⲉⲡⲟⲩ ⲉⲙⲉⲉⲅⲉ ϫⲉ-, ShBMOr
8810 465 *S* ⲙ. ϭⲉ ⲉⲥⲟⲣⲙⲉⲕ ⲙⲁⲅⲁⲁⲕ, El 50 *A* ⲙ.
ⲁⲟⲩⲱϣⲧ ⲡⲉⲓ, ShC 42 145 *S* ⲙ. ⲉⲧⲣⲁⲙⲟⲩ, *cf* PMich
4553 *S* ⲙ. ⲡⲣ ⲕⲟⲅⲓ ϩⲏⲧ. With ϫⲛ- *S*, *or not*: 3
Kg 22 15 shall I go ϫⲛ̄ⲡⲡⲱⲣ ⲧⲁϭⲱ ⲏ̓ ?

ⲙ̄ⲡⲣ- *SAA²*, ⲙ̄ⲡⲉⲣ- *B*, ⲡ̄ⲡⲉⲣ- *SBF*, ⲡⲣ-, ⲡⲉⲣ-
SAF, ⲙ̄ⲡⲉⲗ-, ⲡⲉⲗ-, ⲙ̄ⲃⲉⲗ- (Eccl 7 10) *F* as pref
of neg imperat: Pro 3 11 *SB* ⲙ̄ⲡⲣⲣ ⲕⲟⲅⲓ ⲛϩⲏⲧ (*A*
ⲙ̄ⲡ-), Is 30 10 *SBF* ⲙ̄ⲡⲣⲧⲁⲙⲟⲛ, Mt 6 13 *BF* ⲙ̄-
ⲡⲉⲣⲉⲛⲧⲉⲛ ⲉϩⲟⲩⲛ (*S* diff), Jo 5 45 *SA²* ⲙ̄ⲡⲣⲙⲉⲉⲅⲉ
(*B* diff), PS 33 *S* ⲙ̄ⲡⲣϩⲱⲡⲧ ⲉⲣⲟⲓ, CO 324 *S* ⲙ̄-
ⲡⲣⲥⲕⲅⲗⲗⲉⲓ ⲙ̄ⲙⲟⲕ, CMSS 44 *F* ⲡⲡⲉⲗⲧⲁⲕⲁⲩ, *ib*
47 *F* ⲡⲉⲗⲕⲁⲧⲉⲭⲓ, ST 330 *S* ⲡⲣⲁⲙⲉⲗⲉ, ZNTW 24
86 *F* ⲡⲉⲣ(ⲣ) ϩⲏⲧ ⲥⲛⲟⲩ, *ib* 90 *F* ⲡⲉⲣⲥⲱⲧⲙ̄ ⲛⲥⲱϥ,
Hos 4 15 *A* ⲡⲣⲣ ⲁⲧⲥⲁⲅⲡⲉ. With ⲁⲛ *SB*: C 41
28 *B* ⲙ̄ⲡⲉⲣϫⲉ ⲙⲉⲑⲛⲟⲩϫ ⲁⲛ, *ib* 86 79 *B* ⲙ̄ⲡⲉⲣϯ
ⲁⲥⲟ ⲉⲣⲟⲓ ⲁⲛ (var om ⲁⲛ), Ryl 110 *S* ⲡⲉⲣⲟⲩⲱⲙ
ⲁⲛ. ⲙ̄ⲡⲱⲣ for ⲙ̄ⲡⲣ- *SA²*: Ge 31 35, 2 Kg 13 20,
Ap 19 10 (all var ⲙ̄ⲡⲣ-), BM 1103, CO 271 ⲙ. ⲣ
ⲡⲁⲱⲃ̄ϣ (*cf* 254,338), Hall 73 ⲙ. ϭⲛ ⲁⲣⲓⲕⲉ, Cai 8510
ⲙ̄ⲡⲟⲩⲣ ⲗⲩⲡⲏ; *A²* BM 1224 ⲙ. ⲁϥϣⲕ ⲁⲣⲁⲉⲓ. ⲙⲣ-,
ⲙⲉⲣ- *S* ? error: *v* Ep 1 249, LAl 72 n. Often +
caus ⲧⲣⲉ-, ⲑⲣⲉ-, *let not.*

ⲙ̄ⲡⲁⲣⲉ- *B* *v* ⲙⲉⲣⲉ-.

(ⲙ̄ⲡⲱⲧ) ⲉⲙⲡⲱⲧ *S* nn f, meaning unknown,

part of weaving apparatus : Ryl 238 38 ⲉⲙ. ⲥⲛⲧⲉ
ⲛⲧⲁⲗⲟ ⲕⲁⲙⲁⲥ(ⲓ)ⲟⲛ (καμίσιον).

ⲙⲡⲁⲧⲉ- *SAA²BF*, ⲙⲡⲁⲛⲧⲉ- *B* (Miss 4 97, 108)
pref neg perf of what *has not yet happened* : Nu 11
33 *SB*, Mal 4 5 *AB*, Jo 4 49 *SA²B* πρίν ; Ps 89 2
SB, Mt 6 8 *SBF* πρὸ τοῦ ; Ge 15 16 *SB*, He 2 8
SBF οὔπω ; Sir 32 21 *S* (var ⲉⲙⲡⲉ-) ἕως ; PS 9 *S*
ⲙⲡⲁⲧⲟⲩⲧⲏⲡⲟⲟⲩ ⲛⲁⲓ, C 41 33 *B* ⲙⲡⲁⲧⲉⲡⲓⲟⲩⲱⲓⲛⲓ
ϣⲁⲓⲉ, Aeg 10 *S* he reached 40 ⲙⲡⲁⲧⲟⲩϫⲓ ⲥϭⲣⲓⲙⲉ
ⲛⲁϥ.   With ⲛⲉ- pluperf of same : Nu 15 34 *S*
(*B* ⲙⲡⲁⲧⲉ-), Jo 3 24 *SBF* οὔπω ; PS 78 *S* ⲛⲉⲙⲡⲁ-
ⲧⲟⲩⲥⲱⲧⲙ ⲉⲣⲟⲥⲡⲉ, TT 116 *S* ⲛⲉⲙⲡⲁⲧⲱϣⲕⲡⲉ ϫⲓⲛ-
ⲧⲁϥⲉⲓ = Wess 11 160 *S* = C 89 66 *B* ⲙⲡⲉϥϣⲱⲕ ⲓⲥ-
ϫⲉⲛ- ἐλθὼν γενέσθαι.

ⲙⲡϣⲁ *SABF*, ⲙϣⲁ *S* (BHom, LAl 71) *B*,
ⲉⲙⲡϣⲁ *SBF*, ⲉⲙⲡϣⲉ *F* vb intr, *be worthy, worth*,
a with gen ⲛ- : Ge 23 9 *B*, Job 30 1 *SB*, Pro 3 15
SAB, Mt 10 10 *SB*, Jo 1 27 *S* (*B* ⲛⲓⲙⲁ), 1 Cor 6 2
SB, Ap 5 2 *S* (*B* ⲉ-), Aeg 244 *S* ⲡⲉⲧⲙ. ⲙⲡⲉⲓⲑⲗⲟ-
ⲙⲟⲥ, Z 277 *S* ϥⲙ. ⲡⲣ ϩⲏⲃⲉ ⲉϫⲱϥ ἄξιος (εἶναι),
He 10 29 *SB*, BM 247 8 *S* ⲡⲉⲡⲧⲁ ⲉⲙ. ⲡϣⲱⲡⲉ
ϩⲙⲡϫⲟⲉⲓⲥ, BHom 57 *S* ⲙ. ⲙⲡⲁⲧⲉ ⲙⲡⲧⲁⲓⲟ ἀξιοῦσθαι, ViSitz 172 4 26 *S* ⲥⲉⲙ. ⲡⲣ ϣⲡⲏⲣⲉ ἀξιοθαύ-
μαστος ; Mt 3 11 *S* (*B* ⲉ-), 1 Cor 15 9 *S* (*B* ⲉⲟⲑⲣⲟⲩ-)
ἱκανός ; Pro 14 9 *SA* (*B* diff), Sa 12 15 *S*, BHom
21 *S* ⲧⲡⲙ. ⲡⲣ ⲡⲙⲉⲉⲩⲉ, Mor 18 158 *S* ⲕⲉⲙ. ⲡⲉⲓⲙⲉ
ⲉⲡⲁⲓ ὀφείλειν ; He 2 2 *SBF* ἔνδικος ; Lu 6 2 *B* (*S*
ϣϣⲉ) ἔξεστι ; Mt 20 4 *SBF* (PMich 539 ⲡⲉⲧⲛⲡϣⲁ
ⲛⲧⲙⲉⲉⲓ) ὁ δίκαιον ; Mt 26 66 *B* (*S* = Gk) = Mk
14 64 *S* (*B* = Gk) ἔνοχος ; TRit 284 *B* thy husband
ϥⲉⲙ. ⲡⲥⲱⲧⲙ ⲡⲥⲱϥ يجب ; PS 271 *S* ⲡⲉⲧϥⲙ. ⲙⲙⲟϥ
give him, *ib* 369 *S* ϯⲡⲁⲧⲣⲉⲧⲡⲙ. ⲛⲧⲙⲡⲧⲉⲣⲟ, BG 65
S ⲥⲉⲡⲙ. ⲛⲑⲃⲃⲟⲟⲩ, ShC 73 114 *S* ⲙⲁⲣⲓⲙ. ⲡⲛⲁⲩ
ⲉⲣⲟϥ, J 122 50 *S* witnesses ⲉⲩⲙ. ⲙⲡⲓⲥⲧⲉⲩⲉ ⲡⲁⲩ,
Ep 87 *S* sim, MIE 2 362 *B* ⲉⲓⲡⲁⲙ. ⲡⲧⲁⲓⲙϣϯ
ⲡⲉⲧϥⲱ, C 89 41 *B* sell them ϩⲁⲡⲉⲧⲟⲩⲙ. ⲙⲙⲟϥ,
ST 318 *S* sale of book ϫⲉⲉϥⲙ. ⲡⲱ(=ⲟⲩ), WZKM
14 238 *S* sheep ϥⲉⲙ. ⲡ(ⲟⲩ)ⲧⲣⲓⲙⲓⲥ.   **b** with ⲉ-,
worthy to, or *to be* : Ge 31 28 *B* (*S* ⲡ ⲙ.) ἀξιοῦσθαι, Ap 5 4 *SB* (cf 5 2 *S* ⲛ-), CaiEuch 472 *B* ϥⲉⲙ.
...ⲉϩⲱⲥ ⲉⲣⲟⲛ ἄξιος ; Mt 3 11 *B* (*S* ⲛ-), 1 Cor 15
9 *F* (*S* ⲛ-, *B* ⲉⲟⲑⲣⲟⲩ-) ἱκανός ; Mt 12 4 *B* (*S* ϣϣⲉ)
ἐξόν ; Br 109 *S* make them ⲙ. ⲉϫⲓ baptism, C 43
198 *B* who is not ⲙ. ⲉⲙⲟⲩϯ ⲉⲣⲟϥ ϫⲉ- ; or with
causat ⲉⲧⲣⲉ- : Sa 18 4 *S*, MG 25 6 *B* ἀξ. infin,
1 Cor 16 4 *B* (*S* ϣϣⲉ) ἀξ. τοῦ ; BMis 390 *S* ⲁⲡⲙ.
ⲉⲧⲣⲉⲕⲉⲓ ⲡⲁⲛ = BSM 43 *B* ⲉⲣ ⲙ. ⲙⲡⲉⲕϫⲓⲛⲓ, DeV
2 127 *B* ϯⲙ. ⲁⲛ ⲉⲟⲣⲡⲁⲩ.   **c** with subjunct :
1 Cor 7 36 *B* (*SF* ϣϣⲉ ⲉ-) ὀφείλειν ; R 1 5 49 *S*
this other ⲉⲧⲙⲡⲉⲓⲙ. ⲡϣⲙⲁϫⲉ ⲡⲓⲙⲁⲓ, BSG 195 *S*
ϣⲁⲛⲧⲙ. ⲛⲧⲉⲡⲉⲡⲡⲁ ⲉⲓ, MIE 2 346 *B* ⲙⲡⲓⲙ. ⲡⲧⲁ-
ⲟⲩⲱϣⲧ ; or ϫⲉⲕⲁⲥ *S*, ϩⲓⲛⲁ *B* : Mt 8 8 ἱκ.   **d** *be
meet, entitled, obliged* : BHom 94 *S* ⲟⲩⲕⲟϥⲡ ⲕⲙ.

ⲡⲣ ⲡⲁⲓ ὀφείλ., BG 82 *S* ⲡⲉⲧⲟ ⲡⲏⲧⲛ ⲉⲥⲟⲟⲩⲛ ⲙⲡ-
ⲡⲉⲧⲙ. ⲛⲥⲟⲟⲩⲛ, Ryl 72 358 *S* tale of bricks ⲉⲧⲉϣⲁⲩ-
ⲙ. ⲡⲧⲁ(ⲁ)ⲥ, TT 110 *S* ⲡⲡⲉⲕⲙ. ⲁⲛ ⲡϣⲁϫⲉ thus to
him, C 89 199 *B* ϩⲁⲣⲁ ⲧⲉⲛⲙ. ⲡϩⲟⲥ ⲉⲣⲟⲛ ϫⲉ-, Pcod
9 *S* ϥⲙ. ⲡⲁⲡⲁⲭⲱⲣⲉⲓ ⲡⲁϥ lest blood be shed, BMis
349 *S* ϯⲙ. ⲡⲣⲁϣⲉ to-day = BSM 15 *B* ϥⲧⲟⲙⲓ,
Kr 80 *S* rent ⲉϣⲁⲕⲙ. ⲡⲧⲁⲁⲃ ⲡⲁⲓ, BM 1056 *S* sim,
Va 67 78 *B* my children ⲉⲧⲉⲙ. ⲡⲧⲁⲓⲡⲗⲁⲍ *have a
right to*, RE 9 137 *S* ⲕⲙ. ⲁⲛ ⲉϫⲓ ϣⲁⲭⲉ against
us.   **e** without obj, *be worthy, fitting* : Jer 15 19
B, Mt 22 8 *SB* ⲡⲁϥⲙ. ⲅⲁⲣⲡⲉ ἀξ.,
EpJer 43 *F* (*B* ⲧⲁⲓⲟ) ἀξιοῦσθαι, Cl 50 2 *A* whom
God ⲡⲁⲧⲟⲩⲙ. ⲕⲁⲧⲁⲝ. ; Mt 20 4 *B* (*S*+ⲛ-) δίκαιος ;
Aeg 211 *S* ⲉϣⲱⲡⲉ ϥⲙ. εὔλογος ; AM 226 *B* ⲉⲡ-
ⲡⲁⲭⲱ ⲁⲛ ⲡⲟⲩϩⲗⲓ ⲉϥⲙ. ⲁⲛ, Ep 194 *S* ⲟⲩϩⲱⲃ ⲉϥⲙ.
ⲁⲛ.   **f** impersonal *B*, *it is right, needful* : Mt 18
33 (*S* ϣϣⲉ), Ac 16 30 (*S* do), MG 25 26 δεῖ ; Ro
15 27 (*S* do), 2 Cor 12 11 (*SF* do) ὀφείλ. ; Eph 5
3 (*S* = Gk) πρέπειν ; BSM 32 this bread ⲥⲉⲙ. ⲛ-
ⲧⲉⲛϫⲁϥ ϩⲁⲧⲟⲧⲟⲩ = BMis 374 *S* ⲡⲁⲡϣⲓ ⲛⲕⲱ ϩⲁⲣⲱⲟⲩ, DeV 15 ⲥⲉⲙ. ⲡⲏⲓ ⲉⲟⲣⲓϥⲱⲛ my blood, *ib*
108 ⲉⲡⲁⲥⲙ. ⲛⲱⲧⲉⲛⲡⲉ ⲉⲣⲁϣⲓ, AM 114 ⲥⲉⲙ. ⲡⲁⲛ
ⲡⲧⲉⲙⲙⲉⲡⲣⲓⲧⲟⲩ.

ⲁⲧⲙ. *SB* adj, *worthless, unworthy* : AM 274 *B*
I being ⲡⲁ. ⲙⲡⲁⲓⲧⲁⲓⲟ, CaiEuch 531 *B* thy servants
ⲡⲁ. ἀνάξιος ; Miss 8 30 *S* ϩⲃⲏⲩⲉ ⲡⲁ. παρὰ τὸ προσ-
ῆκον ; *ib* 189 *S* hast ventured to speak ϩⲱⲥ ⲁ. *unworthy as thou art*, Ep 178 *S* ⲡⲓⲉⲗⲁⲭ(ⲓⲥⲧⲟⲥ) ⲡⲁ.
(sc writer).   ⲙⲡⲧⲁⲧⲙ. *SB* nn f, *unworthiness* :
R 2 4 90 *S* shall not deprive them ⲭⲱⲣⲓⲥ ⲙ., AM
238 *B* ⲧⲁⲙ. hast thou made worthy ;   adverbial :
1 Cor 11 27 *B* (*S* vb) ἀναξίως ; CA 95 *S* ⲉϥⲙⲟⲟϣⲉ
ϩⲛⲟⲩⲙ.

———— *SABF* nn m, *worth, desert, fate* : Sa 7 15 *S*,
Ro 16 2 *SB*, 1 Thes 2 12 *SF* (*B* vb), Cl 21 1 *A*
ἀξίως, Job 33 27 *SB*, Lu 23 41 *SB* ἄξιος, BHom
2 *S* ἀξία ; Sa 14 30 *S* ⲡⲉⲙ. ⲙϥⲱⲃ τὰ δίκαια, Ac
28 4 *S* (*B* ϩⲁⲡ) δίκη ; Lev 27 27 *S* (*B* ⲧⲓⲙⲏ) τίμημα ; Z 332 *S* forgiven ϩⲙⲡⲙ. ⲡⲡⲉϥⲛⲟⲃⲉ ἔγκλημα ;
ShBMOr 8810 410 *S* ⲡⲁⲙ. ⲡⲉ ⲙⲕⲁϩ ⲡϩⲏⲧ, J 81
17 *S* brought on child sickness ⲡⲣⲟⲥ ⲡⲙ. of my
sins, R 2 1 70 *S* ⲁϥⲧⲁⲕⲟϥ ⲡⲁⲣⲁ ⲡⲉϥⲙ., C 86 156
B ⲡⲉⲙ. ⲡⲡⲉϥϣⲏⲣⲓ is that thou requite their kindness, *ib* 43 108 *B* buried ϩⲁⲡⲉⲟⲩⲙ. ⲡⲉⲙⲟⲩⲧⲙⲏ,
Miss 4 202 *B* David singeth of us ϩⲁⲡⲉⲟⲩⲙ. *justly*
(Ps 13 3).

ⲣ, ⲉⲣ ⲙ. or ⲣ ⲡⲙ. *SBF*, *become, be worthy, de-
serve* : Ge 31 28 *S* (*B* vb), AM 275 *B* if I shall ⲉⲣ
ⲡⲉⲙ., Bor 253 159 *S* ⲙⲡϥⲁⲁⲧ ⲡⲙ. even of a word,
CaiEuch 453 *B* ⲁⲣⲓⲧⲧ ⲡⲉⲙ. to stand ἀξιοῦν, *ib* 532
B ⲁⲕⲑⲣⲉⲣ ⲉⲙ. of sonship, R 1 1 38 *S* will not
suffer thee ⲉⲧⲣⲉⲕⲣ ⲙ. ⲡⲕⲁⲓⲥⲉ ⲕⲁⲧⲁⲝ., Lu 12 48 *S*
(*B* vb) ἄξια ποιεῖν ; Col 1 12 *B* (*S* diff) ἱκανοῦν ; Va

57 14 *B* ⲉⲥⲉϣⲱⲡⲓ ⲛⲁⲛ ⲉⲑⲣⲉⲡⲉⲣ ⲡⲉⲙ. ⲙⲙⲱⲟⲩ ἐπιτυγχάνειν ; PS 267 *S* ⲉⲙⲡⲉϥⲉⲓⲣⲉ ⲙⲡⲉⲙ. of mysteries, ShC 42 142 *S* ⲙⲡϥϫⲁⲁⲛ ⲡⲙ. ⲡⲉⲓ ϣⲁⲣⲟⲛ *he
deigned not*, BMis 367 *S* ⲁⲛⲣ ⲙ. (var ⲁⲛⲙ.) = BSM
27 *B* ⲉⲣ ⲡⲉⲙ. of great favour, BM 595 *F* I longed
to see thee but (ⲙ)ⲡⲉⲕⲉⲓⲧ ⲡⲉⲙⲡϣⲏⲓ, Pcod 14 *S*
ⲙⲡⲉⲧⲁⲓⲟⲓⲕⲏⲥⲓⲥ...ⲧⲣⲉⲓⲣ ⲡⲙ. *to come*, AM 150 *B*
ⲉⲑⲣⲉⲡⲁⲓⲧ ⲡⲉⲙ. ⲡⲧⲉⲧⲉⲡⲓ to my dwelling. *V* AZ
47 143.

ⲙⲡϣⲁ *S*(once)*AA²* adv, *much, greatly* : Ex 1 7
A(*B* ⲉⲙⲁϣⲱ), AP 47 *A²* σφόδρα ; *ib* 14 2 πολύ ; Cl
1 3 *A* πάνυ ; *ib* 17 2 *A*, Zech 11 2 *A* (*B* do) μεγάλως ; Pro 14 29, 29 35 *A* (*S* ⲉⲙⲁⲧⲉ) ἰσχυρῶς ; *ib*
14 17, 19 16 (19) *A* (*S* do) πολλά ; *ib* 13 24 *A* (*S* do,
B diff) ἐπιμελῶς ; Joel 1 14 *A* (*S* do, *B* ⲉⲙⲁϣⲱ)
ἐκτενῶς ; AP 8 *A²* πικρῶς, *ib* δεινῶς ; Ge 4 5 *A*
(Cl, *B* do) λίαν, Pro 12 13 *A* (*S* do, *B* ⲛⲕⲁⲗⲱⲥ)
λεῖα (? λίαν) ; Jude 20 *A* ⲉⲥⲟⲩⲁⲁⲃⲉ ⲙ. (*S* do, *B* om)
ἁγιώτατος ; BG 20 *S* ⲡⲉⲓⲗⲩⲡⲉⲓ ⲙ. ϩⲣⲁⲓ ⲛϩⲏⲧ.
Cf ⲙⲁϣⲟ (ⲉⲙⲁϣⲟ).

ⲙⲡϣⲓϣ *v* ⲙϣⲓϣ.

ⲙⲁⲣ, ⲙⲏⲣ *S bundle v* ⲙⲟⲩⲣ.

ⲙⲏⲣ *S*(once)*B*, ⲙⲉⲣ DM nn m, *shore of river
esp opposite shore* : Ez 47 8 gloss(*S* ⲕⲣⲟ), O'LearyTh
41 ⲡⲙ. of Jordan (*cf* Mt 4 15 ϩⲓⲙⲏⲣ, *S* do). With
e- as prep, *to the other side* : Nu 21 13 (*S* ϩⲓⲡⲉⲕ.),
Deu 30 13 (*S* ⲙⲡⲓⲕ.), Mt 14 22 (*S* ⲉⲡⲉⲕ., *F* ⲉⲡⲁⲉⲧ)
εἰς τὸ πέραν, Nu 33 44 (*S* ϩⲓⲡⲉⲕ.) ἐν τῷ π. ; Ps 135
14 (*S* om) διάγειν ; Deu 27 2 (*S* ⲝⲓⲟⲟⲣ) διαβαίνειν,
Bar 3 27 διαβ. πέραν, MG 25 344 went ⲉⲙ. ⲉⲡⲓ-
ⲕⲉⲥⲁ εἰς τὸ ἄλλο π. ; ST 330 *S* ⲙⲁⲣⲉⲧⲉⲕⲕⲁⲧⲟ ⲡⲟⲭⲟⲩ ⲉⲙ., N&E 39 338 ⲁⲩⲉⲣ ϭⲓⲡⲓⲟⲣ ⲉⲙ., C 43 79
martyr's heels pierced & cords (?) passed ⲉⲙ. ⲡⲃⲏ-
ⲧⲟⲩ (*cf* AM 166 sim). *Cf* dem *a-mr*, RylDem 3
231 n & DM 9 23 ⲁⲙⲉⲣ. With ϩⲓ-, *on, at other
side* : Ge 50 10 (cit TstAb 256 ϩⲓⲡⲉⲭⲣⲟ ϩⲓⲙ., *S*
ϩⲓⲡⲉⲕ.), Deu 30 13 (*S* ϩⲛⲁⲣⲏⲧⲥ *l* -ⲝⲥ), Is 7 20 (*S*
ϩⲁⲡⲉⲕ.), Mt 19 1 (*S* ⲉⲡⲉⲕ.) πέραν gen, Jer 32 22 (8)
ἐν τῷ π., Nu 21 11 ⲉⲃⲟⲗ ϩⲓⲙ. (*S* ϩⲓⲡⲉⲕ., var ⲉⲃⲟⲗ
ϩⲓⲡⲉⲕ.) ἐκ τοῦ π., MG 25 344 voice reached them
ϩⲓⲙ. ⲙⲡⲓⲕⲉⲥⲁ = Z 316 *S* ϩⲓⲡⲉⲕ. ἐκ τοῦ ἄλλου π.
(var μέρους), EW 108 on reaching ferry found kings
ⲉⲩⲭⲏ ϩⲓⲙ. ⲡϯⲡⲟⲗⲓⲥ. As nn, *on further side* :
Ez 39 11 ϫⲉⲛⲡⲓϩⲓⲙ. ⲡⲁⲃⲁⲣⲙ Gk diff (*cf* Heb).
In place-names : ⲡⲁⲓⲙⲉ ⲧⲙⲟⲩⲙⲏⲣ in nome of
Antinoe (Bodl(P) e 70, *cf* ⲣⲙⲟ), ⲡϣⲁⲙⲏⲣ (Ep 1 121)
= Ψαμῆρις Spg *Petubastis* 24*. *Cf* ⲣ̄ⲙⲣⲱ.

ⲙⲟⲩⲣ *SAA²BF*, ⲙⲣ- *SA*, ⲙⲉⲣ- *SB*, ⲙⲁⲣ- *S͘F*,
ⲙⲟⲣ⸗ *SB*, ⲙⲁⲣ⸗ *S͘AA²F*, ⲙⲁⲗ⸗*F*, ⲙⲏⲣⲧ *SAA²BF*,
ⲙⲉⲗⲧ*F* (JKP 2 134), p c ⲙⲁⲣ- *SF*, ⲙⲉⲣ- *SB*, ⲙⲟⲣ-
B vb I tr, *bind, gird, tie*, ⲁ c acc of thing bound : Ez

16 4 *SB*, Mt 13 30 *SBF*, *ib* 14 3 *S* (*BF* ⲥⲱⲛϩ), Jo
18 12 *SA²* (*B* do), AP 11 *A²* δεῖν, Jos 9 10 *S* ἀποδ ,
Ez 34 4 *SB*, Lu 10 34 *SB* καταδ., Ez 3 26 *SB* συνδ. ;
Ps 146 3 *SB*, Am 2 8 *AB*, Mt 23 4 *SB* δεσμεύειν,
Si 7 8 *S* (Lemm) καταδεσ. ; Job 38 3 *S* (*B* diff),
Z 345 *S* = MG 25 210 *B* ζωννύειν, Joel 1 13 *SAB*,
Lu 12 37 *S* (*B* ⲥⲱⲕ) περιζ., Jer 26 6 *B* reading
ἀναζ., Ac 27 17 *SB* ὑποζ. ; RNC 41 *S* ⲡⲧⲉⲣⲉϥ-
ⲃⲟⲗⲟ (gospels)...ⲁϥⲙⲟⲣⲟⲩ πτύσσειν, BMis 451
S sim ; BG 103 *S* ⲧⲙⲣⲣⲉ ⲡⲧⲉϥϣⲙⲉ (*l* ⲡⲧⲃϣⲙⲉ) ⲁⲥ-
ⲙⲟⲣϥ, ShC 73 154 *S* ⲉϥⲙⲉⲣ ⲉⲧⲡⲱ, Jⲉⲩⲇ 444 *S*
exorcism against one that has ⲙ. ⲡⲟⲩⲙⲁ ⲉⲁϥⲕⲱ
ⲡⲣⲏⲧϥ ⲙⲡⲉⲕⲣⲟϥ, AZ 33 132 *S* spell ⲉⲓⲙ.
ⲡⲧⲡⲏ ⲉⲓⲙ. ⲙⲡⲕⲁϩ, C 43 26 *B* ⲁⲩⲙⲟⲣϥ ⲡⲧⲟⲧϥ, TU
26 1 b 42 *S* ⲡⲉⲧⲙ. ⲙⲡⲕⲓⲙ ⲡⲓⲙⲉⲗⲟⲥ (but Aeg 282
S ⲣⲉϥⲃⲱⲗ) ἑρμηνεύς, P 129¹⁵ 21 *S* ⲁϥⲙⲟⲣϥ *tied it
up* (*sc* χάρτης on which charms written), Mor 28
218 *S* ⲁϥⲙⲁⲣ ⲧⲉϥⲟⲩⲉⲣⲏⲧⲉ when broken. ⲃ c ⲡ-
of that wherewith bound (Gk mostly acc) : Ps 149
8 *S* (*B* ⲥⲱ.), Mt 13 30 *SBF*, Jo 11 44 *S* (var ϩⲛ-)
A²B δεῖν ; Ex 29 9 *S* (*B* ⲥⲱⲕ), Is 3 24 *SB* ζων.,
Jo 13 4 *SB* διαζ., 1 Kg 2 4 *B* (*S* ϯ ϩⲓ-), Ps 29 11
SB, Is 32 11 *BF* (*S* diff), Dan 10 5 *B* (*S* ϩⲛ-), R
1 1 33 *S* ⲁϥⲙⲟⲣϥ ⲡⲟⲩⲗⲉⲡⲧⲓⲟⲛ περιζ. ; EpJer 42 *B*
(*F* + ⲉⲗⲁⳅ), Mor 17 55 *S* ⲉⲩⲉⲙⲟⲣⲧ ⲡⲡⲉⲙⲡⲉⲛⲓⲡⲉ
περιτιθέναι ; PS 106 *S* ⲡϥⲙⲟⲣⲉϥ ⲙⲡⲕⲁⲕⲉ, ShA 2
83 *S* ⲡⲧⲁⲡⲁⲓ ⲙⲟⲣϥ ⲁⲡ ⲡⲧⲉⲓⲁϣⲏ ⲙⲙⲟϩ ShMIF
23 33 *S* girdle of lies ⲡⲉⲛⲧⲁⲕⲙⲟⲣⲕ ⲙⲙⲟϥ, AM
319 *B* rope ⲁⲩⲙⲟⲣϥ ⲙⲙⲟϥ, BSM 115 *B* ⲉϥⲙ.†
ⲡⲟⲩⲙⲟⲭⳅ, Z 628 *S* ⲡⲧⲙⲟⲣⲉ ⲡⲟⲩⲧⲟⲉⲓⲥ, PSBA 27
168 *S* sim., Louvre R 49 *S* ⲁⲩⲙⲟⲣⲧ ⲡⲥⲁⲣⲙⲟⲟⲩ
girt or *constrained me* (*v* ⲙⲟⲟⲩ). ⲥ ϩⲛ-, ϩⲉⲛ-
sim (Gk ἐν or acc) : Jud 16 6 *S*, Ez 3 25 *B* δεῖν,
Bor 100 28 *S* = CaiEuch 484 *B* ⲁⲕⲙⲟⲣⲧ ϩⲙⲡⲁϩⲣⲉ
ⲡⲓⲙ appertaining unto life καταδ. ; Pro 29 35 *SAB*
ἀναζων., Ps 64 6 *SB*, Si 45 12 *S* περιζ. ; 1 Kg 17
38 *B* (*S* ⲛ-) ἐνδύειν ; PS 180 *S* ⲉⲓⲙ.† ϩⲙⲙⲣⲣⲉ,
C 43 166 *B* ⲉϥⲙ.† ⲡⲡⲉϥϭⲓϫ...ϩⲉⲛϩⲁⲡⲡⲉϫⲉⲥ. ⲥ
c ⲡ- of that upon, to, in which bound (Gk dat, ἐπί) :
Nu 19 15 *B* (*S* diff) καταδεῖν ; Is 11 5 *SB* ζων.,
Jo 13 5 *SA²B* διαζ. ; Deu 23 13 *S* (*B* Gk om), Is
3 24 *B* (*S* Gk om) ; ShA 2 65 *S* ⲫⲁⲥⲧⲓⲁ ⲉϣⲁⲣⲉ-
ⲙⲟⲣⲥ ⲙⲙⲟ, EW 101 *B* chains ⲉⲧⲙ.† ⲙⲙⲟϥ, Mor
47 209 *S* garment ⲉⲧⲉⲣⲉⲡⲟⲩϥ ⲙ.† ⲙⲙⲟϥ. ⲥ e-
sim (Gk ἐπί, πρός, dat) : Ge 38 28 *S* (BMis 127) *B*,
Job 40 24 *S* (*B* ⲛ-), Mk 11 4 *S* (*B* ⲥⲱ.), 1 Cor 7 27
SF (*B* do) δεῖν, Jer 28 63 *SB* ἐπιδ. ; Eph 6 14 *S*
(*B* ⲥⲱⲕ ⲉⲭⲉⲡ-) περιζων. ; Nu 27 6 *S* (*B* ϯ ⲡ-), Mt
27 48 *S* (*B* ⲑⲱⲕⲥ) περιτιθέναι ; Lu 17 2 *S* (*B* ⲓϣⲓ)
περικεῖσθαι ; Mt 18 6 *S* (*B* diff) κρεμαννύναι ; Pro
3 3 *SA* (*B* diff) ἀφάπτειν ; Gk om : Jud 15 14 *S*,
Jer 13 4 *B*, Mk 1 6 *SB*, Jo 20 7 *S* (*B* ⲭⲱ) ; P 129¹⁶
68 *S* millstone ⲙ.† ⲉⲣⲟϥ (*ib* ⲙ.† ⲙⲙⲟϥ), Mor 47

208 S ⲁⲥⲙ. ⲙⲡⲣⲟⲗⲟⲕ, ⲉⲅⲣⲃⲟⲟⲥ, BM 527 F charm ⲙⲁⲣⲉϥ ⲉⲡⲉⲕϫⲡⲁⲣ Mus 40 41 S ⲉⲅⲡⲁⳝⲱ ⲉⲅⲙ.† ⲉⲛⲉⲅⲉⲣⲏϥ *jungentur,* Mor 663 A 142 S lest they blame me ⲧⲁϣⲱⲡⲉ ⲉⲓⲙ.† ⲉⲅⲅⲁⲡ before Lord, *ib* 46 26 S accusation ⲛⲧⲁⲩⲙⲟⲣϥ ⲉⲣⲟϥ, Miss 4 772 S ⲉⲅⲙ.† ⲉⲡⲛⲓ ⲙⲡⲡⲉ̄. c ⲉϫⲛ- sim (Gk ἐπί, acc): Ap 9 14 S (B ⲥⲱ.) δεῖν; 1 Kg 17 39 S (B ϭⲱⲕ), Is 11 5 SB ζων., Jud 3 16 S, Ps 44 3 SB περιζ.; Deu 11 18 S (B e-) ἀφάπτειν; Ez 24 17 B (S ⲣⲓϫⲛ-) συμπλέκεσθαι; C 86 145 B ⲉⲥⲙ.† ⲉϫⲉⲛⲧⲉⲥⲧⲏⲓ. c ⲣⲓϫⲛ- sim (Gk ἐπί): Deu 6 8 B (S diff) ἀφάπ.; Ge 27 16 B (Lect Copt Mus Cai, var e-) περιτιθέναι; Ez 44 18 B (S ⲙ.† ⲛ- P 44 115) Gk om, El 50 A ⲡⲁⲩⲙ.†...ⲣⲓϫⲛⲡⲉϥⲕⲉⲓⲃⲉ (*cf* Ap 1 13), BKU 1 26 (1) 13 F ⲙⲁⲣⲁϥ ⲣⲓϫⲟⲡⲉⲕϫⲉⲡⲉ. d c ⲣⲛ-, ϩⲉⲛ- of place where bound (Gk ἐν, εἰς): Ac 20 22 S (B ⲥⲱ.) δεῖν, Pro 6 27 SAB ἀποδ., Si 22 17 SB ἐνδ., Pro 26 8 SA ἀποδεσμεύ., Sa 17 2 S, Eph 4 1 S (B ⲥⲱ.) δέσμιος; PS 13 S soul ⲉⲧⲙ.† ⲣⲏⲓⲱⲣⲁⲡⲡⲏⲥ, BHom 117 S ⲁⲩⲙⲟⲣⲥ ⲣⲛⲁⲙⲛⲧⲉ. c ⲛⲥⲁ- S, *tie behind:* R 1 5 47 bade ⲙⲟⲣϥ ⲛⲥⲁⲟⲩⲅⲧⲟ, BMis 528 sim. e *gird* with monastic habit: Mor 31 89 S of abbot ⲁϥⲙⲉⲣ ⲕⲉⲙ̄ⲧⲥⲁϣϥ ⲛⲥⲟⲡ, Wess 18 3 S rubric ⲉϣⲱⲡⲉ ⲙⲡⲟⲩⲙⲉⲣ ⲣⲱⲙⲉ, BM 1001 S ⲁⲩⲙⲟⲣϥ ⲙⲡⲉⲥϫⲛⲓⲁ, BSM 108 B ⲙⲡⲁⲧⲟⲩⲙⲟⲣⲧ ⲙⲡⲁⲓⲥ̅ϫ̅. ⲉⲑⲟⲩⲁⲃ, Mor 51 36 S degenerate monks are like ⲡⲉⲛⲧⲁⲩⲙⲟⲣϥ ⲛⲃⲣⲣⲉ. *Cf* ⲙ. ⲉϧⲟⲩⲛ of widow's consecration Aeg 251. f *bind, oblige* by oath, *adjure:* Mor 19 20 S ⲕⲙ.†...ⲉⲧⲣⲉⲕϫⲱ what thou sawest = Miss 4 106 B, HL 103 B ⲁϥⲙⲟⲣϥ not to eat, CA 92 S sim (*cf* ⲙ. ⲉϧⲟⲩⲛ), BMOr 7561 43 S ⲁϥⲙⲟⲣⲟⲩ ⲉⲧⲁⲧⲣⲉⲩϩⲟⲡϥ, Z 265 S ⲁϥⲙⲟⲣⲟⲩ to eat with him, J MMA 24 2 3 S ⲁⲓⲙⲁⲣⲟⲩ ⲙⲡⲣⲁⲛ ⲙⲡⲡⲉ̄ to take & give them in alms, BIF 2 67 S every one that entereth ϭⲙ.† ⲉⲧⲣⲉϥⲣ ⲧⲁⲅⲁⲡⲏ & pray for me, Ep 204 S ϯⲙ. ⲙⲙⲟⲕ ⲙⲡⲉⲣⲕⲱ (*l* ϭⲱ).

Qual, *bound, girt:* Job 32 19 SB, Mt 21 2 S (BF ⲥⲱ.) δεῖν, Is 46 1 SB καταδ., Mk 15 7 F (S ϭⲱⲡ, B ⲥⲱ.), Ac 16 25 S (B do) δέσμιος, Ge 39 20 S (B do) δεσμώτης; Lu 12 35 S (B ϭⲱⲕ) περιζων.; Ps 145 7 S (B ⲥⲱ.) πεδᾶσθαι; 3 Kg 20 (21) 11 S ὀρθός opp ⲥⲏϭ; ShA 1 302 S ill built walls come apart ϫⲉⲥⲉⲙ. ⲁⲛ, BMis 389 S ⲛⲉⲩⲙ. ⲡⲉ & stood serving, MIF 9 5 S ⲟⲩⲁ ⲉϥⲙ. = R 1 1 31 S ⲣⲙⲡⲉϣⲧⲉⲕⲟ, JKP 222 S ⲟⲩⲕⲟⲟⲥ ⲉϥⲙ., ShC 73 84 S days of Lent ⲉⲧⲙ. ⲏ ⲉⲧⲉⲣⲉⲛϩⲧⲟⲣⲡⲉ (*cf* ⲙ. ⲉϧⲟⲩⲛ), Ryl 313 S letter sent ⲉⲥⲙ. *tied up* (*cf* BP 12498 S]ⲛⲥⲫⲣⲁⲅⲓⲥ ⲉⲧⲙ. ⲙⲙⲟⲟⲩ *sc* letters, PS 337 S ⲡⲉⲥⲫⲣ. ⲛⲁⲓ ⲉⲧⲙ. ⲉϧⲟⲩⲛ ⲉⲧⲉϥⲯⲩⲭⲏ).

II intr S (rare), *bind:* BHom 51 power ⲉⲃⲱⲗ ⲁⲩⲱ ⲉⲙ., BMis 461 scripture ϣⲁⲥⲙ. ϩⲛⲟⲩⲙⲁ ⲛⲥⲃⲱⲗ in another (*cf* Miss 8 167 sim ⲙ.†...ⲃⲱⲗ).

V also ⲙ. ⲉϧⲟⲩⲛ, ⲙ. ⲙⲛ-.

—— *SB* nn m, *band, girth, strap:* Nu 19 15 B (S ⲙⲣⲣⲉ), Jer 34 2 B δεσμός, Col 3 14 B (S do) σύνδεσ., Is 1 6 B (S do) κατάδεσ. *bandage,* ib 22 12 SB ζῶσις; Mor 17 19 S ⲡⲙ. on her head διάδημα; *bundle:* Ge 42 27 B δεσ.; Bodl(P) e 37 S ⲙ. ⲛⲃⲏⲧ, Kr 247 S ⲛⲡⲟⲩⲣ, BMOr 9525 8 S ⲡⲉⲓⲁⲩ; *magical* (*cf* δεσμός): Cai 42573 1 S title of charm ⲟⲩⲙ. ⲡⲡⲉⲛⲫⲓⲟⲥ (νυμφίος), RChamp 541 S ⲡⲉϯⲡⲁⲉⲣ ⲣⲱⲃ ⲉⲣⲟϥ ⲡⲟⲩⲙ.; *clutch:* Mor 44 37 S laid hands on Jesus with blows, scourges ϩⲛⲡⲙ. ⲡⲡⲉⲩⲧⲏⲛⲃⲉ; *metaph:* TRit 246 B ⲫⲙ. ⲡⲧⲉ ⲟⲩⲁⲣⲏⲃ. Adj: ShIF 104 S for sickness ϩⲉⲛⲧⲣⲟϭ ⲙⲙ.

—— ⲉϧⲟⲩⲛ S, ⲁϧ. AA², ⲉϧ. B, *bind, join to:* Jud 15 4 S δεῖν, AP 15 A² ⲁⲩⲙⲁⲣⲥ ⲁϧ. ⲁⲩⲙⲟⲩⲉⲓ προσδ., Va 66 294 B ⲫⲏ ⲉⲧⲁϥⲙⲟⲣⲉⲛ ⲉϧ. ⲉⲣⲟϥ συνδ.; Ge 22 13 S (B ⲧⲁⲣⲡⲟ) κατέχειν; Ez 41 6 SB ἅπτειν; Tob 6 18 S κολλᾶσθαι; BHom 48 S ϣⲁϥⲙⲉⲣ ⲧⲉϥⲯⲩⲭⲏ ⲉϧ. ⲉⲧⲁⲡⲁⲧⲏ συμπεδᾶν; 3 Kg 2 7 S ἐγγίζειν; PS 121 S ⲁⲓⲙⲟⲣϥ ⲉϧ. to bed post, ShWess 9 139 S fox's claws ⲙ.† ⲉϧⲟⲩⲛ ⲉⲡⲉϥⲟⲩⲉⲣⲏⲧⲉ as amulet, ShC 73 207 S Lord will ⲙ. ⲡⲧⲟⲣϭⲛ ⲉϧ. ⲉⲣⲟⲟⲩ, Mus 35 19 B substances & persons ⲉⲅⲙ.† ⲉϧ. to single Godhead, BKU 1 3 S ⲉⲧⲉⲧⲡⲉⲙ. her mind & body ⲉϧ. ⲉⲣⲟⲓ by spells, Mor 25 202 S these commands ⲥⲉⲙ.† ⲉϧ. ⲉⲡⲉⲛⲟⲥ ⲡⲓⲙ, Miss 4 541 S he saw them not yet inclined ⲉⲙ. ⲉϧ. ⲉⲧⲕⲟⲓⲛⲱⲛⲓⲁ. Of fast which *binds:* ShA 1 418 S ⲉⲓⲡⲁⲙ. ⲉϧ. ⲉⲧ(ⲧ)ⲉⲥⲥⲉⲣⲁⲕⲟⲥⲧⲏ, BM 1128 S come ⲉⲡⲡⲁⲧⲡⲙ. ⲉϧ.; also tr: CO 15 S ⲙ. ⲙⲡⲉⲕⲥⲱⲙⲁ ⲉϧ. & become son of τόπος, RE 9 164 S from nuns to bishop, If thou wouldst ⲉⲧⲣⲉⲡⲙ. ⲡϣⲉⲉⲣⲉ ϣⲏⲙ...ⲛⲧⲛⲙⲟⲣⲟⲩ ⲉϧ. (*sic* MS) till feast of Cross. As nn m, *obligation, fast* (esp lenten): ShMIF 23 105 S ⲡⲙ. ⲉϧ. of 40 days, Mor 31 17 S ate no bread from Sunday of ⲙ. ⲉϧ. till Sabbath of ⲃⲱⲗ ⲉⲃⲟⲗ (*q v* nn a), Saq 226 S list of feasts & fasts ⲡⲙ. ⲉϧ. & ⲡⲃⲱⲗ ⲉⲃ., Leyd 136 S ⲕⲩⲣⲓⲁⲕⲏ ⲙⲡⲙ. ⲉϧ. precedes 1st Sunday of 40 days, Vollers *Katal* '06 421 B ⲡⲓⲥⲁⲃⲃ. ⲡⲧⲉ ⲡⲓⲙ. ⲉϧ. in Mechir, Z 10 B (ⲡⲓ)ⲙ. ⲉϧ. ⲛⲡϣⲓϯ, Ryl 340n S ⲡⲡⲟϭ ⲙⲙ. ⲉϧ. & ⲡⲕⲟⲩⲓ ⲙⲙ. ⲉϧ.

—— ⲙⲛ- S, ⲛⲉⲙ- B, *bind with, be at enmity with:* ShA 1 71 S sayest ⲉⲓⲙ.† ⲡⲙⲙⲁⲥ ϩⲛⲟⲩ ⲏ ϫⲉ ⲙⲡⲧⲁⲓ ⲙⲟⲥⲧⲉ ⲉϧⲟⲩⲛ ⲉⲣⲟⲥ, Mor 663 A 137 S if one angered him he continued ⲉϥⲙ.† ⲡⲙⲙⲁϥ in wrath = MG 17 547 مرتبط معه في الغضب, TT 28n S I determined ⲉⲧⲁⲧⲣⲁⲃⲱⲗ ⲡⲙⲙⲁϥ, then vision appears & asks ⲟⲛⲧⲱⲥ ⲕⲡⲁⲙ. ⲙⲡⲡⲉⲧⲣⲓⲧⲟⲩⲱⲕ remembering not 1 Pet 2 23?, BAp 162 S ⲙⲡⲣⲙ. ⲙⲡⲗⲁⲁⲩ ϫⲉⲡⲉⲧⲙ.† ⲙⲡⲉϥⲥⲟⲡ ϧⲟ ⲡϫⲁϫⲉ with God = لا يُعقد على الناس (*v* ZDMG 68 182 n), *ib* 166 S ⲉϣϫⲉ ⲁⲕⲙ. ⲙⲡⲡⲉⲕⲥⲟⲡ & forgive him not, Miss 4 109 B among sinners some ⲉⲅⲙ.† ⲡⲉⲙⲡⲟⲩⲉⲣⲛⲟⲩ (Mor 18 14 S om).

ⲙⲁⲣ-, ⲙⲣ-, ⲙⲉⲣ- *SB* p c in ⲙⲉⲣⲕⲁⲥ, ⲙⲏⲣ (*l* ⲙⲉⲣ)ⲙⲉⲥⲧⲉⲛϩⲏⲧ, ⲙⲁⲣⲙⲏⲧⲉ, ⲙⲣⲟⲅⲟϭⲉ, ⲙⲁⲣϩⲏⲧ, ⲙⲟⲩⲣ-, ⲙⲁⲣⲭⲡⲁϩ, ⲙⲁⲣⲭⲱϫⲉ (? *q v*). *V* ⲕⲁⲥ, ⲙⲉⲥⲧϩⲏⲧ, ⲙⲏⲧⲉ, ⲟⲩⲟϭⲉ, ϩⲏⲧ *heart*, ϫⲡⲁϩ.

ⲙⲁ ⲙⲙ. *S*, *place of binding, prison* : Is 24 22 (*B* ⲙⲁ ⲡⲥⲱⲛϩ) δεσμωτήριον, Ac ? (only P 44 18) اعتقال. (ⲣⲉϥⲙ.) ⲙⲛⲧⲣⲉϥⲙ. *S*, *magical binding* : Leyd 442 ϩⲉⲛⲙ. ⲛϧⲉⲛⲣⲱⲙⲉ with sicknesses.

ϭⲓⲛ-, ϫⲓⲛⲙ. *SB* nn f m, *binding, that which binds* : PS 32 *S* ⲁⲕⲡⲱⲱⲛⲉ ⲛⲧϭ. ⲛⲡⲁⲣⲭⲱⲛ, AZ 33 132 *S* bound with ϭ. ⲛⲓⲙ *spell*, O'LearyH 12 *B* loosed ⲛⲉϭϫ. *fetters*.

ⲙⲁⲣ, ⲙⲁⲁⲣ *S* nn m, *bundle* : Ryl 88 ϣⲟⲗⲧ ⲙⲙ. ⲛϣⲟⲣⲉⲧ, BMOr 6201 A 72 ⲙ. ⲉⲗⲁⲥ, *ib* 125 ⲙⲁⲁⲣ ⲉⲛⲕⲁϣ, BM 1045 sim.

ⲙⲏⲣ, ⲙⲉⲣ *S* nn m, meaning same : CO 364 ⲥⲛⲁⲩ ⲙⲙ. ⲛⲡⲟⲩϩ, BP 908 sim ϣⲙⲟⲩⲛ ⲙⲙ., Ep 398 ϯⲟⲩ ⲙⲙⲉⲣ, *ib* 353 ⲉⲓⲥⲧ(ⲉ) ϣⲏ ⲧⲁⲓⲟⲩ ⲙⲙ. ⲙⲙⲁⲣⲉ.

ⲙⲁⲓⲣⲉ *S* nn f, meaning same : Cant 1 13 ἀπόδεσμος ; Ryl 291 ⲛϭⲙⲥ, ⲛⲉⲣⲃⲏⲓⲥ, WS 147 ⲛⲕⲁⲙ, Ostr *penes* GJéquier ⲛⲟⲩⲟⲧⲉ.

ⲙⲏⲣⲉ, ⲙⲉⲣⲉ *S*, ⲙⲏⲣⲓ *B* nn f, meaning same : Mt 13 30 *B* (*SF* ϣⲟⲗ) δεσμός ; CO 180 *S* ⲥⲩⲛⲧⲉ ⲙⲙ. ⲛⲃⲁⲗ[ⲟⲧ ?], *ib* 341 ⲙⲙⲁⲣⲉ, Win 71 *S* ⲥⲟⲉ ⲙⲙⲉⲣⲉ of herbs, MG 25 355 *B* stolen chattels ⲁⲅⲁⲓⲧⲟⲩ ⲡⲟⲩⲙ.

ⲙⲁⲣⲓ *B* nn f, ? *part of loaf* or ? *loaf of certain form* (cf ⲙⲁⲓⲣⲉ) : C 86 172 when asked to taste bread ⲁϥϫⲓ ⲡⲟⲩⲙ. & put it in mouth.

ⲙⲁⲣⲙⲁⲣ *B* nn, *bandage* (?) : C 86 177 ⲟⲩⲙ. ⲡⲉⲙⲟⲩϣⲁⲗ applied to wound.

ⲙⲣⲣⲉ *SA*, ⲙⲉⲗⲗⲓ *F* nn f, *chain, bond, joint* : Nu 19 15 *S* (*B* ⲙⲟⲩⲣ), Job 38 31 *S* (*B* ⲥⲛⲁⲩϩ), Ps 116 6 *S* (*B* do), Hos 11 4 *A* (*B* do), Mk 7 35 *S* (*B* do) δεσμός, Is 1 6 *SF* (*B* ⲙⲟⲩⲣ) κατάδ., 4 Kg 11 14 *S*, Job 41 6 *S* (*B* do), Ac 8 23 *S* (*B* ⲥⲛ.) σύνδ. ; Ac 12 7 *S* (*B* = Gk) ἅλυσις ; Pro 5 22 *SA* (*B* = Gk) σειρά ; Job 17 11 *S* (*B* ⲙⲟϯ) ἄρθρον ; *ib* 18 13 *S* (*B* ⲥⲛⲃⲓ) κλών ; Si 40 11 *S* (var ⲥⲛ.) ἐπαγωγή (cf Is 14 17 *SB* ⲥⲛ.) ; PS 34 *S* ⲛⲉϭⲙⲏⲣ ⲛϩⲡⲉⲙ., BHom 118 *S* bound not with ⲛⲉϩⲛⲥ but with ϩⲉⲛⲙ., BG 17 *S* ⲧⲙ. ⲛⲧⲁϩϣⲉ enduring a while, Sh(Besa)Mich 550 22 *S* guileful thoughts & ⲧⲙ. ⲙⲡⲟⲛⲏⲣⲟⲛ, MG 17 319 *S* ⲧⲙ. ⲧⲏⲣⲥ ⲛⲧⲕⲟⲓⲛⲱⲛⲓⲁ was in grief = *ib* 93 *B* ⲑⲱⲟⲩⲧⲥ ⲧⲏⲣⲥ, Miss 4 234 *S* covenant ⲉⲧⲣⲉⲩϣⲱⲡⲉ ⲡⲟⲩⲙ. ⲡⲟⲩⲱⲧ in food, raiment, BMar 99 *S* let us have no ⲙ. ϩⲓⲡⲉⲡⲣⲏⲧ ⲉϩⲟⲩⲛ ⲉⲗⲁⲁⲩ (cf ? ⲙⲁⲣϩⲏⲧ, *v* ϩⲏⲧ), *ib* 182 *S* ⲉⲕϩⲟⲩⲙ. ⲡⲛⲏⲥϯⲁ (cf Esaias Abbas *ed* Jerusalem 39 ἔδησας σεαυτὸν εἰς τ. ὥραν τ. φαγητοῦ).

ⲙⲟⲣⲥ *SB* nn f, **a** *binding, restriction* (of fast) : Wess 18 4 *S* rubric 1st Sunday in Lent ⲧⲕⲩⲣⲓⲁⲕⲏ ⲉϫⲛⲧⲙ.   **b** *bundle, girdle used as purse* : Mor 17

32 *S* ⲟⲩⲛⲟϭ ⲙⲙ. ⲛⲡⲟⲩϧ ἀπόδεσμος = EW 32 *B* ⲟⲩϭⲓⲥⲓ ⲛⲛ., BSM 44 *B* ϯⲙ. sealed & full of money = EW 70 *B*, Va 63 10 *B*, BMis 391 *S* ⲛⲁⲛⲛⲓⲛ (πάννιον), BSM 150 *B* ï̄ⲅⲟ.

ⲙⲁⲣⲉ-*SAA²BF*, ⲙⲁⲗⲉ-*F*, verbal pref optative : Ps 21 8 *SB* ⲙⲁⲣⲉϥⲛⲁϩⲙⲉϥ ῥυσάσθω, Zech 8 9 *A* ⲙⲁⲣⲉⲡⲉⲧⲛϭⲓϫ ϭⲙ ϭⲁⲙ κατισχυέτωσαν, Jo 19 24 *A²* ⲙⲁⲣⲛⲟⲩ[ⲁϩ ⲉ]ⲛⲓⲙ λάχωμεν, Is 5 19 *F* ⲙⲁⲗⲟⲩϭⲣⲱⲛⲧ ἐγγισάτω, *ib* 30 21 *F* ⲙⲁⲣⲉⲡⲛⲱⲧ πορευθῶμεν. Absolute ⲙⲁⲣⲟⲛ *SB*, ⲙⲁⲣⲁⲛ *SᶠAA²F*, *let us (go)* : Ge 4 8 *A*(Cl)*B* διέλθωμεν, Deu 13 2 *S* (*B* ⲙⲁⲣⲉⲛϣⲉ ⲛⲁⲛ) πορευθῶμεν, Mic 4 2 *SA* (*B* do) ἀναβῶμεν, Jo 11 16 *SAA²B* ἄγωμεν ; C 41 34 *B* ⲙ. ⲛⲁⲛ, Leyd 419 *S* ⲙ. ⲧⲛⲃⲱⲕ, Mor 27 32 *Sᶠ* ⲙ. ⲉⲛⲁⲛⲓ, C 41 10 *B* ⲙ. ⲉⲃⲟⲗ. Once ⲙⲁⲣⲟⲕ *S* : Mor 52 39 Anianus to Mark ⲙⲁⲣⲟⲕ ⲛⲓⲙⲁⲓ ⲉⲛⲁⲛⲓ (cf same incident P 129¹⁴ 135 *S* ⲙⲁⲣⲟⲛ).

ⲙⲁⲣⲓ *B*   *v* ⲙⲟⲩⲣ *sf*.

ⲙⲁⲓⲣⲉ *S*   *v* ⲙⲟⲩⲣ *sf*.

ⲙⲉⲣⲉ-*SF*, ⲙⲁⲣⲉ-*SAA²*, ⲙⲡⲁⲣⲉ-*B*, ⲙⲉⲗⲉ-*F*, ⲙⲁ-*SA*, ⲙⲉⳍ*SF*, ⲙⲁⳍ*SA*, ⲙⲡⲁⳍ*B*, pref neg aor, opp ϣⲁⲣⲉ- : Job 5 6 *S* ⲙⲉⲣⲉϭⲓⲥⲉ ⲉⲓ, Si 11 27 *S* ⲙⲉⲕⲣ ⲡⲙⲉⲉⲩⲉ (var ⲙⲁⲕ-), Jo 4 9 *SA²BF* ⲙ. ⲓⲟⲩⲇⲁⲓ ⲧⲱϩ, Mk 7 12 *S* ⲙⲉⲧⲉⲧⲛⲕⲁⲁϥ (var ⲙⲙⲁⲧⲉⲧⲛ-, *B* ⲛ-... ⲁⲛ), Pro 27 24 *S* ⲙⲉⲅⲧⲁⲁϥ *A* ⲙⲁⲅ-, EpJer 11 *F* ⲙⲉⲅⲉϣ ⲟⲩϭⲉⲓ, *B* ⲙⲡⲁⲅ-. With ⲁⲛ : Jth 7 10 *S* ⲙⲉⲅⲕⲱ ⲛⲧⲏⲅ ⲁⲛ. With ⲛⲉ- aor preterite : Ps 100 7 *S* ⲡⲉⲙⲉⲓⲥⲟⲩⲧⲱⲛϥ (*B* ⲙⲡⲁϥ-) οὐ κατεύθυνεν.

ⲙⲁ- (rare) El 98 *A* ⲙⲁⲡⲭ̅ⲥ̅ ϩⲱⲧⲃⲉ ⲇⲓⲕⲁⲓⲟⲥ, PVi 10157 *A* ⲙⲁⲑⲛϫⲟⲡⲏ ⲙⲡⲓⲣⲛ ϩ̅ ⲣ ⲕⲁ[ⲧⲉ]ⲭⲉ ⲙⲙⲁϥ, CO 300 *S* ⲙⲁⲁⲡⲁ ⲃⲓⲕⲧⲟⲣ ⲣ ⲙⲡⲧⲥⲟϭ again, RE 9 137 *S* ⲙⲁⲉⲓⲣⲏⲛⲏ...ϣⲱⲡⲉ, Ep 437 *S* ⲙⲁⲣ ϩⲱⲃ ⲛⲁⲧⲁⲛϩⲁⲗⲱⲙⲁ, PBu 257 *S* we trust ϫⲉⲙⲁⲡⲡⲉ̅ ϯ ⲑⲉ ⲡⲥⲉⲙⲁⲧⲉ ⲙⲡⲁⲓ (sc defraud us).

ⲙⲉⲉⲣⲉ *SA*, ⲙⲉⲣⲓ *B*, ⲙⲏⲣⲉ *F*, ⲙⲉⲣⲉ *O* nn, *midday* : **a** *SB* ⲛⲡⲁⲩ ⲙⲙ., Ge 18 1, Zeph 2 4 (*A* do), Ac 8 26 μεσημβρία ; **b** *S* ⲛⲡⲁⲩ ⲙⲙ. *B* ⲙⲙ., Ge 43 16, Job 5 14, Ps 54 18, Jer 15 8 μεσ., μεσημβρινός, Ac 22 6 *S* ⲛⲛ. ⲙⲙ. *B* ⲛⲕⲱϯ ⲙⲙ. περὶ μ. ; **c** *S* ⲛⲛ. ⲙⲙ. *B* ϩⲁⲛⲙⲙ., Ps 36 6, *ib* 90 6, Is 18 4, *B* ⲁⲛⲙⲙ., Job 11 17, Is 58 10 μεσ. ; **d** *SAB* ⲙⲙ., Is 59 10 μεσ. ; Su 7 *S* (*B* ⲧⲫⲁϣⲓ ⲙⲡⲓⲉϩⲟⲟⲩ) μέσον ἡμ. ; Is 34 10 *B* (*S* ϩⲟⲟⲩ), Lu 2 37 *B* (*S* do), Cl 25 4 *A*, Z 345 *S* = MG 25 210 *B* ⲉϩⲟⲟⲩ ἡμέρα ; *day* opp *night* : 1 Thes 2 9 *B* (*SF* ϩⲟⲟⲩ), CaiEuch 576 *B*, MG 25 204 *B* ἡμ., Mor 30 27 *F* ⲉⲓⲧⲉ ϭⲱⲣϩ ⲉⲓⲧⲉ ⲙ. ; PS 189 *S* light ⲙⲛⲡⲁⲩ ⲙⲙ., Leyd 150 *S* ⲧⲕⲁⲑⲏⲧⲛⲥⲓⲥ ⲙⲙ. ⲙⲛⲡⲥⲁⲃⲃⲁⲧⲟⲛ, MIE 2 358 *B* ϥ̄ⲛ. ⲙⲙ. = BAp 86 *S* ⲕⲁⲓⲣⲟⲥ ⲙⲡⲙⲟⲩϩ ⲙⲡⲙⲟⲟⲩ (so ? *l* ⲙⲙⲏⲣⲓ), AZ 21 100 *O* ⲛⲙ. ⲡϣⲱⲛ, Sh(Besa)Bor 204 246 *S* blind ⲉⲧϫⲟⲡϫⲛ ⲙⲙ. as if midnight, ShA

1 2 S ⲙⲡⲣⲡⲉ ⲙ. ⲡⲁⲣⲁ ⲡϣⲓ paral ⲙⲡⲣϣⲱⲣⲡ, R 1 2 45 S ⲉⲥⲙⲟⲟϣⲉ ⲙⲙ. ϩⲁⲡⲁⲗ., ⲁⲛⲁⲗ. B nn f, besides *ee g* above : HL 113 passed all ϯⲁ. *walking*, ib 121 ϭⲉⲛⲧϥⲁϣⲓ ⲙⲡⲓⲉϩⲟⲟⲩ ⲛϩ. ⲛϯⲕⲁⲩⲙⲁ. *Cf* ϩⲁⲛⲁⲣⲟⲩϩⲓ, ϩⲁⲡⲁⲧⲟⲟⲩⲓ.

ⲙⲉⲉⲣⲉ S nn f, *a tree* : JTS 8 241 ⲃⲛⲛⲉ, ϣⲟⲡⲧⲉ, ⲧⲙ. *Cf* LMis 37, but ? *l* ⲡⲥⲉⲉⲡⲉ.

ⲙⲏⲣⲉ S, **ⲙⲏⲣⲓ** B *v* ⲙⲟⲩⲣ *s f*.

ⲙⲣⲱ S, ⲉ ⲙⲡⲣⲱ S(Z 614), ⲉⲙⲃⲣⲱ B, pl **ⲙⲣⲟⲟⲩⲉ** S nn f, *harbour, landing stage* on sea or river : Ge 49 13 B ⲉⲙⲃ. all MSS (S ⲙⲁ ⲙⲙⲟⲟⲛⲉ) ὅρμος : P 44 128 S ساحل; BHom 89 S ⲡⲗⲉⲙⲏⲛ (λιμήν)... ⲉⲧⲉⲧⲁⲓⲧⲉ ⲧⲉⲙ., R 1 2 31 S ⲧⲉⲙ. ⲛⲑⲁⲗⲁⲥⲥⲁ of Alexandria, BMis 468 S ⲧⲙ. ⲛⲉϫⲭⲓⲥⲥⲁ do (*v* Pcod 66 n), Z 281 S of Constantinople, BIF 14 178 S of Antioch, P 129¹⁴ 128 S ⲁⲩϫⲓⲟⲟⲣ ⲉⲡⲓⲉⲣⲟ ⲁⲩⲉⲓ ⲉⲧⲙ. ⲙⲡⲛϯⲙⲉ ; pl form ShZ 501 S ⲛⲉⲙ. ⲙⲡⲓⲉⲣⲟ, P 44 *lc* S ⲙ. سواحل. ⲁⲡⲉⲙⲣⲱ B nn f, meaning same : K 134 ⲗⲩⲙⲏⲛ (sic) مينا .ا. موردة, C 43 154 sailed to ϯⲁ....ⲉⲧⲁⲅⲁⲙⲟⲛⲓ ⲉⲡⲓⲭⲣⲟ, ib 1 ⲁϥⲁⲙⲟⲛⲓ ⲉϯⲁ., AM 88 ϯⲁ. ⲛⲧⲉ ⲫⲓⲟⲙ, C 43 111, ib 210 *judg-ment-seat* placed ϩⲓⲭⲉⲛ-, ⲉϫⲉⲛϯⲁ. In place-name : ϯⲙⲣⲱ (AM 301 ?دمرو). *Cf* ⲙⲏⲣ *shore*, ⲉⲓⲟⲟⲣ (ⲉⲓⲟⲣ). ⲉⲙⲣⲱ B MG 25 359 *v* ⲣⲟ *ply*.

ⲙⲣⲱⲙ SB, ⲉⲙⲣⲱⲙ, ⲙⲣⲟⲙ B, ⲟⲩⲣⲱⲙ, ⲟⲩⲗⲱⲙ S nn m, *pillow* = ἐμβρίμιον : FestschrEbers 39 S laid it beneath head ⲛⲟⲉ ⲛⲟⲩⲟⲩⲗⲱⲙ = MG 25 213 B ⲟⲩⲙⲣ. ἐμβ., Z 314 S seated upon ⲟⲩⲣⲱⲙ(sic) ⲛⲟⲩⲟⲧ ἐμβ., MG 25 40 B put garments ⲉϫⲉⲛⲟⲩⲙⲣ. (sic), ib not a man but ⲟⲩⲉⲙ.ⲡⲉ *dummy* ; K 134 B ⲡⲓⲙⲣⲟⲙ مرموم Montp 168 B ⲟⲩⲙⲣⲟⲙ رومس, طن, رمموم (*bundle, raft*), prob = ϭⲱⲗⲛ B *q v*.

ⲙⲁⲣⲙⲁⲣ B *v* ⲙⲟⲩⲣ *s f*.

ⲙⲁⲣⲙⲏⲧⲉ S *v* ⲙⲏⲧⲉ *s f*.

ⲙⲁⲣⲟⲛ *v* ⲙⲁⲣⲉ-.

ⲙⲉⲣⲁⲛ, ⲙⲛ. B nn m, *trough, tank* : Ex 2 16 حوض (S *illegible*, A ϭⲱ[ⲧ]) δεξαμένη, K 129 ⲡⲓⲙⲛ. *cook's utensils* جرن هاون, ib 153 *bath furniture* جرن.

ⲙⲣⲣⲉ *v* ⲙⲟⲩⲣ.

ⲙⲉⲣⲣⲉ B nn m, *red of hair* : Ryl 453 336 ⲡⲓⲙ. اشقر (*cf* ⲕⲁⲣⲟⲩⲥ). *Error* ? for ⲙⲉⲣϣ.

ⲙⲁⲣⲏⲥ *v* ⲣⲏⲥ.

ⲙⲁⲩⲣⲉⲥ, -ⲣⲏⲥ, ⲙⲁⲣⲓⲥ (K) B nn f, *jug, jar* : ROC 25 255 drank ⲟⲩⲙ. of water daily κιλικίσσιον, var ib 273 ⲗⲁⲕⲟⲡ ⲡⲕⲉⲗⲏⲕⲓⲥⲓⲟⲛ ⲙⲙ, K 145 ϯⲙ. جر holding 19 اقساط ξέσται.

ⲙⲣⲓⲥ S, ⲉⲙⲃⲣⲓⲥ B nn m, *new wine, must* : Job

32 19 SB, Ac 2 13 SB (var ⲙⲃ.) γλεῦκος ; Mt 9 17 S (B ⲏⲣⲡ ⲙⲃⲉⲣⲓ) οἶνος νέος ; Is 63 2 S ⲙ. ⲡϩⲣⲱⲧ (B Gk diff) ; Kr 234 S ⲙ. = μοῦσθ(ος) opp ⲏⲣⲡ ⲁⲥ, Ryl 158 37 S sim ; P 44 80 S ⲡⲉⲙ. · أ‏ل = 43 54 سلاف, Tri 496, 664 S '—; Va 68 165 B there ⲡⲉⲙ. ⲛⲧⲉ ⲧⲫⲉ welleth not up, ShA 1 246 S ⲡⲉⲙ. *sweet at first becometh good or bad*, BMis 570 S ⲥϯ ⲡⲙ. *in Paradise*, Ryl 137 S ⲧⲁⲩⲣⲓⲛⲉ ⲡⲉⲙⲣⲓⲥ ⲡϣⲉ ⲡϥⲏⲅ *title or name* ? V Dévaud *Études '22* 9.

ⲙⲟⲣⲉ *v* ⲙⲟⲩⲣ *s f*.

ⲙⲉⲣⲓⲧ *v* ⲙⲉ *love*.

ⲙⲟⲣⲧ SB, ⲙⲁⲣⲧ Sᶠ, ⲙⲁⲗⲧ F nn f, *beard* (DM *chin*) : Lev 13 29 SB, Ps 132 2 SB, EpJer 30 BF, MG 25 254 B *hair grew on* ⲡⲓⲑⲟⲩⲥ ⲛⲧⲉ ⲧⲉϥⲙ. πώγων ; R 1 5 13 S ⲙⲡⲣϥⲉⲉⲕⲉ ⲧⲉⲕⲙ., Z 343 S ⲁⲧⲉϥⲙ. ⲁⲣⲭⲉⲓ ⲛⲧⲟⲟⲧϥ = MG 25 208, 284 B ⲁϥϭⲓ ⲁⲣⲭⲏ ⲙⲙ. γένειον ; R 1 2 39 S *whoso shaveth* ⲧⲉϥⲙ. (var Lammayer 41 Sᶠ ⲙⲁⲣⲧ sic MS), AM 175 B *of Baptist* ⲟⲩⲙ. ⲉⲥⲣⲏⲧ ⲡⲕⲁⲗⲱⲥ, *MélCh Moeller* S ⲟⲩⲛⲟϭ ⲙⲙ. ⲉⲥϣⲏⲣ, C 43 196 B ⲧⲉϥⲙ. ⲟⲓ ⲡⲑⲟⲩⲥ ⲉⲡⲉⲥⲏⲧ, P 129¹⁴ 123 S *one seized* ⲡⲉⲥⲡⲓⲣ ⲡⲧⲉϥⲙ. *other* ⲡⲕⲉⲥⲡⲓⲣ, Mor 31 20 S ⲡⲁⲧϩⲟϭ ⲙⲙ., Mor 24 7 F *hair &* ⲙⲁⲗⲧ. ⲁⲧⲙ. S, *beardless* : P 44 68 ⲁⲧⲉⲡⲓⲟⲥ أمرد. ϩⲁⲙ. S, *underpart* (?) of beard : PMich 4949 glossary ⲁⲡⲑⲏⲣⲓⲟⲛ (ἀθήρ.) · ⲧϩⲁⲙ. between κρόταφος & γλῶσσα. ⲣ, ⲉⲣⲙ. SB, *grow beard, be bearded* : BIF 13 101 S = MG 25 284 B, ib 208 B = Z 343 S ⲟⲩⲡ ⲙ. ⲙⲙⲟϥ ⲉⲓϩⲉ γέν. ϣⲉⲡ ⲙ. B, *shave beard* as disgrace : K 162 حلق لحية. ⲙⲟⲣⲧⲓⲟⲥ B, *well bearded* : K 72 الى.

ⲙⲉⲣⲱⲧⲡ B *v* ⲡⲉϩ (ⲡ. ⲙⲙⲉ).

ⲙⲉⲣⲟⲩⲟϭⲉ S *v* ⲟⲩⲟϭⲉ.

ⲙⲣⲟϣ, ⲙⲣⲁϣ S, ⲙⲟⲣϣ† S, ⲙⲁⲣϣ† A vb intr, *be red or yellow* : Lev 13 30†, 31† S (B ⲁⲟⲩⲁⲡ ⲙⲫⲏⲣϣ) ξανθίζειν ; ib 42† S (B ⲑⲣⲉϣⲣⲱϣ), ib 14 37† (ShIF 132, B ⲁⲟⲩⲁⲡ ⲡⲭⲣⲱⲙ) πυρρίζειν, Cant 5 10† S (var ⲧⲣⲉϣⲣⲱϣ) πυρρός ; Est D 5† S ἐρυθριᾶν ; *dark-hued* : Ge 49 12 S κατάκορος (B ⲣⲁϣⲓ) χαροποιός) ; Pro 23 29† A (S ⲟ ⲡⲉⲗⲉⲗⲕⲛⲙⲉ) πελιδνός ; Mus 42 231 S ⲉϥⲙ.† opp ⲉϥⲟⲩⲟⲃϣ, PMéd 307 S cook them ϣⲁⲡⲧⲟⲩⲙⲣⲁϣ.

ⲙⲏⲣϣ SBF, **ⲙⲉⲣϣ** SF, **ⲙⲣϣ** SA adj, *red, ruddy* : 1 Kg 16 12 S (P 44 109 ⲙⲉⲣⲥⲉ) πυρράκης, Zech 1 8 A (B ⲁⲟⲩⲁⲡ ⲡⲭ.) πυρρός ; P 44 83 S *of horse* ⲇⲁⲕⲁⲗⲓⲛ (?) · ξανθός ⲙⲙ. اشقر ; Glos 313 S κιρρός · ⲙⲣϣ ; BM 603 F *of ass* ⲓⲱ ⲡⲙ. (*cf* حمار), AM 136 B *of complexion* ⲟⲩⲙ. ⲡⲉ, Miss 4 738 S ⲧⲉϥϭⲟⲧ ⲙⲙ. ⲣ, ⲉⲣⲙ. SBF, *be ruddy* : BMis 237 S *of hair* ⲉϥⲟ ⲙⲙ. = Mor 30 10 F, C 43 196 B sim, Mor 44 26 S *of Christ's appearance* ϩⲛⲥⲟⲡ ⲉϥⲟ ⲙⲙ. ϩⲛⲥⲟⲡ ⲉϥⲟ ⲡⲟⲩⲱⲃϣ (*cf* Cant 5 10).

ⲙⲟⲩⲣϣ S vb intr (?), *look around, stare about* : Si 9 7 ⲙ. ⲡⲡϭⲓⲣ (var ⲙⲟⲩϣⲧ ⲡⲟⲩ̅ⲣ.) περιβλέπειν ἐν.

ⲙⲣⲱϣⲉ, S nn f, *a vessel of clay* : Bodl(P) b 6 ⲉⲙ. ⲡⲃⲉⲗϫⲉ, BKU 1 140 ⲡⲧⲟⲩϣⲏ (*l* ⲉⲩϣⲏ) ⲉⲙⲡⲁⲧⲉⲧⲙⲣ[ⲱ]ϣⲉ ⲕⲱⲧⲉ ? *water-clock* (*v* Ep 549 n). ? = ⲙⲣⲱⲣⲉ.

ⲙⲣⲟϣⲧ† B vb intr, *stink* : Job 6 7 ⲉⲩⲙ. (S ϣⲟⲩϣ) βρόμος, HL 121 demons' bread ⲥⲉⲙ. As nn m : Job 17 11 (S ⲇⲟ), Joel 2 20 (SA ⲇⲟ) βρόμος.

ⲙⲉⲣⲱϥ B nn, meaning unknown, prob a quantity (? ⲙⲉϩⲣⲱϥ *mouthful*) : C 43 33 ⲁⲓϭⲓⲟⲩⲓ ⲡⲟⲩⲙ. ⲙⲙⲟⲟⲩ in his face.

ⲙⲣⲟϭⲧ B nn, *pipe-clay* : IgR 112 μόροχθος (whence ?),

ⲙⲉⲣⲉϩ SB, ⲙⲉⲣϩ S, ⲙⲉⲣⲏϩ A nn m, *spear, javelin*, cf מרח (IgR) : 1 Kg 17 45 S (B ⲡⲁⲅⲓ), Si 29 16 S, Mic 4 3 SA (B ⲇⲟ) δόρυ ; Hab 3 11 A (SB diff) βολίς *hasta* ; Joel 3 10 S (B = Gk) σιρομάστης ; P 44 58 S ⲕⲟⲡⲧⲁⲣⲓⲡ ⲉⲅⲭⲟⲥ (ἔγχος) ⲙ., K 116 B رمح, P 54 118 B نصل ; Mor 19 28 S ⲙ. = Miss 4 114 B ⲗⲟⲭ̅ⲏ, BMis 214 S Constantine set cross upon ⲡⲉϥⲙ. = Mor 16 64 S ⲕⲟⲡⲧⲁⲣⲓⲟⲡ, C 86 152 B ⲙ.= *ib* ⲕⲟⲡⲧ., Mor 18 54 S ϩⲣⲓⲡ(ⲧ)ⲁⲣⲓⲟⲡ thrown ⲉⲧⲉⲣⲉⲡⲕⲟⲩⲓ ⲙⲙ. ⲡⲉ = Miss 4 130 B, LMär 5 S ⲡⲧⲡⲁⲡⲉϩ ⲙ. ⲁⲡ ⲡⲥⲱⲓ = C 43 60 B ϩⲓ ⲙ., PRain 4741 S ⲟⲩⲙ. ϩⲁⲧⲣⲉⲙⲛⲥⲉ ⲥⲡⲁⲩ. ϣⲥ (ϣⲥⲉ, ϣⲧⲉ) ⲡⲙ. S, ϣⲉ ⲡⲙ. B, *blow with spear* : LMär 3 S ⲉⲁⲕϯ ⲡⲁϥ ⲡⲟⲩϣ. = Mor 39 39 S⁴, C 43 58 B. ϥⲁⲓⲙ. S, *spear-bearer* : Ac 23 23 (B ⲣⲉϥϥⲓ ⲗⲟⲭ̅ⲏ) δεξιολάβος (var -βόλος), BMis 240 δορυφόρος.

ⲙⲣⲏϩ S nn, *pole of waggon* : Mus 40 39 none shall ride on ⲙ. ⲡⲁϭⲟⲗⲧⲉ *temonem plaustri.*

ⲙⲣⲉϩ B nn in ⲙⲁⲙⲣⲉϩ, 20th station of moon, *q v.*

ⲙⲙⲏⲣϩ S *v* ⲙⲟⲩⲗϩ (ⲙⲉⲗϩ) *salt.*

ⲙⲣⲱϩⲉ, ⲉⲙ. S nn f *a vessel prob of metal* : Ep 549 in list of utensils in bronze or brass, *ib* 550 sim, TurM 18 ⲙⲣⲟ. (ϩ altered from ϣ) sim, CO 454 sim, *ib* 251 ⲧⲙ. ⲡⲥⲱⲧϥ *strainer* (?), Gu 51 ⲧⲉⲙⲣⲱϩ[ⲉ] (*sic* MS) covering corpse's face that he might ⲡⲓϥⲉ ⲉⲃⲟⲗ, so ? *strainer* (*v* AZ 39 152). V ⲙⲣⲱϣⲉ. Cf Berl*Wörterb* 2 112 *mrḫt* (1°).

ⲙⲟⲩⲣⲭⲡⲁϩ, ⲙⲁⲣϭⲡⲁϩ *v* ⲭⲡⲁϩ.

ⲙⲁⲣⲭⲱϫⲉ S, pl -ϫⲟⲟϫⲉ nn, *a garment* : CO 472 among napkins, cloths &c ⲟⲩⲙ., P 131⁶ 37 effeminate monks wear ϩⲉⲡⲥⲧⲟⲗⲏ ⲉⲩϣⲟⲡⲧ ⲡⲟⲉ ⲡⲡⲉⲓⲙⲁⲣϫⲟⲟϫⲉ of women. Cf J 76 40 among women's clothing ⲡⲁⲉⲣϣⲱⲡ...ⲙⲡⲟⲩⲙⲓϫⲕⲉ ⲙ̅ⲡⲁⲣⲭⲱϫⲉ (*l* ? ⲡⲁⲙⲁⲣⲭ.) ⲙⲡⲟⲩⲅⲉⲕⲧⲉ, also MG 17

630 برجوج = PO 4 473 τρεῖς μηλωταὶ συνάψαι, which = *ib* 631 ثوب الصوف (Gk om). ⲙⲁⲣ- ? ⲡⲥ of ⲙⲟⲩⲣ.

ⲙⲁⲥ B nn, meaning unknown : C 86 176 sword's blow ⲥⲉϫⲡ (*l* ? ⲥⲉⲗⲡ) ⲟⲩⲙ. ⲡϣⲁⲣ whereby his head hung (obscure, corrupt, cf ? ⲙⲟⲩⲥ or ⲗⲁⲥ).

ⲙⲁⲥ *v* ⲙⲓⲥⲉ.

ⲙⲁⲉⲓⲥ S nn f, *a measure* (?) : Ryl 243 42 ⲥⲛⲏⲧⲉ ⲙⲙ. ⲡϣⲉ, Hall 70 21200 S ⲁⲩⲃⲓ ⲟⲩⲙ. ⲡⲧⲏⲓ (*sic l*). Cf ? ⲙⲟⲩⲥ.

ⲙⲓⲥ S nn : PMéd 233 ϩⲉⲡⲙⲓⲥ, but prob *l* ϩⲉⲡϩⲉⲗⲙⲓⲥ (ἕλμις) as *ib* 283, 318. Cf next word & ⲑⲙⲓⲥ.

ⲙⲟⲥ S nn f, meaning unknown, occurs in recipes : Z 629 ϣⲁⲥⲉⲓⲡⲉ ⲉⲡⲉⲥⲏⲧ ⲡⲧⲙ. ⲙⲙⲟⲟⲩ, PMéd 233 ϩⲉⲡ(ϩⲉⲗ)ⲙⲓⲥ (ἕλμις) called ⲧⲙⲟⲥ (*sic l*) ϣⲟⲉⲓϣ.

ⲙⲟⲩⲥ SAF, ⲙⲟⲩⲥⲉⲣ, -ⲏⲣ B nn m, *strap, band* : Si 30 35 S, Is 5 18 S (B ⳓⲱⲕ), Mk 1 7 SB ἱμάς ; Ge 14 23 SB σφαιρωτήρ (var ἱμ.) ; Lev 26 13 S (B ⲥⲡⲁϩ) δεσμός ; Nah 2 3 AB ἡνία ; *belt, girdle*, soldier's &c : Mor 47 141 S ⲙ. ⲡⲥⲡⲁⲑⲁⲣⲓⲟⲥ, *ib* 38 90 S ⲙ. ⲡⲥⲧⲣⲁⲧⲓⲱⲧⲁ (*sic*), BSG 198 S soldier unbinds ⲡⲉϥⲙ. = *ib* 32 B ⳓⲱⲕ, BMar 36 S soldier-martyr ⲁϥⲧⲣⲉⲩ...ⲥⲱⲗⲡ ⲙⲡⲉϥⲙ. ; *strap in harness* : ShA 1 455 S ⲙⲙ. ⲙⲡⲡⲉⲧⲙⲏⲣ ⲉϩⲟⲩⲡ to yoke of plough-team, R 2 1 73 S sim ; *various straps, thongs* : C 86 276 B martyr stretched out with 4 ⲙ., BAp 80 S visitor pulls ⲙ. of cell's door, RE 14 28 S ⲡⲉⲓⲙ. ⲡⲧⲁⲩⲥⲱⲗⲡ ϩⲓⲡⲉϫⲱⲱⲙⲉ for tying up book, ShC 73 165 S ⲙ. among supplies needed by craftsmen, Sh(Besa)Z 504 S ⲙ. ⲡⲧⲟⲟⲩⲉ as thing of small value, J 37 66 S sim, BM 1103 S sandal & ⲡⲉϥⲙ., *ib* 527 S⁴ recipe ⲧⲁⲁⲩ ⲉϩⲟⲩⲡ (ⲉ)ⲟⲩⲙ. ⲡⲉⲓⲟⲩⲗ *thong of doe hide*, Kr 225 F coins ϩⲓⲭⲱⲙ. ⲉⲃⲁⲗⲉⲃ *in a girdle (that is) to be undone*, Vi 164 ostr S]ϣⲟⲧ ⲡⲙ. *pillow of* (plaited ?) *straps*, ST 118 S ϣⲁⲧⲓⲗⲁ ⲡⲙ. paral ϣ. ⲡⲩⲃⲏⲡⲉ. ⲣⲉϥⲧⲁⲙⲓⲉ ⲙ. S, *girdle-maker* : Mor 38 91.

ⲙⲥⲉ S, ⲉⲙⲥⲓ B *v* ⲱⲙⲥ.

ⲙⲁⲥⲉ S, ⲙⲉⲥⲉ A, ⲙⲁⲥⲓ BF *v* ⲙⲓⲥⲉ.

ⲙⲏⲥⲉ S, ⲙⲏⲥⲓ B one with child *v* ⲙⲓⲥⲉ.

ⲙⲏⲥⲉ SA, ⲙⲏⲥⲓ B, ⲙⲏⲥⲏ F usury *v* ⲙⲓⲥⲉ *sf.*

ⲙⲓⲥⲉ SAA², ⲙⲓⲥⲓ BF, ⲙⲉⲥⲓⲉ O, ⲙⲥⲓⲉ DM (V 16 3), ⲙⲁⲥ- SB, ⲙⲉⲥ- SABF, ⲙⲉⲥⲧ- S, ⲙⲁⲥⲧ⳹, ⲙⲉⲥⲧ⳹ SA, ⲙⲁⲥ⳹ S (Kr 228) B, ⲙⲓⲥⲧ⳹ O, ⲙⲟⲥⲉ† S, ⲙⲟⲥⲓ† B, pc ⲙⲁⲥ- SABF, ⲙⲉⲥ- SAF vb ⲁ intr, *bear, bring forth* : Ge 16 2 SB, Ps 47 6 SB, Is 13 8 SB, Lu 2 5 S (B ⲙⲃⲟⲕⲓ), Jo 16 21 SA²B, Z 296 S = MG 25 205 B τίκτειν, Job 21 10 B (S ϩⲓ ϩⲏ)

ὠμοτοκεῖν; Ge 10 21 B, Lu 23 29 SB, 1 Jo 5 1 B (S ϫⲡⲟ *bis*) ⲅⲉⲛⲛⲁⲛ (γίνεσθαι); Is 34 15 B (SF ⲥⲁⲁⲡϣ), Ez 31 6 B ⲛⲟⲥⲥⲉⲩⲉⲓⲛ; Mun 51 S ⲁⲥⲙ.... ⲁⲥⲭⲡⲟ ⲡⲟⲩϣⲏⲣⲉ, R 2 1 6 S ⲉϣϫⲉⲁⲧⲁⲥⲣⲏⲓ ⲱⲱ... ϯⲡⲁⲙ. ⲣⲱ, C 43 242 B woman ⲉⲑⲛⲁϯϭⲓ ⲙⲙ.

b tr, *bear young*: Ge 3 16 B (S ϫⲡⲟ), 1 Kg 2 5 B (S do), Pro 3 28 B (SA do), Hos 2 5 AB, Ap 12 13 SB τίκ.; Lev 18 9 B (S do), Mt 2 4 B (S do), Ac 7 20 B (SF do) ⲅⲉⲛⲛⲁⲛ, Ez 4 14 S (B ϫ.) γένεσις; Ge 21 5 B (S do), Is 9 6 B (S do), He 11 12 B (S do), MG 25 1 B ⲙⲡⲁⲧⲟⲩⲙⲁⲥϥ γίνεσθαι; Is 59 13 B (S ⲱⲱ) κύειν; Ja 1 15 S (B ϫ.) ἀποκύ.; AM 176 B after ⲡⲓⲉⲙⲃⲟⲕⲓ...ⲁⲥⲙ. ⲙⲡⲉⲥϣⲏⲣⲓ, R 1 2 63 S whoso saith ⲙⲡⲁⲧⲟⲩⲙⲁⲥϥ He was not = JA '75 5 209 S -ϫⲡⲟϥ, Mor 34 24 S king ⲛⲧⲁⲩⲙⲁⲥⲧϥ = BMis 98 S -ϫⲡⲟϥ, Hor 79 O ⲡⲣⲟⲟⲩ ⲡⲙⲓⲥⲧϥ, Kr 228 13 S not thou ⲡⲉⲛⲧⲁⲕⲙⲁⲥ(ⲥ), ShIF 151 S dig up roots ⲉⲧⲙⲉⲥ ⲙⲟⲟⲩ, MG 25 226 B dwelleth with man ⲉⲙⲁⲥ ϣⲏⲣⲓ; of male, *beget*: C 86 107 B have never wedded nor ⲙⲡⲓⲙⲁⲥ ϣⲏⲣⲓ, Aeg 31 B ⲁϥ- ϣⲁⲡⲙ. ⲡⲟⲩϣⲏⲣⲓ. Qual, *be newly delivered, give suck*: Ge 33 13 S (B ϯϭⲓ), Ps 77 71 SB, λοχεύεσθαι; Ps 103 17 S (B diff) ἐννοσσεύειν; ShA 2 272 S ⲉⲣⲉⲡϫⲁⲓⲙⲱⲡ ⲙ. in you, C 41 68 B ⲟⲩϭⲁⲙⲁⲩⲗⲓ ⲉⲥⲙ. foal following her = Miss 4 39 رلد, جد, C 86 116 B sim, PMéd 301 S milk of women ⲉⲥⲙ. ⲡⲟⲩ- ϣⲏⲣⲉ, DeV 194 B ϩⲓⲟⲙⲓ ⲉⲑⲙ., LAl 13 S ⲉⲧⲱⲣ(ⲉ) ⲉⲩⲙ. foals being kept apart.

—— *SABF* nn m, *offspring, generation*: Job 11 3 B (S ⲣⲱⲙⲉ), Mt 11 11 B (S ϫⲡⲟ) γεννητός, Eccl 7 2 S γέννησις, CaiEuch 327 B ⲡⲓⲙ. ⲡⲓⲉⲃⲟⲗ ⲙⲡⲓ- ϣⲱⲓ ἀναγέννησις, Mt 12 34 B (S do) γέννημα, Gal 4 29 B (S do) ⲅⲉⲛⲛⲁⲛ, Deu 30 9 SB ἔκγονος; Hos 9 11 AB τόκος; AM 106 B ⲟⲩⲙ. ⲡⲉ ⲡⲧⲉ ⲡⲁⲏⲓ *child of my house* (cf below ⲙⲉⲥ ϩⲏⲓ), Miss 4 721 S when she reached days of ⲡⲉⲥⲙ. she bore son, Pcod 46 S on 5th day ⲙⲡⲉⲥⲙ. *since her giving birth*.

—— + gen ⲛ-. ⲃ̄ⲗⲗⲉ ⲙⲙ., *born blind*: Jo 9 1 B (SA² diff) τυφ. ἐκ γενετῆς; ϭⲁⲗⲉ ⲙⲙ., *born lame*: MG 25 405 B; ⲉⲃⲟⲧ ⲙⲙ., *birth-month*: Job 39 2 SB μὴν τοκετοῦ, C 43 135 B, WTh 178 S sim; ⲙⲁ ⲙⲙ., *birth-place*: Ge 31 13 B (S diff) γένεσις; ⲟⲩⲟⲉⲓϣ ⲙⲙ., *time of birth*: Eccl 3 2 S καιρὸς τ. τέκειν; ϣⲟⲣⲡ¹, ϣⲣⲡ ⲙ.² or ⲙⲙ.³, ϣⲁⲙ.⁴, *first-born child*: Ex 34 19 S²B¹, Ps 134 8 S²B¹, Zech 12 10 A⁴B¹, He 1 6 S³B¹F¹ πρωτότοκος; or *bearing first child*: 1 Kg 6 7 S, Jer 4 31 SB πρωτοτοκοῦσα, TT 30 S agony of ⲛϣⲁⲙ. (var ⲙⲙ.) ⲙⲡⲧϣⲟⲣⲡ &c ⲙⲙ., *right, position of firstborn*: Ge 25 31 B, Deu 21 17 SB πρωτοτοκεῖον, Mic 6 7 SB πρωτότοκος; ⲣ ϣⲣⲡ ⲙ., *give birthright*: Deu 21 16 S (B diff) πρωτο- τοκεύειν; ϫⲱⲙ ⲙⲙ., *birth-book*: Mt 1 1 B (S diff) γένεσις; ϩⲟⲟⲩ ⲙⲙ., ϩⲟⲩⲙ., *birthday*: Ge

40 20 B, 2 Mac 6 7 A, Mt 14 6 SBF γένεσις, R 1 5 49 S thy father will ⲉⲣ ⲡⲉⲕⲣⲟⲩⲙ., PRain 4705 S good wishes ⲕⲁⲓϣⲉ ⲡⲣ. ⲟⲡ ϩⲁⲡⲉⲧⲡⲉⲣⲟⲩⲙ. As name: ⲣⲟⲩⲙⲓⲥⲉ Miss 4 782, BM 1116, ⲣⲟⲩⲙⲓⲥⲓ *ib* 673, ⲣⲱⲙⲓⲥⲉ Kr 249, ϥⲟⲩⲙⲓⲥⲉ BM 1111.

ⲙ. ⲉϩⲣⲁⲓ S, *bring forth*: 1 Kg 6 1 ἐκζεῖν; ⲙ. ⲉⲡϣⲱⲓ B sim: DeV 2 227 beasts ⲁϥⲟⲣⲉⲡⲕⲁϩⲓ ⲙⲁⲥⲟⲩ ⲉⲡ.

ⲉⲣ ⲙⲉⲥ B, *meaning sim*: C 86 274 ⲫⲏ ⲉⲧⲁϥⲉⲣ ⲙ. ⲥⲁⲁⲣ ⲡⲉⲙⲥⲁⲣϥⲁⲧ ⲅⲉⲛⲛⲁⲛ.

† ⲉⲙ. S, *meaning sim*: 1 Kg 4 19 ⲁⲥϯ ⲉⲙ. τί- κτειν.

ⲙⲁⲥ-, ⲙⲉⲥ- p c, *bearing, producing*: Ps 31 9 S ⲙⲁⲥⲡⲟⲣⲕ (B ⲧⲉⲙⲟⲁⲙ), Zech 14 15 A (B do) ἡμίο- νος; Ap 18 13 S (B om) ῥέδη, Miss 4 227 B Virgin ϯⲙⲁⲥⲡⲟⲩϯ (θεοτόκος), Ge 1 11 B ϣϣⲏⲛ ⲙⲙⲁⲥ- ⲟⲩⲧⲁϩ κάρπινος, Ps 106 34 B sim (S ⲣⲉϥϯ ⲕⲁⲣⲡⲟⲥ) καρποφόρος; ShIF 151 ⲡⲟⲩⲛⲉ ⲙⲙⲉⲥⲙⲟⲟⲩ.

ⲣⲉϥⲙⲓⲥⲉ, -ⲥⲓ SB, *one who bears*: 3 Kg 4 23 S (P 44 110 = 43 105) ⲉⲅⲥⲟⲧⲏ (*sic l*) ⲡⲣ. σιτευτός, νο- μάς (?), Va 58 185 B ⲟⲩⲣ. ⲡⲁⲧⲁⲑⲟⲛ ⲡⲓⲃⲉⲡ; ⲣⲉϥ- ⲙⲉⲥ- S: Br 241 ⲕⲁϩ ⲡⲣ. ⲡⲟⲩⲧⲉ ⲏ ⲣⲉϥⲙϩⲡⲉ ⲡⲉ̄, Bor 240 113 ⲡ. ⲡⲉϩⲟⲟⲩ, ShC 42 143 sim. ⲣⲉϥⲙⲉⲥⲧⲉ, -ⲙⲉⲥ- S, ⲣⲉϥⲙⲓⲥ-(*sic*) A: Pro 21 24 ⲣ. ⲡⲉϩⲟⲟⲩ μνησικακεῖν. ⲙⲛⲧⲣⲉϥⲙ. S, *bearing, birth*: BMis 89 ⲧⲙ. ϩⲱⲡⲏ ⲡⲧⲁϭⲣⲏⲓ, TT 27 due time of ⲧⲙ., BHom 19 ⲙⲛⲧⲣⲉϥⲙⲉⲥⲧ ⲡⲉⲑⲟⲟⲩ μνησικακία, *ib* 36 do, R 2 4 96 do.

ⲁⲧⲙ. S adj, *unborn*: KKS 485 sheep ⲡⲁ. ⲙⲙⲟϥ ϩⲛⲟⲩⲙⲁⲁϥ (v Ge 22 13). ⲙⲉⲧⲁⲧⲙ. B, *barren- ness*: TEuch 2 505 prayer against it.

ϭⲓⲛ-, ϫⲓⲛⲙ. SB, *birth, generation*: Ex 6 24 B (A ⲣⲉⲓⲧⲉ), Ez 16 3 SB, Ja 1 23 B γένεσις; Ex 6 19 B (A do) συγγένεια; BMis 509 S small (young) ϩⲛⲧⲉϥϭ. great in His divinity.

ⲙⲉⲥⲓⲉ O rel in ⲛⲓⲙ ⲡⲙⲉⲥⲓⲉ ⲛⲓⲙ *so & so whom so & so bore* AZ 21 100 & ⲉⲙⲉⲥⲓ: PGM 1 60 O ⲥⲓ ⲕⲁⲧ ⲉ. ⲕⲁⲧ, *ib* 146 εμεσιε. V Griffith *Stories* 94 n, also ⲙⲙⲓⲥⲉ DM V 16 3.

ⲙⲛⲥⲉ S, -ⲥⲓ B nn f, *one with child*: EpJer 28 B (F ⲟⲩⲓ ⲉⲥϩⲛⲏⲡⲧ ⲉⲙⲓⲥⲓ) λεχώς, cf Mor 16 15 S ⲉⲥⲱ ⲡϣⲣⲱ ⲛ ⲉⲥⲟ ⲙⲙ. (BMis 189 S om), Mor 28 60 S ⲡⲁⲣⲑⲉⲛⲟⲥ, ⲙ., ⲙⲉⲥⲓⲱ, ⲙⲁⲁⲩ; *child-birth*: MG 25 69 B pay costs of ⲧⲉⲥⲙ. = GöttAr 114 13 نفقة لدلولدي. ⲙⲛⲥⲉ *usury* v below.

ⲙⲁⲥ SB, ⲙⲉⲥ AF, ⲙⲏⲥ F nn m, *young*, mostly of animal or bird: Deu 22 6 SB, Job 38 41 SB, Is 60 8 B (S ϣⲏⲣⲉ) νοσσός, Nu 24 21 B (S do), Ps 83 4 B (S do), Lu 13 34 S (B ⲙⲟϩ) νοσσιά, Ps 103 17 B (S ⲙ. vb), Jer 22 23 B νοσσεύειν; Deu 28 11 B (S ϫⲡⲟ), Is 30 6 F (SB ϣⲏ.) ἔκγονος; Lam 4 3 SB, Nah 2 12 AB σκύμνος, Pro 15 17 A (S ⲙⲁⲥⲉ) μόσχος; Lu 1 41 B (S ϣⲏⲣⲉ ϣⲏⲙ) βρέφος; Is 34

15 B (SF ϣⲏⲣⲉ) παιδίον; K 168 B ⲡⲓⲙ. فرخ; AM 293 B woman's, MG 25 199 B sheep's, C 41 68 B camel's, Pro 24 52 SAB eagle's, AZ 23 41 F ⲡⲉⲙ. πτερα (? cf τετράβολος Preisigke). V also ⲁⲃⲱⲕ, ⲃⲁⲁⲙⲡⲉ, ⲉⲓⲱ, ⲉⲓⲟⲩⲗ, ⲕⲣⲟⲩⲣ, ⲙⲟⲩⲓ, ⲙⲁⲧⲟⲓ, ⲡⲟⲩⲣⲉ, ⲣⲱⲙⲉ, ϣⲁϣ, ϩⲁⲗⲏⲧ, ϩⲧⲟ, ϩⲟϥ, ϭⲁⲙⲟⲩⲗ, ϭⲣⲟⲙⲡⲉ, ϭⲁⲣⲥⲉ. In names: Μεσῆσε BMEA 26273, Μεσμοῦις (Preis.), Μεσεντριφι POslo 220 (cf PGM 1 140).

ⲙⲁⲥⲉ S, ⲙⲉⲥⲉ Sᵃ A, ⲙⲁⲥⲓ BF, ⲙⲉⲥⲓ F nn m, *young animal,* esp *calf, bull:* Ge 12 16 SB, Ps 105 19 SB, Ez 46 6 SB, Hos 10 5 SAB, He 9 12 SBF, Glos 66 Sᵃ ⲙⲉⲥⲉ μόσχος, Ge 18 7 SB, Lev 9 2 B (S ⲙ. ⲡⲕⲧⲏⲣ), Is 11 6 S (B ⲕⲟⲩϫⲓ ⲙⲙ.) μοσχάριον; Deu 33 17 S (B = Gk), Ps 21 12 S (B do), Is 1 11 SBF, Mt 22 4 SB ταῦρος; Ex 20 10 S (B ⲉⲣⲉ), Nu 7 3 SB, Ps 65 15 S (B do), Lu 13 15 S (B do) βοῦς; of goat: Deu 14 4 S ⲙ. ⲉⲃⲟⲗ ϩⲓⲡⲃⲁⲁⲙⲡⲉ (var ⲙⲁⲥ ⲡⲃ., B ⲃⲁⲣⲏⲧ) χίμαρος ἐξ αἰγ.; of sheep: Ez 46 13 B ⲟⲩϭⲓⲏⲃ ⲟⲩⲙ. ⲡⲟⲩⲣⲟⲙⲡⲓ ἀμνὸς ἐνιαύσιος; of birds: RAL '93 518 S learning to fly like ⲟⲩⲙ. ⲡⲣⲁⲗⲏⲧ, P 131¹ 38 S sim (or ? *l* ⲙⲁⲥ ⲉⲡ-); C 86 274 B ϩⲁⲡⲙⲟⲩⲧ ⲙⲙ. βούνευρον, Mor 17 118 S = GMir 119 ϣⲁⲁⲣ ⲙⲙ. δέρματα βοῶν. ⲙⲁⲡⲉ ⲙ. F, *calf-herd:* CMSS 72. ⲙⲡⲧⲙ. S, *likeness to calf* (cf ταυροειδής): BM 250 31 Christ's ⲙ., paral ⲙⲡⲧⲁⲉⲧⲟⲥ. As name: ⲙⲁⲥⲉ J 2 57, Πμάσε BM 1075, Πμέσι POxy 1917.

ⲙⲛⲥⲉ SA, ⲙⲏⲛⲥⲉ S, ⲙⲛⲥⲓ B, ⲙⲛⲥⲏ F nn f, *off-spring* of money, *usury, interest:* Mt 25 27 SB κομίζειν σὺν τόκ., Sph 10 155 S ⲛ̄ⲧⲁϯⲟⲩ ⲡⲁⲕ ⲙⲡⲧⲉⲩⲙ., J 64 12 S sim, ST 424 S I owe...ⲙⲛⲧⲉⲥⲙ. namely 6 measures of corn (cf Kr 59), AZ 23 34 F ⲑⲟⲗⲟⲕ/...ⲙⲉⲧⲉⲥⲙⲉⲥⲩ (*sic l*), C 86 138 B ϩⲁⲓⲧⲉ ⲑⲙ. of what I formerly sent thee, CO 189 S ⲥⲡⲧⲉ ⲡⲣⲟⲙⲡⲉ ⲙⲙ. ⲁⲓⲧⲁⲁⲩ. ϯ ⲉⲙ. SA, ⲉⲑⲙ. B, *give at* interest: Deu 28 44 SB, Pro 19 14 SA, Is 24 2 S (B ⲉⲡⲟⲩϣⲁⲡ), Lu 6 34 S (B = Gk) δανίζειν, Ex 22 25 B (S om), Deu 23 19 S (B ⲉⲟⲩϣⲁⲡ) ἐκδαν.; Lev 25 37 SB, Ps 14 5 SB ἐπὶ τόκῳ διδόναι. ⲭⲓ ⲙ., ⲉⲙ. SA, ϭⲓ ⲉⲑⲙ. B, *take interest:* Ps 36 21 B (S ϫⲓ ⲉϩⲟⲩ⸗), Pro 20 4 SA δαν.; Lev 25 36 SB, Ez 18 17 B τόκον λαβεῖν. As nn S: Si 29 4 δάνος. ⲧⲁⲗⲉ ⲙ. B, *add interest* to loan: Ex 22 25 τόκ. ἐπιτίθεναι, Jer 9 6 τόκ. no vb. Other vbs: Deu 23 19 S ⲕⲧⲟ...ⲟⲩⲙ., B ϣⲁⲡ...ⲙⲙ. ἐκτοκεῖν; Aeg 223 S ϣⲉⲧ ⲡⲉⲧⲭⲣⲉⲱⲥⲧⲉⲓ ⲡⲁϥ ⲙⲙ. τόκ. ἀπαιτεῖν; ShBM 197 S ⲉϥϣⲁⲛ[ⲧⲙ]ⲡ ⲧⲙ. ⲉϩⲟⲩⲛ ⲡϥⲧⲙⲁⲁⲥ ⲡⲟⲩⲕⲁⲓⲫⲁⲗⲁⲓⲟⲛ ⲡϥϫⲓ ⲙ. ⲟⲛ ⲙⲙ...ⲙⲟⲥ, ShR 2 3 51 S ⲙⲙ. ⲉⲧⲕⲕⲱⲃ ⲙⲙⲟⲟⲩ ⲉⲣⲟⲟⲩ. ⲁⲧⲙ., *without interest:* Bodl Copt inscr 428 S ⲟⲩⲧⲣⲏ- (ⲙⲓⲥⲓⲟⲡ) ⲡⲁ., COAd 17 S sim.

ⲙⲉⲥⲓⲱϯ, ⲙⲏⲥ. B nn f, *womb* in ⲙ. ⲙⲡⲏⲣⲓ ὀρτυγομήτρα = S ϩⲛ ⲙⲡ.: Nu 11 32 ϯⲙ., Ps 104 40;

nursing, having given birth: Job 42 12 ⲉⲓⲱ ⲙⲙ. (S ⲣⲉϥⲙⲟⲟⲛⲉ) νομάς مولد (*ib* 1 3 om). Cf ⲟⲟⲧⲉ.

ⲙⲉⲥ ϩⲛ-, ϩⲉⲡⲏⲓ SB nn m f, *one born in the house:* Ge 15 2 SB f, *ib* 17 12 B m, Eccl 2 7 S οἰκογενής; DeV 1 38 B Herod's feast ⲉⲡⲉϥⲙ. ⲡⲉⲙⲡⲉϥⲙⲉⲧⲓⲥⲧⲁⲡⲟⲥ (Mk 6 21).

ⲙⲉⲥⲟⲣⲏ S (oftenest) B, -ⲱⲣⲏ SB, -ⲟⲩⲣⲏ SB, -ⲟⲣⲉ, -ⲟⲩⲣⲉ, ⲙⲏⲥⲟⲩⲣⲉ, -ⲟⲩⲣⲓ (Ryl 165), -ⲱⲣⲏ, ⲙⲟⲩⲥⲱⲣⲏ (Kr 1), -ⲥⲟⲣⲉ (JdeMorgan Catal 1 137), ⲙⲓⲥⲟⲩⲣⲏ (BM 1031), ⲙⲉⲥⲥⲟⲩⲣⲓ (JA '04 2 118) &c S nn, *name of 12th month, Birth of Re* (Sun), Gk Μεσορή, Ar مسرى.

ⲥⲉⲙⲓⲥⲓ B nn f, lit *birth-place, seat,* so *childbirth, parturition:* Ge 35 16 Va ϣⲱϣⲧ ϩⲉⲛⲧⲉⲥⲥ. (Lag ⲙ. vb, S ⲙ. nn) τοκετός مخاض, Ex 1 16 (A ⲙ. vb) τὸ τίκτειν الخ.

ⲙⲉⲥⲓⲟ (for ⲧⲙⲉⲥⲓⲟ) S, ⲧⲙⲁⲥⲉⲓⲟ A, ⲑⲙⲉⲥⲓⲟ B, ⲑⲙⲉⲥⲓⲉ- B, ⲙⲉⲥⲓⲟ⸗ S vb tr, *bring to birth, act midwife:* Ex 1 16 AB, Job 26 5 B μαιοῦσθαι; Br 259 S ⲡⲧⲟⲕ ⲡⲉⲡⲧⲁⲕⲙⲉⲥⲓⲟⲟⲩ ⲣⲙⲡⲉⲕⲥⲱⲙⲁ & formed them, JAs '05 1 439 S show me a midwife ⲡⲥⲙ. ⲡⲧⲉⲓⲥϩⲓⲙⲉ, BMis 94 S woman ⲉⲥⲥⲟⲟⲩⲛ ⲙⲙ., TT 30 = R 2 4 58 S ⲁⲣⲙ. ⲙⲙⲟ ⲙⲁⲅⲁⲁⲧⲉ, P 44 96 S ⲙⲡⲟⲩⲙ. ⲙⲟⲥ. ⲣⲉϥⲑⲙ., *v* ⲙⲉⲥⲓⲱ.

ⲙⲉⲥⲓⲱ, -ⲓⲟ S, -ⲉⲓⲟⲩ A nn f, *midwife, nurse:* Ge 35 17 S (B ⲣⲉϥⲑⲙ.), Ex 1 15 A (B do) μαῖα; El 80 A ⲧⲙ., Wess 15 152 S ⲁⲧⲙ. ϭⲟⲡϥ (babe); ϭⲣⲓⲙⲉ ⲙⲙ.: FR 20 S, Wess 15 151 S. ⲣ ⲙ. S, *bring to birth:* Z 604 ⲁϥⲣ ⲙ. ⲉⲧⲉϥⲯⲩⲭⲏ ⲉⲧⲣⲉⲥⲙⲟⲩ. As name: Τμεσιῶς, Θμ., Ψεντεμεσιῶς (Preisigke).

(ⲙⲉⲥⲱⲃⲉ), ⲉⲙ., ⲙⲥⲱⲡⲉ (PLond) S, ⲉⲙⲥⲟⲃⲓ, ⲙⲉⲧⲥⲟⲃⲓ B, ⲙⲉⲥⲱⲃⲓ F nn f, *large needle:* K 132 B ϯⲉⲙ. (var Ryl 452 ⲙⲉⲧ.) مسلة, Bodl(P) f 24 S list of tools &c ⲉⲙ., PLond 4 517 S sim ⲯⲓⲧⲉ ⲡⲙ., CMSS 76 F sim ⲙ. ϭⲁⲡⲡⲁⲥ.

ⲙⲟⲩⲥⲕ S, ⲙⲁⲥⲕ⸗ S, ⲙⲟⲥⲕ† B vb tr, a *strike, rub* (?) S: Bor 253 164 = Mor 31 183 Joseph's ⲫⲓⲁⲗⲏ (Ge 44 5) ⲉϥⲙ. ⲙⲙⲟⲥ ϩⲓⲧⲉϥϭⲩⲡⲁⲙ κρούειν, *ib* ⲁϥⲙ. ⲡⲧⲉϥ. ⲉⲡⲣⲁⲛ of each brother. b *be sharpened by whetting* (?) B: C 86 271 ϩⲁⲡⲃⲁϣⲟⲩⲣ ⲉⲩⲙ.† = BSG 205 حادّة, *ib* 275 ⲓϭⲧ ⲉⲩⲙ.† حادّة (cf *ib* ⲓϭⲧ ⲉⲩϫⲏⲣ الخ), BKU 1 130 S]ⲧⲃⲁϣⲟⲩⲣ ⲙⲁⲥⲕⲥ[.

ⲙⲉⲥⲗⲉϩ S nn: P 44 53 ⲕⲟⲛⲓⲟⲣⲧⲟⲡ تراب, ϫⲟⲩⲥ, ϫⲱⲙⲁ, ⲙ. مثل, so ? is مثل, *like it, ditto* transcribed.

ⲙⲟⲥⲛⲉ, ⲙⲟⲥⲡ S nn m, *a vessel or dry measure:* CO 216 ⲡⲓⲙⲟⲥⲡ ⲡⲭⲟⲉⲓⲧ, *ib* 161 ⲙⲟⲥⲡⲉ ⲡⲟⲣⲁϩ (ἄραξ), BKU 1 45 ⲥⲓⲙ ⲙⲡⲟⲩⲙⲟⲥⲡⲉ ⲡⲥⲁⲓⲟⲩ.

ⲙⲁⲥⲡⲟⲣⲕ *v* ⲡⲟⲣⲕ

ⲙⲟⲩⲥⲉⲣ *B* v ⲙⲟⲩⲥ.

ⲙⲉⲥⲟⲣⲏ v ⲙⲓⲥⲉ s f.

ⲙⲟⲥⲧⲉ *S*, ⲙⲁⲥⲧⲉ *AA²*, ⲙⲟⲥ† *B*, ⲙⲁⲥ† *F*, ⲙⲉⲥⲧⲉ- *SB*, ⲙⲥⲧⲉ- *A*, ⲙⲉⲥⲧⲱ- *F* (BM 527), ⲙⲉⲥⲧⲱ= *SAB*, p c ⲙⲁⲥⲧ- *S*, ⲙⲁⲥⲧⲉ- *B*, ⲙⲉⲥⲧⲉ- *S* (?) vb a tr, *hate*: Ge 29 31 *SB*, Ps 17 40 *SB*, Pro 1 22 *SAB*, Is 33 15 *SBF*, Jo 3 20 *SA²BF* μισεῖν, Pro 26 11 *SA*, Sa 14 9 *S* μισητός; Lev 26 30 *SB*, Nu 21 5 *S* (*B* ⲉⲣⲟϣ ⲉ-), Ps 21 24 *S* (*B* do) προσοχθί-ζειν; Job 30 10 *B* (*S* ⲃⲱⲧⲉ) βδελύσσειν; ⲙⲡϣⲁ ⲙⲙ.: Tit 3 3 *B* (*S* ⲟ ⲙⲙⲉⲥⲧⲉ) στυγητός; PS 47 *S* ⲡⲉϭⲙ. ⲙⲙⲟⲓ, ib 69 *S* ⲁϥⲙⲉⲥⲧⲱⲓ, BSM 73 *B* ⲁϥⲑⲣⲟⲩⲙⲉⲥⲧⲱⲟⲩ with great hatred, BM 527 *F* recipe for woman ⲉϣⲁⲥⲙⲉⲥⲧⲱ ⲡⲉⲥϩⲁⲓ, ShMun 117 *S* ⲡⲉⲧⲙ. ⲡⲥⲱⲧⲙ ⲉⲣⲟⲟⲩ, BHom 87 *S* Judas ⲉϥⲙⲉⲥⲧⲉ ⲡⲛ̄, Mor 31 198 *S* sun & moon ⲙⲉⲥⲧⲉ ϣⲁ ⲉⲝⲡⲧⲏⲅⲧⲛ.   b intr (rare): Ps 35 2 *SB* μισεῖν.

—— *SAB* nn m, *hatred, object of hatred*: Ps 108 5 *SB*, Pro 10 12 *SAB*, Jer 24 9 *SB* μῖσος; C 43 228 *B* ⲁⲕϣⲱⲡⲓ ⲡⲟⲩⲙ. before me, BG 57 *S* tree's leaves ⲟⲩⲙ. ⲡⲉ, JKP 2 222 *S* (instances of) *h.*, Z 268 31 *S* ⲡⲧⲕⲟⲩⲙ. ⲡⲙⲙⲁϥ *at enmity with Him*, Cai 42573 2 *Sf* title of recipe ⲟⲩⲙⲁⲥⲧⲉ (to produce) *hatred*.

p c, *hater of*: Ro 1 30 *SB* ⲙ. ⲡⲉ θεοστυγής (*cf* ⲙⲁⲓⲡⲉ), P 129¹⁴ 92 *S* doctrine ⲙⲙⲙ. ⲡⲉ θεομισῶν, ShBor 246 77 *S* devil ⲡⲙ. ⲣⲱⲙⲉ, C 89 144 *B* ⲁⲡⲟⲓ ⲙⲙ. p. toward God's image, BMar 16 *S* father ⲙⲙ. ϣⲏⲣⲉ, DeV 1 23 *B* Herod ⲙ. ⲥⲟⲡ, BMar 193 *S* ⲡⲙ. ⲡⲉⲧⲛⲁⲡⲟⲩϥ μισόκαλος, Miss 4 218 *B* sim, ShA 2 231 *S* we are ϩⲉⲛⲙ. ⲡⲉⲡⲁⲧⲟⲡ, Mor 29 47 *S* that sickness is ⲟⲩⲙ. ⲉⲕⲕⲗⲏⲥⲓⲁ like demon; Sa 19 13 *S* ⲙⲛⲧⲙ. ϣⲙⲙⲟ μισοξενία, BMar 158 *S* ⲙⲛⲧⲙⲁⲥ ϩⲟⲩⲙⲛⲧ (*sic* MS) ἀκτημοσύνη.   ⲙⲉⲥⲧⲉ- *S*: Mor 20 44 (*i e* BP 11965) Nineve ⲡⲙ. ⲗⲁⲍⲁⲣⲟⲥ, Miss 8 180 ⲁϥϣⲱⲡⲉ ⲙⲙ. ϣⲏⲣⲉ.

ⲣⲉϥⲙⲉⲥⲧⲉ v ⲙⲓⲥⲉ (ⲣⲉϥⲙⲓⲥⲉ).

ϣⲟⲩⲙ. *SBF*, *deserving to be hated*: Ge 34 30 *B*, BM 189 168 *S* knowledge of good & evil is not ⲡϣⲟⲩⲙⲉⲥⲧⲱϥ (*sic l*) μισητός; Dan 3 32 *B* (*S* ⲥⲁϫⲉ) ἔχθιστος; ShC 42 64 *S* ϣⲁϫⲉ ⲡϣⲟⲩⲙⲉⲥⲧⲱⲟⲩϥ, Mor 27 9 *F* ⲡϣⲟⲩⲙ. ⲉⲧⲙⲙⲁⲩ.

ⲙⲉⲥⲧⲉ, -ⲧⲏ (rarely m) *S*, ⲙⲉⲥⲧⲟⲩ, ⲙⲥ. *A*, f ⲙⲉⲥⲧⲏ *S* (-ⲧⲏⲧ not found) nn, *hated person*: Pro 24 39 *SA*, Si 20 14, 37 26 *S* μισητός, f Deu 21 15 *S* (*B* vb rel) μισούμενος; f R 2 2 40 *S* wife will ϣⲱⲡⲉ ⲙⲙ. ⲡⲡⲁϩⲣⲁⲕ ἀηδέστερος; ShC 42 25 *S* ϩⲉⲡⲙ. ⲡⲉ ⲁⲩⲱ ⲡⲭⲁⲕⲉ, Mor 43 17 *S* ⲟⲩⲙ. ⲡⲉ ⲡⲟⲩⲟⲛ ⲡⲓⲙ = ib 42 17 *S* ⲙⲁⲥⲧⲉ, BMis 327 *S* ⲡⲙ. ⲁⲩⲱ ⲡⲥⲁⲧⲁⲡⲁⲥ which is devil (*cf*? *Mastema*);   as adj: Pro 24 58 *SA* ⲧⲉⲥϩⲓⲙⲉ ⲙⲙ. (*B* ϣⲟⲩⲙ.) μισητός.   ⲣ ⲙ., *become, be hateful*: Ge 34 30 (P 44 104) *S*, f R 1 5 9 *S* women ⲉⲩⲟ ⲙⲙ. μισητός; Tit 3 3 *S* (*B* ⲙⲡϣⲁ

ⲙⲙⲉⲥⲧ⸗), Cl 45 7 *A* στυγητός; ShHT L 1 *S* ⲉⲧⲉⲧ-ⲡⲟ ⲙⲙ.

ⲙⲉⲥⲧⲟⲩ *S* nn m, meaning unknown. *V* ⲁⲡⲁⲕ.

ⲙⲉⲥⲓⲱ† *B* v ⲙⲓⲥⲉ.

ⲙⲉⲥⲑⲏⲧ *SA²*, ⲙⲉⲥⲧⲡⲣⲏⲧ *S*, ⲙⲥⲧ. *A*, ⲙⲉⲥⲧⲉϩ. *B* nn f, *breast*: Ge 3 14 *SB*, Pro 6 10 *SAB*, Jo 13 25 *SA²B*, BHom 3 *S* ϩⲓⲟϥⲉ ⲉⲣⲟⲩⲡ ϩⲛⲧⲉⲕⲙ., MG 25 10 *B* ⲉϥⲕⲱⲗϩ ϩⲉⲡⲧⲉϥⲙ. στῆθος, Lev 8 28 *B* (*S* = Gk) στηθύνιον; Ps 90 4 *S* (*B* ⲙⲟ†), Is 51 23 *S* (*B* do *sic l*) μετάφρενον; 3 Kg 22 34 *S* θώραξ; PS 94 *S* kissed ⲉⲣⲡⲧⲙⲉⲥⲧϩ. of Jesus, RAl 137 *S* ⲧⲙⲛⲥⲧϩ. of Father, AM 267 *B* ⲡⲉϥⲙⲟ† ⲡⲉⲙⲁϩⲏⲧⲉ ⲡⲧⲉϥⲙ.   ⲙⲏⲣ (*l* ⲙⲉⲣ) ⲙⲉⲥⲧⲉⲡϩⲏⲧ *B* nn f, *girdle*: Jer 2 32 (*S* ⲫⲁⲥⲕⲓⲁ) στηθοδεσμίς.

ⲙⲉⲥⲟⲩⲁϥⲓ *S* nn, meaning unknown: Sh(Besa) Z 511 wast bidden not to transgress, for thou hadst † ϣⲟⲟⲩ ⲁⲩⲱ ⲙ. to a maiden with thee in house. Coptic?

ⲙⲉⲥⲁϩ *SB*, ⲉⲙ- *B*, ⲙⲥⲉϩ DM (3 21), pl ⲙⲥⲟⲟϩ *S* nn m, *crocodile*, cf تمساح: Lev 11 29 *S* ⲡⲉⲙ., *B* ⲡⲓⲙ. ⲡⲧⲱⲟⲩ κροκόδ. χερσαῖος ﺿﺐ, Glos 404 *S* ⲙ. ⲕⲟⲣⲕⲟⲇ. · βαινεφώθ (v ⲉϥⲱⲧ); ShZ 600 *S*, A 1 381 *S* worshipped, PS 259 *S* ἄρχων sim, AM 56 *B* beast devouring souls has head like ⲑⲁⲟⲩⲙ., BMis 559 *S* demons with ϩⲟ ⲙⲙ., BM 279 fr 21 *S* usurer is like ⲙ., P 129¹² 66 = Wess 9 139 *S* ⲡⲁⲁϫⲉ ⲡⲙ. as phylactery, MR 5 37 *S* seal with man & ⲟⲩⲉⲙ. ϩⲁⲣⲁⲧϥ, TT 119 *S* sinners in mouths of ϩⲉⲡⲙⲥⲟⲟϩ, MG 17 319 *S* ⲡⲉⲙⲥⲟⲟϩ = ib 93 *B* ⲡⲓⲙ. in river.

ⲗⲁⲥ ⲡⲙ. v ⲗⲁⲥ d.   As name Πεμσάις, Πεμσᾶς &c (Preisigke), ﻡﺳﺎﻝ martyr (Synax 1 337). *V* Rec 25 156.

ⲙⲉⲥⲱⲗ *S*, ⲙⲁϩⲥⲟⲗ, -ⲥⲱⲗ *B* nn m, ? ﻝﺴﻢ (IgR), *file*: ShZ 637 *S* processes of forging iron ⲡⲟⲭϥ ⲉⲡⲙⲟⲟⲩ, ⲥⲗⲉϭⲗⲱϭϥ ϩⲛⲡⲙ., K 125 *B* ⲡⲓⲙ. ﺲﻤﺒﺮ. Cf ⲃⲉⲣⲓ.

ⲙⲉⲧ- *BF* v ⲙⲏⲧ-.

ⲙⲏⲧ *SAA²B*, f ⲙⲏⲧⲉ *S*, ⲙⲏ† *B*, ⲙⲏⲧ- *SAA²*, ⲙⲉⲧ-, ⲙⲏⲧ- *B*, numeral *ten*: a cardinals m Sa 7 2 *S* ⲙ. ⲡⲉϩⲟⲧ, Ps 143 9 *B* ⲙ. ⲡⲕⲁⲡ, AP 18 *A²* ⲙ. ⲡⲣⲟⲟⲩ; f Ap 13 1 *S* ⲙ. ⲡϣⲣⲏⲡⲉ, Mt 4 25 *B* ⲙ. ⲙⲡⲟⲗⲓⲥ; ⲙⲏⲧ-, ⲙⲉⲧ- (*eleven to nineteen*); 4 Kg 13 1 *S* ⲙⲏⲧⲥⲁϣϥⲉ ⲡⲣⲟⲙⲡⲉ, 2 Chr 4 3 *B* ⲙⲏⲧ-ⲥⲡⲁⲩ ⲙⲙⲁⲥⲓ, Hos 3 2 *A* ⲙⲏ† ϩⲣⲉⲧ, Jo 11 18 *A²* ⲙⲏⲧⲏ ⲡⲥⲧⲁⲇⲓⲟⲛ.   b ordinals with ⲙⲉϩ- *SA* (*BF* use ⲓ̄ = *ten*): Si 25 9 *S* ⲡⲙⲉϩⲙⲏⲧ (ⲡⲣⲱⲃ), Ge 14 5 *S* ⲧⲙⲉϩⲙ̄ⲡⲧⲁϥⲧⲉ (*B* ⲙⲁⲣⲓ̄ⲁ̄) ⲡⲣⲟⲙⲡⲉ, Zech 1 7 *A* ⲡⲙⲁϩⲙⲏⲧⲟⲩⲓⲉ ⲡⲉⲃⲁⲧ.   *Tenth day*: Ex 12 3 *S* ⲥⲟⲩⲙⲏⲧ δεκάτη, or ⲙ. alone: KroppK 29 *S* ⲡⲙⲉⲧ ⲙⲡⲱϩ (*l* ⲟⲟϩ), PS 4 *S* ⲡⲙⲡⲧⲏ ⲙⲡⲟⲟϩ.   *Tenth*

part: ⲣⲉⲙⲏⲧ *SB*, pl ⲣⲉⲙⲁⲧⲉ *S*, -ⲙⲁϯ *B*: sg Lev 23 3 *SB*, Mt 23 23 *SB*; pl Nu 18 24 *SB*, He 7 8 *B* (*S* sg).

ⲙⲏⲧ *SO* v ⲙⲉ *truth s f.*

ⲙⲓⲧ *SB*, ⲉⲙⲓⲧ *B* (Bodl 325 151) nn m, *parsley* or *celery*: P 44 82 πολύτριχον, μακεδόνιον (*sic*) مقدونس, K 195, 269 *B* فجسـ which P 44 *l c* = πετροσέλινον. V Rec 16 4 & *cf* ⲗⲁⲧ.

ⲙⲟⲉⲓⲧ *S*, ⲙⲁⲉⲓⲧ *Sᵃ* (Ep 472) *AA²*, ⲙⲱⲓⲧ *B*, ⲙⲁⲓⲧ *F*, pl ⲙⲓⲧⲱⲟⲩⲓ *B* nn m, I *road*, *path* (mostly *B*): Ge 6 12 *B* (*S* ϩⲓⲏ), Jud 5 6 *S*, Ps 106 40 *B* (*S* do), EpJer 42 *B* (*F* ϩ.), Ro 11 33 (*SF* do) ὁδός, Ez 27 3 *B* (*S* diff), Bel 13 *B* εἴσοδ., Is 51 20 (*S* ϩ.), Lam 2 19 *B* (*S* do) ἔξοδ., Deu 13 16 *B* (*S* do), Pro 7 8 *B* (*SA* ϩⲓⲣ) δίοδ., Ez 16 25 *B* (*S* diff), 1 Cor 16 7 *B* (*SF* diff) πάροδ.; 2 Kg 20 13 *S*, Jer 9 10 *B* (*S* ϩ.), Hos 2 6 *AB* τρίβος; Is 8 11 *B* (*S* do), Ja 1 11 *B* (*S* do) πορεία; Job 11 7 *B* (*S* diff) ἴχνος; Ez 40 10, 42 1 *B* (*S* ϩ.) Gk om *via*; *ib* 40 18 *B* (*S* ϣⲓⲏ, *B* read ϩ ϩⲓⲏ, *cf* 42 6), Va 61 23 *B* ⲟⲩⲙ. ⲉϥⲟⲩⲏⲟⲩ μῆκος, Cl 50 1 *A* ⲙ. ⲡϣⲉⲝⲉ ἐξήγησις; C 43 47 *B* beheld ⲟⲩⲙ. ⲉϥⲧⲁⲭⲣⲏⲟⲩⲧ like ladder, BSM 82 *B* to teach us ⲡⲓⲙ. ⲛϥⲱⲗ ϣⲁϥϯ = BMis 172 *S* ϩ., Ep 200 *S* preserve us from men ⲛⲧⲁ ϭⲛ ⲙ. ⲁⲧⲉⲭⲱⲣⲁ, ST 310 *S* ⲙⲁⲛⲧⲏⲓ ⲙ. ⲉⲣⲟϥ ϩⲁⲣⲱⲃ ⲛⲭⲣⲉⲟⲥ *no occasion against him, cf* CO 168 *S* ⲙⲡⲧⲁⲓ ⲙ. (ⲡ)ⲉⲓ ⲉⲃⲟⲗ ϩⲁⲣⲟϥ, MG 25 285 *B* admirers ⲉⲣ ⲡⲓⲙ. ϣⲁⲡⲓⲁⲧⲓⲟⲥ ⲙⲙⲁ ⲙⲙⲟϣⲓ *made road to be a highway* = BIF 13 102 *S* ϩⲓⲟⲟⲩⲉ.   Pl form *B*: Job 6 19 (*S* ⲙⲁ ⲙⲙⲟⲟϣⲉ) ἀτραπός; Lam 3 9 (*S* do), Ps 24 4 (*S* ϩ.) τρ., BerlOr 599 53 Daniel walked ⲛⲥⲁ ⲡⲉϥⲙ. في الميدان.   ⲙ. ⲡⲉⲓ ⲉϩⲟⲩⲛ *SB*, *entrance*: He 7 19 *B* (*SF* ⲉⲓ ⲉϩ. nn) ἐπεισαγωγή; ShA 2 63 *S*; ⲙ. ⲛ̄ϣⲉ ⲉⲃ.: Ez 46 19 *B* εἴσοδ.   ⲙ. ⲡⲉⲓ ⲉⲃⲟⲗ *SB*, *coming forth*: Ps 113 1 *B* (*S* ⲉⲓ ⲉⲃ. nn) ἔξοδ., Jud 5 18 *S*, Ps 67 21 *B* (*S* ⲟⲟⲉ) διέξ.; MIE 2 416 *B* prepare for thy ⲙ. ⲡⲓ ⲉⲃ. from this life; ⲙ. ⲛ̄ϣⲉ ⲉⲃ.: Ez 43 11 *B* ἔξοδ. With ⲥⲟⲃ̄ϯ *B*: Dan 8 12, Ro 1 10 (*S* ϩ.) εὐοδοῦσθαι; with ⲥⲱⲟⲩⲧⲉⲛ: 3 Jo 2 (*S* om) εὐοδ. ϩⲓϥⲙ. *B*: 2 Cor 11 26 ϩⲁⲡⲙⲟϣⲓ ϩ. (*S* ϩⲓⲏ ⲙⲙⲟⲟϣⲉ) ὁδοιπορία; MG 25 11 ⲉϥ. ἄποντος αὐτοῦ; C 86 333 ⲉⲩⲙⲟϣⲓ ϩ.

ϯ ⲙⲡⲓⲙ. *B, give way, occasion*: C 43 46 to upright ϣⲁϥϯ ⲙⲡⲓⲙ. to attain heaven, DeV 2 208 will narrate them if Lord ϯ ⲙⲡⲓⲙ. ⲛⲏⲓ; ϯⲙ. *S*: PBu 30 dispute as to property ⲁⲛⲟⲕ ⲍⲉ ⲉⲱ ⲩⲁⲓϯ ⲙ. ⲭⲉⲡⲉⲧⲣⲓⲧⲟⲛ ⲡⲉⲧⲟⲩⲭⲓ ⲙⲙⲟϥ (*obscure*).

ⲭⲓ, ϭⲓ ⲙ. *SAA²BF, take road* before, for (mostly ϩⲏⲧⲥ *S*, dat *B*, rarely ϩⲁϩⲏ *S*, ϩⲁⲭⲉⲡ- *B*) *lead*, *guide*: Ex 32 34 *SB*, Pro 11 3 *SAB*, Jo 16 13 *SA²B*, Ac 8 31 *B* (*S* ⲧⲥⲁⲃⲉ ⲉⲓⲁⲧⲥ), Aeg 241 *S* anger

ⲭⲓ ⲙ. ϩⲏⲧⲥ ⲛⲧⲁⲛⲧⲣⲉϥϭⲱⲧⲃ, HL 94 *B* ⲡⲧⲉϥϭⲓ ⲙ. ϩⲁⲭⲱⲓ to desert ὁδηγεῖν, Jer 2 6 *B* καθοδ.; Ps 79 9 *S* (ϩⲁⲑ) *B* (ϩⲁⲭⲉⲡ-) ὁδοποιεῖν; Sa 7 12 *S*, Jth 5 3 *S* ἡγεῖσθαι, Mt 7 13 *S* (*B* ⲙ. ⲉⲧϭⲓ ⲉ-) ἀπάγειν; Ac 7 40 *S* (*B* ⲥⲱⲕ ϩⲁⲭ.) προπορεύεσθαι; *ib* 9 8 *S* (*B* ⲱⲗⲓ ⲉϧⲣⲏⲓ) χειραγωγεῖν; C 89 74 *B* come & ϭⲓ ⲙ. ⲡⲏⲓ = MG 17 328 *S* ⲧⲥⲁⲃⲟⲓ διδάσκειν; PS 79 *S* ⲭⲓ ⲙ. ϩⲏⲧ & let me know, MG 25 360 *B* ϭⲓ ⲙ. ⲡⲏⲓ ⲭⲉⲉⲕⲟⲩⲱϣ ⲟⲩ, TU 24 1 6 *S* bade them ⲭⲓ ⲙ. ϩⲏⲧϥ & bring him, TstAb 168 *B* gate that ϭⲓ ⲙ. ⲉϩⲟⲩⲛ ⲉⲡⲱⲛϩ, Ryl 348 *S* ⲁⲡ̄ⲡ̄ⲉ̄ ⲭⲓ ⲙ. ⲉⲁⲙⲡⲟⲩⲥ ('Amr) he hath reached us safe, BM 592 *F* ⲡⲟ̄ⲥ̄ ⲭⲉ ⲙ. ⲡⲉⲃ.   ⲣⲉϥⲭⲓ, ϭⲓ ⲙ., *leader*, *guide*: Ac 1 16 *SB*, Ro 2 19 *SB* ὁδηγός; Deu 1 15 *S* (*B* om) εἰσαγωγεύς.   ⲙⲉⲧⲣⲉϥϭⲓ ⲙ. *B, leading, guidance*: DeV 2 7 star ⲟⲩⲙ. ⲡⲡⲓⲙⲁⲧⲟⲥ ϣⲁⲣⲟϥ. ⲭⲁⲩ- *S*, ⲭⲁⲓ- *A*, ϭⲁⲩ- *B* (v ⲭⲓ) ⲙ., *leader*, *guide*: Mt 15 14 *SB* ὁδηγός; 1 Cor 4 15 *B* (*S* = Gk) παιδαγωγός; TU 43 21 *A* become ⲭ. for believers, DeV 2 36 *B* became for them ⲉⲧⲓⲟⲥ (αἴτιος) ⲟⲩⲟϩ ⲛϭ., Pcod 13 *S* art not thou ⲛⲭ. ⲛ̄ⲡⲉⲛⲯⲩⲭⲏ? ⲙⲛⲧⲣⲉϥⲭⲁⲩⲙ. *S, leadership*: Bor 248 58 ⲧⲙ. ⲙⲡϣⲟⲥ. ⲣ ⲭⲁⲩⲙ. *S*, ⲉⲣ ϭⲁⲩⲙ. *B, be leader*: Ac 1 16 *B* (*S* ⲣⲉϥⲭⲓ ⲙ.), Ro 2 19 *S* (*B* ⲣⲉϥϭⲓ ⲙ.) ὁδηγός, Gal 3 24 *B* (*S* = Gk) παιδαγ., BSM 15 *B* Michael ⲁϥⲉⲣ ϭ. (*sic l*) ϩⲁⲭⲱⲛ.

ⲭⲁⲭ, ϭⲁⲭ ⲙ. *S, making path rough, difficult (?)*: RE 9 176 ⲛϣⲁⲭⲉ ⲛⲭ. ⲙ. ⲉⲧⲩⲧⲁⲅⲟ ⲙⲙⲟⲟⲩ, *ib* 142 (same scribe) to slay me with ⲛϣⲁⲭⲉ ⲙⲛ[...ⲉⲧ]ⲉⲣⲉϭ. ⲙ. ⲧⲁⲅⲟ ⲙⲙⲟⲟⲩ (*l* ? ⲛϭ.).

ⲙ. ⲉⲃⲟⲗ *B, road (of going) out*: 2 Kg 1 20 (*S* ϩⲓⲏ), Ps 64 9 (*S* do), *ib* 143 13 (*S* ⲙⲁ ⲡⲉⲓ ⲉⲃ.), Pro 1 20 (*SA* ϩⲓⲣ), Is 37 28 (*S* ϭⲓⲛⲉⲓ ⲉⲃ.), Ez 43 11 (var ⲙ. ⲛϣⲉ ⲉⲃ.), 2 Pet 1 15 (*S* ⲉⲓ ⲉⲃ. vb) *decease* ἔξοδος, Lev 23 36 (*S* ⲉⲓ ⲉⲃ. nn) ἐξόδιον, Ps 106 33 (*S* ⲟⲟⲉ) διέξοδος, AM 273 ⲁⲩⲑⲁⲙⲓⲟ ⲙⲡⲓⲙ. ⲉⲃ. πάροδος.

ⲙ. ⲉϩⲟⲩⲛ *B, road (of going) in*: Ge 30 27 (*S* ⲉⲓ ⲉϩ. vb), Ps 73 5 (*S* ϩⲓⲏ ⲡⲉⲓ ⲉϩ.), *ib* 120 8 (*S* ϭⲓⲛⲉⲓ ⲉϩ.), Pro 8 3 (*SA* ⲙⲁ ⲛ̄ⲃⲱⲕ ⲉϩ.), 1 Thes 1 9 (*SF* ⲉⲓ ⲉϩ. vb) εἴσοδος; C 89 153 I have found demon's ⲙ. ⲉϩ.

ⲙ. ⲉⲡϣⲱⲓ *B, going up*: 2 Kg 6 2 (*S* ϩ. ⲡⲃⲱⲕ ⲉϩⲣⲁⲓ), Is 15 5 (*S* ⲉⲓ ⲉϩ. nn) ἀνάβασις.

ⲙ. ⲙⲙⲟⲟϣⲉ, ⲙⲟϣⲓ *SB, track*: Ez 27 19 *SB* τροχίας; CaiEuch 588 *B* ὁδοιπορία, C 89 87 *B* lest he die midway ⲙ̄ⲡⲓⲙ. ⲙ. = Miss 4 548 *S* ϩⲓⲏ.

ⲙ. ⲡⲥⲓⲛⲓ *B, passage*: Is 51 10 (*S* ϩ. ⲛ̄ⲭⲓⲟⲟⲣ) ὁδ. διαβάσεως.

II *place B* (*S* once): Job 28 20 (*S* ⲙⲁ), Pro 15 3 (DeV 1 146, *SA* do), MG 25 13 depart ⲉⲡⲉⲧⲉⲡⲙ. τόπος; Va 57 31 found not ϩⲗⲓ ⲙ̄ⲙ. where to rest χώρα, *ib* 229 ⲁϣ ⲙ̄ⲙ. of prophet hath been read χώριον?; *ib* 174 ⲙ̄ⲙ. ⲛⲓⲃⲉⲛ πανταχόθεν; Va 62

290 will bring thee forth from ⲡⲁⲓⲙ. ἐντεῦθεν ; CDan 89 a man ⲙⲡⲁⲓⲙ. ⲱⲇⲉ ; Nu 33 52 ⲙ. ⲡⲱⲡⲓ (S diff) σκοπιά ; Va 57 276 ⲙ. ⲡⲕⲟⲓ ἀγρός ; MG 25 91 sent each to ⲡⲉϥⲙ. (var ⲙⲁ), Va 63 13 ⲁⲣⲓ ⲫⲣⲱⲟⲩϣ ⲙⲡⲓⲙ. = BMis 385 S ⲙⲁ, BSM 71 ⲙ. ⲛⲓⲃⲉⲛ whither thou goest = BMis 162 ⲙⲁ ⲡⲓⲙ, PO 11 376 wilt thou that I eat ⲙⲡⲁⲓⲙ. ⲓⲉ ⲙⲡⲁⲓⲙⲁ ϣⲁⲡⲡⲁⲓⲙⲁ ⲓⲉ ⲡⲁⲓⲙ.?, ST 286 S have not seen (lost) key ⲛⲧⲡⲥⲟⲟⲩⲛ ⲁⲛ ⲉⲡⲉϥⲙ., ROC 25 255 B demon ϫⲉⲙ ⲙ. ⲉⲣⲟϥ, DeV 2 151 ⲡⲓⲙ. ⲙⲙⲟⲛⲓ of ships. *Cf* ⲙⲁ ⲙⲙⲟⲟⲛⲉ.

ⲙⲟⲩⲧ *SB* nn m, a sinew, nerve : sg Ge 32 32 *SB*, Is 48 4 *S (B pl)*, pl Ge 49 24 *S (B* ⲙⲟϯ*)*, Job 10 11 *S (B do)*, ib 40 12 *S (B do)*, Ez 37 6 *SB* νεῦρον, P 44 69 *S* ⲙⲙ. · ⲡⲉⲩⲣⲱⲡ عرق, K 74 *B* ⲡⲓⲙ. 'ع, C 86 276 *B* ⲙ. ⲙⲙⲁⲥⲓ βούνευρον ; ShP 130² 83 *S* ⲕⲉⲉⲥ ϩⲓⲥⲁⲣⲝ ϩⲓⲙ., ShA 1 40 *S* ⲡⲓⲙ. ⲡⲡⲉⲩⲙⲏⲣⲟⲥ (*sic l, v* ⲕⲱⲃ), SHel 24 *S* ribs flayed ⲛⲥⲉⲉⲓⲡⲉ ⲡⲡⲉϥⲙ. ⲉⲃⲟⲗ, C 43 167 *B*, AM 62 *B* sim, Mor 38 57 *S* of paralysed ⲡⲉⲙⲣⲣⲉ ⲡⲡⲉϥⲙ. loosed & he arose, Leyd 341 *S* ⲙⲙ. ⲛⲧⲉⲩϫⲟⲛⲏ *bonds* ; *joint :* Eph 4 16 *B (S* ⲧⲣⲁ*)* ἁφή. b *sg, neck :* Ez 16 11 *B*, AM 278 *B* he bared ⲡⲉϥⲙ., P 44 *lc S* رقبة, τράχηλος ; Miss 4 634 *S* water reached ϣⲁⲡⲉϥⲙ., C 43 133 *B* collar hung ⲉⲡⲉϥⲙ., MG 25 69 *B* pots ⲉⲧⲟⲓ ⲉⲡⲉϥⲙ. (var ⲡⲉϥⲙⲟϯ), C 86 87 *B* they stretched ⲡⲉϥⲙ. (var ? ⲙⲟϯ), C 43 167 *B* took tongue out ϧⲉⲛⲡⲉϥⲙ. *throat*, Bar 2 34 *B* νῶτος *back* ; BM 917 *B* evading barbarian's hand ⲁϥⲱⲗⲓ ⲡⲛⲉϥⲙ. ⲡⲧⲟⲧϥ *shoulders* = Mor 31 57 *S* ⲙⲁⲕϩ.

ⲙⲟⲧⲉ *S*, ⲙⲁⲧⲉ *S*ᶠ, ⲙⲟϯ *B*, ⲙⲁϯ *F* nn m, (mostly *B* & pl), *neck :* Deu 28 48 *B (S* ⲙⲁⲕϩ*)*, Pro 1 9 *B* sg (var pl, *SA* do), Is 30 28 *F* sg (*S* do, *B* ⲛⲁϩⲃⲓ), Lam 5 4 *B (F* sg*)*, Lu 17 2 *F* sg (*S* do, *B* diff), Z 330 *S* ⲉⲥⲱⲙⲥ ϣⲁⲡⲉⲥⲙ. τράχηλος ; Ps 128 4 *B (S* ⲙⲁⲕϩ*)*, AM 278 *B* αὐχήν ; Mor 18 61 *S* my mother brought low ⲡⲁⲙ. ⲡⲕⲉϩⲁⲥⲓϩⲏⲧ like thee = MR 4 71 *S* ⲙⲁⲕϩ, Mor 16 87 *S* of giraffe ⲡⲉϥⲙ. ⲟ ⲡⲛⲟϭ ⲉⲙⲁⲧⲉ, Mun 46 *S*ᶠ two collars ⲉⲛⲉⲩⲙⲁϯ, C 86 108 *B* she fell upon ⲡⲉϥⲙ., AM 239 *B* stones tied about ⲡⲉϥⲙ. ; *shoulders :* Job 31 36 *B (S* diff*)*, Is 10 27 *B (S* ⲛⲁϩⲃⲉ*)*, Lu 15 5 *B (S* do*)* ὦμος ; Mor 31 240 *S* hair fell upon ⲡⲉϥⲙ. like women's, Ryl 393 *S* ⲙⲡⲣⲱ ⲉⲕⲧⲁⲗⲉ ⲙ. ⲉ[ϩⲣⲁⲓ?, Tri 396 *S* bent ⲡⲉϥⲙⲟⲧⲟⲩ (for rhyme, but *v* AZ 47 43) اعناق ; Deu 32 11 *B (S* ⲛⲁϩⲃ*)*, Ps 90 4 *B (S* ⲙⲉⲥⲧ ϩⲏⲧ*)* μετάφρενον ; *sinew :* Ge 49 24 *B (S* ⲙⲟⲩⲧ*)*, Job 10 11 *B (S* do*)* νεῦρον ; AM 167 *B* ⲡⲓⲙ. of tongue, C 43 146 *B* of feet, K 116 *B* ⲡⲓⲙ. وتر, *bowstring* ; *joint :* Job 17 11 *B (S* ⲙⲣⲣⲉ*)* ἄρθρον, Lev 5 8 *B (S* gloss ⲁⲡⲧⲏⲗⲙ) σφόνδυλος.

ⲙⲁⲧⲉ, ⲙⲁⲁⲧⲉ *S*, ⲙⲉⲧⲉ *S (BG) A*, ⲙⲉⲉⲧⲉ *AA²*,

ⲙⲁϯ *B*, ⲙⲉϯ *F*, ⲙⲁⲧⲱⲟⲩϯ *S (PS)* vb I tr (not *B*), *reach, obtain, enjoy :* Est E 11 *S*, Pro 24 58 *SA (B* ϯ ⲙ.*)* τυγχάνειν, ib 12 27 *SA (B* diff*)*, He 6 15 *S (F* ϯ ⲙ., *B* ϣⲁϣⲡⲓ*)* ἐπιτυγχ. ; Miss 8 84 *S* ⲁⲡⲟⲕⲣⲓⲥⲓⲥ ⲡⲧⲁⲙ. ⲙⲙⲟⲥ λαμβάνειν ; R 2 2 28 *S* ϣⲁⲡⲧⲁⲙ. ⲙⲡⲉϥⲟⲩⲱϣ ἐφικνεῖσθαι ; P 129¹⁷ 76 *S* hasten ⲡⲧⲁⲙ. ⲙⲡⲁⲉⲓⲱⲧ ἀπολαύειν ; BHom 57 *S* worthy ⲙⲙ. ⲙⲡⲧⲁⲓⲟ ἀξιοῦσθαι, ViSitz 172 4 21 ⲉⲧⲣⲁⲙ. ⲙⲡⲉⲛⲕⲗⲏⲣⲟⲥ κατάξ. ; 1 Tim 16 *S (B* ϯ ⲙ.*)*, AP 8 *A²* ⲙⲡⲉϥⲙ. his wife ἀστοχεῖν ; BG 105 *S* ⲉⲩⲉⲙ. ⲡⲡⲟⲩⲧⲓⲙⲏ, J 86 14 *S* ⲧⲁⲣⲟⲩⲙ. ⲙⲡⲕⲱ ⲉⲃⲟⲗ, AZ 21 148 *S* went to apostles & ⲁⲡⲙ. ⲡⲡⲉⲩϭⲟⲙ *benefited by their wonders*, PBu 179 *S* seeing that ⲁⲡⲙ. ⲛⲧⲉⲧⲛⲙⲛⲧ x̅c̅ (*sc* authority to whom petition addressed) & ye have heard our case. **II** intr (rarely *B*), *be successful, hit the mark :* Mor 17 66 *S* ⲉϥϣⲁϫⲉ ⲉϥⲙ. μὴ ἀποτυγχ. ; ib 15 *S* am but beginner ⲙⲡⲉⲓⲉϣ ⲙ. ἀστοχεῖν ; Mor 36 26 *S* when old ⲁⲡⲗⲟ ⲉⲙ. in our affairs, P 131⁴ 150 *S* Abel ⲙ. ⲉϩⲟⲣⲉ ⲉⲡⲣⲉϥϫⲓ ⲛϭⲟⲛⲥ. With ⲉ- : Deu 19 5 *B (S* ⲣⲱϩⲧ*)* τυγχ. ; 2 Mac 5 27 *A* μετέχειν ; HL 112 *B* after long privations ⲁϥⲙ. ⲉⲡⲉϥⲥⲁϭⲟⲩⲛ *was affected in intestines*, PS 280 *S* that mystery ϭⲙⲁⲧⲱⲟⲩ ⲉⲡⲟⲓ ⲙⲙⲟϥ. With ⲛ- : ViSitz 172 4 35 *S* ⲉⲧⲣⲁⲙ. ⲡⲡⲁⲩ (var Leyd 413 ⲉⲧⲣⲁⲡ.) *your face*, Gu 97 *S* ϭⲙ. ⲡⲁⲁϥ (*sic l*) ⲛⲉⲣⲡⲟ *fitted to be.*

ϭⲓⲙⲁⲙ. *S* nn f, *obtaining :* CO 19 ⲉⲧⲃⲉⲧϭ. ⲡⲡⲉⲣⲏⲧ (*cf* He 11 33).

—— *S* nn m, *attainment, success :* Sa 13 19 ἐπιτυχία.

ϯ ⲙ. *SBF* I tr, meaning as ⲙ. : He 6 15 *F (S* ⲙ., *B* ϣⲁϣⲡⲓ*)* ἐπιτυγχ. ; Lev 26 34 *B (S* ⲉⲓⲣⲉ*)* εὐδοκεῖν ; Is 64 5 *B (S* ⲧⲱⲙⲛⲧ*)* συναντᾶν ; Gal 6 16 *BF (S* diff*)* στοιχεῖν ; BG 94 *S* ⲉⲩⲉϯ ⲙⲉⲧⲉ ⲙⲡⲟⲩϫⲁⲓ, Mor 30 49 *F* ⲡⲁϥϯ ⲙ. ⲙⲡⲧⲉⲗϭⲁ = BMis 273 *S* ⲙ. **II** intr *S* (rare) *B*, *attain, consent, agree :* Ro 11 7 (*S* ⲙ. tr) ἐπιτυγχ. ; Ge 24 26, Ps 76 8 (*S* ⲧⲱⲧ ⲡϩⲏⲧ), 1 Cor 1 21 (*S* ⲡ ϩⲛⲁϩ), Col 1 19 (*S* ⲟⲩⲱϣ) εὐδοκ., Ac 22 20 (*S* = Gk) συνευδ. ; Ps 44 5 (*S* ⲥⲟⲟⲩⲧⲛ) κατευοδοῦν ; Ac 20 15 (*S* ⲉⲓ) καταντᾶν ; MG 25 17 *B* ⲁϥϯ ⲙ. ⲙⲙⲁⲩ εὐκαιρεῖν ; P 129²⁰ 133 *S* Son ⲡⲧⲁϥϯ ⲙ. ⲁⲩⲱ ⲁϥⲣ ⲕⲁⲧⲁϫⲓⲟⲩ (*sic l*) & came down, PO 11 349 *B* bishops ⲉⲧⲁⲩϯ ⲙ. ⲙⲙⲁⲩ *had come together there*, Va 67 73 *B* their opinion ⲙⲡⲉϥϯ ⲙ. With ⲉ- *B* : 1 Chr 29 3, Ps 39 14 (*S* ⲣ ϩⲛⲁϩ), ib 67 17 (*S* ⲟⲩⲱϣ), 1 Thes 2 8 (*SF* ⲉⲣϩⲛⲁϩ) εὐδοκ. ; Va 61 23 ⲁⲥϯ ⲙ. ⲉⲣⲱⲟⲩ ⲡϫⲉ ⲟⲩ ⲱⲟϣ ἀπαντᾶν, Phil 3 11 (*S* ⲉⲓ ⲉ-) καταν., Ex 23 4 (*S* ⲧⲱⲙⲛⲧ) συναν., Pro 24 58 (*SA* ⲙ.), He 8 6 (*SF* ⲝⲓ) τυγχ. ; Ac 20 14 (*S* ⲧⲱ.) συμβάλλειν ; HL 92 ⲙⲡⲟⲩϯ ⲙ. to become monks, DeV 2 125 at last ⲁϥϯ ⲙ. ⲉϯⲙⲉⲧⲉⲡⲓⲥⲕⲟⲡⲟⲥ. With ⲉϫⲛ- *B* : Ps 84 2 (*S* ⲟⲩⲱϣ) εὐδοκ. ; Ge 34 19 (*S* ⲕⲱ ⲉϫⲛ-)

ἐγκεῖσθαι dat, N&E 39 335 ⲧⲉⲛϯ ⲙ. ⲁⲛ ⲉⲭⲉⲛⲡϣⲟⲩⲉ of these τόποι; ⲉⲣⲏⲓ ⲉⲭⲉⲛ-: He 10 6 (S ⲣ ⲉⲛⲁⲝ ⲉⲛ-, F ⲟⲩⲱⲩⲩ ⲉⲉⲛ-) εὐδοκ., Ac 8 1 (S = Gk) συνευδ. dat. With ⲙⲛ-ⲑⲡⲉⲙ- SBF: Ge 33 10 B (S ⲣ ⲟⲩⲱⲩⲩ) εὐδοκ., Is 7 2 B (S ϭⲓ ⲙⲛ-) συμφωνεῖν πρός; Gal 5 25 B (S ⲁⲣⲉ ⲉ-) στοιχεῖν dat ; Lev 20 5 B (S no vb) ὁμονοεῖν dat, Ro 2 8 neg BF ἀπειθεῖν dat (S ⲣ ⲁⲧⲥⲱⲧⲙ, cf ⲁⲧϯ ⲙ.); CMSS 7 S ⲉ[ⲣ]ϣⲁⲛ[ⲅⲟⲙ]-ⲓⲗⲓ ⲡϭⲛⲁϯ ⲙ. ⲡⲁⲙⲉ ⲁⲛ, Miss 4 221 B Henoticon ϯ ⲙ. ⲡⲉⲙⲡⲓⲡⲁⲣϯ ⲡⲟⲣⲑⲟⲇⲟⲍⲟⲥ. With ϭⲉⲛ-, ⲉⲉⲛ- BF: Job 14 6 B (S ⲟⲩⲱⲩⲩ), Jer 14 12 B (S ⲧⲱⲧ ⲡⲟⲏⲧ), 2 Cor 12 10 B (S do, F ⲧⲱⲕ ⲡⲟ.) εὐδοκ.; Gal 6 16 BF (S ⲁⲣⲉ ⲉ-) στοιχ. dat ; C 86 359 B golden pomegranates on throne (fell &) ⲁⲩϯ ⲙ. ϭⲉⲛⲡⲉⲩⲃⲁⲗ reached his eyes, BSM 53 B if seest one sick ⲛⲧⲉⲕϯ ⲙ. ϭⲉⲛⲡⲉϥϥⲁϣⲣⲓ = BMis 406 S ⲛⲧⲉⲉⲣⲁⲡⲉⲩⲉ ⲙⲙⲟϥ.

ϯ ⲙ. BF nn m, assent, good pleasure : Ps 18 15 (S ⲥⲙⲟⲩ), ib 50 20 (S ⲟⲩⲱⲩⲩ), Eph 1 5 BF (S ⲧⲱⲧ ⲡⲟⲏⲧ) εὐδοκία; 1 Cor 7 5 (SF ϣⲱⲡϥ) σύμφωνος, 2 Cor 6 15 B (S = Gk) -φώνησις, MG 25 219 B = Z 347 S ⲥⲙⲛ ⲧⲟⲟⲧⲝ -φωνία; Ge 30 11 τύχη; Va 61 26 ⲕⲁⲧⲁ ⲟⲩϯ ⲙ. of God βούλησις, AM 276 sim συγκυρία; MG 25 67 ⲙⲡⲉⲛⲓϯ ⲙ. ϣⲱⲡⲓ that they should wed.

ⲣⲉϥϯ ⲙ. B, obedient person : Tit 3 1 ⲟⲓ ⲡⲣ. (S ⲣ ⲥⲧⲙⲏⲧ) πειθαρχεῖν.

ⲁⲧϯ ⲙ. B, not agreeing : Deu 21 20, 1 Pet 2 8 (S ⲁⲧⲡⲁⲣⲧⲉ) ἀπειθεῖν; Ac 28 25 (S ⲧⲱⲧ ⲡⲟ. ⲁⲛ) ἀσύμφωνος; Rom 1 31 (S om) ἀσύνθετος. ⲙⲉⲧ-ⲁⲧϯ ⲙ., unacceptableness : Miss 4 199 ϯⲙ. ⲡⲧⲉ ⲡⲏ ⲉⲧⲥϭⲛⲟⲩⲧ.

ⲙⲁⲧⲉ in ⲉⲙⲁⲧⲉ (often ⲙⲙⲁϯ) S, (ⲉ)ⲙⲁϯ F (once) advb, greatly, very (here = B ⲉⲙⲁϣⲱ, ⲙ-ⲙⲁϣⲱ if not notified): Ge 12 14, Ps 6 2 (var ⲉ-ⲙⲁϣⲁ), Mt 26 22 (F ⲉⲙⲁϣⲁ) σφόδρα, Ps 37 8, Lam 5 22 (F do) ἕως σφ.; 2 Kg 2 17, Job 29 5, Mt 4 8 λίαν; Sa 17 3, Mt 8 6 δεινῶς; Is 23 16, Mk 15 3 (var ⲉⲡⲉⲣⲅⲟ, B ⲡⲣⲁⲡⲗⲏⲩ) πολλά; Job 15 11 μεγάλως; Ps 30 24 (B om) περισσῶς, Dan 3 22 (B ϭⲉⲡⲟⲩⲙⲉⲧⲣⲟⲩ), 1 Thes 3 10 (B ⲡⲣⲟⲅⲟ ⲡⲣⲟⲅⲟ) ἐκ περισσοῦ; ViSitz 172 4 35 S πλεῖστα; Jude 20 S (A ⲙⲡϣⲁ, B om) ἅγιος superlat; Ps 50 2 (B ⲡⲣ.) ἐπὶ πλεῖον; Lu 23 10 εὐτόνως; BM 173 216 we end fast ⲉⲣⲟⲅϭⲉ ⲉⲙ. (cf ἑσπέρα βαθεία & Mk 16 2 B); Mt 2 3, ib 14 9 (BFGk om); PS 22 ⲟⲩⲛⲟϭ ⲡⲣⲟⲧⲉ ⲉⲙ., BG 29 ⲁⲥⲟⲱϣⲧ ⲉⲅⲟⲩⲡ ⲉⲣⲟϥ ⲉⲙ., ShC 73 127 dark places ⲉⲅϣⲟⲕϭ ⲉⲙ., ShA 2 317 ⲡⲣⲁϣ ⲛⲥⲟⲡ ⲉⲙ., ShMIF 23 146 ⲟⲩⲛⲟϭ ⲉⲙ. ⲛ ⲃⲱ, PRain 4725 ϭⲁⲣⲉϭ ⲉⲣ[ⲟⲥ] ⲉⲙ., J 80 18 sickness ⲉϥϭⲟⲣϣ ⲉⲙ., Mor 41 45 he continued ⲉϥ-ϣⲗⲏⲗ ⲙⲙ., P 129²⁰ 129 fiery river ⲉϥϯ ϭⲣⲟⲟⲩ ⲉⲙ.,

BKU 1 26 (1) 16 F ⲟⲩⲥⲁⲓⲏ ⲙⲁϯⲡ[ⲉ; iterated : PS 7 ⲡⲉϥⲡⲉϫ ⲁⲕⲧⲏ ⲉⲃⲟⲗⲡⲉ ⲉⲙ. ⲉⲙ., Mor 22 22 ⲉϥⲡⲁϣⲱⲡⲉ ⲉⲙ. ⲉⲙ. ϭⲛⲧⲉϥⲕⲁⲕⲓⲁ, Hall 86 ⲉⲡ ⲭⲣⲓⲁ ⲉⲙ. ⲉⲙ. is very needy.

ⲙⲁⲧⲉ in ⲙⲙⲁⲧⲉ (sometimes ⲉⲙⲁⲧⲉ) S, ⲙⲙⲉⲧⲉ A², ⲙⲙⲉϯ F advb, only : Jud 6 37 S, Job 19 3 S (B om), Mt 14 36 SF (B = Gk), Jo 8 16 S (A² ⲟⲩ-ⲁⲉⲉⲧⲝ, B ⲙⲙⲁⲅⲁⲧⲝ) μόνος, -ον; Si 39 1 S πλήν; PS 21 S saw not me but ⲡⲟⲩⲟⲉⲓⲛ ⲙⲙ., Br 91 S ⲡⲟⲩⲥⲟⲡ ⲙⲙ., AP 10 A² ⲉϥⲣ ⲭⲣⲓⲁ ⲙⲙ. of man's salvation, BHom 69 S not only ⲛⲣⲱⲙⲉ ⲙⲙ. but beasts.

ⲙⲁϯ F v ⲙⲟⲩⲧ (ⲙⲟⲧⲉ).

ⲙⲁⲧⲟⲓ SB, -ⲟⲉⲓ SA², -ⲁⲉⲓ A², -ⲁⲓ F nn m, soldier (originally Mede, GöttN '16 124): Mk 15 16 SBF, Jo 19 23 SA²B, AP 49 A², BHom 20 S στρατιώτης, Phil 2 25 SB ϣⲃⲣ, ϣⲫⲏⲣ ⲙ. συνστρ., Ex 14 4 B στρατιά, Jer 48 12 B, Lu 21 20 SB στρατόπεδον; ShZ 505 S ϭⲛⲧⲉⲙⲱⲡ ⲛ ⲙ., BM 346 S ⲡⲡⲟⲟϭ ⲙⲙ. of the legion, C 43 149 B ⲟⲅⲃⲟⲏⲑⲓⲁ ⲙⲙ., AM 52 B ⲁⲡⲁⲓⲱⲧ ϭⲟⲕⲧ ⲙⲙ., Ann 16 250 F ⲟ̄ ⲡϣⲏ ⲙⲙ. C 86 172 B among Muslim officials ⲡⲓⲙ. ⲡⲓⲅⲩⲡⲉⲩⲥ (ἱππεύς) ⲡⲓⲙⲁⲥⲙⲁⲧⲟⲓ young soldiers (?) ⲡⲓⲧⲉⲛⲧⲉⲣⲓⲟⲛ (جاندار v BIF 1 130).

ⲣ, ⲉⲣ ⲙ., become soldier : 1 Cor 9 7 SBF στρα-τεύεσθαι; C 43 2 B ⲉⲓⲡⲁⲉⲣ ⲙ. ϭⲁⲣⲁⲧϥ, BIF 14 134 S sim, AM 156 B ⲧⲉⲛⲡⲁⲉⲣ ⲙ. ⲡⲁⲕ ⲁⲛ.

ⲙⲛⲧ-, ⲙⲉⲧⲙ., soldiery, warfare : Lu 2 13 B (S = Gk) στρατιά, 2 Cor 10 4 SB, Aeg 234 S στρα-τεία, CaiEuch 581 B ⲡⲓⲙ. τὰ στρατιωτικά; SHel 71 S appointed to ⲧⲙ. ⲉ(ⲗ ⲙ)ⲡⲡⲟⲩⲙⲉⲣⲟⲡ ⲡⲡⲁⲡ-ⲕⲁϭ, AM 259 B arms of thy ⲙ., Miss 8 216 S stripped of ⲑⲃⲥⲱ ⲡⲧⲁⲙ.

As name : ⲙⲁⲧⲟⲓ MG 25 323 (= PG 65 289 Ματόη), J 65 95, ⲙⲁⲧⲁⲓ CO 447, -ⲧⲁⲉⲓ LMis 104, Ματόι, -τάει (Preisigke), ⲡⲙⲁⲧⲟⲓ WS 193, ⲧⲙⲁⲧⲟⲓ J 119 1 (v GöttN l c 130). In place-names: J 81 54 ⲉⲡⲟⲓⲕⲓⲟⲛ ⲙ., Alex 281, Cai 8646, ⲙⲁ ⲡⲙⲁⲧⲟⲓ, -ⲱⲓ.

ⲙⲏⲧⲉ SAO, ⲙⲏⲛⲧⲉ S, ⲙⲏϯ BF nn f, middle, a as nn : 3 Kg 8 64 B, Dan 3 50 B τὸ μέσον, Sa 7 18 S μεσότης; Is 3 24 SB μεσο(πόρφυρος) Eph 2 14 SB μεσο(τοιχον); Ge 49 26 S, Ps 7 16 S (both B ⲥⲱⲟⲩⲅⲣⲓ) κορυφή; Glos 297 S σφάκελος · ⲧⲏⲃⲉ ⲡⲧⲙ., ST 109 S ⲡⲙⲉⲣⲟⲥ ⲧⲁⲧⲙ. b as prep : ⲉⲧⲙ., to, into midst, between : Jer 48 7 B τὸ μέσον, Ge 15 10 S (B ϭⲉⲛ-) μ. adj, Ps 77 28 SB, Ez 5 4 SB εἰς μ., Job 2 1 S (B ϭⲉⲛ-), Ez 3 24 SB ἐν μ., Jos 1 11 S κατὰ μ.; PS 34 S ⲡⲉϣⲁϥⲉⲓ ⲉⲧⲙ. ⲡ-ⲡⲁⲓⲱⲛ; come forward : RNC 25 S after hiding ⲁϥⲉⲓ ⲉⲧⲙ. ἔρχεσθαι ἐν τῷ μ., ROC '13 172 S lest any strange word ⲉⲓ ⲉⲧⲙ. ἐγκύπτειν (var παρεμπί-πτειν, cf Leont Neap Gelzer 180), C 43 128 B ⲁϭⲓ

ⲉⲟⲙ. before magistrate, Mich 550 45 S ϣⲁⲣⲉϩⲉⲛⲕⲟⲅⲓ ⲛϯⲱⲡ ⲉⲓ ⲉⲧⲉⲩⲙ.; come *before*, *between*: BHom 137 S I need no man ⲉⲧⲣⲉϥⲉⲓ ⲉⲧⲁⲙ. μεσίτης, J 36 41 S important men came ⲉⲧⲛⲙ. ⲙⲡⲛⲉⲣⲏⲩ; bring *forward*: Va 63 91 B let us begin by ⲓⲛⲓ ⲉⲟⲙ. ⲛⲣⲁⲛⲕⲟⲩϫⲓ ⲛⲥⲁϫⲓ εἰς μ. ἄγειν, ShBor 246 37 S ⲁⲛⲛ ⲡⲉϥⲣ ⲡⲙⲉⲉⲩⲉ ⲉⲧⲁⲙ., DeV 1 191 B I will not be silent ⲉϣⲧⲉⲙⲓⲛⲓ ⲉⲟⲙ. remembrance of…, Miss 4 136 B ⲙⲡⲉⲣⲓⲛⲓ ⲛⲁⲛ ⲉⲟⲙ. blasphemies; Miss 8 58 S forbid to ⲕⲱ ⲉⲧⲁⲙ. ⲡⲕⲉⲣⲱⲃ προτιθέναι. ⲛⲧⲙ., *in midst*: Ps 21 14 S, Pro 5 14 SA, Mt 10 16 S ἐν μ., Ps 103 12 S, Sa 12 5 S ἐκ μ., Ps 67 13 S ἀνὰ μ. (all B ϧⲉⲛ-); PS 171 S said this ⲛⲧⲙ. ⲡⲙⲙⲁⲑⲏⲧⲏⲥ, PGM 1 60 O ⲉⲧⲉⲡⲉϥϩⲟ ⲛⲧⲙ. ⲛ-, FR 180 S Jews wished to hide His cross ⲛⲧⲙ. (BMis 202 om, cf ⲱⲗ, ϥⲓ ⲛⲧⲙ.); *present, in midst*: Ac 19 40 S ⲉⲩⲛ ϩⲱⲃ ⲛⲧⲙ. (B diff) ὑπάρχειν (?), BMis 235 S debated ⲉⲡϩⲱⲃ ⲉⲧⲛⲧⲙ. = Mor 30 8 F ⲉⲧⲣⲛⲧⲙ., ST 412 S agreed ϩⲁⲣⲟⲃ ⲡⲓⲙ ⲛⲧⲡⲉⲙ. (cf Ep 88); *in midst* of two or more, *between*: Ge 13 3 S ⲛⲧⲙ….ⲁⲩⲱ ⲛⲧⲙ. (B ⲟⲩⲧⲉ- ⲡⲉⲙⲟⲩⲧⲉ-), ib 13 8 S ⲛⲧⲁⲙ. ⲙⲛⲧⲉⲕⲙ. (B ⲟⲩⲧⲉ-…ⲟⲩⲧⲉ-), Is 22 11 S (B ⲟⲩⲧⲉ-), Ez 34 22 SB ⲛⲧⲙ. ⲛ-…ⲙⲛ ἀνὰ μ., Lu 11 51 S (B ⲟⲩⲧⲉ-) μεταξύ, R 1 3 29 S rock ⲛⲧⲙ. ⲡⲙⲡⲉⲣⲥⲟⲥ ⲙⲛⲧⲙ. ⲡⲛⲣⲱⲙⲁⲓⲟⲥ; *from midst*: Is 57 2 S (B ⲉⲃⲟⲗ ϧⲉⲛⲟⲙ.), Zech 9 7 S (Bor 246 24, ib 25 ϧⲛⲧⲙ., AB do) ἐκ μ.; AP 12 A² ϥⲓⲧϥ ⲛⲧⲙ. αἱρεῖν, Ps 108 23 S (B diff) ⲗⲟ (var ϥⲓ) ⲛⲧⲙ. ἀνταναιρεῖν, 2 Kg 14 7 S ϥⲓ ⲛⲧⲙ. (ib 11 ϩⲛⲧⲙ.), Cl 48 1 A sim. ἐξαιρεῖν, BM 174 1 S knife ⲁⲥⲗⲟ ⲛⲧⲙ. παύεσθαι, BMis 409 S ⲁϥⲥⲟⲧⲡϥ ⲛⲧⲙ. of brethren; ⲉⲃⲟⲗ ⲛⲧⲙ.: Sa 4 14 S, Mt 13 49 S (BF do) ἐκ μ. ϩⲛⲧⲙ., ϧⲉⲛⲟⲙ., *in midst, between*: Su 59 B μέσον, Lev 25 33 SB, Ps 39 8 SB, Is 5 25 SBF, Ez 19 11 B (S ⲛⲧⲙ.) ἐν μ., Si 34 19 S (var ⲉⲧⲙ.) ἀνὰ μ., Jo 20 19 SA²B εἰς τὸ μ., Jud 18 25 S μετά, Lu 16 26 S (B ⲟⲩⲧⲉ-…ⲡⲉⲙⲟⲩⲧⲉ-) μεταξύ; Br 231 S ⲟⲩⲛ ⲟⲩⲧⲣⲁⲡⲉⲍⲁ ϩⲛⲧⲉⲩⲙ., ShA 1 55 S decide ϩⲛⲧⲙ. ⲙⲡⲉⲓⲣⲱⲃ, C 41 33 B secrets ⲉⲩϧⲉⲛⲧⲟⲩⲙ. ϩⲓⲟⲩⲥⲟⲡ, BAp 172 S whether thou depart or ⲉⲕϧⲛⲧⲙ. *art present*; ϩⲛⲧⲙ.…ⲙⲛ-: Ge 3 15 S (B ⲟⲩⲧⲉ-…ⲡⲉⲙ.-), Lev 11 47 SB, Jth 8 11 S ἀνὰ μ.…καί, Si 19 7 S ἐν…καὶ ἐν; Miss 4 191 B God is ϧⲉⲛⲧⲙ. ⲡⲉⲙⲁⲕ ⲡⲉⲙⲟⲟⲩ (sc those entrusted to thee), BP 5561 F ⲫⲱϥ ⲉⲧϩⲉⲧⲉⲡⲙⲏⲧⲓ, BM 1061 S ⲛⲧⲁⲥϫⲟⲕⲉⲓ ϩⲛⲧⲙ. ⲡⲉⲙⲁⲕ, J 123 4 S God ϩⲛⲧⲙ. ⲙⲛⲧⲙ. ⲡⲡⲉⲛⲧⲁϥⲙⲟⲩ. ⲉⲃⲟⲗ ϩⲛⲧⲙ., ϧⲉⲛⲟⲙ., *from out midst*: Ps 135 11 SB, Jer 51 7 SB, Col 2 14 B (S ⲛⲧⲙ.) ἐκ μ., ἐκ τοῦ μ.; PS 158 S set them apart ⲉⲃ. ϩⲛⲧⲙ. ⲛⲛⲓⲕⲱⲱⲥ, BHom 106 S separate wicked ϩⲛ- (= ⲉⲃⲟⲗ ϩⲛ) ⲧⲙ. ⲛⲛⲁⲇⲓⲕⲁⲓⲟⲥ, PSBA 10 396 B ⲁⲗⲓⲟⲩ ⲉⲃ. ϧⲉⲛⲟⲙ. these impious ones. ϩⲓⲧⲙ., *in, through midst*: Lu 23 45 S (B

ϧⲉⲛ-) μέσον, ib 12 46 S (B do) διχοτομεῖν, ClPr 26 76 S wall ϩⲓⲧⲉⲛⲙ. & God's. In place-names: Νεχήουι τμῆτι (BGU 571).

ⲙⲁⲣⲙⲏⲧⲉ S nn f, *a thing girt about the middle* (?), *belt*: P 131³ 35 sailors have money ϧⲏⲧⲉⲩⲙ., BM 594 S ⲥⲛⲏⲧⲉ ⲡⲙⲁⲣⲙⲏⲧⲉ (sic corrected from -ⲙⲁⲓⲏⲧⲉ).

ⲙⲟⲧⲉ, ⲙⲟϯ v ⲙⲟⲩⲧ.

ⲙⲟⲩⲧⲉ SAA², ⲙⲟⲩⲏⲧⲉ A (v Till 34 j), ⲙⲟⲩϯ BF vb I intr, *speak, call* (of men, animals, things): **a** without obj, Ps 134 17 SB, Is 29 4 SB, EpJer 40 B (F ϣⲉϫⲓ), Zeph 2 14 AB, Mt 26 74 SB φωνεῖν, 2 Chr 5 13 B ἀναφ.; Job 14 15 SB, ViSitz 172 4 14 S without clergy ⲙⲉⲩⲙ. ϫⲉⲉⲕⲕⲗⲏⲥⲓⲁ καλεῖν, Job 5 1 S (B ⲱϣ ⲉϩⲣⲏⲓ) ἐπικ.; Is 8 19 B (S ϣⲁϫⲉ) ⲉⲃⲟⲗ ϧⲉⲛⲟⲩⲉϫⲓ ἐγγαστρίμυθος; 1 Cor 15 52 B (S = Gk trumpet) σαλπίζειν; Si 50 17 S (sim) ἠχεῖν; Jer 31 36 B (flute) βομβεῖν; Si 13 13 S εἰσαγορεῖσθαι; 1 Kg 28 3 S rel γνωστός (var μάγος); Ryl 89 S idols ⲙⲉⲩⲙ. ϩⲛⲧⲉⲩϣⲟⲩⲱⲃⲉ, C 41 79 B ·ⲁϥⲙ. thrice (var Miss 4 181 ⲱϣ ⲉⲃⲟⲗ), HCons 462 S ⲡⲉⲛⲧⲁϥⲙ. *invite* (var Aeg 259 ⲧⲱϩⲙ.), Aeg 282 S paying heed to birds ⲉⲩⲙ. **b c e-**: Ge 3 20 SB, Job 19 16 SB, Is 48 1 B (S ⲧⲱ.), EpJer 29 BF, Hos 1 9 AB, 1 Cor 15 9 SBF, BHom 53 S ⲁⲩⲙ. ⲉⲥⲟⲩⲥⲁⲡⲃ καλεῖν, Jos 4 4 SB ἀνακ., 3 Kg 8 43 B (S = Gk), Ps 88 26 SB, Jer 14 9 B (S ⲧⲁⲅⲟ ⲉϩⲣⲁⲓ), ib 15 16 B (S ⲭⲱ) ἐπικ., Ac 7 14 SB μετακ., Job 19 17 SB, Ps 49 4 S (B ⲙ. ⲟⲩⲃⲉ-), Mt 15 32 S (B do) προσκ.; Mk 3 31 SB, Jo 4 16 SA²BF, Z 339 S = MG 25 216 B φων., Mt 11 16 S (B ⲙ. ⲟⲩⲃⲉ-) προσφ.; Mt 26 36 SBF, 1 Cor 8 5 SBF λέγειν; Sa 14 8 S ὀνομάζειν; Ac 11 26 S (B ϯ ⲣⲉⲛ) χρηματίζειν; in Ez often before Hebr name where Gk om: 23 4, 43 15, 17, 47 10, 17; PS 13 S ⲧⲁⲓ ⲉϣⲁⲩⲙ. ⲉⲣⲟⲥ ϫⲉⲧⲁⲙⲁⲁⲩ, Br 47 S ⲥⲉⲛⲙ. ⲉⲣⲟϥ ⲙⲡⲉⲓⲣⲁⲛ, Z 269 S sim, ShC 73 208 S they hear ⲉⲛⲉⲧⲙ. ⲉⲣⲟⲟⲩ, Mor 30 12 Sf this name ⲙ. ⲉⲣⲟⲕ ⲙⲙⲁϥ, BMis 2 S ⲁⲛⲡⲣⲟ….ⲙ. ⲉⲣⲟⲟⲩ ⲡⲁϥ ⲛⲥⲟⲡ, C 86 231 B bade ⲙ.ⲉⲡⲓⲁⲧⲓⲟⲥ ⲡⲁϥ, BIF 13 118 S ⲙ. ⲉⲡⲣⲁⲛ ⲛⲟⲩⲁ ⲡϩⲏⲧⲟⲩ ⲉϫⲙⲡⲉⲓⲧⲟⲡⲟⲥ = MG 25 311 B, TU 43 20 A ⲥⲉⲛⲙ. ⲁⲣⲱⲧⲛⲉ ϫⲉⲥⲁϥ, PLond 4 494 S Theodosius ⲡⲉⲧⲟⲩⲙ. ⲉⲣⲟϥ ϫⲉⲡⲟⲩⲱⲡϣ (cf ὁ καί indicating 2d name). *Enchant, charm*: Ps 57 5 S (B ⲣⲉϥⲙ.), Jer 8 17 B ἐπάδειν, BMOr 8811 67 S snake & ⲡⲉⲧⲙ. ⲉⲣⲟϥ, Miss 4 109 B enchanters ⲉⲩⲙ. ⲉⲡⲓϣⲱⲓ; cf above 1 Kg 28 3.

—— S nn, *magical call, incantation*: Deu 18 10 (B ϫⲉ ⲙⲧⲁⲩ, var ⲁϣⲉⲃⲉⲓ) ἐπαοιδή; R 1 4 25 I know ⲟⲩⲁⲛⲥ ⲙⲙ. & all magic arts, ib 2 1 76 pouring over selves ϩⲉⲛⲙⲟⲟⲩ ⲙⲙ., ib ϩⲉⲛⲙⲙ. & things (amulets) to bind on heads.

ⲣⲉϥⲙ., *enchanter*: Lev 19 31 *S* (*B* ⲣⲉϥϣⲉⲛ ϩⲓⲛ), 1 Kg 6 2 *S*, Si 12 14 *SB*, Dan 1 20 *S* (*B* ⲣⲉϥϭⲓ ϣⲏⲙ), Aeg 242 *S* ἐπαοιδός, Is 47 9 *S* (*B* ⲙⲉⲧⲣⲉϥϫⲉ ⲙⲧⲁⲩ) ἐπαοιδή, Deu 18 11 *S* (*B v* ⲁϣⲉⲃⲉⲛ), Eccl 10 11 *SF* ἐπᾴδων, K 114 *B* pl ﺣﻮﺍﺓ; ShWess 9 139 *S* healing oil from ϩⲉⲛⲣ. ⲏ ϩⲉⲛⲣⲉϥⲣ ⲡⲁϩⲣⲉ, CA 88 *S* ⲣⲉϥⲕⲁ ⲟⲩⲛⲟⲩ, ⲣ., ⲣⲉϥϣⲓⲛⲉ, C 43 103 *B* ⲉϩⲱⲣⲅⲏⲥⲧⲏⲥ ⲛⲣ., Miss 4 717 *S* went to ⲣ. & was delivered of child, BHom 17 *S* it is no snake's bite that I should go to ⲣ. φάρμακον ἐπιτιθέναι. *V* ⲛⲏϭⲉ. ⲙⲛⲧⲣⲉϥⲙ. *S*, *enchantment*: Leyd 442 ⲙⲛⲧⲣⲉϥⲣ ϩⲓⲕ, ⲙⲛⲧⲣ., R 2 4 96 ⲙⲛⲧⲣ., ⲙⲛⲧⲙⲁⲅⲟⲥ, ⲙⲛⲧⲣⲉϥϣⲓⲛⲉ. *V* also ⲙ. nn.

With following prepositions.

—— ⲉϫⲛ- *S*, ⲁϫⲛ- *A*, ⲉϫⲉⲛ- *B*, *call upon, cry to*: Ge 12 8 *B* ἐπικ., Pro 9 3 *SA* (*B* ⲑⲱϩⲉⲙ) συγκ.; AM 54 *B* standing above ⲁϥⲙ. ⲉϫⲱϥ, Mor 44 37 *S* ⲁϥⲙ. ⲉϫⲙⲡⲙⲏⲏϣⲉ saying, BMis 20 *S* I saw dream ⲉⲩⲙ. ⲉϫⲱⲓ saying; ⲙ. ⲉϧⲣⲏⲓ ⲉϫ. *B*, meaning sim: C 43 87 ⲁϥⲙ. ⲉϩ. ⲉϫⲱϥ (*sc* corpse) saying (*l* ⲉϧ., *cf* AM 330 below), AM 34 sim ⲉϧ. ⲉϫⲱⲟⲩ. *Cf* ⲙ. ⲉⲡⲉⲥⲏⲧ.

—— ⲟⲩⲃⲉ- *SB*, meaning as last: Ge 3 9 *S* (*B* ⲉ-), Ps 49 1 *B* (*S* ⲉ-), Is 21 8 *B* (*S* do) καλεῖν, Ps 41 8 *B* (*S* ⲱϣ ⲟⲩⲃⲉ-), Pro 2 3 *S* (var & *A* ⲉ-, *B* ⲧⲱⲃϩ ⲛⲥⲁ-) ἐπικ., *ib* 9 15 *B* (*SA* ⲉ-), Gu 73 *S* ⲁϥⲙ. ⲟⲩⲃⲏⲓ (var Mor 17 95 ⲉ-) προσκ.; Lu 18 19 *S* (*B* ϫⲱ ⲉ-) λέγ.; Mt 11 16 *B* (*S* ⲉ-) προσφων.; PS 232 *S* ⲉⲓⲙ. ⲟⲩⲃⲉⲧⲏⲩⲧⲛ ϫⲉⲛⲁⲥⲛⲏⲩ, MG 25 393 *B* ⲁϥⲙ. ⲟⲩⲃⲉϯⲥϩⲓⲙⲓ saying, Mor 18 17 *S* ⲙ. ⲟⲩⲃⲏⲓ (var *ib* 19 25 *S* ⲉⲣⲟⲓ, *B* Miss 4 111 ⲟⲩⲃⲏⲓ). ⲙ. ⲉϩⲣⲁⲓ, ⲁϩ. ⲟⲩⲃⲉ- *SA*: Ps 49 15 *A* (Cl, *S* = Gk, *B* ⲱϣ ⲉⲛϣⲱⲓ ϩⲁ-), Pro 1 28 *SA* (*B* ϯ ϩⲟ ⲉ-).

—— ϧⲁϫⲉⲛ- *B*, *call ahead, forward*: MIE 2 411 ⲁⲓⲙ. ϧⲁϫⲱⲓ according to canon, Rec 6 177 sim (*cf* ⲙ. ⲉϩⲟⲩⲛ *announce*).

—— ϩⲁ- *B*, *call to*: Is 21 11 (*S* dat) καλ. πρός.

—— ϩⲓϫⲛ- *S^f*, meaning same: AZ 33 55 ⲉⲩⲙ. ϩⲓϫⲛ(ⲛ)ⲓⲣⲉϥⲉⲣ ⲑⲗⲓⲃⲉ saying.

With following adverbs.

—— ⲉⲃⲟⲗ, ⲁⲃⲁⲗ *SAB*, *call out* (from within): Z 234 *S* ⲁϥⲙ. ⲉⲃ. ⲉⲣⲟⲟⲩ saying (*cf* ⲙ. ⲉϩⲟⲩⲛ), BIF 13 118 *S* = MG 25 311 *B* Macarius ⲙ. ⲉⲃ. ϩⲛⲧⲉⲕⲕⲗⲏⲥⲓⲁ saying; *call* (to come) *out*: Ge 19 5 *S* (*B* ⲙ. ⲉⲛⲥⲁ ⲛⲃⲟⲗ), Deu 20 10 *S* (*B* ⲙ.) ἐκκαλεῖν; ROC 25 248 *B* bade ⲉⲑⲣⲟⲩⲙ. ⲉⲣⲟϥ ⲉⲃ. ἐξέρχεσθαι; TU 43 2 *A* he found us within ⲁϥⲙ. ⲁⲣⲁⲛ ⲁⲃ.; *call out* to, *accost*: BMis 382 *S* ⲙ. ⲉⲃ. ⲉⲡⲉⲓⲟⲩⲱϩⲉ & say = BSM 38 *B* ⲁϫⲟⲥ ⲛ-, Aeg 45 *B* ⲁϥⲙ. ⲉⲃ. ⲉⲡⲁⲉⲓⲱⲧ saying, TEuch 1 311 *B* rubric ⲛⲧⲉⲡⲓⲗⲁⲟⲥ ⲙ. ⲉⲃ. *cry aloud* saying; *resound, echo*: 1 Kg 3 11 *S*, Is 16 11 *S* (*B* ⲱϣ ⲉⲃ., *cf* Jer 19 3) ἠχεῖν.

—— ⲉⲡⲉⲥⲏⲧ *SB*, *call down* from above: C 41 66 *B* raven on wall ⲁϥⲙ. ⲉⲡ. ⲉϫⲱⲟⲩ, KroppA *S* take cup & ⲛⲅⲙ. ⲉⲡ. ⲉϫⲱⲟⲩ saying; from below: PS 129 *S* ⲁⲓⲙ. ⲉⲅⲁⲃⲣⲓⲏⲗ ⲉⲡ.

—— ⲉϩⲟⲩⲛ, ⲉϧ. *SB*, *call* to, *cry* upon: Lu 7 32 *S* (*B* ⲙ. ⲟⲩⲃⲉ-) προσφωνεῖν; *call in* (from without): Z 550 *S* went to house ⲁϥⲙ. ⲉϩ. ⲉⲣⲟϥ saying, Miss 4 749 *S* ⲁϥⲙ. ⲉϩ. ⲉⲧⲉϥⲥϩⲓⲙⲉ in nunnery saying, Mor 18 4 (var *ib* 19 11 & Miss 4 99 *B* ⲙ.) opened door ⲁϥⲙ. ⲉϩ. saying, Aeg 61 *B* ⲁϥⲙ. ⲉϧ. ⲉⲡⲓⲙϩⲁⲩ; *announce* one's presence: BAp 80 *S* after pulling latch ⲁϥⲙ. ⲉϩ. according to canon, saying Bless me, BMis 461 *S* sim (*cf* ⲙ. ϧⲁϫⲉⲛ-), Z 234 *S* ⲁϥⲙ. ⲉϩ. ⲉⲧⲡⲟⲗⲓⲥ saying Open (*cf* ⲙ. ⲉⲃⲟⲗ), Rec 6 169 *B* at door ⲁⲓⲙ. ⲉϧ. = BMar 206 *S* ⲧⲱϩⲙ ⲉϩ., BMar 180 *S* ⲙⲡⲣⲙ. ⲉϩ. ⲉⲣⲱⲙⲉ *make not a call upon a man* for (mere) ease or greed, C 41 25 *B* ⲡⲓⲡⲁⲩ ⲉⲧⲁⲕⲙ. ⲛⲏⲓ ⲉϧ. *visited me*; *invite in, summon*: Ex 2 20 *B* (*S* ⲙ.) καλεῖν, Ac 10 23 *SB* εἰσκ.; C 43 187 *B* ⲁⲥⲙ. ⲉⲣⲟϥ ⲉϧ. saying Be seated, DeV 2 44 *B* ⲡⲁϥⲙ. ⲉⲛⲓϧⲉⲗⲗⲟⲓ ⲉϧ. to this same mourning, Ryl 439 *B* ⲙⲡⲁϥⲙ. ⲉⲓⲱⲁⲛⲛⲏⲥ ⲉϧ. to feast, Mor 22 113 *S* when visitor (f) announced she bade ⲉⲧⲣⲉⲩⲙ. ⲉⲣⲟⲥ ⲛⲁⲥ ⲉϩ. = BSM 102 *B* ⲉⲑⲣⲟⲩⲉⲛⲥ ⲉϧ. ⲙ. ⲉϩ. ⲉϩⲣⲛ- *S*, *cry into face of* (hostility, impudence): ShBM 205 *S* ⲉⲛⲧⲁⲩⲙ. ⲉϩ. ⲉϩⲣⲁⲓ when I withstood them, ShC 42 156 *S* sim.

—— ⲉϧⲣⲏⲓ *B*, *call down* from above: AM 330 ⲁϥⲙ. ⲉϧ. ϩⲓϫⲉⲛ- corpse.

—— ⲉϩⲣⲁⲓ *S*, ⲁϩ. *A*, *call, cry*: Dan 4 11 *S* (*B* ⲙ.) φωνεῖν: Pro 1 28 *SA* (*B* ϯ ϩⲟ) ἐπικαλεῖν.

II tr, *call, pronounce*, mostly of name: Is 45 3 *B* (*S* ⲙ. ⲉ-), *ib* 63 19 *S* (*B* ⲙ. ⲉ-), Jer 41 17 *B* καλεῖν, 2 Kg 6 2 *B* (*S* ⲧⲁⲩⲟ), Ps 113 15 *B* (*S* intr), Is 43 7 *SB*, Dan 9 19 *B* (*S* ⲧⲁⲩⲟ) ἐπικ.; Ac 16 28 *S* (var ⲉ-, *B* ⲱϣ ⲉⲃ.) φων.; ShC 73 134 *S* to wake him ⲉϥⲉⲙ. ⲙⲡⲉϥⲣⲁⲛ, Br 51 *S* first sound ⲉⲛⲧⲁϥⲙ. ⲙⲙⲟϥ, BIF 13 118 *S* ⲡⲙⲁ ⲉⲧⲟⲩⲛⲁⲙ. ⲙⲡⲉⲕⲣⲁⲛ ⲉϩⲣⲁⲓ ⲉϫⲱϥ = MG 25 312 *B*, PO 14 345 *B* ⲛⲧⲟⲩⲙ. ⲙⲡⲉⲕⲣⲁⲛ ⲉϩ. ⲉϫⲱⲥ, *cf ib* ⲛⲥⲉⲙ. ⲉⲡⲁⲣⲁⲛ ⲉϩ. ⲉϫⲱⲥ.

ϭⲓⲛ-, ϫⲓⲛⲙ. *SB*, *calling, naming*: 1 Chr 28 3 *B* ἐπονομάζειν, 1 Kg 28 12 *S* ⲁⲥⲙ. ϩⲛⲧⲉⲥϭ. Gk om.

ⲕⲱ ⲙ. *S*, obscure, ? *supply words*: Ep 169 be kind ⲛⲧⲉⲧⲛⲕⲱ ⲙ. ⲉⲡϩⲏⲧ ⲙⲡⲓϩⲏⲕⲉ & write for him..., may be God will guide him, Tur ostr 5889 thou sentest brother for the *solidus* ⲛⲧⲟⲟⲩ ⲙⲁⲓⲧⲥⲁⲃⲟϥ (or ? ⲛⲧⲟⲟⲩⲛ ⲁⲓ-) ⲉⲥⲛⲁⲩ ⲛⲡⲉⲓⲕⲟⲩ ⲙ. ⲉⲡⲉϥϩⲏⲧ.

ⲧⲁⲓⲉ ⲙ. *B*, *address word to, greet* deferentially: c dat, Deu 23 6 (*S* ϫⲉ ϣⲁϫⲉ), MG 25 212 ⲁⲕⲧ. ⲙ. ⲛⲏⲓ προσαγορεύειν; Lev 19 32 (*S* ⲧⲓⲙⲁ ⲙⲡϩⲟ) πρόσωπον τιμᾶν; Mt 10 12 (*S* = Gk) ἀσπάζειν; C 43 118 maid ⲧ. ⲙ. ⲛⲁϥ ⲉⲙⲁϣⲱ; c ⲉ-, C 86 284 ϧⲉⲛⲡϫⲓⲛⲑⲣⲉϥⲧ. ⲙ. ⲉⲣⲟϥ = BSG 183 *S* ⲁⲥⲡⲁⲍⲉ

C 43 110 ⲁϥⲧ. ⲙ. ⲉⲣⲟϥ (angel).   As nn m, *greeting*: MG 25 11 ⲙⲡⲉⲕϣⲉⲡ ⲡⲁⲧ. ⲙ. ⲉⲣⲟⲕ ἀσπασμός. *V* ⲙⲛⲧ- prefix.

ⲙⲧⲟ *SAA²*, ⲙⲑⲟ, ⲉⲙⲑⲟ *B*, ⲙⲧⲁ, ⲉⲙⲧⲁ *F* nn m, *face, presence* (properly vb, DM 6 31, from same root as ⲙⲡⲧⲣⲉ, ⲙⲉⲉⲣⲉ, ⲙⲏⲧⲉ, AZ 38 145, 45 38, 52 114), *SA* always + art or poss & ⲉⲃⲟⲗ ⲁⲃⲁⲗ, *BF* mostly without ⲉⲃ., *in face of, before* as prep: Nu 3 4 *S* (var ⲙⲡⲣⲱⲧⲉ ⲉⲃ.), Ac 8 21 *S* ἔναντι, Is 17 13 *S*, Mt 27 24 *S* (all *B* ⲙ.) ἀπέναντι, Ez 3 8 *SB*, Mk 12 41 *SF* (*B* do), Ro 4 17 *SF* (JEA 13 26, *B* do) κατέναντι, Ps 17 7 *S* (*B* ⲛⲁϩⲣⲉⲛ-), *ib* 38 2 *SB*, Is 52 2 *SA* (Cl, *B* om), EpJer 31 *BF* ⲙ. ἐναντίον, Ps 34 3 *S* (*B* ⲉϩⲣⲉⲛ-), Mk 15 39 *SF* (*B* ⲙ.) ἐξ ἐναντίας; Ex 23 15 *SB*, Ps 50 3 *SAB*, *ib* 17 12 *S* (*B* ⲛⲁϩⲣⲉⲛ-), *ib* 67 4 *S* (*B* ⲉⲃ. ϩⲁⲡϩⲟ), Eph 1 4 *S* (*BF* do), Ap 3 2 *S* (*B* ⳉⲁⲧⲉⲛ-) ἐνώπιον, Dan 5 22 *B* ⲙ. κατενώπιον; Ps 20 9 *S* (*B* ϩⲟ) πρόσωπον, Ge 15 10 *S* (*B* ⲙ.) ἀντιπρ., Ps 16 9 *S* (*B* do, *F* Mor 33 ϩⲁⲃⲁⲗ ⲙⲡϩⲣⲁ), Ez 3 9 *SB* ἀπὸ πρ., Job 1 11 *S* (*B* do) εἰς πρ., Lev 26 10 *B* ⲙ. (*S* ϩⲓⲑⲏ) ἐκ πρ., Jer 52 25 *B* ⲙ. ἐν πρ., Deu 34 1 *S* (*B* ⲙ.) ἐπὶ πρ., Is 30 28 *SF* (*B* do), Ac 3 13 *S* (*B* do) κατὰ πρ., Ps 56 6 *SB*, Is 62 11 *B* ⲙ. (*S* ϩⲁⲑⲏ), Mal 3 14 *A* (*B* ⳉⲁⲧⲉⲛ-) πρὸ πρ.; Mt 21 42 *S* (*B* ⳉⲉⲛ-) ἐν ὀφθαλμοῖς, Sa 14 16 *S* ἐν ὄψει, Jer 39 12 *S* (*B* ⲙ.) κατ' ὀφθ., Deu 11 18 *S* (*B* do), Cl 5 3 *A* πρὸ ὀφθ.; AM 273 *B* ⲙⲡⲉⲙ. ⲙⲡⲓⲕⲱⲗϩ κατ' εὐθεῖαν; Job 41 13 *S* (*B* ⳉⲁⲭⲉⲛ-), Mt 11 10 *S* (var JTS 8 241 ϩⲓⲑⲏ, *B* ⲙ.), Jo 12 37 *SA²* (*B* do) ἔμπροσθεν; Nu 2 3 *S* (*B* = Gk), Jos 17 9 *S* (var ⲉⳉⲛ-) κατά; Dan 8 3 *B* ⲙ. πρό; Jer 8 2 *B* πρός; Ez 40 13 *B* ⲙ. ⲉⲃ. (*S* ⲡⲣⲟⲧ ⲉⲃ.) ἐπί; Deu 17 1 *B* (*S* ⲙⲙⲁϩ-) Gk dat; PS 151 *S* I am despised ⲙⲡⲉⲙ. ⲉⲃ. ⲡⲟⲩⲗⲏⲛϣⲉ, El 50 *A* standing ⲙⲡⲁⲙ. ⲁⲃ., Miss 4 110 *B* monastery ⲙⲡⲉⲙ. ⲉⲃ. ⲡⲟⲩⲧⲓⲙⲓ, J 105 20 *S* none can sue thee ⲙⲡⲉⲙ. ⲉⲃ. ⲙⲙⲁ ⲛ+ϩⲁⲡ, AP 12 *A²* rejoicing ⲙⲡⲙ. ⲁⲃ. ⲡⲟⲩⲁⲡ ⲡⲓⲙ, RAl 128 *S* ⲡⲥⲉⲡⲱⲧ ⲙⲡⲁⲙ. ⲉⲃ., Aeg 15 *B* wept ⲙⲡⲉⲕⲙ. (*S* ⲙ. ⲉⲃ.), C 86 284 *B* ⲉⲕⲉⲣ ⲙⲉⲟⲣⲉ ⲙ-ⲡⲟⲩⲙ. (var ⲙ. ⲉⲃ.), BSM 39 *B* ⲁϥⲭⲁϥ ⲉⲡⲉⲥⲛⲧ ⲙⲡⲉⲥⲙ. = Va 63 13 *B* ⲙ. ⲉⲃ. = BMis 385 *S* ϩⲓⲑⲏ ⲙⲙⲟⲥ. In *before my* (*his &c*) *eyes* ⲙ. & ⲉⲃ. may be separated: Ps 5 5 *B* ⲙⲡⲉⲙ. ⲡⲛⲉⲕⲃⲁⲗ ⲉⲃ. (*S* ⲙⲡⲉⲙ. ⲉⲃ. ⲡⲛⲉⲕⲃ.), Ro 3 18 *SB*, ShBMOr 8810 367 *S* fear of Christ not ⲙⲡⲉⲙ. ⲡⲡⲉⲧⲃ. ⲉⲃ., C 86 291 *B* ⲭⲏ ⲙⲡⲉⲙ. ⲡⲡⲉϥⲃ. ⲉⲃ.

ⲙⲧⲱ, ⲉⲙⲧⲱ, ⲙⲧⲟ (rare) *S*, ⲉⲙⲑⲱ *B* (once) nn f (2) m (1), *depth* of sea: Mor 37 15 ⲁϥⲙⲟⲩ ⲛⲡⲙⲧⲟ ϩⲛⲑⲁⲗⲁⲥⲥⲁ (? *l* ϩⲙⲡⲙ. ⲛⲑ.), Tri 515 swimming ϩⲙⲡⲙⲟϭ ⲛⲙⲧⲟ ﻋﻤﻴﻖ; ⲃⲱⲕ ⲛⲙ., *go to the depths, founder* (cf ⲃ. ϩⲁ-): Mor 17 8 ⲡⲉⲡⲧⲁⲃ. ⲉⲡⲉⲙⲧⲟ ⲛⲁⲩⲁⲅⲏⲥⲁⲛⲧⲉⲥ, BHom 48 ⲛⲥⲃ. ⲛⲧⲙⲧⲱ ⲁⲩⲱ ϣⲁⲥⲃ.

ϩⲙⲡⲣⲁⲥⲓⲉ (= R 2 2 32 only ⲃ. ⲡϩⲁⲥⲓⲉ) ὑποβρύχιος φέρεσθαι, *ib* 118 ship ⲃ. ⲛⲧⲙ., BMis 160 storm ϩⲱⲥⲧⲉ ⲛϥⲃ. ⲡⲉⲙ. ⲙⲡⲡⲉⲧⲏϩⲧϥ (*sic* MS) = BSM 69 *B* ⲡⲥⲉⲱⲙⲥ, Mus 42 231 *S* of Peter (cf Mt 14 30 ⲱⲙⲥ), P 44 95 (ⲉ)ⲧⲣⲉⲡⲁϭⲉⲡⲓⲛ ⲃ. ⲡⲉⲙ. ﺗﻨﺪﺏ ﺇﻟﻰ ﺍﻟﻴَﻢّ; ϭⲓⲛⲃ. ⲛⲙ. nn f, *shipwreck*: Wess 15 130 ⲛⲧⲁⲓⲃⲱⲕ ⲉϩⲣⲁⲓ ⲉⲁϣ ⲛϭ. = EW 29 *B* ϩⲱⲗ ⲡⲉⲥⲉ ναυάγιον; With other vbs: Mor 18 24 ⲁⲩⲡⲟⲩⳉⲉ ⲙⲡⲉⲧⲡⲧⲁϥ ⲧⲏⲣϥ ⲡⲉⲙ. into wells & tanks (Miss 4 118 *B* om ⲡⲉⲙ.), BAp 94 Pharaoh's host ϣⲁⲛⲧⲉϥⲛⲟⳉⲟⲩ ⲛⲙ. in sea; P 131¹ 21 careful lest ⲛⲥⳉⲉ ⲡⲁϭⲉⲓⲛ ⲉⲃⲟⲗ ⲛⲙ., Va 58 191 *B* hatred ⲟⲩⲱⲣⲡ ⲛ+ⲯⲩⲭⲏ ⲡⲉⲙ. καταβαπτίζειν.   Etymol of ⲙⲧⲟ & ⲙⲧⲱ distinct?, *v* Berlin *Wörterb* 2 174, 184.

ⲙⲉⲧⲑⲓⲃⲥ *B* *v* +ⲃⲥ.

ⲙⲁⲧⲉⲙ *F* nn m, meaning unknown, named with winnowing fan: Is 30 24 (*SB* Gk om) ⲛϩⲣⲉⲓ ⲙⲛⲡⲙ.

ⲙⲧⲟⲛ *SB*, ⲉⲙ. *SB*, ⲙⲧⲁⲛ *AA²F*, ⲉⲙⲧⲁⲛ *F*, ⲙⲟⲧⲛ† *S*, ⲙⲁⲧⲛⲉ† *A*, ⲙⲟⲧⲉⲛ† *B*, ⲙⲁⲧⲛ† *F* vb I intr, *be at rest, at ease, be relieved* (of sickness), a no object *SABF*: Lev 25 2 *S* (*B* ⲉⲣ ⲙ.), Job 3 26 *S* (*B* refl), Is 57 20 *B* (*S* refl), Philem 7 *B* (*S* do), Z 339 *S* ⲡⲙⲁ ⲉϣⲁⲡⲉⲙ. ⲡⲏⲧϥ ἀναπαύεσθαι, Hos 11 6 *B* (*A* diff) καταπ.; Lev 13 18 *S* (*B* ⲕⲁ ϩⲕ) ⲉϣⲁⲡⲙⲁ ⲡⲣⲏⲧϥ, Lu 7 10 *S* (*B* ⲟⲩⳉⲁⲓ) ὑγιάζειν; Deu 28 27 *S* (*B* ⲗⲱⳉⲓ) ἰᾶσθαι; Phil 2 19 *SB* εὐψυχεῖν; Job 3 13 *S* (*B* refl) ἡσυχάζειν; 2 Cor 2 13 *SB* ἄνεσιν ἔχειν; Mk 16 18 *S* (*B* ⲟⲩⳉ.) καλῶς ἔχ.; Jo 4 52 *SA²* (*B* ⲁⲥⲓⲁⲓ, *F* +ⲉⲡⲉⲙ.) κομψότερον ἔχ.; Mk 5 26 *S* (*B* ⳉⲉⲙ ϩⲏⲟⲩ) ὠφελεῖσθαι; 1 Cor 7 35 *B* (*S* ⲕⲁⲗⲱⲥ) εὐπάρεδρος (εἶναι); Va 58 182 *B* ship ϣⲁϥⲙ. ⲡⲣⲱⲗ ῥαδίως; ShWess 9 139 *S* amulets ⲙⲟⲣⲟⲩ ⲙⲙⲟⲕ ⲕⲛⲁⲙ., Z 627 *S* after recipe ϥⲛⲁⲙ. MIE 2 347 *B* +ⲛⲁⲙ. ⲉⲃⲟⲗ ⳉⲉⲛⲡⲙⲁⲥⲧⲓⲅⳉ, CO 228 *S* will tend your ass ⲛⲧⲉⲡⲉⲧⲛⲏⲣ ⲙ., C 43 239 *B* condemn him (martyr) ⲛⲧⲉⲡⲉⲙ. ⲉⲃⲟⲗ ϩⲁⲣⲟϥ *be eased of him* (cf *ib* 245 *B* ⲛⲧⲁⲙ. ⲙⲙⲟⲓ ⲥⲁⲃⲟⲗ ⲙⲙⲟⲕ), Bor 143 25 *S* ⲁⲡⲉⲕⲣⲏⲧ ⲙ. that these should die for thee?, Z 311 *S* ⲙⲉⲙ. ⲉⳉⲓⲧϥ οὐ θέλειν, MG 25 79 *B* after some days ⲁⲡⲉϥⲙⲉⲩⲓ ⲙ. ⲉⲧⲁⲥⲑⲟ *was fain* = GöttAr 114 17 ﻃﺎﺏ, Mor 29 28 *S* ⲁⲣⲏϫ ⲙⲡⲣⲏⲧ ⲙⲡⲇⲓⲕⲁⲓⲟⲥ ⲙ.† ⲁⲛ ⲉⲡⲁⲓ = BMis 258 *S* ⲡⲓⲑⲉ, BM 586 10 *F* (ⲉ)ϣⲱⲡ(ⲓ) ϥ[ⲱϥ] ⲉⲙⲧⲁⲛ (ⲛ)ⲉⲕ.   With ⲉ- as *dat commodi*: Aeg 14 *S* ⲁⲧⲁⲯⲩⲭⲏ ⲙ. ⲉⲣⲟⲓ, AM 52 *B* sim.   ⲃ Qual, *easy, hale, satisfied*; Z 239 *S* she quitted world ⲉⲥⲙ. ἐν ὑγείᾳ, Si 30 14 *S*, JA '75 5 243 *S* sleep on ground if ⲉⲕⲙ. ὑγιής; Mt 9 12 *S* (PS 250, var ⲧⲏⲕ, *B* ⳉⲟⲣ) ἰσχύων; Bor 235 58 *S* ⲉⲛⲕⲁ ⲡⲓⲙ ⲉϥⲙ. ἡδύς, Pro 3 24 *SA* (*B* ϩⲗⲟϭ) ἡδέως; Wess 11 169 *S* +ⲙ. ⲉⲙⲛ ⲡⲟⲗⲉⲙⲟⲥ ϩⲓⳉⲱⲓ ἀναπαυόμενος; Va 57 7 *B* ⲥⲙ. ⲡⳉⲉ ⲑⲙⲉⲧⲥⲱⲧⲡ ῥάδιος;

Si 33 11 *S* ἀγαθός ; Deu 15 16 *S* (*B* ⲡⲓⲡⲉⲑⲛⲁⲛⲉϥ ϣⲟⲡ) εὖ εἶναι ; Va 66 308 *B* ⲉⲕⲙ. in thy body εὐεκτεῖν ; ShC 42 191 *S* if eyes healed man sees ⲡⲕⲁ ⲛⲓⲙ ⲉϥⲙ., ShC 73 172 *S* ⲉⲓⲧⲉ ⲉⲅϣⲱⲡⲉ ⲉⲓⲧⲉ ⲉⲅⲙ., MG 25 127 *B* man & wife at peace ⲉⲅⲙ. ⲛ̄ⲕⲁⲗⲱⲥ, BMar 84 *S* ⲉⲡⲉ ⲕⲙ. ⲙⲉⲕⲣⲓⲙⲉ, JTS 9 383 *S* ⲁϣϣⲉ ⲡⲉⲧⲙ. ⲡⲁⲣⲣⲁⲕ this or that ?　**c** Qual with ⲉ-, *easy to, to be*, Gk εὖ- : Ps 91 14 *SB* -παθεῖν ; Jth 7 10 *S* -χερής ; Pro 24 63 *S*(*A* ⲙ. ⲛ-) -άλωτος ; Ac 27 12 *S* (*B* ⲥⲙⲟⲡⲧ) -θετος ; Mk 2 9 *SB* -κοπος ; AZ 23 104 *S* clay ⲉϥⲙ. ⲉⲃⲱⲗ (*sic l*) ⲉⲃⲟⲗ, ShP 130ˢ 82 *S* ⲉⲣⲙ̄-ⲧⲣⲉⲕϣⲱⲡⲉ ⲉⲕⲙ. ⲉⲥⲱⲧⲙ *hearing easily, readily* ; *dat commodi* : C 89 175 *B* ⲉⲣⲉⲡⲟⲩⲣⲏⲧ ⲙ. ⲉⲣⲱⲟⲩ, Mor 25 8 *S* ⲙ̄ⲙⲟⲛ ⲡϭⲱⲃ ⲙ. ⲉⲣⲟⲓ (var P 131² 82 ⲥⲃ̄ⲧⲱⲧ) = Va 61 91 *B*, TU 24 1 3 *S* God knoweth why ⲡⲉⲥⲥⲱⲙⲁ ⲙ. ⲉⲣⲟⲥ ⲁⲛ.　Impersonal ⲥⲙⲟⲧⲛ, *it is easy* : Si 22 16 *S*, Lu 18 25 *SB* εὔκοπος, -ώτερος, CDan 86 *B* ϩⲁⲣⲁ ⲥⲙ. (? ⲉⲥⲥⲙⲟⲡⲧ) ⲙⲡⲁⲓⲣⲏϯ ἄρα ἀρέσκει τῷ θεῷ, ShC 42 152 *S* ⲥⲙ. ⲉⲧⲣⲉⲡⲛ̄ ⲕⲱ ⲛⲁⲩ ⲉⲃⲟⲗ, AM 127 *B* ⲥⲙ. ⲉⲉⲣⲗⲉⲅⲭⲓⲛ (ἐλέγχειν) ⲙ̄ⲙⲟⲥ = R 1 4 67 *S* ⲥⲙⲟⲡⲧ (*l* ⲥⲙⲟⲧⲛ, *cf* Ac 27 12 *S* & *B*) εὐανάτρεπτος ; DeV 2 214 *B* Eve ⲥⲙ. ⲡⲉⲣ ϩⲁⲗ ⲙ̄ⲙⲟⲥ.　**d** Qual with ⲛ-, meaning as with ⲉ- (or ? is qual of ⲙⲟⲩⲧⲛ *q v*) : Sa 19 20 *S* εὔφθαρτος ; Aeg 246 *S* ⲉⲅⲙ. ⲛ̄ⲭⲟⲟⲩⲥⲟⲩ εὔσκυλτος ; ShMIF 23 30 *S* soft & ⲉϥⲙ. ⲛ̄ⲧⲁⲕⲟϥ, Bor 145 54 *S* this thing ⲣⲱⲙⲉ ⲛⲓⲙ ⲙ. ⲛⲉⲓⲙⲉ ⲉⲣⲟϥ, Cat 31 *B* reed ⲉⲣⲉⲡⲉⲑⲛⲟⲩ ⲙ. ⲛ̄ⲕⲓⲙ ⲉⲣⲟϥ, ROC 25 248 *B* second kind ⲥⲉϩⲟⲥⲓ ⲛ̄ϩⲣⲟ ⲉⲣⲱⲟⲩ, first ⲥⲉⲙ. ⲛ̄ⲟⲉⲃⲓⲱⲟⲩ, BM 1131 *S* ⲡⲉⲧⲉϥⲙ. ⲛ̄ⲧⲉⲕⲙⲛ̄ⲧⲥⲟⲛ send it.

――― ⲉϫⲛ̄-, ⲉϫⲉⲛ- *SB*, ⲉϩⲣⲁⲓ ⲉϫⲛ̄- *S*, *rest upon, be satisfied with* : 2 Cor 7 13 *B* (*S* ⲙ. ⲡⲁϩⲣⲛ̄-) ἀναπαύεσθαι ; 1 Thes 3 7 *S* (*B* ⲑⲱⲧ) παρακαλεῖσθαι ; BMis 32 *S* father's heart ⲟⲩⲱ ⲉϥⲙ. ⲉϩⲣⲁⲓ ⲉϫⲱⲕ ; qual : DeV 1 96 *B* ⲉⲣⲉⲡⲉϥϩⲏⲧ ⲙ. ⲉϫⲱⲓ ⲧⲟⲡⲱ. *V* also tr (refl).

――― ⲙⲛ̄- *SF*, meaning same : ShP 130¹ 141 *S* if his heart ⲙ. ⲙⲛ̄ⲣⲟⲉⲓⲛⲉ ϩⲁⲧⲏⲧⲏⲧⲛ̄, Mor 30 44 *F* if saint's heart ⲙ. ⲛⲉⲙⲁⲛ = BMis 269 *S* ⲧⲏⲧ, J 67 89 *S* ⲙ̄ⲡⲧⲉ ⲡⲉⲥϩⲏⲧ ⲙ. ⲡⲓⲙⲁⲥ.

――― ⲛϩⲏⲧ *S*, *be at rest, be content* : Philem 20 (*B* ⲙ. refl) ὀνίνασθαι ; JA '75 5 264 whoso abideth with wife ⲛⲁⲙ. ⲛϩ. ⲉϩⲣⲁⲓ ⲉϫⲱⲥ ; 1 Kg 22 2 ⲛϥⲙ. ⲁⲛ ⲛϩ. κατώδυνος ψυχῇ.　As nn *SB*, *rest, satisfaction* : Ac 24 10 *S* (*B* ⲟⲩⲛⲟϥ ⲛϩ.) εὐθύμως ; DeV 2 47 *B* ⲟⲩⲙ. ⲛϩ. ⲡⲉⲙⲟⲩⲣⲁϣⲓ, MR 5 42 *B* in letter ⲃⲟⲣⲡ ⲡⲉⲕⲙ. ⲛϩ. ⲡⲏⲓ.

II tr (refl), **a** *rest self* : Ex 23 12 *SB*, Is 32 16 *SBF*, Hab 3 16 *SAB*, Mt 26 45 *SB*, AP 9 *A²* ἀναπαύ., Ge 8 22 *B* (*S* ⲱϣⲡ), Deu 33 12 *SB*, Ru 2 7 *S*, Ps 54 6 *SB*, Ez 1 24 *B* καταπαύ. ; Jth 13 1 *S* ἀναλύειν, Nu 22 8 *S* (var ⲡⲕⲟⲧⲕ, *B* ϣⲱⲡⲓ), Si 14 27 *S*,

Lu 19 7 *B* (*S* ϭⲟⲓⲗⲉ) καταλύ. ; Pro 7 18 *SA* (*B* ⲟⲩⲛⲟϥ), *ib* 13 23 *SA* (*B* diff) ἀπολαύειν ; Ps 38 13 *S* (*B* ⲭⲃⲟⲃ) ἀναψύχειν, Ge 18 4 *S* (*B* do) καταψ. ; Pro 1 33 *SAB* κατασκηνοῦν ; Ru 3 13 *S* αὐλίζεσθαι ; Va 62 285 *B* ⲁϥⲙ. ⲙ̄ⲙⲟϥ from sickness ἀποθεραπεύεσθαι ; BG 26 *S* ⲉϥⲙ. ⲙ̄ⲙⲟϥ ϩⲛ̄ⲟⲩⲕⲁ ⲣⲱϥ, ShA 2 272 *S* demons ⲙ. ⲙ̄ⲙⲟⲟⲩ in your thoughts, BM 342 *S* soul returning to body ⲙ. ⲙ̄ⲙⲟⲥ ⲉⲡⲉⲥⲙⲁ ⲡⲕⲉⲥⲟⲡ, DeV 2 136 *B* ϣⲁⲧⲁⲙ. ⲙ̄ⲙⲟⲓ ⲉⲃⲟⲗ ϫⲉⲛⲡⲓϭⲓⲥⲓ of journey, C 43 245 *B* ⲛ̄ⲧⲁⲙ. ⲙ̄ⲙⲟⲓ ⲥⲁⲃⲟⲗ ⲙ̄ⲙⲟⲕ & these insults.　ⲙ. ⲙ̄ⲙⲟ⸗ ⲉϫⲛ̄- : 4 Kg 2 15 *S*, Ro 2 17 *SB*, Aeg 242 *S* ⲉⲕⲙ. ⲙ̄ⲙⲟⲕ ⲉϫⲛ̄ⲡⲉⲩϣⲁϫⲉ ἐπαναπαύ., C 43 44 *B* ⲁⲅⲙ. ⲙ̄ⲙⲱⲟⲩ ⲉϫⲉⲛ beds ; ⲉϩⲣⲁⲓ ⲉϫⲛ̄- : Nu 11 26 *SB*, Lu 10 6 *S* (*B* om ⲉϩ.) ἐπαναπαύ.　**b** *go to rest, die* : C 89 27 *B* ⲁⲣⲉϣⲁⲛⲟⲅⲓ ⲙ. ⲙ̄ⲙⲟⲥ τελεοῦσθαι ; MG 25 13 *B* ἀναλύειν ; Z 345 *S* = MG 25 211 *B* ⲡⲕⲟⲧ ⲕⲟⲓⲙᾶσθαι ; TU 24 1 6 *S* ⲁⲡⲧⲟⲗⲉⲙⲁⲓⲟⲥ ⲙ. ⲙ̄ⲙⲟϥ & quitted life, ShC 73 212 *S* year ⲡⲧⲁϥⲙ. ⲙ̄ⲙⲟϥ ⲛϩⲏⲧⲥ, Ming 341 *S* he moved not ⲛⲉⲁϥⲙ. ⲙ̄ⲙⲟϥ ⲅⲁⲣⲡⲉ (BMar 205 diff) ;　epitaphs *S* : Cai 8465 ⲁϥⲙ. ⲙ̄ⲙⲟϥ ⲛ̄ⲥⲟⲩ-, CO 492, ST 404 sim.　*Cf AZ* 60 131 & ϭⲓⲛⲙ̄ⲧⲟⲛ.

――― *SAA²BF* nn m, *rest, ease, relief* : Ex 16 23 *S* (*B* ⲥⲁⲃⲃⲁⲧⲟⲛ ⲛⲉⲙ.), Lev 25 8 *B* (*S* = Gk), Job 3 23 *SB*, Ps 131 8 *B* (*S* ⲙⲁ ⲛ̄ⲙ.), Is 32 17 *SBF*, Mt 11 29 *S* (*B* ⲙⲁ ⲛ̄ⲙ.) ἀνάπαυσις, 2 Chr 6 41 *B* κατάπ. ; Ex 8 11 *B*, Ps 65 12 *B* (*S* ⲙⲁ ⲛ̄ⲙ.), CaiEuch 515 *B* ⲟⲩⲙ. ⲛⲛⲏ ⲉⲧϫⲁⲧ ἀνάψυξις ; Pro 6 8 *SA* (*B* ⲟⲩϫⲁⲓ) ὑγίεια, Lev 13 10 *S* (*B* ⲡⲉⲧⲟⲩⲟϫ) ὑγιής ; Mt 10 15 *S* (*B* ϯ ⲁⲥⲟ) ἀνεκτός ; 2 Cor 8 13 *SB* ἄνεσις ; Ps 72 5 *SB* ἀνάνευσις ; Sa 2 1 *S* ἴασις ; *ib* 16 24 *S* εὐεργεσία ; Is 1 6 *SF* (*B* om) ὁλοκληρία ; Ps 15 11 *S* (*B* ⲉⲣⲟⲩⲟⲧ) τερπνότης ; ShA 2 313 *S* ϩⲓⲥⲉ of poverty & ⲙ. of wealth, BSM 78 *B* ϭⲓⲥⲓ is past ⲁⲡⲓⲙ. ϯⲟϩ ⲉⲣⲱⲧⲉⲛ = BMis 169 *S* ⲙ̄ⲛ̄ⲧⲓⲱⲧ (*sic* MS, ? *l* ⲙ̄ⲧⲟⲛ), P 130⁴ 86 *S* servants sent ahead that he may find ⲡⲉϥⲙ. ⲉϥϭⲃ̄ⲧⲱⲧ, ShC 42 46 *S* bees give their labour to kings ⲉⲅⲙ., Z 640 *S* beings created ⲉⲅⲙ. ⲛⲁⲩ (sc men, C 89 127 *B* diff), AZ 21 145 *S* why bewailest thou dead man ? ⲁⲣⲏⲩ ⲛ̄ⲧⲁⲟⲩⲡⲟϭ ⲛⲉⲙ. was between you ? (var ⲙⲟⲧⲛⲉⲥ).　As adj : BMar 126 *S* fire turned ⲉⲅⲉⲓⲱⲧⲉ ⲛ̄ⲙ., RAl 85 *B* ⲟⲩϭⲓⲕ ⲡⲉⲡⲓⲟϩⲙⲓⲁ (Dan 10 3) which is ⲟⲩϭⲓⲕ ⲛⲉⲙ. (DeV 1 192 diff), BSM 27 *B* ⲡⲥⲉϯ ⲧⲁⲓⲟ ⲛⲉⲙ. to their fathers.

ⲙⲁⲓⲙ. *S*, *loving ease* : ShA 2 231 we are ϩⲉⲛⲙⲁⲓⲡⲉⲙⲙ., JKP 2 106 ⲁⲩϣⲱⲡⲉ ⲙ̄ⲙⲁⲓⲡⲉⲅⲙ. ; ⲙ̄ⲛ̄ⲧⲙⲁⲓⲙ. : ShC 73 213 ⲧⲉⲡⲙⲛ̄ⲧⲙⲁⲓⲡⲉⲙⲙ. in all things, BM 224 not from sickness but ⲉⲧⲃⲉⲟⲩⲙ̄ⲛ̄ⲧⲙⲁⲓⲡⲉⲅⲙ.　ⲙⲁⲥⲧⲙ., *hating ease* : ShA *l c*.

ϩⲛ̄ⲟⲩⲙ. *S* (rare), ϧⲉⲛⲟⲩⲙ. *B* as advb, *with ease, easily* : Va 63 80 *B* sowing seed ϧ. μετ' εὐκολίας ;

ShMIF 23 73 S he that would ⲥⲱⲡⲉ ⲛⲟⲩⲧⲉⲛⲏ ϩ.,
Va 58 153 B effeminate rich ⲉϥⲃⲏⲗ ⲉⲃⲟⲗ ⲥ. through
paltry sickness, ROC 25 247 B this heresy all ⲡⲁ-
ⲙⲟϣⲓ ⲡⲥⲱϥ ⲥ. Br 39 = 44 S ϩⲓⲡⲉⲙ. not adverbial.

ⲁⲧⲉⲙ. B, unquiet : Va 57 174 ⲟⲩⲣⲉϥϩⲱⲧⲥⲡⲉ ⲡⲁ.
ἀκατάλλακτος.

ⲙⲁ ⲡⲙ. SB, place of resting : Nu 10 34 S (B ⲙ.),
Ps 114 7 B (S ⲙ.), Mt 12 43 SB ἀνάπαυσις, Deu
12 9 SB, He 4 38 B κατάπ.; Ps 65 12 S (B ⲙ.)
ἀναψυχή; Ex 15 13 B (S diff) κατάλυμα; C 43 180
B ⲫⲙⲁ ⲡⲉⲙ. of righteous.

ⲥⲓⲡⲙ. S, resting, death : BMis 494.

ⲣ, ⲉⲣ ⲙ. SB, be, set at rest, ease : Lev 25 2 B
(S ⲙ.) ἀναπαύ.; ShP 130¹ 140 S nun's garment
heavy, ⲉⲓⲉⲓⲣⲉ ⲙⲡⲉⲥⲙ. I have eased her, ShC 73
172 S no man being verily of the community ⲡⲁⲣ
ⲡⲉⲩⲙ. ⲙⲁⲩⲁⲁⲧⲟⲩ.

† ⲙ. SAA²BF, set at ease, content, set a pause,
c ⲛ- dat : Is 14 3 SB, Mt 11 28 SB, 1 Cor 16 18
SBF, Z 355 S ⲁϥ† ⲙ. to poor with food, Wess
11 169 S sim ἀναπαύ., Ge 5 29 SB διαναπ., Deu 5
33 S (B ⲑⲣⲉⲙ.) καταπ.; 2 Tim 1 16 SB ἀναψύχ.;
Ex 23 11 B (S ⲗⲟ ϩⲁ-) ἄνεσιν ποιεῖν; ib 18 22 S
(B ⲁⲥⲓⲁⲓ) κουφίζειν; Va 57 256 B we must † ⲙ.
ⲙⲡⲓⲥⲁⲭⲓ καταλύειν; Z 289 S beseeching ⲉⲧⲣⲉϥ†
ⲙ. ⲡⲁϥ ἐνδιδόναι; Sa 10 7 S εὐεργετεῖσθαι; Hall
7 S epitaph ⲉⲕⲉ† ⲙ. ⲡⲧⲉⲯⲩⲭⲏ ⲛ-, AM 243 B
ⲉⲧⲁⲩ† ⲙ. ⲙⲡⲓⲁⲅⲓⲟⲥ ⲉⲃⲟⲗ ⲥⲉⲡⲛⲓⲥⲛⲁϩ, PLond 4
454 S we will guard them (returned fugitives) ⲧⲛⲧⲓ
ⲉⲙ. ⲡⲁⲩ relieve their wants (?), ShIF 153 S not
finding new raiment ⲉⲁϥ† ⲙ. ⲡⲁϥ ϩⲓⲣⲉⲡⲥⲗⲡⲉ
ⲛⲧⲟⲉⲓⲥ, C 89 121 B if wouldst † ⲙ. ⲛⲏⲓ, BMar
99 S let us † ⲙ. ⲙⲡϣⲁϫⲉ ϣⲁⲡⲉⲓⲙⲁ, CMSS 23 F
as greeting ⲧⲓ ⲉⲙⲧ. ⲙⲡⲉⲕⲁⲅⲓⲱⲛ ⲙⲡⲛⲁ in Lord,
ib 37 F, 53 S sim.; imperat : CaiEuch 581 B
ⲙⲟⲓ ⲡⲱⲟⲩ ⲡⲟⲩⲙ. ἄνεσις; ib 362 B ⲙⲁ ⲙ. to their
souls ἀνάπαυσις. † ⲉⲡⲉⲙ. SF, become eased :
Jo 4 52 F (SA² ⲙ. vb, B ⲁⲥⲓⲁⲓ) κομψότερον ἔχειν;
ShIF 239 S diseased limbs ⲙⲡⲟⲩ† ⲉⲡⲉⲙ. but
grew worse.

ϫⲓ, ϭⲓ ⲙ. SB, get rest, be at ease : 2 Cor 7 5 B (S
ϫⲓ ⲙⲟⲧⲛⲉⲥ) ἄνεσιν ἔχ.; AP 6 A² ⲥⲉⲛⲁϫⲓ ⲡⲟⲩⲙ.
ἀνάπαυσιν ἔχ.; Lu 6 24 S (B diff) παράκλησιν ἀπέχ.;
ShIF 65 S not granted ⲉⲧⲣⲁϫⲓ ⲙ. in these garments,
MG 25 89 B dismissed them ϫⲉⲁⲩϭⲓ ⲙ. ⲡⲟⲩⲕⲟⲩϫⲓ (var ⲙ. refl), ShC 42 127 S ⲉⲁⲩϫⲓ ⲙⲡⲉⲩⲙ.
apart from community (cf ⲣ ⲙ.).

ⲙⲟⲧⲛ S nn m (rare), health, ease; Si 17 23 ὑγιής;
BMEA 10577 tubs made ⲛⲡⲣⲟⲥ ⲟⲩⲣⲧⲟⲩ ⲡⲥⲟⲩⲟ
ⲙⲡⲙ. ⲉⲡⲙⲁϩⲉ for accomodation of flax (v ⲉⲟⲅⲓⲛ).

ⲙⲉⲧⲙⲟⲧⲛ B, ease : K 92 بّراحة.

ⲙⲟⲧⲛⲉⲥ S, ⲙⲁⲧⲛⲉⲥ Sᵃ (Ep 459) Sᶠ (Bor 253) F,
ⲙⲟⲑⲛⲉⲥ B nn f, ease, contentment : Ecll 6 5 S, Is
34 14 SF (B ⲙⲧⲟⲛ) ἀνάπαυσις; HL 112 B life
ⲉⲥⲙⲉϩ ⲙⲙ. ἀβρότατος; ShMIF 23 198 S Nineve
in hell ⲙⲡⲉⲙ. ⲧⲁⲣⲟϥ, BIF 22 107 F sim, DeV 1
66 B ⲛⲧⲉⲛϫⲓⲙⲓ ⲛ†ⲙ. ⲁⲛ facility, opportunity, Cat
87 B ⲟⲩⲙ. ⲛⲥⲱⲙⲁⲧⲓⲕⲟⲛ without sickness, BMis
178 S ⲧⲙ. ⲙⲡⲙⲁⲥⲉ ⲙⲡⲡⲣⲱⲧ ⲛⲡⲉϩⲓⲉⲓⲃ pleasantness
of ox (as food ?) & wool of lamb; satisfaction,
equivalent of debt &c S : PBu 56 house to be ἐνέχυρον & rent-free ⲛⲧⲙ. ⲙⲡϩⲣⲟⲗⲟⲕ/ which we paid
owner, WS 136 debtor owing 1 solidus offers cheese
ϩⲁⲧⲉϥⲙ., Bodl(P) e 70 ten solidi ϩⲁⲧⲉϥⲙ. †
ⲙⲟⲧⲛⲉⲥ S, give relief : R 1 1 63 S who gave ⲟⲩⲙ.
to Israelites κατάπαυ.; PS 328 † ⲡⲁⲩ ⲡⲟⲩⲙ. in Thy
mercy, Mor 41 11 angel ⲁϥ† ⲙ. ⲡⲁⲓ (sc wounded
man) = DeV 2 259 B ⲙⲧⲟⲛ, BMOr 6201 A 112 S
magical prayer ⲉⲧⲉⲧⲛⲧⲓ ⲟⲩⲙ. to NN. ⲣ ⲙ. S,
set at ease : R 1 4 30 ⲡⲉⲧⲛⲁⲣ ⲧⲙ. of body before
soul's, BMis 179 Michael ⲟ ⲙⲙ. ⲛⲡⲉⲧⲣⲟⲥⲉ. ϫⲓ,
ϭⲓ ⲙ. SB, get relief, satisfaction : 2 Cor 7 5 S (B do)
ἄνεσις; Va 58 181 B ϭⲓ ⲙⲕⲁϩ opp ϭⲓ ⲙ. τρυφᾶν;
BMar 181 light not (cooking) fire for self alone ⲛϭⲓ
ⲡⲟⲩⲙ., P 131³ 34 will not give price to τόπος for
clergy to ϫⲓ ⲡⲧⲉⲩⲙ. therefrom, Pcod 32 poor ⲡⲁϫⲓ
ⲡⲟⲩⲕⲟⲩⲓ ⲙⲙ. in place of riches. ϩⲛ-, ⲥⲉⲡⲟⲩⲙ.
SBF as advb, with ease, easily : RNC 43 S able to
fight ϩ., Bor 253 119 S defeated ϩ. εὐχερῶς; C 89
106 B thorn in foot ϣⲁⲥⲓ ⲉⲡϣⲱⲓ ⲥ. εὐκόλως (cf
PMéd 173); Ep 592 B 17 S healeth all ϩ. ῥᾳδίως;
BHom 30 S fly upward ϩ. εὐπετὴς γίνεσθαι; BM
247 6 S ϣⲁⲣⲉⲙⲡⲁⲑⲟⲥ ⲉⲣ ϩⲱⲃ ϩ. ἀδιαφόρως; ShC
73 137 S grain in oven ⲉⲅⲉⲗⲱⲕ ϩ. (cf ib ⲗⲱⲕ ⲕⲁⲗⲱⲥ), Z 269 S good despiseth not wicked ϩ., Va
63 25 B come to port ⲥ. = Mor 27 43 F ϩ. = BSM
58 B ⲥⲉⲡⲟⲩϩⲓⲣⲏⲛⲏ = BMis 416 S ϩⲛⲟⲩⲥⲟⲟⲩⲧⲛ.

ⲙⲟⲩⲧⲛ S (Ryl, WS), ⲙⲟⲧⲉⲛ B, ⲙⲉⲧⲛ- (Deu 3)
S, ⲙⲟⲧⲛ⸗ S, ⲙⲁⲧⲛ⸗ F (for qual v ? ⲙⲧⲟⲛ I d), ⲣ ⲥ
ⲙⲁⲧⲛ- S, vb tr (S sometimes, B always refl), rest,
set at rest (cf ⲙⲧⲟⲛ) : Ge 29 2 B (S ⲙⲧⲟⲛ), Si 22
10 S (B ⲙⲧⲟⲛ refl), Ez 34 15 B, MG 25 215 B
ⲡⲓⲙⲁ ⲉⲡⲁⲛⲙ. ⲙⲙⲟⲛ ⲙⲙⲁⲩ ἀναπαύειν, Deu 3 20
S (B † ⲙⲧⲟⲛ), ib 12 10 S (B ⲑⲣⲉ-ⲙⲧⲟⲛ refl), Jos 1
13 S καταπ.; Lu 21 37 B (S diff) αὐλίζεσθαι; Ez
37 14 S (ShA 1 371, B diff), ib 40 2 S (B Tatt &
HCons 288 diff) τιθέναι; Z 299 S gift of fish ⲁϥⲟⲩⲱϣ ⲉⲙⲟⲧⲛⲉϥ ⲛⲁⲡⲁ ϩⲱⲣ ποιεῖν dat, apparare
pro; ShIF 91 S bandages ⲛⲧⲁϥⲙⲟⲧⲛⲟⲩ ϩⲁⲡⲉϥⲟⲩⲉⲣⲏⲧⲉ (cf ⲕⲱϩ II), C 86 279 B ⲉⲕⲙ. ⲙⲙⲟⲕ ⲉϫⲉⲛⲡⲓ-
ⲙⲁⲟⲩ, LAp 528 F ⲧⲱⲟⲩⲛ ⲙⲁⲧⲛⲉ (f) arise & be
at rest. Agree upon S : Kr 157 ⲡⲥⲩⲙⲫⲟⲛⲟⲛ (ⲛ)-
ⲧⲁⲓⲙⲟⲧⲛⲏϥ ⲙⲛ(ⲛ)ⲡⲗⲟⲩⲧⲁⲅⲉⲛⲁ (?), WS 96 send
one north ⲡϥⲙⲟⲩⲧⲛ ⲡⲉⲓⲁⲥⲟⲟⲩⲣ, Ryl 188 20 ⲧⲉ-

ⲡⲣⲁⲥⲓⲥ (ⲡ)ⲧⲁⲓⲙⲟⲧⲛⲉⲥ ⲛⲁⲕ, *ib* 387]ⲧⲓⲙⲏ ⲡⲧⲁⲓⲙⲟⲧⲡⲟⲩ ⲡⲁⲕ, *ib* 343 ⲙⲁⲣⲟⲩⲙⲟⲩⲧⲛ ⲫⲱⲗⲧ, *ib* ⲫⲱⲃ ⲡⲉϣⲁϭⲏⲡ ⲙⲗⲟⲧⲛ[ⲉϥ, PMich 3573 I am ready ⲧⲁⲧⲓ ⲥⲡⲁ[ⲩ] ⲛ...ⲉⲛⲁⲕⲙⲟⲧⲛⲏⲧ (ⲙ)ⲙⲟ(ⲟ)ⲩ. pc *S*: BMis 533 Raphael angel ⲙⲙⲁⲧⲛⲏⲣⲓⲧ, Z 614 do paral ⲣⲙⲣⲁϣ.

ⲙⲁⲧⲣ *S*, ⲙⲁⲧⲉⲣ *B* nn, *glue*: Is 44 13 (cit P 131⁶ 104 *S* ⲙⲟⲣⲧ) κόλλα.

ⲙⲉⲧⲣⲏ *F* *v* ⲙⲛⲧⲣⲉ.

ⲙⲁⲁⲧⲥⲉ *S* *v* ⲙⲁⲁϫⲉ measure.

ⲙⲧⲁⲧ *SB* nn f, *bridle, bit*: K 136 *B* رسن , مقود , ROC 25 243, 272 *B* ⲁϥϯ ⲡⲟⲩⲙ. ⲉⲣⲱⲥ like horse & led her φέρβειν; Hall 82 *S* ⲧⲙ. ⲡⲕⲗⲓⲃⲣⲏⲥ (?), Ep 287 *S* I paid 800 ϣⲉ (coin) ϩⲁⲧⲉⲙⲧⲁⲧ.

ⲙⲧⲱⲧⲉ *S* nn, meaning unknown : CO 466 list of varia & duplicate Univ College London.

ⲙⲧⲟⲧϥ *B*, ϥⲧⲱⲧϥ *S* (prob *l* ⲙⲧ.) nn m, *wild rue*: K 195 ⲡⲓⲙ. بري , P 44 83 *S* ⲁⲃⲣⲁϩⲁⲡⲟⲩ (ἀβρότονον)· ⲁⲧⲣⲓⲟⲡⲓⲥⲧⲁⲡⲡⲟⲩ (? *l*-ⲡⲏⲧⲁⲡⲟⲛ) ⲕⲁϣⲟⲩϣ ϩⲟⲟⲣⲧ· ϥ. سداب = 43 59 *S* ⲉⲕⲧⲟⲧϥ فلیا (*cf* penny-royal, Dozy). *Cf* ⲕⲁϣⲟⲩϣ.

ⲙⲧⲁⲧϩ *B* nn f, meaning unknown, ? = ⲙⲧⲁⲧ : MG 25 127 brethren will not heed me. He said ⲁⲣⲏⲟⲩ ⲧⲟⲩⲙ. ⲡⲧⲟⲧϥ ⲡⲕⲉⲟⲩⲁⲓ, wherefore they hearken not. (Not ⲙⲧⲁⲧ ϩⲏⲧⲟⲩ)

ⲙⲧⲁⲩ *B* nn, *wizardry, magic*, lit *words* (?), *v* AZ 59 160 : Deu 18 10 Va ⲉϥϫⲉ ⲙ. ϩⲉⲛⲟⲩⲙ. (var Lag ⲁϣⲉⲃⲉⲛ nn, *S* ⲣⲉϥⲙⲟⲩⲧⲉ ϩⲛⲟⲩⲙⲟⲩⲧⲉ) ἐπαείδων ἐπαοιδήν. ϫⲉ ⲙ., *speak magic* (?): Deu 18 14 Lag (var Va ϣⲉⲛ ϩⲓⲛ, *S* ⲣⲉϥϣⲓⲛⲉ) μαντεία. ⲣⲉϥϫⲉ ⲙ., *magician*: Va 57 108 ⲙⲁⲅⲟⲥ, ⲫⲁⲣⲙⲁⲅⲟⲥ, ⲣ.; ⲙⲛⲧⲣⲉϥϫⲉ ⲙ., *magic*: Is 47 9(*S* ⲣⲉϥⲙⲟⲩⲧⲉ)ἐπαοιδή.

ⲙⲁⲧⲟⲩ, ⲙⲁⲧⲟⲩⲉ (once), ⲙⲁⲧⲉ (do), *S*, ⲙⲉⲧⲟⲩ *A*, ⲙⲁⲑⲟⲩⲓ *B*, ⲙⲉⲧⲃⲓ *F* (?) nn f, *poison*, esp serpent's : Deu 32 33 *S*ᶠ(Mor 54 142) ⲟⲩⲙⲉⲧⲃⲓ ⲡⲇⲣⲁⲕⲱⲡⲡⲉ ⲟⲩⲙ. ⲉⲧⲉⲙⲉⲥⲙⲟⲩ *B*(*S* Gk diff) *fel... venenum*; Ps 13 3 *S* (var -ⲟⲩⲉ) *B*, Pro 23 32 *SA*, Lam 3 13 *B*(*S* diff), Ja 3 8 *SB*, Z 320 *S* ἰός; Ez 28 24 *SB* πικρία; PS 158 *S* ⲧⲙ. ⲙⲡⲣⲉϥϫⲉ ⲡⲉⲑⲟⲟⲩ, Bor 226 174 *S* of dead flies (Eccl 10 1), ShMIF 23 28 *S* ⲡⲉⲕⲙ. ⲧⲁϩⲟ whole world, JKP 2 84 *S* ⲡⲉⲩⲙⲁⲧⲉ ⲉⲧⲣⲟⲟⲩ, ShA 1 134 *S* ⲧⲙ....ⲉⲥⲙⲟⲟϣⲉ ϩⲙⲡⲥⲱⲙⲁ, BMar 37 *S* ⲟⲩⲕⲗⲟ ⲙⲡⲟⲩⲙ. ⲡⲣⲟϥ, AM 60 *B* sim, BG 56 *S* their fruit ⲟⲩⲙ. ⲡⲉ, Mor 38 67 *S* wine blackened by snake's ⲙ., ShR 2 3 81 *S* serpent ⲡⲓϥⲉ ⲉⲡⲉϥⲃⲁⲗ ⲡⲧⲉϥⲙ.

ⲕⲁⲕⲙ. *S*, *sending, casting poison*: Sa 16 10, Z 552 ϫⲁⲧⲃⲉ ⲡⲕ. ἰοβόλος; R 1 3 59 ϩⲟⲩ ⲡⲕ. (*sic* MS).

ⲡⲉϫ ⲙ. *S*, *throw p.* of reptiles : R 1 1 44 ϫⲁⲧϥⲉ

ⲉⲧⲛ. ⲙ.; ⲣⲉϥⲛ. ⲙ., *thrower of p.*: *ib* 1 2 72, My 30.

ϩⲓ ⲙ. *B* in ⲣⲉϥϩⲓ ⲙ., meaning same : Va 57 220 ϭⲉⲡⲧ ⲡⲣ.; Cat 184 ⲙⲉⲧⲣ. of snake.

ϫⲓ ⲙ. *S*, *receive p.*, *be poisoned*: R 1 4 37 wounds wherein ⲡ[ⲧⲁⲩ]ϫⲓ ⲙ.

ⲙⲁⲩ *SB*, ⲙⲱ *S*ᵃ (Ep 1 241), ⲙⲟ *A*, ⲙⲉⲩ, ⲙⲉⲟⲩ *A*²*F*, ⲙⲁⲟⲩ, ⲙⲉⲟⲩ *O* nn, *the place there*, in **I a** ⲙⲙⲁⲩ &c advb, *there, therein*: Nu 13 29 *SB*, 2 Kg 6 7 *B* (*S* ϩⲓⲡⲙⲁ ⲉⲧⲙ.), Ps 47 6 *S* (*B* om), Pro 11 2 *SAB*, Jer 51 8 *B* (*S* ⲡϩⲏⲧϥ), EpJer 2 *BF* (*S* ⲙⲡⲙⲁ ⲉⲧⲙ.), Lu 6 6 *SB*, Aeg 242 *S* ϥⲙ. ⲡϭⲓ ⲡⲭ̅ⲥ̅ ἐκεῖ, Ge 2 11 *SB* ἐκεῖ οὗ; 2 Chr 3 1 *B* οὗ; MG 25 215 *B* ⲡⲙⲁ ⲉⲡⲁⲡⲙⲟⲧⲉⲡ ⲙⲙⲟⲛ ⲙⲙ. ὅπου; Ps 138 8 *B* (*S* diff), MG 25 240 *B* ⲉⲡⲭⲏ ⲙⲙ. παρεῖναι; Ac 9 38 *SBF*, MG 25 230 *B* ⲉϥⲡⲁⲭⲏ ⲙⲙ. ἐν αὐτῷ(-ῇ) εἶναι; PS 204 *S* ⲡⲙⲁ ⲉⲧⲙⲙ., Br 230 *S* ⲉⲣⲉⲁⲫⲣⲏϫⲱⲡ ⲙⲙ., ShBMOr 8810 491 *S* place ⲉⲛⲧⲁⲅⲉⲓ ⲙⲙ. *whence they came*, ShIF 294 *S* day whereon God shall ⲧⲁⲕⲟ ⲡⲡⲉⲧⲡ̅ⲯⲩⲭⲏ ⲙⲙ., Hor 81 *O* ϥⲧⲟⲩⲁⲉⲓⲧ ⲡⲙⲁⲟⲩ, AZ 21 100 *O* ⲡⲛⲉⲟⲟⲙ (? ⲡⲉⲧⲧⲱⲣⲙ) ⲡⲙⲉⲟⲩ (gloss ⲡⲙⲁⲟⲩ), C 43 86 *B* ⲉⲩⲡⲁⲉⲡⲕⲟⲧ ⲙⲙ., BMis 60 *S* are there 5 gospels? yea ⲥⲉⲙⲙ., *ib* 334 *S* ϯⲙⲙ., ShR 2 3 7 *S* ⲕⲙⲙ. ⲁⲛ, BP 5662 *F* ϥⲙⲉⲩ, J 67 129 *S* ⲙⲁ ⲡⲙⲁ ⲉⲩⲡⲁⲛⲧⲉ ⲉⲃⲟⲗ ⲙⲙ., *ib* 75 126 *S* sim ⲡϩⲏⲧϥ; **b** after vb tr *take away* (Gk om): Ge 48 17 *S* (var & *B* om), Jos 24 14 *S* (var om), Ps 136 3 *B* (*S* om), Ez 16 27 *SB*, Jo 19 31 *SA*²(*B* om), PS 155 *S* ⲁⲕϥⲓ ⲟⲩⲗⲏ ⲙⲙ., Va 57 15 *B* ⲡϥⲱⲗⲓ ⲙⲙ. ⲁⲛ ⲙⲡⲓϫⲓⲛⲉⲣ ϩⲱⲃ; & vb intr, *cease*: *v* ⲗⲟ *s f*, ⲕⲏⲛ **I** *s f*. **c** after vbs *have, lack* (Gk om): Ge 43 7 *SB*, Ps 3 2 *S* (*B* om), *ib* 31 9 *B* (*S* om), Lam 5 3 *BF*, Mt 3 9 *SB*(var), Ap 9 4 *S* (*B* diff), TU 43 16 *A* ⲉⲩⲛⲧⲉⲩ ⲙⲙⲟ ⲡⲧⲁⲅⲁⲡⲏ, ZNTW 24 90 *F* ⲟⲩⲛⲧⲏⲧⲛ ⲙⲉⲩ, Br 275 *S* ⲉⲙⲡⲧⲩ ⲣⲁⲛ ⲙⲙ., BG 40 *S* ⲟⲩⲛⲧⲁⲩ ⲙⲙ. ⲡⲡⲟⲩⲥⲧⲉⲣⲉⲱⲙⲁ, Va 57 12 *B* ⲉⲟⲩⲟⲡ ⲡⲧⲱⲟⲩ ⲙⲙ. ⲙⲡⲁⲓϩⲱⲃ; sim C 43 131 *B* ϭⲉⲡⲧⲏ ⲙⲙ. ⲡϫⲉ ⲡⲟ̅ⲥ̅; **d** ⲉⲃⲟⲗ ⲙⲙ., *thence*: Deu 11 10 *B* (*S* ⲡϩⲏⲧϥ), Jud 19 18 *S*, Is 52 11 *S* (*B* ⲉⲃ. ϩⲉⲛⲧⲙⲏϯ), EpJer 2 *B* (*SF* ϩⲙⲡⲙⲁ ⲉⲧⲙ.), Ac 13 21 *B* (*S* ⲙⲡⲡⲥⲱⲥ) ἐκεῖθεν; ShC 73 121 *S* ⲡⲧⲛⲡⲟⲭϥ ⲉⲃ. ⲙⲙ., AM 54 *B* ⲁⲩⲥⲁⲧϥ ⲉⲃ. ⲙⲙ. **e** varies with gen ⲙⲙⲟ⸗ (*v* ⲡ- gen part **I b**): Ge 35 28 *S* (*B* ⲙⲙⲱⲟⲩ), Is 30 32 *F* (*S* ⲙⲙⲟϥ, *B* om), Mt 13 42 *S* (*B* ⲙⲙⲟϥ), *ib* 43 *S* (*BF* do), Ac 25 10 *B* (var ⲙⲙⲟϥ), AM 280-1 *B* ⲡⲙⲁ...ⲙⲙⲟϥ, ⲡⲙⲁ...ⲙⲙ., C 86 271 *B* borers ⲉⲟⲩⲱⲧⲉⲡ ⲡⲛⲕⲁⲥ ⲙⲙ., *cf ib* 191 *B* sim ⲙⲙⲱⲟⲩ. *V* Stern 298, 534. **f** with rel ⲉⲧⲙⲙ. *S*, ⲉⲧⲉⲙⲙ. *B*, *who, which is there* = demonstr *that*: Lev 7 10 (20) *SB*, Pro 6 7 *SA* (*B* ⲫⲏ), Jer 27 4 *SBF*, Zech 14 3 *SAB*, Mt 15 18 *S* (*B* ⲡⲁⲓ, *cf* Mk 7 20 *B* ⲛⲑⲟϥ), ShR 2 3 16 *S* who shall speak ϩⲙⲡⲙⲁ ⲉⲧⲙ. = BM 285 II a, MG 25 5 *B* ⲡⲓⲑⲏⲣⲓⲟⲛ ⲉⲧⲉⲙ. ἐκεῖνος,

Ge 12 7 *S* ⲣⲙⲙⲁ ⲉⲧⲙ̅ⲙ. (*B* ⲙⲙ.), Ps 65 6 *SB*,
Mt 2 13 *S* ⲙ̅ⲡⲙⲁ ⲉⲧⲙⲙ. (*B* ⲙⲙ.) ἐκεῖ, *ib* 9 9 *S* do
(*B* do), AP 11 *A²* ⲁⲃⲟⲗ ϩⲙⲡⲙⲁ ⲉⲧⲙⲙ. ἐκεῖθεν;
Sa 16 25 *S*, Mt 4 17 *SB* ⲡⲉⲟⲩⲟⲉⲓϣ ⲉⲧⲙⲙ. τότε;
Ac 2 29 *B* (*S* diff) οὗτος, MG 25 11 *B* ⲡⲓⲙⲁⲩ ⲉⲧ-
ⲉⲙⲙ. αὐτός, Va 57 14 *B* ⲡⲏ ⲉⲧⲉⲙⲙ. οἱ μέν...ⲁⲡⲟⲛ
ⲍⲉ; BG 20 *S* ⲡⲓⲁⲓⲱⲛ ⲉⲧⲙⲙ. whither we go, PS 5
S when they saw ⲡⲟⲩⲟⲉⲓⲛ ⲉⲧⲙⲙ., El 46 *A* ⲧⲟⲩ-
ⲡⲟⲩⲧⲉ ⲧⲉⲓ ⲉⲧⲙⲙ., AZ 23 39 *F* ⲡⲕⲟⲩⲙⲁⲣⲓ ⲉⲧⲙⲉⲟⲩ,
Miss 8 8 *S* ⲡⲉⲥⲧⲱⲣⲓⲟⲥ ⲉⲧⲙⲙ., Z 286 *S* I asked
archbishop, ⲡⲉⲝⲉ ⲡⲉⲧⲙ̅ⲙ. ⲡⲁⲓ ⲝⲉ-.

ⲣⲉⲙⲙ̅ⲙⲁⲩ *B*, lit *man of there, native*: EW 46
ⲛⲉⲟⲩⲣ. ⲅⲁⲣⲡⲉ by race.

II **ⲉⲙⲁⲩ** *SB*, **ⲉⲡⲙⲁⲩ** *S* (Ryl 387), **ⲁⲙⲟ** *A*, **ⲁⲙⲉⲩ**
A², *thither*: Ge 42 2 *S* (*B* diff), Deu 12 6 *S* (var
& *B* ⲙⲙ.), Jer 51 14 *B* (*S* ⲙⲙ.), Jo 11 8 *SA²B*
ἐκεῖ; Mt 28 16 *S* (*B* ⲉⲣⲟϥ) οὗ; Jo 8 21 *SA²* (*B* do)
ὅπου; Lu 19 5 *S* (*B* ⲉⲝⲉⲡⲡⲓⲙⲁ) ἐπὶ τὸν τόπον; Ac
27 39 *SB* (both var ⲙⲙ.) εἰς ὅν; no Gk: Jud 7 10
S, 1 Kg 24 4 *B* (*S* ⲉ-), Is 5 14 *B* (*S* om), Ac 18 27
S (*B* om); ShZ 592 *S* place ⲉⲧ̅ⲡⲁⲃⲱⲕ ⲉⲙ., ShC
73 51 *S* ere brethren have ⲥⲱⲟⲩϩ ⲉⲙ., El 40 *A*
ⲁⲩϣⲁⲉⲓ...ⲁⲙⲟ, MG 25 241 *B* ϣⲁⲛⲧⲉϥϣⲉ ⲡⲁϥ ⲉⲙ.

ⲙⲁⲩ *AF* *v* ⲙⲟⲟⲩ.

ⲙⲁⲁⲩ *S*, **ⲙⲁⲩ** *SB*, **ⲙⲟ** *Sᵃ* (J 35) *A*, **ⲙⲟⲩ** *Sᵃ*
(Ep 290), **ⲙⲱ** *Sᵃ* (J 31, 38, Ep 561) *A*, **ⲙⲉⲉⲩ** *A²F*,
ⲙⲉⲟⲩ *FO* (AZ 21 100), **ⲙⲛⲟⲩ** *F* nn f, *mother*: Ge
3 20 *SB*, Pro 10 1 *SAB*, Mt 13 55 *SBF*, Jo 19 25
SA²B μήτηρ; church as mother: ShA 1 225, *ib* 2
137 *S*; as title: Z 346 *S* ⲧⲙ. ⲛⲟⲉⲡⲉⲉⲧⲉ ἀμμά,
MG 25 168 *B* ⲁⲙ. (? not title), ShC 73 44 *S* ⲧⲙ.
ⲛ̅ⲧⲉⲩⲛⲁⲅⲱⲅⲏ, Saq 27 *S* ⲧⲙ. ⲛ̅ⲧⲛⲟϭ (prob) ⲙⲙⲟⲡⲏ,
C 89 27 *B* ⲙ. of Pachôm's nunnery, Miss 4 701 *S*
sisters in ⲑⲉⲛⲉⲉⲧⲉ ⲙ̅ⲡⲧⲉⲩⲙ., ShA 2 282 *S* will require your blood of her called ⲙ. ϩⲁⲧⲉⲧⲏⲩⲧⲛ, ShF
285 *S* ⲡⲉⲓⲟⲧⲉ ⲡ̅ⲡⲏⲓ, ⲙⲙ. ⲡ̅ⲡⲏⲓ, Ryl 296 *S* letter to
ⲧϥⲭⲟⲉⲓⲥ ⲙ̅ⲙ.; Virgin as *our mother* on stelae *S*:
Saq 26, 169, 211, WS 60 ff ⲧⲙⲙ. (var ⲧⲉⲙⲙ.) ⲙⲁⲣⲓⲁ;
sim Eve: Saq 203, 226; Sibylla (var ⲁⲙⲁ ⲥ.): *ib*
30, 219, 233; ⲙ. ⲡⲁϥ ⲡⲉⲃⲓⲱ *S* *queen-bee*: JA '88
2 370.

ϣⲙⲙ., ϣⲏⲡ ⲙ̅ⲙ. (Ge 20), **ϣⲏⲙⲙⲙ.** (Mor 31) *S*,
ϣⲉⲛⲙⲙ. *B* nn m, *mother's child*: Ge 20 12 *SB*, Deu
13 6 *SB* (ἀδελφός) ἐκ μ.; Ge 43 16 *S* (Mor 31 182,
var Bor 253 163 ϣⲏⲣⲉ ⲙⲙ.) *B* ὁμομήτριος, BM 920
266 *B* شقيقة (اخو); AZ 21 100 *O* ⲡϣⲉ ⲡⲧⲁⲙ.

ⲙ. ⲙⲙⲟⲡⲓ *B*, *nursing mother, nurse* *v* ⲙⲟⲟⲛⲉ
nurse.

ⲙ̅ⲛ̅ⲧⲙⲁⲓⲙ. *S*, *love for mother*: Mor 37 24.

ⲁⲧⲙ. *SBF* adj, *without mother*: He 7 3 *SBF*
ἀμήτωρ; Ep Append 1 62 *S* of Christ before incarnation, BHom 102 *S* sim.

ⲣ ⲙ. *S*, *be mother*: R 1 2 73 fasting ⲣ ⲙ. ⲛ̅ⲧⲉⲕ-
ⲕⲗⲏⲥⲓⲁ.

—— *SB* nn f, *caul, afterbirth*: Deu 28 57 χόριον
مشيمة.

In name (?): Σενμααῦς (Preisigke).

ⲙⲟⲟⲩ *S*, **ⲙⲁⲩ** *AA²F*, **ⲙⲁⲟⲩ** *A²* DM (13 11),
ⲙⲱⲟⲩ *B* (Suidas μῶυ), **ⲙⲟⲩ-** *SBF* (thus mostly if
constr or where gen ⲛ- follows), **ⲙⲉ-** *Sᶠ* (JKP 2 64),
pl **ⲙⲟⲩⲉⲓⲏ, ⲙⲟⲩⲛⲉⲓⲉ, ⲙⲟⲩⲉⲓⲟⲟⲩⲉ, -ⲡⲉⲓⲟⲟⲩⲉ, -ⲡⲓⲟ-**
ⲟⲩⲉ *S* (*v* Rec 24 206, BIF 20 223 & above ⲉⲓⲟⲩⲉ),
ⲙⲟⲩⲓⲉⲩⲉ, ⲙⲟⲩⲉⲓⲁⲅⲉⲓⲉ (BM 522 2 a) *A* & sg as pl,
nn m, *water*: Nu 5 17 *SBF*, Ps 148 4 *SBF*, Jon 2 6
SAB, Jo 4 11 *SA²BF* ὕδωρ; Job 14 11 *S* (*B* ⲓⲁⲣⲟ),
Sa 11 7 *S* ποταμός; Job 8 11 *S* (*B* ⲥⲱ) πότος; Deu
32 2 *S* (*B* ⲙ. ⲡ̅ⲣⲱⲟⲩ) ὄμβρος; Tob 2 10 *S* λεύκωμα (*cf* BMis 258). sg as pl: ⲙⲙ., Lev 11 9
SB, Ps 17 15 *SB*, Mt 14 28 *SBF*, MG 25 249 *B*
camels carry ⲙⲙ. for journey, MIE 2 398 *B* ⲡⲓⲕⲟⲩ-
ⲝⲓ ⲙⲙ.; ϩⲉⲡ-, **ⲥⲉⲡⲙ**., Deu 5 8 *B* (*S* ⲙⲟⲩⲉⲓⲟⲟⲩⲉ),
Ps 104 41 *SB*, Nah 1 12 *SA* (*B* diff). Pl forms:
S **ⲙⲟⲩⲉⲓⲏ** Ps 77 16, **-ⲉⲓⲟⲟⲩⲉ** Lev 11 9 (var -ⲡⲉⲓⲟ-
ⲟⲩⲉ & *ib* ⲙⲙⲟⲟⲩ), Deu 4 18 (var do), Mt 14 29
(var do, *cf* 28 ⲙⲙ.), Ap 17 15 (var do), Br 100, PS
64, 212, ShZ 593, R 1 2 24, Pcod 14; **-ⲡⲉⲓⲟⲟⲩⲉ**
2 Kg 12 27, Jth 9 12, Ez 32 14, ShC 73 178, BHom
109, BAp 87, Tri 478 مياه الأنهار; *A* Hab 3 10,
El 100. *Hot water*: Jer 38 2 *B* ⲙⲟⲩⲥⲉⲙ θερμόν;
Ap 3 16 *B* (*S* diff) -ⲥⲉⲙⲓ (var ⲥⲏⲙ.) ζεστός, PMéd
257 *S* ⲙ. ⲉϥϩⲏⲙ.; *cold water*: Pro 25 25 *SA*, Mor
37 94 *S* ⲙ. ⲉϥⲕⲏⲃ ψυχρός, PMéd 206 *S* do; Mt
10 42 *S* ⲙ. ⲡⲱⲣϣ, *B* ⲙ. ϩⲱⲝ, Ap 3 15 *B* do ψυ.;
tepid water: Ap 3 16 *SB* ⲙ. ⲡⲥⲗϩⲟ χλιαρός; *filtered, pure water*: Ez 36 25 *SB* ⲙ. ⲉϥⲥⲱⲧϥ καθαρός, Mor 37 94 *S* διειδός.

Inundation of Nile: Z 106 *Sᶠ* God had pity
ⲁⲩⲛⲟϭ ⲙⲙ. ⲉⲓ ⲉϩⲣⲁⲓ, BAp 87 *S* ⲁⲩⲛⲟϭ ⲙⲙ. ϣⲱⲡⲉ
(var Munich Landesbibl Copt LIX ⲁⲡⲁⲃⲁⲥⲓⲥ) =
MIE 2 359 *B*, *ib* 412 *B* river's water ⲙⲡⲉϥⲙⲟϩ
ⲕⲁⲗⲱⲥ, ROC 25 245 *B* foretelling ⲉⲑⲃⲉⲡⲙ. ⲛ̅ⲧⲉ
ⲫⲓⲁⲣⲟ, Sh(Besa)Z 514 *S* Thy yearly mercy ⲉⲧⲉⲡⲙ.
ⲡⲉ ⲙⲡⲉⲓⲉⲣⲟ, Osir pl 36 44 *S* thanks to Thee ⲁⲕⲛ
ⲡⲙ. ⲛⲁⲡ ⲉϩⲟⲩⲛ ⲁⲑⲁⲙⲉ, Saq 340 *S* sim (& *v* ⲙⲏϣⲧ-
ⲧⲉ), Kr 1 25 *S* date when news of ⲡⲙ. (rising) was
brought, Lant 113 14 *S* sim, Leyd 153 *S* rubric
ⲡⲉⲣⲟⲟⲩ ⲉϣⲁⲣⲉⲡⲙ. ⲉⲓ ⲉϩⲟⲩⲛ to monastery, Wess
18 6 *S* sim ⲙⲡⲛ̅ⲥⲁⲧⲣⲉⲡⲙ. ⲥⲱⲕ ϩⲛ̅ⲡⲉⲓⲟⲣ, GFr 361
= Leyd 129 *S* prayer for ⲡϣⲓ ⲙ̅ⲡⲙ. ⲙⲡⲉⲓⲉⲣⲟ, Ep
315 *S* ⲙ̅ⲡⲁⲧⲉⲡⲙ. ⲝⲱⲗⲝ (? belongs here). In
agriculture: Ep 85 *S* sowing contract ⲛ̅ⲧⲛ̅ϯ ⲡⲉⲩⲙ.
ⲉⲣⲟⲟⲩ (lands), CO 172 *S*, ST 41 *S* sim, Ryl 159 *S*
ⲧⲁⲧⲓ ⲡⲉⲩϩⲁⲙⲟⲟⲩ ⲡⲁⲩ, *ib* 340 of water-wheel ⲧⲁⲡⲁⲩ
ⲝⲉϣⲁⲥϯ ⲧⲉⲓϩⲁⲙⲟⲟⲩ ⲧⲁⲓ, Ryl 159 *S* in winter ⲧⲁ-

ⲕⲱⲧⲉ ⲉⲣⲟⲟⲩ ⲡⲙ. ⲙⲙⲏⲧⲛ, in summer ⲡⲙ. ⲙⲙⲛⲧ
ⲥⲡⲟⲟⲩⲥ, *ib* 158 33, Kr 91, J 57 10, 59 9 *S* sim
(periodical waterings, *cf* ποτισμός).

ⲙ. ⲡⲁⲗⲃⲟⲩⲗ *S water of beans* (? الفول) AZ 23 108,
ⲡⲁⲗⲗⲟⲉⲓⲥ *S* Cai 42573 1, ⲡⲃⲛⲛⲉ *S* C 73 136, ⲡ
ⲃⲁϣⲟⲩϣ *S* PMéd 296, ⲡⲉⲗⲟⲟⲗⲉ *S ib* 306, ⲡⲏϭⲉ
S ib 56, ⲡⲕⲉⲡⲧⲉ *S ib* 111, ⲡⲉⲙϫⲱⲗ *S* WS 52, ⲡ
ⲥⲧⲁⲕⲧⲏ *S* Mor 25 13 = *B* Va 61 95, ⲡⲥⲟⲟⲩϭⲉ *S
white of egg* PMéd 172, AZ *l c*, ⲡⲣⲙⲟⲩ *S* ShC 73
136, ⲡⲣⲧⲓⲧ *S* PMéd 235, ⲡⲭⲟⲉⲓⲧ *S* ما الزيتون P 43
233 ; *juice* after boiling &c: BKU 1 26 (4) *F boil
bat* ϭⲁⲡ (ⲡ)ⲉϥⲙ., Bodl(P) a 1 *a S* ϫⲓ ⲡⲡⲉⲩⲙ. ⲡⲁⲕ,
PMéd 318, 319 *S* sim ; ⲙ. ⲃⲱⲱⲛ, ⲙ. ⲡⲃ. *S bad
water*, diseased exudation (v ⲃⲱⲱⲛ): Montp 177 *B*
ⲙⲟⲩⲃⲟⲛ ذابل, قى (prob *sic l* K 159 ⲙⲟⲩⲑⲟⲙ do),
ⲡⲓⲁⲃⲓ *B* sim (v ⲉⲓⲁⲃⲉ), ⲡⲕⲱⲱⲥ (v ⲕⲱⲱⲥ), ⲙⲙⲟⲩⲧⲉ
(v ⲙⲟⲩⲧⲉ nn), ⲉⲃⲟⲟⲩ *S* from herbs ShA 1 257, ⲙ.
ⲡⲗⲓⲃⲓ *B w. of madness* AM 316, ⲙ. ⲛϭⲣⲟϭ *S semen
virile* Nu 5 2 (*B* diff) γοννορυής, *cf* Br 100 *S* ⲙⲟⲩ
ⲉⲓⲟⲟⲩⲉ ⲡⲛⲣⲟⲟⲩⲧ ; as eye disease : ⲡⲙ. *S cataract*
(Chassinat) PMéd 66, 342, ⲙ. ⲡⲣⲟⲩⲡ *S* sim *ib*, Mor
30 27 *F* ⲁⲡⲙⲟⲩ ⲡⲣ. ϣⲟⲩⲁ ⲉⲡⲉⲛⲧ from within ἐγκέ
φαλος = Mor 29 22 *S* ⲡⲉϩⲗⲟⲥⲧⲡ. ⲙ. ⲡⲃⲉⲉϩⲉ *SB
fountain* (v ⲃⲉⲉϩⲉ), ⲡⲉⲓⲱⲧⲉ *S dew* (v ⲉⲓⲱⲧⲉ), ⲡⲥⲱⲣⲙ
SB torrent (v ⲥⲱⲣⲙ), ⲡⲣⲁⲧⲉ *S flood* (v ⲣⲁⲧⲉ), ⲡⲱϣⲓ
B (v ⲱϣⲓ), ⲡⲣⲱⲟⲩ *SABF rain* (v ⲣⲱⲟⲩ) ; *urine* :
Is 36 12 *B* (*S* ⲙⲏ ⲙ., *F* ⲓϣ) οὖρον.

ⲁⲧⲙ., ⲁⲑⲙ. *S* (rare) *AB* adj, *waterless* : Job 30
3 *SB*, Ps 77 40 *B* (*S* ⲙⲛ ⲙ.), Pro 9 12 *SAB*, Is 35
7 *B* (*SF* do), Mt 12 43 *B* (*S* do) ἄνυδρος ; Kr 127,
132 *S* leases of ⲥⲉⲧⲓⲱϭⲉ ⲡⲁⲧⲙ. (*cf* ἄνυδ. PLond 5
94 n) ; ⲙⲉⲧⲁⲑⲙ. *B*, *drought* : TSBA 9 367.

ⲃⲟ, ϥⲟ ⲙⲙ. *canal* (v ϥⲟ), ⲃⲉⲣⲱ ⲙⲙ. *whirlpool*
(v ⲃⲉⲣⲱ), ⲡⲟⲩⲧ ⲙⲙ. *pool* (v ⲡⲟⲩⲧ), ⲟⲟⲉ ⲙⲙ. *water
spring* (v ⲟⲟⲉ), ϩⲟⲛⲃⲉ ⲙⲙ. sim (v ϩⲟⲛⲃⲉ).

ⲕⲁ ⲙ. *S, cease* (to give) *water* : Is 58 11 (*B*
ⲙⲟⲩⲛⲕ) ἐκλείπειν ; Z 354 hand held in flame ϣⲁⲛ
ⲧⲉⲥⲕⲁ ⲙ. *dried up* (?).

ⲙⲉⲥ ⲙ. *S, water-bearing, containing* : ShIF 151
dig up ⲡⲡⲟⲩⲛⲉ ⲙⲙⲉⲥ ⲙ.

ⲙⲉϩ, ⲙⲁϩ ⲙ. *SBF, draw water* : Ex 2 19 *B* (*SA*
ⲥⲱⲕ), Is 12 3 *B* (*S* ⲟⲩⲱⲧϩ), Jo 4 7 *SA²BF* ἀντλεῖν ;
Ge 24 11 *B*, 1 Kg 7 6 *S* ὑδρεύειν ; Jos 3 15 *SB*
πληροῦν ; BMis 195 *S* ⲙⲙ. ⲡⲧⲁⲅⲙⲁⲣⲟⲩ ⲙⲡⲗⲁⲕ
ⲕⲟⲥ, DeV 2 69 *B* ⲉϥⲙⲁϩ ⲙ. ϩⲉⲛⲟⲩⲡⲩⲧⲛ. ⲙⲁ
ⲙⲙⲉϩ ⲙ. *S, place of drawing water* : Miss 4 700
jars ϩⲓⲭⲛⲙⲙ., BM 1167 send camels ⲉⲡⲙ. ⲣⲉϥ
ⲙⲉϩ, ⲙⲁϩ ⲙ. *SB, water-drawer* : Deu 29 11 *SB*,
Jos 9 33 *S* ὑδροφόρος.

ⲣ, ⲉⲣ ⲙ. *SA²B, become water, liquify* (mostly in
recipes) : AZ 23 111 *S* bury in dung ϣⲁⲛⲧⲉϥⲉⲣ
ⲙ., Bodl(P) a 1 *b* ⲧⲁⲁⲩ ⲉϩⲟⲩⲛ ⲉⲡⲁⲗϩⲁⲗ (? الحل

ϣⲁⲛⲧⲉⲩⲃⲱⲗ ⲉⲃⲟⲗ (ⲛ)ⲧⲉⲩⲣ ⲙ., *ib* a 2 49 *S* ⲉⲓϣⲧϥ
...ϣⲁⲛⲧⲉϥⲉⲣ ⲙ. ⲧⲏⲣϥ, PMéd 296 *S* eye ⲉϥⲟ ⲙⲙ.,
Miss 8 255 *S* diseased eyes ⲁⲩⲣ ⲙ., AP 33 *A²*
ⲉϥ]ⲟⲉⲓ ⲙⲙ.

ⲥⲉⲕ ⲙ. *S, draw water* : Ex 2 16 *S* (*A* om ⲙ., *B*
ϯ ⲙ.), Z 308, 313 ἀντλεῖν ; but ⲙ. ⲉⲧⲥⲱⲕ, *flowing
water* (v ⲥⲱⲕ). ⲥⲁⲕ ⲙ. *S* nn f, meaning unknown,
? water conduit : BM 487.

ⲥⲣ ⲙ. *SB, scatter, distribute water* : Miss 4 242
S = *ib* 39 *B* ⲉⲩϭⲃⲧⲱⲧ ⲉⲥⲣ (*sic l*) ⲙ. = *ib* 381 لينادر.
ⲥⲁⲣⲙ. *S* ⲛⲛ, *water-distributor* (?) : Louvre R 49 ⲁⲩ
ⲙⲟⲣⲧ ⲡⲥ. ϩⲛⲡ[ϣⲁ ⲉⲧⲟ]ⲅⲁⲁⲃ ⲡⲡⲉⲥⲧⲁⲩⲣⲟⲥ *obliged
me* (to be) *water-distr on Holy Cross day.*

ϯ ⲙ. *SB, give water* : BAp 66 *S* ⲡⲩⲧⲛ ⲉⲧϯ ⲙ.
to 4 rivers, C 89 13 *B tree* ⲉⲩϯ ⲙ. ⲉⲣⲟⲥ *with hands*,
Va 57 34 *B* ⲉϥϯ ⲙ. ⲉⲃⲟⲗ ϧⲉⲛ ⲡⲁⲓⲙⲟⲩⲙⲓ εἴς τινα
ἀντλίαν (PG 58 738 *l* πηγαῖς), BMEA 10577 *S* ⲧⲃⲟⲟ
(*l* ⲃⲟ) ⲡⲱⲛⲉ ⲉⲧϯ ⲙ.ⲉϥⲟⲗ ⲉⲡⲓⲱϭⲉ. *V* above, *Inundation*. ⲙⲁ ⲛϯ ⲙ. *SAB, place of giving* (*forth*)*water* :
Joel 3 18 *SAB* ἄφεσις, Z 634 *S hath closed* ⲡⲓⲙⲁ
ⲛϯⲙ. ⲧⲁⲓⲙ. *F* nn m, *irrigator* (?) : CMSS 77.

ⲧⲥⲉ ⲙ. *SB, slake with water* : Nu 5 24 *SB*, Mor
37 99 *S* ⲁⲩⲧⲥⲟϥ (canal) ⲙⲙⲙ. ποτίζειν.

ϥⲓ ⲙ. *S, carry water* : Mor 16 15 went to tank ϫⲉ
ⲕⲁⲥ ⲉⲩⲉϥⲓ ⲙ. & drink ; ϥⲁⲓⲙ. (always so) nn f, *water-
carrier, -holder, conduit* (?) : TurM 16 ⲧⲃ. ϩⲛⲑⲛⲉⲓⲧ
(*sic* ostr), *ib* ⲧⲃ. ⲡⲟⲛⲉ(ⲓ)ⲧ, J 24 127, 35 33 ϩⲛⲉⲓⲧ,
ⲧⲱⲣⲧ, ⲃ. to be in common, CO 149, 150, 151 sim.

ϩⲓ ⲙ. *S, rain* : BM 1089 ⲛⲧⲁⲧⲛⲉ ϩⲓ ⲙ.

ϫⲓ, ϭⲓ ⲙ. *SB, take, receive water* : Ez 22 24 *S*
(C 42 159) *B* βρέχεσθαι, BMis 461 *S* ⲡⲧⲉⲡⲥⲱϣⲉ
ϫⲓ ⲙ., J 104 19 *S* ⲁⲓϫⲓ ⲙ. from holy tank. As nn
m *S, watering* (?) : Ryl 158 28 annual rent for each
of ϫⲓ ⲙ., BM 1172 *S* we owe Victor 4 ϫⲓ ⲙ. ⲙⲁ
ⲛϫⲓ ⲙ. *SF, water conduit, cistern* (?) : Is 36 2 *F* (*S*
ϥⲟ, *B* = Gk) ὑδραγωγός ; BIF 14 186 *S* city's walls
towers & ⲡⲉⲥⲙ. ⲉⲣ ϭⲓ ⲙ. (1 var ⲣⲉϥϭⲓ ⲙ.) *B* nn
m, *urine* : K 161 ⲡⲓⲉⲣ. اراقة, بول. In names : Παπ
μόουν, Σαυμόουν (Preisigke) ; in place-names : Πμοῦ
νλακων (*ib*).

ⲙⲟⲩⲙⲉ *S* (once), ⲙⲟⲩⲛⲙⲉ *A* (Hos 13 15), ⲙⲟⲩ
ⲙⲓ *B* nn f, *spring, fountain* : Ge 8 2, Lev 20 18,
Ps 73 15, Pro 4 21, Is 35 7, Jo 4 6 (all *SAF* =
Gk), Ps 41 2 (*S* ϩⲟⲛⲃⲉ), Jer 9 1 (*S* ⲙⲟⲩ ⲡⲥⲱⲣⲙ
BHom 36), Va 57 177 of Job ϩⲁⲡⲙ. ⲡϭⲉⲡⲧ πηγή ;
Lam 3 48 ἄφεσις ; Ja 3 11 *SA* (ϯⲙ[, *B* ⲟⲩⲱⲧⲉⲛ)
ὀπή ; Va 67 88 ϯⲙ. ⲙⲙⲱⲟⲩ ⲉⲁⲥϭⲱϫⲓ ⲉⲡϣⲱⲓ (*cf
ib* 87 ⲟⲩϣⲟϯ ⲙⲙⲱⲟⲩ ⲃⲉⲃⲓ ⲉⲡϣ.), Aeg 9 thou art
ϯⲙ. of all good.

V ⲙⲏⲛ, ⲯⲉⲣⲙⲟⲟⲩ.

ⲙⲁⲩⲁⲁ⸗ *S*, ⲙⲁⲩⲁⲧ⸗ *S* (Sh) *B* (rare), ⲙⲙⲁⲩⲁⲧ⸗
B, ⲙⲁⲩⲉⲉⲧ⸗ *F* adj, *alone, single* (ⲙ + ⲟⲩⲁⲁ⸗ *q v*) :

Ge 7 22 *SB*, Ps 50 4 *SB* (*A* Cl ⲟⲩⲁⲉⲉⲧⲋ), Is 10 8
SB, Su 15 *B* (*S* ⲙⲙⲁⲧⲉ), Mt 21 19 *S* (varr ⲙⲙⲁⲧⲉ,
ⲙⲙ. ⲙⲁⲩⲁⲁⲋ) *B*, Mk 9 8 *SB* (*F* ⲟⲩ.), Jo 6 15 *SB*
(*A²* ⲟⲩ.), Jude 25 *B* (*S* ⲟⲩ.), Z 316 *S* ⲉⲡⲉⲛⲧⲟⲋ
ⲙⲁⲩⲁⲁϥⲡⲉ = MG 25 230 *B* impossible
ⲉⲧⲣⲉϥⲣ ⲡⲁⲓ ⲙⲁⲩⲁⲁϥ, BHom 49 *S* ⲉⲩⲡⲁϩⲉ ⲉⲣⲟⲋ
ⲙⲁⲩⲁⲁⲥ μόνος, Ps 32 15 *SB*, Jer 15 17 *SB*, Lu 9
18 *SB* κατὰ μόνας, Ps 21 21 *B* (*S* ⲟⲩⲱⲧ), Jo 3 16 *B*
(*S* ⲇⲟ, *F* = Gk) μονο(γενής), Ps 151 tit *B* (*S* om)
μονο(μαχεῖν); Mk 2 7 *SB*, Ro 3 10 *B* (*S* ⲟⲩⲁ),
BHom 50 *S* ⲟⲩⲥϭⲓⲙⲉ ⲙⲁⲩⲁⲁⲥ εἷς; Br 258 *S* blessing ⲉⲡⲓⲟⲩⲁ ⲙⲁⲩⲁⲁϥ, ShC 73 3 *S* ⲡⲓⲙⲁ ⲙⲁⲩⲁⲧϥ,
ib 153 *S* ⲡⲉⲧⲟⲩⲏϩ ⲙⲁⲩⲁⲁϥ, Pcod 37 *S* showing it
ⲉⲡϣⲉ ⲙⲁⲩⲁⲁϥ (var ⲙⲙⲁⲧⲉ), BMar 47 *S* Creator
called ⲡⲧⲉⲭⲛⲓⲧⲏⲥ ⲙⲁⲩⲁⲁϥ, TEuch 1 334 *B* ⲛⲑⲟⲕ
...ⲡⲓⲙⲁⲩⲁⲧϥ ⲛⲛ̄ϯ, BSM 14 *B* ⲟⲩϣⲏⲣⲓ ⲙⲙⲁⲩⲁⲧϥ
= BMis 348 *S* ⲟⲩⲱⲧ, DeV 2 112 *B* none knoweth
Trinity except ⲑⲁⲣⲓϩⲁⲣⲟⲥ ⲙⲙⲁⲩⲁⲧⲥ; *own* :
Pro 5 18 *B* (*SA* ⲟⲩ.), Ac 1 7 *S* (*B* om), 2 Pet 3 16
B (*S* ⲙⲙⲓⲛ ⲙⲙⲟⲋ) ἴδιος, Job 7 13 *S* (*B* ϩⲁⲣⲓϩⲁⲣⲟⲋ)
ἴδια, Mt 14 13 *S* (*B* om, *F* ⲛⲥⲁⲟⲩⲥⲁ), *ib* 20 17 *S*
(*B* ⲟⲩⲧⲱⲋ ⲡⲉⲙ-) κατ᾽ ἰδίαν;   as pron, *self* : Pro
15 27 *S* (var & *A* ⲟⲩ.), Is 5 21 *S* (var ⲟⲩ., *F* ⲙⲙⲓⲛ
ⲙⲙⲁⲋ), Ro 2 14 *S* (*B* ⲙⲙⲓⲛ ⲙⲙⲟⲋ), *ib* 15 1 *B* (*S*
ⲟⲩ.), Z 274 *S* agreeth not ⲛⲙⲙⲁⲥ ⲙⲙⲓⲛ ⲙⲙⲟⲥ
ⲙⲁⲩⲁⲁⲥ ἑαυτοῦ, Jo 3 27 *SB* (*F* ⲟⲩ.), *ib* 5 19 *SB*
(*A²* ⲟⲩ.) ἀφ᾽ ἑαυ., EpJer 71 *B* (*F* diff) ἀπ᾽ αὐτῶν,
Ac 21 23 *S* (*B* om) ἐφ᾽ ἑαυ., EpJer 26 *B* (*F* ⲟⲩ.)
δι᾽ ἑαυ., Zech 12 12 *S* (*B* ϩⲁⲣⲓϩⲁⲣⲟⲥ) καθ᾽ ἑαυ.,
Nu 32 24 *S* (*B* om), Ro 2 1 *SB*, MG 25 217 *B* ⲡ-
ⲧⲉⲕⲧⲁⲕⲟⲕ ⲙⲙⲁⲩⲁⲧⲕ σεαυτοῦ, Jo 8 28 *SB* (*A²* ⲟⲩ.)
ἐμαυτοῦ; Lev 25 5 *S* (*B* ⲡⲟⲩⲁⲧⲋ), Jos 6 5 *S*, Mk
4 28 *SB* αὐτόματος; PS 21 *S* gates ⲁⲩⲟⲩⲱⲛ ⲙⲁⲩⲁⲁⲩ, Br 228 *S* being father ⲉⲣⲟϥ ⲙⲁⲩⲁⲁϥ, ShA 1
193 *S* ⲧⲙⲛⲧⲉⲣⲟ...ⲧⲁⲡⲉⲧⲙⲡϣⲁ ⲙⲁⲩⲁⲁⲧⲟⲩⲧⲉ, ShC
73 13 *S* sword ⲉⲧⲧⲱⲕⲙ ⲙⲙⲟⲥ ⲙⲁⲩⲁⲁⲥ from sheath,
BMis 458 *S* verily thou art a saint. (answer) ⲛⲧⲟⲕ
ⲙⲁⲩⲁⲁⲕ ⲉⲡⲉϩⲟⲩⲟ, AM 153 *B* ϣⲉⲛϩⲏⲧ ϩⲁⲣⲱⲧⲉⲛ
ⲙⲙⲁⲩⲁⲧⲉⲑⲏⲛⲟⲩ; no Gk : 1 Kg 31 5 *S*, Jer 51 14
B (*S* om), Ac 27 22 *SB*;   ⲙⲙⲁⲩⲁⲧϥ *B* indecl,
as advb, *only, merely* (cf μόνον) : Va 57 174 ⲉⲥⲟⲩⲟⲧⲉⲃ ⲉⲃⲟⲗ ⲙⲙ., ⲉⲩⲟⲩⲟⲧⲉⲃ ⲙⲙⲟⲥ ⲉⲃⲟⲗ ⲙⲙ. μετέ-
βαινε μόνον; MIE 2 402 ⲁⲕϣⲁⲛⲥⲓⲛⲓ ⲙⲙ. ⲉⲃⲟⲗ
ϩⲉⲛⲡⲓⲙⲁ, C 86 297 ⲛⲧⲉⲕⲟⲩⲱϣⲧ ⲛⲡⲛ̄ϯ ⲙⲙ., Va
63 89 ⲛⲁⲥⲟⲓ ⲛⲁϥ ⲛⲉϩⲣⲓⲙ ⲙⲙ. ⲁⲛⲡⲉ, *ib* 92 ⲡⲓⲥⲁϫⲓ
ⲉⲧⲣⲟⲃⲥ ⲙⲙ.

ⲙⲉⲉⲩⲉ *SAA²*, ⲙⲉⲩⲉ *SAA²* (once), ⲙⲉⲉⲩ *S*
(rare), ⲙⲉⲟⲩⲉ *A*, ⲙⲉⲩⲓ *BO*, ⲙⲛⲟⲩⲓ, ⲙⲛⲏ., ⲙⲉⲉⲩⲉⲓ
F vb intr, *think*, **a** no obj : 1 Cor 13 11 *SB* λογίζεσθαι, Mt 16 7 *S* (*B* & Mk 8 16 *S* ⲙⲟⲕⲙⲉⲕ), Lu 5
22 *S* (*B* ⲇⲟ) διαλ.; Ro 12 3 *SBF* ὑπερφρονεῖν; Si
17 5 *S* διανοεῖν; Mt 5 17 *B* (*S* ⲱⲡ) νομίζειν; BHom

90 *S* ⲛⲧⲁⲁϣ ⲛⲛⲟⲩⲥ ⲙ. ⲡⲧⲉⲓϩⲉ. **b** + ϫⲉ-, *think
that* : Ge 19 14 *B* (*S* diff), Job 15 21 *SB*, Jo 5 45
SA²B, He 10 29 *B* (*S* ϫⲱ) δοκεῖν; Sa 14 20 *S*, Ro
8 18 *SB* λογ., Lu 3 15 *S* (*B* ⲙⲟⲕⲙⲉⲕ) διαλ.; Ac
17 29 *S* (*B* diff), 1 Cor 7 26 *SBF*, MG 25 219 *B*
ⲡⲁⲓⲙ. ϫⲉϩⲁⲡⲓⲛⲁⲛⲉ νομ.; Job 20 2 *SB*, Lu 7 43
SB ὑπολαμβάνειν; Job 40 3 *S* (*BAp* 79) *B*, Is 57
8 *SB*, Ja 1 7 *SB* οἴεσθαι; PS 121 *S* ⲡⲉⲓⲙ. ϫⲉⲡ-
ⲧⲟⲕⲡⲉ, ShA 2 50 *S* ⲡⲓⲙ. ⲡⲉⲧⲛⲙⲁ....ϫⲉⲧⲛⲕⲱⲛⲥ
ⲡⲓⲉⲩⲉⲣⲏⲩ, Ryl 385 *S* ⲧⲓⲙⲉⲉⲩ ϫ(ⲉ)-, C 43 243 *B*
ϫⲙ. ϫⲉϫⲡⲁⲥⲣⲟ ⲉⲣⲟⲓ. **c** + ethic dat : C 89 68 *B*
ⲡⲁⲓⲙ. ⲛⲛⲏⲡⲉ ϫⲉ- (*S* MG 17 320 om dat) νομ.;
BIF 13 116 *S* ⲡⲉⲓⲙ. ⲛⲁⲓⲡⲉ ϫⲉ- = MG 25 308 *B*
ⲡⲁⲓⲙ. ⲁⲡⲟⲕⲡⲉ, AM 187 *B* ⲡⲁⲩⲙ. ⲡⲱⲟⲩⲡⲉ ϫⲉ-.
d c ⲉ- : Mt 24 44 *S* (*B* ⲥⲱⲟⲩⲛ), He 4 1 *B* (*S* diff),
BHom 52 *S* those ⲉϥⲙ. ⲉⲣⲟⲟⲩ ϫⲉ- (var R 2 2 35
ⲉϥⲣ ⲙ.), Va 57 13 *B* ⲛⲏ ⲉⲧⲉⲙⲙ. ⲉⲣⲱⲟⲩ ϫⲉⲧⲟⲩⲉⲣ
ⲉⲛⲉⲣⲅⲓⲛ δοκεῖν, Sa 18 17 *S* ⲉⲡⲥⲉⲙ. ⲉⲣⲟⲟⲩ ⲁⲛ
ἀδόκητος; 1 Kg 1 13 *S*, Ps 35 4 *S* (*B* ⲙⲟⲕ.), Hos
7 15 *SA* (*B* ⲥⲟϭⲛⲓ), 1 Cor 4 1 *B* (*S* ⲱⲡ) λογ., Ps 9
22 *S* (*B* ⲇⲟ), Pro 17 12 *SA* διαλ.; Mk 8 33 *SB* (*F*
ϭⲓ λⲟⲟⲩϣ), Ro 12 16 *SF* (*B* diff), Z 273 *S* ⲉⲩⲙ.
ⲉⲛⲉϩⲃⲏⲩⲉ of Manichaeans, Miss 8 35 *S* sim φρονεῖν.; EpJer 39 *BF*, Z 345 *S* = MG 25 210 *B* νομ.;
Ge 6 5 *S* (*B* diff), Jer 19 5 *B* διανοεῖν, Job 1 5 *SB*
ἐννο., *ib* 4 18 *S* (*B* ⲙⲟⲕ.) ἐπινο., Dan 7 25 *B* ὑπονο.;
Ps 69 2 *S* (*B* diff), Is 31 6 *SF* (*B* ⲥⲟϭ.), ROC 17
407 *B* ⲛⲛⲟⲩⲙ. ⲉⲟⲩϩⲱⲃ βουλεύειν; Ps 49 21 *SB*,
Bor 305 97 *S* lest any ⲙ. ⲉⲡⲁⲓ ⲉⲛⲡⲉ ⲡⲗⲟⲩⲟⲥ that
He died ὑπολαμβ.; Sa 3 14 *S*, Mt 1 20 *S* (*B* ⲙⲟⲕ.);
Ps 118 39 *S* (*B* ⲉⲣ ϭⲓ ⲥⲁⲡⲓⲥ) ὑποπτεύειν; Ps 62 7
B (*S* ⲣ ⲡⲙ.) μνημονεύειν; Ge 50 15 *B* (*S* ⲇⲟ), Joel
3 4 *SAB* μνησικακεῖν; Jer 2 33 *B* (*S* = Gk), Su 43
B πονηρεύειν; Si 11 35 *S* τεκταίνεσθαι; Ge 43 25
B (*S* fut), CaiEuch 588 *B* ⲛⲏ ⲉⲑⲙ. ⲉⲩϣⲉ μέλλειν;
Job 24 23 *S* (*B* = Gk) ἐλπίζειν, Sa 11 8 *S* neg
ἀνελπίστως; PS 44 *S* ⲁⲥⲙ. ⲉⲃⲱⲕ, BG 136 *S* ⲉϥⲙ.
ⲉⲧⲣⲉϥⲧⲱⲟⲩⲛ, ShBM 204 77 *S* hunter & ⲡⲉⲧϥⲙ.
ⲉⲣⲟⲟⲩ ⲉϩⲟⲡⲟⲩ, DeV 2 16 *B* ⲡⲏ ⲉⲑⲙ. ⲉϣⲱⲡⲓ ⲙ-
ⲙⲟⲓ *about to befall* (cf below **f**), J 65 20 *S* ϣⲁⲩⲙ.
ⲉϩⲛⲉ ⲉⲟⲩⲡⲁ *expecting*, BAp 111 *S* ⲙⲡⲣⲙ. ⲉⲣⲟⲓ
ϫⲉⲛⲧⲁⲓϫⲉ ⲡⲁⲓ= MIE 2 389 *B*, Mor 29 12 *S* ⲛϯⲙ.
ⲁⲛ ⲉⲣⲟⲕ ϫⲉⲁⲕⲧⲁλϭⲟⲕ *without magic*, Wess 15 19
S ⲡⲧⲁϥⲙ. ⲉⲛϩⲟⲩⲙⲁ of Nestorius, P 131³ 20 *S*
ⲉⲙ. ⲉⲩⲥⲱϣϥ ⲉϩⲟⲩⲛ ⲉⲧⲙⲡⲧⲡⲉ, AZ 21 106 *O* ⲡⲉⲧ-
ⲉⲙⲡⲉⲥ(ϩ)ⲏⲧ...ⲙⲉⲛⲡⲉⲧⲉⲙ. ⲉⲣⲟϥ (*sic* !), AM 28 *B*
ⲟⲩ ⲉⲧⲉⲕⲙ. ⲉⲣⲟϥ ? **e** sim c ⲉ- (refl dat) : Pro 26
12 *SA*, Su 5 *B* (*S* ϫⲱ), 1 Cor 14 37 *BF* (*S* om dat)
δοκεῖν; Pcod 27 *S* ⲉⲓⲙ. ⲉⲣⲟⲓ ϫⲉⲧⲛⲁⲩ ⲉⲃⲟⲗ, ShR
2 3 68 *S* ⲉⲕⲙ. ⲉⲣⲟⲕ ϫⲉⲙⲡⲧⲁⲕ λⲁⲁⲩ, DeV 2 281
B ⲉⲧⲓ ϫⲉ ⲉϥⲙ. ⲉⲣⲟϥ to do this; as nn *S* : Bor 226
176 ⲡⲙ. ⲉⲣⲟⲕ ϩⲱⲥ ϣⲙⲙⲟ to world.   **f** + ⲛ-
(Stern 456), *meditate* doing, *be about to* do (cf

above **d**): Bor 263 25 *S* ⲉⲕⲙ. ⲛⲃⲱⲕ to heaven, C 43 184 *B* ⲣⲱⲥϫⲉ ⲉϥⲙ. ⲡⲥⲁϫⲓ, PO 11 382 *B* summoned him ⲉϥⲙ. ⲡⲉⲣ ⲡⲉⲧϩⲱⲟⲩ ⲡⲁϥ.

—— ⲉⲣⲟⲩⲛ, ⲉⲋ. ⲉ- *SB, think, design against*: Ps 82 3 *S* (*B* ⲥⲟϭⲛⲓ ϩⲁ-) βουλεύ. κατά; Sa 14 30 *S* φρον. περί; MIF 9 89 *S* ⲡⲉⲡⲧⲁⲕⲁⲣⲓⲱⲥ (Quirinius) ⲙ. ⲉⲣⲟϥ ⲉϩ. ⲉⲓ̅ⲥ̅, Va 59 3 *B* ⲡⲁϥⲙ. ⲉⲣⲁⲛⲥⲟϭⲛⲓ... ⲉⲋ. ⲉ-.

—— ⲉⲃⲟⲗ *SB, think upon, consider*: Wess 11 160 *S* = C 89 65 *B* ⲉϥⲙ. ⲉⲃ. ⲉⲡⲕⲟⲧⲥ of devil λογ., BHom 9 *S* ⲙⲁⲣⲛⲙ ⲉⲃ. ⲉⲡⲉⲡⲧⲁϥⲟⲣⲅ ⲡⲟⲗⲓ ⲡⲉ ἀναλ.; Va 57 216 *B* ⲉϣⲱⲡ ⲁⲕϣⲁⲛⲙ. ⲉⲃ. ⲉⲡⲁⲓ ἐννο., Bor 253 163 *S* ⲉⲓⲙ. ⲉⲃ. ⲉⲧⲉⲕⲑⲗⲓ̈ⲯⲓⲥ κατανο.; Aeg 240 *S* ⲡⲡⲉⲕⲙ. ⲉⲃ. ⲉⲡⲡⲉⲑⲟⲟⲩ μνησικακ.; Bor 280 55 *S* ⲡⲉϫⲙ. ⲉⲃ. as to dream's meaning, DeV 2 33 *B* ⲉⲩⲙ. ⲉⲃ. ⲉⲡⲁϣⲁⲓ of iniquities, BMis 379 *S* ⲉϥⲙ. ⲉⲃ. ϫⲉⲟⲩ ⲡⲉⲧⲉϥⲛⲁⲁⲁϥ, ShR 2 3 4 *S* ⲉⲕⲙ. ⲉⲃ. ϫⲉ- why have I not repented, Ryl 94 (33 3) *S* ⲙⲁⲣⲛⲙ. ⲉⲃ. ϫⲉ- what peril we incur, Va 57 90 *B* ⲉⲓⲙ. ⲉⲃ. ⲋⲉⲡⲡⲁⲡⲟⲩⲋ, TU 20 4 8 *S* ⲉⲓⲙ. ⲉⲃ. ⲣⲙⲡⲁⲣⲏⲧ ⲉⲧⲃⲉⲡϫⲓⲱⲧⲙⲟⲥ, AM 6 *B* ⲡⲁϥⲙ. ⲉⲃ. ⲡⲉ ⲉⲑⲃⲉⲡⲓⲣⲱⲃ, ROC 7 146 *S* ⲉⲩⲙ. ⲉⲃ. ⲡⲧⲛⲟϭ ⲛⲁⲣⲉⲧⲏ of dead woman (? *l* ⲉⲧⲛⲟϭ).

—— *SAA²BF* nn m, *thought, mind*: Ps 32 10 *S* (*B* ⲥⲟϭⲛⲓ), Ro 2 15 *B* (*S* ⲙⲟⲕ.), Z 296 *S* = MG 25 204 *B* λογισμός, Ps 55 5 *S* (*B* ⲥⲟϭ.) διαλ.; Bar 2 8 *B*, 2 Cor 11 3 *B* (*S* ⲣⲏⲧ) νόημα, Is 55 9 *SB* διαν.; Pro 4 1 *SA* (*B* ⲕⲁϯ), Si 2 14 *S* (*B* ⲟⲩⲱϣ) ἔννοια, Jer 38 33 *B*, He 8 10 *SBF* διάνοια, Sa 9 14 *S* ἐπίν., CaiEuch 465 *B* ⲟⲩⲙ. ⲡⲟⲩⲱⲧ ὁμόν.; Ps 144 7 *B* μνήμη, Lev 2 2 *B* μνημόσυνον, Phil 1 3 *B* μνεία, Ps 37 tit *B* ἀνάμνησις (all *S* ⲣ ⲡⲙ.); Jer 3 17 *B* (*S* ⲟⲩⲱϣ) ἐνθύμημα; Ro 8 6 *SB* φρόνημα, ib 12 16 *SBF* ⲙ. ⲉⲩⲙ. φρονεῖν; Ps 13 1, 27 4 *S* (*B* diff) ἐπιτήδευμα; Pro 25 1 *SA* ⲁⲭⲙ. ἀδιάκριτος; PS 184 *S* ⲟⲩⲁⲓⲥⲑⲉⲛⲥⲓⲥ ⲙⲡⲟⲩⲙ., Sh(?)C 73 VIII *S* ⲙ. & ⲡⲟⲩⲥ, Miss 8 252 *S* ⲗⲟⲅⲓⲥⲙⲟⲥ & ⲙ., ROC 25 257 *B* maniac healed ⲉⲣⲉⲡⲉϥⲙ. ⲥⲙⲟⲛⲧ ⲉⲣⲟϥ, J 75 46 *S* ⲙ. ⲉϥⲧⲟⲩϫⲏⲩ *sound in mind*, Ep 435 *S* ⲛⲧⲕⲁ ⲡⲁⲙ. ⲡⲁⲕ *let thought of me be with thee*, AM 83 *B* devil ⲥⲁⲧ ⲙ. ⲉⲣⲟⲥ, Mor 38 86 *S* ⲕⲁⲧⲁ ⲡⲁⲙ. *in my opinion*.

ⲙ. ⲛϩⲏⲧ *SAB* nn, meaning as last: 2 Cor 3 14 *S* (*B* ⲙ.) νόημα, Lu 11 17 *S* (*B* do) διαν., Eph 2 3 *B* (*S* ⲙ.) διάνοια; Ez 14 5 *B* ἐνθύμημα, Is 44 9 *S* (*B* ⲟⲩⲱϣ ⲛϩ.) καταθύμιος; Hos 11 6 *AB* διαβουλία; Si 3 24 *S* ὑπόληψις; Miss 8 106 *S* φρόνημα; ShC 42 41 *S* confused in their ⲙ. ⲛϩ., C 89 65 *B* followed his vain ⲙ. ⲛϩ.

(ⲁⲧⲙ. adj), ⲙⲛⲧⲁⲧⲙ. *SB, absence of thought*: Mk 11 25 tit *S* (H p 645) ⲡⲁϩⲏⲧ(*l* ⲧⲙⲛⲧ)ⲁⲧⲙ. ⲉⲡⲡⲉⲑⲟⲟⲩ, HL 75 *B* sim ἀόργητον.

ⲣⲉϥⲙ. *SA, one who thinks*: Pro 15 22 βουλεύων; ib 12 2 ⲣ. ⲉⲡⲡⲉⲑⲟⲟⲩ (*B* Gk diff, cf Vulg).

ϯ ⲙ., ⲡⲙ., ⲙⲡⲙ. *SB, cause thought, suggest, remind*: Ps 118 49 *B* (*S* ⲣ ⲡⲙ.) μιμν., Z 317 *S* = MG 25 231 *B* ὑπομιμν.; Bor 235 58 *S* if demons ϯ ⲙ. ⲡⲁⲕ πείθειν, Pcod 24 *S* sim, C 86 291 *B* ⲁⲕϯ ⲙⲫⲙ. ⲡⲏⲓ ⲙⲡⲓⲉϩⲟⲟⲩ.

ϫⲓ ⲙⲡⲙ. *F, esteem*: EpJer 44 ⲡⲥⲉϫ. ⲉⲗⲁⲩ ⲉⲡ (*B* ⲙ. ⲉ-) νομιστέος.

ϫⲓⲙⲙ. *B* nn, *thinking, esteem*: Va 57 160 ⲙⲉⲧⲁⲥ-ⲑⲉⲛⲏⲥ opp ⲟⲩⲕⲟⲙⲡⲟⲥ ⲡⲉⲙⲟⲩϫ. ⲉⲣⲟϥ *self-esteem*.

ⲣ ⲙ. *S, think, esteem*: R 2 2 35 those ⲡⲉϯⲣ ⲙ. ⲉⲣⲟⲟⲩ ϫⲉ- my shepherds (var BHom 52 ⲙ. ⲉ-) δοκεῖν (? *l* ϯⲙ.).

ⲣ ⲡⲙ., ⲉⲣ ⲫⲙ. *SAA²BF, have mind of, remember* **a** *no obj*: Job 21 6 *SB*, Ps 24 7 *SB* μιμν., Is 23 16 *SB* μνεία γίνεσθαι; 2 Cor 13 11 *B* (*SF* ⲙ. ⲉⲡⲉⲓⲙ.) φρονεῖν. **b** ϯ ϫⲉ-, *remember that*: Deu 5 15 *SB*, Job 4 7 *SB*, Ps 77 39 *SB*, Jo 2 17 *SA²B* μιμν.; C 86 290 *B* ϯⲓⲣⲓ ⲙⲫⲙ. ⲁⲡ...ϫⲉⲁϥⲓ; ϯ ϫⲉⲕⲁⲁⲥ: Sa 12 2 *S* ὑπομιμν. ἵνα. **c** ϯ gen ⲛ-: Ge 8 1 *SB*, Ps 54 24 *S* (Rahlfs *Septuag Stud* 2 157, *B* diff), Hos 8 13 *AB*, Ps 108 14 *SB*, 2 Cor 7 15 *SB* ἀναμιμν., Jo 14 26 *A²* (*SB* ϯ ⲙⲡⲙ.) ὑπομιμν.; Lu 17 32 *SB* μνημονεύειν; Sa 12 22 *S* μεριμνᾶν; Is 32 10 *SBF* μνείαν ποιεῖν; Sa 1 1 *SB* φρον. περί; PS 75 *S* ⲉⲕϣⲁⲡⲣ ⲡⲙ. ⲙⲡⲁⲡⲟⲃⲉ, DeV 2 54 *B* ⲉⲡⲓⲣⲓ ⲙⲫⲙ. ⲛⲛⲉⲡⲙⲉⲧⲁⲙⲉⲗⲉⲥ; or with poss pron: Ps 41 4 *SB* ⲁⲣⲓ ⲡⲉⲩⲙ. μιμν., Eph 1 16 *SB* ⲉⲓⲉⲓⲣⲉ ⲙⲡⲉⲧⲛⲙ. μνείαν ποι. Wess 11 169 *S* fathers ⲉⲧⲟⲩⲉⲓⲣⲉ ⲙ-ⲡⲉⲩⲙ. (ἀεί)μνηστος; BSM 8 *B* ⲉⲡⲁⲅⲓⲣⲓ ⲙⲡⲉϥⲙ. ⲁⲡ ϫⲁⲧⲉⲡⲡⲉⲟⲩⲣⲟ = BMis 325 *S* ⲙⲛⲉⲉⲩⲉ, J 65 34 *S* sim ⲡⲓϣⲟⲩⲣ ⲡⲉⲩⲙ., J&C 95 *A²* ⲉⲉⲓⲕⲉⲓⲣⲉ ⲙⲡⲁⲙⲉⲉⲩ(ⲉ added), Lant 74 2 *S* ⲁⲣⲓ ⲡⲁⲙⲉⲉⲩ.

ⲣ ⲡⲙ. *SABF* nn m, *remembrance*: Lev 23 24 *S* (*B* ϫⲓⲡⲉⲣ ⲫⲙ.), Nu 5 15 *SF* (ⲛⲗ ⲡⲓⲙⲟⲩ, *B* ⲙ.), Ps 33 16 *SA* (Cl, *B* ⲙ.), Mt 26 13 *SF* (*B* do), Z 294 *S* commemoration μνημόσυνον, Pro 1 12 *SA* (*B* do), 2 Pet 1 15 *S* (*B* ⲙ. vb) μνήμη, Deu 9 22 *S* (var & *B* ⲙⲣⲁⲁⲩ) μνῆμα, Nu 10 10 *SB*, He 10 3 *SF* (*B* vb) ἀνάμνησις, 2 Tim 1 5 *SB*, Aeg 240 *S* ὑπόμνησις; BAp 75 *S* day of ⲡⲉϥⲣ ⲡⲙ. ⲉⲧⲟⲩⲁⲁⲃ, BSM 32 *B* ⲡⲉⲣ ⲫⲙ. ⲉⲧⲧⲁⲓⲏⲟⲩⲧ of Michael, Osir pl 37 *S* ⲡⲁⲡⲉⲓⲣ ⲡⲙ. ⲉⲧⲁⲡⲟⲩϥ Apa..., Lant 104 *S* whoso shall read ⲡⲓⲣ ⲡⲙ. (*sc* dedicated book), Miss 4 232 *S* brought ϩⲉⲛⲣ ⲡⲙ. to monastery, J 106 66 *S* this small ⲣ ⲡⲙ. (*sc* gift to monastery). ϯ ⲡⲉⲣ ⲡⲙ. *SB, remind*: Jo 14 26 *B* (*SA²* ⲧⲣⲉⲣ ⲡⲙ.), Aeg 245 *S* ⲁⲧⲉⲧⲛϯ ⲡⲉⲣ ⲡⲙ. ⲡⲁⲓ, Miss 8 79 *S* go ⲛⲧⲛϯ ⲡⲣ ⲡⲙ. ⲙⲡⲉⲡⲓⲥⲕⲟⲡⲟⲥ ὑπομιμν.; TstAb 173 *B* Enoch as scribe ⲉϥϯ ⲙⲡⲓⲉⲣ ⲫⲙ. to judge, ShC 73 141 *S* we wish ⲉϯ ⲡⲣ ⲡⲙ. ⲡⲏⲧⲛ as to how &c, Ep 168 *S* here is the brother ⲉⲛⲧⲁϯ ⲡⲣ ⲡⲙ. ⲡⲁⲕ ⲉⲧⲃⲏⲏⲧϥ. ϭⲓ ⲟⲩⲉⲣ ⲫⲙ. *B, get remembrance, be remembered*:

Va 58 136 thief begged Thee ⲉϭⲓ ⲡⲟⲩⲉⲣ ⲫⲙ. ⲙ-
ⲙⲁⲩⲁⲧϥ (cf Lu 23 42). ϣⲉ ⲡⲉⲣ ⲫⲙ. B, nn m,
remembrance : AM 220 ⲡⲉⲕϣ. shall endure, ib 77
all who ⲉⲣⲉϫⲓⲥⲓ ⲓⲉ ϣ. ⲛⲧⲱⲟⲩ ⲛϭⲛⲧϥ (sc dedicated
book), Miss 4 186 book given is ⲟⲩϣ. ϣⲁⲉⲛⲉϩ. For
ϣⲉ cf? ϣⲉ ⲛⲛⲁ (v ⲛⲁ pity). ⲣⲉϥⲉⲣ ⲫⲙ. B, remem-
brancer : BSM 8 may enter without ⲙⲉⲥⲓⲧⲏⲥ ⲓⲉ ⲣ.
= BMis 325 S ⲉⲝⲡⲏⲛⲉⲩⲉ ; ⲙⲉⲧⲣⲉϥⲉⲣ ⲫⲙ., remembrance : CaiEuch 461 ϯⲙ. ⲛⲧⲉ ϯⲕⲁⲕⲓⲁ μνησικακία, MG 25 32 sim. ϫⲓⲡⲉⲣ ⲫⲙ. B nn m f,
meaning same : Lev 2 9 m (S ⲣ ⲡⲙ.) μνημόσυνον,
1 Cor 11 24 m (S ⲇⲟ) ἀνάμνησις ; K 215 chapter-
heading ϫⲉⲛⲡⲓϫ. ⲛⲧⲉⲕⲕⲗⲏⲥⲓⲁ في ذكر (var ib 105
ⲡⲓⲉⲣ ⲫⲙ.) ; DeV 2 55 f ϯⲭ. ⲙⲫϯ.

ⲙⲟⲩⲙⲉ S, ⲙⲟⲩⲛⲙⲉ A, ⲙⲟⲩⲙⲓ B   v ⲙⲟⲟⲩ.

ⲙⲁⲟⲩⲥⲉ (gloss -ⲥⲓ) O nn m, an internal organ,
? liver : AZ 21 100 (III 2). Cf DM 21 31 n, Berl
Wörterb 2 44.

ⲙⲟⲩⲟⲩⲧ SA² (Jo), ⲙⲟⲩⲧ Sᵃ (ST 227) A, ⲙⲱⲟⲩⲧ B (Ez only), ⲙⲉⲩⲧ- S, ⲙⲟⲩⲧ- A, ⲙⲟⲟⲩⲧⲥ S,
ⲙⲁⲩⲧⲥ A, ⲙⲁⲟⲩⲧⲥ A² vb **I** tr, kill : Pro 24 11 SA
κτείνειν, Ge 18 25 S, Ex 4 23 A, Ps 93 6 S, Ez 7
16, 33 27 SB, Mt 14 5 S (F ϧⲱⲧⲉⲃ), Jo 8 22 SA²
(all B ϧⲱⲧⲉⲃ), Ps 138 19 S (B ⲧⲁⲕⲟ) ἀποκτείνειν, Pro
10 3 SA (B ϭ.) (λιμο)κτονεῖν ; Deu 17 7 S, Job 5
2 S, Mt 10 21 S, Ro 8 13 S (all B ϭ.) θανατοῦν ;
Lev 23 30 S, Pro 15 1 S (Aeg 246, var & A ⲧⲁⲕⲟ),
Mk 9 22 S (all B ⲧⲁⲕⲟ) ἀπολλύναι ; Mt 2 16 S, Ac
25 3 S (both B ϭ.) ἀναιρεῖν ; Deu 19 6 S (B ⲇⲟ)
φονεύειν ; Col 3 5 S (B ⲇⲟ) νεκροῦν ; ShC 42 S ⲉⲅⲙ.
ⲙⲙⲟϥ before his time, ShA 1 167 S sought ⲡⲥⲁⲙ.
ⲙⲡⲭⲥ, Pcod 31 S will not ⲙⲉⲩⲧ ⲟⲩⲯⲩⲭⲏ, ST
227 S ⲙⲡⲁⲧϥⲙ. ⲙⲙⲟⲓ, Cl 45 4 A ⲁⲩⲙⲁⲩⲧϥ.
ShA 1 169, 2 124 S for ⲙⲟⲟⲩⲧ prob l ⲙⲟⲩⲟⲩⲧ.
II intr (rare) : Deu 32 39 SA (Cl, B ϭ.), Sa 16 14
S, 2 Cor 3 6 S (B ⲇⲟ) ἀποκτ., 1 Kg 2 6 S θαν.
ⲣⲉϥⲙ. S, killer : BHom 110 ⲣⲉϥⲙⲉⲩⲧ ⲯⲩⲭⲏ ; as
adj, deadly : Job 33 23 (B ⲛⲧⲉ ⲫⲙⲟⲩ), R 2 2 23
θανατηφόρος, Nu 21 6 (B ϭ.) θανατοῦν, RNC 42
ⲙⲁⲧⲟⲩ ⲡⲣ. θανάσιμος. V ⲙⲟⲩ.

ⲙⲫⲏ B   v ⲙⲡⲉ- II.

ⲙⲫⲱⲣ B   v ⲙⲡⲱⲣ.

ⲙⲉⲭⲓⲣ SB   v ⲙϣⲓⲣ.

ⲙⲟⲭⲥ   v ⲙⲕⲁϩ (ⲙⲟⲕϩⲥ).

ⲙⲉⲭϩ A   v ⲙⲁⲕϩ.

ⲙⲛⲏϣ B   v ⲙⲛⲏϣⲉ.

ⲙⲁϣⲉ S, ⲙⲁϩⲉ A, ⲙⲁϣⲓ B, ⲙⲉϣⲓ F (?) nn f
m (once), balance : Lev 19 35 SB, Job 6 2 SB, Pro

11 1 B (SA ϣⲓ, ϩⲓ), Mic 6 11 AB, Ap 6 5 SB
ζυγός ; Ez 5 1 SB ζ. στάθμιον, Lev 26 26 B (S ϣⲓ)
σταθμός ; Sa 11 23 S πλάστιγξ ; K 50 B in Zodiac
ϯⲙ. الميزان, P 44 19 S ⲙⲁⲁϣⲉ do ; C 86 277 B
ⲟⲩⲥⲁ ⲡⲧⲉ ϯⲙ. wherein ox weighed, Va 58 135 B
ⲟⲩⲙ....ⲣⲁⲕⲥ ϥⲟⲛϫⲥ, ShC 73 57 S ⲉϥϣⲏⲩ ϩⲛⲧⲙ.,
Vi ostr 164 S ⲟⲩⲙ. ⲙⲡⲉⲛⲓⲡⲉ, WS 94 S ring ϩⲟⲩⲣ
of ⲙ., Ryl 239 S ⲟⲩⲙ. ⲛϣⲓ ϩⲏⲡⲉ, Rec 6 66 S ⲧ]ⲙ.
ⲡⲡⲧⲓⲙⲉ (cf ζυγῷ τῆς κώμης, ⲛϣⲓ ⲙⲡⲕⲁⲥⲧⲣⲟⲛ), BM
598 F ϫⲓ ⲧⲁⲙ....ⲟⲩⲁⲁⲧⲉⲥ ⲡⲉⲛ. ⲡⲓⲙⲁϣ ⲡⲧⲉ ⲡⲓ-
ⲕⲁⲡ B, plumb-line : K 124 الخيط ⲙⲓⲍⲁⲛ. ⲥⲁ ⲡⲙ.
B, balance maker, seller : K 114 ⲡⲓⲥ. موازني.

ⲙⲁϣⲓ B axe   v ⲙⲁϫⲉ.

ⲙⲁⲁϣⲓ F   v ⲙⲟⲟϣⲉ.

ⲙⲁϣⲟ in ⲉⲙⲁϣⲟ S (? archaic), -ϣⲱ (often ⲙ-
ⲙⲁϣⲱ) B, -ϣⲁ SꟻF advb, greatly, very : Ge 7 17 B
(S ⲉⲙⲁⲧⲉ), Ps 6 2 S (var ⲉⲙⲁⲧⲉ) B, Lam 5 22 BF
(S ⲇⲟ), Mt 26 22 BF (S ⲇⲟ), Va 57 11 B ⲉⲧⲟⲓ ⲛϭⲁⲉ
ⲙⲙ. σφόδρα ; Ge 4 5 B (A Cl ⲙⲡϣⲁ), Mk 16 2 BF
(S diff) λίαν ; Job 19 11 B (S ⲡⲟϭ) δεινῶς ; 1 Cor
16 12 B (S ⲉⲙⲁⲧⲉ) πολλά ; Nu 6 2 S (B ϫⲉⲛⲟⲩ-
ⲙⲉⲛⲓϣϯ) μεγάλως ; 1 Pet 1 2 S (B ⲁϣⲁⲓ vb) πληθύνειν ; Ge 6 5 B ἐπιμελῶς ; 2 Cor 12 15 F (S ⲇⲟ,
B ⲛϩⲟⲩⲟ) περισσοτέρως ; Ac 25 10 B (S ⲛϩⲟⲩⲟ)
κάλλιον ; PS 178 S ⲁⲥⲧⲉⲗⲏⲗ ⲉⲙ., ib 190 ⲟⲩⲛⲟϭ
ⲡⲣⲁϣⲉ ⲉⲙ., ib 229 S ⲥⲉⲛⲁⲣ ϩⲟⲧⲉ ⲉⲙ. (cf ib 21 ⲉ-
ⲙⲁⲧⲉ), ib 101 S ⲉⲩⲛⲁϣⲧ ⲉⲙ. (ib 44 sim ⲉⲙⲁⲧⲉ),
DeV 2 33 B such thoughts ⲟⲩⲟⲛ ⲣⲏϯ ⲉⲙ. ⲉⲑⲣⲉⲛϭⲓ
ⲡⲟⲩϫⲓⲟⲣⲱⲥⲓⲥ ⲛϩⲏⲧⲟⲩ, MIE 2 402 B door ⲉϥⲟⲩⲏⲛ
ⲉⲙ., BSM 44 B ⲉϥⲟⲓ ⲛⲛⲓϣϯ ⲉⲙ. = BMis 391 S
ⲉⲙⲁⲧⲉ, C 43 99 B ⲟⲩⲛⲓϣϯ ⲡⲉⲙⲕⲁϩ ⲙⲙ., BSM
128 B ⲉⲩϭⲟϫⲓ ⲉⲙ. ⲉϫⲉⲛⲡⲟⲩⲉⲣⲏⲟⲩ, Mor 53 6 Sꟻ
ⲁϥⲣⲓⲙⲉ ⲙⲙⲁⲧⲉ (l ⲉⲙⲁⲧⲉ) ⲉⲙⲁϣⲁ, BKU 1 31 (9)
S ϯⲣⲏⲛⲏ ⲛⲏⲧⲛ ⲉⲙ., Ryl 113 S glossary ϩⲁⲕⲟⲧⲟⲡ ·
ⲡⲣⲁϭⲱⲡⲧ ⲉⲙ. Iterated S : PS 7 ⲉϥⲣ ⲟⲩⲟⲉⲓⲛ ⲉⲙ.
ⲉⲙ., Br 108 ⲟⲩⲛⲟϭ ⲡⲣⲁϣⲉ ⲉⲙ. ⲉⲙ. Cf ⲙⲡϣⲁ A.

ⲙⲉϣⲉ, ⲙⲉϣⲁ S, ⲙⲉϩⲉ A (once) vb, a not
know : Sh(?)Ep 66 ⲙⲉⲓϩⲉ ⲉⲑⲉ ⲡⲉⲓⲙⲉ...ⲙⲉϣⲁⲓ ϫⲉ-
ⲉⲛⲁϫⲉ ⲟⲩ, ShLeyd 411 ⲡⲟⲉ ⲟⲛ ⲉⲧⲉⲙⲉϣⲉ (f) ⲉⲛ-
ⲧⲱⲱϣ (v CR Acad Leningrad '25 23), ShA 1 76
ⲙⲉϣⲉ (f) ϫⲉⲡⲓⲙⲉ ⲏ ⲟⲩⲛⲉ ϫⲉⲉⲣⲉ (f) ⲥⲟⲩⲱⲛⲟⲩ, ib
78 he saith ⲡⲉⲧⲉⲙ. (f) ⲉⲣⲟϥ ϫⲉⲡⲓⲙⲉ, ShBMOr
8800 6 ⲉϥⲥⲟⲟⲩⲛ ϫⲉⲙⲉϣⲁϥ ⲙⲡⲛⲁⲩ when he shall
leave world (var R 2 3 11 ⲙⲉϣⲁⲕ), ShIF 180 ⲙⲡⲣ-
ⲧⲁⲡⲣⲉⲧ ⲡⲉⲧⲉⲙⲉϣⲁⲡ ⲉⲣⲟⲟⲩ ϫⲉⲟⲩⲡⲉ ⲉⲓⲙⲏⲧⲓ ⲛⲧⲛ-
ⲥⲟⲩⲱⲛⲟⲩ ⲛϣⲟⲣⲡ. b ⲙ. ⲡⲓⲙ as indef pron,
anyone, such & such, so & so : Z 296 ⲙ. ⲡ. ⲡϣⲏⲣⲉ
ϣⲏⲙ = MG 25 71 B ⲡⲁⲫⲙⲁⲡ (v ⲙⲁⲡ), ib 339
addressing corpse ⲙ. ⲡ. where didst thou &c ?,
KKS 24 addressing woman ⲙ. ⲡ. = MG 25 213 B
ⲧⲁⲛⲓⲙ, Wess 18 104 ⲁⲙ. ⲡ. ⲡⲣⲱⲙⲉ ⲣ ϩⲁϩ ⲙⲡⲉ-

ⲑⲟⲟⲩ ὁ δεῖνα; Z 302 go to ⲙ. ⲡ. ⲡⲁⲡⲁⲭⲱⲣⲓⲧⲏⲥ
(PL 73 963 *illum*), BKU 1 5 loose bonds of ⲙ. ⲡ.,
Mor 28 230 saw him with ⲙ. ⲡ. ⲡⲉⲣⲙⲉ, BMis 456
ⲙⲓϣ ⲡⲡ. ⲛϫⲓⲁⲕⲟⲡ.

ⲙⲉϣⲁⲕ, ⲙⲏ. S, ⲙⲉϩⲉⲕ A, *thou knowest not*, so
perhaps (v AZ 32 128): Job 1 5 (B ⲙⲏⲡⲱⲥ), Si 19
12 (but 13 ⲙⲉϣⲁϥ), Lu 3 15 (B = Gk) μή ποτε,
1 Thes 3 5 (B ⲙⲏⲡⲱⲥ ⲁⲛ, F ⲡⲁⲡⲧⲱⲥ) μή πως, Jos
9 13 μή; Ge 32 20 (B diff), Jer 5 4 (B ⲁⲣⲏⲟⲩ), Lu
20 13 (B do) ἴσως; Ps 30 22 (B = Gk), Is 56 3 (B
do) ἄρα; Philem 15 (B do) τάχα; Jos 2 5 εἰ; Miss
4 653 ⲉϥⲁⲣⲡⲁ ϫⲉⲙ. ϥⲡⲁⲣⲱⲡ λαθεῖν πειρωμένου;
Gk om: BHom 14 38 ⲁⲗⲗⲁ ⲙ. ⲕⲡⲁⲭⲟⲟⲥ ἀ. λέ-
γεις; PS 6 they thought ⲙ. ⲉⲅⲡⲁⲥⲗ ⲡⲕⲟⲥⲙⲟⲥ,
ShC 73 160 ⲙ. ⲡⲧⲉⲟⲩⲁⲡⲁⲡⲧⲏⲙⲁ ϣⲱⲡⲉ (var ⲉⲓⲙⲏⲧⲉⲓ), ib 72 ⲙ. ⲣⲱ ⲟⲩⲡ ⲣⲉⲛϣⲁϫⲉ ⲡⲣⲏⲧⲟⲩ that
are not seemly, ShA 2 147 men deposit not treasure in house ⲙ. ⲡⲥⲉⲡⲁⲡⲁⲣⲁⲧⲉ...ⲁⲛ *unless they have
(first) visited it*, ShBor 246 55 ⲙⲏⲡⲱⲥ ⲡⲧⲉⲡⲉⲡ-
ⲧⲁⲩϫⲟⲟⲩ...befall us ⲏ ⲙ. ⲣⲱ ⲡⲧⲓⲧⲁⲣ ⲃⲟⲗ ⲉⲣⲟϥ,
BHom 46 ⲙ. ϥⲡⲁⲧⲁⲓⲉ poor (var R 2 2 30 ⲧⲁⲭⲁ
ⲣⲱ), TU 43 3 A doubted ϫⲉⲙ. ⲡⲧⲁϥ ⲉⲡⲡⲉ, Miss
8 255 ⲁⲣⲏⲩ ⲕⲡⲁⲉϣ ⲧⲱⲟⲩⲡ & I bring thee to shrine
ⲙ. ⲡⲧⲉⲡⲉϥⲡⲁ ⲧⲁϩⲟⲕ, BMis 571 I fear ϫⲉⲙ. ⲁⲣⲏⲩ
ⲡϥⲧⲙ̄ⲡϣⲁ ⲁⲛ; ShC 42 48 ⲙ. ⲡⲉⲓϫⲱⲟⲡ... & *now*
or & *as to* (v BIF 28 69). V ⲉⲙⲉϣⲙⲓⲉ.

ⲙⲏⲏϣⲉ SA²F, ⲙⲏϣⲉ A², ⲙⲉⲓϣⲉ, ⲙⲓϣⲉ A,
ⲙⲏϣ B, ⲙⲏⲏϣⲓ, ⲙⲉϣⲓ F (BKU 1 26 (1)) nn m,
a *multitude* (persons or things), *crowd, troop*: Job
4 3 SB, Ps 70 7 S sg B pl, 2 Cor 12 21 SBF, He
12 15 S pl B sg πολύς, πολλοί; Ex 12 6 SB, Lev
25 36 B (S ⲣⲟⲅⲟ), Ps 43 12 S (B ⲁϣⲁⲓ), Ac 14 4
SB πλῆθος, Deu 7 7 B ⲟϣ ⲙⲙ. (S ⲟϣ ⲉⲙⲁⲧⲉ) πο-
λυπληθεῖν, Ez 26 2 B ⲉⲑⲙⲉϩ ⲙⲙ. πλήρης; Ge 19
4 B (S = Gk), Is 10 22 B (S do), Ez 17 15 B λαός;
Sa 6 27 S, BHom 51 S δῆμος, ib 47 S ⲉⲧⲙⲉϩ ⲙⲙ.
πάνδημος: EpJer 5 SBF, Dan 10 6 SB, Mk 15 15
SBF ὄχλος, Am 7 16 SAB ὄχλ(ἀγωγεῖν); Job 30 28
S (B ⲑⲱⲟⲩⲧⲉ) ἐκκλησία; Ez 37 10 B συναγωγή; Jud
8 6 S δύναμις (var στρατεία); 1 Kg 4 10 S τάγμα;
PS 151 S despised in sight of ⲟⲩⲙ., Miss 4 604 S
general & ⲡⲉϥⲙ. = C 89 164B, JTS 10 397 S throng
of servants ⲡⲁⲣ ⲡⲙ. ⲡⲟⲩⲡⲟⲗⲓⲥ *population*, MG 25
260 B I wished to say ⲟⲩⲙ. ⲡⲱⲧⲉⲡ, DeV 2 162 B
who cast ⲟⲩⲙ. into treasury, Miss 4 113 B ϣⲁⲡϭⲓ
ⲟⲩⲙ. from ashes;   pl: Ex 4 30 B, Ps 59 10 S,
Pro 5 23 SA, Ez 16 40 B (S sg); CDan 87 B appointed for him ⲡϥⲁⲡⲙ. περισσότερον ἀνάλωμα.
b +gen ⲛ- as adj, *many, great*: Ge 40 4 S (B om),
Ps 21 12 S (B ⲑⲟ), Ac 1 3 B (S ϩⲁϩ), Ro 12 4 S
(PS 254, var ϩⲁϩ) B πολύς, Jer 19 6 B πολυ(ἀν-
δρ ιον), EpJer 46 B (F ⲡⲁϭ) πολυ(χρόνιος); Ge 48
19 SB, Is 5 13 SBF, Ez 23 42 B (S ⲁϣⲏ) πλῆθος,

EpJer 2 B (S ⲡⲁϣⲉ, F ⲁⲧⲁ), Ac 14 17 B (S ϩⲁϩ),
ib 27 20 B (S ⲁⲡⲥ) πλείων, Ps 105 43 B (S do), Is
42 20 B (S do) πλεονάκις; Ac 9 23 SB, Ro 15 23
B (S do) ἱκανός; Lu 15 29 S (B ⲟⲩⲏⲣ), BHom 2
S ⲡⲉⲓⲙ. παρετὴ τοσοῦτος; PS 46 S what I have
told ⲡⲟⲩⲙ. ⲛⲥⲟⲡ, R 1 3 64 S ⲟⲩⲙ. ⲡⲉⲟⲟⲩ around
him, Va 63 2 B ⲟⲩⲙ. ⲡⲁⲅⲁⲑⲟⲡ = BMis 364 S
ⲁϣⲏ, C 43 220 B ⲡⲁⲓⲙ. ⲡⲥⲡⲟϥ, BSM 118 B ϩⲉⲛⲟⲩⲙ. ⲙⲙⲁ.   **c** as advb, *greatly*: Mk 5 10 B
ⲡⲣⲁⲡⲙ. (S ⲉⲙⲁⲧⲉ) πολλά; MG 25 338 B ⲉⲧⲁⲅ-
ϫⲉⲙ ⲣⲏⲟⲩ ⲡⲟⲩⲙ. = ROC 17 365 ⟨⟩, C 86 274
B ⲫⲏ ⲉⲧⲟⲓ ⲡⲣⲉϣϣⲓⲡⲓ ⲡⲟⲩⲙ.

Concord: sg with sg predicate: Nu 21 6 S ⲁϥⲙⲟⲩ (var ⲁⲩ-) ⲛ̄ϭⲓ ⲟⲩⲙ. B, Zeph 1 11 A ⲡⲉⲓⲙ....
ⲉϥⲧⲓⲧⲁⲡⲧ, Mk 4 1 S ⲡⲙ....ⲉⲡⲉϥⲁϩⲉⲣⲁⲧϥ (B ⲁⲩ-
ⲑⲱⲟⲩⲧ), Ac 15 12 B ⲁϥⲭⲁ ⲣⲱϥ ⲡϫⲉ ⲡⲓⲙ. (S ⲡⲙ.
ⲕⲁ ⲣⲱϥ), AP 21 A² ⲡⲙ....ⲁϥⲣⲓⲙⲉ, P 129¹⁵ 19 S
ⲁⲩⲡⲟϭ ⲙⲙ. ⲟⲩⲁϩϥ (var BMis 235 S ⲟⲩⲁϩⲟⲩ),
BMOr 8811 225 S ⲟⲩⲙ. ⲡⲣⲱⲃ...ⲉⲓⲣⲉ ⲙⲙⲟϥ;
sg with pl predicate: Pro 7 26 SAB ⲟⲩⲙ. ⲁⲥⲧⲁⲩ-
ⲟⲟⲩ ⲉϩⲣⲁⲓ, Jo 4 41 A² ⲟⲩⲙ....ⲁⲩⲣ ⲡⲓⲥⲧⲉⲩⲉ (B ⲙ.
pl), Cl 5 4 A ⲟⲩⲙ....ⲁϥϥⲓ ϩⲁⲣⲁⲩ; ShC 73 82 S
ⲟⲩⲙ. ⲉⲅⲥⲟⲟⲩϩ, BMis 46 S ⲡⲉⲓⲙ. ⲡⲥⲡⲟϥ ⲡⲧⲁⲓⲡⲁⲣ-
ⲧⲟⲩ, C 43 6 B ⲡⲓⲙ....ⲁⲩⲧ ⲱⲟⲩ;   pl with pl
predicate: Mt 4 25 SB, Ac 2 6 B (S sg); PS 172
S ϩⲉⲛⲙ. ⲡⲁⲣⲭⲱⲡ...ⲁⲩⲡⲱⲧ, C 43 98 B ⲡⲓⲙ. ⲁⲩⲱϣ ⲉⲃⲟⲗ, MIE 2 396 B ϩⲁⲡⲙ. ⲡⲣⲁⲗⲏⲧ ⲉⲅⲟⲩⲉϩ
= BAp 122 S sg.

ⲉⲣ ⲟⲩⲙ. B, *be a crowd*: Ac 28 23 (S diff) πλείων,
Ge 30 30 (S Gk diff).

V ⲗⲉⲙⲏⲏϣⲉ.

ⲙⲓϣⲉ SA², ⲙⲉⲓϣⲉ S, ⲙⲓⲉⲓϣⲉ, ⲙⲉⲓϣⲉ, ⲙⲓϣⲉ A,
ⲙⲏϣⲓ BF, ⲙⲉϣ-, ⲙⲁϣ-, ⲙⲁϣϥ, ⲙⲁϣⲓ† B vb I intr,
fight: Lev 24 10 S (B ⲙⲗⲁⲃ), Is 28 20 S (B †),
Ja 4 2 S (B ϣϭⲡⲏⲡ) μάχεσθαι, Ac 23 9 S (B ⲙⲗⲁⲃ)
διαμ.; Ap 19 11 S (B om) πολεμεῖν, Ps 101 5 B
(S ϣⲱϣⲉ), Ap 8 12 B (S do) πλήσσειν; Jo 18 36
SA² (B † ⲉϩⲣⲏⲓ ⲉϫⲉⲡ-) ἀγωνίζεσθαι; El 74 A goeth
forth ⲁⲙⲉⲓϣⲉ, BMis 287 S none receiveth crown
except ⲡⲉϥⲙ. ⲕⲁⲗⲱⲥ, AM 145 B take courage ⲡⲧⲉ-
ⲧⲙ. ϩⲉⲡⲡⲓⲁⲅⲱⲡ.

—— ⲉ- SB, a *fight for* (? *dat commodi*), or in-
tensive *fight bravely*: Est 9 16 S βοηθεῖν dat; R 1
3 17 S hitherto ⲉⲕⲙ. ⲉⲣⲟⲕ ⲙⲁⲅⲁⲁⲕ fight now
ⲉⲭⲱⲟⲩ *for them*, BAp 170 S ⲙⲁⲣⲡⲙ. ⲉⲣⲟⲛ whilst
repentance is to be had (= BMOr 4523 182 ...جاهد
نفوسنا (على), Mor 31 92 S ⲙ. ⲉⲣⲱⲧⲛ in purity &
peace, AM 305 B martyr to fellow-prisoners ⲙ.
ⲉⲣⲱⲧⲉⲛ for ἀγών is not every day (cf C 43 73);
v also ⲙ. ⲉϫⲉⲡ-.   **b** *fight against, attack*: 1·Cor
8 12 B (but var ⲡ-, SF ⲣⲱϥⲧ) τύπτειν; Bor 226 171
S vices ⲙ. ⲉⲣⲟⲥ (sc soul), R 1 5 26 = BM 337 S
shepherd & sheep-stealers ⲁϥⲙ. ⲉⲣⲟⲟⲩ ⲁϥϫⲓⲧⲟⲩ

(= *ib* 25 he smote 3 of them & took sheep from them, *cf* Synax 1 324).

—— ⲉϫⲛ- *SBF, fight for, on behalf of*: Deu 3 22 *S* (*B* = Gk) πολεμ. περί, Si 29 16 *S* πολ. ὑπέρ ; Sa 10 21 *S* ὑπερμάχ.; Si 4 29 *S* (*B* ✝ ⲉϫⲉⲛ-) ἀγων. περί, Jude 3 *S* (*B* ⲉⲣ ⲁⲧⲱⲛ.) ἐπαγων. dat ; Jud 9 17 *S* παρατάσσεσθαι ὑπέρ ; BM 300 *S* ⲛⲧⲁϫⲙ. ⲁⲛ ⲉⲧⲃⲉⲣⲉⲡⲭⲣⲏⲙⲁ ⲟⲩⲇⲉ ⲉϫⲡⲣⲉⲡⲏ, PS 49 *S* I await him ⲡϭⲙ. ⲉϫⲱⲓ, R 1 3 17 *S* (as above)...ⲉϫⲱⲟⲩ ⲛⲁⲙ-ⲙⲁⲕ ; *strike upon*: Mk 15 19 *F* (*SB* ϩⲓⲟⲩⲉ) τύπτ. dat ; Mus 40 187 *B* waves ⲙ. ⲉϫⲉⲛϯⲡⲉⲧⲣⲁ.   ⲙ. ⲉϩⲣⲁⲓ ⲉϫⲛ- *SB, fight for*: Jos 1 14 *S* συμμάχ. dat, Bor 248 8 *S* ⲉϫⲙ. ⲉϩ. ⲉϫⲁⲡⲗⲗⲟⲩ συνήγορος εἶναι ; Pey *Gram* 166 *S* Jesus ⲙ. ⲉϩ. ⲉϫⲱⲓ, AM 21 *B* that we ⲙ. ⲉϩ. ⲉϫⲉⲛⲡⲉϥⲣⲁⲛ.

—— ⲙⲛ-, ⲛⲉⲙ- *SA²BF, fight with, against, chide*: Ge 31 36 *S* (*B* ϣⲱⲡⲧ) μάχ. dat, Jo 6 52 *SA²* (*B* ✝ ⲟⲩⲃⲉ-), BHom 50 *S* ⲉϥⲙ. ⲙⲡⲟⲩϭⲣⲓⲙⲉ μάχ. πρός, Ps 151 tit *S* (*B* ✝ ⲛⲉⲙ-) μονομάχ. dat, AP 16 *A²* ⲙ. ⲙⲡⲛⲑⲏⲣⲓⲟⲛ θηριομάχ.; Ex 17 8 *S* (*B* = Gk), Is 30 32 *SF* (*B* ⲃⲱⲧⲥ), Z 347 *S* ⲉⲓⲙ. ⲙⲡⲡⲁ-ⲙⲉⲉⲩⲉ = MG 25 219 *B* (var) ✝ ⲛⲉⲙ- πολ., Ex 1 10 *A* (*B* do) ἐκπολ.; Ge 32 24 *S* (*B* ✝ ⲛⲉⲙ-) πα-λαίειν μετά ; Jud 5 20 *S* παρατάσσ. μετά ; Miss 4 634 *S* parents ⲙ. ⲙⲡⲡϣⲱⲥ saying Why hast not &c = C 41 9 *B* ⲉⲙⲗⲁϭ, MG 17 307 *S* ⲛϥⲙ. ⲙⲡ-ⲡⲉⲅⲣⲙⲡⲏ if found careless = C 89 179 *B* do, AM 122 *B* will teach you ⲉϣⲧⲉⲙⲙ. ⲛⲉⲙⲡⲓⲡⲣⲟⲥⲧⲁⲅⲙⲁ.

—— ⲟⲩⲃⲉ- *S, fight against*: Jer 41 7 (*B* ✝ ⲟⲩⲃⲉ-) πολ. ἐπί.; BHom 50 ⲉⲥⲙ. ⲟⲩⲃⲉⲣⲟⲟⲩⲧ παλαίειν ; BMar 50 ⲁⲕⲙ. ⲟⲩⲃⲉⲙⲡⲁⲑⲟⲥ.

—— ϩⲓϫⲉⲛ- *B, fight on behalf of*: AM 26 will not ⲙ. ϩ. a renegade king.

II tr *B, strike*: Deu 21 1 (*S* ϩⲱⲧⲃ), 2 Kg 1 25 (*S* diff) τραυματίζειν ; Ps 77 20 (*S* = Gk) πατάσσ.; Jer 5 6 (*S* ϣⲱⲱϭⲉ) παίειν ; Ryl 453 337 ⲧⲉϥϫⲫⲉ ⲙ.✝ ; MG 25 121 ⲁⲕⲙⲁϣⲧ ϩⲓⲧⲉⲛⲡⲉⲕⲑⲉⲃⲓⲟ, C 89 105 ⲁϥⲙ. ⲙⲙⲟϥ (*sc* staff) ϩⲓϫⲉⲛⲡⲓⲕⲁϩⲓ, Cat 49 ⲡⲧⲉⲛϣⲧⲉⲙⲙⲁϣ ⲧⲟⲩⲥⲩⲛⲉⲓⲇⲏⲥⲓⲥ. With ⲛ- of instrument : Ex 17 5 (*S* ϩⲱⲣⲧ) πατάσσ. ἐν ; Is 22 2 (*S* diff) τραυματίας ἐν, Pro 7 23† (*SA* ϣⲱ.) πλήσσ. dat ; Jer 18 21 (*S* Gk diff). *Cf* ⲙ. ⲉ-.   With ϫⲉⲛ- of instr : Nu 20 11 (*S* ⲣⲱ.) πατάσσ. dat ; Pro 10 3 (*SA* do) τύπ. dat ; Va 57 191 resounding goblets ⲉⲩⲙ. ⲙⲙⲟⲩ ϫⲉⲛⲡⲟⲩⲧⲏⲃ ἐνείρων κυμβα-λίζειν.

—— ⲉⲃⲟⲗ *B, meaning same*: Is 14 29 (*S* ϣⲁⲁⲣⲉ) παίειν.

—— *SAB* nn m, *fight, quarrel*: Ge 13 7 *S* (*B* ϣⲟⲛⲧ), Pro 15 18 *SA* μάχη ; Eph 6 12 *S* (*B* ✝) πάλη ; Pro 21 9 *A* (*S* ϣⲟⲛⲧ) ἀδικία ; Cl 30 1 *A* συμπλοκή ; 2 Tim 4 6 *S* (*B* Gk diff), ShMun 94 *S* ϩⲉⲛⲙ. ⲙⲡϩⲉⲛϯⲧⲱⲛ ; K 54 *B* ⲡⲓⲙ. of sun .

---

eclipse.   + gen ⲛ- *S*: Deu 1 41 (*B* = Gk) ϩⲛⲁⲁⲩ ⲙⲙ., 2 Kg 1 27 (*B* do) ⲥⲟⲧⲃⲉϥ ⲙⲙ.

ⲙⲁ ⲙⲙ. *S, fighting place*: Jud 6 26 παράταξις ; Jer 40 4 (*B* diff) χάραξ ; Ryl 62 1 athlete ⲉϥϩⲙⲡⲙⲁ ⲙⲙ.

ⲁⲧⲙ. *B, not attacked, unhurt*: AM 272 keep people ⲛⲁ. ἄτρωτος ; TEuch 1 213 keep her (nun) ⲛⲁ. παρρεπηικοτⲥ .

ⲣⲉϥⲙ. *SAB, fighter*: Jos 5 6 *S* μάχιμος, Joel 3 9 *SA* (*B* ⲣⲉϥϩⲱⲧⲥ) μαχητής, ClPr 30 7 *S* ⲣ. ⲙⲛⲡⲛⲉ θεομάχος, Is 13 4 *S* ⲣ. ⲙⲛϭⲗ (*B* ⲣⲉϥϯ ⲙⲡⲣⲟⲡⲗⲟⲛ) ὁπλομάχος ; Sa 18 15 *S* πολεμιστής, Is 27 4 f *S* (*B* ⲃⲏⲧⲥⲉ) πολεμία, BMar 104 *S* ⲟⲩⲣ. ⲉⲙⲁⲧⲉ πολεμικώ-τατος ; C 43 235 *B* Christ calls martyr ⲡⲁⲣ. ϫⲉⲡⲓⲁⲧⲱⲡ, BM 232 253 *S* ⲧⲉⲓⲣ. ⲧⲁⲡⲟⲗⲓⲁ.   As adj, *hostile, quarrelsome*: ⲣⲱⲙⲉ ⲡⲣ., Jud 12 2 *S*, ⲥϩⲓⲙⲉ ⲡⲣ. Pro 21 19 *SA* μάχιμος ; Jer 52 7 *S* (*B* ⲣ. ⲛⲃⲉⲧⲥ) πολεμιστής ; ShBMOr 8810 372 *S* ⲗⲁⲥ ⲡⲣ.   ⲣ ⲣⲉϥⲙ., *be quarrelsome, hostile*: JA '75 5 238 *S* ⲙⲡⲣⲣ ⲣ. μάχ. γίνεσθαι, C 86 90 *B* became ⲣ. ⲛ-ⲕⲁⲗⲱⲥ.; P 131³ 33 *S* among vices ⲧⲙⲛⲧⲣⲉϥⲙ.

ϭⲓⲛ-, ϫⲓⲛⲙ. *SB, art of fighting*: Bor 226 166 *S* knowing not ⲧϭ. τὸ πῶς πολεμῆσαι ; Va 58 147 *B* ⲟⲩⲙⲛϣ ⲛϫ. whereby to catch thief, ShR 2 3 12 *S* ⲙⲡⲧⲁϥ ⲕⲉϭ. more potent than sickness & poverty, BMis 293 *S* ⲧϭ. (*l* ⲧⲉⲕϭ.) ⲉϫⲱⲓ in war, Z 295 *S* if hast ⲟⲩϭ. let us cast it on corpse παλαίωμα (mis-understood, *cf* παλαίειν.   V LMis 170).

ⲙⲟⲟϣⲉ, ⲙⲟϣⲉ (Psalt ViSitz 155 1 11) *S*, ⲙⲁⲁϩⲉ *AA²*, ⲙⲁϩⲉ *Sᵃ*, ⲙⲟϩⲉ *Sᵃ* (J 68, ST 359), ⲙⲟϣⲓ *B*, ⲙⲁⲁϣⲓ, ⲙⲁϣⲓ *F*, imperat ⲙⲁⲁϣ, ⲙⲁϣ *F* vb intr, *walk, go* on land or water, *cf* ? مشـﯽ : Hos 5 15 *SA* (*B* ϣⲉ), Jo 4 50 *BF* (ⲙⲁⲁϣⲓ, *SA²* ⲃⲱⲕ) πορεύεσθαι, Lu 4 37 *S* (*B* ⲥⲱⲣ ⲉⲃⲟⲗ) ἐκπορ.; Pro 6 22 *SAB*, Jo 5 8 *SAF*, 1 Cor 3 3 *SBF* περιπατεῖν ; Deu 5 30 *S* (var ⲃ., *B* ϣⲉ), Is 26 20 *S* (*B* do) βαδί-ζειν ; Dan 3 48 *B* (*S* ⲉⲓ ⲉⲃⲟⲗ) διοδεύειν ; Jer 10 5 *SB* ἐπιβαίνειν, Lev 16 22 *S* neg (*B* ⲁⲧϩⲱⲙⲓ), Jer 6 8 *SB* neg ἄβατος (*cf* ⲁⲧⲙ.); Mt 13 25 *F* (*S* ⲃ., *B* ϣⲉ) ἀπέρχεσθαι, Ps 65 6 *S* (*B* ⲥⲓⲛⲓ), Hab 1 11 *SA* (*B* do), Lu 5 15 *S* (*B* ⲥⲱⲣ ⲉⲃ.) διέρχ., Tob 8 17 *S* ἐξέρχ., Lu 17 7 *S* (*B* diff) παρέρχ., Sa 6 17 *S* περιέρχ.; 2 Thes 3 1 *S* (*B* ϭⲟϫⲓ), BHom 30 *S* overfed horse ⲙⲉϥⲉϣ ⲙ. τρέχειν ; 1 Cor 12 2 *B* (*S* ⲃ.) ἀπάγειν, Mk 15 21 *S* (*B* ⲥⲓ.) παράγ., Jo 4 16 *F* ⲙⲁϣ (*S* ⲃ., *B* ϣⲉ) ὑπάγ.; Ac 20 13 *SB* πεζεύειν ; Lu 15 13 *S* (*B* ⲱⲛⲓ) ζῆν ; BAp 26 *S* ⲁϥⲙ. ⲁϥⲃⲱⲕ into city, BMis 574 *S* ⲙ. ⲛⲧⲉⲧⲛⲃⲱⲕ & preach, PBu 6 *S* ⲁⲥⲃⲱⲕ ⲛⲁⲥ ⲉⲥⲙ. there being no ship, J 68 16 *S* ⲉⲓⲁⲛⲣ ⲉⲓⲙ. ⲉⲓϩⲛ ⲣ(ⲟ)ⲟⲩϣ (*cf* PLond 5 180 ἐπὶ ποδῶν βαδίζων), ShA 2 276 *S* I came ⲉⲓⲙ. ϩⲛⲛⲁⲟⲩⲉ-ⲣⲏⲧⲉ, C 89 201 *B* ⲁϥⲙ. ⲡⲉϥϭⲁⲗⲁⲩϫ, ST 228

S^a ϭⲙ. ⲡⲣⲁⲧϥ, AM 259 B ⲉⲓⲙ. ⲕⲁⲧⲁ ⲙⲁ recruiting, ShA 1 434 S I will desist for I see ϫⲉⲧⲉⲧⲛ-ⲟⲩⲱϣ ⲙ., LMär 39 S ⲙ. ϣⲁⲣⲧⲟⲟⲩⲉ *depart till morning*, AM 64 B ⲉⲧⲁϥⲡⲟⲅⲓ ⲉⲙ., EW 61 B that word may ⲙ. ⲁⲧϭⲡⲉⲧⲁϩⲛⲟ, BMis 161 S ⲁⲡϩⲟⲓ ⲙ. till reached city = BSM 70 B, ShC 73 15 S ⲡⲉⲧⲣⲟ-ϫⲟⲥ ⲉⲧⲙ., C 43 4 B ⲡⲁϭⲙ. ⲡⲉ ⲉϥⲉⲣ ⲯⲁⲗⲓⲛ, ShC 73 3 S titles & rank we abandon ⲛⲧⲛⲙ. *depart* (die), COAd 64 S thy share thereof ⲛⲟⲉ ⲡⲡⲉⲛⲧⲁⲩⲙ. *those departed.*   *Be about to, proceed to*: Ge 26 13 B ⲡⲁϭⲙ. ⲉⲁⲓⲁⲓ προβαίν.; Lev 13 53 S ⲙ. ⲉⲛⲱⲣϣ ⲉⲃⲟⲗ (B om) διαχεῖν; Mor 37 33 S ⲁⲡⲥⲏⲩ…ⲙ. ⲉⲟⲩⲉⲓⲡⲉ συγκλείειν, DeV 66 B ⲁⲡⲓⲕⲣⲡ ⲙ. ⲉⲕⲏⲛ. With ethic dat S: ShC 42 192 ⲙ. ⲛⲁⲕ ⲉϩⲣⲁⲓ ϩⲓ-ⲡⲧⲱⲧⲣ, Mor 40 41 ⲙ. ⲛⲏⲧⲛ ⲉⲡⲉϥⲙⲁ, CO 133 ⲙ. ⲡⲏ.   *Var with* ⲙⲟⲩϣⲧ SB: Job 1 7 B ἐμ-περιπατ.; Lu 9 6 B (var ⲙⲟϣⲓ), 19 1 S διέρχ.

—— SAB nn, *going, pace, journey*: 2 Cor 11 26 B ϩⲁⲡⲙ. ϩⲓⲫⲙⲱⲓⲧ (S ϩⲓⲏ ⲙⲙ.) ὁδοιπορία; Cl 25 4 A ⲃ̄ⲱⲕ ϩⲓⲡⲉϭⲙ. ἀφορμᾶν; P 131⁶ 37 S degenerate monks ⲕⲱ ⲡⲥⲱⲟⲩ ⲙⲡⲙ. ⲡⲓⲧⲟⲩⲉⲓⲛ, ShC 73 158 S striving to ⲣ ⲡⲉⲓⲙ. ⲛⲟⲩⲱⲧ *same pace*, Z 580 S cattle turning mill ϣⲁⲅⲉⲣ ϯⲁϣⲏ ⲙⲙ.   With following preposition.

—— ⲉ- SB, *go to*: Ge 22 3 S (B ϣⲉ + ⲓ), MG 25 5 B ⲡⲟⲣ.; Ac 27 3 S (B ⲓ) κατάγ. εἰς, Z 343 S ⲁⲡⲙ. ⲉⲥⲓⲟⲟⲩⲧ ὁδεύειν εἰς; Br 127 S ⲛⲧⲉⲧⲛⲙ. ⲉⲧⲡⲉ, ShA 2 165 S (on He 13 2) angel ⲡⲉⲧⲙ. ⲉⲣⲟϥ, CA 89 S readmitted cleric ⲉϥⲉⲙ. ⲉⲡⲟⲣⲁⲙⲟⲛ of junior deacon, DeV 2 9 B ⲉϥⲙ. ⲉⲙⲁⲩ, JTS 4 395 S may thy perfume ⲙ. ⲉⲡⲟⲩⲉ (cf ⲙ. ϩⲓ-).

—— ⲉϫⲛ-, ⲉϫⲉⲛ- SBF, *walk upon, go toward*: Ge 3 14 SB ⲡⲟⲣ. ἐπί, Lev 26 33 B (S ⲙ. ⲉϩⲟⲩⲛ ⲉ-) ἐπιπορ.; Ps 103 3 S (B ⲙ. ϩⲓϫⲉⲛ-) περιπατ. ἐπί; BIF 13 112 S ϩⲙⲡⲧⲣⲉⲩⲙ. ⲉϫⲛⲡϭⲁⲗⲟⲩⲗ = MG 25 302 B ϣⲱⲡⲧ ⲉ-, Mor 30 36 F saw man ⲁϥⲙ. ⲉϫⲱϥ = BMis 261 ⲙ. ⲉ-, AM 91 B ⲙ. ⲉϫⲉⲛⲡⲉⲛ-ⲥⲫⲟⲧⲟⲩ of river.   ⲙ. ⲉϩⲣⲁⲓ ⲉϫⲛ- S: Ryl 24 *tread upon* serpents (cf Lu 10 19 ϩⲱⲙ).

—— ⲙⲛ-, ⲛⲉⲙ- SA^2B, *walk, agree, consort with*: Ge 13 5 SB συμπορ., Ap 3 4 SB περιπατ. μετά; Ac 1 21 S (B diff) συνέρχ. dat; AP 4 A^2 συνοδεύ.; Lu 8 38 S (B ⲟϩⲓ ⲛⲉⲙ-) εἶναι σύν; Si 13 1 SB κοινωνεῖν dat; Lu 12 58 S (B ϣⲉ ⲛⲉⲙ-) ὑπάγ. μετά; Sa 19 21 S παριστάναι; Miss 8 37 S bishops that ⲙ. ⲙⲡⲛⲉⲥⲧⲱⲣⲓⲟⲥ σχισματικός; Mor 18 8 S brother that ⲙ. ⲙⲛ- Macarius = Miss 4 102 B ⲟⲩⲟϩ ⲛⲥⲁ-, BAp 97 S whilst Pesenthius in hiding ⲛⲉⲙ. ⲛⲙⲙⲁϥ, RE 9 164 S I will make hoods ⲛⲥⲉⲙ. ⲙⲡⲛⲣⲟⲓⲧⲉ, MG 25 357 B unless humility ⲙ. ⲛⲉⲙⲱⲟⲩ.

—— ⲛⲥⲁ- BF (= S ⲟⲩⲟϩ refl ⲛⲥⲁ-), *go after, follow*: Is 45 14 B, Mt 10 38 B ἀκολουθεῖν ὀπίσω,

Mt 14 13 F (B ⲙ.) ἀκ. dat, Is 55 3 B ἐπακ. dat, Jer 2 2 B ἐξακ. dat, Ac 16 17 B κατακ. dat; Ge 32 19 B ⲡⲟⲣ. ὀπ., Ex 16 4 B ⲡⲟⲣ. dat; Mt 16 24 B (S ⲉⲓ ⲉⲡⲁϩⲟⲩ), Mk 8 34 F (B ⲓ ⲥⲁⲙⲉⲡϩⲏ) ἔρχ. ὀπ.; ROC 25 247 B all Egypt ⲡⲁⲙ. ⲡⲥⲱϥ (heretic), MG 25 332 B ⲁⲕⲙ. ⲡⲥⲁⲧⲁⲙⲉⲧⲣⲉϥϯ ⲥⲃⲱ.

—— ⲥⲁⲙⲉⲡϩⲏ B, *meaning same*: Jer 16 11 (S ⲙ. ϩⲓⲡⲁϩⲟⲩ) οἴχεσθαι ὀπ., DeV 2 66 ⲁⲅⲙ. ⲥⲁⲙⲉⲡ-ϩⲏϥ.

—— ⲥⲁⲫⲁϩⲟⲩ B, *meaning same*: Jer 42 15 (S ⲙ. ϩⲓⲡⲁϩ.) ⲡⲟⲣ. ὀπ.

—— ϩⲓⲡⲁϩⲟⲩ, -ⲫⲁϩⲟⲩ SB, *meaning same*: Jer 15 6 B (S ϯ ⲉⲡⲁϩ.) ⲡⲟⲣ. ὀπ.; ShC 73 62 S ⲙ. ϩ. ⲛⲡⲉⲥⲛⲏⲩ.

—— ϣⲁ- SB, *go to*: Ez 1 8 B (S ⲙ. ϩⲓ-) Gk om, C 43 58 B ⲁⲅⲙ. ϣⲁⲛⲓⲟⲩⲣⲱⲟⲩ, BIF 14 153 S ⲙ. ϣⲁⲡⲉⲕⲡ̄ⲉ̄.

—— ϩⲓ- SAB, *walk on, in* (cf ⲙ. ϩⲛ-): Pro 2 20 SAB, Is 33 21 B (SF om ϩⲓ-) ⲡⲟⲣ., Ps 8 9 S (B ⲥⲓⲛⲓ) διαπορ.; Is 59 8 B (S ⲙ. ϩⲛ-) διοδεύ.; Jer 6 16 B βαδίζ. ἐν; Ro 4 12 B (S diff) στοιχεῖν dat; AZ 21 141 S ⲉϥⲙ. ϩⲓⲡⲉⲕⲣⲟ, BSM 36 B ⲉϥⲙ. ϩⲓ-ⲡⲉϥⲙⲱⲓⲧ = BMis 379 S ⲉϥⲙ., Va 61 101 B perfume ⲙ. ϩⲓⲫⲟⲩⲉⲓ *spread abroad* (cf ⲙ. ⲉ-).

—— ϩⲛ-, ⲑⲉⲛ- $SABF$, *go, walk in* (cf ⲙ. ϩⲓ-): Job 29 3 SB, Is 33 15 SBF, Cl 1 3 A ⲡⲟⲣ. ἐν, Ac 14 16 S (var ⲃ̄ⲱⲕ) B ⲡⲟⲣ. dat, Ps 38 6 SB, Ez 33 15 SB διαπορ. ἐν; Ge 3 10 SB, Job 38 16 S (B ⲙ. ϩⲓϫⲉⲛ-), 2 Cor 4 2 SB περιπατ. ἐν; BM 172 40 S ⲙ. ϩⲛⲟⲩϩⲣⲓⲛ ὁδεύ., Zeph 3 6 AB διοδεύ.; Ps 103 10 S (B ⲥⲓⲛⲓ) διέρχ., Ez 29 11 SB δ. ἐν; Jos 3 17 SB διαβαίν., Jer 18 15 SB ἐπιβαίν.; ib 30 3 SB βαδίζ. ἐν; 2 Cor 1 12 SB ἀναστρέφ. ἐν; Jer 31 11 B οἴχεσθαι; KKS 667 S that rain ⲙ. ϩⲛⲙⲁ ⲛⲓⲙ, AM 138 B ⲁⲅⲙ. ⲑⲉⲛϯϩⲟⲙ of Christ, BM 849 32 B prayer for those ⲉⲑⲛⲁⲙ. ⲑⲉⲛⲫⲓⲟⲙ, Bodl(P) b 4 S awaiting letters (ⲛ)ⲧⲛⲙ. ⲡⲣⲏⲧⲟⲩ *act accordingly*.

—— ϩⲓⲧⲛ- SS^a, *go through, quit* (cf below ⲙ. ⲉⲃⲟⲗ ϩⲓⲧⲛ-): ST 308 S ⲕⲁⲧⲁ ⲑⲉ ⲛⲧⲁⲕⲙ. ϩⲓⲧⲟⲟⲧ, CO 181 S^a ⲉⲡⲉⲓⲇⲏ ⲁⲕⲙ. ϩⲓⲧⲟⲧ, Ep 225 S ⲁⲕⲙ. ϩⲓⲧⲟ[ⲟⲧ] ϫⲉⲉⲕⲡⲁϫⲟⲟⲩ ⲡⲣⲱⲙⲉ.   V Ep 431 n.

—— ϩⲁϫⲛ- S, ϩⲁϫⲏⲛ- A, ⲑⲁϫⲉⲛ- B, *go before*: Is 58 8 SB ⲡⲣⲟⲡⲟⲣ. ἔμπροσθεν; Mt 2 9 B (S ϩⲏⲧⲥ̄) προάγ.; Mic 2 13 SA (B ⲓ ⲉϩ. ⲙⲡⲉⲙⲑⲟ) ἐξέρχ. πρὸ προσωπ.; Mor 27 35 S ⲁⲅⲙ. ϩⲁϫⲱϥ of archon (BMis 289 BSM 42 diff), C 86 90 B champions ⲙ. ⲑⲁϫⲱϥ ⲙⲡⲟⲩⲣⲟ.

—— ϩⲓϫⲛ-, ϩⲓϫⲉⲛ- $SABF$, *go upon*: EpJer 61 B (F ϣⲏ) ἐπιπορ.; Job 9 8 SB, Mt 14 25 SBF περιπατ. ἐπί; Jer 12 10 S neg (B ⲙⲁ ⲡⲁⲑⲙ.) ἄβατος; Ge 1 26 S (B ⲕⲓⲙ ϩ.) ἕρπειν ἐπί; Cl 33 3 A beasts ⲉⲧⲙ. ϩⲓⲭⲱϥ φοιτᾶν; J 71 20 S ⲉⲓⲧⲏⲕ ⲉⲓⲙ. ϩ. ⲡⲕⲁϩ (cf PLond 1 232 ἐπὶ γ. βαδίζων), C 43 111 B ⲉϥⲙ.

ⲋ. †ⲁⲡⲉⲙⲣⲱ. ϭⲓⲛ-, ϫⲓⲛⲙ. ⲋ.: Mk 6 45 tit *S*
(H p 648), Mt 14 24 *F* sim ⲧϭ. ⲋ. ⲑⲁⲗⲁⲥⲥⲁ, ShBor
247 121 *S* ⲧⲉⲛϭ. ⲋ. ⲟⲩⲉⲣⲏⲧⲉ ⲥⲛⲧⲉ.

With following adverb.

—— ⲉⲃⲟⲗ *SAA²BF, go forth*: Ge 8 5 *S* (*B* ⲙ.),
Hos 14 7 *SA* (*B* do), Leyd 132 *S* ⲙ. ⲉⲃ. in peace
ⲡⲟⲣ., Nu 26 2 *S* (*B* ⲡⲛⲟⲩ ⲉⲃ.), ι Kg 17 20 *B* (*S*
ⲃⲱⲕ ⲉⲃ.) ⲉ̓ⲕⲡⲟⲣ., *ib* 29 2 *S* ⲡⲁⲣⲁⲡⲟⲣ.; *ib* 22 1 *S*
ⲁ̓ⲡⲉⲣⲭ.; ClPr 54 46 *S* fame ⲙ. ⲉⲃ. διαφοιτᾶν; Br
51 *S* voice ⲉⲥⲙ. ⲉⲃ. ⲛⲥⲁⲡⲉⲥⲉⲣⲏⲧ *resounding* (?),
ShC 73 151 *S* ⲡⲉⲧⲛⲁⲙ. ⲉⲃ. ϧⲓⲑⲏ of brethren, AP
55 *A²* ⲁⲉⲓⲙ. ⲁⲃ. ϧⲓⲭⲛⲑⲁⲗⲁⲥⲥⲁ, DeV 2 100 *B*
apostles ⲙ. ⲉⲃ. ϩⲉⲛⲡⲓⲕⲟⲥⲙⲟⲥ, AM 289 *B* so saying ⲁϥⲙ. ⲉⲃ., BKU 1 181 *F* to Adam expelled ϫⲉ-
ⲙⲁⲁϣ ⲉⲃ., BMis 141 *S* pregnant womb ⲙ. ⲉⲃ.,
EW 52 *B* sim (*cf* ⲙ. ⲉⲑⲏ & ⲃⲱⲣⲉ ⲉⲃ.), Mor 51 27
S ⲁⲡⲉϥϩⲏⲧ ⲙ. ⲉⲃ. & he became dropsical, Gu 94
S when tomb opened ⲥϯⲃⲱⲛ ⲙ. ⲉⲃ.

—— ⲉⲃ. ϩⲓⲧⲛ- *SAA²B*, a *go forth from, quit*: ι
Kg 10 2 *S* ⲁ̓ⲡⲉⲣⲭ. ⲁⲡⲟ́; Pcod 38 *S* when about to
ⲙ. ⲉⲃ. ϩⲓⲧⲟⲟⲧ, J&C 97 *A²* ⲕⲁⲧⲁ ⲑⲉ ⲉⲧⲉⲁⲕⲙ. ⲉⲃ.
ϩⲓⲧⲁⲧⲛ, ST 363 *S* ⲁⲓⲙ. ⲉⲃ. ϩⲓⲧⲟⲟⲧⲕ going south;
sim ⲙ. ϩⲓⲧⲛ- *q v.* b *pass through*: Nah 1 15 *A*
(*B* ⲥⲓⲛⲓ ⲉⲃ.) διέρχ. διά; Zech 9 8 *S* (Bor 248 29) *A*
(*B* do) διαπορ.; Ap 21 24 *S* (*B* ⲙ. ⲉⲃ. ϩⲉⲛ-) περιπατ. διά (var ⲉ̓ⲛ). ϫⲓⲛⲙ. ⲉⲃ. *B* nn m, *going forth,
departure*: Deu 28 6 (*S* ⲉⲓ ⲉⲃ.) ⲉ̓ⲕⲡⲟⲣ.; Ps 104 38
(*S* do) ⲉ̓ξⲟδⲟς; Is 30 11 (*S* ⲙⲁ ⲙⲙ., *F* ϩⲓⲁ ⲛⲙ.)
τρίβος.

—— ⲉⲡⲉⲥⲏⲧ *S, go down*: Deu 9 12 (*B* ϣⲉ) καταβαίν.; BMar 116 ⲁϥⲙ. ⲉⲡ. ϩⲓⲡⲙⲁ κατέρχ. ⲁⲡⲟ́.

—— ⲉⲡϣⲱⲓ *B, go up*: Ez 41 7 (*S* ⲙ. ⲡⲥⲁⲧⲡⲉ)
ⲁ̓ⲛⲁβⲁίⲛ. ⲉ̓ⲡὶ τὰ ⲩ̔ⲡⲉⲣⲱ̣ⲁ; ϫⲓⲛⲙ. ⲉⲡ. nn m: EW 187.

—— ⲉⲑⲏ *SB, go forward*: Ex 19 19 *B*, Mt 4 21
S (*B* ⲥⲓⲛⲓ ⲉ-) ⲡⲣⲟβⲁⲓⲛ.; Mk 14 35 *S* (var ⲃⲱⲕ, *B* do)
ⲡⲣⲟⲉⲣⲭ.; Z 274 *S* ⲛⲧⲉⲣⲉⲡϣⲁϫⲉ ⲙ. ⲉ. ⲡⲣⲟⲓⲉ́ⲛⲁⲓ
when letter had proceeded further; Miss 4 232 *S*
ⲡⲉⲩⲙ. ⲉ. daily (spiritual progress), DeV 2 78 *B*
drunkard ⲁϥϣⲁⲡⲙ. ⲉ. ⲡⲟⲩⲕⲟⲩϫⲓ ϩⲉⲛⲡⲏⲣⲡ...
ϣⲁϥϭⲓⲥⲓ, ShBerlOr 1613 1 *S* if Mary conceived
Christ ⲟⲩⲕⲟⲡ ⲁⲣⲏⲧⲥ ⲙ. ⲉ.? (*cf* ⲙ. ⲉⲃⲟⲗ).

—— ⲉϩⲟⲩⲛ, ⲉϩ. *SBF, go in, approach*: Lev 26
23 *S* (*B* ⲙ. ⲛⲉⲙ-) ⲡⲟⲣ. ⲡⲣⲟ́ς, Nu 18 7 *S* (*B* ⲓ ϩⲁ-)
ⲡⲣⲟⲥⲡⲟⲣ.; Ru 3 15 *S*, Mt 6 6 *F* (*S* ⲃⲱⲕ ⲉϩ., *B* ϣⲉ
ⲉϩ.) ⲉ̓ⲓⲥⲉ́ⲣⲭ.; Si 12 14 *SB* ⲡⲣⲟⲥⲁ́ⲅ. dat; P 129¹⁸
106 *S* ⲁⲩⲙ. ⲉϩ. ϩⲓⲡⲧⲟⲟⲩ to their χⲱ́ρα, MIE 2
402 *B* ⲉⲧⲁⲛⲙ. ⲉϩ. 3 miles (*cf* Ep 1 183), BMis
455 *S* arose & ⲙ. ⲉϩ. ⲉⲡⲉⲥⲗⲟϭ of sick, Va 59 121
B ⲁⲡⲓϫⲉⲗⲗⲟ ⲙ. ⲉϩ. ⲉϫⲱϥ (var *ib* 156 ⲥⲱⲕ ⲉϫ.),
TEuch 1 299 *B* ϣⲁⲩⲙ. ⲉϩ. ⲡⲉⲙⲡⲓⲙⲓⲧⲣⲟⲡ (*cf*
ب ⲭⲁⲣ), J 106 33 *S* ⲉⲓⲙ. ⲉϩ. ⲉⲃⲟⲗ & am hale (*cf* ⲙ.
ϩⲓϫⲛ- J 71).

—— ⲉϩⲣⲁⲓ *S*, ⲁϩⲣ. *A*, ⲉϩⲗ. *F, go up*: Jud 13 20
S (var ⲙ.), Ac 21 15 *S* (*B* ⲛⲁ ⲉϩ.) ⲁ̓ⲛⲁβⲁⲓⲛ.; Jon 3
2 *A* (*S* ⲃⲱⲕ ⲉϩ., *B* ϣⲉ ⲉϩ.) ⲡⲟⲣ. ⲉ̓ⲓⲥ; *go down*:
Is 30 2 *F* (*S* ⲃ. ⲉⲡⲉⲥⲛⲧ, *B* ϣⲉ ⲉⲃ.) κατⲁβⲁⲓⲛ.; Eccl
1 7 *S* ⲡⲟⲣ. ⲉ̓ⲓⲥ; BMis 100 *S* ⲁⲩⲙ. ⲉϩ. & went to
Egypt (*cf* Mt 2 14); doubtful: Jud 19 18 *S* ⲡⲟⲣ.
ⲉ̓ⲓⲥ, Joel 3 17 *SA* (prob, *B* ⲥⲓⲛⲓ ⲉⲃ. ϩⲓⲧⲉⲛ-) διⲉ́ⲣⲭ.
διⲁ́; ϫⲓⲛⲙ. ⲉϩ. *S, ascent*: P 131² 118 wings
ⲛⲧϭ. ⲉϩ.

—— ϩⲁⲑⲏ *SAA²B, go before*: Ps 96 3 *S* (*B* ⲉⲣ
ϣⲟⲣⲡ ⲙⲙ. ⲙⲡⲉϥⲙⲑⲟ), *ib* 88 15 *SB*, Hab 3 5 *SA*
(*B* ϩⲁϫⲉⲡ-) ⲡⲣⲟⲡⲟⲣ.; Jo 10 4 *SA²* (*B* do) ⲡⲟⲣ. ⲉ̓ⲙ-
ⲡⲣⲟⲥⲑⲉⲛ; Pro 16 18 *S* (*A* ϩⲁⲣⲧⲡ-), Mt 21 9 *S* (*B*
ϩⲁϫⲉⲡ-) ⲡⲣⲟⲁ́ⲅ.; Lu 1 17 *S* (*B* ⲉⲣ ϣⲟⲣⲡ ⲛⲓ ϩⲁϫ.)
ⲡⲣⲟⲉⲣⲭ. ⲉ̓ⲛⲱ́ⲡⲓⲟⲛ. *go toward, accomodate S* in
documents: Ep 93 ⲁⲕⲙ. ϩⲁⲧⲁϩⲛ & didst lend me
&c, ST 41 sim. *Cf* CO 140 ⲁⲕⲙ. ϩⲁϩⲏⲧⲛ.

—— ϩⲓⲑⲏ *SAB, go before*: Lu 1 76 *S* (*B* ⲉⲣ ϣ.
ⲙⲙ. ⲙⲡⲉⲙⲑⲟ) ⲡⲣⲟⲡⲟⲣ. ⲡⲣⲟ́; Jos 8 10 *S* ⲁ̓ⲛⲁβⲁⲓⲛ.
κατⲁ ⲡⲣⲟ́σⲱⲡⲟⲛ; Ge 33 3 *S* (*B* ⲥⲱⲕ ϩⲁϫ.) ⲡⲣⲟⲉⲣⲭ.
ⲉ̓ⲙⲡⲣⲟⲥ.; 2 Mac 6 7 *A* ⲡⲟⲙⲡⲉⲩⲉⲓⲛ dat (in 2 Kg 12 31
S ⲡⲟⲙⲡ. = διⲁ́ⲅⲉⲓⲛ); AM 96 *B* ⲁϥⲙ. ϩⲓⲧⲏ ⲙⲙⲟⲟⲩ.

—— ϩⲓⲑⲏ *S, meaning same*: Jud 1 2 ⲁ̓ⲛⲁβⲁⲓⲛ.,
Eccl 8 3 ⲡⲟⲣ. ⲁ̓ⲡⲟ́ ⲡⲣⲟⲥⲱ́ⲡⲟⲩ; Am 9 4 (*A* ϩⲓⲧⲉⲣⲓ, *B*
ⲙⲡⲉⲙⲑⲟ) ⲡⲟⲣ. ⲡⲣⲟ̀ ⲡⲣⲟⲥ.

—— ϩⲓⲧ⳯ *S, meaning same*: Jth 12 15 ⲡⲣⲟⲥⲉ́ⲣⲭ.,
Lu 22 47 (var ϩⲁⲑⲏ, *B* ϩⲁϫ.) ⲡⲣⲟⲉⲣⲭ.; Mt 2 9 (*B*
do) ⲡⲣⲟⲁ́ⲅⲉⲓⲛ.

ⲁⲧⲙ., ⲁⲑⲙ. *SB, pathless*: Ps 62 1 *SB*, Jer 12
10 *B* (*S* vb neg) ⲁ̓βⲁⲧⲟς.

ⲙⲁ ⲙⲙ. *SAB, place of walking, path*: Ps 24 4 *S*
(*B* ⲙⲱⲓⲧ), Pro 3 17 *SAB*, Is 30 11 *S* (*B* ϫⲓⲛⲙ., *F*
ϩⲓⲁ ⲛⲙ.) τρⲓ́βⲟς; *ib* 11 16 *B* (*S* ϩ.) διⲟδⲟς, Ps 106 33
B (*S* ⲟⲟⲉ) διⲉ́ξⲟδⲟς; Ps 67 25 *SB* ⲡⲟⲣⲉⲓ́ⲁ; Pro 2 15
SA (*B* ⲙⲱ.) τⲣⲟⲭⲓⲁ́; Job 6 19 *S* (*B* do) ⲁ̓ⲧⲣⲁⲡⲟ́ς;
Nu 33 2 *S* (*B* diff) ⲁ̓ⲡⲁⲣⲟⲓⲥ; BIF 13 102 *S* = MG
25 285 *B* pilgrims made roads to saints ⲙⲙⲁ ⲙⲙ.
ⲛⲁⲩ (*worn, familiar*) *paths*, Miss 8 46 *S* ⲙⲙⲁ ⲙⲙ.
ⲙⲡⲉⲑⲁⲗⲁⲥⲥⲁ opp ϩⲓⲏ ⲙⲙ., C 89 6 *B passer-by*
ϩⲓⲟⲩϭⲟⲓ ⲓⲉ ⲟⲩⲙⲁ ⲙⲙ. = MG 17 344 ...الب سفینة,
Dan vis 14 49 *B* ⲛⲓϭⲓⲣ ⲡⲉⲙⲡⲓⲙⲁ ⲙⲙ. ⲙⲁ ⲙⲙ.
ⲉⲡϣⲱⲓ *B, path upward*: Ps 83 6 (*S* diff) ⲁ̓ⲛⲁ́βⲁⲥⲓς;
ⲙⲁ ⲙⲙ. ⲉϩⲟⲩⲛ *B, path inward*: Ez 8 5 ⲉ̓ⲓⲥⲡⲟⲣⲉⲩ́-
ⲉⲥⲑⲁⲓ; ⲙⲁ ⲙⲙ. ϩⲓϫⲉⲛ- *B, path upon*: Ps 103 3
(*S* diff) ⲉ̓ⲡⲓ́βⲁⲥⲓς.

ⲙⲟⲉⲓⲧ, ⲙⲱⲓⲧ ⲙⲙ. *SB, road, journey*: Ez 27 19
τⲣⲟⲭⲓ́ⲁ *SB*, CaiEuch 588 *B* ⲟ̔δⲟⲓⲡⲟⲣⲓⲁ; DeV 2 151
B days spent in ⲡⲓⲙ. ⲙⲙ. = MG 25 423 *S* ϩⲓⲟⲟⲩⲉ.

ϩⲓⲏ, ϩⲟ, ϩⲓⲁ ⲙⲙ. *SAF, road, path*: Ps 16 5 *F*
(*S* ϩ., *B* ⲙⲱ.), Sa 4 3 *S* τⲣⲓ́βⲟς; Nah 1 3 *SA* (*B*
ⲙⲱ.) ⲟ̔δⲟ́ς; Cl 60 2 *A* διⲁ́βⲏⲙⲁ; Jos 10 13 *S* στⲁ́σⲓς;
ROC 20 56 *S* ⲛϭⲓⲣ, ⲡⲉϩ. ⲙⲙ. ⲣ ϩ. ⲙⲙ. *S, go,
walk*: Deu 2 27 (*B* ⲥⲓⲛⲓ) ⲡⲁⲣⲉ́ⲣⲭ. TT 142 ⲣ ⲡⲁϣⲉ
ⲡⲧⲉϩ. ⲙⲙ.

ⲣⲟⲟⲩ, ⲉⲣ. ⲙⲙ. *SAB, day's journey* : Nu 11 31 *B*
(*S* ⲣⲓⲛ ⲛⲟⲩⲣⲟⲟⲩ), Lu 2 44 *SB* ἡμέρα ; Jon 3 4 *SA*
(*B* ⲙⲱⲓⲧ ⲙⲙ. ⲡⲧⲉ ⲟⲩⲉⲣ.) πορεία ἡμ. ; ShRE 10
163 *S* in to desert ⲛⲣⲉⲣⲡ. ⲙⲙ. Ac 1 12 *B* ⲥⲁⲃⲃⲁⲧⲟⲛ ⲙⲙ. (*S* diff) σαβ. ὁδός. EW 170 *B* distant
ⲡⲟⲩⲙⲟⲡⲏ ⲙⲙ.

ϣⲫⲏⲣ ⲙⲙ. *B, fellow-traveller* : CaiEuch 588
συνοδοιπόρος ; Bar 3 35 ⲉⲣ ϣ. ⲙⲙ. συναναστρέφεσθαι, TRit 244 sim συμπορ.

ⲣⲉϥⲙ. *S, goer* (on foot), *walker* : BMis 34 (con-
temptuous) ⲡⲓⲙⲡⲉ ⲟⲩⲙⲁⲧⲟⲓ...ⲡⲓⲙⲡⲉ ⲟⲩⲣ. ⲡⲛⲉϥⲟⲩⲉⲣⲏⲧⲉ ? (*cf* πεζός).

ϭⲓⲛ-, ϫⲓⲙⲙ. *SBF, going, gait, conduct* : Si 19 26
S, R 2 2 25 *S* Potiphar's wife ⲧⲉϥϭ. βῆμα ; Nu 33
2 *S* (var ⲣⲓⲛ) *B*, Is 3 16 *B* (*S* ⲣ.), CaiEuch 588 *B*
πορεία ; Gal 1 13 *B* (*S* ⲣⲃⲏⲅⲉ), Eph 4 22 *B* (*S* do)
ἀναστροφή ; Pro 14 24 *B* (*SA* diff) διατριβή ; Ex
23 16 *B* (*S* ⲣⲁⲛ) ἔξοδος ; Mt 14 22 tit *F* ⲧϭ. ⲣⲓⲭⲉⲛ-
ⲑⲁⲗⲁⲥⲥⲁ, Va 57 227 *B* vain woman's ϫ. & ϫⲓⲛ-
ⲥⲟⲙⲥ σχῆμα ; PS 35 *S* beholding ⲥⲭⲏⲙⲁ ⲛⲡϭ.
ⲡⲡⲁⲓⲱⲛ, Cat 99 *B* of heretical companionship ϫⲉϫ
ⲡϫ. ⲉⲧⲙⲙⲁⲩ, Tri 382 *S* sun's ϭ. شمس .

ⲙⲟⲟϣⲉ nn *v* ⲙⲟⲩϣⲧ (ⲙⲟϣⲧⲉ).

ⲙⲉϣⲑⲏⲃⲥ *B v* ⲙⲉϣϯⲃⲥ.

ⲙⲁϣⲑⲱϯ *B v* ⲙϣⲧⲱⲧⲉ.

ⲙⲉϣϫⲁⲕ *v* ⲙⲉϣⲉ.

ⲙⲉϣⲕⲟⲗ *S* nn, *rump, buttocks* (? *anus, cf* ϣ-
ⲕⲟⲗ) : P 43 41 طينة , است, between ⲃⲓⲗⲧⲓ (*q v*)
& ⲙⲟⲣⲓⲟⲛ ; EW 222 *S* (scala p 153 parts of body)
ϣⲕⲟⲗ منقب prob for this.

ⲙⲉϣⲡⲉⲗⲧ *S* nn as pl, meaning unknown : BM
538 ⲣ ⲣ]ⲱⲃ ⲡⲡⲉⲙ. ⲡⲥⲉⲥⲙⲡⲧⲟⲩ.

ⲙⲉϣⲡⲱⲛⲉ *S v* ⲙⲉⲭⲡⲱⲛⲉ.

ⲙϣⲓⲣ *SB*, ⲉⲙϣⲓⲣ *SB*, ⲙⲉϣⲓⲣ *SSᶠ*, ⲙϣⲏⲣ *F*
(Kr 158), ⲙⲉⲭⲓⲣ *SB*, ⲙⲡϣⲓⲣ *S* (Miss 8 92), ⲙⲉ-
ⲭⲓⲗ *F* (Cai 8522) nn, name of 6th month, Gk
Μεχείρ, Ar أمشير . *V* AZ 39 130.

ⲙϣⲓⲣ, ⲉⲙ- (ⲉⲙϣⲓ AZ 12 157) *B* nn m, *pot,
box* for incense : K 216 church utensils ⲡⲓⲙ. حق
البخور (var P 51 *B* درج البـ).

ⲙⲁϣⲣⲧ *S*, -ⲉⲣⲧ *SB* nn m f, *cable* of palm fibre :
Cat 54 *B* (on Mt 19 24) ship's great ropes to which
anchors are bound ⲉⲧⲉⲡⲓⲙ. ⲡⲉ, *ib* 100 (on same)
camel explained as ⲟⲩⲛⲟϭ ⲙⲙ. (*cf* جمل cable) ; WS
96 *S* go to the palm-fibre workers (ⲥⲁⲡϣⲏⲡⲡⲉ) for
the sailors need ⲧⲙ. ⲙⲡⲡⲗⲉⲃⲁⲛ ⲙⲡⲛⲕⲟⲩⲓ ⲙ. (*sic*
m & f), Kr 240 *S* ⲡⲉⲙⲁϣⲓⲣⲧ, PLond 4 129 μασζέρτ,
μασέρτ named with other kinds of rope. *Cf*? Almk
2 103 شال one of ship's cables.

ⲙⲟⲩϣⲧ *SAA²BF*, ⲙⲉϣⲧ- *SB*, ⲙⲁϣⲧ- *BF*,
ⲙⲟϣⲧ⸗ *SB*, ⲙⲁϣⲧ⸗ *Sᵃ*, ⲙⲟϣⲧ† *S* (once), pc ⲙⲁϣⲧ-
A² vb **I** tr, *examine, search out, visit* : Ge 31 33 *S* (*B*
ϩⲟⲧϩⲉⲧ), Pro 20 27 *S* (*A* ⲣⲉϥⲙ.), Bor 253 265 *S*
undo your sacks ⲧⲁⲗⲙⲟϣⲧⲟⲩ ἐρευνᾶν, Glos 221 *Sᶠ*
ἐραυνητής (*sic l*) · ⲡⲉⲧⲙⲁϣⲧ (*l* ? ⲙⲟ.), Ps 108 11
S (*B* ϩⲟⲧ.) Zeph 1 12 *A* (*S* cf Ps 49 6, *B* do)
ἐξερ. ; Ps 110 2 *S†* (*B* ϩⲟⲧ.†) ἐκζητεῖν ; Nu 13 16
B (*S* ⲡⲁⲩ) κατασκέπτεσθαι, Jud 21 9 *S* ἐπισκεπτ.,
Jos 2 1 *S* κατασκοπεύειν ; Ge 3 6 *S* (P 44 101, *B*
ϯ ⲡⲓⲁⲧ⸗), Ps 118 15 *S* (*B* ⲕⲁϯ), Is 5 12 *S* (*B* ⲡⲁⲩ,
F ϯ ϩⲏⲧ) κατανοεῖν ; Jer 2 10 *B*, Lu 19 1 *S* (*B*
ⲙⲟϣⲓ), Ac 13 6 *S* (*B* ϭⲓⲛⲓ), Miss 4 531 *S* = C 89
49 *B* ⲁⲕⲙ. ⲡⲕⲁⲗⲅⲃⲏ διέρχεσθαι, Job 1 7 *SB*, R 1
1 48 *S* ⲁⲡⲙ. ⲡⲧⲟⲟⲩ ⲡⲓⲙ περιέρχ. ; Job 2 2 *S* (*B*
ⲙⲟϣⲓ ⲉⲃ. ⲣⲓϫⲉⲛ-) διαπορεύεσθαι ; Ge 12 6 *SB*, Ac
17 1 *S* (*B* ϭⲓⲛⲓ ⲉⲃⲟⲗ) διοδεύειν, Zech 1 10 *AB* περ-
ριοδ. ; Mt 9 35 *S* (*B* ⲕⲱϯ) περιάγειν ; Si 9 5 *S*,
BMis 240 *S* bade ⲉⲧⲣⲉⲩⲙ. ⲙⲡⲉϥⲥⲱⲙⲁ καταμανθάνειν ; Job 12 11 *S* (*B* ϩⲟⲧ.) διακρίνειν ; Lev 13
7 *S* (*B* ⲡⲁⲩ) ἰδεῖν ; Jos 19 49 *S* ἐμβατεύειν ; Job 13
9 *S* (*B* ϩⲟⲧ.) ἐξιχνιάζειν ; EW 148 *B* ⲉⲩⲙ. ⲙⲡⲓⲥⲁϫⲓ ⲡⲉⲙⲡⲟⲅⲉⲣⲟⲩ διεξιέναι ; ShA 1 217 *S* ⲉⲕϣⲁⲛⲙ.
ⲡⲉⲧⲅⲣⲁⲫⲓ, ShC 73 73 *S* none may kindle fire ⲙ-
ⲡⲟⲩⲙ. ⲡⲣⲱⲃ ⲡϣⲟⲣⲡ with the superior, ShP 130⁵
19 *S* moth devoured it ⲁⲥⲙⲟϣⲧϥ & made it in
holes, P 129¹⁶ 96 *S* sick queen ⲁⲥⲙ. ⲡⲡⲧⲟⲟⲩ yet
found not healing (*v* Synax 1 145 داري), C 89 152
B ϯⲛⲁⲙ. his body (medically), AM 81 *B* suffer me
to ⲙ. ⲡⲡⲁⲙⲉⲅⲓ, CO 249 *S* send books ⲡⲧⲙⲟϣⲧ-
ⲧⲟⲩ, *ib* 253 *S*, Ep 383 *S* sim, Mor 33 11 *S* of Mary's
virtues ⲙⲡⲉⲥⲙ. ⲡⲧⲉⲥⲁⲡⲉ with comb (BMis 77 om),
BM 274 *S* let us ϩⲟⲧⲣⲧ ⲁⲩⲱ ⲡⲧⲙⲙ. ⲙⲡⲛⲧⲉⲛⲟⲥ ⲡ-
ⲡϩⲁⲗⲁⲧⲉ. With ethic dat *S* : AZ 52 126 ⲙ. ⲡⲉ
ⲡⲑⲓⲗⲏⲙ̄ ⲡⲧⲉ.

p c *A²*, *examiner, prover* : AP 13 God ⲡⲙⲁϣⲧ-
ⲣⲏⲧ καρδιογνώστης.

Refl *SB*, *examine self, reflect* : BM 247 5 *S* ⲙⲁⲣ-
ⲉⲛⲙⲟϣⲧⲛ ϫⲉ- whether we bear Christ ἐρευν. ; Gal
6 1 *B* (*S* ϭⲱϣⲧ) σκοπεῖν ; BHom 18 *S* ⲙⲟϣⲧⲕ
ⲡⲧⲡⲁⲩ λογίζεσθαι ; JA '75 5 238 *S* ⲙⲟϣⲧⲕϭⲉ ⲙ-
ⲙⲓⲛ ⲙⲙⲟⲕ σκέπτ. ; C 89 8 *B* ⲡⲧⲉⲕⲙⲟϣⲧⲕ in all
things δοκιμάζειν ; *ib* 22 *B* he stood ⲉϥⲙ. ⲙⲙⲟϥ
διαλογίζειν ; 1 Cor 11 31 *S* (*B* = Gk) διακρίνειν ;
ShC 42 110 *S* let each ⲙⲟϣⲧϥ ⲁⲩⲱ ϥⲡⲁⲉⲓⲙⲉ, Ep
264 *S* ⲁⲓⲙⲟϣⲧ(ⲧ) ⲕⲁⲧⲁ ⲡⲡⲉ that it is not right,
J 70 10 *S* ⲁⲓⲙⲟϣⲧ(ⲧ) ϩⲛⲟⲩⲥⲕⲉⲯⲓⲥ ⲙⲙⲛⲧⲣⲱⲙⲉ
(that) it was fitting &c.

— ⲉⲃⲟⲗ *SB* refl, *consider, ponder* : J 81 28 *S*
ⲉⲁⲓⲙⲟϣⲧ(ⲧ) ⲉⲃ. ϫⲉⲁⲛⲧⲟⲩⲅⲣⲉϥⲣ ⲡⲟⲃⲉ, *ib* 89 32 *S*
sim, DeV 2 274 *B* go & ⲙⲟϣⲧⲕ ⲉⲃ. = Mun 69 *S*
om ⲉⲃ.

II intr *SAB*(rare), *consider, visit* : Eccl 7 26 *S*

κατασκέπτ.; *wander* (? confused with ⲙⲟⲟϣⲉ): Si 31 (34) 10 *S* πλανᾶν, *ib* 11 ἀποπλ.; Wess 18 38 *S* shall come to Egypt ⲛϥⲙ. ⲕⲁⲧⲁ ⲡⲟⲗⲓⲥ, *cf* Lu 9 6 *B*. With prep: JKP 2 94 *S* word spoken ϣⲁϥⲙ. ⲉⲧⲉϣⲃⲉ ⲥⲛⲟⲟⲩⲥ ⲛⲭⲱⲣⲁ, J 106 79 *S* ⲅⲁ-ⲛⲡⲧⲣⲁⲙ. ⲟⲩⲛ ⲉⲡⲁⲓ, Bor 240 54 *S* ⲉⲥⲁⲓ ϣⲟϫⲛⲉ ⲁⲩⲱ ⲉⲥⲙ. ⲉⲧⲃⲏⲏⲧⲟⲩ, ShBMOr 8810 465 *S* ⲛⲧⲙ. ⲡⲥⲱⲕ like woman seeking coin (Lu 15 8), C 86 161 *B* ⲁϥⲙ. ⲡⲉⲙⲡⲓⲉⲑⲛⲟⲥ (but Ps 105 35 *B* ⲙⲟⲩⲭⲧ), Cl 25 5 *A* (Rösch) ⲟ̇ⲁⲣⲟⲩⲙ. ⲟ̇ⲓⲛ̇ⲭⲙⲉ (var = Gk) ἐπισκέπτ., Mich 550 45 *S* ⲡⲥⲉⲙ. ⲙⲡⲡⲉϭⲉⲣⲏⲅ ⲟ̇ⲓⲛⲡϣⲁϫⲉ of scriptures, Mor 40 35 *S* ⲉϥⲙ. ⲟ̇ⲓⲛ̇ⲭⲱⲱⲙⲉ ⲡⲧⲁⲩⲣ ⲟ̇ⲟⲟⲗⲉ, Mus 40 41 *S* word ⲉⲩⲛⲁⲙ. ⲡⲣⲏⲧϥ *inter se ruminare*, HL 113 *B* letting mind ⲙ ϭⲉⲡⲛⲓⲭⲓⲛ-ⲡⲁⲩ ⲉⲧⲥⲙⲟⲡⲧ.

—— nn m *SB*, *consideration, opinion*: MG 17 325 *S* ⲁϣ ⲙⲙ. ⲡⲉⲧⲡⲏⲣⲧⲧⲏⲩⲧⲛ (*B ib* 100 diff) λο-γισμός; EW 146 *B* ⲉⲃⲟⲗ ⲟ̇ⲓⲧⲉⲛⲟⲩⲙ. of whole race κρίσις; ShA 2 256 *S* ⲟⲩⲙ. ⲉⲣⲟⲩⲛ ⲉⲡⲕⲱⲧ ⲛⲧⲡⲓⲥⲧⲓⲥ, Mor 56 20 *S* he was ⲟ̇ⲛⲟⲩⲛⲟϭ ⲙⲙ. ⲉⲧⲃⲉⲡϣⲏⲣⲉ ϣⲏⲙ *in great concern*, BHom 28 *S* vain words ⲁⲭⲛⲙ.

ⲁⲧⲙ. *SB* adj: Tatt 27 *S* ἄπειρος (whence ?, not in My), P 44 47 *S* ⲡⲁⲧⲙⲟϣⲧϥ ἀψηλάφητος *intangible*, Va 59 3 *B* devilish errors & ϯⲙⲉⲧⲁⲧⲙ. *thoughtlessness*.

ⲣⲉϥⲙ. *A, examiner*: Pro 20 27 (var Cl ⲉϥⲟ̇ⲁⲧⲟ̇ⲧ, *S* ⲡⲉⲧⲙ.) ἐρευνᾶν.

ⲟ̇ⲓⲛⲙ. *S, examination, deliberation*: Miss 8 58 ⲧϭ. of your holy synod διάσκεψις, ShBor 247 116 ⲧϭ. ⲙⲡⲡⲉⲑⲟⲟⲩ ⲙⲛⲡⲉⲧⲛⲁⲛⲟⲩϥ, *ib* 117 ⲡϭⲣⲓⲥⲉ ⲛⲧϭ. ⲙⲡϣⲁϫⲉ.

ⲙⲟϣⲧⲉ, ⲙⲟⲟ. *S* nn as pl, *parts, neighbourhood*: Mt 2 22 (var ⲙⲟⲟϣⲉ, *B* ⲥⲁ), *ib* 15 21 (var do, *B* do), paral Mk 7 24 *S* ⲧⲟϣ, *cf* Mt 16 13 ⲙⲟⲟϣⲉ (*B* do) μέρος, P 129¹⁷ 74 Seleucia ⲟ̇ⲛⲙⲙⲟⲟϣⲉ of Antioch (var Mor 17 8 ⲧⲟϣ) ἡ κατά; Ep 382 will come south ϣⲁⲙⲙⲟϣⲧⲉ ⲙⲡⲙⲟⲩⲣ ⲉⲟ̇ⲟⲩⲛ *about* (? *the season of*) *Lent*.

ⲙⲉϣⲧⲉ *A²* *v* ⲙⲁⲁϫⲉ *ear*.

ⲙⲏϣⲧⲉ, ⲙⲓϣ[ⲧⲉ] *S* nn f, *ford, ferry* (?) in records of Nile's rise: J G Wilkinson's note book ¹⁷⁄ᵥ (in Bodl) p 98 ⲁⲡⲙⲟⲟⲩ ⲥⲱⲕ ⲟ̇ⲁⲧⲙⲏϣⲧⲉ [?] ⲟ̇ⲛⲙⲉⲥⲟⲩⲣⲏ ⁻ⲓⲍ, Hall 66 sim ⲟ̇ⲁⲧⲙⲓ. *Cf* Berl *Wörterb* 2 158 *mšdt* & ? place-name (Siût) [Arabic].

ⲙⲟϣⲧⲉ *S v* ⲙⲟⲩϣⲧ *sf*.

ⲙⲉϣϯⲃⲥ, -ⲑⲃⲥ *B* nn m, *hinge* of door: Ex 12 7 *B* Lag between ⲟⲩⲉⲭⲣⲟ & ⲑⲟⲩⲁⲓ (Va 1 *S* Gk om); Pro 26 14 *S* (*A* ⲕⲟⲩⲣ) στρόφιγξ; Z 233 *S* ⲧⲉⲓⲗⲁⲕⲙ...ⲟⲩⲙ. ⲧⲉ ⲟ̇ⲛⲡⲣⲟ of Hell, Mor 48 94 *S* = C 43 146 *B* sim, BAp 9 = MIF 9 46 *S* gates

broken ⲉⲣⲉⲡⲉⲩⲙ. ⲡⲏⲟ̇ ⲉⲃⲟⲗ; Am 8 3 *S* (*B* ⲥⲉⲛϯ) φάτνωμα but Vulg *cardo* (*v* ⲙⲉⲗⲱⲧ).

ⲙⲉϣⲧⲱⲗ *B v* ⲙⲉϭⲧⲱⲗ.

ⲙϣⲧⲱⲧⲉ, ⲙⲓϣ. (BM 1096) *S*, ⲙⲁϣⲑⲱϯ *B* nn f, *comb*: K 125 *B* among weaver's tools [Arabic] (*cf* ? ⲙⲟⲩϣⲧ); Mor 33 11 *S* Mary's virtues ⲙⲡⲉⲥⲙⲟⲩϣⲧ ⲡⲧⲉⲥⲁⲡⲉ ⲡⲟⲩⲙ. (varr *ib* 34 6 om ⲡⲟⲩⲙ., BMis 77 om all), Ryl 139 *S* among bridal gifts ⲟⲩⲙ., BM 1096 *S* list ϣⲟⲙⲧⲉ (ⲙ)ⲙ.; *comb of foot, metatarsus*: K 79 *B* ⲡⲓⲙ. (var -ⲑⲱⲟⲩϯ) [Arabic].

ⲙⲉϣⲫⲱⲛⲓ *B v* ⲙⲉⲭⲡⲱⲛⲉ.

ⲙⲉϣⲓϣ *BF* (Ac 7), ⲉⲙ., ⲙⲡϣ. *B* nn m, *vengeance*: Ge 4 15 (var Cat 51 ϭⲓ ⲙ.) ἐκδικούμενον.

ⲓⲣⲓ ⲙ-, ⲉⲣ ⲡⲙ., *do vengeance for, requite*: Hos 8 13 (*A* ϫⲓ ⲕⲃⲁ) ἐκδικεῖν; DeV 2 141 ⲉϥⲓⲣⲓ ⲙⲡⲉⲙ. ⲛⲛⲏ ⲉⲑⲟⲩⲁⲃ, Va 61 106 could he not ⲉⲣ ⲡⲉϥⲙ. ⲡⲉⲙⲛⲏ who do him violence ?

ϭⲓ ⲙ., *take vengeance, be avenged* a with poss pron: Ps 36 28 ⲥⲉⲛⲁϭⲓ ⲙⲡⲟⲩϭⲓ ⲙ. (*S* ⲣ ⲟ̇ⲁⲡ), Ro 12 19 (*S* ⲣ ⲕⲃⲁ) ἐκδ.; Is 59 16 (*S* ⲃⲱⲱⲣⲉ) ἀμύνειν. b with prep: c ⲛ-, Ex 21 20 (*S* ϫⲓ ⲕ.), 2 Cor 10 6 (*S* do) ἐκδ.; MIE 2 378 lest he ϭⲓ ⲙ. ⲙⲙⲟⲛ, Va 58 72 ⲥⲉⲛⲁϭⲓ ⲙ. ⲛⲧⲉϥϣⲉⲣⲓ *avenge his daughter*, Aeg 35 whoso transgresseth ϯⲛⲁϭⲓ ⲙ. ⲙⲙⲟϥ; c ⲉⲃⲟⲗ ⲛ-, Deu 18 19 (*S* do) ἐκδ. ἐκ, Jer 20 10 ἐκδίκησιν λαμβάνειν ἐκ, Ps 42 1 (*S* ⲣ ⲟ̇ⲁⲡ) δικάζειν ἐκ. c ⲉϫⲉⲛ-, Jer 23 2 (*S* ϫⲓ ⲕ. ⲟ̇ⲛ-), Zeph 1 8 (*A* ϫⲓ ⲕ. ⲛ-) ἐκδ. ἐπί; c ⲡⲉⲙ-, Lu 18 3 (*S* ⲣ ⲟ̇.) ἐκδ. ἀπό; Ps 117 10 (*S* ⲃⲱⲱⲣⲉ) ἀμύν. dat; C 43 78 ϭⲓ ⲙⲡⲁⲉⲙ. ⲡⲉⲙⲕⲁⲓⲛ my brother; c ϭⲉⲡ-, Jer 15 3 ⲉⲓⲉϭⲓ ⲙ. ⲛⲟ̇ⲏⲧⲟⲩ ἐκδ. ἐπί, *ib* 5 9 ἐκδ. ἐν.

ϭⲓ ⲙ. nn m, *taking vengeance, retribution*: Ex 7 4, Is 59 17 (*S* ϫⲓ ⲕ.) ἐκδίκησις; DeV 1 162 sword that shall punish ϭⲉⲡⲟⲩϭⲓ ⲙ.

ⲓⲣⲓ ⲙ-, ⲉⲣ ⲡⲓϭⲓ ⲙ., ⲟⲩϭⲓ ⲙ., *do vengeance*: Nu 33 4 (*S* ⲉⲓⲣⲉ ⲙⲡⲭⲓ ⲕ.), Ac 7 24 *BF* (ⲓⲗⲓ ⲡⲟⲩϭⲓ ⲙ. sic, *S* do) ἐκδ. ποιεῖν; Va 58 71 ϯⲛⲁⲓⲣⲓ ⲡⲟⲩϭⲓ ⲙ. ϭⲉⲡⲟⲏⲡⲟⲩ & leave none alive.

ϯ ⲡⲟⲩϭⲓ ⲙ., *give requital, take vengeance on*: Ps 17 48 (*S* ϯ ⲡⲣⲉⲡϫⲓ ⲕ.), 2 Thes 1 8 (*S* ϯ ⲡⲟⲩⲕ.) ἐκδ. διδόναι.

ⲣⲉϥϭⲓ ⲙ., *taker of vengeance, avenger*: Ps 8 3 (*S* ⲣⲉϥϫⲓ ⲕ.) ἐκδικητής; 1 Thes 4 6 (*S* do) ἔκδικος; 1 Kg 24 16 (*S* = Gk) δικαστής.

ⲙⲓϣϣⲉ *S v* ϣϣⲉ.

ⲙⲉϣϣⲱⲧ (ⲙⲉⲛϣⲱⲧ) *B*, pl ⲙⲉϣϣⲟϯ, ⲙⲉⲛ-ϣⲟϯ & sg as pl, nn m, *plain, field*: Ge 14 17 (*S* ⲥⲱϣⲉ), Deu 1 7 (*S* do), Hab 3 5 (*S* do, *A* ⲕⲁⲓⲉ) πεδίον, Is 32 19 (*SF* do) πεδινός; Ez 36 6 νάπη; TEuch 2 312 ⲡⲓⲙ. ⲡⲧⲉ ⲭⲏⲙⲓ [Arabic], Vi *Denkschr*

46 16 sim opp ⲫⲗⲁⲣⲏⲥ.   ⲉⲣ ⲙ., *be like a plain*: Is 13 2 (*S* ⲟⲩⲱϣⲥ ⲉⲃⲟⲗ) πεδινός.   As place-name: ⲡⲓⲙⲉⲡϣⲟ† C 43 223, 237, ⲡⲓⲙⲉϣⲟ† *ib* 200, ⲡⲓⲙⲉϣϣⲱⲧ *ib* 63 اسفل الأرض one of Delta nomes (MIF 36 8, Amélineau *Géog* 64).

ⲙⲁϣϫ *B* v ⲙⲁⲁϫⲉ *ear*.

ⲙⲟⲩⲅ *A* v ⲙⲟⲩⲣ *look*.

ⲙⲁϭⲉ *A* v ⲙ ϣⲉ.

ⲙϭⲉ *A* v ⲙⲓϣⲉ.

ⲙⲉϧⲉⲕ *A* v ⲙⲉϣⲉ (ⲙⲉϣⲁⲕ).

ⲙⲁϭⲓ *B* vb(?): Va 57 124 ⲓ̅ⲁ̅ⲟ̅ⲥ̅ ⲛⲓⲃⲉⲛ ⲙⲙ. πᾶν εἶδος μάχης.   Prob Gk μάχη.

ⲙⲁϭⲟⲩⲗ *B* nn m, *chisel, pick*: K 123 among carpenter's tools منقار, Bodl 325 152 ⲡⲓⲙ. sim, also = سندال *anvil* (but ? misread for 'ⲙⲛ).

ⲙⲁϭⲧ *B* v ⲙⲁⲣⲧ.

ⲙⲁϩ-, always ⲙⲙⲁϩ- *S* prep, *before* (v ϩⲁⲣ), of sacrifices offered before a god (only in Lev, Deu, Kg): ⲙ. ⲡϫⲟⲉⲓⲥ Lev 1 9, 4 3, 17 5 &c (all *B* ⲙ̅ⲡ̅ϭ̅ⲧ̅), Deu 17 1 (*B* ⲙ̅ⲡⲉⲙⲑⲟ ⲙ-), 1 Kg 6 14 τῷ κυρίῳ; ⲙ. ⲙⲡⲉⲧⲛ̅ⲡⲉ, -ⲛⲉⲩⲡⲉ Lev 22 25, 23 14 (var ⲙ. ⲛ., *B* ⲡⲧⲉ), Deu 12 31 (Mor ⲙ. ⲉⲡⲉⲩⲡⲉ, *B* ⲛⲡⲟⲩ-), τῷ θεῷ, τ. θεοῖς.   Cf sim phrase Nu 15 3, 7, 18 17 &c *S* ⲙ̅ⲡϫⲟⲉⲓⲥ.

ⲙⲁϩ, ⲙⲁⲁϩ *S*, ⲙⲁⲁⲣⲓ *Sf* (Is), ⲙⲏϩⲉ *A*, ⲙⲟϩ *B* nn m, *nest, brood* of young: Deu 22 6 SB, Pro 27 8 SA, Is 10 14 *S* (varr ⲙⲙⲁϩ, -ϩⲓ) *B*, Lu 13 34 *B* (*S* ⲙⲁⲥ pl) νοσσιά; Ge 6 14 *B* (*S* ⲟⲩⲛⲧ) vo. *cubicle*; Mt 8 20 *S* (*B* ⲙⲁ ⲡⲟⲩⲱϩ) κατασκήνωσις; Mor 22 29 *S* ⲟⲩⲙ. ⲡⲣⲁⲗⲏⲧ, MG 25 271 *B* ⲙ. of snake = Mor 40 45 *S* ϩⲃⲃ.   ⲙⲁϩⲟⲩⲁⲗ, -ⲃⲁⲗ SB, ⲙⲉϩⲟⲩⲏⲗ, ⲙⲉⲡⲟⲩⲁⲗ (BMis 87) *S* nn m, *nest, dovecot*: P 44 23 *S* pl ارجة, اوكار, Aeg 48 *B* ⲡⲓⲙ. ⲉⲧⲁⲡⲓϭⲣⲟⲙⲡⲓ ⲟⲩⲟϩ ⲛϧⲏⲧϥ, Mor 48 94 *S* souls like doves ⲉⲩⲣⲏⲏⲩ ⲉⲃⲟⲗ ϩⲛⲡⲉⲩⲙⲉϩ., Cai 42573 1 *S* dung of dove ⲛϣⲁϥⲣⲱⲗ ϩⲓⲡⲉϥⲙⲉϩ. in recipe.

ⲙⲉϩ-, ⲙⲁϩ- pref of ordinals v ⲙⲟⲩϩ *fill*.

ⲙⲟϩ *B* v ⲙⲁϩ *nest*, ⲙⲟⲩϩ *fill, burn, look*.

ⲙⲟⲉⲓϩ, ⲙⲟⲓⲁϩ *S*, ⲙⲁⲓⲁϩ *F* nn m, μοεῖ, μώιον (WS 147 n), measure for fodder &c: Ryl 319 *S* ⲟⲩⲙ. ⲡⲧⲱⲁⲣ, PRain 4721 *S* sim, PStras 124 *S* ⲛϥⲣⲉⲣⲉ, BM 602 15 *F* ⲛ̅ⲣⲣⲏ, WS *lc S* ⲡⲟⲓⲕ (reeds); or grain: BM 1055 *S* ⲛⲥⲟⲅⲟ; Kr 247 *S* ? a vessel.

ⲙⲟⲩϩ *SAA²F*, ⲙⲟϩ *B*, ⲙⲉϩ- *SF*, ⲙⲁϩ- *S* (Kr 238) *AA²B*, ⲙⲁϩ⳿ *SAB*, ⲙⲟϩ⳿ *S* (Ep 484, PLond 4 499, PJkôw), ⲙⲉϩ⳿, ⲙⲉ(ϩ)⳿ *F*, ⲙⲉϩ† *SBF*, ⲙⲏϩ†

SAA² vb **I** tr, *fill*: Ge 1 28 *SA* (Cl) *B*, Ps 80 10 *SB*, Jo 16 6 *SA²B* πληροῦν, Is 63 3 *SB*, Mt 14 20 *SBF* πλήρης; no Gk: Is 32 12† *B* (*SF* om), Jer 24 2† *SB*, Mk 8 8† *S* (*B* om); PS 133 *S* ⲁⲥⲙⲉϩ ⲛⲕⲁ ⲛⲓⲙ, CA 105 *S* barns ⲛϥⲙⲁϩⲟⲩ, C 43 5 *B* fame ⲙ. ⲛ†ⲡⲟⲗⲓⲥ, PMéd 268 *S* powder (ξηρόν) for abcesses (?) ⲛϥⲙⲁϩⲟⲩ *fills them* (brings to head, Chassinat, cf ⲙ. ⲉϩⲣⲁⲓ), ShIF 197 *S* ⲡⲁϩⲟ ⲉⲧⲙ.†, ShC 73 38 *S* heart heavy ⲛ ⲉϥⲙ.†, *ib* 162 *S* edges (? sleeves) of garment ⲉⲩϭⲟⲭⲉⲃ ⲛ ⲉⲩⲙ.†, Kr 190 *S* ⲥⲉⲙ.† ⲥⲉϣϣⲁⲧ, Ryl 162 *S* sim (cf πλέον ἔλασσον).   c ⲡ- of thing *wherewith* filled: Ps 109 6 SB, Ez 28 16 SB, Ro 15 13 *B* (*S* ϫⲱⲕ ⲉⲃⲟⲗ) πλη., Ge 2 21 *SB* ἀναπλ., Pro 8 21 SAB, Mic 3 8 SAB ἐμπλ., Nu 7 14† SB, Job 14 1† SB πλήρης; Ps 13 4† SB, Mk 15 36 SBF, AP 4 *A²* ⲉⲩⲙ.† ⲛⲅⲩⲡⲟⲕⲣⲓⲥⲓⲥ, γέμειν; Pro 6 34† SAB, Jo 19 29 *SA²B* μεστός; Br 240 *S* ⲉⲩⲙ. ⲙⲡⲧⲏⲣϥ ⲡⲟⲩⲟⲉⲓⲛ, BG 26 *S* ⲡⲟⲩⲟⲓⲛ ⲉⲧⲙ.† ⲛⲧⲃⲃⲟ, BHom 128 *S* moon ⲙ.† ⲡⲟⲩⲟⲉⲓⲛ, BMis 350 *S* ⲁϥⲙⲁϩⲧ ⲛϭⲟⲙ = BSM 15 *B*;   c ϩⲛ-: Lev 16 12 *S* (var ⲡ-, *B* ⲉⲃⲟⲗ ϧⲉⲛ-), Ps 32 5 *S* (var ⲡ-, *B* do) πλήρης, Is 22 2 *S* (*B* ⲡⲧⲉ) ἐμπλ.; Mor 30 25 *F* ⲁϥⲙⲉϩ ⲡⲉϫⲙⲉⲣⲉϩ ϩⲛⲧⲁⲡⲏ of Julian;   c ⲉⲃⲟⲗ ϩⲛ-: Jer 28 34 *B*, Ac 2 4 *SB* ⲡⲓⲙⲡⲗⲁⲛⲁⲓ; PS 117 *S* ⲉⲩⲙ.† ⲉⲃ. ϩⲙⲡⲉⲕⲟⲩϫⲁⲓ.   Qual + nn translates Gk adj: Ps 65 5 *B* ⲙ. ⲛⲣⲟϯ (*S* ϯ ϩⲟⲧⲉ) φοβερός, CaiEuch 317 *B* ⲙⲃⲁⲗ πολυόμματος, Jer 38 12 *SB* ⲡⲟⲩⲧⲁϩ ἔγκαρπος, *ib* 31 17 *B* ⲛⲱⲟⲩ εὐκλεής, Bor 100 27 *S* ⲛⲭⲣⲟ ἐπινίκιος, BHom 47 *S* ⲙⲙⲛⲏϣⲉ (var ⲟϣ ⲙⲙ.) πάνδημος, Pro 17 1 *SA* ⲡϣⲱⲟⲧ πολλῶν... θυμάτων; here ? belongs *B* ⲙ. ⲛⲭⲣⲱⲙ (v ⲙⲟⲩϩ *burn*, Qual);   of payment *in full S*: ST 92 received a *solidus* ⲉϥⲙ.†, CO 174 *tremis* ⲉϥⲙ.† ϩⲓⲛϣⲓ ⲙⲡⲁⲗⲉⲕⲧⲱⲣ, J 1 72 sim;   *fulfil, complete*: C 41 70 *B* ⲛⲧⲁⲙⲁϩ ⲡⲁⲓ ⲛ̅ ⲛⲉϩⲟⲟⲩ ⲛⲉⲣ ϩⲱⲃ, Kr 67 *F* ⲧⲁⲙⲉϩ ⲧⲁⲗⲁⲙⲓⲡ[ⲓ;   with numerals *amount to, reach*: Ge 35 22 *S* (*B* om), Mt 14 21 *F* (*SB* ⲉⲓⲣⲉ), Ac 19 7 *S* (*B* do) εἶναι; Ex 12 37 *B* εἰς, 2 Macc 5 27 *A* ποῦ γίνεσθαι; PS 340 *S* ⲡⲗⲓⲧⲟⲩⲣⲅⲟⲥ...ⲉⲩⲙⲉϩ ⲧ̅ϫ̅ⲉ̅ (cf ϫⲱⲕ e g BMar 21), Pcod 28 *S* ⲡⲉϫⲙⲉϩ ⲙ̅ⲡⲧⲛ ⲛⲣⲱⲙⲉ, Miss 4 651 *S* ⲛⲉⲧⲉϥⲙⲉϩ ϭⲙⲉ ⲛ̅ⲣⲟⲙⲡⲉ in cave, BM 706 *F* ⲁⲩⲙⲉϩ ⲟⲩⲙⲉⲧⲣⲟⲩ ⲉⲡⲟⲩⲉ.   *pay SB* (mostly ⲙ. ⲉⲃⲟⲗ) *F*: Ac 11 29 *B* (*S* diff) εὐπορεῖν; BMar 47 *S* farmers ⲙⲉϩ ⲡⲉⲩⲇⲏⲙⲟⲥⲓⲟⲛ from fields, Bor 248 62 *S* not able ⲉⲙⲉϩ ⲡⲉⲧⲉⲣⲟⲓ, BMis 310 *S* give here the bill ⲛⲧⲁⲙⲁϩⲕ ⲙⲙⲟϥ, ShR 2 3 58 *S* among charitable deeds ϩⲉⲛⲥϭⲁⲓ ⲉⲡⲁϩⲟⲩ (sic MS) ⲉⲩⲉⲣⲟⲩ ⲛⲡⲣⲏⲕⲉ ⲉⲙ̅ⲛ ϭⲟⲙ ⲙⲙⲟⲟⲩ ⲉⲙⲁϩⲟⲩ, ShA 2 267 *S* men ⲙⲉϩ ⲡⲉⲩⲛⲟⲃⲉ ϩⲛⲧⲕⲟⲗⲁⲥⲓⲥ *pay for sins with punishment*, ShHT *H* 24 *S* sim, BMar 12 *S* devil to martyr led to death ⲉⲕⲡⲁⲙⲉϩ ⲡⲉⲓⲡⲉⲑⲟⲟⲩ ⲧⲱⲛ *repay* ? (var CodLeningrad ⲙⲉϩ ⲉⲃⲟⲗ ϣⲁ[ⲁ]ϣ

ⲛⲟⲩⲟⲉⲓⲛ), Bodl(P) d 20 *S* debts ⲧⲁⲣⲡⲙⲁϩⲕ ⲙⲙⲟⲟ-
ⲟⲩ, CO 51 *S* ⲁⲕ]ⲙⲟϧⲧ ⲙⲡⲁⲃⲉⲕⲉ, Ep 94 *S* ⲁⲡⲙⲁϧⲕ
ⲛⲛⲕⲁ ⲛⲓⲙ ⲉⲩⲡⲧⲏⲕϥ ⲉⲣⲟⲛ; c ⲉ- of things *for
which* payed *F*: Kr 10 ⲧⲓⲉ ⲡⲉⲧⲛⲙⲱ(ⲥ) ⲧⲁⲙⲉ(ϩ`ⲕ
(ⲉ)ⲗⲁⲩ at harvest, BP 3241 when thou requirest
them ⲧⲉⲙⲙⲉ(ϩ)ⲕ ⲉⲗⲁⲩ, Cai 8075 ⲉϣⲟⲡⲉ ⲙⲡⲓⲙⲉϧⲕ
ⲉⲗⲁⲟⲩ.

ⲙⲉϩ ⲉⲓⲁⲧ⳯ *v* ⲉⲓⲁ *eye*.

ⲙⲉϩ ⲙⲟⲟⲩ *v* ⲙⲟⲟⲩ.

ⲙⲉϩ, ⲙⲁϩ ⲣⲱ⳯ *SB*, **a** *fill mouth*: BMis 312 *S*
struck by heaven ⲁⲡⲉϥⲗⲁⲥ ⲙ. ⲣⲱϥ, Miss 4 158 *B*
sim. **b** *seize, bite*: c ⲛ- of thing seized, Job 13
14 *S* ἀναλαμβάνειν; Ac 28 3 *S* (*B* ϫⲱⲕϧ) καθάπτειν; ShMich 550 15 *S* beast seeks to ⲙ. ⲣⲱϥ ⲛ-
ⲡⲉϥⲙⲉⲗⲟⲥ; or c ϧⲛ-, ϫⲉⲛ-, Mor 37 135 *S* horse
ⲙ. ⲣⲱϥ ϧⲛⲧⲟⲩⲉⲣⲏⲧⲉ δῆγμα; AM 56 *B* ⲁϥϣⲁⲡⲛ.
ⲣⲱϥ ⲛϩⲏⲧⲟⲩ (cf MIE 2 409 *B*), C 43 187 *B* ⲉⲣⲉⲣⲱϥ ⲙ.† ϫⲉⲛⲧⲉϥϣⲃⲱⲃⲓ; or c ⲉ-, MG 25 236
B hyena ⲙ. ⲣⲱⲥ ⲉⲡⲉⲥⲙⲁⲥ λαμβ., BSM 77 *B* scorpion ⲙ. ⲣⲱⲥ ⲉⲣⲟⲥ = BMis 168 *S* ⲗⲟⲕⲥϥ; or
c ⲉϫⲛ- *S*, Mor 31 72 idiot ⲉⲁϥⲙ. ⲣⲱϥ ⲉϫⲛⲡⲉϥ-
ϧⲟⲓⲧⲉ. As nn *S*: BMOr 8811 209 snake ⲡⲉⲛⲧⲁϥϯ ⲙⲉϩⲣⲟ ⲡⲉ.

ⲙⲉϩ ⲧⲟⲟⲧ⳯, ⲧⲁⲧ⳯ *SF*, ⲙⲁⲣⲧⲟⲧ⳯ *B*, *fill hand, lay hold
on*: Ps 128 7 *B* (*S* ⲙ. ϭⲓⲝ) πληροῦν; Lev 2 2 *S* (*B*
ϫⲟⲣⲡⲥ) δράσσεσθαι; Ez 29 7 *SB* ἐπιλαμβ.; RicciL
260 *F* ⲁϥⲙ. ⲧⲁⲧϥ ⲛⲛⲓⲧⲉⲛ (cf C 43 211 *B* ⲙ. ϫⲓⲝ),
LAl 14 *S* ⲁϥⲙ. ⲧⲟⲧⲉϥ & took 4 (stones, cf ib 107).

ⲙⲉϩ ϧⲏⲧ⳯ *SA*, ⲙⲁϩ ϧⲏⲧ⳯ *B*, *fill belly*: Pro 14 14
B (*SA* ⲥⲉⲓ), ib 18 20 *SA* πιμπλάναι; Ac 2 13 *B* (*S*
ϧⲏⲧ⳯ ⲙ.†) μεστοῦν; Ps 16 14 *SB* (*F* ⲥⲓ), Lam 3 29
B χορτάζειν; MG 25 196 *B* ⲙⲡⲓⲙ. ϧⲏⲧ ⲡⲱⲓⲕ κόρον
λαμβ.; C 43 141 *B* drank ϣⲁⲧⲉϥⲙ. ϧⲏⲧϥ.
As nn *B*, *satiety*: Dif 1 115 not beguiled by ⲫⲙ.
ϧⲏⲧϥ ⲛⲧⲉ ⲟⲩϩⲉϫⲓ.

II intr *SABF*, *be full*: 4 Kg 4 4 *S* (BP 10623,
cf Miss 4 782), Mt 13 48 *SBF*, 2 Cor 10 6 *B* (*S*
ϫⲱⲕ ⲉⲃ.) πλη.; Si 39 29 *S* ἐπικαλύπτειν (*l*? ἐπικλύζειν cf inundare); Lu 14 23 *SB* γεμ.; C 89
159 *B* water (Nile) ⲁϥⲙ. ⲉⲛϣⲱⲓ, BMis 494 *S* river
stayed ⲉϥⲙ. ϧⲛⲟⲩⲙⲟϧⲛ ⲉⲃⲟⲗ, CR ’87 376 *S* recipe
for breast ⲉⲥⲙ., (or ? *burning*, *v* next word & BKU
1 25 vo). c ⲛ-: Ps 64 9 *SB* πλη., Ge 6 11 *SB*,
Pro 12 21 *SA*(*B* ⲥⲓ), Lu 5 26 *SB* πιμπλ., Ez 7 23 *SB*
πλήρης; PS 57 *S* ⲁⲣⲱⲓ ⲙ. ⲡⲉⲟⲟⲩ, ShA 1 256 *S*
coins ⲉⲧⲙ. ⲙⲡⲉⲩϣⲉⲓ, BSM 42 *B* ϣⲁⲧⲉⲙⲙⲁ ⲙ.
ⲡⲣⲱⲟⲩⲧ ⲡⲉⲙϧⲓⲟⲙⲓ = BMis 389 *S*; c ϧⲛ-:
Eccl 1 8 *F* (*S* ⲥⲉⲓ) πλη.; c ϧⲁ-: ShC 42 63 *S*
hell ⲛⲁⲙ. ⲁⲛ ϧⲁⲡⲉⲧⲟⲩⲛⲁⲣⲟⲕϧⲟⲩ therein, Miss 4
697 *S* ship & ⲡⲉⲧϩⲓⲱⲱϥ ⲛ ⲡⲉⲧϥⲙ.† ϧⲁⲣⲟⲟⲩ; c
ⲉϫⲛ-: C 73 213 (not Sh) ⲉⲣⲉⲡⲟⲩⲁ ⲡⲟⲩⲁ ⲙ. ⲉϫⲱϥ
ⲉⲃⲟⲗ ⲡⲉϥϩⲣⲟⲧⲉ (= ⲙ. ⲉⲃⲟⲗ); c ϧⲓⲧⲛ-: ShC 42
63 *S* sea ⲙⲉⲥⲙ. ϧⲓⲧⲛⲙⲙⲟⲟⲩ flowing into it.

Of moon, *wax SB*: Si 39 16 *S* πλη.; R 1 4 66 *S*
ⲉⲧⲟⲱⲭⲃ ⲁⲩⲱ ⲉⲧⲙ. = AM 126 *B* ⲉⲑⲙⲉϧ αὐξάνειν;
ShP 130⁴ 105 *S* moon’s light ⲙ., BKU 1 25 ro *S*
recipe ⲃⲓⲧϥ ⲉⲩⲛⲟⲩϧⲉ…[ⲉⲣⲉ]ⲡⲟⲟϧ ⲙ., KroppK *sf*
sim; *be paid S*: Ep 177 will deliver you (to
justice) ϣⲁⲛⲧⲟⲩⲙ. *till debts paid*, PJkôw ⲉⲧⲁϥⲓⲧϥ
(sc field) ⲛⲧⲟⲟⲧϥ ϣⲁⲡⲧⲉⲧⲉϥⲙⲓⲥⲱⲥ(ⲓⲥ) ⲙ., ST 38
ⲧⲉⲃⲣⲓ ⲥⲱϣⲉ ⲙ. ϧⲛⲡⲕⲟⲓⲛⲟⲛ, CO 169 ⲁⲓϫⲓ ⲁⲓⲙ.
ⲡⲧⲟⲟⲧⲕ the rent, ST 46 ⲁⲛⲙ. ⲙⲙⲟⲟⲩ (wages) ⲛ-
ⲧⲟⲟⲧⲕ, J 15 57 ⲁⲓϫⲓ ⲁⲓⲙ. ϧⲓⲧⲟⲟⲧⲕ full price.

With following adverb.

—— ⲉⲃⲟⲗ *SBF* **a** tr, *fill*: Phil 2 2 *B* (*SF* ϫⲱⲕ
ⲉⲃ.) πλη., Ex 23 26 *B* (*S* do) ἀναπλ., Is 65 20 *B*
(*S* ϫⲱⲕ) ἐμπλ.; Jo 2 7 *S* (var ⲙ. ⲉϩⲣⲁⲓ, *B* om ⲉⲃ.)
γεμίζειν; MG 25 336 *B* ⲉⲁⲩⲙⲁϩϥ ⲉⲃ. ϫⲉⲛⲟⲩⲛⲓϣϯ
ⲡⲉⲩϥⲣⲟⲥⲩⲛⲏ; *pay*: P 129¹⁶ 85 *S* money borrowed ϣⲁⲛϯⲙⲁϥ ⲉⲃ. = C 86 348 *B*, C 43 116 *B*
ⲁⲣⲉⲧⲉⲡⲁ. ⲛⲛⲁⲓϫⲏⲙⲟⲥⲓⲟⲛ ⲉⲃ., Va 63 16 *B* ϯⲛⲁ-
ⲙⲁϩⲑⲏⲛⲟⲩ ⲉⲃ. ⲙⲡⲓⲕⲉⲫⲁⲗⲉⲟⲛ = BMis 395 *S* ⲛⲧⲁ-
ⲡⲗⲏⲣⲟⲩ. **b** intr, *be full, filled, paid*: Ge 25 24 *B*,
Z 356 *S* store-room ⲉϥⲙ.† ⲉⲃ. ⲉⲣⲱϥ πλη., Ps 74 8 *S*†,
Jo 2 7 *S* (*B* om ⲉⲃ.) sim πλήρης; CaiEuch 394 *B*
ⲁⲩⲙ. ⲉⲃ. ⲛϫⲉ ⲡⲓϩⲙⲟⲧ τελειοῦν; Va 61 208 *B* ⲁⲓⲟⲩⲱ
ⲉⲓⲥⲓ…ⲁⲓⲙ. ⲉⲃ., Wor 268 *S* ⲣϣⲁⲡⲡⲉϣϣⲟⲣ ⲙ.
ⲉⲃ. *when rent due*, ShC 42 160 *S* rivers ⲉⲩⲙ.† ⲉⲃ.
ⲉⲣⲱⲟⲩ (cf ⲙ. ⲉϩⲣⲁⲓ), Kr 72 *F* ⲁⲅⲓ ⲧⲁⲛ (= ⲉⲧⲁⲧⲛ)
ⲉⲩⲙ.† ⲉⲃ., AZ 23 35 *F* sim; c ⲛ-: 2 Tim 1 4
S (*B* do) πλη. gen, Ps 89 14 *S* (*B* ⲙ. ϫⲉⲛ-) ἐμπλη.
gen, Cl 2 3 *A* ⲉⲧ-ⲉⲧⲛⲙ.† ⲁⲃ. ⲙⲡϣⲁϫⲡⲉ μεστός
gen, CO 396 *S* send thy news ⲉⲓⲉⲙ. ⲉⲃ. ⲡⲣⲁϣⲉ;
c ϧⲛ-, ϫⲉⲛ- Ps 103 24 *SB*, Lu 1 15 *S* (var ⲙ. ⲛ-) *B*
πλη. gen, Is 31 4 *SBF* ἐμπλη.; Ps 103 13 *S* (*B* do)
χορτ., Is 6 3 *B*† (*S* om ⲉⲃ.) πλήρης gen; BSM 41
B chests ⲉⲩⲙ.† ⲉⲃ. ϫⲉⲛⲥⲙⲟⲧ ⲛⲓⲃⲉⲛ = BMis 387 *S*
ⲙ.† ⲛ-, DeV 2 43 *B* ⲁⲥⲙ. ⲉⲃ. ϫⲉⲛⲡⲓⲣⲓⲱⲓϣ. As
nn *B*, *fulfilment, limit*: DeV 2 45 end of our life
ⲫⲙ. ⲉⲃ. ⲡⲕⲉⲧ ⲡⲉⲣⲟⲟⲩ.

—— ⲉϩⲟⲩⲛ, ⲉϧ. *SB* tr, *fill up, supplement*: Va
57 265 *B* ⲛⲧⲟⲩⲙ. ⲉϧ. ⲙⲡⲉⲧⲉⲛϣⲣⲟϧ (Phil 2 30 ⲙ.
ⲉϧ.) ἀναπλ.; MG 25 369 *B* ⲉϥⲙ. ⲛⲁϥ ⲉϧ. ⲙⲛ-
ⲭⲣⲉⲟⲥ of priesthood, BAp 149 *S* devil’s attacks
ϣⲁϥⲙⲁϩⲟⲩ (sc evil spirits) ⲉϧ. ⲉⲣⲟⲓ to fight with
me. ϫⲓⲛⲙ. ⲉϧ. *B*, *completion*: Va 57 86 ⲛϫ.
ⲛⲛⲏ ⲉⲧⲁϥϣⲁⲧ ⲙⲙⲟⲟⲩ.

—— ⲉϩⲣⲁⲓ *S* tr & intr, *fill up*: ShA 2 113
wounds ⲉⲓ ⲉϩⲟⲩⲛ ⲛ ⲁⲩⲙ. ⲉϩ. by much treatment,
ib 234 sim, PMéd 259 old wound ⲉⲕⲟⲩⲱϣ ⲉⲙⲟϧⲥ
ⲉϩⲣⲁⲓ, Mor 22 61 Nile ⲙ. ⲉϩ. ⲕⲟϯ ⲕⲟϯ till
covers earth, Kr 1 4 diary of inundation ⲁⲛⲙⲟⲟⲩ
ⲙ. ⲉϩ.

—— *SAB* nn m, *fullness, contents*: Ps 49 12 *B*
(*S* ϫⲱⲕ ⲉⲃ.), Eccl 4 6 *S* (*F* ϧⲁⲣⲡⲥ), Ro 15 29 *B* (*S*

do), CaiEuch 507 *B* ϥⲙ. ⲧⲏⲣϥ ⲛⲧⲉⲕⲕⲗⲏⲥⲓⲁ πλήρωμα, Col 2 2 *B* (*S* ⲧⲱⲧ ⲛϩⲏⲧ) πληροφορία, Deu 33
23 *B* (*S* ⲥⲉⲓ) πλησμονή; ShC 73 133 *S* ⲡⲥⲉⲡⲣⲟⲥⲉⲭⲉ
ⲁⲛ ⲉⲡⲙ. ⲛⲧⲉⲯⲩⲭⲏ, TU 43 7 *A* ⲡⲙ. as attribute
of God, BMEA 44720 *S* payment of ϩⲟⲗⲧ ⲡⲁⲕ
ϩⲁⲡϥⲙ.;　of moon, stars: Job 38 32 *B* (*S* om)
κόμη; Si 43 8 *S* αὐξάνειν; ShP 130⁴ 126 *S* moon's
ⲙ. ⲉϥⲁⲩϫⲁⲡⲉ ⲡⲡϣⲏⲛ;　of river's rise: BMis 474
S season of ⲡⲙ. ⲙⲡⲙⲟⲟⲩ, BAp 86 *S* sim, P 54
119 *B* ϩⲁⲡⲙ. جاري، سواقي, *channels, conduits.*

ϭⲓⲙⲙ. *S, filling, completion*: Bor 248 58 ⲧϭⲓⲙⲙⲉϩ
ⲡϣⲱⲧ (*cf* Col 1 24 ϫⲱⲕ ⲉⲃ. ἀναπληρ.); ShP 130⁴
105 ⲧϭ. ⲙⲛⲧϭⲓⲛϭⲱⲕⲃ of moon; ϭ. ⲉⲃⲟⲗ: PS 31
that they should be affrighted ϩⲛⲧⲉⲩϭ. ⲉⲃ. ⲧⲏⲣⲥ.

ⲙⲉϩ- *SF*, ⲙⲁϩ- *S* (archaic) *AA²BF* pref to ordinal numerals, lit *filling, completing*: a ⲛⲛ not
expressed, Ge 4 19 *SB* δεύτερος, Is 19 24 *SB* τρίτος, Ps 11 tit *SB* ὄγδοος; C 43 208 *B* one blow
enough, I should not add ⲙⲡⲓⲙⲁϩⲃ̄, MG 25 26 *B*
ϯⲙⲁϩϯ̄.　b followed by ⲛ+ⲛⲛ, Lev 23 8 *SB*,
Jer 25 1 *SB*, Mk 14 41 *SBF*, PS 46 *S* ⲡⲙⲉϩ-
ⲙⲛⲧⲥⲛⲟⲟⲩⲥ ⲡⲁⲓⲱⲛ, El 84 *A* ⲧⲙⲁϩⲥⲱⲉ ⲡⲣⲁⲙⲡⲉ,
Lant 51 22 *S* ⲧⲙⲁϩ⳨ⲙ̄ⲧ̄ ⲡⲣⲟⲙⲡⲉ, Z 106 *Sⁱ* ⲧⲙⲉϩ-
ⲯ̄ⲗ̄ ⲡⲣⲁⲙⲡⲉ, Br 83 *S* ⲧⲙⲉϩⲟⲩⲏⲣ ⲡⲧⲁϫⲓⲥ;　prefixed to ⲛⲛ (only with *two*), Nu 29 17 *S* ⲡⲙ. ϩⲟⲟⲩ
ⲥⲛⲁⲩ (*B* ⲉϩ. ⲙⲙⲁϩⲃ̄) ἡ ἡμέρα ἡ δευτ., Hag 1 1
SA ⲧⲙⲉϩⲣⲟⲙⲡⲉ ⲥⲛⲧⲉ (*B* ⲙⲁϩⲃ̄ϯ ⲡⲣ.), Jo 9 24
SA²B ⲡⲙⲉϩⲥⲉⲡ ⲥⲛⲁⲩ ἐκ δευτέρου, PS 271 *S* ⲡⲙⲉϩ-
ⲭⲱⲣⲏⲙⲁ ⲥⲛⲁⲩ ⲏ ⲡⲙⲉϩϣⲟⲙⲛⲧ.　c following
ⲛⲛ *B*, Ge 1 19 ⲡⲓⲉϩⲟⲟⲩ ⲙⲙⲁϩⲝ̄ (*S* ⲡⲙⲉϩϥ. ⲛϩ.)
τέταρτος, AM 261 ⲕⲉⲭⲗⲟⲙ ⲙⲙⲁϩϥ̄;　rarely *S*:
Nu 10 6 ⲥⲛⲙⲁⲥⲓⲁ ⲙⲙⲉϩϣⲟⲙⲛⲧⲉ, Eccl 4 15 ϩⲉⲣϣⲓⲣⲉ ⲙⲙⲉϩⲥⲛⲁⲩ, Ap 211 ⲙⲟⲩ do.　d ⲙⲁϩ- *S*:
Est 7 2 ⲙⲁϩⲣⲟⲟⲩ ⲥⲛⲁⲩ, PS 193 ⲙⲉϩⲥⲛⲁⲩ ⲡϣⲏⲛ
& ⲙⲁϩⲧⲟⲟⲩ do, *ib* 224 ⲙⲁϩϣⲟⲙⲛⲧ & ⲙⲉϩϣ.,
BG 16 ⲙⲁϩⲧⲟⲉ & ⲙⲉϩϥⲧⲟⲉ, My 88 ⲙⲁϩϣⲉ &
ⲙⲉϩϣⲉ;　*F*: BM 591 ⲙⲁϩⲥⲛⲉⲩ, CMSS 39 ⲙⲁϩ-
ⲥⲛⲟⲩⲧⲓ.

ⲙⲟⲩϩ *SAA²F*, ⲙⲟϩ *B*, ⲙⲉϩ†(?) *B* vb intr, *burn,
glow*: Job 31 12 *SB*, Ps 49 3 *SB*, Is 30 27 *SBF*,
Jo 5 35 *SA²B*, Va 62 277 *B* without fire ⲙⲡⲁⲣⲉ-
ⲡⲓⲥⲱⲟⲩϩⲃⲉⲛ ⲙ. καίειν, Hos 7 6 *AB* ἀνακ. Nu 11
1 *SB*, Ps 77 38 *B* (*S* ϫⲉⲣⲟ), Is 9 19 *B* (*S* ⲣⲱⲕϩ)
ἐκκ.; Ex 24 17 (P 131⁷ 43, var ϯ ϣⲁϩ, *B* ϩⲓ ϣⲁϩ),
Dan 7 9 *S* (*B* ⲟⲓ ⲡϣⲁϩ) φλέγειν, Ps 104 32 *SB*
καταφ., ClPr 54 41 *S* youth ⲙ. ⲛⲑⲉ ⲡⲟⲩⲕⲱϩⲧ
φλεγμαίνειν; Ps 77 21 *SB*, Jer 21 12 *B* (*S* ϫ.), Lu
12 49 *S* (PS 300 & *B*, *S* H ϫ.) ἀνάπτειν; EstD 7
S πυροῦν (var πληροῦν), BMis 233 *S* ⲁⲩⲙ. ⲉⲃⲟⲗ
ϩⲙⲡⲉⲡⲛⲁ ἀναζωπυρεῖν (but *cf* Ac 4 8 *S* πληροῦν);
Nu 11 1 *S* (var & *B* ϭⲱⲡⲧ) θυμοῦν; Job 29 3 *S* (*B*
ⲉⲣ ⲟⲩⲱⲓⲛⲓ) αὐγεῖν; 2 Pet 1 19 *S* (*B* do) φαίνειν; Si

26 17 *S* ἐκλάμπειν; Gk om: Eccl 7 7 *S* (*F* ⲧⲱⲕ),
Mt 13 42 *SB*; PS 373 *S* demons perish ⲛⲧⲉⲡⲉⲩ-
ϣⲁϩ ⲙ., BIF 13 113 *S* ⲟⲩϣⲁϩ ⲡⲕⲱϩⲧ ⲉϥⲙ. =MG
25 304 *B* ϯ ⲙⲟⲩϩ, MIE 2 351 *B* at prayer fingers
ⲙ. like torches, BAp 162 *S* stone on steel ϣⲁⲣⲉⲡ-
ⲕⲱϩⲧ ⲙ.　With ⲉ- *SB*, *burn at, for*: TT 89 *S*
ϩⲏⲃⲥ ⲉⲧⲙ. ⲉⲡⲙⲁ, AM 138 *B* basin of holy water
ⲉⲣⲉⲟⲩⲫⲁⲛⲟⲥ ⲙ. ⲉⲣⲟϥ, BSM 101 sim = Mor 22
112 *S* ⲙ. ⲙⲡⲉϥⲙⲧⲟ ⲉⲃⲟⲗ.　With ⲉϩⲟⲩⲛ ⲉ- *S*,
burn against: Ob 18 (*A* ϫ., *B* ⲣⲱⲕϩ) ἐκκαί. εἰς,
ShA² 279 God's wrath ⲉϥⲙ. ⲉϩ. ⲉⲣⲱⲧⲛ.　With
ϩⲛ-, ϩⲉⲛ-, ⲛ- of thing burnt, fuel: Deu 4 11 *S* ⲙ.
ϩⲛⲟⲩⲥⲁⲧⲉ = *B* ⲙ. ⲛⲭⲣⲱⲙ πυρί, Jud 15 14 *S*
ϩⲛⲟⲩⲕⲱϩⲧ ἐν π., Job 41 11 *S* (*B* om) ϩⲛϩⲉⲛϫⲃⲃⲉⲥ
πυρὶ ἀνθράκων, Pro 26 20 *S* (*A* ϫ.) ϩⲛϩⲁϩ ⲡϣⲉ ἐν,
BSM 100 *B* ϩⲉⲛⲟⲩϫ̄. ⲡⲉⲙⲟⲩⲑⲏⲡ; Ex 3 2 *B* ⲛⲭ.
πυρί, ShA 2 100 *S* ⲁⲩⲙ. ⲡⲕⲱϩⲧ;　or ϩⲓⲧⲛ-: Is
5 24 *S* ϩ. ⲟⲩϫⲃⲃⲉⲥ (*B* ⲣⲱⲕϩ ⲉⲃⲟⲗ ϩ., *F* ϫⲉⲗⲁ ϩ.),
ib 30 33 *SF* ϩ. ⲟⲩⲑⲏⲡ (*B* ⲡⲧⲉⲡ-) ὑπό.

—— ⲉⲃⲟⲗ *SB*, meanings as ⲙ.: Lev 13 38 *S*
(*B* ⲉⲣ ⲟⲩⲱⲓⲛⲓ) αὐγάζειν, DeV 1 103 *B* face ⲙ. ⲉⲃ.
like fire.

Qual *B*: Eph 6 16 (var ⲙⲟϩ, *S* ϫ.) πεπυρωμέ-
νος. Or ? in following is ⲙⲟϩ *fill*, C 43 113 ⲑⲣⲓⲣ
ⲉⲥⲙⲉϩ ⲡⲭⲣⲱⲙ, AM 102 ⲓϭⲧ ⲉⲩⲙ. ⲛⲭ., C 86 296,
RAl 101 sim.

—— *S* ⲛⲛ m, *burning, inflammation* (Chassinat):
PMéd 271 recipe for ⲡⲙ. ⲛⲧⲁⲡⲉ.
V ⲧⲙϩⲟ.

ⲙⲟⲩϩ *S*, ⲙⲟⲩϩ *A*, ⲙⲟϩ *B* vb intr, *look*: Ac
11 6 *S* (*B* ϯ ⲡϩⲏⲧ) ἀτενίζειν εἰς; Pro 4 25 *A* (*SB*
ⲉⲓⲱⲣⲙ, *B* var ϭⲱⲣⲉⲙ) νεύειν; ShC 42 116 *S* like
man ⲉϥⲙ. ⲉⲡⲟⲩⲉ or upon whom others look (ϭⲱϣⲧ, ? Lam 3 11), MG 25 163 *B* sick man after
vision ⲁⲓⲙ. (*sic*) ⲉⲡϣⲱⲓ in great joy, TU 43 3 *A*
ⲙ. ⲁⲡⲁⲟⲩⲣⲏⲧⲉ ⲕⲡⲟ ϫⲉ-, ShHT H 29 *S* ⲉⲡⲙ. ⲉ-
ϩⲉⲡⲙⲛⲏϣⲉ but saints ⲛⲁⲩ ⲉⲡϩⲛⲧ, ShC 73 63 *S*
ⲉⲧⲣⲉⲩⲙ. ⲉϩⲟⲩⲛ ⲙⲡⲥⲱⲟⲩϩ by chinks of door,
ShBMOr 8810 448 *S* some they respect, others
ⲉⲩⲙ. ⲛⲥⲱⲟⲩ ⲣⲱ ⲁⲛ ϩⲟⲗⲱⲥ, WZKM 26 339 *S* corn
I ground (but) ⲙⲡⲓⲙ. ⲛⲥⲱⲟⲩ [ϩⲟ]ⲗⲟⲥ took no heed
of.　As ⲛⲛ m *B*, *appearance*: Lev 21 5 (*S* diff)
ὄψις (*cf* 19 27 *B* ϩⲟ ὄψ.).

ⲙⲁϩⲉ *SA*, ⲙⲁϩⲓ *BF*, ⲙⲉϩⲓ *F* nn m, *ell, cubit*
(*forearm*): Nu 11 31 *SB*, Pro 31 19 *B* (*SA* diff),
Ez 40 7 *SB*, Zech 5 2 *SAB*, Ap 21 17 *S* (*B* diff)
πῆχυς; K 77 *B* ⲡⲙ. ذراع *forearm*; Mus 40 37 *S*
(Reg Pachom) ⲉⲕⲡⲁⲕⲁ ⲟⲩⲙ. between thee & him,
BM 170 *S*, ShC 73 168 *S* sim, BMis 219 *S* κοπρία
overtopping city ⲡⲁϣⲉ ⲙⲙ., C 43 172 *B* hung ⲙ.
ⲥⲛⲁⲩ above ground, ShBor 247 118 *S* how to know
good & evil κατὰ θε ⲡⲣⲉⲛⲟⲓⲕⲟⲍⲟⲙⲏ ⲉⲣⲉⲟⲩⲙ. ⲏ

ⲕⲉⲥⲟⲧϩⲉϥ ⲧⲣⲉϥⲥⲟⲟⲩⲧⲛ ⲛϭⲓ ⲡⲉⲧⲉⲓⲣⲉ ⲙⲙⲟϥ *foot-rule* (?), Z 106 *S* ⲓⲏ ⲙⲁϧⲣⲓ ⲡⲙⲟⲟⲩ, BM 1114 *S* 6th ⲙ. ϫⲱⲕ (inundation), Kr 1 27 *S* sim, BM 528 no 18 *F* ⲡⲙⲉⲣⲓ among measures. *half-cubit*: Ez 43 17 *B* ⲟⲩⲫⲁϣⲓ ⲙⲙ. (var ϫⲉⲙⲁ.) ἥμισυ π., Ex 25 17 *B* ⲟⲩϩⲟⲥ ⲙⲙ. ἥ. π.; LMär 5 *S* ⲟⲩϭⲓⲥⲙ. = C 43 60 *B* ⲟⲩϥⲁϣⲙ., Mor 40 31 *S* ⲟⲩϭ. ⲙ. = ib 41 146 *S* ⲟⲩⲡⲁϣⲙ. *Lion's cubit*, 7th lunar station: K 51 *B* ⲡⲙⲙ. ذراع الأسد (v IgR 164).

ⲙⲁϧⲉ *SA*, ⲙⲁϧⲓ *B* nn m, *flax*: Ex 9 31 *B*, Pro 31 13 *S* (var Mor 43 255 & *B* ⲉⲓⲁⲁⲩ) *A* λίνον, Jos 2 6 *SA* (Cl) λινοκαλάμη, Is 19 9 *SB* ⲙ. ⲡⲕⲱⲕ ⲗ. σχιστόν (P 43 111) (كتان الشنور); Is 1 31 *SB*, ClPr 30 16 *S* ⲥⲁⲁϭⲉ, ⲙ., ϭⲗⲱ ⲥⲧⲓⲡⲡⲓⲟⲛ (cf ⲗⲁⲥ); Dan 3 46 *S* (& cit Cai 8027, *B* ⲑⲏⲡ) νάφθα (in other reff to this ⲙ. omitted: Bor 264 39, P 44 115, Tri 526); P 129¹⁶ 11 *S* dealer bought all ⲥⲓⲡⲡⲟⲛ (ⲥⲧⲓⲡ.) of fields sown with ⲙ., ShIF 188 *S* ⲟⲩⲕⲁϣ ⲙⲙ., EW 73 *B* ⲡⲓϫⲁϫⲓⲱⲗⲡⲉ ⲡⲓⲧⲟϭ *straw* that comes from ⲙ., ShC 73 51 *S* season of ⲡ ⲣⲱϩ ⲉⲡⲙ., J 59 4 *S*, ST 422 *S*, Kr 92 *S* fields of ⲙ., RE 14 23 *S* fields ⲛⲧϫⲁⲓⲧⲟⲩ (ⲙ)ⲙ. (*sic l*, cf CO 304), Ann 21 74 *S* see to ⲡⲕⲟⲩⲓ ⲙⲙ. ⲛⲧⲣⲉⲩϭⲁⲗⲉϥ, v BMOr 6201 A 72 sv ⲗⲁⲥ, BKU 1 268 *S* ⲡⲉⲕⲟⲩⲓ ⲙⲙ. ... ⲡⲧⲉⲧⲛⲥⲟⲙⲛϥ (*l* ⲥⲟⲙⲥ) ⲕⲁ[ⲗⲱⲥ, Bodl(P) b 9 *S* ⲙ. ⲉⲩⲥⲛⲙ ϧⲏⲡⲡⲩⲣⲅⲟⲥ, Kr 106 *S* rent for κοίτων ⲡⲧⲁⲧⲡⲉⲱⲧⲡ ⲡⲉⲙ. (ⲉ)ⲣⲟϥ (cf ⲕⲟⲓ. BM 1089), CO 453 *S*, ST 216 *S* ⲙ. ⲡⲥⲡⲟⲩϥ of *last year's crop*, Ep 353 *S* ⲙⲏⲣ ⲙⲙ., C 43 80 *B* martyr wound about with ϧⲁⲡⲧⲉⲃⲓ ⲡⲙ. & burnt (cf AM 319 sim ⲡⲟϭ ⲡⲥⲓⲡⲡⲉⲡ). ⲉϧⲣⲁ ⲙ. *S*, *linseed*: PMéd 114 λινόσπερμον (Chassinat), Bodl(P) 2 64 *S* oil of ⲉϧⲣⲉ ⲙ.; cf ⲑⲉⲣϣ. ⲣⲉϥϯ ⲙ. *B*, *flaxseller*: C 86 162 ⲟⲩⲣ. ⲡⲁⲡⲓϧⲓⲟⲙⲓ (*l* ⲡⲡⲓ-).

ⲙⲁⲁϧⲉ ⲙⲁϧⲉ *A* v ⲙⲟⲟϣⲉ.

ⲙⲁϧⲉ *S*, ⲙⲉϧⲓ *F* v ⲁⲙⲁϧⲧⲉ **II** s f.

ⲙⲉϧⲓ *F* v ⲙⲁϧⲉ ell.

ⲙⲁϩϧⲉ, ⲙⲉϧⲉ *S*, ⲙⲉϧⲓ *B* nn m, *feather*: Lev 1 16 *B* (Va ⲡⲙⲙ., *S* diff), Aeg 276 *S* ϩⲉⲡⲙ. ⲡⲧⲁⲱⲥ πτερόν, Tri 724 *S* fans ⲉⲃⲟⲗ ϧⲣⲉⲡⲙⲙ. ريش, PMéd 240 *S* ibis's used for applying liniment, Cat 147 *B* raven's ⲛ̄ϫⲁⲙⲉ, Leyd 274 *S* ⲙ. ⲣⲱⲧ ⲉⲣⲟϥ as birds, Mun 180 *S* ⲡⲉⲡⲧⲁⲡⲉϥⲙ. ⲣⲱⲧ *lancet B*: K 135, P 55 10 ⲡⲓⲙ. (1 var ⲡⲓ-) ريش الفصاد.

ⲙⲁϩϧⲉ *S* nn f, *tumour, abscess* (? Chassinat PMéd 126): ib 130 in eye, ib 304 in anus, ib 130, 273 causing ⲙ. to come up (?) ⲉⲓ ⲉϧⲣⲁⲓ, ib 126 to extract or destroy it ⲡⲟⲣⲉϧ (*l* ⲡⲟⲣⲕⲥ), ib 268 to cleanse ⲕⲁⲑⲁⲣⲓⲍⲉ.

ⲙⲏϩϧⲉ *A* v ⲙⲁϩ.

ⲙⲟⲉⲓϧⲉ, ⲙⲟⲓ. *S*, ⲙⲁⲉⲓ. *AA²*, ⲙⲁⲓ. *S*ᶠ*AF*, ⲙⲁⲓϧⲓ *F* nn f m, *wonder*; Ps 88 5 *S* (*B* ϣⲫⲏⲣⲓ) θαυμάσιος, Pro 6 30 *A* (*SB* ϣⲡⲏⲣⲉ), Cl 50 1 *A* f, ib 43 1, 60 1 m θαυμαστός; Jo 4 48 *A²* (*SBF* ϣ.) τέρας; Cl 25 1 *A* σημεῖον; Sa 5 2 *S* f (*B* ϣ.) παράδοξος; ShA 2 346 *S* ⲡⲙⲙ. of God in Egypt, ShC 42 103 *S* ⲟⲩⲙ. ⲁⲡⲧⲉ that they should malign thee, ShMIF 23 142 *S* garment ⲉⲟⲩⲙ. ⲧⲉ ⲉⲡⲁⲩ ⲉⲣⲟⲥ, ShRE 10 161 *S* ⲡⲙ. ⲧⲏⲣϥ, Mor 38 95 *S*ᶠ ⲡⲉⲓⲛⲟϭ ⲙⲙ.

ⲣ ⲙ. *SAA²F*, *wonder, be astonished*, no object: Jo 5 20 *A²* (*SB* ⲣ ϣ.) θαυμάζειν; Mor 56 31 *S* looking round ⲉϥⲟ ⲙⲙ. + ϫⲉ-: Jo 4 27 *A²F* (*SB* ⲣ ϣ.) θαυμ.; ib 13 22 *A²* (*S* = Gk, *B* diff) ἀπορεῖν; Pcod 12 *S* ϯⲣ ⲙ. ϫⲉⲓⲱⲣⲁⲡⲡⲏⲥ...ⲁϥϧⲁⲗⲉⲓ. ⲉ ⲡ-, *wonder at*: Jth 10 19 *S*, Lu 24 12 *S* (var & *B* ⲣ ϣ.), Cl 1 2 *A* who hath not ⲣ ⲙ. ⲙⲡⲉⲧⲛⲙⲙⲏϣⲉ? θαυμ. acc; FR 72 *S* ⲁⲓϯ (ἔτι) ⲉⲡⲉⲣ ⲙ. ⲉⲙⲡⲉⲡⲧⲁϥϣⲱⲡⲉ (var ⲉϫⲡ-). ⲉ ⲉϫⲡ-: Mic 7 17 *A* (*S* ⲣ ϣ., *B* ⲧⲱⲙⲧ) ἐξιστάναι; Mor 17 20 *S* ⲉⲩⲟ ⲙⲙ. ⲉϧⲣⲁⲓ ⲉϫⲡⲡⲓⲛⲟϭ ⲡⲣⲏⲃⲉ θαυμ.; ShC 73 189 *S* ⲉⲕⲉⲣ ⲙ. ⲉϫⲡⲡⲉⲧⲉⲕⲛⲁⲩ ⲉⲣⲟⲟⲩ. ⲉ ϧⲡ-: ShMich 550 20 *S* ⲙⲡⲟⲩⲣ ⲙ. ⲟⲛ ϧⲛⲡⲁⲓ.

ⲙⲟⲓϧⲓ *B* v ⲕⲟⲓⲣⲓ.

ⲙϧⲱ *A* v ⲙϧⲁⲁⲩ.

ⲙⲁϩⲃⲁⲗ v ⲙⲁϧ.

ⲙϧⲁⲗ *B* v ϩⲙϧⲁⲗ.

ⲙⲉϧⲏⲗ *A* in ϣⲁⲧⲙ., *bald place* on head: El 90 among marks of Antichrist = ib 120 *S* ϭⲁⲗⲟⲩϩⲓϧ q v. For ϣⲁⲧ cf ? ϣⲁⲧⲃⲟⲓ (ϥⲱ) *B*,

ⲙⲉϧⲙⲟⲩϧⲉ, -ϧⲓ *SB* nn f, *purslane*: P 43 34 *S* ϩⲣⲁ ⲙ. بزر رجلة (cf 44 82 ⲁⲡⲁⲣⲁⲭⲡⲏ (رجلة)), K 196 ϯⲙ. رجلة; in recipes: BKU 1 25 (*bis*), PMéd 207, 233 &c, CR '87 376 (*sic l*).

ⲙⲉϧⲣⲟ *S*, ⲙⲁϧ. *B* nn m, *manure*: Lu 13 8 *SB* κόπρια (pl); Va 57 268 *B* ⲡⲓⲕⲟⲡⲣⲟⲥ ⲉⲧⲉⲡⲙ. ⲡⲉ, K 395 *B* ⲡⲓⲙ. زراعة تفليح; BMOr 8811 209 *S* devil planted thee (f) ⲡⲉⲛⲧⲁϥϯ ⲙ. ⲡⲉ, C 89 105 *B* ϯ ⲙⲱⲟⲩ & ϯ ⲙ. تزبل, Miss 8 222 *S* seed watered ⲡⲥⲉϯ ⲙ. ⲡⲁϥ, BMar 36 *S* sim ⲡⲧⲉϥⲥⲱϧⲉ. ⲣⲉϥϯ ⲙ. *S*, *one who manures*: P 44 80 = 43 54 ⲡⲓⲣ. عزاقين.

ⲙⲁϧⲥⲟⲗ *B* v ⲙⲉⲥϧⲱⲗ.

ⲙⲁϧⲧ *S*, ⲙⲁϧ̄ⲧ *B*, ⲙⲉϧⲧ *SF* nn m, *bowels, intestines* (sg rare): Ge 43 30 *B* ἔντερα (var ἔγκατα); Job 21 24 *B* (*S* ⲥⲁ ⲡϩⲟⲩⲡ), Ps 108 18 *SB* ἔγκ.; Jer 28 13 *B* σπλάγχνα; BHom 8 *S* κοιλία; Ep 592 *S* ⲡⲉⲕⲙ. γαστήρ; P 44 70 *S* ⲙⲙ. · (ⲉ)ⲡⲧⲉⲣⲁ أمعا, مصران; Aeg 13 *S* ⲙⲙ. ⲙⲡⲟⲏ, R 2 1 71 *S* among parts of body ϧⲉⲡⲙ. ϩⲓϩⲟⲩⲡ ⲉⲩϭⲗⲙⲗⲱⲙ ⲉⲩⲅⲕⲟⲧⲉ,

DeV 1 123 B worms ✝ ϭⲓⲥⲓ ⲙⲡⲉϥⲙ., Mor 30 46 F ⲁⲡⲉϥⲙ. ⲉⲓ ⲉⲃⲟⲗ, Z 261 S Arius ⲡⲉϥⲙ. ⲧⲏⲣⲟⲩ ⲙⲛ- ⲡⲉⲧⲁⲡⲉϥϩⲟⲩⲛ collapsed, C 43 77 B martyr torn so that ⲡⲉϥⲙ. ⲓ ⲉⲃⲟⲗ ϩⲉⲛⲧⲉϥⲛⲉϫⲓ, Mor 55 84 S Miriam ⲧⲥⲱⲛⲉ ⲙⲙ. of Moses (cf ὁμοκοίλιος), Wess 15 152 S midwife ties babe's ⲙⲁ[ϩ]ⲧ navel (?), P 43 234 S ⲁⲓⲁⲣⲟⲓⲁ · ⲙⲙ. ⲉⲧⲥⲱⲕ. ⲙⲉϩⲧ ⲟ, ⲱ S, *great intestine*: Glos 51, 52 ⲙⲙ. ω κῶλον, κῶλιξ, PMéd 316, 317; ib 187, Br 267 S ⲡⲛⲟϭ ⲙⲙⲁϩⲧ. ⲙⲁϩⲧ ϣⲏⲙ S, *small intestine*: P 44 70 [Arabic]; ⲡⲕⲟⲩⲓ ⲙⲙ. Br *lc.* Cf DM 21 31.

ⲁⲧⲙ. B, *without bowels* of compassion: Va 61 199 Abraham overcame natural feelings ⲙⲫⲣⲏϯ ⲛⲟⲩⲁ.

ⲗⲁⲃ-, ⲗⲁⲙ. SB *v* ⲗⲓⲃⲉ.

ϣⲁⲡⲙ. B nn as pl, *dysentery*: Ac 28 8 (var ϣⲉⲡ-, S ϣⲱⲡⲉ ϩⲣⲏⲧ⸗, var ⲉⲣⲏⲧ⸗) δυσεντερία, but among bodily organs K 78 ⲡⲓϣ. (1 var ϣⲙⲁϭⲧ) [Arabic].

ϣⲁⲛⲑⲙ. B, *compassionate person*: Orat Manas 7 εὔσπλαγχνος, Ja 5 11 ⲟⲩⲡⲓϣϯ ⲛϣ. (S ϣⲛϩⲧⲏϥ) πολύσπλ., AM 267 ⲁⲛⲟⲕ ⲟⲩϣ. ⲁⲛ ἄσπλαγχνος; Va 57 208 ⲡⲓϣ. ⲡⲧⲉ ⲧⲟⲩⲛⲉϫⲓ οἰκτίρμων (cf Lam 4 10); Va 63 26 = BMis 418 S ϣⲛϩⲧⲏϥ. ⲙⲉⲧϣ., *compassion*: Dan 9 18 (S ⲙⲛⲧϣⲛϩ.) οἰκτιρμός; Phil 1 8 (SF do) σπλάγχνα, CaiEuch 487 εὐσπλαγχνία.

ⲙⲟⲓⲧ SAO, ⲙϩⲓⲧ A, ⲙⲉϩⲓⲧ A (Zech 6 6) A²F, ⲉⲙⲓⲣⲓⲧ SBF, ⲙⲉⲛϩⲣⲓⲧ F nn m, *north*: Ge 13 14 SB, Job 37 22 S (B ⲥⲁⲡⲉⲙ.), Jer 27 3 F (B do), Joel 2 20 SAB, Ap 21 13 S (B do) βορρᾶς; CaiEuch 578 B ἄρκτος; BMis 570 S ϫⲓⲡⲡⲙ. ϣⲁⲡⲣⲏⲥ, P 131² 89 S ⲡⲙⲉⲣⲟⲥ ⲧⲏⲣϥ ⲡⲉⲙ. called Scythia, Kr 222 F ⲡⲙⲉⲣⲟⲥ ⲡⲡⲙⲉⲛ., ib 36 F door opens ⲉⲡⲙⲉ.; rare with vb of motion (*cf* ϩⲣⲏⲧ *north*): C 89 4 B ⲁⲩϣϭⲛⲏⲣ ⲉⲡⲉⲙ. = MG 17 316 S ⲉⲡⲥⲁ ⲙⲡⲉⲙ., Miss 4 566 S sim, RNC 69 S come forth ⲉⲡⲉⲙ. of city, Wess 18 37 ⲡⲧⲉⲣⲟⲩⲉⲣ ⲡⲉⲙ. ⲙⲡⲧⲙⲉ, Ryl 364 n S ⲡⲧⲟϣ ⲡⲉⲙ. of Shmoun (cf βορρινὴ μερίς), BM 1015 S ⲡⲉⲙⲡⲧ ⲡⲡⲉⲙ. *northwest*. ⲙⲡⲉⲙ. ⲛ-, *on north of*: AZ 21 100 O ⲉⲡⲉⲙ. ⲡⲡⲁϩⲱⲧ, ShC 73 120 S ⲡⲉⲓⲁ ⲉⲧⲙⲡⲉⲙ. ⲡⲧⲕⲱⲗⲛ, Ryl 156 S Pamata ⲙⲡⲉⲙ. ⲡϣⲙⲟⲩⲛ, BM 1041 S sim ⲡⲉⲙ. ϣⲙⲟⲩⲛ, Ryl 165 S ⲡⲡⲉⲙ. ⲡⲧⲭⲟ of house. With ⲥⲁ: Ex 26 35 S ⲥⲡⲓⲣ ⲉⲧⲥⲁⲙ. (B ⲥⲁⲡⲉⲙ.) πρὸς β., Eccl 11 3 S ϩⲁⲡⲥⲁ ⲙⲡⲉⲙ. ἐν τῷ β., Is 14 31 B ⲉⲃⲟⲗ ⲥⲁⲡⲉⲙ. (S ⲉⲃ. ϩⲁⲡⲥⲁⲙ.) ἀπὸ β.; El 64 A from south ϣⲁⲡⲥⲁⲙ., P 129¹² 47 S village ⲉⲧⲥⲁⲙ. ⲙⲙⲟⲕ, ShC 42 210 S ⲟ̄ϯ ⲙⲡⲉϥⲟⲩⲟⲉⲓ ⲛⲥⲁⲡⲥⲁ ⲙⲡⲉⲙ., BM 1008 S ⲯⲁⲙ....ⲛⲧⲁⲡⲧⲓⲟⲭⲓⲁ.

ⲧⲏⲩ ⲙⲙ., ⲧⲟⲩⲙ. SA, *north wind*: Pro 25 23 SA ἄνεμος β., Cant 4 16 S β.; PS 214 S ⲡⲧⲟⲩⲙ., ib 348 S ⲟⲩⲧⲏⲩ ⲙⲙ.; Si 43 17 S ϩⲁⲧⲏⲩ ⲙⲡⲉⲙ. καται- γὶς βορέου.

In place-names: Πρεμιτ RylDem 3 149 n, ⲡⲥⲁ ⲡⲉⲙϩⲓⲧ [Arabic] *Lower Egypt* (v MIF 36 227). V Ep 1 105.

ⲙϩⲟⲧ B nn m, shoemaker's *last* or *mallet*: K 132 [Arabic].

ⲙⲉϩⲧⲟ *v* ⲙⲁⲣⲧ.

ⲙⲉϩⲧⲱⲗⲡ F, ⲙⲉϩⲧⲱⲡ S *v* ⲧⲱⲣⲡ *sew*.

ⲙϩⲁⲁⲩ, -ⲁⲟⲩ, -ⲁⲩⲉ S (1 Kg 22 1, Lu 23 53, 24 9), -ⲁⲟⲩⲉ O, ⲙϩⲱ A, ⲙϩⲉⲉⲩ A², ⲙϩⲁⲩ, ⲉⲙ. B, ⲉⲙϩⲉⲟⲩ F nn m, *tomb, cavern*: Deu 9 22 S (var p ⲡⲙⲉⲉⲩⲉ) B, Ez 37 12 B (S ⲧⲁⲫⲟⲥ), Lu 8 27 SB μνῆμα, Is 26 19 SB, Mk 6 29 SBF, Jo 12 17 AB (SA² ⲧ.) μνημεῖον; Job 5 26 B (SA Cl do), Ro 3 13 B (S do) τάφος, ROC 17 404 B fire upon ⲙ. ἐπι- τάφιος; 1 Kg 24 4 S (B ⲃⲏⲃ), Is 2 19 S (B = Gk), ib 32 14 SF (B ⲃ.), ib 65 4 S (B = Gk), Jo 11 38 A² (B ⲃ., S = Gk) σπήλαιον; C 86 289 B ⲟⲩⲙ....in rock λάρναξ; MG 25 213 B entered ⲟⲩⲙ. to sleep ἱερόν (PL 73 894 *monumentum*); BHom 120 S ⲛⲧ- ⲁⲫⲟⲥ ⲙⲡⲉⲙ., BMis 243 S Saviour's ⲙ. (var ⲧ.), C 86 97 B thy throne ⲟⲩⲧ. ⲛⲙ. ⲡⲉ, AM 275 B arisen ⲉⲃⲟⲗ ϩⲁⲡⲙ., Hor 84 O ⲡⲓϩⲣⲁⲟⲩⲉ (or -ⲟⲩ). ⲙⲁ ⲛⲙ. S meaning same: Ge 49 30 ⲟⲩ[ⲙⲁ] ⲛⲙ. (B ⲉⲙ.), BAp 54 ⲟⲩⲙⲁ ⲛⲙ. μνημεῖον. *Cf* AM 277 B ⲫⲙⲁ ⲛⲡⲓⲙ. τὰ μνημεῖα.

ⲙⲁϩⲟⲩⲁⲗ *v* ⲙⲁϩ.

ⲙⲉϩⲭ O *v* ⲙⲁⲕϩ.

ⲙⲁⲉⲓϩϭ F nn, meaning unknown, object sent (?) by writer of letter BM 628. Cf? ⲙⲟⲓⲁϩ (ⲙⲁⲓⲁϩ).

ⲙⲁϫ- *v* ⲙⲁⲁϫⲉ measure.

ⲙⲟⲩϫ S *v* ⲙⲟⲩϫϭ (ⲣⲉϥⲙ.).

ⲙⲁⲁϫⲉ S, ⲙⲉⲉϫⲉ AF, ⲙⲉϫⲉ, ⲙⲏϫⲓ F (Ps 101), ⲙⲉϣⲧⲉ A², ⲙⲉϣⲧ (Glos) Sᵃ, ⲙⲁϣϫ B nn m, *ear*: Lev 14 14 SB, Job 4 12 SB, Is 30 21 SBF, 1 Cor 12 16 SB οὖς, Mt 26 51 SB, Jo 18 10 SA²B, Glos 30 Sᵃ ὠτίον; 2 Tim 4 4 SB ἀκοή; PS 239 S ⲡⲉϥⲙ. ⲥⲡⲁⲩ, C 43 208 B Christ ⲡⲙ. ⲡⲣⲉϥⲥⲱⲧⲙ; recipes for painful ear: PMéd 237 S ⲟⲩⲙ. ⲉϥϯ ⲕⲕⲁⲥ (l ⲧⲕⲁⲥ), ib 288 ⲉϣⲱⲡⲉ, ib 239 ⲙⲙ. ⲉⲧⲣⲟⲣϣ ⲉⲥⲱⲧⲙ (cf Is 6 10). ϭⲁϫⲉ ⲙⲙ. ὠτότμητος MR 4 128 S. ⲕⲁ, ⲭⲁ ⲙ., *give ear, listen* c ⲉ-: JKP 2 82 S ϫⲓ ⲥⲙⲏ ⲕⲁ ⲙ. ⲉⲧⲁⲥⲟⲫⲓⲁ, Mich '25 (v Lant 81 b) S ⲙⲡⲣⲕⲁ ⲙ. ⲉⲗⲁⲁⲩ ⲉϥϣⲧⲣⲧⲱⲣ, MIE 2 349 B ⲉϥⲭⲁ ⲙ. ⲉⲣⲟϥ whilst he recited. ⲣⲓⲕⲉ ⲙⲡⲙ., *incline ear* c ⲉ-: Ps 16 6 SBF, Jer 17 23 SB κλίνειν; Pro 4 20 SA (B diff) παραβάλλειν. As *handle* of basket: Z 310 S for ⲛϩⲓⲣ ⲱⲧ., BM 536 S writer about to weave asks for ϩⲉⲛⲕⲟⲩⲓ ⲙ.; of jar: MG 25 203 B ϩⲁⲡⲙ. ⲡⲕⲟⲩϥⲟⲡ ⲱⲧ., K 244 B ⲙⲟⲕⲓ

ⲛⲃⲉⲗϫ ⲉⲣⲉⲡⲓⲙ. ⲧⲟⲓ ⲉⲣⲟϥ;   ⲁⲧⲙ., *without handle*:
Ryl 238 *S* ⲗⲉⲕⲁⲡⲏ ⲡⲁ., BMOr 6796 *S* ϭⲁⲗⲁϩⲧ
ⲡⲁ.   In names: Ταμύσθα Spg *AegMitteil* 1925
ii, Μυσθαρίων, ⲙⲟⲩⲥⲟⲁⲣⲓ CMSS 20.

—— ⲛⲕⲗⲏ, *cat's ear* v ⲕⲗⲏ.

—— ⲙⲡⲓⲛ *S*, *mouse's ear, myosotis*: P 44 83
ⲁϫⲉⲗⲫⲁⲧⲟⲥ (= 43 59 -ⲕⲟⲥ) وذن الفار, BKU 1 9 sim.

ⲙⲁⲁϫⲉ, ⲙⲁϫⲉ, ⲙⲁⲁⲧⲥⲉ (?ST 116), ⲙⲁϯ (Win
5, Ep 176), ⲙⲁϫ- *S*, μάτιον (v CO 165 n) nn f, a
measure of grain, fruit &c ; its capacity : 12 to the
ⲣⲧⲟⲃ (PLondV 157), but COAd 18 ⲉⲧⲉⲙⲛⲧⲉ (*sic l?*)
(ⲙ)ⲙ. ⲉⲡⲉⲣⲧⲁ[ⲃ] (*cf* PLond 159 n, 15 to ⲣⲧⲟⲃ), Ep
305 ϥⲧⲟⲉ ⲛϭⲓϫ of corn ⲉⲩⲟ ⲛϥⲉ ⲙⲙ., Turin ostr
5875 ϯⲟⲩ ⲛⲣⲧⲟⲃ ⲡⲁⲣⲁ ⲟⲩⲙ., CO 462 sim.   Of
corn ⲥⲟⲩⲟ ShC 42 83 (only here in literature), ST
246, Ep 305 ; barley ⲉⲓⲱⲧ Ep 176 ; seed-corn ⲉⲃⲣⲁ
CO 306 ; milled corn ⲧⲉϣ CO 239, ST 354 ; radish
ⲥⲓⲙ WS 134 ; sesame ⲥⲓⲙⲥⲓⲙ Hall 130, ST 90 ;
lentils ⲁⲣϣⲓⲛ Hall 130 ; lupins ⲧⲁⲣⲙⲟⲥ Ep 543 ;
dates ⲃⲛⲛⲉ ST 123, WS 121 ; salt ϩⲙⲟⲩ CO 217,
ST 255.   ⲙⲁϫ-: ST 316 ⲧⲙⲁⲭϭⲟⲥ ⲛⲉⲃⲣⲁ, CO
476 ⲟⲩⲙ]ⲁⲭϭⲁⲥ, *cf* Hall 84 ⲧϥ[ⲟ] ⲙⲁⲭⲉⲓⲟⲩⲧ.
The measuring vessel (?): ST 116 ⲥⲛⲧⲉ ⲙⲙⲁⲁⲧⲥⲉ
(in Ep 547, 548, WS 122 ⲙ. ? ⲁⲭⲉ q v) ; Hall 106
corn weighed ⲛⲧ]ⲙ. ⲛϫⲓⲕⲁⲓⲟⲛ (*cf* Ryl 162 ⲟⲓⲡⲉ
ⲛϫⲓⲕ.), CO 206 ⲧⲙ. ⲛⲡⲥⲉⲕⲉ (ζυγόν). *V* ⲙⲱϫⲉ.

ⲙⲁϫⲉ *S*, ⲙⲁϫⲓ, ⲙⲁϣⲓ *B* nn m, *axe, pick*: Ps
73 6 *B* (*S* ⲥⲟⲧⲃⲉϥ) λαξευτήριον معول, paral ⲕⲉⲗⲉⲃⲓⲛ,
C 86 266 *B* sim, K 123 *B* carpenter's tools ⲡⲓⲙⲁ-
ϣⲓ قدوم = P 55 9 *B* ⲙⲁϫⲓ, C 86 219 *B* carpenter
splits martyr's head with ⲙ. ⲙⲃⲉⲛⲓⲡⲓ, Mor 28 154
S sim ⲙ. ⲛⲣⲁⲙϣⲉ, Ep 547 *S* list of implements ⲙ.
ⲛⲣⲁⲙ, *ib* 548 *S* sim ⲟⲩⲙ., WS 122 *S* sim ⲙ. ⲙⲡⲉⲛⲓⲡⲉ, ST 118 *S* ⲟⲩϩⲁⲗⲁⲕ ⲙⲙ. (? same).

ⲙⲉϫⲉ-, ⲙⲁϫⲉ-, ⲙⲡⲁϫⲉ- *SA* v ⲡⲉϫⲉ-.

ⲙⲱϫⲉ (*sic l?* or -ⲉⲛ) *B* nn as pl, *modius* μόδιος
measure : Cat 160 κόρος of corn (equals) Λ̄ ⲙⲙⲱ-
ϫⲉⲡⲡⲉ (v PG 43 272).   *Cf ?* ⲙⲁⲁϫⲉ measure.

ⲙⲁϫⲟ *S*   v ϫⲡⲟ.

ⲙⲁϫⲃ *F*   v ⲙⲟϫϩ.

ⲙⲟⲩϫⲏ   v ⲙⲟⲩϫϭ.

ⲙⲁϫⲕⲉ[1], ⲙⲓ.[2], ⲙⲓϫⲉⲕⲉ[3], ⲙⲉⲕϫⲉ[4], ⲙⲓϫϭⲉ[5] *S* nn,
a woman's garment : J 76 40 woman's bequests
ϩⲟⲓⲧⲉ ⲡⲭⲏⲕⲉ, ⲉⲣϣⲱⲛ ⲡⲭⲏⲕⲉ, ⲙ.[2] (*ib* 66 38 om),
CO 465 wife's ϩⲟⲓⲧⲉ, ⲣϣⲱⲛ, ⲡⲉⲥⲙ.[3], ST 119 ⲗⲱⲧⲓϫ, ⲗⲉ(ⲃⲓ)ⲧⲱⲡ, ⲙⲙ.[3], ⲥⲉⲛⲧⲱⲡ[ⲉ, Tor 43 ⲗⲱⲧⲓϫ,
ⲙ.[1] ⲍ̄, ⲙⲁⲡⲡⲁ, Win 51 ⲉⲣϣ[ⲱⲛ], ⲙ.[4], ST 178 ⲙ.[5].
Cf ? ϫⲱⲱϭⲉ.

ⲙⲁϫⲁⲕⲓⲛ *S* nn as pl, meaning unknown,
named with embroiderers : ShP 130[4] 109 = *ib* 130[2]
84 ⲙⲙ. ⲁⲩⲱ ⲙⲡⲗⲟⲙⲁⲣⲓⲟⲥ ⲏ ⲙⲡⲟⲓⲕⲓⲗⲧⲏⲥ said
Who is Mary that hath borne God ?   Termination
-ⲓⲛ as if semitic.   *Cf ?* مشاق *writer* (Bevan), or *v*
Dozy 2 595 مشاق *tow*, so ? *tow-workers*.

ⲙⲟϫⲕϥ   v ⲙⲟϫϩ.

ⲙⲉϫⲏⲗ *S* nn as pl, meaning unknown, part of
oven : P 129[18] 168 ⲗⲁⲕⲛⲧ heated so that became
like ⲡⲉⲓⲙ. ⲛⲣⲣⲱ.

ⲙϫⲱⲗ *SB*, -ⲱⲣ (PMéd) *S*, ⲉⲙϫⲱⲗ *SB*, ⲙ-
ϫⲟⲩⲗ *B* nn m, *onion*, cf בצל (IgR) : Nu 11 5 *SB*
κρόμμυον, P 44 82 *S* ⲡⲉⲙ. · ⲕⲟⲗⲙⲉⲥⲓⲟⲥ (? κρομμύ-
διον) · ϩⲧⲓⲧ &c = 43 57 (om ϩⲧⲓⲧ) بصل, K 194 *B*
ⲡⲉⲙ. 'ϫ ; Aeg 261 *S* among herbs not to be blessed,
R 1 4 68 *S* = AM 128 *B* worshipped by heathen,
Ryl 106 54 *S*, ST 316 *S* ⲉⲃⲣⲁ ⲉⲙ., PMéd 291 *S*
ⲡⲟⲩⲛⲉ ⲡⲉⲙ., Mor 51 34 *S* ⲕⲟⲩⲕⲉ ⲡⲉⲙ., WS 52 *S*
ⲙⲟⲟⲩ ⲡⲉⲙ., *ib* 56 *S*, Sph 10 1 *S* ϭⲟⲟⲩⲛⲉ ⲡⲙ.,
Hall 67 *S* ⲑⲁⲗⲓⲥ ⲡⲉⲙ., CO 210 *S* ⲙ. ⲉⲧⲙⲁⲗϩ.
ⲉⲙ. ϩⲉϩⲧ (ϩⲟⲟⲩⲧ) *S*, *wild onion* : P 43 235 ⲉⲩⲉ-
ⲑⲓⲁⲥ · ⲉⲣⲥⲓⲁ (*quid ?*) بصل عنصل *squill*.

ⲙⲭⲛϩ, ⲉⲙϫⲛϩ   v ⲉⲛϩ.

ⲙⲉϫⲛⲡⲱⲛⲉ, -ⲡⲱⲱⲡⲉ, ⲙⲉϣⲡⲱⲛⲉ *S* (Lev var),
ⲙⲁϣⲡⲱⲛⲉ *A*, ⲙⲉϣⲫⲱⲡⲓ, ⲙⲉⲧϣ. (Tatt 847) *B* nn
m f, *ulcer, eruption* : Lev 21 20 *S* (*B* om), *ib* 22 22
SB λιχήν قوب, Tri 531 *S* ⲡⲙ. 'ϫ, K 160 *B* ϯⲙ.
قوب, ShA 1 105 *S* ⲧⲙ. ⲉⲧⲣⲙⲡϣⲁ *in nose*, Mor 36
19 *S* ⲟⲩⲙ. ⲧⲉ ⲡⲁⲧⲉⲣ ⲡⲁϩⲣⲉ ⲉⲣⲟⲥ ; paral ψωρα
ⲡⲁϯⲣⲓⲟⲛ as in Lev : R 2 1 54 *S*, Mor *lc S* : RChamp
539 *A* ⲁⲕⲁⲡⲧϣ (*l* ⲛⲧⲥ) ϩⲛⲡⲟⲩϭⲉⲉ ⲉⲡⲙ. ;   PMéd
308 *S* ⲟⲩⲙ. ⲛⲣⲟⲟⲩⲧ λ. ἄγριος (*ib* 275).   *Cf* Berl
Wörterb 2 157 *mšpnt* (Dévaud).

ⲙⲁϫⲁⲁⲧ (or *l* -ⲉⲁⲧ) *S* nn f, meaning unknown :
ST 298 ⲡϫⲁⲗⲁϫⲱⲙ ⲉⲧⲛⲧⲡⲉ ⲛⲡⲕⲁⲧⲁϩ ⲛⲡϣⲁϣⲟⲧ
ⲛⲧⲙ. ⲥⲛⲧⲉ.   Scarcely = ⲙϫⲁϩⲧ.

ⲙⲟⲩϫⲧ   v ⲙⲟⲩϫϭ.

ⲙϫⲁⲧϩ   v ⲙϫⲁϩⲧ.

ⲙⲟϫϩ[1], ⲙⲁϫϩ[2], ⲙⲟⲧϩϥ[3], ⲙⲟϫⲕϥ[4], ⲙⲟϫϥ[5],
ⲙⲟϫⲕϥ[6], ⲙⲟϫϥϩ[7], ⲙⲟϫϥ[8], ⲙⲁϫϥ[9], ⲙⲁϫⲕϥ[10] *S*,
ⲙⲁϫϩ *A*, ⲙⲟϫϭ, ⲙⲟⲩϫϭ[11], ⲙⲟϫϫ[12] *B*, ⲙⲁϫⲃ[13] *F*,
ⲙⲟϫ[14] *SF*, ⲙⲁϫ[15] *F* nn m, *girdle* of soldier or monk:
Ex 29 9 *S*¹*B*, Lev 16 4 *B* (*S* ⲉⲡϩⲱⲡⲛ), Is 5 27 *S*¹
(var²) *B*, Ez 9 2 *S*¹ *B*¹¹, Mt 10 9 *S*¹ (varr⁵ ¹⁵) *B*, Mk
1 6 *S*¹ (var⁴) *B*, Ac 21 11 *S*¹ (var⁵) *B* (var¹¹), Ap 1
13 *S*¹ (var⁵) *B* ζώνη ; 1 Kg 17 38 *B* (*S* ϩⲱⲣ) μανδύας ; Z 345 *S* monk's ⲉⲡϩⲱⲡⲛ, ⲙ.³ ζ. = MG 25
210 *B* ⲙⲁⲣϭⲁϫ ἀνάλαβος ; BMis 338 *S*⁶ (var⁵)=
Mor 27 14 *F*¹⁵, BAp 125 *S*⁶ = MIE 2 418 *B* monk's,

El 50 *A*, Va 62 153 *B*¹², TSBA 9 376 *B* do, Mor 36 47 *S*¹⁴, KroppK 56 *S*¹⁰, ShA 1 270 (= Z 438 n) *S*⁷, Mor 51 38 *S*⁸ monk's, Mich 601 *S*⁹, JKP 2 134 *F*¹³.   Oath by monk's ⲙ.⁸ Mor 51 41 *S*.   ⲙⲟⲭ ⲣⲥ (*sic* as Pey for ⲙⲟⲭⲣⲥ, though var ⲙⲟⲕⲣⲥ) Si 30 35 *S* στρέβλη.

ⲙ̄ⲕⲁϩⲧ *S* (oftenest) *B*, ⲙⲕⲁⲧϩ *SB*, ⲙⲕⲁⲣϫ *S* (*Z*) nn f, *mortar*: Nu 11 8 *SB* θυία, K 149 *B* ϯⲙ. صلاة; AZ 23 108 *S* recipe ⲑⲛⲟϣ ϧⲓⲧⲙ., PMéd 174 *S* sim, Z 630 *S* pour mixture ⲛⲧⲙ. & pound (τρίβειν), ST 118 *S* ⲟⲩⲉⲙ. ⲙ̄ⲡⲧⲉⲥⲁⲡⲟⲑⲟⲏⲕⲉ (ἀγγοθήκη), BM 1109 *S* ⲧⲉⲙ. ⲡ̄ⲕⲟⲧ *socket* (?) *of mill-wheel*.   *V* Rec 39 171.   *Cf* ⲙⲁⲕⲣⲟ.

ⲙⲟⲩϫ̄ⲥ¹ *SA*, -ϫⲕ² *S*, -ϫⲧ³ *SAB*, ⲙⲉϫⲧ- *S*, ⲙⲟϫϩ⳿, -ⲕ⳿ *S*, ⲙⲟϫⲧ⳿ *SB*, ⲙⲟϫϭ⳿⁴ *S*, -ϫⲧ⳿⁵ *SB*, ⲙⲁϫⲧ⳿⁶ *SA* vb **I** intr, *be mixed, cf* מזג (IgR): Ex 12 38 *B* ἐπίμικτος, Dan 11 6 *B* συμμιγνύναι; ShA 1 250 *S* wine ⲉⲧϩⲟⲗϭ ⲉⲧⲙ.⁵   c ⲉ- *be mixed with*: Jer 32 20 *B* συμμικτός gen, Dan 11 23 *B* συνανάμιξις πρός; ShR 2 3 47 *S* wine ⲉⲧⲙ.⁴ ⲉ[ⲡⲉⲥ]ϯ ⲡ̄ⲏⲡⲉ, AM 14 *B* I will not ⲙ. ⲉⲣⲟⲕ in anything;   ⲉⲥⲟⲩⲛ ⲉ-: Va 57 251 *B* devil ⲉϥⲙ.⁵ ⲉϩ. ⲉⲣⲱⲟⲩ συμπλέκεσθαι dat.   c ⲛ̄- *meaning same*: Ex 28 14 *B* καταμιγ. ἐν, Ez 22 18 *B* (var ⲛⲉⲙ-) ἀναμιγ. dat.   c ⲙⲛ-, ⲛⲉⲙ- *meaning same*: Ps 105 35 *B*, Is 36 8 *B*, Mt 27 34 *B*⁵ (all *S* ⲧⲱϩ) μιγ., Dan 2 43 *B* ἀναμιγ. dat, Pro 14 10 *B*(*SA* do) ἐπιμιγ. dat, Ex 14 20 *B* συμμιγ., Ez 27 17 *B* (*S* do) συμμικτός gen, 1 Cor 5 9 *B* (*S* do) συναναμιγ. dat; Jo 4 9 *B* (*SF* do, *A*² ϫⲱϩ) συγχρᾶσθαι dat; Is 30 24 *B* (*SF* do) ἀναποιεῖν ἐν; Jos 23 12 *B* (*S* ⲣⲓⲕⲉ) προστιθέναι dat; PS 14 *S* ⲧϭⲟⲙ...ⲉⲧⲙ.⁴ ⲁⲡⲡⲁϩⲟⲣⲁⲧⲟⲥ, BG 51 *S* fire & earth ⲁⲩⲙ.¹ ⲙ̄ⲡⲡⲁⲗⲟⲟⲩ, ShMIF 23 78 *S* demons & ⲡⲉⲧⲙ.⁴ ⲛ̄ⲙⲙⲁⲩ, BM 835 7 *B* angels ⲁⲩⲙ. ⲛⲉⲙⲡⲓⲣⲱⲙⲓ, Mor 28 160 *S* streams ⲥⲉⲙ.⁶ ⲙ̄ⲛⲛⲉⲩⲉⲣⲏⲩ; ⲉⲥⲟⲩⲛ ⲛⲉⲙ-: DeV 2 56 *B* no sin ⲙ.⁵ ⲉϩ. ⲛⲉⲙⲡⲉⲛϣⲏⲗ.   c ϩⲓ- *meaning same*: Nah 3 14 *S*⁵ (var⁴ Z 425) *A*⁶ (*B* diff) συμπατεῖσθαι ἐν, Mk 15 23 *S*¹*B*⁵ (*F* ⲧⲱϩ) Gk diff, Pcod 34 *S* if fornication ⲙ.⁵ ϩⲓⲛⲁⲓ (var ⲙⲛ-), Mor 43 86 *S* wine ⲉϥⲙ.⁵ ϩⲓϣⲁⲗ.   c ϩⲛ-,

ϧⲉⲛ- *meaning same*: Ap 8 7 *B*⁵ (*S* ⲧ.) μιγ. ἐν, Dan 2 43 *B* συμμιγ. ἐν; Jos 23 12 *B* (*S* ⲧ. ⲙⲛ-) συγκαταμιγ. dat; Pro 20 3 *S*³*A*¹ συμπλέκειν dat; Miss 4 235 *S* ⲉⲣⲉⲡⲉⲣⲟⲩⲟ...ⲙ.⁴ ϧⲛ̄ⲥⲩⲛⲏⲑⲉⲓⲁ ⲡⲁⲣⲭⲁⲓⲟⲥ; ⲉⲃⲟⲗ ϧⲛ-: P 131⁶ 12 *S* incense ⲉⲧⲙ.⁵ ⲉϩ. ϧⲛⲟⲩ ⲥⲧⲁⲕⲧⲏ ⲙ̄ⲡⲟⲩⲉⲓⲉⲓϩ *compounded of*.

   II tr, *mix*: Is 1 22 *B* (*S* ⲧ.), Hos 4 2 *B* (*SA* diff) μίσγειν, Lu 13 1 *B* (*S* ⲧ.) μιγ.; Z 355 *S* ⲁⲩⲙⲉϫⲧ ⲡⲉⲩⲱⲡⲁϩ ⲙ̄ⲡⲛⲉⲩⲉⲣⲏⲩ, CO 235 *S* wines ⲙⲟⲭⲥ̄ⲟⲩ ⲙ̄ⲡⲛⲉⲩⲉⲣⲏⲩ, PMéd 185 *S* ⲙⲁϫⲕⲟⲩ ⲙ̄ⲡⲟⲩⲏⲣⲡ; refl: Va 57 3 *B* cold & heat ⲛ̄ⲧⲟⲩⲙⲟⲭⲧⲟⲩ ⲛⲉⲙ ⲡⲟⲩⲉⲣⲏⲟⲩ.

  —— nn m, *mixture*: Nu 11 4 *B* (*S* ⲙ̄ⲛⲏⲩϣⲉ ⲉⲧⲛ̄ⲧⲏϥ) ἐπίμικτος, Jer 32 34 *B* συμμικ., Z 313 *S* ⲟⲩⲙ.⁵ ⲙ̄ⲡⲟⲡⲟⲛⲏⲣⲟⲛ συμμιγῆ, Va 57 247 *B* ϯⲙⲓϫⲓⲥ ⲉⲧⲉⲡⲓⲙ.; Nu 4 16 *B* (*S* ϭⲱⲣϭ) σύνθεσις; Ez 22 19 *B* σύγκρασις; Deu 22 11 *B* (*S* ⲥⲛⲏϣ) κίβδηλος; ShIF 146 *S* ⲁⲩϣⲱⲡⲉ ⲉⲩⲙ.⁵...ⲁⲧⲉⲧⲛ̄ϣⲱⲡⲉ ⲉⲩⲙ.¹ ⲡⲟⲩⲱⲧ, P 130⁵ 27 *S* sim ⲙ.², P 131¹ 18 *S* Eve answered serpent ⲁϫⲛⲙ.³ *without duplicity* (or ? = ⲙⲟⲩϣⲧ), MG 25 172 *B* ⲟⲩⲙ. ⲡⲉ with Ishmaelites, K 89 *B* among vicious ϥⲁⲡⲓⲙ. ذو التخاليط.

   (ⲁⲧⲙ. *B*), ⲙⲉⲧⲁⲧⲙ., *unmixedness*: CaiEuch 407 took flesh ϧⲉⲛⲟⲩⲙ. μὴ ἐν μίξει.

   ⲣⲉϥⲙ. *S*, *mixer, confuser, disturber*: Mor 25 46 among vicious ⲣⲉϥⲙⲟⲩϫ (*sic, cf* R 2 4 11 *S* ⲙⲟⲭϩ).

   ϭⲓⲛ-, ϫⲓⲛⲙ. *SB* nn f, *mixture, intercourse*: Va 57 35 *B* ϫ. ⲛ̄ⲥⲱⲙⲁⲧⲓⲕⲟⲛ μίξις, Mor 17 106 *S* ⲧϭ.³ πολυμιξία; Bor 248 54 *S* ⲧϭ.³ of crops together, Mun 171 *S* ⲧϭ.³ ⲧⲉ ⲧⲉⲩⲡⲟⲩⲅⲓⲁ ⲡⲣⲁϩ ⲛ̄ⲥⲟⲡ.

ⲙⲉⲥⲧⲱⲗ & varr *SB* nn m, *tower, cf* מגדל: Is 5 2 ⲙⲉϭⲧ. (cit P 131⁸ 98 ⲙⲉⲕⲧ., ShP 130² 95, P 44 58 ⲙⲉϭⲧ. برج, *B* = Gk) πύργος; Ryl 158 ⲡⲉⲙⲁ ⲡⲣⲟⲉⲓⲥ ⲡⲁⲓⲥⲧ. in vineyard (*cf Fay Towns* 154). In place-names: Ex 14 2 *B* ⲙⲉϣⲧ. مجدول (*cf* مشتول), Jer 26 14 *S* ⲙⲉⲥⲧ. *B* do, Ez 29 10, 30 6 *S* ⲙⲉⲭⲧ. *B* ⲙⲓⲭⲧ. all Μάγδωλος; village near Shmûn *S*: BM 1031 ⲙⲓⲕⲧ., ib 1042, 1065 ⲙⲓⲕⲧⲁ., Lant 42, Bodl(P) e 7 *F* ⲙⲓⲕⲧⲁⲁⲗ, Kr 53 *F* ? ⲙⲓⲧⲱⲗ (*cf* مطول), PMich 3553 *S*, Baouit 2 44 *F* ⲙⲓⲭⲟⲗ.   *Cf* Kr 63 *F* ⲡⲓⲡⲩⲣⲅⲟⲥ.

ⲛ

ⲛ, 13th letter of alphabet, called *S* ⲛⲉ (My 34), ⲛⲛⲏ (TT 13, *cf* ROC 19 82 النّي), ⲛ (Leyd 434), *B* ⲛⲉ (Stern p. 418), ⲛⲓ (K 1), نا (P 43 242, 44 124), نيا (Stern *l c*). As numeral *BF*, rarely *S* = *fifty* (ⲧⲁⲓⲟⲩ). Derived from hierogl *n*, as ⲛⲏⲃ, ⲛ̄ⲧⲟⲕ, ⲥⲟⲡⲧⲉ, ⲧⲏⲣ, ϩⲱⲱⲡ, ⲧⲁⲡⲛ. Varies with ⲙ, as ⲛⲙⲟⲥ ⲙⲙⲟⲥ, ϩⲛⲕⲉ

ϧⲉⲗⲕⲓ, ⲥⲱⲡⲕ ⲥⲱⲙⲕ; with ⲣ, as ⲡⲁⲡⲡⲉ -ⲣⲉ, ⲧⲉⲡ ⲣⲟⲙⲡⲓ ⲧⲣⲣⲟⲙⲡⲉ; with ⲗ, as ⲧⲡⲟⲙ ⲧⲗⲟⲙ, ⲃ̄ⲗ̄ⲃⲓⲛⲉ (Lu 13 19 *S* var), ⲡⲁⲗⲁⲧⲓⲥ (Mor 30 51 = ⲡⲉⲡⲁⲧⲓⲥ, ib 29 44 πινακίς), ⲛⲓⲗⲁⲙⲙⲱⲛ ⲗⲓⲗⲁⲙⲟⲩ.   Replaces ϧ in ⲥⲟⲟϩⲉϥ, ⲗ in ⲥⲩⲙⲃⲟⲛⲉⲩ (ST 254 συμβουλεύειν). Written ⲛ̄ to represent ⁿ*n*, as ⲛ̄ⲡⲁⲩ, ⲛ̄ⲧⲉ, ϩⲓⲧⲛ̄, but

becomes ⲙ̄ (°m) before ⲙ ⲡ (ⲫ ⲯ) S (Stern 66), as
ⲙⲙⲁⲩ, ⲁϥⲙ ⲡⲉϥⲥⲟⲡ (Nu 25 6), ϩⲙϥⲏⲧ, ⲙⲛⲧ
ⲙⲯⲩⲭⲏ. Assimilated before ⲃ ⲗ ⲣ S (archaic),
as ⲃⲃⲟⲗ (PS 33), ⲗⲗⲁⲁⲩ (Ac 10 47), ⲣⲣⲉϥ- (Ps 72
12). Inserted before ⲧ ϫ ⲁ S, as ⲙⲛⲧ- (B ⲙⲉⲧ-),
ϩⲟⲙⲛⲧ (B ϩⲟⲙⲉⲧ), ⲡⲁϩⲙⲛⲧ (Worr 273), ⲕⲣⲙⲛⲧⲉ
(BG 62), ⲙⲛ̄ⲡⲥⲁⲡⲧⲣⲉ- (ib 67 &c), ⲥⲙⲁⲙⲁⲁⲡⲧ (Ps 67
36 Rahlfs), ⲛⲧϥⲉ- (ⲉⲧⲃⲉ- PLond 4), ϫⲓⲛϫⲉⲉⲩⲉ ; also
A ⲙⲟⲩⲛⲧⲉ, ⲡⲟⲩⲛⲧⲉ & rarely B ⲙⲡⲁⲛⲧⲉ- (Miss 4 97
&c), ⲥⲡⲁⲡⲁⲗⲁⲛ (Va 63 89) ; in many Gk words
SBF, as ⲁⲗⲏⲛⲑⲓⲛⲟⲥ (Va 65 12), ⲉⲡⲧⲏⲙⲁ (αἴτημα
Wess 18 47), ⲕⲟⲛⲧⲣⲁⲡⲧⲏⲥ (Mt 5 26), ⲙⲉⲛⲧⲣⲟⲛ
(Mor 31 101), ⲭⲣⲏⲥⲟⲗⲓⲛⲑⲟⲥ (BMis 10), ⲥⲱⲡⲁⲓⲟⲛ
(ζῴδιον Mor 30 52 F). Before (or replacing) ⲃ,
as ⲧⲉⲡⲃⲱⲣⲁ (Δεββῶρα Sph 10 3), ⲧⲏⲃⲟ (BMEA
10587), ⲧⲥⲁⲡⲃⲟ (Mor 37 12) or ⲙ: ⲙⲟⲩⲛⲙⲉ A
(Hos 13 15) ; before ⲧ, ⲕ, as ⲁⲡⲕⲣⲁⲧⲱⲣ (ἄκρατος
BMis 10), ⲕⲓⲡⲧⲗⲟⲥ (κύκλος AZ 23 106), ⲟⲩⲛⲧ ⲟⲩⲛ
(οὔκουν Mor 22 117), ⲕⲟⲣⲓⲛⲫⲉⲟⲥ (κορυφαῖος Va 67
83), ⲙⲁⲛϭⲁⲗⲉ q v, ⲙⲡⲕⲉⲣ (Mt 14 9 F), ⲥϥⲓⲡⲓϩ
(σφήξ P 44 56) ; also in ⲁⲡⲧⲏⲛ (ἀγγεῖον), ⲁⲡⲧⲉⲗⲟⲥ,
ⲛⲕⲣⲁⲧⲏⲥ & sim ; before ⲣ B in ⲙⲉⲡⲣⲉ, ⲙⲉⲡⲣⲓⲧ
(v ⲙⲉ love) ; in ϭⲟⲛϥ -ⲙⲉϥ B ϫⲟⲟⲩϥ S (cf ⲙ before
ⲡ ⲫ). Doubled S (archaic) A as initial : ⲛⲛⲧⲟⲕ
(El), ⲛⲡⲁ, ⲛⲛⲏⲩ S (Sa Si) A (El) A² (AP Jo) F
(ZNTW 24 86), ⲛⲛⲓⲙ S (BAp 5), ⲛⲛⲁⲡⲟⲩϥ S (Cai
8485) ; as particle : ⲛⲛ̄ⲱⲡⲉ Deu 5 22 S (Ciasca),
ⲛⲛⲉⲣⲱⲟⲩ S (Sa 10 16), ⲛⲛⲁⲓⲱⲛ S (Ps 41), ⲛⲛⲁⲩϣ
S (Ap 3 3), ⲛⲛⲁⲧⲛⲁⲩ S (BG 125), other e e g in
Rahlfs *Psalter* 33. For F v Asmus 41, 72, also
J&C 98 ⲡⲉⲧ ⲛⲡⲉⲙⲉⲩ, ⲁⲛⲡⲉⲟⲩ, ⲥⲛⲡⲉⲟⲩ. Final ⲛ
omitted F, as ⲉⲙⲧⲁ- (BM 586), ⲥⲁⲟⲩ- (ib), ⲟⲩ- (ib
601), ϩⲓⲧ- (ib 591), ⲉⲓⲭⲉ- (MR 5 37), ⲙⲉ- (ib 550,
BM 548), ⲡⲉⲧ- (Kr 236). Transcribes Ar ن, as
ⲉⲛⲟ انت, ϣⲉⲓⲧⲁⲡ شيطان, ⲡⲉϥⲥⲟⲣ نفسة (EW 234 ff) ;
transcribed by ن, as فانة ⲃⲁⲛⲉ (name Ryl 214),
اهناس (ⲉ⳿ⲣⲡⲏⲥ), فش (ⲡⲃⲏ ⲡⲛⲛ WS).

ⲛ- *SAA²BFO* (often ⲉ- in S² F), ⲙⲙⲟ⸗ (archaic
& often B ⲛⲙⲟ⸗), mostly ⲙ- before ⲃ ⲙ ⲡ ⲫ ⲯ ;
in certain early S texts assimilated to initial ⲃ ⲗ ⲣ ;
rare & archaic ⲡⲉ- (ϣⲉⲡⲉⲧⲱⲙ, ϫⲉⲡⲉⲡⲱⲣ, ? ⲥⲁⲡⲉ-
ϩⲟⲩⲣ), **I** particle of gen (often = B ⲛⲧⲉ q v), **a**
Ge 27 39 S ϯⲱⲧⲉ ⲛ̄ⲧⲡⲉ (B ⲛⲧⲉ), Ps 7 17 SB ⲡⲣⲁⲛ
ⲙ̄ⲡ̄ϫⲟⲉⲓⲥ, Lu 15 29 S ⲙⲁⲥ ⲛ̄ⲃⲁⲁⲙⲡⲉ B ⲛⲃ̄., AZ
21 96 O ⲡⲡⲛⲃ ⲡⲧⲕⲁⲛⲥⲉ, Miss 4 547 S ⲣⲱⲙⲉ ⲡⲟⲩⲟⲉⲓⲛ, Eccl 3 4 S ⲟⲩⲟⲉⲓϣ ⲡⲣⲓⲙⲉ, CA 92 S ⲙⲁ
ⲡⲟⲩⲱⲙ, JKP 2 154 F ⲡⲟ̅ⲥ̅ ⲉⲥⲁⲣϫ ⲡⲓⲙ (156 ⲡⲥ.),
CO 192 S ⲟⲩⲡⲣⲏϣ ⲡⲟⲩϭⲟⲗⲟⲕ/ (*at price*) *of* ; after
construct : ⲣⲙ ⲡⲏⲓ, ϣⲣⲡ ⲙⲙⲓⲥⲉ. **b** partitive :
Ge 3 22 S ⲟⲩⲁ ⲙⲙⲟⲛ (B ⲉⲃⲟⲗ ⲛ-) = ἐκ, Deu 30 13
S ⲡⲓⲙ ⲙⲙⲟⲛ (B Gk diff), PS 107 S ϩⲓⲣⲟⲩⲛ ⲙ̄ⲙⲟⲓ,
ShA 1 107 S ⲧⲡⲉ ⲙⲙⲟϥ ; after rel (complement-

ary) : Ja 1 24 *SB* ⲑⲉ ⲉⲡⲉϥⲟ ⲙⲙⲟⲥ, ShC 73 96 *S*
bird ⲉⲣⲉⲡⲧⲏϥ ⲙⲙⲟϥ, BMis 488 *S* ⲟⲩⲃⲁⲗ ⲡⲟⲩⲱⲧ
ⲡⲉⲧⲙⲙⲟϥ, 1 Kg 13 21 *S* ⲡⲉⲓϣⲓ ⲡⲟⲩⲱⲧ ⲙⲙⲟⲟⲩⲡⲉ,
HL 98 *B* ⲡⲓⲉⲣⲟⲟⲩ ⲉⲧⲁⲓ ⲉⲡⲁⲓϣⲁϫⲉ ⲙⲙⲟϥ, PS 42
S ⲡⲟⲩⲟⲉⲓⲛ ⲉⲡⲉϥϣⲟⲟⲡ ⲙⲙⲟⲓ, *ib* 8 *S* ⲧⲉⲕⲇⲓⲁⲕⲟⲡⲓⲁ
ⲛⲧⲁⲕⲃⲱⲕ ⲙⲙⲟⲥ, Z 334 *S* ⲧⲉⲩⲛⲟⲩ ⲉⲡⲁϥⲛⲕⲟⲧⲕ
ⲙⲙⲟⲥ, C 43 224 *B* ⲡⲓⲙⲟⲩ ⲉⲧⲉϥⲛⲁⲙⲟⲩ ⲙⲙⲟϥ
ⲧⲉⲛⲛⲁⲙⲟⲩ ⲛϩⲏⲧϥ ; esp local with ⲙⲁ *B* : Deu 12
11 ⲡⲓⲙⲁ…ⲉⲙⲟⲩϯ ⲉⲡⲉϥⲣⲁⲛ ⲙⲙⲟϥ (var ⲙⲙⲁⲩ, *S*
ⲡϩⲏⲧϥ) ἐκεῖ, Mt 24 28 ⲡⲓⲙⲁ ⲉⲧⲉϯϣⲟⲗⲥ ⲙⲙⲟϥ
(*S* ϣⲱⲡⲉ ⲙⲙⲟϥ) ὅπου, v ⲙⲁⲩ e ; with vbs ⲟⲩⲟⲛ,
ⲙⲙⲟⲛ : ShA 1 251 *S* ⲉⲩⲛ ϥⲧⲟ ⲛⲁⲡⲉ ⲙⲙⲟϥ, EpJer
7 *BF* ⲙⲙⲟⲛ ϣϫⲟⲙ ⲙⲙⲱⲟⲩ. **c** adjectival, (1)
adj after nn : Sa 16 3 *S* ϩⲣⲉ ⲃⲃⲣⲣⲉ, Ac 4 9 *SB*
ⲣⲱⲙⲉ ⲛϭⲱⲃ, Lu 1 58 *B* ⲡⲉϥⲛⲁⲓ ⲡⲛⲓϣϯ, Nu 17 10
S ⲡϣⲏⲣⲉ ⲡⲁⲧⲥⲱⲧⲙ ; (2) nn after adj : Lev 19 25
S ⲧⲙⲉϩϥ ⲡⲣⲟⲙⲡⲉ, Mt 15 34 *S* ϩⲉⲛϣⲏⲙ ⲛ̄ⲧⲃ̄ⲧ,
MG 25 211 *B* ⲡⲓⲕⲟⲩϫⲓ ⲛϣⲉⲙⲙⲟⲩϥ, *ib* 40 *B* ⲟⲩ ⲙ-
ⲡⲉⲧϩⲱⲟⲩ. **d** attributive : Jos 4 7 *B* ⲡⲓⲓⲟⲣⲇⲁⲛⲏⲥ
ⲡⲓⲁⲣⲟ, Si 36 6 *S* ϣⲃⲏⲣ ⲣⲣⲉϥⲥⲱⲃⲉ, Jo 18 17 *SA²*
ⲧⲙⲁⲅⲁⲗ ⲡⲁⲡⲟⲟⲧⲉ, Miss 4 644 *S* ⲡⲉⲡⲉⲓⲱⲧ ⲙⲡⲣⲟⲫⲏⲧⲏⲥ, C 89 30 *B* ⲟⲩⲥⲟⲡ ⲙⲙⲟⲛⲁⲭⲟⲥ. Here ?
belong BM 658 *F* ⲁⲛⲁⲕ ⲡⲡⲁⲡⲁ ⲉⲓⲥⲓⲧⲣⲟⲩ, ⲁⲛⲁⲕ ⲡ-
ⲕⲁⲥⲉⲙ &c (joint authors), J 15 36 *S* ⲡⲧⲟϥ ⲡⲡⲁϩⲱⲙ.

II indicating obj of vb, **a** tr : Ge 1 26 *B* ⲙⲁ-
ⲣⲉⲛⲑⲁⲙⲓⲟ ⲡⲟⲩⲣⲱⲙⲓ, Nah 1 9 *A* ϥⲛⲁⲉⲓⲣⲉ ⲡⲟⲩ-
ϩⲁⲉⲓ, P 129¹⁴ 104 *S* ⲁϥⲕⲱⲗϫ ⲡⲡⲉϥⲡⲁⲧ, BKU 1 23
F ⲡⲉⲧⲉⲛⲥⲁⲩⲛ ⲉⲙⲁⲩ (*S* ⲙⲙⲟⲟⲩ). **b** intr & qual :
Sa 2 1 *S* ⲉϥⲙⲉⲣ ⲗⲗⲩⲡⲏ, *ib* 19 12 *S* ⲡⲉϥⲙ ⲡϣⲁ
ⲛϣⲉⲡ ⲡⲁⲓ, PS 45 *S* ⲉⲓⲉϣ ϭⲙ ϭⲟⲙ ⲛⲃⲱⲕ, ShC 42
71 *S* ⲉⲩϣⲁⲁⲧ ⲛⲗⲁⲁⲩ, AM 186 *B* ϣⲁⲣⲉⲣⲱⲙⲓ
ⲥⲱⲃⲓ ⲙⲙⲱⲟⲩ, Tob 11 15 *S* ⲡⲉϥⲟ ⲛϣⲏⲣⲉ ⲙⲙⲟϥ,
Br 227 *S* ⲙⲟⲩⲧⲉ ⲉⲣⲟϥ ϫⲉⲛⲙⲓⲟⲩⲣⲅⲟⲥ ⲁⲩⲱ ⲡⲉⲓⲱⲧ
(Stern 482 *sf*) ; *as, for*, εἰς : Ez 11 20 *B* ⲉⲩⲉ-
ϣⲱⲡⲓ ⲛⲏⲓ ⲡⲟⲩⲗⲁⲟⲥ (*S* ⲉⲩ-), Sa 5 3 *S* ⲉϥϣⲟⲟⲡ ⲛⲁⲡ
ⲙ̄ⲡⲁⲣⲁⲃⲟⲗⲏ, CaiEuch 540 *B* ⲉⲩϯ ⲙⲙⲟⲥ ⲉϫⲱⲛ
ⲡⲟⲩⲥⲱⲧ εἰς λύτρωσιν ; sim Lev 13 25 *S* ⲟ ⲙⲙⲁⲉⲓⲛ,
Ro 4 17 *SB* ⲕⲱ ⲙⲙⲟϥ ⲡⲉⲓⲱⲧ acc. **c** refl : Lu
1 29 *S* ⲡⲉⲥⲙⲟⲕⲙⲉⲕ ⲙⲙⲟⲥ, Jo 5 35 *SA²B* ⲁⲧⲉ-
ⲧⲛⲟⲩⲱϣ ⲉⲧⲉⲗⲏⲗ ⲙⲙⲱⲧⲛ, C 43 10 *B* ⲁⲩϣⲟⲩϣⲟⲩ
ⲙⲙⲱⲟⲩ.

ⲛ- *SAA²BFO* prep, **a** instrument, agent (often var
ϩⲛ-, ϧⲉⲛ-), *with, by*, Gk dat or ἐν : Ps 21 7 *A* (Cl)
ϣⲉϫⲉ ⲡⲡⲟⲩⲥⲡⲁⲧⲟⲩ (*SB* ϩⲛ-), Job 1 17 *B* ϧⲱⲧⲉⲃ
ⲡⲧⲥⲏϥⲓ (*S* ϩⲛ-), Ac 12 2 *B* sim (*S* do), Jer 26 9 *S*
ϩⲏⲕ ⲛϩⲉⲛⲣⲟⲡⲗⲟⲛ (*B* ϧⲉⲛ-), Sa 13 14 *S* ⲁϥⲥⲟⲗϭⲟⲩ
ⲛⲟⲙⲉ, Mt 13 15 *B* ⲛⲁⲩ ⲛ̄ⲡⲟⲩⲃⲁⲗ (*S* do), *ib* 7 6 *S*
ⲣⲟⲙⲟⲩ ⲛⲡⲉⲩⲟⲩⲉⲣⲏⲧⲉ (BG 126 *S* ⲣⲱⲙ ϩⲛ-), Ps 76
2 *B* ⲱϣ ⲛⲧⲁⲥⲙⲏ (*S* ϩⲛ-), Ez 23 29 *B* ⲓⲣⲓ…ⲡⲟⲩ-
ⲙⲟⲥϯ (*S* do), Z 317 *S* ⲉⲕⲣ ⲟⲩ ⲡⲡⲉⲓⲣⲏⲁⲁⲩ (MG 25
231 *B* diff) ἵνα τί σοι ?, Mt 26 63 *SB* ϯⲧⲁⲣⲕⲟ ⲙⲙⲟⲕ
ⲙⲡⲛ̅ⲧ̅, Jer 28 14 *B* ⲱⲣⲕ…ⲙⲡⲉϥϣⲱϣⲛ κατά, Lu
24 47 *S* preached ⲙⲡⲉϥⲣⲁⲛ (*B* ϧⲉⲛ-) ἐπί dat ; Br

47 S shall call him ⲙⲡⲉⲓⲣⲁⲛ, C 43 41 B ⲗⲟϣⲓ ⲡⲡⲉⲕϭⲁⲗⲁⲩⲝ, ShIF 67 S cut ⲡⲟⲩⲡⲕⲁ ⲉϥϩⲏⲣ, BKU 1 1 vo S ϣⲁⲁⲧϥ ⲡⲁⲧϭⲟⲣⲧⲉ, Mus 41 241 S ϭⲟⲗⲉⲧ ⲡⲟⲃⲥⲱ, BM 583 F die ⲙⲡⲉⲣⲕⲁ; with ⲉⲃⲟⲗ: P 129¹⁵ 24 S ⲁⲩⲡⲕⲟⲧⲕ ⲉⲃ. ⲡⲧⲗⲩⲡⲏ. **b** local, *in, to, from*: He 2 6 SB ⲡⲟⲩⲙⲁ (F ϩⲛ-), Z 344 S ⲡⲡⲉⲓⲙⲁ = MG 25 208 B ⲱⲇⲉ, Cl 21 2 A sim, PS 4 S ϣⲟⲟⲡ ⲙⲫⲟⲩⲛ, Lu 16 24 SB dip finger ⲙⲙⲟⲟⲩ Gk gen, Sa 14 3 S ⲣⲓⲛ ⲡⲟⲁⲗⲁⲥⲥⲁ... ϩⲛⲡⲣⲟⲉⲓⲙ ἐν...ἐν, Ap 2 12 S ⲧⲛⲁ ⲙⲡⲣⲟ ⲥⲛⲁⲩ (var ⲉ-, B ϩⲓⲟⲩⲓ ⲡⲣⲟ ⲃ̅), Jer 39 10 B ⲥϭⲁⲓ ⲡⲟⲩⲭⲱⲙ (S ⲉ⳿ⲅⲭ.) εἰς, ShC 73 4 S ⲣ ⲣⲣⲟ ⲙⲡⲱⲡⲣ everlasting, PS 113 S ⲧⲟⲡⲟⲥ ⲉⲧⲡⲥⲁ ⲡⲧⲡⲉ, ROC 17 406 B bury ⲙⲡⲕⲁϩⲓ, Deu 5 4 S ⲡⲧⲙⲏⲧⲉ (var ϩⲛ-), Jos 3 16 S ⲡⲏⲩ ⲙⲡϫⲓⲥⲉ (*sic? l*) ἄνωθεν, AZ 21 94 O who art ⲡⲡⲣⲏⲥ ⲡⲧⲡ, *ib* 100 O ⲡⲉⲧⲡⲕⲟⲩ ⲡⲡⲧⲟⲟⲩ *to* (?) *hill*, Ryl 320 S ⲃⲱⲕ ⲡⲡⲙⲁ *to*, ShC 73 44 S may not ⲃⲱⲕ ⲡⲗⲁⲁⲩ ⲡⲣⲱⲃ *to*, 2 Thes 2 7 S ⲗⲟ ⲡⲧⲙⲏⲧⲉ (B ϭⲉⲡ-) ἐκ; with ⲉⲃⲟⲗ, ⲥⲁⲃⲟⲗ, *from, from out*: Su 13 B ⲫⲱⲣⲝ ⲉⲃ. ⲡⲡⲟⲩⲅⲉⲣⲏⲟⲩ ἀπό, Ex 30 2 B horns ϣⲱⲡⲓ ⲉⲃ. ⲙⲙⲟϥ ἐκ, Br 228 S ⲉⲓ ⲉⲃ. ⲙⲙⲟϥ ⲛ ⲉⲃ. ⲡⲣⲏⲧϥ, Cl 25 3 A ⲧⲱⲡⲉ ⲁⲃ. ⲡⲧⲭⲱⲣⲁ (var ⲁⲃ. ϩⲛ-) ἀπό, *ib* 57 2 A ϯⲕ ⲁⲃ. ⲡⲧϥϩⲉⲗⲡⲓⲥ ἐκ, PS 14 S ⲡⲧⲥ ⲉⲃ. ⲙⲙⲟⲓ, Jer 40 10 B ⲥⲁⲃ. ⲡⲓⲗⲏⲙ̅ ἔξωθεν. **c** temporal, *in, on*: Ez 12 4 SB bring them forth ⲙⲡⲉϩⲟⲟⲩ Gk acc, CaiEuch 407 B ⲡⲟⲩⲥⲟⲩⲥⲟⲩ ⲡⲟⲩⲱⲧ ἐν (cf 1 Cor 15 52 ϭⲉⲡ-), PS 376 S ⲡϣⲟⲙⲧⲉ ⲡⲣⲟⲙⲡⲉ *during*, Z 285 S ⲙⲡⲉϩⲟⲟⲩ ⲉⲧⲙⲙⲁⲩ, *ib* 286 ϩⲙⲡⲉϩ. ⲉⲧⲙ., AZ 21 100 O ⲡ-ⲙⲉⲣⲉ, Eccl 10 17 F ⲙⲡⲡⲉⲩ ⲉⲧⲉϣϣⲏ, πρὸς καιρόν, C 89 58 B what doth he ⲡⲡⲁⲓⲉϩⲟⲟⲩ τὰς ἡμ. ταύτας?, PS 63 S ⲙⲡⲙⲉϩⲥⲟⲡ ⲥⲛⲁⲩ, C 43 1 B ⲡⲥⲟⲩ ⲓ̅ⲍ̅ of month, ShMIF 23 136 S ϩⲁⲧⲉϥϩⲏ ⲡⲣⲉⲡϩⲟⲟⲩ *some days before him*, ShRE 10 163 S going in to desert ⲡⲣⲉⲡϩⲟⲟⲩ ⲙⲙⲟⲟϣⲉ. **d** in compound prep, as ⲡⲥⲁ-, ⲡⲟⲩ(ϩ)ⲉ- F ⲡϩⲁ- F (LAp 541 *sic l*), ⲡϣⲁ- (Ryl 314), ⲡϩⲓ- A, ⲡϩⲣⲏⲓ, ⲡϩⲏⲧϥ, also ⲙⲡⲁ-ⲣⲁ: ShC 73 162 S ⲙⲡⲁⲣⲁ ⲡϣⲓ, LMis 464 S ⲥⲟⲧⲡ ⲙⲡⲁⲣⲁ ⲧⲡⲉ, BM 586 F no one ⲙⲡⲁⲗⲉⲗⲁⲕ; *v* Ep 1 251 n. **e** in advbs, as ⲡⲁ (*v* ⲁ- advb), ⲡⲟⲉ (cf ⲕⲁⲧⲁ ⲑⲉ), ⲙⲫⲣⲏϯ, ⲡⲣⲟϩⲟ, ⲙⲡⲕⲱⲧⲉ, ⲙⲡⲉⲥⲡⲁⲩ, ⲡⲟⲩⲱϣⲙ, ⲡⲟⲩⲁ ⲟⲩⲁ, ⲡⲟⲩϣⲛⲙ, ⲡϣⲟⲣⲡ, ⲡϣⲁ-ⲃⲟⲗ, ⲡⲧⲡⲁⲩ, ⲡⲕⲁⲗⲱⲥ (after vb), ⲡⲥⲭⲉϩⲟⲡ (C 86 206), ⲡⲣⲟⲗⲟⲥ (Bodl(P) c 11), ⲡⲁⲣⲏⲩ (Ep 392), ⲡⲧϣⲉⲃⲓⲱ, ⲙⲙⲁⲩ, ⲙⲡⲁⲣⲣⲏⲥⲓⲁ, ⲡⲭⲓⲟⲩⲉ; or adverbial phrases: BKU 1 8 34 S ⲉⲕⲡⲓⲥⲧⲉⲩⲉ ⲡⲁⲧ-ⲟⲩⲱⲙ (*sic l*). Here ? belong B ⲉⲣ ⲡⲭⲣⲓⲁ (MG 25 24, C 86 75), ⲙⲃⲟⲕⲓ (*v* ⲃⲟⲕⲓ). **f** before conjunctions (archaic) SAA²F: ⲡⲧⲁⲣ, ⲡϫⲉ Deu Budge, AP, ZNTW 24 84, 90, Ryl 6, 292, ⲡϫⲉ- A (TU 43 5); or interj S: BIF 13 44 ⲱ ⲡϩⲓⲁ = MG 25 270 B ⲱ ϩⲓⲁ.

ⲛ- SAA²BFO, ⲡⲁ⳿ SBO, ⲡⲏ⳿ SᵃFO, ⲡⲉ⳿ AA²F

(for forms *v* Stern 502, Ep 1 248, Till 154, Asmus 27), **ⲛⲁ-** for **ⲛ-** S (Theban, *v* Ep *lc*, J Index, CO Index) prep of dative *to, for*: Deu 7 9 SB keeping mercy ⲡⲡⲉⲧⲙⲉ ⲙⲙⲟϥ τοῖς, Ac 2 30 SB ⲁⲡⲡⲉ̅ ⲱⲣⲕ ⲡⲁϥ αὐτῷ, 1 Thes 2 15 B ⲣ ⲁⲡⲁϥ ⲙϥϯ θεῷ, Jon 4 8 SAB ⲁϥⲟⲩⲁϩⲥⲁϩⲛⲉ ⲡⲟⲩⲡⲡ̅ⲁ̅ πνεύματι, Jo 4 15 F ⲙⲁⲓ ⲡⲏⲓ μοι, Ez 33 12 B ⲁϫⲟⲥ ⲡⲡⲉⲡϣⲏⲣⲓ πρός, Ps 6 1 S ϯ ⲥⲃⲱ ⲡⲁⲓ ⲙⲉ, *ib* 9 24 SB ϯ ⲡⲟⲩϭⲥ ⲙⲡⲭⲟⲉⲓⲥ τόν, Sa 11 24 S ⲉⲕⲡⲁ ⲙⲡⲧⲏⲣϥ πάντας, Ps 62 7 SB ϣⲱⲡⲉ ⲡⲁⲓ ⲡⲃⲟⲏⲑⲟⲥ βο. μου; AZ 21 100 O ⲡⲉⲭⲁϥ ⲡⲁⲥ, PS 113 S ⲁⲕⲧⲏⲡⲟⲟⲩ ⲡⲁⲓ, ShC 73 5 S ⲡⲉⲧⲡⲁⲣ ⲣⲁϣⲉ ⲡⲁϥ from sorrow, AM 172 B ϯ ϭⲓⲥⲓ ⲡⲱⲧⲉⲡ, Hor 80 O ⲡⲡⲉϣⲏⲣⲓ ϭⲱⲡⲉ ⲡⲏϥ, El 100 A ⲥⲉⲧⲉⲉⲥ ⲡⲉⲩ, Ep 84 S ⲉⲓϣⲁⲡϫⲟⲟⲩⲕ ⲡⲟⲩϩⲱⲃ *for an affair, on business*; in address of letter; BM 1122 S ⲧⲁⲁⲥ ⲡⲑⲉⲟⲇⲟⲥⲉ, CMSS 39 F ⲧⲉⲉⲓⲧⲥ ⲡⲡ-ⲙⲉⲗⲓⲧ ⲥⲁⲡ. With *give, pay* S (Theban) sometimes dat **ⲛ-** only, vb omitted: ⲁⲓⲡⲁϥ, ⲉϥϣⲁⲡ ⲡⲁⲕ, *v* Ep 532 n. Ethic dat: Ge 33 18 S ⲁϥⲟⲩⲉϩ ⲡⲁϥ, Ex 2 18 B ⲁϥϣⲉ ⲡⲱⲟⲩ, Mich 550 39 S ⲁϥϭⲱ ⲡⲁϥ ϩⲙⲡⲙⲁ, Z 347 S ϩⲙⲟⲟⲥ ⲡⲁⲕ = MG 25 220 B om ⲛ-, BAp 51 S ⲉⲓⲙⲉϣⲉ ⲡⲏⲧⲛ, MIE 2 355 B ⲡⲁⲓ-ⲙⲉⲣⲓ ⲡⲏⲡⲉ ϫⲉ- = BAp 80 S om ⲛ-.

ⲛⲁ- S: J 79 53 ⲟⲩⲕ ⲉϫⲓⲥⲧⲁⲓ (ἔξεστι) ⲡⲁⲓ ⲟⲩⲇⲉ ⲡⲁⲗⲁⲁⲅⲉ ⲡⲣⲱⲙⲉ, *ib* 36 25 ⲁⲡⲥⲙⲏ ⲉⲩⲅⲣⲁⲫⲟⲡ ⲡⲁ-ⲡⲉⲅⲉⲣⲏⲩ, CO 165 ⲥϩⲁⲓ ⲡⲁⲡⲁⲉⲓⲱⲧ, Ep 398 ϫⲟⲟⲩ ⲡⲁⲓⲁⲕⲱⲃ, BKU 1 97 oath sworn ⲡⲁⲡϣⲓⲣⲉ ⲡⲓⲱⲁⲡ-ⲡⲏⲥ. Once F: PMich 606 ⲡⲉⲧⲥϭⲉⲓ ⲡⲁⲁⲡⲁ ⲓⲱⲥⲏⲫ.

ⲡⲁ⳿, ⲡⲏ⳿ + obj suff S: 1 Kg 21 9 ⲙⲁ ⲡⲁⲓⲥ (var ⲁⲡⲓⲥ ⲡⲁⲓ) δός μοι αὐτήν, 2 Kg 20 21 ⲙⲁ ⲡⲁⲓϥ, Hall 87]ϥ ⲉⲡⲧⲁⲕ ⲡⲏⲓⲥⲟⲩ (vb om as above). *Cf* ⲟⲩⲡ-ⲧⲁⲓϥ, ⲙⲡⲧⲁϥ &c.

ⲛ- neg pref (ⲛ-...ⲁⲛ) *v* ⲁⲛ

ⲛ-, ⲡⲉ-, ⲡⲓ-, ⲡⲉⲡ- pl art *v* ⲡ-.

ⲛ- (ᵉⲛ) SAA², ⲉⲛ- SBF *v* ⲉⲓⲛⲉ *bring*.

ⲛⲁ, ⲛⲁⲁ (Deu 13 17, Si 44 11) S, **ⲛⲁⲉ** SAA², **ⲛⲁⲓ** S (CO) B, **ⲛⲁⲉⲓⲛ** S (ST), **ⲛⲉⲓ, ⲛⲉⲉⲓ** F, ⲣ ⲥ ⲡⲁ- (ⲡⲁϩⲣⲓⲧ, ⲡⲁⲛⲧ) SABF vb intr, *have pity, mercy* **a** no obj: Tob 13 2 S, Ps 36 26 SB, Ro 12 8 SBF ἐλεεῖν, BHom 63 S ⲉⲩⲡⲁ ⲉⲩϯ. **b** c **ⲛ-** dat = Gk acc: Deu 13 17 S (B ϯ ⲡⲛ., var ⲡⲟⲩⲛ., Job 27 15 SB, Ps 50 3 SA (Cl) B, EpJer 37 BF, Mt 20 30 SF (B ϭⲁ-), Ro 11 30 S (var ⲡⲁⲧⲏⲩⲧⲛ *sic?*) BF ἐλ.; AP 40 A² Lord ⲡⲁ ⲡⲉⲛ, Ryl 270 S ⲁⲕⲡⲁⲉ ⲡⲁⲓ, Pcod 18 S ⲡⲥⲡⲁⲡⲁ ⲁⲛ ⲙⲡⲉⲧϩⲓⲧⲟⲩⲱⲕ, C 43 88 B ⲡ. ⲡⲡⲓⲣⲉϥⲉⲣ ⲡⲟⲃⲓ. **c** c ϩⲁ-, ϭⲁ- Gk acc: Is 30 19 F (S ⲛ-, B diff), Mt 15 22 B (S ⲛ-) ἐλ., R 1 1 28 S ⲁⲩⲡⲁ ϩⲁⲣⲟⲓ κατελ.; PS 122 S ⲁϥⲡⲁ ϩⲁⲡⲡⲉ-ⲡⲟⲥ, PO 11 344 B ⲡⲁⲓ ϭⲁⲡⲁⲥⲟⲡ.

—— SABF nn m, *pity, charity*: Ge 19 19 B

(S diff), Ps 31 10 SA (Cl) B, Mic 6 8 SAB, Mt 12
7 SA (Hos 6 6) BF ἔλεος, PS 23 5 S (B ⲙⲉⲧⲛⲁⲏⲧ)
ἐλεημοσύνη; BG 51 S ⲛⲁϣⲉ ⲡⲉϥⲛⲁⲉ (ib 53 ⲛⲁ),
CA 99 S gavest me naught ⲛ̄ⲡⲁ, BSM 2 B ⲙⲉϩ ⲛ̄-
ⲡⲁⲓ ⲉϩⲟⲩⲛ ⲉⲧⲣⲓⲕⲱⲛ, BMis 20 S who gavest ⲛⲁⲡⲁ
ⲉⲡⲉⲕⲣⲏⲧ, ST 262 S ⲉⲓϣⲱⲡⲉ ⲁⲛⲛⲁ ϣⲱⲡⲉ & we be
not asked, Bodl(P) d 20 S ⲁⲡⲉⲕⲛⲁ ⲧⲁⲣⲟⲛ & didst
lend, BM 601 F ⲛ̄ⲧⲉⲡⲉⲃⲛⲉⲉⲓ ⲧⲁⲣⲁⲓ; in witness's
signature : J 38 63 S ⲁⲛⲟⲕ...ⲣⲁⲛⲡⲁ ⲙ̄ⲡⲛ̄ⲧ̄ hum-
blest priest (cf ἐλέει θεοῦ PLond 1 235, Wess 3 343).

ⲉⲓⲣⲉ, ⲣ ⲛⲡ., ⲟⲩⲛ. SBF, do charity, kindness : Ps
108 16 SB ἐλ. ποιεῖν; c ⲙⲛ̄- : 2 Kg 3 8 S, Lu
10 37 SB ἐλ. ποι. μετά; DeV 2 166 B ⲁϥⲉⲣ ⲡⲉϥⲛⲁ.
ⲡⲛⲓϣϯ ⲡⲉⲙⲁⲛ, AZ 21 150 S ⲁⲧⲉⲧⲛⲉⲓⲣⲉ ⲡⲁⲛⲁⲓ
ⲡⲟⲩⲛⲁ, Ep 377 S ⲣⲉⲡⲕⲟⲩⲓ ⲡⲟⲉⲓⲕ ⲣ ⲡⲛⲁ ⲡⲁⲛⲁⲛ,
CMSS 23 Sᶠ ⲛⲉⲣⲛⲙⲉⲭ ⲉⲛϣⲁⲕⲉⲣ ⲛⲁ ⲡⲉⲙⲁⲓ ⲙ̄-
ⲙⲟⲟⲩ, RE 14 30 S ⲁⲣⲓ ⲡⲛⲁ ⲡⲁⲛⲙⲁⲛ ⲡⲟⲩⲭⲱⲱⲗⲉ,
BM 589 F ⲉⲕⲓⲗⲓ ⲡⲓⲉⲓ ⲡⲉⲙⲛⲓ & forgive me, CO
278 S pray that God ⲣ ⲟⲩⲛⲁⲓ ⲡⲉⲙⲁ(ⲓ), Ep 660 S
sim ⲡⲁⲉ (v ib 1 247), ST 287 Sᵃ ⲁⲣⲛⲟⲩ ⲥⲁⲛⲣ ⲟⲩ-
ⲡⲁⲉⲓⲏ ⲙⲉⲡⲁⲓ, CO 240 S send cauldron for ϣⲁⲡⲣ
ⲡⲡⲁ ⲙ̄ⲡⲉⲥⲓⲏⲩ.   c ⲉϩⲣⲁⲓ ⲉϫⲛ̄- S sim : Ge 47
29 (B ⲙⲉⲑⲛⲁⲏⲧ) ἐλεημ. ποι. ἐπί.   c ϩⲁ- B sim :
BSM 61 ⲉⲣ ⲟⲩⲛⲁ ϩⲁⲡⲉϥⲗⲁⲟⲥ.   c ϩⲉⲛ- B sim :
Ge 40 14 ἐν ἐμοί.   c conjunct : CO 256 S ⲣ ⲡ̄ⲡⲁ
ⲛ̄ⲧⲟⲩϯ ⲟⲩⲕⲟⲩⲓ.

ϣⲉⲡⲛⲁ S, mercy? (cf ϣⲉ ⲡⲉⲣ ϥⲙⲉⲅⲓ) : Ryl 339
I am a taxpayer ⲧⲓⲉⲣ χρεια ⲡϣⲉⲡⲛⲁ ⲉⲣⲟⲓ.

ϣⲡ ⲛⲁ S, receive charity : BMar 17 ⲛ̄ϥϣⲱⲡⲉ
ⲉϥϣⲡ ⲛⲁ at city gate.

ϣⲟⲩⲛⲁⲓ B, worthy of pity, pitiable : Va 66 294
ϩⲁⲡ̄ϣ. ⲡⲱⲟⲩ ἐλεεινός.

ϫⲓ ⲛⲁ Aᵃ, ϭⲓ ⲛ. BF, get pity, take alms : 1 Cor 15
19 BF (S diff) ἐλεεινός, BM 1224 Aᵃ may I see
them (whom I curse) ⲉⲩϫⲓ ⲛ̄ⲡⲁ ⲙ̄ⲡⲕⲟⲥⲙⲟⲥ (cf
ϫⲓ ⲙ̄ⲛ̄ⲧⲛⲁ, ϫⲓ ⲁⲅⲁⲡⲏ).

ⲁⲧⲛ., ⲁⲑⲛ. SABF, pitiless : Pro 5 9 SAB ἀνελεήμων, Ja 2 13 SB ἀνέλεος; PS 100 S entreated
ⲉⲡⲓⲁ. ⲉⲧⲙⲙⲁⲩ, BG 122 S ⲡⲓⲁⲧⲛⲁⲉ.   As adj :
ShR 2 4 46 = BM 214 S ⲁⲅⲅⲉⲗⲟⲥ ⲛⲁⲧ., AM 185
B ⲣⲁⲙⲁⲟ ⲛⲁⲑ.   ⲣ ⲁⲧⲛ., ⲟ ⲛⲁⲧ., be pitiless : Ro
1 31 B ἀνελεή., BMis 557 S ⲉⲅⲟ ⲛⲁ. ⲉϩⲟⲩⲛ ⲉⲡⲉ-
ⲯⲩⲭⲏ, BM 586 F ⲙ̄ⲡⲉⲗⲉⲗ ⲁ. (ⲉ)ⲗⲁⲡ.   ⲙⲛ̄ⲧ-,
ⲙⲉⲧⲁⲧⲛ., pitilessness : Job 6 21 SB ἀνελεημόνως
C 43 100 B striking him ϩⲉⲛⲟⲩⲙ., Pcod 6 S at
sight of demon man's bones ϣⲧⲟⲣⲧⲣ ϩⲛⲟⲩⲛⲟϭ ⲛⲁⲙ.

ⲙ̄ⲛ̄ⲧⲛⲁ. SAAᵃ, ⲙⲉⲧ-, ⲙⲉⲑⲛ. B nn f, pity, charity :
Ps 32 5 S (B ⲙⲉⲑⲛⲁⲏⲧ), Pro 3 3 SA (B do), Ac 9
36 S (BF do) ἐλεημοσύνη; BHom 87 S Judas stole
ϩⲉⲛⲛⲁ.   ⲣ ⲛⲁ., do charity S : Ps 102 6 (B do),
Mt 6 3 (BF do) ἐλεημ. ποι.   ⲥⲣ ⲛⲁ. S, distribute charity : Z 350.   ϯ ⲛⲁ. S, give charity :
Lu 12 33 (B do) ἐλεημ. διδόναι, Si 32 2, Z 355 ϯ

ⲙ. from own labour ἐλ. ποι.; ST 56 bequests
ⲛ̄ⲧⲁⲁⲩ ⲛ̄ⲁ. ϩⲁⲣⲟⲓ.   ϣⲁⲁⲧ ⲛ̄ⲁ. S, ϣⲉⲧ, ϣⲁⲧ
ⲛ̄ⲁ. SB, ask pity, charity : Ac 3 2 SB ἐλεημ. αἰτεῖν;
Ps 108 10 B (S diff) ἐπαιτ., Jo 9 8 SB (Aᵃ ϫⲓ ⲛ̄)
προσαιτ.; BMis 359 S = BSM 21 B those ⲉⲧϣ. ⲛ̄ⲁ.
at gate, AZ 21 153 S ⲁⲩⲥⲟⲣϥ ⲛ̄ⲡⲉⲧϣⲁⲁⲧ ⲛ̄ⲁ.
As nn B, one asking charity : Ps 34 10 (S ⲉⲃⲓⲏⲛ)
πένης, Jo 9 8 (SAᵃ ⲣⲉϥⲧⲱⲃϩ) προσαίτης; adj : C 43
187 ⲟⲩⲣⲱⲙⲓ ⲛϣ.

ϫⲓ ⲛ̄ⲁ. SAᵃ, receive charity : Mk 10 46 S (B ⲣⲉϥⲧⲱⲃϩ) προσαίτης, Jo 9 8 Aᵃ ut sup, JKP 2 100 S.

ⲣⲉⲙ̄ⲛ̄ⲡⲛⲁⲓ B, pitiful, charitable person : Ṣalib 142
ⲟⲩⲁⲅⲁⲡⲏⲧⲟⲥ ⲡⲣ.

ⲣⲉϥⲛⲁⲓ B, meaning same : Is 49 10 (S ⲛⲁ vb)
ἐλεεῖν; K 43 God ⲡⲓⲣ.

ϫⲓⲛⲛⲁⲓ B nn m, pity, act of pitying : Is 30 18
(SF ⲛⲁ vb) ἐλεεῖν.

ⲛⲁϩⲏⲧ B (rare v inf), ⲛⲁⲏⲧ SABF, ⲛⲁⲉⲓⲏⲧ Sᶠ,
pitiful of heart, compassionate : Ex 22 27 S (B ϣⲉⲡ-
ⲣⲏⲧ), Tob 6 17 S, Ps 110 4 SB, Jon 4 2 SAB, He
2 17 SF (B ⲟⲓ ⲛⲡ.) ἐλεήμων; Pro 2 8 SA (B diff)
εὐλαβούμενος (read ? as ἐλεημόνων); PS 8 S Jesus
ⲛⲡ. ⲁⲩⲱ ⲡⲣⲁⲗϭⲣⲏⲧ, ShBor 246 38 S ⲛ. opp ⲁⲧⲛⲁ,
Pcod 45 Sᶠ ⲟⲩⲛⲁⲉⲓⲏⲧ, BMOr 6201 A 114 S Christ
ⲡⲓⲛⲁⲏⲧ.   As adj : Pro 11 17 SAB, CaiEuch 399
B ⲟⲩⲛⲟⲩϯ ⲛⲡ. ἐλεήμων; BM 214 S ⲛⲁⲅⲅⲉⲗⲟⲥ
ⲛⲡ.   ⲣ ⲛⲁⲏⲧ SB, be pitiful : Lu 6 36 B (S ϣⲁⲛ-
ϩⲧⲏϥ) οἰκτίρμων, Mun 49 S ⲟ ⲛⲡ. ⲉϩⲟⲩⲛ ⲉⲡⲉⲛ-
ⲕⲉ.   ⲙⲁⲓⲛ. S, charity-loving : Tob 14 8 φιλε-
λεήμων.

ⲙⲛ̄ⲧ-, ⲙⲉⲑⲛⲁⲏⲧ SBF nn f, pity, charity : Is 38
18 B, Dan 9 16 B, Lu 11 41 B (all S ⲙⲛ̄ⲧⲛⲁ) ἐ-
λεημοσύνη; Ps 99 S ⲉⲓϣⲟⲟⲡ ϩⲛⲟⲩⲙ. ⲉϩⲟⲩⲛ ⲉⲣⲟⲥ,
Mor 24 24 F, BSM 48 B = BMis 398 S ⲁⲅⲁⲡⲏ.

ⲉⲓⲣⲉ, ⲣ ⲙⲛ̄ⲧⲛ. S (rare) BF, do charity, have pity :
Ps 102 6 B, Mt 6 3 B, Ac 9 36 BF (all S ⲙⲛ̄ⲧⲛⲁ)
ἐλεημ. ποι.; BMis 164 S ⲧⲙ. ⲉⲧⲟⲩⲉⲓⲣⲉ ⲙ̄ⲙⲟⲥ, AM
220 B ⲛ̄ⲧⲉϥⲉⲓⲣⲓ ⲛⲟⲩⲙ. ⲛ̄ⲛⲏ ⲉⲧⲉⲣ ϩⲁⲓⲉ.   ϯ ⲙⲉⲧⲛ.
B, give charity : Va 67 78 ⲉⲛϯ ⲙ. in Lord's name.

ⲛⲁϩⲣⲏⲧ B : AM 288, Miss 4 159, TSBA 9 384, Z
54; ⲙⲛ̄ⲧ]ⲛⲁ ⲛⲁϩ [ⲛⲧ A Cl 19 3 Rösch (var ⲙⲛ̄ⲧ-
ϩⲁⲣϣϩⲏⲧ).

ⲛⲁ SAB, ⲛⲡⲁ AAᵃ vb intr (qual Stern 348,
Jernstedt CR Russian Acad 1927 33), go : Pro 8 20
A (S ⲃⲏⲕ, B = Gk) ἀναστρέφεσθαι; Ex 4 21 A (B
ϣⲉ ⲛ-) πορεύεσθαι; Sa 13 18 S ϩⲓⲛ ⲉⲧϥⲛⲁ ⲙ̄ⲙⲟⲥ
ὁδοιπορία; ShA 1 206 S it is written ⲉⲕⲛⲁⲃⲱⲕ
ⲉⲡⲛⲁ...ⲉⲓⲙⲉ ϫⲉⲉⲩⲛⲁ ⲉⲧⲃⲉⲟⲩ.   With ⲛⲏⲩ, go
& come : Ge 1 2 S (BMis 551, B ⲡⲛⲟⲩ only), ib
7 18 SB (Va) ἐπιφέρεσθαι for both, Mk 6 31 B (S
ⲃⲏⲕ) ἔρχεσθαι...ὑπάγειν; BG 45 S (on Ge 1 2)
ⲡⲉⲥⲛⲁ ⲉⲥⲡⲏⲩ ⲡⲉ, ⲡⲉⲥⲛⲁ ⲇⲉ ⲙ̄ⲡⲡⲉⲥⲉⲓ ⲡⲁⲡⲉ ⲉⲡ-
ⲫⲉⲣⲉ, ShMIF 23 18 S breath ⲉϥⲛⲁ ⲉϥⲡⲏⲩ, ShC

42 76 S familiar friend ⲉϥⲛⲁ ⲉϥⲛⲏⲩ in house, BKU 1 92 S wilt meet no man ⲉⲕⲛⲏⲩ ⲛ̄ ⲉⲕⲛⲁ, Bodl Marsh 32 125 B ⲉϥⲛⲁ ⲉϥⲛⲏⲟⲩ ⲁⲛ in things of world يجر. V also ⲛⲁ ⲉⲡϣⲱⲓ, ⲉⲧⲱⲛ, ⲉϩⲟⲩⲛ, ⲉϩⲣⲁⲓ. With following preposition.

—— ⲉ-, often *be in act of going to*: Eccl 3 20 S, Bel 33 B, Ac 16 16, 22 5 B (S ⲃⲱⲕ) πορ. εἰς; Jo 13 36 SA² (B ϣⲉ) ὅπου ὑπάγεις; Si 41 10 S(ⲓ ⲉⲩⲛⲁ) Gk om, ShA 1 207 S ⲡⲧⲉⲧⲛ̄ⲃⲱⲕ ⲉⲣⲟⲟⲩ ⲛ̄ⲑⲉ ⲉⲧⲉⲧⲛⲁ ⲉⲧⲉⲕⲕⲗⲏⲥⲓⲁ, ShBor 246 48 S maketh preparation ⲉϥⲛⲁ ⲉⲡϣⲙⲙⲟ, C 41 27 B when reached Chereu ⲉϥⲛⲁ ⲉⲣⲁⲕⲟϯ, Gu 30 S middle piece of cross nailed upon ⲡϣⲉ ⲉⲧⲛⲁ ⲉⲡⲉⲓⲥⲁ ⲙⲡⲡⲁⲓ, DeV 2 268 B when they ⲓ ⲉϫⲉⲛⲡⲓⲧⲣⲓⲥⲁⲧⲓⲟⲥ & ⲁⲅⲛⲁ ⲉⲡⲓⲥⲧⲩⲗⲟⲥ; *befit, suit* : Job 6 20 S (var ⲣ ⲉ-, B ϣⲱⲡⲓ ⲛ-) ὀφείλειν; ShC 73 209 S drugs ⲉⲧⲛⲁ ⲉⲡϣⲱⲡⲉ.

—— ⲉⲣⲁⲧ⸗ SA², *go to* God : 1 Kg 10 3 S ἀναβαίνειν πρός; Jo 13 3 SA² (B ϣⲉ ϩⲁ-) ὑπάγ. πρός; ClPr 41 28 S came from God & ϥⲛⲁ ⲉⲣⲁⲧϥ, ShIF 197 S righteous ⲉⲧⲛⲁ ⲉⲣⲁⲧϥ, cf ib ⲉⲧⲃⲱⲕ ⲉⲣⲁⲧϥ.

—— ⲉϫⲛ- S, *go up to, approach* : ShA 2 68 one that ⲛⲁ ⲉϫⲙ̄ⲡⲉⲑⲩⲥⲓⲁⲥⲧⲏⲣⲓⲟⲛ to communicate. With following adverb.

—— ⲉⲡⲉⲥⲏⲧ B, *go down* : Ps 113 25 (S ⲃⲏⲕ ⲉⲡ.), Is 14 19 (S ⲃⲏⲕ ⲉϩⲣⲁⲓ) καταβ. V next.

—— ⲉⲡϣⲱⲓ B, *go up* : Ge 28 12 ⲛⲁ ⲉⲡ....ⲡⲛⲏⲟⲩ ⲉⲡⲉⲥⲏⲧ, Ps 106 26 sim (S ⲃⲱⲕ...ⲉⲓ) ἀναβ....καταβ.; Va 66 301 sim ἄνω κάτω φέρεσθαι; MG 25 211 flame ⲉϥⲛⲁ ⲉⲡ. ⲉⲧⲫⲉ (S Z 345 ꞓ.) ἀναβ.; C 43 50 ⲉⲩⲛⲁ ⲉⲡ. ⲓⲉ ⲉⲩⲛⲁ ⲉⲡⲉⲥⲏⲧ(S Mor 39 27 ⲡⲛⲏⲩ...ⲡⲛⲏⲩ)

—— ⲉⲧⲱⲛ, ⲉⲑ. SAA²B, *go whither* : Ge 32 17 SB, Zech 2 2 A (B ⲙⲟϣⲓ), MG 25 231 B (S Z 317 ⲃⲏⲕ) ποῦ πορ.; Jud 19 17 S ⲛⲁ ⲉ....ⲉⲓ ⲧⲱⲛ πορ.... ἔρχεσθαι; Jo 3 8 SA² ⲉⲓ...ⲛⲁ ⲉ., B ⲡⲛⲏⲟⲩ...ⲛⲁ ⲉ. (F ⲡⲛⲏⲟⲩ...ϣⲏ) ἔρχ...ὑπάγ., ib 14 5 SA² (B ϣⲉ) ὑπάγ.; ShMIF 23 200 S ⲉϥⲛⲁ ⲉ. ⲏ ⲉϥⲃⲱⲕ ⲉⲁϣ ⲙⲙⲁ?, BMis 380 S ⲉⲕⲛⲁ ⲉ.= BSM 36 B ⲟⲛⲗ, BIF 13 107 S = MG 25 291 B.

—— ⲉϩⲟⲩⲛ, ⲁϧ., ⲉϩ., SAA²B, *go in, enter* : Lev 16 23 S (B ϣⲉ ⲉϧ.), EpJer 16 B (F ⲡⲛⲏⲟⲩ) εἰσπορ., Ac 9 28 B ⲛⲁ ⲉϧ. ⲡⲉⲙⲉⲃⲟⲗ (S ⲃⲏⲕ, ⲡⲛⲏⲩ) εἰσέκπορ., Zech 8 10 A ⲡⲛⲏⲟⲩ ⲁϧ....ⲛⲁ ⲁϧ. (B ⲡⲛⲏⲟⲩ ...ⲡⲛⲏⲟⲩ) εἰσπορ., Mk 7 15 S ⲛⲁ (var ⲃⲱⲕ) B ⲉϩ.... ⲡⲛⲏⲩ ⲉⲃ. εἰσ- ἐκπορ.; Pro 6 29 AB (S ⲃⲏⲕ), AP 8 A² ⲡⲉⲧⲛⲁ ⲁϩ. εἰσέρχ.; Ac 3 3 B (S ⲃⲱⲕ) εἰσιέναι; He 4 12 B (ϫⲱⲧⲉ) διικνεῖσθαι; ShEp 65 S ⲃⲱⲕ ⲉϩ. through wide gate ⲛⲁ ⲉϩ. through narrow (Mt 7 13), ShWess 9 141 S demons ⲉⲧⲛⲁ ⲉϩ. ϣⲁⲧⲉⲯⲩⲭⲏ, MG 25 271 B road ⲉⲑⲛⲁ ⲉϧ. ⲉⲓⲕⲟⲡⲓⲟⲛ, Z 234 S ⲁⲩⲃⲱⲕ ϫⲉⲉⲩⲛⲁ ⲉϩ.

—— ⲉϩⲣⲁⲓ, ⲁϧⲣⲓ, ⲉϩⲣⲏⲓ SAA²B, *go up* : Deu 1 41 S (var ⲛⲁⲃⲱⲕ, B ϣⲉ), Mk 10 32 S (B ⲡⲛⲏⲟⲩ), Ac 21 15 B (S ⲙⲟⲟϣⲉ ⲉϩ.), Jo 6 62 SA²B ἀναβ., Ge 28 12 S ⲛⲁ ⲉϩ.....ⲡⲛⲏⲩ ⲉⲡⲉⲥⲏⲧ (BAp 83, var ⲃⲏⲕ, B ⲛⲁ) ἀναβ. καταβ.; El 106 A ⲉϥⲛⲁ ⲁϧ. [ϥ]ⲡⲛⲏⲩ ⲁϧⲣⲏⲓ, AP 29 A² ⲉϥ]ⲡⲛⲁ ⲁϧ. ⲁⲧⲩⲣⲟⲥ.

—— ⲉϩⲣⲁⲓ, ⲉϧ. SB, *go down* : Ps 27 1 B (S ⲃⲏⲕ ⲉⲡⲉⲥⲏⲧ), Is 31 1 B (S do, F ⲡⲏⲧ) καταβ.; ShC 42 212 S ⲉⲣⲉⲧⲉⲩϫⲁⲏ ⲛⲁ (var ⲃⲏⲕ) ⲉϩ. to hell.

—— *as vbal pref* 1 & 2 fut in SAA²BO (AZ 21 100 ⲉⲧⲕⲛⲁⲁⲓⲧⲟⲩ), in F ⲡⲉ-.

ⲛⲁ- poss v ⲡⲁ-.

ⲛⲁ- SF, ⲛⲁⲩ- B v ⲁ- *about*.

ⲛⲁⲁ SB, ⲛⲁⲉ SF, ⲛⲁⲁ⸗ SB, ⲛⲁⲁⲁ⸗ S, ⲛⲉⲉ⸗ AA² *nominal vb, be great*, cf ⲁⲓⲁⲓ, o : Deu 1 19 B (S ⲛⲟϭ), Ps 18 14 B (S do) μέγας, 1 Cor 14 5 S ⲛⲁⲉ ⲡⲉⲧ- B ⲛⲁⲁ ⲡⲉⲧ-, ib 12 31 B (S do), 1 Jo 3 20 S ⲛⲁⲉ (B ⲛⲓϣϯ), ROC 17 398 B ⲙⲙⲟⲛ ⲡⲉⲑⲛⲁⲁϥ μείζων, Mt 23 5 S (B ϣⲓⲁⲓ) μεγαλύνειν, 2 Pet 1 17 B μεγαλοπρεπής; Jer 13 9 B (S ⲛⲁϣⲉ) πολύς; Eccl 7 13 F (S diff) περισσεία; P 131⁴ 143 S ⲛⲉϥϧⲃⲏⲩⲉ ⲉⲛⲁⲁⲩ, Mich 550 40 S garments ⲉⲣⲉⲡⲉⲩⲧⲟⲟⲙⲉ ⲛⲁⲁⲁⲩ, DeV 2 23 B ⲟⲩϭⲓϣⲱⲟⲩ ⲉⲛⲁⲁϥ, Bor 311 98 S ϧⲉⲛⲥⲙⲟⲧ ⲉⲛⲁⲟⲩⲟⲩ. c ⲉ-, *greater than* : Hag 2 9 SA (B ⲛⲓϣϯ) μέγ. ὑπέρ; Jos 19 9 S, Jo 4 12 SA² (B do, F ⲛⲁϭ), He 6 13 S ⲛⲁⲁϥ (B do) μείζ.; Philem 16 S ⲛⲁⲁϥ (B ⲟⲩⲱϯ) ὑπέρ; 2 Kg 24 3 S ⲛⲁⲁⲣⲟⲟⲩ (ⲓ ⲉⲣⲟⲟⲩ) ὥσπερ αὐτούς; Mk 12 28 S (B ϣⲟⲣⲡ) πρῶτος; ShC 42 222 S no rest o ⲛ̄ⲛⲟϭ ⲉⲛⲉⲧⲛⲁϣⲱⲡⲉ...no labour ⲉⲛⲁⲁⲁϥ ⲉⲛⲉⲧⲛⲁϣⲱⲡⲉ, Mor 40 47 S ϧⲛⲕⲉⲣⲙⲟⲧ ⲉⲛⲁⲁⲁϥ ⲉⲛⲁⲓ = MG 25 273 B only ⲉⲑⲛⲁⲁⲩ, Mor 40 8 S shalt see ⲡⲉⲧⲛⲁⲁⲩ ⲉⲛⲁⲓ = C 43 38 B, Mor 18 96 = 19 98 S ⲙⲏ ⲛⲁⲁⲁⲕ ⲉⲣⲟⲟⲩ? c ⲛ- S: Ap 2 19 (var & B ⲉ-) πλείων gen. c ⲉⲣⲟⲧⲉ ⲉ- B : He 11 26 (S ⲉϩⲟⲩⲟ) μείζ. gen, BSM 61 no one ⲉⲛⲁⲁϥ ⲉϩⲟⲧⲉⲣⲟϥ (cf Mt 11 11 ⲛⲁⲁϥ ⲉ-). c ϧⲉⲛ- B, *greatest* : 1 Cor 13 13 (S ⲛⲟϭ ⲉ-) μείζ. gen. No concord with subj : Mk 12 31 S ⲙⲙⲛ ⲉⲛⲧⲟⲗⲏ ⲉⲛⲁⲁϥ ⲉⲛⲁⲓ, Jo 15 13 SA² ⲗⲁⲁⲩ ⲁⲅⲁⲡⲏ ⲉⲛⲁⲁϥ ⲉⲧⲁⲓ, PS 187 S ⲧⲛⲟϭ ⲛϭⲟⲧ ⲉⲧϥ̄ⲛⲁⲁⲩ ⲉⲣⲟϥ, PO 11 306 B ⲛ̄ⲑⲟⲕ ⲙⲙⲁⲩⲁⲧⲕ ⲉⲑⲛⲁⲁϥ. V also ⲉⲓⲁ (ⲛⲁⲓⲁⲧ⸗), but cf AZ 64 64 inf.

ⲛⲁⲉⲓⲱ, ⲛⲁⲓⲱ, ⲡⲉⲓⲱ, (ⲡ)ⲉⲓⲱ S, ⲁⲡⲁⲓⲱ (? ⲁⲡⲡⲁⲓⲱ) B nn f, *peg, stake* for ship's hawsers, tent ropes : Si 14 24 S ⲧⲉϭⲡ., ib 26 12, Is 33 20 S(P 44 113 ⲡⲉⲓⲱ, B ϣⲙⲟⲩ), ib 54 2 S (B do) πάσσαλος; Tri 528 S ass clave to wall like ⲉϣⲁⲩⲧⲉϭ ⲟⲩⲉⲓⲱ وتد, C 89 121 B bind ship ⲉϯⲁⲡ. = Va ar 172 69 في الوتد P 54 115 B ϯⲁⲡ. موردن (مينا) (wharf), MG 25 160 B bind hawser ⲉϯⲁⲡ., PMich '24 S about repair (φιλοκαλία) of dyke ⲡⲉⲓⲡ. ⲙⲡⲡⲉⲩⲥⲟⲧⲁϥϥ ⲙⲡⲡⲉⲩⲃⲁⲁⲣⲉ, BMOr 6201 B 56 S]ⲙⲡⲧⲁⲥⲉ ⲡⲡ. As place-name: Cai stele 8595 S ⲧⲡ., R 1 5 27 S ⲧⲡ.

ﻗﺎﺏ (v Amélineau *Géog* 453, 478) & thence in names
Πατναιῶς, Τροντναιῶς (Preisigke).

ⲛⲉ- *SB*, ⲛⲁ- *ABF* vbal pref **I a** of imperf before
vbal subj : Gen 39 23 *B* ⲛⲁϥⲉⲙⲓ ⲁⲛⲡⲉ ; before
nominal subj ⲛⲉⲣⲉ- *S*, ⲛⲁⲣⲉ- *AB* : *ib S* ⲛⲉⲣⲉⲡⲉⲧⲣⲓ-
ⲭⲡⲡⲉϣⲧⲉⲕⲟ ⲥⲟⲟⲩⲛ ⲁⲛ ἦν ;   **b** plupf : 4 Kg 15
5 *S* ⲛⲉⲁϥⲥⲱⲃⲣⲡⲉ ἦν ;   **c** past aorist : Ps 118 62
S ⲛⲉϣⲁⲓⲧⲱⲟⲩⲛ ἐξεγειρόμην ;   **d** neg plupf with
ⲁⲙⲡⲉ- *q v.*

II ⲛⲉ- in nominal clause indicates past : Ps 151
1 *S* ⲛⲉⲁⲛⲅⲟⲩⲕⲟⲩⲓ ἤμην, Jo 18 18 *B* ⲛⲉⲧⲉϥⲣⲱⲧⲉ
ἦν ; or with vbs ⲟⲩⲟⲛ, ⲙⲙⲛ- : Lu 4 27 *B* ⲛⲉⲟⲩⲟⲛ
ⲟⲩⲙⲏϣ ἦσαν, Ps 106 2 *S* ⲛⲉⲙⲛ ⲡⲉⲧⲃⲟⲏⲑⲉⲓ.

ⲛⲉ- *SF* art pl   v ⲛ-.

ⲛⲉ- *S* poss pron f   v ⲛⲁ-.

-ⲛⲉ *SB* pl suff as copula   v -ⲡⲉ.

ⲛⲉ *SA* interrog   v ⲉⲛⲉ.

ⲛⲉⲓ, ⲛⲏⲓ *B* nn f, *time* : Ex 8 8 ὁρισμός ; Gal 4
2 (*S* = Gk) προθεσμία ; FR 112 ϯⲛ. ⲛⲧⲉ ⲧⲉⲥⲁⲡⲁ-
ⲗⲩⲙⲯⲓⲥ.   ⲉⲣ ⲛ., *make, reach time* : Job 15 32
(*S* ⲟⲩⲛⲟⲩ) ὥρα, Is 65 20 ⲁⲙⲡⲁⲧⲉⲥⲣ ⲛ. (*S* ϣⲁⲣⲁϥⲉ)
ἄωρος.   ϯ ⲛ., *give, appoint time* : Ex 9 5 ὅρος ;
Job 14 13 (*S* ⲟⲩⲟⲉⲓϣ), Dan 2 16 χρόνος ; Su 14 (*S*
do) καιρός ; C 89 42 ⲙⲁ ⲟⲩⲛ. ⲛⲁⲛ = Miss 4 522
S = Gk προθ. ; DeV 2 191 ϯⲛⲁϯ ⲡⲟⲩⲛ. ⲛⲱⲧⲉⲛ
till 10th of month ;   *appoint (without time)* : Mt
28 16 mount where Jesus ϯ ⲛ. ⲛⲱⲟⲩ ⲉⲣⲟϥ (*S* =
Gk), Ac 28 23 (*S* do) τάσσειν dat.   In ⲓⲥ ⲟⲛⲉⲓ,
then in apodosis, v ⲉϣϫⲉ ⲉ.

ⲛⲓ, ⲛⲓⲧⲋ *F*   v ⲉⲓⲛⲉ *bring.*

ⲛⲟ *AO*   v ⲛⲁⲩ *see*, ⲛⲁⲩ *hour.*

ⲛⲟⲉⲓ *S*, ⲛⲁⲉⲓ *Sᵃ* nn m, meaning unknown, place
where loaves (?) & wine deposited : Ep 531 baskets
of loaves ⲁⲥⲉⲓⲛⲉ ⲟⲩⲁⲉ (ⲉ)ⲣⲟⲩⲡ (ⲉ)ⲡⲁⲛⲓ ⲡⲥⲉⲕⲱ (*l*
ⲡⲥⲕⲱ) ⲕⲟⲩ(ⲟⲩ)ⲁⲉ ⲣⲉⲛⲛⲟⲉⲓ, *ib* 338 ⲡⲉⲛⲣⲡ ⲉⲧⲁⲓⲉⲛⲧϥ
ⲣⲓⲛⲛⲁⲉⲓ.

ⲛⲟⲩ *SF*, ⲛⲟⲩⲉ *SA²*, ⲛⲟⲩⲓ *B*, qual v below, vb
intr, *go, be going to, about to* c ⲉ-, ⲁ- : Tob 6 18 *S*,
Mk 13 4 *SB*, Ac 12 6 *S* (*B* fut), P 129¹³ 53 *S*
ⲉⲕϣⲁⲛⲛ. ⲉⲟⲩⲱⲙ μέλλειν ; AP 15 *A²* ⲛⲧⲁⲣⲟⲩⲛ.
ⲛⲁⲉ ⲁⲡⲟⲙⲡⲉⲅⲉ ἡνίκα (var ὡς δέ) ; Ez 3 27 *S* (*B*
diff) ἐν τῷ, Aeg 243 *S* ⲉⲕϣⲁⲛⲛⲟⲩ ⲉⲝⲓ πρὸς τό ;
neg : Jo 7 8 *SA²* (*B* fut) οὔπω ; Gk om (*when about
to*) : Ex 1 16 *B* (*A* ⲉⲓ), Lev 10 9 *S* (*B* fut), Jo 16 21
B (*SA²* ⲉⲓ + fut), Ac 28 10 *S* (*B* fut) ; ShC 73 161 *S*
ⲉϥϣⲁⲛⲛ. ⲉⲭⲱ, Bor 239 77 *S* ⲉⲥϣⲁⲛⲛ. ⲉⲃⲱⲕ (var
ⲛⲟⲩⲉ), MG 25 268 *B* ⲉⲧⲁϥⲛ. ⲉⲉⲙⲧⲟⲛ ⲙⲙⲟϥ (*cf*
below), BM 591 *F* ⲉϣⲱⲡ ⲁⲕⲛⲟⲩ ⲉⲓ ⲉⲃⲁⲗ ; Gu 51
S ⲁⲡⲁⲡⲟⲥⲧⲟⲗⲟⲥ ⲛ. ⲉⲩⲡⲣⲟⲥⲉⲩⲭⲏ (? = ⲉⲟⲩⲡⲣ.).

c ⲛ- : Ex 34 34 *B* Gk om ; AM 280 *B* ⲁⲅⲛ. ⲛϯ
ⲛⲉⲙ- μέλ. ; Mun 89 *S* ⲛⲧⲉⲣⲉϥⲛ. ⲛⲭⲟⲟⲩⲥⲟⲩ ⲉⲃⲟⲗ,
Z 349 *S* ⲉⲩϣⲁⲛⲛ. ⲛⲥⲩⲛⲁⲩⲉ, AM 255 *B* ⲉⲧⲁϥⲛ.
ⲛⲉⲙⲧⲟⲛ (*cf* above).

ⲛⲏⲩ† *SA²F*, ⲛⲏⲟⲩ† *SABFO* (AZ 21 100), ⲛⲏⲅⲉ†
S (Jud 1 14), ⲛⲛⲏⲩ *S* (Sa Si) *A²F* ⲛⲛⲏⲟⲩ† *AF*,
ⲛⲁⲩ† *S* (Ep 304 n), *be (in act of) coming, about to
come*, as qual of ⲉⲓ *q v*, mostly with fut sense (*S* ⲛ.†
often = *B* ⲓ fut) : Ge 42 5 *B* ⲁⲅⲓ...ⲛⲉⲙⲡⲏ ⲉⲟⲛ.,
Job 23 3 *S* (*B* ⲓ), Ps 21 31 *SB*, Si 21 6 *S* ⲛⲛ., Is
5 26 *S* (*B* do), Zech 9 9 *B* (*SA* ⲉⲓ), Lu 13 35 *SBF*,
Jo 5 7 *SA²* ⲛⲛ. *B*, Z 347 *S* ⲛⲉⲩⲛ. = MG 25 219 *B*
ⲁⲅⲓ ἔρχεσθαι, Pro 27 12 *SA*, Is 45 11 *B* (*S* ϣⲱⲡⲉ
fut), Ez 33 4 *B* (*S* ⲉⲓ), Cl 24 3 *A* ἐπέρχ. ; Ps 39 7
S (*B* ⲓ), Hab 2 3 *A* ϥⲛⲁⲉⲓ ⲁϥⲛ. (*B* ⲓ...ⲓ fut), Mt 24
14 *S* (*B* ⲓ fut), Jo 8 42 *SA²* ⲉⲓ...ⲛ. (*B* ⲓ...ⲓ) ἤκειν ;
Mt 12 32 *SBF*, Ro 5 14 *B* (*S* ϣⲱ. fut) μέλ. ; Cai
Euch 489 *B* ⲧⲡⲁⲣⲟⲩⲥⲓⲁ...ⲉⲧⲉⲕⲛ. ⲛⲃⲏⲧⲥ μέλ. ἔρχ. ;
Deu 13 6 *S* (*B* = Gk) ἴσος ; Jo 3 23 *SBF* παραγίνεσθαι ; Ac 23 11 *SB* ἐπιέναι ; Is 29 6 *B* (*S* ⲥⲱⲕ)
φέρεσθαι ; with rel ⲉⲧ- : Lev 22 27 *B* (*S* diff) ἐπέκεινα, EstB 7 *S* μετέπειτα, Ac 13 42 *SB* μεταξύ ;
Gk om : Ez 40 29 *SB*, *ib* 41 9 *SB* ; J&C 92 *S* if
thou find brother ⲉϥⲛⲏⲟⲩ, PS 367 *S* ⲙⲡⲛ ⲗⲁⲁⲩ
ⲉⲓⲛ. *when I came*, *ib* 289 *S* ⲛϯⲛ. ⲁⲛ henceforth,
BG 16 *S* ⲉⲣⲉⲛ. ⲭⲓⲛⲧⲱⲛ ⲉⲣⲉⲃⲏⲕ ⲉⲧⲱⲛ?, PS 13
when Christ ⲉⲓ ⲉϥⲛ. ϥⲛ. ⲛϭⲓ ⲣⲏⲗⲓⲁⲥ *before Him*,
Hall 59 *S* ⲁⲓⲛ. ⲉⲁⲓⲉⲓ (*sic* prob), AP 42 *A²* ϥⲛⲛ. ⲣⲛ-
ⲟⲩϭⲉⲛⲛ, ShZ 595 *S* ⲣⲛⲟⲩⲅⲉⲓ ⲕⲛ. (*cf* He 10 37), Miss
8 81 *S* if proper ϯⲛ., paral *ib* 80 ϯⲛⲁⲉⲓ, AM 261 *B*
this world & ⲛⲉⲟⲛ., PLond 4 500 *S* will pay due
ⲣⲛⲧⲭⲏⲣⲉ ⲉⲧⲛ. (*cf* ⲛ.† ⲉⲣⲟⲩⲛ).

With 2d vb (continued or future action), without
prep : Ps 125 6 *B* ⲉⲩⲛ. ⲉⲩⲉⲓ (*S* ⲛ....ⲛ.), Lu 13 7 *B*
ἔρχ., C 41 67 *B* lo for years ϯⲛ. ⲉⲓⲥⲓⲛ. ;   with
ⲉ-, *increase in doing* : 2 Kg 3 1 *S* ⲛ. ⲉⲧⲁⲭⲣⲟ (var ⲛ-)
κραταιοῦν impf, Mor 31 75 *S* ⲛⲁⲥⲛ. ⲉⲑⲟ ⲉⲡⲉⲣⲟⲩⲟ,
PO 11 359 *B* sim ;   sim with ⲛ- : Ge 7 17 *B* ⲛ.
ⲛⲁϣⲁⲓ (*S* om) πληθύνειν impf, Ac 9 22 *B* sim (*S* do)
ἐνδυναμοῦν impf, Pro 11 24 *B* ἐλαττονοῦν pres, Gal
3 23 *B* ⲛ. ⲛϭⲱⲣⲛ ⲉⲃⲟⲗ (*S* ⲥⲱⲗⲛ fut) μέλ. ; Mor
25 11 *S* fire ⲛ. ⲛⲭⲉⲣⲟ ⲕⲟⲩⲓ ⲕⲟⲩⲓ = Va 61 94 *B*
ⲛⲁϥϭⲉⲣⲛⲟⲩⲧ, PSBA 32 200 *S* ⲉⲓⲛ. ⲛⲭⲓ προκοπη
in wisdom = Mor 41 188 *S.*

Qual with following preposition.

——— ⲉ- *SB*, *be coming, be on road to*, **a** with vb :
Ge 32 6 *S* (*B* ⲛⲓ. ⲉⲃⲟⲗ), Is 66 18 *SB*, Mt 27 49 *SB*
ἔρχ. ; Ex 18 6 *S* (*B* ⲛ. ⲣⲁ-) παραγίν. ; Aeg 256 *S*
ϥⲛ. ⲉⲕⲣⲓⲛⲉ ;   **b** with nn : Is 3 13 *S* (*B* ⲓ ⲉ-)
καθιστάναι εἰς ; PS 91 *S* ⲉⲩⲛ. ⲉⲛⲭⲓⲥⲉ, DeV 2 112
B women ⲉⲟⲛ. ⲉⲛⲓⲉⲙⲣⲁⲩ, AM 74 *B* ⲉⲧⲓ ⲉϥⲛ. ⲉⲣⲏⲥ
whilst coming south, PBu 149 *S* ⲁⲓⲉⲓ ⲉⲓⲛ. ⲉⲣⲏⲥ from
Babylon.

—— ⲛ- dat *SAB*, meaning same: Ap 2 16 *SB* ⲉⲣⲭ. dat; Pro 24 49 *SA* ἥκειν; BG 67 *S* ⲉⲣⲉⲡⲉⲡⲡⲁ̄ ⲛ. ⲡⲁⲩ.

—— ⲉⲣⲁⲧ⸗ *S*, come to: Su 6 (*B* diff), Mk 1 45 (*B* ⲛ. ϩⲁ-) ⲉⲣⲭ. ⲡⲣⲟⲥ; PS 139 ⲉⲓⲛ. ⲉⲣⲁⲧⲕ.

—— ⲉⲧⲛ- *S*, come upon, befall: PMéd 204 sickness ⲉⲧⲛ. ⲉⲧⲟⲧⲕ.

—— ⲉϩⲛ- *S*, come to, agree with: Ps 54 13 (*B* ϣⲏϣ ⲡⲉⲙ-, cf Deu 13 6 *S*) ἰσόψυχος; Sa 16 20 πρός; sic *l*? Ac 13 22 (*B* = Gk) κατά (cf Cl 18 1 *A* ⲛ. ⲡⲣⲛ-); ShBMOr 8810 428 wicked ⲁⲡⲁⲧⲁ ⲛⲡⲉⲧⲛ. ⲉϩⲙⲡⲉⲩϩⲏⲧ.

—— ⲉϫⲛ- *SAA²B*, come upon, to: Pro 21 6 *SA*, Jo 18 4 *SA²* (*B* ⲛ. ⲉϩⲣⲏⲓ ⲉϫ.), MG 25 210 *B* = Z 345 *S* ϩⲱⲗ ⲉϫ. ⲉⲣⲭ. ἐπί, Job 21 17 *S* (*B* ⲓ fut ⲉϩⲣ. ⲉϫ.), Ez 47 9 *B* (*S* ⲉⲓ ⲉ- fut) ἐπέρχ.; Pro 24 40 *SA* ἥκ.; Eccl 2 4 *SB* ἐπάγεσθαι; Ez 7 26 *SB* εἶναι fut; Si 43 22 *S* καταλύειν; Gk om: Nu 21 4 *S* (var & *B* om), Jer 28 11 *B*; ShC 73 82 *S* ⲟⲩ ⲡⲉⲧⲛ. ⲉϫⲱϥ, BMis 377 *S* brethren ⲉⲧⲛ. ⲉϫⲱⲛ = Va 63 7 *B* (BSM 34 *B* ⲛ. ϩⲁ-), MG 25 140 *B* parable ⲉⲣⲉⲡⲉⲥⲃⲱⲗ ⲛ. ⲉϫⲉⲛⲟⲩ suits, befits.

—— ⲉϩⲣⲁⲓ ⲉϫⲛ- *S*, ⲉϩⲣⲏ ⲉϫ. *B*, meaning as last: Is 21 2 *SB*, Mt 24 30 *S* (*B* ⲛ. ⲉϫ.) ⲉⲣⲭ. ἐπί, Is 47 13 *SB*, Ap 3 10 *S* (*B* ⲓ ⲉϩ. ⲉϫ. fut) μέλ. ⲉⲣⲭ., Ez 5 17 *SB* διέρχ. ἐπί; Jer 31 35 *B* ἀναβαίν. ἐπί, Aeg 242 *S* συμβαίν. dat; Lu 19 43 *S* (*B* ⲓ ⲉϩ. ⲉϫ. fut) ἥκ. ἐπί; BG 65 *S* whom ⲡⲉⲡⲡⲁ̄ ⲛ. ⲉϩ. ⲉϫⲱⲟⲩ.

—— ⲙⲛ- *SB*, come with, bring: FR 112 *B* ϯⲛ ⲡⲉⲙⲧⲉⲥ...ⲯⲩⲭⲏ, ST 50 *S* man ⲉⲧⲛ. ⲛⲁⲕ ⲙⲛϯ-ⲃⲗϭⲉ (cf ib 309 ⲛ ϯϩ. ⲛⲁⲕ), Ep 303 *S* sim.

—— ⲛⲥⲁ- *SB*, come after, for: Mun 43 *S* ϯⲛ. ⲛⲥⲱⲕ to-morrow, C 43 170 *B* sim, Pcod 49 *S* what ἐξουσία ⲧⲉⲧⲛ. ⲛⲥⲁⲧⲁⲯⲩⲭⲏ? MG 17 296 *S* (*B* ib 41 ⲉⲃⲟⲗ ⲥⲁ-), come from (? *l* ⲛⲡⲥⲁ ⲛ-).

—— ⲙⲛⲛⲥⲁ- *SB*, come after, follow: Mk 1 7 *SB* ⲉⲣⲭ. ὀπίσω; Sa 8 13 *S* μετά; BHom 34 *S* what come ⲙⲛⲛⲥⲁⲡⲁⲓ τὰ ἑξῆς, AM 261 *B* children ⲉⲑⲛ. ⲙⲉⲛⲉⲛⲥⲱⲕ.

—— ϣⲁ- *SA²BF*, come to, reach, of persons: Ge 48 2 *S* (*B* ⲛ. ϩⲁ-), Jo 6 5 *SA²* (*B* do) ⲉⲣⲭ. ⲡⲣⲟⲥ, ZNTW 24 90 *F* every one ⲉⲧⲛ. ϣⲁⲣⲁⲧⲉⲛ, Z 344 *S* ⲛ. ϣⲁⲣⲟⲓ...ⲃⲏⲕ ϣⲁⲕⲉⲟⲩⲁ = MG 25 209 *B* ⲛ. ...ϩⲏⲗ ⲉⲣⲭ....ὑπάγ.; Ps 100 2 *S* (*B* ⲓ ϣⲁ-), Jer 2 31 *S* (*B* ⲛ. ϩⲁ-) ἥκ. ⲡⲣⲟⲥ; C 43 195 *B* thereafter ϯⲛ. ϣⲁⲣⲟⲕ.

—— ϩⲁ- *B*, meaning same: Jer 39 7 (*S* ⲛ. ϣⲁ-), 2 Cor 13 1 (*SF* do) ⲉⲣⲭ. ⲡⲣⲟⲥ, 1 Kg 17 43 (*S* ⲛ. ⲉⲃⲟⲗ ⲉ-) ⲉⲣⲭ. ἐπί; Su 4 (*S* ⲥⲱⲟⲩϩ ⲉ-) προσάγ. πρός; TstAb 228 ϯⲛ. ϩⲁⲣⲟⲕ without delay.

—— ϩⲁ- *S*, come under: Est E 9 ⲉⲣⲭ. ὑπό acc.

—— ϩⲓϫⲛ- *SB*, come upon, over: Ge 1 2 *S* (cit

My 24) *B* ἐπιφέρεσθαι ἐπάνω; Mor 31 52 *S* knew ϫⲉⲛⲃⲁⲣⲃⲁⲣⲟⲥ ⲛ. ϩⲓϫⲱⲟⲩ.

Qual with following adverb.

—— ⲉⲃⲟⲗ *SAA²B*, come forth: Job 23 11 *S* (*B* ⲙⲟϣⲓ ⲉϩ.), Pro 24 68 *SA* (*B* ⲓ ⲉϩ.), AP 8 *A²*, MG 25 211 *B* ⲉⲓⲛ. ⲉϩ. = Z 345 *S* ⲁⲓⲉⲓ ⲉϩ. ἐξέρχ.; Nu 1 20 *SB*, Ps 87 8 *B* (*S* ϩⲱⲕ) ἐκπορ., Ac 9 28 *S* ⲃⲏⲕ ⲉϧⲟⲩⲛ, ⲛ. ⲉϩ. (*B* ⲛⲁ ⲉϩ. ⲉϩ.) εἰσπορ. ἐκπορ.; Ps 64 tit *S* (*B* ϣⲉ fut) ἥκ.; Ac 20 7 *S* (*B* ⲓ ⲉϩ. fut) μέλ. ἐξιέναι; PS 315 *S* none shall ⲃⲱⲕ ⲉϧⲟⲩⲛ nor ⲛ. ⲉϩ., TU 43 6 *A* prison opens ϣⲛ. ⲁϧ., CO 297 *S* ⲡⲣⲁⲡ ⲉⲧⲛ. ⲉϩ.   ⲛ. ⲉϩ. ⲉ- *SB*, c. forth to, against, sue (v ⲉⲓ ⲉϩ. ⲉ-): Jud 9 33 *S* ἐκπορ. πρός, Jer 21 9 *B* ἐκπορ. inf, J 18 68 *S* ⲛⲡⲉⲧⲛ. ⲉϩ. ⲉⲣⲟⲕ he that shall sue thee.   ⲛ. ⲉϩ. ⲉⲣⲁⲧ⸗ *S*, c. forth to: Mk 1 5 (var ⲃⲱⲕ, *B* ⲛ. ⲉϩ. ϩⲁ⸗) ἐκπορ. πρός.   ⲛ. ⲉϩ. ⲉϩⲛ- *SB*, meaning as last: Jud 11 34 *B* (*S* ⲉⲓ. ⲉϩ. ϩⲏⲧ⸗) ἐκπορ. εἰς; BIF 14 124 *S* she saw saint ⲉϧⲛ. ⲉϩ. ⲉϩⲣⲁⲥ.   ⲛ. ⲉϩ. ⲉϫⲛ- *SA*, c. forth upon: Zech 5 3 (*B* ⲛ. ϩⲓϫⲉⲛ-) ἐκπορ. ἐπί.   ⲛ. ⲉϩ. ⲛ-(ⲙⲙⲟ⸗) *SB*, c. forth from: Lu 6 19 *S* (var ϩⲛ-) *B* ἐξέρχ. παρά; C 43 79 *B* wonders ⲛ. ⲉϩ. ⲙⲙⲟϥ, Va 61 13 *B* stink ⲛⲁϧⲛ. ⲉϩ. ⲙⲙⲟϣⲡⲉ.   ⲛ. ⲉϩ. ⲥⲁ- *B*, c. forth from beside, from: Is 14 31 (*S* ⲉϩ. ϩⲛ-), Dan 8 5 ⲉⲣⲭ. ἀπό; v ⲛ. ⲛⲥⲁ-.   ⲛ. ⲉϩ. ϩⲁⲣⲁⲧ⸗ *S*, c. forth at foot of, below: Jth 7 12 ἐκπορ. ἐκ.   ⲛ. ⲉϩ. ϩⲁⲑⲏ *S*, c. forth before, to meet: Br 134 ⲛⲁⲓ ⲉⲧⲛ. ⲉϩ. ϩⲁⲧⲉⲧⲏⲣ.   ⲛ. ⲉϩ. ϩⲁϫⲛ-, ϩⲁϫ. *SB*, meaning as last: Mor 18 78 *S* ⲥⲉⲛ. ⲉϩ. ϩⲁϫⲱⲛ (var ib 19 86 ϩⲁⲧⲉⲕⲣⲏ) = Miss 4 149 *B* ⲓ ⲉϩ. ϩⲁϫ., BMis 68 *S*, C 41 44 *B* sim.   ⲛ. ⲉϩ. ϩⲓ- *SB*, c. forth from: Is 49 12 *B* (*S* ⲛ. only) ἥκ. πόρρωθεν; Ez 9 2 *B* ⲉⲣⲭ. ἀπό, Ac 8 7 *B* (*S* ϩⲛ-) ἐξέρχ. only; BMis 555 *S* ⲡⲥⲁϣ ⲉⲧⲛ. ⲉϩ. ϩⲓⲱⲧ exiebant de.   ⲛ. ⲉϩ. ϩⲛ-, ϧⲉⲛ- *SABF*, meaning as last: Nu 24 7 *S* (*B* ⲓ ⲉϩ. ϧⲉⲛ-), Nah 1 11 *SA* (*B* do), Jo 4 30 *SB* (*A²F* ⲓ ⲉϩ. ϩⲛ-) ἐξέρχ. ἐκ; Ps 18 6 *SB*, Mt 15 18 *SBF* ἐκπορ. ἐκ.; 1 Kg 28 13 *S* (var ⲉϩⲣⲁⲓ ϩⲛ-), Ap 7 2 *S* (*B* ⲓ ⲉϩ. ϧⲉⲛ-) ἀναβαίν. ἐκ, ἀπό, Ac 8 26 *SB* καταβαίν. ἀπό; Jer 4 15 *S* (*B* ⲓ fut) ἥκ.; Cai Euch 497 *B* advent ⲉⲑⲛ. ⲉϩ. ϧⲉⲛⲡⲓⲫⲛⲟⲩⲓ μέλ. ἀπὸ οὐρ.; Is 63 1 *SB* παραγίνεσθαι ἐκ; Pro 16 23 *SA* (Gk om), Lu 8 27 *S* (*B* Gk om); Br 118 *S* ⲛⲧⲉⲧⲛ-ⲉⲓ ⲉⲧⲉⲧⲛ. ⲉϩ. ϩⲛⲥⲱⲙⲁ, C 43 213 *B* blood ⲉⲧⲛ. ⲉϩ. ϧⲉⲛⲣⲱϥ.   ⲛ. ⲉϩ. ϩⲓⲧⲛ- *SB*, c. out through, from: Ps 123 5 *S* (*B* ⲥⲓⲛⲓ) διέρχ., Si 39 6 *S* διέρχ. ἐν; Jud 3 26 *S* παρέρχ.; Ac 16 4 *S* (*B* ⲕⲱϯ ϧⲉⲛ-) διαπορ.; Mor 28 109 *S* oath sworn ⲉⲕⲛ. ⲉϩ. ϩⲓⲧⲟⲟⲧⲉ as thou didst quit her, C 43 126 *B* peace he gave me ⲉⲓⲛ. ⲉϩ. ϩⲓⲧⲟⲧϥ.

—— ⲉⲡⲉⲥⲏⲧ *SBF*, come down: Deu 9 21 *SB*, Job 17 16 *S* (*B* ⲓ ⲉϩⲣⲏⲓ), Mk 9 9 *SF* (*B* ⲛ. ⲉϧ.) καταβαίν.; Mic 1 4 *SB* (*A* ⲛ. ⲁϧ.) καταφέρεσθαι;

Lu 9 37 *S* (*B* ı eϭ.) κατέρχ.; BMar 13 *S* Isaac saw knife ecn. en. exωϥ.

—— enψωı *S* (once) *B, come up*: Dan 8 3, MG 25 211 ἀναβαίν., Mor 39 27 *S* angels eı eγn. en. = C 43 50 *B* nа en.

—— eϩoγn, аϧ., eϭ. *SAB, come in, enter*: Ge 30 16 *SB*, Ps 70 16 *S* (*B* ı eϭ. fut), *ib* 117 20 *SA* (Cl, *B* ϣe eϭ. fut), He 3 11 *S* (*B* do) εἰσέρχ.; ı Kg 18 13 *S*, Jer 17 19 *B* (*S* ϩωn eϧ.), Mk 4 19 *S* (var *B.*, *B* ɯoϣı ϧen-) εἰσπορ.; C 89 80 *B* eϥn. ϫe eϭ. *as he entered*, PS 219 *S* neтn. eϧ. encooγn, Ep 675 A *S* (graffito) every one eтn. eϧ. eneɯа, CO 160 *S* will pay at harvest eтn. eϧ. (*cf* BM 1041), ST 253 *S* I found no man eϥn. eϧ. nаĸ.

—— eϩраı, аϧ., eϩрнı *SAA²BO, come up*: Nu 13 32 *S* (*B* ϣe enψωı fut), Ps 105 7 *SB*, Hos 10 8 *SA* (*B* ı enϣ. fut), Mk 1 10 *S* (var eı eϧ., *B* n. enϣ.) ἀναβαίν.; 2 Kg 6 16 *S* (var n. eϩoγn, *B* ı enϣ.), AP 4 *A²* (prob) παραγίνεσθαι; MIE 2 335 *B* when (Nile) water n. eϧ., PS 9 *S* ereрpн n. eϧ. in east, Hor 82 *O* n. аϧ. of star, COAd 26 *S* neтn. eϧ. ϩаnnoγϩ *result from*.

—— eϩраı, аϧр., eϭр. *S* (rare) *AB, come down*: Ps 132 3 *B* (*S* n. enecnт) καταβαίν.; Cl 46 7 *A* ἔρχ., Ez 21 4 *SB* ἐξέρχ., BMis 510 *S* Jesus eϥn. eϧ. eneϥϭıϫ, *cf* AM 20 *B* God eϥn. eϭ. eneϥxıϫ, Aeg 265 *S* drops eγn. eϧ. ϩıoγnнтn, El 106 *A* eϥnn. аϧ. [ϥ]nn. аϧ. *S often doubtful if up or down.*

V тınooγ.

noγ *S* nn   *v* naγ *hour.*

noγ *SF*   *v* noγϩe *vb.*

nω *Sᵃ*   *v* naγ *see*, naγ *hour.*

neeϥ   *v* neeϥ.

nнϧ *BO*, neϩ- *B* DM nn m f, *lord*: *B* in Ge 15 2, Pro 6 7, Jer 4 10, Ac 4 24, 2 Tim 2 21, Ap 6 10 (all *S* ϫoeıc), CaiEuch 388 ϥn. noϭ̄ nennoγϯ, C 86 285 nenn. nıpн, AM 266 nenn. ϥϯ δεσπότης; Jon 4 3 (*SA* ϫ.) δ. κύριος, Jer 44 20 κύ., Ez 35 14 ϥn. noϭ̄ (*cf* ıı nϫecn. noϭ̄) κύ. κύ.; AM 139 nennoϭ̄ oγoϩ nenn., AZ 21 86 *O* Osiris nn. nтĸаnce, DM 28 ı *O* v ϧaı *spirit*. *master, owner B*: Ex 21 29 (*cf* 28 oϭ̄, *S* ϫ.), MG 25 216 owner of borrowed money = Z 239 *S* ϫ. κύ.; C 89 14, MIE 2 392, DeV 2 272 (*cf* 273 oϭ̄) sim, *ib* 2 168 nenn. of slain workmen; *mistress B*: CaiEuch 406 Virgin тenoϭ̄ nn. δέσποινα.

аtn. *B* adj, *lordless*: DeV 2 173 mother bewailing son аıϣωnı (var eıoı) nа.

ɯeтn. *B, lordship*: Ps 144 13 (*S* ɯnтϫ.) δεσποτεία.

ep n. *B, be lord*: ı Chr 29 11, Ps 21 29 (*S* o nϫ.) δεσπόζειν; ı Tim 5 14 (*S* p ϫ.) οἰκοδεσποτεῖν.

neϩаϧı *B, longlived*, *v* аϧe *length of life*.

neϩнı *B*, nenнı *S* (P 44 27), *lord of house, householder*: Mt 10 25 (*S* ϫ. only), Mk 14 14 (= Lu 22 11 n. nтe nнı, *S* ϫ. ɯnнı) οἰκοδεσπότης (also = neϩıoрı); *lady of h.*: 3 Kg 17 17 (K. al-Tagnîz 206, var oϭ̄) κύρια.

neϩıoрı *B, lord of the field, landowner* (or ? *v* oϧe *s f*): Mt 13 27 (*S* ϫ., *F* = Gk), *ib* 21 33 (*S* рɯɯаo) oıκoδ.; EW 92 Christ to martyr ϯnаını noγрωɯı (n)neϩıoрı (*sic l*) to Egypt to tend thy relics (*cf* C 38 95 Pereira).

neϩрнт, neϩnт *B, lord of mind, man of sense*: Pro 1 5, 10 19 (*SA* рɯnϧнт) νοήμων.

In names: Νεβιήβ (KKS 77), Πνεβσῆις, Φνεβσῆς, Πνεβτῦνις (Preisigke), Φνεβεννοῦνι (POslo 44).

nнϧ *S* nn, *meaning unknown*: Cai 67324 (*v* PCai 3 119) in list of σκεύη, ϫoϫ cneγ ɯnoγnнϧ.

nнϧ *S*, nıɯ *B* in ϧınнϧ, -nıɯ.

noγϧ *SAA²BF*, -ϥ *SF*, noϧ (ST 54), noϥ (Ryl 259) *S* nn m, *gold*: Ge 2 11 *SB*, Pro 3 14 *SAB*, Ac 17 29 *SB*, He 9 4 *SBF* χρυσός, -σίον, Is 30 22 *SF* (*B* diff) περιχρυσοῦν; PS 212 *S* ϑγλн (ὕλη) ɯnn., ShC 73 43 *S* n. н ϩoɯnт, BHom 2 *S* ask not oγn. oγϫe oγраt, AZ 23 106 *S* in alchemy nn. ncаn, DeV 2 145 *B* oγn. eϥcoтn, AP 23 *A²* oγλaaγene nn. As *money, coin*: BMis 381 *S* ɯn n. nтooт = BSM 37 *B*, *ib* 393 *S* аıcoγn neın. = *ib* 45 *B* nаın., BMar 15 *S* hath king adjudged thee eγn. *money fine* ?, J 68 40 *S* paying tax ϩnneın. eтɯɯω, Ryl 284 *S* send me nннoγϥ, *ib* 292 *S* payment in n. or corn, Ep 260 *S* ϧeнĸoγı nn., BM 528 34 *F* n. ϧıĸec *solidi & carats*, CO 44 *S* oγonтıа nn., ST 183 *S* λıтра nn. As *adj*: Ex 20 23 *SB*, Pro 1 9 *SAB*, Ap 5 8 *SB* χρυσοῦς; Hor 82 *O* ĸλɯ ɯnn. (*v* ĸλoɯ), El 50 *A* oγɯaaϧ nn., AZ 33 56 *F* aγan nn., EW 38 *B* nıϧнϫ nn., PMich 597 *S* nxω nn. of Isis nаnoт ϧраt of Osiris, BM 1013 *S* ϩoλoĸ/ nn., Ryl 463 *S*, C 86 322 *B* do, CMSS 44 *F* ṽ ϛ nn.

ɯаın. *S, gold-loving*: Br 102 bid him not p ɯаın., Z 271 neтo ɯɯ.

p n. *S*, meaning uncertain, *have money dealings?*: ST 172 men nϣaıep n. nтooтoγ, Ryl 372 аıep n. ṽ ĸβ (reading doubtful).

eıen-, ıeϩn. *SB* v eıone, adding 2 Kg 1 24 *S* oγeı. (var ϧneı., *B* coλceλ nn.) κόσμος χρυσοῦς, Is 30 22 *B* oı nı. (*SF* ϭooλe nn.) περιχρυσοῦν.

ϧаɯn.¹ *SBF*, ϧаγn.², ϧoγn. *S*, nn m, *goldsmith*: Is 40 19 ϧ.¹ *S* (var ²) *B*, Jer 10 14 *S* ϧ.² *B*, EpJer 45 *BF* χρυσοχόος, Sa 15 9 ϧ.² *S* χρυσουργός; Mor 41 27 *S* one of the ϧ.² of city = DeV 2 282 *B* to make gold εἰκών, Mor 38 90 ϧ.¹ *S*, *ib* 91 ϧ.² *S*, Kr 199 ϧ.² *S*, Ryl 118 ϧ.² *S*, Cai 67324 *S* ϥoγnoγϥ,

O Wulff *Altchr...Bildwerke* 3 no 95 ϥⲟⲅⲛⲟⲩⲃ; ⲥⲁϧ ⲛϧ. : JKP 2 178 ϩ.[2] *S* makes gold cross, BMar 187 ϩ.[2] *S* decorates gospel book.

In place-names : τόπος Φοννοῦβ PLond 4 428, ⲑⲛⲟⲅⲃ (?) Baouit 114, 116, ⲡⲁⲅⲟⲛ ⲡⲛ. Χρυσόρροα (a river) Z 336.

ⲛⲁⲃⲓ *B v* ⲛⲁⲅⲓ.

ⲛⲏⲏⲃⲉ[1], ⲛⲏ.[2], ⲛⲓⲃⲉ[3], ⲛⲓϥⲉ[4] *S*, ⲛⲏⲃⲓ[5], ⲛⲉ.[6], ⲛⲓⲡⲓ[7], ⲛⲉϥ(ⲓ)[8] *B*, ⲛⲓⲃⲓ[9] *BF* vb intr, *float, swim* : Job 11 12[1] *S* (*B* ϩⲉⲗϩⲉⲗ) νήχειν, Mor 37 106 *S* ⲉϥⲛ.[4] ϩⲁⲙ-ⲙⲟⲟⲩ διανή. ; Ac 27 42 *S*[1]*B*[5] ἐκκολυμβᾶν ; Sa 14 4[1] *S* (Gk diff) ; Ez 47 5 *S* ⲙⲟⲩ ⲛⲛ.[2] ἐξυβρίζειν (prob *l* ⲛⲃⲉⲉⲃⲉ) ; BMis 324 *S* would I knew ⲛⲛ.[2], BSM 3 *B* ⲛϯⲥⲟⲟⲩⲛ ⲛⲛ.[5] ⲁⲛ = Mor 27 6[9] *F*, Miss 4 202 *B* ⲧⲉⲛⲛ.[6] ϫⲉⲛϥⲛⲟⲅⲛ, Va 57 242 *B* ⲡⲧⲉϥⲛ.[7] in fiery river, BIF 13 113 *S* ⲉϥⲛ.[8] and is submerged in water.   As nn m *B*, BSM 4 ⲛⲛ.[5] ⲉⲡϣⲱⲓ *float-ing on surface* = BMis 324 *S* ϭⲓⲛⲛ., K 335 ⲛⲛ.[5] عوم, Lacr 59 ⲛⲛ.[6] ⲣⲉϥⲛ.[2] *S, swimmer* : Mus 40 45 = Mun 78 ⲉⲛⲟⲩⲣ. ⲁⲛⲛⲉ *non nutet et fluctuat*. ϭⲓⲛ-[1], ϫⲓⲛⲛ.[8] *SBF, floating, sailing* : BMis, Mor 27 *ut sup*, Dif 1 64 *B* knoweth not ϯϫ. in sea.

ⲛⲓⲃⲉ *O*, ⲛⲓⲃⲓ *F v* ⲛⲓⲙ *every*.

ⲛⲟⲃⲉ *S*, ⲛⲁⲃⲉ *Sf* (ALR '06 473) *AA*[2], ⲛⲟⲃⲓ *B*, ⲛⲁⲃⲓ, -ϥⲓ *F* nn m, *sin* : Ge 15 16 *SB*, Pro 10 16 *SAB*, Is 30 13 *SBF*, Ro 7 13 *SB*, Cl 44 4 *A* ἁμαρ-τία, Lev 4 29 *SB*, Hos 10 8 *SAB*, Mk 3 28 *SB* ἁμάρτημα ; Sa 10 1 *S*, Eph 1 7 *S* (*B* = Gk) παρά-πτωμα ; Lev 14 12 *S* (*B* ⲙⲉⲧϣⲁϥⲧ), Ps 67 22 *S* (*B* ⲙⲉⲧⲁⲙⲉⲗⲏⲥ) πλημμέλεια ; Sa 5 24 *S* κακοπρα-γία ; Ps 50 2 *SA* (Cl, *B* ⲁⲛⲟⲙⲓⲁ) ἀνόμημα ; Ez 22 9 *B* (*S* ϫⲱⲣ̄) ἀνόσιος ; PS 48 *S* ⲛⲛ. ⲉⲡⲧⲁⲓⲁⲁϥ, *ib* 12 *S* baptism ⲛⲕⲁ ⲛ. ⲉⲃⲟⲗ, ShRE 10 161 *S* ⲛ. ⲡⲉ ⲡⲉⲡⲣⲁⲛ ⲣⲱⲙⲉ ⲁⲛ, AM 182 *B* I knew not ϫⲉⲟⲩⲛ. ⲛⲉ, Lant 5 *S* book dedicated ϩⲁⲡⲥⲱⲧⲉ ⲛⲡⲉϥⲛ., PBu 47 *S* ⲕⲛⲁⲕⲱ ⲛⲛ. ⲛⲧⲁⲡⲣⲟⲥⲫⲟⲣⲁ ϩⲓϫⲱⲕ *re-sponsibility, blame.*

ⲁⲧⲛ., ⲁⲑⲛ. *SABF* adj, *sinless, innocent* : 1 Kg 19 5 *S*, Job 9 28 *B* (*S* ⲟⲩⲁⲁⲃ), Ps 17 25 *SA* (Cl) *B*, Mt 27 24 *B* (*S* do) ἀθῷος ; Deu 21 9 *SB*, Mt 12 7 *BF* (*S* ⲙⲛ ⲛ. ⲉ-) ἀναίτιος ; Sa 4.9 *S* ἀκηλίδωτος ; Z 339 *S* = MG 25 216 *B* ἀναμάρτητος ; DeV 1 202 *B* ⲫϯ ⲛⲓⲁⲧⲛ. ⲙⲛⲧ-, ⲙⲉⲧⲁⲧⲛ., *sinlessness* : ShA 1 175 *S*, BSM 89 *B*.

ⲙⲁⲓⲛ. *SB, sin-loving* : Pro 17 19 *SA* φιλαμαρτή-μων ; ShRec 7 90 *B* shall be called ϩⲁⲡⲛ.

ⲣ, ⲉⲣ, ⲉⲗ ⲛ. *SAA*[2]*BF, commit sin* : Ge 4 7 *A* (Cl) *B*, Ps 38 1 *SB*, Jo 5 14 *SA*[2]*B*, Ro 2 12 *SBF* ἁμαρτάνειν ;   with ⲉ-, *against* : 1 Kg 24 12 *SB*, Pro 8 36 *SAB*, 1 Cor 8 12 *SBF* ἁμ. εἰς ; Ex 23 33 *SB*, 1 Jo 5 16 *B* (*S* ϫⲓ ⲉϧⲟⲩⲛ ⲉ-) ἁμ. πρός ; Ps 77 17

SB, Is 42 24 *SB*, Hos 4 7 *SAB* ἁμ. dat ; Lev 5 26 *S* (*B* ϣⲱϥⲧ), Jos 7 1 *S*, Si 49 5 *S* πλημμελεῖν ; Job 9 20 *S* (*B* ⲉⲣ ⲙⲉⲧⲁⲥⲉⲃⲏⲥ) ἀσεβεῖν ; El 128 *S* shall seek to ⲣ ⲛ. ⲉⲡⲗⲁⲟⲥ = *ib* 94 *A*, BM 217 21 *S* he that feeds enemy ⲉⲣ ⲛ. ⲉⲣⲟϥ ⲙⲙⲓⲛ ⲙⲙⲟϥ, AM 94 *B* ⲁⲓⲉⲣ ⲛ. ⲉⲣⲱⲧⲉⲛ in ignorance, JKP 2 142 *F* ⲙⲡⲓⲉⲗ ⲛ. ⲗⲉⲕ.

ⲣⲉϥⲣ ⲛ. *SAA*[2]*BF, sinner* : Ge 13 13 *SB*, PS 49 16 *SA* (Cl) *B*, Is 1 4 *SBF*, Jo 9 25 *SA*[2]*B* ἁμαρτω-λός ; Pro 1 10 *SA* (*B* = Gk), Ez 33 11 *SA* (Cl, *B* do) ἀσεβής ; Pro 4 17 *SA* (*B* do) παράνομος ; PS 208 *S* punishments of ⲛⲣ., BM 511 *F* Jesus sat ⲙⲡⲡⲉⲗⲉϭⲉⲗ ⲛ., *ib* 517 *F* ⲗ. ⲡⲁϥⲓ, DeV 1 200 *B* ⲡⲓⲟⲩⲏⲓ ⲛⲉⲙⲡⲓⲣ., BSM 4 *B* ⲥⲁⲣⲝ ⲛⲣ. ; expressing writer's humility : CO 330 *S* ϩⲁⲣⲱⲡ ⲛⲓⲣ. ⲉϥϩⲁⲓ, Lant 22 *F* ⲁⲛⲁⲕ ⲛⲓⲣ. beyond all men, ST 300 *S* ⲧⲉⲕⲣⲙⲅⲁⲗ ⲛⲣ.   ⲙⲛⲧⲣⲉϥⲣ ⲛ. *SF, sinfulness* : PS 210 *S*, MR 5 33 *F*.

ϫⲓ, ϭⲓ ⲛ. *SB, bear sin* : Lev 19 17 *SB* ἁμ. λαμ-βάνειν, Pcod 20 *S* if traders be moderate ⲛⲥⲉⲛⲁϫⲓ ⲛ. ⲁⲛ.

ⲛⲓⲃⲉⲛ *B v* ⲛⲓⲙ *every.*

ⲛⲟⲃⲣⲟⲩ *S* nn, *marsh mallow* : P 43 33 خطمية (Νούφρα *nenufar* نوفر is different. With it *cf* K 187 ⲡⲁⲗⲉⲛⲟⲃⲉⲣ حب عروس *nenufar*).   *Cf* ? DM vo 2 4 *nfr ḥr*, despite different use of name.

ⲛⲟⲩⲃⲥ *O* nn m, *a tree* (*v* Berlin *Wörterb* 2 245) : AZ 21 94 Osiris ⲡⲉⲧⲣⲁ (om ? ϣϥⲁ‾) ⲛⲛ. ⲡⲡⲉⲣⲟⲩⲉ (*l* ⲙⲉⲣ.), with which *cf* DM 21 3 *pnt ḥr pnbs nmrwe* (*v* AZ 38 86).

ⲛⲟⲩⲃⲧ, ⲛⲟⲩⲧⲃ, ⲛⲟⲩⲧⲡ *B*, ⲛⲟⲃⲧ̄ *S* vb tr, *weave* : HL 95 ⲉϥⲛ. ⲡⲣⲁⲛⲃⲏⲧ, Wess 11 170 *S* ⲁⲩⲛⲟⲃⲧⲟⲩ (*sc* ⲃⲏⲧ), MG 25 243 ⲉϥⲛ. ⲛⲉⲃϯ (made of ⲃⲏⲧ) ; intr *ib* 31 ⲉϥⲛ. ϫⲉⲛⲟⲩⲛⲉⲃϯ πλέκειν.

ⲛⲏⲃⲧⲉ *S*, ⲛⲉⲃϯ *B* nn f, *plait, tress* : Z 344 *S* ⲉϣⲁⲩⲣ ϩⲱⲃ ⲉⲧⲛ. = MG 25 209 *B*, Z 319 *S* hid self ϩⲁⲣⲛⲛ., MG 25 76 *B* ⲉϥⲉⲣ ϩⲱⲃ ⲉϯⲛ. & sold baskets made thereof, BIF 13 109 *S* taught them ⲧⲁⲣⲭⲏ ⲛⲧⲛ. = MG 25 296 *B* σειρά, K 138 *B* ϯⲛ. ضفيرة.

ⲛⲉⲟ, ⲛⲑⲟⲕ, ⲛⲑⲟϥ *B v* ⲁⲛⲟⲕ.

ⲛⲟⲉⲓⲕ *S*, ⲛⲁⲉⲓⲕ *A*, ⲛⲱⲓⲕ *B*, ⲛⲁⲓⲕ *F* nn m, *adulterer* : Job 24 15 *B*, Pro 6 32 *SAB*, He 13 4 *SB* μοιχός, Ro 7 3 *S* (*B* ϭⲣⲓⲙⲓ ⲛⲛ.) μοιχαλίς ; PS 320 *S* ⲫⲟⲛⲉⲩⲥ, ⲛ., ⲫⲁⲣⲙⲁⲕⲟⲥ, ShA 2 59 *S* ⲡⲟⲣ-ⲛⲟⲥ, ⲛ., ⲣⲉϥϫⲓ ⲛϭⲟⲛⲥ, MG 25 377 *B* fear hindered ⲛⲛ. ⲉϣⲱⲡⲧ.   As adj : Pro 24 55 *SA* (*B* ⲟⲓ ⲛⲛ.), Si 25 4 *S*, Mk 8 38 *SBF* μοιχός, -αλίς ; C 43 21 *B* ϭⲱϫⲉⲙ ⲛⲛ.

ⲣ, ⲉⲣ ⲛ. *SAB, commit adultery* : Ez 16 32 *SB*,

Mt 19 9 *SB* μοιχᾶσθαι, Hos 4 13 *AB* μοιχεύειν, Miss 8 250 *S* some fornicate others εγρ π.;   c e-: Lev 20 10 *SB*, Jer 36 23 *B*, Mt 5 32 *S* (*B* ϫϥε π.) μ. acc, ShA 1 239 *S* κπλερ π. εθιλε, Va 58 175 *B* αϥπ. (prob *l* ερ π.) ετεϥςϲιλι;   c εϫπ-: Mk 10 11 *SB* μ. ἐπί;   c ʌπ-: Ap 2 22 *SB* μ. μετά, Ep 315 A *S* πετο ππ. πλλ[λς;   c ϭεπ-: Jer 3 9 *B* μ. acc.   ρεϥερ π., *committer of adultery*: Ez 6 9 *B* (*S* = Gk) πορνεύων.

    ʌπτ-, ʌετπ. *SABF, adultery*: Jer 5 7 *SB*, Hos 2 2 *AB*, Mt 15 19 *SBF*, Aeg 227 *S* πορπιλ, ʌ. μοιχεία; JA '75 5 259 *S* signs of τʌ. are curls & braids of hair, Mor 24 4 *F* devil filled Salome with ʌʌʌ., R 1 5 27 *S* ʌʌʌ. πτλκλλγ πηεριοʌε.

    ΝΛΑΚΕ *S*, πεεκε, πεκε, πεκϭε *A*, πλκϱι *B* nn f, *pains of travail*: Job 2 9 *SB*, Is 66 7 *SB*, Mic 4 9 *AB*, 1 Thes 5 3 *SB* ὠδίν; BHom 103 *S* Virgin's π. λχπλλ ππκοτκ, Sh(Besa)Z 503 *S* who cried out εϫπτεςπ., MG 25 70 *B* πιπ. were heavy on her, PSBA 26 178 *S* ογϱλοπλεπ ππ., BMis 106 *S* Virgin says ππ. εϥϣοϙο εϫωι like raindrops; *pains of death, hell*: Ps 17 5 *SB* ὠ., CaiThe 435 *B* πιπ. ʌϥʌιογ طلقان;   *pains in general*: Ex 15 14 *SB*, Ez 7 7 *SB*, Nah 2 10 *AB* ὠ.; Mor 31 230 *S* λϱππ. τλϱοϥ (*sc* king), MIE 2 416 *B* πεππ. π̄ϯϭλπ.

    ϯ π. *SAB, be in travail*: Ps 7 14 *SB*, Hab 3 10 *SAB*, Ap 12 2 *SB* ὠδίνειν; ShC 42 150 *S* τετϯ π. about to bear, MG 25 139 *B* απερ ϧοκι απϯ π. απʌιςι, R 1 2 27 *S* Virgin αςϯ π. πογεϣ πϯ τκλς, Aeg 27 *S* dying εϥϯ π. like one giving birth, Mor 50 47 *S* of efforts to relieve nature, BKU 1 1 *S* gazelle εϭτι πλκες (*sic*) ετρεςʌιςε, Z 603-4 *S* αϥϯ π. εροϥ...ʌπτλκο, ShBMOr 8810 380 *S* your fathers ετϯ π. ϱλπετʌψγχη;   *be in travail of child* c π-: Is 51 2 *SB*, Gal 4 19 *SB* ὠδίν. acc; Br 254 *S* children εϯϯ π. ʌʌοογ, ShBMOr 8800 199 *S* what madness πεπταϥϯ π. ʌπιϫι πϭοπε? As nn, *travail*: Cat 107 *B* πιʌϧοκι, πιϯ π.

    ΝΚΑ, πκο (rare) *S*, πϫλι, επ. (& *v* b) *B*, πκε *A*, πκεει (AP), πκεεπ (Jo) *A²*, πκει *F*, πκη (DM 20 31, *cf* 24 4) *O*, κεεπι, κλπε (BM 651) *F* nn m, *a thing in general*: ShC 73 122 *S* money, clothing or κελλγ ππ., ShA 2 293 *S* ογπ. that wind beareth away, Va 61 93 *B* κερ χριλ πογπ. I will cause bring it = P 131³ 83 *S* ειλος; +rel Gk om, Ex 16 14 *S* π. εϥποκ (*B* om) λεπτόν, Aeg 276 *S* fan of ϱεππ. εϥϣοʌε ὑμένων λεπτῶν, Lev 6 3 *S* π. εϥςορʌ (*B* diff) ἀπώλεια, ib 22 8 *S* π. εαϥʌιογ (*B* om) θνησιμαῖος, Va 66 308 *B* π. ετϭλϧεʌ ἄγος; ShIF 67 *S* clothes cut πογπ. εϥμηρ, PMich 593 G *S* ογπ. εϥϱολϭ to be eaten, C 89 96 *B* πλιπ. εταϥϥλςϥ;

or + π- gen, Deu 15 17 *S* π. πογωτϥ (*B* diff) ὀπή- τιον, GPar 2 6 *S* ʌπεπιπε ξυρόν, ShZ 637 *S* π. πςλοϧλεϭ = ib ϲοϧεϥ πϲ. *plane*, BM 329 *S* π. πϭωϫε *spade*, Leyd 343 *S* π. πϯ ϲοτε *quiver* (*cf* ϱπλλγ πϯ ϲ.), LAl 11 *S* πεπ. πτϲωϣε *plants* (*cf* Va 57 214 *B* θπογπι πογπ.).   b *thing to eat, food* π. πογωλ (*cf* λλλγ πογ.): Dan 6 18 *B*, Ge 27 4 &c *B* ογχογωλ, ϱλπχογωλ (? for πϫλι πογ.) ἔδεσμα; Jo 21 5 *B* (*S* diff) προσφάγιον; 1 Kg 30 12 *S* (Mor), Jth 10 5 *S* παλάθη; 2 Kg 17 19 *S* gloss on ἀραφώθ; DeV 2 262 *B* ϱλπκογϫι πεπ. πογ. = Mor 41 13 *S* ϭιπογωλ, Aeg 260 *S* wine & ογ. πογ., DM 24 4 *O* put drugs upon a κπογʌ (? = π. πογ.).   c as *vessel*: Si 50 15 *S* π. πογ- ωτπ εϧολ σπονδεῖον, Jo 19 29 *A²* (*S* ϱπλλγ, *B* ʌοκι) σκεῦος, Z 311 *S* π. πειω νιπτήρ; TT 157 *S* π. full of dates, ShC 73 137 *S* π. of pottery, Miss 4 671 *S* πκοπιλ *plaster pail*, ib 536 *S* π. πολε = MG 17 570 شاش, KKS 57 n *S*, Miss 8 258 *S* (πκο) sim;   d *property, belongings*: Pro 1 13 *S* (*A* ϱπο, *B* = Gk) κτῆσις, Sa 13 17 *S*, Mk 10 22 *S* (*B* ϫϥο) κτῆμα; Pro 19 11 *S* (*A* do) ὕπαρξις, Job 21 19 *S* (*B* = Gk) ὑπάρχοντα; Pro 29 32 *S* (*A* do), Lu 15 12 *S* (*B* ωπϧ) βίος *substantia*; Ge 31 1 *S* (*B* π. πιϧεπ), Job 18 19 *S* (*B* πη ετεπογϥ), Aeg 232 *S* πεπ. ʌππῑπε τά +gen; Sa 11 25 *S*, Is 5 8 *B* (*S* om), ZNTW 24 90 *F* τι, τινα; Pcod 30 *S* ππ. of Laban given to Jacob, C 43 193 *B* πεϥεπ. re- nounced, Lant 79 *S* bought it with πεϥπ., RNC 50 *S* hast paid all πεκπ. to physicians, C 86 341 *B* stole πιεπ. of τόπος.

    —— πιλ, πιϧεπ, -ϧι *SAA²BF, everything*, mostly inanimate: Ge 31 43 *S* (*B* πλι τηρογ), Nu 3 10 *S* (*B* ϱωϧ πι.), Si 1 4 *SB*, Mk 8 25 *S* (*B* πτηρϥ, *F* ϱωϧ πι.), Jo 13 3 *SA²B*, 1 Cor 2 15 *BF* (*S* ογοπ πιλ), He 1 2 *F* (*S* πτηρϥ, *B* ογ. πι.) πᾶν, πάντα, ἅπαντα, Ps 103 28 *B* (*S* τηρογ) σύμπαντα, Lev 27 28 *SB*, Is 39 2 *SB*, Mt 13 46 *S* (*B* πετεπ- τλϧ, *F* ϱωϧ πι. ετ-) πάντα ὅσα, Cl 55 6 *A* behold- ing π. πιλ παντεπόπτης (*cf* ib 64 1 πτηρϥ); ShR 2 3 10 *Ṣ* lacking bread ʌππ. πιλ, AP 25 *A²* I be- held π. πιλ, Mor 48 32 *S* God named π. πιλ (var BMar 219 λλλγ πιλ) = Rec 6 185 *B* ογ. πι., BM 651 *F* κλπε πιλ that is thine, AM 163 *B* distri- buted π. πι. to poor;   animate: Ge 7 22 *S* (*B* ογ. πι.), Ps 68 35 *B* (*S* πετ- τηρογ), Ez 47 9 *B* (*S* ψγχη πιλ) πᾶν, πάντα, Lev 11 27 *S* (*B* θηριοπ πι.) πᾶς ὅς, ib 18 6 *B* (*S* ογ. πιλ) πᾶς οἰκεῖος; J 65 42 *S* my quitting of body προς πτωϣ ππ. πιλ.

    ΝΚΕ *O* *v* ϭε *S* ϫε *B*.

    ΝΚΕΕΝ *A* *v* πκλ.

    ΝΟΗΝΕΚ *S* vb intr, *have affection, inclination*

+ ⲉⲣⲟⲩⲡ ⲉ- : Ro 12 10 (B ϫⲏ ⲥⲉⲡⲟⲩⲙⲉⲓ ⲉⲃ. ⲉ-, F
ⲣⲱⲗϭ ⲉⲣ. ⲉ-) φιλόστοργος εἰς, ShP 130¹ 102 ⲉⲣⲉⲡ.
ⲉⲣ. ⲉⲡϣⲏⲣⲉ ⲙⲡⲥⲁⲧⲁⲡⲁⲥ ⲩⲡϩⲗⲟϭ ⲡⲓⲙ.   As nn,
affection : Mor 48 34 their kindness & ⲡⲡ. ⲙⲡⲉⲩϩⲏⲧ ⲉⲣ. ⲉⲣⲟⲓ, var BMar 220 ⲑⲉ ⲉⲧⲟⲩϩⲗⲟⲗⲉ ⲉⲣ.
ⲉⲣⲟⲓ = Rec 6 186 B diff, P 44 51 ⲡⲁⲡⲟⲩ ⲡⲉϥⲏ.
بشاشة (*v* AZ 24 97).

ⲛⲟⲩⲕⲉⲣ B vb tr, *prick, incise*, of unripe syca-
more-figs, *cf* נקר (IgR): Am 7 14 (S ⲟⲩⲟⲩⲕⲉ, A
ⲡⲟⲩⲟⲩϫⲉ) κνίζειν (explained as κεντεῖν, var χαράσσειν).   As nn, *incision* of this fruit : K 178 ⲡ.
ختان الجميز . *Cf* BIF 28 57 ff.

ⲛⲟⲩⲕⲥ A *v* ⲡⲟⲩϭⲥ.

ⲛⲕⲟⲧⲕ, ⲉⲡ., ⲛⲕⲟⲧⲉ S, ⲛⲕⲁⲧⲉ SSᵃA, (ⲛ)ⲕⲁⲧⲉ
O, ⲛⲕⲁⲧⲕⲉ A²O, ⲉⲡⲕⲟⲧ B, ⲛⲕ. SB, ⲉⲡⲕⲁⲧ, ⲉⲡⲕⲁⲧⲕ
F, ⲛⲕⲁⲧ SᵃF, ⲛⲕⲱⲟⲧ O vb intr, a *sleep* : Ge 2 21 B
(S ⲱⲃϣ), Ps 43 23 SB, *ib* 120 4 B (S ⲱ.), Pro 4
16 B (S do, A ϩⲱⲣⲡ) ὑπνοῦν, Ge 41 5 B ἐνυπ., Pro
24 48 SA καθυπ.; Jon 1 5 SAB, Mt 13 25 SBF,
Lu 8 52 SB, 1 Thes 5 7 SB καθεύδειν, Mk 14 37 S
ⲱⲃϣ...ⲡ. BF ⲡ....ⲡ. ⲕⲁⲑ.,ⲕⲁⲑ.; Mt 28 13 SB, Jo 11
11 SA²B, MG 25 210 B = Z 345 S ⲱ. κοιμᾶσθαι;
ShC 73 26 S ⲉⲓⲧⲉ ⲉϥⲡ. ⲉⲓⲧⲉ ⲉϥⲏⲣⲥ, BAp 98 S ⲉⲓⲡⲏϫ
ⲉⲃⲟⲗ ⲉⲡ., TU 43 21 A ⲁⲅⲣⲁⲉⲓⲥ ⲡⲡⲟⲅⲡ., BG 58
S ⲁϥⲧⲣⲉϥⲡ. (on Ge 2 21), C 86 327 B bewitched
them ϣⲁⲧⲟⲩⲉⲡ. then robbed them, KroppK 65 Sᵃ
ⲙⲡⲡⲁⲩ ⲉⲧⲉϣⲁⲕⲛⲕⲁⲧⲉ, PNolot 16 S ⲛⲧⲁϥⲛⲕⲁⲧⲉ in
Lord, AZ 21 100 O fire ⲉⲧⲉⲙⲉⲥⲕⲁⲧⲉ (*cf* ? ἀκάμα-
τον πῦρ).   **b** *lie down* : Jos 6 11 S, 3 Kg 19 5 S,
Ps 3 5 SB, Dan 8 27 SB κοιμ.; Jo 5 6 SB (A²
ⲡⲏϫ) κατακεῖσθαι; Pro 3 24 SA ⲡ....ⲱⲃϣ B ⲡ....
ⲡ. ⲕⲁⲑ., ὑπ.;   Rec 4 154 S ⲛⲧⲉⲣⲉⲡⲣⲱⲙⲉ ⲉⲡ. he
raised voice & sang, R 1 2 41 S Virgin ⲡⲉⲥⲡ. only
for getting sleep, MR 5 49 F ⲧⲓⲉⲡ. ⲧⲓϣⲱⲡⲓ, AZ 33
57 F ⲟⲩⲣⲱⲙⲉ (ⲡ)ⲕⲟⲧ ⲉϥϣⲟⲡⲉ, Brussels Mus Cinq
E 6346 F ϯⲕⲁⲧ ⲉⲓϣⲱⲡⲓ, PMéd 235 S give 3 (doses)
ⲉϥⲡⲁⲡⲕⲟⲧⲉ, AM 172 B camels ⲁⲩⲉⲡ.   **c** *die* :
3 Kg 2 10 SB, Mt 27 52 SB, 1 Cor 7 39 B (SF
ⲙⲟⲩ), Cl 44 2 A ϩⲉⲛϩⲁⲉⲓⲡⲉ ⲡ., CaiEuch 515 B
remember them ⲉⲧⲁⲩⲉⲡ. ⲕⲟⲓⲙ.; Eccl 7 16 F (S ⲙ.)
ἀπόλλυσθαι; ShC 73 213 S when they heard ϫⲉ-
ⲁϥⲡ., DeV 2 13 B resurrection of ⲛⲏ ⲉⲧⲁⲩⲡ., CMSS
49 F ⲁⲩⲥⲁⲡ (ⲡ)ⲕⲁⲧ ϩⲁϩ[ⲧⲏⲡ, Cai 8519 S epitaph
ⲁϥⲛⲕⲟⲧ, EW 55 B ⲡⲉⲥϩⲟⲟⲩ ⲡⲉⲡ. drew nigh.   *Cf*
ⲗⲧⲟⲡ II **b**.
With following preposition.
—— ⲉ-, *sleep, lie upon* : Is 51 20 SB καθεύδ.
ἐπί, Dan 12 2 B ⲕ. ⲉⲛ; ShMIF 23 157 S ⲧⲉⲧⲛⲡ.
ⲉⲡⲕⲁϩ, ShC 73 82 S I will not ⲡ. ⲉϭⲗⲟϭ, BMar
6 S sim, R 1 5 52 S ϣⲁⲡⲛ. ⲉⲩⲡⲟⲓ, & *ib* ϩⲓⲟⲩⲡⲟⲓ;
lie down to, for : Miss 4 736 S on 4th of month
ⲁϥⲡ. ⲉⲡϣⲱⲡⲉ, *ib* 785 S sim.

—— ⲉϫⲡ-, ⲉϩⲣⲁⲓ ⲉϫⲡ-, *lie upon* : Ez 4 4 S ⲉϫⲡ-,
B ⲉⲣ. ⲉϫⲉⲡ- ⲕⲟⲓⲙ. ἐπί, Am 6 4 B (A ϩⲓϫⲡ-) καθεύδ.
ἐπί, R 1 5 13 S when fasting if canst ⲣ ϩⲉⲡⲣⲉⲃϩⲟ-
ⲙⲁⲥ ⲉⲕⲡ. ⲉϫⲱⲥ = JA '75 5 239 S ⲣ ⲟⲩϩⲉⲃϩ. ⲉⲕⲥⲉⲕ ⲥⲡⲁⲩ *sleep upon it* & so *fast 2 days together*
(but Gk ἑβδομάδα ὑπερθῆναι νηστείαις), TstAb 231
B ⲉⲡ. ⲉϫⲉⲡⲟⲩⲙⲁ ⲡⲉⲡ. ⲟⲩϫⲉ ϩⲓϫⲉⲡⲟⲩϭⲗⲟϫ, MG
25 172 B king shall ⲉⲡ. ⲉϫⲱⲟⲩ *oppress*, C 43 46 B
army ⲉⲡ. ⲉϫⲉⲡⲫⲓⲁⲣⲟ.

—— ϩⲓϫⲡ-, *meaning same* : Lev 15 20 B κοιτάζειν ἐπί, Job 39 9 SB ⲕⲟⲓⲙ. ἐπί, Lu 5 25 B (S diff)
κατακεῖσθαι ἐπί.

—— ⲉⲃⲟⲗ ϩⲓϫⲡ-, *meaning same* : PS 384 S sinners ⲉⲣⲉⲧⲁⲙⲉⲗⲓⲁ ⲡ. ⲉⲃ. ϩⲓϫⲱⲟⲩ (*cf* ? *ib* 375 ⲃⲱⲕ
ⲉⲃ. ϩⲓϫⲡ-).

—— ϩⲓ-, *meaning same* : Job 8 17 S (B ϩⲓϫⲉⲡ-)
ⲕⲟⲓⲙ. ἐπί; MG 25 210 B ⲁϭⲉⲡ. ϩⲓⲟⲩⲙⲁ = Z 345
S ϩⲡⲟⲩⲧⲙⲏ τιθέναι ἑαυτ. εἰς; Mor 31 50 S ass
ⲁⲥⲉⲡ. ϩⲓⲡⲉⲥⲏⲧ, Ep 162 S ⲉⲓⲡ. ϩⲓⲡⲉϣⲗⲟϭ.

—— ϩⲡ-, ϩⲉⲡ-, *lie in, on* : Ge 28 11 S (var ⲛ-)
B ⲕⲟⲓⲙ. ⲉⲛ; 1 Kg 3 3 S καθεύδ. ⲉⲛ; Ps 103 22 SB
κοιτάζεσθαι ⲉⲛ; Job 21 26 S (B ϩⲓϫⲉⲡ-) ⲕⲟⲓⲙ. ἐπί;
Z 351 S ⲉϥⲉⲡ. ϩⲙⲡⲕⲁϩ.

—— ϩⲁ-, *lie below* : Nu 22 27 S (B ϩⲉⲙⲥⲓ ⲉⲡⲉⲥⲏⲧ ϩⲁ-) συγκαθίζ. ὑποκάτω; Jo 5 3 SA² (B ⲣⲱϫⲡ
ϩⲉⲡ-) κατακεῖσθαι ⲉⲛ; BMis 9 S pillar where children ⲡⲕ. ϩⲁⲣⲟϥ.

—— ϩⲁⲣⲧⲡ-, *lie, stay by, with* : Nu 22 8 S (B
diff) καταλύειν; 2 Kg 13 11 S κοιμ. μετά.

—— ⲛ- *lie in* : MG 25 210 B ⲁⲓⲡⲁⲉⲡ. ⲙⲡⲁⲓⲙⲁ
ⲕⲟⲓⲙ. ὧδε, HSt 464 S ⲛⲧⲡ. ⲙⲡⲉⲕⲙⲁ (var Aeg
264 ⲉ-).

—— ⲙⲡ-, ⲡⲉⲙ-, *lie with* : Lev 18 22 SB, Is 57
8 SB κοιμ. μετά; Ge 39 10 SB καθεύδ. μ.; AZ 21
100 O Nephthys ⲉⲥⲉⲡⲕⲁⲧⲕⲉ ⲡⲉⲙⲟⲩⲥⲓⲣⲓ, *ib* 106 O
ⲉϣⲟⲡⲉ (= ⲉϣⲱⲡⲉ) ⲉⲥⲡⲕⲱⲧ ⲙⲉⲡⲕⲉⲟⲩⲉ; PS 380
S man ⲉⲧⲟⲩⲡ. ⲡⲓⲙⲁϥ.   ⲉϩⲣⲁⲓ ⲙⲡ- S, *lie down
on bed* : Mor 29 25 ⲉϥⲡ. ⲉϩ. ⲙⲡⲧⲉⲥϩⲓⲙⲉ.

—— B mostly, SA² rare nn m, *sleep* : Ge 28 16
B, Ps 126 2 B (S ϩⲓⲡⲏⲃ), Is 29 7 B (S ⲱⲃϣ vb)
ὕπνος; Jo 11 13 SA²B κοίμησις; ShRE 10 160 S
wake from ⲡⲣⲓⲡⲏⲃ ⲁⲩⲱ ⲡⲉⲡ., Va 61 89 B we dream
ⲥⲉⲡⲡⲉⲡⲛ., TRit 214 B sick man ⲡⲓⲉⲡ. ⲡⲧⲉ ⲧⲉϥⲓⲁⲃⲓ
قاب (*cf* 219 ϭⲗⲟϫ, ϣⲱⲡⲓ);   *death* : Si 38 25 S
ἀνάπαυσις; Z 263 S ⲡⲉⲡ. of Athanasius, BMis 69
S she told them not of ⲡⲉⲥⲡ., J 68 64 Sᵃ ⲉⲓⲁⲡϩ ⲛ
ⲙⲡⲛⲥⲁⲡⲁⲛⲕⲁⲧ.

ⲁⲧⲡ. SB adj, *sleepless* : BHom 55 S eye ⲡⲁ. (var
ⲁⲧⲱⲃϣ) ἀκοίμητος; ShR 2 3 66 S, BAp 10 S, C
43 203 B worm ⲡⲁ. (*cf* Mk 9 48), Z 63 B ⲉϥⲟⲓ ⲡⲁ.
two years, PMich 601 S love charm ⲁ(ⲁ)ⲥ ⲡⲁⲧⲡ-
ⲕⲟⲧⲉ ⲁ(ⲁ)ⲥ ⲡⲁⲧⲟⲩϣⲡ.

ⲙⲁ ⲛ̄. *SABF, place of lying, couch*: 2 Kg 11 2 S, Ps 35 5 B (S ϭⲗⲟϭ), Is 17 2 B (S ϣⲁⲓⲣⲓ), Hos 7 14 *SAB* ⲕⲟίⲧⲏ; BHom 52 S θάλαμος; Ge 48 2 S, Lu 5 18 S (both var & B ϭⲗ.) ⲕⲗίⲛⲏ; Ac 9 33 F (SB ϭⲗ.) ⲕⲣάⲃⲃⲁⲧⲟⲥ; PS 121 S tied to foot of ⲛ̄., ShA 2 268 S ⲟⲩⲙ. ⲉⲧⲧⲃ̄ⲃⲏⲩ, CO 30 &c S ordinand shall keep watch over his ⲙ., BMis 273 S in church for martyr's relics, SHel 25 S iron ⲙ. torture-bed (*cf* ἑⲣⲙⲏⲧάⲣⲓⲟⲛ), AM 143 B sim, Aeg 264 S ⲛⲉϭⲗⲟϭ ⲙⲡⲉⲕⲙ. *sleeping room*;   *sexual cohabitation*: Lev 22 4 S, Job 36 28 S, Ro 9 10 S (all B ϣⲁⲓⲣⲓ) ⲕⲟίⲧⲏ; Mor 33 123 S begotten without ⲙ. ⲡⲣⲟⲟⲩⲧ, AM 182 B pure from ⲫⲙ. ⲛⲧⲉϥⲥϩⲓⲙⲓ, P 129¹⁴ 99 S wage of ⲡⲁⲙ. *concubinage*.

ⲣⲉϥⲛ̄. *SB, one who lies* in ⲣ. ⲙⲡⲣⲟⲟⲩⲧ: 1 Cor 6 9 SB, 1 Tim 1 10 SB ἀⲣⲥⲉⲛⲟⲕⲟίⲧⲏⲥ; TstAB 253 B, Aeg 281 S (var ⲥⲟⲝⲟⲙⲓⲧⲏⲥ).

ϭⲛ̄-, ϫⲓⲛⲛ̄. *SB, act of lying, sleeping*: Nu 5 20 S (B ϣⲁⲓⲣⲓ) ⲕⲟίⲧⲏ; BHom 39 S ⲧϭ. ϩⲓⲡⲉⲥⲛⲧ-χαμευνία, MG 25 180 B I know not ⲧϫ. ⲛⲧⲁⲓⲥϩⲓⲙⲓ, *ib* 333 B ⲡⲓϫ. ⲉⲡⲕⲁϩⲓ, Z 271 S sim; *of death*: BIF 13 104 S after king's ϭ., CDan 99 B commemoration of ⲡⲉϥϫ.

ⲡⲁⲕϩⲓ *B*, ⲡⲉⲕϩⲉ *A*   *v* ⲡⲁⲁⲕⲉ.

ⲡⲁⲙ   *v* ⲡⲟⲙ.

ⲡⲉⲙⲙ- *SBF*   *v* ⲙⲛ-.

ⲛⲓⲙ *SAA²BF, interrog pron, a who?* sg: Ge 3 11 SB, Job 13 19 SB, Is 33 14 SBF, *ib* 53 1 SA (Cl) B, Jo 8 53 SA²B, 1 Cor 9 7 SBF, Va 57 10 B ⲛ. ϭⲉⲡⲉⲛⲡⲟⲩ, MG 25 354 B ⲛⲑⲟⲕ ⲛ. ⲧίⲥ; PS 178 S knew not ϫⲉⲁⲛⲟⲕ ⲛ., Br 235 S ⲛ. ⲡⲉ ⲡⲁⲓ, C 89 93 B ⲁⲩⲥⲟⲩⲱⲛϥ ϫⲉⲛ. ⲡⲉ, ShBor 246 50 S their possessions ⲛⲁⲛ. ⲡⲉ if not God's, Miss 8 190 S ⲁⲡⲛⲡϣⲏⲣⲉ ⲛⲛ̄.;   pl: Job 25 3 SB, Is 42 19 SB, He 3 17 SB, Ap 7 13 SB ⲧίⲥ; Pcod 11 S after these ⲛ. ⲡⲉ, BHom 52 S ⲡⲧⲉⲧⲛⲛ̄.   *b what?*: Ge 32 27 SB, Eccl 10 14 S, Hos 11 8 A (B ⲁϣ), Mt 23 17 SB, as obj Lu 1 62 SB ⲧί; BMis 60 S 4 gospels ⲛ. ϩⲱⲱϣⲡⲉ ⲡⲙⲉϩⲧⲟⲩ, Z 317 S ⲛ. ⲡⲉ ⲡⲉϥⲣⲁⲛ = MG 25 232 B ⲛ. ⲉⲣⲉⲛϥ.   As adj + ⲛ-: Job 25 4 SB, Is 50 1 B (Lacr, var & S ⲁϣ), Dan 3 15 B, Lu 14 31 SB ⲧίⲥ; PS 3 S ⲛ. ⲁϥϥⲩⲗⲁⲝ ⲡⲉⲧϭⲓⲣⲛ-, ShA 2 18 S ⲛ. ⲛ̄ϣⲱⲥ leaveth sheep, Mor 25 3 S ⲉⲓⲛⲁⲣ ⲛ. ⲙⲡⲣⲟⲅⲟⲓⲙⲓⲟⲛ = Va 61 87 B.

—— *SBFO, a certain person* or *thing, so & so*: Leyd 131 S pray for patriarch ⲁⲡⲁ ⲛ., Va 66 295 B ⲡⲁⲣⲉⲛ. ⲥⲱⲟⲩⲛ ⲙⲙⲟⲓⲛⲉ δεῖνα; TRit 220 B ⲡⲉⲕⲃⲱⲕ ⲛ. ὅδε ⲩⲗⲓ, Z 315 S unto whom? Some said ⲛ. ⲡⲉ ὅⲥⲇⲉ, others ⲛ. ⲡⲉ ἕⲧⲉⲣⲟⲛ; AZ 21 100 O ⲑⲏ ⲛⲛ̄. ⲡⲙⲉⲥⲓⲉ ⲛ., PSBA 19 214 S ⲁⲡⲟⲕ ⲛ. ⲩ̄ⲥ (ⲩⲓόⲥ) ⲛⲛ̄., BAp 134 S ⲛ. ⲛ̄ϣⲏⲣⲉ ⲛⲛ̄., Kr 3 F, BM

524 F ⲛ. ⲧϫⲉⲓⲗⲓ ⲛ. (ⲧϫⲏⲗⲓ ⲛⲛ̄.), BMis 274 = Mor 29 43 S ⲙⲡⲛⲥⲁⲡⲁⲩ ⲛ. ⲉⲕⲡⲁϫⲡⲉ ⲉⲓ, *ib* 30 53 F ⲙⲡⲥⲁⲡⲉⲩ ⲛⲓⲃⲓ, BMis 1199 S must needs quit world ⲙⲡⲛⲥⲁⲡⲁⲩ ⲛ.

ⲛ. ⲙⲛⲛ̄. *S, so & so*: Sh 73 125 ⲉⲣⲉⲛ. ⲙⲛⲛ̄. ϣⲱⲗ ⲙⲙⲟⲟⲩ ⲉⲃⲟⲗ, ShIF 242 wherefore is not this ⲧόⲡⲟⲥ filled with Christ's beloved ⲛⲑⲉ ⲛⲛ̄. ⲙⲛⲛ̄. *like such another*.   As adj + ⲛ-: Mt 26 18 S (B ⲡⲁⲫⲙⲁⲛ), Va 66 295 B mother of ⲛ. ⲡⲣⲱⲙⲓ δεῖνα; ShA 1 204 S ⲁⲛ. ⲡⲥⲱⲛⲉ ⲙⲟⲩ.   ⲡⲁⲛ., ⲧⲁⲛ., *belonging to whom*: Jo 19 24 SA²B, Va 61 216 B ⲧίⲛⲟⲥ; J 67 80 S they will tell thee ϫⲉⲧⲁⲛ. (ⲧ)ⲉ ⲧⲁϫⲟⲉ; *so & so*: MG 25 213 B ⲧⲁⲛ. = KKS 24 S ⲙⲉϣⲉ ⲛ. ἡ δεῖνα, TRit 244 B thy servants ⲡⲁⲛ. ⲡⲉⲙⲧⲁⲛ. ὅⲇⲉ, Bodl Marsh 32 152 B church of ⲧⲁⲛ. ⲙⲡⲟⲗⲓⲥ, Va 57 234 B nature of ⲡⲁⲛ. evil.   MG 25 366 B ⲡⲁⲛ. ⲛ̄ϩⲉⲗⲗⲟ ὁ δεῖνα ὁ γέⲣⲱⲛ, Va 61 219 B ⲡⲁⲛ. ⲡⲣⲱⲙⲓ ὁ δεῖνα, MIE 2 391 B ⲡⲁⲛ. ⲡⲣⲱⲙⲓ = BAp 114 S ⲛ. ⲡⲣ.

ⲙⲉϣⲉ ⲛⲓⲙ   *v* ⲙⲉϣⲉ.

ⲛⲓⲙ *SAA²FO*, ⲛⲓⲃⲉⲛ *B*, -ϭⲉⲛ *F* (Kr 116), ⲛⲓ-ⲃⲓ *FO*, ⲛⲓⲃⲉ *O* *adj, every*   **a** *as pl* (oftenest): Ge 6 17 S ⲥⲁⲣⲝ ⲛ. ⲉⲟⲩⲛ ⲡⲓϫⲉ ⲡⲣⲏⲧⲟⲩ (B ⲡϫⲏⲧϥ), Ps 11 3 SB ⲥⲡⲟⲧⲟⲩ ⲛ., Ez 24 4 B ⲫⲁϫⲓ ⲛ. ⲉⲡⲁⲡⲉⲩ, Jo 1 3 SBF ⲡⲕⲁ ⲛ. ⲁⲩϣⲱⲡⲉ ⲡⲁ̂ⲥ; PS 368 S ⲉϥⲥⲱⲕ ϩⲛⲧⲟⲩ ⲙ̄ⲯⲩⲭⲏ ⲛ., ShBor 246 113 S ⲁⲅⲁ-ⲑⲟⲛ ⲛ. ⲡⲟⲩϭⲡⲉ, Kr 116 F, ⲗⲁⲩ ⲛ. ϣⲁⲣⲉⲡⲟⲩⲣⲟ ⲟⲣⲓ[ϫⲉ] ⲙⲟⲟⲩ, J 84 35 S ⲉϩⲟⲩⲥⲓⲁ ⲛ. ⲉⲩϩⲟⲥⲉ.   **b** *as sg*: Lev 3 16 B ⲱⲧ ⲛ. ⲁⲡⲓⲧϥ (S pl), Pro 11 25 S ⲯⲩⲭⲏ ⲛ. ⲉⲧⲟⲩⲥⲙⲟⲩ ⲉⲣⲟⲥ (A ⲧⲏⲣⲥ, B diff), Mt 13 52 SB ⲅⲣⲁⲙⲙⲁⲧⲉⲩⲥ ⲛ. ⲉⲁϥϫⲓ (F ⲛ̄ⲧⲁϫⲓ), Ja 1 19 SAB ⲣⲱⲙⲉ ⲛ....ⲉϥϣⲥⲕ ⲡⲁ̂ⲥ; ShZ 505 S ⲧⲟ-ⲟⲩⲉ ⲛ. ⲉⲩⲡⲁⲥⲁⲛⲧϥ, but *ib* ϩⲡⲟ ⲛ. ⲉⲩⲡⲁⲧⲁⲙⲓⲟⲟⲩ, DeV 1 104 B ⲣⲱⲙⲓ ⲛ. ⲉⲧⲟⲩⲡⲁϧⲟⲩ;   *with sg art or pron*: Nu 15 13 B ⲡⲓⲣⲉⲙⲛ̄ⲧϥⲙⲓ ⲛ. (S ⲟⲩⲟⲛ ⲛ.), Lev 3 3 B ⲡⲓⲱⲧ ⲛ. (var om ⲛ., S om), 2 Tim 4 2 S ϩⲙ̄ϩⲁⲣⲱϣϩⲏⲧ ⲛ. (? error, var ⲙⲛⲧϩ.) ⲡⲁ̂ⲥ; ShA 2 333 S ⲡⲉϩⲟⲟⲩ ⲛ., ZNTW 24 84 F sim, Lev 21 18 B ⲟⲩϩⲱⲙⲓ ⲛ. (var om ⲛ.), *ib* 6 11 B ⲫⲏ ⲛ. ⲉⲧⲁ- (S ⲟⲩ. ⲛ.) ⲡⲁ̂ⲥ; Va 57 207 B ⲫⲏ ⲛ. wherein thou shalt sin ὅⲥⲟⲥ; EW 159 B ⲡⲟⲩⲁⲓ ⲡⲟⲩⲁⲓ ⲛ.   **c** *sg & pl* S: ShMIF 23 186 ⲣⲱⲙⲉ ⲛ. ⲉϥⲟⲩⲉϣ... ⲉⲩⲛⲁϯ, JKP 2 86 ⲣⲱⲙⲉ ⲛ. ⲉϣⲁϥⲥⲱⲧⲙ...ϣⲁϥϫⲓ-ⲧⲟⲩ, TT 43 ϩⲡⲟ ⲛ. ⲉϥⲡⲁⲣ ⲁⲥ ⲡⲥⲉⲧⲁⲕⲟ, J 68 90 ϩⲡⲟ ⲛ. ⲉϥϣⲟⲡ ⲡⲁⲓ...ⲉⲧⲁⲁⲩ.   **d** *no concord shown*: Deu 5 14 B (S ⲗⲁⲁⲩ), Ps 8 7 SB, 1 Cor 7 17 S (BF ⲧⲏⲣϥ) ⲡⲁ̂ⲥ; Ps 34 27 S ⲡⲟⲩⲟⲉⲓϣ ⲛ. B ⲛ̄ⲥⲛⲟⲩ ⲛ. ⲇⲓⲁⲡⲁⲛⲧόⲥ, Is 11 9 SB ⲙⲁ ⲛ. ⲥύⲙⲡⲁⲥⲁ, Sa 14 31 S ⲛⲥⲟⲡ ⲛ. ἀεί; AZ 21 100 O ⲥⲁⲧⲓ ⲛⲓⲃⲉ (gloss -ⲃⲓ) ⲡⲓⲥⲓ ⲛⲓⲃⲓ (gl -ⲃⲉ), PGM 1 60 O ⲡⲟ ⲛⲓⲙ, PS 239 S ⲧⲟⲡⲟⲥ ⲛ....ⲛⲧⲟⲡⲟⲥ ⲧⲏⲣⲟⲩ, Mor 30 3 F ⲣⲱⲙⲉ

пıвε, *ib* пıвı MR 2 56 *F* ⲗⲱⲙⲙ пιειвı, Mor 24 7 *F* ϣⲏⲡ пıₐₐ, *ib* 10 пıвı, AP 25 *A²* beheld пкεει п.
V also ⲗⲁⲁⲩ, ⲟⲩⲟⲡ.

пıₐₐ *B* in ⲣⲓⲡⲓₐₐ. *v* ⲣⲓⲡⲏв.

поₐₐ *SB*, ⲡⲁₐₐ *SAB* nn m, *pine, tamarisk, cypress* (?): Zech 11 2 *A* (*B* = Gk) πίτυς, TstAB 160 *B* tree was ⲟⲩⲡⲟₐₐ (*cf* Ge 18 1 δρῦς), P 44 81 *S* ⲡⲟₐₐ · ⲙⲉⲣⲓⲕⲓⲟⲡ (μυρίκη) جزل, P 43 56 *S* (ₐₐ)ⲉⲣⲓⲕⲓⲟⲡ جزل· ⲡⲟₐₐ جرس, K 175 *B* пıⲡⲁₐₐ جزل; Baouit 1 130 *S* ⲥⲟ пвⲏⲧ пıⲡⲁₐₐ, Hall 80 *S* ⲟⲩϣⲁⲡ пϣⲏ пⲡⲁₐₐ; ⲉⲗⲕⲟ пⲡⲟₐₐ (var ⲡⲁₐₐ) *S*, *gall of tamerisk* (?): PMéd 233, 315 (*v Acta Or* 6 294). In place-names: Θερσω πναμ, PLond 4 593, Πιωρε πναμ (var νομ) *ib* 596.

пⲁₐₐ *v* ₐₐε truth.

пⲉₐₐ *O* nn f, *flame* (?) as goddess: DM 2 16 ⲧϣⲧ пⲧп.

пⲉₐₐⲟⲩⲣⲉ (? or ⲉₐₐⲟⲩⲣⲉ) *S* nn m, meaning unknown, among iron (?) σκεύη: Hall 131 ϣⲟₐₐⲧ пп. with ⲕⲣⲓⲕⲟⲥ, ⲕⲗⲁⲗ, ⲕⲁⲡⲓϫⲉ. Coptic?

пⲟₐₐⲧⲉ *S*, ⲡⲁₐₐⲧⲉ *A*, ⲡⲟₐₐϯ *B*, ⲡⲁₐₐϯ *F* nn f, *strength, power*: Deu 3 24 *SB*, Ps 21 15 *B* (*S* ϭⲟₐₐ), *ib* 32 16 *S* (*B* ₐₐⲉⲧϫⲱⲣⲓ), Zech 4 6 *SA* (*B* ϫⲟₐₐ), Am 2 14 *S* (*AB* do) ἰσχύς, Dan 3 20 *B* men ⲉⲩϫⲟⲣ пп. ἰσχυροὶ ἰσχύι; Job 40 11 *SB*, Ez 28 5 *B* (*S* ϭ.) δύναμις; ShR 2 3 69 *S* ⲧп. ппⲉϥⲥⲁⲣϫ, C 86 217 *B* touched him & ⲁϥₐₐⲟⲣϩ пп., BMis 262 *S* leaped up ϩпⲟⲩпⲟϭ пп. = Mor 30 37 *F*; *encouragement, comfort B*: Is 30 7 (*S* ⲥⲟⲗⲥⲗ, *F* ⲧⲱвⲁϩ), He 6 18 (*SF* ⲥⲟпⲥ) παράκλησις; Col 4 11 (*S* = Gk) παρηγορία; 1 Thes 1 5 (*SF* ⲧⲱⲧ пϩⲏⲧ) πληροφορία; BSM 2 ⲥⲟⲗⲥⲉⲗ ϩⲓп. = BMis 322 *S* παραμυθια, Va 57 2 ⲁϣ пп. пⲧⲉ ⲟⲩₐₐⲁ ₐₐⲟпⲓ shall be theirs ?, PO 11 326 ⲉⲩϭⲓ п. ⲉвⲟⲗ ϩⲓⲧⲟⲧϥ. As adj *B*: Zech 1 13 (*SA* ⲥⲟⲗⲥⲗ) παρακλητικός, MG 25 141, AM 271 sim. As advb *F*: Is 30 30 пϣϣⲁⲗⲟⲩ пп. (*SB* diff) βιαίως.

ⲁⲧп. *B* adj, *without strength*: Job 41 18 (*S* ⲟⲩⲟϣϥ) σαθρός.

ϯ п. *B* (*S* once), *fortify, comfort*: Ge 24 67 (*S* ⲥⲟⲗⲥⲗ), Job 4 3 (*S* ⲥⲟпⲥ), *ib* 29 25 *SB*, Ps 76 3 (*S* ⲥⲟⲗ.), *ib* 118 82 (*S* ⲥⲟпⲥп), Ro 12 8 (*S* = Gk) παρακαλεῖν; Ge 49 24 (*S* ϯ ϭⲟₐₐ), Is 50 11 (*S* do) κατισχύειν, Deu 3 28 (*S* ⲧⲁϫⲣⲟ), Ez 34 4 (*S* ϯ ϭ.) ἐνισχ., *ib* 34 27 (*S* do) ἰσχ. διδόναι; 1 Tim 1 12 (*S* do) ἐνδυναμοῦν; MG 25 290 пⲁⲩϯ п. each to other = BIF 13 106 *S* ₐₐпⲧϫⲁⲣϩⲏⲧ, BSM 53 ϯ п. to prisoners = BMis 406 *S* ⲥⲟⲗ.; ⲣⲉϥϯ п., *comforter*: BSM 15 χⲱⲣⲓⲥ ⲣ. пⲏ = BMis 349 *S* ⲁⲧⲣⲱₐₐⲉ; ₐₐⲉⲧⲣⲉϥϯ п., *comfort, encouragement*: Ro 15 4 (*S* ⲥⲟпⲥ) παράκλησις; Cat 99 visiting nunnery

εⲟвⲉⲟⲩₐₐ. of inmates.   ϯ п. nn m, *consolation* Ps 93 19 (*S* ⲥⲟⲗ.), Jer 16 7, Lu 2 25 (*S* do) παράκλησις.

ϫⲉₐₐ п. *B* (ϭₐₐ п. *S* once), *find strength, comfort*: Deu 31 6 (*S* ⲧⲁϫⲣⲟ), Is 8 9 (*S* ϭₐₐ ϭⲟₐₐ) ἰσχύειν, Ge 43 1, Jer 6 1 ἐνισχ., Ex 17 11 (*S* do), Ez 3 8 (*S* do) κατισχ.; Bar 4 5, Mt 9 2 (*S* ⲧⲱⲕ ₐₐₐₐⲟ?) θαρσεῖν; Jer 18 12 *S* (ShIF 208) *B*, Nah 2 1 (*A* ⲧⲱⲕ) ἀνδρίζεσθαι, Job 27 14 (*S* ϭₐₐ ϭ.) ἀνδροῦν; Col 2 2 (*S* ₐₐⲧⲟп) παρακαλ.; 1 Cor 16 13 (*S* ϭₐₐ ϭ.) κραταιοῦν; Ge 26 16, 2 Cor 12 10 (*S* do) δυνατὸς γίνεσθαι, εἶναι; PO 11 381 ϫ. п. *fear not*, AM 313 ₐₐⲁⲣⲉпⲉⲕϩⲏⲧ ϫ. п.

пⲉₐₐⲱⲟⲩ *B*, Is 59 5 having broken eggs ⲁϥϫⲓₐₐ пⲟⲩп. (*sic* 3 MSS) ⲟⲩⲣⲓⲟⲛ εὗρεν (*S* ⲁϥϭⲉ ⲉⲩⲟⲩⲣⲓⲟⲛ). But ? *l* ϫⲓₐₐⲓ пⲟⲩ пⲉₐₐⲱⲟⲩ ماذا اصاب فيها

пⲟⲉⲓп *S*, ⲡⲁⲓпⲉ *A*, ⲡⲟⲓпⲓ, пⲱ. *B*, ⲡⲁⲉⲓп *S*ᶠ*A²* (prob) *F*, ⲡⲁⲁпⲉ *S*ᶠ vb **a** intr, *shake, tremble*: Jud 5 4 *S*, 2 Kg 22 8 *S* (*cf* Ps 17 8 *S* ⲥⲧⲱⲧ, *B* ⲥⲟⲟⲣⲧⲉⲣ), Joel 2 10 *SA* (*B* ₐₐⲟпₐₐⲉп), Mt 28 4 *S* (*B* do), AP 18 *A²* пⲁ]ⲉⲓп σείειν; Jer 23 9 *S* (ShA 2 98, *B* ⲕⲓₐₐ), Mic 1 4 *SA* (*B* do), Ac 16 26 *SS*ᶠ (*B* do) σαλεύεσθαι; *ib* 21 30 *S* (*B* do) κινεῖσθαι; 3 Kg 1 40 *S* ῥηγνύναι; PS 6 *S* ⲁⲅп. ϩⲓпⲉⲧⲉⲣⲏⲩ, ShBMOr 8800 2 *S* when ⲕпⲁп. ⲧⲏⲣ ϩⲓⲧⲟⲗⲓⲯⲓⲥ, ShHT *H* 23 *S* drink not lest пⲧⲥⲣⲟₐₐⲣₐₐ пⲧп., MIE 2 359 *B* fish ⲉϥп. ⲥⲁпⲓϣⲱⲓ пⲡₐₐⲱⲟⲩ = BAp 87 *S* ⲉϥпⲟⲩϣⲥ, Miss 4 169 *B* dying ⲉⲩпⲱпⲓ (*sic* MS) ⲉпⲁⲓⲥⲁ пⲉₐₐϥⲁⲓ, PcodMor 54 *F* foundations of hills ⲁⲩпⲁⲉⲓп ⲁⲩϣⲧⲁⲣⲧⲏⲣ (*cf* Ps 17 8). **b** tr, *shake*: Job 9 28 *S* (*B* ⲕⲓₐₐ intr), Is 14 16 *S* (*B* ₐₐⲟп.) σεί., Mor 17 59 *S*ᶠ ⲉⲁϥпⲁⲁпⲉ ₐₐₐₐⲟⲓ ⲉₐₐⲁⲧⲉ *waking me* διασεί., Ps 59 2 *S* (*B* do), C 89 20 *B* demons п. ₐₐпⲉϥₐₐⲁ пϣⲱпⲓ συνσεί., ShA 2 326 *S* ϣⲁпⲧⲟⲩп. пⲧⲥⲩпⲁⲣⲱⲥⲓⲥ ⲧⲏⲣⲥ, Va 58 131 *B* at Judgment ⲗⲟⲅⲟⲑⲉⲧⲏⲥ ⲉϥп. ₐₐпⲁϫⲓⲣⲟⲅⲣⲁϥⲟп *brandish*.

ⲁⲧп. *S* adj, *unshaken*: Mor 17 119 ἀσάλευτος.

—— *SAB* nn m, *shaking*: Jer 29 3 *S* (*B* ₐₐⲟп.), Nah 3 2 *A* (*B* diff) σεισμός; K 158 *B* as malady пıпⲱпⲓ خران (*crisis, climax* Lane); Ryl 94 103 *S* пп. пⲡⲉⲩₐₐⲉⲗⲟⲥ from cold.

ϭⲓпп. *S*, *trembling, tremor*: ShIF 100 пⲉⲑₐₐⲕⲟ пⲧⲉϥϭ. ⲁⲩⲱ ⲧⲉϥϭⲓпⲕⲓₐₐ.

пⲟⲩп *SABFO* (PGM 1 64) nn m, *abyss of hell, depth of earth, sea*, f Lu 5 *S* & ⲛⲟⲩпⲓ (POslo), Ναῦνι (PLeyd 1 143), as sg: Ge 7 11 *SB*, Is 51 10 *SB*, Ro 10 7 *SB*, Cl 28 3 *A* ἄβυσσος; Ez 32 18 *B* (*S* ϣⲓⲕ), Lu 5 4 *S* (var ⲧп., *B* пⲉⲧϣⲏⲕ) βάθος; Ps 68 16 *SB*, 2 Cor 11 25 *S* (*B* ϣⲱⲕ) βυθός; BIF 22 107 *F*, El 50 *A* пп. ₐₐпⲁₐₐⲡⲧⲉ, KroppG *S* ₐₐⲙⲟⲟⲩ ₐₐпп. ₐₐппⲁпⲣ, My 39 *S* ⲕⲁϭ, п., ⲕⲁϭ ⲉⲧⲥⲁпⲉⲥⲏⲧ, Br 226 *S* пвⲁⲑⲟⲥ ппⲓпⲧⲏⲣϥ...ппⲟϭ ⲣϣⲁпп.;

ⲡϣⲓⲕ ⲙ̄ⲡⲏ. Job 41 23 *S* τάρταρος τῆς ἄ., Sa 10 19 *S* βάθος ἄ., ⲧⲙ̄ⲱⲧⲉ ⲙ̄ⲡⲏ. Ap 9 1 *SB* φρέαρ ἄ., J 110 28 *S*; as pl : Deu 33 13 *SB*, Ps 70 20 *SB*, *ib* 105 9 *SB*, Dan 3 54 *SA*(Cl)*B* ἄ.; ShA 1 303 *S* heavens, earth & ⲛ̄ⲡⲏ., *ib* 2 84 *S* where ⲡⲡ. ⲏ ⲡⲡ. ⲟⲩⲱⲛ ⲡⲣⲏⲧϥ, EW 5 *B* ⲁⲩϣⲑⲟⲣⲧⲉⲣ ⲛ̄ϫⲉ ⲡⲡ. In magical names : Βαινφνοῦν (PLeyd 2 145), Κομνοῦν (PGM 1 116), Φνεβεννοῦνι (POslo 44).

ⲛⲁⲛⲟⲩ- *SAA²F*, ⲛⲁⲛⲉ- *SAB*, ⲛⲁⲛⲟⲩ⸗ *SAA²F*, ⲛⲁⲛⲉ⸗ *B* vb intr (nominal vb), *be good, fair*, cf ⲁⲛⲁⲓ: Ge 1 25 *SAB*, Pro 2 10 *SAB*, Is 5 20 *SBF*, Su 2 *B* (*S* ⲛⲉⲥⲉ-), 1 Cor 5 6 *SB* καλός; Ps 53 6 *S* (*B* = Gk), Pro 1 7 *SAB*, Ro 7 12 *B* (*S* = Gk) ἀγαθός; translates εὖ- : Deu 9 2 *B* (*S* diff) εὐμήκης, Pro 11 25 *SA* εὐσχήμων; Ez 47 12 *B* ⲛⲁⲛⲉϥ ⲉⲟⲩⲱⲙ βρώσιμος; PS 49 *S* ⲛⲁⲛⲟⲩ ⲡⲉⲕⲛⲁ, ShC 73 174 *S* ⲡ. ⲧⲏⲛⲏⲥⲧⲓⲁ, *ib* 176 *S* ⲡ. ⲡⲉⲣⲃⲏⲅⲉ, C 43 29 *B* ⲡ. ⲡⲥⲁϫⲓ, RO 11 333 *B* ⲡ. ⲑⲁⲓ (*sc* ⲉⲡⲓⲥⲧⲟⲗⲏ), Aeg 251 *S* testifieth of him ϫⲉⲛⲁⲛⲟⲩϥ, PMéd 154 *S* recipe ⲛⲁⲛⲟⲩϥ ⲕⲁⲗⲱⲥ for every malady, *ib* 276 *S* ⲡ. ⲡⲓⲡⲁⲣⲣⲉ ⲉⲙⲁⲧⲉ, AM 87 *B* ⲡⲓⲥⲱⲧⲉⲙ...ⲛⲁⲛⲉϥ, Miss 4 721 *S* if I sell child ⲛⲁⲛⲟⲩϥ ϩⲁⲟⲩⲏⲣ ⲛ̄ϯⲙⲏ ? (*cf* Synax 1 322 10); impersonal + -ⲥ, *it is good, right* : Ex 16 3 *S* (*B* ⲁⲙⲟⲓ), Job 14 13 *S* (*B* do), 2 Cor 11 1 *S* (*B* do) ὄφελον; Ge 2 18 *B* (*S* ⲛⲁⲛⲟⲩ), Mt 15 26 *SB*, Gal 4 18 *SB* καλόν; ShA 1 55 *S* ⲛⲁⲛⲟⲩⲥ ⲉⲣⲱ ⲡⲧⲉⲓⲣⲉ, RNC 73 *S* ⲛⲉⲛ. ⲉⲡⲉⲁⲕϫⲟⲟⲥ (*v* ⲉⲡⲉ-), BMis 371 *S* ⲡ. ⲛ̄ⲧⲏⲙⲁⲩ = BSM 30 *B*, Aeg 252 *S* ⲡ. ⲉⲧⲣⲉϥϭⲗⲟ (var ⲛⲁⲛⲟⲩ ⲡⲣⲱϩ); *better than* c ⲉ- : Num 14 3 *SB*, Jer 22 15 *B* βελτίων; Jud 11 25 *S* ἀγαθώτερος; Pro 19 22 *SA* κρείσσων; c ⲉϩⲟⲩⲟ, ⲛ̄ϩ., ⲉϩⲟⲧⲉ : Ps 36 16 *SB*, Pro 12 9 *SA* (*B* ⲥⲟⲧⲡ̄), *ib* 24 5 *SA* ⲛⲁⲛⲟⲩ (var ⲛⲁⲛⲉ) ⲕⲣ., *ib* 8 19 *SA* (*B* ⲛⲁⲛⲉⲥ), MG 25 3 *B* βελ.; BMis 375 *S* ⲛⲁⲛⲟⲩⲥ ⲉⲧⲣⲏϯ...ⲡⲣⲟⲩⲟ ⲉⲣⲟⲥ ⲉ- = BSM 33 *B* ⲛⲁⲛⲉⲥ...ⲉϩⲟⲧⲉ ⲡⲧⲉⲡ-, LMär 11 *S* ⲙⲏ ⲛⲁⲛⲟⲩⲕ ⲡⲁⲣⲁⲣⲟⲡ, DeV 2 207 *B* your lips ⲛⲁⲛⲉϥ ⲡⲏⲓ...ⲡⲁⲣⲁ ⲟⲩⲙⲏϣ.

Rel ⲉⲛ., ⲉⲧⲛ. as adj *SAA²BF*, *good, fair* : Ge 25 8 *SB*, Is 5 9 *S* (var ⲛⲉⲥⲉ-) *BF*, AM 8 13 *SAB*, Mt 12 33 *SBF*, Jo 10 11 *SA²B* ⲕⲁⲗ.; Sa 2 7 *S* πολυτελής; BMar 190 *S* ἐπιτήδειος; Job 31 31 *S*, Ez 28 13 *SB* χρηστός; 1 Kg 24 20 *SB*, Ps 44 1 *S* (*B* = Gk), Dan 1 15 *B* (*S* ⲛⲉⲥⲉ-), Cl 30 7 *A* ἀγ.; translates εὖ- : Ps 77 11 *B* (*S* ⲡⲉⲧⲛ.) εὐεργεσία; *ib* 144 15 *B* (*S* om) εὐκαιρία, Ez 23 12 *B* (*S* ⲛⲉⲥⲉ-) εὐπάρυφος; CaiEuch 503 *B* ⲱⲛϧ̄ ⲉⲧⲛ. εὐζωΐα; Br 102 *S* ⲛⲉⲡⲧⲟⲗⲟⲟⲩⲉ ⲉⲧⲛⲁⲛⲟⲩⲟⲩ, BM 511 *F* showering ⲓⲱϯ ⲉⲧⲛⲁⲛⲟⲩⲟⲩ (*sic*), Cai 8521 *S* epitaph ⲛⲁⲡⲏ (*l* ⲁⲡⲉ) ⲉⲧⲛⲁⲛⲟⲩϥ, BMis 411 *S* ⲟⲩϣⲓ ⲉⲛⲁⲛⲟⲩϥ = BSM 56 *B*, AM 79 *B* ϯⲟⲙⲟⲗⲟⲅⲓⲁ ⲉⲑⲛⲁⲛⲉⲥ, WZKM 14 234 *S* 4 *solidi* ⲉⲛⲁⲛⲟ(ⲩ)ⲟⲩ, Tor 33 *S* sim (*cf* PAmh 89 ἄριστον), BM 1031 n 2 *S* of grain (*cf* POxy 2017 καλός opp ῥυπαρός), *wine*. Adverbial :

COAd 57 *S* ϯⲛⲁⲟⲩⲟϩⲉⲥ ⲛⲁⲕ ⲉⲛⲁⲛⲟⲩⲥ (*ib paral* ⲕⲁⲗⲱⲥ).

ⲡⲉⲧⲛ. *SAA²BF*, ⲫⲏ ⲉⲑⲛ. *B*, *that which is good* as nn sg & pl : Lev 27 14 *SB* ⲛ̄ⲡⲉⲧⲛ., Ps 34 12 *SB* ϩⲉⲛⲡⲉⲧⲛⲁⲛⲟⲩ, *ib* 132 1 *SB* ⲟⲩⲡⲉⲧⲛⲁⲛⲟⲩⲥ, Sa 4 12 *S* ⲡⲉⲧⲛⲁⲛⲟⲩⲥ, Ro 12 17 *S* ⲙ̄ⲡⲉⲧⲛⲁⲛⲟⲩϥ *B* ϩⲁⲡⲉⲑⲛⲁⲛⲉϥ ⲕⲁⲗ.; sim ἀγ. Ps 37 20 *SB*, Hos 8 3 *A*, Ro 3 8 *SB*, ἀγαθωσύνη Ps 51 3 *SB*, Eccl 7 15 *F* (*S* ⲟⲩⲡⲟϥ); translates εὖ- : Si prol *S* εὔνοια, Deu 6 3 *SB* εὖ εἶναι; ShC 73 68 *S* meditating ϩⲉⲛⲡⲉⲧⲛⲁⲛⲟⲩ, Cl 21 1 *A* ⲧⲛⲉⲓⲣⲉ ⲡ̄ⲙ̄ⲡⲉⲧⲛⲁⲛⲟⲩϥ (var -ⲛⲟⲩⲟⲩ), *ib* ⲡⲉϥⲡⲉⲧⲛⲁⲛⲟⲩϥ, C 86 353 *B* ⲟⲩⲡⲓϣϯ ⲙ̄ⲡⲉⲑⲛⲁⲛⲉϥ, *ib* 193 ⲛⲓⲡⲓϣϯ ⲡ̄ⲡⲉⲑⲛⲁⲛⲉϥ, Ap 23 *A²* sated with ⲡⲉⲧ[ⲉ]ⲛⲁⲛⲟⲩϥ ⲛⲓⲙ, BKU 1 37 *S* will help thee ϩⲏⲣⲱⲃ ⲛⲓⲙ ⲉⲛⲡⲉⲧⲛⲁⲛⲟⲩ (*cf* ἐπ’ ἀγαθῷ), BM 661 *F* that thou wouldst add ⲡⲉⲓⲡⲉⲧ(ⲛⲁ)ⲛⲟⲩϥ ϩⲓϫⲱⲡⲉⲓ ⲧⲏⲗⲟⲩ. ⲙⲁⲓⲡⲉⲧⲛ. *SB*, *loving the good* : Tit 1 8 φιλάγαθος.

ⲣ ⲡⲉⲧⲛ., ⲉⲓⲣⲉ ⲙ̄ⲡⲡⲉⲧⲛ. *SAA²BF*, *do good*; Tob 12 7 *S*, Ps 36 27 *SB*, Jo 5 29 *SA²B* ἀγαθὸν ποιεῖν, Cl 2 2 *A* desire ⲁⲣ ⲡⲉⲧⲛ. ἀγαθοποιΐα; Is 1 17 *SB*, 2 Cor 13 7 *SBF* καλ. ποι.; Ac 10 38 *SB* εὐεργετεῖν; C 43 136 *B* ⲡ̄ⲡⲉⲑⲛⲁⲛⲉϥ ⲉⲡⲁⲥⲓⲣⲓ ⲙ̄ⲙⲱⲟⲩ; c ⲛ- dat : Jud 17 13 *S*, Ps 48 18 *S* (*B* = Gk) ἀγαθύνειν; EpJer 37 *BF* εὖ ποι.; BG 138 *S* ⲁϥⲉⲓⲣⲉ ⲛⲁⲩ ⲛ̄ⲙ̄ⲡⲉⲧⲛⲁⲛⲟⲩⲟⲩ; c ⲉ- : Ge 12 16 *B* (*S* ⲙ̄ⲡ-) εὖ χρᾶσθαι; c ⲙ̄ⲡ- : Nu 10 32 *S* (*B* ⲉⲣ ⲁⲅⲁⲑⲟⲛ) εὖ ποι., Ps 12 6 *F* (MR 5 34, *SB* ⲡ-) εὐεργ. acc ; BSM 59 *B* ⲁⲕϣⲁⲡⲉⲣ ⲡⲉⲑⲛ. ⲡⲉⲙⲏⲓ = BMis 418 *S* ⲣ ⲡⲡⲁ, AZ 23 38 *F* ⲉⲗ ⲡⲉⲧⲛⲁⲛⲟⲩⲃ ⲙⲉⲡⲉⲓⲕⲁⲡⲗⲱⲙⲓ. ⲣⲉϥⲣ ⲡⲉⲧⲛ., *doer of good, benefactor* : Sa 19 13 *S*, Lu 22 25 *SB* εὐεργέτης; BG 54 *S* Father is ⲟⲩⲣⲉϥⲣ ⲡⲡⲉⲧⲛ., AM 268 *B* Christ ⲡⲉⲣⲡ. ⲙ̄ⲡⲧ-, ⲙⲉⲧⲣⲉϥⲣ ⲡⲉⲧⲛ., *beneficence* : Z 330 *S* εὐεργεσία; C 86 272 *B* ϯⲙ. of gods, J 86 13 *S* law admonisheth ⲉⲅⲙ. ⲥⲁ ⲙ̄ⲡⲉⲧⲛ. *B*, *doer of good, righteous* : 1 Pet 2 14 (*S* ⲣⲉϥⲣ ⲡⲉⲧⲛ.) ἀγαθοποιός; Mt 13 49 (*SF* = Gk) δίκαιος.

ⲛⲏⲛⲓ *B* nn m f (once), *honeycomb* : Ps 18 10 (*S* ⲙⲟⲩⲗϩ̄) κηρίον, cit MG 25 159, 198 (ⲛⲏⲛⲓ sic MS), AM 61, C 89 172, Va 63 26; K 199 ⲛⲏⲛ. مـح ; Cat 84 plants whence bees ⲑⲁⲙⲓⲟ ⲛ̄ⲫⲏⲛ.

ⲛⲓⲛⲉ *F* nn, *nothing* (?) : Hos 7 16 (JEA 11 245) ⲁⲩϣⲱⲡⲉ ⲉⲅⲛ. (*SA* ⲡⲉⲧϣⲟⲩⲉⲓⲧ, *B* ϩⲗⲓ) οὐδέν. Cf ? *ib* 2 10 (*lc* 244) (ⲡ)ⲡⲉϩⲓⲛⲉ ϣ ⲡⲉϩⲙⲥ (*A* ⲗⲁⲅⲉ, *B* ϩⲗⲓ) οὐδείς.

ⲛⲟⲛⲓ (5 MSS, var ⲛⲟⲡⲓ 5 MSS) *B* vb intr, *fall down* : K 234 ⲁϥⲛ. طـفـ انهدم.

ⲛⲟⲩⲛⲉ *SA*, -ⲛⲓ *BF* nn f, *root* : Deu 29 18 *SB*, Job 13 27 *B* (*S* ⲁⲣⲏϫ⸗), Pro 12 3 *SAB*, Is 5 24 *SBF*, Mt 13 21 *SBF*, Va 57 214 *B* ⲟⲩⲣⲓⲥⲁ ⲡⲧⲉ ⲑⲛ. ῥίζα,

Ps 51 5 *SB* ῥίζωμα; PS 157 *S* ϣоϥ...теϥп. (*v* Harris & Mingana *Odes Solom* 2 326 & *cf* Is 14 29 Vulg), El 64 *A* every tree ипточп., AM 73 *B* descended евоλ ϫепочп. естаιночт, PMéd 292 *S* тп. of tooth, *ib* 308 *S* in recipe п. пϫпп, TurM 9 *S* sim п. пкепаріс.　　пеϫ п. евоλ *S*, put forth root : Job 5 3 (*B* ϩι- ев.), Hos 14 6 (*A* ϫо ав., *B* do) ῥ. βάλλειν;　　рет п. *B*, meaning same : Is 37 31 (*S* ϫе п.) ῥίζαν φύειν;　　ϫε, ϫι п. *S*, ϭе п. *B*, take root : Job 31 8 *S* (*B* рωт) Gk diff, C 43 123 *B* devil ϭе п. пϩнтк;　　+ евоλ *SB* : Is 40 24 *S* (*B* п. ϣωπι), Col 2 7 *SB*, CaiEuch 502 *B* may concord ϭе п. ев. in us ῥιζοῦν; Sa 12 10 *S* ἔμφυτος (γίν.); ShC 42 141 *S* tree that would ϫι п. ев. пϩнточ, BSG 184 *S* if dead wood ϫι п. ев. = *ib* 15 *B* ϣεп п.;　　ϭеп, ϣеп п. *B* meaning same : Jer 12 2 (*S* ϫе п. ев.) C 86 293 wooden pillar аϥϣ. п. ῥιζοῦν; Va 57 176 φύ.;　　р п. *S*, meaning same : ShMIF 23 74 lest it be planted ϫεеспар п.

—— *B* nn m, *radish*: K 194, Bodl 325 151 пιп. فجل.

ппе- *SA²BF*, пе- *S* (Si) *AA²* pref neg 3 fut: Ex 20 15 *SB*, Ps 33 20 *SB* оὐκ; Job 5 21 *SA*(Cl)*B*, Zeph 1 12 *AB*, Lu 9 27 *S* (*B* псепа- ап) оὐ μή; PS 106 *S* ппеϥпточ еϩраι until now, J 75 23 *S* епекеϣ поϫϥ евоλ.　　vetitive : Ge 44 6 *B*, 2 Kg 1 21 *S* (paral иптре-), Ps 40 2 *SB* μή.　　final : Ps 118 37 *S* (*B* еϣтеи-) тò μή, *ib* 9 38 *S* (*B* ϩιпа птеϣтеи-), Jo 4 15 *SA²* (*B* do, *F* кес птеϣ.), AP 8 *A²* ϫекаасе епочϫι ϩеι ἵνα μή, Ps 77 44 *S* (*B* ϩопωс птеϣ.) ὅπως μή, *ib* 16 4 *SF* (*B* птеϣ.) ὅπ. ἂν μή, PS 49 *S* паϫиет...ϫеппаωис, BMar 43 *S* I have bought shroud ϫεкас ппеϥкост ϩпочкаісе пϣииο, JKP 2 236 *S* art exalted like elect ϫип- пιϫ οос ϫекϫосе ероοч *not to say*.

пно *S* neg imperat of 3 fut, *it shall not be, no*: Mt 21 30 (*B* п ϯΟуωϣ ап) оὐ θέλω, cit Tri 393 Ϥ; TT 98 what is word thou hast said ϫеп. ? = MG 17 396 Ϥ.

пепеве, пепеев *O* nn, *styrax* (?): DM 11 22, *cf* لبنى (*v* Rec 16 148).　　In place-name (?): Σενινήβις (BGU 557).

пοунн *v* епп.

пοунте *A* *v* пοуте.

папаι *B* Is 41 7, prob *l* п-апаι. *V* Addenda.

папре, папне (PS), пепре *S*, паϥрι *B*, пепрι *F* nn f, *grain, seed*: Mt 13 31 *BF* (*S* вλвιλе) of mustard, Jo 12 24 *B* (*SA²* do) of wheat κόκκος; Lev 19 10 *B* (*S* do), Is 65 8 *B* (*S* do) single *grape* ῥώξ; Bor 265 93 *S* οуп. пте песиаϫ, PMéd 190 *S* пιпι (*l* ? кικι) пепре, P 129¹⁴ 124 *S* found оуп. псоуο on palace floor = C 41 16 *B*, PS 187 ff *S* shall seem (as small) as оуп. пϣοιϣ *grain, speck*

of dust, DeV 85 *B* пιп. пϣω of sand on shore. In name (or ? place) : Κουννεπρεῖ (Preisigke).　　*Cf* ? евра.

паре-, пере- *v* пе- verbal prefix.

пοупре, -λе(PMéd)*S*, пοупрι *BF* nn f m, *vulture*: Lev 11 13 *B* (*S* = Gk) γρύψ (var γύψ) مرحم (*l* رخم), but *ib* 14 *S* п. ικτίν; Deu 14 12 *B* (Lag пιп., Va ϯп., *S* = Gk) γρύψ (var γύψ) عقاب, Job 5 7 *S* (*B* аϫωи), *ib* 15 23 *S* (*B* поϣер *sic l*) γύψ; K 168 *B* ϯп. رخم, AZ 3 48, Ann 1 52 *B* пιп. عنذب griffon, (*cf* K 169 ϯпрιψ عنقاب); PS 318 *S* оуϩο пп., BMar 58 *S* demon darted forth пϭе пοупοупре (*cf* Byz Z 30 327), BAp 122 *S* birds & ϩепп. gathered at carcase, PMéd 56 *S* gall of тп., *ib* 299 *S* blood of п., BKU 1 26 (8116 b) *F* тп.;　　иас пп. : Job 5 7 *SB* νεοσσὸς γυ.　　*V* Spg 78 n.

пас *B* : Is 13 22 еγеϫϥе пас ϭеппеспι (*S* иιсе) νοσσοποιεῖν. ? *l* иас (Dévaud) or ϫϩо пас (dat).

пΟус *S* nn m, meaning unknown, among abusive terms : ShC 73 59 none may call his brother пοуϫ, λакуϣа, п., потнс, ипο &c.　　Or *l* ? оус *q v*.

песе- *SB*, песо∞ *SAA²BF*, песо∞ *SAF* vb intr (nominal vb), *be beautiful, cf* са vb : Ge 3 6 *B*, Si 15 9 *S*, Is 63 1 *S* (*B* саι), Mt 23 27 *SB* ὡραῖος, 2 Kg 1 26 *B* (*S* сωтп) ὡραιοῦσθαι; Ge 12 14 *S* (*B* папе-), Cant 1 15 *S*, Su 2 *S* (*B* do) καλός, Deu 21 11 *S* еп. ϩрас (*B* епапес ϭеппессаι) κ. τῷ εἴδει; translates εὐ- : Ge 12 11 *SB* εὐπρόσωπος, 2 Kg 1 23 *S* (*B* diff) εὐπρεπής, Ps 150 5 *SB* εὔηχος, Aeg 245 *S* п. пеϥсиот εὔτροπος, AP 14 *A²* пто песω, GFr 440 *S* еп. ϩрас εὔμορφος;　　Ex 2 2 *A* (*B* = Gk), Ac 7 20 *S* (*BF* do) ἀστεῖος; 2 Kg 14 25 *S* (var glossed еϥтнϣ) αἰνετός; ShZ 600 *S* п. пеγκos- иос, ShBor 246 18 *S* песω (O soul), TstAb 177 *B* епесωк ипаιрнϯ *how fair art thou*, Mor 30 36 *F* епесωϥ ϩипеϥсеι = BMis 261 *S*, opp песе- *q v*; *more beautiful than* с е-, еϩоуе, еϩоте : Sa 13 3 *S* βελτίων, Aeg 40 *B* етп. еуепос пιвеп, Ez 28 3 *S* песωк е- (whence *B* οι псаιе, but prob *l* песвωк) σοφώτερος, Sa 7 29 *S* п. еϩоуепрн (*B* саιе еϩоте) εὐπρεπέστερος.

Rel еп., етп. as adj, *beautiful*: Is 3 25 *S* (*B* сωтп), Ez 16 13 *SB* καλ., Sa 5 17 *S* τοῦ κάλλους; Lev 23 40 *S* (*B* саι), Ac 3 10 *S* (*B* саιе) ὡρ.; Zech 10 3 *AB* εὐπρεπής; Dan 1 15 *S* (*B* папе) ἀγ.; Ps 80 3 *B* (*S* потι) τερπνός; El 44 *A* (оу)поλιс епе- сωс, BHom 32 *S* пеϫорос етпесωϥ of stars, AM 228 *B* flowers еθпесωоу.　　петп., *that which is beautiful* as nn : Lam 2 2 *S* (ShC 73 77) петпесω- оу (*B* иетсаιе), Ac 3 2 *S* про...петпесωϥ (*B* саιе)

ⲱⲣ.; Bor 253 266 S Joseph ⲡⲉⲧⲛⲉⲥⲱϥ πάγκαλος ;
PS 33 S ⲧⲉⲧⲡⲉⲥⲱⲥ in her speech.

ⲛⲏⲥⲉ S nn f, *bench, seat* (?): BM 329 ⲧ]ⲛ. [ⲉⲧ-
ϩⲁ]ⲣⲧⲁⲓⲡϣⲏⲓ of church, *ib* lay blinded ϩⲁ·ⲣ[ⲧⲏ]ⲧⲛ.
ⲁⲡ[ⲧⲟ]ⲡⲟⲥ both = BMOr 4723 40 باب البيعة
(though scarcely a translation), J 43 25 house ⲉⲧ-
ⲉⲣⲉⲧⲡⲟϭ ⲡⲛ. ϩⲓⲱⲱϥ, Ryl 252 builder's account
ϩⲁⲧⲛ. ⲡⲧⲁⲓⲕⲟⲧⲉ spending 2 days thereon, PMich
3591 6 wine account ϩⲁⲧⲛ. ⲕⲟⲗⲗ[ⲁθⲁ x (? place-
name).

ⲛⲟⲩⲥⲉ (or ? ⲟⲩⲥⲉ) S nn f, meaning unknown :
KroppA Hôr weepeth & crieth ⲁⲓϣⲓⲥⲉ ⲟⲩⲟϩ ⲉⲥⲁϣϭⲉ ⲡⲛ. & not one of them hath slept, *ib* ⲉⲓⲟⲩⲱϣ
ⲉⲥⲁϣϭⲉ ⲡⲟⲩⲥⲉ (*sic bis*). Charm to bring sleep.

(ⲛⲉⲥⲃⲟ), ⲡⲉⲥⲃⲱⲟⲩ S vb intr, *be wise*, cf ⲥⲃⲟ :
Deu 4 6 ⲗⲁⲟⲥ ⲉⲡⲉⲥⲃⲱⲟⲩϥ (B ⲥⲁⲃⲉ) ἐπιστήμων, 3
Kg 3 12 ⲟⲩϩⲏⲧ ⲡⲥⲁⲃⲉ ⲉⲡⲉⲥⲃⲱⲟⲩϥ σοφός, Sa 14 2
ⲧⲥⲟⲫⲓⲁ ⲉⲧⲡⲉⲥⲃⲱⲟⲥ σ. τεχνίτης. *Cf* ⲡⲉⲥⲉ- (Ez
28 3).

ⲡⲟⲩⲥⲑ O *v* ⲡⲟⲩϣⲡ.

ⲡⲟⲩⲥϩ A *v* ⲡⲟⲩⲱϣⲥ.

ⲡⲁⲧ SB, ⲡⲏⲧ, ⲡⲉⲧ S nn m, *a loom*: Is 38 12
SB, *ib* 59 6 SB, Va 57 142 B ⲡⲉⲥⲡ. ⲉⲡⲁⲥⲉⲣ ϩⲱⲃ
ⲉⲣⲟϥ ἱστός; K 125, 257 B منسج , نول ; ShIF 148
S ⲡⲉⲧⲡⲛ. ⲡⲁⲣ ϭⲟⲓⲧⲉ ⲛⲏⲧⲛ ⲁⲡ, ShP 131⁴ 111 S garments ⲡⲡⲉⲧ ⲉⲧⲟⲩⲥⲱϩⲉ ϩⲓⲱⲱϥ, Ep 351 S ⲟⲩⲛⲧⲁⲓ
ϩⲉⲛⲕⲁⲓⲣⲉⲁ (κειρίαι) ⲧⲁⲗⲏⲩ ⲉⲡⲛ., *ib* 352 S will
bring 2 camels & set up ⲡⲛ., Miss 4 232 S ⲡ.
ⲡⲧⲁⲗⲉ ϩⲃⲟⲟⲥ fixed in clay, J 27 26 ff S sale of ⲡⲏⲧ
ⲧⲏⲣϥ situate in yard ϫⲓⲡⲡⲉϥⲥⲡⲧⲉ ϣⲁⲣⲁⲧⲏⲩ, Osir
11, 12 S nun's title ⲧⲁⲡⲉ ⲡⲡⲛⲏⲧ (*cf* ἱστωνάρχης),
ib 16 S guard Thou ⲡⲣⲱⲙⲉ (*sc* nuns) ⲙⲡⲉ(ⲡ)ⲡⲏⲧ,
R 1 5 42 S weaver laid the needle upon ⲡⲛ. (*cf*
Synax 2 119 18, *l* حائكا , not حاذق), CO 466 S ⲕⲉⲗⲕⲓⲗ ⲡⲡⲉⲧ, var Univ College Lond ⲕ. ⲡⲡⲉⲧ ⲡⲡⲟⲩ-
ⲱϫⲉ ⲕⲉⲣϩ, COAd 46 S send me ⲡⲛ., Mor 51 38 S
v ⲕⲗⲗⲉ ⲁ. ϣⲉ ⲡⲛ. S some wooden part of
loom (weaver's beam 1 Kg 17 7 S ϩⲟ ⲛⲥⲱϩⲉ): ShP
130⁴ 157 ⲟⲩϣⲉ ⲡⲛ. ⲡⲟⲩⲉϩ ⲧⲁⲓⲛ, CO 355 give…
& ⲡϣⲉ ⲡⲡⲏⲧ to bearer of this, Hall 98 send ⲟⲩϣⲉ
ϫⲉ(ⲉ)ⲡⲁⲧⲟⲟⲕ (ⲧⲱϭ) ⲡⲉⲓⲁⲁⲧ. b *web* : Is 59 5
SB ⲓⲟ. of spider, Mor 18 123 S wool & linen ⲉⲩⲡ
ϩⲉⲡⲡ. ⲡⲣⲏⲧⲟⲩ ⲙⲡⲟⲩϫⲛⲟϥⲉ ἱστῶνες καὶ βάμματα.
V Ep 1 68, 155.

ⲡⲁⲓⲁⲧ *v* ⲉⲓⲁ *eye* s f & ⲡⲁⲁ-.

ⲡⲁⲏⲧ *v* ⲡⲁ *have pity*.

ⲡⲏⲧ, ⲡⲉⲧ *v* ⲡⲁⲧ.

ⲡⲟⲉⲓⲧ, ⲡⲁⲉⲓⲧ, ⲡⲱⲓⲧ, ⲡⲁⲏⲧ *v* ⲡⲟⲩⲧ.

ⲡⲟⲩⲧ SABF, ⲡⲁⲧⲟⲩ S, ⲡⲟⲧⲟⲩ B, ⲡⲉⲧⲟⲩ F, ⲡⲁⲧ† (?)

F vb a tr, *grind, pound* corn &c : Nu 11 8 SB, R
1 4 73 S ⲉⲩⲡⲁⲛ. ⲁⲙⲟⲓ by beast's teeth ἀλήθειν,
Is 47 2 SB ἀλεῖν, Deu 9 21 B (S ⲣ ϣⲏⲙ ϣⲏⲙ)
καταλεῖν; Bodl(P) a l d S mill ⲉϣⲁⲥⲡ. ⲡⲥⲱⲙⲁ ⲡⲓⲙ,
Ep 297 S ⲡⲥⲉⲥⲓⲕⲧ ⲟⲩⲙⲁⲭⲉ ⲡⲥⲟⲩⲟ ⲡⲥⲉⲡⲁⲧⲉ ⲡⲡⲟⲉⲓⲧ
ⲉϥϣⲟⲟⲙⲉ *grind…pound* (cf Reil *Beiträge* 151 κόπτειν, ἀλεῖν), ST 285 S ⲡⲥⲟⲩⲟ ⲁⲓⲡⲁⲧⲟⲩ, BM 527
F raven's blood ⲉⲕⲁⲡⲉⲧⲉϥ ϩⲓⲣⲉⲙϫ. b *intr* :
Eccl 12 3 S, Mt 24 41 SB ἀλήθειν, Deu 24 6 S
ⲡⲉϣⲁⲩⲡ. ϩⲓⲱⲱϥ that whereon is ground cf Ps & Si
below (B diff as Gk) ἐπιμύλιον, Lam 5 13 SB Gk
om ; El 34 A ⲉⲩⲡ….ⲡⲟⲩⲙⲏⲭⲁⲡⲛ, ShC 42 210 S
turning about like ⲧⲉⲧⲛ., DeV 2 91 B Zedekiah
in captivity ⲉⲩⲡ. ϩⲉⲛⲡⲓⲧⲣⲓⲙⲩⲗⲗⲓⲟⲛ, CO 145 S
ⲡⲱⲡⲉ ⲡⲛ., CO 361 S ⲡⲁⲡϩⲁⲗⲱⲙⲁ ⲙ[ⲡ]ⲡⲃⲉⲕⲉ ⲡ.
milling wage, PMich 3593 F ⲧⲓⲁⲧⲓ ⲟⲩⲉⲗⲧⲁⲃ ⲉⲥⲟⲩⲁ
ⲡⲉⲃ ⲉⲧⲡⲁⲧ [ⲁϩ]ⲁ ⲥⲡⲉⲩ ⲗⲁⲕ (ⲉ)ⲡⲉϩ ⲡⲉⲃ ⲛⲧⲡⲁⲧ.
As nn, *grinding, mill* (?): Lam *l c* B (S ⲙⲁ ⲡⲛ.) Gk
om ; ShC 73 146 S ⲡⲥⲓⲕⲉ (var ⲡⲟⲉⲓⲕ *l*? ⲥⲉⲓⲕ(ⲉ)) ⲛ
ⲡⲛ.; *receptacle* : Ps 113 8 S (B = Gk) λίμνη
of waters, Si 39 24 (17) S sim ἀποδοχεῖον (cf *ib* 50
3 ⲥⲟⲟⲩϩⲥ), Miss 4 634 S ⲟⲩⲡ. ⲙⲙⲟⲟⲩ in desert
= C 41 9 B ϣⲏⲓ (same ?) V Spg *Kopt Etym* 41).
ⲙⲁ ⲡⲛ., *milling place, mill* : Nu 11 8 S (B ⲉⲩⲡⲓ)
μύλος, Va 63 89 B serving maid ϩⲉⲛⲟⲩⲙ. μυλωθρίς
BAp 158 S ⲡⲙ. where Samson wrought, Bor 264
38 S Hezekiah (*sic*) ran after horses' dust in ⲡⲙ.
(cf DeV above), P 131⁶ 33 S in hell ⲥⲉⲧⲁⲁⲡ ⲙⲙ.
ⲙⲡⲧⲁⲣⲧⲁⲣⲟⲥ. ⲣⲉϥⲡ., *grinder* : P 44 62 S ἀλέτης,
cf ⲫⲏ ⲉⲧⲡ. K 112 B طحان .

ⲡⲟⲉⲓⲧ S, ⲡⲁⲉⲓⲧ A, ⲡⲱⲓⲧ B, ⲡⲁⲏⲧ, ⲡⲁⲓⲧ F nn m,
meal of any kind : Jud 6 19 S, 2 Kg 17 28 S, Is 47
2 SB, Hos 8 7 AB, Mt 13 33 SBF ἄλευρον, Nu 5
15 S ⲡ. ⲡⲉⲓⲱⲧ (B om) ἄ. κρίθινον ; 1 Kg 25 18 S,
Jth 10 5 S ἄλφιτον ; Ge 18 6 S (var ⲥⲁⲙⲓⲧ, B =
Gk) σεμίδαλις ; P 55 8 B ⲡⲡⲛ. دقيق , P 44 85 S
ⲕⲟⲗⲗⲁⲣⲓⲟⲛ · ⲡ. خبز , قرصة *loaf*, Z 630 S ⲡ.
ⲡⲟϩⲁⲣⲙⲟⲩⲥ, PMéd 111 S ⲡ. ⲛⲁⲣϣⲓⲛ, *ib* 185 S ⲡ.
ⲡϣⲱⲃⲉ, *ib* 318 S ⲡ. ⲛⲥⲟⲩϭ ; ShC 73 146 S ⲃⲓⲣ
ⲡⲛ., *ib* 147 ⲡⲉϫ ⲡⲛ. ⲉⲧⲗⲁϩⲙ, BSM 32 B we have
not ⲡ. ⲟⲩⲇⲉ ⲥⲟⲩⲟ=Mor 27 28 F ⲡⲁⲓⲧ=BMis 375
S ⲟⲉⲓⲕ, Ep 297 S ⲡ. ⲉϥϣⲟⲟⲙⲉ (*v* above), ST 282
S ⲛⲧⲡⲟⲩⲟϣⲙ ⲡⲕⲟⲩⲓ ⲡⲛ., Montp 207 B ⲭⲱ ⲁⲡⲛ.
الكنبوت (?) (Bevan κιβωτός كيبوت) وهو موضع الدقيق .
ⲣ ⲡ., *become, produce meal* : ShZ 503 S a sheaf not
full (enough) ⲉⲧⲣⲉϥⲣ ⲡ. In place-names (?) :
Σασνοειτ (PLond 4 258), ⲡⲉⲣϭ·ⲡⲟⲉⲓⲧ S. of Antinoe
(Mor 47 195).

ⲛⲧⲁ F, ⲛⲧⲟ S *v* ⲁⲛⲟⲕ.

ⲛⲧⲉ-, SA²BFO (Hor 82,,83), ⲧⲉ- SABF, pref of
conjunct. *V* Stern 440 ff, Sdff 280 ff, Till 139,
Mallon 249 ff, *V* also ϣⲁ- prep (ϣⲁⲛⲧⲉ-).

ⲛⲧⲉ *SA* (rare) *B*, ⲛⲧⲁⳅ *SB*, ⲛⲧⲉⳅ *A*[2], ⲛⲧⲏⳅ *SfF*, particle of gen (oftenest in *B* & PS, Br), used **a** for greater precision than ⲛ- (Stern 295): Nu 18 2 *SB* ⲡⲁⲏⲙⲟⲥ ⲛ. ⲡⲉⲕⲉⲓⲱⲧ (var ⲛ-), Deu 22 17 *SB* ⲡⲛⲟϭ ⲛ. ⲧⲡⲟⲗⲓⲥ, Cant 1 tit *S* ⲡϫⲱ ⲛ. ⲛⲉϫⲱ, Jo 12 34 *S* ⲡϣⲏⲣⲉ ⲙⲡⲣⲱⲙⲉ... ⲡⲉⲓϣⲏⲣⲉ ⲛ. ⲡⲣⲱⲙⲉ, AM 175 *B* ⲧϥⲁϣⲓ ⲛ. ⲡⲓⲉⲭⲱⲣⲅ (144 sim ⲙⲡⲓ.); or ? ceremoniously: Zech 4 6 *SB* ⲡϣⲁϫⲉ ⲛ. ⲡϫⲟⲉⲓⲥ (*A* ⲛ-), Mt 25 34 *SB* ⲛⲉⲧⲥⲙⲁⲙⲁⲁⲧ ⲛ. ⲡⲁⲉⲓⲱⲧ, PS 46 *S* ⲡⲟⲩⲟⲉⲓⲛ ⲛ. ⲡⲓⲟⲩⲟⲉⲓⲛ, *ib* 333 *S* ⲡⲛⲓϥⲉ ⲛ. ⲧⲉⲩⲧⲁⲡⲣⲟ (but *ib* 36 ⲛⲛ. ⲛⲧⲉⲩⲧ.), Bor 263 36 *S* call Thee ϣⲏⲣⲉ ⲛ. ⲡⲡⲛⲉ̄, them ⲡϣ. ⲙⲡⲡⲛⲉ̄. **b** where preceding word has indef art: Ps 101 6 *S* ⲟⲩϭⲣⲓⲙ ⲛ. ⲡϫⲁⲓⲉ (*B* diff), He 1 3 *B* ⲟⲩⲧⲟⲩⲃⲟ ⲛ. ⲡⲛⲟⲃⲓ (*SF* ⲛ-), Is 19 11 *B* ϩⲁⲛϣⲏⲣⲓ ⲛ. ⲡⲓⲟⲩⲣⲱⲟⲩ (*S* ⲛ-), BG 123 *S* ⲟⲩⲭⲁⲣⲓⲥ ⲛ. ⲡⲉⲓⲱⲧ, CA 89 *S* ϩⲉⲛⲉⲡⲧⲟⲗⲏ ⲛ. ⲡⲡⲛⲉ̄, C 43 162 *B* ⲟⲩⲙⲁⲧⲟⲓ ⲛ. ⲡⲁϭⲥ̄, *ib* 86 91 *B* ϩⲁⲛϣⲏⲣⲓ ⲛ. ⲧⲙⲉⲧⲟⲩⲣⲟ. **c** between 2 names (persons or places): Nu 13 23 *S* ϫⲁⲁⲡⲉ ⲛ. ⲕⲏⲙⲉ (*B* diff), AM 86 *B* ⲛⲣⲁⲓ ⲛ. ⲧⲁⲙⲙⲱⲟⲩ, EW 46 *B* ⲣⲁⲕⲟϯ ⲑⲛ ⲛ. ⲡⲓⲫⲁⲣⲟⲥ; less often with one: Jud 12 5 *S* ⲛⲉⲧⲧⲟⲩϩⲏⲩ ⲛ. ⲉⲫⲣⲁⲉⲙ, Ez 21 19 *B* ⲡⲟⲩⲣⲟ ⲛ. ⲃⲁⲃⲩⲗⲱⲛ; in episcopal list Miss 8 61 ff ⲛ. & ⲛ- vary: ⲟⲩⲁⲗⲉⲣⲓⲟⲥ ⲛ. ϩⲓⲕⲟⲡⲓⲟⲥ = ⲟⲩⲁ. ⲛⲣⲓⲕ. **d** after foregoing gen or after attribute (adj or rel): Ps 46 9 *S* ⲡϣⲱⲣⲉ ⲙⲡⲕⲁϩ ⲛ. ⲡⲡⲛⲉ̄, Mt 1 1 *B* ⲡϫⲱⲙ ⲙⲙⲓⲥⲉ ⲛ. ⲓⲏ̄ⲥ (var ⲛ-), Jo 3 18 *SA*[2] ⲡⲣⲁⲛ ⲙⲡϣⲏⲣⲛⲟⲩⲱⲧ ⲛ. ⲡⲡⲛⲉ̄, Z 273 *S* ⲧⲉⲓⲭⲁⲣⲓⲥ ⲛⲧⲉⲓϭⲟⲧ ⲛ. ⲡⲉⲭⲥ̄; Jud 7 8 *S* ⲣⲱⲙⲉ ⲛⲓⲙ ⲛ. ⲡⲓⲏ̄ⲗ, Is 30 13 *BF* ⲟⲩⲥⲟⲃⲧ ⲉϥⲛⲁϩⲉ ⲛ. ⲟⲩⲃⲁⲕⲓ (*S* ⲛ-), Br 90 *S* ⲡⲛⲟϭ ⲡⲣⲁⲛ ⲛ. ⲡⲉⲕⲓⲱⲧ, Va 57 13 *B* ϯⲙⲉⲧⲗⲁⲧⲟⲓ ⲡⲣⲟⲩⲟ ⲛ. ⲧⲡⲗⲉⲟⲛⲉⳅⲓⲁ τὸ πλεονέκτειν, *ib* ϯⲁⲕⲧⲏⲙⲟⲥⲩⲛⲏ ⲛ. ⲡⲓϫⲱⲗ ⲉⲃⲟⲗ ἀκτημοσύνη (often in this MS in such redundant phrases), ShC 73 42 *S* ϩⲱⲃ ⲛⲓⲙ ⲉⲧⲉⲁϩⲉ ⲛⲁⲩ ⲛ. ⲡⲥⲱⲙⲁ; often after ⲧⲏⲣ: Deu 28 1 *SB* ⲡⲉⲑⲛⲟⲥ ⲧⲏⲣⲟⲩ ⲛ. ⲡⲕⲁϩ, El 60 *A* ⲛⲓⲃⲛⲟⲩⲉ ⲧⲏⲣⲟⲩ ⲛ. ⲡⲡⲛⲉ̄, PS 199 *S* ⲛⲧⲉⲡⲟⲥ ⲧⲏⲣϥ ⲛ. ⲡⲣⲱⲙⲉ. **e** *B* after strong art: Ps 115 3 ⲛⲓⲡⲁⲕⲣⲓ ⲛ. ⲫⲓⲟⲩ (*S* ⲛ-), Jer 26 24 ⲡⲓⲗⲁⲟⲥ ⲛ. ⲡⲉⲙⲣⲓⲧ, Va 57 15 ϯⲥⲡⲟⲩⲁⲛ ⲛ. ⲡⲓⲧⲉⲡⲟⲥ, MG 25 273 ⲡⲓⲭⲓⲛⲛⲁⲩ ⲛ. ⲡⲓⲃⲁⲗ.

ⲛⲧⲁⳅ &c, indicating possession, ownership (esp in *B*): Ge 34 15 *S* ϩⲟⲟⲩⲧ ⲛⲓⲙ ⲛⲧⲉⲧⲏⲩⲧⲛ ὑμῶν, Jud 11 34 *B* ⲟⲩϣⲉⲣⲓ... ⲙⲙⲉⲣⲓⲧ ⲛⲧⲁϥ (*S* ⲛⲁϥ) αὐτῷ, Lev 11 8 *S* ⲛⲉⲧⲙⲟⲟⲩⲧ ⲛⲧⲁⲩ *B* ⲛⲧⲱⲟⲩ (*S* var ⲛϩⲏⲧⲟⲩ) αὐτῶν, Ps 16 14 *BF* ⲛⲏ ⲉⲧϩⲛ ⲛⲧⲁⲕ (*S* ⲡⲉⲕⲡⲉⲑⲛⲡ) σου, 1 Kg 17 40 *B* ϥⲏ ⲉⲡⲁⲩⲛⲧⲁϥ ⲙⲙⲁⲩ (*S* ⲉϥϣⲟⲟⲡ ⲛⲁϥ) τῷ ὄντι αὐτῷ, Is 54 10 *B* ⲡⲓⲛⲁⲓ ⲛⲧⲏⲓ (*S* ⲡⲁⲕⲉ-) παρ' ἐμοῦ, Am 9 11 *SB* (*A* ⲛⲧⲛ-) αὐτῆς, Mt 13 44 *SBF* ὅσα ἔχειν, Jo 5 37 *SA*[2]*B* αὐτοῦ, C 89 27 *B* among nuns ⲟⲩⲓ ⲛⲧⲁϥ ἴδια αὐτοῦ, 1 Cor 8 9 *SF* ⲧⲉⲓⲉⳅⲟⲩⲥⲓⲁ ⲛⲧⲉⲧⲏⲩⲧⲛ (*B* ⲛⲉⲧⲉⲛ- ⲫⲁⲓ) ὑμῶν; Br 125 *S* ⲟⲩⲛⲟϭ ⲛⲁⲩⲡⲁⲙⲓⲥ ⲛⲧⲁϥ, ShC

73 71 *S* Abel offered ⲛⲉⲧⲥⲟⲧⲡ ⲛⲧⲁϥ, AM 29 *B* ϥⲣⲁⲛ ⲙⲡⲁϭⲥ̄ ⲓⲏ̄ⲥ ⲛⲧⲏⲓ, Mor 27 8 *F* ⲙ(ⲛ) ⲙⲛⲧⲭⲉⲕⲓ ⲛⲧⲏⲩ = BMis 327 *S* ϩⲁⲣ̄ⲧⲏⲩ = BSM 10 *B* ⲍⲉⲡⲧⲟⲩⲙⲏ(ϯ), C 43 131 *B* ϥⲉⲡⲧⲏⲓ ⲙⲙⲁⲩ ⲛϫⲉ ⲡⲁϭⲥ̄, Sph 10 142 *S* ⲛⲧϫⲟⲟⲥ ⲛⲁⲡⲁⲡⲓⲁⲥ ⲛⲧⲁⲕ *thy* (*friend, man* ?) *A.*, J 5 52 *S* ⲧⲉ(ⲓ)ⲡⲣⲁⲥⲓⲥ ⲛ ⲙⲉⲣⲟⲥ ⲛⲧⲁⲥ. With ⲟⲩⲟⲛ, ⲙⲙⲟⲛ (*S* as ⲟⲩⲛ-, ⲙⲙⲛ-, ⲙⲛ-), *there is, is not..., have, not have*, v ⲟⲩⲟⲛ, ⲙⲙⲛ-. Rel ⲉⲧⲛⲧⲁⳅ, ⲡⲉⲧⲛⲧⲁⳅ *S*, ⲉⲧⲉⲛ., ⲡⲉⲧⲉⲛ., ϥⲏ ⲉⲧⲉⲛ. *B*, *that which is (mine, his &c)*: Ge 31 18 *SB* τὰ αὐτοῦ, Job 1 11 *SB*, Mt 25 29 *S* (var ⲉⲧⲉⲟⲩⲛⲧⲁⳅ, *B* ⲉⲧⲉⲛⲧⲟⲧⲩ) ὅ, ἃ ἔχειν, Ps 108 11 *S* (*B* ⲉⲧϣⲟⲟⲡ ⲛ-) ὅσα ὑπάρχειν dat, Mk 5 26 *SB* τὰ παρ' αὐτῆς; PS 247 *S* types only ⲡⲉⲧⲛⲧⲁⲩ, Z 614 *S* ⲡⲉⲧⲛⲧⲁϥ (*l* -ⲁⲥ) ⲛⲧⲙⲛⲧⲉⲣⲟ *what belongeth to kingdom*, C 86 194 *B* ⲡⲉⲧⲉⲛⲧⲁϥ, *cf* 195 ϥⲏ ⲉⲧⲉⲛⲧⲁϥ, Mor 31 10 *Sf* all ⲉⲧⲉⲛⲧⲏⲓ = Miss 4 773 *S* ⲉⲧϣⲟⲟⲡ ⲛⲁⲓ, Kr 116 *Sf* we will pay ϩⲉⲛⲡⲓⲧⲉⲛⲧⲁⲛ; ⲡⲉⲧⲛⲧⲉ- *S* (rare): Mor 41 24 ⲛ. ⲡⲉⲓⲣⲱⲙⲉ. Sometimes confused with ⲛⲧⲛ- (*v* ⲧⲱⲣⲉ *hand*).

ⲛⲟⲩⲧⲉ *SAA*[2]*O*, ⲛⲟⲩϯ *BF*, ⲛⲟⲩⲛⲧⲉ *A*, ⲫϯ (*i e* ⲫⲛⲟⲩϯ) *BF*, f ⲛⲧⲱⲣⲉ only in name Ψεντεντῶρις (Preisigke) & place-name ⲛⲧⲉⲛⲧⲱⲣⲉ, ⲧⲉⲛⲧⲱⲣⲓ, Τεντυρίς, -ρα (Sethe *Verbum* 3 100, its Coptic forms Amélineau *Géog* 140), pl ⲉⲛⲧⲏⲣ &c (*v* below, for possible dual AZ 47 57) & sg as pl, nn m f, *god*: throughout literature *pass* θεός; in Pro Cl BM 1224 *A* mostly ⲛⲟⲩⲧⲉ (*v* AZ 45 79); in *F* mostly ⲫϯ: 2 Cor He Thes ⲛⲫϯ (with ⲛⲛⲟⲩϯ He 9 14, Kr 236), AZ 23 28 ⲓⲏ̄ⲥ ⲡⲉⲛⲫϯ (*cf* ⲡⲉⲛⲥⲱⲧⲏⲣ *F* AZ 33 55); in *O* ⲛⲛ.: Hor 79, AZ 21 94, PGM 1 38, 58, 180; in My 20, 124 *S* ⲛⲡⲛⲉ̄. As f: Ac 19 37 *S* (*B* diff) ἡ θ., EW 31 *B* ⲁⲧⲁⲛ. ϩⲉⲛⲥ ⲥⲁⲃⲟⲗ, BMar 22 *S* Artemis ⲧⲛⲟϭ ⲛⲛ., *cf* AM 78, C 43 200 *B* ⲛ. ⲛⲥϩⲓⲙⲉ, TT 84 *S* sim, *cf* name ⲧⲛⲟⲩⲧⲉ. Pl forms: RAl 141 *S* among demons exorcised ⲉⲛⲧⲏⲣ ⲡⲣⲟⲟⲩⲧ, ⲉ. ⲛⲥϩⲓⲙⲉ, BP 11347 *S* among maladies to be dispelled ⲁⲛⲟⲓⲣ ⲛⲓⲙ ⲡⲣⲟⲟⲩⲧ, ⲁ. ⲛ. ⲛⲥϩⲓⲙⲉ, Journ Soc Or Res 12 27 *S* sim ⲁⲛⲁⲉⲉⲣⲉ ϩⲟⲟⲩⲧ, ⲁ. ⲛⲥ., AZ 21 94 *O* ⲛⲧⲉⲣ ϩⲟⲟⲩⲛⲧ, ⲛ. ϩⲥⲓⲙⲉ (*l* ⲥϩⲓⲙⲉ), DM 7 21 *O* magic name ⲥⲁⲣⲓⲡⲧⲏⲣ, PS 371 *S* sim ⲉⲛⲧⲁⲓⲣ, PGM 1 38 *O* ⲡ[ⲛ]ⲟⲩⲧⲉ νεντηρ τηρ[ου], *ib* 124, 180 *O* sim νινθηρ, *ib* 112, 116 ενθηρ, BM 524 *F* prayer against ⲙⲛⲣⲁ ⲛⲓⲃⲓ ⲙⲡⲉⲛⲑⲏⲣ ⲛⲓⲃⲓ, *ib* magic name ⲙⲓⲕⳅⲁⲛⲑⲏⲣ; as constellation: BAp 73 *S* 7 stars named ⲛⲉⲉⲛⲧⲏⲣ forerunners of pestilence (prob comets J K Fotheringham), distinct from *ib* 7 stars rising in north, LCyp 3 *S* ⲧϭⲓϩⲣⲟⲩⲧ ⲙⲡⲛⲛⲧⲏⲣ = Mor 18 109 *S* ⲛⲧⲉⲉⲣ, TT 88 *S* water demons ⲛⲧⲁⲓⲣⲉ whom Gk poets call Children of Poseidon (= *Vita Pachom* § 2 φαντάσματα δαιμονίων); *v* also below in names.

ⲛⲛ. ⲟ *O*, *the great god*: AZ 21 98, PGM 1 58,

60, DM 17 11 ⲃⲁⲓⲛⲟⲩϯ ⲱ, *cf ib* 16 12 *p ntr* ⲱ ⲱ.
ⲉⲓⲥ ⲡⲛ. ⲙⲛ- *S, lo, God is with...*, implying freedom of choice : J 70 41 ⲉ. ⲡⲛ. ⲙⲛⲡⲉⲧⲉϣⲁϥϥⲓⲧⲟⲩ ⲛ̄ϥⲧⲁⲁⲩ ⲙ̄ⲡⲣⲟⲥⲫⲟⲣⲁ, *ib* 91 24 ⲡⲛ. ⲛⲕⲙⲁⲕ ⲉⲧⲕⲉⲗⲉⲅⲉ ; *as thou wilt*: Leyd 483 ⲡⲗⲏⲛ ⲉ. ⲡⲛ. ⲛⲕⲙⲁⲕ, CO 327 *sim*, MMA 14 1 113 *letter ends* ⲉⲓⲥ ⲡⲛ. (ⲛⲕⲙⲁⲕ ?) ⲭⲉⲧⲉⲟⲩⲱϣ ⲉⲡⲓϩⲉ ⲙⲙⲟⲕ. *V* ⲙⲛ- **I** *s f*.
As adj, *godly, divine* : CaiEuch 651 *B* ⲡⲓⲣⲱⲧ ⲛⲛ. θεῖος ; HL 78 *B book filled with* ⲫⲁϩⲣⲓ ⲛⲛ. σεμνός ; Miss 8 158 *S crying with his* ⲧⲁⲡⲣⲟ ⲛⲛ., BP 11346 *S becoming* ⲥⲱⲙⲁ ⲛⲛ. ϩⲓⲥⲛⲟϥ ⲛⲛ.
ⲁⲧⲛ. adj, *godless*: 2 Jo 9 *B* (*S diff*) θεὸν οὐκ ἔχειν, ViSitz 172 4 14 *S* ⲡⲕⲉⲁ. ⲡⲁϣⲓⲡⲉ ⲣ̄ⲏⲧϥ ἄθεος ; ShRE 10 163 *S* ⲡⲁ. ⲙ̄ⲡⲛⲣⲙⲛⲛ. ; ⲙⲛⲧⲁⲧⲛ., *godlessness*: ShC 42 48 *S your unbelief &* ⲧⲉⲧⲛⲙ., Z 623 *S* ⲍⲟⲩⲙⲁ ⲙⲛ. ; ⲣ ⲁⲧⲛ., *be godless*: Eph 2 12 *SB* ἄθ. ; ShC 42 51 *S* ⲁⲧⲉⲧⲛⲣ ⲁ.
ⲙⲛⲧ-, ⲙⲉⲧⲛ., *divinity* : Ro 1 20 *SB* θειότης ; Cl 15 1 *A* ⲡⲉⲧⲉ ⲡⲉⲓⲣⲏⲛⲛ ϩⲛⲟⲩⲙ. εὐσέβεια ; EpApp 1 5̄ *S* ⲟⲩⲙ. ⲛⲟⲩⲱⲧ *in Trinity*, PS 240 *S* ⲧⲙ. ⲛ̄ⲧⲁⲗⲏⲑⲓⲁ, DeV 2 106 *B* ⲁϯⲙ. ϣⲉⲡ ⲉⲙⲕⲁϩ.
ⲙⲁⲓⲛ., *godloving, rarely bibl* : 2 Tim 3 4 *B* (*var* ⲙⲁⲓ ⲙⲫϯ, *S* ⲙⲉⲣⲉ ⲛⲛ.) φιλόθεος ; Miss 8 40 *S kings* ⲙⲁⲓⲛ. ⲁⲩⲱ ⲡⲉⲩⲥⲉⲃⲏⲥ εὐσεβ. ⲕ. θεοφιλέστατος, BSM 82 *B* ⲡⲓⲟⲩⲣⲟ ⲙⲙ., Leyd 131 *S* ⲡⲉⲡⲛ. ⲡⲉⲓⲱⲧ θεοφ. *archimandrite*, RE 9 158 *S* ⲭⲟⲉⲓⲥ ⲡⲉⲓⲱⲧ ⲉⲧⲟⲩⲁⲁⲃ ⲙⲙ. *bishop*, Ryl 294 *S* ⲡⲙ. ⲁⲩⲱ ⲉⲧⲧⲁⲓⲏⲩ *abbot*, J 75 137 *S* ⲙ. ⲡⲉⲓⲱⲧ, BM 547 *Sf* ⲙⲁⲓⲛⲟⲩⲧ (*sic & ib* 609) ⲛⲟⲧ ⲡⲓⲱⲧ *monks*, BAp 106 *S* ϩⲉⲡⲕⲗⲏⲣⲓⲕⲟⲥ ⲙⲙ. ⲙⲛⲧ-, ⲙⲉⲧⲙⲁⲓⲛ., *godliness, piety* : Pro 1 7 *SA* (*B* ⲙⲉⲧⲉⲩⲥⲉⲃⲏⲥ) εὐσέβεια εἰς θ. ; Miss 4 535 *S*, C 89 55 *B Pachôm called* ⲧⲉⲕⲙ.
ⲙⲁⲥⲛ., *God-bearing, of Virgin* : Miss 4 227 *B*, EW 64 *B* ⲑⲏ ⲉⲧ[..]ⲙⲁⲥ ⲫϯ ; ⲣⲉϥⲙⲉⲥ ⲛ., *God-bearer* : Br 241 *S*. *Cf below* ⲭⲡⲉ ⲛ.
ⲙⲁⲥⲧⲉⲛ., *God-hater* : Ro 1 30 *SB*, *v* ⲙⲟⲥⲧⲉ.
ⲣ, ⲉⲣ ⲛ., *be god*: EpJer 47 *BF* θεὸς εἶναι ; Ming 334 *S let not thy heart* ⲉⲣ ⲛ. ⲛⲁⲕ.
ⲣⲙⲛⲛ., *man of God, godly person* : Pro 13 19 *SA* (*B* = Gk), Is 26 7 *S* (*BF do*) Ac 10 7 *S* (*B do*) εὐσεβής ; Job 2 3 (*B om*), Jo 9 31 *SA²* (*B* ϣⲁⲙϣⲉ ⲛ.) θεοσεβής ; ShC 42 220 *S* ⲡⲣ. *opp* ⲛⲁⲧⲛ. ;
ⲙⲛⲧⲣ., *godliness* : Is 33 6 *SF* (*B* ⲙⲉⲧⲉⲩⲥ.) εὐσέβεια ; ⲣ ⲣ., *be godly*: ShC 42 51 *S* ⲁⲡⲧⲓ ⲧⲣⲉⲧⲉⲧⲛⲣ ⲣ. ⲁⲧⲉⲧⲛⲣ ⲁⲧⲛ.
ϩⲁⲧⲃ, ⲋ. ⲛ., *god-slaying* : My 106 *S Jews* ⲛ̄ϩ., DeV 2 100 *B sim* ⲛ̄ⲣⲉϥϩ.
ϣⲁⲙϣⲉ ⲛ. *B, serving God, as nn, God-server* : Jo 9 31 *ut sup*, DeV 2 163. ⲙⲉⲧϣ. ⲛ. *B, God-service, piety* : Ge 20 11 (*S* ⲙⲛⲧⲣⲉϥϣ. ⲛ.) θεοσέβεια ; HL 91 ⲗⲉⲝⲓⲥ ⲉⲧⲙⲉϩ ⲙⲙ. εὐλάβεια λέξεων, *as title* : DeV 1 87. ⲣⲉϥϣⲉⲙϣⲉ ⲛ. *SB, God-serving, pious person* : Z 308 *S* ⲥⲟⲛ ⲥⲛⲁⲩ...ⲡⲣ. εὐλαβής, Miss 8

---

30 *S* ⲡⲣ. ⲡⲉⲡⲓⲥⲕⲟⲡⲟⲥ θεοσεβ., RNC 88 *S* ⲡⲓⲣⲱⲙⲉ ⲡⲣⲉϥϣ. ⲙ̄ⲡⲛ., C 43 91 *B true men* ⲡⲣ. ⲙⲛⲧⲣⲉϥϣ. ⲛ., *piety*: Miss 8 43 *S* ⲧⲉⲧⲛⲙ. θεοσέβεια ; Wess 15 135 *S* προσκυνητός (? misunderstood).
ⲭⲡⲉ, ⲭⲫⲉ ⲛ., *God-bearing* : BMis 112 *S* ⲛ̄ⲧⲁⲥⲭ. ⲛⲛ. (*paral ib* ⲛ̄ⲧⲁⲥⲙⲓⲥⲉ ⲙ̄ⲡⲛ.) ; ⲣⲉϥⲭ. ⲛ., *God-bearer* : Z 278 *S*, FR 76 *S*, EpApp 1 59 *S*, EW 55 *B*. *Cf* ⲙⲁⲥⲛ.
In many names : Πνούθιος (PGM 1 4), ⲡⲓⲛⲟⲩⲧⲉ (ST 138), Πινοῦθις, Πινουτίων (Preisigke), ⲁⲛⲟⲩⲧⲉ (Ryl 200, Kr 252), Ἀνοῦθις (Pr), ⲡⲁⲡⲟⲩⲧⲉ (Miss 4 630, ST 169), ⲡⲁⲡⲡⲟⲩⲧⲉ, Παπνούθιος, ⲧⲛⲟⲩⲧⲉ (BM 1223), ⲧⲛⲟⲩⲡⲧⲉ (LMis 101), Τινοῦθις (Pr), ⲧⲁⲡⲡⲟⲩⲧⲉ (ST 145), ⲧⲁⲃⲛⲟⲩⲧⲉ (Cai 8551), ⲧⲁⲡⲛⲟⲩⲧⲓ (MR 5 26), Πανινούθιος (PG 25 292), ϣⲉⲛⲟⲩⲧⲉ, ϣⲛ. (Ryl 222), ⲥⲉⲛ. (*ib* 256), ⲥⲓⲛ. (Kr 5), ⲥⲓⲛⲟⲩⲑⲓⲟⲥ, ⲥⲉⲛⲟⲩϯ (AM 100), ⲥⲉⲙⲛⲟⲩⲧⲉ (ST 148), ⲡϣⲙⲛⲟⲩⲧⲉ (Hall 143, Cai 8497), ⲯⲉⲙⲙ. (*ostr olim* EW), ⲯⲉⲛⲡⲛⲟⲩⲑ/ (Bodl(P) d 45), Ψενπνούθης (Pr), ⲧϣⲉⲛⲟⲩⲧⲉ, ⲧⲥⲉⲛ. (J 35 13, 36 5), ⲭⲓⲛⲟⲩⲧⲉ (Miss 4 680), ⲭⲉⲡⲛ. (Cai 8445), ⲁⲣⲟⲡⲛⲟⲩⲧⲉ (Ryl 271), Ἁρπνοῦτις (Pr) ; *with pl form*: Νεντῆρις, Πανθῆρ, Τανεντῆρις, Ψενεντῆρις, Ψενου., Σενεντῆρις, Σενουδῆρ, Πετενεντῆρις, Τετενεντῆρις, Τατενοντῆρις (Pr).
In place-names : ⲡⲉⲣⲡⲛⲟⲩⲧⲉ (P 131³ 39, Lant 45), Τεβενοῦθις (PGiss 1 31), ⲧⲉⲙⲉⲛⲟⲩⲧⲉ (J 23, 44, *cf* Θεμενούθιον Tait 1 76), Τεμγενοῦθις (POxy 99 &c), ⲧⲉⲣⲉⲛⲟⲩϯ Τερενοῦθις (Amél *Géog* 493), ⲭⲉⲃⲉⲛⲟⲩⲧⲓ (Kr 72), ⲭⲉⲙⲛⲟⲩϯ دنوس (Amél *Géog* 411), *for* ⲡⲓⲧⲉⲛⲧⲱⲣⲓ *v above*.
Also in ϩⲉⲛⲉⲉⲧⲉ, ϩⲟⲛⲧ.

ⲛⲧⲟⲕ, ⲛⲧⲁⲕ *v* ⲁⲛⲟⲕ.

ⲛⲧⲱⲕ *S v* ⲧⲱⲕ *bake*.

ⲛⲟⲩⲧⲙ *SF*, -ⲧⲙⲉ *A*, -ⲧⲉⲙ *B* (these not as vb), ⲛⲟⲧⲙ† *S*, -ⲧⲉⲙ† *B*, ⲛⲁⲧⲙ† *F* vb intr, *be sweet, pleasant* : Ps 134 3 *S* (*B* ϩⲟⲗϭ), Si 23 17 *B* (Va 57 215, *S* ϩⲗⲟϭ), *ib* 40 23 *S* ἡδύς ; Pro 16 21 *S* (*var & A* ϩⲗ.) γλυκύς ; Ps 80 2 *S* (*B* ⲡⲉⲥⲉ-), BHom 50 *S* τερπνός ; *ib* 48 *S voice* ⲉⲧⲛ. καλλιφωνία ; RNC 10 *S face* ⲉϥⲛ. ἱλαρός ; Jer 52 32 *B spake* ⲉϥⲛ. χρηστός ; *translates* εὐ- : Jth 4 7 *S* εὐχερῶς, Ez 33 32 *S* (*B* ⲛ. adj) εὐάρμοστος, RNC 25 *S face* ⲉϥⲛ. εὐμενής ; EW 118 *B* ⲉⲣⲉⲛⲥⲟⲟⲓⲛⲟⲩϥⲓ ⲛ., MG 25 257 *B pottage* ⲛ̄ⲥϭⲟ ⲉⲧⲛ., PMéd 293 *S wine* ⲉϥⲛ., R 1 5 33 *S* ⲁⲛⲧⲏⲩ ⲛⲓϥⲉ ⲉϥⲛ., PS 213 *S air* ⲉⲧⲛ., *ib* 214 *S* ⲧⲉⲭⲁⲗⲁⲍⲁ ⲁⲩⲱ...ⲡⲉⲭⲓⲱⲛ ⲉⲧⲛ., P 129¹⁴ 101 *S pomegranate seed* ⲉϥϩⲟⲗϭ ⲁⲩⲱ ⲉϥⲛ., C 41 75 *B* ϩⲁⲡⲥⲙⲛ ⲉϥⲛ., Mor 30 18 *F* ⲕⲓⲑⲁⲣⲁ ⲉⲧⲛ.
ⲛⲟⲩⲧⲉⲙ *B as adj, sweet* : Ge 30 14 *B* (*S* = Gk) ⲭⲉⲙⲫⲉⲣ ⲛⲛ. μανδραγόρας ; Ez 33 32 *ut sup*.
As nn *S, sweetness* : P 44 96 = 43 84 ⲧⲛ. ⲛ̄ϯϩⲣⲁ طرب الطنابير (*l ?* ⲧⲙⲛⲧⲛ.). ⲙⲛⲧⲛⲟⲩⲧ[ⲙ] *S nn f,*

meaning same : BM 1123 ⲉⲕⲟⲩⲣⲱⲡϧ (*sic*) ⲡⲧⲉⲕⲙ. ⲁⲣⲟⲩ(ⲡ) ⲉⲟ(ⲅⲟ)ⲡ ⲡⲓⲙ. ⲭⲓⲧⲛ. *SAF*, ⲭⲱⲓⲧ ⲛⲛ. *B*, *sweet olive* (v ⲭⲟⲉⲓⲧ): Ro 11 24 *SBF* (opp ⲭⲓⲧ-ϧⲣⲟⲟⲩⲧ) καλλιέλαιον; Zech 4 14 *SA* (*B* diff) πιότης Vulg *olei*.　　In place-name Χοιβνῶτμις (PHibeh 68, 112).

ⲛⲧⲏ-, ⲛⲧⲉⲛ- *v* ⲧⲱⲣⲉ *hand*.

ⲛⲧⲏⲣ, ⲛⲧⲁⲓⲣⲉ *v* ⲛⲟⲩⲧⲉ.

ⲛⲧⲁⲣⲉ- *v* ⲧⲁⲣⲉ-.

ⲛⲧⲉⲣⲉ- *S*, (ⲛ)ⲧⲁⲣⲉ- *A* verbal pref in temporal clause, *when, after* : Ge 39 18 *S* ⲛⲧⲉⲣⲉϥⲥⲱⲧⲙ ⲭⲉ- (*B* ⲉⲧⲁϥ-), Jo 4 1 *S* ⲛⲧⲉⲣϥⲉⲓⲙⲉ ⲭⲉ- (*B* ϧⲟⲧⲉ ⲉⲧⲁϥ-, *F* ⲉⲧⲁϥ-) ὡς; BMis 1195 *S* ⲛⲧⲉⲣⲓϣⲉ ⲉⲧⲉⲅⲕⲁⲓⲣⲓⲁ... ϯⲡⲁⲉⲓⲣⲉ, TU 43 2 *A* ⲧⲁⲣⲟⲩϧⲛⲁⲡ ⲭⲉ ⲁϧⲟⲩⲡ.

ⲛⲧⲱⲧⲛ, ⲛⲧⲁⲧⲉⲛ *v* ⲁⲛⲟⲕ.

ⲛⲧⲟⲟⲩ, ⲛⲧⲁⲩ *v* ⲁⲛⲟⲕ.

ⲛⲧⲟⲟⲩⲛ, ⲛⲧⲱⲟⲩⲛ *S*, ⲛⲧⲁⲩⲛ *A* conjunct, *then* : Job 31 8 *S* (*B* om), Ps 72 13 *S* (*B* = Gk), Ro 7 21 *S* (*B* do) ἄρα, Gal 3 7 *S* (*B* do) ἄ. var γάρ; Z 306 *S* my labour is vain ϯⲡⲁϩⲱⲕ ⲛ. ⲱⲁⲟⲩⲥⲟⲡ, *ib* 337 *S* he cometh not ⲙⲁⲣⲛⲣ ⲡⲁⲓ ⲛ. οὖν, Lu 20 25 *S* (*B* ϯⲛⲟⲩ) οὖν var τοίνυν, Job 36 14 *S* (*B* om), Is 27 4 *S* (*B* do) τοίνυν; Job 24 22 *S* (*B* ⲟⲩⲛ) τοιγαροῦν; 1 Kg 15 30 *S*, Job 19 4 *S* (*B* ⲭⲁⲥ ⲭⲉ-), Is 7 13 *S* (*B* om) δή, Pro 2 22 *SA* (*B* om) δέ, ViSitz 172 4 63 *S* ⲉⲧⲃⲉⲟⲩ ⲁⲉ ⲛ. τί δέ; 2 Cor 2 7 *S* (var ⲛⲧⲟϥ, *B* ⲡⲉⲧⲟⲩⲃⲏϥ) τοὐναντίον μᾶλλον; Lu 18 26 *S* (*B* ϧⲱϥ) καί; Gk om : 2 Kg 18 30 *S* ⲁⲙⲟⲩ ⲛ. ⲡⲧⲁϧⲉⲣⲁⲧⲕ, Job 7 13 *S* ⲡⲁϭⲗⲟϭ ⲛ. ⲡⲁⲥⲗⲱϭⲧ, Pro 15 11 *SA* ⲡⲁ⳿ ⲛϧⲉ ⲛ.; ShA 1 267 *S* ⲙⲁⲧⲁⲙⲟⲛ ⲛ. ⲭⲉⲛⲓⲙⲡⲉ, R 1 3 30 *S* ⲁⲙⲟⲩ ⲛ. ⲛⲧⲟⲩⲱϣⲧ, ShA 2 46 *S* ϧⲁⲙⲟⲓ ⲛ. ⲉⲡⲉ(ⲙ)ⲡⲉⲡⲛⲟⲩⲃ ϣⲱⲡⲉ, ShP 131⁴ 90 *S* admonition is vain ϯⲡⲁϧⲱ ⲛ.;　　after -ϭⲉ: Mk 11 31 *S* (ⲛⲧⲟⲟⲩ), Gal 3 19 *S* (*B* -ⲭⲉ), ViSitz 172 4 19 *S* ⲉⲓⲡⲁⲙⲟⲩϭⲉ ⲛ. ⲉⲡⲭⲓⲛⲭⲏ οὖν; Eccl 2 15 *S* καί; P 131⁴ 104 *S* ⲉϣⲭⲉ ⲕⲟⲩⲱϣϭⲉ ⲛ. ⲉⲉⲓⲱ ⲙⲡⲉⲕϧⲟ, *cf* also Mt 22 21 *S*, Mk 12 17 *S*;　　in apodosis after ⲉⲓⲉ-: Sa 5 6 *S* ἄρα, ShA 2 192 *S* ⲉⲓⲉ ⲁⲙⲟⲩ ⲛ. ⲡⲧⲟⲩϧⲁⲣⲕ;　　after ⲉⲧⲃⲉⲟⲩ: KKS 483 *S* ⲉ. ⲛ. ⲙⲡⲉⲕⲭⲓ ⲡⲓⲥⲙⲁⲏⲗ ?, or ⲉⲓⲉ ⲉⲧⲃⲉⲟⲩ: ShZ 592 *S*, BHom 108 *S*;　　after ⲟⲩⲕⲟⲩⲛ: ShZ 600 *S* king's chariot & horses good ⲟⲩ. ⲭⲟⲟⲥ ⲟⲛ ⲉⲣⲟⲟⲩ ⲛ. ⲭⲉⲡⲣⲣⲟⲡⲉ *doth one then call them ' the king '* ?, Bor 241 149 *S* ⲟⲩ. ⲛ. ⲁϥϣⲱⲡⲉ ⲡⲣⲙϧⲉ *is he not then free* from punishment (δίκη) ?　　after ⲉϣⲭⲉ, ⲉϣⲱⲡⲉ: Ge 43 11 *S* ⲉϣⲭⲉ ⲧⲁⲓ ⲛ. ⲧⲉ ⲑⲉ (Gk om), Bess 7 63 *S*, BM 343 *S* sim, *ib* 250 32 *S* ⲉϣⲱⲡⲉ ⲙⲡⲉϥⲧⲱⲟⲩⲛ ⲛⲧⲁⲟⲩⲛ why doth world keep festival ?

ⲛⲟⲩⲧϥ, -ⲟⲩⲧ *SB*, ⲡⲉⲧϥ-, ⲡⲉⲧⲃ- *SB*, -ⲟⲩⲧ- *B*, ⲡⲁϥⲧ-

S, ⲡⲁⲧⲉϥ- *F*, ⲡⲟϧⲧ⳿ *B*, ⲡⲟⲧϥ†, -ⲧⲃ† *S* vb **I** tr, *loosen, dissolve, settle, make terms for* (v AZ 53 131): Ex 18 16 *B* ⲡⲉⲧϥ- (*S* diff) διακρίνειν, Va 57 250 *B* thy daughter ⲉⲁⲕⲡⲟⲩⲧⲉⲥ ⲉϥⲃⲉⲭⲉ ϩⲁⲟⲩⲙⲁ ⲡⲡⲟⲣⲛⲏ ἐκμισθοῦν;　　esp *loosen mouth, face* in smiles: Si 21 21 *S* (Lemm), C 86 303 *B* μειδιᾶν; Si 7 25 *S* (P 44 118) ⲡⲉⲧϥ ⲡⲉⲕϧⲟ ἱλαροῦν; BMar 244 *S* ⲁϥⲡⲉⲧⲃ ⲣⲱϥ ⲡⲥⲱⲃⲉ, C 41 36 *B* sim, Mor 24 25 *F* Saviour ⲡⲁⲧⲉϥ ⲗⲱⲃ ⲡⲥ., BM 1008 *S* ⲁϥⲡⲁⲧ ⲣ. ⲡⲥ., C 43 137 *B* ⲁϥⲡⲉϥⲧ ⲣ. ⲡⲥ.; or in tears: Z 535 n *B* ⲁϥⲡⲉϥⲧ ⲣ. ϩⲉⲛϩⲁⲡⲉⲣⲙⲱⲟⲩⲓ.　　As nn : Si 19 30 *B* (HL 91) ⲡⲓⲡⲉϥⲧ ⲣ. ⲡⲥ. (*S* ⲥⲱⲃⲉ) γέλως.　　**II** intr, *be relaxed, released* : Is 10 7 *B* (*S* diff), Lu 12 58 *B* ⲉⲃⲟⲗ ϧⲁ- (*S* ⲛⲱⲗϭ) ἀπαλλάσσειν; Pro 6 35 *B* (*SA* ⲃⲱⲗ) διαλύεσθαι; of smiles: Sa 17 4 *S* ⲛϧⲟ... ⲡⲥⲉⲡ.† ⲁⲛ ἀμείδητος; BMis 555 *S* ⲡⲉϥϧⲟ...ⲉϥⲛ.† ⲛⲥⲱⲃⲉ *subridens*, Mor 41 163 *S* sim ⲛ.† ϩⲛⲟⲩⲣⲁϣⲉ; of air *changed* after winter : TT 19 *S* ⲛⲧⲉⲡⲁⲏⲣ ⲡⲟⲩⲧϥ & sun shineth (var Mich 550 24 ⲡⲟⲩⲟⲣ, *l* ? -ϥⲧ).　　As nn, *relaxation* : ShC 73 131 *S* ⲟⲩⲥⲱⲃⲉ ⲙⲡⲟⲩⲛⲟⲩⲧϥ in face, Va 57 *lc B* our body ⲁⲛⲧⲏⲓϥ ⲉⲡⲟⲩϧⲧ ⲉⲁⲛϯ ⲡⲧⲉⲛⲥⲁⲣⲝ ⲉⲃⲟⲗ to devil ἐκμισθ. (for both).　　ⲭⲓⲛⲡⲉⲧϥ ⲣⲱ⳿ *B*, *act of smiling* : MG 25 129 mirror reflects ⲡⲓⲭ. ⲣⲱϥ.　　*Cf* ⲛ. in ⲗⲁⲧ ⲡⲟⲩⲧϥ (but ? *l* -ⲧⲙ).

ⲛⲧⲟϥ *S*, ⲛⲧⲁϥ *AA²F*, ⲛⲑⲟϥ *B* 3 sg m of pers pron (v ⲁⲛⲟⲕ) used without concord for contrast, opposition, *rather, but,* or merely *again* : Ps 32 10 *S* (*B* ⲁⲉ ⲛ.), Pro 3 7 *SA* (*B* om), Mt 12 31 *SB*, Jo 3 21 *S* (*B* ⲁⲉ, *F* ⲁⲉ ⲛ.), 1 Cor 13 6 *S* (*B* do) δέ; ⲁⲉ + ⲛ.: Ge 41 54 *S* (*B* diff), Ps 140 5 *SA* (Cl, *B* om), Jer 8 7 *B*, Mt 15 18 *S* (*BF* ⲁⲉ), ZNTW 24 90 *F* ⲉϣⲱⲡⲓ ⲁⲉ ⲛ. ⲁϥϣⲁⲡ- δέ;　　Mt 10 28 *B* (*S* om), Mk 15 11 *S* (*B* = Gk) μᾶλλον; Lu 23 28 *S* (*B* do) πλήν; Gal 2 7 *S* (*B* ⲡⲉⲧⲟⲩⲃⲏϥ), 1 Pet 3 9 *S* (*B* do) τοὐναντίον, 2 Cor 2 7 *S* (var ⲛⲧⲟⲟⲩⲛ ? error, *B* do + ⲙⲁⲗⲗⲟⲛ) τοὐν. μᾶλ.; Nu 15 40 *S* (*B* ⲟⲩⲟϩ), Mk 4 20 *S* (*B* ϧⲱ⳿), Jo 14 22 *A²B* (*S* om) καί, BHom 139 *S* ⲙⲡⲛⲁⲩ ⲛ. when centurion came καί...μέν; Aeg 214 *S* ⲉϣⲱⲡⲉ ⲙⲉⲛ...ⲛ ⲛ., BM 174 1 *S* of stone or bronze ⲛ ⲛ. ϩⲛⲕⲉϩⲩⲗⲏ ἤ;　　Gk om, after ⲁⲗⲗⲁ: Deu 9 4 *S* (var & *B* om), Jos 22 27 *S*, 2 Kg 10 3 *S*, Mk 16 7 *S* (*B* do), Ro 12 3 *SF* (MR, om BM, *B* do), BHom 136 *S* ⲁⲗⲗⲁ ⲉⲕⲉⲡⲓⲥⲧⲉⲩⲉ ⲁⲉ ⲛ. ⲛϧⲟⲩⲟ ἀλ. πίσ.;　　after ⲁⲉ: Ac 13 39 *B* (*S* om), MG 25 19 *B* others asked ⲡⲓⲕⲉⲟⲩⲁⲓ ⲁⲉ ϧⲱϥ...ⲛϣⲓⲛⲓ ⲉⲑⲃⲉϧⲗⲓ ⲛ. ⲁⲛ ὁ δὲ εἷς ...μηδὲν ἐρωτῶν;　　after ⲉⲓⲉ: Sa 13 9 *S* ⲉⲓⲉ... ⲉⲧⲃⲉⲟⲩ ⲛ.;　　PS 326 *S* ⲁⲗⲗⲁ ⲉϣⲱⲡⲉ ⲉⲣⲉⲡⲣⲉϥⲣ ⲛⲟⲃⲉ ⲛ. ⲡⲉ, *ib* 185 *S* ⲉϧⲟ ⲡⲁϣ ⲛⲧⲩⲡⲟⲥ ⲛ ⲙⲙⲟⲛ ⲛ. ⲉϧⲟ ⲡⲁϣ ⲛⲥⲙⲟⲧ, ShC 73 13 *S* ⲉⲅⲕⲉⲗⲉⲩⲉ ⲛⲁⲥ ⲁⲛ, ⲛⲧⲟⲥ ⲛ. ⲉⲧⲕⲉⲗⲉⲩⲉ, Pcod 19 *S* is it good to build church ⲛ. ⲉⲡⲣⲁⲛ ⲙⲡⲭ̅ⲥ̅ rather than make

gifts ? DeV 2 51 *B* rejoice not at...ⲁⲗⲗⲁ ⲑⲉⲗⲏⲗ
ⲛ. ⲉⲝⲉⲛ-, Bor 233 232 *S* that he be not wroth
ⲁⲗⲗⲁ ⲉⲧⲣⲉϥϭⲣⲟϣ ⲛϧⲏⲧ ⲛ., PS 186 *S* ⲟⲩ ⲛ. ⲡⲉ
ⲉϥⲛⲁϫⲟⲟϥ ?, BM 258 1 *S* showeth us ⲉⲃⲟⲗ ⲛϧⲏⲧⲟⲩ ⲛ. (ⲛ)ⲡⲉⲧⲅⲣⲁⲫⲏ ϫⲉ-, C 89 92 *B* soul cast ⲉⲛⲓ-
ⲕⲟⲗⲁⲥⲓⲥ ⲓⲉ ⲛ. ⲉⲡⲉⲥⲏⲧ to hell, AM 87 *B* worldly
obedience is naught ⲡⲓⲥⲱⲧⲉⲙ ⲇⲉ ⲛ. ⲛⲧⲉ ⲡⲁⲟ̄ⲥ̄ is
good, JKP 2 64 *F* ⲁⲡⲕⲁϩ ⲉⲛⲧⲁϥ ⲁⲃϯ ⲅⲁⲣⲡⲱⲥ.

ⲛⲧⲟⲥ *S* 3 sg f sometimes sim, but concording
with subj : Ps 34 9 (*B* ⲇⲉ) δέ, Si 40 14 (var ⲇⲉ)
καί, PS 91 ⲧⲁϭⲟⲙ ⲛ. ⲛⲁⲟⲩⲣⲟⲧ (paral *ib* 95 ⲧⲁⲯⲩⲭⲏ ⲇⲉ), TU 24 3 having healed others ⲉⲧⲃⲉⲟⲩ ⲛ.
ⲧⲉⲕϣⲉⲉⲣⲉ...why hast not helped her ? BHom 140
ⲟⲩ ⲛ. ϯⲉⲃⲓⲏⲛ why didst not answer her ? (Mt 15
23), *ib* 2 some rejoice in riches ⲧⲛⲁⲣⲑⲉⲛⲟⲥ ⲇⲉ ⲛ.
ⲙⲁⲣⲉⲥⲉⲩϥⲣⲁⲛⲉ in Lord.

ⲛⲧⲟⲟⲩ *SB* 3 pl sim : Ro 3 29 *SB* καί (var δὲ καί);
Ps 33 21 *S* (*B* Gk om); BHom 95 *S* ϣⲁⲣⲉⲛⲧⲁϭⲥⲉ
...ⲡⲟⲩϩⲉⲣⲏⲧⲉ ⲇⲉ ⲛ. ⲙⲡⲁⲝ̄ⲥ̄....

ⲛⲑⲟⲩ, -ⲥ, -ⲱⲟⲩ, *likewise, again*, in titles of
prayers, hymns, sermons *B* : HCons 463 after Gk
prayer ⲛⲑⲟⲥ ⲟⲛ هي ايضًا & Coptic transl, EW 7
ⲛⲑⲟⲩ ⲟⲛ (ⲛϫⲟⲥ) آدم ايضًا, Dif 1 65 ⲛⲑⲱⲟⲩ ⲟⲛ, Va 57 (*v* Z 5, 6) ⲛⲑⲟⲩ ⲟⲛ ⲡⲓⲁⲅⲓⲟⲥ ⲓⲱⲁⲛⲛⲏⲥ (var ⲟⲙⲟⲓⲱⲥ ⲛ. ⲟⲛ, *S* mostly ϩⲟⲙⲟⲓⲱⲥ or ⲧⲟⲩ
ⲁⲩⲧⲟⲩ); *S* in Glos *pass* ⲛⲑⲟϥ ⲟⲛ, *same again* as
last, ⲛⲑⲟⲥ 96, 194, ⲛⲑⲟⲟⲩ 19, 20, 49 (*cf* مثلا in
P 43, 44).

ⲛⲑⲟϥ ⲛⲑⲟϥ *S*, ⲛⲑ. ⲛⲑ. *B*, *he* (*is*) *he*, (*is*) *same* ; He
13 8 *B* (*S* ⲛ. ⲡⲉ) ὁ αὐτός ; ShC 42 31 *S* sun ⲛ. ⲛ.
ⲟⲛⲡⲉ ϩⲙⲡⲉϥⲟⲩⲟⲉⲓⲛ, MG 25 205 *B* eating or fasting ⲡⲉⲕⲥⲱⲙⲁ ⲛ. ⲛ. ⲡⲉ ⲉϥϣⲟⲩⲟⲩⲟⲩ Gk om, My 26
S God & man at once ⲉⲧⲉⲛ. ⲛ. ⲡⲉ ;   sim ⲛⲧⲟⲕ:
Ps 101 27 *SB* ὁ αὐ., ShMIF 23 21 *S* ⲛⲉⲕⲣⲙⲡⲉ ⲛⲉⲕⲣⲙⲡⲉ
ⲟⲛⲡⲉ ⲁⲩⲱ ⲛ. ⲛ. ⲟⲛⲡⲉ ; or ⲛⲧⲟⲟⲩ : ShC 42 42 *S*
His decrees ⲛ. ⲛ. ⲟⲛⲡⲉ from beginning.

ⲛⲧϥⲉ- *v* ⲉⲧⲃⲉ-.

ⲛⲧⲏϭ *SA*, ⲉⲛ. *S*, ⲉⲛⲧⲏϫ, ⲛⲧⲏϫ *B*, ⲉⲛⲧⲏϭ *F*
nn m, *plant, herb, weed* : Job 8 12 *S* (*B* ⲥⲓⲙ), Is
58 11 *S* (*B* ⲥⲓⲙ), He 6 7 *S* (*B* ⲥⲓⲙ), LCyp 10 *S*
βοτάνη (*cf* PS 212 *S* ⲛⲃⲟⲧ. ⲉⲛⲉⲛⲉⲛ. ⲛⲉ), Job 5 25
A (Cl, *S* ⲣⲱⲧ, *B* ⲥⲙ.) παμβότανον ; Deu 32 2 *S*
(*B* = Gk), Is 37 27 *S* (*B* ⲥⲱⲟⲩⲃⲉⲛ), Hos 10 4 *SA*
(*B* = Gk) ἄγρωστις ; Job 31 40 *SB* κνίδη ; *ib* 30
4 *S* (*B* ⲁⲣⲁⲣⲓⲙ) ἅλιμον ; *ib* 30 7 *S* (*B* ⲗⲉⲃϣ) φρύγανον ; Sa 7 20 *S* ῥίζα ; Mor 18 107 *S* πόα ; speci-
fically *darnel* Mt 13 25 *SBF* ζιζάνια وان ; K 197
B, Tri 601 *S* '; Br 106 *S* ⲡⲓⲉⲛ. ϫⲉⲕⲩⲡⲟⲕⲉⲫⲁⲗⲟⲛ,
PMéd 292 *S* ⲡⲓⲉⲛ. ϫⲉⲙⲁⲗⲁⲃⲁⲑⲣⲟⲛ, ShC 42 63 *S*
ⲧⲱϩ, ⲣⲟⲟⲩⲉ, ⲕⲉⲉⲛ., ShR 2 3 44 *S* ⲟⲩⲣⲧ, ϣⲗϩ,
ⲕⲉⲉⲛ. sweet smelling, ShP 129¹² 10 *S* ϩⲉⲛⲟⲩⲟⲟⲧⲉ

ϩⲱⲥ ⲉⲛ. ⲉⲩⲛⲟⲥⲉ, ShMing 87 *S* drugs from ⲛ., SHel
41 *S* ⲟⲩⲉⲛ. ⲛⲁⲧⲣⲓⲟⲛ in poison draught, Va 58 186
B ⲛⲛ. in cooking pot (4 Kg 4 40), EpApp 1 138 *S*
ⲉⲛ. ⲉⲧⲙⲉϩ ⲛϣⲱⲛⲉ, Miss 4 762 *S* ⲡⲓⲉⲛ. ⲛⲧⲉ ⲧⲥⲱϣⲉ
ⲙⲡⲛⲉⲓⲟⲅⲟⲧⲟⲩⲉⲧ, Rec 6 174 *B* ϫⲱⲃⲓ ⲛⲉⲛ. as covering, ClPr 54 43 *S* ϩⲛⲧⲟⲩⲱ ⲛⲛ. λειμών.   ⲣ ⲛ.
SA, *become weedy* (of ground): Pro 24 46 *SA* χορ-
τομανεῖν, Mor 51 37 *S* men ⲉⲧⲟ ⲛⲉⲛ. in their
deeds.   ϫⲉ, ϫⲓ ⲛ. *S*, *sow herbs* : HengB 6* wine
supplied to ⲛⲛⲟϭ ⲛⲣⲱⲙⲉ ⲉⲩϫⲓ ⲛ. in big garden,
Mor 51 37 season of ⲛϫⲓ ⲉⲛ. ;   *weed-sower* : Z
271 ⲡⲣⲉϥϫⲉ ⲛ. (*cf* Mt 13 25).

ⲛⲁⲩ *SB*, ⲛⲉⲩ *A²F*, ⲛⲟ *AA²*, ⲛⲱ *Sᵃ* (Ep 1 241),
ⲛⲁⲟⲩ *O*, imperat ⲁⲛⲁⲩ *SB*, ⲁⲛⲉⲩ *A²F*, ⲉⲛⲟ *A* (Ex)
vb I intr, *look, behold*   **a** no obj : Ge 13 14 *A* (Cl)
B (*S* om), Ps 34 21 *B* (*S* ⲙⲉϩ ⲉⲓⲁⲧ), Is 33 11 *SBF*,
Mt 12 2 *SBF* ὁρᾶν (ἰδεῖν), Ps 5 3 *S* (*B* ⲛ. ⲉ-) ἐφορ.,
Ac 2 31 *B* (*S* ⲉⲓⲙⲉ) προορ. ; Ps 39 13 *B* (*S* ⲛ. ⲉⲃⲟⲗ),
Mt 13 14 *SBF* βλέπειν, AM 267 *B* ⲁⲛ. ⲙⲡⲉⲣϣⲱⲡⲓ
ⲉⲣⲟⲕ βλ. μή, 1 Kg 16 7 *B* (*S* ϭⲱϣⲧ) ἐμβλ. ; Dan 7
6 *SB*, Lu 23 35 *SB* θεωρεῖν ; Ps 93 9 *B* (*S* ⲛ. ⲉ-),
Ac 7 31 *S* (*B* ϯ ⲛⲓⲁⲧ) κατανοεῖν ; Ps 78 10 *S* (*B*
diff) γινώσκειν, Job 4 16 *S* (*B* ⲥⲱⲟⲩⲛ) ἐπιγιν. ;
EpJer 4 *B* (*S* ϯ ϩⲧⲏⲧ, *F* ⲉⲣ ϩⲁⲧ) εὐλαβεῖσθαι ; ShC
73 100 *S* ⲛⲧⲟⲟⲩ ⲉⲧⲛⲁⲛ., AM 258 *B* ⲉⲧⲁⲩⲛ. they
wondered, BM 605 *F* ⲁⲛⲉⲟⲩ ⲙⲡⲉⲗⲧ(ⲣ)ⲉⲗⲱⲙⲓ
ⲥⲱ[ⲧⲙ ;   with ϫⲉ-, *see that, how* : Ge 1 8 *B*, Ps
13 2 *SB*, Is 40 26 *SB*, Mk 15 36 *SB* ὁρ. (ἰδ.) ; Ps
9 35 *SB*, 2 Cor 7 8 *B* (*S* ϭⲱ.), Cl 56 16 *A* βλ. ;
Gk & *B* om : Ac 27 39 *S* ⲁⲩϭⲓ ϣⲟⲝⲛⲉ ⲉⲛ. ϫⲉ-,
ib 22 26 *S* sim ; PS 78 *S* ⲁⲥⲕⲟⲧⲥ ⲉⲛ. ϫⲉⲁⲩⲕⲱ ⲛⲁⲥ
ⲉⲃⲟⲗ, C 43 101 *B* ⲙⲁⲣⲓⲛ. ϫⲉϥⲛⲁϩⲁⲣⲙⲉⲕ, AP 23
A² ⲁⲧⲣⲟⲩⲛ. ϫⲉϥⲁⲣⲏ [ⲁϩⲟⲩⲛ].   **b** ⲉ-, sometimes
+ethic dat : Nu 1 49 *SB*, Is 5 19 *SBF*, Hab 3 7
AB, Jo 8 51 *SA²B*, Z 316 *S* = MG 25 231 *B* ⲁϥⲛ.
ⲉⲡⲥⲁⲧⲁⲡⲁⲥ ὁρ., Ro 1 20 *SB* καθορ., Ps 138 3 *S* (*B*
ⲉⲣ ϣⲟⲣⲛ ⲛⲛ.) προορ. ; Sa 2 17 *S* (*B* ϫⲟⲩϣⲧ), Mt
7 3 *S* (var ϭⲱ.) *B* βλ., Is 5 12 *B* (*S* ϭⲱ., *F* ⲥⲁⲙⲥ),
Mk 8 25 *SB* (*F* ⲓⲱⲣϩ) ἐμβλ., Dan 3 54 *B* (*S* ϭⲱ.)
ἐπιβλ., Pro 31 16 (29 34) *SAB*, Su 20 *SB*, Ap 11
11 *SB* θεω., Mt 22 11 *SB*, MG 25 243 *B* θεᾶσθαι ;
Ge 41 33 *S* (Bor 304 51, *B* ⲥⲟϭⲛⲓ) σκέπτεσθαι, Nu
14 38 *S* (*B* ϫⲉⲣ-) κατασκ. ; Mt 7 3 *S* (*B* ϯ ⲛⲓⲁⲧ)
κατανο. ; Ps 137 6 *S* (*B* ⲥⲱⲟⲩⲛ) γιν. ; Gal 1 18 *SB*
ἱστορεῖσθαι ; Ez 41 8 *SB* videre ; Gk & *B* om : Lu
18 24 *S* ⲁⲛ. ⲉⲑⲉ ; Br 118 *S* ϭⲱϣⲧ...ⲛⲧⲉⲛⲛ. ⲉⲛⲉ-
ⲣⲓⲟⲟⲩⲉ, BMis 464 *S* ϯⲛ. ⲉⲧⲉⲛⲕⲁⲥⲡⲉ that it is like
ours, Bor 143 21 *S* ⲛⲧⲉⲣⲉϥⲉⲓ ϫⲉ ⲉⲛ. ⲉⲡⲁⲛⲥⲉ *to
visit*, J 36 38 *S* ⲛⲧⲉⲣⲛⲛ. ⲉⲣⲱⲧⲛ ⲉⲧⲉⲛⲟⲩⲱϣ ⲉ-, C
86 148 *B* ⲁⲛ. ⲛⲁⲕ ⲉⲛϣⲑⲟⲣⲧⲉⲣ ⲙⲡⲁⲥⲱⲙⲁ, BM
1224 24 *A²* ⲁⲉⲓⲛⲟ ⲁⲣⲁϥ (*l* ⲁⲓⲁⲛⲟ ⲁⲣⲁⲩ) ⲉⲩϫⲓ ⲛⲛⲁ
may I see them begging alms, Hor 82 *O* ⲛⲧϥⲛ.
ⲁϩⲁⲛ ;   with ⲉ- *dat commodi* : Ge 41 17 *S* (*B*

om) οἴεσθαι, PSBA 25 269 S ⲁⲛ. ⲉⲣⲟⲓ in vision
= Miss 4 98 B, JKP 2 240 S sim, MG 25 28 B
ⲉⲕⲛ. ⲉⲣⲟⲕ ⲉⲕⲟⲓ ⲡⲁϣ ⲡⲣⲏϯ ? *provide, seek out*:
Ex 4 13 SA (B ϩⲓ ⲧⲟⲧ⸗ ⲉⲭⲉⲛ-) προχειρίζειν, 1 Kg
20 36 S ⲛⲧⲛ. ⲡⲁⲓ ⲉⲛⲥⲟⲧⲉ (var ⲛⲧⲛ. ⲉⲧⲃⲉⲛⲥ.) εὑρίσκειν dat; ShC 73 167 S ⲉϥⲛⲁⲛ. ⲡⲁϥ ⲉⲟⲩⲣⲱⲙⲉ,
BKU 1 126 S ⲁⲣⲓ ⲧⲁⲅⲁⲡⲏ ⲛⲕⲛ. ⲉⲩⲧⲱϣ ⲡⲉⲙⲁⲓ,
Aeg 51 B ⲁⲛ. ⲉⲭⲉⲛⲡⲓⲙⲁ ⲡⲉⲣϣⲱⲟⲩϣⲓ & bring
thence &c.

—— ⲉⲃⲟⲗ SAA²B (oftener ⲙⲃ.) F, *see opp not
see, be blind*: 1 Kg 9 9 S, Ps 39 12 S (B ⲛ.), Ez
13 3 SB, Mt 13 13 S (BF do), Ap 3 18 S (B ⲛ.
ⲙⲃ.) βλέπειν, Mk 10 52 S (B do) ἀναβλ., Ac 22 11
S (B do) ἐμβλ.; Nu 24 3 S (var ⲉⲓⲱⲣϩ, B ⲛ.), Pro
20 10 S (A ⲛ.), Cl 21 1 A ⲡⲟ ⲁⲃ. ⲙⲏⲡⲱⲥ (var
ⲥⲱⲡⲧ) ὁρᾶν, EpJer 36 F (B ⲛ. ⲙⲃ.) ὅρασις, Z 324
S, Miss 4 526 S (B ⲛ. ⲙⲃ.) διορατικός; Sa 13 5 S
θεωρεῖν; ShA 1 111 S ⲡⲉⲧⲛ. ⲉⲃ. shall be blind,
ShC 73 171 S opp be asleep, BIF 13 112 S when
blind touched ⲁϥⲛ. ⲉⲃ. = MG 25 303 B ⲛ. ⲙⲃ.
ⲛ. ⲉⲃ. ⲉ-: Ac 13 11 S (B ⲛ.) βλ., Lu 6 42 S (B ⲛ.
ⲙⲃ.) διαβλ., Bor 226 164 S ⲡⲧⲁⲛ. ⲉⲃ. ⲉⲡⲉϫⲉⲟⲟⲩ
ⲕⲁⲧⲁⲛⲟ., PS 50 S in darkness ⲛⲥⲉⲧⲙⲛ. ⲉⲃ. ⲉⲡⲟⲩⲟⲉⲓⲛ, AP 25 A² ⲁⲉⲓⲛ. ⲁⲃ. ⲁⲡⲕⲉⲉⲓ ⲡⲓⲙ. As nn
S, *sight, power to see*: Is 61 1 (B ⲛ. ⲙⲃ.), ἀνά-
βλεψις; Pcod 9 ⲛⲛ. ⲉⲃ. = ib ⲡⲉⲓⲱⲣϩ prophetic *insight* as ἀρετή. ⲣⲉϥⲛ. ⲉⲃ. S, *seer*: Z 335 διορατικός (cf ⲣⲉϥⲛ.).

—— ⲙⲃⲟⲗ B, meaning as last *q v*: Ge 48 10
(S ⲉⲓⲱ.) βλ.; AM 274 ⲉⲧⲁⲕⲛ. ⲙⲃ. ϩⲉⲛϯϫⲓⲁⲕⲱⲛⲓⲁ
ἐκπληροῦν, MIE 2 384 eyes being open ⲉϥⲛ. ⲙⲃ.
As nn: Ez 23 16 (S ⲛ.) ὅρασις; CaiEuch 487 Thou
gavest ⲫⲛ. ⲙⲃ. to blind τὸ βλέπειν. ⲙⲉⲧⲁⲑⲛ.
ⲙⲃ., *sightlessness*: Deu 28 28 (S ⲕⲣⲟⲙⲣⲙ) ἀορασία.

II tr, rare (? incorrect): Dan 10 7 B (S ⲛ. ⲉ-) ὁρ.,
Ac 13 11 B (var & S ⲉ-) βλ.; ShA 2 176 S ϥⲛ.
ⲙⲡⲣⲟ of father, Tri 321 S ⲛⲧⲛ. ⲡⲡⲉⲡⲧⲁⲅⲉⲓ, ib 512
S apostle ⲛ. ⲉⲭⲓⲧⲉⲥⲁⲡⲉ ⲡⲟⲩⲙⲓⲧⲣⲁ.

—— nn m SB, *sight, view, vision*: Lev 13 12 S
(B ϫⲓⲛⲛ.), Jer 23 16 B ὅρασις, Deu 26 8 B (S =
Gk), Eccl 6 9 S ὅραμα, Ac 26 19 B (S ⲥⲱⲗⲡ ⲉⲃ.)
ὀπτασία, 2 Cor 5 7 S (B ⲥⲙⲟⲧ) εἶδος, Mor 37 108
S came merely ⲉⲧⲃⲉⲡⲛ. ⲉⲣⲟϥ τὸ ἰδεῖν; 2 Pet 2 8
S (B ⲥⲟⲙⲥ) βλέμμα, MG 25 19 B ⲛⲛ. ⲉⲣⲟⲕ τὸ
βλέπειν; Is 2 16 S (B ϫⲓⲛⲛ.), ib 27 11 SB θέα;
ShC 73 5 S ⲛⲛ. ⲉⲡⲣⲟ of angel, Mor 40 46 S ⲛⲛ.
ϩⲛⲡⲃⲁⲗ better than hearing = MG 25 273 B ϫⲓⲛⲛ.
(cf Aeg 44 B, FR 2 S, BMis 236 S sim).

ⲁⲑⲛ. SB, *unseen, unseeing* + ⲉ-: Ge 1 2 B, Is 45
3 B (S vb neg), Ro 1 20 B (S ⲡⲉⲑⲏⲡ) ἀόρατος;
BG 22 S ⲛⲓⲁ. ⲉⲣⲟϥ, BM 187 130 S seeking in
ⲡⲉⲓⲁⲟⲣⲁⲧⲟⲛ enquiring in ⲡⲉⲓⲁ. ⲉⲣⲟⲟⲩ, CaiThe
122 B ⲡⲓⲁⲧϣ ⲛ. ⲉⲣⲟϥ. ⲉⲣ ⲁⲑⲛ. B: ROC 23 280

she having thus spoken ⲁⲓⲉⲣ ⲁ. ⲉⲣⲟⲥ *lost sight of
her*. V also ⲛ. ⲙⲃⲟⲗ.

ⲣⲉϥⲛ. SB, *seer*: Job 34 21 B (S vb) ὁρατής;
MG 25 63 B ⲛⲉⲟⲩⲣ. ⲡⲉ having revelations from
God, P 129²⁰ 122 S Thou hast created me ⲛⲣ. ⲉⲣⲟⲓ
ⲁⲩⲱ ⲡⲁⲧⲛ. ⲉⲣⲟⲓ in same φύσις (cf Renaudot *Lit²*
2 422), ROC 25 258 B some of ⲛⲣ. beheld soul
borne upward. Cf ⲣⲉϥⲛ. ⲉⲃⲟⲗ. As adj B, *seeing*:
AM 290, C 43 208 prayer to Christ ⲛⲓⲃⲁⲗ ⲛⲣ.
ⲉⲣ ⲣ. B, *become seer, spectator*: 2 Pet 1 16 (S ⲛ. vb)
ἐπόπτης γίνεσθαι.

ϭⲓⲛ-, ϫⲓⲛⲛ. S (rare) B nn f m, *sight, vision*: Dan
9 23 B (S ⲥⲱⲗⲡ ⲉⲃ.), 2 Cor 12 1 B (S ⲟⲩⲱⲛϩ ⲉⲃ.).
HL 108 B sent angel in ϫ. ⲡⲧⲉ ⲡⲓⲉϫⲱⲣϩ ὀπτασία,
Dan 2 31 B ὅρασις, MG 25 254 B ϯϫ. ⲉⲣⲟϥ *his
aspect* εἶδος; HL 110 B ϯϫ. seen in night ἔκστασις;
Sa 2 15 B (S ⲛ.) βλέπειν, CaiEuch 393 B ϫⲓⲛⲕⲓⲙ,
ϫ., ϫⲓⲛϫⲟⲙϫⲉⲙ βλέμμα; BIF 13 108 S palms &
pools & other such ϭ. = MG 25 293 B, Bor 226
181 S hateful ϩⲏⲧϭ. ⲉⲣⲟϥ, C 86 105 B strong
ϫⲉⲛⲡⲉϥϫ. ⲉⲣⲟϥ.

ⲛⲁⲩ SB, ⲛⲟⲩ S (v below), ⲛⲱ SᵃF, ⲛⲟ AO,
ⲛⲉⲩ A²F nn m, *hour, time*: Jos 11 6 S, Su 13 SB,
Si 35 11 S, Mt 14 15 SBF, Jo 4 52 SA² (B ⲟⲩⲛⲟⲩ)
ὥρα; Mk 11 13 S (var & B ⲥⲛⲩ), Aeg 210 S ⲛⲛ.
ⲛⲧⲉⲡⲣⲟⲥⲫⲟⲣⲁ καιρός; Ge 29 7 S (B diff) ἡμέρα;
1 Kg 20 41 S (var ⲕⲁⲩ) συντέλεια; Ps 89 4 B ⲛ.
ⲡⲁⲣⲉϩ (S ⲟⲩⲣϣⲉ), Bar 3 31 B ⲛ. ⲡⲣⲱⲓⲥ φυλακή;
Gk om: Su 15 B ⲫⲛ. ⲙⲡⲓⲕⲁⲩⲙⲁ (var om ⲫⲛ.);
ShBM 992 S (let) each speak ⲙⲡⲉϥⲛ., J 79 31 S
when he attained ⲡⲛ. ⲛⲑⲓⲗⲓⲕⲓⲁ, PS 26 S she gazed
ⲙⲡⲛ. ⲡⲟⲩⲟⲩⲛⲟⲩ, C 86 290 B sim (var ⲫⲟⲩⲱϣ),
AM 153 B ⲁϥⲉⲣ ⲟⲩⲛ. gazing, Miss 4 187 B ⲙⲫⲛ.
ⲛⲧⲟⲩⲛⲟⲩ ⲡⲁⲡⲁⲛⲕⲏ, J 65 3 S ϣⲁⲣⲉⲧⲉⲩⲛⲟⲩ ⲙⲡⲙ-
ⲙⲟⲩ ⲉⲓ ⲡⲁϣ ⲛⲛ., ib 85 30 S since ⲛⲛ. of prophet
Samuel, BMis 388 S ⲁⲛⲛ. ϣⲱⲡⲉ for us to go =
BSM 42 B; iteration: ShA 2 278 S to see one another ⲙⲛⲛ. ⲛⲛ., MIE 2 404 B ⲡⲉⲕϣⲗⲏⲗ ⲛⲁⲡⲛ.
ⲛⲛ.; *daylight*: 2 Kg 3 35 S ⲉⲣⲉⲡⲛ. ⲛⲃⲟⲗ (var
ⲉⲟⲩⲛ ⲡ. ⲛⲃ.) ἔτι οὔσης ἡμέρας; Mor 53 75 S didst
come ⲉⲩⲛ ⲡ. ⲛⲃⲟⲗ ? (v ⲃⲱⲗ, ⲛⲃⲟⲗ II c).

With ϫⲛ-, ⲁϫⲛ-: Mk 15 25 SBF, Jo 1 39 SB,
MG 25 210 B ὥρα, Lu 23 44 SB ὡσεὶ ὥ.; PS 7 S,
AP 2 A² sim, C 43 226 B ⲉⲧⲁⲫⲛ. ⲡⲁϫⲡⲥ̅ ϣⲱⲡⲓ.

Morning, early hour: ⲛⲛ., ⲫⲛ. ⲛ̄ϣⲱⲣⲡ 3 Kg 17
6 B, Ps 142 8 S (B ϩⲁⲛⲁⲧⲟⲟⲩⲓ) τὸ πρωί, Ex 19 16
B, Ac 5 21 S (B diff) ὄρθρος; ⲛⲛ. ⲛⲣⲧⲟⲟⲩⲉ, ⲡϩⲁ-
ⲡⲁⲧⲟⲟⲩⲓ, ⲧⲟⲟⲩⲓ Lev 6 13 S (B ϫⲉⲛⲛⲛ. ⲛⲧⲉ ϩ.), Ez
12 8 SB τὸ π., Ps 72 14 SB εἰς τὰς πρωίας, ib 21
tit S (B ⲛ. ⲛϣ.) ἑωθινός, LCyp 27 S = Mor 18 176
S ⲛⲛ. ⲛϣ.; ⲛⲛ. ⲙⲡⲟⲩⲟⲉⲓⲛ FR 84 S, C 43 47, 60
B sim; ⲛⲛ. when cock croweth Mk 13 35 S (B
diff) ἀλεκτοροφωνία, MG 25 400 B ⲫⲛ. ⲙⲡⲓⲁⲗⲉⲕ-

ⲧⲱⲣ. *Midday*: ⲡⲛ. ⲙⲙⲉⲉⲣⲉ Job 5 14 *S* (*B* om ⲛ.), Ps 90 6 *S* (*B* do) μεσημβρινός, Su 7 *S* (*B* diff) μέσον ἡμέρας; BSM 66 *B* ⲫⲛ. ⲙⲙⲉⲣⲓ. *Evening*: ⲡⲛ., ⲫⲛ. ⲡⲣⲟⲩϩⲉ, -ϩⲓ, ϩⲁⲡⲁⲣⲟⲩϩⲓ Ge 8 11 *SB*, Ez 33 22 *SB*, Lu 24 29 *S* (*B* om ⲛ.) ἑσπέρα, Jer 31 33 *B* δείλη; ⲫⲛ. ⲡⲣⲱⲧⲡ ⲙⲫⲣⲏ Ge 15 17 *B* (*S* Gk om ⲛ.) πρὸς δυσμάς.

ⲛⲟⲩ *S* only for periods of day as above: ⲛ. ⲡϣⲱⲣⲡ Ps 87 13, *ib* 89 14, Cant 6 9, Is 58 8 (all var ⲛⲁⲩ); ⲛ. ⲙⲙⲉⲉⲣⲉ Si 31 17, Jer 15 8, Zeph 2 4, Ac 22 6 (*B* ⲕⲱϯ); ⲛ. ⲡⲣⲟⲩϩⲉ Ex 12 6 (WS 47, var ⲛⲁⲩ), Deu 16 6 ⲛ. ⲙⲡⲛⲁⲩ ⲛⲣ., Is 17 13.

ⲛⲟϭ, ⲛⲓϣϯ ⲛⲛ., *great, long time*: Mk 6 35 *S* (*B* ⲟⲩⲛⲟⲩ) ὥ. πολλή; BMar 131 *S* stood at door ⲛⲟⲩⲛ. ⲛⲛ., MIE 2 399 *B* ⲉⲣ ⲟⲩⲛ. ⲛⲛ. = BAp 98 *S* ⲕⲱⲟⲩ, AM 280 *B* ⲉⲧⲁⲟⲩⲛ. ⲛⲛ. ϣⲱⲡⲓ, *ib* 278 *B* standing ϣⲁⲟⲩⲛ. ⲛⲛ. ἐπὶ φανεράς; ⲕⲟⲩϫⲓ ⲛⲛ. *B*, *little time*: C 89 63 hid himself ⲉⲛⲟⲩⲕ. ⲛⲛ. πρὸς ὀλίγον.

Adverbial expressions **a** *every hour, always*, ⲛ. ⲛⲓⲙ, ⲛⲓⲃⲉⲛ &c: Lev 16 2 *S* (*B* ⲟⲩⲛⲟⲩ), 1 Cor 15 30 *S* (*B* do) πᾶσαν ὥ.; MG 25 233 *B* look upward ⲛⲛ. ⲛ., BM 181 2 *S* mind darkened ⲛⲛ. ⲛ. πάντοτε; PS 25 *S* gazing leftward ⲛⲛ. ⲛ., C 43 73 *B* ⲙⲙⲟⲛ ⲁⲧⲱⲛ ⲛⲛ. ⲛ., PGM 1 60 *O* ⲛⲟ ⲛⲓⲙ ⲟⲩⲛ[ⲟⲩ] ⲛⲓⲙ, J 68 77 *S* ⲕⲁⲛ ϯⲛⲟⲩ ⲛ ϣⲁⲡ. ⲛ., ST 42 *Sᵃ* ϣⲁⲡⲱ ⲛ., AZ 33 54 *F* ⲡⲱ ⲛⲓⲙ, BP 3241 *F* ⲛ. ⲛⲓⲃⲓ ϣⲁⲕ ϣⲱⲡⲓ [ⲉ]ⲥⲱⲟⲩ; ⲛⲛ. ⲧⲏⲣⲟⲩ: MG 25 39 *B* read Scriptures ⲛⲛⲛ. ⲧ. **b** *when* ϩⲁ ⲛⲛ. ⲛ-: Mk 1 32 *S* (*B* = Gk) ὅτε, AM 51 *B* ϭⲉⲛⲛⲓⲛ. ⲉⲧⲟⲩⲛⲁⲓ ⲛⲓ; ⲛⲁϣ ⲛⲛ.: Jo 6 25 *S* (*B* ⲛⲟⲏⲛ.) πότε (*cf* ⲧⲛⲁⲩ below); ⲙⲛⲛ., ⲙⲛⲛ. + rel: CO 228 *S* we asked thee ⲙⲛⲛ. ⲛⲧⲁⲕⲉⲓ ⲉϩⲟⲩⲛ *at time of thy coming*, C 43 132 *B* ⲙ. ⲉⲧⲁⲩⲁϣⲕ on cross, J 67 43 *S* sitting by him ⲙ. ⲉϥⲛⲁⲙⲟⲟⲩ; om ⲙ-: Ep 260 *Sᵃ* ⲛⲡⲱ ⲛⲧⲁⲓϣⲱⲡⲉ, ST 91 *Sᵃ* ⲛⲡⲱ ⲉⲧⲕⲛⲁϫⲡⲟⲩⲛ; **c** *then* ⲙⲛⲛ. ⲉⲧⲙⲙⲁⲩ: Aeg 284 *S* gave sentence ⲙ. ⲉⲧ., MG 25 11 *B* ϭⲉⲛⲛⲓⲛ. ⲉⲧ. he fell on face. **d** *just now, meanwhile, forthwith*, of past or fut ⲙ ⲡⲉⲓⲛ., ⲙⲛⲁⲓⲛ.: Miss 4 531 *S* hast visited brethren's cells ⲙ. ?, AM 82 *B* I have drunk ⲙ., Ep 243 *S* ϯⲛⲏⲩ ⲉⲡⲣⲏⲧ ⲙ., *ib* 335 *Sᵃ* bring it us (ⲙ)ⲡⲉⲛⲱ, ST 389 *S* neglect not to send ⲙⲡⲉⲛ. (*sic* l) **e** *at this* (*same*) *time* ⲡⲁⲓⲛ.: Ex 9 18 *B* ταύτην τὴν ὥ., AM 305 *B* ⲛⲁⲓⲛ. ⲡⲣⲁⲥⲧ ye shall end your fight. **f** *up to the hour, until* ϣⲁ ⲛⲛ.: Mk 15 33 *SBF* ἕως ὥ. CO 221 *S* I will work ϣ. ⲉϥⲛⲁⲃⲱⲕ, PGol 47 *A* ϣⲁⲡⲛⲟ ⲉⲧⲟⲩⲛⲏⲩ ⲉⲡⲉⲕϭⲓϫ. **g** *before now* (?) ϩⲁ ⲑⲏ ⲙⲛⲛ.: Miss 4 581 (Ming 208) *S* as he said ϩ. ⲙ. when teaching them. **h** *from the hour* ϫⲓⲛ ⲛⲛ., ⲓⲥϫⲉⲛⲫⲛ.: BMis 386 *S* ϫ. ⲛⲧⲁⲡⲉⲛ ⲧⲁⲡⲁⲣⲭⲏ ⲉⲃⲟⲗ = BSM 41 *B*; *henceforth* ϫⲓⲛⲙ ⲡⲉⲓⲛ., ⲓⲥϫⲉⲛ ⲡⲁⲓⲛ.: Ez 16 63 *SB* ἔτι, Tob 10 8 *S* οὐκέτι; ShC

73 166 *S* have no share therein ϫ., AM 21 *B* whose soldier I am ⲓⲥϫ.

ⲣ ⲛ. *S, be time*: Ge 29 7 (*B* ⲛ. ϣⲱⲡⲓ) οὔπω ὥ.; ShA 1 420 I will taste naught ⲙⲡⲁⲧⲣ ⲛ., R 1 3 39 arise, go ϫⲉⲁϥⲣ ⲛ. ⲛⲛⲟⲩⲥⲩⲛⲁϫⲓⲥ.

ⲧⲛ. *SF*, ⲧⲛⲛⲁⲩ *S*, ⲛⲟⲏⲛ. *B*, ⲛⲧⲛ. *S* (rare) *F*, *when?*: Ge 30 30 *S* ⲛⲧⲛ. *B*, Job 2 9 *SB*, Ps 93 8 *B* (*S* ϭⲉ), Pro 6 9 *SB* (*A* ϣⲁⲧⲉⲟ ϩⲱⲡⲉ), Mk 13 35 *BF* (*S* ⲛⲁϣ ⲛⲛ.), He 1 5 *B* (*SF* ⲉⲛⲉϩ) πότε; Deu 28 67 *S* (var ⲛⲧⲛ.) *B* πῶς ἄν; PS 815 *S* know not ϫⲉⲉϥ ⲡⲁϣⲱⲡⲉ ⲧⲛ., BG 66 *S* expecting ϫⲉⲉⲩⲛⲁⲡⲧⲟⲩ ⲉⲃⲟⲗ ⲧⲛⲛⲁⲩ, BP 9445 *S* inform me ϫⲉⲉⲕⲛⲁⲃⲱⲕ ⲧⲛⲛⲁⲩ, Mun 167 *S* ⲛⲧⲁⲡⲭⲟⲉⲓⲥ ⲣ ⲣⲣⲟ ⲛⲧⲛ. *since when*, BSM 46 *B* ⲛⲟⲏⲛ. ⲁϥⲓ ϣⲁⲣⲟⲛ = BMis 395 *S* ⲁϣⲱⲡⲉ ⲡⲉϩⲟⲟⲩ ⲛⲧⲁⲕⲉⲓ, BSM 47 *B* will tell you ϫⲉ ⲑⲛ. ⲡⲉ ⲉⲧⲁⲓⲓ = BMis 396 *S* ⲛⲧⲁⲉⲓ...ⲛⲁϣ ⲛⲟⲩⲟⲉⲓϣ, BM 597 *F* ⲉⲛⲧⲉⲛⲏⲩ (as if ⲛⲧⲉⲩⲛⲟⲩ).

ϣⲁⲧⲛ., ϣⲁⲟⲛ., *until when?*: 1 Kg 16 1 *S*, Ps 73 10 *SB*, Jo 10 24 *SB* (*A²* ϣⲁⲡⲧⲉⲉⲩ ϣⲱⲡⲉ), Mt 17 17 *S* ϩⲉⲱⲥ ϣ. *B* ϣ. ἕως πότε; Ex 16 28 *SB*, Hab 1 2 *SB* (*A* ϣⲁⲧⲉⲟ ϩⲱⲡⲉ) ἕως τίνος, Job 8 2 *SB* μέχρι τ.; Mor 40 26 *S*, C 43 55 *B* ϣⲁⲟⲛ. = Mor 39 35 *S* ϣⲁⲟⲩⲏⲣ ⲛⲟⲩⲟⲉⲓϣ, MMA 14 1 170 *S* ϣⲁⲧⲛⲛⲁⲩ ⲉⲕⲉϯ ⲟⲥⲉ [ⲉⲧⲉⲕ]ⲯⲩⲭⲏ? Etymol of ⲧⲛ. Spg 148 (but ? from dem *tn*, & not related to ⲛⲁⲩ HT).

ⲛⲁⲩ- *B* about *v* ⲁ- advb.

ⲛⲁⲁⲩ *v* ⲉⲓⲁⲁⲩ.

ⲛⲁⲟⲩ *O* *v* ⲛⲁⲩ vb.

ⲛⲏⲩ, ⲛⲏⲟⲩ, ⲛⲛⲏⲩ *v* ⲛⲟⲩ.

ⲛⲟⲩ *S hour* *v* ⲛⲁⲩ nn.

ⲛⲁⲩⲓ, ⲛⲁⲃⲓ, ⲛⲁⲣⲃⲓ *B* nn m, *spear*: 1 Kg 17 45 (*S* ⲙⲉⲣⲉϩ), Job 41 17 (ⲛⲁⲣ.), Mic 4 3 (*SA* do) δόρυ; Is 2 4 (ⲛⲁⲣ., *S* ϫⲉⲃⲏⲗ), Jer 6 23 ζιβύνη; K 116 ⲛⲛ. مزرق (l سفود), *javelin, spike* (between σειρομάστης رمح & ὀβελός سنان).

ⲛⲟⲩⲉ- *F* *v* ⲟⲩⲃⲉ-.

ⲛⲟⲩⲟⲉⲓ *S* *v* ⲟⲩⲟⲓ.

ⲛⲁⲩⲃⲉⲛ *B*, ⲛⲉⲩϩⲟⲩ *F* nn as pl, *footstep*: Ps 16 5 *BF* (Mor 33 2 ⲛⲁϣ ⲛⲛⲉⲩϩⲟⲩ), *ib* 17 36, 118 133 *B* (all *S* ⲧⲁϭⲥⲉ) διάβημα.

ⲛⲱⲟⲩϯ *B* nn, *swaddling bands*: Va 57 115 (*v* AZ 13 109) time when no longer manger nor ϩⲁⲛⲛ., cave, guiding star nor flight to Egypt, but Son of Man appearing in glory, K 118 ⲡⲓⲟⲩⲛⲱⲟⲩϯ (so MSS, *l* ? ⲡⲓⲟⲩⲁⲓ ⲛⲛ. or om ⲡⲓ-) قماط, *ib* 259 مياقيط (Bevan ? مقاميط), اطناب.

ⲛⲟⲟⲩϩⲉ *S* nn f, *meaning unknown*: Mor 51 39 (parable) take sickles moving to & fro ⲉⲣⲉⲧⲉⲩⲛ

ⲕⲱⲧⲉ ⲉⲡⲟⲉⲓⲕ, (interpret) take men ⲉⲣⲉⲡⲉⲩϩⲏⲧ ⲡⲟ-
ⲟⲩⲣⲉ (? = ⲡⲟⲩϫⲉ) ⲉⲡϫⲟⲉⲓⲥ *whose hearts turn* (?) *to
Lord* (? play upon 2 words).

ⲛⲁϥⲣⲓ *B v* ⲡⲁⲡⲣⲉ.

ⲛϫⲁⲓ *B v* ⲡⲕⲁ.

ⲛⲉϣ *F v* ϣ vb.

ⲛⲟⲉⲓϣ *S,* ⲛⲁⲓϣ *Sᵃ,* ⲛⲱⲓϣ *B* nn m, *spleen*: P
44 70 = 43 41 *S* ⲥⲡⲗⲏⲛ · ⲡⲛ. طحال, Glos 55 *Sᵃ* ⲡⲛ.,
K 78 *B* 'ⲧ, PMéd 173 *S* ⲛⲉⲧϣⲱⲡⲉ ⲉⲡⲉⲅⲛ.

ⲛⲁϣⲉ-, ⲛⲁϣⲱ⸗ *SAA²BF,* ⲛⲁⲁϣⲱ⸗ *A* (Cl) vb
intr (nominal vb), *be many, much,* cf ⲁϣⲁⲓ: Deu 3
19 *S* (*B* ⲙⲏⲛϣ), Job 5 25 *S* (*B* ⲁϣⲁⲓ), Joel 2 11 *A*
(*B* do), Mk 6 31 *S* (*B* do) πολύς, 2 Kg 18 8 *S*
πλεονάζης; Ps 139 10 *B* ⲛ. ⲡⲉϥⲗⲁⲥ (*S* ⲁϣ ⲟⲉⲓⲛ)
γλωσσώδης; PS 277 *S* ⲛ. ⲡⲉⲧⲡⲏⲧ ⲛⲥⲱⲡ, DeV 2
215 *B* ⲛ. ⲡⲏ ⲉⲧⲁⲩⲙⲟⲩ, BHom 82 *S* ⲛⲉⲩϩⲃⲏⲕⲉ
ⲛⲁϣⲱϥ.

Rel ⲉⲧⲛ. as adj, *many, great*: Ex 2 23 *S* (*B* ⲁϣⲁⲓ),
Ps 35 6 *S* (*B* ⲛⲁⲁ⸗) ⲡⲟ., Pro 1 13 *SA* (*B* ⲉⲧⲛ. ⲛ-
ⲥⲟⲩⲉⲛ⸗) πολυτελής; 2 Cor 9 14 *S* (*B* ⲉⲣ ϩⲟⲩⲟ), Cl
19 2 *A* ὑπερβάλλων; BG 46 *S* ⲡⲙⲏⲏϣⲉ ⲉⲧⲛⲁϣⲱϥ,
Mor 30 44 *F* ϣⲡⲏⲣⲓ ⲉⲧⲛⲁϣⲱⲟⲩ = BMis 268 *S*
ⲉⲛ.; or ⲉⲛ. sim: Gen 15 14 *S* (*B* ⲛⲓϣϯ), Ps 18
11 *SB,* Is 30 33 *SF* (*B* do), Mic 4 2 *SA* (*B* do),
Jo 6 2 *SA²* (*B* ⲁϣⲁⲓ), Cl 6 1 *A* ⲡⲟ.; Sa 4 13 *S*
μακρός; PS 342 *S* distant ⲣⲛⲟⲩⲟⲩⲉ ⲉⲛⲁϣⲱϥ, DeV
2 13 *B* filled with ⲟⲩⲛⲟⲙϯ ⲉⲛⲁϣⲱⲥ, El 46 *A* ⲉⲥϯⲕ
ⲥⲉⲉⲧⲉ ⲁⲃⲁⲗ ⲉⲛⲁϣⲱϥ. With ⲥⲟⲩⲛⲧ⸗, ⲥⲟⲩⲉⲛ⸗,
price: 1 Chr 29 2 *B,* Is 28 16 *S* (*B* diff) πολυτελής;
Mt 13 46 *SBF,* Jo 12 3 *SAA²B* πολύτιμος; Ez 27
22 *SB* χρηστός; BMar 3 *S* jewels ⲉⲛ. ⲥⲟⲩⲉⲛⲧⲟⲩ,
C 43 180 *B* perfume ⲉⲛ. ⲛⲥⲟⲩⲉⲛϥ.

ⲛⲟⲟϣⲉ (IF), ⲛⲟϣⲉ (A) *S* vb qual, meaning unknown, paral *stinking* of disease: ShIF 101 sickness
ⲉϥϣⲟⲡϣ ⲉϥⲛ., ShA 1 128 ϩⲉⲛϣⲛⲟⲩϣ ⲉⲩⲛ. ⲉⲛⲁϣⲱⲟⲩ of wounds.

ⲛⲟⲩϣⲡ *SAB,* ⲛⲟⲩⲥⲉ *O,* ⲛⲉϣⲡ- *SB,* ⲛⲁϣⲡ- *S,*
ⲛⲟϣⲡ⸗ *SB,* ⲛⲁϣⲡ⸗ *SA,* ⲛⲟϣⲡϯ *B,* ⲣⲉ ⲛⲁϣⲡ- *BF*
vb **I** *blow* of wind *B* (v Spg *Kopt Etym* 5), cf ϣⲱ⸗,
intr: Va 68 164 breezes of youth ⲉⲩⲛ. ⲛⲁϩⲣⲁϥ
ῥιπίζειν, BMOr 8775 108 ⲣⲓⲛⲓⲍⲓⲛ · ⲉϥⲛ. نافر جافل
(cf next meaning); tr *B*: Jer 22 14 ϩⲁⲛⲙⲁ
ⲉⲩⲛⲉϣⲡ ⲕⲁⲃⲱⲟⲩ ῥιπιστός, as nn P 55 17 ⲣⲉⲛⲓⲁⲓⲁ
(ῥιπίδιον) · ϯⲛⲉϣⲡ ⲑⲏⲟⲩ مرؤح. Hence **II** *agi-
tate, frighten, overawe SABO* a tr: Ru 2 16 *S,* Mk
10 48 *S* (*B* = Gk) ἐπιτιμᾶν, ib 10 14 *S* (*B* ⲧⲁϩⲛⲟ)
κωλύειν; Jer 21 13 *B* (*S* ϣⲧⲟⲣⲧⲣ) πτοεῖν; Job 7
14 *S* (*B* ϣⲟⲣ.) καταπλήσσειν, Pro 24 65 *SA* (*B*
ⲉⲣ ϩⲟϯ ⲃⲁ⸗) καταπτήσσειν (reading ? -πλήσσειν),
Deu 28 26 *SB* ἐκφοβεῖν; Jer 7 33 *B* ἀποσοβεῖν;

Ac 4 17 *B* (*S* ⲡⲁⲣⲁⲅⲅⲉⲓⲗⲉ) ἀπειλεῖν; 1 Kg 25 7 *S*
(var ⲛ. ⲉⲃⲟⲗ) ἐντέλλεσθαι (var ἐνοχλεῖν, cf ib 15);
Ez 7 21 *B* (*S* diff) διαφθείρειν; Ge 32 25 *B* (*S* l
ⲛⲟⲩⲱϣⲥ q v); JA '05 1 434 *S* ⲁⲅⲛⲟϣⲡϥ saying Get
thee gone (cf ⲛ. ⲉⲃⲟⲗ), Mor 47 135 *S* sim (cf Amélineau *Contes* 2 45), MG 25 81 *B* let us affright
him ⲁⲣⲏⲟⲩ ⲧⲉⲛⲛⲁϣ ⲛⲟϣⲡϥ, PGM 1 114 *O* may
your power protect (?) NN ⲥⲁⲧⲉⲧⲉⲛⲛⲟⲩⲥⲉ ⲡⲁⲓ ⲡⲁ-
ⲕⲁⲑⲁⲣⲧⲟⲥ (l ⲡⲁⲓ ⲁⲕ.). **b** intr, *be frightened BF*:
Deu 31 6, Jer 34 4, Hab 3 7 (*A* ϩⲧⲁⲣⲧⲣⲉ), Lu 21
9 (all *S* ϣⲧ.) ⲡⲧⲟ., Jer 27 2 neg ἀπτόητος; Lev 26
6 (*S* ⲫⲣϣⲟ) ἐκφ.; Hos 4 16 (*A* ⲡⲱⲥϩ ⲁⲃⲁⲗ) παρ-
οιστρᾶν; Phil 1 28 (*SF* ⲣ ϩⲟⲧⲉ) πτυρεῖν; AM 267
ⲁⲓⲛ. on a sudden θροεῖν; C 89 21 demon as crow-
ing cock, but Pachôm ⲙⲡⲉϥⲛ. ⲉⲡⲧⲏⲣϥ, Mor 30 31
F ⲁⲛⲙⲟⲅⲗⲗⲁ (= BMis 257 ⲧⲁⲙⲟⲩⲗⲓⲥ) ⲛ., DeV 2
184 sim.

With following preposition. **c** ⲉ- (obj) *S, shake,
disturb*: ShP 130³ 15 enemies ⲛ. ⲉⲡⲛⲁϩⲃ ⲛⲧⲕⲟⲓⲛⲱⲛⲓⲁ, Tri 429 ⲙⲡⲣⲛ. ⲉⲣⲟϥ حقر *contemn.* **c** ⲉⲃⲟⲗ
ⲛ- *SB*: Job 23 15 *B* (no *S*) ⲡⲧⲟ. ἐξ; Z 321 *S* ἀπο-
σείειν; ShIF 88 *S* sin devoureth wicked ⲉⲁⲛ ⲡⲉⲧ-
ⲛⲁⲡⲟϣⲡϥ ⲉⲃ. ⲙⲙⲟⲟⲩ ⲏ ϩⲓⲭⲱⲟⲩ. **c** ⲉⲃ. ϩⲓϫⲉⲛ-
S, scare from off: Deu 28 26 *SB* ἐκφοβεῖν, Job 38
13 *S* (*B* ϩⲓⲟⲩⲓ ⲉⲃ. ϩ.) ἐκτινάσσειν; Mich 550 24 *S*
ⲛⲉⲧⲛ. ⲡⲛⲉⲑⲏⲣⲓⲟⲛ ⲉⲃ. ϩⲓⲭⲱⲛ; ⲉⲃ. ϩⲁ- *B* sim: AM
254 ⲛ. ⲛⲛⲁⲓⲟⲩⲱⲛϣ ⲉⲃ. ϩⲁⲣⲟⲛ. **c** ϩⲁ-, ϣⲁ- *SB,
be scared away from*: Mor 40 13 *S* horse ⲛ. ϩⲁⲣⲟϥ
= C 43 43 *B* = Wess 15 122 *S* ⲉⲃⲟⲗ ϩⲁ-. **c** ϩⲓ-
S: Z 627 ⲛⲟϣⲡϥ (sc sick man) ϩⲓϩⲣⲡ, l ? ⲛⲟϣϥϥ.
c ⲛⲥⲁⲃⲟⲗ, ⲥⲁⲃⲟⲗ ⲛ-, *S, scare, drive away from*:
Z 345 ⲉϥⲛ. ⲡⲡⲉⲍⲉⲗⲙⲱⲛ ⲥ. ⲙⲙⲟϥ διώκειν; ib 264
ⲛⲧⲛ. wolves ⲛⲥⲁⲃⲟⲗ ⲙ.ⲛⲟϩⲉ, GFr 306 may this
liturgy ⲛ. ⲥ. ⲙⲙⲟⲟⲩ all mischief. **c** ϣⲉⲛ- *B,
awake from* CDan 89 *B* ⲁⲓⲛⲟⲩϣ ϣⲉⲛ-
ⲡⲓϩⲟⲣⲁⲙⲁ διυπνίζειν; ⲉⲃⲟⲗ ϣⲉⲛ- *B*: Va 58 183
birds ⲉⲩϣⲁⲛ. ⲉⲃ. ϣⲉⲛⲟⲩⲡⲉⲧⲣⲁ *scared from.* **c**
ϣⲁϫⲉⲛ- *B, be scared by, at*: Is 31 4 (*SF* ϣⲧ.) ⲡⲧⲟ.

With following adverb. **c** ⲉⲃⲟⲗ intr *B, be scared
away*: BMAdd 39583 devil would that they ⲛ. ⲉⲃ.
ϩⲓⲧⲉⲛⲡⲉϥⲫⲁⲛⲧⲁⲥⲓⲁ; tr *SB, scare away*: Ps 108
23 *SB,* ib 126 4 *SB* ἐκτιν.; Si 22 21 *SA* ἀποσοβ.;
Va 58 193 *B* smoke ⲉⲩϣⲁϥⲛ. ⲉⲃ. ⲛⲛⲓⲁϥ ⲛⲉⲃⲓⲱ ἀπο-
διώκειν; Jer 23 2 *S* (*B* ϩⲓⲟⲩⲓ ⲉⲃ.) ἐξωθεῖν; Z 610 *S*
σάρδιον stone ϣⲁϥⲛ. ⲉⲃ. ⲛⲛⲡⲁⲑⲟⲥ, Sh(?)Mor 54 93
S ⲛⲛⲉⲩⲛⲁϣⲡ ϣⲉⲡⲧⲟⲩ ⲉⲃ. *blow nose* in sanctuary
(cf ⲛⲓϣⲉ **I**), Leip 24 17 *B* ⲁⲩ]ⲛⲟⲃϣϥ ⲉⲃ. saying Get
thee gone (Miss 4 185 om); **c** ⲉⲫⲁϩⲟⲩ *B* intr,
be scared back: C 86 224 on hearing this ⲁⲩⲛⲟⲃϣⲡ
(l ⲛⲟⲩϣⲡ) ⲉⲫ. for were afraid.

—— *B* nn m, *fright*: Pro 3 25 (*S* ϩⲟⲧⲉ, *A* ϩⲛⲱ-
ⲱⲣⲉ) πτόησις, Bodl 325 (Lacr) ⲛⲡⲛ. خوف.

ⲛⲁϣⲡⲏⲣⲓ *B* (sic prob) *F* for ⲛⲁϣⲡ ⲛⲏⲣⲓ nn m,

scare-quail, scare-crow (v пнре): EpJer 70 προβα-σκάνιον.

Cf пoүщс.

нoшp S, -ep B nn m, *vulture, falcon, cf* נשר (IgR): Lev 11 14 B (S om) عنقاء, Deu 14 12 B (S prob пoүpe) 'ع, Job 15 23 B пoүeщep (S do) γύψ; نسر; P 44 55 S ἀγριέραξ (*sic*) · пп. باز (but 43 22 ἀγρ. 'ب · пп. 'ـس), K 167 B 'ب. Prob not in place-name ϯaпoщep (Amélineau *Géog* 143).

нoүщc SF, пoүce A², нoщc⸗ S vb intr, *grow numb*: Ge 32 32 S (B пoүщп انفرز), *ib* 25 S пoү-xc (*l* -щc, B do tr) ναρκᾶν; Ez 18 2 S (BMis 219, var Miss 8 152, 187 -⸗c, B cоepтep) γομφιάζειν, αἰμωδιᾶν, cit Tri 700 S تفرس; *tr* S, *benumb*: ShRE 10 161 devil hath scattered them aчпoщcoү & subdued them, Z 627 *v* пoүщп ϩi-; 1 Tim 5 1 мпрпoщcoү *rebuke*, ἐπιπλήσσειν. As nn m, *numbness*: Si 30 10 S (var -⸗c) γομφ., Am 4 6 S (*sic l*, B ⸗ϫpιϫ) γομφιασμός; Si 21 5 S καταπληγμός; Eccl 7 6 F (S ϫпιo) ἐπιτίμησις; ClPr 40 1 S eчϫωϩ eпп. мпeчмнpoc (*cf* Ge 32 25); Deu 28 22 S (but *l* -⸗c, B щϭпнп) ἐρεθισμός whence BM 1223 A² пoүce (*v* apoщ).

нoщcч S nn m, *striker*: 1 Tim 3 3, Tit 1 7 (both B peчϯ тeпщi) πλήκτης.

V LAl 82 on confusion пoүщc, -⸗c, -щп.

нoүщт S, пoүϭт A vb intr, *become heavy, hard*: Is 6 10 S (B oүмoт) παχύνειν (cit Mt 13 15 S where пщoт & Ac 28 27 S do, var βαρύνειν); BG 75 S aчтωм ппeϩнт aүп. eвoλ ϩмпoүщт of the ἀντίμιμον πνα; *tr* (refl), meaning uncer-tain: Pro 19 25 SA щape пaϩнт п. ммoч πανουρ-γότερος γίνεσθαι. As nn, *strength, violence*: Mor 37 234 S high tide ϯ мпeсoүoi ϩпoүп. to destroy Alexandria, BG *ut sup*. пaщт qual of this or ? of пщoт *q v*.

нщiт S (or ? щiт) nn as pl, meaning unknown: Mor 51 35 (parable) aпкω пeпщ. eүтoϭc пoүωϭ мпeпϫeкϫωкoү (interpret) shelves full of books, yet we read not.

нщoт eп. SB, пϩaт A, пaщт† SA²BF, пaϩт† A, пeщт† F, p c пaщт- SBF, пaϩт- A vb intr, *be hard, strong, difficult* & related meanings: Deu 15 18 S (B†), Ps 16 4† SBF, Pro 27 16† SA, Jo 6 60† SA²BF σκληρὸς εἶναι, Ex 4 21 B (A ϯ п.), Ro 9 18 B (var пщωт, S ϯ п.), Cl 51 3 A σκληρύ-νειν, Job 39 16 B ἀποσκλ.; Deu 21 4† SB, Is 40 4† SB, Lu 3 5† SB τραχύς, Ps 90 3† S (reading ? τραχώδης, B peчщoopтep), Si 34 25† S (reading ? ἐντραχύς); Ge 48 17† S (B ϩpoщ), Si 34 2† S βαρύς, Ac 28 27 S (B oүмoт) βαρύνειν (*cf* пoүщт); Job 2 13† S (B мokϩ), Sa 5 2† S (B пiщϯ) δεινός,

ib 18 17† S δεινῶς; Nu 13 28† B (S пaщт ϩнт), Pro 13 17† B (SA пa. ммe) θρασύς; Is 18 2† S (B om), 2 Tim 3 1† S (B ϩwoү) χαλεπός; Deu 28 27† S (B = Gk) ἄγριος; Is 17 5† S(B ϫop), Jer 15 18† SB στερεός, Deu 15 7† B (S diff) ἀποστερίζειν; 1 Kg 23 19† S αὐχμώδης; Jos 6 20† S, Pro 6 2† SA (B diff) ἰσχυρός; Mor 37 98 S кaмa eчп.† σφοδρό-τατος; Ps 47 8 B (S пϭoпc), Sa 19 7 S βίαιος; Deu 6 22†, 28 60† S (B ϩwoү) πονηρός; Deu 8 15† S, Ps 113 8†, 135 16† S (all B пщωт as from щωт *cut*), Sa 11 4† S ἀκρότομος; Gk om: Ez 16 22† SB, Ap 6 6† B (S om), BHom 51 S oүнp пpwϩ eчп.† πόσα; PS 260 S darkness eтп.† eмaщo, C 86 270 B sim, ShZ 473 S winds eтп.†, Mor 40 5 S strong in body & eчп.† ϩптeγψүхн = C 43 35 B = Mor 39 7 F, BM 888 B monk's life eтп.†, JTS 4 391 S persecution п.† eмaтe, ShA 1 258 S fruit eчп.† opp кiωoү, PChas 1 23 S recipe тaaч eγкωϩт eчп.† (*cf* к. eткeрa PMéd 148, eтϭнп AZ 23 111), R 2 1 76 S щωпe eчп.† needs ϩeппaϩpe eγп.†, C 41 79 B voice ecп.†, Va 61 114 B sabbath day of rest & чп.† *solemn, important* (?, S paral Mor 25 lost), ShC 42 43 S if man be eчп.† shall die un-timely, P 131⁷ 52 S ппeoүa п. ϩптaпaтн мппoвe.

With following preposition. c e-: Ge 35 17 B п. eмici (S п. nn) σκληρῶς; *dat commodi*: El 98 A фнт пaп. apaү = *ib* 134 S пωщc epooч, Gu 23 S his heart eп. epoч like beast's ἀγριαίνειν, TT 55 S sim; c eϫп-: 1 Kg 31 3 S βαρύνειν ἐπί; Mor 40 11 S eчп.† eϫмпeнoc of Christians = C 43 41 B; eϩpai eϫп-: Jos 19 47 S βαρ. ἐπί; BMis 160 S caused waves to п. eϩ. eϫмпϫoi; c птeп-: Ge 45 5 B σκληρός dat.

пaщтeiмe, -iмe *presumptuous v* eiмe.

пaщтмaкϩ *stiff-necked v* мaкϩ.

пaщтпaϩвi sim *v* пaϩвi.

пaщтϩpa⸗ (ϩo) S, *hard of face, impudent*: Deu 28 50 (B aтщфiт ⸗eппeчϩo) ἀναιδὴς προσώπῳ; P 129¹⁸ 106 ϩaмoi eщωпe пoүϩiϩaλ (п)п. ϩpaч aппe = EW 44 B oүвωк eпaпeч aппe, BMis 244 when saw that oүп. ϩpaчпe = Patr History *ed* Seybold 62 شديد القوة, BAp 94 ϩeϩпoc пп. ϩpaч пaтщiпe ϩaпeчϩo. мнтп. ϩpooү (*l* ϩpa⸗), *im-pudence*: Mor 25 45.

пaщтϩнт SAB, п. ϩpнт S, *strong, hard of heart*: Nu 13 29 S (B п.†) θρασύς, Pro 14 14 SAB θρασυ-κάρδιος; Ez 3 7 S σκληροκ. мнтп. ϩ., *hard heartedness*: Mt 19 8 SBF σ. καρδία, Ro 2 5 B (S п.) σκληρότης; RNC 25 θράσος; BHom 87 тм. мфaρaω, MR 2 55 A пiмптпaϩтϩ. p, ep п. ϩ., *be hard hearted*: Ac 19 9 B (S п. пϩ.) σκληρύ-νειν; ShA 2 304 S eϫo пп. пϩ., Leip 24 12 B м-пeрep п. ϩ. eϩpнi epωoү.

пϣⲟⲧ *SABF* nn m, *hardness, boldness*: Deu 9 27 *SB*, Is 4 6 *SB* σκληρότης, Mk 10 5 *S* п. ⲡⲣⲏⲧ (*B* ⲙⲉⲧⲛⲁϣⲧⲣ.) σ. καρδία; Ac 27 41 *S* (*B* ϭⲓ ⲡϫⲟⲡⲥ) βία; Ez 19 7 *SB* θράσος; Jer 29 16 *B* (*S* ⲙⲛⲧⲁⲧ-ϣⲓⲡⲉ) ἰταμία; P 45 73 = 44 22 *S* ⲡⲉⲡ. قسال, فجاجة; Sh(Besa)Mich 550 22 *S* God putteth in me ⲟⲩⲛ. ⲡⲣⲏⲧ opp ⲙⲛⲧϭⲁⲃϩⲏⲧ, ShBMOr 8810 428 *S* ⲡⲉⲡ. ⲡⲣ. opp ⲙⲛⲧⲣⲙⲣⲁϣ, DeV 1 130 *B* пп. of wind, Z 265 *S* ⲡⲉⲡ. of demons. Once f *S* (same?) meaning unknown: Ryl 254 account of expenses ϩⲁⲧⲉⲡϣⲟⲧ. ϩⲛ-, ϩⲉⲛⲟⲩⲛ. as advb, *roughly, hardly*: Ge 35 17 *S* (*B* vb), Is 22 3 *B* (*S* ⲉⲙⲁⲧⲉ) σκληρῶς; Hab 2 6 *AB* στιβαρῶς; Sa 17 17 *S* βία; HCons 460 *S* αὐθαδῶς; Pro 24 67 *B* (*SA* diff) μετὰ μάχης; C 89 8 *B* he said ϩ., ShBor 233 245 *S* not seemly to raise voice ϩ., Mor 19 63 *S* attacking him ϩ., var Mor 18 55 ϩⲛⲟⲩϭ ⲡϩⲟⲣⲙⲏ, MG 25 70 *B* pains overtook her ϩ., BMar 202 *S* paralysed feet strike each other ϩⲛⲟⲩϩⲣⲟⲧ (*l*? п-ϣⲟⲧ), *ib* 42 martyr bound between 2 palms ⲡⲥⲉ-ⲕⲁⲁⲩ ⲉⲃⲟⲗ ϩ. *released violently*. ⲙⲛⲧⲡⲁϣⲧ *S*: ShA 1 71 (= Z 397), prob *l* ⲙⲛⲧⲡⲁⲛⲧ.

✝ п. *SAB*, *make hard* (mostly with ϩⲏⲧ), *encourage*: Ex 4 21 *A* (*B* ⲑⲣⲉ п.), He 3 8 *SB*, HL 110 *B* devil ✝ п. ⲉⲡⲉϥϩⲏⲧ σκληρύνειν; 1 Kg 6 6 *S* βαρύνειν; PS 362 *S* ⲡⲥⲉ✝ п. ⲙⲡⲉⲩϩⲏⲧ, Mor 31 24 *S* officer ✝ п. ⲡⲁⲩ saying Smite him.

ⲡⲁϣⲧⲉ *S*, ⲡⲁϣⲧⲉ *A*, ⲡⲁϣ✝ *B*, ⲡⲉϣ✝ *F* nn f *SA*(?), m *B*, *strength, strengthener, protector*: Sa 18 22 *S* ἐνέργεια; Ps 17 2 *S* (*B* ⲣⲉϥ✝ ⲉϩⲣⲏⲓ ⲉϫⲉⲡ-), *ib* 83 9 *S* (*B* ⲣⲉϥ✝ ⲉⲃⲟⲗ ⲉϫ.) ὑπερασπιστής; Si 31 16 *S*, Cl 56 16 *A* -ⲥⲙⲟⲥ; 2 Kg 18 3 *S* βοήθεια, Sa 17 11 *S* -θημα; Ps 70 6 *B* (*S* diff) σκεπαστής, Nah 3 11 *A* (*B* diff) στάσις auxilium; Ps 118 114 *B* (*S* ⲣⲉϥ-ϣⲱⲡ ⲉ-) ἀντιλήμπτωρ; Mor 22 95 *S* Michael ⲧⲛ. of Christians, C 43 247 *B* Jesus ⲡⲁⲡ., RE 9 152 *S* ⲁⲓϭⲱⲡ ⲡⲅⲁⲅⲓⲟⲥ ⲕⲩⲣⲓⲁⲕⲟⲥ пп., BSM 125 *B* set it in my house пп., Wor 309 *S* image ϣⲁⲥϣⲱⲡⲉ пп. for city. As adj: Ps 30 2 *SB* ὑπερασπιστής.

ⲣ, ⲉⲣ п. *SABF*, *be protector*, c ⲉ-: Ps 19 1 *S* (*B* ✝ ⲉϩ. ⲉϫ.), Pro 2 7 *SAB*, Is 31 5 *SF* (*B* do) ὑπερασπίζειν; BAp 82 *S* bishop o пп. ⲉⲡⲉⲡⲧⲟϣ = MIE 2 344 *B* ϣⲱⲡⲓ пп. п-; c п- dat: Ge 15 1 *S* (*B* ⲉϫ.), Sa 5 17 *S* ⲩⲡ.; Deu 32 38 *B* (*S* = Gk) σκεπ. γίνεσθαι; ShR 2 3 32 *S* trusting ⲉⲧⲣⲉⲩⲣ п. ⲡⲁϥ from trouble, AM 118 *B* ⲡⲧⲉϥⲉⲣ п. ⲡⲏⲓ ϩⲉⲡ-ⲧⲉϥⲥⲕⲉⲡⲏ; c ⲉϫⲉⲡ-: Ge *lc B* (*S* п-).

ⲡⲉϣⲧⲉ *B* nn m, *hard, rough person*: Is 48 4 (*S* п.✝) σκληρός; Cat 150 he inciteth пп. by teaching (on Lu 12 42), Va 57 235 ⲡⲓⲉⲡⲓ(ⲉⲓ)ⲕⲏⲥ opp пп. As adj: *ib* 128 ⲣⲉϥ✝ ϩⲁⲡ пп. ὠμός; Cat 132 ⲙⲉⲧ-ⲁⲑⲛⲁⲓ & ϫⲓⲛⲥⲁϫⲓ пп. ⲙⲉⲧп., *roughness*: Va 57 192 ⲙ. & ⲙⲉⲧⲡⲁϣⲧⲣⲏⲧ ὠμότης; ⲉⲣ п., *become*

hard: Job 22 21 (*S* п.✝) σκλ. γίνεσθαι; MG 25 393 idolator ⲉϥⲟⲓ пп. ϩⲉⲡⲟⲩⲙⲉⲧⲧⲓⲣⲁⲡⲡⲟⲥ.

пⲓϣ✝ *B* v ⲡⲟϭ.

ⲛⲉⲉϥ *SA*, ⲡⲉⲉⲃ, ⲡⲉⲉⲩ (PLond), ⲡⲏⲏϥ, ⲡⲏⲏⲃ, ⲡⲏϥ (Ep 681), ⲡⲉϥ, ⲡⲉⲃ *S*, ⲡⲉϥ *B*, ⲡⲏⲏϥ, -ⲃ (BM 546) *F* nn m, *sailor*: Ac 27 27 *SB*, Ap 18 17 *S* (*B* diff) ναύτης, Jon 1 5 *SAB* ναυτικός; Pro 23 34 *SA* κυβερνήτης; Tri 428 *S* ship provided with п. ملاح (var نوتي); MG 25 423 *S* пп. ⲉⲧⲣⲙⲡϫⲟⲓ = DeV 2 151 *B*, Miss 4 729 *S*, *ib* 185 *B* пп. ⲙⲡϫⲟⲓ, WS 104 *S* sim ⲡⲉϥ, DeV 2 206 *B* пп. ⲉⲧⲉⲣ ϩⲱⲧ ϩⲉⲡϥⲓⲟⲙ, Z 633 *S* ⲡⲉⲓⲡⲏⲏⲃ ⲡⲣⲉϥⲁⲙⲥⲭⲟⲓ; BM 1148 *S* пп. ⲉⲁⲕⲧⲁⲗⲟ ⲡⲉⲧⲏⲧⲁⲕ ⲡⲁϥ, Ep 401 *S* give it to пп. ⲡϥϥⲓⲧϥ ⲉⲡϩⲣⲏⲧ, Ryl 347 *S* give jar of wine to ⲡⲉп. for transport of beans, ST 63 *S* ⲉⲩϣⲁⲡⲧⲁⲗⲟⲕ пп. as recruit, JLeip 1 *S* writers will oppose fine (ζημία *l* ζημιοῦν) ϩⲁϣⲱⲡⲉ пп. *for impressing as sailor*, PLond 4 442 *S* п. ⲡⲧⲕⲟⲩⲣⲥⲟⲡ recruited for the *cursus*, Ann 8 89 *S* monk as sailor, AZ 60 108 *S* guild of п., Miss 4 750 *S* ⲣⲱⲙⲉ пп.; *head sailor*: BMar 189 *S* ⲡⲟϭ пп. ⲙⲡϫⲟⲓ ναύκληρος, C 41 18 *B* ⲡⲡⲓϣ✝ пп. = Miss 4 328 رئيس (*cf* Mor 37 200 *S* ⲡⲟϭ ⲡⲡⲁⲅⲕⲗ., Miss 4 101 *B* sim), Ming 328 *S* ⲡⲉⲓⲥⲁϩ пп. ⲉⲧⲣ ϩⲙⲙⲉ. (*cf* P 131³ 34 ⲥⲁϩ п-ⲡⲁⲅⲕⲗ.); *sailor at prow, pilot*: Ez 27 29 *S* (*B* diff) п. ⲡⲑⲏ, Jon 1 6 *SA* п. ⲉⲧϩⲓⲣⲏ, *B*-ϩⲓⲧϩⲏ, LAp 566 *F* пп. ⲙⲡ[ϫⲁⲓ?] (*cf* Gu 55) πρωρεύς; *on various ships*: PLond 4 435, 438 *S* п. ⲕⲁⲣⲁⲃⲏ (καράβιον) recruited for *cursus*, BM 1090 *S* sim, Ryl 144 *S* I engage with thee as п. ⲉⲧⲕⲟⲩⲓ ⲕⲁⲣⲁⲃⲏ; WS 96 *S* пп. ⲙⲡⲗⲓⲃⲉⲣⲡⲟⲥ, BM 1110 *S* пп. ⲉⲧⲕⲁⲧⲟ as letter-carrier; *ferryman*, v ⲉⲓⲟⲟⲣ (ϫⲓⲟⲟⲣ).

ⲁⲧп. *S*, *without sailor*, i e without forced service on ship(?): Kr 145 wage to be paid ⲡⲁⲧⲁⲗⲱⲧ ⲡⲁⲧⲣⲟⲩⲥ(ⲟⲡ) ⲡⲁⲧⲡ., Bodl(P) d 39 δημόσιον paid ⲡⲁ(ⲧ)ⲧⲏⲡⲉ ⲡⲁⲧⲡⲉϥ *without dyke* (-service χωματικά), *without sailor* (-service? ναῦλον). *Cf* TurM 6, though п. not there.

ⲙⲛⲧп. *S*, *condition, trade of sailor*: ShBor 247 120 among various trades.

ⲕⲁⲧⲁп. *F* nn m, *list of sailors, crew*: BM 675. *Cf* PLond 4 450 ⲡⲕⲁⲧⲁⲉⲣⲅⲁⲧⲏⲥ, Ryl 338 ⲡⲕⲁⲧⲁⲧⲓⲙⲉ.

пⲓϥ *SBF* v ⲡⲓϥⲉ nn.

пⲓϥⲉ *SAA²*, -ⲃⲉ *S*, -ϥⲓ *BF*, -ⲃⲓ *F*, ⲡⲁϥⲧ⸗ *S*, ⲡⲉϥⲧ⸗ *SA*, ⲡⲓϥⲧ⸗ *S* vb I intr, *blow, breathe* of wind, breath: Ps 147 18 *SB*, EpJer 60 *BF*, Mt 7 25 *SB* πνεῖν, Job 9 18 *B* (*S* ⲁⲡϣⲧⲏⲩ) ἀναπ., Ac 27 13 *B* (*S* diff) ὑποπ.; *ib* 28 13 *S* (*B* diff) of wind ἐπιγί-νεσθαι; Ryl 94 102 *S* north wind п.; Ez 47 5 *S* (*B* diff) ⲙⲟⲩ пп. ῥοῖζος, Job 32 19 *B* (*S* diff) ϩⲟⲓ пп. φυσητήρ.

With following preposition. ⲥ ⲉ-, *blow upon*:
Is 10 24 *S* (*B* ⲛⲥⲁ-), Jo 3 8 *SBF* πν.; Si 28 13 *S*,
Is 54 16 *S* (*B* ⲇⲟ) φυσᾶν, Job 4 21 *S* (*B* ⲇⲟ) ἐμφ.;
ShIF 147 *S* ⲛⲥⲉⲡ. ⲉⲧⲥⲁⲧⲉ, C 43 213 *B* wind ⲛ.
ⲉⲡⲓⲗⲁⲃⲟ, Aeg 264 *S* ⲉⲕϣⲁⲡⲛ. ⲉⲡⲉⲕⲥⲓⲝ instead of
washing. ⲥ ⲉⲣⲟⲩⲛ, ⲉⲥ̇. ⲉ-, *blow into*: Jo 20 22
A²B (*S* ⲉⲣ. ⲟⲛ-)ἐμφ., Ez 22 21 *B* ἐκφ.; Cant 4 16
S (cit TT 19 ⲉⲣ. ⲟⲛ-) διαπ.; PS 335 *S* ϣⲁⲡⲛ. ⲉⲣ.
ⲉⲧⲙⲛⲧⲉ of soul, ShBor 246 114 *S* God ⲛ. ⲉⲣ. ⲉⲣⲟϥ
(*l* ⲣⲱϥ) ⲡⲟⲩⲡⲡⲟⲛ; ⲉⲣ. ⲉⲣⲣⲁⲝ: Sa 15 11 *S* ἐμπ.;
Ac 27 14 *B* (*S* ⲟⲓⲟⲩⲉ) βάλλειν; ShA 1 448 *S* fire ⲛ.
ⲉⲣ. ⲉⲣⲣⲁⲩ, C 86 122 *B* wind ⲛ. ⲉⲥ̇. ⲉⲣⲣⲁⲩ; ⲉⲣ.
ⲟⲛ-: Ge 2 7 *SB*, Jo 20 22 *S*(*A²B v* above) ἐμφ.; BG
51 *S* ⲛ. ⲉⲣ. ⲟⲛⲡⲉⲕⲣⲟ from thy spirit; PS 336
S ϣⲁⲡⲛ. ⲉⲣ. ⲉⲣⲡⲧⲉⲯⲩⲭⲏ. ⲥ ⲉⲥⲣⲏⲓ ⲉ- *B, blow
down upon*: Dan 7 2 προσβάλ.; PO 11 329 demon
ⲛ. ⲉⲥ̇. ἐπεχμαϣⲝ. ⲥ ⲉϫⲛ-, ⲟⲓϫⲛ-, *blow upon*:
Ap 7 1 *S* ⲉ. *BF* ⲟ. π.; Bodl(P) a 2 40 *S* ⲛ. ⲉϫⲱϥ
ⲕⲟⲩⲓ ⲕⲟⲩⲓ ⲟⲛⲡⲡⲓⲃⲉ & it will melt. ⲥ ⲛⲥⲁ-,
blow after, upon: Is 40 24 *B* (*S* ⲉ-) π., Hos 13 3 *B*
(*A tr*) ἀποφ., Ez 21 31 *B* (Mich Pasc Lect 247),
Mor 37 83 *S* ⲁⲓⲛ. ⲛⲥⲱϥ ἐμφ.; ROC 17 403 *B* ⲉϥⲛ.
ⲛⲥⲁⲡⲙⲙⲉⲩⲓ ἀναρριπίζειν; ShR 2 3 6 *S* coals ⲉⲩⲛ.
ⲛⲥⲱⲟⲩ, MG 25 396 *B* ⲡⲁϥⲛ. ⲛⲥⲱⲟⲩ (*sc* demons),
Cat 98 *B* ambition ϫⲉⲙ ϫⲟⲙ ⲛⲛ. ⲛⲥⲱⲟⲩ, CaiThe
56 *B* ⲁϥⲛ. ⲛⲥⲁⲡⲓϣϣⲏⲛ till they blossomed.

With following adverb. ⲥ ⲉⲃⲟⲗ, *breathe*: MG
25 6 *B* hyena running & ⲉⲥⲛ. ⲉⲃ. ⲉⲙⲁϣⲱ πνίγεσθαι
anhelare; Gu 51 *S* ⲙⲣⲱϩⲉ covering corpse's face
so that ⲉϥⲉⲥⲛ ⲟⲉ ⲛⲛ. ⲉⲃ.

II *tr, blow*: Si 43 4 *S* ἐμφ., Hos 13 3 *A* (*B* ⲛⲥⲁ-)
ἀποφ.; ShR 2 3 81 *S* as serpent ⲛ. ⲡⲧⲉϥⲙⲁⲧⲟⲩ
ⲉⲡⲉϥⲃⲁⲗ, ShA 2 169 *S* poison ⲉⲁⲣⲡⲉϥⲧⲥ (var ⲡⲟⲭⲥ)
ⲉⲃ. ϩⲛⲣⲱ, ShMIF 23 29 *S* ⲉⲛⲧⲧⲥⲟ ⲁⲡ ⲉⲛⲁⲩⲧⲟⲩ
(*sc* poison), PMich 593 E *S* speak it (*sc* charm)
ⲉⲭⲛⲟⲩⲅⲏⲡ ⲛⲡⲛⲓϥⲧⲉ (indicates ? whispering or hissing enunciation, but *cf* ⲛⲟⲩϣⲉ Z 627 sim recipe),
MIE 2 374 *B* none may spit nor ⲛ. ⲙⲡⲟⲩϣⲁⲓ (*cf*
ⲛⲟⲩϣⲡ *sf*). ⲥ ⲉⲃⲟⲗ, *blow away*: Hag 1 9 *A* (*B*
ⲛⲥⲁ-) ἐκφ.; BHom 134 *S* chaff ⲉⲁⲩⲡⲉϥⲧϥ ⲉⲃ. ἀναρριπίζειν; ShC 42 49 *S* scattered by wind ϩⲙⲛ-
ⲧⲣⲉⲡⲉⲡⲛⲁ̄ ⲡⲉϥⲧⲟⲩ ⲉⲃ.

—— *SABF*, ⲛⲓϥ *SBF* nn m, *breath*: Ge 7 22 *S*
(*B* ⲑⲛⲟⲩ), Job 27 3 *SB*, Pro 24 12 *SA* πνοή, Cai
Euch 406 *B* ϣⲁⲡⲛ. ⲛⲥ̄ⲁⲉ ἀναπ.; Ge 6 17 *S* (*B* =
Gk) πνεῦμα, Ps 17 15 *SB* ἔμπνευσις; Sa 11 19 *S*
ἄσθμα; BM 247 10 *S* ⲛⲛ. ⲉⲣⲟⲥ (*sc* soul) of Spirit
ἐμφύσησις; Job 24 20 *SB*, Si 24 3 *S* (*B* ⲛⲓϥ), Joel
2 2 *B* (*SA* ⲕⲣⲙⲧⲥ), 2 Pet 2 17 *S* (*B* ⲛⲓϥ) ὁμίχλη;
Deu 32 2 *S* ⲛⲓϥ (var & *B* ⲛⲓϥⲉ) νιφετός; Mic 5 7
A (*B* Gk diff) *stillae*; Nu 21 35 *S* (*B* ⲉϥⲟⲛⲃ̄) ζω-
γρεία; Va 58 29 *B* ⲉⲧϣⲁⲡϣ ⲛⲛ. ⲛⲓⲃⲉⲛ, PS 25 *S*
dead ⲉⲙⲛ ⲛ. ⲛⲣⲏⲧⲟⲩ, Br 230 *S* ⲛⲛ. ⲡⲣⲱϣ, RAl

137 *S* issuing from ϫⲉϥϣⲁ (*l* ⲟⲉⲃ-), Va 61 94 *B*
ⲁⲙⲟⲛ ⲛ. ⲛⲭⲃⲟⲃ in hell, R 1 3 6 *S* warmed by
ⲧⲁⲩⲏ ⲛⲡⲛ. of animals (*cf* ⲗⲣⲱⲃ), Mor 48 88 *S* fire
became as ⲛⲓϥ ⲡⲓⲱⲧⲉ = C 43 143 *B*, PS 114 *S* may
ⲟⲩⲛⲓϥ ⲛⲁⲏⲣ darken them (Od Solom 5 5 ادحنوا ilí),
Bodl(P) a 2 40 *S ut sup* ⲛⲛ. *breath* or *blow-pipe*(?).

ⲣⲉϥⲛ. *B, blower, blow-pipe*: Jer 6 29 φυσητήρ.

ϫⲓⲛⲛ. *B, blowing*: Va 66 305 ⲧϫ. of wind ῥεῦμα;
Cat 229 ⲡⲉϫϫ. ⲉⲥⲟⲩⲛ ⲝⲉⲛⲡⲟⲩⲣⲟ (Jo 20 22).

ϣⲉ ⲛⲛ. *B, blow of breath*, drawing of breath,
breathing: MG 25 142 ⲕⲁⲧⲁ ϣⲉ ⲛⲛ. of our nose.

ⲡⲉⲛⲕ ⲛ. *S, draw breath*: Mor 31 25 sick man ⲉϥⲛ.
ⲛ. ⲉⲛⲙⲟⲩ *drawing breath as if dying* (*v* Ep 297 n).

ϯ ⲛ. *SB, give breath*: Ryl 72 325 *S* of God ⲁϥ
ϯ ⲛ. ⲛⲥⲱⲡⲧ ⲛⲓⲙ; *take breath*, rest, doze: MG
25 371 *B* stone cell ⲛⲉϣⲁϥϯ ⲡⲟⲩⲕⲟⲩϫⲓ ⲛⲛ. ⲛϩⲏⲧⲥ
(ROC 18 285 سلمط).

ϩⲙ-, ϫⲁⲙⲛ. *SB, difficult breathing* (*v* ⲣⲱⲱⲙⲉ):
K 158 *B* ⲡⲓⲝ̄. ضيق النفس, P 44 94 *S* ⲡⲧⲉⲡⲉⲡⲛⲉⲩ-
ⲙⲟⲛ (*l* ⲡⲉⲡ.) ⲟⲩⲁϩϥ ⲛⲥⲁⲡⲛⲓϥⲉ نفس, ⲡⲧⲉⲡ. منفس
ⲟⲩⲁϩϥ ⲛⲥⲁⲧⲥⲁⲣⲝ = 43 81 *S* ⲡⲛⲓϥⲉ, EW 222 scala
S p 15 among parts of body ⲛⲣ. نفن, ϣⲕⲟⲗ (*v*
ⲙⲉϣⲕⲟⲗ), ⲡⲉⲭⲟⲗⲟⲥ, PMich 610 *S* recipe ⲧ]ⲣⲟ-
ⲭⲓⲥⲕⲟⲥ ⲉⲧⲃⲉⲡⲉ[?]ⲉ ⲉⲩⲣⲉⲙⲛⲓⲃⲉ (as ? vb).

ⲛⲟⲩϣⲉ, -ϣⲓ *v* ⲛⲟⲩϣⲣ *sf*.

ⲛⲟⲩϥⲣ *S*, ⲛⲉϥⲣ- (Lu 5), ⲛⲟϥⲣ† *S*, ⲛⲟϥⲉⲣ† *B*,
ⲣ ⲡ ⲛⲁϥⲣ-, ⲛⲁⲃⲉⲣ- (in names) vb intr, *be good,
profitable*: Lu 5 39 *S* (*B* ϩⲟⲗϫ) χρηστός; GFr 361
S ⲡϩⲱⲟⲩ ⲙⲛⲧⲱⲧⲉ ⲉⲩⲛⲟϥⲉⲣ (sic MS) ὠφέλιμος;
Mich 550 24 *S* in spring ⲡⲧⲉⲡⲁⲏⲣ ⲛⲟⲩϥⲣ (var TT
19 ⲛⲟⲩⲧϥ), Va 61 203 *B* ⲡⲁⲉⲣⲟⲩⲟⲧ ⲉϥⲛ.† in doing
thy bidding; impers: MG 25 197 *B* ⲥⲛ.† ⲛⲥⲟϫⲓ
ⲛⲥⲁⲡⲡⲁⲑⲟⲥ.

ⲛⲟⲩⲣⲉ, ⲛⲟⲃⲣⲉ *S*, ⲛⲁϥⲣⲉ *AA²*, ⲛⲟⲩⲣⲓ *B*, ⲛⲁⲃⲣⲉ,
-ⲃⲣⲓ, -ϥⲓ *F* nn f, *good, profit, advantage*: Nu 20
3 *S* (var ⲛⲁⲡⲟⲩⲥ, *B* diff) ὄφελον, 1 Tim 4 8 *S* (*B*
ⲉⲣ ⲛ.), C 89 79 *B* ὠφέλιμος, Z 361 = Mor 37 91 *S*
ⲧⲛⲛ. ⲙⲛⲧⲁⲣⲉⲡⲕⲟⲟⲩⲉ, Aeg 267 *S* ⲉⲩⲛ. ⲡⲁⲡ, Ep 592
A 12 *S* ⲕⲛⲁⲁⲓⲥⲟⲁⲡⲉ ⲉⲧⲉⲥⲛ. ὠφέλεια, Cl 48 6 *A* ⲧⲛ.
τὸ κοινωφελές; Deu 23 6 *S* (*B* ⲉⲣ ⲛ.), He 12 10 *S*
(*B* ⲇⲟ), Miss 8 34 *S* ⲧⲛ. ⲛⲧⲡⲓⲥⲧⲓⲥ συμφέρον; He 13
17 *S* (*B* ⲇⲟ) λυσιτελής, Miss 8 76 *S* ⲧⲛ. ⲛⲡⲁⲏⲙⲟⲥⲓⲟⲛ δημοσίων λυσιτέλεια; Phil 2 4 *S* (*B* as Gk)
τὰ ἑαυτῶν; ShZ 603 *S* reaping out of season ϥⲓ
ⲡⲧⲟⲟⲧϥ ⲛⲧⲛ., ShC 73 161 *S* ⲧⲛ. ⲁⲩⲱ ⲛⲣⲏⲩ of souls,
Miss 4 584 *S* ⲟⲩⲛⲟⲥ ⲛⲛ. = C 89 176 *B* ⲛⲟⲩⲟⲩ, ShBor
246 115 *S* vessels differing ϩⲙⲡⲉⲩⲥⲁ ⲙⲛⲧⲉⲩⲛ.,
TT 156 *S* ⲛ ⲟⲩⲛ. [ⲁⲛ]ⲧⲉ ⲙⲡⲉⲓⲥⲟⲛ = C 89 84 *B*
ⲥϣⲉ ⲛⲁϥ ⲁⲛ, Mor 25 17 *S* arguing with thee ⲉⲧⲉⲕⲛ.
= Va 61 100 *B*, Mor 24 25 *F* this became ⲛⲛⲁⲃⲣⲓ
ⲛⲏⲧⲉⲛ, Ep 540 *S* ⲉⲩⲛ. ⲡⲟⲩⲕⲟⲩⲓ (context obscure).

ⲣ ⲛ. *SAA²BF, be profitable*, *a* no obj: 1 Cor 6

12 SB συμφέρειν; Pro 28 3 SA neg, Is 44 10 B neg (S ⲙⲡ ϩⲏⲩ), Wess 15 137 S dogmas ⲡⲥⲉⲣ ⲡ. ⲁⲡ ἀνωφελής, Ro 2 25 S(B ϩⲏⲟⲩ) ὠφελεῖν; ShC 73 72 S words ⲉⲩⲣ ϩⲟⲟⲛⲉ opp ⲉⲩⲣ ⲡ.; with rel: Pro 31 19 B(SA ϣϣⲉ), Jer 33 14 SB συμφ., Phil 1 10 SBF διαφ.; Aeg 213 S ⲟⲩⲁⲓⲧⲓⲁ ⲉⲥⲣ ⲡ. εὔλογος; Miss 8 56 S everything ⲉⲩⲣ ⲡ. συντελεῖν; ClPr 54 38 S counselled young ⲉⲛⲉⲧⲣ ⲡ. σύμμετρον; C 42 101 S (Esaias Scet) abide in cell ⲉⲕⲇⲟⲕⲓⲙⲁⲍⲉ ⲛ-ⲡⲉⲧⲣ ⲡ., BM 310 S ⲁⲩⲥⲟⲡⲉ ⲉⲛⲉⲧⲣ ⲡ. = LAp 532 F e]ⲛⲟϭ .. ⲉⲛⲧⲉⲗ ⲡ. (frag now lost, Jernstedt) = Gu 22 S ⲡϫⲟⲉⲓⲥ, Cat 190 B God provides for each ⲕⲁⲧⲁ ⲡⲉⲧⲉⲣ ⲡ. c e-, *be profitable to* do so & so: Mt 19 10 S (var ⲛ-) B συμφ.; ShC 73 100 S ⲥⲣ ⲡ. ⲉⲕⲁⲁⲩ, Aeg 263 S ⲧⲁⲅⲉ ⲡⲉⲧⲣ ⲡ. ⲉⲟⲩⲟⲛ ⲛⲓⲙ; Jo 18 14 SA² ⲉⲧⲣⲉ- (B conjunc) συμφ., AP 20 A² ⲥⲣ]ⲡ. ⲡⲉϥ ⲁⲧⲣⲉϥⲙⲟⲩ. c ⲛ- dat, *be profitable for*: Deu 23 6 S(B ⲡ. nn), Pro 19 7 SA, Ac 20 20 SB συμφ.; C 89 23 B commandments ⲉⲩⲉⲣ ⲡ. ⲛⲓⲟⲩⲯⲩⲭⲏ ὠφέλιμος, Mor 37 114 S ⲡⲉⲧⲣ ⲡ. ⲡⲁϥ τὰ πρὸς ὠφέλειαν; Si 20 8 S λυσιτελεῖν; Aeg 219 S things ⲉⲧⲣ ⲡ. ⲙⲡⲉϥⲧⲟϣ ἐπιβάλλειν; Jos 23 14 B (S ϫⲓ ⲉϩⲟⲩⲛ) ἀνήκειν; TU 24 1 4 S ⲡⲁⲓ ⲡⲉⲧⲣ ⲡ. ⲛⲉ, RAl 83 = DeV 1 183 B ⲙⲡⲉⲥⲉⲣ ⲡ. ⲛⲁϥ ⲡϩⲗⲓ.

ⲙⲉⲧⲛ. B, *good things*: Ge 45 20 ἀγαθά. ⲙⲛⲧ-, ⲙⲉⲧⲁⲧⲛ. SBF, *unprofitableness*: He 7 18 τὸ ἀνωφελές.

In many names: ⲡⲁϥⲣϩⲟ (CR '04 525), ⲡⲁϩⲉⲣϩⲟ (BM 1020), abbrev? ⲡⲁϩⲉⲣ (ib, CMSS 77), Νεφερῶς, Πνεφερῶς, Tv.(Preisigke), ⲡⲁϩⲣⲁϩⲁ F(BIF 15 230), cf ⲛⲟϩⲣⲟⲩ above, Ναβερϣάι (PLond 4), Πατνεφερσόις (Preis), Νεφερσοῦχις, Νεφερπρῆς (Preis), Ἀρσενόφρη (PLeyd 2 23), Ὀρσενόφρη (PGM 1 124), ⲟⲩⲉⲛⲁϥⲣⲉ O (AZ 21 104), ⲟⲩⲛⲁϥⲣ (Hall 22) ⲓⲱⲛⲟϥⲣ (Ryl 159), ⲟⲩⲁⲛⲟⲩⲣⲉ (BP 5178), ϩⲉⲛⲟϥⲉⲣ (Rec 6 168), ϩⲁⲛⲁϥⲣⲉ (MMA 24 6 19) ⲟⲩⲉⲛⲁϩⲗⲓ (BM 1235), ⲟⲩⲉⲛⲁϩⲉⲗ (Kr 72), Ὀννῶφριος & other varr, Ὀσαρνῶφρι (PGM 1 192). In place-name Ψεννῶφρις (Fay Towns 118).

ⲡⲟⲩϥⲉ SAA²O, ⲡⲟⲩϥⲓ BF adj, *good*: rare except in ⲥⲧⲛ. (v ⲥⲧⲟⲓ), ϣⲉⲙⲛ., ϣⲉ(ⲛ)ⲡ. (v ϣⲓⲛⲉ), ϩⲉⲛ. (v ϩⲉ season). Further He 13 16 B ⲙⲉⲧⲣⲉϥⲉⲣ ϩⲉⲛⲡ. (S ⲡⲉⲧⲛⲁⲡⲟⲩϥⲉ) εὐποιία, 1 Tim 6 2 B ϩⲉⲛⲡ. (S ⲣⲱⲃ ⲉⲧⲛⲁⲡⲟⲩϥⲉ) εὐεργεσία, Va 57 176 B ⲉϩⲣⲟⲟⲩ ⲡ. εὐημερία; ⲡⲉⲣⲡ. q v, Hor 81 O ⲥⲟⲩⲛ.ⲡ. opp ⲥⲟⲩϩⲱⲛ, Ming 328 S ⲧⲏⲩ ⲡⲡ. opp ⲡⲣⲉⲃⲱⲱⲛ (so? l ⲡⲣⲉⲡ.). In names: Οἰνοῦφις (Preisigke), ϣⲉⲡⲟⲩϥⲉ (Mor 41), ⲟⲩⲉⲣϣⲉⲡⲟⲩϥⲉ Οὐερσενούφιος (PLond 4), Βαρσανούφιος. In place-names: ⲡⲁⲡⲟⲩϥⲓ (BM 1237), ϣⲉⲧⲉⲡⲟⲩϥⲉ (BM 321), ϣⲉⲧⲛⲟⲩϥⲓ (Amélineau Géog 424), ⲡⲁⲑⲉⲟⲡⲟⲩϥⲃⲉ (Ryl 340).

ⲡⲟⲩϥⲧ SB, -ϥⲧ S vb intr, *swell, be distended*: BIF 13 98 = BM 339 S angel smote him so that skin ⲛ. like ἀσκός = MG 25 277 B = GöttAr 114 190 انتفخ, K 255 B ⲧⲃ (sic MS), ورم. Cf P 54 168 ⲑⲓϥⲓ, طخ ,وام ,تزتر.

ⲡⲉϥⲧⲉ (sic MS) S nn as pl, *swelling* or *wind* (intestinal): PMéd 187 ⲡⲡ. ⲡⲗⲁⲉⲓ ⲉⲡⲉⲥⲏⲧ.

ⲡⲟⲩϩⲧ A v ⲡⲟⲩϣⲧ.

ⲡϩⲁⲧ, ⲡⲁϩⲧⲉ A v ⲡϣⲟⲧ.

ⲡⲉϩϫⲓ B v ⲡⲟⲩϫⲕ s f.

ⲡϩ v ⲉⲡϩ.

ⲡⲉϩ SABF DM (19 28), ⲡϩ S, ⲡⲛⲏϩ SAF nn m, *oil*: Lev 24 2 SB, Is 1 6 SBF, Joel 2 19 SAB, Ap 6 6 SB ἔλαιον; K 269 B زيت ,دهن; ShC 73 119 S, C 43 113 B, BM 511(4) F; as pl: BM 1090 S, ib 1122 S, CO 380 S, K 131 B; ⲡ. ⲉϥⲕⲓⲱⲟⲩ S, ⲕⲉⲡⲓⲱⲧ B, *fat, thick*: Ps 91 11 ἐ. πῖον; ⲡ. ⲉⲑⲟⲡⲧⲉⲗ B, *sweet*: Bodl 325 151 زيت طيب (cf ⲡ. ⲙⲙⲉ); ⲡ. ⲉϥϩⲉⲣϩⲉⲣ B, *boiling*: C 43 140; ⲡ. ⲛⲥⲙⲟⲩ S, *of blessing*: GPar 24; ⲡ. ⲉⲧⲟⲩⲁⲁⲃ SB, *holy*: BM 1121 S (baptismal); ⲛⲧⲉ ⲡⲓⲑⲉⲗⲏⲗ *of joy*: AM 21 B (cf TEuch 1 336 ⲁⲅⲁⲗⲗⲓⲉⲗⲁⲓⲟⲛ); ⲡ. ⲡⲧⲱϩⲥ SB, *of anointing*: Lev 21 12 ἐ. τὸ χριστόν; ⲡ. ⲡϣⲗⲏⲗ S, *of prayer*: COAd 48; ⲡ. ⲛϩⲣⲓⲕ S, *of enchantment*: PMich 594. Various sorts: true, genuine i e olive (v ⲙⲉ *truth* adj) ShC 42 71 S ⲡ. ⲙⲉ = Miss 4 399 طيب, BMOr 920 242 B ⲡ. ⲙⲙⲉ (cf K 200 ⲙⲉⲣⲱⲧⲡ i e μυρώδης), Tri 437 S ⲡ. ⲛⲁⲗⲏⲑⲓⲛⲟⲛ الحقيقي; PMéd pass S ⲡ. ⲙⲉ & ⲙⲙⲉ, Z 626 S, AZ 23 103 S sim, EW 98 B ⲙⲙⲛⲓ, KroppJ S ⲡ. ⲙⲛⲏ ⲉϥⲁⲡⲟⲥ; olive Lev 24 2 S ⲡϫⲟⲉⲓⲧ (B ⲉⲃⲟⲗ ϩⲉⲛⲑⲣⲁϫ.) ἐλάινον; radish Z 629 S, PMéd 239 S, Ep 574 S ⲡⲥⲓⲙ (cf DM 20 21); cabbage CO 347 S ⲛϭⲗⲟϭ; garden ib S ⲛϭⲱⲙ; rose RAl 125 S, Z 627 S ⲡⲟⲩϩⲣⲧ, PMéd 297 S ⲛϩⲣⲟϯⲛⲟⲛ; perfume Cai 42573 1 S ⲉⲥⲧⲟⲓ, BKU 1 26 (8117) F ⲉⲧⲓⲁⲥⲙⲛ (δίοσμος); myrtle Z 630 S, PMéd 314 S ⲙⲟⲩⲣⲥⲓⲛⲉ; camomile Z 628 S ⲡⲭⲁⲙⲉⲙⲉⲗⲱⲛ (χαμαίμηλον); nuts Ryl 106 11 S ⲡⲕⲁⲓⲣⲉ (κάρυον); aloes Bodl(P) a 1 g S ⲡⲁⲗⲗⲱⲏⲥ; linseed ib a 2 64 S ⲛⲉⲃⲣⲉ ⲙⲁϩⲉ; doubtful PMéd 244 S ⲛⲕⲗⲓ (v ⲕⲣⲓ), PGen S (magical) ⲛⲥⲣⲓⲙⲉ (cf? ϩⲉⲛⲓⲡⲉ ⲛⲣⲟⲟⲩⲧ, ⲛⲥⲣⲓⲙⲉ). Oil vessels, measures: ⲁⲡⲕⲓⲟⲡ &c (ἀγγεῖον) BM 305 S, CO 347 S, ⲁⲓⲡⲉ (ⲟⲓⲡⲉ) ST 121 S, ⲃⲁⲥ q v, ⲕⲁⲙⲧⲉ q v, ⲕⲉⲗⲏ BKU 1 133 S]ⲧϥⲉ ⲡⲕ. ⲡⲡ. (cf CO 212 S ⲥⲩⲡⲕⲓⲗⲉ), ⲕⲟⲩⲡϩⲟⲩ q v, ⲗⲟⲕ q v, ⲗⲁⲕⲱⲡ (v Ep 283 n), ⲗⲁϩⲛ q v, ⲍⲉⲥⲧⲏⲥ ShC 42 70 S, BM 711 F, Ryl 159 S, ⲧⲏⲃ MG 25 144 B, ϫⲓ WS 146 S, ϭⲁⲗⲓⲧⲉ ib 88 S.

ⲉϩⲣⲁ ⲡ. v ⲉϩⲣⲁ & ϩⲁⲣⲛⲉϩ.

ⲁⲧ-, ⲁϩⲛ. SB, *oilless*: Ps 108 24 B (S Gk not neg), Bor 254 175 S lamps without light ⲉⲧⲃⲉⲧⲙⲛⲧⲁ.

ⲙⲁ ⲙⲛⲏ. *B, oil cellar*: BSM 41 = BMis 387 *S*
= Va 63 14 *B* ⲕⲉⲗⲗⲁⲣⲓⲟⲛ.

ⲣ ⲛ. *S, oil-making* place, press (or ? *v* ⲡⲉⲣ-): J 44
64 house & ⲡⲉⲣ ⲛ., Kr 244 radishes (ⲥⲓⲙ) which I
took ⲉⲛⲣ ⲛ., BM 1107 oil ϩⲁⲛⲓⲣ ⲛ., BP 9421 *v* ⲃⲁⲥ,
ib 3267 ⲛⲉϩ ϩⲓⲛⲁⲣⲛⲉϩ, Saq 132 Victor ⲛⲁⲡⲉⲣ ⲛ.

ϯ ⲛ. *S, pour oil*: Num 4 9 *S* ⲁⲛⲥⲛⲛ ⲛϯ ⲛ. (*B*
Gk om vb), ShC 73 55 forbidden to ϯ ⲛ. ⲉⲡϫⲓⲣ ⲛ
ⲉⲡⲉⲣⲙⲟⲩ, PLond 4 517 ⲕⲟⲅⲭⲟⲩ ⲡϯ ⲛ., BMOr
6230 45 ⲗⲁⲕⲱⲛ do. *Cf* ST 116 ⲗⲁⲕⲱⲛ ⲛⲃⲱⲕ ⲛ.
wherein *to put oil*.

ⲥⲁ ⲛⲛ. *S, oil dealer*: Ryl 249 Peter ⲛⲥ., BM
1049, ST 290 sim, Ep 667 ⲥⲁⲙⲛ., AZ 60 110 guild
(ⲕⲟⲓⲛⲟⲧⲏⲥ) of ⲛⲥ., PLond 4 266 ⲧⲟⲡⲟⲥ Ψⲁⲛⲛⲉ́ (*cf ib*
200 ⲧ. Ἐⲗⲁⲓⲟⲩⲣⲅⲟⲩ̂).   ⲥⲁ ⲣ ⲛ. *S, oil-maker* (?):
BMOr 6201 A 179 ⲛⲥ. to supply ἄⲣⲁⲕⲟⲥ to labourers, OWulf *Altchr…Bildw.* 3 no 258, Baouit 1 160
sim.

ⲛⲟϩ *B* nn as pl, *eyelid*: Pro 6 25 (Lacr, LectP
70, Ryl 424, bible ⲃⲟⲩϭⲓ = *SA*) βλέφαρον. *Cf* ? ⲉⲛϩ.

ⲛⲟϩ *B* *v* ⲛⲟⲩϩ & ⲛⲟⲩϩⲉ vb.

ⲛⲟⲩϩ *SAA²F*, ⲡⲁⲩϩ *Sᵃ* (Ep 438), ⲛⲱϩ *S*, ⲛⲟϩ
B, ⲁⲛⲟⲩϩ, ⲁⲛⲛ- *F* nn m, *rope, cord*: 2 Kg 8 2 *S*,
Job 36 8 *B* (sic l), Ps 139 5 *S* (*B* ⲥⲛⲁⲩϩ), Is 5 18
SBF, Am 7 17 *SAB*, Jo 2 15 *SA²B* σχοινίον, Is 54
2 *S* (*B* ϣⲉ ⲛⲛ.) σχοίνισμα; Nu 3 37 *S* (*B* = Gk)
κάλος, Jud 15 13 *S* καλῴδιον;   form ⲁⲛⲟⲩϩ *F*:
CMSS 47 send ⲥⲡⲉⲩ ⲡⲁⲛⲟⲩϩ…ⲡⲓⲥⲛⲉⲩ ⲡⲁⲛⲛⲟⲩϩ,
BM 592 I wrote thee ⲉⲧⲁⲃⲉⲛⲁⲛ., *ib* ⲉϣⲱⲡⲓ ⲁⲕϭⲁⲛ
ⲛⲁⲛ. (but *ib* (ⲛ)ⲧⲉⲃⲟⲩⲁⲧ ⲛⲉⲛ., so ? here ⲛⲁ-ⲛ. *my
ropes*);   ship's cables: DeV 2 206 *B*, BMis 564
S, BM 711 *F*, Cat 100 *B* ⲛ. ⲙⲙⲁϣⲉⲣⲧ *q v*, C 41
18 *B* ⲁϥϯ ⲛ. ⲉϩⲟⲩⲛ ⲉⲡⲓⲱⲛⲓ & made ship fast;
well-bucket rope: BAp 88 *S* = MIE 2 359 *B*, MG
25 346 *B*;   acrobat's tight-rope: Aeg 39 *B* ⲣⲉϥ-
ⲥⲱⲃⲓ ϩⲱⲗ ⲉⲡϣⲱⲓ ⲉⲭⲉⲛϩⲁⲛⲛ.;   in land measure-
ment (*cf* σχοινίον): Ps 77 55 *SB* σχ., TurM 16 *S*
ⲛⲥⲟⲩ(ⲟⲩ)ⲱϩ ⲛⲛ. ϫⲓⲛⲡⲛⲧⲓϫⲉ…ϣⲁⲧⲛϫⲉ, CO 139,
ib Ad 26 *S* ⲡⲣⲟⲥ ⲡⲉⲧⲛⲏⲩ ⲉϩⲣⲁⲓ ϩⲁⲛⲛ., J 107 12 *S*
gift of ⲟⲩⲛⲱϩ ⲛⲕⲁϩ, Kr 228 vo *S* ⲛⲛ. ⲛⲧⲡⲟⲗⲓⲥ
town's customs-boundary (?), *cf* ⲥⲕ ⲛ., ϣⲉ ⲛⲛ.;
net rope: PSBA 33 115 *S* trembling like ⲟⲩⲛ.
ⲛⲁⲃⲱ; made of (or ? for binding) twigs: ST 232
S ⲛϭⲗⲱ;   of tow: AM 319 *B* ⲡⲥⲓⲡⲡⲉⲛ (στίππιον, sim C 43 80 *B* ⲧⲉⲃⲓ ⲛⲙⲁϩⲓ), Ez 40 3 *S* ⲛⲗⲁⲥ
σπαρτίον;   of palm-fibre: Va 61 12 *B*, AM 166
B ⲛϣⲉⲛⲃⲉⲛⲓ, Hall 117 *S* ⲛⲱϩ ⲛⲧⲱⲡ ⲛϣⲃⲃⲏⲛⲉ *sow-
ing-thread of fibre*;   of rags: ShIF 153 *S* ⲛⲛⲗϭⲉ
beneath ϩⲉⲛⲛⲗϭⲉ ⲛⲧⲟⲉⲓⲥ (*cf* Jer 45 11);   made
by monks: MMA 24 2 6 *S* monks going north to
sell ⲧⲉⲩⲕⲟⲩⲓ ⲙⲡⲣⲁⲅⲙⲁⲧⲉⲓⲁ ⲛⲛ.; for pulling (part

of loom): ShP 131⁴ 111 *S* ⲛⲛ. ⲛⲥⲱⲕ;   for measuring: ⲡⲣⲱϣ *B* Ps 15 6 (*S* ⲥⲛⲁⲩϩ) σχ., Zech 11
7 (*SA* ⲥⲕ ⲛ.) σχοίνισμα, Is 34 11 (*SF* ⲛ. ⲛϣⲓ ⲓⲱⲣⲉ)
σπαρτίον γεωμετρίας, Zech 2 1 (*A* ⲛ. ⲛϩⲓⲱⲣⲉ) σχ.
γεωμετρικόν; ⲛϣⲓ Tri 675 *S* قياس, Job 38 5
B (*S* ϩⲱⲥ) σπαρ.; ⲛϣⲓ ⲉⲓⲱⲣⲉ Mic 2 4 *SA* (*B* ⲣ.)
σχ., ShC 73 90 *S* breaches in dyke ⲣ ϩⲉⲛⲛ. ⲛϣ.;
obscure: Mor 51 33 *S* (parable) ⲁⲛⲕⲁ ⲛⲛ. ⲛⲁⲧⲏⲣ
ⲉϩⲣⲁⲓ ⲁⲛϩⲉⲗⲉⲙ ⲛⲛ. ⲛⲛⲟⲃⲗⲥ, (interpret) we have
abandoned commands for entreaties.

ⲥⲣ ⲛ. ⲉⲃⲟⲗ *SA, lay out* (measuring) *cord*: Deu
21 2 (*B* ⲣⲱϣ) ἐκμετρεῖν; 2 Kg 17 13 σχ. λαμβάνειν; Mic 2 5 *SA* (*B* ϩⲓⲟⲩⲓ) σχ. βάλλειν;   ⲥⲕ ⲛ.
SA, nn m, *stretching of cord*, portion so bounded:
Deu 32 9 *S* (*A* Cl ⲧⲁϣ, *B* ⲛ. ⲡⲣⲱϣ), 2 Kg 8 2 *S*
(Mor), Ps 104 11 *S* (*B* do), Zech 11 7 *SA* (*B* do)
σχοίνισμα.   ϣⲉ ⲛⲛ. *B* nn m, meaning sim: Is
54 2 (*S* ? diff), Zeph 2 5 (*SA* ⲧⲟϣ) σχοίνισμα.

ϣⲉϣ ⲛ. *SB, twist rope*: C 89 37 *B* sitting ⲉϥϣ.
ⲛ. = MG 17 404 يفتل حبال, BMis 486 *S* hermit's
occupation ⲉϥϣ. ⲛ., RNC 90 *S*, ST 283 *S* sim,
Mor 51 37 *S* monks ⲉⲩϣ. ⲛ. whilst reciting scriptures (μελετᾶν). *V* Ep 1 155.

ⲕⲁⲛ ⲛⲛ., *strand, thread, v* ⲕⲁⲛ *string*.   ⲕⲁⲙ
ⲛⲛ. *S, reeds* (used for) *rope*: P 131⁶ 37 formerly
used by monks as mat (*cf* Ep 1 72).   ⲙⲟⲩⲣ, ⲙⲏⲣ
ⲛⲛ. *S, bundle of rope, v* ⲙⲟⲩⲣ.

ϣⲁⲡⲟⲩϩ *S* nn f, meaning unknown: ShC 73 50
ⲟⲩϣ. ⲛⲛⲟⲩϩ paral ⲟⲩⲧⲙⲏ, CO 471 so ⲛϣⲁⲡⲱϩ,
ϣⲙⲟⲩⲛⲉ ⲛϣ.

ⲛⲟϩⲓ *B* nn m, *rope-maker*: K 138 ⲛⲏ. حبّال.

ⲛⲟⲩϩⲉ, ⲛⲱϩⲉ (Ep 181) *S*, ⲛⲟⲩϩ *SABF* (ⲛⲟⲩ-
ⲟⲩϩ *A*), ⲛⲟϩ *B*, ⲛⲟⲩ *SF*, ⲛⲉϩ- *SBF*, ⲛⲁϩϯ *SB*,
ⲛⲁⲩϩϯ *ASᵃ*, ⲛⲉϩϯ *B*, ⲛⲏϩ† *SB*, ⲛⲉϩ† *SB* vb **I** tr,
shake, cast off, set apart, separate: Lu 9 5 *S* (*B* ⲛ.
ⲉⲃⲟⲗ), Ac 28 5 *B* (*S* ⲛⲟⲩϩⲉ) ἀποτινάσσειν, Is 28
27 *B* (*S* ⲛ. ⲉⲃ.), Dan 3 49 *B*, Ac 13 51 *S* (*B* do)
ἐκτιν.; Lev 4 6 *S* (HT, *B* ⲛⲟⲩϫϭ ⲉⲃⲟⲗ) προσραί-
νειν; Ex 21 27 *S* (*B* ⲱⲗⲓ) ἐκκόπτειν; Dan 7 8 *S*
(*B* ϥⲱϫⲓ ⲉⲃⲟⲗ) ἐκριζοῦν; Ps 7 13 *B* (*S* ⲥⲟⲃⲧⲉ)
ἑτοιμάζειν اتقن; Ez 48 17 *B* διάστημα εἶναι dat;
Mor 17 117 *S* ⲁϥⲛ. ⲡⲧⲉϥϭⲓϫ ⲛⲧⲟⲟⲧⲉ σπαράσσειν
ἑαυτόν; Ac 27 17 *S* (*B* ϫⲱ ⲉⲡⲉⲥⲏⲧ) χαλᾶν; BKU 1
21 37 *Sꟊ* ϣⲁⲕⲛⲉϩ ⲡⲁⲡⲉⲓ ⲉⲡⲉⲥⲏⲧ ⲉⲡⲙⲁⲩ, Tri 353
S yoke ⲛⲧϭⲉⲡⲏ ⲉⲛⲁⲣϥ ⲉⲡⲉⲥⲏⲧ رمي; Gk om: Jud
3 24† *S* (or ? *l* ⲉϥⲛⲏⲩ); Mor 28 27 *S* elders ⲛ. ⲙⲡⲉⲩ
…ⲕⲗⲟⲙ ϩⲓϫⲛⲛⲉⲩⲁⲡⲏⲅⲉ (*cf* Ap 4 10 *S* ⲛⲟⲩϫⲉ),
Tri 719 *S* must ⲛ. ⲛⲟⲉⲃⲥⲱ ⲛⲁⲡⲁⲥ خلع; ShMich
550 13 *S* virtuous women ⲉⲧⲛ. ⲙⲡⲉⲩⲕⲟⲥⲙⲟⲥ,
BMar 18 *S* ⲁϥⲛ. ⲙⲡⲉϥϩⲟⲩⲣ from finger, Ep 181
S ⲉⲧⲉⲧⲛⲛⲱϩⲉ ⲙⲡⲛϣⲉ ϩⲓⲉⲓⲱⲧ *loosen stocks*, BMis 271
S ⲛⲉϩ ⲡⲉⲕⲕⲟⲩⲛⲧⲁⲣⲓⲟⲛ ϩⲓⲱⲱϥ (var Mor 30 47 ⲛ.

ⲉⲃ.), Z 352 *S* ⲁⲡⲥⲟⲛ ⲛⲉϩ ⲡⲉⲥϩⲉ ⲙⲡⲣⲟ & *bore it off*, R 1 3 81 *S with sword* ⲁϥⲛⲟⲩϩⲉ ⲙⲡⲡⲙⲁⲕϩ *of maiden*.

Refl, **a** *separate self S*: Nu 16 3 (P 44 107, var & *B* ⲧⲱⲟⲩⲡ ⲉϩⲣ. ⲉϫⲡ-) ⲕⲁⲧⲁⲛⲓⲥⲧⲁⲛⲁⲓ, *ib* 21 (*l c*, var & *B* ⲡⲱⲣϫ ⲉⲃⲟⲗ) ⲁⲡⲟⲥⲭⲓⲍⲉⲓⲛ; **b** *turn, return A*: Ge 4 7 (Cl Rösch, var ⲕⲧⲁ, *B* ϫⲓⲛⲧⲁⲥⲑⲟ) ⲁⲡⲟⲥⲧⲣⲟⲫⲏ, Ps 50 13 (Cl, *SB* ⲕⲱⲧⲉ), Hos 2 9 (*B* ⲧⲁⲥⲑⲟ) ⲉⲡⲓⲥⲧⲣⲉⲫⲉⲓⲛ, TU 43 2 ⲁⲥⲛⲁϩⲣⲥ ϣⲁⲡⲕⲟⲉⲓⲥ, El 44 ⲁⲩⲛⲁⲧⲣⲟⲩϩⲉ ⲁⲡⲁⲣⲟⲩ; **c** ⲉϫⲡ- *Sª*, *return to* (?): CO 381 *if ye persuade him not* ⲙⲁⲉⲓⲛⲁⲩⲧ ⲉϫⲱⲧⲛ, Ep 286 ϯⲛⲁⲡⲁⲩⲧ ⲁⲛ ⲉϫⲱⲧⲛ, *ib* 307 ⲁϥⲛⲁⲟⲩϩⲩ ⲉϫⲱϥ.

ⲛⲉϩ ⲗⲁⲅⲟ *S*, *shake out* (?) *sail, set sail v* ⲗⲁⲅⲟ.

ⲛⲉϩ ⲏⲣⲡ *S*, *throw off* effects of (?) *wine*: Z 285 *at supper* [ⲛⲧ]ⲉⲣⲉⲡⲣⲣⲟ ⲛ. ⲡⲏⲣⲡ, Mor 32 29 *despite tortures lo, thy face is ruddy* ⲙⲡⲁⲧⲉⲕⲛ. ⲏⲣⲡ, P 129[16] 50 sim ⲛ. ⲏⲣⲡ, ShA 1 280 ⲛⲉⲡⲧⲁⲩⲛⲉϩ ⲡⲉⲩⲏⲣⲡ ⲏ ⲡⲉⲧⲙⲡⲟⲩϩⲧϩⲉ ⲣⲱ ϩⲙⲡⲏⲣⲡ (*cf* sim phrases C 43 81, AM 67).

ⲛⲉϩ ⲙⲁⲕϩ *S*, *be stiff-necked* (lit meaning?): Job 15 25 (*B* ⲧⲱⲟⲩⲛⲟⲩ ⲡⲧⲛⲁϩⲃⲓ) ⲧⲣⲁⲭⲏⲗⲓⲁⲛ, cit Z 268, Mor 40 27, P 131[1] 44 &c.

ⲛⲉϩ ⲣⲙⲟⲡⲧ, ⲛ. ⲣⲁⲧ, ⲛ. ⲥⲟⲩⲣⲓ, ⲛ. ⲧⲟⲟⲧ⸗, ⲛ. ϣⲗϩ, ϣⲗϥ *v* ⲣⲙⲟⲡⲧ, ⲣⲁⲧ, ⲥⲟⲩⲣⲉ, ⲧⲱⲣⲉ *hand*, ϣⲗⲁϩ.

—— ⲉⲃⲟⲗ *SBF*, *shake off, cast out, set apart, assign*: 1 Kg 10 2 *S* ⲁⲡⲟⲧⲓⲛ., Is 28 27 *S* (*B* ⲛ.), Dan 7 20 *B*, Ac 18 6 *SB* ⲉⲕⲧⲓⲛ.; Si 22 13 *SB* ⲉⲛⲧⲓⲛⲁⲅⲙⲟⲥ; Lu 10 11 *B* (*S* ϭⲱⲧⲉ) ⲁⲡⲟⲙⲁⲥⲥⲉⲓⲛ; Lev 4 17 *S* (*B* ⲛⲟϫϩ) ⲣⲁⲓⲛⲉⲓⲛ; Is 30 22[†] *S* (*BF* diff), Ez 22 10[†] *SB* (prob *sic l*) ⲁⲡⲟⲕⲁⲑⲓⲥⲧⲁⲛⲁⲓ; Mor 17 114 *S* ⲁⲥⲡⲉⲣ ⲡⲁⲓ…ⲉⲃ. ⲇⲓⲁⲃⲁⲗⲗⲉⲓⲛ, RNC 38 *S* ⲛⲧⲛⲡⲉ-ⲣⲉ (*sic*) ⲡⲁⲓ ⲉⲃ. ⲉⲕⲃⲁⲗ.; Deu 10 8 *S* (*B* ⲟⲩⲱ̇ϯ ⲉⲃ.) ⲇⲓⲁⲥⲧⲉⲗⲗⲉⲓⲛ; Jud 13 19 *S* (var om ⲉⲃ.) ⲇⲓⲁⲭⲱⲣⲓⲍⲉⲓⲛ; Ac 22 14 *S* (*B* ⲥⲱⲧⲡ) ⲡⲣⲟⲭⲉⲓⲣⲓⲍⲉⲓⲛ; 1 Kg 17 10 *S* ⲇⲓⲇⲟⲛⲁⲓ, *ib* 5 4[†] *S* ⲁⲫⲁⲓⲣⲉⲓⲛ, Lev 1 12 *S* (*B* diff) ⲇⲓⲁⲓⲣ.; Jos 18 20 *S* ⲟⲣⲓⲍⲉⲓⲛ, *ib* 21 27 *S* ⲁⲫⲟⲣ.; Ez 41 12 *SB* ⲁⲡⲟⲗⲟⲓⲡⲟⲥ *separatus*; Jos 7 14 *S* ⲇⲉⲓⲕⲛⲩⲛⲁⲓ; *ib* 18 8 *S* ⲉⲕⲫⲉⲣⲉⲓⲛ; Ps 1 4 *B* (*S* ⲑⲗⲟ ⲉⲃ.) ⲉⲕⲣⲓⲡⲧⲉⲓⲛ; Ez 5 2 *B* (*S* ϫⲱⲱⲣⲉ ⲉⲃ.) ⲇⲓⲁⲥⲕⲟⲣⲡⲓⲍⲉⲓⲛ; Aeg 289 *S* ⲁⲡⲛ. ⲉⲃ. ⲡⲁⲩ *high priesthood* ⲛⲉⲙⲉⲓⲛ, *ib* 288 *S* ⲁϥⲛ. ⲉⲃ. ⲙⲡⲉⲧⲣⲉⲡⲉⲓ ⲁⲡⲟⲛ.; JA '75 5 248 *S let them pray* ⲉϫⲛ.[†] ⲉⲃ. ⲓⲇⲓⲁ; ShA 1 77 *S* ⲛⲥⲓϣⲉ…ⲉϫⲛ[†] ⲉⲃ. ⲙ-ⲡⲉϩⲗⲟϭ, ShMIE 23 78 *S harlots* ⲉϫⲛ.[†] ⲉⲃ. ⲉⲩϯ ⲥⲟⲉⲓⲧ, AM 218 *B* ⲉⲁϥⲛⲉϩ ⲡⲓϣⲁϩ ⲛⲭⲣⲱⲙ ⲉⲃ. (*v* Dan 3 49 & *cf* C 43 80 *B* ⲑⲣⲉ…ⲫⲱⲧ ⲥⲁⲃⲟⲗ), PS 324 *S dragon* ⲛⲁⲡ. ⲙⲡⲉϥⲥⲁⲧ ⲉⲃ. ϩⲓⲣⲱϥ, ShZ 471 *S robbers* ⲛ. ⲉⲃ. ⲙⲡⲉϣϣⲧ ⲙⲡⲉⲃ̄ϩⲉ, Bodl g 1 *B* (Theotokia) *birds' wings* ⲁⲩϣⲁⲛⲛⲉϩⲟⲩ ⲉⲃⲟⲗ *Almighty smelleth their perfume*, C 43 108 *B executioner* ⲛ. ⲧⲉϥⲁⲡⲉ ⲉⲃ., P 129[14] 129 *S archbishop* ⲛ. ⲉⲃ. ⲙⲡⲟⲗⲗⲁⲣⲓⲟⲛ (? ⲃⲟⲩⲗⲗⲁⲣⲓⲟⲛ) *from neck*, BAp 9 *S gate's hinges* ⲛⲏϩⲉ (var ⲛⲏϩ) ⲉⲃ. *dislodged*, P 44

116 *S* ⲛⲗⲉϩⲓⲥ ⲉⲧⲛ.[†] ⲉⲃ. *from Minor Prophets* مختزع, *ib* 119 sim منتزع, JA '75 5 256 *S Nicene fathers finding selves* 319 ⲙⲡⲟⲩⲉ̄ϣ ⲛ. ⲡⲣⲱϣ ⲉⲃ. *as to what their number was*, BM 1076 *S* (heading of tax-register) *God watch over NN* ϣⲁⲡⲧϥⲛ. ⲡⲛⲙⲟ-ⲥⲓ(ⲟ)ⲛ ⲉⲃ. *account for*, Kr 81 *S* ⲁⲡⲛ. ⲉⲃ. ⲙⲡⲉⲫⲟⲣⲓⲥ (ⲫⲟⲣⲟⲥ) *of 13th* (indiction), sim ? CO 62 *S*, Kr 228 *S*[ꞌ] ⲁⲣⲏⲩ ϣⲁⲡⲡⲟⲩ ⲉⲃ. ⲙⲫⲱϥ.

Refl, *separate, remove self*: PS 222 *S* ⲁⲩⲡⲉϩⲟⲩ ⲉⲃ. *into 3 parts*, MG 25 371 *B if he dozed* (*v* ϯ ⲡⲓϥⲓ) *forthwith* ⲛⲧⲉϥⲛⲉϩϥ ⲉⲃ. (ROC 18 285 محاله *reading* ? ⲛⲉϩⲥⲓ), Pcod 37 *S* (var) ⲡⲉⲧⲛⲁⲡⲉϩϥ ⲉⲃ. ⲙⲡⲕⲟⲥⲙⲟⲥ.

—— ⲉⲃ. ϩⲛ-, ϫⲉⲛ- (*i e* ⲉⲃ. ⲉⲃ. ϩⲛ-) *SB*, *separate from, out of*: 1 Kg 1 14 *S* ⲡⲉⲣⲓⲁⲓⲣⲉⲓⲛ ⲁⲡⲟ, Is 33 15 *SF* (*B* ⲉⲃ. ϩⲁ-) ⲁⲡⲟⲥⲉⲓⲉⲓⲛ ⲁⲡⲟ; Jth 10 17 *S* ⲉⲕⲗⲉⲅⲉⲓⲛ ⲉⲕ; Br 125 *S* ϥⲡⲁⲛ. ⲡⲟⲩϫⲩⲡⲁⲙⲓⲥ ⲉⲃ. ⲛϩⲏⲧϥ *bring forth from self*, AM 319 *B* ⲁϥⲛ. ⲡⲓⲭⲣⲱⲙ ⲉⲃ. ϫⲉⲛ-ⲡⲓⲥⲱⲙⲁ.

II *intr*, *be shaken out*: BMar 85 *S in old age* ⲁⲛⲡⲁⲭ(ⲉ) ⲛ. *fall out*; K 233 *B* ⲁϥⲛⲟϩ, قفز وثب, نط, *jump*.

—— ⲉⲃ. *come apart, be loosed*: BMis 262 *S quarrelsome ox* ⲁⲡⲉϥⲧⲁⲡ ⲛ. ⲉⲃ. ⲁⲩϩⲉ, EW 101 *B martyr racked till bones* ⲛ. ⲉⲃ., BM 1144 *S* ⲛⲡⲟⲩ-ⲕⲁⲁⲧ ⲧⲁⲛⲟⲩ ⲉⲃ. *& go home*, *ib* 598 *F send Mena* ⲛϣⲁⲡⲧⲁⲛⲟⲩ (ⲉ)ϩ[ⲁ]ⲗ ϩⲓⲡⲉⲛⲓⲱϩⲓ; ⲛ. ⲉⲃ. ϩⲛ-: Deu 19 5 (*B* ϩⲉⲓ ⲉⲃ. ϫⲉⲛ-) ⲉⲕⲡⲓⲡⲧⲉⲓⲛ ⲁⲡⲟ; Job 31 22 *S* (*B* do) ⲁⲫⲓⲥⲧⲁⲛⲁⲓ ⲁⲡⲟ. Va 58 152 *B* ϣⲁϥⲛ. ⲉⲃ. ϩⲓϫⲉⲛⲡⲓⲕⲁϩⲓ *scattered from off earth* like dust, LAI 10 *S* ⲁⲩⲡ. ⲉⲃ. ϩⲓϫⲱⲛ ⲛϭⲓ ⲡⲡⲁⲣⲉϩ.

—— *S nn, some form of labour, paid for*: Ep 532 ϩⲁⲛ., paral ϩⲁⲣⲓⲥⲉ. *Cf next*.

ⲛⲉϩϥ *B* (var ⲛⲉϩ) nn m, *what is shaken* or ? *that wherewith is shaken*, of dust, chaff: K 269 تذرية, ذفض.

V ⲛⲟϩⲉ.

ⲛⲟⲩϩⲉ *S*, -ϩⲓ *BF* nn f, *sycamore* (*ficus sycomo-rus*), *fig-mulberry*: Ps 77 47 *SB*, Is 9 10 *SB*, Lu 17 6 *SB* ⲥⲩⲕⲁⲙⲓⲛⲟⲥ all جوزة; Tri 474 *S*, C 41 9 جميز, P 44 81 *S* ⲥⲩⲕⲟⲙⲱⲣⲓⲁⲥ· ⲥⲩⲕⲁⲙⲓⲛⲟⲥ· ⲛ. 'ج, P 43 55 *S* ⲥⲉⲕⲁⲙ· ⲥⲩⲧⲧⲟⲙ. 'ج, ⲛ. 'ج, 'ج, K 348 *B* 'ج; in recipes TurM 9 *S* ϣⲉ ⲛⲛ. (*cf* Ep 326), PMéd 204 *S ashes of* ϣⲉ ⲛⲛ., *ib* 145 *S milk of* ⲛ., *ib* 236 *S syrup* (ⲉϥⲓⲱ) *of* ⲛ., BKU 1 25 *S* ⲟⲩⲛ. ⲙⲡⲁⲣⲑⲉ-ⲛⲟⲥ; AZ 23 39 *F* ⲛ. ⲥⲓⲛⲧⲓ, CMSS 78 *F list of expenses* ⲉϩⲟ(ⲩ)ⲡ (ⲟⲩ)ⲧⲉⲗ ⲛ. *branch* (?) *of syc.* In name: Παⲧⲟⲩⲛⲉⲓ̂ (Preisigke). In place-names: ⲧⲛⲟⲩϩⲉ (Ep 520 n, *ib* 1 122), كفر دنوهية (near Zaga-zig), بردنوهة (Abû Ṣâliḥ 74 a, *cf* Amélineau *Géog* 455 n). *Cf* ⲉⲗⲕⲱ, ⲗⲱⲱⲥ nn.

ⲡⲟⲩϩⲃ *SA*, ⲡⲟⲣⲉⲃ, ⲡⲱ. *B*, ⲡⲁⲣϩ- *S*, ⲡⲉϩⲡ- *B*, ⲡⲁⲣϩ⸗, ⲡⲟⲣϩ⸗ *S*, ⲡⲁⲣϩ† *S* vb **I** tr, **a** *make ready wagon by yoking* beasts: Ge 46 29 *SB*, Jth 15 11 *S* ζευγνύναι; Nah 2 4 *A* (*B* ⲥⲟⲃϯ ⲛⲛ) ἑτοιμασία; Mor 31 239 *S* arise ⲡ. ⲡⲛⲉⲕϩⲁⲣⲙⲁ, C 89 181 *B* ⲁⲡⲟⲡ ⲉⲧⲡⲁⲡ. ⲡⲡⲟⲩⲛ (*sc* wagons), WS 99 *S* thou constrainest ⲡⲕⲟⲩⲧⲉⲥ ⲉⲡ. ⲉϥⲟⲓ (*l* ⲙϥ.) *to yoke* (beasts) *to the water-wheel*, Ryl 340 *S* ⲁⲓ(ⲧ)ⲣⲉⲩⲡⲁⲣϩ ϥⲟⲓ & I let water into gardens. **b** *yoke* beasts: C 89 23 *B* who would ⲡ. ⲙⲡⲉϥⲧⲉⲃⲡⲏ ⲉⲟⲩⲓⲟϩⲓ ζευ. εἰς μηχανήν, *ib* 86 288 *B* ⲁⲡⲁϣⲏⲣⲓ ⲡ. ⲙⲡⲉϥⲙⲁⲥⲓ ϩⲉⲡⲧⲕⲟⲓ ζευ., *ib* 89 117 *B* working in field ⲙ[ⲛ]ⲁⲓⲡⲉⲣϩ ϧⲗⲓ ⲡⲣⲁⲡⲏⲓ ὑδραγώγειν = Va ar 172 67 على بهايما في دوالب. ⲡ. ⲉⲣⲟⲩⲡ, ⲉϩ. ⲉ-, *yoke to, join to*; 1 Kg 6 7 *S* (var om ⲉϩ.) ζευ. ἐν, Ez 1 11 *B* (var HCons 280 ⲡⲉⲣⲡ) gloss on ϩⲱⲧⲡ συνζυγήν, Z 580 *S* beasts ⲉⲧⲙ.† ⲉϩ. (ⲉ)ⲙⲙⲉⲭⲁⲡⲏ.

II intr, *be yoked, harnessed*: R 1 3 49 *S* chariot with 4 mules ⲡ.† ⲉⲣⲟⲩ. ⲡ. ⲙⲛ-, *be united with*: BG 38 *S* ⲁⲥⲡ. ⲡⲓⲙⲁϥ ⲡⲟⲩⲕⲗⲟⲟⲗⲉ (= ϩⲡⲟⲩ-), *ib* 65 ⲉⲁⲩⲡ. ⲙⲛⲧϭⲟⲙ.

ⲡⲁⲣϩ, -ϩⲉⲃ *S*, -ϩⲉϥ *SA²B*, -ϩϥ *A*, ⲡⲉⲣϩⲉϥ *F* nn m, *yoke*: Ge 27 40 *S*, -ϩⲉϥ *B*, Lev 26 13 *SB*, Ps 61 9 *S* (var -ϩⲉϥ) *B*, Is 5 18 *S* -ϩⲉϥ (var -ϩⲉ) *BF*, Zeph 3 9 *AB*, Mt 11 29 *S* (var do) *B* ζυγός; ShA 2 130 *S* ⲡⲥⲉⲙⲟⲣⲟⲩ ⲉϩⲟⲩⲛ ⲉⲡⲛ., ShP 130³ 15 *S* ⲡⲛ. ⲡⲧⲕⲟⲓⲡⲱⲡⲓⲁ, C 89 136 *B* ϥⲡ. of monkhood, Cl 16 17 *A* ⲡⲛ. of His grace, BMOr 6201 A 90 *S* ⲡ. ⲡⲕⲱⲧⲉ *for irrigation*, ⲡ. ⲡⲥⲕⲁⲓ *for ploughing*. ⲡⲁⲣϩⲉϥ *B* (1 var -ⲡⲉϥ), *cross-beam in loom*: K 126 ⲡⲡ. نير .

ⲧⲟⲩⲣⲡⲁⲣϩⲉ (or ? ⲧ-ⲟⲩⲣⲡ.) *S* nn, *yoke-strap*: Glos 113 ⲧ.· ζυγοδέσμιον.

ϥⲁⲓⲡ. *S*, -ⲡⲁⲣϩⲉϥ *S* (BM 174 1) *A* nn m, *yoke-bearer, beast of burden*: Ex 20 10 *S* (*B* ⲉⲱ), Deu 5 14 *S* (*B* ⲓⲱ), Zech 9 9 *SA* (*B* do), Mt 21 5 *S* (*B* ⲉⲱ) ὑποζύγιον; Tri 353 *S* اثان opp ⲧⲃⲡⲏ.

ⲡⲁϩⲃ (oftenest), -ϥ, -ϩⲉ *S*, -ϩⲓ, -ⲟⲩ (AM 113) *B*, ⲡⲉⲣϩⲓ *F* nn f, **a** *shoulders, back*, sg or pl: Ge 21 14 *SB*, Jos 4 5 *SB*, Job 31 20 *S* (*B* ⲭϥⲟⲓ), *ib* 22 *S* (*B* ϣⲱⲃϣ), Is 10 27 *S* (*B* ⲙⲟϯ), EpJer 3 *BF* (*S* diff), ROC 11 305 *S* ⲉⲣⲉⲟⲩⲡⲓⲣⲁ ϩⲓⲧⲉϥⲡ. ὦμος, P 44 69 *S* ⲡⲡ.· ὦ.· ἀκρώμιον; Deu 32 11 *S* (*B* ⲙⲟϯ), Ps 67 14 *S* (*B* do), P 44 *lc* ⲡⲡ. (*sic*) μετάφρενον; Br 236 *S* ten δέκαδες encircling ⲡⲉⲥⲡ., ShA 1 53 *S* woman ⲉⲥⲟⲩⲟⲗⲥ ⲉϩⲡⲡⲉϥⲡ., Mor 30 42 *F* lifted plank ⲉⲧⲉϥⲡ. = BMis 266 *S* ⲉϫⲱϥ, Ryl 94 106 *S* she lifted him ⲉϩⲡⲡⲉⲥⲡ., ShMIF 23 18 *S* hands lopped off ϣⲁⲡⲉϥⲡ., Tor 28 *S* orphans have no ⲣϣⲱⲡ ⲉⲧⲉϥⲡ. **b** *neck*, mostly sg: Ge 33 4 *B* (*S* ⲙⲁⲕϩ), Is 30 28 *B* (*S* do, *F* ⲙⲁϯ), Ez 21 29 *B* (var ⲙⲟϯ), Hos 10 11 *B* (*A* ⲙⲉⲭϩ) τράχηλος; ShC

---

42 38 *S* chain ϩⲓⲧⲉϥⲡ., AM 133 *B* stretched out ⲧⲉϥⲡ. to executioner, Mor 25 83 *S* if thou be strong ⲙⲉϩ ⲙⲟⲟⲩ ϩⲡⲧⲉⲕⲡ., DeV 1 63 *B* sim, C 89 62 *B* ⲁⲕⲡⲁϯ ⲡⲧⲉⲕⲡ. ϩⲁⲡⲁⲓⲥⲟⲡ = Miss 4 546 *S* ⲙⲁⲕϩ *q v*, Miss 4 107 *B* ϩⲁⲡⲡ. (*sic* MS) like writing-tablets (πυξίον) = Mor 18 13 *S* ϩⲡⲁⲁⲩ, *ib* 19 22 *S* ⲥⲕⲉ(ⲩ)ⲟⲥ (diff word ?).

ϣⲓ ⲡⲡ. *SB* nn, *shoulder-measure, height of shoulders*: 1 Kg 9 2 *S* (var ⲉϩⲟⲩⲉ ⲟⲩⲡ.) ὑπερωμία; AM 305 *B* ⲟⲩϣⲓ ⲡⲡ. ⲡⲣⲱⲙⲓ.

ϩⲃⲥ ⲡ. *S* nn m, *shoulder-covering*, vestment: Ex 29 5 (*B* = Gk) ἐπωμίς.

ⲡⲁϣⲧ ⲡ. *B*, *stiff-necked*: Deu 9 6 (*S* ⲡⲁϣⲧ ⲙⲁⲕϩ), Ac 7 51 (*S* do) σκληροτράχηλος; ⲙⲉⲧⲡ. ⲡ., *obstinacy*: C 41 37 answered ϩⲉⲡⲟⲩⲙ.

ϫⲁⲣⲉⲃ ⲡ. *B*, *bare-necked*: He 4 13 (*S* ϣⲁⲁⲧ) τραχηλίζειν; Va 57 67 sad & humbled ⲉⲡⲟⲓ ⲡϫ. in fear & trembling.

ϭⲁⲥⲓ ⲡ. *B*, *high-necked*, conceited: 2 Tim 3 4 (var ϭⲁⲥ-, *S* ϫⲁⲥⲓϧⲏⲧ) τυφοῦσθαι.

ⲱⲗⲓ ⲡⲧⲡ. *B*, *take off neck*, behead: 1 Kg 17 46 (*S* ϥⲓ ⲁⲡⲉ) κεφαλὴν ἀφαιρεῖν, Mk 6 16 (*SF* do) ἀποκεφαλίζειν.

ⲡⲟⲩϩⲃ *S* vb **a** intr, *copulate, engender*, if not same as last (so Dévaud: *cf* Berlin *Wörterb* 2 284 *nhp*): Lev 19 19 (*B* ϭⲓ ϫⲣⲟϫ ⲉⲃⲟⲗ ϩⲉⲡ-) κατοχεύειν, Si 36 6† (HT) εἰς ὀχείαν. **b** tr, *fertilize*: BG 105 that she be no longer lacking ⲁⲗⲗⲁ ⲉⲩⲉⲡⲁϩⲃⲉⲥ ⲉⲃⲟⲗ ϩⲓⲧⲟⲟⲧ.

ⲡⲁϩⲃⲓ *B*, *spear* *v* ⲡⲁϫⲓ.

ⲡⲉϩⲃⲏⲗ, -ⲃⲉⲗ, -ⲃⲁⲗ *B* nn m, *wine-skin* νέβελ נבל, containing 150 ξέσται (PG 43 284): K 144 ⲡⲡ. ⲡⲏⲣⲡ زق الخمر الكبير . 1 Kg 1 24 *S*, Hos 3 2 *SA* νέβελ = ϣⲓ.

ⲡⲁϩⲃⲉϥ &c *v* ⲡⲟⲩϩⲃ.

ⲡϩⲁⲗ *S* vb intr, ? *be soaked, impregnated*: AZ 23 108 (recipe) put it in liquid ϣⲁⲡⲧϥⲡ. then set it to dry. Prob Ar انل .

ⲡⲁϩⲗⲉⲡ- *F* *v* ϩⲟ (ⲡⲁϩⲣⲡ-).

ⲡⲟⲩϩⲙ *SA²*, -ϩⲙⲉ *A*, ⲡⲟϩⲉⲙ *B*, ⲡⲟⲩϩⲉⲙ *F*, ⲡⲉϩⲙ- *S*, ⲡⲁϩⲙⲉ- *A*, ⲡⲁϩⲙ- *SA²*, ⲡⲟϩⲉⲙ- (Ro 11 14), ⲡⲁϩⲉⲙ- (Jer 21 12) *B*, ⲡⲉϩⲙⲓ- (Is 36 20 *sic* MS) *F*, ⲡⲁϩⲙ⸗ *SAA²B*, ⲡⲉϩⲙ⸗ *F*, ⲡⲁϩⲙ† *SF*, ⲡⲟϩⲉⲙ† *B*, ⲡⲉϩⲉⲙ† *F* vb **I** intr, *be saved, safe*: 1 Kg 19 12 *S* (var refl), Job 1 15 *B* (*S* ⲟⲩϫⲁⲓ), Is 30 15 *B* (*SF* do), Eph 2 5 *B* (*S* ⲧⲟⲩϫⲏⲩ), MG 25 214 *B* ⲭⲟⲩⲱϣ ⲉⲡ. σώζεσθαι, Ez 6 9 *SB* ἀνασω., EpJer 54 *B* (*F* refl) διασω.; Ps 70 11 *B* (*S* refl), Dan 11 45 *B* (*S* do) ῥύεσθαι; Is 31 5 *SF* (*B* tr) ἐξαιρεῖν; Pro 19 5 *SA* διαφεύγειν; PS 133 *S* ⲁⲩⲡ.

ⲣⲓⲧⲡⲟⲩⲙⲟⲟⲩ, ShC 73 2 *S* ⲁⲣⲁ ⲧⲛⲛⲁⲡ. at Judgment ?, AM 99 *B* ⲁⲥⲡ. ⲁⲥⲓ ⲉⲃⲟⲗ. Qual *S*: MR 5 29 I hope ϫⲉⲕⲛ., *ib* 47 by God's will ⲧⲛⲛ., Bodl(P) c 13 pray that I arrive ⲉⲓⲛ.; *sim* + ⲉⲃⲟⲗ *S*, *be wholly saved*, *cf* ϩⲱⲗ (ⲉⲃⲟⲗ *init*): BMar 16 *S* found all ⲉⲩⲛ. ⲉⲃ. *Cf also* **II.**

With following preposition, all same meaning.

—— ⲉ- *SBF*, **a** *be saved, escape from*: Ez 6 8 *B* (*S* ⲟⲩ.) ⲁⲛⲁⲥⲱ. ἐκ; Ps 17 29 *S* (*B* ⲛ-) ῥύ. ἀπό, *ib* 123 7 *S* (*B* ⲉⲃⲟⲗ ϩⲉⲛ-) ῥύ. ἐκ; Aeg 270 *S* ⲛⲧⲁϫⲛ. ⲉⲛⲉⲓⲛⲉⲑⲟⲟⲩ περιγίνεσθαι; PS 256 *S* ⲛⲧⲉⲧⲛⲛ. ⲉⲛ-ⲕⲟⲗⲁⲥⲓⲥ, ST 186 *S* ⲉⲓⲛ.† ⲉϣⲱⲡⲉ, MR 5 47 *F* this I write ⲉⲓⲛⲉⲣⲉⲙ ⲉⲛⲉⲑⲁⲩ. **b** *escape safely to*: MG 25 19 *B* ship ⲛ. ⲉⲡⲓⲭⲣⲟ ⲥⲱ. ἐπί, Is 37 38 *B* (*S* ⲡⲱⲧ ⲉϩⲣⲁⲓ ⲉ-) ⲇⲓⲁⲥⲱ. εἰς; MG 25 20 *B* ϥⲛⲁⲡ. ⲉⲟⲩⲗⲓⲙⲏⲛ ἥκειν εἰς; BM 323 *S* ⲁϫⲛ. ⲉϩⲣⲁⲓ ⲉⲡⲉⲅⲙⲁ.

—— ⲛⲧⲛ- *SB*: 2 Kg 22 3 *S* (var ⲉⲧⲛ-) ⲥⲱ. ἐκ, Is 20 6 *B* (*S* ⲉⲃ. ϩⲓⲧⲛ-) ⲥⲱ. ἀπό.

—— ⲉⲃⲟⲗ ϩⲁ- *B*: EpJer 11 (*F* ⲟⲩ- ⲉ-) ⲇⲓⲁⲥⲱ. ἀπό; Ro 15 31 (*S* ⲉⲃ. ϩⲓⲧⲛ-) ῥύ. ἀπό.

—— ϩⲛ-, ϩⲉⲛ- *SB*: Ez 14 15 *B* διοδεύειν ἀπὸ προσώπου; PS 118 *S* ⲉⲧⲣⲉϩⲛ. ϩⲙⲡⲉⲭⲁⲟⲥ.

—— ⲉⲃ. ϩⲛ- *SAB*: Ps 17 4 *B* (*S* ⲟⲩ.) ⲥⲱ. ἐκ, Is 45 20 *B* (*S* ⲟⲩ.) ⲥⲱ. ἀπό; Pro 10 2 *SAB* ῥύ. ἐκ; 2 Cor 11 33 *B* (*S* ⲣ ⲃⲟⲗ ⲉ-) ἐκφύγ. acc; BMis 416 *S* ⲉⲓⲉⲛ. ⲉⲃ. ϩⲛⲧⲙⲏⲧⲉ of abyss = BSM 58 *B*.

—— ⲉⲃ. ϩⲓⲧⲛ- *S*: Is 20 6 (*B* ⲛⲧⲉⲡ-) ⲥⲱ. ἀπό; Lu 1 74 (*B* ⲉⲃ. ϩⲉⲛ-) ῥύ. ἐκ χειρός, 2 Thes 3 2 (*B* ⲉⲃ. ϩⲁ-) ῥύ. ἀπό.

II tr, *save, preserve*: Ps 108 26 *B* (*S* ⲧⲟⲩϫⲟ), Is 33 22 *B* (*SF* ⲧⲁⲛϩⲟ), Hab 1 2 *SAB*, Mk 8 35 *SBF* ⲥⲱ., Jer 28 6 *B* ⲁⲛⲁⲥⲱ., Zech 8 13 *AB* ⲇⲓⲁⲥⲱ.; Ps 21 8 *SA*(Cl)*B*, Is 36 14 *B* (*SF* ⲧⲟⲩ.) ῥύ.; Job 5 4 *SB*, EpJer 36 *BF* ἐξαιρ.; Ac 7 24 *S* (*BF* ϣⲉⲛ ϩⲏⲧ) ἀμύνειν; PS 90 *S* ⲁⲙⲟⲩ ⲛⲧⲛⲁϩⲙⲉⲧ, El 100 *A* hast not power ⲁⲛ. ⲙⲙⲁⲕ, AP 23 *A*² ⲁϥⲛⲁϩⲙ ⲡⲁⲉⲓⲱⲧ, AM 118 *B* ⲛⲧⲉϥⲛⲁⲣⲉⲙⲟⲛϩⲟⲩ; without obj: Ps 17 41 *SB* none ⲛⲉⲧⲛ., R 2 2 37 *S* ⲡⲁⲓ ⲉⲧⲛ. (var BHom 56 ⲧⲟⲩ.).

Refl: 1 Kg 19 12 *S* (var intr) ⲥⲱ., EpJer 54 *F* (*B* intr) ⲇⲓⲁⲥⲱ.

—— ⲉⲃⲟⲗ *SB*, implying completion (*cf* **I**): PS 92 *S* I know ϫⲉⲕⲛⲁⲡⲁϩⲙⲉⲧ ⲉⲃ., CaiThe 370 *B* those in trouble ⲛⲁϩⲙⲟⲩ ⲉⲃ.

With following preposition, all same meaning.

—— ⲉ- *SA*, *save from*: Job 5 20 *S* (*B* ⲛⲧⲉⲡ-) ⲥⲱ. ἐκ; *ib* 81 4 *S* (*B* ⲉⲃ. ϩⲉⲛ-) ῥύ. ἐκ, Pro 2 12 *SA* (*B* ⲉⲃ. ϩⲁ-) ῥύ. ἀπό; Eccl 7 27 *S* ἐξαιρ. ἀπό; BMar 38 *S* ⲁⲕⲛ. ⲡⲟⲩⲯⲩⲭⲏ ⲉⲡⲙⲟⲩ.

—— ⲉⲧⲛ- *S*: 1 Kg 7 3 (var ⲛⲧⲛ-) ἐξαιρ. ἐκ χειρῶν; Ps 16 13 (*B* ⲉⲃ. ⲛⲧⲉⲛ-) ῥύ. ἀπό, PS 87 ⲛⲁϩⲙⲉⲧ ⲉⲧⲟⲟⲧⲟⲩ ⲛⲡⲉⲡⲣⲟⲃⲟⲗⲟⲟⲩⲉ.

—— ⲛⲧⲛ- *SAB*: Hos 13 14 *A* (*B* ⲥⲱϯ) ῥύ. ἐκ, Is 25 4 *B* (*S* ⲉ-) ῥύ. ἀπό; 1 Kg 17 37 *S* (varr ⲉⲧⲛ-, ⲉⲧϭⲓϫ ⲛ-, *B* ⲉⲃ. ϩⲉⲛ-) ἐξαιρ. ἐκ; PS 175 *S* ⲛⲁϩⲙⲉⲧ ⲛⲧⲉⲧⲏⲩⲧⲛ, TstAb 247 *B* ⲉⲧⲁⲓⲛⲁϩⲙⲉⲕ ⲛⲧⲟⲧϥ ⲛ-... ⲉⲧⲁⲓⲛ. ⲉⲃ. ϩⲉⲛⲛⲉⲛϫⲓϫ ⲛ-.

—— ⲉⲃⲟⲗ ⲛⲧⲉⲛ- *B*: Ps 105 10 (*S* ⲧⲟⲩ. ⲉⲧϭⲓϫ) ⲥⲱ. ἐκ χ.; *ib* 16 13 (*S* ⲉⲧⲛ-, *F* ϩⲁⲃⲁⲗ ⲛ-) ῥύ. ἀπό; Dan 6 27 ἐξαιρ. ἐκ χ.

—— ϩⲁ- *B*: BSM 24 able ⲉⲛⲁϩⲙⲉϥ ϩⲁⲡⲉⲛϩⲉϫⲓⲥ = BMis 364 *S* ⲧⲟⲩ. ϩⲛ-.

—— ⲉⲃ. ϩⲁ- *B*, meaning same: Ac 2 40 (*S* ⲟⲩ. ⲉⲃ. ϩⲛ-) ⲥⲱ. ἀπό; Mt 6 13 (*S* ⲉⲃ. ϩⲓⲧⲛ-, *F* ϩⲁⲃⲁⲗ ⲛ-) ῥύ. ἀπό, Ro 7 24 (*S* ⲉⲃ. ϩⲛ-) ῥύ. ἐκ; BSM 67 ϭⲛⲁⲛⲁϩⲙⲉⲕ ⲉⲃ. ϩⲁⲡⲉⲧϩⲱⲟⲩ = BMis 159 *S* ⲉ-.

—— ϩⲁⲃⲁⲗ ⲛ- *F*: Mt 6 13 v above, ZNTW 24 84 sim ῥύ. ἀπό.

—— ϩⲛ-, ϩⲉⲛ- *SB*: Ro 7 24 *S* (Mun 182, var ⲉⲃ. ϩⲛ-, *B* ⲉⲃ. ϩⲁ-), 2 Tim 3 11 *S* (*B* ⲉⲃ. ϩⲉⲛ-) ῥύ. ἐκ; Is 57 13 *B* (*S* ⲧⲟⲩ. ϩⲛ-) ἐξαιρ. ἐν; Mor 31 129 *S* ⲁϫⲛ. Three Children ϩⲛⲧⲉϩⲣⲱ (var ⲉⲧⲉϩ. Miss 4 788).

—— ⲉⲃ. ϩⲛ-, ϩⲉⲛ- *SAA²BF*: EpJer 49 *BF*, Jo 12 27 *B* (*SA*² ⲧⲟⲩ.) ⲥⲱ. ἐκ, Mt 1 21 *B* (*S* ⲇⲟ) ⲥⲱ. ἀπό; Ps 50 14 *B* (*SA* ⲇⲟ), Pro 10 2 *SAB* ῥύ. ἐκ, Ez 37 23 *SB* ῥύ. ἀπό; Nah 2 1 *A* (*B* intr), Gal 1 4 *B* (*S* ⲧⲟⲩ.) ἐξαιρ. ἐκ; AP 10 *A*² ⲉⲓⲛⲁⲛⲁϩⲙⲟⲩ ⲁⲃ. ϩⲙⲡⲧⲉⲕⲟ ἀποσπᾶν ἀπό; AM 295 *B* ⲉⲧⲁϥⲛ. ⲛⲇⲁ-ⲛⲓⲏⲗ ⲉⲃ. ϩⲉⲛⲫⲗⲁⲕⲕⲟⲥ.

—— ⲉⲃ. ϩⲓⲧⲛ- *SB*: Ex 2 17 *S* (*B* om ⲉⲃ. ϩ.) ῥύ. ἀπό, Ps 17 tit *S* (*B* ⲉⲃ. ϩⲉⲛ-) ῥύ. ἐκ; AM 115 *B* ⲛⲧⲉϥⲛⲁϩⲙⲉⲛ ⲉⲃ. ϩⲓⲧⲟⲧϥ of Satan.

—— ⲥⲁⲃⲟⲗ ⲛ- *B*: Ps 139 2 (*S* ⲧⲟⲩ. ⲉ-) ῥύ. ἀπό.

—— *SB* nn m, *safety*: Lev 3 1 *B* (*S* ⲟⲩ.), Ps 11 6 *B* (*SA*(Cl)ⲇⲟ) σωτήριος, Ro 1 16 *B* (*S* ⲇⲟ), MG 25 19 *B* σωτηρία; *ib* 17 2 *SB* ῥύστης; *ib* 48 8 *B* (*S* diff) ἐξίλασμα; PMich 593 *S* charm for ⲛⲛ. ⲡⲣⲉⲡⲉⲭⲏⲩ, PO 11 363 *B* ⲁϥϯ ϯ ⲡⲟⲩϫⲡ. ⲛⲁϥ before king, C 41 22 *B* gift made ϩⲁⲡⲁⲛ.; vbal form as nn *B*: Ps 118 173 ⲉϥⲛⲁϩⲙⲉⲧ (*S* ⲡⲧⲟⲩϫⲟⲓ) τοῦ σῶσαί με, Jer 49 11 ⲉϥⲛⲁⲣⲉⲙⲟⲛϩⲟⲩ ἐξαιρεῖσθαι ὑμᾶς.

ⲣⲉϥⲛ. *SB*, *saviour*: Ps 69 6 *B* ⲣⲉϥⲛⲁϩⲙⲉⲧ (*S* ⲡⲁϣⲧⲉ) ῥύστης μου; PS 91 *S* ⲙⲛϭⲉⲣ. ⲡⲥⲁⲃⲗⲗⲁⲕ, BMis 509 *S* ⲡⲣ. ⲙⲙⲟⲓ, BSM 122 *B* Michael ⲡⲓⲣ.; ⲉⲣ ⲣ. *B*: Nu 25 13 (*S* ⲥⲟⲡⲥ) ἐξιλάσασθαι.

ϫⲓⲛⲛ. *B* nn m, *salvation, safety*: Ps 108 31 (*S* ⲛ. vb) τὸ σῶσαι; Dan 6 14 ⲡϫⲓⲛⲛⲁϩⲙⲉϥ τὸ ἐξελέσθαι αὐτόν.

(**ⲛⲟϩϩ**), ⲛⲉϩⲛⲟⲩϩ⸗, ⲛⲉϩⲛⲟⲩϩ† *S* vb tr, *shake*: Lu 6 38† (*B* ϥⲉⲛⲣⲱⲛ) σαλεύειν, cit BMis 411; ⲛ. ⲉⲃⲟⲗ refl, *shake self out, break out*: 2 Kg 23 16 ⲁⲩⲛⲉϩⲛⲟⲩϭⲉ (*l* -ϩⲟⲩ) ⲉⲃ. διαρρηγνύναι, R 1 5 51 ⲁϥⲛⲉϩⲛⲟⲩϭϥ ⲉⲃ. like a mighty man. *V* ⲛⲟⲩϩⲉ.

ⲛⲉϩⲡⲉ *SA*, -ⲡⲓ *BF* vb intr, *mourn*, lit *smite self* :
2 Kg 3 31 *S*, Ez 6 9 *S* ⲡ. ⲉⲣⲟⲩⲏ ϩⲙⲡⲉϩⲣⲟ (*B* ⲡ.
ⲉⲃⲟⲗ ⲉϩ. ϧⲉⲛ-, *cf* ⲕⲱⲗϩ ⲉϩ., ϩⲓⲟⲩⲉ ⲉϩ.), Joel 1 13
SAB, Mt 11 17 *SB* κόπτεσθαι; AM 279 *B*, MG
25 20 *B* ὀδύρεσθαι; BHom 53 *S* θρηνεῖν; ShR 2
3 8 *S* ⲡⲉⲧⲛ. *mourners* cry aloud, DeV 1 124 *B* ⲧⲛⲁ-
ⲑⲣⲟⲩⲉⲣ ϩⲏⲃⲓ...ⲛⲥⲉⲛ., R 2 4 61 *S* sim.   c ⲉ-,
mourn for : Ge 50 10 *SB*, Jer 41 5 *B* (*S* ⲛ- dat),
Lu 8 52 *SB* κόπ. acc ; Jer 22 10 *B*, Ez 32 16 *B*
(*S* ⲧⲟⲉⲓⲧ) θρη.; JTS 10 400 *S* on death-beds ⲉⲣⲉⲡⲉⲩϭⲓϫ ⲡ. ⲉⲣⲟⲟⲩ because they had not gotten
wisdom, ShBor 246 88 *S* ⲥⲉⲛ. ⲉⲡⲉⲧⲙⲟⲩ.   c ⲉϫⲛ-,
meaning same : Is 32 12 *SB* (*F* ϩⲓϫⲛ-), Zech 12 10
A (*B* ⲉϩⲣⲏⲓ ⲉϫ.) κόπ. ἐπί; Ez 32 18 *B* (*S* ⲧⲟ.) θρη.
ἐπί;   c ⲉϩⲣⲁⲓ ⲉϫⲛ- *SB* : Ap 18 9 κόπ. ἐπί.
c ⲛ- *S*, meaning same : Jer 41 5 *v* above.   *Cf*
ⲕⲱⲱⲣⲉ **II**.

—— ⲉⲃⲟⲗ *B*, meaning as ⲡ. : Ez 7 12 (*S* ⲧⲟ.)
θρη., ib 6 9 *v* above.

—— *SAB* nn m, *mourning* : Est 4 3 *S*, Ps 29 12
SB, Joel 2 12 *AB* κοπετός; Jer 9 18 *B* (Lacr, var
ϩⲏⲃⲓ) θρῆνος, Ez 27 32 *B* (*S* ⲧⲟ.) θρήνημα; Ge 50
11 *B* (*S* ϩⲏ.), Bar 4 11 *B* πένθος; ShA 2 315 *S*
weeping & ⲟⲩⲛ., ShC 42 164 *S* ϩⲉⲛⲛ. ⲉⲣⲟⲩⲛ ϩⲙⲡⲉϩⲣⲟ (*cf* Ez 6 9 above), C 86 143 *B* ⲁⲩϣⲱⲡⲓ ϧⲉⲛ-
...ⲟⲩⲛⲓϣϯ ⲛⲡ.

ⲉⲓⲣⲉ, ⲣⲓ ⲛⲟⲩⲛ. *SB*, *make mourning* : Ac 8 2 *SB*,
RNC 46 *S* κοπ. ποιεῖν.

ϭⲓ ⲡ. *B*, *take mourning, mourn* : Jer 9 10 (*S* ⲭⲱ
sic ⲧⲟ.) κοπ. λαμβάνειν, Is 14 4 (*S* ϫⲓ ⲧⲟ.), Ez 19 1
(*S* ⲇⲟ) θρ. λαμβ.

ⲣⲉϥⲛ. *B* ; *mourner* : Jer 9 17 (*S* ⲣⲉϥⲧⲟ.) θρηνῶν.

ⲛⲟⲩϩⲣ, -ⲣⲉ (J 67) ⲉⲃⲟⲗ, ⲛⲁϩⲣⲉ† ⲉϩ. *S* vb intr,
meaning unknown : CO 114 give him 240 bundles
of flax ⲡⲁⲓ ⲉⲧⲛⲁϩⲣⲉ ⲉϩ. ⲛⲧⲁϥ ⲙⲁⲩⲁⲁϥ. As nn
m, ? part of dowry or bridal outfit (? *movable* belongings, *cf* next word) : J 67 59 Susanna coming
to me (as wife) brought naught given her by parents
ⲉⲡⲉⲥⲛ. ⲉϩ., ib 37 58 all property has been divided
including ⲥⲭⲁⲁⲧ, ϣⲉⲗⲉⲉⲧ, ⲣⲟⲙⲡⲉ ⲛⲟⲩⲱⲙ, ⲡ. ⲉϩ.,
ib 44 73 sim.   *Cf* ? παράφερνα (A Schiller).

ⲛϩⲟⲩⲣ, ⲉⲛ. *B* vb intr, **a** *tremble* : ROC 17 403
ϯⲉⲛ., TEuch 2 270 depths ⲉⲧⲟⲩⲉⲛ. ϧⲁⲧⲉⲕϩⲏ, Va
58 187 ⲛⲕⲉⲛ. ⲁⲛ nor be troubled φρίσσειν; Va 57
97 demons ⲥⲑⲉⲣⲧⲉⲣ, devil ⲉⲛ. τρέμειν; DeV 1 87
when thou hearest, thy body ⲛⲁⲉⲛ., TstAb 174 when
death touched him ⲁⲡⲉϥⲥⲱⲙⲁ ⲛ. ⲉⲣⲟϥ.   **b** *cause
to tremble, be terrible* : Dan 7 7 ἔκθαμβος, Va 68 178
God's βῆμα ⲉⲧⲉⲛ. ⲉⲙⲁϣⲱ. As nn, *shuddering* :
Job 4 14 (*S* ⲛⲉϩ ϣⲗϥ) φρίκη; K 405 دُهش *fear*;
with ⲙⲉϩ ⲛ- : MIE 2 400 ⲟⲩϩⲟⲧⲡⲉ ⲉⲥⲙ. ⲛⲉⲛ. =
BAp 99 *S* ϩⲟⲧⲉ ⲙⲡⲟⲩⲥⲧⲱⲧ, AM 255, FR 94 sim.

ⲁⲧⲛ., *unshakable, immovable* : BM 908 = O'Leary
Th 13 ἀναφορεῖς for bearing ark ⲉⲩⲧⲁϫⲣⲏⲟⲩⲧ ⲛⲁⲧⲛ.
(*cf* Ex 25 14 ἀκίνητος ⲁⲧⲕⲓⲙ).

ⲛⲁϩⲣⲛ-, ⲛⲁϩⲣⲉⲛ-   *v* ϩⲟ *face*.

ⲛⲉϩⲥⲉ *SAO*, -ⲥⲓ *S^f BFO* vb **I** intr, *awake, arise* :
1 Kg 26 12 *S*, BM 247 6 *S* ϣⲁⲣⲉⲡⲛⲟⲩⲥ ⲛ. ἐγεί-
ρεσθαι, Ge 41 21 *S* (*B* ⲧⲱⲛ), Jon 1 11 *B* (*SA* ⲧⲱⲟⲩⲛ) ἐξέγ., Jo 6 18 *B* (*SA²* ⲇⲟ) διεγ.; Jud 3 31 *S*,
3 Kg 3 12 *S*, Z 316 *S* sinking & ⲛⲉⲛ. ἀνιστάναι,
Jud 5 7 *S* ἐξαν. (paral ⲧⲱⲟⲩⲛ ἀν.); Z 345 *S* like
those ⲛⲧⲁⲩⲛ. = MG 25 211 *B* ⲉⲓⲣⲟⲣⲡ διυπνίζειν;
Deu 32 17 *S* (*B* ϧⲁⲉ) πρόσφατος; ShR 2 3 47 *S*
may not speak lest ⲛⲛⲉϥⲛ., MG 17 306 *S* = 241 *B*
ⲙⲡⲉⲕⲉϣⲏⲣⲉ ⲛ....except Theodore, Aeg 262 *S* at
time ⲉⲧⲟⲩⲛⲁⲛ. (paral 263 ⲧⲱ. ⲛϣⲱⲣⲡ), MG 25 182
B ⲛⲛⲉⲛϣⲁⲣϧⲁ ⲛ. ⲉⲣⲟⲕ.

With following preposition.   c ⲉϫⲛ- *SB*, *rise
against* : Wess 15 143 *S* trials ⲛⲧⲁⲩⲛ. ⲉϫⲛⲡϣⲏⲣⲉ
ⲛ̄ϯⲣⲏⲛⲏ, Dif 2 63 *B* ⲁⲛⲥⲁⲧⲁⲛⲁⲥ ⲛ. ⲉϫⲱⲕ; Miss
8 181 *S* persecution ⲁϥⲛ. ⲉϩⲣⲁⲓ ⲉϫⲛ- Christians,
Cat 22 *B* waves ⲛ. ⲉϩ. ⲉϫⲱⲟⲩ.   c ϩⲁ- *SF*, *arise
from* : LAl 10 *S* ⲁⲕⲛ. ϩⲁⲡⲉⲣⲉⲛ (*l* ⲛⲣⲡ, *cf* ⲛ. ⲉⲃⲟⲗ
ϩⲛ-), Mor 30 28 *F* ⲁϥⲛ. ϩⲁⲡϩⲓⲛⲏϥ.   c ϩⲛ-, ϧⲉⲛ-
SB, *arise from, in* : Pro 28 2 *S* (var & *A* ⲉⲧⲃⲉ-) ἐγ.
δία; Lev 13 21 *S* (varr ⲛ. ⲉⲃⲟⲗ ϩⲛ-, ϣⲱⲡⲉ ⲉϩ. ϩⲛ-,
B diff) εἶναι; P 131⁴ 99 *S* like smoke ⲉϥϣⲁⲛⲛ. ϩⲛ-
ⲟⲩϣⲉ & rising spreadeth into a cloud, P 129¹⁶ 62 *S*
glowing awls into his ears till ⲕⲁⲡⲛⲟⲥ ⲛ. ϩⲙⲡⲉϥⲁⲡⲕⲉⲫⲁⲗⲟⲥ, BMar 28 *S*, EW 83 *B*, C 43 173 *B*,
ib 86 208 *B*, AM 34 *B* sim (*cf* ⲛ. ⲉϩⲣⲁⲓ), Z 270 *S*
ⲁϥⲃⲱⲕ ⲉϩⲟⲩⲛ ⲉⲣⲁⲕⲟⲧⲉ...ⲉⲁϥⲛ. ϩⲛⲕⲏⲙⲉ.   c ⲉⲃⲟⲗ
ϩⲛ-, ϧⲉⲛ- *SB*, *awake, arise from* : Ge 9 24 *B* ἐκνήφειν ἀπό (*cf* Lam 3 49 *B* ἔκνηψις); Job 14 12 *B* (*S*
ⲧⲱ.) ἐξυπνίζειν ἐκ; Jer 28 64 *S* (*B* ⲧⲱ.) ἀνιστ. ἀπό.

With following adverb.   c ⲉⲛϣⲱⲓ *B*, *rise up,
awake* : HL 110 ⲁϥⲛ. ⲉ. ϧⲉⲛϯϫⲓⲛⲛⲁⲩ ἐπανέρχεσθαι
ἀπό; CDan 88 ⲁⲓⲛ. ⲉ. διυπν.; DeV 2 34 ⲉⲁⲛⲛ. ⲉ.
from sleep.   c ⲉϩⲣⲁⲓ, ⲉϩⲣⲏⲓ *SBF*, meaning same :
Jud 2 10 *S* ἀνισ., Ru 3 8 *S* ἐξαν.; Ez 38 9 *B* ἀναβαίν.; 3 Kg 3 15 *S* ἐξυπν.; AZ 52 120 *S* = C 89
19 *B* crocodile ⲛ. ⲉϩ. ⲛⲓⲙⲁϥ = MG 17 363 قفز
= Va ar 172 15 وثب إليه *came, leaped up at him*,
BIF 15 245 *S^f* till smoke ⲛ. ⲉϩ. ϩⲙⲡⲉϥⲁⲡⲕⲉⲫⲁⲗⲟⲥ
(*cf* ⲛ. ϩⲛ-), Mor 30 50 *F* ⲁϥⲛ. ⲉϩⲗ. ϩⲁⲡϩⲟⲣⲟⲙⲁ =
BMis 274 *S* ⲉϩⲙⲡϩⲟⲣ. ⲉϩⲣⲁⲓ.

II tr *SABO*, *waken, raise up* : Jth 14 13 *S*, Cant
8 4 *S*, Mt 8 25 *B* (*S* ⲧⲱ.) ἐγ., 2 Kg 12 11 *S* (var
ⲧⲱ.) ἐξεγ.; Va 58 171 *B* sin ⲛ. ⲛⲟⲩⲏⲣ ⲛϧⲓⲥⲓ (PG
55 571 no vb); BM 981 *S* if wouldst ⲛ. ⲡⲉⲕⲗⲟ-
ⲧⲓⲥⲙⲟⲥ (PG 47 313 no vb); PS 362 *S* demons ⲛ.
ⲛⲡⲓⲡⲟⲗⲉⲙⲟⲥ, AZ 21 104 *O* ⲉⲕⲉⲛⲉϩⲥⲓ ⲛⲫⲏⲧ ⲛⲛⲓⲙ,
ib 105 *O* ⲛⲉϩⲥⲉ (*sic*) ⲛϣⲟⲓ, Miss 4 534 *S* God hath

ⲡ. ⲙⲡⲉⲓⲛⲟϭ. ⲡⲥϯ ⲛⲟⲩϭⲉ = MG 17 568 ابل, MG
25 250 *B* overloaded camel ⲙⲡⲉⲧⲉⲛϣ ⲡ. ⲙⲙⲟⲥ,
MIE 2 414 *B* fountain ⲥⲉⲛⲁⲡ. ⲙⲙⲟⲥ, WTh 184 *S*
sim. Refl: BAp 147 *S* ⲡ. ⲙⲙⲟⲕ delay not, PVi
10157 78 *A* ⲡ. ⲙⲙⲱⲧⲛⲉ, KroppM *S* sim, C 41 70
to withered plant ⲡ. ⲙⲙⲟ ⲉⲡϣⲱⲓ (71 sim ⲉϩⲣⲏⲓ =
Miss 4 435 افسد).   ⲡ. ⲉϩⲣⲁⲓ *S*, *raise up*: Jud
20 38 ἀναφέρειν, ShP 130⁵ 100 neglectfulness ⲉⲧⲡ.
ⲉϩ. ⲉϫⲱⲡ ⲙⲡⲉϩⲟⲟⲩ ⲛⲓⲙ, LCyp 5 ϣⲁⲡ. ⲡⲧⲟ-
ⲣⲧⲛ ⲉϩ.

ϫⲓⲛ. *B* nn m, *awakening, arising*: TDi 297 ⲡⲓϫ.
ⲡⲧⲉ ⲡⲁϫⲁϫⲓ.

ⲛϩⲟⲧ, ⲡϩⲟⲩⲧ *v* ⲛⲁϩⲧⲉ.

ⲛⲁϩⲧⲉ *SAA²*, -ϯ *B*, ⲛⲉϩϯ *F*, ⲛϩⲉⲧ- *S*, ⲛϩⲟⲩⲧ-
A, ⲛϩⲟⲩⲧⲥ *A*, ⲛϩⲟⲧ†, ⲛϩⲟⲩⲧ† *S*, ⲛϩⲁⲧ† *AA²*, ⲉⲛϩⲟⲧ†
B, ⲉⲛϩⲁⲧ† *F* (*v* Sdff 248, Sethe *Verbum* 2 87, AZ
56 61) vb **I** intr, *trust, believe*: Is 7 9 *B* (*S* =
Gk), Ac 2 44 *B* (*S* do) πιστεύειν; Hab 2 18 *A* (*B*
ⲭⲱ ϧⲏⲧ ⲉϫⲉⲛ-) πείθειν, Ac 14 2 *S* neg (*B* ⲉⲣ ϩⲱⲧ
ⲡϩⲏⲧ) ἀπει.; Ps 21 4 *S* (*B* = Gk), *ib* 55 3 *S* (*B* do)
ἐλπίζειν; C 43 12 *B* I know ϫⲉⲭⲛⲁⲡ. ⲁⲡ, *ib* 225
B every one that ⲡ. ⲉⲃⲟⲗ ϧⲓⲧⲟⲧⲛ. With ϫⲉ-:
Is 43 10 *B* (*S* = Gk), MG 25 4 ϯⲡ. ϫⲉϥϯ ⲛⲁ-,
CaiEuch 408 *B* ϯⲡ. ϫⲉⲑⲁⲓⲧⲉ in truth πισ.; AP 40
A² ⲧⲛⲡ....ϫⲉ-, AM 226 *B* ⲧⲉⲛⲡ. ϫⲉⲥⲉⲛⲁⲟⲩⲱⲛ ⲛⲁⲛ.

With following preposition. ⲉ ⲉ-, *believe, trust
in*: Ge 15 6 *B* (*S* = Gk), Si 2 6 *B* (*S* do), Is 28 16
SB, Ro 4 3 *B* (*S* = Gk) πισ.; Job 27 8 *S* (*B* ⲭⲱ
ϧⲏⲧ ⲉ-), Pro 3 5 *SA* (*B* do), Is 30 12 *SF* (*B* ⲉⲣ ϩⲉⲗⲡⲓⲥ ⲉ-) πείθ.; Ps 21 8 *SA* (Cl) *B*, Is 51 5 *S* (*B* ⲉⲣ ϩ.),
ViSitz 172 4 26 *S* ⲉⲛⲉϩⲡ. ⲉⲣⲟϥ ⲉⲗⲡ.; PS 80 *S* name
is ⲡⲁⲡⲉⲧⲛ. ⲉⲣⲟϥⲡⲉ, AM 52 *B* ⲉⲕⲡ. ⲉⲟⲩ? ⲉ ⲉϫⲛ-,
trust to: Is 36 6 *SF* (*B* ⲭⲱ ϩ. ⲉ-) πείθ. ἐπί. ⲉ
ϧⲛ-, ϧⲉⲛ-, *trust in*: Ps 77 37 *B* (*S* ⲧⲁⲛϩⲟⲩⲧ, *A* ⲡ-
ϩⲟⲩⲧ tr) πισ.; *ib* 32 21 *S* (*B* ⲉⲣ ϩ.) ἐλπ., Eph 1 12
S (*BF* ⲉⲣ ϩ.) προελπ.

Qual, *trustworthy, faithful*: Nu 12 7 *B* (*S* = Gk),
Ps 18 7 *SB*, Pro 14 25 *SAB*, Is 33 16 *SBF*, Mt
25 21 *B* (*S* = Gk) πιστός, Jo 12 3 *A²* (*SB* do) πιστικός, Ps 92 5 *B* (*S* ⲧⲁⲛϩ.) πιστοῦν; AM 272 *B*
ⲟⲩⲁⲓ ⲙⲡⲓⲥⲧⲟⲥ ⲉϥⲉⲛ. γνήσιος; Ps 32 17 *S* neg (*B*
ⲙⲉⲑⲛⲟⲩϫ) ψευδής; AM 249 *B* ⲡⲓⲉⲃⲓⲁⲓⲕ ⲉⲧⲉⲛ.
ⲉ ⲉ-, *trustworthy for, fit to be entrusted with*: ShClPr
24 354 *S* ⲙⲡⲉⲧⲛϣⲱⲡⲉ ⲉⲧⲉⲧⲛ. ⲉⲡⲥⲁⲣⲕⲓⲕⲟⲛ, ROC
25 240 *B* foretold things to ⲛⲏ ⲉⲧⲉⲛ. ⲉⲡⲉϥⲥⲁϫⲓ,
Tri 654 *S* chain of sins ⲉⲕⲡ. ⲉⲃⲟⲗⲥ خبر. ⲉ ⲉϩⲣⲁⲓ ⲉϫⲛ-, *responsible for* (?): BM 1008 *S* thou ⲉⲧⲛ.
ⲉϩ. ⲉϫⲛⲡⲙⲉⲣϥⲓⲥ ⲛⲧⲉⲛⲟⲥ ϩⲟⲟϥ. ⲉ ⲛ- dat, *trust
to*: ShC 42 33 *S* ϧⲛ. ⲡⲛⲉϥⲇⲓⲕⲁⲓⲱⲙⲁ, *ib* 128 ⲉⲩ-
ⲛϩⲟⲩⲧ ⲙⲡⲁⲇⲁⲓⲙⲟⲛⲓⲟⲛ that speaketh in them. ⲉ
ⲛⲧⲛ-, *trusted by*: RNC 23 *S* ⲡⲉⲧⲛ. ⲛⲧⲟⲟⲧϥ πιστό-
τατος αὐτοῦ.

II tr, *believe*: MG 25 9 *B* ⲡⲁⲓⲣⲏϯⲡⲉ ⲉⲧⲡ. ⲙ-
ⲙⲟⲥ (sic) πισ., C 86 243 *B* ⲡ. ⲡⲉ ⲡϯⲑⲱⲣⲓⲁⲥ (or *l*
? ⲉϯ);   construct *S*, Sh only: C 73 20 ⲛⲁⲡⲟⲩ
ⲛϩⲉⲧ ⲡⲉⲧⲟⲩⲣ ⲙⲛⲧⲣⲉ ⲛⲁϥ, *ib* 172 ship ⲉⲡⲛⲁϣ ⲛϩ-
ϩⲉⲧ ⲛⲉϥⲥⲟⲛⲣ ⲁⲡ, P 130³ 7 ⲙⲡⲟⲩⲛϩⲉⲧ ⲡⲉⲧⲭⲱ ⲙ-
ⲙⲟⲟⲩ, ClPr 24 353 ⲉⲩⲛⲁⲡϩⲉⲧⲧⲏⲩⲧⲛ ⲉⲡⲉⲡⲡⲁⲧⲓⲕⲟⲛ;
A Ps 77 37 (Cl) ⲙⲡⲟⲩⲛϩⲟⲩⲧ ⲧϥⲇⲓⲁⲑⲏⲕⲏ;   with
suff *A*: Ex 4 5 ⲁⲩⲛ[ⲁ]ⲛϩⲟⲩⲧⲕ (*B* ⲡ.), Mic 7 5 ⲙⲡ-
ⲡⲣⲟⲩⲧⲧⲏⲛⲉ (*SB* ⲧⲁⲛϩⲣⲉⲧ-), Cl 43 1 ⲡⲉⲧⲁⲛϩⲣⲟⲩⲧⲟⲩ.

As nn m, **ⲁ** ⲛⲁϩⲧⲉ *SAB*, *trust, faith*: Deu 32 20
SB, 4 Kg 12 15 *S*, Si 22 23 *SA*, Mt 8 10 *B* (*S* =
Gk) πίστις; Jud 9 26 *S* ⲉⲗⲡⲓⲍⲉⲓⲛ; Nu 33 52 *S* (var
ⲡⲉⲧⲟⲩϯ ⲛϩⲧⲏⲩ ⲉⲣⲟⲟⲩ, *B* diff) σκοπιά; C 43 54 *B*
ⲛⲟⲩⲛ. ⲉⲑⲟⲩⲟϫ;   once f: Sh hom *ed* Burmester *B*
ϯⲡ. ⲁⲥⲉⲣ ϩⲱⲃ for salvation;   with prep: Ac 26
18 *B* ⲛⲏ. ⲉ- (*S* diff) εἰς, DeV 2 161 *B* ⲛⲏ. ⲉϩⲟⲩⲛ
ⲉ-, LAp 548 *F* ⲛⲏ. ⲙⲡⲉⲭ̅ⲥ̅.   **ⲃ** ⲛϩⲟⲧ *S* (rare),
meaning same: 4 Kg 16 2 ϩⲛⲟⲩⲛ. πιστῶς, Ap 21
5, 22 6 words ϩⲉⲛⲛ. (*B* ⲡ.†) πιστός: ⲣ ⲛϩⲟⲧ *S*,
be trusty: Aeg 231 ⲙⲡⲓⲥⲧⲟⲥ ⲁⲩⲱ ⲉⲩⲟ ⲛϩⲟⲧ (sic)
ἀξιόπιστος; Bor 263 16 his word ⲉϥⲟ ⲛϩⲟⲧ (sic)
ⲛⲧⲟⲟⲧϥ, BMis 13 ⲡⲉⲩⲱ ⲛϩⲟⲧ (sic) ⲉⲡⲉⲑⲣⲟⲡⲟⲥ *responsible for.*

ⲙⲉⲧⲛⲁϩϯ *B*, *faith*: BSM 49 Theopiste means
ⲑⲙ. ⲉϥϯ = BMis 399 *S* ⲧⲉⲧⲡⲓⲥⲧⲉⲩⲉ ⲉⲡⲡ̅ⲉ̅.

ⲁⲧ-, ⲁⲑⲛ. *SBF* adj, *unbelieving*: Is 17 10 *B* (*S*
= Gk), Mk 9 19 *SB*, 1 Cor 7 12 *B* (*SF* = Gk) ἄπι-
στος, Sa 10 7 *S* ἀπιστεῖν; Jer 5 23 *S* (*B* ⲁⲑⲱⲧ)
ἀπειθής; Aeg 264 *S* ⲡⲓⲁ. ⲛⲓⲟⲩⲇⲁⲓ.   ⲙⲛⲧ-, ⲙⲉⲧⲁⲧⲛ., *unbelief*: Mt 13 58 *SB* (*F* = Gk), Ro 11 23
SBF ἀπιστία; BM 172 40 *S* ἀπείθεια.   ⲣ ⲁⲧⲛ.,
be unbelieving, mistrustful: Sa 1 2 *SB*, Ac 28 24 *SB*
ἀπιστεῖν; Nu 14 43 *S* (*B* ⲁⲧⲥⲱⲧⲉⲙ), Ps 67 19 *S*
(*B* ⲁⲧϩⲱⲧ ⲛϩⲏⲧ), Is 30 12 *SF* (*B* ⲁⲧⲥⲱ.), 1 Pet 2
8 *S* (*B* ⲁⲧϯ ⲙⲁϯ) ἀπειθεῖν; Pcod 24 *S* ⲛⲥⲉⲣ ⲁ.
[ⲉ]ⲙⲙⲟⲣⲫⲏ (var ⲧⲙⲡⲓⲥⲧⲉⲩⲉ).

ⲣⲉϥⲛ. *S*, *believer*: Mor 17 28 ⲁⲁⲩ ⲛⲣ. τὸ πιστεύειν.

ϣⲟⲩⲛ. *B*, *worthy of belief*: BSM 66 men ⲛϣ.
ⲉⲣⲱⲟⲩ. *Cf S* ⲛϣⲟⲩⲡⲓⲥⲧⲉⲩⲉ BAp 111, J 6 7.
V ⲧⲁⲛϩⲟⲩⲧ.

ⲛⲉϩ ϣⲗϩ, -ϣⲗϥ *v* ϣⲗⲁϩ.

ⲛⲉϧϥ *B* *v* ⲛⲟⲩϭⲉ vb *s f.*

ⲛⲟϫ *BF*, ⲛⲁϫ *F* *v* ⲛⲟϭ.

ⲛⲟⲩϫ *SABF* adj, *lying, false*: Pro 24 43 *SA*,
Is 30 9 *B* (*S* ϭⲟⲗ, *F* ⲗⲉϫϩⲓ ϭ.) ψευδής; transl
ψευδο-: 1 Cor 15 15 *SBF* ψ.μάρτυς, Mt 15 19 *SBF*
ψ.μαρτυρία, Ex 20 16 *SB*, Mk 14 56 *SBF* ψ.μαρ-
τυρεῖν, Ap 19 20 *S* (*B* = Gk), ZNTW 24 86 *F*
ψ.προφήτης, Gal 2 4 *SB* ψ.ἀδελφός, Aeg 271 *S* ⲣⲁⲛ
ⲛⲛ. ψευδώνυμος, MG 25 204 *B* ⲁⲓⲣⲓ ⲗⲁ ⲛⲛ. ⲉⲣⲟϥ

αἰτιᾶσθαι ψευσαμένη (for S v ⲗⲁ); Sa 14 25 S, CaiEuch 400 B ⲱⲣⲕ ⲛⲛ. ἐπιορκία; Sa 4 3 S, He 12 8 B (S ⲛⲛ) νόθος; PS 256 S ⲡⲗⲁ ⲛⲛ., Mor 22 113 S = BSM 102 B clothed with ⲟⲩⲥⲭⲏⲙⲁ ⲛⲛ.
As nn, *liar*: Ps 61 9 S (B ⲥⲁ ⲙⲉⲑⲛ.), Hos 12 11 A (B ⲣⲉϥϫⲉ ⲙⲉⲑⲛ.) ψεῦδος; as f: Nah 3 1 A ⲧⲛ. (B ⲙⲉⲑⲛ.) ψευδής; with rel: 2 Thes 2 9 B ⲡⲉⲑⲛ. (S ϭ.) ψεῦδος; ShC 73 59 S as abusive name ⲛⲛ. As advb, *falsely*: Sa 14 28 S, Mt 5 33 SB ἐπιορκεῖν; ShP 130² 60 S feigning sickness ⲛⲧⲛⲕⲟⲧⲕ ⲉϩⲣⲁⲓ ⲛⲛ., Pcod 33 S swearing by God's name ⲛⲛ. Cf AZ 61 110 on ⲛ. & ⲟϫⲓ.

ⲙⲛⲧ-, ⲙⲉⲑⲛ., *lie, falsity*: Pro 6 19 B (SA ϭ.), Is 30 12 B (SF ϭ.), Hos 7 13 SAB, Jo 8 44 B (S ϭ., A² ⲣⲉϥϫⲉ ϭ.) ψεῦδος, Jer 8 8 B ψευδής, Ro 3 7 B (S ϭ.) ψεῦσμα; Eccl 7 8 F (S ⲙⲛⲧⲗⲁ) συκοφαντία; BSM 105 B God hateth ϯⲙ., SHel 90 S hypocrisy & ⲥⲁⲕ ⲙⲙ., Z 281 S ⲉⲕϣⲁⲛⲣ ⲙ. ⲉⲣⲟⲥ *deny* faith.
ϫⲉ ⲙ. B, *say falsehood*: Is 59 13 (S ϫⲓ ϭ.), Hab 3 17 (A diff), He 6 18 (SF ϫⲓ ϭ.) ψεύδειν; c ⲉ-, *against*: Is 57 11 (S do), Ac 5 3 (S do), MG 25 205 = Z 296 S do ψεύ.; c ϩⲁ- sim: Bel 12, Ja 3 14 (S do) ψεύ. ⲣⲉϥϫⲉ ⲙ. B, *liar*: 1 Tim 1 10 (S ⲣⲉϥϫⲓ ϭ.) ἐπίορκος; C 89 45 = Miss 4 526 S do. ⲁⲑⲙ. B, *without lie*: TEuch 1 324 Thy promises ⲛⲁ., Miss 4 150 ⲣⲱⲕ ⲟⲩⲁ. ⲥⲁ ⲡⲙⲛⲧⲛ. S, ⲥⲁ ⲙⲉⲑⲛ. B, *dealer in, maker of lies*: Ps 116 2 SB, Jo 8 44 B (SA² ⲣⲉϥϫⲓ ϭ.), Tit 1 12 B (var ⲣⲉϥϫⲉ ⲙ., S do) ψεύστης; Ps 71 4 B (S ⲣⲉϥϫⲓ ⲗⲁ) συκοφάντης; ShRyl 67 399 S (A 2 174 om) ⲁⲛⲣ ⲥ. ⲧⲏⲣⲛ, DeV 2 39 B that he become not ⲥⲁ ⲙ. ϭⲉⲛϥⲏ ⲉⲧⲉϥⲛⲁϫⲟϥ.

ⲛⲟⲩϫ *SBF, throw* v ⲛⲟⲩϫⲉ.

ⲛⲟⲩϫ *S, sprinkle* v ⲛⲟⲩϫⲕ.

ⲛⲁ(ⲁ)ϫⲉ S v ⲡⲁϫⲣⲉ.

ⲛϫⲉ BF v ⲛϭⲓ.

ⲛⲉϫⲉ SA v ⲡⲁϫⲣⲉ.

ⲛⲉϫⲓ B v ⲛⲏϭⲉ.

ⲛⲏϫⲓ B v ⲛϭⲉ.

ⲛⲓϫⲉ S nn f, meaning unknown, point in wall whence measurements taken: TurM 16 ⲛⲥⲟⲩ(ⲟⲩ)ⲱϩ ⲡⲛⲟⲩϫ ⲛⲓⲛⲧⲛ. ⲛⲧϫⲟⲉⲓ ⲧⲁⲣⲏⲥ ϣⲁⲧⲛ. ⲛⲧϫⲟⲉ ⲧⲁⲡⲣⲏⲧ & they shall build it (wall) in common.

ⲛⲟⲩϫⲉ SA², ⲛⲟⲩϫ SB (rare) F, ⲛⲉϫ- SB, ⲛⲁϫ- A², ⲛⲟϫⲋ SB, ⲛⲁϫⲋ SᵃA²F, ⲛⲏϫⲧ† SAA²BF vb I tr, *throw, cast* (all examp S unless otherwise marked): Ps 147 17 (B ϩⲓⲟⲩⲓ), Is 19 8 (B do), Mt 17 27 (B do), Ap 4 10 (B ⲭⲱ ⲉϩⲣⲏⲓ, cf ⲛⲟⲩϫⲉ I) βάλλειν, Ac 25 17 (B diff) ἀναβολὴν ποιεῖν; Sa 5 23 ῥίπτειν; Ez 5 11 (B ⲙⲟⲩⲛⲕ) ἀπωθεῖν; AP 37 A² ⲉⲩⲛⲁⲡ.

ⲙⲡⲕⲉⲡⲁⲅⲗⲟⲥ ⲡⲛⲙⲉⲥ, C 86 313 B ⲁϥⲛ. ⲛϥϩⲉⲙⲓ ⲡⲉⲗⲱⲟⲩ & went aboard, PS 132 souls ⲉⲩⲛ. ⲙⲡⲛⲏⲩ about to *cast out breath*, expire (Od Solom 6 15 ܐܒܐ ܦܘܩܗ), CO 61 ⲁⲡⲣⲱⲙⲉ ⲛⲉϫ ⲡⲥⲕⲩⲗⲙⲟⲥ & came. V also ⲁⲃⲱ, ⲗⲟⲩⲗⲁⲓ, ⲙⲁⲧⲟⲩ, ⲥⲟⲧⲉ, ⲧⲏⲙⲣ, ϩⲣⲟⲟⲩ. Refl: Lu 14 10 (BF ⲣⲱⲧⲉⲃ), Jo 13 12 SA² (B do) ἀναπίπτειν; Nu 24 9 (B do) κατακλίνειν; ib 2 2 (B ϧⲓ ⲕⲟⲧ) παρεμβάλ.; ShMIF 23 131 ϥⲛ. ⲙⲙⲟϥ with disciples, Miss 8 220 ϯⲛⲁⲧⲣⲉⲕⲛⲟϫⲕ at table. Qual, *thrown down, lying, reclining*: Mt 8 14 (B ⲣⲁϣⲧ) βάλ.; ib 22 10 (BF ⲣⲟⲧⲉⲃ) ἀνακεῖσθαι, Pro 6 9 SA (B ⲉⲛⲕⲟⲧ), Jo 5 6 A² (SB ⲛⲕ.) κατακεῖ.; Ps 87 5 (B ⲣⲟϧⲡ), Is 33 12 SF (B do) ῥίπ.; TU 24 1 3 paralytic ⲥⲛ.

With following preposition.

—— ⲉ- SA²F, *throw at, put into*: Ge 39 20 (B ϧ.), Is 19 8 (B do), Mt 13 50 (BF do), Ex 15 1 F (B ⲃⲟⲣⲃⲉⲣ) ῥίπ., Ps 54 22 (B ϧ.) ἐπιρρ.; Jo 10 32 A² ⲛⲁϫ ⲱⲛⲉ (SB ϧ.) λιθάζειν; Ac 4 3 (B ϧ. ⲉϧⲟⲩⲛ ⲉ-) τιθέναι, Deu 28 48 (B ⲧⲁⲗⲟ ⲉϫⲛ-) ἐπιτιθ.; Si 30 37 καθιστάναι; ClPr 30 3 stone ⲉⲁⲩⲛⲟϫϥ ⲉⲡⲕⲱⲧ πηγνύναι; PS 107 ⲁⲩⲛ. ⲙⲙⲟⲓ ⲉⲡⲓⲥⲁ ⲙⲡⲡⲁⲓ, ShC 73 137 ⲡⲉⲧⲟⲩⲛⲁⲛⲟϫϥ ⲉⲧⲉⲧⲣⲓⲣ, ShMIF 23 45 ⲛ. ⲉⲡⲙⲟⲟⲩ of ships *launched*, R 1 3 51 ⲁⲥⲛ. ⲉⲣⲟϥ (corpse) much incense, Miss 4 743 ⲁⲡⲉϥⲉⲓⲟⲧⲉ ⲛⲟϫϥ ⲉⲧⲁⲛϩⲏⲃⲉ, ib 8 11 emperor's *sacra* examined ⲙⲡⲁⲧⲟⲩⲛⲟϫⲥ ⲉⲡⲉⲭⲁⲣⲧⲏⲥ ⲛⲕⲁⲑⲁⲣⲟⲛ, J 98 2 ⲁⲡⲡⲉ ⲛ. sickness ⲉⲡⲁⲙⲉⲣⲓⲧ ⲡϣⲏⲣⲉ, ib 80 53 ⲁⲓⲛⲉϫ ⲙⲁⲣⲧⲩⲣⲟⲥ...ⲉⲣⲟϥ (sc witnesses to deed). Qual: Job 18 8 (B ⲣⲁⲟⲩⲱ ϣⲉⲛ-) ἐμβάλ.; RChamp 371 lo the matter ⲛ. ⲉⲧⲉⲕⲁⲅⲁⲡⲏ to see that &c, ShA 1 453 sim, Mus 42 227 Word ⲉⲧⲉⲧⲛ. ⲉⲣⲟϥ *on whom ye rely*, BMar 71 his hope ⲛ. ⲉⲡϫⲟⲉⲓⲥ. Refl: Ps 21 10 (B ϧ. ⲛⲥⲁ-) ἐπιρρ., Tob 2 2 ἀναπίπ.

—— ⲉϫⲛ- S, *cast, impose upon, put* (clothes) *on*: Job 38 6 (B ⲭⲱ ⲉϩⲣⲏⲓ ⲉϫ.), Lu 12 49 (var ⲉϩⲣⲁⲓ ⲉϫ., B ϧ. ⲉϫ.) βάλ., Ge 2 21 (B do) ἐπιβ., Ru 3 9 περιβ.; Jth 9 1 ἐπιτιθ.; Ex 21 22 (B ϯ ⲟⲥⲉ) ζημιοῦν; ShA 2 132 ⲁⲧⲉⲧⲛ. ⲉϫⲛⲡⲏⲕⲉ your bad (wine), Ep 84 ⲧⲕⲁⲧⲁϫⲓⲕⲏ ⲉⲧⲟⲩⲛⲁⲛⲟϫⲥ ⲉϫⲱⲓ, COAd 60 not right ye should ⲛⲉϫ ⲡⲕⲁⲙⲟⲩⲗ ⲉϫⲙⲡⲥⲛⲁⲩ ⲛⲣⲱⲙⲉ but should distribute its cost, Miss 4 528 garment ⲙⲛⲥⲛⲟϫⲥ ⲉϫⲱⲥ = C 89 46 B ⲧⲛⲓⲥ ϩⲓⲱⲧⲥ, J 87 25 ye it is feed & ⲛⲉϫ ϩⲃⲥⲱ ⲉϫⲱϥ, Mor 28 191 to auditors ⲙⲡⲣⲛⲉϫ ⲕⲣⲁⲩⲅⲏ ⲉϫⲉⲛⲡⲁϣⲁϫⲉ *raise a shout*. Qual: Jth 10 21 ἀναπαύεσθαι; BAp 2 ⲉϥⲛ. ⲉϫⲙⲡⲕⲁϩ. Refl SA²: Jo 21 20 (B ⲣⲱⲧⲉⲃ) ἀναπίπ.; AP 37 A² ⲁϥⲛⲁϫϥ ⲁϫⲛⲡⲉϥⲡⲉⲧ.

—— ⲛ- dat SA²F, *throw to*: Mt 25 27 (B ϯ) βάλ., Jos 18 10 ἐμβ., Is 34 17 SF (B ⲓⲛⲓ ⲉϫⲉⲛ-) ἐπιβ.; Job 16 11 (var ⲛⲥⲁ-, B ⲃⲟⲣⲃⲉⲣ) ῥίπ., Ex 22 31 (B do) ἀπορρ.; AP 15 A² condemned ⲁⲛⲁϫⲉ ⲛⲛⲑⲏⲣⲓⲟⲛ.

—— ⲛⲥⲁ- *SB*, *throw after*, *cast upon*: Sa 18 18†, RNC 40 ⲛⲉϫ ⲡⲓⲁⲣⲓⲕⲉ ⲡⲥⲁⲉⲡⲓϥⲁⲡⲓⲟⲥ ῥίπ.; BM 247 frag ⲙⲡⲉϥⲛⲉϫ ϩⲟⲟⲩ ⲛⲥⲁ ϩⲟⲟⲩ ἀναβάλ. (*cf* ⲛ. ⲉϩⲟⲩⲛ), C 86 152 *B* ϩⲓⲟⲩⲓ ⲙⲡⲉⲕⲕⲟⲛⲧⲁⲣⲓⲟⲛ ⲛⲥⲱϥ...ⲁϥⲛⲟϫϥ ⲛⲥⲱϥ, Pcod 45 *let us not* ⲛⲉϫ ϥⲩⲥⲓⲥ ⲥⲛⲧⲉ ⲛⲥⲁⲧ-ⲙⲛⲧⲛⲉ *attribute to*, RNC 52 *S sim*.

—— ϩⲁ- *S*, *cast*, *put beneath*: Ge 21 15 (*B* ϩⲟⲣ.) ῥίπ.; RNC 55 *laid on rack* ⲛⲥⲉⲛⲉϫ ⲗⲁⲙⲡⲁⲥ ϩⲁ-ⲡⲉϥⲥⲡⲓⲣⲟⲟⲩⲉ, Mun 37 *martyr* ⲛⲥⲉⲡⲟϫϥ ϩⲁⲡϣⲉ *put in stocks* = C 86 284 *B* ⲧⲟⲥϥ ⲉ-.   Refl: Mt 15 30 (*B* ϩ. ⲉϩⲣⲏⲓ ϩⲁ-) ῥίπ.; Mk 7 25 (var ⲡⲱϩⲧ, *B do*) προσπίπ.

—— ϩⲓ- *S*: Mk 7 30† *lying upon* (*B om*) βάλ.

—— ϩⲓϫⲛ- *S*, *throw (self) upon*: Mt 15 35 (var ⲉϩⲣⲁⲓ ⲉϫⲛ-, *B* ⲣⲱⲧⲉⲃ) ἀναπίπ.; Mk 9 2† (*B* ϣⲧⲟ) βάλ.; Jud 3 25† πίπ.; R 1 1 28 ⲉϫⲛ.† ϩⲓϫⲛⲟⲩⲙⲁ ⲛⲛⲕⲟⲧⲕ κατακεῖ.

With following adverb.

—— ⲉⲃⲟⲗ *SBF*, *cast forth*, *discard*: Ap 6 13 (*B* ϥⲟⲣϥⲉⲣ) βάλ., Ex 2 17 (*A* ϯⲕⲉ ⲁⲃ., *B* ϩ. ⲉⲃ.), Ps 16 10 (*B do*, *F* ⲥⲓϯ ⲉⲃ.), Aeg 210 *bishop may not* ⲛⲉϫ ⲧⲉϥⲥϩⲓⲙⲉ ⲉⲃ. ἐκβ., Miss 8 97 *though incarnate* ⲛⲧⲁϥⲓ. ⲁⲛ ⲉⲃ. *divinity* ἀποβ.; Sa 11 15, Z 338 ⲁϥⲛⲟϫⲧ ⲉⲃ. *& departed* ῥίπ., Ps 37 20 (*B* ϩⲟⲣ. ⲉⲃ.) ἀπορρ.; Si 29 13, Mt 5 31 (*B* ϩ. ⲉⲃ.) ἀπολύειν; 1 Cor 7 12 *F* (*S* ⲗⲟ ϩⲁ-, *B* ⲭⲱ ⲛⲥⲁ-), Miss 8 41 ⲛⲉϫ ϣⲁϫⲉ ⲉⲃ. ἀφιέναι; Deu 22 19 (*B* ϩ. ⲉⲃ.) ἐξ-αποστέλλειν, Aeg 218 ⲙⲁⲣⲟⲩⲛⲟϫϥ ⲉⲃ. ἀφορίζειν; Deu 6 19 (*B* ϭⲟϫⲓ ⲛⲥⲁ-) ἐκδιώκειν; Ez 21 10 (*B* ϩ. ⲉⲃ.) ἀπωθεῖν; *ib* 22 15 (*B* ⲙⲟⲩⲓⲕ ⲉⲃ.) διασπείρειν; Ps 68 31 (*B* ⲧⲁⲟⲩⲟ) ἐκφέρειν; Pro 17 27 (*A* ⲧⲱⲕ ⲁⲃ.) προίεσθαι; PS 5 *light* ⲉϥⲛ. ⲉⲃ. ⲛⲣⲉϥⲁⲕⲧⲓⲛ, ShZ 602 *for hope of gain* ϣⲁⲥⲛ. ⲉⲃ. ⲙⲡⲣⲓⲙⲛⲃ, MIE 2 374 *B let no priest* ⲛⲉϫ ⲑⲁϥ ⲉⲃ., BHom 67 *limbs* ⲛⲉϫ ϯⲟⲩⲱ ⲉⲃ. *like tree*   Qual: Is 34 3 *F* (*S om* ⲉⲃ., *B* ϩⲟⲣ. ⲉⲃ.) ῥίπ.; 1 Kg 20 30 αὐτομολῶν *abandoned*; ShA 1 371 *bones* ⲉⲧⲛ. ⲉⲃ. *in tomb*, Miss 4 169 *B sick* ⲛ. ⲉⲃ. *on beds*, MIF 9 55 *whoso not ordained by* (?) *Peter's throne* ⲧⲉϥϭⲓϫ ⲛ. ⲉⲃ. (var *ib* 63 ⲥⲧⲛⲩ ⲉⲃ.), J 65 29 *things of this life* ⲉⲩⲛ. ⲉⲃ. *&* *dreams*, BM 1113 *wine jars* ⲛ. ⲉⲃ. ϣⲁⲛⲟⲟⲩ *still lie neglected*.   As nn: Jer 12 12 (*B* ⲡϩ. ⲉⲃ.) διεκ-βολή.   ⲉⲃ. ⲉ-, *cast*, *send forth*: Mt 8 12 (*B* ϩ. ⲉⲃ. ⲉ-), *ib* 9 38 (*B* ⲧⲁⲟⲩⲟ ⲉⲃ. ⲉ-) ἐκβ.; Ps 70 9 (*B* ϩⲟⲣ. ⲉ-) ἀπορρ.;   ⲉⲃ. ⲛ-, *cast out from*, *repulse*: Job 30 22 (*B* ϩⲟⲣ.), Ez 18 31 (*B* ϩ. *om* ⲛ-) ἀπορρ.; Mk 10 50 (*B* ⲥⲓϯ ⲉⲃ.) ἀποβ.; Lev 20 23 (*B* ⲟϭⲱⲣⲡ ⲉⲃ. ϩⲁ-) ἐξαποστέλλειν; BMis 132 ⲙⲉϥⲛⲉϫ ⲗⲁⲁⲩ ⲉⲃ. ⲙⲙⲟϥ *who cometh to him*;   ⲉⲃ. ϩⲁ-, *out from*: Ps 77 55 ἐκβ. ἀπό; BMis 337 *sim*;   ⲉⲃ. ϩⲓ-: Ep 84 ⲉⲓϣⲁⲛⲛⲟϫⲕ ⲉⲃ. ϩⲓⲡⲕⲁⲙⲟⲩⲗ *put thee forth from camel* (*contrary to contract*);   ⲉⲃ. ϩⲛ-*SA*², *cast forth from* (*often for* ⲛ. ⲉⲃ. ⲉⲃ. ϩⲛ-): Nu

22 6 (*B* ϩ. ⲉⲃ. ϩⲓϫⲉⲛ-), Ps 108 10 (*B* ϩ. ⲉⲃ. ⲥⲉⲛ-), Mt 7 5 (*B do*) ἐκβ. ἐκ; Ex 32 19 (*B* ϩⲟⲣ. ⲉⲃ. ⲥⲉⲛ-) ῥίπ. ἀπό; Aeg 215 ⲡⲟϫϥ ⲉⲃ. ϩⲛⲧⲕⲟⲓⲛⲱⲛⲓⲁ ἀφορί-ζειν; AP 3 *A*² ⲁⲅⲛⲁϫϥ ⲁⲃ. ϩⲛⲧⲉⲩⲡⲟⲗⲓⲥ, RNC 75 *heels pierced* ⲁϥⲛⲟϫ (? ⲛⲉϫ) ϩⲉⲡⲙⲟⲩⲥ ⲉⲃ. ⲡⲣⲏⲧⲟⲩ;   ⲉⲃ. ϩⲓϫⲛ-, *upon*, *over*: 2 Kg 20 12 ἐπιρρ. ἐπί, Mor 50 10 ⲉϥϣⲁⲛⲛⲉϫ ⲧⲏⲛⲃⲉ ⲉⲃ. ϩⲓϫⲱϥ *pointeth finger at him*;   *from off*: Ps 2 3 (*B* ϩ. ⲉⲃ. ϩⲓϫ.) ἀπορρ. ἀπό; BMis 214 ⲁϥⲛⲟϫϥ ⲉⲃ. ϩⲓϫⲙⲡϥⲟⲣⲟⲡⲟⲥ.

—— ⲉⲡⲉⲥⲏⲧ *SA*², *cast down*: Jo 12 31 (*A*² ⲉⲃ., *B* ϩ. ⲉⲃ.) ἐκβ. ἔξω, Ap 12 10 (*B* ϩ. ⲉⲡⲓⲕⲁϩⲓ ⲕⲁⲧⲁⲃ.; Jud 15 15† ἔκριπ.; AP 27 *A*² ⲡⲧⲁⲣⲉϥⲛⲁϫϥ ⲁⲡ.; ⲉⲡ. ⲉ-: Jo 5 7 (*A*² ⲁϩⲣⲏⲓ ⲁ-, *B* ϩ. ⲉϩⲣ. ⲉ-) β. εἰς, BHom 47 ⲛⲧⲛⲛⲟϫϥ ⲉⲡ. ⲉⲣⲉⲛⲧⲁϫⲟϥ ϥⲩⲗⲁⲕⲓⲟⲛ ⲕⲁⲧⲁⲃ. (*ib* 46 *sim* ⲛ. ⲉ-);   ⲉⲡ. ϩⲓϫⲛ-, *down from*: Mt 4 6 (*B* ϩ. ⲉⲃ. ⲧⲁⲓ) β. κάτω.

—— ⲉⲡⲁϩⲟⲩ, ϩⲓⲡ. *S*, *cast behind*, *postpone*: Ac 24 22 (*B* ϩ. ⲉϥⲁϩⲟⲩ) ἀναβάλλειν; ShBM 253 56 ⲁⲧⲉⲧⲛⲛⲉϫ ⲡⲉⲩϣⲁϫⲉ ⲉⲡ. ⲙⲙⲱⲧⲛ, Ps 49 17 ϩⲓⲡ. (*B* ϩ. ⲥⲁϥⲁϩⲟⲩ) ἐκβ. ὀπίσω.

—— ⲉϩⲟⲩⲛ *SA*², *cast*, *put in*, *introduce*: Ac 6 11 (*B diff*) ὑποβ.; *instigate*: *ib* 19 33 (*B* ⲓⲛⲓ ⲉⲃ.) συμβι-βάζειν (var ⲕⲁⲧⲁⲃⲓⲃ.);   ⲉϩ. ⲉ-: Mk 12 41 (*B* ϩ. ⲉ-, *F* ⲕⲱ ⲉϩⲗⲏⲓ ⲉ-), AP (BerlSitz '09 218) *A*² β. εἰς, Nu 4 6 (*B* ϩ. ⲥⲁⲡϣⲱⲓ ⲛ-) διεⲙⲃ., Pro 26 18 (*A* ⲧⲱⲕⲉ ⲁϩ. ⲁ-) προβ. εἰς; Ex 32 24 (*B* ⲑⲟⲡⲧⲉⲛ), Mt 27 5 (*B* ϩⲟⲣ. ⲉϩ. ⲉ-) ῥίπ. εἰς; Ex 26 29 (*B* ϩ. ⲉϩ. ⲥⲉⲡ-) εἰσάγειν εἰς; Z 314 *bread* ⲁϥⲛⲟϫϥ ⲉϩ. ⲉⲣⲱϥ μεταλαμβάνειν; PS 12 *soul* ⲁⲩⲛⲟϫⲥ ⲉϩ. ⲉⲧⲕⲁⲗⲁϩⲏ *of Elizabeth*, *ib* 315 ⲙⲡⲣⲡ. ⲡⲟⲩϩⲣⲟⲟⲩ ⲉϩ. ⲉϩⲣⲟⲟⲩ (*cf* ⲛ. ⲛⲥⲁ-), ST 181 *S*ᵃ]ⲡⲁⲭⲃ ⲉϩ. ⲁⲡⲏⲉⲓ, P 129¹⁴ 127 ⲉϩⲛ. ⲡⲡⲉⲩⲧⲏⲛⲃⲉ ⲉϩ. ⲉⲡⲉⲩϩⲃⲁⲗ;   ⲉϩ. ⲉϩⲣⲡ-: Deu 25 9 (*B* ϩ. ⲉϩ. ⲥⲉⲡ-), Mk 10 34 (*B do*) ἐμ-πτύειν;   ⲉϩ. ϩⲛ-: 2 Kg 16 13 πάσσειν dat, CO 8 *captains* ⲛⲉϫ ϣⲁϫⲉ ⲉϩ. ϩⲛⲏⲗⲓⲁⲥ (*cf* 4 Kg 1);   ⲉϩ. ϩⲁ-, *in under*: Mor 48 15 ⲁϥⲛⲟϫϥ ⲉϩ. ϩⲁⲡ-ⲕⲟⲟⲩ (var BMar 210 *om* ⲉϩ.), BMar 39 *caused* ⲛ. ⲉϩ. ϩⲁⲣⲟϥ 6 *lamps*.

—— ⲉϩⲣⲁⲓ *S*, *a throw up*, *put forth*: Bor 260 121 *seed* ⲛ. ⲉϩⲣ. *its fruit*, LMär 40 O *sea*, *Lord bids thee* ⲛ. ⲉϩⲣ. ⲡⲉⲓⲥⲓϩⲱⲣⲟⲥ, PMéd 321 ⲉϥⲛ. ⲥⲛⲟϥ ⲉϩⲣ. ϩⲓⲡⲣⲱϥ, PLond 4 474 (*tax returns*) *have not omitted one* ⲛⲡⲉⲛⲟϫϥ ⲛⲏⲧⲛ ⲉϩⲣ. (= 473 ⲧⲁⲥⲥⲉ ⲉϩⲣ.);   ⲃ, *throw down*: Jud 7 12† β., Nu 5 17 (*B* ϩ. ⲉϩⲣ., *F* ⲥⲓⲧⲓ ⲉϩⲗ.) ἐⲙⲃ.; J 26 5 ⲁⲡⲛ. ⲕⲗⲏⲣⲟⲥ ⲉϩⲣ., TT 157 ⲁϥⲛⲉϫ ⲧⲟⲟⲧϥ ⲉϩⲣ. *to jar of dates* (*cf* Miss 4 531);   ⲉϩⲣ. ⲉ-: Mt 13 42 (*BF* ⲉ-), Ap 19 20 (*B* ϩ. ⲉϩⲣ. ⲉ-) β. εἰς, Ge 43 22 (*B do*) ἐⲙⲃ. εἰς; Zech 9 4 (ShA 2 334, *A* ϯⲕⲉ ⲁϩⲣ., *B* ⲓⲛⲓ ⲉϩⲣ.) πατάσσειν εἰς;   ⲉϩⲣ. ⲉϫⲛ-: Mt 10 34 (*B* ϩ. ϩⲓϫ., ⲉϫ.) β. ἐπί, Ap 12 4 (*B* ϩ. ⲉⲡⲉⲥⲏⲧ ϩⲓϫ.) β. εἰς; Jer 15 8 (*B* ϩⲟⲣ. ⲉϫ.) ἐπιρρ. ἐπί; Mt 14 19 (*B* ⲣⲱⲧⲉⲃ

ⲣⲓⲝ., F ⲗⲱⲧ. ⲉⲝ.) ἀνακλίνειν ἐπί; Deu 26 6 (B diff)
ἐπιτιθέναι dat, J 45 24 ⲁⲡⲡ. ⲕⲗⲏⲣⲟⲥ ⲉ̅ⲣ̅ⲣ̅. ⲉⲝⲡⲡⲏ.

—— ⲡⲃⲟⲗ ⲛ- S, *cast outside of*: Mk 12 8 (B ⲣ.
ⲥⲁⲃ.) ⲉⲕⲃ. ⲉⲝⲱ; ⲥⲁⲃⲟⲗ, ⲛⲥⲁⲃ. ⲛ-: Mt 5 29 (B
ⲣ. ⲉⲃ. ⲣⲁ-) β. ἀπό; PS 103 (cf Ps 51 5) root ⲛϥ-
ⲡⲟⲝⲥ ⲥ. ⲡⲡⲉⲧⲟⲣ, Aeg 269 ⲁⲡⲡ. ⲛⲥ. ⲙⲙⲟⲡ ⲙⲡ-
ⲣⲏⲃⲉ ἀπορρ., BIF 13 109 ⲙⲡⲣⲛⲟⲝⲡ ⲛⲥ. ⲙⲙⲟⲕ =
MG 25 295 B ⲣ. ⲉⲃ. ⲣⲁ-; ⲣⲓⲃⲟⲗ ⲛ-: BP 12486
to bishop ⲁⲕⲛⲟⲝⲧ ⲣ. ⲙⲡⲱⲁ, CO 80 sim.

II intr S ⲛ. ⲉⲃⲟⲗ, *cast forth*: Is 5 29 (B ⲣ. tr)
ⲉⲕⲃ.; Z 629 recipe for fingers ⲛϣⲁⲡ. ⲉⲃ. *that
swell* (?, or = ⲡⲟⲩϣⲧ) ⲉⲃ. ⲉ-, *reach out to* of
boundaries: Jos 15 3 ἐκπεριπορεύεσθαι, ib 18 14
τὸ πρὸς (θάλασσαν); ⲉⲃ. ⲉⲝⲡ-: ib 8 ἐκβ. ἐπί.

—— ⲉⲣⲣⲁ ⲉ-, *extend over*: Jos 15 6 παραπορ.
ἐπί; 1 Kg 13 18 εἰσκύπτειν ἐπί.

—— ⲉⲝⲡ-, *pass over*: Jos 16 2 παρέρχεσθαι ἐπί.

—— S nn m, *throw*, *cast* of stone, arrow: Ge
21 16, Lu 22 41 (B both ⲟⲩⲱϣ) βολή; sim BAp
122 = MIE 2 396 B ⲡⲣ. ⲉⲃⲟⲗ, Wess 15 134,
ShBM 194 ι ⲟⲩⲡⲉⲝ ⲥⲟⲧⲉ.

ⲁⲧⲡ. S adj: BMis 187 (divine) flesh ⲛⲁⲧⲡ. ⲉⲣⲟⲥ
ⲡⲟⲩϭ̅ⲣⲟϭ *whereon no seed is cast*.

ⲙⲁ ⲡⲡ. S, *place of throwing*: Ez 4 2 ⲙⲁ ⲡⲛⲉⲝ
ⲥⲟⲧⲉ (B ⲛ̅ⲭⲁ ⲥ.) βελόστασις; Mk 12 39 ⲙⲁ ⲡⲛⲟⲝ-
ⲟⲩ ⲛϣⲟⲣⲡ (BF ⲙⲁ ⲡⲣⲉⲙⲥⲓ) πρωτοκλισία.

ⲣⲉϥⲛⲉⲝ- S, *thrower*: Z 233 inf ⲣ. ϣⲏⲣⲉ ⲕⲟⲩⲓ
ⲉⲡⲙⲟⲟⲩ, R 1 2 72 snakes ⲛⲣ. ⲙⲁⲧⲟⲩ, RNC 75 ⲣ.
ⲥⲟⲧⲉ.

ϭ̅ⲓⲡⲡ. S, *throwing, attack*: Leyd 351 evil spirits
[ⲧ]ⲉⲩϭ. ⲉⲧⲟϣ ⲛⲡⲗⲟ[ⲩⲓⲥ]ⲙⲟⲥ, SHel 81 ⲧϭ. ⲉⲃⲟⲗ]
of demons, LDi 274 ⲧϭ̅ⲓⲡⲡⲏⲝ ⲧⲁϥ.

ⲛⲁⲝϥ S nn m, *place into which to throw* (?):
PRain 4736 ⲧⲁⲗⲟ ϣⲉ ⲡⲗⲁⲣⲏ ⲣⲛⲡⲡ. ⲉ(ⲗ ⲛ)ⲧⲕⲁⲧⲱ
into boat's hold. Or ? verbal (Stern 468).

ⲛⲟⲩⲝⲕ, -ⲝϭ, ⲛⲟⲩⲝ SF(?), -ⲝⲣ A, -ⲝϭ, -ϭⲝ B,
ⲡⲟⲝⲕⲍ, -ⲝϭⲍ, ⲡⲟⲝⲍ, ⲡⲁⲝⲍ(?) S, ⲡⲟⲝϭⲍ, -ϭⲝⲍ B,
ⲡⲟⲝϭ† B vb **I** intr, *sprinkle, asperge*: cf نضف
(IgR): Nu 19 4 B (S ϭⲟⲩϭϣ), He 10 22† (SF
do†) ῥαίνειν, Lev 4 6 B (S ⲕⲱ) προσρ., Ge 30 32†
B (S ⲥⲟⲩϭⲓⲟⲩ) ῥαντός; Ap 19 13† (S ⲝⲱⲱϭⲉ)
βάπτειν; P 129^{18} 102 S they set me (idol) in temple
ⲉⲩⲥⲱⲣ ⲉⲅⲡ. before me = LAp 541 F ⲉⲩⲥⲁⲕⲃⲓ
ⲉⲩⲛⲟⲩ[ⲝⲕ] ⲛⲣⲁⲗⲁⲓ (sic MS), BMar 9 S I girt self
ⲉⲓⲥⲱⲣⲣ ⲉⲓⲡ. in temple, J 93 32 S oblate shall ⲥⲟⲣⲣ
ⲛϥⲡ. in monastery (cf Griffith *Stories* 127). ⲡ.
ⲉⲃⲟⲗ, meaning same: Nu 19 19 B (S ϭ.) περιρ.,
Lev 4 6 B (S ⲡⲟⲩϭⲉ) προσρ. ⲡ. ⲉⲡϣⲱⲓ B, *be
scattered upwards*: C 43 151 drops from cauldron
ⲡ. ⲉⲡ. ⲡ. ⲉⲝⲡ- SB, *sprinkle, scatter upon*: Ex
29 21 B ῥ. ἐπί, He 9 13† B (S ϭ.) ῥ. acc.; Lev 8
30 SB προσρ. ἐπί; Ex 24 8 B (S do) κατασκεδα-

ζειν; Mor 52 53 S Mark's brains ⲛ. ⲉⲝⲡⲡⲉⲃⲗⲁϭ
(cf BM 298 b), J 91 11 S ⲁⲡⲡⲟⲩⲝ ⲛⲡⲗⲱⲧⲏⲣⲓⲟⲡ
we sprinkled from basin...ⲁⲝⲙⲡϭⲥⲱⲙⲁ, C 86 356
B lamp broke ⲁϥⲡ. ⲉ̅ⲣⲏ̅ ⲉⲝⲱϥ.

II tr, *sprinkle, scatter*: Is 45 8 B (S ϣⲟⲩⲟ ⲉⲣⲣⲁⲓ)
ῥαίν., Pro 7 17 SAB διαρρ., Ez 43 20 B (HCons 304,
var diff) περιρ.; He 9 19 B (SF ϭⲟϣ.) ῥαντίζειν;
TEuch 2 122 B rubric ⲡ. ⲙⲡⲓⲙⲱⲟⲩ ⲛⲡⲓⲭⲟⲓ رش;
ShWess 9 145 S hath swept paths ⲁⲩⲱ ⲡⲟⲝϭⲟⲩ
with blood, ShA 1 301 S men to ⲥⲉⲣⲣ ⲡⲁⲡⲃⲟⲗ
ⲁⲩⲱ ⲉⲡⲟⲝ(ⲕ)ϥ, BMis 10 S road ⲡⲥⲉⲡⲟⲩⲝ ⲙⲙⲟⲥ
ⲙⲙⲟⲩⲥⲧⲕⲟⲡ (cf WTh 152 ⲙⲓⲥⲧⲓⲕⲟⲡ, BAp 142
ⲙⲟⲩⲥⲭⲁⲧⲱⲡ), Ryl 159 S will water vines ⲡⲙⲟⲩ
ⲡⲁⲡⲧⲥⲡⲟⲟⲩⲥ ⲁⲩⲱ [ⲡⲡ m ⲧⲁ]ⲡⲁⲭϥ ⲡⲙⲟⲩ ⲡⲉϣ-
ⲙⲟⲩⲡ, MélOr 6 515 B ϯⲡⲁⲡ. ⲙⲡⲣⲟ ⲡⲧⲁϣⲏⲣⲓ ϭⲉⲡ-
ⲡⲁⲓⲥⲡⲟϥ, Mor 31 244 S drawing water ⲉⲩⲡⲟⲩⲝ
ⲡⲓⲧⲁⲡⲍⲏⲃⲓ (245 do & ⲉϥⲡⲟⲩⲝⲉ ⲙⲙⲟⲥ, cf Amélineau *Contes* 2 138). ⲡ. ⲉⲝⲡ- SB, *sprinkle upon*:
Ez 36 25 S ⲡⲟⲩⲝ (var ShA 2 72 -ⲝϭ) B ῥ., Nu 8
7 B (S ϭ.) περιρ.; Ps 50 9 B (SA do), ῥαντίζειν;
Ez 43 24 B (var ⲧⲁⲗⲟ ⲣⲓⲝ., l ? ⲡⲟⲩⲝ) ἐπιρίπτειν;
BAp 114 S bring water ⲡⲧⲁⲡⲟⲝϥ (sic MS) ⲉⲝⲙⲡⲉⲓ-
ϣⲏⲣⲉ ϣⲏⲙ = MIE 2 390 B ⲡⲟϝϥ ⲉⲝ., AM 104
B water ⲁϥⲡⲟϭϥ ⲉⲝⲡⲡⲓⲙⲁϣ, BMis 479 S take
water & ⲛ̅ⲧⲡⲟⲝϥ ⲉⲝⲱϥ, ib ⲡⲟⲝⲕϥ. ⲡ. ⲉⲃⲟⲗ B,
scatter out: Ez 10 2 ⲡⲟⲝϭⲟⲩ (coals) ⲉⲃ. ⲉⲝⲉⲡ̅ϯⲃⲁⲕⲓ
διασκορπίζειν; AM 323 dipped fingers in water
ϣⲁϥⲡⲟⲝϭⲟⲩ ⲉⲃ. ⲣⲓⲭⲱⲟⲩ *shook them out*.

—— nn m SB, *sprinkling*: Zech 13 1 B (SA om),
1 Pet 1 2 B (S ϭ.) ῥαντισμός; J 79 47 S being servant of monastery for its sweeping & ⲡⲉϥⲡ.

ⲡⲉⲝⲝⲓ B (l ? ⲡⲉⲝϭⲓ) nn f (v following words) as
pl, *what is scattered, splashed* (?): C 86 287 ⲡⲓⲡ.
ⲡⲧⲉ ⲡⲓⲗⲉⲃⲏⲥ اطراف المرجل (var a Cai MS اطواق).
Cf BSG 185 11 & v ⲃⲉⲣϣⲟ.

ⲡⲉⲝⲡⲉⲝ S vb intr, *meaning unknown*: ShC
73 99 = ClPr 37 2 who neglect & mock sick saying ⲧⲡⲡ. or (ἤ) we cannot suffer stink.

ⲡⲟⲝⲡⲉⲝ B v ⲡⲟϭⲡⲉϭ.

ⲡⲁⲝⲡ B nn, *stone, kernel* of fruit: P 54 116,
BMOr 8775 118 نواة.

ⲡⲟⲩⲝⲥ S v ⲡⲟⲩϣ.

ⲡⲁⲝϥ S v ⲡⲟⲩⲝⲉ sf.

ⲡⲟⲩⲝⲣ A, ⲡⲟⲧⲝϭ B v ⲡⲟⲩⲝⲕ.

ⲡⲁⲝϩⲉ, ⲡⲁⲁⲝⲣⲉ (R 2 3 69), ⲡⲁⲭⲉ, ⲡⲁⲁⲭⲉ S,
ⲡⲉⲭⲉ SA, ⲡⲉⲉ. A, ⲡⲁⲭⲣⲓ B nn f, *tooth* a of man:
Ge 49 12 B (S ⲟⲃϩⲉ), Nu 11 33 S (var ⲟ.) B, Ps
56 4 SB, Mic 3 5 B (SA ⲟ.), Zech 9 7 S (ShA 2
335, var ib 334 ⲟ.) B, Mt 13 42 B (SF ⲟ.) ὀδούς;
Job 29 17 SB, Pro 24 37 SA μύλη paral ⲟ.; ShA

2 341 *S* ⲧⲁⲗϭⲉ ⲡⲉϥⲛ....ⲁⲩⲱ ⲡⲉϥⲟⲃϩⲉ (ref to Ps 33
13), C 43 151 *B* pulled out ϣⲟⲗ & ⲛ., *ib* 4 sim,
PMéd 292 *S* ⲟⲩⲡⲁⲁϫⲉ ⲉⲓ ⲟⲩϣⲟⲗ, Mor 22 50 *S*
Christ's body ⲁⲧⲉⲡⲟⲩⲉϭⲟⲩⲱϭϥ ϩⲛⲡⲉⲧⲡⲛ., C 43
100 *B* ⲁϥⲥⲣⲁⲭⲣⲉⲭ ⲛⲡⲉϥⲛ., PMéd 272 *S* ⲛ. extracted without pincers, *ib* 273 *S* ⲡⲉϫⲉ ⲡⲉϥⲟⲩϣ as
drug (? ivory), *ib* 290 *S* ⲁϥ ⲛⲡⲛ. *gums*.   **b** of
beasts : Deu 32 24 *B* (*S* ⲟ.), Si 39 38 *S* ⲟ̄ⲇ. ; Ps 57
7 *SB*, Joel 1 6 *AB* μν. paral ⲟ.; Mor 52 26 *S*, Z
600 *S* of serpent, Wess 9 139 = P 129¹² 66 *S* of
crocodile as amulet, AM 122 *B* of wild beast ;
c of saw : C 86 221 *B* ⲡⲉⲡⲡⲁⲣϫⲓ (*sic*) ⲛϯⲃⲁϣⲟⲩⲣ.
V Rec 38 206.

ⲛⲟⲩϫϭ *S*   *v* ⲛⲟⲩϫⲕ.

ⲛⲟϭ *S*, ⲛⲁϭ *AA²F*, ⲛⲁⲕ *Sᵃ*, ⲛⲟⲩϭⲧⲉ *S* (Sh),
ⲛⲓϣϯ *B*, ⲛⲟϫ *BF*, ⲛⲟⲧ *F* (BP 8095), ⲛⲟⲩϫ *B*, ⲛⲁϫ
S(MR)*F*, ⲛⲓϭⲧⲏ (?) *O* adj, *great, large*, **I** before nn :
Ge 10 11 *SB*, Ps 20 5 *SB*, Joel 2 11 *SAB*, Mk 15 37
SBF, Jo 19 31 *SA²B*, MG 25 214 *B* ⲛ. ⲛϩⲉⲗⲗⲟ
μέγας, Ja 3 5 *SA* (*B* ⲙⲉⲧⲛ.) μεγαλαυχεῖν, Ps 34 26 *S*
(*B* ϫⲉ ⲙⲉⲧϩⲉⲣⲟⲩⲱ) μεγαλορρημονεῖν, Ez 16 26 *S*
(*B* ⲥⲁⲣⲝ ⲉⲧϩⲟⲁⲓ) μεγαλόσαρκος, Jer 39 19 *B* (*S*
ⲛⲁϣⲉ) μεγαλώνυμος ; Job 29 18 *SB*, Ps 34 18 *S*
(*B* ⲟϣ), Is 36 2 *SBF*, Ac 16 16 *S* (*B* ⲗⲛⲏϣ) πολύς,
Job 32 10 *S* (*B* ⲙ. ⲛⲭ.) πολυχρόνιος ; Mt 28 12 *S*
(*B* diff), Lu 23 8 *S* (*B* ⲙ.) ἱκανός ; Sa 17 2 *S* μακρός, Is 53 10 *S* (*B* om) μακρόβιος, Eccl 7 9 *F* ⲛⲁϫ
ⲡϩⲏⲧ (*S* ϩⲁⲣϣ ϩ.) μακρόθυμος, *cf* 1 Cor 9 12 *F* ⲁⲓ
ⲛⲛ. ⲡϩⲏⲧ ; Ps 49 3 *S* (*B* ⲉⲙⲁϣⲱ) σφόδρα ;   approx transl : Ps 138 22 *S* (*B* ϫⲏⲕ) τέλειος, Sa 13 14
S ἄγριος, *ib* 16 11 *S* βαθύς, *ib* 10 16 *S* φοβερός, Mt
9 16 *S* (*B* ⲡⲣⲟϭⲟ) χείρων, Ac 15 2 *S* (*B* as Gk) οὐκ
ὀλίγος, Ap 18 17 *SB* τοσοῦτος, Jos 10 2 *S* ⲛ. ⲙⲡⲟⲗⲓⲥ μητρόπολις, CDan 84 *B* ⲛ. ⲡⲓⲱⲧ of Shiet ἡγούμενος, BMar 189 *S* ⲛ. ⲡⲛⲉⲉϥ ναύκληρος, Va 57 10
B ⲛ. ⲛⲟⲥⲓ ἄφατος, MR 4 128 *S* ⲛⲁϫ ⲛⲟⲃⲣⲉ ὀδούς,
Glos 358 *S* ⲛ. ⲛⲁⲡⲟⲧ · θηρίκλειον, *ib* 406 *S* ⲛ.
ⲡⲧⲏⲧ · ἰχθύς ;   PGM 1 60⁶³⁵ *O* ⲧ]ⲛⲓϭⲧⲏ ⲛⲥⲁⲧⲏ,
Br 135 *S* ⲡⲙⲉⲣϩ̄ ⲛⲛ. ⲛⲁϩⲟⲣⲁⲧⲟⲥ, El 7 6 *A* ⲟⲩⲛ.
ⲛⲑⲁⲗⲁⲥⲥⲁ, BSM 42 *B* ⲟⲩⲛⲟϫ ⲙⲫⲣⲏϣ = BMis
388 *S*, C 86 128 *B* ⲟⲩⲛⲟϫ ⲡⲣⲁϣⲓ, CO 196 *Sᵃ* ⲟⲩ-
ⲛⲁⲕ ⲛϣⲱⲛⲉ, Miss 4 181 *B* ⲟⲩⲛ. ⲛⲥⲗⲏ (var C 41
79 ⲥ. ⲉⲥⲛⲁϣⲧ), Kr 22 *F* ⲛⲁⲧⲛⲁϫ (ⲛ)ⲉⲕ(ⲕ)ⲗⲏ(ⲥⲓⲁ),
BM 346 112 *S* ⲛⲛ. ⲙⲙⲁⲧⲟⲓ of the legion, Hall 86
S have pity for ⲟⲩⲛ. ⲡⲣⲏⲕⲉⲡⲉ *is very poor*, Kr 3 *F*
ⲛⲉⲛ. ⲛⲧⲉⲭⲛⲓⲧⲓⲥ *full-grown craftsmen* opp ⲕⲟⲩ-
ⲛⲧⲉⲭ., AZ 23 41 *F* ⲛⲉⲛⲁϫ ⲃⲁ(ⲙ)ⲡⲓ, BM 889 4 *B*
ⲡⲁⲓⲛⲟⲩϫ ⲛⲱⲟⲩ, O'LearyTh 19 *B* ϯⲛⲟⲩϫ ⲙⲡⲉⲣⲥⲟⲥ
(*sic* MS) ;   Va 57 13 *B* ⲟⲩⲛ. ⲛⲱⲧⲉⲡⲡⲉ ⲧⲉⲧϥⲱ
μείζων ; PS 80 *S* my trespass ⲟⲩⲛ. ⲧⲉ, R 1 1 64 *S*
ⲟⲩⲛ. ⲡⲉ ⲡⲉⲕⲣⲁⲛ.

   ⲛ. ⲡⲣⲱⲙⲉ *SBF* **a**, *grown* or *old man* opp youth :

ShC 42 207 *S* ⲛ. ⲡⲣ. opp ϣⲏⲣⲉ ϣⲏⲙ, *ib* 199 sim,
BHom 122 *S* youth & elder ϩⲣⲣⲉ ϩⲓⲛ. ⲡⲣ., Bor 134
4 *S* (Vita Sinuth) ⲁϥⲣ ⲛ. ⲡⲣ. = C 41 34 *B* ⲉⲣ ϩⲉⲗⲗⲟ ⲡⲣ., MG 25 256 *B* was actor by trade ϣⲁⲧⲉϥⲉⲣ
ⲛ. ⲡⲣ.   **b** as title, *elder, notable* (*v* CO 119 n,
Ep 1 131) : Est A 1 *S* ἄνθρωπος μέγ. ; Ac 13 50 *S*
(*B* ϩⲟⲩⲁϯ) πρῶτος ; Z 340 *S* ἀββâ ; Leyd 163 *S*
festival of ⲛⲛ. ⲡⲣ. ⲙⲡⲛⲉⲩⲧⲉⲗⲁⲣⲓⲟⲥ (δευτερ.),
Wess 9 79 *S* ⲛⲛ. ⲡⲣ. *sc* archbishops & archimandrites, BAp 107 *S* ⲛⲛ. ⲡⲣ. *sc* bishop = MIE 2 383
B ⲡⲓϩⲉⲗⲗⲟ, Miss 4 245 *S* ⲛⲛ. ⲡⲣ. *sc* Shenoute, C
41 22 *B* do, BM 601 *F* ⲛⲛ. ⲛⲗ. *sc* abbot, RE 9 149
S ⲛⲛ. ⲡⲣ. opp ⲛⲕⲗⲏⲣⲓⲕⲟⲥ, J 36 35 *S* lashanes &
ϩⲉⲛⲕⲉⲛ. ⲡⲣ., MMA 24 6 4 *S* ⲛⲛⲁⲕ ⲡⲣ. ⲙⲡⲧⲓⲙⲉ,
ST 300 *S* sim, CO 342 *S* ⲛⲁⲡⲛⲅⲉ ⲙⲡ(ⲛ)ⲡ. ⲡⲣ.,
Mor 41 19 *S* ⲛ. ⲡⲣ. = DeV 2 270 *B* ⲣ. ⲡⲣⲁⲙ-
ⲁⲟ. (*Cf* μεγάλοι τῆς μονῆς Vita Pachom § 35,
μέγ. of ascetes Usener *Theodos*. 107, μέγ. ἀνήρ
anchorite PG 42 192, ὁ μέγ. *sc* Antony *Hist Laus*
65).   ⲙⲛⲧⲛ. ⲡⲣ. *S*, *old age* : ShC 73 49 ⲧⲉⲛⲛ.
ⲛ ⲧ(ⲉ)ⲛⲛⲧⲏⲣⲣⲉ, ShA 1 108 ⲧⲉⲛⲛ. ⲛ ⲧⲉⲛⲣⲁⲛ,
PSBA 32 200 spare thyself in thy ⲙ. ⲡⲣ.   ⲛ.
ⲛⲥϩⲓⲙⲉ *S*, *elder, aged woman* : 1 Tim 5 2 (*B* ϩⲉⲗ-
ⲗⲱ) πρεσβυτέρα ; ShC 73 74 ⲛ. ⲛⲥ. opp ϣⲉⲉⲣⲉ
ϣⲏⲙ, *ib* 62 ⲑⲗⲗⲱ (abbess) ⲛⲕⲉⲥⲟ ⲛⲛ. ⲛⲥ. that
are aged (*cf* CDan 26 ἡ μεγάλη).   ⲛ. ⲛϣⲏⲣⲉ *SB*,
elder son : Lu 15 25 *SB* πρεσβύτερος ; BAp 83 *S*
Esau her ⲛ. ⲛϣ., DeV 2 90 *B* Joachaz ⲛⲓⲛ. ⲛϣ.
of Josiah ; as monastic title (*cf* ⲛ. ⲡⲣⲱⲙⲉ, ⲛⲥⲟⲡ) :
C 41 54 *B* convoked ⲛⲓⲛ. ⲛϣ. & superintendants
of monastery, GMaspero *Musée Eg*. 2 pl 16 *S* saints
& rest of ⲛⲛ. ⲛϣ. commemorated, J 39 21 *S* ϩⲉⲛⲛ.
ⲛϣ. of *castrum* as umpires, BP 11937 *S* prior will
not act without consulting ⲛⲉⲛ. ⲛϣ. of monastery.
  ⲛ. ⲛⲥⲟⲛ *SB*, *elder brother* : Ge 10 21 *B* μείζων,
BIF 13 106 *S* ⲡⲉϥⲛ. ⲛⲥ. ; as title (*cf* ⲛ. ⲡⲣⲱⲙⲉ,
ⲛϣⲏⲣⲉ) : Bodl(P) g 15 *S* rest of ⲛⲉⲛ. ⲛⲥⲛⲏ[ⲩ, *il*
d 20 *S* sim.   ⲛ. ⲛⲥⲱⲛⲉ, *elder sister* : Ez 16 46
SB πρεσβυτέρα opp ⲕⲟⲩⲓ ⲛⲥ.

  II with 2nd adj intervening *S* : PS 248 ⲛⲉⲓⲛⲟϭ
ⲧⲏⲣⲟⲩ ⲛⲁϩⲟⲣⲁⲧⲟⲥ, CA 98 ⲛ. ⲡⲓⲙ ⲡⲁⲅⲁⲡⲏ, TT 149
ⲛ. ⲥⲡⲁⲩ ⲡⲁⲣⲭⲁⲅⲅⲉⲗⲟⲥ (*cf* Si 41 12 ϣⲟ ⲡⲁϩⲟ ⲛⲛ.,
PS 359 ϯⲟⲩ ⲛⲛ. ⲡⲁⲣⲭⲱⲛ).   Before name, without ⲛ- *SB* : RNC 8 *S* ⲛⲛ. ϩⲓⲗⲗⲁⲣⲓⲱⲛ, P 129¹⁴
131 *S* ⲛⲛ. ⲇⲓⲟⲛⲩⲥⲓⲟⲥ = AM 271 *B* ⲇ. ⲡⲓⲛⲓϣϯ ὁ
μέγας, Gu 68 *S* ⲧⲛ. ⲁⲣⲧⲉⲙⲓⲥ ἡ μ., BIF 13 116 *S*
ⲛⲛ. ⲁⲡⲁ ⲙⲁⲕⲁⲣⲉ = MG 25 307 *B*.

  III after nn, both with art *SB* : Ex 23 31 *B*
ⲫⲓⲁⲣⲟ ⲡⲓⲛⲟϭ (*S* ⲛⲛ. ⲡⲉⲓⲉⲣⲟ) μέγ. ποτ., Is 36 4 *B*
ⲡⲟⲩⲣⲟ ⲡⲛ. (*SF* ⲛⲛ. ⲡⲣ.) ὁ βασ. ὁ μ., Jer 39 18 *SB*
ⲡⲡⲉ̄ ⲡⲛ. ὁ θ. ὁ μ., Ac 2 20 *S* = Joel 2 31 *SA* ⲡϩⲟⲟⲩ
ⲙⲡϫⲥ̄ ⲡⲛ. (*B* ⲛⲓⲛ. ⲡⲉϩ.) ἡμ. ἡ μ. ; LMär 40 *S* ⲱ
ⲑⲁⲗⲁⲥⲥⲁ ϯⲛ. ;   or after name : Si 48 26 *S* ὁ μ.,

FR 148 S ϩηρωϫηϲ пп. = Aeg 6 B, BKU 1 23 F
ⲃⲁⲕⲑⲓⲟⲅⲑⲁϩ пп.　　After nn with п- SB: Nu
11 33 S ογπλησι пп. (var п. ⲙⲛ., B п. пербϭⲟⲧ),
Si 46 2 S пеϥⲣⲁп ип., Ez 17 6 B ογⲃⲱ пп., Ac
15 22 S ϩепⲣⲱⲙⲉ пп. (B = Gk), Z 315 S ογϩⲗⲟ
ип., Bor 154 111 S εγⲣⲱⲙⲉ пп. ϩптеϥϭⲟⲧ, Z 10
B ϯⲕγⲣⲓⲁⲕη...пп.;　　or without п- SF(?): Nu
14 12 ογϩⲉⲑⲛⲟⲥ п. (var & B п. пϩ.), Is 27 1 тсиϥⲉ
п. ⲉⲧⲟγⲁⲁⲃ (B теϥⲥ. ⲉⲑ. ϯп.), Ap 16 19 тⲃⲁⲃγ-
λⲱп п. (B ⲃ. ϯп.); PS 48 пепⲣⲟⲃⲟⲗⲟⲟγⲉ п., BAp
64 ογпηⲥⲛ ⲙⲙⲟογ п., WS 132 ⲁпⲁ ⲁпⲟγп п.
(or l пп.), Bal ⲃⲁⲣⲑⲟⲗⲟⲙⲉⲟⲥ п. (cf ϣηⲙ, ⲕⲟγⲓ
after names), J 96 72 пеⲕⲣⲓⲙⲁ п., CMSS 70 F
ογⲙⲁпⲡⲁ ⲅⲁⲗⲗⲁⲉⲓⲛ(η) п. (καλλάϊνος).

—— e- SBF, greater, older than: Jo 4 12 BF
(SA² пⲁⲁ⸍) μείζ.; Philem 9 S (B ϩⲉⲗⲗⲟ) πρεσβύτης; BMar 235 S was пп. еⲣⲟογ тηⲣογ; LMär
29 S ⲁпⲧⲟγп. ϩⲣⲟγⲟ еⲣⲱⲧп, sim AZ 52 121 S I
am пп. παραρόκ.

—— nn SAA²BF, great, old person, thing: 3 Kg
22 31 S, Job 42 3 SB, Is 33 4 SBF, Ac 8 10 SB,
Z 339 S this is пп. = MG 25 216 B μέγ., Ge 29
16 SB, Ro 9 12 SB μείζ. MG 25 208 B μειζότερος,
Pro 8 16 SA (B diff), Ap 6 15 S (var) F (B om)
μεγιστᾶνες; 1 Kg 9 22 S, Mk 6 21 S (B ϩⲟγⲁϯ),
AP 15 A² πρῶτος, Aeg 273 S пп. of bishops πρό-
κριτος; Mic 3 9 SA (B = Gk), He 13 7 S (B do)
ἡγούμενος; Jos 9 17 S, Jer 39 8 SB πρεσβύτερος;
Dan 7 9 S (B ⲁпⲁⲥ) παλαιός; Deu 22 15 S (B
ϩⲉⲗⲗⲟ) γερουσία; Pro 24 72 SA (B ϫⲱⲣⲓ) δυνάστης; 1 Kg 29 3 S, Ez 32 30 SB στρατηγός; Mor
17 69 S пⲧⲟⲗⲓⲥ πολιτάρχης; Nu 16 2 S (B
= Gk) σύγκλητος; Mor 56 10 S ἐμφανής; BMis
233 S пп. ⲉⲧϩⲓϫⲱⲟγ ῥήξ; Eccl 5 11 S, Lu 16 10
SB πολύς; C 86 301 B George пⲁп. пте пиⲅⲁ-
λⲓⲗⲉⲟⲥ = BSG 195 S сⲁϩ ⲙⲙγⲥⲧηⲣⲓⲟп μύστης
τῶν Γ., R 1 5 50 S пⲧⲟⲕ ογп. пϣпп., C 89 30 B
sim, BMar 103 S пп. ⲙⲡⲡⲁⲗⲗⲁⲧⲓⲟп, BAp 133 S
hast obtained ογп. above all honours, J 38 25 S
all property ϫⲓⲡⲟγⲕⲟγⲓ ϣⲁⲟγп., BM 511 F bless
пеⲕⲟγⲓ ⲙⲡпеп., Miss 8 53 S only 30 condemn
Cyril, but ϯп. majority Nestorius;　　as advb
greatly: Bor 263 22 S ϣⲁϥⲙⲉ поγп. (cf Lu 7 47
ⲉⲙⲁⲧⲉ πολύ), Jth 13 1 S ⲉγп. ἐπὶ πλεῖον.

ⲙпⲧ-, ⲙⲉⲧп. SA²BF, greatness, seniority: Deu
32 4 SB, Ps 78 11 SB, He 8 1 SBF μεγαλοσύνη,
Sa 13 5 S, Eph 1 19 BF (S ϭⲟⲧ), BMar 105 S μέγεθος, Ps 70 19 SB, AP 11 A² μεγαλεῖος, Ps 28 5
S (B п.), ib 144 12 S (B ⲙⲉⲧп. ⲙⲙⲉⲧⲥⲁⲓⲉ) μεγαλο-
πρέπεια, Jer 40 9 B, Lu 9 43 SB μεγαλειότης, Ps
105 21 SB, Va 57 15 B ⲙⲉⲅⲓ ⲉⲟγⲙ. μέγας, Nu 6
2 B ϩⲉпⲟγⲙ. (S ⲉⲙⲁϣⲟ) μεγάλως; Ge 43 33 B,
JA '75 5 219 S ⲙⲙ. precedence among the churches

τὰ πρεσβεῖα; Si 7 2 S ἡγεμονία; 1 Tim 2 2 S (B
ⲉⲧϭⲟⲥⲓ) ὑπεροχή; 2 Cor 4 7 B (S ϩⲟγⲟ) ὑπερβολή;
Z 301 S ἀρχή; Dan 4 8 B κύτος (reading κῦδος);
ShC 73 167 S rendering account ϩⲁпⲉⲓϩⲱⲃ ϫⲉⲙ.
sc office of abbot, DeV 2 5 B ⲑⲙ. ⲙпⲁϫⲓⲱⲙⲁ of
Word, Bor 256 152 S to king ⲁⲧⲉⲕⲙ. ϫⲟⲟγ, BSM
16 B ⲙⲉⲧпⲟϫ old age, BIF 14 169 S what thy craft
ⲉⲕⲧⲁⲅⲟ пⲡⲉⲓⲙ. makest these boasts?　　ϩ ⲙпⲧп.
S, do great things: Ps 103 1 (B еⲣ п.) μεγαλύνειν,
Si 50 24 μεγαλοποιεῖν.

ϩ, еⲣ п. SABF, a become, be great: Ex 11 3 B,
Mk 10 43 SB μέγ. γίνεσθαι, Ge 12 2 B (S ϫⲓⲥⲉ),
Lam 2 13 B (S ⲁϣⲁⲓ), 2 Cor 10 15 B (S ⲁⲓⲁⲓ) μεγαλύνειν, 2 Pet 2 11 SB μείζων εἶναι; Jud 11 6 S,
Nah 3 4 A (B = Gk) ἡγούμενος; Ge 15 1 B (S ⲟϣ)
πολὺς εἰ.; 1 Kg 10 1 S (var ϩ ⲁⲣⲭⲱп) ἄρχειν;
ShBor 246 115 S some ⲉγⲟ пп. others ⲉγⲥⲟⲃⲕ,
BSM 24 B ϩⲁпⲧⲁⲓⲟ ⲉγⲟⲓ ппⲟϫ, MG 25 94 B hair
& nails ⲁγⲉⲣ п., Mor 16 87 S giraffe's neck ⲟ пп.
ⲉⲙⲁⲧⲉ, BMis 289 S ⲁϥⲁⲁϥ пп. ⲉϫпⲡⲁⲣⲓⲟⲙⲟⲥ,
WTh 141 S none ⲟ пп. пⲑⲉ ⲙпеϥϣⲏⲣⲉ so important as his son, J 67 92 S пⲉⲧⲟ пп. the superior
(of monastery) at that time;　　with art ογ-: Mt
7 27† S (B om vb), Lu 1 15 S (B om art) μέγ. εἰ.
(cf ϣⲱⲡⲉ поγп.)　　ⲃ grow old, be of age: Ex 2 11
B (A ⲁⲓⲉγ) μέγ. γίν.; Ru 1 13 S ἁδρύνειν; Jo 9 23 S
(A² ϩ тⲉ, B diff) ἡλικίαν ἔχειν; 1 Cor 7 36 SF (B еⲣ
ⲁⲕⲙⲛ) ὑπέρακμος εἰ., Si 42 11 S παρακμάζειν; Mk
4 27 S (B ϣⲓⲏ) μηκύνειν; BMar 85 S пⲧⲉⲕⲣ п.
ипⲉⲓ ⲉⲑⲏⲗⲩⲕⲓⲁ, Aeg 4 B ⲉⲁⲥⲉⲣ п. ϣⲁⲓⲃ пⲣⲟⲙⲡⲓ,
Wess 18 33 S пⲉⲧⲉϣⲁⲣⲉпⲁⲣⲑⲉпⲟⲥ ϩ п. ⲙⲙⲟϥ
ϣⲁⲣⲉⲧⲉⲥϩⲃⲥⲱ ϩ п. ⲙⲙⲟϥ as Virgin grew her raiment grew, FR 10 S Zacharias serving Lord ⲉϥⲟ
пп.　　c be greater, older than c e-: Ge 48 19 B
(S ϫⲓⲥⲉ ⲉϩⲟγⲉ-), Mt 12 6 S (B ϩⲟγⲟ e-), He 6 16
SF (B om vb) μείζ. εἰ., Lam 4 6 B (S ⲁϣⲁⲓ) με-
γαλύν.; Mt 10 24 S (B ογⲟⲧ e-) ὑπὲρ εἰ.; Va 58
180 B fasting ⲟⲓ пп. ⲉпⲓпⲟⲙⲟⲥ πρεσβύτ. gen; BMis
133 S Baptist ⲟ пп. ⲉпепⲥⲱⲧηⲣ by 6 months, PO
11 336 B thy good deeds еⲣ п. еⲣⲟⲓ surpass me.
ⲙⲉⲧⲉⲣ п. B, greatness: Va 66 288 to know ⲑⲙⲉⲧⲟⲓ
пп. ϩⲉпⲛⲁⲣⲉⲧη ἡ νικῶσα.　　ⲙⲁⲓⲣ п. S, loving
greatness, ambitious: BAp 174 congregations are
become ⲙⲙ.

ϣⲱпⲉ поγп. S, become, be great: 2 Kg 18 7 ϣ.
ⲉγп. (var ϩ поγп.), Su 63 (penes HT, B еⲣ ογп.)
μέγ. γίν., Lu 1 32 (B do) μέγ. εἰ.; Pcod 28 so that
discussion ϣ. поγп. ⲉⲙⲁⲧⲉ;　　ϣⲱпⲓ пп. B sim:
Jer 36 26 ἐπιστάτης γίν.

поγϭⲧⲉ S: ShA 1 234 пп. ппⲣⲟⲫⲏⲧηⲥ Ezekiel.

As name: ноϭ (BM 1172, WS 76), Νόκις (BM
1077). Cf Μέγας.

(пєсє-), пєσωϩ, -ωωϩ S vb intr (nominal vb), *be ugly, unseemly, disgraceful*: Ge 41 20 (*B* ϫαιο) αἰσχρός, BHom 2 епесωωϩ н ечсннϩ αἰσχρότερος; Ge 34 7 (*B* пшιпι), Deu 24 1 (*B* щωш) ἀσχήμων; Lev 13 4 gloss on ѳⲃⲃⲓⲏⲧ (*B* Gk om); ShA 1 374 пєсωϥ поνнр...пєσωϥ ϫє ϩωωϥ поνнр, ShWess 9 110 stone пϫαιє н єтпєσωϥ (Mt 21 42?), ROC 19 73 declaring it оγрωⲃ єпєσωⲃ that God should accept human birth, COAd 13 I will not hear any ϩωⲃ єпєσωϥ ϩαрωτп.

ⲚⲎⲤⲈ *S* (once), пєϫι *B* nn f, *belly, womb*: Ge 3 14, Job 2 9, Ps 131 11 (*S* all ϩн), Jon 2 1 (*SA* ϩн). Mt 15 17 (*S* do, *F* кαλαϩн) κοιλία opp оϯ μήτρα: Ps 21 10 коι.; Job 3 10, Ps 16 14 (*F* кαλ.), Tit 1 12 (all *S* do), P 44 70 = 43 41 *S* ѳн · тп. بطن γαστήρ; AM 327 who entered ѳн. of Virgin, MIE 2 387 child that ϫн ϩєптєсн. = BAp 111 *S* пϩнтс, EW 142 ѳн. поγσριαι containing child (var RAl 88 ϫнтс), Va 61 93 тєчп. пατсι, C 43 8 tore (his flesh) till bowels ι єⲃⲟⲗ ϩєптєчп, P 55 13 тп. of ship 'ϩ. ⲙⲟγϯ єⲃⲟⲗ ϩєпѳп. ἐγγαστρίμυθος(εἶναι): Lev 20 6, Is 19 3 (both *S* do); In Ps 39 9 *S* BMOr 7561 37 (*ed* Maspero) has ϩнтⲙ[нтє, not п[нσє. In place-names: PLond 4 179 Πατνєϫι, ϯпєтрα пкоγппєϫι, *v* коγпϩ.

ⲚⲞ⳪ *SAA*[2](AP)*F*, пⲧι *S* (BKU 1 8), σι, пσє, σє, ϫє *A*, ϫι *A*[2] (Jo), пϫє *BF*, пσє *Sf* (Gu 66 ff) *F*, пσн (LAp 513), пϫι, ϫє *F*, cf DM V 13 11 nge, particle preceding nominative in proleptic vbal clause (Stern 482, Sdff 448, Mallon 350, Till 203): Ge 1 25 *B* ачпαγ п. ϕϯ (*S* αппє пαγ), Ps 16 5 *SBF* ппєγкιⲙ п. пατασсє, Ap 10 10 *S* ачсιщє п. ϩнт (*B* αταпєϫι єр сαшι), PS 52 *S* ачпнⲃє ⲙⲙⲟι п. пєкппⲁ, Cl 18 8 *A* сєпατєλнⲗ σє пкєєс (var пσι), El 80 *A* асαрєщє σє тαϩрнι, ib 44 *A* ачϩωϫ αрαγ ϫє пαппєλος, AP 12 *A*[2] ачоγαϩσαϩпє п. ϕнσєⲙωп, Jo 6 7 *A*[2] ачоγωшⲃ ϫι ϕιλιппос, ib 61 *F* єчсαϩп ϫє пϫι ιⲥ, EpJer 58 *F* ϥсαпт пϫє оγєррα, BM 1224 *A*[2] αγαєι αϩрн αϫωϥ пσι пєтснр, ZNTW 24 86 *F* єчппєι єⲃⲁⲗ пϫє пιαпωстωλος, cf ib 84 ϫє, 90 пϫι, Gu 74 *Sf* птєрєϥєι...пσι ιωϩαппнс асⲙιсι пσє тєϥσριⲙє. Similarly used with subj of vbal pref трє-, ѳро, ѳрє-: Ac 2 1 *S* ϩⲙптрєϥϫωк ϫє єⲃⲟⲗ п. пєϩооγ, Va 57 191 *B* єγѳро ⲙⲙⲟγ єоγпоσ п. ϩαпрωⲙι, C 86 274 *B* αϥѳроγσωλкϥ єⲃⲟⲗ п. ⲙⲙατοι. In documents only where narrative, in letters hardly ever (*v* J p 375, Ep 1 251): PLond 5 132 *S* тєптαϥϫпос п. пєγєιωт, J 106 224 *S* асαιтєι ⲙⲙοι п. ιωⲁⲛⲛ, PBu 232 *S* птєроγсωтⲙ пαι п. пαпⲙєрос ⲙϥιλⲛⲙⲱⲛ. Irregularly used: Mor 28 34 *S* ϯсωтⲙ єроϥ п. ιωϩαппнс ϫє- (Ap 8 1), Is

60 4 *B* (HCons 270) αιтнιтоγ п. пєщнрι єϥоγєι, CaiThe 491 = TThe 243 *B* ѳн єтαγоγωрп щαрос п. ⲅⲁⲃⲣⲓⲏⲗ, P 44 31 *S* пαι пταγϫп ριсє пⲣⲏⲧоϥ ...п. псαϥ.

ⲚⲞ⳪ⲚⲈ⳪ *S*, пⲁ⳪ⲛ⳪, -пє⳪ *AF*, поϫпєϫ *B* (once), пє⳪пє⳪- *S*, пє⳪поγ⳪ *SA* vb I tr, *reproach, mock*: 1 Kg 17 10 *S*, Ps 34 7 *S* (*B* ϯ щωш), Pro 20 4 *S* (var сωщ) *A*, Si 22 21 *SA*, Mt 11 20 *S* (*B* ϩι ϫοϩ єⲃⲟⲗ є-), ib 27 44 *S* (*B* ϯ щѳпнн пєⲙ-), Lu 6 22 *S* (*B* щωш) ὀνειδίζειν; Sa 11 15 *S* χλευάζειν; BMar 199 *S* ὑπερηφανεῖν; ShA 2 106 *S* єтєтпαпє⳪пє⳪ пⲙоγ saying (1 Cor 15 55), KKS 634 *S* pagans пє⳪поγ⳪оγ saying Ye cannot deceive us, C 86 110 *B* angry wife єсн. ⲙⲙоϥ єсⲃорⲃєр ⲙ ⲙⲟϥ. II intr *S*: Ps 73 10 (*B* ϯ щωш), Ja 1 5 (*B* щωщϥ) ὀν.; Ac 17 32 (*B* сωⲃι) χλ., ib 2 13 (*B* єр щєрщι) διαχλ.; ShC 73 59 єγсωⲃє н єγп.

—— nn m, *reproach*: Ge 34 14 *S* (*B* щιпι), 1 Kg 17 36 *S* (*B* щωш), Ps 78 4 *S* (*B* щϥιι), Is 30 6 *SF* (*B* щωш), Mic 6 16 *A* (*B* do) ὄνειδος, Jos 5 9 *S*, Ps 68 7 *S* (*B* щϥ.), He 10 33 *S* (*B* щωш) ὀνειδισμός, Pro 27 11 *SA* ἐπονείδιστος; Ps 37 7 *S* (*B* сωⲃι) ἐμπαιγμός; ShA 1 99 *S* if this one say ϩαпп. птєϥψγχн...let me die, Aeg 241 *S* demons cause soul to щωпє ϩαп.

р п., *be reproach*: Ps 21 6 *SA* (Cl ϩооп пп., *B* щϥ.), Ez 16 57 *S* (*B* ϩι ппιщϯ, reading *S* по⳪) ὄνειδος εἶναι.

ноү⳪c *SF*, -кc *A*, пє⳪с- (Job 27), по⳪сϯ *S*, пαксϯ *A* vb I intr, *be wroth*: Ex 22 24 *S*, Ps 4 4 *S*, Zech 1 15 *SA*, Lu 15 28 *S* (all *B* ϫωпт) ὀργίζειν; Nu 11 1 *S* (varr σωпт, ⲙоγϩ), θυμοῦν; 1 Pet 2 23 *S*ϯ ἀπειλεῖν (cit Aeg 216ϯ, BHom 130ϯ, both *B* do); BIF 14 138 *S* αϥп. єⲙατє (var LMär 35 σωпт), Miss 4 539 *S* when he heard αϥп. ϩрнт, JTS 4 395 *S* (on αλλωн *q v*) єпєιп.ϯ αп in telling thee this = Mor 25 18 *S* ϥγσιολоⲅєι = Va 61 101 *B* єр ϕιλософιп (*l* ? поϩс). с є-, *be wroth at, against*: Ge 40 2 *S*, Job 32 2 *S*, Is 64 5 *S*, Mt 5 22 *S* (all *B* ϫ.) ὀρ. ἐπί, ἐν, dat; Jo 7 23 *S* χολᾶν; Col 3 19 *S* πικραίνειν (all *B* ϫ.); Ps 54 3 *S* (*B* ⲙⲃоп) ἐγκοτεῖν; Mk 10 14 *S* (var σω., *B* ϩнт ⲙкαϩ) ἀγανακτεῖν; PS 360 *S* ⲙпрн. єрои, ShP 130[2] 100 *S* єтⲙ...п.ϯ єтєтрιтоγωс, BAp 83 *S* єιс пєксоп п.ϯ єрок, Mun 23 *S* lest пϥп. єроп (var BMis 55 σω.). с єϫп-, *meaning same*: Jud 2 14 *S* (cf 3 8 sim є-), Ps 73 1 *S* (*B* ϫ.) ὀρ.; Nu 24 10 *S* (var σω., *B* do) θυμ.; Is 5 25 *S* (*BF* do), Zech 10 3 *A* (*B* do) παροξύνειν; єϩрαι єϫп-: Ex 16 20 *S* (*B* ϫ. є-) πικραίνειν.

II tr, *make wroth*: Job 27 2 *S* (*B* diff) πικρ.

—— nn m, *wrath*: Jer 21 5 *S* (*B* ⲙⲃоп) θυμός;

Pro 20 2 *SA* ἀπειλή; Nu 35 21 *S* (*B* do) μῆνις; Eph 4 26 *S* (*B* do) παροργισμός; Deu 28 22 *S* ноүще (*B* щϭнн) ἐρεθισμός; Job 7 11 *S* (*B* щащι), Eph 4 31 *S* (*B* do) πικρία.

р п., *make wroth*: Si 13 4 *S* προσεμβριμᾶσθαι.

реϥп., *wrathful person*: Ps 17 47 *S* (*B* реϥჯ.), Pro 22 24 *SA* ὀργίλος; Bor 260 *penult S* р....реϥ-ϭωпт.

ϯ п., *give, cause wrath* c dat: Deu 9 7 *S* (*B* ϯ ჯ.), Pro 14 31 *SA*, Is 5 24 (*BF* do), Aeg 287 *S* сеϯ п. мпеⲭⲥ παροξ.; Ps 77 58 *S* (*B* ჯ.), Is 1 4 *SF* (*B* ϯ ჯ.), Mic 2 7 *A* (*B* do) παρορ.; Ps 105

33 *S* (*B* do), Hos 10 5 *SA* (*B* do) παραπικρ.; Pro 25 23 *SA* ἐρεθίζειν; Lu 11 53 *S* ϯ п. е- (*B* diff) δεινῶς ἐνέχειν; without dat: Ps 65 7 *S*, 105 7 *S* (both *B* ϯ ჯ.) παραπικρ.; El 66 *A* = BerlSitz '25 313 *S* ϯ ϭω., PS 180 *S* аιϯ п. мпτωщ of light, paral *ib* ϯ ϭωпт. мпτреϥϯ п., *incitement to wrath*: Sh(Besa)BMOr 8810 437 *S* keep far from пιм. мппⲉ, ShIF 279 *S* sim.

пαϭсе *S* nn, *wrath*: Job 9 18 (*B* щащι) πικρία, P 44 59 = 43 27 пп.· псащ جراح, جُرْج *wounds*.

V also ноүщс.

ноүϭте *S v* ноϭ.

ⳤ, 14th letter of alphabet, called ⳤι *S* (My 155) *B* (K 1, Stern p 418), الكسا (P 43 243, Stern *l c*). As numeral *BF*, rarely *S* = *sixty* (ⲥе). In Coptic only for кⲥ, as ѳоүⳤ, лωⳤ, тωⳤ (Mor 52 38), елⳤ (Ac 26 26 *B*), пореⳤ (PMéd 126), ⳤоүр, ⳤсооүп (Ryl 385), ⳤмарωоүт (CaiThe 462), ⳤнрϥе (Ryl 266); in Greek conversely, as ексоүсιа (BKU 1 26

35), акⲥıпе (ἀξίνη P 44 87), ⳤекⲥıⲥ (C 89 135), or as initial with е- om, as ⳤесϯ (Ryl 266), ⳤорıⳤе (P 44 23), ⳤапıпа (CaiThe 447), sim ⳤерıⳭос ('Οξύρυγχος Mor 41 103). Strengthened by т-, к-, as еⲛⳤапе (ксооүп Ryl 396), лотеⳤ (ST 315), апотıкⳤıⲥ (Kr 100), (е)кⳤорıсϯа (BMis 302). Ⳮ for ⳤ in ѣıпаⳭ (πίναξ). *Cf* к f.

о, 15th letter of alphabet, called оү *S* (My 74, P 44 124), оү, о *B* (K 1, Stern p 418) ,و, او (Stern *l c*, P 43 244). As numeral *BF*, rarely *S* = *seventy* (щ̄е). On relation to hierogl. half-consonants & vowels *v* Sethe *Verbum* 1 40-43, Sdff 63. Dialectal equivalents: *S* оеıк *AF* аıк *B* ωıк, *SB* аⳤом *AF* -ам, *SB* еѣол *AF* -ал, *B* ϭоⳣ *SAF* ჯωⳣ, *S* соооүп *AF* саү *B* сω-, *SAB* тащо *F* -а. Doubled о *S* = single *B*, as елооле алолı, сооⳋе соⳋı. Often doubled in Esne-Edfu texts *S*, as еıооте (BMis 333), ⳋıооме (*ib* 349), ⳋоосе (*ib* 473), ჯоосе (BMar 57). *S* аү, оү = *A* о, as ммаү, паү, оү. In Theban *S* (*v* Ep 1 239) о often for а, as ко-, моⳋ-, ⳋоп; for оү, as еⳋоп, о (art); for оүо-, as опⳋ, оⳭ.

In Eccl *F* (Berl) о for ĕ: кωлом, сωтом.

о, ω *SBO*, оү *SSᵃ*, аү *Sᵃ*, ω *DM*, а *F*, а- *O* (*v* паⳋте) adj, *great* (*cf* аıаı) archaic, follows nn: PGM 1 58 *O*, AZ 21 98 *O* ппоүте о, DM 16 12 p ntr ω ω, Glos 51 *S*, PMéd 316 *S* пмеⳋт о, ω (*v* маⳋт), PGM 1 60 *O* псıт о, Hos 9 5 *B* щаı о (*A* паϭ)

πανήγυρις, CO 60 *S* пща ω opp ща щнм, BP 9446 *S* тıнⲥтıа ω, RE 9 155 *S*, ST 261 *S* sim оү, *ib* 231 *Sᵃ* sim аү (*cf* тı. щнм), J 35 31 *S* теⳤ(е)ⳋра оү, CO 116 *S* ⳋеⲕсоı ω, *ib* 450 *S* оүтннѣе оү, Ep 540 *S* оеıк оү opp оеıк щнм, *ib* 532 *S* плакωп оү, Hall 129 *S* апⳋıн ω, K 168 *B* ѳерⳭ ω (*v* ерⳭ);

after art without nn: PGM 1 46 *O* Thôth пıω пıω, AZ 21 94 *O* sim пıо пıо; forming compound with nn: еıеро, ıаро, ıера (*v* еıоор), рро, оүро, саⳭо (*v* саⳋ), ⳋлло, Ⳍелло f -ω, ртω, ⳋроⳋо, Ⳍероⳋω, оⳋаıω (WS 137 or ? name); as а- before nn: AZ 21 94 *O* апаⳋте, *cf* name пⳋепапаⳋ-те Va ar 172 35 = C 89 55, Ψεναπάτης (Preisigke).

In names: паⳋωмо, -ω, -а (*v* PSBA 21 247, KKS 76), ıсаак ω (Cai 8382), ıоүлı ω (Cai 8411), пⳋнре ω (ST 158), *cf* BKU 1 22 ⳋωр пⳋнре о ⲡпессе (*l* пⳋⲥе), парѳепоп ω (Ann 8 82). *Cf* ап- *great one*.

о *A v* оү interrog.

о *S*, оı *B v* еıре.

oι *SBO*, ⲁⲉⲓ &c *AO*   *v* ⲁⲓⲁⲓ.

oϩ̄ *S* nn (?): Nu 21 5 (P 44 107 = 43 96, var ⲙⲟⲥⲧⲉ, *B* ϩⲣⲟϣ ⲉ-) ⲁⲧⲉⲡⲯⲩⲭ̄ⲏ ϯ oϩ̄ ⲙⲡⲓⲟⲉⲓⲕ مَلَّت προσοχθίζειν.

oϩ̄ε *S* nn, *channel, watercourse*: BMis 543 ⲉⲩ-ⲣⲟⲕⲉ ⲉⲃⲟⲗ ⲉϫⲛⲟⲩⲟ. ⲙⲙⲟⲟⲩ canales aquae. Prob *l* oⲟⲉ (*v* ⲱⲧϩ).

oϩ̄ε, oϩ̄ⲓ   *v* ⲉⲓϩ̄ε.

oϩⲏⲛ[1], -ⲉⲛ[2], -ϩⲛⲉ[3], ⲁϩⲉⲛ[4] *S*, ⲱϩⲉⲛ *B* nn m, *alum*: K 204 *B* ⲡⲓⲱ. شَبّ , ⲡⲓⲥⲧⲩⲯⲓⲙ يماني شَ , PMéd 64 *S* o.[1], ib 265 *S* o.[2] ⲛ̄ⲗⲁⲥ (*cf* στυπτηρία & ⲗⲁⲥ στύπ-τιον, not ⲗ. *tongue* as proposed 144 *b* above, con-fusion also *s v* ⲉⲙⲓⲥⲉ between شَبّ & شِبْت), ib 134 *S* o.[3] ⲛⲥⲓϣⲛ *flaked a.* prob = AZ 23 109 *S* ⲁ.[4] ⲛϣⲓϣ (*cf* σχιστός مشقّق) or this ? = PMéd 290 *S* o.[1] ⲛⲥⲛϫⲉ, BM 1135 *S* piece of o.[2] ⲛⲁⲗⲁⲩ *white a.* for dyeing (*cf* στ. βαφική PHolm), TurM 9 *S* o.[2] ⲛⲥⲓⲣ (*sic l* prob) *greasy a.* (*cf* زفر) in recipe for haemor-rhoids, PSBA 27 168 *S* ψιμύθιον & o.[1] in prepara-tion of parchment.

oϩ̄ϣⲉ   *v* ⲱϩ̄ϣ *s f.*

oϩϩε, oϩϩ *S*, ⲁϩϩε *A*, ⲁϩⲁϩ, ⲁϩϩ *F* nn f, *tooth*, **a** of man: Ex 21 27 *S* (*B* ⲛⲁϫϩⲓ), Nu 11 33 *S* (var & *B* ⲛ.), Mic 3 5 *SA* (*B* do), Mt 13 42 *SF* (*B* do), Ap 9 8 *S* BerlOr 408 oϩϩ (*B* do) ὀδούς; ShA 2 335 ff *S* ⲛⲉⲩⲛⲟϩϩ̄ⲉ (*sic*), *cf* P 44 69 *S* ⲧⲓⲛⲟϩϩ̄ⲉ · ⲕⲩ-ⲛⲟϫⲟⲛⲧⲉⲥ ناب = 43 39 *S* do أسنان , Mor 25 10 *S* chattering of ⲛⲛⲟϩϩ̄ ϩⲁⲡⲱϭϩ̄; **b** of animals: Job 41 5 *S* (*B* ϣⲟⲗ) leviathan, BM 174 1 *S* lion, Sa 16 10 *S* serpent ὀδ., PMéd 316 *S* wolf in re-cipe ; **c** *hoe, ploughshare* (?): 1 Kg 13 21 *S* ⲧⲟ. ὀδ.

oⲉⲓⲕ *S*, ⲁⲉⲓⲕ *AA[2]F*, ⲁⲓⲕ *S"F*, ⲱⲓⲕ *B* nn m, *bread, loaf*: Ge 14 18 *SB*, 2 Kg 6 19 *SB*, Pro 6 26 *SAB*, Is 30 20 *SBF*, Jo 6 32 *SA[2]BF*, Cl 34 1 *A* ἄρτος ; Job 24 10 *SB* ψωμός, MG 25 209 *B* ψωμίον; Ac 7 11 *S* (*B* ⲥⲟⲩⲟ) χόρτασμα ; Z 344 *S* ⲕⲟⲩⲓ ⲛⲟ. = MG 25 210 *B* ⲱ. παξαμᾶς ; PS 370 *S* ϩⲉⲛⲟ. *loaves*, ShC 73 57 *S* ⲟⲩⲟ. ϣⲏⲙ, ϩⲉⲛⲕⲟⲩⲓ ⲛⲟ., Ep 540 *S* o. ⲱ & o. ϣⲏⲙ, BM 583 *F* ⲕⲁⲡⲁ. (*v* ⲕⲟⲩⲓ constr), C 43 180 *B*, Tri 493 *S* ⲛⲕⲁⲑⲁⲣⲟⲥ, Ryl 110 *S* ⲟⲩⲟ. ⲙⲡⲣⲟⲥⲫⲟⲣⲁ ⲗⲟⲕ, BMar 218 *S* loaves ⲉⲩ-ϩⲏⲙ ⲉⲩⲣⲟⲟⲩⲧ = Rec 6 184 *B* ⲉⲩϩⲏⲙ ⲉⲩϩⲏⲡ, CA 101 *S* sim, *ib* ⲛⲥⲕⲁⲡ *stale* (?), Cai 8010 *S* ϣⲟⲩⲱⲟⲩ, Tri 496 *S* ϣⲟⲟⲩⲉ *dry, stale*, Wess 18 16 *S* (rubric) day whereon brethren ⲧⲱϭ ⲙⲡⲉⲩⲟ., Miss 4 583 *S* ϣⲁⲡⲧⲓⲧⲁⲙⲓⲉ ⲡⲉⲛⲕⲟⲩⲓ ⲛⲟ. in bakery, *ib* 584 *S* ⲉⲕ-ⲛⲁⲥⲙⲛⲉ ⲛⲛⲟ., ShC 73 143 *S* sim, C 41 53 *B* ϯϫⲏⲣⲓ ⲙⲫⲟⲣϣ ⲱ. *floor for spreading b.* before bak-ing (*v* Miss 4 413 n), C 43 180 *B* ⲟⲩⲱ....ⲉⲩϥⲓⲥⲓ ⲙⲙⲟϥ, J 93 34 *S* ⲛⲟ. ⲛϣⲙⲙⲟⲓ given in alms,

BM 464 *S* tale (κανών) to be supplied ⲉϥϣⲁⲁⲧ ⲁⲛ ⲛⲟⲩⲟ. ⲛⲟⲩⲱⲧ, CO 90 *S* ⲛⲉⲓⲟ. to be blessed by bishop, BP 4982 *S* ϩⲉⲛⲟ. ⲛⲥⲙⲟⲩ, ST 121 *S[a]* ⲟⲩ-ⲁⲓⲕ, Ep 253 *S* have sent ⲛⲟ., ST 331 *S* ϫⲟⲩⲱⲧ ⲛⲟ.   *V* ⲕⲟⲟϩ̄ ⲥ, ⲗⲟⲙ.   *Receptacles, measures* &c.: bushel ROC 25 273 *B* ⲙⲉⲛⲧ, sack MG 25 208 *B* ⲥⲟⲕ = Z 344 *S* ϫⲡⲟⲩ ἀναβολίδιον, BM 1166 *S*, CO 197 *S* ϭⲟⲟⲩⲛⲉ, Bodl(P) c 15 *S* ⲑⲁⲗⲗⲓⲥ; basket ShC 73 144, CO 199, 498, ST 288, Hall 92 *S* ϩ̄ⲓⲣ *q v*; ϩⲉⲣⲥⲓϯ *q v*, PO 11 339 *B* ⲡⲓϣϯ ⲙⲡⲗⲁ͡ϩ ⲛⲱ., Aeg 259 *S* ⲕⲗⲁⲥⲙⲁ ⲛⲟ.

ⲙⲁ ⲛⲕⲁ, ϯ, ⲟⲩⲉϩ o., *bread storeroom, pantry*: C 41 61 *B* ⲙⲁ ⲛⲭⲁ ⲱ. of monastery = Miss 4 648 *S* ⲕⲁⲧⲁⲅⲏ (κατάγειον), *ib* 636 *S* ⲡⲁϩⲟ ⲛⲛⲟ. = 20 *B* ⲙⲁ ⲛⲭⲁ ⲱ., R 1 3 74 *S* ⲙⲁ ⲛⲕⲁ o., BMis 387 *S* sim (var ⲛϯ o.), Z 356 *S* ⲙⲁ ⲛⲟⲩⲉϩ o. ἀρτοθέσιον.

ⲣ o., *become bread*: Mt 4 3 *SB* ἄρ. γίνεσθαι.

ⲁⲧⲟ. adj, *without bread*: BM 596 *F* ⲁⲩⲉⲣ ⲁⲧⲟ.

ⲣⲉϥⲧⲁⲙⲓⲉ o., *baker*: Mor 31 169 *S* ⲛϣⲟⲣⲡ ⲡⲣ. (*cf* Gen 40 ⲁⲙⲣⲉ).

ⲥⲁ ⲡⲱ. *B*, *bread-seller*: K 111 خبّاز .   On bread *v* Ep 1 146.

—— nn, *dung*: Ez 4 12 *S* (var ⲙⲏ o., *B* ϩⲁⲗⲙⲓ) βόλβιτος.   *V* ⲙⲏ.

In name: ⲡⲉⲓⲟⲉⲓⲕ (PBu 148).

oⲉⲓⲕ *S* nn m, *reed*: ShC 73 152 take heed not to root up ϩⲁϩ ⲛⲟ. ϩⲛⲛⲃⲟ, *ib* & not to break ⲛⲥⲛϫⲉ ⲛⲛⲟ., ShZ 501 ⲙⲙⲁ ⲛⲟ. where cattle pasture, Mor 51 40 will not go to reap o. with brethren, *ib* 39 *v* ⲛⲟⲟϩⲣⲉ, Z 340 from modesty he plunged ϩⲛⲛⲟ. ⲉⲧⲣⲏⲧ, BP 11349 in neglected field ⲛⲟ. ⲉⲩⲣⲱⲕϩ̄ ϩⲁ-ⲛⲓⲃⲉ, WS 147 ⲙⲟⲓⲁϩ ⲛⲟ.

ⲟⲕⲉ, ⲁⲕⲉ (Z 627 same?) *S* nn m, *sesame*: P 44 83 ⲥⲓⲛⲁⲙⲓⲛ · ⲥⲓⲁⲙⲟⲥ · ⲥⲓⲥⲁⲙⲓⲟⲩ (σησάμιον) o. ﺳﻤﺴﻢ = 43 59 ⲥⲓⲛⲁⲙⲟⲥ · o. '؎, CR '87 376 alternative to ϩⲁⲗ ⲛⲁⲃⲱⲕ in recipe, Z 629 leaves of o.

ⲟⲗⲉ in ⲁϣⲟⲗⲉ (var -ⲱⲗⲉ) *v* ⲁⲗ *S* nn.

ⲟⲗⲉⲓⲉ, ⲟⲓ. *S*, ⲁⲓⲗⲉ *A*, ⲱⲓⲗⲓ, ⲟⲓ. (Ez) *B*, ⲁⲓⲗⲓ, ⲁⲓⲗ *F* nn m, *ram* cf אֵל : Ge 31 38 *SB*, Ps 113 4 *SBF* (-ⲗⲓ PcodMor), Is 1 11 *SBF* (ⲁⲓⲗ), Ez 34 22 *SB*, Mic 6 7 *S* (ShA 1 413) *B* (*A* ϩⲓⲉⲓϩ̄) κριός; Sa 19 9 *S*, Zech 10 3 *AB* ἀμνός; BHom 54 *S* πρόβατον; MR 2 46 *S* o. ⲟⲡⲡ ⲉⲥⲱ ⲛⲥϩⲓⲙⲉ, PMich 584 *F* ⲛⲉⲁⲓⲗ, ⲛⲁϭ ⲛⲁⲓⲗ.

ⲟⲗⲃ̄ⲉ   *v* ⲟⲣⲃ̄ⲉ.

ⲟⲗⲟⲕⲟϫⲓ   *v* ⲗⲟⲅⲕⲟϫⲓ.

ⲟⲗⲥ   *v* ⲱⲗ.

ⲟⲙⲉ, ⲟⲟ. *S*, ⲁⲙⲉ *SS[a]AA[2]*, ⲁⲁ. *A*, ⲟⲙⲓ *B*, ⲁⲙ- *S* nn m f (Ps 68 *SB*), *clay, mud*: Ex 1 14 *AB*, Job 27 16 *S* (ⲟⲟ.) *B*, Ps 68 14 *SB*, Mic 7 10 *SA* (ⲁⲁ.) *B*,

Jo 9 6 *SA²B*, BHom 135 *S* (ⲟⲟ.) πηλός ; Ps 39 2
SB π. ἰλύος, Is 14 23 *SB* π. βάραθρον, LCyp 7 *S*
sim, Job 4 19 *SB* πήλινος ; Sa 15 7 *S* γῆ ; Ge 2 7
B χοῦς ; K 157 *B* ⲡⲓⲟ.(*sic*) الطبن, 204 *B* ⲡⲓⲟ. ⲉⲧ-
ⲧⲟ̅ⲃ̅ الخــز 'ⲃ̅; ShBor 246 115 *S* potter's ⲟ. ϩⲓⲃⲗ̅ⲝⲉ,
ShC 73 162 *S* ⲉϥⲣ ϩⲱⲃ ⲉⲅⲟ., ShP 130² 6 *S* ϩⲗ ⲟ.
ⲛ ⲡⲱⲡⲉ, ShP 130 37 *S* ⲛ ⲃⲱⲗ ⲕ, Pcod 27 *S* ⲥⲱⲙ
ⲟ. *knead clay*, Ryl 72 348 *S* Hebrews oppressed
ϩⲙⲛⲟⲟ. & brick-making, BMis 121 *S* city built of
ⲧⲱⲃⲉ ϩⲓⲟ., ⲛ also ⲡⲱⲡⲕ ⲃ, BSM 57 *B* we are ⲟⲩⲕⲁϩⲓ ⲡⲉⲙⲟⲅⲟ., Miss 4 232 *S* loom fixed in ⲟ., Ep
392 *S* ⲟ. used in book-bindings (*v* note there), ST
37 *S*, 38 *Sᵃ* contracts to sow ⲙⲉⲣⲟⲥ ⲡⲁ., BKU 1
48 *S* sim, BP 9419 *Sᵃ* come & work at thy ⲙⲉⲣⲟⲥ
ⲡⲁ., Hall 119 *Sᵃ* receipt for ⲡⲧⲓⲙⲟⲥⲓⲟⲛ (δημόσιον)
ⲙⲡⲁ., ST 111 *S* sim (ⲟⲟ.), Miss 8 258 *S* wall-
builder's ⲡⲕⲁ ⲡⲟ., Lemm *Patriarchengesch* 26 *S*
sim, PMéd 262 *S* ⲁ. ⲡⲣⲁϩⲧ *fuller's earth*, AZ 23
108 ff *S* smear (stop) bottle with ⲟ. ⲡⲥⲟϥⲟⲥ, *cf*
Bodl(P)a 1 *a*, *e S* sim ⲕⲁϩ ⲡⲥⲟϥⲟⲥ *ie* ... الطين 'ⲃ̅(Dozy).

As adj : BAp 134 *S* flood brought ⲕⲁϩ ⲡⲟ. ⲉⲭⲱϥ
& covered it, KroppK 46 *S* ⲁⲡⲕⲏⲛ (ἀγγεῖον) ⲡⲁ.,
Z 614 *S* ⲥϥⲣⲁⲅⲓⲥ ⲡⲟ.

ⲣ ⲟ., ⲟⲓ ⲡⲟ., *become clay, mud* : Va 57 194 *B* who
is in rags & ϥⲏ ⲉⲧⲟⲓ ⲡⲟ. ῥύπος, Miss 4 539 *S* stood
all night on brick so that it ⲣ ⲟ. ϩⲁⲡⲉϥⲟⲩⲉⲣⲏⲧⲉ,
C 89 12 *B* sim, Mor 37 159 *S* vessels ⲉⲧⲓ ⲉⲅⲟ ⲡⲟ.
before baking.

ⲁⲙ-*S* : PGen ⲁⲙⲡⲏⲣϣ *red clay*, KroppJ ϣⲟⲩⲣⲏ
ⲡⲁⲙϩⲁⲧ *white clay* (*cf* γήϊνος PGM 1 6 &c).

ⲟⲩⲁⲙⲟ. *SB* (once), ⲛⲟⲙⲉ *S* (PMéd) nn f, *earth-
eater*, a rodent or devouring animal : ShAZ 13 111
S canal bank where ⲡⲉⲧⲟⲩⲙⲟⲩⲧⲉ ⲉⲣⲟⲟⲩ ϫⲉⲟⲩ.
burrow (*v* ⲃⲟⲗⲃⲗ ⲃ & *cf* ⲕⲁϩ (ⲟⲩⲁⲙⲕⲁϩ)), ? =
اكال الطين worm living in mud in Upper Egypt
(Sobhy). rodent ulcer, gangrene : P 43 50 *S*
اكلا, (in 44 79 confused), *ib* 235 sim, Mor 36 43 *S*
knife cuts out ⲡⲟⲩ., BMar 209 *S* ulcers (πληγή)
in liver he scraped ⲁϥϯ ⲡⲡⲉⲩⲟⲩ. ⲉⲅⲧⲟⲉⲓⲥ = Rec 6
172 *B*, BIF 13 98 *S* ⲧⲟⲩ. ⲉⲧⲟⲅⲱⲙ ⲡⲥⲱϥ = MG
25 277 *B* ⲟⲩⲁⲙⲉⲧϥ, PMéd 242 *S* recipe for ⲡⲛⲟⲙⲉ
ⲉⲑⲟⲟⲩ ; ⲣ ⲟⲩⲁⲙⲟ. *S*, *eat, spread as gangrene* :
2 Tim 2 17 (*B* ϫⲉⲙ ⲙⲁ ⲡⲛⲓⲟⲡⲓ) νομὴν ἔχειν, cit
Aeg 245 νέμεσθαι ; ShA 2 224 wounds left to ⲣ ⲟⲩ.,
Z 351 feet ⲉⲣ ⲧⲟⲩ.(*sic* MS) ⲉⲣⲟϥ, BMar 43 wounded
foot shall ⲣ ⲟⲩ. ⲉⲣⲟϥ ⲡϥⲙⲟ., BAp 164 fornication
ⲟ ⲡⲟⲩ. ⲉⲧⲉⲕⲯⲩⲭⲏ.

ϫⲁⲭⲟ. *B*, nn as pl, metal agricultural tool, hoe ?
pick ? : AZ 13 144 (original not found) smith makes
sickles, plough's parts, ⲡⲓϫ. & spades.

oeiɯe, ⲟⲓ., ⲟⲉⲓⲙ *S*, ⲁⲉⲓⲙⲉ *A*, ⲱⲓⲙⲓ *B* nn f,
hook : Is 19 8 *SB*, Hab 1 15 *S* (Wess 9 106) *AB*,

Mt 17 27 *SB*, Va 57 190 *B* ϩⲁⲡϩⲱⲓⲙⲓ (*sic*) of iron,
BHom 135 *S* ⲁⲥⲉⲓ ⲡϫⲓ ⲧⲟⲉⲓⲙ ⲁⲥⲥⲉⲗⲕ ⲡⲉⲭⲙⲁ-
ⲗⲱⲧⲟⲥ ἄγκιστρον, TThe 125 *B* thou (Virgin) art
ϯⲟ. ⲡⲡⲟⲛⲧⲉ (νοητός) catching Christians صناد ; ShA
1 279 *S* fisher puts ϩⲉⲡϩⲱⲡ ϩⲡⲧⲉϥⲟ. as bait, Va
57 146 *B* fish ϫⲱⲗⲝ ⲉϯ ⲱ., Mor 22 51 *S* fish's death
ϩⲡⲧⲟⲉⲓⲙ, Bor 258 104 *S* curls of Judith's hair
ϣⲱⲡⲉ ⲡⲁϥ ⲡⲟⲉⲓⲙ (*ib* ⲟⲓⲙⲉ), BSG 183 = Mun 38 *S*
long nails & ⲟ. as torture.

oɴ *SB*, ⲁⲛ *AA²F* adv, *again, also, still*: Ge 8 12 *S*
(*B* ⲡⲁⲗⲓⲛ ⲟⲛ), Job 14 14 *S* (*B* ⲡⲕⲉⲥⲟⲡ), Is 30 18 *SF*
(*B* = Gk), Jo 10 31 *SAA²* (*B* om), AP 16 *A²*, MG 25
16 *B* ϭⲱⲗⲕ ⲟⲛ πάλιν ; Nu 32 14 *S* (*B* = Gk), Ps 77
17 *B* (*S* om), Jer 2 33 (*S* ϫⲓⲡⲧⲉⲡⲟⲩ), He 11 4 *B* (*S*
ⲉⲧⲓ ⲟⲛ), 1 Cor 15 17 *BF* ⲉⲧⲓ ⲟⲛ (*S* = Gk) ἔτι ; Ps 55
8 *SB*, Sa 14 3 *S*, EpJer 9 *B* (*F* om), Jo 8 19 *SA²* (*B*
ⲕⲉ-), Va 57 9 *B* wherefore ⲁϥⲟⲩⲁϩ ⲧⲟⲧϥ ⲟⲛ, ZNTW
24 90 *F* ⲡⲧⲉⲓϩⲏ ⲁⲛ καί ; Jer 31 33 *B* neg, Ap 9 20
S (*B* = Gk) neg οὐδέ, -τέ ; AM 271 *B* ⲁⲙⲡⲁⲭⲟⲥ ⲟⲛ
δέ ; Ac 15 27 *S* (var & *B* ϫⲉ) οὖν ; Sa 3 18 *S* τε ;
no Gk : *ib* 15 17 *S*, Jer 41 16 *S* (*B* ⲧⲁⲥⲑⲟ ⲉ-), Hag
2 13 *S* (*AB* om), Ac 1 11 *B* (*S* om) ; *also, further* : PS 97 *S* not ye alone but ⲟⲩⲟⲛ ⲡⲓⲙ ⲟⲛ ⲉⲧ-,
ShC 73 149 *S* ⲕⲉϩⲱⲃ ⲟⲛ ⲉϣϣⲉ ⲉⲁⲁϥ, BMis 365 *S*
ⲕⲁⲧⲁ ⲑⲉ ⲟⲛ ⲙⲡⲉⲥϩⲁⲓ (var & Va 63 4 *B* ⲡⲉⲥⲕⲉϩ.;
BSM 26 *B* om), *ib* 137 *S* lo heaven is prepared, lo
ⲧⲅⲉⲉⲡⲛⲁ ⲟⲛ, DeV 2 48 *B* ⲟⲩⲟϩ ⲥⲁⲧⲟⲧϥ ⲟⲛ he bade,
C 43 186 *B* ⲥⲱⲧⲉⲙ ⲟⲛ ⲉⲧⲁⲓⲕⲉ, CMSS 35 *F* send
them ϩⲓϫⲟⲕⲉⲥⲁⲡ ⲁⲛ, R 1 3 19 *S* not alone these
ⲁⲗⲗⲁ ⲟⲩⲙⲏⲏϣⲉ ⲟⲛ ; *again* : PS 78 *S* ⲁⲥⲕⲟⲧⲉ
ⲟⲛ ⲉⲡϫⲓⲥⲉ, ShA 2 346 *S* Moses' serpent ϣⲱⲡⲉ ⲟⲛ
ⲡϩⲉⲣⲱⲃ, J 7 26 *S* boundary to south ⲡϩⲓⲣ, to north
ⲡϩⲓⲣ ⲟⲛ, C 43 99 *B* hath delivered me & ϥⲡⲁⲡⲁϩ-
ⲙⲉⲧ ⲟⲛ ; *still, yet* : PS 37 *S* wished to detain it
ϫⲉⲉⲅⲉⲱⲥⲕ ⲟⲛ ϩⲡⲧⲉϥⲙⲡⲧⲉⲣⲟ, DeV 2 212 *B* Virgin
bare not without male & ⲡⲧⲉⲥϩⲉⲙⲥⲓ ⲟⲛ ⲉⲥⲟⲓ ⲙⲡⲁⲣⲑⲉⲛⲟⲥ, Rec 39 96 *S* ⲙⲡⲁⲧⲉⲕⲡⲓⲑⲉ ⲟⲛ ⲉⲑⲩⲥⲓⲁⲍⲉ ? ;
C 43 131 *B* ⲉⲧⲓ ⲕⲟⲡϥ ⲟⲛ ?, Miss 4 766 *S* sim, Gu
63 *S* have escaped men ⲧⲉⲡⲟⲩ ⲁⲡⲉⲓ ⲉⲧⲟⲟⲧⲩ ⲙⲡⲕⲱⲣⲧ ⲟⲛ ; *even if* : ShBor 246 43 *S* knoweth not
ⲏ ϭⲉⲓⲙⲉ ⲟⲛ ϭⲱⲃϣ ⲙⲙⲟϥ, BMis 135 *S* ⲉⲣϣⲁⲛ-
ⲧⲁϭⲣⲏⲡ ⲱⲱ ⲟⲛ habit of nature (yet) remaineth,
BMar 11 *S* ⲉⲕϣⲁⲡⲡⲁⲣⲁϫⲓϫⲟⲩ ⲙⲙⲟⲓ ⲟⲛ (yet) have
I a helper.

ⲁⲩⲱ, ⲟⲩⲟϩ ⲟⲛ, ⲟⲩⲁⲛ (*A*) : Ps 77 56 *S* (*B* om)
καί ; Sa 10 4 *S* πάλιν ; Ac 4 14 *S* (*B* ⲕⲉ- ϫⲉ) τε ;
Br 103 *S* ϯⲛⲁϯ...ⲁ. ⲟⲛ ϯⲛⲁϯ, PS 8 *S* ⲁⲡϣⲧⲟⲣⲧⲣ
ⲁ. ⲟⲛ ⲁϥϣⲧⲟⲣⲧⲣ, TU 43 11 *A*...ⲁⲟⲩ ⲉⲧϭⲏⲩ ⲟⲩⲁⲛ
ⲉⲧⲗⲁϫϩ, AM 215 *B* ⲟⲩⲟϩ ⲁⲥⲓ ⲟ. ⲟⲛ ⲁⲥϣⲉⲡ ϩⲙⲟⲧ,
ShC 73 15 *S* ⲙⲙⲡⲧϩⲁⲣϣϩⲏⲧ ⲁ. ⲟⲛ ⲧⲁⲡⲟⲭⲏ(var ⲁ.)
V also ⲁⲩⲱ **VI**. ⲟⲛ ⲡⲕⲉⲥⲟⲡ : LCyp 19 *S* ⲁϥⲕⲟⲧϥ
...ⲟⲛ ⲡ., MG 25 358 *B* ⲡ. ϫⲉ ⲟⲛ. ⲡⲁⲗⲓⲛ ⲟⲛ :
Mt 4 8 *SB* π.; El 64 *A* π. ⲁⲛ ϩⲁⲣⲉϥⲣ ⲥⲁⲗⲡⲓϫⲉ, Br

48 S, сепамоүте...п. оп сепаморте, AM 81 B п. оп ечоүωш *further wishing to.* ομοιως оп: PS 30 S, Ep 309 S, AM 215 B, оп ϩ. R 1 3 6 S.   ᴣε оп : PS 234 S ачоγωρᴍ...асоγωρᴍ ᴣε оп, ShC 42 34 S аιϫω ᴣε оп ᴍпειкеоγа, BMar 137 S spoke of...ачшаϫε ᴣε оп етбе-, MG 17 325 S пτереч- паγ ᴣε оп = C 89 72 B ᴣε.   ρω оп (S once) *same:* DeV 2 26 through whom we trust to attain епιωнϩ ρω оп пепεϩ, AM 301 some from паιϫοω ρω оп, Mus 42 222 S каιτοι ρω оп ечϫι ϭολ.   ϩωωϩ оп : AP 12 A² аτроγпτε ϩωωс ап авал καί, PS 16 S we all пᴍᴍак ϩωωк оп, MG 17 326 S пτоч ᴣε ϩωωч оп = C 89 73 B пϥ. ϩωч.   ᴍппсωс оп : Ep 110 S ϯшιпе...ᴍ. оп ϯпωϧτ ᴍᴍоει, AM 153 B ᴍ. ᴣε оп ᴍаωϫε.   паιρηϯ оп: BSM 102 they did ᴍп. оп, DeV 2 48 ᴍп. оп ϩως ереϥϯ тсаво;   ϑε пϣорп оп, ϥρηϯ пш. оп : Gu 8 S ετεтп(п)ар ϑ. оп, Miss 4 110 B ϯ ϫоᴍ пнι ᴍϥ. оп.   пτоч пτоч оп *v* пτоч sf.   оп ϯпоγ, *now again:* TU 43 3 A whom didst deny аоγ ап ϯ. dost deny, C 43 107 B ᴍнιс пнι оп ϯ. еϩрι-, AM 35 B who hath healed thee оп ϯ. ?   ϩамоι оп: Gal 5 12 S (B om оп) καί, ShBor 246 41 S ϩ. оп епεγпар пеγωϣϫ, BM 268 S ϩ. оп ереппᴇ паϯ пак.   repeated: BIF 13 101 S палιп оп ᴣε оп пеϫач = MG 25 284 B п. ᴣε оп, *ib* 104 S пτειρε оп ϩωογ оп, ShC 73 150 S аγω оп пчсᴍоγ оп.

ωпι *B v* еιпе *resemble.*

ωпτε S *nn as pl,* meaning unknown: ShP 130² 24 let us slay sin, piercing its head or breast пτепечωпτε п печᴍаϩτ еι евол, so ? *brain* or as equivalent of ᴍ. *bowels.*

ωпшс S *v* ωпϣ.

ωпϩ *ṠB nn v* апϩ.

ωειпе, оι. S, ᴣеιпе A, аιпе SᵃF, ωιпι B, аιпι F *nn f,* οἰφί ἴφι (PCai 3 80) whence אֵיפָה ويبة, *ephah* a measure of grain &c, less than пτов (*v* PLond 5 158): Lev 5 11 B (S шι), Nu 15 4 B (S do) οἰφί; Is 5 10 F (S do, B ᴍепт) μέτρον; of corn Ep 191, 301 S, CO 499 F; barley Ryl 388 S, WS 150 S; radishes *ib lc*; dates *ib* 87 S; raisins ST 118 S; lentils *ib* 219 S; clover (ораϫ) Ep 323 S; τаш CO 467 S; ϭоγϫ Sph 10 4 S;   also liquids: oil ST 121 S.   Vessel in which measured: Lev 19 35 S (B шι), Deu 25 14 S (B ᴍепт), Pro 20 10 SA μέτρον, Z 355 S ιματιον (*l* μάτιον) *modius;*   CA 96 S two о. оγ- коγι ᴍпоγпоϭ; in grain contracts &c S: Kr 77, BM 1043 τкоγι по., *ib* 1066 τакоγι по., Ryl 162 то. поγооιе паιкаιоп, Kr 60 τεко., *ib* 128 тεтпо., Ryl 169 то. of the headman Pegôsh, ST 118 оγо. естоове, BMOr 6230(44) оγо. пше есϭооле (ᴍ)-

---

пепιп[е.   In S Jud 6 19, Ru 2 17, 1 Kg 1 24, *SB ib* 17 17 οἰφί = ϣι.   *V AZ* 41 143.

орве, олве (PLond) S *nn, wafer, thin cake:* Ex 29 2 (B = Gk) رِقَاقَة, Lev 8 26 (B do) رُقَاقَة, 2 Kg 6 19 λάγανον, *cf* Lev 2 4, 7 12 ϩепλакапоп п ϩепϭωωλε.   In P 44 110 = 43 103 о. لُوبِيَة (confused with ὄροβος, *cf* K 197 олові оос لُوبِيَا); PLond 4 517 оγлакнпт птι о., BMOr 6230 (45) do;   са по., *wafer-seller* (or ? = ὀροβοπώλης, ὀροβοπ.): BM 1095, TurO 7.

орввϲ S *v* ωрв.

ωсе S, асе SᵃA, оси B, асι F *nn m, loss, damage, fine:* Ac 27 21 SB, Phil 3 7 SB, Va 57 10 B, BHom 3 S по. пρепхрнᴍа, JA '75 5 229 S not to look at women ϫεппεоγо. шωпе паγ ζημία, Ex 21 22 S ἐπιζήμιον; Aeg 211 S be cause of оγо. ᴍпλаос βλάβη; Ex 21 30 B (S сωтε) λύτρον; Lu 3 14 S ттε о. (var ϯ о., B λεωϫ) διασείειν; ShA 1 219 S not only ϩεпо. паγпе алла ϩεпкекрιᴍа, Mor 30 59 F паϑγвιа ᴍппаа., BMis 261 S ploughman's ox injured ϩамоι...пτεпеᴍоϭ по. таϭоι, Va 57 75 B по. of riches, BAp 168 S по. етпашωпе етϩεпнрп, ShC 42 188 S поγо. паγ аппе етреγᴍελета *it were no harm to them,* Pcod 28 S н ϩнγ н о., COAd 14 S sim, ShC 73 37 S пето пнтп по. such as shows & theatres, MG 25 25 B everything ετοι по. пτεкϥγхн;   *fine:* ShR 2 3 51 S usury ᴍппо. тнроγ thou layest upon them, ShWess 9 123 S poor man аιшаатч поγо., Ep 162 S ϩепкео. еаγшιт(т) ᴍᴍооγ, BP 11349 S crop's price ачтаαγ ϩапечо. птаγшатч ᴍᴍоч, DeV 1 74 B brought to judgment псешετоγ п- ϩапкео., Tor 12 S thou hast paid year's δημόσιον ετεγо. пε, Bodl Copt insc 428 S account по. псара псне κερ/ ιβ.   As adj: BMar 180 S ϩепшаϫε по....ϩрнγ.

ϯ о., *suffer loss, hurt, be fined:* Ex 21 22 B (S поγϫε еϫп-), Pro 17 26 SA, 1 Cor 3 15 SBF, Z 303 S if overpraised шаϥϯ о. тωпоγ ζημιοῦσθαι, LCyp 25 S поγεш пϯ о. ἀζημίως; BHom 48 S оγоϩ еϯ о. ἀβλαβής; ShMiss 4 281 S if hast pro- fited by this it were good ετιτρεкϯ о. ϩппεικεо- оγа, ShC 73 92 S I would not any ϯ о. н скапᴣа- λιζε, Mor 41 331 S ᴍпрϯ о. етвепшаϫε (*cf* Synax 1 389 تَغْفَل لَا), BAp 78 S when discovered at de- votions аιϯ поγпоϭ по. ᴍпооγ & vain my labour, Miss 4 154 B well art come ᴍпекϯ о. ϫεакι, PLond 4 462 S authorized to stay ϩппечᴍа (п)- тчτι пϥоосе *tax(?),* J 67 115 S trespasser shall ϯ оγпоϭ по. to magistrate, Z 261 S [ϯ]паϯ о. пт(е)к- клнсια ташатс поγϭιпϩωр *lay fine upon;*   с п-

of thing lost: Deu 22 19 B (S ⲛⲟⲝⲍ ⲉⲃⲟⲗ ⲛⲟⲩⲟ.), Mk 8 36 SBF, 2 Cor 7 9 B (S ϣⲱⲱⲧ), Bor 253 168 S ⲧⲏⲡⲁϯ ⲟ.ⲡⲉ ⲙⲡⲃⲉⲕⲉ ζημ.; Z 314 S ⲛϭⲧⲙϯ ο. ⲙⲡⲉϥϧⲓⲥⲉ ἀπολλύναι; C 41 57 B ⲁⲕϯ ο. ⲛⲟⲩⲛⲓϣϯ ⲛⲥⲙⲟⲩ, BIF 15 245 S[f] blinded martyr ⲛⲁⲃⲁⲗ ⲛⲧⲁⲓⲧⲉⲓ ο. ⲙⲙⲁϥ for Thy name, Ep 472 S[a] (ⲡ)ⲛⲉϥⲧ ⲁ. ⲡⲧⲉϥⲯⲩⲭⲏ; c ⲉ-: Sa 10 8 S ⲁⲩϯ ο. ⲉⲉⲓⲙⲉ (var ϯ ο. ⲙⲡⲟⲩⲥⲟⲩⲛ-) βλάπτειν τοῦ μή; Mor 25 200 S let him not ϯ ο. ⲉⲣⲟⲕ *suffer loss through thee* (refers to withdrawing from agreed bargain), Miss 4 152 B we suffered him not ⲉϯ ο. ⲉⲣⲟⲛ *to cause us injury*, rather ⲁϥϯ ϩⲛⲟⲩ unto our souls.

ⲙⲛⲧⲟ. S, *loss*: Tri 531 ⲛⲡⲉⲡϭⲉ ϩⲛⲧⲙ. خسارة.

ocı B nn in K 175 ⲡⲓϣⲉ ⲛⲟ. (var ⲟⲥ) طرفا *tamarisk*. Cf اثل.

ocκ S nn m, meaning unknown, among metal objects: CO 459 ϣⲟⲙⲛⲧ ⲛⲟ. Cf ? ⲁⲥⲕ ib 482.

ocϭ B v ⲱⲣⲥ.

ocϧϥ S v ⲱⲣⲥ.

oeıⲧ S vb qual: ShC 73 72 all good things ⲉⲃⲟⲗ ϩⲣⲏⲛⲗⲁⲩ ⲛⲓⲙ ⲉⲧⲟ. ⲛⲧⲁⲛ. Prob = ⲟⲓ[t] (ⲁⲓⲁⲓ), but cf AZ 62 44.

oot S vb qual, *snort, groan*: Jo 11 33 (A ϣⲧⲃⲟ, A[2] ⲙⲕⲁϩ ⲡϩⲏⲧ, B ⲙ.), ib 38 (A[2] ⲙ. ⲡϩⲏⲧ, B ϣⲉⲛϩⲏⲧ) ἐμβριμᾶσθαι; Mor 17 77 they marvelled & ⲉⲡⲉϥⲟ. ϩⲣⲁⲓ ⲡϩⲏⲧⲟⲩ & spake not because of astonishment (Gk Zahn 88 om).

ooⲧⲉ, ⲟⲧⲉ S, ⲁⲧⲉ A, ⲟϯ B, ⲱⲧⲓ F, ⲧⲟⲧⲉ S, ⲧⲟϯ B (error) nn f, *womb*: Ge 29 31 SB (var ⲧⲟϯ), ib 30 22 S ⲧⲟⲧⲉ (P 44 103) B, Nu 3 12 SB (var do), Ps 21 9 SBF(PMich 1192), Hos 9 14 AB, Ro 4 19 S (B = Gk) μήτρα; K 270 B رحم; ShC 73 29 S ϣⲧⲁⲙ ⲉⲣⲏⲧⲟ. of their souls, TEuch 2 505 B ⲁⲟⲩⲱⲛ ⲡⲧⲉⲥⲧⲟϯ, ClPr 47 4 S born ϩⲛⲧⲕⲁⲗⲁϩⲏ ⲛ ⲧⲟ. of Mary, Va 60 90 B ⲉⲓⲥⲉⲡⲧⲟϯ...ⲉⲓⲥⲉⲡⲑⲉⲛⲉⲭⲓ, PMéd 284 S ⲧⲟ. ⲛⲟⲩⲥ(ϩ)ⲓⲙⲉ. Cf ⲙⲓⲥⲉ (ⲙⲉⲥⲓⲱϯ).

ooⲉ S v ⲱⲧϩ.

ooⲩϣ S, ⲱⲟⲩϣ B nn m, *gruel* of bread or lentils, cf بوش (ⲡⲱⲟⲩϣ): Miss 4 529 S = C 89 48 B cooked him a little ο. ϩⲛⲟⲉⲓⲕ ⲉⲧⲙⲙⲁⲩ ἀθήρα = MG 17 560 = زريد = Va ar 172 29 بوش, C 89 96 B cooked for them ⲱ. = MG 17 472 = Va ar 172 56 بوش with gloss قمح دشيش pottage of crushed corn & oil (Dozy), BMOr 8775 123, P 54 127 B ⲡⲓⲱ. عصيد (cf P 44 85 ⲁⲗⲉⲩⲣⲟⲡⲓⲕⲧⲟⲛ 'ε), PMéd 318 S flour & grapes ⲡⲉⲥⲧⲟⲩ ⲛⲟ., ShC 73 212 S ⲗⲁϧⲙⲉⲥ, ⲟⲩⲟⲟⲧⲉ ⲛ ο., cf ib 73 ⲟⲩⲟⲟⲧⲉ ⲛ ⲁⲑⲁⲣⲁⲡ, MG 25 267 B ⲱ. ⲛⲥⲟⲩⲟ ⲉϥⲛⲟⲧⲉⲙ cooked in water.

oeıϣ SB, ⲁⲉⲓϣ A, ⲁⲓϣ A[2]F, ⲱⲓϣ B nn, *cry*: Mor 17 39 S heralds ⲉⲧϯ ⲟⲩⲟⲉⲓϣ (*l* ? ⲉⲧϯ ο.) = EW 34 B ⲉⲧⲣⲓ ⲱ. Otherwise only in compounds.

ⲁϣⲟ. S, *much crying, loquacious* (v ⲁϣⲁⲓ): Ps 139 10 (B ⲛⲁϣⲉ ⲡⲉϥⲗⲁⲥ) γλωσσώδης.

ⲧⲁϣⲉ ο. SAA[2]F, *increase crying, proclaim, preach* (v ⲧⲁϣⲟ): Ge 41 43 S (B ⲱϣ ⲉⲃⲟⲗ), Ex 32 5 S, Pro 8 1 SA, Mic 3 5 A (S = Gk, all B ϩⲓ ⲱ.), Mk 16 20 S (BF ϩⲓ ⲱ.) κηρύσσειν; Lev 25 9 S, Lu 9 60 S διαγγέλλειν, Ac 17 23 S, 1 Cor 9 14 SF καταγγ. (all B ϩⲓ ⲱ.), Ps 95 2 S, Ac 14 15 S (both B ϩⲓ ϣⲉⲛⲡⲟⲩϥⲓ) εὐαγγελίζεσθαι; PS 12 S able ⲛⲧ. ϩⲁⲧⲛⲉϩⲏ, AP 20 A[2] ⲡⲉⲉⲓ ⲉⲧⲉⲕ. ⲙⲙⲁϥ, R 2 1 34 S ⲉⲧⲧ. ⲡⲁⲩ ⲡⲟⲩⲛⲟϭ ⲡⲣⲁϣⲉ, Mor 48 71 S ⲉⲧⲧ. ⲙⲡⲥⲟⲉⲓⲧ of saint = C 43 136 B ⲥⲱⲣ ⲙⲡⲓϣⲓⲛⲓ ⲉⲃⲟⲗ. As nn, *preaching, proclamation*: Pro 9 3 S (B ⲝ̅ⲣⲱⲟⲩ), Mt 12 41 S (B ϩⲓ ⲱ.), 1 Cor 15 14 SF (F var & B do) κήρυγμα; Ryl 86 S ⲡⲧ. of Resurrection; ⲣⲉϥⲧ. S, *preacher, herald*: Ac 21 8 (B ⲣⲉϥϩⲓ ϣ.) εὐαγγελιστής; Aeg 218 κῆρυξ; ⲣ ⲣⲉϥⲧ., *be herald*: Ricci (v PSBA 26 178) magi ⲣ ⲣ. ⲡⲧⲟⲩϭⲓⲛ ⲭⲛⲟ, BHom 136 S woman ⲛⲧⲁⲥⲣ ⲣ. (Mt 15 22). ⲙⲛⲧⲣⲉϥⲧ., *proclamation*: Mor 52 45 ⲙ. suffced not for apostles, they died for Him.

ϩⲓ ⲱ., ⲁ. BF (S once), *throw a cry, proclaim, preach*: v examples in ⲧⲁϣⲉ ο. κηρύσσειν; Ps 18 2 (S ⲝⲱ), Is 3 9 (S ⲟⲩⲱⲡϩ ⲉⲃⲟⲗ), ib 48 20 (S ⲝⲱ) ἀναγγ., Ps 104 1 (S do) ἀπαγγ., ib 2 7 (S do) διαγγ., Phil 1 18 BF (S ⲧⲁϣ.) καταγγ.; BIF 14 156 S ⲁⲡⲡⲣⲟ ⲧⲣⲉⲩϩⲓ ο. ϩⲓⲧⲡⲟⲗⲓⲥ, C 86 353 ⲁⲩϩ. ⲛϯⲡⲟⲗⲓⲥ, DeV 2 9 should find him ⲉⲧⲁϩ. ⲙⲙⲟϥ ⲡⲁϥ. As nn, *preaching, announcement*: Ro 16 25 (S ⲧⲁϣ.) κήρυγμα; AM 274 ⲁⲕⲥⲉⲣ ⲡⲓϩ. ⲉⲃⲟⲗ, DeV 2 32 ⲡⲓϩ. that hath reached us; ⲣⲉϥϩ., *preacher*: Ac 17 18 (S ⲧⲁϣ. vb) καταγγελεύς, CaiEuch 352 κῆρυξ; ⲝⲓⲛϩ., *annunciation*: Abû Ṣâliḥ p 36 ⲡⲓⲝ. ⲛⲧⲉ ϯⲁⲅⲓⲁ ⲙⲁⲣⲓⲁ. (cf ϩⲓ ϣⲉⲛⲡⲟⲩϥⲓ Mus 41 95).

oⲩϥ S v ⲱϥ.

oıϩ S nn m, meaning unknown: WS 85 letter to ⲑⲉⲅⲛⲁ ⲡⲁⲡⲟⲓϩ.

ooϩ SA, ⲟϩ S, ⲱϩ SO(Hor 81), ⲓⲟϩ B, ⲁⲁϩ, ⲁϩ F, ⲓⲱϩ DM 82 nn m, *moon*: Deu 17 3 SB, Is 30 26 SBF, Joel 2 10 SAB, Mt 24 29 SB, σελήνη; PS 4 S day ⲉϣⲁⲣⲉⲡⲟ. ⲝⲱⲕ ⲡϩⲏⲧϥ, Job 31 26 S ⲡⲟ. ϭⲱⲕⲃ (B ⲙⲟⲩⲛⲕ), Si 39 16 S ⲙⲟϩ like moon, BKU 1 25 ro S ⲉⲣⲉⲡⲟ. ⲙⲟⲩϩ ⲉϥϣⲏϣ, AM 126 B moon ⲉⲧⲟⲝⲉⲃ ⲉⲑⲙⲉϩ, ShP 130[t] 105 S ϭⲓⲛⲙⲟⲩϩ, ϭⲓⲛϭⲱⲕⲃ ⲙⲡⲟ.; in calendar: PS 6 S ⲡⲁⲛⲧⲛ ⲙⲡⲟ., Cai 42573 1 S ⲥⲟⲩ ⲓⲉ̅ ⲙⲡⲟ., KroppK 24 S ⲡⲝⲟⲩⲧⲉ ⲙⲡⲱϩ, LDi 275 S ⲡⲟⲩⲏⲣ ⲙⲡⲟ., ib 270 S I noted day & ⲡⲟ. & month, BM 523 F ⲡⲉϩⲁⲩ ⲛⲧⲉ ⲡⲁϩ, ib ⲡⲁⲁϩ. *Silver* in recipes: AZ 23 110 S ⲡⲟ.

ⲡⲧⲁⲕⲣⲟϩⲧ (ⲙ)ⲙⲱϥ, *ib* 107 ϣⲁϥⲉⲣ o. ⲙⲉⲧⲓⲟϩ *B*
nn f, *moon's course*: K 50 stations of ϯⲁⲙ. منازل
القمرية.

oϩⲉ, ooϩⲉ, ⲱϩⲉ *SA*, oϩⲓ, ⲓoϩⲓ *B*, ⲁϩⲓ *F*, ⲉⲓⲁϩ- *A²*
nn m, **a** *yard* of house, *fold* for cattle, sheep: Ge
25 16 *B*, Nu 22 39 *B* oϩⲓ (var ⲓo., *S* ⲣⲱ), *ib* 32 16
B (*S* ⲣϩⲉ) ἔπαυλις, but *ib* 31 16 *B* ⲙⲁ ⲛⲑⲱⲟⲩϯ ⲛⲧⲉ
ⲡⲟ. ἔπ., 2 Kg 17 18 *S*, Is 34 13 *SF* (*B* = Gk), Jo
10 1, 16 *SA²* (*B* do) αὐλή; Ez 34 14 *B* μάνδρα;
Leyd 444 *S* parts of house o., ⲧⲣⲓⲕⲗⲓⲡⲟⲛ, ⲁⲩⲗⲏ,
Kr 125 *S*, BM 1023 *S* sim, Z 349 *S* o. of hermit's
cell (cf MG 25 99 ⲁⲩⲗⲏ, Ep 1 45), ShA 2 18 *S*
sheep in ⲡⲟ. ⲁⲩⲱ (var ⲏ) ⲧϣⲁⲓⲣⲉ, BAp 6 *S* sheep's
o. = MIF 9 43 *S* ϣⲁⲓⲣⲉ, Mor 56 27 *S* to build
oⲩo. for cattle, CMSS 33 *F* sim ⲡⲉⲓⲕⲁⲡⲁ., Mor 31
59 *S* ⲡⲟ. ⲛⲡⲉϥϭⲁⲙⲟⲩⲗ. **b** *pasture*: Job 30 1 *S*
(*B* ⲉⲥⲱⲟⲩ) νομάς, Ps 73 1 *SB*, Jer 23 1 *B* (*S* ⲙⲁ
ⲙⲙⲟⲟⲛⲉ), Am 1 2 *A* ⲱ. (*B* ⲙⲁ ⲡⲙⲟⲛⲓ), νομή. **c**
flock, herd: Ge 30 40 *SB*, Job 24 2 *SB*, Zech 10 3
AB, Lu 12 32 *SB*, Cl 16 1 *A* o. (var ⲱ.) ποίμνιον, Jo
10 16 *SB* (*A²* ⲉⲓⲁϩⲉⲥⲁⲩ), 1 Cor 9 7 *SBF* ποίμνη; Deu
28 4 *B* (*S* ⲣⲱ) of cattle βουκόλιον; ShWess 9 127 *S*
ⲡⲟ. ⲡⲉⲥⲟⲟⲩ;   ⲓoϩⲓ *B*: 1 Kg 16 11 (*S* ⲉⲥⲟⲟⲩ), Is

27 10 (*S* o.), Zeph 2 6 (*A* ϣⲱⲥ) ποίμνιον & ? in
ⲡⲉϩⲓoϩⲓ (*v* ⲡⲛϩ); 1 Kg 17 34 (*S* diff), Mt 8 30 (*S* =
Gk) ἀγέλη; Pro 24 66 *SA* (ooϩⲉ) αἰπόλιον; AM
228 *B* ⲡⲓⲓoϩⲓ ⲡⲗⲟⲧⲓⲕⲟⲛ of Christ. In name: ⲡⲁ-
ⲡⲟϩⲉ (AZ 40 61) = ? Πάπο. As place-name: ⲡoϩⲉ
(Mor 47 191, Ryl 255), ⲡⲉϣϭⲉⲡoϩⲉ (Mor *ib* 174,
Miss 4 763), ⲡⲉⲥϭⲟϩⲉ (WS83).

oϩⲓ *B* vb & nn   *v* ⲱϩⲉ.

oϩⲉ *S*   *v* ⲱϩⲥ.

oϫ *S*   *v* ⲱϫ.

oϫⲓ *B* nn f, *iniquity*: PS 118 118 (*S* ϫⲓ ⲛϭⲟⲛⲥ)
ἄδικος; He 1 9 (*SF* do) ἀνομία; Va 57 137 ⲗⲁⲥ
ⲉⲑⲙⲉϩ ⲡⲟ.;   *iniquitous person*: Mt 5 45 (*S* ⲣⲉϥϫⲓ
ⲛϭ.), 1 Pet 3 18 (*S* do) ἄδ.; as adj : Ex 23 1 (*S*
ϫⲓ ⲛϭ.), Ps 17 49 (*S* do), Pro 6 17 (*SA* do) ἄδ.;
Mus 34 186 ⲣⲉϥϯ ϩⲁⲡ ⲡⲟ.; ⲙⲉⲧo., *iniquity*: Lev
19 12, Job 6 30, Is 58 6 (all *S* do) ἄδ., Pro 1 17 (*A*
do, *S* ⲉⲡⲣⲁ) ἀδίκως; Job 35 13 (*S* ϩⲱⲃ ⲉⲙⲉϣϣⲉ)
ἄτοπος.

oϫⲓ *v* ⲥoⲩⲣⲉ (ⲥⲉⲣoϫⲓ).

oϭⲉ *S*   *v* ⲡⲱϭⲉ.

oϭⲃⲥ *S*   *v* ⲱϭⲃ.

Π

Π, 16th letter of alphabet, called ⲡⲓ *S* (My 34,
76), *B* (Stern p. 418, K 1), بي (P 44 124, 43 245).
As numeral *BF*, rarely *S* = *eighty* (ϩⲙⲉⲛⲉ). Derived from hierogl *p*, as ⲛⲓⲥⲉ, ⲥⲡⲓⲣ, ϣⲱⲡⲉ, ⲕⲱⲡ;
when initial of word or syllable in *B* mostly ⲫ, as
ⲡⲱϣ ⲫ., ⲣⲡⲉ ⲉⲣⲫⲉⲓ, but also ⲉⲓⲉⲡ oⲩoⲉⲓⲉ ⲓⲉⲫ oⲩ.,
ⲣⲟⲙⲡⲉ -ⲡⲓ, ⲡⲓⲣⲉ -ⲣⲓ, ⲫoⲡⲡⲉⲛ var -ⲫⲉⲛ. Varies
with ⲃ, as ⲁⲡo ⲉⲃⲱ, ⲡⲡⲏ ϩⲉⲡⲡⲏ, ⲡⲉⲡⲓⲡⲉ ϩⲉⲡⲓⲡⲓ,
ϣⲱⲡϣ ϣⲱⲃⲉϣ; or erroneously, as ⲡoⲩⲡ (Cat 158),
ⲁⲣⲏⲡ (Va 66 304), ϩoⲡⲥoⲩ (Job 21 26), ⲡⲗⲁⲡⲧⲉⲓ
(BMis 531), ⲧⲉⲡⲁⲓⲥ Θεβαίς (Abû Ṣâliḥ p 36), ⲕⲣⲁⲙⲡⲏ
(BM 1095); converse (rare), as ⲗⲉⲃⲧoⲡ;   with ⲫ
erroneously, as ⲁⲡⲑⲁⲣⲧoⲥ (BMis 270), ⲉⲩⲡⲣoⲥⲩⲡⲏ
(DeV 1 167), ⲡⲗⲁⲅⲉⲓⲁⲛoⲥ *Flavian* (Mor 46 4), ⲥⲡo-
ⲣⲁ (P 43 14).   Strengthens ⲫ, as ⲡⲫⲑⲟⲡⲟⲥ (Mor
26 12), ⲡⲫⲓⲡⲛⲃ (BKU 1 22); or ⲯ, as ⲡⲯⲁⲡ (CO
301).   Doubled, as oⲩⲡⲡⲉϣ, ⲧⲁⲡⲡⲟⲩⲧⲉ (*v* Ep 1
246).   Inserted between ⲙ & following consonant
as ⲙⲡⲣ- (hierogl *m'r*), ⲉⲙⲡⲗⲁϩ (1 Kg 17 1), ⲧⲙⲡⲧⲣⲉ-
(PMéd 212), ⲙⲡϣⲓⲣ (Wess 9 79).   Transcribes Ar
ب, as ⲉⲡⲡ اب, ⲡⲉϩⲉ بي (EW 234 ff), ϫⲓⲡⲣⲓⲧ كربت
(AZ 23 117), ϩⲁⲡⲓⲡ حبيب (DeV 2 164); transcribed by ب, as بشنس ⲡⲁϣoⲡⲉ, بلاص ⲡⲁⲗⲗⲁⲥ,

بارقليط ⲯⲓⲧ, باراقليط ⲡⲁⲣⲁⲕⲗⲏⲧ(oⲥ BM 786n), rarely
ف, as اطفيم (ⲡⲉ)ⲧⲡⲏⲣ (Amél *Géog* 557). ⲙⲡ, ⲛⲡ,
ϩⲡ = ς, as ⲙⲡⲛⲓⲧⲉ فضة (*v* ⲡⲁⲓⲧⲏ), ⲙⲡⲉⲗϩⲓⲡ بلهيب
Z 546, PLond 4 506 ⲡⲡⲛⲉⲓ, Kr 11 ⲉϩⲡⲡⲉ ابن.

ⲡ- *SAA²BFO*, ⲡⲉ- *SA²F*, ⲡⲓ- *SABFO*, ⲫ- *B*
defin art m, its f ⲧ-, ⲧⲉ-, ϯ-, ⲑ-, pl ⲛ-, ⲛⲉ-, ⲛⲓ-,
ⲛⲉⲡ- (*BF*). In *S* ⲡⲉ- before double consonants :
ⲡⲉⲗⲧo, ⲧⲉϥⲣⲟⲙⲡⲉ, ⲡⲉⲥⲡⲏⲩ or words for time :
ⲡⲉϩⲟⲟⲩ, ⲧⲉⲩⲛoⲩ. *S* ⲡⲓ- archaic : ⲡⲓoⲩoⲉⲓϣ, ϯϭoⲙ,
ⲡⲓoⲩoⲉⲓⲛ (PS), ⲡⲓⲧⲉⲗⲓoⲥ, ϯⲙⲡⲛoϭ, ⲡⲓⲁⲧⲛⲁⲩ (BG),
ⲡⲓⲥⲱⲙⲁ, ⲡⲓⲣⲓoⲙⲉ (El), also *O* : ⲡⲓo, ⲧⲓⲥⲁⲧⲓ, ⲡⲓⲧⲓⲃⲥ
(AZ 21), ⲡⲓⲣⲉ (PGM 1). *B* ⲫ-, ⲑ- (for ⲡ-, ⲧ-) before
liquids & half-consonants : ⲫⲣⲁⲛ, ⲫⲓⲱⲧ, ⲑⲙⲁⲩ,
ⲑⲛⲉϫⲓ, ⲑⲟⲩoϫⲓ. *B* ⲛⲉⲡ- mostly before gen : ⲛⲉⲡ-
ϣⲏⲣⲓ ⲛⲡⲣⲱⲙⲓ, but *F* ⲛⲉⲙⲡⲛoⲩⲓ, ⲡⲓϣⲉϫⲓ (Asmus 62). In vocative : Pro 6 6 *SA* ⲡⲣⲉϥϫⲛⲁⲁⲩ,
B ⲡⲓϭⲉⲡⲛⲉ, Mt 15 28 *SB* ⲧⲉⲥϩⲓⲙⲉ, Miss 4 126 *B*
ϯⲡⲁⲣⲑⲉⲛoⲥ, Ez 34 2 *S* ⲡϣoⲟⲥ, Leyd 447 *S* ϯⲧⲁⲣⲕo
ⲙⲙⲱⲧⲛ ⲛϫⲓⲛϭⲟⲛⲥ ⲛⲓⲙ.   On *B* art *v* BIF 13 1.

ⲡⲁ-, ⲧⲁ-, ⲛⲁ- *SAA²FO*, ⲫⲁ-, ⲑⲁ-, ⲛⲁ- *B* possess pron, with suffixes ⲡⲉⲓ &c, as ⲡⲉⲕⲙⲁ, ⲡⲉⲡoⲃⲉ,
ⲧⲉϥⲥϩⲓⲙⲉ, ⲡⲉⲧⲡⲉⲓⲱⲧ, ⲡⲉⲩϣⲏⲣⲉ.   *V* Stern 252,
Sdff 90, Till 58, Mallon 86.

ⲡⲁ-, ⲧⲁ-, ⲛⲁ- *SAA²FO*, ⲫⲁ-, ⲑⲁ-, ⲛⲁ- *B* possess art, *the...belonging to*, the (man) *of* : ⲡⲁⲧϣⲉ ⲗⲉⲉⲧ *he of the bride, bridegroom*, ⲡⲁⲧⲥⲉⲕⲱⲧ *S*, ⲫⲁ ⲛⲥⲱⲧⲉⲙ *B* (MG 25 22), ⲡⲁⲡⲙⲉⲣⲭ ⲛϣⲉ *O* (AZ 21 98), ⲧⲁⲉⲫⲣⲁⲉⲓⲙ *S* ἡ ἐν ’Ε. (Jud 6 11), ⲧⲁⲡⲓⲙ *S* (J 67 80), ⲡⲁⲡⲓⲙ *B such an one* (TEuch 1 129), ⲛⲁⲡⲕⲉⲣⲓ *F* (Jo 3 12), ⲛⲁⲡⲉⲥⲧⲟⲣⲓⲟⲥ *doctrines of N.* (P 129¹⁴ 127), ⲟⲩⲡⲁⲧⲁⲓⲁⲕⲟⲛⲓⲁ (ShC 73 46), ⲡⲁⲕⲉⲃⲧ *man of Keft* (J 91 36), ⲡⲁⲡⲕⲁⲗⲁⲛⲕⲉⲣ (Kr 10). With gen ⲛ- rare *S* : ⲡⲧⲟⲟⲩ ⲡⲁⲛⲧϫⲟⲉⲓⲧ (BG 79). In many names as ⲡⲁⲛⲥⲉ, ⲧⲁⲛⲥⲉ, ⲡⲁⲗⲓⲛ, ⲧⲁⲗⲓⲛ, ⲡⲁⲡⲉⲥⲛⲏⲩ, Τανεσνεῦς, ⲧⲁⲃⲓⲕⲧⲱⲣ, ⲡⲁⲃⲓⲕⲧⲱⲣ (J 94 53 *son of ? Vic* or ⲁⲡⲁ ⲃ̅.) *V* Stern 250, Sdff 94, Till 59, Mallon 87.

ⲡⲁⲓ, ⲧⲁⲓ, ⲛⲁⲓ *S*, ⲫⲁⲓ, ⲑⲁⲓ, ⲛⲁⲓ *B*, ⲡⲉⲓ, ⲧⲉⲓ, ⲛⲉⲓ *AF*, ⲡⲉⲉⲓ &c *AA²* demonst pron **a** absol, *this* (cf ⲡⲏ) : ⲁⲩϣⲁⲛⲣⲓ ⲙⲫⲁⲓ *B*, ⲡⲉⲓ ⲛϯⲙⲓⲛⲉ *A*, ⲧⲁⲓⲧⲉ ⲑⲉ *S*, ⲡⲁⲓ ϫⲉ ⲛⲧⲉⲣⲉϥϫⲟⲟⲩ *S*, ⲟⲉⲓⲙⲟⲩϯⲛⲉ ⲡⲉⲓ *F*. **b** construct ⲡⲉⲓ-, ⲧⲉⲓ-, ⲛⲉⲓ- *SAF*, ⲡⲉ- &c *S* (Theban), ⲡⲉⲉⲓ- &c *A²*, ⲡⲁⲓ-, ⲧⲁⲓ-, ⲛⲁⲓ- *BO*, ⲡⲓ-, ϯ-, ⲛⲓ- *SABFO* : ⲡⲉⲓⲕⲁⲥ ⲡⲁⲓ, ⲣⲱⲃ ⲛⲧⲉⲙⲓⲛⲉ *S*, ⲡⲉⲓⲛⲉⲓ, ϯⲟⲩⲛⲟⲩ *A*, ⲡⲁⲓⲡⲉⲣ ⲫⲁⲓ *B*, ⲡⲉⲓⲗⲱⲙⲓ *F*, ⲡⲓⲕⲟⲩⲓ, ⲡⲁⲓⲁϣ ⲛⲥⲁⲧⲓ *O*. *V* Stern 242, Sdff 95, Till 49, Mallon 92.

ⲡⲉ *SAO*, ⲫⲉ *B*, ⲡⲏ *AF*, pl ⲡⲏⲩⲉ *S* (cf PS) *A²*, ⲡⲏⲟⲩⲉ *A*, ⲫⲏⲟⲩⲓ *B*, ⲡⲏⲟⲩⲓ *F* nn f, *heaven, sky* : Ge 1 26 *SAB*, Job 11 8 *SB*, EpJer 54 *BF*, Jo 3 13 *SA²B* οὐρανός ; BG 41 *S* ⲧⲥⲁϣϥⲉ ⲙⲡⲉ, FR 14 *S* ⲛⲉϥⲫⲱⲥⲧⲏⲣ ⲛⲧⲡⲉ, ib 90 *B* lifted eyes ⲉⲡϣⲱⲓ ⲉⲧⲫⲉ, El 98 *A* sent ⲁⲃⲁⲗ ⲛⲧⲡⲉ, AZ 21 105 *O* ϣⲟⲓ ⲉⲧⲡⲉ ; pl : Ps 8 4 *SB*, Is 44 23 *SB*, He 9 23 *SBF* οὐρ. ; PS 7 *S* go up ⲉⲙⲡ., cf ib 32, 33 *S* ⲛⲉⲩⲡⲏⲩⲉ, AP 16 *A²* ⲛⲡⲏ̅ ⲛⲁⲡ. Adjectival phrases : Ps 67 15 *S* ⲡⲉⲧϩⲛⲙⲡ. = *B* ⲫⲏ ⲉⲧⲣ̅ⲭⲉⲛⲧϥⲉ, 1 Cor 15 40 *S* ⲉⲧⲣ̅ⲧⲡⲉ = *B* ⲛⲧⲉ ⲧⲫⲉ, Eph 1 3 *S* sim = *B* ⲛⲁⲛⲓⲫ. ἐπουράνιος.

Compounds : ⲁⲩⲁⲛ ⲙⲡⲉ *S*, *sky-coloured, blue* : P 44 104 *S* ⲁ. ⲙⲡⲉ ⲛⲥⲁⲣⲇⲓⲟⲛ = 43 88 ⲛⲥⲁⲣ. ⲛⲟⲉ ⲙⲡⲉ لازورد (v ⲁⲩⲁⲛ) ; ⲁⲗ ⲙⲡⲉ *SBF*, *hailstone* (v ⲁⲗ ⲃ) ; ⲣⲙⲙⲡⲉ *S*, ⲣⲉⲙⲙⲫⲉ *B*, *man of heaven* : 1 Cor 15 49 *B* (*S* ⲉⲃⲟⲗ ϩⲛⲧⲡⲉ) ἐπουράνιος ; Mor 22 106 *S* who can ⲣ ⲡⲉϥⲛⲟⲩⲥ ⲛⲣ.? = BSM 95 *B*, DeV 2 11 *B* thou ⲛⲓⲣ. art become ⲣⲉⲙⲛⲕⲁϩⲓ ; ϩⲣⲟⲩ ⲙⲡⲉ *S*, *voice of h., thunder* : Jo 12 29 (*A²* ϩⲣⲁⲩ, *B* ϧⲁⲣⲁⲃⲁⲓ), Ap 6 1 (*B* do) βροντή ; Gu 70 ἦχος, BSG 190 = ib 24 *B* ϧⲁⲣ. ; ⲣⲱⲟⲩ ⲙⲡⲉ *S*, *rain* : Lev 26 4 (*B* ⲙⲟⲩ ⲛⲱϣⲓ), Job 38 28 (*B* ⲙ. ⲛⲣⲱⲟⲩ), Joel 2 23 (*A* ϩ., *B* do) ὑετός, BHom 125 ⲛⲣ. ⲙⲡⲉ ⲙⲛ̅ϯⲟⲧⲉ.

—— *SF* (v c ⲥⲁ- below), *what is above* : Cant 6 6 ⲧⲡⲉ ⲛⲛⲟⲩⲟⲟϭⲉ μῆλον ; Si 50 2 ⲧⲡⲉ ⲙⲡⲛϫⲓⲥⲉ ἀνά-

λημμα ὑψηλόν ; ShA 1 107 of veil ⲧⲡⲉ ⲙⲙⲟϥ, ⲡⲓⲧⲛ ⲙⲙⲟϥ, ⲧⲉϥⲙⲏⲧⲉ *its top, bottom, middle*, J 39 31 ⲧⲭⲏⲣⲉ ⲉⲧⲁⲡⲉ (*sic, l ?* ⲉⲧⲁⲧⲡⲉ, but *cf* CO 204, Ep 102 ⲧⲁϩⲣⲁⲓ & J 24 124 (ⲧ)ⲧⲟⲓ ⲉⲧⲁⲡϩⲣⲏⲧ).

With preposition, ⲥ ⲉ-, *upward* : Eccl 3 21 ἄνω, Lev 27 7 (*B* ⲉⲡϣⲱⲓ) ἐπάνω, Ps 8 2 (*B* ⲥⲁⲡϣ.) ὑπεράνω ; Ps 74 5 (*B* ⲉⲡϭⲓⲥⲓ) εἰς ὕψος ; PS 5 ϫⲓⲛⲙⲡⲉⲥⲛⲧ ⲉⲧⲡⲉ, BHom 48 wave ϩⲉⲉⲃⲉ ⲉⲧⲡⲉ (var ϩ. ⲉϩⲣⲁⲓ). ⲥ ⲛ- adj, *upper* : ⲙⲁ ⲛⲧⲡⲉ Jud 3 23 (cf 24 ⲉⲧⲣⲓⲧⲡⲉ), Ac 9 37 (*B* ⲉⲧⲥⲁⲡϣ.) ὑπερῷον ; Lu 22 12 (*B* ⲉϥⲥⲁⲡϣ.) ἀνώγεον ; J 106 112 house & ⲛⲉϥⲙ. ; ⲥⲁ ⲛ. 4 Kg 15 35 ἐπάνω, Nu 4 25 (*B* ⲥⲁⲡϣ) ἄνωθεν ; PS 155 ⲉⲧⲙⲡⲥⲁ ⲛ. (cf 157 ⲉⲧⲥⲁⲧⲡⲉ), ShA 1 245 herbs whose roots go downward others ⲉⲩⲙⲡⲥⲁ ⲛ., BKU 1 94 ⲡⲕⲁⲧ ⲛ. paral ⲡⲕ. ⲙⲡⲓⲧⲡⲉ ; +gen, *above* : Zech 4 3 (*A* ⲛⲡⲥⲁϩⲣⲉ, *B* ⲥⲁⲡϣ.) ἐπάνω, Ez 11 22 (*B* do) ὑπεράνω, Nu 4 6 (*B* do) ἄνωθεν, Ps 77 23 (*B* do) ὑπεράνωθεν ; BHom 93 God ⲉⲧⲛ. ⲙⲫⲩⲥⲓⲥ ⲛⲓⲙ ὑπέρ, ib 37 setting naught ⲛ. ⲙⲡⲉⲥⲟⲩϫⲁⲓ προκρίνειν ; BMis 225 cross ⲛ. ⲙⲡⲧⲁⲫⲟⲥ = Mor 16 84 ⲙⲡⲉⲧⲡⲉ ⲙ., ib 395 words ⲉⲩⲛ. ⲛⲛⲉⲛⲙⲉⲧⲣⲟⲛ, J 58 10 house ⲉⲧⲛ. ⲙⲡϣⲏⲓ (cf 16 ⲉⲧⲣⲡϣⲏⲓ). As advb, *above* : BHom 53 those in theatre ⲛⲉⲧⲛ. opp ⲉⲧⲙⲡⲉⲥⲛⲧ, CO 482 he that wrote ⲛ. ⲥ ϩⲛ-, *in upper part, above* : Dan 6 10 (*B* do) ὑπερῷον ; Jth 1 8 ⲧⲅⲁⲗⲓⲗⲁⲓⲁ ⲉⲧϩ. ἄνω, cf JA ’75 5 212 ⲧⲗⲓⲃⲏ ⲉⲧⲛ. ἀνώτερος. + gen : Lev 11 21(var ⲛⲧⲡⲉ, *B* ⲥⲁⲡϣ.) ἀνώτ. ⲥ ⲥⲁ-, ⲛⲥⲁ-, *on upper side, over* : Ps 148 4 *SF* ⲉⲧⲥⲁⲧⲡⲉ ⲛⲙⲡⲏⲩⲉ (*B* do) ὑπεράνω ; ShA 1 150 water pouring ⲛⲥ. ⲙⲙⲟϥ (sc fire) ; as advb, *upward, above* : PLond 4 438 which we set forth ⲥⲁⲧⲡⲉ, J 106 68 whom I named ⲛⲥ. ⲙⲡⲉⲓϩⲱⲣⲓⲥⲧⲓⲕⲟⲛ ; ShA 1 256 plants bearing fruit ⲛⲥⲁⲛϩⲣⲁⲓ others ⲛⲥ., ST 442 *Sᵃ* ⲣ ϩⲱⲃ ⲙⲡⲓⲧⲛ ⲥⲉⲧⲡⲉ. ⲥ ϩⲓ-, *above* : Ex 20 4 (*B* ⲛ̄ϩⲣⲏⲓ) ἄνω, Ge 6 16 (*B* ⲥⲁⲡϣ.), Is 45 8 (*B* ⲙⲡϣ.) ἄνωθεν ; ShC 73 137 cover fuel ϩⲓⲧⲡⲉ ; + gen : Si 45 20 ἐπάνω, Deu 28 1 (*B* do) ὑπεράνω, Nu 4 25 (var ⲙⲡⲉⲥⲥⲁ ⲛⲧⲡⲉ, *B* ⲥⲁⲡϣ.) ἄνωθεν ; Z 339 fire below us & ϩ. ⲙⲙⲟⲛ ἕως κεφαλῆς ; Mic 3 2 (*A* ⲙⲡⲥⲁϩⲣⲉ, *B* ⲉⲃⲟⲗ ϩⲁ-) ἀπό ; BSG 178 wheel with swords ϩ. ⲙⲙⲟϥ, knives ϩⲓⲡⲉⲥⲛⲧ, LMis 385 head ϩ. ⲙⲡⲙⲁⲕϩ, Miss 4 238 shalt stand ϩ. ⲙⲡⲃⲛⲙⲁ, cf 239 ⲙⲡⲭⲓⲥⲉ ⲙⲡϩ., BMis 135 what thou tellest ϥϩ. ⲛϣⲡⲏⲣⲉ ⲛⲓⲙ. ⲥ ϫⲓⲛ-, *from above* : Mk 15 38 (FR 70 ϫⲓⲛⲉⲧ., *B* ⲓⲥϫⲉⲛⲡϣ.) ἀπὸ ἄνωθεν ; J 57 12 ⲡⲧⲁⲥⲉⲧⲛⲡⲉⲩⲉ (κινδυνεύειν) ⲁⲣⲟⲥ (sc ⲥⲧⲱϩⲉ ⲛⲕⲁϩ) ⲛⲁⲕ ⲉⲙⲛⲧⲉ ⲉⲛϫⲓⲛⲧⲡⲉ (obscure).

ⲣ ⲧⲡⲉ, *be above, surmount* : ShA 1 306 through scriptures ⲛϥⲧⲣⲉϥⲣ ⲧ. ⲙⲙⲟⲟⲩ *cause* mind *to overcome* them (sc vices) ; ⲣ ⲥⲁⲧⲡⲉ, meaning same : PS 150 ⲁⲓⲣ ⲥ. ⲛⲛⲁϩⲩⲗⲏ (cf 151 ⲁⲓⲣ ⲡⲉⲧⲡⲉ ⲛ-) ; ⲣ ϩⲓⲧⲡⲉ, sim ; Mor 37 112 ⲁⲩⲣ ϩ. ⲙⲙⲟϥ ὑπερπέτεσθαι.

With m art + prep є- (пєтпє, whence Spg's derivation from tp, tpe 'head', *Kopt Etym* 15): ⲙⲡ ⲛ-, *above, over* Ge 22 9 (*B* ⲥⲁⲡϣ.) ἐπάνω, 4 Kg 25 28 ἐπάνωθεν, Z 318 trees ⲙⲡ. ⲡⲛⲉⲩⲣⲓ (*l* ? ⲣⲟ) = MG 25 136 *B* ϩⲓⲣⲉⲛⲛⲓⲣⲱⲟⲩ ἐπὶ θυρῶν; 1 Esd 8 72 (Pap *penes* GHorner) ⲁⲅⲁϣⲁⲓ ⲙⲡ. ⲡⲡⲉⲛⲁⲡⲏⲅⲉ ὑπέρ; PS 112 place ⲉⲧⲙⲡ. ⲙⲡⲉⲭⲁⲟⲥ (*cf ib* ⲙⲡⲥⲁ ⲛⲧⲡⲉ), Mor 43 74 ⲥⲙⲡ. ⲛⲥⲟⲫⲓⲁ ⲛⲓⲙ (var R 2 4 17 ⲛⲧⲡⲉ), *ib* 25 12 ⲉϥⲙ. ⲛⲧⲁⲁⲡⲉ (var P 131³ 84 ϩⲓⲧⲡⲉ, Va 61 94 *B* ⲥⲁⲡϣ.), Mor 44 38 thing ⲉϥⲙⲡ. ⲡⲛⲉⲕⲙⲉⲧⲣⲟⲛ (var BMis 395 *ut sup*); ϩⲙⲡ. ⲛ-: Bor 228 48 voice ϣⲱⲡⲉ ϩⲙⲡ. ⲙⲙⲟϥ, BMis 183 cross appeared ϩⲙⲡ. ⲙⲡⲧⲁⲫⲟⲥ. With poss pron: Deu 28 23 heaven ⲉⲧⲙⲡⲉⲕⲛⲧⲡⲉ (*B* ⲥⲁⲡϣ. ⲛⲧⲉⲕⲁⲫⲉ) ἐπὶ τ. κεφαλῆς σου, Ps 73 5 their road ⲙⲡⲉⲩⲉⲧ. (*B* ⲉⲧⲥⲁⲡϣ.) ὑπεράνω, PS 44 ⲧⲡⲓⲥⲧⲓⲥ ⲉⲧⲙⲡⲉⲩⲉⲧ., BAp 36 cloud over throne ⲙⲡⲉⲩⲛⲧⲡⲉ (*l* ⲉⲧ.). *Cf* ⲉⲥⲏⲧ I *s f*, ⲟⲛ *front* (ⲉⲧϩⲏ *A²*).   ⲣ ⲡⲉⲧⲡⲉ, *be above, surmount*: Mic 4 1 (*A* ⲣ ⲡⲣⲣⲉ, *B* ϭⲓⲥⲓ ⲥⲁⲡϣ.) μετεωρίζεσθαι; Z 329 ⲉⲧⲙⲣ ⲡ. ⲡⲛⲉⲣϩⲏⲅⲉ that we have seen ὑπερβαίνειν; PS 151 ⲁⲓⲣ ⲡ. ⲡⲛⲉϣⲧⲏⲛ ⲛϣⲁⲁⲣ (Od Solom 25 8 diff), P 131⁵ 103 what I tell thee ⲁⲓⲣ ⲡ. ⲛ̇ⲭⲟⲟⲩ *I have already told* thy father.

-ⲡⲉ *SAA²BF* vbal enclitic following imperf: ⲡⲉϥⲙⲉⲉⲩⲉⲡⲉ, ⲡⲉⲣⲉϥϯ ⲭⲏ ⲛⲉⲙⲁϥⲡⲉ; pluperf: ⲛⲉⲁⲩϣⲧⲟⲣⲧⲣⲡⲉ; less often fut: Jud 16 11 *S*, Ps 123 4 *S*, Pro 23 35 *SA*, Ap 3 2 *S*, Ez 32 6 *B*; R 1 4 19 *S* ϯⲛⲁϯ ⲡⲟⲩϭⲥ ⲙⲡⲡⲉⲛⲉ, AM 159 *B* ⲁϥⲛⲁⲉⲣ ⲟⲩ ⲡⲱϣⲛⲡⲉ, HL 75 *B* ⲡⲁϥⲛⲁⲭⲟⲥ ⲁⲛⲡⲉ; or perf (after ⲉϣϫⲉ, ⲉⲓⲥ ϩⲏⲏⲧⲉ &c): ShA 1 95 *S* ⲉⲓⲥⲡⲉ ⲁⲩⲕⲟⲡⲥⲟⲩⲛⲉ, ShZ 591 *S* ⲉϣⲭⲡⲉ ⲁⲅⲟⲡⲟⲩⲛⲉ, R 1 4 14 *S* ⲉⲓⲥ ϩⲏⲏⲧⲉ ⲁⲣⲗⲟⲡⲉ. After place-names *B*: C 86 75 ⲁϥϭⲱⲗ ⲉⲧⲁⲩⲃⲁⲣⲡⲉ (var om), AM 135 ϣⲁ ⲡⲓⲗⲁⲕⲱⲡⲉ, Amélineau *Géog* 558 ff often. *Cf* AM 148 n. *V* Stern 373–376, Sdff 295, Till 136, Mallon 242, 243.

-ⲡⲉ pronom enclitic *v* ⲡⲏ demonst.

ⲡⲉ- *S* interrog or condit pref expressing doubt, *perhaps* (?): BMOr 8810 458 Besa to discontented monk ⲡⲉⲡⲉⲓϩⲃⲏⲅⲉ ⲣ ϣⲁⲩ ⲛⲁⲕ ⲛⲧⲟⲕ ⲉⲧⲥⲟⲟⲩⲛ... ⲡⲉⲁⲡⲉⲕϩⲏⲧ ⲙⲕⲁϩ ⲛ ⲁⲓⲗⲩⲡⲉⲓ ⲙⲙⲟⲕ unwittingly, why didst not tell me?... ⲡⲉⲉⲕϫⲱ ⲙⲙⲟⲥ ⲉⲧⲃⲉ ⲡⲉⲕϣⲏⲣⲉ who but own evil deeds pursueth them? *Cf* ? ⲉϣϫⲡⲉ, ⲉⲓⲥⲡⲉ, ⲉⲓⲣⲡⲉ.

ⲡⲉⲓ *S*, ⲡⲓ *SAF*, ⲡⲓⲉⲓ *A*, ⲫⲓ *B*, ⲡⲉ *F* nn f, *kiss*: Pro 27 6 *SA*, Lu 22 48 *SB*, 2 Cor 13 12 *SBF* φίλημα; Bor 241 211 *S* ⲧⲉϥⲡⲓ ⲟⲩⲛⲓⲧⲉ ⲡⲁⲅⲁⲡⲏ, KroppB *S* ⲙⲡⲉⲥⲟⲩⲱϣ ⲉϫⲓ ⲡⲧⲁⲡⲓ; ϯ ⲡ., ⲫ. *SABF*, *give kiss c* ⲉ-: Job 31 27 *B* (*S* ⲟⲩⲱϣⲧ) φιλεῖν, Lu 7 38 *SB*, BMis 561 *S* ⲉϥϯ. ⲉⲣⲟⲓ, MG 25 10 *B* ⲉϥϯ. ⲉⲣⲱϥ ⲡⲉⲙⲡⲉϥⲃⲁⲗ καταφ.; *ib* 25 7 *B* ⲁⲩϯ. ⲉⲡⲟⲩⲉⲣⲏⲟⲩ

ἀσπάζειν; PS 275 *S* ⲁⲥϯ. ⲉⲣⲟⲟⲩ (*sc* feet), AM 294 *B* ⲉⲩϯ. ⲉⲛⲉϥϫⲓϫ;   *c* ⲉⲣⲡ-, ⲉⲣⲉⲡ-, ⲉⲣⲱ: Ge 29 13 *SB*, Pro 7 13 *SAB*, Mt 26 48 *SB* φιλ., Ge 31 28 *S* ⲉⲣⲡ- *B* ⲉⲣⲱⲟⲩ ⲡ-, Mk 14 45 *SBF* καταφ.; PS 94 *S* ⲁϥϯ. ⲉⲣⲡⲧⲙⲉⲥⲧⲱⲛϩⲏⲧ, *ib* 122 *S* ⲁϥⲱⲗⳝ ⲉⲣⲟⲕ ⲁϥϯ. ⲉⲣⲱⲕ, ShA 2 108 *S* ⲁⲧⲉⲧⲛϯ. ⲉⲣⲡⲛⲉⲧⲛⲉⲣⲏⲩ, BSM 80 *B* ⲁϥϯ. ⲉⲣⲱϥ ⲛⲓⲱⲁⲛⲛⲏⲥ = BMis 171 *S* ⲉⲣⲱⲟⲩ;   *c* ⲉϩⲣⲉⲛ- *B*: Ge 31 55 (*S* ⲉⲣⲡ-) καταφ. acc;   *c* ⲉϧⲟⲩⲛ ϧⲉⲛ- *B*: AM 327 ⲉϥϯ. ⲉϧ. ϧⲉⲛⲣⲱϥ;   *c* ⲉϫⲛ-, ϩⲓϫⲉⲛ-: BMEA 10578 *F* ⲁϥϯ ⲡⲉ ⲉϫⲛⲧⲁⲡⲓ ⲛ-, WTh 141 *S* ⲁϥϯ. ⲉϫⲛⲧⲁⲡⲉ of devil, AM 110 *B* sim, Miss 4 109 *B* ϩⲓϫⲉⲛⲧⲉϥⲁⲫⲉ, BMis 452 *S* fell at feet ⲉϥϯ. ⲉϫⲱⲟⲩ.   *c* ⲛ- (prob for ⲉ-): *B* AM 150 ⲁϥϯ. ⲛⲡⲓⲉⲣϭⲱⲧ.

ⲡⲏ, ⲧⲏ, ⲛⲏ *SA²F*, ⲫⲏ, ⲑⲏ, ⲛⲏ *B* demonst pron, *that* (*cf* ⲡⲁⲓ): Job 15 28 *S*, Sa 14 2 *S*, Jo 10 6 *SA²* (all *B* diff), BHom 54 *S* ἐκεῖνος; Is 26 19 *S* (*B* diff) ἥ, Mt 13 11 *SB*, *ib* 3 29 *BF* (*S* ⲡⲉⲧ-) ὁ, Sa 14 8 *S* ⲡⲁⲓ ⲙⲉⲛ...ⲡⲏ ϫⲉ ὁ...τό. *V* Stern 242, Sdff 96, Mallon 95.

-ⲡⲉ, -ⲧⲉ, -ⲛⲉ *SAA²BFO*, enclitic of ⲡⲏ &c, joins subj & predic in nominal clause: ⲁⲡⲁⲣⲧⲉⲡⲉ ⲡⲁⲣⲉⲛ, ⲡⲁϣⲏⲣⲉⲡⲉ ⲡⲁⲓ, ⲧⲁⲓⲧⲉ ⲑⲉ, ⲟⲩⲛⲓϣϯⲡⲉ ⲡⲉⲛⲛⲟⲩϯ, ⲟⲩⲅⲁⲓⲃⲉⲥ ⲉⲁⲥⲟⲩⲉⲓⲛⲉⲡⲉ, ⲙⲡⲱϥ ⲁⲛⲡⲉ, ⲛⲓⲙⲛⲉ ⲛⲁⲓ? *V* Stern 300, Sdff 422, 427, Till 49, Mallon 356.

ⲡⲏⲓ *SF*, ⲡⲏⲏⲓ *Sᶠ*, ⲫⲉⲓ, ⲫⲏⲓ *B* nn, a *leap*, with vb, *take a leap*: Mor 31 50 *Sᶠ* camel ⲁⲥϩⲱⲧⲉ (*i e* ϥⲟϭⲥ) ⲉϩⲣⲁⲓ...ⲁⲥϥⲓ ⲡⲏⲏⲓ;   with ϭⲓ *BF* (once): Job 6 10 (*S* ϫⲓ ϥⲟϭⲥ), Is 35 6 (var & *SF* do), Jo 4 14 *BF* (*SA²* ϥⲱϭⲉ ⲉϩⲣⲁⲓ) ἅλλεσθαι, Nah 3 17 (*A* ϭⲓ ϭⲁⲕⲥ), Ac 3 8 (*S* ϥⲱϭⲉ) ἐξάλ., Va 57 190 heart ϭⲓ ⲫ. ἐφάλ.; Joel 1 17 (*A* = Gk) σκιρτᾶν; Ez 47 9 (var BM 1247 ⲃⲉⲣⲃⲉⲣ, *S* ϥ. ⲉϩⲣⲁⲓ) ἐκζεῖν; DeV 2 9 ⲛⲁϥϭⲓ ⲫ. ⲛⲉ from joy, MG 25 405 ⲁϥⲥⲟϫⲓ ⲉϥϭⲓ ⲫ.   b *leaper, flea*: 1 Kg 24 15 *SB* (ⲫⲏⲓ) ψύλλος, *ib* 26 20 *S* (Gk om) *pulex*, K 172 غوث.

ⲡⲟⲓ *S*, ⲫⲟⲓ *B* nn m *S* f *B*, *bench*: Ez 46 2 *B* (*S* ⲡⲓⲛⲏ) πρόθυρον; Tri 461 *S* درج; K 155 *B* ϯⲫ. (var ⲫⲟⲓ) طبقة; ShC 73 84 *S* ⲡⲉϭⲙⲁ ⲛ̇ⲛⲕⲟⲧⲕ... ⲛ ⲙⲡ., PSBA 10 197 *S* ϣⲁⲥⲛⲕⲟⲧⲕ ϩⲓⲟⲩⲡ. ⲡⲟⲩⲟⲧ ⲡⲓⲙⲁⲥ (*cf* Synax 1 388 دخل 'ده), Miss 4 732 *S* ⲡⲕⲟⲩⲓ ⲙⲡ. whereon I sit at work.   In name (?): ϩⲁⲙⲡⲟⲓ, ϩⲁⲛⲡⲟⲉⲓ (BM 1075).

ⲡⲱⲍ, ⲧⲱⲍ, ⲛⲟⲩⲍ *SAA²F*, ⲫⲱⲍ, ⲑⲱⲍ ⲛⲟⲩⲍ *B* possess pron as nn, *mine, his* &c: Ex 19 5 *SB* ⲡⲱⲓ ⲡⲉ ⲡⲕⲁϩ, Jo 7 16 *SB* ⲧⲁⲥⲃⲱ ⲡⲧⲱⲓ ⲁⲛⲧⲉ, Ps 49 10 *SB* ⲛⲟⲩⲓ ⲧⲏⲣⲟⲩ ⲡⲉ ⲛⲉⲑⲏⲣⲓⲟⲛ, Wor 325 *F* ⲧⲱⲕⲧⲉ ⲧϭⲁⲙ, Ge 20 7 *B* ⲛⲑⲟⲕ ⲡⲉⲙⲡⲉⲧⲉⲫⲱⲕ, AP 3 *A²* ⲡⲱⲡⲉ ⲡⲉⲁⲩ, Zech 9 17 *A* ⲁⲅⲁⲑⲟⲛ ⲛⲓⲙ ⲡⲱϥⲛⲉ, Ryl 99 *S* ⲡⲉⲡⲡⲁⲑⲟⲥ ⲡⲟⲩⲓ, ShBM 195 *S* ⲧⲉⲩϩⲁⲛ ⲁⲩⲱ ⲧⲱⲧⲛ.

Emphatic use *B*: C 86 252 hail ⲫⲏ ⲉⲧⲉⲫⲱⲓ

ⲅⲉⲱⲣⲅⲓⲟⲥ *my own George*, Va 65 1 ⲟⲏ ⲉⲧⲉⲑⲱⲥ
ⲡϥⲩⲥⲓⲥ *her own nature.*   Here ? belongs ⲧⲱⲋ *S*
in Lu 1 9 (*B* diff) ⲁⲥⲣ ⲁⲧⲱϥ ⲉⲧⲁⲗⲉ λαγχάνειν, cit
R 1 3 69 ⲣ̄ ⲁ-, Tri 448 ⲣ ⲉⲧⲱϥ, P 129²⁰ 122 celestial
beings ⲁⲥⲣ ⲁⲧⲱⲟⲩ ⲉⲧⲣⲉⲩⲁϩⲉ ⲣⲁⲧⲟⲩ. *V* Stern 251,
Sdff 89, Till 57, Mallon 36.

ⲡⲟⲕ *S* *v* ⲡⲁⲕⲉ & ⲡⲱϭⲉ.

ⲡⲱⲱⲕ *S* vb tr: BMOr 6201 B 205 ⲧⲁϭⲟⲗⲧⲉ
ⲉⲓ...ⲉⲥⲡ. ⲧⲱⲋ ⲉⲣⲟⲩⲛ[, *l* ? ⲡⲱⲛⲕ (ⲡⲱⲡⲕ).

ⲡⲁⲕⲉ, ⲡⲁⲗ., ⲡⲟⲕⲉ† (Mor 37), ⲡⲟⲕ† *S*, ⲣ ⲥ ⲡⲁⲕ·
A (once) vb intr, *be light, thin*: Ex 16 14† (*B* ϣⲙⲁ),
Mor 37 74 bodies ⲉⲩⲡ.† παρα ⲡⲣⲱⲙⲉ λεπτός, Ps
17 42 (*B* do) λεπτύνειν; ShIF 152 some garments
ⲉⲩⲟⲩⲟⲙⲧ others ⲉⲩⲡ.†, ShA 2 158 ϩⲉⲛⲧⲟⲟⲩⲉ ⲉⲩⲡ.†
on feet, PSBA 27 168 write on it (parchment) ϩⲛⲟⲩ-
ⲕⲁϣ ⲉϥⲡ.†, BG 69 ⲡⲱⲥ ϣⲁⲣⲉⲧⲉⲯⲩⲭⲏ ⲡ. ⲡ. *grow
small (gradually)*?   *Be small, poor at heart*: Jud
16 16 ⲁϥⲡ. ⲡϩⲏⲧ, Hab 2 13 *A* ⲣ ⲡⲁⲕϩ. (*B* ⲉⲣ ⲕⲟⲩⲭⲓ ⲛϩ.) ὀλιγοψυχεῖν; BAp 148 evil spirits plagued
me ϣⲁⲛⲧⲉⲡⲁϩ. ⲡⲁⲁⲕⲉ.   As nn, *lightness*: ShIF
180 ⲡⲉⲩⲡ. ⲡⲉⲩⲟⲩⲙⲟⲧ.

ⲡⲟⲕϥ *S* nn m, *thin sheet, plate*: Ex 29 6 ⲡⲡ. gloss
on ⲡⲉⲧⲁⲗⲟⲛ (*B* = Gk), Nu 17 4 made them into
ϩⲉⲡⲡ. ⲡⲣⲟⲙⲛⲧ (*B* Gk om), *cf ib* 3 ⲃⲛⲧⲉ λεπίς; Jud
6 37 πόκος (? misled by Gk); Ryl 238 ⲟⲩⲥⲁⲕⲓⲛ
ⲙⲯⲓⲙⲓⲑⲓⲟⲛ ⲙⲡ., Bodl(P) a *l* e spread garment to
be dyed & ⲁⲁϥ ⲙⲡ.

ⲡⲁⲕⲉ *Sf* *v* ⲡⲟϭⲉ.

ⲡⲟⲕϥ *v* ⲡⲁⲕⲉ.

ⲡⲉⲗⲏⲕ *S*, -ⲏϭ *A* nn or adj, meaning unknown,
epithet of Antichrist, ? *thin* (*cf* M R James *Lost Apocr*
59): El 120 *S* ⲟⲩⲡ. ⲡⲟⲩⲕⲟⲩⲉⲓ, youthful (?), thin-
legged &c = *ib* 90 *A*.

ⲡⲱⲗⲕ *v* ⲡⲱⲗϭ.

ⲡⲗⲁⲗⲉ *F* vb intr (?), meaning unknown: BM
642 letter ⲗⲓⲡⲟⲛ ⲁⲡⲗⲱⲙⲓ ⲡ. ⲉⲧⲉ[.

ⲡⲱⲗϣ *S* *v* ⲡⲱⲣϣ.

ⲡⲱⲗϩ *SAF*, ⲫⲱ. *B*, ⲡⲟⲗϩ⳯ *S*, ⲫⲟⲗϩ⳯ *B*, ⲡⲟⲗϩ†,
-ⲣϩ† (PMéd) *S* vb **I** tr, *wound*: Mk 12 4 *B* (*S*
ⲕⲱⲗϩ) κεφαλιοῦν; Ac 19 16 *S* (*B* ϫⲱⲟⲩ ⲫⲏϩ⳯) τραυματίζειν; Tri 330 *S* Job ⲛⲧⲁϥⲡ. (ⲛ)ⲡⲉϥⲥⲁϣ with
nails طبّ; ShIF 152 *S* ⲡⲉⲡⲗⲏⲅⲏ ⲡⲧⲁⲩⲡⲟⲗϩⲟⲩ,
PMéd 268 *S* ⲛⲃⲁⲗ ⲉⲧⲡ.†;   **II** intr, *be wounded*:
Mun 66 *S* feet bound with thongs ϫⲉⲡⲉⲩⲡ., ShA
2 120 *S* thou fearest ϫⲉⲡⲡⲉⲧⲉⲕϭⲓⲝ...ⲡ., CO 346 *S*
ϫⲟⲟⲩ ⲛⲃⲁⲗⲟⲧ ⲡⲁⲓ ϫⲉⲁⲡϭⲁⲙⲟⲩⲗ ϩⲱⲛ ⲉⲡ. (meaning ?);   c ⲉ-: *be wounded, offended by*: BAp 173
S if art vexed with a brother ⲛⲧⲉⲡⲉⲕϩⲏⲧ ⲡ. ⲉⲩ-
ⲥⲟⲛ, Va 57 65 *B* shameful lusts ⲉⲩϥⲟⲗϩ (*l* ⲫⲱ.)

ⲉⲣⲱⲟⲩ...ⲡⲭⲉⲑⲙⲉⲧⲙⲉⲑⲣⲉ of thy conscience (*l* ?
ⲉⲥϥ.).

—— *SABF* nn m, *wound*: Pro 27 6 *SA*, Si 34
33 *S*, Is 1 6 *B* (*SF* ⲥⲁϣ) τραῦμα; Is 30 26 *F* (*S* do,
B ⲉⲣϩⲟⲧ) πληγή; BMis 240 *S* there is no ⲡ. ϩⲓ-
ⲡⲉⲕⲥⲱⲙⲁ μώλωψ; ShC 73 83 *S* ⲉⲁⲩⲣ ⲡⲕⲉⲡ. ⲡ-
ⲡⲉⲩⲟⲩⲉⲣⲏⲧⲉ & they limped, DeV 2 107 *B* ⲛⲫ. ⲛϯϣⲉ
ⲡⲗⲟⲥⲭⲏ, Mor 30 14 *F* ⲙⲛ ⲗⲁⲡϯ ⲙⲛ. in martyr's
body = BMis 240 *S* ⲧⲁⲕⲟ, Mor 25 81 *S* ⲛⲥⲁϣ
ⲙⲡⲁⲡ. in sick body.

ϫⲓⲛϥ. *B* nn : OrChrNS 3 44 ϩⲓⲧⲉⲛⲟⲩⲕⲟⲩϫⲓ ⲛϫ.
they wrote 'Zacharias' in place of 'Azarias' (=
PO 14 86 ـذحـمـل *change*, so prob *l* ⲫⲟⲛϩ).

ⲫⲟⲗϩϥ *B* nn m, *wounded person*: PasH 228
wounds healed of those ⲉⲧⲟⲓ ⲙⲫ.

ⲡⲱⲗⲝ *F* *v* ⲡⲱⲣϫ.

ⲡⲉⲗⲏϭ *A* *v* ⲡⲉⲗⲏⲕ.

ⲡⲱⲗϭ, -ⲗⲕ, -ⲗⲝ *S*, ⲫⲱⲗⲝ *B*, ⲡⲁⲗⲕⲏ *Sᵃ* (J 38),
ⲡⲁⲣⲕⲉ *S* (BM 1116), ⲡⲗϭ-, ⲡⲉⲗⲕ- *S*, ⲫⲟⲗⲝ- *B*,
ⲡⲁⲗⲝ- *F*, ⲡⲟⲗϭ⳯, -ⲕ⳯, -ⲝ⳯, ⲡⲁⲗϭ⳯ *S*, ⲡⲁⲗⲝ⳯ *S/F*,
ⲫⲟⲗⲝ⳯ *B*, confused with ⲡⲱⲣϫ, vb **I** intr *S*, *be a-
greed, reach satisfaction, decide*: CO 128 ⲉϥϣⲁⲡⲡ.
ⲕⲁⲡ ⲙⲡϩⲡ. we will release the men, ST 352 here
is bishop's judgment ϫⲉⲧ(ⲉ⳯ⲡ)ⲡⲁⲉⲓ ⲡⲧⲉⲧⲡ. & remain in your house, *ib* 359 ⲏ ⲛⲧⲡ. ⲏ ⲛⲧⲣⲁϣⲥ *either
be agreed or be content*, Mor 28 238 they signed
deed ⲡⲣⲟⲥ ⲑⲉ ⲡⲧⲁⲩⲡⲱⲣⲝ, Ep 253 *S* ⲡϣⲁⲣ ⲉⲧⲛⲁ-
ⲡⲱⲣⲝ (for -ⲗϭ), J 100 62 as the steward shall
ⲡ., Lant 80 34 taught me (scribe) till I finished
book ⲕⲁⲧⲁ ⲡϣⲓ ⲡⲧⲁⲓϣ ⲡ. *so far as I could attain*
(in skill, *cf* ⲡ. ⲙⲛ- sim), Mor 663 *A* 142 (Pachôm)
ϯⲛⲁⲡⲱⲗⲝ ⲛϩⲉ ⲡⲓⲙ *will endeavour in all ways that
I may go to Lord* = Va ar 172 96 اعطي باي شيء كأن
انعطي الى الرب (*cf* MG 17 645), BAp 124 Pesenthius dying ⲁⲓϭⲱⲡ ⲉⲡ. *am about to be relieved i e
die* (*cf* MIE 2 419 *B* ⲁϥϫⲱⲛⲧ ⲛϫⲉ ⲡⲁⲥⲛⲟⲩ), Pcod
49 sim. *Cf* ⲡ. ⲉⲃⲟⲗ.

II tr *SBF*, *deliver, decide, settle* an affair : He 2
15 *SF* (*B* ⲧⲁⲗϭⲟ) ἀπαλλ.; 2 Kg 14 6 *S* (var ⲡⲟⲗ-
ϫⲟⲩ ⲉⲃ.) ἐξαιρεῖσθαι; ClPr 54 39 *S* disputes ⲛⲉⲩⲡ.
ⲙⲙⲟⲟⲩ by his counsel διαλύεσθαι; CaiEuch 431
B ⲫ. ⲙⲯⲩⲭⲏ ⲡⲓⲃⲉⲛ ⲉⲧⲣⲉϩϫⲱⲕ فرج; ShA
2 338 *S* Sodomites ⲁⲣⲁ ⲙⲡⲟⲩⲡⲟⲗϭⲟⲩ...ⲛϭⲓ ⲡ-
ⲕⲱϩⲧ?, Mor 32 35 *Sf* martyrs say World is naught
ⲁⲡⲟⲛ ϫⲉ ⲁⲡⲡⲁⲗϫϥ, ShMIF 23 71 *S* devil's power
ⲙⲡⲉϥϫⲟⲉⲓⲥ ⲡⲟⲗϭϥ ⲣⲱ ϩⲓⲡⲉⲥϯⲟⲥ ?, Mus 42 230 *S*
Christ died ⲛϥⲡⲗϭ ⲟⲩⲟⲛ ⲡⲓⲙ that dreaded death,
C 89 80 *B* this dispute ⲉⲑⲣⲓϥⲟⲗⲝϥ = MG 17 458
حكم على, Va ar 172 48 فصل (*cf* TT 155), Mus 40 43
S if sin found ⲛϥⲛⲁⲩ ⲉⲡⲉϣⲧⲁ ⲛϥⲙⲡⲟⲗϭϥ *non*

increpaverit delinquentem, J 38 28 *Sᵃ* ⲡⲣⲟⲥ ⲑⲉ ⲛⲧⲁⲡ-
ⲛⲟϭ ⲡⲣⲱⲙⲉ ⲡⲁⲗⲕⲏ ⲡⲓⲙⲟⲥ, CO 244 *S* ⲙⲡⲡⲱⲣⲝ
ϣⲁⲣ ⲡⲓⲙⲁⲕ ϩⲟⲗⲱⲥ, Hall 77 *S* ⲡϣⲁⲣ ⲁ̀ⲡⲟⲣⲭϥ,
(for -ⲗϭϥ), BM 1116 *S* ⲡⲡⲉϭⲁⲃⲁⲣ ⲡⲁⲣⲕⲉ ⲉⲙⲟⲛ
ϩⲁⲕⲁϩ, Ep 188 *S* ⲁⲧⲉⲧⲡⲡ. ⲙⲡⲣⲏⲕⲉ *who is ill
used.*   ϥⲟⲗϫ ⲣⲟ *B, expand mouth, yawn* (? for
ϥⲱⲣϫ): Va 57 126 *pray steadfastly* ⲛϥ. ⲣⲟ ⲁⲛ
χασμᾶν, DeV 2 56 ⲧⲉⲛϥ. ⲣⲟ (*sic l*) ⲧⲉⲡⲉⲗϫ ⲕⲁⲥ,
sim ϥⲉⲣϫ ⲣⲟ (=*S* ⲁϣ ⲥⲟⲗϥ, *v* ⲕⲱⲣϫ).

With following preposition.

—— ⲙⲛ- *SB* (twice), *agree, come to terms with,
settle* intr : Lu 12 58 *SB* (varr ϥ. only, ⲡⲟⲩⲧϥ)
ἀπαλλάσσεσθαι ἀπό ; EW 44 *B* ⲁⲩϥ. ⲡⲉⲙⲧⲉϥⲧⲓⲙⲏ
= Lewis *Horae Sem* 3 60 بينهما تقرب الثمن ; Mor 28
137 ⲧⲡⲡⲁⲡ. ⲡⲓⲙⲙⲉ *as to passage-money,* Gu 49 *king
to saint,* Let us make peace ⲛⲧⲁⲡ. ⲙⲡⲡⲁⲣϩⲏⲅⲉ (*cf
π. ⲉⲃⲟⲗ*) = BM 312 59 ⲡⲧⲁϫⲓⲛⲕⲉⲓ (διοικεῖν) ⲡⲡⲉ-
ϩⲣⲏⲅⲉ *of kingdom,* CO 239 ⲡⲧⲉⲧⲡⲡ. ⲡⲓⲙⲙⲁϥ *as to
rent,* Ryl 283 ⲁⲓϣ ⲡ. ⲙⲡⲡⲁⲡⲟⲕⲣⲓⲥⲓⲥ *cannot settle
the business,* Tor 31 ⲁⲩⲡ. ⲙⲡⲡⲉϩⲱⲃ ⲡⲁⲓ, PBu 151
ask him to π. ⲙⲡϥⲓⲗⲏⲙⲱⲡ ϩⲁⲡⲏⲓ. *Cf* ἀπαλλ.
πρός *eg* PMon 23, PLon 5 168.   tr *S* : BMar
188 *to sailor* ⲡⲉⲗⲕ ⲧⲣⲉⲙⲉ ⲡⲓⲙⲙⲁⲛ, PBu 41 *imprisoned* ϣⲁⲡⲧⲁⲡ. ⲡⲁⲣⲱⲃ ⲡⲓⲙⲙⲁϥ, ViNatBibl ostr
ϣⲁⲛϯⲡⲱⲣⲕ ⲡⲁⲣⲱⲃ ⲡⲏⲙⲉⲕ, PLille(Sottas) l 69 ⲁⲕ-
ⲡⲟⲗϭⲡ ⲙⲡⲡⲣⲓⲁⲡⲧⲓⲡⲟⲟⲩ.

—— ⲡ- dat *SB* : CaiEuch 430 *B give them grace
in presence of rulers* ϥ. ⲡⲱⲟⲩ فرج عنهم *relieve them,*
BM 1155 *S* ⲉϣⲱⲡⲉ ⲙⲉⲕⲛⲓϣ ⲡⲱⲗⲉϫ ⲡⲓⲓⲡⲧⲥ *if canst
not manage to bring it.*

—— ⲡⲧⲡ- *S* : ShA 1 58 *let none know lest they
hear* ⲡⲧⲡⲧⲙⲉϣ ⲡ. ⲡⲧⲟⲟⲧⲟⲩ & *we be not able to
satisfy them.*

With following adverb.

—— ⲉⲃⲟⲗ *SB, reach conclusion, make an end,
a* intr : Hall 96 *S* ϣⲁⲡⲧⲁⲡ. ⲉⲃ. ⲉⲓⲣ ϩⲱⲃ ⲡⲡⲁⲉⲣⲏⲩ,
BMOr 9525 8 vo *S send us tow* (σίππιον) ⲡⲥⲉⲣⲓⲧⲟⲩ
(*l* ? ⲣⲓⲥⲧⲟⲩ) ⲙⲡⲁⲧⲉϥⲱϩ (*l* ? ϩⲱⲃ) ⲡ. ⲉⲃ., AM 41 *B
martyr tortured* ϩⲓⲥⲁ ⲡⲧⲉϥϥ. ⲉⲃ. ⲡⲧⲉϥⲙⲟⲩ (? for
ϥⲱⲣϫ), RNC 82 *S* ⲁⲡⲉϥⲧⲟⲟⲩ ⲡⲕ[ⲟⲟϩ ?] ⲡⲧϣⲏⲛⲉ
ⲡ. ⲉⲃ. *came apart* (*cf* π. ⲉⲃ. ⲡ-) & *fire came forth,*
K 46 *B* ϥⲏ ⲉⲧϥ. ⲉⲃ. فرج *dissipater* of cares, *con-
soler* ;   c ⲉⲃ. ⲉ- *S, be freed from* : Bor 252 303
ϫⲉⲕⲁⲥ ⲡⲡⲁⲡ. ⲉⲃ. ⲉⲧⲕⲟⲗⲁⲥⲓⲥ ;   c ⲉⲃ. ⲙⲡ- *S, come
to agreement with* : BM 1059 ⲁⲓⲡ. ⲉⲃ. ⲡⲉⲙⲁⲕ...
ϩⲁⲡⲉⲓⲣⲱϥ, ST 412 ⲁⲡⲡ. ⲉⲃ. ⲙⲡⲡⲉⲡⲉⲣⲏⲩ ϩⲁϩⲱⲃ
ⲛⲓⲙ ;   c ⲉⲃ. ⲡ- *S, be freed from, transferred* : GFr
438 *that ye should* ⲡ. ⲉⲃ. ⲡⲧⲗⲟⲓϭⲉ (*l* -ϩⲉ) *of sin*
ἀπαλλάσσεσθαι, Job 36 28 (*B* ϣⲟϥⲧ ⲉⲃ. ϩⲁ-) διαλλ. ;
ShA 1 302 *walls crack* & ⲡ. ⲉⲃ. ⲡⲡⲉϩⲉⲣⲏⲩ ϫⲉⲥⲉ-
ⲙⲏⲣ ⲁⲛ, R 1 4 71 *thrown to beasts* & ⲡϥⲡⲁⲡⲱⲣϭ
(*prob sic*) ⲉⲃ. ⲙⲡⲉϥϣⲱⲡϩ, Aeg 22 ⲁⲩϩⲱⲛ ⲉϩⲟⲩⲡ ⲉⲡ.
ⲉⲃ. ⲙⲡⲓⲃⲓⲟⲥ (*cf* π. BAp 124 *above*);   c ⲉⲃ. ϩⲁ- *B,*

be freed from : Va 68 180 ⲁϥϥ. ⲉⲃ. ϩⲁⲡⲧⲁⲕⲟ ;   c ⲉⲃ.
ϩⲡ-, ϫⲉⲛ- *SB, be transferred, relieved from* : Va 57
128 *B I seek not* ⲉϥ. ⲉⲃ. ⲡϩⲏⲧⲟⲩ (*sc troubles*)
ἀπαλλ., ShMIF 23 91 *S sins* ⲙⲡⲡ. ⲉⲃ. ⲡϩⲏⲧⲟⲩ,
BM 985 *S* ⲙⲡⲁⲧⲉϥⲡ. ⲉⲃ. ϩⲙⲡⲉⲓⲕⲟⲥⲙⲟⲥ.

b tr *SB, settle, make an end of* : ShA 2 350 *S whoso
would get things* ⲙⲡⲟⲩⲡⲗϭ ⲡⲉⲩϣⲁⲁⲣ ⲉⲃ. *without
settling price* (*cf* ⲡⲱⲣϫ I), Mor 32 17 *S take them
to prison* ϣⲁⲡⲧⲁⲡⲉⲗϭ ⲡⲧⲉⲗⲉⲙⲏ (Ptolemy) ⲉⲃ.,
BMar 44 *S to executioner* ⲡⲟⲗϭⲧ ⲉⲃ. ⲧⲁⲭⲏ (*cf
ⲡⲱⲣϫ ⲉⲃ. tr*);   *take off, out* : Dan 4 11 *B* ἐκτίλλειν (*of branches*), KKS 484 *S Abraham about
to slay Isaac* ⲉϥⲟⲩⲱϣ ⲉⲡⲟⲗϭϥ ⲉⲃ.   c ⲉⲃ. ⲉ- *S* :
Ryl 285 ⲡⲥⲟⲩⲡⲟⲗϭⲟⲩ ⲉⲃ. ⲉⲡⲉⲩϫⲓⲁⲅⲣⲁϥⲟⲛ.   c ⲉⲃ.
ⲙⲡ- *S, bring to terms with* : J 36 23 *magistrates have*
ⲡⲟⲗϭⲧ ⲉⲃ. ⲙⲡⲡⲉⲡⲉⲣⲏⲩ ϩⲁⲧⲉⲓⲕⲗⲏⲣⲟⲡⲟⲙⲓⲁ.   c ⲉⲃ.
ⲡ- *S, relieve from, satisfy* : Miss 8 141 ⲡⲧⲁⲡⲟⲗⲉ-
ⲉϭⲕ (*cf* ST 172) ⲉⲃ. ⲡⲧⲙⲧⲣⲉϥϫⲓ ⲗⲁ ἀπαλλ. gen,
ShMiss 4 279 *delay not* ⲉⲡⲗϭ ⲡⲟⲩⲁ ⲡⲟⲩⲁ ⲉⲃ. ⲡ-
ⲡⲉⲡⲧⲁϥⲉⲓ ⲉⲧⲃⲏⲏⲧⲟⲩ, Wess 18 108 *miracles could
not* ⲡⲉⲗϭ ⲡⲉⲧⲙⲙⲁⲩ ⲉⲃ. ⲡⲛⲕⲟⲗⲁⲥⲓⲥ (*cf* Mt 7 22),
ST 234 ⲁⲩⲡⲟⲗⲕⲧ ⲉⲃ. ⲙⲡⲉⲕϩⲟⲗⲟⲕ/ *have paid me
thy solidus.*   c ⲉⲃ. ϩⲁ- *B, deliver from* : TEuch 1
464 ⲉⲁⲕϥⲟⲗϫⲉⲡ ⲉⲃ. ϩⲁⲡϫⲓⲡⲱⲛϩ *of beasts.*   c ⲉⲃ.
ϩⲡ- *S sim* : P 131⁶ 50 ⲡⲟⲗϭⲥ (*sc soul*) ⲉⲃ. ϩⲙⲡϣⲓⲡⲉ.

—— *B* ⲡⲛ m, *ease, liberty* : K 100 ⲡⲓϥ. انسياط.

ⲡⲗⲟϭ *S* ⲡⲛ m, *portion, part* : Mor 19 51 *smote
him* ⲡⲥⲉⲁⲁⲩ ⲙⲡ. ⲥⲛⲁⲩ = *ib* 18 43 *S* ⲙⲉⲣⲟⲥ ⲥⲛⲁⲩ =
Wess 18 60 *S* ⲧⲉⲭⲏ (? πτυχή) ⲥⲡⲧⲉ.

ⲡⲟⲗϭⲥ *S* ⲡⲛ as pl, *clod, lump* : Job 7 5 ϩⲉⲛⲛ.
ⲡⲕⲁϩ (*B diff*) βῶλαξ (? *imitates Gk word*).

ⲡⲗϭⲉ, ⲡⲉⲗ., ⲡⲣϭⲉ, ⲡⲉⲗϫⲉ *S*, ϥⲉⲗϫⲓ *B* ⲡⲛ m
(f once) *split, torn cloth, rag* : Is 64 6 *B* (*S* ⲧⲟⲉⲓⲥ)
ῥάκος, Va 57 194 *B* ⲉⲑⲙⲏⲣ ⲡⲡⲓϥ. ῥάκιον ; Pro 23
21 *B* (DeV 1 75, *SA* do) διερρηγμένον, Tri 389 *S*,
P 55 14 *B* (خرق) ; P 131³ 83 *S* ⲉϥⲡⲟⲩϫⲉ ⲡⲟⲩⲡ. *on
his sores* = Va 61 93 *B* ϥⲉⲗϫ (*sic*) ⲡϩⲃⲱⲥ, JA '05
1 431 *S wearing* ϩⲉⲛⲡ. (ⲉ)ⲧⲗⲁⲁⲙ, Faras 3 lxviii 16
S ⲁϥϯ ⲧⲏⲣϭⲉ ϩⲡⲓⲱϣ (*l* ϩⲓⲱⲱϣ).   ⲡ. ⲡⲧⲟⲉⲓⲥ *S*, ϥ.
ⲡⲧⲱⲓⲥ *B, rag of cloth* : Jer 45 11 *B* ῥάκος παλαιόν,
ShIF 153 *S* ϩⲉⲛⲡ. ⲡⲧ. *as pads below ropes* (*cf* Jer
l c) opp ⲧⲟⲉⲓⲥ ⲡϣⲁⲓ, Miss 4 828 *S* ϩ(ⲉⲛ)ⲡⲉⲗϫⲉ ⲡⲧ.
& *other wretched chattels,* Va 61 95 *B* ϩⲁⲡϥ. ⲡⲧ. =
P 131³ 84 *S* ⲡ. ⲡϩⲟⲓⲧⲉ.   ⲡ. ⲡϩⲃⲟⲥ *B, ragged garment* : Mt 9 16 (*S* ϣⲧⲏⲡ ⲙⲡ.) ἱμάτιον παλ. ; Va 66
296 ῥ. διεσπασμένον.   ⲡ. ⲡϩⲟⲓⲧⲉ *S sim* : BMar
196 ἱμάτιον διερρηγός.   As adj *SB, worn, old* :
Mk 2 21 *S* (*B* ϩⲃⲱⲥ ⲡⲁⲡⲁⲥ) παλαιός, Wess 11 165 *S*
ϩⲉⲛϣⲧⲏⲡ ⲙⲡ. ⲉⲅⲟⲡⲧⲟⲉⲓⲥ παλ. πολύρραφα ; BMar
202 *S* ϩⲟⲓⲧⲉ ⲙⲡ. ἱⲙ. ῥακώδες ; RChamp 541 *S limp
as* ⲟⲩⲧⲟⲉⲓⲥ ⲡⲡ., Va 58 159 *B* ⲟⲩϩⲃⲟⲥ ⲡϥ.

ⲣ ⲡ., ϥ. *SB, become, be ragged, old* : Jos 9 19 *S*,
Is 50 9 *S* (*B* ⲉⲣ ⲁⲡⲁⲥ), He 1 11 *S* (*B* do, *F* ⲉⲗ ⲁⲥ),

Mor 37 141 *S* given me new, lo ⲁϥⲣ ⲡ. παλαιοῦσθαι; Mor 31 210 *S* shoes ⲡⲁⲥⲱⲗⲡ ⲡⲥⲉⲉⲣ ⲡ., EW
160 *B* garments ⲁⲩϭⲓϯ ⲁⲩⲉⲣ ⲫ.   ⲣ ⲡ. ⲡ. *S, become
rags*: ShA 1 108 veils ⲛⲧⲁⲩⲣ ⲁⲥ ⲛ ⲡ. ⲡ., ShMiss
4 279 girdle ⲉⲧⲟ ⲙⲡ. ⲡ.

Prob not in *F* place-names ⲡⲉⲗϭⲉⲛⲥⲓ (*cf Περ-
κεῆσις* PLond 2 227), ⲡⲉⲗϭⲉⲥⲱⲕ BM 692, CMSS
67, ⲡⲉⲣⲕⲉⲑⲁⲗⲩⲧ Lant 5 25 (*cf Περκεθαυτ* Wess 10
165).

ⲡⲁⲙⲛϩⲁⲧⲡ, ⲫⲁⲙⲉⲛⲁⲧⲡ   *v* ⲡⲁⲣⲙϩⲟⲧⲡ.

ⲡⲟⲙⲡⲉⲙ *S* vb intr, *swell*: BMar 56 woman's
breasts ⲁⲩⲱⲓϥⲉ (*l* ⲱⲁϥⲉ) ⲁⲩⲡ. ⲉⲙⲁⲁⲧⲉ.   But *cf* P
129¹⁵ 22 *S* sim ⲁⲅⲡⲟⲙⲡⲉⲩⲉ ⲉⲙⲁⲧⲉ (*v* ByzZ 30 327)
& prob *l* so here.

ⲡⲉⲛ *S   v* ⲡⲓⲡ.

ⲡⲓⲡ *SA*, **ⲫⲓⲛ** *B* nn m, *mouse*: Lev 11 29 *SB*,
Is 66 17 *SB* μῦς; P 44 56 *S* ⲡⲡ.· ποντικός· فار; C
89 214 *B* ⲛⲓⲫ. eat lamp wick, Miss 4 700 *S* cast
forth ⲡⲉⲓⲡ. ⲉⲱⲁⲩⲱⲱⲡⲉ ϩⲙⲡⲏⲧ, BMis 519 *S*
neither ⲡ. nor ⲡⲏⲣⲱ in his fields, DeV 2 227 *B*
ⲕⲁⲗⲏ & ⲫ. are enemies.   ⲡⲟϭ ⲙⲡ. *S, rat*(?): Glos
261 σατυρίσκος (*sic l*)· ⲡϩⲁ ⲡⲟϭ ⲡⲡ.; ⲉⲟⲩⲉⲛ ⲙⲡ.
A, ⲁⲟⲩⲁⲡ ⲙⲫ. *B, mouse-coloured*: Zech 1 8 ψαρός; ⲙⲁⲁⲭⲉ ⲙⲡⲡ. *S, myosotis*: P 44 83 ودن الفار,
BKU 1 9 sim.   ⲙⲟⲟⲩ ⲡⲡⲉⲛ ⲉⲧⲛⲡⲱⲱ, *water of split*
(& cooked) *mouse* (so Chassinat citing Dioscorides)
PMéd 297 *S, cf ib* 275 ⲙⲟⲩⲛⲉⲧⲛⲡⲱⲱ.   *V* also
ⲕⲉⲗⲕⲉⲃ.   As name: *Ππῖν* (Preisigke).

ⲡⲱⲛ, ⲡⲱⲱⲛ, ⲡⲱⲱⲡⲉ *S*, **ⲡⲟⲩⲛⲉ** *A*, **ⲫⲱⲛ** *B*, ⲡⲓⲡ-,
ⲡⲉⲓⲡ-, ⲡⲉⲉⲛ-, ⲡⲉⲡⲉ- *S*, **ⲫⲉⲛ-** *B*, ⲡⲟⲡ⳹ *S*, ⲡⲁⲡ⳹ *SF*,
ⲫⲟⲡ⳹ *B*, ⲡⲏⲡ† *S*, ⲫⲏⲡ† *B* vb **I** intr, *be poured, flow*:
Ps 21 13 *S* (*B* ⲫ. ⲉⲃ.) ἐκχέεσθαι, Lam 3 54 *B* ὑ-
περχ.   ⲥ ⲉⲃⲟⲗ *SB, be poured out*: Deu 19 10 *S*
(*B* tr), Ps 72 2 *B* (*S* ⲭⲱⲱⲣⲉ ⲉⲃ.), Mt 9 17 *S* (var
ⲡⲱⲱⲡⲉ) *B*, Ac 1 18 *S* (ⲡⲱⲱⲡⲉ) *B* ἐκχ., Lam 4 21
B ἀποχ., Job 21 24 *S*†*B* διαχ., Pro 5 16 *S* (*A* ⲡⲱⲣⲧ
ⲁⲃ., *B* ⲫⲟⲡⲡⲉⲛ ⲉⲃ.) ὑπερεκχ.; Ps 136 7 *B* (*S* diff),
C 89 60 *B* ἐκκενοῦν; Mor 18 195 *S* his inwards
ⲁⲩⲡ. ⲉⲃ. (var ⲡⲱⲱⲡⲉ) γυμνοῦσθαι;   ⲥ ⲉⲃ. ⲉⲭⲉⲛ-
B, flow out upon: Joel 2 28 (*SA* ⲡⲱⲣⲧ), Ac 10 45
ⲉϩⲣ. ⲉⲭ. (*S* do ⲉϩⲣ. ⲉⲭ.) ἐκχ. ἐπί;   ⲥ ⲉⲃ. ϩⲓⲭⲛ-
SB, meaning same: Hos 4 2 *B* (*SA* ⲡⲱⲣⲱ ⲉⲃ. ϩ.)
χ. ἐπί; 2 Kg 14 14 *S* (var ⲉⲭⲛ-) καταφέρεσθαι ἐπί;
C 86 205 *B* his inwards ⲫ. ⲉⲃ. ϩ. ⲡⲕⲁϩⲓ;   ⲥ ⲉⲃ.
ϩⲛ- *SB, a flow into*: Lev 13 22 *S* (var ⲡⲱⲣⲱ, *B*
ⲭⲱⲣ) διαχ. ἐν, Lam 4 1 *B* ἐκχ. ἐπί, Ro 5 5 ϩⲣ. ϭ.
B (*S* ⲡⲱⲣⲧ ⲉⲃ. ϩⲛ-) ἐκχ. ἐν;   *b flow out from B*:
Ac 2 17 (*S* do ⲡ-) ἐκχ. ἀπό; C 41 63 much bread ⲫ.
ⲉⲃ. ⲡϩⲏⲧϥ (*sc* cupboard);   ⲥ ⲉⲃ. ϩⲁ- *SA, overflow by reason of, with*: Joel 2 24 (*B* ⲫⲟⲡ.) ὑπερχ.
gen;   ⲥ ⲉⲃ. ϩⲓ- *S, flow upon, in*: Ps 44 2 (*B* ⲭⲱⲱ
ⲉⲃ. ϩⲉⲛ-) ἐκχ. ἐν.

II tr, *pour out*: Lev 4 18 *S* (*B* ⲭⲱⲱ), Ac 2 33 *B*
(*S* ⲡⲱⲣⲧ) ἐκχέειν; AM 87 *B* ⲉⲑⲣⲟⲩⲫⲉⲛ (*sic l*) ⲡⲁ-
ⲥⲡⲟϥ, C 86 159 *B* ⲡⲓⲫⲉⲛ ⲥⲛⲟϥ;   ⲫⲉⲛ ⲣⲁⲥⲟⲩⲓ
v ⲡⲱⲱⲣⲉ *a*.

With following preposition.

ⲥ ⲉ- *B, pour into*: Ez 24 3 (*S* do) ἐγχέειν εἰς, C
43 120 boiling pitch ⲁϥⲑⲣⲟⲩⲫⲟⲡⲟⲩ ⲉϩⲣⲏⲓ ⲉⲧⲉϥⲱ-
ⲃⲱⲃⲓ, or *over*: *ib* 30 23 λικμᾶν εἰς;   ⲥ ⲉⲭⲉⲛ- *BF*,
p. upon: Ez 9 8 ἐκχ. ἐπί, Mt 26 7 *F* (*S* do, *B* ⲭ.)
καταχ.; C 86 81 ⲁϥⲫⲟⲡϥ (var ⲫⲟⲡϥ) ⲉⲭⲉⲛⲟⲩⲁⲓ;
Ez 43 18 ⲉϩ. ⲉⲭ. προσχ.; DeV 1 15 ⲉⲑⲣⲓⲫ. ⲙⲡⲁ-
ⲥⲛⲟϥ ⲉϩ. ⲉⲭⲉⲛⲧⲉϥϫⲓⲁⲕⲟⲛⲓⲁ;   ⲥ ϩⲓⲭⲉⲛ- *B*, meaning same: Job 16 14 (*S* do) ἐκχ. εἰς, Ez 22 22 (var
ⲭ.) ἐκχ. ἐπί; C 86 205 ⲡⲥⲉⲫⲟⲡⲟⲩ ϩ. ⲡⲉϥⲉⲣϭⲟⲧ;   ⲥ
ϩⲉⲛ- *B, p. into, over*: Ez 29 12 (*S* ⲱⲱⲱ ⲉ-) λικμᾶν
εἰς (*cf above*); AM 154 ⲡⲥⲉⲫⲟⲡⲟⲩ ⲉϩⲣ. ϩⲉⲛⲣⲱⲟⲩ.

With following adverb.

ⲥ ⲉⲃⲟⲗ *SB, p. out, away*: Ge 9 6 *B* (*S* ⲡⲱⲣⲧ ⲉⲃ.),
Ps 13 4 *SB*, Is 57 6 *S* (var ⲡⲱⲱⲡⲉ ⲉⲃ., *B* ⲟⲩⲱⲧⲉⲡ),
Zeph 1 17 *B* (*SA* do) ἐκχ., Job 21 24† *S* (*B* ⲫⲟⲡ-
ⲡⲉⲛ) διαχ., Lu 6 38† *S* (*B* do) ὑπερχ.; Cant 1 2†
SB (TEuch 1 332) ἐκκενοῦν; Ez 22 13 *SB* effundi;
Ps 143 13† *S* (*B* ⲃⲉⲃⲓ ⲉⲃ.) ἐξερεύγεσθαι; Aeg 15 *B*
(*S* do) ⲉⲓⲫ. ⲡⲛⲁⲉⲣⲙⲱⲟⲩⲓ ⲉⲃ., ST 261 *S* corn ⲛⲧⲃⲱⲕ...ⲛⲧⲛⲁⲡⲟⲩ ⲉⲃ.   ⲫⲉⲛ ⲙⲱⲟⲩ ⲉⲃ. *B, pour
out water, urinate*: MG 25 243 went forth ⲉⲫ. ⲙ.
ⲉⲃ. εἰς τὴν χρείαν αὐτοῦ, *ib* 156 pots ⲛⲫ. ⲙ. ⲉⲃ.,
HL 112 ⲡⲉϥⲙⲁ (*sic*) ⲛⲫ. ⲙ. ⲉⲃ. ⲡⲣⲉⲙⲥⲓ *anus,
rectum* (?)   ⲁⲧⲫⲉⲛ- ⲉⲃ. *B adj, without shedding*:
Dif 1 84 martyr ⲛⲁⲧⲫ. ⲥⲛⲟϥ ⲉⲃ.   ⲥ ⲉⲃ. ⲉⲭⲛ- *SB*,
pour out upon: Deu 12 16 *SB* ἐκχ. ἐπί, Mt 26 28
B (*S* ⲡⲱⲣⲧ) ἐκχ. ὑπέρ; TEuch 1 5 *B* ⲉⲕⲫ. ⲉⲃ. ⲡ-
ⲡⲉⲕⲭⲱⲣⲉⲁ ⲉⲭⲉⲛⲡⲉⲕⲉⲃⲓⲁⲓⲕ, C 43 214 *B* ⲡⲧⲁⲫ.
blood ⲉⲃ. ⲉϩⲣⲏⲓ ⲉⲭⲉⲛⲡⲉϥⲣⲁⲛ;   ⲥ ⲉⲃ. ϩⲓⲭⲉⲛ- *B*,
meaning same: Mt 23 35 (*S* do) ἐκχύνειν ἐπί; AM
195 ⲁϥⲫ. ⲙⲡⲓⲁⲫⲟⲧ ⲉⲃ. ϩ. ⲡⲕⲁϩⲓ;   ⲥ ⲉⲃ. ϩⲁ-, ϩⲁ-
SB, p. out for: PS 368 *S* blood ⲉⲧⲟⲩⲛⲁⲡⲟⲡϥ ⲉⲃ.
ϩⲁⲣⲱⲧⲛ, BSM 95 *B* sim ϩⲁⲣⲟⲛ;   ⲥ ⲉⲃ. ϩⲉⲛ- *B*,
p. forth into: Va 57 278 words of mouth ⲉϥⲫ.† ⲉⲃ.
ϩⲉⲛⲡⲓⲁⲏⲣ τῷ ἀέρι διαχεῖται; Ez 30 26 λικμᾶν εἰς
(*cf* ⲫ. ϩⲉⲛ-).   As nn m *SBF, outflow*: Va 63
88 *B* ⲛⲫ. ⲉⲃ. of blood ἔκχυσις, He 11 28 *SF* (both
ⲡⲱⲱⲡⲉ) *B* πρόσχ.; Lev 15 13 *B* ῥύσις.   *V* ⲫⲟⲡⲡⲉⲛ.

ⲡⲁⲱⲛⲉ, -ⲛⲓ (BM 1031, J 21 7, Saq 31), -ⲟⲩⲛⲓ
(Tor 30), -ⲏⲡⲉ (COAd 21), ⲡⲟⲟⲡⲉ (Z 565, BMOr
6954 55) *S*, **ⲡⲁⲱⲡⲓ** *BF* (Kr 63) nn, name of 10th
month, Gk *Παῦνι*, Ar بؤونة.

ⲡⲟⲛⲓ *B   v* ⲡⲟⲛⲓ.

ⲡⲟⲩⲛⲓ *B* nn f, *anus*: Bodl 325 156 among
man's parts ϯⲡ. جمر (*cf* Tatt 857).

ⲡⲱⲱⲛⲉ, ⲡⲱⲛⲉ *SA²*, **ⲡⲟⲩⲛⲉ** *A*, **ⲡⲱⲛⲓ** *Sᶠ*, **ⲡⲱⲱⲡⲓ**,

пλλпє *F*, пєєпє-, пєпє-, пппє- (Ac 19 26) *S*, поу-
пє- *A*, папє- *F*, поопє⸗, пєп⸗ (Mor 53) *S*, пλλпє⸗
SAF, папє⸗ *AA²*, поопє† *S*, p c папє- *S* vb **I** intr,
change, turn, cf ϥωпϧ *B* (Sethe *Verbum* 1 359) : Lev
13 20 *S* (*B* оуωтєꙟ, cf ib 3 ϣⲓꙟє), Si 18 25 *S* μετα-
βάλλεσθαι ; 1 Kg 10 6 *S* στρέφεσθαι, Ryl 99 *S* words
єуп.† = Ac 20 30 ϭооⲙє διαστ., 1 Kg 14 21 *S*
ἐπιστ., Hos 7 8 *SA* (*B* ϭⲓ) μεταστ.; R 1 2 63 *S*
ϣαϣп. αυω ϣαϥϣⲓꙟє τρεπτός, ἀλλοιωτός ; Is 54
10 *S* (*B* оу.), He 6 17 *SF* (*B* do) μετατίθεσθαι ;
Mor 37 67 *S* сєсꙟтωт єп. μετασχηματίζεσθαι ; ClPr
54 45 *S* lake асп. & became dry μετασκευάζεσθαι ;
Z 336 *S* αуп. ἐναλλάσσεσθαι ; ShA 2 24 *S* єрє-
пєϥϧо п.† or reversed, ShIF 298 *S* αϥп. тнрϥ &
became demon, ShBor 246 58 *S* єϥп.† оп ϧнтпⲓс-
тⲓс, Aeg 11 *S* (*B* ϥωпϧ), Br 256 *S* truth ⲙєсп.,
Kr 164 *F* verdict ппєϥϣ пλλпє, Mor 40 25 *S*
dragon єϥп.† ⲛαϧραϥ = ib 39 34 *S* сⲭнⲙατⲓзє.

II tr *SF*(Kr), *turn* : 4 Kg 14 25 ἀφιστάναι, Ac
13 22 (*B* оуωтєꙟ єꙟ.) μεθεστ. ; 1 Kg 31 9 ἀποστρέφειν, Eccl 7 14 (*F* кωϯ) διαστ.; Ge 48 14 (*B* ϣⲓꙟϯ)
ἐναλλάσσειν ; 1 Cor 15 58 neg (*B* ατκⲓⲙ) ἀμετα-
κίνητος ; BMar 121 αупєпє пєϥран μετονομάζε-
σθαι ; BM 177 17 able to пєєпє пєꙟнϫє μετα-
πλάσσειν ; Mor 17 112 пτєроуп. ⲙпⲣнтєⲙωп
transfer διαδέχεσθαι ; PS 32 птⲁⲓп. птєуϭⲓⲙⲙо-
оϣє, ShA 2 52 ⲙпⲣп. ⲙпєтпхω ⲙⲙоϥ, Miss 8
187 who setteth up kings & єϥп. ⲙⲙооу, BMar
49 tortures could not п. ⲙпєкλотⲓсⲙос, Mor 48
41 devil αϥп. ⲙпєϥϧнт = C 43 120 *B* сωрєⲙ, Mor
19 4 †папєєпє пϣαϫє *alter, adapt* = Miss 4 93 *B*
хⲓⲛϥєпϧ, BMar 189 monk understood that John
wished єпоопϥ *to change* (give other meaning to
his words ?), Kr 36 *F* пєтпєпапє пєⲓхωⲙє (sc
deed) shall pay fine, Bor 248 10 I composed discourse αⲓпоопϥ *copied* & sent it you (= Brooks
Sel Lett Severus 1 207 ‎ﻭﺍﺳـﻠـﻪٮ‎), Mor 53 70
Athanasius & Nicene canons єαϥпєпоу *translated*
(?) *them* for Tabennesiotes, My 132 Hebrew scriptures птαуєр пкєпωпоу птαспє of Greeks ; ϥєп
расоуⲓ *v* пωωрє **a**.   p c *S*, *perverter* (?) : Cai
42573 1 title of recipe оупапєрωⲙє ϧⲓ (*ie* ϧп-)
пєϥϧωꙟ.

With following preposition.

—— є- *S* intr, *be changed to, turn toward* : Lev
13 13 (*B* оу.) μεταβάλ. acc, Miss 8 94 *μ. εἰς* ; Aeg
268 Moses' rod єпταϥп. єуроꙟ ἐμψυχοῦσθαι *εἰς* ;
ShA 2 141 wool п. єϥнпє псⲙот паϧαп, Miss 4
537 if drowsy ϣαуп. єкєϧωꙟ пϭⲓх = C 89 10 *B*
оу ;   iterated : JKP 2 26 *Sf* pillar borne through
air єϥп. п. єпⲓса ⲙє(п)паⲓ ; єϧоуп є- : Mor 17
11 аⲓп. єϧ. єуϧⲓнꙟ τρέπειν *εἰς* ; ib 37 115 heretics
п. єϧ. to godliness μεταβολὴ *εἰς* ; ShWess 9 171

ψωρα…єасп. єϧ. єрооу, R 1 4 62 Epicureans say
soul ϣасп. єϧ. to asses, apes ;   єϧраⲓ є-, *cross
over to* : 1 Kg 5 8 μετέρχεσθαι *εἰς* ; BHom 6 let us
п. єϧ. єтпоλⲓс in heavens ;   as nn : 3 Kg 8 47
μετοικία ;   tr *SA²* (AP), *turn to, transfer* : BMar
200 єсп. ⲙⲙоϥ (sc book) єпєⲓса ⲙппаⲓ ἀναστρέφ.
εἰς, Am 6 13 (BMOr 8810 493, *B* ϥωпϧ) єкот., *ib*
8 10 (*B* do) μεταστ. *εἰς* ; R 1 1 11 these words п-
сєпоопоу єкєхωⲙє *copy*, BHom 33 пϥп. ⲙпрнт
єуоупоу μεταβάλ. ; Est E 14 μετάγειν *εἰς* ; Jude 4
(*B* ϣⲓꙟϯ), AP 16 *A²* μετατⲓθ. *εἰς* ; PS 323 псєпоо-
пєϥ єусωⲙа паⲓкаⲓос, ShA 1 264 ппаєϣ пєєпє-
тнуп ап єєр ϧєλλⲓп, ShClPr 23 = P 130⁴ 131
words written on πίνακες αппоопоу єпєⲓхартⲓс,
Lant 91 when птапп. пⲓϣахє in old book єпєⲓ-
хωⲙє written afresh, Mun 115 sim (*transcribing
from papyrus to parchment*) ;   єϧоуп є- : Col
1 13 (*B* оуωтєꙟ) μεθⲓст. *εἰς*, Bor 260 99 пϥпоопоу
єϧ. *from* bestiality єпхωп пλотⲓкоп ;   єϧраⲓ
є- : Ac 7 16 (*BF* do) μετατⲓθ. *εἰς* ; P 131⁶ 55 Israelites аϥпооу єϧ. єтꙟаꙟуλωп ; єпєснт є- :
ShBor 247 101 plucketh out eyes пϥпоопоу єп.
єпкаϧ.

—— єхп- *S*, *turn over upon* intr : R 1 3 22 Diocletian's throne п. єхωϥ (cf ib 23 єптауп. ⲙпаꙟр.
ϧароⲓ & C 86 359 *B* αуϥωпх ⲙпⲓꙟр. ꙥароϥ) ;   tr :
Mor 25 81 prisoners in stocks пⲥпоопоу єхⲙпса
єтпаϯ ⲙтоп паϥ ϧⲙпϣє.

—— п- *S*, *move from* : ShR 2 3 67 thy riches
єкп. ⲙⲙооу ⲙⲙа єⲙа ; or *to* : BIF 13 106 пϥп.
ппєⲓтооу…пⲣєпλⲓⲙⲓн = MG 25 290 *B* ϥωпϧ є-.

—— пса- *S*, *turn continuously* : BKU 1 21 45
put thing (to be dyed) in hot water пкп. псωϥ lest
it burn, cf ib 31 sim пкп. пλаϥ.

—— птп- *S*, *turn from* : Gal 1 6 (*B* саꙟоλ
п-) μετατⲓθ. *ἀπό* ; ShBMOr 8810 477 to nun тєп.
птⲙпєптаϥταⲙє, Mus NS 12 13 let not пϥωꙟ
п. птоотєп *be perverted for us*.

—— ϧа- *S* intr, *move from, be displaced* : P 129¹⁶
3 shall go to bath птєоупλаϧ п. ϧароϥ & shall
die ; *v* also tr.   tr, *overset* : Mor 48 106 аϥп.
ⲙпєθропос ϧароϥ (sc magistrate = C 43 151 *B*
ϥωпх ꙥа-), Mor 23 97 at Satan's revolt God bade
cherub п. ⲙпєωп (αἰών) ϧароϥ…& thus τάξεις of
angels п. ϧапєϧєрну *were upset*, disorganized.

—— ϧⲓ- *S*, *move from, transcribe* (?) : RE 14 28
when ye have finished єтєтпп. ϧⲓпλакⲓхас send
it (story of Eustathius Placidus ? *v* BMar 102), Lant
86 dwelt there ⲙппсатрап. ϧⲓпнⲓ (of) Callinicus.

—— ϧп- *S* intr, *be changed from* : ShP 130⁵ 38
ⲙпоуп. ϧⲙпєупєтⲓапоуϥ (cf below єꙟ. ϧп-), R 2
1 10 Mary asks птапаϧо п. ϧⲙпаϧап of virginity?,
ShA 2 260 єтⲙтрєуп. ϧпоуϧωꙟ єϧωꙟ, Br 88 аⲓп.

ϩⲣⲁⲓ ⲛϩⲏⲧϥ (*sc* a thought), *cf ib* 93 ⲡ. ⲉⲃⲟⲗ;   tr, *move from*: Miss 4 537 ⲛⲥⲉⲡ. ⲙⲡϣⲱ...ϩⲛϩⲉⲛⲙⲁ ⲉϩⲉⲛⲙⲁ = C 89 10 *B* ⲟⲩⲱⲧⲉⲃ ⲙⲉⲧⲁⲫⲉⲣ. ἀπό, ShC 73 164 whom they ⲛⲟⲟⲡⲟⲩ ϩⲛⲟⲩⲏⲓ ⲉⲩⲏⲓ, R 2 4 81 cleric expelled or [ⲛ]ⲥⲉⲡⲟⲟⲡⲉϥ [ϩ]ⲛⲧⲉϥⲧⲁϫⲓⲥ (*v* PSBA 26 58).

With following adverb.

—— ⲉⲃⲟⲗ *SA²* (once), *move out* intr: Ge 13 18 (*B* ⲟⲩ.) ἀποσκηνεῖν; Ps 45 2 (*B* do) μετατίθεσθαι, Aeg 213 ϩⲙⲧⲣⲉϥⲛ. ⲉⲃ. (cleric *migrating* without leave) μεθιστάναι; Mk 11 23 (*B* ϥⲓ refl) αἴρεσθαι, cit AP 55 *A²*; ShBMOr 8810 489 martyrs long ⲉⲛ. ⲉⲃ. & be with God;   c ⲉⲃ. ⲉ- *S*, *move over to*: ShBKU 1 180 vo place ⲉⲧⲁϥⲛⲁⲡ. ⲉⲃ. ⲉⲣⲟϥ;   c ⲉⲃ. ⲉϫⲛ- *S*, *go forth upon*: Ps 10 1 (*B* do) μεταναστεύειν ἐπί;   c ⲉⲃ. ϩⲓ- *S*, *go forth from*: ShIF 295 bidding ⲡ ⲉⲃ. ϩⲓⲡⲉⲓⲧⲟⲟⲩ & go to river;   c ⲉⲃ. ϩⲛ- *SAA²*, meaning same: 2 Macc 6 1 *A*, Mt 12 9 *S* (*BF* do) μεταβαίν. ἐκ, ἐκεῖθεν, Jud 8 8 *S* ἀναβ. ἐκ.; Deu 10 7 *S* (*B* do) ἀπαίρ. ἐκ., Mt 13 53 *S* (*BF* do) μεταίρ. ἐκ.; 1 Kg 22 3 *S* ἀπέρχεσθαι ἐκ.; BHom 43 *S* ⲡ. ⲉⲃ. ϩⲙⲡⲁⲓ ⲉⲡⲁⲓ μεταπηδᾶν; Mor 18 118 *S* ⲁⲓⲡ. ⲉⲃ. ϩⲛⲕⲏⲙⲉ ⲉϩⲣⲁⲓ ⲉ- στέλλεσθαι παρά; ShBMOr 8810 474 *S* ϣⲁϥⲡ....ⲉⲃ. ϩⲙⲡⲉⲧⲛⲁⲛⲟⲩϥ to evil;   c ⲉⲃ. ϩⲓϫⲛ- *S*, *move from off*: BMis 107 ⲛⲁⲡ. ⲉⲃ. ϩⲓϫⲙⲡⲕⲁϩ (var Mor 33 68 ⲉⲃ. ϩⲙ-) up to heaven;   tr *SAF*: Ge 5 24 *S* (*B* ⲟⲩⲱⲧⲉⲃ), Hos 5 10 *A* (*B* do), He 7 12 *SF* (*B* do) μεταⲧιθ.; Cl 44 6 *A* ⲁⲧⲉⲧⲛⲡ. ϩⲉⲛϩⲁⲉⲓⲛⲉ ⲁⲃ. μετάγειν; Job 22 8 *S* (*B* diff) κομίζειν; Si 29 21 *S* ἀποικίζειν; Jud 2 3 *S* μετοικ., Ac 19 26 *S* (*B* ⲟⲩ. ⲉⲃ.) μεθιστ., Ps 108 10 *S* (*B* do) μεταναστ.; Ps 77 52 *S* (*B* diff) ἀπαίρ., Pro 22 28 *SA* μεταίρ.; PS 241 *S* when man dies ⲛⲥⲉⲡⲟⲟⲡⲉϥ ⲉⲃ. & hand him to Virgin, BIF 13 107 *S* ⲡⲉⲛⲧⲁϥⲡ. ⲡⲉⲡⲱϫ ⲉⲃ. = MG 25 ⲁ92 *B* ⲟⲩ. ⲉⲃ., PLond 4 457 *S* ⲡ. ⲉⲃ. of *migration* of (deserting) peasants, BM 596 14 *F* ⲉϣⲱⲡⲉ ϣⲁⲕⲡⲁⲁⲡⲉ ϩⲉⲛⲕⲁⲡⲙⲟⲩϫⲱⲗ (sic=ⲙⲁϫ.) ⲉⲃ. ⲉϩⲟⲩⲛ (ⲉ)ⲧⲙⲡ(ⲏ);   c ⲉⲃ. ⲉ- *S*, *carry out, remove to*: S 28 15 διαστ. ἀπό, εἰς; Ac 7 43 (*B* ⲟⲩ.) μετοικ. ἐπέκεινα, Mor 50 16 delayed not ⲙⲛⲟⲟⲡⲉϥ (corpse) ⲉⲃ. ⲉⲡⲕⲁϩ of fathers;   c ⲉⲃ. ⲛ- *SA*, *carry out from*: Hos 10 5 (*B* do ϩⲁ-) μετοικ. ἀπό;   c ⲉⲃ. ϩⲓ- *S*, meaning same: 2 Kg 7 15 ϩⲓⲣⲏ (var ϩⲓⲑⲏ) ἀφιστ. ἐκ.; ShA 2 114 ⲡⲉⲧⲡ. obstacles ⲉⲃ. ϩⲓⲧⲉϩⲓⲏ;   c ⲉⲃ. ϩⲛ- *S*, meaning same: 2 Kg 6 3 (*B* ⲱⲗⲓ) αἴρ. ἐκ., Ps 79 8 (*B* ⲟⲩ.) μεταίρ. ἐκ.; Si 47 33 ἀφιστ. ἀπό.; 2 Kg 20 12 ἀποστρ. ἐκ., Ps 51 5 (*B* do) μεταναστεύειν ἀπό; PS 158 ⲁⲕⲛⲟⲟⲡⲟⲩ ⲉⲃ. ϩⲛⲧⲁⲙⲛⲧⲉ of corpses (Od Solom 22 8), ShC 42 21 builders of Babel ⲛⲧⲁϥⲡ. ϩⲣⲉⲛⲧⲱⲃⲉ ⲉⲃ. ϩⲙⲡⲕⲁϩ (*cf ?* ⲡⲱⲛⲕ **II** b), Miss 4 240 asked ⲉⲧⲣⲉϥⲛⲟⲟⲡⲉϥ ⲉⲃ. ϩⲛⲥⲱⲙⲁ;   c ⲉⲃ. ϩⲓϫⲛ- *S*, *remove from*: Si

48 17 προνομεύεσθαι ἀπό; Ez 4 8 (*B* ⲫⲱϩⲣ ϩⲓϫ.) στρ. ἀπό. *V* also nn.

—— ⲉⲡⲁϩⲟⲩ *S*, *be turned back*: Z 340 face ⲡ. ⲉⲡ. στρέφεσθαι ὀπίσω.

—— ⲉϩⲣⲁⲓ *S*: Mor 50 65 dug & found body ϩⲱⲥ ϫⲉⲛⲧⲁⲡⲕⲁϩ ⲡⲟⲟⲡⲉϥ ⲉϩ. *had covered it over* (?) without hand of man.

—— *SF* nn m, *removal, change, death*: He 7 12 *SF* (*B* ⲟⲩ.) μετάθεσις; ShC 73 98 *S* ⲡⲛ. of man's unstable heart, Cai 42573 *S* ⲟⲩⲡ. title of recipe, object not stated;   ⲡ. ⲉⲃⲟⲗ *SF*: 4 Kg 25 27 *S* ἀποικία, Jer 9 11 *S* (*B* ⲟⲩ.) μετοικία, Jud 18 30 *S* μετοικεσία; Bor 226 157 *S* ⲡⲡ. ϣⲁϫⲉ ⲉⲃ. μεταφέρειν; LAp 520 *F* preaching & ⲡⲡ. ⲉⲃ. of apostle, BIF 13 118 *S* = MG 25 311 *B* ⲟⲩⲱⲧⲉⲃ sim.

ⲁⲧⲡ. *SF* adj, *immovable, unchangeable*: He 6 18 *SF* (*B* ⲁⲑⲟⲩ.), BMis 242 *S* ⲟⲩⲁⲧⲡ. ⲡⲉ ⲡⲉϥⲗⲟⲅⲓⲥⲙⲟⲥ ἀμετάθετος; ShC 73 113 *S* endurance ⲛⲁⲧⲡ. ⲁⲩⲱ ⲡⲁⲧⲕⲓⲙ.; J 14 22 *S* ⲟⲩⲗⲟⲅⲓⲥⲙⲟⲥ ⲉⲛⲁⲧⲡⲟⲟⲛϥ ⲉⲃ.; ⲙⲛⲧⲁⲧⲡ. *S*, *unchangeableness*: ROC 19 72 became man ϩⲛⲟⲩⲙ. ⲙⲛⲟⲩⲙⲛⲧⲁⲧϣⲓⲃⲉ.

ⲣⲉϥⲡ. *S*, -ⲡⲟⲟⲡⲉϥ *SA*, *changeable person*: Pro 17 20 *S* (var -ⲉϥ) *A* εὐμετάβολος; Miss 8 251 *S* ⲣⲉϥⲡⲉⲉⲡⲉ ⲧⲱϣ ⲉⲃ. ⲙⲛⲧⲣⲉϥⲡ. *S*, *changeableness*: Z 579 of bat's erratic flight.

ϭⲓⲛⲡ. *S*, *changing, alteration*: P 44 120 ⲧϭ. ϩⲛⲡⲉϩⲣⲓⲟⲟⲩⲉ تراويح, ShBor 247 109 naught is stable ⲟⲩϭ. ⲡⲉ ϩⲱⲃ ⲛⲓⲙ; ϭⲓⲛⲡ. ⲉⲃ.: FR xxvii to Virgin dying ⲧⲟⲩϭ. ⲉⲃ. ϩⲙⲡⲉⲓⲁⲓⲱⲛ.

ⲡⲱⲱⲡⲉⲥ, ⲡⲟⲟ. *S* nn f, *movement*: P 131² 117 = P 44 122 when drunk seest everything ⲉϫⲓ ⲡⲱ. ϩⲁⲣⲟⲕ = Va 58 193 *B* ϭⲓ ⲫⲟϩⲣⲥ, Mor 25 149 earth shall not cease ⲉϥϯ ⲡⲟ. ⲡⲟ. till he come.

Cf ⲫⲱϩⲣ.

ⲡⲱⲛⲕ, -ⲛⲧ, -ⲛϭ *S*, ⲫⲱⲛⲕ *B*, ⲡⲏⲛⲕ-, ⲡⲉⲛⲕ-, ⲡⲟⲛⲕ- also ⲡⲱⲛϭ- *S*, ⲫⲉⲛⲕ- *B*, ⲡⲁⲛⲕ- *F*, ⲡⲟⲛⲕⲁ *S*, ⲫⲟⲛⲕ† *B* vb **I** intr, a *S* *draw, bail, empty out* water &c: 3 Kg 7 26 (P 44 111 = 43 107) ⲡⲉⲥⲑⲉⲣⲙⲁⲥⲧⲣⲓⲟⲛ ⲉⲧⲉⲡⲉⲭⲣⲓⲛⲡⲉ (*l ?* ⲭⲣⲓ ⲡⲉ) ⲙⲛ. غارف للنشل, Gloss 377 ἀντλητής · ⲡⲉⲧⲡ., ShLeyd 320 ⲛⲧⲡⲡ.... ⲧⲏϩⲟ ⲉⲃⲟⲗ as it were water, ShA 2 49 steersman giveth heed (παρατηρεῖν) to ⲡⲉϥⲟⲩⲟⲡⲧ ⲙⲡ.(*cf* Almk 2 103 خن hold whence water bailed), ·BM 1115 ⲡⲏⲕⲱⲧⲉ (ⲧ)ⲧⲟ ⲛϭⲟⲙ (*l* ϭⲱⲙ)...till I come ⲧⲁⲡⲟⲟⲛⲧ (*l* -ⲛⲧ) ⲉⲕⲉⲥⲡⲓⲣ. b *S* *transfer, carry over*: ShBor 300 70 when building ⲉϥϥⲓ ⲱⲡⲉ ⲛ ⲉϥⲡ., TT 119 ⲉϥⲡ. *whilst he loaded* (boat) = MG 17 413 اوسقوا السفينة, Mor 51 35 ⲥⲙⲛ ⲛⲣⲱⲙ at even ⲥⲙⲛ ⲙⲡ. at dawn.   c ⲉⲡϣⲱⲓ *B*, *bring up*: MG 25 152 sheep ⲁϥϣⲁⲛϥ. ⲉⲡ. *ruminating, cf* MG 25 39 ⲛⲓ ⲉⲡ.;   c ⲉϩⲟⲩⲛ *S*, *transfer, bring over into*: CA 105 of corn ϥⲛⲁⲡ. ⲉϩ. ⲉⲡⲉϥⲁⲡⲟⲑⲏⲕⲏ, LAl 11

when parents bring food young birds rejoice ϩⲓ-
τεπτϭⲓⲛ[πο]ⲛⲉⲕ εϩ. εⲣⲟⲟⲩ (l εⲣⲱⲟⲩ);   c ⲛⲥⲁ-
S, *draw* (water) *from*: BMar 91 man at well eϥ-
ⲭⲱⲗϩ ⲁⲩⲱ eϥⲡ. ⲛⲥⲁⲧⲡⲩⲧⲛ, BP 10589 if ye send
camels ⲛⲁⲓⲛⲁⲡ. ⲛⲥⲱⲟⲩ *draw for them* (?);   c ϩⲛ-
S, *draw from*: ShA 1 78 gall in vessel ⲛⲉⲧϥⲓ ⲛ
ⲛⲉⲧⲡ. ⲛⲣⲏⲧϥ.   c B *hollow, cut out* (? same word,
cf ⲡⲱⲣⲕ I): C 86 283 great stone eϥϥ.† = BSG
182 S ⲛⲥⲉϣⲧϣⲱⲧϥ γλυφθῆναι, C 86 219 carpenter
ⲡⲧⲉϥϥ. ⲡⲟⲙⲛ† of martyr's head with axe. *V*
ⲣⲉϥϥ.

    II tr, **a** *SB draw, bail* water &c: Hag 2 16 B
(*SA* ⲭⲱⲗϩ) ἐξαντλεῖν; FR 26 S = Mor 33 129 S
dig for water or π. ⲛⲟⲩⲡⲓⲧⲛ = BMis 64 S diff (*cf*
I c), BMis 194 S πετⲡⲓⲧ ⲙⲟⲟⲩ from cistern,
ShA 2 48 S eⲭⲱⲗϩ ⲛ eⲡ. eⲃⲟⲗ ⲡⲙⲙⲟⲟⲩ, Mor
31 25 S eϥⲡⲉⲛⲕ ⲛⲓⲃⲉ eⲡⲙⲟⲩ *drawing breath as if
dying*.   **b** *SBF, transfer, carry*: ShP 130² 6 S
builders eⲧⲣeⲩϭⲗ ⲟⲙⲉ ⲁⲩⲱ eⲧⲣeⲩⲡⲓⲧ ⲧⲱⲃⲉ, (*cf*
? ShC 42 144 ⲡⲱⲛⲉ ⲡⲣⲉⲡⲧⲱⲃⲉ), ShC 73 209 S
eⲩⲡ. ⲡⲣⲉⲡⲉⲃⲣⲏⲅⲉ or bricks, Mor 30 44 F eϥⲡⲁⲡⲕ
ⲧⲱⲃⲓ, BMis 270 S ⲡⲟⲡⲉ ⲟⲙⲉ = Mor 30 45 F ⲧⲁⲗⲁ
ⲕeϩⲓ, Ryl 252 S, BM 1089 S sim, BMOr 6201 A
54 S ⲡeϣⲉ ⲡeⲗⲟⲟⲗⲉ ⲡⲧⲡⲟⲡⲕⲟⲩ eⲡⲛⲓ, FR 96 B
slaying them & eⲩϥ. (? ⲙⲙⲟⲟⲩ) ϩⲉⲛⲟⲩⲏⲛⲉ *carrying* (them) *off*, Kr 92 S ⲡⲧⲡⲟⲟⲩϥ (*sic* for ⲡⲟⲡⲕϥ);   c
eⲭⲡ- S, *pile upon*: ShC 42 88 eⲩⲡⲓⲧ ⲕⲁϩ eⲭⲱⲟⲩ
& weeping, ShZ 595 ⲡⲥeⲡⲓⲧ ϣⲟeⲓϣ eⲭⲱⲟⲩ;   c
ϩⲛ- S, *transfer from*: CA 107 wine eⲧⲕⲡⲁⲡⲟⲡⲕϥ
ϩⲙⲡeⲕeⲓⲟⲙ =*ib* ⲣⲓ تقدح من ;   c eⲃⲟⲗ S, *remove*:
BMis 218 dirt eϣⲁⲩⲡⲟⲡⲧⲟⲩ eⲃ. from houses, Mor
31 214 golden ephod aϥⲧⲣⲟⲩⲡⲟⲡⲕϥ eⲃ. & make
of it crown;   c eϩⲟⲩⲛ S, *transfer into*: BM
1122 give him house ϣⲁⲛⲧϥⲡ. ⲡeϥⲥⲕⲓⲛ eϩⲟⲩ(ⲡ)
eⲣⲟϥ;   c eϩⲣⲁⲓ S, *transfer, bring up*: Deu 23
13 (B ⲓⲛⲓ eⲭeⲡ-) ἐπάγειν; Miss 4 522 corn is in
ship, send ⲡⲧeⲧⲡⲡⲟⲡⲕϥ eϩ. = C 89 42 B eⲡϥ
eⲡϣⲱⲓ = Va ar 172 26 انقاد, *ib* aϥⲡⲟⲡⲕϥ eϩ. = B
aϥϣⲧⲏϥ eϩ. = Va ar حملو .

    ⲣⲉϥϥⲱⲡⲕ (*sic* MSS) B, *sculptor*: K 113 نقاش,
Montp 172 مهندس . *V* **I c**.

    ⲡⲟⲡⲕϥ S nn m, *bottle, tube* (?): Mor 31 211
Jeremiah's pit ϭⲏⲅ ⲡⲧϣⲓⲛ (l ? ⲡⲑⲉ) ⲡⲟⲩⲡ. ⲡⲁϣe-
ϭⲉⲉⲛⲉ = BMOr 3599 91 حافتر رقيقة مثل القدح الزجاج .

    ⲡⲉⲡⲙⲉ, -ⲛⲏ S nn, *bug*: Tri 495 bed full of π.,
P 44 57 = BM 491 ψύλλος (*sic* l) · π. برغوث (*cf* ⲡⲏⲓ
leap ⲃ).

    ⲡⲛⲛⲏ, ⲡⲛⲏ S, ⲃⲉⲡⲛⲏ B nn f, *doorpost, threshold,
step*: Ex 21 6 B (S ⲟⲩeϭⲣⲟ), Deu 15 17 B (var ⲟⲩ-
eⲭⲣⲟ, S om) σταθμός; 1 Kg 1 9 S, MG 25 252 B
φλιά; Jud 19 27 S, Ez 46 2 S ⲡⲛⲛⲏ (B ϥⲟⲓ), R 2
2 39 S ⲡeⲡ. ⲡⲣⲟ πρόθυρον, R 1 4 22 S charms

buried below ⲧⲡ. ⲙⲡⲣⲟ *limen*; Lev 8 35 S (B ⲣⲟ)
θύρα; Pro 9 18 B (*SA* ⲡⲁϣ) πέταυρον; 1 Kg 5 5
S, Si 6 37 S βαθμός; Tri 492 S درج ; Mor 40 20 S
ⲧϣⲟⲣⲡⲉ ⲙⲡ. ⲙⲡⲧⲱⲣⲧⲣ = C 43 49 B †ϩⲁⲛ ⲡⲃ.
ⲡⲧⲉ ⲡⲓϩⲁⲉ ⲡⲧⲱⲣⲧⲉⲣ, ShP 131⁶ 57 S foot on ladder
ⲣ ⲧⲡⲉ ⲡϣⲟⲙⲧⲉ ⲙⲡ., RChamp 373 S suffer him not
to come within π. of monastery, C 86 350 B entered
ϩⲓⲧ̄ϥ̄. of τόπος, C 41 49 B seated ϩⲓⲣⲉⲛⲉϥⲣⲟ...e-
ⲭeⲡϥ̄ϥ̄.   But π. & ϥ. ? distinct words (Dévaud
Études 59 n).

    ⲡⲉⲡⲓⲡⲉ *v* ⲃⲉⲡⲓⲡⲉ.

    ⲡⲱⲱⲡⲉⲥ, ⲡⲟⲟⲡⲉⲥ *v* ⲡⲱⲱⲡⲉ *s f*.

    ⲡⲓⲡeϭ *v* ⲃⲓⲡⲁϫ.

    ⲡⲁⲟⲡⲉ (oftenest), **ⲡⲟⲟⲡⲉ** (C 73 xi, Mor 27 25),
ⲡⲁⲁⲡⲉ (BMis 422, Lant 114 21, CO 27, 478), **ⲡⲁⲁⲡⲓ**
(BM 468) S, **ⲡⲁⲱⲡⲓ, ⲡⲁⲟⲡⲓ** (Va 63 4), **ⲡⲁⲟⲡⲏ** (C
43 22) B, **ⲡⲁⲁⲡⲓ** (Sph 10 2, CMSS 58) F nn, name
of 2d month, Gk Φαωφί, Ar بابه . *V* AZ 39 129.

    ⲡⲁⲡⲟⲓ, -ⲁⲓ S nn m, *bird, chicken* (?): 3 Kg 4 23
(P 44 110) ὄρνις. Lev 14 4 (B eⲣϫ) ὀρνίθιον, MR 4
128 ⲟⲣⲡⲓⲉⲓⲙ · ⲧⲡⲁⲡⲟⲓ (*sic*), Tri 517 gathering young
like ⲙⲡ. دجاجة (*cf* Mt 23 37), Miss 4 532 ⲟⲩϩⲁⲗⲏⲧ
ⲙⲡ. (C 89 50 B & Gk diff), *ib* 533 do (var *ib* 810,
B 51 Gk diff), BAp 95 rich man fed upon ϩⲉⲛⲱⲃⲧ
ⲙⲡϩⲉⲡ., Mor 25 13 sim, PMich 3568 d ϭⲣⲟⲟⲙⲡⲉ
ⲙⲡⲡ. ⲥⲡⲁⲩ, AZ 30 39 ⲟⲩⲣⲟ ⲙⲡ(ⲡ)ⲉⲥⲡ., *ib* 40 ⲡⲓⲣⲟ
ⲙⲡ(ⲡⲓ)ⲡ., *cf* Ryl 267 ⲡⲁⲙⲉⲥⲛⲓ ⲙⲡ. (l ?? ⲙⲉⲥ ⲙⲡ.)
& *ib* ⲡⲡ., Kr 242 ⲃⲧⲟⲟⲩ ⲡⲡ., Cai 42573 1 in recipe
dung (ϩⲁϭ) eⲡⲁⲡⲁⲓ, Ep 574 egg ⲙⲡⲁⲡⲁⲓ, Ryl 107
sim.   ⲥⲁ ⲡⲡ., *chicken seller*: PLond 4 192 Ψαν-
παπόι.   As name: Παπάει (Preisigke).

    ⲡⲱⲱⲡⲉ S, **ⲡⲁⲡⲓ** F (?), **ⲡⲁⲡⲉ**- SA, **ⲡⲁⲡ**- SS[f],
ϥⲁⲡⲉ-B, **ⲡⲁⲡⲱ**- S[f]F, **ⲡⲁⲡⲱ⸗** S vb intr, *knead* (clay),
make bricks: ShP 130² 6 S workmen eⲧⲣeⲩⲡ. ⲁⲩⲱ
eⲧⲣeⲩϭⲗ ⲟⲙⲉ (*v* ⲡⲟⲡⲕ **II ⲃ**), CMSS 63 F]eϥ-
ⲡⲁⲡⲓ;   tr with ⲧⲱⲃⲉ: Ge 11 3 B πλινθεύειν;
ShC 42 21 S ⲡⲧⲁⲡⲛ. ⲡⲣeⲡⲧ. eⲃⲟⲗ ϩⲙⲡⲕⲁϩ, BMis
260 S arise & ⲡⲧⲡⲁⲡⲉ ⲧ. = Mor 30 34 F ⲡⲁⲡⲱ ⲧ.,
ib 29 29 S[f] eⲕⲡⲁⲡⲱ ⲧ., PMich 3532 S ⲡⲉⲧⲣⲙⲙⲛ-
ⲥⲛⲏ (τριμήσιον) ⲡⲧ. ⲁⲩⲡⲁⲡ ⲱϥ, JKP 2 46 S craft
of ⲡⲁⲡⲧ.   As nn: Ex 1 14 B ⲡⲓϥ. ⲧ. (A ⲙⲛⲧⲡ.
ⲧ.) πλινθεία, cit Ryl 72 358 S, Bor 295 98 S.   ⲙⲛⲧ-
ⲡⲁⲡⲉ ⲧ., *making of bricks*: Ex 1 14 A (*v* above),
PMich 4937 S working at ⲧⲙ., JKP 2 52 S[f]
ⲧⲙⲉⲧⲡⲁⲡ ⲧⲱⲃⲓ.   ⲣⲉϥⲡⲁⲡⲉ ⲧ., *brick-maker*: Mor
38 80 S builders & p. & workmen.   ⲙⲁ ⲙⲡⲁⲡⲉ
ⲧ., *place for brick-making*: BMis 263 S.

    ⲡⲁⲡⲉⲓⲧ, *brick-maker*: BM 217 S ϩⲙⲡ. eⲩⲧⲁ-
ⲙⲓⲉ ⲧ.   **ⲡⲉⲡⲓ**, meaning ? same: BMEA 10577 S
ⲙⲡⲓϩⲉ ⲗⲁⲟⲩ eⲧⲓ ⲡeⲡ. ⲧⲁⲣⲟⲩⲥⲙⲛⲧⲟⲩ (ⲡ)ⲧ. ⲡⲁⲓ.
V also ⲕⲟⲉⲓϩ.

пер-, *house* in перепειτι J 43 26, περιπεροι &
in place-names: προγωπϣ Ryl Suppl 43, *Πέρκωψ*
POxy 1278, перппоутε Lant 45, περογωτ Kr 169,
Περοῦεν POxy 2038, *Περσεβοῦλ* ib 1989, περϭιποειτ
Mor 47 195, прϭоуϣ Miss 4 763, (*пертпоуϫε)
Φερετνοῦιϲ ادیری Ryl 430 n.   *V* also names in
(RChamp 728) поу- & ϫεπεпωр, ? перιεϩ (v пεϩ).

пара *S* nn m, meaning unknown: BMOr 6201
A 94 tax account ϩαππ. мпεϫακε(ἐξάγιον). Coptic?
Hall 65 ϩмоу мп. (*bis*).   Same?

пαρε *S* nn m, meaning unknown: Ep 449 be
so kind пϲϯ пп. пαϥ.   *V* n there & *cf* ? аре *pail*.

перε *S* nn m, *scurf*: Tri 532 جرب.

пηрε, -ра *S*, пηρι *BF* nn m, *quail*, *cf* ٱری (AZ
30 26): Kr 242 *S* presents to eparch ϣмоуп пп.,
тαιου пп., *ib* 139 *S* ϥτооу пп. in rent;   ϩη мп.
S, мεсιωϯ мп. *B*, *flock, brood of quails*: Ex 16 13
SB, Ps 104 40 *SB*, Sa 16 2, 19 12 *S* -ра ὀρτυγομήτρα; Tri 259 *S* -ра سلوی, MIF 9 6 *S* -ра;   пαϣ-
пηρι *v* поуϣп.

пειρε, пι. *S*, ϥιρι, ϥερ- *B*, поре† *S*, ϥορι† *B*,
преιωоуⳁ *SA*, пер.† *S*, ϥεριωоуⳁ, -ωоутⳁ (DeV)
B, also пррε *S* (He 7), пррιε *A*, пррειε, прιε *A²* vb
I *intr*, *come forth* of light, *blossom &c* : Is 61 11 *B*
(*S* ϯ оуω), Zech 6 12 *A* ϥпαпριε (sic ?, *B* diff), 2
Pet 1 19 *B*(*S* ϣα) ἀνατέλλειν; AP 19 *A²* light п. пнει
λάμπειν; Ps 91 13 *B* (*S* ϫιсε) ἀνθεῖν; Ez 21 28 *B*
(var ιελελ) στίλβειν; Mk 9 3 *S* (*BF* оуωⳃⳃ) λευκαίνειν; Va 63 79 *B* пη ετεϣαϥϥ. in corn field
φύεσθαι; Job 9 27 *B* (*S* ϫω) εἰπεῖν (*cf* с ε- &c below); ShA 1 405 *S* stars ετп. поуоειϣ пιм, AM
132 *B* ακϣρεϥϥ. пϣηтс пϫε пιмустηριон of
Christ's birth, Mor 41 66 *S* hair & beard αϥп.
ппαϣ пϩε.   Qual α поре, ϥ.: Mk 9 3 *B* (*S* тоуо
var моуϩ, F сϯ ηλλι στίλ.; Ap 15 6 *B* (*S* оуωⳃⳃ) λαμπρός; *ib* 3 18 *B* (*S* do) λευκός; Lev 13
19 *S* gloss on оуоⳃⳃ (*B* om) τηλαυγής; C 86 271
B ϩαпснϥι εϥϥ.;   ♭ преιωоу, ϥ.: Ja 2 2 *SA*
(*B* ϥорι), BMar 164 *S* raiment εсп., Wess 18 107
S orator's peroration εсп. & easily acceptable λαμπρός; BMis 233 *S*, Va 61 16 *B* sim λευχείμων; Is
3 22 *S* (*B* оуоϩϩ εⳃол) διαφανής; Va 66 297 *B*
ἐμπρέπειν; R 1 4 66 *S* sun's light εтп. = AM 126
B ετϥ., DeV 2 207 *B* сϫημα ετϥεριωоуⳃ, ShC
42 209 *S* animal εϥп. η εϥоуоⳃⳃ, BM 180 376 *S*
beryl εсп. & variegated, P 131⁶ 60 εкоуооλε αуω
εкп. in thy life.

With following preposition.
   с ε- *as obj B, put forth, announce, tell*: Ps 101
22 (*S* ϫω) ἀναγγέλλειν, Job 21 31, Ps 70 18 (*S* do)
ἀπαγ., Ro 9 17 (*S* do) διαγ.; Va 61 28 пαϥϥ. ε-
τεϥмετϫωρι λαλεῖν; Ps 47 14 (*S* do) διηγεῖσθαι;

CaiEuch 466 Thy mercy пαтⳃ ϥ. ερос ἀνεκδιήγητος; Ge 6 4 ετεϣαуϥ. εпоуран ὀνομαστός;
MG 25 266 ϥη ετапер ϣорп пϥ. ероϥ = Mor
40 40 *S* ϣαχε ε-, C 43 129 will cut out thy tongue
мпαптεкϥ. εпαιραп = Mor 48 57 *S* тαϭо п-,
DeV 2 67 εϥϥ. ερωоу *celebrating them*, Miss 4 132
мαреϥϥ. εпипαу *tell of time* when we went to...
= Mor 18 56 *S* нтоп εχппαу;   с εⳃⳃε- *B*,
tell of, talk of: He 11 32 (*S* ϣαχε), HL 94 асϥ.
пεⳃни εоⳃηтϥ διηγ.; *ib* 104 птεпϥ. εоⳃεпεϥα-
ретη;   с εχп- *SB*, εϩρηι εχ. *B*, αϩ. αχп- *A*,
come forth, shine upon: Ps 131 18 *B* (*S* ϯ оуω)
ἐξανθ. ἐπί; Is 60 1 *A* (PVi 10157, *SB* ϣα εχ.) ἀνατέλλ. ἐπί; ShMIF 23 152 *S* on what land did ever
sun set αϥп. εχпκεоуει ?, El 66 *A* sim;   с п-
dat *SB*, *come forth, shine for*: Job 11 17 *B* (*S* ϣα
dat), Sa 5 6 *S* (*B* ϣαι εχ.) ἀνατέλλ.; P 44 100 *S*
Virgin тεптαсп. пαп βλαστεῖν; Ep 56 *S* sun пεп-
тαϥп. птоικоумεпη;   с ϫαтεп- *B*, *tell to*: C
86 291 hearken птαϥ. ϫαтотк ϫε- διηγ., Job 12 8
(*S* ϫω dat) ἐκδιηγ. dat, *ib* (*S* оуωϣⳃ) ἐξηγ.

With following adverb.
   с εⳃол *SB*, *come, blossom forth*: Ge 2 5 *B*, Is 43
19 *B* (*S* оуωпϩ εⳃ.), Hos 10 4 *B* (*SA* ϯ оуω) ἀνατέλλ., Job 14 2 *B* (*S* ϩρηρε), Is 35 1 *B* (*SF* ϯ оуω)
ἀνθ., Lev 13 12 *SB* ἐξανθ.; Job 8 11 *B* (*S* do) θάλλειν, Ps 27 7 *B* (*S* do) ἀναθάλ.; He 9 4 (*SF* do)
βλασ.; Am 9 13 *B* (*SA* пωϩ) περκάζειν; ShA 2 223
S sickness αϥп. εⳃ. in limbs, C 41 71 *B* αϯⳃоιϯ ϥ.
εⳃ. again;   с εⳃ. ε- *B*, *come forth for*: Is 17 11
(*S* ϯ оуω) ἀνθ. εἰς; Phil 4 10 (*S* оурот ε-) ἀνα-
θάλλ.   с εⳃ. ϩп-, ϫεп- *SB*, *come forth from*: Ps
71 16 *B* (*S* ϯ оуω) ἐξανθ. ἐκ; He 7 14 *B* (*S* пррε
Z 596, var ϣα) ἀνατέλλ. ἐκ; Gu 48 *S* Son of God
птαϥпιра (*l* -ре) εⳃ. ϩапειωт, Mor 40 37 *S* Nitria
where ϩмоу пλоуικоп п. εⳃ. ϩρηтϥ = MG 25
263 *B*.   ϥ. εⳃ. qual *B* (*S* once), *blooming*: Ex
28 33, Nah 1 4 (*SA* ϯ оуω) ἐξανθ., Va 58 180 re-
newed & εϥϥ. εⳃ. ἐπανθ.; Dan 4 18 εὐθάλλ.; Ps 187
3 (*S* рооут) εὐθηνεῖν; Ricci *S* (v PSBA 26 177) of
Judith εϣχεпαтωп преιωоу εⳃ.

II *tr B, put forth, proclaim*: Ps 74 2 (*S* ϫω) διηγ.;
C 43 228 heard thee εкϥ. (м)пαιраn, Mani 1
A² αϥпр. мпεϥ[пα]ϩтε ϩпμιμεεу, CaiThe 362
Lord ϥ. поуⳃω пαλоλι رجل.   с εⳃол: Nu 17
23 (*S* тαϭо εⳃ.) ἐξανθ., C 86 219 trees ϥ. εⳃ. пϫωⳃι.

—— *SB*, nn m, *coming, shining forth, tale*: Is 60
3 *SB* (var + εⳃол) λαμπρότης; Ex 24 10 *B* (*S* оуоп)
καθαριότης; Deu 28 37 *SB* διήγημα; K 82 *B* пιϥ.
titles, epithets of man طرب; ShC 42 52 *S* пп. п
поуωпϩ εⳃол of light, BMis 435 *S* of silver, MG
25 402 *B* saint among blessed ϫεпоуϥ. пϣηρι.
с εⳃол: Bar 5 3 *B* λαμπ., My 116 *S* of flowers.

ⲙⲁ ⲙⲡ., *place of coming forth* of sun: Nu 34 10
S (var ⲥⲁ ⲙⲡ., B ⲙⲁ ⲡϣⲁⲓ), Cl 5 6 A (var do) ἀνατολή opp ⲙⲁ ⲡⲣⲱⲧⲡ. V also ⲉⲓⲉⲃⲧ, ϣⲁ vb.

ⲥⲁ ⲙⲡ. A, *side of coming f.*: El 86. Cf ⲙⲁ ⲙⲡ.
ⲥⲓⲡⲡ., ϫⲓⲛⲫ., *coming, showing forth*: Ps 91 3 B
(S ⲭⲱ) ἀναγγέλλειν; Va 66 297 B ϯⲭ. πρoγο τὸ
περιττὸν κ. περίεργον; Mich 550 25 S of sun (ⲡⲉ-
ⲫⲱⲥⲧⲏⲣ *sic*) ⲧⲉϥϭ. ⲙⲛⲧⲉϥϭⲓⲙⲡⲱⲧ.

поро S nn, *vessel holding oil*: ST 117]ⲛⲡⲟⲟ⳽
ⲙⲡ. ⲡⲛⲉⲣ sealed. Coptic?

пωⲱⲣⲉ S, ⲡⲟⲩⲣⲉ A, ⲫⲱⲣ B, ⲡⲉⲣⲉ- S, ⲫⲉⲣ- B,
ⲡⲟⲟⲣ⳽ S vb tr, *dream* ⲉ + ⲣⲁⲥⲟⲩ a dream (oftenest):
Ge 28 12 S ⲁϥⲡ. ⲡⲟⲩⲣ. (B ⲡⲁⲩ), Is 29 7 S (B do),
Dan 2 3 S (B ϫⲓⲙⲓ), Joel 2 28 SA (B ⲉⲣ ⲡ.), Jude
8 S (var ⲡⲉⲉⲡⲉ-, B ⲫ. nn) ἐνυπνιάζεσθαι, Mic 3 7
SA (B ⲡⲁⲩ) ἐνύπνια ὁρᾶν; Mor 25 6 S snoring &
ⲉⲛⲡ. ⲣ. ϩⲙⲡⲉⲛⲕⲟⲧⲕ = Va 61 89 B ⲫⲉⲡ ⲣ., cf TSBA
9 363 B ⲁⲣⲏⲟⲩ ⲉⲩⲫⲉⲡ ⲣ. (3 Kg 18 27 καθεύδειν). **b**
without ⲣ. S: Job 20 8 ⲡⲉϣⲁⲩ ⲡⲟⲟⲣⲟⲩ ⲡⲧⲉⲩϣⲏ
(B diff) φάντασμα; Is 56 10 (B ⲫ. ⲣ.) ⲉⲩⲡ. ⲡⲙⲙⲁ
ⲡⲡⲕⲟⲧⲕ ἐνύπ. As nn B: Jude *ut sup*. ⲣⲉϥⲡ.
ⲣ., ⲫ. ⲣ. SB, *dreamer of dreams*: Ge 37 19 B ἐνυ-
πνιαστής, Deu 13 1 SB ἐνυπνιαζόμενος. Cf ? ⲃⲟⲩⲣⲉ.

пⲣⲱ SA²F, ⲡⲣⲟⲩ A, ⲫⲣⲱ B nn f, *winter*: Cant
2 10 SA (Vi 10157), Mt 24 20 SB, Jo 10 22 SA²BF
χειμών, Pro 27 15 SA, Cl 20 9 A χειμερινός; Miss
4 762 S ⲙⲉⲕⲱϫⲉⲃ ⲡⲧⲉⲡ., BSM 90 B ⲉϥⲟϫⲉⲃ ϩⲉⲡ-
ϯⲫ., ST 94 S will pay corn even as ⲉⲧⲟⲩⲧⲓ ⲉⲭⲡ-
ⲥⲟⲩⲟ ϩⲛⲧⲡ. ⲣ ⲧⲉⲡ., ⲫ. SB, *pass winter*: 1 Cor
16 6 παραχειμάζειν.

поⲣⲕ S, ⲫⲱⲣⲕ, ⲫⲟ. B, ⲡⲁⲣⲉⲕ F nn m, *outer
mantle of clerics, monks, pallium*: TEuch 1 190 B
monk invested with σχῆμα, then with ⲫ. برنس, var
ib 85 & BodlMarsh 32 99 مِزر (*l* مِزْر) which = K 120
μηλωτή & P 44 91 ϫⲁⲗⲟⲧ (سطو *v* ϩⲁⲗⲟⲧ), K 119 B
clerical garments ⲡⲓⲫ. دلق (ragged cloak Lane 905),
P 54 149 B برجوج (*v* ⲙⲁⲣⲭⲱϫⲉ), برك, دلق, ROC
27 164 B monk's dress ϩⲓⲣⲣⲟⲥ, ⲕⲟⲗⲟⲃⲓ ⲙϫⲱ, ⲫⲟ.,
Bod(P) f 19 S sim ⲗⲉϩⲓⲧⲟⲡ, ϣⲧⲏⲛ, ⲡ., C 43 111 B
garments for (divine) service ⲉⲧⲉⲡⲉϥⲫ. ⲡⲉ, BM 699
F ⲡ. ⲡⲗⲁⲩ, *ib* 583 F ϭⲁⲡ ⲡⲕⲁⲡⲡ. ⲉⲧ[ⲕⲏ] ϩⲁⲑⲏⲕ
(or ? is ⲡ. *mule*); among armour: K 116 B
جوشن *cuirass*; *boat's sail*: K 268 B ⲫⲟⲣⲕ (*sic*)
قلع (var قطع *piece cut off*, cf ⲡⲱⲣⲕ vb). As nickname (?); hermit Pamoun ⲡⲁⲙⲡⲟⲣⲕ (BMar 130,
in Ethiop version *Zap Imp Russ Arkheol Obš* 15 05
epithet om), invoked (*D. el-Gebrawi* 2 pl 29 3), his
τόπος (BMOr 6206, 6202); cf ? Pamoun ⲡⲁⲧⲣⲉⲃⲥⲱ
ⲙⲙⲓⲛⲉ ⲙⲓⲛⲉ (Miss 4 759).

поⲣⲕ, -ⲉⲕ S, ⲡⲁⲣⲕ S^f AF, ⲫⲟⲣⲕ B (once) nn m
f, *a foal, calf*: ShC 42 91 ϩⲉⲡⲡ. ⲡⲧⲃⲡⲏ, *ib* ⲙⲡ. ⲡ-

ⲡⲉⲧⲛⲧⲃⲛⲟⲟⲩⲉ, CO 221 will tend camel ⲛⲧⲁⲣ ϩⲱⲃ
ⲉⲧⲡ. Also ? in ϩⲁⲡⲟⲣⲕ. **b** with ⲙⲁⲥ- SAB,
ⲙⲉⲥ- S (*v* ⲙⲓⲥⲉ) *mule, cf* ? פֶרד: Ge 12 16 (B ⲧⲉⲙ-
ⲑⲁⲗ), 2 Kg 18 9 f, *ib* m, 3 Kg 1 33 f, Is 66 20 S/
(B do), Zech 14 15 A (B do) ἡμίονος; Ap 18 13
(B om) ῥέδη; ShBor 246 19 ⲡⲙⲉⲥⲡ., JA '88 2 368
ⲡⲉⲙⲟⲩⲗⲓⲁⲣⲏⲥ (cf μουλάρι) ⲙⲡⲡⲉⲙⲙⲁⲥⲡ. (ref Ps 31
9), Mor 31 254 horses & ⲙⲁⲥⲡ. = BMEA 10578 F,
Z 269 not a thorough gentleman (ἐλεύθερος) but of
mixed breed like ⲡⲉⲙⲙⲁⲥⲡ., TstAb 160 B ⲟⲩⲙⲁⲥ
ⲙⲫ. m.

пⲱⲣⲕ SA, ⲫ. B, ⲡⲣⲕ-, ⲡⲉⲣⲕ- S, ⲫⲉⲣⲕ- B,
ⲡⲟⲣⲕ⳽ S, ⲡⲁⲣⲕ⳽ A, ⲫⲟⲣⲕ⳽ B, ⲫⲉⲣⲕ† B vb **I** intr,
be plucked out, destroyed: Pro 12 3 SA (B ϥⲱϯ)
ἐξαίρεσθαι; Mt 15 13 S (B ⲕⲱⲣϫ) ἐκριζοῦσθαι;
Job 4 7 S (B diff) ὁλόριζος ἀπόλλυσθαι; P 131⁴ 145
S tents of wicked ⲡⲁⲡ. (cf Pro 14 11 ⲧⲁⲕⲟ ἀφανί-
ζεσθαι); El 138 S = *ib* 64 A trees & their roots
ⲡⲁⲡ., ShC 73 10 S sim of thoughts, MIE 2 336 B
eyes ⲡⲁⲫ. ⲡⲥⲉⲓ ⲉⲃⲟⲗ from weight of stone about
neck = P ar 4785 119 تنزع, BMar 40 S *dux* bade
ⲡ. ⲙⲡⲉϥⲃⲁⲗ...ⲁⲧⲉϥϭⲁⲗⲱ ⲡ. & fell to ground, PMéd
126 *v* ⲙⲛϩⲉ *tumour*, Tri 522 S ⲁⲧⲉⲥⲯⲩⲭⲏ ⲡ. &
she died انفصل, CDan 91 B ⲁϥⲫ. ⲙⲙⲁⲩ (*sc* in rock,
l ? ⲫⲱⲡⲕ) κρούειν. ⲡⲓⲉⲧⲫ.† B, *with wide-set
teeth* or *with split upper lip*: K 72 (var ⲫⲣⲉⲕ) ابل,
Montp 123 ⲫⲏ ⲉⲧⲫ. فل.

II tr, *pluck, root out*: Lev 14 40 S (ShIF 132,
B ⲑⲱⲕⲉⲙ), Eccl 10 9 S (F ⲥⲓϯ ⲉⲃⲁⲗ), Mt 5 29 SB
ἐξαιρ.; Ps 51 5 S (var & B ϥⲱϫⲉ), Jer 24 6 S (B
do) ἐκτίλλειν; Zeph 2 4 S (prob) A (B do), Mt 13
29 S (B do, F ⲧⲱⲕⲉⲙ) ἐκριζ.; Nu 16 14 S (B ϣⲱⲧ
ⲉⲃⲟⲗ) ἐκκόπτειν; Job 3 21 B (*l* ? ⲫⲱⲡⲕ, S ϣⲓⲕⲉ)
ἀνορύσσειν; ShA 2 341 S why not ⲡⲟⲣⲕⲟⲩ (*sc*
teeth)?, ShBM 196 ⲉϥⲡ. ⲡⲡⲱⲡⲉ, ShBerlOr 1613
2 320 S axes & tools for ⲡⲣⲕ ϣⲱⲡⲧⲉ, Mor 25 25 S
ⲁⲡϫⲥ̅ ⲡ. ⲙⲡⲥⲉⲉⲡⲉ ⲡⲡⲉⲓϫⲱⲗⲟⲡ = Va 61 120 B
ϥⲱϫⲓ, C 43 97 B bade ⲫ. ⲡⲡⲓⲉⲃⲧ (*l* ⲓϥⲧ).
With following preposition.

ⲥ ⲡⲥⲁ- S, *pluck at*: Mor 41 164 demon's claws
ⲡ. ⲡⲥⲁⲡⲉⲃⲁⲗ;   ⲥ ϩⲡ- SAB tr, *pluck from*: PVi
10157 84 A vices ⲡⲁⲣⲕⲟⲩ ϩⲣⲧⲏ[ⲡⲉ, BM 358 S
plants ⲙⲡⲓⲉϣ ⲡⲟⲣⲕⲟⲩ ϩⲛϯⲡⲟⲗⲓⲥ; intr, *delve, burrow in* (cf ? ⲡⲱⲡⲕ): BerlOr 1607 4 104 S anchor
of orthodoxy (in parable) ⲣⲟⲉⲓⲥ...ⲉⲧⲙⲧⲣⲉⲕⲕⲁⲁϥ ⲉⲡ.
ϩⲛⲡⲓⲥⲧⲓⲥ (*l* ? -ⲣⲭ), Va 61 101 B animal ⲉϥⲫ. ϫⲉⲡ-
ⲡⲓϩⲱⲣⲓ = Mor 25 19 S ⲥⲣⲟϥⲣⲉϥ;   ⲥ ϩⲓϫⲡ- S:
Mor 46 18 passing beneath it ⲡⲧⲉⲧⲃⲉⲡⲡⲉ ⲡ. ϩⲓϫⲱϥ
shall be rooted up upon (?) *him* & he shall die.
With following adverb.

ⲥ ⲉⲃⲟⲗ SB tr, *pluck out*: Gal 4 15 SB ἐξορύσσειν; Pro 24 52 B (SA ϣⲟⲕϣⲕ) ἐκκόπ.; C 43 167

B ϥ. ⲛⲛⲉϥⲃⲁⲗ ⲉⲃ., ST 394 *S* ⲁⲧⲉⲧⲛⲡⲱⲣⲕ ⲙⲙⲟϥ ⲉⲃ. (obscure);   intr, *be plucked out, start out*: C 43 218 *B* till eyeballs ϥ. ⲉⲃ., PLond 4 457 *S* will not suffer that any man ⲡ. ⲉⲃ.[(*cf ?* ⲡⲱⲗϭ ⲉⲃ. intr), ST 378 *S* when about to ⲡ. ⲁⲃ. *migrate* (?);   c ⲉⲃ. ϩⲛ-, ϩⲉⲡ-, *pluck out from*: ShC 42 140 *S* ⲁⲕⲡⲟⲣⲕⲛ ⲉⲃ. ϩⲛⲧⲥⲩⲡⲁⲅⲱⲅⲏ, AM 56 *B* ⲁⲩϥ. ⲛⲧⲁⲯⲩⲭⲏ ⲉⲃ. ϩⲉⲛⲡⲁⲥⲱⲙⲁ;   c ⲉⲡⲉⲥⲛⲧ *B*, *drag down*: C 86 359 fell into eyes ⲁⲩϥ. ⲛⲡⲉϥⲁⲗⲗⲟⲩ ⲉⲡ.;   c ⲉⲡϣⲱⲓ *B*, *pull up*: C 89 92 with hook they ϥ. ⲛⲧⲉϥⲯⲩⲭⲏ ⲉⲡ. from body.

—— *SB* nn m, *plucking out*: Leyd 271 *S* ⲡⲡ. ⲛⲛⲃⲁⲗ, Montp 125 *B* ⲙⲟⲣⲧ, ⲥⲭⲓⲙ, ⲡⲓϥ. نتف *depilation*, R 1 3 74 *S* ⲙⲟⲕⲣⲉⲥ, ⲡⲟⲗⲓⲧⲓⲁ, ⲡ. ⲛϩⲏⲧ *breaking of heart*.

ⲡⲟⲣⲕ *S* nn f, a dimension (?) in measurements: CO 473 ϣⲙⲟⲩⲛ ⲛϣⲟⲡ ⲉⲧⲛⲟϭⲉ ϣⲟⲙⲛⲧ ⲛϣⲟⲡ ⲉⲧⲡ., Hall 121 ⲛ]ϣⲟⲟⲡ ⲉⲧⲉϥⲡⲟⲣϭ.

In place-names (?): ⲡϣⲁⲡⲁⲣⲉⲕ, Ψααπάρεκ in Fayyûm (Wess 10 40, POxy 1917, *cf* ⲯⲁϩⲣϣⲏⲅⲉ, ⲡⲥⲁϩⲃⲏⲥ &c), Φερκω (PSI 932).

ⲡⲉⲣⲕⲓⲃⲉ *v* ⲕⲓⲃⲉ.

ⲡⲉⲣⲗⲱⲕ *v* ⲗⲱⲕ (ⲉⲣ ⲗⲱⲕ).

ⲡⲣⲓⲙⲓⲣ *S*[a] vb intr, meaning unknown: Kropp K 71 recipe ⲛⲥⲧⲁⲁⲥ ⲙⲡⲉⲙⲧⲟ ⲉⲃⲟⲗ ⲙⲡⲣⲏ ⲭⲉⲡⲛ. (*l* ?? ⲭⲉⲉϥⲉⲛⲡⲓⲣⲣⲉ *when about to rise, cf* ⲡⲉⲓⲣⲉ).

ⲡⲉⲣⲙⲟⲩ, ⲡⲉⲣⲉ. *B* nn, *lunatic*: C 86 323 ⲁⲛⲟⲕ ⲟⲩⲡⲉⲣ. (var ⲡⲉⲣⲉ.), ib 339 do; ⲟⲓ ⲛⲡ., *be lunatic*: Mt 4 24, 17 15 (*S* both ϩⲓⲧⲉ) σεληνιάζεσθαι. BM 920 207 Samanûdi says ⲡ. means beginning of month & of lunation راس الشهر وراس الهلال as ⲁⲗⲕⲉ its end.

ⲡⲣⲓⲙⲙⲉⲛⲟⲩ *S* nn, plant *artemisia*: P 44 83 ⲁⲃⲣⲟⲧⲓⲡⲟⲡ· هندبا = ⲡ. Prob a Gk word miswritten.

ⲡⲁⲣⲙⲟⲩⲧⲉ, ϥⲁⲣ. (Bor 251 296, PSBA 33 pl 50), ⲡⲁⲣⲙⲟⲩⲧ̇ (Ryl 265, Saq 275) *S*, -ⲙⲟⲩⲧⲓ (BM 580, Kr 217) *F*, ϥⲁⲣⲙⲟⲩⲑⲓ *B*, name of 8th month, Gk Φαρμοῦθι, Ar برمودة.

ⲡⲁⲣⲙϩⲟⲧⲡ, ⲡⲁⲣⲉⲙ. (oftenest), -ϩⲁⲧⲡ (J 9 5, Ep 537, DeBock *Matér* 69, Cai 8608), -ϩⲟⲧ (BMis 1192, BM 173) ⲡⲁⲣⲙϩⲟⲧ (Strzygowski *Kopt Kunst* 119), -ϩⲁⲧ (FR 8, J 38 6), ⲡⲁⲙⲡϩⲁⲧⲡ (Alex stele 175), ϥⲁⲙⲉⲛⲁⲧⲡ (Cai 8465) *S*, ⲡⲁⲣⲙⲁϩⲁ̅ⲧ̅ (*l* ? -ϩⲁⲧ BP 5561) *F*, ϥⲁⲙⲉⲛⲱⲑ *B*, name of 7th month, Gk Φαμενῶθ, Ar برمهات. *V* AZ 39 130.

ⲡⲉⲣⲛⲟⲩϭⲉ *S* nn, a plant ?: PMéd 204 ⲙⲟⲟⲩ ⲛⲡ. *Cf* برنوف *conyza* (Chassinat).

ⲡⲣⲛⲉϩ *v* ⲛⲉϩ.

ⲡⲣⲁⲡⲉ *S* nn f, meaning unknown, an object

of wax (?): Kropp K 48 ⲧⲁⲙⲉⲓⲟ ⲛⲛⲕ ⲛⲟⲩⲡ. ⲙⲙⲟⲩⲗ(ϩ) & write charm thereon (ⲉⲣⲟⲥ).

ⲡⲉⲣⲓⲡⲉⲣⲟⲓ *S* nn m, *royal palace*: Est 4 5 ϩⲁⲧⲉⲙ(ⲡⲉ)ⲡ., Nah 2 7 ⲛⲉⲡⲣⲓⲡⲉⲣⲟⲓ (P 44 116, *A* ⲛⲛⲟⲩ ⲛⲡⲣⲣⲁⲓ, *B* ⲛⲓⲙⲉⲧⲟⲩⲣⲱⲟⲩ) τὰ βασίλεια; Est 7 8 ⲡⲉⲡ. οἰκία (of king); P 43 70 ⲙⲡⲉⲣⲓⲡⲣⲟⲓ = 44 88 ⲡⲉⲣⲓⲡⲉⲣⲟⲥ ايوانات; Mor 25 101 built chapels like ϩⲉⲛⲡ. ⲙⲡⲣⲣⲟ, ib 28 23 sitting before Lord ⲉⲩⲡⲣⲟⲥⲉϩⲣⲉⲅⲉ ⲉⲛⲉϥⲡⲉⲣⲓⲡⲉⲣⲱⲓ. *V* HT *Copt Palimp* 384, OLZ 14 552, Spg *Kopt Etym* 19, Gardiner *Gram* 481.

ⲡⲣⲣⲉ *S*, ⲡⲣⲣⲓⲉ *A* *v* ⲡⲉⲓⲣⲉ.

(ⲡⲱⲣⲥ), ⲡⲣⲥ-, ⲡⲟⲣⲥ† *S* vb intr, *stretch, strain* (?): JTS 9 373 ⲡⲧⲉⲣⲉⲙⲁⲣⲉⲁ ⲡ.† ⲉⲃⲟⲗ ⲉⲡⲉϩⲟⲩⲟ yet made not progress (Lu 10 40), Mor 22 121 hair ⲡ.† ⲉϩⲣⲁⲓ like wild swine's = BSM 110 *B* ⲧⲉⲥ ⲉⲛϣⲱⲓ (*cf* ⲡⲣⲟⲥⲣⲉⲥ);   tr, *look boldly* (lit ? *stiffen eyes*): Mich 166 8 (Paul of Tammah) ⲉⲕⲉⲡⲣⲥ ⲡⲉⲕⲃⲁⲗ ⲉϫⲛⲛⲉⲕϩⲁϫⲉ like lion.

ⲡⲟⲣⲥ *S*, ⲡⲁⲣⲥ, -ⲉⲥ *F* nn f, *thing stretched?*, *mat?, curtain?*: Z 352 *S* hung ⲟⲩⲡ. on door of cell until should make one of ϥⲁ palm branches, Wess 15 151 *S* monk to porter ϫⲓ ⲡⲁⲕ ⲛ[ⲧⲉⲓ]ⲡ. & these reeds, CMSS 31 *F* money ⲛⲧⲁⲩϫⲓⲧⲟⲩ ⲙⲡ. ⲡⲉⲩ, ib 47 *F* send ϩⲉⲛⲡ., BM 546 *F* ⲧⲡ.

(ⲡⲱⲣⲥ), ⲡⲁⲣⲥ- *A* vb tr, *slaughter*: Is 53 7 (Cl) ⲁⲡⲁⲣⲥϥ (var & *S* ⲡⲕⲱⲛⲥ, *B* ϭⲟⲗϭⲉⲗ) σφαγή, 2 Mac 6 9 ⲁⲩⲡⲁⲡⲁⲣⲥⲟⲩ κατασφάζειν. Hardly same as last.

(ⲡⲣⲟⲥⲣⲉⲥ), ⲡⲣⲉⲥⲣⲁⲥⲧ† *S* vb intr, *become stiff of hair* (? *cf* ⲡⲱⲣⲥ): BHom 138 ⲡϥⲱ ⲉⲧⲡ. ϩⲁⲡⲓⲧⲉ Gk diff (πλοκάμους λυομένους).

ⲡⲣⲁϣ *S* nn m, meaning unknown, relates to irrigation: ShC 73 152 ⲉⲧⲙⲡⲉϣ ⲡⲙⲟⲟⲩ ⲉⲡ. ⲥⲡⲁⲩ ...ⲉⲣⲉⲡ. ⲥⲡⲁⲩ ⲡⲁⲥⲱ...ⲉⲧⲙⲕⲁ ϩⲁϩ ⲙⲙⲟⲟⲩ ⲉⲡⲉⲡ. *Cf* ? ⲡⲱⲣϣ, so *division, branch* of canal.

ⲡⲏⲣϣ *SA*, ϥⲏⲣϣ *B* nn m, *red-coloured substance*: Sa 13 14 *S*, Jer 22 14 *SB* μίλτος; ⲁϭⲁⲡ ⲙⲡ.: Lev 13 30 *B* (*S* ⲙⲣⲟϣⲧ†) ξανθίζειν, BP 11349 *S* crop withers & ⲁϥⲣ ⲡⲁϭⲟⲡ (sic) ⲙⲡ., PMéd 281 *S* in recipe for shingles (*ἀνζώνη). *rust, red blight*: Deu 28 42 *S* (*B* ⲉⲧⲏϣⲓ *q v*), Hos 5 7 *A* (*B* do), Joel 2 25 *S* (*A* ϩ ⲧⲱⲣϣ, *B* do) ἐρυσίβη; BMis 519 *S* nor mouse nor ⲡ. shall harm fields, BAp 65 *S* when dew fails dust & ⲡⲡ. ϣⲱⲡⲉ.   ⲁⲙⲡⲏⲣϣ *S*, *red earth*, *v* ⲟⲙⲉ.

ⲡⲱⲣϣ *SAF*, ⲡⲱⲣϩ *A*, ϥⲱⲣϣ *B*, by error ⲡⲱⲣϫ *S*, ϥⲱⲣϫ *B*, ⲡⲣϣ-, ⲡⲉ. *S*, ⲡⲣϩ- *A*, ϥⲉⲣϣ- *B*, ⲡⲟⲣϣ⳰ *S*, ⲡⲁⲣϩ⳰ *A*, ϥⲟⲣϣ⳰ *B*, ⲡⲁⲣϣ⳰ *A*[2] (Mani 1) *F*, ⲡⲟⲣϣ† *S*, ⲡⲁⲣϩ†, ⲡⲁⲣϫ† (Hos 5) *A*, ϥⲟⲣϣ† *B*, ⲡⲁⲣϣ† *F* vb I intr, *be spread*: Joel 2 2 *SB* (*A* ⲡ. ⲁⲃ.) χέειν,

Lev 13 22 S (var ⲡ. ⲉⲃ., B ϫⲱⲣ) διαχ.; LCyp 12 S
light ⲡ. ⲙⲡⲙⲁ ⲧⲏⲣϥ καταυγεῖν; BMis 385 S prepare place ⲡ. ⲕⲁⲗⲱⲥ (varr & BSM 40 B om, cf Mk
14 15), Mor 19 16 S went ϫⲉⲉϥⲛⲁⲡ. spread (bed)
at evening (var ib 18 8 ⲡ. ⲡⲛⲉϥϭⲣⲟⲓⲧⲉ) = Miss 4 103
B, Ryl 243 S ⲙⲁⲧⲧⲏⲗⲉ (μαντήλιον) ⲙⲡ., PMich
4567 S ⲧⲁⲡⲓⲥ (τάπης) ⲡⲡ.

II tr SAB, spread, cf فرش : Job 17 13 SB, Pro
7 16 SAB, Mk 14 15† SB στρωννύειν; Ps 104 39
B (S ⲡ. ⲉⲃⲟⲗ) διαπετάζειν; Jth 4 11 S ἐκτείνειν; Bel
14 B κατασείειν; Ez 40 17† SB stratus; BMar 34 S
bade ⲉⲧⲣⲉϥⲡ. ⲙⲡⲉⲃⲏⲙⲁ, C 43 4 B sim, BSM 42 B
ⲁⲩϥ. ⲡⲟⲩⲛⲟϫ ⲙⲫⲣⲏϣ, Aeg 52 B garments ⲉⲧⲁⲓ-
ⲫⲟⲣϣⲟⲩ, BMis 571 S throne ⲉϥⲡ.†, Leyd 386 S
ⲡϣⲁ ⲉⲧⲡ.†, Mor 28 6 S ⲡϣⲁϫⲉ ⲉϥⲡ.† ⲡϣⲟⲩⲓⲧⲉ ⲡϭⲓⲛ
& I know not ⲉⲓⲡⲁⲡⲟⲣϣⲧ ⲉⲁⲩ ⲙⲙⲟⲟⲩ, C 41 53 B
†ⲭⲏⲣⲓ ⲙⲫⲟⲣϣ (l ⲫⲉ.) ⲱⲓⲕ = Miss 4 413 تسطح
(v n there).

With following preposition. ⲉ ⲉ- S, stretch toward : R 1 4 57 S my reason ⲡ† ⲉⲡⲡⲉ ἀνατείνειν,
Phil 3 13 (cit BHom 9 -ⲗⲱ, B ⲥⲱⲟⲩⲧⲉⲡ) ἐπεκτείν.
dat (cf ⲡⲱⲣⲝ ⲉ ⲉ·); ⲉ ⲉϫⲛ- SAB, spread upon :
Hos 5 1 B (A ⲡ. ⲁⲃⲁⲗ) ἐκτείν. ἐπί; Pro 25 22
S (var ⲅⲓϫⲛ-) A σωρεύειν ἐπί; Am 9 6 A (S ⲡⲱⲣⲧ,
B ϫⲱϣ) ἐκχέειν ἐπί; Lu 19 35 S (B ⲃⲟⲣⲃⲉⲣ)
ἐπιρρίπτειν ἐπί; R 1 4 59 S fire ⲛⲧⲉⲧⲛⲡⲟⲣϣϥ
ⲉϫⲙⲡⲕⲁϩ ἁπλοῦν εἰς; Ez 12 13 B ⲉϩⲣⲏⲓ ⲉϫ. (S ⲡ.
ⲉⲃ.) ἐκπετ. ἐπί; ShRyl 67 404 S throne & ⲡⲉⲧⲡ.†
ⲉϫⲱϥ; ⲉ ⲅⲓϫⲛ- SB, meaning same : Ex 40 4 B
προτιθέναι; Mk 11 7 S (B ⲧⲁⲗⲟ) ἐπιβάλλειν dat;
Ryl 94 S ⲡⲥⲉⲡⲉⲣϣ ⲟⲩⲙⲏⲏϣⲉ ⲛⲝⲃⲃⲥ ⲅⲓϫⲙⲡ-
ⲕⲁϩ; ⲉ ⲡ.- dat SB, spread for : 1 Kg 9 25 S
(var ⲅⲁⲣⲟϥ ⲡ-) διαστρωννύναι dat; CDan 94 B were
about to ϥ. ⲡⲁϥ on roof, BSM 41 B ⲡⲧⲉⲡϥ. ⲙⲡⲁⲣ-
ϫⲱⲡ = BMis 388 S ϩⲁ-. ⲉ ⲡⲁ ϥⲣⲡ- S, spread
before : R 1 4 72 ⲁⲓⲡ. ⲙ[ⲡⲁ]ⲙⲉⲉⲩⲉ ⲛⲡⲁϩⲣⲁϥ ἐκτείν.
πρός; ⲉ ϩⲁ-, ϣⲁ- SBF intr, spread beneath, prepare couch : Ac 9 34 SBF στρω. dat; PO 11 325 B
serving them & ⲉϥϥ. ϣⲁⲣⲱⲟⲩ, Mor 25 193 S ⲁⲩⲡ.
ϩⲁⲣⲟϥ & laid him on bed, AM 99 B sim, BMis
386 S & Va 63 13 B how shall we ⲡ. ϩⲁⲡⲁⲣⲭⲱⲡ?
= BSM 40 B what shall we ⲫⲟⲣϣϥ ⲥⲁϩⲣⲏ ⲙ-
ⲡⲁⲣ.?; tr SB : Ez 27 30 SB στρω., Is 58 5
SB ὑποστ.; ShC 73 84 S ⲡϣⲟⲩⲡⲟⲣϣϥ ϩⲁⲣⲟⲟⲩ
(skin or pillow), BMar 24 S ⲁϥⲡ. ϩⲁⲣⲟϥ ⲛⲁⲡⲁ ⲃⲓⲕⲧⲱⲣ ⲛⲧⲉϥⲥⲧⲟⲗⲏ, C 43 119 B ⲁⲥϥ. ϩⲁⲣⲟϥ ⲛⲟⲩⲙⲁ
ⲡⲉⲡⲕⲟⲧ; ⲉ ϩⲓ- SB, spread on, in : Mt 21 8 B
(S ⲡ. ϩⲣⲁⲓ ϩⲛ-) στρω. ἐν; ⲉ ϩⲛ-, ϣⲉⲡ- SB,
meaning same : Jth 7 14 S καταστ. ἐν; BMis 69 S
sheets ⲁⲥⲡⲟⲣϣⲟⲩ ϩⲙⲡⲕⲁϩ, C 43 147 B bade ϥ.
ⲙⲡⲉⲃⲏⲙⲁ ϣⲉⲡⲟⲩⲧⲟⲡⲟⲥ; ⲉ ϩⲁⲧⲛ-, ϣⲁⲧⲉⲛ- SB,
spread beside : R 1 3 36 S ⲡ. ⲙⲡⲉⲥⲟⲣⲟⲡⲟⲥ ϩⲁⲧⲙ-
ⲡⲱϥ, C 43 206 B ϥⲟ. ⲡⲓⲃⲏⲙⲁ ϣⲁⲧⲉⲛⲫⲣⲟ.

With following adverb.

—— ⲉⲃⲟⲗ intr, SAB, be spread out : Ez 1 11 B
(var tr) ἐκτείνεσθαι; ib 31 5 B πλατύνεσθαι; Lev
14 48 S (ShIF 134, B ϫⲛⲱϣ) διαχέεσθαι; 1 Chr 28
18 B whose wings ϥ. ⲉⲃ. διαπετ., Ez 34 12 B δια-
χωρίζεσθαι; BM 893 B sim (not ϥ.†), Miss 4 813 S
will cause thy name to ⲡ. ⲉⲃ. in all land; ⲉⲃ. ⲉ-
SB, spread to : Is 54 3 B (S tr) ἐκπετ. εἰς; Z 323
S ⲉⲣⲉⲡⲉϥϫⲓϫ ⲡ. ⲉⲃ. ⲉϩⲣⲁⲓ ⲉⲧⲡⲉ ἁπλ. εἰς; ⲉ ⲉⲃ.
ⲉϫⲛ- SB, spread upon, over : Hos 4 2 S (var & A
ϩⲓϫⲛ-, B ⲫⲱⲡ) χέ. ἐπί; Lev 13 13 S (var & B ⲣⲱϩⲥ),
Ez 30 18 B καλύπτειν; 3 Kg 8 7 B διαπετ. ἐπί; Ez
37 8 SB extendi desuper; Mk 9 7 S (var ⲣⲱϩⲥ, BF
ⲉⲣ ϧⲁⲓⲃⲓ) ἐπισκιάζειν dat; ⲉⲃ. ϩⲓϫⲛ- SB, meaning same : Si 47 20 S καλύπ.; C 89 6 B dew fell
& ⲁⲥϥ. ⲉⲃ. ϩ. ⲡⲣⲟ of ground, Bor 256 153 S cloud
ⲁⲥⲡ. ⲉⲃ. ϩ. ⲡⲉⲃⲁⲣⲃⲁⲣⲟⲥ; ⲉⲃ. ⲡ- S, be spread
with (clouds) : Deu 33 28 (B ⲙⲉϩ ⲡ-) συννεφὴς
(γίνεσθαι). tr, SABF, spread out, abroad : Nu
14 16 S (B om ⲉⲃ.) καταστρω.; Ps 103 2 S (B ⲥⲱⲗⲕ),
Pro 1 24 SAB, Hos 5 1 A†B†(Lacr), Jo 21 18 S
(B ⲥⲱⲟⲩⲧⲉⲡ) ἐκτείν., Is 40 32 S (B ⲥ.) διατ., Ac 20
7 B (S ⲥⲱⲕ) παρατ.; 3 Kg 8 38 B διαπετ.; MG 25
11 B hands ϥ.† ⲉⲃ. ἁπλοῦσθαι; Ap 20 12 S (B ⲟⲩⲱⲡ)
ἀνοίγειν; Jud 8 25 S ἀναπτύσσειν; Z 309 S ⲁϥⲡ.
ⲉⲃ. ⲛⲧⲡⲏⲥⲧⲓⲁ ἐπιμένειν dat; PS 242 S ⲉϥⲡ.† ⲉⲃ.
ⲙⲡⲡⲉϥⲙⲉⲗⲟⲥ ⲧⲏⲣⲟⲩ lying spread out (?) paral 243
ⲡⲱⲣϫ ⲛⲡⲉϥⲙⲉⲗⲟⲥ, Z 587 S formerly rare now
ⲉϥⲟϣ ⲁⲩⲱ ⲉϥⲡ.† ⲉⲃ., AM 264 B fame ϥ.† ⲉⲃ. everywhere, Mor 24 27 F festival ⲉⲧⲡ.† ⲉⲃ., BHom 50 S
great fight ⲡ.† ⲉⲃ., El 52 A ⲡⲧⲁⲣⲉϥⲡⲁⲣϧ ⲁⲃ. (sc
roll), Va 58 73 B ⲡⲁϥⲫⲟⲣϫ (l ⲫⲱⲣϣ) ⲉⲃ. ⲛⲧⲧⲣⲁ-
ⲡⲉⲍⲁ, BKU 1 26 (8116 a) F bird's heart (ⲡ)ⲧⲉⲕ-
ⲡⲁⲣϣϥ ⲉⲃ., BMar 218 S ⲁⲓⲡⲉⲣϣ ⲧⲟⲟⲧ ⲉⲃ. = Rec
6 183 B; refl S : ShA 1 452 ⲁϥⲡⲟⲣϣϥ ⲉⲃ. lay
stretched out in road, ShRE 10 164 dragon ⲛϥⲡⲟⲣϣϥ
ⲉⲃ. ⲡⲧⲉϥϣⲓⲡ, Mun 127 ⲧϭⲟⲙ...ⲁⲥⲡⲟⲣϣⲥ ⲉⲃ. &
rested upon Virgin; ⲉⲃ. ⲉ- SAB, s. out to : Ps
43 20 S (B ⲉⲃ. ⲟⲩϩⲉ-) διαπετ. πρός, Lam 1 13 B
δ. dat, Is 65 2 S (B do) ἐκπετ. πρός, Pro 1 17 SA (B
ⲉϫⲉⲡ-) ἐκτείν. dat; AM 161 B ⲁⲩϥ. ⲛⲡⲟⲩϫⲓϫ ⲉⲃ.
ⲉⲡⲥⲁ of east : ⲉⲃ. ⲉϫⲛ- SB, s. out upon : Ez 37
6 S (ShA 1 370) B ἐκτ. ἐπί; Job 38 24 S (B ⲥⲓⲣ ⲉⲃ.)
διασκεδαννύναι εἰς; Si 37 35 S ἐκχέειν ἐπί; MG
25 38 B snares ϥ.† ⲉⲃ. ⲉϫ. ⲡⲓⲕⲟⲥⲙⲟⲥ ἁπλ. ἐπί;
Deu 32 11 S refl (B ⲣⲱϩⲥ) σκεπάζειν; Lev 3 3 S (B
Gk om); ShC 42 146 S ⲉⲓⲡ.† ⲉⲃ. ⲉϫⲙⲡⲕⲁϩ on my
face, Aeg 32 B refl ⲁⲓⲫⲟⲣϣⲧ ⲉⲃ. ⲉϫⲉⲡⲡⲉϥⲥⲱⲙⲁ,
BMar 92 S disease ⲉⲧⲡ.† ⲉⲃ. ⲉϫⲡⲛⲁⲟⲩⲣⲏⲧⲉ; Ez 12
13 S ⲉϩⲣⲁⲓ ⲉϫⲡ- (B om ⲉⲃ.) ἐκπετ. ἐπί; ⲉⲃ.
ϩⲓϫⲛ- SBF, meaning same : Ge 15 11 S (var ⲉϫ.,
B ϧⲉⲙⲥⲓ ϩ.) συγκαθίζειν dat; 2 Kg 17 19 S (var
ⲉϫ.) ψύχειν ἐπί; Pro 8 27 SA (B ⲟⲩⲱϯ ⲉⲃ.) ἀφορί-

ζειν ἐπί; ShA 2 299 S ⲁϥⲡⲟⲣϣϥ ⲉⲃ....ⲅ. ⲡⲕⲁϩ for could not stand, AM 314 B �ⲛⲁⲡ. ⲉⲃ. ϩⲓⲭⲱϥ ⲛ̄ⲧⲁⲥⲧⲟⲗⲏ, Mor 24 5 F grief ⲉⲧⲡ.† ⲉⲃ. ϩⲓⲭⲉⲡⲡⲕⲟⲥⲙⲟⲥ; ⲉⲃ. ⲟⲩⲃⲉ- B, v ⲉⲃ. ⲉ- above; ⲉⲃ. ϩⲁⲧⲏ ⲥⲃ, s. before: Si 4 28 SB ὑποστρω. dat; Ez 16 25 S (B ⲓⲛⲓ ⲉⲃ.) διάγειν dat; ⲉⲃ. ⲉⲡϣⲱⲓ B, s. forth upward: 2 Chr 6 12 διαπετ. only.

—— ⲉⲡϣⲱⲓ B, spread upward: 3 Kg 8 22 διαπετ. εἰς, Is 1 15 (SF ⲉϩⲣⲁⲓ) ἐκτείν. πρός.

—— ⲉϩⲟⲩⲛ S, penetrate: Jth 4 7 ϩⲓⲏ ⲙⲡ. ⲉ. πρόσβασις.

—— ⲉϩⲣⲁⲓ SF, spread upward: Ps 87 10 S (B ⲉⲡϣⲱⲓ) διαπ. πρός, Is 1 15 SF ut sup.

—— SB nn m, thing spread, mat, coverlet, cf فرش; Ps 131 3 B (S ⲡⲣⲏϣ, Am 6 4 B (var ⲫⲣⲏϣ, A ⲡⲣⲉϩ) στρωμνή, C 89 41 B = Miss 4 521 S ϩⲃⲥⲱ στρῶμα; BSM 39 B = BMis 384 S do, Ryl 243 S ⲟⲩⲡ. ⲡⲁⳠⳠⲡⲁⲇ (الديباج). ⲡ. ⲉⲃⲟⲗ S, spreading out: Br 227 ⲡⲡ. ⲉⲃ. of hands.

ⲙⲁ ⲙⲡ., ⲫ. SB, place spread, couch: Ez 26 14 B ψυγμός for nets; FR 38 S sheets spread like ⲟⲩⲙⲁ ⲡ̄ⲕⲟⲧⲕ ⲏ ⲟⲩⲙⲁ ⲙⲡ.

ϫⲓⲛⲫ. B, act of, place of spreading: Am 2 8 (A = Gk) παραπέτασμα, AM 110 garments ⲉⲡⲝ. ϩⲁⲣⲱⲟⲩ.

ⲫⲟⲣϣ B nn f, spread table: MG 25 210 ⲁϥϫⲁ ⳿ϯⲫ., ib 378 sitting ϩⲉⲛ⳿ϯⲫ., ib eating ϩⲓ⳿ϯⲫ. τράπεζα, P 54 170 ⳿ϯⲫ. حصير, برش . ⲡⲟⲣϣⲥ S nn f, meaning same: BMar 181 if thou need aught (at meals) ϩⲣⲧⲡ., ib 182 if visitor come ⲕⲱ ⲉϩⲣⲁⲓ ⲛ̄ⲧⲕⲡ. & eat with him. Cf ? ⲡⲁⲣϩⲥ.

ⲡⲣⲏϣ SF, ⲡⲣⲁϣ S (PStras 41), ⲡⲣⲏϩ A, ⲫⲣⲏϣ B nn m, thing spread, mat, cloak: Ge 49 4 SB, Job 17 13 SB, Am 6 4 AB (var ⲫⲱⲣϣ) στρωμνή, Pro 22 27 SA, Miss 4 521 S = C 89 41 B ⲫ., ib 530 S ⲡ. ⲡϧⲱ = ib 49 B ϩⲃⲟⲥ στρῶμα opp ⲧⲙ̄ⲏ; Z 307 S ⲡ. ⲡⲕⲁⲙ ψίαθος; Deu 27 20 S (B ϩⲱⲃⲥ) συγκάλυμμα; Jer 15 12 B (S diff) περιβόλαιον; Is 3 23 S (B = Gk) κατάκλιτον, Va 66 298 B lying on ϩⲁⲡϣⲫ. ⲉⲅⲑⲁⲙⲓⲏⲟⲩⲧ ἐπίβλημα; Jth 12 15 S κώδιον; Mor 37 141 S ἱμάτιον; Mus 40 38 S ⲉⲣⲉⲡⲉⲡⲛ. ϭⲟⲟⲗⲉ ⲙⲙⲟϥ palliolum lineum; Tri 426 S, TRit 219 B فراش; ShC 73 113 S ⲡ. ⲏ ϩⲟⲓⲧⲉ not to be changed without leave, Sh(Besa)Z 504 S ϩⲟⲉⲓⲧⲉ, ⲡ., ⲕⲗⲁϥⲧ, BM 585 F ⲕⲁⲙⲓⲥⲓ & ⲡ., ShP 130⁵ 34 S variegated ⲡ. covering rich man's dogs, BSM 42 B spread ⲡⲟϫ ⲙⲫ. for ἄρχων = Va 63 14 B & BMis 388 S ⲁⲕⲟⲩⳠⲓⲧⲱⲛ, Z 352 S lay down & ⲁϥⲡⲟⲩⲝ ⲙⲡⲉⲡ. ⲉϫⲱϥ, BMis 315 S ⲡⲉⲡ. ⲉⲧϩⲓⲭⲱϥ on bed, Va 67 80 B ⲁⲓⲉⲡⲕⲟⲧ ⲉϫⲉⲡⲡⲁⲫ., TT 158 S ⲡ. ⲡⲥⲟⲣⲧ, ST 294 S ⲡ. ⲡϫⲁⲕ, TurM 18 S ⲡ. ϣⲏⲙ ⲡ̄ϩⲏⲕⲉ (sic l). V also ⲕⲗⲙⲉ.

ⲙⲁⲫⲣⲏϣ B nn m: C 86 180 king (al-Kâmil) was sleeping in ⲡⲓⲙ. فراش ? .

ⲡⲱⲣϩ, ⲡⲁⲣϩ, ⲡⲣⲏϩ A v ⲡⲱⲣϣ.

ⲡⲁⲣϩⲥ SF nn f, covering for jar: Ep 351 S ⲧⲉⲡ. ⲡ̄ⲧⲓⲥ (= ⲧⲁⲁⲥ) ⲉⲣⲱϥ ⲙ̄ⲡⲓⲑⲟⲥ, BP 908 S in list ⲟⲩⲡ., BM 707 F ⲡⲗⲟⲩ(ⲟⲥ) ⲙⲡⲡ. (l ⲡ̄ⲙⲡ.). Cf ⲡⲱⲣϣ (ⲡⲟⲣϣⲥ).

ⲡⲱⲣⲝ SAA²FO, ⲫⲱⲣⲝ B, ⲡⲱⲗⲝ, -ⲉⲝ F, ⲡⲣⲝ, ⲡⲉⲣⲝ- S, ⲫⲉⲣⲝ- B, ⲡⲟⲣⲝ⳰ S, ⲡⲁⲣⲝ⳰ AF, ⲫⲟⲣⲝ⳰ B, ⲡⲁⲗⲝ⳰ F, ⲡⲟⲣⲝ† S, ⲡⲁⲣⲝ† A, ⲫⲟⲣⲝ† B, often confused with ⲡⲱⲣϣ, vb I intr, divide, be divided: Is 31 28 B (SF ⲡⲱϣ) διαιρεῖσθαι; Ez 24 14 SB, Nah 1 12 A (B ⲫ. ⲉⲃ.) διαστέλλειν; Ex 14 21 B σχίζειν, Ps 34 15 S (var ⲭⲱⲱⲣⲉ ⲉⲃ.) B διασχ.; 1 Cor 7 15 SBF χωρίζειν; Mk 3 26 S (B ⲫⲱϣ) μερίζεσθαι; BSM 34 B ⲁⲡⲫ. & become two = BMis 377 S ⲡⲱϣ.

II tr SABF; divide, separate: Lev 5 4 B (S diff), Si 16 26 S διαστ.; Ps 135 13 B (S ⲡⲱϣ) καταδιαιρεῖν; Ex 19 12 S (B ⲟⲩⲱ⳿ϯ) ἀφορίζειν; Job 28 10 B (S ⲡⲱϩ) ῥηγνύναι, Ps 77 13 B (S do) διαρρ.; Deu 18 8† S (B ⲫⲱϣ) μερίζειν; ib 14 8† B (S ⲡⲱⲧⲥ) διχηλεῖν; Mt 19 6 SB χωρ., Pro 16 28 SA διαχ.; Mt 24 51 B (S ⲡⲱϣ) διχοτομεῖν; Ge 11 7 B συγχέειν; Is 7 15 S (B om) προαιρεῖν; Lev 2 14 B (S ? ⲡⲱϩ) φρύγειν, cf ib 23 14 sim (S ⲟⲩⲱϣⲙ); BHom 67 S ⲡϭⲡ. ⲡ̄ⲡⲉⲡⲧⲏ⳰, Mus 42 223 S bade ⲉⲧⲙⲡⲣⲝ ⲡ̄ⲧⲁⲙⲟⲥ, BSM 48 B Michael says ⲉ ⲫ. ⲙ̄ⲡⲓⲡⲟⲗⲉⲙⲟⲥ before king (l ? ⲫⲱⲗⲝ) = Va 63 17 B & BMis 397 S ϭⲱⲧⲡ, BM 583 F lest we starve ϣⲁⲡⲧⲉⲡⲡⲉ̄ ⲡⲁⲣⲭⲉⲡ, Kr 247 S ⲫⲁⲥⲓⲗⲉ (φάσηλος) ϭⲡ.†, ⲫⲁⲥ. ϭⲧⲙⲁ, ib ⲁⲣϣⲓⲛ do (cf Lev 2 14 above); ⲫⲉⲣⲝ ⲣⲟ B, ⲡⲣⲝ ϣⲁⲣ S v ⲡⲱⲗⲇ II.

With following preposition.

—— ⲉ- SAA²BFO intr, a be divided from: Pro 18 1 SA, 1 Cor 7 10 SBF χωρ. ἀπό, 2 Kg 1 23 S (var + ⲉⲃⲟⲗ, B ⳿ϯ ⲟⲩⲱ ⲉⲃ.) διαχ.; ShC 42 130 S ⲉϥϩⲟⲩⲉϣ ⲡ. ⲉⲡⲉϥϣⲃⲉⲉⲣ, Mun 56 S ⲉⲕⲡⲁⲡ. ⲉⲣⲟⲓ ? = C 89 18 B, Mor 30 27 F ⲕⲡⲉⲡ. ⲉⲗⲁⲓ, Hor 83 O ⲡ. ⲁⲣⲁⲥ, BMar 190 S wishing ⲙⲡ. ⲉⲡϩⲙϩⲁⲗ be rid of, C 43 13 B body began ⲙ̄ⲫ. ⲉⲡⲉϥⲁⲣⲟⲩ come to pieces; tr, divide from: Sa 1 3 S (B ⲉⲃⲟⲗ ϩⲁ-), Ro 8 35 S (B ⲥⲁⲃⲟⲗ ⲛ-) χωρ. ἀπό; Ru 1 17 S διαστ. ἀνὰ μέσον; 2 Cor 6 17 S (B ⲉⲃ. ⲛ-) ἀφορ.; Mt 10 35 SB διχάζειν; AP 8 A² στερεῖν; ShBor 246 90 S if eye whole ⲉⲣⲉⲡⲟⲩⲟⲉⲓⲛ ⲡ.† ⲉⲣⲟϥ ⲡⲟⲩ ?, C 41 74 B ⲉⲫ. ⲡ̄ⲧⲁⲯⲩⲭⲏ ⲉⲡⲁⲥⲱⲙⲁ, Mor 24 3 F to Herodias ⲡ. ⲡ̄ϩⲏⲣⲱⲁⲛⲥ ⲉⲗⲁ, cf ib 4 sim ϩⲁⲃⲁⲗ ⲛ-; b intr, be divided into: Ge 2 10 SB ἀφορ. εἰς, Ez 37 22 S (B ϣⲱⲡⲓ ⲛ-), Dan 11 4 B διαιρεῖν εἰς, BMar 42 S woman ⲁⲥⲡ. ⲉⲧⲉⲥⲙⲏⲧⲉ; tr, divide into: Ge 32 7 B (S ⲡⲱϣ ⲉ-) διαιρ. εἰς, Miss 8 96 S cannot ⲡ. ⲙ̄ⲡⲟⲩⲁ...ⲉϣⲏⲣⲉ ⲥⲛⲁⲩ διαίρετος εἰς; PS 299 S spirit & body ϣⲁϥⲡⲟⲣⲭⲟⲩ ⲉⲩⲙⲉⲣⲟⲥ

but soul ⲉⲕⲉⲙⲉⲣⲟⲥ;   for ⲡⲱⲣϣ *S*: BMis 413 ⲡⲧⲓⲡⲟⲣⲝⲡ ⲉⲡⲁⲑⲏ (*cf* Phil 3 13), *ib* 140 Virgin & child ⲉⲣⲉⲡⲛⲉ ⲡ.† ⲉⲡⲉⲥⲡⲓⲣ raising face to hers.

—— ⲉⲭⲉⲛ- *B* intr, *be divided from*: Lu 12 53 (*S* ⲡⲱϣ ⲙⲛ-) διαμερ. ἐπί.

—— ⲛ- *SB* intr, *part from*: Philem 15 *B* (*S* ⲟⲩⲉ) χωρ., Gu 23 *S* ⲁⲥⲡ. ⲙⲡⲉⲅⲙⲁ ⲡⲉⲡⲕⲟⲧⲕ χωρισμός; Mor 34 58 *S* turned aside ϧⲱⲥ ⲉϥⲛⲁⲡ. ⲙⲙⲟⲟⲩ, C 89 22 *B* ⲥⲉⲛⲁϣ ϥ. ⲛⲛⲟⲅⲓⲟϯ = Miss 4 543 *S* ⲡ. ⲉ-;   tr, *separate from*: AM 107 *B* ⲙⲡⲓϥⲟⲣⲭϥ ⲙⲙⲟⲓ since my youth.

—— ϧⲛ-, ϩⲉⲛ- *SBO* intr, *divide in, between*: Lev 10 10 *S* (*B* ⲟⲩⲱϯ), Ez 22 26 *B* διαστ. ἀνὰ μέσον; Hor 80 *O* ⲡⲁϥⲁⲡ. ϩⲛⲟⲩⲉⲓⲉⲡϣⲱⲧ.

With following adverb.

—— ⲉⲃⲟⲗ *SABF* intr, *separate, divide*: Jos 15 12 *S* ὁρίζειν, Is 52 11 *B* (*S* refl) ἀφορ., Aeg 285 *S* ἀφιστάναι; ShBM 209 35 *S* thus did every heresy ⲡ. ⲉⲃ. from the first;   tr, *divide, set apart*: Nu 8 11 *SB*, Is 52 11 *S* (*B* intr), Mt 13 49 *S* (*BF* ⲉⲃ. ϩⲉⲛ-), Lu 6 22 *S* (*B* ⲟⲩⲱϯ ⲉⲃ.), Ro 1 1 *S* (*B* ⲑⲱϣ) ἀφορ, Ez 20 31 *SB* ἀφόρισμα, Is 45 18 *S* (*B* ⲟⲩ.) διορ., Ro 8 29 *S* (*B* ⲑ.) προορ.; Lev 7 34 *B* (*S* = Gk) ἀφαίρεμα; Lev 13 46† *S* (*B* ⲥⲁⲡⲥⲁ), He 7 26† *B* (*SF* ⲥⲟⲟϩⲉ ⲉⲃ.), Wess 15 137 *S* Nestorius hath ⲡⲁⲣⲭⲟⲩ ⲉⲃ. χωρ.; Deu 19 7 *S* (*B* ⲟⲩ.) διαστ., Hab 2 4 *A* (*B* ϧⲉⲛ-); Va 57 231† *B* διασπᾶν; Su 55 *B* (var om ⲉⲃ.) σχίζειν; R 1 1 59 *S* ⲁⲩⲡⲟⲣⲝⲟⲩ ⲉⲃ. αἰρ. ἀπ᾽ ἀλλήλων; Aeg 274 *S* book ⲡ.† ⲉⲃ. on his head ἀναπτύσσειν (*l* ⲡⲟⲣϣ); Lam 4 7† *S* (*B sic l*) Gk om (? gloss on Ναζειραῖος); ShC 73 89 *S* ⲁϥⲡⲣⲭ ϩⲉⲡⲕⲟⲩⲓ ⲡⲁϥ ⲉⲃ., BMis 349 *S* ⲁϥⲡ. ⲡⲁⲓ ⲉⲃ. ⲙⲡⲁⲃⲉⲕⲉ = BSM 14 *B* ⲥⲉⲙⲡⲓ (*v* Ge 30 31), Mor 24 11 *F* ⲡⲥⲉⲡⲁⲗϫⲟⲩ ⲉⲃ., R 1 5 51 *S* martyr prays hegemon will ⲡⲟⲣⲝϥ ⲉⲃ. speedily = Mor 32 28 *S* ⲡⲁⲗϭϥ ⲉⲃ. (*cf* ⲡⲱⲗϭ ⲉⲃ. tr), AM 288 *B* ⲁϥϥ. ⲡ. ⲡⲉϥϫⲓⲝ ⲉⲃ. (*l* ϥⲟⲣϣ);   c ⲉⲃ. ⲉ- *S* intr, *be divided into*: PS 221 ⲁϥⲡ. ⲉⲃ. ⲉⲥⲁϣϥ mysteries; tr, *separate from*: PS 343 limbs ⲁⲩⲡⲟⲣⲭϥ (*l* ?-ϫⲟⲩ) ⲉⲃ. ⲉⲧⲯⲩⲭⲏ, BM 358 ⲉⲁϥⲡⲉⲣⲉϫ ϩⲁϩ ⲉⲃ. ⲉⲧⲡⲓⲥⲧⲓⲥ;   c ⲉⲃ. ⲉⲭⲛ- *S* intr: Am 8 9 (Z 217) grief & sadness ⲡⲁⲡ. ⲉⲃ. ⲉⲭⲛⲧⲟⲓⲕⲟⲩⲙⲉⲛⲏ, but prob *l* ⲡⲱⲣϣ;   c ⲉⲃ. ⲛ-, *part from* intr: Jud 4 11 *S* χωρ. ἀπό, Ac 13 13 *SB* ἀποχ. ἀπό, Lu 9 33 *SB* διαχ. ἀπό; Ge 31 49 *B* (*S* ⲥⲟⲟϩⲉ ⲉⲃ. ⲡ-) ἀφιστάναι ἀπό; Ez 37 11 *SB* διαφωνεῖν; ShHT *K* 2 *S* Satan ⲉⲁϥⲡ. ⲉⲃ. ⲡⲡⲉⲧⲣⲙⲙⲓⲛⲅⲉ fell to earth, BMis 66 *S* ⲁϥⲡ. ⲉⲃ. ⲙⲙⲟⲛ = FR 30 *S* ⲥⲟⲕϥ ⲡⲥⲁⲃⲟⲗ ⲛ-;   tr: Lev 25 34 *S* (*B* ⲟⲩ. ⲉⲃ. ⲛ-), Mt 25 32 *S* (*cf* R 2 3 16 [ⲡⲟⲩ]ϩⲣⲉ ⲉⲃ., *B* ⲉⲃ. ϩⲉⲛ-) ἀφορ. ἀπό, Job 35 11 *S* (*B* ⲉⲃ. ϩⲉⲛ-), Is 45 24 *S* (*B* ⲟⲩ. ⲉⲃ. ϩⲁ-) διορ. ἀπό; Su 52 *B* διαχωρ. ἀπό; ShC 42 147 *S* ⲉⲉⲓⲡ.† ⲉⲃ. ⲡⲧⲥⲩⲛⲁⲅⲱⲅⲏ, ShA 2 276 *S* ⲡ. ⲙⲡⲉⲥⲟⲩ ⲉⲃ.

ⲙⲡⲧⲱⲣ, Pcod 37 *S* ⲡⲣⲝ ⲡⲉⲕⲙⲁ ⲡϣⲱⲡⲉ ⲉⲃ. ⲙ- ⲡⲕⲟⲥⲙⲟⲥ;   c ⲉⲃ. ϩⲉⲛ- *B*, meaning same, intr: C 89 111 ⲡⲧⲉϥϥ. ⲉⲃ. ϩⲉⲛⲡⲓⲥⲛⲏⲟⲩ & depart, *cf ib* ϥ. ⲉⲡⲓⲥⲛⲏⲟⲩ;   tr *SBF*: Si 47 2 *S* ἀφορ. ἀπό, Is 29 22 *S* (*B* ⲟⲩ. ⲉ-), Mt 13 49 *SBF* ἀφορ. ἐκ; Ge 30 32 *S* (*B* ϥ. ⲙⲙⲁⲩ) διαχωρ. ἐκεῖθεν; Nu 16 21 *S* (*B* intr) ἀποσχ. ἐκ μεσου; DeV 2 21 *B* ϥⲏ ⲉⲧⲁϥϥ. ⲡⲉⲡⲓⲟϯ ⲉⲃ. ϩⲉⲛⲡⲓⲡⲁⲣⲁⲇⲓⲥⲟⲥ;   c ⲉⲃ. ⲡⲧⲉⲛ- *B* tr, *separate in respect of*: Ex 29 28† ἀφαίρεμα παρά;   c ⲉⲃ. ⲟⲩⲧⲉ- *B* intr, *divide between*: Ge 1 4 διαχ. ἀνὰ μέσον; tr *S*: BMis 558 ⲙⲏ ⲁⲓⲡⲟⲣϫⲉ ⲉⲃ. ⲟⲩⲧⲉⲡⲁⲇⲓⲕⲁⲓⲟⲥ?   c ⲉⲃ. ϩⲁ- *B* tr, *part from*: Is 56 3 (*S* ⲉⲃ. ϩⲛ-) ἀφορ. ἀπό; C 89 204 time ⲉⲑⲣⲓϥ. ⲉⲃ. ϩⲁⲡⲁⲓⲱⲧ;   c ⲉⲃ. ϩⲓ- *S* tr, *remove from off*: ShC 73 90 ⲡⲣⲝ ⲟⲩϩⲡⲁⲁⲩ ⲉⲃ. ϩⲓⲧⲉⲧⲣⲁⲡⲉⲍⲁ;   c ⲉⲃ. ϩⲓⲭⲉⲛ- *B* (*l* ?ϥⲟⲣϣ): AM 118 ⲁϥϥ. ⲡⲉϥϫⲓⲝ ⲉⲃ. ϩⲓⲡⲓⲗⲁⲟⲥ.

—— ⲥⲁⲃⲟⲗ ⲛ- *B* part from, intr: 1 Cor 7 10 (*SF* ⲡ. ⲉ-) χωρ. ἀπό, Ge 13 11 (*S* ⲧⲱⲟⲩⲛ ⲉⲃ. ϩⲛ-) διαχ. ἀπό; C 43 49 let not brother ϥ. ⲥ. ⲙⲙⲟⲓ = Mor 39 26 *S* ⲡ. ⲉ-;   tr: Ro 8 35 (*S* ⲉ-) χωρ. ἀπό, C 43 31 ⲉⲧⲁϥⲫⲟⲣⲭⲧⲉⲡ ⲥ. ⲙⲡⲭ̅ⲥ̅;   ⲥⲁⲃⲟⲗ ⲉ- *S* intr: BMis 62 ⲙⲉϩⲡ. ⲥ. ⲉⲡⲉⲡⲧⲁⲩϫⲡⲟϥ.

—— ϩⲁⲃⲁⲗ ⲛ- *S[f]F* intr, meaning same: Mor 23 30 *S[f]*, *ib* 24 21 *F* ⲁⲓⲟⲩⲁⲥ ⲡ. ϩ. ⲙⲙⲟⲟⲩ; tr: Ps 16 14 *F* (*SB* ⲡⲱϣ ϩⲛ-) διαμερίζειν ἐν; Mor 23 31 *S[f]* ⲁϥⲡⲟⲣⲭⲉⲡ ϩⲁⲃⲟⲗ ⲙⲙⲟϥ.

—— ⲉϩⲣⲁⲓ ⲉⲭⲛ- *SB*, divide, scatter upon: Ps 67 15 *S* (*B* ⲑⲱϣ) διαστ. ἐπί, Cat 101 *B* heretics ϥ. ⲡⲛⲓⲥⲙⲏ ⲉϩ. ⲉⲭⲉⲡⲡⲓⲫⲩⲥⲓⲥ.

—— *SBF*, ⲡⲣⲁⲝ *A*² nn m, *separation, parting*: Jo 7 43 *SA*² (*B* = Gk), 1 Cor 11 18 *SB* σχίσμα; Ro 16 17 *SB* διχοστασία; 1 Cor 14 7 *S* (*B* ϣⲓⲃϯ) διαστολή; *ib* 33 *B* (*S* ϣⲧⲟⲣⲧⲣ) ἀκαταστασία; Zech 14 4 *B* (*A* diff) χάος; He 2 4 *SF* (*B* ⲧⲟⲓ ⲙϥⲱϣ) μερισμός; Mor 13 138 *S* took flesh ⲁⲭⲡⲡ., MIE 2 367 *B* ⲡⲓϥ. & heresies, AJSL 46 249 *S* charm ⲙⲁⲥⲕⲁ ⲡ. to be in thy house; ⲉⲓⲣⲉ ⲡⲟⲩⲡ. *S*, *make division*: Ge 32 16 (*B* ⲟⲩⲱϣ) διάστημα; Aeg 243 ⲡⲓⲉⲕⲉⲓⲣⲉ ⲡϩⲉⲡⲡ. σχ.;   ϯ ⲡ., ⲡⲟⲩⲡ. *S*, meaning same: Ac 15 9 (*B* ϣⲓⲃϯ) διακρίνειν; ShC 42 22 ⲁⲣϯ ⲟⲩⲡ. ⲡⲁⲡ ⲡⲙⲙⲉ, ShA 1 333 ⲡⲉⲧϯ ⲡⲟⲩⲡ. between Father & Son.   ⲡ. ⲉⲃⲟⲗ *SB*, *separation*: Ex 8 19 *B* διαστολή; Nu 18 26 *S* (*B* = Gk) ἀφαίρεμα; Lev 10 14 *SB* ἀφόρισμα; Ge 11 9 *B* (*S* ⲭⲱⲡⲣⲉ ⲉⲃ.) σύγχυσις; J 65 27 *S* ⲡⲡ. ⲉⲃ. ⲡⲧⲉⲯⲩⲭⲏ ⲉⲃ. ϩⲡⲡⲥⲱⲙⲁ.

ⲁⲧⲡ., ⲁⲑϥ. *SB* adj, *undivided, indivisible*: Miss 4 138 *B* ⲙⲉⲧⲟⲅⲁⲓ ⲡⲁ., J 65 13 *S* Trinity ⲡⲁ.; ⲁⲧ- ⲫⲟⲣⲭ *B*: Cat 91 ⲡⲓⲁ. ⲡ̅ⲭ̅ⲣ̅ⲥ̅;   ⲁⲧⲡ. ⲉⲃ. *S*: Mus 42 238 thou art ⲟⲩⲁ. ⲡⲡⲉⲧⲙⲉ ⲙⲙⲟ;   ⲣ ⲁⲧⲡ. *S*, *be inseparable*: BMis 140 Spirit ⲁϥⲣ ⲁ. ⲉⲣⲟ (Virgin);   ⲙⲛⲧⲁⲧⲡ., ⲙⲉⲧⲁⲧϥ. *SB*, *indivisibility*:

BM 174 2 *S* ϩпоуⳉ. ἀδιαστάτως; DeV 2 102 *B* sim.
ⳉⲁ пп. *S*, *place of dividing, frontier*: Mor 31
226 пⳉ. of Jerusalem & тⲏⲁпⲱпⳉⲁ (*l* ? тⲃⲁⳉⳉⲗⲱпⳉⲁ,
cf Amélineau *Contes* 2 121).

реⳡп. *S*, *divider*: Lu 12 14 (*B* реⳡϥⲱϣ) μεριστής; ViSitz 172 4 25 whoso followeth p. σχίζων.
ϭⳁпп., ⳉⳁпⳡ. *SB*, *separation, parting*: Cat 220
B пⳉ. п†ⳡⳡⲭⲏ епⳁⲥⲱⳉⲁ, FR 84 *S* тϭ. ероп
птпⲁⲣⲑⲉⲛⲟⲥ; ϭ., ⳉ. еⳉⲃⲟⲗ: My 108 *S* тϭ. еⳉ.
пⲁⲥпе, PO 11 346 *B* пеⳡⳉ. еⳉ. ⳅⲉппⲁⲓⲕⲟⲥⳉⲟⲥ.

пеес *F* nn, *meaning unknown*: BKU 1 26
(8116 b) recipe пекⲏⲥ епⲉⲥⲁⲥⲁⲧⲉⲣ (*v* ⲥⳉⲁⲩ) поу-
пⲁⳉ ⳉⲁⲣⲟⲩ ⳉⳁⳅⲉⳉⲟⲩⳟ. *right to right, left to left*.

пⳁⲥⲉ *SA*, пⳁⲥ *S*, ⳡⳁⳁ *B*, пⳁⳁ *FO*, пес-, пест-
S, пⳁⳁ- *SA*, ⳡⲉⳁ-, ⳡⲁⳁ- *B*, пⲁⲥⳁⳉ *SF*, пⳁⳁⳁ *S*
(Hall 64), пест⳽ *SA*, ⳡⲁⳁ⳽ *B*, поⳁⲉ†, пⳁⳁ† (Ps 11
ed Rahlfs) *S*, пⲁⲥⲉ† *A*, ⳡⲟⳁⳁ† *B*, р ⳁ пⲁⳁ- *S*, ⳡⲁⳁ-
B vb **I** intr *be cooked, melted*: Deu 16 7 *SB* opp
ϭⲱϭ, Zech 14 21 *SB*† ἕψειν; Dan 12 10 *B*, πυροῦν;
BMis 503 *S* ⲁⲕⲧⲟϭⳁ like egg еⳉⲁⲥп. in fire. **II**
tr, *boil, bake, melt*: meat Ex 12 9† *B* in water,
manna *ib* 16 23 *SB* opp тⲱϭ, ⳅⲱϭ, cakes 2 Kg 13
8 *S* ἕψ., bread Is 44 15 *SB* πέσσειν, 1 Kg 8 13 *S*
пеⲥⲥⲟⳟп (var пест), Si 38 8 *S* пⲁⲥⲥ., Ex 30 25 *B*
ⳡⲁⲥⲥ. μυρεψός; bricks Ge 11 3 *B* ὀπτᾶν; sim Job
8 16 neg *SB* ὑγρός; silver Ps 11 6† *S* (пⳁⳁ) *B*, Pro
10 20† *B* (*SA* ⲥⲟⲧп), bronze Ap 1 15† *SB* πυρ.;
ib 2 18 *S* bronze еⳡⳟ.† ⳅⲛⲟⲩⳅⲣⲱ (*B* Gk om), El
50 *A* ⳅⲁⲣⲱⳁ еⳡⳟ.† in fire, glass DeV 2 86 *B*, pots
Pcod 27 *S* тⲁпⲁⲥⲧⲟⳁ, metals AZ 23 112 *S* пⲁⲥⲧⲟⳁ
ⳉⲛⲛⲉⲩⲅⲣⲏⳁ, sim Bodl(P) 2 70 *S* пⲉⲥⲧⲟⳁ оⳁⲁ оⳁⲁ,
sheep Bor 295 99 *S* пⲧⲁⳁпⲉⲥ пⲉⲥⲟⲟⳁ ⲁп ⲁⲗⲗⲁ
пⲧⲁⳁⳅⲉⳉⲱⳡⳡ, oil PMéd 105 *S* пⳁⲥ пⲛⲉⳅ with
the wax, raven's blood BM 527 *F* пⲁⲥⲧⲉⳉ, Mor 24
30 *F* пⳡпⲉⲥⲧⲟⳁ, RE 10 150 (10) *S* оⳁⲟⲧⲉ пⲛⳁⲥⲉ,
Bal wine list ⲗⲁⲕⲟп еⳅⳉⲟⲥ, ⲗ. ⳉⳁпⳁⲥ, P 43 63 *S*
пⲉⲧп.· μάγειρος طبّاخ, Mor 51 36 *S* пⲁⲥⲧⲁⲣⳉⳉⲟⳁ.
п. еⳅⲣⲁⳁ *S*, *boil down* (?): CO 335.

—— *SBO* nn m, *thing cooked*: Ge 25 30 *B*, MG
25 210 *B* ἕψημα; Ge 43 16 *B* (var ⳡⲁⲥⳁ) θῦμα;
Hos 3 1 *B* (*A* рⲁⲭⲏ) πέμμα; AZ 21 100 *O* ⲥⲁⳁⳁ
paral п., C 41 77 *B* pot еⲥⳅⲉⲣⳅⲉⳁ пⲧⲉ пⳡ., Bodl(P)
1 *f S* end of recipe еⳁⲥ пп. ⲁⳡⲧⲁⳉⲟⳁ ероⳡ.
ⲁⳁⳡ. *B*, *unmolten*: Is 13 12 gold (*S* ⲥⲟⲧп as Pro
10 20) ἄπυρος.

реⳡⳡⲟⳁⳁ (*l* ⳡⳁ.) *B*, *metal-founder*: K 111 سبّاك;
реⳡпⲉⲥⲥⲟⳟп *S*, *perfume-boiler*: Si 49 1 μυρεψός.
ϭⳁпп., ⳉⳁпⳡ. *SB*, *boiling, melting*: Dan 11 35 *B*
пⳅⳁпⳡⲁⲥⲟⳁ πυρῶσαι; AZ 23 109 *S* тϭ. ⳉпⳅⲁⲗⲏⳁ.
пⲁⲥⲉ *S*, ⳡⲁⳁⳁ *B* nn, *cooking, cooked food*: ShC
42 70 *S* herbs ⳉⳁп., WS 217 *S* † оⳁп. пⲁⳁ, Ge 43
16 *B* as above.
Also in тⲉⲣпⲟⲥⲉ, ⲥⲕⲉпⳁⲥⲉ (*v* ⲥⲟϭп).

ⳡⲉⲣⳉⲟⲟⳁ, ⳡⲣ. *S* nn as pl: Z 629 recipes
еⳁⳉⲉⲣпⳡ., еⳁⳉⲉпⲉⳡ., ... ⲥⲱⲗϭ ероⲟⳁ. Prob =
ⳡⲱⲣⲁ ⳉⳉⲟⲟⳁ kind of scurvy, as *ib* 628 (Zoega).

ⳡⲓⲥ *SA*, ⳡⲓⳁ *S* (rare) *B* (K 67, *cf* أبسيط Synax 1
234 18) m, ⳡⳁⲧⲉ *SA*², -ⲥⲉ *S*'f nn, *nine* (*BF* mostly
as ꙋ): m Deu 3 11 *S*, Si 25 9 *S* (var ⳡⳁⳁ), Lu 17 17
S (var do); ⳉⲛⲧ ⳡ. 2 Kg 2 30 *S*, пⲥⲧⲁⳁⲟⳁ ⳡ. (var
еⳡⳁⲥ) Mt 18 12, 13 *S*; f Nu 34 13 *S* (*B* †ꙋ),
Br 230 *S* ⳡ. ⳟⲣⲉппⲁⲥ; ⳉⲛⳡ. Ge 46 22 *S*;
ⳉпⳡⳁⲧⲉ AP 2 *A*², ⳉпⳁⳁⲧⲉ BG 136 *S*; ⳡⲓⲥⲉ Ge 5
11, 27 *S*, P 131⁶ 63 *S*, BIF 14 162 *S*; тⲉⳡⲓⲥ (*sic*)
пϣⲉ пⲣⲟⳉпⲉ, Bor 239 82 = R 1 2 46 *S*; ⳉⲉⳅⳡ.,
ninth: Hag 2 11 *A* пⳉ. пⲉⳅⲁⳁ, PS 364 *S* пⳉ. п-
ⲁⳁⲱп, *ib* 318 пⳉⲉⳅⳡⲓⳁ, Lev 25 22 *S* тⳉ. пⲣⲟⳉпⲉ.

пⲥⲧⲁⳁⲟⳁ *S*, пⲓⲥⲧⲁⳁ (K 67) *B*, but mostly ⳝ (пⳁⲥ-
тⲉⲟⳁ Dan 12 was added by Tuki in Va 46), ⳡⲁⳁⲧⲉ
S, *ninety*: 1 Kg 4 15, Ez 4 5, Miss 4 820, Ge 5 9
-ⲁⳁⲟ; Ep 562 ⳡⲁⳁⲧⲁⲥⲉ пⲛⲕⲁⲥⳁ. ⳉⲉⳅп. *S*,
ninetieth: Bor 260 106. *Cf* Lu 15 4 *B* gloss بضايو.

пⲱⲥⳡ *S*, пⲱⲥⳅ *A* *v* пⲱϣⳡⲥ.

пⲁⲥⳅⳡ *A* *v* пⲁϣ.

пⲁⳁ *S*, пⲉⳁ *SᶠAA*²*F*, ⳡⲁⳁ *B* nn f, *a knee* as pl:
Ge 30 3 *S* (*B* ⲁⲗⲟⳅ), Deu 28 35 *S* (*B* ⲕⲉⲗⳁ), Is 35
3 *SF* (*B* do), *ib* 45 23 *S* п. пⳁⳉ (*B* do), Nah 2 10
AB, Glos 175 *Sᶠ*, RNC 27 *S* diseased ⳉⳁпⲛⲉⳡп.
епⲉⲥⳁ γόνυ; ShA 2 87 *S* mud reached пⲛⲕⲗⲗⲉ or
ⳉп. or ⳉⳁⳉⲣⲟⲥ, Aeg 12 *S* ⳉп. whereon I sat =
ib *B* ϭⲁⲗⲁⳅ, BMis 149 *S* trembling & оⳁⳅⳁⲟⳁⲉ
пп. one against other, ShA 1 431 *S* horse falls
ⳅⳁⳅⳉⳅⲃⲱⲗ пⲛⲉⳡп. пⲏⳁ opp оⳁⳅⲉⲣⳁⲧⲉ, BMar 125
S lion bent пⲛⲉⳡп. **b** *foot* sg or pl: Ge 29 1 *B*
(*S* оⳁⳅⲉⲣⳁⲧⲉ), Lev 11 21 *B* (*S* рⲁⳁ), Pro 3 27 *B*
(*SA* оⳁ.), Ez 1 7 *B* (var ϭⲁⲗ., *S* do), MG 25 216
B foot of bed πούς; ShC 42 143 *S* idols without
п., MR 5 49 *F* cannot stand ⳅⳁⳅⳉⲟпⲁⳁ., BMOr
6201 A 157 *S* ⲁⳁⲕⲁ пⲁⳁ. еⳉⲃⲟⲗ ⲁⳁⲉⳁ, BMis 518 *S*
cast self еⳅⳁⳉп. of father, AP 37 *A*² sim, PMéd
302 *S* hoof of ass's п., BSM 119 *B* ⳁⲉⳉ ⳉⳡ. bird's
claw. **c** *leg, shin, thigh*: Ez 24 4 *B* (*S* оⳁ.) σκέλος;
PSBA 10 399 *B* ἀντικνήμιον; Ez 47 4 *S* ⳉⲟⳁ пп.
(*B* om) μηρός; Glos 176 *Sᶠ* ἰγνύα.

ϥⲧⲉ ⳡ. *B*, *quadruped*: Ge 1 24 (*S* тⳉⳁⲏ), Is 30
5 (*SF* do) τετράπους. *Cf* Lev 11 20 *SB*.

рⲁⳁⳡ. *B* nn m, *long-footed, hare*: Lev 11 5 (*S*
еⲣеⲣⲁⳁⳡ рⳁⳁ) δασύπους; K 164 أرنب (also = ⲥⲁⲣⲁ-
ϭⲱⲟⳁⳡ). *V* рⲱⳁ р ⲥ.

ϣⲉ пⳡ. *B*, *blow, stamping, kick with foot* c †:
Ac 26 14 (*S* тⳉⲏⲣ) λακτίζειν πρός, C 86 292 ⲗ. εἰς,
Miss 4 151 ⲁⳁ† поⳁⳡ ⳅⲉппⲉⳡⲁпⲁⲥⲕⲉⲟп = Mor
18 82 *S* ⲁⳡⲗⲁⲕⲧⳁⳅⲉ: Dan 8 4 κερατίζειν κατά;
Ez 6 11 (prob *l* † ⳡ., *S* р ⳅⲣⲟⳁ) ψοφεῖν dat *alli-*

dere; AM 308 ⲁϥϯ ⲛⲟⲩϣ. ϩⲉⲡⲡⲓⲕⲁϩⲓ *stamped on ground*, *ib* 195 ϩⲓϫⲉⲛϯⲧⲣⲁⲡⲉⲍⲁ *kicked table*.

ⲕⲱⲗϫ, ⲕⲗϫ ⲡ., ϥ. *SA²B, bend knee*, v ⲕⲱⲗϫ **II**, adding AP 13 *A²* ⲡⲉⲣⲉⲡⲁⲅⲗⲟⲥ [ⲕ]ⲗϫ ⲡ. γ. κλίνειν.

ⲡⲱⲧ *SAA²F*, ⲫⲱⲧ *B*, ⲡⲟⲧ *F*, ⲡⲏⲧ *SAA²F*, ⲫⲏⲧ† *B* vb intr, *run, flee, go* : Lev 26 36 *SB*, Is 30 16 *SBF*, Mk 14 52 *SBF*, Jo 10 12 *SA²B*, BHom 10 *S* if pursued ϣⲁϥⲡ. φεύγειν, Am 9 1 *B* (*SA* ⲣ ⲃⲟⲗ) διαφ.; Ge 29 12 *S* (*B* ϭⲟϫⲓ), Mk 5 6 *S* (var ⲃⲱⲕ, *B* do), BHom 30 *S* ⲡ. opp ⲙⲟⲟϣⲉ τρέχειν, Sa 3 7 *S* διατρ., Nu 11 27 *S* (*B* do) προστρ., Miss 8 77 *S* συντρ.; Is 35 10 *SBF* ἀποδιδράσκειν; Jer 4 29 *B* (*S* = Gk) ἀναχωρεῖν; Ps 70 11 *S* (*B* ϭ. ⲡⲥⲁ-) καταδιώκειν; Jth 14 17 *S* ⲡ. + ⲉⲓ ⲉⲃⲟⲗ ἐκπηδᾶν; Job 20 8 *S* (*B* ϩⲱⲗ) πέτεσθαι; Ez 23 6† *SB* on horse ἱππάζειν; PS 92 *S* ⲁⲅⲡ. ⲁⲅⲗⲟ ϩⲁⲣⲟⲓ, ShC 73 64 *S* ⲛⲉⲧⲡ.† ⲙⲡⲟⲩϫⲟⲟⲩⲥⲉ, Miss 4 640 *S* ⲁⲧⲉⲥϩⲓⲙⲉ ⲡ. ϣⲁ- = *ib* 246 *S* ⲉⲓ ϣⲁ-, BIF 13 98 *S* ϣⲁϥⲡ. & stood at altar = MG 25 276 *B* ϩⲱⲗ, AP 42 *A²* ⲥⲉⲡ.† *speedily*, FR 78 *S* ⲁⲅⲉⲓ ⲉⲅⲡ.† *came running*, Mor 30 8 *F* begged ⲉϣⲧⲁⲡ. = BMis 235 *S* ⲃⲱⲕ, DeV 1 37 *B* secure him ⲙⲏⲡⲱⲥ ⲛⲧⲉϥ.ϥ., ST 432 *S* guarantee to returned fugitive ⲛⲡⲉⲣ ⲡⲉϥⲟⲟⲩ ⲡⲁⲕ ϫⲉⲁⲕⲡ., JKP 2 224 *S* I fear lest ⲡⲁⲭⲟⲓ ⲡ. & cargo perish (? for ⲡ. ⲡⲣⲁⲥⲓⲉ, cf ⲡ. ϩⲁ-), AZ 23 111 *S* molten metals ϣⲁⲣⲉⲡϣⲓ ⲛⲃⲁⲣⲟⲧ ⲡ. & silver remains :   with ethic dat, *depart* : ShC 73 121 *S* whoso wisheth ⲉⲡ. ⲛⲁϥ ⲉⲛϫⲁⲓⲉ, Mor 24 22 *F* arise ⲛⲧⲉⲡⲡ. ⲛⲏⲛ, J 93 16 *S* when healed ⲁϥⲡ. ⲛⲁϥ *secretly*;   with cogn acc : Ps 18 5 *S* ⲡ. ⲛⲧⲉϥϩⲓⲏ (*B* ϩⲓ-) τρ. ὁδόν.

With following preposition.

—— ⲉ- *SAA²BF, run, flee, go to* : Ex 21 13 *SB* φεύ. οὖ, Ps 138 7 *S* (*B* ϣⲉ) φ. ποῦ, Mt 10 23 *B* (*S* ⲉϩⲣⲁⲓ ⲉ-), Mk 13 14 *S* (*B* ⲉϫⲉⲛ-) φ. εἰς, EpJer 67 *B* (*F* ϩⲁ-) ἐκφ. εἰς, Is 54 15 *B* (*S* ⲉⲣⲁⲧϥ) καταφ. ἐπί; Ge 18 7 *S* (*B* ϭ.) τρ. εἰς, Pro 1 16† *SA* τρ., Nu 24 14 *S* (*B* ϣⲉ) ἀποτρ. εἰς, Lu 19 4 *S* (*B* do) προτρ. εἰς; Hos 12 12 *A* (*B* = Gk) ἀναχ. εἰς; Ez 30 9† *SB* σπεύδειν; Is 17 2† *S* (*B* ϭ. ⲡⲥⲁ-) διώκ.; PS 24 *S* ⲁϥϭⲱ ⲉϥⲡ.† ⲉⲡⲓⲥⲁ ⲙⲛⲡⲁⲓ, Mor 48 5 *S* ⲉⲧⲣⲁⲡ. ⲉⲛϫⲁⲓⲉ = BMar 205 *S* ⲃⲱⲕ ⲉⲣⲟⲩⲛ ⲉ- = Rec 6 168 *B* ϩⲱⲗ ⲉ-, AP 28 *A²* ⲁⲅⲡ....ⲁⲡⲣⲡⲉⲉⲓ, BM 1001 *S* I see that my words are about ⲉⲡ. ⲉⲟⲏ ⲛⲧⲟⲟⲧ *to outrun me*, Z 301 *S* tree ⲉϥⲡ.† ⲉⲡϫⲓⲥⲉ, Miss 4 722 *S* those wishing to ⲡ. ⲉⲡⲙⲟⲛⲁⲥⲧⲏⲣⲓⲟⲛ *on ship*, CMSS 39 *F* was told ϫⲉⲁⲕⲡ. ⲉⲡⲁϩⲅⲗⲱⲛ, BM 691 *F* wine ⲛⲧⲁⲃⲡ. ⲉⲡⲟⲩⲁⲓⲧ.

—— ⲉⲣⲁⲧϥ *S*, *meaning same* : Mk 9 15 (*B* ϭ.) προστρ., Z 355 ⲛⲉⲣⲉϩⲁϩ ⲡ.† ⲉⲣⲁⲧϥ συντρ.; Job 23 14 (*B* ⲓⲱⲥ) σπουδ. ἐπί; BM 152 Jesus help of ⲛⲉⲡⲧⲁⲅⲡ. ⲉⲣⲁⲧϥ;   ⲉⲣⲁⲧϥ ⲛ- *SB* : Nu 22 13 *S* (*B*

ⲧⲁⲥⲑⲟ ϩⲁ-) ἀποτρ. πρός; Est C 12 *S* καταφ. ἐπί; C 43 186 *B* ⲁⲥⲫ. ⲉⲣⲁⲧⲥ ⲛϯⲃⲟⲏⲑⲓⲁ.

—— ⲉⲧⲛ- *S*, *run, go to* : BMis 46 let not my sword ⲡ. ⲉⲧⲟⲟⲧϥ ⲛⲕⲉⲟⲩⲁ, Z 282 ⲡ.† ⲉⲧⲛⲡⲉⲧⲁⲓⲱⲕⲉⲓ (prob for ⲛⲧⲛ-).

—— ⲉϫⲛ- *SB*, *meaning same* : Mt 24 16 *B* (*S* ⲉ-) ϥ. εἰς; Lammayer 50 *S* ⲛⲉⲧⲡ.† ⲉϫⲛⲡⲥⲱⲙⲁ of Christ (var R 1 2 47 ⲃⲏⲕ ⲉⲣⲟⲩⲛ ⲉϫⲛ-), BMis 313 *S* ⲁⲅⲡ. ⲉϫⲱϥ & asked him, Mor 22 137 *S* crowd ⲉⲅⲡ.† ⲉϫⲛⲡⲉⲅⲉⲣⲏⲩ = BSM 128 *B* ⲉⲩϭⲟϫⲓ ⲉⲙⲁϣⲱ ⲉϫⲉⲛ-.

—— ⲙⲛ- *S*, *run, go with* : Ps 49 18 (*B* ϭ.) συντρ. dat; R 1 3 62 ⲁⲓⲡ. ⲛⲙⲙⲁⲕ ⲉⲧⲉⲣⲛⲙⲟⲥ...ⲉⲓⲡ.† ⲛⲙⲙⲁⲕ ϩⲛⲧⲉⲣ., Z 263 seized bones ⲁⲅⲡ. ⲛⲙⲙⲁⲩ.

—— ⲛ- (ⲛⲃⲉⲗⲧⲟ) *S*, *run from* : Ge 16 6 (*B* ⲉⲃⲟⲗ ϩⲁ-), Ps 56 tit (*B* do) ἀποδιδρ. ἀπό; or *in* : *ib* 18 5 (var ϩⲛ-, *B* ϭ. ϩⲓ-) τρ. acc;   dat : BM 659 *F* badest me take barley ⲧⲁⲡ. ⲛⲉⲃ.

—— ⲛⲥⲁ- *SAA²F*, *run after, pursue* : Ps 33 14 *SA* (Cl, *B* ϭ.), Is 30 16 *SF* (*B* do), Jo 5 16† *A²* (*S* = Gk, *B* do), Ro 12 13† *SF* (*B* do) διώκ., Deut 1 44 *S* (*B* do) καταδ.; Z 318 *S* ⲡ. ⲛⲥⲱⲟⲩ ⲉⲃⲟⲗ ϩⲙⲡⲉⲓⲙⲁ φυγαδεύειν; PS 175 *S* ⲁⲅⲣⲱⲧⲛ ⲧⲉⲧⲡ.† ⲛⲥⲱⲓ ?, BAp 92 *S* ⲛⲧⲁϥⲡ. ⲁⲛ ⲛⲥⲁⲡⲧⲁⲓⲟ, MG 17 315 *S* caused them to ⲡ. ⲛⲥⲱⲓ ϩⲓⲛⲙⲁ = C 89 3 *B* ϭ. ⲉⲃ. ϩⲉⲛ-.

—— ⲛⲧⲛ- *SBF*, *flee from* : Va 61 219 *B* ⲁϥⲫ. ⲛⲧⲉⲛⲛⲓⲣⲑⲛⲟⲩⲓ of towns ϥ., Aeg 272 *S* ⲡ. ⲡⲧⲟⲟⲧϥ ⲙⲡⲣⲁⲡ ἐκφ., LAp 360 *S* there is no kingdom ⲛⲁⲡ. ⲡⲧⲟⲟⲧϥ διαφ.; Jth 11 3 *S* ἀποδιδρ. ἀπό; ShC 42 145 *S* ⲁⲅⲡ. ⲛⲧⲟⲟⲧ ⲁⲩⲃⲱⲕ, Wess 15 23 *S* servant ⲛⲧⲁϥⲡ. ⲛⲧⲟⲟⲧϥ of master, C 43 114 *B* ⲛⲁⲓⲫ.† ⲁⲛ ⲛⲧⲟⲧⲥ ⲛⲧⲉⲕⲟⲓⲕⲟⲡⲟⲗⲓⲁ, AM 291 *B*, GMir 187 *S* sim, Mor 31 24 *S* whip ⲡ. ⲛⲧⲟⲟⲧϥ *flew* (dropped) *from his hand*, BM 585 *F* ⲙⲡⲉⲗⲕⲉⲟⲩ ⲧⲟⲩⲡ. ⲡⲧⲁⲁⲧⲕ.

—— ⲛⲁϩⲣⲛ- *S*, *flee from* : Ge 35 7 (*B* ⲉⲃ. ϩⲁ-) ἀποδιδρ. ἀπό.

—— ϣⲁ- *SB*, *run, go to* : Aeg 259 *S* (var ⲃⲱⲕ ⲉⲣⲟⲩⲛ), BMis 135 *S* arise & ⲡ. ϣⲁⲉⲗⲓⲥⲁⲃⲉⲧ, BSM 14 *B* ⲁⲓⲫ. ϣⲁⲗⲁⲃⲁⲛ = BMis 349 *S* ⲃⲱⲕ ⲉⲣⲁⲧϥ ⲛ-.

—— ϩⲁϫⲉⲛ- *B*, ϩⲁ. *F*, *flee from* : Is 31 8 *F* (*S* ϩⲏⲧϥ ⲡ-, *B* ⲉⲃ. ϩⲁⲡϩⲟ ⲡ-) ϥ. ἀπό; MG 25 129 *B* judgment ⲡⲁⲧϣ ϥ. ϩⲁϫⲱϥ.

—— ϩⲁ- *S*, *go from under* : Miss 8 217 ship ⲡ. ϩⲁⲣⲟϥ (cf 2 Cor 11 25 *S* ⲃⲱⲕ ϩⲁ-), BMar 132 ⲡ. ϩⲁⲡϩⲟ ⲛ-.

—— ϩⲁ- *B*, *run, go to* : Ps 142 9 (*S* ⲉⲣⲁⲧϥ), Is 10 3 (*S* do) καταφ. πρός, Ac 3 11 (*S* ⲥⲱⲟⲩϩ ⲉ-) συντρ. πρός.

—— ϩⲁⲧϩⲏ ⲛ- *S*, *flee from before* : Jos 8 6, Ps 59 4 (*B* ⲉⲃ. ϩⲁⲧϩⲏ), Ap 20 11 (*B* do) ϥ. ἀπό;   ϩⲁⲧϩⲏ ⲛ- *B* : Is 24 18 (*S* ⲣ ⲃⲟⲗ ⲉ-) ϥ.

—— ϩⲓ- *SBF, go upon*: Is 30 16 *SBF* ϥ. ἐπί; ShC 42 212 *S* blind ⲉⲩⲡ.† ϩⲓⲛϩⲓⲟⲟⲩⲉ.

—— ϩⲛ- *SA, go in, upon*: Ps 118 32(*B* ϭ.)ⲧⲣ. acc, Jer 5 1 (*B* ⲇⲟ) περιτρ. ἐν; Hos 9 17† *A* (*B* ⲥⲱⲣⲉⲙ) πλανήτης εἶναι ἐν; Aeg 281 ⲉϥⲡ.† ϩⲙⲡⲉⲥⲧⲁⲇⲓⲟⲛ σταδιοδρόμος; ShP 130⁴ 126 heretics say Almighty ⲡ.† ϩⲙⲡⲉⲇⲣⲟⲙⲟⲥ of sun & waxeth with moon, ShC 42 159 those that ⲡ.† ϩⲛⲡⲉⲣϩⲏⲅⲉ ⲡⲧⲇⲓⲁⲕⲟⲛⲓⲁ, Miss 8 225 we hasten to bury dead ⲛⲧⲡⲡ. ϩⲛⲡⲉⲣϩⲃⲏⲅⲉ ⲉⲧϣⲟⲩⲉⲓⲧ; ϩⲛ- = ⲉⲃⲟⲗ ϩⲛ- *S, from*: Job 30 3† (*B* ⲉⲃ. ϫⲉⲛ-) ϥ.; Bor 100 40 whence sorrow ⲡ. ⲡⲣⲏⲧϥ (*cf* Is 35 10), Ryl 289]ⲕⲟⲩⲓ ⲡϣⲏⲣⲉ ⲡ. ϩⲙⲡⲙⲟⲛⲁⲥⲧⲏⲣⲓⲟⲛ.

—— ϩⲏⲧⲍ, ϩ. ⲛ- *S, flee before, from*: Mor 37 47 ⲛ†ⲡ.† ϩⲏⲧⲟⲩ ⲛⲛⲉⲧⲛⲥⲁϣ ϥ., Sa 10 10† φυγὰς (εἶναι); Ps 3 tit (*B* ⲉⲃ. ϫⲁⲧϩⲏ ⲛ-) ἀποδιδρ. ἀπό; ShMIF 23 177 ⲛⲉⲧⲡ. ϩⲏⲧⲥ ⲛ ϩⲁⲧⲉⲥϩⲏ.

—— ϩⲁϩⲧⲡ- *SF, go to*: BM 530 *S* ⲡ. ϩⲁⲧⲧⲏϥ, CMSS 39 *F* ⲁⲓⲡⲟⲧ ϩⲁⲑⲛϥⲗⲁ (= ϩⲁϩⲧⲙⲡⲉⲗⲗⲟ).

—— ϩⲓϫⲉⲡ- *F, go upon*: Mor 24 3 when Saviour ⲡ. ϩ. ⲡⲧⲁⲩ = *ib* 23 5 *S* ⲉⲓ ⲉϫⲡ-.
With following adverb.

—— ⲉⲃⲟⲗ *SAA²B, run, go forth*: 4 Kg 9 10 *S*, BHom 136 *S* Jews ⲡ.† ⲉⲃ. woman ⲡ.† ⲉϩⲟⲩⲡ (*cf* Mk 7 24) ϥ., 2 Pet 2 18 *S* (*B* om ⲉⲃ.) ἀποφ., Ac 16 27 *S* (*B* ⲇⲟ) ἐκφ.; Am 2 16 *S* (*B* ⲇⲟ) διώκεσθαι; Ez 19 3 *SB* ἀποπηδᾶν; MG 25 243 *B* ἀναχω.; Mk 6 55 *S* (*B* ⲇⲟ), AM 268 *B* ⲉⲓϥ.† ⲉⲃ. ϫⲉⲛⲙⲁ ⲉⲙⲁ περιτρ.; ⲉⲃ. ⲉ-, *run out to*: Ac 14 14 *S* (var ϩⲛ-, *B* ϭ. ϣⲁ-) ἐκπηδ. εἰς; Kr 116 *Sᵇ* fugitives ⲉⲩⲡ.† ⲉⲃ. ⲉⲡⲓⲧⲓⲙ; ⲉ- for ⲛ-: BMis 65 *S* ⲛⲉⲥⲡ.† ⲉⲃ. ⲉⲡⲉⲟⲟⲩ, Bor 262 121 *S* ⲡ. ⲉⲃ. ⲉϫⲓ ϩⲣⲁϥ; ⲉⲃ. ⲛ-, *flee forth from*: Ps 103 7 *S* (*B* ⲉⲃ. ϫⲉⲡ-), Jo 10 5 *SA²* (*B* ⲉⲃ. ϩⲁ-) ϥ. ἀπό, Sa 1 5 *SB* ϥ. acc, BHom 37 *S* διαφ.; Sa 4 14 *S* ⲥⲡⲉⲩⲇ. ἐκ; Hos 7 13 *SA* (*B* ⲥⲁⲃⲟⲗ) ἀποπηδ. ἀπό; ShC 42 118 *S* ⲛⲧⲡⲡ. ⲉⲃ. ϩⲙⲡⲧϧⲁⲭⲉ ⲡⲓⲙ, Br 256 *S* ⲁⲩⲡ. ⲉⲃ. ⲙⲡⲉⲧⲡ.† ⲛⲥⲱⲟⲩ; ⲉⲃ. ϩⲁⲑⲏ, ϫⲁⲧϩⲏ ⲛ-, *flee from before*: BMis 70 *S* ⲙⲁⲣⲟⲩⲡ. ⲉⲃ. ϩⲁⲧⲁϩⲏ, Mt 3 7 *B* (*S* ϩⲏⲧϥ ⲛ-) ϥ. ἀπό; DeV 2 39 *B* ⲁϥϥ. ⲉⲃ. ϫⲁⲧϩⲏ ⲙⲡⲉϥϩⲟ; ⲉⲃ. ϩⲁ- *B, meaning same*: Ps 138 7 (*S* ⲉⲃ. ⲛ-), Is 31 8 (*S* ϩⲏⲧⲍ ⲛ-, *F* ϩⲁϫⲱⲥ ⲛ-) ϥ. ἀπό, Ac 27 30 (var ⲉⲃ. ϫⲉⲛ-, *S* diff) ϥ. ἐκ; Ge 16 6 (*S* ⲛ-) ἀποδιδρ. ἀπό; Jer 48 17 Gk om; BSM 27 ⲉⲩϥ.† ⲉⲃ. ϩⲁⲡⲓⲱⲟⲩ; ⲉⲃ. ϩⲓⲣⲁⲧⲍ *S, run out after*: Jos 2 5 καταδιωκ. ὀπίσω; BHom 16 ⲉϥⲡⲁⲡ. ⲉⲃ. ϩⲓⲣⲁⲧⲛ *toward us*; ⲉⲃ. ϩⲓⲧⲛ- *S, go forth from*: Miss 8 223 having said this ⲁϥⲡ. ⲉⲃ. ϩⲓⲧⲟⲟⲧϥ; ⲉⲃ. ϩⲛ-, ϫⲉⲛ-, *meaning same*: Is 48 20 *SB*, Mt 23 33 *B* (*S* ⲣ ⲃⲟⲗ ⲉ-) ϥ. ἀπό, Jer 11 15 *B* διαφ. dat, Su 22 *B* ἐκφ. acc; ShC 73 104 *S* ⲉⲩⲡ.† ⲉⲃ. ϩⲛⲡⲉⲓⲥⲩⲛⲁⲅⲱⲅⲏ, DeV 2 50 *B* ϥ. ⲉⲃ. ϫⲉⲛⲡⲓⲡⲉⲧϩⲱⲟⲩ; ⲉⲃ. ϩⲏⲧⲍ ⲛ- *S, run from*: BHom

31 ⲙⲁⲣⲡⲡ. ⲉⲃ. ϩⲏⲧϥ ⲙⲡϣⲓⲡⲉ ϥ.; *run toward*: Ge 33 4 (*B* ϭ. ⲉⲃ. ⲉϩⲣⲉⲡ-) προστρ.

—— ⲥⲁⲃⲟⲗ ⲛ- *B, run from*: Ps 30 12 (*S* ⲟⲩⲉ ⲡⲥⲁⲃ.) ϥ. ἀπό, 1 Cor 6 18 (*S* ⲉⲃ. ⲛ-) ϥ. acc; Va 66 308 ⲙⲡⲉⲣϥ. ⲥ. ⲙⲡⲉⲕⲥⲟⲡ παρατρ.

—— ϩⲁⲃ. ⲛ- *SF, meaning same*: Sh (?) Mor 54 131 *S* ⲡ. ϩ. ⲡⲧⲙⲡⲧⲡⲟⲉⲓⲕ (*cf* BM 189 169 *S* sim ⲉⲃ. ⲛ-), BM 511 *F* ⲉⲧⲣⲟⲩⲡ. ϩ. ⲡⲡⲁⲃⲓ ⲛⲓⲃⲓ.

—— ⲉⲡⲉⲥⲛⲧ *SF, go down*: Is 31 1† *F* (*S* ⲃⲱⲕ†, *B* ⲡⲁ) καταβαίνειν; BIF 14 187 *S* steps ⲉⲩⲡ.† ⲉ-. to sea.

—— ⲉⲫⲁϩⲟⲩ *B, run, go back*: Jo 18 6 (*S* ⲉⲓ ⲛⲥⲁⲡ., *A²* ϩⲁⲉⲓⲉ ⲥⲁⲡ.) ἀπέρχ. εἰς τὰ ὀπίσω.

—— ϩⲓⲡⲁϩⲟⲩ ⲛ- *S, run behind, after*: BSG 190 ⲁϥⲡ. ϩ. ⲙⲡⲉⲩⲩⲡⲏⲣⲉⲧⲏⲥ = *ib* 25 *B* ϭ. ⲥⲁϥ.

—— ⲉϩⲟⲩⲛ, ⲉϩ. *SSᶠBF, run, go in*: Ac 12 14 *S* (*B* ϭ.) εἰστρ.; MG 25 243 *B* ϣⲁϥⲡ. ⲉϩ. ⲡⲭⲱⲗⲉⲙ εἰσιέναι; Mor 39 10 *Sᶠ* ⲡⲧⲉⲣⲉϥⲡ. ⲉϩ. = C 43 37 *B* ϣⲉ ⲉϩ., Miss 4 721 *S* child playing ⲛⲉϥⲡ.† ⲉϩ. ⲉⲃⲟⲗ; ⲉϩ. ⲉ-: Deu 19 11 *S* (*B* om ⲉϩ.), Jer 27 16 *B* (*S* ⲉϩⲣⲁⲓ ⲉ-, *F* ⲕⲱ† ⲉ-) ϥ. εἰς, He 6 18 *SF* (*B* ϩⲁ-) καταφ.; Job 16 14 *S* (*B* ϭ. ⲉϫⲉⲡ-) ⲧⲣ. πρός; Is 36 6 *F* (*S* ⲃⲱⲕ, *B* ϣⲉ) εἰσέρχ. εἰς; PS 118 *S* ⲧϭⲟⲙ ...ⲉⲥⲡ.† ⲉϩ. ⲉⲣⲟⲓ, ShC 42 155 *S* ⲡⲉⲧⲡⲁⲡ. ⲉϩ. ⲉⲡⲉⲧⲣⲓⲧⲟⲩⲱⲟⲩ, Ep 395 *S* letter begins ⲡ. ⲉϩ. ⲉⲡⲁ(ⲉⲓⲱ)ⲧ & fetch &c; ⲉϩ. ϩⲁ-: R 1 5 30 *S* snakes ⲡ. ⲉϩ. ϩⲁⲣⲁⲧϥ & he trod thereon, BKU 1 26 (8116 a) *F* virtues of diamond (ⲁⲗⲙⲱⲉⲥ المّاس *v* LAl 35) ⲉϥⲡ.† ⲉϩ. ϩⲁⲣⲟⲩⲙⲉϣⲓ ⲡⲧⲉⲭⲛⲏ *is applicable to*.

—— ⲉϩⲣⲁⲓ *SBF, run up, away*: Ac 7 29 *S* (*B* om ⲉϩ.) ϥ.; Br 240 *S* aeons shall ⲡ. ⲉϩ. ⲙⲡⲡⲁϩⲟⲣⲁⲧⲟⲥ, Miss 8 260 *S* sore will ⲡ. ⲉϩ. ϩⲛⲧⲉⲕⲟⲩⲅⲉⲣⲛⲧⲉ into body; ⲉϩ. ⲉ-: Ap 12 6 *S* (*B* ⲇⲟ) ϥ. εἰς; Jos 7 22 *S* ⲧⲣ. εἰς; DeV 2 112 *B* ⲡⲧⲟⲩϥ. ⲉϩ. ⲉ†ⲃⲁⲕⲓ, LAp 524 *F* ⲁⲃⲡⲟⲧ ⲉϩ. ⲉ[ⲡⲉⲙⲡⲏ]ⲟⲩⲓ; ⲉϩ. ⲉϫⲡ-: Ac 21 32 *S* (*B* ϭ. ⲉϫ.) καταⲧⲣ. ἐπί, Su 19 *S* (*B* ϭ. ϩⲁ-) ἐπιⲧⲣ. dat; Deu 34 1 *S* (var ⲃⲱⲕ, *B* diff) ἀναβαίν. ἐπί; ShC 73 200 *S* trap which beasts ⲡ. ⲉϩ. ⲉϫⲱⲥ.

—— *SB* nn m, *course, flight*: 2 Tim 4 7 *S* (*B* = Gk) δρόμος; Is 52 12 *SB*, Mt 24 20 *SB* φυγή; BHom 103 *S* ⲡⲡ. of winds opp ⲡⲉⲥϭⲣⲁⲧ.

ⲙⲁ ⲙⲡ. ϥ. *SAA²B, place of refuge*: Ex 17 15 *SB*, Ps 17 2 *SB*, AP 17 *A²* καταφυγή, Nu 35 6 *SB* φυγαδευτήριον, 1 Kg 22 23 *S* (var & Gk om ⲙⲡ.); BMis 92 *S* ϣⲓⲡⲉ ⲡⲥⲙ. ⲉⲣⲟϥ, AM 289 *B* ⲃⲟⲏⲑⲟⲥ ⲡⲉⲙⲙ.; *race-course*: Mor 17 93 = Gu 71 *S* ⲙ. ⲛⲡⲉⲣⲧⲱⲣ ἱπποδρόμιον; doubtful BM 449, 450 *S* in boundaries ϫⲓⲛⲡⲙⲁ ⲡϩⲙⲟⲟⲥ ... ϣⲁⲙⲁ ⲙⲡ.   ⲙⲁ ⲙⲡ. ⲉⲃⲟⲗ, *outgoing, exit*: Ob 14 *SA* (*B* ⲙⲱⲓⲧ ⲙϥ.) διεκβολή.

ⲙⲁⲓϥ. *B, loving to flee*: Rec 6 171 ⲁⲓⲉⲣ ⲙ. ⲡⲧⲉⲛⲫⲛⲟⲃⲓ = BMar 208 *S* ⲣ ϩⲛⲁⲓ ⲙⲡ.

ⲣⲉϥⲡ. *SA, runner*: Job 9 25 *S* (*B* ϫⲓⲛϭⲟϫⲓ), Pro 6 11 *SA* (*B* ⲣⲉϥϭ.) δρομεύς, Mor 37 75 *S* ταχυδρόμος, BMar 172 *S* ὀξυδρόμος; ShRE 11 15 *S* life ⲉⲧⲁⲥⲱⲟⲩ ⲉⲟⲩⲣ.

ϭⲓⲛⲡ. *S, running, course*: BHom 31 δρόμος, *ib* 103 of stars, P 131² 156 ship's course, Miss 8 239 ⲧⲉⲕϭ. ⲉⲣⲁⲧⲅ, ROC 20 53 ⲟⲩϭ. ⲉⲃ. ⲙⲡⲛⲟⲃⲉ.

ⲡⲁⲓⲧⲏ, ⲡⲏⲓⲧⲉ, ⲡⲉⲓϫⲉ (written ⲙⲡ. in P 44 82, 43 57, EW 222 *S* scala 164), *i e* Ar بيفة *eggplant, solanum*. *V* ⲃⲟⲛⲧⲉ *s f*.

ⲡⲓⲧⲁ *v* ⲣⲓⲧⲁ.

ⲡⲓⲧⲉ *SA*, ⲫⲓϯ *B* nn f, *bow (arcus)*: Ge 9 13 *SB*, Job 20 24 *B* (*S* ⲥⲟⲧⲉ), Hos 7 16 *SAB*, Ap 6 2 *SB* τόξον, Ge 49 23 *SB*, Jer 27 14 *SB* τόξευμα (also = ⲥⲟⲧⲉ); K 60 *B* ϯⲫⲏⲧⲧⲉ (var ϥⲉⲧ.) قوس قزح *rainbow*. *Bend* bow: *S* ⲥⲱⲗⲧ, ϫⲱⲗⲕ, *B* ϭⲱⲗⲕ. ⲣⲁ ⲙⲡ. *S* nn, *loop-hole*: Jud 5 28 ϣⲟⲩϣⲧ ⲉⲧⲟ ⲡⲣ. (in P 43 97 الروشن الذي بابه يفتح الى اسفل).

ⲡⲉⲧⲃⲉ *v* ⲧⲱⲱⲃⲉ *requite*.

ⲡⲁⲧⲁⲗⲁⲥ *SB*, -ⲁⲗⲟⲥ, -ⲧⲁⲗⲟⲥ *B* nn, meaning unknown, ? ethnic: MG 25 212 *B* near Shiêt a Gentile ⲡⲉⲟⲩⲟⲩⲏⲃ ϫⲉ ⲙⲡ. τινι ἱερεῖ τῶν Ἑλλήνων (*cf* PG 26 821 σχολαστικὸς παταλᾶς...Ἕλλην ὤν, paral σχολ. τῶν κυνικῶν), *ib* 91 *B* deaf mute ⲡⲥⲙⲟⲧ ⲙⲡ. = Gött ar 114 22 b نجسة فيه ارواح, ShBM 199 361 *S* ye are worse than ⲡⲡ. for ye do deeds of beasts, ShMIF 23 191 *S* ϩⲉⲛⲡ. & very offensive to God in their filth, ShA 1 216 *S* bones unduly revered ⲛⲁϩⲉⲛⲡ. ϭⲉⲡⲉ ⲛ ⲡⲟⲣⲛⲟⲥ ⲛ ⲁⲥⲉⲃⲏⲥ, *ib* 2 165 *S* if he do charity with ⲟⲩⲡ. shall receive again manifold.   As name (?): Παταλᾶς, -λος (Preisigke).

ⲡⲉⲧⲉⲡⲏⲡ (most MSS), -ⲏⲧ *B* nn as pl, *hoopoe*: K 169 ⲡⲏⲡ. هدهد. *Cf* ⲕⲣⲁⲡⲉⲡ, ⲕⲁⲕⲟⲩⲡⲁⲧ. *V* BIF 30 322.

ⲡⲟⲧⲡⲧ *S*, ⲡⲁⲧ. *A*, ϥⲟⲧϥⲉⲧ, ϥⲉⲧϥⲱⲧⲅ, ϥⲉⲧϥⲱⲧ† *B* vb **I** intr, *fall away*: Zech 14 12 *S* (ROC 20 55) *A* (*B* ⲃⲱⲗ ⲉⲃⲟⲗ) τήκειν; Va 57 193 *B* beggars ⲉⲣⲉⲡⲟⲩⲙⲉⲗⲟⲥ ϥ.† διεστραμμένος; C 86 208 *B* flesh ϥ. & fell on ground;   c e-, *S, fall to, upon*: ShC 73 19 limbs ⲡⲁⲡ. ⲉⲡⲕⲁϩ, ShA 1 375 dead limbs perish & ⲁⲩⲡ. ⲉⲡⲉⲥⲏⲧ, R 1 5 31 tortured till flesh ⲡ. ⲉⲡⲉⲥⲏⲧ ⲉⲡⲕⲁϩ.   **II** tr, *make fall, drop, cut down*: ShC 42 98 *S* woman that cuts own flesh & ⲉⲥⲡ. ⲙⲙⲟⲟⲩ ⲉϩⲣⲁⲓ ⲉⲡⲧⲁⲕⲟ, ROC 20 55 *S* sword ready ⲉⲡ. ⲉⲡⲉⲥⲏⲧ ⲙⲡⲉⲧⲛⲥⲱⲙⲁ, C 43 78 *B* soldiers ϥⲉⲧϥⲟⲧⲟⲩ with axes, *cf ib* 176 caused them to ϥ. ⲡⲥⲁⲡⲉϥⲥⲱⲙⲁ with knives (or ? *v* ϥⲱⲧⲅ).

ⲡⲱⲧⲥ *SF*, ⲡⲟⲧⲥ† *S*, ⲡⲁ.† *F* vb tr, *divide, split*,

crack: Lev 11 3† *S* (*B* ϥⲱⲣϫ), Deu 14 7 *S* (*B* do) διχηλεῖν; Is 36 6† *SF* (*B* ϩⲟⲙϩⲉⲙ), *ib* 42 3† (*B* do, *cf* Mt 12 20 *S* ⲟⲩⲱϣϥ) θλᾶν; Mor 30 13 *F* bade ⲡ. ⲉⲡⲉϥⲥⲱⲙⲁ with knives τέμνειν = BMis 239 *S* ϣⲱⲗϭ; P 131⁶ 47 *S* camel ⲡϭⲡⲱⲧⲥ (*sic*) ⲉⲓⲃ ⲁⲡ; TT 77 *S* ⲙⲡⲛⲥⲁⲧⲣⲉϥⲡ. ⲡϭⲉⲛⲙⲟⲩⲥ from martyr's back (*cf* C 43 73 *B* sim ⲥⲱⲗⲡ ⲉⲃⲟⲗ), BMar 150 *S* with knife ⲁⲥⲡ. ⲡⲧⲉⲥⲉⲛⲕⲃⲉ & drew drops of blood.   ⲁⲧⲡ. *S, unbroken, not cracked*: KroppE prayer for voice ⲡⲁⲧϩⲱⲗⲉ ⲡⲁ. ⲡⲁⲧϫⲁϫⲉ.   ⲣ ⲡ. *S, be cracked* (?): Mor 27 34 wine jar ⲉⲁϥⲣ ⲡⲱⲧⲥ = BMis 387 ⲟⲩⲟⲗⲥ (var + ⲉϩⲟⲩⲛ) = Va 63 14 *B* ⲃⲟⲗⲥ (*l* ⲟⲩⲟⲗⲥ) ⲉⲃⲟⲗ.

ⲡⲁⲧⲥⲉ *S*, ϥⲁⲧⲥⲓ, ⲡⲁⲧⲥⲓ (DeV 1 131) *B* nn f, *thing divided, split off, plank*: Ac 27 44 *S* (*B* = Gk), C 86 285 *B* ϥ. of which thrones built = BSG 184 *S* ⲡⲟϣⲉ, P 44 54 *S* σανίς درمس (*v* BIF 20 58, K 133); BMOr 8775 141 *B* ⲛⲓϥ. فلقات وهو للخشب المنشور *public stocks* (*cf* ϥⲟⲭⲓ); Mus 40 40 *S* in bakery ⲡⲉⲧⲅⲣⲓⲡ. *tabula* on which loaves ranged, ShC 73 144 *S* sim ⲡⲉⲧϩⲙⲟⲟⲥ ⲉⲧⲡ. (var ⲡⲟϭⲉ).

ⲡⲉⲧϣⲁ-, ⲡⲉϣⲁ- *O* *v* ⲡⲉϫⲉ-.

ⲡⲱⲧⲅ *S* (My), ϥⲱⲧⲅ *B*, ϥⲟⲧⲅ- *B* (ⲣⲉⲙϥ.), ⲡⲟⲧϩ *S*, ϥⲟⲧϩ- *B*, ⲡⲟϩⲧ† *S* (Sa 18), ϥⲟⲧϩ† (rarely ϥⲟϩⲧ) *B* vb tr, *carve, engrave, depict* by carving or painting, *cf* ⲡⲏⲡ (IgR): Ex 28 9, 2 Chr 3 7, Is 44 9 (*S* ϣⲱϫⲧ) γλύφειν; Job 19 24 (*S* ϣⲟⲧϣⲧ) ἐγγλ.; Ex 25 11† στρεπτός (*cf ib* 25 ⲙⲟⲡⲙⲉⲛ ⲥⲧⲣ.); Is 51 1 (*S* ⲕⲁϥⲕⲉ) λατομεῖν, Nu 21 18 (*S* do) ἐκλατ.; Is 9 10 (*S* do) λαξεύειν; *ib* 44 12 (*S* diff) τετραίνειν; Jer 10 4† (*S* diff) τορευτός; Ex 32 16† (*S* ϣⲟⲧ.) κολλᾶν; Sa 18 24† *S* (var ⲙⲟⲡⲧ) Gk om; Va 57 244 impossible ⲉϥ. ⲡⲡⲏ ⲉⲧϭⲓ ⲉϩⲟⲩⲡ ⲉⲣⲟⲥ ζωγραφία; ROC 23 279 ϯⲡⲗⲁϫ...ⲉⲟ̄ⲣⲉⲕϥ. ⲉⲣⲟⲥ ⲡϯϩⲓⲕⲱⲛ of Virgin, WTh 43 sim on stele = *ib S* ⲥϩⲁⲓ, BSM 101 board ⲛⲧⲉⲧϩⲓⲕⲱⲛ ϥ.† (*sic l*) ⲉⲣⲟⲥ = Mor 22 112 *S* do, BSM 113 portrait ⲉⲥϥⲟⲧⲅ (*sic l*) ϩⲉⲛⲣⲁⲛ ϥⲁϩⲣⲓ, MG 25 177 fingerprints ⲉⲩϥ.† ⲉⲑⲟⲩⲟⲝⲓ, C 43 186 saint's portrait on wall ⲉⲣⲉⲡⲓϫⲁⲣⲁⲕⲱⲛ ϥ.† beneath his feet, My 108 *S* ⲁϥⲡ. ⲡⲟⲩⲡⲗⲁϫ...ⲡⲡⲓⲭⲁⲣⲁⲕⲧⲏⲣ of alphabet, *ib* 119 *S* ⲁⲩⲡⲟⲧⲅⲟⲩ by Creator.   ϥ. ⲉⲃⲟⲗ, meaning same: C 43 182 ⲁⲩϥ. ⲡⲧⲣⲓⲕⲱⲡ ⲉⲃ., DeV 2 275 place where portrait ϥ.† ⲉⲃ. ⲉⲣⲟϥ = Mun 69 *S* ⲥϩ., BSM 98 ϥ. ⲡⲏⲓ ⲉⲃ. ⲙϥⲗⲩⲙⲏⲡ = Mor 22 109 *S* ζωγραφει.

—— *B* nn m, *thing carved, graven, wrought*: Ex 34 13 (*S* ⲙⲟⲩⲡⲧ ⲡϭⲓϫ), Is 10 10 (*S* do), Hos 11 2 (*A* ⲙ. ⲡϭ.) γλυπτός, Is 60 18 (*S* = Gk) γλύμμα, Ex 25 7 γλυφή; *ib* 39 6 ἐκκόλαμμα (*cf* 28 11), Is 44 12 ⲥⲕⲉⲟⲥ ⲙϥ. (*S* ⲥⲁϥ) τέρετρον; Hos 13 12 (*A* ⲥⲁϥⲥ) συστροφή (*cf* Ex 25 11 above); Is 21 9 (*S* ⲧⲟⲩⲣⲱⲧ) ἄγαλμα;   *thing molten, cast*: Nu 33

52 (S ⲟⲩⲱⲧϩ), Dan 11 8 χωνευτός, Hab 2 18 (A = Gk) χώνευμα.   As adj: Lev 19 4 (S ⲟⲩ. vb) χωνευτός; 2 Chr 4 5 διαγεγλυμμένος.

ⲣⲉⲙϥⲟⲧϩ ⲛⲟⲩ B, *house-carver* (? v ⲛⲓ pl): Tuki 46.

Cf name of god ⲡⲧⲁϩ (Hephaestus): ShA 1 385. In place-names: Κερκέφθα (POxy 2017) Θμοίφθα (BGU 1285): Σενέφτα (POxy 72).

ⲡⲟⲟⲉ S vb tr (?), meaning unknown, ? *catch* as fisherman: Mor 47 192 devil says ⲁⲓⲡⲟⲩϫ ⲛ̄ⲁⲟⲓⲙⲉ ⲙ̄ⲡⲉⲓⲡⲟⲟⲉ ⲛ̄ⲗⲁⲁⲩ = P ar 4776 136 ولم اصيد شى. Or ? *l* ⲙ̄ⲡⲉⲡⲟⲧϩ ⲉⲛ ⲗ.

ⲡⲟⲟⲩ, ⲫⲟⲟⲩ v ϩⲟⲟⲩ *day*.

ⲡⲁⲩⲣⲉ A vb intr, *increase, grow* of animal, plant: Cl 24 5 (Rösch) seeds when sown ⲡ. ⲥⲉϯ ⲟⲩⲟⲩ (var ⲣ ⲁⲩⲝⲁⲛⲉ) αὔξειν, ib 25 4 (Berl) by degrees worm ϭⲛ. (var ⲣ ⲁⲩⲝ.) Gk om.

ⲡⲁϣ S, ⲫⲁϣ B nn m, *trap, snare*: Job 18 8 SB, Ps 34 8 B (S ϭⲟⲣϭⲥ), Pro 7 23 SB (A ⲡⲁⲥϩϥ), Si 27 20 S (var ⲡⲁϣϥ), Hos 5 1 S (Mun 176, A do) B, Am 3 5 S (B ϫⲟⲣϫⲥ) παγίς, Ro 11 9 B ϥ....ϫ. (S ϭ....ⲡ.) π., θήρα; Ps 34 8 S (B ϫ.) θ.; Va 57 133 B flee from ⲡⲉϥϥ. λαβή; Pro 9 18 S (A do, B ⲃⲉⲛ-ⲡⲏ) πέταυρον *profunda*; ShC 73 7 S ⲟⲩⲛ ⲡ. (var ⲡⲁϣϥ) ⲟⲩⲛ ⲕⲉϭⲟⲣϭⲥ, BMar 36 S ⲙ̄ⲡ. ⲙ̄ⲛ̄ⲛϭ. of devil, ShA 1 458 S for birds ⲟⲩⲛ. ⲉⲡⲁϣⲉ ⲛⲉϥ̄ⲁ-ⲗⲟⲟⲩⲉ, ROC 25 259 B ⲡⲓϥ. ⲉⲧⲉⲧⲛ̄ϣⲱⲕ ⲉⲣⲟϥ, Mor 34 35 S ⲡ. = BMis 110 S ϩⲧⲟⲡ, BMis 1195 S ⲧⲓ-ⲥⲉⲣ ⲡ. ⲉⲃⲟⲗ ⲉⲣⲟⲕ.

ⲣⲉϥϫⲁ ϥ. B, *trap-setter*: C 86 162 prostitutes ⲕⲓⲣ. ⲛ̄ⲛⲓⲣⲱⲙⲓ (sic l).

ⲡⲁϣϥ S, ⲡⲁⲥϩϥ A, *trap*: Pro 7 23 A, Si 27 20 S, Hos 5 1 A (all S var ⲡⲁϣ) *ut sup*, R 1 5 10 S (var ϭ.) παγίς; ShBM 204 77 ⲛ̄ⲁⲗⲟⲟⲩⲉ ⲛ̄ ⲙ̄ⲡ., ShMun 165 ⲛ̄ⲡ. ⲙ̄ⲡⲉⲑⲏⲣϭ.

ⲡⲟⲉⲓϣ S nn m, *rung, step* of ladder: TT 39 ϭⲗⲟⲟϭⲉ...ⲡⲉⲥⲡ. ϫⲟⲥⲉ ⲉⲡⲉϥⲉⲣⲏⲩ, ib 40 setting foot upon ⲡϣⲟⲣⲡ ⲙ̄ⲡ. of ladder, Mor 37 161 mounting ϩⲛ̄ϩⲉⲛⲧⲱⲣⲧⲣ ⲛ̄ ϩⲉⲛⲡ.

ⲡⲱϣ SAF, ⲡⲱϣⲉ SAA², ⲫⲱϣ B, ⲡⲉϣ- SA, ⲫⲉϣ- B, ⲡⲁϣ- F, ⲡⲟϣ⸝ S, ⲡⲁϣ⸝ AF, ⲫⲁϣ⸝ B, ⲡⲏϣ† SSᶠ, ⲫⲏϣ† B, vb **I** intr, *divide, be separate*: 1 Kg 15 29 S, Is 30 28 SF (B ⲫⲱⲣϫ) διαιρεῖσθαι; CaiEuch 528 B ⲫⲏ ⲉⲧⲁϥⲫ. κλᾶσθαι, Lam 4 4 B διακ.; Is 34 17 SBF διαμερίζεσθαι; Ac 14 4 S (B ⲫⲱⲣϫ) σχίζεσθαι; Si 47 27 S δίχα γίνεσθαι; 1 Kg 9 24 S ἀποκνίζειν; BHom 117 S soul and body ⲁⲩⲡ. at death, Aeg 264 S ⲁⲡⲉϩⲟⲟⲩ (of crucifixion) ⲡ. & darkness fell = PO 8 618 انقسم, Miss 8 159 S Jeroboam's kingdom ⲛⲁⲡ. ⲛ̄ⲧⲟⲟⲧϥ ⲁⲡⲡⲉ.

II tr, *divide*: Nu 26 53 SB, 1 Kg 23 28 B (S ⲡⲱⲣϫ), Hos 10 2 SAB, Ro 12 3 B (SF ⲧⲱϣ) μερίζειν, Ge 49 7 SB, Ps 16 14 SB (F ⲡⲱⲗⲉϫ), Ac 2 3† B (S ⲡⲱⲣϫ) διαμερ., Job 40 25 S (B ⲉϩⲣⲉⲛ-) μερι-τεύεσθαι; Lev 1 17 SB, Ps 67 13 SB διαιρ., ib 135 13 S (B ⲫⲱⲣϫ) καταδιαιρ.; Mt 14 19 SBF, BAp 54 S ⲛ̄ⲧⲉⲣⲉϥⲡⲉϣ ⲡⲟⲉⲓⲕ κλᾶν, Lu 9 16 SB κατακ.; Ge 15 17† SB, Mt 24 51 S (B do) διχοτομεῖν; Lev 2 6 S (B om) διαθρύπτειν; PS 341 S ϣⲁⲩⲡⲟϣⲟⲩ & make 2, AP 55 A² ⲁⲉⲓⲡ. ⲛⲣⲉⲡⲛⲟⲩⲉⲓ ⲡⲁⲉⲓⲕ, ClPr 46 S ⲡⲉϣⲁϥⲡⲉϣ ⲡⲣⲟⲟⲩϣ ⲙⲡⲉϩⲟⲟⲩ *apportion duties*.

With following preposition.

—— ⲉ- SB, *divide at, into*: Ge 15 10 S (var ⲉⲃⲟⲗ ϩⲛ-) B διαιρ. μέσος, ib 32 7 S (B ⲫⲱⲣϫ) δ. εἰς; Si 44 28 S μερίζειν ἐν; Ac 1 18 S (var ϩⲛ-, B ⲕⲱϣ) λακεῖν; BHom 100 S ⲉⲡⲛ. ⲁⲛ ⲛ̄ⲡⲉϥⲅⲥⲓⲥ ⲉⲥⲡⲧⲉ, BMar 160 S veil ⲡ. ⲉⲧⲩⲙⲏⲧⲉ. V also ⲡ. ⲡ- sf.

—— ⲉϩⲣⲛ- SAB, *divide between, share with*, intr: Mt 12 25 B (S ⲉϩⲣⲁⲓ ⲉϫⲛ-) μερ. κατά, 1 Cor 9 13 B (SF ⲉϫⲛ-) συμμερ. dat; tr: Nu 26 53 B (S dat), Pro 8 21 B (var ⲫⲱⲣϣ, SA ⲉϫⲛ-) μερ. dat, Lu 12 13 B (S do) μερ. μετά, Mk 15 24 SB (F ϩⲓ-) διαμ., Lev 25 46 B (S do) καταμ. dat; Joel 3 2 SAB καταδιαιρ.; Cat 69 B ⲉⲧϥ. ⲉϩⲣⲁϥ ⲙ̄ⲫⲟⲩⲁⲓ ⲫⲟⲩⲁⲓ.

—— ⲉϫⲛ- SAA²BF, meaning same, intr: Is 17 11 S (B ϯ ⲕⲗⲏⲣⲟⲥ ⲡ-) κληροῦν dat, *cf* Pro 13 22 SA, Va 58 168 B David might not use Saul's armour, lest king should ϥ. ⲉϫⲛⲡⲉϥϩⲟⲡⲗⲟⲛ & boast, Et Leem 92 S laid out booty ⲁⲩⲡ. ⲉϫⲱⲟⲩ; tr: Pro 14 18 SA (B ⲉϩⲣⲉⲛ-) μερ., Jer 12 14 S (B ⲡ-) μερ. dat, Lu 12 52† S (cf PS 301, B ⲫⲟⲣϫ) διαμερ. ἐπί, Jo 19 24 SA² (B ⲉϩⲣⲉⲡ-) δ. dat, Nu 32 18 S (B ϭⲓ ⲙⲉⲣⲟⲥ) καταμερ.; Ex 21 35 S (B ⲉϩⲣⲉⲡ-) διαιρ.; Aeg 280 S let deacons ⲡⲟϣⲟⲩ ⲉϫⲙ̄ⲡⲉⲕⲗⲏ-ⲣⲟⲥ διανέμειν dat; CaiEuch 333 B body ⲉⲧⲟⲩⲡⲁ-ⲫⲁϣϥ ⲉϫⲉⲡⲉⲑⲏⲡⲟⲩ κλᾶν ὑπέρ; ShR 2 3 29 S many shall ⲡ. ⲉϫⲱⲟⲩ ⲛ̄ⲡⲉⲕⲛⲕⲁ, TEuch 2 388 B tongues of fire ⲡⲁⲩⲡ.† ⲉϫⲉⲛⲫⲟⲩⲁⲓ ⲫⲟⲩⲁⲓ; + ⲙ̄ⲡ-, ⲡⲉⲙ-: Va 61 98 B ⲁϥⲫⲁϣⲥ ⲉϫⲱϥ ⲡⲉⲙⲡⲓϩⲛⲕⲓ, J 45 20 S ⲧⲁⲣⲉⲡⲡⲟϣⲥϥ ⲉϫⲱⲛ ⲙ̄ⲛⲉⲛⲉⲣⲏⲩ. ⲉϩⲣⲁⲓ ⲉϫⲛ- S: Mt 12 25 *ut sup*. V also ⲉⲃⲟⲗ ⲉϫⲛ-.

—— ⲙⲛ- S, *divide with, among*: Lu 12 53 (var ⲉϫⲛ-, B ⲫⲱⲣϫ ⲉϫ.) διαμερ. ἐπί; Mor 18 153 war-ring demons ⲁⲓⲧⲁⲩ ⲉⲡ. ⲙ̄ⲛ̄ⲡⲉⲩⲉⲣⲏⲩ τοὺς κάτω πρὸς τὰ ἄνω συνέβαλον, J 122 51 ⲉⲁⲩⲡ. ⲡⲉⲕⲁϩ ⲙ̄ⲛ̄-ⲡⲉⲛⲅⲉⲓⲟⲧⲉ, ClPr 54 40 bade ⲡ. ⲙ̄ⲡⲉⲧⲟⲛϩ ⲙ̄ⲛ̄ⲡⲉⲧ-ⲙⲟⲟⲩⲧ.

—— ⲡ- dat SB, *divide for, share with*: Is 58 7 S (B ϯ) διαθρύ.; Jer 12 14 B (S ⲉϫⲛ-). Qual SSᶠ, *streaked with* (?): Z 314 S piece of flesh ⲉϥⲡ.

пспоϥ ἡματωμένος, BHom 122 S mouth п. ихір
ріеітп, Mor 40 27 S devil's face п. испоϥ = ib 39
36 Sᶠ = C 43 56 B мер пс., cf MIF 9 15 S their
words п.† епбоλ are half lies (?).

—— рп- SAB, divide in, among: Ge 15 10 B
(S є-, var єѣ. рп-) διαιρ. μέσος, Pro 17 2 SA δ. ἐν;
ib 18 18 SA ὁρίζειν ἐν; ShC 73 32 S епп.† ρ̅мпеп-
рнт one toward other, MG 25 50 B єϥп.† бепе-
пеϥλοτісмос.

—— ріхп- Sᶠ, divide between: JKP 2 64 аѣпаϣ
пехрωпωс ріхωѣ пемаѣ.
With following adverb.

—— єѣоλ B, separate, part: intr, Aeg 24 dying
soul ф. єѣ. = ib S оуωϣ єєі єѣ.; tr, Ez 13 18
διαστρέφειν; MG 25 228 фаϣоу єѣ & give me
part; єѣ. єхп- SᶠB, divide among: PcodMor
25 Sᶠ arithm problem ϣакпоуϣ (sc money) єѣ.
єхωтапс псоуа, MIE 2 405 B аϥфоϣоу (sc corn)
єѣ. єхеппіп̄ перооу; єѣ. рп- S, from: 1 Kg
15 28 διαρρηγνύειν ἐκ.

—— nn m SB, division: He 4 12 B (S ма мп.)
μερισμός, Mic 7 12 B (SA vb) διαμ.; Lu 24 35 SB
κλάσις; K 167 B birds пемпеϥф. اقتسم, ShC 73
93 S loss (of bread) етϣооп рітамп мппtако.
атп., атф. SB, indivisible, undivided: Br 231 S
па …етемпϥп. епер, BMOr 9525 (2) unity па.,
C 86 94 B Trinity єсоі па.; атп. єѣоλ S: P
129²⁰ 122 фусіс па. єѣ. рпспау; атпоϣϥ, -ф.
BMOr 8775 82 B па· амарістос (ἀμέρ.), Z 281
S поуа пеіа.
ма мп. S, place of dividing: He 4 12 ut sup.
реϥп., -ф. SB, divider: P 44 50 S διανομεύς;
Lu 12 14 B (S реϥпωрх) μεριστής.
хіпф. B, dividing, division: Cat 147 рапх. пте
рапtоі іе рапіклнропоміа, K 61 піх. of day,
time &c قسام, Abû Ṣâliḥ Churches 36 lections ау-
фаϣоу бепт пх.; біпп. єѣоλ: PcodMor 25
Sᶠ arithm тб. поуϥ єѣ. єхωоусоуа.
паϣє SF, -ϣі Sᶠ, пеϣє SAA², піϣє S (esp
Theban), піϣє S, фаϣі B, пеϣі F, паϣ- SF,
пϣ-, пеϣ-, піϣ- S, фаϣ- B nn f, division, half:
2 Kg 10 4 S, Ez 40 42 B (S бос) ἥμισυ; Jo 6 12
F (Mich 3521, SA² λакм, B λакр) κλάσμα; Ez 45
3 B ѳѣа ѣ пелоуф. к̅є χιλιάδες; PS 46 S єретєпп.
о пкωрт, AP 28 A² тп. of temple, DeV 2 137 B
tower destroyed ϣатеϥф., BM 528 56 F arithm
таλа птекеп. ріхωоу, Bodl(P) 1 c S recipe хі
тєупа.= ib 3 58 пе., ST 437 S оуп. (i e оуп. про-
λок/); п. п-, пте: Ex 24 6 SB, Zech 14 2 SAB,
Mk 6 23 SB ἥμ.; Z 293 S ϣатп. птеріп μέσος;
AM 297 B оуф. пте оустуλλос, JKP 2 26 Sᶠ
тпаϣі пхемопіоп spirit serving Solomon, COAd
42 S тп. проλок/, J 21 36 S тпн. мпапні, PMich

3547 S оупеϣє поптіа; п. of day: Jer 15 9
SB μεσοῦν, Su 7 B (S пау мееρе) μέσος; BSM
37 B тф. мпεрооу = BMis 381 S do, TT 16 S
darkness птп. мпεрооу, Mor 30 26 F тпеϣі мпεр.
= ib 29 22 S па.; п. of night: Ps 118 62 SB,
Mk 13 35 SBF μεσονύκτιον, Mt 25 6 SB μέσης
νυκτός; AZ 21 147 S рптп. птеуϣн, C 43 229 B
єтатф. мпіехωрр ϣωпі. As adj (or advb) S:
ST 37 sowing contract птхооу пеіωρε пп., BP
11349 I sold field піар мп. (cf BKU 1 48 птпр
рωѣ єроϥ птп. є(п)оуа). Adverbial S: BMis
1198 whoso communicates without lessons heard
єϥсупате мпіϣε.
паϣ- &c, half-: C 43 60 B оуф. маρі, Tor 2 S
тпϣтрімпсе, BKU 1 99 S паϣ птрнмпсіоп, WS
116 S оупϣмпт (= мпт), Kr 227 F оупаϣаіпі,
PLond 4 447 S тпаϣертатнс (cf ib тпаϣε пερг.),
Ryl 386 S send пеϣпер спау; с р, ер, о, оі
dividing, halving, half-: Sa 18 18 S пϣмоу ἡμίθνητος, Lu 10 30 SB sim ἡμιθανής; Is 51 20 S
пϣλωρм B фаϣλ. ἡμίεφθος; BMis 239 S єϥо
мпаϣмоу, C 86 334 B аує р фаϣмоу. Cf
next.

р паϣе, ер ф. SB, be half, be midway: Jo 7 14
B (S рітмпте п-) μεσοῦν; Ps 54 24 B (S diff)
ἡμισεύειν; Mor 19 45 S аϥр п. ммоу, ib 43 161 S
апка пϣахе єѣоλ єϥо мп., PChass 1 24 S recipe
аас мп., C 86 321 B єтаує р ф. поуωм, RNC 80
S sack єϥо мп. пϣω half (full) of sand; iteration: Mor 16 97 S ϣакхω мпекϣахе єϥо мп.
п., R 2 1 47 S sim (sic l), BMis 257 S broken idol
о ппн. пн. = Mor 29 27 S па. па. = ib 30 32 F
пеϣі п., C 41 57 B broke them & аітоу мф. ф.

паіϣє, паϣє, пеϣε, піϣε S, піре Sᵃ, фаіϣі
B (Lab whence?), DM 13 24 пλеіϣε nn f m (?),
a disease producing pustules, swelling: P 43 51
тпаі. حبة, حبة (venereal disease AZ 25 62), PMéd
306 оупа. єс† ϣар пкωрт that burns, AJSL 46
247 charms for тпі. пкωрт & тп. прωλ, Z 627
charm for тпаі. in margin (later) الورم جيدة على النمل,
ib 628 recipe, ShC 73 73 only external maladies as
оупе., оухеуте (sic MS) to be treated by physician,
ST 297 orpiment (ἀρσενικόν) for hand which о ппі.,
Hall 65 Sᵃ fragm recipe піρε пім…єϣаϥпωϣ…
пт]бпте бо пспоϥ…по]б ппіρε пϥϥі п[. In
name (?) Τρονтπαῖσις (Preisigke).

пеϣε v пωϣ(паϣε) & паіϣε.

пωϣп SO, -еп F, фωϣεп B, пеϣп-, поϣп-
S, фоϣп- B, поϣп† S, фоϣп† B vb I intr, do
service, serve as priest: Nu 4 39 S (var & B ϣεм-
ϣε), ib 43 B (S ϣ.) λειτουργεῖν, Ps 102 21† B (S

ϣⲁϣϥⲧ) λειτουργός; Mor 41 34 S archons & captains ⲙⲡⲛⲕⲟⲟⲩⲉ ⲉⲧⲛ.† *officials*, ShC 73 165 S ⲣⲱⲙⲉ ⲛⲓⲙ ⲉⲩⲛ.† *whether priest or deacon*, *ib* 63 S ⲡⲣⲱⲙⲉ ⲉⲧⲛ.† *serving* at funeral.   With following prep. Lu 10 40 S ⲡ. ⲉ- (B ϯ ⲧⲟⲧⲥ) συναντιλαμβάνειν; MIF 9 55 S Christ to Peter ⲡⲉⲧⲉⲛⲉϧⲛⲁⲡ. ⲁⲛ ⲉⲡⲉⲕ-ⲑⲣⲟⲛⲟⲥ (*cf* below ⲡⲁϣⲛⲉⲥ), ShC 73 108 S ⲉⲩⲛ.†... ⲛⲥⲟⲃⲧⲉ ⲛⲓⲙ *due to altar*.

II tr, **a** *serve*: Nu 16 9 SB λειτ.;   **b** *ordain to office*: Z 297 S ϯⲛⲁⲡⲟϣⲛⲉϥ, Aeg 217 S ⲡⲉⲛ-ⲧⲁϥⲡⲟϣⲛⲉϥ χειροτονεῖν, Mor 18 56 S bishop forbidden ⲭⲉⲛⲛⲉϥⲡⲉϣⲛ ⲗⲁⲁⲩ = *ib* 19 65 S ⲭⲓⲣⲟ-ⲧⲟⲛⲉⲓ = Miss 4 132 B ϥ. ⲡⲟⲩⲭⲉⲓⲣⲟⲧⲟⲛⲓⲁ; BMis 468 S ⲁϥⲡⲟϣⲛϥ ⲛⲇⲓⲁⲕⲟⲛⲟⲥ, ⲁϥⲁⲁϥ ⲙⲡⲣⲉⲥⲃ., ⲁϥ-ⲭⲓⲣⲟⲧⲟⲛⲉⲓ ⲙⲙⲟϥ ⲛⲉⲡⲓⲥⲕ., Mor 31 100 S ⲁϥⲡⲟϣⲛ-ⲛⲟⲩ & *made them deacons*, *cf* ⲓⲃ ⲁϥⲭⲓⲣⲱⲧⲱⲛⲉⲓ ⲙⲙⲟϥ ⲙⲡⲣⲉⲥⲃ., Gu 13 S ⲉⲁϥⲡ. ⲛⲁⲩ ⲛⲅⲉⲡⲓⲥⲕ. (var *ib* ⲕⲁⲑⲓⲥⲧⲁ), BIF 13 118 S ⲁⲩⲡ. ⲛⲁⲡⲁ...ⲙ-ⲡⲣⲉⲥⲃ. = MG 25 311 B ⲑⲱϣ, LAp 549 F ⲁⲩⲡ. ⲛⲉϥ ⲛⲟⲩⲉⲡⲓⲥⲕⲟⲡⲟⲥ.

Hor 82 O ⲡ. (obscure).

—— *SB* nn m, *service*: Nu 4 28 B (S ϣⲙϣⲉ ⲛⲗⲓⲧⲟⲩⲣⲅⲓⲁ, var om ⲡϣ.), Phil 2 17 B (S = Gk) λειτουργία; *ordination*: BerlOr 1611 1 S ⲛϣⲟⲣⲡ ⲙⲡ. at Chrysostom's hands = BSM 125 B, TEuch 1 105 B ⲉⲡⲓⲕⲗⲏⲥⲓⲥ ⲛⲧⲉ ⲡⲓϥ.

ⲣⲉϥⲡ., -ϥ. *SBF*, *servant*: Ro 13 6 B (S = Gk), He 8 2 B (var ⲣⲉϥϯ ϥ., S do) λειτουργός; HL 121 B ⲣⲁⲛⲡ. of church κληρικός; PMich 4932 f S incantation ⲛⲣ. ⲙⲡⲣⲏ ⲙⲟⲩⲧⲉ ⲉⲣⲟⲕ, Kr 13 F ⲗⲉⲃⲛ. ⲭⲟ (χωρίον) Καρπε, *ib* 53 F ⲗⲉⲃⲛ. ⲙⲛⲙⲓⲧⲱⲗ (so ? attached to a place), *ib* 11 F ⲗⲉⲙⲛ.

ⲭⲓⲛⲫ. B, *service*: Nu 4 27 (S ϣ.) λειτουργία; ROC 11 67 ⲛⲭ. ⲛⲟⲩⲙⲟⲛⲁⲭⲟⲥ (TEuch 1 151 ـــ).

ⲡⲁϣⲛⲉ S, ⲫⲁϣⲛⲓ B nn f, *service*: Nu 7 8 S (B ⲫⲟϣⲛⲉⲛ), He 8 6 B (var & SF ϣ.) λειτουργία; BM 1031 S ⲛⲉⲣⲓⲉⲣⲉⲩⲥ...ⲙⲛⲧⲛ. ⲧⲏⲣⲥ ⲛⲓⲉⲣⲟⲩⲣⲁⲧⲉ as witnesses; *ordination*: P ar 203 153 B in patriarch's ⲧⲁⲕⲗⲓⲇ we bishops ⲁⲛⲑⲁⲙⲓⲟ ⲛⲧⲉϥϥ. ـــ & enthronement, TEuch 1 125 sim ـــ.

ⲡⲁϣⲛⲉⲥ S nn f, *ordination* (?): MIF 9 63 Christ to Peter ⲡⲉⲧⲉϥⲛⲁϣⲱⲡⲉ ⲁⲛ ⲣⲁⲧⲛ. of thy throne his (imposition of) hands ⲥⲧⲏⲩ ⲉⲃⲟⲗ *is abhorrent* (*cf* above MIF 9 55).

ⲫⲟϣⲛⲉϥ B nn m, *ordination*: BodlMarsh 32 136 ⲡⲓϥ. ⲙⲃⲉⲣⲓ of new bishop ـــ (*cf* 138 ⲑⲱⲝⲉⲛ ⲙⲃ. 'ـــ).

ⲡⲁϣⲟⲛⲥ (oftenest), -ⲱⲛⲥ, -ⲁⲛⲥ, ⲡⲁⲭⲟⲛⲥ (WTh 185), -ⲭⲁⲛⲥ (Alex 281), -ⲣⲁⲛⲉⲥ (Win 61), -ⲣⲟⲛ[ⲥ (CO 478), ⲁⲡϣⲟⲟⲥ (Ryl 265) S, ⲡⲁϣⲟⲛⲥ (C 43 220) B, ⲡⲁϣⲁⲛⲥ (BM 596, Ann 23 58), ⲡⲁϣⲁⲥ (Kr 193) F nn, name of 9th month, Gk Παχών, Ar بشنس.

ⲡⲱϣⲥ *SA²F*, -ⲥϣ S, -ⲥⲣ A, ⲡⲉϣⲥ-, ⲡⲟϣⲥⲥ, ⲡⲁϣⲥⲥ, ⲡⲟϣⲥ†, -ⲥϣ† S, ⲡⲁ.† SF, ⲡⲁⲥⲣ† A vb I intr, *be amazed, beside oneself*: Ge 27 33 S (B ⲧⲱⲙⲧ), Is 28 7 S (B ⲥⲱⲣⲉⲙ), *ib* 32 11 SF (B ⲧ.), Dan 2 1 S (B ϣⲑⲟⲣⲧⲉⲣ), Hos 5 8 SA (B ⲧ.), Mk 3 21 S (B ⲥⲓⲣ̅ⲓ), AP 15 A² ἐξιστάναι, Si 16 8 S ἀφισ.; Z 288 S on seeing him ⲁⲥⲡ., BMar 174 S who would not ⲡ.? καταπλήσσειν, AP 7 A² being afraid ⲛⲑⲉ ⲛⲧⲁⲥⲡ. ἔκπληξις; He 12 13 S (B ⲣⲓⲕⲓ), Aeg 288 S (*cf* 1 Tim 5 15) ἐκτρέπεσθαι; Z 302 S seeing hermit herding swine said ⲉⲁⲡⲉϥϩⲏⲧ ⲡ. *stupere*; ShWess 9 160 S worshipping idols like ⲛⲉⲣⲱⲟⲩ ⲛⲧⲁⲩⲡ., ShBMOr 8800 200 S Origen's words ⲉⲩⲛ.†, Miss 8 233 S ⲛϯⲡ.† ⲁⲛ...ⲛⲧⲟⲕⲡⲉ ⲛⲧⲁϥⲗⲓⲃⲉ, GuDorm 5 S ⲁⲣⲏⲩ ⲉϥⲛ.† or is fool, BMar 43 S whilst coming down ϥⲛⲁⲡ. *be diverted, slip* (*cf* ⲡ. ⲉⲃⲟⲗ).

II tr, *SA*, *amaze, turn aside*: Ex 23 27 S (B ⲧ.), Job 12 17 S (B do), Lu 24 22 S (B ⲉⲣ ϣⲫⲏⲣⲓ), Ac 8 9 S (B ⲟⲩⲱⲧⲉⲃ ⲉⲃⲟⲗ) ἐξισ., Nu 32 9 S (B ⲣⲓⲕⲓ), Deu 1 28 S (B ⲫⲱⲛⲣ), 1 Kg 19 10 S refl ἀφισ., Jos 14 8 S μεθισ., Hos 9 7 A (B ⲧ.) παρεξισ.; Mic 3 9 SA (B ⲫ.), Cl 47 5 A διαστρέφειν; Joel 2 7 A (B ⲣ. ⲉⲃⲟⲗ) ἐκκλίνειν; 1 Kg 21 13 S ⲣ ⲑⲉ ⲛⲓⲉⲧⲛ.† προσποίεσθαι; ShC 42 187 S ⲁϥⲡ. ⲙⲡⲉⲧⲛϩⲏⲧ ϩⲛ-ⲟⲩϩⲃⲁ, GFr 312 S ⲁϥⲡ. ⲙⲡⲉⲥⲗⲟⲅⲓⲥⲙⲟⲥ ⲁϥⲡⲱⲛⲉ ⲙⲡⲉⲥⲛⲟⲩⲥ, Pcod 29 S ⲁϥⲡⲉϣⲥ ⲟⲩⲙⲏⲏϣⲉ.

With following preposition.

—— ⲉ- dat *SA*, *be turned to*: 1 Kg 6 12 μεθι-στάναι; dat commodi: Jos 2 11 ἐξισ.; El 134 heart of multitude ⲛⲁⲡ. ⲉⲣⲟⲟⲩ = *ib* 98 A ⲛϩⲁⲧ ⲁⲣⲁⲩ, Miss 4 713 whose heart ⲡ. ⲉⲣⲟⲟⲩ, *ib* var ⲗⲟ ⲙ-ⲙⲁⲩ;   tr Cl 12 4 A Rahab & king's men ⲉⲥⲡ. ⲙⲙⲁⲩ ⲁⲕⲉⲥⲁ ἐναλλάσσειν.

—— ⲉϫⲛ- S, *be amazed at*: Sa 5 2 (B diff) ἐξισ. ἐπί; ShR 2 3 24 ⲁⲩⲡ....ⲉϫⲛⲧⲉⲙⲛⲧⲣⲉϥⲣ ⲛⲟⲃⲉ; ⲉϩⲣⲁⲓ ⲉϫⲛ-: Jth 12 16 ἐξισ. ἐπί, Ac 3 10 (B ⲙⲉⲧ-ⲉⲃⲛ) ἐκστάσεως πληθῆναι ἐπί, Sa 13 4 ἐκπλήσ. dat; ShA 1 437 ⲁⲛⲡ. ⲉϩ. ⲉϫⲱⲓ ⲙⲁⲩⲁⲁⲧ, Miss 8 166 judge & martyr ⲁϥⲡ. ⲉϩ. ⲉϫⲛⲡⲉϥⲁⲡⲟⲗⲟⲅⲓⲁ (*cf* 205 sim ⲡ. ⲉϫⲛ-).

—— ⲛⲥⲁ- S, *be silly after*: ShLeyd 303 women ⲉⲧⲛ.† ⲁⲩⲱ ⲉⲧⲗⲟⲃⲉ ⲛⲥⲁⲡⲣⲟⲟⲩⲧ.

—— ϩⲛ- S, *be dazed, bemused*: ShP 130⁵ 92 ⲙⲡⲛⲕⲗⲓⲃⲉ ⲁⲩⲱ ⲛⲥⲡ. ϩⲙⲡⲏⲣⲡ, Mus 40 276 ⲛⲡⲉⲓⲡ. ϩⲛⲟⲩⲇⲟⲡⲏ; *turn aside, about*: ShA 1 246 fish ⲉϣⲁⲩⲡ. ϩⲛⲡⲙⲟⲟⲩ, BAp 87 sim ⲉϥⲡⲟⲥϣ ϩⲁⲛ-ⲙⲟⲟⲩ ⲉϥⲣⲗⲟⲓⲗⲉ = MIE 2 359 B ⲛⲟⲓⲛⲓ.

With following adverb.

—— ⲉⲃⲟⲗ *SAF* meanings as ⲡ., intr: Is 33 3 SF (B ⲧⲱⲙⲧ) ἐξισ.; Hos 4 16 A (B ⲛⲟⲩϣⲡ) παρ-οιστρᾶν; Eccl 7 17 S ἐκπλήσ.; Jer 18 14 S (B ⲣⲓⲕⲓ) ἐκκλίν.; Tit 3 11 S (B ⲫⲱⲛⲣ) ἐκστρέφ., Deu

32 35 S (B ϣⲱϧⲧ) σφάλλειν; ViSitz 172 4 15 S
lest ye cannot bear to hear ⲛ̄ⲧⲉⲧⲛ̄п. ⲉϧ. στραγγαλοῦσθαι; ShRE 11 18 S in whom demons spake
ϣⲁⲛⲧⲟⲩп. ⲉϧ.; tr: Ez 13 22 S (ShA 2 22, B
т. ⲉϧ.) διαστρ.; 2 Kg 6 6 S refl (B diff) περισπᾶν; c ⲉϧ. e- intr (cf п. e-), turn away from:
1 Kg 4 13 S ἐξισ.; P 131¹ 17 S devil misleads man
ⲉⲁ̣ϥп.† ⲉϧ. ⲉⲧⲉⲡⲧⲟⲗⲏ (cf next); c ⲉϧ. п-: 2 Kg
5 23 S ἀποστρ. ἀπό; Cl 47 7 A ⲉⲅⲡ.† ⲁϧ. ⲙ̄ⲙⲁⲛ
ἑτεροκλινὴς ἀπό (cf ib 11 1 ⲣⲓⲕⲉ ⲁϧ. ἑτεροκ.);
ShWess 9 87 S sons of Ham п. ⲉϧ. ⲙⲡ̄п̄ⲉ, P 44
97 S ⲁϥп. ⲉϧ. ⲛ̄ⲧⲉⲡⲧⲟⲗⲏ; c ⲉϧ. ϩⲛ-, as last intr:
ShA 1 246 S ⲛⲉⲧп. ⲉϧ. ϩ̄ⲛⲡⲉⲧⲅⲣⲁⲫⲓ, Bor 240 87 S
causing to stumble ⲉⲧⲣⲉⲅп. ⲉϧ. ϩⲛⲧⲉϩⲓⲏ.

—— SA nn m, amazement: Dan 10 7 (B ⲧⲱ.),
Zech 12 4 A (B ⲇⲟ) ἔκστασις; Mor 17 27 his words
ϩⲁⲛп. пⲉ λῆρος; ClPr 54 39 ⲟⲩⲛⲟϭ ⲙ̄п. at wonders
ἐκπλήσ., Ming 292 tight-rope walking ⲉⲅⲙⲉϥ ⲙ̄п.
ϩⲓⲣⲟⲧⲉ, BMar 172 ⲕⲗⲟϧⲉ ϩⲛⲟⲩпⲱϣ.

—— п̄ϩⲏⲧ SF, be disturbed in mind, amazed: Ro
4 19 F (JEA 13 26, S ϭⲛ̄ϧⲉ, B ϣⲱпⲓ) ἀσθενεῖν;
ShC 42 96 suddenly as if п̄ⲧⲁⲅп. п̄ϩ., Bor 134 4
(Vita Sin) looked at Shenoute ⲉⲁⲅп. п̄ϩ. = C 41 34
B ⲥⲱⲣⲉⲙ п̄ϩ., Z 282 ⲉⲁ̣ⲅп. п̄ϩ. ⲉⲡⲉⲅⲟⲩⲟ at his
boldness, Ep 592 11 ⲉⲅ̄ϣⲱпⲉ ⲉⲅ̄ⲥⲱ (l ? пⲱϣⲥ or
ϣⲥ) п̄ϩ. φρενοβλάβεια; qual: 1 Kg 21 14 S ἐπίληπτος, Mor 37 41 ἐξισ.; c ⲉⲝп-: ShA 1 128
whereat wast astonished п̄ⲧⲉⲡ. п̄ϩ. ⲉϫⲱϥ; c
п̄ⲥⲁ-: ShA 2 278 if ye see not kindred ϣⲁⲧⲉⲧⲛ̄п.
п̄ϩ. п̄ⲥⲱⲟⲩ. As nn S, amazement: Deu 28 28 (B
ⲥⲓϩⲓ п̄ϩ.) ἔκστ. διανοίας; ShC 42 125 ϣⲧⲟⲣⲧⲣ, п.
п̄ϩ., GuDorm 6 п. п̄ϩ., ϩⲃⲁ.

пⲁϣⲥ S nn m, landing plank (Budge): BMar 43
quitting ship ⲉⲅ̄пⲏⲩ ⲉⲡⲉⲥⲛ̄ⲧ ϩⲁⲙ̄пп. & shall slip
(пⲱϣⲥ).

V Dévaud Études 12.

пⲁϣⲟϣ S Ryl 104 §3 v ⲃⲁϣⲟⲩϣ.

пⲁϣⲥ S v пⲁϣ.

пⲱϩ A v пⲱϩ break.

пⲁϩⲣⲉ A v ⲫⲱϩⲉⲣ.

пⲁϩⲥ A v пⲱϩ break пⲁϩⲥ.

пⲱϩⲧ A v пⲱϩⲧ.

пⲱϩ SA²F, пⲱϩ A, ⲫⲱϩ B, пⲉϩ- SF, пⲁϩ- S,
ⲫⲁϩ- (AM 267), ⲫⲉϩ- (Ge 22 3) B, пⲁϩ⸗ SA²,
пⲟϩ⸗ S, ⲫⲁϩ⸗ B, пⲏϩ† SF, пⲉϩ† S, ⲫⲏϩ† B vb
I intr, break, burst, tear: Ge 7 11 S (B ⲫⲱϧⲓ), Job
32 19 SB, Hab 3 9 SA (B ⲇⲟ) ῥηγνύναι, Lu 5 6 SB,
Va 57 39 B ⲙ̄пⲉϥⲫ. п̄ϫⲉ ⲧⲉϥⲙⲉⲧⲟⲩⲣⲟ (3 Kg 11 12)
διαρρ.; Mk 15 38 SBF, Jo 21 11 SB σχίζειν; Va
63 82 B ⲁпⲓⲭⲁⲣⲧⲏⲥ ⲫ. διασπᾶν; Lev 2 16 S (B

ⲫⲱⲣⲝ) χίδρον; RNC 20 S until water in font п.
ταράσσειν; ShZ 637 S ships п̄ⲥⲉⲣ ϩⲙ̄ⲙⲉ ⲙ̄ⲙⲟⲟⲩ
ⲉⲧ̄ⲁⲩп., BHom 127 S ⲁⲙ̄ⲙпⲧⲉ п., C 86 277 B brazen
bull ⲁⲅⲫ., BMar 65 S tumour п. ϩⲙ̄пⲉⲅⲥⲁ п̄ⲣⲟⲩп,
Mus 42 237 S walkest in purity ϣⲁⲩп. п̄ϭⲓ ϩⲟⲉⲓⲛⲉ
(sc demons).

II tr SAA²BF, meanings same: Job 1 20 SB,
ib 28 10 S (B ⲫⲱⲣⲝ), Is 13 16 S (reading ῥήξουσιν,
B ⲣⲱϧⲧ), Mt 7 6 SB ῥηγ., Jud 11 35 SB, Ps 77
15 S (B ⲫⲱϭⲓ), EpJer 30† B (F пⲱϭⲓ), Hos 14 1
AB, Lu 8 29 S (B ⲥⲱⲗп) διαρρ.; Eccl 10 9 SF, Is
36 22† SBF, Jo 19 24 SA²B σχ., AM 267 B who
hath ⲫⲁϩ ⲧⲉⲕϣⲏп ?, AP 15 A² sim περισχ.; BMar
105 S stag ⲉⲁⲅпⲉϩ ⲧⲁⲧⲉⲗⲏ & departed ἀποσπᾶν,
Is 58 6 S (B † ⲟⲩⲱ) διασп.; Mk 5 5 S (B ϣⲱⲧ)
κατακόπτειν; Sa 5 12 S τέμνειν; ShA 1 2 S work
by rule ⲙ̄пⲣпⲉϩ ⲙⲉⲉⲣⲉ пⲁⲣⲁ пϣⲓ…ⲙ̄пⲣ̄ϣⲱⲣп оп
пⲁⲣⲁ пⲛⲁⲩ, Sh(Besa)Bor 206 575 S ⲉп̄пⲁп. ⲙ̄
пⲉпϩⲏⲧ & weep, ShMIF 23 198 S in hell ⲕⲁп
ⲉⲁⲅпⲉϩ пⲉⲅ̄ϩⲏⲧ who heedeth ?, BHom 101 S heretics ⲗⲓϧⲉ Jews п. п̄пⲉⲅϩⲏⲧ (ALR '96 194 ⲗⲁ),
Bor 134 (Vita Sin) 1 S ⲁⲕпⲉϩ ϩⲏⲧⲥ with sword =
C 41 23 B ⲫ. п̄ⲧⲉⲥпⲉϩⲓ, El 82 A п. п̄пⲉⲧϩⲁⲓⲧⲉ,
BM 1249 B ⲫ. ⲙ̄пⲓϭⲓ п̄ϫⲓⲝ of our sins, Ann 16
250 F ⲧⲅⲙⲟⲣⲫⲏ(ⲣⲁ) ⲁⲅпⲉϩⲥ, ShC 73 143 S beast
(ox) ⲉⲅⲛⲁпⲁⲣϭ ϩⲓⲧпⲟⲩⲑⲏⲣⲓⲟп (l ? пⲁⲣⲥⲅ), EW 92
B п̄ⲧⲁⲫ. ⲙ̄пⲉⲅⲥⲱⲙⲁ with fever, PRain 4796 S
ⲁⲓⲡⲁϩ ⲧⲉⲅⲕⲟⲩⲕⲁⲙⲓⲥⲩⲛ (καμίσιον).

With following preposition. c e- S, divide in,
at: BHom 56 ⲉⲅпⲁпⲁⲣϭ ⲉⲧⲉⲕⲙⲏⲧⲉ (var R 2 2 37
ⲟⲩⲁⲥⲧ ϩⲓ-) σχ. μέσον; c ⲉϫⲉп- B, divide between: Va 66 300 ⲫ. пⲉпϩⲅпⲁⲣⲭⲟпⲧⲁ ⲉϫⲱп
пⲉⲙ̄п‾ⲭ‾ⲥ‾ συμμεριστέον; c ϩⲓϫп- S, divide upon:
Ps 140 7 (B ⲫⲱϭⲓ ϩ.) διαρρ. ἐπί; c п̄ⲥⲁ- adds emphasis SB: Va 58 191 B when angry ⲅ† ⲧⲉпϣⲓ ⲅⲫ.
п̄ⲥⲱⲅ διαρρήγνυσθαι, P 131⁵ 4 S ⲉпп. п̄ⲥⲁпⲉⲡⲉⲣⲏⲩ
like beasts; c ϩⲓ- S, divide in, at: Lu 23 45 (B
ⲫ. ⲝⲉп-) σχ. μέσον; RNC 48 may beast п. ϩⲓⲧⲉⲅ̄
ⲙⲏⲧⲉ, BM 223 tree ⲉϣⲁⲅпⲁⲣϥ ϩⲓⲧⲉⲅⲙ.; qual:
2 Kg 1 2 διαρρ.; BMis 477 п. ϩⲓⲱⲱⲅ rent garments
(being) on him, cf п. e-, п. ϩп-; c ϩп-, ⲝⲉп-
SB, divide at, into: intr Mk 15 38 B (SF ⲣ̄ ⲥпⲁⲩ)
σχ. εἰς; AM 104 B ⲁпⲓⲥⲱⲁⲓⲟп (ζῴδιον) ⲫ. ⲝⲉпⲧⲉⲅ̄
ⲙⲏⲧ; tr ShBM 253 S angels will beg ⲉпⲉϩ̄ⲧⲏⲧⲛ̄
ϩⲓⲧⲉⲛ̄ⲙ., TstAb 236 B sim; Jer 48 5 B ϩⲃⲱⲥ ⲫ.†
п̄ϩⲏⲧⲟⲩ διαρρ. (cf п. ϩⲓ-).

With following adverb. c ⲉϧⲟⲗ intr S, meaning as п.: KKS 166 ⲁпϫⲟⲓ п. ⲉϧ. διαρρ.; ⲉϧ. п-B:
Job 26 8 ῥηγ. ὑποκάτω; tr S: Z 341 snakes ϣⲁⲅ̄
пⲁϩⲟⲩ ⲉϧ. in their middle σχ.; ⲉϧ. ϩп-, ⲝⲉп-
SB, tear out: Lev 13 56 S (B ⲉϧ. ϩⲁ-) ἀπορρ. ἀπό,
Ez 13 20 B διαρρ. ἀπό; c ⲉпⲉⲥⲛ̄ⲧ S, tear downward: Mor 28 261 garments п.† ⲉп. ϩⲓⲱⲱⲥ; c

ⲉϧⲟⲩⲛ, ⲉϣ. *SB, split up to, as far as*: GMir 257
S ⲧⲟⲩⲉⲣⲏⲧⲉ...ⲁⲩⲡⲁϩⲥ ⲉϩ. ⲉⲡⲉϥⲙⲏⲣⲟⲥ (*sic l*) =
C 86 46 *B*.

—— *SB* nn m, *division, piece*: Is 2 19 *S* (*B*
ⲫⲱⲝⲓ), Mt 9 16 *SB* σχίσμα; Ex 21 25 *B* (*S* ⲥⲁϣ)
τραῦμα; Is 7 19 *S* (*B* do) ῥαγάς; Mt 5 22 *S* (*B*
= Gk) ῥακά (? as if ῥαγάς); Va 57 79 *B* ϩⲁⲡϥ.
ⲛⲉⲙϩⲁⲛⲯⲟⲫⲟⲥ of chariots & horses (*cf* Mic 1
13); ⲣ ⲡ., ⲉⲣ ⲫ. *SB* iterated, *become, be in pieces*:
MG 25 27 *B* body ⲟⲓ ⲙⲫ. ⲫ. διεσπαραγμένος; Mor
16 19 *S* sim, P 129¹⁶ 12 *S* beaten till ⲡⲉϥⲥⲟⲓ ⲉⲣ ⲡ.
ⲡ. (*cf* below ⲣ ⲡⲁⲣⲉ, ⲣ ⲡⲁⲣⲥ).

ⲣⲉϥⲡⲉϩ-, ⲫⲉϩ-, ⲫⲁϩ- *SB, divider, splitter*: Deu
29 11 *B* ⲣ. ⲣⲟⲕϩ (*S* ⲋⲗ-), Jos 9 27 *S* ⲣ. ϣⲉ ξυλοκόπος, Cat 204 *B* ⲣⲉϥⲫⲉϩ ⲯⲩⲭⲏ, Miss 4 126 *B* sim
-ⲫⲁϩ ⲯ., R 1 2 72 *S* sim.

ⲡⲁⲣⲉ *S*, ⲫⲏϣⲓ *B*, pl ⲡⲟⲟⲣⲉⲩⲉ (Tri, for ⲡⲁⲣⲉⲩⲉ)
S nn f, *fragment*: AM 267 *B* ϯⲫ. ⲥⲡⲟⲩϯ of colo-
bium ῥῆγμα, Mor 52 46 *S* ⲣⲉⲡⲡ. ⲛϣⲉ (*cf* 3 Kg 18
33 σχίδαξ), Montp 101 *B* ⲫ. ⲡⲣⲱⲕϩ نشقة, Tri
520 *S* ⲣⲉϥⲥⲏⲧ ⲣⲛⲡⲟⲟⲣⲉⲩⲉ (Ar misunderstands),
Mor 51 38 *S* whilst tailors stitch ⲡⲉⲧⲙⲡ., PLond
4 499 *S* ⲡⲡ. ⲛⲥⲟⲓ, BMOr 6201 A 168 *S* distribution of wood ⲉ̅ⲧⲟ ⲡⲡ. ⲙⲛϣⲏⲧ ⲛⲃⲁ; ⲣ ⲡ. ⲡ. *S*
(*cf* ⲣ ⲡⲱϩ): PMich 4945 mountain ⲉϥⲫⲟⲣϫ ⲛⲣⲉⲡⲡ.
ⲡ. (PO 8 106 ܠܡܦ܇ ܠܒ̈ܕ), ShIF 67 clothes ⲁⲁⲩ
ⲙⲡ. ⲡ., others ⲉⲧⲡⲏϩ ⲉⲧⲟ ⲙⲡⲁϣⲉ ⲡⲁϣⲉ.

ⲡⲁⲣⲥ *S*, ⲡⲉⲣⲥ *Sᶠ*, ⲡⲁⲣϩ *A* nn f, *thing torn, prey*:
Ex 22 13 *S* (*B* ϣⲟⲗⲣⲥ), Ps 16 12 (*BF* ϩⲟⲣϫⲥ),
Is 31 4 *SF* (*B* do), Nah 2 12 *A* (*B* do) θήρα; Job
10 16 *S* (*B* ⲋⲟⲗⲋⲉⲗ) σφαγή; ShC 73 200 *S* ⲟⲩⲡ.
whereon birds pounce, Mor 41 80 *S* eating ⲡ. like
beasts, ShR 2 3 89 *S* stink of ⲧⲡ.; ⲣ ⲡ. *S, become, make prey*: ShC 73 197 dead & ⲉⲁⲩⲣ ⲡ.,
ShR 2 3 53 ⲛⲧⲉⲡⲉⲑⲏⲣⲓⲟⲛ ⲁⲁⲩ ⲙⲡ.; Hos 13 8 *A*
ⲉⲩⲉ ⲡⲡ. ⲡ. (*cf* ⲣ ⲡⲱϩ, ⲣ ⲡⲁⲣⲉ) διασπᾶν; Leyd
216 *S* in calendar ⲧⲡ. ⲛⲁⲡⲟⲗⲗⲱ ⲙⲛ(ⲁ)ⲡⲁ ⲡⲉⲣⲓⲉⲓ̈ⲃ
(*i e* ⲫⲓⲃ, 25th Paope, obscure).

ⲡⲁⲣϥ *S* nn m, *cleft or fragment, splinter*: Miss
4 730 ⲟⲩⲡ. ⲙⲡⲉⲧⲣⲁ in desert.

In place-names (?): ⲡⲉⲣⲡⲧⲁⲗ (Ryl 173 Πεεντᾶλις),
ⲡⲉϩⲣⲥⲁⲙⲟⲩⲡ (or ? ⲡⲉⲣⲥ-ⲁⲙⲟⲩⲡ Kr 147 سمود),
ⲡⲉⲣⲡϣⲏⲙ (BM 585), ⲥⲱⲡⲉⲣⲥ (Lant 21 &c).

ⲡⲱϩ *SAF*, ⲫⲟϩ *B*, ⲡⲟϩ, ⲡⲉϩ *F* (BM 581), ⲡϩ *S*
(*v* II), ⲡⲉϩ- *SF*, ⲫⲉϩ- *B*, ⲡⲏϩ† *SA*, ⲫⲉϩ† *B*, vb I intr,
reach: Si 30 26 *S*, 1 Thes 4 15 *B* (*S* ⲣ ϣⲟⲣⲡ ⲉ-)
φθάνειν, Ps 67 26 *B* ⲉⲣ ϣⲟⲣⲡ ⲙⲫ. (*S* ϣ. only)
προφθ.; Sa 7 24 *B* (*S* ⲭⲱⲧⲉ, var om) διήκειν; Mt
26 35 *B* (*S* ϣⲱⲡⲉ) δεῖ; Aeg 23 *B* hour of death
ⲫ. = *ib S* ⲉⲓ, EW 159 *B* demons ⲛⲁⲩϣ ⲫ. ⲁⲡⲡⲉ
attained not to affright him; *reach* maturity,
ripen: Ge 40 10 *SB*, Cl 23 4 *A* πέπειρος; Am 9

13 *SA* (*B* ⲫⲓⲣⲓ) περκάζειν; Ap 14 18 *S* (*B* om) ἀκμάζειν; Lev 2 14 *S* (*B* Gk ?); R 1 4 66 *S* causing
fruits to grow ⲛⲥⲉⲡ. = AM 126 *B* ⲉⲫⲟⲩⲅⲫ. =
Mart Ign VII πεπαίνειν; Ex 9 31 *B* παριστάναι;
Hos 9 10 *A* ⲡ. ⲛϫⲁⲣⲡ σκοπὸς πρώιμος, Mic 7 1
SAB sim πρωτόγονος; Mk 4 29 *B* (*S* ϯ ⲕⲁⲣⲡⲟⲥ)
παραδιδόναι; Gu 60 *S* ⲕⲁⲣⲡⲟⲥ ⲉϥⲡ.†, Pcod 4 *S*
fruit that ⲡ. ⲡⲁⲣⲁ ⲡⲕⲁⲓⲣⲟⲥ opp ⲉⲡⲧⲁϥϫⲉⲕ ⲡⲉϥ-
ⲟⲩⲟⲉⲓϣ ⲉⲃⲟⲗ; ⲡ. ⲉⲃⲟⲗ *S*: BSG 184 ⲛⲥⲉϯ ⲕⲁⲣⲡⲟⲥ ⲉϥⲡ.† ⲉ̅ⲃ̅. = *ib* 15 *B* ⲫⲟⲣⲓ ⲉ̅ⲃ.

With following preposition.

—— ⲉ- *SBF, attain to*: Mt 12 28 *BF* (*S* ⲉϩⲣⲁⲓ
ⲉϫⲛ-) ⲫⲑ. ἐπί, Ps 94 2 *B* (*S* ⲉⲓ ⲉ̅ⲃ̅. ϩⲏⲧ⳽) προφθ.;
Ge 22 3 *S* (*B* ⲓ ⲉ-) ἔρχεσθαι ἐπί, Pro 14 12 *SA* (*B*
ⲡⲛⲟⲩ ⲉϩⲣⲏⲓ ⲉ-) ⲉⲣ. εἰς, MG 25 241 *B* ⲉⲧⲁⲩⲫ. ⲉⲡⲓ-
ⲡⲓϣϯ ⲡⲁⲏⲧ ⲉⲣ. ἐν; Job 13 27 *S* (*B* ϣⲉ ⲉ-) ἀφικνεῖσθαι εἰς, 2 Cor 10 14 *B* (*S* ϣⲁ-) ἐφικ. εἰς; ROC
18 36 *B* sword ⲫ. ⲉⲧϣⲱⲃⲓ ἅπτεσθαι; Ge 33 3
S (*B* ⲋⲱⲡⲧ ⲉ-) ἐγγίζειν ἕως; 1 Cor 14 36 *B* (*SF*
ϣⲁ-) καταντᾶν εἰς; Ac 17 10 *S* (*B* ⲓ ⲉ-) παραγίνεσθαι εἰς; He 4 13 *B* (*S* ϫⲓ ⲉϩⲟⲩⲛ ⲉ-) (εἶναι) πρός;
PS 21 *S* ⲛⲧⲉⲣⲓⲡ. ⲉⲧⲡⲩⲗⲏ, *ib* 341 *S* ϣⲁⲩⲡⲱⲣⲧ ⲉⲡⲕⲟⲥⲙⲟⲥ (*l* ? ⲡ., *cf* ⲡ. ⲉϫⲛ-), C 89 3 *B* ran ϣⲁⲧⲉϥⲫ.
ⲉⲡⲉϥⲏⲓ = MG 17 315 *S* ⲧⲁϩⲟ, PSBA 10 197 *S*
ⲙⲡⲉⲓⲛ. ⲉⲛϣ of things such as this, MG 25 237 *B*
ⲁⲣⲉϥ. ⲉⲑⲱⲡ *where hast been ?*, Cat 131 *B* give ⲕⲁⲧⲁ
ⲫⲏ ⲉⲧⲉⲣⲉⲧⲟⲧⲕ ⲡⲁⲫ. ⲉⲣⲟϥ ⲡⲉⲙⲁϥ, BM 581 *F* ill-
treatment allowed me not ⲧⲁⲡⲉϩ ⲉⲡⲣⲱⲃ...ⲛⲡⲓϣ
ⲡⲉϩ, CMSS 41 *Sᶠ* ⲡⲉϣϣⲉ ⲡⲧⲁⲩⲡ. ⲉⲣⲁⲡ; *v* also
below auxil; *c* ethic dat: MG 25 409 *B* ⲫⲏ ⲉⲧⲫ.†
ⲓⲁϥ ⲉⲫⲟⲩⲱϣ ⲙⲫϯ; ⲉⲡⲉⲥⲏⲧ ⲉ- *SB, reach down
to*: Dan 6 24 *B* ⲫⲑ. εἰς τὸ ἔδαφος, BMis 539 *S* stone
dropped into pit ⲙⲟⲧⲥ ⲛⲥⲡ. ⲉⲡ. ⲉⲣⲁⲧϥ; ⲉⲡϣⲱⲓ
ⲉ- *B, reach up to*: AM 330 ϣⲁⲧⲟⲩⲫ. ⲉⲡ. ⲉⲡⲓⲫⲛⲟⲩⲓ; ⲉϩⲟⲩⲛ, ⲉϣ. ⲉ- *SB, reach, arrive within*:
Ez 17 7 *B* πρός (no vb), Miss 4 584 *S* ϣⲁⲡⲧⲟⲩⲡ.
ⲉϩ. ⲉⲑⲉⲡⲉⲉⲧⲉ, TstAb 160 *B* ⲉⲧⲁⲩⲫ. ⲉϣ. ⲉⲧⲡⲟⲗⲓⲥ; ⲉϩⲣⲁⲓ, ⲉϩⲣ. ⲉ- *SB, reach up, down*: Ez 47
15 *B* (Gk diff) venire; Mun 52 *S* ϣⲁⲡ[ⲧⲉⲕ]ⲡ. ⲉϩ.
ⲉⲡ[ϣⲓ] ⲛⲧⲁⲡⲧⲧⲉⲗ[ⲓⲟⲥ]; ϣⲁⲣⲁⲓ ⲉ- *SA, reach
up to*: Ge 28 12† *S* (*B* ⲋⲓ ϣⲁⲉϩⲣ. ⲉ-) ἀφικ. εἰς;
Deu 29 7 *S* (*B* ⲓ ϣⲁ-) ἔρχ. ἕως; Mic 4 10 *A* (*B*
ⲋⲱⲡⲧ ⲉϣ. ⲉ-) ἥκειν ἕως; Pcod 16 *S* fame ⲡ. ϣⲁϩ.
ⲉⲧⲡⲉ.

—— ⲉϫⲛ- *SB, reach, come upon*: Dan 4 25 *B*,
Lu 11 20 *S* (*B* ⲉ-) ⲫⲑ. ἐπί; 2 Kg 17 1 *S* ⲡⲱⲣⲧ
(*l* ? ⲡ., *cf* ⲡ. ⲉ-) ἐπέρχ. ἐπί; Ac 21 35 *S* (*B* ⲁⲗⲏⲓ
ⲉϩⲣ.) γίν. ἐπί; BMis 246 *S* ⲛⲧⲉⲣⲟⲩⲡ. ⲉϫⲙⲡⲓϣⲁⲁⲩ
(var Z 263 ⲉ-); ⲉϩⲣⲁⲓ ⲉϫⲛ- *SF*: 1 Thes 2 16 (*B* ⲓ
ⲉϩⲣ. ⲉϫ.).

—— ⲛ- *B, arrive at*: BSM 66 ⲁϥⲫ. ⲛⲥⲟⲩⲧⲁ̅ of
month = BMis 158 *S* ⲡ. ⲉⲡϣⲁ, EW 227 ⲁⲥϣⲁⲡϥ.

ⲡⲧⲉⲡⲙⲉⲧⲟⲩⲣⲟ ; AM 200 ⲉⲧⲁⲩϥ. ⲙⲡⲉⲙⲑⲟ ⲙⲡⲟⲩ-
ϯⲙⲓ, AM 291 *B* prayer ϥ. ϣⲁϩ. ⲛⲛⲉⲙⲙⲁϣϫ; ϩⲁ-
ⲣⲁⲧ⸗ ⲛ- *B, reach, arrive at* : TstAb 160 ϣⲁⲛⲧⲟⲩϥ.
ϩⲁⲣⲁⲧϥ ⲡⲟⲩϣϣⲏⲛ.

—— ϣⲁ- *SBF, reach to* : Eccl 8 14 *F* (PMich,
S ⲧⲁϧⲟ) ϥⲑ. πρός, Phil 3 16 *B* (*S* do) ϥⲑ. εἰς ; Job 38
11 *SB* ἔρχ. μέχρι ; Lu 16 16 *S* (*B* Gk no vb) μέχρι,
Ro 10 18 *S* (*B* Gk no vb) εἰς ; Job 15 8 *S* (*B* ⲉ-)
ἀφικ. εἰς ; Jon 3 6 *SAB* ἐγγίζ. πρός ; Job 20 6 *S*
(*B* ϭⲓ ⲡⲉⲙ-) ἅπτειν, Is 15 8 *B* (*S* ⲧⲱϭⲉ) συνάπ. ;
Ps 35 5† *S* (*B* Gk no vb) ἕως ; BIF 13 105 *S* ⲡⲧⲉ-
ⲣⲟⲩⲡ. ϣⲁⲡⲉⲡⲁⲣⲭⲟⲥ = MG 25 287 *B* ϥ. ⲉ-),
BMOr 8811 220 *S* ⲉⲣⲉⲡⲅⲁⲡ ⲡⲡⲁⲓ ⲡ.† ϣⲁⲧⲱⲡ ?
ⲉϥⲡ.† ϣⲁⲡϣⲏⲣ ⲡⲁⲙⲉⲡⲧⲉ ; *touch, refer to* : ShP
130⁵ 33 *S* this word ⲡ.† ⲁⲛ ϣⲁⲟⲩⲱⲙ ⲙⲁϩⲁⲁϥ
ⲁⲗⲗⲁ ϭⲡⲏⲅ ⲉⲭⲡⲣⲁϩ ⲡⲣⲱϩ, MG 25 143 *B* ⲁⲣⲉϯ-
ⲙⲉⲧⲁⲡⲟⲓⲁ ϥ.† ϣⲁⲡⲓⲕⲉⲗⲁ ⲕⲉⲗⲓ ⲙⲁϭⲁⲧϥ ⲁⲡ, Bor
234 4 *S* ⲡⲉⲧⲡ.† ϣⲁⲣⲟⲕ *do it as best thou canst,*
TT 188 *S* ⲡⲉⲧⲡ.† ϣⲁⲣⲟⲛ *tell it us.*

With following adverb.

—— ⲉⲃⲟⲗ *B, reach out* : Dif 2 24 his teaching
ϥ. ⲉⲃ. *to world's ends* ; *v* also above ⲡ. *ripen.*

II as auxil *SB*(rare), *attain to, succeed* in doing,
just do, do for once. ⲥ ⲡ- : Lu 13 25 *S* ⲉϥϣⲁⲡϩ
ⲡⲧⲱⲟϩⲡ (*B* ⲉ-) ἀφ' οὖ ἄν *when once hath* ; Gal 6 1
S ⲉⲣϣⲁⲡ...ϩ ⲡⲅⲉ (*B* om) ἐὰν καὶ προληφθῇ, R 2
2 45 *S* ere flame ⲡϩ (*sic* l) ⲡⲭⲓⲥⲉ πρὶν ἀρθῆναι ;
BHom 42 *S* ⲉⲣϣⲁⲛⲟⲩⲯⲩⲭⲏ ⲡϩ ⲡϩⲁⲓ ϯⲡⲉ ἅπαξ
γευσαμένη ; *ib* 22 *S* ⲡⲉⲡⲧⲁϥⲡϩ ⲡⲥⲗⲁⲁⲧⲉ ὁ φθάσας
ὀλισθῆσαι, Z 232 *S* ⲁⲓⲡϩ ⲡⲁⲁⲥ *have just managed
to* or *succeeded in doing it,* ShZ 593 *S* ⲉⲩϣⲁⲡϩ
ⲡⲱⲣϫ ⲙⲡⲣⲟ *when once door be fastened,* Mor 46 8
S ⲉⲓϣⲁⲡϩ ⲉⲛⲭⲟⲟϩⲕ *when once I have sent thee* to
κόμης *then can I no longer save thee,* TEuch 1 665
ⲁϥϣⲁⲡϥ. ⲡⲭⲱ ⲁⲙⲏⲛ (var HCons 378 ϥ. ⲉϥⲙⲱⲓⲧ
ⲡⲧⲉ ⲁ.) ; ⲥ ⲉ- : Mt 10 23 *B* ϥ. ⲉⲙⲉϣⲧ *already
visited* (*S* Gk diff) ; Mor 17 109 *S* ϯⲡ.† ⲉⲧⲟⲩⲡⲉⲥ
going to raise fallen temple (var Ming 309 ϯⲡⲁⲧ.)
μέλλειν, *ib* 83 *S* ⲧⲓⲡ.† ⲉⲡⲁⲑⲉ ⲙ. ; PS 220 *S* ⲡⲥⲟⲟⲩⲡ
...ϯⲡ.† ⲉⲭⲟⲟϥ *am going to tell you,* *ib* 315 *S* delay
not (saying) ϫⲉⲧⲉⲧⲡ.† ⲉϫⲓ *when we come again,*
TstAb 238 *B* eyes will not ϥ. ⲉⲡⲁⲩ ⲉⲣⲱⲟⲩ.

III tr *SᶠB* : BSM 48 *B* will not cease ϣⲁⲧⲁϥⲉⲣ-
ⲑⲏⲧⲟⲩ ⲉⲡⳉⳅ = BMis 398 *S* ⲡⲣⲟⲥⲉⲡⲉⲕⲏ ⲙⲙⲱⲧⲡ,
ib 56 *B* ⲙⲁⲣⲉⲡϥ. ⲙⲙⲟⲛ *draw nigh* to archangel
= BMis 412 *S* ϯ ⲡⲉⲡⲟⲩⲟⲓ ; *stretch* : BM 512
Sᶠ ⲛϥⲡⲉⲣ ⲧⲉϥϭⲓϫ ⲉⲥⲙⲟⲩ.

—— *B* nn m, *maturity* : K 102 بلغ, *ib* γλικια ʹ.
ⲙⲁ ⲡϥ. *B, goal* : Ps 18 7 (*S* ⲙⲁ ⲡⲃⲱⲕ ⲉϩⲟⲩⲡ)
κατάντημα.

ⲡⲁϧⲉ *S,* ϥⲏϭⲓ *B* *v* ⲡⲱϩ *break.*

ⲡⲓϧⲉ *S* *v* ⲡⲁⲓϣⲉ.

ⲡϧⲉ- *F* *v* ⲑⲡⲟ.

ϥⲟ (ϥⲁ⸗) *SF* *v* ⲑⲡⲟ.

(ϥⲱϣⲉⲣ) *B,* ⲡⲟⲭⲣⲓ *DM,* ⲡⲉϧⲉⲣ- *O,* ϥⲁϣⲉⲣ†
B vb intr & tr, *charm, bewitch* : AZ 21 106 *O* ⲉⲓⲉ-
ⲡⲉϧⲉⲣ ⲉⲣⲉⲧⲏⲥ...ⲛⲧⲁⲡ. ⲧⲉⲥϣⲟⲙⲧⲉ ⲡϣⲉ ⲥⲉⲧⲏ ⲡⲕⲉⲗⲓ
(*sic* l), DM 16 21, 17 26 ⲁⲗⲟⲩ ⲁⲡ. *boy who enchants*
(*ie* medium HT) : Dan 1 20† *B* (*S* ⲥⲟⲟⲩⲡ) Gk om
(but LXX σοφώτερος).

ⲡⲁϧⲣⲉ *SA²O,* -ϧⲣ *S* (Ryl 106 31, 65), -ϧⲣⲉ *A,*
ϥⲁϩⲣⲓ *B,* ⲡⲉϧⲗⲓ *F* nn m f(twice), a *drug, medicament* :
Ps 57 5 *SB,* Nah 3 4 *B* (*A* ⲙⲛⲧⲣⲉϥⲣ ϧⲓⲕ), Va 57 110
B ⲟⲩϥ. *healing wounds,* CaiEuch 484 *B* ⲁⲕⲙⲟⲣⲧ
ϩⲉⲡⲡϥ., Leyd 463 *S* ⲧⲁⲗϭⲟ ⲭⲱⲣⲓⲥ ⲡ., BHom 10
S ⲡⲡ. ⲡⲧⲙⲉⲧⲁⲡⲟⲓⲁ, LAp 558 *F* φάρμακον, Ap 9 21
B ϥ. ⲡϧⲓⲕ (*S* ϧⲓⲕ) ϥ. ; Jer 26 11 *B* (*S* ⲧⲁⲗϭⲟ) ἴαμα ;
Ap 3 18 *S* (*B* = Gk) κολλούριον ; Mor 38 52 *S* ⲟⲩⲡ.
ⲡⲥⲁⲉⲓⲛ ⲉϥⲧⲁⲓⲏⲩ = *ib* 29 ⲉⲙⲡⲗⲁⲥⲧⲣⲟⲛ, BIF 14 152 *S*
ⲧⲟⲉⲓⲥ ⲙⲡ. *bandage,* PMéd 239 *S* ⲟⲩⲛⲟϭ ⲙⲡ., Ryl 106
30 *S* title of recipe ⲟⲩⲡ. ⲡⲥⲁⲓⲉ, BSM 53 *B* ⲡⲧⲉⲕϯ
ⲙⲁϯ ϩⲉⲡⲡⲉϥ. = BMis 406 *S* ⲡⲧⲑⲉⲣⲁⲡⲉⲅⲉ ⲙⲙⲟⲩ,
BAp 69 *S* ⲙⲡ. ⲙⲡ...ⲡϩⲟⲧⲁⲡⲓ, PMéd 56 *S* ⲡ. ⲉⲧ-
ϩⲉⲛⲃⲁⲗ, Ryl 106 *S* ⲡⲉⲡⲁⲓϧⲣⲉ ϧⲉⲡⲕⲱⲗⲁϭ, ShZ 601 *S*
honey wherein ⲟⲩⲡ. ⲉϥⲧⲁⲕⲏⲩ, BMar 38 *S* ⲡ. *poison
mixture,* AM 60 *B* sim, *ib* 321 *B,* C 43 82 *B* ingredients of incense, BM 331 *S* demons took forms of
ϩⲉⲡⲡ. & roses, ShC 73 89 *S* ⲟⲩϩⲗⲃⲓⲗⲉ ⲙⲡ. ; BHom
12 *S* ⲡ. ⲡⲟⲩϫⲁⲓ, ShZ 637 *S* ⲡ. ⲡϯ ⲕⲃⲟ, TstAb 224 *B*
sim, Miss 4 200 *B* ϧⲁⲡϥ. ⲥⲩⲡⲛⲟⲩⲧ, Gu 61 *S* heads
smeared with ⲡ. ⲡⲟⲩⲁⲙⲥⲁⲣϥ, Sa 1 14 *S* ⲡ. ⲙⲙⲟⲩ
ϥ. ὀλέθρου, Mk 16 18 *S* sim (*B* ⲉⲡⲭⲁⲓ ⲉϥⲙⲟⲩ)
θανάσιμος ; ⲃ *paint, colour* : MG 25 156 *B* jars
decorated with ϩⲁⲛϩⲱⲧⲣⲁϥⲓⲁ ⲡⲧⲉ ϩⲁⲛϥ., Mor 29
22 *S* portrait painted ϧⲡⲣⲉⲡⲡ. = *ib* 30 26 *F,* BSM
113 *B* sim ϩⲁⲡϥ. ⲡⲁⲟⲩⲓⲁⲃⲁⲡ, R 1 3 12 *S* ⲟⲩϧⲓ-
ⲕⲱⲛ...ⲟⲩϣⲉⲧⲉ ⲙⲡϧⲉⲡⲡ., My 45 *S* ⲡⲡ. used in
painting letter ⲁ ; AZ 23 104 ff *S,* Bodl(P) a 1 *S* for
dyeing ; *v* ϫⲓ ⲡ. ; ⲡ. f *S* : Sa 16 12 μάλαγμα ;
ALR '93 525 ⲧⲁⲓⲧⲉ ⲧⲡ. (ⲡ)ⲡⲉⲡⲥⲁϣ, Miss 8 256
ⲟⲩⲡ. ⲉⲡⲁⲡⲟⲩⲥ.

ⲣ ⲡ., ⲉⲣ ϥ. *SAA²B, use drugs, heal* : Si 38 7 *S,*
BHom 135 *S* ⲟⲩⲥⲁⲉⲓⲛ...ⲣ ⲡ. θεραπεύειν ; HL 89 *B*
food ⲟⲓ ⲙϥ. ⲡⲧⲉ ⲡⲓⲙⲕⲁϩ ; ⲥ ⲉ- : Mt 4 23 *SB,*
Ac 28 9 *S* (*B* ⲧⲁⲗϭⲟ) θερ. ; Ac 10 38 *S*(*B* do)
ἰᾶσθαι, Jer 28 9 *SB* ἰατρεύειν ; Hos 6 2 *SAB* μοτοῦν ;
ShC 73 160 *S* no child may ⲣ ⲡ. ⲉⲣⲱⲙⲉ (var ϯ ⲡ.),
AP 20 *A²* ⲡⲉ ⲉⲧⲁⲩⲣ ⲡ. ⲁⲣⲁϥ, DeV 2 64 *B* ⲡⲧⲟⲩⲉⲣ ϥ.
ⲉⲡⲟⲩⲉⲣϩⲟⲧ ; ⲣⲉϥⲣ ⲡ., *drug-maker, magician* : Ex
22 18 *S*(*B* = Gk) φαρμακός, Nah 3 4 *A* (*B* do) -κον ;
ShWess 9 139 *S* p. gave charmed water ; ⲙⲛⲧⲣⲉϥⲣ ⲡ., *magic, wizardry* : Mic 5 11 *A* (*B* ϥ.)
φάρμακον, Sa 18 13 *S,* Gal 5 20 *S* (*B* ⲙⲉⲧⲣⲉϥϯ ϥ.)
φαρμακεία ; R 1 1 66 *S* ⲙ. ⲡϧⲓⲕ.

ϯ ⲡ., ⲫ. *SB, give drugs, heal*: Va 58 178 *B* ⲉⲩϯ
ⲫ. ⲉⲣⲟⲕ θερ.; ShMun 112 *S* physicians ⲉⲑⲉⲣⲁⲡⲉⲩⲉ ⲏ ⲉϯ ⲡ. ⲉⲭⲱⲟⲩ;   ⲣⲉϥϯ ⲫ. *B, drug-giver,
magician*: Dan 2 2 (*S* ⲣⲉϥⲣ ⲡ.) φαρμακός;   ⲙⲉⲧⲣⲉϥϯ ⲫ. *B* ʋ ⲙⲛⲧⲣⲉϥⲣ ⲡ.

ϫⲓ ⲡ., ϭⲓ ⲫ. *SB, take drugs, be healed*: Jer 28 9
S (*B* ⲗⲱϫ) ἰᾶσθαι, Si 18 18 *S*, Lu 9 11 *S* (*B* ⲉⲣ ⲫ.
ⲉ-) θερ.;   *take colour, be dyed*: Mor 52 18 *S*
πρῖνος applied to wool ϣⲁⲡⲧⲟⲩϫⲓ ⲡ.   ⲙⲁ ⲡϫⲓ
ⲡ., ϭⲓ ⲫ., *place of healing*: ShA 2 231 *S* ⲙ. ⲏ ⲡⲣ
ⲡ. ⲉⲣⲟⲛ ⲡⲣⲏⲧϥ, MélOr 6 499 *B* God's house ⲟⲩⲙ.

In place-name (?) ⲡⲙⲁϯⲡⲡⲉϩⲣⲉ (Wess 20 218,
cf ShA 2 231 above).

For ⲡⲁϩⲣⲉ (?) Ge 41 18, Is 19 7   ʋ ⲁϩⲣ

ⲡⲁϩⲥ, ⲡⲁϩⲥ, ⲡⲉϩⲥ   ʋ ⲡⲱϩ *break* s f.

ⲡⲱϩⲥ *SA*, -ⲥϩ *A*, ⲡⲉϩⲥ- *S*, ⲡⲁϩⲥ⸗ *A*, ⲡⲟϩⲥ† *S*,
ⲡⲉϩⲥ† *F* vb **a** intr, *bite*: ShMIF 23 28 *S* when
snake springs or ⲛϥⲡ....ⲉϫⲛⲁⲡⲉϩⲥ ⲟⲩⲏⲣ?   **b** tr:
Am 9 3 *A* (*S* ⲗⲱⲕⲥ, *B* ϫⲱⲕⲣ), Mic 3 5 *A* (*S* ⲇⲟ, *B* ϭⲓ
ⲗⲁⲡⲥⲓ) δάκνειν; Pro 23 32 *A* (*S* ⲇⲟ) πλήσσειν; ShA
1 458 *S* beasts ⲉⲩⲡ. ⲙⲙⲟⲕ ⲙⲡⲥⲁⲧⲣⲉⲕϣⲱⲡⲉ ⲙ-
ⲡⲁϩⲥ;   *stumble, go wrong* (? same or = ⲡⲱϩⲥ) *S*:
Job 18 7 (*B* ϣⲱϥⲧ) σφάλλειν; Mor 41 15 woman in
travail ⲡ. ϩⲛⲧⲉⲥⲕⲁⲗⲁϩⲏ & in pain 11 days before
bearing.   As nn *SA*, *bite*: Mic 5 5 *A* (*B* ⲗⲁⲡⲥⲓ)
δῆγμα; ShP 130² 28 *S* ⲡⲡ. ⲛⲟⲩϩⲟϥ.

ⲡⲱϩⲧ *SA²*, -ϩⲧ *A*, ⲫⲱϣⲧ *B*, ⲡⲉϩⲧ- *SF*, ⲡⲁ. *S*,
ⲫⲁϣⲧ- *B*, ⲡⲁϩⲧ⸗ *SA²*, ⲡⲁϩⲧ⸗ *A*, ⲫⲁϣⲧ⸗ *B*, ⲡⲉϩⲧ⸗ *F*,
ⲡⲁϩⲧ† *S*, ⲡⲁϩⲧ† *A*, ⲫⲁϣⲧ† *B*, ⲡⲉϩⲧ† *F* vb, **A** *bend*
tr: Tri 286 *S* ⲡⲉⲛⲧⲁϥⲡⲉϩⲧ ⲁⲡⲉ; refl, *bend self, fall*:
Mt 2 11 *S* (*B* ϩⲓⲟⲩⲓ ⲉϩⲣⲏⲓ) πίπτειν, Ps 71 9 *S* (*B*
ⲇⲟ) προπ.; *ib* 9 30 *S* (*B* ⲕⲱⲗϫ) κύπτειν; PS 40 *S*
ⲁⲩⲡⲁϩⲧⲟⲩ ϩⲓⲡⲉϥⲉⲣⲏⲩ, Mor 24 15 *F* ⲡⲧⲉⲙⲓⲭⲁⲏⲗ
ⲡⲉϩⲧⲃ;   qual: ShBMOr 8800 2 *S* ⲉⲕⲉⲡ. ⲡⲥⲟⲩ-
ⲱϣⲧ ⲛⲁⲩ, BSM 113 *B* ⲉϥⲧⲱⲃϩ ⲉϥⲫ., BM 511 *F*
ⲧⲉⲡⲡ. ⲧⲉⲡⲥⲁⲡⲥ.
With following preposition.

—— ⲉ-, *bend to, toward*: Jos 7 10 refl πίπ. Gk
om prep; BSM 36 *B* face ⲫ. (*l* ⲫ.†) ⲉⲡⲕⲁϩⲓ =
BMis 380 *S* ⲡ.† ⲉⲡⲉⲥⲏⲧ.

—— ⲉϫⲛ- *SF, bend, bow upon*: Nu 16 22 *S* (*B*
ϩ. ⲉϫ.) ⲡ. ἐπί; BM 278 *S* ⲉⲥⲡ.† ⲉϫⲙⲡⲥⲱⲙⲁ =
Mor 30 56† *F*;   refl: Ge 46 29 *S* (*B* ϩ. ⲉϩⲣ. ⲉϫ.)
ⲡ. ἐπί, Job 1 20 *S* (*B* ϩ. ⲉⲡⲉⲥⲏⲧ) ⲡ. χαμαί; PS 61
S ⲁⲥⲡⲁϩⲧⲥ ⲉϫⲛⲡⲉϥⲟⲩⲉⲣⲏⲧⲉ;   ⲉϩⲣⲁⲓ, ⲉϩ. ⲉϫ.
SAB: Dan 10 9 *S* (*B* Gk om vb); ShC 73 67 *S*
face ⲡ.† ⲉϩ. ⲉϫⲛⲡⲉϥⲡⲁⲧ, C 86 128 *B* ⲉⲣⲉⲑⲉⲟⲇⲱⲣⲟⲥ
ⲫ.† ⲉϩ. ⲉϫⲱϥ;   refl: Mt 26 39 *S* (*B* ϩ. ⲉϫ.) ⲡ. ἐπί;
Ex 34 8 *S* (*B* ⲇⲟ) ⲕ. ἐπί; El 46 *A* ⲁⲉⲓⲡ.† ⲁϩⲣⲏⲓ
ⲁϫⲛⲡⲁϩⲱ.

—— ϩⲓϫⲛ- *S, meaning same*: Ryl 290 ϯⲡ.†
ϩⲓϫⲙⲡⲁϩⲟ.

—— ⲛ- dat *SB, bend toward, bow to*: P 129¹⁴
122 *S* ⲉⲩⲡ.† ⲡⲁⲓ = DeV 1 77 *B* ⲉⲩⲫ.† ϩⲁⲡⲁϭⲁ-
ⲗⲁⲩϫ, BHom 74 *S* ceasing not ⲉⲩⲡ.† ⲙⲡⲛ̄ⲧⲉ̄;   refl:
Ps 94 6 *S* (*B* ϩ. ⲉϩⲣ. ⲛ-) προσπ. dat; Z 343 *S*
ⲁⲩⲡⲁϩⲧⲟⲩ ⲡⲁⲓ = MG 25 208 *B* ϯ ⲙⲉⲧⲁⲛⲟⲓⲁ ⲙⲉⲧ.
βάλλειν, *ib* 337 *S* ⲁⲓⲡⲁϩⲧ(ⲧ) ⲡⲁϥ μετανοεῖν dat; *ib*
305 *S* sim προσκυνεῖν dat (PO 8 169), AM 81 *B*
ⲁⲥⲫⲁϩⲧⲥ ⲡⲁϥ ϩⲓϫⲉⲛⲡⲓⲕⲁϩⲓ, Miss 4 763 *S* ⲁⲡⲡⲁϩⲧⲛ
ⲡⲁϥ & saluted him;   ⲙⲡⲉⲙⲑⲟ ⲉⲃⲟⲗ ⲛ- *SB,
bend, bow before*: BSM 100 *B* ⲉⲧϥ.† ⲙⲡ. ⲉⲃ. ⲙⲫⲓⲱⲧ;
refl: Ps 21 29 *S* (*B* ϩ. ⲉϩⲣ.) προπ. ἐνώπιον; Mt 27
29 *S* (*B* ϩ. ⲉϫ. ⲕⲉⲗⲓ) γονυπετεῖν ἔμπροσθεν; PS 21
S ⲁⲩⲡⲁϩⲧⲟⲩ ⲙⲡⲁⲙ. ⲉⲃ.

—— ϩⲁ- *B, overturn under*: AM 316 ⲁⲩⲫ.
ⲙⲑⲣⲟⲛⲟⲥ ϩⲁⲣⲟϥ (cf ⲡⲱⲡⲉ ϩⲁ-), *ib* 308 they
cast stones ⲁⲛⲓⲱⲛⲓ ⲫⲁϣⲧ ⲛⲉⲣ. ϩⲁⲣⲟϥ;   ⲥ ϩⲁ-
ⲧⲉⲛ- *B, bow before*: AM 145 ⲁϥⲫⲁϣⲧⲟⲩ ϩ. Lord's
feet;   ⲥ ϩⲁ-, ϩⲁ- *SB* refl, *bow under, at feet*:
BMar 194 *S* ⲡ. πρός, Lu 5 8 *S* (*B* ϩ. ϩⲁⲧⲉⲛ-) προσπ.
dat, *ib* 8 41 *S* (*B* ⲇⲟ) προσπ. παρά; MIE 2 382 *B*
sim;   ⲥ ϩⲁⲣⲁⲧ⸗ *SA²* refl, *meaning same*: Mk 3
·11 *S* (*B* ϩ. ⲉϩⲣ. ϩ.) προσπ. dat; AP 20 *A²* ⲧⲡⲡ.
ⲙⲙⲁⲛ ϩⲁⲣⲉ[ⲧⲕ].

—— ϩⲓⲣⲏ *S, bow before*: Mk 10 17 (*B* ϩ. ⲉϫ.
ⲕⲉⲗⲓ) γονυⲡ. acc; ϩⲓⲑⲏ: 2 Kg 9 6 ⲡ. ἐπὶ πρόσωπον.
With following adverb.   ⲥ ⲉⲃⲟⲗ, *meaning as* ⲡ.:
Ps 74 8 *S* (*B* ⲣⲓⲕⲓ ⲉⲃ.) κλίνειν, ROC 17 405 *B* ⲡⲁⲥ-
ⲡⲁⲫⲁϩⲧⲥ ⲉⲃ. ⲉϫⲉⲛⲡⲉϣⲏⲣⲓ περιχέεσθαι dat;   ⲥ
ⲉⲡⲉⲥⲏⲧ *SA²B, bend down*: Lu 24 5 *S* (*B* ⲣⲓⲕⲓ) ⲕⲗ.;
Si 19 23 *S* συγκύπ.; Mich 550 39 *S* sack ⲁϥⲡⲁϩⲧϥ
ⲉⲡ., BMis 55 *S* faces ⲡ.† ⲉⲡ. ⲉϫⲙⲡⲕⲁϩ;   refl: AP
19 *A²* ⲡ. εἰς τὸ ἔδαφος, Ep 247 *S* ϯⲡ. ⲙⲙⲟⲉⲓ ⲉⲡ.
ⲉⲡⲕⲁϩ ϯⲟⲩⲱϣⲧ.

ⲡⲁϩⲧⲉ *S* nn f, *bowing, prostration*: P 129¹⁴ 61
(Can Ancyr) fulfilled time of ⲧⲉⲩⲡ. ὑπόπτωσις.

ⲡⲁϩⲧⲩ *S* nn, *meaning uncertain*: P 131⁶ 37
monks of old would traverse desert & stay in ϩⲉⲛⲙⲁ
ⲙⲡ. ⲛⲏⲡⲧⲟⲟⲩ in heat, (shady) *places to lie in*.

B *pour, flow*, **I** intr *SAA²* with preposition: Joel
2 28 *S* ⲉϫⲛ- (*B* ⲫⲱⲡ), Ac 10 45 *S* ⲉϩⲣⲁⲓ ⲉϫⲛ- (*B*
ⲇⲟ) ἐκχέειν ἐπί, Z 311 *S* ϣⲁⲩⲡ. ⲉϩ. ⲉϫⲱϥ καταχ.
ἐπάνω, Lam 3 54 *S* ⲉϫⲛ- (ShA 2 95, *B* ⲇⲟ) ὑπερχ.
ἐπί; AP 20 *A²* much water ⲡⲱϩⲧ[, Z 628 *S* recipe
ⲛⲥⲡ. ...ϩⲓϫⲙⲡⲉⲧϣⲱⲡⲉ.

II tr *SB*: BHom 136 *S* ⲡ. thy tears ἐκχ.; Si 13
6 *S* ἀποκενοῦν, Is 51 17 *S* (*B* ϣⲟⲩⲟ ⲉⲃⲟⲗ) ἐκκ.;
BHom 87 *S* blood that Joab ⲡⲁϩⲧⲟⲩ, PMéd 278,
316 *S* ⲡⲁϩⲧⲟⲩ (? into mortar, ʋ ⲡ. ⲉ-, ϩⲓϫⲛ-); *draw
sword*: Ps 34 3 *S* (*B* diff) ἐκχ., Ez 5 12 *SB* ἐκκεν.
With following preposition.

—— ⲉ- *S, pour upon, into*: Lev 4 12 *S* ⲡⲉϩⲧ
(var ⲡⲁ., *B* ⲫⲱⲡ) ἐκχ. no prep, Job 16 13 *S* (*B*
ⲫⲱⲡ ϩⲓϫⲉⲛ-) ἐκχ. εἰς; PMéd 260 *S* ⲡⲁϩⲧⲟⲩ ⲉⲧⲉ-

ⲙⲭⲁⲑ ; ⲉϩⲣⲁⲓ ⲉ- S BM 344 ⲡⲁⲣⲧ ϧⲉⲙⲝ ⲉϧ. ⲉⲣⲟⲟⲩ (sc wounds).

—— ⲉⲝⲛ- SA, meaning same: Hos 12 14 A (B ⲫⲱⲛϣ), Ap 16 17 S (B ⲭⲱϣ) ἐκχ. ἐπί, Lev 11 38 S (B ⲫⲱⲛ intr) ἐπιχ. ἐπί, R 1 4 70 S ⲡ. ⲡⲟⲩⲣⲙⲟⲩ…ⲉⲝⲛⲡⲉϥⲥⲁϣ = MartIgn 877 B ⲭ. ⲕⲁⲧⲁⲭ. gen ; ShZ 589 S ⲙⲉⲩⲡⲉⲣⲧ ⲥⲟϭⲛ ⲉⲝⲛⲧⲉⲥⲁⲡⲉ, Bor 143 41 S ⲟⲩⲥⲕⲉⲟⲥ…ⲁⲥⲡⲁⲣⲧϥ ⲉⲝⲛⲧⲁⲡⲉ ; ⲉϩⲣⲁⲓ ⲉⲝⲛ- S, ⲉϧ. ⲉⲝ. B : Ps 41 4 S (B ⲭ. ⲉϧ.) ἐκχ. ἐπί, Ge 35 14 S (B ⲟⲩⲱⲧⲉⲛ ⲉϧ.) ἐπιχ. ἐπί, Mt 26 7 S (B ⲭ., F ⲡⲱⲡ) ⲕⲁⲧⲁⲭ. ἐπί ; Jud 6 3 S ⲡⲁⲣⲉⲙⲃⲁⲗⲗⲉⲓⲛ ⲉⲓⲥ ; BG 47 S ⲁϥⲡ. ⲉϧ. ⲉⲝⲱⲥ ⲡⲟⲩⲡⲛⲁ, C 86 324 B crowd ⲫ. ⲉϧ. ⲉⲝⲱϥ rushed upon him.

—— ⲙⲡⲉⲙⲧⲟ ⲉⲃⲟⲗ ⲛ- S, pour forth before: Ps 61 8 (B ⲭ.) ἐκχ. ἐνώπιον ; Job 15 13 S (l ⲡⲱϩ, B diff) ῥηγνύναι ; Aeg 15 S ⲉⲓⲡ. ⲛⲁⲣⲙⲉⲓⲟⲟⲩⲉ ⲙⲡⲉⲕⲙ. ⲉϧ. = ib B ⲫⲱⲛ.

—— ϩⲓⲑⲏ ⲛ- S, meaning same : TT 45 ⲡ. tears ϩⲓⲑⲏ ⲙⲡⲉⲭⲥ.

—— ϩⲁⲣⲧⲛ- S, meaning same : Lev 4 7 (B ⲭ. ⲉⲝⲉⲛ-) ἐκχ. παρά, Nu 18 17 (varr ⲉϧ. ϩⲁⲣⲁⲧ⸗, ϣⲱⲗ ⲉϧ. ⲙⲡⲁⲧⲟ, B ⲫⲱⲛ) προσχ. πρός.

—— ϩⲓⲝⲛ- S, pour upon : PMéd 270 ingredients ⲡⲁⲣⲧⲟⲩ ϩ. ⲛⲉⲧϣⲟⲟⲩⲉ in mortar.
With following adverb.

—— ⲉⲃⲟⲗ SAF, pour forth, shed intr : Job 38 38† (B ⲭ.†) χέεσθαι, Z 323 S ἐκχ., Pro 5 16 A (S ⲡⲱⲛ, B ⲫⲟⲡⲡⲉⲛ) ὑπερεκχ. ; BHom 120 S corpses ⲡ.† ⲉϧ. ϩⲙⲡⲕⲁϩ, Pcod 9 S lest blood ⲡ. ⲉϧ. ; tr : Ge 9 6 S (B ⲫⲱⲛ) ἐκχ. ; Phil 2 7 S (B ϣⲟⲩⲟ) κενοῦν ; Pro 29 11 SA ἐκφέρειν ; ShC 73 35 S let none ⲡ. ⲉϧ. ⲙⲡⲉⲣⲙⲟⲧ of Lord, Mor 56 6 S Decius ϩⲙⲡⲧⲣⲉϥⲡ. ⲉϧ. ⲡⲧⲙⲡⲧϩⲉⲗⲗⲏⲛ promulgating Gentile (religion) bade people sacrifice ; ⲉϧ. ⲙⲛ- S, abandon (self) with : Z 284 Lot ⲁϥⲡ. ⲉϧ. ⲙⲛⲧⲉϥϣⲉⲉⲣⲉ ⲥⲛⲧⲉ ; ⲉϧ. ⲉⲝⲛ- SA : Jth 15 3, Joel 2 28 A ἐκχ. ἐπί, Lev 8 12 (B ⲭ.) ἐπιχ. ἐπί ; ClPr 30 6 ⲁϥⲡ. ⲉϧ. ⲙⲡⲉϥϣⲁϫⲉ ⲉⲝⲛⲛⲉⲧⲟⲩⲛⲁⲩ ⲉⲣⲟⲟⲩ κεν. ἐπὶ τὰ ὁρώμενα ; ⲉϧ. ϩⲛ- S, shed into : Ro 5 5† (B ⲫⲱⲛ) ἐκχ. ἐν ; ⲉϧ. ϩⲓⲝⲛ- S : Mt 23 35 (B do) ἐκχ. ἐπί. V also nn.

—— ⲉⲡⲉⲥⲏⲧ S, pour down : AZ 23 111 ⲡⲁⲣⲧϥ ⲉⲡ. ⲉⲣⲟϥ sc mixture into cup.

—— S nn m, effusion : P 46 238 parts & functions of body ⲡⲡ. انفذ, between ⲗⲟⲅ⳽ & ⲥⲁⲣⲝ. ⲡ. ⲉⲃⲟⲗ, meaning same : Mor 22 46 ⲡⲡ. ⲉϧ. of my tears, ShClPr 44 20 ϧⲉⲛⲡⲉⲣⲧ ⲥⲡⲟϥ ⲉϧ. sheddings.

ⲁⲧⲡ. ⲉⲃⲟⲗ S adj, not pouring : BM 1127 ⲛⲁⲧⲥⲱⲗⲡ ⲛⲁⲧⲡⲁⲣⲧⲟⲩ ⲉϧ., Ryl 21 sacrifices ⲡⲁ. ⲥⲡⲟϥ ⲉϧ.

ⲙⲛⲧⲡ. ⲉϧ. S, pouring out, shedding : JTS 10 390 blood-shedding.

ʼⲣⲉϥⲡ. ⲉϧ. S, shedder : ShBor 246 20 ⲣⲉϥⲡⲉⲣⲧ ⲥⲡⲟϥ ⲉϧ. ; ShC 42 73 ⲙⲛⲧⲣ., shedding.

ⲡⲁⲣⲧⲉ O nn, strength, valiance : with ⲁ- (v o great) AZ 21 94 ⲛⲟⲩ ⲟ, ⲁⲡⲁⲣⲧⲉ great Eou, very valiant (AZ 38 88, PGM 1 67, cf Ryl Dem 3 274 n). In names ⲡϣⲛⲁⲡⲁⲣⲧⲉ S (Va ar 172 35 gloss on بشناپهـ) = ⲡϣⲉⲛⲁⲡⲁⲣⲓ B (C 89 55), Ἀπάθης, Ψεναπάθης, -της, Σεναπάθης, -της (Preisigke).

ⲡⲁⲣⲧⲥ, -ⲧϥ v ⲡⲱⲣⲧ A.

ⲡⲁϩⲟⲩ SAA²O, ⲫⲁⲣ. B, ⲡⲉϧ., ⲡⲁϩⲁⲩ F nn m, originally dual buttocks, so hinder part, back : Ex 33 23 S (B ⲥⲁⲙⲉⲛϩⲏⲓ) opp ϧⲟ, Jer 13 26 S (B ⲡⲉⲧⲥⲁⲫ. ⲙⲙⲟ), Phil 3 13 SB τὰ ὀπίσω, 2 Chr 4 4 B τὰ ὀπίσθια (v ϧⲓⲡ. nn) ; Ac 27 41 S (B ⲫ. ⲙⲙⲟϥ) πρύμνα ; Wess 18 60 S smote him ⲉⲡⲉϥⲡ. (var Mor 18 43 ⲛⲥⲁⲡ.), PO 4 580 S dog wags ⲡⲉϥⲡ. ⲛ ⲡⲉϥⲥⲁⲧ, Mor 51 37 S ϧⲉⲣⲃⲱⲧ ⲙⲡⲁϩⲕⲏ. broad-backed staves. As adj, hinder, past : TT 45 S forgive ⲛⲛⲟⲃⲉ ⲙⲡ., BMis 386 S ϩⲁⲙⲟⲓ (ⲉ)ⲡⲉⲡⲉϩⲟⲟⲩ ⲙⲡ. ⲛⲉ, Hor 84 O ⲛⲡ.

Forming adverb or preposition.

ⲉ- SAA²BF, to back, backward : Is 30 21 SB (F ϧⲓⲡ.), Mt 24 18 SB ὀπ., 2 Kg 1 22 SB, Ps 77 66 S (B ⲥⲁⲫ.), Pro 25 9 A (S ϧⲏⲧ⳽), Jo 20 14 SA²B εἰς τὰ ὀπ., Lu 8 44 S (B ϧⲓⲫ.) ὄπισθεν ; behind, backward in compound Gk vbs : Ex 16 19 S (B diff) καταλείπειν, Ps 6 10 SB ἐπιστρέφειν, Ac 24 22 SB ἀναβάλλειν, Jos 21 45 S διαπίπτειν, Pro 10 30 SA (B diff) ἐνδιδόναι ; PS 175 S ⲁⲥⲕⲟⲧⲉ ⲉⲡ., ShBor 300 71 S ⲁϧⲉ ⲉⲡ. opp ⲙⲟⲟϣⲉ ϩⲓϩⲏ (sic), El 44 A ⲁⲅⲡⲁⲅⲣⲟⲩⲉ ⲁⲡ., BMis 275 S sick man † ⲉⲡ. ⲙⲙⲏⲛⲉ went back (in health, v Rec 37 20), BMis 369 S ⲙⲡⲟⲩⲉⲓ ⲉⲡ. ⲡⲗⲁⲁⲩ reduced naught = BSM 29 B ⲭⲱϫⲓ, CA 104 S ⲉϥⲉϣⲱϫⲡ ⲉⲡ. ⲡⲟⲩⲙⲉⲣⲓⲥ, DeV 2 39 B ϥⲛⲁⲧⲁⲥⲑⲟ ⲉⲫ. ⲛⲧⲁⲡⲟⲫⲁⲥⲓⲥ, BKU 1 26 (8116 a) F ⲥⲧⲁⲥ ⲉⲡⲉϩⲟⲩ ⲉϩⲟⲩ(ⲛ ⲉ)ⲛϧⲁⲡⲛⲗⲁⲩ, ShR 2 3 58 S among good deeds ϧⲉⲛⲥϧⲁⲓ ⲉⲡ. ⲉⲅⲉⲣⲟϥ ⲛⲡⲏⲛⲕⲉ backing bills (?), Miss 8 219 S bade bind hands ⲉⲡ. ⲙⲙⲟⲓ, J 76 48 S ⲝⲛⲛⲡⲟⲟⲩ ⲉⲡ., cf ST 101 S ⲝⲛⲛⲡⲟⲟⲩ ⲥⲉⲡ.

ⲥⲁ- SA²B(mostly)F, behind, after : 1 Kg 17 35 B (S ϧⲓⲡ., ⲉⲡ.), Mk 8 33 B (S ⲉⲡ., F ⲛⲥⲁϧⲏ⳽) ὀπ., Ps 49 17 B (S ϧⲓⲡ.), Jo 18 6 A² (S ⲛⲥⲁⲡ., B ⲉⲫ.) εἰς τὰ ὀπ. ; Ez 40 18 B (HCons 293, S diff) κατὰ νώτου ; Ac 27 29 B (S ϧⲓⲡ.) ἐκ πρύμνης ; BMis 257 S mule ⲃⲱⲕ ⲥⲁⲡ., Mor 30 31 F ⲁϥⲃⲁⲭϥ ⲥⲁⲡ., MG 25 250 B jar ⲉϥⲥⲁⲫ. ⲙⲡⲓⲣⲟ, PO 11 330 B saint ⲉⲣ ⲥⲁⲫ. ⲛⲛⲓⲥⲛⲏⲟⲩ.

ⲛⲥⲁ- SBF, behind, from behind : 2 Kg 2 23 S ἐν τῷ ὀπ., Jo 18 6 S (A² ⲥⲁⲡ., B ⲉⲫ.) εἰς τὰ ὀπ., Lu 19 14 F (S ϧⲓⲡ., B ⲥⲁⲫ.), 2 Pet 2 10 B (S ϧⲓⲡ.) ὀπ., Ez 41 15 S (B ⲥⲁⲫ.) τῶν κατόπισθεν ; PS 382 S ⲉⲓ ⲡⲥ. ⲙⲙⲟⲥ, BMis 478 S fell ⲡⲥ. ϩⲓϫⲙⲡⲕⲁϩ.

ϩⲁ- *S, at back, formerly*: Wess 18 77 sins ϩⲁⲡ. betterment ⲛⲥⲁϩⲏ, BMis 181 sim ϩⲓⲡ.

ϩⲓ- *SAA²BF, behind, after, before* (in time), mostly as prep: Ge 35 5 *S* (*B* ⲥⲁϥ.), Joel 2 3 *SAB*, Ap 1 10 *S* (*B* ⲛⲥⲁⲙⲉⲛϩⲏⲓ) ὄπ., EpJer 5 *BF*, AP 13 *A²* ὄπισθεν, Ps 77 71 *SB* ἐξόπισθεν; Mk 4 38 *SB* ἐν τῇ πρύμνῃ; Aeg 283 *S* as we bade ϩⲓⲡ. (var ϩⲣⲏⲓⲉⲧ-ϩⲓⲡ.) ἐν τ. προλαβοῦσι; Deu 25 18 *S* ⲡⲉⲧϩ. (*B* ⲥⲁⲧ) οὐραγία; PS 370 *S* set cup ϩ. ⲛⲡⲟⲉⲓⲕ, AM 254 *B* faces turned ϩ. ⲙⲙⲟⲟⲩ, MIF 9 89 *S* spake accusations ϩ. ⲡⲛⲥ, Mor 25 17 *S* many rich ϩ. ⲙⲙⲟⲓ = Va 61 99 *B* ⲥⲁϫⲱⲓ *behind me* (in past), Mor 19 75 *S* ⲡⲉⲛⲧⲁⲛϣⲁϫⲉ ⲉⲣⲟϥ ϩ. = *ib* 18 66 *S* ϩⲁϩⲏ = Miss 4 140 *B* ⲉⲣ ϣⲟⲣⲡ ⲛⲥⲁϫⲓ, CMSS 23 *F* letter ⲟⲩⲁⲡⲟⲕⲣⲉⲥⲓⲥ ⲉⲕ[ⲉ]ⲣ ⲭⲣⲓⲁ [ⲙ]ⲁⲥ ϩⲉⲡⲁϩⲁⲩ an answer *back* (?), JAOS 48 148 *S* all that befell ϩ. ϣⲁⲧⲉⲛⲟⲩ *hitherto*, Ep 348 *S* there are other 7 pair ⲛⲡⲁϩⲉⲛ. *of the former lot*; in rubric after *incipit* of prayer, hymn *S*: Leyd 132 29 ⲉⲓⲥ ⲡⲉϥⲃⲱⲗ ϩ. *lo its translation is above* (v 132 10), *ib* 317 ⲉⲓⲥ ⲧⲉϥ ϩ. on 20th of Hathor, *cf ib* ⲉⲓⲥ ⲧⲉϥ ϩⲓⲟⲏ on 10th of Pashons, P 129²⁰ 116 after 2 hymns ⲉⲓⲥ ⲧⲉⲩ ϩ. on middle Sabbath of Fast, where ⲧⲉϥ, ⲧⲉⲩ = ? ⲧⲉϥⲅⲉⲣⲙⲏⲛⲓⲁ (*cf* ⲃⲱⲗ nn), Leyd 140, 150, 222, Ryl 53 sim. As nn m *B*: Ex 39 19, Jer 13 22 (*S* ⲛⲁⲡⲛ.) ὀπίσθιος. ⲉⲣ ϩ. *B, be behind, follow after*: C 41 9 ⲁϥⲉⲣ ϩ. ⲙⲙⲟϥ, C 86 118 let half of us ⲉⲣ ϩ. ⲙⲡⲁⲓⲍⲱⲟⲛ.

ⲡⲟⲟϩⲉⲩⲉ *S*   *v* ⲡⲱϩ *break* (ⲡⲁϩⲉ).

ⲡⲟϫ *S* vb qual, *amorous* (?): Marucchi *Mus Eg Vatican* 301 (Menander) ⲟⲩϩⲗⲗⲟ ⲉϥⲡ. ⲧⲉϥⲯⲩⲭⲏ ⲛⲁϫⲟ ⲉⲡϩⲁⲉ γέρων ἐραστής (Recto of fragt ends with ⲡ., nothing missing).

ⲡⲱϫ *F*   *v* ⲡⲱϫϭ.

ⲡⲁϫⲓ *F*, ⲡⲟⲩⲟⲩϫⲉ *A*   *v* ⲡⲱϭⲉ.

ⲡⲉϫⲉ- *SBF*, ⲡⲁ. *AA²*, ⲡⲉⲧϣⲁ-, ⲡⲉϣⲁ- *O* (lit *what…saith*, v Sdff 267), *say* + suff *S* ⲡⲉϫⲁⲓ, -ⲁⲕ, -ⲁϥ -ⲁⲥ, -ⲏⲧⲛ (Lu 7 33), -ⲉⲧⲛ (Mor 33 134), -ⲁⲧⲛ (Mor 41 114), -ⲁⲩ; *SᵃAA²* ⲡⲁϫⲉⲓ, -ⲉⲥ, -ⲉϥ, -ⲉⲛ (TU 43 2), -ⲏⲧⲛⲉ (Mal 1 2), -ⲉⲩ (Br 43); *B* ⲡⲉϫⲏⲓ (Ge 24 47), -ⲁϥ, -ⲁⲥ, -ⲁⲛ (*ib* 26 28), -ⲱⲧⲉⲛ (Mal *l c*), -ⲱⲟⲩ; *SᵃF* -ⲉϥ (-ⲏϥ), -ⲉⲥ, -ⲉⲩ; *O* ⲡⲉⲧϣⲁϥ (AZ 23 100, *ib* ⲡⲉϣⲁϥ); with initial ⲙ-: *S* ⲙⲡⲉϫⲁⲩ (BM 483), ⲛⲡⲉϫⲁϥ (Mor 36 8), *F* ⲙⲡⲉϫⲉ-, -ⲉϥ (LAp 513, 564, Mor 30 12, 29), *A²* ⲙⲡⲁϫⲉϥ (AP 44), *SF* ⲙⲉϫⲉ (Russian Acad *Nauk* '24 99, CMSS 44, RChamp 543), ⲙⲉϫⲁϥ (BM 1118), *A* ⲙⲁϫⲉ- (Zeph 1 2, Ryl 396 *sic l*). With following nn: ⲡⲉϫⲉ ⲡϫⲟⲉⲓⲥ, ⲡ. ⲙⲁⲣⲑⲁ (Jo 11 39), ⲡ. ⲛⲁⲡⲟⲥⲧⲟⲗⲟⲥ (Gu 97), ⲡⲉϫⲁϥ ⲛϭⲓ ⲓⲱϩⲁⲛⲛⲏⲥ ⲙⲡⲙⲁⲑⲑⲁⲓⲟⲥ (Aeg 239, LMis 269), Va 61 111 *B* ⲁⲙⲟⲩ

ⲡⲉϫⲁϥ ⲛϫⲉ ⲫϯ; mostly + ϫⲉ-: BAp 78 *S* ⲡⲉϫⲁⲩ ϫⲉⲁⲡⲉⲓ ϫⲓⲛⲛϣⲱⲣⲡ, C 43 230 *B* ⲡⲉϫⲁϥ ϫⲉϩⲣⲟ ⲙⲙⲟⲕ; ⲥ ⲛ- dat: AZ 23 100 *O* ⲡⲉⲧϣⲁϥ ⲛⲁⲥ, PS 15 *S* ⲡⲉϫⲁϥ ⲛⲁⲩ ϫⲉ-, AP 56 *A²* ⲡⲁϫⲉ ⲥⲓⲙⲱⲛ ⲛⲉϥ, C 43 233 *B* ⲡⲉϫⲁϥ ⲛⲟⲩⲁⲓ ⲛⲡⲓⲣⲟϥ; ⲥ ⲉϩⲟⲩⲛ ϩⲛ- *SF*, more emphatic or formal than ⲛ-: Nu 17 12 *S* ⲡ. ⲡϣⲏⲣⲉ ⲙⲡⲓⲏⲗ ⲉϩ. ϩⲁⲙⲱⲩⲥⲏⲥ (var ⲉ-, *B* ⲛ-) πρός, PS 371 *S* ⲡ. ⲓ̄ⲥ̄ ⲉϩ. ⲉϩⲣⲛⲡⲉϥⲙⲁⲑⲏⲧⲏⲥ, Ann 16 249 *F* ⲡⲉϫⲉϥ…ⲉϩ. ϩⲁⲙⲡⲓϣ ⲛⲧⲟⲩⲱⲧ; ⲉϩ. ⲉϩⲣⲛ- *S*: Nu 9 7 (*B* dat) πρός. Gk εἰπεῖν: Ge 7 15 *B* (*S* ϣⲁϫⲉ), Mt 14 28 *BF* (*S* ϫⲱ), Ac 5 29 *B* (*S* do); λέγειν: Job 1 17 *SB*, *ib* 6 1 *B* (*S* ϫⲱ), Jo 4 7 *SA²BF*, Ap 10 8 *S* (*B* ϫⲱ); φάναι Ex 2 6 *A* (*B* do), Jer 38 31 *SB*, He 8 5 *SBF*.

ⲡϫⲱ *S* nn m, meaning uncertain, *hard, tough flesh or nightshade*: Job 20 18 (*B* = Gk) στρύφνος var στρύχνος. Text ?imperfect, *l* ⲟⲩⲡ[… ⲉϥϩⲁ]ϫⲱ.

ⲡⲁϫⲥ, ⲡⲱϫⲧ *S*, ⲡⲱϫϩ *A*   *v* ⲡⲱϫϭ.

ⲡⲱϫϭ, -ϫⲕ, -ϫⲧ, ⲡⲟϫⲧ†, ⲣ ⲥ ⲡⲁϫϭ-, ⲡⲁϫⲕ- *S* vb tr, *beat flat, broad*: Is 41 7 (var -ϫⲧ, *B* ⲕⲱⲗϩ) ἐλαύνειν; Mor 37 65 phantoms ⲉⲩⲡ.† ϩⲛⲧⲉϭϭⲟⲧ πλατύς; Ryl 238 ⲟⲩⲥⲟⲩⲙⲁⲣⲓⲥⲧⲟ(ⲛ) ⲉⲥⲡ.† *flat (or beaten) ladle*; ⲣⲥ: Gu 37 ⲛⲛ.ⲟⲩⲉⲣⲏⲧⲉ πλατύπους (AZ 25 63 ⲡⲁϩⲟⲩⲉⲣⲏⲧⲉ الرجلين أخمخ ? for ϭⲁⲃ-), Mor 51 37 ϩⲉⲣⲃⲱⲧ ⲙⲡⲁϫⲕⲛⲡⲁϩⲟⲩ *v* ⲡⲁϩⲟⲩ.

——, -ϫⲕ *S*, -ϫϩ *A*, -ϫ *F* nn m, *flat part, breadth*: Ge 32 25 (var -ϫⲥ, *B* ⲟⲩⲛϣϭⲓ), Pro 7 3 *SA* (*B* do), Mor 37 114 -ϭⲕ πλάτος; Job 11 9 (*B* ⲟⲩⲟⲥⲑⲉⲛ) εὖρος; Dan 4 17 (*B* diff) κύτος (*cf* Ps 64 7); Mor 29 47 struck him with ⲛⲛ. of sword = *ib* 30 54 *F* ⲛⲉⲥⲛ., Ep 564 measurements ⲟⲩⲙⲁϩⲉ ⲛⲛ.

ⲡⲁϫⲥ *S* nn f, meaning unknown: J 108 5 ⲧⲛ. ⲡⲣⲱⲙⲟⲟⲩ, CO 48 ⲧⲡⲁϫⲥ ⲉⲧϩⲣⲓⲡⲉⲓⲉϥⲧ (ⲛⲧ)ϫⲏⲣⲉ (*sic l* ?).

ⲡⲁⲓϭⲉ *A* nn f, *mouth*: Ex 4 11 (*S* ⲧⲁⲡⲣⲟ, *B* ⲣⲟ), Ps 61 5 (Cl, *SB* do), Mic 4 4 (*SB* do).

ⲡⲓϭⲁ, -ϭⲕ, -ϭⲓ *S*, -ϭⲉ (Eccl 4, Hos), -ϭⲉⲓ (Is), -ϫⲉⲓ (Eccl 7) *F* nn, *vanity*: Is 30 7 *SF* (*B* ⲉϥⲫⲗⲏⲟⲩ), Hos 6 8 (JEA 11 245, *SA* ⲡⲉⲧϣⲟⲩⲉⲓⲧ, *B* ⲙⲉⲧⲉϥ.) μάταιος, Eccl 4 4 (Mich, *S* do), *ib* 7 7 (CSchmidt, *S* do) ματαιότης; ⲙⲉⲧⲡ.: Is 30 5 *F* (*S* ϫⲓⲛϫⲏ, *B* ⲉϥ. as advb) μάτην, Eccl 7 16 *F* ⲙⲛⲛⲡⲉⲓϫⲉⲓ (CSchm, *S* ⲙⲛⲧⲡⲉⲧϣ.) ματαιότης; PcodMor 6 *S* ⲙⲧⲡⲓϭⲏ, *ib* 4 -ϭⲓ ματαίως (? Ps 34 19).

ⲡⲟϭⲉ *S* nn, prob *battlefield* (so Spg, *v* Berl *Wörterb* 1 562): ShC 73 5 (ref Eph 6 16) ⲁⲩⲉⲓ ⲉⲃⲟⲗ ⲉⲛ. ⲁⲩⲙⲓϣⲉ.

ⲡⲱϭⲉ *S*, ⲡⲟⲩⲟⲩϫⲉ *A*, ⲫⲱϫⲓ *B*, ⲡⲟϭ⸗, ⲡⲟⲕϭ⸗, ⲡⲟⲧϭ⸗, ⲡⲟⲧⲉ† *S*, ⲫⲟϫⲓ† *B*, ⲡⲏϭ† *F* vb I intr, *break, burst*: Nu 16 31 *B* (*S* ⲡⲱϩ), Is 35 6 *B* (*SF* ⲥⲱⲕ)

ῥηγνύναι, Ps 140 7 B (S πωϩ) διαρρ.; Mt 27 51 B (S do) σχίζειν; Jer 10 20 B διασπᾶν; Ac 28 6 B (S ϣωϩϐ) πιμπράναι; ShRyl 68 270 S devil's wickedness πωϩ н пєсп. пϩнтк, LMis 468 S when pierced ⲁⲡⲉϥⲥⲛⲓⲣ п., TurM 9 S tumour ⲁⲥп. ⲁⲥⲉⲣ ⲥⲛⲟϥ, C 89 123 B thinking ϫⲉⲁⲧⲉϥⲁⲫⲉ ⲫ, R 1 5 35 S martyr to blasphemer п. пⲥⲉϩⲱⲱⲗⲉ ⲙⲡⲉⲕⲗⲁⲥ. п. ⲉϐⲟⲗ S, burst into leaf: JKP 2 18 all trees п. ⲉϐ.

II tr: Is 59 5 B (S ⲟⲩⲱϭп) ῥηγ., Ps 77 15 B (S πωϩ), Jer 5 5 B (S ⲥⲱⲗп), EpJer 30† F (B ⲫⲱϭ†) διαρρ.; Am 7 14 A v ⲛⲟⲩⲕⲉⲣ; BKU 1 3 S ⲡⲱⲡⲉ ϣⲁⲓⲡⲟϭϥ, ib 7 19 S sim, Hall 127 S ⲙⲁϯ ⲡⲭⲁⲣⲧⲏⲥ ⲡⲁⲕ ⲧⲕⲡⲟⲕϥ. ⲫ. ⲉϐⲟⲗ B, tear out: Dif 1 63 ⲁϥⲫ. ⲉϐ. ⲛϯⲥⲟⲩⲣⲓ قلع.

ⲡⲟϭⲉ[1], ⲡⲱ.[2], ⲡⲟⲕⲉ[3], ⲡⲁϭⲉ[4], ⲡⲁⲕⲉ[5] S, ⲫⲱϫⲓ[6], ⲫⲟ.[7], ⲫⲁ.[8] B, ⲡⲁϫⲓ F, ⲡⲱⲕⲉ O (place) nn f, broken piece, fragment: Is 2 19 B[6] (S πωϩ), Jon 2 7 B[6] (SA ⲟⲩⲱϣ) σχίσμα; Is 7 19 B[6] (S πωϩ) ῥαγάς, 4 Kg 2 12 S[1] (PMich 607) ῥῆγμα; Jer 16 16 B[6] (S ϣⲕⲟⲗ) τρυμαλιά; Ob 3 B[6] (A ⲕⲗⲟ) ὀπή; P 44 71 = 43 42 ⲧп.[2] · βάσις, ἀστράγαλος, σφυρά (l -όν) · شط الرجل, sole of foot (same ? or cf ⲡⲱϫϭ); K 156 B[6] (var[7]) قرم, فلقات (cf ⲡⲱⲧⲥ, ⲫⲁⲧⲥⲓ); ShC 73 205 S garments ⲉⲁⲓⲁⲁⲩ ⲙп.[1] ⲥⲛⲧⲉ, C 86 212 B wheel made ⲛⲫ.[7] ϐϯ, MG 25 255 B ⲡⲓⲫ.[8] ⲧⲏⲣⲟⲩ of broken cup, Mor 47 49 S building materials ϣⲉ, ⲥⲟⲓ, п.[1], BMis 275 S bier of ϩⲉⲛⲡⲉⲩⲕⲓ(ⲛ)ⲟⲛ ⲁⲩⲥⲙⲛⲧⲟⲩ ⲙп.[1] wood-inlay (?) v below п. ϣⲉ, ShC 73 144 S[1] v ⲡⲱⲧⲥ (ⲡⲁⲧⲥⲉ), AZ 25 63 (Marciana Or 193) S book wherein could read ⲟⲩп.[1] ⲙⲙⲁⲧⲉ, Leyd 139 S rubric ⲉⲓⲥ ⲧⲉϥ (cf ⲡⲁϩⲟⲩ, ϩⲓ-) ϩⲛⲧⲉⲓп.[1] ⲛⲟⲩⲱⲧ section of book, CO 473 S measurements ⲧп.[1] paral ⲧⲡⲟⲣⲕ (obscure), BMOr 6201 B 60 S camels loaded with ⲛⲉп.[3] & ⲡⲗⲁⲅⲟⲛ, Baouit 1 162 S list ⲗⲁⲕⲟⲛ, п.[3], ϩⲛⲁⲁⲩ; pieces of clothing &c: Ryl 213 n S п.[1] ⲡⲗⲉϐⲓⲧⲱⲛ, Bodl(P) g 17 S п.[1] ⲡⲕⲁⲙⲓⲥⲉ, Ryl 243 S п.[4] ⲛⲁⲛⲛⲁⲛⲁⲗⲉ (ἀνάλαβος), Deu 25 9 S[1]B[7] п ⲡⲧⲟⲟⲩⲉ ὑπόδημα, Mor 52 38 S п.[1] ⲡⲧⲟⲟⲩⲉ = PO 1 142 شسع حذاء shoe-strap, Miss 4 236 S σκηνή of skins, ropes & ϩⲉⲛп.[1] ⲛϭⲟⲟⲩⲛⲉ; pieces, portions of other things: Mor 37 94 S ⲟⲩп.[1] ⲛⲕⲁϩ πεδιάς, BMOr 6201 A 90 S п.[1] ⲛϩⲟⲓ, Ryl 189 S п.[1] ⲛϩⲟⲓ ⲛϣⲉ part of wooden water-wheel, Mor 55 64 S п.[1] ⲙⲙⲟⲩⲗϩ in beehive, AZ 23 39 F п. ⲥⲛⲛⲧⲓ ⲛϐⲁⲣⲛⲉϩ (linseed); piece of wood: Ez 27 5 SB п.[4] ⲫ.[8] ⲛϣⲉ, ROC 27 155 B ⲫ.[7] σανίς, Mor 18 126 S п.[1] ⲛϣⲉ ⲙⲡⲣⲟ σανίδιον, Tri 345 S ⲧп.[2] ⲛϣⲉ of Cross لوح, Dif 1 27 B picture on ⲟⲩⲫ.[1] ⲛϣⲉ 'ل, Z 612 S[4] sim, BSG 184 S throne ⲧⲏϭ ϩⲛϩⲉⲛп.[1] ⲛϣⲉ = ib 15 B ⲫⲁⲧⲥⲓ (cf above BMis 275); iterated, in pieces: Ez 24 6 B[8] (S ϣⲁⲩ) μέλος; ShA 1 108 S garments torn п.[1] п. н ⲗⲁⲕⲙ ⲗⲁⲕⲙ, ShIF 67 S sim ⲟ ⲙп.[4] п. paral ⲡⲁϩⲉ ⲡⲁϩⲉ, DeV 2 184 B his head ⲉⲣ ⲫ.[6] ⲫ, C 86 225 B ⲉⲕⲟⲓ ⲛⲫ.[8] ⲫ.

ⲣⲉⲙⲫ.[7] B, what is in pieces, two-leafed tablet (?): BMOr 8775 90 ⲇⲓⲡⲧⲩⲭⲟⲥ · ⲡⲓⲣ. دراسين.

As name (?): Τπακε κεμ POxy 2033. In place-names: John of ⲡⲁⲕⲉ, -ⲕⲏ invoked (Saq 226 &c, also PO 14 356), κώμη Πακή (Hermopol, Wess 20 68), Πακί (PStras, PFior 2), ⲡⲁϭⲓ ⲛⲛⲓⲁⲙ (PMich 777, cf باجة Aṣ-Ṣafadî 63, Ibn Duḳmâḳ 4 131). Only J 66 81 with art ⲧⲡⲁⲕⲉ. AZ 21 104 O ⲟⲩⲡⲱⲕⲉ at Abydos (so Möller PGM 1 74, cf DM 12 17, Berl Wörterb 1 561)

ⲡⲟϭⲗⲉ S nn as pl, meaning unknown, part or quantity of vegetables: ShHT E 342 fragt begins]ⲥⲉⲥⲙⲛ[......]ⲁⲛⲉϥп. ⲛⲥⲉⲥⲙⲛⲧⲟⲩ ⲙⲛⲉⲧⲁⲓⲧⲉⲓ ⲁⲗⲗⲁ ⲉⲩⲛⲁⲡⲁⲥⲧϥ ⲙⲡⲟⲩⲁ ⲡⲟⲩⲁ ⲡϭⲉ ⲛⲧⲁⲡⲣⲱⲙⲉ ⲙⲡⲟⲩⲟⲟⲧⲉ ⲛⲧϥ, ShP 130[2] 62 ϩⲉⲛⲕⲁⲣⲡⲟⲥ ⲛϣⲏⲛ, ϩⲉⲛп. ⲛⲟⲩⲟⲧⲉ. Cf ? Berl Wörterb l c pḳr, a herb (?).

ⲡⲱϭⲙ S nn, meaning unknown: BM 1137 ⲁⲓⲁⲡⲟⲗⲟⲅⲓⲍⲉ ⲡⲙⲟⲟⲩ (sc money) ϩⲁϩⲛⲉп. (l ? ϩⲉⲛ-) ⲁⲓϫⲓⲧⲟⲩ ⲛϐⲏⲛⲉ. Cf place ⲡⲉп. = ἐποίκιον Kr 145, also Ryl 340.

ⲡⲱϭⲥ S vb intr, meaning unknown, ? sweat, drip: Miss 4 753 ⲡⲧⲉⲡⲉⲑⲩⲥⲓⲁⲥⲧⲏⲣⲓⲟⲛ п. & shed tears from the pillars.

ⲡⲁϭⲥⲉ, ⲡⲁⲧⲥⲉ (IsKropp) S, ⲡⲉϭ. A[2] nn f, spittle: Job 7 19 (B ⲑⲁϥ), πτύελος, Is 50 6 (B do) ἔμπτυσμα; Z 571 ⲫⲗⲉⲅⲙⲁ н ⲟⲩп. φλέγμα; Aeg 265 ⲧп. ⲉⲧⲉⲕⲛⲁⲡⲧⲥ ⲉϐⲟⲗ ϩⲛⲧⲉⲕⲧⲁⲡⲣⲟ, Mor 43 218 ⲙп. in His mouth are healing salve, KroppR 16 20 τп. that came forth from Father's mouth; cast spittle ⲛⲟⲩϫⲉ, ⲛⲉϫ п.: Jo 9 6 SA[1] πτύειν, Nu 12 14, Mt 26 67 (all B ϩⲓ ⲑ.) ἐμπτ.; ShBor 247 107 ⲉⲩп. ⲙⲙⲟϥ ⲉϐⲟⲗ ⲙⲛⲉⲥⲙⲟⲧ ⲛⲟⲩп., ShIF 95 hateful sickness ⲛⲥⲉⲛⲉϫ п. ⲉϐ. ⲉϫⲱϥ н ⲉⲧϐⲏⲛⲧϥ, Mor 31 57 ⲁϥⲛⲉϫ п. ⲛⲥⲁⲛⲣⲏ = BM 917 B ⲥⲁⲧ ⲑ., Mor 19 16 ⲛⲉϫ п. = ib 18 8 S ⲛⲉϫ ⲧⲁϥ.

ⲣ

ⲣ, 17th letter of alphabet, called ⲣⲱ (My 34, 90), ⲉⲣⲟ (P 131ʻ 77) S, ⲣⲟ B (Stern p 418, K 1), رّ, (Stern lc), اٜ, (MG 17 368), اهرٍ (P 43 247). As numeral BF, rarely S = hundred (ϣⲉ). Derived from hierogl r, as ⲣⲱⲙⲉ, ⲣⲡⲉ, ⲡⲉⲓⲣⲉ, ⲙⲟⲩⲣ; rarely from n, as ⲣⲓϧⲉ (?), ⲅⲉⲣⲙⲁⲛ, ⲡⲁⲣⲙⲟⲧⲡ (RChamp 721). Often lost, as ϣ, ⲉϣ vb, ⲙⲉ love, ϩⲟⲟⲩ day, ⲛⲟⲩⲧⲉ, ⲥⲁϩⲟⲩ (Sethe Verbum 1 235 ff), less often palatalized, as ⲕⲁⲓⲥⲉ, ⲟⲩⲟⲉⲓϣ, ϩⲓⲏ, ϩⲕⲟⲉⲓⲧ (lc 243, AZ 27 106). Varies with λ, q v ⲁ b & Ep 1 243. ⲛ before ⲣ assimilated S (archaic), as ⲣⲣⲟⲙⲡⲉ (Ap 20 5), ⲣⲣⲟⲟⲩϣ (PS 219), ⲣⲣⲁⲥⲟⲩ (Sa 18 19) & A, as ⲣⲣⲙⲡⲕⲏⲙⲉ (Ex 1 15), ⲣⲣⲟ (Pro 14 19), but for λλ sometimes ⲣλ, as ⲫⲟⲣ̀ⲗⲟⲥ (PLond 4 464), ⲥⲓⲕⲉⲣⲗⲛ (ib 523), ⲡⲏⲣλⲁϯⲟⲡ (JKP 2 54), ⲃ̄ⲣⲗⲉ (Faras 3 pl 68 15). Intrusive in ⲙⲁⲣⲕⲉⲑⲟⲡⲓⲟⲥ (BMis 443). Transcribes Ar رٍ, as ⲁⲭⲡⲁⲣ اكبرٍ, ⲉⲣⲣⲁⲡ الربٍ, ⲣⲁϩⲙⲉϥ رحمةٍ (EW 234 ff), ⲕⲁⲣⲟⲟⲣⲉ قارورةٍ, ϩⲁϭⲁⲣ حجرٍ (AZ 23 117, 118); transcribed by رٍ, as ⲉⲣⲙⲟⲡⲧ ارمنتٍ, ⲙⲁϣⲓⲣ امشيرٍ, ϩⲁⲧⲣⲉ, ⲡⲉⲣⲡⲟⲩⲍ برنوجٍ.

ⲣ-, ⲣⲁ v ⲉⲓⲣⲉ.

ⲣⲁ SB(rare). ⲣⲟ S(Mor 17), ⲣⲁ- SB nn m, state, condition, v AZ 47 149: Z 580 reaching not ⲉⲡⲣⲁ ⲉⲧϣ̄ϣⲉ. With following nn or inf giving local or generic sense: Lev 16 14 ⲣⲁ ⲛϣⲁ (var & B ⲙⲁ), Lu 13 29 ⲣⲁ ϣⲁ (var & B ⲇⲟ) ἀνατολή; Jud 5 28 ⲣⲁ ⲙⲡⲓⲧⲉ τοξική; ShC 73 141 that none quarrel ϩⲙⲡⲣⲁ ⲣ ϩⲱⲃ, ib 150 ⲣⲁ ⲛⲣ ϩ., Mor 51 37 findest them not ϩⲙⲡⲣⲁ ⲉⲣ ϩ. nor at weeding time, Sh lc ⲡⲣⲁ ⲱϩⲥ, ib 152 ⲡⲣⲁ ϣⲗⲏϩ, J 4 53 from foundations to ⲣⲁ ⲧⲏⲩ, paral ib 106 139 ⲡⲁⲏⲣ (cf PMon 132 ἕως ἀέρος), Va 61 111 B ⲛⲟⲩⲣⲁ ⲧⲱⲙⲓ their joints, P 44 71 ⲣⲁ ⲧⲱϭⲉ · ⲙⲟⲣⲓⲟⲛ · ⲟⲅⲓⲟⲛ · مفصلٍ = P 54 125 B sim (v below, place-name), ⲣⲁⲙⲱⲡⲉ (?) q v, Ep 86 ⲟⲩⲣⲁ ϣⲁⲧ loss, deficit (?); & in ⲥⲁⲣⲁⲕⲱⲧⲉ. With prep: ϣⲁⲡⲣⲁ, ⲁ with nn, to the extent, as far as, Mor 17 27 casting stones ϣⲁⲡⲣⲟ ⲡⲟⲩⲟⲩⲛⲟⲩ ὡς ἐπὶ ὥραν, Bor 240 89 ϣⲁⲡⲉⲓⲣⲁ ⲙⲙⲁⲧⲉ ⲁⲡⲡⲉ ⲧⲉⲃⲗⲁϩⲏ...ⲁⲗⲗⲁ, ib 248 58 ⲙⲡⲁⲧⲉⲓⲭⲱϩ ⲉⲡⲉⲥϭⲣⲁϩⲧ ⲟⲩⲇⲉ ϣⲁⲡⲣⲁ of my finger tips, Mus 42 215 took thought for body ϣ. ⲛⲧⲁⲡⲁⲧⲕⲏ ⲙⲙⲁⲧⲉ, Ep 101 jars] found (only) ϣ. ⲡϭⲙⲉ ⲛϩⲓⲛⲗⲁ. ⲃ with vb, until, even: Mus 40 40 (Reg Pach) none may kindle oven ϣ. ⲉⲧⲟⲩⲛⲁⲟⲩⲉϩⲥⲁϩⲛⲉ ⲛⲡⲉⲥⲛⲏⲩ, Ryl 94 110 could not endure ⲟⲩⲇⲉ ϣ. ⲛⲥⲱⲧⲙ, ST 292 send me answer ϣ. ⲉⲛⲧⲁⲓⲉⲓ ⲁⲃⲟⲗ, Bor 248 55 gossiping in church ϣ.

ⲙⲙⲁⲧⲉ ⲙⲟⲛⲥ ⲉⲧⲣⲉⲡⲥⲱⲧⲙ ⲉⲡⲉⲡⲉⲣⲏⲩ; ϩⲁⲡⲣⲁ, as to, in respect of: BG 17 say your say ϩ. ⲛⲡⲉⲡⲧⲁⲥⲍ[ⲟ]ⲟⲩ; ϭⲁⲣⲁ- B distributively: Ap 22 2 ϭ. ⲁϩⲟⲧ (var & Gk ⲕⲁⲧⲁ), but S ϩⲣ- q v.

In place-names: ⲣⲁⲕⲟⲧⲉ (Berl Wörterb 2 403), cf ⲣⲁⲕⲟϯ (MG 25 158), Σαρατωκε, -τοκε (PLond 4).

ⲣⲁ v ⲉⲓⲣⲉ.

ⲣⲁ-, ⲣⲉ-, part v ⲣⲟ, after III.

-ⲣⲉ S interrog enclitic: Pcod 8 (v ⲛ there) of thief & things stolen ⲉ]ⲩϣⲁⲛⲧⲁϩⲟϥ ⲛⲓⲙⲁⲩⲣⲉ?, ib 11 of heretic bidden to a feast ⲉⲓⲉ ⲉⲩⲧⲙⲕⲁⲁϥ ⲉⲃⲟⲗⲣⲉ?

ⲣⲏ SBO DM, ⲣⲉ FO DM, ⲣⲉⲓ, ⲣⲓ A nn m, sun: Deu 4 19 SB, Eccl 7 12 SF, Ap 9 2 SB, Cl 20 3 A ⲣⲉⲓ, Joel 2 10 A ⲣⲓ ἥλιος; Ac 27 20 S ⲟⲩⲣⲏ; PGM 1 102 O Φρῆ Οὔσιρι, AZ 21 104 O crown of ⲡⲣⲏ, PGM 1 58 O ⲛⲧⲟⲕ ⲉⲧⲉⲡⲓⲣⲉⲡⲉ, DM 12 15 ⲣⲏ, 7 21 ⲣⲉ; sun's light: Is 30 26 SBF ⲡⲟⲩⲟⲉⲓⲛ ⲙⲡⲣⲏ; shine: Job 31 26 SB, Ap 1 16 SB ⲣ ⲟⲩⲟⲉⲓⲛ, Sa 5 6 S ⲡⲓⲣⲉ; rise: Ps 103 22 SB, Mt 13 6 SB ϣⲁ, PS 16 S ⲉⲓ ⲉϩⲣⲁⲓ, ib 4 S ⲉⲓ ⲉⲃⲟⲗ; set: Ge 28 11 SB, Eph 4 27 SB ϩⲱⲧⲡ, Ge 15 17 S ⲃⲱⲕ ⲉⲡ., BAp 124 S ⲛⲛⲁⲩ ⲙⲡⲣⲏ ⲉϥⲡⲁϩ.; sun = gold (alchemy): AZ 23 115 S the compound ϣⲁϥⲣ ⲣⲏ ⲛⲥⲁⲛ; sun tree: P 44 83 = 43 59 S ⲡϣⲏⲛ ⲙⲡⲣⲏ · ⲁⲣⲧⲉⲙⲓⲥⲓⲁⲥ; ⲙⲁ ⲙⲡⲣⲏ, sun-god's sanctuary (?): Mor 31 260 S whence Jeremiah recovers hidden treasures. V also ⲁⲛⲁϣ S plant.

In place-names: ⲡⲁⲡⲉⲫⲣⲏ (C 86 69), Ταχενεφρῆ (PSI 544).

ⲣⲏⲓ SB nn m, a fish, alestes dentex: P 46 168 S ⲡⲣⲏⲓⲗⲉ (l ? ⲡⲗⲉ) بلطيٍ (by error, v ⲣⲁⲙⲉ), ib 237 S (in margin) ⲡⲗⲓ رايٍ, K 171 B ⲡⲓⲣ. ٍ,. Cf M1F 51 118, AZ 30 29, JEA 14 33 (? = ῥαῖα).

ⲣⲓ SB, ⲣⲉⲓ S (Mor 37 13, Baouit 120), λⲓ F nn f, not biblical, cell, room a monk's, hermit's· Z 343 S = MG 25 208 B ⲧⲣⲓ of Abba Macarius, HL 98 B I built ⲧⲁⲓⲣⲓ κέλλα, Z 344 S = MG lc B sim, ROC 25 240 B ⲟⲩⲣⲓ ⲉⲥⲟⲣϥ, Z 294 S wherein hermit & disciple dwell, EW 194 B ⲛⲧⲉⲕϩⲉⲙⲥⲓ ϭⲉⲛⲧⲉⲕⲣⲓ κελλίον; Mor 48 30 S = BM 364 S ⲕⲟⲩⲓ ⲛⲣⲓ built on mount (desert) = Rec 6 183 B, ib S = ib B same called ⲥⲡⲏⲗⲁⲓⲟⲛ, ShC 73 58 S inspection of ⲣⲓ ⲛⲓⲙ in monastic houses, C 89 32 B cell in

monastery = Va ar 172 20 خزانة = MG 17 390
كيبة (l كيبة κύπη); BAp 80 *S* dwelt in small ⲣⲓ
within ⲃⲏⲃ (equivalence of ⲣⲓ & ⲃ. *v* Ep 1 128),
PSBA 10 194 *S* in ⲣⲓ on south of church, AM 180
B small ⲣⲓ built in his dwelling (τόπος), BM 346 *S*
hermit arrested in ⲡⲙⲁ ⲡⲧⲉϥⲣⲓ, Gött Nachr '99 38
B ϥⲙⲁ ⲡⲉⲣⲓ ⲙⲡⲓϩⲉⲗⲗⲟ, Saq 48 *S* ⲧⲣⲓ ⲡⲁⲡⲁ *abbot's
cell*, Baouit 105 *S* sim, EW 106 *B* bishop's, BM
1130 *S* ⲧⲣⲓ ⲡⲡⲉⲕⲟⲩⲓ *novice house*, BMOr 6204 *B S*
ⲡⲓⲱⲧ ⲉⲧⲣⲓ (ⲡ)ⲡⲉⲕⲟⲩⲓ, Miss 4 163 *B* ϯⲛⲓϣϯ ⲛⲣⲓ in
monast of Macarius = PSBA 29 290 دنشتري, BAp
124 *S* Pesenthius dying in ⲧⲛⲟϭ ⲣⲓ, BM 727 *B*
ⲑⲣⲓ ⲛⲧⲉⲕⲕⲗⲏⲥⲓⲁ of Macarius. ⲃ *room in house*:
MG 17 321 *S* = C 89 68 *B* house with ϣⲉ ⲛⲣⲓ
τόποι ἤ κελλία, PBu 3 *S* house contains ⲟⲩⲣⲓ, συμπόσιον, κοιτών (cf κέλλα *eg* PMon 97), J 35 27 *S*
ⲧⲣⲓ beneath staircase, *ib* 73 21 *S* share in ⲧⲣⲓ
(ⲉ)ⲧⲁϭⲉⲓ ⲉϫⲱⲓ, BM 673 *F* ⲧⲥⲏⲡⲉ (ⲉ)ⲗⲓ…ⲉⲧⲥⲁⲡⲓⲏⲃⲧ,
ⲧⲗⲓ (ⲉ)ⲧⲥⲁϥⲓⲗ; cf PLille 1 84;   *prison cell*:
C 43 243 *B* cast into ϯⲣⲓ ⲉⲧⲥⲁϩⲟⲩⲛ, *ib* 115 *B* ⲟⲩⲣⲓ
ⲛ̄ϫⲁⲕⲓ, Mor 41 339 *S* ⲣⲓ *filled with dung*; WTh
175 *S* cast into ⲣⲓ ⲛⲥⲉϯ ⲕⲱϩⲧ ⲛⲁϥ, Ep 466 *S* ⲛⲣⲓ
ⲙⲡⲙⲁ ⲛⲧⲱⲕ, GFr 430 *S* sick sheep cast into ⲟⲩⲣⲓ
ⲛ ⲕⲉⲧⲟⲡⲟⲥ. As *place-name*: ⲛⲣⲓ *S* (BM 216 80,
Z 309), ⲛⲓⲣⲓ *B* (HL 111) τὰ Κελλία in Nitria.

ⲣⲓ *A v* ⲣⲏ.

ⲣⲟ *SAA²B*, ⲣⲁ *S ͵*, ⲗⲁ *F*, ⲣⲁ- *S*, ⲣⲉ- *SB*, ⲗⲉ- *F*, ⲣⲱ⸗
SAA²BO, ⲗⲱ⸗ *F*, pl ⲣⲱⲟⲩ *SAA²B*, ⲣⲟⲟⲩ *A*, ⲗⲱⲟⲩ
F nn m, **I** *mouth*: Ex 4 11 *B* (*S* ⲧⲁⲡⲣⲟ, *A* ⲡⲁⲓⲥⲉ),
Job 3 1 *SB*, Pro 3 16 *SAB*, Is 5 14 *SBF*, Ac 1 16
B (*S* do) στόμα; *Gk diff or om*: Jud 9 52 *S* ⲉⲓ
ϣⲁⲣⲱϥ ⲙⲡⲡⲩⲣⲅⲟⲥ ἕως, Cl 20 6 *A* ⲛⲕⲗ ⲉⲧⲁⲅⲧⲉⲅⲉ
ⲁⲣⲱⲥ (*sc* sea) περιτεθειμένα, Mt 22 34 *S* ϣⲧⲙ ⲣⲱⲟⲩ
B ⲑⲱⲙ ⲡⲣⲱⲟⲩ φιμοῦν, Ps 74 8 *S* ⲙⲉϩ ⲉⲃⲟⲗ ⲉⲣⲱϥ
πλῆρες, Jo 2 7 *S* sim ἕως ἄνω; PS 57 *S* ⲁⲣⲱⲓ ⲙⲟⲩϩ
ⲡⲉⲟⲟⲩ, Br 106 *S* put herb ⲉϩⲟⲩⲛ ⲛⲣⲱⲟⲩ, Mor 41
31 *S* words come forth ϩⲛⲣⲱⲧⲛ. AZ 21 100 *O* ⲡⲉⲧⲓ
ⲡⲉⲧⲣⲱⲥ ⲉⲣⲱⲓ, DeV 2 57 *B* set bit ⲛⲣⲱϥ ⲛⲁⲙⲉⲛϯ,
BM 1133 *S* ⲧⲁⲣϥϣⲁϫⲉ ⲛⲉⲙⲁⲕ ⲡⲣⲱϥ *by word of
mouth*, Ep 431 *S* ⲛⲧⲁⲅⲟ ⲧⲁⲡⲟⲕⲣⲓⲥⲓⲥ ⲉⲣⲟϥ ⲛⲣⲱⲕ, 2
Jo 12 *B* speak ⲡⲣⲟ ⲟⲩⲃⲉⲣⲟ σ. πρὸς σ., Ryl 106 61
S drug will cleanse ⲡⲣⲟ ⲙⲡⲉⲕϩⲏⲧ, cf PMéd 176 *S*
ⲟⲩⲥⲧⲟⲙⲁⲭⲟⲥ…ⲉⲣⲉⲧⲉϥⲗⲟ (*sic*) ⲛⲓⲃⲉ, ShC 73 147 *S*
ⲣⲱϥ ⲙⲡⲉϩⲓⲣ, BAp 88 *S* water rose ⲉⲣⲱⲥ ⲛⲧϣⲱⲧⲉ,
cf 89 ⲧⲁⲡⲣⲟ ⲛⲧϣ.;   with suff -ϥ *as if absol S*
(*rare, v* **III**) *B*: Lu 6 45 ⲡⲓⲣⲱϥ (var ⲣⲟ), Ap 13
2 ⲣ. ⲛⲟⲩⲙⲟⲩⲓ, Va 63 26 word of ⲛⲁⲣ. = BMis 417
S ⲧⲁⲧ., Mus 34 206 ⲡⲉⲕⲣ. ⲛⲁⲧⲥⲓ, DeV 2 118 ⲣ.
ⲛⲛⲓϫⲉⲙⲱⲛ, BM 834 37 ⲣ. ⲛⲓⲃⲉⲛ, EW 169 greet
thee ⲛⲣ. ⲛⲉⲙⲣ., AZ 23 114 *S* ⲧⲟⲙ ⲛϥⲣⲟϥ *sc* of
vessel;   ⲕⲁⲥⲣⲟ *v* ⲕⲁⲥ *bone*; ⲕⲏⲡⲉ ⲡⲣⲟ *v* ⲕⲏⲡⲉ;
ⲙⲁ ⲙⲡⲣⲟ *v* **III**.   ⲁⲧ-, ⲁⲑⲣⲱϥ, *mouthless, not*

---

speaking the language: Mor 19 7 *S* = Miss 4 96 *B*.

ⲕⲱ, ϫⲱ ⲡⲣⲱ⸗, ⲕⲁ, ϫⲁ ⲣⲱ⸗ *SABF*, ⲕⲁⲣⲁⲉⲓⲧ† *S*
(*v below*), *place, leave mouth, be silent*: Deu 27 9
SB, Mt 20 31 *SBF*, MG 25 243 *B* ⲉϥϫⲱ ⲡⲣⲱϥ
σιωπᾶν, Nu 13 30 *B* ⲑⲣⲉ-…ϫⲁ ⲣⲱϥ (*S* ϫⲓ ⲣⲱϥ ⲛ-)
κατασ., Ge 34 5 *SB* παρασ.; Ps 31 3 *SB*, 1 Cor 14
34 *SBF* σιγᾶν; Lu 14 4 *SBF* ἡσυχάζειν, Pro 11 12
SA(*B*=Gk) ἡσυχίαν ἄγειν; Job 13 13 *SB* κωφεύειν;
ib 18 2 *S* (*B* ⲕⲏⲡ), παύεσθαι; Aeg 259 *S* let every
one ⲕⲁ ⲣⲱⲟⲩ, TstAb 230 *B* ϫⲁ ⲣⲱⲕ ⲉⲕⲣⲓⲙⲓ, BM
511 *F* ⲁϫⲉⲡⲕⲁ ⲗⲱⲟⲩ;   ⲥ ⲉ-, *be silent toward,
about*: Nu 30 15 *B* (*S* ⲱⲃϣ) παρασιω. dat, Ps 27
1 *SB* ⲡ. ἐπί; Ro 16 25 *SB* σιγ.; BMis 6 *S* ⲛϯⲛⲁⲕⲁ ⲣⲱⲓ ⲁⲛ ⲉⲡⲉⲣ ⲡⲙⲉⲉⲩⲉ;   ⲥ ⲉϫⲛ sim: Job
29 21 *S* (*B* ⲉϩⲣⲏⲓ ⲉϫ.) σιω. ἐπί;   ⲥ ⲉⲧⲃⲉ- sim:
Z 273 *S* ϯⲛⲁⲕⲁ ⲣⲱⲓ ⲉ. ⲛⲥⲃⲃⲉ σιω. acc.   ⲥ ⲉⲃⲟⲗ:
C 41 73 *B* ⲉⲧⲁϥϫⲁ ⲣⲱϥ ⲉⲃ. *when had opened mouth*
(to eat) *he found* (food) *to stink* = Miss 4 469
لما كشفنا *when we examined it*, Z 345 30 (*sic* MS,
print om) *S* in repeating Psalter ⲕⲁⲧⲁ ⲥⲟⲡ ⲛⲕⲁ
ⲣⲱϥ ⲉⲃ. *he made 3 genuflections* κατὰ ψ. ἐποίει
εὐχήν;   ⲥ ⲉⲡϣⲱⲓ, *open mouth upward, lift up
voice*: MG 25 153 *B* wolf ϫⲁ ⲣⲱϥ ⲉⲡ. ⲁϥⲉϣ ⲟⲩⲛⲓϣϯ ⲛⲥⲣⲱⲟⲩ ⲉⲃⲟⲗ.

ⲕⲁ, ϫⲁ ⲣⲱϥ nn, *silence*: Ac 21 40 *B* (*S* ⲥϭⲣⲁϩⲧ)
σιγή; CA 96 *S* ⲉⲣⲉⲟⲩⲕ. ϣⲱⲡⲉ in church, DeV 2
208 *B* ⲛⲧⲉⲧⲛϯ ⲛⲟⲩϫ. ⲙⲡⲓⲥⲁϫⲓ, BP 8503 *S* let him
(? *adversary*) ϫⲓ ⲉⲡⲟⲩⲕ. ⲛⲑⲉ ⲛⲛⲁⲡⲉⲧⲙⲟⲟⲩⲧ.

ⲁⲧⲕⲁ, ϫⲁ ⲣⲱ⸗ *SB*, *without leaving mouth shut,
never silent*: P 129²⁰ 127 *S* ⲟⲩϩⲏⲧ ⲛⲁ., TEuch 1 314
B ⲟⲩⲥⲙⲏ ⲛⲁⲧϫⲁ ⲣⲱⲥ, Leyd 471 *S* sim.

ⲙⲛⲧⲣⲉϥⲕⲁ ⲣⲱϥ *S*, *silence*: Miss 8 140 σιωπή.

ⲕⲁⲣⲁⲉⲓⲧ† *SA²*, *be silent*: Bor 253 171 ⲉⲓⲕ. σιω.,
Ge 24 21 ⲉϥⲕ. (P 44 103, *B* ϫⲱ ⲡⲣⲱϥ) παρασιω.,
BHom 67 ⲉϥⲕ., Mani 1 *A²* sim, GMir 262 half
speaketh ⲉⲣⲉⲧⲡⲁϣⲉ ⲕ. (Va 59 19 *B* diff);   as
nn: SitzVi 172 4 23 ⲡⲉϥⲕ. σιγῶν.

ⲙⲉϩ ⲣⲱ⸗ *v* ⲙⲟⲩϩ *fill* **I** *s f*.

ⲡⲉⲧϥ ⲣⲱ⸗ *v* ⲡⲟⲩⲧϥ.

ϯ ⲣⲱ⸗ *B*, *give mouth, word, promise*: MG 25 248
ⲉⲧⲁϥϯ ⲣⲱϥ ⲙⲡⲓϩⲉⲗⲗⲟ, HL 111 ⲙⲁ ⲣⲱⲕ ⲛⲏⲓ λόγον
διδόναι; P 54 168 ⲁϥϯ ⲣⲱϥ دعاه, انذر; C 86 334
ⲉⲁⲅϯ ⲣⲱⲟⲩ ⲉϥϯ.

ⲟⲩⲱⲛ ⲛⲣⲱ⸗ *SB*, ⲟⲩⲛ ⲣⲟ *S*, *open mouth*: Ps 108
2 *S* (PS 107) *B* ⲥⲧ. ἀνοίγειν, PS 93 *S* ⲁⲅⲟⲩⲱⲛ
ⲡⲣⲱⲟⲩ ⲉϩⲟⲩⲛ ⲉⲣⲟⲓ (cf Ps 34 21): 1 Kg 4 19 *S ͵*
ⲁⲥⲟⲩⲉⲛ ⲣⲁ (*sic*) ⲁⲥⲣⲓⲙⲉ κλαίειν; Mk 5 38 *S* ⲉⲩⲟⲩⲛ
ⲣⲟ ⲉⲃⲟⲗ (var ϯ ϩⲣⲟⲟⲩ ⲉⲃ., *B* ϣⲗⲏⲗⲟⲩⲓ) ἀλαλάζειν;   as nn: 2 Kg 19 4 *S* ⲁϥⲉⲡ ⲟⲩⲡⲣⲟ κράζειν
(or *l*? ⲁϥⲟⲩⲛ ⲣⲟ).

ϥⲟⲗϫ, ϥⲉⲣϫ ⲣⲟ *v* ⲡⲱⲗϭ **II**.

ϫⲓ, ϭⲓ ⲣⲱ⸗ *SB*, *deprive, prevent, anticipate*: Jud
7 24 *S* ⲁⲩϫⲓ ⲣⲱϥ ⲙⲡⲙⲟⲟⲩ καταλαμβάνειν, *ib* 12

5 *S* sim προκ.; Nu 13 31 *S* (*B* ѳре- ϫⲁ ⲣⲱⲋ) κατασιωπᾶν; ROC 25 243 = *ib* 271 *B* she ate neither sort ⲁⲗⲗⲁ ⲁⲩϭⲓ ⲣⲱⲥ ⲛ⳨ϯⲣⲉ ⲉ̄ϯ στερεῖσθαι; MR 4 70 *S* Flavian answered ⲉⲁϥϫⲓ ⲣⲱϥ ⲙⲡⲣⲣⲟ = Mor 19 69 *S* ⲟⲩⲉϩⲙ ⲡϣⲁϫⲉ ⲉⲣⲡⲣⲱϥ ⲙⲡ. = Miss 4 136 *B* ⲥⲁϫⲓ ⲛⲧϣⲟⲣⲡ ⲉⲡⲟⲩⲣⲟ, ShR 2 3 8 *S* friends beg dying man to answer ⲁⲩϫⲓ ⲣⲱϥ ⲉⲧⲙϣⲁϫⲉ (var BMOr 8800 3 ϫⲉ ⲣ.), Ostr Moskow *olim* Golenischeff *S*, send for (*nomina*) ⲛϫⲓ ⲣⲱⲟⲩ ⲛϫⲟⲟⲩ ⲛⲥⲁ-.

ϫⲉⲕ ⲣⲱⲋ *B, fill mouth, satisfy*: Dan 5 26 πληροῦν, 1 Cor 16 17 (*SF* ϫⲉⲕ ϣⲱⲧ ⲉⲃⲟⲗ) ἀναπ.

II *edge of weapon*: of sword BSG 178 *Sᶠ* wheel ⲉϥϫⲓ ⲣⲁ ⲡⲥⲏϥⲉ = *ib* 9 *B* ⲟⲓ ⲡⲣⲟ ⲛⲥ.; ⲣⲱⲥ ⲡⲧⲥⲏϥⲓ *B* Jer 21 7 (*S* ⲧⲁⲡⲣⲟ), Lu 21 24 (*S* do), C 43 191; two-edged s. *B*: He 4 12, Ap 1 16 (both *S* ⲣⲟ) δίστομος, Aeg 44 c. ⲡⲓⲃⲉⲛ ⲡⲣⲟ ⲃ̄; of saw *v* ⲃⲁϣⲟⲩⲣ; further 1 Kg 17 5 *S* ⲣⲱⲕ ⲡⲣⲉ ⲛⲥⲓⲛϭⲉ (P 44 109 ⲥⲓⲛϭⲉ) θώραξ ἀλυσιδωτός, *ib* 6 *S* ϩⲟⲡⲗⲟⲛ ⲡⲣⲉ ⲛⲣⲟⲩ ἀσπὶς χαλκῆ (ἀσ. as snake, P 44 *lc* المية), or ? pe here = pa *state* in generic sense.

III *door, gate*: Ex 29 4 *SB*, Ps 140 3 *S* (*B* ⲥ̄ⲃⲉ), Pro 5 8 *SAB*, Mk 13 29 *SBF*, Jo 10 1 *SA²B*, AP 11 *A²* θύρα, Ez 46 3 *SB* ⲡⲣⲟ ⲛⲧⲡⲩⲗⲏ πρόθυρα τῆς π.; Sa 6 15 *S* πύλη (π. is rarely translated); Cl 43 3 *A* κλείς; Gk & *B* om: Ge 7 16 *S* κλείειν, Job 12 14 *S* ἀνοίγειν; ShC 73 63 *S* ⲡⲣⲟ ⲙⲡⲥⲱⲟⲩϩ, ShZ 598 *S* ⲉϩⲱⲣϫ ⲉⲣⲱⲕ ⲡⲓⲣⲱⲟⲩ ⲙⲡⲏⲓ, Miss 4 115 *B* ⲁⲩϯ ⲙⲡⲓⲣⲟ ⲉⲣⲱⲛ = Mor 19 29 *S* ϣⲧⲁⲙ ⲙⲡⲣⲟ ⲉⲣⲱⲛ, TU 43 6 *A* ⲡⲣⲱⲟⲩ of prison, BMar 30 *S* ⲡⲣⲟ ⲙⲡⲕⲁⲥⲧⲣⲟⲛ, DeV 2 84 *B* ⲫⲣⲟ of furnace, Kr 36 *F* ⲉϫⲉ⳿ⲁⲣⲁ...ⲡⲉⲥⲗⲁ, P 131⁶ 64 *S* entered ⲡⲣⲟ ⲛⲧⲡⲩⲗⲏ ⲏ ⲡⲣⲟⲩⲛ ⲙⲡⲥⲟⲃⲧ; Z 352 *S* ⲣⲟ ⲛⲃⲁ *door of palm-branches*; J 50 43 *S* ⲣⲟ ⲉϩⲟⲩⲛ *entrance door*, *ib* 106 123 *S* ⲣⲟ ⲛⲃⲟⲗ, MG 25 99 *B* ⲣⲟ ⲉⲃⲟⲗ *outer d.*, Ryl 252 *S* ⲣⲟ ⲛⲫⲓⲣ, J 1 63 *S*, CO 150 *S* ⲣⲟ ⲛⲁⲩⲑⲉⲛⲧⲏⲥ *main d.* (cf θύρα αὐθεντική); with suff -ϥ as in **I**: Gu 60 *S* ⲧⲉⲧⲣⲓⲣ ...ⲡⲉⲥⲣⲱϥ, PMéd 105 *S* ⲥⲁϣ ⲡⲓⲙ ⲉⲙⲛ ⲣⲱϥ ⲛϩⲏⲧⲟⲩ (*meaning ?*); ⲡⲙⲁ ⲙⲡⲣⲟ = ⲡⲣⲟ: ShA 2 327 *S* elder appointed for ⲡⲙ., ShC 73 71 ⲡⲙⲁ ⲡⲓⲣⲱⲟⲩ (but *ib* 130 ⲙⲁ ⲡⲣⲱⲛ *mouth*), R 2 4 69 *S* accompanied us ϣⲁⲡⲙ., *cf* 70 ϣⲁⲡⲣⲟ, Miss 4 528 *S* ⲡⲙ. = C 89 46 *B* ⲛⲡⲓⲣⲟ, C 89 123 *B* looked toward ⲫⲙ. = Va ar 172 71 مكان باب, MG 17 480 باب; door key ϩⲟⲩⲣ: Ep 397 *S*, ϣⲟϣⲧ BM 1017 *S*; d. hinge ⲕⲟⲩⲣ: CO 233 *S*; d. post (?) ⲣⲁⲙϣⲓⲛⲉ ST 120 *S*; d. curtain ⲟⲩⲏⲗⲟⲛ *velum*: Ryl 238 *S*. *V* also ⲡⲩⲗⲏ, ⲥⲃⲉ, ⲟⲩⲟϭⲉ(ⲟⲩⲉϭⲣⲟ).

ⲁⲧⲣⲟ, *doorless*: MG 25 239 *B* cells ⲉⲩⲟⲓ ⲛⲁⲑⲩⲣίⲇⲱⲧⲟⲥ.

ⲡⲁ-, ⲫⲁⲡⲣⲟ *SB, he of the door, doorkeeper*: P 44

61 *S* ⲑⲩⲣⲱⲣⲟⲥ · ⲡ., Miss 4 522 *S* = C 89 42 *B* = MG 17 554 بواب (opp 41 *B* ⲙⲡⲟⲩⲧ خادم), BM 355 152 *S* ⲡⲥⲟⲡ ⲉⲧⲟ ⲙⲡ.

ϩⲁⲡⲣⲟ *SB*, ⲁⲡⲣⲟ, ϩⲟ ⲡⲣⲟ *B* nn m *porch*(?): Is 6 4 *B* (*S* ⲧⲟⲩⲁ) ὑπέρθυρον, Ez 46 3 *S* (*B* ϩⲟ ⲙⲡⲓⲥⲃⲉ) πρόθ.; *ib* 40 6 *S* ⲛϩ. (*B* do) αἰλάμ, *ib* 7 *S* (*B* ⲙⲁ ⲉⲧⲥⲁⲓⲉ) θεέ, *ib* 41 16 *S* (*B* ϩⲟ ⲡⲧⲉ ⲡⲓⲣⲟ) limen; Ex 26 4 *B* ϩⲁⲡⲣⲟ (var ⲁⲡ.) χεῖλος حافة.

ⲣⲁ- *S*, ⲣⲉ- *SB*, ⲗⲉ- *F* nn m, *part, fraction*: Nu 15 7 *S* ⲣⲁϣⲟⲙⲛⲧ, *B* ⲣⲉⲅ̄ τρίτον, J 9 53 *S*; Nu 28 7 *S* ⲣⲁϥⲧⲟⲟⲩ (var ⲟⲩⲉⲛ-), *B* ⲣⲉⲇ̄, Ez 5 2 *B* ⲣⲉⲇ̄ (*S* ⲟⲩⲉⲛ-) τέταρτον, Ryl 106 2 *S*, J 6 26 *S*; Lev 5 24 *B* ⲣⲉⲉ̄ (*S* do) πέμπτον; J 24 49 *S*, CO 220 *S* ⲣⲁⲥⲟⲟⲩ, -ⲥⲟⲩ; Ge 14 20 *SB*, He 7 4 *SBF* ⲣⲉ-, ⲗⲉⲙⲏⲧ δεκάτη, pl ⲣⲉⲙⲁⲧⲉ *S*, -ϯ *B*, *v* ⲙⲏⲧ. Ex 29 40 *B* Va 1 ⲣⲉⲅ̄, Lag ⲣⲉϥⲅ̄.

ⲧⲣⲉ- *S* (once), ⲧⲉⲣⲉ- *B* nn m f (once), meaning same: Nu 28 14 *S* ⲡⲧ. ϥⲧⲟⲟⲩ (var ⲟⲩⲛ-, *B* ⲣⲉ-), Lev 23 13 ⲡⲓⲧ. ⲅ̄ ⲧⲉⲧ., Cat 48 ϯⲕⲓϯ ⲡⲓⲧ. ϫⲡⲉ of ounce, C 86 331 ϯⲧ. ⲋ̄ (var ⲧⲉⲣⲓ-) ⲡⲧⲉ ⲡⲓⲡⲉⲣⲥⲓⲥ.

ⲉⲣⲛ- (ⲉⲣⲟ ⲛ-) *S*, ⲁⲣⲛ- *AA²*, ⲉⲗⲉⲛ- *F*, ⲉⲣⲱⲋ *SB*, ⲁⲣⲱⲋ *AA²*, ⲉⲗⲱⲋ *F* prep, *to mouth of, to, upon* mostly with vb of motion: Ex 29 4 *S* (*B* ϩⲁ-), Lev 17 4 *S* (*B* ⲉϩⲣⲉⲛ-), Deu 21 10 *S* (*B* ⲉϫⲉⲛ-), Ac 12 12 *S* (*B* ⲉ-) ἐπί acc, Job 31 27 *S* (*B* ϩⲓⲣⲉⲛ-), Mk 13 29 *SF* (*B* ⲉ-) ἐπί dat, Ge 19 6 *S* (*B* diff) πρός, AP 11 *A²* εἰς, Job 40 21 *S* (*B* ⲉ-) περί acc; *against* mostly ⲉⲣⲱⲋ ⲛ-: Jud 4 7 *S*, Zech 12 9 *A* (*B* ⲉϫ.) ἐπί acc; Deu 20 10 *S* (*B* ⲉ-) πρός acc; Jos 8 3 *S* εἰς; Job 12 14 *S* (*B* ⲉϩⲣⲉⲛ-) κατά gen; 4 Kg 15 37 *S* ἐν; no Gk prep, as ϯ ⲡⲓ ⲉⲣⲛ- Ge 31 28 *SB*, ⲉⲣⲱⲋ *ib* 29 13 *SB* acc, ϣⲧⲁⲙ ⲉⲣⲛ- Job 3 10 *S* (*B* = Gk) acc; ⲥⲕⲟⲣⲕⲣ ⲉⲣⲛ- *ib* 27 60 *S* (*B* ⲉⲣⲱⲋ ⲛ-) dat, ϩⲱⲃⲥ ⲉⲣⲛ- Ps 68 7 *S* (*B* = Gk) acc; PS 20 *S* ⲉⲓ ⲉⲣⲛⲧⲡⲩⲗⲏ, Mor 30 61 *F* ⲉⲓ ⲉⲗⲉⲙⲡⲏ, RNC 49 *S* ⲧⲱϩⲙ ⲉⲣⲙⲡⲣⲟ, AM 49 *B* ⲙⲁϣⲑⲁⲙ ⲙⲡⲓⲣⲟ ⲉⲣⲱϥ, Miss 4 115 *v* above **III**, P 131⁶ 17 *S* Daniel ϣⲧⲁⲙ ⲉⲣⲉⲛⲙⲙⲟⲩⲓ, ShZ 598 *S* ⲉϩⲱⲣϫ ⲉⲣⲱⲕ ⲡⲓⲣⲱⲟⲩ, PS 328 *S* key opening ⲉⲣⲗⲡⲧⲏⲣϥ, BMis 117 *S* ϯ ⲧⲟⲟⲧⲟⲩ ⲉⲣⲛⲡⲉⲩⲙⲁⲁϫⲉ, PS 94 *S* ϯ ⲡⲓ ⲉⲣⲛⲧⲙⲉⲥⲧ ⲛϩⲏⲧ, AM 86 *B* ϯ ⲫⲓ ⲉⲣⲱϥ ⲙⲫⲛⲏⲃ.

ⲛⲣⲛ- *A*, meaning same: Ac 13 22 (Cl, *S* ⲉϩⲛ-, *B* = Gk) ⲉϥⲛⲏⲟⲩ ⲛⲣⲙⲡⲁϩⲏⲧ.

ϩⲁⲣⲛ- (ϩⲁⲣⲟ ⲛ-) *S*, (ϧⲁⲣⲉⲛ- *B*), ϩⲁⲣⲱⲋ *S*, ϧⲁⲣⲱⲋ *B* prep, *under mouth of, beneath, before* mostly = Gk dat: set food *before* Ge 18 8 *SB*, Si 34 17 *S*, Mk 6 41 *S* (*B* ⲛⲁϧⲣⲉⲛ-); 1 Kg 28 22 *S* ἐνώπιον; Mt 7 6 *S* ϩⲁⲣⲱⲋ ⲛ- (*B* ⲙⲡⲉⲙⲑⲟ ⲛ-) ἔμπροσθεν; ShA 2 166 *S* setting food ϩⲁⲣⲱⲃ ⲙⲡϣⲙⲙⲟ; *table before* Lu 11 6 *S* (*B* ϧⲁⲧⲉⲛ-), BHom 134 *S* (ϩⲁⲣⲱⲛ *sic*), C 89 47 *B* food ⲁϥⲭⲁⲩ ϧⲁⲣⲱϥ ⲙⲡⲉϥϣⲏⲣⲓ; BMis 361 *S* food on table ϩⲁⲣⲱⲕ = Va 63

ı B ϩⲓⲧⲛ ⲙⲙⲟⲕ = BSM 23 B ⲙⲡⲉⲕⲙⲑⲟ; make answer *to* ı Kg 20 28 S (var ⲛ-), Mk 12 34 S (var ⲛ-, B Gk om); AM 236 B ⲥⲁⲣϯ ϩⲁⲣⲱⲟⲩ, R 2 ı 22 S sitting ϩⲁⲣⲙⲡⲣⲟ (cf Ge 18 ı S ϩⲓⲣⲙ-); ⲣ ϩⲁⲣⲡ϶(?): Ps 17 18 S ⲣ ϩⲁⲣⲱⲓ (var ϩⲁⲣⲟⲓ, *sic l*?) προφθάνειν.

ϩⲓⲣⲛ- (ϩⲓⲣⲟ ⲛ-) *SAA²* ϩⲓⲣⲉⲛ- B, ϩⲓⲗⲉⲛ- F, ϩⲓⲣⲱ⸗ *SAA²B*, ϩⲛⲗⲱ⸗, ϩⲓⲗⲉ⸗, ϩⲉⲗⲉ⸗(?) F prep, *at mouth, door of, at, upon*: Ex 16 14 S (B ϩⲓⲭⲉⲛ-), Mic 7 6 *SAB* ἐπί acc, Nu 11 10 *SB*, Jer 19 2 B (S ⲉⲛⲃⲟⲗ ⲛ-) ἐπί gen, Pro 8 34 *SAB*, Jo 11 38 *SA²* (B ⲉ-) ἐπί dat; Lev 1 3 B (S ϩⲁⲧⲛ-), Ac 3 2 S (B ϩⲁⲧⲉⲛ-) πρός acc; Ja 5 9 *SB*, Z 320 S sat ϩ. ⲧⲉⲕⲕⲗⲏⲥⲓⲁ πρό; BMis 560 S ϩ. ⲧⲡⲩⲗⲏ ἔμπροσθεν; Jos 5 13 S (var εἰς), Is 66 17 *SB* ἐν; 2 Kg 11 25 S, MG 25 216 B laid finger ϩ. ⲣⲱϥ εἰς; Z 583 S = Ge 22 17 *SB* ϩⲁⲧⲛ-, Ps 88 28 B (var ⲛⲁϩⲣⲉⲛ-, S = Gk) παρά; Ge 29 3 S (B ⲉⲃⲟⲗ ϩ.), 2 Kg 10 14 S ⲉϩ. ϩ. (var ϩⲛ-) ἀπό, ib 20 21 S ϩⲓⲣⲱⲥ ⲛ- (var ϩⲓⲣⲛ-) ἀπάνωθεν; Mk 16 3 *SB* (F ϩⲁⲃⲁⲗ) ἐκ; no Gk prep Jos 10 5 S acc, Jer 52 4 S acc, Ps 38 1 *SB* dat, Sa 19 3 S dat, Hab 1 10 *SA* κρατεῖν αὐτοῦ (B acc); PS 45 S ϥⲩⲗⲁⲝ ⲉⲧϩ. ⲙⲡⲩⲗⲏ, Z 349 S axe floats ϩ. ⲡⲙⲟⲟⲩ (cf 4 Kg 6 6), BMar 131 S ⲡⲉⲓⲁϩⲉ ⲣⲁⲧ ϩ. ⲡⲣⲟ, cf 129 sim ϩⲓⲡⲣⲟ, TU 43 22 A ⲉⲓ ⲁϩⲓⲣⲛ ⲡⲣⲟ, Mor 30 42 F ⲡⲱⲧ ϩⲓⲗⲁⲙⲡⲗⲁ = BMis 266 S ⲉⲣⲙ-, C 41 57 B ϩⲱⲗ ϩ. ⲡⲓⲣⲟ, Mor 28 145 S ⲟⲩⲛⲟϭ ⲛⲭⲁⲣⲓⲥ ϩ. ⲡⲉϩⲣⲟ, ShIF 307 S multitudes ⲉϥϩⲓⲣⲱϥ crying for pity, P 129¹² 47 S ⲁϥϭⲱ ϩⲓⲣⲱⲟⲩ, Miss 4 536 S dost journey north & south ϩⲓⲣⲱϥ ⲙⲡⲉⲕⲉⲣⲉⲡⲉⲉⲧⲉ (*sic*, prob ⲡⲉⲕⲣ.) visiting brethren, BMOr 11289 3 F ϩⲛⲗⲱϥ ⲙⲯⲁⲭⲁ, PCol 2 F ⲁⲩⲃⲁϣ ⲡⲃⲓⲛⲓⲃⲓ ϩⲓⲗⲉⲓ *loosed irons from off me*, BM 582 F ⲕⲉ ⲡⲉⲕϩⲁ ϩⲉⲗⲉⲛ (cf 580 15), ib 643 F ⲧⲉⲕⲉⲣ ⲧⲉⲕϭⲁⲙ ⲧⲏⲣⲉⲥ ϩⲓⲗⲉ (*i e* ϩⲓⲣⲁⲓ); ⲉⲃⲟⲗ ϩⲓⲣⲛ- *SB*, *from before*: ShR 2 3 51 S cast them ⲉⲃ. ϩ. ⲡⲉⲕⲣⲟ, MG 25 335 B sim, BMar 2 S affixed ⲟⲩⲥϩⲁⲓ ⲉⲃ. ϩ. ⲡⲣⲟ.

ⲣⲟ *SB*, ⲣⲁ F nn m, *strand, ply of cord*: Eccl 4 12 *SB* (MG 25 127) ϣⲟⲙⲛⲧ ⲡⲣⲟ (var Mor 18 27 S ⲕⲁⲡ) ἔντριτος; Mor 30 16 F thong ⲉⲥⲁⲓ ⲛⲅ̄ ⲉⲣⲁ = ib 29 14 S ⲕⲱⲃ = BMis 241 S ϣⲗⲟⲡ. ⲉⲙⲣⲱ B MG 25 359 this word? *Cf* ? ⲣⲟ *mouth* **III.**

ⲣⲟ S nn m, *goose*: AZ 30 39 among things stolen ⲟⲩⲣⲟ ⲙⲡⲉⲥ(*l* ⲡⲉϥ)ⲡⲁⲡⲟⲓ, ib 40 ⲡⲓⲣⲟ, (cf AZ 35 108), ST 344 (?) ⲡⲣⲟ ⲉⲧⲓⲧⲟⲟⲧⲕ to be sent.

ⲣⲱ *SA²B*, ⲣⲱⲱ (PS 17) S, ⲣⲟⲩ A, ⲣⲟ B (Cat), ⲗⲱ F enclitic particle, emphatic or explicative, often untranslatable **a** *same, again, also* esp B: Ex 36 9 (37 2) B (Va, Lag ⲣⲱ ⲣⲱ), EpJer 60 B ⲡⲁⲓⲡⲛⲁ̄ ⲣⲱ (F ⲡⲉⲓⲡⲛⲁ̄ *bis*), Mt 26 44 B (S ⲟⲩⲱⲧ), Ac 15 27 B (S ϩⲱⲱ⸗ ⲟⲛ), Gal 2 10 S (B ⲟⲩⲟϩ) ὁ αὐτός; MG 25 168 B who labour & who labour not ⲟⲩ-

ⲡⲁⲓⲣⲏϯ ϩⲱⲟⲩ ⲣⲱⲡⲉ, TstAb 243 B on 28th ⲙⲡⲁⲓ- ⲁⲃⲟⲧ ⲣⲱ ⲟⲛ, Cat 16 B careless ⲙⲫⲣⲏϯ ⲣⲱ ⲟⲛ ⲡⲡⲓⲉⲑⲛⲓⲕⲟⲥ. *V* also ⲟⲛ.

b emphasis or contrast, *indeed, but*: ı Kg 20 2 S ⲡⲉϥϣⲟⲟⲡ ⲣⲱ ⲁⲛ (var ⲁⲛ ⲣⲱ) τοῦτο, 2 Kg 12 18 S ⲉⲓⲥ ϩⲏⲏⲧⲉ ⲣⲱ ἔτι, Eccl 4 3 S ⲙⲡⲉϥϣⲱⲡⲉ ⲣⲱ ⲟⲩⲡⲱ, Mk 8 26 S ⲙⲡⲣⲃⲱⲕ ⲣⲱ μηδέ, Si 18 5 S ⲛⲧⲁϥⲉⲓ ⲣⲱ ⲉϩⲟⲩⲛ τότε; Gk om: 2 Kg 16 11 S ⲡⲁϣⲏⲣⲉ ⲣⲱ, Ac 19 2 *SB* ⲙⲡⲛⲥⲱⲧⲙ ⲣⲱ, Va 57 186 B ⲟⲩⲇⲉ ⲡⲓⲕⲉⲥⲟⲡ ⲣⲱ οὐδὲ ἅπαξ; PS 57 S ⲛⲧⲁⲓ- ⲡⲁⲣⲧⲉ ⲣⲱ ⲉⲡⲉⲕⲟⲩⲟⲉⲓⲛ *from beginning*, ShRec 7 143 S ϯⲙⲡϣⲁ ⲣⲱ ⲙⲡⲥⲱϣ *for have sinned*, Mun 63 S *are there no virgins*? ⲙⲡⲉⲓⲙⲁ ⲣⲱ ⲙⲛ ⲟⲩⲟⲛ, Va 61 95 B *have heard* ⲁⲗⲗⲁ ⲙⲡⲓⲧⲉⲛⲥⲟⲟⲩⲧⲉ ⲣⲱ = P 131³ 84 S om, Wess 18 36 S *one made priest other deacon* ⲁⲩⲱ ⲣⲱ ⲡⲁⲡⲓⲛⲉ *was held worthy of priesthood*, R 1 5 38 S ⲧⲉⲕⲭⲁⲣⲓ[ⲥ ⲣ]ⲱ ⲛⲧⲟⲕ ⲟⲩ- ⲗⲁⲁⲩⲛⲉ *but my Lord's…*, BM 307 S ⲡⲓϩⲱϥ ⲣⲱ ⲭⲉⲣⲙⲟⲟⲥ ⲙⲡϩⲁⲓ *is against my wish* = BSM 106 B, C 43 113 B *why wilt not sacrifice*? ϣⲟⲩϣⲟⲩϣⲓ ⲣⲱ ϯⲛⲁⲉⲣ ϣ. ⲁⲛ, Ep 327 S *perhaps we may find whole* solidus ⲧⲡⲁϣⲉ ⲣⲱ ⲟⲩⲏϩ, Z 352 S *I gave thee cloak* ⲁⲛⲟⲕ ⲣⲱ ϯⲛⲁϯⲛ ⲕⲉⲟⲩⲁ, Wess 15 10 S ⲛⲧⲟⲕ ⲣⲱ ⲡⲧⲕⲟⲩⲉⲗⲗⲟ = Miss 4 117 B om, C 89 60 B ⲁⲛⲟⲕ ⲣⲱ ϯⲛⲁϣ ⲙⲟⲩⲛ ⲉⲃⲟⲗ ⲁⲛ, Cat 209 B ⲟⲩⲉⲧ ⲣⲟ ⲑⲁⲓ ⲟⲩⲉⲧ ⲣⲟ ⲡⲏ ⲉⲧⲉⲙⲙⲁⲩ, ib 141, 215 sim; translates or accompanies advbs, ὅλως: 1 Cor 5 1 S ⲥⲉⲥⲱⲧⲙ ⲣⲱ ⲉⲩⲡⲟⲣⲛⲉⲓⲁ (B om), ib 15 29 SF ⲉϣϫⲉ ⲡⲉⲧⲙⲟⲟⲩⲧ ⲣⲱ (B om), MG 25 27 B ⲡⲓⲣⲡ ⲣⲱ ⲫⲁⲡⲓⲙⲟⲛⲁⲭⲟⲥ ⲁⲡⲉ ὅλ. οὐκ ἐστίν, Aeg 223 S ⲉϣⲱⲡⲉ ⲣⲱ ϩⲟⲗⲱⲥ εἴγε; ShA 2 278 S ϩⲟ. ⲣⲱ ϯⲛⲁⲩ ⲉⲣⲱⲧⲛ, C 41 58 B ϩⲟ. ⲣⲱ ⲛⲑⲟⲕ ⲟⲩⲉⲡⲓⲥⲕⲟⲡⲟⲥ ⲁⲛ, Bor 245 63 S *Gentiles know not virginity* ϩⲟ. ⲣⲱ ⲡⲥⲉⲥⲟⲟⲩⲛ ⲁⲛ ⲙⲡⲛⲉ̄. πάντως: ShC 42 196 S ⲡ. ⲣⲱ ⲙⲡⲉⲛⲛⲟⲉⲓ ⲙⲡϣⲁϫⲉ; δή: Jer 18 13 B ϣⲓⲡⲓ ⲣⲱ, Dan 12 1 B (S om) ϭⲟⲡⲧⲉⲛ ⲣⲱ; ⲙ- ⲙⲟⲛ, *but indeed*: ShA 2 283 S ⲙ. ⲣⲱ ⲉⲃⲟⲗ ϩⲙ- ⲡⲁϣⲁⲓ ⲛⲧϣⲏⲃⲉ *that mislead you*, AM 232 B ⲙ. ⲛⲟⲟϥ ⲣⲱ *let us not torture him here*; πλήν: Job 9 21 S ⲡ. ⲣⲱ (B om) π. (var διό), PS 298 S ⲡ. ⲣⲱ ⲙⲉⲩⲉϣ ϫⲓⲧⲟⲩ ⲉⲃⲟⲗ; μόνον: Ge 24 8 B ⲙ. ⲣⲱ ⲛⲟⲟϥ (var om ⲛ.); τέως, *meanwhile, at present*: Z 317 S *how goes it*? ⲧⲉⲛⲟⲩ ⲣⲱ ϯⲣ ϣⲁⲩ = MG 25 232 B & Gk τ. (cf Ep 299 ⲧⲉⲛⲟⲩ ⲣⲱ), BM 351 33 S ⲧⲉⲱⲥ ⲣⲱ ⲃⲱⲕ *& visit thy children*, DeV 2 162 B *found not time to build* ⲧ̄ ⲣⲱ ⲛⲁⲣⲉ- ⲡⲓⲥⲓϣ ϣⲱⲟⲩ *remained in his heart*.

c explicative: Jo 9 30 *SB* (A²+ⲟⲩⲛ) γάρ; PS 17 S *we sent thy robe* ⲉⲧⲉⲡⲱⲕ ⲣⲱⲱⲡⲉ, ShLMis 414 S *want & hunger* ϩⲕⲟ ⲃ ⲣⲱⲡⲉ ⲡⲁⲓ *of prophets*, ShA 1 389 S *knowing no god but Thee* ⲟⲩⲧⲉ ⲣⲱ ⲙⲛ ⲟⲩⲟⲛ, Cat 14 B *treasure in heaven* ⲉⲧⲉⲡⲁⲓ ⲣⲱⲡⲉ ⲡⲓⲁⲣⲉⲧⲏ, RNC 73 S ⲛⲧⲟϥ ⲣⲱ *for he it was*

gave him his clothes, P 131⁵ 49 S was ordinary man else ⲉⲡⲉⲙⲉϥϫⲓ ⲉϩⲓⲙⲉ ⲣⲱⲡⲉ; ⲉⲧⲃⲉⲡⲁⲓ ⲣⲱ : 2 Mac 6 16 A διόπερ; BHom 3 S e. ⲣⲱ ⲁⲡⲥⲱⲧⲏⲣ ⲙⲁⲕⲁⲣⲓⲍⲉ καί, Lu 7 7 S (B ⲁⲡⲟⲕ) Gk om; PS 10 S e. ⲣⲱ ⲁⲓⲥⲉⲧⲡⲧⲏⲩⲧⲛ, Va 63 99 B Christ came to save man e. ⲣⲱ ⲙⲡⲉϥϥⲟⲣⲓ heavenly guise.

d emphasis, *even, at all, at last*: 1 Cor 6 3 S ⲙⲡⲁⲧⲛⲡⲱⲣ ⲣⲱ (B = Gk) μήτιγε, Va 66 297 B clad in rags ⲓⲉ ⲧⲁⲭⲁ ⲣⲱ quite naked μᾶλλον δέ, MG 25 13 B ⲡⲱⲥ ⲣⲱ ϯⲕⲉⲫⲩⲥⲓⲥ of beasts should know καί, Ge 27 36 B ⲙⲡⲉⲕⲥⲉϫⲡ ⲟⲩⲥⲙⲟⲩ ⲣⲱ ⲡⲏⲓ ⲁⲡⲟⲕ Gk om, Jth 11 13 S none may ϫⲱϩ ⲣⲱ ⲉⲣⲟⲟⲩ Gk om, MG 17 326 S when made abbot was as if ⲙⲡⲟⲩⲧⲟϣϥ ⲣⲱ = ib 101 B ⲉⲡⲧⲏⲣϥ, Br 102 S not swear falsely ⲟⲩⲇⲉ ⲉⲧⲙⲧⲣⲉϥⲱⲣⲕ ⲣⲱ ⲉⲡⲧⲏⲣϥ, ShMIF 23 18 S cannot move ϫⲉⲉϥⲛⲁⲧⲱⲟⲩⲛ ⲣⲱ *far less rise*, ShWess 9 142 S woe is me ϫⲉⲁⲩϫⲡⲟⲉⲓ ⲣⲱ, ShP 130³ 2 S drank so much that ⲛⲥⲉⲧⲙϣ ϭⲙ ϭⲟⲙ ⲣⲱ ⲉⲙⲟⲟϣⲉ, PO 2 179 S burn it ϫⲉⲛⲛⲉⲩϭⲉⲡⲧⲥ ⲣⲱ ⲉⲡⲧⲏⲣϥ, Mor 22 46 S if soldier without wounds ⲙⲡϭⲙⲓϣⲉ ⲣⲱ (var R 24 41 om), ROC 9 321 B Constans so pious that almost might be said ϫⲉⲙⲡⲉϥⲙⲟⲩ ⲣⲱ ⲛϫⲉ ⲕⲱⲥⲧⲁⲛⲧⲓⲛⲟⲥ, *ib* 23 273 B ⲙⲡⲉⲟⲩⲛⲟⲩ ⲥⲛⲟⲩϯ ϣⲱⲡⲓ ⲣⲱ ϣⲁⲧⲉⲥ-;   after ἤ S : Mor 37 100 ⲟⲩⲛⲟⲃⲉ...ⲏ ⲟⲩⲙⲉⲉⲩⲉ ⲣⲱ ⲉϥϩⲟⲟⲩ ἤ ὅλως; ShC 73 89 mercy better than possessions ⲛ ⲣⲱ ⲛϩⲟⲩⲟ ⲉⲩⲟⲩⲥⲓⲁ, ShLeyd 370 ⲙⲁⲣⲟⲩϣⲱⲡⲉ ⲛϫⲁⲓⲉ ⲛ ⲥⲉϣⲟⲟⲡ ⲣⲱ.

e in question, *then* : 2 Kg 11 10 S ⲙⲏ ⲛⲧⲁⲕⲓ ⲣⲱ ⲁⲛ (var -ⲉⲓ ⲁⲛ ⲛⲧⲟⲕ) σύ ?, Jer 20 18 B ⲉⲑⲃⲉⲟⲩ ⲣⲱ ⲁⲛ τοῦτο ?, Ac 21 37 B ⲕⲥⲱⲟⲩⲛ ⲣⲱ (S Gk om) ?, Va 57 209 B ⲓⲥϫⲉ ⲅⲉⲉⲛⲁ ϣⲟⲡ ⲁⲛ ⲣⲱ ἂν μὴ ἦ ?; El 124 S ⲛ̄ⲕϣⲓⲡⲉ ⲣⲱ ⲉⲛ ⲛⲧⲟⲕ ?, ShA 1 283 S ϣⲁⲣⲉⲟⲩⲧⲃⲛⲏ ⲣⲱ ⲣ ⲛⲟⲃⲉ ?, C 86 318 B ⲕⲱⲛⲥ ⲣⲱ ⲡⲁⲟ̄ⲥ̄ ?, BM 343 75 S ⲁϩⲣⲟϥ ⲣⲱ ⲡⲁϩⲱⲙ ?

f after various particles, ⲁⲣⲏⲩ, *perhaps indeed* : PS 265 S ⲁ. ⲣⲱ ⲛⲧⲉⲧⲛϯ ϩⲑⲟⲩ ⲛⲧⲉⲯⲩⲭⲏ, ShBMOr 8810 372 S ye fight them ⲁ. ⲣⲱ ⲧⲉⲧⲛϫⲓ ϩⲉⲛϣⲃⲁⲧⲉ & smite them, MG 25 242 B accept me ⲁ. ⲣⲱ ϯⲛⲁⲉⲣ ⲙⲟⲛⲁⲭⲟⲥ ⲣⲱ;   ⲙⲉϣⲁⲕ sim : ShC 42 26 S ⲙ. ⲣⲱ ⲉⲧⲃⲉⲡⲁⲓ came this great curse;   τάχα sim : R 2 2 30 S ⲧ. ⲣⲱ ϣⲁϥⲧⲁⲓⲟ (var BHom 46 ⲙⲉϣⲁⲕ ϥⲛⲁⲧ.) πολλάκις δέ, v also **d** Va 66; ⲉϣⲱⲡⲉ, *even if, if indeed* : 1 Cor 14 7 S e. ⲣⲱ (B = Gk) ὅμως; ShA 2 68 S murmurers e. ⲣⲱ ⲉⲩⲧⲁⲙⲙⲉⲥⲧⲉ ⲡⲉⲧϫⲡⲓⲟ, Va 63 1 B e. ⲣⲱ ϩⲟⲗⲱⲥ ⲁⲓϣⲁⲛϯ = BMis 363 S om;   ⲉϣϫⲉ sim : Tri 649 S ليس . ⲉⲛⲉ- sim : ShA 1 111 S e. ⲛⲧⲉⲧⲛⲣⲉⲛⲃⲗⲗⲉ ⲣⲱ ye would not have sin, AM 89 B e. ⲉⲑⲃⲉⲡⲉⲕⲥⲭⲏⲙⲁ ⲁⲛ ⲣⲱⲡⲉ I had sworn thou wert... ϩⲁⲙⲟⲓ, ⲁⲙ., *would that* : Wor 295 S ϩ. ⲣⲱ ⲉⲡⲉⲟⲩⲣⲱⲙⲉⲡⲉ ⲡⲧⲏⲣ ϩ (*l* ϩⲉ), Mor 27 31 S/ ϩ. ⲣⲱ ⲧⲁⲙⲡϣⲁ = BMis 381 S ⲙⲁⲣⲉⲓⲣ ⲡⲙ.

ⲣⲱ +suff (error ?): ShA 2 286 S ϩⲱⲥⲧⲉ ⲉⲧⲣⲉⲩⲭⲟⲟⲥ ⲣⲱⲟⲩ ⲉⲩⲗⲩⲡⲉⲓ ϫⲉ-, DeV 2 114 B ⲉⲑⲃⲉϥⲁⲓ ⲣⲱⲥ when devil saw Eve inclined.

ⲣⲏⲃ   *v* ⲁⲣⲏⲃ.

ⲣⲁⲃⲏ   *v* ⲣⲁⲩⲉ.

ⲣⲃⲉ, ⲉⲣⲃⲓ   *v* ⲱⲣⲃ.

ⲣⲓⲃⲏ, -ⲃⲓ B nn f, *rope with belt* for hauling ship's cable : K 134 ϯⲣ. ⲓ̄, خلاب (1 MS وهو شنوطة اللبان). *Cf* BIF 20 70 n, Almk 2 105, Dozy 1 791.

ⲣⲃⲧ, ⲉⲣ., ⲣϥⲧ S nn epithet of ϣⲧⲏⲛ: Jud 3 16, 1 Kg 17 38 (B ⲙⲟϫⲃ, *cf* 39 S ϩⲱⲕ), 2 Kg 20 8 ϣ. ⲛⲣ. μανδύας (which 2 Kg 10 4 = ϩⲟⲓⲧⲉ S), P 44 57 ⲍⲁⲣⲁ · (*l* ⲍⲁⲃⲁ) ϣ. ⲛⲣ. زرد *coat of mail*.

ⲣⲁⲃⲛⲟⲩⲧ   *v* ⲣⲁⲟⲩⲱ.

ⲣⲓⲕⲉ SAA², -ⲕⲓ B, ⲗⲓⲕⲓ F, ⲣⲉⲕⲧ-, ⲣⲁⲕⲧ- S; ⲣⲉⲕ- SB, ⲣⲓⲕ- (?) A, ⲣⲁⲕ- B (AM), ⲗⲉⲕⲧ- F, ⲣⲉⲕⲧ⸗ SA, ⲣⲁⲕⲧ⸗, ⲣⲁⲕ⸗ (Va 61) B, ⲗⲉⲕⲧ⸗ F, ⲣⲟⲕⲉ† S, ⲣⲁⲕⲉ† SA, ⲣⲁⲕⲧⲉ† S (1 Pet), ⲣⲁⲕⲓ† B vb **I** intr, *bend, turn*: Ps 45 6 SB, Is 33 23 SBF, Lu 24 29 SB κλίνειν, Si 2 7 SB ἐκκ.; Nu 30 6 B (S ⲕⲧⲟ) ἀνανεύειν; He 12 13 B (S ⲡⲱϣⲥ) ἐκτρέπεσθαι; BMar 217 S ⲡⲡⲉⲕⲣ. ⲟⲩⲇⲉ ⲡⲡⲉⲕⲣⲉ = Rec 6 182 B, JKP 2 106 S where child rules ⲡⲉⲙⲛⲧⲉⲣⲱⲟⲩ ⲁⲩⲣ. *totter*, C 41 38 B day ⲉⲣϩⲧⲥ ⲛⲣ. *began to decline*.

II tr: Ps 85 1 SB, Jo 19 30 SA²B ⲕⲗ., Deu 24 17 B (var ⲕⲱⲗϫ), Is 10 2 B (S ⲣ. ⲉⲃⲟⲗ) ἐκκ., Ge 24 14 B ἐπικ.; Lev 26 21† B (S ϣⲱⲙ† neg) πλάγιος; Jo 8 6 B (SA² om) κάτω κύπτειν; R 1 1 16 S ⲛⲧⲁⲣ. ⲡⲡⲓⲥⲓϣⲟⲡ κάμπτειν; PS 283 S ϣⲁϥⲣ. ⲡⲧⲉⲯⲩⲭⲏ & constraineth it to transgress, TEuch 1 8 B not to do ⲛⲏ ⲉⲑⲣ.† *what is perverse*;   refl : Nu 24 9 S (var ⲛⲟⲩϫⲉ, B ⲣⲱⲧⲉⲃ) κατακ.

With following preposition.

—— ⲉ- intr SAB, *bend toward, incline* : Zech 14 4 AB ⲕⲗ. πρός, Ge 19 2 B (S ⲣ. ⲉϩⲟⲩⲛ ⲉ-) ἐκκ. π., Jos 23 6 B (S ⲣ. ⲉⲃ. ⲉ-), Is 66 12 B (S ⲣ. ⲉϫⲛ-) ἐκκ. εἰς, Nu 20 17 SB ἐκκ. δεξιά; 1 Tim 1 6 B (S ⲃⲱⲕ ⲉϩⲣⲁⲓ ⲉ-) ἐκτρεπ. εἰς; BSG 192 S sun ⲣ. ⲉϩⲱⲧⲡ, Mor 43 76 S ⲁϥⲣ. ⲉⲣ ⲡⲟⲩⲱϣ ⲙⲡⲗⲁⲟⲥ, Rec 6 177 B saw cave & ⲁⲓⲣ. ⲉⲣⲟϥ = BMar 212 S refl ⲉϫⲛ-;   tr SABF : Ps 16 6 SBF ⲕ. dat, *ib* 30 2 SB ⲕ. πρός, *ib* 118 36 SB ⲕ. εἰς, Su 9 S ⲣ. ⲉⲧⲙ- (B diff) ἐκκ. τοῦ μή; Pro 4 20 SA (ⲣⲓⲕ-) B παραβάλλειν dat; Ps 33 15† S (var 1 Pet 3 12 ⲣⲁⲕⲧⲉ) A (Cl, B ⲛⲥⲁ-) εἰς no vb, BHom 23 S flesh ⲣ.† ⲉⲡⲕⲁϩ ῥέπειν; Miss 4 240 S ⲉⲡⲣ.† ⲉⲧⲕⲁⲕⲓⲁ, Va 63 101 B ⲉϥⲣ.† ⲉⲡⲉϥⲟⲩⲱϣ;   refl : Jud 14 8 S, Pro 4 15 A (SB ⲣ. ⲉⲃ.) ἐκκ., MG 25 196 B ϣⲁⲓⲣⲁⲕⲧ ⲉⲧϫⲟⲓ παρακ.; Jos 22 5 S προσκεῖσθαι, Mun 24 S ⲁⲩⲣⲁⲕⲧⲟⲩ ⲉⲡⲱⲧ τρέπ.; Z 641 S priest ⲣⲁⲕⲧϥ ⲉⲡϫⲓⲥⲉ.

—— ⲉϫⲛ- *SB*, meaning same, intr : Is 66 12 *S* (*B* ⲉ-) ἐκκ. εἰς ; AM 21 *B* ⲁⲡⲟⲩϭⲏⲧ ⲣ. ⲉϫⲉⲛⲡⲓⲥⲁϫⲓ, Bor 252 304 *S* let us not ⲣ. ⲉ. ⲟⲩⲁ ⲛⲥⲁ more than other ; tr : Ps 54 4 *S* (*B* ⲉϩⲣⲏⲓ ⲉϫ.) ἐκκ. ἐπί ; Ge 8 21† *B* (*S* ⲕⲱ ⲉϫⲛ-) ἐγκεῖ. ἐπί ; Est D 7 *S* κατεπικύπτειν ἐπί ; DeV 2 52 *B* ⲡⲏ ⲉⲟⲣ.† ⲉ. ϥⲛⲟⲃⲓ ; Mor 55 96 *S* eyes ⲣⲁⲕⲉ ⲉ. ⲡⲉϫⲓⲕⲁⲓⲟⲥ ; refl : Est D 3 *S* ἐπερείδειν dat ; FR 30 *S* ⲁϥⲣⲁⲕⲧϥ ⲉ. ⲡⲧⲟⲟⲩ ⲙⲡⲓⲛⲉⲃⲧ, P 131³ 83 *S* ⲙⲡⲉⲡⲓⲡⲉⲅⲏ ⲣⲁⲕⲧϥ ⲉ. ⲗⲁⲍⲁⲣⲟⲥ = Va 61 93 *B* ⲣⲁⲕϥ ⲉϫⲱϥ.

—— ⲛ- dat *SB*, bend to, toward : R 1 4 29 *S* ⲉⲩⲣ. ⲙⲡⲉⲩⲙⲁⲕϩ ⲛⲁϥ, Z 269 *S* I ought ⲉⲣ. ⲙⲡⲧⲁⲓⲟ of neighbour rather than to his blame, PO 11 363 *B* ⲁϥⲣ. ⲛϧⲣⲉⲓ through age.

—— ⲛⲥⲁ- *SB*, meaning same : Ge 34 3 *S* (*B* ϯ ϩⲑⲏⲥ ϫⲉⲛ-) προσέχειν dat ; BHom 48 *S* eye ⲣ. ⲛⲥⲁⲛⲥⲁ of maiden ῥέμβεσθαι ; TRit 174 *B* ⲉⲩⲣ. ⲛⲥⲁⲡⲓⲡⲉⲧϩⲱⲟⲩ (var BM 857 ⲣ.† ⲉ-) ; Gu 95 *S* ear ⲣ.† ⲛⲥⲁⲡⲉϥϩⲣⲟⲟⲩ, DeV 2 114 *B* Eve's heart ⲣ.† ⲛⲥⲁⲡⲓⲟⲩⲧⲁϩ ; tr : Pap olim GHorner *S* women cause men to ⲣⲉⲕⲧ ⲡⲉⲩⲃⲁⲗ ⲛⲥⲱⲟⲩ ; refl : 2 Tim 4 4 *B* (*S* ϩⲱⲕ ⲉ-) ἐκτρέπ. ἐπί.

—— ⲛⲁϩⲣⲉⲛ- *B*, meaning same : 2 Kg 6 10 (var ϩⲁ-, *S* ⲣ. ⲉϧⲟⲩⲛ ⲛ-) ἐκκ. πρός.

—— ϣⲁ- *SA*, meaning same, refl : Ge 18 5 (*B* Va ϩⲁ-), Pro 9 16 *SA* (*B* do) ἐκκ. πρός ; Wess 11 163 show me a saint ⲧⲁⲣⲁⲕⲧ ϣⲁⲣⲟϥ = C 89 103 *B* ϣⲉ ϣⲁ-.

—— ϩⲁ- *B* v ⲣ. ϣⲁ-.

—— ϩⲓϫⲛ- *SBF*, bend upon, tr : Ps 16 11 *F* (*SB* ϩⲛ-) ἐκκ. ἐν. ; BMis 191 *S* when Lord ⲡ. ⲡⲧⲉϥⲁⲡⲉ ϩⲓϫⲱϥ (sc cross), Bess 7 7 *B* my heart ⲣ. ϩ. ⲛⲉⲣⲥⲁϫⲓ ; refl : ShMIF 23 157 *S* ⲁϥⲣⲁⲕⲧϥ ϩ. ⲡⲧⲟⲟⲩ. With following adverb.

—— ⲉⲃⲟⲗ *SB*, turn from, away, intr : Ps 13 3 *SB*, C 89 169 *B* if one ⲣ. ⲉⲃ. will be lost ἐκκ. ; Ez 13 18 *B* διαστρέφειν ; He 2 1 *B* (*S* ϩⲁⲁⲧⲉ, *F* ⲥⲗⲉϫⲗⲉϫ) παραρρέειν ; SHel 2 *S* devil's plan ⲉⲧⲣⲉⲡⲕⲟⲥⲙⲟⲥ ⲣ. ⲉⲃ. as hitherto ; tr : Is 10 2 *S* (*B* om ⲉⲃ.), Joel 2 7 *B* (*A* ⲡⲱϩϧ) ἐκκ. acc ; Tit 1 11 *B* (*S* ϣⲟⲣϣⲣ) ἀνατρέπειν ; Mor 38 77 *S* ⲡⲉⲧⲣ. ⲉⲃ. ⲛⲧⲗⲁϣⲉ, AM 279 *B* ⲁⲩⲣⲁⲕ ⲡⲥⲱⲙⲁ ⲉⲃ. laid down, My 66 *S* limbs of letter ⲗ ⲉⲧⲣ.† ⲉⲃ. ; refl : R 1 1 16 *S* standards ⲣⲁⲕⲧⲟⲩ ⲉⲃ. ⲙⲁϩⲁⲁⲩ κάμπ. ; C 41 64 *B* after praying ⲁϥⲣⲁⲕⲧⲩ ⲉⲃ. = Miss 4 451 [ﻝﻳﻡ] ; ⲉⲃ. ⲉ-, turn to, intr : Jos 23 6 *S* (*B* ⲉ-) ἐκκ. εἰς ; JTS 10 396 *S* all ⲣ. ⲉⲃ. ⲉⲡⲧⲁⲕⲟ ; tr & refl : Pro 28 9 *SA* ἐκκ. τοῦ μή, ib 16 17 *S* ⲣⲁⲕⲧⲛ ⲉⲃ. ⲉ- (*A* ⲉⲃ. ⲛ-) ἐκκ. ἀπό ; ⲉⲃ. ⲉϫⲛ- *S*, bend upon, overhang : BMis 543 ⲉⲩⲣ.† ⲉⲃ. ⲉϫⲛⲟⲩⲟⲃⲉ ⲙⲙⲟⲟⲩ pendentes super, Ryl 85 22 will bid demons ⲛⲥⲉⲣ. ⲉⲃ. ⲉϫⲱⲓ & trample me, KroppJ unicorn ⲉⲩⲣ.† ⲉⲃ. ⲉϫⲛⲟⲩϩⲟⲓ *lying on meadow* ; ⲉⲃ. ⲛ-, turn from intr : Pro 5

12 *SA* (*B* ⲥⲁⲃⲟⲗ ⲛ-) ἐκκ. acc, Bar 4 12 *B* ἐκκ. ἐκ ; tr : Sh(Besa)Bor 206 556 *S* ⲁⲩⲣ. ⲛⲛⲁⲓ (sc sins) ⲉⲃ. ⲙⲙⲟⲛ ; refl : Nu 22 33 *S* (*B* ⲥⲁⲃ. ⲛ-), Ps 118 21 *S* (*B* do), Pro 3 7 *SA* (*B* ⲉⲃ. ϩⲁ-) ἐκκ. ἀπό ; PS 180 *S* ⲁⲕⲧⲣⲁⲣⲁⲕⲧ ⲉⲃ. ⲙⲡⲧⲟⲡⲟⲥ ; ⲉⲃ. ϩⲁ- *B*, meaning same : Hos 5 6 (*A* ⲥⲱϣⲉ ⲁⲃ. ⲛ-), Zeph 1 6 (*A* ⲗⲁϣⲉ) ἐκκ. ἀπό ; ⲉⲃ. ϩⲓ- *SAB*, as last : Pro 1 15 *AB* (*S* ⲉⲃ. ϩⲛ-), Ez 16 27 *S* (*B* ⲧⲁⲥⲑⲟ ⲉⲃ. ϩⲁ-) ἐκκ. ἐκ ; ⲉⲃ. ϩⲛ- *SB*, as last intr : Job 31 7 *S* (*B* ⲉⲃ. ϩⲓ-) ἐκκ. ἐκ., BHom 117 *S* ⲁⲥⲣ. ⲉⲃ. ϩⲛⲡⲉⲣⲓⲟⲟⲩⲉ ; tr : Ps 43 19 *S* (var ⲉⲃ. ϩⲓ-, *B* ⲥⲁⲃ. ⲛ-) ἐκκ. ἀπό ; Is 29 21 *B* (*S* ⲕⲧⲟ) πλαγιάζειν ἐν ; P 129¹⁶ 89 *S* devil ⲣⲕⲧ ⲟⲩⲟⲛ ⲛⲓⲙ ⲉⲃ. ϩⲁⲙⲡϣⲓϣⲉ ; refl : 2 Kg 2 17 *S* ἐκκ. ἐκ.

ⲥⲁⲃⲟⲗ ⲛ- *B*, meaning same, intr : Ps 33 15 (*SA* refl ⲉⲃ. ⲛ-), Dan 9 5 (*S* do) ἐκκ. ἀπό ; Ez 20 8 (*S* ⲥⲟⲟϩⲉ ⲉⲃ. ⲛ-) ἀφιστάναι ἀπό, ib 18 28 (*S* ⲕⲧⲟ ⲉⲃ. ϩⲛ-) ἀποστρέφειν ἐκ ; tr : Ps 43 19 (*S* ⲉⲃ. ϩⲛ-) ἐκκ. ἀπό ; refl : Va 61 92 ϥⲡⲁⲣⲁⲕϥ ⲥ. ⲙⲡⲓϧⲏⲟⲩ ⲡϣⲗⲟϥ = P 131³ 82 *S* ⲉⲃ. ⲛ- ; ⲛⲥⲁⲃⲟⲗ *S* : ShC 73 152 reeds on canal bank ⲉⲩⲣⲉⲅⲣⲁⲕⲧⲟⲩ ⲛⲥ. ; ⲛⲥ. ⲛ- : Jer 5 25 (*B* ⲥⲁⲃ. ⲛ-) ἐκκ. ἀπό ; ϩⲁⲃⲟⲗ ⲛ- *S* : Mor 54 32 ⲁⲩⲣ. ϩ. ⲛⲧⲉⲣⲓⲛ.

—— ⲉⲡⲉⲥⲏⲧ *SB*, bend down, tr : R 1 4 16 *S* ⲣⲉⲕⲧ ⲧⲉⲕⲁⲡⲉ ⲉ. *inclinare*, Va 57 120 *B* sim ; refl : LMär 37 *S* idol ⲣⲁⲕⲧϥ ⲉ. (var BIF 14 139 ⲡⲁ]ϧⲧϥ om ⲉ.).

—— ⲉⲫⲁϩⲟⲩ *B*, turn back : Ps 43 19 (*S* ⲥⲟⲟϩⲉ ⲉⲡ.) ἀφιστ. εἰς τὰ ὀπίσω.

—— ⲉϧⲟⲩⲛ *S* (rare), ⲉϣ. *B*, turn in, toward, c ⲉ- : 2 Kg 6 10 *B* (*S* refl) ἀποκ. εἰς, 4 Kg 4 10 *B* ἐκκ. ἐκεῖ ; C 89 84 *B* ⲉⲩⲣ. ⲉϣ. ⲉϩⲧⲟⲓ ; refl : Jer 14 8 *B* (*S* ⲉ-) ἐκκ. εἰς ; Mor 41 2 *S* reached monastery ⲁⲡⲣⲁⲕⲧⲛ ⲉϩ. = DeV 2 248 *B* ; c ⲛ- *S*, refl : 2 Kg 6 10 (*B* ⲛⲁϩⲣⲉⲛ-) ἐκκ. πρός ; c ϣⲁ- *S*, refl : ShA 2 166 begged ⲉⲧⲣⲉⲩⲣⲁⲕⲧⲟⲩ ⲉϩ. ϣⲁⲣⲟϥ (cf Ge 18 5 om ⲉϩ.).

—— *SAB* nn m, turning, inclination : 1 Tim 5 21 *B* (*S* ϫⲓ ϩⲟ) πρόσκλισις ; Ja 1 17 *SA* (*B* diff) τροπή ; Nu 31 16 *B* (*S* ⲥⲟⲟϩⲉ ⲉⲃ. vb) τὸ ἀποστῆσαι ; ShMIF 23 68 *S* ⲟⲩⲣ. ϣⲏⲙⲡⲉ whether man become child of God or of devil, ShC 42 215 *S* toppling house sways ϣⲁⲡⲧⲉⲡⲉⲓⲣ. ⲧⲏⲣⲟⲩ ϣⲱⲡⲉ, P 129¹⁴ 98 *S* Christ above ⲫⲩⲥⲓⲥ ⲛⲓⲙ ϩⲓⲣ. ⲛⲓⲙ & every name, MG 25 328 *B* right resolve without ϩⲗⲓ ⲡⲣ. ; ⲣ. ⲙⲙⲁϣⲉ, weight that turns scale : Pro 16 11 *SA*, Is 40 15 *SB* ῥοπή ; ⲣ. ⲙⲃⲁⲗ, blink, wink of eye : 1 Cor 15 52 *SB* ῥιπή ; BMis 532 *S* have never quitted thee ϣⲁⲡⲣ. ⲡⲟⲩ⳿., TstAb 242 *B* signing him to be silent ϫⲉⲛⲫⲣ. ⲡⲛⲉϥⲃ., N&E 39 339 *B* ⲡⲓⲣ. ⲛⲃ. ⲡⲧⲉ ⲫϯ *God's approval* came to meet them, MG 25 112 *B* sim, Miss 4 711 *S* scarce turned face toward them ϩⲓⲧⲙⲡⲣ. ⲛⲛⲉϥⲃ.

атр. *SB, without turning, unwavering* : He 10 23 B(S ахпр.)ἀκλινής ; DeV 1 57 B balance πα., ROC 19 75 S apostles' faith πα. ;   ρ ατр. : P 129²⁰ 133 S thoughts ε϶ο πα., DeV 1 151 B ϩιος ε϶οι πα.

сϣр. *B, unbending* : Ex 37 15(Lag 224 10)ε϶соϒтωн επϣωι пс. (var ϣтр.) مستقيمة (gloss غير متحركة) Gk om, *l* ?? поϒεϣнепр.

реϥр. *B, turner, bender* : Jer 31 12 κλίνων ; ллптреϥр. *S, inclination* : P 129¹⁴ 101 Barnabas inclined not to Mark ετϩεο϶лл. εϫπτлλετапоіа but in true sympathy.

ϭιπ-, ϫιπр. *SB, inclination, perversion* : Lam 3 35 B ἐκκλῖναι ; ROC 20 53 S тϭ. лппоϧε, J 75 6 S that we may find тϭιπрактп εϧολ пταταпактнсіс.

ракте *S nn f, bent, direction, perversion* : Lu 9 53 (B ϩο) πρόσωπον ; Miss 4 812 son of iniquity humbled him not ϩιтр. пташϣωпе ппаϒпатос who rose up against Horsiesi.

Cf ркріке.

ракрек, λεκλωκ⸗ *Sᶠ vb intr & tr, meaning uncertain, cf* λωκ (λοκλκ **II**) : Bodl(P) a 1 d екϣапти ппарре εϫωс (sc iron μηχανή) псракрек ϣаϧωλ псωлла тнро϶ εϧολ = *ib* a 3 68 ϣа(п)тексет о϶парре ϩιϫω(п)пепіпе текλεκλωκϥ.

(рокрек), рекрωκ† *B vb intr, become, be putrid or scorched* (?) : Va 61 94 B Ninive (Dives)'s tongue р.† ϫапіϣаϩ = P 131⁵ 84 S λεϥλωϣ ϩιтп- (Mor 25 12 om), K 232 = P 54 177 B εϥр.† عفن *putrid*, قف *scorched*.

ркріке *SA*, ϩр. *S*, рекрікі *BF*, λεκλικι *F* (once each) *nn f, bending, nodding* of head in sleep, *cf* ріке : Si 34 2 S νυσταγμός ; Mor 30 24 F о϶λ. асі εϫлπϩатіос ;   † р. с п-, *give sleep to* : Ps 131 4 S (B сролл) v. διδόναι, Pro 6 4 *SA* (B ϩіпілл) ἐπινυστάζειν ; ϫι, ϭι р., *take to nodding, doze* : Ps 75 6 S, Is 56 10 S, Nah 3 18 A, Mt 25 5 S (all B ϩιпілл) νυστάζειν ; K 90 B піϭі р. نعاس ; NC 89 S soldiers ϫι р. аϒωϧϣ, BMis 534 S лпеіϫі о϶р. ϩολωс, Mor 24 27 F лпелϫі р. ;   form ϩр. *S* : BAp 148 (Ps 131), BHom 6, 78 (do), Ep 592 A 20 ϩрік. (*cf* Is 5 27 var рік.).

рωϫ *v* λωκс (nn).

ракте *v* ріке *sf.*

рωκϩ *SAA²B*, λ. *F*, рекϩ- *SB*, рокϩ⸗ *SB*, ракϩ⸗, рокϫ⸗ (C 73 94), роϫ⸗ *S*, раϫϩ⸗ *A*, раϫ⸗ *S* (PMéd) *AA²*, λакϩ⸗ *F*, рокϩ† *SB*, роϫ† (Saq 103), рωϫ† (PMéd), роϩϫ† *S* (AZ 23), ракϩ† *AF*, роϫϩ† *SF* (Job) *vb* **I** *intr, burn* : Deu 32 22 *SB*, 2 Pet 3 10 *SB*, Z 347 S лερεπετісωлла р. = MG 25 220 B р.† καίειν, Deu 29 23 S (B ϫоϥϫеϥ), Is 33 12† *SBF*, He 13 11 *SB* κατακ., Is 5 24 *SB* (F

лоϒϩ), Jon 4 8† *SAB* σννκ., Job 30 17 *BF* (WS, S ϭωϭ, reading σνγκέκανται), Is 1 7 *SF* (B tr) πνρίκανστος ; 1 Cor 7 9 *SF* (B ϭι ϫрωлл) πνροῦσθαι ; Nu 5 21 S (B о϶ісі, reading πρίειν) πίμπραναι ; ShA 1 449 S branches аϒр. & became as cinders, PMéd 162 S ϩосл εϥрωϫ, BKU 1 21 vo F sim, Mich 136 1 S тап εϥроϧϫ, AZ 23 112 S пϧарот εтро϶ϫ, Miss 4 667 S village εϥр.† ϩιтлпкаллпнсос (Cambyses), LCyp 30 S аϥр. аϥлло϶, Ryl 313 S sick woman петпесϩо϶п р.†

II *tr* : Lev 4 12 *SB*, Si 28 23 S роϫо϶, Jo 15 6 *SA²* (B *intr*) καί., Ez 5 2 *SB* ἀνακ., Pro 29 8 *SA* ἐκκ., Ac 19 19 *SB* κατακ., Is 5 11 *BF* (S тлро϶) σννκ., He 6 8 *SBF* καῦσις ; Ps 73 7 *SB* ἐμπνρίζειν ; Mal 4 1 *AB* φλέγειν, Ps 82 14 *SB* διαφ., ib 105 18 S(B телϩро) καταφ., Is 42 25 *SB* σνμφ. ; PS 299 S fire пϥрекϩ ппоϧе, Mor 32 27 S εϒερакрек, *ib* 24 18 F птетплакϩо϶, C 43 153 B εϥо϶ωϣ εрокϩтеп.

With following preposition.   с е- *SB, burn toward, after* : Bor 100 22 S пепϩорлн εтр.† еппоϧе, Va 63 101 B екр.† ео϶порпіа, BM 247 5 S sim ϣаϥр. εϩо϶п εроϥ ἐκκ. εἰς ; RAl 86 B εср.† εϧ. εϥ† ;   *dat commodi* : 1 Tim 4 2† S (B р. пϫнрі ϫεп-) καντηριάζεσθαι acc ;   с пса- *SB emphasis* : Va 57 253 B сер. псωо϶ катакαίονται *devoured* by greed, Z 319 S poison р. псапе϶ϩнт катак. acc ; ShRyl 71 93 S петр.† псапеіϧоте, Mor 31 93 S εϒр. псапетпϫпа϶ (var Miss 4 780 р. п-), PBu 123 S ϭе εтϥр.† псапні ллос *covet* ;   с птеп- *B, burn by, through* : Lev 10 6 (S р. пп) ἐμπιμπ. ὑπό, MG 25 195 εір.† птеппіϧі φλ. ὑπό ;   с ϩп- *SAA²BF, burn with, by* : Ro 1 27 B (S ло϶ϩ) ἐκκ. ἐν, Lev 21 9 S (B ϩіϫеп-) катак. ἐπί, Ps 45 9 *SB* ἐν, Mt 13 40 *SBF* dat, Ge 31 40 *SB* σννκ. dat ; Si 8 13 S ἐμπνρίζεσθαι ἐν ; Mic 1 7 *SAB* ἐμπιμπ. ἐν, Mt 22 7 *SB* om ἐν ; AP 33 *A²* атлтроϒр. ϩλ[п]кωрт, ShIF 108 S петр.† ϩнтϥ (sc disease), BHom 13 S εϥр.† ϩпо϶λιϧε εϩраι εϫптесϫіне ;   с ϩітеп- *B, meaning same* : Mart Ign 867 Heracles аϒрокϩϥ ϩ. о϶ϫрωлл ἀναλίσκειν dat, MIE 2 335 mount р.† ϩ. пікаϒлла.

——— *SB nn m, burning, fervour* : Nu 19 6 B (S ϣаϩ), Jer 31 34 B κατάκανμα ; Nu 11 3 *SB* ἐνπνρισμός ; Is 4 4 *SB* καῦσις ; Ap 18 18 *SB* πύρωσις ; BHom 49 S пр. птеϒепіϧνлла φλόξ ; 2 Chr 6 28 B gloss ? on іктерос ; Miss 4 531 S пеϥр. ϩрнт εϩрϩп еппē = C 89 150 B ἐπιποθεῖν ; ShC 73 1 S пр. of Sodom, DeV 2 143 B пір. of serpents' poison, AZ 21 143 S пр. ппекспλаϫпоп toward him.

реϥр. *SB, who burns, burning* : R 1 4 58 S кωϩ[т] пр. = Mart Ign 870 B, AM 122 B πῦρ καντικόν.

рокϩ, рω.(*l* ро.)B *nn m, fuel, firewood* : Lev 1 8 pl, Jer 5 14 (S BMis 198), 1 Cor 3 12 (all S ϣe)

ξύλον; ROC 17 407 σχίδαξ; Cat 129 ϩⲁⲡⲣ. cut with axe, C 89 7 load of p. from ⲡⲓϣⲟⲡϯ; *gather fuel* ϭⲱⲕⲓ, ϭⲉⲕ-: Nu 15 32 (S v TT 52 ϭⲗ ϣⲉ), 3 Kg 17 10, cit RAl 86 ξ. συλλέγειν; *split f.* ϥⲉϭ-: Ge 22 3 (S diff) ξ. σχίζειν; ⲣⲉϥϥ. p.: Deu 29 11 (S ⲣⲉϥϭⲗ ϣⲉ) ξυλοκόπος.

ⲣⲟⲕϩⲉ, ⲣⲁ. S, ⲣⲁⲕϩⲓ B nn f, *fuel*: Jer 43 22 B ἐσχάρα; Jo 21 9 B (S ϣⲁϩ) ἀνθρακιά; ShC 73 137 S ⲡⲣ. to be stamped into oven, Va 61 200 B will cut wood ⲙⲡϣⲁϥ ⲡϯⲣ.; ⲣⲟϫⲛ m S ? same: Sh *lc* when oven opened ⲉ(ⲩ)ⲛⲁϩⲉ ⲉⲡⲣ. ⲧⲏⲣϥ or = ϩⲁϫⲛ (MS ⲣⲁϫⲛ) A, *baked cake*: Hos 3 1 (B ⲫⲓⲥⲓ) πέμμα.

In place-name (?): Πκεμρόχ (POxy 1913).

ⲣⲱⲙⲉ *v* ⲙⲣⲱⲙ.

ⲣⲁⲙⲉ, -ⲙⲏ, ⲣⲁⲁⲙⲉ S, ⲣⲁⲙⲓ B nn m f, *a fish tilapia*: Glos 422 S ⲣⲁⲁⲙⲉ · κοριαξός, P 46 237 S ⲡⲣⲁⲙⲏ طلبا (cf ἀβραμίς), EW 222 scala S ⲧⲣⲁⲙⲉ طلب, K 171 B ⲛⲓⲣ. 'ⲋ (var + رومي). *V* JEA 14 24.

ⲣⲓⲙⲉ SAA², -ⲙⲓ BF, ⲗⲓⲙⲙ F vb intr, *weep*: Ge 21 16 SB, Is 30 19 SBF, Jo 11 31 SA²B, Ro 12 15 SBF, MG 25 215 B wherefore ⲧⲉⲣ.? κλαίειν; Job 3 24 SB, Jo 11 35 SA² (B diff) δακρύειν; Mt 11 17 B (S ⲧⲟⲉⲓⲧ) θρηνεῖν; PS 61 S ⲁⲥⲣ. ϩⲛⲟⲩⲁϣⲕⲁⲕ, AP 21 A² ⲁϥⲣ. as he looked, AM 279 B ⲉⲅⲣ. ⲉⲅⲡⲉϩⲛⲓ; c ⲉ-, *w. about, for*: Lev 10 6 SB, Jer 41 5 SB, Mk 5 39 S (var ⲉⲧⲃⲉ-) B κλ. acc; BM 174 1 S ⲉϥⲣ. ⲉⲡⲉϥⲙⲟⲩ ὀδύρεσθαι acc; AZ 21 142 S ⲁⲅⲣ. ⲉⲡⲉⲧⲙⲟⲟⲩⲧ, TT 35 S ⲧⲏⲣ. ⲉⲣⲟⲛ ⲙⲙⲁⲅⲁⲁⲡ, Miss 4 179 B ⲁⲅⲣ. ⲉⲣⲟϥ (sc dying man); *w. to*: Bor 265 88 S forgive them ⲉⲧⲣ. ⲉⲣⲟⲕ, CO 254 24 S (?); c ⲉϩⲟⲩⲛ ⲉ-, *w. to*: PS 7 S ⲉⲅⲣ. ⲉϥ. ⲉⲡⲉⲅⲉⲣⲏⲩ, BMis 481 S ⲁϥϭⲱ ⲉϥⲣ. ⲉϥ. ⲉⲣⲟϥ saying; ⲉϥ. ⲉϩⲣⲛ-: Jud 14 16 S κλ. πρός; BKU 1 181 F ⲁϥⲗ. ⲉϥ. ⲉϩⲗⲉⲅ ⲡⲡⲉⲁⲅⲅⲉⲗⲟⲥ κλ. ἔμπροσθεν τῶν; ⲉϭ. ϩⲉⲛ-: DeV 1 48 B all creatures ⲣ. ⲉϭ. ϩⲉⲛⲡϩⲟ of one another: c ⲉϫⲛ-, *w. about, for*: Jud 11 37 S (B ⲉϩⲣⲏⲓ ⲉϫ.), 2 Kg 1 24 SB κλ. ἐπί, Jer 9 1 B κλ. acc; Si 38 16 S δάκρυα κατάγειν ἐπί; Mor 18 76 S ⲉⲓⲣ. ⲁⲛ ⲉ. ⲡⲉⲕⲡⲱϣⲉ ⲉⲃⲟⲗ = ib 19 84 S ⲉⲧⲃⲉ- = Miss 4 147 B ⲉϫ., C 86 37 B ⲙⲡⲉⲣⲣ. ⲉⲣⲟⲓ ...ⲣ. ⲉϫⲉⲛⲑⲏⲛⲟⲩ; ⲉϩⲣⲁⲓ, -ⲛⲓ ⲉϫ.: Nu 11 13 S (var ⲉ-)B, Lu 19 41 SB κλ. ἐπί; TstAb 179 B ⲁϥⲣ. ⲉϥ. ⲉ. ⲡⲉϥⲓⲱⲧ; FR 76 S ⲁϥⲣ. ⲉⲡⲉⲥⲛⲧ ⲉϫⲱⲥ; c ⲉⲡϣⲱⲓ ϩⲁ-, *w. toward*: C 89 68 B ⲣ. ⲉⲡ. ϩⲁⲡϭⲉ; c π-, *weep about, for*: Deu 34 8 S (var & B ⲉ-) κλ. acc, Lu 23 28 S (B ⲉϫ.) κλ. ἐπί; ShLeyd 410 S ⲉⲧⲛⲁⲣ. ⲙⲡⲁⲓ ⲏ ⲉϫⲙⲡⲁⲓ, ShA 1 259 S ϩⲉⲛⲡϣⲟⲩⲣ. ⲡⲁⲩ, DeV 2 173 B ⲣ. ⲛⲉⲙⲁⲓ ⲛⲡⲁⲙⲟⲛⲟⲅⲉⲛⲏⲥ (var ⲉϫ.); c ⲛⲥⲁ-, *w. after*: ShMIF 23 199 S ⲉϣⲁⲩⲣ. ⲡⲥⲱϥ because he hath gone, AM 65 B at departure ⲉⲅⲣ. ⲡ. ⲥⲱϥ ⲧⲏⲣⲟⲩ.

—— SABF nn m, *weeping*: Job 16 16 SB, Mt 13 42 SBF κλαυθμός; Ps 115 8 S (B pl) δάκρυον; Mt 2 18 SB θρῆνος, Zech 11 3 A (B ϩⲛϩⲓ) θρηνεῖν; BG 136 S ϩⲁϩ ⲡⲣ. ⲉϥⲉⲓⲣⲉ ⲙⲙⲟⲟⲩ, ShA 1 284 S ϩⲉⲛⲡⲣ. ⲙⲡⲉⲛⲣⲙⲉⲓⲟⲟⲩⲉ *weeping & tears* (cf Mal 2 13), R 1 2 58 S sign of repentance is ⲡⲣ., BSM 36 B eyes heavy ⲉⲑⲃⲉⲡⲓⲣ.

ϫⲓ, ϭⲓ ⲣⲓⲙⲉ, SBF, *weep*: 2 Kg 1 24 S κλ., Lam 5 13 BF (S ⲣ.) κλαυθμὸν λαμβάνειν; Tob 10 6 S θρηνεῖν.

ⲣⲙⲉⲓⲏ, -ⲉⲓⲉ S, ⲣⲙⲙⲓⲏ Sᶠ, ⲣⲙⲓⲉⲓ A, ⲉⲣⲙⲏ B, ⲗⲉⲙⲓⲏ F, ⲉⲙⲣⲏ O, pl ⲣⲙⲉⲓⲟⲟⲩⲉ S, ⲣⲙⲏⲉⲅⲉ, ⲣⲙⲓⲉⲅⲉ A, ⲉⲣⲙⲱⲟⲩⲓ B, ⲣⲉⲙⲓⲁⲅⲓ, ⲗⲉⲙⲓⲁⲅⲉ, -ⲁⲅⲓ F, ⲉⲣⲙⲟⲟⲩ O & sg as pl, nn f, *tear*: Ps 38 12 SB, Si 22 20 SA ϩⲉⲛⲣⲙⲓⲉⲓ, Jer 13 17 SB, Ap 7 17 SB δάκρυον; ShBMOr 8800 4 S ⲧⲣ. ⲕⲱⲧⲉ ϩⲛⲡⲉϥⲃⲁⲗ, R 2 1 48 S ⲡⲉⲙⲕⲁϩ ⲙⲛⲧⲣ., Mor 27 27 Sᶠ ⲧⲡⲏⲧⲛ ⲡⲣⲙⲙⲓⲏ, MG 25 167 B ⲟⲩⲉⲣ., C 89 175 B eyes ⲙⲉϩ ⲉⲡⲉⲣ., Mor 30 27 F ϩⲛⲗⲉⲙⲓⲏ, AZ 21 100 bis O ⲉⲓⲁⲧⲉ ϫⲁ ⲉⲙⲣⲏ; pl forms: Ps 6 6 SB, 2 Tim 1 4 SB δά.; BHom 136 S ⲡⲱϣⲧ ⲛⲛⲉⲕⲣ., DeV 1 117 B speaking ϫⲉⲛϩⲁⲡⲉⲣ., Mal 2 13 A ϩⲉⲛⲣⲙⲓⲉⲅⲉ, Mic 2 6 A ⲟⲩⲣⲙⲏⲉⲅⲉ (S ϩⲉⲛⲣ.), He 5 7 F ϩⲛⲗⲉⲙⲓⲁⲅⲉⲓ, Mor 24 26 F -ⲁⲅⲓ, AZ 21 100 O ⲡⲉⲣⲙⲟⲟⲩ ⲡⲓⲉⲧⲉ.

ϯ ⲣⲙⲉⲓⲏ, ⲉⲣⲙⲏ SB, *give tears, weep*: Si 34 14 S, Jo 11 35 B (SA² ⲣⲓⲙⲉ) δακρύειν; Job 16 20 S (B ⲧⲁϩⲟ ⲉⲣ.) στάζειν; Bor 256 149 S ⲁⲡⲁⲃⲁⲗ ϯ ⲣ., C 89 27 B sim, KKS 518 S ⲉⲥⲣⲓⲙⲉ ⲉⲥϯ ⲣⲙⲉⲓⲉ.

ⲣⲱⲙⲉ SAA²O (Hor 79, PGM 1 52), ⲣⲱⲙⲓ BF, ⲗⲱⲙⲓ, ⲗⲟ.(MR 5 37)F, ⲣⲱⲙ- S, ⲣⲟⲙ- O, ⲣⲙ- SAA², ⲣⲉⲙ- SBF, ⲗⲉⲙ-, ⲗⲉ(ⲙ)- F (cf ⲉⲣⲙⲟ- AZ 43 89) nn m f, *man, human being*: ἄνθρωπος pass, ἀνήρ pass; Is 56 2 SB ⲣ....ⲣ. ⲁⲛ....ⲁⲛⲑ.; Job 36 25 SB βροτός; f Pro 7 4 SA (B diff) γνώριμος; m & f: ShA 2 213 S ⲣ....ⲉⲓⲧⲉ ϩⲟⲟⲩⲧ ⲉⲓⲧⲉ ⲥϩⲓⲙⲉ, BSM 51 B ⲡⲁⲓⲣ. Dorotheus & Theopiste, Miss 4 715 S ϩⲉⲛⲣ. brought their daughter; *inner man*; Eph 3 17 S ⲡⲣ. ⲉⲧϩⲓϩⲟⲩⲛ B ⲉⲧⲥⲁϧⲟⲩⲛ ὁ ἔσω ἄνθ.; adj *human*: Nu 5 6 B ⲛⲧⲉ ⲡⲓⲣ. (S ⲙⲛⲧⲣ.), ib 19 18 S (B diff), Ez 4 12 SB, 1 Cor 4 3 S (B ⲙⲉⲧⲣ.) ⲛⲣ., Ro 6 19 S ⲕⲁⲧⲁ ⲣ. (B do) ἀνθρώπινος; cf ϧⲱⲥ ⲣ., *because of human frailty*: Leyd 468 S, BIF 13 106 S, C 41 47 B (cf BMar 114 ϧⲱⲥ ⲥϩⲓⲙⲉ); *any one, no one*: Mk 11 25 S (B diff) τις, Ez 44 2 B (S Baouit 55 ⲗⲁⲁⲩ) οὐδείς, Pcod 18 S ⲙⲙⲉϥⲕⲁ ⲣ. ⲉⲉⲓⲙⲉ, Cai ostr 46304 49 S ⲙⲡⲣⲧⲁⲁⲥ ⲛⲣ., ShR 2 3 61 S ⲡⲣ. ⲡⲣ. *every one in whom God dwelleth* (cf Nu 30 3 S), ShC 73 73 S sim; *kinsman, friend, serving-man*: Mk 3 21 S (B ⲡⲏ ⲉⲧⲉⲛⲟⲩϥ) οἱ παρ' αὐτοῦ, ib 5 19 S (B do) οἱ σοί, Si 40 25 S ⲡⲉⲕⲣ. ἑταῖρος; ShA 2 277 S your children, brethren & ⲡⲉⲧⲡⲣ. ⲧⲏⲣⲟⲩ, Miss 4 546 S ⲡⲁⲣ. = C 89 61 B ⲡⲁⲡⲁⲛⲓ, TT 109 S ⲡⲉϥⲣ. ⲕⲁⲧⲁ

ⲥⲁⲣⲝ, Wess 11 164 S ⲛⲉⲕⲣ. = C 89 103 B ⲡⲉⲕⲓⲟϯ,
BSM 72 B made feast ϥ ⲛⲟⲩⲣ., J 89 7 S we grieved
I & ⲡⲁⲣ. ⲧⲏⲣⲟⲩ, COAd 63 S greets brother &
ⲡⲉϥⲣ. ⲧ., Ep 268 S ⲡⲉⲓⲣ. ⲉⲡⲱⲡⲉ, CMSS 45 F ⲡⲁⲗ.;
PLond 4 490 S ⲡⲉⲓⲣ. *fellow townsman* (?), BM 545
6 B ⲁⲡⲟⲩ ⲓⲁⲕⲱⲃ ⲡⲉϥⲣ.; rarely *husband*: AM 174
B.   ⲫⲣ. ⲙⲡⲓⲃⲁⲗ B *pupil* (image reflected in) *of
eye*: K 75 انسان العين. *Cf* ⲁⲗⲱ *pupil*. With ⲛ-
of apposition: Ge 9 20 SB ⲣ. ⲡⲟⲩⲟⲓⲛ ἄνθ. γεωργός,
Ps 36 37 B ⲣ. ⲛϭⲓⲣⲏⲛⲓⲕⲟⲥ S ⲣ. ⲛⲣⲉϥⲣ ⲉⲓⲣⲏⲛⲏ ἄνθ.
εἰρ., Is 41 7 SB ⲣ. ⲛⲣⲁⲙϣⲉ ἀν. τέκτων, Ez 3 26 SB
ⲣ. ⲛⲣⲉϥⲥⲟⲟⲣⲉ ἀν. ἐλέγχων; Miss 4 708 S ⲣ. ⲙⲡⲣⲟⲫⲏⲧⲏⲥ, J 104 15 S ⲣ. ⲛⲁⲡⲓⲥⲧⲟⲥ; without ἄνθ., ἀν.:
Ez 31 12 B ⲣ. ⲛϣⲉⲙⲙⲟ ἀλλότριος, Va 63 81 B ⲣ.
ⲛⲟⲩⲣⲟ βασιλικός, AP 8 A² ⲣ. ⲛⲡⲗⲁⲛⲟⲥ πλανῶν;
Wor 293 S ⲣ. ⲛⲣⲕⲁⲧⲏⲥ, MIE 2 386 B ⲣ. ⲛⲙⲁⲛ-
ⲉⲥⲱⲟⲩ = BAp 106 S ϣⲱⲥ, DeV 2 284 B ⲣ. ⲛϩⲁⲙ-
ⲛⲟⲩⲃ(With these *cf* PCai 1 119 γραμματηφόρος ἄνθ.,
Synax 1 312 رجل شيخ, Miss 4 437 زجاج (',); with
preceding nn or adj: Mt 13 28 SBF ⲭⲁϫⲉ ⲛⲣ.
ἐχθρὸς ἄνθ., MG 25 241 B ⲉⲣⲅⲁⲧⲏⲥ ⲛⲣ. ἐργ., Miss
4 750 S ⲉⲗⲗⲟ ⲛⲣ., BMEA 10585 F ϩⲉ(ⲛ)ⲗⲉⲃⲉⲗ
ⲛⲁⲃⲓ (ⲛ)ⲗ., Va 59 154 B ⲙⲟⲛⲁⲭⲟⲥ ⲛⲣ., Ryl 273 S
ⲁⲡⲁⲅⲅⲉⲟⲛ ⲛⲣ.   ⲛⲟϭ ⲛⲣ. *v* ⲛⲟϭ.

ⲙⲁⲥ ⲛⲣ. S, *born of man*: ShIF 288.

ⲁⲧⲣ. SA²B, *without man, friendless*: AP 16 A²
ϣⲙⲙⲱ ⲛⲁ. ἐρῆμος, P 44 73 S ⲁⲡⲁⲡⲣⲟⲥ · ⲛⲁ.;
Mor 40 5 S Diocletian was ⲁ. = C 43 36 B, Miss
4 729 S ⲟⲩⲉⲃⲓⲏⲛ ⲛⲁ., MIF 9 16 S linen cloths in
tomb ⲉⲩⲕⲏ ⲉϩⲣⲁⲓ ⲛⲁ., Ann 23 221 S lion ⲁϥⲣ
ⲛⲉⲣⲓⲟⲟⲩⲉ ⲛⲁ., BM 1224 A² ⲉϥⲉ ⲛⲁ. ϩⲛⲡⲉⲓⲕⲛⲟⲛ *in
prison*; ⲙⲛⲧⲁⲧⲣ. S, *friendlessness*: BAp 82, TT
75, Z 231.

ⲙⲁⲓ ⲣ., *man-loving, kind*   *v* ⲙⲉ *love*.

ⲙⲁⲥⲧⲉ ⲣ., *man-hating*   *v* ⲙⲟⲥⲧⲉ.

ⲙⲛⲧ-, ⲙⲉⲧⲣ. SB, *humanity*: 1 Cor 4 3 B (S ⲣ.),
Ro 6 19 B (S ⲕⲁⲧⲁ ⲣ.) ἀνθρώπινος, CaiEuch 407 B
ⲧⲉⲕⲙⲉⲧⲛⲟⲩϯ...ⲧⲉⲕⲙ. ἀνθρωπότης; PS 10 S ⲡⲛⲉⲡ-
ⲛⲟⲥ ⲛⲧⲙ., Mus 42 227 S ⲟⲩⲙⲉⲉⲩⲉ ⲙⲙ., BSM 7
B *father of* ϯⲙ. ⲧⲏⲣⲥ, CA 94 S ⲧⲉϥⲙ. ⲉⲧⲛⲁⲛⲟⲩⲥ
good disposition;   *company of men* (?): ShC 73 158
S when brethren go anywhere ϣⲁϩⲣⲁⲓ ⲉⲩⲙ. all
shall walk together, *ib* 61 nuns may not visit monks
nor ⲃⲱⲕ ⲉⲧⲉⲩⲙ., *ib* 65 none may chant where
corpse lieth nor ϩⲛⲧⲙ. whilst walking to burial;
ⲙⲛⲧⲕⲁⲧⲁⲣ.: Pcod 31 S heart wherein is not ⲙ.

ⲣ, ⲉⲣ ⲣ. SB, *become man*: Z 242 S took flesh
ⲁϥⲣ ⲣ. = CaiEuch 292 B ἐνανθρωπεῖν;   ϫⲓⲛⲉⲣ
ⲣ. B, *act of becoming man*: Cat 119 ϯϫ. ⲙⲡⲉⲛⲥⲱⲧⲏⲣ.

ⲣⲙ- &c as above, *man* (m or f) *of, from*, pref
of nn, a + ⲛ- (ⲉ-): 1 Cor 15 48 B ⲣⲉⲙⲛⲕⲁϩⲓ χοϊκός,
Ge 16 12 B ⲣⲉⲙⲛⲕⲟⲓ ἄγροικος, Zech 13 7 SA

ⲣⲙⲛϯⲙⲉ (B ⲣⲉⲙⲃⲁⲕⲓ) πολίτης, Ps 38 12 SB ⲣⲙ-
ⲛϭⲟⲓⲗⲉ πάροικος, Ez 23 23 S ⲣⲙⲛⲥⲟⲉⲓⲧ (B ⲣⲉⲙ-
ⲥⲏⲛ) ὀνομαστός, Deu 1 13 S ⲣⲙⲛⲣⲏⲧ συνετός,
ⲣⲙⲙⲙⲉ *v* ⲙⲉ *truth*, Ac 10 7 S ⲣⲙⲛⲛⲟⲩⲧⲉ εὐσεβής,
Is 37 9 B ⲣⲉⲙⲛⲣⲱⲃ ἄγγελος, Nu 11 21 SB ⲣⲙ-
ⲛⲣⲁⲧⲟⲩ πεζός (Jth 1 4 ⲣⲙⲣⲁⲧⲟⲩ); PS 52 S ⲣⲙ-
ⲛⲟⲩⲟⲓⲛ, ShC 73 46 S ⲣⲙⲛⲣⲁⲛ, BM 1008 S
ⲣⲙⲉⲛⲡⲱϣ, Mor 24 17 F ⲗⲉⲙⲉⲥⲁⲣⲝ, EW 46 B
ⲣⲉⲙⲙⲙⲁⲩ *native there*, BMis 89 S ⲣⲙⲛϭⲓⲛ (var
Mor 33 32 ⲣⲙϭⲓⲛ);   f: ShC 73 61 S ⲧⲣⲙⲛⲏ (*v*
p 66 above), PS 124 S Mary ϯⲣⲙⲛⲕⲁϩ;   or with
adj: Rom 6 6 S ⲣⲙⲛⲁⲥ παλαιός ἄνθ.;   rarely with
vb: BMis 530 S ⲟⲩⲣⲙⲛϩⲓⲁⲕⲟⲛⲉⲓ ⲕⲁⲗⲱⲥ, ShC 73
101 S ⲣⲙⲛⲟⲩⲉⲣϣⲁⲣⲡⲉ...ⲣⲙⲛⲡⲉⲓⲣⲉ.   **b** without
ⲛ-: Ps 36 11 SB ⲣⲙⲣⲁϣ, -ⲣⲁϣⲛ πραΰς, Jo 10 12 B
ⲣⲉⲙⲃⲉⲭⲉ μισθωτός (*cf* ⲗⲉⲃⲉⲕⲏ), Lu 15 15 S ⲣⲙ-
ϯⲙⲉ (var ⲣⲙⲛ-) B ⲣⲉⲙⲃⲁⲕⲓ (var ⲣⲉⲙⲙ-) πολίτης,
Bor 225 2 S ⲣⲙⲟⲩϯⲙⲉ, MG 25 241 B ⲣⲉⲙⲟⲩⲱⲓ
ἐργάτης, ⲣⲙⲙⲁⲟ *q v*; Rec 6 186 B ⲣⲉⲙⲟⲱⲡ (*cf*
Bor 256 149 S ⲣⲙⲛⲧⲱⲡ), CMSS 63 F ⲣⲉⲙⲡⲱⲗⲓⲥ,
BM 834 36 B ⲣⲉⲙⲫⲓⲁ, *ib* 663 F ⲗⲉⲙϣⲧⲟⲗⲓ;
obscure ⲣⲙⲕⲗⲕⲙ (*v* ⲕⲗⲕⲙ), ⲣⲙⲣⲛⲉⲣ *q v*.   **c**
with place-name: Deu 23 7 S ⲣⲙⲛⲕⲏⲙⲉ, Ac 7 24
F ⲗⲉⲙⲛⲕ., Is 30 7 F ⲗⲉⲙⲕ. Αἰγύπτιος (*cf* ἐρμοχύ-
μιος AZ 43 158), Job 42 18 S ⲣⲙⲧⲁⲣⲁⲃⲓⲁ Ἀρά-
βισσα, Jer 35 1 B ⲣⲉⲙⲧⲁⲃⲁⲱⲛ ἀπὸ Γ.; BMEA
10576 F ⲗⲉⲙⲕⲏⲙⲓ, Kr 22 F ⲗⲉⲙⲗⲁⲕⲁⲧⲓ, *ib* 226 F
ⲗⲉⲙⲁⲣⲏⲥ, BM 1234 F ⲗⲉ(ⲙ)ⲛⲟⲩϭⲓⲣⲓ, J 34 2 S
ⲣⲙⲛⲕⲏⲙⲉ, *ib* 67 130 S ⲣⲙⲛⲡⲟⲗⲓⲥ ⲕⲱⲥ, J&C 92 S
ⲣⲙⲛⲧⲱⲣⲉ, WS 64 S ⲣⲙⲛⲣⲁϭⲉ, CO 392 S ⲧⲣⲙⲥⲛⲏ;
without art S (Theban): ST 54 ⲕⲁⲣⲁϣⲓⲣⲉ ⲣⲙⲉⲛ-
ⲁⲡⲏ, *ib* 435 ⲕⲩⲣⲓⲕⲱⲥ ⲣⲙⲛⲭⲏⲙⲉ, BM 478 ⲕⲩⲣⲟⲥ
ⲣⲙⲛⲁⲡⲁⲣⲓ;   ⲣⲱⲙ- S, ⲣⲟⲙ- O: PLond 4 441
ⲣⲱⲙⲧⲕⲛⲟⲟⲩ, *ib* 492 ⲣⲱⲙⲃⲁⲃⲩⲗⲱⲛ, Ryl 218 ⲣⲱⲙ-
ⲥⲃⲏⲣⲧ, CO 404 ⲣⲱⲙⲭⲏⲙⲉ, Bodl(P) c 12 ⲡⲉⲣⲱⲙ-
ⲁⲡⲁ ⲓⲉⲣ(ⲉ)ⲙⲓⲁⲥ, Ny Carlsberg stele 337 ⲧⲣⲱⲙⲧⲃⲱ,
CO 449 ⲣⲟⲩⲙⲧⲁⲃⲉⲛⲉ;   rarely + ⲛ-: AZ 28 50 O
ⲧⲣⲟⲙⲛⲁⲧⲣⲓⲛⲉ, BKU 1 35 ⲣⲱⲙⲛⲁⲡⲉ, Ryl 194 ⲣⲱⲙ-
ⲛⲣⲁϭⲉ;   seldom ⲣⲱⲙⲉ except with ϣⲙⲟⲩⲛ (*l* ?
ⲣⲱⲙ ⲉϣ.): Kr 74, 85, Ryl 120, 158 f, BM 1013,
1068 ⲛⲣ. ϣ., PMich 593 H ⲣ. ⲛϯⲙⲉ (var ⲣⲙⲛ-).

ⲣⲉϥ- SAA²B, ⲣϥ- SA, ⲗⲉϥ-, ⲗⲉⲃ- F (from ⲣⲙ
ⲉϥ-, *v* below) pref forming agent of vb (rarely qual):
Jo 4 23 SA²B ⲣⲉϥⲟⲩⲱϣⲧ προσκυνητής, Ex 4 10 SA
-ϣⲁϫⲉ εὔλογος, Sa 9 15 S -ⲧⲁⲕⲟ φθαρτός, Ap 3 3
SB -ϫⲓⲟⲩⲉ κλέπτης, Is 14 4 B -ϣϯ ἀπαιτῶν, Cl
20 11 A -ⲥⲱⲛⲧ δημιουργός, Ps 37 20 SB -ⲙⲟⲟⲩⲧ
νεκρός, Z 278 S -ϫⲡⲉ ⲡⲉ θεοτόκος, Ps 9 20 S -ⲥⲙⲛ
ⲛⲟⲙⲟⲥ νομοθέτης, Si 23 11 S -ⲁϣⲁⲓ ⲛⲱⲣⲕ πολύορκος, Is 1 4 SBF -ⲣ ⲛⲟⲃⲉ ἁμαρτωλός, Ac 8 9 S
-ⲣ ϩⲓⲕ μαγεύων, Ex 2 14 SAB -ϯ ϩⲁⲡ δικαστής,
Mt 14 2 SB -ϯ ⲱⲙⲥ βαπτιστής, Sa 14 31 S -ϫⲓ
ⲛϭⲟⲛⲥ ἄδικος, Ps 8 3 B -ϭⲓ ⲙⲡϣⲓϣ ἐκδικητής, Jo

8 44 *SA²B* -ϫⲓ, -ϫⲉ ϭⲟⲗ ψεύστης, Ps 11 3 *S* -ϫⲉ
ⲛⲟϭ ⲛϣⲁϫⲉ μεγαλορρήμων; PS 91 *S* -ⲛⲟⲩϭⲙ,
CaiEuch 361 *B* -ⲃⲏϣ, PS 107 *S* -ϣⲟⲟⲣ, Tri 383
S -ϫⲟⲟⲣ (cf 1 Kg 2 4 ⲛϫⲱⲱⲣⲉ), ShZ 463 *S* -ⲧⲁⲕⲉ
ϩⲏⲧ ⲡⲣⲱⲙⲉ, P 129²⁰ 122 *S* hast created me ⲡⲣ.
ⲡⲁⲩ ⲉⲣⲟⲓ, R 1 ι 80 *S* -ϫⲓ ⲣⲱⲙⲉ ⲉϩⲣⲁⲓ to heaven,
Mor 24 26 *F* ⲗⲉϩⲉⲗ ⲡⲁϩⲓ, ib 15 ⲗⲉ(ϩ)ⲥⲱⲧⲙ, CMSS
78 *F* ⲗⲉⲃⲱϣ, Kr 13 *F* ⲗⲉⲃⲡⲟϣⲛ, ⲗⲉⲗⲡ.; wrongly
(late) with nn: PSBA 29 193 *S* Barsoma son of
ⲡⲣⲉϥⲧⲱϩ = *ib* 143 التَّبَّان *straw-seller*, or not agent:
Job 15 16 *B* ⲣⲉϥⲥⲱ ποτός.

    ⲣⲙ ⲉϥ- *AA²*: El 88, 98 *A* -ⲙⲁⲧ, Jo 9 8*A²* -ⲧⲱϩⲣ
(*S* ⲣⲉϥⲧ.), ib 25 -ⲣ ⲡⲁⲃⲉ (*S* do).   ⲙⲛⲧⲣⲉϥ- *S*:
BMar 99˙ ⲧⲉϥⲙ. ⲣ ϣⲁ; ⲙⲉⲧⲣⲉϥ- *B*: Ro 1 18 ⲙ.
ϭⲓ ⲛϫⲟⲛⲉ (*S* ⲛϫⲓⲛϭ.) ἀδικία.

    In names: Πρεμεβῦθις, Πρεμπαμοῦνις, Πρωμ-
πετό, Τρομπαβεῖτις, Τροντναιῶς, Τρωβλακότη (?
ⲧⲣⲱⲙⲣⲁⲕⲟⲧⲉ) (Preisigke).

    ⲣⲙⲙⲁⲟ *SAA²*, ⲣⲁⲙⲁⲟ *B*, ⲣⲉⲙⲙⲉⲁ, ⲗⲉⲙⲙⲉⲁ,
-ⲁⲁ, ⲗⲉⲙⲉⲁ, -ⲁⲁ, ⲗⲉⲙⲁⲁ, ⲗⲓⲙⲙⲁ (Eccl 10 6) *F*,
f (?) ⲣⲙⲙⲁⲱ *A²* (AP 15), pl ⲣⲙⲙⲁⲁⲉⲓ, -ⲁⲁⲓ *A*,
ⲣⲙⲙⲁⲟⲓ, -ⲱⲓ (Jer 24 ι), -ⲟⲩ *B* & sg as pl, *great
man*, whence *rich man*, v ⲣⲱⲙⲉ (ⲣⲙ-): Ge 13 2
SB, Is 53 9 *SA*(Cl ⲣⲙⲙⲁⲁⲓ) *B*, Ja 2 6 *SB* (-ⲁⲟⲓ
var -ⲁⲱⲟⲩ), Ap 6 15 *SBF* (ⲗⲉⲙⲉⲁⲁ) πλούσιος; Pro
23 ι *S* (var ϫⲱⲱⲣⲉ) δυνάστης; Job 1 3 *SB* εὐγενής;
Ac 17 4 *S* (*B* ϩⲟⲩⲁ†) πρῶτος; Mt 13 52 *S* (*B* diff)
οἰκοδεσπότης; TT 49 *S* ⲟⲩⲛⲟϭ ⲡⲣ., DeV 2 10 *B*
ⲡⲓⲣ. ⲉⲁⲕⲉⲣ ϩⲏⲕⲓ, TU 43 13 *A* ⲛⲣⲙⲙⲁⲁⲉⲓ, C 86
100 *B* ⲡⲉⲥⲣⲁⲙⲁⲟⲓ, Ryl 436 *B* ⲟⲩⲣ. ⲛⲥϩⲓⲙⲓ; as
adj: Is 32 9 *SBF* ⲣⲉⲙⲙⲉⲁ), ib 33 20 *SBF* (ⲗⲉⲙⲙⲉⲁ) πλούσιος; Z 611 *S* ⲡⲣⲱⲙⲉ ⲛⲣ.

    ⲙⲛⲧ-, ⲙⲉⲧⲣ. λ. *SABF*, *riches, wealth*: Deu 33
19 *SB*, Pro 3 16 *SAB*, EpJer 34 *BF* (-ⲗⲉⲙⲉⲁ),
Ro 11 33 *SSƒ* (-ⲣⲉⲙⲙⲁⲟ MR 2 70)*F* (-ⲗⲉⲙⲁⲁ Mor
43 299), Eph 1 18 *SBF* (do Mich 550) πλοῦτος;
Pro 8 21 *SA* (*B* = Gk), He 10 34 *SB* ὕπαρξις; Ez
38 12 *B* κτῆσις; BM 217 22 *S* ⲧⲙ. opp ⲧⲙⲛⲧϩⲏⲕⲉ,
BSM 51 *B* ⲟⲩⲛⲓϣⲧ ⲡⲙ. = BMis 403 *S*.   ⲣ ⲙ.:
Ro 11 12 *S* ⲣ ⲙ. *B* ⲉⲣ ⲟⲩⲙ. πλοῦτος.

    ⲣ, ⲉⲣ ⲣ. *SB*, *become, make rich*: Ps 48 17 *SB*,
Lu 1 53 *SB* πλουτεῖν, 1 Kg 2 7 *B* (*S* † ⲙⲛⲧⲣ.), Pro
10 4 *SAB*, 2 Cor 6 10 *SB* πλουτίζειν; Sa 10 10 *S*
εὐπορεῖν; AM 184 *B* ⲡⲁϫⲟⲓ ϥⲁⲓ ⲡⲁⲁⲓⲧ ⲡⲣ., EpApp
1 123 *S* soul ⲁⲥⲣ ⲣ. ϩⲣⲉⲛⲉⲛⲉⲣⲅⲓⲁ ⲡⲓⲙ.

    In names: ⲡⲣⲙⲁⲟ (Hall 143), ⲡⲣⲱⲙⲁⲟ (BIF 3
208), Πρωμαῶς, Πρωμό (Preisigke), Πρωμοου
(PLond 4 234).

    In place-name (?): ⲣⲱⲙⲁⲩ (ST 213), ⲣⲁⲙⲁⲟⲩ
(TurO 4), ⲣⲱⲙⲟⲟⲩ (J 108 9) &c. *Cf* RylDem 3
161 n, 435.

    ⲣⲁⲙⲱⲡⲉ, -ⲙⲟⲩⲡⲉ, or ? ⲣⲁⲙⲱⲡ, -ⲙⲟⲩⲡ *S* nn m,
part of door, post?: BP 9446 letter asks ϣⲁⲙ to make

ⲡⲓⲕⲟⲩⲓ ⲡⲣⲁⲙⲟⲩⲡⲉ[, ⲡⲣⲁⲙⲟⲩⲡ ⲉⲡⲁⲡⲟⲩϥ, sends its
measurements & refers to ⲡϩⲃⲥ, ⲧⲡⲡⲏ & ⲧϫⲟ,
ST 120 list of *varia* ⲟⲩⲣⲁⲙⲱⲡⲉ ⲛ̄ⲣⲟ (or ? ⲉⲛ̄ⲣⲟ).
Cf ? Berl *Wörterb* 2 420 rmn.

    ⲣⲙⲟⲛⲧ, ⲣⲙⲟⲟⲧ *S* nn f, *shivering, ague*: Miss
4 530 ⲉⲣⲉⲡⲉϥⲥⲱⲙⲁ ⲡⲉϩ ⲣ. (cf ⲡⲉϩ ϣⲗϥ) = C 89 49
B ϩⲟⲣϣ ⲉⲣⲟϥ (v ⲁⲣⲟϣ) αὐτῷ ῥίγωντι = MG 17
552 مريضا الحُمَّة, BM 355 317 body enfeebled by
ⲡⲉϩⲙⲟⲙ ⲙⲛⲧⲣⲙⲟⲟⲧ, Ryl 104 ⲧⲉⲣ. ⲙⲡⲁⲥⲓⲕ.

    ⲣⲁⲙⲡⲉⲓ, -ⲡⲓ, ⲣⲁⲡⲡⲓ *S* nn as pl, *ring*: Ex 25 12
ⲣⲁⲙ. (P 44 104, *B* ϣϭⲟⲩⲣ), ib 26 29 ⲣⲁⲡ. δακτύλιος, ShIF 182 ϩⲉⲟⲩⲁϩ...ⲉⲩⲟⲩⲧ ⲉϩⲟⲩⲛ ⲉϩⲉⲣⲡⲁⲙ

    ⲣⲟⲙⲡⲉ *S*, ⲣⲁⲙ. *SAA²O*, ⲣⲟⲙⲡⲓ *B*, ⲗⲁⲙⲡⲓ,
ⲣⲁⲙ. *F*, ⲣⲙⲡⲉ- *SA*, ⲣⲙⲡ- (in ⲣⲙⲡϣⲓⲣⲉ) *S*, pl ⲣⲁⲙ-
ⲡⲟⲟⲩⲉ *S*, -ⲡⲉⲟⲩⲉ *A* (on these v Rec 35 74), ⲣⲁⲙⲡⲉ
O (?) & sg as pl, nn f (art *S* often ⲧⲉ-), *year*: Lev 25
11 *S* (*B* om), Is 14 28 *S* ⲧⲉⲣ. *B*, Lu 13 8 *SB*, MG
25 232 *B* ⲧⲁⲓϩⲡⲓ ⲛⲣ. ἔτος; Deu 11 12 *S* ⲧⲉⲣ. *B*,
Sa 7 19 *S* ⲧⲉⲣ., Is 34 8 *S* ⲧⲉⲣ. *BF*, Jo 11 49 *SA²B*
ἐνιαυτός, Lev 9 3 *S* (*B* ⲉⲣ ⲟⲩⲣ.), Ez 46 13 *B* ἐνιαύσιος; TU 43 6 *A* after ⲕⲉⲟⲩⲏⲣ ⲛⲣ., AM 176 *B*
child shall be born ϫⲉⲡⲧⲁⲓⲣ., AZ 44 72 *S* ⲡⲉϥⲣ.
ϫⲉ ⲧⲏⲣⲟⲩ ⲉⲧⲓ ⲡ̄ⲏ̄, CO 98 *S* ⲧⲉⲣ. ⲙⲡⲁⲉⲓⲱⲧ *anniversary*, MMA 23 3 701 *S* knowest thou not ϫⲉⲧⲉⲓⲣ.
ϩⲁⲥⲉ ? (cf CO 132, BKU 1 316), Kr 140 *F* hired for
ⲟⲩⲗ. ⲛϩⲁⲟⲩ;   pl forms: Lev 25 27 *S* (var ⲣⲟⲙⲡⲉ), Ps 60 6 *S*, Joel 2 2 *A*; Hor 82 *O* ⲛⲣⲙⲡⲉ ⲡⲣⲓ-
ⲛⲟⲩ.   With ordinal *second* ⲣ. (ⲣⲙⲡⲉ-) *SA* follows
ⲙⲉϩ-, v ⲙⲟⲩϩ (ⲙⲉϩ- ⲃ), ⲥⲡⲁⲩ sf.

    ⲙⲛⲧⲛⲟϭ ⲛⲣ. *S*, *great age*: Gu 87.
    Prepositional phrases. ⲉⲓⲥ: ShA 2 342 *S* one
asked me ⲉⲓⲥ ϩⲉⲛⲣ. *years ago*, sim ShA 1 391 *S*
ϩⲁⲑⲏ ⲛⲛⲉⲓⲣ.;   ⲛ-: BM 174 ι *S* serving thee
ⲛⲧⲉⲣ. ⲧⲏⲣⲥ διὰ τοῦ ἐν., ShA 2 278 *S* had not seen
brethren ⲛⲟⲩⲣ. *for a year*, J 93 17 *S* no news of
him ⲛϩⲁϩ ⲛⲣ., Lev 25 53 *S* ⲛⲟⲩⲣ. ⲉⲣ. *B* ⲛⲟⲩⲣ.
ⲉⲃⲟⲗ ϫⲉⲟⲩⲣ. ἐν. ἐξ ἐν., ShA 1 11 *S* to visit them
ⲡⲣⲉⲛⲣ. ⲉϩⲉⲛⲣ.;   ϫⲓⲛ-: ShA 2 112 *S* have heard
ϫⲓⲛⲡⲓⲣ. ⲉⲡⲓⲣ., Hor 83 *O* ⲛⲡⲭⲓⲣ. ⲛⲃ̄ ⲁϩⲣⲏⲉⲓ;   ϩⲛ-,
ϫⲉⲛ-: J 36 16 *S* ϩⲛⲧ†ⲣ. that is past, *ib* 68 26 ϩⲛ-
ⲡⲉⲓⲣ. sim; Lev 23 12 *S* ⲉϥϩⲡⲟⲩⲣ. (*B* ⲉⲣ ⲟⲩⲣ.)
ἐνιαύσιος, Is 65 20 *B* ⲉϥϫⲉⲛⲣ̄ ⲛⲣ. (*S* ⲣ ϣⲉ ⲛⲣ.)
ἐτῶν; ⲕⲁⲧⲁ: J 78 24 *S* a *solidus* ⲕ. ⲣ.;   ϫⲁ-:
Ez 15 4 *B* ⲡⲉⲥⲕⲗⲏⲙⲁ ϫⲁⲣ. κατ᾽ ἐν.   ⲧⲣ., ⲛⲧⲣ.,
this year: BAp 157 *S* as last so ⲑⲉ ⲛⲧⲣ., BM 581 (2)
F ⲙⲡⲉⲧϣⲱϣⲓ ⲟⲩⲱⲗⲉ ⲧⲣ. ShP 130⁴ 140 *S* service
(διακονία) increased ⲛⲧⲣ. beyond all, Mus 11 215
S epistle written us ⲛⲧⲣ. = C 89 176 *B*, C 41 51 *B*
forbade rain ⲛⲉⲣ., MG 25 339 *B* hath rained often
ⲛⲉⲣ. = ROC 18 174 *S* ⲧⲉⲣ., RE 9 156 *S* ⲡϣⲟϣⲟⲩ
(of wine) ⲛⲧⲣ. ⲧⲁⲕⲛⲟⲩ.   †ⲕⲉⲣ. *B*, next year:
Ge 17 21 ἐν. ἕτερος.

тпр.¹, трр.², тер.³ *S*, тепр.⁴, темр.⁵, тер.⁶ *B*, тел.⁷, тл.⁸ *F*, also пт., ет., *each year, annually*, v LMis 377 : Deu 14 21 *S*¹ (var e-³) *B* п-⁴, Tob 1 7 *S*³, He 10 3 *S*²*B* e-⁵ (var п-⁵) *F* e-⁷, Mor 37 95 *S* e-³ κατ᾽ ἐν., Lu 2 41 *S*²*B* п-⁴ κατ᾽ ἔτος, Lev 23 40 *S*³*B* пте †р. τοῦ ἐν., Aeg 220 *S*³ τοῦ ἔτ., R 1 1 56 *S* ρпт.³ τοῦ ἐν., Jud 11 40 *S*²*B* ⲥ̄епте. ἐν τῷ ἐν., Deu 15 18 *S*² (var³) *B* ката р. ἐφέτιος ; Hall 113 *S* a *solidus* т.¹ & тмр., ShC 73 74 *S* four times т.², MG 17 333 *S* twice ет.³, *ib* 327 *S* sim т.³ = C 89 73 *B* п-⁴, MG 25 236 *B* once пт.⁵ (*cf ib* once п†р.), Mor 23 59 *S* when we reach this day пт.³, *ib* 48 sim³, Rec 6 17 *B* tree's 12 shoots пт.⁵ = BMar 208 *S* ката р., BP 3248 *F* rent of кес б̄ т.⁸, BM 1073 *S* rent т.³ пр. пим, Mor 24 14 *F* we rejoice this day ет.⁷

р, ер, ел р *SA²BF*, *reach year* of age, *spend year* : Ge 15 9 *B* (*S* пшомт, шмт р.) τριετίζειν, Is 15 5 *B* (*S* do) τριετὴς εἶναι, Jo 5 5 *SA²B* ἔτη ἔχειν, *ib* 2 20 *SBF* Gk no vb, Nu 28 3 *B* (*S* п- var ρп-) ἐνιαύσιος ; PS 1 *S* адр мптоүе пр. speaking with them, ShBM 209 42 *S* old men епатр ⲅⲁⲅ пр.

V also ⲉ̄рре, оүⲱм, ϣⲓре, ⲣⲱⲃ.

ромеіп *B* nn m, a plant : K 198 пир. قضاب (*sic l, cf* Schweinfurth *Ar Pfl* 74, 75. Dozy 2 361 ق *clematis*, whereof one species κλ. μυρσινοειδής, so ?? *l* морсіп μυρσίνη).

рмⲅе *SA²*, рем. *B*, ремⲅп, лемⲅп *F*, рмпϣе (R) *S* nn m, f -ⲅп *SB*, pl -ⲅееⲅе *S*, -ⲅеⲩ, -ⲅпоⲩ *B*, *free person*, v AZ 53 116, RChamp 722 : Eccl 10 17 *SF*(λιμ.), Mt 17 26 *SB*(-ⲅеⲩ), 1 Cor 7 39 *SB* f *F*, Ap 6 15 *SB* (-ⲅеⲩ) *F*, Va 57 277 *B* пиⲃⲱⲕ... пиремⲅпоⲩ ἐλεύθερος ; 1 Tim 1 10 *B*(*S* diff) реⲩ† р. еⲃол ἀνδραποδιστής ; K 163 *B* beasts wild, tame, four-footed поⲩремⲅеⲩ пемпоⲅапаⲑпма وحراً الحلال ; BMar 2 *S* еіте ⲅⲓⲅⲁⲗ еіте р., P 131¹ 86 *S* Virgin тр. *the lady* тмаⲩ епепремⲅееⲅе (ⲉⲗ. in this sense mostly untranslated : Z 269, Bor 286 48, Miss 4 239, 820, BAp 118, AM 211, ST 192, exception : ROC 25 242), DeV 2 236 *B* ye are ⲅапремⲅеⲩ еⲃол ⲥ̄епкⲩпаⲏпос пиⲃеп.

мпт-, метр. *SA²BF*, *freedom* : Lev 19 20 *SB*, Ro 8 21 *SB*, ἐλευθερία ; Aeg 269 *S* тм. еⲃол ⲅптаⲥеⲃⲓⲁ ἀπαλλαγῆναι gen, AP 33 *A²* оⲅм., BM 153 *S* тм. Prayer of *Absolution, ib* 511 (3) *S*f do, DeV 2 227 *B* beasts saved in ark, who gave them таⲓм.?

ⲕⲱ пр. *S*, *set free* : Job 39 5, Jth 16 23 ⲕⲱ еⲃол пр. ⲉⲗ. ἀφιέναι.

р, ер р. *SA²BF*, *make free, become free* : Jo 8 32 *SA²B*, MG 25 216 *B* = Z 339 *S* ϣⲱпе пр. ἐλευθεροῦν, Ex 21 2 *SB* ⲉⲗ. ἀπέρχεσθαι, 1 Cor 7 21 *SBF* ⲉⲗ. γίνεσθαι, 1 Kg 17 25 *B* (*S* ⲕⲱ еⲃол пр.), EW 194 *B* slave аріⲧⲩ пр. ⲉⲗ. ποιεῖν ; BMis 206 *S* ser-

vants аⲅаⲩ пр. = Mor 16 48 *S* адкаⲁⲩ еⲃол еⲅо пел., R 1 1 66 *S* souls пⲥⲁⲁⲩ прмⲅе (*sic* MS) Aeg 254 *S* candidates to bathe пⲥеаⲁⲩ пр. *be freed*, exorcised (Ar *pray* HSt 100 5, but Ethiop ተፍታ: *ib* 20 19), AM 220 *B* if bewitched went to shrine ϣⲁⲅер р., PSBA 19 214 *S* I adjure thee & †еіре ⲙⲙоⲕ пр. ап until thou &c, BSM 35 *B* if I bring not price take this garment, ⲕⲟⲓ пр. ⲙⲙоⲩ = BMis 379 *S* †аптаⲥⲥе ⲙⲙоⲥ пак, BMOr 6201(*sic*)*S* тетпо пр. птетпмоⲩⲅ моⲩ ⲅеплаккос, AZ 23 37 *F* аⲧⲧⲏⲥ пеі...†(е) петемоⲥ таеіⲥ (п)лемⲅп пеⲕ, BM 545 (2) *F* ϥⲱ премⲅп еп теⲩⲥⲩпаⲕⲓ *shall not be free to communicate* ; *be free, freed from*, ⲅп- *S* : 1 Cor 9 19 (*B* еⲃол ⲅⲁ-) ἐλεύθερος εἶναι ἐκ ; еⲃол ⲅп-, ⲥ̄еп- *SB* : Ro 8 2 *S* (*B* еⲃ ⲅⲁ-) ἐλευθεροῦν ἀπό, BM 247 6 *S* unless soul р р. еⲃ. ⲅптетⲅⲓⲃⲁⲗ ⲉⲗ. gen, ShC 73 5 *S* пето пр. еⲃ. ⲅптмптⲅмⲅал, DeV 2 57 *B* ϣасаⲓϥ пр. еⲃ. ⲥ̄епптпмⲱрⲓⲁ ; еⲃ. ⲅⲁ- *B* : CaiEuch 399 арітеп пр....еⲃ. ⲅапоⲃⲓ пиⲃеп ⲉⲗ. ἀπό, MIE 2 367 who оⲓ пр. еⲃ. ⲅапаⲓ (*sc* vices) ? ; Cat 13 пⲓхіпер р. еⲃ. ⲅапипаⲑоⲥ ; е- *SB* : BMis xxxix *S* мекр оⲩсооⲩпе пр. епмоⲩ, Va 61 104 *B* ϥпаер р. епиколаⲥⲓⲥ, LCyp 18 *S* sim.

As name (?) : Ῥέμη (POxy 1862).

рмⲅеⲅ *S* nn m, *pole, shaft* of cart : Glos 115 ῥυμός · пр.

ран *SBO*, рıп (Br 139, Ep 169, CO 126) *S*, реп *AA²FO*, леп *F*, реп- *SB*, рпт⸗ *SA*, репт⸗, рıпт⸗, рапт⸗ *S*, рıп⸗ *SO*, реп⸗ *BO* nn m, *name* : Ex 23 13 *S* рıпоⲩ, Pro 10 7 *SAB*, Is 30 27 *SBF*, Ap 2 17 *SB* ὄνομα, Jer 39 19 *B* ϥапипϣⲧ пр. μεγαλώνυμος, Ge 6 4 *S* (P 44 101) паϣе рıпоⲩ ὀνομαστός ; Pro 21 24 *S* ерпⲧⲩ (var рапⲧⲩ, *A* рпⲧⲩ) καλεῖσθαι ; PS 52 *S* partaken of mysteries ⲅпмеⲩр., ShRE 10 161 *S* those that are thine еаⲅⲅелоⲥ рпоⲩ ппарⲣаⲕ, ShC 42 34 we run after пр. еⲧхоⲥе, Pcod 19 *S* ⲕⲁ оⲩр. пак *leave n.* (*fame*) *behind thee*, Miss 8 55 *S* лⲓп р. ϣооп п.... пеⲥⲧⲱрⲓⲟⲥ, MIE 2 365 *B* паⲓр. хеоⲅпⲃ, BM 915 18 *B* seek not to еп оⲩр. еⲃол пⲥⲱⲕ *make repute for self*, El 40 *A* write in book поⲩр., AP 55 *A²* епеⲩр. пе ⲥⲓмⲱп, Kr 10 *F* ⲅеппл. еппоⲩтⲓ, Hor 82 *O* прмпе прıпоⲩ *years named* (*cf* DM 18 28), Wess 18 45 *S* Virgin's name о пр. ріхⲙпепмопаⲥⲧⲏрⲓⲟп, J 5 28 *S* lands come to us ⲅапр. of our father, C 43 50 *B* baptized еⲫр. ппⲥⲱⲧⲏр, Ep 149 *S* write to him епар., ST 352 *S* sim, Ep 201 *S* beg him ппар. ; Ge 32 27 *S* пıм рпⲧⲕ (varr ер., BAp 84 прапⲧⲕ, *B* пıмпе пеⲕр.) τί τὸ ὄν. σού ἐστιν ?, Mk 5 9 *S* пıм ерепⲧⲕ (*B* do) τί σοι ὄν. ?, ShA 2 118 *S* hath told you хепıм рпⲧⲩ, MG 25 232 *B* пıм ерепⲩ = Z 317 *S* пıмпе пеⲩр. ?, BIF 13 101 *S* пıм ерепппрⲱме = MG 25

284 (*sic*) *B* ;   magical uses : POslo 312 *O* Horus
αρ-χεφρε νεψουφι ριγχ, PGM 1 124 ανοχ ριγχ, *ib* 60
O ⲛⲓ ⲣⲓⲡⲕ ⲛⲓⲡⲉ ⲡⲉⲕⲣ., AZ 21 99 *O* ⲣⲁⲣⲕⲟ ⲉⲣⲓⲡⲧ
ⲣⲁⲣⲕⲟⲡⲉ ⲡⲁⲣⲉⲛ ⲛⲁⲙⲛⲧ (*cf* DM 7 31, PGM 1 4
αὐθεντικὸν ὄν.), *ib* 89 *O* sim ⲉⲣⲉⲡⲧ, *cf* PS 357 *S*
ⲭⲱⲥⲓ ⲉⲣⲓ ⲧⲁϥⲣⲱⲁⲧⲏ, KroppM *S* I adjure you
ⲙⲡⲉⲧⲛⲣ. ⲙⲡⲉⲧⲛϭⲟⲙ, BKU 1 1 vo *S* hast not
found my name ⲡⲣⲉⲙⲛⲧ (*i e* ⲣⲉⲛ ⲙⲁⲙⲛⲧ, *cf* PGM
1 48 ? ⲣⲓⲙⲛⲧ), RAl 134 *S* adjure thee ⲙⲡⲛⲟϭ ⲡⲣ.
ⲙⲡⲓⲱⲧ, Mor 41 180 *S* wizard invoked ⲛϭⲉⲡⲣ. upon
broken pieces, P 129¹⁴ 129 *S* sim ⲡⲛⲟϭ ⲡⲣ. ⲉⲧⲣⲁⲣⲟⲧⲉ
of Christ, PS 367 *S* spake ⲡⲛⲟϭ ⲡⲣ. ⲉϩⲣⲁⲓ ⲉⲭⲡⲧⲉⲅ-
ⲁⲛⲉ, Br 91 *S* ⲁⲓⲟⲡⲟⲙⲁⲍⲉ ⲙⲡⲛⲟϭ ⲡⲣ. that God told
us, BMar 38 *S* earth trembled ϩⲓⲧⲙⲡⲣ. ⲡⲛⲉϥⲙⲁⲅⲓⲁ.

✝ⲣⲉⲛ⸗ &c *SBF*, give name, call, c ⲭⲉ- : Lu 6 14
S(var ? ⲉ-, *B* ⲙⲟⲩ✝) ὀνομάζειν, Ex 16 31 *B*(*S* ⲙⲟⲩⲧⲉ) ⲉⲡⲟⲛ. ; Is 48 8 *B*(*S* do) καλεῖσθαι, Ac 1 23 *SB*
ⲉⲡⲓⲕ. ; *ib* 11 26 *B* ⲁⲩ✝ⲣⲉⲛ ⲡⲓⲙⲁⲑⲏⲧⲏⲥ(*S* do)χρημα-
τίζειν; BG 35 *S* ⲁϥ✝ⲣⲓⲛϥ ϫⲉⲁⲁⲙ, *cf ib* 53 ✝ⲣⲓⲛϥ &
✝ⲣⲡⲧⲥ, Mor 20 8 *S* ⲡⲉⲛⲧⲁⲩ✝ⲣⲓⲛϥ ϫⲉ-, MG 25 322
B ⲁⲩⲉⲣ ⲡⲕⲉ✝ⲣⲉⲛϥ ϫⲉ-, J 86 23 *S* ⲛⲧⲁⲓ✝ⲣⲁⲛϥ...ϫⲉ-,
BG 38 ⲁⲥ✝ ⲙⲡⲉϥⲣ. ϫⲉⲓⲁⲗⲁⲃⲁⲱⲑ;   with p.
as 2d acc : Ge 4 17 *S* ⲁϥ✝ⲣⲁⲛ ⲡⲣ. ⲛⲧⲡⲟⲗⲓⲥ (*B* ✝
ⲫⲣ.), *ib* 25 *B* ⲁⲥ✝ⲣⲉⲛ ⲡⲉϥⲣ. ϫⲉ- (*S* ⲙ.) ⲉⲡⲟⲛ. τὸ
ὄν., MG 25 90 *B* ⲁⲩ✝ⲣⲉⲛ ⲫⲣ. ⲛ✝ϣⲱ✝...ϫⲉ-;   c
ⲉ-, give name to : Ge 2 20 *SB*, Ps 146 4 *SB* καλ.
ὀν. dat ; Mk 3 14 *S* ⲛⲧⲁϥ✝ⲣⲓⲛⲟⲩ ⲉⲛⲁⲡⲟⲥⲧⲟⲗⲟⲥ (*B*
✝ⲣⲉⲛⲟⲩ ϫⲉ-) ὀνομάζ. acc, Eph 1 21 *BF* (*S* ⲧⲁⲅⲟ)
ὀνομάζεσθαι; ShA 1 212 *S* ⲉⲩ✝ ⲛⲟⲩⲣ. ⲉⲣⲟⲟⲩ ϫⲉ-,
C 86 273 *B* name ⲡⲉⲧⲁⲩⲧⲓⲩ ⲉⲣⲟⲓ;   c ⲉϫⲛ-,
ⲉϩⲣⲁⲓ ⲉϫ. *S*, meaning same : Ge 48 16 ⲉϩ. ⲉϫ. (*B*
ⲙⲟⲩ✝ ⲉ-...ϫⲉⲛ-) ⲉⲡⲓⲕ. ⲉⲛ; Mun 26 ⲡⲧⲁⲓ✝ ⲙⲡⲁⲣ.
ⲉϫⲱⲥ;   c ⲉϩⲟⲩⲛ *B*, give in, inscribe name : Lu
2 1 (*S* diff) ἀπογράφεσθαι.

ⲁⲧ✝ ⲣ. *S*. unnamed : BG 84 ⲟⲩⲁⲧ✝ ⲣ. ⲡⲁϥⲡⲉ.

ⲙⲟⲩⲧⲉ ⲉⲡⲣ., call a name, name, denominate : Ac
1 19 *B*(*S* om ⲡ.) καλ. ; further with ⲙⲟⲩⲧⲉ ShA
1 77 *S* knowest not ⲡⲉϥⲛⲟϭ ⲡⲣ. ⲉⲙ. ⲉⲣⲟϥ ⲙⲙⲟⲟⲩ,
BG 41 *S* ⲁⲥⲁⲕⲗⲁⲥ ⲙ. ⲉⲣⲟⲟⲩ ⲡⲛⲓⲣ. *Cf* ✝ⲣⲉⲛ⸗.

ⲧⲁⲩⲉ ⲣⲓⲛ⸗ *S*, pronounce name : Jos 23 7 (*B* ϫⲱ),
Eph 5 3 (*B* do) ὀνομάζ., Lev 24 11 (var ✝ ⲣ., *B*
ⲙⲟⲩⲧ) ⲉⲡⲟⲛ., Deu 32 3 (*B* do) καλ. ; BM 173 216
such things ⲙⲡⲣⲧⲣⲉⲩⲧ. ⲣⲓⲛⲟⲩ ⲡⲟⲏⲧⲡ ; Mus 40 275
God's fatherhood ⲛⲁⲧⲧ. ⲣⲓⲛⲥ (*cf* ἀνονόμαστος) ;
BM 525 *S* wherever they shall ⲧⲁⲟⲩⲱ ⲡⲓⲣ. ⲉϩⲣⲁⲓ
ⲉϫⲟϥ ;   c ϫⲉ- : Lev 23 35 (*B* ⲙ.) καλεῖσ. ;   c ⲡ-
dat : Is 19 17 (*B* ϫⲱ) ὀνομάζειν.

ϫⲓ ⲣ. *S*, take name, be named : Miss 8 248 Jacob
ⲛⲧⲁⲡⲓⲏⲗ ϫⲓ ⲣ. ⲉⲃⲟⲗ ⲙⲙⲁϥ (*cf* BMar 50), Mor 51
34 elders been silenced ⲁⲙⲙⲁⲓⲁⲣⲭⲉⲓ (*l* -ⲏ) ϫⲓ
ⲙⲡⲉⲩⲣ. their office.

ⲣⲁⲙⲡⲣ. *S*, office-bearer, dignitary : Mus 40 38
(Reg Pachom) none shall...ⲉⲓⲙⲏⲧⲓ ⲉⲡⲣ. ⲙⲙⲁⲧⲉ *cui*

hoc ministerium delegatur, ShP 130² 10 ϩⲉⲡⲣⲱⲙⲉ
ⲡⲟⲡⲟⲙⲁⲥⲧⲟⲥ ⲉⲧⲉⲡⲣ. ⲡⲉ, ShC 73 46 ⲟⲩⲣⲁⲙⲡⲏⲓ ⲏ
ⲟⲩⲡⲁⲧⲁⲓⲁⲕⲟⲛⲓⲁ ⲏ ⲥⲉⲗⲁⲩ ⲡⲣ.

ϩⲟⲟⲩ ⲡⲣ. *S*, official, important day : Mk 6 21 (*B*
= Gk) ἡμ. εὔκαιρος ; 1 Kg 9 12 Gk om ; name day,
commemoration : R 1 3 67 ⲉⲓⲣⲉ ⲡⲟⲩϩ. ⲡⲣ., BMar
126 remember us (martyrs) ⲙⲡⲉⲣ. ⲙⲡⲉⲣ., J 65 65
ⲡϩ. ⲡⲣ. of holy fathers.

In names : Πράν (Preisigke), ⲡⲉⲕⲣⲁⲛ (ST 242
or ? *thy namesake*), ⲡⲁⲡⲓⲣⲁⲛ (MIF 59 288, or ⲁⲡⲁ
ⲡⲓⲣⲁⲛ, *cf* Zoega 350), *cf* Πανιρέν (Preisigke), Οὐ-
σερραννουφι (PLond 1 98).

ⲣⲱⲛ *B* nn, rampart : Ez 17 17 ⲥⲉⲙⲛⲉ ⲡⲟⲩⲣⲱⲛ
ϩⲓⲣⲱϥ χαρακοβολία منجنيقات (*i e* μάγγανον P
2A 55). Or *l* ? ⲡⲟⲩⲟⲩⲣⲱⲛ (for θυρεός as Ps 34
2 *S* &c).

ⲣⲁⲛⲁ *v* ⲁⲛⲁⲓ.

ⲣⲏⲛⲉ *S* nn m, youth (?), prime (?) : Glos 334
ἀφῆλιξ · ⲡⲉⲧ[?] ⲛⲡⲃⲣ.   *Cf* ? PSBA 19 213 *S* I
am Gabriel ⲡⲉⲛⲧⲁϥⲉⲓⲛⲉ (*l* ? -ϭⲓ ⲡⲉ) (ⲙ)ⲡϣⲁⲙⲡⲟⲩⲃⲉ
ⲙⲡⲟⲩⲣⲏⲛⲉ & am come to thee (Mary) to fulfil thy
request, but *l* ? ⲡⲟⲩⲣⲏ ⲡⲉ. Ethiop ALR '97 465 76
om these words.

ⲣⲡⲉ *S*, -ⲉⲓⲉ, -ⲉⲉⲓⲉ *A*, -ⲉⲉⲓ *A*², ⲉⲣⲫⲉⲓ *B*,
ⲉⲣⲡⲏⲉⲓ, ⲉⲗⲡⲏⲓ, -ⲏⲛⲓ, -ⲏ *F*, pl ⲣⲡⲏⲩⲉ *SA*, -ⲛⲟⲩⲉ
A, ⲉⲣⲫⲏⲟⲩⲓ *B* & sg as pl, nn m, temple : Is 66 6
SB, Ez 41 25 *B* (*S* = Gk), Joel 3 5 *SAB* pl, 2 Macc
6 2 *A* -ⲉⲉⲓⲉ, Mk 14 58 *F* -ⲏⲛⲓ, Jo 2 21 *F* -ⲏ, 1 Cor
3 16 *F* -ⲏⲓ ναός ; Ez 27 6 *SB* pl, Mt 4 5 *SB*, Jo 5
14 *A*² -ⲉⲉ ἱερόν ; Ez 6 4 *SB* pl, Hos 8 14 *AB* pl
τέμενος ; R 1 1 16 *S* ϩⲉⲙϩⲁⲗ ⲡⲣⲡⲏⲩⲉ ἱερόδουλος ;
ShR 2 3 44 *S* ⲡⲉⲣ. of Atripe, Miss 4 686 *S* ⲡⲣ. of
Apollo, *ib* 113 *B* ⲡⲓⲉⲣ. of Kothos, AM 74 *B* ⲡⲓⲉⲣ.
ⲛⲧⲉ ⲥⲛ, Mun 148 *S* ⲡⲉⲣ. ⲡϣⲟⲣⲡ ⲡϣⲙⲓⲛ infected
by Origenism, so ? *church*, P 129¹⁶ 37 *S* martyr's
memorial chapel, BM 1100 *S* among churches in
Hermopolis ⲙⲓⲭ(ⲁⲏⲗ) ⲉⲡⲉⲣ., El 84 *A* -ⲉⲉⲓⲉ, *ib*
ⲣⲡⲏⲩⲉ, AP 28 *A*² -ⲉⲉⲓ, Mor 30 8 *F* -ⲛⲉⲓ.

ϣⲱⲗ, ϣⲁⲗ-, ϣⲗ- ⲣ. *SA*², rob temple : Ro 2 22
(*B* ⲟⲓ ⲛⲕⲁⲗⲡⲉⲣ.) ἱεροσυλεῖν, Ac 19 37 (*B* do), AP
15 *A*² ἱερόσυλος ; R 1 2 44 be judged as ϣⲁⲗⲣ.,
BMar 27 robbers & ϣⲁⲗⲣ. = Miss 8 205 ⲣⲉϥϣⲉⲗ
ⲉⲣ.   ⲣⲉϥϣⲗ ⲣ. sim as adj : Z 277 ⲥⲏⲱ ⲡⲣ.

In place-names : Miss 4 667 village called ⲛⲣⲡⲉ,
cf البربا (Amél *Géog* 322), PLond 3 92 Περπισναυ,
cf البربا الكبير & البُرْ المعير (Ibn Giʾân 175) & ⲡⲕⲟⲩⲓ
ⲣⲡⲏⲩⲉ (WS 115) ; AM 185 ⲡⲥⲉⲙⲉⲣⲫⲉⲓ سبرباي
(*Survey*), سمرباية (Amél *Géog* 376).

(рпⲱ), ⲉⲣ. *SF* nn, meaning uncertain, related to
vine leaves, *twig* ? : Is 34 4 *SF* ⲥⲱϩⲉ ⲡⲉⲣ. (*B* ϫⲱϩⲓ
alone) φύλλον, cit P 44 113 = 43 112 اغصان للقبو ;
ShR 2 3 44 *S* strewn in heathen temples ϩⲉⲛϣⲗϩ

ⲙⲡⲣⲉⲡⲕⲟⲡ (sic) ϩⲓⲉⲣ. ⲛϭⲱⲃⲉ ⲡⲉⲗⲟⲟⲗⲉ, P 44 80 = 43 54 S ⲑⲉⲣⲥⲁ (? θύρσα) · ⲟⲅⲥⲗⲁ (l ⲑⲅⲗⲥⲁ i e ⲟⲅⲣⲥⲁ) · ⲡⲉⲣ. زرجⁿ which P 55 8 = ϣⲉ ⲡⲁⲗⲟⲗⲓ (v ⲉⲗⲟⲟⲗⲉ II); v also ⲥⲁⲣϭⲉ.

ⲣⲁⲁⲣ S nn f, a basket or vessel (?): *Raccolta Lombroso* 283 (*cf* TurM tab xxii 1) things I sent ⲉⲅϩⲟⲩⲅⲣ. ⲉⲥⲧⲟⲣⲡ, Ryl 391 sim?

ⲣⲓⲣ SAB, ⲣⲏⲗ S (PLond 4 516), ⲗⲓⲗ SF, ⲣⲣ- S (Ps 79) nn m, *swine, pig*: Lev 11 7 SB ὗς; Mt 8 30 SB (*cf* 31 S ⲉϣⲁⲩ B ⲣ.), Lu 15 15 S (B ⲉ.), Kr 34 S χοῖρος; ShA 1 385 S Ares who took form of ⲟⲩⲕⲁⲡⲣⲟⲥ ⲡⲣ., Mor 16 55 S ⲣ. = BMis 209 S ϣⲁⲩ, ShP 130⁶ 72 S ⲡⲟⲩϩⲟⲟⲣ ⲏ ⲡⲣ. as abusive names, BM 1112 S send me ⲡⲉⲓⲣ....ⲝⲉⲫⲓⲗⲓⲡⲡⲟⲥ, BM 1252 F list of animals ⲥⲁⲩ ⲡⲗ., ⲛ̄ ⲡⲛⲉϣⲟⲩ, AM 319 B ⲟⲩⲕⲉⲡⲓ ⲡⲣ. as fuel, PMéd 260 S ⲗⲓⲗ sim in recipe, *ib* 261 ⲣ., Cai 42573 2 S recipe ϭⲱ ⲡⲣ.; ⲁϥ ⲡⲣ.: Ps 16 14 B(S ϣⲉ), Is 65 4 S(B ⲉϣⲱ), 2 Macc 6 18 A ὕειον κρέας, Mor 51 19 S ⲕⲣ. χοιρέων caten cures cancer, Z 270 S ὑποδοχεύς ⲛⲡⲁϥ ⲡⲣ., AM 59 B used by magician.

—— ⲛⲧⲟⲟⲩ, ⲧⲱ., *mountain, wild swine*: Ps 79 14 B (S ⲣ. ϩⲟⲟⲩⲧ) σῦς ἐκ δρυμοῦ; PS 318, 380 S demon with face of, Mor 31 68 S angry like ⲣ. ⲛⲧ., MG 25 405 B snorted like ⲣ. ⲛⲧ., WTh 138 S sim ⲣ. ⲛⲁⲧⲣⲓⲟⲛ; ⲣ. ⲛϩⲟⲟⲩⲧ S: 2 Kg 17 8 ὗς τραχεῖα; SHel 63 ⲣ. ⲛϩ. ⲛⲧⲟⲟⲩ, ⲣⲣϩ. Ps 79 14 (Rahlfs, var ⲣⲓⲣ) v above.

ⲙⲁⲛⲉⲣ. S, *swineherd*: ShC 73 147 offscourings from bakery given to ⲛⲙ., BMis 33, Cai 8074.

ⲥⲁ ⲡⲣ. S, *pig-dealer*: BM 6201 A 165 ⲁⲓⲡⲱⲗϭ ⲛⲛⲉⲥ.

As name ⲡⲉⲣⲓⲣ (BP 11922), Φρῆρ (Preisigke), ⲫⲣⲣⲏⲣ (Hall 143).

ⲣⲁⲁⲣ, ⲣⲁⲁⲣⲉ, ⲣⲁⲓⲣⲉ S nn m(?) f, *sucking pig*: Ryl 159 in rent ⲟⲩⲣⲁⲁⲣ at 2 carats, *ib* 158 sim at 1½, *cf* Wess 20 218 χοιράς, Aegyptus 9 292 δελφάκιον, WS 98 ⲉ̅ⲧⲟ ⲛⲣⲁⲓ. to be fattened, Letter *penes* HT ⲁⲡⲉⲓ ⲧⲣⲁⲁⲣⲉ when thou comest, ⲧⲁⲣⲉⲓ [...] ⲉⲡⲉⲥⲏⲧ ⲛⲡⲡⲁⲛⲟϭ ⲡⲣⲓⲣ, Kr 242 among presents ⲟⲩⲣⲁⲁⲣⲉ, PMich 1539 in list of edibles ⲛⲟϭ ⲛⲣⲁⲁⲣ, BM 1111 ⲧⲣⲁⲁⲣⲉ; Mich 136 3 Amoun in guise of ⲡⲉⲓⲣⲏⲣⲉ, same? *Cf* ? DM 21 38 *Tryrt*.

ⲣⲣⲟ SAA², ⲉⲣⲣⲟ Sᶠ, ⲉⲣⲟ SO, ⲟⲩⲣⲟ S (AZ 23 150) B, ⲣⲣⲁ, ⲉⲣⲣⲁ, ⲓⲣⲣⲁ (Eccl 10), ⲉⲣⲁ F, f ⲣⲣⲱ SA², ⲉⲣⲱ SSᶠ, ⲟⲩⲣⲱ B, pl ⲣⲣⲱⲟⲩ¹ SA, ⲉⲣⲣⲱⲟⲩ² SF, ⲉⲣⲱⲟⲩ³ SO, ⲣⲣⲟⲟⲩ⁴ S, ⲣⲣⲁ(ⲉ)ⲓ⁵ SᶜA, ⲟⲩⲣⲱⲟⲩ B nn m f, *king, queen*: Ge 14 1 SB, Eccl 10 16 SF, EpJer 34 BF ⲉⲣⲣⲁ, 2 Macc 5 tit A, Mk 15 18 F ⲉⲣⲁ, Jo 12 13 SA²B βασιλεύς; Ez 37 24 B ἄρχων *rex*; Sa 14 21 S τυραννίς; Ac 17 7 SB καῖσαρ; Cl 5 7 A ἡγούμενος; Br 122 S, PS 195 S, JKP 2

52 Sᶠ ⲉⲣⲣⲟ, El 86 A, AP 36 A², C 86 24 B, BSM 55 B, BIF 22 107 F ⲣⲣⲁ, JKP 2 30 F ⲉⲣⲁ, AZ 21 94 O ⲡ. ⲟⲩϭⲓⲣⲓ; pl forms: Jos 10 40 S² (var³), Ps 47 4 S¹ (var²), *ib* 104 30 S¹ (var³), FR 70 S⁴, J 1 41 S⁴, El 114 S⁵, *ib* 74 A⁵, Pro 6 8 A⁵, Is 13 4 B, C 43 106 B, Ap 10 11 F², AZ 23 104 O³.

queen: Est 1 12 S, Mt 12 42 S ⲣⲣⲱ, Jer 51 17 S, Lu 11 31 S, JKP 2 188 Sᶠ ⲉⲣⲱ, AP 15 A², Ps 44 10 B, MG 25 284 B.

As adj, *royal*: Nu 20 17 S ϩⲓⲏ ⲡⲣ. (sim Bor 240 57, PBu 218) B ⲙⲱⲓⲧ ⲛⲟⲩ., Ja 2 8 B(SA diff) ⲛⲟⲙⲟⲥ ⲛⲟⲩ., Job 18 14 S(B = Gk) ⲗⲁ ⲡⲣ., Va 63 81 B ⲣⲱⲙⲓ ⲛⲟⲩ. βασιλικός; Rec 6 65 S ⲃ̄ⲉⲕⲉ ⲛⲟⲩ., DeV 2 143 B ϣⲉⲡⲥ ⲛⲟⲩ., PMéd 159 S ϩⲙⲟⲩ ⲡⲉⲣⲟ, Bor 252 187 S ⲧⲣⲁⲡⲉⲍⲁ ⲡⲣ., LMär 2 S ϣⲉⲉⲣⲉ ⲛⲣⲣⲱ = C 43 41 B *princess*, J 2 16 S ⲡⲉⲛⲭⲓⲥⲟⲟⲩⲉ ⲛⲉⲣⲣⲟⲟⲩ that now rule us (*i e* khalifs).

ⲙⲛⲧⲣ., -ⲉⲣⲟ (oftenest), ⲙⲉⲧⲟⲩ., *kingdom, reign*: Ex 19 6 SB, Is 62 3 SB, AM 7 13 AB, Jo 3 5 SA²BF βασιλεία; Si 47 27 S τυραννίς; PS 90 S ϯⲛⲁⲥⲙⲓⲛⲉ ⲛⲙⲛⲧⲏ ⲛⲟⲩⲙ., Aeg 271 S ⲡⲧⲙⲛⲧⲉⲣⲟ (var -ⲣⲣⲟ) ⲡⲁⲉϣ ⲁϩⲉ ⲣⲁⲧⲥ ⲁⲡ, C 43 200 B ⲑⲙ. ⲛⲇⲓⲟⲕⲗⲏⲧⲓⲁⲛⲟⲥ, Aeg 235 S ⲧⲉϥⲧⲟⲉ ⲙⲙ. books of *Kingdoms*; pl ⲙⲛⲧⲣⲣⲱⲟⲩ, -ⲉⲣ. S, -ⲣⲣⲁⲓ A, ⲙⲉⲧⲟⲩⲣⲱⲟⲩ B: Deu 3 21 SB, Lu 4 5 SB, Hab 3 9 A, Mun 38 S fame spread through ⲙⲙ. ⲧⲏⲣⲟⲩ, BSM 121 B sim, Pcod 36 S ⲙⲙ. books of *Kingdoms*, DeV 2 90 B sim.

ⲣ ⲣⲣⲟ, ⲉⲣ ⲟⲩⲣⲟ, ⲉⲗ ⲉⲣⲣⲁ, *be king, reign*: Ps 9 37 SB, Pro 1 1 S.AB, Is 32 1 SBF, 1 Cor 15 25 SBF, CaiEuch 314 B ⲉⲧⲟⲓ ⲛⲟⲩ. for ever βασιλεύειν; PS 37 S ⲉⲩⲉⲱϣⲕ ⲉⲅⲟ ⲡⲣ., AM 192 B ⲁϥⲉⲣ ⲟⲩ. in his stead; ⲥ ⲉϫⲛ-, *reign over*: Ez 20 33 SB, Mt 2 22 SB β. ἐπί; ⲉϩⲣⲁⲓ, -ⲛⲓ ⲉϫ.: 1 Kg 8 9 S, Lu 19 14 S (var om ⲉϩ.) BF β. ἐπί, Sa 3 8 S β. acc. ⲥ ϩⲓϫⲛ-: BG 41 S 7 kings ⲣ ⲣ. ϩⲓϫⲛⲙⲡⲏⲅⲉ; ⲥ ⲛ- of time: Jer 52 1 SB, Ap 20 6 SB β. acc. ⲉⲓⲣⲉ ⲡⲣ., ⲓⲣⲓ ⲛⲟⲩ. tr, *make king*: Jer 44 1 B βασιλεύειν, Jo 6 15 SA²B βασιλέα ποιεῖν, BHom 98 S ⲁϥⲁⲁϥ ⲛⲣ. ⲉⲡⲉϥⲥⲉⲡⲟⲥ, BSM 15 B ⲁϥⲁⲓⲧ (*sc* Joseph) ⲛⲟⲩ. ⲛⲭⲏⲙⲓ.

ⲣⲉⲣⲙⲏ S nn m, quantity, measure of land: ST 41 sowing contract ⲛⲧⲁϣⲟ ⲟⲩⲣ. ⲛⲕⲁϩ...ⲡⲉⲣ. ⲛⲕⲁϩ ⲉⲧϩⲓⲃⲟⲗ. From ⲣⲉ- (*v* ⲣⲟ *mouth*) & ⲣ ⲙⲏ (*v* ⲙⲏ)??

ⲣⲣⲏⲧ *v* ⲉⲣⲏⲧ.

ⲣⲏⲥ SABFO nn m, *south*, places in the south: Jud 1 14 S, Job 9 9 SB, Dan 11 40 SB, Zech 6 6 AB, Mt 12 42 S (B ⲥⲁⲣ.) νότος; Mor 40 3 S ⲛⲡⲟⲗⲓⲥ ⲙⲡⲣ. = C 43 34 B, WS 118 S ⲫⲟⲓ ⲙⲡⲣ., J 3 9 S ⲡⲣ. ⲙⲛⲧⲙⲉ, PRain 4726 S ⲁⲩⲉⲣ ⲡⲣ.; in boundaries: J 21 40 S ⲡⲣ. ⲛⲉⲓⲣ ⲇⲏⲙⲟⲥⲓⲟⲛ, Kr 127 S ⲡⲉⲥⲣ. ⲡⲓⲟⲟⲣ, *ib* 130 S ⲡⲉⲅⲣ. ⲫⲟⲟⲩⲧⲛ (*cf* PLond

5 170 νότου, PCai 1 141 ἐπὶ ν.). As adj : BIF
13 106 S ⲡⲉⲥⲡⲟⲧⲟⲩ ⲡⲣ. of sea = MG 25 290 B
ⲡⲉⲣⲛⲥ, N&E 39 344 B ⲧⲁⲓⲉⲕⲕⲗⲏⲥⲓⲁ ⲡⲉⲣ., DeV 2
160 B sim.

Prepositional phrases. ⲉ ⲉ-, motion to south ;
Eccl 1 6 F (S ⲉⲡⲥⲁ ⲙⲡⲣ.) πρὸς ν. ; Z 282 S sailed
ⲉⲣ. ⲉⲑⲉⲃⲁⲉⲓⲥ, Ryl 321 S ⲧⲁⲗⲟⲟⲩ ⲡⲁⲓ ⲉⲣ., AZ 21
100 O]ⲉⲣ. ⲡⲡⲉ, BAp 105 S κήρυγμα sent ⲉⲣ.
ⲟⲣⲛⲕⲏⲙⲉ ⲧⲏⲣϥ southward throughout all Egypt, AM
74 B as he went ⲉⲣ. ⲋⲉⲛⲭⲏⲙⲓ ; without motion :
Ez 41 11 SB πρὸς ν., J 71 57 S ⲡⲣⲟ ⲉⲧⲟⲩⲏⲡ (sic l)
ⲉⲣ., Kr 36 F sim, J 39 29 S ⲭⲓⲡⲙⲡⲣⲁⲯⲓⲥ ⲉⲣ., ib
1 62 S ⲛⲟⲓⲣ ⲃⲉⲗⲗⲉ ⲉⲣ., BerlOr 1611 5 40 S ⲡⲉⲓⲉⲃⲧ
ⲉⲣ., DeV 2 83 B sim south-east : ⲉ ⲛ-, on south :
Ps 125 4 S (B ⲟⲓ-) νότῳ ; BMis 442 S island ⲙⲡⲣ.
ⲙⲙⲟⲛ, J 43 35 S cellar ⲉⲧⲙⲡⲣ. ⲙⲡⲉⲣⲉⲓⲡⲉⲧⲛ, AZ
21 94 O ⲡⲉⲧⲛⲡⲣ. ⲡⲧⲓⲛ ; om ⲛ- : Ryl 325 S ⲡⲣ.
ⲛϣⲙⲟⲩⲛ ; ⲉ ϣⲁ-, to, as far as south : CaiEuch 578
B from north ϣⲁⲫⲣ. μέχρι μεσημβρίας ; Miss 4 761
S accompanied us ϣⲁⲡⲣ. ⲉ(l ⲙ)ⲡⲧⲟⲡⲟⲥ, J 45 27 S
ⲭⲡⲡⲧⲡⲛϣⲉ ⲡⲧⲕⲁⲙⲁⲣⲉ ϣⲁⲣ. ⲉⲭⲟⲩϥ ⲙⲡⲏⲓ ; ⲉ ⲟⲁ-
S, as last : ST 199 ⲉⲓⲏⲩ ⲟⲁⲣ. ; not motion : Ex 26
35 (B ⲟⲓⲡⲥⲁ ⲡⲧⲉ ⲫⲣ.) πρὸς ν. ; ShC 73 74 brethren
ⲉⲧⲟⲁⲣ., J 67 85 house ⲟⲁⲣ. ⲟⲙⲛⲧⲓⲙⲉ ; ⲉ ⲟⲓ-, on
south : Ps 125 B as above, J 29 25 S house ⲟⲓⲙⲣ. ⲉⲡⲧ-
ⲕⲁⲑⲟⲗⲓⲕⲏ ⲉⲕⲕⲗ., AM 287 B soldier ⲉϥⲃⲏⲕ ⲟⲓⲫⲣ.
enrolled, quartered (?) in south ; ⲉ ⲛⲥⲁ ⲛ-, ⲡⲥⲁ-,
southern side : Nu 2 3 S ⲟⲓⲛⲥⲁ ⲙⲡⲣ. (B ⲡⲥⲁⲫⲣ.)
κατὰ ν., Eccl 1 6 S ⲉⲡⲥⲁ ⲙⲡⲣ., Jer 13 19 S ⲙⲡⲥⲁ
ⲙⲡⲣ. (B ⲉⲧⲥⲁⲫⲣ.) πρὸς ν., Ez 40 2 S do (B ⲋⲉⲛ-
ⲡⲉϥⲥⲁ ⲡⲧⲉ ⲫⲣ.) ad austrum ; Nu 34 11 S ⲉⲭⲙⲡⲥⲁⲣ.
ἐπὶ ν. (B diff) ; El 64 A ⲟⲣⲙⲙⲥⲁⲣ. ϣⲁⲡⲥⲁⲙⲟⲉⲓⲧ,
Kr 161 S church ⲟⲓⲡⲡⲥⲁⲣ. ⲡⲧⲡⲟⲗⲓⲥ, MIE 2 381 B
sent clerics ⲋⲉⲛⲛⲓⲥⲁⲡⲉⲣ. (v above adj) ⲡⲧⲉ ⲭⲏⲙⲓ
= BAp 160 S ⲉⲣ., C 89 100 B sim ; ⲥⲁ-, on
south side : Ge 12 8 B ⲥⲁⲫⲣ. (S diff) κατὰ ν., Nu
13 30 S ⲉⲧⲥⲁⲣ. (B ⲉⲧⲥⲁⲫⲣ.) πρὸς ν., AM 277 B
ⲁⲩⲟⲗϥ ⲥⲁⲣ. ⲙⲡⲓⲙⲁⲣⲧⲩⲣⲓⲟⲛ ἐκ ν., Jer 13 19 B as
above, Lu 13 29 B (S ⲡⲣ.) (ἀπό) ν. ; Et Leem 91
S ⲧⲉⲧⲛⲥⲁⲣ. ⲡⲁⲡⲧⲡⲱⲟⲩ, Worr 287 S ⲟⲩⲁⲡⲟⲑⲏⲕⲏ
ⲛⲥⲁⲣ. ⲛⲧⲡⲟⲗⲓⲥ, C 89 44 B convent ⲉⲥⲥⲁⲣ. ⲛⲧⲁⲃⲉⲛ-
ⲡⲛⲏⲥⲓ = Miss 4 525 S ⲉⲥⲙⲡⲣ., C 43 91 B Babylon
ⲥⲁⲣ. ⲛⲱⲛ, P 44 1 S ⲧⲁⲥⲡⲉ ⲉⲧⲥⲁⲣ. صعيدية, MG 25
112 B ⲥⲁⲣ. ⲛⲉⲙⲉⲛⲧ south-west of village ; ⲉ ⲧⲁ-
S (Theban), on southern side, in s. quarter (v ⲧⲟ
land) : Lant 1 194 ⲧⲛⲉⲭⲓⲁⲥ ⲧⲁⲣ. ⲛⲧⲡⲟⲗⲓⲥ (cf ib
190) : Ep 102 ⲡⲁⲛⲟ ⲧⲁⲣ., ib 562 ⲡⲏⲓ ⲧⲁⲣ., ImpRuss
ArS ⲡⲧⲟⲟⲩ ⲧⲁⲣ., J 35 44 ⲧⲧⲁⲉ ⲧⲁⲣ. In place-
name : Πιαταρῆς (Ostr Stras Viereck 696).

ⲣⲙ-, ⲣⲉⲙⲣ. SB, man of south : MG 25 2 B Paul
ⲡⲓⲣ. Θηβαῖος, Ostr penes EES ⲁⲡⲟⲕ ⲧⲁⲅⲁⲡⲏ ⲧⲣ.,
C 86 161 B ⲟⲩⲣⲱⲙⲓ ⲡⲣ. In names : Πρημῆς,
Προμρῆσις, Τρομρῆσις (Preisigke).

ⲙⲁⲣⲏⲥ SBF nn m, Southern Country, Upper
Egypt : MG 25 241 B went from Nitria ⲉⲫⲙ.
Θηβαίς, C 89 5 B went from Antinoe ⲉⲫⲙ., Mor
37 93 S Antony would go ⲉⲡⲙ. ⲡⲕⲏⲙⲉ ἡ ἄνω Θ.
صعيد ، ّ، ، ، MG 17 296 S = C 89 29 B from
Denderah ⲉⲡⲙ. '،، C 89 149 B Pachom returning
ⲉⲃⲟⲗ ⲋⲉⲛⲫⲙ. = Va ar 172 85 من قبلي ، Z 550 S
from Fayyûm ⲋⲡⲙ. (sc to Achmîm), Amél Géog
571 B ⲭⲛⲏⲓ ⲡⲉ(ⲙ)ⲫⲙ. '.والص، Bonjour Monum
11 B ⲡⲓⲙⲉϣϣⲟϯ ⲡⲧⲉ ⲭ. ⲡⲉⲙⲫⲙ., P 131¹ 62 S
ⲑⲏⲃⲁⲓⲥ ⲙⲡⲙ. ⲡⲕⲏⲙⲉ, RChamp 372 S towns of
ⲑ. ⲉⲓⲧⲉ ⲟⲓⲡⲙ. ⲉⲓⲧⲉ ⲟⲓⲙⲡⲥⲁⲙⲡⲉⲙⲣⲓⲧ, Miss 4 148
B ϣⲁⲫⲙ. ⲡⲓⲃⲁⲣⲃⲁⲣⲓⲕⲟⲛ ⲡⲧⲉ ⲭ. = Mor 18 78 S
ϣⲁⲣ. ⲙⲡⲃ. (v Preisigke Wbuch s v β.), C 43 121 B
Philae last town of ⲫⲙ., AM 195 B Philae of ⲫⲙ.
ⲡⲭⲛⲏⲓ (cf ib 200 Philae ⲉⲧⲥⲁⲃⲟⲗ ⲡⲧⲉ ⲭ.), C 43
90 B ⲫⲙ. ⲡⲓⲛⲓϣϯ as far as Ethiopians (cf below),
WTh 187 S from Alexandria to ⲡⲙ. ⲡⲕ. ⲧⲏⲣϥ, P
131⁶ 103 S Pachom's monastery (Pboou) ⲟⲓⲡⲙ., C
41 29 B Shenoute's ⲋⲉⲛⲫⲙ. ⲡⲭ., BMis 31 S Psoi
in ⲡⲙ., Ryl 461 B Ashmûnain in ⲫⲙⲁⲣⲓⲥ ; without art : Mor 37 75 S set out ⲭⲓⲡⲙ., HL 78 B
dwelling ⲋⲉⲛⲙ. ⲡⲉⲙⲥⲟⲩⲁⲡ (v Preuschen Pallad
u Rufin 251 n) Θηβαίς ; EW 99 B Arian governor
ⲡⲧⲉ ⲙ. (elsewhere of Thebaid : RNC 83, BM 346,
C 43 95), C 43 148 B ⲍⲟⲩⲭ ⲉⲙ., AM 263 B ⲙ.
ⲡⲓⲛⲓϣϯ (cf above), Ryl 227 S ⲁⲡ[ⲁ ⲕ]ⲓⲣⲓ ⲡⲁⲙ.,
Kr 54 F ⲁⲡⲁ ϣⲉⲡⲟⲩⲧⲓ ⲙ. (l? ⲁⲙⲙ.), BM 1153 S
came north ⲟⲩⲙⲙ., ib 1098 S ⲧⲉⲡⲣⲁⲅⲙ(ⲁⲧⲓⲁ) ⲡⲙ.,
Cai 42573 1 S in recipe ⲥⲟⲩⲟ ⲙ. (cf hyphene
thebaica). Northern Nubia called المريس (Abû
Ṣâliḥ 94 a) or Upper Ṣa'îd as far as Nubia (Mas'ûdi
6 273), hence مريس suburb of Fustât (Ibn Dukmâk
4 121) ; Copts of Ṣa'îd called مريس (? for ّٰ، اهل,
Quatremère Rech 176). ⲣⲉⲙⲙ., ⲗⲉⲙⲙ., ⲣⲉⲙⲡⲙ.,
southerner : Z 610 S ⲟⲩⲣⲉⲙⲙⲙ. Θηβαῖος, CMSS
78 F ⲡⲗⲉⲙⲙ., Kr 226 F ⲗⲉⲙ., Aeg 238 B ϯⲁⲥⲡⲓ
ⲡⲣⲉⲙⲙⲁⲣⲓⲥ opp ⲣⲉⲙⲡⲉⲙⲟⲓⲧ. Etymology of ⲙ.
v BerlSitz '28 620.

In place-names v Ep 1 118 n & add Παθούρης,
Φαθωρῆς (Jer 15 15, Ez 29 14), ⲧⲟⲩⲣⲏⲥ (CO 160
sic l, cf ib Ad 17 ⲡⲡⲡⲟⲗⲟⲥ, Hall 106 ⲉⲡⲛ.).

ⲧⲟⲩ-, ⲑⲟⲩⲣ., south wind v ⲧⲏⲩ.

ⲣⲟⲉⲓⲥ S, ⲣⲁ. S/A, ⲣⲱⲓⲥ, ⲣⲱⲥ B, ⲣⲁⲓⲥ A²F, ⲗⲁⲉⲓⲥ, ⲗⲁⲓⲥ F, ⲣⲏⲥ† SB vb I intr, be awake, watch :
Mk 13 34 SBF, Ap 3 3 S (B ⲣ.† ⲉⲃⲟⲗ) γρηγορεῖν,
Lu 9 32 S (B ⲉⲣ ϣⲣⲱⲓⲥ) διαγρ., Bor 226 165 S
ⲉⲕⲣ.† ⲉⲕⲣⲓⲛⲏⲃ ἐν γρηγορήσει ; Cant 5 2 S†, Mk 13
33 SB (F ⲁⲓ ⲛⲡⲟⲩϣⲏ ⲛⲗ.) ἀγρυπνεῖν ; Ez 27 11 SB
φύλαξ ; 1 Cor 15 34 B† (SF ⲡⲛⲏⲫⲉ) ἐκνήφειν, 1 Tim
3 2 B† (S ⲧⲟⲣⲟ), BM 168 S ⲡϣϣⲱⲡⲉ ⲉⲏⲣ.† νηφά-
λιος ; ShC 73 24 S who slay sin ⲭⲉⲥⲉⲣ.† ⲁⲩⲱ ⲥⲉⲣ.,

TU 43 21 *A* unable пр., Va 58 174 *B* Nathan αϥρωс пαϣ пρнϯ…ογοϩ εταϥρωс *expectant* how he should be answered (2 Kg 12 13), PSBA 25 269 *S* кр.† = Miss 4 98 *B art awake?*, AM 287 *B* пαϥр.† кαλωс in Christ's teaching, HL 107 *B* пαϥр.†пε ϫεппιϲγραφн διαλεκτώτατος ὤν, PLond 4 436 *S* we swear ετρпϩαρϩ τнρ. as written above, KroppC 11 *F* magic αкλ. καλεϩ пεϥ⳪ пϲε.

With following preposition.

—— ε- SS^fAA²BF, *watch over, keep, be careful*: Nu 31 47 *S*(*B* αρεϩ), Ps 126 1 *B*(*S* ϩαρεϩ), Ez 23 24 *SB*, BMar 114 *S* пϭр. επκαρпос φυλάσσειν; R 1 1 40 *S* ετρεγρ. επταϕος τηρεῖν; PS 81 *S* р. εταϭολι. El 100 *A* ϲε]р. αρα[γ = *ib* 138 *S*, Mani 1 *A²* εγρ. αραι, ShC 42 83 *S* ye compel poor ετρεγρ. ερωтι in ships, PGol 53 *S* пεкϣнλ р. εροι, MG 25 39 *B* camel's food ϥρ. εроϲ ϲαϩογп λιλιοϥ, MIE 2 341 *B* ϯпαρ. επαιλιγϲτнριοп till death, P 131⁴ 112 *S* Epiphany water εγρ. εροоγ for a year, DeV 1 74 *B* thief αϥρωϲ εроϥ & slay him, Kr 236 *F* εлεппоγτι λ. ελακ, Mor 39 27 *S*^f εϥρ. εϣτελικε ρωλιε εϐωк = C 43 50 *B* αρεϩ; *preserve (someone) from*, ε-…ε- *S*: BHom 116 р. ερωтι επεто пϫαϫε, AJSL 46 249 spell пαρ. εροк εϕαρλιαϲια πιλι, P 129¹² 13 р. ερωтι εταγε ϣαϫε; ε-…εϐоλ ϩп-: р. επεγϧнт εϐ. ϩпϫωρλι πιλι; εϐ. ϩα- *B* · Cat 95 р. εроп εϐ. ϩαпαι.

—— εϫп-, *watch over*: Jer 1 12 *SB*, Dan 9 14 *B*(*S* ϯ ϩнт εϩραι εϫ.) γρηγ. ἐπί.

—— ογϐε- *S*, *keep watch against*: ShMIF 23 24 to devil пετρ. ογϐнк εγρ.†, ShC 73 94 пετρ. ογϐεпετϩпиειτοпос *watch over* (?).

—— п- dat, *watch, keep on behalf of*: BM 1041 *S* I swear тαρειр. пнтп прос тεϲϭολι, Ryl 144 *S* do, *cf* BM 1060 *S* тαρпϥγλαϲ(ϲ)ε пαк, C 86 195 *B* ερεп⳹⳩Ⳬ р. εроϥ пαϥ, Bibl Marciana Or 193 6 *S* shares ετογр. εрооγ λιпϫоειϲ птϲωϣε, P 129²⁰ 125 *S* be not wroth for ever пϭтαρ. пαι επαπεθооγ. *V* also **II**.

With following adverb. ϲ εϐоλ *B*, *wake up*: Ap 3 2 (*S* om εϐ.) γρнγ.; C 86 330 пн ετεпкот ρωϲ εϐ. & arise. ϲ επϣωι *B*, meaning sim: Va 57 70 λιαρεпρωϲ επ. ϫεппαιϩιλιιλι.

II tr *S* (rare), *keep, observe*: Kr 91 тαр. λιπεϲκαρпоϲ пαк, Ep 149 εϥпαр. πλоϲоϲ пαϥ, CO 166 ready to р. пεкαϲнλιοϲ (ἀζήμιον) ϩιтпρωλιε пιλι that shall sue thee, BKU 1 79 sim, PBu 111 we know you impartial птετпр. п̇αικαιоп пαп, Bodl(P) d 44 ειр. пαк птιαϲϕαλεια, BM 1076 God р. п петρα ϐонθоϲ *keep Peter the* βοηθός.

—— nn m *SB*, *watch, guard*: Dan 5 12 *B*(*S* т' BAp 151) γρнγόρηϲιϲ; CaiEuch 654 *B* νῆψις, Lam 2 18 *B*(*S* diff) ἔκν.; Va 58 193 *B* пεϥρωϲ is

as one dreaming = P 131² 117 *S* пεϥрнϲ; *ib* 93 *S* εϲо пϲελιпоϲ ϩλι…пр. ппεϲϐαλ, C 89 30 *B* listened with attention пελιογρωϲ, Ryl 102 *S* amulet огр. ϩпϧωϐ пιλι, KroppM 66 *S* sim; рнϲ *S*: ShA 1 301 птγпоϲ пϥрεпϩαп, пιλιεıп птεκριϲιϲ, пıпε λιпр., P 131² as above.

реϥр., *watchman, guardian*: 1 Kg 17 20 *S* (*B* реϥαρεϩ) φύλαξ, Jth 12 7 *S* σωλιατоϕ., R 1 1 52 *S* παραϕ.; Lam 4 14 *B* ἐγρήγορος; CaiEuch 633 *B* ϕρουρός; Leyd 313 *S* αγϯ р. ελιпγλн, DeV 1 157 *B* пıр. standing at door, BIF 14 122 *S*^f пεреϥϥραιϲ of prison, BSM 78 *B* пιр. of city = BMis 168 *S* пεϩрнпαριоϲ, BM 1130 *S* пεрнϐнρоιϲ (? confused with ῥιπάριος), sim C 43 183 *B*, Ryl 322 *S*, BM 623 *F* λεϐλ., *ib* 656 *F*, CMSS 64 *F* реϥλ., BSM 75 *B* αρχпр. = BMis 166 *S* проϲоγроϲ (*cf* ἀρχιϕύλαξ), PMich 3593 a *F* пιϲαϭα πλεϐλ.; R 1 2 69 *S* prayer & fasting пειр. εроп.

λια пр. *SAB*, *place of watching*: Is 21 11 *S* (*B* ϲоϐт) ἔπαλξις; Nah 2 5 *A*(*B* λια пαρεϩ), Jth 10 11 *S* λι. пϣорп προϕυλακή; ShMIF 23 144 *S* ϩεппγρϲоϲпε ϫελιλι.пε, Ryl 158 24 *S* пελι. πλιιϲϩωλ on farm land, ShA 2 48 *S* *watch towers* of city, C 86 116 *B* пιλι. at foot of hill.

ϐεκε р., *watchman's wage*: Bodl(P)d 32 *S* account ϩαпϐ.

пαγ пр., *time of watch, vigilia*: Bar 3 34 *B* ϕυλακή; R 1 1 40 *S* earthquake λιпп. пр. (*cf* Mt 28 2) τηρούντων ἡμῶν.

огϣн пр. *SABF*, *night of waking, vigil*: Si 42 10 *S*, 2 Cor 6 5 *S* (*B* ϣρωιϲ) ἀγρυπνία; р, ог. пр., do, *keep vigil*: 2 Kg 12 21 *S*, Pro 8 34 *SA* (*B* εр ϣ.), Mk 13 33 *F* (*SB* р.) ἀγρυπνεῖν; Job 2 9 *S* (*B* εр ϣ.), Lu 6 12 *SB* διανυκτερεύειν; Ps 118 28 *S* (*B* diff) νυστάζειν; BHom 42 *S* shepherds р ог. пр. ἐϕιστάναι; Aeg 254 *S* λιαроγερ тεγϣн тнрϲ εγр. *Cf* εϫωρϩ пϣ.

ϣρωιϲ *B* vb, *watch, guard* c ε-: Ac 28 16 (var & *S* αρεϩ) ϕυλ. As nn m: 2 Cor 11 27 (*S* ог. пр.), Va 57 122 ϯαγрιппιпια пте пıϣ. ἀγρυπνία; C 86 284 remained ϫεппιϣ. = Mun 38 *S* εϥр.† ἄϋπνος; CaiThe 223 αϥϫокϥ εϐоλ ϫεпоγпιϣϯ пϣ. *zeal*: εϫωρϩ пϣ., as огϣн пр.: Va 66 290 αγр., C 89 140 prayers & fastings (ἄσκησις) & ϩαпλιпϣ пε. εр ϣ., *keep vigil*: Ps 101 8 (*S* р ог. пр.), Eph 6 18 (*S* do), C 89 22 εϥоι пϣ., MG 25 207 кεр ϣ. ἀγρυπνεῖν; Col 4 2 (*S* do) γρηγ.; Ps 126 1 (*S* do) νυϲτ.; Lu 6 12 (*S* do) διανυκτ.; AM 256 ειоι пϣ. through sickness.

рнϲε *A*, рнιϲι, -ϲεп *B* nn m, *dust*: Lev 14 41 χοῦς; Ps 1 4 (*S* ϣоειϣ), Is 5 24 (*SF* do) χνοῦς; Hos 13 3 *A* (*B* αоλιϲ) χν. var χ.; Va 57 203 earth

εϥⲙⲟϫⲧ ⲡⲣⲏⲓⲥⲉⲡ, *ib* 205 ⲕⲉⲣⲙⲓ ⲡⲉⲙⲣⲏⲓⲥⲉⲡ κόνις ;
Κ 60 ⲡⲓϣⲱⲓϣ, غبار, ⲡⲓⲣ. ها .

ρcω *S*, ⲉⲣ. *SF*, ⲣⲥⲟⲩ *A*, pl ⲣⲥⲟⲟⲩⲉ, ⲉⲣ. *S*, ⲉⲣ-
ⲥⲱⲟⲩ *B* (Is) nn f, *fold* for cattle or sheep : Lev 25
31 *S* (*B* ⲉⲣⲃⲓ), Nu 22 39 *S* (*B* ⲟⲣⲓ), Pro 3 33 *SA*
(*B* ⲉⲣ.), Is 35 7 *SB* (v Pey) *F*, *ib* 34 13 *S* (*B* ⲙⲁ ⲛ
ⲓϣⲱⲡⲓ, cf Ac 1 20 & Ps 68 26) ἔπαυλις ; Deu 28 18
S (*B* ⲓⲟⲣⲓ) βουκόλιον ; Tri 297 *S* زرب ; ShA 2 33 *S*
ϣⲁⲓⲣⲉ, ⲣ., ⲥⲟⲃⲧ, Ryl 158 *S* ⲧⲣ. in agricultural
property, BMOr 6201 A 22 *S* rent for house & ⲧⲣ.,
BM 1073 *S* property containing ⲡⲉϥⲃⲏⲡⲉ ⲙⲡⲉϥ-
ⲉⲣⲥⲟⲟⲩⲉ, Cai 42573 2 *S* charm buried in ⲧⲉⲣ. of
cattle.   As place-name : ⲧⲉⲣⲥⲱ ⲉⲧϣⲏϥ (Lant 36).

ρατε *S*, ⲣⲏ. *Sᵃ*, ⲣⲉ. *SᵃAA²*, ⲣⲁⲥϯ *Sf* (Mor 27
25) *B*, ⲗⲉⲥϯ *F* nn m, *morrow* : **a** no art : Ex 32 5
SB, 1 Kg 28 19 *S*, Pro 3 28 *SA* (*B* ⲛⲣ.), 1 Cor 15
32 *BF* (*S* ⲛⲣ.), R 1 1 55 *S* ⲡⲥⲁⲃⲃⲁⲧⲟⲛ ⲣ. αὔριον ;
Pro 27 1 b *SA* (*B* DeV 2 238 ⲧⲟⲟⲩⲓ) ἐπιέναι, Mt 6
11 *BF* (*S* ⲉⲧⲏⲩ) ἐπιούσιος ; BMis 373 *S* knowest
not ϫⲉⲁϣ ⲡϣⲁⲡⲉ ⲣ. ? = BSM 31 *B* ⲣ. ⲡⲉ ⲡⲓϣⲁⲓ ?,
AM 188 *B* ⲣ. ϯⲛⲁϯ ⲡⲁⲕ, Till Oster 29 *A*]ⲣ. ⲛⲧⲕⲩⲣⲓⲁⲕⲏ (or ⲛ]ⲣ.), BM 1133 *S* ⲕⲁⲛ ⲣ. ⲕⲁⲛ ⲥⲁⲣ., PRain
4720 *S* ⲡⲟⲟⲩ ⲣ. *to-day or to-morrow* ; **b** with art :
Est 9 13 *S* αὔ., Lev 23 15 *B* (*S* ⲡⲉϥⲣ.) ἐπαύριον ;
BMis 555 *S* ⲛⲣ. ⲛⲧⲕⲩⲣⲓⲁⲕⲏ, PStras 226 *S* ⲛⲣ.
ⲛ(ⲧ)ⲥⲓⲣⲁⲥⲛ, ⲡϣⲟⲙⲉⲧ, P 44 21 *S* ⲛⲣ. b̄ (Theotokia
of) *morrow sc* Monday يوم الاثنين = *B* ⲡⲉϩⲟⲟⲩ ⲙⲡⲃ̄,
P 45 68 *S* ⲑⲉⲱⲇⲟⲕⲓⲁ ⲛⲣ. do (cf ⲥⲁⲣ.) ; **c** with
poss : Lev 19 6 *SB*, Pro 27 1 a *SA* αὔ., Jo 12 12 *SB*
(*A²* ⲙⲡⲉϥ-), Ac 10 24 *S* (var ⲙⲡⲉϥ-) *B* ἐπαύ. ; BSM
68 *B* ⲡⲉϥⲣ. he came to them, cf BMis 159 *S* ⲙⲡⲉϥⲣ.
BSM 31 *B* ⲥⲟⲩⲓⲁ̄ ⲙⲡⲓⲁⲃⲟⲧ ⲉⲧⲉⲡⲉϥⲣ. ⲡⲉ ⲥⲟⲩⲓⲃ̄. **c**
ⲉ-, ⲟⲛ *the morrow* : CO 229 *Sᵃ* ϯⲛⲏⲩ ⲉⲣⲓⲥⲧⲉ, AM
82 *B* ⲁⲓϣⲁⲡⲓ ⲉⲣ. ; Lev 23 11 *B* ⲉϥⲣ. (*S* ⲙⲡⲉϥⲣ.),
Su 28 *B* τῇ ἐπαύ., AP 16 *A²* she should fight ⲁⲡⲉϥⲣ.
εἰς τὴν αὔ. ; MG 25 288 *B* ⲉⲡⲉϥⲣ. = BIF 13 105
S do, C 86 332 *B* when arose ⲉⲡⲉϥⲣ. (var ⲙⲡ.) ; **c**
ⲡ- & ⲉ- for ⲛ-, meaning same : Jos 4 6 *SB*, Ac 23
20 *SB* αὔ. ; ShA 1 92 *S* to-day that is come ⲏ ⲛⲣ.
ⲉⲧⲛⲏⲩ, C 43 75 *B* ⲡⲁⲓⲛⲁⲩ ⲛⲣ., MR 5 54 *F* ϣⲁϣⲟ-
ⲣⲉⲡ ⲉⲗ., Hall 79 *S* ϩⲓⲣⲟⲩϫⲉ ⲛⲣ., Ep 233 *S* ⲛϭⲉⲓ
ⲛⲁⲡ ⲛⲣ., MR 5 48 *F* ϯⲛⲏⲩ ⲡⲉⲕ ⲉⲗ. ; **ⲙⲡⲉϥⲣ.** :
Nu 33 3 *S* (var ϩⲁⲡⲉⲥⲛⲁⲩ) *B* τῇ ἐπαύ., Mk 11 12
S (*B* ⲉⲡⲉϥⲣ.) ἐπαύ. ; Ac 7 26 *SF* (*B* ⲡⲉϥⲣ.) τῇ
ἐπιούσῃ ἡμ., *ib* 25 17 *S* (*B* do) τῇ ἑξῆς ; Ex 2 13 *A*
(*B* ⲉϩⲟⲟⲩ ⲙⲙⲁⲣⲃ̄) τῇ ἡμ. τῇ δευτ. ; PS 6 *S* ϫⲡⲡϥⲓⲧⲉ
ⲙⲡ., Miss 8 18 *S* ϩⲧⲟⲟⲩ(ⲉ) ⲙⲡ., AM 19 *B* ⲁⲥϣⲱⲡⲓ
ⲇⲉ ⲙⲡ. **c ⲡⲥⲁ-, ⲥⲁ-** *S*, *after to-morrow* : Lu 13
32 (*B* ⲡⲓⲙⲁⲣϥ̄) τῇ τρίτῃ ; ST 285 ⲉⲡⲁⲧⲱϭ (*sic* ?)
ⲛⲥⲁⲣ., so send flour to-morrow, BMOr 6201 B 70
ⲕⲁⲡ ⲣ. ⲕⲁⲡ ⲥⲁⲣ., RNC 69 ⲕⲁ ⲡⲟⲟⲩ ⲙⲛⲣ. ⲡⲉⲧⲉⲧⲛ
ⲥⲁⲣ. ⲁⲙⲏⲓⲧⲛ, P 45 69 Theotokia ⲛⲥⲁⲣ. يوم التلت (*cf*

P 44 21 ⲙⲡⲛ̄) ; ⲙⲡⲛⲥⲁⲣ., ⲡⲉϥⲣ. : Ex 32 30 *SB*, 1
Kg 11 11 μετὰ τὴν αὔ., Miss 8 11 ⲙ. ⲁϥⲟⲩⲉϩⲥⲁϩⲛⲉ,
PLond 4 522 ⲧⲓⲛⲉⲩ ⲉϩⲣⲏⲧ ⲙⲉⲛⲉⲛⲥⲁⲣ. **c ϣⲁ-,**
till to-morrow : Lev 23 16 *B* (*S* ϣⲁⲡⲉϥⲣ.) ἕως τῆς
ἐπαύ. ; ϣⲁⲡⲉϥⲣ. : Ac 4 3 *SB* εἰς τὴν αὔ. ; AM 22
B let them adorn palace ϣⲁⲡⲉϥⲣ. *against the morrow* ; **c ϩⲛ-, ϫⲉⲛ-,** *on morrow* : Ge 30 33 *S* ϩⲛⲣ.
ⲡⲣⲟⲟⲩ *B* ⲉϩⲟⲟⲩ ⲡⲧⲉ ⲣ. ἐν τῇ ἡμ. τῇ αὔ., C 86 351
B will bring a man ϫⲉⲛⲣ. ; ϫⲉⲛⲡⲉϥⲣ. : 1 Chr 29
21 *B* τῇ ἐπαύ.

ρacoⲩ *S*, ⲣⲉ. *A*, ⲣⲉcⲟⲅⲉ *A²*, ⲣⲁⲥⲟⲩⲓ *B* ⲗⲉⲥⲃⲓ
F (Pcod 39) nn f, *dream* : Ge 40 5 *SB*, Joel 2 28 *SAB*
ἐνύπνιον, Nu 12 6 *SB*, AP 16 *A²* saw it ⲛⲣ. ὕπνος ;
Mt 1 20 *SB*, AP *lc* ϩⲛⲟⲩⲣ. ὄναρ, Sa 18 17 *S* ὄνειρον ;
Is 28 7 *S* (*B* ϩⲟⲣⲧϣ) φάσμα ; PS 283 *S* ϣⲁϥⲕⲓⲙ
ⲉⲣⲟⲥ ϩⲛⲣⲉⲡⲣ., Mun 57 *S* ⲧⲣ. ⲛⲧⲁⲕⲛⲁⲩ ⲉⲣⲟⲥ, C 86
351 *B* hath told me ϫⲉⲛⲡⲟⲣ., Aeg 252 *S* ⲡⲉⲧⲃⲱⲗ
ⲛⲣⲉⲡⲣ. ; **ⲉⲣ ⲣ.,** *have, dream a dream* : Is 29 8 *B*
(*S* diff) ἐνυπνιάζειν ; **ⲣⲉϥⲟⲩⲉϩ ⲣ.,** *interpreter of
dreams* : Ge 41 8 *S* (*B* ⲥϥⲣⲁⲧϣ) ἐξηγητής. *V* also
ⲡⲱⲣⲉ.

ρατ⸗ *SB*, ⲣⲉⲧ⸗ *SᵃAA²FO*, ⲣⲏⲧ⸗ *Sᵃ* (Ep 1 238),
ⲣⲉⲉⲧ⸗ *A* (El 46, 58), ⲗⲉⲧ⸗ *F* nn m, *foot* : Ex 12 11
S (*B* ϭⲁⲗⲁϫ), Lev 11 21 *S* (*B* ⲫⲁⲧ), Ps 90 12 *B*
(*S* ⲟⲩⲉⲣⲏⲧⲉ), Jo 13 14 *SB* (*A²* ⲟⲩ., cf *ib B* ϭⲁ.)
πούς, Mic 1 8 *S* ⲉⲣⲉⲣⲁⲧⲥ ϭⲓⲡⲉⲥⲏⲧ (*B* ⲁⲧⲑⲱⲟⲩⲓ)
ἀνυπόδετος ; Jos 9 11 *S* sandals ⲉⲧⲟⲧϥ ⲉⲣⲁⲧⲟⲩ ὑπόδημα ; Ez 16 25 *SB* σκέλος ; Lev 11 3 *S* (*B* ϭⲟⲡ)
ὁπλή ; ShIF 160 *S* ⲡⲉⲧⲛⲟⲩⲅⲉⲣⲏⲧⲉ...ⲣⲁⲧⲧⲏⲩⲧⲛ, Mor
18 78 *S* pour tears ϩⲁⲣⲁⲧⲧⲏⲩⲧⲛ = *ib* 19 85 *S* ϩⲁ-
ⲡⲉⲧⲛⲟⲩⲉⲣ. = Miss 4 148 *B* ϫⲁⲧⲉⲧⲉⲛϭⲁⲗ., C 43 26
B ⲁⲩⲙⲟⲣϥ ⲡⲧⲟⲧϥ ⲡⲉⲙⲣⲁⲧϥ, BMar 14 *S* ⲟⲩⲡⲁⲓⲇⲁⲓⲥ
(πέδη) ϩⲛⲡⲉϥⲟⲩⲣⲏⲧⲉ, ⲟⲩⲫⲓⲙⲓⲡⲁⲣⲓⲟⲛ (φιμινάλιον)
ϩⲛⲣⲁⲧϥ, AZ 21 100 *O* ⲉϥϣⲟⲟⲙⲉ ⲡⲣⲉⲧⲃ, cf El 120 *S*
ϣⲁⲙⲁⲣⲉⲧϥ ; *lowest part, bottom S* : Jth 7 12 ῥίζα
of mountain, ShC 73 147 ⲣⲁⲧⲥ ⲡⲧⲗⲁϩⲙ, *ib* 137
ⲣⲁⲧⲥ ⲡⲧⲉⲧⲣⲓⲣ, BMis 540 ⲣⲁⲧϥ of deep pit, P 131²
89 ⲣⲁⲧϥ ⲙⲡⲉⲓⲁ *solum convallis*, BAp 157 ⲁϣⲡⲉ ⲣⲁⲧⲥ
ⲡⲧⲉⲕⲁⲙⲉⲗⲉⲓⲁ *limit*, LMis 92 ⲉⲓⲙⲉ ⲉⲣⲁⲧϥ ⲙⲡⲣⲱⲃ,
BMis 493 ⲧϭⲗⲟⲟϭⲉ...ⲣⲁⲧⲥ ; ⲉⲓⲉⲓⲃ ⲛⲣ., *foot* (*toe*)
nail : Deu 28 35 *S* ἴχνος π. ; HTZ a *S* = C 89 130 *B* ;
ⲕⲗⲗⲉ ⲛⲣ. *v* ⲕⲗⲗⲉ c ; ⲕⲁϣ ⲛⲣ. *v* ⲕⲁϣ ; ⲥⲛⲃⲉ ⲛⲣ. *v*
ⲥⲛⲃⲉ *reed*. ϭⲟⲡ ⲛⲣ. *B, sole of foot* : Ac 3 7 (*S* diff)
σφυρόν ; C 86 275 nails into ⲡⲓϣⲟⲡ ⲡⲧⲉ ⲣⲁⲧϥ.

ⲣⲙⲛⲣ. *SB, footman* : Nu 11 21 *SB*, 4 Kg 13 7 *S*
ⲡⲉϫⲟⲥ ⲛ ⲣ. πεζός ; **ⲣⲙⲛⲣ.** *S* : Jth 1 4 πε., Mor 31
225, P 131⁵ 3.

With prep ⲛ- : MG 25 234 *B* ϩⲱⲙⲓ ⲛⲣⲁⲧ, Bor
264 38 *S* ⲡⲏⲧ ⲛⲣⲁⲧϥ, Ps 90 12 *B* ϭⲓ ϭⲣⲟⲡ ⲛⲣⲁⲧⲕ,
Is 20 2 *S* ⲙⲛ ⲧⲟⲟⲩⲉ ⲛⲣⲁⲧⲕ ; *v below* ⲙⲟⲟϣⲉ
ⲛⲣ. ; with ⲛⲥⲁ- : KroppB *S* came in ⲛⲥⲁϫⲱⲓ
went out ⲛⲥⲁⲣ.

ⲕⲁ p. *S, lay, set foot*: Deu 28 56 (*B diff*) βαίνειν;
2 Kg 2 23 ἐπιστρέφειν; **c ⲉⲃⲟⲗ**, *step, set forth*:
1 Kg 26 20 ἐξέρχεσθαι, 3 Kg 10 1 *Gk om*; BM 216
80 ⲙⲡⲉⲥⲕⲉ ⲣⲁⲧⲥ ⲉⲃ. ⲉⲛⲁⲩ παρακύπτειν; ShC 73 80
some ⲕⲁ ⲣⲁⲧⲟⲩ ⲉⲃ. ϧⲡⲡⲉϭⲏⲓ ⲛⲥⲉⲉⲓ, Miss 4 705
ⲁⲩⲕⲁ ⲣⲁⲧⲥ ⲉⲃ. ⲁⲩⲃⲱⲕ.

ⲙⲟⲟϣⲉ ⲛⲣ. *SBF, go on foot*: Ps 65 6 *S* (*B* ϭⲁ.)
ποδί; Ac 20 13 *SB* πεζεύειν; 2 Kg 15 4 *S*, Mt 14
13 *BF* (*S* = Gk), Z 336 *S* πεζῇ; Mor 33 57 *S* ⲉϥⲙ.
ⲡⲣⲟⲧⲩ (*sic*) = BMis 101 *S* ⲡⲛⲉϥⲟⲩⲉⲣⲏⲧⲉ, RAl 99
B ⲉⲟⲙ. ⲡⲣⲁⲧⲩ...ⲉⲧⲧⲁⲗⲏⲟⲩⲧ *on horse*.

ⲡ (ⲉⲓⲛⲉ) p. *SA, bring, follow foot, trace (cf ϭⲛ p.)*:
Ro 11 33 (*F* MR ϭⲉⲛ ⲗ., *B* FRyl ϭⲓ ⲧⲁⲧⲥⲓ), Cl 20
5 *A* ⲙⲁⲩⲛ (*var* ⲙⲁⲩϩ ⲡ) ⲣⲉⲧⲟⲩ (ἀν)εξιχνίαστος;
Br 97 *is it thy will* ⲉⲧⲣⲉⲩⲛ ⲣⲁⲧⲕ *therein*? ShA 1
150 ⲙⲡⲟⲩⲉϣ ⲛ ⲣⲁⲧⲩ *in the depths*; **ⲁⲧⲛ p.** *SA²,*
untraceable: PS 243 *God* ⲛⲁ. ⲣⲁⲧⲩ, Br 125 *sim*,
R 1 3 78 *hell* ⲛⲉⲓⲁ. ⲣⲁⲧⲩ Mani 1 *A²* ⲡⲱⲛϩ ⲛⲁ.

ⲡⲉϧ p. ⲉⲃⲟⲗ *S, disengage foot*: P 44 96 عزل قدم.

ⲥⲱⲣ ⲛⲣ., ⲥⲣ p. *S, spread feet* & *so ventrem pur-*
gare: Jud 3 24 πόδας ἀποκενοῦν, 1 Kg 24 4 ⲥⲉⲛ
(*l* ⲥⲉⲣ, *B* ⲉⲣ ⲓⲩ ⲛ̅ⲣⲉⲙⲥⲓ) παρασκευάζεσθαι; ShC 73
95 *none may lift raiment* ⲉϥⲛⲁⲥⲁⲣ ⲣⲁⲧⲩ, *ib* 125
ⲉⲩϣⲁⲛⲥⲣ ⲣⲁⲧⲟⲩ ⲉϩⲣⲁⲓ ϧⲓⲗⲁⲁⲩ ⲛⲣⲏⲁⲁⲩ, *ib* 124 *sim*
ⲉⲗⲁⲁⲩ; MG 25 131 *B beast springs on prey*
ⲛ̅ⲧⲉϥⲥⲟⲣ (*sic MS*) ⲣⲁⲧⲩ ⲉⲣⲟⲩ *get astride* (?).

+ ⲉⲣ. *SB, put on foot, shoe*: Ez 36 10 *SB* ὑποδύειν; Mk 6 9 *B* (*S* ⲱⲧϩ), Ac 12 8 *SB*, Bor 239 58
S if need be ⲉⲧⲣⲉⲕ+ ⲉⲣⲁⲧⲕ ὑποδέεσθαι; C 43 16 *B*
sandal ⲉⲧⲧⲟⲓ ⲉⲣⲁⲧⲩ.

ⲟⲩⲉϩ p. *SF, set foot*: Ac 20 18 (*B* ⲓ ⲉ-) ἐπιβαίνειν;
ShA 1 97 *not even* ⲉⲟⲩⲉϩ ⲣⲁⲧⲛ ϧⲓϫⲱϥ, BAp 171
ⲛ̅ⲧⲟⲩⲉϩ ⲣⲁⲧⲕ *on his neck*, MR 5 49 *F* ⲙⲡⲓⲛⲉϣⲟⲩϩ
ⲣⲉⲧ ϧⲓϫⲱⲛⲁⲡⲉⲧ (*l?* ⲟϩⲓ ⲣⲉⲧ).

ϫⲓ p. *S, hold foot, impede*: Ep 244 ⲁⲩⲕⲟⲩⲓ ⲛ̅ⲣⲱⲃ
ϫⲓ ⲣⲁⲧ & *I had not leisure to come*.

ϭⲛ p. *SF, find foot, base, search (cf ⲡ p.)*: Job
11 7 (*B* ϫⲉⲙ ⲙⲱⲓⲧ) ἴχνος εὑρίσκειν; Pcod 34 *can-*
not ϭⲛ ⲣⲁⲧⲟⲩ ⲛ̅ⲡⲉϥϩⲓⲟⲟⲩⲉ (*sc God's*), LMis 92
I seek to ϭⲛ ⲣⲁⲧⲩ ⲙⲡϩⲱⲃ; **ⲁⲧϭⲛ p.,** *untrace-*
able, unattainable: Ro 11 33 *F as above*, P 44 47
ἄφθαστος, *ib* 48 ἀνεξιχν.; CO 4 ⲛⲁⲧϭ. ⲡⲁⲧϧⲉⲣⲱⲧϥ,
Mor 41 26 *send* ⲟⲩⲃⲟⲏⲑⲟⲟⲥ ⲛⲁⲧϭ. (? *error*) = DeV
2 281 *B* ⲃⲟⲏⲑⲓⲁ ⲛ̅ⲭⲱⲗⲉⲙ.

ⲁϧⲉ p. *v* ⲱϧⲉ.

ⲉⲣⲁⲧ⸗ *SAA²BF, to foot of, to, mostly of persons*:
Ge 28 5 *S* (*B* ϧⲁ-), Hos 5 13 *SA* (*B* do), Jo 6 37 *F*
(Mich P 3521, *SA²* ϣⲁ-, *B* ϧⲁ-), BHom 35 *S go*
ⲉⲣⲁⲧⲩ ⲙⲡⲉⲕⲣⲓⲧⲏⲥ πρός, BMar 108 *S* προσέρχ. *dat*;
Deu 1 17 *S* (*B* do), Job 23 14 *S* (*B* ⲉϩⲣⲏⲓ ⲉϫⲉⲛ-)
ἐπί, Mk 9 25 *S* (*B om*) ἐπισυντρέχειν; Ru 1 10 *S*
εἰς; Ez 46 17 *B dat*; Ac 17 17 *S* (*B Gk om*); Ez
4 14 *S* ϣⲁⲣⲟⲩⲛ ⲉⲣⲁⲧⲩ ⲙⲡⲟⲟⲩ (*B* ϣⲁⲉϧⲟⲩⲛ ⲉ-)

ⲉⲱⲥ; PS 8 *S* ⲁϩⲉⲓ ⲉⲣⲁⲧⲩ ⲛ̅ⲓ̅ⲥ̅, *ib* 148 *S when she had*
ⲡⲓⲥⲧⲉⲩⲉ ⲉⲣⲁⲧⲩ ⲙ̅ⲡⲟⲩⲟⲉⲓⲛ, MIE 2 368 *B brought*
ⲉⲣⲁⲕⲟϯ ⲉⲣⲁⲧⲩ *of archbishop*, BM 661 *F written*
ⲉⲗⲉⲧⲩ ⲙ̅ⲡⲉⲧⲁⲙⲡϣⲏ *of all honour*, Ep 145 *S write*
for me ⲁⲣⲁⲧⲩ ⲙ̅ⲡⲉⲡⲓⲥⲕⲟⲡⲟⲥ, BM 340 *S who came*
ⲉⲣⲁⲧⲩ ⲙ̅ⲡⲉⲕⲧⲟⲡⲟⲥ (*cf* ⲉⲓ ⲉⲣⲁⲧ⸗).

ϧⲁⲣⲁⲧ⸗, *SA²,* ϧⲁⲣ. *A,* ϧⲁⲣ. *B,* ϧⲁⲗ. *F, under foot,*
beneath: Ex 32 19 *S* (*B* ⲥⲁⲡⲉⲥⲏⲧ), Deu 33 3 *S* (*B*
ϧⲁⲧⲉⲛ-), Ps 17 39 *B* (*S* ϧⲁ-), Mt 8 9 *SB*, Jo 1 48
F (PcodMor, *SB* do) ὑπό, Deu 28 23 *S* (*B* ⲥⲁⲡ.),
Dan 4 18 *B* (*S* do), Mk 7 28 *S* (*B* ⲉϧⲣⲏⲓ) ὑποκάτω,
Mic 1 4 *SA* (*B* do) ὑποκάτωθεν, Sa 14 15 *S* ⲛⲉⲧϧⲁⲣ.
ὑποχείριος; Ex 24 6 *S* (*B* ϧⲁⲧⲉⲛ-), Mk 5 11 *S* (*B*
do) πρός; *ib* 33 *SB* προσ(πίπτειν); Nu 34 7 *S* (*B*
do) παρά; Ac 10 25 *SB* ἐπί; Ez 40 15 *B* (*S* ϧⲓϧⲣⲁ⸗)
ante; Eccl 7 15 *F* (*S* ⲙ̅ⲛ̅ⲛⲥⲁ-) ὀπίσω, Ru 2 2 *S*
κατόπισθεν; 1 Kg 8 11 *S* ἐν; Si 50 16 *S* εἰς θεμέλια;
BHom 142 *S* ⲛⲉⲧϧⲁⲣⲁⲧⲩ διάκονος; BG 46 *S spirit*
ⲣ ϩⲱⲃ ϧⲁⲣⲁⲧⲩ ⲙ̅ⲡⲉⲥⲡⲉⲣⲙⲁ, ShC 42 38 *S following*
him as if ⲉϥϧⲁⲣⲁⲧⲩ ⲙ̅ⲡⲁⲓ, BHom 83 *S sim*, Mun
18 *S disciples* ϧⲁⲣⲁⲧⲩ ⲛⲟⲩϧⲁϩ, TU 43 21 *A went*
forth ϧⲁⲣⲉⲧⲩ ⲙ̅ⲡⲭ̅ⲥ̅ (*cf* Mt 25 1), AP 29 *A²* ⲁⲩ]-
ⲥⲁⲡⲉⲛ ϧⲁⲣⲉⲧⲩ ⲙ[ⲡⲁⲩⲗⲟⲥ; C 43 163 *B enrolled*
ϧⲁⲣⲁⲧⲩ ⲙ̅ⲡⲁⲥⲧ̅, BMar 11 *S sim*, Mor 50 6 *S hid-*
den ϧⲁⲣⲁⲧⲟⲩ ⲛ̅ⲛⲉⲡⲉⲧⲣⲁ, J 106 37 *S will witness* ϧⲁ-
ⲣⲁⲧⲥ ⲛ̅ⲧⲉⲓⲡⲣⲁⲥⲓⲥ, Miss 4 221 *B* ⲥϩⲁⲓ ϧⲁⲣⲁⲧⲩ *of*
Henoticon; Mor 51 36 *S* ⲁϧⲁⲕⲱⲥ ⲉⲣ ⲑⲉ ⲛ̅ϧⲁⲣⲁⲧⲥ.

ϧⲓⲣⲁⲧ⸗ *SAA², toward*: Jo 12 13 *A²* (*S* ⲉⲧⲱⲙⲛⲧ,
A ϧⲏⲧ⸗, *B* ⲉϩⲣⲁ⸗) εἰς ὑπάντησιν, *ib* 18 *A* (*SA²* ϧⲏⲧ⸗,
B ϧⲁ-) ὑπαντᾶν; Jos 2 5 *S* ὀπίσω; BHom 16 *S will*
run forth ϧⲓⲣⲁⲧⲛ, Br 239 *S* ⲁⲡⲉⲧϣⲟⲟⲡ ⲉⲓ ⲉⲃⲟⲗ ϧⲓ-
ⲣⲁⲧⲟⲩ, BMOr 6201 A 119 *S* ⲉⲓⲟⲩⲱϣ ⲃⲱⲕ ϧⲓⲣⲁⲧⲩ,
PLond 4 445 *S wrote northward* ϧⲓⲣⲁⲧⲩ ⲛ̅ⲑⲉⲟⲇⲟ-
ⲥⲓⲟⲥ.

In name (?): Ταυρατω (PBad 93 32).

ⲣⲏⲧ *S nn m, a title*? : BM 1160 ⲡⲣ. ϣⲉⲛⲟⲩⲧⲉ.
In ? name Παχομ πρῆτ (Preisigke).

ⲣⲏⲧ *vow v* ⲉⲣⲏⲧ.

ⲣⲟⲧ *in* ⲥⲟⲩⲣⲟⲧ *v* ⲥⲓⲟⲩ.

ⲣⲱⲧ *SAB,* ⲗⲱⲧ *F,* ⲣⲉⲧ- *SB,* ⲣⲟⲧ⸗ *B* (Cat 78),
ⲣⲏⲧ† *SAB,* ⲗⲏⲧ† *F,* ⲣⲥ ⲣⲁⲧ- *SB vb* **1** *intr, grow,*
sprout, be covered with a growth as vegetation, hair:
Ps 1 3† *SB, ib* 91 14† *B* (*S* ⲧⲏϭ), Pro 11 30 *AB* (*S*
om), Is 34 13 *SBF*, Lu 8 6 *SB* φύειν, Job 24 18†
B (*S* ϣⲏⲡ) φυτόν; Lev 13 37 *B*, Ps 64 11 *B* ἀνατέλλειν, Mt 13 5 *B* ἐξαν.; *ib* 26 *BF* βλαστάνειν;
Job 5 6 *B* (*all S* + ⲟⲩⲱ) ἀναβλ., *ib* 15 30 *B* (*S* do
nn) βλαστός; Is 5 6 *SB* ἀναβαίνειν; Hos 7 9 *B*
ἐξανθεῖν, Mt 13 32 *F* (*B* ⲁⲓⲁⲓ, *S* = Gk) αὐξάνειν;
2 Kg 18 9† *S* δάσος, Lev 11 5† *S* (*B* ⲣⲁⲧϥⲁⲧ) δασυ-;
Jud 15 5† *S* ὀρθός (*var* ἑστώς); Ez 17 10 *B plantari*;

PS 226 *S* ⲡⲉⲧⲣ.† ϩⲣⲁⲓ ⲡⲣⲏⲧⲟⲩ, R 1 3 73 *S* ⲡⲉⲧⲣ. ⲣⲏⲡⲧⲟⲟⲩ, El 64 *A* trees ⲉⲧⲣ.† on earth, C 41 42 *B* island whereon ϩⲁⲡϣⲱⲙ ⲣ.†, AM 158 *B* ⲡⲟⲩⲓⲏⲃ ⲁⲩⲣ., RNC 83 *S* touched wounded lips ⲁⲧⲉϥⲧⲁⲡⲣⲟ ⲣ. ⲡⲧⲉϣⲉ, P 131⁷ 25 *S* ⲡⲉⲓⲱⲣⲉ ⲉⲧⲣ.† ⲕⲁⲗⲱⲥ opp ⲉⲑⲟⲟⲩ, Ryl 402 *S* ⲉⲣⲉⲡⲉϥⲉⲙⲕⲁϩ ⲣ.† *with bushy eyebrows*, BMis 269 *S* wooden canopy bears fruit as if ⲉϥⲣ.† = Mor 30 44† *F*, KroppM 91 *S* write with reed ⲉϥⲣ.† *from growing plant*, Ryl 346 *S* ϩⲣⲉ ⲉϥⲣ.† *standing fodder*. MIE 2 409 *B* ⲉⲣⲉⲡⲟⲩⲥⲱⲙⲁ ⲣ† like scorpion's = PO 22 426 نَشَ, AZ 33 56 *Sᶠ* tree ⲉϥⲣ.† ϩⲓⲱⲡⲓ [ⲙⲙ]ⲉ, BMis 442 *S* large stones ⲣ.† ϩⲁⲡⲙⲟⲟⲩ *stuck up*, Mor 30 47 *S* thy spear ⲣ.† ⲡϩⲏⲧ = BMis 271 *S* ⲧⲟⲕⲥ ⲉⲣⲟⲓ;   c ⲉⲃⲟⲗ *SB*, *grow forth*: ShC 73 171 *S* hairs ⲉⲧⲣ. ⲉⲃⲟⲗ in armpits, C 86 295 *B* tree ⲉⲧⲁϥⲣ. ⲉⲃ.;   c ⲉϩⲣⲁⲓ *S*, *grow upward*: Lev 25 5 (*B* ⲣ.) ἀναβαίν.; ShA 2 141 lilies ⲉⲧⲣ. ⲉϩ. ⲣⲏⲧⲥⲱⲙⲉ;   c ⲉⲡϣⲱⲓ *B*, meaning same: Deu 29 18† (*S* ϯ ⲟⲩⲱ ⲡⲥⲁⲧⲡⲉ), He 12 15† (*S* ⲣ. ⲉϩⲣ.) φύ. ἄνω; Ge 19 25† (*S* ϯ ⲟⲩⲱ) ἀνατέλ.; Va 57 226 ϣⲁⲩⲣ. ⲉⲡ. ϩⲉⲛⲡⲓⲕⲁⲣⲓ βλαστ.; TEuch 2 199 rained on earth ϣⲁⲛⲧⲉϥⲣ. ⲉⲡ. & gave fruit;   c ⲉϩⲟⲩⲛ *B*, *stick in*: C 89 16 if thorn ⲣ. ⲉϩ. ϩⲉⲛⲡⲉϥⲥⲁⲗⲁⲅϫ;   c ⲛ-, *overgrown, covered with* (v ⲛ- partic II **b** & *cf* ⲁϣⲁⲓ, ⲟϣ ⲛ-): Ge 27 23† *S* (*B* ⲟϣ ⲛ-) δασύς; Jer 4 29 *B* ⲙⲁ ⲉⲟⲣ.† ⲡϣϣⲏⲛ (*S* ⲙⲁ ⲡϣ.) ἄλσος; Ez 1 7† *SB* ⲡⲧⲉⲣⲱⲧⲟⲥ; Z 328 *S* whole body ⲣ.† ⲡⲗⲁⲥ γλῶσσαν ὑπάρχειν; MG 25 248 *B* head ⲣ....ⲡϣⲱⲓ τριχοῦν; BAp 81 *S* ⲉϥⲣ.† ⲡϣⲱ = MIE 2 356 *B*, HL 90 *B* ⲉⲩⲣ.† ⲡⲉϫⲓⲙ *wholly bald*, ShA 1 424 *S* land had been as if ⲁϥⲣ. ⲡⲣⲡⲉ, Mor 48 18 *S* ⲥⲉⲛⲁⲣ. ⲡⲧⲏⲣ (var BMar 211 ⲣⲉⲧ ⲧ. Is 40), P 131⁶ 47 *S* lamb ⲙⲡⲁⲧⲉϥⲣ. (ⲡ)ⲥⲟⲣⲧ, Ryl 72 360 *S* phoenix grows ϣⲁⲛⲧϥⲣ. ⲙⲙⲛϩⲉ;   ⲣ. ⲉⲃⲟⲗ ⲛ- *S*: Sa 13 13 wood ⲉⲧⲣ.† ⲉⲃ. ⲡⲉⲓⲃ συμφύ.; BMis 546 pit ⲉⲥⲣ.† ⲉⲃⲟⲗ ⲡⲧⲁϭ ⲧⲁϭ ⲡⲕⲱϩⲧ *massas igneas ex omni parte*.

II tr *SB*, *bring forth*: Ge 3 18 *B* (ⲉϥⲉⲣⲱⲧ P 1, *S* ⲧⲁⲩⲟ), Is 45 8 *B* (*S* ϯ ⲟⲩⲱ) ἀνατέλ.; *ib* 32 13 *B* (*SF* ⲧⲁⲩⲟ ⲉϩⲣ.) ἀναβαί.; *ib* 40 31 *SB* (ⲡⲧⲉⲣⲟ)φύειν; Tri 423 *S* land ⲣ. ⲡⲁϥ ⲡⲟⲩϩⲁⲣⲟⲟⲩⲉ اينب; PS 287 *S* ϣⲁⲥⲣ(ⲧ?) ⲧⲏϩ, PMéd 226 *S* eyes ⲉⲧⲣⲉⲩⲣ. ϩⲟⲩϩⲉ, Cat 210 *B* sown seed ϣⲁⲥⲣ. ⲙⲡⲓⲥⲉⲗⲥ, *ib* 78 *B* thorns ⲉϥⲉⲣⲟⲧⲟⲩ ⲡⲁⲕ (*cf* Ge 3);   c ⲉⲃⲟⲗ *S*: P 131⁴ 148 ⲉⲧⲉⲡⲣⲏⲧ (*l.* ⲣⲉⲧ) ⲙⲛϩⲉ ⲉⲃ. in church;   c ⲉⲡϣⲱⲓ *B*: Cat 223 land ⲣ. ⲉⲡ. ⲛϩⲁⲡⲥⲟⲩⲣⲓ, C 89 105 sim;   c ⲉⲡⲉⲥⲏⲧ *B*: Is 37 31 (*S* ϫⲉ ⲡⲟⲩⲡⲉ ⲉⲃ.) φύ. κάτω.   ⲣ c *SB*: Is 27 6 *B* ⲉ(ⲣ) ⲣⲁⲧⲧⲁⲣ ⲉⲃⲟⲗ (or ? *l* ⲣⲉⲧ, *S* ⲧⲉⲕ ϯⲟⲩⲱ ⲉⲃ.) βλαστ., ShMing 325 *S* ⲣⲱⲙⲉ ⲡⲣⲁⲧϥⲙ (*cf* 4 Kg 1 8 δασύς), ⲣⲁⲧϥⲁⲧ ⲟ ⲡⲁⲧ.

—— nn m *SAB*, pl ⲣⲁⲧⲉ *S*, ⲣⲟϯ *B*, *a growth*: Deu 28 33 *S* ⲣⲁⲧⲉ (*B* ⲟⲩⲟϯ) ἐκφόριον; Ez 16 7 *SB*

ἀνατολή; Job 5 25 *S*(*B* ⲥⲙⲁϩ) παμβότανον; Is 61 11 *B*(*S* ϩⲣⲏⲣⲉ) ἄνθος; Joel 1 19 *A*(*B* diff) ὥραιος; Mt 12 1 *B* & paral ⲣⲟϯ (*S* ⲙⲁ ⲉⲧϫⲏⲩ) σπόριμα; Lev 23 17 *S* ⲣ. ⲡϣⲟⲣⲡ (*B* ϣ. ⲡⲟⲩⲧⲁϩ) πρωτογένημα; Ann 1 54 (K 172 om) *B* ⲛⲓⲣⲱϯ حَشَائِش (*l* حَشَائِش), K 180 *B* ⲛⲓⲣ. نَبَات, P 55 2 *B* الزُّرُوع, TEuch 2 99 *B* ⲡⲓⲥⲙ ⲣ. of field ʾ﮲ʿ; Br 275 *S* ⲁⲩⲧⲟⲫⲩⲏⲥ ⲛ ⲡⲓⲣ. ⲙⲁⲅⲁⲁϥ, Mor 50 6 *S* bones hidden in ⲛⲉⲣ. ⲡⲕⲁⲙ, BSM 88 *B* ⲡⲣ. ⲡⲛⲓⲭⲣⲱϣ;   *cicatrization*: ShC 42 195 *S* after treatment of wound ϣⲁⲣⲉⲣ. ⲟⲩⲱⲡϩ ⲉⲃⲟⲗ...ϫⲉⲁⲧⲉⲡⲗⲏⲅⲏ ⲉⲓ ⲉϩⲟⲩⲡ;   **b** wool *S*: Lev 13 59 (*B* ⲥⲟⲣⲧ) ἔρεος, BP 419 ⲗⲱⲧⲓⲍ ⲡⲣ., *cf* BMis 178 ⲡⲣ. of lambs, ⲡⲣ. ⲡⲥⲟⲣⲧ of sheep, ⲡⲣ. of fruits.

In place-name(?) Φερετνουῖς (POxy 937, *cf* ﺏﺩﻧﺭ, v ⲛⲟⲩϩⲉ *sycamore*).

V also ⲥⲓⲙ.

ⲣⲁⲧⲉ *S* nn as adj, meaning unknown: BMis 533 Raphael warns Chrysostom that Arcadius will build him (R.) chapel, ⲉⲓⲥ ⲡⲣⲣⲟ ⲡⲁⲭⲡⲟⲩⲕ ⲉⲩϣⲁϫⲉ ⲡⲣ. ϫⲉ ϥⲛⲁⲕⲱⲧ &c.

ⲣⲁⲓⲧⲉ *S*, ⲣⲉⲓ. *A²*, ⲣⲉⲉⲓ. *AA²* nn f, *kindred*: Ex 6 24 *A*(*B* ϫⲓⲛⲙⲓⲥⲓ) γένεσις, *ib* 14 *A*(*B* ⲅⲉⲛⲟⲥ), *ib* 19 *A* ⲣⲉⲉⲓ. (*B* = Gk), Nu 1 20 *S*(*B* do), Jos 6 23 *S*, Lu 1 61 *S*(*B* do) συγγένεια; P 131¹ 20 *S* Nazareth ⲧⲣ. ⲙⲏⲧⲡⲟⲗⲧⲉⲓⲁ of Elizabeth, Mor 33 107 *S* ⲡⲉⲥⲣ. = BMis 55 *S* ⲛⲉⲧⲥⲟⲟⲩⲛ ⲙⲙⲟⲥ, Mani 2 *A²* ϯⲣ. ⲡϣⲙⲙⲟ, P 44 95 *S* laying foundations ⲡⲧⲣ. ⲡⲡⲣⲉϥⲛⲟⲃ خُنْس; ⲕⲁⲧⲁⲣ. *S*, *kinship* (*cf* ⲕ.ⲥⲁⲣϩ): P 131¹ 62 I would establish ⲧⲕ. ⲡⲧⲉⲓⲡⲁⲣⲑⲉⲛⲟⲥ;   ⲣⲙⲣ. *S*, *kinsman*: Lu 1 58 (varr ⲣⲙⲙⲣ., ⲣⲙⲣⲁⲩⲏ, *B* = Gk) περίοικος, JA '05 1 422 (on Lu *lc*) ⲡⲉⲥⲣⲙⲣⲁⲩⲏ ⲙⲡⲡ[ⲉⲥ]ⲣⲙⲣ., Mor 28 1c4 Paêse's friend Paul ⲉⲩⲣⲙⲣ. ⲡⲉ = Synax 1 143 صَدِيق.   ϫⲓ ⲣ. *S*, *have kinship, be akin*: P 44 96 ⲡⲉⲧϫⲓ ⲣ. ϩⲛⲁⲁⲅⲉⲓⲁ خُنْس.

ⲣⲏⲧⲉ *S*(rare, mostly = ϩⲉ) *AA²*, -ϯ *B*, ⲣⲉⲧⲉ *O* nn m, *manner, fashion, likeness*: J&C 92 *S* ⲡⲣ. ⲡⲟⲩⲗⲉⲩⲓⲧⲏⲛ, *ib* ⲡⲣ. ⲛⲓⲡⲧⲟⲟⲩⲉ, Ac 4 21 *B*(*S* ϩⲉ) τὸ πῶς, MG 25 209 *B* ⲡⲓⲣ. ⲡϣⲱⲗⲕ (*S* Z 344 om) πῶς; Dan 1 15 *B* beheld ⲡⲟⲩⲣ. (*S* ϩⲟ) εἰδέα, Zech 12 9 *A*(*B* Gk om); DeV 2 166 *B* ⲉϩⲟⲧⲉ ⲡⲓⲣ. ⲉⲡⲁⲡⲙⲉⲩⲓ ⲉⲣⲟϥ, Mus 42 222 *S* ⲡⲣ. ⲟⲡⲡⲉ ⲡⲁⲓ ⲉⲧⲣⲉⲩϫⲟⲟⲥ *this is like as if they should say*, ShC 73 152 *S* ⲡⲣ. ⲉⲧⲉⲣⲉⲡⲣⲁϣ ⲥⲡⲁⲩ ⲛⲁⲥⲱ, Aeg 44 *B* ⲡⲓⲣ. ⲉⲧⲁⲥϫⲁ ⲥⲱⲙⲁ ⲉϩⲣⲏ ⲙⲙⲟϥ, Miss 4 140 *B* will tell thee ⲉⲡⲓⲣ. ⲉⲧⲥϣⲉ Hor 78 *O* ⲟⲩⲛϥⲣ.; ⲡⲁⲓⲣ. *B*, (*in*) *this manner, thus*: Job 1 10 (*S* ϩⲓⲛⲁⲓ), Ez 23 44 (*S* ⲧⲁⲓⲧⲉ ⲑⲉ), Mt 1 18 ⲟⲩⲛ. (*S* ϩⲉ) οὕτως, CaiEuch 642 ὡσαύτως; EpJer 16 (*F* ⲣⲏ) τοιοῦτος; Job 5 8 neg (*S* diff) οὐ μὴν δέ; BSM 73 ⲡ. ⲁⲩⲧⲱⲟⲩⲛⲟⲩ = BMis 163 *S* ⲡⲧⲉⲓⲣⲉ, Va 63 12 ⲓⲥϫⲉ ⲡ. ⲡⲉ ⲓⲉ &c = BMis 382 *S* ⲉϣϫⲉ ⲧⲁⲓⲧⲉ ⲑⲉ, DeV 2 143 when saints turned toward demons ⲡ. ⲁⲩϥⲱⲧ, C 86 355 when τόπος

destroyed п. оп єкєϣорϣєр churches, AM 62 oүп.
πє пαγλoc ;   лпр. A, лϥр. B, *in form, manner,
like as* : Pro 2 4 (SA ϧє), Ac 1 10 (S om) ὡς, ib 2 3
(S ϧє) ὡσεί, EpJer 26 (F ϧн), Jo 5 21 (SA² дo)
ὥσπερ, Su 15, Hag 2 3 (SA єϣxє) καθώς ; Jer 40
11 κατά ; Ez 12 11 (S дo), Am 9 9 AB, Zech 11 13
AB (both S cлoт) ὃν τρόπον ; DeV 2 43 єϥлι.
xєєϥxω лмoc пαϥ xє-, ib 169 found them єγлι.
ϧωc єγcoбϯ, C 86 22 л. єγпα єϩрнι єoγпнcн ;
лпαιρ.B, лпιр. AA² adjectival, *of this sort, like this,
thus* : Jer 9 9 (S лιнє), Ro 2 2 (S дo) τοιοῦτος, Lu 6
26 (S ϧє) κατὰ τὰ αὐτά ; C 86 282 пθoκ пιл л. τίς
εἶ συ?, ib 195 пαιιϣϯ п̄γнатoc л. ; adverbial, *in
this manner, thus* : Ge 1 6, Ez 20 44 (S дo), Nah 1 12
AB οὕτως ; El 52 A who this angel standing л. ?,
Mani 2 A²]єιрє пєγ л.   лпєκ-, лпєϥр. &c B,
like thee, him &c : EpJer 43 (F ϧн) ὥσπερ, Ro 13 9
(S дo), Ap 6 11 (S дo) ὡς, ib 16 18 (S дo) οἷος ; Bodl
Marsh 32 87 oγєγχн лпєcр. ⟨ق⟩ *like last*, Cat 127
preserved virginity лпєcр. *in its condition* as before,
DeV 2 50 do they not know me лпєκр., believe on
me птєκ̅ѕ̅є, serve me лпєκcлoт ?   κатα фр. B,
according to the manner, as : Ex 32 28 (S ϧє), Bar 1
6 καθά, Ac 2 4 (S дo) καθώς, Ez 20 32 (S дo) ὃν τρ.,
Va 57 15 κ. пαιр. єпαϥxω лмoc (due to S original κ. θє, *l* лмoϥ, MG 25 9 sim) οὕτως ;   cα
πр. B, *meaning same* : Ge 24 1 κατα c. пιбєп κ.
πάντα, Ro 3 2 (S cлoт) sim κ. п. τρόπον, Dif 2
49 єϥϩoϧєx лмoϥ псαc. пιбєп ;   ϣαπр. S,
up to likeness of, in respect of : Z 269 ϣ. пєпϣαxє
(*l* пп-) αппє пєϥϩo *his badness was not (merely) in
respect of words*, but deeds made clear &c, BMOr
9525 8 αγтαлoι xєϣ. лпєтєκαγαπн ϣoγп (*l*
ϣωп) гєωргιoc єрoc ;   αϣ пр. B, *what sort,
manner* : Ez 26 17 oγα. ?, Va 57 11 ϧαпα. пє ?, MG
25 233 єκєр пнcтєγіп пα. (S ϧє) πῶς ?, Pro 6 8a
(SA = Gk) ὡς ; Va 63 12 αιпαєр α. ?   ανϣ пр.
B, *many sorts* : 2 Tim 3 6 (S ϣoбє), Va 61 217
doctrine of oγл. ποικίλος, PO 11 356 grace of
healing пoγл. ;   ато, θo пр. SB, *meaning same* :
Ex 27 16 ποικιλία, Ez 16 18 (S пαγєιпαγαн), 1 Pet
1 6 (var лнϣ, S ϣoбє) ποικίλος ; CaiEuch 651
єтoι пoγθ. πολυμερής ; BKU 1 9 S пoγα]тo пє-
рнтє ;   р. пιбєп B, *every sort, way* : CaiEuch
588 journeying пр. п. οἵῳ δήποτε τρόπῳ, DeV 2
138 demons єγoι пр. п.

ιрι, oι лϥр. B, *be in manner, likeness, be as* :
Ez 18 14 ποιεῖν κατά ; 1 Jo 3 2 (S єιнє) ὅμοιος
εἶναι ; Is 44 7 (S ϧє) ὥσπερ no vb, MG 25 220 cannot єр пєтєпр. ὡς ; C 86 17 limbs єр пoγр. птє
ϣoрп ;   єр лϥр. : Job 8 14 (S Gk om), Is 1 9 (S
ϣωпє пθє п-) γίνεσθαι ὡς, Ez 31 8 ὅμοιος dat ; C 43
11 αϥєр л. пoγϣαϩ пχρωл. V also cωпт *custom*.

ϯ лϥр. B, *give means* : C 89 126 птє пc̅̄ ϯ л.
пϣoγ to do good = Z 640 S ϯ θє, MIE 2 372 αγϯ
л. пнι to speak.

xєл р., пιр. B, *find means* : MG 25 197 cx. р.
αп єϯ, EW 105 лпєϥx. пιр. лϥωт.

oγoп, лмoп р. AB, *there is, is not means* : Si 22
22 A oγп р. пιαγϩ (S ϧє) διαλλαγή, DeV 2 33
oγoп р. єпαϣϣo єoрєпϭι, Jer 43 5 л. р. лмoι
єϣє (S пϯпαϣ бωκ αп) οὐ μὴ δύνωμαι, 2 Macc 6
6 A пєлп р. αр cαββατoп Gk om.

ριтα B, *a plant* : K 191 пιтα (all MSS р.) رَهِى,
رَهِى flower of *laurus nobilis*. But cf رِيتَج *sapindus*
(Schweinfurth Ar Pfl 41, 76).

ρтω S, єр. SB nn f, *span* lit *great hand* : Ex 28
16 B, Jud 3 16 S, Is 40 12 SB σπιθαμή ; P 44 70
S тєр. شِبْر ; K 142 B ϯєр. 'شِ. ; C 89 95 B = MG
17 469 'شِ. ; Miss 4 637 S pot єϣαcр oγєр. пϣιп
= C 41 21 B, P 129¹⁷ 83 S tablet єcпαр oγтртω
(sic), Mor 52 53 S seeing Mark's steadfastness at
death αпϫιαбoλoc ϯ птєϥєр. (meaning ?).

(ρωтб S), -тєб B, λωтєб F, ротбϩ S (once),
рoєбϩ B, λатбϩ F, ротєбϯ B, λатєбϯ F vb I intr,
recline : Va 57 110 B at king's feast ϣακр. in fear,
Mt 14 19 BF c ϧιxєп- (S пoγxє єϩрαι єx.) ἀνα-
κλίνεσθαι, Lu 14 8 BF c ϧєп- (S п. refl) κατακλ. ;
Mt 22 10 B(S п.†), ib 26 7† BF(S дo) ἀνακεῖσθαι,
1 Cor 8 10 B(S дo), Mk 14 3 B†F(S дo) κατακεῖ. ;
Ge 49 9 B(S п. refl), Mt 15 35 B(S дo) ἀναπίπτειν,
Ex 26 17† B ἀντιπίπ. ; AM 17 B αγр. & ate &
drank, ROC 23 154 B at feast ϣαγр. & call for
music, Miss 4 225 B vision пαϥр.† пє ϧιxєппιбι-
пαx ;   р. єбoλ B, *meaning same* : Dif 2 72 р. єб.
ϧєппιϫιппoп.

II tr BF, *make to recline* : C 43 216 B ϯпαрoє-
бєϥ ϧєппιϫιппoп, Ann 23 55 F пкλатбєc ϧικoγп-
тϥ ;   refl : Mt 8 11 B(S п. refl) ἀνακλ., Jo 21
20 B c єxєп- (S дo) ἀναπίπ. ; HSt 462 S let not
catechumen ротбєϥ лмпєпιcтoc (var Aeg 259 пo-
xoγ).

лα пр. BF, *place of reclining* : Lu 14 7 (S лα
пп.) (πρωτο)κλισία.

ρтoб¹, єр.², ρтoϥ³, єр.⁴, ρтαб⁵, єр.⁶, αρтoб⁷,
-αб⁸ S(⁵⁻⁸ Theban), єртoб⁹, -oп¹⁰, -ωб¹¹ B, єртαб¹²,
єλ.¹³, -αϥ¹⁴ F nn m, *measure of grain &c*, ἀρτάβη
اَرْدَب : Is 5 10 S¹B¹⁰F¹⁴, Bel 3 B¹⁰ ἀр. ; K 143 B¹¹ اَرْ;
HL 103 B⁹, PLond 4 500, CO 463 S², BM 1056,
1065 S³, ShC 42 70, ST 319 S⁴, CO 180, ST 87 S⁵,
ib 120, Hall 77 S⁶, CA 98, RE 9 158 S⁷, BM 476,
ST 117 S⁸, CMSS 71 F¹², ib 75 F¹⁴, Kr 11 F¹³.
Cf Gött Nachr '16 112. V αрϣιп, бппє, єιωт
barley, рooγє, coγo, ϣωпє *gourd*, ϩлoγ, also лпт,
лααxє *measure*.

ⲣⲓⲧⲓⲟⲓ *B* nn m, zodiacal sign *Aquarius*: K 50 ⲁⲣⲭⲱⲟⲥ (ie ὑδροχόος) دالي, ϥⲣ. ʼⲇ; horns of Scorpio: ib 52 ⲡⲣ. زبانان. Coptic ?

ⲣⲁⲧϥⲁⲧ *v* ⲡⲁⲧ.

ⲣⲁⲅⲏ, -ⲉ, -ⲉⲓ (JA'05 1 422), ⲣⲏⲅⲉ *S*, ⲣⲁⲟⲅⲏ, ⲣⲁⲃⲏ *B*, ⲗⲁⲅⲉⲓ *Sᶠ* (PMéd), ⲗⲁⲅⲏ, ⲗⲁⲟⲅⲏ *F* nn f, *quarter* of town, *neighbourhood*: Jer 30 16 *B* ἄμφοδος; LMis 370 *B* ⲁⲙⲟⲩ ⲉⲧⲁⲓⲣⲁⲃⲏ دار, P 44 190 *B* حارة; BMis 104 *S* ⲣ̄ⲙⲉ (ῥύμη), ⲛϭⲓⲣ, ⲛⲣ. of town, Miss 4 242 *S* from house to house & from ⲟⲩⲣ. ⲉⲕⲉⲣ., DeV 2 197 *B* built church in ⲧⲉϥⲣ. for τόπος was distant, Baouit 44 *F* ⲣⲛⲧⲉⲡⲗ. ⲧⲏⲣⲛ, Kr 36 *F* ⲧⲗ. ⲛϣⲁⲅⲙⲟⲩϯ ⲗⲁⲥ ⲭⲉ-, C 86 147 *B* we met ⲟⲩⲣⲁⲃⲏ...ⲉⲩ ⲭⲱ ⲙϥⲁⲓ *company*, MG 25 66 *B* youth dwelt in ⲧⲉⲥⲣ. = Gött Ar 114 11 بقر, ib 87 *B* tomb-cave & cells round it called ⲑⲣⲁⲃⲏ (var -ⲟⲩⲏ) ⲛⲛⲓⲣⲱⲙⲁⲓⲟⲥ = lc 20 دير الروم, ib 311 *B* = BIF 13 118 *S* sim, Mor 31 12 *S* ⲧⲣ. of Macarius in Shiêt, N&E 39 337 *B*, PO 14 338 *B* sim, MG 25 98 *B* ⲣⲁⲡⲕⲉⲣ. named after hermits dwelling there, J 24 67 *S* house ⲣⲓⲧⲣⲏⲅⲉ of St Ananias = 106 128 ⲣⲓⲣ, Amélineau *Géog* 577 *B* ⲧⲣⲁⲃⲏ ⲛⲡⲉⲃⲅⲗⲱⲛ حارت زويلة; ⲣⲙⲣ., *neighbour*: Job 19 15 *S* -ⲉ (*B* ⲑⲉϣⲉ), Ru 4 17 *S*, BHom 57 *S* (= R 2 2 37 ⲣⲙⲛⲏⲓ) γείτων; Lu 1 58 *S* περίοικος *v* ⲣⲁⲓⲧⲉ; MG 25 127 *B* ⲑⲉϣⲉⲩ, ⲣ., Mor 51 27 *S* ⲡⲉⲥⲣⲱⲙⲉ, ⲡⲉⲥⲣ., ⲡⲉⲥⲣⲙⲣⲁⲗ, JA '88 2 378 *S* fire fell from sky as if ⲛⲧⲁⲟⲩⲣ. ⲛⲟⲭϥ, PMéd 230 *Sᶠ* household, kin & ⲣⲙⲗ.; ⲙⲉⲧⲣⲉⲙⲣ. *B*, *neighbourhood*: MG 25 67 ⲥⲩⲛⲅⲉⲛⲓⲁ & ⲙ.

ⲣⲏⲓⲟⲅⲉ *v* ⲣⲟⲟⲩⲉ.

ⲣⲁⲟⲩⲱ, ⲣⲁⲟⲩⲛⲟⲩⲧ†, -ⲃⲛⲟⲩⲧ† *B* vb intr, *happen, fall, be subject, be caught*: Ex 22 3† (*S* ϭⲱⲡ†) ἔνοχος; Pro 6 30 (*SA* ϭⲱⲡ), Is 31 9 (*SF* ϭ.) ἁλίσκεσθαι; Pro 1 10 (var & *SA* ⲟⲩⲱϣ) βούλεσθαι; 2 Tim 2 26† (*S* ϭ.†) ζωγρεῖσθαι; TEuch 1 362 save us from trials ⲉⲧⲣ.† حاضر *present* opp ⲉⲑⲛⲏⲟⲩ, ib 2 19 this time ⲉⲧⲁϥⲣ. ح.; MG 25 89 ⲁϥⲣ. ⲉⲁϥϣⲱⲕⲓ *chanced to be digging*, HL 97 ⲁⲥⲣ. ⲙⲙⲁⲩ *as he was dying*, PO 11 370 heretic ⲁϥⲣ.† ⲙⲙⲁⲩ, Miss 4 209 ⲧⲉⲛⲛⲁⲣ. ⲉⲩⲉⲣ ⲕⲁⲑⲉⲣⲓⲛ ⲙⲙⲟⲛ *shall fall to be deposed*, BSM 14 ⲁⲙⲓⲭⲁⲏⲗ ⲣ. = BMis 348 *S* ⲉⲓ ⲛⲧⲉⲩⲛⲟⲩ; ⲥ ⲉ-, *fall upon, into, be liable for, chargeable with*: Ge 26 11† ἔνοχος; Pro 1 23† (*SA* ϭ.†) ὑπεύθυνος; ib 13 17 (*S* ϥⲉ ⲉϩⲣⲁⲓ, *A* ⲧⲱⲙⲧ), He 10 31 (*S* do) ἐμπίπτειν, Ja 1 2 (*S* ⲉⲓ ⲉϩⲣ.) περιπ.; Is 24 18 (*S* ϭⲱⲗⲭ) ἁλίσκ.; Pro 9 18 (*SA* ⲧⲱ.) συναντᾶν; Va 57 206 ⲁⲩⲣ. ⲉϥⲕⲁⲧⲁⲇⲓⲕⲏ δίκην διδόναι; AM 270 ⲁϥⲣ. ⲉⲟⲩⲏⲣ ⲛⲕⲩⲛⲁⲓⲡⲟⲥ ὑπομένειν; C 89 83 ⲉⲕⲣ.† ⲉⲣⲁⲡⲛⲟⲃⲓ = MG 17 448 مطلوب; Miss 4 134 shall be ⲣ.† ⲉϥⲙⲟⲩ *liable to*, AM 306 taxes if paid ⲥⲉⲛⲁⲣ. ⲉⲣⲱⲧⲉⲛ ⲁⲛ again = C 43 116

ⲥⲉⲛⲁϣ ⲱⲡ ⲉⲣⲱⲧⲉⲛ ⲁⲛ, BSM 42 is time ⲉⲑⲣⲉⲛⲣ. ⲉⲧⲁⲡⲁⲫⲟⲣⲁ = BMis 388 *S* ⲃⲱⲕ; ⲥ ⲥⲉⲛ-, *fall into, suffer*: He 2 15† (*SF* = Gk) ἔνοχος; Su 23 ⲉⲙⲡⲓⲡ., Pro 11 5 (*SA* ϭⲉ ⲉϩⲣ.) περιπ.; Job 18 8 (*S* ⲛⲟⲩϭⲉ†) ἐμβάλλεσθαι; Va 57 199 ⲁⲩϣⲁⲛⲣ. ⲥⲉⲛ ⲣⲁⲡⲓⲕⲁⲩ πάσχειν; HL 84 ⲁⲩⲣ. ⲥⲉⲛⲣⲁⲡⲡⲁⲑⲟⲥ, Miss 4 221 will learn from ⲡⲏ ⲉⲧⲁⲣ. ⲥⲉⲛⲧⲁⲓⲃⲁⲕⲓ; ⲥ ⲥⲁ-, ⲥⲁⲧⲉⲛ-, *happen to be with*: TRit 242 this pledge ⲉⲧⲁⲩⲣ. ⲥⲁⲣⲟⲛ لدينا, MG 25 400 that none should ⲣ. ⲥⲁⲧⲟⲧϥ, BSM 47 ϣⲁⲧⲉⲛⲣ. ⲥ. ⲡⲁⲥⲧ = BMis 396 *S* ⲉⲓ ⲉ-; ⲥ ⲥⲁⲭⲉⲛ-, meaning sim: PO 11 350 others ⲉⲧⲁⲩⲣ.† ⲥⲁⲭⲱⲟⲩ. As nn m, *presence, event*: K 99 حضور, ib 463 حصول ووقوع.

ⲣⲟⲟⲩⲉ, ⲁⲣ. (1 Cor), ⲣⲟⲉⲓⲟⲩⲉ (Ep) *S*, ⲣⲏⲓⲟⲩⲉ (El) *Sᵃ*, ⲣⲉⲓⲟⲩⲉ, ⲁⲣ.(Ob)*A*, ⲣⲱⲟⲅⲓ, ⲁⲣ. (Joel sic BM 729) *B*, ⲗⲁⲟⲅⲓ *F* nn m, *stubble*: Job 24 24 *B* (*S* ⲥⲃⲣⲟⲟⲩⲉ), Is 1 31 *B*(*S* ⲕⲁϣ), ib 5 24 *SBF*, Joel 2 5 *AB*, Nah 1 10 *B*(*SA* ⲙⲁ ⲡⲕⲁϣ), 1 Cor 3 12 *S* (var ⲁⲣ.) *B* καλάμη; K 256 *B* ⲛⲓⲣ. قصل (Lab برويةة, cf Kremer *Beitr* s v, land of inferior quality; transcribes ? ⲡⲓⲣⲱⲟⲅⲓ); El 144 *Sᵃ* fire shall devour them ⲛⲑⲉ ⲛⲟⲩⲣ., ShEp 56 *S* ⲟⲩⲣ. ⲉϥⲙⲟⲩⲣ (cf Mal 4 1), ShZ 504 *S* ⲥⲗⲙ, ⲣ., Sh ib 596 *S* ⲣ., ϣⲟⲩⲕⲣⲉ, Budge *Bibl Texts* 270 *S* fire ⲉϥⲛⲏⲧ ⲣⲛⲟⲩⲣ. (var El 68 *A* ⲟⲩⲣⲣⲁⲩ); Hall 130 *S* in account of corn ϯⲟⲩ ⲛⲁⲣⲧⲟⲃ ⲛⲣ., Turin pap A 8 *S*]ⲛⲥⲉϯⲱⲣⲉ ⲛⲣ. (cf ⲕⲁϣ); ⲥⲃⲣ. *S* nn f, *stalk of corn*: Ge 41 22 (*B* ⲗⲁⲃⲉⲙ), Job as above πυθμήν; ShZ 603 grain drops from off ⲧⲥ. In place-name Ψβρουε (PLond 4 188). Distinct from ⲁⲣⲟⲟⲩⲉ q v. V ⲥⲛⲃⲉ.

ⲣⲟⲟⲩⲛⲉ *S*, ⲣⲁⲩ. *Sᵃ*, ⲣⲁⲟⲩ. *A*, ⲗⲁⲩⲛⲓ *F* nn m, *virgin, virginity*: EpJer 8 *F*(*B* = Gk), Z 296 *S* he took ⲛⲣ. ⲛⲧⲓϣⲉⲉⲣⲉ = MG 25 204 *B* ⲥⲉϥ ⲧⲉⲛϣⲉⲣⲓ παρθένος; as adj: Kropp K 67 *Sⁿ* ⲣⲉⲛⲃⲛⲛⲉ ⲛⲣ., ib 56 ⲃⲛⲣ., ib J *S* ⲃⲛⲧ ⲛⲣ. *virgin palm*; ⲙⲛⲧⲣ., *virginity S*: Deu 22 14(*B* ⲙⲉⲧⲡⲁⲣⲑ., cf BMar 145 sim), Lu 2 36 (*B* do) παρθενία, Si 42 12 παρθενεία, Joel 1 8 (*B* do) παρθενικός *pubertas*; Ez 23 11 (*B* ⲡⲁⲣⲑⲉⲛⲓⲁ) Gk diff, Tri 700 ⲛⲛⲓ ⲛⲧⲉⲥⲙ. بكور; Wess 18 62 ⲑⲩⲗⲓⲕⲓⲁ ⲛⲧⲙ. = Mor 19 52, Cai 42573 2 will tell everything that befell her ⲭⲓⲛⲛⲧⲉⲥⲙⲛⲧⲣⲟⲟⲩⲛ (sic).

ⲣⲟⲟⲩⲧ, ⲣⲱ., ⲣⲁⲩⲧ, ⲣⲱⲟⲩⲧϥ *v* ⲟⲩⲣⲟⲧ.

ⲣⲁⲟⲩⲧⲉ *S* nn, among bronze utensils: BP 9421 ⲥⲛϩⲟⲩ, ⲭⲉⲣⲉ, ⲣ., ⲕⲁⲧⲟⲩⲥ &c. (Not ⲣⲁϩⲧⲉ).

ⲣⲁⲩϣ *B* *v* ⲣⲁϣ.

ⲣⲟⲟⲩϣ *S*, ⲣⲁⲩϣ *A*, ⲣⲁⲟⲩϣ *Sᶠ A²F*, ⲣⲱⲟⲩϣ *B*, ⲗⲁⲟⲩϣ *F*, vb intr (rare), *have care for, be intent on*,

c e- *B*: Jo 6 6, 15, 71 (all *SA²* om) μέλλειν (? confused with μέλει); Cat 111 ⲉⲑⲣ. ⲉⲉⲣ ⲛⲟⲃⲓ, Va 61 205 where is sheep ⲉⲧⲉⲕⲣ. ⲉϣⲁϯϥ ? (Ge 22 7); c ⲅⲁ- *S*: BMis 256 gods ⲉⲧⲟⲩⲅ. ⲅⲁⲣⲟⲛ.

—— nn m *SAA¹BF*, a care, concern: Job 11 18 *SB*(P 104 103), Mt 13 22 *SBF* μέριμνα, Va 58 169 *B* ⲛ̇ϣⲟⲡ ⲝⲉⲛⲅⲁⲛⲣ. ἐμμέριμνος; Job 15 20 *SB*, Sa 8 9 *S* φροντίς, Ps 39 17 *S*(*B* ϥⲓ ⲣ.) φροντίζειν; Mk 4 38 *S*(*B* = Gk), Jo 10 13 *SAA²*(*B* do), 1 Cor 9 9 *SF*(*B* do), Mor 37 82 *S* ⲟⲩⲛⲉ ⲡⲉⲧⲣ. ⲅⲁⲡⲁⲓ? μέλει; P 44 15 *S* ἀδολεσχία ⲓ̣ⲱ; ROC 18 173 *S* prayer ⲁϫⲛⲣ. ἀπερισπάστως; PS 365 *S* ⲡⲣ. ⲉⲧⲉⲙⲛ ⲅⲏⲩ ⲡⲣⲏⲧⲩ, ShA 2 28 *S* that kept vigil ⲉⲧⲃⲉⲡⲉⲕⲣ. *care for things of God*, MIE 2 414 *B* whilst praying ⲉⲣⲉⲡⲉϥⲣ. ⲧⲏⲣϥ ⲝⲉⲛⲡϭⲓⲥⲓ, J 65 64 *S* ⲡⲣ. ⲛ̇ⲡⲣⲏⲃⲥ at shrine, PS 219 *S* everyone ⲉⲧⲅⲁⲣ., P 131³ 79 *S* got wealth & ⲁϥϣⲱⲡⲉ ⲅⲛⲟⲩⲛⲟϭ ⲡⲣ., DeV 2 166 *B* ⲟⲩⲟⲛ ⲟⲩⲙⲏϣ ⲡⲣ. ⲭⲏ ⲅⲓⲭⲱ, Wess 15 21 *S* ⲉⲙⲛ ⲗⲁⲁⲩ ⲡⲣ. ⲅⲓⲭⲱϥ; *in neg phrase* *S*: ShC 42 83 ⲡⲉⲡⲣ. ⲁⲡⲡⲉ ⲅⲱⲃ ⲡⲧⲉⲓⲣⲉ, RNC 68 judge asks ⲙ̇ⲡⲉⲕⲣ. ⲁⲡⲡⲉ ⲭⲉⲃⲁⲥⲁⲡⲓⲍⲉ ⲙ̇ⲙⲟⲛ?, Mor 38 15 ⲙ̇ⲡⲁⲣ. ⲁⲡⲡⲉ ⲅⲁⲣⲟⲕ *am not concerned with thee*.

b —— *SB* nn, *cause of anxiety, so* ? overwhelming height, billow: Job 28 18 *B* μετέωρος, Ps 87 7 *SB*, ib 92 4 *B*(*S* ⲭⲓⲥⲉ), Jon 2 4 *B*(*S* ⲅⲟⲧⲉ, *A* ⲅⲛⲱⲱⲣⲉ), μετεωρισμός; Ps 41 7 *SB* καταρράκτης. *Cf* Lu 12 29 *SB* ϥⲓ ⲣ. μετεωρίζεσθαι.
As obj of various verbs.

ⲕⲁ ⲣ. *S*, *set as a care, be careful, intent*, c following dat: Mk 13 11 (var & *B* ϥⲓ ⲣ.) (προ)μεριμνᾶν; ShC 73 145 superintendant ⲛ̇ⲁⲕⲁ ⲡⲣ. ⲡⲁϥ ... ⲡϥⲧⲣⲉⲩ-, ib 42 35 when summoned ⲙ̇ⲡϥⲕⲁ ⲗⲁⲁⲩ ⲡⲣ. ⲡⲁϥ ⲁϥⲧⲁⲣⲟ ⲧⲁⲭⲏ (*sic* l), P 131² 89 (Epiph *De Gem*), scripture useth jewels ⲉⲁⲥⲕⲁ ⲡⲉⲩⲣ. ⲡⲁⲥ ⲉⲅⲕⲟⲥⲙⲟⲥ *curans ad ornatum...uti*, BKU 1 151 ⲡ̇ⲧⲕⲱ ⲡⲣ. ⲡⲁⲕ...ⲛ̇ⲧϣⲓⲡⲉ, ST 388 ⲕⲁ ⲡⲣ. ⲡⲁⲕ ⲅⲁ-ⲡⲧⲣⲓⲙⲛⲥⲉ; ⲡⲉⲭ ⲣ. *SF*, *cast care, depute*, c e-: Ps 54 22 *S*(*B* ⲅⲓⲟⲩⲓ), 1 Pet 5 7 *S*(*B* ⲟⲩⲟⲅ)μⲉⲣ. ἐπιρρίπτειν; GFr 305 *S* remember all ⲛ̇ⲧⲁⲩⲛⲉⲭ ⲡⲉⲩⲣ. ⲉⲣⲟⲛ saying 'Remember us in our (your) prayers' (*cf* AZ 40 29), BM 643 *F* ⲁⲓⲛⲁϭ(*sic* MS) ⲡⲁⲣⲁⲟ(ⲩ)ϣ ⲉⲣⲁⲕ; ⲡⲉϣ ⲡⲣ. *S*, v ⲡⲱϣ II; ⲣ ⲣ., ⲟ, ⲟⲓ ⲡⲣ. *SBF*, *make care, be anxious*: Tob 10 1 *S* λογίζειν, ib 5 λόγον ἔχειν; c dat: *become care for*: 1 Cor 7 21 *SF*(*B* = Gk) μέλει; Bor 170 84 *S* ⲙ̇ⲡⲉⲓⲣ ⲣ. ⲡⲁϥ φροντίζειν; Mor 37 129 *S* ⲙ̇ⲡⲉⲛⲉⲥⲅⲁⲓ ⲣ ⲣ. ⲛⲁϥ περὶ πολλοῦ τινος ποιεῖν; ShA 1 458 *S* ⲙ̇ⲡⲣ ⲣ. ⲡⲁⲕ ⲉⲙⲉⲧⲁⲡⲟⲓ, ShC 73 21 *S* ϭⲟ ⲡⲣ. ⲡⲁⲩ ⲅⲁⲡⲧⲃⲃⲟ, BMar 202 *S* seeing her fate ⲧⲟⲧⲉ ⲁⲡⲉⲓⲣⲱⲃ ⲣ ⲣ. ⲡⲁⲩ & they obeyed, BMEA 10585 *F* ⲙ̇ⲡⲉⲕⲕⲉ ⲡⲁⲣⲱⲃ ⲉⲃⲉⲗ ⲗ. ⲡⲉⲛ, Va 61 119 *B* ⲡⲁⲣⲉⲡⲅⲱⲃ...ⲟⲓ ⲡⲣ. ⲡⲱⲟⲩ, BM 581(2) *F* ϥⲱⲃ...ⲱ ⲡⲗ. ⲡⲉⲓ; *take care of, give heed to*: TstAb 226 *B*

ⲁⲣⲓ ⲡⲉⲕⲣ. for I am sent to fetch thee, Mor 41 330 *S* sim, *ib* 31 110 *S* ⲃⲱⲕ ⲁⲣⲓ ⲡⲣ. ⲡⲡⲉⲥⲡⲏⲩ *ie* feed them; ⲟⲩⲁⲅ ⲣ. *B*, *lay care*: 1 Pet 5 7 as above, C 43 184 ⲁⲓⲟⲩⲁⲅ ⲡⲁⲣ. ⲉⲣⲟⲕ; ϣⲱⲡⲉ ⲡⲣ. *S*, *be a care*: ShMing 325 Moses ⲙⲏ ⲡⲉϥϣ.† ⲡⲁϥ ⲁⲡ ⲡⲣ. ⲉϥⲟⲣⲉⲓ ⲡ̇ⲧⲍⲱⲡⲏ ?, R 1 3 67 let not this ϣ. ⲛⲁⲡ ⲡⲣ.; ϥⲓ ⲣ. *SAA²BF*, *take care, thought*: Pro 14 23 *SAB*, Lu 12 25 *SB* ⲙⲉⲣ.; Job 3 25 *SB* φρον.; Mor 31 111 *S* ⲉⲓⲡⲁϥⲓ ⲙ̇ⲡⲣ. ⲅⲛⲟⲩ?, J 75 45 *S* ⲉⲡⲟⲛⲃ ⲉⲛⲡⲟⲓ ⲉⲡϥⲓ ⲣ. (*cf* PLond 1 232 φρονῶν); c poss: Ps 39 18 *B*(*S* diff) φρον., Aeg 220 *S* let bishop ϥⲓ ⲡⲉⲕⲣ. φροντίδα ἔχειν; Lu 10 34 *SB* ἐπιμελεῖσθαι; Nu 23 9 *SB*, Sa 3 16 *S* προνοεῖν; Job 22 4 *S*(*B* ϥⲓ ⲱⲡ) λόγον ποιεῖσθαι; Bor 239 60 *S* others ϥⲓ ⲡⲉⲕⲣ. ὑπ' ἄλλων τρέφεσθαι; Rec 6 179 *B* caused angel to ϥⲓ ⲡⲁⲣ. ⲝⲉⲛⲡⲧⲁⲧⲣⲟⲫⲏ = BMar 213 *S* ⲇⲓⲁⲕⲟⲛⲉⲓ; c ⲭⲉ-: Mt 10 19 *SB* ⲙⲉⲣ.; Sa 15 9 *S* φροντὶς εἶναι; Ep 198 *S* how often ⲁⲡϥⲓ ⲣ. ⲭⲉ-ⲉⲡⲁⲉⲓ; c e-, *take care for*: 1 Cor 7 33 *S*(*B* ⲝⲁ-, *F* ⲅⲁ-) ⲙⲉⲣ. acc; 1 Tim 3 5 *B*(*S* = Gk) προιστάναι gen; Mor 33 66 *S* ⲉϥϥⲓ ⲣ. ⲉⲣⲟⲓ ⲅⲛⲟⲩⲛⲉⲅ (var BMis 106 ⲅⲁ-), MG 25 339 *B* ⲉϥϥⲓ ⲣ. ⲉⲉⲙⲓ ⲉⲧⲕⲁⲧⲁⲥⲧⲁⲥⲓⲥ = ROC 17 366 ⲗⲟ, BSM 26 *B* ϣⲁϥϥⲓ ⲣ. ⲉϥⲟⲩⲥⲓⲁ = Va 63 3 *B* ϥⲓ ⲫⲣ. ⲡ- = BMis 366 *S* ⲧⲁⲥⲥⲉ; c ⲉⲧⲃⲉ- *S*, *meaning same*: 1 Kg 10 2 ⲙⲉⲣ. περί; R 2 2 25 angels ϥⲓ ⲣ. ⲉⲧⲃⲉⲓⲱⲥⲏⲫ φροντὶς εἶ. περί; c ⲡ-, *meaning same*: Ro 12 17 *SBF* προνοεῖν acc; Si 41 12 *S* φρον. περί; Pro 27 24 *SA* ἐπιμελ. gen; Job 14 3 *S*(*B* ϥⲓ ⲱⲡ) λόγον ποι. gen; PS 71 *S* entrusted to me to ϥⲓ ⲡⲣ. ⲙ̇ⲡⲓⲕⲟⲥⲙⲟⲥ *provide for, supply*, ShC 73 40 *S* ⲕⲡⲁϥⲓ ⲡⲣ. ⲡ̇ⲧⲉⲕ-ϭⲓⲛⲁⲡⲁⲛⲧⲁ ⲉⲛⲡⲉ, DeV 2 265 *B* ⲁⲥϥⲓ ⲫⲣ. ⲙ̇ⲡⲓⲕⲟⲩⲭⲓ ⲛ̇ⲭⲓⲛⲟⲩⲱⲙ, Miss 4 195 *B* ⲡⲓⲣⲱⲙⲓ ⲉⲧⲁϥϥⲓ ⲫⲣ. ⲙ̇ⲡⲓⲕⲱⲧ of chapel; of dedicated book *provided for* church: Lant 5 *S* ⲡⲣⲱⲙⲉ ⲡ̇ⲧⲁϥϥⲓ ⲙ̇ⲡⲣ. ⲙ̇ⲡⲓⲕⲉ-ⲫⲁⲗⲁⲓⲟⲛ ⲛ̇ϫⲱⲱⲙⲉ & gave it to monastery, *ib* 101 17 *S* ⲡ̇ⲧⲁϥϥⲓ ⲙ̇ⲡⲉⲩⲣ. ϣⲁⲡⲧⲟⲩⲥⲁⲅⲩ, C 86 269 *B* ⲉⲧⲁϥϥⲓ ⲫⲣ. ⲡⲡⲁⲓⲭⲱⲙ ⲁϥⲑⲁⲙⲓⲟϥ by own labour, PMich 3572 *S* this is book that John (?) ϥⲓ ⲡⲉϥⲣ. ⲉⲡⲧⲟⲡⲟⲥ; c ⲅⲁ-, ⲝⲁ-, *meaning same*: Mt 6 28 *SB* ⲙⲉⲣ. dat, Ps 37 18 *S*(*B* ⲉⲭⲉⲡ-), ⲙⲉⲣ. ὑπέρ; 1 Kg 9 5 *S* φρον. acc; Ro 13 14 *B*(*S* ⲡ-) προν. gen; Sa 12 13 *S* μέλει περί; ShC 73 2 *S* ⲡⲉⲧⲉⲣⲉⲡ⳨ⲥ ϥⲓ ⲣ. ⲅⲁⲣⲟⲛ ⲡⲅⲏⲧⲟⲩ, TstAb 260 *B* ϥⲓ ⲣ. ⲝⲁⲛⲥⲁⲭⲓ ⲙⲫϯ, BM 603 *F* (ⲙ)ⲡⲉⲗϥⲓ ⲗ. ⲅⲁⲗⲁⲅ; as nn, *care, anxiety*: Pro 3 8 *SA*(*B* ⲟⲩⲭⲁⲓ) ἐπιμέλεια; Ac 24 2 *B*(*S* = Gk) πρόνοια; Va 57 11 *B* μέριμνα; BSM 31 *B* hour of ⲡⲓϥⲓ ⲣ. ⲉϥⲟⲩⲥⲓⲁ = BMis 373 *S* hour ⲉⲧⲣⲉⲩⲧⲁⲥⲥⲉ ⲡ-, CaiThe 147 *B* Magdalen at angel's words ϣⲱⲡⲓ ⲝⲉⲛⲟⲩϥⲓ ⲣ. ⲟⲡⲟⲓⲁ; ⲭⲓⲛϥⲓ ⲣ. *B*, meaning same: Va 57 12 ⲟⲩⲭ. ⲁⲡⲡⲉ ⲡⲁⲓⲣⲱⲃ μεριμνῶν; C 86 180 day of ⲡⲓⲭ. ⲙ̇ⲡⲱϣⲁⲓ; ϥⲁⲓ-, ⲃⲁⲓⲣ., *care-taker, guardian*: PO 4 581 *S* God is

ⲡⲉⲕϥ., BSM 30 *B* ⲡⲓϥ. ⲛⲁⲅⲁⲑⲟⲥ, BHom 1 *S* Paul
ⲡϥ. ⲡⲡⲉⲕⲕⲗⲏⲥⲓⲁ, Mor 48 93 *S* executioner ⲛⲕ̅.
ⲙⲡⲁⲇⲓⲕⲁⲥⲧⲏⲣⲓⲟⲛ;   as adj : Sa 9 15 *S* ϥⲏⲧ ⲡϥ.
πολύφροντις;   R 1 2 72 *S* ⲡϣⲟⲟⲥ ⲡϥ., Lant 74 *S*
ⲡⲉⲡⲃ̅. ⲡⲥⲟⲡ;   c ϩⲁ-, ϩⲁ-, *taking thought for*:
BAp 53 *S* ⲡϥ. ϩⲁⲡⲉϥϩⲙϩⲁⲗ κηδεμών, BSM 60 *B*
ⲡⲓⲛⲓϣϯ ⲡϥ. ϩⲁⲣⲟⲛ = BMis 419 *S* προστατης;   ⲟ,
ⲟⲓ ⲡϥⲁⲓⲣ. : Bor 253 155 *S* ⲉⲣⲉⲡⲡⲉ ⲟ ⲡⲁⲕ ⲡϥ. προνοεῖν dat, AM doxol *B* Julius of Kbehs ⲟⲓ ⲙϥ. ⲡⲡⲏ
ⲉⲟⲩ̅;   ⲙⲛⲧ-, ⲙⲉⲧϥⲁⲓⲣ., *care, providence*: Wess
15 130 *S* do duty ϩⲛⲟⲩⲙ. = EW 29 *B* ⲉⲣⲟⲅⲟⲧ
ἐπιμέλεια; BMar 112 *S* ⲧⲙ. of God πρόνοια; Cai
Euch 488 *B* ⲧⲉⲕⲙ. ϩⲁⲣⲟⲓ κηδεμονία; BM 185 *S*
calling to us ϩⲛⲟⲩⲙ. ϫⲉ- (Eph 5 14), Lant 98 3 *S*
in zeal & ⲙ. ⲁϥϫⲁⲙ ⲡⲓⲭⲱⲙⲁ, DeV 2 167 *B* ϩⲉⲛ-
ⲟⲩⲛⲓϣϯ ⲡⲙ. he laid money in treasury.

ⲁⲧⲣ., *care-free, not liable*, always with ⲣ, ⲉⲣ : Sa
7 23 *S*, Mt 28 14 *SB*, 1 Cor 7 32 *SBF*, C 89 23 *B*
ⲁϥⲁⲓⲧⲟⲩ ⲡⲁ., Z 305 *S* ⲧⲉⲧⲛⲟ ⲡⲁ. ϩⲙⲡⲉⲓⲕⲟⲥⲙⲟⲥ
ἀμέριμνος; Deu 24 5 *B*(*S* ⲙⲛ ⲣⲱⲃ ϫⲓ ⲉⲣⲟϥⲛ ⲉ-)
ἀθῷος; Si 41 1 *S* ἀπερίσπαστος; AM 269 *B* I wrote
often ⲙⲡⲓⲉⲣ ⲁ. ἀρκεῖσθαι; EW 32 *B* ⲁⲣⲓ ⲁ. ⲡⲁⲕ
ἀφρόντιστος; Bor 226 159 *S* enemies ⲟ ⲡⲁ. ⲉⲣⲟⲕ
ⲁⲛ οὐ σιωπῶσιν ἀπὸ σοῦ; ShZ 596 *S* at leisure &
ⲧⲏⲟ ⲡⲁ., Mor 40 38 *S* I would have kept silence
about them (Max & Domet) ⲧⲁⲣ ⲁ. ⲉⲛⲉⲓⲣⲣⲱⲟⲩ,
Z 281 *S* ⲁϥϣⲱⲡⲉ ⲉϥⲟ ⲡⲁ. ϩⲁⲧⲉϥⲯⲩⲭⲏ;   ⲙⲛⲧⲁ.
S, freedom from care: BHom 26 ἀμεριμνία; Mus
40 274 silence & ⲧⲙ. save many souls.

As name : Προοῦς, Πρωοῦς &c (Preisigke), Πε-
ρούϣ (same ? BM 1075).

ⲣⲁϧⲛⲉ *S* nnf, a garment : Pap *penes* RG Gayer-
Anderson ϫⲟⲟⲩ ⲧⲣ. ⲉϩⲏⲧ ⲧⲁⲧⲁⲁⲥ (ⲡ)ⲥⲟⲩⲧⲁⲡⲟⲥ. *Cf*
ῥάχνη (Preisigke *Wbuch*), ῥάχνι (POxy 2058).

ⲣⲁϣ *S*, ⲣⲉ(ⲉ)ϩϥ *A*, ⲣⲁϥϣ *B*, ⲗⲏⲩϣ *F*, only with
ⲣⲙ- ⲣⲉⲙ-, ⲗⲉⲙ-, *mild, gentle person*: Nu 12 3 *SB*,
Ps 24 9 *SB*, Zech 9 9 *SAB*, Mt 11 29 *SB* πραΰς;
Si 25 22 *S* ἥσυχος, Is 66 2 *SA*(Cl ⲣⲉⲉ.)*B*, 1 Tim 2
2 *B*(*S* ϩⲟⲣⲕ), -χιος; 1 Thes 2 7 *SF*(*B* diff) ἤπιος;
Bor 253 164 *S* came forth ϩⲱⲥ ⲣ. ἱλαρῶς (cf Ge 43
31); PS 220 *S* ⲟⲩⲣ. ⲡⲉ ⲡⲁⲡⲁϩⲃⲉϥ (cf Mt 11 30),
BMis 351 *S* David ⲡⲣⲣⲟ ⲡⲣ. (var ⲇⲓⲕⲁⲓⲟⲥ), Mor
51 26 *S* woman ⲡⲉⲩⲣ. ⲉⲥⲥⲱⲃⲉ;   ⲙⲛⲧ-, ⲙⲉⲧⲣ.,
gentleness: Ps 44 5 *SB*, Si 1 26 *SB*, Gal 5 23 *SB*,
Cl 21 7 *A* πραΰτης; Aeg 283 *S* ⲟⲩⲙ. toward slaves
εὐμενῶς; EW 148 *B* voice ⲙⲙ. ἠρεμαῖος; BHom
68 *S* thou art fair in thy ⲙ. ⲉⲧϭⲏⲡ, C 43 64 *B* beloved for ⲧⲉϥⲙ.;   ⲣ, ⲉⲣ ⲣ., *become, be gentle*:
1 Thes 4 11 *B*(*S* ⲥϭⲣⲁϩⲧ)ἡσυχάζειν; Aeg 246 *S* ⲟ
ⲡⲣ. ἐπιεικής; Pcod 18 *S* ϣⲁϥⲣ ⲉⲣⲟⲩⲛ ⲉⲡⲣⲉϥⲣ
ⲛⲟⲃⲉ, DeV 2 179 *B* smiling & ⲉⲥⲟ ⲡⲣ. ⲡⲉⲙⲁϥ.

ⲣⲱϣ, ⲣⲁϣ⳱ *B*, vb intr, *measure*: Deu 21 2 ⲣ.

ⲉϫⲉⲡ- (*S* ⲥⲣ ⲡⲟⲩϩ ⲉⲃⲟⲗ) ἐκμετρεῖν;   tr : Am 7
17 (*S* ϣⲓ), Mic 2 4 (*SA* ⲇⲟ) καταμ.; *cf* ⲣⲱϣⲉ (adverbial);   ⲡⲟϩ ⲡⲣ., *measuring cord*: Deu 32 9
(*S* diff), Ps 104 11(*S* ⲥⲕ ⲡⲟⲩϩ) σχοίνισμα;   *v* also
ⲡⲟⲩϩ (for measuring).

ⲣⲁϣⲉ *S*, ⲣⲉ. *AA²*, ⲣⲁϣⲓ *B*, ⲗⲉϣⲓ *F* vb **I** intr,
rejoice: Ps 95 11 *SB*, Joel 2 21 *SAB*, Jo 3 29 *SBF*,
ib 8 56 *SA²B*, MG 25 205 *B* χαίρειν, Ez 25 15 *B*
ἐπιχ., Job 3 22 *SB*, AP 6 *A²* περιχαρὴς γίνεσθαι;
Ps 103 15 *B*(*S* ⲟⲩⲣⲟⲧ) ἱλαρύνειν; 2 Cor 2 2 *B*(*S* =
Gk) εὐφράινειν; PS 8 *S* ⲣ. ⲡⲧⲉⲧⲛⲧⲉⲗⲏⲗ, Mor 50 29
S will ye take us aboard ? ⲧⲏⲡⲁⲧⲁⲗⲉⲧⲏⲧⲛ ⲉⲛⲣ.
gladly, BHom 124 *S* died on cross ⲉϥⲣ., BM 610
F ⲙⲁⲗⲉⲡⲉⲕⲡⲉⲉⲓ ϣⲱⲡⲓ ⲉⲕⲗⲉϣⲉ, Kr 127 *S* ⲧⲓⲣ. ⲧⲓ-
ϩⲟⲙⲟⲗⲟⲅⲉⲓ...ⲉⲓⲙⲓⲥⲟⲟⲩ (*cf* ὁμολογῶ ἑκουσίως or
? misunderstanding of formula...χαίρειν. Ὁμολογῶ
κτλ as PMon 9 5, PLond 5 17), ST 46 *S* ⲁⲛⲟⲛ...
ⲉⲩⲅⲣⲁⲓ ⲡ-...ⲣ. *greeting*, Ep 327 *S* ⲁⲡⲣ. ⲉⲙⲁⲧⲉ at
hearing of your welfare, J 66 66 *S* they read it to
me ⲁⲓⲣ. ⲉⲙⲁⲧⲉ ⲁⲓⲡⲟⲉ.

With following preposition.   c ⲉ- *B*, *at, over*:
BSM 35 ⲁϥⲣ. ⲉⲡⲧⲁⲭⲣⲟ of her faith = BMis 378 *S*
ⲉϩⲣⲁⲓ ⲉϫⲛ-, *dat commodi* DeV 2 207 ϥϩⲟⲣⲟ ⲙⲡⲁϩⲏⲧ ⲣ. ⲉⲣⲟⲓ;   c ⲉϫⲛ-, meaning same : Lu 1 14
SB, 1 Cor 16 17 *SBF* χαί., Pro 2 14 *B*(*SA* ⲥⲱⲃⲉ
ⲡⲥⲁ-) χ. ἐπί, Ob 12 *SAB* ἐπιχ. ἐπί or dat, Job 31
29 *SB* ἐπιχαρὴς γίν. dat; Sa 1 13 *S* τέρπειν ἐπί;
ib 7 12 *S* εὐφραίνεσθαι ἐπί; ShBM 202 177 *S* ⲉⲩⲣ.
ⲉⲭⲛⲣⲉⲡⲣⲱⲙⲉ ϫⲉⲁⲩⲙⲟⲟⲩⲧⲟⲩ, AM 9 *B* ⲉⲩⲣ. ⲉϫⲉⲡ-
ⲡⲓϩⲣⲟ;   ⲉϩⲣⲁⲓ, -ⲛⲓ ⲉⲭ.: Is 39 2 *SB*, Mt 18 13
SB χαί. ἐπί, Ps 34 19 *B*(*S* ⲡ-) ἐπιχ. dat; Br 122 *S*
ϥⲛⲁⲣ. ⲉⲣ. ⲉⲭⲡⲧⲏⲅⲧⲛ, DeV 2 105 *B* ⲁϥⲣ. ⲉⲣ. ⲉⲭ-
ⲉⲡⲧⲟⲩⲕⲁⲧⲁⲡϩⲝⲓⲥ;   c ϩⲓϫⲉⲛ- *B*, meaning same :
MG 25 5 ⲉϥⲣ. ϩ. ⲡⲱⲟⲩ of Christ χαί. ἐπί; Va 63
9 ⲡⲁϥⲣ.ⲡⲉ ϩ. ⲡⲉⲥⲡⲓϣϯ ⲡⲡⲁϥϯ = BMis 378 *S* ⲉⲣ.
ⲉϫⲛ-;   c ⲉⲑⲃⲉ- *B*, meaning same : DeV 1 123
when I die all ⲛⲁⲣ. ⲉⲑⲃⲏⲧ;   c ⲙⲛ-, ⲛⲉⲙ-, *with* :
Ro 12 15 *SBF* χαί., Lu 1 58 *SB* συγχ., Bor 235 57
S think not ⲥⲉⲛⲁⲣ. ⲡⲓⲙⲁⲕ χαρῆναι ἔχειν μετά; Miss
8 102 *S* Cyril's letter ϯⲣ. ⲡⲓⲙⲁⲥ ἄγασθαι; ShC
42 76 *S* ⲡⲉⲥⲡⲁⲣ. ⲁⲡⲡⲉ ⲙⲛⲡⲉⲧⲟ ⲛⲡⲟⲉⲓⲕ ⲉⲧⲉⲥϣⲉⲉⲣⲉ,
Miss 4 184 *B* king dismissed us ⲉϥⲣ. ⲛⲉⲙⲁⲛ, R 1
3 60 *S* angels around him ⲉⲩⲣ. ⲛⲙⲙⲁϥ, C 43 230
B sim;   c ethic dat : Leyd 460 *S* ⲣ. ⲛⲏⲧⲛ all
creatures, C 86 144 *B* ⲣ. ⲛⲁⲕ for they shall take
thy soul.

II tr, *SAB* rejoice at, deride : Ap 11 10 *S*(*B* ⲉϩⲣ.
ⲉϫ.) χαίρ. ἐπί; Bor 235 58 *S* demons persuade him
ⲡⲥⲉⲣ. ⲙⲙⲟⲩ χ. acc, Ps 34 19 *S*(*B* ⲇⲟ), RNC 30 *S*
art come ⲉⲣ. ⲙⲙⲟⲓ with thy words ? ἐπιχ. dat, Pro
11 3 *SAB* ἐπίχαρτος γίν., Ex 32 25 *SB*, Si 6 4 *S*
ἐπίχαρμα, Pro 1 26 *SA*(*B* om obj) καταχαίρ., Ps 40
11 *S*(*B* refl) περιχ. ἐπί; PS 47 *S* ⲡⲁⲣⲭⲱⲡ...ⲉⲩⲣ.

ⲙⲙⲟⲓ, ShMich 550 18 *S* enmity ⲡⲁⲣ. ⲙⲙⲟⲟⲩ ⲁⲩⲱ ⲥⲱⲃⲉ ⲡⲥⲱⲟⲩ;   refl: Ps 40 11 *B* as above;   redundant acc: 1 Thes 3 9 *SB*, EW 115 *B* this is joy ⲉϯⲣ. ⲙⲙⲟϥ.

—— nn m *SA²BF*, *gladness, joy*: Si 1 12 *SB*, Mt 13 20 *SBF*, Phil 1 4 *SBF*, AP 12 *A²* χαρά, Job 3 7 *SB* χαρμονή, Jer 40 11 *SB* χαρμοσύνη; Job 8 21 *B*(*S* ⲥⲱⲃⲉ) γέλως; Sa 8 16 *S* εὐφροσύνη; Ro 12 8 *B*(*S* ⲟⲩⲣⲟⲧ) ἱλαρότης; ShC 73 210 *S* ⲡⲉϥⲣ. ⲉⲣⲟⲩⲡ ⲉⲡⲉⲥⲏⲏⲩ, BMis 333 *S* ⲡⲉⲓϣⲟⲙⲛⲧ ⲡⲣ. *greetings* = BSM 8 *B* ⲭⲉⲣⲉⲧⲓⲥⲙⲟⲥ, Lant 15 32 *Sᶠ* ⲡⲣⲁϣⲓ ⲙⲡⲡⲟⲩⲡⲁϥ, AM 196 *B* do as bidden ϫⲉⲡⲟⲩⲣ.;   ⲣ ⲣ. *SF*, ϭⲓ ⲣ. *B*: Philem 7 χ. ἔχειν, BM 1238 *F* ⲁⲣⲓ ⲡⲁⲙⲉⲩ(ⲓ) ⲙⲁⲛ ⲥⲉⲣ ⲡⲁⲗⲉϣⲓ; ϭⲓ ⲣ. ⲉⲃⲟⲗ *S*: BMis 571 ⲟⲩⲥⲧⲟⲗⲏ ⲉⲥϭ. in ineffable splendour.

As name: ⲣⲁϣⲉ (Hall 6), ⲡⲣⲁϣⲉ (Ryl 321), ⲡⲣⲏϣⲉ (J 51 11 = ⲡⲣⲉⲥⲉ *ib* 1), ⲡⲣⲁⲥⲉ (J 39 81 = ⲡⲣⲏⲥⲉ *ib* 85), ⲧⲣⲁϣⲉ (Ryl 204, Ann 8 87), ⲧⲁⲣϣⲉ (? CO 167), ⲧⲏⲣϣⲉ (Ny Carlsberg stele 336), Τρασέ, Ταρσέ (Preisigke), though names formed of f art + m nn are rare.

ⲣⲱϣⲉ *SA²F*, -ϣⲉ *A*, -ϣⲓ *B*, ⲗⲱϣⲓ, ⲣⲁϣⲏ (BM 660)*F*, ⲣⲉϣⲧ-, ⲣⲁϣⲧ- *S*, ⲣⲁϣ-, ⲣⲉϣ- *B*, ⲣⲁϣⲧ⸗ *SB*, ⲣⲁϣ⸗ *SB*, ⲣⲱϩⲧ⸗ (? ⲧⲉⲣⲱϩⲧ) *A*, ⲗⲉϣ⸗ *F*, ⲣⲁϣⲓᵗ *B* vb I intr, a *suffice*: BHom 22 *S* if sins small ϥⲣ. ⲛ̅ϭ̅ⲓ ⲟⲩⲕⲟⲩⲓ ⲡⲣⲓⲙⲉ ἄρκειν, Nu 11 23 *SB* ἐξάρ., Phil 4 11 *S*(*B* ⲣ. ⲉ-) αὐτάρκης εἶναι, Pro 24 50 *SA* (*B* ⲕⲏⲡ), Lu 22 38 *SB* ἱκανός; ShBor 246 89 *S* all time ⲡⲁⲣ. ⲁⲡⲡⲉ, KKS 582 *S* ⲟⲩⲥⲟⲡ ⲡⲟⲩⲱⲧ ⲡⲁⲣ., Cai 42573 2 *S* after recipe ⲁϥⲣ., Bodl(P) ⲁ 1 b *S* sim ϣⲁϥⲣ., BM 660 *F* ⲙⲁⲣⲉⲡϣⲁϫⲓ ⲣ., BMis 26 *S* ⲁⲡⲣⲱⲃ ⲣ. ⲉⲡⲉϣⲟⲟⲡ ⲡⲧⲉⲓⲭⲱⲣⲁ, Mor 50 62 *S* ⲁⲡⲣⲱⲃ ⲣ. ⲉⲓⲁⲡⲉⲧⲉⲓⲙⲁ (ἐπιτιμᾶν) ⲡⲡⲣⲱⲙⲉ; impers: ShWess 9 140 *S* ϥⲣ. ⲉⲭⲟⲟⲥ ⲙⲙⲁⲧⲉ ϫⲉ-, BSM 35 *B* ϥⲣ. ϩⲁⲟⲩⲧⲉⲣⲙⲏⲥ (BMis 379 *S* Va 63 9 *B* diff).   b *be concerned, responsible*: Mt 27 4 *SB*, Ac 18 15 *SB* ὁρᾶν (ὄψεσθαι); ShHT *B* 65 *S* ⲥⲉⲣ. ⲁⲡⲟⲕ ϯⲟⲩⲁⲁⲃ, ShP 130¹ 141 *S* if elder wish to expel any ϥⲣ., CO 298 *S* if he punish me ... if he forgive ⲛ̅ⲧⲟϥ ⲉⲧⲣ., ShBMOr 8810 409 *S* ⲱ ⲧⲉⲧⲛⲣ. ⲛ̅ⲧⲱⲧⲛ who give place unto Satan, ShC 73 149 *S* if one have fever ⲉⲧⲣⲉⲩⲡⲣⲟⲥⲉⲭⲉ ⲉⲣⲟϥ ⲛ̅ϭ̅ⲓ ⲡⲉⲧⲣ.

With following preposition.   c ⲉ-, *suffice for, be fit to, responsible for*: Nu 11 22 *S*(*B* tr), Jo 6 7 *A²* (*SB* tr), C 89 58 *B* ⲁⲩⲣ. ⲉⲣⲟⲓ, Aeg 281 *S* man & wife ⲉⲧⲣⲉⲩⲣ. ⲉⲣⲟⲟⲩ, EW 29 *B* ⲧⲭⲣⲓⲁ ⲙⲡⲓⲥⲱⲙⲁ ⲣ. ⲉⲣⲟⲓ ἀρκ. dat, Deu 32 10 *S*(*B* ⲉⲣ ϥⲣ. ⲛ-) αὐταρκεῖν, Si 5 1 *SB* αὐτάρκης εἶναι, 1 Tim 5 10 *S*(*B* ϣⲱⲡⲓ ϩⲁⲭⲉⲛ-), CaiEuch 515 *B* those in straits ⲣ. ⲉⲣⲱⲟⲩ ⲉⲡⲓⲁⲅⲁⲑⲟⲛ ἐπαρκ.; Ex 12 4 *SB*, Is 40 16 *S*(*B* = Gk) ἱκ., Nu 16 7 *S*(*B* tr) ἱκανοῦσθαι; R 1 1 19 *S* ⲡⲧⲟⲟⲩ ⲥⲉⲣ., answer ⲧⲏⲣ. ⲉⲟⲩ? ὁρ.; 3 Kg 21

10 *S* *sufficere*; Br 90 *S* give us a name ⲛϥⲣ. ⲉⲡⲧⲟⲡⲟⲥ ⲧⲏⲣⲟⲩ, ShC 42 30 *S* ⲧⲉⲧⲛⲙⲛ̅ⲧⲥⲁⲃⲉ ⲣ. ⲉⲡⲟⲉⲓ, BHom 99 *S* tongue ⲡⲁⲣ. ⲁⲛ ⲉⲧⲁⲅⲟ, BSM 32 *B* ϥⲣ. ⲉϥⲛ ⲉⲧⲉⲡϣⲁⲧ ⲙⲙⲟϥ, ShP 130² 55 *S* send disobedient to me ⲁⲛⲟⲕ ⲡⲉⲧⲡⲁⲣ. ⲉⲣⲟⲟⲩ *I will deal with them*, ShC 73 110 if I live ϯⲡⲁⲣ. ⲉⲕⲱⲧ ⲛ ⲉⲧⲁⲕⲱⲧ, *ib* 146 *S* ⲡⲉⲧⲣ. ⲉⲡⲙⲁ ⲡⲟⲩⲱϣⲙ (*cf ib* ⲡⲉⲧⲡⲣⲟⲥⲉⲭⲉ), Ostr *penes* GJéquier *S* ⲡⲧⲟⲟⲩ ⲉⲧⲣ. ⲉⲙⲁϥ *it is they are due to pay him*;   *adjudge* or sim: ShA 1 193 *S* hell fire shall p. ⲉ- disobedient, BHom 72 *S* terrific beings summon dying ⲥⲉⲣ. ⲉⲣⲟⲛ;   c ⲉϫⲉⲛ- *B*, meaning same (?): Ge 32 10 (*S* ⲣ ⲡⲁϣⲧⲉ) ἱκανοῦσθαι dat;   c ⲙⲛ- *S*, *be concerned with, deal with*: ShBM 8810 522 my accusers ⲉϣⲱⲡⲉ ⲡⲉⲩϩⲏⲧ ⲡⲁⲙⲧⲟⲛ...ⲥⲉⲣ. ⲙⲡⲛⲛⲧⲉ *they (must) settle it with God*, ShA 1 67 whoso rekindleth fire ⲣ. ⲙⲛⲡⲛⲧⲉ, Sh(Besa)Z 504 inf sim;   c ⲛ- dat, *suffice for*: Sa 14 22 *S* ἀρκ.; Nah 2 12 *A* (*cf* Ob 5, *B* nn) ἱκ.; BSM 33 *B* corn ⲛⲧⲉϥⲣ. ⲙⲡⲓϩⲱⲣⲟⲡ = BMis 375 *S* ⲉ-; temporal: ShC 73 136 *S* ⲉϥⲉⲣ. ⲛⲣⲟⲟⲩ ⲥⲡⲁⲩ, PMéd 207 *S* ⲉϥⲡⲁⲣ. ⲛ̅ⲟⲩⲥⲟⲡ ⲉⲡⲉⲃⲟⲧ.

II tr *SABF*, *suffice, content*: Nu 11 22 *B*(*S* ⲣ. ⲉ-), Jos 17 16 *S*, Lu 3 14 *B*(*S* ϩⲱ ⲉ-), Cl 2 1 *A* Christ's wage ⲣ. ⲙⲙⲱⲧⲛⲉ, HL 81 *B* ⲙⲡⲉⲥⲣⲁϣϥ ⲛ̅ϫⲉ ϯϫⲓⲛⲥⲱⲧⲉⲙ, C 86 295 *B* ⲫⲁⲓ ⲣ. ⲙⲙⲟϥ ϯⲛⲟⲩ = *ib* 231 *B* ⲣ. ⲉ- ἀρκ., Z 328 *S* riches ⲛⲉⲩⲣ. ⲙⲙⲟⲛ ⲁⲛ, ROC 25 273 *B* all he ate ⲙⲡⲁⲣⲁϣϥ ἐπαρκ.; Ob 5 *A*(ⲧⲉⲣⲱϩⲧⲟⲩ, *cf* Nah 2 12) *B* ἱκ.; 3 Kg 8 64 *B* altar could not ⲣⲁϣϥ ⲛⲡⲓⲧⲁⲓⲟ ὑποφέρειν; 1 Kg 26 8 *S* I will let once ⲣⲁϣⲧϥ (var ⲣ. ⲉⲣⲟϥ) Gk diff; Tob 12 4 *S* δικαιοῦν dat; R 1 3 74 *S* locusts ⲛⲉⲩϣⲣ. ⲙⲙⲟ⸗ⲛⲉ (Mt 3 4), Mor 31 45 *S* have abandoned world to thee ⲙⲡⲉϥⲣⲁϣⲧⲕ, Mor 37 232 *S* ⲣⲁϣⲧⲕ ⲙⲁ̅ⲅ̅ⲁ̅ⲁ̅ⲕ *mind thine own affairs*, Miss 8 233 *S* ⲙⲁⲣⲉⲟⲩϣⲁϫⲉ ⲣⲁϣⲧⲕ, BMis 293 *S* sim ⲣⲁϣⲕ, AM 157 *B* ϣⲁⲣⲉⲟⲩⲥⲁϫⲓ ⲣ. ⲡⲟⲩⲥⲁⲃⲉ, C 43 234 *B* sim ⲣⲁϣ ⲟⲩⲥ., Pcod 26 *S* sim ⲣⲉϣⲧ ⲟⲩⲥ., TEuch 2 33 *B* no place ⲣⲁϣϥ ⲙⲙⲟϥ (var HCons 467 ϣⲱⲡ), AM 177 *B* ϯⲡⲁⲣⲁϣ ⲡⲓϩⲱⲃ *will attend to matter*, ST 359 *S* ⲛ ⲛ̅ⲧⲡⲱⲗⲕ ⲛ ⲛ̅ⲧⲣⲁϣⲥ ⲛ̅ⲕⲟⲩϩⲟⲩⲃ ⲡⲉⲙⲁϥ, Ryl 159 *S* am ready ⲧⲁⲣⲁϣⲧ ⲡⲙⲁ ⲧⲏⲣϥ (*cf* PMon 2 14 ἱκανὸν ποιεῖν), Pcod 19 *S* humbler vessels ⲡⲁⲣⲁϣⲧ ⲧⲉⲑⲩⲥⲓⲁ, BM 591 *F* ϣ(ⲁⲗⲉ)ⲁⲃⲣⲁϩⲁⲙ ⲗⲉϣⲕ *Ab. will (?) suffice thee*, CMSS 39 *F* if Virgin help us ⲃⲗⲉϣ(ⲛ ?) *it sufficeth (us ?)*.

—— nn m *SAB*, *sufficiency, enough, plenty*: Pro 24 31 *SA* αὐτάρκης, 2 Cor 9 8 *SB* αὐτάρκεια; Lev 12 8 *B*(*S* ⲧⲱϣ), Pro 25 16 *SA*, Nah 2 12 *B*(*A* vb) ἱκανός; Ex 16 21 *B*(*S* ⲡⲉⲧⲏⲡ) καθῆκον; Va 57 13 *B* ⲛⲓⲣ. in all things συμμετρία; PO 14 363 *B* sim, Miss 8 250 *S* ⲟⲩⲛ ⲡⲣ. ⲡⲣⲏⲧⲛ without food;   c gen ⲛ-: Lev 25 26 *SB* ἱκ.; BMar 193 *S* ⲡⲣ. ⲡⲉⲧⲕⲣⲁϯ πολύς; Va 57 245 *B* ⲫⲣ. ⲛⲧⲟⲩϩⲣⲉ κόρος;

ShMIF 23 173 *S* ⲁⲡⲭⲉ ⲡⲣ. ⲛ̄ϯⲡⲁⲣⲁⲃⲟⲗⲏ elsewhere, ShP 131ᵉ 49 *S* vine with ⲡⲣ. ⲛⲃⲗⲃⲓⲗⲉ, Miss 8 15 *S* supply us with ⲡⲣ. ⲛⲟⲉⲓⲕ, ST 192 *S* sent him ⲡⲣ. ⲡⲉⲡⲓⲥⲧⲟⲗⲏ, Bor 145 49 *S* ⲡⲣ. ⲛϣⲁϫⲉ = Mor 53 92 *S* ⲟⲩⲙⲏⲛϣⲉ ⲛϣ., Z 629 *S* recipe ⲡⲣ. ⲡⲛⲉϩ, *ib* ⲡⲉϩ ⲉⲡⲉϥⲣ., PMéd 173 *S* pound with ⲡⲉⲩⲣ. ⲛⲉ- ⲃⲓⲱ, Miss 4 678 *S* coming ⲙⲡⲣ. ⲛⲥⲟⲡ, J 93 11 *S* we deemed him ⲙⲡⲣ. ⲛⲥⲟⲡ ϫⲉⲁϥⲙⲟⲩ, MG 25 359 *B* ϥⲣ. ⲛⲃ̄ ⲙⲃⲓⲣ *enough* (plaited rope) *for 2 baskets.*

Adverbial ⲉⲡⲣ., *sufficiently* : MG 25 244 *B* hast edified us ⲉϥⲣ. ⲁⲩⲧⲁⲣⲕⲱⲥ, Ryl 110 *S* onions soaked ⲉⲡⲣ. ϧⲛ-, ϧⲉⲛⲟⲩϧ., *moderately* : 1 Tim 6 6 *SB* ⲙⲉⲧⲁ ⲁⲩⲧⲁⲣⲕⲉⲓⲁⲥ, Si 34 31 *S* ⲁⲩⲧⲁⲣⲕⲏⲥ; *ib* 30 *S* (var ϧⲛⲟⲩϣⲓ) ⲙⲉⲧⲣⲱ, EW 149 *B* ϫⲉ ⲡⲓⲥⲁϫⲓ ϧ. ⲥⲩⲙⲙⲉⲧⲣⲟⲥ; Aeg 259 *S* eat ϧⲛⲟⲩⲉⲡⲓⲥⲧⲏⲙⲏ ⲙⲡⲟⲩϣ. *Cf* ⲣⲱϣ.

ⲣ ⲡⲣ., ⲉⲣ ϥⲣ., *be, do enough* : Deu 32 10 *B* (*S* ⲣ. vb) ⲁⲩⲧⲁⲣⲕⲉⲓⲛ; Si 34 21 *S* ⲙⲉⲧⲣⲓⲟⲥ; ShBM 198 29 *S* worldly works not evil ⲉⲛϣⲁⲛⲣ ⲡⲣ. *if we do* (*them*) *moderately,* Mor 27 26 *S* poverty ⲣ ⲡⲣ. ⲡⲣⲱⲃ ⲉⲑⲟⲟⲩ = BMis 371 *S* ϧⲁϧ ⲛ- = BSM 30 *B* ⲟⲩⲙⲏⲛϣ ⲛ-, J 68 76 *S* ⲁⲓⲣ ⲡⲣ. ⲙⲡⲉⲧⲛⲁⲡⲟⲩϥ ⲛⲙⲙⲁϥ.

ⲣϣⲱⲛ *SA²,* ⲉⲣ. *SSꟼBF* nn m, *cloak, covering* : Ge 49 11 *SB* (man's) ⲡⲉⲣⲓⲃⲟⲗⲏ, He 1 12 *SBF,* Is 59 17 *S* (*B* ϧⲃⲟⲥ man's), 1 Cor 11 15 *SB* (woman's), BMar 173 *S* ϣⲧⲏⲛ, ⲣ. ⲡⲉⲣⲓⲃⲟⲗⲁⲓⲟⲛ; Ps 103 5 *S* (*B* ϧ.) ⲡⲉⲣⲓⲃⲗⲏⲙⲁ; Jo 19 23 *A²* (*S* ϧⲟⲉⲓⲧⲉ, *B* do man's) ⲓⲙⲁⲧⲓⲟⲛ; Ge 24 65 *SB* (wom), Cant 5 7 *S* (wom), Is 3 23 *SB* ⲑⲉⲣⲓⲥⲧⲣⲟⲛ; Ex 26 7 *B* ⲇⲉⲣⲣⲓⲥ; 1 Cor 11 10 *B* (wom, *S* diff) ⲕⲁⲗⲩⲙⲙⲁ; R 1 4 22 *S* ⲣ. ⲉⲧϧⲓϫⲛⲧⲉⲥⲁⲡⲉ *amictus*; P 55 14 *B,* Tri 431 *S* ⲓϧ., Ryl 453 336 *B* do & مئزر; Br 259 *S* ϧⲟⲉⲓⲧⲉ, ϣⲧⲏⲡ, ⲣ., ShMun 109 *S* ϣⲧ., ⲣ. (man's), BSM 33 *B* ϧⲃⲱⲥ...ⲉⲣ. = Va 63 8 *B* ϣⲑⲏⲡ...ⲉⲣ., Tor 43 *S* ϧⲟ., ⲣ., ⲗⲟⲧⲓϫ, CO 465 *S* ϧⲟ., ⲣ. (wom), J 66 38 *S* do, ShC 42 71 *S* ⲡⲣⲏϣ, ⲣ., ϧⲃⲟⲥ ⲡⲕⲱⲱⲥ, Mor 33 11 *S* ⲉⲣ. fell down on her eyes (var BMis 77 ⲡⲁⲗⲗⲏⲡ), Va 63 8 *B* ⲉⲣ. wherewith coverest head, Mor 44 40 *S* ⲉⲣ. ⲡϣⲏⲥ, CMSS 70 *Sꟼ* ⲉⲣ. ⲉϥϫⲓ ⲥⲧⲁⲩⲣⲟⲥ (*cf* ϫⲓ Ryl 244).

ⲣⲁϣⲣⲉϣ *S* vb intr, meaning unknown : ShP 130² 130]ϥⲛⲁϯ ⲙⲉϩⲣⲟ ⲛⲁⲩ ⲛϥ̄ⲧⲣⲉⲩϣⲱⲡⲉ ⲉⲩⲣ. ⲉⲃⲟⲗ in midst of trees in orchard; as nn *A²*: Mani 1 ⲧⲥⲫⲁⲓⲣⲁ ⲣⲉϭⲣⲉϭ ⲡⲕⲉⲕⲁϩ ⲟⲩⲣⲉϣⲣⲉϣ. For ? ⲡⲣⲁϣⲣⲉϣ, *cf* ⲡⲱⲣϣ ⲉⲃⲟⲗ.

ⲣⲉϣⲧ-, ⲣⲁϣⲧ- *v* ⲣⲱϣⲉ.

ⲣⲱϥ *v* ⲣⲟ **I** & **III**.

ⲣⲟϥⲣⲉϥ *v* ⲥⲣⲟϥⲣⲉϥ.

ⲣϧⲉ *A* vb intr, *be willing* : Cl 2 3 ⲉⲧⲉⲧⲛ̄ⲣϧⲉ ⲉⲡ (var ⲉⲣⲏⲛⲧⲡ[ⲉ ⲉⲡ) ⲁⲕⲟⲛⲧⲉⲥ. Or ?*l* ⲣ ϧⲉ.

ⲣⲱϧⲉ *A* *v* ⲣⲱϣⲉ & ⲣⲱϧⲉ.

ⲣⲉϥ, ⲣⲙ- *A* *v* ⲣⲁϣ.

ⲣⲁϭⲓ, ⲣⲱϭⲓ *B* *v* ⲣⲱϧⲉ.

ⲣⲱϣⲧ, ⲣⲁϣⲧ nn *B* *v* ⲣⲱϣⲧ.

ⲣⲟⲩϧⲉ *SA²,* -ϧⲓ *B,* ⲗⲟⲩϧⲓ *F* (ϧⲓⲣ. *v* below) nn m, *evening* : Ge 1 19 *B,* Jth 9 1 *S* ⲡⲉⲣ., Ps 54 17 *B* (*S* ⲡⲛⲁⲩ ⲡⲣ.), Ac 4 3 *SB* ⲉⲥⲡⲉⲣⲁ; Is 5 11 *SBF,* MG 25 233 *B* ⲟⲯⲉ, Mk 15 42 *SBF* ⲟⲯⲓⲁ; MG 17 297 *S* ⲡⲧⲉⲣⲉⲣ. ϣⲱⲡⲉ = C 89 30 *B* ⲣ. ϫⲉ of that day, BSM 77 *B* ⲡⲉⲣ. ϩⲁⲣⲡⲉ; adverbial, *at evening* : Ez 12 7 *SB* ⲉⲥⲡⲉⲣⲁⲥ; Mt 28 1 *SB* ⲟⲯⲉ, Jo 20 19 *SA²B* ⲟⲯⲓⲁⲥ ⲟⲩⲥⲏⲥ, 1 Kg 17 16 *B* (*S* ⲉⲣ.) ⲟⲯⲓⲍⲉⲓⲛ; BM 706 *F* ⲗ. ⲡⲧⲁⲅⲉⲓ; c ⲉ- : Ps 58 6 *SB,* Is 21 13 *S* (*B* ⲡⲣ.) ⲉⲥⲡ; ShC 73 60 *S* ⲡⲉϥⲃⲱⲕ ⲉⲣ.; c ⲡ- : BAp 109 *S* gave them him ⲡⲣ., AM 175 *B* ⲁⲕⲧⲱϧϥ ⲡⲣ., BM 631 *F* ⲡⲗ.; c ϣⲁ- : Job 4 20 *SB* ⲙⲉⲭⲣⲓ ⲉⲥⲡ., Ac 28 23 *SB* ⲉⲱⲥ ⲉⲥⲡ. c ϧⲁ- *F* : BM 664; c ϧⲓ- *S* : ShMich 550 16 synaxis ϧⲓⲣ., Miss 4 530 (*B* ⲡⲁⲡⲁⲣ.).

ⲡⲛⲁⲩ ⲡⲣ., *time of evening* : Lev 23 5 *S* (*B* ⲁⲡⲁⲣ.), Ps 140 2 *S* (*B* ϧⲁⲡⲁⲣ.) ⲉⲥⲡⲉⲣⲓⲛⲟⲥ; with prep, ⲡ- : Ex 16 6 *S* (*B* om ⲡ-), Ps 89 6 *S* (*B* ⲣ.) ⲉⲥⲡⲉⲣⲁⲥ; Mk 13 35 *S* (*B* ϧⲁ., *F* ⲗ.) ⲟⲯⲉ; Jer 31 33 *B* ⲇⲉⲓⲗⲏⲥ, Ge 3 8 *B* ⲇⲉⲓⲗⲓⲛⲟⲛ; c ϣⲁ- : Jos 8 29 *S,* Ps 103 23 *S* (*B* ϣⲁⲣ.) ⲉⲱⲥ ⲉⲥⲡ.

ϧⲁⲣ., ⲁⲣ. as nn f; Cai 42573 2 *S* ϧⲉⲗϧⲱⲗϥ ⲉⲡⲉⲥⲣⲟ ⲛⲑⲁⲣ., Job 9 9 *B* ⲡⲓⲥⲓⲟⲩ ⲛⲧⲉ ⲁⲣ. (*cf* 38 32 *B*).

ϧⲓⲣ. *SAA²* as nn (*cf* ϧⲓⲧⲁⲩⲉ) : Zech 14 7 *A* (*SB* ⲣ.) ⲉⲥⲡⲉⲣⲁ, Pro 7 9 *A* (*S* ⲣ., *B* ϧⲁⲡⲁⲣ.) ⲉⲥⲡⲉⲣⲓⲛⲟⲥ; *ib* 16 15 *A* (*S* do) ⲟⲯⲓⲙⲟⲥ, Jo 6 16 *A²* (*SB* ⲣ.) ⲟⲯⲓⲁ; Zeph 2 7 *A* (*S* ⲣ., *B* ϧⲁ.) ⲇⲉⲓⲗⲏ; ShC 73 92 *S* ⲉϭⲱ ϣⲁⲣ. (var ϣⲁⲣ.)

ϧⲁⲡⲁⲣ., ⲁⲡⲁⲣ. *B* nn f, meaning as ⲣ. (*cf* ϧⲁⲡⲁⲧⲟⲟⲩⲓ) : Nu 28 4 (*S* ⲣ.), Ps 64 9 (*S* do), Ac 20 15 (*S* diff), TEuch 2 355 ⲧⲁⲓϧ., ⲡⲁⲓⲉϫⲱⲣϧ ⲉⲥⲡ., Dan 9 21 (*S* ⲡⲁⲩ ⲡⲣ.) ⲉⲥⲡⲉⲣⲓⲛⲟⲥ; C 89 49 came in ⲡⲁⲡ. = Miss 4 530 *S* ϧⲓⲣ., *ib* 193 one followed him ⲉⲡⲟⲩϧ ⲁ ⲡ., AM 174 ⲡⲓⲗⲩⲅⲭⲡⲓⲕⲟⲡ ⲛⲧⲉ ϧ., BSM 31 ϯⲟⲩϭⲓⲁ ⲛⲁⲡ. = Va 63 6 ⲛⲣⲁⲡ., BMis 373 *S* ⲣ.; ϥⲡⲁⲩ ⲡϧ. : Ex 12 6 (*S* ⲡⲁⲩ ⲡⲣ.), Ez 46 2 (*S* do) ⲉⲥⲡ.

ϫⲓ ⲣ. *S, spend evening* : Si 36 35 ⲟⲯⲓⲍⲉⲓⲛ (*cf* 1 Kg 17 16 *B*).

ⲁⲧⲣ. *S* : 2 Kg 13 16 ⲟⲩⲁ. (var ⲟⲩⲡⲟⲣⲛⲏ) ⲉⲧⲁⲓⲣⲁ (reading ? ⲉⲥⲡⲉⲣⲁ), cit P 44 110 لا مساء ⲛⲟ.

ⲣⲱϧⲉ *S,* -ϧⲉ *A,* -ϭⲓ *B,* ⲣⲁϭ *B,* ⲣⲁϧⲉ† *S,* -ϭⲓ† *B* vb **I** intr, *become, be clean* : Mal 3 2 *AB* ⲡⲗⲩⲛⲉⲓⲛ; Va 58 186 *B* if besprinkled ϣⲁϥⲣ. ⲕⲁⲑⲁⲣⲟⲥ ⲅⲓⲛⲉ- ⲥⲑⲁⲓ; Tri 706 *S* ⲡⲉⲧⲣ. طّاهر. **II** tr, *cleanse, wash* : Ex 19 10 *SB,* Lev 11 25 *B* (*S* ϣⲱⲙ), Ps 50 4 *B* (*SA* Cl ⲉⲓⲱ), C 89 46 *B* ϣⲑⲏⲡ ...ⲉⲧⲁⲥⲣⲁϭ = Miss 4 805 *S* ϣⲟⲗⲥ ⲡⲗ.; Zech 3 5

S†(A ογλλβε, B τογβηογτ), Mt 27 59† S(B ογλβ) καθ. ; Ps 50 7 B(S ϫωκμ) ῥαντίζειν ; Z 320 S πεϩρο p.† λαμπρός ; Cant 5 10† S ἐκλελοχισμένος (reading ? ἐκλελουμένος) ; ShP 130¹ 37 S εϩρ. ππεϩροιτε ϩμπεπλγμιοπ, C 41 49 B πεϥλεβιτογ ετρ.†, LMis 449 S ταϣϧηπ εϲρ.† = Miss 4 120 B.   As nn, *cleansing* : Va 57 35 B ογρ. πτε ϩλπϩῶϲ ἀποπλ. Cf ρλϩρεϩ.

ρλϭι B nn m, *bleacher, fuller* : K 110, 139 πιρ. قصّار, مبيّض, *ib* 113 ρλϭιτης ᷍ω.

ρλϩτ SF, -ϭτ B, ρεϩτ, λε., -τε F, nn m f, *cleaner, fuller* : Is 36 2 SBF γναφεύς ; Gu 15 S ογρ. slew James with ϣε πωϣε, Hall 32 S clothes sent to πρ., *ib* 80 S πρ. not to handle roughly sacramental μάππαι but merely to wash them, Ep 366 S ππλτ μπρ., Saq 241 S πιωτ μπμλ πρ., *ib* 16 S πμλ πμοοϲ ππερ., PMéd 262 S λμε πρ. *fuller's earth*, Petrie *Hawara* pl 22 F Peter πλ., Strzygowski *Kopt Kunst* 118 B-S πιρ., Saq 16 S ψλϩ…πρ., J 23 23 S Thecla τρ., CMSS 63, 64 F πλεϩτε, TT 165 n ? saint's epithet.   πρ. πτωϭϲ : Is 7 3 S(P 44 112, var p. only), Mk 9 3 S(BF p. only) γν.   In place-name : τϣηπ περλϩτ (BMOr 6201 B 204).

V also cιμ.

(ρλϩρεϩ), ρεϩρωϩ⸗ Sᶠ vb tr, *wash* (?) : BKU 1 21 19 take thing to be dyed to river πτογρεϩρωϩϥ εβλλ & spread to dry. Cf ρωϩε.

ρωϩτ SAA², ρωϩε A²(AP), -ϭτ B, λωϩτ F, ρεϩτ- SF, ρεϭτ- B, ρλϩτ⸗ SAF, ροϩτ⸗ S, ρλϭτ⸗ B, λεϩτ⸗ F, ρλϩτ† S, ρλϭτ† B vb I intr, *strike, be struck, so fall* : Jer 4 7 B καθαιρεῖν ; 2 Kg 21 9 S πίπτειν ; Mt 8 14† B(S πηϫ) βάλλεσθαι ; Ez 32 20 SB κοιμᾶσθαι ; Jth 7 25 S καταστρωθῆναι ; Ez 32 30† B(S ϣοοϲε) τραυματίας ; Sa 17 10 S συνέχεσθαι ; BMOr 8800 200 S εαπεϥϩητ ρ. ϩπογηρπ *corde conciderit* (PL 22 782), ShA 1 128 S wounds ππετρ.† η πετϣοοϲε, Cat 143 B praying εϣτεμρ. πϩητϥ (sc temptation), C 43 130 B πλϥρ.† πε from much torture.   With following preposition. c ε-, εϩρλι ε-, *be struck to* earth &c S : 2 Kg 2 16 πίπ. ; *ib* 12 15 ρ. επϣωπε ἀρρωστεῖν ; ShMIF 23 187 επρ. εϩ. επιϩογεβοτε ; c εϫπ- SA, *strike upon* : Am 9 1 A(SB ϩιογε) πατάσσειν ἐπί ; Ryl 94 103 teeth ρ. εϫππεϥερηϥ ; εϩρλι εϫπ- : Is 9 11 (B tr) ῥάσσειν ἐπί ; ShC 42 98 εϩρ. εϩ. εϫμπκλϩ ; c ϩιϫεπ- B : Dan 8 10 πίπ. ἐπί ; c πεμ- B, *lie with* : Va 58 67 εϲρ. πεμλϥ & so conceived ; c ϩπ-, ϭεπ-, *cast upon, lie in* : Deu 21 1† S(B ϩει) πίπ. ἐν, 1 Kg 31 8† S π. ἐπί ; Mt 8 6† B(S πηϫ) βάλ. ἐν ; εϩογπ ϩπ-, *be cast, lying upon* : Pro 26 22 S(var εϩ. ε-)A τύπτειν εἰς ; AP 27 A² εϥρωϩε λϩ ϩμπεϥϩο, R 1 75 S rays p. εϩ. ϩμπεϩγο (cf Jo 18 6), *ib* 2 1 56 S in ship λϩρ. εϩ. ϩιτπετρλ.

With following adverb. c επεϲητ, *be struck down* : ShA 2 274 S πτετϩε εϩρλι λγω πτετπρ. επ. by demons, *ib* 1 92 εϩρ † επ. weeping, FR 120 B λπρ. επ. through fear ; c εϩρλι, εϩρηι, meaning same : ShWess 9 180 S τηρ. εϩ. ϫεπτπορϫ λπ, ShP 130⁶ 101 S †ρ.† εϩ. εμλτε in sorrow, Miss 4 212 B εiρ.† εϭ. ε†ϩερεϲιϲ ; as nn : ShA 1 41 S in wrath & in ϩεπρ. εϩ. *abasement* of stubborn.

II tr, *strike, cast* : Ge 32 11 S(B ϣλρι), Ex 17 5 S(B μιϣι), Is 10 24 S(B † ερϭοτ), Zech 10 11 A(B ϣ.), Lu 22 50 S(B ϩιογι πϲλ-) πατ. ; Ex 21 15 S(B † ϣλϣ), 1 Cor 8 12 SF(B μι.) τύπ. ; 2 Kg 6 7 B(S πατασσε), Job 16 9 S(reading ἔπαι., B diff), Jo 18 10 S(A² ϣωϲε, B ϩι. πϲλ-) παίειν, Lam 3 11 S(reading κατέπαι., B diff) ; Is 13 16 B(S πωϩ reading ῥήξ.) ῥάσσειν, Jo 18 22 S(A² ϣωϲε, B †) ῥάπισμα διδόναι ; Lu 9 42 SB(reading ἔρραϩ.)ῥηγνύναι, Ps 144 14 S(B ρ. εϩρηι) καταρρήγν. ; Jer 27 30 B ῥίπτεσθαι ; BHom 48 S wind ρλϩτε ῥιπίζειν (reading ? ῥιπτ.), BM 182 2 S λγρλϩτκ ϩιτπεϲ†οϲ βάλλεσθαι, Pro 18 8 SA, Is 26 5 B(S ταϩο επεϲητ) καταβάλ. ; Deu 32 42 S(B ϣλρι), Ez 30 11 B(S ϣω.) τραυματίας ; Ps 88 23 S(B ϭοτϭετ) συγκόπτειν ; Is 5 5 B ἀφαιρεῖν, Ps 51 7 B, Lu 1 52 B(all S ϣορϣρ) καθαι. ; Ge 13 10 B(S do) καταστρέφειν, Si 11 36 S διαστ. ; Mor 17 57 S λϩρ. ππιρο διακρούειν ; Bor 267 103 S setting up πεπτλγρλϩτογ, BSM 12 B εταϩλιπ ρ. πλβηλ, PMich 1191 S εϩρ. μπεϣϣη εγπογϫε πρεππομε (sic), BM 287 S took a staff ϫεεϥπαρλ[ϩ]τϲ (sc dove) μμοϥ, MIF 14 47 S λϥρεϩτ ιϲ πογϫϲ πλλϲ.   With following preposition. c ε-, εϩογπ ε- S, *strike, throw upon* : Mk 9 18 (B εiπε επεϲητ) ῥήσσειν ; Mt 5 39 (B † κογρ) ῥαπίζειν ἐπί ; 2 Kg 8 2 κοιμίζειν ἐπί ; ShA 1 448 cut boughs λϥρλϩτογ επκλϩ, Z 579 unstable soul εϩρ. μμοϲ επιϲλ μππαι, *ib* 302 λϥρ. πογμοπλχοϲ … εϩογπ ετεϥογοϲε ; c εϫπ-, meaning sim : Sa 4 19 S ῥηγν. ; Ps 88 44 S(B φωπϫ) καταρράϲ. ; Hos 10 14 B(A ρ. λϩρηι)ἐδαφίζειν ἐπί ; Lu 6 29 S(B ϩι.) τύπ., Job 16 10 S(B ρ. εϩρηι)παι. εἰς ; Wess 11 159 S seized log ϫεεϥπαρλϩτϥ εϫπτεϥλπε = C 89 65 B τηιϥ εϫεπ- διδόναι κατά ; ShR 2 3 29 S εϫρ. ππεϭιϫ εϫππεϥερηγ, BHom 76 S reed επλγρ. μμοϥ εϫπτεϥλπε ; εϩρλι εϫπ- : Mt 27 30 S(B ϩι.) τύπ. εἰς ; ShRyl 70 249 S λϩρ. πτεγϣηπ εϩρλι εϫμπκλϩ ; c π-, *with* (agent) : R 1 3 62 S λϥρλϩτϥ πτϲηϥε, Mor 23 14 S sim πογλ ππεϥτηρ = *ib* 24 10 F λεϩτβ, MIE 2 373 B sim, LAl 18 S Alexander ρεϩετ πρηηριτης…πογϭεροϥ ; c ϩπ-, ϭεπ- S, meaning same : Nu 35 16 (B † ερϭοτ), Is 10 24 (B do) πατ. ἐν ; R 1 2 56 λιρ. ππετϣηρε…ϩπογμογ ; c εϩογπ ϩπ- S, *throw, smite upon* : 2 Kg

22 24 πατ. ἐπί; ShC 42 106 επⲁⲅⲣⲟϩⲧϥ ⲉϥ. ⲟⲛ-
ⲧⲉϥⲟⲩⲟϭⲉ, Miss 8 218 servant ⲣⲁϩⲧ(ⲧ) ⲉϥ. ⲉⲙ-
ⲡⲁϩⲟ ; c ϩⲓϫⲉⲛ- B, meaning same: Ob 3 (A ⲥⲱⲕ)
κατάγειν ἐπί; C 41 37 ⲉϥⲣ. ⲙⲙⲟϥ ϩ. ⲡⲓⲕⲁϩⲓ.
With following adverb.   c ⲉⲡⲉⲥⲏⲧ, *strike, throw
down*: Hos 14 1 B(A ⲣ. ⲁⲡⲕⲁϩ), Lu 19 44 SB ἐδαφίζειν ; Jer 10 18 S(B om ⲉⲡ.) σκελίζειν; AP 27 A[2]
let him not ⲣ. ⲙ̄ⲙⲁⲛ [ⲁⲡ]ⲉⲥⲏⲧ, R 2 2 28 S clothes
ⲁϥⲣⲁϩⲧⲟⲩ ⲉⲡ. ⲉϫⲙ̄ⲡⲕⲁϩ, C 43 134 B ⲁϥⲣ. ⲙ̄ⲡⲓ-
ⲣⲱⲙⲓ ⲉⲡⲉⲥⲏⲧ ;   c ⲉϩⲣⲁⲓ (once), ⲉϩⲣⲏⲓ, meaning
same: Sa 11 21 S πίπ.; Ps 73 6 (S ⲧⲁϭⲟ ⲉϩ.)
καταρρηγν.: Job 16 10 (S diff), 2 Cor 4 9 (S ⲧ. ⲉⲡⲉⲥⲏⲧ) καταβάλ., ib 10 4 (S ϣⲟⲣ.) καθαιρ., Nu 33 52
(S ⲟⲩⲱϣϥ) ἐξαιρ., Lu 9 39 (S ϩⲓⲧⲉ) σπαράσσειν ;
C 89 214 mice ⲣ. ⲙ̄ⲡⲓⲕⲉϣⲏϭ ⲉϭ. & break it.

ⲣⲉϥⲣ. B, *epileptic*: K 89 ⲡⲓⲣ. ﺻﺮﻉ.

ϫⲓⲡⲣ. B, *casting down*: Ps 36 14 (S ⲧⲁϭⲟ ⲉϩⲣⲁⲓ),
ib 105 26 ⲡ̄ϫⲓⲡⲣⲁϩⲧⲟⲩ (S ⲣ. ⲧⲣ) καταβάλ.

—— SB nn m, *stroke, blow*: 2 Cor 10 8 B(S
ϣⲟⲣ.) καθαίρεσις ; K 158 B ⲡⲓⲣⲱ. (sic) ﺻﺮﻉ *epilepsy*;
AZ 21 142 S ⲡⲣ. ⲡⲓⲙ̄ⲟⲩⲡⲉⲓⲟⲟⲩⲉ ;   ⲣⲁϩⲧ B :
Ez 32 29 (S ϣⲱϭⲉ) τραῦμα.

ⲣⲁϩⲧⲥ S, ⲗⲉϩ. F nn f, *striking, slaughter*: Jos 10
20 (sic prob) κοπή; 1 Kg 4 17 πληγή; 2 Kg 17 9
θραῦσις ; Am 8 3 (B diff) πεπτωκώς; ShR 2 3 5
mourning for ⲧⲣ. ⲡ̄ⲧⲁⲥ[ϣ]ⲱⲡⲉ (?), Mor 39 14 ⲁⲩⲛⲟϭ
ⲡⲣ. ⲧⲁϩⲁ ⲡⲉⲡⲉⲣⲥⲟⲥ = C 43 40 B ϩⲱⲧⲉⲃ, Mor 30
22 F died ⲉⲧⲛⲟϭ ⲛ̄ⲗ. that befell him.

ⲉⲣϩⲟⲧ B, pl ? -ϩⲱⲧ & sg as pl nn m, *blow, wound*:
Jud 11 33 (S=Gk), Is 1 6 (SF do), ib 30 26 (S ⲥⲁϣ,
F ⲡⲱⲗⲁϩ), Mic 1 9 (SA=Gk), Ac 16 33 (S ⲥⲛϣⲉ)
πληγή; Ge 4 23 (S ⲥⲁϣ), Ps 68 27 (S do) τραῦμα;
Ex 21 18 (S ⲇⲁⲭⲉ) πυγμή; Lev 13 18 (S ⲥⲣⲁϩ)
ἕλκος ; 1 Pet 2 24 (S do) μώλωψ; 3 Kg 8 38 ἀφή
plaga ; Miss 4 146 smote him ϩⲉⲛⲟⲩⲡⲓϣⲧ̄ ⲡⲉⲣ.,
AM 34 ⲁϥⲧⲁⲗϭⲟ ⲛ̄ⲡⲓⲉⲣϩⲟⲧ, ib 150 ⲁϥϯ ϥⲓ ⲛ̄ⲡⲓ-
ⲉⲣϩⲱⲧ, Va 57 76 plague, drought & ⲛⲓⲉⲣ. on fruit
& trees ;   ⲉⲣ ⲉⲣ., *be, become wound*: MG 25 277
whole body ⲉⲣ ⲉⲣ. = BIF 13 98 S ⲣ ⲡⲗⲩⲅⲏ, AM
311 skin ⲉⲣ ⲟⲩⲡⲓϣⲧ̄ ⲡⲉⲣ. ;   ϯ ⲡⲟⲩⲉⲣ., ϯ ⲉⲣ.,
give wound, wound: Lev 24 17 (S = Gk), Deu 19
4 (S ⲣⲱϩⲧ), Is 27 7 (S ϣⲁⲁⲣⲉ) πατάσσειν ; Job 5 18
(S do) παίειν, Lu 10 30 (S ⲥⲁϣ) πληγὰς ἐπιτιθέναι,
MG 25 212 ⲡⲗ. διδόναι; FR 118 fire ϯ ⲉⲣ. ⲡⲟⲩⲙⲏϣ,
ROC 25 250 ⲉⲧⲁϥϯ ⲙ̄ⲡⲉⲣ. (var ϣⲁϣ) ϩⲉⲛⲡⲓⲣⲟ
with staff ;   ϭⲓ ⲉⲣ., *receive blow, be smitten*: Ex
16 3 (S ϣⲱϭⲉ), Is 1 5 (SF c.) πλήσσειν; C 89 149
saw one ⲉⲁⲩϭⲓ ⲉⲣ. ϩⲉⲛⲟⲩⲛⲟⲃⲓ, DeV 2 168 ⲁⲩϭⲓ
ⲉⲣ. ⲉϥⲓⲟⲩ.

ⲣⲁϩⲧⲉ[1], ⲣⲟ.[2], ⲗⲟ.[3], ⲣⲱ.[4], ⲣⲁϩⲧ[5] S, ⲗⲁϩϯ[6], ⲣⲉⲣⲧⲉ[7].

F nn f, *cauldron*: Eccl 7 7[6] F(S ϫⲁⲗⲕⲓⲟⲡ) λέβης;
ShC 73 138 S not to neglect ⲟⲩⲣ.[4] lest it spoil in
fire, AZ 13 136 S bade cast him ⲉⲩⲣ.[1] & set fire
below it, P 129[16] 51 S ⲡ̄ⲃ̄ⲣ̄ⲃ̄ⲣ ⲡ̄ⲧⲣ.[1], PMich 1291 F
lept forth from ⲧⲣ.[7], Ryl 88 S drew forth wool from
ⲧⲣ.[2], BM 1147 S ⲟⲩⲣ.[2] ϩⲁⲛ ⲁϫ, PLond 4 516 S
ⲟⲩⲛⲟϭ [ⲛ]ⲗ.[3], Ostr Univ Coll Lond (dupl of CO
466) S ⲟⲩⲣ.[5]

ⲣⲁϩⲧⲥ v ⲣⲱϩⲧ.

ⲣⲁϩⲧⲟⲩ S nn, *a monkish garment*: Mus 40 36
(Reg Pach) none may walk in convent ⲡⲟⲩⲉϣ ⲡⲣ.
ϩⲓⲧⲟⲗⲟⲙⲱⲡ (τελαμών) *cucullo et pellicullo*, ShBMOr
8810 491 if I desire to quit (monastery) ⲉⲓⲁⲙⲟⲣⲧ
ⲡⲟⲩⲣ. ⲡ̄ⲧⲁⲃⲱⲕ, Mich 550 40 degenerate monks have
ϩ̄ⲛⲣ. ⲉⲣⲉⲡⲉⲩⲧⲟⲟⲙⲉ ⲡⲁⲁⲩ *with large pouches*, so ?
ⲣ. leather apron, v Ep 1 76.

ⲣⲉϫ v ⲱⲣϫ.

ⲣⲁϫⲏ A   v ⲣⲱⲕϩ (ⲣⲟⲕϩⲉ).

ⲣϫⲛⲟⲟⲩ, ⲣⲉϫⲡⲁⲩ v ϫⲛⲟⲟⲩ.

ⲣⲱϫⲡ, ⲣⲉϫⲡ- (2 pl). ⲣⲟϫⲡ̄, ⲣⲟϫⲡ̄[†] B vb I intr,
be thrown down, sink down: Ps 87 5[†] (S ⲛⲏϫ), Is 33
12[†] (SF do), EpJer 71[†] (F ⲥⲏⲧ ⲉⲃⲁⲗ) ρίπτεσθαι ;
Va 63 97 sick ⲉϭⲣ.[†] ϩⲓϫⲉⲛⲟⲩⲙⲁ ⲡⲉⲛⲕⲟⲧ κεῖσθαι,
Jo 5 3 (SA[2] ⲛⲕⲟⲧⲕ) κατακ., CDan 85 lo 15 years ⲕⲣ.[†]
ϩⲉⲛϯⲡⲟⲣⲛⲓⲁ, MG 25 291 ⲉⲩⲣ.[†] like dead = BIF
13 107 S ⲡ. ⲉⲃⲟⲗ, DeV 2 166 restoring churches
ϫⲉⲁⲩⲣ. (var ⲟⲩⲱϫⲡ) ⲉⲡⲉⲥⲏⲧ, CDan 87 after long
fast ⲁⲓⲣ. ⲉⲡ. ⲁⲓⲉⲛⲕⲟⲧ, BMAdd 39583 let none ⲣ.
ⲉϩⲟⲩⲛ ⲉⲟⲩⲙⲁ ⲉϥⲛⲁϣⲧ ⲡ̄ⲧⲉ ⲫⲓⲟⲃⲓ.

II tr, *throw down*: Nu 35 20 (S ⲧⲱϭⲛ) ὠθεῖν ;
MG 25 195 ⲁⲡⲣ. ⲡ̄ⲧⲉⲡⲙⲉⲧϫⲱⲃ ϩⲁⲣⲁⲧⲟⲩ, DeV 2
53 let us not ⲣ. ⲡ̄ⲧⲉⲛⲯⲩⲭⲏ ⲉϩⲣⲏⲓ ⲉⲡϣⲓⲕ, C 89
136 ⲡⲥⲉⲣ ⲡⲛⲓⲙⲟⲕⲓ = Bor 296 4 S ⲟⲩⲱϫⲡ = MG
17 507 ﺍﺭﻛﺲ ;   refl: Jer 28 6 ⲣⲉϫⲡⲟⲑⲏⲛⲟⲩ ἀπορ-
ρίπ., Ps 83 11 (S do) παραρίπ.   As nn: Cat 207
humility, self-blame & ⲡⲓⲣ. ϩⲁⲧⲉⲡϥϯ, MG 25 131
sim.

ⲣⲟϫⲣⲉϫ S, ⲣⲉϭⲣⲉϭ A[2] vb, *wash* (?), *polish* (?):
as nn Sh(Besa)Z 505 among malpractices ϩⲉⲛⲣ.
ⲉⲃⲟⲗ ⲡⲓⲉⲟⲩⲉⲣⲏⲧⲉ ⲙ̄ⲡⲡⲉⲩϩⲟ so as to beautify
them, lc n 10 paral ⲉⲓⲱ ⲉⲃⲟⲗ, Mani 1 A[2] ⲡⲁⲏⲣ
ⲧⲣⲟⲩⲅⲁⲓⲡⲉ ⲧⲥⲫⲁⲓⲣⲁ ⲣ.

ⲣϫⲱϫⲉ v ⲙⲁⲣϫⲱϫⲉ.

ⲣⲁϭⲣⲉϭ S vb intr, *hiss* (?) of bones or flesh in
fire: Ryl 94 109 (AZ 25 65) noise of bones ⲉⲩⲣ.
ⲉⲃⲟⲗ ϩⲓⲧⲙ̄ⲡⲕⲱϩⲧ, ib sticks ⲉⲩⲣ. ϫⲉⲥⲉⲗⲏⲕ, ib ⲡⲥⲱⲙⲁ ⲉϣⲁϥⲣ. ϩⲁⲧⲁϭⲃⲉⲥ ⲡ̄ⲧⲥⲁⲣⲝ.

C

c, 18th letter of alphabet, called сниаа (Leyd 434), сүниаа (My 90) *S*, сниаа (K 1, Stern p 1), сниаа (Stern p 418) *B*, ا۔ (Stern *l c*, P 43 247= 44 127). As numeral *BF*, rarely *S* (Br 128) = 200 (щнт *S*). Derived from hierogl *ś* & *s*, as соп, снипе, иосте, ιωс, ϩωⲃс. Varies with ӡ *q v* (σӡ = щ in transcribed texts) & with initial щ, as *S* сааⲛⲯ, саще *B* щаⲛⲯ, щаⲯⲓ; *S* щаⲝⲉ, щⲱⲝⲛ *B* саⲝⲓ, сⲱⲝⲛ, *v* also Ep 1 244; represents щ *O* (rarely) сасфⲓ, сⲱⲃⲓ (PGM 1 114); init dropped, as коркр, ⲗоϥⲗϥ(?), ϩⲃⲏⲛⲉ, ϭⲣⲉϣⲧ. On metathesis *v* Sethe *Verbum* 1 275 ff. Transcribes Ar س, as ⲝⲉⲗⲉс جالس , ⲉⲛⲥⲉⲛ انسان , ⲥⲉⲉⲗ سأل (EW 234 ff); or ز, as сⲓⲛⲓⲛ زبيب (Ryl 106), ⲁⲛсⲁⲣⲱ روت عنز (PMéd); or ص, as сⲁⲛⲧⲁⲗ صندل (*ib*), ⲁсⲃⲁⲣ أصفر (AZ 23 118), ⲓⲟⲝⲗос خلص (EW); transcribed by س , as بسندة ⲡⲉсⲡⲧⲉ, طوبي ⲥⲓⲟⲟⲩⲧ; or ص, as ابوصير ⲡⲟⲩⲥⲓⲣⲉ, قوص ⲕⲱс. Appended to vb it forms nn f, as ⲁⲡс, ⲕоⲧс, ⲙоⲕϩс, ⲡⲁⲣс, ⲣⲁⲩⲥ, сооⲩϩс, щоⲗс, ϭорϭс. Ancient causative с- survives in сааⲛⲯ, сⲓⲛⲉ, сооϩⲉ, сⲁϩⲛⲉ, сⲱⲣⲡ, сⲁⲝⲓ, сⲟϭⲛⲓ, сϭⲣⲁϩⲧ &c (Sdff 251 ff).

сⲁ *SAA²B*, **се** *Sⁿ*(S̊T 101)*F* nn m, *side, part*: Ex 32 15 *SB*, Ez 1 8 *SB*, Dan 2 33 *B*, Ac 19 1 *S* (*B* ⲙⲁ) μέρος; Is 11 12 *S*(*B* ⲗⲁⲕϩ)πτέρυξ; Ro 15 23 *B*(*S* = Gk) κλίμα; Va 61 17 *B* sought him ϩⲉⲛⲡⲓсⲁ ⲧⲏⲣоⲩ τόπος; Ge 19 9 *S* ⲉⲡⲉⲓсⲁ (*B* ⲙⲙⲁⲩ), Z 338 *S* lo he is сⲁⲡⲓсⲁ ἐκεῖ; TU 24 1 3 *S* ⲡⲉсⲟⲩⲁ сⲁ сⲛϭ, Bor 252 304 *S* incline ⲉⲝⲙⲡⲟⲩⲁ ⲡⲛсⲁ, ShC 42 215 *S* ϩⲉⲛⲥⲁ ⲉⲩⲗⲱⲕⲯ of new house, Va 58 145 *B* guide me to ⲡⲓсⲁ where he is, Dan Vis 14 53 *B* ⲡⲓсⲁ ⲉⲧсⲁⲡⲉⲙⲛⲧ, Miss 4 111 *B* ⲡⲓсⲁ ⲛ̅ of my robe, C 86 280 *B* ⲡⲓⲧⲛ̅ ⲡⲥⲁ ⲛⲧⲉ ⲫⲓоⲙ (*cf* BSG 180 *S* оⲩⲛϣоⲙⲛⲧ), Pcod 2 *S* Judas ⲡ ϩⲁⲉ ⲉⲡсⲁ сⲡⲁⲩ, ShR 2 3 82 *S* ⲉⲩсⲱⲕ ⲙⲙоϥ ⲉⲡсⲁ сⲡⲁⲩ, BMis 556 *S* ⲡⲉϥⲧоⲩсⲁ, BM 524 *F* ⲡⲉϥⲝ̅ ⲛсⲉ; ⲕесⲁ *v* below, ⲗⲁⲁⲩ ⲛсⲁ, сⲁ ⲛⲓⲙ *v* ⲛсⲁ- **I.** **a** *this side & that*: Jos 9 6 *S* ⲡⲓсⲁ...ⲡⲁⲓ, Ez 41 19 *B* sim (*S* ⲛсⲁⲡⲁⲓ ⲙⲛⲡⲁⲓ), *ib* 40 10 *S* ⲡсⲁ ⲡⲥⲁ (*B* ⲡсⲁⲥⲁ ⲛⲓⲃⲉⲛ) ἔνθεν κ. ἔν., Nu 11 31 *S* ⲡⲉⲓсⲁ...ⲡⲁⲓ (*B* сⲁⲙⲡⲁⲓ *bis*), Ap 22 2 *S* sim (*B* do), 2 Kg 2 13 *S* ⲡⲓсⲁ...ⲡⲓⲕесⲁ ἐντεῦθεν κ. ἐντ., 4 Kg 2 14 *S* sim ἔνθα κ. ἔν.; Ex 2 12 *A* ⲡⲓсⲁ ... ⲡⲉⲓ (*B* ⲉⲙⲡⲁⲓ *bis*) ὧδε κ. ὧ.; PS 24 *S* ⲉϥⲡⲏⲧ ⲉⲡⲓсⲁ ⲙⲙⲡⲁⲓ, AM 99 *B* could not move ⲉⲡⲁⲓсⲁ ⲛⲉⲙⲫⲁⲓ, Mor 23 18 *S* stood ⲛсⲁⲡⲓсⲁ ⲙⲡсⲁⲡⲁⲓ ⲙⲙоϥ. **b** сⲁ ⲛ-, ⲛⲧⲉ :

Ex 16 35 *S*(*B* = Gk), Mt 15 21 *B*(*S* ⲙооⲩⲧⲉ), Ac 23 9 *S* (*B* ⲉⲃоⲗ ϩⲉⲛ-) μέρ.; often with preceding prep & art = Gk prep : Lev 1 15 *S* ⲉⲡсⲁ ⲛ- (*B* ϩⲁⲧⲉⲛ-) ἐπί, πρός, Nu 13 22 *B* sim (*S* ⲉ-) κατά, Ge 35 16 (21) *S* ⲙⲡⲓсⲁ ⲛ- (*B* do), Ac 7 43 *S* ⲉⲡⲓсⲁ ⲛ- ἐπέκεινα, 1 Kg 20 38 *S* ϩⲓⲡⲓсⲁ ⲛ- ἀπό; PS 113 *S* ⲡⲧоⲡос ⲉⲧⲙⲡⲥⲁ ⲛⲧⲡⲉ, Mani 1 *A²* ⲡсⲁ ⲛⲡⲓⲧⲛ, El 86 *A* щⲁⲡсⲁ ⲛⲣⲱⲧⲡ, BMis 132 *S* table ϩⲁⲡⲉⲓсⲁ ⲙⲙоⲓ, MG 25 336 *B* looked ⲉⲡсⲁ ⲛⲁⲃⲃⲁ ⲓⲱⲁⲛⲛⲏс; кⲁⲧⲁ сⲁ ⲣⲏ† *v* ⲣⲏ†; esp in phrases of geogr direction : Jos 18 14 *S* ⲉⲝⲙⲡсⲁ ⲛ- παρά, Mk 3 7 *S* ⲉⲡсⲁ ⲛ- (*B* ⲉсⲕⲉⲛ-) πρός (var παρά), Nu 3 23 *S* ϩⲓⲡсⲁ ⲛ- (var ϩⲁⲧⲡ-, *B* сⲁⲡсⲁ ⲛ-) παρά (var κατά), Ez 43 1 *B* ⲉⲡⲓсⲁ ⲡⲧⲉ (*S* ⲉ-) κατά, *ib* 2 *B* ϩⲉⲛⲡсⲁ ⲛ- (*S* ϩⲓⲛ, *cf* 40 44) ὁδός, 1 Kg 30 14 *S* ⲉⲡсⲁ ⲛ- ἐπί, Ez 40 46 *S* do (*B* ⲙⲡсⲁ ⲛ-) πρός; MG 17 316 *S* sailed ⲉⲡсⲁ ⲙⲡⲉⲙϩⲓⲧ = C 89 4 *B* ⲉⲡⲉⲙ., C 43 127 *B* turned ⲉⲡсⲁ ⲛ†ⲁⲡⲁⲧоⲗⲏ, P 131¹ 62 *S* reacheth ⲛсⲁ ⲙⲡⲣⲏс of Egypt; or without prep where no motion : Ez 47 19 *B* ⲡсⲁ ⲙⲫⲣⲏс τὰ πρός *plaga*, Zech 14 4 *A* ⲡсⲁ ⲙⲡⲙϩⲓⲧ (*B* ⲉⲡсⲁ ⲛ-) πρός; RChamp 372 *S* ⲡсⲁ ⲙⲡⲉⲙϩⲓⲧ opp ⲡⲙⲁⲣⲏс. **c** without ⲛ-, ⲛⲧⲉ (in *B* often = ⲛсⲁ- *S*): Ps 148 4 *S* ⲉⲧсⲁⲧⲡⲉ (*B* сⲁⲡϣⲱⲓ) ὑπεράνω, Ge 6 16 *B* сⲁⲡсⲫⲓⲣ ⲛ- (*S* ⲡсⲁ-) ἐκ πλαγίων, 2 Kg 21 14 *S* sim ἐν τῇ πλευρᾷ, Deu 33 2 *B* сⲁоⲩⲓⲛⲁⲙ ⲛ- (*S* ⲡсⲁ-) ἐκ δεξιῶν, Ez 16 46 *B* сⲁϩⲃоⲩⲣ (*S* do) ἐξ εὐωνύμων; FR 38 *S* ⲡⲉⲧсⲁϩⲃоⲩⲣ (var BMis 70 ϩⲓϩ.); geogr : Ge 2 8 *B* κατά, Nu 13 30 *SB*, Is 14 13 *B* (*S* ⲛ-) πρός, Nu 32 19 *B*(*S* ϩⲛ-)ⲉⲛ, Ez 1 4 *B* ⲉⲃоⲗ сⲁⲡⲉⲙϩⲓⲧ(*S* ϩⲛ-), Ap 21 13 *B*(*S* ⲉ-) ἀπό; Miss 4 533 *S* village ⲉⲧсⲁⲙϩⲓⲧ ⲙⲙоⲕ = C 89 51 *B* ⲉⲧⲥⲁⲡⲉⲙ., Mor 31 5 *S* χώρα ⲉⲧсⲁϩⲣⲓⲧ (var Miss 4 771 ⲙⲡⲙϩⲓⲧ), Miss 4 719 *S* ⲡⲣⲱⲙⲉ ⲛⲧⲉ сⲁϩⲣⲧ, C 89 44 *B* convent ⲉссⲁⲣⲏс of Tabennesi = Miss 4 525 *S* ⲙⲡⲣ., *Mél Charles Mœller* 1 227 *S* ⲙⲙⲉⲣос ⲙⲡсⲁⲉⲓⲙⲏⲧ, AM 168 *B* brought them сⲁⲡⲉⲓⲉⲃⲧ of city, Wor 294 *S* ⲡϥⲣ сⲁⲡⲓⲉⲃⲧ of city, BM 1008 *S* ⲯⲁⲙϩⲓⲧ, Z 639 *S* ⲧсⲱϣⲉ...ⲡⲉ(с)сⲁⲣⲏс.

ⲉⲃоⲗ сⲁ- *B*, *from the side, from* : Is 14 31 (*S* ⲉⲃ. ϩⲛ-), Jer 27 3 (*F* ⲉⲃ. ϩⲛ-), Mt 2 1 (*S* do) ἀπό; C 89 30 coming ⲉⲃ. сⲁⲡⲉⲙϩⲓⲧ = MG 17 296 *S* ⲛсⲁⲡⲙ.

ⲕесⲁ *SB*, *other part, apart, elsewhere* ; Jo 10 1 *S* ϩⲓⲕ. (*B* ⲛϩоⲩⲧⲉⲛ) ἀλλαχόθεν ; BMis 79 *S* ⲡⲡⲉⲛⲕⲧⲉ ⲡϣⲁⲝⲉ ⲉⲕ., MG 25 375 *B* departed сⲁⲕ., Rec 6 70 *S* if I give my daughter ⲛсⲁⲕоⲩсⲁ (instead of to thee) ; of menstruous woman ο ⲡⲕ. *S* Lev 20 18

(B ⲕⲉⲙⲁ) ἀποκαθημένη, ib 18 19(B ⲟⲩⲱϯ ⲉⲃⲟⲗ)ἐν
χωρισμῷ.

ⲡⲥⲁ- *SA²BFO*, ⲥⲁ- *A²*(Mani, BM 1223) *B*(Jer 14
3, 44 2), ⲉⲥⲁ- *F*, ⲡⲥⲉ- *A*, ⲥⲉ- *AF*, ⲡⲥⲱ⸗ *SAA²BF* (2
pl *S* ⲡⲥⲱⲧⲛ BAp 92, ⲡⲥⲁⲧⲏⲩⲧⲛ *ib*, PS 372) prep.

I *behind, after* lit or figur *S* (*cf* c above), independent of vb : Lu 13 33 ⲛ. ⲣⲁⲥⲧⲉ ἐχόμενος ; Mor 22 93
seized Habakkuk ⲛ. ⲛⲃ̄ⲱ ⲛⲧⲉϥⲁⲡⲉ, *ib* 52 53 dragged
him ⲛ. ⲛⲉϥⲟⲩⲉⲣⲏⲧⲉ, KroppB went in ⲛ. ϫⲱⲓ came
forth ⲛ. ⲣⲁⲧ, *ib* ⲛ. ⲟⲩ ⲛⲧⲉⲟⲩⲱϣ ⲧⲁⲣⲓⲙⲉ ⲁⲛ *wherefore ?*, Gu 106 wilt go to catch fish ⲛ. ⲟⲩ̄?, *ib* 79
sharpen sword ⲛ. ⲕⲱⲡⲥ *for slaughter*, BMis 3 their
chapels ⲕⲏⲧ ⲛ. ⲡⲉⲩⲉⲣⲏⲩ *side by side*, ShBMOr 8810
402 food ⲁⲧⲉⲛⲡϣⲓⲧⲉ ⲛⲭⲓⲟⲩⲉ ⲛ. ⲡⲉⲧⲡⲉⲣⲏⲩ, RNC 85
doors ⲟⲩⲱⲛ ⲛ. ⲡⲉⲩⲉⲣⲏⲩ ;   *against* : Ex 21 17 *B*
(*S* ⲉ-)acc, BHom 87 accusations of Judas ⲛ. ⲡⲥⲱⲧⲏⲣ, CO 221 *S* ⲡⲡⲉⲕⲕⲛ ⲕⲁⲧⲁⲫⲣⲟⲛⲏⲥⲓⲥ ⲛⲥⲱⲓ, BM
604 *F* ϣⲁⲓⲥⲡ ⲗⲁⲟⲩ ⲥⲉⲕ ;   *without vb* : Jer 18 14
ⲉⲣⲉⲟⲩⲅⲏⲩ ⲛⲥⲱϥ (*B* Gk diff) ;   rarely *from* : Nu
5 2 *S* γονορρυής ; MG 17 296 *S* coming ⲛ. ⲡⲁⲣⲓⲧ
(*v* ⲉⲃⲟⲗ ⲥⲁ-), Va 64 180 *B*(HL 120 om) ⲁⲥϥⲉⲓ ⲛ-
ⲥⲁⲟⲩⲁⲓ *fallen from* (been dropped by) *some one.*

Verbs oftenest with ⲛⲥⲁ-, meaning, more or less
lit, *after* : ⲉⲓⲁ ⲧⲟⲟⲧ⸗, ⲉⲓⲱϣ, ⲕⲱ, ⲕⲱⲧⲉ, ⲙⲟⲟϣⲉ,
ⲡⲱⲧ, ⲣⲓⲕⲉ, ⲥⲱⲃⲉ, ⲥⲱⲧⲙ, ⲥϩⲁⲓ, ϯ, ⲟⲩⲱϩ, ⲟⲩⲱϣ,
ϣⲓⲛⲉ, ϣⲁϫⲉ, ϩⲓⲟⲩⲉ, ϫⲟⲟⲩ, ϫⲓⲟⲩⲉ, ϭⲓⲛⲉ ; many
others, as Is 55 1 *S* ⲃⲱⲕ *go for*, Miss 4 104 *B* ⲓⲛⲓ
ⲉⲃⲟⲗ *bring against*, Mk 15 29 *S* ⲕⲓⲙ *shake at,
against*, PS 380 *S* ⲙⲟⲩⲣ *tie by* the tongue, ShA 2
278 *S* ⲡⲱϣⲥ ⲛϩⲏⲧ *be amazed at*, Miss 4 170 *B*
ϣⲑⲟⲣⲧⲉⲣ *be troubled on account of*, AZ 21 105 *O*
ⲡⲉϫⲥⲓ *incite toward*, MG 25 303 *B* ϥⲱϯ *wipe down*,
Ac 27 19 *B* ϩⲓ ⲧⲟⲟⲧ⸗ *lay hands on*, Sa 19 16 *S*
ϭⲟⲙϭⲙ *feel after* ;   emphasizes ? meaning, as
BKU 1 21 45 *S* ⲡⲱⲛⲉ *stir about, keep stirring*,
ROC 27 143 *B* ⲣⲱⲕϩ *burn up*, *ib* 25 255 *B* ⲥⲱⲗⲡ
tear up, Mor 32 20 *S*, Miss 4 170 *B* ⲟⲅⲉⲓⲥ *saw
in pieces*, Mor 52 32 *S* ϣⲱϥ *devastate*, *ib* 54 53 *S*,
Miss 4 126 *B* ϩⲱⲧⲉⲃ *slaughter*, Mor 55 72 *Sf* ⲥⲉⲑⲃⲉ
keep chewing.

ⲛⲥⲁⲥⲁ, ⲥⲁⲥⲁ ⲛⲓⲙ *S*, ⲥⲁⲥⲁ ⲛⲓⲃⲉⲛ *B*, ⲛⲥⲁⲥⲉ ⲛ. *F*,
on every side : Job 31 12 *SB* ἐπὶ πάντ. τ. μερῶν, Si
51 8 *S*, Jer 20 9 *B*, He 9 4 *SBF*, R 2 2 34 *S* ϯⲣⲏϣ
ⲛ. ⲛ. (var BHom 51 ⲥⲁⲥⲁ ⲛ. = Su 22 *B*) πάντοθεν,
Miss 8 57 *S* πανταχόθεν, Ac 24 3 *B*(*S* diff) πάντῃ ;
Z 320 *S* holding him ⲥ. ⲛ. παρ' ἑκάτερα ; ShA 1
302 *S* solid walls ⲥⲉⲙⲛⲣ ⲛ. ⲛ., Bor 258 41 *S* Virgin ⲉⲧⲕⲟⲥⲙⲉⲓ ⲛ. ⲛ., ROC 27 144 *B* woe is me ⲥ.
ⲛ., DeV 1 123 *B* ⲙⲉϩ ⲡⲓⲁϩⲓ ⲥ. ⲛ. ⲛⲧⲁϥ, BM 1211
S shall be thy servant ⲛ. ⲛ.

ⲛⲥⲁⲟⲩⲥⲁ *SF*, ⲥⲁⲟⲩⲥⲁ *SB*, ⲥⲁⲛⲥⲁ *B*, *on a side,
apart* : Is 18 7 *S*(*B* = Gk), AM 267 *B* ἐν μέρει ;
Mt 14 13 *F*(*S* ⲙⲁⲩⲁⲁ⸗, *B* om), Lu 9 10 *S*(*B* c.

ⲙⲙⲁⲩⲁⲧ⸗) κατ' ἰδίαν ; Ge 30 40 *S*(*B* om) καθ'
ἑαυτόν ; Sa 18 18 *S* ἀλλαχῇ ; Jer 15 17 *S* ⲛ. ⲙⲁⲅⲁⲁ⸗
(*B* ⲙⲙ.) καταμόνας ; Lev 13 46 *B* (*S* ⲡⲟⲣϫ ⲉⲃⲟⲗ)
κεχωρισμένος ; ShC 42 147 *S* to eat ⲛ., ShBerlSitz
'29 430 *S* isle ecc. ⲛⲑⲁⲗⲁⲥⲥⲁ, C 43 194 *B* ⲁϥⲥⲟⲕϥ
ⲥⲁⲡ., *ib* 58 *B* ⲥⲟⲕ ... ⲥⲁⲟⲩ., Cat 94 *B* if fingers &
spittle (Mk 7 33) ⲛⲛ ⲉϥⲙⲉⲧⲣⲱⲙⲓ ⲥⲁⲡ. *alone, who
healed diseases ?*

ⲛⲥⲁ-, ⲥⲁⲗⲁⲩ ⲛⲥⲁ *S* -ϩⲗⲓ ⲛⲥⲁ *B* *on any (no) side* :
Sa 17 9 *S* μηδαμόθεν, Job 21 9 *SB*, Z 325 *S* ⲙⲛ
ⲁⲅⲅⲉⲗⲟⲥ ⲥⲁⲗ. ⲛ. οὐδαμοῦ ; ShMun 110 *S* no fruit
ⲛ. ⲗ. ⲛ., BSM 130 *B* ⲙⲡⲁϥⲕⲓⲙ ⲛ. ϩⲗⲓ ⲛ.

II *except, beyond SAB*(rare)*F* : Eccl 3 12 *S*, Mt
14 17 *S*(*BF* ⲉⲃⲏⲗ ⲉ-), 1 Cor 8 4 *SF*(*B* do), BHom
25 *S* naught therein ⲛ. ⲗⲩⲡⲏ εἰ μή ; Job 25 2 *S*
(*B* do), Mal 2 15 *A*(*B* do)ἤ, Jos 17 3 *S*, Si 22 15 *S*,
Is 66 2 *S*(*B* do) ἀλλ' ἤ ; Ro 4 24 *F* ⲛ. ⲉⲧⲃⲏⲧⲛ (*SB*
ⲁⲗⲗⲁ) ἀλλὰ καί ; Nu 11 6 *S*(*B* do), Ac 15 28 *S*(*B*
= Gk) πλήν ; Si 31 25 *S* πλεῖον ἤ ; 1 Kg 21 9 *S*
παρέξ ; PS 376 *S* having never sinned ⲛ. ⲣⲱⲧⲃ,
ShIF 259 *S* wherein differ we from them ⲛ. ⲟⲩⲣⲁⲛ ?, Mor 18 72 *S* ⲙⲡⲉⲓⲉⲓⲙⲉ ⲛ. ⲡⲟⲟⲩ *only to-day*
= Miss 4 145 *B* ϣⲁⲫⲟⲟⲩ, Ryl 316 *S* I have no one
(ⲛ)ⲥⲁⲣⲱⲧⲛ, Miss 8 203 *S* none other ⲛ. ⲛⲧⲟϥ, Mor
30 49 *F* begᵗ none ⲛ. ⲛⲧⲁⲥ = BMis 273 *S* ⲛ. ⲕⲉⲗⲗⲁⲥ,
JKP 2 154 *F* ⲙⲡⲉⲩⲉⲣ ⲡⲉⲑⲁⲩ ⲉⲥⲁⲡⲉⲧⲛⲁⲛⲟⲩϥ *but
rather good*, DeV 2 228 *B* no hope ⲛ. ϯⲃⲟⲏⲑⲓⲁ of
Lord ;   with ⲧⲣⲉ- & vb *SA* : Deu 10 12 *S*(*B*
ⲉⲃⲏⲗ), Ps 132 1 *S*(*B* do), Mic 6 8 *A*(*B* = Gk) ἀλλ'
ἤ, Lu 12 49 *S*(PS 300 reading ? εἰμήτι, var ⲉⲧⲣⲉ-,
B = Gk), Jo 15 13 *S*(BM 8810 449, var & *A²* ϫⲉⲕⲁⲥ
ⲉϥⲉ-, *B* = Gk) ; ShMIF 23 71 *S* how shall I profit
ⲛ. ⲧⲣⲁϯ ⲟⲥⲉ ⲙⲙⲟⲓ ?, Bor 282 164 *S* ⲛⲕⲉⲗⲁⲁⲩ ⲁⲛⲡⲉ
ⲛ. ⲧⲣⲉϥϫⲟⲟⲥ ϫⲉ-.

III with impers ⲉⲥ-, *it is* (incumbent, depends)
upon S : ShC 73 24 ⲉⲥⲡⲥⲱⲡ ⲉⲧⲙⲣ ⲛⲟⲃⲉ, P 131²
155 ⲉⲥⲡⲥⲱⲡ ⲉⲧⲣⲉⲥⲥⲱ (sc ⲧⲉⲭⲁⲣⲓⲥ) ⲛⲙⲙⲁⲛ, Z 603
birth and death ⲛϩⲱⲃ ⲉⲧⲉⲛⲥⲉⲡⲥⲱⲛ ⲁⲛ ⲉⲣⲟϥ.

ⲙⲛⲛⲥⲁ- *SA²FO*, ⲙⲡⲛⲥⲁ- *S*(Ac 15 13 Budge), ⲙ-
ⲡⲛⲥⲉ-*A*, ⲙⲉⲛⲉⲡⲥⲁ-*BF*, ⲙⲉⲛ(ⲛ)ⲉⲥⲁ-*F*, -ⲥⲱ⸗ *SABF*,
after of time   ⲁ with nn or pron : Nu 13 26 *SB*, Ps
15 4 *SB*, Mt 1 12 *SB* μετά ; 1 Kg 24 21 *SB*, Jo 1
15 *SB* ὀπίσω ; Nu 32 19 *S*(*B* ⲥⲁⲙⲡⲏ), Su 64 *B*
ἐπέκεινα ; 1 Cor 15 46 *B*(*S* ⲙⲛⲛⲥⲱⲥ) ἔπειτα ; Jer
27 17 *SF*(*B* ⲛϭⲁⲉ), Mt 22 27 *S*(*B* do) ὕστερον ;
Jud 11 39 *SB* ἐν τῷ τέλει ; AM 274 *B* ⲉⲧⲁϥⲓ ⲙⲉⲛ-
ⲡⲥⲱϥ οἱ καθεξῆς ; Mk 2 1 *SB* διά gen ; PS 245 *S*
ⲉⲅⲛⲁϭⲱ ⲙ. ⲡϥⲟⲩ ⲙⲙⲩⲥⲧⲏⲣⲓⲟⲛ, ShBor 246 33 *S*
ⲡⲉⲧⲙⲛⲛⲥⲱϥ opp ⲡⲉⲧϣⲟⲣⲡ, AM 261 *B* ⲉⲑⲛⲏⲟⲩ
ⲙⲉⲛⲉⲡⲥⲱⲕ, Va 59 14 *B* finger ⲉⲑⲙ. ⲡⲓⲕⲟⲩϫⲓ, BM
586 *F* ⲙⲛⲡⲉⲥⲁⲡⲉⲓ, *ib* 592 *F* ⲙⲉⲛⲉⲥⲁⲡⲁⲓ ;   ⲙ.
...ⲉⲃⲟⲗ *S*, meaning same : R 2 4 71 ⲙ. ⲡⲡⲉ ⲉⲃ
thou art the physician, BMis 417 O my lord ⲙ.

ⲛⲡⲉ ⲉⲃ., BIF 13 103 let none sit on my throne ⲙⲛⲡϭⲱⲓ ⲉⲃ.   ♭ with ⲧⲣⲉ- (ⲉⲧⲣⲉ-, ⲛⲧⲣⲉ-) S, ⲡⲧⲉ- A, ⲧⲉ- A², ⲑⲣⲉ- B, ⲉⲧⲣⲉ- F + vb : Ge 5 4 SB, ib 7 S ⲉⲧ. B, Ps 126 2 SB, Ac 15 13 S(B ⲙ. ⲉⲧⲁ-) ⲙⲉⲧⲁ ⲧⲟ, AP 4 A² ⲙ. ⲧⲉϥⲡⲱⲧ μ. τὴν φυγήν, Cl 51 5 A ⲙ. ⲡⲧⲟⲩϣⲱⲡⲉ διὰ τό; TU 43 5 A ⲙ. ⲡⲧⲁ-ⲃⲱⲕ, BG 67 S ⲙ. ⲛⲧⲣⲉⲩϫⲟⲟⲥ, PS 1 S ⲙ. ⲧⲣⲉⲓⲥ ⲧⲱϭⲡ, AM 174 B ⲙ. ⲑⲣⲟⲩⲕⲏⲡ, Mor 30 17 Sᶠ ⲙ. ⲉⲧⲣⲉⲡⲙⲁⲣⲧⲩⲣⲟⲥ ϫⲱⲕ ⲉⲃⲟⲗ;   other verbal forms : Jos 23 1 S ⲙ. ⲡⲧⲉ-, Ac 1 3 B ⲙ. ⲉⲧⲁ- (var & S ⲧⲣⲉ-) μ. τό; Mor 23 15 S ⲙ. ⲡⲧⲁⲅⲡⲟⲩϫ, CMSS 35 F ⲙ. ⲡⲧⲁⲓϭⲣⲁⲓ, Mor 24 31 F ⲙ. ⲁⲩϣⲁⲡⲙⲉϥ = ib 23 43 S ⲙ. ⲡⲥⲉ-, Hor 81 O ⲙ. ϣⲧⲁⲙ ⲡⲧⲏϥ, Lu 12 5 S ⲙ. ⲙⲟⲩⲧⲧⲏⲅⲧⲛ (B ⲉⲑⲣⲉϥ-, ⲑⲣⲟⲩ-) μ. τό, JMMA 24 2 3 S ⲙ. ⲧⲁⲁⲩ, Lakân 262 B ⲙ. ⲙⲛⲡ-ϫⲓⲛⲡϣⲉ;   ⲙⲛⲡⲥⲱⲥ SAA², ⲙⲉⲛⲉⲡ. BF, ⲙⲛ(ⲡ)-ⲥⲟⲥ F, afterward : Jo 11 7 SA²(B ⲙⲉⲛⲉⲡⲥⲁⲫⲁⲓ) μ. τοῦτο; Cl 23 4 A εἶτα, 1 Cor 15 7 SF(B ⲓⲧⲁ) ἔπει-τα, Ez 43 27 B ἐπέκεινα; Pro 5 4 SA (B ⲉⲡⲥⲁⲃ), Ro 11 31 SF(B diff) ὕστ.; Lu 8 1 S(B ⲙⲉⲛⲉⲡⲥⲁ-ⲡⲁⲓ) ἐν τῷ καθεξῆς; Ex 15 18 F(B = Gk), Mk 12 34 S(B ϫⲉ) ἔτι; PS 9 S ⲙ. ϭⲉ...ⲁϥⲧⲛⲡⲟⲟⲩ, ib 73 S come forward & ⲙ. ϩⲙⲟⲟⲥ ⲉϩⲣⲁⲓ, AM 94 B ⲙ. ϯⲉⲙⲓ ϫⲉ-, J 1 15 S ⲉⲡϯ ⲙ. ⲡⲟⲩⲅⲩⲡⲟⲅⲣⲁⲫⲉⲩⲥ to subscribe.   V also on s f.

V also ⲃⲱⲗ (ⲡⲥⲁⲃⲏⲗ, ⲥⲁⲃⲟⲗ), ⲉⲥⲏⲧ, ⲙⲡⲁⲓ, ⲙⲡⲏ, ⲙⲉⲛⲣⲏ, ⲙⲣⲓⲧ, ⲡⲁϩⲟⲩ, ⲣⲏⲥ, ⲥⲡⲓⲣ, ⲧⲱⲣⲉ (ⲧⲟⲟⲧ⳽), ⲟⲩⲛⲁⲙ, ϣⲱⲓ, ϩⲣⲏⲓ, ϩⲏ front, ϩⲃⲟⲩⲣ. ϩⲟⲩⲛ, ϩⲣⲉ upper part, ϫⲱ⳽, ϭⲁϩⲏ.

ⲥⲁ S, ⲥⲁⲓ B(once), ⲥⲁⲉⲓⲟⲟⲩ† S(once), ⲥⲁⲓⲱⲟⲩ†, ⲥⲁⲓⲉ† (Ez)B vb intr, be beautiful : Cant 7 2 S, Si 25 1 S ὡραιοῦσθαι, Lev 23 40† B(S ⲛⲉⲥⲉ-), Is 63 1† B (S do) ὡραῖος; Job 18 15† B εὐπρεπής, Tit 2 1† B (S ⲉⲧⲉϣϣⲉ) πρέπειν; Cant 4 10 S καλλιοῦσθαι; 1 Cor 12 24† B(S ⲛⲉ.) εὐσχήμων; Gal 6 12 S(B ⲥⲕⲉⲡⲣⲟ) εὐπροσωπεῖν; EstD 2 S ἐπιφανὴς γίνεσθαι; Ez 40 7 &c ⲥⲁⲓⲉ B(S ⲛⲉ.) θεέ; Mus 42 226 S not wishing ⲉⲧⲣⲉⲡⲉϥⲡⲁⲣⲑⲉⲛⲟⲥ ⲥⲁ with outward beauty, DeV 2 216 B devil & forbidden fruit ⲑⲣⲉϥⲥ. ⲡⲁϩ-ⲣⲁⲥ, R 1 3 60 S ⲉⲣⲉⲡⲉϥϭⲟ ⲥⲁ, Bodl(P) g 1 S cattle ⲉⲩⲥ.† ⲣⲛⲧⲉⲩϭⲟⲧ, BSM 57 B garments ⲉⲩⲥ.†;   ⲥⲁⲓ-ⲱⲟⲩ B wrongly for ⲁⲥⲓⲱⲟⲩ v ⲁⲥⲁⲓ init, converse 3 Kg 8 53.

ⲥⲁ SF, ⲥⲁⲉⲓⲉ A, -ⲓⲉ AA²B, ⲥⲁⲓ S(CMSS)B, ⲥⲉⲓ Sᶠ F, pl ⲥⲁⲓⲱⲟⲩ B & sg as pl, nn m, beauty : Ge 49 21 S(B ⲙⲉⲧⲥⲁⲓⲉ), Ps 44 4 B(S ⲁⲡⲁⲓ), Pro 6 25 SA(B do), Ez 16 15 SB, BHom 42 S ⲟⲩⲥⲁ wither-eth κάλλος; 2 Kg 1 23 B pl (S ⲛⲉ.) ὡραῖος, Ps 49 2 SB ὡραιότης, Jer 4 30 S(B ⲥⲟⲗⲥⲉⲗ) ὡραισμός; Si 22 18 SA κόσμος; 1 Cor 12 23 B(S = Gk) εὐ-σχημοσύνη; Ps 25 8 S(B ⲙⲉⲧⲥ.) εὐπρέπεια, ib 20 5 S(B do) μεγαλοπρ.; Sa 7 10 S εὐμορφία; Eccl 12 6 S ἀνθέμιον; Deu 21 11 B(S ⲛⲉ.), Is 53 2 a S(B

ⲥⲙⲟⲧ) εἶδος; 1 Kg 16 7 S(B ϩⲟ) ὄψις; Br 238 S ⲡⲉϥⲥⲁ ⲙⲡⲉϥϩⲁⲡⲁⲓ, ShMIF 23 98 S ⲡⲥⲁ ⲙⲡⲣⲁ-ⲙⲁⲟⲡⲉ ⲡⲁ, R 2 4 82 S garments adorned ϩⲛⲟⲩⲥⲁ, CMSS 7 S to woman ⲡⲟⲩⲥⲁⲓ, ib ⲡⲟⲩⲥⲁ, Mani 1 A² ⲡⲣⲏⲣⲉ...ⲡⲟⲩⲥ., EW 191 B ⲡⲥⲁⲓ of body, WTh 198 S to martyrs ⲙⲡⲣⲧⲁⲕⲟ ⲙⲡⲉⲧⲛⲥⲁ, Mor 30 36 Sᶠ ⲉⲡⲉⲥⲱϥ ϩⲙⲡⲉϥⲥⲉⲓ = BMis 261 S ⲥⲁ, Aegyptus 11 444 S monk's epitaph ⲉⲧⲣⲟⲟⲩⲧ ϩⲙⲡⲉϥⲥⲁ.

ⲥⲁⲉⲓⲉ¹ S, -ⲓⲉ² SBF, -ⲉⲓⲏ³ S, -ⲓⲏ⁴ SBF, ⲥⲁⲏ⁵ S (-ⲏ sometimes f), beautiful person : 1 Kg 16 12 B ⲟⲩⲥ.² ϩⲉⲛⲡⲉϥⲃⲁⲗ (S ⲥ.⁴ ⲛⲃ.) μετὰ κάλ. ὀφθ., Ps 44 3 B² (S ⲛⲉ.) ὡρ.; Ez 17 3 B² μεγαλο(πτέρυγος); Su 31 B⁴ f τρυφερός; R 1 2 38 S ⲡⲓⲥ.¹ ⲧⲏⲣⲟⲩ in tombs, Lammeyer 40 S ⲡⲉϩⲟ ⲡⲥ.³ f, Kropp M 15 S ⲟⲩⲥ.³ ⲉⲥⲙⲟⲟⲥ on seat, BKU 1 26 (8116) F ⲡⲱⲡⲓ ...ⲟⲩⲥ.⁴, BMis 213 S ⲉⲩⲥ.² ⲧⲱⲡⲟⲩⲡⲉ.   As adj : Ez 28 12 B²(S ⲥⲁ), Dan 1 4 B²(S ⲛⲉ.); Si 9 8 S⁴ f εὔ-μορφος; Miss 8 244 S ϣⲏⲣⲉ ϣⲏⲙ ⲡⲥ.⁵, Ryl 106 30 S ⲟⲩⲡⲁⲣⲣⲉ ⲡⲥ.² καλῶς, BM 613 F ⲏⲣⲡ ⲉⲥ.²;   be-fore nn : Ac 3 10 B⁴ f (S ⲉⲧⲛⲉ.) ὡρ.; R 1 5 50 S ⲡⲉⲓⲥ.² ⲡⲣⲱⲙⲉ, BMis 266 S ⲡⲉⲓⲥ.⁵ ⲡϣⲉ, C 86 196 B ⲧⲁⲥ.² ⲡⲡⲟⲗⲓⲥ, Miss 4 738 S ⲟⲩⲥ.⁴ ⲛⲃⲁⲗ, C 43 63 B² sim (cf following);   without ⲡ- : 1 Kg 17 42 S ⲟ ⲡⲥ.¹ ⲃⲁⲗ μετὰ κάλ. ἀφθ.; Mél Charles Mœller 1 228 S ⲟⲩⲥ.³ ⲃⲁⲗ εὐόμματος, P 129¹⁶ 10 S ⲟⲩⲥ.⁵ ϩⲣⲁⲥ.   Adverbial ⲡⲥ. (ⲉⲥ.), fairly, thoroughly esp in recipes SF (cf ⲕⲁⲗⲱⲥ, ⲡ.ⲕ.) : AZ 23 103 ⲧⲁϩⲟⲩ ⲡⲥ.⁵, ib 115 ϣⲁϥⲣ ⲣⲏ (become gold) ⲡⲥ.⁵ ⲕⲁⲗⲟⲟⲥ (καλῶς), Cai 42573 2 ⲟⲩⲧⲁⲉⲓⲥ...ⲙⲁⲣⲉ ⲡⲥ.⁴, Ryl 106 3 ϣⲁⲡⲧⲉϥⲗⲱⲕ ⲉⲥ.², sim PCol 2 F ⲉⲓⲙⲓ ϫ(ⲉ)ⲁⲕⲗ ⲟⲩⲛ ⲉⲥ.⁴ ⲥ.⁴ be very sure thou knowest what thou doest.

ⲉⲓⲉⲡ-, ⲓⲉⲃⲥⲁ   v ⲉⲓⲟⲡⲉ.

ⲙⲛⲧ-, ⲙⲉⲧⲥⲁⲓⲉ SB, -ⲥⲉⲓ F, beauty : Ez 28 8 B (S ⲥⲁ), EpJer 23 BF κάλλος, Lev 23 40 B(S = Gk) κάλλυνθρον, Ps 46 5 B(S ⲁⲡⲁⲓ) καλλονή; ib 25 8 B (S ⲥⲁ) εὐπρέπεια, ib 110 3 B(S do) μεγαλοπρ.; Is 44 13 B(S do) ὡραιότης; 1 Tim 2 9 B(S diff) ⲙ. ⲡϩⲏⲧ κατὰ καταστολὴ κόσμιος; ShC 42 51 S ⲧⲙ. of souls opp ⲙⲛⲧⲅⲁⲓⲉ, AM 155 B ⲧⲟⲩⲙ. destroyed in fire, Pcod 5 S was Moses raised ? ⲟⲩⲙ. ⲧⲉ ϫⲟⲟⲥ ϫⲉⲁϩⲉ, ROC 25 241 B handicraft ⲟⲓ ⲙⲙ. ⲡⲱⲟⲩ was adorn-ment to them.

ⲣ ⲥ., ⲟ ⲡⲥ., become, be beautiful : Ez 16 13 S³B² κοσμεῖσθαι; TU 24 1 3 S daughter ⲟ ⲡⲥⲁⲓⲏ, DeV 2 250 B youths ⲉⲧⲟⲓ ⲡⲥ.² ϩⲉⲛⲡⲟⲩϩⲟ, AZ 23 106 S recipe ends ⲛⲧⲓⲙⲉ ϫⲉⲁϥⲣ ⲥⲁⲏ.

✝ ⲥⲁ S intr, beautify, become beautiful (cf KKS 677) : Z 571 when making book ⲙⲡⲣϯ ⲥⲁ ⲉⲧⲉϥ-ⲕⲟⲥⲙⲏⲥⲓⲥ καλλωπίζειν; Ep 72 ⲉⲕⲣⲓⲥⲉ ⲉⲕϯ ⲥⲁ ⲉⲡⲉⲕ-ⲧⲁⲓⲟ, Mich 550 29 topaz ϣⲁϥϯ ⲥⲁ ⲉϥϩⲓϫⲡⲧⲉⲥⲧⲟⲗⲏ of kings, MG 17 328 mat-making ⲉⲣⲉⲡⲧⲙⲏ ⲕⲱⲗϩ ⲕⲁⲗⲱⲥ ⲡⲥⲉϯ ⲥⲁ = ib 103 B ⲡⲧⲟⲩⲥⲁⲓ = ib 441 ز ;

† мпсаι B sim: BSM 95 scriptural thoughts ει†
м. = Mor 22 101 S † мпапαι.

In names: Ψάιε, Σαιέ (Preisigke), cει (Leyd 190),
κγρасει (Kr 149, CMSS 78), маρισει (PGol 44),
or ? these from cει vb.

V песе-, тсаιο.

ca SABF nn m, man + gen n-, man of, maker of,
dealer in. V абачнεın, апот, ач, ннпе, евιω, нрп,
нбе, кнснр, кап, зоγр, лаıхатп, мащε, пес,
оеıк, орве, папоι, рıр, солч, сас awl, твт, тапп,
тнтч, оγρω, оγоотε, шар, шхнн, шхωт, салωм,
смоγ, сомпт, снпе, сат, соγч, хоι, хωωве (хн-
ве), бедвесıтε, бадıтε, сооγне, боγч. With
Gk words: MIF 59 253 -катапетасма, BM 1095
S -кражпн (κράμβη), BMOr 6201 A 23 S -ла-
ханоп, N & E 39 341 B -малакı (μαλάκιον), К
109 B -плотıс (? πλόκος) بزّار (l ? قزّاز), ib 110 B
-плаконхı (πλακόντιον) فرّان (sic MS, l ? فرّان, if so,
misplaced), PMich 4552 S -тозарıп (τοξάριον),
ROC 25 239 B -тракнмата тр. πιπράσκων, LMis
131 S -фоγска, EES Report '06 -'07 10 -серωı
(? Coptic); Of moral qualities: ca мпеопа-
печ (v папоγ-), ca мпетсооγ (v сооγ evil), ca
ммпетпоγх (v поγх), ca пхесал (v сол), ca п-
котс (v кωтс, котс), ca пкроч (v кроч), ca пша-
хе (v шахе), ca пхιоγе (v хιоγе). Without
п-: салашειε (?), саракωтε. ca р- S, meaning same (or ? сар- distributer): Ryl 215 -воптε,
Baouit 1 160 -пес, Pap penes HT -камаркс. Also
in солме; v AZ 53 84.

ca A v соı.

ca F сооγ & co († co).

caı v соı.

ваιε &c v ca vb.

ce- SAA²BO, сн S/F particle m (Mt 5 37 var),
yea a answers questions: Mt 9 28 SB, ib 17 25 B
(S шо), Jo 11 27 SA²B(var), Z 309 S is there repentance? ce, ib 345 S = MG 25 211 B wouldest
thou? I said ce, Mor 17 103 S dost believe? ce
топоγ ναί, ROC 18 172 S wilt remain? ce тωпоγ
ναί καὶ πάνυ; Gk vb only: 1 Kg 9 12 S ἐστί, Mt
20 22 S(B оγоп шхом) δυνάμεθα, Gu 36 S art yet
alive? ce †опс ζῶ, LAp 568 F kindly take us сн
ам[ωп]н ἀνέλθατε; PS 292 S know ye? ce, El 62
A are there bodies here? ce, BM 173 213 S will
they dare? ce ce сепатолма, Mor 30 11 S/ doth
this suit thee? сн, BSM 77 B if one pay shall they
be freed? ce = BMis 168 = Mor 26 23 S ммоп,
DeV 2 152 B is he well? ce = MG 25 424 S ce
топω. b answers μή: R 1 4 64 S мн мпе-...?

ce ναί, Cl 43 6 A мн пачсаспе еп? ce μάλιστα;
DeV 1 70 B мн оγоп шхом...? ce топоγ. c
contradictory(?): BMis 460 S па]поγ печсωв ап,
reply ce папоγ печсωв, C 89 76 B thou canst not
...ce оγоп шхом ммоι. d after condit ешхе,
ιсхе: Job 32 22 S(B ммоп) εἰ δὲ μή; ShA 2 285
S e. ce еıε етвеоγ? (cf 284 e. се), AM 306 B ı. ce
ıε мощı псωı, Pcod 26 S e. ce еıε таλοι (var e.
есе мат.). e verily, indeed: Is 48 7 SB, Lu 11
51 SB, 2 Cor 1 19 SF(B сса), Phil 4 3 B(S саιо),
Ap 16 7 B(S асе), CaiEuch 664 B ce теп† со
ерок ναί; PS 93 S saying ce тппачı песоγоıп
(paral 97 ειτε), TU 43 19 A ce †пасωтме, AZ
21 100 O ce певсω lieth with Osiris, MG 25 337
B ce пашнрı hearken (ROC 17 365 ܠܝܢܐ), ib 71 B
ce †ımпша (var тафмнı), AM 222 B ce псс take
my spirit; шωпе псе S: Mt 5 37 (B сса) ναί,
cf Br 102 S маρепеγпсе (l пεγсе) ш. псе печм-
моп пımмоп & Ja 5 12 (B do) петпсе. f introduces question S: BMOr 7561 85 ce пток коγωш
етра-?, Mor 18 51 сн тетпкеλεγε паı етра-?
(var ib 19 59 om). Cf есе yea.

ce, cı also се-, cı- nn f, seat, place in секωт
(v кωт), семıсı (v мıсе), сесвор, сıооγп & prob
in place-names: Τσεκρουχ (PLond 4), тсесıω (Ryl,
BM), тсе-, тсγмоγλот (WS), тсепашıщ (Kr 84,
127), тсıпверест (BM) = †сıхерест (EW), тсıп-
бωрб (do), тсγпсωр (WS), perhaps in Τασε (POxy
2037) & in тсн (Miss 4 535 = Ταση ActaSS Maii
iii 33*, MG 25 324, WS 117, CO 492, J 59, Ep 1
123, cf ετсн MIF 59 114 & إسنا eg Miss 4 419).

ce sixty v сооγ.

ce blow v сωш (саш).

cει SAA²F, cı SA²BF, caι B (nn), снγ† SA²,
сноγ† B vb intr, be filled, satisfied, enjoy: Si 42 31
S, Jer 27 19 S(ShA 2 344) B πιμπλάναι, Deu 6 11
SB, Hab 2 5 AB, Jo 6 12 SA²BF ἐμπ.; Ps 16 15
SBF, Mt 14 20 SB χορτάζεσθαι; 1 Cor 4 8 S†B
κορεννύναι; Is 24 20† B(S † бλο) κραιπαλᾶν; Z
347 S еıε пкосмос с.† as of old? εὐθηνίαν ἔχειν;
ShIF 106 S меγс. еγωш есраı ероч, AP 33 A² am
not hungry ееιс.†, C 43 29 B ıε мпекı shedding
blood? ShC 73 23 S not to drink ес., AZ 23 110
S pound in water шαптечсı till saturated; filled
with с п-: Ex 16 12 SB, Ps 16 14 F(SB мес
снтс), Pro 5 10 SAB, Eccl 1 8 F(Mich 3520, S са-)
πλ. gen, Job 19 22† SB ἀπό, Is 34 6 SBF, Ro 15
24 SB ἐμπλ. gen, 1 Kg 2 5 SB πλήρης gen; PS 94
S атепбом с. мпесоγоıп, ShBor 246 50 S inherited wealth чпасı ммос ап for long, TstAb
163 B suffer me птасı ммок yet once, AM 314 B

admit us ⲛⲧⲉⲛⲥı ⲙⲡⲉⲕⲡⲟⲩϯ *be filled with* (? benefit by) *thy god*, AP 23 A² ⲡⲉϥⲥ.† ⲙⲡⲉⲧ[ⲉ]ⲡⲁⲡⲟⲩϥ
ⲡⲓⲙ, Mor 16 55 S water ⲉⲧⲉⲣⲉⲡⲣⲓⲣ...c.† ⲙⲙⲟϥ
(var BMis 209 cı ⲉⲃⲟⲗ ⲛ-);   c ⲛ- & vb S: ShLeyd
358 ⲡⲥⲁⲃⲉ c. ⲁⲛ ⲡⲥⲱⲧⲙ, ShC 73 99 ⲙⲉⲅⲥ. ⲡⲧⲱⲣⲡ,
BHom 77 ⲡⲉⲡⲧⲁϥⲥ. ⲡⲣⲓⲙⲉ;   c ⲣⲁ-: Eccl 1 8 S
(F ⲡ-) πλ. gen;   c ⲣⲛ-, ϩⲉⲛ-: Ru 2 18 S, Ps
103 28 S(B ⲙⲟϩ) ἐμπλ. gen, AM 318 B ⲉϥⲥ.† ϩⲉⲛ-
ⲡⲓⲏⲣⲡ; ⲉⲃⲟⲗ ⲣⲛ-, ϩⲉⲛ-; Ps 64 4 SB ἐν, Is 27 6 B
(S ⲙⲟⲩϩ) πλ. gen, Lu 16 21 S(B ⲙⲁϩ ϩⲏⲧⲋ) χορτ.
ἀπό, Ap 19 21 S(B ⲟⲩⲱⲙ) χ. ἐκ; Ps 35 8 S (var
ⲡ-, B ⲑⲓϭı), μεθύσκεσθαι ἀπό; Lu 15 16 S(B ⲙ.
ϭ.) κοιλίαν γέμειν ἐκ; PO 11 323 B let bellies cı
ⲉⲃ. ϩⲉⲡⲏ ⲉⲧⲉⲛⲟⲩⲧⲉⲛ.   Obscure: Lant 80 1 S
colophon ⲱⲛϩ c. ⲙⲙⲟϥ ϩⲓⲡⲣⲁϣⲉ...my holy fathers
(var *ib* 53 67 ϩⲙⲡⲣⲁϣⲉ).

—— nn m SABF, *fullness, surfeit*: Ge 41 30 S
(cf BMis 368) B, Deu 33 23 S(B ⲙⲟϩ), Si 14 SB
(ⲥⲁı), Is 30 23 SF(B ⲕⲉⲡⲓⲱⲟⲩⲧ) πλησμονή; Pro 24
15 SA χορτασία; Ps 35 8 S(B ⲕⲉⲡⲓ) πιότης; Va
58 179 B ⲡⲥı of food κόρος; Lu 21 34 S(B ϭⲓⲙⲉ)
κραιπάλη; PS 215 S ⲡⲥ. paral ⲙⲏⲧⲁⲓϩⲏⲧⲥ, ShBor
246 35 S ⲙⲡⲧⲁⲩ c. ⲙⲙⲁⲩ ⲉⲡⲉϩ ⲉⲩϣⲁϫⲉ *never
enough of talking*, Va 57 84 B ⲡⲓⲥı ⲙⲙⲉⲑⲟⲩϫ
whereinto he is fallen, MG 25 251 B have not
eaten ⲉⲡⲥı, Leyd 303 S ⲧⲉⲧⲣⲩϥⲏ ⲙⲡⲉϩⲟⲩⲉⲥⲉı.

ⲁⲧⲥ. SBF adj, *insatiate*: Ps 100 5 SB, Pro 23 2
SA ἄπληστος; ShA 1 57 S ⲡⲓⲙⲡⲉ ⲡⲁ. ⲏ ⲡⲁ.?,
Mus 34 206 B ⲡⲉⲕⲣⲱϥ ⲡⲁ. ⲙⲙⲟϥ;   ⲙⲛⲧ-,
ⲙⲉⲧⲁⲧⲥ., *unsatedness, greed*: Bor 239 60 S πλεόνασμα; ShMIF 23 26 S *she attaineth not to thee*
ϩⲓⲧⲙ. (Pro 24 50), C 41 43 B *begged yet again*
ϩⲉⲛⲟⲩⲙ.;   ⲣ ⲁⲧⲥ., *make unsated, be insatiable*:
Si 34 18 S ἀπληστεύεσθαι; BM 524 F(*bis*) expel
demons ⲉⲛⲣ ⲁⲧⲥⲁⲓⲉı (ⲙ)ⲙⲁⲟⲩ ⲧⲏⲣⲟⲩ (? not this
word).

ceı SA, ⲥⲓⲉ(Tri)S, cı A nn f, *a tree*: 2 Kg 18 9
S(var ⲥⲓⲥⲟⲩ, P 44 110 ﺩﺭﻩ), Hos 4 13 A(B = Gk,
P 44 116 ﺑﻠﻪ), Am 2 9 A(B do), Zech 11 2 A(B
ϣϣⲏⲛ, P 44 *lc* ’ﺵ) δρύς; 3 Kg 5 8 S κέδρινος
(confused with ⲥⲓϣⲉ) ’ﺵ (P 44 110), Tri 530, 673 S
’ﺵ; so *terebinth* (oak) or *lotus-tree* (LöwF 3 134).

cı- O *v* ϣⲏⲣⲉ.

cо SA, ⲁⲥⲟ B, ⲥⲁ S^f F nn (cf ? DM 2 8 cⲱ),
with ϯ forms vb intr, *spare, refrain*: Job 6 10 SB,
Pro 6 34 SAB, 2 Cor 13 2 SBF, Mor 17 106 S
ⲙⲡⲉϥϯ cо ⲉϥϣⲁϫⲉ φείδεσθαι; PS 232 S ⲙⲡⲓϯ cо
ⲉⲓⲙⲟⲩⲧⲉ (cf He 2 11), AM 185 B ⲙⲡⲉⲕϯ ⲁ. ⲉⲕϭı
ⲡ̇ϩⲟⲡⲥ;   c ⲉ- with nn, pron: Ge 22 12 SB, Job
33 18 SB, Joel 3 16 SAB, 1 Cor 7 28 SBF, R 1 4 57
S ϯ cо ⲉⲣⲟⲕ ⲙⲁⲅⲁⲕ φ.; Pro 28 14 SA καταπτήσσειν; *ib* 21 23 S(ShC 73 59, var ϩⲁⲣⲉϩ) φυλάσσειν;

ShR 2 39 S ⲉϥϯ cо ⲉⲡⲉϥⲭⲣⲏⲙⲁ & *gives not alms*,
Bor 241 150 S ⲡϥⲛⲁϯ cо ⲉⲣⲟⲛ ⲁⲛ ⲉⲧⲙⲡⲟϫⲓ, MG
25 142 B *nurse & dirty babe* ⲙⲡⲁⲥϯ ⲁ. ⲉⲡⲓⲥⲟⲩⲃⲱⲛ
shuns not stink but lifts him, Mus 40 276 S wine
unbridles tongue so that ⲡⲛⲉⲕϯ cо ⲉⲗⲁⲁⲩ;   with
vb: 2 Kg 12 4 S, Pro 21 14 SA, Mor 17 54 S ⲛⲧϯ
cо ⲉⲧⲁϫⲉ ⲧⲉⲓⲥⲃⲱ φεί.;   4 Kg 4 3 S (BP 10623)
ὀλιγοῦν; Ac 9 38 F(SB ⲝⲡⲁⲁⲩ) ὀκνεῖν; ShA 2 269
S ⲙⲡϥϯ cо ⲉⲭⲱ ⲛⲏⲧⲛ, MG 25 195 B ⲙⲡⲁϥϯ ⲁ.
ⲉϩⲓⲧⲟⲩ ⲉϩⲟⲩⲛ, ST 339 S ϣⲁϥϯ cо ⲉⲙⲟⲟϣⲉ ⲉϩⲱϥ
forbear to go thither, Mor 28 37 S^f ⲛⲥⲉϯ ⲥⲁ ⲁⲛ
ⲉⲱⲣⲕ...ⲙⲡⲟⲩϫ; ShA 2 283 S ⲙⲡⲉⲓϯ cо ⲉⲧⲣⲁⲉⲓ
(var ⲉⲉı), ShC 73 138 S ⲙⲡⲏϥϯ cо ⲡϭı ⲡⲣⲣⲟ ⲉⲧ-
ⲣⲉⲩⲙⲟⲩⲣ (Mt 22 13);   c ⲛ-: Mor 31 76 S ⲁϥϯ
cо ⲛⲣⲱⲛ ⲉϩⲟⲩⲛ;   c ⲉⲧⲃⲉ-: Miss 8 75 S ⲁⲡϯ
cо...ⲉⲧⲃⲉⲡⲉⲥⲕⲩⲗⲙⲟⲥ ὀκνηρότερος γίνεσθαι περί;   c
ⲉϫⲛ-: Is 13 18 SB φεί. ἐπί, Ro 11 21 B(Sf e-)
φεί. gen.

—— nn SBF, *forbearance*: Job 16 13 S(B vb)
φεί. vb;   ϩⲛⲟⲩϯ cо adverbial: Sa 12 18 S φειδώ;
ib 20 προσοχή; 2 Cor 9 6 S(B vb) φειδομένως;   c
·ⲁϫⲛ-, ⲁϣⲛⲉ-, *without sparing, unhindered*: Est B 6
S φειδώ; Ez 7 22 SB ἀφυλάκτως; Ac 28 31 S(B
ϣⲱϣⲧ vb) ἀκωλύτως; P 129¹⁴ 72 S *ships to use
ports* ⲁ. ϯ cо, BIF 22 107 F *slaughter them* ⲁ. ϯ
cⲁ, C 43 90 B *every punishment* ⲁ. ϯ ⲁ., Pcod 15
S *went* ⲁ. ϯ cо *without delay*.

ⲁⲧϯ ⲁ. B, *unsparing*: Is 14 6 (S vb neg) φεί.
neg;   ⲙⲛⲧ-, ⲙⲉⲧⲁⲧ., *unrestrainedness*: Col 2
23 SB ἀφειδία; C 89 57 B *eating* ϩⲉⲛⲟⲩ. μὴ
ἐγκρατεῖς ὄντες; ShA 2 259 S *not destroying aught*
ϩⲛⲟⲩⲙ., Pcod 33 S *swearing falsely* ϩⲛⲟⲩⲙ., DeV
1 124 B *worms devouring* ϩⲉⲛⲟⲩⲙ.

ⲙⲛⲧⲣⲉϥϯ cо S, *sparingness, parsimony*: BM 185
1 *table spread* ϩⲓⲧⲛⲧⲙ.

cо *v* cⲟⲟⲩ *six*.

cоı SB, ⲥⲁı SF nn m, *back of man or beast*:
Ge 9 23 B(S ϫⲓⲥⲉ), 4 Kg 17 14 S, Ps 20 13 B(S
diff), Ez 1 18 B, Glos 35 S ⲥⲁ., Z 339 S ⲟⲩⲥ ⲉϥ-
ⲕⲧⲏⲩ ⲉϩⲟⲩⲛ ⲉⲩⲥ. νῶτον; Job 40 14 B(S ⲕⲁⲥ ⲡⲧⲝ.)
ῥάχις; Ez 8 16 B ὀπίσθιος; R 1 3 76 S *belly clave*
ⲉⲡⲉϥⲥ. *from hunger*, TT 77 S *slicing strips* ⲉⲃⲟⲗ
ϩⲓⲡⲉϥⲥ., C 43 208 B *laid him* ⲉϫⲉⲛⲡⲉϥⲥ., MG 25
361 B ⲙⲡⲁϥⲉⲛ ⲡⲉϥⲥ. ⲛⲁϥ *straightened not his back*
(ROC 18 62 ﺃﻝ ﻟﻪ), Mor 30 40 F ⲡⲉⲕⲥ. = *ib* 29
34 S ϫ., Worr 220 S *set him on* ⲡⲥ. ⲙⲡⲙⲟⲩⲓ.

cоı SB, ⲥⲁ A, ⲥⲁı S^f, -ⲉı F nn m f, *beam of wood*:
4 Kg 6 5 S, EpJer 18 B(F c. ⲡⲟⲩⲟϩ), Mt 7 3 SB
δοκός; Nu 33 9 S(var & B ⲕⲁϥ) στέλεχος; TurO
7 S ⲉⲓⲥ ⲡⲥ....ⲙⲡⲉⲓϣⲛ ⲕⲁⲙⲟⲩⲗ ⲡⲧⲁⲧⲁⲗⲟϥ, J 106
113 S *house* ⲙⲡⲛⲉϥⲥ., *ib* 67 80 S *suffered thee not*
ⲉⲟⲩⲉϩ c. ⲉⲣⲟⲥ (*sc* wall), BM 479 S ⲕⲟⲟϩ ⲉⲥ., PLond

4 499 S пαρε пс., Ryl 338 S rent (πάκτον) of c.,
CO 116 S ρεпс. ω, BMOr 6201 A 90 S in account
c., ib c. псιще (quid?); f S (cf ογερсοι) ST
324...ллерос рпте. етепалларте ерос, Bodl(P) d
30 (about building лла пщωпе) тс. есογохп,
BMEA 10136 ρатс. спте.

ογερс. SS/F, ογαρс. AB nn f, *addition of beams,
roof* (cf above c. пογορ): Ge 19 8 SB, Is 38 7 B
(S нι), Mt 8 8 SB, Cl 12 6 A ογαρсλ, Z 345 S
στέγη, -os; Eccl 10 18 F δόκωσις; CaiEuch 481 B,
Va 63 96 B птеφсолсел пφογ. ὀροφος; Cant 1 17
S φάτνωμα; Tri 403 S سقف, P 44 60 S пογ. of
church ʾ—; P 131' 35 S/ pillars φι ρатογερсαι, Z
350 S песογ. *roof-beams,* Va 66 297 B houses whose
ραρсοι λαλнογт with gold, BMis 106 S = Mor 33
68 S/.

соι B nn m, *among trees, between* ллιсι &
ραллос: P 55 2 пιс. سارية (*pillar, ? misplaced*).

соγ- v снγ & сιογ.

соγ- in согнвепне v внпе (щпв.).

сω S nn, *soaked reed, mat of reeds*: ShC 73 136
not to tread on псω етκн ραρωογ ппеснηγ cf Reg
Pach §4 *juncos qui aqua infusi,* Mus 40 41 сω ещщщ
ib § 124 *j. inf. ad operandum,* ShC 73 60 вωκ есωр
ппсω епсωορ, ShMich 550 18 ппαγ псωр псω,
AZ 52 120 lay in water (river) ογщηλλ пкαλλ...
хееγпλααφ псω = Va ar 172 15 ليفتلوا حبال = MG
17 362 يصنعا حبال, ShC 73 109 filling jars псωλλ
сω *for soaking reeds,* P 44 91 сω حلفا paral тλλε
حصير. Same word ? Ep 168 begs ογκογι псω
for sick brother who cannot reap & has no other
craft, also Ming 321 екф огвепексαρ ρптексω
(but f). V AZ 64 93.

сω SA²BF, согγ SAA², се- SABF, са- SF, сеγ-
(Job 15 16), соγ- S, сооς SAA², соς B, саас F,
p с саγ- SAB vb, *drink* I *intr*: Ge 24 14 B, Job
8 12 SB, Jo 4 7 SA²BF, ib 12 A² & AP 7 Aʾ соγ,
πίνειν; Ge 13 10 B(S тсо) ποτίζεσθαι, 2 Kg 3 20
S ρооγ псω πότος; PS 132 S αγсω & thirst
quenched, ShC 73 152 S leaving no place пογещ
псω, C 43 238 B етαφκип еφсω, CR '87 376 S
recipe ллαр(с)огγ пⲡ̄ περооγ; c ρеп- B, *drink
of, from*: Jer 28 7 πί. ἀπό; DeV 2 77 began псω
ρеппιрп; евол ρп-, ρеп-: Ge 9 21 SB, Mt 26
27 S(B σι сω), Jo 4 12 SA²BF πί. ἐκ, 1 Cor 10 21
B(S се-) πί. acc.

II *tr*: Is 36 12 SBF са-, Lam 5 4 BF саас, Joel
3 3 SAB, Zeph 1 13 A соγ B, He 6 7 SB πί., Job 6
4 B(S сωпк), Is 51 17 SB, Zech 9 15 B(A сωρп)
ἐκπί.; 1 Tim 5 23 SB се ллооγ ὑδροποτεῖν; PS 374
S пллооγ...пессооγ, ShIF 268 S апкαρ ол̄κογ н

сооγ, MG 25 235 B се ерωφ пακ, BM 527 F
raven's blood сααφ пακ, FR 6 S dove ессα ллооγ,
CR lc S ллαрогсογ пеγллооγ, BMOr 6230 45 S
vessel псογ ллооγ, PMéd 111 S sim, DeV 2 38 B
water φер щαγ епсογ; p c, *drinker*: Mt 11 19
B саγирп (S ρеφсе-) οἰνοπότης, Pro 23 21 SA
ὑπνώδης (reading ? οἰνοπ.); ллит-, ллетсαγ-,
drinking: Va 58 181 B οἰνοποσία; Ep 51 47 S; р
саγ-, *be drinker* S: Si 34 28 ἀνδρίζειν ἐν οἴνῳ.

—— nn m SA²BF, *drinking, potation*: Ge 19 3
B(S щопс), Job 8 11 B(S ллооγ), ZNTW 24 84 F
со πότος, Jer 28 39 B πότημα, Jo 6 55 SA²B πόσις,
Ps 101 10 B(S vb), He 9 10 B(SF σипсω) πόμα;
PS 132 S птероγφ пαγ ллпсω (= Od Solom 6 12
ܠܡܫܐ), BSM 27 B pouring for them щαтогхωк
евол ρεппιсω = Va 63 3 B щαтогсι; σι сω B
Mt 26 27 (S сω) πί. ἐκ.

лла псω SB, *drinking place, bout*: Est C 28 S
συμπόσιον, Pro 23 30 SA πότος; Sa 14 23 S κῶμος; ShZ 507 S огαристои н оглла псω, Va 61
118 B made ραпл. пαтщαγ in streets, R 1 3 58 S
she entered пл. of Herod = DeV 1 39 B; лла п-
се нри: Si 34 34 S συμπ.

ρеφсω B, *drinker*: Job 15 16 (S ллооγ) reading
ποτός; ρеφсе нри SB, *wine-drinker*: Mt 11 19
S(B саγ-) οἰνοπότης, JKP 2 114 S сριλλε пр. (cf
Si 26 8 ρеφфге μέθυσος), Aeg 246 S ρеφсе ρας
пн. οἴνῳ χρώμενος, 1 Tim 3 3 B(S ρеφфге) πάροινος.

ллптса ири S, *wine-drinking*: Mus 40 276 (l ?
ллптсαγ-, but cf са ллооγ above).

атсω B, *without drinking*: AM 64 еφοι...па.,
C 86 351 агχαφ...па.; MG 25 206 огερооγ
патсе ллооγ.

σип-, хипсω, *drink*: He 9 10 SF(above) πόμα;
Cat 61 B τροφη огλе х.

сωωφ S, сωφ B nn as pl, *drinking*: 1 Pet 4 3 πότος.
In names: Σανειώρ(PMG 1 80)& place-name:
τόπος Σαγμόου, cf τόπ. Тσεμαοῦ(Preisigke).

V тсо.

сωι B vb intr, *become hairless (?)*: Lev 13 40
арещαптαφе с. (S φω ρωλ евол), 41 (S σωλ ев.)
μαδᾶν انتثر; as nn m relating to eye: K 75 пιс.
(var соι قذا (var قذى), l قذا an eye-disease (Dozy
2 318).

св in св псете A nn as pl, *burnt offerings*: Ps
150 16 (Cl 18 16, S σλιλ, B σ. пхоφхеφ). V
Klio 6 291.

сев B, снв F v саве.

сιв S, сιп B nn m, *tick, insect*: P 44 57 S
φθ(е)ιφα · ерεсιвη · пс. قرد, ib κονδιλα (cf κονίς)

κροτων ⲡⲥ., HL 116 *B* stayed in open until whole body ⲙⲟϩ ⲉⲃⲟⲗ ϩⲉⲛϥⲁⲓⲥ. ⲕⲣ.; PMéd 215 *S* recipe ⲧ̄ ⲡⲥ. ϩⲓⲟϥⲉⲣⲉ ⲡⲕⲁⲙⲉ (*v* note), Cai 42573 2 *S* title of magical recipe ⲟⲩⲥ. ⲉⲕⲟⲩⲱϣ ⲉⲟⲩϩⲁⲣϥ ⲉⲡⲉϩⲉϥ.

ⲥⲁⲃⲉ SABO, -ⲃⲏ SABF mostly f, pl ⲥⲁⲃⲉⲉⲩ[1] *SA*, -ⲉⲉⲅⲉ[2] *SA*, -ⲏⲅ[3] *Sf*, -ⲉⲩⲉ[4] *AA*[2], -ⲉⲩ *B*, -ⲏⲟⲩ *F* & sg as pl, nn m, *wise person*: Deu 32 6 *SB*, Ps 57 6 *B*(*S* = Gk), Is 31 2 *SB*(*F* = Gk) σοφός, Ex 7 11 *B* σοφιστής; 1 Kg 2 10 *SB*, Pro 11 29 *SAB*, Ro 11 25 *SBF* φρόνιμος; Ps 13 2 *S*(*B* ⲡⲉⲧⲕⲁϯ) συνίων, Jer 4 22 *SB* συνετός; Si 19 25 *S* νοήμων; AZ 21 94 *O* ⲡⲥ. ⲟⲩⲧⲱⲩⲛⲉⲧ ϩⲟⲟⲩⲡⲧ, BAp 111 *S* is not yet marriageable ⲁⲩⲱ ⲟⲩⲥ. ⲡⲉ, Mor 51 28 *S* husband accuses wife ⲛⲧⲉⲟⲩⲥ. ⲁⲛ ϩⲙⲡⲟⲩ-ⲥⲱⲙⲁ, Miss 8 189 *S* ⲡⲁϩⲏⲧ ⲉⲧⲉⲟⲩⲥ. ⲁⲡⲡⲉ, AM 157 *B* ⲟⲩⲥⲁϫⲓ ⲣⲱϣⲓ ⲡⲟⲩⲥ. *verbum sap.*, C 43 139 *B* sim, PSBA 32 200 *S* ⲁⲣⲓ ⲥ. & sacrifice, reply ⲁⲡⲟⲕ ⲟⲩⲥ. ⲙⲙⲏⲛⲉ *always wise*, Mor 41 188 *S* same, *cf* C 43 20, AM 61; pl forms: *S* Deu 16 19[1](var[2]), Pro 15 1[1], Lu 10 21[1], ShC 42 132[1], 220[1], Pro 24 59[2], Miss 228[2], ShC 73 139[2](var[1]), Mt 25 2[3]; *A* Pro 14 6[1], 16 21[1], 15 1[2]; *A*[2] Mani 1, *B* Ps 48 11, Ro 1 14; *F* Is 5 21; f: Jer 9 17 *S*(TT 137)*B* σοφός, Tit 2 5 *SB* σώφρων; Mt 25 2 *S*(var pl[3])*B* φρ.; ShC 42 22 *S* women ϩⲉⲛⲥⲁⲃⲏ. As adj after nn : 3 Kg 3 12 *S*(*v* ⲡⲉⲥⲃⲟ), Hos 13 13 *AB*, Lu 12 42 *SB* φρ.; Si 37 25 *S* πανοῦργος; PS 77 *S* ⲕⲱϩⲧ ⲡⲥ., AZ 21 158 *S* ⲁϥ ⲡⲉϩⲓⲱ ⲡⲥ., DeV 2 54 *B* λογισμος ⲡⲥ.; f ⲥⲁⲃⲏ Jud 5 29 *S* σοφ. (but 2 Kg 14 2 *S* = Gk); Si 22 4 *S* φρ.; ShC 42 22 *S* ⲙⲁⲁⲩ ⲡⲥ., Bor 239 76 *S* παρθενος ⲡⲥ., BSM 97 *B* ⲥϩⲓⲙⲓ ⲡⲥ. (*ib* 101 -ⲃⲉ); before nn : Is 3 3 *B*, Aeg 268 *S*; f Pro 14 1 *SB*, BHom 113 *S* ϩⲉⲡⲥ. ⲡⲥϩⲓⲙⲉ.

ⲙⲛⲧ-, ⲙⲉⲧⲥ. *SABF*, *wisdom*: Job 12 16 *S*(*B* ⲕⲁϯ), Pro 2 2 *SA*(*B* do), Eph 3 4 *S*(*B* do) σύνεσις, Is 32 8 *SBF* συνετός; Pro 3 13 *SAB*, Ez 28 4 *SB* φρόνησις; Is 40 20 *B*(*S* ⲙⲛⲧⲣⲙⲛϩⲏⲧ) σοφῶς; Deu 32 28 *S*(*B* = Gk), Job 21 22 *S*(*B* do) ἐπιστήμη; BHom 137 *S* φιλοσοφία; Hos 7 11 *A*(*B* as Gk) καρδία; BG 52 *S* ⲁⲧⲉϥⲙ. ⲧⲁⲭⲣⲟ, ShC 42 30 *S* addressing a dignitary ⲧⲉⲧⲛⲙ. (*cf* 31 ⲧⲉⲧⲛⲙⲛⲧⲣⲙⲛ-ϩⲏ.), AM 210 *B* ⲧⲁⲙ. ⲡⲉⲙⲧⲁⲙⲉⲧⲕⲁⲧⲟⲣϩⲏⲧ, CA 97 *S* eating & drinking ϩⲛⲙ. ⲛⲓⲙ.

ⲣ, ⲉⲣ ⲥ, *SAB*, *become, be wise*: Pro 6 6 *SAB* σοφ. γίνεσθαι, Ro 16 19 *B*(*S* ϣⲱⲡⲉ ⲡⲥ.) σ. εἶναι, Pro 8 33 *B*(*SA* ⲣ ⲥοϕⲟⲥ), Si 7 5 *S* σοφίζειν; Is 44 28 *B*(*S* ⲙⲉⲉⲅⲉ) φρονεῖν; R 1 4 61 *S* teach you ⲉⲣ ⲥ. σωφρ., Mt 10 16 *B*(*S* ϣ. ⲡⲥ.)φρόνιμος γίν.; Is 5 21 *SB*(*F* nn) συνετός; BG 58 *S* ⲥⲟ ⲡⲥⲁⲃⲏ, ShIF 248 *S* brethren & sisters ⲡⲁⲣ ⲥ. ⲁⲩⲱ ⲥⲁⲃⲏ, C 43 175 *B* have spared him ϫⲉⲁⲣⲏⲟⲩ ϥⲛⲁⲉⲣ ⲥ.; ϫⲓⲡⲉⲣ ⲥ. *B*, *becoming wise, instruction*: Va 57 80.

As name (?): Σαβεῦ (Preisigke).

ⲥⲉⲃ *B*, ⲥⲏⲃ *F* nn m, *knowing, cunning person*: Pro 14 24 *B*(*SA* diff) πανοῦργος; ⲙⲉⲧⲥ., *craftiness, guile*: 1 Cor 3 19 *B*(*S* ⲕⲟⲧⲥ), Eph 4 14 *B*(*S* = Gk) πανουργία, Ps 82 4 *B*(*S* ⲉϥϩⲟⲟⲩ)καταπα-νουργεύεσθαι; 2 Pet 1 16 *B* (var -ⲥⲁⲃⲉ, *S* om) σοφί-ζεσθαι, Ac 7 19 *F*(*S* ϫⲓ ϣⲟⲭⲡⲉ, *B* ϫⲉⲙ ⲥⲃⲱ) κατασοφ.

ⲥⲃⲟ *v* ⲧⲥⲁⲃⲟ.

ⲥⲃⲟⲩⲓ *SBF* nn m, *disciple, apprentice*: Mt 10 24 *S*(*B* = Gk) μαθητής; WS 82 *S* ⲯⲁϩ...ⲡⲉⲃⲥ., Mun 18 *S* ϩⲉⲡⲥ. ⲉⲅϩⲁⲣⲁⲧϥ ⲡⲟⲩⲥⲁϩ, Lant 5 28 *S* I know not well, am but ⲟⲩⲥ., *ib* 56 13 *S* ⲡⲓⲥ. ⲡϧⲙϩⲁⲗ, C 43 109 *B* ⲡⲓⲥ. ⲡⲁⲧⲉⲙⲡϣⲁ, BM 1065 *S* carpenter & apprentice ⲧⲁⲣⲉⲕⲣ ϩⲱϥ ⲡⲁⲓ ϩⲱⲥ (ⲥ)ⲃⲟⲩⲓ, *ib* 1063 *S* wage of c., Ryl 369 *S* ⲯⲁⲡⲁⲡⲟⲧ & ⲡⲉϥⲥ., Z 549 *S* ⲛ]ⲡⲟⲥ ⲡⲥ. in school, Mor 30 22 *F* ⲡⲉϥϣⲏⲣⲓ ⲡⲥ. (l ? ϣⲃⲏⲗ, *cf* BMis 244 *ult*); K 231 *B* ⲡⲓⲥ. بﺎﺱ , حقﯾر (expressing humility as in colophons); ⲙⲛⲧ-, ⲙⲉⲧⲥ., *state of pupilage*: Lant 104 18 *S* have written according to my poverty & ⲧⲁⲙ., *ib* 98 20 *S*, BMar 155 *S* sim, Cat 150 *B* beguileth unlearned (ἰδιώτης) ⲕⲁⲧⲁ ⲧⲉϥⲙ.

ⲥⲃⲱ *SA*[2]*BF*, ⲥⲃⲟⲩ *AA*[2], pl ⲥⲃⲟⲟⲩⲉ, -ⲱⲟⲩⲉ *S*, ⲥⲃⲁⲩⲉ *A*, ⲥⲃⲟⲩⲉⲓⲉ *A*[2], ⲥⲃⲱⲟⲩⲓ *B*, ⲥⲃⲁⲟⲩⲓ, ⲥϥⲁⲩⲓ *F* & sg as pl, nn f, *doctrine, teaching*: Ro 12 7 *SF* (*B* ⲙⲉⲧⲣⲉϥϯ ⲥ.), AP 4 *A*[2] διδασκαλία, Mt 7 28 *SB*, Ac 2 42 *SB*, He 6 2 *B*(*SF* ⲧⲥⲁⲃⲟ) διδαχή; Pro 1 2 *SAB*, Ez 13 9 *SB* παιδεία; Nu 24 16 *S*(*B*=Gk), Job 12 16 *S*(*B* ⲉⲙⲓ), Jer 3 15 *SB* ἐπιστήμη; Is 29 24 *F*(*S* ⲙⲛⲧⲣⲁⲛϩⲏⲧ, *B* ⲕⲁϯ) σύνεσις; 1 Cor 10 11 *SB*, Aeg 240 *S* νουθεσία, Pro 2 2 *SAB* νουθέτησις, Job 5 17 *SB* νουθέτημα; 1 Kg 2 10 *B*(*S* ⲙⲛⲧⲥⲁⲃⲉ), Is 40 28 *B*(*S* ⲙⲛⲧⲣⲙⲛϩ.) φρόνησις; Dan 1 4 *B*(*S* = Gk), 1 Cor 3 19 *B*(*S* do) σοφία; Jer 13 21 *B* μάθημα; Jud 5 14 *S* διήγησις; PS 259 *S* ⲡⲉⲥ. ⲙⲡⲗⲁⲡⲏ, Miss 4 728 *S* ⲧⲁⲥ. ⲙⲛⲧⲁ-ⲉⲡⲓⲧⲓⲙⲓⲁ, AM 102 *B* ϯⲥ. ⲡⲟⲩϫⲁⲓ, BAp 107 *S* I may not ⲁϫⲛⲧⲉⲥ. ⲙⲛⲡⲟϭ ⲡⲣⲱⲙⲉ = MIE 2 383 *B* ⲥⲟϭⲛⲓ; as adj: Aeg 269 *S* ⲟⲩϣⲁϫⲉ ⲡⲥ. διδα-κτικός; TstAb 245 *B* sim; pl forms: *S* Is 29 13, ShC 73 6, Tri 239 -ⲱⲟⲩⲉ; *A* Pro 25 1, El 70; *A*[2] AP 43; *B* AM 116, 275, BSM 96; *F* ZNTW 24 86, LAp 570.

ⲁⲧⲥ. *SAB*, *without teaching, ignorant*: Zeph 2 1 *SAB*, 2 Tim 2 23 *S*(*B* ⲙⲉⲧⲁⲧⲥ.) ἀπαίδευτος; Eph 5 15 *B*(*S* ⲁⲑⲏⲧ) ἄσοφος; Ro 1 21 *S*(*B* ⲁⲧⲕⲁϯ) ἀσύνετος; Ps 48 10 *S*(*B* do) ἄνους; Aeg 285 *S* ⲁⲧⲁ-ⲕⲧⲉⲓⲛ; ShC 42 133 *S* disobedient & ⲡⲓⲁ., DeV 2 37 *B* ⲟⲩⲙⲉⲧⲁⲗⲟⲩ ⲡⲁ.; ⲙⲛⲧ-, ⲙⲉⲧⲁⲧⲥ.: Si 21 25 *S* ἀπαιδευσία; 2 Thes 3 6 *B* (*S* = Gk) ἀτάκτως; ShC 73 127 *S*.

ⲙⲁⲓⲥ. *S*, *loving instruction, docile*: Si prol φιλο-

μαθής; ShA 2 4 ммастевω...ммм., BM 173 220 пaιпε пмaειп пммм. тaιτε тεϙιн птмε; as adj B: Va 63 20 пιмкрωaтнс ммм.

рмпс. S, *instructed, knowledgeable person*: Tob 4 14 πεπαιδευμένος; Deu 1 13 (B as Gk) ἐπιστήμων; p p.: Eccl 7 17 σοφίζειν.

† c. SAA²BF, *teach, chastise*: Job 21 22 S(B † кa†), Ps 24 4 B(S тсaбо), Mt 13 54 SBF, Jo 9 34 SA²B, Aeg 281 S † c. пaϥ етмптεϥсεбнс, ZNTW 24 86 F пϥ† c. нитп пнει διδάσκειν; Deu 8 5 SB, Ps 117 18 SA(Cl)B, Lu 23 16 B(S = Gk) παιδεύειν, BHom 32 S παιδαγωγεῖν; Job 4 3 SB, Ac 20 31 SB, Cl 7 1 A νουθετεῖν; Ps 118 98 B(S тсaбо) σοφίζειν; CaiEuch 503 B the young мa c. пωoγ σωφρονίζειν; Mt 14 8 F(S тоγп ειaтϩ, B тс.) προβιβάζειν; Ps 24 9 B(S тс.) ὁδηγεῖν; Ac 14 21 SB μαθητεύειν; Sa 7 15 S διορθωτὴς εἶναι; Va 57 13 B εϥ† c. ппн етεр схолaζιп διαλέγειν dat; Br 44 S ептаϊϲ † c. ммос ппεϥaпостолос, ShA 2 320 S етрa† c. мпaмεεγε ερaктϥ εбол, Aeg 265 S † c. ппετпεрнϥ тсaбε пкaтнхоγмεпос, C 41 10 B εϥ† c. пωoγ επн етεр поϥρι, AM 219 B †пa† c. пaк with punishments; мa п† c. S, *teaching place*: Aeg 280 διδασκαλεῖον, R 2 2 23 virtuous life as м. παιδευτήριον; ShA 2 76 who speaketh in пм. *Cf* мa пхι c.; рεϥ† c. SB, *teacher*: Mt 8 19 B(S сaϙ) διδάσκαλος; Si 37 25 S, Ro 2 20 SB παιδευτής; Mt 23 10 S(B сaб)καθηγητής; Aeg 253 S when p. λο εϥкaθнгει; мпт-, мετρ., *teaching*: Col 2 22 B(S c.), Miss 8 115 S тм. profitable to souls διδασκαλία, 1 Cor 2 13 BF (Mor 38 104, S do) διδακτός; Cat 99 B θм. ппоγомнλια; бп-, хпп† c., meaning same: Ps 104 22 B(S † c.) παιδεύεσθαι; ROC 20 49 S тεγϭ. пaϥ ϙпоγλωкщ.

хι, бι c. SAA²BF, *get teaching, be taught*: Ps 2 10 SB, Jer 5 3 SB παιδεύεσθαι; Job 34 16 SB νουθ.; Dan 12 4 B διδάσκεσθαι; Ro 12 3 BF(BM 506, var & S p рмпϙнт) σωφρονεῖν; Job 36 3 S (B бι мпкa†) ἐπιστήμην ἀναλαμβάνειν; c e-† nn or vb: Ps 105 35 S(B тсaбо), ib 118 7 S(B εмι), Pro 22 25 SA, Ez 19 3 B(S тс.), Mt 13 52 SBF, He 5 8 F(S сбо, B do), Aeg 235 S children х. ερooγ μανθάνειν; MG 25 2 B пaϥϭ. επισбaι παιδ.; Bor 235 118 S εкщaпх. εгϙωб пϭιх διδ.; ShC 73 194 S every virtue х. ερooγ, PSBA 10 395 B пн етaϥϭ. ερωoγ from apostles, Mani 2 A² men х. aрaγ, AP 32 A² п]тaεϊхι сб[ω, Lant 14 44 S we are not yet skilled ἀλλὰ επх., CO 385 S see aιхι тεкс. aιрмоoс; рεϥхι, бι c., *one taught*: Is 54 13 SB, Jo 6 45 SA²B διδακτός; CO 401 S оγр. επϙωб επaпoγϥ, C43 124 B ϙaпр. птε ф†; aтбι c. B, *untaught*: HL 73 none oι

па. except God ἀδίδακτος; мa пхι, бι c., *learning place*: BHom 50 S παιδευτήριον, BMar 102 S διδασκαλεῖον, ROC 17 401 B παλαίστρα. *Cf* мa п† c.

хεм c. B: Ex 1 10 (A мεεγε aγϙωб aϙoγп a-), Ac 7 19 (S хι щохпε, F бεп мετснб) κατασοφίζεσθαι.

сaбо B *v* тсaбо.

сεбι B *circumcise v* сббε.

снбε, сιбε, сιϙι, сιϥ *v* сιϥε *tar*.

снбε, -ϙε S, -бι, сεбι B, снϙι F, сб- S nn f, *reed*: Ex 30 23 B κάλαμος; KroppM 91 S оγс. пкaщ εϥϙрнт for writing, ShC 73 152 S пс. п[по]ειн *stalks of rushes*; *greave*: 1 Kg 17 6 S κνημίς (*v* c. прaτϩ); *shin-bone*: PMéd 293 S пс. еткнк, *cf* name PStras 555 F Chael пкaк c.; Lev 11 21 B(-бι, -ϙι, S ϙрб) σκέλος (*v* c. прaτϩ); as *flute*: Is 5 12 B(SF c. пхω q *v*) αὐλός (*cf* tibia Dévaud); among weaver's (? *cf* сa man s f) tools: K 126 B пιс. ورامل; *kohl bottle*: K 258 B †c. لاسك (*v* Lane *Mod Eg*¹ 1 52).

сброоге *v* рооге.

c. прaτϩ SB, *pipe, stalk of leg, shin-bone*: Deu 28 35 SB, Ps 146 10 SB, Is 47 2 SB κνήμη; Job 18 13 B(S мрре пр.) κλών; Aeg 22 SB feet & пс. прaтϥ, LMis 468 S breaking of пс. прaтϥ (Jo 19 33), Va 61 14 B blood ran down upon пιс. птε рaтϥ; *greave*: Dan 3 21 B what are bound επεпс. прaтoγ (S оγεрнтε) περικνημίς.

c. пхω SBF, *reed for singing, flute*: 2 Kg 6 5 SB, Is 30 29 BF(S c.), 1 Cor 14 7 SB αὐλός; ShA 1 200 S птaп мппс., ROC 23 154 B drums, cymbals & ϙaпс., BAp 134 S aтειс. ωщ εбол, RNC 70 S c. of χοραύλης.

cwбe SA, -бι BF vb **I** intr, *laugh, play*: Ge 18 12 SB, Lu 6 25 SB γελᾶν; Ex 32 6 SB, Pro 26 19 SA, 1 Cor 10 7 SB παίζειν, Bar 3 16 B ἐμπ.; Ac 17 32 B(S пoсϭπεϭ) χλευάζειν; Aeg 248 S μειδιᾶν; ShA 1 244 S сεс. сεрaщε сεрooγт, TstAb 168 B weeping & then επaϙс.пε, BMis 269 S they spake пθε (п)пετс., BHom 128 S εγс. εγхнр, C 89 182 B етaγс. ϙιτεн мпιмaсι (2 Kg 6 5), Va 58 179 B actor етс. етεр ϙaл, Miss 1 406 S casting dice (βόλος) εγс., GPar 3 18 B мпεпaιωт щεпoγ† c. επεϥ; ethic dat: RNC 83 S c. пнтп тεпoγ.

II tr, *deride, mock*: Job 40 24 SB παί., MG 25 247 B διαπ., Ge 39 14 SB, Mk 15 20 SBF(prob sic I), LeipBer '02 144 S aγс. ммoϥ (*sc* Kronos) ϙιτпрεa ἐμπ., Jer 9 5 S(BMOr 8810 462)B κατaπ., Job 41 24 SB ἐγκαταπ., Sa 15 12 S щоγс. ммoϥ παίγνιον εἶναι; Va 63 92 B c. ммoп γελ., Ps 2 4

B(S c. ncλ-) ἐγγ., Job 5 22 B(S do) καταγ.; Pro
16 29 A(S p ϩλλ) ἀποπειρᾶν; 4 Kg 4 16 B δια-
ψεύδειν; ROC 25 271 B was not able ec. λλoc
δελεάζειν (cf ib 242), Aeg 284 S eγc. λλoϥ (sc
Jesus, var cωϣ) ὕβρις; TU 24 1 4 S epeфopoλλ
c. λλoi, ShC 42 188 S each nλc. λπeϥϣнpi,
Wess 15 142 S кc. λλoi (var BAp 5 ncωi), BSM
46 B λпepc. λλoп = Va 63 17 B = BMis 395 S
p ϩλλ.

With following preposition.   c e- S dat commodi:
RNC 83 c. nнтn nтeтnp [ϩo]γo c. epon;   eϩoγn
e-, laugh at: BMis 45 S aϥc. nкpoϥ eϩ. epoϥ;   c
eϩ., eϣ. eϩpн-: Mor 34 43 S eϥec. eϩ. eϩpλ (Virgin), ROC 27 146 B laid hold of him & acc. eϣ.
eϩpλϥ;   c exn- SAB, meaning sim: Pro 2 14
SA(B pλϣi) χαίρειν ἐπί; Mun 177 S eγc. ex-
λпeγтaкo, Dif 2 54 B eϑpoγc. exnпoγϣeλ-
ϣi; eϣoγn ex. B: DeV 1 117 gazing up at soldiers eγc. eϣ. exωoγ; eϩpλi, -нi ex.: Ps 51 8
SB, Lam 1 8 B γeλ. ἐπί, Pro 1 26 B ἐπιγ. dat;   c
λп-, пeλ- SBF, sport with: Ge 26 8 B πaί. μeтά,
Si 47 3 S π. ἐν, Mk 15 31 BF(S ncλ-) ἐμπ. πpóc,
Si 8 5 S πpoσπ. dat; Job 29 24 SB γ. πpóc, Si 13
7 S πpoσγ. dat; JTS 10 398 S λпeϥc. eпeϩ λп-
oγϣeepeϣнλ as rich man doth;   c ncλ- SAB,
laugh at: Ps 36 13 S(B acc) ἐкγ. acc, Aeg 241 S ἐπιγ.
dat, Mic 3 7 SA(B do) Lu 8 53 S(B do), каταγ. gen,
Sa 5 3 S(B ϯ ϣωϣ) eἰς γéλωтa ἔχειν; GFr 425 S
eкc. ncωк oγaaк π. intr, Mk 10 34 S(var & B acc)
ἐμπ. dat; Lu 23 35 S(ShRyl 70 245, H кωλϣ,
B eλк ϣai) ἐкμυκтηρίζειν; BHom 94 S aϥc. ncλ-
тλнтпoϭ of prophecy кωδωνeῖν acc; PS 79 S beheld archons eγc. ncωc, ShA 1 378 S eγкωλϣ
aγω eγc. ncλ-, R 1 4 69 S кc. ncωn eпeϩoγo =
AM 129 B, Leyd 402 S those eтc. ncaпeγωпϩ;   c
ϩn-, sport with: Is 3 16 S(B n-) πaί. dat; ShR 2
3 75 S birds eтγc. nϩнтoγ in idleness.   With
advb eпϣωi B: DeV 2 180 babes c. eп. ϣaпaϩo.

—— nn m SABF, laughter, derision: Job 8 21
S(B pλϣi), Eccl 7 7 SF, Mic 1 10 SAB γéλωc,
Ps 43 13 SB каταγ.; Jer 29 16 B(S хнp) πaiγvía,
He 11 36 SB ἐμπaiγμóc; Job 12 4 SB χλeύaσμa;
Va 57 96 B c. nϣepϣi λaγveía; ShWess 9 131 S
Origen mixed with Christianity λнтp ϩaλ & c.,
ShA 2 342 S oγc. пe хooc it is ludicrous to say,
HL 85 B oγc. nтe пiϩeλλωn laughing-stock, P 131³
81 S unprofitable men eтoγeϩ c. ϩiϑн λλoк (var
Mor 25 8 peϥc.).   As adj: P 129¹⁷ 76 S фaп-
тacia пc. μaγiкòν ἐμπaiγμa; ϩωб пc. SB, laugh-
able thing: Lu 24 11 S(B eбϣi) λῆρoc; Va 66 300
B пipбнoγi пc. that children make in sand πaí-
ζovтec тυпoῦv, Aeg 288 S πaiδiá; BHom 31 S
каταγeλaστóc; BM 331 16 S I knew serpent how

aϥϣωпe каta oγϩ. пc. ὅтi фavтáζei; ShA 1 455 S
wrought as one eϥp ϩ. пc.;   v also ϣхcωбe
below.

eipe noγc. SB, make sport, mock: Ge 21 6 SB
γéλωтa πoieῖv; RNC 76 S wroth because of пc.
nтaϥaaϥ naϥ, Cat 113 B пic. пeλпiϣepϣi eтaγ-
aiтoγ naϥ, BIF 14 131 S bid me тaeipe noγc.
before thee (causes idols to slay their priests), BMis
270 S пc. that Christians have made (sc miraculous
fruit in shrine).

λa пc. B, jesting place: MIE 2 394 = BAp 121
S λa пхλeγaзe, Va 58 154 man's frailty oγλ.
птe пiбωλ play-ground for fevers.

peϥc. SB, jester, mocker: Is 3 4 SB, Jude 18 B
(var peϥep ϩaλ, S peϥхнp, A -хpхpe) ἐμπaίктηc;
Job 31 5 SB γeλoiaστήc; Si 36 6 S μωкóc; Aeg
39 B ϩanp. go up upon (tight) ropes.

ϣхc. S, ridiculous, jesting talk: Bor 226 170 γe-
λωтoпoiòc λóγoc; Wess 18 110 λнтϣna, ϣ., oγ-
eλλнб;   BMar 79 S answerable even for oγ-
кoγпϣaхe пc., AM 81 B oγcaхi пc.

бin-, хinc. SB, laughter: BM 178 87 тб. of
Mary is angels' joy, DeV 2 54 B oγх. ecбнλ eбoλ.

cωбe, -пe S, -пi B nn f, edge, fringe of garment
&c, cf שׁפח (IgR): Ex 28 32 B, Ps 132 2 SB, cit
Mor 31 239 S -пe ϣa; TEuch 1 302 B (ib 331
cωoγϩi), ShA 1 107 S nтoп н пc. λпкataпeтac-
λa, ib 218 пpoeiтe...пeγcωпe, тeγaпe, тeγλнтe,
ShIF 67 S sim;   Job 38 38 S aiтaбc пϑe пoγ-
ωпe пc. (B = Gk) λίϑω кύβoν. Cf λcωбe needle for
stitching edges, so ? stone joining another; or c.
is ? play & кύβ. dice.   V LMis 397.

cбe S(once)B, -н F (once) nn m, door: Ps 140
3 (S po), EpJer 58 F, Ez 41 11 (S do), Jo 10 7
(var DeV 2 223 & A² po, SA diff) ϑύpa, Ez 8 16
πpóϑυpoν, ib 46 2 пpo λпic. (S ϩaпpo) πpóϑ.; ib
40 9 sim (S do) aἰλáμ; ib 40 38 (S po) ϑύpωμa;
ib 40 13 (S do) πύλη, ib 41 2 (S do) πυλών; 2 Chr
4 21 πυpeῖa (reading ? πύλai); P 55 12 among
wooden objects пic. باب; Z 352 S I have no c. eϯ
eпaλa пϣωпe, so brother gave him пec. λпpo
λпϩip & hung mat (? пopc) there until he could
make po nбa.

cбe S nn, meaning unknown: Hall 115 хi c.
naϥ пpoc ϑe[.   Cf ? cбω.

cбe A   v ϣϥe.

cбo   v тcaбo.

cбω, cбoγi   v caбe.

cββe¹ SA, ceбi² B, cнббi³ F, ϲббe-⁴ SA, coγбe-⁵

B, cⲩⲃⲃⲏ-⁶F, cⲃⲃⲏⲧⲥ̄⁷S, cⲟⲩⲃⲏⲧⲥ̄⁸B, cⲉⲃⲏⲧⲥ̄⁹F, cⲃⲃⲏⲩ†¹⁰S, -ⲏⲩⲧ†¹¹S, cⲟⲩⲃⲏⲧ†¹²S, cⲟⲩⲛⲧ†(P 54 134)B, cⲉⲃⲛⲟⲩⲧ†F¹³ (for B cⲉⲃⲛⲟⲩⲧ GMir clviii l ϣⲉⲃⲓⲛⲟⲩⲧ, v C 86 240) vb tr, *circumcise*: Ge 21 4 S¹B⁵, Ex 4 25 A¹B⁵, Lu 2 21 S⁷B⁸, Jo 7 22 S⁴B², 1 Cor 7 18 S¹⁰B¹²F¹³, Gal 5 3 S¹¹B², ib 6 13 b S⁴B⁵F⁶ περιτέμνειν, VSitz 172 4 27 S oⲩⲣⲱⲙⲉ eϥⲥ.¹⁰ περιτομὴν ἔχειν; R 1 1 38 S ⲛϥⲥⲃⲃⲏⲧ (l -ⲏⲩⲧ) ⲁⲛ ἀκρόβυστος; Z 308 S ⲁⲩⲥⲃⲃⲏⲧⲟⲩ for kingdom of heaven εὐνουχίζειν (Mt 19 12 misunderstood). Intr (once): Va 57 121 B ⲙ̄ⲫⲣⲏ† ⲉⲧⲁⲓⲥ. ⲡⲁⲓⲣⲏ† oⲛ †ⲛⲁϭⲓ ⲱⲙⲥ (cf Mt 3 15). As nn m *SBF*: Jo 7 22 SB, 1 Cor 7 18 SBF, Col 2 11 SB (var⁹) περιτομή, Phil 3 2 S(BHom 140, var ϣⲱⲱⲧ ⲉⲃⲟⲗ, B ϣ. ⲛⲥ.) κατατ.

ⲁⲧⲥ. *SBF, uncircumcised* as nn: 2 Kg 1 20 SB, Is 52 1 SB, Ac 7 51 SB ἀπερίτμητος; as adj: Lev 26 41 SB, 1 Kg 17 36 SB ἀπ.; Ac 11 3 *SB* ἀκροβυστίαν ἔχειν; o, oⲓ ⲛⲁⲧⲥ., *be unc.*: Ex 28 10 SB ἀπ.; 1 Cor 7 18 SBF ἐν ἀκρ.; ⲙⲛⲧ-, ⲙⲉⲧⲁⲧⲥ. *SABF, uncircumcisedness*: Ge 34 24 B(S = Gk), Ex 4 25 AB, 1 Kg 18 27 S, 1 Cor lc SBF ἀκροβυστία.

cⲟⲩⲃⲏⲧ, -ⲛⲟⲩⲧ (Pro) B adj (AZ 20 200, Sethe *Verb* 2 91, 658 n), *well-looking, decent*: Pro 11 25 (var ⲧⲟⲩⲃⲏⲟⲩⲧ, SA ⲛⲁⲛⲟⲩ-), 1 Cor 7 35 (SF ⲕⲁⲗⲱⲥ) εὐσχήμων, 1 Thes 4 12 (var cⲟⲩⲛⲧ, S ⲧⲥⲁⲛⲏⲩ) εὐσχημόνως; *peculiar*: Ex 19 5 (S ⲧⲟⲩⲏⲧ) περιούσιος (var ἐκλεκτός) مطهّر.

cⲃⲃⲉ S nn m, *meaning unknown*, part of property bequeathed: J 66 30 fifth part of church ⲙ̄ⲡⲉⲥ. ⲙ̄ⲡⲉϥϭⲣⲟⲓ ⲙ̄ⲡⲉϥⲁⲓⲙⲟⲥ(ⲓⲟⲛ) &c, ib 76 27 (duplicate) ⲡϭⲣⲟⲓ ⲙⲛ[ⲛⲉϥ]ⲁⲅⲟⲩ ⲙ̄ⲡⲥ. &c.

cⲃⲟⲕ SB, -ⲁⲕ AF, cⲟⲃⲕ† SB, cⲁ.† S/AA²F, vb intr, *become, be small, few*: Nu 26 56† S(B ⲕⲟⲩ-ϫⲓ), Is 21 17 S(B ⲉⲣ ⲕ.), Mt 9 37† S(B ⲕ.) ὀλίγος, Ex 12 4 S†B, Pro 10 27 SA(B ⲉⲣ ⲕ.), Is 60 22 S†B ὀλιγοστός, Ps 11 2 SB, Nah 1 4 SA(B ⲉⲣ ⲕ.) ὀλιγοῦσθαι; 2 Kg 12 8† S, Mk 4 31† S(B ⲕ.) μικρός, Nu 26 54† S(B do), Jo 2 10 B(S ⲥⲟϫⲃ) ἐλάσσων, Mt 25 40† S(B do) ἐλάχιστος, Lev 25 16 B(S ⲧⲥⲃⲕⲟ), Jer 51 18 S(B ⲉⲣ ⲕ.) ἐλαττοῦν; Jth 8 9 S cⲃⲏⲕ (? cf ib 11 12 cⲃⲟⲕ) σπανίζειν; Hos 4 3 SAB σμικρύνειν; Mt 24 22 S(B ⲉⲣ ⲕ.) κολοβοῦσθαι, Lev 21 18 S ϣⲁⲁⲡⲧϥ c.† (B ϫⲁϫϣⲁⲓ) κολοβόριν, ib 22 23 B c. ⲡⲥⲏⲧ (S ⲥⲁⲗⲡⲥⲁⲧ) κολοβόκερκος; Job 5 4 B(S ϭⲑⲃⲃⲓⲟ, Is 23 8 B(S ⲕ.) ἥσσων; Ge 8 11 S(B ⲣⲟⲩⲣⲟⲩ) κοπάζειν; Z 355 S ⲡⲟⲉⲓⲕ ⲉⲁⲥ. λείπειν, Ge 8 13 S(var ⲱϫⲛ, B ⲙⲟⲩⲛⲕ) ἐκλ.; Ps 151 1† S (B ⲁⲗⲟⲩ) νεώτερος εἶναι; Mor 18 106† S νήπιος; 2 Tim 3 15† S(B ⲉⲣ ⲁⲗ.) βρέφος; PS 245 S ⲙ̄-ⲙⲩⲥⲧⲏⲣⲓⲟⲛ eⲧⲥ.† opp ⲙⲙ. eⲧⲟⲅⲟⲧⲃ, ib 69 S ⲁⲡⲁ-

oⲩⲟⲉⲓⲛ c. ϩⲣⲁⲓ ⲛϩⲏⲧ, ShA 1 173 S some reach great age others die eⲩⲥ.†, ib 373 S driving off wolves ⲛ̄ϥⲧⲣⲉⲩⲥ.† eⲃⲟⲗ ϩⲓⲧⲙ̄ⲙⲏⲧⲉ, C 43 41 B ⲡⲓⲡⲟⲗⲉⲙⲟⲥ ⲁϥⲥ. ⲡⲟⲩⲣⲟⲙⲡⲓ = Mor 39 15 S ⲕⲁⲧⲁⲥⲧⲉⲗⲓ, Mor 24 9 F ⲡⲉⲧⲥ.† eⲗⲁⲓ, ib 43 213 S/ moon eⲓⲥ.† ⲙⲛ̄ⲡⲉⲱⲥ ⲁⲓⲣ ⲛⲟϭ, BM 256 221 S wedlock c.† ⲛ̄ⲡⲁⲣ̄ⲡⲡⲁⲣⲑⲉⲛⲓⲁ, Mani 2 A² ⲡⲉⲧⲥ.† eⲅⲟ ⲛ̄ⲕⲟⲩⲓ, C 86 103 B eϥⲥ. ϫⲉⲛ†ⲙⲁⲓⲏ; ⲡⲏⲩ ⲛⲥ., *go on diminishing*: Ge 8 3 S(B † ⲡⲧⲟⲧⲥ̄) ἐνδιδόναι, ib 5 B eⲙⲙⲟϣⲓ ⲡⲁϩⲛ ⲛⲥ. (S c.) ἐλαττονοῦν.

tr, *make less*: C 43 48 B ⲡⲧⲉⲕⲥ. ⲙ̄ⲡⲭⲱⲛⲧ = Mor 39 25 S † ϩⲣⲁⲕ.

—— nn m *SB, smallness, few*: Ps 101 23 S(B ⲙⲉⲧⲕⲟⲩϫⲓ) ὀλιγότης; Lev 25 16 B(S cⲃⲕⲉ) ἔλαττον; Job 13 10 B ἧττον; 2 Cor 4 17 S(B ⲁⲥⲓⲁⲓ) ἐλαφρός; ShZ 513 S ϩⲟⲩⲟ eⲛⲁⲓ ⲛ̄ ⲡⲉⲥ., Cat 125 B ⲡⲥ. ⲡⲧⲟⲩⲛⲗⲓⲕⲓⲁ.

cⲃⲕⲉ S nn m, *meaning same*: 1 Kg 14 6 ϩⲓϩⲁϩ ⲛ̄ ϩⲡⲥ. ὀλίγος, Lev as above.
V ⲧⲥⲃⲕⲟ.

cⲃⲗⲧⲉ, cⲗⲃⲧⲉ, cⲗϥ. S vb intr, *roll over, about*: Jud 4 21 c.(var cⲗⲃ.) ϩⲓⲡⲉⲥⲏⲧ ἀποσκαρίζειν, ib 5 27 ⲁϥⲥ. ⲁϥⲕⲉⲕⲱⲥϥ eⲃⲟⲗ συγκάμπτειν; BHom 33 will lift thoughts to heaven ⲧⲁⲧⲙⲥⲗⲃ̄. ϩⲛ̄ⲡⲁⲛⲕⲁϩ περισπᾶσθαι; ShA 2 87 mud...cⲗϥ. ⲡ̄ⲣⲓⲧϥ like swine, P 131⁶ 89 ill-behaved clerics eⲩⲣ ⲡⲕⲉⲥ. ϩⲓⲡⲉⲛⲕⲁ of church, Mor 51 33 ⲁⲡⲧⲱⲟⲩⲣ ϩⲓⲧⲉⲣⲱⲧⲉ ⲁⲡⲥⲃⲗⲧⲉ ϩⲙ̄ⲡϩⲁⲟⲩⲟⲛ *clave unto milk* (cf He 5 12) & *wallowed in servitude*.

cⲉⲃⲉⲛ B nn, *bandage, selvage*: Pro 7 16 (SA = Gk), Jo 11 44 (SAA² do) κειρία; K 390 ϩⲁⲡⲥ. لفائف, ib 126 ⲡⲓⲥ. among weaver's (قزّاز) furniture (v Almk 1 313); ROC 25 251 bade loose ⲡⲓⲥ. eⲡⲁⲅⲙⲏⲣ ⲙ̄ⲙⲟϥ (sc corpse). Cf *sabanum* (Stern 137).

cⲉⲃⲟⲟⲛ S nn as pl, *support, prop*: Tri 508 ⲗⲩⲭⲛⲓⲁ ⲧⲁⲧⲁϩⲣⲉ ⲡⲉⲥⲥ. دعائم. Coptic?

cⲟⲃⲛ S vb intr, *make breeze, make cool* or sim, with fan: Mor 663 A whilst Pachôm lay in fever one sat eϥⲥ. eⲣⲟϥ ϩⲓⲧϥⲕⲗⲁϥⲧ = Va ar 172 93 عليه رَوّح, ib ⲙ̄ⲡⲉⲕϣⲉ eⲩⲥⲁⲧⲱ ⲛ̄ⲥ. eⲣⲟϥ ⲙ̄ⲙⲟⲥ? = مروحة تُرَوّح عليه بها?, P 155 Cherubs' wings c. eⲡⲟⲩϩⲣⲟ (cf PSBA 26 178). Cf ? determ of *sbn*, Hess *Setne* 174.

cⲃⲛⲥⲉⲧⲉ A v cⲃ.

cⲟⲃⲥⲉⲃ B v cⲟⲡⲛ.

cⲓⲃⲧ SAF nn f, *hill*, often paral ⲧⲟⲟⲩ: Ps 64 12 S(B ⲕⲁⲗⲁⲙⲫⲟ), Pro 8 25 SA(B do), Is 30 25 SF(B do), Hos 10 8 S(A = Gk, B ⲑⲁⲗ), Lu 3 5 S (B do) βουνός; Deu 32 13 S ⲡⲉⲧⲣⲁ ⲡⲥ. (B ⲡ. eⲥ-ϫⲟⲣ) στερεὰ π., Ap 6 16 S(B diff) πέτρα; P 44 54

S ⲡⲥ. اكلي (اكلي), ShA 2 90 *S* ⲧⲡⲉⲧⲣⲁ ⲛ ⲧⲥ., Miss 4 685 *S* ⲁⲩⲧⲁⲗⲉ ⲉϩⲣⲁⲓ ⲉϫⲛⲧⲥ. As place-name: ⲧⲥⲓⲃⲧ (BKU 1 158), ⲧⲥⲛⲃⲧ, ⲧⲥⲃⲧ (TurO 7 *sic* l).

сⲟⲃⲧ *SB*, ⲥⲁ., ⲥⲁⲃⲧⲉ *A*, ⲥⲁⲃⲉⲧ *F*, pl ⲥⲃⲑⲁⲓⲟⲩ *B* nn m, *wall often of town, fence*: Ex 14 22 *B*, 1 Kg 31 12 *S*, Ps 50 20 *SB*, Is 30 13 *SBF*, Joel 2 7 *AB*, He 11 30 *SBF* τεῖχος, Lam 2 8 *B*, Ez 42 20 *B*(HCons 296, *S* ⲥ. ⲉϥⲣⲙⲡⲉϥⲕⲱⲧⲉ) προτείχισμα; Ez 40 5 *SB* περίβολος; Jer 31 18 *B* ὀχύρωμα; Nu 22 24 *B*(*S* ⲭⲟⲗⲭⲗ), Ps 88 41 *B*(*S* ⲭⲟ) φραγμός; 3 Kg 20 12 *S*, Ez 26 8 *B* χάραξ; *ib* 4 2 *SB* προμαχών; Is 21 11 *B*(*S* ⲙⲁ ⲡⲣⲟⲉⲓⲥ) ἔπαλξις; P 46 147 5 ⲥ., رور, ⲭⲟ حائل, C 89 134 *B* ⲥ. of vineyard = MG 17 502 حصن, ShP 130² 25 *S* ⲣⲉⲛⲭⲟ ⲁⲅⲱ ϩⲉⲛⲥ., RNC 90 *S* outside ⲡⲥ., Ep 70 *S* ⲡⲥ. ⲉⲧⲕⲱⲧⲉ ⲉⲧⲡⲟⲗⲓⲥ, Miss 4 117 *B* ⲥ. ⲛⲭⲣⲱⲙ encircled temple & its ⲭⲟⲓ fell, Kr 92 *S* ⲛⲥⲟⲃⲉⲧ around flax field, DeV 2 260 *B* building ⲡⲥ. ⲙⲡⲟⲩⲥⲓⲁⲥⲧⲏⲣⲓⲟⲛ (var ⲛ̄ϯⲉⲕⲕⲗⲏⲥⲓⲁ), BM 915 18 *b B* astride ⲛⲓⲥ. as if on horse; pl form *B*: Ps 54 10, Pro 1 21, Is 49 16, Lam 2 5; with ⲕⲧⲟ, ⲧⲁⲕⲧⲟ, ⲕⲱⲧ, *surrounded, built with wall(s)*: Lev 25 29 *SB*, Nu 32 17 *S*(var ⲟⲅⲟⲛ)*B*, Hos 8 14 *AB* τειχίζεσθαι, Nu 13 19 *SB*, Jos 19 35 *S* τειχήρης; Jer 52 4 *SB* περιχαρακοῦν; ClPr 30 15 *S* ⲁϥⲕⲧⲉ ⲥ. ⲉⲣⲟⲟⲩ, DeV 2 36 *B* city ⲧⲁⲕⲧⲏⲟⲩⲧ ⲛⲥ.; ⲣ, ⲉⲣⲥ., ⲟⲓ ⲛⲥ., *be wall*: Till Oster 8 *A* ⲧⲁⲣⲉⲥⲣ ⲟⲩⲥⲁⲃⲧ ⲁⲧⲉⲧⲛⲡⲁⲣⲑⲉⲛⲓⲁ, TEuch 1 240 *B* ⲁⲣⲓ ⲥ. ⲉⲣⲱⲟⲩ, BSM 110 *B* ⲉⲕⲟⲓ ⲛⲥ. ⲉⲃⲟⲗ ϩⲁⲉⲛⲓⲃⲟⲅⲗⲛ ⲛⲓⲃⲉⲛ.

In place-names: ⲡⲥⲟⲃⲧ [ⲙⲡ]ϩⲟⲓ (EW 92), ⲡⲥⲁⲃⲧ, -ⲉⲧ(CMSS 54 &c), Ψεβθενκυρινου(PLond3), Ψεβτομιτ (PEleph), Ψεβθονεμβη (PHib 1). Cf حصن.

сⲟⲃⲧⲉ-, -ⲱⲧⲉ *S*, ⲥⲁⲃⲧⲉ *S*ᶠ*AA*², ⲥⲟⲃϯ *B*, ⲥⲁⲃϯ, -ⲱϯ *F*, ⲥⲃⲧⲉ- *SA*, ⲥⲉⲃ. *SB*, ⲥⲃⲧⲱⲧ† *SAA*²*F*, ⲥⲉⲃ. *B*, ⲥⲃⲧⲱⲧ† *SA*(once), ⲥϥ.† *S*, ⲥⲃⲧⲁⲧ† *A*, -ⲧⲁⲓⲧ *A*², ⲥⲉⲃⲧⲱⲧ† *B* vb **I** intr, *be ready, prepare, set in order*: Ps 88 3 *B*(*S* tr), Jer 26 14 *S*(*B* tr), C 89 57 *B* ⲁⲩⲥ. ⲭⲉⲁⲅⲡⲁⲟⲩⲱⲙ, Miss 4 530 *S* ⲥ. ⲡⲡⲉⲥⲏⲏⲩ *prepare (food) for* = C 89 49 *B* tr: ἑτοιμάζειν, Lu 14 17 *S*(*B*†) ἕτοιμος εἶναι; 2 Cor 13 11 *B*(*SF* tr), He 11 3 *B*(*S* do) καταρτίζεσθαι; Pro 23 5 *SA* κατασκευάζεσθαι, Ac 10 10 *SB* παρασκ.; Ro 1 10 *B*(*S* ⲥⲟⲟⲩⲧⲛ) εὐοδοῦσθαι, Dan 8 11 *B* κατευ.; Ez 21 15 *SB* εὖ γίνεσθαι; Pro 8 30 *SAB* ἁρμόζειν; Is 35 6 *B*(*SF* ⲥⲟⲟⲩⲧⲛ) τρανὸς εἶναι; PS 35 *S* ϣⲁⲥ....ϣⲁⲡⲧⲟⲩ ⲧⲁⲁϥ, ShMiss 4 283 *S* ⲡⲉⲧⲥ. ϩⲁⲡⲙⲁ ⲛⲟⲩⲱⲙ, *ib* 282 ⲡⲉⲩϩⲣⲁⲁⲩ ⲛⲥ., Sh(Besa)Z 513 *S* crowds ⲉⲧⲟⲥ. ⲡⲁⲩ, DeV 2 195 *B* prayed ⲉⲑⲣⲉⲡⲉϥⲙⲱⲓⲧ ⲥ., MR 2 57 *B* God keep thee & ⲧⲉϥⲥⲱⲡⲓ ⲡⲱⲧⲉⲛ, BM 604 *F* ⲁⲡϭⲟⲓⲥ ⲥⲁϥⲧ ⲡⲉⲕ, Baouit 138 *S*ᶠ may Lord ⲧⲁϣ ⲧⲉⲡϩⲓⲏ ⲡⲥⲁⲃⲧⲓ ⲛⲏⲛ, COAd 67 *S* ⲁⲡⲡⲉ ⲥ. ⲁⲕⲧⲱⲥⲅ, BMis 383 *S* question ⲁⲛϩⲱⲃ ⲙⲡⲁⲣⲓⲥⲧⲟⲛ ⲥ

(var ⲥⲟⲟⲩⲧⲛ) ? = BSM 38 *B* ⲕⲏⲛ ⲡⲭⲱⲕ ? ⲥ ⲉ-, *make ready to, for*: Jer 6 23 *B* παρατάσσεσθαι εἰς; PS 325 *S* ⲉⲩϣⲁⲡⲥ. ⲉⲥⲱⲕ veils, *ib* 175 *S* ⲁϥⲥ.... ⲉⲧⲣⲉϥϥⲓ, BMis 382 *S* lo, sheep ⲁϥⲥ. (ⲉ)ⲧⲉⲭⲣⲓⲁ of great man = Mor 27 31 *F* = BSM 37 *B* ⲁϥⲥ. ⲉⲑⲃⲉⲛϩⲱⲃ ⲛ-; ⲉⲣⲟⲩⲛ, ⲉⲝ. ⲉ- : 1 Chr 29 2 *B* ἑτοιμάζειν εἰς.

Qual, *ready*: Nu 16 16 *SB*, Mic 4 1 *AB*, Jo 7 6 *SA*²*B* ἕτοιμος; Is 26 7 *SB* παρασκ.; 1 Cor 1 10 *SB* καταρτ.; Deu 7 6 *B*(*S* ⲧⲁⲓⲏⲟⲩ)περιούσιος; Ps 31 6 *S*(*B* ⲥⲟⲩⲧⲱⲛ)εὔθετος; Pro 14 6 *SA*(*B* ⲙⲟⲧⲉⲛ) εὐχερής; Ez 23 41 *B*(*S* ϭⲟⲣϭ)κοσμεῖσθαι; PS 366 *S* ⲡⲕⲟⲗⲁⲥⲓⲥ etc. for sinners, Till Oster 25 *A* ⲡⲕⲉ ⲡⲓⲙ ⲥ., Bor 248 11 *S* footsteps ⲥ. ϩⲛⲟⲩⲥⲟⲟⲩⲧⲛ, WHatch 762 *B* ⲩⲥ. ⲛⲭⲉ ⲡⲁⲙⲱⲓⲧ = PO 1 142 جهل, C 86 185 *B* ⲉϥⲥ. ϩⲉⲛⲡⲉϥϩⲏⲧ, Mani 1 *A*² ⲛⲛⲗⲁⲙⲡⲁⲥ ⲥ.; ⲥ ⲉ-, *ready to, for*: Ex 19 11 *SB*, Ps 16 12 *SBF*, Lu 22 33 *SB* ἕτοιμος εἰς, 2 Cor 12 14 *SF*(*B* tr) ἑτοίμως inf; Ro 9 22 *SB* καταρτ. εἰς; Hab 1 8 *SB* (*A* ⲣⲁⲩⲧ) πρόθυμος εἰς; ShC 73 45 *S* ⲡⲣⲓⲣ etc. ⲉⲕⲟⲛⲥϥ, AZ 14 59 *S* ⲡⲭⲟⲓ...ⲥ. ⲉⲱⲙⲥ = BSM 98 *B*, El 96 *A* ⲡⲉⲓ etc. ⲁϥⲟⲩⲛⲟⲩ (*sic* ?), AM 121 *B* ⲧⲉⲡⲥ. ⲉϥⲁⲓ ϩⲁⲃⲁⲥⲁⲛⲟⲥ, C 43 8 *B* ϯⲥ. ⲉⲑⲣⲓⲙⲟⲩ, Pcod 7 *S* one ⲉϥⲥ. ⲉⲕⲁⲁϥ ⲉⲃⲟⲗ another ⲉϥⲥ. ⲉⲕⲟⲗⲁⲍⲉ ⲙⲙⲟϥ; ⲉϩⲟⲩⲛ ⲉ- : Va 63 88 *B* heart etc. ⲉϣ. ⲉⲡⲓϩⲱⲃ; ⲥ ⲉϫⲉⲛ- : Ex 28 7 *B* ἐξαρτίζ. ἐπί.

II tr, *prepare, set in order*, often refl : Ge 43 25 *SB*, Job 38 25 *S*(*B* ⲥⲉⲗⲙⲓ), Pro 8 27 *SAB*, Is 30 33 *SF*(*B*†), Jo 14 2 *SA*²*B*; ZNTW 24 84 *F* kingdom ⲉⲧⲁⲛ[ⲥ]ⲃⲧⲟⲧⲥ, CaiEuch 530 *B* ⲁⲕⲥ. ⲡⲁⲡ ⲡⲟⲩⲱⲓⲕ ⲉⲧⲟⲓⲙⲁⲍ., Mic 6 8 *A*(*B*†) ⲉⲧⲟⲓ. εἶναι; Ps 16 5 *SBF*, Mt 4 21 *SB*, He 10 5 *SBF* καταρτ.; Nu 21 27 *SB*, Is 45 7 *SB* κατασκευ., Ac 21 15 *SB* ἐπισκευ., Pro 29 5 *SA*, 1 Cor 14 8 *SB* παρασκευ.; Z 317 *S* each one ⲥⲃⲧⲱⲧϥ = MG 25 232 *B* εὐτρεπίζεσθαι; Ps 139 3 *B*(*S* ⲥⲣ ⲙⲗⲁϩ) παρατάσσειν; Ac 23 24 *S* (*B* ϭⲓ) παριστάναι; Ro 1 13 *B*(*S* diff) προτιθέναι; 2 Cor 11 2 *S*(*B* diff) ἁρμόζ.; Ps 67 20 *B* ⲥ. ⲡⲙⲱⲓⲧ (*S* ⲥⲟⲟⲩⲧⲛ dat) κατευοδεῖν; 1 Thes 3 11 *B* sim (*S* do) κατευθύνειν; TU 9 1 6 *S* ⲩⲥ. ⲙⲡⲡⲉⲧⲛⲁⲡⲟⲩϥ for each, Sh(Besa)Bor 206 583 *S* ⲙⲡⲟⲩⲥⲉⲃⲧⲉ ⲡⲉϩ in jars (Mt 25 4), C 43 149 *B* ⲥⲉⲃⲧⲱⲧⲕ ⲱ ⲡⲓϣⲱⲭ = Mor 48 104 *S* ⲥ. ⲉⲃⲟⲗ, Mani 1 *A*² ⲡⲧⲉⲥⲃⲧⲱⲧⲉ, Miss 4 522 *S* wait ϣⲁⲡⲧⲉⲡⲭ̅ⲥ̅ ⲥⲃⲧⲉ ⲥⲟⲩⲧⲛ̄ϥ & we pay thee = C 89 42 *B* ⲑⲁⲓϣⲧⲉⲛ ⲉⲡⲥⲟⲩⲉⲡϥ, Va 63 8 *B* ⲡ̅ⲟ̅ⲥ̅ ⲁϥⲥ. ⲡⲏⲓ ⲙⲡⲓⲣⲱⲃ = BMis 376 *S* ⲥⲟⲟⲩⲧⲛ, *ib* 3 *B* ⲡⲥⲉⲥ. ⲡⲣⲁⲡⲭⲁⲗⲕⲓⲟⲛ = BMis 366 *S* ⲥⲙⲓⲛⲉ, Va 61 202 *B*(Sarah to Isaac) I believe God ⲡⲁⲥⲉⲃⲧⲉⲑⲏⲛⲟⲩ & bring you again (*cf* **I** MR 2 57). ⲥ ⲉ-, *prepare for*: Si 2 1 *SB* ἑτοιμάζ. εἰς; Ep 71 *S* etc. ⲙⲙⲟⲕ ⲉϩⲟⲩⲛ ⲉϩⲉⲡⲁⲣⲉⲧⲏ; ⲥ ⲉⲃⲟⲗ *SB*, as ⲥ.: Ez 21 10 *SB* ἕτοιμος; Z 345 *S* ⲥⲃⲧⲱⲧⲉ (f) ⲉⲃ. προσδοκεῖν; ShP 130⁵ 127 *S* ⲧⲉⲧⲛⲥ. ⲙⲙⲱⲧⲛ ⲉⲃ.

ⲉⲙⲓϣⲉ, Mor 25 79 *S* ⲉⲅⲥ. (*sic l*) ⲛϧⲉⲛⲁⲣⲓⲥⲧⲟⲛ ⲉⲃ.
ⲉⲛⲉⲅⲉⲣⲏⲅ, Mor 31 120 *S* gird yourselves ⲛⲧⲉⲧⲛⲥⲃ-
ⲧⲱⲧⲧⲏⲩⲧⲛ (*sic*) ⲉⲃ., TurM 13 *S* tell Martha ⲛⲧⲉⲥⲃ-
ⲧⲱⲧⲥ ⲉⲃ. & *forewarn her*, Miss 4 147 *B* ⲁⲛϣⲁⲛⲥ.
ⲉⲃ. ⲙⲡⲉⲓⲣⲱⲃ we will take him.

—— ⲛⲛ m *SABF*, *preparation*, *things prepared*,
furniture: Nah 2 4 *B*(*A* ⲛⲟⲩϧⲃ), Zech 5 11 *AB*,
Eph 6 15 *SB* ἑτοιμασία, Mor 17 80 *Sᶠ* ⲣϩⲟⲩⲛⲟⲃ
ⲡⲥⲁ. ἕτοιμος πολύ; Nu 10 12 *B*(*S* ⲛⲉⲧϣⲟⲟⲡ ⲛ-),
Ez 25 4 *B* ἀπαρτεία, 2 Cor 13 9 *SBF* κατάρτισις,
Eph 4 12 *SB* καταρτισμός; Ps 96 2 *S*(*l*? ⲥⲟⲟⲩⲧⲛ,
B ⲥⲱⲟⲩⲧⲉⲛ) κατόρθωσις; Ge 31 18 *SB* ἀποσκευή
(cf ⲁⲥⲏⲣ), EW 151 *B* ⲛⲥ. ⲡⲛⲉϥⲙⲉⲗⲟⲥ διασκ., Nu
8 4 *B*(*S* ⲙⲟⲩⲛⲕ) κατασκ., Va 63 88 *B* ⲛⲥ. ⲙⲡⲓⲣⲏⲧ
παρασκ., Ac 27 17 *S*(*B* = Gk) σκεῦος; Is 3 20 *B*
(*S* ⲥⲙⲓⲛⲉ) σύνθεσις; 4 Kg 12 5 *S* ⲛⲥ ⲧⲏⲣϥ πάντα;
ShP 130² 95 *S* wood, stones &c ⲡⲕⲉⲅⲗⲏ ⲧⲏⲣⲟⲩ
ⲙⲡⲥ. ⲙⲡⲕⲱⲧ, ShC 73 14 *S* virtues ⲛⲉⲧⲣⲙⲡⲉⲥⲥ. ⲛ
ⲛⲉⲥⲧⲱϣ ⲧⲏⲣϥ, BMis 174 *S* all c. of baptistry, table,
napkins, gospels = BSM 83 *B*, P 44 54 *S* of ship
ⲛⲥ. ⲓⲥ *tackle*, Mus 42 214 *S* having ⲛⲥ. ⲛⲧⲉⲥⲯⲩⲭⲏ
ⲉϣϣⲏϣ *equable disposition*; ⲣ, ⲉⲣ ⲥ., *make preparation*: BG 25 *S* ⲡⲉⲧⲙⲉⲧⲉⲭⲉ ⲉⲅⲁⲓⲱⲛ ϩⲛ̄ⲟⲓⲕⲟⲩⲙⲉ-
ⲛⲉ ⲣ ⲥ. ϩⲁⲣⲟϥ, ShC 42 178 *S* ⲉⲁⲅⲉⲓⲣⲉ ⲙⲡⲥ. ⲧⲏⲣϥ
ⲙⲡⲉⲩϣⲛ̄ϩ, Mor 41 9 *S* whilst ⲉⲅⲉⲓⲣⲉ ⲙⲡⲥ. ϫⲉ-
ⲉϥⲛⲁ- = DeV 2 255 *B*, MIE 2 421 *B* ⲁⲓⲣⲓ ⲙⲡⲁⲥ.
so saying he died, BMis 385 *S* ⲁⲣⲓ ⲥ. ⲙⲡⲙⲁ = Va
63 13 *B* ϥⲣⲱⲟⲩϣ, CMSS 33 *F* send him to ⲣ
ϩⲛ̄ⲕⲟⲓⲥ. ⲉⲛⲉⲓⲧⲉϥⲙⲟⲟⲩⲉ.

ⲁⲧⲥ. *B*, ⲁⲧⲥⲃ̄ⲓⲱⲧⲥ *S*, *unprovided*: Ge 1 2 *B* ἀκατα-
σκεύαστος; My 24 *S* ⲡⲕⲁϩ...ⲛⲁⲧⲥⲃ̄ⲧⲱⲧϥ.

ⲙⲁ ⲛⲥ. *B*, *place of preparing* or *storing*: BSM
41 ⲫⲙ. ⲙⲡⲓⲱⲓⲕ = BMis 387 *S* & Va 63 14 *B* ⲙⲁ
ⲛ̄ⲕⲁ (var ⲛ̄ϯ) ⲟⲉⲓⲕ.

ⲣⲉϥⲥ. *S*, *preparer*: BMOr 7028 (*v* BMis li) of
Raphael ⲡⲁⲡⲟⲩⲅⲙⲟⲥ ⲛⲣ. ⲡⲓⲅⲙⲫⲁⲧⲱⲧⲟⲥ ⲡⲣⲉϥⲣ
ϩⲙ̄ⲙⲉ.

ϫⲓⲛⲥ. *B*, *preparation*: Va 57 238 ⲛⲓϫ. ϩⲁⲭⲱⲛ
ⲙⲡⲥⲟⲃϯ ⲙⲡⲥⲁϫⲓ κατασκ., HCons 463 who shared
in ⲡϫ. ⲙⲡⲁⲓⲛⲓ κατασκευή.

ⲥⲃⲏⲏⲧⲉ *v* ⲥϧⲃⲏⲏⲧⲉ.

ⲥⲃ̄ϣⲉ, ⲥⲩⲃⲉ, ϣⲃ̄ϣⲉ *S*, ϣⲉⲃϣⲓ *B* nn f, *shield*:
2 Kg 1 21 *B*, Ps 45 10 *B*, Eph 6 16 *B* (all *S* = Gk)
θυρεός; Job 41 6 *S* (varr ϣ., ⲥϣ., *B* ϩⲟϥ Gk misunderstood) ἀσπίς; Ez 38 4 *B* πέλτη; MG 25 321
B ⲑⲟⲛⲑⲉⲓⲁ ⲛ̄ⲧϣ., TRit 522 *B* body (of dead)
withered, senses destroyed, heart ceased ⲁⲥϣⲱⲡⲓ
ⲛⲁⲧⲙⲟϣⲓ ⲛϫⲉ ϯϣ. قتال *strength* or sim (Bevan,
but ? *l* ϣⲟϣⲡⲓ).

ⲥⲱⲃϩ, ⲥⲟⲃϩ-, ⲥⲟⲃϩⲥ, ⲥⲟⲃϩ.† *S*, ⲥⲁ.† *SᵃSᶠA* vb intr,
become, be leprous: Lev 14 2† (*B* ⲕⲁⲕ ⲥⲉϩⲧ), Nu 5

2† (var ϫⲁϩⲙ, *B* do), Mt 26 6† (*B* do, *F* ⲉⲧⲕⲏⲕ
ⲙⲡⲥⲁⲃϩ), Aeg 287 (var ⲥⲱⲟϣ) λεπρός, R 1 1 29
ⲛⲉⲓⲥ.† ⲛⲉ λ. γίνεσθαι; Nu 12 10 (*B* do) λεπρᾶν, 4
Kg 15 5 λεπροῦσθαι; Deu 23 1 (*B* ⲗⲱⲱⲥ) θλαδίας;
El 88 *A* ⲛⲉⲧⲥ.† = *ib* 120 *S*, ShBor 246 82 ⲛⲑⲉ ⲉⲛ
ⲧⲁⲩⲉϫⲉⲓ ⲥ. ⲉⲛϧⲥ.† ⲁⲛ, ShA 2 26 *Sᵃ* ⲟⲩⲣⲱⲙⲉ ⲉϥⲥ.†
Gu 72 *Sᶠ* sim, Mor 18 87 ⲁϥⲥ. like snow = Miss
4 153 *B* ⲁϥⲕⲱⲕ ⲛⲥⲉϩⲧ; *tr S*, *make leprous*: Lev
13 3 ⲛϥⲥⲟⲃϩϥ gloss on ϫⲁϩⲙⲉϥ (var *B* Gk om).

—— *SA*, ⲥⲁⲃϩ *F* nn m, *leprosy*: Lu 5 12 *S*(*B*
ⲥⲉϩⲧ) λέπρα, Lev 13 2 *S*(*B* do), Mk 14 3 *F*(*S* ⲛⲉⲧⲥ.†,
B do) λεπρός; Mor 16 101 *S* ⲉϥϣⲟⲟⲡ ϩⲛ̄ⲟⲩⲥ. (var
Worr 271 ϩⲛ̄ⲟⲩⲥⲟⲟϣ), Z 629 *S* recipe for ϣⲱⲡⲉ ⲛⲓⲙ
ⲛⲥⲱⲃϩ, El 90 *A* ⲟⲩⲕⲟⲕ ⲛⲥ. = *ib* 120 *S*, BAp 118
S water caused body to ⲕⲱⲕ ⲉⲛⲥ., Mus 41 231 *S*
ⲉϥⲥⲛⲟϭ ⲉϥⲕⲏⲕ ⲉⲛⲥ., Mor 41 29 *S* sim = DeV 2 285
B ⲟⲓ ⲛⲥⲉϩⲧ, Cai 42573 1 *S* recipe to produce ⲟⲩ
ⲕⲱⲕ ⲉⲛⲥⲟⲃϩ.

ⲥⲓⲁ *F* nn, meaning unknown: Kr 30]ᵛ ⲁ ⲉⲭⲉ
ⲥⲓⲁ ⲕⲁⲧⲁ ⲁⲣ̄ ⲓⲃ[. (? *l* ⲥⲓ, δ).

ⲥⲑⲟ *SB* *v* ⲧⲥⲧⲟ.

ⲥⲑⲟⲓ *B* *v* ⲥⲧⲟⲓ.

ⲥⲑⲃⲁⲓ *B* *v* ⲥⲧⲉⲃⲁⲉⲓϩ.

ⲥⲑⲏⲙ *B* *v* ⲥⲧⲏⲙ.

ⲥⲁⲑⲙⲓ *B* *v* ⲥⲁⲧⲃⲉ.

ⲥⲑⲉⲓⲛⲓ *B* *v* ⲁⲡⲁⲓ *s f*.

ⲥⲟⲑⲛⲉϥ *B* *v* ⲥⲟⲧⲃⲉϥ.

ⲥⲁⲑⲉⲣⲓ *B* *v* ⲥⲁⲧⲉⲉⲣⲉ.

ⲥⲑⲉⲣⲧⲉⲣ *B* *v* ⲥⲧⲣⲧⲣ.

ⲥⲁⲕ *SB* nn m, *adornment, appearance, capacity*:
HL 108 *B* wished to flee ⲛⲁϥϫⲓⲙⲓ ⲙⲡⲓⲥ. ⲁⲡⲡⲉ οὐκ
ἴσχυεν; P 131³ 47 *S* ⲙⲡⲉⲡϩⲉ ⲛⲥ. ⲉⲧⲁⲥⲥⲉ ⲙⲙⲟⲥ
non ea visa est assumenda; K 71 *B* ⲛⲓⲥ. ⲡⲉⲙⲡⲓ-
ⲧⲉⲛⲧⲱⲛ والاشكال; HL 114 *B* when rest gone
let him ask ϫⲉⲛⲟⲩⲥ. ⲥⲁⲡⲥⲁ ⲟⲩⲧⲱϥ ⲡⲉⲙⲏⲓ *freely*
(?) *aside, between him & me*, ROC 25 248 *B* went
toward him ϫⲉⲛⲟⲩϫⲱⲕ ⲡⲉⲙⲟⲩⲥ. ⲛⲧⲉ ⲟⲩⲙⲉⲧⲣⲉⲙ
ⲣⲁⲩϣ (var Va 59 121 ϫⲉⲛⲟⲩⲥ. ⲡⲉⲙⲟⲩⲅⲕⲱⲧ, Preuschen *Pall. u. Ruf.* 126 om) *appearance of mildness*;
SHel 90 *S* without hypocrisy ϩⲓⲥ. ⲙⲙⲛ̄ⲧⲛⲟⲩϫ,
Mor 41 106 *S* Salome & ⲛⲉⲥⲥ. ⲛⲁⲡⲁⲧⲏ, FR 16 *S*
Virgin sought not ϩⲉⲛⲥ. like women; ⲁⲧⲥⲟⲕ
(*sic*) *S*, *shapeless*: BIF 13 114 fleets ϩⲛ̄ⲟⲩϩⲱⲗ ⲉⲃⲟⲗ
ⲙⲡⲟⲩⲙⲛ̄ⲧⲁ. *collapse & unrestraint*; ϯ ⲥ. *SB*,
make a show, give appearance: Si 10 27, *ib* 37 26 *S*
σοφίζειν; HL 121 *B* ⲛⲁⲩϯ ⲥ. ⲉⲣⲱⲟⲩⲡⲉ so as not to
let him know them εὐφυῶς ἑαυτ. συνσκενάζεσθαι;
MG 25 233 *B* when had ϯ ⲙⲡⲓⲥ. ⲙⲡⲓⲥⲟⲛ = Z 318
S ϯ ⲥⲃⲱ τυποῦν *corrigere*; RNC 74 *S* judge asks

martyr екоүеш ✝ c. ⲙⲙⲟⲕ ⲡⲟⲩⲕⲟⲩⲓ *wouldst take occasion, have liberty* (?) *that mayest learn* ?, Mor 54 137 *S* no woman shall ✝ c. ероc *when going to church*; ϭⲓ c. *B, take opportunity, give occasion*: Va 58 67 *when met the maiden* ϩⲉⲛⲟⲩⲙⲱⲓⲧ ⲉϥϭⲓ c. *in a likely place he fell with her.*

сак- *S v* сѡк *s f.*

сек *S nn as pl, meaning unknown*: Mor 25 71 *here no respect of persons*, ⲁⲡⲉⲥⲉⲕ ⲡⲁⲧⲕⲁⲣⲟⲥ ⲟⲩⲱ ⲙⲡⲟⲟⲩ, *face that (used to) put to shame appears to-day itself ashamed.* ? *Sf* for сак.

сⲓⲕ *v* асⲓⲕ.

сⲟⲕ[1], сⲱⲕ[2] *SB*, сак[3], сⲟⲟⲕ[4], сⲱⲱⲕ[5] *S, nn m, sack, sackcloth, bag*: Lev 11 32 *S*[1](var[4])*B*[1], Jos 9 10 *S*[4] pl, Ps 29 12 *B*[1](var[2], *S* ϭⲟⲟⲩⲛⲉ), Is 32 11 *B*[1] (*SF* do), Mt 11 21 *B*[1](var[2], *S* do), Is 3 24 *B*[1](*S* ⲡⲟⲩϩ) σάκκος; Ge 42 27 *B*[1](*S* ϭ.) μάρσιππος; BIF 13 106 *S* ⲟⲩⲥ.[1] = MG 25 289 *B* ϩⲁⲛⲥ.[1], BKU 1 306 *S* ⲡⲓⲥ.[1], Bodl(P)g 17 *S* ⲟⲩⲥ.[4], DeV 2 168 *B* ⲟⲩⲥ.[1], WS 124 *S* ϩⲁⲗⲟⲧ ⲃ̄ c.[4] ⲃ̄, Vi ostr 34 *S* c.[3] ⲧ, RNC 79 *S* ⲟⲩⲥ.[5];   *contains bread*: MG 25 208 *B*[1] = Z 344 *S* ⲭⲡⲟϥ ἀναβολίδιον; *corn*: Ge 42 25 *B* (var ⲙⲟⲕⲓ) ἀγγεῖον, BKU *ut sup*; *money*: MG 25 103 *B*[1]; *sand*: Tri 615 *S* ϩⲉⲛⲥ.[1] غرائر;   c. ⲙϭⲱⲓ *B, hair sacking*: Zech 13 4[1] (*A* ϭ.) δέρρις τριχίνη, Ap 6 12 *B*[2](*S* ϭ.) σ. τρ., C 86 274 ϩⲁⲛⲥ.[2] ⲙϭ. *to cast body into.*   *Cf* ϫⲁⲕ *hair cloth*.

сⲟⲕ (*sic* MS)*A vb intr, be content, satisfied*: Hab 2 4 ⲧⲁⲯⲩⲭⲏ ⲛⲁⲥ. ⲉⲡ(*B* ✝ ⲙⲁ✝) εὐδοκεῖν. *Belongs* ? *to next.*

сⲱⲕ *SAA*[2]*BF*, сⲱⲕⲓ *B*, ск- *SAF*, сек- *SA*[2](AP) *BF*, сак- *SA*[2](Jo)*F*, сⲟⲕ- *B*(CDan 87, MG 25 394, C 43 58, *ib* 86 149), сⲟⲕⲝ *SB*, сек⳽ *AF*, сакⳃ *SʃA*[2]*F*, снⲕ[1] *S, p c* сак- *S vb* **I** *intr, flow as water, hair, blow as wind, smoke, generally move on swiftly, glide, also draw, be drawn*: Jud 5 14 *S*, Dan 7 10 *SB* ἕλκειν; BHom 43 *S torrent* ⲉϥⲥ. παραρρεῖν; Ps 77 20 *S*(*B* ϫⲱⲗⲕ)κατακλύζειν, Is 66 12 *S*(*B* do)ἐπικλ.; Sa 13 2 *S* βίαιος; Is 5 24 *S*(*B* diff, *F* ⲭⲉⲗⲛⲟⲩⲧ) ἀνειμένος; Si 43 17 *S* πνεῖν; Is 30 28 *SF*(*B* ⲱⲙϯ)σύρειν; Ps 104 41 *S*(*B* ⲙⲟϣⲓ)πορεύεσθαι, Is 30 25 *SB*(var ⲉⲗ ϩⲁϯ)*F* διαπ.; *ib* 32 2 *SF*(*B* ϩⲁϯ), Ac 27 15 *B*(*S* ⲣ ϩⲱⲧ)φέρεσθαι; Pro 25 26 *SA* ἔξοδος ὕδατος, Si 25 28 *S* διέξ.; Ps 103 28 *B*-ⲕⲓ (*S* ⲥⲱⲟⲩϩ ⲉϩⲟⲩⲛ)συλλέγειν; Ex 2 16 *A*(*S* tr, *B* ✝ ⲙⲟⲟⲩ) ἀντλᾶν; Cant 5 11[1] *S* (reading ἐλατός); ShZ 593 *S* ⲛⲉⲓⲉⲣⲱⲟⲩ c. ⲡⲙⲟⲩⲉⲓⲟⲟⲩⲉ ϩⲁⲧⲉ, El 84 *A* ⲟⲩⲥⲛⲁϥ ⲛⲁⲥ., Va 63 7 *B tears* c. ϩⲉⲛⲛⲁϩⲃⲁⲗ, Miss 4 550 *S* ⲉⲧⲥ. ϩⲛⲧⲉϥϭⲓⲛⲙⲟⲟϣⲉ *like water* ⲉϥⲥ. = C 89 89 *B*, Mor 51 37 *S* ⲧⲙⲉⲗⲉⲧⲏ ⲉⲧⲥ. *like flowing water*, R 1 2 73 *S* ⲁⲧⲟⲩⲗⲗⲉ c. (*cf* FR 12), ShBor 247 119

S ⲡⲉⲭⲣⲟⲛⲟⲥ c.[1], Mus 40 41 *S* ⲉⲣϣⲁⲛⲟⲩⲥⲟⲡ c. *dormierit* (*die, v* c. ⲉⲃⲟⲗ), P 43 234 *S* ϫⲓⲁⲣⲟⲓⲁ · ⲙⲙⲁⲣⲧ ⲉⲧⲥ. اعماء ابحري ; ShMun 110 *S* ⲡⲧⲏⲩ ⲉⲧⲥ., ShC 73 199 *S smoke* c. ⲉⲃⲟⲗ ϩⲡⲣⲱⲟⲩ, Mor 23 35 *S* ⲁϩⲉⲛϩⲏⲛⲉ c., C 43 143 *B* ⲟⲩⲛⲓϭ ⲉϥⲥ., LMär 8 *S* ⲉⲧⲥ. ϩⲙⲡⲁⲏⲣ, PSBA 32 30 *S ships* ⲉⲧⲥ.[1] ϣⲁⲣⲣⲁⲓ ⲉⲕⲛⲏⲗⲉ, PS 41 *S veils* ⲁⲩⲥ. ⲙⲁⲩⲁⲁⲩ, Br 122 *S veils* ⲉⲧⲥ.[1] ⲉⲣⲡⲓⲡϩⲟϭ ⲡⲣⲣⲟ, MG 25 239 *B seized serpent* ⲁϥⲥ. ⲁϥϩⲟⲣϫϥ, TT 9 *S Enoch weighing sins* ⲡⲛⲟⲃⲉ ⲉⲧⲥ. ⲡⲁⲣⲁ ⲡⲁⲅⲁⲑⲟⲛ *outweigh* (*cf* below c. ⲉ-), PMich 1522 *S sale of corn* ⲉⲣϣⲁⲛⲡϣⲁⲁⲣ c. ⲧⲁⲁⲩ ⲉⲃⲟⲗ, BM 180 375 *S beryl* ⲉϥⲥ. ⲙⲡⲉⲓⲛⲉ ⲙⲡⲁⲏⲣ *tends to likeness* (colour) *of sky*, Mor 28 241 *S man challenged to swear in* τόπος *says* c. ⲧⲁⲱⲣⲕ ⲛⲁⲕ *go on, proceed*, K 44 *B epithet of God* ⲉⲧⲥⲱⲕⲓ سالب (var ساكب), Hall 69 *S* ϣⲏⲧ ⲛⲁⲡⲟⲩ ⲉⲧⲥ.[1] (meaning?).

II tr, *draw, beguile, gather, impel*: Deu 21 3 *B* (*S* ϥⲓ), Job 39 10 *S*(*B* сⲭⲁⲓ *q v*), Jo 6 44 *SA*[2]*B*, Ac 16 19 (*S*(*B* ⲱⲙϯ), R 1 1 33 *S* ⲉⲧⲣⲉⲥ. ⲙⲡⲟⲩⲛⲏⲗⲟⲛ ἕλκ., Pro 24 68 *SA*(*B* c. ⲉⲃⲟⲗ), Ja 1 14 *SB* ἐξέλ., EpJer 43 *BF*(*l* ? сек-)ἐφέλ.; Ja 3 4 *B*(*S* ⲣ ϩⲣⲱⲧ) ἐλαύνειν; Is 5 18 *SBF*, Nah 3 14 *A*(*B* ⲙⲟⲩϩ), 1 Cor 7 18 *BF* (*S* ϩⲱϩⲥ)ἐπισπᾶν, Ac 20 30 *B*(*S* ⲡⲱϩⲥ)ἀποσ.; Jo 21 8 *SB*, Ap 12 4 *S*(*B* ⲱ.)σύρειν; Jer 29 10 *S*(*B* ⲱ.)κατασ.; Ac 20 7 *S*(*B* ϥⲱⲣϣ ⲉⲃ) παρατείνειν; Ez 27 26 *S*(*B* diff), BHom 4 *S* ⲧⲉϥⲛⲏⲑⲓⲁ c. *him that followeth it* ἄγειν, 4 Kg 11 15 *S* ἐξάγ., Lu 5 11 *B*(*S* ⲙⲟⲟⲛⲉ) κατάγ., Ja 3 3 *B*(*S* ⲕⲧⲟ) μετάγ., Ez 38 4 *B* συνάγ.; Is 32 2 *SF*(*B* ⲓⲛⲓ) φέρεσθαι, Ac 20 9 *SB* καταφ.; Dan 12 10 *B* ἐκλέγειν (*cf* Lu 22 31 below), Ex 16 17 *B*-ⲕⲓ (*S* ⲥⲱⲟⲩϩ ⲉϩⲟⲩⲛ), Mt 13 29 *B*-ⲕⲓ (*S* do, *F* ⲕⲱⲧϭ), Ps 128 7 *B* (var -ⲕⲓ, *S* ⲥⲱⲟⲩϩ) συλλ.; Lev 25 5 *B* (var & *S* ⲱⲥ) ἐκθερίζειν; Ex 2 17 *SA*(*B* om), Pro 9 12 *SAB*, Z 213 *S* ⲉϥⲥⲉⲕ ⲙⲟⲟⲩ (*cf ib* ⲙⲉϩ ⲙ.) ἀντλᾶν; Ge 19 6 *B*(*S* ϣⲧⲁⲙ) προσοίγειν; Mt 13 48 *B*(*SF* ⲉⲓⲛⲉ ⲉϩⲣⲁⲓ) ἀναβιβάζειν; Aeg 273 *S* ⲡϣⲁϫⲉ c. ⲙⲙⲟⲛ ἐπείγειν; Lu 22 31 *S*(*B* ϣⲟⲗϣⲉⲗ) σινιάζειν; Jer 50 12 *B*-ⲕⲓ (*S* ⲙⲟⲩϣⲧ) φθειρίζειν; сек ⲁϭⲁⲛ, *v* ⲁϭⲁⲛ **II**; сек ⲟⲩⲟⲥⲣ Ez 27 26 *S* κωπηλάτης; сек ϩⲁⲏ 2 Kg 19 11 *S* ἔσχατος γίνεσθαι; ск ϭⲱⲟⲩ Eccl 7 14 *F* κοσμεῖσθαι (*cf* below c ⲛⲥⲁ-); сек ⲟⲩⲥⲧⲁⲩⲣⲟⲥ Z 341 *S* σφραγίζειν; c. ⲡⲭⲛⲁⲣ Ac 16 15 *S* παραβιάζειν; сек сϫⲁⲓ, *v* сϫⲁⲓ (ⲣⲉϥⲥ.);   PS 361 *S* ϣⲁⲩⲥ. ⲡⲛⲕⲁⲧⲁⲡⲉⲧⲁⲥⲙⲁ *to left & right*, BIF 13 101 *S* ⲁⲩⲥⲉⲕ ⲛϩⲁⲗⲩⲥⲓⲥ *drew back chains* = MG 25 282 *B*, BIF 22 107 *F* ⲁⲩⲥ. ⲡⲛⲟⲩ ⲙⲡⲗⲁ = Mor 41 194 *S* ⲁⲩⲥⲉⲕ ⲛⲕⲟⲗⲗⲁ, TStAb 235 *B* ⲁϥⲥⲉⲕ ⲡⲓⲣⲃⲟⲥ & *covered face*, BMis 380 *S* ⲁϥⲥⲉⲕ ⲡⲉⲭⲁⲗⲓⲛⲟⲥ *of horse* = Mor 27 30 *F* сак-, El 80 *A* сес. ⲛⲡⲟⲩⲥⲡⲱϥ *from breasts*, Cai 8329 *S epitaph* ⲛⲧⲁⲅⲥ. ⲛⲉⲡⲥⲟⲡ *draw* (? *to grave*), Z 638 *S ships* ϣⲁⲩⲥⲟⲕⲟⲩ ϩⲛⲣⲉⲡⲡⲟⲩϩ, Bor 143 40*S* ⲧⲗⲁⲩⲟ c. ⲙⲡϫⲟⲓ, BIF 15 248 *Sʃ*

north wind cⲁⲕⲉⲛ ⲉⲣⲏⲥ *drove us*, JKP 2 44 *S* ⲁⲓcⲉⲕ ⲡⲓⲡⲟ ⲉⲡⲉⲗⲁⲧⲟⲥ *traverse*, C 41 22 *B* ⲉ̣ⲕⲥ. ⲙⲡⲓϣⲱ *comb* (*S* c. ⲛⲥⲁ- *q v*) = Miss 4 358 ‿, ShMIF 23 146 *S* vine ⲉⲁⲩcⲉⲕ ⲟⲩϣⲗϩ ⲡⲣⲏⲧⲥ, Rec 6 186 *B* ⲉⲩ-cⲱⲕⲓ ⲡⲡⲓⲕⲁⲣⲡⲟⲥ = BMar 220 *S* ⲕⲱⲧⲥ, Mich 136 7 *S* palm ⲉⲙⲡⲟⲩcⲕ ϧ̇ⲁ ⲡⲣⲏⲧⲥ, BMOr 6201 *B* 29 *S* brethren ⲉⲩcⲉⲕ ⲁⲡⲁⲣⲭⲏ ϧⲁⲡⲉⲙⲙⲉⲣⲓⲧ ⲡⲉⲓⲱⲧ Mena, Aeg 2 *B* my father will cⲉⲕ ⲗⲟⲅⲟⲥ ⲡⲉⲙⲱⲧⲉⲛ at Judgement, BM 1103 *S* ⲧⲁⲣⲉⲕⲥ. ⲡⲉⲕⲗⲟⲅⲟⲥ ⲡⲉⲙⲁⲕ, *ib* 530 *S*, AZ 23̄ 105 *S* sim, Bor 263 36 *S* ⲡ(ⲉ)ⲓ-ⲟⲩⲱϣⲡⲉ ⲡⲥ. ⲙⲡϣⲁϫⲉ *prolong discourse* but this shall suffice, Bodl(P) a 2 7 *S* cⲉⲕ ⲡⲭⲁⲗⲕⲟⲥ ⲕⲁⲗⲱⲥ ⲟⲩⲱϣⲙⲉⲕ ⲙⲡⲙⲟⲟⲩ *sift*(?), BKU 1 26 (81 16 b) *F* bird's liver, dry it, cⲉⲕⲥ *strain, sift it* (?), let patient drink it, *cf ib* cⲉⲕⲟⲩ & apply to patient, BIF 13 98 *S* sores cⲉⲕ ϧⲡⲧ ⲉⲃⲟⲗ ϧⲁⲣⲟⲕ = MG 25 277*B*, Cat 158 *B* passions cⲉⲕ cⲟⲩ̄ⲣⲓ ⲛⲧ̄ⲯ̄ⲩⲭ̄ⲏ *make tremble* (? *cf* c. ⲉⲃⲟⲗ *tr*), Aeg 26 *B* river cⲉⲕ ϧⲁϯ, C 86 205 *B* sim, P 131³ 37 *S* ⲁⲩⲥⲕ ⲟⲩⲛⲟϭ ⲡⲁϣ ϧⲟⲙ, Miss 4 671 *S* ⲉⲕⲥⲉⲕ ϧⲣⲟⲟⲩ ϧⲛϣⲁⲡⲧⲕ *snort*, C 43 56 *B*, Mor 24 10 *F* sim cⲁⲕ ⲟⲩϧⲗⲁⲟⲩ (*cf* c. ⲉⲃⲟⲗ), Miss 4 158 *B* could not c. ⲡⲁⲕ ⲙⲡⲉϥⲛⲓⲕⲓ, FR 12 *S* taught her ⲉcⲉⲕ ⲟⲩⲉⲗⲗⲓ (*cf* cⲉϧ ⲟⲩ.), Mor 38 87 *S* can hardly bear up ⲡⲧⲉⲡⲥⲉⲕ ⲡⲉⲓⲛⲟϭ ⲡⲥⲕⲩⲗⲙⲟⲥ, ST 294 *S* let him not c. ⲡⲥⲕⲩⲗ. (in vain), BSM 21 *B* lest ye c. ⲡⲱⲧⲉⲛ ⲡⲟⲩϭⲓⲥⲓ, BM 1118 *S* until thy letter come ⲙⲉⲣ(ⲉ)ⲡⲁϧⲏⲧ cⲕ ⲙⲧⲱⲛ, ShBor 233 241 *S* ⲉⲩⲥ. ⲙⲙⲟⲕ ϧⲓⲧⲡⲗⲟⲅⲓⲥⲙⲟⲥ, BMis 1195 *S* ⲁⲧⲁⲙⲉⲗⲓⲁ...c. ⲙⲙⲟⲕ & *he forgot*, *ib* 275 *S* ⲉⲕⲟⲩⲱϣ (ⲉ)c. ⲙⲡⲟⲩⲥ of parents = Mor 30 52 *F* cⲁⲕ ⲛⲡ., BAp 151 *S* ⲙⲡⲉⲕⲉϣ cⲟⲕⲟⲩ (*sc* 3 Children) ϧⲛⲡⲉⲩ-ⲟⲩⲉⲗⲗⲉ ; *protract the fast, fast SB* (*cf* HistLaus 63 ⲭⲣⲟⲛⲟⲛ ἕⲗⲕⲉⲓⲛ) : ROC 18 171 *S* ⲁⲩcⲉⲕ ⲡⲥⲁⲃⲃ̇ⲁ-ⲧⲟⲛ ⲧⲏⲣⲕ, Z 306 *S* weeks ⲡⲧⲁⲕcⲟⲕⲟⲩ, BM 915 18 *B* ⲡⲧⲟⲩⲥⲉⲕ ⲡⲁⲥⲭⲁ ⲡⲟⲩϧⲉⲃϧⲟⲙⲁⲥ ⲛⲏⲥⲧⲉⲩⲉⲓⲛ ; CDan 87 *B* ⲁⲓⲥⲟⲕ ϯⲉⲃ̇ⲇ. ⲧⲏⲣⲥ ⲥⲩⲛⲁⲡⲧⲉⲓⲛ ; MG 25 243 *B* ⲉⲩcⲉⲕ ϣⲁⲣⲟⲩϧⲓ ἐⲥⲑⲓⲱⲛ ἐⲥⲡⲉ́ⲣⲁⲥ ; Z 349 *S* ⲁⲩⲥⲉⲕ ⲡⲛⲓⲁⲥⲧⲏⲙⲁ of 40 days, RAl 108 *B* ϯⲥⲉⲕ ⲡⲛⲏⲥⲧⲓⲁ from sabbath to sab. (*cf* BMar 6), C 86 178 *B* ⲁⲡⲥ. ⲙⲡⲓⲉϧⲟⲟⲩ *without eating* ; JA '75 5 234 *S* if canst cⲉⲕ cⲛⲁⲩ *2 days together* ὑⲡⲉ́ⲣⲑⲉⲥⲓⲛ ⲡⲟⲓⲉⲓ̂ⲛ, C 89 33 *B* ⲡⲁⲩⲥⲉⲕ ⲃ̄ ⲧⲁ̀ⲥ ⲇⲩ́ⲟ ⲛⲏⲥ., Mor 31 16 *S* ⲉⲕⲥⲉⲕ cⲡⲁⲩ cⲡⲁⲩ, BIF 13 109 *S* ⲉⲩⲥⲉⲕ cⲡⲁⲩ = MG 25 296 *B* cⲉⲕ ⲃ̄ⲃ̄, MIE 2 338 *B* sim يومين, Mor 37 257 *S* cⲁⲕ ϣⲟⲙⲛⲧ, MIE 2 399 *B* cⲉⲕ ⲅ̄ⲅ̄ = BAp 98 *S* ⲡⲛⲏⲥⲧⲉⲩⲉ ϣⲟⲙⲛⲧ ϣⲟⲙⲛⲧ, ShBMOr 8810 453 *S* cⲉⲕ ϥⲧⲟⲟⲩ, Z 310 *S* cⲉⲕ cⲟⲟⲩ ἕⲗⲕ. ⲧⲁ̀ⲥ ἕⲝ (*v* ⲯⲁⲕ-cⲟⲟⲩ at end of this art) ; Mor 53 34 *S* cⲉⲕ ϣⲟⲙⲡⲧ ⲡⲣⲱⲙⲉ *fasting* = TstAb 231 *B* ⲓⲣⲓ ⲛⲅ̄ ⲛ̄ⲣⲱⲙ(ⲉ). cⲟⲕⲥ (once cⲟⲕ) *B* marginal rubric, ? *continue, start* (*here*), *opp* ⲭⲁⲕ or ⲭⲁⲕ ⲉⲃⲟⲗ, *cease, pause* (*here*), or ? refers to mode of recital : Va 64 152, *ib* 59 9 (cⲟⲕ), MG 25 154 n.

Refl *SA²B, draw aside, induce* : 2 Kg 3 27 *S* ⲁⲕ-cⲟⲕⲕ ⲡⲥⲁⲡⲓⲣ ἐⲕⲕⲗⲓ́ⲛⲉⲓⲛ ; Z 308 *S* ⲉⲩⲥ. ⲙⲙⲟⲟⲩ in zeal ⲫⲉ́ⲣⲉⲥⲑⲁⲓ ; C 89 5 *B* ⲁⲩⲥⲟⲕⲕ cⲁⲟⲩⲥⲁ = MG 17 317 *S* cⲉⲣⲧⲩ ⲁⲛⲁⲭⲱⲣⲉⲓ̂ⲛ ; Br 127 *S* ⲡⲥⲉⲥⲟⲕⲕ ⲡⲁⲩ & *flee*, DeV 2 154 *B* cⲉⲕⲑⲏⲛⲟⲩ ⲡⲱⲧⲉⲛ, Mor 17 98 *S* ⲁⲩⲥⲟⲕⲕ ⲉⲟⲩⲁ *of bystanders*, C 43 239 *B* ⲁⲩ-cⲟⲕⲕ ⲉⲣⲟⲕ & *said*, Mani 2 *A²* ϣⲁⲣⲉⲡⲡⲟⲩⲥ cⲁⲕⲕ ⲁⲣⲁⲕ, Mor 22 76 *S* ⲁⲩⲥⲟⲕⲕ ϧⲁⲧⲛⲡⲣⲱⲙⲉ cⲡⲁⲩ = *ib* 26 9 *S* ϧⲱⲕ ϣⲁ- = BSM 67 *B* ϯ ⲙⲡⲉϥⲟⲩⲟⲓ ⲉ-. With following preposition.

―― ⲉ- *SA²B intr, be drawn, flow, tend toward* : Ge 30 37 *S*(*B* diff) ⲡⲉⲣⲓⲥⲩ́ⲣⲉⲓⲛ acc ; 1 Kg 17 40 *B* -ⲕⲓ ⲥⲩⲗⲗⲟⲅⲏ́ ; Si 24 30 *S* ἐⲝⲉ́ⲣⲭⲉⲥⲑⲁⲓ ⲉⲓ̓ⲥ ; R 1 1 18 *S* ecc.† ⲉⲡⲥⲁ *of Jews* ⲓ̓ⲟⲩⲇⲁⲓ̈́ⲍⲉⲓⲛ ; Z 609 *S* colour c.† ⲉⲡⲉⲧⲟⲩⲉⲧⲟⲩⲱⲧ, Cat 61 *B* food etc. ⲉⲡⲓⲙⲁ ⲡⲣⲉⲙ-ⲥⲓ, BAp 36 *S* curtains c.† ⲉⲡⲟⲩⲁ ⲡⲟⲩⲁ ⲡⲡⲉⲑⲣⲟ-ⲡⲟⲥ, C 86 277 *B* in balance ⲡⲧⲟⲩϣⲧⲉⲙⲟⲩⲧⲱⲓ c. ⲉⲟⲩⲧⲱⲓ (*cf* I TT 9), Mor 31 27 *S* ⲁⲩⲥ. ⲉⲣⲏⲥ ⲉⲩ-ⲙⲟⲟϣⲉ, KroppE *S* voice etc. ⲉⲡϫⲓⲥⲉ, ST 177 *S* ⲉⲕⲥ.† ⲉⲡⲙⲟⲟⲩ ; *tr, draw to* : Jo 12 32 *SA²B* ἕⲗⲕ. ⲡⲣⲟ́ⲥ ; Lu 12 58 *S*(*B* ϧⲁ-) ⲕⲁⲧⲁⲥⲩ́ⲣ. ⲡⲣⲟ́ⲥ ; 2 Kg 13 11 *S* ἐⲡⲓⲗⲁⲙⲃ. gen ; Gal 5 26 *B*(*S* = Gk)ⲡⲣⲟⲕⲁⲗⲉⲓ̂-ⲥⲑⲁⲓ acc ; BHom 94 *S* sun ⲁⲕⲥ. ⲉⲣⲟⲕ ⲡⲛⲉⲕⲁⲕⲧⲓⲛ ⲥⲩⲥⲧⲉ́ⲗⲗⲉⲓⲛ ; Aeg 243 *S* ⲡⲧⲥ. ⲧⲟⲟⲧⲕ ⲉⲣⲟⲕ ⲥⲩⲥⲡⲁ̂ⲛ ; C 41 39 *B* ⲁⲡⲁⲓⲱⲧ c. ⲧⲉϥϫⲓϫ ⲉⲣⲟⲕ *withdrew hand*, AP 20 *A²* ⲉⲁⲩⲥⲉⲕ ⲧⲟⲟⲧⲕ ⲁⲡⲓⲧⲛ, PS 8 *S* c. ⲉⲣⲟⲕ ⲙ̄-ⲡⲉⲕⲟⲩⲟⲉⲓⲛ, BG 75 *S* ⲁⲩⲥⲁⲕⲟⲩ ⲉⲩⲡⲓⲣⲁⲥⲙⲟⲥ, BM 353 *S* ⲡⲉϣⲁⲩⲥ. ⲉⲣⲟⲟⲩ ⲙⲡⲕⲟⲥⲥⲉ (ⲕⲟ́ⲥⲥⲟⲥ).

―― ⲉⲣⲁⲧⲥ *B, follow after* : DeV 2 77 runaway sheep ⲁⲩⲥ. ⲉⲣⲁⲧⲕ & found it.

―― ⲉϫⲛ- *SB intr, flow, drag upon, approach* : Jos 16 8 *S* ⲡⲟⲣⲉⲩ́ⲉⲥⲑⲁⲓ ἐⲡⲓ́, Is 30 25 *SF*(*B* ⲉⲗ ϧⲁϯ ϧⲓⲭⲉⲛ-)ⲇⲓⲁⲡ. ἐⲡⲓ́ ; ROC 25 248 *B* ⲁⲡⲓϫⲉⲗⲗⲟ c. ⲉϫⲱⲕ ⲡⲣⲟⲥⲉ́ⲣⲭ. ; ShC 42 104 *S* tears c. ⲉϫⲛⲡⲉⲕ-ⲟⲩⲟϧⲉ, C 86 326 *B* seized neck ⲁⲓⲥ. ⲉϫⲱⲕ, *cf* 324 sim ⲁⲩⲥⲟⲕⲕ, *ib* 43 72 *B* martyr cast upon torture wheel ⲡⲥⲉⲥ. ⲉϫⲱⲕ, *ib* 13 sim ; ⲉϧⲣⲁⲓ ⲉϫⲛ- : ShA 1 153 *S* water c. ⲉϧ. ⲉϫⲱⲟⲩ ; *tr, bring upon, to* : Lev 17 13 *S*(*B* ϧⲱⲃⲥ) ⲕⲁⲗⲩ́ⲡⲧⲉⲓⲛ dat, Wess 15 134 *S* c. ⲙⲡⲕⲁϧ ⲉϫⲱⲓ ἐⲡⲓⲥⲩ́ⲣ., Va 57 111 *B* that we c. ⲉϫⲱⲡ ⲡⲡⲓⲙⲉⲧϣⲉⲡϧⲏⲧ ἐⲝⲓⲗⲁ́ⲥⲕⲉⲥⲑⲁⲓ ; ShMIF 23 90 *S* ϣⲁⲩⲥⲉⲕ ⲡⲉⲡⲡⲟⲃⲉ ⲉϫⲱⲟⲩ as theirs, Hall 109 *S* seller of camel to buyer ⲙⲛ ϭⲟⲙ ⲙⲙⲟⲓ ⲉⲥⲁⲕⲕ ⲉϫⲱⲓ ; ⲉϧⲣⲁⲓ, ⲉϧ. ⲉϫⲛ- : ShLeyd 297 *S* ⲉⲧⲉⲧⲛⲥ. ⲉϧ. ⲉϫⲱⲧⲛ ⲡⲟⲩⲟⲣⲅⲏ (*cf* Ro 2 5 cⲱⲟⲩϧ ⲉϧⲟⲩⲛ), TEuch 2 274 *B* ⲉⲁⲕⲥ. ⲉϧ. ⲉϫⲱⲟⲩ ⲙⲡⲉⲕⲛ̄ⲛ̄ⲁ̄.

―― ⲙⲛ-, ⲛⲉⲙ- *SB intr, go forward with* : Mor 31 48 *S* setting him on camel ⲁⲩⲥ. ⲡⲙⲙⲁⲕ ϧⲙⲡ-ⲧⲟⲟⲩ, AM 325 *B* ⲁⲩⲥ. ⲡⲉⲙⲁⲕ ϧⲉⲛⲫⲓⲁⲣⲟ, ShBor 247 122 *S* length of everything ⲕⲥ.† ⲡⲙⲙⲁⲕ ⲛϭⲓ ⲡⲛⲓⲁⲥⲧⲏⲙⲁ ⲙⲡⲉⲭⲣⲟⲡⲟⲥ *therein is involved extent of time* ; *tr, bring together* : Ps 27 3 *SB* ⲥⲩⲛⲉ́ⲗⲕ. ⲙⲉⲧⲁ́ ; ShIF 305 *S* who was it counselled him ⲉⲁⲩ-

ⲥⲉⲕ ⲡⲉϥⲣⲟ ⲛⲙⲙⲁϥ, so that he learnt what had befallen ?

—— ⲛ- *S, flow with*: Job 29 6 (*B* ϥⲟⲛⲡⲉⲛ†) χέειν dat, Mor 16 22 rivers c. ⲙⲙⲟⲟⲩ ⲉϥϩⲟⲗϭ = BMis 192 ϩⲁⲧⲉ ϩⲛ-.

—— ⲛⲥⲁ- *SB, draw, follow after*: Ap 6 8 *B*(*S* ⲟⲩⲱϩ) ἀκολουθεῖν μετά, 2 Pet 2 2 *B*(*S* do) ἐξακ.; Z 273 *S* ⲛⲉⲧⲥ.† ⲛⲥⲁⲡⲣⲁⲛ παρασύρ. dat ; Bor 134 2 *S*(Vita Sin) one of men c. ⲛⲥⲁⲡϧⲱ of head = C 41 25 *B* c. ⲛ- (*v* above II), Va 58 151 *B* fisherman c. ⲛⲥⲁ†ⲥⲁⲣⲉⲡⲏ ⲉⲡϣⲱⲓ, AM 180 *B* ⲉϥⲥⲱⲕ ⲛⲥⲁⲡⲓ‑ⲇⲏⲙⲟⲥⲓⲟⲛ *seeking, gathering taxes*, HCons 390 *B* let him turn east ⲉϥⲥ. ⲛⲥⲁ†ⲭⲟⲓ ⲡⲉⲣⲏⲥ *following south wall*, BSM 74 *B* ⲁⲩⲥ. ⲙⲙⲟⲟⲩ ⲛⲥⲁⲡⲓϣⲱⲓ *dragged by hair* ; ⲛⲥⲁⲡⲁϩⲟⲩ *S, draw back*: ShBor 247 110 ⲁⲓⲥⲟⲕⲥ ⲛ. with bridle.

—— ϩⲁ-, ϧⲁ- *SB, flow, draw before, beneath, submit to*: Si 28 20 *S* ἕλκ. acc ; PS 354 *S* powers c. ϩⲁⲣⲟϥ like horses, C 43 235 *B* cherubs c. ϧⲁⲛⲉϥ‑ϩⲁⲣⲙⲁ, BMis 539 *S* fiery river c. ϩⲁⲣⲟⲟⲩ (*sc* souls), Pcod 7 *S* sim c. ϩⲁⲧⲉϥϭⲏ (*cf* Dan 7 10), MG 25 402 *B* ⲡⲁⲓ...ⲉⲧⲥ. ϧⲁⲧⲟⲩϭⲏ, C 86 274 *B* blood c. ϧⲁ‑ⲣⲟϥ like water, P 131ᵉ 68 *S* clouds ⲉⲧⲥ. ϩⲁⲧⲏⲉ, FR 6 *S* ⲡⲧⲉⲣⲉⲥⲥ. ϩⲁⲡϩⲓⲛⲏϥ, Ryl 128 *S* if contract not fulfilled ⲧⲏⲥ. ϩⲁⲣⲱϥ ⲛⲓⲙ ⲡϣⲁϥⲉⲓ ⲉⲃⲟⲗ (*cf* c. ⲉϩⲣⲁⲓ), PLond 4 435 *S* ⲧⲁⲣⲏⲥ. ϩⲁⲡⲣⲟⲥⲧⲓⲙⲟⲛ ⲛⲓⲙ (*cf ib* 454 sim ⲁⲡⲟⲗⲟⲅⲓⲍⲉ ϩⲁ-) ; ⲉⲃⲟⲗ ϩⲁ- *B*: Jer 12 14 (*S* ⲧⲱⲕⲙ ⲉⲃ. ϩⲛ-) ἀποσπᾶν ἀπό ; ϩⲁⲣⲁⲧ⸗ *S go along beside*: Mor 31 83 her foal c. ϩⲁⲣⲁⲧⲥ ; *be drawn beside*: Br 86 signs ⲉⲧⲥ.† ϩⲁⲣⲁⲧⲟⲩ ⲛⲛⲉϥⲧⲟⲡⲟⲥ.

—— ϩⲏⲧ⸗ *SA, lead on, go before*: Pro 24 66 *SA* (*B* ϧⲁⲭⲉⲛ-) ἡγούμενος ; Wess 18 89 *S* shame shall c. ϩⲏⲧⲟⲩ ⲉⲧⲣⲉϩⲉⲛⲛⲁ προάγειν ; PS 368 *S* ⲉϥⲥ. ϩⲏⲧ‑ⲟⲩ ⲙⲯⲩⲭⲏ ⲛⲓⲙ, Till Oster 11 *A* fear of God c. ϩⲏⲧⲕ ⲁϩⲟⲩⲛ ⲁ-, Mor 41 29 *S* ⲛⲉⲧⲥ. ϩⲏⲧϥ = DeV 2 285 *B* ⲉⲧϭⲓ ⲙⲱⲓⲧ ϧⲁⲭⲱϥ.

—— ϩⲓⲑⲏ ⲛ- *SB, meaning same*: BIF 13 116 *S* ⲉⲧⲥ. ϩ. ⲡⲧⲉⲯⲩⲭⲏ = MG 25 308 *B* ϧⲁⲭⲱⲥ ⲛ-, MIE 2 334 *B* pillar c. ϩ. ⲙⲙⲟϥ, *cf ib* ⲙⲟϣⲓ ϩ. ⲙ., BAp 99 *S* river c. ϩ. ⲙⲡⲉⲕⲣⲓⲧⲏⲥ ; ϩⲓⲑⲏ ⲛ-: PO 2 181 *S* ⲡⲕⲱⲣⲧ ⲉⲩⲥ. ϩ. ⲙⲙⲟⲛ

—— ϩⲁⲭⲛ-, ϧⲁⲭⲉⲛ- *SB, meaning same*: Ex 32 1 *B*(*S* ⲙⲟⲟϣⲉ ϩⲁⲧⲏⲛ) προπορεύ., Mt 14 22 *B*(*S* ⲣ ϣⲟⲣⲡ ⲉ-), 1 Tim 5 24 *B*(*S* ⲭⲓ ⲙⲟⲉⲓⲧ ϩⲏⲧ⸗)προάγ., Va 58 186 *B* fasting c. ϧⲁⲭⲱⲟⲩ *leadeth* saints to godliness χειραγωγεῖν ; Deu 1 33 *S*(*B* ϭⲓ ⲙ.) ὁδη‑γεῖν ; Mor 18 48 *S* ⲡϩⲗⲗⲟ...c. ϩⲁⲭⲱⲟⲩ = *ib* 19 56 *S* ⲙⲟⲟϣⲉ ϩⲁⲭ., C 89 28 *B* father ⲙⲟϣⲓ ϩⲓⲫⲁϩⲟⲩ ...mother c. ϧⲁⲭⲱⲟⲩ.

—— ϩⲓⲭⲛ- *SB, draw, flow upon*: ShC 73 136 *S* let water c. ϩⲓⲭⲱⲟⲩ, MG 25 134 *B* tears c. ϩⲓⲭⲉⲛ‑ⲡⲓⲕⲁϩⲓ, Mor 28 119 *S* bones come apart ⲉⲩⲥ. ϩⲓ-

ⲭⲱϥ, PO 2 165 *S* ⲥⲉⲥ. ϩⲓⲭⲱⲟⲩ *make selves answerable for* one greater than these.

With following adverb.

—— ⲉⲃⲟⲗ *SB* intr, *be drawn, come forth*: Lu 8 22 *B*(*S* ⲣ ϩⲱⲧ)ἀνάγ. ; BMis 541 *S* worms c. ⲉⲃ. from mouth ἀνέρχ. διά ; Ex 12 38 *B*(Gk om) ; C 89 10 *B* ⲁⲩⲥ. ⲉⲃ. ϫⲉⲛⲡⲓϣⲣⲱⲓⲥ = Miss 4 537 *S* tr = MG 17 350 ﺍﺯﺩﺍﺩ, Miss 4 565 *S* sim, ShC 73 200 *S* ⲟⲩⲭⲁⲙⲱⲥ (κημός) c. ⲉⲃ. ϩⲛⲛⲉϥϭⲃϣⲁ, C 43 211 *B* blood c. ⲉⲃ. ϫⲉⲛⲛⲓⲡⲗⲁⲧⲉⲁ, AM 141 *B* sim ϩⲓ‑ⲭⲉⲛ-, My 46 *S* ⲡϣⲟⲗ ⲉⲧⲥ.† ⲉⲃ. *line drawn*; *pass out, die* (*cf* I Mus 40) *S*: Tob 14 3 ἀποτρέχειν, *ib* 3 6 ἀπολύεσθαι ; Est 2 7 μεταλλάσσειν ; BMar 182 if brother c. ⲉⲃ. go weep for him, BM 981 ⲉⲓϣⲁⲛⲥ. ⲉⲃ. ϩⲙⲡⲓⲃⲓⲟⲥ ; tr, *draw forth*: Ac 8 3 *S*(*B* ⲱϣⲧ ⲉⲃ.)σύρ. ; Pro 24 68 *B*(*SA* c. only)ἐξέλκ. ; PS 282 *S* ϣⲁⲣⲉⲧϭⲟⲙ c. ⲡⲁⲥ ⲉⲃ. ⲙⲡⲙⲉⲣⲟⲥ ⲛⲧϭⲟⲙ, C 43 224 *B* ⲉⲧⲁⲩⲥ. ⲙⲡⲓⲱⲛⲓ ⲉⲃ., WTh 138 *S* ⲉϥⲥⲉⲕ ϩⲣⲟⲟⲩ ⲉⲃ., (*cf* above II Miss 4), AM 178 *B* body ⲥⲉⲕ ⲥⲟⲩⲣⲓ ⲉⲃ. *sweat thorns, shiver* (*cf* C 89 78 ⲛⲉϩ ⲥⲟⲩⲣⲓ & above II Cat 158) ; refl : BMar 197 *S* ⲁϥⲥⲟⲕϥ ⲉⲃ. ⲡⲟⲩⲕⲟⲩⲓ ; as nn m : Jer 26 20 *B* ⲥⲉⲕ ἀπόσπασμα ; Cat 86 *B* ⲡⲓⲥⲱⲕ ⲉⲃ. of apostles (Mk 3 14) ; in liturg rubrics *S*: Leyd 150 the *incipits* of ⲡⲥ. ⲉⲃ. ⲙⲡⲛⲥⲧⲁⲩⲣⲟⲩ ⲙⲡⲛϩⲣⲙⲏⲛⲓⲁ ⲙⲡ‑ⲟⲩⲱϩⲙ, then ⲡⲥ. ⲉⲃ. ⲁ̅, ⲡⲥ. ⲉⲃ. ⲃ̅ each followed by Ps & Gospel, *ib* 153 ⲃ̅ⲗ ⲡⲥ. ⲉⲃ., Balestri lviii, Vict & Albert Mus 434ᵃ, P 129²⁰ 164 sim (*cf* below c. ⲉⲧϩⲏ *B*) ; *going forth, death S*: P 129¹⁷ 30 ⲡⲥ. ⲉⲃ. ⲡⲧⲉⲕⲙⲁⲁⲩ the Virgin, Miss 4 576 wept for ⲡⲥ. ⲉⲃ. of Petronius.

—— ϩⲁⲃⲟⲗ *S* tr, *draw forth, along*: LMär 27 ⲁϥⲥⲁⲕϥ ϩ. ⲉⲧⲉϩⲓⲏ.

—— ⲉⲡⲉⲥⲏⲧ *SAB* intr, *flow down*: Mich 550 39 *S* sweat c. ⲉⲡ. upon brick, Mor 31 24 *S* blood c. ⲉⲡ. like water ; tr, *bring down*: Jer 29 10 *S*(*B* ⲱϣⲧ) κατασύρ. ; Lam 5 10 *S*(*BF* diff) συσπᾶσθαι ; Hos 7 12 *A*(*B* ⲓⲛⲓ), Ob 3 *A*(*B* ⲣⲱϭⲓ) κατάγ. ; BHom 48 *S* συνέλκ. ; Z 351 *S* bowels ⲥⲉⲕ ⲥⲡⲟϥ ⲉⲡ.

—— ⲉⲡϣⲱⲓ *B* intr, *bring up*: MG 25 11 ⲉϥⲥ. ⲡⲉⲙⲱⲟⲩ ⲉⲡ. to heaven ἀνέρχεσθαι εἰς ; tr, Jo 21 6 (*S* ⲉϩⲣⲁⲓ) ἕλκ. ; Is 46 4 ἀναλαμβ. ; Hab 1 15 (*A* ⲧⲱⲕⲙⲉ) ἀνασπᾶν ; TstAb 254 ⲁϥⲥⲉⲕ ⲡⲉϥⲥⲁ‑ⲗⲁⲩϫ ⲉⲡ. (Ge 49 33 *B* ϥⲁⲓ ⲉⲭⲉⲛ-), Va 61 94 ⲥⲟⲕⲕ ⲉⲡ. *draw back, aside* till he pass thee = P 131ᵃ 83 *S* ⲥⲁϩⲱⲕ ⲉϩⲣⲁⲓ, C 86 146 ⲁⲥⲥⲟⲕⲥ ⲉⲡ. on road ; as nn : Ex 37 19 ἐκτείνειν ἄνωθεν.

—— ⲉⲡⲁϩⲟⲩ, ⲉⲫ. *SB, draw back*: Cant 1 3 *S* ἕλκ. ὀπίσω ; Aeg 241 *S* your wrath ⲥⲟⲕϥ ⲛⲏⲧⲛ ⲉⲡ. ἀνακρούειν ; C 89 126 *B* worldly cares ⲉⲧⲥ. ⲙⲙⲟⲟⲩ ⲉⲫ., Sh(Besa)Bor 205 701 *S* ⲉⲡⲥ. ⲛⲛⲉⲡⲉⲣⲏⲩ ⲉⲡ.

—— ⲉⲑⲏ *S*, ⲉⲧϩⲏ *B, go forward*: J 91 13 *S* child

recovered ⲁϥⲥ. ⲉ. ⲕⲟⲅⲓ ⲕⲟⲅⲓ, EW 218 B rubric c. ⲉ. ⲯⲁⲗⲓ *continue with* (?) chant from Theotokia.

—— ⲉϧⲟⲩⲛ S, ⲉ̅ⲥ. B *intr, draw, go in*: Ge 24 65 B(S ⲙⲟⲟϣⲉ ⲉⲧⲱⲙⲡⲧ) πορεύεσθαι εἰς συνάντησιν, Jer 17 20 B(S ⲡⲏⲩ ⲉϧ.) εἰσπ., Va 57 210 B must needs ⲥⲱⲕⲓ ⲛⲁⲛ ⲉ̅ⲥ. ⲉⲡⲉⲫⲣⲏⲧ συλλέγειν; ShC 42 159 S water c. ⲉϧ. ⲉϧⲉⲛⲥⲱϣⲉ, BMis 472 S footprints ⲉⲩⲥ. ⲉϧ. ϧⲁⲟⲩⲕⲱϣ ⲙⲡⲉⲧⲣⲁ; tr, *draw, lead in*: CaiEuch 393 B ⲡⲓϧⲟⲣⲙⲏ ⲉⲧⲥ. ⲙⲙⲟⲡ ⲉ̅ⲥ. to sin πρός no vb; Aeg 242 S ϣⲁⲥⲥ. ⲙⲡⲣⲱⲙⲉ ⲉϧ. to blasphemy ἄγειν πρός, ShA 2 117 S not ashamed ⲉⲥ. ⲉϧ. ⲡⲁⲩ ⲛⲛ̄ⲧⲟⲡ of garments, ShC 42 160 S trenches ⲉⲩⲥⲉⲕ ⲙⲟⲟⲩ ⲉϧ. ⲉϧⲉⲛⲥⲱϣⲉ, Va 63 10 B ⲥⲉⲕⲟⲏⲡⲟⲩ ⲉ̅ⲥ. ⲉⲣⲟⲓ= BMis 393 S ϧⲱⲡ ⲉϧ. ⲉⲣⲟⲓ; as nn: Hos 4 19 A(B ϥⲟⲛϧ) συστροφή.

—— ⲉϩⲣⲁⲓ S, -ⲏⲓ B, *draw up*: tr, Ez 29 4 S(B ⲛϣ̄ⲣ-ⲏⲓ *sic* ?) ἀναγ.; Jo 21 6 S(B ⲉⲡϣⲱⲓ) ἕλκ.; LCyp 8 S ⲡⲉⲧⲥ. ⲉϧ. earth & stones ἀνιμᾶν; ShA 2 73 S shepherd ⲥⲉⲕ ⲙⲟⲟⲩ ⲉϧ. for flock, Va 58 151 B ⲉⲥϭⲟⲥⲓ ⲡⲥⲟⲕⲉ ⲉϧ. (*sc net*), BIF 14 166 S ⲥⲉⲕⲧⲏⲩⲧⲛ̄ ⲉϧ.... ⲁⲩⲥⲉⲕⲟⲩ & gave him place; intr, ShP 130¹ 37 S sitting ⲉⲩⲥ. ⲉϧ. ⲉϫⲡⲟⲩⲙⲁ ⲉⲩϫⲟⲥⲉ; ⲉϩⲣⲁⲓ S, ⲉϧ̄ⲣ-ⲏⲓ B, ⲉϧ. BF, *draw down*: intr, Eccl 1 5 SF(PMich 3520) ἕλκ. εἰς, Mor 16 22 S rivers c. ⲉϧ. ⲉⲣⲟⲥ (*sc sea*), var BMis 192 ϧⲁⲧⲉ ⲉⲡⲉⲥⲏⲧ ⲉ-), C 43 72 B honey ⲉⲩⲥ. ⲉ̅ⲥ. ⲉⲧⲁϣⲃ̄ⲃⲓ, J 80 46 S ⲉϥⲡⲁⲥ. ⲉϧ. ϧⲁⲡⲉⲕⲣⲓⲙⲁ; tr, Va 57 265 B ⲉϧ. καθέλκ.; MG 25 21 B if thou see one going up to heaven in thoughts ⲥⲟⲕϥ ⲉϧ.; doubtful: Mor 52 53 S ⲁⲩⲥⲟⲕϥ ⲉϧ. ⲡⲥⲁⲡⲉϥⲟⲩⲉⲣⲏⲧⲉ *dragged him along by feet*, PLond 4 435 S conscripts ⲧⲁⲣⲟⲩⲥ. ⲡⲉⲩⲧⲁϩⲓⲧ(ⲓⲟ)ⲡ ⲉϧ. ϧⲱⲥ ⲛⲉⲉϥ *submit to, perform*.

—— nn m SB, *drawing, attraction*: BG 65 S ⲡⲥ. ⲛⲧⲡⲟⲣⲛⲓⲁ, K 12 B ⲡⲓⲥ. جذب (*sic l*). V c. ⲉⲃⲟⲗ.

ⲣⲉϥⲥ. SB, *drawer*: Ez 27 8 SB ⲣ. ⲛⲡⲟⲩⲟⲥⲣ (κωπ)ηλάτης; Deu 16 18 S ⲣ. ϧⲛⲧⲧⲏⲩⲧⲛ -εισαγωγεύς; ⲣⲉϥⲥⲉⲕ-: FR 26 S ⲣ. ⲟⲩⲉⲗⲗⲉ, BMOr 8775 88 B ϩⲉⲣⲉⲧⲁⲣⲓⲟⲥ · ⲣ. ⲥ̄ϧⲁⲓ.

ϭⲓⲛ-, ϫⲓⲛⲥ. SB, *drawing, flowing*: Mk 6 48 B(S ⲥⲟϩⲣ) ἐλαύνειν; ClPr 54 46 S of river ῥεῦμα, Mor 19 4 S ⲧⲟ̄. of archer's bow = Miss 4 93 B, Lakân 43 B ⲡⲭ. ⲛⲁⲡ ⲡⲟⲩⲡⲓϧⲓ.

ⲥⲁⲕϩⲏⲧ S belongs ? here, v ϩⲏⲧ I s f; also ? ⲥⲁⲕⲥⲟⲩⲣⲉ S: PMich 3571 I sent ϣⲟⲗⲧⲉ ⲡⲥ.

ⲥⲁⲕⲥⲟⲩⲟ S nn, obscure: Ryl 289.

ⲥⲁⲕⲥⲟⲟⲩ S, epithet: MIF 59 348 ⲡⲉⲧⲣⲉ ⲯⲁⲕⲥⲟⲟⲩ *the 6-day faster* (?). In name (?) Ψακϧόι (PLond 4 376).

ⲥⲕ ⲡⲟⲩϩ nn v ⲡⲟⲩϩ.

V ⲥⲟⲕⲥⲉⲕ.

ⲥⲓⲕⲉ SA, -ⲕⲓB(C41), ⲥⲉⲕⲧ-S', ⲥⲓ., ⲥⲁⲕⲧ∕S, ⲥⲉⲕⲧ∕ S', ⲥⲟⲕⲉ†, ⲥⲟⲟⲕⲉ† S, ⲥⲁⲕⲓ S' vb intr, *grind, pound*: Lev 24 2 ⲥⲟ.† (var ⲥⲟⲟ., B ⲧⲉⲡⲡⲏⲟⲩⲧ) κόπτειν; Mor

31 243 set him in ⲙⲁ ⲡⲡⲟⲩⲧ ⲉϥⲥ., WS 89 send us ⲥⲟⲩⲟ ⲡⲥ., RE 9 176 ⲁⲣϣⲓⲛ ⲉϥⲥⲟⲕⲉ, BKU 1 21 12 S' ⲡⲁⲡⲉⲓ ⲉⲧⲥ.†; tr: LAp 334 ⲡⲧⲉⲣⲉϥⲥ. ⲡ...ⲙⲁⲥⲧⲓⲭⲉ κόπ.; ShA 2 172 sickness ⲉϥⲥ. ⲡⲡⲉϥⲥⲁⲣϧ, C 41 16 B ⲉⲩⲥ. ⲙⲡⲓⲱⲓⲕ, Ep 297 ⲡⲥⲉⲥⲓⲕⲧ ⲟⲩⲙⲁ̄ⲭⲉ ⲡⲥⲟⲩⲟ ⲡⲥⲉⲡⲁⲧⲉ ⲛ̄ⲡⲟⲉⲓⲧ (*dele* n 2 there), BKU 1 21 20 S' ⲡⲧⲉⲥⲉⲕⲧ (l ⲡⲧⲥ.) ⲡⲁⲡⲉⲓ ⲕⲁⲗⲟⲥ, AZ 23 109 ingredients ⲥⲁⲕⲧⲟⲩ ⲙⲡⲡⲉⲩⲉⲣⲏⲩ, Bodl(P) a 32 ⲥⲉⲕⲧϥ (var ib a 1 a ⲉⲛⲟϥ), Miss 8 219 ⲁⲩⲥⲁⲕⲧⲩ (*sc martyr*) in mill-wheel.

ⲕⲟⲧ ⲡⲥ. S, *mill-wheel i e stone*: WTh 199 ⲟⲩⲕ. ⲡⲥⲉⲕⲱⲧⲉ ⲙⲙⲟϥ ϩⲓϫⲱⲟⲩ (martyrs), BIF 14 163 weight basket with ⲟⲩⲕ. ⲙⲁ ⲡⲥ. S, *grinding place, mill*: BMOr 6201 B 202; ⲱⲡⲉ, -ⲓ ⲡⲥ. SAB, *grinding stone*: Deu 24 6 S(B ⲙⲏⲭⲁⲡⲏ) μύλος, Lu 17 2 SA(Cl, B ⲱ. ⲙⲙⲟⲩⲅⲗⲟⲡ) λίθος μυλικός, Jud 9 53 S ἐπιμύλιον; C 41 16 B cast grain into ⲡⲓⲱ. ⲡⲥ., BKU 1 21 1 S' ⲡⲱ. ⲡⲥⲉⲕⲧ ⲟⲩϫⲛϭⲉ ⲉϥⲧⲁⲣϣⲡⲉ ⲡⲱⲡⲉ ⲡϫⲉϫ ⲟⲩϫⲛϭⲉ ⲉϥⲕⲏⲙⲡⲉ.

—— nn S, *grinding*: ShC 73 146 overseer of ⲡⲥ. ⲛ ⲡⲡⲟⲩⲧ.

ⲥⲱⲕⲓ B v ⲥⲱⲕ.

ⲥⲕⲁⲓ S, ⲥⲕⲉ A A² F, ⲥϫⲁⲓ B, ⲥⲉⲕ-, ⲥⲟⲕ∕ S, ⲥϫⲏⲧ∕ B vb intr, *plough*: Job 1 14 SB, Is 45 9 SB, Lu 17 7 SBF(Mor 30 1) ἀροτριᾶν, Hos 10 11 A(B Gk diff) arare; R 2 4 61 S ⲉⲩⲥ. ϧⲡⲡⲉⲩⲥⲱϣⲉ; Mun 66 S lame feet ⲉⲩⲥ. ϧⲓⲡⲕⲁϩ (l ⲥⲱⲕ), Mani 1 A² ⲡⲉⲧϫⲟ ⲉⲧⲥ.; tr: Is 7 25 S ⲥⲉⲕ- B, Mic 3 12 SAB ἀρ.; BMis 261 S ⲉⲧⲣⲉϥⲥ. ⲙⲡⲕⲁϩ with plough; Job 39 10 B (l ⲥⲱⲕ as S) ἕλκειν; c ⲡ- *plough with, by means of*: Deu 22 10 SB ἀρ. ἐν, Ryl 438 B ⲉϥⲥ. ϩⲛ̄ ⲡⲣⲉϩⲓ of oxen (3 Kg 19 19); c ϩⲛ-, ϫⲉⲛ- sim: Jud 14 18 S ἀρ. ἐν; BerlOr 1607 1 109 S ⲉϥⲥ. ϩⲛⲟⲩⲥⲟⲉⲓϣ of oxen, C 43 5 B sim ϫⲉⲛⲡⲉϥⲧⲉ̄ⲃⲛⲱⲟⲩⲓ, cf ib c. ⲡⲉⲙⲡⲉϥⲧ.; as nn: DeV 2 237 B no tilling nor c. nor vintage, Kr 92 S undertakes to ⲧⲓ c. ⲥⲡⲁⲩ to field. ϧⲃⲃⲉ ⲡⲥ. S; Berl lc 110, ST 118; ⲥⲓⲛⲉ ⲡⲥ. SA, *ploughshare* (?): Joel 3 10 SA(B ϧⲉⲃⲓ), Mic 4 3 S(A ⲉⲙⲉ, B do) ἄροτρον, Jud 3 31 S ἀροτρόπους (var ἄροτρον); ⲣⲉϥⲥ. SB, *ploughman, who ploughs*: Is 61 5 SB ἀροτήρ, Bodl copt g 1 S ⲧⲃⲡⲟⲟⲩⲉ ⲛⲣ.

ⲥⲕⲉ v ⲥⲕⲉⲡ.

ⲥⲁⲕⲃⲓ F vb intr: LAp 541, var ⲥⲱϧⲣ. V ⲡⲟⲩϫⲕ.

ⲥⲕⲁⲗⲕⲗ F v ⲥⲕⲟⲣⲕⲣ.

ⲥⲕⲉⲗⲁⲕⲓⲣ v ⲥⲕⲟⲣⲕⲣ (ⲥⲕⲁⲣⲁⲕⲓⲣ).

ⲥⲕⲓⲙ SS'AF, ⲥϭ. S, ⲥϫⲓⲙ B nn m, *discoloured, grey hair*: sg Sa 4 9 S, Va 61 220 B ⲡⲥ. ⲁⲡⲡⲉ ⲡⲓϣⲱⲓ ⲉⲑⲟⲩⲟⲃϣ ⲁⲗⲗⲁ ⲡⲥ. ⲡⲉ ϯⲁⲣⲉⲧⲏ πολιά; K 76 B ⲡⲥ.

شيب, ShBor 246 85 *S* great age & ογc. επαϣωϥ, Cl
Pr 47 3 *S* αcογⲃⲁϣ ϩⲁⲡⲉc., MG 25 325 *B* grown old
ϫⲁⲧϥϩ ⲗⲙⲓc.;   pl Sa 2 10 *S*, Is 47 2 *SB*, Hos 7 9
S(ShC 73 182)*B* π., MG 25 254 *B* ⲉⲧⲁϥⲟⲩⲱⲙ ⲛ-
ⲡⲉϥc. πολιόφαγος, AM 219 *B* sim (but *l* ? πολυφά-
γος, *v* MélOr 5 567); ShA 1 102 *S* ⲧⲉⲩⲙⲛⲧϧⲉⲗⲗⲟ
ⲛ ⲡⲉⲩc., MG 25 129 *B* ⲡⲉⲕc. ceoⲩⲃⲁϣ, ClPr 29
244 *S* ⲡⲉc. of his head;   as adj : El 120 *S* ⲟⲩⲧⲥⲉ
ⲛⲥ̇. = *ib* 90 *A*, Va 58 140 *B* our age & ⲡⲉⲛϫⲁⲉ
ⲛc., PMich 4946 *Sf* ⲛⲛⲏⲓ ⲛⲥ. ⲛⲛⲏⲓ ⲛⲁⲧϣⲁⲗ *grey-
haired fleas, toothless fleas*;   with vb : R 2 2 26 *S*
face young but heart ⲡ c., HL 90 *B* ⲉⲩⲣⲏⲧ ⲛⲥ.,
Mor 41 55 *S* ⲉⲧⲣⲉⲟⲩⲃⲁϣ ⲛⲥ.;   ⲣⲙ-, ⲗⲉⲙc.
SF, grey-haired man : Mor 40 11 *S* in likeness of
ⲟⲩⲣ. ⲡⲉⲕⲏⲡⲧⲓⲟⲥ = *ib* 39 15 *F* = C 43 41 *B* ⲣⲱⲙⲓ
ⲛc., Mor 31 11 *S* ϧⲗⲗⲟ ⲡⲣ.; ⲣⲙⲛ-, ⲣⲉⲙc. *SB* :
Lev 19 32 *SB* πολιός, Si 25 6 *S* πολιά; BMOr
6954 (35) *S* ⲣⲱⲙⲉ ⲡⲣ.

сκ̇ϫ̇κ̇ιϫ̇ *S* nn m: Mor 51 41 insubordinate
monk called ⲡⲉϩⲧⲟ ⲛϣⲉ ⲡⲉc., latter explained as
ⲡⲉⲧⲟ ⲛⲥⲙⲟⲧ ⲙⲡⲁⲣⲧⲁⲗⲓc, so ? *spotted* (? redupl from
сκ̇ιϫ̇).

соκ̇ⲙⲁϫⲓ *B* nn m, *long table* : K 151 among
furniture ⲟⲩc. (var ⲛⲓc.) طبلداش طويل (var om '.b).

сκ̇ⲉⲡ (? сκⲉ ⲡ-), сκⲉⲡϩ *B* nn, *side* (?), with ⲉ-,
ⲉcκⲉⲡ, prep *beside* : Ge 41 17 (var ϧⲓc., *S* ⲉϫⲛ-)ἐπί,
Ex 19 17 ὑπό, Deu 2 36(*S* ϩⲁϧⲧⲛ-), Pro 7 8 (*SA* do),
Mk 3 7 (var & *S* ⲉ-) παρά, Jer 29 7 ⲉϫⲉⲛⲉc. ⲫⲓⲟⲙ
(so all MSS, *l* ? ⲉϫ. ⲛⲓc. ⲛⲫ., *S* ⲉϫⲛⲙⲙⲁ ⲉⲧϩⲓϫⲛ-)
ἐπὶ τὰς παραθαλασσίους; MG 25 92 ⲉϥⲉⲛⲕⲟⲧ ⲉc.
ⲛⲓⲣⲱⲙⲓ, *ib* 251 cell ⲉc. ⲛⲛⲓϣϯ ⲛϣⲁϥⲉ, C 41 67
came south ⲉc. ϣⲙⲓⲛ, PO 11 365 standing ⲉcⲕⲛ-
ⲧⲕ;   with ϧⲓ-: Is 19 5 (*S* ϩⲁⲧⲛ-), Mt 4 13 (*S*
do), or ⲓ-: Ge 36 37 παρά, MG 25 236 ⲁϥϩⲱⲗ ⲓc.
ⲧⲉϥⲙⲁⲩ.

сκⲉⲡϩⲟ, *good appearance* (?): Gal 6 12 ϭⲓ c.(var
ϭⲓ ⲛⲥ., *S* ⲧⲣⲉⲡϩⲟ ca) εὐπροσωπεῖν.   Same word ?
V Rec 34 157.

сκⲉⲛⲉⲡⲓcⲉ *v* coϧⲛ.

сκ̇ⲛⲁⲡ *S* nn, *stale* (?) of bread : CA 101 oⲉⲓⲛ ⲛⲥ.
not to be used as offering but fresh & newly baked
= *ib* ⲣo *inf* قد فضل من امس.

сκⲟⲩⲣ *S* ? = ϣϭⲟⲣ, ϣκⲁⲣ *q v*.

сκⲟⲣκⲣ *S*, сκⲁⲣκⲣⲉ *A*, сκⲉⲣκⲉⲣ *B*, сκⲁⲗκⲗ
(also сⲗⲉϭⲗⲉϭ), сκⲁⲣκⲣ *F*, сκⲣⲕⲣ- *S*, [сκⲉⲗ]κⲱⲗ-
F, сκⲣⲕⲱⲣϩ *S*, сκⲉ.ϩ *B*, сκⲉⲣκⲱⲣϯ *SB*, -ⲟⲣⲧϯ *S*,
сκⲣⲕⲣϯ (?) *A²* vb I intr, *roll, be rolled* : Am 5 24 *B*
κυλίειν; Ps 16 13 *F* сⲗ. (*SB* ⲧⲁϧⲟ ⲉϩⲣⲁⲓ) ὑποσκελίζειν; He 2 1 *F* сⲗ. (*S* ϩⲁⲁⲧⲉ, *B* ⲣⲓκⲓ ⲉⲃⲟⲗ) παραρρέειν; ShA 2 299 *S* ⲉϥc.ϯ & weeping, ROC 23 285

B pillars ⲁⲩc. till reached stadium, ShBM 263 3 *S*
slew him & left him ⲉϥcκⲣ[κⲟ]ⲣⲧ ⲙⲙⲁⲩ, ShMun
96 *S* fell sick & ⲡⲉϥcκⲣⲕⲟⲣⲧ ⲉϥⲙⲟκϩ, BM 185 *S*
mount (? monastery) of Pelusium is ⲟⲩⲧⲟⲟⲩ ⲉϥc.ϯ
steep (?), Va 58 177 *B* c. as rubric in margin, *ib* later
ϫⲁⲕ ⲉⲃⲟⲗ (*cf* cⲱκ II *sf*).

II tr : Pro 26 27 *SA*, Am 2 13 b *B*(*S* intr, *A* [ϯ-
κⲉ]) κυλ., Mt 28 2 *SBF* ἀποκ.; Ryl 94 *S* ⲛcⲉcκⲣκⲣ
ⲡⲕⲟⲧ upoⲛ which martyr bound, BM 1145 *S* ⲁⲩ-
(c)κⲉⲣκⲟⲣ ϩ(ⲉ)ⲡκⲟⲩⲓ ⲧⲉϥⲡⲟⲟⲩⲉ[(meaning ?).

   With following preposition. c ⲉⲣⲡ- *S*, roll at,
upon : Jos 10 18 κ. ἐπί, Mk 15 46 (*B* ⲉⲣⲱϫ ⲛ-) προσκ.
ἐπί = Mt 27 60 (*B* ⲉⲣⲱϫ) προσκ. dat ; c ⲉϫⲉⲛ- *B*
intr, *roll, loll upon* : Va 57 129 ⲉⲩc. ⲉ. ϩⲁⲡcⲧⲣⲟⲙ-
ⲡⲏ κατακλίνεσθαι ; tr. *roll upon* : AM 143 ⲛcⲉc. ⲛⲛⲏ
ⲉⲑⲟⲩⲁⲃ ⲉϫⲱϥ (*i e* torture bed) ; c ϫⲁⲣⲁⲧϫ *B*,
roll below : Va 63 97 ⲉcc. ϫⲁⲣⲁⲧc ⲛϯκⲁκⲓⲁ ῥίπτεσθαι
ἐπί ; c ϩⲁ- *F*, Am 2 13 sim (JEA 11 246, *S* tr, *B*
cⲁⲡⲉcⲛⲧ ⲛ-, *A* ϯκⲉ ϩⲁ-) κ. ὑποκάτω ; c ϩⲛ-,
ϧⲉⲛ- *SB*, roll in intr : Pro 7 18 *B*(*S* ϩⲱⲗϭ) ἐγκυλ.
dat ; ShA 2 97 *S* ⲡⲉⲧc.ϯ ϩⲓⲙⲡϣⲱⲡⲉ, *ib* 322 *S* ⲉⲓⲛⲏϫ
ⲉⲓc.ϯ ϩⲓⲙⲙⲁ ⲡⲓⲕⲟⲧⲕ, *ib* 30 *S* ⲉⲩc.ϯ in dwellings like
burnt bush ⲉⲧⲛⲏϫ in field, Va 61 96 *B* ⲉκc.ϯ ϧⲉⲛ-
ⲡⲓⲙϩⲁⲩ, Mor 25 17 *S* ⲉκc.ϯ ϩⲓⲙⲡⲉⲓⲟⲙⲉ = Va 61
99 ⲟⲩⲉcⲟⲱⲡ ⲉⲃⲟⲗ, P 131¹ 74 *S* Jordan ⲡⲏⲧ ⲛ ⲉϥ-
(c)κⲣⲕⲱⲣ ϩⲛ- its channel ; tr : BMar 80 *S* ⲁⲩcκⲣ-
κⲱⲣϥ ϩⲛⲡⲧⲁⲫⲟc ; ϩⲣⲁⲓ ϩⲛ-, ⲛϩⲣⲏⲓ ϧⲉⲛ- : 2 Pet 2
22 *B*(*S* c. nn) εἰς κυλισμόν ; ShA 2 113 *S* ⲉⲧⲉⲧⲛc.ϯ ϩ.
ϩⲓⲙⲡⲉϣⲁⲛϣ ; ⲉⲃⲟⲗ ϩⲛ-, ϧⲉⲛ-, roll from : Lu 24 2
S(*B* cⲁⲃⲟⲗ, var ⲉⲃ. ϩⲓⲣⲉⲛ-) ἀποκ. ἀπό, Jer 28 25 *B*
κατακ. ἀπό ; c ϩⲓⲣⲡ- *S*, meaning same : Ge 29
3 *S*(*B* ⲉⲃ. ϩⲓⲣⲉⲛ-) ἀποκ. ἀπό ; ⲉⲃ. ϩⲓⲣⲉⲛ- *B* : BSM
18 ⲉⲁⲩc. ⲙⲡⲓⲱⲛⲓ ⲉⲃ. ϩⲓⲣⲱϥ of tomb ; c ϩⲓϫⲛ-
SA²B, roll upon intr : Jth 14 15 *S* ῥίπ. ἐπί, AP 11
A² ⲡⲉc(c)κⲣκⲣⲡⲉ ϩ. ⲡⲙⲁ where Paul was κυλ. ἐπί
gen ; tr : ShA 1 44 *S* tortured them ϣⲁⲛⲧⲟⲩcκⲣ-
κⲱⲣⲟⲩ ϩ. ⲡκⲁϩ, C 43 140 *B* caused them c. ⲙϥⲛ
ⲉⲑⲟⲩⲁⲃ ϩⲓϫⲱc (sc fiery trench) ; ⲉⲃⲟⲗ ϩ. *S*, *from
off* : Jth 13 9 ἀποκ. ἀπό ; ShC 42 162 stone fallen
on some, others cκⲣκⲱⲣϥ ⲉⲃ. ϩⲓϫⲱⲟⲩ.

   With following adverb. c ⲉⲃⲟⲗ *S*, *roll away* :
ShA 1 461 like stone he will cκⲣκⲱⲣκ ⲉⲃ. ⲉⲡⲟⲩⲉ,
Gu 103 about to die κⲛⲁcκⲣⲕⲱⲣκ ⲉⲃ. shalt stretch
forth hands, be bound & borne to tomb ; c ⲉⲡ-
ⲉcⲏⲧ *S*, *roll down* : Miss 4 767 ⲁϥcκⲉⲣκⲱⲣⲉϥ ⲉⲡ.
ⲉⲩⲉⲓⲁ, BSG 182 rolled stone ϩⲛⲟⲩⲙⲁ ⲉϥc.ϯ ⲉⲡ. c
ⲉϩⲣⲁⲓ *S*, meaning same : ShC 73 150 not suffering
us ⲉc. ⲉϩ. ⲉⲡⲉϩⲉⲓⲧ, BMOr 8802 6 (Severus Ant)
ⲛⲏc. ⲉϩ. ⲉⲩϩⲱⲃ ⲉⲙⲉϣϣⲉ.

ⲣⲉϥc. *S*, *roller* : ShWess 9 145 ⲛⲣⲉϥcκⲣκⲣ ⲱⲡⲉ
ⲉϩⲣⲁⲓ ⲉⲡⲉⲓⲟⲟⲩⲉ.

—— nn m *S*, *rolling* : 2 Pet 2 22 *S*(*B* vb) κυλι-
σμός.

ⲥⲕⲁⲣⲁⲕⲓⲣ[1], ⲥⲕⲟⲣ.[2], ⲥⲕⲉⲗ.[3] *S*, ⲥⲕⲉⲣⲁⲕⲓⲣ *B* nn,
steep place, slope : Si 25 22[1] *S* ἀνάβασις, cit R 2 4
84[3] *S*, P 44 119[1] = 43 126[1] *S* غزِ (misunderstood),
Mic 1 4 *B* ⲙⲁ ⲛⲥ. (*S* ⲙⲁ ⲛⲉⲓ ⲉⲃⲟⲗ) καταβ., BIF 13
111 *S* reached place ⲉϥⲟ ⲛⲥ.[2] = MG 25 301 *B* ⲟⲓ
ⲛϩⲁⲗⲁⲓ = P ar 4793 146 حدَ (Polotsky). *V* KKS
331.

ⲥⲕⲟⲣⲕⲉⲣ *B* nn m, *beer* : K 131 *B* ⲛⲓⲥ. (var ⲥⲕⲉⲣ.)
مزر (*sic* MS). Same ? Cai 42573 2 *S* throw ingredients into wine or ⲟⲩⲥⲕⲟⲩⲣⲕⲟⲩⲣ, *ib* 1 ⲡⲉⲥⲕⲟⲩⲣⲕⲣ.

ⲥⲉⲕⲥⲓⲕ *B* nn, *sunny place, room* : Montp 207
مشرقة .

ⲥⲟⲕⲥⲉⲕ *SB*, ⲥⲉⲕⲥⲉⲕ- *SB* (?), ⲥⲉⲕⲥⲟⲕⲋ *S* vb tr,
pull (v ⲥⲱⲕ), *gather* : Aeg 17 *S* ⲡⲉⲕⲙⲁⲁϫⲉ ⲁⲓⲥⲟⲕϥ
...ⲁⲕⲥ. ⲡⲁⲙⲁⲁϫⲉ, Ryl 102 *S* adjuration of iron
ⲡⲉⲛⲧⲁⲩⲥⲟⲕϥ ⲁⲩⲥⲉⲕⲥⲟⲕϥ & made thereof a spear,
K 233 *B* = P 54 107 *B* ⲁⲩⲥⲉⲕⲥⲉⲕ (obj of vb om)
حسبوا , لقطوا ; as nn m *B*, *yawn* (stretching mouth) :
K 160 ⲡⲓⲥⲟⲕⲥⲉⲕ (*sic*) تشاوب . ⲣⲉϥⲥ. *B*, *collector* :
K 111 (var ⲣⲉϥϭⲓ ⲱⲡ) جابي للحسوب .

ⲥⲉⲕⲧ- *v* ⲥⲓⲕⲉ.

ⲥⲉⲕⲱⲧ *v* ⲕⲱⲧ *s f*.

ⲥⲉⲕⲉϩ *B* vb tr, *clear out* a house : Lev 14 36 (*S*
wanting) ⲥ. ⲙⲡⲏⲓ ἀποσκευάζειν فرّغ . Same ? WS
90 *S* send camels ⲛⲥⲉⲥⲉⲕⲉϩ ⲛⲛⲉⲓⲃⲏⲧ.

ⲥⲓⲕⲏϩⲉ *S* vb tr, meaning unknown : PMéd 230
ⲟⲩⲭⲣⲏⲙⲁⲡⲉ ⲉⲕⲱ ⲟⲛⲛⲉⲕⲧⲁⲙⲓⲟⲛ...ⲥ. ⲙⲙⲟϥ ⲛⲧⲟⲟ-
ⲟⲧⲕ ϩⲱⲥ ⲭⲣⲏⲙⲁ *put it aside, treasure it* (?).

ⲥⲉⲓⲗ *F* *v* ⲥⲓⲣ.

ⲥⲟⲗ *SB*, ⲥⲁⲗ *AF* nn m, *wick* : Is 42 3 *SB*, Mt
12 20 *SB* λίνον ; Tri 508 *S* ⲛⲥ. ⲛⲧⲁⲗⲩϫⲛⲓⲁ فتل ;
ShIF 273 *S* ⲛⲥ. ⲉⲧⲣⲧⲙⲧⲱⲙ, DeV 2 153 *B* ⲛϥⲁⲛⲟⲥ
fitted with oil &c., Mor 50 14 *F* sim, HL 117 *B*
ⲉⲣⲉⲛⲥ. ⲙⲟϩ, C 89 214 *B* mice eat c. of ϩⲏⲃⲥ ; ⲙⲁ
ⲛϯ c. Zech 4 12 *SAB* μυξωτήρ ; PMéd 126, 162
S wad, plug as suppository &c (v 129 n) ; cf ⲥⲁϩ *awl*.

ⲥⲱⲗ *SB*, ⲥⲟⲗⲋ *B*, ⲥⲏⲗ† *S* vb tr, *dissipate, pervert* :
Job 21 18 *B* (*S* ϥⲓ) ὑφαιρεῖσθαι ; ⲥ ⲉⲃⲟⲗ *S* : ShZ
516 ⲟⲩⲅⲏⲧ ⲉϥⲥ.† ⲉⲃ. (cf Pro 6 14 διεστραμμένος,
not 18 τεκταινόμενος, *B* ⲫⲟⲛⲭ), Mus 42 234 sim
(AZ 25 68 *l* ⲃⲱⲗ) ; intr ⲥ ⲉϩⲣⲏⲓ *B* : RAI 84 ⲁϥⲥ.
ⲉⲃ. in thoughts of his heart (var DeV 1 192 ⲉⲣ
ⲥⲁⲃⲟⲗ ⲙⲡⲓϣⲓ).

ⲥⲗⲁ *v* ⲣⲡⲱ.

ⲥⲗⲏ *B* nn f, *coffin* : Ge 50 26 (*S* ⲧⲁⲓⲃⲉ), Job 21
32, Lu 7 14 (*S* ϭⲗⲟϭ) σορός ; K 135 نعش , ⲑⲉⲃⲓ
نقير , *ib* 254 do, ⲕⲁⲓⲥⲓ كفن ; C 86 225 ⲟⲩⲥ. ⲛⲱⲛ
wherein corpses, FR 112 sim.

ⲥⲁⲗⲟ, -ⲱ, ⲥⲁⲣⲟ *S* nn f, *basket* : Kr 247 ⲥⲛⲧⲉ ⲛⲥ.,
PMich 529 ⲟⲩⲥ. ⲛⲁⲡⲁ...ⲟⲩ ⲙⲛⲥⲟⲛ, Win 28 ⲉⲧⲁⲛ-
ⲡⲟⲛⲟⲩ ⲉⲃⲟⲗ ⲉⲣⲟ]ⲧⲛ ⲉⲛⲥ., Ep 531 -ⲱ ⲛⲕⲁⲕⲉ, ST
263 -ⲱ, PLond 4 508 ⲕⲟⲩⲓ ⲛⲥⲁⲣⲟ ⲉⲥⲙⲏϩ ⲡⲉⲧⲧⲉⲓ.
Cf قفة , ܠܡ (κανοῦν in Ge 40 16) & Almk 2 63.

ⲥⲓⲗⲓ *B* nn f, meaning uncertain : K 126 ϯⲥ. للاَ
(var للاَ) rod fixed in drum of loom to secure lower
end of web (so Kabis AZ 13 137). Is ? the Ar
word.

ⲥⲟⲩⲗⲓ, ⲥⲟⲗⲓ *B* nn f, *veil, covering* : K 118 ⲥⲟ.
(so all MSS) ملاءة , مقنعة ; *saddle-cloth* : *ib* 136 ϯⲥⲟⲩ.
مرشحة (1 var + بردعة). In P 45 144 مر ⲕⲟⲡⲣⲓⲧⲟⲩⲣⲓⲛ
(κοπριτόριον coopertorium, cf P 44 84).

ⲥⲛⲗⲃⲓ *F* *v* ⲥⲣϫⲉ.

ⲥⲱⲗⲕ *B*, -ⲗϫ *S* (once), ⲥⲟⲗⲕⲋ *B* vb intr, *cleave,
adhere* : AM 171 he set heads on bodies ⲁⲩⲥ. ; ⲥ
ⲉ- : Va 61 15 cord ⲁϥⲥ. ⲉⲣⲱⲟⲩ (sc ⲡⲉⲡⲥⲁⲣϩ) κολλᾶσθαι ; ShC 42 76 *S* causeth not blood of unruly
children to c. ⲉⲛϭⲉⲣⲱⲃ but permitteth punishments worse than whippings, C 86 221 flesh c. ⲉ-
ⲡⲉⲛⲁϩϫⲓ of saw, Aeg 57 grave-clothes c. ⲉϩⲟⲩⲛ
ⲉⲡⲉⲥⲥⲱⲙⲁ ; tr, *make cleave, join* : Rec 6 173
ⲁϥⲥⲱⲗⲕ (*sic* MS) ⲙⲙⲁ that he had opened =
BMar 209 *S* ⲧⲱϭⲉ, C 86 155 dragon's skin ⲁⲩⲥⲟⲗⲕϥ
ⲉⲛⲓⲡⲩⲗⲏ. *Cf* ⲥⲱⲗϫ *smear*.

ⲥⲁⲗⲟⲩⲕⲓ *B* nn as pl, fish *petrocephalus* : K 171
ⲛⲥ. راس الجر (P 54 150 merely حيتان). *V* MIF 51
17, 33, cf JEA 14 30.

ⲥⲓⲗⲟⲩⲕⲓ *B* nn as pl, meaning unknown : MG 25
293 ϩⲁⲛⲕⲟⲩϫⲓ ⲛⲥ. ⲛⲃⲉⲛⲓ growing near swamp =
MIF 13 108 *S* ⲕⲟⲩⲓ ⲛϩⲛⲛⲉ = Gött Ar 114 201
merely نخيل .

ⲥⲓⲗⲓⲗ (not ⲉⲓⲗ.) *A*[2] nn, meaning unknown, ?*gleam* :
Mani 1 ⲡⲁⲏⲣ ϯ ⲟⲩⲛⲓⲣⲉ, ⲛⲟⲩⲁⲓⲛⲉ ϯ ⲟⲩⲥ., ⲡⲙⲁⲩ
ϯ ⲟⲩⲕⲃⲟ, *ib* ?c]ⲓⲗⲓⲗ ⲙⲡⲟⲩⲁⲓⲛⲉ.

ⲥⲗⲱⲗϫ *F* vb tr, meaning unknown : BP 3248
v ⲙⲓⲕⲉ a. *l* ?ⲥⲗⲱⲗⲉϥ (v ⲥⲟⲗⲥⲗ *adorn*).

ⲥⲱⲗⲁⲗⲉ *S* vb ?, meaning unknown : PStras 171
abusive references in letter ⲛⲧⲟϥ ⲡⲉⲧⲟ ⲛⲥⲁⲧⲁⲡⲁⲥ...
ⲟⲩⲣⲱⲙⲉ ⲛⲁⲧⲕⲗⲏⲡⲉ ⲟⲩϫⲉ ⲥ. ⲛⲧⲁϥ[ⲟⲩ]ⲱⲙ ⲁϥ ⲉⲧ-
ⲛⲏⲟ.

ⲥⲉⲗⲓⲗⲉⲛ, -ⲓⲛ *S* nn, *vulture* : P 44 56 = 43 23
ⲥ. ⲧⲁⲓⲁ · ⲧⲣⲉ اذخ . Coptic ?

ⲥⲱⲗⲙ, ⲥⲁⲗⲙ† *S*[f] vb intr, meaning unknown,
?*boil* : BKU 1 21 set fire beneath water till it be
hot ⲛⲃⲥ...., put dye-stuff ⲉⲛⲙⲁⲩ ⲉⲧⲋ.† & stir it.

ⲥⲱⲗⲡ *SAA*[2]*F*, -ⲉⲛ *B*, ⲥⲗⲡ-, ⲥⲉ. *S*, ˙ⲥⲁⲗⲉⲡ- *A*[2],
ⲥⲟⲗⲡⲋ *SB*, ⲥⲁ. *S*[f]*AF*, ⲥⲟⲗⲡ† *SB*, ⲣ c ⲥⲁⲗⲡ- *S* vb

I intr, *break, burst* (cf لسـ Dévaud): Is 33 23 *SBF* ῥηγνύναι, Eccl 4 12 *SB* (Miss 4 120) ἀπορ., EpJer 43 *B*(*F* tr), Va 57 227 *B* garments ⲉϣⲧⲉⲙⲥ. ⲓⲉ ⲛⲧⲟⲩϥⲱϣ διαρ., MG 25 16 *B* if brethren be overstrained ⲥⲉⲛⲁⲥ. προσρ.; Jer 4 20 *B* διασπᾶν; Ez 17 22 *B* ἀποκνίζειν; ShM!F 23 150 *S* cords ⲛⲧⲁⲩⲥ., AM 191 *B* ⲁϯϩⲱⲡⲛ ⲥ., TurM 9 *S* tumour ϣⲁⲥⲥⲱⲗⲡ, Bodl(P) e 13 *S* ⲡⲣⲟⲥ ⲛϣⲁⲁⲣ ⲉⲧⲁ(ϥ)ⲥ. *price that was decided* (?). ⲥ ⲛⲥⲁ- *B, tear at* or merely emphatic: Mt 12 1 (*S* ⲧⲱⲗⲕ, *F* ⲧⲱⲕⲗ ⲛⲥⲁ·) τίλλειν, C 86 155 ⲁⲩⲥ. ⲛⲥⲁⲡⲓϭⲱⲓ of beards, *ib* 275 nails ⲛⲁⲩⲥ. ⲛⲥⲁⲡⲓⲥⲁⲣⲝ. *V* also ⲥ. ⲉⲃⲟⲗ. ⲥ ϩⲓ- *S, cut, tear from*: Lu 5 36 (*B* ⲫⲱϣ ⲉⲃ. ϩⲉⲛ·) σχίζειν ἀπό, RE 14 28 thongs ⲛⲧⲁⲩⲥ. ϩⲓⲛⲉϩⲱⲱⲗⲉ. ⲥ ϩⲛ-, ϩⲉⲛ-, *be broken, separated from*: BAp 109 *S* ⲙⲡⲁⲧⲉⲛϣⲁϫⲉ ⲥ. ϩⲛⲣⲱⲓ (var BmOr 7561 62 ⲟⲩⲱ), Ryl 94 *S*, Miss 4 757 *S* (*sic l*) sim; *break in* midst: AM 43 *B* machine ⲥ. ϩⲉⲛⲧⲉϥⲙⲏϯ, KKS 542 *S* sim.

Qual *SB*: Lev 21 18 *S*(*B* ϫⲏϫⲓ ⲉⲃⲟⲗ) -τμητος, Ryl 374 *S* that thou depart not ϣⲁⲛⲧⲉⲙⲙⲟⲟⲩ ⲥ. ⲁⲛ (*i e* ⲟⲛ) refers? to irrigation; ⲥ ⲉ-: ST 251 *S* ⲛϣⲁⲁⲣ...ⲉⲩⲥ. ⲉⲧⲉϥⲙⲏⲧⲉ (cf ϩⲛ- above); ⲥ ⲉⲃⲟⲗ: Jud 1 7 ἀποκόπτεσθαι; BMis 542 *S* feet ⲥ. ⲉⲃ., C 43 8 *B* ⲉⲣⲉⲡⲉϥϭⲛⲁϩ ⲥ. ⲉⲃ.

II tr *SAA²BF, break, cut off*: Jer 5 5 *S*(*B* ⲫⲱϫⲓ), EpJer 43 *F*(*B* intr), Nah 1 13 *AB* διαρ.; Is 58 6 *B*(*S* ⲡⲱϩ), Mk 5 4 *SB* διασπ.; Z 300 *S* ⲙⲡⲉϥⲥ. ⲙⲡⲥⲉⲉⲡⲉ of fish κόπτειν, Jo 18 26 *SA²*(*B* ϫⲱϫⲓ ⲉⲃ.) ἀποκ., Mt 5 30 *S*(*B* ⲇⲟ) ἐκκ.; Ez 5 2 *B*(*S* ⲥⲟϫⲥϫ) κατακ.; Jo 15 2 *S*(*A* ϣⲱⲧ, *B* ⲕⲱⲣϫ) αἱρεῖν, 1 Kg 17 51 *S*(*B* ⲱⲗⲓ ⲉⲃ.) ἀφαι.; PS 180 *S* ⲁϥⲥ. ⲛⲡⲁⲙⲣⲣⲉ, BG 104 *S* ⲁⲓⲃⲱⲗ ⲙⲡⲥⲱⲛⲧ ⲁⲓⲥ. ⲙⲫⲱϩ ⲙⲡⲓⲣⲁⲟⲩ, DeV 2 283 *B* tool wherewith ⲉϣⲁⲩⲥ. ⲙⲡⲓⲣⲁⲧ ⲛϩⲏⲧϥ, PO 2 176 *Sᶠ* ear ⲛⲧⲁⲡⲉⲧⲣⲟⲥ ⲥⲁⲗⲡϥ, BM 1146 *S* about sale of wine & local taxes ⲧⲏⲧⲡⲉⲥ. ⲡⲁⲛⲙⲟⲥⲓⲟⲛ ⲉⲛⲓⲱⲣⲉ.

ⲡ ⲥ *S*: Lev 22 23 ⲥⲁⲗⲡⲥⲁⲧ (*B* ⲥⲃⲟⲕ ⲡⲉⲛⲧ) κολοβόκερκος, cit P 131¹ 52.

—— ⲉⲃⲟⲗ *SBF* a intr, *be cut, broken off*: Va 57 174 *B* wave ⲉⲩⲥ. ⲉⲃ. by winds διακόπ.; ShA 1 135 *S* limbs ⲁⲩⲥ. ⲉⲃ. from body, ShC 73 111 *S* hasten ⲉⲥ. ⲉⲃ. *break off* (work) & return to τόπος, Gu 61 *S* heads ⲥ. ⲉⲃ. ϣⲁⲡⲉⲩⲕⲉⲗⲉⲡⲕⲉϩ, EW 58 *B* ⲁⲡⲉϥ ϭⲛⲁϩ ⲥ. ⲉⲃ. ⲙⲙⲟϥ, BMEA 1057 8 *F* sim = Mor 31 254 *S* ϩⲱⲣⲃ, J 122 44 *S* ⲙⲡⲡⲥ. ⲉⲃ. ⲙⲡⲡⲉⲣⲏⲩ ϩⲁⲡⲉⲙⲉⲣⲟⲥ. b tr, *cut off, decide*: Deu 25 12 *S* (*B* ϫ. ⲉⲃ.) ἀποκ., Va 57 11 *B* ⲁϥⲥ. ⲉⲃ. ⲡⲗⲟϫⲓ ⲡⲓ ⲃⲉⲛ ἐκκ.; AM 279 *B* ⲁⲡⲓⲗⲁⲟⲥ ⲥⲟⲗⲡⲟⲩ ⲉⲃ. (sc garments) κατατιλ., Z 344 ⲥⲉⲗⲡ ⲱⲡⲉ ⲉⲃ. = MG 25 208 *B* ϫ. intr λατομεῖν; AZ 21 152 *S* ⲉⲣⲉⲟⲩⲥⲛⲏϥⲉ ⲥ. ⲉⲃ. ⲛⲡⲁⲙⲉⲗⲟⲥ, Va 61 200 *B* ϯⲛⲁⲥ. ⲛⲣⲁⲡⲣⲟⲕϩ ⲉⲃ., ̕BM 1124 *S* ⲁⲓⲟⲩⲱ (ⲉ)ⲓⲥ. ⲛⲁⲣⲱϣ ⲉⲃ. ⲛⲉⲙⲁϥ (cf intr); ⲉⲃ. ⲛⲥⲁ-*S*, ⲛⲥⲁ- ⲉⲃ. *B* (cf ⲥ. ⲛⲥⲁ-): Mor 17 20 *S* ⲡⲉⲥⲥ. ⲉⲃ. ⲛⲥⲁⲡⲉⲥϭⲃⲟⲓ κατατέμνειν; EW 31 *B* ⲁⲥⲥ. ⲉⲃ.

ⲛⲥⲁⲡⲓϭⲱⲓ ἐπιλαμβάνεσθαι gen, Miss 4 780 *S* passions ⲥ. ⲉⲃ. ⲛⲥⲁⲡⲟⲛⲏⲣⲉⲙⲱⲡⲓⲕⲟⲛ; as nn *S, separation*: My 100 ⲇⲓⲁⲕⲟⲡⲏ ⲉⲧⲉⲡⲁⲓⲡⲉ ⲡⲥ. ⲉⲃ. *V* also qual.

—— ⲉⲡⲉⲥⲏⲧ *B, cut off* (& fall) *down*: C 86 274 beaten until flesh ⲥ. ⲉⲡ.

ⲁⲧⲥ. *B, unbroken*: DeV 2 13 ⲡⲓⲥⲛⲁⲩϩ ⲛⲁ.

ⲥⲗⲡⲉ *S* nn, *strip*: ShIF 155 ϩⲉⲛⲧⲟⲉⲓⲥ ⲡⲥ. ⲉⲁⲩⲥⲟⲗⲛⲟⲩ from ragged garments; iterated: ShA 1 108 ϩⲉⲛϩⲃⲟⲟⲥ ⲛ ϩⲉⲛⲥ. ⲥ. *Cf* ⲥⲗⲟⲡⲗⲉⲛ.

ⲥⲗⲉⲡⲗⲓⲛ *S* nn f, *meaning unknown, part of a snake*: BKU 1 3 in magic recipe ⲧⲉⲥ. ⲡⲟⲩϩⲟⲃ ⲡⲟⲩⲱⲥ ⲡⲟⲩⲧⲣⲁⲕⲟ[ⲛ].

ⲥⲗⲟⲡⲗⲉⲛ *SB*, ⲥⲗⲁⲡ. *Sᶠ*, ⲥⲗⲉⲡⲗⲱⲡ⳿ *S*, ⲥⲗⲉⲡⲗⲱⲛⲧ *B* vb tr, *tear asunder*: ShR 2 3 66 *S* ⲁⲛⲛⲟⲃⲉ (l? ⲟϩⲣⲉ) ⲥ. ⲡⲛⲉ[ⲕϩ?]ⲃⲱⲱⲥ, Ryl 453 337 = BM 920 266 *B* ⲉⲩⲥ.† مستخي *limp, foolish* (same? word); ⲥ ⲉⲃⲟⲗ, *meaning same*: R 1 4 56 *S* Dionysus ⲡⲉⲧⲟⲩⲥ. ⲙⲙⲟϥ ⲉⲃ. ϩⲓⲧⲛⲛⲧⲓⲧⲁⲡⲟⲥ = Mart Ign 868 *B* διασπᾶν; Mor 17 27 *Sᶠ* ⲛⲉⲩⲥ. ⲙⲙⲟⲟⲩ ⲉⲃ. κατατέμνειν, BHom 101 *S* ⲉⲩϣⲁⲡⲥⲗⲉⲡⲗⲱⲡⲟⲩ ⲉⲃ paral ⲗⲓⲃⲉ, ⲡⲱϩ ⲛϩⲏⲧ (cf ⲥ.† above); intr ⲥ ⲛⲥⲁ- *Sᶠ*: Mor 1c ⲉⲩⲥ. ⲡⲥⲱⲟⲩ ⲙⲁⲩⲁⲁⲩ ὀλέσκειν. *Cf* ⲥⲱⲗⲡ.

ⲥⲉⲗⲉⲡⲓⲛ *S* nn m, *spleen* or organs around it (? σπλήν which in P 43 41 ⲥⲉⲡⲗⲏⲛ): 1 Kg 31 3 ⲡⲥ. ⲡⲣⲏⲧϥ τὰ ὑποχόνδρια (var τὸ μέρος τὸ ἔγγυς τ. ἥπατος), Mor 18 55 do = Miss 4 131 *B* ⲥⲫⲓⲣ, P 44 70 ⲡⲥ. ·ⲕⲁⲣⲇⲓⲁ· ⲡⲣⲏⲧ قلب, *ib* 87 ⲡⲥⲩ. ارب. (ⲥⲡⲗⲏⲛ = ’ʒ BAp 79–MIE 2 352–PO 22 338, C 89 17–Va ar 172 12).

ⲥⲉⲗⲉⲡⲓⲛ, ⲥⲁⲗⲁ. (TT)*S*, ⲥⲉⲗⲟⲩ. *B, little finger* (so Ar), *toe*: K 77 *B* ⲡⲓⲥ. خنصر, ShC 42 106 *S* ⲡⲥ. of hand or foot (as smallest part of body), TT 188 *S* I have not told you 10th part of ⲡⲁⲥⲁⲗ. *V* DM 13 18 n.

In name Σελεπῖνις (Preisigke).

ⲥⲉⲗⲥⲓⲗ *B* v ⲥⲟⲗⲥⲗ (both).

(ⲥⲟⲗⲥⲗ *S*), ⲥⲟⲗⲥⲉⲗ *B*, ⲥⲗⲥⲗ- *S* (Tri), ⲥⲉⲗⲥⲱⲗ⳿ ⲥⲉⲗⲥⲱⲗⲧ *B*(*F* v nn) vb tr, *adorn*: Mic 6 9 (*A* = Gk), Mt 25 7 (*S* ⲧⲥⲁⲛⲟ) κοσμεῖν, Ex 38 28 ⲕⲁⲧⲁⲕ.; Ge 38 14, Va 63 96 ⲁϫⲟⲕ ⲕⲥ. ⲙⲡⲏⲓ? καλλωπίζειν; AM 22 send to ⲥ. ⲙⲡⲓⲡⲁⲗⲁⲧⲓⲟⲛ, TEuch 2 129 bride ⲉⲧⲁⲩⲥⲉⲗⲥⲱⲗⲥ ⲙⲡⲓⲣⲓⲛⲃ; ⲥ ϩⲛ-, ϩⲉⲛ-, *adorn with*: EpJer 10 (*F* ⲧⲁⲃⲧⲉⲃ) ⲕⲟⲥ. dat, 1 Tim 2 9 (*S* ⲧⲥ.) ⲕ. μετά, Is 61 10 (*S* ⲕⲟⲥ.) κατακ. acc; Tri 428 *S* ⲁϥ ⲥⲗⲥⲗ ⲡⲉϥϫⲟⲓ ϩⲓⲛⲡⲉⲉϩ & oars زي, BSM 59 honour ⲉⲧⲁϥϯ ⲥⲉⲗⲥⲱⲗⲕ (sic l) ⲛϩⲏⲧϥ = BMiss 417 *S* ⲥⲧⲟⲗⲓⲍⲉ, C 41 13 ⲛⲁⲩⲥ. ⲙⲡⲉϥⲃⲓⲟⲥ ϩⲉⲛⲡϫⲱⲕ ⲉⲃⲟⲗ of monastic work, *ib* 43 146 ⲥⲉⲗⲥⲱⲗⲟⲩ ϩⲉⲛϩⲁⲛⲙⲁⲛⲡⲁ

for Mor 48 94 *S* ⲥⲟⲩⲗⲱⲗⲟⲩ; ⲉⲃⲟⲗ ϧⲉⲛ-: Lu 21 5 (*S* = Gk) κοσ. dat; intr (once): BSM 90 houses ⲉⲩⲥ. (*l* c.†).

Qual, *adorned*: Mt 12 44 (*S* ⲧⲥ.†), Ap 21 2 (*S* ⲧⲁⲙⲓⲟ†) κοσ.; Ps 143 12 (*S* do) καλλ.; Ex 35 35 ποικιλία, Ez 16 10 (*S* ⲁⲩⲉⲓⲛ ⲁⲩⲁⲛ) ποικίλος; Va 63 1 going to feast ⲉⲕⲥ. = BMis 361 *S* ⲣⲟⲟⲩⲧ; c ϧⲉⲛ-: Jer 10 4 (*S* = Gk) καλλ. dat; Va 66 297 houses ⲉⲩⲥ. ϧⲉⲛϩⲁⲛⲙⲁⲣⲙⲁⲣⲟⲛ διανθίζειν; C 43 36 ⲉϥⲥ. ϧⲉⲛⲟⲩⲫⲟⲃⲟⲥ ⲛⲫⲁⲛⲧⲁⲥⲓⲁ.

—— ⲉⲃⲟⲗ, meaning same: CaiThe 141 ⲥⲕⲏⲛⲏ ⲉⲧⲁϥⲥⲉⲗⲥⲱⲗⲥ ⲉⲃ., AM 172 shrine ⲁⲩⲥⲉⲗⲥⲱⲗϥ ⲉⲃ. ϧⲉⲛⲙⲉⲧⲥⲁⲓⲉ ⲛⲓⲃⲉⲛ; qual: Va 59 31 ⲙⲁ ⲉϥⲥ. ⲉⲃ. ⲉⲙⲁϣⲱ = Mor 41 3 *S* ⲉϥⲕⲁⲗⲗⲓⲟⲛⲓⲍⲉ, Bodl copt g 1 discourses ⲉⲩⲥ. ⲉⲃ., C 86 253 ⲉϥⲥ. ⲉⲃ ϧⲉⲛⲟⲩⲛⲟⲩⲃ.

—— nn m *BF*(once), *adornment*: Ge 2 1 (*A* = Gk), 2 Kg 1 24 (*S* = Gk) κόσμος, He 9 1 (*SF* do) κοσμικός; Ez 16 13 (*S* ⲁⲩ.) ποικίλος; Jer 4 30 (*S* ⲥⲁ) ὡραισμός; Is 34 4 (*SF* om) δύναμις *militia*; Va 66 305 ⲡⲓⲥ. of heaven κάλλος; C 43 7 ⲡⲥ. of stars, PMich 580 *F* repast spread with much honour ⲙⲛⲟⲩⲥⲁⲗⲥⲉ[ⲗ; as adj: Dif 1 16 ⲟⲩϫⲗⲟⲙ ⲡⲥ. مزيّن; as advb: Lu 16 19 ϧⲉⲛⲟⲩⲥ. (*S* ⲕⲁⲗⲱⲥ) λαμπρῶς.

ⲁⲧⲥ., *unadorned*: Va 68 170 Prodigal son ϫⲏ ⲛⲁⲧⲥ.

ⲙⲁⲓⲥ., *fond of adornment*: EpJer 8 (*F* ⲙⲁⲓⲧⲁⲃⲧⲉⲃ) φιλόκοσμος.

ⲣⲉϥⲥ., *adorner*: TEuch 1 10 ϩⲁⲛⲣ. ⲙⲡⲓⲉⲣⲫⲉⲓ being guardians of vessels مزيّنين, K 245 ⲡⲉⲱⲕⲉⲣⲟⲥ· ϯⲣ. (*sic*) مزيّنة.

ⲥⲉⲗⲥⲓⲗ *B* adj, *orderly*: 1 Tim 3 2 (*S* ⲕⲟⲥⲙⲉⲓ), Va 57 265 ⲉϥⲣⲏⲥ ⲛⲥⲁⲃⲉ ⲡⲥ. κόσμος, C 86 105 ⲟⲩⲡⲟⲗⲉⲙⲁⲣⲭⲟⲥ ⲡⲥ. ⲛϫⲱⲣⲓ.

In place-names: Σαλσελτόϩ, Σαρσωρ. &c, Σελσελσῖρ, Σελσῖλ (Preisigke, prob belong here, not to next word).

ⲥⲟⲗⲥⲗ *S*, ⲥⲁⲗⲥⲗⲉ *A*, ⲥⲁⲗⲥⲗ *A*², ⲥⲟⲗⲥⲉⲗ *B*, ⲥⲁⲗⲥⲉⲗ *F*, ⲥⲗⲥⲗ-, ⲥⲉⲗⲥⲱⲗ- (Mor 28) *S*, ⲥⲗⲥⲗⲉ- *A*, ⲥⲉⲗⲥⲉⲗ- *B*, ⲥⲗⲥⲱⲗ⸗ *SA*², ⲥⲗⲥⲟⲗ⸗ *A*, ⲥⲉⲗⲥⲱⲗ⸗ *BF*, ⲥⲗⲥⲱⲗ† ⲥⲗⲥⲟⲗⲧ† *S* vb **I** intr, *be comforted, encouraged*: Ps 118 52 *S*(*B* ϫⲉⲙ ⲛⲟⲙϯ) παρακαλεῖν; 1 Thes 2 12 *SF*(*B* ⲑⲱⲧ ⲙⲡϩⲏⲧ) παραμυθεῖσθαι, R 1 4 34 *S* on seeing him ⲁϥⲥ. ⲉⲙⲁⲧⲉ *consolari*, C 89 61 *B* sim; BM 255 *S* Jacob ⲙⲡⲉϥⲟⲩⲱϣ ⲉⲥ. (Ge 37 35 *B* ϯ ⲛ.), Ryl 449 *B* sim, BAp 80 *S* depart not ϣⲁⲛϯⲥ. ⲡⲕⲉⲕⲟⲩⲓ = MIE 2 354 *B* tr, TT 14 *S* ⲙⲡⲥⲥ.ⲡϩⲏⲧ; qual *S*: ShR 2 3 8 sick man ϥⲥⲗⲥⲟⲗⲧ by daylight, BMar 214 ⲛⲥⲉϭⲱ ⲉⲩⲥⲗⲥⲱⲗ a long while.

II tr, *comfort*: Deu 3 28 *S*(*B* ϯ ⲛ.), Job 2 11 *S* (var ⲥⲟⲡⲥⲡ, *B* do), Lu 16 25 *S*(*B* ⲑ. ⲙⲡϩ.), AP 5 *A*² ⲥⲗ]ⲥⲱⲗⲟ[ⲩ παρακ.; Jo 11 31 *SA*²(*B* do), Va 63 90 *B* ⲉⲓⲥ. ⲛⲛⲓϩⲏⲕⲓ παραμυ.; Z 318 *S* wishing ⲉⲥ. ⲡⲉⲥⲛⲏⲩ παρηγορεῖν; Si 30 23 *S* *misereri* (Gk diff); ShP 131⁴ 89 *S* ⲛⲧⲉⲛⲟⲩⲉϣ ⲥⲗⲥⲱⲗⲛ ϩⲓⲧⲛ...ⲛϩⲉⲗⲗⲏⲛ, BMar 214 *S* ⲛϥⲥⲩⲛⲁⲅⲉ ⲙⲙⲟⲟⲩ ⲛϥⲥⲗⲥⲱⲗⲟⲩ = Rec 6 180 *B*, Till Oster 13 *A* ⲛⲧϩⲉ ⲛⲥⲗⲥⲗⲉⲧⲏ[ⲛⲉ, Mor 24 29 *F* continued ⲉϥⲥ. ⲙⲙⲁⲩ, *ib* 28 88 *S* wished ⲛⲥⲉⲗⲥⲱⲗ ϩⲣⲱⲙⲁⲛⲟⲥ, BKU 1 291 *S* ⲥⲗⲥⲗⲧⲏⲩⲧⲛ be not sad, Pcod 39 *S* ⲙⲡⲉⲛⲡⲉ ⲥⲗⲥⲱⲗⲧ, *ib F* ⲥⲉⲗ.

With following preposition. c ⲉ-, *console for*: BMis 17 *S* ⲛⲓⲙ ⲡⲉⲧⲛⲁⲥⲗⲥⲗ ⲛⲁⲉⲓⲱⲧ ⲉⲡⲁⲙⲕⲁϩⲛϩⲏⲧ?; c ⲉⲧⲃⲉ- sim: Ge 24 67 *S*(*B* ϯ ⲛ. ⲉⲑⲃⲉ-) παρακ. περί; Jo 11 19 *SA*²(*B* om) παραμυ. περί; c ⲉϫⲛ- *S* sim, intr: ShA 2 304 ⲛⲧⲛⲥ. ⲉϫⲙⲡⲉⲛϩⲓⲥⲉ; tr: Deu 32 36 (*B* ϯ ϩⲟ ⲉϫ.) παρακ. ἐπί, Si 38 25 π. ἐν; c ϩⲁ- sim *S*: 2 Kg 10 2 (var ⲉϫⲛ-) παρακ. περί; c ϩⲛ- *S*, *take comfort from*: Pcod 35 ⲙⲁⲣⲉⲛⲁⲓ ⲥⲗⲥⲱⲗϥ ϩⲛⲓⲱⲥⲏⲫ; ⲉⲃⲟⲗ ϩⲛ- *console from, for*: Sa 8 9 παραίνεσις gen, Wess 18 59 ⲁⲓⲥ. ⲉⲃⲟⲗ ϩⲛⲧⲗⲩⲡⲉⲓ.

—— nn m *SAA*²*BF*, *consolation, amusement*: Is 57 18 *S*(*B* ⲑⲱⲧ ⲛϩⲏⲧ), Nah 3 7 *A*(*B* = Gk), Lu 2 25 *S*(*B* ⲛⲟⲙϯ) παράκλησις; Phil 2 1 *SF*(*B* ⲑ. ⲛϩ.) παραμύθιον, Mor 37 94 *S* ⲟⲩⲕⲟⲩⲓ ⲛⲥ. from the dates -θία; ShC 42 148 *S* weeping with tears ⲉⲛⲥⲱⲃⲉ ϩⲛⲟⲩⲥ., *ib* 73 113 *S* to give ⲟⲩⲥⲙⲟⲩ ⲏ ⲟⲩⲥ. *gift or gratuity*, TT 27 *S* ⲛⲥ. of market-place & enjoyments (?) of feasts, Rec 7 91 *B* we hope for ⲁϣ ⲛⲥ. (var ⲥⲉⲗⲥⲓⲗ)?, Mor 41 320 *S* rich monks ϭⲓⲛⲉ ⲛⲧⲉⲩⲙⲟⲧⲛⲉⲥ ⲙⲛⲡⲉⲩⲥ. = Synax 1 386 13 ما يتعزون, TEuch 1 648 *B* rubric ⲡⲓⲥ. التعزية or HCons 346 *B* ⲡⲓⲉⲩϫⲏ ⲛⲥ. نيسلسل (*i e* prayer for peace, patriarchs & congregation); as adj: Zech 1 13 *SA*(*B* ⲛ.), Aeg 275 *S* ϣⲁϫⲉ ⲛⲥ. παρακλητικός, C 89 180 *B* sim.

ⲣ c. *S*, *make, have comfort*: Philem 7 (*B* ⲛ.) παράκλησιν ἔχειν; *be, give comfort B*: BSM 2 ⲫⲏ ⲉⲧⲟⲓ ⲛⲥ. ⲛⲏⲓ.

ϣⲱⲡⲉ ⲛⲥ. *SA*²*B*, *become, be com.*: Job 21 2 *S*(*B* ⲛ.) παρακ. εἶναι; Ez 26 5 *B* προνομή (*cf* ? 34 28 *S* ϣⲟⲗⲥ); AP 15 *A*² παραμυ.; Aeg 51 *B* ϣ. ϧⲉⲛⲡⲓⲥ. ⲛⲉⲙⲡⲓⲟⲩⲛⲟϥ, J 96 31 *S* children ϣⲟⲟⲡ ⲛⲥ. to parents.

ϫⲓ, ϭⲓ c. *SB*, *take comfort*: Job 22 22 *S*(*B* diff) ἐξηγορίαν ἐκλαμβάνειν; C 89 35 *B* ⲛⲧⲟⲩϭ. ⲉⲃⲟⲗ ϩⲓⲧⲟⲧϥ, Ep 162 *S* sent this book ⲧⲁⲣⲉⲕϫ. ϩⲓⲱⲱϥ.

ⲣⲉϥⲥ. *SB*, *comforter*: Job 16 2 *S*(*B* ⲣⲉϥϯ ⲛ.) παρακλήτωρ, BAp 104 *S* ⲡⲣ. ⲙⲙⲉ, HCons 502 *B* ⲫⲣ. ⲛⲛⲓϩⲏⲧ معزي; ⲣⲉϥϯ c. *B*, meaning same: Bodl Marsh 32 40 priest's qualities ⲣⲉⲙⲣⲁⲩϣ, ⲣ. ⲛ̅.

ⲥⲉⲗⲥⲓⲗ *B* nn as ⲥⲟⲗⲥⲉⲗ: EW 130 ⲥ. ⲡⲣⲉⲙⲣⲁⲩϣ ⲛⲉⲡⲓ(ⲉⲓ)ⲕⲏⲥ (*cf* PO 1 514), Rec 7 91 tears of wicked ⲙⲙⲟⲛ ϩⲗⲓ ⲛⲥ. followeth them.

ⲥⲗⲁⲁⲧⲉ *SAA*², ⲥⲗⲁⲧⲉ *S*(rare), ⲥⲗⲁϯ *B*, -ⲧⲓ *F* vb intr, *stumble, slip*: Ps 36 31 *SBF*(PcodMor), Pro 26 18 *S* (var ⲥⲗⲟⲟ.) *A* ὑποσκελίζεσθαι; Ps 106 39 *S* (reading ? ὠλίσθησαν, *B* diff), Pro 14 19 *B*(*SA* ϩⲉ), Si

14 1 *S* c. ϧⲏⲣⲱϧ ὀλισθάνειν, Z 325 *S* ⲉⲁⲥⲥ. ⲉ....
ⲡⲗⲟⲓϥⲉ ⲕⲁⲧⲟⲗ., with ethic dat Ps 34 6 *S*(*B* ⲛⲛ), Jer
23 12 *B* ὀλίσθημα; Ro 11 11 *B*(*S* ϫⲱⲣⲡ), 2 Pet 1
10 *B*(*S* ϧⲉ) πταίειν; Am 5 2 *S* ⲁⲥϥⲉ(ShBMOr
8810 411, *B* ϣⲱϥⲧ) σφάλλειν; BG 68 *S* a spirit
grew upon them ϧⲙⲡⲧⲣⲉⲅⲥ., ShA 1 114 *S* he all
but c. ⲙⲡⲉⲣⲱⲡⲉ ⲉϥⲥⲕⲟⲣⲕⲣ ⲙⲙⲟⲟⲩ, BIF 13 111
S camel ⲁϥⲥ. ⲁϥⲣⲉ = MG 25 301 *B*, C 89 191 *B*
feet c. ⲉⲃⲟⲗ ϧⲁⲡⲓⲙⲱⲓⲧ; c ⲉⲡⲉⲥⲛⲧ, *slip down*:
BHom 48 *S* soul c. ⲉⲡ. ⲉⲅⲣⲅⲍⲟⲡⲉ σκελ.; R 1 4 35
S water ϣⲁϥⲥ. ⲉⲡ. from hills *delabi*, DeV 2 33 *B*
ⲉⲩⲡⲁⲥ. ⲉⲡ.... ⲡⲥⲉϥⲉⲓ ⲉϩⲣⲏⲓ; c ⲉϩⲣⲁⲓ, ⲉϩⲣⲏⲓ,
meaning same: ShBerlOr 1613 4 4 *S* giving occasion ⲡⲥ. ⲉϧ. ⲉⲡⲛⲟⲃⲉ, BMOr 7561 (99) *S* ϣⲁⲡⲧⲡⲥ.
ⲉϧ. ⲉⲡⲓⲡⲉⲑⲟⲟⲩ, TEuch 2 7 *B* ϫⲉⲛⲡϫⲓⲛⲑⲣⲉϥⲥ. ⲉϧ.
ⲉⲡⲓϧⲏϫⲟⲡⲏ.

ⲣⲉϥⲥ., *one that stumbles*: BMis 412 *S* our nature
ⲟⲩⲣ. = Va 63 24 *B*, MIE 2 371 *B* sim.

ⲁⲧⲥ. *B*, *not stumbling*: Jude 24 (*S* ⲧⲁϫⲣⲏⲩ) ἄ-
πταιστος; TEuch 2 369 establish my thoughts ⲛⲁ.

—— nn m *SAA²BF*, *stumbling, falling*: Ps 55 13
S(*B* ⲥⲗⲁⲧⲗⲉⲧ), ib 115 8 *SBF*(PcodMor) ὀλίσθημα;
Pro 24 17 *SA* ὑποσκέλισμα; ShMun 111 *S* rejoicing in ⲡⲉⲥⲥ. ⲛ ⲡⲉⲥϧⲉ, ShIF 271 *S* ⲁⲧⲉⲧⲛⲧⲁϣⲟ
ⲙⲡⲉⲥ. ⲡⲡⲉⲧⲛⲉⲣⲏⲩ ϧⲛⲡϧⲓⲣ; ✝ c. *SAA²*, *cause
to stumble*: Ps 139 4 *S*(*B* vb) ὑποσκ.; Si 3 24 *S*
ὀλισ.; Pro 29 25 *SA* σφάλμα διδόναι; AP 27 *A²* ✝
ⲡⲟⲩⲥ. ⲡⲉⲡ, P 131¹ 17 *S* devil ✝ ⲡⲟⲩⲥ. ⲡⲁϥ ⲉⲩⲙⲛⲧ-
ⲁⲧⲥⲱⲧⲙ. *Cf* ⲥⲗⲁⲧⲗⲉⲧ.

ⲥⲗⲁⲧⲗⲉⲧ *B* nn m, *slip, stumbling*: Ps 55 *ut sup*
ὀλίσθημα, Dan 11 21 &c -θρημα; C 86 162 harlots
(who are) ⲫⲙⲱⲓⲧ ⲙⲡⲓⲥ.

ⲥⲁⲗⲁϣⲓⲉ *S* nn, *tall* (?, *cf* ⲥⲁ *man* & ⲗⲁϣⲓⲉ):
El 120 describing Antichrist c. ⲡϣⲁⲙⲁⲣⲉⲧϥ = *ib*
90 *A* ϧⲣϣⲓⲣⲉ ⲡϣⲁⲙⲟⲩⲣⲏⲧⲉ, where ϧ. (without
correspondent in paral versions) may be this word
distorted or misread (as *ib* ϣⲁⲧⲙⲉⲗⲏϧ? for ϭⲁⲗⲟⲩ-
ϧⲓϧ). *Cf* MRJames *Catal MSS Corpus Chr Coll 2
270 longus, macris pedibus*.

ⲥⲟⲗϥ, -ⲣϥ, -ⲗⲓⲃ, ⲥⲱⲗϥ *S* nn m, *sieve*: Si 27 4
κόσκινον; PMéd 89 ϣⲗⲱϣⲱⲣⲟⲩ ϧⲛⲟⲩⲥⲟⲣϥ ⲉϥϣⲟⲙⲉ,
BIF 14 165 carrying basket & millstone as if ⲟⲩⲥ.
ⲉϥϣⲟⲩⲉⲓⲧ, Ryl 106 6 recipe ⲧⲁⲗⲟ ⲡⲉϣⲁϥⲉⲓ ⲉⲡⲉⲥⲛⲧ
ϧⲓⲡⲥ., *ib* 44 ϧⲓϫⲛⲟⲩⲥⲟⲗⲓⲃ, Bodl(P) a 2 30 recipe
ⲧⲁ(ⲁ)ϥ ⲉⲩⲥⲱ. ⲡⲥⲓⲣ ⲉⲛⲑⲱⲣ (? اتٮر Bevan) ⲡⲙⲟϥ
ϧⲓⲡⲥⲱ., MIF 59 27 ⲫⲓⲃ ⲡⲥⲁ ⲡⲥ. *sieve seller*; ⲁϣ
c., *yawn* (same?): P 131² 117 after drinking ⲉⲕⲟⲩ-
ⲉϣⲡ ⲕⲉⲉⲥ ⲉⲕⲁϣ ⲥ. = Va 58 192 *B* ⲕⲉⲣϫ ⲕⲁⲥ ⲉⲕⲫⲉⲣϫ ⲣⲟ χασμώμενος (*cf* ⲁϣ ⲁϧⲟⲙ χάσμη), cit P 44
122 = 43 131 ⲉⲕⲡⲉϧ ⲁⲥⲥⲱ. خطم عن مزول (misunderstood). *Cf* ? ⲥⲱⲗ (Bsciai).

ⲥⲗⲓϥⲓ *B* nn f, *lung*: K 78 ✝c. ⵣⵊ, but P 54 152
ⲡⲓⲗⲥⲓϥⲓ, whence Bodl 325 156 ⲡⲓⲗⲉⲓϥⲓ *q v*.

ⲥⲗϥⲧⲉ v ⲥⲃⲗⲧⲉ.

ⲥⲗϧⲟ, ⲥⲉⲗϧⲱ *S*, ⲥⲉⲗϧⲟ, ⲥⲁⲗ. (P 44 190, K 394)
B nn, *warm water* (?): Ap 3 16 ⲙⲟⲩ ⲡⲥ. *S*, ⲙⲟⲩⲥ.
B χλιαρός; PMéd 285 *S* mixture ⲧⲥⲟⲟⲩ ϧⲓⲥⲉⲗϧⲱ
(*cf* 235 ϧⲓⲑⲉⲣⲙⲱⲡ).

ⲥⲗⲓϫ *B* nn, state of *being on edge* (?) of teeth:
Jer 38 29 ⲉⲣ c. αἱμωδιᾶν *obstupescere*; as vb: P 54
174 ⲁⲩⲥ. (prob *l* ⲉⲣ c.) *set on edge*. ⲥⲗⲏϫⲓ nn m
sim: Montp 206 ⲡⲓⲥ. ضرس. *Cf* ⲡⲟⲩϣⲥ (Ez 18 2); as
vb: Dif 1 102 ⲁⲡⲡⲁϫⲣⲓ...ⲥⲗⲏϫⲓ.

ⲥⲱⲗϫ *B* v ⲥⲱⲗϭ.

ⲥⲗⲁϫⲗⲉϫ *B* v ⲥⲗⲟϭⲗϭ.

ⲥⲱⲗϭ *SA*, -ⲗϫ *B*, ⲥⲁⲗϭ-, ⲥⲗϭ- *A²*, ⲥⲉⲗϫ- *B*,
ⲥⲟⲗϭ- *S*, ⲥⲁ. *SᵃA²*, ⲥⲁⲗⲕ⸗ *Sᵃ*, ⲥⲟⲗϫ⸗ *B*, ⲥⲟⲗⲉϭᵗ *S*,
ⲥⲁⲗⲕᵗ *Sᵃ* vb **I** intr, *smear, wipe, obliterate*: Nu 27
4 *B*(*S* ϥⲱⲧⲉ ⲉⲃⲟⲗ) ἐξαλείφειν; ShP 130² 104 *S* they
built, dug, ⲁⲩⲥ. *plastered*, traded, Va 63 82 *B* paper
torn but ⲙⲡⲉⲛⲓⲥⲃⲁⲓ c. μένειν; qual *S*, *smeared
with clay for seal*: Ep 253 ⲡⲟⲉⲓⲕ...ⲉⲩⲥ. ⲉⲩⲧⲟⲟⲃⲉ,
Sph 10 1 ⲧϭⲟⲟⲩⲡⲉ...ⲉⲥⲥ. ⲉⲥⲧ., Ep 549 *Sᵃ* vessels
ⲉⲩⲥⲁⲗⲕ ⲉⲩⲧ.

II tr: Lev 14 42 *S*(ShIF 133, *B* ⲱϣϫ), Ps 50
3 *B*(*SA* ϥⲱⲧⲉ ⲉⲃⲟⲗ), CaiEuch 452 *B* c. ⲡⲡⲁⲡⲁ-
ⲣⲁⲡⲧⲱⲙⲁ ἐξαλ.; Va 61 218 *B* ⲉϥⲥ. ⲥⲁⲃⲟⲗ ⲙⲙⲟⲕ
ⲡⲛⲉⲕⲛⲟⲃⲓ διακρούεσθαι; C 43 236 *B* bid Enoch to
c. ⲙⲡⲓⲭⲓⲣⲟⲅⲣⲁⲫⲟⲛ of his sins, CO 348 *Sᵃ* vessels
ⲡⲥⲁⲗⲕⲟⲩ ⲡⲧⲁⲃⲟⲩ.

With following preposition. c ⲉ- *S* intr, *smear
upon, anoint*: CR '87 376 for painful breasts [ⲉ]ⲕⲥ.
ⲉⲣⲟⲟⲩ till they cease (aching), Z 629, PMéd 274
sim, PLond 5 134 ⲥⲕⲉⲅⲏ ⲡⲓⲙ...ⲁⲡⲥ. ⲁⲡⲧⲱⲃⲉ ⲉⲣⲟⲟⲩ; tr *SA²*: Jo 9 6 *A²*(*S* ϫⲱϧ, *B* ⲗⲁⲗⲉ) τιθέναι ἐπί;
Mor 16 38 c. ⲙⲡⲉϥⲥⲡⲟϥ ⲉⲡⲉⲧⲟⲩⲁ (var BMis 199
ϫⲱϧ, *cf* Ex 12 7 *S* ⲱⲥϭ), RNC 77 earth ⲥⲟⲗϭϥ ⲉ-
ⲡⲉⲕⲃⲁⲗ. c ⲛ-, ϧⲛ- *S*, *smear with*: Sa 13 14 ⲛ-
καταχρίειν; AZ 23 108 ⲥⲟⲗϭϥ ⲉⲡⲟⲙⲉ (*cf* 109 ϫⲁⲣⲥ
ⲉⲡⲟ.); Bor 264 39 firewood ⲥⲱⲗϭⲟⲩ ϧⲛⲟⲩⲙⲟⲅⲗϧ.

With following adverb. c ⲉⲃⲟⲗ *B*, *wipe out*:
Deu 29 20 (*S* ϥ. ⲉⲃ.), Ap 3 5 (*S* do) ἐξαλ.; TDi 182
c. ⲉⲃ. ϧⲁⲣⲟⲡ ⲙⲡⲓⲥϭⲓ ⲛϫⲓϫ (Col 2 14 om ⲉⲃ.).

—— nn m *S*, *obliteration*: P 44 88 محو.

ⲁⲧⲥ. *B*, *unobliterated*: Va 57 273 good thoughts
ⲟⲓ ⲛⲁ. ϫⲉⲛⲡⲓⲧⲁⲙⲓⲟⲛ of heart.

ⲣⲉϥⲥ. *B*, *one who wipes out*: MG 25 162 Jesus
ϥⲣ. ⲙⲡⲓⲛⲟⲃⲓ.

Cf ⲥⲱⲗⲕ.

ⲥⲗⲉϭⲗⲉϭ *F* v ⲥⲕⲟⲣⲕⲣ.

ⲥⲗⲟϭⲗϭ *S*, ⲥⲗⲁϫⲗⲉϭ *Sᶠ*, ⲥⲗⲁϫⲗⲉϫ *B*, ⲥⲗⲉⲥⲗⲱϭ-,

ⲥⲗⲉⲥⲗⲱϭ†, ⲥⲗⲕⲗⲱⲕ† S, ⲥⲗⲉϩⲗⲁϭ† A, ⲥⲗⲉϫⲗⲱϫ† B vb I intr, *be, make smooth* : Ge 27 11† S(P 44 103, B ϫⲏⲛ), 1 Kg 17 40† B(S ⲟⲩⲟϩ τέλειος), Pro 2 20† SA(B do) λεῖος; Deu 28 54† S(B ⲗⲏⲕ q v) τρυφερός; Is 40 4† S(B ϫ.) πεδίον; Ez 24 7† S(B do) λεωπετρία; Tri 304 S gourd shaded Jonah's body ⲉⲧⲁϥⲥⲗⲉϭⲗⲱϭ (l ⲥⲗⲟϭⲗϭ) *delicate* (انسل *be hot* by error); ShR 2 3 63 S ⲡⲉϥⲥⲱⲙⲁ ⲉⲧⲥ.†, BMar 166 S *flesh* ⲉⲧⲥ.† by washing & anointing, ShBM 202 184 S *trees* ⲉⲩⲥ.† others ⲉⲩⲭⲁⲥⲱ, Mich 550 29 S *jacinth* ⲉⲩⲥ.† & glittering, Va 57 167 B *stones* ⲉⲩⲥ.†, ShZ 637 S ⲥⲟⲧⲃⲉϥ ⲡⲥ. opp ⲕⲉⲗⲉⲃⲓⲛ (cf ⲡⲓⲁ a); BMar 209 S ⲁϥⲥ. ⲉϫⲙⲡⲁⲥⲱⲙⲁ with hand = Mor 48 12 S ⲁϥⲥⲗⲉϭⲗⲱϭ ⲡⲁⲥ. = Rec 6 172 B c. e-.

II tr: Job 14 19 B λεαίνειν; Is 45 2 S(B ϣⲱϣ) ὁμαλίζειν; Mor 48 12 S v above, ib 28 117 Sᶠ sim ⲥⲗⲁϩⲗⲉϭ ⲛ-, SHel 53 S sim ⲥⲗⲉϭⲗⲱϭ ⲡⲉϥ-. V ⲙⲉⲥϭⲱⲗ.

—— nn SB, *smoothness* : BMar 147 S ⲡⲉⲥ. ⲙⲡⲉⲥⲥⲱⲙⲁ ⲉⲧϭⲏⲡ, JTS 10 400 S sim, K 72 B c. طبى, جرد *bald*, Montp 160 B ⲡⲓⲥ. *bald, peeled place* سلخ, cf K 161 (same context) ⲡⲓϩⲁⲧ '–.

Cf ? ⲗⲁⲕⲗⲏ.

ⲥⲉⲗϭⲁⲙ v ϣⲗϭⲟⲙ.

ⲥⲓⲙ SABF, ⲥⲙ-S, ⲥⲓⲙ-SB nn m, *a grass, fodder, herbs in general* : Ge 1 29, 30 B, Ps 36 2 B(S=Gk), Mt 14 19 BF(S do) χόρτος; Ex 9 25 B, Job 8 12 B(S ⲡⲧⲏϭ), He 6 7 B(S do) βοτάνη; Mal 3 2 A(B =Gk) πόα; CaiThe 322 B sown seed & ⲡⲓⲥ. عشب, K 180 B ⲡⲓⲥ. كلأ, بقولات (var 'ⲉ), P 54 143 B ⲡⲓⲥ. 'ⲃ, 'ⲉ, Ann 1 62 B ⲡⲓⲟⲩⲟϯ ⲡⲓⲥ. بقول, K 364, P 55 2 B ⲡⲓⲥ. طرب (as *clover* AIssa 116), PO 11 315 B ⲟⲩϣⲟⲗ ⲡⲥ. for ass, C 41 72 B spreading like ⲟⲩⲥ. ⲡⲧⲉ ⲡⲕⲁϩⲓ, WS 90 S camels loaded with c. **b** *radish* S: P 44 82 = 43 57 ⲣⲉⲡⲁⲡⲓⲁ · ⲣⲓⲡⲁⲡⲟⲡ · ⲡⲥ. فجل; ShC 42 71 for oil, Kr 244 ⲡⲉⲥ. ⲡⲧⲁⲃⲓⲧⲟⲩ ⲉⲡⲡⲣⲉ, BKU 1 45, WS 132 as wages with corn, barley, ib 150 ⲉⲣⲧⲟϥ ⲡⲥ., ib 134 ⲙⲁⲭⲉ ⲡⲥ.; **c** doubtful : BM 1110 S ⲡⲉⲥ., ib 1127 S sim, CMSS 63 F husbandmen ⲉⲩⲕⲁⲣⲉ ⲥ.; various: Ge 1 29 B ⲥ. ⲡⲉⲓϯ ϫ. σπόριμος, PMich 593 S ⲡⲥ. ⲡϣⲣⲟⲟⲙⲡⲉ which is περιστερεών, P 43 233 S ⲣⲁⲡⲱⲥ · ⲥ. ⲡϣⲛϩⲉ دهن الاوز *goose fat* (plant ? goosegrass), ib 245 S ⲥ. ⲡⲟⲅⲟⲟⲣⲉ حشيشة العقرب, Hall 65 S ⲡⲥ. ⲡⲧⲟⲩⲟϣⲣⲉ, BP 11349 S ⲥ. ⲡⲗⲁⲧ ⲡⲟⲩⲧϥ (v ⲗⲁⲧ), DM 24 27 *sym n* ⲕⲗⲟ (v ⲕⲗⲟ).

ⲥⲙ-, ⲥⲓⲙ- : Jer 2 22 S ⲥⲙⲣⲱϩⲉ (Z 511, B ϩⲟⲥⲉⲙ) πόα, cf Mal 3 2 A, TEuch 2 99 B ⲥⲓϯ, ⲥⲓⲙ, ⲥⲓⲙⲣⲱⲧ نبات, Bodl(P) b 7 S ⲥⲓⲙⲉⲛϩ (l ⲥⲓⲙⲡⲉϩ or ? ⲡⲡⲉϩ), Mor 51 31 S harvest of ⲡϭⲉⲗⲃⲟⲟⲩ ⲙⲡⲥⲓⲙⲟⲩⲅ (cf ? σιμαίς Preisigke *Wörterb*), K 197 B ⲥⲓⲙⲓⲁⲙ (var -ⲁⲛ) كتبى (? كتيبة); ⲡⲉϩ ⲡⲥ. S, *radish oil* : PMéd

239 n, Z 629, Ryl 106 11, Ep 574 all in recipes; ϭⲗⲟϭ ⲡⲥ. S, *radish seed* (?) : Ryl 106 54 (= ϭⲣⲟϭ).

ⲟⲓ ⲡⲥ. B, *be in grass, be green* : C 89 117 sown field ⲉⲧⲓ ⲉⲥⲟⲓ ⲡⲥ. = MG 17 581 وهو عشب ὅτε χόρτος γέγονεν (cf Sethe *DemUrk* 12).

ⲃⲉⲣⲥⲓⲙ S, *seed* (?) of one of above plants v p 43. In place-names: ⲧⲙⲟⲩ ⲡⲥⲓⲙ (WS 167 &c), Νιαⲅⲟⲥⲓⲙⲟⲩⲕⲓ (? ⲟⲕⲉ, PLond 4 200).

ⲥⲱⲙ, ⲥⲟⲙ⸗S, ⲥⲁⲙ⸗SA(once), ⲥⲏⲙ† vb I tr, *subdue, press, pound* : Ja 3 7 SA(B ϭⲛⲉ ϫⲱ⸗) δαμάζειν, Si 30 8 ἀδάμαστος; Pcod 27 potter ϣⲁⲓⲥ. ⲙⲡⲉⲩⲟⲙⲉ ⲕⲁⲗⲱⲥ, PSBA 27 168 white lead ⲡⲧⲥⲟⲙϥ ϩⲙⲡⲉⲕⲧⲏⲛⲉ ⲉⲣⲟ[ⲩⲡ] ⲉⲣⲟⲥ (sc parchment), PMéd 105 ⲡⲧⲥⲁⲙⲟⲩ ⲙⲡⲡⲉⲅⲉⲣⲏⲩ, AZ 23 114 ⲥⲟⲙ ⲡⲁⲓ ⲧⲏⲣⲟⲩ ⲙⲡⲡⲉⲅⲉⲣⲏⲩ (cf ⲑⲛⲟ sim TurM 9), BKU 1 268 flax ⲡⲧⲉⲧⲡⲥⲟⲙⲙⲩ (sic) ⲕⲁ[ⲗⲱⲥ, Bodl(P) b 9]ⲙⲁϩⲉ ⲉⲩⲥ.† ϩⲙⲡⲡⲩⲣⲅⲟⲥ, Ryl 160 ⲧⲁϩⲟⲟⲗⲉϥ ⲧⲁⲥⲟⲙⲉϥ ⲧⲁⲕⲟⲕϥ (? flax, v Blümner[1] 1 180), ShC 73 109 ⲡⲉⲣⲡⲟ ⲡⲥ. ⲥⲱ. II intr: PMéd 155 ⲉⲕⲥ. ⲉⲣⲟϥ (sc mixture), ib 222 sim ⲉⲕⲥ. ⲡⲥⲱⲟⲩ.

ⲥⲱⲙⲉ, ⲥⲟⲙⲉ⸗S, ⲥⲁⲁⲙⲉ-, ⲥⲁⲁⲙⲉ⸗Sᶠ, *rub, polish* (same ?) : Bor 253 152 after ⲡⲕⲉⲥ. of rusted vessel γάνωσις, ib if one ⲥⲁⲁⲙⲉ ⲡⲣⲟⲙⲡⲧ γανοῦν, 153 bronze ⲉⲕϣⲁⲡⲧⲓⲥⲁⲁⲙⲉϥ ὑγρόν ἐάν, 151 ⲉⲩϣⲁⲡⲧⲓⲥⲟⲙⲉϥ.

ⲥⲉⲙⲉ F v ⲥⲡ-.

ⲥⲉⲙⲓ B v ⲥⲓⲙⲉ.

ⲥⲓⲙⲉ, ⲥⲓⲙⲓ v ⲥϭⲓⲙⲉ.

ⲥⲱⲙⲉ S v ⲥⲱⲙ sf.

ⲥⲙⲁ S nn, *unknown substance, measured in* ⲙⲁϫⲉ *& related to oil* : TurM 13 ⲡⲧⲃⲱⲕ ⲟⲩⲙⲁϫⲉ ⲡⲥ. ⲉϫⲙⲡⲛⲉϩ.

ⲥⲙⲏ SAA²BF, ⲥⲙⲏⲉ(PO 4 186), ⲥⲙⲉⲓ, ⲥⲙⲓ A nn f, *voice*, **a** of men : Ge 15 4 SB, Ps 28 3 S(B ϩⲣⲱⲟⲩ), Is 30 17 SBF, ib 65 19 B(S ϩⲣⲟⲟⲩ), Hag 1 12 AB, Jo 5 25 SA²B φωνή, BHom 35 S ϩⲣⲟⲟⲩ of trumpet ἦχος, c. of judge φ.; Is 33 19 B c. ϣⲏⲕ (SF ϩⲁϣⲃⲉ.) βαθύφωνος, 2 Tim 2 16 SB c. ϣⲟⲩⲉⲓⲧ κενοφωνία, Ex 4 10 A (Cl) c. ϩⲛⲙ (cf 6 30, S ϩⲁ c., B ϣⲟⲙ) ἰσχνόφωνος, Ez 3 6 B c. ϩⲟⲣϣ *profundi sermonis*, Ps 113 15 B(S diff) ⲙⲟⲩϯ ⲡⲟⲩⲥ. φωνεῖν; Mt 25 6 S(B ϩ.), Lu 1 42 SB κραυγή; Job 42 5 SB, Mt 4 24 B(S ⲥⲟⲉⲓⲧ), Ro 10 16 B(S ϩ.) ἀκοή; 1 Cor 14 7 B(S do) φθόγγος; Lu 4 37 B(S ⲥⲟ.) ἦχος; El 102 A ⲧⲥⲙⲓ ⲡⲣⲱⲙⲉ, AP 38 A² all said ϩⲛⲟⲩⲥ. ⲡⲟⲩⲱⲧ, PS 126 S ⲧⲉⲥ. ⲉⲡⲧⲁⲡⲣⲱⲙⲉ ⲕⲓⲙ ⲉⲧⲃⲏⲛⲧⲥ, ShZ 638 S c. ⲡϣⲁⲕⲉ, BIF 14 166 S raised ⲧⲉⲩⲥ. ϣⲁⲡⲧⲉⲡⲉⲩϩⲣⲟⲟⲩ shook foundations, R 1 3 74 S heard c. like ⲟⲩⲥ. ⲉϥⲱϣ ⲉⲃⲟⲗ, MIE 2 369 B ⲉⲩⲧⲁⲟⲩⲟ ⲡⲡⲓⲥ. ⲉⲑⲡⲉⲥⲱⲟⲩ Holy, holy, BKU 1 181 F ϩⲉⲡⲥ. ⲡϩⲁϯ, C 43 99 B ⲡⲓⲥ. ⲉⲧⲟⲩⲱϣ ⲙⲙⲟⲟⲩ ⲉⲃⲟⲗ,

AM 166 *B* unable to ⲙⲟⲩϯ ⲛⲟⲩⲥ. from throats, MG 25 238 *B* praising God ϩⲉⲛϯⲥ. ⲙⲙⲉⲧⲣⲉⲙ- ⲛⲭⲏⲙⲓ *language*, Miss 4 199 *B* ⲁⲕⲙⲉⲅⲓ ϩⲉⲛⲟⲩⲥ. ⲉⲥⲗⲟⲃⲓ to depose me.   **b**, *of animals* : Job 4 10 *SB* lioness, Sa 17 18 *S*(var ϩ.) bird, Jer 26 22 *B* serpent φ.   **c**, *sound* of things : Ex 32 17 *B* battle, Ps 41 8 *B* torrent, Is 18 3 *B* trumpet, Eccl 7 7 *F* burning thorns φ.; Jer 29 3 *B* wheels ἦχ. (all *S* ϩ.) Ap 6 1 *SB* thunder φ.; Mor 51 35 *S* c. ⲛϥⲱⲙ, c. ⲛⲛⲱⲛⲧ, Mus 35 28 *B* c. of feet approaching, My 34 *S* letters ⲉⲧⲉⲟⲩⲛⲧⲟⲩ c. vowels.   As adj *B*, *famed* : Ez 39 11 ⲙⲁ ⲛⲥ. ⲧⲟⲡ. ὀνομαστός.

ϯ c. *SB*, *give voice* : men Nu 14 1 *SB*, Ps 17 13 *SB* φ. διδόναι, Mor 17 45 *S* why ⲉϥϯ ⲛⲡⲉⲓⲥ.? φ. ἀποδ., Ex 24 11 *S*(*B* diff) διαφωνεῖν; ShWess 9 140 *S* babe ⲉⲧⲣⲉϥϯ ⲛⲧⲉϥⲥ., ShA 1 431 *S* spared not ⲉϯ ⲛⲧⲉⲥⲥ. ⲉϩⲣⲁⲓ ⲉⲛⲡ̄ⲥ̄ *raise voice against*, ShC 42 55 *S* ⲁⲥϯ ⲛⲧⲉⲥⲥ. ⲉϩ. ⲉϫⲱⲓ crying out;   animals Ps 103 12 *SB* φ. δ., Is 53 7 *S* neg (*A* Cl ϣⲉϫⲉ ⲉⲛ, *B* ⲟⲓ ⲛⲁⲧⲥ.) ἄφωνος; C 41 57 *B* none of beasts ϯ ⲛ- ⲧⲟⲩⲥ.;   things 1 Cor 14 7 *SB* φ. δ., Is 51 15 *B*(*S* diff) ἠχεῖν; Leyd 420 *S* ⲟⲩⲕⲁⲧⲟ ... ϯ ⲛ- ⲧⲉⲥⲥ.;   ⲣⲉϥϯ c. *S*, *vocal* : My 153 letters ⲛⲣ. vowels.

ⲝⲓ, ϭⲓ c. *SABF*, *receive sound, listen* : Nu 28 18 *SB*, Ps 48 1 *S*(*B* ⲣⲉⲕ ⲙⲁⲩϫ), Is 1 2 *SBF*, Jer 13 15 *B*(*S* ϯ ϩⲏⲧ), Hos 5 1 *AB* ἐνωτίζειν; Si 14 23 *S* ἀκροᾶσθαι; Is 32 4 *SF*(*B* ⲥⲱⲧⲉⲙ) ἀκούειν; PS 34 *S* ⲥⲱⲧⲙϫⲉ ⲁⲅⲱ ϫ., JKP 2 82 *S* ϫ. ⲕⲁ ⲙⲁⲁϫⲉ (cf Pro 5 1), C 43 219 *B* ϭ. ⲛⲓⲃⲁⲗ ⲛⲣⲉϥⲛⲁⲩ; *take, speak with voice* : LMär 32 *S* idol ϫ. ⲛⲣⲱⲙⲉ & cried;   c ⲉ-, *listen to* : Job 32 11 *SB*, Is 51 4 *SB*, ⲉⲛⲱ.; Ac 15 12 *S*(*B* ⲥⲱ.) ἀκού.; R 2 2 32 *S* ⲛⲛⲉϫ. ⲉⲣⲉⲛⲟⲩⲉⲗⲗⲉ (var BHom 47 ⲕⲁ ⲙⲁⲁϫⲉ ⲉⲥⲱⲧⲙ ⲉ-), MIE 2 406 *B* ⲁⲓϭ. ⲉⲡⲁⲓⲱⲧ; c ⲛ̄ⲧⲉⲛ- *B* meaning sim : C 41 66 do not ϭ. ⲛⲧⲟⲧϥ ⲙⲡⲁⲓⲣⲁⲗⲏⲧ;   as nn : Is 21 8 *B*(*S* ϣⲁϫⲉ) ἀκρόασις; ⲙⲁ ⲛϭ. *B*, *place of hearing, of trial* : Ac 25 23 (*S* ⲙⲁ ⲛϯ ϩⲁⲡ) ἀκροατήριον; ⲣⲉϥϫⲓ, ϭⲓ c., *listener, obeyer* : Is 3 3 *B*(*S* ⲣⲉϥⲥⲱ.), Ja 1 22 *B*(*SA* do) ἀκροατής; ⲙⲛⲧ- ⲣⲉϥϫ. : PS 210, ib 256 *S* (as a fault ?).

ⲁⲧⲥ. *SB*, *voice-, soundless* : Mor 17 90 *S* ⲁⲩϣⲱⲡⲉ ⲛⲁ. ἄφωνος, My 34 *S* letters ⲛⲁ.;   ⲉⲣ. ⲁⲧⲥ. *B*, *be voiceless, without speech* : Is 53 7 (*S* ϯ c. neg), 1 Cor 14 10 (*S* ⲙⲛⲧϥ ⲥ.) ἄφ.

ⲉⲣ c. *B*, *be famed* : Ez 24 14 (*S* ⲟ ⲛⲥⲟⲉⲓⲧ) ὀνομαστός.

ⲣⲉⲙⲥ. *B*, *famed person* : Ez 23 23 (*S* ⲣⲉⲙⲛⲥⲟ- ⲉⲓⲧ) ὀνομαστός.

ϩⲁⲥⲃⲉ. *S* v above a Is 33 19, Ex 4 10.

ϫⲁⲥⲧⲥ. *S*, *loquacious* : Si 8 4 γλωσσώδης.

ⲥⲙⲟⲩ *SAA²BF*, ⲥⲓⲱ *S*(Theban), ⲥⲙⲁⲙⲉ *A²*, ⲥⲙⲁⲙⲁⲁⲧ†, -ⲛⲧ†, ⲥⲙⲁⲁⲧ† *S.A²*, ⲥⲙⲁⲙⲁⲧ† *AB*,

ⲥⲙⲁⲅⲁⲧ† *B* (? Jer 17 7), ⲥⲙⲁⲙⲉⲧ, -ⲉⲉⲧ† *F*(Mor 24 16), ⲥⲙⲁⲣⲱⲟⲩⲧ† *B* vb intr, *bless, praise* : Ps 48 13 *SB*, Mk 6 41 *B*(*S* + ⲉ-), Ro 12 14 *BF*(*S* do) εὐλογεῖν; Ps 105 12 *S*(*B* ϩⲱⲥ) αἰνεῖν; ib 64 13 *SB* ὑμνεῖν; El 56 *A* ⲉⲩⲥ. ϩⲁⲧⲁⲉϩⲓⲉⲓ, BSM 64 *B* ⲛⲧⲉⲛϩⲱⲥ ⲟⲩⲟϩ ⲛⲧⲉⲛ.;   c ⲉ-, *bless* : 2 Kg 6 18 *SB*, Pro 24 34 *SA*, Dan 3 24 *B* (*S* ϯ ⲉⲟⲟⲩ), Mt 14 19 *SBF*, AP 13 *A²*, Aeg 279 *S* bishop ϣⲁϥⲥ. ⲙⲉⲩⲥ. ⲉⲣⲟϥ ⲉⲩⲗ.; Ps 68 30 *SB*, Joel 2 26 *SAB*, Lu 2 20 *S*(*B* ϩ.) αἰ., Ps 144 4 *SB* ἐπαι.; He 2 12 *SBF* ὑμ.; Ps 67 33 *S*(*B* do) ᾄδειν; Br 238 *S* ⲉⲩⲥ. ⲉⲣⲟϥ saying Holy, holy, C 43 197 *B* ⲁⲛⲁⲧⲓⲟⲥ c. ⲉⲡⲓⲣⲱⲙⲓ, ShBor 300 75 *S* ⲧϭⲁⲓⲉ ⲟⲩⲣⲱⲙⲉ opp c. ⲉⲣⲟϥ, Aeg 260 *S* ⲧⲉⲛⲥ. ⲉⲣⲟⲕ ⲉϩⲣⲁⲓ ⲉϫⲛⲛⲁⲓ *thank*, BP 3270 *F* ⲉⲗⲉⲛⲛⲟⲩⲧ(ⲉ) c. ⲗⲁⲏ, Lant 4 1 *S* in colophon c. ⲉⲣⲟⲓ ϯϯ ⲙⲉⲧⲁⲛⲟⲓⲁ, BAp 175 *S* ending text c. ⲉⲣⲟⲛ (cf εὐλόγησον), Bor 235 117 *S* lay not hold of aught on table except thou say c. ⲉⲣⲟⲓ εὐλόγησον;   as greeting : P 129¹⁴ 124 *S* Cyril to Shenoute sailing on cloud c. ⲉⲣⲟⲓ, DeV 2 174 *B* greeting his mother c. ⲉⲣⲟⲓ, BAp 80 *S* knocked at door & cried c. ⲉⲣⲟⲓ = MIE 2 354 *B*, Miss 4 177 *B* on entering said c. ⲉⲣⲟⲓ ⲁⲛⲟⲕ ϫⲉ ⲁⲓⲥ. ⲉⲣⲟϥ, BM 536 *S* letter begins c. ⲉⲣⲟⲛ ⲡⲉⲛⲓⲱⲧ; or in reply : BAp 124 *S* he cried 'John', I answered c. ⲉⲣⲟⲓ = MIE 2 419 *B*, DeV 2 128 *B* sim (cf Callinicus *Vita Hypat* 15 φωνεῖ αὐτὸν Ὑπάτιε, ὁ δὲ ἀπεκρίνατο Εὐλόγησον).

ⲥⲙⲁⲙⲉ *A²* : Mani 1 ⲙⲁⲣⲡⲟⲩⲱϣⲧ ⲙⲡⲓⲡⲛⲁ ... ⲙⲁ]ⲣⲓⲥ. ⲙⲡⲓⲛϫⲁⲓⲥ ⲓ̄ⲥ̄. Hence :

ⲥⲙⲁⲙⲁⲁⲧ &c, *blessed* : Ge 9 26 *SB*, Ps 17 46 *S* (var -ⲛⲧ, *B* ⲥⲙⲁⲣ.), Mk 14 61 *SF*(*B* do), 2 Cor 1 3 *SB*(var ⲥⲙⲁⲣ.) εὐλογητός, Ge 12 2 *SA*(Cl)*B*, Job 11 3 *B*(*S* ⲛⲁⲓⲁⲧϥ), Mt 25 34 *S*(BHom 63 ⲥⲙⲁⲁⲧ, *B* ⲥⲙⲁⲣ.), Lu 13 35 *SF*(*B* do), Jo 12 13 *S.A²*-ⲛⲧ, (*B* do), AP 5 *A²* ⲥⲙⲁⲙ. εὐλογημένος; Ps 47 1 *S*(*B* do) αἰνετός, Dan 3 26 *S* c....c. *B* ⲥⲙⲁⲣ....c. ⲉⲩⲗ. ⲁⲓⲛ., ib 53 *S* (*B* do) ὑπεραιν.; ShRE 10 161 *S* ⲕⲥ. ⲉⲝⲡⲛⲉⲕⲁⲅⲁⲑⲟⲛ, AP 29 *A²* ϥ]ⲥⲙⲁⲁⲧ ⲛϭⲓ ⲛⲡⲉ, ClPr 36 198 *S* ⲉⲩⲥ. ⲙⲡⲡⲉ, Mich 166 9 *S* ϥⲉⲥⲙⲁⲙⲁⲁⲧ (*sic*).

—— nn m *SA²BF*, ⲥⲙⲁⲙⲉ *A²*, *blessing, praise* : Lev 25 21 *SB*, Ps 108 17 *SB*, Ap 5 13 *SB* εὐλογία; Ps 50 15 *SA*(Cl)*B*, Is 35 10 *SBF* αἴνεσις, Ps 90 tit *SB*, Mt 21 16 *SB* αἶνος; Ps 6 tit *S*(*B* ϩⲱⲥ), Col 3 16 *SB* ὕμνος; 2 Cor 6 8 *SB* εὐφημία; Job 8 21 *S* (*B* diff) ἐξομολόγησις; Bor 151 128 *S* whom godly shall bless ⲛⲁϣⲱⲡⲉ ϩⲁⲡⲉⲥ., Mani 2 *A²* ⲡⲛⲟϭ ⲛ- ⲥⲧⲩⲗⲟⲥ ⲛⲧⲉ ⲡⲥⲙⲁⲙⲉ, DeV 2 190 *B* give me ⲟⲩⲥ. ⲉⲃⲟⲗ ϩⲉⲛⲣⲱⲕ & heal my son, ShA 2 326 *S* ruined by their sweet words & ⲡⲉⲩⲥ. *flattery* (?), Kr 227 *F* Lord grant them ⲉⲃⲓⲛ ⲡⲉⲩⲥ. ϩⲓϫⲱⲛ ⲡⲕⲁⲡⲓ (ⲁⲅⲁ- ⲡⲏ), BM 547 *S* introductory greetings, then ⲙⲡⲉ-

сапаіс.; liturgical: BSM 33 B ϩⲱⲥ...ⲉⲑⲃⲉⲡⲓⲥ. = Va 63 7 B ϣⲱⲡ ⲛϭⲓ ⲥ. = BMis 375 S ϣⲧ. ⲛⲉϥⲡⲁⲅⲉ, C 43 204 B ⲡⲓⲥ. (sc ⲉⲩⲗⲟⲅⲓⲁ) in his mouth, JTS 4 389 S ⲡⲉⲥ. ⲛⲛⲉⲡⲧⲁⲡⲕⲗⲁⲥⲙⲁⲧⲓⲍⲉ ⲙⲙⲟⲟⲩ distributed, Aeg 259 S ⲥ. opp ⲉⲩⲭⲁⲣⲓⲥⲧⲓⲁ, BM 626 B letter to clerics ϫⲁ ⲡⲓⲥ. ⲡⲛⲓ till I come, BKU 1 313 S ⲡⲥ. ϫⲉⲉⲓⲛⲁⲟⲩϣϥ, cf ? Ryl 423 100 B ⲡⲓⲥ. prayer so called; cf also ϫⲓ ⲥ.; as gift, benevolence, often blessed by saint, cleric: Ge 33 11 SB ⲉⲩⲗ.; ShC 73 113 S extra victuals ⲉⲓⲱⲡ ⲙⲙⲟⲟⲩ ⲉⲩⲥ., ShHT B 65 S emperor's gift ⲟⲩⲥ. ⲡⲉ, Miss 4 800 S ϩⲉⲛⲕⲟⲩⲓ ⲛⲥ. of vegetables, bread &c = C 89 42 B ϩⲁⲛⲉⲩⲗⲟⲅⲓⲁ, Gu 4 S ⲡⲥ. ⲙⲡⲁⲧⲟⲡⲟⲥ for sick man, Hall 92 S ⲁⲧⲉⲧⲛϫⲟⲟⲩ ⲛⲥ. ⲛⲁϥ (? eulogies from church), BP 4982 S ⲟⲉⲓⲕ ⲛⲥ., Ep 201 S send him ⲟⲩⲥⲙⲟⲩ, BM 1114 S ⲡⲛⲟϭ ⲛⲥ. (sc 2 fishes), ST 274 S be kind & give ⲟⲩⲥ. to boy (who had brought letter), J 65 65 S ⲡⲉⲥ. ⲉⲡⲣⲟ ⲛⲡⲏⲛⲕⲉ alms, Ep 84 S priest's contract with camelherd ϯⲛⲁϯ ⲡⲉⲥ. ⲙⲡⲧⲟⲡⲟⲥ ⲡⲁⲕ ϩⲛⲡϣⲁ, Kr 247 S ⲧⲛⲱⲥⲓ(ⲥ) ⲛⲛⲕⲟⲩⲓ ⲛⲥ. list of varia (cf ib 242 ⲧⲁⲓⲟ), C 41 22 B ⲟⲩⲕⲟⲩϫⲓ ⲛⲥ. given to ⲧⲟⲡⲟⲥ ϩⲁⲡⲁⲛⲟⲣⲉⲙ; as abundance, treasure: C 41 16 B ⲟⲩⲛⲓϣϯ ⲛⲥ. ⲁϥϣⲱⲡⲓ in corn-mill, Miss 4 648 S great ⲥ. of bread in storeroom, C 86 319 B dig there ϫⲛⲁϫⲓⲙⲓ ⲙⲡⲓⲥ., Mor 20 8 S he traded ⲉϥϭⲓⲛⲉ ⲡⲟⲩⲛⲟϭ ⲛⲥ. v Ep 201 n, 245 n, 378 n.

As adj, with ⲑⲩⲥⲓⲁ: Lev 7 13 SB, Ps 49 14 SA (Cl)B ⲁⲓⲛⲉⲥⲉⲱⲥ; Miss 4 183 B ⲡⲁⲓⲗⲟⲅⲕⲟϫⲓ ⲛⲥ. as offering, Hall 72 S ⲙⲟⲩ ⲛⲥ. for sprinkling cattle.

ⲁⲧⲥ. B, without blessing: PO 11 328 ⲧϥⲉⲣⲉⲥⲓⲥ ⲛⲛⲓⲁ. those not taking communion (?).

ϯ ⲥ. SB, give blessing, sacrament: P 83 6 SB, Si 50 22 S ⲉⲩⲗ. ⲇⲓⲇⲟⲛⲁⲓ; DeV 1 83 B patriarch brought to church to ϯ ⲥ. ⲛϩⲏⲧⲥ, EW 166 B priest ⲉϥϯ ⲥ. in church = PO 8 63 ⲁⲗⲟ; ⲥ ⲛ- dat: MG 25 253 B ⲙⲡⲓϯ ⲥ. ⲙⲙⲁⲣⲕⲟⲥ ⲡⲣⲟⲥⲫⲟⲣⲁⲛ δ.; TEuch 1 25 B after ordination bishop ϯ ⲥ. ⲡⲁⲩ & gives mysteries, AM 117 B bishop ϯ ⲥ. ⲙⲡⲗⲁⲟⲥ from body & blood, Va 58 67 B priest sent to ϯ ⲥ. ⲛⲛⲓⲡⲁⲣⲑⲉⲛⲟⲥ, CO 66 S bishop bids ϯ ⲡⲥⲙⲟⲩ ⲛⲁⲥ.

ϫⲓ, ϭⲓ ⲥ. SABF, take blessing, hence salute a superior: 4 Kg 4 29 S(Bor 226 166 Esaias, bibl ⲁⲡⲟⲕⲣⲓⲛ.), Ps 48 18 S(B ⲥ. ⲉ-), Pro 28 20 SA, Is 36 16 SF (B do), Z 355 S visitor ⲁϥϫⲓ ⲥ. saluted & returned home ⲉⲩⲗⲟⲅⲉⲓⲥⲑⲁⲓ, Ac 3 25 S(B ϣⲱⲡⲓ ⲉⲩⲥⲙⲁⲣ.) ⲉⲛⲉⲩⲗ.; CaiEuch 656 B ⲡⲧⲉϥ. ⲩⲙⲛⲉⲓⲥⲑⲁⲓ; BAp 106 S ⲁⲩⲭ. ϩⲛⲡⲉϥⲥⲓϫ = MIE 2 381 B ⲉⲃⲟⲗ ϩⲉⲛ-, BM 983 S bishop says ⲁⲩⲭ. ⲛⲧⲟⲟⲧ, BIF 13 112 S seized saint's hand ϫⲉⲉϥⲛⲁϫ. ⲛⲧⲟⲟⲧϥ, Miss 4 750 S ⲛⲧⲁϥϫⲓ ⲙⲡⲉⲥ....ⲉⲡⲉⲥⲛⲧ ⲉⲡⲉϥϭⲓϫ; equivalent to please (imperat): CMSS 30 Sʲ ϫⲓ ⲡⲉⲥ. ⲛⲁⲕ & buy some wine, BM 590 B ϭⲓ ⲡⲓⲥ. & bring, ib 545

(2) B ⲟⲩⲱϣ ⲧⲉⲕϫⲓ ⲡⲉⲥ. ⲧⲉⲕⲥⲙⲉⲛ ⲡⲉϥϩⲱⲃ; take sacrament S B: Va 63 15 B in church ⲁⲩⲥ. = BMis 389 S ⲥⲩⲡⲁⲅⲉ, Miss 4 144 B ⲙⲡⲉⲣϭ. ⲛⲧⲟⲧϥ = Mor 18 72 S ⲥⲩⲛ., BSG 187 S pilgrims ϫ. in ⲧⲟⲡⲟⲥ, AM 185 B sim, DeV 1 91 B asks hermit ⲉϥϭ. ⲛⲱⲡ, C 41 27 B man carrying ⲧⲣⲁⲡⲉⲍⲁ ⲛϭ. portative altar (?), Va 63 7 B ϣⲱⲡ ⲛϭ.; ⲥ ⲉϫⲉⲛ- B, take sacrament for, in memory of: C 89 109 suffered not to chant nor ⲉϭ. ⲉϫⲱϥ ⲡⲣⲟⲥⲫⲟⲣⲁ ⲅⲓⲛⲉⲥⲑⲁⲓ ⲩⲡⲉⲣ; Va 58 78 after burial ⲉⲩϭ. ⲉϫⲱϥ daily.

ϫⲓⲛⲥ. B, act of blessing: 1 Chr 16 35 m ⲧⲟ ⲁⲓⲛⲉⲓⲛ; Ps 70 6 B f (S diff) ⲩⲙⲛⲏⲥⲓⲥ.

In name: ⲡⲥⲙⲟⲩ (CO, Ep), ⲯⲙⲱ (J, ST).

ⲥⲁⲙⲃⲉϩⲓ B nn f, testicles: K 78 ϯⲥ. انشيان.

ⲥⲁⲙⲁⲑⲉ S nn f, cistern, tank: Z 313 ⲇⲉⲝⲁⲙⲉⲛⲏ into which water poured, BM 1114 m. Gk word? or cf ⲥⲁⲙⲡⲧ?

ⲥⲱⲙⲕ v ⲥⲱⲡⲕ.

ⲥⲙⲙⲉ SA, ⲥⲙⲙⲁ A, ⲥⲉⲙⲓ B, ⲥⲛⲙⲙⲓ (He 7 25), -ⲏ F vb intr, appeal, make application ⲥ ⲛ- of person to whom: Va 68 173 B singest me psalms & ⲕⲥ. ⲛⲏⲓ with angels, LAp 326 S my spirit seeth thee & ⲉϥⲥ. ⲛⲁⲕ (var ⲉⲣⲟⲕ) ⲉⲛⲧⲩⲅⲭⲁⲛⲉⲓⲛ, AZ 34 86 S ϯⲥ. ⲛⲁⲕ ϫⲉⲉⲕⲁⲉⲓⲣ ⲡⲁⲣⲁⲡ, BKU 1 23 F ⲧⲓⲥⲛⲙⲙⲏ ⲡⲉⲕ Almighty; ⲥ ϩⲁⲣⲧⲛ- S, meaning same: Mor 47 135 going ⲉⲥ. ϩⲁⲧⲙⲡⲗⲟⲩϫ, Leyd 276 sim; ⲥ ⲉ-, appeal against, accuse: Ac 19 38 B (var & S ⲛ-) ⲉⲅⲕⲁⲗⲉⲓⲛ dat, Ro 8 33 B(S ⲟⲩⲃⲉ-) ⲉⲅ. ⲕⲁⲧⲁ; ib 11 2 B(S ⲉϩⲣⲁⲓ ⲉ-) ⲉⲛⲧ. dat, Z 308 S, HL 109 B ⲉⲛⲧ. ⲕⲁⲧⲁ; Ac 25 15 S(B ⲟⲩⲱⲛϩ) ⲉⲙⲫⲁⲛⲓⲍⲉⲓⲛ ⲡⲉⲣⲓ; Mor 17 79 S ⲁⲛⲥ. ⲉⲣⲟϥ ⲙⲡⲛϩⲣⲉⲙⲙⲱⲡ ⲡⲣⲟⲥⲉⲣⲭⲉⲥⲑⲁⲓ dat; BHom 22 S ⲥ. ⲉⲣⲟϥ ⲙⲡⲉϥⲭ̅ⲥ̅ ⲡⲣⲟⲥⲁⲛⲁⲫⲉⲣⲉⲓⲛ dat; BMis 544 S ⲡⲉⲩⲥ. ⲉⲣⲟⲟⲩ ⲙⲡⲁⲅⲅⲉⲗⲟⲥ interpellare; Miss 4 207 B ⲉⲕⲥ. ⲉⲣⲟⲓ ⲙⲫϯ, COAd 52 S if ye meet me not ⲧⲁⲥ. ⲉⲣⲱⲧⲛ ⲡⲧⲉⲡⲉⲧⲛϩⲏⲧ ϩⲓⲥⲉ; ⲁϩⲟⲩⲛ ⲁ- A, appeal to: BM 1224 20 ⲁⲧⲉⲧⲛⲁⲥⲙⲙⲁ ⲁⲣ. ⲁⲡⲡⲉ; ⲉϩⲣⲁⲓ ⲉ- or ⲛ- S: Ro 11 2 (B ⲛ-) ⲉⲛⲧ. dat, ShP 130¹ 6 ⲉⲩⲥ. ⲉ. ⲉⲡⲡⲉ ϩⲁⲡⲉⲧⲡⲁⲣⲁⲃⲁ, ShClPr 23 voice ⲉⲥⲥ. ⲉ. ⲙⲡⲉⲧϫⲟⲥⲉ ϫⲉⲙⲁⲧⲛⲃⲟⲟⲩ, ShC 42 43 ⲥ. ⲉ. ⲉⲡⲡⲉ (var ⲙ-); ⲥ ϩⲁ-, ϩⲁ- SB, appeal concerning, for; Ac 24 1 B(S ⲉ-) ⲉⲙⲫ. ⲕⲁⲧⲁ, He 7 25 S(B ⲉϩ. ⲉⲝ.) ⲉⲛⲧ. ⲩⲡⲉⲣ; ShC 73 74 S ⲉϥⲥ. ϩⲁⲣⲟⲡ ϫⲉ-, Gu 4 S ⲡⲉⲕⲉⲓⲱⲧ ⲥ. ⲙⲡⲡⲉ ϩⲁⲧⲉϥⲡⲣⲟⲥⲫⲟⲣⲁ that hast stolen, AM 214 B ⲉⲩⲥ. ⲙⲫϯ ϩⲁⲛⲓⲁⲥⲉⲃⲏⲥ; ⲉϩⲣ. ϩⲁ-, ϩⲁ- SB: Ro 8 26 S(B ⲉ. ⲉⲝ.) ⲩⲡⲉⲣⲉⲛⲧ.; BHom 71 S ⲉⲩⲥ. ⲉϩ. ⲙⲡⲡⲉ ϩⲁⲣⲟⲡ, Va 66 311 B ⲩⲥ. ⲉϩ. ϩⲁⲛⲓϩⲏⲕⲓ; ⲥ ⲉϫⲉⲛ- B, meaning same: Ro 8 27 (S ⲉϩ. ϩⲁ-) ⲉⲛⲧ. ⲩⲡⲉⲣ, Va 68 166 ϥⲣⲱϣⲓ ⲉⲥ. ⲉϫⲱⲓ ⲡϫⲉ ⲫⲣⲁⲡ ⲙⲡⲁⲓⲱⲧ ⲡⲣⲟⲥ ⲧⲏⲛ ⲡⲣⲉⲥⲃⲉⲓⲁⲛ; ⲉϩⲣⲏⲓ ⲉϫ.: Ro 8 34 (S do) ⲉⲛⲧ. ⲩⲡ.; DeV 1 118 B souls ⲥ. ⲉϩ.

ⲣⲁⲡⲟⲧ ⲉⲧ. ⲡⲓⲡⲁⲣⲁⲡⲟⲙⲟⲥ; ⲥ ⲉⲧⲃⲉ- *SB*, meaning same: Ac 25 24 *SB* ἐντ. *περί*; Miss 4 238 *S* ⲁⲅⲉ. ⲉⲡⲉⲡⲉⲓⲱⲧ ⲉ. ⲡⲉⲣⲡⲏⲅⲉ *against…concerning*, Ryl 273 *S* ⲥ. ⲛϥⲏⲅⲉⲙⲱⲛ ⲉ. ϩⲉⲛⲕⲟⲟⲩⲉ; ⲥ ⲟⲩⲃⲉ-, *appeal against*: Ro 8 33 *S*(*B* ⲉ-) ἐγκ. *κατά*; Job 7 20 *B* (*S* ⲕⲱ ⲟⲩⲃⲉ-) κατεντευκτὴν τιθέναι.

—— nn m *SB*, *petition, accusation*: 1 Tim 2 1 *B*(*S* ⲧⲱⲃϩ), ib 4 5 *B*(*S* ϣⲗⲏⲗ) ἔντευξις, ShMIF 23 94 *S* ⲡⲥ. ⲡⲧⲁⲕⲉ. ⲉⲣⲟⲓ ⲙⲙⲟϥ *in judgment hall*, MG 25 139 *B* προσευχη, ⲥ., ϭⲓ ϩⲣⲟⲙ.

ⲁⲡⲥⲙⲙⲉ *SA* nn, *ordinance*: Pro 1 8 *SA*(*B* ⲥⲟϭⲛⲓ), ib 6 20 *SA*(*B* ⲑⲱϣ) θεσμός; ib 29 43 *SA* τάξις; Ex 12 14 *S*(*B* ⲡⲟⲙⲟⲥ) νόμιμον; Br 261 *S* gave them ⲛϩⲣⲉⲡⲁ., ShBMOr 8810 412 *S* ⲥϭⲟⲟⲩⲉ…ⲁ. of fathers, AJSL 46 251 *S* ⲛⲁ. ⲙⲡⲉⲓⲛⲟϭ ⲛⲗⲓⲧⲟⲅⲣⲧⲟⲥ preserve the world, Ryl 94 100 *S* ⲛⲁ. ⲡⲧⲁⲡⲥⲙⲛⲧⲟⲩ with king.

ⲣⲉϥⲥ. *B*, *advocate, accuser*: AM 275 ⲟⲩⲣ. ⲡⲧⲉ ⲡⲁⲧⲁⲓⲕⲁⲑⲉⲇⲣⲁ (*sc* St Mark) πρεσβεία; BSM 9 ⲡⲓⲣ. ⲉⲧⲣⲱⲟⲩ = BMis 326 *S* κατηγορος. *Cf* ⲥⲙⲓⲛⲉ (ⲣⲉϥⲥ.)

ϭⲓⲛⲥ. *S*, *accusation*: P 44 57 شكوى.

ⲥⲙⲁⲙⲉ *A²* *v* ⲥⲙⲟⲩ.

ⲥⲓⲙⲙⲁⲙ *B* *v* ⲥⲓⲙ *sf*.

ⲥⲙⲓⲛⲉ *SA*, ⲥⲙⲓⲛⲉ *A²*(Jo), ⲥⲉⲙⲛⲓ *BF*, ⲥⲙⲓⲛⲓ *F*, ⲥⲙⲛ- *SA*, ⲥⲙⲉⲛ- *SF*, ⲥⲙⲓⲛ- (PLond 4 436 &c), ⲥⲙⲛⲧ- (Lant 112, 117) *S*, ⲥⲙⲙⲛ- *A²*(AP), ⲥⲉⲙⲛⲉ- *B*, ⲥⲙⲛⲧ⸗ *SAF*, ⲥⲉⲙⲛⲏⲧ⸗ *BF*, ⲥⲙⲟⲡⲧ† *SB*, ⲥⲙⲟⲧ† *B* (C 41 71), ⲥⲙⲁⲛⲧ† *AA²F*, ⲥⲙⲁⲁⲛⲧ† *A²*, ⲥⲉⲙⲛⲏⲟⲩⲧ† *B* vb **I** intr, *be established, set right, in order*: 1 Kg 24 21 *B*(*S* ⲁϩⲉ ⲣⲁⲧ⸗), Pro 14 11 *B*(*SA* do) ἱστάναι, Ps 96 tit *SB* ⲕⲁⲑⲓⲥ., Deu 28 65 *S*(*B* diff) στάσις γίνεσθαι; Dan 4 3 *B* τίθεσθαι; EpJer 26 *F*(*B* ⲟϩⲓ ⲉⲣⲁⲧ⸗) ὀρθοῦσθαι, Z 313 *S* διορθ.; Pro 8 25 *B*(*SA* ⲧⲁϫⲣⲟ) ἑδράζεσθαι; Eccl 11 6 *S* στοιχίζειν; Job 15 21 *S*(*B* = Gk) εἰρηνεύειν; ShA 2 4 *S* demon ⲙⲉϥⲕⲁ ⲣⲱⲙⲉ ⲉⲥ. ⲉⲡⲉϩ (Miss 4 694 same), ShBor 247 123 *S* ⲡⲉⲛⲧⲁϥⲣ ϩⲗⲗⲟ opp ⲡⲉⲧⲉⲙⲡⲁⲧϥⲥ., Mor 41 162 *S* ⲁⲩⲥ. ⲛϭⲓ ⲡⲉϥϩⲏⲧ *came to senses*, PO 11 383 *B* ⲉⲧⲁⲡⲉϥϩⲏⲧ ⲥ., Mor 18 7 *S* blind healed ⲁⲧⲉϥⲟⲣⲁⲥⲓⲥ ⲥ. = Miss 4 102 *B*, BIF 14 176 *S* ⲁⲡⲧⲏⲩ ⲥ. & sea calmed, C 86 123 *B* sim, MG 25 76 *B* ⲁⲕⲙⲧⲁⲛⲥ. *when art settled* (in abode) I will visit thee, Lant 80 vo 23 *S* ⲡⲉⲧⲉⲙⲡϥⲥ. *what is not correct* in copy, TRit 522 *B* tongue (of corpse) is idle ⲁⲩⲥ. ⲛⲑⲉ ⲡⲓϫⲓϫ اشل.

Qual: Lev 13 5 *S* gloss on ϭⲉⲉⲧ (*B* om), 1 Cor 13 13 *SB* μένειν, Ps 5 6 *B*(*S* ⲙⲟⲩⲛ ⲉⲃⲟⲗ) διαμ., Pro 12 7 *B*(*SA* do) παραμ., Job 15 31 *B*(*S* do) ὑπομ.; EstB 7 *S* εὐσταθεῖν, He 9 8 *B*(*SF* ⲧⲁϩ.) στάσιν ἔχειν, Nu 3 32 *B*(*S* = Gk) καθισ.; Ac 27 12 *B*(*S* ⲙⲧⲟⲛ) εὔθετος; Mk 14 59 *SF*(*B* = Gk) ἴσος εἶναι;

Ac 17 11 *S*(*B* ϣⲱⲡⲓ) ἔχειν *se habere*; Jud 18 27 *S* πείθειν; Lu 8 35 *S*(*B* ⲟⲓ ⲛⲥⲁⲃⲉ) σωφρονεῖν; Bel 17 *B* σῶος; Tob 7 4 *S* ὑγιαίνειν; Cl 3 4 *A* ⲧⲣⲉ ⲉⲧⲥ. (var ⲉⲧⲉϣϣⲉ) καθῆκον; Ac 19 36 *B*(*S* c. refl) καταστέλλεσθαι; Si 41 1 *S* εἰρηνεύειν; 1 Tim 6 17 *B* neg (*S* ⲧⲁϫ.) ἀδηλότης; Ez 42 4 *SB* Gk om; Sh Ming 316 *S* ⲡϥⲛⲁϣⲱϥⲧ ⲁⲛ ⲙⲡⲉⲧⲥ. *what is right*, ShMIF 23 167 *S* soul ⲉⲥⲥ. ⲛ ⲉⲥⲟⲩⲟⲝ, ShP 130³ 7 *S* ⲁⲥⲕⲟⲥ…ⲉϥⲥ. ⲁⲛ (*cf* ⲗⲱⲱϭⲉ), El 72 *A* ⲥⲉⲥ. ⲉⲛ in faith = Budge *Bibl Texts* 271 *S*, Va 63 13 *B* ⲉⲣⲉⲧⲉⲛⲥⲃⲉ ⲥ. = BMis 386 *S* ϩⲓⲛ ⲧⲛϣ, Mor 41 25 *S* through prayers all creation c. = DeV 2 280 *B* ⲧⲁϩⲣⲟⲩⲧ ⲉⲣⲁⲧⲥ, ClPr 54 38 *S* that church c. *is standing* to-day, Mani 2 *A²* ⲡϫⲁⲓ…ⲧⲉϥⲥⲕⲏⲛⲏ ⲥ. ⲡ-ϩⲏⲧϥ, ib sim ⲥⲙⲁⲁ., Mor 29 58 *S* ⲉⲣⲉⲡⲁⲏⲣ ⲥ. *calm*, J 66 1 *S* ⲉⲣⲉⲡⲁⲗⲟⲅⲓⲥⲙⲟⲥ ⲥ. (*cf* PMon 97 λογισμοῦ σῶς), C 89 168 *B* clad not in ϩⲉⲃⲥⲱ ⲉϥⲥ., R 1 3 10 *S* ϯⲗⲉⲝⲓⲥ ⲥ. ⲁⲛ *not correct*, Kr 36 *F* this deed ϭⲱ ⲉⲃⲥ.; ⲥⲉⲙⲛⲏⲟⲩⲧ *B*: 1 Cor 4 11 neg (*S* diff) ἀστατεῖν; Va 57 122 calm sea etc., MG 25 236 his simplicity ⲉϥⲥ.

II tr, a *establish, construct, set right*: Ex 26 35 *S*(*B* ϫⲱ), Ps 16 11 *BF*(*S* ⲕⲱ), MG 25 206 *B* ⲡⲁϥⲥ. ⲡⲟⲩⲟⲱϣ τιθ., Hos 10 4 *SAB*, He 9 16 *BF*(*S* ⲕⲱ ⲉϩⲣⲁⲓ) διατ., Job 36 15 *S*(*B* ⲓⲛⲓ ⲉⲃⲟⲗ) ἐκτ., Ex 40 25 *B* ἐπιτ., Ps 40 8 *SB* κατατ., Pro 29 24 *SA* προτ., Jo 9 22 *SA²B*, Ac 23 20 *B*(*S* ⲧⲁⲥⲥⲉ) συντ., Ps 24 12 *SB* c. ⲡⲟⲙⲟⲥ νομοθετεῖν; Lev 27 17 *SB*, Jer 42 14 *B*(*S* ⲧⲁϩⲟ ⲉⲣ.), AP 10 *A²* ἱστάναι, Pro 22 17 *SA* ἐφισ., Nu 21 15 *S*(*B* ⲧⲁϩⲟ), Tit 1 5 *B*(*S* ⲧⲁϩⲟ ⲉⲣ.) καθισ., Lev 13 16 *S*(*B* diff) ἀποκ.; Ez 4 2 *SB*, Hab 3 19 *SA*(*B* ⲑⲱϣ) τάσσειν, Dan 6 10 *SB* ⲉⲛⲧ., Job 38 12 *S*(*B* ⲑⲁⲙⲓⲟ) συντ.; ib 25 *B*(*S* ⲥⲟⲃⲧⲉ) ἑτοιμάζειν; Mal 2 10 *S*(ShA 1 281, *B* om) κτίζειν; Jos 18 1 *S* πηγνύναι, Hos 9 8 *S*(R 2 1 59) *A*(*B* ⲧⲁϫ.) καταπ.; Lu 9 51 *B*(*S* ⲧⲁϫ.) στηρίζειν; Ac 23 13 *S* (*B* ⲓⲣⲓ) ποιεῖν; Jos 11 23 *S* refl καταπαύειν; Si 43 25 *S* κοπάζειν; Jud 15 19 *S* ⲁⲡⲉϥⲡⲛⲁ ⲥⲙⲧϥ ἐπιστρέφειν; Deu 2 24 *S* ⲥⲙⲛ ϫⲱ ἐνάρχεσθαι; ShC 73 163 *S* novices shall c. ⲙⲡⲉⲩϣⲁϫⲉ before altar, ib 195 *S* God ⲡⲧⲁϥⲥⲙⲛ ⲡⲟⲩⲟⲙ, ShP 131⁷ 45 *S* ⲙⲁ ⲛⲥⲙⲛ ⲛⲉϩ, ShA 1 300 *S* workers in wood & ⲡⲉⲧⲥ. ⲛⲓⲡⲉⲛⲓⲡⲉ, Sh(Besa)Z 505 *S* ⲧⲟⲟⲩⲉ ⲡⲓⲙ ⲉⲩⲡⲁⲥⲙⲛⲧϥ, R 2 4 11 *S* wool ⲡⲥⲉⲥⲙⲛⲧ ⲛϩⲟⲓⲧⲉ, BSM 42 *B* ⲁⲩⲥⲉⲙⲛⲉ ϩⲁⲛⲧⲣⲁⲡⲉⲍⲁ = BMis 388 *S* ⲕⲱ ⲉϩⲣⲁⲓ, R 1 2 62 *S* creed ⲡⲧⲁⲩⲥⲙⲛⲧⲉ at Nicæa, AM 211 *B* c. ⲙⲡⲁⲓⲛⲓϣϯ ⲛⲓⲱⲧⲙⲟⲥ, BM 545 (2) *Bꞔ* ⲥⲙⲉⲛ ⲡⲉϥϩⲱⲃ *for he is wretched*, HT N 80 *S* ϫⲱⲱⲣⲉ ⲉⲃⲟⲗ of tongues opp c., C 86 122 *B* moor ship till God c. ⲙⲡⲁⲓⲧⲛⲟϥⲟⲥ, ib 260 *B* ⲁⲩⲥ. *set up* relics in ⲧⲟⲡⲟⲥ, BAp 98 *S* ⲁⲧⲁϩⲉϩⲓⲥ ⲥⲙⲛⲧⲉ & thirst ceased, BMar 218 *S* ⲥⲙⲛ ⲡⲉⲕϩⲏⲧ with bread = Rec 6 184 *B*. **b** *compose, write* book *S*: Mor 17

128 when I had ⲥⲙⲛ ⲡⲉⲩⲁⲅⲅⲉⲗⲓⲟⲛ ⲛ̄ⲕⲁⲑⲁⲣⲟⲛ (var Gu 78 ⲥϩⲁⲓ) καθαρογράφειν, *ib* 107 books that demons ⲥⲙⲛⲧⲟⲩ κατασκευάζειν (var συντιθ.), *ib* 124 ⲁϥⲥ. ⲡⲟⲩϫⲱⲱⲙⲉ ϣⲁⲓⲱⲣⲁⲡⲏⲥ βιβλίον ποιεῖν, Bor 248 10 ⲁⲓⲥⲙⲛ ⲟⲩⲕⲟⲩⲓ ⲡⲗⲟⲧⲟⲥ = Brooks *Sel Lett Severus* 207 ⲥⲟⲃⲟ ; ShZ 506 ⲥϩⲁⲓ ⲛ ⲥ. ⲛ̄ⲛ̄ϫⲱ., TT 88 poets ⲛ̄ⲧⲁⲩⲥ. ⲛ̄ⲛ̄ϫⲱ. ⲛ̄ⲛ̄ϩⲉⲗⲗⲏⲛ, Imp Russ Ar S 18 026 Psalter he hath written ⲙⲁⲣⲉϥⲥⲙⲛⲧϥ *complete* & price it ;   *provide, pay for* book (mostly in colophons) *S* : BMar 186 ⲥ. ⲡⲟⲩⲉⲩⲁⲅⲅⲉⲗⲓⲟⲛ ἀγοράζειν ; Lant 111 4 ⲁϥⲥⲙⲛ ⲡⲉⲓϫⲱ. by own labour & gave it, *ib* 120 (2) 2 sim, *ib* 13 ⲁⲛⲥ. ⲙ̄ⲡⲓϫⲱ. ⲉϩⲟⲩⲛ to church (in these scribe also named) ; *ib* 113 (1) 3 ⲁϥϥⲓ ⲡⲣⲟⲟⲩϣ for book ⲁϥⲥⲙⲛⲧϥ & gave it, *ib* 10, 72, 88 8, 98 4, 121 sim (in these & generally provider only named) ; *B* paral is ⲑⲁⲙⲓⲟ (Z 64, 66) or ϣⲟⲡ (DeV 1 52, also *S* Balestri lxv).   **c** *draw up deed* (cf τιθέναι) *SB* : EW 30 *B* can I ⲥ. ⲕⲉⲡⲣⲁⲥⲓⲥ ? ποιεῖν ; Miss 4 234 *S* ⲧⲣⲉⲩⲥ. ⲡⲟⲩϩⲟ ⲙⲟⲗⲟⲅⲓⲁ in writing, Mor 44 41 *S* ⲁⲩⲥ. ⲡ[ⲟⲩ]ⲭⲁⲣⲧⲏⲥ & wrote thereon as follows, TstAb 227 *B* ⲥ. ⲛ̄ⲧⲉⲕⲇⲓⲁⲑⲏⲕⲏ, J 35 76 *S* ⲁⲓⲥⲙⲛ ⲧⲓⲧⲓⲁⲗⲏⲥⲓⲥ (scribe also named), ST 48 *S* ⲁⲓⲥⲙⲛ ⲡⲓⲉⲅⲅⲣⲁⲫⲟⲛ (do) ;   also *write* : J 42 57 *S* scribe says ⲁⲓⲥⲙⲛⲧⲥ, *ib* 76 90, CO 424 *S* (cf *ib* 425 ⲉⲧⲣⲁϣⲥ) sim ; with prep *S* : PBu 37 ⲉⲧⲁⲥⲙⲛ ⲡⲣⲁⲥⲓⲥ ⲉⲡⲏⲓ *respecting*, J 66 79 sim, BP 11938 ⲧⲣⲉϥⲥⲙⲛ ⲙⲓⲥⲑⲱⲥⲓⲥ ⲉⲣⲟⲟⲩ (sc fields), BMis 309 ⲥⲙⲛ ⲡⲉⲕⲣⲁⲙⲙⲁⲧⲟⲛ ⲡⲁⲓ ⲉ ⲡⲉⲧⲕⲣ ⲭⲣⲓⲁ ⲙ̄ⲙⲟϥ, Ryl 325 ⲛϥⲥⲙⲛ ⲟⲩⲥⲓⲕⲉⲗⲉⲛ (σιγίλλον) ⲛ̄ⲡⲓⲣⲱⲙⲉ.   **d** *set up, construct* building &c *SB* (rare) : Ge 12 8 (*B* ⲧⲁϩⲟ), Si 47 18 ἱστ., Job 8 6 (*B* ✝) ἀποκαθιστ. ; Ge 35 16 (*B* ⲧⲁ.) πήγ. ; R 1 4 7 exstruere ; ShA 1 301 ⲥ. ⲡⲣⲉⲡⲕⲁⲑⲉⲇⲣⲁ, PO 14 352 *B* ⲁϥⲥ. ⲡⲱⲟⲩ ⲛ̄ⲟⲩⲙⲁ ⲛ̄ⲑⲱⲟⲩϥ, Ryl 252 ⲡⲉⲥⲡⲏⲗⲁⲓⲟⲛ ⲛ̄ⲧⲁⲡⲉⲕⲱⲧ ⲥⲙⲛⲧϥ, Miss 4 533 ⲥⲙⲛ ⲟⲩⲅⲉⲛⲉⲉⲧⲉ = C 89 51 *B* ⲕⲱⲧ, BSG 178 bade ⲥⲙⲛ ⲟⲩⲛⲟϭ ⲛ̄ⲧⲣⲟⲭⲟⲥ = *ib* 9 *B* ⲑⲁⲙⲓⲟ, BMis 272 ⲧⲣⲉⲩⲥ. ⲙ̄ⲡϩⲗⲓⲙⲛⲏ ⲛ̄ⲛⲟⲩⲃ, *ib* 274 ⲥ. ⲙ̄ⲡⲉⲓⲃ̄ⲗⲟϭ ;   ⲥⲙⲛ ⲥⲡⲧⲉ, v ⲥⲱⲡⲧ *be created* (ⲥⲡⲧⲉ).

ⲥⲙⲛ ⲧⲟⲟⲧⲥ ⲙⲛ- *S, lay hand with, agree with* : Ex 23 1 (*B* diff) συγκατατιθ. μετά ; Z 347 συμφωνία γίνεσθαι dat = MG 25 219 *B* ✝ ⲙⲁ✝ ϣⲱⲡⲓ ; BHom 49 κοινωνίαν τιθ. (var R 2 2 33 ⲥⲙⲛⲧⲥ ⲙⲛ-) ; Miss 8 239 ϣⲁⲩⲥⲙⲛ ⲧⲟⲟⲧⲟⲩ with harlots, PNolot 35 ⲁⲩⲥⲙⲛ ⲧⲟⲩⲧⲟⲩ ⲙ̄ⲡⲛⲉⲩⲉⲣⲏⲟⲩ ⲉⲧⲣⲉ- ;   qual : 1 Kg 22 17 ἡ χεὶρ μετά ; Bor 134 3 (Vita Sin) harlot to-day with thee, to-morrow ⲧⲟⲟⲧⲥ ⲥ. ⲙ̄ⲛⲕⲉⲟⲩⲁ = C 41 29 *B*.

With following preposition.

—— ⲉ- *SAB* intr, *dat commodi* : BSM 80 *B* ⲁⲡϩⲏⲧ ⲙ̄ⲡⲟⲩⲣⲟ ⲥ. ⲉⲣⲟϥ = BMis 171 *S* ϣⲱⲡⲉ ⲙ̄ⲙⲟϥ, AM 322 *B* ⲁⲡⲉϥϩⲏⲧ ⲥ. ⲉⲣⲟϥ ⲉⲃⲟⲗ ϩⲉⲛⲡⲓⲃⲓⲥⲓ, ShC 73 166 *S* ⲉⲣⲉⲧⲉϥϩⲏⲧ ⲥ.✝ ⲉⲣⲟϥ ⲉⲧⲙⲧⲁⲕⲟ, CO 467 *S*

things written in this list ⲥⲟⲩⲥ.✝ ⲉⲣⲟⲕ ⲛ̄ⲧⲧⲁⲁⲩ ⲡⲁⲓ ;   tr, *set up for, against, fabricate* : Ps 108 5 *SB* ⲧⲓⲑ. κατά ; Pro 27 23 *SA* ⲉⲫⲓⲥ. dat, Ps 140 9 *B* (*S* ⲧⲁⲣⲟ ⲉⲣⲁⲧ⸗ ⲉ-) συνισ. ; Job 7 12 *S*(*B* ⲑⲱϣ ⲉϩⲣ. ⲉⲝ.) κατατασ. ἐπί ; ShC 42 26 *S* ⲧⲉⲧⲛⲥⲙⲛ ϩⲉⲛ ϣⲁϫⲉ ⲙ̄ⲡⲁⲣⲁⲛⲟⲙⲟⲛ ⲉⲣⲟⲓ, BAp 152 *S* ⲉⲩⲥⲙⲛ ⲕⲣⲟϥ ⲉⲣⲟⲕ, CO 218 *S* about tending camel ⲛ̄ⲧⲁⲥⲙⲛ ⲧⲉϥϭⲩⲗⲏ ⲉⲣⲟϥ, WTh 178 *S* ⲁⲡⲉϥϩⲏⲧ ⲥⲙⲛⲧϥ ⲉⲣⲟϥ *mind righted itself* (cf intr), BMis 294 *S* ⲁⲓⲥⲙⲛ ⲡⲉⲕϩⲏⲧ ⲉϩⲟⲩⲛ ⲉϩⲉⲛϣⲁϫⲉ of folly, Va 57 77 *B* evil things ⲛ̄ⲧⲉϥⲥⲙ̄ⲛⲧⲟⲩ ⲉⲃ. ⲉⲕⲉⲟⲩⲓ *transform* ;   neuter -ⲥ & vbal ⲉ-, *resolve to* : ShC 42 20 *S* ⲁⲩⲥⲙⲛⲧⲉ ⲉⲧⲣⲉⲩⲣ ⲟⲩⲣⲱⲃ, Z 622 *S* archbishop ⲥⲙⲛⲧⲉ ⲉⲧⲁⲅⲉ ϩⲱⲃ ⲛⲓⲙ, C 43 194 *B* ⲁϥⲥⲉⲙ ⲛ̄ⲛⲧⲥ ϩⲉⲛⲡⲉϥϩⲏⲧ ⲉⲣⲱⲗ ; or ⲉ- +ⲛⲛ : Mt 26 15 *S* ⲁⲩⲥⲙⲛⲧⲉ ⲉⲙⲁⲁⲃ ⲛ̄ϩⲁⲧ ἱστ. acc.   *V* also **II c.**

—— ⲉϫⲛ- *SABF*, *set, fix upon*, intr : Va 57 205 *B* hills ⲉⲧⲁⲥⲥ. ⲉϫⲱⲟⲩ (sc ark) ἱδρύεσθαι ; Miss 4 630 *S* peace ⲥ. ⲉϫ̄ⲙⲡⲕⲁϩ ;   tr : Pro 23 5 *SA* ⲉⲫⲓⲥ. πρός, Ez 18 12 *B* ⲧⲓⲑ. εἰς, Ex 39 18 *B* ⲉⲡⲓⲧ. ἐπί (*ib* 7 ϩⲓϫⲉⲛ-), He 8 6 *SBF* νομοθετεῖν ἐπί ; Mor 38 94 *S* ⲁϥⲥ. ⲡⲟⲩⲕⲗⲟⲙ ⲉϫⲱϥ for self & ⲉϫⲙ̄ⲡⲉϥϣⲏⲣⲉ.

—— ⲙⲛ-, ⲛⲉⲙ- *SAB*, *settle with* intr : Lu 22 29 *B* (*S* tr) διατ. dat ; Su 14 *S*(*B* ✝) συντασ. ; Ps 72 14 *B* (*S* ⲛ-) ἀσυνθετεῖν ;   tr : Ge 6 18 *SB* ἱσ. μετά, Mt 26 15 *SB* ἱσ. dat ; Si 44 18 *S* ⲧⲓⲑ. πρός, Hos 12 1 *AB* διατ. μετά, He 10 16 *SBF* δ. πρός ; Is 28 15 *SB* ποι. μετά ; Mt 20 2 *SB* συμφωνεῖν μετά ; Ex 8 5 *B* ⲧⲁⲥ. πρός ; Is 28 18 *B*(*S* Gk no vb) πρός ; Ez 16 60 *SB* (Gk do) μετά ; ShC 73 72 *S* ⲥⲙⲛ ⲃⲉⲕⲉ ⲛⲙⲙⲁⲩ, Bor 262 122 *S* ⲁϩⲣⲟ ⲧⲉⲣⲥⲙⲛ ϩⲟⲙⲉⲗⲓⲁ ⲙ̄ⲡⲣⲟⲟⲩⲧ ?, Miss 4 749 *S* ⲁⲩⲥⲙⲛⲧⲉ ⲙ̄ⲡ ⲡⲉⲅⲉⲣⲏⲩ ⲉⲡⲉⲓϩⲱⲃ, BSM 30 *B* oaths ⲉⲧⲁⲛⲥⲉⲙⲛ ⲏⲧⲟⲩ ⲛⲉⲙⲱϥ.   *V* also ⲥⲙⲛ ⲧⲟⲟⲧ⸗ ⲙⲛ-.

—— ⲛ- dat *SAB* intr : Ps 72 18 *SB* ⲧⲓⲑ. ; TEuch 2 270 *B* Thou (God) ⲉⲧⲟⲩⲥ. ⲡⲁⲕ ⲡⲛ̄ϫⲉ ⲡⲓⲥⲓⲟⲩ اليلٌ موّرٌ ;   tr : 4 Kg 4 13 *B* ἐξισ., Ps 9 20 *S*(*B* ⲧⲁⲣⲟ) καθισ. ; Ex 15 25 *SB* ⲧⲓⲑ., Hos 2 18 *AB* διατι. ; Job 14 13 *S*(*B* ✝) ⲧⲁⲥ. ; Ac 14 23 *S*(*B* ⲭⲁ ϫⲓϫ ⲉϫ.) χειροτονεῖν ; ShRyl 70 247 *S* branches ⲥⲙⲛⲧⲟⲩ ⲛ̄ⲟⲩⲕⲗⲟⲙ, Mor 41 27 *S* ⲥ. ⲡⲁⲓ ⲙ̄ⲡⲗⲟⲓⲙⲏⲛ (ⲗⲓⲙⲏⲛ) = DeV 2 282 *B* ⲑⲁⲙⲓⲟ, BSM 14 *B* ⲁϥⲥ. ⲡⲁⲃⲉⲭⲉ ⲡⲏⲓ, BMis 531 *S* ⲁϥⲥⲙⲛ ⲡⲧⲃ̄ⲧ ⲙ̄ⲡϣⲏⲣⲉ ϣⲏⲙ (sc Tobit), *ib* 308 *S* employed him to ⲥⲙⲛ ⲡⲉϥⲗⲟⲅⲟⲥ ⲛⲁϥ *keep his accounts*, *ib* 153 *S* ⲥⲙⲛ ⲡⲉⲕⲛⲟⲩⲥ ⲡⲁⲓ *give attention*, JTS 10 402 *S* fathers were continent ϣⲁⲛⲧⲟⲩⲥⲙⲛ ϫⲱⲟⲩ ⲛ̄ⲛⲉⲩϣⲏⲣⲉ (cf **II a** Deu 2 24).

—— ⲟⲩⲧⲉ- *B*, *set up between* : Ge 9 17 διατιθ. ἀνὰ μέσον ; BSM 24 ⲥ. ⲡⲟⲩⲙⲉⲧϣⲫⲏⲣ ⲟⲩⲧⲱⲥ ⲛⲉⲙ ⲟⲩⲁⲓ = Va 63 2 *B* = BMis 363 *S* ⲕⲱ ⲛⲁϥ.

—— ϩⲛ-, ⲭⲉⲛ-, *be established in* : ShR 2 3 21 *S* ⲁⲕⲥ. ⲏ ⲁⲕⲧⲱϣ ⲡⲁⲕ ϩⲛ̄ⲡⲉⲕⲣϩⲏⲅⲉ ⲉⲑⲟⲟⲩ, PO 11 366 *B* suffered him not ⲉⲥ. ⲭⲉⲛⲡⲉϥⲉⲡⲓⲥⲕⲟⲡⲓⲟⲛ ; *be*

settled, at rest from: Jos 11 23 *S* refl καταπαύειν (or ? εὐσταθεῖν).

—— nn m *SB*, *confirmation, agreement, putting together, adornment*: Sa 7 29 *SB* θέσις, Eph 1 11 *B*(*SF* τωϣ) προθ., Ex 31 11 *B*, Is 3 20 *S*(*B* со́ϯ) συνθ., Z 322 *S* συνθήκη; Dan 6 15 *B* στάσις, Sa 6 26 *S* εὐστάθεια; Va 63 80 *B* пс. of your hearts τὸ ἀσάλευτον, GFr 361 *S* пес. (*sic l*) пнанр εὐκρασία; BM 174 *S* пес. of aged κόσμος; ShA 1 302 *S* parts of ill-built house εϥϣαατ мпеүс., ShWess 9 124 *S* let оүс. ϣωпε among you, ShA 1 107 *S* veil perfect in косннсıс ϩıс., ShIF 102 *S* no blemish ϩıпса мпеүс., TstAb 261 *B* grant me пıс. плаϩпоϩı, DeV 2 166 *B* health & peace & оүс. to all churches, BMis 178 *S* пес. of vine & εγϥросγпн of wine; *adverbial*: BMis 160 *S* апхоı аϩε ратϥ ϩпоүс., MIE 2 349 *B* ер мелетап ϫεпоүс., EW 159 *B* saint spake to demons ϫεпоүс. *calmly*.

атс. *B*, *unstable*: Ja 1 8 (*S* ϣτртωр) ἀκατάστατος; 2 Tim 3 3 (*S* diff) ἄσπονδος; метатс., *instability*: Cat 189 monastic vices ϭı ϩраϥ, ϯм., метмаıϭγλн.

ма пс. *B*, *standing-place*: 1 Chr 28 2 στάσις; Ps 98 5 (*S* = Gk) ὑποπόδιον; ма псмп пеϩ *oil press* (?): ShP 131⁷ 45 *S*.

реϥс., смп- *SB*, *one who sets up, prepares*: P 43 47 *S* р. мпаϥре = 44 74 реϥр п. φάρμακος, 43 62 *S* реϥсмеп сепϫαλıоп · καλικωτнс (καλιγωτής *blacksmith*), Mus 40 257 *S* Jesus преϥсмп ϫро; Va 68 167 *B* constrained his eyes еϯ пϭапр. (*l* ? семı) пемаϥ *sc* tears συμπρεσβευτής; реϥс. полос: Ps 9 20 *S*(*B* реϥϯ сбω п-) νομοθέτης; Va 57 113 *B* реϥсемпе п.; метреϥс. п.: Cat 52 *B*.

ϭıп-, ϫıпс. *SB*, *setting up, depositing*: Dan 6 7 *B* m στῆσαι; My 167 *S* тϭıпсмеп ппγрос of Babel, N&E 39 330 *B* ϯϫ. of martyrs relics.

In place-name: тсмıпе C 89 56 = Τωμηναί ASS Maii 3 38* = MG 17 574 دشميني = Va ar 172 35 اتصمونا (*sic prob*), or MG 646 اشميني = Va 96 اسمينا (*gloss* смпе).

сиоүпе *S* DM nn f, *Nile goose (chenalopex aeg)*: ShC 42 45 heretics raising hands in church compared to birds often found (? painted) there spreading wings пτaoc(ταῶс)мпτес., DM 10 31 (cypher) сиоүпе. Cf سماني (Lab). In names: Τεσμοῦνε (Wess 10 25), Τσμοῦνıς, Τεσμοῦνα (Preisigke). V *Arch du Mus d'Hist Nat Lyon* 14 21, OLZ '27 353.

соүмаıп (var со., -епı) *B* nn f, *sexual organs, parts*: K 78 ϯс. فرج var ذكر between ϣωı & колıωп (cf ? κωλῆ).

смпт *SA*, -мет *S* (once) nn f, *a pool, tank*(?): Mor 17 103 *S* as I was in bath demon еı еϩраı ϩптс. ἔμβασις, which P 44 86, 45 167 = زن, (*basis* Sobhy); BMEA 10577 *S* псамет птаıсмптоү мп(п)еγεεγıп...еγτı мооγ еϩоγп ероoγ (*sc* пс.), *ib* то]ϯı псампт...тоϯı, BMOr 6201 A 53 *S*]ϩıтс. (no context). b *collecting place* (?): El 86 *A* Anointed shall come like оүс. пϭрампе with crown of doves about him, Mor 51 35 *S* (parable) пс. про ϭромпе апϫа моγλαϫ мıсе пϩптоγ, (interpr) convents once filled with holy men, (now) foul men dwell there, BP 11349 *S* among crops ϣомте пс. псıм плат поγтϥ. Cf ? ST 378 4, also сапмт, сомте, самаϥе.

смопт *B* nn *v* смот.

сωмпт *v* сωмт.

сıмепϩ *v* сıм *sf*.

самепϩн *v* мепϩн.

самрϯ *S* vb tr, *meaning unknown*: Hall 65 recipes псамрϥ поγта[(*sic*, *text altered*).

смоγр *B* nn m, *moustache*: K 76 пıс. شارب, Bodl 325 156 пıс. شوارب, BMOr 8775 118 пıс. دردور.

сıмрωт, сıрωϩе *v* сıм *sf*.

смарωoγт *B* *v* смоγ.

смас *S* nn as pl, *meaning unknown, a marble object*: BMis 571 there were ϩепс. мммармароп over the throne.

сıмоγс *v* сıм *sf*.

сомс *S*(rare) *B*, са. *S/F* vb intr, *look, behold*: Ac 1 9 (*S* еıωрм), 1 Cor 3 10 (*S* ϭωϣт, *F* с. ебaл) βλέπειν, Va 57 11 ἐμβ., Ps 12 4 (*S* diff) ἐπιβ., Job 7 8 περιβ.; He 8 5 *F*(*S* ϭ., *B* паγ) ὁρᾶν; MG 25 6 аϥс. аϥпаγ, C 86 295 етаϥс....аϥпаγ ἀτενίζειν; Job 23 15 κατανοεῖν; Lu 11 53 (*S* diff) ἐνέχειν; MIE 2 360 аϥс. аϥпаγ епıмоoγ *spreading* = BAp 89 *S* ϑεωреı мпм., TstAb 238 с. ппекбaл & see.

With following preposition. с е-, *look at, consider*: Su 9 (var ϫоγϣт) β. εἰς, Ez 40 6 (*S* ϭ.) β. κατά, *ib* 45 (*S* do) β. πρός, Lu 19 5 (*S* ϥı еıατϥ) ἀναβ., Is 5 12 *F*(*S* ϭ., *B* п.) ἐμβ., Ez 10 11 (*S* κте еıατϥ) περιβ. acc; Ac 11 6 (*S* ϭ.) ἀτ. acc; Va 57 126 еϣтемс....епн етϫaoγωп ὁρ. acc, Ge 16 13 ἐφορ. acc, Ez 7 19 neg (*S* ϭ. пса-) ὑπερορ.; 1 Jo 1 1 (*S* еıωрϩ) θεᾶσθαι; Ro 12 16 *F*(*S* ϭ., *B* меγı) φρονεῖν acc; Mt 16 3 διακρίνειν acc; C 89 94 bade him с. епıспноγ = MG 17 468

اهتم ب =Va ar 172 55 تواضب حال, MIE 2 383 етаqс.
ероı = BAp 107 S ϭ. еϩоүп еϩраı, Mor 27 38 F
as vanishes еүс. ероq = BMis 402 S ϭ. псωq, Cat
28 еıпаϫоүϣт ап е...алла еıпас. ететепгүпо-
мопн;   с еϫп- SB, *look upon, at*: Ps 118 6 (S
ϭ. еϫп-) ἐπιβ. εἰς; Ez 9 9 ἐφορ. acc; Tri 500 S ϭ.
аүω птс. еϫптаψγχΗ أبصر; BSM 16 аqс. е.
пепϑевıо; еϩрнı еϩ.: Ez 20 46 (S ϭ. еϩ. еϫп-)
ἐπιβ. ἐπί.; C 43 19 с. еϩ. еϫωı;   с пса- BF,
look after, at: TstAb 235 let not eye с. псаоү-
сϭıмı, Mor 30 49 F еүс. есос as if seeing God =
BMis 273 S ϭ. псωс, C 43 206 ascended to heaven
ерепıатос с. псωq;   с ϫаϩеп-, *look toward*:
Lu 12 46 (S diff) προσδοκᾶν;   с ϩатϩн F, meaning sim: He 9 28 (S ϭ. евол ϩнтq, B ϫ.еϩ. ϫаϩ.)
ἀπεκδέχεσθαι;   с ϩıϑе Sˢ, *look in front*: Mor 27
30 аqс. ϩ. ммоq аqпаγ = BMis 379 S ϭ. ϩıϩн
= Va 63 9 B ϫ. ϩıтϩн.

With following adverb.   с евол BF, *look forth,
expect*: Ez 40 19 B(HCons, var & S diff) βλ. ἔξω,
Mk 13 33 F (S ϯ ϩнт, B ϫ. еϩ.), 1 Cor 3 10 F (S
ϭ., B с.) βλ.; Ac 27 33 (S моγп еϩ.), MG 25 174
еqс. еϩ. when he should come προσδοκ.; He 10
13 F(S ϭ. еϩ., B ϫ.) ἐκδέχεσθαι; *ib* 12 15 (S do)
ἐπισκοπεῖν; Bess 7 5 ϯс. еϩ. оγоϩ еıхорϫ, DeV
2 10 етаqс. еϩ. ппеqвал; as nn: Ac 12 11 (S =
Gk) προσδοκία, Phil 1 20 F(S ϭ. еϩ., B ϫıпϫ.) ἀποκαραδοκία;   еϩ. ϫеп-, *look forth from*: DeV 2 84
аqс. еϩ. ϫеппıϣоγϣт; еϩ. ϫатϩн, *look toward, expect*: Ro 8 19 (S ϭ. еϩ. ϩнтч) ἀπεκδέχ., EW 111 ете.
еϩ. ϫ. мпıхлом; еϩ. ϫаϩеп-, meaning sim: Ac
17 16 (S ϭ. ϩнтч) ἐκδέχ., *ib* 10 24 (S do) προσδοκ.;
Va 57 176 с. еϩ. ϫаϩепоγϣωпı ἀναμένειν; BSM
42 еүс. еϩ. ϫаϫωq of archon = Va 63 15 ϫ. еϩ.
ϫ. = BMis 389 S προσϫокеı ϩаϑн; as nn: Lu 21
26 (S ϭ. ϩнтч vb) προσδοκία; еϩ. ϩа-, *beware of*:
Cat 95 с. ерωтеп еϩ. ϩа- (cf Mk 8 15 ϫ. еϩ. ϩа-)
β. ἀπό; еϩ. ϩıϫп- F, *look forth upon*: Mor 24 14
апс. еϩ. ϩ. пкеϩı = *ib* 23 21 S ϭ. еϩр. еϫп-;   с
ϩавал F: Mk 12 38 (S ϯ ϩнт, B паγ еϩ. ϩа-) β.
ἀπό;   с епеснт, *look down*: TstAb 238 с. еп.
птекпаγ;   с епϣωı, *look up*: Ac 1 11 (S ϭ.
еϩр.) β. εἰς, Is 8 22 (S ϫı еıат еϩраı) ἐμβ. εἰς,
CaiEuch 491 акс. еп. етϥе νεύειν ἄνω;   с еϩоγп,
look in, into: Ez 21 2 (S с. еϩ.) ἐπιβ. ἐπί, MG 25 6
етаqс. еϩ. аqпаγ ἐμβ. ἔσω; Ac 6 15 (S еıωрϩ
еϩ.) ἀτεν. εἰς; MIE 2 361 апс. еϩ. ϫепоγаı пппı-
ϣоγϣт, AM 155 аqс. еϩ. епıхрωм, EW 109
етаqс. еϩ. еϩреп Apa Krajôn;   с еϩрнı, еϩ.
BF, *look down*: C 86 291 пϭϲ с. еϩр. епıколасıс
(var еϩ. еϫ.) ἐπιβ. ἐπί; Mor 24 11 F еqс. еϩр.
еϫωϩ;   с еϩрнı, *look up*: Lu 9 16 (S ϫı еıат
еϩ.) ἀναβ. εἰς.

—— nn, *looking*: 2 Pet 2 8 (S паγ) βλέμμα;
Va 57 85 пс. ϫпепвал ефоγωıпı.

ϫıпс. m f, *looking, look*: Va 57 193 пϫ. θέα (cf
ib ϫıппаγ θ.), C 43 218 ϯϫ. пкакωс of Satan,
TRit 375 пıϫ. етоı проϥ пте пекϩап, Ro 8 19 пϫ.
евол (S пϭ. еϩ.) ἀποκαραδοκία.

семıсı   *v* мıсе *s f*.

сıмсıмм[1], **сıмсм**[2] **сıмсм**[3], **семснм**[4] S nn m,
sesame: P 44 66 сасıмнп(*sic*) · с.⁴ سمسم;   с.² Ep
329, с.³ BKU 1 306, с.¹ Ep 327.   Ep 332 if wouldst
buy с.¹ мoϣтч калωс ϫеqоγ пϩар ϫпеqϣаϩ[;
measured in мааϫе Ostr Jéquier¹, Win 56²; ртоϥ
CO 187¹, MMA 14 1 134¹;   ϩо ST 90¹, *ib* 140¹;
(B سمسم K 197 сıсамнп, which *ib* 175 is ساسم, *ib*
178 سبستان; *ib* 194 '.مـ = P 55 146 ϥакı *i e* φάκος).
V Löw F 3 1.   Cf ? сıсмн.

смıт SB (once) F (do) nn m, *fine flour* σεμί-
δαλıς دقيق (Fraenkel 32, PMéd 277): Ge 18 6 (var
поеıт, B = Gk), Si 39 33 пс., Is 1 13 SF(B do),
Ez 16 13 SB σεμ.

сωмт, **-мпт** S, **сомт-** SB, **-мпт-** S, **сомт†** SB,
-мпт† S, vb intr, *be stretched, wait* S: Ps 77 9 (var
-мпт, B ϭωлк) ἐντείνειν; Sa 5 22† εὔκυκλος; Tri
705 bows еүс.† موتور; WTh 134 martyr crucified
еqс.† пеıϩт, CO 386 wouldst that I depart or ет-
рас. ?, *ib* 379 екпас. yet 2 days, Ep 97 mayst come
птс. ϫмпекнı;   tr, *stretch, bind* S: Pro 7 16
(var -мпт, AB do) τείν., Ps 36 14 (B do) ἐντ., *ib*
84 5 (B сωоγтеп) διατ., Ac 22 25 (B do) προτ.;
Nu 24 8 (var ϫωлк, B ϩı соϑпеч) κατατοξεύειν;
ShP 130⁴ 150 canons аıмороγ аıсомтоγ opp кω
псωоγ;   с е-, *be bound to* S: BMis 15 еqсмопт
(*sic*, l ? сомпт) епеqклал like dog, J 87 37 пqϩωп
пϫс. еϩωϩ пıм written in this deed, *ib* 66 64 sim
пγсопт (*ie* сωмт) етϫом (cf PMon 83, PCai 3 4
στέργειν κ. ἐμμένειν); еϩоγп е-: Lev 8 8 (var -мпте,
B ϭ. еϩрнı еϫп-) συσφίγγειν ἐν;   с ϩа-, *stretch
bow against* S: Tri 383 пϫс. ϩароq птпıте ϫداد على;
с евол, *stretch, extend* SB: RNC 87 S bade с.
ϫпмакарıос еϩ. ϩрепмоγс (cf Ac 22 25), C 43
172 B martyr аqсомтq еϩ. hung up above ground,
Va 58 73 B bound between pillars еqс.† еϩ. п-
калωс.

сопτq nn m S, *stretching*: P 44 59 punishments
пс. Ⅹ., пхωлк евол تشبيم.

смнт   *v* сωтм *s f*.

смот SB, **-оγт** (J 3 50), **-ωт** (*ib* 71 46) S, **-ат**
AA²F, **-опт** B, pl сıмωт (EpJer) F nn m f (ShA
1 264), *form, character, likeness, pattern*: Nu 18

7 *SB*, Deu 13 17 *S*(*B* рнϯ), Pro 9 11 *SA*(*B*=Gk), Zech 4 1 *SB*(*A* рнтє), He 1 1 *SBF*, Va 66 289 *B* Lot оⲩсоⲑоⲙⲓⲧнс ⲁⲡⲉ ⲍⲉⲛⲡⲉⲩⲥ., ZNTW 24 88 *F* if пєꞓ. ⲙⲛ̄ⲝ̄ⲥ̄ are his, R 1 4 52 *S* having ϩєпꞓ. поⲏрⲓоⲛ = Mart Ign 865 *B*, Mor 37 106 *S* asked to know пєꞓ. ⲛⲧⲁϥϫⲓоор ⲙⲙоϥ *how he had crossed*, BHom 135 *S* how or ϩⲓⲛⲁϣ пꞓ. τρόπος, Aeg 245 *S* єпєꞓє пєꞓꞓ. єⲩτρ., Mor 17 16 *S* ⲡⲁⲡⲉꞓ. єⲑооⲩ = EW 30 *B* κακότρ., BMar 104 *S* пєⲓꞓ. поⲩⲱⲧ ὁμοιότρ.; Ac 7 43 *SB*, 1 Thes 1 7 *SF*(*B* = Gk), C 89 58 *B* ꞓ̄ пꞓ. of keeping vigil τύπος, He 9 24 *SF*(*B* τυπ.), Z 313 *S* bread not His body but пєϥꞓ. пє ἀντίτυ.; Ge 29 17 *B*(*S* єⲓпє), Is 53 3 *B*(*S* do, *A* ϩⲣⲃє), 2 Cor 5 7 (*S* пⲁⲩ) εἶδος, Ge 5 3 *B*, EpJer 62 *BF*, Mt 28 3 *B* (*S* єⲓ.) ἰδέα; Sa 19 6 *S* γένος; Is 44 13 *SB*, Mk 16 12 *SBF* μορφή, Ro 8 29 *B* ϣфнр пꞓ. (*S* ϣ. єⲓпє) σύμμορφος; He 8 5 *SBF*, Cl 6 1 *A* ὑπόδειγμα, Ex 25 9 *B*, 1 Chr 28 18 *B* παράδ.; Deu 28 37 *S* (*B* оⲩⲱп пꞓⲁϫⲓ), 3 Kg 10 1 *S* ꞓ. пϣⲁϫⲉ αἴνιγμα; 1 Pet 2 21 *S* (*B* = Gk) ὑπογραμμόν; Deu 4 12 *B* (*S* ϩⲣⲃ), Is 40 18 *B*(*S* ⲙⲓⲛⲉ), Phil 2 7 *S* (*B* ⲓⲏⲓ) ὁμοίωμα, He 4 15 *B* (*S* ϩє) ὁμοιότης; Est 2 20 *S*, 2 Tim 3 10 *SB* ἀγωγή; Lev 13 30 *S* (*B* ϩо), Ez 23 15 *SB* ὄψις; Tob 12 19 *S* (*cf* DeV 2 212 *B*), Dan 3 92 (25) *B* ὅρασις; 1 Kg 21 13 πρόσωπον; Va 68 173 *B* blaming not in word nor ꞓⲉпоⲩꞓ. σχῆμα; Bor 248 7 *S* ϩⲛоⲩꞓ. τὸ δοκεῖν; He 1 3 *B* (*S* єⲓ.) χαρακτήρ; Tit 2 3 *B* (*S* diff) κατάστημα; Jud 6 4 *S* ὑπόστασις; Va 61 216 *B* оⲩꞓ. пꞓⲃⲱ ὑπόθεσις διδασκαλίας; auxiliary uses: Ex 38 16 *B* ꞓ. пⲕⲁⲣⲓⲁ καρνωτός, Deu 14 9 *S* ꞓ. пⲧⲏⲣ πτερύγιον, Aeg 214 *S* ꞓ. пϩооⲩⲧ τὰ ἀνδρῶν (*cf* DeV 1 123), Deu 22 15 *S* ꞓ. пⲧⲙⲛⲧⲣооⲩпє (*B* ⲙⲉⲧпⲁрⲑⲉⲛоꞓ) παρθένια, 1 Kg 19 13 *S* ꞓ. пⲧⲕⲁⲓⲥⲉ κενοτάφιον (*cf* AM 194), Sa 17 4 *S* ꞓ. ϩⲣо πρόσωπον, Lev 11 23 *S* ꞓ. пⲣⲁⲗнⲧ πετεινός, 2 Cor 11 13 *B* ϣⲓⲃϯ ⲙпꞓ. μετασχηματίζεσθαι, 1 Kg 28 8 *S* ϣⲉⲃⲧⲩ пꞓ. συγκαλύπτεσθαι; adverbial &c: Ez 16 26 *S* ϩⲛϩⲁϩ пꞓ. *B* ꞁⲉпоⲩⲗⲏϣ пꞓ. πολλαχῶς, Col 3 20 *S* ⲕⲁⲧⲁ ꞓ. ⲛⲓⲙ κ. πάντα, Is 56 11 *B* ⲕⲁⲧⲁ пєϥꞓ. κ. τὸ ἑαυτοῦ; Job 40 3 *S* (*B* р.) ⲕⲉꞓ. ἄλλως; Phil 3 15 *S* (*B* do) ἑτέρως; Deu 4 32 *S* ꞓ. пϯⲙⲓⲛⲉ (*B* ϩⲱⲃ ⲙпⲁⲓрнϯ), ROC 17 403 *B* names ⲙпⲁⲓꞓ. τοιοῦτος, Va 57 109 *B* пⲁϣ пꞓ. ποῖος, BHom 36 *S* sim ποταπός, Deu 12 30 *S* (*B* р.) sim πῶς, Jude 10 *S* ⲙпєꞓ. п- (*B* р.), Jud 9 36 *S* пⲑє ⲙпєꞓ. п-, Is 4 5 *B* ⲙфрнϯ поⲩꞓ. пⲧє (*S* пⲑє ⲙпєⲓ.) ὡς, Aeg 289 *S* ⲙпꞓ. п- ὥσπερ, Deu 22 26 *S* (*B* р.) sim ὡσεί; ShC 73 33 *S* ⲁϣпє пꞓ. of prophets but to suffer ?, JTS 10 399 *S* like calves decked out so is пꞓ. пⲧєⲓꞓⲓⲙⲉ, WTh 134 *S* took on оⲩꞓ. ⲙⲙⲛⲧⲣⲙⲛⲕⲉ *appearance*, MG 25 59 *B* оⲩꞓ. пⲁⲅⲅⲉⲗоꞓпє пⲁⲓꞓⲉⲗϣⲓⲣⲓ *sort of angel*, BAp 66 *S* what fruit ? оⲩꞓ. пⲭⲙⲡⲉϩ *sort of apple*,

ShIF 192 *S* destroy them with sword, spear or ϩⲛ ꞓⲉпⲕⲉꞓ. пⲧєⲓϩⲉ, Va 61 6 *B* пⲁⲓⲃⲓоꞓ пꞓ. пꞓⲛⲓⲃⲓ *doleful life*, Mor 52 45 *S* оⲩꞓ. пⲑⲁⲗⲁꞓⲥⲁ *around altar* (3 Kg 18 32), ShA 1 264 *S* Hekate тєꞓ. ⲙпоⲣпⲏ, P 44 89 *S* тꞓ. пєпєпⲧⲓⲁ (αἰτία) пⲓⲙ ⲗⲁ, C 41 79 *B* пⲓꞓ. ϩⲣоϯ *apparition*, ST 289 *S* loaves ϩєпꞓ. єⲛⲁпоⲅоⲩ єⲙⲁⲧє, Miss 4 107 *B* ϣⲁϥⲫєϩ пⲓꞓⲁϫⲓ ꞓєпⲕєꞓ. *not wishing to tell*, ALR '93 525 *S* thinkest thou I did thus to thee єⲕєꞓ. ⲁⲗⲗⲁ ⲝєⲕєоⲩⲱпϩ єⲃоⲗ пⲁⲓⲕⲁⲓоꞓ ?, Mani 1 *A²* ⲙⲛ ⲕⲁⲓꞓ. ⲁⲙоⲩⲣ пⲭⲁⲝⲉ, C 89 35 *B* пⲁⲅⲭоϩ єпєⲩꞓ. *envied his character* = MG 17 406 ⳿, AP 25 *A²* пєⲩꞓ. єⲧоⲩⲁⲁⲃ, PS 332 *S* vapour ⲙпꞓ. поⲩⲕⲁпⲛоꞓ, C 86 198 *B* adorned ꞓєпⲉⲩꞓⲙⲟⲛⲧ, Rec 6 183 *B* wrapped therein ⲙпⲉⲙⲟⲛⲧ поⲩⲕⲁⲓꞓⲓ, C 43 49 *B* gave them ⲙпꞓ. поⲩпⲁⲣⲁⲑⲏⲕⲏ *as deposit*, BMis xxxiv *S* devil ⲙпꞓ. пⲧⲙⲟⲛⲁⲭⲏ = BSM 106 *B* оⲓ ⲙпꞓ. п- *guise*, AM 84 *B* пⲧⲉϥϣⲓⲃϯ ⲙпⲉⲩꞓ. *disguised self*, ST 192 *S* use him пꞓ. ⲛⲓⲙ єⲓоⲩⲱϣ *as I would*, Mor 53 86 *S* mute makes signs ϩⲓⲧⲙпєꞓ. ⲙпⲉϥⲧⲛⲛⲏⲃⲉ, *ib* 37 18 *S* пꞓ. пⲛⲉϩⲓоⲙⲉ *sc menstruation* (*cf* ꞓⲱпⲧ *custom*), ROC 23 276 *B* do no ϩⲱⲃ пꞓ. пⲧєⲭⲛⲓⲧнꞓ, ShClPr 22 356 *S* Christ ⲕⲁⲁϥ пꞓ. поⲩⲟⲛ ⲛⲓⲙ, Bor 234 9 *S* ϫⲓ ⲍⲁⲅⲉⲓⲁ пⲁⲕ пꞓ., ShC 73 200 *S* passed 2 days ϩⲛпꞓ. єⲧⲙⲙⲁⲩ *in that state*, DeV 2 50 *B* why is face sad ⲙпⲁⲓꞓ. ?, Mani 1 *A²* didst devise пꞓ. ⲙⲙоⲩⲣ ⲙⲙⲁⲩ *how to*, Z 610 *S* stone tested ϩⲛоⲩꞓ. пⲧєⲓⲙⲓⲛⲉ *as follows*, P 131³ 23 *S* spake ⲕⲁⲧⲁ оⲩꞓ. *in a figure*, CO 93 *S* єⲧⲧⲁⲉⲓⲏⲩ ⲕⲁⲧⲁ ꞓ. ⲛⲓⲙ (*cf* πανένδοξος), Ming 297 *S* ϩⲓⲧⲙпⲉⲓꞓ. *by this behaviour*, EW 166 *B* Timothy enthroned that ϩⲓⲧєⲙпⲁⲓꞓ. *thus* city might get confidence.

ⲁⲧꞓ. *S, without form*: Sa 11 18 (var ⲁⲧє-) ἄμορφος; P 44 48 оⲩⲁ. ⲁꞓⲭⲏⲙⲁⲧⲓꞓⲧоꞓ, (Va 66 305 *B* пⲓⲕⲁⲣпоꞓ ⲛⲁ. prob for ⲁⲧо *q v*).

єⲓⲣⲉ, о пꞓ. *SBF, have appearance, be like, be pattern*: 2 Kg 14 2 *S* εἶναι ὡς; Cant 8 14 *S* ὁμοιοῦσθαι; 1 Tim 1 16 *S* (*B* ꞓ.) ὑποτύπωσις; *ib* 5 25 *S* о пⲕєꞓ. (*B* ⲕⲉⲣⲏϯ) ἄλλως ἔχειν; Jo 13 15 *SB* ὑπόδειγμα διδόναι; 1 Cor 9 22 *S* р ꞓ. ⲛⲓⲙ (*B* ϣⲱпⲓ пⲣ. п.) πάντα γίνεσθαι; 1 Kg 21 15 *S* р пєⲓꞓ. Gk diff *behave thus*; Ez 42 6 *SB* о пϣоⲙⲛⲧ пꞓ. τριπλοῦς; C 89 206 *B* єϥоⲓ пꞓ. оⲩоϩ єϥϯ ⲙⲏⲓⲛⲓ σημεῖον εἶναι, *ib* 72 *B* єⲓоⲓ пꞓ. ⲁⲛ = MG 17 326 *S* οὐ σχήματι; LAp 566 *F* є[ⲩ]ⲁⲓ ⲙпєꞓ. [пꞓⲉп]ⲗⲱⲙⲓ φανῆναι ποιεῖν ὡς; Miss 4 580 *S* єϥо поⲩꞓ. ὑπογραμμός; Miss 8 93 *S* р ꞓ. ⲛⲓⲙ єⲧⲣⲉ- ἀπάσης εὐτεχνίας καθιστάναι (*cf* TurM below), BHom 49 *B* р пꞓ. of thief (var р ⲑє ⲙпєꞓ. conflate ?) δίκην; ShC 42 219 *S* men єⲁⲩⲣ ꞓ. поⲏⲣⲓоⲛ, ShP 130⁴ 135 *S* if abbot wish єⲣ ϩєпꞓ. ⲙпⲣоⲉⲓⲛⲉ *by granting extra food* (? ϩєпϩⲙоⲧ), ShC 73 169 *S* cursed whoso пⲁⲣⲧϥ єⲭⲡⲣⲏⲧϥ єⲣ ϩєпꞓ. єⲩϩⲣоⲩ, C 89 94 *B* єпоⲓ

пс. ммаѓатq *we do but seem,* C 86 319 B in dream
аqер пс. ӿееqпатшӣq, Bor 143 40 S пеаѓр оѓс.
ӿепеоѓѡм (var Mor 28 141 о ӣпес. ѓшс), TurM
13 S p с. пим птѣѡ[к *do utmost,* Louvre R 1780
S пср с. пим мӣптрмнсе & *send it,* JTS 10 395
S Sodomites p с. поѓоп пим *set example.*

✝с. S *give form* c e-: Si 38 38 (30) τυποῦν.

ӿι, сι с. SABF, *become, be like*: Zeph 1 11 B
(A тантн✝) ὁμοιοῦσθαι, EpJer 5 S (B ιιιι) ἀφομ.;
Ro 12 2 F (S ӿι ѻрѣ, B ер ш̄фнр псхнма) συν-
σχηματίζειν, ib F (S do, B ш̄еѣт с.)μεταμορφοῦσθαι,
1 Cor 4 6 S (B do) μετασχ., C 89 63 B he withdrew eqсι c. σχήματι ἀναχωρεῖν; 2 Tim 1 13 S
(B ха с.) ὑποτύπωσιν ἔχ.; Cl 5 1 A ὑπόδειγ. λαμβάνειν; ShA 2 15 S *devil* ӿι пес. *of man,* C 43
187 B *sim,* Miss 4 699 S *empty corn ears* eѓӿι c
пѻмс.

солте S (*sic* collated) nn f, *meaning unknown*:
WS 94 *varia to be sent to* тс.   *Cf*? самӣт.

смаѓ SS͛BF, -ааѓ S(PMéd) nn m dual, *temples
(tempora), eyelids*: Jud 4 21 S пеѓс., Ps 131 4 SB
pl, P 44 68 S κρόταφος صدغ; K 75 B пис. 'ʚ,
TEuch 1 5 B амонι ппеѓс. 'ʚ; Jer 9 18 B pl βλέφαρον; Mor 28 26 S аqка теѓсιӿ поѓӣам ӷапеѓс.
& *turned face as if to look,* Ryl 107 S *maladies of*
тапе мӣпс., PMéd 277 S ѻепс. eѓ✝ ккас (*sic*),
BKU 1 26 (8116 b) S͛ с. поѓпам (*cf ib* асатер =
? المضغ).

соmѻ S nn m, *axle*: Glos 116 *parts of cart* ἄξων
тторе етепс.

смаѻ SAB, -еѻ BF nn m, *bunch of fruit,
flowers*: *of grapes* Ge 40 10 SB, Mic 7 1 SAB,
Ap 14 18 SB βότρυς; ShA 2 10 S пес....qι тѣл-
ѣιле ммаѓ пѻнтq, ShHTH 28 S кѡтѓ пѻепхлле,
ӿшѧле пѻепс., DeV 2 79 B пис. малолι (*forbidden
fruit* Ge 3 6), Kr 239 S *sim,* BMis 562 S тѣа....пс.
ѻипш̄елѻ, тѣа пѣлѣιле ѻапес., C 86 95 B оѓ-
смеѻ *hanging from vine;*   *other trees*: Cant 1
14 S с. пкоѓпер, cit Mor 24 7 F, P 131⁶ 41 S
оѓѣппе...пеѓс. мӣпеqкарпос (*cf* Cant 7 7).

смеѻ B nn m, *mostly as pl, herb*: Ge 1 11, Is
58 11 (S птнѕ) βοτάνη, Job 5 25 смаѻ (S рѡт)
παμβότανον; Ps 104 35 (S = Gk), Ap 9 4 (S do)
χόρτος; P 55 2 пис. نبات.

семрем S͛ vb tr, *meaning unknown,* ? *devastate*: Z 106 = ALR '06 473 = Hyvernat *Alb* 15 пικε-
рос птаѓс. ппек(к)лнсια аѓа пемѡпастнрιоп.

смаѻнр S nn, *fennel*: P 43 34 شمار, ib 233
τοιρι شمر بري, 44 82 τοѓннтιоп اسفانج *spinach* (in *ib*
66 & K 185 γεγγίδιον is شاهترج *fumitory*); Z 628

in recipe;   ш̄амар, -мер, ш̄емар S *same*?:
P 44 83 малаѣаѻроѓ (*l* мараѻ.) ш̄. ѻооѓт = 43
60 -мер شمار بري (*cf* K 193), PMéd 321 ш̄. ѻооѓт
(*cf* DM vo411). Mor 51 34 ш̄е пемпсе, ш̄е пш̄ем.,
ib affairs of monastery are become like пш̄ам.   In
place-names Σαμαχῆρ, -ρε, Σαμαῆρ (PLond 4 597).
V Almk 1 393 n.

смιӿ S nn *meaning unknown, among metal
utensils*: PLond 4 517 оѓс.

смеιп, смιпе (Baouit 93) S, сееιпе A, сеιпе
A², снιпι BF (Mor 30 14), снеп (*ib* 15), снιп (BM
511) F nn m f (Sh), *physician*: Job 13 4 SB, Pro
14 30 SA, Mt 9 12 SB ἰατρός; ShC 73 72 S *carpenter, smith, mason* or оѓс., *ib* 42 69 S самq пс.
eѓ✝ пафре, BMis 530 S оѓс. преqталѓо, AM 293
B *brought her* оѓмιпш̄ пс., C 89 17 B саѻ пс.,
DeV 2 176 B оѓмеркас оѓоѻ пс., Bodl (P) d 32
S с. пѻртѡр, AM 99 B *Colluthus* пис. мӣпресѣѓ-
теρос, DeV 2 168 с. *wearing* соκ, Rec 11 135 S
оѓхшмле пс. Mani 1 A² пафре пс., ShC 73 161
S сѻιме пс. ѻιпεισѓпатѡсн, ShIF 260 S *suffer
not* тс. eeι eѻоѓп *to sick girl*: мӣтс. SB, *physician's craft, skill*: Ex 21 19 S (B ѻомт пс. *fee*),
Miss 8 141 S *hearken to me* eѓм. *for (thy) healing,*
Va 58 173 B *hinder him* eeр теѓм. *to do his part as
ph.* ἰατρεία; Z 278 S тесѣѡ пↄм. ἰατρικός; ShBor
247 121 S мӣτοѓоeιп, мӣτпееq, м., ShRE 10
159 S техпн мм., BAp 129 S пафре мм., P 44
94 S сотⳡq пↄм.;   ма пс. B, *place for medical
treatment*: Va 68 176 ἰατρεῖον;   реqс. B, as с.:
Abst 447.   In *names*: Ψέειпε (Preisigke), ? сеιпε
f (R Champ 541).

соп SBO, сап S͛AA²FO DM, сп-, сеп- S, pl
спнѓ SAA²F, -поѓ ABF, -еѓ, -еоѓ F nn m, *brother
literal & figur*: Ge 4 2 SB, Ob 10 SAB, Jo 6 8
SA²B, Eph 6 21 SBF ἀδελφός; AZ 21 100 O пас.
Osiris, DM 7 25 сап, Mor 43 220 S пеιш̄омпт
пс. *brother & sisters*;   pl Pro 6 19 SAB, Jo 2 12
SA²B, Ro 2 25 SBF, Ac 7 26 F -поѓ ἀδ., BM 580
F -еѓ, *ib* 582 (2) -еоѓ F; PS 43 S песс. тнроѓ,
C 43 226 B пекс. мↄмартѓрос; *as sisters*: ShC
73 139 S пеѓс. *foolish virgins, ib* 74 S пес...етем-
монахнпе, Gu 91 S, MG 25 130 B пес. *of Lazarus;*   спнѓ ѻрооѓт PS 377 S, J 76 50 S (*cf
сѡпе пↄριме*);   поↄ, пιш̄✝ пс., *elder b., senior
brethren,* v поↄ I s f, с. поↄ Job 1 13 S (var сп п.
BMOr 6807 4), B пιш̄✝ пс.;   коѓι, коѓхι пс.,
younger b. v коѓι II A s f; с. коѓι v *ib* B & Ge 43
3 S спк.(B к. пс.), Mor 50 40 S псⳡп к.;   с. ш̄нм
S, *young, small (humble*?) *b.*: ShA 2 275 пεтпс.
ш̄. sc *present writer,* Ep 297 пспнѓ ш̄.;   с.
пеιѡт S, *uncle*: J 18 53;   ш̄пс. S, *nephew*: *ib.* 18

47, cf PBu 25 S letter from aunt to ⲡⲁⲙⲉⲣⲓⲧ
ⲛⲥ.;   as cousin : BMar 145 S we are ⲥⲛⲏⲩ ⲛⲛⲉⲛⲉⲣⲏⲩ;   as husband : BMis 369 S ⲡⲁⲥ. = BSM 29 B,
Mor 18 70 S ⲡⲁⲥ. = Miss 4 142 B ⲡⲁϧⲁⲓ, BMar 200 S
ⲡⲁⲭ̅ⲥ̅ ⲛⲥ. κύριός μου;   ⲥⲛ ⲟⲩⲁ S, meaning ?; ST
34 on? prohibited matrimonial degrees (? = ϣⲡⲟⲩⲁ
ⲩ ϣⲏⲣⲉ);   c. ⲙⲙⲟⲟⲛⲉ, foster b. : Ac 13 1 S(B
ϣⲫⲏⲣ ⲛϣⲁⲛϣ) σύντροφος.

As title pass in monastic narratives, epitaphs &c :
c. ⲙⲙⲟⲛⲁⲭⲟⲥ : MG 17 296 S, C 41 22 B, c. ⲡⲁ-
ⲛⲁⲭⲱⲣⲓⲧⲏⲥ : MG 17 319 S, c. = διακονητής of ϧⲗⲗⲟ
Z 294 S, ⲁⲡⲟⲗⲗⲱ ⲡⲥ. Samuel's διακ. Mor 31 89 S,
c. opp ϧⲗⲗⲟ Z 304 S;   ⲡⲁⲥ. without concord of
persons S (cf ⲡⲁⲉⲓⲱⲧ) : RAC 100 ⲁⲛⲟⲕ ⲡⲁⲥ. ⲓⲱϩⲁⲛⲛⲏⲥ, Baouit 42 ⲁⲛⲟⲕ ⲡⲁⲥ. ⲓⲉⲣⲉⲙⲓⲁⲥ, ib ⲡⲕⲉⲡⲁⲥ.
ⲏⲛⲁ, WS 146 ⲉϥⲥϩⲁⲓ ⲙⲡⲁⲥ. ⲉⲛⲱⲭ, ib 88 writer
signs ϩⲓⲧⲛⲡⲁⲥ. ⲡⲁⲡⲛⲟⲩⲧⲉ.

ⲥⲱⲛⲉ SAA²F, -ⲛⲓ BF nn f, sister, pl v above &
sg as pl : Ex 2 4 AB, Jo 11 1 SA²B, 1 Cor 7 15
SBF ἀδελφή;   ⲛⲟϭ, ⲡⲓϣⲧ ⲛⲥ., elder s. v ⲛⲟϭ
I s f;   ⲕⲟⲩⲓ, ⲕⲟⲩϫⲓ ⲛⲥ., younger s. : Jud 15 2
S, Ez 16 46 SB;   c. ⲙⲙⲁⲣⲧ, blood-sister : Mor
55 84 S;   c. ϧⲁⲉⲓⲱⲧ, sister by father (step-s.) :
PLond 5 132 S;   c. ⲛⲥϩⲓⲙⲉ SBF (cf ϣⲉⲉⲣⲉ
ⲛⲥϩ., ⲥⲛⲏⲩ ⲛϩⲟⲟⲩⲧ) : Mt 13 56 SB(F ⲥⲛⲏⲟⲩ ⲛⲥϩ.),
Jo 11 3 B(SA² c.) ἀδ., 1 Cor 9 5 SBF ἀδ. γυνή,
J 66 49 S, C 43 136 B;   as wife : BMar 199 S,
BMis 375 S = BSM 32 B;   as cousin : Mor 31
78 S ⲧⲁⲥ. my father & hers were brothers.   As
title (?) : WS 65, 79 ⲧⲁⲥ.; female disciple : Ac 9 36
S(B ⲙⲁⲑⲏⲧⲏⲥ ⲛⲥϩ.) μαθήτρια.

ⲙⲛⲧⲥ. SB(rare)F, brotherhood, brotherliness : 1
Pet 5 9 S(B c. pl), Z 273 S ἀδελφότης; HL 92 B
to whom ⲧⲙ. ⲧⲏⲣⲥ testified, ShA 2 341 S noised
abroad ϩⲓⲧⲙ., Mus 42 265 S ⲧⲙ. in Christ, ST 267
S ⲣ ⲧⲙ. ⲛⲧⲉⲓ, Ep 351 S sim, CO 239 S I greet
ⲧⲉⲧⲛⲙ. ⲉⲧⲛⲁⲡⲟⲩⲥ, AZ 23 30 F sim;   ⲙⲛⲧ-
ⲥⲱⲛⲉ S : ST 201;   ⲙⲛⲧⲙⲁⲓⲥ. SBF, brotherly
love : Ro 12 10 φιλαδελφία, BM 1102 S ⲧⲉⲕⲙ. toward all, BSM 89 B be in ⲟⲩⲙ. ⲛⲟⲩⲱⲧ.

ⲣ c. SB, be brother : Job 30 29 ἀδ. γίνεσθαι; Ep
278 Sᵃ ⲉⲓⲛⲱ ⲛⲥ. ⲙⲛⲛⲉⲡⲉⲣⲉⲩ.

In many names, as ⲡⲥⲟⲛ, ⲯⲟⲛ, ⲯⲁⲛ, ⲥⲁⲓⲥⲛⲱ,
-ⲥⲡⲁⲩ (El Gebrawi 2 pl 29), Σανσνάυ, -σνεῦς &c,
Ψονσναῦς &c, ⲥⲟⲛϣⲏⲙ (Ryl 300), -ⲭⲏⲙ, ⲥⲁⲡϧⲏⲙ,
Κουισόν, ⲡⲁⲡⲉⲥⲛⲏⲩ, ϣⲙⲧⲥⲡⲛⲏ, Χεμτονεῦς &c,
Φθοσνεῦς, ⲧⲥⲱⲡⲉ, Τσανκουι, Τσανσναῦς, Θαπσοσ-
σναῦς, Τανεσνεῦς, Θινιψανσνῶς.   In place-name :
Ανεσνοῦτος gen (PSI 80).

ϭⲱⲱⲛ S nn m, meaning unknown : Mor 28 32
(on Ap 7 13) those of heaven enquiring of those of
earth ⲡⲣⲱⲙⲉ ⲅⲁⲣ ⲟⲩϭ. ⲡⲉ ⲙⲙⲁⲓⲉⲟⲟⲩ ⲁⲩⲱ ⲙⲙⲁⲓ-
ⲁⲣⲭⲉⲓ ϩⲓⲟⲩⲥⲟⲛ.

ⲥⲛⲓⲉ, ⲥⲉⲛⲏ, ⲥⲉⲡⲉ S, ⲥⲛⲏⲓ B nn f, granary, bin :
Miss 4 748 S ⲟⲩⲥⲩ(ⲛ)ⲏ ⲛⲟⲉⲓⲕ closed with clay seal,
ib 749 as much as they ate by so much ⲧⲥ. ϣⲱⲧ
daily = Synax 1 412 صَوْمَعة silo (cf ϧⲏⲡⲓ), C 41 71
B ⲛⲥ. ⲛⲱⲓⲕ ϩⲓⲥⲟϩⲉ = Miss 4 435 مَخزَن, AZ 66 64
S in corn-delivery notes (? this word);   hence ?
heap, collection : Lu 9 14 S(B ⲙⲁ) κλισία (cf Mk
6 39 S ⲁⲩⲏⲧ).

ⲥⲓⲛⲉ S.A, ⲥⲛⲏⲓ B nn f, ploughshare : c. ⲛϧⲉⲃⲓ Is
2 4 B(S ϩⲃ̅ⲃⲉ) ἄροτρον; ShA 1 455 S ⲡϣⲟϣⲧ ⲛⲧϧⲃ-
ⲃⲉⲙⲛⲧⲉ.   V also ⲥⲕⲁⲓ.

ⲥⲓⲛⲉ SSᶠA, -ⲛⲓ BF, ⲥⲛ-¹, ⲥⲓⲧ- (ⲥⲉⲛⲧ-)², ⲥⲁⲁⲧ-³
(for these forms Sdff 228), ⲥⲁⲧ-⁴ S, ⲥⲉⲛ-⁵ SB, ⲥⲁⲁⲧϩ⁶
S, ⲥⲁⲧϩ⁷ SA, ⲥⲟⲧϩ⁸, ⲥⲟⲟⲧϩ⁹, ⲥⲓⲧϩ¹⁰ S, ⲥⲉⲛϩ BF, ⲥⲓ-
ⲛⲓⲱⲟⲩ† B vb I intr, pass by, through : Ps 143 4 B
(S ⲟⲩⲉⲓⲛⲉ), 1 Cor 7 31 BF(S = Gk), Aeg 284 S
ⲁϥⲧⲣⲉⲧⲉⲩϣⲏ c. (var ⲟⲩ.) παράγειν; EpJer 43 BF,
Zeph 2 2 B(SA ⲧⲁⲕⲟ) παραπορεύεσθαι; Lev 27 32
B(S ⲉⲓ) ἔρχεσθαι, MG 25 231 B ἀπέρ., Ps 17 13 SB,
Is 41 3 B(S ⲙⲟⲟϣⲉ) διέρ., Ps 36 36 B(S trᶻ, A Cl
ⲛⲟⲩ), Is 34 16 B(SF ⲉⲓ ⲉⲃⲟⲗ), Mt 14 15 BF(S ⲟⲩ.)
παρέρ.; ROC 17 399 B ⲁⲟⲩⲛⲓϣⲧ ⲛⲥⲛⲟⲩ c. διαβαίνειν; Ez 5 14 B(S ⲡⲁⲣⲁⲧⲉ) διοδεύειν; Ac 14 16 B
(S ⲟⲩ.) παροίχεσθαι; AM 241 B ⲉⲧⲁⲡⲓⲉⲭⲱⲣϩ c.,
C 89 160 B ⲙⲡⲓϧⲗⲓ c. of all he had said, Mor 30
7 Sᶠ ⲟⲩϩⲁⲍⲓⲱⲙⲁ ⲉⲧⲉⲙⲉϥⲥ. = BMis 234 S ⲟⲩ., ib
34 67 S things of world c. ⲛⲛⲁϩⲣⲁⲕ pass by, beyond
thee, Bor 263 30 S if unworthy ⲙⲁⲣⲉϥⲥ., C 43 226
B ⲉⲧⲁⲛ ⲉⲓⲥ. †ⲛⲟⲩ.   Qual B : Mk 2 14 (var ⲥⲓⲛⲓ,
S = Gk) παράγ.; Va 57 216 corpse ⲉⲩⲥ. ⲡⲉⲙⲁϥ
φέρεσθαι; MG 25 231 Satan ⲉϥⲥ. = Z 316 S ⲛⲏⲩ
παρέρ., DeV 2 176 ⲁϥⲓ ⲉϥⲥ.;   wrongly : Ac 5 15 ⲉϥⲡⲁⲥ. (var ⲥⲓⲛⲓ, S ⲉⲓ ⲉϥⲏⲣⲏ) ἐρ., AM 242 ⲉⲧⲁⲩⲥ.,
BSM 35 ϫⲉⲛⲡϫⲓⲛⲑⲣⲉϥⲥ. = BMis 378 S ⲙⲟⲟϣⲉ.

II tr, pass through, across : Deu 2 7 B(S ⲙⲟ. ϧⲛ-),
Jth 13 10 S³, Job 41 7 Sⁿ(B ⲟⲩⲱⲧⲉⲛ), Ps 123 4 B
(S ⲉⲓ ⲉⲃⲟⲗ ϩⲓⲧⲛ-) διέρ. (cf ⲥⲓ† B διέρ. Mic 2 13),
Ge 18 3 S⁴(var²)B, ib 32 31 Sⁿ(BAp 84) B Ex 23
5 B(S ⲕⲱ), Pro 27 13 SⁿAⁿ, Is 33 22 SⁿBF, Ac 16
8 S³(BF c. ⲉϧ. ϫⲉⲛ-), MG 25 38 B who may ⲥⲉⲛ
ⲛⲁ? παρέρ., Mor 17 96 S cannot c.³ ⲛⲛⲁ ⲉⲧⲙⲙⲁⲩ
(var Gu 74 c.¹) μετέρ., Ac 12 10 B(S ⲛⲱϧ ϣⲁ-)
προέρ.; Pro 9 18 B(SA ϫⲓⲟⲟⲣ) διαβαίν., Job 14 5
SⁿᶜB ὑπερβ.. Mk 14 36 Sⁿ (B c. ⲉϧ. ϧⲁ-) παραφέρειν
ἀπό; Job 23 11 Sⁿ(B ⲣⲓⲕⲓ ⲉⲃⲟⲗ ϫⲉⲛ-) ἐκκλίνειν
ἀπό; ShP 130⁴ 104 S ⲟⲩⲧⲱϣ ⲛⲡⲉⲩⲉϣ ⲥⲁⲁⲧϩ, Va 63
12 B ⲉⲧⲁⲩⲥ. ⲙⲙⲱⲧⲉⲛ †ⲛⲟⲩ = BMis 382 S ⲉⲓ
ⲉϥⲛⲁⲣⲁⲧⲉ ⲙⲙ., Tri 604 S ⲙⲡⲉⲕⲥ.² ⲡⲉⲕⲙⲛⲧϣⲏ-
ⲣⲉⲧⲛϥ omittted, ClPr 40 2 S ⲉⲁϥⲥ.³ ⲧⲉⲣⲱⲧⲉ & out-
grown childhood, C 86 359 B ⲁⲧⲉⲕⲙⲉⲧⲟⲩⲣⲟ ⲥⲉⲡⲕ
& is given to another, Miss 8 257 S great marvel
ⲛⲟⲩϣⲟⲩⲥⲁⲁⲧⲉ ⲁⲛ, AM 329 B ⲛⲡⲉϥⲥⲉⲛ ⲡⲁⲓⲙⲁ

ернс, Ryl 374 *S* пнєксаат щантє *shalt not quit me until*; сєп рат⳽ *v* рат⳽ (сшр п-).

With following preposition. с є- *B*, *pass over to*: Ps 72 7 (*S* єі євол) διέρ. εἰς, Nu 34 4 (*S* ⳉіо-ор) παρέρ.; 4 Kg 4 8 διαβ. εἰς, Mt 4 21 (*S* ло.) προβ.; с єⳉєп- *B*, *pass by*: Ez 16 8 (*S* пар.) διέρ. διά; MIE 2 389 аⳓі єⳅс....єⳉ. пієкклнсіа (*cf ib* кш+ єⳉ.); с ⳉатєп- *B*: BM 849 36 пн єѳпас. ⳉатотⳉ поⳓоⳓтаⳉ & *bring it to priest* من نبرة عند; с ⳉа-, *B*, *pass over to*: Ge 31 52 (*S* єі ща-) διαβ. πρός, Is 45 14 (*S* пнⳉ єрат⳽) δ. ἐπί; с ⳉі- *B*, *pass by on*: Ps 8 9 (*S* ло. ⳉі-) διαπορεύ. acc, Lam 2 15 (*S* δο) παραπ. acc; Ps 88 42 (*S* δο) διοδεύειν acc; C 89 6 єⳅпас. ⳉіоⳓⳉоі *or on road*, Bodl Copt g 1 *Virgin is door* лпєⳉлі с. ⳉішⳅє *across it except Lord*; с ⳉп-, ⳅєп- *SB*, *pass through*: Ge 41 46 *B*(*S* єі єⳉ. ⳉітп-) διέρ. acc, Ac 20 25 *B*(*S* δο), Ps 103 20 *B*(*S* ло. ⳉп-) δ. ἐν; MG 25 168 *B* єⳅс.†...ⳅєпоⳓ+лі παρέρ. διά; Is 11 15 *B* (*S* δο) διαπορ. acc; Deu 23 14 *S* (*B* лощі ⳅєп-) ἐμπεριπατεῖν ἐν; DeV 2 151 *B* roads єтаіс. пⳅнтоⳓ = MG 25 423 *S* єі пⳉ.; с ⳉітєп- *B*, *meaning same*: Is 43 2 (*S* єі ⳉ.) διαβαίν. διά; с ⳉіⳅєп- *B*, *pass by*: Ps 72 9 (*S* єі єⳉ. ⳉп-) διέρ. ἐπί; BSM 37 єтаⳅс. ⳉіⳉшк = Va 63 11 с. ллок = BMis 381 *S* παραγε.

With following adverb. с євол *B*, *pass out, away, die*, intr: Ps 67 8 (*S* єі єⳉ.) ἐκπορ.; Mt 9 9 (*S* = Gk) παράγ. ἐκεῖθεν; MG 25 350 *when came nigh* єⳅ. єⳉ. = ROC 18 54 ومضى ضى, Cat 100 *innocents* єѳпас. єⳉ., Miss 4 161 аⳓщапс. єⳉ. *may He give souls rest* (*cf* ⳉпс.); tr, *pass out of, leave SB*: Ex 33 11 *B*(*S* єі єⳉ. ⳉп-) ἐκπορ. ἐκ; Jos 1 8 *S*(BMar 227, *var* cooⳉє єⳉ.) ἀφιστάναι ἐκ; R 1 4 12 *S* лєісєп тарі єⳉ. єпєⳉ *egredi de*; PS 297 *S* *cannot* сєп пєⳉаос єⳉ., Gu 85 *S* лпєⳅп поⳓєрнтє пс̄ єⳉ. (*var* KKS 264 сєпт), Miss 8 256 *S* *will not* сєпт пєктопос єⳉ. *till I die*, BMis 555 *S* лєⳓсєптоⳓ єⳉ. *parted not from each other*, BAp 5 *S* *will not* сіптк єⳉ., Ryl 277 *S* пнⳓсаатк єⳉ. щантⳓ-, Rec 6 185 *B* єтаісєпоⳓ єⳉ. поⳓкоⳓⳉі = BMar 219 *S* оⳓєллооⳓ, HL 115 *B* *so hospitable that* щтєлтєⳅрі сєп...щєлло єⳉ. ллннⳅ *lacked not*; єⳉ. єⳉєп- *B*, *pass by*: MIE 2 349 аоⳓсоп с. єⳉ. єⳉшⳅ; єⳉ. птєп- *B*, *pass through*: Ez 44 2 (HCons, *var* щє єⳅоⳓп ⳅєп-) διέρ. διά; єⳉ. оⳓтє- *B*, *pass out through*: Lu 17 11† (*S* пнⳓ єⳉ. ⳉітп-) διέρ. διά; єⳉ. ⳉа- *SB*, *pass, bring forth from*: Jer 5 6 ἐκπορ. ἀπό; Leyd 453 *S* сіптк єⳉ. ⳉароⳓ (*sic l*) лпірасⳅос піл; єⳉ. ⳉп-, ⳅєп- *SBF*, *pass out from, through*: Jo 4 4 *BF*(*S* єі єⳉ. ⳉітп-) διέρ. διά, Ps 104 13 *B*(*S* єі єⳉ ⳉп-) δ. ἐκ, Lam 5 18 *BF*(*S* ло. єⳉ.) δ. ἐν, Mt 19 24 *F*(PMich 538, *S* єі єⳉ. ⳉітп-, *B* і єⳅоⳓп ⳅєп-)

єісєр. διά, Ac 16 8 *BF*(*S*³ om єⳉ.) παρέρ. acc, MG 25 206 *B* π. ἀπό; PGen *S* *suffer him not* єс. єⳉ. ⳉлⳅні; єⳉ. ⳉітєп- *B*, *meaning sim*: Nu 20 18 (*S* єі єⳉ. ⳉ.), Ac 9 32 (*var* с. ⳉіⳅ., єⳉ., *S* δο) διέρ. διά; Zeph 2 15 (*A* лаⳅє аⳉ. ⳉ.) διαπορ. διά; Jer 27 13 (*S* пар. єⳉ. ⳉп-) διοδ. διά; TstAb 169 єⳓс. єⳉ. ⳉітотⳓ *passing before him*; єⳉ. ⳉіⳅєп- *B*, *pass by*: DeV 2 72 аⳓс. єⳉ. ⳉ. пієлⳉраⳓ; с єⳅоⳓп *B*, *pass in through*: Miss 4 123 ⳉпасєп +пⳓлн єⳅ. ан = Mor 19 39 *S*² = *ib* 18 30 *S* р προⳓп; с єⳅрні *B*, *pass downward*: Is 38 8 (*S* єі єпєснт ⳉі-) καταβαίν.; с єⳉраⳓ *S*, *pass from, quit*: Sa 17 19 neg συνέχειν dat.

—— пп m *B*, *passing, decline of day, afternoon*: K 61 піс. زوال.

атс. *SB*, *impassable, not passing*: CaiThe 48 *B* оⳓлшіт па. (*sc* Red Sea), BP 10587 *S* плнⳅн па.

рєⳅс. *S*, *one that passes*: P 129¹⁶ 81 *fruits of earth* ⳉєпр. пє (*var* R 1 4 67 рєⳅщіⳉє) φθαρτός.

ла пс. *B*, *passage, path crossing (desert?)*: Cat 30 піл. іє піла пщаⳓєⳓ *where no water*; лшіт пс. *B* sim: Is 51 10 (*S* ⳉін пⳉіоор) διάβασις.

ⳉіпс. *B*, *passing by, crossing*: Ge 32 22 (*S* ⳉіо.) διάβασις; Va 61 93 пєⳓⳉ. ллоⳓ *his passing by him* = P 131³ 83 *S* ⳓіппараⳅє, Va 57 71 пєкⳉ. *passing away, death, ib* 59 165 ⳉ. євол sim.

соопє, сопє *S*, сапє *AA*², -пі *A*², сопі *B*, са-апі *F*, pl сіпшоⳓі *B* & sg as pl пп m, *robber*: EpJer 14 *BF*, Mt 26 55 *B*(*S* шⳉ), Jo 10 1 *SAA*²*B* λῃστής; EpJer 57 *BF*, Hos 7 1 *AB*, Mt 24 43 *B*(*S* рєⳓⳉі-оⳓє) κλέπτης; Job 25 3 *S*(*B* рєⳓєр ⳉроⳓ) πειρατής; 2 Tim 2 9 *S*(*B* рєⳓєр пєтⳉшоⳓ) κακοῦργος; R 1 5 26 *S* лп лнстнс оⳓⳅє с. *in village*; BG 121 *S* єⳓтаⳉо ппісопє, *ib* соопє, AP 22 *A*² сапі, ShA 1 114 *S* ршлє пс., CDan 93 *B* піаⳅє пс., *ib* 94 ⳉшⳉ пс.; pl *B*: Jer 18 22, Lu 10 30, MG 25 249 ⳉапс. пфаіат, *ib* 264 піс. прєⳓⳉшлєл; sg as pl: EpJer 17, Mt 6 19.

оі пс. *B*, *be robber*: Ryl 439 *a man* єⳓоі пс.

ла пс. *S*, *place of robbers*: Job 16 9 (*B* diff), Ps 17 29 *S*(*B* ла пⳉшпт) πειρατήριον; Lu 10 30 *S* (BMOr 8811 206, *B* с. pl) λῃστής.

лєтсіпшоⳓі *B*, *robber's trade*: EW 106 *all that* лощі ⳅєп+.

сєно　*v* тсаⳅо.

сшпє　*v* соп.

спо *A*　*v* спаⳓ.

сшпк¹, -пⳅ², -лк³, -лⳅ⁴ *S*, сшпк, сєпк-, сопⳅ *B* vb intr, *suck*: Is 66 11 *S*²(*B* щапєщ) θη-λάζειν; P 44 23 *S*³ ارتفع, JA '05 2 116 *S* аⳓс.² ⳉі.пєсєкіⳉє; tr: Cant 8 1 *S*³ (*var*⁴), Is 60 16

$S^2(B$ оⲩⲱⲙ) θ.; Job 6 4² $S(B$ сⲱ) ἐκπίνειν; El 122 S ϥпас.² ⲙпессⲡооⲩ, ShIF 148 S^2 sim, BMar 17 S еіс.² ⲡпоⲅекіⲃе, MG 25 135 B аⲅсепк ерⲱ+, Va 61 22 B пⲓерⲱ+ еⲧаксопкоⲩ ϫеппаⲙпоⲧ, AM 104 B с. ⲙпекⲱⲟⲩ *suck up*, Mor 25 40 S mice с.⁴ ⲙппеϩ of lamp; с пса- B: MG 25 161 fish с. пса+ⲣⲟⲓⲙⲓ, *ib* 146 bee с. псапіеⲃіⲱ; ϭ̄пе. S^3, *sucking*: P 44 121 тϭ. ппеⲃрефос. *Cf* тспкⲟ.

снкоⲩ S nn, meaning unknown: Cai 42573 1 recipe for scab ϭап пескоⲩркр ϩіс. таρⲥ пеϥсⲱⲙа & it shall become white.

саⲙⲙⲧ S nn f, meaning unknown: KroppK 47 recipe (charm) еⲧⲃеоⲩс. еⲕарρϫ (*i e* ϭарϭ). Or *l* ? саⲙⲙⲧ *q v*.

снаеін S, снⲏⲓⲛⲓ B vb intr, *skip, stroll, wander*: Ps 113 4 $S(B$ ⲑⲉⲗⲏⲗ) σκιρτᾶν, Sa 19 9 S διασ.; Ge 24 63 $B(S$ BM 2 ϫⲓ ϩраϩ) ἀδολεσχεῖν نُزَّ; HL 113 B yard еϥс. пϧⲏⲧϥ; refl: C 86 288 B +с. ⲙⲙоⲓ in city διάγειν تَفَخَّر, *ib* 295 B еⲩс. ⲙⲙⲱоⲩ in streets περιπατεῖν = *ib* 231 B еⲩсіні ϫⲉⲛ-. As nn m B, *swaying gait*: K 100 пⲓс. (*sic*) تَفَخَّتَر (*sic*, var تَفَخَّط), *ib* 263 оⲩс. تَفَخَّط رفق في المشى.

снⲏⲓⲛⲓ B nn f, *irrigation machine*: K 153 +с. خطّارة (*v* Dozy), ساقية, *ib* 263 do, P 55 1 с. ⲙⲙⲱоⲩ سقاية الماء.

саⲛⲛⲉϩ S nn m, *grasshopper*: ShA 1 254 small beast called in Egypt с....оⲩϭалⲏⲧ еϥⲃⲱϭⲉⲡⲉ (depicted Z tab vii).

саⲛⲓс S(once) B nn, with vb ϫⲓ, ϭⲓ, *doubt* (related to снаⲩ Stern 99, AZ 47 13): Mk 11 23 (S р ϩⲏⲧ снаⲩ) διακρίνεσθαι; Mt 28 17 (S = Gk) διστάζειν; HL 110 апеϥϩⲏⲧ ϭⲓ с. ἐνδυασμὸς γίνεσθαι; Aeg 15 апаϫⲛⲧ ϭⲓ с. ероⲓ (S diff), P 44 94 S аⲩϫⲓ с. ерооⲩ شَكّ. As nn: PasH 39 аϭⲛеϭⲓ с.; ер ϭⲓ с., *doubt*: Ps 118 39 (S ⲙееⲩе) ὑποπτεύειν; Cat 47 throng оⲓ пϭⲓ с. because of demons, *ib* 73 паⲅер ϭⲓ с. ϫⲉппоⲩⲙеⲅⲓ; ⲙⲉⲧреⲩϭⲓ с., *doubt* (nn): Cat 81 *d*. as to resurrection.

снсн S, сепсеп SB vb intr, *resound*: Job 30 4 SB, Is 17 12 B (S ⲱϣ еⲃол), 1 Cor 13 1 B (S + ϩрооⲩ) ἠχεῖν; MG 25 225 B пекⲙаϣϫ с., FR 126 B voice с. ϫеппекⲙаϣϫ; с. еⲃол S, *echo*: Mor 52 16 testing stone ϫеϧⲱⲣϥ пϥс. еⲃ. As nn SB: Is 13 21 $B(S$ ϩр.), He 12 19 $B(S$ do) ἠχώ; Br 226 S пϣорп пс. ϣаⲡⲧепⲧⲏⲣϥ аісⲱⲃⲛⲉ, O'LearyH 35 B ϩапс. пϫⲱ.

сⲱⲛⲧ SAA^2BF, сⲱⲱ. SA^2(AP), снⲧ- S, сенⲧ- SB, сопⲧϥ SB, соопⲧϥ S, саⲛⲧϥ A, сопⲧ† S vb **I** intr, *be created*: Ps 32 9 SB, Ro 1 25 SB κτίζειν;

Ex 21 22 $B(S$ ϫⲓ ϩеіⲕⲱп) ἐξεικονίζειν. **II** tr, *found, create*: Ge 14 19 $S(B$ ⲑаⲙⲓо), Ps 50 10 SA (Cl)B, Hos 13 4 AB кт.; Mt 19 4 $B(S$ таⲙⲓо), LAp 564 F еⲧаⲃсⲱпⲧ (*sic* ?) [ⲙⲙаⲛ ποιεῖν; Is 27 11 $B(S$ = Gk) πλάσσειν; Sa 11 25 S κατασκευάζειν; BG 46 S angels пⲧаϥсопⲧоⲩ, TillOster 24 A пе]ⲧаϥсапⲧϥ, AP 38 A^2 аϥⲱⲱпⲧ пⲧⲡ[е, BHom 106 S world епⲧаϥсоопⲧе, C 86 300 B аϥⲑаⲙⲓо пⲧфе аϥс. ⲙпрⲏ, ShA 2 32 S аⲕⲕеⲧ пкосⲙос аϥсⲱпⲧ all therein, DeV 2 107 B Christ еⲧаⲩс. ⲛϩⲱⲃ ⲛⲓⲃеⲛ еϧоⲩⲛ ероϥ *for whom all was created*.

—— nn SAA^2BF, *creature, creation*: Mk 10 6 $SB(F$ ϣа пс.), He 9 11 SBF, Cl 59 3 A κτίσις, Sa 9 2 S κτίσμα; Eccl 11 5 S ποίημα; Ge 7 4 SB, Zech 7 9 S(ShA 2 339)$A(B$ таϩо ераⲧϥ) ἀνάστημα; Sa 1 14 S γένεσις, Aeg 276 S пс. еⲧⲣⲏⲗ ζῷον; PS 375 S пс. ⲙпкосⲙос, R 1 2 26 S Christ оⲩс. ап, Aeg 262 S mouse ⲛ кес., KroppE 22 S псⲱⲱпⲧ ⲛⲧпе, Leyd 455 S I conjure you ⲛⲓс. that arise with moon, Mani 1 A^2 пс. ⲧⲏроⲩ, C 86 148 B оⲩс. called onocentaur.

аⲧсопⲧϥ SB, *uncreated*: JA '75 5 224 S пеⲡⲡⲁ ...оⲩаⲧсопⲧϥ ἄκτιστος, Leyd 442 S паⲧсопⲧϥ ἀχειροποίητος (Kropp 2 169); Dif 2 14 B Trinity паⲧсопⲧе.

ⲙаⲓс. B, *loving offspring* (?): Va 57 197 φιλόστοργος оⲩⲟϩ ϩапⲙ.

реϥс. SB, *creator*: Jth 9 12 S κτίστης, Ro 1 25 S (ShBor 246 64, var & B vb) κτίζων; Sa 13 1 S τεχνίτης; BMis 134 S пр. ⲙпка ⲛⲓⲙ, AM 127 B ϥр. ⲛⲧфе.

оⲩаϩⲙ̄с. B, *re-creation*: Mt 19 28 (S ϫпо ⲛкесоп, F оⲩ. ϫпа) παλιγγενεσία.

ϣас. S, ϣа пс. F, *first creation*: Mt 13 35 S пϣ. ⲙпкосⲙос (BF = Gk) καταβολή; Mk 10 6 F (Mor 21 141, SB с.) κτίσις.

ϭⲓⲛ-, ϫⲓⲛс. SB, *creation*: My 30 S тϭ. ⲙпкосⲙос, Va 57 78 B кеϩ. ⲛⲃерⲓ.

сⲛⲧⲉ SAA^2, сⲛⲧⲓ S (place-name), сенⲧ B, снⲛⲧ F nn f, *foundation*: Deu 32 22 SB, Is 13 5 SB, 1 Cor 3 12 SBF θεμέλιον, Aeg 239 S тс. of church θεμελίωσις; Sa 4 3 S βάσις; Job 28 9 SB ῥίζα; Am 8 3 $B(S$ ⲙеϣ+ⲃс), Zeph 2 14 $B(A$ ⲙелⲱⲧ) φάτνωμα; ShA 2 144 S псⲱр еⲃол ⲛⲛеⲩс., Ryl 90 S sim, Mani 1 A^2 тс. ⲙⲛϭро, DeV 2 167 B mason digging ϫⲉⲛⲧϥ, J 4 53 S ϫⲓⲛⲛеⲩс. ϣараⲧⲏⲩ (*cf* PMon 11 30 ἀπὸ θεμελίων); кⲱ, ϫⲱ с. SBF, *lay found.*: Lu 6 48 B ϩⲓⲭⲉⲛ- (S саⲙⲓⲛе) θ. τιθέναι ἐπί, cit Tri 395 S еϫⲛ-; +еϩраⲓ, еϩр.: He 6 1 $SF(B$ рⲱϣⲧ) θ. βάλλειν; Z 613 S began еⲕа тс. еϩ., AM 62 B аϥⲭⲱ ⲛоⲩс. еⲃ.; ϭⲓⲛка, ϫⲓⲛⲭа с., *laying found.*: My 25 S тϭ. of church, ROC 23 271 B sim m; р с. S, *be a found.*: PS 158 thy

light ⲣ ⲥ. ⲛⲁⲩ (= Od Solom 22 12) ; ⲥⲙⲛ ⲥ. *SA*, *lay found.*, mostly ⲥ acc : Job 38 4 (*B* ϩⲓⲟⲅⲓ), Zech 4 9 *SA*(*B* do), He 1 10 (*BF* do) θεμελιοῦν, Lu 14 29 (*B* ⲭⲱ) θ. τιθ. ; Ps 135 6 (*B* ⲧⲁⲭⲣⲟ) στερεοῦν ; BMis 246 to clear temple site ϣⲁⲛⲧⲥⲉ. ⲥ. ⲙⲙⲟϥ, TurM 41 ⲥ. ⲥ. ⲙⲡⲉⲓⲧⲟⲡⲟⲥ ; † ⲥ. *S*, meaning same : 1 Pet 5 10 (*B* ϩ.) θ. ; Bor 205 359 † ϭⲟⲙ ⲛⲁⲩ ⲙⲡⲛ† ⲥ. ⲛⲁⲩ ; ⲟⲩⲉϩ ⲧⲥ. *S*, same : BMis 177 = BSM 86 *B* ϩ. ; ϭⲓ ⲥ. *BF*(once) same, ⲥ acc : Ps 86 5 (*S* ⲥⲙ.), Am 9 6 (*SA* do), He 1 10 *BF*(*S* do) θ. ; ROC 23 154 ⲁⲩϣⲁⲡϩⲓ ⲥ. ⲛ̄ⲣⲁⲡⲡⲁⲗⲁⲧⲓⲟⲛ, BSM 93 festival which saint ϩⲓ ⲥ. ⲙⲙⲟϥ ϫⲉⲛ- ⲡⲥⲁϫⲓ : ⲣⲉϥϩⲓ ⲥ. *B*, *founder* : Lacr 82, AZ 13 139. *Cf* ⲥⲉⲧⲛ.

As place-name : ⲧⲥⲉⲛⲧⲉ الاساس (Ep 1 108), var ⲧⲥⲓⲛⲧⲓ (Lant 97).

ⲥⲱⲛⲧ *SAA²*(Jo)*B*(once), ⲥⲱⲱ. *A²* (AP) nn m, *custom* : Ac 6 14 *S* (*B* ⲥⲩⲛⲏⲑⲓⲁ), He 10 25 *S* (*B* ⲕⲁϩⲥ), Z 311 *S* ⲡⲥ. of fathers ἔθος ; Jo 18 39 *SA²* (*B* = Gk) συνήθεια ; Lev 18 3 *S*(*B* = Gk), Mic 6 15 *A*(*B* ⲛⲟⲙⲟⲥ) νόμιμον ; Sa 14 23 *S* θεσμός ; 2 Mac 6 9 *A* ⲡⲥ. ⲛⲣⲉⲗⲗⲏⲛ τὰ Ἑλληνικά ; AP 44 *A²* ⲡⲥ. ⲛ̄ⲧⲛⲏⲥⲧⲓⲁ, Bor 282 174 *S* ⲡⲥ. ⲛ̄ⲧⲉⲅⲣⲁⲫⲏⲡⲉ ⲉⲧⲣⲉⲥ- ⲙⲟⲩⲧⲉ ⲉⲡⲁⲏⲣ ϫⲉⲧⲡⲉ, BMar 127 *S* ⲕⲁⲧⲁ ⲡⲥ. of Christians ; ⲡⲥ., ⲡⲥ. ⲛ̄ⲛⲉϩⲓⲟⲙⲉ *SB*, *custom of women* (sc menstruation, *cf* ⲥⲙⲟⲧ) : Ge 18 11 *S*(*B* ⲣⲏ†), ROC 17 400 *B* τὰ γυναικεῖα, Ge 31 35 *S*(*B* do) ἐθισμός ; Aeg 254 *S* ⲉⲥϣⲟⲟⲡ ϩⲓⲡⲥ. ⲛ̄ⲛⲉϩ., BMis 78 *S* feared lest ⲡⲥ. ⲛ̄ⲛⲉϩ. ϣⲱⲡⲉ ⲙⲙⲟⲥ (Virgin) in temple, *cf ib* 135 *S* ⲡⲥ. ⲛ̄ⲧⲉϥⲫⲩⲥⲓⲥ ; ⲉⲓⲣⲉ ⲙⲡⲥ. *S, follow custom* : Lu 2 27 (*B* ⲕⲁⲧⲁ ⲡⲉⲧⲥϣⲉ) εἰθι- σμένον ; ShHT *L* 1 ⲉⲩⲉⲓⲣⲉ ⲛⲡⲥ. of demons.

ⲥⲱⲛⲧ *S*(Sh only) *A*, ⲥⲟⲛⲧ† *S*, ⲥⲁ. † *A* vb intr, *look*, with preposition. ⲥ ⲉ- look at : Pro 4 25 (*SB* ϭⲱϣⲧ) βλέπειν acc (20 16 *SA* confused ? with this) ; *ib* 7 6 (*SB* do) παρακύπτειν εἰς ; Ex 2 4 (*B* † ⲡⲓⲁⲧⲥ) κατασκοπεύειν ; Cl 17 2 ἀτενίζειν εἰς ; Sh C 73 92 ⲉⲩⲛⲁⲩ ⲁⲩⲱ ⲉⲩⲥ.† ⲉⲣⲟⲉⲓⲡⲉ ; ⲁⲛⲣⲏⲓ ⲁ- : Mic 7 7 (*S* ϭ. ⲉϩⲣ., *B* ϫ. ⲉϫⲉⲛ-) ἐπιβ. ἐπί ; ⲥ ⲉϫⲛ-, ⲁϫⲛ-, *look upon* : Ge 4 4 (Cl, *B* ϫ. ⲉϩ. ⲉϫ.) ἐπιδεῖν ἐπί ; Hos 3 1† (*B* ϫ. ⲉϫ.) ἐπιβ. ἐπί ; Pro 5 21† (*SB* ϭ. ⲉϫⲛ-) σκοπεύειν εἰς ; ShClPr 22 360 ⲉϥⲥ. ⲉϫⲱⲧⲛ, ShWess 9 154 ⲛ̄ⲑⲉ ⲉϣⲁⲕⲛⲁⲩ ⲉⲣⲟⲓ …ⲛ̄ⲑⲉ ⲉϣⲁⲕⲥ. ⲉϫⲱⲓ, ShIF 302 ⲕⲥ.† ⲉϫⲱⲛ ⲕⲛⲁⲩ ⲉⲣⲟⲛ ; ⲉϩⲣⲁⲓ ⲉϫⲛ- : ShP 130¹ 37 ⲉⲩⲛⲁϭⲱϣⲧ ⲛ̄ ⲛⲥⲉⲥ. ⲉϩ. ⲉϫⲙ̄ⲡϭⲱⲗⲡ ⲉⲃⲟⲗ of fellows ; ⲥ ⲡⲥⲁ-, meaning sim : ShC 42 39 brethren ⲉⲩⲥ.† ⲛⲥⲱⲓ (var ϭ.), El 90 transformed before ⲡⲉⲧⲥ.† ⲛⲥⲱϥ ; ⲥ ϩⲛ-, *look from* : ShA 2 240 windows ⲉϥⲥ. ⲉⲃⲟⲗ ϩⲛⲧⲟⲩ into heaven (*cf ib* 1 388 sim ⲉⲃⲟⲗ ϩⲛ-).

With adverb. ⲥ ⲉⲃⲟⲗ, *look forth, await* : ShA 2 322 ⲉⲓⲥ.† ⲉⲃ. ⲛ̄ⲧⲉⲩϣⲏ ⲧⲏⲣⲥ longing for sunrise,

ShC 73 80 hypocrite's fast if faster ⲥ. ⲉⲃ. ϫⲉⲉⲩⲛⲁ- ⲥⲱⲕ ⲙⲙⲟϥ *wait to be constrained* to eat, ShA 1 388 ⲡⲉⲧⲥ.† ⲉⲃ. ϩⲓⲡϣⲟⲩϣⲧ ; ⲁⲃ. ⲁϫⲛ- : Hos 11 4 (*B* ϫ. ⲉϫ.) ἐπιβ. πρός ; ⲉⲃ., ⲁⲃ. ⲣⲏⲧⲥ : Cl 23 5† προσδοκᾶν ; ShC 73 94 ⲡⲉⲧⲟⲩⲥ.† ⲉⲃ. ⲣⲏⲧϥ shall come ; ⲥ ⲉⲣⲟⲅⲛ ⲉⲃ., *look this way & that* (?) : ShMiss 4 280 ⲉⲥ. ⲉϩ. ⲉⲃ. ϩⲓⲡⲛⲁ ⲉⲧⲙⲙⲁⲩ (*cf* p 34 *b supra*).

ⲙⲁ ⲡⲥ., *look-out place* : Hos 5 1 (*S* Mun 176 ⲛ̄ϭ. ⲉⲃ., *B* ⲡⲁⲣⲉϩ) σκοπιά.

V Rec 28 206.

ⲥⲛⲁⲧ *S* vb intr, *fear* : Sa 12 11 ⲥ ⲣⲏⲧⲥ ⲛ- (var ⲣ ϩⲟⲧⲉ) εὐλαβεῖσθαι ; Vi ostr ⲙⲡⲣⲥ. ϫⲉⲉⲕⲉⲓ ⲁⲣⲏⲥ.

ⲥⲛ̄ⲧⲉ *foundation v* ⲥⲱⲛⲧ *be created*.

ⲥⲛ̄ⲧⲉ *two v* ⲥⲛⲁⲩ.

ⲥⲟⲛⲧⲉ *S*, ⲥⲁ. *SᵃF*, ⲥⲟⲛ† *B* nn m, *resin* : Ge 37 25 *S* (P 44 104 صنور) *B* (لطم), Jer 8 22 *S*(BHom 12) *BF*(Mor 54 6), Ez 27 17 *SB* ῥητίνη ; P 44 93 *S* (ⲉ)ⲙⲡⲗⲁⲥⲧⲣⲟⲛ · ⲡⲥ. · ⲙⲙⲁⲗⲁⲅⲙⲁ درياق, Tri 440 *S* ⲡⲉⲓⲥ. ʾⲟ ; K 175 *B* ⲡⲓⲥ. ʾⲱ ; Br 112 *S* ϣⲁⲗ, ⲥ., ⲉϩⲓⲱ, ShIF 94 *Sᵃ* found not ⲥ. nor healer, AM 310, 322 *B* ingredient in torture cauldron. In name(?) : Πεσόντε (Preisigke).

ⲥⲟⲛⲧϥ *v* ⲥⲱⲛⲧ.

ⲥⲛⲁⲩ *SAB*, -ⲁⲁⲩ *S*(WS), -ⲉⲩ *AA²F*, ⲥⲛⲟ *A*, ⲥⲛⲱ *Sᵃ* (Ep 1 241), ⲥⲛⲉⲟⲩ *SᵃFO*, ⲥⲛⲡⲉⲟⲩ (J&C 98), ⲥⲛⲟⲩ *Sᵃ* (*l c*), -ⲁⲟⲩ *O*, f ⲥⲛ̄ⲧⲉ *SA*, ⲥⲛⲟⲩⲧⲉ *Sᶠ* (Pcod Mor), ⲥⲛⲟⲩ† *BF*, ⲥⲛⲏ† *F*, compounds & ordinals *v below*, nn, *two* (*BF* mostly ⲃ̄, f ⲃ̄†) Ⅰ as nn : 1 Kg 11 11 *S* ⲥ. ⲗⲁⲁⲩ, Is 47 9 *SB*, Mt 24 41 *SB* f, Phil 1 23 *S*(*B* ⲡⲓⲥⲛⲟⲩ†, *F* ⲡⲓⲃ̄) δύο ; Nu 7 13 *SB* ἀμφότερος ; GPar 2 10 *B* ⲟⲩⲃ̄ ⲉⲃⲟⲗ ϫⲉⲛⲛⲉϥϭⲁⲗⲱ- ⲟⲩϫⲓ ; with *days* implied : Ps 47 1 *B* ⲛⲃ̄ ⲙⲡⲥⲁⲃⲃⲁ- ⲧⲟⲛ (*S* ⲥⲟⲩⲥ.) δεύτερος, Ac 28 13 *SB* ⲡⲉⲛⲥ. δευτε- ραῖοι ; Nu 33 3 *S* (var & *B* ⲣⲁⲥⲧⲉ) ἐπαύριον ; BM 216 109 *S* Ⅰ eat ⲙⲡⲁⲥ. διὰ δύο ; ShMiss 4 281 *S* ⲡⲉϫⲥ., EW 215 *B* ⲡⲥ. ⲛ̄ⲧⲉⲃⲇⲟⲙⲁⲥ ; iterated : Ge 7 15 *SB*, Mk 6 7 *SB* δύο, Si 42 30 *S* δισσός ; ShC 73 84 *S* compelled to fast ⲥ. ⲥ. *2 (days) together*, sim ShBMOr 8810 453 *S* ⲉⲓⲣⲉ ⲥ. ⲥ., C 89 130 *B* ⲉϥⲥⲉⲕ ⲃ̄ ⲃ̄.

Ⅱ as adj **a** before nn : Nu 7 89 *S*(*B* after), Aeg 240 *S* ⲥ. ⲡⲣⲓⲛ (*ib* ϩⲓⲛ ⲥ.), *ib* 276 *S* ⲕⲉⲥ. ⲛ̄ⲇⲓⲁⲕⲟⲛⲟⲥ ⲇ. ; BHom 37 *S* ⲥ. ⲛ̄ⲃⲁⲗ, PCodMor 22 *Sᶠ* (arith) ⲧⲓⲥⲛⲟⲩ† ⲛ̄ϭⲓϫ (*l* ϭⲓⲝ), *ib* 25 ⲥⲛⲟⲩⲧⲉ, CMSS 47 *F* ⲡⲓⲥ. ⲛ̄ⲛⲓⲟⲩϩ ; with ⲛⲟϭ : EstA 5 ⲛ. ⲥ. ⲛ̄ⲡⲁⲣⲁⲕⲱⲡ, PS 246 ⲛ. ⲥ. ⲛ̄ϣⲱⲙⲉ, KKS 28 ⲛⲛ. ⲥ. ⲛ̄ⲥⲧⲩⲗⲗⲟⲥ …ⲉⲩⲧⲁⲭⲣⲏⲩ. **b** after nn (oftenest) : Ge 22 3 *SB*, Ex 31 18 *SB*, Am 1 1 *AB*, Ez 37 22 *B* ⲟⲩ- ⲙⲉⲧⲉⲣⲟ ⲛ̄† ⲥ., Ap 11 10 *S* ⲡⲓ-...ⲥ., *B* ⲡⲓ-...ⲥ. ⲇ., Aeg 246 *S* ⲗⲁⲥ ⲥ. ⲇⲓ- ; Sa 14 30 *S* ἀμφ. ; Lev 5 11 *S*(*B*

ни) ζεῦγος; PS 17 *S* ечо пеⲛ̇агⲙⲁ с., Br 106 *S* теⲅϭιⲝ спте, Hor 77 *O* ппо̇ⲩте спаоⲩ, AZ 21 105 *O* пико спеоⲩ, Mani 1 *A²* поⲩаіпе с., AM 135 *B* оⲩсоп б̄, ib 267 *B* тоі споⲩϯ, BMOr 6948 1 *F* ολокоті споⲩті, AZ 23 39 *F* поⲩϱі сниті, AP 8 *A²* рⲱⲙⲉ снеⲩ; ϱо с. *S*, *two-edged*: Ps 148 (149) 6 (*B* ро б̄), Ap 1 16 (*B* do) δίστομος. ϱнт с. *SB*, *two hearts, doubt*: J 106 27 *S* ахнϱ. с; Ja 1 8 *S* рⲱⲙⲉ пϱ. с. (*B* оі пϱ. б̄) δίψυχος; р ϱ. с., *be doubtful*: Aeg 240 *S* δίγνωμος; ⲙⲛⲧϱ. с., *state of doubt*: Si 1 27 *S* καρδία δισσή.

спооⲩе m f, -се f *S*, спаⲩе *A*, -аоⲩе, -аⲩсе f (Mani 2)*A²* in ⲙⲛⲧе. *twelve*, хоⲩте. *twenty-two* &c: -спооⲩе Ex 15 27 f, Jud 10 3 f, Ps 59 tit, Jon 4 11 *SA*, AP 12 1, PS 24 ⲙⲛⲧе. паіⲱⲛ, *ib* 14 ⲙⲛⲧе. пϭоⲙ; -спооⲩсе Ge 14 4, Nu 35 6, Mk 5 42 (var -с), Jo 11 9 (do); but J&C 98 ⲙⲁⲃ̄снпеоⲩ. *V* AZ 47 12.

ⲙпеспаⲩ *SB*, птеспте *S* adverbial, *both together*: Lev 20 11 *SB*, Ru 1 19 *S*, Su 10 *SB*, Lu 6 39 *SB* ἀμφ.; Jo 20 4 *SB* οἱ δ.; PS 299 *S* ϱптеⲩⲙⲛⲧе ⲙпес., AM 249 *B* ϱапⲟⲙⲛⲓ ⲙпес., J 66 37 *S* daughters птес. shall inherit *together*, Ep 165 *S* send to тⲙⲗⲡ(т)ϱнке ⲙпес. *to both of us*, HSt 464 *S* pray ⲙппетпеϱнⲩ ⲙпес. (var Aeg 264 ϱіоⲩсоп).

соп, сеп с., ⲙерсеп с. *v* соп.

р с., ер б̄ *SB*, *become, be two*: Ge 41 32 *B* f, Jer 2 27 *B* δευτεροῦν, Mt 27 51 *SB* σχίζεσθαι εἰς δ., Ge 25 9 *S*(*B*=Gk) διπλοῦς; BMis 205 *S* оⲩраще ечо пс., C 43 78 *B* broke in middle ачер с.; ⲙптρечр с., *duality*: P 131⁵ 70 *S* Christ's nature without ⲙ.

ⲙер-, ⲙарс., -спте *S.A²F*, *second* (v ⲙоⲩϱ *fill* sf), before nn: Nu 7 18 *S*(*B* after), Jo 4 54 *SA²* (*B* do), Ap 20 6 *S* (*B* do) δεύτερος; PS 127 *S* пⲙ. птоⲗⲟⲥ, Mani 2 *A²* пⲗⲁϱснеⲩ пϱооⲩе, Lant 75 *S* тⲗⲉрⲙⲛтспооⲩсе пϱιстоρια, CMSS 39 *F* тⲗⲁϱ-споⲩті кⲩріакн, also Nu 10 11 *S* тⲗⲉрⲣⲁⲙⲡⲉ спте, Ge 45 6 *B* ⲑⲙⲁϱроⲙпι б̄ϯ, Jon 3 1 *SAB* sim; after nn: Ap 2 11 *SB* m, Nu 10 6 *SB* f; as monastic title: Miss 4 533 *S* ϱепрⲗⲁⲛі ⲙⲡⲗ. = C 89 51 *B* δεύ., WS 216 *S* проестⲱс & пⲗ., Leyd 131 *S* sim = *ib* ⲇⲉⲩтеларιос (δευτεράριος), ShC 73 44 *S* пеіⲱт ... печⲙ., *ib* тⲙааⲩ ... тесⲙ. *Cf* сⲱоⲩϱ(сооⲩϱ sf).

р ⲙерс. *SB*, *be second*: Nu 2 16 *S*(*B* om vb) δεύ.; ShZ 603 *S* suckling, youth, пептачр ⲙ., full grown (τέλειος), waxing feeble.

Cf сапіс.

In names: Σονσνάυ, -σναῦς, -σνῶς, Ψονσναῦς (Preisigke). In place-name: PLond 3 92 Περπι-σνάυ.

споⲩⲱп *A²* *v* сооⲩп.

сааⲛϣ, саⲛϣ, -пⲭ (J 116) *S*, саⲛϱ, саа (Pro 23) *A*, сапещ *A²*, щаⲛϣ, -ещ *B*, щнⲛϣ, ще. *F*, сааⲛϣ-, са. *S*, щапоⲩщ-, щапещ, щепещ-(Hos 9) *B*, сапоⲩщ- *F*, сапоⲩщ⸗ *SA²*, -оⲩϱ⸗ *A*, щапоⲩщ⸗ *BF*, сапащт†, -аϱт† *A*, щапеⲩщ†, -оⲩщт† (Ez 39) *B* vb **I** intr, *make live, be alive*: Ge 50 20 *SB*, Lu 23 29 *B*(*S* тспко), Va 61 24 *B* snake ачщ. ϭептеспехі τρέφειν, Pro 23 24 *SA* ἐκτ., Ps 36 11 *S*(*B* оⲩпоϥ) катат.; Job 40 25 *S*(*B* щ.†) ἐνσιτεῖσθαι; ShBor 246 34 *S* псес. ϱппечⲇıкаιⲱⲗⲁ, Z 270 *S* петс. ϱⲙпсⲱⲗⲁ, *ib* 641 *S* seeds етреⲩс. by rains = C 89 127 *B*, ROC 23 278 *B* sell it псещ. пϱнтоⲩ (*sc* its price); с е- *SB*: BM 217 (1) *S* петс. епечха-хе, Aeg 57 *B* ϥн етщ. епісⲱпт тирϥ, *ib* 40 *B* sim.

Qual, *nourished, well fed*: Dan 4 9 *B* τρέφεσθαι, 1 Tim 4 6 *SB* ἐντ., Mic 1 16 *A* (*l*? сапаϱт, *SB* ϭнп) τρυφερός, Mor 18 116 *S* εὔτροφος; Jud 6 28 *S*, Lu 15 23 *SB* σιτευτός, Mt 22 4 *SA*(TillOster 25) *B* σι-τιστός; Ez 39 18 *B* στεατοῦσθαι; *ib* 34 3 *B* παχύς; Ps 21 12 *S* (*B* кепιⲱоⲩт) πίων; Pro 15 17 *SA* *saginatus*; Ge 49 21 *S* (*B* фоρі ебоⲗ) ἀνειμένος; ShP 130² 38 *S* етс. ϱϱрепаϥ, Va 57 142 *B* waters where fish щⲱпі еⲩщ.

II tr, *nourish, rear, tend*: Nu 6 5 *SB*, Ac 12 20 *SB* τρέφ., Sa 7 4 *S*, Ac 7 20 *SBF* ἀνατ., Ps 30 4 *SB*, Pro 22 9 *SA* διατ., Hos 9 12 *AB*, Eph 5 29 *SB* ἐκτ., Miss 8 122 *S* птаⲩсапоⲩщт ϱιпιстіс ἐντ., Ps 36 4 *S*(*B* оⲩпоϥ) κατατρυφᾶν, Deu 1 31 *SB* τροφοφορεῖν, Aeg 246 *S* еⲩс. ппеⲩщнре τεκνοτρ-φος, Nu 32 4 *SB* с. теⲃпн κτηνοτρ.; Job 20 16 *B*, Is 66 11 *B*(*S* сⲱпк) θηλάζειν; Lam 4 5 *B*(*S* ϱⲗоо-ле) τιθηνεῖν; Is 34 15 *SF*(*B* ⲗісі) νοσσεύειν; Si 14 11 *S* εὖ ποιεῖν; AM 274 *B* етачщапоⲩщт ἀνάγειν; ShA 2 280 *S* аⲩсапоⲩщп ϱιоⲩсβⲱ, AP 44 *A²* ϥпас. поⲩⲗⲡще, BM 512 *F* ечсапоⲩщ перⲱⲗⲓ, Pcod 40 *F* етщепщ ⲗⲗаі (*S* саа.), BM 244 *S* паⲛр...с. ппекарпос, C 43 105 *B* sim, Wess 18 25 *S* nurse ассапоⲩщϥ, BSM 12 *B* mother's milk еⲟресщапоⲩщт = BMis 345 *S* тспко, BM 445 *S* ϱптеⲩпоⲩ птапсапоⲩщϥ ечеι еіс ϱнⲗικιап, J 116 4 *S* we agree to сапⲭ ⲗⲗок *maintain*, Bor 100 42 *S* петсааⲛϣ щнре, Mani 1 *A²* ппⲗⲗерıт са-поⲩщϥ.

щⲃнр с. *S*, щϥ. пс. *B*, *reared with, akin*: Ac 13 1 *B* (*S* соп ⲗⲗоопе) σύντροφος; BM 187 130 *S* mounts to sky пϥр щ. с. ⲗппаⲛр.

—— nn m *SBF*, *nourishment*: BM 183 *S* пс. ⲗптако τροφή, Z 330 *S* пс. птаісапоⲩще пϱн-тоⲩ τροφεῖα, MG 25 69 *B* пщ. ⲗпесщнрі τὸ τρέ-φειν, Z 273 *S* пс. ⲗпоⲩгел ерⲱте γαλακτοτροφία; Mus 42 233 *S* ye have пс. ϱιтппетпеιоте, Wess 11

155 *S* нс....птачтилооγ, Kr 143 *F* his wage [&]
певшннш;   *nursling B*: Jo 4 12 (*SA²* тѣнн, *F*
ш. vb) θρέμμα; Va 61 5 ye are пиш. of church.

ла нс., ш. *SF, nursing, feeding place*: Nu 32 1
S(*B* ла only) τόπος for cattle, R 1 3 52 *S* ла нс.
of child Jesus, BM 178 87 *S* Mary's breasts лла
нс. for famished, BMis 235 *S* sea ла нс. нптѐт =
Mor 30 7 *F*.

речс., ш. *SB, nourisher, nurse*: Ge 46 32 *SB*
-τρόφος, Ex 2 7 *B*(*A* лаане) τροφεύειν; Is 49 23
B(*S* речуслооле) τιθηνός; Aeg 252 *S* речс. преп-
порнн -βοσκός; TstAb 164 *B* Rebecca ꝉр. ннаі-
каіос; лптречс. *S, rearing*: BHom 30 тл.
шнре.

бинс., хиш. *SB, nourishment, education*: MG
25 26 *B* пих. of body τὸ τρέφειν; Wess 15 127 *S*
тб. лпечсар, Mor 22 83 *S* parents' care of теч5.,
Va 61 6 *B* течх. еөапес.

снɔч *SBF*, -оѣ *SO*, -ач *SⁱAA²F*, -оγч *Sⁱ*,
pl -ωωч *S*, -ооч *A*, -ωч *AB* & sg as pl, nn m,
blood: Ex 4 9 *AB*, Ps 50 7 *SA*(*B* om), Is 34 3
SBF, Jo 6 53 *SA²B*, He 9 12 *F* -оч αἷμα; PS
367 *S* оγрп лноγс, AZ 21 100 *O* сωп [п]лоч
реппес., ShA 2 329 *S* young girl рнптоеіс, then
рлпес. (? attaining puberty), then есшапаγζапе,
BKU 1 25 ro *S* woman ереπес. рарос (cf Lev 15
33 *S* ереπесс. шоγо лнос, *B* телтел рарос, Mt
9 20 *S* шооп ра., *B* шат еѳол ѕа.), ShA 2 338 *S*
речсерп с., AP 23 *A²* аеіпωт псаоγс, C 43 220
B паімнш нс., Z 282 *S* wolves поγллс., ib 629 *S*
аγап нс., Miss 4 767 *Sⁱ* псетаγа с. еѳол, Kropp
M 60 *S* recipe for оγрреγла н о(γ)кω нс., BM
525 *Sⁱ* for пкωл пспоγ;   blood in recipes: of
аѣωк BM 527, апшеγле Cai 42573 1, какоγпат
ib 2, поγре PMéd 299, реѣωі AJSL 46 247, бро-
лпе KroppK 59, поб птннѣе Cai lc 2, лааxе
паре ib 1;   pl forms: *S* Jer 2 34 (*B* sg), Ez 16
36 (*B* do), ShR 2 3 18; *A* El 80 -ωч, Nah 3 1
-ооч; *B* Ps 15 4 (*S* sg), Va 57 268;   sg as pl:
Ps 77 44 *S*(*B* sg), Ac 15 20 *B*(*S* sg), BMis 476 *S*
пес. етсωк, C 43 99 *B* печсарζ...печс.

атс. *SB, bloodless*: CaiEuch 577 *B* паіщелшı
па. ἀναίμακτος; Mor 43 90 *S* corpse ачшооγе
ачр а., cf Dif 1 84 *B* martyr патфеп с. еѳол.

пωп *S*, фωп *B* с. еѳол, *shed blood*: Ps 13 4 *SB*,
Pro 1 16 *S*(*A* рωл), Mt 26 28 *B*(*S* пωрт) ἐκχέειν.
V also пωрт.

р с. *SB, become blood*: Ap 8 8 аꝉ. γίνεσθαι.

ꝉ с. *F, give blood, bleed* (intr): BM 527 елепеч-
карı ꝉ с.

ωл, ωлı с. *SB, staunch, mop up blood*: R 1 5 46
S асω. лпечс., PMéd 146 *S* колл(γр)іоп пωл с.,

---

ib 265 sim палс., 288 sim, but P 54 116 *B* ел с.
ꝓ *let blood*.

xı с. *S, take blood, bleed*: ShC 73 73 none may
xı с. лнооγ етѣеоγткас; *be blooded*: ShP 130²
2 cannot draw forth sword елпатсхı с.

In name Κουισνοβ (BM 1075).

сноγч *SB*(once), -ѣ *S* nn, *last year*: 2 Cor 8
10 *SB* xıп-, ісхепс. ἀπὸ πέρυσι; Ep 566 xıпс.,
ib 81 с. леп ... тепоγ оп, CO 453 пшωл нс.,
PMich 3571]нкоγфоп (? κουφίζειν) ероч рас.,
BM 1111 рас., ратролпе, BAp 157 пое нс. таı
оιпте өе птр.;   нс. adverbial: ShA 1 387 went
to Ephesus нс., ShBor 246 109 what I declared
нс., ST 418 пепт[ак]тааγ нс.;   р с.: BM 1117
акеір сноγѣ екоγωл with thy wife.

сωης *SAA²BO*, сепр- *B*, сопрⲍ *SB*, са. *SⁱA*
A²F, сопрꝉ *SB*, са.ꝉ *AF* vb **I** intr (rare), *be bound,
fettered*: Dan 3 23 *B*(*S* лоγрꝉ), ib 3 91 *B* πεδᾶσθαι; Ps 19 9 *B*(*S* блоллı) συμποδίζεσθαι; AZ
21 98 *O* апок etc. еттı оγω, BG 72 *S* аγс. рпоγ-
шı лпепснγ, AM 248 *B* power ес.   Qual: Is
22 3 *SB*, Mt 21 2 *BF*(*S* л.)δεῖσθαι; Zech 9 11 *SAB*,
He 10 34 *B*(*S* л.) δέσμιος; Lu 4 18 *B*(*S* = Gk)
αἰχμάλωτος; ShBor 233 226 *S* еγс. paral еγлнр,
C 86 134 *B* he heard xепечшнрı с.;   с ероγп *S*,
be in bonds: ShA 2 305, 315.   **II** tr, *bind*: 2 Kg
3 34 *S* сопроγ (var са.), Hos 10 6 *SAB*, Mt 14 3
BF (сапарⲍ, *S* л.), Mk 15 1 *SB* δέειν, Zeph 2 1
B(*A* л. ароγп, *S* diff) συνδ., ROC 17 409 *B* ач-
сопреч δεσμοῖς διαλαμβάνειν, Pro 7 22 *B*(*SA* ꝉ еп-
клал) ἐπὶ δεσμούς; Dan 3 20 *B* πεδᾶν, Ge 22 9
SB, Zech 13 3 *SAB* συμπ.; DeV 2 57 *B* шасс.
лпаролос пꝉаıωріа, ShC 42 104 *S* аγсопреч
like thief, Mani 1 *A²* аγс. ллаı, Mani 2 *A²* пꝉ-
лароγ пγсапроγ.

With following preposition.   с е- *SB*, *bind to*:
1 Cor 7 27ꝉ *B*(*SF* л.) δ. dat; MG 25 160 *B* сепр
піле̄ѣап еꝉапаıω, BM 346 1 *S* аγс. ллоч епсат
of horse; ероγп, еѕ. е-: BMis 279 *S* еч с.ꝉ ер.
епеѕлоб, C 86 275 *B* ачөроγсопреч еѕ. ероч;
bind as to limbs: ShC 73 199 *S* есс.ꝉ етоотс, Mor
48 87 *S* псесопреч епеꝉхıх = C 43 143 *B* ечс.ꝉ
п-;   с п-, *as to B*: Mt 22 13 (*S* л. acc) δ. acc;
AM 311 өроγс. напа...пхωч пелратч, ib 36
псес. лпаıтос ппечхıх;   *with*: ROC 25 255
ечс.ꝉ лѣепıпı;   с птп- *SB*, *to*: R 1 4 53 *S* еıс.ꝉ
птоотоγ ллнт ѐпδ. dat; Miss 8 183 *S* son с.ꝉ
птоотоγ прплаατоı, BSM 124 *B* ечс.ꝉ птотч of
Michael = Mor 22 133 *S*.   с рп-, ѕеп- *SAB*,
as to (cf above): ShMIF 23 72 *S* сопреч рппечбıх;
in, with: Jud 16 8 *S* δ. ἐν; Pro 20 14 *SA* συμποδ.
ἐν; ShRyl 71 92 *S* с.ꝉ ррепллрре, C 86 279 *B* с.ꝉ

ⲍⲉⲛϩⲁⲛⲥⲛⲁⲩϩ, ST 30 S ⲙⲏⲣ ϩⲓⲟⲩⲡⲓⲛⲓⲡⲉ…ⲥ.†
ϩⲓⲟⲩϣⲉ ; ⲥ ϩⲓⲡⲁϩⲟⲩ, ϩⲓϥ. ⲛ-, *behind* : ROC 18
36 B hands ⲥ.† ϩ. ⲙⲙⲟϥ περιάγεσθαι εἰς τοὐπίσω ;
BSG 198 S ⲁⲩⲥⲟⲡϩϥ ϩ. ⲙⲙⲟϥ = C 86 305 B ⲁⲩⲥ.
ⲡⲛⲉϥϫⲓⲝ ϩ. ⲙⲙⲟϥ.

—— nn m S, *bond, fetter* : BG 55 ⲡⲥ. ⲛⲑⲩⲗⲏ,
ib 69 ⲛⲟⲝⲟⲩ ⲉϩⲛⲥ.

ⲙⲁ ⲡⲥ. B, *place of binding, prison* : Ge 39 22 (S
ϣⲧⲉⲕⲟ), Is 24 22 (S ⲙⲁ ⲙⲙⲟⲩⲣ), Ac 5 21 (S ϣ.)
δεσμωτήριον ; AM 216 ⲣⲉϥϩⲁⲣⲉϩ ⲡⲧⲉ ⲡⲓⲙ.

ϫⲡⲥ. B nn m, *binding* : Ps 149 8 (S ⲙ.) δεῖσθαι.

ⲥⲛⲁⲩϩ SB, -ⲟⲟⲩϩ S (? pl), ⲥⲛⲱϩ, -ⲟⲟϩ A, ⲥⲛⲁϩ
A²B, -ⲉⲩϩ, -ⲉⲩⲁϩ(Eph)F, nn m, *bond, fetter* mostly
as pl : Lev 26 13 B (S ⲙⲟⲩⲥ), Ps 115 7 B(S ⲙⲣⲣⲉ), Is 42 7 SB, Hab 3 13 S (ShC 73 19) A -ⲱϩ
B, Phil 1 17 BF(S do), Cl 55 2 A -ⲟⲟϩ δεσμός, Is
58 6 B(S do), Col 2 19 B(S do) συνδ.; Eph 6 20
F(S do, B = Gk) ἅλυσις ; Ps 139 6 B (var ⲥⲛⲁϩ, S
ⲛⲟⲩϩ) σχοινίον ; Si 40 11 S (var do), Is 14 17 SB
ἐπαγωγή ; BG 121 S ⲃⲱⲗ ⲉⲃⲟⲗ ⲛⲛⲥⲛⲟⲟⲩϩ, BMis
327 S ϩⲉⲛⲥⲛⲟⲟⲩϩ (var ϩⲁⲗⲁⲥⲓⲥ), C 43 24 B ⲥⲱⲗⲡ
ⲛⲛⲓⲥ., CO 474 S ⲡⲗⲟⲧⲥ ⲛⲓⲥ. (contains ⲟⲩⲙⲏⲣ,
ϣⲟⲙⲛⲧ (ⲙ)ⲙⲏⲣ) ; as sg A²B : Is 52 2 ⲛⲓⲥ. δ.,
Jer 11 9 ⲟⲩⲥ. συνδ. ; MG 25 222 bound ⲍⲉⲛⲟⲩϩ
ⲡⲧⲉ ⲟⲩⲁⲥⲕⲏⲥⲓⲥ, *ib* 223 var ⲥⲛⲁϩ, DeV 2 22 do,
Mani 1 A² ⲛⲓⲙⲣⲣⲉ ⲙⲛⲡⲥ.

ⲥⲛⲁϩ B : Mk 7 35 (S ⲙⲣ.), Lu 13 16 (var -ⲁⲩϩ,
S do), Va 63 91 ⲛⲓⲥ. δ. ; Miss 4 201 ⲛⲓⲥ. of unbelief, C 43 144 ⲁⲡⲓⲥ. ⲃⲱⲗ ⲉⲃⲟⲗ.

ⲥⲓⲛⲁϩⲃⲓ B nn, ingredient in boiling cauldron :
AM 322 ⲟⲩⲥ. ? σίναπι (but P 44 82 ⲥⲓⲛⲏⲡⲓ,
-ⲁⲡⲉⲛ, PMéd 176 ⲥⲓⲛⲁⲡⲉ, KroppM 77 ⲥⲓⲛⲁⲡⲟⲩ ;
cf DM 27 10 snwpt).

ⲥⲉⲛϩⲟⲩⲧ B *v* ⲥⲁϩⲛⲉ.

ⲥⲁⲡ S nn, meaning unknown : J 5 R 5 ⲡⲣⲁⲙ
ⲡⲥ. ⲡⲁⲣⲡⲁⲣⲓⲁ (البريم). *Cf* ? ⲥⲟⲡ a measure.

ⲥⲡ-, ⲥⲉⲡ-SF, ⲥⲉⲙⲉ F nn f, *year* in dating events,
documents : Est A 1 S ⲧⲥⲡ ⲥⲡⲧⲉ, *ib* F 11 S ϩⲣⲥⲡ
ⲯⲧⲟ, Dan 1 21 S ⲧⲥⲉⲡ (*sic* l) ⲟⲩⲉⲓ (B ⲁⲥϥⲟⲩⲓ), Lu
3 1 S ⲧⲥⲡ ⲙⲛⲧⲏ (B ⲣⲟⲙⲡⲓ) ἔτος ; Kr 164 F ⲧⲥⲉⲡ
ⲓⲉ ⲛⲗⲁⲙⲡⲓ ⲙⲡⲕⲏⲕⲗⲟⲥ, *ib* 12 F ⲧⲥⲉⲡ ⲙⲛⲧⲏ ⲛⲗⲁⲙ-
[ⲡⲓ, BP 3241 F ⲥⲟⲩⲕ̄ [month] ⲗⲁⲙⲡ[ⲓ] ⲧⲥⲉⲡ ⲍ̄,
ib 5561 F ⲡⲧⲉⲙⲟⲥⲓ (δημόσιον) ⲡⲧⲥⲉⲡ ⲁ̄, BM 671 F
ⲕⲓⲁⲭ ⲡⲥⲉⲡ ⲛ̄, Ny Karlsberg stele 1544 F ⲡⲕⲁⲣⲡⲟⲥ
ⲡⲧⲥⲉⲙⲉ (*sic*) ⲓⲃ̄, Fitzwilliam Cambr stele ⲡⲁϣⲁ(ⲛ)ⲥ
ⲡⲥⲉ ⲛ̄ ⲡⲓ(ⲛⲁ ?) ; *hour* F : Mor 27 27 ⲡⲛⲁⲩ ⲛⲥⲡ
ⲟⲩⲉⲓ ⲙⲡⲟⲟⲩ = BMis 374 S ⲭⲡ = Va 63 7 B ⲁⲭⲡ,
Mor 24 12 ⲧⲥⲉⲡ ⲓⲁ̄ = *ib* 23 17 S ⲭⲉⲡ. V ⲁⲥϥⲟⲩⲓ
& AZ 50 125, 51 138

ⲥⲓⲡ B *v* ⲥⲓⲃ.

ⲥⲟⲡ SB, ⲥⲁⲡ S^a (J 92) S^f (PLond 4) AA²F, ⲥⲓ-
ⲥⲉⲡ- S (only + ⲥⲛⲁⲩ), pl (?) ⲥⲱⲡ S.A, ⲥⲱⲟⲡ, ⲥⲟⲟⲡ
S (v III), nn m, *occasion, time (vices), turn* (καιρός
in Dan 6 10 S) **I** independently : ShBor 246 72 S
ⲁϣⲧⲉ ⲧⲉⲩⲛⲟⲩ ⲉⲧⲙⲙⲁⲩ ⲡⲥⲁⲡⲛⲁⲩ ⲁⲩⲱ ⲡⲥ. when
was crucified, ShZ 637 S ⲟⲩⲉⲧ ⲡⲥ.…ⲟⲩⲉⲧ ⲡⲛⲁⲩ,
ShMIF 23 97 S ⲡⲥ. ⲁⲛⲡⲉ ⲡⲁⲓ for many words,
Hall 4 S foreign land ⲉϥⲟⲩⲏⲩ ⲡⲁⲣⲁ ⲡⲥ. ⲧⲏⲣⲟⲩ
(var Imp Russ Ar S 10 80), ShBM 203 76 S ⲟⲩⲥ.
ⲉⲃⲟⲗ ϩⲓⲟⲩⲥ. (cf sim ϩⲟⲟⲩ), Mani 2 A² ⲡⲥ. ⲉⲧⲉⲣⲛⲉϥ,
Mor 31 114 S Lent overtook him ⲙⲡⲥ. ⲉⲧⲙⲙⲁⲩ,
ShZ 598 S ⲟⲩⲥ. ⲧⲉⲣⲟⲙⲡⲉ ;   ⲥⲟⲡ…ⲥⲟⲡ, *now…
again* : R 1 4 52 S ⲥ. ⲙⲉⲛ by road ⲥ. ⲥⲉ by sea,
ShA 1 249 S ⲥ. ϣⲁⲩⲥⲱⲧⲙ ⲥ. ⲥⲉ ϣⲁⲩⲣ ⲁⲧⲥⲱⲧⲙ,
ib 12 S ⲥ. ⲙⲱϩⲥⲛⲏⲡⲉ…ⲥ. ⲟⲛ ⲁⲁⲣⲱⲡⲉ, AM 127
B ⲥ. ⲙⲉⲛ ⲉⲥϫⲱ ⲙⲙⲟⲥ ϫⲉ-…ⲟⲩⲥ. ⲟⲛ ϫⲉ- ; pl: Sa
16 18 S ϩⲉⲛⲥ. ⲙⲉⲛ…ϩ(ⲉ)ⲛⲥ. ϫⲉ πότε…πότε ; ShC
42 197 S ϩⲉⲛⲥ. ⲙⲉⲛ ϫⲉ-…ϩⲉⲛⲥ. ϫⲉ ⲟⲛ ϫⲉ-, C 89 81
B ϩⲁⲛⲥ. ⲙⲉⲛ it riseth ϩⲁⲛⲥ. ϫⲉ ⲟⲛ sinketh ; *sometimes* S: Sh(Besa)Z 513 ⲥ. ϩⲟⲩⲟ ⲉⲛⲁⲓ, BAp 98 ϩⲉⲛⲥ.
ϫⲉ ;   *turn, round* of prayer or reading (cf μέρος
eg Miss 4 142 n): BP 1248Q S ordinand shall say
ϣⲉ ⲡⲥ. ⲡϣⲗⲏⲗ daily, Mus 40 43 S ⲥⲟⲟⲩ ⲡⲥ. ⲡϣ.
sex orationes, C 89 9 B ⲝ̄ ⲡⲥ. ⲡϣ. in day = MG
17 348 ⲁⲝⲓ, ShC 73 52 S ⲡⲥⲟⲟⲩ ⲡⲥ. ϩⲓⲣⲟⲩϩⲉ, *ib*
129 S canon of prayers ϩⲙⲡⲥⲱⲟⲩϩ, ϩⲙⲡⲥⲟⲟⲩ ⲡⲥ.
or ϩⲛⲛⲏⲛⲓ, *ib* 109 S shall first pray ⲛⲟⲩⲥ. before
work, Wess 18 3 S ⲡⲥ. ⲡⲟⲱϣ ⲙⲙⲉⲉⲣⲉ, BM 147 S
sim ⲡⲧⲉⲩϣⲏ, Cai 8313 S ϥⲛⲁⲱϣ ⲟⲩⲥ. ⲛⲣⲏⲧⲉ (*sc*
Epistle), TEuch 1 662 B ϩⲁⲛⲙⲏϣ ⲡⲥ. ⲛⲡⲓϣϯ ⲛ̄ⲕⲉ
ⲉⲗⲉⲛⲥⲟⲛ, Rec 6 181 B ⲉⲣ ⲅ̄ ⲡⲥ. ⲛϣⲗ. = BMar 216
S ϫⲉ ϣⲟⲙⲛⲧ ⲡⲥ., BM 291 S ⲧⲁⲣ ⲟⲩⲥ. ⲛϣⲗ., TstAb
233 B ⲧⲁⲟⲅⲟ ⲡⲣ̄ ⲡⲥ. ⲛϣ.   *Obscure* Ep 373 S
forget me not ⲧⲉⲧⲛⲙⲉⲣ (l ? ⲙⲉⲣⲉⲣ) ⲥ. ⲉⲡⲁⲣ ⲡⲙⲉⲉⲩⲉ ⲛⲁ ⲉⲡⲉⲧⲛⲉϩⲣⲧ.

II adverbial, **a** with help of prep. ⲥ ⲉ- SA² :
Mor 37 93 ⲛⲑⲉ ⲉϣⲁⲩⲙⲟⲩⲧⲉ ⲉⲣⲟϥ ⲉⲛⲥ. πολλάκις ;
P 131³ 28 will relate whole matter ⲕⲁⲧⲁ ⲑⲉ ⲉϣⲁⲓ-
ⲁⲁⲥ ⲉⲛⲥ. *often*, Miss 4 664 none might visit him
ⲉⲓⲙⲏⲧⲉⲓ ⲡⲥⲁⲃⲃⲁⲧⲟⲛ ⲉⲛⲥ. *now & then*, CO 287
ⲉⲥⲡⲁ ⲉⲣⲟⲓ ⲉⲛⲥ. *often*, ShC 73 54 shall not cook
enough ⲛϩⲟⲟⲩ ⲥⲛⲁⲩ ⲉⲛⲥ. *at one time, at once*,
CO 106 undertakes to come ⲙⲫⲓⲥⲟⲛ ⲡⲟⲩⲉϩⲟⲩ
ⲛⲡⲣⲟⲟⲩ ⲉⲛⲥ., sim, Mani 2 A² ⲡⲉⲧⲉϣⲁϥⲉⲓ ⲁⲡⲥ.
ⲛϥⲣ ϥⲟⲣⲉ ⲡⲧⲉⲕⲕⲗⲏⲥⲓⲁ, Sh 73 66 ⲛⲧⲉⲧⲛⲥⲩ-
ⲁⲅⲉ ϩⲁⲧⲓⲧⲏⲩⲧⲛ ⲛⲟⲩⲥ. ϣⲁⲛⲧⲛⲕⲱⲧⲉ ⲉⲃⲟⲗ ⲉⲛⲥ.
(obscure), BAp 60 archons of aeons each ruling
ⲉⲝⲡⲧⲉϥⲣⲟⲙⲡⲉ ⲉⲛⲥ. (do) ;   ⲉⲩⲥ. *v* ϩⲓⲟⲩⲥ. ⲥ ⲛ-,
ⲙⲡⲥ. SA², *at the time* : Deu 9 8 (B Gk om), ShA
1 402 thus I spake ⲙ. ⲉⲛⲉϥϩⲁⲣⲧⲛ, ShP 130⁶ 127
ⲙ. ⲛⲧⲁϥⲧⲟⲩⲛⲉⲥ ⲗⲁⲍⲁⲣⲟⲥ, ShC 42 195 giveth drug
ⲙ. ⲏ ⲡⲛⲁⲩ when needed, Aeg 262 take sacrament
ⲙ. ⲉⲧⲟⲩⲡⲁⲧⲁⲗⲟⲥ ⲉϩⲣⲁⲓ, Mani 2 A² ⲙ. ⲉⲧϥⲛⲏⲩ

ⲁⲃⲁⲗ; *now & then*: 1 Kg 20 25 (var ⲕⲁⲧⲁ ⲥ.) ὡς ἅπαξ κ. ἅπ.; ⲙⲡⲉⲓⲥ., -ⲡⲁⲓⲥ. *SB, this time*: Z 329 S choose life thou willest ⲙ. τηνικαῦτα; PS 347 S ⲁⲓⲥⲕⲩⲗⲗⲓ ⲙⲙⲟⲓ ⲙ., P 129¹⁵ 20 S for father's sake ⲁⲓⲕⲁⲁⲕ ⲉⲃⲟⲗ ⲙ., C 43 221 B ⲁϥⲙⲟⲩ ⲙ., Hall 102 S send them ⲙ. ⲛⲡⲟⲅⲱⲧ (*sic*), ST 227 Sᵃ ϭⲉⲛⲧⲁϭⲉⲓ ⲁⲣⲏⲥ ⲙⲡⲉⲥ. ⲡⲁⲓ; ⲛⲟⲩⲥ. *SBF, once*: Ps 88 35 S(B ⲟⲩⲥ.), He 10 2 SBF, Z 306 S eating ⲛ. ⲕⲁⲧⲁ ϩⲉⲃⲇⲟⲙⲁⲥ ἅπ.; MG 25 218 B ⲉⲓⲣⲉⲙⲉⲓ ⲛ. ϩⲉⲛⲧⲣⲓ ποτέ; PS 264 S if he sin ⲛ. ⲏ ⲥⲛⲁⲩ, BMis 158 S ⲁⲥϣⲱⲡⲉ ⲇⲉ ⲙⲙⲟϥ ⲛ., CMSS 28 F ⲙⲡⲉⲕⲟⲩⲁⲧⲉ ⲡⲉⲛ[ⲟⲩϫⲉⲓ ⲛ.; ⲛⲟⲩⲥ. ⲛⲟⲩⲱⲧ: Nu 16 21 S(B ⲛⲓⲟⲩⲥ.) εἰς ἅπ., 1 Cor 15 6 SF(B ⲉⲩⲥ.) ἐφ' ἅπ.; PS 383 S shall suffer all punishments ⲛ., C 43 116 B blot out sins & crimes ⲛ.; ⲛⲟⲩⲥ. ⲉⲩⲥ. S, *from time to time*: ShC 73 57 if they need food ⲛ. ⲉ., ST 101 sim; om ⲛ- B: Ps 88 (above), C 86 284 ⲟⲩⲥ. ⲁⲕⲙⲟⲩ ⲙⲙⲟϥ; pl ⲛⲡⲁⲓⲥ. B: AM 24 came not ⲛ. ⲧⲏⲣⲟⲩ; ⲛⲣⲉⲛⲥ. SB: Si 37 20 S ἐνίοτε, ROC 18 169 S ⲛ. πυκνά, Z 297 S keeping vigil ⲛ.; iterated: Jud 20 30 S ⲛⲑⲉ (ⲛ)ⲛⲓⲥ. ⲥ. ὡς ἅπαξ κ. ἅπ.; MG 25 16 B ⲉϣϣⲉ ⲛⲣⲁⲓⲥ. ⲥ. ⲉⲓ ⲉϩⲣⲏⲓ, ROC 18 170 S came to him ⲛⲣⲏⲥ. ⲥ. μίαν μίαν; ShC 42 33 S sim; om ⲛ-: Mich 550 39 S ⲙⲟⲛⲥ ϩⲉⲛⲥ. ⲥ. *hardly ever*; ϩⲓⲟⲩⲥ. SAB(mostly = ⲉⲩⲥ.)F, *at one time, together*; Ge 22 6 S, Is 11 7 S(B ϩⲓⲟⲩⲙⲁ), ib 31 3 SF ἅμα; Deu 22 11 S, Nah 1 9 S(A ϩⲓⲙⲟⲩⲉⲣⲏⲟⲩ, all B ⲉⲩⲥ.) ἐπὶ τὸ αὐτό; Jo 4 36 S(A² ϩⲓ]ⲙⲟⲩⲉⲣ., BF do) ὁμοῦ, Job 2 11 S(B do) ὁμοθυμαδόν; Nu 7 19 S (var & B ⲡⲉⲥⲛⲁⲩ), Mt 13 30 SF(B ⲡⲉⲙⲛⲟⲩⲉⲣⲏⲟⲩ) ἀμφότεροι; Is 66 8 S(B ⲉⲩⲥ.) εἰς ἅπ.; Cl 51 1 A ⲧⲓⲣⲉⲗⲡⲓⲥ ϩ. τὸ κοινὸν τῆς ἐλ.; Sa 14 9 S ⲉⲛ ⲓⲥⲱ; Z 277 S ⲡⲉⲧⲛⲟⲩϫⲁⲓ ϩ. ἁπάντων; 4 Kg 14 9 S ϩⲱⲱ ϩ. συμπατάσσειν, Jth 14 3 S ⲡⲱⲧ ϩ. συντρέχειν, Ez 30 4 S ϩⲉ ϩ. (B do) συμπίπτειν; Jud 11 10 S ⲟⲩⲧⲱⲛ ϩ. ἀνὰ μέσον ἡμῶν, Zech 6 13 A sim, Job 1 4 S ⲙⲛⲛⲉⲅⲉⲣⲏⲩ ϩ. (B om) πρὸς ἀλλήλους; PS 17 S ⲁⲛⲟⲛ ⲧⲏⲣⲛ ϩ., El 34 A women grinding ϩ. (cf Lu 17 35 S), ShBor 281 100 S ⲁϥⲧⲁⲕⲟ ⲙⲡⲉⲅⲕⲉⲱⲥ ϩ., BHom 50 S preparing ⲉⲙⲓϣⲉ ϩ. (var R 2 2 34 ⲙⲡⲛⲉⲅⲉⲣⲏⲩ), BAp 29 S no division ⲟⲩⲧⲱⲟⲩ ϩ., Kr 197 F ⲁⲡⲁⲛ ϩ., C 43 46 B ⲡⲧⲉⲧⲉⲛⲉⲣ ϣⲫⲏⲣⲓ ϩ.; ⲉⲩⲥⲟⲡ B: DeV 1 173 dead all alike ⲛⲓⲙⲡⲉ ⲫⲏ ⲉⲧⲧⲁⲓⲏⲟⲩⲧ ⲓⲉ...ⲉⲧϣⲱϣ ⲉ.?, Bess 7 15 ⲡⲧⲉⲥϭⲱϫⲉⲙ ⲙⲡⲓⲁⲏⲣ ⲉ. *befouled whole air*, RO 14 356 ϣⲁⲡⲧⲉⲩⲉⲣ ⲡⲓϣⲱⲙ ⲧⲏⲣϥ ⲉ. *entire summer*, ib 352 bade each pray ϩⲁⲣⲓϩⲁⲣⲟϥ ⲉ. ϩⲙⲡⲥ. S, *at time, when*: ShC 73 69 ϩ. ⲏ ϩⲙⲡⲓⲁⲩ, ShBMOr 8811 246 ϩ. ⲉⲧⲟⲩⲛⲏⲩ ⲡⲥⲱⲕ. ⲕⲁⲧⲁ ⲥ. *SBF, from time to time*: 1 Kg 20 25 S (var ⲙⲡⲥ.) ὡς ἅπ. κ. ἅπ.; PS 265 S ϯ ⲡⲁϥ ⲕ. ⲥ. ⲡⲙⲩⲥⲧⲏⲣⲓⲟⲛ, C 41 13 B making 24 obeisances ⲕ. ⲥ., Aeg 259 S let them remember ⲕ. ⲥ. ⲛⲓⲙ ⲉⲩϭⲱⲙ, BM 601 F ⲕ. ⲥ.

ⲡϣⲁⲕⲱϣⲏⲗ; ⲡⲣⲟⲥ ⲟⲩⲥ. S, *at one time*: PLond 4 460 surety for a *solidus* ⲛ. (ib ⲥⲁⲛ, var ⲡⲣⲟⲥ ⲁⲡⲁⲝ), 461 ⲛ. ⲛⲟⲩⲱⲧ.

b other combinations. ⲕⲉⲥⲟⲡ SAA²B, *another time, again*: AM 181 B would read Psalter ⲕⲉⲥ. ⲇⲉ ⲟⲛ ⲛⲓⲡⲣⲁⲝⲓⲥ; oftener ⲡⲕⲉⲥ.: Ge 2 19 S(B = Gk), Job 14 7 S(B ⲟⲛ) ἔτι; Phil 1 26 B (SF ⲟⲛ) πάλιν, Mt 19 28 SF ϫⲡⲟ ⲛⲕ. (B ⲟⲩⲁϩⲉⲙ ⲥⲱⲛⲧ), Cl 9 4 A παλιγγενεσία; Ps 103 30 SB ⲣ ϩⲣⲣⲉ ⲛⲕ. ἀνακαινίζειν; Gu 68 S stay not in this city ⲛⲕ. τοῦ λοιποῦ; BMar 122 S have told thee ⲛⲕ. *already*, ib 189 sim, AP 13 A² (in these Gk om); ShC 73 82 S ⲁⲓϫⲟⲟⲥ ⲛⲕ. ϫⲉ-, BAp 69 S ⲙⲡⲟⲩϭⲉ ⲉⲣⲟⲟⲩ ⲛⲕ. *no more*, BSM 119 B ⲙⲡⲁⲥϩⲉⲙⲥⲓ ⲛⲉⲙϩⲁⲓ ⲛⲕ.; ⲙⲡⲉⲓ-, ⲙⲡⲁⲓⲕⲉⲥ. SB, *yet once more, again*: Ge 18 32 B(S ⲛⲕ.) ἔτι ἅπ., Jud 16 18 S ἔτι τὸ ἅπ. τοῦτο, GMir 19 S let me fill them ⲙⲛ., C 43 12 B ⲡⲧⲉϥⲧⲁⲗϭⲟⲕ ⲙ.

ⲁⲡⲥ ⲛⲥ. *v* ⲁⲡⲥ.

ⲕⲱⲃ ⲛⲥ. *v* ⲕⲱⲃ.

ⲙⲏⲛϣⲉ, ⲙⲏϣ ⲛⲥ. SB, *multitude of times, often*: Is 42 20 B(S ⲛϩⲁϩ ⲛⲥ.), Ro 1 13 B(S do) πολλάκις, ib 15 22 B(S do) τὰ πολλά; PS 11 S have told you ⲛⲟⲩⲙ. ⲛⲥ., AM 24 B once & again ϣⲁⲣⲁⲛ ⲛ. ⲛⲥ.

ϩⲁϩ ⲛⲥ. S, *meaning same*: Mt 17 15 (B ⲙⲏϣ ⲛⲥ.) πολλ.; Ps 105 43 (B do) πλεονάκις; Lu 5 33 (B diff) πυκνά; PS 58 ⲉⲥϣⲁϫⲉ ⲛϩ. ⲛⲥ.

ⲧⲙⲡⲥ. S(only PS) A² meaning sim, lit *not counting times* ⲧⲙ ⲉⲡ ⲥ. (so Sethe *Verb* 2 1003 n): PS 7 ⲉⲣⲉⲟⲩⲉⲓ ⲟⲩⲟⲧⲃ ⲉⲟⲩⲉⲓ ⲧ. *one surpassing other countless times*, ib 203 ⲉⲟⲩⲛ ⲟⲩⲁ ⲟ ⲛⲛⲟϭ ⲉⲟⲩⲁ ⲧ., Mani 2 A² ⲛⲛⲁϭ ⲧ. *countless times great*. Hardly same is BMEA 10579 S without your kindness ⲛⲧⲛⲉϣ ⲡⲟⲗϭ ⲁⲛ ⲧⲉⲡⲥⲟⲡ.

ⲣⲱϣⲉ ⲛⲥ. *v* ⲣⲱϣⲉ ⲛⲛ.

ⲥ. ⲛⲓⲙ, ⲛⲓⲃⲉⲛ SB, *everytime, always*: 1 Cor 11 25 B(S ⲁⲡⲥ ⲛⲥ.), CaiEuch 336 B ὁσάκις; Sa 14 31 S ἀεί; R 1 2 41 S ⲡⲉⲥϩⲙⲟⲟⲥⲡⲉ ⲛⲥ. ⲛⲓⲙ *facing eastward*.

III With numerals. **a** cardinals, precedes ⲥⲛⲁⲩ: Nu 20 11 S ⲥⲛ ⲥ. B ⲥⲟⲛ ⲥ., Ps 61 11 SB, Nah 1 9 SAB do; follows others: Dan 6 10 S ϣⲟⲙⲛⲧ ⲛⲥ. (B ⲛⲥⲟⲩ) καιρός; Jo 13 38 SA² ϣⲟⲙⲛⲧ ⲛⲥ. B ⲅ̄ ⲛⲥ., Ez 16 30 S ϣⲙⲧ ⲥ. B do, Mt 18 21 S ⲥⲁϣϥ ⲛⲥ., B ⲍ̄ ⲛⲥ. **b** ordinals, BSG 183 S ϣⲟⲣⲡ ⲛⲥ., AM 193 B sim, ib 43 B ⲥ. ⲛϩⲟⲩⲓⲧ, Deu 9 18 S ⲙⲉⲣⲥⲉⲡ ⲥⲛⲁⲩ, Job 33 14 S ⲙⲉⲣⲥ. ⲥⲛⲁⲩ B ⲥ. ⲙⲙⲁϩⲃ̄, Ge 27 36 B ⲙⲁϩⲥ. ⲃ̄, He 9 28 F sim, Cat 80 B ⲙⲁϩⲅ̄ ⲛⲥ., Mt 26 44 S ⲙⲉⲣϣⲟⲙⲛⲧ ⲛⲥ., B ⲙⲁϩⲅ̄ ⲛⲥ.; ⲥⲱⲡ SA, ⲥⲱⲱⲛ S only +ϣⲙ(ⲛ)ⲧ-: Pro 22 20 S ϣ. ⲥⲱⲡ (var ϣⲟⲙⲛⲧ ⲛⲥⲟⲡ) A, Lu 22 34 ϣ. ⲥⲱⲱⲛ (var do, B ⲅ̄ ⲛⲥ.), Ac 10 16 do (var ⲥⲟⲟⲛ, B do).

соп *S* nn, a measure? : BMis 263 ϣε пс. (*sic* MS) птωвε = Mor 29 32 *S*, *ib* 30 38 *F* апе, BMOr 6201 B 22 оутрамма пара с. оуа[, PRain 4714 пс. ϣнм плас (*sic l, v* лас *flax*). *Cf* ? Lev 24 6 *S* с. θέμα (*B* хιптало).

сωп *SBO*, -в *B*, сп- *SF* (Jo 13), сеп- *SB*, сап- *A²*, сев- *B*, соп⸗ *SB* vb intr (once) *dip, soak*: Ex 12 22 *B* βάπτειν ;   tr : Lev 4 6 *SB*, Deu 33 24 *B* (*S* ϩωрп), Ru 2 14 *SB* (Paris Inst Cath 133), Jo 13 26 *SA²BF* в., Mt 26 23 *SB* ἐμβ. ; BHom 10 *S* пет-пасеп пеутнвε ммооу ἐπιστάζειν, C 41 69 *B* sim, R 1 5 31 *S* sim ϩапеусноу, AZ 21 100 *O* с. [п]моу ϩеппеспов, KroppJ *S* аусопе пϩнмхр (Mt 27 48 мар?), Mor 21 111 *S* сеп пестнвε ппеϩ, P 44 134 *S* сеп пеівнт j̄, PMéd 244 *S* сеп оуϭемε, Bodl(P) a l f *S* ппркаϥ (*sc* mixture) еϣта c. *let it not lack soaking*, AM 323 *B* ϣаϥсωв ппеутнв, *ib* 311 *B* аϥсев пеут. ;   as nn m, *dipped, moistened food* &c ; DeV 1 156 *B* пιс. етϩеппоу-вιпаϫ, *ib* 173 пιс. пте пеуϭιпоуωм, Bodl *lc S* soak them ϩιппептаусепе ϩιпс.

сωп *B* nn m, *kohl-stick* for applying *k.* to eyes : K 257 пιс. درم (*sic, v* AZ 13 139). *Cf* ? last or next.

сωп, -пε *S* nn m, *eyelid* : P 43 233 ганθος (κανθός) · пс. пвал جفون العين , PMéd 219 eyes ере-пеусωпε оуомт. *Cf* кωλм.

сеепε *SAA²F*, сепε *SA*, сιпε *S*, сепι *B*, снн-пι *F* vb I intr, *remain over, be remainder* : Lev 10 12 *S*(*B* сωϫп), Is 37 4 *SB* καταλείπεσθαι, 1 Kg 25 34 *S*, Zech 12 14 *SA*(*B* do) ὑπολ. ; Mt 14 20 *S*(*B* diff, *F* ελ ϩоуа), Jo 6 12 *SA²*(*BF* ер ϩоуо) περισ-σεύειν ; Ex 34 25 *S*(*B* пкот) κοιμᾶσθαι ; ShC 73 213 *S* food еаус. мпеϩооу *remained from Sabbath day*, Ryl 310 *S* пкеϣωϫп ептаус., Kr 236 *F* пет-ϣаус. With following preposition. с е- *SA²BF*, *remain over from, for* : Ps 16 14 *F*(*S* nn, *B* сω.) καταλοιπος, 1 Thes 4 15 *SB* περιλείπ. εἰς, Ex 23 11 *S*(*B* do) ὑπολ. gen ; Sa 13 12 *S* ἀπόβλημα gen, Jo 6 13 *A²*(*SB* р ϩоуо, *F* сω.) περισ. dat ; ShLeyd 319 *S* еус. (*sic* ? l) епмоу *by choosing life*, CA 100 *S* shall eat петпас. епеθусιастнрιоп, Va 61 105 *B* they eat ϕн еθпас. ероϥ *his leavings*, BM 1124 *S* ϣареоуоп сιпε ерок *I will fetch it* ; с п- dat : BSM 33 *B* garments аукнι пс. пап = BMis 375 *S* ϣωϫп = Va 63 7 *B* сω. ; с ϩп-, ϫеп- *SB*, *remain over from* : Jos 11 22 *S* катал. gen, Is 4 3 *B*(*S* ϣ. nn) к. ἐν ; ShA 2 296 *S* ϣε пептаус. ϩιпϣо (*cf* Am 5 3), Wess 15 147 *S* only this с. ϩп(п)поув ; евол ϩп- : Lev 2 10 *S*(*B* сω. ев. ϫ.) катал. ἀπό, 2 Kg 9 1 *S* ὑπολ. ἐν. With adverb. с епа-

ϩоу *S*, *remain behind* : J 3 36 no other claim (δίκαιον) с. еп.

II tr *S* (once), *leave remaining, spare* : BIF 14 181 пϯпас. ап поуψухнποуωт.

——, *SAA²BF*, снипε, сн. *S*, сιпι *B*, сепι *F*, сепε DM (1 20) nn m f (BM 528), *remainder* : Lev 2 3 *SB*, Is 44 15 *B*(*S* ϣ.), 1 Cor 7 12 *SBF*, Cl 25 2 *A* λοιπός, Jer 15 9 *SB* катал., Ps 20 12 *S*(*B* сω. vb) περιλ., 1 Kg 9 24 *S* ὑπόλιμμα ; ShIF 199 *S* архн еппа пс., ShA 1 430 *S* wood & stone ауω пкес. *et caetera*, CO 8 *S* аϥпеϫ пеус. пмтω, BM 584 *F* псепι, *ib* 528 63, 72 *F* (arith) тесс. еiв екес (*ie* ааϥ пкас), Pcod 20 *S* пкес. ϫе *for the rest*, BHom 63 *S* sim (*cf* Gal 6 17 *B* пс. ϫе ппаι τοῦ λοιποῦ) ; with gen п-, пте : 2 Cor 12 13 *SBF*, Cl 32 2 *A* пеупес. пϭрнпε λοι., Jer 51 14 *B*(*S* ϣ.) ἐπιλ., Nu 3 26 *SB*, Mic 3 9 *SA*(*B* сω.) катал., Jer 34 19 *B* ὑπολ. ; PS 196 *S* пкес. папттелос, AP 40 *A²* пкес. папостолос, ShC 73 212 *S* оуем оус. пϭιпоуωм, HCons 463 *S* ϩιснипε *remains of feast*, DeV 2 65 *B* пс. ппеϥевιаιк, MG 17 298 *S* thou art пс. ппепрофнтнс *last remnant*, Ryl 155 *S* пснипε тнрϥ (п)перωм [? пептιмε, C 89 181 *B* like пικес. ппιрωмι *rest of mankind*.

сωпε *v* сωвε *edge* & сωп *eyelid*.

спеi *A* nn as pl, *chosen, elect* : Cl 6 1 ммιеϣε пс., 46 8 оуε ппас., 49 5 пс. мппⲉ̄ ἐκλεκτός ; TU 43 14 пс.   Related ? to сωтп (*v* Rec 31 80).

сплнλιп, спелеλιп *S* nn, meaning unknown, ? *poultice* (*splelyn* DM V 9 9) : PMich 593 β recipe птксаас (*quid* ?) ϩιϫωоу пспл., Z 630 boil оуарϣιп пткаталассе ммоу поуспел. *on his belly*. Coptic ?

спір *SAA²*, сϥιр *B*, спιλ *F*, pl спιрооуε *S*, -еуε *A*, -рωуι *B*, -раϩε *Sf* -λаϩеι *F*, & sg as pl, nn m, a *rib* : 2 Kg 2 16 *S*, Jo 19 34 *SA²B* πλευρά, Ez 4 4 *SB* -ρόν ; TU 43 3 *A* *blow of lance* ппас., BMEA 10578 *F* *side split* ϣапеуспιλ (Mor 31 254 *S* om) ;   pl forms : Nu 33 55 *SB*, Job 40 13 *S* (var sg) *B*, Pro 22 27 *SA* πλ. ; BM 257 327 *S* п-таутϭек пеус., P 131³ 82 *S* *poor man's rags* етϩа-пеус. = Va 61 91 *B*, Mor 30 13 *F* *set coals* ϩапеус. = BMis 329 *S* ϩароϥ, AM 213 *B* пιкепι пте пеус., PMich 4946 *Sf* (hymn) арке ϩаiϯ ϩппеутеве арке пни ϩапнус. арке ав ϩппеуλакоп ; b *side* : Ex 26 25 *SB* μέρος ; *ib* 28 *SB*, Ps 127 3 *B*(*S* кλе) κλίτος ; Ez 41 2 *SB* ἐπωμίς ; *ib* 8 *SB* *latus* ; Ez 40 41 *SB* νῶτον ; Z 618 *S* *ark's door* ϩιпесс., Mor 30 52 *F* ϩпоус. пте тесапі = *ib* 29 45 *S* са, P 129¹⁴ 123 *S* пес. птеϥморт = DeV 1 79 *B*, P 129¹⁶ 4 *S* *standing* ϩапеус., Mich 136 7 *S* *move not* ελ[аа]у пс. ; pl Ez 41 6 *SB* πλ.

ⲃⲏⲧ c. *SF*, rib v ⲃⲏⲧ **II**, adding Mor 24 8 *F* one of ⲛⲉϥⲃ. ⲥⲡⲓⲗ.

As prep + ⲥⲁ-, *beside* : 2 Kg 21 14 *S* (var ⲛⲥⲁⲥ.) ἐν τῇ πλ., 3 Kg 6 13 *S* (P 44 111) ⲉⲧⲥⲁⲥ. τῆς πλ.; BMis 47 *S* brought hands ⲥⲁⲥ. ⲙⲙⲟϥ & level with body, MIE 2 337 *B* sitting ⲥⲁⲥ. ⲙⲡⲓⲣⲱⲙⲓ; or ⲛⲥⲁⲥ., ⲛⲥⲁⲡⲉⲓⲥ. *S*, ⲥⲁⲡⲓⲥ. *B*: Ge 6 16 *SB*, Deu 31 26 *SB* ἐκ πλαγίων, Ex 26 35 *S*(*B* ϧⲓⲡⲓⲥⲁ-) ἐπὶ μέρους; Ez 40 39 *SB* ἔνθεν; 2 Kg 13 34 *S* ἐκ πλευ-ρᾶς; Jos 15 10 *S* ἐπὶ νώτου; R 1 3 34 *S* stone ⲛⲥⲁⲥ. ⲙⲡⲣⲟ; ϧⲓⲥ. *S*, *on side*: ShC 73 152 reeds grow-ing ϧ. ⲛⲧⲃⲟ; ϧⲓⲟⲩⲥ. *S*, *aside*: Z 233 ⲧⲟⲡⲟⲥ ϧ. ϧⲛⲁⲙⲛⲧⲉ.

In place-name (?): Πίσπιρ (*Hist Laus* § 21 & note 37).

ⲥⲟⲡⲥ *SF*, ⲥⲁⲡⲥ *SᵃF*, ⲥⲡⲥ-, ⲥⲉⲡⲥ- *S* vb **I** intr, *pray, entreat, comfort* (cf ⲥⲟⲡⲥⲡ) : Ex 32 11 *S*(*B* ⲧⲱⲃϩ), Job 19 16 *S*(*B* ϯ ϧⲟ) δέεσθαι, Lu 5 33 *S* (var ϣⲗⲏⲗ, *B* ⲧ.) δεήσεις ποιεῖν; 2 Cor 13 11 *F*(*S* ⲥⲟⲗⲥⲗ, *B* ϫⲉⲙ ⲛⲟⲙϯ) παρακαλεῖν; 1 Thes 4 1 *S* (*B* ϯ ϧⲟ) ἐρωτᾶν; ShR 2 3 17 *S* ⲧⲉⲧⲛⲥ. ⲧⲉⲧⲛⲧⲱⲃϩ, BM 600 *F* ⲧⲉⲛⲥ. ⲧⲉⲛⲡⲁⲣⲁⲅⲁⲗⲓ, AZ 21 157 *S* ⲁⲩⲥ. ⲙⲡⲁⲩⲧⲟ ⲉⲃⲟⲗ of Baptist saying &c.

II tr : Ge 43 20 *S*(*B* ϯ ϧⲟ), Ps 29 8 *S*(*B* ⲧ.), Z 314 *S* ⲁⲩⲥ. ⲙⲡⲛⲉ (& *ib* ⲙⲁⲣⲉⲡⲛ.) δ.; Job 4 3 *S* (*B* ϯ ⲛⲟⲙϯ), 1 Thes 2 11 *SF*(*B* ϯ ϧⲟ) παρ.; Jo 14 16 *S*(*Aᵃ* ⲥⲁⲡⲥⲡ, *B* do) ἐρ.; Sa 19 3 *S* ἱκετεύειν; Ps 44 12 *S* (*B* = Gk) λιτανεύειν; Ge 32 20 *S*(*B* ⲟⲩⲱϣⲧ) ἐξιλάσκειν; 1 Thes 5 14 *S*(*B* ϯ ⲛ.) παρα-μυθεῖσθαι; Mt 17 14 *S* (var ⲥⲟⲡⲥⲡ, *B* as Gk) γονυπετεῖν; FR 84 *S* ⲡⲉⲡⲥ. (var ⲥⲟⲡⲥⲡ) ⲙⲡⲛⲉ, Ryl 270 *Sᵃ* ϯⲥ. ⲙⲙⲟⲕ, J 16 8 *S* ⲉⲓⲥ. ⲛⲛⲙⲛⲧⲣⲉ (15 8 & mostly ⲉⲓⲛⲡⲁⲣⲁⲕⲁⲗⲉⲓ).

With ϫⲉ- : Ro 1 10 *S*(*B* ⲧ.) δ.; Lu 7 3 *S*(*B* ϯ ϧⲟ) ἐρ.; Mun 22 *S* ⲉϥϫⲱ ⲙⲙⲟⲥ ⲉϥⲥ. ϫⲉ- (var BMis 55 ⲧ.); ϫⲉⲕⲁⲥ : Lu 21 36 *S*(*B* ⲧ.) δ. ἵνα; Mor 48 12 *S* ⲁⲓⲥ. ⲙⲙⲟϥ ϫ. ⲉϥⲉ- (var BMar 209 ⲕⲱⲣϣ).

With following preposition. c ⲉ-, *pray to*: Leyd 436 *S* c. ⲉⲛⲡⲛⲉ for people; verbal, *pray that*: Ac 28 20 *S*(*B* ⲧ.) παρ. inf, BHom 76 *S* ⲉⲩⲥ. ⲙⲙⲟⲛ... ⲉⲣ ⲡⲓⲥⲧⲟⲥ, Ac 11 23 *S* ⲉⲧⲣⲉ- (*B* ϯ ⲛ.) παρ. inf; Aeg 248 *S* ϯⲥ. ⲙⲙⲱⲧⲛ ⲉⲧⲣⲉⲧⲉⲧⲛϩⲁⲣⲉϩ ⲉⲛⲉⲡⲧⲟⲗⲏ; c ⲉⲧⲃⲉ- *S*, *pray for*: Si 30 29 δ. περί; Jo 16 26 (*Aᵃ* ⲥⲁⲡⲥⲡ, *B* ϯ ϧⲟ) ἐρ. περί; Sa 13 18 ἀξιοῦν περί; ViSitz 172 4 38 ⲥⲡⲥ ⲡⲭ̅ⲥ̅ ⲉⲧⲃⲏⲏⲧ λιτ. ὑπέρ; c ⲉϫⲛ- *SF*, meaning same : Ps 105 30 (*B* diff) ἐξιλ.; Deu 9 20 (var ϣⲗ., *B* ⲧ.) εὔχεσθαι περί; BMis 157 ⲡⲉⲧⲥ. ⲙⲡⲛⲉ ⲉϫⲱⲛ ϣⲁⲡⲉⲧϥⲧⲟⲩ-ϫⲟⲛ, LAp 528 *F* ⲛⲥⲉⲥ. ⲉϫⲛⲧⲏ[ⲛⲟⲩ, R 1 1 32 Moses c. ⲉϫⲱⲧⲛ (var MIF 9 6 ⲙⲉⲧⲁⲛⲟⲉⲓ ⲉϩⲣⲁⲓ ⲉϫⲛⲧⲏⲩ-ⲧⲛ); Lev 4 26 c. ⲉϩⲣⲁⲓ ⲉϫⲛ- (*B* ⲧ.) ἐξιλ. περί; c

ⲡⲧⲛ- *S*, beg of: Lev 1 4 (*B* ϣⲱⲡ) δεκτός (? mis-understood) : c ϧⲁ- *S*, *pray for, about* : Ac 8 24 (*B* ⲧ.) δ. ὑπέρ; Ex 32 30 (*B* ⲥⲉϧϩⲟ ⲉϧⲣⲏⲓ ⲉϫ.), Nu 25 13 (*B* ⲉⲣ ⲣⲉϥⲡⲟⲣⲉⲙ ⲡⲧⲉ-) ⲉϫⲓⲗ. περί; 1 Thes 3 2 (*B* ⲧ. ⲉϧⲣ. ⲉϫ.) παρ. ὑπέρ; Ep 199 ⲉⲧⲣⲉⲕⲥⲉⲡⲥ ⲡⲛⲉ ϧⲁⲣⲟⲓ; c ϧⲓϫⲛ- *S*, meaning same : PSBA 30 277 ⲡⲱϣⲡⲉ c. ϧⲓϫⲱⲕ; *pray over* : Pcod 14 ⲉⲩⲥ. ϧⲓϫⲛⲧⲕⲟⲗⲩⲙⲃⲏⲑⲣⲁ.

—— nn m *S*, *entreaty, prayer* : Job 8 6 (*B* ⲧ.), Ps 16 1 (*B* ϯ ϧⲟ), He 5 7 *SF*(*B* ⲧ.) δέησις; Ac 9 31 (*BF* ϣⲟⲧ ⲛϩⲏⲧ), Ro 12 8 *SF*(*B* do), 2 Thes 2 16 (*B* ⲛⲟⲙϯ) παράκλησις; Ps 65 19 (*B* ⲧ.) προσ-ευχή; Ac 26 7 (*B* ⲙⲟⲩϩ ⲉⲃⲟⲗ) ἐκτένεια; ShC 73 150 ⲟⲩⲛⲟϭ ⲛⲥ. & weeping, R 1 5 38 martyr to judge ϯⲣ ⲭⲣⲓⲁ ⲁⲛ ⲙⲡⲉⲕⲥ.

ⲣ c. *SF*, *make prayer* : Phil 1 4 (*B* ⲉⲣ ⲧ.) δ. ποιεῖν. ϫⲓ c. *SF*, *receive comfort* : He 6 18 (*B* ϭⲁ ⲛ.) παρ. ἔχειν.

ⲣⲉϥⲥ. *S*, *intercessor, petitioner* : BMis 48 ⲡⲣ. ⲉϥ-ⲥⲟⲡⲥ ⲙⲡⲣⲣⲟ for us.

ⲥⲟⲡⲥⲡ *S*, ⲥⲁⲡ. *AAᵃF*, ⲥⲡⲥⲡ *A*, ⲥⲟⲡⲥⲉⲡ, ⲥⲟⲃ-ⲥⲉⲃ *B*, ⲥⲡⲥⲡ- *SA*, ⲥⲟⲡⲥⲱⲡ- *SAᵃ*, ⲥⲉⲡⲥⲉⲡ- *B*, ⲥⲡⲥⲱⲡⲝ *S*, ⲥⲉⲡ. *SAAᵃ*, ⲥⲉⲡⲥⲱⲡ† *S* vb **I** intr, meanings as ⲥⲟⲡⲥ: Mal 3 14 *A* (*B* ⲧⲱⲃϩ) ἱκέτης; BAp 173 *S* ⲉⲕⲥ. ϫⲉⲕⲱ ⲡⲁⲓ ⲉⲃⲟⲗ; c ⲉ- *B*: MG 25 12 ⲉⲩⲥ. ⲉⲁⲡⲁ ⲁⲛⲧⲱⲡⲓ κολακευτικῶς τῷ, FR 102 ⲙⲁⲣⲉⲥ. ⲉⲧⲁⲯⲩⲭⲏ comfort, AM 99 ⲉⲩⲥⲟⲃⲥⲉⲃ ⲉϯⲡⲁⲣⲑⲉⲛⲟⲥ enticing; c ⲉϩⲣⲁⲓ ⲉϫⲛ- *S*: Aeg 276 priest c. ⲉϩ. ⲉ. ⲧⲉⲛⲡⲣⲟⲥⲫⲟⲣⲁ εὔχεσθαι; c ϧⲁ- *S*: PSBA 22 249 c. ϧⲁⲙⲙⲟⲩ ⲡⲉⲓⲟⲟⲩⲉ; ϧⲁⲣⲁⲧⲝ : AP 29 *Aᵃ* ⲁϥ]ⲥ. ϧⲁⲣⲁⲧϥ ⲙ[ⲡⲁⲩⲗⲟⲥ.

II tr : Ex 4 10 *A*(*S* ⲥⲟⲡⲥ, *B* ϯ ϧⲟ), Lu 5 12 *S* (*B* do), AP 48 *Aᵃ* ⲁ]ⲩⲥⲉⲡⲥⲱⲡϥ δέεσθαι, Is 57 10 *S* καταδ.; Deu 13 6 *S*, Pro 1 11 *SA* (all *B* ϯ ϧⲟ), Job 2 11 *S* (var ⲥⲟⲗⲥⲗ, *B* ϯ ⲛⲟⲙϯ) παρακαλεῖν, Is 51 3 *S* ⲁⲓⲥⲉⲡⲥⲱⲡⲝ... ⲁⲓⲥⲉⲡⲥ- (*B* ϯ ⲛ. *bis*) π.... π., 1 Cor 1 2 *S*(*B* ⲙⲟⲩϯ) ἐπικ.; Jo 4 31 *SAᵃ*(*B* ϯ ϧⲟ, *F* diff) ἐρωτᾶν; Ps 36 7 *S*(*B* ⲧ.) ἱκετεύειν; Ja 1 14 *B*(*S* ⲁⲡⲁⲧⲁ) δελεάζειν; Ex 22 16 *B*(*S* ⲣ ϧⲁⲗ) ἀπατᾶν; Z 295 *S* ⲁⲥⲥⲡⲥⲱⲡϥ & drew him in προτρέπειν; FR 84 *S* ⲡⲉⲡⲥ. ⲙⲡⲛⲉ (var ⲥⲟⲡⲥ), Ming 344 *S* Holy Spirit ⲛⲁⲥⲉⲡⲥⲱⲡⲉⲛ ⲡⲩⲥⲉⲗⲥⲱⲗⲛ, Rec 11 147 *A* ⲧⲓⲥⲡⲥⲡ (*sic l*) ⲛⲟⲩⲁⲡ ⲛⲓⲙ to pray, BKU 1 30 *F* ϯⲥ. ⲉⲙⲁⲕ release my lord; with ϫⲉ- : Lu 8 31 *S*(*B* ϯ ϧⲟ) παρακ. ἵνα, Pcod 12 *S* ⲁⲩⲥⲉⲡⲥⲱⲡⲛ ϫⲉⲉⲛⲉⲧⲛⲡⲟⲟⲩⲥⲟⲩ; ϫⲉⲕⲁⲥ- : Mt 14 36 *S*(*B* do, *F* ⲧ.) π. ἵνα; Mk 7 26 *S*(*B* do) ἐρ. ἵνα; TU 24 1 4 *S* ⲁⲩⲥⲉⲡⲥⲡ ⲡⲉⲧⲣⲟⲥ ϫ. ⲉϥⲛⲁ-.

With following preposition. c ⲉ- *S* : 2 Kg 8 10 ἐρ., ViSitz 172 4 14 ⲛⲧⲁⲩⲥⲉⲡⲥⲱⲡⲧ ⲁⲛ ⲉⲡⲁⲓ οἴε-σθαι; verbal : Jo 4 40 *SAᵃ*(*B* ϯ ϧⲟ) ἐρ. inf, 1 Tim 1 3 ⲉⲧⲣⲉ- (*B* do) παρ. inf, Z 318 παρ. ἵνα, TU 20 4 b 6 ⲁⲩⲥⲉⲡⲥⲱⲡⲧ ⲉⲧⲣⲁⲭⲉⲓⲣⲟⲧⲟⲛⲉⲓ; c ⲉⲧⲃⲉ- *S* :

Lu 4 38 (*B* ⲇⲟ) ἐρ. περί; ClPr 54 37 *S* when others had ⲥⲉⲡⲥⲱⲡϥ ⲉⲧⲃⲉⲡⲁⲓ *ἐκ*.; ⲥ ⲉϫⲛ- *S*: Ps 89 13 (*B* ϭⲓ ϯ ⲉ̅ⲟ) π. ἐπί; BAp 224 ⲁϥⲥⲉⲡⲥ ⲡⲭ̅ⲥ̅ ⲉϫⲱⲟⲩ, Ep 162 4 ⲛⲥⲉⲥⲉⲡⲥⲱⲡ ⲡⲭ̅ⲥ̅ ⲉϫⲱⲓ, BMis 73 ⲥ. ⲙⲡⲉⲥϣⲏⲣⲉ ⲉϩⲣⲁⲓ ⲉϫⲱⲟⲩ;   ⲥ ϩⲁ- *S*: RNC 14 ⲁϥⲥⲉⲡⲥⲱⲡϥ ϩⲁⲡⲕⲉⲟⲩⲁ π. ὑπέρ.

—— nn m *SAB*, ⲥⲉⲡⲛ *A*: Ps 33 15 *A*(*S* ⲥⲟⲡⲥ, *B* ⲧ.) δέησις; 1 Thes 2 5 *B* (var -ⲥⲉⲃ, *SF* ⲕⲱⲣϣ) κολακία; Br 232 *S* ⲡⲛⲟⲩⲥ ⲙⲡⲧⲏⲣϥ ⲡⲥ. ⲡⲟⲩⲟⲡ ⲛⲓⲙ *consolation*, Worr 317 *S* hear our ⲥ. (var Mor 16 124 ⲥⲟⲡⲥ), Till Oster 13 *A* ⲙⲛ ϩⲛⲁⲛ ⲁϩⲟⲩⲛ ⲁⲡⲉⲥⲥⲉⲡⲛ, O'LearyH 19 *B* turned ear to ⲛⲥⲟⲃⲥⲉⲃ (*sic l*) *allurements* of serpent; K 101 *B* ⲥⲟⲃⲥⲉⲃ خذاع.

ⲣⲉϥⲥ. *B*, *beguiler*: 2 Tim 3 13 (*S* ⲡⲗⲁⲛⲟⲥ) γόης.

сапт, ⲥⲱⲡⲧ *F* *v* ⲥⲱⲧⲡ.

ⲥⲟⲡⲉⲧ *S* nn, *meaning unknown*: PRain 4741 list ⲙⲉⲧⲟⲩⲉ ⲡⲗⲓⲧⲣⲁ ⲡⲥ. For ? ⲥⲟⲧⲡ.

ⲥⲡⲟⲧⲟⲩ *S*, ⲥⲡⲁ. *AF*, ⲥⲫⲟⲧⲟⲩ *B*, ⲥⲡⲁⲧ DM (9 16) nn m, *lips* (dual), *edge*, *shore*, ⲁ as pl: Ge 11 9 *B*(*S* ϭⲓⲛϣⲁϫⲉ), Job 15 6 *SB*, Ps 16 4 *SBF*, Si 22 30 *SA*, Is 30 27 *SBF*, Mk 7 6 *SA*(Cl)*B* χεῖλος; Jos 3 15 *B*(*S* ⲥⲧⲱ) κρηπίς; 2 Kg 19 24 *S* μύσταξ; C 86 281 *B* ⲡⲉⲡⲥ. ⲙⲡⲓⲗⲁⲕⲕⲟⲥ στόμα = BSG 180 *S* ⲧⲁⲡⲣⲟ MG 25 346 *B* sim = ROC 17 372 لسوه, BHom 72 *S* ⲡⲣⲱⲙ ⲡⲡⲉⲩⲥ. ⲃ as sg: Ge 11 1 *B* ⲟⲩⲥ., Deu 3 12 *S* ⲡⲉⲥ. (*B* pl), Job 40 21 *SB* ⲡⲉⲩⲥ. χ.; RNC 82 *S* ⲡⲉⲩⲥ. ⲥⲡⲁⲩ (but *ib* ⲡⲁⲥ.), Mor 37 93 *S* ⲡⲉⲥ. of river ὄχθαι; BIF 13 106 *S* ⲡⲉⲥ. ⲡⲣⲏⲥ of sea = MG 25 290 *B*.

ⲥⲁⲣ (ⲥⲁ ⲣ) *v* ⲥⲁ *man*.

ⲥⲣ, ⲥⲉⲣ *v* ⲥⲱⲣ & ⲥⲟⲩⲣⲉ.

ⲥⲓⲣ[1], ⲥⲁⲉⲓⲣ[2], ⲥⲁⲉⲓⲣⲉ[3], ⲥⲏⲣⲉ *S*, ⲥⲉⲉⲣⲉ *A*, ⲥⲉⲓⲣⲉ *A*[2] nn m, *first milk* (colostrum), *butter*: Deu 32 14[3] (*B* ϭⲉⲗⲓ) لبأ (var سمن), 2 Kg 17 29[3] (var ⲥⲟⲉⲓⲣⲉ), Job 20 17[3] (*B* ⲇⲟ), Pro 24 68 *S*[3]*A*, Is 7 15[3] (*B* = Gk) βούτυρον; 1 Kg 17 18 ⲟⲉⲓⲕ ⲡⲥ.[2] (*B* ϭ. ⲡⲉⲣⲱϯ) στρυφαλὶς γάλακτος (var τύρου) = P 44 109[2] در *fine flour*; BMis 141 Virgin *loq* my womb swelled, breasts ⲡ ⲥ.[3], Cai ostr 46304 79 ⲟⲩϫⲉ ⲉⲣⲱⲧⲉ ⲟⲩϫⲉ [ⲥ]ⲏⲣⲉ; ⲟⲃⲉⲛ ⲡⲥ.[1] *v* ⲟⲃⲛ.; ϭⲃ ⲥ. *A*[2], nn f, *cooled*(?) *butter*: Mani 1 ⲧϭ. ⲁϥⲛⲧⲥ ⲁⲡⲉⲣⲱⲧⲉ ⲉⲧⲣϩⲙ.

ⲥⲓⲣ, ⲥⲉⲣ, ⲥⲉⲣⲉ *S*, ⲥⲉⲉⲣⲉ *A*, ⲥⲉⲓⲗ *F* nn m, *leaven* cf שׂאר (*v* Dévaud *Ét* 50): Mt 13 33 *F* ⲟⲩⲥ. ⲉⲁⲟⲩⲥⲣⲙⲙ ϫⲓⲧϥ (cf *S* ⲟⲩϭⲁⲃ ⲉⲁ-, *B* ϣⲉⲙⲏⲣ) ζύμη; ShC 73 190 *S* ⲛⲥⲉⲣⲉ (var ⲥⲉⲣ) ϩⲁⲡⲛϣⲱⲧⲉ, AZ 33 133 *S* ⲟⲉⲓⲕ ⲡⲁⲧⲥⲓⲣ, TU 43 6 *A* ⲡϫⲁⲉ ⲛⲡⲁⲧⲥ. (cf Lu 22 1);   doubtful: Ep 296 *S* baker skilled ⲛⲣ ⲥ., ST 282 *S* ⲡⲕⲟⲩⲓ ⲡⲥ....make it & knead the flour. Leaven can be made from soured milk (Berggren *Guide Fr-Ar* 524). In place-name (?) Σελσελσῖρ (Preisigke).

ⲥⲓⲣ *S* nn m, *hair, line, stripe*: Mor 55 65 anathema on whoso saith Son inferior (ϭⲟϫⲃ) to Father ⲡⲟⲩⲥ. ⲛⲃⲱ, PMich 602 3 write charm on papyrus ⲛⲧⲙⲟⲣϥ ⲡⲥ. ⲡⲉⲓⲱ, Bodl(P) ⲁ 2 30 ⲟⲩⲥⲱⲗϥ ⲡⲥ., Z 611 ⲕⲟⲩⲓ ⲡⲥ. ⲛ ⲙⲁⲉⲓⲛ ⲡⲕⲣⲟⲕⲟⲥ in onyx, Mor 40 42 garments ⲉⲩⲟ ⲡⲥ. ⲥ. ⲡⲕⲁⲙⲛ = MG 25 268 *B* ϩⲓⲣ ϩⲓⲣ; PMéd 111 ⲟⲩⲥ., a malady, *cf ib* 105 ff ⲟⲩⲁⲙⲥ., Z 630 ⲟⲩⲟⲙⲥ. sim ?

ⲥⲓⲣ *B* nn, *jar*: Bodl 325 154 (Tatt 864) طسث (*v* Almk 2 51). Prob is زر.

ⲥⲱⲣ *SBF*, ⲥⲱⲱⲣⲓ *F*, ⲥⲣ- *SA*, ⲥⲉⲣ- *SB*, ⲥⲱⲣ- *A*, ⲥⲟⲣ- *B* (C 86 317), ⲥⲁⲣ- *F*, ⲥⲟⲣ⳨ *SB*, ⲥⲟⲟⲣ⳨ *S* (Ann '17 151), ⲥⲁⲣ⳨ *S*[f]*AA*[2]*F*, ⲥⲁⲁⲣ⳨ *F*, ⲥⲛⲣⳁ *SB*, ⲡ ⲥ ⲥⲁⲣ- *S* vb **I** intr, *scatter, spread*, esp of sun's light: Jud 19 26 *S* διαφαύσκειν; 1 Kg 9 26 *S* ἀναβαίνειν; BMis 155 *S* ⲡⲟⲩⲟⲉⲓⲛ ⲁϥⲥ. & sun began to rise, Mor 30 58 *F* until light ⲥⲱⲱⲣⲓ = *ib* 29 50 *S* ϣⲁ, BMar 103 *S* whilst idolatry yet ⲥ.†; K 112 *B* ⲫⲏ ⲉⲧⲥ. سواق *trader*.

II tr: Lu 11 22 *S*(*B* ϫⲱⲣ) διαδιδόναι; ShC 73 66 *S* ⲉⲡⲁⲥⲣ ⲁⲅⲁⲡⲏ for dead, JTS 8 241 *S* sim, ShC 73 138 *S* ⲡⲉⲧⲛⲁⲥⲉⲣ ⲙⲟⲟⲩ, Miss 4 242 *S* = C 41 39 *B* sim (*cf* ⲡ ⲥ), GFr 308 *S* when they shall ⲥⲉⲣ ⲡⲉⲕⲗⲟⲙ, AP 24 *A*[2] alms ⲁⲩⲥⲁⲣⲟⲩ, C 41 20 *B* ⲫⲏ ⲉⲧⲥ. ⲛⲛⲓⲱⲓⲕ, C 86 317 *B* ⲁϥⲟⲩⲟⲥⲟⲣ ⲧⲟϥ in foundations (*v* below Mor 30 40), BKU 1 26(8116a) *F* receipe ⲡⲉⲕⲁⲕ of bird ϣⲁⲩⲥⲁⲣ ⲡⲉⲧⲥⲉⲗ ⲉⲃⲁⲗ (or ? ⲥⲁⲣ ⲉⲃ.).

ⲡ ⲥ *S*, *distributer*: Louvre R 49 God ordained ⲁⲩⲙⲟⲣⲧ ⲡⲥⲁⲣⲙⲟⲟⲩ ϩⲓⲡ[ϣⲁ ⲉⲧⲟ]ⲅⲁⲁⲃ ⲡⲡⲉⲥⲧⲁⲩⲣⲟⲥ (but meaning doubtful). *Cf* ⲥⲁ *man* s f.

—— nn m *B*, *distribution*: 1 Cor 16 1 (*S* ⲟⲩⲱϣⲥ) λογία. *V* also ⲥ. ⲉⲃⲟⲗ.

With following preposition. ⲥ ⲉ- *spread for, against*: Ps 26 3 *S*(*B* ⲧⲱⲛ ⲉϩⲣⲏⲓ ⲉϫⲉⲡ-) παρατάσσεσθαι ἐπί; ShC 73 60 *S* ⲥⲱⲣ ⲛⲡⲥⲱ ⲉⲡⲥⲱⲟⲩϩ, PSBA 19 212 *S* veils etc.† ⲉⲧⲉⲥⲕⲩⲛⲏ, Mor 41 98 *S* ⲉⲕⲛⲥⲣ (*l* ⲥⲉⲣ) ⲡⲁϣ ⲉⲡⲉⲕⲥⲟⲡ, Mor 30 40 *F* straw ϣⲁϥⲥⲁⲁⲣϥ ⲉⲧⲥⲩⲛϯ (*v* above), AM 152 *B* ⲥⲟⲣⲟⲩ ⲉⲡⲓϩⲏⲕⲓ;   *divide into*: Mani 1 *A*[2] ⲛϭⲁⲙ...ⲁⲩⲥⲁⲣⲟⲩ ⲁⲙⲛⲧⲉ ⲙⲡⲉ;   ⲥ ⲉϩⲣⲉⲛ- *B*; *scatter upon, among*: C 86 251 thought to ⲥ. ⲙⲡⲁⲥⲱⲙⲁ ⲉϩⲣⲁⲩ after death;   ⲥ ⲉϫⲛ-, *spread, stretch upon*: Job 38 5 *S*(*B* ⲓⲛⲓ ⲉϩⲣ. ⲉϫ.) ἐπάγειν ἐπί; Is 34 11 *SF* (*B* ⲇⲟ) ἐπιβάλλειν ἐπί; BMis 234 *S*[f] riches ⲁϥⲥⲁⲣⲟⲩ ⲉϫⲛⲡⲙⲁⲧⲟⲓ = Mor 30 6 *F* do ⲉⲃⲁⲗ ⲉϫⲛ-, C 89 5 *B* ⲥ. ⲉϫⲱⲟⲩ ⲉⲃⲟⲗ ϩⲉⲛⲡⲓⲁⲛⲛⲟⲛⲁ;   ⲥ ⲛ- dat: Lu 18 22 *B*(*S* ϯ) διαδ. dat; BMar 202 *S* property ⲁϥⲥⲟⲣϥ ⲡⲡⲛⲕⲉ, C 43 196 *B* sim;   ⲥ ⲡⲉⲙ- *B*, *scatter with, to, upon*: RAl 102 ⲧⲉϥⲕⲉⲣⲙ ⲛⲥⲉⲥⲟⲣⲉ ⲡⲉⲙⲡⲓⲑⲛⲟⲩ;   ⲥ ⲡⲥⲁ- *S*, *spread* report *against*: Deu 22 14 (*B* ϫⲱ ⲛⲥⲁ-) καταφέρειν dat, *ib* 19 (*B*

ιιι нса-) ἐκφ. ἐπί;   с εβολ ϩα- B, *dispel from*: HL 113 εϥс. мпіϩιιιιι εβ. ϩароϥ.

With following adverb.   с εβολ *SAA²BF*, intr *spread out, abroad, prepare*: Nu 2 34 *S*(*B* ϩι коτ) παρεμβάλλειν; Ru 1 19 *S* ἠχεῖν, 1 Thes 1 8 *B*(*SF* † соеіτ) ἐξηχ.; Ps 111 9 *B*(*S* ϫωрε εβ.) σκορπίζειν; Is 31 4 *SF*(*B* ϭωκ εϫεп-) ἐπιστρατεύεσθαι ἐπί; Lu 4 37 *B*(*S* мооϣе) ἐκπορεύεσθαι; PS 100 *S* пϭорϭ с.† εβ.; ShA 1 302 *S* ill-founded house εϥс.† εβ. ап калωс, Bor 256 153 *S* апεϥсоеіτ с. εβ. ϩιша пім, CA 96 *S* deacons пас. εβ. ϩιϫм пиаос *be distributed about*, MIE 2 412 *B* grief с.† εβ. throughout world, ROC 27 148 *B* torturing self although ммоп ϫικαστηριοп с.† εβ.;   tr: Jud 9 44 *S*, Zech 1 16 *SA*(*B* ϥωрϣ εϫεп-) ἐκτείνειν; 2 Kg 6 19 *S*(*B* †) διαμερίζειν; Ez 36 19 *S* (*B* ϩιоϩι) λικμᾶν; Mt 9 31 *B*(*S* † соеіτ) διαφημίζειν; AM 274 *B* акεр пϭι шιϣ εβ. κηρύσσειν; ShC 73 141 *S* ср шаϫε εβ., Br 49 *S* form εптаιоϒω еіс. ммоϥ εβ., ShA 2 114 *S* building пταϒcopϭ εβ. from foundations upward, ShP 131⁴ 111 *S* garments петс. ммооϒ εβ. н ет† шι ероϒ, Mani 1 *A²* аϒс. ммеіλιоп аβ., AM 185 *B* аϥεр пеϥϣιпі εβ., C 86 115 *B* піхроϥ етаксорϭ εβ. against Christians, Leyd 158 *S* петс. мпша εβ. *distributes communion*, ST 99 *S* none shall с. лааϒ пϭωβ εβ. еіϫωк (*l* еϫ-) allot tax;   с е-: Deu 21 2 *S*(*B* рωϣ εϫεп-) ἐκμετρεῖν ἐπί; Pro 29 5 *S* (var om εβ.) *A* περιβαλ. dat; Ac 8 1 *B*(*S* ϫωωре εβ.) διασπείρειν κατά; ShC 73 159 *S* brethren с.† εβ. εϩпаα пεр ϩωβ, BMOr 11289 18 *S* еϒср кроϥ εβ. ерок *against thee*.

—— εβ. nn *S*, *spreading, setting forth, laying out*: PS 264 telling you of пс. εβ. мптнрϥ, ShA 2 144 пс. εβ. ппеϒсптε; *allotment* of tax: CO 406 receipt for меρос пс. εβ., Hall 147 sim, PLond 4 473 пі[сω]р εβ. (sic prob) = 474 піа[іαстаλмос].

реϥс. εβ. *S*, *layer out, founder*: Wess 18 85 Christ пр. ппаιωп, AZ 25 70 do.

ϭιпс. εβ. *SA²*, *laying out*: Br 85 птопос...теϥϭ. (cf ib ϭіпкω еϩраі), ShWess 9 108 пϭ. мппоβе аϒω пеϥϫωк, Mani 2 *A²* тϭ. мппоλεмос.

V мλаϩ, раτϭ, соρср.

сдеіре, сере &c *v* сір.

сдро *v* сало.

соϒре *SAA²*, -рі *BF*, соϒр-, сар-, ср- *S*, сер- *SB* nn f, *thorn, spike, dart*: Ps 31 4 *B*(*S* шопте), Is 32 13 *B*(*S* do), Mt 13 22 *B*(*SF* do) ἄκανθα; Hos 2 6 *S*(ShA 2 336)*A*(*B* серβеιι); 2 Cor 12 7 *S* (*B* do), BHom 33 *S* date-palm hath ϩеіс. σκόλοψ; Ge 3 18 *B*(*S* арооϒе), He 6 8 *BF*(*S* do) τρίβολος; Zech 12 6 *B*(*A* реιоϒе) καλάμη; Hos 13 14 *B*(*A*

еіβ), Ac 26 14 *SB*, Ap 9 10 *B*(*S* еіβ) κέντρον; Jos 23 13 *B*(*S* соте) βολίς; Tri 338 *S* assassin пеϥпаϣ, теϥс., теϥеіоме شول, Dif 1 86 *B* rose grew on †βω пс. شول; MG 25 12 *B* on seeing lions атеϥс. оϩі ерате ναρκᾶν *exhorrescere* (cf пеϩ с.); Mani 1 *A²* пϣа]пте мпіс., C 43 226 *B* пікам, піс., Mun 20 *S* crown of шопте еϒрнт пс., BAp 32 *S* пеϩс пс. of crown of thorns, C 43 173 *B* шβωт еϒмеϩ пс.;   *needle &c*: ShP 130⁴ 157 *S* оϒс. пϫελϭ тооϒе, RE 14 28 *S* тс. пϣωβ for stitching thongs, Mor 52 38 *S* cobbler's awl, R 1 5 42 *S* shuttle (?) of пат loom, WS 123 *S* with ϭорте, Ryl 243 *S* оϒс. ппоϒϥ;   ер с. *B*, *produce, grow thorns*: Is 7 23 (*S* р шопте) еіς ἄκ. еἶναι, ib 5 2 (*S* таϒе ш.) ἄκ. ποιεῖν; пеϩ с. *B*: C 89 78 in terror body п. с. ероі *shuddered* = Va Ar 172 47 اقشعر جسمي; сек с. εβολ *B* sim: AM 178 = Synax 2 220 1 تعبّ. *Cf* MG 25 12 above.

Compounds. срβпе *S*, серβ. *B*, *thorn of date-palm*: Nu 33 55 *S*(var с.)*B*, Hos, 2 Cor as above σκ.; Jer 9 8 *B*(*S* соте)βо.; MélOr 6 504 *B* оϒс. іе оϒапωп; сер-, сар-, соϒрϭамоϒλ *S*, *leucacanthus* شُ للمال (Dozy 1 804, Löw 293): 2 Kg 12 31 τρίβ. (as iron instrument), P 44 83 = какτλιος (? κάκτος); сραрооϒе *v* арооϒе; серо-ϫι *B*, *thistle*: Mt 7 16 (*S* ар.) τρίβ.; Va 63 79 соϒрі пемс. ἄκ.; C 86 159 -ωϫι sim, K 339 піс. عوج; cf ? place-name Σαρουτσει (PLond 4 225);   сакс. *S*, meaning?: PMich 3571.

сро nn, *ram*: DM 14 13 (cf ib 1 12 n), PGM 1 60 *O* моϒι пс., ib 160, ib 2 25, POslo 351, μουι σρω.

серεβ *v* сраϥ.

срβпе, серβеιι *v* соϒре.

срεβроϒβе *S* nn as pl, *handfuls*: P 46 237 пс. حفن, between βоϒϭе & алоϒ. But prob *l* جفن *eyelid*.

соϒрωθ *B* *v* соϒрот.

сараθноϒ *B* *v* тнϒ.

сароϒкі *B* nn m, *one bald on temples*: K 72 піс. انزع, between слахλех & фалакрос.

сдрдкωτе¹, -коте², -котте³, -косте⁴ *S*, -кω† *B* nn as pl, *wanderer, vagrant* (v са man & ? еіре), whence ?misread *Sarabaita* (PRE³ 17 480), cf *gyrovagus*, κυκλευτής AZ 25 70, Ep 1 125 n & Z 579): P 44 64 *S* мпараситос · пс.¹ رتّالين, ib 77 *S* пехλωп (*l* ? кекλωп κυκλῶν) · пс.¹ мпар. ´, ib 90 *S* пахλоп (*l* ? -оп) · пс.¹ ´ = 43 73 *S³*, P 45 189 *S* мпар. · пс.⁴ اربعين (for اربعين as if σαρακοστή), Tri 471 *S* еітптωп пϩеіс.² ´;   CA ιλ books

of Meletius & للبلا with ⲥⲁⲣⲁⲕⲱϯ *B* as gloss, so here *ignorant*.

ϭⲟⲣⲙ, ϭⲁ. *S*, ϭⲁⲣⲙⲉ *A²* (Mani 1), ϭⲟⲣⲉⲙ *B* nn m, *lees, dregs* of wine, oil &c : Ps 74 9 *SB* τρυγίας ; PS 37 *S* eating ⲡϭ. ⲡⲧⲉⲩⲅⲩⲗⲏ, ib 333 ⲟⲩϭ. ⲧⲉ ⲛⲧⲉ ⲡⲥⲱⲧϥ ⲙⲡⲟⲩⲟⲉⲓⲛ, ib 334 ϣⲁⲟⲩⲱϣⲙ ⲙⲡⲥ. ϩⲓ ⲡⲉϥⲉⲣⲏⲩ, Z 629 *S* ϭⲁ. ⲛⲟⲙϫ ⲉϥⲣⲁⲕⲉ, ib 630 ϭ. ⲛⲏⲣⲡ ; ⲁⲧϭ. *B*, *clarified* : Ex 27 20 *B* ἄτρυγος (var ⲁⲧϭⲱⲗ ἀτρύγητος). *V AZ* 50 89.

ⲥⲱⲣⲙ *S*, -ⲙⲉ *A*, -ⲉⲙ *BF*, ⲥⲉⲣⲙ- *S*, ⲥⲁⲣⲙⲉ- *A²*, ⲥⲉⲣⲉⲙ- *B*, ⲥⲟⲣⲙⲉ *SA²B*, ⲥⲁⲣⲙⲉ⸗ *A*, ⲥⲟⲣⲙ† *S*, ⲥⲁⲣⲙⲉ† *AA²*, ⲥⲟⲣⲉⲙ† *B*, ⲥⲁⲣⲉⲙ† *F*, ⲣ ϭ ⲥⲁⲣⲙ- *S*, vb **I** intr, *go astray, err, be lost* : Ex 23 4† *SB*, Job 38 41 *B(S* ⲕⲱⲧⲉ*)*, Pro 14 22† *SA*, Jer 27 17 *SBF*, Mt 18 12 *SB* πλανᾶν ; Ex 22 9 *S(B* ⲧⲁⲕⲟ*)*, Ps 30 13 *S (B* do*)*, Is 34 16 *SF(B* do*)*, Mt 10 6 *SB* ἀπόλλυσθαι ; Mt 9 36 *B(S* = Gk*)* ἐκλύεσθαι ; Ac 27 9 *B (S* om*)* ἐπισφαλὴς εἶναι ; Aeg 222 *S* ⲡⲉⲧⲙⲡⲉⲛⲕⲁ …ϭ. διαπίπτειν ; BMis 554 *S* my labours ⲁⲩϭ. εἰς οὐδὲν λογίζεσθαι ; PS 31 *S* shall be misled & ϭⲉⲡⲁⲥ.; ShA 1 111 *S* eyes ⲛⲧⲁⲡⲉⲩⲟⲩⲟⲉⲓⲛ ϭ., DeV 2 56 *B* ⲉⲣⲉⲡⲟⲩϩⲏⲧ ϭ.†, C 43 25 *B* ⲡⲁⲓⲙⲁⲅⲓⲁ ⲉⲧϭ.†, Mor 40 22 *S* dumbfounded as one ⲉⲧϭ.† = ib 39 30 *Sᶠ* ⲉⲓⲁⲣⲙ, Pcod 41 *F* ⲛⲉϥⲉⲣⲉⲥⲓⲥ ϭ.† *(S* ϭⲉ ⲉⲃⲟⲗ*)*, Mani 1 *A²* ⲡⲉⲧϭ.† ; ϭ. ⲛϩⲏⲧ : Gal 6 9† *B(S* ϣⲱⲥⲙ*)* ἐκλύ.

II tr, *lead astray, lose* : Pro 12 26 *SAB*, Is 19 13 *B(S* = Gk*)*, Ap 12 9 *B(S* do*)* πλ. ; Mk 9 41 *S(BF* ⲧⲁ.*)*, Jo 12 25 *SA²(B* do*)*, Mor 37 140 *S* ⲙⲡⲣϭ. ⲛⲧⲉⲧⲛⲁⲥⲕⲏⲥⲓⲥ ἀπολλύναι ; ShA 2 46 *S* Judas ⲁϥϭⲟⲣⲙⲉϥ for money, P 129¹⁷ 62 *S* ⲛϭⲉⲥ. ⲙⲡⲉⲟⲩ ϫⲁⲓ, C 43 106 *B* ϥⲛⲁⲥⲟⲣⲙⲉⲛ ⲧⲏⲣⲟⲩ ; ⲣ ϭ, BHom 78 *S* ⲡϭⲁⲡⲕⲟⲧⲉ ⲛⲥⲁⲣⲙϩⲏⲧ (*sic l*).

With following preposition. ϭ ⲉ- *S*, *err toward* : BG 67 ⲙⲉϭϭ. ⲉⲧⲡⲟⲛⲏⲣⲓⲁ ; ϭ ⲛⲧⲛ- *S*, *send astray from*, so *lose* : Deu 22 3 *(B* ⲧⲁ.*)* ἀπ. παρά, Jer 18 18 (ShC 42 15, *B* do*)* ἀπ. ἀπό ; Mor 52 28 ⲟⲩⲣⲱⲙⲉ (sc Adam) ⲛⲉⲡⲧⲁϥϭⲟⲣⲙⲉϥ (sc virginity) ⲛⲧⲟⲟⲧϥ ; intr ShA 1 54 fled from him ⲁϥϭ. ⲛⲧⲟⲟⲧϥ & *was lost to him* ; ϭ ϩⲓ- *B* *stray in* : Ps 106 4 *(S* = Gk*)*, Is 16 8 *(S* acc*)* πλ. ; ϭ ϩⲛ-, ϭⲉⲛ- *SAB* intr, *stray in, by reason of* : Si 9 9 *S* πλ. ἐν, Pro 21 16† *SA* πλ. ἐκ, Is 29 24† *SF(B* ϭ.*)* πλ. dat ; ib 27 13 *S(B* ⲧⲁ.*)* ἀπ. ἐν ; Mus 40 43 *S* everything ⲉϥϭⲁⲥ. ϩⲙⲡⲏⲓ *perire in* ; PS 179 *S* ⲁⲓⲥ. ϩⲛⲣⲉⲡⲧⲟⲡⲟⲥ ; tr : Job 12 24 *SB*, Pro 28 10 *SA* πλ. ἐν ; BMar 29 *S* ⲁⲕϭ. ⲛⲧⲉⲕⲯⲩⲭⲏ ϩⲛⲣⲉⲡⲑⲗⲓⲯⲓⲥ ; ϭ ϩⲓⲧⲉⲛ- *B*, *go astray through* : Ez 7 26 *(S* ⲛⲧⲛ-*)* ἀπ. ἐκ ; DeV 2 76 ⲁⲩϭ. ϩ. ⲛⲓⲟⲓϭⲓ ; ϭ ϩⲓϫⲛ-, *stray upon* : Is 22 5 *S†B* πλ. ἐπί.

With following adverb. ϭ ⲉⲃⲟⲗ *SBF* intr, *wander forth, about, be idle* : Mor 17 33 *S* ϯϭ.† ⲉⲃ. in strange land πελάζεσθαι εἰς ; Sa 14 22 *S* πλ.

περί, Z 277 *S* ⲉⲩϭ.† ⲉⲃ. in his comments πλ. ἐκ (? ἐν) ; Ming 329 *S* ⲙⲡⲣϣⲱⲡⲉ ⲉⲕϭ.† ⲉⲃ., but give heed (νήφειν), Miss 4 814 *S* what hast seen ⲉⲕϭ.† ⲉⲃ. (*sic l*) so long ? (cf ⲉⲓⲱⲣⲙ ⲉⲃ.), Bor 134 1 *S* (Vita Sin) ϯϭ.† ⲉⲃ. ϣⲁⲧⲉⲟⲩ = C 41 25† *B* = Miss 4 357 يسهو , BM 580 *F* ⲉⲓⲣⲙⲁ(ⲥ) ⲡⲁⲧⲣⲟϥ ⲛⲁⲧ[ⲓ]ⲁⲡⲓ ⲉⲓϭ.† ⲉⲃ. ; *v* also nn ; tr, *mislead* : Ps 106 40 *B (S* = Gk*)* πλ. ἐν, BM 216 109 *S* ⲧⲁⲥⲟⲣⲙⲉⲧ ⲉⲃ. in desert πλάζ. (reading ? πλάν.) ἐν ; Bor 234 3 *S* beware ϫⲉⲛⲛⲉⲩϭⲟⲣⲙⲉⲕ ⲉⲃ. ; ⲉⲃ. ⲉ- *S*, *wander toward* : P 130¹ 85 heart ϭ.† ⲉⲃ. ⲉⲡⲁⲡⲕⲟⲥⲙⲟⲥ ; ⲉⲃ. ϩⲁ- *B* intr, *stray from* : Ps 118 110 *(S* diff*)* πλ. ἐκ, 1 Tim 6 10 *(S* = Gk*)* ἀποπλ. ἀπό ; tr : Is 63 17 *(S* do*)* πλ. ἀπό ; AM 40 ⲁⲕϭ. ⲡⲧⲉⲕⲯⲩⲭⲏ ⲉⲃ. ϩⲁϥⲙⲱⲓⲧ ; ⲉⲃ. ϩⲛ- *SB*, tr, *set astray from* : ShA 1 386 *S* ⲉⲩϭ. ⲙⲙⲱⲧⲛ ⲉⲃ. ϩⲛⲧⲙⲉ, ROC 25 245 *B* ⲁϥⲥⲟⲣⲙⲉϥ ⲉⲃ. ϫⲉⲛⲡⲓⲛⲁϩϯ πλανήσας ἀπέστησε τῆς πίστεως ; ⲉⲃ. ϩⲓⲧⲉⲛ- *B*, *stray from* : Bar 4 28 πλ. ἀπό ; *by means of* : C 43 95 ⲥⲉϭ.† ⲉⲃ. ϩ. ⲛⲓⲙⲁⲅⲓⲁ. ϭ. ⲉⲃ. as nn *S*, *derangement* : BP 8503 invocation ϯ ⲉⲡⲟⲩⲕⲁⲣⲱϥ ⲙⲛⲟⲩϭ. ⲉⲃ., KroppM 80 title of charm ⲟⲩϭ. ⲉⲃ., J 74 26 ⲉⲣⲉⲡⲁⲗⲟⲅⲓⲥⲙⲟⲥ ⲧⲁⲭⲣⲏⲩ ⲁⲝⲡⲗⲁⲁⲩ ⲡϭ. ⲉⲃ.

ϭ ⲥⲁⲃⲟⲗ ⲛ- *B*, ⲡⲥⲁⲃ. ⲛ- *S*, *send astray from* : C 43 63 *B* devil ϭ. ⲙⲡⲉϥϩⲏⲧ ⲥⲁⲃ. ⲙⲫϯ, BMar 1 *S* sim ⲡⲥⲁⲃ. ; ϭ ϩⲁⲃⲟⲗ ⲛ- *S*, *meaning sim* : LMär 37 ϭ. ⲙⲡⲉⲩϩⲏⲧ ϩ. ⲙⲡⲡⲉ ; ϭ ⲉⲫⲁϩⲟⲩ *B*, ϩⲓⲡⲉϩⲟⲩ *F*, *cause to stray backward* : Is 30 20 *(S* Gk πλ. no advb*)*.

—— nn m *SAB*, *error* : TU 43 17 *A* their end is ⲡϭ. (Phil 3 19 *SB* ⲧⲁⲕⲟ), ShA 2 334 *S* ⲉⲧⲣⲉⲛⲉⲓ ⲉⲃⲟⲗ ϩⲙⲡϭ., DeV 2 26 *B* ⲡϭ. ⲛϥⲙⲉⲧⲁⲧⲉⲙⲓ.

ⲙⲟⲩ ⲡϭ., *torrent* : Ge 32 23 *B(S* = Gk*)*, Ps 109 7 *SB*, Jo 18 1 *B(SA²* = Gk*)* χείμαρρος ; Ez 6 3 *B (S* ⲕⲣⲱⲟⲩ*)* νάπη (s v ⲕⲣⲟ *B* is wrong) ; ib 31 12 *B* φάραγξ ; BHom 36 *S* ϩⲉⲡⲙ. ⲡⲣⲙⲉⲓⲛ, ROC 27 158 *B* perish in ⲛⲓⲁⲙ. (sc sea).

ⲁⲧϭ. *B*, *clear, unerring* : Cat 99 ⲡⲓⲕⲁϯ ⲛⲁ.

ⲣⲉϥϭ. *SA²B*, *one who leads astray* : Sa 4 12 *S* ῥεμβασμός ; BSG 195 *S* ⲡⲣ. ⲛⲁⲓⲙⲟⲛⲓⲟⲛ, C 89 132 *B* ⲣ. opp ⲣⲉϥⲧⲟⲩϫⲟ ; Mani 1 *A²* ⲣⲉϥⲥⲁⲣⲙ ⲣⲱⲙⲉ.

ⲥⲣⲙⲉ *S*, ⲥⲉⲣⲙⲏ *SB* nn, *wanderer, vagrant* : Peet Abydos 3 pl 13 *S* Joseph ⲡⲥⲉⲣⲙⲏ, Dendera graffito same saint ⲡⲥⲛⲣⲙⲉ ; ⲙⲛⲧⲥⲣⲙⲉ : JA '75 5 229 *S* warning against ⲟⲩⲙ. ῥέμβος ; ⲉⲣ ϭ. *B* : Job 2 9 *(S* ⲕⲱⲧⲉ*)* πλανῆτις.

ⲥⲟⲣⲙⲉⲥ *SB*, ⲥⲁⲣ. *SF* nn f, *error, wandering* : Jude 11 *B(S*= Gk*)*, ROC 25 247 *B* ⲉⲩϫⲉϣ ϭ. into soul πλάνη, Is 22 5 *B(S* ⲥⲱⲣⲙ*)* πλάνησις, Deu 29 19 *B(S* ⲟⲩⲱϣ*)* ἀποπλάνησις ; BIF 14 184 *S* destroyed by Diocletian in ⲧⲉϥϭ., Faras 3 pl 67 6 *S* ⲡⲥⲁⲣ. ⲧⲏⲣⲟⲩ of devil, Mor 40 48 *S* ⲧϭ. ⲉⲧⲡⲣⲏⲧⲕ

= MG 25 275 *B*, C 43 86 *B* God brought upon them oⲩⲥ. so that they strayed, Mor 24 6 *F* ⲅⲃⲉ …c. As adj *B* : Is 19 14 (*S* cⲱⲣⲙ) πλάνησις.

cⲣⲟⲙ *B* nn m, *unconsciousness, moment of sleep* : Ps 131 4 (*S* ⲣⲉⲕⲣⲓⲕⲉ)νυσταγμός; MG 25 196 leaned against wall ϣⲁ†ⲅⲱⲗⲉⲙ ⲡⲟⲩⲕⲟⲩϫⲓ ⲡⲉ. μικρόν τι τοῦ ὕπνου; PO 14 342 ⲡⲁϥⲅⲓⲙⲙ ⲁⲡⲡⲉ…ⲉⲃⲏⲗ ⲉⲟⲩⲕⲟⲩϫⲓ ⲡⲉ.; c. ⲣⲱⲙⲙ : Ge 2 21 (*S* ⲣⲓⲛⲏⲃ) ἔκστασις; ROC 23 286 oⲩⲥ. ⲡⲅ. ⲁϥⲓ ⲉⲅⲣⲏⲓ ⲉϫⲱⲓ, PO 11 341 ϭⲓ oⲩⲥ. ⲡⲅ. *Cf next.*

cⲣⲟⲙⲣⲙ *S*, cⲣⲁⲙ. *S′A*, cⲣⲙⲣⲱⲙ⳽ *SA*, cⲣⲉⲙⲣ. *SB*, cⲣⲙⲣⲱⲙ⳾ *S*, -ⲣⲟⲙⲧ† *S*(Sh), cⲣⲉⲙⲣⲱⲙ† *B* vb **I** intr, *be obscured, dazed, stupefied* : P 44 95 *S* ⲧⲉⲥⲏⲱ…(c)c.† سدر, ShHT *H* 23 *S* drink not lest ⲛⲡⲉⲥ. ⲡⲉⲡⲟⲉⲓⲙ, ShC 42 210 *S* ⲉⲩⲥ.† ⲏ ⲉϣϫⲉⲁⲩⲣ ⲃⲗⲗⲉ, *ib* 73 113 *S* ⲡⲥⲱⲙⲁ ⲟⲩⲟⲅ…ⲙⲡⲉⲥ. ⲡϭⲓ ⲧⲁⲡⲉ, DeV 2 190 *B* ⲉⲥⲥ.† like corpse knowing no one, R 2 1 47 *S* drunkard ⲡⲉϥϩⲏⲧ c.† With preposition. c ⲉϫⲛ- *S*: Jer 8 21 (ShA 2 98, *B* ⲉⲣ ϫⲁⲕⲓ) σκοτοῦν ἐπί; c ⲅⲁ- *S*: ShA 1 205 ⲉⲩⲥ.† ⲅⲁⲏⲣⲡ; c ⲅⲛ- *SAB*: Mic 6 14 *A*(*B* ϫⲱⲣ ⲉⲃⲟⲗ) σκοτάζειν ἐν; Va 58 193 *B* ⲫⲏ ⲉⲧⲥ.† ϫⲉⲡⲡⲓⲏⲣⲡ κραιπάλη; ShRE 11 17 *S* ⲁⲩⲧⲥⲉ ⲁⲩⲥ. ⲅⲛⲧⲁⲡⲁⲡⲓⲥⲧⲟⲥ. *Wander, sway owing to stupefaction* (*cf* cⲱⲣⲙ): Hab 2 16 *A*(*B* ⲕⲓⲙ or ? ⲙⲟⲡⲙⲉⲛ) σαλεύεσθαι; Mor 18 37 *S* ⲁⲡϣⲱⲡⲉ ⲉⲡⲥ.† = Miss 4 129 *B* ⲅⲉⲭⲅⲱⲭ, P 44 94 *S* eye c. ⲅⲛⲧⲟⲡⲟⲥ جاب.

II tr *SA, daze, bemuse* : BMar 175 *S* darkness ⲡⲁⲥⲣⲙⲣⲱⲙⲟⲩ κατέχειν; ShC 42 200 *S* sheep ⲉⲁⲩⲥⲣⲙⲣⲱⲙϥ by demon, *ib* 73 154 *S* ⲥⲉⲥ. (*l* cc.) ⲡⲡⲉⲡⲧⲁⲩ†ⲥⲉ ⲡⲅⲏⲧⲥ, BM 1223 *A* invoking evil upon woman ⲁⲕⲁⲥⲣⲙⲣⲱⲥⲙ (*l* -ⲙⲥ).

—— nn m *S, stupefaction* : ShRyl 67 400 †ⲥⲉ, c., cⲱⲣⲙ, R 2 1 42 head ⲥⲕⲟⲧⲟⲩ ⲁⲡ through ⲡⲉⲥ. ⲙⲡⲧⲥⲉ; *error, straying* : Tri 518 ⲁϥⲥⲉ ⲅⲁⲡⲉⲥ. تيه, J 74 38 ⲉⲙⲡ cⲱⲣⲙ ⲉⲃⲟⲗ ⲅⲓⲥ. in me, KroppK 62 *S*ᵃ recipe headed ⲉⲧⲃⲉⲟⲩⲥ., ends (ⲡ)ⲡⲉⲣⲁⲥⲙⲟⲥ ⲡⲁⲡⲱⲧ. *Cf* cⲱⲣⲙ.

(cⲣⲟⲙⲣⲉⲙ), cⲣⲉⲙⲣⲱⲙ⳽ *B* vb tr (refl ?), *enforce, admonish* : Mk 1 43 ⲉⲧⲁϥcⲣⲉⲙⲣⲱⲙϥ ⲉⲃⲟⲩⲛ ⲉⲣⲟϥ (var ⲉϫⲱϥ, *S* ⲅⲱⲡ) ἐμβριμᾶσθαι dat (*cf* Mt 9 30 *B* ⲅⲟⲩϩⲉⲡ). Hardly same as last.

cⲟⲣⲙⲉⲥ *v* cⲱⲣⲙ *s f.*

cⲁⲣⲙⲟⲟⲩ *v* cⲱⲣ ⲣⲥ.

cⲣⲏⲅ *S* nn as pl, *eyebrow* : P 44 68 ⲙⲉⲥⲟⲫⲣⲓⲡⲟⲛ (var 43 38 -ⲫⲣⲓⲟⲛ)· ⲧⲙⲏⲧⲉ ⲡⲡⲉⲥ. بين الحواجب. Misspelt ? *v* ⲉⲡⲅ.

cⲉⲣⲡ *S* nn (? incomplete), *meaning unknown*, mixed with white-lead, used in preparing parchment : PSBA 27 168 ⲉⲕⲡⲁ† cⲉⲣⲡ ⲉⲣⲟⲥ.

cⲟⲣⲡ (*sic* MS) *S* nn as pl, *meaning unknown* : Kr 6 litres ⲡⲥ. ⲉⲩⲉⲓⲏ ⲡⲁⲧϭⲱⲃⲉ γι/ ⲉⲣ/ λ κγ, so *l* ? cⲟⲣⲧ ἐρ(έας).

cⲁⲣⲁⲡⲟⲓ *S* nn, meaning unknown, with myrtle, olive-oil &c : KroppH 109. Coptic ?

cⲁⲣⲡⲟⲧ nn f, *lotus* : DM 2 17 ⲧⲥ., PGM 1 60 *O* cⲉⲣⲡⲱⲧ, *cf* C 86 274 *B* cⲁⲣⲫⲁⲧ. *V* AZ 46 124.

(cⲟⲣcⲣ), cⲉⲣcⲱⲣ† *S* vb, *spread abroad, display* : ClPr 56 11 at festivities ⲉⲣⲉⲅⲉⲡcⲓⲧⲙⲁⲧⲓⲟⲛ c. ⲉⲃⲟⲗ ⲅⲓϫⲛⲡⲉⲭⲏⲩ. *Cf* cⲱⲣ ⲉⲃⲟⲗ.

cⲣⲓⲧ *SB*, cⲗ. *F*, cⲣⲁⲧ⳽, cⲣⲓⲧ⳽ *S* vb intr, *glean* : Ru 2 2 *S* συνάγειν; *ib* 15 συλλέγειν; Si 30 26 *S* καλαμᾶσθαι; Lam 3 51 *F* ἐπιφυλλίζειν; tr : Lev 19 10 *S* gloss on ϫⲱⲗⲉ (var & *B* om) ἐπανατρυγᾶν; Deu 24 20 (*B* ϭⲱⲗ), Is 24 13 *S* cⲣⲁⲧⲟⲩ *B* κⲁⲗ.; CA 106 *S* ⲡⲡⲉⲕⲕⲧⲟⲕ ⲉcⲣⲓⲧ, Lant 102 34 *S* ⲁⲩⲥ. ⲙⲡⲕⲁⲅ ⲧⲏⲣϥ *ravaged*.

cⲟⲣⲧ *SB*, cⲁ. *SSᵃS′AF*, cⲁⲣⲉⲧ *F*, cⲣⲧ- *A* nn m f, *wool* of sheep, goat &c : Lev 13 48 *SB*, Pro 29 31 *SAB*, Is 1 18 *SA* (Cl cⲣⲧ-) *B*, He 9 19 *SBF* ἔριον; Nu 31 20 *B*(*S* om) αἰγία; Ps 71 6 *SB* πόκος; Deu 18 4 *S*(*B* ϭⲱⲕ) κουρά; K 122 *B* صوف, PSBA 29 193 *S* shrouded in ⲅⲟⲓⲧⲉ ⲡⲥ.; ثياب صوف ; ShC 73 43 *S* bartered, ShMiss 4 278 *S* sim; BAp 112 *S* c. ⲡⲟⲩⲱⲃϣ of calf, BMis 568 *S* hair like oⲩⲥⲁ. ⲡⲟⲩⲱⲃϣ, Ryl 107 *S* c. ⲡⲁⲗⲁⲅ, Hall 43 inf *S* ⲡcⲟⲣⲧ (*sic l*) ⲉⲛⲁⲡⲟⲅⲟⲩ as rent (*cf* PLond 5 99), Kr 242 *S* among presents oⲩⲥ., Mor 29 54 *S* priests wear ⲫⲩⲗⲟⲡⲓⲟⲥ (φελώνιον) ⲡⲥ., deacons ⲉⲡⲱⲙⲓⲥ ⲡⲉⲓⲁⲁⲩ, BSM 36 *B* ⲅⲁⲡⲥ. as garment, ST 116 *S* ⲕⲁⲙⲛⲥⲉ ⲡⲥ., AZ 23 41 *F* sim, Ryl 243 *S* ⲕⲁⲗⲗⲁⲥⲉ (قلنسوة) ⲡⲥ., BP 4977 *S* ⲙⲁⲡⲧ]ⲛⲗⲉ ⲡⲥ. opp ⲡⲅⲃⲟⲟⲥ, TT 158 *S* ⲡⲣⲛϣ ⲡⲥ. = C 89 49 *B* ⲙϥⲱⲓ, ST 117 *S* ϣⲟⲧ ⲡⲥ., PMéd 244 *S* ⲕⲗⲙⲉ ⲡⲥ., BMis 178 *S* ⲣⲱⲧ ⲡⲥ., EW 64 *B* Gideon's ϭⲗⲁⲡ ⲡⲥ., CO 320 *S*ᵃ ⲗⲓⲧⲣⲁ ⲡⲥⲁ., Ryl 88 *S* ⲙⲁⲣ ⲡⲥ. *bundle of w.*, R 1 2 43 *S* ⲡⲁⲅⲁⲡ ⲙⲡⲥ. (var Lammayer 46 *S*ᶠ cⲁⲣⲧ *sic l*), BM 585 16 *F* ⲁⲩⲅⲉⲥⲧ ⲡⲉⲥⲁⲣⲉⲧ; f *S* Jud 6 37 πόκ., Mor 34 13 ⲧⲥ. ⲉⲧⲛⲉⲥⲱⲥ = BMis 85 *S* ⲡⲥ., BMar 138 rain upon ⲧⲥ. ⲡⲡⲟⲏⲧⲏ, BM 1102 how much paid ⲅⲁⲧⲥ. In place-name ⲡ[..]ⲙⲟⲩⲡⲉⲡcⲟⲣⲧ (stele Turin).

cⲟⲩⲣⲟⲧ, -ⲣⲱⲧ *B* nn m, *myrobalan* : K 184 ⲡⲉⲥ. (var ⲡⲓⲥ.) هليلج كابلي (var هندي ه′); P 54 139 cⲟⲩⲣⲱ نبات، زهر، نعش scarcely same.

cⲟⲩⲣⲟⲧ *B* *v* ⲥⲓⲟⲩ.

cⲉⲣϥⲱⲧ *B* nn f, *insect* (?) depositing worm (maggot) in sheep : MG 25 155 †ⲥ. cⲁⲧ ϫⲉⲡⲧ ⲉⲡⲓⲉⲥⲟⲟⲩ which are cured by ⲫⲁϭⲣⲓ.

(cⲱⲣϣ), cⲟⲣϣ† *S* vb, *meaning unknown* :

Bodl(P) d 47 among vegetables ⲟⲩⲣⲱ ⲉϥⲥ.†, ⲁⲣϣⲓⲛ ⲉϥⲥ.† *Cf* ϣⲱⲣⲝ & ? Kr 247 ⲡⲟⲣⲝ.

сраϥ, ⲥⲉⲣⲉⲃ *S* nn m, *wound, sore*: Lev 13 18 ⲟⲩⲥⲁⲣⲝ ⲛ ⲟⲩⲥⲣ. ⲡⲣⲉⲗⲕⲟⲥ (var om gloss ⲛ ⲟⲩⲥⲣ., *B* ⲉⲣⲃⲟⲧ) σάρξ...ἕλκος; Tri 531 ⲡⲥⲉ. ⲙ̄ⲡⲡϩⲉⲣⲓⲕⲟⲥ (ἕλκος) جرح.

сⲓⲣⲉϥⲉ, ⲥⲓⲗ. *S* nn f, ? same or *scab*: PMéd 265 ⲟⲩⲥⲓⲣ. ⲡⲧⲁⲥⲱⲥⲕ, *ib* 262 ⲟⲩⲡⲗⲏⲅⲏ ⲡⲧⲁⲥⲣ ⲥⲓⲗ., remedy for which laid upon ⲧⲉⲛⲣⲁⲝ (σάρξ).

ⲥⲁⲣϥⲉ, -ⲉϥ *S* nn in c. ⲛⲥ̄ⲱⲙ P 44 81 زرجون الكرم = 43 56 ⲥⲁⲣⲉϥ ⲉⲥ. *vine-twig* (?, cf ʹϳ ⲥⲗⲱ κληματίς). Gk equivalents prob misplaced (cf P 45 157 b). *Cf* صريف *rope of halfâ or vine-twigs* (Lab) & *v* ⲣⲡⲱ.

ⲥⲣϥⲉ *SA²*, -ⲃⲉ, ⲥⲏⲣϥⲉ *S*, (*B* uses qual), ⲥⲏⲗⲃⲓ *F*, ⲥⲣⲟϥⲧ† *SB*, -ⲃⲧ† *S*, ⲥⲣⲁⲃⲧ† *Sᶠ*, -ϥⲧ *A²*, ⲥⲣⲱϥⲧ† *B* vb intr, *be at leisure, unoccupied*: Ps 45 10 *SB*, Mt 12 44† *SB*, Z 322 *S* ⲛ̄ⲧⲥ.† ⲁⲛ σχολάζειν, AP 11 *A²* εὐσχολεῖν; Am 282 *B* if ⲡⲓⲙⲁ ⲥ.† εὐκαιρεῖν; ShA 1 2 *S* do naught ϣⲁⲛ†ⲥ. ⲡⲧⲁⲙⲉϣⲧ ⲡⲉⲓⲣⲱⲃ, WTh 150 *S* ϣⲁⲛⲧⲁⲥ. ⲝⲉⲉⲓⲁⲣ ⲟⲩ, Mor 18 39 = 19 47 *S* ⲛ̄ⲧⲁⲕⲥ. ⲧⲉⲡⲟⲩ from shedding blood, C 41 36 *B* †ⲥ.† ⲁⲛ †ⲛⲟⲩ = Miss 4 639 *S* ⲥⲭⲟⲗⲁⲍⲉ, MR 5 49 *F* ⲡⲡⲓⲥ. ⲧⲁⲉⲓ, BMEA 10585 *F* ϣⲱⲡ ⲙⲉⲕⲥ. ⲡⲕⲓ.

With following preposition. ⲉ ⲉ- *SA²BF*, *have leisure for, be occupied with*: 1 Cor 7 5 *SBF*, Z 362 *S* ⲉϥⲥⲛ. ⲉⲧⲁⲥⲕⲏⲥⲓⲥ, Aeg 223 *S* ⲉⲧⲥ.† ⲉϩⲉⲛⲧⲁⲃⲗⲁ, MG 25 360 *B* if thou need baskets here are they ⲁⲡⲟⲕ ⲝⲉ †ⲥ.† ⲁⲛ ⲉⲃⲓⲣ = ROC 18 61 لا ... , Wess 18 94 *Sᶠ* ⲉϥⲥ.† ⲉⲡⲡⲉ σχ. dat, C 86 250 *B* hast destroyed queen, now ⲁⲕⲥ. ⲉⲣⲟⲛ ⲣⲱⲛ *wilt deal with us* (cf *ib* 308 *B* περὶ ἡμᾶς ἀσχολῇ & BM 346 112 *S*, AM 64 *B* sim); 1 Cor 9 13† *S* (var CA 93 ϩⲟⲥⲉ, *B* ⲙⲛⲡ) παρεδρεύειν dat; Mk 6 31 *S* (*B* = Gk) εὐκαι. inf; Ac 6 4 *SB* προσκαρτερεῖν dat; Mk 3 20 *S* (*B* ϣ ⲝⲉⲙϫⲟⲙ) δύνασθαι inf; ShC 42 82 *S* ye suffer them not ⲉⲥ. ⲉⲁⲁϥ (sc Pascha), Mani 1 *A²* ⲉϥⲥ.† ⲁⲧⲥⲟⲫⲓⲁ, AP 24 *A²* ⲡⲧⲡⲥ. ⲁⲛ.[, Cat 142 *B* ⲉⲑⲣⲉⲥⲥ. ⲉⲥⲱⲧⲙ ⲉⲡⲥⲁϫⲓ; ⲉ ⲡ- *S*, meaning same: ShBor 247 114 ⲉⲧⲥ.† ⲉⲣⲏⲧϥ ⲙⲙⲁⲧⲉ, *heeds belly only*, BP 10589 ⲙⲡⲟⲩⲥ. ⲡⲉⲓ ⲉⲧⲉⲡⲟⲩ; ⲉ ϩⲛ- *S*, meaning sim: Si 39 2 ἀσχ. ἐν; CA 92 ⲙⲉⲩⲥ. ⲡⲣⲏⲧⲟⲩ (sc trades) at hour of mass, ShC 42 111 heart ⲥ.† ϩⲛⲧⲉⲥⲡⲟⲩⲇⲏ of piety; ⲉ ⲉⲃⲟⲗ ⲛ-, ⲉⲃ. ϩⲛ- *S*, *have leisure, be idle from*: Mor 17 12 none could ⲥ. ⲉⲃ. ϩⲙⲡⲱⲃ σχ. dat; ShMIF 23 21 ⲉⲧⲥ.† ⲉⲃ. ⲡⲡⲉⲕⲥⲱϣϥ (sc devil's), ShA 2 280 ⲧⲉⲧⲡⲥ.† ⲉⲃ. ϩⲙⲡⲣⲟⲟϣ.

—— *S*, ⲥⲣⲱϥⲧ *B*, ⲥⲏⲣϥⲓ *F* nn m, *leisure, perseverance*: Si 38 26 *S* σχολή, Z 327 *S* ⲉϥⲉⲓⲣⲉ ⲙⲡⲉϥⲥ.

βίον ἀπασχολεῖν; Eph 6 18 *SF* (? Mus 35 4, *B* ⲙⲟⲩⲛ) προσκαρτέρησις; Va 57 125 *B* ⲟⲩⲥ. ⲡⲧⲉ †ⲡⲣⲟⲥⲉⲩⲭⲏ νῆψις; ShBM 230 157 *S* God gave ⲟⲩⲥ. ⲉⲧⲣⲉⲡⲣⲡ ⲣⲱⲃ, ShP 130² 7 *S* ⲡⲥ. ⲙⲡⲉⲥⲙⲟⲩ ⲙⲡⲡⲉ thou puttest to unfitting uses, ShA 2 189 *S* ⲡⲟⲩⲱⲙ ⲙⲡⲥ. ⲉⲧⲟϣ, Va 61 114 *B* day of c., Cai ostr 44674 126 *S* ⲟⲩⲡ ⲥⲣⲟⲩϥⲉ ⲙⲙ[ⲁⲩ]; ϩⲛⲟⲩⲥ. *S, at leisure*: ShC 42 99 hear the word ϩ., Bor 240 94 ϩ. ⲙⲡⲟⲩⲕⲁⲙⲏ.

ⲁⲧⲥ. in ⲙⲛⲧ-, ⲙⲉⲧⲁⲧⲥ. *SB, lack of leisure*: Si 40 1 *S* ἀσχολία, ShR 2 3 50 *S* ⲧⲉⲕⲙ. ⲙⲡⲡⲁϣⲁⲓ ⲡ ⲡⲉⲕϩⲓ[ⲥⲉ], P 129¹⁶ 78 *S* worldly things & ⲧⲙ ⲙⲡⲃⲓⲟⲥ = Va 59 16 *B*.

ⲣⲉϥⲥ. *B, idler*: Ex 5 17 σχολαστής.

ϭⲓⲛ-, ϫⲓⲛⲥ. *SB, leisure*: P 44 31 *S* have laboured ϩⲡⲟⲩϭ. ⲙⲡⲟⲩⲕⲁⲧⲁⲥⲧⲁⲥⲓⲥ خلوا بال, Va 58 123 *B* †ϫ. ⲉϥ†.

сⲓⲣⲉϥⲉ *v* ⲥⲣⲁϥ.

ⲥⲣⲟⲩⲣⲉϥ, -ⲣϥ, ⲥⲣⲟⲃ., ⲥⲣⲟϥⲣⲃ *S*, ⲥⲣⲁϥⲣⲉϥ *A*, ⲥⲣⲉϥⲣⲱϣ, ⲥⲣⲃⲣⲱⲃ *S* vb intr, *fall, wither*: Pro 11 14 *SA* (*B* ϩⲉⲓ) πίπτειν, Ps 36 2 *S* (*B* ϩ. ⲉⲃⲟⲗ) ἀποπ., Job 15 30 (*B* ϭⲟⲣϥⲉⲣ) ἐκπ.; Ps 1 3 (*B* do) ἀπορρέειν, Is 64 6 (*B* do) ἐκρ.; ShZ 594 ϥⲡⲁⲥ. ⲛϭⲓ ⲡⲉⲟⲟⲩ, BMar 113 ⲁⲓϣⲟⲟⲩⲉ ⲁⲓⲥ., BHom 119 corpse ⲥ. ϩⲙⲡϣⲱ, Mor 53 21 bones c., *ib* 25 19 where filth is ⲉϥⲥ. ⲡⲣⲏⲧⲟⲩ = Va 61 101 *B* ϥⲱⲣⲕ (meaning ?, cf ⲥ. ⲛⲥⲁ-); tr, *make to fall, dissipate*: ShA 1 440 rich man ⲡⲧⲁⲓ ⲥ. ⲡⲧⲉϥⲙ̄ⲡⲧⲣⲙⲙⲁⲟ, *ib* 94 to be avenged on them ⲛ ⲉⲥⲣⲉϥⲣⲱϣⲟⲩ, Mor 53 22 property ⲁⲩⲥⲣⲃⲣⲱⲃⲟⲩ & devoured them.

With following preposition. ⲥ ⲉ-, *fall upon*: Deu 28 40 (*B* ϥ.) ἐκρ.; ⲉϩⲣⲁⲓ ⲉ-: Miss 4 695 all he doth shall ⲥ. ⲉϩ. ⲉⲡⲕⲁϩ, ShLMis 415 †ⲛⲁⲥⲣⲉϥⲣⲱϥϥ ⲉϩ. ⲉⲡⲕⲁϩ; ⲥ ⲉϫⲛ-, *let fall upon* (?): TurM 9 recipe ⲡⲧⲥ. ⲉϫⲱⲥ (sc boil) ⲙⲡⲓⲡⲁϩⲣⲉ, PMéd 259 ⲣⲟⲩϥⲣⲉϥ (*l* ? ⲥⲣ.) ⲉϫⲱⲥ (sc wound); ⲥ ⲛⲥⲁ- Mor 25 19 (cf *ib* intr) ⲉϥⲥ. ⲡⲥⲁⲡⲟⲉⲓⲣⲉ = Va *l* ⲥ ϥⲱⲣⲕ ϩⲉⲛ-.

With following adverb: ShA 1 372 ⲁⲩⲥ. ⲉⲡⲉⲥⲏⲧ like leaves, ShHT *H* 4 ⲙⲡⲣⲧⲣⲉⲡⲥⲣⲉϥⲣⲱϥϥ ⲉⲡ.

—— nn m, *falling, withering*: BAp 168 ⲡⲉⲥ. ⲡ ⲡⲕⲁⲣⲡⲟⲥ.

ⲁⲧⲥ. in ⲙⲛⲧⲁⲧⲥ., *unwithered state*: Tri 514 increase fruits ϩⲛⲟⲩⲙ.

ⲥⲣ(ⲉ)ϥⲣⲓϥⲉ, -ⲃⲉ *S* nn as pl, *what falls, droppings*: Mt 15 27 (var -ⲣⲓϥ, *B* ⲗⲉϥⲗⲓϥⲓ) ψιχίον; Mor 31 112 ⲕⲟⲩⲓ ⲡⲗⲁⲕⲙⲉ, ⲕⲟⲩⲓ ⲡⲥ. of bread, P 131³ 62 ⲥ. ⲡⲟⲉⲓⲕ.

ⲥⲣⲉϥⲣⲉϥ *S* sim: BHom 140 cit Mt 15 ⲡⲉⲥ., *ib* ⲥⲣⲉϥⲣⲓϥ, P 130⁴ 85 ⲡⲉⲥ. of your table.

Cf ⲗⲟϥⲗϥ.

ⲥⲣⲱϥⲧ *B* *v* ⲥⲣϥⲉ.

ϭⲁⲣϩ, ϭⲣⲁϩ *B* *v* ϭⲱϩⲣ.

ϭⲣⲁϩ *S*(once)*B* nn, *example* : Jer 8 2, Nah 3 6 (*A* = Gk) παράδειγμα; Bar 3 7 ὄφλησις; P 54 168 varia ϭⲁⲣϩ (prob *l* c.) ا.ﺨﻔﺾ *object of shame*; ⲣ, ⲉⲣ ⲥ., ⲟⲓ ⲛⲥ., *display as example*, put to shame : Mt 1 19 (*S* ϯ ⲥⲟⲉⲓⲧ) δειγματίζειν; He 6 6 (*S* = Gk) παραδ.; Col 2 15 (*S* ϫⲁⲓⲟ), Va 68 169 ϯⲙⲉⲧⲁⲧⲟⲩ-ϫⲁⲓ (? ἀσωτία) ⲉⲓⲣⲓ ⲙⲙⲟⲓ ⲛⲥ. θριαμβεύειν; Ps 88 24 (*S* ⲟⲩⲱⲗⲥ) τροποῦσθαι قهر (var فض Tuki); HL 108 she pursued him ϣⲁⲧⲉⲥⲉⲣ ⲥ. (*sic l*) λυττᾶν; P 44 94 *S* ⲣ ⲧⲉϥⲯⲩⲭⲏ ⲛⲥ. مقفرة; Cat 22 evil powers ⲁϥⲁⲓⲧⲟⲩ ⲛⲥ. by His death, PO 11 350 ill reputed & thus ⲁϥⲁⲓϥ ⲛⲥ.

ϭⲣⲁⲙⲉ *S* nn m, meaning unknown, epithet or name of occupation? : Win 30 ⲇⲓⲕⲧⲱⲣ ⲡⲥ., Bodl ostr 428 list of names &c ⲡⲁⲡⲟϩϫⲉ ⲡⲥ.

ϭⲱⲣϫ *B* nn, meaning unknown : C 86 83 ⲁϥ-ⲑⲣⲟⲩϭⲓⲣⲓ ⲙⲡⲥⲱⲙⲁ...ⲛⲥ. ⲥ. with iron knife. *Cf*? ϣⲱⲣϫ.

ϭⲉⲣⲟϫⲓ *v* ϭⲟⲩⲣⲉ.

ϭⲉⲣ-, ϭⲁⲣϭⲁⲙⲟⲩⲗ *v* ϭⲟⲩⲣⲉ.

ϭⲁⲣϭⲁⲧⲥⲉ *S* nn f, *flatus ventris* : Glos 53 φύσσα · ⲧⲥ. *Cf* ϫⲟⲕⲥⲓ. With ϭⲁⲣ- *cf* ϭⲁⲣⲑⲛⲟⲩ (Dévaud).

ϭⲁⲣⲁϭⲱⲟⲩϣ¹, -ϭⲱϣ², ϭⲁⲣⲁⲡϭⲱϣ³, ϭⲁⲗⲁ-ϭⲱⲟⲩϣ⁴, ϭⲁⲗⲁⲡϭⲱϣ⁵ *S*, ϭⲁⲣⲁϫⲱϥ (K), ϫⲁⲣⲁ-ϭⲱⲟⲩⲧⲉ *B*, ϭⲁⲡϭⲱϣ *F* nn m, *hare, cf* Pers خرگوش (IgR) : Mor 54 5 *S*⁵ beside picture of long-eared animal (seized by leg by ⲡⲁⲗⲥⲱⲗⲱⲅⲕⲓ السلوقى) cer-tainly intended for h., ib 31 6 *S*³ sim, BM 528 4 *a* *F* sim; Lev 11 6 *S*¹(*B* = Gk), Pro 24 61 *S*¹ (var⁴ PMich 4566, *A* = Gk) *B* χοιρογρύλλιον, Ps 103 18 *SB* χ. (var λαγωός); K 164 *B* ⲣⲁⲧϥⲁⲧ (*q v*), ϭⲁⲣⲁ-ϫⲱϥ (all MSS, BM 934 gloss صعيدى), ϭ. all أرنب; ShA 2 129 *S* hunting ⲥ.¹, foxes, bubalus, gazelles in desert, Cai 42573 2 *S* gall of ⲛⲥ.² in recipe. Lab 2 96 ورل *hyrax* (D'Arcy Thompson), but cf ϣⲟϣ.

ϭⲓⲱⲥ *S* nn, epithet of *day*, meaning? : BMis 93 Joseph & Mary inscribed their names on 27th (Koiahk) ⲙⲡⲉϩⲟⲟⲩ ⲛⲥ., 28th being Great Fast = Mor 33 42, but ib 34 19 inscribed on 28th ⲧⲡⲁⲣⲁⲥ-ⲕⲉⲩⲏ ⲡϣⲟⲣⲡ ⲡⲥⲟⲩⲕⲏ̅, so not = παρασκευή.

ϭⲱⲥ *SBF*, -ⲥⲓ, ϭⲟⲥⲓ *B*, ϭⲟⲥⲉ *S*, ϭⲁⲥⲉ *F*, ϭⲏⲥⲧ⁺ *S* vb intr, *be thrown down, upset* : Am 9 11 *B*(C 89 113, Tatt & *SA* ϩⲉⲓ) πίπτειν; Job 12 14 *B*(*S* ϣⲟⲣϣⲣ) καταβάλλειν, Ac 15 16 *B*(*S* do) καταστρέφειν; K 316 *B* ϭⲱⲥⲓ هدم; BIF 14 *S* ⲡⲉⲧⲕⲱⲧ ⲡⲉⲧⲥ., DeV 2 194 *B* sim, TEuch 2 58 *B* old church ⲁϭϣⲁⲡⲥ. &

is rebuilt, Rec 6 183 *B* palm-tree ⲁϭϭⲉⲓ, hut ⲁⲥⲥ., J 106 101 *S* wished to make plain my affair lest I leave it ⲉϥϭⲥ.⁺; tr, *overthrow* : Eccl 10 8 *F*(*S* ϣⲗ.), cit Mor 54 31 *S*, Lam 2 2 *F*(*B* ⲟⲩⲱϫⲡ) καθαί-ρειν; Mk 11 15 *B*(*S* ⲧⲁⲩⲟ ⲉⲡⲉⲥⲏⲧ) κατάστ. (*cf* Mt 21 12 *B* ϥⲱⲛϫ, *S* ϣⲗ.), Ac 27 40 *B* ϭⲟⲥⲓ (*S* ϭⲓ ⲉϩⲣⲁⲓ) ἐπαίρειν; PasH 52 *B* ⲁϥϭ. ⲡⲡⲟⲩⲕⲉⲣⲙⲁ دكّ; Ez 13 14 *B*(*S* ϣⲗ.) κατασκάπτειν; Mor 54 31 *S* ⲛϭⲉ ⲡⲧⲁⲥ. ⲡⲣⲓⲉⲣⲓϫⲱ. As nn m *S* : ShA 1 302 walls all fall ⲉⲁⲩⲣ ⲡⲉⲓϭ. ⲡⲟⲩⲱⲧ.

ϭⲁⲁϭⲉ¹, ϭⲁϭⲉ² *S* nn, *tow* (*cf* ساس De Sacy) : Dan 3 46¹ (*B* ϫⲁϫⲓⲑⲱⲗ) στιππύον, cit P 44 115² سراقة, Tri 462 2 ⸍ⲥⲱ (*cf* ܐܣܪ Lemm), ClPr 30 16¹, Bor 264 39², Cai 8027²; ShMIF 23 77 cast ⲥ.¹ ϩⲓϭⲗⲱ on flames. *Cf* C 43 70 *B* ϭⲁϩⲥ, prob this.

ϭⲁϭⲉ, ϭⲉ. *S* vb, meaning unknown : ShClPr 22 363 murmurers say ϯⲡⲁϭⲁ. ⲉⲧⲉϥⲙⲟⲣⲧ *will pull* (?) *his beard*, for he hath not cooked for me this or that (var P 130³ 13 ϭⲉ. ⲧⲉϥⲙ.).

ϭⲓϭⲉ *S* nn, meaning unknown : PMéd 91 powder called ⲟⲩⲥ.

ϭⲓⲥⲟⲩ *S* *v* ϭⲉⲓ nn.

ϭⲱⲥⲓ *B* *v* ϭⲱⲥ.

ϭⲉⲥⲃⲟϩ *B* nn f, *place of atonement*, *cf* DM 15 9 : Lev 16 2, Nu 7 89 (both *S* = Gk) ἱλαστήριον. As vb intr, *make atonement* with following preposition : Ex 30 10 ⲉϫⲉⲛ- ἐξιλάσκειν ἐπί, ib 32 30 ⲉϩⲣⲏⲓ ⲉϫ. (*S* ⲥⲟⲡⲥ) ἐξ. περί; Ez 43 20 ϭⲉⲡ- (HCons, Tatt ⲧⲟⲩⲃⲟ) ἐξ. acc; tr : ib 26 (HCons, Tatt ⲧⲱⲃϩ ⲉϫ.) ἐξ. acc. As nn m, *atonement* : Ex 30 10, Ez 43 23 (HCons, Tatt diff) ἐξιλασμός; ⲉⲣ ⲥ. : Ex 30 15 ἐξ. περί. *V* ϭⲉ *place* & Rec 28 208.

ϭⲁⲥⲉⲗ *B* vb qual (?), *demented* : P 54 125, BMOr 8775 122 مجنون. Or? *cf* σαλός.

ϭⲓⲥⲙⲏ *S*ᶠ nn, meaning unknown : Cai 67324 vo ⲗⲉⲕⲙⲏ ⲛⲥ., ib ⲧⲉϭⲥⲏ ⲡⲥ[ⲓ]ϭⲙⲏ. *Cf* ? ϭⲓⲥⲁⲙⲉⲛ (*v* ϭⲓⲙϭⲓⲙ).

ϭⲧ-, ϭⲉⲧ- *v* ϭⲱⲧ *measure* & ⲉⲓⲟⲣⲉ.

ϭⲁⲧ *SB*, ϭⲉⲧ *AA²B*, ϭⲏⲧ *SSᶠB* nn m, *tail* : Deu 28 44 *SB*, Job 40 12 *SB* ϭⲏⲧ, Is 19 15 *SB*, Ap 12 4 *SB* (varr ϭⲉⲧ, ϭⲏⲧ), MG 25 12 *B* ⲡⲁⲩⲕⲓⲙ ⲡⲡⲟⲩϭ. οὐρά, Deu 25 18 *B*(*S* ⲡⲉⲧϩⲓⲡⲁϩⲟⲩ) οὐραγία; Ex 4 4 *AB*, Pro 26 17 *SA* κέρκος; Tri 519 *S* moon in ⲡⲥ. called ⲡⲕⲁⲧⲁⲃⲓⲃⲁⲍⲱⲛ (moon's descending node οὐρὰ δράκοντος Fotheringham), ShIF 267 *S* ϭ. ⲛ-ⲟⲩⲟⲟϩ, Mani 2 *A*² ⲡⲉϥϭ. like fish's, BM 264 1 *S* lion's, Miss 8 251 *S* dog's, BMar 14 *S* horse's, P 131² 89 *S* (Epiph *De Gem*) λιγούριον explained as ⲡⲥ. ⲡⲟⲩⲗⲓⲧⲧⲓⲣⲓⲟⲛ (οὖρον mistaken for οὐρά D'Arcy Thompson), PMich 4946 *S*ᶠ ⲡⲡⲏⲓ ϭⲏⲧ ⲡⲡⲏⲓ ⲡⲁⲧⲥ.

fleas tailed & tailless, CO 472 *S* in list ⲟⲩⲥⲏⲧ ⲛⲃⲉⲧⲛ same ? ;   ⲥⲁⲗⲡⲥⲏⲧ *S*, ⲥⲃⲟⲕ ⲛⲥⲏⲧ *B*, *dock-tailed* : Lev 22 23 κολοβόκερκος.

ⲥⲏⲧ *SB*, ⲥⲉⲉⲧ *S*, *penis* : P 43 41 *S* ⲡⲥⲉ. ذكر, مَحْشَم, 44 71 *S* ⲫⲁⲗⲟⲥ (*l* φαλλός) · ⲧⲁⲡⲉ ⲙⲡⲥ. رأس الذكر, = 43 41 ', عضو التناسل, Bodl 325 157 *B* ذ. الاحليل.

ⲥⲁⲁⲧ   *v* ⲥⲓⲡⲉ.

ⲥⲉⲧ, ⲥⲉⲉⲧ   *v* ⲥⲁⲧ.

ⲥⲉⲧ, ⲥⲏⲧ *F*   *v* ⲥϩⲁⲓ.

ⲥⲏⲧ, ⲥⲟⲧⲉ *S*, ⲥⲁⲧ *B* vb qual, *spun* : Ex 26 31 *SB*, Lev 14 4 *B*(*S* ϣⲛⲏϣ) κεκλωσμένος (var νενησμένος), Ex 26 31 *S*(*B* ⲉⲣ ⲓⲛⲃ) νεν., Nu 15 38 *S* ⲕⲁⲡ ⲉϥⲥⲟⲧⲉ, (P 44, var ⲧⲱⲧⲉ, *B* ϩⲃⲱⲥ) القزّ var + المبروم, var ⲭⲓⲧⲁ مِن القزّ, κλῶσμα ; CaiThe 113 *B* ⲡⲓϣⲉⲛⲥ ⲉⲧⲥ. مَزول var ⲥⲛⲥ, R 1 5 42 *S* ⲡⲭⲏⲥ[ⲉ] ⲉⲧⲥⲏⲧ ; Cant 5 11 *S* ⲥⲉⲥⲏⲧ (Ming 139, var ⲥⲛⲕ better) Gk om ;   ⲣⲉϥⲥⲏⲧ *S*, *spinner* f : Tri 519 الغزّال.

ⲥⲏⲧⲉ *S* nn f, *spun* fabric : P 44 21, 45 70 ⲧⲥ. مبروم (but var Va 75 86 ⲉⲧⲥⲉⲧⲉ, *l* ? ⲉⲧⲥⲏⲧ).

ⲥⲏⲧ *tail*   *v* ⲥⲁⲧ.

ⲥⲓⲧ *SO*, ⲥⲓⲧⲉ *S*, -ⲧ *B* (once) nn m, *basilisk* : Ps 90 13 (*B* = Gk), Is 59 5 *S*-ⲧⲉ *B* (Va 98 202) βασιλίσκος ; PGM 1 60 *O* ⲡⲥ. ⲟ (*cf* DM 14 3), PS 318 ⲟⲩⲅⲟ ⲛⲥⲓⲧ (*sic* MS), ShC 42 179 (var -ⲧⲉ), BMis 514 ϩⲉⲡⲣⲃⲟⲩⲓ ⲙⲡⲣⲉⲡⲥ., Cai 42573 1 recipe ⲙⲟⲟⲩ ⲛⲥ. ;   ϩⲟϥ ⲛⲥ., lit *basilisk-snake* : PS 156, BMis 191 ⲛϩ. ⲛⲥ. (in Nu 21 6) ⲉⲧⲉⲧⲁⲓⲧⲉ ⲧⲣⲃⲱ (viper), PS 141 ⲥ. ⲛϩ.   Cf ? ⲁⲥⲓⲑ AZ 38 93 (more prob = ⲉⲥⲏⲧ, PGM 1 117 n).

ⲥⲟⲧ, ⲥⲟⲟⲧ *S*, ⲥⲁⲧ *SB* (once), pl ⲥⲁⲁⲧⲉ *S* (v LMis 396) nn m, *dung, excrement* : Lev 4 11 (var & *B* ϩⲟⲉⲓⲣⲉ), 4 Kg 6 25 ⲥⲁⲧ (P 44 111 = 43 108), LCyp 26 ϩⲉⲡⲥ. κόπρος, Si 22 2 ϩⲟⲉⲓⲣⲉ ⲛⲥ. κόπριον ; K 257 *B* ⲛⲓⲥ. بَرز ; PSBA 32 286 martyr in cell filled with ⲥ. ⲡⲉⲓⲱ ⲉⲧⲗⲏⲕ, PMéd 219 sim, AZ 23 110 bottle of chemical mixture buried in ⲡⲥ. ⲛⲓⲱ, Bodl(P) a 1 f sim in ⲡⲥ. ⲛⲡⲉⲣⲓⲥⲧ(ⲉⲣⲁ) ϩⲓⲣⲧⲱ, PChass 1 bury in ⲡⲕⲱϩⲧ ⲛⲥ., GMir 181 as fuel, ShC 73 137 sim, *ib* 152 for repairing canal-banks, Saq 227 ⲡⲁ]ⲧⲗⲉ ⲉϥⲧⲁⲗⲟ ⲥ., *ib* 302, 322 ⲛⲁⲡⲥ. as title, ShA 2 74 digging for metals or things less valuable ϣⲁϩⲣⲁⲓ ⲉϩⲉⲛⲥⲁⲁⲧⲉ ;   ⲟⲩⲉⲙ ⲥ., *dung-eating* : Z 336 κόπρον ἐσθίων, cf *ib* ⲟⲩⲉⲙ...ϩⲟⲓⲣⲉ, ShBM 196 154 sim ;   ⲣ ⲥ., *make, deposit dung* : CO 294 ⲉⲓϣⲁⲛⲣ ϭⲉⲥⲟⲟⲧ ϩⲁⲣⲟⲓ I will pay fine (*cf* Ep 176 ⲣ ⲙⲛ ϩⲁⲣⲟⲓ).

ⲥⲟⲉⲓⲧ *S*, ⲥⲁ. *Sf*/*A*, ⲥⲁⲓⲁⲓⲧ *A²* (Mani 2), ⲥⲱⲓⲧ *B*, ⲥⲁⲓⲧ *AF* nn m, *fame, report* : Ps 111 6 *S*(*B* ⲥⲙⲏ), Mt 14 1 *SF* (*B* do) ἀκοή ; Pro 16 2 *SA*, Mt 9 26 *S*(*B* do) φήμη ; Lu 4 37 *S*(*B* do) ἦχος ; Pro 29 49

SA ϫⲱ ⲙⲡⲥ. ὑμνεῖν ; Wess 15 129 *S* ⲛⲧⲁⲡⲉⲥⲥ. ⲡⲱϩ ϣⲁⲣⲱⲙⲛ = EW 29 *B* ἀκούεσθαι ; ShC 42 225 *S* ⲟⲩⲛ ⲟⲩⲛⲟϭ ⲛⲥ. & clergy have written that &c, Mor 40 40 *Sf* ⲡⲉϥⲥ. filled Syria = MG 25 267 *B*, DeV 1 31 *B* when heard of saint's ⲥ. ⲉⲑⲛⲁⲛⲉϥ, Z 614 *Sf* sim, RNC 53 *S* ⲛⲥ. ⲡⲣⲟⲧ ⲁⲛ ;   as adj, *famous* : Si 44 3 *S*, Is 56 5 *S*(*B* = Gk) ὀνομαστός, 2 Kg 8 13 *S* ⲣⲁⲛ ⲛⲥ. ὄνομα only ; C 43 4 *B* thy martyrdom ⲡⲁϣⲱⲡⲓ ⲛⲥ. in world.

ⲙⲉⲧⲥ. *B*, *fame* : AZ 13 140.

ⲣ ⲥ., ⲟ ⲛⲥ. *SABF*, *become, be famous* : Deu 26 19 *S*(*B* = Gk), Ez 22 5 *SB*, *ib* 24 14 *S*(*B* ⲟⲓ ⲡⲥⲙⲏ) ὀνομασ. ; Hab 1 7 *SA*(*B* ⲟⲩⲟⲛϩ ⲉⲃⲟⲗ) ἐπιφανής ; Jth 10 18 *S* διαβοᾶσθαι, BMar 104 *S* διαβόητος ; 1 Thes 1 8 *SF*(*B* ⲥⲱⲣ ⲉⲃⲟⲗ) ἐξηχεῖσθαι ; Mt 27 16 *S*(*B* om) ἐπίσημος ; Va 63 80 *B* λάμπειν ; ShA 1 248 *S* ⲉϩⲟ ⲛⲥ. ϩⲛⲡⲉϩⲃⲏⲩⲉ ⲛⲁⲓⲕⲁⲓⲟⲥⲩⲛⲏ, C 43 134 *B* will cause thy name to ⲣ ⲥ. ; *make famous* : Nu 25 4 *B*(*S* = Gk) παραδειγματίζειν ; ShA 1 192 *S* God ⲁⲁϥ ⲛⲥ. in world, R 1 4 46 *S* city which poets ⲁⲁⲥ ⲛⲥ.

ⲧ ⲥ., ⲛⲥ. *SABF*, *be, make famed* : Mt 28 15 *S*(*B* ⲥⲱⲣ ⲉⲃ.) διαφημίζειν ; 1 Thes 1 8 *SF*(*B* do) ἐξηχεῖν ; Cl 1 1 *A* περιβόητος ; Mk 6 14 *S*(*B* ⲟⲩⲱⲛϩ ⲉⲃ.) φανερὸς γίνεσθαι ; Ac 21 39 *S*(*B* ⲁⲧⲟⲩⲟⲛϩ ⲉⲃ. ⲁⲛ) οὐκ ἄσημος, Miss 8 42 *S* bishops ⲉⲩⲧ ⲥ. ἐπίση. ; ShMIF 23 78 *S* harlots ⲉⲩⲛⲉϩ ⲉⲃⲟⲗ ⲉⲩⲧ ⲥ., MG 25 324 *B* Oxyrhynchus ⲧⲡⲟⲗⲓⲥ ⲉⲧⲧ ⲥ. (*cf* ἡ λαμπρά), PMéd 271 *S* ⲟⲩ(ⲉ)ⲙⲡⲗⲁⲥⲧⲣⲟⲛ ⲉⲥⲧ ⲥ. ;   with art *SAB* : Deu 29 19 *S*(*B* ϩⲓ ⲱⲓϣ) ἐπιφημ. ; Mt 1 19 *S* (*B* ⲓⲣⲓ ⲛⲥⲣⲁϩ) δειγ., Jer 13 22 *B*(*S* ⲟⲩⲱⲛϩ ⲉⲃ.) παράδ. ; Mk 7 36 *S*(*B* ϩⲓ ⲱ.) κηρύσσειν ; Pro 29 46 *SA* αἰνεῖν ; ShRyl 68 259 *S* ⲥⲉⲧ ⲡⲣⲉⲡⲥ. ⲉⲩⲣⲟⲟⲩ about godly, BMis 452 *S* ⲁⲩⲧ ⲛⲥ. ⲙⲡⲡⲉⲧⲟⲩⲁⲃ.

With prep of person, thing *famed*. ⲥ ⲉ- *S* : Mor 18 199 ⲟⲩⲙⲁ ⲉⲩⲧ ⲥ. ⲉⲣⲟϥ ⲉⲡⲓⲥⲏ. ;   ⲥ ⲉⲑⲃⲉ- *B* : C 89 105 ⲥⲉⲧ ⲥ. ⲉϥϩⲱⲟⲩ ⲉⲑⲃⲏⲧⲟⲩ ;   ⲥ ⲡ- (dat or gen) *SB* : Mk 1 45 *S*(*B* ⲥⲱⲣ ⲉⲃ.) διαφη., Ro 1 8 *S* ⲛⲧⲉ (var ⲉ-, *B* ϩⲓ ⲱⲓϣ) καταγγέλλεσθαι ; ShC 73 3 *S* ⲥⲉⲧ ⲥ. ⲛⲧⲉⲩⲁⲓⲕⲁⲓⲟⲥⲩⲛⲏ *are famed for*, DeV 1 155 *B* ⲉⲩⲧ ⲥ. ⲛⲑⲙⲉⲧⲣⲁⲙⲁⲟ sim, Miss 8 40 *S* ⲛⲛⲓⲧⲁⲩⲡⲣⲁⲥⲥⲉ...ⲉⲩⲧ ⲥ. ⲙⲙⲟⲟⲩ in city ; *ib* 4 688 ⲁϥⲧ ⲛⲡⲥ. ⲛⲧⲉⲡⲣⲟⲫⲏⲧⲓⲁ ;   ⲥ ϫⲁ- *B* : C 86 91 king ⲧⲥ. ϫⲁⲛⲓϣⲏⲣⲓ ⲕⲟⲩⲓ (*sic*) *proclaim, celebrate* ;   ⲥ ϩⲛ- *S* : ShA 1 431 horse ⲉⲩⲧ ⲥ. ϩⲛⲧⲉϥϭⲓⲛⲙⲟⲟϣⲉ *noted for*, *ib* 419 ⲩⲧ ⲥ. ϩⲛⲧⲉⲡⲟⲗⲓⲧⲉⲓⲁ by strict fasting, ShIF 102 ⲉⲩⲧ ⲥ. ϩⲓⲡⲥⲁ ⲙⲡⲉϥⲥⲙⲛⲉ ;   with ϫⲉ- *SB* : C 86 52 *B* ⲧⲉⲧⲉⲛⲧ ⲥ. ⲧⲟⲛⲱ ϫⲉⲛⲑⲱⲧⲉⲛ &c φημίζ. ὡς, Miss 8 23 *S* ⲁⲩⲧ ⲥ. ϫⲉⲁⲣⲏⲩ *it was rumoured*, ShA 1 228 *S* ⲁⲛⲧⲉⲓ ⲥ. ϫⲉⲁⲩϭⲉ ⲉϩⲣⲁⲓ *drunken upon altar*, *ib* 2 158 *S* ⲁⲩⲧ ⲛⲥ. ϫⲉⲡⲁⲣⲭⲏⲅⲟⲥ ⲛⲏⲩ, Va 58 142 *B* things ⲉⲩⲧ ⲙⲡⲟⲩⲥ. ϫⲉϣⲁⲩϫⲉⲙⲟⲩ with barbarians.

ρмпс. *S, famous person*: Si 39 3, Ez 23 23 (*B* ρεмсмн) ὀνομαστός.

сωτ *SA*, сотⲍ¹, сооⲧⲍ², сааⲧⲍ³, сωⲧⲍ⁴ *S* vb **I** intr, *return, repeat*, in neg clause = *not…again*: Job 40 27 (*B* ⲭⲉ) μηκέτι, Zech 14 21 *A*(*B* ⲇⲟ) οὐκ ἔτι; ShBM 209 36 could not с. ⲉⲧⲱⲟⲩⲛ ⲉⳅⲣⲁⲓ, ShA 1 153 fire пас. ан ехеро, ShC 42 163 ⲉⲧⲁⲧⲣⲉⲩⲕⲁⲁⲩ ес. ехе лаау пщахе, *ib* 42 183 ⲁпс. анхооⲩ, *ib* 73 88 пеⲧпас. еⳅⲓ мпетсотп & to give worse to neighbour, ShMiss 4 285 none shall с. еⳅⲓ ⲟⲉⲓⲕ (*sic l*) for self; TU 43 2 *A* м]пс. ⳅⲉ ери ме. **II** tr (refl): Job 10 21¹ (*B* ⲧⲁⲥⲑⲟ ⲭⲉ) ἀναστρέφειν, Ps 38 13¹ (varrᵃ⁴, *B* ⲭⲉ) οὐκέτι, Si 31 27 πάλιν; ShHT *J* 1 harvest past ⳍпасооⲧⳅ ап еⲉⲓ (? Jer 8 20), BMOr 8811 76 мпепλаос…сотоⲩ ⲉⳅⲁⲩ епⲱⲣⲉ.

―― *SAA²*, stretch, reach, с е-: ShA 2 52 at communion I put Christ's body into thy hands ⲕⲥ. ероⲓ мпеⳃсноⳃ; с еⳘⲟⲗ, ⲁⳙ.: Zeph 2 13 *A*(*B* сⲱⲟⲩⲧⲉⲛ) ἐκτείνειν; Mani 1 *A²* с. птооⲧⲉ ⲁⳙ.; с еⳅⲟⲩⲛ: ShIF 93 мн еⲓпас. ⳅⲉ еⳃ. епаса пⳅоⲩп & tear out this malady?; с еⳅⲣⲁⲓ: ShP 130¹ 37 those baking bread еⲩс. еⳅ. епетⲣⲓⲣ. *Cf* C 73 88 above.   Same word?

сωτ *S* nn, *a measure of land*: TU 24 1 6 оⲩс. пⳃⲱм bequeathed. For сⲧ- *S*, сеⲑ-, сеⲧ- *B*, сιⲧⲓ *F* v еⲓⲱⲣⲉ. V PSBA 39 184.   сⲧⲱⲧⲉ *S* nn f, same?: BM 1013 11 ⲧⲓс. пеⲓⲱⲣⲉ, *ib* 1061 ⲧес. пⲓⲱⲣⲉ, Ryl 158 7 сⲧ]ⲱⲧⲉ мⲉп пⲕⲁⳅ ⲕⲁⲓс. ⲭⲉ пⳙⲁⳃ (*cf ib* 11 се]ⲧⲓⲱⲣⲉ пⳙⲁⳃ), Ryl 188 3 сⲧⲱⲧⲉ(?) пⲓⲱⲣⲉ.

сатⲉ *SA*, саⲁ., со. *S*, се. *AA²O*, сеⲉ. *A*, саⳃ *B* (Jer, elsewhere ⳍⲣⲱм) *F*, саⲧⲓ *O* nn f, *fire*: Lev 4 12 *S* (var со.), 2 Kg 22 9 *S* (in Ps 17 8 ⲕⲱⳃⲧ), Ps 20 9 *S*, Joel 1 19 *A* се., Mt 3 12 *S* (var ⲕ.) πῦρ; AZ 21 100 *O* ⲧⲓсаⲧⲓ (gloss се.) ⲉⲧⲉⲙⲉс(п)ⲕⲁⲧⲉ, El 46 *A* sea есⳃⲕ сⲉⲉ. ⲁⳙⲁⲗ, Mani 2 *A²* sacrificing to ⲧⲥ., BMis 503 *S* ⲧⲩⳅⲉⳍⲛⲛⲁ псаа.; ⳙⲁⳃ пс., *flame of fire*: Ps 28 7 *S*(*B* ⳙ. пⳍ.), Is 66 15 *S* со., He 1 7 *SF* φλὸξ πυρός; ма пс. *S*, *oven*(?): BM 1130 pay 2 (wine measures) па(м)ма пс. τόπου καμ(ί)νου;   ⲣ с. *S*, *be fiery*: AZ 25 71 о пс.   ⳅⲓ с. *B*, *throw fire, set on fire* с е-: Jer 28 25 ἐμπυρίζειν.   сⳙ псеⲧⲉ *A* v сⳙ.

сатⲉ *S* vb, *fan*: ShA 1 136 if sick ⲣ ⳍⲣⲉⲓⲁ пс. ероⳃ ⳅⲛⲟⲩⲅсатⲱ.

сатⲱ, -о *SB* nn f, *fan*: Aeg 276 *S* ⳅⲉпс. ⲣⲓⲡⲓⲇⲓⲟⲛ, Mor 663 A *S* مِرْوَحة (v соⳙⲛ), P 44 87 *S* псато 'ⲁ, Tri 724 *S* пеⲓс. еⳘⲟⲗ ⳅⲣⲉпмⲛⳅⲣⲉ 'ⲁ, Ryl 241 *S* с. пⲁⳙⲣⲁп. н[, PMich 4538 4 *S* Apa Noub ⳋсаⲧо пноⳙ in thy hand, Dif 2 36 *B* same ⳃⲁⳋс. пноⳙ пхаⳅ (v PO 11 792 n).

саⳋ vb *B*   v снⲧ vb.

сеⲧⲏ, сⲓ. *S*, спⲧⲉ *SB*, сеⳋ *A* nn prop f, a condition of the fig, ? *early fig*: Nah 3 12 *A* fig-trees еⳅⲡ ⳅⲉпс. ⳅⲓⲱⲟⲩⲉ (*B* = Gk) σκοπός (var καρπός), Hos 9 10 *A* ⲕпⲧⲉ пс. (*B* ⲇⲟ) σκ. (var σῦκον) ἐν συκῇ; Is 28 4 *S* оⲩсⲉ. пⲕпⲧⲉ (var & *B* P 70 198 сп., Tatt ⳙⲟⲣп пⲕ.) πρόδρομος, cit P 129¹⁴ 101 (var сι. *ib* 102, *cf* Bargès *St Marc* ٣٥ أساس, as if спⲧⲉ *foundation*).

снⲧⲉ nn   v снⲧ vb.

сιⲧⲉ *SAA²*, сιⳋ *BF*, снⳋ *F* (Mk 12), сеⲧ- *SBF*, саⲧ- *SB*, сιⲧ- *S*, снⲧ- *F*, саⲧⲍ *SB*, сеⲧⲍ *SF*, сιⲧⲍ *S*, снⲧ† *SF*, снⳋ†, саⳋ† *B* vb **I** intr, *throw, sow* (oftener) & related meanings (*cf* ? *B* ⳙⲓⳋ): Ps 125 5 *B*(*S* ⳍⲟ), Mic 6 15 *B* (*A* ⳍⲟ), Mt 13 18 *BF*(*S* ⲇⲟ) σπείρειν; Ps 77 9 *B*(*S* пⲟⲩⳍⲉ tr) βάλλειν, Mk 1 16 *B* ⳙпепс. (*S* om) ἀμφίβληστρον; Va 57 11 *B* φυτεύειν.

II tr: Ex 23 10 *B*(*S* ⳍⲟ), Is 5 10 *B*(*SF* do), Mt 13 27 *BF*(*S* do) σπ.; Ac 22 23 *B*(*S* ⳃⲓ еⳅⲣⲁⲓ) ῥιπτεῖν; *ib* *B*(*S* п.) βάλ.; Mic 2 13 *B* (*cf* ? сⲓпⲓ, *SA* Ⳙⲱⲕ еⳅⲟⲩⲛ ⳅп-) فى دخل διέρχεσθαι; Mk 9 3 *F* v ⲓⲉⲗⲗⲉ; BKU 1 1 (II) *S* аⳃс. пеⳃоⲩⲉⲗⲗⲉ (meaning?), BIF 14 154 *S* аⳃс. пеⳃмⲁⲁⳍⲉ & spake not with him, PRain 4749 *S* п]соⲩсⲓⲧ пⲣⲱⳃ ⳍ[, AZ 23 28 *F* аⲩс. оⲩⲱⲗⲟⲕⲟⲧⲥⲓ пⲧеⳃ еⳍⲱп, Kr 233 *F* ⲁпⲁⲕ etc. ⳅⲁⲁⳙⲓ мⲉⲛⲏⳃ (*sc* corn).

With following preposition.   с е- *SBF*, *throw at, put to* intr: AM 316 *B* аⲩс. еⲧⳅⲓⲕⲱп (*cf* с ⳅⲓ-), MR 5 52 *F* whatever God shall сеⲧ еⲧⲉⲕⳏⲩⳍⲏ; tr: Lu 4 35 *B*(*S* п.) ῥίπ.; Va 63 79 *B* ready to с. мпеⳃⳍⲣⲟⳍ еⲧⲕⲟⲓ καταβάλ.; MG 25 214 6 *B* (*sic* MS) аⳃсет ⲱпⲓ ероⲟⲩ λιθάζειν; AM 317 *B* sim аⲩсат, R 1 5 51 *S* еⲧⲣеⳃсет пеⳃпⲁ епⳅⲏⲧ, PMich 1190 *S* еⲓⳙⲁпсаⲧⲕ еппⲟⲩп, Va 61 93 *B* пн еⳙⲁⲩсаⲧоⲩ епⳍⲓⲣ = P 131³ 83 *S* п., EW 30 *B* ессат ⲓⲧⲉп ероⳃ, LMär 25 *S* еⲩс. ммоⳃ еⲧоⲟⲧоⲩ of one another, C 43 93 *B* sim, Mor 24 20 *F* пⲕсет пⲓⲛⲟⳅⲓ епеⳘⲣⲏⲧ, MG 25 192 *B* аⳃсатⲧⲉп емⲓⲣ, *ib* 155 *B* if insect сат ⳍⲉпⲧ епⲓесⲱоⳃ;   с еⳍп- *SB*, *throw, put upon, add to*, intr: Is 32 20 *B*(*SF* ⳍⲟ) σπειρ. ἐπί; AM 104 *B* аⲩс. еⳍ. пⲓⳅⲛⲧⲉмⲱп;   tr: Lev 24 23 *B*(*S* ⳅⲓⲟⳅⲉ е-) λιθοβολεῖν; Ez 27 30 *B*(*S* п. еⳍ.) ἐπιτιθέναι ἐπί, Mor 25 10 *S* пⳃсет оⲩпеⲗⳍⲉ еⳍⲱⳃ (var P 131³ 83 п.) = Va 61 93 *B*, AZ 23 109 *S* recipe сат оⲩⳙⲓ еⳍпⳏ пⲕⲁ[сⲓⲧⲏⲣⲉ (*cf ib* 113), C 41 42 *B* еⲩс. ппⲓⳅⲣп…еⳍ. пⲓоⲩⳅⲏ *dispose of to*, BM 1127 *S* sim;   с пса- *SB*, *throw after, upon*: 1 Kg 20 33 *S* (var п-) Gk diff, Mor 39 42 *S* сет ⳙⲉ пмⲉⲣеⳅ псⲱⲓ = C 43 60 *B* ⳅⲓ. м. пс., ROC 27 155 *B* waves с. псⲱс, Cat 231 *B* аⳃсет ⳍⲱⳙ

ⲡⲓⲃⲉⲛ ⲡⲥⲁⲫϯ; ⲥ ⲣⲁ-, ⲃⲁ-, *throw, put beneath*:
Mor 41 147 *S* ⲙⲉⲕⲥ. ⲙⲡⲉⲕⲙⲉⲣⲉϩ ϩⲁⲣⲁⲧ ⲡⲕⲉⲥⲟⲡ,
C 43 30 *B* ⲁⲩⲥⲁⲧϥ ϩⲁⲡⲉⲛϭⲁⲗⲁϫ of beast; ⲥ ϩⲓ-
SB, throw, put upon, in: Cai 42573 1 *S* charms (?)
for fishing-net ⲥⲁⲧⲟⲩ ϩⲓⲡⲉϥⲑⲉⲏ, AZ 23 111 *S*
ⲥⲁⲧ ⲟⲩⲧⲉⲣϩ(ⲁⲙ) ϩⲓⲟⲟϥ, AM 308 *B* ⲁⲩⲥⲁⲧ ⲱⲡⲓ ϩⲓⲧⲣⲓⲕⲱⲛ (*cf* ⲥ ⲉ- & C 43 81 ⲥ. ⲉϫⲟⲩⲡ ⲉ-), Kr 228
S ⲡⲡⲓⲣⲥⲓⲁ ⲡⲉⲥⲱϧ ϩⲓⲡⲁϩⲟⲩ ⲡⲙⲟⲕ, Va 61 94 *B*
ⲉⲩⲥ. ⲡⲓⲣⲏⲕⲓ ϩⲓⲫⲟⲅⲉⲓ = P 131³ 83 *S* ⲃⲱⲣⲉ ⲡⲥⲁⲃⲟⲗ, AM 56 *B* ⲉⲩⲥ. ⲡⲡⲓⲯⲩⲭⲏ ϩⲓⲧⲉⲛ ⲙⲙⲟϥ; ⲥ
ϩⲓⲭⲛ- *SB, meaning same*: AM 307 *B* ⲁϥⲥⲁⲧⲩ ϩ.
ϯϣⲛⲟⲩⲓ, Bodl(P) a 3 40 *S* dyeing recipe ⲥⲉⲧ ⲟⲩϣⲓ
ϩⲛⲡⲉⲕⲡⲁϩⲣⲉ ϩⲓⲭⲱⲣⲕ ⲡⲩⲓ=*ib* 1 ⲉ 6 ⲧⲓ ⲟⲩⲁ...ⲉϫⲛ-,
AZ 23 110 *S* sim.

With following adverb.

—— ⲉⲃⲟⲗ *SA²BF, throw out*: Mt 13 48 *F*(*S* ⲛ.,
B ϩ.) βάλ. ἔξω, Ps 16 11 *F*(*SB* do) ἐκβ., Mk 10 50
B(*S* do) ἀποβ.; Ac 27 19 *B*(*S* ⲛ.) ῥίπτειν; Jer 27
17 *F* (Louvre 10052, *SB* ⲭⲱⲣⲉ ⲉⲃ.) ἐξωθεῖν; Eccl
10 9 *F*(*S* ⲡⲱⲣⲕ) ἐξαίρειν; BM 1008 99 *S* ⲉⲧⲥⲁⲧ ⲉⲃ-
ⲣⲏϭ ⲉⲃ., Mani 1 *A²* ⲛⲕⲁⲧ ⲉⲧⲥⲓⲧⲉ ⲉⲡ[ ]ⲁⲃ., C 89 66
B ⲁⲩⲥⲁⲧ ⲧⲉϥⲉⲧϥⲱ ⲉⲃ.=MG 17 318 *S* ⲛ., Gu 22 *S*
women with child ⲥⲉⲧ ϩⲓⲧⲟⲩ ⲉⲃ. through fear, MG
25 201 *B* ⲟⲩⲟⲁϥ ⲡⲥⲁⲧⲩ ⲉⲃ., PcodMor 25 *F* arithm
ⲥⲉⲧⲟⲩ ⲉⲃ. ⲉⲓⲥ ϩⲉⲕⲁⲧⲱⲡ (*cf* ⲉⲓⲡⲉ ⲉⲃ.); qual,
cast forth, lying: WHatch 317 *B* ⲉϥⲥⲏ. ⲉⲃ. dead
κεῖσθαι; EpJer 70 *F*(*B* ⲣⲟⲭⲡ) ῥίπτεσθαι; Mor 18
115 *S* tongue ⲉϥⲥ. ⲉⲃ. (var LCyp 8 ⲉϥϣⲏⲩ) προφέρειν; ShC 73 200 *S* sim ⲥ. ⲉⲃ. ⲡⲣⲱϥ, C 43 221 *B*
ⲁⲩⲭⲁϥ ⲉϥⲥⲏ. ⲉⲃ., *ib* 240 *B* corpse ⲉϥⲥⲓ. (*l* ⲥⲏ.)
ⲉⲃ., DeV 1 29 *B* ⲉⲓⲥⲏ. ⲉⲃ. ϫⲉⲛⲡⲁϣⲱⲡⲓ, C 89 124
B ⲉⲥⲥⲁ. ⲉⲃ. ϫⲁⲛⲉϥϭⲁⲗⲁϫ; ⲉⲃ. ϩⲛ-, ϫⲉⲛ-, *cast
out from*: MIE 2 369 *B* ⲁⲩⲥ. ⲙⲡⲉϥϑⲁϥ ⲉⲃ. ϫⲉⲛⲡ-
ⲣⲱϥ, P 131² 88 *S* ⲉⲩⲥ. ⲙⲡⲱⲡⲉ ⲉⲃ. ϩⲛⲡⲙⲁ ⲉⲧⲙⲙⲁⲩ; ⲉⲃ. ϩⲓⲭⲛ-, *cast out upon*: Va 57 49 *B*
ⲉϥⲥⲏ.† ⲉⲃ. ϩ. ⲡⲕⲁϩⲓ, *ib* 61 120 *B* ⲉϥⲥⲁ.† ⲉⲃ. ϩ. ⲡⲓⲕ.;
out from: BMEA 10578 *F* ⲁⲩⲥⲉⲧⲩ ⲉⲃ. ϩ. ⲡⲉϥϩⲧⲁ
= Mor 31 254 *S* ⲁϥⲥⲉ ⲉϫⲛ-, P 131² 89 *S* ⲉⲣϣⲁⲛ-
ⲟⲩⲁ ⲥⲁⲧ ⲡⲉϩⲣⲟ ⲉⲃ. ϩ. ⲧⲁⲡⲉ ⲡⲡⲓⲧⲟⲩⲉⲓⲛ *a summit.
mont. aspiciat*; ⲥ ⲡⲥⲁⲃⲟⲗ *S, cast out from*: PS
36 ⲡⲥⲉⲥ. ⲡⲧϭⲟⲙ ⲡⲥ. ⲙⲙⲟⲟⲩ; ⲥ ϩⲁⲃⲁⲗ *F, meaning sim*: KroppC 19 ⲥ. ϩ. (ⲙ)ⲙⲁⲥ ⲡⲉⲡⲉⲣϭⲓⲁ ⲡⲓⲃⲓ
ⲉⲧϩⲁⲟⲩ, *ib* ⲥⲉⲧⲟⲩ ϩ.

—— ⲉⲡⲉⲥⲏⲧ *SBF, throw down*: Ac 27 28 *B*(*S*
ⲛ.) βολίζειν; Mor 18 20 *S* ⲁⲩⲥⲉⲧ ⲱⲡⲉ ⲉ. = *ib* 19
29 *S* ⲛ. = Miss 4 114 *B* ϩⲓ., Mor 24 10 *F* ⲁϥⲥⲉⲧⲩ
ⲉ. = *ib* 23 14 *S* ⲛ., *ib* 38 77 *S* wishing to ⲥⲁⲧⲩ ⲉ.
ⲡⲥⲁϫⲱϥ (*cf* Lu 4 29), C 86 325 *B* ⲁⲩⲥⲁⲧⲩ ⲉ. ϩⲓ-
ϫⲉⲛⲡⲓⲡⲗⲁϩ.

—— ⲉⲡϣⲱⲓ *B cast, bring up*: EW 12 hell ⲁⲩⲥ.
ⲉ. the dead, DeV 2 230 ϥⲛⲟⲩⲡ ⲉⲧⲥ. ⲉ. intr.

—— ⲉϩⲟⲩⲛ, ⲉϫ. *SSⁱB, cast in*: AM 49 *B* ⲁⲩⲥⲁⲧⲩ ⲉϫ. & shut door, PS 12 *S* ⲁⲓⲥ. ⲡⲟⲩϭⲟⲙ ⲉ.

ⲉⲣⲟⲥ, CMSS 36 *Sⁱ* man sent ⲡⲃⲥⲉⲧ ⲡⲉⲛⲏⲣⲡ ⲉ. *deposit*(?), C 89 68 *B* ϣⲁⲓⲥⲁⲧ ⲟⲩⲙⲉⲩⲓ ⲉ. ⲉⲣⲟϥ =
MG 17 321 *S* ⲛ. ⲙⲉⲉⲩⲉ ⲉ., C 43 81 *B* ⲁⲩⲥ. ⲉ.
ⲉϥⲣⲓⲕⲱⲛ *cast stones at*, AM 156 *B* ⲁⲩⲥⲁⲧⲟⲩ ⲉ.
ϫⲉⲡⲡⲣⲟ ⲙⲡⲓⲣⲏⲧⲉⲙⲱⲛ, Ricci L 260 *F* sim ⲥⲉⲧⲩ.

—— ⲉϩⲣⲁⲓ *S*, ⲁϩⲣⲏⲓ *A*, ⲉϩⲣ. *B*, ⲉϩⲗ. *F*, *cast
down*: Mk 12 43 *F* (Mor 46 63, *S* ⲛ., *B* ϩⲓ.), Cl
24 5 *A* sower ⲁϥⲥ. ⲁ. ⲁⲡⲕⲁϩ (var ϯⲕⲉ) βάλ. εἰς;
Sa 17 19 *S* (var ⲥⲓⲡⲉ ⲉ.) συνέχεσθαι dat; Va 57 175
B ⲡⲧⲉⲕⲥⲁⲧⲉ ⲉ. ⲉⲑⲛⲉϫⲓ of poor διασπείρειν εἰς;
ShBM 8810 480 *S* thoughts ⲉⲧⲟⲩⲥ. ⲙⲙⲟⲟⲩ ⲉ. ⲉ-
ⲡⲉⲡϩⲏⲧ, C 41 57 *B* ⲁⲩⲥⲁⲧⲟⲩ ⲉ. ⲉϥⲓⲁⲣⲟ, Va 61 116
B ⲁϥⲥⲁⲧⲩ ⲉ. ϩⲓⲭⲉⲛⲡⲓⲕⲁϩⲓ = JTS 4 396 *S* ⲛ. ⲉϩⲣⲁⲓ
ⲉϫ., C 43 27 *B* ⲥ. ⲉ. ⲉϫⲱϥ ⲡⲟⲩϑⲏⲓ; ⲥ ⲉϩⲣⲁⲓ
S, -ⲛⲓ *B*, *throw up*: Z 570 *S* cerastes ⲕⲁ ⲡⲉϥⲧⲁⲡ
ⲉⲩⲥ.† ⲉ., Ryl 106 27 *S* drink it ⲉⲕⲥ. ⲉ. *wilt vomit*,
PMéd 323 *S* ⲉϥⲥⲓⲧ ⲥⲡⲟϥ ⲉ. ϩⲣⲱϥ, MIE 2 378 *B*
ⲁⲩⲥ. ⲙⲡⲓⲁⲡⲑⲟⲩⲥ ⲉ., PMich 2066 *S* ⲡϣⲏⲓ ⲛⲧⲁⲩ-
ⲥⲁⲧⲩ ⲉϩⲣ[ⲁⲓ (meaning ?), Ryl 233 *S* list of names,
money, grain ⲡⲛⲧ(ⲁ)ⲓⲥⲁⲧⲉ ⲉ. (*cf* ⲡⲟⲩϫⲉ ⲉϩⲣⲁⲓ *make
return* PLond 4 474).

—— ⲛⲛ m *B, thing thrown, seed*: Ex 34 21 (*S*
ϫⲟ), Am 9 13 (*SA* do) σπόρος; Va 66 307 sinners
& those ⲉⲧⲉⲣ ϩⲁⲗ ⲙⲙⲟⲩ ϫⲉⲡⲡⲉ. ⲡϯⲧⲣⲟⲫⲏ ⲉⲧⲟϣ; as adj: Ge 1 29 σπόριμος.

ϫⲓⲡⲉ. *B, sowing*: 1 Pet 1 23 (*S* ϫⲡⲟ, *l* ? ϫⲟ),
Va 57 30 ⲡϫ. σπόρος (Mt 6 26); TRit 86 ϯϫ. of
enemy ϩⲣϫ·

ⲥⲉⲧ ⲉⲃⲣⲏϫ *B, lightning*: Jer 10 13 (*S* ⲉⲃ. only)
ἀστραπή; ⲟⲓ ⲡⲥ.: Ez 1 4 (HCons, var ϯ ⲡⲟⲩⲥ., *S*
ϯ ⲉⲃ.) ἐξαστράπτειν. *V* ⲉⲃⲣⲏϭⲉ, ⲥⲓⲧⲉ nn below.

ⲥⲟⲧⲉ, ⲥⲟⲟ *S*, ⲥⲁ. *SⁱA*, ⲥⲁϯ *B* (once) *F*, pl ⲥⲟⲟⲧⲉ
S & sg as pl, nn m f, *arrow, dart*: Job 6 4 *S*, Is
5 28 *S* (var ⲥⲁ.), Eph 6 16 *S* (all *B* ⲥⲟⲟⲛⲉϥ), BHom
23 *S* ⲧⲥⲟⲟⲧⲉ βέλος, Jos 23 13 *S*(*B* ⲥⲟⲩⲣⲓ), Hab 3
11 *SA*(*B* ⲥⲟⲟ.), Jer 9 8 *S*(*B* ⲥⲉⲣⲃⲉⲡⲓ), *ib* 27 9 *S*
(*B* ⲃⲉⲣⲃⲓⲣ) βολίς; Job 41 19 *S*(*B* ϥⲓϯ) τόξον, Pro
7 23 *SA*(*B* ϣⲉ ⲡⲥⲟ.) τόξευμα; PS 140 *S* ⲟⲩⲥ.
ⲉϥϩⲏⲗ, Mor 39 12 *Sⁱ* he shot ⲥ. ⲥⲛⲧⲉ, *ib* 30 31 *F*,
K 116 *B* ⲡⲓⲥ. قش *arrow-head*; pl form *S*: Nu 33
55 (*B* ⲟⲃⲟⲗⲓⲥⲕⲟⲥ) βολ., Cant 4 4, Job 16 9, BHom
44 βέλ.; ⲡⲉϫ ⲥ. *S, throw dart, shoot arrow*: Ps
77 9 (*B* ⲥⲓϯ ϫⲉⲛⲫⲓϯ) τόξ. βάλλειν, *ib* 63 4 (*B* ϩⲓ
ⲥⲟⲟ.) κατατοξεύειν; BM 257 368 ⲥⲉⲡⲉϫ ⲥ. ⲉⲣⲟⲥ,
BHom 8 demons ⲡⲉϫ ⲥⲟⲟ. ⲉⲡⲉⲛⲙⲁⲭⲉ; 2 Kg 11
24 ⲉⲃⲟⲗ ⲉϫⲛ- τοξεύειν πρός; as nn: BM 194 1
with sword or ⲟⲩⲛ. ⲥ., Ge 21 16 ⲡⲡⲟⲩϫⲉ ⲡⲟⲩⲥ.
(*B* ϣⲉ ⲡⲥⲟⲟ.) τόξου βολή; ⲙⲁ ⲡⲡ. ⲥ. *S, place
for shooting arrows*: Ez 4 2 (*B* ⲙⲁ ⲡⲭⲁ ⲥⲟⲟ.)
βελόστασις; ShA 1 300; ⲣⲉϥⲡ. ⲥ. *S, shooter of
arrows*: Am 2 15 (*Sⁱ* ⲣⲉϥϩⲓ ⲥ. JEA 11 248, *A* ⲣⲉϥϯⲕ
ⲥ., *B* ⲣⲉϥϩⲓ ⲥⲟⲟ.) τοξότης; RNC 75; ⲣⲉϥⲧⲕ ⲥ.

SA sim: Ge 21 20 *S*(*B* do), Am *lc A* τοξότης; ϫι c. *S, receive, be struck by arrow*: ShC
42 69 ⲛⲉⲡⲧⲁⲅϫⲓ c. ⲛ ⲁ ⲩ ϣ ⲟ ⲟ ⲅ ⲟ ⲩ; ⲅⲡⲁⲁⲩ ⲡⲕⲁ
c. *S, quiver*: Is 49 2 (*B* ⲙⲟⲕⲓ ⲡ ⲭⲁ ⲥ ⲟⲃ.) φαρέτρα; ⲅ. ⲛ ϯ c. *S*, sim: Ps 10 2 (*B* ⲙⲟⲕⲓ) φ.;
ⲉⲡⲕ[ⲁ] ⲛϯ c. *S* Leyd 343.   *V* also ⲕⲗⲟ.

ⲥⲓⲧⲉ *S*, ⲥⲓϯ *B* basilisk *v* ⲥⲓⲧ.

ⲥⲓⲧⲉ *S* nn f, meaning unknown, *? beam* of light:
PS 7 ⲧϣⲟⲣⲡ ⲛⲥ.   *V* AZ 22 71. Same *?* in ⲥⲉⲧⲉⲃ-
ⲣⲏⲭ (*v* ⲉⲃⲣ ⲏ ϭ ⲉ), but *cf* ⲥⲓⲧⲉ ⲉⲃⲟⲗ BM 1008.

ⲥⲓⲧⲓ   *v* ⲉⲓⲱⲅⲉ (ⲥⲧⲉⲓⲱⲅⲉ).

ⲥⲟⲧⲉ   *v* ⲥⲏⲧ, ⲥⲁⲧⲉ *fire* & ⲥⲓⲧⲉ *throw s f.*

ⲥⲟⲧⲉ, ⲥ ⲁ. *S* nn, a measure (?): Z 583 ϣⲉ ⲡⲥ.
(*sic* MS, altered to ⲉⲥ.) ⲡⲉⲓⲱⲧ (Ge 26 12 *B* ⲣ̄ ⲛⲕⲱⲃ
ἑκατοστεύων); PB 11349 neglected fields ϣⲁⲩⲣ
ⲁⲥⲁ. ⲉⲙⲁⲧⲉ (*l* ⲙⲙ ⲁ.), same ?

ⲥ ⲟⲟⲧⲉ *S* nn m, meaning unknown: Leyd AC
23 wine (?) account ⲅⲙⲡⲥ. (*sic*) ⲥⲁ ⲩ ϣⲉ ⲛϣⲉ ϣϥⲉ
ⲧⲁⲥⲉ.   *Cf ?* last or is *?* place-name.

ⲥⲱⲧⲉ *SA*, ⲥⲱⲧ *A*, ⲥⲱϯ *S͗BF*, ⲥⲉⲧ- *SB*, ⲥⲟⲧ- *S*,
ⲥⲱⲧ- *SA*, ⲥⲟⲧⲍ *SB*, ⲥⲟⲟⲧⲍ *S*, ⲥ ⲁⲧⲍ *SAF*, ⲥⲁⲁⲧⲍ *SA*
vb **I** intr (rare) *redeem, rescue*: Ps 7 2 *SB* λυτροῦσθαι; Hos 5 14 *B*(*SA* ϥⲓ ⲛⲧⲛ-) ἐξαιρεῖσθαι; ShBM
252 56 *S* ⲉⲙⲛ ϣⲁϫⲉ ⲉ ϫ ⲱ ⲉⲙⲛ ⲣ ⲱ ⲃ ⲉⲥ.   **II** tr:
Nu 18 15 *SB*, Is 35 9 *SBF*, Hos 7 13 *SAB*, Cl 55
2 *A* ⲥⲱⲧ ⲅ ⲉ ⲛ ⲕ ⲉ ⲕ ⲉ ⲅ ⲉ λυ., Ex 21 8 *SB* ἀπολυ.; Pro
24 11 *SA* ⲥⲱⲧ ἐκπρίασθαι; EpJer 53 *BF* ῥύεσθαι;
Is 31 5 *B*(*BF* ⲛⲟⲩⲅⲙ) ἐξαιρ.; Br 79 *S* c. ⲙⲙⲉⲗⲟⲥ
ⲛⲓⲙ ⲛⲧⲁⲓ, Mor 27 36 *S͗* ⲛⲧⲉⲧⲛⲥ. ⲛⲧⲉ ϣ ⲧ ⲏ ⲛ = BMis
393 *S*, *ib* 394 *S* sim = BSM 46 *B* ⲃ ⲱ ⲗ ⲉⲃⲟⲗ, P
131⁵ 45 *S* gave self for sinners ϣ ⲁ ⲛ ⲧ ⲉ ϥ ⲥ ⲁ ⲧ ⲟ ⲩ, Ep
178 *S* have pity ⲅ ⲱ ⲥ ⲉ ⲧ ⲉ ⲧ ⲛ ⲥ ⲱ ⲧ ⲛ ⲟ ⲩ ⲁ ⲓ ⲭ ⲙ ⲁ ⲗ ⲱ ⲧ ⲟ ⲥ,
J 10 19 *S* bade us pay ⲛⲧⲛⲥⲱⲧ ⲡ ⲉ ⲡ ⲕ ⲁ ⲅ, Ann 22
270 *S* I pawned a hammer ⲙⲡⲓ ϭⲙ ϭⲟⲙ ⲛⲥⲟⲧϥ.

With following preposition.   c ⲉ- *S, save from*:
Ps 118 134 (*B* ⲉⲃⲟⲗ ⲅⲁ-) λυ. ἀπό; PS 260 ⲛⲥⲉⲡⲁ-
ⲥⲉⲧⲧⲏ ⲩ ⲧ ⲛ ⲁ ⲛ ⲉ ⲡ ⲕ ⲟ ⲥ ⲙ ⲟ ⲥ, CO 254 ⲁ ⲕ ⲥ ⲟ ⲧ ⲥ ⲟ ⲉ ⲙ-
ⲯ ⲩ ⲭ ⲏ ⲉ ⲡ ⲙ ⲟ ⲩ.; ⲉ ⲅ ⲟ ⲩ ⲛ ⲉ-: ShMich 550 13 pious
women etc. ⲉ ϥ. ⲉ ⲛ ⲉ ⲧ ⲉ ⲛ ⲟ ⲩ ⲟ ⲩ ⲛ ⲉ; c ⲛⲧⲛ- *SAB*,
meaning same: Hos 13 14 *A*(*B* ⲉ ⲃ. ϫ ⲉ ⲛ-) λυ. ἐκ,
1 Chr 16 35 *B* ἐξαιρ. ἐκ; PS 337 *S* ϣⲁⲅ ⲥ. ⲙ ⲙ ⲟ ⲥ
ⲛⲧⲟⲟⲧⲟⲩ ⲛⲡⲉⲥⲉⲓⲟⲧⲉ, Mor 23 95 *S* ϣ ⲁ ⲛ ⲧ ⲉ ϥ ⲥ ⲁ ⲁ ⲧ ϥ
ⲛⲧⲟⲟⲧϥ of enemy, J 50 48 *S* ground ⲛⲧⲁⲓ ⲥ ⲟ ⲧ ⲩ
ⲛⲧⲟⲟⲧϥ of monastery;   c ϫ ⲁ- *B, redeem (in exchange) for*: Ex 34 20 (*S* ϣ ⲓ ⲃ ⲉ ⲛ-) λυ. dat, Is 52 3
(*S* ⲅ ⲛ-) λυ. μετά;   c ⲅ ⲛ-, ϫⲉ ⲛ-, meaning sim:
1 Pet 1 18 *SB* λυ. dat, Ps 48 7 *SB* λυ. only;   *redeem from* (= ⲉⲃⲟⲗ ⲅ ⲛ-): BMis 88 *S* ⲥ ⲟ ⲧ ⲛ ⲅ ⲛ ⲡ ⲉ ⲛ-
ⲛ ⲟ ⲃ ⲉ, AM 114 *B* sim.

With following adverb.   c ⲉⲃⲟⲗ *B*: Cai The 406

ⲟⲏ ⲉ ⲧ ⲁ ⲕ ⲥ. ⲙ ⲙ ⲟ ⲥ ⲉⲃ.; ⲉⲃ. ⲙ ⲙ ⲁ ⲩ *B, thence*: Mic
4 10 (*A* ⲛⲟ ⲩ ⲅ ⲙ) λυ. ἐκεῖθεν; ⲉⲃ. ⲛⲧⲉⲡ- *B*: Ps 58
2 (*S* ⲉⲃ. ⲅ ⲛ-) λυ. ἐκ; ⲉⲃ. ⲅ ⲁ- *B*: Ps 54 19 (*S* do)
λυ. ἀπό; TEuch 1 652 ⲉ ⲟ ⲣ ⲉ ⲡ ⲥ. ⲉⲃ. ⲅ ⲁ ⲡ ⲓ ⲡ ⲓ ⲣ ⲁ ⲥ ⲙ ⲟ ⲥ;
ⲉⲃ. ⲅ ⲛ-, ϫ ⲉ ⲡ-: Deu 7 8 *SB*, Ps 24 22 *S* (var ⲥ ⲱ ⲧ-)
B, Mic 6 4 *AB* λυ. ἐκ; CaiEuch 632 *B* ⲥ ⲟ ⲧ ⲧ ⲉ ⲛ
ⲉⲃ. ϫ ⲉ ⲛ ⲛ ⲉ ⲛ ⲛ ⲟ ⲃ ⲓ ῥύ. ἀπό; PS 158 *S* ⲁ ⲕ ⲥ ⲟ ⲧ ⲟ ⲩ ⲉⲃ.
ⲅ ⲛ ⲧ ⲁ ⲫ ⲟ ⲥ (Od Solom 22 8 ⟿ reading *?* ⲥ ⲟ ⲧ-
ⲡ ⲟ ⲩ), Aeg 240 *S* ⲛ ⲧ ⲁ ϥ ⲥ ⲟ ⲟ ⲧ ⲕ ⲉⲃ. ⲅ ⲛ ⲙ ⲟ ⲩ, Mus
34 192 *B* ⲉ ⲧ ⲁ ⲩ ⲥ. ⲉⲃ. ϫ ⲉ ⲛ ⲧ ⲡ ⲗ ⲁ ⲛ ⲏ; ⲉⲃ. ⲅ ⲓ ⲧ ⲛ-: Ps
135 24 *S*(*B* ⲉⲃ. ϫ ⲉ ⲛ ⲛ ⲉ ⲛ ϫ ⲓ ϫ) λυ. ἐκ χειρ. (var ἐκ);
BSM 134 *B* c. ⲙ ⲙ ⲟ ⲛ ⲉⲃ. ⲅ ⲓ ⲧ ⲟ ⲧ ⲥ ⲛ ⲧ ⲉ ϫ ⲙ ⲁ ⲗ ⲱ ⲥ ⲓ ⲁ.

—— nn m *SAA²BF*, ⲥⲱⲧ *A, ransom, price*: Ex
21 30 *SB*, *ib B*(*S* ⲟ ⲥ ⲉ), Pro 6 35 *SAB*, Mk 10 45
SB, BM 182 2 *S* ⲙ ⲉ ⲩ ϯ ⲡ ⲉ ⲓ ⲥ. ⲡ ⲗ ⲁ ⲁ ⲩ λύτρον, Cai
Euch 327 *B* gave self ⲛⲥ. ϫ ⲁ ⲣ ⲟ ⲛ ἀντιλ., Nu 18 16
SB, He 9 12 *SBF*, Cl 12 7 *A* ⲥⲱⲧ λύτρωσις, Ro 3
24 *SB* ἀπολ.;   Job 5 3 *B* (prob *l* ⲥ ⲟ ⲃ ϯ as 5 24, *S*
diff) δίαιτα; 4 Kg 12 7 *S* πρᾶσις; *ib* 4 συντίμησις;
PS 271 *S* there is no c. ⲛ ⲧ ⲉ ϥ ⲯ ⲩ ⲭ ⲏ (*cf* 268 ⲧ ⲥ ⲧ ⲟ),
Mani 1 *A²* sent thee ⲁ ⲛ ⲥ. of thy churches, ShLeyd
246 *S* ⲛ ⲉ ⲓ ⲛ ⲟ ϭ ⲛⲥ. ⲛ ⲧ ⲁ ϣ ϣ ⲱ ⲡ ⲉ ⲛ ⲁ ⲛ, AM 115 *B* ⲛⲥ.
of captives, J 13 31 *S* offerings are ⲅ ⲉ ⲛ ⲥ. ⲛ ⲯ ⲩ ⲭ ⲏ.

ⲉ ⲓ ⲣ ⲉ, ⲟ ⲓ ⲛ ⲥ. *SB*, *be, make redemption*: Lu 1 68
SB λύτρωσιν ποιεῖν, Ryl 21 *S* ⲡ ⲉ ⲡ ⲧ ⲁ ϥ ⲉ ⲓ ⲣ ⲉ ⲙ ⲡ ⲥ.
of sinners, BSM 60 *B* Michael's name ⲟ ⲓ ⲛ ⲥ. ⲛ ⲏ ⲓ
= Va 63 27 *B* ⲅ ⲉ ϥ ⲧ ⲟ ⲩ ϫ ⲟ = BMis 419 *S* ⲥ ⲧ ⲟ ⲗ ⲏ.

ϯ c. *S, redeem*: Lev 19 20 (*B* c.) λυτροῦσθαι; ϯ
ⲉ ⲛ ⲥ., ⲙ ⲛ ⲥ. *S, pay for, as ransom*: Aeg 243 ϯ ⲉ ⲛ ⲥ.
ⲛ ⲛ ⲉ ⲕ ⲛ ⲟ ⲃ ⲉ εἰς λύτρωσιν (var ἄφεσιν); ShA 1 256
sim.

ϫⲓ, ϭ ⲓ c. *SB, get ransom*: Nu 35 32 *SB* λύτρον
λαμβάνειν.

ⲣⲉ ϥ ⲥ. *SA²B, redeemer*: Ps 18 15 *SB* λυτρωτής;
PS 64 *S* ⲁ ⲛ ⲉ ⲕ. ϣ ⲓ ⲛ ⲉ ⲛ ⲥ ⲁ ⲧ ϭ ⲟ ⲙ in my soul, Mani
1 *A²* ⲡ ⲣ. ⲡ ⲁ ⲯ ⲩ ⲭ ⲁ ⲅ ⲉ, AM 274 *B* ⲡ ⲓ ⲣ. ⲛ ⲧ ⲁ ⲛ;
ⲣⲉ ϥ ⲥ ⲉ ⲧ ⲯ ⲩ ⲭ ⲏ *S* Gu 86.

ⲥⲧⲟ, ⲥ ⲧ ⲁ   *v* ⲧ ⲥ ⲧ ⲟ.

ⲥⲧⲟ ⲓ *S*, ⲥ ⲧ ⲁ ⲓ *AS͗F*, -ⲁ ⲉ ⲓ *A²*, ⲥ ⲟ ⲟ ⲓ *B*, ⲥ ϯ- *SAF*,
ⲥⲧⲟ ⲓ-, ⲥ ⲧ ⲁ ⲓ-, ⲥ ⲧ ⲉ- *S*, ⲥ ⲟ ⲟ ⲓ-, ⲥ ⲟ ⲓ-, ⲥ ⲟ ⲩ- *B*, ⲥ ⲑ ⲉ- *O*
nn m, **I** *smell*: Lev 26 31 *SB*, Is 34 3 *SBF*, Jo 12
3 *SA²B*, 2 Cor 2 14 *SB* ὀσμή, Hos 14 7 *SAB* ὀσφρα-
σία; K 332 *B* ﺷﻢّ ; ShC 73 136 *S* c. of foul
water, Pcod 17 *S* ⲛⲥ. of fasting in your mouth,
Va 58 193 *B* of wine, PGM 1 140 *O* ⲥ ⲑ ⲉ ⲛ ⲉ ⲡ ⲓ ⲱ
(ⲉ ⲃ ⲓ ⲱ), SHel 47 *S* of fire (as Dan 3 94), Miss 4
814 *S* of death, DeV 2 66 *B* ⲙ ⲡ ⲓ ⲁ ⲣ ⲱ ⲙ ⲁ ⲧ ⲁ;   as
adj *S*: PMéd 175 ⲏ ⲣ ⲡ ⲛ ⲥ., Cai 42573 1 ⲛ ⲉ ⲅ ⲉ ⲥ.
(*l* ⲛ ⲥ.).

ⲥ ϯ ⲛ ⲟ ⲩ ϥ ⲉ *SAF*, ⲥ ⲟ ⲟ ⲓ-, ⲥ ⲟ ⲩ ⲛ. *B, good smell, perfume*: Ge 8 21 *SB*, 2 Cor 2 15 *SB* εὐωδία, Ez 16
19 *SB*, *ib* 20 28 *B*(*S* ⲑ ⲩ ⲥ ⲓ ⲁ) ὀσμή εὐωδίας, Is 3 24

S ⲥⲧⲁⲓ- (var ⲥϯ-) *B* ὀσ. ἡδεῖα ; Gu 42 *S*, Tri 309
S ⲥⲧⲟⲓⲙ., Br 111 *S* ϣⲟⲩ̅ⲏⲛⲉ ⲡⲉⲥϯⲡ., JTS 4 394 *S*
ⲉⲣⲏⲣⲉ ⲡⲥϯⲡ., MIE 2 379 *B* forsook ⲡⲓⲥⲑⲟⲓⲡ. loved
ⲡⲓⲥⲟⲩⲃⲱⲛ, Kr 238 *S* ⲡⲉⲥϯⲡ. of virtue, ShR 2 3
44 *S* ⲉⲡⲧⲏϭ ⲉⲅⲟ ⲡⲥϯⲡ., DeV 2 75 *B* wine sim ;   c.
ⲡⲥϯⲡ. *SB, smell of perfume* : Nu 15 7 *SB*, Eph 5
2 *B*(*S* ⲥϯⲡ.) ὀσ. εὐω., AM 275 *B* εὐω. ; Va 63 2 *B*
c. ⲡⲥⲑⲟⲓⲡ. = BMis 364 *S* ⲥⲧⲉⲡ.

ⲥϯⲃⲁⲛ *SAB* *v* ⲁⲃⲁⲓ *s f.*

ⲥϯⲃⲱⲱⲡ *S*, ⲥⲑⲟⲓⲃ. *B, bad smell* : Z 311 *S* δυσ-
ωδία ; Va 66 308 *B* of putrifaction μίασμα ; *ib* 57
108 *B* ⲙⲁ ⲉⲧⲟⲓ ⲡⲉ. βόρβορος ; AZ 21 151 *S* body
ϣⲉϣ c. ⲉⲃⲟⲗ, Pcod 18 *S* c. of sins.

ⲥϯⲕⲉⲙⲉ, -ⲕⲁⲙⲉ *v* ⲕⲙⲟⲙ(ⲕⲁⲙⲉ), adding P 44
82 *S* ⲥⲧⲓ ⲡⲧⲁⲙⲏ.

ⲥϯϩⲏⲡⲉ *v* ϩⲏⲡⲉ.

II *fragrant plant* : P 44 81 *S* ϩⲩⲥⲥⲟⲡⲟⲡ · ⲡⲉⲥ.
زوⲛ, ريⲕⲁⲛ ; PO 11 330 *B* ⳛⲱ ⲡⲥ., *ib* ⲡⲓⲥ. ⲡⲧⲱⲟⲩ
growing in ⲕⲟⲓ, *phot penes* En Paterson 1930 *S*
ⲡϣⲏⲛ ⲙⲡⲥ., BMis 259 *S* ϩⲉⲡⲕⲗⲁⲍⲟⲥ ⲡⲥ., N & E
39 340 *B* ϩⲁⲡϩⲁⲗ ⲡⲧⲉ ⲡⲓⲥⲑⲟⲓⲛⲟⲩϥⲓ in garden, BKU
1 181 *F* ⲅⲁⲣⲡⲟⲥ ⲡⲥϯⲡ. ; *fragrant substance, in-*
cense : Lu 23 56 *S*(*B* ⲥⲟⳝⲉⲛ) μύρον ; Miss 4 721 *S* c.
= 722 ϣⲟⲩ̅ⲏⲛⲉ, *ib* ⲡⲭⲱⲱⲙⲉ ⲡⲥ , TurM 5 *S* ϣⲟⲗ
ⲡⲗⲁⳝⲁⲡⲟⲡ, ϣ. ⲡⲟⲩⲟⲟⲧⲉ, ϣ. ⲡⲥ., CO 362 *S* c. for
τόπος ; Ryl 243 33 *S* ⲟⲩⲗⲁⲁⲩ ⲡϯ c. ⲉϩⲣⲁⲓ *censer*
or *incense-box* ; ⲥϯ-, ⲥⲑⲟⲓⲛ. : Est C 13 *S* ἥδυσμα ;
Ez 27 17 *B*(*S* ϩⲏⲡⲉ), ZNTW 24 84 *F* μύρον ; Mk 16
1 *B*(*S* do) ἄρωμα ; Ez 16 18 *B*(*S* ϣⲟⲩⲅⲏⲛⲉ) θυμίαμα, Is 43 24 *B*(*S* do) θυσίασμα ; WTh 185 *S*, CO
335 *S* ⲥⲧⲉⲡ., Cl 25 4 *A* phoenix offers self as ⲥϯⲡ.,
BHom 68 *S* anoint with ⲡⲉⲥϯⲡ.

ϩⲁϭⲓⲛ, ⲁϭⲓⲛ ⲡⲥ. *v* ϩⲁϭⲓⲛ.

ⲣ c., ⲟ ⲡⲥ. *SA*² , *be ill smelling, make smell* : Jo
11 39 *SA*²(*B* ⳝⲱⲛⲥ) ὄζειν, Z 311 pus ⲉϥⲟ ⲡⲥ.
σαπρὰ ὀσμή ; BHom 44 mouth ⲣ c. ϩⲁⲧⲡⲏⲥⲧⲓⲁ.

ⲥⲧⲱ *S* nn f, *bank of river* : Jos 3 15 ⲧⲉⲥ. ⲧⲏⲣⲥ
(*B* ⲥⳃⲟⲧⲟⲩ) κρηπίς (in 4 18 untranslated) *alveus* ;
ClPr 54 46 river ⲟⲩⲱⲧⳃ ⲉⲃⲟⲗ ϩⲓⲭⲡⲉⲥ. ὄχθη.   As
place-name Τέστω (PFior 3 340).

ⲥⲁⲧⳃⲉ *S*, ⲥⲉⲧ. *Sf*, ⲥⲁⲑⲙⲓ *B* vb **a** intr, *chew,*
ruminate : Deu 14 7 *SB* μηκυρισμὸν ἀνάγειν ; Sh
Mun 109 *S* cattle ⲉⲧⲥ., Mor 55 72 *Sf* sheep ceaseth
not ⲉϥⲥ. ;   c ⲉⲡϣⲱⲓ *B, ruminate, bring up* : Lev
11 3 (*S* c.) μ. ἀ. ;   c ⲉϩⲣⲁⲓ *S*, meaning same :
Lev 11 6 (*B* ⲓⲛⲓ ⲡⲟⲩⲥ. ⲉⲡϣⲱⲓ) μ. ἀ. ;   c ⲉⳝⲉⲡ-
B, chew upon food : MG 25 39 camel's food ⲡⲧⲉϥ-
ⲓⲛⲓ ⲙⲙⲟⲥ ⲉⲡϣⲱⲓ ⲡⲧⲉⲥ. ⲉⳝⲱⲥ, *ib* 133 mastic which
women c. ⲉⳝⲱϥ,...ⲉⲟⲥ. ⲟⲩⲟϩ ⲉⲑⲟⲩⲟⳝⲟⳝⲉⳃ ⲉⳝⲱϥ,
HL 98 speak not except first ⲡⲧⲁⲥ. ⲉ. ⲡⲓⲥⲁⳝⲓ ;   c
ⲡⲥⲁ-*Sf*, as c. : Mor *l c* ⲉⲕⲥ. ⲡⲥⲁⲡⲕⲱⲙⲁ of God.   **b**
tr *S* : R 1 3 71 camel ϥⲥⲁⲧⳃ(ⲉ) ⲡⲧⲉϥⲧⲣⲟⲫⲏ.

—— ⲛⲛ m *B, cud* : Lev 11 6 above, MG 25 153
ⲡⲓⲥ. in sheep's mouth.

ⲥⲟⲧⳃⲉϥ *S*, ⲥⲁⲧⳃⲉϥ *SSfA*, ⲥⲟⲧϥ (ShA 1 301),
ⲥⲟⲧϥ̄ (P 155 = PSBA 26 176) *S*, ⲥⲟⲑⲛⲉϥ *B* nn m,
tool, weapon (*B* mostly where *S* ⲥⲟⲧⲉ) : Ex 20 25
S(*B* ⳃⲉⲛⲓⲡⲓ) ἐγχειρίδιον ; *ib* 32 4 *S*(*B*=Gk) γραφίς ;
Ps 73 6 *S*(*B* ⲙⲁⳝⲓ) λαξευτήριον ; Is 44 12 *S*(*B* ⳃⲉⲡ.)
σίδηρον, 3 Kg 6 7 *S*(BHom 106) c. ⲙⲡⲉⲛⲓⲡⲉ σκεῦος
σιδ. ; Is 21 17 *B*(*S* ⲡⲓⲧⲉ, *cf* ⲥⲟⲧⲉ) τόξευμα ; ShBM
Or 8810 390 *S* ye (nuns) steal ⲡⲥ. ⲛⲡⲉⲧⲡⲉⲣⲏⲩ even
very clothes, BMis 472 *S* ⲡⲁⲥ. ⲙⲡⲛⲁⲥⲕⲉⲩⲏ ⲧⲏⲣⲟⲩ,
CO 270 *S* c. ⲡⲣ ⲣⲱⳃ, El 74 *A* husbandman's tool,
ShZ 637 *S* ⲡⲥ. ⲡⲉⲗⲟϭⲗⲉϭ = *ib* ⲡⲕⲁ ⲡⲥⲗ. *plane,*
ShA 2 332 *S* scraping teeth with ϩⲉⲡⲥ. ⲙⲡⲉⲛⲓⲡⲉ,
P 44 94 *S* ⲡⲥ. of physician ; ϣⲉ ⲡⲥ. *B, stroke,*
cast of weapon : Ge 21 16 (*S* ⲡⲟⲩ̅ⳝⲉ) βολὴ τόξου ;
MG 25 121 ⲁⲓϣⲁⲡⲙⲁⳝⲕ ⳝⲉⲡⲟⲩⳝⲉ ⲡⲥ.   c. ⲙ-
ⲙⲓϣⲉ *S*, c. ⲡϯ *SB, weapon for fighting* : 1 Kg 8 12
(var ⲥⲁ.), Jth 14 2 σκεῦος πολεμικόν, RE 9 162 ⲥⲁ.
ⲙⲙ. ; Miss 4 604 = C 89 165 *B* c. ⲡϯ, BMOr
6230 44 *S* ⲟⲩⲥⲟⲧⳃ (*sic*) ⲡⲧⲓ [.

· ϩⲓ c. *B, cast dart, shoot arrow* : Jer 27 14 (*S* ⲡⲉⳝ
ⲥⲟⲧⲉ) τοξεύειν ; Nu 24 8 (*S* ⳝⲱⲗⲕ, ⲥⲱⲙⲧ), Ps 63 5
(*S* ⲡ. c.) κατατ. ; Is 37 33 (*S* do) βέλος βάλλειν ;
C 43 39 ⲁϥϩⲓ c. ⲉⲣⲟϥ ; ϩⲓ c. ⲉⲃⲟⲗ : C 86 357
ⲉϥϩⲓ c. ⲉⳃ. ⳝⲉⲡⲡⲓⲁⲡⲣ, MIE 2 396 ϣⲁⲡϩⲓⲟⲅⲓ ⲉⳃ.
ⲡⲟⲩⲥ. = BAp 122 *S* ⲡⲡⲟⲩ̅ⳝⲉ ⲡⲟⲩⲥ. ;   ⲙⲁ ⲡϩⲓ
c., *place for shooting arrows* : Jer 28 27 βελόστασις ; ⲣⲉϥϩⲓ c., *shooter of arrows* : Ge 21 20 (*S*
ⲣϥⲧⲕ ⲥⲟⲧⲉ), Am 2 15 (*S* ⲣⲉϥⲛ c., *A* ⲣⲉϥϯⲕ c.).

ⳝⲁ c. *B* : ⲙⲁ ⲡⳝⲁ c. Ez 4 2 (*S* ⲙⲁ ⲡⲛ. ⲥⲟⲧⲉ)
βελόστ., ⲙⲟⲕⲓ ⲡⳝⲁ c. Is 49 2 (*S* ϩⲡⲁⲁⲩ ⲡⲕⲁ c.)
φαρέτρα.

ⲥⲧⲉⳃⲁⲉⲓϩ *S*, ⲥⲉⳃⲁⲓϩ, ⲥⲟⳃⲁⲓ *B*, pl ⲥⲉⳃⲁⲓⲟⲩ *B*
nn only as pl, *tool, utensil* : Ex 38 30 (39 10) *B* -ⲁⲓ
ἐργαλεῖον ; Jer 26 3 *B* -ⲁⲓϩ, ἀσπίς ; *ib* 31 7 *B* -ⲁⲓⲟⲩ
ὀχύρωμα *munitio* ; C 86 271 *B* ⲡⲓⲥⲟⳃⲁⲓ ⲡⲧⲉ ⲡⲓⳃⲁ-
ⳅⲁⲡⲓⲥⲧⲏⲣⲓⲟⲡ, *ib* -ⲁⲓⲟⲩ, MG 25 310 *B* silence &
tribulation ϩⲁⲡⲥⲟⳃⲁⲓ of our race (*S* BIF 13 117
diff), J 38 23 *S* ϩⲏⲡⲉ. (*sic* MS) ⲡⳃⲉⲥⲏⲛⲧ, Ep 264 *S* ;
J 113 6 *S* ⲧⳃⲁⲓⲉⲓϩ prob same, *cf* ? also PMich '24
ⲥⲟⲧⲁϩϥ (*v* ⳃⲁⲁⲣⲉ).   *Cf dem sṭbḥ* (var Ryl Dem 3
258 *sbt* ⲥⲟⳃⲧⲉ nn *q v*).

ⲥⲱⲧⲙ *SA*²*F*, -ⲙⲉ *AA*², -ⲉⲙ *BF*, ⲥⲉⲧⲙ-, ⲥⲟⲧⲙ⸗
S, ⲥⲁⲧⲙ⸗ *SaAA*², ⲥⲟⲑⲙ⸗ *B*, ⲥⲱⲧⲙ⸗ *F* (nn He 5) vb
I intr, *hear* : Is 30 15 *SBF*, *ib* 32 4 *B*(*SF* ⳝⲓ ⲥⲙⲏ),
Jo 5 30 *SA*²*B* ἀκούειν ; PS 72 *S* c. ⲧⲁⳝⲟⲟⲥ, BSM
65 *B* c. ⲡⲧⲁ(ⲧⲁ)ⲙⲱⲧⲉⲡ, J 95 21 *S* ⲉϥⲥ. ϩⲡⲣⲱⳃ ⲡⲓⲙ ;
with ⳝⲉ- : Ps 84 8 *SB*, Ap 2 7 *SB* ἀκ. ; AM 48 *B*
ⲙⲡⲉⲕⲥ. ⳝⲉⲁⲡⲟ̅ⲥ̅ ⳝⲟⲥ.   **II** tr : Ge 29 13 *S* (var
& *B* ⲉ-), Ps 77 3 *SB*, Mt 2 18 *B*(*S* ⲉ-), Cl 23 3 *A*
ⲁⲡⲥⲁⲧⲙⲟⲩ, AP 16 *A*² ἀκ., Job 11 2 *S* ⲥⲉⲧⲙ- (*B*

e-) ἀντακ., 3 Kg 8 30 B εἰσακ.; BG 101 S πεϥ-
εοου...ⲙⲡⲟⲩⲥⲟⲧⲙⲉϥ, J 122 12 S ⲁⲡⲥⲉⲧⲙ ⲡⲁⲓ,
PLond 5 132 S invited me ⲉⲧⲣⲁⲥ. ⲡⲉⲩⲣⲱⲃ (judi-
cially), J 13 68 Sᵃ ⲁⲅⲁⲱϫ ⲁⲣⲟⲓ ⲁⲓⲥⲁⲧⲙⲉⲥ, BSM
125 B ⲫⲏ ⲉⲧⲥ. ⲡⲟⲩⲟⲡ ⲡⲓⲃⲉⲡ.

With following preposition.

—— e- SAA²BF, *listen to*: Ex 18 19 S(B ⲡⲥⲁ-),
Pro 1 33 SA (var Cl & B do), Is 32 9 SBF, Jo 4 42
SA²(B om e-), Aeg 211 S c. επεγραφη ἀκ. gen,
Ps 33 17 SA(Cl)B, He 5 7 SBF εἰσακ., Ps 16 6
SBF ἐπακ.; ib 85 6 S(B ϫⲁ ⲙⲁⲱϫ) ἐνωτίζειν;
PS 29 S c. ⲉⲣⲟⲓ ⲧⲁϫⲡⲟⲩⲕ, TU 43 21 A c. ⲁⲡⲟⲩ-
ⲣⲉⲡ, BMis 112 S babel of tongues that none might
c. ⲉⲧⲁⲥⲡⲉ ⲙⲡⲉⲧϭⲓⲧⲟⲩⲱϭ, TstAb 245 B ⲉⲧⲁϥ-
ⲥⲡⲁⲓ, AM 5 B ⲙⲡⲓⲥ. ⲉⲟⲩⲟⲡ (sc perfume) like
it; c e-...e-: Job 15 17 S(B diff) ἀκ. gen acc.

—— ⲉⲧⲃⲉ- SB, *hear concerning*: MG 25 244 B
ⲁⲓⲥ. ⲉⲑⲃⲏⲧⲕ τὰ περί; PS 40 S c. ⲉ.ⲡϣⲁϫⲉ ⲉⲡⲧⲁ-
ⲩϣⲱⲡⲉ ⲙⲙⲟⲓ.

—— ⲉⲧⲛ- S, *at hand of, from*: Z 234 ⲡⲧⲉⲣⲟⲩⲥ.
ⲉⲧⲟⲟⲧϥ (? for ⲡⲧ.) ⲙⲡϩⲁⲗⲏⲧ.

—— ⲛ- dat, *SB listen to, obey*: Tob 6 16 S ἀκ.
gen, Deu 1 43 S(B ⲡⲥⲁ-) εἰσακ. gen, Ge 30 33 SB
ἐπακ. dat, Pro 8 1 SA(B do) ὑπακ. dat; Ja 3 3 SB
πείθεσθαι acc; Br 45 S ⲁϫⲓⲥ ⲉⲣⲟⲡ ⲛⲧⲁⲣⲡⲥ. ⲡⲁⲕ,
BSM 9 B heavenly hosts c. ⲡⲁϥ.

—— ⲡⲥⲁ- SAA²BF, *meaning same*: Ex 18 24
SB, Is 36 16 SBF ἀκ. gen, Nu 14 22 S(var e-)B
εἰσακ. gen, Mt 18 17 SB neg παρακ., Pro 2 2 SA(B
e-), Ro 10 16 SB ὑπακ.; Pro 26 25 SA πειθ., Ac
5 29 SB πειθαρχεῖν; Lu 2 51 S(B ϭⲡⲟ ⲡⲭⲱϥ) ὑπο-
τάσσεσθαι dat; PS 48 S ⲙⲡϥⲥ. ⲡⲥⲁⲧⲉⲕⲕⲉⲗⲉⲩⲥⲓⲥ,
LAp 513 F ⲧ[ⲡ]ⲉⲥ. ⲉⲥⲱⲕ, AP 27 A² ⲁ]ⲡⲟⲩⲥ. ⲡⲥⲱϥ.

—— ⲡⲧⲡ- SAB, *hear at hand of, from*: Jo 8 26
SA²B ἀκ. παρά, Ac 1 4 SB ἀκ. gen; AM 261 B
ⲁⲩⲥⲟⲟⲙⲟⲩ ⲡⲧⲟⲧⲟⲩ.

—— ϩⲁ- S, *hear about* (?): Ps 91 11 (B ϩⲉⲡ-)
εἰσακ. ἐν.

—— ϩⲛ-, ϩⲉⲡ- SB, *hear with* ears: Ps 43 1 SB,
Jer 33 11 SB ἀκ. ἐν.

—— ϩⲓⲧⲛ- SA²B, *hear through, from*: Jo 8 40
SA²(B ⲡⲧⲉⲛ-) ἀκ. παρά; AM 270 B ⲫⲣⲏⲧ ⲉⲧⲁⲓⲥ. ϩ.
ⲡⲁⲓⲧⲣⲓⲃⲟⲩⲅⲟⲥ, PLond 4 436 S I sign προς θε ⲡⲧ-
ⲁⲓⲥⲱⲧⲙ (sic) ϩ. ⲡⲉⲧⲥⲙⲓⲡⲉ ⲙⲙⲟⲥ (sc deed); ⲉⲃⲟⲗ
ϩ.: Jer 29 15 SB ἀκ. παρά; AP 40 A² ⲉⲡⲁⲥ. ⲁⲃ.
ϩⲓⲧⲟⲟⲧⲕ.

—— ⲛⲛ ⲙ SA²BF, *hearing, obedience*: 1 Kg 15
22 S, Jer 10 22 B ἀκοή, Ro 1 5 SB, 2 Kg 22 36 S
ⲡⲉⲕⲥ. ⲉⲣⲟⲓ, He 5 8 F ⲡⲥⲱⲧⲙϥ (S c., B ⲙⲉⲧⲣⲉϥⲥ.)
ὑπακ.; Mor 40 46 S ⲡⲥ. ⲛⲡⲙⲁⲁϫⲉ = MG 25 273
B ⲡⲭⲓⲥ., Mani 2 A² ⲡⲧⲱⲣⲙⲉ ⲙⲡⲡⲥⲱⲧⲙⲉ, AM
252 B ϩⲱⲥ ⲉϥϫⲱⲕ ⲡⲟⲩⲥ. ⲉⲃⲟⲗ, MG 25 22 B ⲫⲁ-
ⲡⲓⲥ. = ib ⲟⲩⲣⲉϥⲥ., Baouit 1 108 S ⲓⲁⲕⲱⲃ ⲯⲁϩ ⲡⲉⲥ.

ⲁⲧⲥ. SABF, *unhearing, disobedient*: Jer 6 28 B
ἀνήκοος; ShMun 100 S ⲡⲉⲓⲁ. ⲉⲧⲙⲙⲁⲩ, Mor 22
127 S ⲁ. ⲡⲓⲙ shall go to perdition = BSM 116
B; as adj: Nu 17 10 S(B as nn), Jer 5 23 SB
ἀνή.; Is 30 9 SF(B diff) ἀπειθής, Ro 10 21 B(S
ⲁⲧⲡⲁϩⲧⲉ) ἀπειθεῖν; ⲙⲡⲧ-, ⲙⲉⲧⲁⲧⲥ. SBF, *disobedience*: Ro 5 19 SB, He 2 2 SBF, CaiEuch 458
B ⲧⲙ. ⲡⲥⲁⲧⲉⲕⲉⲡⲧⲟⲗⲏ παρακοή; Dan 9 7 SB
ἀθεσία; ⲣ ⲁⲧⲥ. SABF, *be disobedient*: Is 48 8
B(S = Gk) ἀθετεῖν; Ac 19 9 SB, Cl 58 1 A ἀπει.;
BM 915 17 B ⲟⲓ ⲡⲁ. ἄτακτος; PS 102 S ⲡⲥⲉⲧⲙⲣ
ⲁ.; + ⲡⲥⲁ-: Pro 1 25 SA(B ⲧ ϩⲏⲧ e-), Jer 13 25
B(S ⲁⲧⲡⲁϩⲧⲉ), Ro 11 30 B(SF do) ἀπει. dat; Jer
3 20 B(S = Gk) ἀθ. εἰς; Va 57 8 B ⲟⲓ ⲡⲁ. ⲡⲥⲱⲟⲩ
παρακούειν; Pcod 8 S ⲉⲁϩⲣ ⲁ. ⲡⲥⲁⲡⲉϥϫⲟⲉⲓⲥ.

ⲙⲁⲓⲥ. S, *loving to hear, to obey*: P 131⁶ 33 ⲡⲉⲯⲩⲭⲏ ⲙⲙ.

ⲙⲁ ⲡⲥ. S, *place of hearing, music room*: Si 35 4
ἀκρόαμα.

ⲣⲉϥⲥ. SB, *hearer*: Is 3 3 S(B ⲣⲉϥϭⲓ ⲥⲙⲏ), Ro
2 13 B(S c. rel) ἀκροατής; PO 14 355 B ⲣⲱⲥ ⲣ.
ⲡⲥⲁⲡⲉϥⲓⲱⲧ; as adj: BMis 505 S ⲡⲡⲉ ⲡⲣ., C
43 208 B ⲡⲓⲙⲁϣϫ ⲡⲣ.; ⲙⲡⲧ-, ⲙⲉⲧⲣ. SB,
obedience: Ro 16 19 B(S ⲙⲡⲧⲥⲧⲙⲏⲧ) ὑπακοή; C 89
18 B ⲧⲁⲓⲡⲓϣⲧ ⲙⲙ. = Mun 56 S do; ⲟⲓ ⲡⲣ.
B, *be obedient*: 2 Cor 2 9 (S ⲥⲧⲙⲏⲧ) ὑπήκοος εἶναι.
V also ⲥⲧⲙⲏⲧ.

ϭⲓⲡ-, ϫⲓⲡⲥ. SB, *hearing, report*: Ex 23 1 B(S
ϣⲁϫⲉ) ἀκοή; HL 81 B ⲧϫ. ⲉⲧⲁⲣⲉⲧⲓ φήμη; R 1
2 54 S shun ⲡⲓϭ. ⲉⲧϩⲟⲟⲩⲧ, ib 46 S teach children
ⲧϭ. ϩⲡⲟⲩⲅⲕⲁⲣⲱϥ.

ⲥⲧⲙⲏⲧ¹, ⲥⲉⲧⲙ.² S, ⲥⲙⲏⲧ³ SA for ⲥⲉⲧⲙ ⲣⲏⲧ (cf
ⲡⲁⲛⲧ, ⲟⲩⲁϩⲣⲏⲧ), *obedient as nn*: 2 Cor 2 9¹ (B
ⲣⲉϥⲥ.) ὑπήκοος, Z 295 ⲟⲩⲥ.¹ ⲡⲉ = MG 25 22 B
ⲣⲉϥⲥ. ὑπακοὴν ἔχειν; ShC 42 119 ⲉⲁⲩϣⲱⲡⲉ ⲡⲥ.¹,
Mus 40 254 ⲡⲥ.³ ⲡⲧⲉ ⲧⲙⲉ ⲙⲡⲡⲉ̄; as adj: Pro
21 28 S¹ (var³) A, Phil 2 8¹ (B do) ὑπήκοος, Z 318
ⲟⲩⲡⲧⲁⲓⲥⲩ ⲡⲥ.¹ = MG 25 234 B ⲉⲧⲥ. ⲡⲥⲱⲓ ὑπακού.
dat; Mor 17 112 a Jew ⲡⲥ.³ σώφρων; ⲁⲧⲥ.,
disobedient: P 44 79 ⲁⲡⲓⲕⲟⲟⲥ · ⲟⲩⲁⲧⲥ.³; ⲙⲡⲧⲥ.,
obedience: Ro 5 19¹ (var³, B ⲙⲉⲧⲣⲉϥⲥ.), Cl 9 3 A
ⲙⲡⲧⲥⲙⲏⲧ, MG 17 318 ⲡⲡⲁ̄ ⲙⲙ.³ = C 89 66 B
ⲙⲉⲧⲣⲉϥⲥ. ὑπακοή; ShC 73 127 ϩⲩⲡⲟⲧⲁⲥⲡ ϩⲓⲙ.¹,
Mor 34 64 ⲧⲙ.³ = 43 175 ⲧⲙ.¹, Ryl 62 3 ⲧⲙ.² ⲉ-
ϩⲟⲩⲛ ⲉⲡⲉⲭ̄ⲥ̄; ⲣ ⲥ., *be obedient*: Tit 3 1¹ (B ⲣⲉϥⲧ
ⲙⲁⲧ) πειθαρχεῖν, Aeg 245 ⲟ ⲡⲥ.² εὐπειθής.

In name (?) Τσαμῆτ (Preisigke).

ⲥⲧⲏⲙ SB DM, ⲥⲑⲏⲙ B nn m, στίμι (PGM 1
108), στείμι (PLond 1 67), στίβι (Jer), ⲥⲧⲓⲙⲉⲟⲥ
(PMéd), ⲥⲟⲉⲙⲉⲟⲥ (P 43), *stibium, antimony, kohl*:
Jer 4 30 SB σ., Ez 23 40 S ⲡⲟⲩⲥ. B ⲡⲉⲥ. (2 sg f),
Mor 17 12 S στιβίζειν: P 44 88 S ⲡⲉⲥ. كحل, K 204

B пιст. اسل *'S*, DM V 18 8 c. пκвт (*cf σ. κοπτικόν*
PGM, PLond), P 43 248 cⲟ.· κεπτικος اصبهاني *'S*
(*v* Dozy 2 446); ShA 1 201 *S* your mothers ϯ…
пεтс. επεγвαλ, R 1 2 39 *S* c. made of пκερмεс
ппрнвс *lamp soot*, CA 89 *S* космι ммос…ⲣноγс.,
AZ 23 114 *S* pound all together пϭε мпс., TurM
9 *S* sim, Ryl 243 *S* паλмаλаϥ (الالف) пaоγεп εc.
wrappers of c. *colour* (dark blue ? purple ? Dozy 2
447 كلⳋ), *ib* 244 *S* ⲣвос папаⲣ пс. sim, BM 1103
S пιвас εc.   *V* BerlAkadAbh '14 5 13.

сТнмоу *S* nn, meaning unknown, in list of
vegetables : Ryl 291 7½ litres пс.

сωтп *SAA²BF*(сωпт), сετп- *SB*, сω. *A*(Pro 8
10), са. *A²F*(сапт-), сотп⳽ *SB*, са. *AA²F*(сапт⳽),
сотп† *SB*, са.† *AF*(сапт†), сω.† *B*(often) vb **I** intr,
choose.   c ethic dat : Ps 83 10 *B*, 2 Cor 9 7 *B*(*S*
тωщ); Mus 42 219 *S* прωмε επтаус. паγ *made
their choice* ;   c ⲣп-, *choose from* : Z 577 *S* not
to seek to c. ⲣппроιτε.
II tr : Ps 64 4 *SB*, Mk 13 20 *SBF*(-пт), Jo 6 70
SA²BF (PMich 3521) ἐκλέγειν ; 2 Thes 2 13 *SB*,
Phil 1 22 *SBF* αἱρεῖσθαι, Deu 7 6 *SB* προαιρ., Ez
20 5 *SB* αἱρετίζειν ; Is 66 4 *SB* ἐκδέχεσθαι ; PS 10
S аιсεтптнутп ϫιппщорп, Mani 2 *A²* псεсатпϥ
аⲣоγн аппаⲅτε, DeV 2 42 *B* every one εтεϥпасотп-
поγ, J 39 21 *S* апс. ⲣεппоϭ пщнрε as judges, Kr
164 *F* εапсапт апа ιоγλι ;   c ethic dat : 2 Kg
24 12 *S*, Lu 10 42 *SB* ἐκλ. ; Aeg 291 *S* пεптаγ-
сотпε паγ εερ паι προаιρ. ; 2 Mac 6 19 *A*(*sic l*)
ἀναδέχεσθαι ; EW 150 *B* аϥсотпε паϥ εорεϥщωпι
&c ἀντὶ πάντων ποιεῖσθαι ; ShC 73 33 *S* εγсотпε
паγ εщп ⲣιсε, C 43 128 *B* c. пак поγаι ;   c
ⲣп-, *choose from* : Mor 27 41 *F* аϥсатпоγ ⲣмпкос-
мос ; εвоλ ⲣп- : Jo 15 19 *SA²B* ἐκλ. ἐκ ; Aeg 248
S εаγсотпϥ εв. ⲣмпмннщε :   c εвоλ оγтε-,
meaning same : BMis 410 *S* аϥсотпоγ εв. оγтεп-
космос = BSM 55 *B* εв. ⳥εп-.
—— εвоλ *B*, meaning as c. : Ex 18 25 аϥс. εв.
…εв. ⳥εппιλαос ἐπιλέγειν ἀπό.

Qual, **a** *chosen, exquisite* : Ez 27 20 *SB*, Ap 17
14 *S*(*B* c. nn) ἐκλεκτός, Lu 9 35 *SB* ἐκλεγ., Jos 17
16 *S* ἐπίλεκτος ; Zech 11 13 *S*(сω. *l* со.) *AB* δόκιμος, Ps 11 6 *SB* δοκίμιον, Ge 43 23 *S*(*B* as Gk)
εὐδοκιμεῖν ; AM 282 *B* ⲣаιсγпⳝопιоп εγс. ἐξαί-
ρετος ; Pro 10 24 *SA*(*B* щнп) δεκτός ; Ro 2 18 *B*
(*S* р поϭре) διαφέρειν ; Am 5 11 *B* ἐπιθυμητός ;
PSBA 10 402 *B* оγωιλι εϥс. ἐπίσημος ; Mk 14 3
S(*B* = Gk) πιστικός ; 2 Kg 1 26 *S*(*B* пεсε-) ὡραιοῦσθαι ; Is 3 25 *B*(*S* пεсε-) κάλλιστος ; PS 195 *S*
поγоειп εтс. (*cf ib* s.m ετсотⳋ), ShA 1 188 *S* resurrection εтс., ShC 73 72 *S* пεтс. opp пετϭовв,
ib 42 128 *S* food εтс. opp εⲑооγ, C 86 204 *B* is

it Elijah εтс. or Poseidon ? BSM 27 *B* нⲣп εϥс.
= Va 63 3 *B* папεϥ = BMis 366 *S* пащωϥ ;   **b**
choicer, better : Si 18 15 *S*, Phil 1 23 *SBF*, He 7
19 *SBF* κρείσσων ; Jer 42 15 *B*(*S* апаι ?) βελτίων ;
BHom 52 *S* cc. паι ετмεıрε (var R 2 2 34 папоγс)
αἱρετός ; *ib* 60 *S* кс. ⲣоγо εмпкарпаⳝε *hadst
done far better not to seize*, DeV 2 50 *B* мн пεпрωв
c. пε *were it better* not to relieve them ?, RE 9 158
S your health εтс. пап пара ⲣωв пιм ;   c ε-,
better than : Is 56 5 *B*(*S* папоγⳋ) кр. gen, 3 Kg 19
4 *S* кр. ὑπέρ ; Va 57 10 *B* πλεῖον (Mt 6 25) ; Is 17
3 *S*(*B* εⲣотε) βελ. gen ; Mk 12 33 *S*(*B* оι ппιщϯ
ε-) περισσότερος gen ; Si 36 26 *S* καλ. gen ; R 1 4
56 *S* ἀμείνων gen ; Ps 18 10 *S*(*B* εⲣ.) ἐπιθυμητός
ὑπέρ ; ShMun 105 *S* ravens c. ап εⲣωтп, PS 5 *S*
εⲣεоγа c. εоγа, SHel 33 *S* wizard εϥс. εрок ;   c
пⲣоγо ε-, εⲣоγε- *SAF*, meaning same : Ps 62 3 *S*
(*B* εⲣотε) кр. ὑπέρ, Pro 3 14 *SA*(*B* папεⳋ) кр. ἤ,
He 1 4 *SF*(*B* do) кр. gen ; Si 30 15 *S* βελ. gen ;
Tob 3 6 *S* λυσιτελεῖν ἤ ; ShA 1 59 *S* псс. ап ετмт-
трεпϯ … пⲣ. ετрεпϫı, Mun 44 *S* shall find no
punishment εcc.…εⲣ. тасаϥ ;   c εⲣотε *B*, meaning same : Pro 8 10 (*S* εⲣ., *A* пⲣ. а-) ἀνταναιρ. gen ;
Lam 4 7 *pulchrior* abl ; BSM 128 garment εcc. εⲣ.
ⲑапιоγⲣωоγ.

—— nn m *SAA²BF*, f сотп *B* (adj), *chosen,
elect* person or thing : Ps 104 6 *SB*, Lam 5 13
SBF, Hag 2 7 *SA* pl, Mt 22 14 *B*(*S* c. rel), Cl 46
4 *A* пс. of God ἐκλεκ., Ez 23 7 *SB* ἐπίλεκ. ; Nu
26 9 *B*(*S* поϭ) ἐπίκλητος ; Ro 16 10 *SB* δόκιμος ;
Job 1 1 *SA* (Cl, *B* атарıκı) ἄμεμπτος ; He 7 4 *B*
(*SF* щωλ) ἀκροθίνιον ; Bor 294 121 *S* пειποϭ пс.
Peter, Mani 1 *A²* пεрεпс. тнроγ рıмε, EW 112
B governor to martyr амоγ пас., Ryl 12 *S* пс.
ппапрстоλос *the choosing* (Lu 6 13) ;   as adj, **a**
before nn : Jer 26 15 *B*(*S* rel), Lu 23 35 *S*(*B* nn)
ἐκλ., Ex 15 4 *B* ἐπιλ. ; Si 2 5 *S*(*B* nn) δεκτός ; Va
57 6 *B* оγс. псннп ἄριστος ; Mor 18 194 *S* оγс.
поγннв πρῶτος ; ROC 9 327 *B* ye are ⲣапс. м-
матос.   **b** after nn : Jud 20 34 *S* ἐκλ., Si 24
16 -тϥ *S*, Ac 9 15 *SB*, Cl 29 1 *A* ἐκλογῆς ; 1 Chr
29 4 *B* δόκ. ; Sa 10 15 *S* ἄμεμ. ; R 1 3 49 *S* пεϥ-
ⲣарма пс., WS 121 *S* впнε пс.   сотпı *B* f :
1 Pet 5 13 (varr сωтпı, с.†, *S* = Gk), 2 Jo 1 (var
сωтп, *S* do) ἐκλεκτή.

мпт-, мεтс. *SA²BF*, *election, choice, superiority* :
Ro 11 5 *SB*, 1 Thes 1 4 *SBF*(-сωпт) ἐκλογή ; 1
Pet 1 7 *SB* δοκίμιον ; Ps 77 61 *S*(*B* апаı) καλλονή ;
BHom 41 *S* be changed εγм. βελτιοῦν ; ShWess
9 156 *S* good deeds done ⲣпεтпм., Mani 1 *A²*
тапархн птм., P 131¹ 75 *S* clergy addressed as
тεтпм., ROC 23 271 *B* sim, TEuch 1 22 *B* confirm пıϫıпⲑωрεм пте тεϥм. نيⳋ.

ⲝⲓⲛⲉ. *B*, meaning sim : Dan 11 35 ⲡⲝ. τὸ ἐκλέξασθαι ; TEuch 1 37 var ⲙⲉⲧⲥ. as above.

Cf ⲥⲡⲉⲓ.

ⲥⲁⲧⲉⲣ *F* nn m, meaning uncertain : BKU 1 26 (8116 b) in recipe ⲡⲉⲕⲏⲥ ⲉⲡⲉⲥⲁⲥⲁⲧⲉⲣ ⲡⲟⲩⲛⲁⲙ = ? الصدغ *temple.*

ⲥⲱⲧⲣ *S*, -ⲧⲣⲉ *A*, -ⲧⲉⲣ, -ⲧⲏⲣ *B*, ⲥⲟⲧⲣ† *S*, -ⲧⲉⲣ†, ⲥⲟⲧⲏⲣ†, ⲥⲁⲧⲏⲣ† *B* vb **I** intr, *be turned, twisted* : BHom 137 *S* eyes ⲉⲡⲧⲁⲩⲥ. ϩⲁⲡⲉⲥⲧⲱⲧ διαστρέφεσθαι ; ShC 42 215 *S* in new house rooms ⲁⲩϭⲱⲟⲩϭ ⲏ ⲥⲱⲧⲣ, P 131³ 84 *S* eyes ⲥ.† ⲛⲥⲁⲥⲁ ⲛⲓⲙ = Va 61 95 *B* = Mor 25 12 *S* ϭⲱϣⲧ, TillOster 11 *A* eyes]ⲛⲁⲥ. ϩⲁⲡϩⲧⲁⲣⲧⲣⲉ ⲙⲡⲉⲓ ⲁⲃⲁⲗ, Mus 35 35 *B* in darkness eyes ⲥ.† ϫⲉⲛⲡⲟⲩϫⲓⲛⲛⲁⲩ, BSM 131 *B* eye c. & almost protrudes from head = Mor 22 140 *S* ϭⲱⲟⲩϭ, BMar 78 *S* when dying eyes cease ⲉⲅⲕⲱⲧⲉ ⲛⲥⲉⲥ., BHom 123 *S* sim ⲁⲩⲥ. ⲁⲩϣⲧⲁⲙ, Mor 40 46 *S* face ⲥ.† ϩⲓⲡⲁϩⲟⲩ ⲙⲙⲟϥ = MG 25 272 *B*. **II** tr *B* (once) : C 43 136 devil ⲁϥⲥ. ⲙⲡⲉⲥⲥⲱⲙⲁ ⲧⲏⲣϥ = Mor 48 72 *S* ⲁϥⲧⲣⲉⲥⲥⲓϭⲉ ϩⲙⲡⲉⲥⲥ. As nn : K 159 *B* ⲥⲁ.† لَيّ *curvature* (?), *cf ib* ⲭⲱⲟⲩⲭ ⸍J.

ⲥⲁⲧⲉⲉⲣⲉ *S*, ⲥⲧⲁⲧ. *A*², ⲥⲁⲑⲉⲣⲓ *B* nn f, στατήρ *stater*, coin & weight : Lu 15 8 *S(cit* Sh BMOr 8810 465, *SB* ϭⲓⲥⲕⲓⲧⲉ) δραχμή ; Ge 20 14 *S(B* ⲕ.), Ex 21 32 *S(B* do), Lev 27 3 *S(B* ⲥ. ⲉⲥⲕⲏϫ) δίδραχμον ; Mt 17 27 *SB* ⲥⲧ. ; Jo 12 5 *SA*²*B*, Ap 6 6 *SB* δηνάριον ; P 44 58 *S* ⲡⲟⲗⲓⲥⲙⲁ · ϩⲟⲗⲟⲕⲟⲧⲁⲓⲡⲟⲥ· ⲥ. دينار ; ShHT *H* 4 *S* ⲧϫⲁ ⲛⲥ. ⲏ ⲛϭⲓⲛϣⲱⲣ, C 86 322 *B* ⲗⲟⲅⲕⲟⲩϫⲓ ⲛⲡⲟⲩϫ, ⲥ. ⲡϩⲁⲧ, Mor 16 49 *S* ⲟⲩⲥ. ⲡϩⲁⲧ = BMis 206 *S* ⲟⲩⲧⲣⲁⲭⲙⲏ ⲡⲣⲟⲙⲡⲧ, PS 292 *S* ϯⲥ. ⲉⲥⲟ ⲡϩⲁⲧ ϩⲓⲣⲟⲙⲡⲧ, P 131² 150 *S* ⲟⲩⲁϣⲏ ⲛⲥ. ⲛⲡⲟⲩϫ ; as weight : Lev 5 15 *S* ⲉⲧⲉⲧⲥ. ⲧⲉ gloss on ⲥⲓⲕⲗⲟⲥ (*B* = Gk), 4 Kg 15 20 *S* same gloss σίκλος, Ez 45 12 *B* στάθμιον *siclus*, 1 Kg 9 8 *S* ⲟⲩϭⲓⲥⲕⲓⲧⲉ ⲛⲥ. τέταρτον σίκλου ; Cat 48 *B* ϯⲥ. is half ounce (on Mt 17 27), Z 630 *S* ⲙⲟⲅⲗϫ ⲥ. ⲁ̄, Mich 136 1 *S* ϥⲧⲟ ⲛⲥ. ⲛⲣⲟⲥⲙ. *V* Gött N '16 115 n.

ⲥⲧⲣⲧⲣ *S* (nn only) *A*², -ⲧⲣⲉ *A*, ⲥⲑⲉⲣⲧⲉⲣ *B*, ⲥⲧⲉⲣⲧⲉⲣ *F*ᵇ (nn), vb intr, *tremble* : Ge 4 12 *B*, Is 66 2 *B* (*S* ⲥⲧⲱⲧ) τρέμων εἶναι, Ps 76 19 *B(S* do), He 12 21 *B(S* do) ἔντρομος γίνεσθαι, εἶναι ; Jer 2 12 *B*(ⲥⲑⲟⲣ. *l* ⲥⲑⲉⲣ. or ? ϣⲑⲟⲣⲧⲉⲣ, *cf* Ez 27 28), Dan 7 15 *B*(*S* ϣⲧⲟⲣⲧⲣ) φρίττειν ; *ib* 5 6 *B* συγκροτεῖν ; C 86 296 *B* ⲡⲓⲧⲱⲟⲩ ⲥ. σαλεύεσθαι = BSG 190 *S* ⲡⲟⲉⲓⲛ ; Ez 18 2 *B(S* ⲡⲟⲩϩⲥ) γομφιάζειν ; *ib* 3 9 *B*(*S* ϣ.) πτοεῖν ; Mal 3 17 *A(B* ⲉⲣ ϩⲟϯ) εὐλαβεῖσθαι ; Mani 2 *A*² at his cry ϣⲁⲩⲥ., C 41 24 *B* ⲉⲧⲁⲡⲁⲥⲱⲙⲁ ⲥ.... ⲟⲩⲟϩ ⲛⲁⲓϣⲉⲣⲧⲱⲣ, DeV 1 42 *B* ⲁϥⲥ. ⲉϥⲛⲁⲩ, Tst Ab 167 *B* ⲉⲣⲉⲡⲁϩⲏⲧ ⲥ. ⲉⲣⲟⲓ ; C 86 358 *B* ⲉϥⲥ. ⲛⲛⲓⲙⲁⲧⲟⲓ (prob *l* ⲓϣⲉⲣ.). nn m, *trembling* : Ex 15 15 *BF*ᵇ(CMSS 14), Is 33 14 *B(SF* ⲥⲧⲱⲧ), Hab

3 16 *B(A* ⲭⲁⲗⲉⲥ), Cl 12 5 *A* τρόμος ; Jer 5 30 *B* φρικτός ; *ib* 30 2 *B* θόρυβος ; Ez 30 4 *B(S* ϣⲧⲟⲣⲧⲣ) ταραχή ; Lev 26 16 *B(S* ϩⲓⲟⲅⲉ ⲛⲥⲁ-) σφακελίζειν ⲓⲛⲉ ; Mt 13 42 *B(S* ϭⲁϩϭ, *F* ϣⲕⲏⲕⲉⲗ) βρυγμός ; Ryl 94 103 *S* c. of bodies & ⲡⲟⲉⲓⲛ of limbs through cold, BMar 99 *S* ⲡⲉⲥ. ⲙⲡϭⲁⲣϭⲉϩ of teeth, MIE 2 383 *B* ⲥ. ϫⲉⲛⲡⲁⲕⲁⲥ = BAp 107 *S* ⲡⲁⲣϣⲗϭ, C 86 286 *B* ⲥ. (var ϣⲑⲟⲣ.) = BSG 184 *S* ϣⲧⲟⲣ., DeV 1 77 *B* terrible oaths ⲟⲩⲥ. ⲡⲉ ⲡⲥⲱⲧⲉⲙ ⲉⲣⲱⲟⲩ = P 129¹⁴ 122 *S* ⲟⲩϭⲟⲧⲉ. Confused sometimes with ϣⲧⲟⲣⲧⲣ. *Cf also* ϣⲕⲉⲗⲕⲓⲗ.

(ⲥⲟⲧⲥⲉⲧ), ⲥⲉⲧⲥⲱⲧ† *B* vb, *be shot, projected* (?) : N&E 39 343 martyr's corpse ϩⲱⲗ ⲉⲃⲟⲗ ϫⲉⲛⲡⲓⲁⲛⲣ ⲙⲫⲣⲏϯ ⲡⲟⲩⲥⲓⲟⲩ ⲉϥⲥ. *like shooting star.* *Cf* ⲥⲓⲧⲉ.

ⲥⲧⲱⲧ *SA*²(*BF* nn only) vb intr, *tremble* : 1 Kg 15 32, Jer 4 24 (*B* ⲥⲟⲉⲣⲧⲉⲣ), Lu 8 4 (*B* do) τρέμειν, Ps 76 18 (*B* do) Ac 16 29 (*B* ϫⲉⲛⲟⲩⲥⲉ.) ἔντρομος γίνεσθαι ; BHom 91 hell ⲥ. ⲉⲧⲃⲉⲡⲉⲧⲙⲙⲁⲩ φρίσσειν ; Job 38 17 (*B* diff) πτήσσειν ; Dan 7 15 (as if tr, *B* ϣⲟⲣⲧⲉⲣ) ταράσσειν ; Ps 96 4 (*B* ⲕⲓⲙ) σαλεύεσθαι ; Mor 16 33 ⲁⲡⲉϥⲥⲱⲙⲁ ⲧⲏⲣϥ ⲥ., Mani 1 *A*² ⲉⲥⲥ. ϩⲙ[. ⲥ ϩⲏⲧ̄, *tremble at* : 2 Pet 2 10 (*B* ⲥⲱ.), Aeg 242 ⲥ. ϩⲏⲧⲟⲩ ⲡⲡϣⲁϫⲉ ⲧⲣ. ; *ib* 270 sim φⲣ. ; Ps 32 8 (*B* ⲉⲣ ϩⲟϯ) ⲥⲁⲗ. ; PS 140 ⲙⲡⲉⲥⲥ. ϩⲏⲧⲥ ⲡⲧϭⲟⲙ ; ⲥ ϩⲁ-, *meaning same* : Gu 95 hell ⲥ. ϩⲁⲡⲉϥϩⲣⲟⲟⲩ.

—— nn m *SB*(K)*F*, *trembling* : Deu 11 25, Ps 2 11, Is 33 14 *SF*, Mk 16 8 (var BMis 501 ϩⲟⲧⲉ, all *B* ⲥⲱ.) τρόμος, 1 Cor 2 3 (*B* do) ἐντρ. ; Sa 17 9 ἐκσοβεῖσθαι ; K 163 *B* ⲡⲓⲥⲧⲟⲧ (sic) خوف ; ShR 2 3 82 ⲡⲁⲣ ϩⲟⲧⲉ ⲁⲡ ⲟⲩϫⲉ ⲉⲙⲡ ⲥ. ⲡⲁϫⲓⲧⲛ.

ⲥⲧⲁⲁⲧⲉ *v* ⲧⲁⲁⲧⲉ.

ⲥⲧⲱⲧⲉ *v* ⲥⲱⲧ measure.

ⲥⲁⲧϩⲟⲩⲧ *B* vb qual, prob incorrect : Lev 16 12 ⲡⲓⲥⲟⲩⲡⲟⲩϭⲓ ⲉⲧⲥ. συνθέσεως طِيب (*S* ⲙⲡϭⲱⲣϭ), *cf ib* 4 7 sim ⲉⲧⲥⲁⲡⲉⲥⲛⲧ, also Nu 4 16 ⲛⲧⲉ ⲡⲓⲙⲟⲩ- ϫⲧ (*S* do), Ex 31 11 ⲛⲧⲉ ⲡⲓⲥⲉⲙⲡⲓ all συνθ. Or *l*? *ⲉⲧ(ⲧ)ⲥⲁⲧϩⲟⲩⲧ, or cf Si 49 1 *S* ⲧⲥⲁⲡⲏⲩ ἐσκευασμένος.

ⲥⲧⲟⲩⲏⲧ *S* vb qual, meaning unknown : BM 311 103 Simon Cleophas ⲟⲩⲣⲱⲙⲉ ⲉϥϫⲟⲥⲉ ⲉϥⲥ. ϩⲙⲡⲉϥⲥⲱⲙⲁ *tall & ...in body.*

ⲥⲱⲧϥ *SB*, -ϩⲧ *F*, ⲥⲉⲧϥ- *SBF*, ⲥⲱ. *S*, ⲥⲟⲧϥ⸗ *S*, ⲥⲟⲧϥ† *SB*, ⲥⲁ.† *AA*² vb **I** intr, *be pure, clear, purified* : Job 11 15† *S(B* ⲧⲟⲩⲃⲟ), Ez 36 25† *S* (so ShA 2 72, P 131¹ 55, *B* ⲥⲱⲧⲡ) καθαρός ; Am 6 6† *A(B* do, *l* ⲥⲟⲧϥ) διυλίζειν ; Mor 37 94 *S* ⲙⲟⲟⲩ ⲉϥⲥⲟⲧⲃ ⲉⲙⲁⲧⲉ διειδέστατος ; Mk 8 25 *S* ⲁⲉⲓⲁⲧϥ ⲥ. (*B* ⲁϥ- ⲟⲩϫⲁⲓ, *F* ⲗⲁ) ἀποκαθίστασθαι ; Sa 11 7† *S* Gk diff ; PS 70 *S* chaos ⲉⲧⲉⲡⲡⲁⲥ. ⲁⲡ ⲡⲣⲏⲧϥ, *ib* 156 *S* ⲟⲩ- ⲟⲩⲟⲉⲓⲛ ⲉϥⲥ.†, Bor 267 103 *S* ⲁϥⲧⲣⲉⲡⲁⲏⲣ ⲥ., Mani

1 *A²* clouds ⲙⲙⲁⲩ ⲉⲩⲥ.†, MG 25 182 *B* ϣⲁⲧⲉⲡⲉⲕⲙⲱⲟⲩ ⲥ., ClPr 56 12 *S* wines ⲉⲩⲥ.† ⲡⲣⲉⲡⲁϣⲏ ⲡⲥϯⲡⲟⲩϥⲉ, CO 215 *S* ⲙⲣⲱϥⲉ ⲡⲥ. *strainer* (?).

II tr, **a** *purify, strain* (?): PS 51 *S* leaving no ὕλη ⲉⲙⲡϥⲥⲟⲧϥⲟⲩ, *ib* 117 *S* body ⲉⲛⲧⲁⲓⲧⲃ̅ⲃⲟϥ ⲁⲩⲱ ⲁⲓⲥⲟⲧϥ, *ib* 360 ⲛⲟⲩⲟⲉⲓⲛ ⲉⲧⲟⲩⲥ. ⲙⲙⲟⲟⲩ ϩⲛⲡⲁⲣⲭⲱⲛ, BKU 1 27 *S* cook it ⲛⲧⲥ. ⲡⲉϥⲙⲟⲟⲩ, CO 235 *S* wines to be mixed ⲛⲧⲉⲛⲥ. ⲥⲩⲛⲧⲉ ⲛⲁⲓⲡⲗⲏ ⲛⲁⲩ (or *l*? ⲥⲱⲧⲛ).   **b** *cause to drip, pour*: Mor 19 26 *S* ⲉⲩⲥ. ⲙⲡⲉϥⲥⲛⲟϥ ⲉⲧϣⲏⲩⲉ, *ib* sim ⲉϫⲛⲧϣ. = Miss 4 113 *B*, Aeg 36 *B* ⲛⲧⲉϥⲥⲉⲧϥ-...ϭⲓϫⲉⲛ-, PSBA 27 168 *S* ⲥⲉⲧϥ ⲟⲩⲗⲧⲓⲗⲉ of water ⲉϫⲛ- *on the ink*, LAp 541 *F* ϣⲁⲩⲥ. (*sic* MS) ⲛⲏⲓ ⲛⲟⲩⲏⲗⲡ = P 129¹⁸ 102 *S* ⲟⲩⲱⲧⲛ ⲉⲃ., *ib* *S* ⲉⲩⲥ. ⲡⲁⲓ ⲙⲡⲉϥⲥⲛⲟϥ = *ib* *F* ϭⲁ̣ϣϭⲉϣ, BKU 1 20 *F* ⲥⲉⲧϥ ⲡⲙⲁⲩ ⲉⲧϩⲛⲧⲙⲛ.   *Cf* ⲥⲱϥ *B*.

—— ⲉⲃⲟⲗ *S* intr, *be purified, separated*: PS 159 ⲁⲕⲧⲣⲉⲥⲥ. ⲉⲃ. ⲛϭⲓ ⲟⲩⲗⲏ. ⲉⲃ. ⲛ-, ϩⲛ-, *from, through*: PS 115 ⲡⲣⲩⲗⲏ...ⲁⲩⲥ. ⲉⲃ. ⲛⲣⲏⲧⲥ, Br 139 earth ⲥ. ⲉⲃ. ϩⲛⲧⲙⲛⲧⲉ ⲙⲡⲱⲕⲉⲁⲛⲟⲥ; tr, *purify, strain*: PS 154 ⲁⲓⲥ. ⲉⲃ. ⲙⲙⲟⲓ ⲛⲛⲁϩⲩⲗⲏ, *ib* 148 sim ⲉⲃ. ⲛⲣⲏⲧ, PMéd 197 rub it down ⲥⲟⲧϥ(ϥ) ⲉⲃ. ϩⲛⲟⲩⲧⲟⲉⲓⲥ, Bodl(P) a 1 c ⲥ. ⲛⲣⲏⲙⲁ ⲉⲃ. ⲛⲣⲏⲧϥ;   AZ 23 107 sim ⲉⲃ. ϩⲓⲟⲟⲩ.

—— ⲉⲡⲉⲥⲏⲧ, *pour down*: Mor 36 16 *S* ⲁϥⲥ. ⲉ. ⲉⲡⲡⲟⲧⲏⲣⲓⲟⲛ His blood, AM 326 *B* till his blood ⲥ. ⲉ. ϩⲓϫⲉⲛⲡⲕⲁϩⲓ.

—— nn m *SA²B*, *what is purified, purity*: PS 34 *S* will take ⲡⲥ. ⲙⲡⲟⲩⲟⲉⲓⲛ from the archons, Mani 1 *A²* ⲡⲥ. opp ⲛ]ⲥⲁⲣⲙⲉ, BSM 13 *B* ⲡⲥ. ⲛⲛⲉϥⲣϩⲱⲥ.   As adj: Mor 25 13 *S* water ⲡⲥ. ⲛⲥⲧⲁⲕⲧⲏ = Va 61 95 *B* ⲉⲧⲥ.†

ⲣⲉϥⲥ. *S*, *purifier*: PS 250 mysteries ⲛⲣ., Br 251 powers ⲛⲣ. ϫⲉⲕⲁⲁⲥ ⲉⲩⲉⲥⲟⲧϥⲟⲩ.

сатче *S* nn f, meaning unknown, ? name of a canal: J 107 13 ϫⲛⲡⲉⲓⲱⲣ ⲛⲧⲥ. ⲉϩⲣⲁⲓ ⲉⲡⲧⲟⲟⲩ. In place-name *Τσάτφε* (PSI 1025). *Cf*? last.

ⲥⲟⲧϩ(?) *S* nn, meaning unknown: PLond 4 517 in list of utensils ⲟⲩⲥⲟⲧϩ[(or ? complete).   *Cf*? ⲥⲟⲧⲁϩϥ.

ⲥⲧⲉⲓⲱϩⲉ, ⲥⲧⲱϩⲉ, ⲥⲉⲑⲓⲱϩⲓ *v* ⲉⲓⲱϩⲉ & ⲥⲱⲧ *measure*.

ⲥⲟⲧⲁϩϥ or ⲥⲟⲧⲁϩ[.]ϥ *S*, meaning doubtful. *V* ϩⲁⲁⲣⲉ, ⲥⲟⲧϩ.

ⲥⲧⲁϫⲟⲩⲗ *B* nn m, *spider*: Job 27 18, Ps 89 9, Is 59 5 (all *S* ϭⲁⲗⲟⲩⲥ) ἀράχνη; Va 57 116 Arius like ⲥ. or ϣⲝⲉ;   its *web* (*cf* ⲛⲁⲧ b): Job 8 14, Ps 38 12 (*S* do), Va 63 86 worldly honours as ϩⲁⲡⲥ. & smoke ἀρ., K 173 ⲡⲓⲥ. عنكب; BSM 110 devil disappeared like ⲟⲩⲥ.

ⲥⲁⲉⲓⲟⲟⲩ, ⲥⲁⲓⲱⲟⲩ *v* ⲥⲁ *be beautiful*.

ⲥⲁⲓⲟⲩ *S* nn, meaning unknown (word ? incomplete): BKU 1 45 among wages in kind ⲟⲩⲙⲟⲥⲡⲉ ⲛⲥ.   ⲟⲩ ? = ⲟ(ⲱ) *great*.

ⲥⲁⲓⲱⲟⲩ *B v* ⲁⲥⲁⲓ.

ⲥⲁⲩ *AF v* ⲥⲟⲟⲩ.

снγ *SAA²*, снⲟⲩ *A* (Zech 10)*A²B*, ⲥⲟⲩ- *SABF*, ⲥⲱ- *S*(Kr 249) nn m, *time, season* (oftenest *B*): Ex 23 14 *B*(*S* ⲟⲩⲟⲉⲓϣ), Job 19 4 *B*(*S* ⲧⲏ), Is 33 2 *B* (*SF* do), Hos 2 9 *AB*, Mk 11 13 *S* (var ⲛⲁⲩ)*B*, καιρός; Is 65 20 (*B* ⲥ., *S* ⲁϩⲉ), Gal 4 4 *B*(*S* do) χρόνος, Ac 7 23 *B* ⲛ̅ ⲡⲣⲟⲙⲡⲓ ⲛⲥ. (*F* ⲗⲁⲙ. ⲛⲟⲩ., *S* ⲛⲣ. only) τεσσ.-ετης χ., Is 33 20 *B* ⲡⲥ. ⲛⲧⲉ ⲉⲛⲉϩ (*SF* ⲉⲛⲉϩ ⲛⲟⲩ.) αἰὼν χ., Sa 8 8 *S* ⲟⲩⲟⲉⲓϣ...ⲥ. ⲕ....χ.; Va 57 238 *B* ⲥ. ⲛⲱⲛϩ βίος; Zech 10 1 *AB* ⲥ. ⲛϣⲁⲣⲡ πρώιμος; Am 9 13 *SA* ⲥ. ⲙⲡϫⲟ (*B* ⲥⲓϯ) σπόρος; MG 25 244 *B* ⲟⲩⲏⲣ ⲛⲥ. πολλὰ ἔτη; BG 72 *S* ⲟⲩϣⲓ ⲙⲡⲣⲏⲥ. ⲙⲡⲣⲏⲛⲟⲩ., ShMIF 23 174 *S* ⲡⲕⲁⲓⲣⲟⲥ of Patriarchs, ⲡⲥ. of Judges, ⲡⲉϩⲟⲟⲩ of Prophets, C 43 32 *B* ⲡⲥ. of childhood, Aeg 211 *S* ⲡⲉⲁⲣ ⲛ ⲡⲥ. of equinox, BM 337 *S* ⲡⲕⲁⲓⲣⲟⲥ ⲙⲡⲥ. ⲉⲧⲛⲁⲡⲟⲩϥ, C 43 55 *B* not to destroy him ϩⲁϫⲉⲛⲡⲉϥⲥ., *ib* 86 262 *B* trusted in saint ⲛⲡⲉϥⲥ. ⲧⲏⲣϥ, DeV 2 162 *B* ⲡⲁⲣⲉⲛⲓⲥ. ϯ ⲙⲙⲟϥ ⲁⲛⲡⲉ *time suffered him not*, TEuch 2 270 *B* four ⲥ. *seasons*, C 43 159 *B* ϯⲛⲟⲩ ϫⲉⲛⲓⲥ. ⲡⲉ.

Adverbial phrases.   ⲙⲡⲓⲥ. *S*, ⲙⲡⲁⲓⲥ. *B*, *at this time*: Ge 17 21 *B* εἰς τ. κ. τοῦτον; HT N 80 *S* who pulled down ⲙⲡⲓⲟⲩ. buildeth ⲙⲡⲓⲥ.; ϩⲙⲡⲉⲓⲥ. *SB* sim: Jer 16 21 *SB*, Ro 3 26 *B*(*S* ⲡⲉⲓⲟⲩ.) ἐν τῷ κ. τούτῳ, τῷ νῦν κ.; ⲙⲡⲓⲥ. ⲛⲧⲉ ϯⲛⲟⲩ *B* sim: *ib* 6 21 (*S* ⲙⲡⲉⲓⲟⲩ. ⲧⲉⲛⲟⲩ) τότε; ϩⲙⲡⲉⲓⲥ. ⲧⲉⲛⲟⲩ *S*: ShC 42 141 who departed ϩ. ⲧ.; ⲙⲡⲓⲥ. *B*, *at that time, formerly*: CaiEuch 528 ϧⲏ ⲉⲧⲁϥⲥⲙⲟⲩ ⲙ. bless now, MIE 2 379 as He did to Pharaoh ⲙ. = BAp 95 *S* ⲙⲡⲉⲟⲩ.; ⲙⲡⲓⲥ. ⲉⲧⲧⲏ *B*, sim: Is 45 21 (*S* ⲧⲛⲁⲩ) τότε; ϧⲉⲛⲡⲓⲥ. ⲉⲧⲉⲙⲙⲁⲩ *B*: *ib* 38 1 ἐν τῷ κ. ἐκείνῳ; ⲙⲡⲓⲥ. ⲉⲧⲙ. Mani 1 *A²*; ⲛⲟⲩⲥ. *SA²B*, *on a time, once, at times*: Gal 1 23 b *B*(*S* ⲛ̅ⲡⲓⲧⲉ) ποτέ; Ro 5 6 *B*(*S* ⲕⲁⲧⲁ ⲡⲉⲓⲟⲩ.) κατὰ κ.; ShC 73 70 *S* ⲉⲩⲉⲅⲕⲣⲁⲧⲉⲩⲉ ⲙⲙⲟⲟⲩ ⲛ., Mani 1 *A²* ⲁϥⲧⲁⲡⲟⲩ ⲁϩⲟⲩⲛ...ⲛ., Rec 6 176 *B* ⲁⲛϣⲁⲛⲉⲣ ⲁⲧϭⲟⲙ ⲛ.; ϧⲉⲛⲟⲩⲥ. *B*: 2 Cor 6 2(*S* ϩⲛⲟⲩⲟⲩ.) καιρῷ, Is 41 7 (*S* ⲟⲩⲥⲟⲡ) ποτέ;   ⲛⲥ. ⲛⲓⲙ, ⲛⲓⲃⲉⲛ *SA²B*, *at all times, always*: Ps 68 23 *SB*, Is 30 29 *B*(*SF* ⲛⲟⲩ. ⲛ.), Ro 11 10 *SB* διὰ παντός; Jo 7 6 *SB*(*A²* ⲛⲟⲩ. ⲛ.) πάντοτε; Is 51 13 *B*(*S* do), Ac 7 51 *B*(*S* do) ἀεί; He 7 25 *B*(*S* do) εἰς τὸ παντελές, CaiEuch 519 *B* ⲡⲁⲣⲑⲉⲛⲟⲥ ⲛⲥ. ⲛ. ἀειπάρθ.; BMis 418 *S* will honour thee ⲛⲥ. ⲛ. = BSM 59 *B* = Va 63 26 *B* Mani 2 *A²* helping him ⲛⲥ. ⲛ.;   ⲙⲡⲥ. *S*, ⲙⲡⲓⲥ. *B*, *at the time, when*: Gal 1 23 a *B*(*S* ⲙⲡⲓⲟⲩ.) ποτέ; Ryl 76 *S* ⲙⲡⲥ. ⲉⲓⲛⲏⲩ *at Last Day*;   ϩⲁⲙⲡⲥ. *SB*

sim: Ge 30 41 *B*(*S* ϩⲙⲡⲉⲟⲩ.), Ps 36 39 *B*(*S* do)
ἐν κ.; ShA 1 330 *S* ϩⲙⲡⲉ. when multitude was
with us, ShC 73 43 *S* ϩⲙⲡⲉⲟⲩ. ⲏ ⲡⲉⲅⲥ. ⲡⲭⲓⲧⲟⲩ
(sc wages), ShZ 602 *S* corn-ears ⲙⲡⲁⲧⲟⲩϫⲁⲁⲧⲉ
ϩⲙⲡⲉⲥ.; ⲕⲁⲧⲁ ⲥ. *SB*, *at times, from time to
time*: Nu 23 23 *B*(*S* ⲙⲡⲉⲟⲩ.), Is 60 22 *B*(*S* ⲕⲁⲧⲁ
ⲡⲉⲟⲩ.) κατὰ κ.; ShBMOr 8810 474 *S* ϣⲁϥⲡⲱⲡⲉ
ⲕ. ⲥ. ⲁⲩⲱ ⲕ. ⲕⲁⲓⲣⲟⲥ, Rec 6 179 *B* brought it ⲙ-
ⲙⲏⲡⲓ ⲕ. ⲥ. = BMar 214 *S* ⲙⲙ. only, AM 228 *B*
bishops ⲕ. ⲥ. until Sarapion; ⲕ. ⲡⲉⲓⲥ., *as, at this
time*: Ge 18 10 *SB*, Ro 9 9 *B*(*S* ⲕ. ⲡⲉⲓⲟⲩ.) ⲕ. τὸν
κ. τοῦτον; Nu 9 3 *B* ⲕ. ⲡⲉⲥ. (*S* ⲕ. ⲡⲉϥⲟⲩ.) ⲕ. ⲕ.
αὐτοῦ; ⲡⲁⲣⲁ ⲡⲉϥⲥⲟⲩ *A²*: Mani 2; ⲡⲣⲟⲥ
ⲟⲩⲥ. *B, for a time*: Pro 5 3 (*SA* ⲡ. ⲧⲉⲩⲛⲟⲩ), Mt
13 21(*SF* ⲡ. ⲟⲩⲟⲩ.) π.κ.; AM 17 worldly kingdom
ⲟⲩⲡ. ⲟⲩⲥ.; ϣⲁⲟⲩⲥ., -ⲡⲓⲥ. *B, until, for a time*:
Ez 4 10 (*S* ϣⲁⲟⲩⲟⲩ.) ἕως κ.; AM 6 ϣⲁⲡⲓⲥ. when
I require them.

ⲁⲧⲥ. *SB, timeless*: P 44 48 *S* of God, CaiEuch
473 *B* ἄχρονος; Va 57 71 *B* ⲟⲩⲉϩⲟⲟⲩ ⲡϩⲟϯ ⲙⲡⲟⲡⲏⲣⲟⲛ ⲡⲁ.

ⲉⲣ ⲥ. *B, pass time*: Va 57 199 beasts ⲉⲣ ⲥ. ⲙ-
ⲡⲕⲱⲧ ⲡⲡⲓⲣϩⲛⲟⲩⲓ ⲡϥⲥⲓⲕⲟⲛ.

ϫⲓ, ϭⲓ ⲥ. *SB, take time*: Ps 74 3 *B*(*S* ϭⲓⲛⲉ) ⲕ.
λαμβάνειν; MR 5 55 *S* ϫⲓ ⲡⲥ. ⲡⲁⲕ *take occasion*
(when occasion offers) & give &c.

ϭⲉⲡ ⲥ. *B, meaning uncertain*: Cat 23 what *time*
is meant Mt 8 29? clearly ⲉⲩϭⲉⲡ ⲥ. ⲛϯⲕⲟⲗⲁⲥⲓⲥ.
? = ϣⲉⲡ.

ⲥⲟⲩ- *SABF* with a date of month or festival:
ⲥⲟⲩⲁ (*ie* ⲥⲟⲩⲟⲩⲁ) *S*, ⲥⲟⲩⲉ *A*, ⲥⲟⲩⲁⲓ *B*, ⲥⲟⲩⲉⲉⲓ *F*:
Ps 23 tit *S*(*B* ϥⲟⲩⲁⲓ), Mt 28 1 *S*(*B* do) μία; Ge
8 5 *SB* πρώτη; Nu 28 11 *SB*, Is 1 14 *SBF*, Ez 23
34 *SB* ⲥⲟⲩⲁϯ pl (prob error), Hos 2 11 *AB* νουμηνία; AM 180 *B* ⲥ. ⲙⲫⲁⲣⲙⲟⲅⲑⲓ, Win 61 *S*
ⲥⲉⲩⲁⲓ (*bis*) ⲡⲁⲱⲡⲉ, CO 221 *S* ⲥ. ⲡⲁⲡⲁ ⲡⲁⲡⲡⲟⲩⲧⲉ; ⲥⲟⲩⲥⲛⲁⲩ *S*: Ps 47 tit (*B* ⲡⲥⲛⲁⲩ) δευτέρα;
ⲥⲟⲩⲧⲟⲩ *S*: Ez 1 1 (*B* ⲥⲟⲩⲉ̄) πέμπτη; ⲥⲟⲩⲉ̄ *F*: BM
671; ⲥⲟⲩⲙⲏⲧ *S*: Lev 23 27 (*B* ⲥⲟⲩⲓ̄) δεκάτη, ⲥⲟⲩϫⲟⲩⲧⲉϥⲧⲉ *A*: Hag 2 1 (*B* ⲥⲟⲩⲕ̄ⲁ̄) τετρὰς κ. εἰκ.;
KroppK 68 *S* ⲥⲟⲩϫⲟⲩⲧⲯⲓⲥ ⲙⲡⲱ (*l* ⲟⲟϩ), ShP
130⁵ 49 *S* ϩⲛⲥⲟⲩⲏⲣ ⲡⲁϣ ⲡⲉϩⲟⲧ. b other words:
ⲥⲟⲩϩⲱⲛ v ϩⲱⲱⲛ I.

In names (?) ⲥⲟⲩⲁ, ⲥⲟⲩⲁⲓ m f, ⲯⲁⲟⲩⲁ (ST 94,
Ryl 222).

ⲥⲓⲟⲩ *SABF*, -ⲟⲟⲩ *Sᵃ*, ⲥⲉⲩ, ⲥⲓⲩ *F*, ⲥⲟⲩ- *SBO*
nn m, *star*: Ge 15 5 *SA* (Cl) *B*, Is 13 10 *SB*, 1 Cor
15 41 *SBF*(ⲥⲓⲩ), Ap 8 10 *SB* ἀστήρ, Nu 24 17 *SB*,
Joel 2 10 *SAB*, Lu 21 25 *SB* ἄστρον; Is 33 18 *SF*
(*B* Gk diff); PS 384 *S* ⲡⲉⲓⲥ. ⲥⲛⲁⲩ ⲡⲟⲩⲟⲉⲓⲛ, BKU 1
1 vo *S* six ⲥ. ⲛϩⲓⲗⲁⲥⲧⲏⲣⲓⲟⲛ under sun (Pleiades),
BAp 73 *S* 7 ⲥ. rising in west & 7 called ⲉⲛⲧⲏⲣ (*v*

ⲛⲟⲩⲧⲉ pl forms), Leyd 456 *S* beings rising with
ⲡⲡⲟϭ ⲛⲥ., DeV 2 7 *B* ⲡⲓⲥ. ⲉⲧⲁϥϣⲁⲓ, Mor 30 7 *F*
ϩⲛⲥⲉⲩ shining, BKU 1 3 *S* crown of c. on Jesus'
head, ViK 9541 *S* ⲡⲁⲅⲁⲛ ⲛⲛⲉⲥ., N&E 39 343 *B*
ⲟⲩⲥ. ⲉϥⲥⲉⲧⲥⲱⲧ *shooting* (?) *star*; morning star:
Si 50 6 *S* ⲥ. ⲛϩⲧⲟⲟⲩⲉ ἀ. ἑωθινός, Job 3 9 *S* ⲥⲟⲩⲛ̄ϩ.
B ⲥ. ⲛⲧⲉ ϩ., ib 9 9 *B* ⲥ. ⲛⲧⲉ ϣⲱⲣⲡ (*S* Gk om), Is 14
12 *S* ⲥⲟⲩⲛ̄ⲧⲟⲟⲩⲉ (var ϩⲧ.) *B* ⲛⲧⲉ ⲧⲟⲟⲩⲓ ἑωσφόρος,
2 Pet 1 19 *S* ⲥ. ⲛϩ. (*B* diff) φωσφ.; Jud 16 2 *S* ⲥ. ⲛⲧ.
ὄρθρος; KroppK 39 *Sᵃ* ⲥ. ⲛⲧⲁⲩⲉ; evening s.: Job
9 9 *S* ⲥⲟⲩⲛ̄ⲣⲟⲩϩⲉ *B* ⲥ. ⲛⲧⲉ ⲁⲣⲟⲩϩⲓ ἕσπερος, P 44 52
S سُهَيْل; Orion: Job 38 31 *S* ⲥⲟⲩⲛ̄ϩⲱⲣ(*B*=Gk), Is
13 10 *SB* do, P 44 52 *S* do جَبّار 'Ωρείων; Venus:
K 49 *B* ⲥⲟⲩⲣⲟⲧ زُهَرة; ⲥⲟⲩⲕⲏ *O*, planet Mercury:
Hor 76; ⲥⲟⲩⲛⲟⲩϥⲉ *O, propitious star*: Hor 81;
ⲥⲟⲩϩⲁϫⲉ *O, hostile star*: ib 77; ⲥⲟⲩϩⲱⲛ *O* sim:
ib 78 (but cf ϩⲱⲱⲛ I). V also ? ⲥⲓⲟⲩ ⲥⲓⲟⲩ.

—— *S, spot, blot* of disease on eye: PMéd 196
ⲟⲩⲥ. ⲉϥⲣⲛⲟⲩⲃⲁⲗ, ib 301 ⲃⲁⲗ ⲉϥⲱ ⲛⲥ. (ib 157, 166
opp ⲡⲙⲟⲟⲩ cataract).

As name (?): Hall 122 Ψιου.

ⲥⲓⲟⲩ ⲥⲓⲟⲩ, ⲥⲟⲩⲥ. *S* nn, *star-spangled, speckled
thing*: Ge 31 12 ⲥⲓⲟⲩ. (var ⲥⲟⲩⲥ., *B* ⲡⲟϫϫ) ῥαντός;
Mor 54 99 ⲁⲅⲁⲡ ⲙⲡⲏ ⲛⲥⲓⲟⲩ ⲥ. As name ⲧⲥⲓⲟⲩ-
ⲥⲓⲟⲩ (WZKM 26 339).

ⲥⲟⲟⲩ *SB*(K 67), ⲥⲁⲩ *Sᵃ AA²F*, ⲥⲉⲩ- *S*, f ⲥⲟ,
ⲥⲟⲉ, ⲥⲟⲟⲩⲉ (ST) *S*, ⲥⲱⲉ *A*, ⲥⲟⲉ *A²*, ⲥⲁ *F* nn, *six*
(*B* ⳉ̄): m Ex 20 9 *S*, Pro 6 17 *SA*, Cl 56 8 *A*, Ap
4 8 *S* ἕξ; JA '75 5 232 *S* παρασκευή (6th day);
PS 41 *S* ⲥ. ⲛⲉⲃⲟⲧ, ClPr 26 69 *S* ⲛⲥ. ⲛϩⲟⲟⲩ of
Pascha, BodlCopt g 1 *S* ⲛⲉϩⲟⲟⲩ ⲙⲡⲥⲟⲟⲩ in 3d
week, KroppK 37 *Sᵃ* ⲡⲥⲁⲩ ⲙⲡⲱϩ(ⲟⲟϩ), BM 1252
F ⲥ. ⲛⲗⲓⲗ; f Ge 31 41 *S*, Jo 4 6 *SA²F* ἕξ; ST
125 *S* ⲥⲟⲟⲩⲉ ⲛⲕⲟⲩⲛⲭⲟⲩ; Mt 20 5 *S* ϫⲡⲥⲟⲉ ἕκτη
ὥρα, Mor 31 235 *S* ϫⲉⲡⲥⲟ; *sixteen* ⲙⲛⲧⲁⲥⲉ:
Ex 26 25 *S*, 4 Kg 13 10 *S*; *twenty-six* &c ϫⲟⲩⲧⲁⲥⲉ: Aeg 11 *S* ⲥⲟⲩϫ. of Eⲡⲉⲡ, Mani 1 *A²* ϫⲟⲩⲧⲉⲥⲉ, Br 234 *S* ⲙⲁⲁⲃⲧⲁⲥⲉ, Ex 6 20 *A* ϩⲁⲙⲧⲉⲥⲉ;
sixty &c ⲥⲉ (*B* K 67): Lev 27 3 *S*, Ap 11 3 *S*,
ⲥⲉⲧⲁⲥⲉ Ge 46 26 *S*, ⲥⲉⲧⲏ AZ 21 106 *O*, ⲥⲉ ⲛⲧⲃⲁ
Cl 43 5 *A*; *six hundred* ⲥ. ⲛϣⲉ: Ge 7 6 *S*, 1 Kg
13 15 *S*, ⲥⲉⲩϣⲉ: Nu 1 27 *S*, Jud 3 31 *S*, ⲥⲉ ⲛϣⲉ:
Sh(Besa)Z 513 *S*; *six thousand* ⲥ. ⲛϣⲟ: Job 42 12
S, Br 130 *S*, ⲥⲉⲩϣⲟ 4 Kg 5 5 *S*.

ⲙⲉϩⲥⲟⲟⲩ, -ⲥⲟ &c, *sixth*: m Jos 19 32 *S*, Ap 9
13 *S*, Mani 2 *A²* ⲙⲁϩⲥⲁⲩ; f Lev 25 21 *S* -ⲥⲟ, BG
16 *S* -ⲥⲟⲉ, El 84 *A* -ⲥⲱⲉ; ⲙⲉϩⲥⲉ, *sixtieth*: Si 16
11 *S*. V ⲙⲟⲩϩ *fill s f*.

ⲥⲉⲕ ⲥ., *fast during 6 days, v* ⲥⲱⲕ II *protract*.
V AZ 47 17.

ⲥⲛⲟⲩⲉ *O* nn f, meaning unknown: DM 9 31
will put fire about this c. V AZ 46 128 (? *bandage*).

СНОⲨⲒ *F* nn as pl, meaning unknown : BM 589 13 ⲉⲙⲁⲛ ⲁⲃ̄ⲕⲁⲧ ⲅ̄ⲡⲕⲟⲨⲒ ⲛⲥ. (context obscure).

ⲤⲞⲨⲞ *SAA²B*, **ⲥⲟⲨⲁ** *F* nn m, *corn, wheat* : Deu 7 13 *SB*, Pro 3 10 *SAB*, Is 36 17 *SBF*, Jo 12 24 *SA²B* σῖτος ; Ex 29 2 *SB*, Job 31 40 *SB*, Joel 1 11 *AB* πυρός ; Ge 43 20 *S(B ⲥ̄ⲣⲉ)* βρῶμα ; K 192 *B* ⲛⲥ. قمح ; as pl : Jer 12 13 *SB* πυ. ; BM 1031 *S* ⲛⲥⲉⲟⲨⲟ (*sic*), Ep 531 *S* ⲅⲉⲛⲥ. ; ⲓⲁⲅ ⲥ. : Deu 23 25 *B(S* diff) ἄμητος ; as tax : Ryl 188, 319 *S* ; as rent : *ib* 165 *S* ; as wage : BM 1064 *S*, WS 132 *S* ; measures or containers : ⲣⲧⲟⲃ̄ PLond 4 499 *S* ⲉⲣⲧⲟϥ ⲛⲥ. ⲥⲓⲁⲣⲧ/, CO 129, 460 *S*, BM 1043 *S* ; ⲟⲓⲡⲉ *ib* 1055 *S*, Ep 301 *S*, CO 499 *F* ; ⲙⲁⲁϫⲉ *ib* 165 *S*, WS 121 *S* ; ⲙⲛⲧ Hall 83 *S* ; ⲅⲟ *ib* 87 *S* ; ⲕⲁⲡ AZ 30 39 *S* ; ⲥⲟⲕ Gen 42 25 *B* (var ⲙⲟⲕⲓ) ; ⲥⲟⲟⲩⲡⲉ WS 148 *S*, Bodl(P) g 17 *S*, BP 5567 *F* ; ⲑⲁⲗⲗⲓⲥ Ep 304 *S* ; ⲙⲟⲓⲁⲅ BM 1055, 1066 *S* ; ⲱ̄ϣⲧ CO 204 *S* ; ⲥ̄ⲁⲙⲟⲩⲗ camel's load WS 155 *S* ; prices : CO 257, ST 94, 388, Kr 10 15 (*v* Ep 1 146) ; ⲥ. ⲛⲃ̄ⲣⲣⲉ *S* : BM 1043, Kr 59 ; ⲥ. ⲛⲗⲱⲕ : J 117 5 *S* ; ⲥ. ⲉϥⲧⲃ̄ⲃⲏⲩ *S* : Miss 8 227, Ryl 204 (*cf* σ. καθαρός) ; ⲥ. ⲙⲡⲱⲣϫ : ST 189 *S* (*cf* Lev 2 14 *B*) ; ⲥ. ⲉϥⲥⲁⲣⲙ : Ep 309 *S* ; ⲥ. ⲛⲥⲓⲕⲉ : WS 89 *S* ; ⲱⲟⲩϣ ⲛⲥ. : MG 25 267 *B* ; wheat & barley (ⲉⲓⲱⲧ) : Ru 2 23 *S*, Is 28 25 *SB*, CA 105 *S*, Kr 80, 152 *S*, WS 132 *S*, Hall 106 *S* ; *corn-coloured S* : Mor 44 26 ⲁⲩⲁⲛ ⲛⲥ. (*cf* ⲙⲟⲩⲛⲉ (2)), P 44 67 ⲥ(ⲓ)ⲧⲟⲭⲣⲱⲡ · ⲁⲩ. ⲛⲥ.

In place-name : ⲧⲟⲩⲅⲱ ⲛⲉⲥⲟⲩⲟ (stele from Siut *penes* FPetrie), ? ⲧⲟⲩ̄ⲃⲱ ⲛⲉⲥⲟⲩⲟ (Kr 98).

V ⲃ̄ⲗⲃⲓⲗⲉ, ⲉⲃⲣⲁ, ⲡⲁⲡⲣⲉ, ⲛⲟⲩⲧ, also AZ 47 21 n.

ⲥⲟⲩⲃⲉ- *B v* ⲥⲃⲃⲉ.

ⲥⲱⲟⲩⲃⲉⲛ *B*, **ⲥⲁⲩⲃⲟⲩ** (? *cf* ⲛⲁⲩⲃⲉⲛ, ⲡⲉⲩⲃⲟⲩ) *F* nn m, *grass* (*S* mostly ⲭⲟⲣⲧⲟⲥ) : Job 40 10, Ps 105 20, Is 32 13, Ja 1 10, ROC 27 143 ⲛⲓⲥ. burneth not without fire χόρτος, Ge 24 25 χόρτασμα ; Is 37 27 *B(S* ⲛⲧⲏⲅ) ἄγρωστις ; K 180 حشيش , *ib* 387 عشب ; PO 11 314 ⲟⲩⲙⲟⲗ ⲛⲥ., *ib* 315 opp ϣⲟⲗ ⲛⲥⲓⲙ ; CMSS 20 *F* ϯ ⲣⲱⲙⲉ ⲛⲁⲓ ⲧⲁⲧⲁⲗⲁ ⲛⲉⲥ.

ⲥⲟⲩⲃⲏⲧ, **-ⲛⲟⲩⲧ** *B v* ⲥⲃ̄ⲃⲉ.

(**ⲥⲟⲩⲟⲗⲟⲩⲗ**), **ⲥⲟⲩ(ⲉ)ⲗⲟⲩⲱⲗⲍ**, **ⲥⲟⲩⲗⲱⲗⲍ**, **ⲥⲟⲩⲗⲟⲗⲍ**, **ⲥⲗⲟⲩⲗⲱⲍ** (Tri), **ⲥⲗⲟⲩⲗⲟⲗⲍ** (do)*S*, **ⲥⲟⲩⲗⲱⲗ†** *SS ʃ* vb tr, *wrap*. ⲥ acc & ⲛ-, *wrap someone in* : Ez 16 4 (*B* ⲭⲟⲗϫ) ⲥⲟⲩⲗⲱⲗⲍ σπαργανοῦσθαι ἐν ; R 1 1 38 ⲥⲟⲩⲗⲱⲗⲁϥ ⲡⲟⲩⲥⲓⲛⲇⲱⲛⲓⲟⲛ ἐντυλίσσειν ἐν ; Mor 48 6 garment ⲁⲓⲥⲟⲩⲗⲱⲗⲁϥ ⲙⲙⲟϥ (var BMar 206 ⲥⲟⲩⲉⲗⲟⲩⲱⲗⲥ ⲉⲣⲟϥ), *ib* 34 49 ⲁⲣⲥⲟⲩⲗⲟⲗⲧ ⲛⲣ̄ⲛⲧⲟⲉⲓⲥ = FR 66 *S* ⲥ̄ⲱⲱⲗⲉ ⲙⲙⲟⲓ ⲛ- = Aeg 49 *B* ⲭⲟⲗϫⲧ ⲛ-, CA 94 ⲁϥⲥⲟⲩⲗⲟⲩⲱⲗⲥ ⲙⲡⲥⲟⲩⲅⲁⲣⲓⲟⲛ (Lu 19 20) ; ⲥ ⲅⲛ-, as last : P 131² 88 ⲉⲕϣⲁⲛⲥⲟⲩⲗⲱⲗⲁϥ ⲅⲙⲙⲓⲛⲉ ⲛⲓⲙ ⲛⲣⲟⲓⲧⲉ κατακρύπτειν ; Tri 481 ⲁⲩ-

ⲥⲗⲟⲩⲗⲟⲗⲥ ⲅⲛⲣⲉⲛⲥⲟⲩⲁ., *ib* ⲡⲉⲩⲥⲗⲟⲩⲗⲱⲟⲩ لف , BMar 45 ⲥⲟⲩⲉⲗⲟⲩⲱⲗⲥ ⲅⲛⲣⲉⲛⲙⲁⲡⲡⲁ ; Mor 48 94 *S* ⲁⲩⲥⲟⲩⲗⲟⲩ ⲛⲣⲛⲙⲁⲡⲡⲁ, C 43 146 *B* ⲛⲧⲟⲩⲥⲉⲗⲥⲱⲗⲟⲩ (*sic*) ⲥ̄ⲛⲅⲁⲛⲙⲁⲡⲡⲁ = Mor 48 94 *S* ⲥⲟⲩⲗⲱⲗⲟⲩ ; ⲥ ⲉ-, wrap *about* : AZ 21 142 ⲁϥⲥⲟⲩⲉⲗⲟⲩⲱⲗⲟⲩ (*sc* clothes) ⲉⲛⲕⲉⲉⲥ of corpse, BMar 206 sim ; qual : Mor 33 53 ⲉϥⲥ. ⲛⲣⲉⲛⲧⲟⲉⲓⲥ = BMis 99 ⲥ̄ⲟⲟⲗⲉ ⲛ-, Bor 267 48 napkin ⲉⲧⲥ. ⲉⲛⲉϥⲅⲟ ; Mich 550 44 loaves ⲉⲩⲥ. ⲉⲅⲉⲛⲙⲁⲡⲡⲁ (*l* ⲛⲣⲉⲛ-), Mor 30 29 *Sʃ* ⲛⲁⲥⲱⲙⲁ ⲉϥⲥ. = *ib* 29 24 *S* ⲉϥⲥ. ⲛⲣⲉⲛ(ⲅ)ⲃⲱⲱⲥ.

ⲥⲟⲨⲉⲛ *S*(?)*B*, **ⲥⲟⲩⲛⲧⲍ** *SA²*, **ⲥⲟⲩⲉⲛⲍ** *B*, **ⲥⲟⲩⲉⲛⲧⲍ** *F* nn m, *value, price* (*v* Sethe *Dem Urk* 118) : Ps 48 9 *B* ⲛⲥ. (*S* ⲁⲥⲟⲩ), Is 55 1 *B(S* do) ; Ac 19 19 *S(B* = Gk) τιμή, Pro 6 26 *B* ⲛⲧⲁⲓⲟ...ⲥⲟⲩⲉⲛ ⲟⲩⲱⲓⲕ (*SA* ϣⲁⲟⲩ-) ⲧ....ὅση ; Ep 286 *S* ⲙⲁⲧⲉⲛⲧⲁⲓ ⲥⲟⲩⲉⲛ ⲡⲁ-ⲭⲱⲙⲉ, C 89 42 *B* ⲛⲥⲟⲩⲉⲛϥ of corn = Miss 4 522 *S* ⲥⲟⲩⲛⲧⲥ, AM 185 *B* ⲥⲟⲩⲉⲛϥ of horse, ST 248 *S* ⲥⲟⲩⲛⲧⲟⲩ of jars ; ⲛⲁϣⲉ ⲥ. *SA²F*, ⲛⲥ. *B*, *of great value* : Est D 6 *S*, Job 31 24 *B* ⲱⲛⲓ ⲉⲛ. (*S* ⲙⲙⲉ), Mk 14 3 *SBF* πολυτελής ; Mt 13 46 *SBF*, Jo 12 3 *SA²B* πολύτιμος, Mt 26 7 *SB* βαρύτιμος ; Ez 27 22 *SB* χρηστός ; ShC 73 162 *S* ⲧⲣⲟⲉⲓⲧⲉ ⲉⲧⲉⲛ. ⲥⲟⲩⲛⲧⲥ ⲁⲛ, AP 27 *A²* ⲛⲧⲣⲟⲫⲏ ⲉⲛ. ⲥⲟⲩⲛⲧⲟⲩ, C 43 180 *B* ⲥⲟⲭⲉⲛ ⲉⲛ. ⲛⲥⲟⲩⲉⲛϥ.

ⲥⲟⲨⲒⲚ, **-ⲏⲛ** *v* ⲥⲟⲟⲨⲚ.

ⲥⲓⲟⲟⲨⲚ¹, **-ⲡⲉ²**, **ⲥⲓⲁⲟⲩⲡ³** *S*, **ⲥⲓⲁⲩⲡⲉ⁴**, **ⲥⲓⲉⲓⲁⲩⲡⲉ⁵**, **ⲥⲉⲁⲩⲡⲉ⁶** *Sᵃ*, **ⲥⲓⲱⲟⲩⲡⲓ⁷**, **ⲥⲉⲓ.⁸**, **ⲥⲉ.⁹** *B* nn f, *bath* ; BHom 11 *S* heat of ⲟⲩⲥ.², KKS 24 *S* ⲧⲥ.¹ = MG 25 213 *B⁷*, EW 28 *B⁷⁸*, Va 57 247 *B⁸* βαλανεῖον ; JA '75 5 242 *S²* λουτρόν ; Mor 17 103 *S¹* πριβᾶτον ; Mor 48 87 *S* ⲧⲥ.¹ ⲙⲡⲇⲉⲙⲟⲥⲓⲟⲛ, BMar 10 *S* ⲙⲡⲉⲓ-ϫⲱⲕⲙ ⲅⲛⲟⲩⲥ.¹, GMir 181 *S* ⲛⲙⲁ ⲛⲧⲱⲕ ⲛⲧⲥ.¹, C 43 143 *B⁸* sim, KroppK 25 *Sᵃ* ⲡⲉⲡⲧⲱⲕⲉ ⲛⲧⲥ.⁵, AM 311 *B* ⲡⲓⲭⲁⲗⲕⲓⲟⲛ ⲛⲧⲉ ϯⲥ.⁷, *ib* 50 *B* ⲡⲓⲑⲟⲗⲟⲥ of ⲥ.⁷, KroppM 95 *Sᵃ* ⲟⲩⲙⲟⲩ ⲛⲥ.⁴, Cai 42573 1 *S* water ⲛⲁⲩⲉⲓⲛ ⲛⲥ.¹ ⲛⲉⲅⲓⲙⲉ, C 43 186 *B* fresco on wall of ⲥ.⁷ Mor 17 103 *S* ⲧⲥⲁⲙⲛⲧ of ⲥ.¹, PMéd 277 *S* medical treatment in ⲧⲥⲓⲟⲩⲡⲉ (*ib* 316 ⲧⲥ.¹) ; Z 627 *S³* sim, AJSL 46 250 *Sᵃ* to be eaten when leaving ⲧⲥ.⁶, AM 311 *B* at dinner hour went to ϯⲥ.⁹ ; as pl : ShMIF 23 192 *S* ⲛⲉⲩⲥ.¹, ShC 73 37 *S* heat ⲅⲛⲛⲥ.¹, DeV 1 168 *B⁷* ; ⲛⲁⲧⲥ.² *S*, *bathman* : P 44 86 βαλανεῦς · ⲡ. حمامي ; ⲥⲓⲱⲟⲩⲡⲛⲧⲏⲥ *B* sim : K 113 '۔ (*cf* Stern 169). *V* ⲥⲉ seat & DM 13 15 n.

ⲥⲓⲟⲨ[ⲛ], **ⲥⲓⲟⲟⲛ** *S* nn m, as title, meaning unknown : Saq 98 (*cf ib* 1908 p 66), 133. *Cf* ? ⲉⲓⲟ-ⲟⲩⲛ.

ⲥⲟⲟⲨⲚ *SF*, **ⲥⲁⲩⲡⲉ** *AA²*, **ⲥⲡⲟⲩⲱⲛ** *A²* (Mani), **ⲥⲱⲟⲩⲛ**, **-ⲛⲟⲩ** *B*, **ⲥⲁⲟⲩⲛ**, **ⲥⲁⲟⲩ** (BM 586), **ⲥⲟⲩⲉⲓ** (*ib* 613) *F*, **ⲥⲟⲩⲛ-**, **ⲥⲟⲩⲙ-** *S*, **ⲥⲟⲩⲱⲛ-** *SAA²BF*,

соүеп- *SBF*, соүшп⸗ *SAA²BF*, сеоү. *S* (BHom 120 *bis*), споүшп⸗ *A²* vb **I** intr, *know*; Ge 19 33 *S* (*B* еιме), Job 8 9 *S*(*B* do), Ap 7 14 *S*(*B* tr) εἰδέναι; Ez 37 3 *SB* ἐπίστασθαι, Is 5 21 *F*(*SB* о псаве) ἐπιστήμων; PS 371 *S* sins done еүс., ShP 130¹ 141 *S* if he wish to lessen punishment птоц етс., Mani 1 *A²* сесаүпе рш птаү еп, AM 261 *B* ката фрнϯ ететпс.;   c е-: Ge 29 5 *SB*, Hos 5 3 *AB* γινώσκειν; Jo 4 10 *SA²F*(*B* е.) εἰδ.; PS 92 *S* ϯс. епмүстнріоп, C 73 209 *S* псаеіп етс. епшшпе, ShA 2 267 *S* will tell thee пеϯс. ероц;   +vb : Lu 11 13 *SB* c. е-(var п-), 1 Tim 3 5 *B*(*S* п-)еιδ.;   c етве-: Mk 13 32 *SF*(*B* е.) εἰδ. περί;   c п- + vb : Pro 29 7 *SA*, Is 29 11 *SB* ἐπίσ.; Job 11 2 *B* етс. псаχι (var χш поүмнш псаχι, *S* о пваз пшаχе) εὔλαλος; ShC 73 209 *S* етс. пр пазре, BSM 3 *B* пϯс. ппнві ап (v еіме g), J 94 4 *S* петс. псраι (cf ib 7 поι), Imp Russ Ar S 1080 *S* еүс. есраι (*l* псраι).

II tr : Deu 34 10 *SB*, 3 Kg 8 43 *B*(*S* еιме), Hab 3 2 *SA*(*B* ϯ піатⲥ), Jo 3 10 *SA²F*(*B* е.) γι., Ge 31 31 *SB*, Hos 2 20 *AB*, Mt 14 35 *SBF* ἐπιγι.; Ac 13 27 *S* соүшп паι (var соүеп, *B* еми) ἀγνοεῖν; Ex 32 22 *SB*, Pro 3 28 *SAB*, Is 5 13 *SBF*, Mk 9 6 *SF*(*B* е.) εἰδ., 1 Cor 4 4 *SB* συνειδ.; Deu 28 33 *SB*, Pro 9 13 *SAB* ἐπίσ.; Deu 32 29 *S*(*B* каϯ), Ps 35 3 *S*(*B* do) συνιέναι; He 3 1 *SF*(*B* ϯ піатⲥ) κατανοεῖν; Sa 11 14 *S* αἰσθάνεσθαι; Br 258 *S* none able есоүшпц, BG 68 *S* мпоүсоүшп птнрц, Sh BM 253 58 *S* соүшпеп *let us know ourselves & condemn selves*, Mani 1 *A²* споүшп мпмеіпе, ib 2 *A²* петпасоүшпоү пцр поіе ммаү, AP 9 *A²* аιсоүшп ппе, Hall 98 *S* прwме етапс. ппе етвннтоү, Aeg 11 *B* ммоп зли с. ммоц = ib *S* еι. ероц, Pcod 23 *S* language екс. ммос (var поι), Miss 8 211 *S* пеıс. ммоıпе еıсw пзпнрı епашшоү *I have known myself drinking*, ib 224 *S* = BMar 35 *S* sim, ib 175 *S* кпасоүеп ппро паı мппрмзаλ *distinguish* (corpse of) *king from slave*, Mor 24 7 *F* пшни псоүшп петпапоүв (Ge 2 17 *S* соүп-), Miss 4 236 *S* етреүсоүм ппе, ROC 20 418 *S* ere child соүп моүте епецıшт;   *know sexually*: Ge 4 17 *SB*, Jud 11 39 *SB*, Lu 1 34 *SB* γι.; AP 14 *A²* εἰδ.; Mt 1 18 *B*(*S* зwк ероүп ша-) συνέρχεσθαι; DeV 2 179 *B* апıрwмı с. тецсзıмı, R 1 3 32 *S* емпсс. ма пнкотк прооүт;   *with* χе-, a intr : Ge 18 19 *S*(*B* е.), Mt 22 16 *S*(*B* do), Aeg 281 *S* еүс. χеецпорпеүе εἰδ.; Is 48 4 *B*(*S* еı.), Jo 10 38 *SA²B* γι., Nu 22 34 *S*(*B* е.), Aeg 270 *S* сес. χептаүпоүрм ап ἐπίσ.; PS 84 *S* песс. аппе ...χеапокпе, BG 15 *S* аıсоүшп χе-, ShIF 66 *S* тетцсооүм (*sic*) птоц χепмте, CA 99 *S* bishop cannot еıме ероц but God петс. χе-, AM 229 *B*

тепс. χецшоп, BM 586 *F* еıксаоү(п) χеме(п) зааπı птаат, ib 613 *F* аксоүеı(п) χепшапе.   **b** tr : Jo 7 27 *SB* еıδ.; Ge 37 32 *B*, Ac 4 13 *S*(*B* е.) ἐπιγι.; BMis 4 *S* ϯс. ммооү χе зепрwме патзмотпе, C 43 184 *B* аксоүшпт χеапок пıм? сwоүпоү *B* : Dan 1 4 (*S* еı.) γι.; AM 31 апок етс. птхом, C 86 193 еүс. мпıтаıо & v nn.

—— nn m *SAA²BF*, соүеп- *B*, *knowledge*: 1 Kg 2 3 *S*(*B* еми), Pro 8 10 *SA*(*B* = Gk), Ro 11 33 *SF*(*B* е.), Cl 1 2 *A*, MG 17 315 *S* told пс. мпеıшаχе = C 89 3 *B* вwл γνῶσις, Hos 4 1 *SAB* соүеп-, Col 1 9 *SB* do ἐπίγν., Ac 25 21 *B* do (var сwоүп, *S* diff) διάγν.; Pro 9 10 *SA*(*B* каϯ) σύνεσις, Ac 7 25 *F* ϯ поүсаоүп (*S* еı., *B* к. verbs) συνιέναι; ShBM 230 158 *S* sins done змпс., Mani 1 *A²* tree of пс., AM 124 *B* Christianity оүсwоүпоү пте Фϯ, C 89 187 *B* псоүеп Фϯ, J 65 32 *S* зепс. етвептопос етоүаав *familiarity with*;   шрпс. *S*, *foreknowledge* : Jth 9 6, 1 Pet 1 2 (*B* шорп пе.) πρόγνωσις; мптш. : ClPr 35; сıпш. : BMis. 529 теүⲥ. *of what should befall*.

соүнп, -ıп *B*, *well known, famous person* : Ro 16 7 (var -ıп, *S* ϯ маеıп е-) ἐπίσημος; Va 59 2 оүеүгепнс оүоз пс., PO 14 366 ω пıс. ешапец, BMOr 8775 119 пс. [Arabic] ;   ер с. : Jo 18 15 (*SA²* vb tr) γνωστός εἶναι, Job 18 19 (*S* do) ἐπίγν.; HL 107 ецоı пс. *in city* ἀνθεῖν.

атс. *SBF*, -соүеп *B*, *without knowledge* : HL 86 *B* шшпı патсоүеп Фϯ ἀγνοεῖν, Pcod 24 *S* зепа. (var апонтос);   мпт-, метатс., *ignorance* : Lev 22 14 *S*(*B* еми neg), Ps 24 7 *S*(*B* метате.), Ac 3 17 *S*(*B* do) ἄγνοια, He 9 7 *SF*(*B* do) ἀγνόημα; R 1 2 71 *S*, Br 227 *S* тмптатсоүшпс, Cat 20 *B* ϯмететсоүеп Фϯ;   р, о патс., *be ignorant* : Sa 14 18 *S* ἀγνοεῖν;   c е- : Lu 9 45 *S*(*B* wвш), 1 Cor 14 38 *SF*(*B* оı пате.) ἀγν., Aeg 261 *S* ацр атс. епезооү;   c п- : Sa 13 1 *S* ἀγνωσία παρεῖναι, 1 Cor 15 34 *F* аı патсооү(м) мппϯ ἀγνωσίαν ἔχειν; ShC 73 2 *S* о па. ммоц, DeV 2 78 *B* шацер атсоүшп пецıшт, AM 128 *B* sim атсwоүпоү.

рмпс. *SB*, *one known, acquaintance* : Ru 2 1 *S*, P 129¹³ 44 *S* γνώριμος, Lu 23 49 *B*(*S* vb tr) γνωστός; Mor 34 31 *S* no р. змоос заρтн = BMis 105 мп рwме заρте рс. ммоц.

рецс. *B*, *one who knows* : Pro 12 26 (*S* om, *A* саве) ἐπιγνώμων;   мптрецсоүеп- *S*, *knowledge* : IFEpiph *De Gemm* on amethyst пеıм. пеоүоеıш мпеχıмшп *praedicere tempestates*.

χı с. *S*, *get knowledge* : BG 69 псχı поүс., ALR '93 523 not that еүеχı с. but that they might be proved.

ⲥıпсоүп-, χıпсоүеп- *SB*, *knowing, knowledge* : Ge 3 22 *B*(*S* vb tr), Ps 66 3 *B*(*S* еı. vb) γινώσκειν,

BMar 123 *S* ⲧⲋ̅. ⲡⲉϥⲉⲣⲏⲩ ἀναγνωρισμός ; Am 128 *B* ⲡϫ. ⲫ†.

ⲥⲓⲟⲩⲣ *SA²BF*, -ⲣⲉ pl(?) *S* nn m, *eunuch* (art *S* mostly ⲡⲉ-, ⲛⲉ-): Ge 40 2 *SB*, Mt 19 12 *SBF* εὐνοῦχος, Dan 1 7 *B* ⲭⲱⲭ ⲛⲥ. (*S* ⲥ.) ἀρχιευ.; Ge 37 36 *B*, Is 39 7 *SB* σπάδων; Glos 172 *S* ⲥ. (Gk lost), ὄρχιες ⲛⲧⲟϥ ⲟⲛ, P 44 71 *S* ⲟⲣⲭⲉⲓⲥ · ⲛⲥ.; Z 285 *S* ⲡⲉⲥⲓⲟⲩⲣⲉ, but *ib* ⲛⲉⲥⲓⲟⲩⲣ, PSBA 10 195 *S* Hilarion ⲛⲉⲥ., MIF 59 59 *S* Apa Jacob ⲯⲓⲟⲩⲣ, BM 359 *S* ⲟⲩⲅⲕⲉⲟⲩⲕⲗⲁⲣⲓⲟⲥ ⲛⲥ., C 43 37 *B* ⲛⲓⲥ. ⲡⲉⲙⲡⲓⲕⲟⲩⲃ. that is ⲡⲓⲙⲁⲑⲣⲱⲡⲁ, Mani 1 *A²* ⲛⲥ.; ⲣ̄ⲥ. Mt *lc* εὐνουχίζειν.

As name Πισιουρ (*sic* prob), Ψιοῦρις (Preisigke).

ⲥⲟⲩⲥⲟⲩ *S* vb tr, meaning uncertain, *guide, lead* (?): Mor 47 193 ϣⲁⲡⲧⲉⲡϣⲏⲣⲉ ⲛⲣⲱⲙⲁⲛⲟⲥ (Victor) ⲥ. ⲡⲓⲉⲗⲁⲟⲥ ⲉⲡⲉⲅⲙⲁ ⲉϥⲙⲟⲟϣⲉ ⲛⲓⲙⲁⲩ after festival at his τόπος, *ib* 22 57 those sailing on sea or river Michael ⲥ. ⲙⲙⲟⲟⲩ.

ⲥⲟⲩⲥⲟⲩ *SB* nn m, *point, atom, moment*: Is 29 5 *S*(*B* ϣⲱⲗⲅ) στιγμή; 1 Cor 15 52 *B*(*S* ϣⲡⲉⲛϣⲱⲡ) ἄτομον; P 44 53 *S* ⲗⲉⲡⲧⲁⲥ · ⲛⲥ., فلس; WTh 137 *S* ⲟⲩϭⲓⲥⲟⲩⲛⲟⲩ ⲙⲛⲟⲩⲥ.=C 86 55 *B* ⲟⲩⲥⲛⲟⲩ ⲡⲉⲙⲟⲩⲥⲛⲟⲩ (*cf* Dan 12 7), Cat 90 *B* ⲟⲩⲕⲟⲩϫⲓ ⲛⲥ. ⲙⲙⲁⲩⲁⲧϥ ⲡⲧⲉ ⲟⲩⲣⲓⲕⲓ ⲛⲃⲁⲗ, *ib* 114 *B* ⲟⲩⲥ. ⲡⲧⲉ ⲟⲩⲟⲩⲛⲟⲩ, BMis 36 *S* Diocletian given ⲟⲩⲥ. by Lord (*cf* Ap 12 12), BM 1104 *S* we have no care more pleasant than ⲉⲡⲁⲩ ⲉⲣⲱⲧⲛ ⲕⲁⲧⲁ ⲥ. [ⲥ]ⲭⲉ-ⲗⲟⲡ. As title: DeV 2 201 *B* monk ⲙⲁⲕⲁⲣⲓ ⲛⲓⲥ. As name (?): ⲥⲟⲩⲥⲟ (J 61 11). *Cf*? ⲥⲏⲩ.

ⲥⲟⲩⲥⲓⲟⲩ *S* nn, *wine measure*: PMich 1539 list ⲥ. ⲛⲏⲣⲡ, *ib* 604 wine account ⲥ. ⳽ ⲗ, *ib* 4545 list ⲅⲁⲗⲕⲟⲩ ⲅ, ⲥ. ⲃ⳽, Baouit 1 8 list ⲗⲁⲕⲟⲟⲧⲉ, ⲗⲁⲉ̣ⲏ, ⲥ.

ⲥⲟⲩⲥⲓⲟⲩ *speckled v* ⲥⲓⲟⲩ.

ⲥⲟⲩⲥⲟⲟⲩϣⲉ *v* ϣⲟⲩⲥⲟⲟⲩϣⲉ.

ⲥⲟⲩⲏⲧ *B v* ⲥⲃⲃⲉ.

ⲥⲟⲟⲩⲧⲉ *F v* ⲥⲟⲟⲩⲧⲛ nn s f.

ⲥⲟⲟⲩⲧⲛ *SA²F*, ⲥⲁⲩⲧⲛ *S f*, ⲥⲁⲩⲧⲛⲉ *A*, ⲥⲱⲟⲩⲧⲉⲛ, ⲥⲟⲩⲧⲱⲛ *B* (prob *l* ⲥⲟⲩⲧⲱⲛ-), ⲥⲁⲩⲧⲉⲛ *F*, ⲥⲟⲩⲧⲛ- *SA*, ⲥⲟⲩⲧⲱⲛ- *SABF*, ⲥⲁⲩⲧⲛⲉ- *A*, ⲥⲟⲩⲧⲉⲛ- *B*, ⲥⲟⲩⲧⲱⲛⲋ *SAB*, ⲥⲟⲩⲧⲱⲛ† *SABF*, ⲥⲟⲩⲧⲛⲧ† *AA²* vb **I** intr, *be straight, upright, stretch*: Jud 14 7 *S* εὐθύνειν, Ps 58 4 *SB*, Dan 8 25 *SB* ⲕⲁⲧⲉⲩ.; Jos 1 8 *S*, 2 Chr 7 11 *B* εὐοδοῦν, Ps 1 3 *S*(*B* † ⲙⲁ†) ⲕⲁⲧⲉⲩⲟⲇ.; Ac 21 1 *B*(*S* om) εὐθυ(δρομεῖν); Ps 19 8 *S*(*B* ⲟⲣⲓ ⲉⲣⲁⲧⲋ) Lu 13 13 *S*(var ⲥⲟⲟϭⲉ)*B* ἀνορθοῦσθαι, Pro 16 1 *SA* διορ., *ib* 2 9 *SA*(*B* ⲧⲁⲣⲟ ⲉⲣⲁⲧⲋ), 1 Kg 20 31 *S* (var ⲥⲟⲟϭⲉ) ⲕⲁⲧⲟⲣ.; Is 35 6 *SB*(var ⲥⲟⲃ†)*F* τρανὸς εἶναι; 1 Cor 8 1 *S*(BMis 411, var & *B* ⲕⲱⲧ) οἰκοδομεῖν; Si 14 13 *S* ἐκτεί-

ⲛⲉⲓⲛ; ShA 2 25 *S* ploughman ⲛⲧⲉⲡⲉϥⲧⲓⲟⲙ ⲥ., ALR '93 524 *S* ⲉϥⲛⲁⲧⲣⲉⲧⲕⲁⲕⲓⲁ ⲥ. through punishment, BKU 1 8 *S* that my tongue ⲥ. to chant well, AM 258 *B* crippled hands ⲥ., Mor 40 46 *S* ⲁⲡⲉϥϭⲣⲟ ⲥ. opp ⲥⲟⲧⲣ = MG 25 272 *B*.

II tr, *straighten, stretch*: Si 2 6 *SB* εὐθ., Mk 1 3 *SB* εὐθὺν ποιεῖν, Jer 21 12 *B*(*S* intr) ⲕⲁⲧⲉⲩ.; Is 48 15 *SB* εὐοδ., CaiEuch 588 *B* ⲥ. ⲛⲟⲩⲙⲱⲓⲧ ⲕⲁⲧ-ⲉⲩⲟⲇ.; Ps 118 9 *SB* ⲕⲁⲧⲟⲣ.; Lu 3 4 *SB* -ⲧⲱⲛ ⲉⲧⲟⲓⲙάζειν; *ib* 7 27 *S* (var & *B* ⲥⲟⲃⲧⲉ) κατασκευάζειν; Ge 3 22 *B*(*S* ⲥ. ⲉⲃⲟⲗ), Pro 29 37 *SA* ἐκτείν., Ps 84 6 *B*(*S* ⲥⲱⲙⲛⲧ) διατ.; ROC 17 400 *B* ⲁⲥⲥ. ⲙⲙⲟϥ (*sc* breast) ἐπέχειν; ShA 1 405 *S* ships ⲥ. ⲙⲡⲉⲩⲥϭⲏⲣ by stars, FR 162 *S* ⲉϥⲥ. ⲙⲙⲟϥ *setting him up* before altar, Va 61 ϥ4 *B* had not hands or feet ⲉⲑⲣⲉϥⲥⲟⲩⲧⲱⲛⲟⲩ. Qual: Ps 50 10 *SA*(Cl) -ⲁⲛⲧ *B*, Dan 3 27 *SB*, Hos 14 10 *A* -ⲁⲛⲧ *B* εὐθ., Ming 306 *S* ⲉⲕⲥ. ⲣⲙⲡⲉⲕⲣⲓⲧ εὐθύτης, Pro 9 15 *SA* -ⲱⲛ *B*, *ib* 15 8 *SA*-ⲁⲛⲧ ⲕⲁⲧⲉⲩⲑ.; Ez 1 7 *SB*(var ⲟⲣⲓ ⲉⲣⲁⲧⲋ), He 12 13 *SB* ὀρθός, Deu 18 17 *SB*, ὀρθῶς, Mic 7 2 *SA*-ⲁⲛⲧ ⲕⲁⲧⲟⲣ.; Jer 12 1 *SB* εὐοδ., Pro 24 64 *B*(*SA* ⲕⲁⲗⲱⲥ) εὐόδως, Ps 36 7 *S* (*B* ⲥⲉⲃⲧⲱⲧ) ⲕⲁⲧⲉⲩⲟⲇ.; Sa 5 22 *S* εὔστοχος; J 14 22 *S* ϫⲓⲁⲡⲟⲛⲥⲓⲥ ⲉⲥⲥ. (*cf* PMon 105 ὀρθῇ διανοίᾳ); Z 274 *S* ὀρθόδοξος; ROC 25 248 *B* of faith καλῶς (ὀρθῶς) φρονεῖν (*cf ib* ⲥⲙⲟⲛⲧ); Pro 27 16 *SA* ἐπιδέξιος; PS 80 *S* ⲉϥⲥ. ⲡⲉ ⲛⲟⲩⲟⲉⲓⲛ, ShMIF 23 87 *S* his hand ⲥ. ⲁⲛ ⲁⲥⲣ ϭⲱⲃ, ShC 73 94 *S* ⲡⲉⲧⲙⲉ-ⲉⲩⲉ ⲉⲡⲉⲥ., ShBM 230 147 *S* ⲉⲧⲥ. in speech ⲉⲧ-ϭⲟⲟⲗⲉ in deeds, Mani 1 *A²* ⲛⲃⲛⲓⲙⲁ ⲉⲧⲥ., P 129¹³ 61 *S* ⲛϥⲉⲣⲱⲃ ⲉⲧⲥ. whereon he leaned, *ib* 131⁵ 44 *S* perfume ⲉⲧⲥ. to 7th heaven.

With following preposition.

—— ⲉ- intr *S*, *right, fitted for*: Lu 9 62 (*B* ⲥ.†) εὔθετος dat, Jud 12 6 κατευθύνειν gen; BMis 382 sheep ⲁϥⲥ. ⲉⲧⲉⲭⲣⲓⲁ (var & BSM 37 *B* ⲥⲟⲃⲧⲉ); *stretch toward SB*: MIF 9 25 *S* when Saviour ⲥ. ⲉⲩϭⲓⲛⲟⲩⲱⲙ, BMar 73 *S* foods on table ⲙⲁⲣⲛⲥ. ⲉⲣⲟⲟⲩ, MélOr 6 505 *B* ⲁⲥⲥ. ⲉⲛⲓⲟⲩⲏⲃ & took mysteries; tr *SAA²BF*, *stretch* a thing *to*: Ps 137 7 *S*(*B* ⲥ. ⲉⲃⲟⲗ ⲉϫ.) ἐκτ. ἐπί, Pro 31 20 *B*(*SA* ⲛ-) ⲉⲕⲧ. dat, Va 57 10 *B* ϥⲥ. ⲉⲣⲱⲟⲩ ⲙⲡⲓⲟⲩⲁϩⲥⲁϩⲛⲓ ⲉⲡⲓⲧ., Phil 3 13 *B*(*S* ⲡⲱⲣϣ) ἐπεκτ. dat; Jo 19 29 *SA²*(*B* ⲅⲓⲧϥ ⲅⲁⲧⲉⲛ-) προσφέρειν dat; Ez 47 14 *B* αἴρειν εἰς; BMis 115 *S* ⲉⲩⲥⲟⲩⲧⲛ ⲧⲛⲛⲃⲉ ⲉⲡⲉϥⲉⲣⲏⲩ, *ib* 379 *S* ⲁϥⲥ. ⲉⲣⲟϥ ⲛⲧⲉϣⲧⲏⲛ = BSM 35 *B* ⲛⲁϥ, BAp 123 *S* ⲉⲕⲥ. ⲙⲡⲉⲕϫⲟⲓ ⲉⲅⲙⲁ ⲙⲙⲟⲟⲡⲉ, BM 661 *F* ⲧⲉⲕⲥⲁⲩⲧⲱⲛ (ⲉ)ⲗⲁⲓ ⲙⲡⲉⲧϣⲁⲗⲉⲡⲛ̅ⲛ̅ ⲧⲉⲉⲓϥ ⲉ-ⲧⲉⲕⲯⲩⲭⲏ; *make fit for, direct toward*: Jth 13 18 *S*, Lu 1 79 *S*(*B* ϫⲓⲛⲥ.) ⲕⲁⲧⲉⲩⲑ. εἰς; ShA 2 52 *S* hearts ⲥ.† ⲁⲛ ⲉⲛⲉϥⲉⲣⲏⲩ (*ib* sim ⲙⲛ-), TT 126 *S* found him ⲉϥⲥ.† ⲉⲡⲣⲱⲃ; ⲉϩⲣⲁⲓ ⲉ-: Ge 14 22 *S*(*B* ⲉϩⲣⲏⲓ ϩⲁ-) ⲉⲕⲧ. πρός.

—— ехп-, *stretch over* : Ps 59 8 *S*(*B* евол ех.), Ez 13 9 *B*(*S* ев. ех.) ἐκτ. ἐπί; еҩраı, -нı ех.: Dan 11 42 *SB* ἐκτ. ἐπί; Is 54 17 *S* intr *B* tr εὐοδ. ἐπί.

—— мн-, *be right with* : Ps 77 37† *SA*(Cl)*B* εὐθ. μετά; ShA 2 52 *S* v c е- tr.

—— ша-, *stretch to, as far as* : Ge 49 13 *B*(*S* пшрш ев. шаҩраı е-) παρατ. ἕως; Mor 48 107 *S* аıс. мпаҩнт шароц = C 43 152 *B* е҂оүп е-.

—— ҩн-, ҂еп-, *be upright in, stretch with* : ShC 42 120 *S* мерепетамаү с. ҩппеҩвнҩе, AM 167 *B* асс. ҂еппесмашх, Pcod 28 *S* ҁпас. ҩптеҷ҂ıпшнҩ, C 43 240 *B* аҷс. паҷ ҂ептеҷснҷı.

With following adverb.

—— евол intr, *stretch out* : Leyd 130 *S* c. ев. ye presbyters ἐκτ.; DeV 1 66 *B* аҷс. ев. аҷоүшм, Miss 4 764 *S^f* sim, R 1 1 67 *S* withered hands аҷтреүс. ев.; tr : Ge 3 22 *S*(*B* c.), 1 Kg 14 27 *S*(var c.), Hos 7 5 *AB*, Mt 14 31 *SB* ἐκτ.; BM 355 123 *S* angel c. ев. поүноҁ пҩвос = C 89 88 *B*, AM 85 *B* соүтен текхıх ев., *ib* 113 *B* ассоүтшп птеспаҩоүı (neck) ев., Mor 27 36 *S^f* аҷсоүтшп теҷ҂ıх ев., Miss 4 188 *B* апсоүтшп пеҷсшма ев. еѳрепкшс ммоҷ, MG 25 403 *B* sim, JSch 2 21 *S* if official find this deed пҷтмс. ев. мпҩап птме *maintain*; as nn : EW 148 *B* пс. ев. ппеҷтнв εὐθεῖα; qual : Jer 21 5 *SB* ἐκτ.; Ex 26 28 *B*(*S* хште оүте-) διικνεῖσθαι; ShC 42 140 *S* оүҩнт еҷс. ев., C 43 8 *B* wounded arm c. ев.; c е-, *stretch out to* : 2 Kg 6 6 *SB*, Pro 29 37 *S*(var & *A* c. е-) ἐκτ. ἐπί, Ac 4 30 *SB* ἐκτ. εἰς; Bor 288 172 *S* babe c. пеҷ҂ıх ев. to breast, Miss 4 761 *S^f* аҷс. ев. еоүшм, *ib* 589 *S* I marvel that ατετιταπρο c. ев. ехоос; c ехп-: Ps 59 10 *B* (*S* c. ех.), Zeph 1 4 *AB* ἐκτ. ἐπί; c ҩıхеп-: Ez 14 9 *B* ἐκτ. ἐπί.

—— епшшı, *stretch upward* : Ex 37 16 (38 15) *B* ἐξέχειν.

—— еҩоүп, е҂., *stretch into, forward* : BIF 13 111 *S* аҷс. е. ҩмпеҷҩо with weapon = MG 25 300 *B*, Mor 40 20 *S* атаүпамıс с. еҩ. ҩапестнҩ & drew forth book = C 43 50 *B*; c е-: Jos 24 23 *S* εὐθ. πρός, 1 Chr 29 18 *B* -тшп п- κατευθ. πρός; 1 Kg 7 3 *S* ἕτοιμ. πρός; Aeg 276† *S* ὀρθὸς εἶναι πρός; PS 26 *S* heart c.† еҩ. етмптеро of heaven, Va 61 214 *B* hands еүс.† е҂. еоүсҏос *stretched upon*, BMis 339 *S* ҭпас. мпаоүшш еҩ. ерок, *ib* 403 *S* апйе соүтшп теҷаҩапн еҩ. ершоү = BSM 51 *B*.

—— пн m *SABF*, *uprightness* : Ps 36 37 *SA*(Cl, *B* петс.†), He 1 8 *SBF* εὐθύτης, Is 40 4 *SB* εὐθεῖα; Si 10 5 *S* εὐοδία; Pro 24 73 *SA* ὀρθά; PS 96 2 *B* (*S* совте) κατόρθωσις; Sa 5 12 *S* σκοπός; ShA 2 234 *S* eyes етҁшшт епс., Va 63 26 *B* Michael is

пс. нте паҩнт = BMis 417 *S* солсл, ROC 7 145 *S* мпелааү пс. таҩоı *naught hath gone well*, P 129[16] 84 *S* when cripple touched relics апс. шшпе паҷ, BMis 316 *S* sim, Brussels E 6346 *F* паı҂е(п) псооүтн такоү ҩнт *when I find right* (occasion) & *come north*; ҩп-, ҂епоүс. adverbial, *uprightly, forthwith* : Ge 4 7 *A*(Cl, *B* vb), Lu 7 43 *SB* ὀρθῶς, CaiEuch 505 *B* етҁшшт евол...҂. ὀρθοτομεῖν; Ps 9 8 *SB* ἐν εὐθύτητι; Ex 33 13 *B*(*S* оүшнҩ евол) γνωστῶς, Ro 1 28 *S*(*B* емı) ἐπίγνωσις; Lev 26 28 *S* ҩ. ап (*B* diff) πλαγίῳ; BMar 113 *S* аүхоос ҩ. στοχαζόμενος; Jos 6 20 *S* ἐξ ἐναντίας; PS 307 *S* faith ҩ. ахпҩүпокрıсıс, ShC 73 105 *S* аүптоү ҩ., BMis 416 *S* that I come to port ҩ. = Va 63 25 *B* мооııес = BSM 58 *B* ҩıрннı, BM 528 V *F* ҩмпсооүте епйе (bis).

пс. *SF*(?), *forthwith, just now* : Ge 33 12 (*B* c.†) ἐπ᾽ εὐθεῖαν; 1 Kg 29 10 шерптнүтп п. (var & Gk om), BAp 116 ҁнаҁп апапаүсıс п., LMär 26 тнпактоп п., BMis 311 п. аıеıме ҂епток, *ib* 381 птаҁпараҭе ммок п. = BSM 37 *B* ҭпоү = Mor 27 31 *F* ҩеıоүкоүı, ST 267 амоү еҩоүп п., CO 199 мпҩҁш п. for we wait, ST 393 iterated п. п., BM 580 11 *F* аүтала соүа саҩтеп (*l* ? ec.), Kr 233 *F* пктнаоүтҷ пнı п.

метс. *B*, *rectification*, astrologer's reckoning table: K 129 ҭм. تقف.

реҷс. *B*, *straightener* : 1 Tim 6 18 (*S* реҷҭ) εὐμετάδοτος.

҂ıп-, хıпс. *SB*, *uprightness, establishment* : Lu 1 79 *B*(*S* vb tr) κατευθύνειν; Is 37 29 *B*(*S* om) var εὐθεῖα; ShC 73 14 *S* sword тес҂. евол *drawing forth* from sheath, Cat 76 *B* not to use sword or оүх. псаҩлı.

алаксшоүтеп *v* алос҂.

сшоүҩ *SAA²F*, -оүаҩ *S^f*, сеүҩ- *S*, сшоүҩ- *A*, сооүҩ҂ *S*, саүҩ҂ *AA²F*, сшҩ *A*, саоүҩ҂ *A²*, сооүҩ† *S*, саүҩ† *A*, саоүҩ† *A²*(*B* mostly ѳшоүҭ) vb **I** intr, *be gathered, collected* : Ge 29 3 *S*, Is 43 9 *S*, Mt 6 26 *S* συνάγειν, Mk 1 33 *S* ἐπισ.; Ac 10 27 *S* συνέρχεσθαι; *ib* 12 12 *S* συναθροίζεσθαι; Nah 3 14 *A* Gk diff (all *B* ѳшоүҭ); PS 269 *S* ҩпеҩернү еүс.†, Aeg 262 *S* fail not to c. ппаү пıм, JKP 2 54 *S^f* аүс. тнроү, BMar 125 *S* аүс. епаү епаҭшп.

II tr, *gather, collect* : Job 20 15 *S*, Is 34 16 *SF*, Jo 6 13 *SA²*(all *B* ѳ.) συνάγ., Zech 12 3 *A* ἐπισ.; Ps 128 7 *S*(*B* сшкı) συλλέγειν; AP 27 *A²* еүпас. птполıс, Kr 236 *F* петшаҷтеıҷ пнк саҩроү.

With following preposition.

—— е- *SAA²F*, *collect at, to* : Ps 2 2 *S*(*B* ѳ. е-) συνάγ. ἐπί, Mt 13 2 *S*(*B* ѳ. ҩа-) с. πρός, Jo 18 2 *SA²F*(P 129[18] 124, *B* ѳ. е-) с. ἐκεῖ, MG 17 325 *S*

place ⲉⲧⲉϣⲁⲡc. ⲉⲣⲟϥ = C 89 71 B σ. ὅπου, Su 4 S(B ⲡⲕⲟⲩ ϩⲁ-) προσάγ. πρός; Mk 2 13 S(B do) ἔρχεσθαι πρός, Job 6 29 S(B ϯ ⲙⲁϯ ⲡⲉⲙ-) συνέρ. dat; Ac 21 18 S(B ⲓ ϩⲁ-) παραγίνεσθαι; Mk 10 1 S(B do) συμπορεύεσθαι πρός; Pro 4 15 SA(B ⲑ. ⲉ-) στρατοπεδεύειν ἐν; Mk 15 16 S(BF ⲙⲟⲩϯ ⲉϩⲣⲏⲓ ⲉⲭⲉⲛ-) συγκαλεῖν; PS 93 S in midst of ⲡⲉⲧc.† ⲉⲣⲟⲓ, ShHT L 1 S place ⲉⲧⲟⲩc. ⲉⲣⲟϥ, Miss 8 25 S ⲉϥⲡⲁⲣⲁⲓⲧⲉⲓ ⲉc. ⲉⲧⲥⲩⲛϩⲟⲍⲟc, Aeg 17 S men c. ⲉⲣⲟⲕ = ib B ⲕⲱϯ ⲉ-, JKP 2 48 Sˢ ϣⲁⲡcⲟⲟⲩϩⲁ ⲧⲏⲣⲡ ⲉⲧⲉⲕⲕⲗⲏcⲓⲁ, ib 46 sim; against: Ps 30 13 S(B ⲑ. ⲉϩⲣ. ⲉⲭ.) cⲩⲛⲁⲅ. ἐπί; Ez 2 6 S(B do) ἐπισυνιστάναι ἐπί; tr: Lu 12 17 S(B ⲑ. ⲉ-) cⲩⲛⲁⲅ. ποῦ; ShMIF 23 153 S ⲛⲧⲁϥcⲟⲟⲩϩⲟⲡ ⲉⲡⲉⲡⲉⲣⲏⲩ; as nn: 2 Thes 2 1 S ⲡⲉⲡc. ⲉⲣⲟϥ (B ⲑ.) ἐπισυναγωγὴ ἐπί.

—— ⲉⲭⲛ- S, gather to: Jth 7 23 ἐπισυναγ. ἐπί; Jer 33 9 (B ⲑ. ⲉⲭ.) ἐξεκκλησιάζεσθαι ἐπί; ShC 73 9 ⲁⲩc. ⲉⲭⲙⲡⲭⲥ, ShR 2 3 38 Lord shall c. ⲙⲛⲧⲱϣ ⲉⲭⲙⲡⲧⲱϣ; ⲉϩⲣⲁⲓ ⲉⲭ.: Mt 27 27 (var om ⲉⲭ., B ⲑ. ⲉϩⲣ. ⲉⲭ.) cⲩⲛⲁⲅ. ἐπί; Nu 20 2 (B ⲑ. ⲉⲭ.) ἀθροι. ἐπί; against: Z 243 heretics ⲛⲧⲁⲩc. ⲉⲭⲛⲧⲕⲁⲑⲟⲗ. ⲉⲕⲕⲗⲏcⲓⲁ.

—— ⲙⲛ- SA, meet with: Pro 23 35 SA συνέρχ. μετά; Tri 341 ⲧⲁc. ⲙⲛⲧⲁϣⲉⲗⲉⲉⲧ اجتمع, Mor 22 103 Eve c.† ⲡⲓⲙⲁⲛ to-day, Miss 8 82 ⲛϥc. ⲙⲛⲧⲉⲓⲥⲩⲛϩⲟⲍⲟc.

—— ⲛ- S, gather at: Miss 8 39 synod ⲛⲧⲁcc. ⲛⲧⲙⲉⲧⲣⲟⲡⲟⲗⲓc (cf 40 ⲉⲧⲙ.).

—— ϩⲛ S, ϩⲓ- F, gather at, for: Ac 20 7† S(B ⲑ. ⲉ-) cⲩⲛⲁⲅ. inf; Z 274 S ⲛⲧⲁⲩc. ϩⲛⲡⲓⲕⲁⲓⲁ συνέρχ. ἐν; ShC 73 173 S ⲡⲉⲓⲧⲟⲡⲟc...ⲡⲉⲧc.† ⲡⲣⲏⲧⲟⲩ, Mor 30 40 F crowd c. ϩⲓⲡⲉⲓⲙⲉ.

With following adverb.

—— ⲉϩⲟⲩⲛ SAA²F, gather together, a intr: Ps 47 4 S, Is 33 4 SF, Lu 22 66 S cⲩⲛⲁⲅ., Is 9 5 S ⲉⲡⲓⲥ. (all B ⲑ.); Aeg 273 S let people c. ⲉϩ. συνέρχ.; Ps 38 6 S(B ϩⲓⲟⲩⲓ ⲉⲥ.), 2 Cor 12 14 SF(B do) θησαυρίζειν; Aeg 245 S ⲉϥc. ⲉϩ. on Sunday cⲩⲛⲇⲣⲟⲙⲟc; ShC 42 148 S ⲉⲡc.† ⲉϩ. talking, TU 24 1 3 S ⲁⲩⲙⲏⲛϣⲉ c. ⲉϩ.; ⲉϩ. ⲉ-, gather to, for: Mt 6 26 S(B ϩⲓ. ⲉ-) cⲩⲛⲁⲅ. εἰς, Ac 4 27 S(B ⲑ. ⲉⲭⲉⲛ-) c. ἐπί; Si 11 10 S συνεδρεύειν ἐν; Bor 100 102 S heresy ⲛⲧⲁcc. ⲉϩ. ⲉⲡⲉⲕⲕⲗⲏcⲓⲁ; ⲉϩ. ⲙⲛ-, foregather with: Mt 28 12 S(B ⲑ. ⲡⲉⲙ-) cⲩⲛⲁⲅ. μετά; Lu 24 33† S(B do) ἀθροι.; ShA 2 81 S ⲉc. ⲉϩ. ⲙⲛⲧcⲩⲛⲁⲅⲱⲅⲏ for prayer; c ethic dat: Ex 16 26 S(B cⲱⲕⲓ) συλλέγειν; Lu 12 21 S(B ϩⲓ. ⲉⲥ.) θησ. dat. b tr: Ge 29 22 S, Job 27 16 S, Mic 4 12 A cⲁⲩⲅⲟⲩ (all B ⲑ.), Mt 13 47 S(BF do), Jo 4 36 SA²(B do) cⲩⲛⲁⲅ., Mt 24 31 S(BF do) ἐπισ.; Mt 13 28 S(B cⲱⲕⲓ, F ⲕⲱⲧϥ) συλλέγ.; Zech 9 3 SA cⲱⲣⲟⲩ (B ⲑ.),

Ro 2 5 SA (El 72, B ϩⲓ. ⲉⲥ.) θησαυρίζειν; Am 7 16 SA(B ⲑ. ⲉⲭ.) ὀχλαγωγεῖν ἐπί; 4 Kg 15 30 S συστρέφειν; Pro 29 11 SA ταμιεύεσθαι; ShC 42 144 S c. ⲡⲁⲓ ⲉϩ. ⲡⲡⲁcⲱϣⲉ reap, Br 79 S ⲛⲧcⲟⲟⲩϩⲟⲩ ⲧⲏⲣⲟⲩ ⲉϩ.; ⲉϩ. ⲉ-: Mt 13 30 S(BF ⲑ.) cⲩⲛⲁⲅ. εἰς; c ethic dat: Pro 10 10 SA(B ⲑ. ⲛ-) cⲩⲛⲁⲅ. dat; ShBM 230 158 S ⲧⲏc. ⲡⲁⲛ ⲉϩ. ⲡⲟⲩϣⲱϥ; as nn m, gathering, congregation: Ex 34 22 S(B ⲑ.) συναγωγή; 4 Kg 15 15 S συστροφή; Leyd 129 S ⲛc. ⲉϩ. of this monastery, sim ShC 73 59 S, Lant 47, 48 S, BAp 127 S, J 106 17 S, BM 588 F, CMSS 25 Bˢ.

—— nn m SF, a gathering: Lu 21 25 (B diff) συνοχή; CMSS 23 F I greet ⲡⲉⲕc. ⲧⲏⲣϥ; for divine service (σύναξις): Mus 40 44 ⲡⲧⲱϣ ⲙⲡc. collecta major; ShC 73 60 ⲡc. of morn & evening, ib 133 ere (board) be struck for ⲡc., ib 132 when ⲡc. is dismissed; ⲣ ⲡc., do, attend service: Bor 134 4 (Vita Sin) ⲁϥⲣ ⲡc. ⲙⲡⲡⲉⲥⲛⲏⲩ = C 41 33 B cⲩⲛⲁⲝⲓc, Mor 37 13 came to community on Sunday ⲛϥⲣ ⲡc. with brethren, CO 41 (ⲉ)ⲡⲉⲣ ⲡc. ϩⲓⲣⲟⲩϩⲉ. b meeting-place for service: BAp 114 went in to ⲡc. = MIE 2 390 B ⲉⲕⲕⲗⲏcⲓⲁ, Mor 18 90 sim = Miss 4 154 B do, Miss 4 630 he built ⲡc., ShC 42 142 house of God ⲉⲧⲉⲡⲉⲛc. ⲡⲉ, ShC 73 83 corpse taken to ⲡc., ST 354 entered ⲡc. & stole lamp, Mich 550 46 washed out ⲡc. ⲧⲏⲣϥ.

ⲙⲁ ⲡc. S, place of meeting: Deu 22 15 (B = Gk) πύλη; 1 Kg 7 17 S (var ⲙⲁ ⲛⲉcⲱⲁ ie cⲧⲟ) ἀποστροφή; store-house: R 1 2 44 ⲡⲙ. ⲡⲟⲩⲛⲁⲣⲑⲉⲛⲟcⲡⲉ ⲡⲁⲣⲟ (var ⲧⲁⲡⲣⲟ) ⲡⲧⲉⲥⲯⲩⲭⲏ.

ⲣⲉϥcⲉⲩϩ- S, collector: BMis 301 David ⲡⲣⲉϥcⲉⲩϩ ⲟⲩⲉⲗⲗⲉ collector of songs, FR 26 sim, cⲉϩ- Mor 19 3 do, P 44 92 cⲉⲩϩ- جامع النغمات (cf cⲱⲕ II FR 12).

ⲥⲓⲛc. S, gathering: ROC 20 46 ⲧⲉⲧⲛⲥ. ⲉⲡⲉϥⲧⲟⲡⲟc, My 22 ⲧⲥ́. ⲡⲓⲙⲟⲟⲩ (cf Ge 1 10).

cⲟⲟⲩϩc, -ⲁϩc (Ac) S, cⲁⲩϩc AA², cⲁⲟⲩϩc F nn f, congregation, collection: Pro 5 14 SA, Ac 19 39 S (var -ⲁϩc), 1 Cor 16 19 SF(all B = Gk) ἐκκλησία; Is 22 6 S(B ⲑⲱⲟⲩⲧc), Ob 13 SA(B = Gk) συναγωγή; Jth 11 9 S συνεδρία; Nu 32 14 S(B ⲑ.) σύστρεμμα; Hos 13 12 A(B ϥⲱⲧϩ) συστροφή; Pro 21 6 SA θησαύρισμα, Jos 7 26 S σωρός; Lu 5 9 S (B ϫⲟⲣⲭc) ἄγρα; Pro 22 22 SA πύλαι; Jth 14 11 S σπεῖρα; Ps 139 9 S(B diff) κύκλωμα; R 1 4 51 S ⲟⲩc. of monks approached him, Mani 2 A² ⲧc. [ⲉⲧ]ϩⲙⲉⲥⲧ ϩⲓⲧⲉϥϩⲉϩ, BIF 13 114 S c. ⲛⲁⲛⲛⲉ; monastic congregation S: ViK 9516 ⲧc. of Evagrius (var 9454 cⲱⲟⲩϩ) συνωδία, BMar 210 ⲟⲩc. of monks = Rec 6 175 B ⲁⲃⲏⲧ, Mor 51 33 ⲡⲉϥc. ⲉⲧⲉⲡⲁⲓⲡⲉ ...ⲡⲉϥϩⲉⲛⲉⲉⲧⲉ, MG 17 308 ⲡc. = C 89 180 B ⲙⲟⲛⲱⲟⲩⲓ, ShC 73 129 observe canon of prayer in

ⲡⲥⲱⲟⲩϩ or field or ⲧⲥ., BMis 150 ⲟⲩⲁⲡⲉ ⲛⲥ. that is father of monastery, MG 17 330 ϩⲏⲧⲟⲩⲙⲉⲡⲟⲥ ⲛⲥ., Mus 40 40 ⲡⲣⲱⲙⲉ ⲡⲧⲥ. *pater monasterii*, ShC 73 142 sim, Miss 4 598 ⲡⲟⲓⲕⲟⲛⲟⲙⲟⲥ ⲉⲧϩⲓϫⲛⲧⲕⲟⲓ-ⲛⲱⲛⲓⲁ ⲡⲡⲥ. ⲧⲏⲣⲟⲩ, ShC 73 167 ⲡⲙⲉϩⲥⲛⲁⲩ ⲛⲥ., Cai stele 8724 Kalashire ⲡⲙⲉϩⲥⲛⲁⲩ ⲛⲥ. (cf ⲥⲛⲁⲩ *sf* δευτεράριος).

p c., *be collected*: Am 7 10 *A*(*B* ⲉⲣ ⲑ.), Ac 23 12 *S*(*B* ⲑ. vb) συστροφὰς ποιεῖν. *Cf* sauhes (Rec 28 211, where *l* ⲥⲟⲟⲩϩⲥ).

ⲥⲉⲩϩⲓ *F* v ⲥⲁϩⲟⲩ.

ⲥⲟⲟⲩϩⲉ *S*, ⲥⲁⲩ. *SSf*, ⲥⲁⲩϩ(ⲉ) *AA²Sᵃ*(Ep 333), ⲥⲱⲟⲩϩⲓ *B* nn f, **a** egg: Is 10 14 *SB*, Lu 11 12 *SB*, JA '75 5 242 *S* if sick man ϫⲓ ⲉⲃⲟⲗ ϩⲓⲟⲩⲥ. it is no sin ᾠόν; ShBor 247 126 *S* ⲟⲩⲣⲓⲟⲡ ⲉⲧⲉⲡⲁⲓⲡⲉ ⲥ. ⲡⲧⲉ ⲡⲧⲏⲩ (cf Is 59 5 & الريض), PMéd 287 *S* ⲟⲩⲥ. ⲡⲧⲉ ⲡⲣⲟⲟⲩ, Mich 136 3 *S* ⲉⲓⲧⲣⲉⲥ. ⲛⲓⲙ ⲣ ϣⲁⲩ, *ib* ⲥ. ⲛⲁϩⲣⲏⲛ *unfertile*, Ryl 107 *S* ⲧⲥ. ⲙⲡⲁⲡⲟⲓ, AJSL 46 244 *S* ⲥ. ⲛⲃⲏϭ ⲛⲧⲏⲥⲁⲡⲓϫⲉ ⲙⲙⲟⲥ, BMis 503 *S* ⲟⲩⲥ. ⲉϣⲁⲥⲡⲓⲥⲉ, ShC 73 173 *S* ⲧⲥ. ⲉⲥ-ⲙⲟⲗϩ, Mani 2 *A²* ϩⲁⲗⲱⲙ ϩⲓⲥ.; ⲙⲟⲟⲩ ⲡⲥ. *S*, *white of egg* (cf ᾠῶν ὑγρότης Galen-Kuhn 10 937): PMéd 172, CR '87 376, AZ 23 108; ⲏⲗⲗⲉ ⲡⲥ. *S*, *yolk*, v ⲏⲗⲗⲉ; Bodl(P) f 78 *S* list of utensils (?) ⲟⲩⲥ. ⲛⲃⲁⲣⲱⲧ; ⲥⲱⲟⲩϩⲓⲧⲉ *B* f, *white of eye*: K 75 ϯⲥ. بيضة (v Stern 169); ⲉⲓⲉⲛⲥ. *S*, *egg-shaped ornament*: P 44 104 = 43 88 سوسانية (Ex 25 32 ? σφαιρωτήρ); ⲥ. ⲡⲕⲟⲩⲙⲁⲣⲓ (AZ 23 33, MIF 9 61) *B* m, *garden egg-plant*: P 55 6 = Montp 148 باذنجان, cf ⲡⲁⲓⲧⲏ. **b** *crown* of head: Deu 28 35 *SB*, 2 Kg 14 25 *S* (var om), Ps 7 17 *B*(*S* ⲙⲛⲧⲉ), *ib* 67 22 *B* var m κορυφή; ShA 2 268 *S* your blood on you & ⲧⲥ. ⲡⲭⲱⲧⲛ, ShC 42 26 *S* ⲧⲥ. ⲛⲧⲉⲧⲛⲁⲡⲉ, PGol 47 *A* ⲧⲥⲁⲩϩ(ⲉ) ⲛⲭⲱⲟⲩ, C 86 275 *B* drove nails into his ⲁⲫⲉ ϣⲁⲧⲟⲩϭⲟⲩϫⲉⲙ ⲛⲧⲥ. ⲛⲭⲱϥ, Va 61 98 *B* ⲧⲥ. ⲛⲧⲉϥⲁⲫⲉ = Mor 25 15 *S* (prob). In name: Πατσοουρε (BM 1075).

ⲥⲁⲩϩⲥ *S* nn f, woman's title (?): Ostr N de G Davies ϫⲉⲛⲁⲣⲟ ⲧⲥ.

ⲥⲟⲟⲩϩⲥ v ⲥⲱⲟⲩϩ *sf*.

ⲥϥⲓⲣ *B* v ⲥⲡⲓⲣ.

ⲥϥⲣⲁⲛϣ *B*, *soothsayer*: Ge 41 8 (*S* ⲣⲉϥⲟⲩⲉϩ ⲣⲁⲥⲟⲩ) ἐξηγητής (var κρυφιαστής) معبّر; K 114 ساحر. *V* JEA 4 252.

ⲥϥⲏⲓϯ *B* v ⲥⲣⲃⲏⲛⲧⲉ.

ⲥϥⲟⲧⲟⲩ *B* v ⲥⲡⲟⲧⲟⲩ.

ⲥϫⲁⲓ *B* v ⲥⲕⲁⲓ.

ⲥⲁϫⲟ v ⲥϫⲁⲓ (ⲥⲁϩ).

ⲥⲁϫⲟⲗ *B* nn m, *muzzle*, with vb ϯ: Deu 25 4 (*S* ϣⲧⲁⲙ vb), 1 Cor 9 9 (*S* do, *F* ϯ ϭⲗⲏϭ) φιμοῦν; K 127 ⲡⲥ. اكمة.

ⲥϫⲓⲙ *B* v ⲥⲕⲓⲙ.

ⲥϫⲁⲁⲧ v ⲥϭⲁⲧ.

ⲥⲁϣ, ⲥⲁϩ *blow* &c v ⲥⲱϣ *strike*.

ⲥⲁⲓϣ *A²* nn m, incorporeal being accompanying man, 'double' (?): Mani 2 ⲡⲥ....ⲉϥⲟ ⲡⲉϥ ⲡϣⲏⲣⲁⲟⲩϩⲧ ⲉϥⲗⲁϫⲧ ⲁⲣⲁϥ ⲁⲙⲁ ⲡⲓⲙ, Mani 1 ⲡⲉⲡⲁⲣ-ⲙⲉ ⲁⲡⲁⲥ. ϩⲛⲡⲁⲃⲉⲗ. Related ? to ⲥⲟⲉⲓϣ.

ⲥⲛϣ *rigid* v ⲥⲱϭ.

ⲥⲟⲉⲓϣ, ⲥⲟⲉⲓⲣ *S*, ⲥⲁⲉⲓϣ *Sᵃ*, ⲥⲁⲉⲓϩ *Sᵃf*, ⲥⲁⲓϩ *A*, ⲥⲁⲓϣ *A²*, ϣⲱⲓϣ *B* (once), ϣⲁⲓϣ *F* nn m, *pair of animals*: 2 Kg 16 1 *S*, Job 1 3 *S*(*B* ϩⲉⲃⲓ), Is 5 10 *SF*(*B* do), Lu 2 24 *SB* ζεῦγος; Ryl 113 *S* ζευγος· ⲡⲥ. ⲡⲣⲱⲧⲣ ⲡϣⲱⲛⲃ, BerlOr 1607 1 109 *S* ⲥ. ⲛⲉϩⲉ, *ib* *Sf* -ⲉⲓⲣ, RE 9 136 *Sᵃ* sim, BIF 14 143 *S* ⲙⲙⲁⲥⲉ, BMis 59 *S* ⲡⲥⲛⲏ, Win 62 *Sᵃ* -ϣ ⲛϣⲣⲟⲙⲡⲉ; of persons, things, clothes: Lev 3 4 *S*(*B* ⲃ̄) kidneys, δύο; TU 43 1 *A* ⲡⲥ. ⲡⲗⲏⲥⲧⲓⲥ, ShC 73 61 *S* ⲛϩⲃⲟⲟⲥ as shroud, CO 68 *S* ⲡⲕⲉⲣⲉⲁ (κειρία), ST 268 *Sᵃ* sim, Ep 348 *S* ⲥ. & -ⲉⲓⲣ, BM 1066 *S* ⲡⲉⲕⲥⲩⲛ-ⲑⲓⲁ ⲉⲧⲉⲟⲩⲥ. ⲛϭⲓϫ (of cloth ?), Bodl(P) b 5 *S* ⲥⲟⲉⲓϩ ⲛⲟⲉⲓⲕ (cf Wess 20 218 ψωμίων ζεύγη).

ⲥⲟⲉⲓϣ, ϣⲟⲉⲓⲥ *S*, ϣⲁ. *Sf* nn, a measure: PRain 4723 *S* ⲥ. ⲛⲏⲣⲡ, PCai 67324 vo *Sf* list of σκεύη, ⲏⲓⲣ ⲡⲗⲉⲕⲙⲛ, ϣⲁⲉⲓⲥ ⲡⲗ., BMOr 6201 *B* 47 *S* about dates, loaves &c ⲁⲓⲙⲉϩ ⲟⲩⲛⲟϭ ⲛϣⲟⲉⲓⲥ ⲛⲃⲁⲧϩⲁϣ.

ⲥⲱϣ *S*, (ϣⲱϣ) ϣⲁϣ *B*, ⲥⲉϣ-, ϣⲉⲥ-, ⲥⲟϣ⸗ *S* vb intr *B*, tr *S*, *strike*: C 86 175 *B* ⲡⲉⲭⲁϥ ϫⲉϣ. in Lord's name (? corrupt), LAp 366 *S* ⲁⲩϣⲉⲥ ⲡⲙⲁⲕϩ ⲙⲡⲁⲩⲗⲟⲥ τραχηλοκοπεῖν, BHom 126 *S* ⲉⲩⲥ. ⲙⲙⲟⲩ ϩⲛⲣⲉⲙⲁⲥⲧⲓⲅ⳹, ShHT K 11 *S* ⲡⲉⲧⲣ-ⲡⲟⲃⲉ ⲉⲣⲟϥ ϣⲁϥⲥⲟϣϥ; ⲣⲉϥⲥⲉϣ ⲉⲓⲱⲧ *S*, *father-striker*: 1 Tim 1 9 (*B* ϩⲁⲧⲉⲃ-) πατραλῴας.

ⲥⲁϣ *S*, ⲥⲁϩ *A*, ϣⲁϣ, -ϣⲓ *B*, ϣⲉϣ, ϣⲛϣ *F*, ⲥϣ-, ϣⲥ- *S*, ϣⲥⲉ- *SF*, ⲥⲥ- *S*, ⲥⲉ- *Sf*, ⲥϩ- *A*, ϣⲉ- *SBF*, ϣ- *F*, ϣⲧⲉ- *SF*, pl (rarely sg) ⲥⲛϣⲉ *SA²*, -ϩⲉ *A*, ϣⲛϣⲓ *B* f, nn m f, *stroke, blow, sore*: Ex 21 25 *S* (*B* ϥⲱϣ⳿), Is 1 6 *SF*(*B* ⲉⲣϭⲟⲧ) τραῦμα; Lev 13 19 *S*(*B* do), Job 2 7 *SB*, Pro 25 20 *S*(var ⲡⲗⲏⲅⲏ)*A* Ap 16 2 *SB*(var -ϣⲓ) ἕλκος; Is 30 26 *S*(*B* ⲉⲣ., *F* ⲡⲱⲗⲁϩ), Ac 16 23 *B*(*S* ⲥⲛϣⲉ) πληγή; Is 53 5 *S*(*B* ⲗⲉⲗⲉⲭⲛⲁⲓ) μώλωψ; Ps 146 3 *S*(*B* ⲧⲉⲛⲡⲟ) σύν-τριμμα; *ib* 38 2 *S*(*B* ⲙⲕⲁϩ) ἄλγημα; Sa 11 20 *S* βλάβη; Deu 7 15 *S*(*B* ϣⲱⲛⲓ) νόσος; BMis 555 *S* ⲡⲥ. ⲉⲧⲛⲏⲩ ⲉⲃⲟⲗ ϩⲓⲱⲧ like grain of corn *vulnus*; Till Oster 13 *A* ⲡⲉⲥⲥ....ⲧⲛⲡⲗⲏⲧⲛ, AM 112 *B* ⲟⲩϣ. ⲉⲛⲟⲩⲱⲧ of sword, Mor 30 41 *F* Lord touched

ⲡⲉϥϣⲏϣ, *ib* 24 *F* ⲟⲩϣⲉϣ ⲉϥϩⲣⲁⲩ, DeV 1 173 *B* body λεϣⲗⲱϥ ⲉⲃⲟⲗ ϫⲉⲡⲟⲩⲡϣⲏϯ ⲡϣ., BP 10587 *S* ⲟⲩⲥ. ⲡⲁⲧⲕⲁⲑⲁⲣⲓⲍⲉ, PMéd 320 *S* ϩⲱϩ ⲡⲥ.; pl forms: Deu 25 2 *SB*, Zech 13 6 *SA*(*B* ⲉⲣ.), Ac 16 23 *S*(*B* sg) πλ.; Si 23 2 *A*(Cl, *S* = Gk) αἴκισμα; *ib* 23 10 *S* ⲙⲱ.; ShA 1 81 *S* ⲡⲁϣϭⲁ ⲛ ⲡⲁⲥ., Mani 2 *A²* ⲡⲉⲧⲙⲡϣⲁ ⲡⲥ., R 1 2 48 *S* ϩⲉⲛⲡⲟϭ ⲡⲥ. (var Lammeyer 51 ϩⲛⲥⲁϣ), Va 58 77 *B* ⲡⲉⲕϣ. ⲡⲉⲙⲡⲉⲕϫⲫⲓⲟ; as sg f: Job 10 17 *S*(*B* ⲉⲧⲁⲥⲙⲟⲥ) ἔτασις; MélOr 6 505 *B* ⲧⲁⲓⲡⲓϣϯ ⲡϣ.   *V* ⲡⲟⲩϭⲥ (ⲡⲁϭⲥⲉ).

ⲣ ⲥ., ⲟ ⲡⲥ., ⲟⲓ ⲡϣ. *SB*, *cover, be covered with wounds, sores*: Lu 16 20 *SB* ἑλκοῦσθαι; Deu 8 4 *B*(P 104 92, Tatt ϣⲁϣⲣ, *S* ⲗⲱⲟⲧⲉ) τυλοῦσθαι; Va 63 97 *B* ⲟⲓ ⲡϣ. ἕλκη ἔχειν; R 1 3 77 *S* healing them ⲉⲧⲟ ⲡⲥ., PMéd 320 *S* ⲉⲣⲉⲧⲉϥⲁⲡⲉ ⲟ ⲡⲥ. ϩⲓ ψⲱⲣⲁ, Mor 55 73 *S* ⲉⲕⲱϣⲁⲡⲣ ⲡⲉϥⲥⲱⲙⲁ ⲧⲏⲣϥ ⲡⲥ.

ϯ ⲥ., ϣ. *SB*, *give a blow*: Ex 21 12 *B*(*S* ⲣⲱϩⲧ) πατάσσειν; Mk 14 47 *B*(*S* do) παίειν; Lev 24 20 *S*(*B* ⲁϭⲡⲓ) μῶμον διδόναι; ROC 25 250 *B* ⲁϥϯ ⲡⲟⲩϣ. ϫⲉⲡⲡⲓϣⲃⲱⲧ κρούειν; C 86 339 *B* ϯ ⲛϩⲁⲛⲡⲓϣϯ ⲡϣ. (var -ϣⲓ) ⲡⲁϥ.

ϫⲓ ⲥ. *S*, *receive wound, be wounded*: Lu 12 47 *S* ϫⲓ ⲥ. (*B* ϯ ϣⲁϣ) δέρεσθαι; BM 257 328 they shoot arrows but ⲙⲉⲥϫⲓ ⲥ.

Construct forms (*v* above, on gender Spg 130 n). ϣⲥ ⲡⲁⲁⲥ Miss 4 642 *S* = ϣⲉ ⲡⲕⲟⲩⲣ C 14 40 *B*, ϣⲉ ⲡⲁ. BIF 13 111 *S* = ⲕⲟⲩⲣ MG 25 300 *B*, ϣⲉⲡⲡⲉⲉⲥ Mor 30 59 *F*, ϣⲥⲉ ⲡⲁ. MIF 9 47 *S*, ⲥ ⲡⲁ. Mor 17 21 *S*, f in LMär 12 *S*; ϣⲉ ⲡⲃⲁⲓ C 41 42 *B*; ϣⲉ ⲡⲁⲉⲙⲱⲡ *B* MG 25 91, C 43 86 (*cf* δαιμονιόπληκτος); ϣⲉ ⲡⲕⲉⲗⲉⲃⲓⲛ C 89 173 *B*; ϣⲥ ⲡⲕⲟⲩⲙⲡⲟⲥ (κόμβος) R 1 5 50 *S*; ϣⲉ ⲡⲕⲁϣ Cat 113 *B* (Mt 27 30); ϣⲥ ⲡⲗⲟⲩϭⲛ ShC 73 x *S*, ⲥϩ TU 43 3 *A*, ϣⲉ DeV 2 109 *B*, f in BAp 32 *S*, Bor 260 *ult S*, MG 25 178 *B*, DeV 2 107 *B*, Mél Or 6 517 *B* (but P 54 154 *B* among weapons ϯϣⲉ πλ. الخرابة *spear-shaft*); ϣⲥ ⲡⲗⲱⲕⲥ ShZ 601 *S*; ϣⲥ ⲡⲗⲁⲕⲧⲏⲥ (λακτίζειν) Mor 46 18 *S* = *ib* ϣⲥ ⲡⲡⲁⲧ, ϣⲥⲉ πλ. Mor 19 98 *S* = ϣⲉ ⲡϥⲁⲧ Miss 4 157 *B*, ⲥⲉ πλ. Mor 32 19 *S*, ϣⲧⲉ πλ. Ricci L 260 *F*; ϣⲥ ⲡⲗⲁⲥ Job 5 21 *SA*(Cl, *B* = Gk) μάστιξ γλώσσης; ϣⲥ, ϣⲉ ⲡⲙⲉⲣⲉϩ *v* ⲙⲉⲣⲉϩ adding ϣⲧⲉ ⲙ. Mor 39 39 *Sf*, ϣⲥⲉ ⲡⲙ. *ib* 43; ⲥϣ ⲡⲗⲟⲩⲅ ShA 1 49 *S*; ⲥⲉ ⲙⲙⲉⲣⲧⲱⲡ *v* ⲧⲱⲣⲛ *sew*; ϣⲛⲡⲉⲩⲃⲟⲩ (collated) *v* ⲡⲁⲩⲃⲉⲛ; ϣⲉ ⲡⲛⲓϭⲓ *v* ⲛⲓϭⲉ adding MG 25 161 *B*; ϣⲉ ⲡⲥⲉⲣⲃⲉⲡⲓ 2 Cor 12 7 *B* (*v* ⲥⲟⲩϩⲉ) σκόλοψ; *v* also ⲁϫⲉ, ⲕⲟⲩⲣ *blow*, ⲕⲉϩ, ⲥⲟⲧϩⲉϥ, ⲥⲛϥⲉ, ⲧⲏⲛⲃⲉ, ⲧⲁⲡ, ⲧⲱⲛ *stop up*, ⲧⲁϭⲥⲉ, ⲱϥⲧ (ⲉⲓϥⲧ), ϣⲃⲱⲧ, ϩⲱⲱⲕⲉ *scrape*, ϩⲏⲧ *heart*, ϩⲁⲧⲏⲣ, ϭⲉⲣⲱⲃ.

ϭⲱϣ *S*, ϣⲟⲥ *SAA²*, ϣⲱϣ *BF*, ⲥⲉϣ-, ϣⲉⲥ- *S*, ϣⲱⲥ- *A²*, ϣⲉϣ-, ϣⲁϣ- (*v* ⲣⲉϥⲥ.) *B*, ⲥⲟϣⲝ, ϣⲟⲥⲝ *S*, ⲥⲁϣⲝ *Sf*, ϣⲁⲥⲝ *A*, ϣⲟϣⲝ *B*, ϣⲁϣⲝ *F*, ⲥⲏϣⲧ *S*,

ϣⲏⲥⲧ *SA*, ϣⲛϣⲧ *BF*, ⲣ ⲥ ϣⲁϣ- *B* vb **I** intr, *be despised, humbled*: Ge 16 4 *SB*, Is 53 3ᵗ *A*(Cl)*B* (*S* ⲥⲱϣϥ), Mk 12 4ᵗ *S*(*B* ϣⲱϣϥ) ἀτιμάζεσθαι, Job 30 4 *S*(*B* ⲁϫⲟⲕⲓⲙⲟⲥ), Is 3 5 *SA*(Cl)*B*, Mt 13 57 *SBF* ἄτιμος (εἶναι); Ps 30 12ᵗ *B*, Is 30 3 *B*(*S* ⲡⲟϭⲛⲉϭ, *F* ϩⲱⲙⲧ) ὄνειδος (εἰ.); 1 Kg 16 7ᵗ *S*(*B* ϣⲱϣϥ) ἐξουδενοῦν, 1 Cor 6 4 *B*(*S* ⲥⲱϣϥ) ἐξουθενεῖν; Sa 2 20ᵗ *SB* ἀσχήμων; Is 13 3 *S*(*B* ϯ ϣ.) ὑβρίζειν; Si 25 11ᵗ *S*(var ϣ.) ἀνάξιος; Deu 22 11ᵗ *S*(*B* ⲙⲟⲩϫⲧ) κίβδηλος; Va 58 167 *B* weapons ⲥⲉϣ.ᵗ εὐτελής; ShBM 194 4 *S* at incarnation ⲛⲧⲁⲡⲉⲕⲱⲧ c. ϩⲛⲟⲩ entering house He built ?, ShA 2 283 *S* ⲉⲓⲥ.ᵗ ⲉⲓⲧⲙⲁⲓⲏⲩ, Ryl 186 *S* ϫⲓⲛⲡⲉⲧ]ⲧⲁⲓⲏⲩ ϣⲁⲡⲉⲧⲥ.ᵗ (*cf* PLond 5 119 ἄτιμος, PMon 53 εὐτελής, *ib* 80 ἐλάχιστος, KKS 660 *S* David ⲡⲉⲧⲥ.ᵗ among Jesse's sons;   c e- comparat *S*: ShIF 105 ⲡⲉⲧⲥ.ᵗ ⲉⲣⲟⲟⲩ, R 2 4 64 I will not stay ⲛⲛⲁϩⲣⲛⲡⲉⲧⲥ.ᵗ ⲉⲣⲟⲓ.

II tr, *despise*: Pro 28 7 *S*(var ϯ ϣⲓⲡⲉ)*A*, Mic 7 6 *SB*(*A* ϩⲱⲥϥ), Jo 8 49 *SA²B* ⲁⲧⲓⲙ.; Ps 43 6 *B*(*S* ⲥⲱϣϥ), Mk 9 12 *SBF* ἐξουδ.; Jer 12 6 *B*(*S* = Gk), He 9 26 *B*(*SF* ⲟⲩⲟⲥϥ) ἀθετεῖν; Ac 14 5 *SB*, 1 Thes 2 2 *SBF*, BHom 14 *S* ⲡϥϣ. ⲙⲙⲟϥ ὑβρίζειν, He 10 29 *SB* ἐνυβ.; Mt 5 11 *B*(*S* ⲡⲟϭⲛ.) ὀνειδίζειν; 1 Pet 2 4 *B*(*S* ⲧⲥⲧⲟ) ἀποδοκιμάζειν; Job 42 6 *S* (var ⲥⲱϣϥ, *B* ϯ ϣⲟϣ) φαυλίζειν; 2 Cor 8 20 *B*(*S* ⲧⲉϥ ⲧⲱⲗⲙ) μωμεῖσθαι; Aeg 214 *Sf* ⲟⲩⲉⲓ ⲉⲁⲩⲥⲁϣⲥ ἐκβάλλεσθαι; ShC 73 46 *S* ⲉϥⲥ. ⲙⲡⲉⲧⲣⲓⲧⲟⲩⲱϥ, *cf* 47 ⲁⲩⲥⲉϣϥ ⲡⲉⲧϩⲓⲧⲟⲩⲱⲟⲩ, El 74 *A* ⲁϥϣ. ⲙⲡⲱϥⲓⲕⲓⲟⲡ = *ib* 114 *S* ⲥⲱϣϥ, Mani 1 *A²* ⲉⲩϣⲁⲡϣⲱⲥⲧⲛⲏⲉ, C 43 117 *B* ⲁⲓϣⲉϣⲑⲏⲛⲟⲩ & cast you into prison, Mor 30 16 *F* ⲡⲉⲛⲧⲁϥϣ. ⲛⲡⲉⲛⲉ.

ⲣ ⲥ *B*: ϣⲁϣⲣⲱⲙⲓ Pro 6 17 (*SA* ⲣⲉϥⲥ.), Is 2 12 (*S* do) ὑβριστής.

—— nn m *SABF*, *shame, contempt, scorn*: Job 10 15 *SB*, EpJer 25 *BF*, Hos 4 7 *SAB* opp ⲉⲟⲟⲩ, 1 Cor 15 43 *SBF* ἀτιμία; Lev 26 19 *S*(gloss ϣⲟⲩϣⲟⲩ, *B* ϣⲱⲃⲏ ﻋﺮ), Zech 9 6 *S*(ShA 2 335)*AB*, 2 Cor 12 10 *SBF* ὕβρις; Ps 68 21 *B*(*S* ⲡⲟϭⲛ.), Lam 5 1 *BF* ὀνειδισμός, Mic 2 6 *SAB* ὄνειδος; Ps 106 40 *S* (var ⲥⲱϣϥ) *B* ἐξουδένωσις; Hos 7 16 *AB* φαυλισμός; 1 Cor 11 6 *B*(*S* ϣⲗⲟϥ) αἰσχρόν; Ps 30 13 *B*(*S* ⲥⲱϣϥ) ψόγος; Deu 23 13 *B*(*S* = Gk) ἀσχημοσύνη, Ps 34 26 *B*(*S* ⲟⲅⲱⲗⲥ) ἐντροπή; He 7 18 *B* (*SF* ⲟⲩⲱⲥϥ) ἀθέτησις; ShP 130⁵ 16 *S* ⲡⲉⲛϣⲓⲡⲉ... ⲡⲉⲛⲥ., BIF 14 134 *S* ⲉⲁϥⲧⲁⲅⲟ ⲛ̄ⲡⲥ. to king's face, TThe 322 *B* ⲡϣ. ⲛⲉⲗⲓⲥⲁⲃⲉⲧ (*sc* barrenness), C 43 240 *B* ⲟⲩϣ. ⲛⲥⲱⲙⲁ *malady* (? *l* ⲕⲱϣ, *v ib* 85); as adj: Ro 1 26 *B* ⲡⲁⲑⲟⲥ ⲡϣ. (*S* ⲥ.ᵗ) ἀτιμία.

ⲣⲉϥⲥ., ϣ. *SAB*, *scorner*: Pro 6 17 *S* (Bor 206 570) *A* (*B* ϣⲁϣⲣⲱⲙⲓ), Is 16'6 *S*(*B* ⲣⲉϥϯ ϣ.) ὑβριστής; RNC 52 *S* ⲣⲉϥⲥ. ⲛⲛⲡⲉ, ShC 73 99 *S* ⲣⲉϥⲥⲉϣ ⲣⲱⲙⲉ, DeV 1 164 *B* ⲣⲉϥϣⲁϣ ⲓⲱⲧ (or ? *cf* ⲥⲱϣ *strike* 1 Tim); ⲙⲛⲧⲣ., *scorn S*: BHom 19 λοι-

δορία; ShC 42 156 abusing others ϩⲛⲟⲩⲙ.; ⲙⲉⲧⲣⲉϥϣⲁϣ ⲣⲱⲙⲓ B: Pro 11 2 (S ⲥⲱϣϥ) ἀτιμία.

† ⲥ., ϣ. SBF, despise, scorn: EpJer 40 BF, Ez 16 59 SB ἀτιμάζειν; Is 13 3 B(S ⲥ.) ὑβ.; ib 37 4 B(S ⲛⲟϣⲡ.) ὀνειδ.; Mor 18 9 S ⲉⲩ† ⲥ. ⲙⲡⲥⲟⲡ (var 19 16 ⲥ.) = Miss 4 103 B † ϣ., BIF 15 250 S if disobedient †ⲛⲁ† ⲥ. ⲡⲁⲕ ϩⲱⲥ ⲡⲗⲁⲛⲟⲥ, AM 32 B man ⲛⲡϣⲟⲩ† ϣ. ⲛⲁϥ; ⲣⲉϥ† ϣ. B, scorner: 1 Tim 1 13 (S ⲣⲉϥⲥ.) ὑβριστής, 1 Cor 6 10 (S ⲣⲉϥⲥⲁϩⲟⲩ) λοίδορος; ⲙⲉⲧⲣ. B: Zeph 2 8 (SA ⲛⲟϣⲡ.) ὀνειδισμός; Va 58 189 satiety is beginning of †ⲙ. ὕβρις; ⲭⲓⲛ† ϣ. B: Cat 218 ⲛⲓⲝ. of Jews toward apostles.

ϣⲁⲡ ϣ. B: MG 25 125 humility counting self naught & ⲟⲩϭⲛⲓϣϯ ⲙⲙⲉⲧϣ. acceptance of scorn, ib 139 sim.

ⲭⲓ ⲥ., ϭⲓ ϣ. SAB, be scorned: Is 5 15 SBF ἀτιμάζεσθαι, Ez 16 54 S(B ϣ.) ἀτιμοῦσθαι, ib 36 7 B ἀτ. λαμβάνειν; Ps 34 4 B(S ⲟⲩⲱⲗⲥ) ἐντρέπεσθαι; Jer 15 15 B(S ⲭⲓ ⲛⲟϣⲡ.) ὀνειδ. λαμβ.; Deu 25 3 B(S = Gk) ἀσχημονεῖν; Is 44 11 B(S ⲭⲓ ϣⲓⲡⲉ) αἰσχύνεσθαι; Cl 1 1 A βλασφημεῖσθαι; PS 151 S ⲁⲓⲭⲓ ⲥ., cited ib 153 ⲁⲓⲥ., ClPr 56 5 S martyr shall ⲭⲓ ⲛⲡⲣⲉⲡⲛⲟϭ ⲛⲥ.

ⲥⲱϣϥ S, ϩⲱⲥϥ A, -ϣϥ A, ϣⲟϣϥ B, ⲥⲉϣϥ- S, ϣⲉϣϥ- B, ⲥⲟϣϥ⸗ S, ϣⲟϣϥ⸗ B, ⲥⲟϣϥ† S, ϩⲁⲥϥ† A, ϣⲟϣϥ† B, ⲥⲁϣϥ† S/F vb I intr, meanings as ⲥⲱϣ with which it varies: Ps 21 24 SB, ib 72 22† S(B ϣⲱϣ) ἐξουδενοῦσθαι; Is 53 3 S(ACl ϣⲱⲥ, B ϣⲱϣ) ἀτιμάζεσθαι; ib 52 14 S(B ϭⲓ ϣⲱϣ) ἀδοξεῖν; Job 6 25† S(B ϩⲱⲟⲩ) φαῦλος, Is 33 19† SF (B ⲇⲟ) φαυλίζεσθαι; Pro 29 27† SA βδέλυγμα; Tit 1 11 B(S ϣⲗⲟϥ) αἰσχρός; Aeg 289† S/ κίβδηλος; PS 153 S ⲁⲓⲥ.† ⲛⲡⲁⲣⲣⲁⲅ, ShA 2 276 S †ⲥ.† ⲁⲩⲱ †ⲧϭⲁⲉⲓⲏⲩ, AM 253 B ⲡⲓⲕⲟⲩϭⲓ ⲉⲧⲏⲩ† ⲛⲇⲏⲧⲟⲩ; ⲥ e- comparat S: Sa 15 10 εὐτελέστερος ἤ.

II tr: 2 Kg 6 16 B(S ⲕⲱⲙϣ ⲛⲥⲁ-), Job 30 1 S (B ϣⲱϣ), Pro 1 7 SAB, Si 34 34 S (var ⲥⲱϣ), Ro 14 3 SB ἐξουδ.; Pro 21 12 SA, ib 22 12 A -ϣϥ, Mal 1 6 AB φαυλίζ.; Mic 7 6 A(SB ⲥⲱϣ), Ja 2 6 S(B ϣⲱϣ) ἀτιμάζ.; Ps 54 20 S(B ⲥⲱϥ), ib 88 31 S (var ⲥⲱⲟϥ, B ⲥⲱⲃⲉⲙ) βεβηλοῦν.; ib 32 10 B (S = Gk, A Cl 59 3 ϩⲱⲗ ⲁⲃⲁⲗ), Gal 3 15 B (var ϣⲱϣ, S ⲇⲟ) ἀθετ.; Si 14 9 S (l ? ⲥⲉϣϣ) ἀναξηραίνειν; Aeg 286 S ⲉⲧⲣⲉⲡⲥⲉϣϣ (var ⲥⲉϣ) God's creature ὑβρίζ.; ib 225 S sim διαβάλλειν; ShC 42 142 S ⲁϥⲥ. ⲙⲡⲁⲓ...ⲉⲛⲧⲁⲅⲥⲱϣ ⲛⲡⲉⲡⲉⲓⲟⲧⲉ, MG 17 324 S dared ⲉⲥⲉϣϥ ⲛⲉⲡⲛⲁ̄ = C 89 71 B.

—— nn m SAA²B: Ps 21 6 SB ἐξουδένημα, ib 106 40 S(B ϣⲱϣ) -νωσις; Pro 11 2 S ⲥⲱϣ A ϣⲱⲥ B ϣⲱϣ...S ⲥⲱϣϥ A ϩⲱⲥϥ B ⲙⲉⲧⲣⲉϥϣⲁϣⲣⲱⲙⲓ ὕβρις...ἀτιμία; Zeph 3 11 A -ⲥϥ (B ⲙⲉⲧⲣⲉϥ† ϣⲱϣ) φαύλισμα; Ps 30 13 S(B ϣⲱϣ) ψόγος; Si

27 28 S ἐμπαιγμός; ShIF 179 S ⲡⲉⲩⲧⲥⲁⲉⲓⲟ ⲛⲛⲡⲉⲩⲥ., Miss 4 549 S they exploit poor ⲕⲁⲧⲁ ⲡⲉⲩⲥ. = C 89 88 B, ib 36 B ⲟⲩϣ. ⲉϩⲟⲩⲛ ⲉⲡⲉⲕⲥⲟⲡ.

ⲥⲙϣⲉ A²B v ϣⲙϣⲉ.

ⲥⲁϣⲉ v ⲥⲱϭⲉ s f.

ⲥⲛϣⲉ, ⲥⲛϭⲉ v ⲥⲱϣ strike.

ⲥⲓϣⲉ S, -ϭⲉ Sa, ⲥⲁϣⲉ† SA², ⲥⲁϭⲉ† A, -ϣⲓ† A², ϣⲁϣⲓ† (rare), (ⲉ)ⲡϣ.† B, ϣⲉϣⲓ† F vb intr, be like gall, bitter: Ex 15 23† SB, 2 Kg 2 26 S, Zeph 1 14† SAB πικρός (εἶναι), Is 24 9 S(B ⲉⲣ ϣ.) π. γίνεσθαι, Sa 8 16 S πικρίαν ἔχειν, Ap 10 9† SBF πικραίνειν, Mt 26 75† B(S ϩⲛⲟⲩⲥ.) πικρῶς; BG 56 S ⲧⲉⲩⲧⲣⲟⲫⲏ ⲥ.†, COAd 49 Sa lest ⲛⲏⲣⲡ ⲥⲓϭⲉ; with rel: Is 5 20† SBF, Hab 1 6† SAB, AP 15 A² ⲟⲩⲙⲟⲩⲉⲓ ⲉⲥⲥⲁϣⲓ πικρός, Nu 33 8† S(B ⲛⲛ) πικρία; ShC 42 199 S ⲡⲉⲓϩⲣⲏ ϩⲉ ⲉⲧⲥⲛϣⲓ ⲁⲩⲱ ⲉⲧⲥ.†, BAp 103 S ⲁϥⲧⲣⲉⲡⲉⲧⲥ.† ϩⲗⲟϭ, Mus 40 275 S ⲡⲣⲟⲉⲓⲙ ⲉⲧⲥ.†, MIE 2 417 B ⲟⲩⲣⲓⲙⲓ ⲉϥⲉⲛⲡϣ.†, Mani 1 A² ⲡⲉⲧϩⲁⲗ[ϭ]...ⲡⲉⲧⲥ.†, PMich 1545 S among names Ⲏⲟⲣ ⲡⲁⲡⲉⲧⲥ.†

ⲥⲓϣⲉ SA², -ϭⲉ A, ϣⲁϣⲓ, (ⲉ)ⲡϣ. B, ϣⲓϣⲓ F, ⲥⲁϭⲉ, ⲥⲉ. DM ⲛⲛ m, a bitterness: Deu 29 18 SB (sic l), Job 21 25 SB, Is 28 28 B(S ⲛⲟⲩϭⲥ), Lam 3 15 SB ⲛϣ., Eph 4 31 B(S ⲇⲟ) πικρία, Ex 12 8 SB πικρίς; Mus 40 45 S ⲙⲉϥϩⲉⲣⲧ ⲥ. ⲉⲃⲟⲗ before blind man, HL 112 B ⲡⲓⲛϣ. of old age, Mani 2 A² ⲡⲉϥϩⲁⲓⲉ ⲡⲉⲧⲥ. ⲡⲉⲧⲣⲱⲭϩ; as adj: Jer 23 15 B(S ShC 42 171 ⲭⲟⲗⲏ) πικρός; Ro 11 17 B ⲭⲱⲓⲧ ⲛϣ. (S -ϩⲟⲟⲩⲧ) ἀγριέλαιος; PMéd 70 S ⲱϩ ⲛⲥ. b gall: Job 16 13 SB, Pro 5 4 SA(B = Gk), Mt 27 34 SB χολή; AZ 52 124 S ⲡⲉⲭ ⲥ. ⲉⲅⲉⲃⲓⲱ, SHel 41 S ⲛⲥ. ⲙⲡⲉϩⲣⲁⲕⲱⲡ, Z 630 S ⲥ. ⲛⲙⲁⲥⲉ, PMéd 147 S ⲛⲉⲣⲟⲟⲩ, ib 296 S ⲡⲗⲁⲃⲏⲥ, ib 56 S ⲛⲁⲃⲟⲩⲕ, Ryl 412 F sim, PMéd 283 S ⲛⲉⲣϭⲟⲓ, BKU 1 26 (8116 b) F of bird; advb ϩⲛⲟⲩⲥ., ϫⲉⲟⲩⲛϣ. SA²BF, bitterly: Is 33 7 SBF, Lu 22 62 SB, AP 14 A² cried out ϩ. πικρῶς; CA 88 S repenting ϩ., TstAb 164 B weeping ϭ., Ryl 94 103 S wind blowing ϩ.

ⲉⲣ ⲉⲡϣ. B, be bitter: Ap 8 11 (S ⲥ. vb) πικραίνειν, ib (S ⲇⲟ) εἰς ἄψινθον γίνεσθαι. Cf Is 24 9 above.

† ⲥ. S, make bitter: Ru 1 20 πικραίνειν.

ⲥⲱϣⲉ SA², -ϩⲉ A vb I intr, drag, creep: Mor 37 48 snake ⲉϥⲥ. ἔρπειν; Is 33 23 (BF ⲭⲱ ⲉϩⲣⲏⲓ) χαλᾶν (cf PS below); ShP 131[6] 57 climbing ladder ⲉϥⲥ. ϣⲁⲛⲧϥⲃⲱⲕ ⲉϩⲣⲁⲓ; ⲥ ⲉⲡⲉⲥⲛⲧ: PS 359 hair ⲥ. ⲉ. ⲉⲭⲛⲡⲉϥⲟⲩⲉⲣⲏⲧⲉ; ⲥ ϩⲓⲡⲉⲥⲛⲧ: Mic 7 17 SA (B ⲱⲟⲩ† ϩⲓⲭ.) σύρειν acc; ⲥ ⲡⲥⲁ-: Mun 66 cripple's feet ⲥ. ⲛⲥⲱϣ; ⲥ ϩⲓ-: ShC 73 84 would go ⲕⲁⲡ ⲉⲩⲡⲁⲥ. ϩⲓⲧⲉϩⲓⲏ; ⲥ ϩⲓϫⲛ-: Ge 7 8 (B

om) ἐρ. ἐπί; Deu 32 24 (B ω.) σύ. ἐπί; ShA 2 245 cripple ⲉϥϭ. ⲣ. ⲡⲕⲁⲣ, Mor 38 56 ⲉϥϭⲏϭ ⲉϥϭ. ⲣ. ⲡⲕⲁⲣ.   **II** tr: Is 3 16 (B ω.) σύ.; ShC 73 112 (ⲉ)ⲡϭ. ⲙⲡⲥⲱⲙⲁ [ⲅⲓ]ⲡⲁⲣⲟⲩ, ShR 2 3 53 dead sheep ϣⲁⲩϭ. ⲙⲙⲟⲟⲩ ⲉⲡⲟⲩⲉ, GMir 22 ⲡⲉϥϭ. ⲙⲡⲉϥⲥⲱⲙⲁ ⲣⲙⲡⲕⲁⲣ, Mani 1 A² some they beat others ⲁⲩϭ. ⲙ[ⲙⲁⲩ]; nn(?): ShA 2 254 bitten by asp because ⲙⲡⲉϥϯ ⲣⲧⲏϥ ⲉⲡⲉϥϭ., ib n ⲡϭ. ⲙⲡⲣⲟⲩ trail.

ϭⲱϣⲉ S, -ϫⲉ, -ϣⲉ Sᵃ, ϣⲱϣⲓ F, pl ? ϭⲟⲟϣⲉ S (BM 470) nn f, *field, meadow, country* opp town: Ge 2 19 (B ⲕⲟⲓ), Is 32 12 SF(B ⲓⲟⲣⲓ), Mt 13 24 SF(B do) ἀγρός, Jos 21 12 sg ἀγ. pl; Deu 1 7 (B ⲙⲉϣϣⲱⲧ), Job 42 18 (B ⲕ.), Pro 27 24 (A ⲕ.) πε- δίον, Z 329 ϭ. wherein gardens & trees πεδιάς, Jos 10 40 πεδινή; Ex 23 10 (B ⲓ.), Job 31 39 (B ⲕⲁⲣⲓ) γῆ, Pro 6 7 (A ⲕ., B ⲓⲉⲫⲟⲣⲱⲓ) γεώργιον; Ps 73 5 (B ⲓⲁⲣϣϣⲏⲡ), Is 32 19 SF (B = Gk) δρυμός; Ps 131 6 (B ⲓⲁⲣϣ.) δάσος; Sa 17 16 ἐρημία; Ja 5 4 (ShA 1 412, B = Gk) χώρα; Jud 6 3 ϫⲉ ϭ. σπεί- ρειν; Tri 732 ⲧⲉϭϭ. ⲉⲧⲉⲡⲉϭⲣⲟⲓ ساقه ...; ClPr 54 43 ϭ. ⲛⲥⲕⲁⲓ ἄροσις; ShMIF 23 92 ⲡⲧⲁϭⲱⲣϭ ⲛ- ⲡⲉⲧⲡⲥ., ShA 1 454 seed growing in ⲡⲉϭⲥ., ST 437 Sᵃ ⲧⲥⲱⲣⲉ (ⲙ)ⲙⲁⲣⲉ, WS 99 ⲱⲗ ⲧϭ., ⲡⲕⲁⲓⲣⲟⲥ ⲡⲧϭ., BM 581 F ⲙⲡⲉⲧϣ. ⲟⲩⲱⲗⲉ this year, ShC 73 93 ⲛϯⲙⲉ...ⲡϭ., ib 18 ⲡϭ....ⲡⲧⲟⲟⲩ, Mor 51 30 ⲛⲧⲟ⳽ϣ ⲁⲩⲱ ⲡϭ., ib 41 131 not city with laws but ⲟⲩϭ. ⲧⲉ ⲡⲁⲧⲥⲃⲱ, BMOr 6201 B 188 ⲧϭ. ⲙⲡⲁⲧⲙⲉ, Ep App 1 40 returning to city ⲉⲃⲟⲗ ⲣ̇ⲓⲧⲥ., Kr 152 whether in ⲧϭ. or in ⲧⲡⲟⲗⲓⲥ, CO 129 I lack papyrus ⲉⲓⲣ̇ⲓⲧϭ., BKU 1 48 Sᵃ ⲉⲃⲣⲓ ⲥⲱϫⲉ (v ⲉⲃⲣⲁ); ⲣⲙⲡϭ., *countryman*: Mor 17 75 ⲣⲙⲡⲟⲗⲓⲥ...ⲣ. ἀπὸ τ. ἀγροι- κίας, R 1 4 43 ⲡⲣ. ⲙⲡⲛⲕⲉϣⲟⲟϭ *agricola*; ib 2 2 51 lying in manger like ⲟⲩ[ⲉⲣⲅ]ⲁⲧⲏⲥ ⲡⲣ.

ϭⲱϣⲉ vb   v ϭⲱⲣⲉ.

ϭⲱϣⲙ, -ⲣⲙ (Kr), ϣⲟⲥ(ⲉ)ⲙ SF, ϣⲱⲥⲙⲉ A, ϭⲟ- ϣⲙⲧ, ϣⲟⲥⲙⲧ S, ϭⲁ.ᵗ Sᶠ, ϭⲁϫⲉⲙ⸱ᵗ B vb intr, *be faint, undone, disheartened*: 2 Kg 17 29ᵗ (var ϣ.), Pro 3 11 (var & A ϣ., B ⲃⲱⲗ ⲉⲃⲟⲗ), Lam 2 19 (B ϯ ⲟⲩϩⲟⲩⲧ), ib 2 12 SF(B ⲃ. ⲉⲃ.) ἐκλύεσθαι, Ez 23 33 (B l ϣⲱϣⲉⲙ imitating S) ἐκλύσις; Deu 28 65ᵗ B(S ⲭⲟⲧⲣ), Jud 8 5ᵗ ἐκλείπειν; Deu 32 24ᵗ(B do) τήκειν; ib 28 34ᵗ (B ϣⲱ- ⲡⲓ ⲛ̇ⲉⲛⲟⲩϭⲓⲣⲓ ⲡⲣⲏⲧ) παράπληκτος; Pro 10 5 (var & A ϣ., B ⲉⲣ ϫⲓⲛϥⲉⲣ)ἀνεμόφθορος γίνεσθαι; Wess 11 168 ὀλιγωρεῖν; PS 236 ⲥⲉⲡⲁⲥ. ⲛⲥⲉⲣⲉ ⲉⲭⲙⲡⲉⲅⲣⲟ, Miss 8 249 Sᶠ ⲉϥⲟⲃⲉ ⲉⲩϭ., ib 4 762 ⲙⲉⲕⲥ. ⲙⲡϣⲱⲙ.   ϭ e-, *fatigue, annoy*: Z 323 ⲡⲥⲟⲡ ϣ.ᵗ ⲉⲣⲟⲕ, ib 307 ⲁⲩⲥⲟⲡ ϣ. ⲉⲣⲟⲩⲡ ⲉⲩⲥⲟⲡ λυπεῖσθαι κατά; Mich 166 8 ⲙⲡⲣϭ. ⲉ(ⲡ)ⲡⲟⲗⲉⲙⲟⲥ;   ϭ ⲙⲛ-, *be annoyed with*: BAp 173 ⲉⲕϣⲁⲡϭ. ⲙⲡⲟⲩⲥⲟⲡ;   ϭ ⲡⲥⲁ-, *faint for*: Ps 118 81 (B ⲙⲟⲩⲡⲕ ⲡⲥⲁ-) ἐκλείπειν εἰς; Deu 28 32ᵗ (l ϭⲟϣⲙ, var ϣ., B ⲓϣⲓ ⲡⲥⲁ-) σφακελίζειν εἰς; ShBM 192 ⲟⲓϣ. ⲡⲥⲱϭ (*sc* love of Christ), Bor 234

3 ⲙⲡⲣⲧⲥⲁⲃⲟⲕ ⲉϭ. ⲡⲥⲁⲣⲱⲙⲉ;   ϭ ⲣⲁ-, ⲥⲁ-, *faint on account of*: Va 66 297 B ⲉⲩϭ.ᵗ ⲥⲁⲡⲓⲣⲕⲟ ἐκλύε- σθαι; ShC 73 43 S some ϭ.ᵗ ⲛ ϣⲟⲃⲣ ⲣⲁⲡϭⲱⲡⲧ of God, BAp 98 S ⲉⲕϭ.ᵗ ⲣⲁⲡⲉⲓⲃⲉ, Kr 1 S ⲁⲡϯⲙⲉ ϭ. ⲣⲁⲡⲙⲟⲟⲩ;   ϭ. ⲡⲣⲏⲧ SAF, as ϭ.: Lam 2 12 (B ⲃ. ⲉⲃ.) ἐκλύ.; Jud 10 16, Jon 4 8 SA(B ⲉⲣ ⲕⲟⲩϫⲓ ⲛⲣ.), Z 323 ⲁϥϣ. ⲛⲣ. ⲁϥϯ ⲡⲧⲉϥⲯⲩⲭⲏ ὀλιγοψυ- χεῖν;   as nn: Est D 7 ἔκλυσις.

• —— nn m S, *faintness, exhaustion*: Is 21 3 (var ϣ., B ⲃ. ⲉⲃ.) ἔκλυσις; P 44 78 ⲡⲉⲧⲕⲁϭⲉⲓ (ἐγκα- κεῖν)· ⲡϣ. ⲿٮⵥ; Bor 265 87 ⲁⲩϭⲓⲥⲉ ⲣⲙⲡϭ. ⲙⲡⲛⲕⲱⲣⲧ, Mor 53 63 ⲡϭ. ⲡⲛⲉⲧⲟⲃⲉ.

V also ϭⲱⲣⲙ.

ϭⲓϣⲡ, -ⲃ   v ϭⲓϣϥ.

ϭⲁϣⲧ, ϭⲱϣⲧ   v ϭⲱⲣⲉ *weave*.

ϭⲱϣⲧ, -ⲣⲧ(RNC)S, ϣⲱϣⲧ SᶠB(F), ϭⲉϣⲧ-, ϭⲱ. S, ϣⲱϣⲧ- F, ϭⲟϣⲧ⸱, ϭⲟϫⲧ⸱ (P 44), ϭⲁϣⲧ⸱ SA², ϭⲁϣⲧ⸱ S, ϣⲁϣⲧ⸱ B, ϣⲉϣⲧ⸱ BF, ϭⲟϣⲧᵗ, ϭⲁ.ᵗ S, ϣⲟϣⲧᵗ, ϣⲁ.ᵗ B vb **I** intr, *stop, be impeded, hindered*: Mor 84 104 S ⲙⲡⲧⲃⲛⲟⲟⲩⲉ ϭ. & went not forward = C 43 150 B, RNC 67 S ship ϭⲱⲣⲧ in midstream, Mor 31 253 Sᶠ horses & men ⲁⲩϣ. = BMEA 10578 F, C 86 78 B his chariot ϣ., BHom 85 S all creation ϭⲁ.ᵗ waiting for thee, TU 24 1 3 S cripple ⲥⲡⲛϫ...ⲉϭϭ.ᵗ, WTh 178 S at childbirth ⲁⲡⲉⲥϣⲏⲣⲉ ϭ. ⲣⲣⲏⲧⲥ, AM 159 B sim, PSBA 27 168 S if pen ϭ. ⲡ̇ⲧⲙⲙⲟⲟϣⲉ ⲡⲥⲁⲏⲛ, Pcod 13 S ⲧⲉⲟⲩϭⲓⲁ ϭ.ᵗ, RE 9 152, 153 S obscure;   ϭ ⲉ- SB, *be hindered from*: Ge 35 16 B ⲉⲙⲓⲥⲓ δυστοκεῖν; 1 Cor 14 39 F(S = Gk, B ⲧⲁⲣⲡⲟ) ⲉⲙϫⲉⲓ κωλύειν; CaiEuch 483 B ⲉⲩⲧⲉⲙⲟⲩⲱⲙ ἀπ- αγορεύειν; PS 29 S ⲉⲡⲉⲣⲃⲏⲅⲉ (? l ⲡⲛⲉ-) ⲉⲧⲛⲁⲡⲟⲩ- ⲟⲩ, CO 61 S bishop's edict ⲉⲓⲥ ⲡϣⲁ ϭ.ᵗ ⲉⲡϯⲙⲉ;   ϭ ⲉϩⲟⲩⲛ ⲉⲣⲣⲉⲡ- B: Va 57 179 ⲉⲧϣ. ⲉⲃ. ⲉ. ⲡⲉϥⲥⲁϫⲓ ἐμποδίζειν dat; ib 248 ϣ. ⲉⲃ. ⲉⲣⲣⲁⲅ κατέχειν;   ϭ ⲟⲩⲃⲉ- B: Cat 84 ⲉⲡϣ.ᵗ ⲟⲩⲃⲉⲛⲉϥⲡⲁⲟⲥ (*sc* devil's).

II tr, *stop, impede*: Mic 2 4 B(SA = Gk), Ac 16 6 F(S = Gk, B ⲧⲁⲣⲡⲟ) κωλ., ib 28 31 B neg (S ⲁⲭⲡϯⲥⲟ) ἀκωλύτως, ROC 25 247 B I had come but ⲁⲡⲁⲡⲁⲕⲗⲏⲣⲟⲥ ϣⲁϣⲧ διακ., HL 110 B God ϣ. ⲙⲡⲓⲧⲁⲕⲟ ⲉⲃⲟⲗ ⲣⲁⲡⲉϥⲣⲱⲙⲓ, MG 17 32ᵟ S evil spirit ⲁϥϭⲉϣⲧ ⲡⲉⲓⲣⲱⲃ = C 89 68 B ἐμπ.; Si 48 3 S ἀνέχειν; Ap 11 6 S(B ϣⲑⲁⲙ) κλείειν; Z 288 Sᶠ ⲁϭⲣⲓⲥⲉ ⲉϭϣ. ⲙⲙⲟϥ πολλὰ σπουδάζειν *resistere* (cf ϭ. ⲉⲃⲟⲗ); Jth 8 16 S(Gk diff); ShC 42 31 S clouds ⲙⲉⲩϭⲁϣⲧϥ (*sc* sun) in his course, ShA 1 267 S Eli- jah ⲁϥϭⲉϣⲧ ⲧⲡⲉ, DeV 2 282 B angel ϣ. ⲛϯⲥⲕⲁⲫⲏ in sea, BKU 1 314 S bishop's edict ⲉⲓⲥ. ⲙⲙⲱⲧⲛ ϫⲉⲡ- ⲡⲉⲧⲛⲁ(ⲣ)ϣⲁ ⲉⲧⲕⲁⲑⲟⲗⲓⲕⲏ;   of magical influence: Mor 46 16 S ⲁϥϭ. ⲙⲡⲣⲉ (*sic*) in midst of heaven, ib 48 108 S ⲡⲉϥⲙⲁⲅⲓⲁ ϭ. ⲙⲙⲟⲛ not allowing us to go = C 43 152 B ⲧⲁⲣⲡⲟ, RNC 67 S ⲁϥϭⲁⲣⲧⲧ in midstream, KroppM 109 S ⲡⲉⲡⲧⲁϥϭ. ⲛⲧⲡⲉ...ⲉⲕⲁⲥ.

ⲛϩⲁ (?), PSBA 25 330 *B* ⲉⲕⲉϣ. ⲉⲕⲉⲙⲟⲩⲣ mouth & tongue of NN., ST 398 *S* am come to ⲥⲁϣⲧⲕ ϩⲛⲟⲩⲥⲱ[ϣⲧ] ⲧⲁⲟⲃⲕ ϩⲛⲟⲩⲱϩ, P 44 121 *S* ϥⲛⲁⲉⲍⲁⲧⲉ ⲙⲙⲟⲓ ⲛⲥⲟϫⲧ سجت (*l* ? ⲥⲟϫⲧⲧ); c ⲉ- verbal, *hinder from*: Ac 27 43 *B(S* = Gk), Z 341 *S* ⲁⲩⲥⲟϣⲧ ⲉⲧⲙⲧⲣⲁⲡⲁⲣⲁⲅⲉ ⲕⲱⲗ.; ShA 1 117 *S* ⲁⲩⲥⲟϣⲧϥ ⲉⲧⲙⲧⲣⲉⲡⲉⲕⲣⲓⲧⲏⲥ ϣⲓⲡⲉ, PO 11 349 *B* Lord ϣⲁϣⲧϥ ⲉϣⲧⲉⲙⲉⲣ ⲟⲩⲛⲃ; c ⲡⲧⲛ-, *withhold from, deny to*: PHeidelb 578 *S* crops of certain fields ⲁⲡⲥⲁϣⲧⲟⲩ ⲛⲧⲉⲧⲏⲧⲛ; c ϩⲓⲣⲛ-, *stop at*: ShClPr 44 29 *S* ⲉⲧⲣⲉⲩⲥⲉϣⲧⲧⲏⲩⲧⲛ ϩ. ⲙⲡⲩⲗⲏ ⲙⲡⲏⲅⲉ.

—— ⲉⲃⲟⲗ *S*, emphatic of c.: BM 286 123 sent ⲉⲧⲣⲉⲩⲥ. ⲙⲡⲙⲏⲛϣⲉ ⲉⲃ. till he had taken counsel, Miss 4 618 (cf above Z 288) ⲉⲥⲥ. ⲙⲙⲟϥ ⲉⲃ., PMéd 208 ϩⲉⲛⲃⲁⲗ ⲉⲧϣ. ⲉⲃ. obscure.

—— ⲁⲡⲁϩⲟⲩ *A²*, *repel*: Mani 2 ⲁⲧⲣⲟⲩⲥⲁϣⲧϥ ⲁⲡⲁϩⲟⲩ.

—— nn *B*, *impediment*: C 41 41 charms buried so as to ϯ ⲟⲩϣ. ⲙⲡⲓⲙⲱⲓⲧ ⲙⲙⲟϣⲓ. ⲥⲁϣⲧ *S* same?: KroppK 25 charm (prayer) ⲉⲧⲃⲉⲟⲩⲥ.

ϭϣⲟⲧ v ⲥϧⲁⲧ.

ⲥⲁϣϥ *SA²*, -ϩϥ *A*, ⲥⲉϣϥ *S* (R 1 1 49), ϣⲁϣϥ *B* (K 67), ϣⲉϣⲃ *F*, f ⲥⲁϣϥⲉ *SA²*, -ϩⲃⲉ *Sᵃ*, -ϩϥⲉ *A²*, -ϩⲃⲉ *A*, ⲥⲁⲥⲫⲉ, -ⲓ *O* nn, *seven* (*BF* mostly ⲍ̄ m f, not ⲍ̄ϯ), as nn: 2 Kg 21 9, Eccl 11 2, Mk 12 23 ἑπτά; Wess 15 134 ⲡⲥⲁⲃⲗⲗⲁⲡ ⲙⲡⲥ., Win 1 ⲡⲥ. ⲙⲡϣⲁ *7th (day) of festival*, Ge 29 27 ⲧⲥ., PGM 1 114 *O* ⲛⲓⲥ.; as adj, before nn m: 1 Kg 2 5, Pro 6 31 *SA*, Ap 5 6; CMSS 49 *F* ϣ. ⲉⲡⲗⲉⲙⲧⲟⲥⲉ; f: Ge 5 7, Ex 2 16 *SA*, Ap 5 1, PS 3 ⲧⲥ. ⲛϥⲱⲡⲛ, PGol 47 *A²* ⲧⲥ. ⲛⲡⲗⲏⲅⲏ, KroppB ⲥⲁϣϥ(ⲉ) ⲙⲡⲁⲣⲑⲉⲛⲟⲥ; after nn: Jo 4 52 *SA*, Bor 168 151 *S* ϫⲡ ⲥ.; iterated (distributive): P 129¹⁶ 68 ⲥ. ⲥ. ⲕⲁⲧⲁ ⲡⲉⲩⲧⲉⲛⲟⲥ (cf Ge 7 2); *seventeen, twenty-seven* &c: ⲙⲛⲧⲥⲁϣϥ Ge 8 4, ⲙ. ⲥⲁϣϥⲉ 4 Kg 13 1, ⲙ. ⲥⲁϥⲃⲉ ⲛⲥⲟⲡ KroppK 13, ϫⲟⲩⲧⲥⲁϣϥ Ge 7 11, ϫ. ⲥⲁϥⲃⲉ Ep 537, ⲙⲁⲁⲃⲥⲁϣϥ 2 Kg 23 39, ⲙ. ⲥⲁϥⲃⲉ *A* Ex 6 16, ⲧⲁⲓⲟⲩ ⲥⲁϣϥ Nu 1 29. Ordinals: Hag 2 1 *A* ⲙⲁϩⲥ., Ap 10 7 ⲙⲉϩⲥ., Mani 2 *A²* ⲙⲁϩⲥ., 4 Kg 16 1 ⲧⲙⲉϩⲙⲛⲧⲥⲁϣϥⲉ; PS 73 ⲡⲙⲉϩⲣⲙⲉⲛⲉ ⲥⲁϣϥⲉ.

ϣϥⲉ¹, ϣⲃⲉ², ⲥϣϥⲉ³ *S*, ϩⲃⲉ⁴, ⲥϥ.⁵, ϭⲃⲉ (Ex 1 5) *A*, ϣⲃⲏ *F* m f, *seventy* (*B* ⲝ̄): Ge 4 24², Ac 7 14 ϣ.¹ ⲧⲏ, BMis 570 ⲥ.³ ⲥⲛⲟⲟⲩⲥ, Zech 7 5⁴, ib 1 12⁵, BMar 66 *S* ϣⲉ (*sic*) ⲡⲣⲟⲙⲡⲉ; PS 58 ⲙⲉϩϣ.¹, Lange in Griff Stu *F* ⲡⲓϣⲃⲏ ⲡⲟⲩϯ.

ⲥⲓϣϥ, -ⲃ, -ⲡ, ϣⲓϥ *S* nn, *fragment, flake*: ShC 42 110 servants hand him palm twigs ⲉϥϣⲁⲛⲣ ⲟⲩⲉⲓ ⲛⲥ. c. & drop pieces on ground, ShIF 85 garment ⲁⲁϥ ⲙⲡⲁϣⲉ ⲡⲁϣⲉ ⲛ ⲥⲓϣⲃ ⲥ., AZ 23 108 ⲡⲁⲧⲧⲟⲗⲕ (الطلق) ...ⲁⲁϥ ⲉⲥ. ⲥ. & put in cloth, PMéd 134 ⲟⲃⲛⲉ ⲡ-ⲥⲓϣⲡ, AZ 23 109 ⲁⲃⲛ ⲛϣ. *flaked alum* (cf σχιστός).

ⲥⲱⲱϥ, ϣⲱϣϥ v ⲥⲱϣ *be despised*.

ⲥⲁϥ *SB*, ⲥⲛϥ *Sᵃ*, ⲥⲉϥ *AF* nn m, *yesterday*: Ex 4 10 *SB*, Ps 89 4 *SB*, Jo 4 52 *SBF* ἐχθές; c. ⲡ-ϩⲟⲟⲩ: Miss 8 40 *S* χθὲς ἡμέρα; BMis 240 *S* c. ⲙⲉⲛ...ⲙⲡⲟⲟⲩ ϩⲱⲱϥ = Mor 30 14 *F*, FR 32 *S* ⲧⲉⲩϣⲏ ⲛⲥ., Kr 236 *F* ⲡⲉⲕⲥⲟⲉⲓ ⲛⲥⲉϥ...ⲙⲡⲁⲟⲩ, Mor 42 53 *S* ye died with me ϩⲁⲑⲏ ⲛⲥ., BSM 29 *B* ⲓⲥϫⲉⲡⲥⲁⲧϥ ⲛⲥ. = BMis 369 *S* ⲉⲓⲥ ⲕⲉϩⲟⲟⲩ ⲥⲡⲁⲩ, AM 190 *B* c. ⲁⲓⲥⲱⲧⲙ, ST 265 *S* ⲉⲓⲥⲁⲃ (*l* ⲉⲓⲥ c.) ⲁⲃⲟⲅⲱ, Win 2 *S* ⲡⲕⲉⲥ.; ⲡⲁⲥ.: Job 8 9 *B* (*S* ⲛⲥ.) χθιζός; ⲛⲥ.: Ex 2 14 *SAB*, Job 30 3 *SB*, Ac 7 28 *SB* χ.; ShA 1 92 *S* ⲙⲡⲟⲟⲩ ⲛ ⲛⲥ., BMis 398 *S* I stood listening ⲛⲥ. = BSM 48 *B*, BMis 158 *S* what hath happened ⲛⲥ. ⲙⲛϣⲙⲧⲉⲡⲟⲟⲩ?, Ep 169 *Sᵃ* ⲧⲉⲛϣⲁϫⲉ ⲉⲣⲟϥ ⲛⲡⲕⲟⲩⲥ., CO 373 *S* sim.

ⲥⲁϥ *S* nn as pl, *a measure or vessel?*: Mich 136 1 recipe ϯ ⲉϩⲣⲉ.

ⲥⲱϥ *B* vb tr, *strain*: Mt 23 24 (*S* ⲑⲗⲟ ⲉⲃⲟⲗ) διυλίζειν. *L* ? ⲥⲱⲧϥ.

ⲥⲱϥ v ⲥⲱ sf.

ⲥⲱⲓϥ *B* nn, *meaning unknown*: PO 11 332 David ⲁϥⲓ ⲓϥ ⲛⲥ. before Anchous (1 Kg 21 13).

ⲥⲱⲱϥ *SAA²F*, ⲥⲱϥ *BF*, ⲥⲉⲉϥ-, ⲥⲉⲉⲃⲉ-, ⲥⲟⲟϥ- *S*, ⲥⲉϥ- *SB*, ⲥⲁⲁϥ- *F*, ⲥⲟⲟϥϩ, -ⲃϩ *S*, ⲥⲟϥϩ *SB*, ⲥⲟⲟϥϯ *SA*, ⲥⲁⲁϥϯ *Sᶠ*, ⲥⲟϥϯ *B*, p c ⲥⲁϥ- *B* vb **I** intr, *be defiled, polluted*: Nu 6 9 *S(B* ϭⲱϫⲉⲙ), ib 19 20 *B* (*S* ϫⲱϩⲙ), Jo 18 28 *SA²B* μιαίνεσθαι; Lev 10 10ϯ *SB*, He 12 16ϯ *S(B* ⲥⲁϥϩⲧ) βέβηλος; Ac 10 14ϯ *B* (*S* = Gk) ἀκάθαρτος; Ro 14 14ϯ *S(B* ϭ.) κοινός; Cl 14 1ϯ *A* μυσερός; R 2 2 32 *S* songs ⲉⲩⲥ.ϯ πορνικός; Jer 2 22 *B* κηλιδοῦν; Ge 6 11 *B(S* ⲁⲡⲟⲙⲉⲓ) φθείρεσθαι; ShA 1 368 *S* ⲉⲩϫⲁϩⲙ ⲁⲩⲱ ⲉⲩⲥ., Leyd 399 *Sᶠ* ⲡⲓⲟⲩϫⲁⲓ ⲉⲧⲥ.ϯ, C 86 192 *B* ⲛⲓⲡⲟⲩϯ ⲉⲧⲥ.ϯ, Mani 1 *A²* ⲧⲛϩⲁⲡⲛ ⲉⲧⲥ.ϯ

II tr, *defile, pollute*: Lev 18 23 *S* ⲥⲉⲉⲃⲉⲧⲏⲩⲧⲛ (*B* intr), Job 31 11 *SB*, Jer 2 7 *SB* ⲙⲓ.; Ex 31 14 *SB*, Ps 54 20 *B(S* ⲥⲱⲱϥ), Ez 43 7 *B* (var ⲱⲣⲉⲃ), Mt 12 5 *B(S* ⲃⲱⲗ ⲉⲃⲟⲗ) βεβηλοῦν; Ro 2 22 *B(S* ⲃⲱⲧⲉ) βδελύσσεσθαι; Mt 15 18 *SBF* κοινοῦν; 1 Cor 3 17 *SBF* ⲫⲑ., Ge 6 12 *B(S* ⲧⲁⲕⲟ) καταφθ.; ShA 2 305 *S* ⲛⲧⲁϥⲥⲟϥϥ ⲙⲙⲓⲛ ⲙⲙⲟϥ, JKP 2 140 *S* great sin to ⲥⲉⲉⲃⲉ ⲧⲉⲥϩⲓⲙⲉ.

p c *B* in ⲥⲁϥϩⲏⲧ, *defiled in heart*: Jer 15 21 λοιμός; Ap 21 8 (*S* ⲃⲏⲧ) βδελ.; He 12 16 (*S* ⲥ.ϯ) βέβηλος; DeV 2 166 ⲛⲓⲥ. ⲛⲟⲩⲣⲟ.

—— nn m *SA²BF*, *pollution, abomination*: Deu 17 4 *B(S* ⲃⲟⲧⲉ), Mt 24 15 *B(S* ⲇⲟ) βδέλυγμα; 2 Cor 12 21 *SBF*, Z 295 *S* drawing him ⲉⲩⲥ. ἀσέλγεια; Jer 51 4 *B(S* ⲧⲱⲗⲙ) μόλυνσις; ShC 42 177

S minds defiled with ϧⲉⲛⲥ (var ⲭⲱⲣⲙ), AP 26 A²
ⲧⲱⲗⲙ ⲛⲓⲙ ⲣⲓⲥ ⲛⲓⲙ, BMis 520 S amulet not to be
left ϧⲓⲟⲩⲙⲁ ⲉⲟⲩⲛ ⲥ ⲛ̄ϧⲏⲧϤ ; as adj : ShC 73 124
S ⲉⲛⲓⲟⲩⲙⲁⲓⲁ ⲛⲥ.

ⲁⲧⲥ. B, undefiled : He 7 26 (S ⲁⲧⲧⲱⲗⲙ) ἀμίαντος.

ⲣⲉϥⲥⲉϥ- SB, ⲥⲉⲉⲃⲉ- S, defiler : Leip Ber '02 146
S Zeus ⲣⲉϥⲥⲉⲉⲃⲉ ϣⲉⲉⲣⲉ ϣⲏⲙ παιδοφθόρος ; ShC
42 203 S ⲣⲉϥⲥⲉϥ ϣ. ϣ., R 1 4 56 S sim = Mart Ign
868 B ⲣ. ⲕⲟⲩϫⲓ ⲛⲁⲗⲟⲩ ; ⲙⲛⲧⲣⲉϥⲥⲉⲉⲃⲉ ϣ. ϣ. S :
Mor 37 120 παιδοφθορία.

CHϤE SAA², -ⲃⲉ S, -ϥⲓ BF, -ⲃⲓ F nn f m(once),
sword, knife : Ps 16 14 SBF, Hos 2 18 SAB ῥομ-
φαία ; Job 3 14 SB, Sa 18 16 S ξίφος ; Pro 5 4 SAB,
Mk 14 48 S(var -ⲃⲉ)BF, Jo 18 10 SA²B μάχαιρα ;
Ep Jer 14 BF, Ez 21 3 SB ἐγχειρίδιον ; Job 15 22
S(B ⲃⲉⲛⲓⲡⲓ) σίδηρος ; Ap 14 14 B(S ⲟϧⲥ) δρέπανον ;
P 44 7 = 75 27 S ⲧⲥ. سيف, ⲛⲥ. سكين (v AZ 50
62 n) ; PS 177 S ϥⲛⲁⲭⲱⲣ ⲛ̄ⲧⲉϥⲥ., KroppH S ⲧⲥ.
ⲉⲧⲧⲏⲕ, ib R 9 11 S ⲧⲉϥⲥ. ⲃⲏϣϥ in his hand, AP 22
A² ⲟⲩⲥ. ⲉⲥⲧⲁⲕⲙ, ShC 73 158 S ⲥ. ⲛϣⲱϥ razor (?),
BAp 208 S knife, C 86 278 B ⲍⲟⲟⲃⲉϥ ⲛ̄ⲧⲥ. = BSG
178 S ⲧⲁⲅⲟⲩ ⲉϩⲣⲁⲓ ϧⲛⲟⲩⲥ., Mich 550 24 S ⲧⲉϥⲥ.
...ⲉⲥⲱⲗⲡ ⲙⲡϣⲩⲗϩ, Mor 41 81 S ⲧϣⲛⲥ., ib 39 44 S
ⲅϣⲥ ⲛⲧⲥ. Edge of s. v ⲣⲟ II, sheath v ⲕⲟⲉⲓϣ.

CHϤE, ⲥⲏϥⲓ reed v CHⲃE.

CIϢE¹, ⲥⲏ.², ⲥⲓⲃⲉ³, ⲥⲏ.⁴ S ⲥⲓϥⲓ⁵ BF, -ⲃⲓ⁶, ⲥⲓϥ⁷ F
nn m, a tar : P 43 33 S³, K 256 B, Bodl 325 152
B ⲛⲓⲥ. قطران ; in martyr's tortures AM 34 B ⲟⲩ-
ⲟⲏⲡ ⲡⲉⲙⲟⲩⲥ., C 43 72 B ⲡⲁⲓⲥ. ⲛⲉⲙⲡⲁⲓϧⲉⲙⲝ ; in
recipes PMéd 300 S¹ for eyes (cf Hunain b. Ishaq
Meyerhof 120), Z 629 S³, BKU 1 28¹, ib 26 (8116)
F ⲁⲙⲥⲉϥ ⲉⲥ.⁶, Ryl 113 S vocab ζγλαμⲟ̄(?) · ⲡ-
ⲙⲟⲩ ⲛⲥ.⁴ tar water (? wood acid), PMéd 290 S ⲟⲃⲛ
ⲛⲥ.² (cf Chassinat) ; KKS 508 S some worked in
quarries others ⲣ ϧⲱⲃ ⲉⲛⲥ.³, AZ 23 27 S ⲟⲩⲱⲣⲉⲡ
ⲥ.³ ⲛⲁⲓ.   b tar tree, cedar : Tri 720 S ϧⲉⲛⲥ.³
أرز ; ϣⲉ ⲛⲥ., cedar wood : Ps 36 35 B(SA Cl =
Gk), Is 9 10 B(S do), Jo 18 1 BF⁷(P 129¹⁸ 124)
κέδρος, Nu 19 6 S⁴(P 44 107, var ϣⲉ ⲛⲕ.) B, 2
Chr 3 5 ξύλον κέδρινον ; K 175 B ⲡⲓϣⲉ ⲛⲥ. أرز.

ⲥⲟϥⲧⲉ, ⲥϥⲧⲱⲧ v ⲥⲟⲃⲧⲉ.

ⲥϥⲱϯ B nn, meaning unknown, relates to ship :
Montp 173 ⲁⲣⲃⲟⲧ, ⲅⲁⲙⲓⲟⲛ, ϣⲙⲟⲩ, ⲥ. اسفودية (not
in Almk 2 or BIF 20).

ⲥⲁϧ A v ⲥⲱϣ strike & ϧⲣⲁⲓ (ⲥⲁϧ).

CHϧⲉ A v ⲥⲱϣ strike (CHϢⲉ).

CIϧⲉ A v ⲥⲓϣⲉ.

ⲥⲱϧⲉ A v ⲥⲱϣⲉ vb.

ⲥϧⲉⲓ A v ⲥϧⲁⲓ.

ⲥϧⲃⲉ A v ⲥⲁϣϥ (ϣϥⲉ).

ⲥϧⲛⲉ A v ϣⲥⲡⲉ.

ⲥⲱϧⲡ A v ⲥⲱⲣⲡ.

ⲥⲁϧϥ A v ⲥⲁϣϥ.

ⲥⲁϭ, ⲥϭⲁⲓ, ⲥϭⲓ B v ⲥϧⲁⲓ.

ⲥϭⲟ B v ⲥϧⲟ.

ⲥⲱϭⲓ B v ⲥⲱϧⲉ.

ⲥⲁϭⲉⲙ B v ⲥⲱϣⲙ sink & pluck.

ⲥⲱϭⲉⲙ B v ⲥⲱϧⲙ.

ⲥⲁϭⲱⲧ, -ⲟⲧ B nn as pl, treasury (?) : 1 Chr 28
11, 20 ⲛⲉϥⲥ. σακχώ (var ζα.) روقات.   Coptic ?

ⲥⲁϧ writer v ⲥϧⲁⲓ.

ⲥⲁϧ SBF, ⲥϧ S᷑ ⲥⲁϧϥ S, nn m, awl, borer : Is
44 12 (B ⲥⲕⲉⲩⲟⲥ ⲙϥⲱⲧϧ) τέτρετον ; P 44 84 ⲡⲥⲁϧϥ ·
ⲧⲣⲩⲡⲓⲧⲏⲣⲓⲛ (τρυπητήριον) مثقاب, K 123 B carpenter's ⲥ. مثقب ; El 128 ⲥ. ⲛⲡⲉⲛⲓⲡⲉ = ib 94 A
ϣⲗⲓϭ, TT 77 heels pierced with ⲟⲩⲥ. ⲉϥⲗⲟⲃⲱ, C
43 218 B sim, LAp 558 F eyes torn out ϧⲙⲡⲉⲩⲥ.,
C 86 271 B iron ⲥ. ⲉⲅⲟⲩⲱⲧⲉⲡ ⲛ̄ⲛⲓⲕⲁⲥ, BMar 28
ϧⲉⲛⲥⲁϧ of iron, BKU 1 130 ⲡⲥⲁϧϥ ⲛ̄ϧⲱ[ⲙⲛⲧ, Ep
547 ⲥⲁϧϥ ⲱ ; CO 459 metal objects ϣⲟⲙⲧⲉ ⲛⲥϧ
ⲡϣⲱⲃ...for shaving (same ? cf ⲥⲛϧⲉ) ; suppository
(? from shape) : PMéd 187 ⲁⲁⲩ (sc drugs) ⲛⲥ. &
put into anus (κάθισμα) ; cf ⲥⲟⲗ.   ⲥⲁ ⲛⲥⲁϧ S,
awl maker (?) PMich 3553 ϥⲓⲃⲁ]ⲁⲓⲱⲛ ⲯⲁⲙⲥⲁϧ.

ⲥⲱϧ S, -ϧ A nn m, deaf person : Ex 4 11 A(S
ⲁⲗ), El 88 A let ⲛⲥ. hear = ib 118 S paral κωφός ;
ShP 78 45 shutting ears like ⲟⲩϧⲟϥ ⲛⲥ., ShC 73 59
abusive names ⲛⲃⲗⲗⲉ, ⲛⲥ., CO 40 John ⲡⲣⲉⲥⲃ/ ⲛⲥ.,
JSch 7 20 ⲡⲁϧⲁⲙ ⲥⲱⲭ̄ (same ?), Mor 51 34 ⲁⲡ-
ⲱϣ ⲉⲩⲥⲟϧ & lit lamp for blind ; P 44 87 ⲛⲥ. ·
ⲧⲙⲛⲧⲁⲗ طرش deafness ;   ⲣ ⲥ., be deaf : ShZ 599
ear ⲟⲩⲟⲭ ⲉⲣ ⲥ.

CIϧⲉ S᷑ v ⲥⲓϣⲉ.

CIϧⲉ S, -ⲟⲓ B, ⲥⲉϧ-, ⲥⲁϧⲧⲉⲛ S, ⲥⲉϧⲧⲉⲛ SAA² vb
I intr, be removed, displaced B : Mk 3 21 (S ⲡⲱϣⲥ),
2 Cor 5 13 (S do) ἐξιστάναι ; MG 25 293 were as
if ⲉⲁⲡⲉⲛϩⲏⲧ ⲥ. = BIF 13 108 S ⲁⲧⲟⲛ ;   ⲥ ⲉϫⲛ-
S : Mor 47 197 cross hanging from chain ⲁⲩⲥ. ⲉ-
ϫⲱϥ ϣⲁⲛⲧⲟⲩⲥⲟⲗⲡϥ ;   ⲥ ⲉⲃⲟⲗ S : J 66 47 = 76
50 if one ⲥ. ⲉⲃ. pass away brethren shall inherit ;   as
nn ⲥ. ⲛϩⲏⲧ B, derangement of mind : Deu 28 28 (S
ⲡ. ⲛϩⲏⲧ) ἔκστασις διανοίας ; 34 (S ⲥⲱϣⲙ†) παράπληκτος ; 2 Cor 11 23 (S ⲙⲛⲧⲁⲑⲏⲧ) παραφρονεῖν.

   II tr, move, remove self, withdraw, refl SAA² : 2
Macc 5 27 A, Jo 6 15 SA²(B = Gk), MG 17 317
ⲁϥⲥⲉϧⲧϥ ⲛ̄ⲥⲁⲟⲩⲅⲁ = C 89 5 B ⲥⲟⲕϥ ⲥⲁ- ἀναχωρεῖν,

Lu 9 10 (*B* ϣⲉ ⲉⲃⲟⲩⲛ dat) ὑποχ.; 2 Cor 8 20 (*B*
ⲱⲣϥ) στέλλεσθαι, Gal 2 12 (*B* ϧⲉⲛ⳽ dat) ὑποστ.; Jo
5 13 *SA*²(*B* ⲓ ⲉⲃⲟⲗ) ἐκνεύειν; Si 13 11 ⲥⲁⲣⲧⲕ ⲙⲙⲟϥ
ὑποχωρῶν γίνεσθαι; 1 Tim 6 20 (*B* ⲣⲓⲕⲓ ⲥⲁⲃⲟⲗ) ἐκτρέπεσθαι; Leip Ber '02 143 ⲉⲁⲩⲥⲉⲣⲧⲟⲩ ⲉⲟⲅⲟⲡ
ⲡⲓⲙ ἐξοκέλλειν; ShA 1 467 ⲙⲙⲁ ⲉⲧⲕⲥ. ⲙⲙⲟⲕ ⲉ-
ⲣⲟⲟⲩ, Mor 51 5 ⲁϥⲥⲉⲣⲧϥ ⲉϩⲟⲩⲛ ⲉⲡⲉϥⲏⲓ *withdraw to*,
ShC 73 41 ⲥⲉⲣⲧⲕ...ⲉϧⲉⲛⲡⲙⲛⲏⲧϣⲉ ⲡϣⲁϫⲉ *withdraw
from*, ShA 1 61 not fitting ⲉⲧⲣⲉϥⲥⲉⲣⲧⲟⲩ ⲙⲙⲟⲟⲩ, Miss
4 616 ϣⲁϥⲥⲉⲣⲧⲩ ⲙⲡⲣⲱⲙⲉ *move toward*;   not
refl: BMis 565 ⲛⲧⲁⲥⲥⲁⲣⲧⲟⲩ suffering them not to
enter *prohibere*, ShC 73 211 they might not touch
aught ϣⲁⲡⲧⲟⲩϩⲙⲟⲟⲥ ⲉⲥⲉϥ ⲟⲩⲙⲁ ⲛⲭⲟⲡ ⲏ ⲟⲩⲙⲁ
ⲛⲟⲩⲟⲟⲧⲉ, Ryl 239 ⲟⲩⲗⲁⲉⲓⲛ ⲛⲥϥ ⲕⲱⲣⲧ.   Sometimes confused ? with next.

ⲥⲟⲟϩⲉ (Ps 38)*S*, ⲥⲁⲁ- *S*ᶠ, ⲥⲱϧⲓ *B* (?), ⲥⲁϧⲉ- *S*,
ⲥⲉ. *A*, ⲥⲁϩⲱ⳽ *SB*, -ⲱⲱ⳽ *SF*, ⲥⲉϧⲱ⳽ *A*, ⲥⲁϧⲏⳮ† *S*,
-ⲛⲟⲩⲧ† *BF* vb tr, *remove* (mostly refl).   With
following prep. ⲥ ⲛⲥⲁ-: LMär 3 *S* ⲁⲩⲥⲁⲣⲱⲟⲩ ⲛⲥⲁⲟⲩⲥⲁ = *ib B* ⲥⲟⲕ- ⲥⲁⲟⲩⲥⲁ;   ⲥ ϧⲛ-: Bor 154 111
S of Eusignius aged 110, ⲉϥⲥⲁϧⲏⲩ ϩⲓⲧⲉϥϧⲏⲗⲓⲕⲓⲁ
advanced (?) *in age*.   With following advb. ⲥ ⲉⲃⲟⲗ
S: Ge 14 4 (*B* ϣⲉ dat), Is 52 11 (*B* ϧⲉⲛ-), BHom
141 ⲙⲡⲣⲥⲁϩⲱⲛ ⲉⲃ. ἀφιστάναι; Ps 43 9 (*B* ⲭⲱ ⲛⲥⲁ-)
ἀπωθεῖν; ShA 1 73 ⲥⲁϩⲱⲧⲛ ⲉⲃ. ⲏ ⲁⲛⲁⲭⲱⲣⲉⲓ
ⲛⲏⲧⲛ;   ⲉⲃ. ⲛ-, *remove from*: Nu 14 9 *S*(*B*
ⲙⲟⲩⲛⲕ), Jud 16 17 *S*, Job 7 16 *S*(*B* ϧ.), Ps 37 21
S(*B* ⲟⲩⲉⲓ), *ib* 118 118† *S*(*B* ⲣⲓⲕⲓ), Lu 4 13 *S*(*B*
ϣⲉ dat) ἀφισ. ἀπό; Job 13 21 *S*(*B* ⲱⲗⲓ), Sa 2 16†
S(*B* ⲟⲩ.), Pro 9 18 *SA*(*B* ϣⲉ ⲉⲃ.), Mal 3 6 *A*(*B*
ϧ.) ἀπέχεσθαι ἀπό; Ro 16 17 *S*(*B* ϧ.) ἐκκλίνειν
ἀπό; He 7 26† *SF*(*B* ⲫⲱⲣⲝ) χωρίζεσθαι ἀπό;
ShA 2 330 *S* ϣⲁϥⲥⲁⲣⲱϥ ⲉⲃ. ⲙⲙⲟⲥ, Bor 171 59
S ⲉϥⲥ.† ⲉⲃ. ⲛⲕⲣⲟϥ, MIE 2 364 *B* ⲁϥⲥⲁⲣⲱϥ ⲉⲃ.
ⲙⲡⲓⲙⲁ;   ⲉⲃ. ⲉ- *S*, sim: Nu 8 25 (*B* ϧ. ⲉⲃ.) ἀφισ.
gen; Aeg 245 ⲉⲩⲥ.† ⲉⲃ. ⲉⲧⲙⲧⲣⲉⲩⲥⲱ ἀπέχ. gen;
TT 11 ⲥ.† ⲉⲃ. ⲉⲡⲉⲑⲟⲟⲩ;   ⲉⲃ. ϧⲁ- *B*, sim: PO
14 325 ⲥ.† ⲉⲃ. ϧⲁⲣⲱⲟⲩϣ;   ⲉⲃ. ϧⲛ- *S*, sim:
BMis 473 ⲁϥⲥⲁϩⲉ ⲡⲉϥⲙⲁⲕϩ ⲉⲃ. ϩⲙⲡⲡⲟⲩϫ;   ⲉⲃ.
ϩⲓϫⲛ- *S*, *from off*: Nu 12 10 (*B* ϣⲉ ⲉⲃ.) ἀφισ.
ἀπό;   ⲥ ⲡⲥⲁⲃⲟⲗ, ⲥⲁⲃ., *from*: Ps 38 10 *S* ⲥⲟⲟϩⲉ (*B* ⲱⲗ), *ib* 34 22 *S*(var & *B* ⲟⲩⲉ) ἀφισ. ἀπό;
ViK 9543 *S*ᶠ ⲥ. ⲙⲡⲣⲙ̄ⲛⲏ ⲡⲥ., C 43 10 *B* ⲥⲁϩⲱⲕ
ⲥⲁⲃ. ⲙⲙⲟⲓ;   ϩⲁⲃⲟⲗ *S*: Mor 54 65 ⲥⲁϩⲱⲡⲛ
ϩ. ⲡⲡⲉⲣⲑⲏⲩⲉ of devil;   ⲥⲱϧⲓ ⲉⲡⲉⲥⲏⲧ *B*, *throw
down*: Dan 4 11 ἐκτινάσσειν (this vb?);   ⲥ ⲉⲡⲁϩⲟⲩ *SA*, *move backward*: Ps 43 18 (*B* ϧ.), Is 59 14
(*B* ⲧⲁⲥⲑⲟ) ἀφισ. εἰς τὰ ὀπίσω; Pro 25 9 *A*(*S* ϧⲏⲧ⳽)
εἰς τὰ ὀπ. ἀναχωρεῖν.   ⲥ ⲉϩⲟⲩⲛ *S*: 1 Kg 14 19
συνάγειν, Nu 18 2 ⲥⲁϩⲟⲩ ⲉϩ. (var ϩⲉⲡⲧⲟⲩ, *B* ⲑⲱⲟⲩⲧ) προσάγ. πρός (*l* ? ⲥⲱⲟϩϩ);   ⲥ ⲉϩⲣⲁⲓ *S*, ⲉⲃ.
B, *withdraw, draw back*: R 1 1 21 bade Jesus ⲥⲁϩⲱϥ ⲉϩ. χωρίζεσθαι; P 131³ 83 to Lazarus ⲥⲁϩⲱⲕ

ⲉϩ. till he pass by = Va 61 94 *B* ⲥⲟⲕⲕ ⲉⲡϣⲱⲓ, C
86 151 *B* war horse ⲥⲁϩⲱϥ ⲉⲃ. ϩⲱⲥ ⲉϥϭⲓⲟⲅⲓ ⲃⲉⲡ-
ⲡⲓⲡⲟⲗⲉⲙⲟⲥ.

As nn *S*, *removal, departure*: Job 28 28 ⲡⲥⲁϩⲱⲕ
ⲉⲃ. ⲛ- τὸ ἀπέχεσθαι ἀπό, BHom 38 sim ἀποχή;
GFr 438 ⲡⲥⲁϩⲱⲛ ⲉⲃ.

ϭⲓⲛⲥ. *S*, *removal, avoidance*: BMis 126 ⲧϭⲓⲛ-
ⲥⲁϩⲱⲟϥ ⲉⲃ. ⲙⲡⲉⲓⲣⲱⲃ.

ⲥⲟⲟϩⲉ *SA*, ⲥⲟϩⲉ *S*, ⲥⲁⲁϩⲉ *S*ᶠ, ⲥⲁϧⲉ-, ⲥⲁϧⲱ⳽ *S*,
ⲥⲉ. *AA*² vb I intr, *be set up, upright* (caus of ⲱϩⲉ):
Lu 13 13 (var & *B* ⲥⲟⲟⲩⲧⲛ) ἀνορθοῦσθαι; 1 Kg 20
31 (var do) ἑτοιμάζεσθαι; ShClPr 36 198 ships in
tempest ⲣⲓⲕⲉ ⲁⲩⲱ ⲟⲛ ⲁⲩⲥ. ⲉⲩⲟⲩⲟⲭ ⲉⲣⲓⲕⲉ, Mor
32 6 ship ⲡⲁⲥⲁⲁϩⲉ ⲛⲧⲉϥⲣⲉ;   ⲥ ⲉ-: Zech 4 7
SA(*B* do) κατορθοῦν.   **II** tr: Ps 145 8 (*B* ⲧⲁϩⲟ
ⲉⲣⲁⲧ⳽, cf 144 14 *SB* ⲧⲁϩⲣⲟ), BHom 22 ⲥ. ⲡⲡⲉⲧϧ-
ϧⲏⲩ. ἀνορ.; ShBor 246 106 ⲩⲥⲟⲟϩⲉ ⲛⲡⲉⲡⲧⲁϩⲉ, Sh
Leyd 360 † ⲛⲧⲟⲡ ⲛⲟⲩⲡⲟⲗⲓⲥ, ⲥⲁϩⲉ ⲟⲩⲭⲱⲣⲁ (citing
Pro 29 4 ⲧⲟⲩⲛⲉⲥ-), Bor 306 34 words that ⲥ. ⲛⲡⲉⲧⲥⲱⲧⲙ opp ϣⲟⲣϣⲣ, BIF 14 143 ⲁⲡⲣⲁⲛⲓⲟⲥ ⲥⲁϩⲉ
ⲡⲱⲛⲉ & set it at gate;   ⲥ ⲉⲣⲁⲧ⳽ (cf ⲧⲁϩⲟ ⲉⲣ.): Pr
24 3 *SA* ἀνορ.; Mani 1 *A*² ⲟⲩⲗ]ⲁⲕⲛⲧ ⲁⲩⲥⲉⲣⲱϥ ⲁ-
ⲣⲉⲧϥ ϩⲓⲭ[ⲱⲥ;   ⲥ ⲉϩⲣⲁⲓ: ShBMOr 8800 3 sick man
ⲁⲓⲧⲉⲓ ⲉⲥⲁϩⲱϥ ⲉϩ. ⲏ ⲉⲕⲁⲁϥ ⲉⲡⲉⲥⲏⲧ. Gu 35 to Peter
lying on ground ⲥⲁϩⲱⲕ ⲉϩ., Miss 4 571 sim.   As
nn m, *setting up, uprightness*: 2 Tim 3 16 (*B* ⲧⲁϩⲟ
ⲉⲣ.) ἐπανόρθωσις; ShClPr 36 158 ⲡⲉⲩⲥ. ⲙⲡⲉⲩⲥⲟ-
ⲟⲩⲧⲛ; as adj: GFr 364 ⲟⲩⲥ. ⲙⲡⲓⲥⲧⲓⲥ στελειγμους
(? στηριγμός AZ 25 136) πίστεως;   ⲙⲁ ⲛⲥ., *place
of setting up, support*: JTS 10 401 he became ⲙ. for
everyone;   ϭⲓⲛⲥ., *argument*: My 122 revealed to
me in 3 ϭ. (or ? *v* next word).

Prob same as next.

ⲥⲟⲟϩⲉ, ⲥⲟϩⲉ *S*, ⲥⲁⲁϩⲉ *S*ᶠ (Ann 18 69), ⲥⲱⲱϩⲉ
A, ⲥⲟϧⲓ *B*, ⲥⲁⲁϧⲓ, ⲥⲁϩⲉ- *F*, ⲥⲁϧⲱ⳽ *B* vb I intr, *reprove, correct B* (in *SA* bible = ϫⲡⲓⲟ except rarely):
Ge 31 37, Ps 93 10, Hos 4 4 ἐλέγχειν;   ⲥ ⲉ- *S*:
Deu 19 16 (*B* ⲭⲱ ⲛⲟⲩⲙⲉⲧⲁⲥⲉⲃⲏⲥ ϫⲁ-) καταλέγειν;
ShA 2 271 ⲧⲓⲛⲁⲥ. ⲉⲣⲱⲧⲛ ⲛϩⲟ ϩⲓϩⲟ, ShC 73 201
angel ⲥ. ⲉⲣⲟϥ ⲛϩⲓϫⲓⲟⲩⲉ that hath done;   ⲥ ⲉ-
ϩⲣⲏⲓ ⲉϫⲉⲛ- *B*, *reprove for*: Cat 92 ⲉⲥⲥ. ⲉϧ. ⲉϫⲉⲛ-
ⲫⲟⲅⲁⲓ ⲫⲟⲅⲁⲓ of sins;   ⲥ ⲡⲉⲙ- *B*, *dispute with*:
Mic 6 2 (*A* ϣⲉϫⲉ) διαλέγχ. (reading ? διαλέγ.).   **II**
tr: Lev 5 24 *B*, Ps 140 5 *B*(*A* Cl), Mic 4 3 *B*, Mt
18 15 *S*(PS 268, var ϫ.)*B*, Jo 3 20 *BF* ἐλ.; Is 1 18
B(*S* ϧⲱⲧⲡ) διελ. (cf Mic 6 above), Ac 18 28 *B* διακατελ.; MG 17 323 *S* ⲁϥⲥ. ⲙⲙⲟϥ ϩⲙⲡⲉⲛⲧⲁϥⲁⲁϥ
= C 89 80 *B* ⲉⲑⲃⲉ- διορθοῦσθαι; PS 298 *S* ⲙⲛ-
ⲧⲟⲩϧⲱⲃ ⲉⲥ. ⲙⲙⲟⲟⲩ, El 92 *A* ⲉⲥⲥ. ⲙⲙⲁϥ = *ib*
122 *S*, Cat 7 *B* who can ⲥⲁϩⲱϥ ⲛⲧⲉϥⲧⲁϩⲟϥ ⲉⲣⲁⲧϥ?,
LMär 31 *S* ⲁϥⲥ. ⲙⲙⲟϥ & his gods = BIF 14 134
ϫ., BAp 94 *S* ⲉϥⲥⲟϩⲉ ⲙⲙⲟⲟⲩ ϫⲉ-, AM 127 *B* †-
ⲥⲃⲱ ⲉⲧⲉⲙⲡⲟⲩⲥⲁϩⲱⲥ = R 1 4 68 *S* ϫ.

—— nn m *SBF*, *reproof, correction*: Pro 1 23 *B* (*SA* ⲝ.), Ez 13 14 *B*, Va 58 174 *B* ⲟⲩⲥⲁϩⲓ ⲛⲥⲁⲣⲱϥ ἔλεγχος, Nu 5 18 *BF*, 2 Tim 3 16 *B*(*S* all do) ἐλεγμός; ClPr 30 1 *S* ⲛⲥ. ⲁⲩⲱ ⲡⲧⲁϩⲟ ⲉⲣⲁⲧϥ διόρθωσις; BM 242 *S* ⲛⲥ. ⲡⲁⲍⲁⲙ ϩⲓⲧⲙⲡϫⲟⲉⲓⲥ, Miss 4 204 *B* ⲟⲩⲥ. ⲛⲛⲓⲁⲑⲛⲁⲣϯ, Va 61 20 *B* pricking their hearts ⲍⲉⲛⲛⲓⲥ.

ⲣⲉϥⲥ. *SB*, *reprover*: Sa 2 14 *B*(*S* ⲝ.) ἔλεγχος, Ez 3 26 *SB* ἐλέγχειν.

ϫⲓⲛⲥ. *B*, *reproval*: MG 25 237 beasts given understanding ⲉⲛⲡϫⲓⲛⲥ. ⲙⲙⲟⲛ.

ϭⲓ ⲥ. *B*, *receive reproof*: AM 260 ⲁϥϫⲓ ⲛⲟⲩⲥ. ⲡⲧⲉϥⲙⲉⲧⲡⲁⲣⲁⲛⲟⲙⲟⲥ, PO 11 349 sim ⲡⲧⲉ ⲧⲉϥⲙ. Prob same word as last.

ⲥⲱϩⲉ, -ϣⲉ (R), -ϩⲧ *S*, -ϣⲓ *B*, ⲥⲁϩⲧ- *SBF*, ⲥⲁϩⲧⲍ *S*, ⲥⲁⲍ̅ *B*, ⲥⲁϩⲧ†, -ϣⲧ† *S*, ⲥⲏϫⲓ†, -ϣ† *B*, p c ⲥⲁϩⲧ- *SA²F* vb **I** intr, *weave*: Ex 38 23 *B*, 2 Chr 3 14 *B* ὑφαίνειν; Tob 2 11 *S* (l ⲥⲱϩⲉ ϩⲛⲛⲉⲣⲓⲟⲙⲉ) ἐριθεύεσθαι; BM 1020 *S* rent of ⲛⲁⲧ (prob *sic* l) ⲛⲥ., R 1 5 42 *S* workshop [ⲉ]ⲧϥ[ⲥ]ⲱϣⲉ ⲛϩⲏⲧϥ. **II** tr: P 131⁴ 109 *S* ⲟⲩϫⲓⲡⲗⲟⲉⲓⲥ ⲉⲩⲥⲱϩⲧ ⲙⲙⲟϥ without hands, DeV 2 102 *B* spirit ⲉⲧⲁϥⲟⲩⲟϫⲥ (*sc* flesh) ⲟⲩⲟϩ ⲁϥⲥ. ⲙⲙⲟⲥ. With prepositions. ⲥ ⲉ-, *weave at, be occupied in weaving* something: Is 38 12 *B* ⲟⲩⲛⲁⲧ ⲉⲩⲥ. ⲉⲣⲟϥ (*S* ⲟⲙ) ἔριθος, ib 59 5 *B* (*S* ⲧⲁⲗⲟ) ὑφ.; ShA 1 395 *S* ⲉⲩⲥ. ⲉⲡⲉⲓⲡⲣⲏϣ, BM 217 22 *S* garment ⲉϥϯⲥ. ⲉⲣⲟϥ; *weave upon*: Mor 43 251 *S* ⲡϣⲛⲥ ⲉⲧⲥ.† ⲉⲛⲛⲟⲩⲃ, ib 28 80 sim (*cf* 28 69 ⲉϥⲥ.† ⲛⲛⲟⲩⲃ), R 1 3 32 *S* ⲟⲩϩⲣⲟⲉⲓⲧⲉ ⲉⲥⲥⲁϣⲧ ⲉⲛⲛⲟⲩⲃ; ⲉϩⲟⲩⲛ ⲉ- *S*, *weave on to*: ShP 130⁵ 49 ⲕⲣⲟⲕⲓⲟⲛ & ⲥⲧⲏⲙⲱⲛ ⲥ.† ⲁⲛ ⲉϩ. ⲉⲛⲉⲅⲉⲣⲏⲩ (*cf* in ⲥⲱⲣⲙ), ShA 1 107 craftsmen ⲥⲁϩⲧⲟⲩ ⲉϩ. ⲉⲣⲟϥ (*sc* veil); ⲥ ϩⲓ-, *weave with B*: Is 3 22† (*S* ⲧ.) συγκαθυφ. σύν; ⲥ ⲉⲃⲟⲗ ⲛ-, ϫⲉⲛ- *B*, *weave from, of*: Jo 19 23 ϯϣⲧⲏⲛ ⲛⲥ. ⲉⲃ. ⲙⲡϣⲱⲓ (*SA²* diff) ἐκ τ. ἄνωθεν ὑφ., Lev 19 19 ⲥ.† ⲉⲃ. ϫⲉⲛⲥⲛⲁⲩ (*S* ⲧ. ⲛ-), Va 68 170 ⲥⲧⲟⲗⲏ ⲉⲧⲁⲩⲥⲁⲥ ⲉⲃ. ϫⲉⲛⲡⲓⲙⲱⲟⲩ of font ὑφ. ἐκ, Ex 28 32 ⲥ.† ⲉⲃ. ⲙⲙⲟⲥ ⲥⲩⲛⲩϥ.

p c, *weaver*: Jo 19 23 *SA²* ⲟⲩⲥ. ϥⲓⲟⲟⲩ (*BGk* v above, *cf* τετράστιχος, τετραύφαντός); Sh(Besa)Z 506 *S* ⲛⲥ. ϩⲃⲟⲥ, ⲛⲥ. ϭⲟⲟⲩⲛⲉ, CMSS 39 *F* ⲥⲁϩ(ⲧ) ϭⲁϭⲛⲓ, PMich 3553 *S* ⲡⲙⲁ ⲛⲉⲥ. (ⲧ)ⲙⲏ.

—— nn m *SB*, *weaving, weaver's craft* & ? *weaver*: Ex 28 8 *B*, ib 36 10 *B*, Job 38 36 *SB* -ϩⲓ, ClPr 54 40 *S* ⲛⲥ. of garment known by its border ὕφασμα, Ex 26 31 *SB* ὑφάντης, 1 Kg 17 7 *S* ὑφαίνων, Ex 38 23 *B* ⲓⲉⲃ ⲛⲥ. ὑφαντός; Bal *Sⁱ* ⲧⲉⲙⲟⲥⲓⲟⲛ (ⲛ)ⲛⲥ. *weaving tax* (*cf* Bodl(P) d 36 ⲧⲉⲙⲟⲥⲉ ⲛⲧⲁⲗⲉ ϣⲧⲏⲛ); ⲥⲁϣⲉ *S* belongs ? here: 3 Kg 7 18 (P 44 111) ϣⲧⲉ ⲛⲥ. ϊﻮﻟ δικτυοῦσθαι.

ⲣⲉϥⲥⲟⲟϩⲉ *S*, *weaver*: P 43 37 ὑφάντης; ⲙⲉⲧⲣⲉϥⲥ. *B*, *weaving*: AZ 13 144.

ϭⲓⲛⲥⲱϩⲉ *S*, *weaving*: ShA 1 155 of clothes ⲧⲉⲩⲥ.

ⲥⲁϩⲧ (Ryl) *S*, *weaver*, ⲥⲁϣⲧ *S*, ⲥⲉ. *Sⁱ*, same?: Ryl 238 n ϣⲧⲏⲛ ⲛⲥ., Mor 51 38 knock at door of ⲛⲉⲥ. to get bandages for wounds, whilst ϩⲁⲕ *tailors* stitch your rags; as title: AZ 16 25 n ⲛⲥ., Saq 290 ⲡϫⲁϣⲧ, ST 130, Baouit 80 *Sⁱ* ⲛⲥ. *V* AZ 54 132. ⲥⲱϣⲧ, co. *S*, same?: BP 11349 ⲁϥϫⲓ ⲥⲟⲩⲛⲧⲟⲩ (*sc* of fields) ⲛⲧⲛⲛⲥ., *ib* ⲥⲓⲧⲓⲱϩⲉ...ⲁϥⲧⲁⲁⲩ ⲛⲛⲥ. *Cf* ϣⲧⲓⲧ.

ⲥⲱϩⲓ *B* v ⲥⲟⲟϩⲉ *remove*.

ⲥϩⲁⲓ *SA²*, ⲥⲁϩⲉⲓ (BM 1123, Kr 116) *S*, ⲥϩⲉⲓ, -ⲉⲉⲓ *A*, ⲥϩⲉⲉⲓ *A²*, ⲥϩⲏⲧ *SF*, ⲥϫⲁⲓ, ⲥⲁⲓ (BM 1227) *B*, ⲥϩⲉⲓ, ⲥⲉⲓϩⲉⲓ (Kr 181), ⲥⲉⲓϩ, ⲥϩⲉ, ⲥⲉⲓ, ⲥⲉⲧ *F*, ⲥϩⲁⲓ-, ⲥⲉϩ- *S*, ⲥⲁϩ- *A²*, ⲥϩⲉⲓ- *A*, ⲥϫⲉ-, ⲥϫⲏⲧ-, ⲥⲏⲧ- (BM 1227) *B*, ⲥϩⲉ-, ⲥϩⲏ-, ⲥⲏ-, ⲥϩⲉⲧ-, ⲥⲉⲧ-, ⲥⲏⲧ- *F*, ⲥϩⲁⲓⲥ, ⲥϩⲁⲓⲧ, ⲥⲁϩ, ⲥϩⲁ(ⲉ)ⲓ, ⲥⲁϩⲧ, ⲥⲉϩⲧⲍ *S*, ⲥⲁϩⲍ, ⲥϩⲉⲓⲧⲍ *A*, ⲥⲁϩⲍ *A²*, ⲥϫⲏⲧ *B*, ⲥϩⲉⲧⲍ, ⲥϩⲏⲧⲍ, ⲥⲉⲧⲍ *F*, ⲥⲏϩ† *SA²*, -ϩ† *A*, ⲥϫⲏⲟⲩⲧ† *B*, ⲥϩⲏⲟⲩⲧ† *F* vb **I** intr, *write*: Ro 10 5 *SB*, Ap 21 5 *SB* γράφειν, Ps 44 1 *S* ⲣⲉϥⲥϩⲉⲡⲓ ⲉϥⲥ., *B* ϣⲉⲛϣⲱⲡ ⲉϥⲥ. ὀξυγράφος, Is 29 12 *SB* ⲥⲟⲟⲩⲛ ⲛⲥ. γράμματα ἐπιστάναι, Dan 1 4 *B* ⲧⲥⲁⲃⲟ ⲛⲥ. (*S* ⲉ̅ⲛⲥ̅. nn) γράμ. διδάξαι; PLond 4 436 *S* ⲡⲣⲟⲥ ⲑⲉ ⲛⲧⲁⲡϣⲣⲡ ⲥ., JKP 2 42 *S* sent to school ⲉⲥ., AM 268 *B* I ceased not ⲉⲓⲥ. ⲛϫⲱⲡ; qual: Job 42 18 *SB*, Mk 9 12 *BF*, Jo 10 34 *SAA²B*, Cl 13 1 *A* ⲧⲛⲉⲓⲣⲉ ⲙⲡⲉⲧⲥ. γράφεσθαι; CA 100 *S* their number ϩⲛⲧⲉⲕⲕⲗⲏⲥⲓⲁ ⲉⲩⲥ., Mor 30 55 *F* he said (ⲥ)ⲥ. ⲡⲁϣⲧ̅, J 1 29 *S* ⲧⲓⲡⲣⲁⲥⲓⲥ ⲉⲧⲥ., RE 9 145 *S* letters ⲉⲩⲥ. ⲧⲁⲣⲉⲟⲩⲥⲩⲛⲅⲣⲟϫⲟⲥ ϣⲱⲡⲉ.

II tr: Ps 68 28 *S* ⲥϩⲁⲓⲥⲟⲩ *B*, Jo 21 25 *S* ⲥⲁϩⲟⲩ *B*, ib 19 21 *SA²* ⲥⲁϩϥ *B*, 2 Cor 2 3 *S* ⲥⲉϩⲧϥ (var ⲥⲉϩ ⲛⲁⲓ) *B* γρ., Is 44 5 *S* ⲥϩⲁⲓϥ *B* ἐπιγρ., Si 48 10 *S* ⲥϩⲁⲉⲓϥ καταγρ., Ez 43 11 *B* ⲥϫⲏⲧⲟⲩ διαγρ.; PS 71 *S* ⲥⲉϩ ϣⲁϫⲉ ⲛⲓⲙ, ib 73 ⲕⲛⲁⲥϩⲁⲓϥ, ShC 73 160 *S* ⲉⲩⲛⲁⲥϩⲁⲓⲥⲟⲩ (var ⲥⲁϩⲟⲩ), P 130⁵ 126 *S* ⲁϥⲥϩⲁⲓⲥⲟⲩ...ⲡⲧⲁϥⲥⲁϩⲟⲩ ⲁⲛ, Cl 45 8 *A* ⲥϩⲉⲓⲧⲟⲩ, ib 63 2 *A* ⲥⲁϩⲟⲩ, PSBA 27 168 *S* ⲥⲁϩⲥ *write (upon)* it, ST 115 23 *S*, J 12 21 *S* ⲁⲓⲥϩⲁⲓⲧⲥ, BMOr 6201 A 55 *S* ⲥϩⲁⲓⲥϥ, Ryl 277 *S* ⲥϩⲁⲓⲛⲥϥ, BMar 187 *S*, J 67 101 *S* ⲥϩⲁⲓϥ, BM 1116 19 *S* sim, ib 1045 *S* ⲥϩⲁⲓⲥ, My 130 *S* ⲡⲗⲁⲓⲥⲁϩⲧϥ, MR 5 25 *S* ⲥϩⲁⲓ ⲟⲩⲡⲓⲧⲧⲁⲕⲉ, WZKM 16 259 *S* ⲥϩⲁⲓ ⲡⲉⲛⲡⲗⲁϩ, Mani 1 *A²* ⲥⲁϩ ⲡⲓϫⲱⲙⲉ, AM 169 *B* ⲥϫⲉ ⲡⲉⲧⲉⲛⲣⲁⲛ, PO 11 332 *B* ⲥϫⲏⲧ ϯⲉⲡⲓⲥⲧⲟⲗⲏ, BM 1227 *B* ⲥⲏⲧ ⲡⲁⲓϫⲱⲙ, Mor 30 21 *F* ⲥϩⲏⲧⲥ, Kr 227 *F* ⲥϩⲉⲧⲃ, Lant 7 (2) *F* ⲥϩⲉⲧ ⲛⲓⲥϩⲁⲓ, PMich 575 *F* ⲥϩⲉⲧ ⲡⲗⲉⲓ, MR 5 36 *F* ⲥϩⲏ ⲡⲉⲧⲛⲉⲟⲩϫⲉⲓ, Jern 15 *F* ⲁⲓⲥⲏ ⲡⲉⲓϫⲱⲙⲉ, BM 616 *F* ⲥⲉⲓ (ⲙ)ⲙⲁⲁⲩ, ib 603 *F* ⲥⲉⲓϩ ⲡⲉⲓ, ib 617 *F* ⲥⲉⲧ ⲡⲉⲕϣⲓⲛⲓ, CMSS 39 *F* ⲥⲉⲓ ⲉⲧⲃⲏ(ⲧ)ⲕ; *register S*: Ryl 321 bade ⲧⲁⲣⲟⲩⲥ. ⲛⲉⲣⲱⲙⲉⲃⲁⲃⲩⲗⲱⲛ ⲧⲏⲣⲟⲩ; *draw, paint SB*: Is 49 16 *B*(*S*=Gk), Ez 23 14† *SB* ζωγρ., ib 4 1 *SB* διαγρ., Cai Euch 482 *B* ⲁⲕⲥ. ⲡⲉϩⲏⲧ ⲛⲧϩⲣⲓⲕⲱⲛ = Bor 100 27 *S* ⲁⲕϩⲱⲧⲣⲁ-

φει ὑπογρ. ; ShA 1 397 _S_ likeness ⲡⲧⲁⲛⲥⲁϧϥ ⲉϥⲉⲡⲣⲓⲕⲱⲛ, Cat 65 _B_ statue ⲉⲣⲉⲧⲟⲩⲕⲱⲛ ⲥ.† ⲉⲣⲟϥ, WTh 43 _S_ ⲁⲩⲥ. ⲙⲡⲣⲓⲥⲟⲡ on stele = _ib B_ ⲫⲱⲧϩ.
With following preposition.

—— ⲉ- _SABF, write,_ as acc : Lu 16 6 _SB_ ⲥ. ⲉⲧⲁⲓⲟⲩ (var _SB_ ⲡ-) γρ. acc, Mor 18 146 _S_ ϯⲥ. ⲉⲣⲟⲓ ⲡⲁϥ ⲡϧⲙϧⲁⲗ ⲕⲁⲧⲁⲅⲣ. δοῦλον αὐτῷ, Ryl 310 _S_ imprisoned ϣⲁⲛⲧϥⲥ. ⲡⲁϥ ⲉⲡⲉϥϣⲏⲣⲉ ; _upon, in_ : Nu 5 23 _S_(_B_ ⲉϩⲣⲏⲓ ⲉ-) εἰς, Deu 4 13 _S_(_B_ ϧⲓ-), Is 30 8 _SF_(_B_ ⲇⲟ) ἐπί, Jer 28 60 _S_(_B_ ϩⲉⲡ-), Jo 20 30 _S_(_B_ ⲡϧⲣⲏⲓ ϩⲉⲡ-) ἐν ; ShC 42 110 _S_ ϣⲁⲡⲥⲏϥ'(_l_ ⲥⲉϧ) ϧⲉⲛⲥϧⲁⲓ ⲉⲡⲕⲁϩ, RNC 4 _S_ ⲡⲁⲓ ⲉⲧⲥ.† ⲉⲡⲉⲓⲭⲱⲙⲉ, AJSL 46 248 _S_ ⲥϧⲁⲉⲓϧ ⲉⲩⲭⲁⲣⲧⲏⲥ, AM 10 _B_ ⲉϥⲥ. ⲙⲡⲉⲧⲓⲣⲁⲛ ⲉⲡϫⲱⲙ, J 35 71 _S_ ⲣⲱⲃ ⲉϥⲥϧⲁⲓ ⲉⲣⲟⲥ (_sc_ deed) ; ⲉϩⲣⲁⲓ ⲉ- _S_ : Ex 34 1 (_B_ ϧⲓ-) ἐπί, 2 Kg 11 15 ἐν ; _respecting, against_ : Job 13 26 _S_(_B_ ϧⲁ-) ⲕⲁⲧⲁⲅⲣ. κατά ; Ep 300 _S_ ⲥ. ⲡⲁⲓ ⲉⲣⲟⲟⲩ (corn owed)...each shall ⲥ. ⲉⲡⲉϥⲙⲉⲣⲟⲥ, PO 2 198 _S_ ⲥⲉϧ ⲡⲣⲁⲥⲓⲥ ⲡⲁⲓ ⲉⲣⲟϥ, Ep 387 _S_ ⲉⲧⲣⲁⲥⲉϩ ⲡⲁϥ ⲡϫⲱⲙⲉ ⲉⲣⲟϥ, PLond 4 519 _S_ field ⲥ.† ⲉⲡⲉϥⲣⲁⲡ ; _to_ (direction) : PSBA 10 196 _S_ ⲁϥⲥ. ⲉⲣⲁⲕⲟⲧⲉ ⲙⲡⲉⲥⲧⲣⲁⲧⲏⲗⲁⲧⲏⲥ, AM 108 _B_ ⲉⲧⲁⲩⲥϧⲉ ⲡⲉϥⲣⲁⲡ ⲡⲁⲕ ⲉⲭⲛⲏⲙⲓ, Ep 358 _S_ ⲥ. ⲉⲣⲏⲥ ; _for_ : Ps 101 18 _S_ (_B_ ϣⲁ-), Is 4 3 _SB_ εἰς, Hos 8 12 _A_(_B_ ⲡ-) dat ; C 43 242 _B_ ⲥϩⲏⲧⲉ ⲉⲅⲉⲣ ⲫⲗⲉⲅⲓ, DeV 1 114 _B_ ⲡⲥⲉⲥϩⲏⲧⲟⲩ...ⲉⲡⲓⲧⲁⲙⲓⲟⲛ of king to be nurtured there ; Cl 58 2 _A_ ⲉϥⲥ.† ⲁϧⲟⲩⲛ ⲁⲧⲏⲡⲉ ⲉⲛⲧάσσεσθαι εἰς ; _for, to_ (bequest) : ShBMOr 8810 490 _S_ novice's property ⲡϥⲥϧⲁⲓⲥⲟⲩ ⲉⲧⲕⲟⲓⲡⲱⲛⲓⲁ, TU 24 1 6 _S_ ⲁϥⲥ. ⲡⲟⲩⲥⲱⲧ ⲡϣⲱⲙ ⲉⲡⲣⲁⲛ of daughter, DeV 2 189 _B_ ⲥ. ⲡⲧⲁⲟⲩⲥⲓⲁ ⲉⲡⲧⲟⲡⲟⲥ ; _cf_ ⲥ. ⲡ-.

—— ⲉⲣⲁⲧⲋ ⲛ- _SB, to_ (direction) reverential : Miss 4 661 _S_ ⲁϥⲥ. ⲉⲣⲁⲧϥ ⲙⲡⲣⲣⲟ, BM 1101 _S_ ⲉϥⲥ. ⲉⲣⲁⲧⲟⲩ of saints, AM 208 _B_ wrote letter ⲉⲣⲁⲧϥ ⲡⲁⲣⲙⲏⲡⲓⲟⲥ, Ep 163 _S_ ⲁⲡⲧⲟⲗⲙⲁ ⲁⲛⲥ. ⲉⲣⲁⲧϥ of your paternity.

—— ⲉⲧⲛ- _SB, for, on behalf of_ : Ps 151 tit _S_ ⲡⲧⲁⲍⲁⲅⲉⲓⲁ ⲥⲁϧϥ ⲉⲧⲟⲟⲧϥ (_B_ ⲙⲙⲁⲩⲁⲧϥ) ἰδιόγραφος ; Mor 37 106 _S_ ⲁⲩⲥ. ⲙⲡⲉϩⲟⲟⲩ ⲉⲧⲟⲟⲧⲟⲩ σημειοῦσθαι, EW 149 _B_ ⲁϥⲥ. ⲡⲓⲥⲁϫⲓ ⲉⲧⲟⲧϥ ἐνσημαίνεσθαι ; MG 17 302 _S_ ⲁⲩⲥ. ⲙⲙⲟⲟⲩ ⲉⲧⲟⲟⲧⲟⲩ = C 89 191 _B_, Ep 323 _S_ give him ⲟⲩⲁⲓⲡⲉ...ⲛ(ⲧ)ⲥϧⲁⲓⲧⲟⲩ ⲉⲧⲟⲧⲕ ; _to_ : CO 43 _S_ ⲉϥⲥ. ⲉⲧⲟⲟⲧϥ ⲙ[ⲡⲁⲉⲓⲱⲧ.

—— ⲉϫⲛ- _SBF, upon_ : Jos 9 5 _S_, Ap 22 4† _S_ (_B_ om vb) γρ. ἐπί, He 8 10 _SF_(_B_ ⲉϩⲣ. ⲉϫ.) ἐπιγρ. ἐπί ; _concerning_ : Jer 28 60 _SB_, Mk 9 12 _SB_(_F_ ⲉⲧⲃⲉ▪) γρ. ἐπί ; BMis 33 _S_ bribed them ⲙⲡⲁⲧⲟⲩⲥ. ⲉϫⲱⲥ ⲛⲙⲙⲁϥ *ere they had inscribed her with him* (in marriage, _cf_ C 38 115).

—— ⲛ- _SAA²BF, a to_ : Dan 6 25 _B_, 2 Cor 13 2 _SF_(_B_ diff), Ap 2 1 _SB_ γρ. dat ; ShClPr 22 357 _S_ ⲁⲩⲥⲁϩⲟⲩ ⲡⲁⲛ, JEA 13 20 _S_ ϧⲁⲓⲥϧⲏⲧ ⲡⲁⲕ, TU 43 1 _A_ ⲉⲁⲛⲥ. ⲛⲏⲧⲛⲉ, AP 40 _A²_ ⲉⲩⲥ. ⲙⲡⲁⲩⲗⲟⲥ,

DeV 2 54 _B_ ⲉⲩⲥ. ⲡⲁⲡ ⲙⲡⲓⲙⲱⲓⲧ, PMich 1193 _F_ ⲕⲁⲧⲁ ⲡⲉⲧⲁⲓⲥⲉⲧ ⲡⲉⲕ, MR 2 48 _F_ ⲉⲓⲥϧⲉ ⲡⲭⲁⲏⲗ, BM 650 _F_ ⲥϧⲉ ⲡⲉⲕϣⲓⲡⲓ ⲡⲉⲓ, _ib_ 1227 _B_ ⲁⲡⲥⲏⲧ ⲡⲁⲓϫⲱⲙ ⲡⲁⲕ, AZ 23 105 _S_ drug ⲡⲧⲁⲓⲥⲁϧϥ ⲡⲁⲕ ; _without_ ⲡ-: _F_ Kr 129 ⲉⲉⲓⲥ. ⲓⲱⲁⲛⲛⲏⲥ, _ib_ 134, MR 5 48 sim, _S ib_ 31 ⲉⲩⲥ. ⲡⲉⲩϫⲟⲉⲓⲥ, WS 142 ⲡⲉⲧⲥ. ⲡϣⲏⲣⲉ ; _bequeath to_ : BMis 274 _S_ ⲡⲧⲁⲓⲥ. ⲡⲁϥ ⲡⲧⲁⲡⲣⲟⲥϧⲟⲃⲟⲥ, J 15 30 _S_ ⲉⲓⲥ. ⲡⲁⲕ...ⲙⲡⲏⲓ ; _cf_ ⲥ. ⲉ-. **b** _with, by means of_ _S_ : Deu 9 10 (var & _B_ ϧⲛ-) ἐν, Philem 19 (_B_ ⲇⲟ) dat ; KroppK 30 ⲁⲩⲥⲁϧⲟⲩ ⲡⲥⲡⲟⲩϥ (_l_ ⲥⲡⲟϥ), PLond 4 463 ⲉⲩⲥ. ⲡⲧⲉⲩϭⲓϫ, J 106 217 ⲁⲩⲥⲁϧϥ ⲡⲧⲁⲥⲡⲉ of Egyptians, EW 106 _B_ learnt ⲉⲥ. ⲡⲟⲩⲉⲓⲡⲓⲡ, KroppK 28 ⲥ. ⲡⲟⲩⲧⲉⲃⲉ ⲡⲕⲟⲥ (_l_ ⲛⲏⲃⲉ ⲡⲕⲱⲥ), _cf_ ⲥ. ϧⲛ- ; ⲉⲃⲟⲗ ⲛ-, _from out_ : BM 1227 _B_ ⲁⲓⲥⲁⲓ ⲉⲃ. ⲉⲡⲣⲱϧ ⲡⲡⲓⲣⲱⲙⲉⲙⲟⲅⲓ *at bidding, dictation of.*

—— ⲛⲥⲁ- _SA²B,_ ⲥⲉ- _A, ascribe to, inscribe, write down_ : Lu 2 1 _S_(_B_ diff) ἀπογράφεσθαι, Mor 37 54 _S_ ⲁⲩⲥϧⲁⲓⲥⲟⲩ ⲡⲥⲁⲧⲡⲟⲗⲏϯⲁ ⲛⲏⲙⲡⲏⲅⲉ ἀπ. acc, AP 15 _A²_ ⲧⲗⲁⲉⲓϭⲉ ⲉⲛⲧⲁⲥⲁϧⲥ ⲡⲥⲱⲥ ἐπιγραφή ; ShC 73 71 _S_ at novice's arrival ⲉⲩⲥ. ⲡⲥⲁⲡⲕⲁ ⲡⲓⲙ ⲉⲁϥⲡⲧϥ, El 40 _A_ angels ⲥ. ⲥⲉⲛⲛⲁⲃⲉ, BMis 79 _S_ ⲁⲕⲥ. ⲧⲉⲥϭⲓⲙⲉ ⲡⲥⲱⲕ *inscribed her as thine, ib* 396 _S_ your offerings ϥⲥ. ⲙⲙⲟⲟⲩ ⲡⲥⲱⲧⲛ (var _ib_ ⲥ. ⲡⲛⲉⲧⲓⲣⲁⲛ ⲉϫⲱⲟⲩ) = BSM 47 _B_ ϧⲓϫⲱⲟⲩ, Z 350 _S_ scribe ⲉ- ϣⲁϥⲥ. ⲡⲥⲁⲡⲉⲥⲟⲩⲟ, Mor 17 127 _S_ ⲁⲓⲥ. ⲡⲥⲁⲡⲉⲧⲉϥⲭⲱ ⲙⲙⲟⲟⲩ, Miss 4 92 _B_ ⲉⲩⲥ. ⲡⲥⲱϥ *acted as his scribes.*

—— ϣⲁ- _SB, to_ (cf ⲉⲣⲁⲧϧ) : Miss 8 44 _S_ letter ⲉⲁϥⲥⲁϧⲋ ϣⲁⲛⲉⲥⲧⲱⲣⲓⲟⲥ πρός, BMis 20 _S_ ⲁⲡϧⲁⲧⲓⲟⲥ...ⲥ. ϣⲁⲡⲉϥⲉⲓⲱⲧ, AM 72 _B_ ⲁⲩⲥ. ϣⲁⲡⲟⲩⲣⲟ.

—— ϧⲁ- _B, write about, report upon_ : AM 296 ⲥ. ϧⲁⲣⲟϥ (_sc_ martyr) & send to Rakote, Va 68 169 I need no judge to condemn nor ⲕⲁⲧⲏⲅⲟⲣⲟⲥ ⲉⲥ. ϧⲁⲣⲟⲓ.

—— ϩⲁ- _S, for, subscribe to_ : J 3 69 ⲁⲓⲥ. ϩⲁⲣⲟϥ since he cannot, BKU 1 103 I beg thee ⲥ. ϩⲁϯⲁⲥⲫⲁⲗⲉⲓⲁ, Mor 54 36 ⲁⲩⲥ. ϩⲁⲣⲟϥ ϫⲉⲟⲩⲁⲓⲕⲉⲟⲥⲡⲉ *wrote of him.*

—— ϩⲓ- _SB, on, upon_ : Ps 138 16 _B_(_S_ ⲉ-), Is 30 8 _B_(_SF_ ⲇⲟ) γρ. ἐπί ; Si 50 29 _S_ χαράσσειν ἐν ; Deu 29 21 _B_ ⲡϧⲣⲏⲓ ϩⲓ- (_S_ ϧⲛ-) γρ. ἐν, Ac 17 23 _B_ ⲉϥⲣ. ϩⲓ- (_S_ ⲉ-) ἐπιγρ. ἐν ; ShC 73 72 _S_ books ⲉⲙⲟϣⲧⲟⲩ ⲏ ⲥ. ϩⲓⲱⲟⲩ, MG 25 282 _B_ names ⲥ.† ϩⲓⲡⲉⲧⲉⲡⲗⲁⲟⲩⲟ = BIF 13 101 _S_ ⲉ-, AM 19 _B_ ⲉⲩⲥ.† ϩⲓⲟⲩⲭⲁⲣⲧⲏⲥ.

—— ϩⲛ-, ϩⲉⲡ- _SB, in_ : Ps 39 7 _SB_, Ez 13 9 _B_ (_S_ ⲉ-) γρ. ἐν, Lu 10 20 _SB_ ἐγγρ. ἐν, Ex 32 15 _S_ ⲥ.† ϧⲓⲡⲥⲁ ⲥⲡⲁⲩ (_B_ ⲥⲁⲙⲡⲁⲓ) ἔνθεν ἔνθ. ; PS 13 _S_ ϥⲥ.† ϩⲛⲧⲉⲧⲣⲁⲫⲏ ϫⲉ-, DeV 2 94 _B_ ⲁϥⲥ. ⲡⲧⲕⲁⲑⲉⲣⲉⲥⲓⲥ ϧⲉⲛϯϫⲟⲓ (Dan 5 5) ; _with_ (agent) : ShMich 550 13 _S_ ⲉⲩⲥ.† ϩⲛⲟⲩⲥⲛⲟϥ, P 44 95 _S_ pictures ⲥ.† ϩⲛⲟⲩⲙⲟⲩⲗϩ, C 43 142 _B_ ⲡⲧⲉϥⲥ. ϧⲉⲛⲧⲉϥϫⲓϫ, J 67 13 _S_ ⲁⲓⲥ....ϩⲛⲧⲁⲅⲓϫ (J mostly ⲛ-).

—— ϩⲁⲣⲁⲧ⸗ ⲛ- S, *under (orders of)*: Miss 4 598 ⲡⲗⲟⲩⲟⲅⲣⲁⲫⲟⲥ ⲉⲧⲥ. ϩⲁⲣⲁⲧϥ ⲙ̅ⲡⲟⲓⲕⲟⲛⲟⲙⲟⲥ.

—— ϩⲓⲧⲛ- S, *through, by*: J 123 2 S ⲁⲕⲥ. ϩⲓⲧⲟⲟⲧϥ ⲡⲕⲟⲙⲟⲥ ⲉⲧⲃⲉ-; ⲉⲃⲟⲗ ϩ. B: 1 Chr 28 19† ἐν.

—— ϩⲓⲥⲛ- SB, *upon, over*: Mk 15 26† S(B om) ἐπιγρ.; BSM 16 B ⲟⲩⲯⲁⲗⲙⲱⲇⲓⲁ...ⲥ.† ϩ. ⲡⲁϩⲏⲧ. With following adverb.

—— ⲉⲃⲟⲗ SB, *write outward, publish*: Leyd 276 S ⲥ.ⲉⲃ. ϩ̅ⲛⲧⲟⲓⲕⲟⲩⲙⲉⲛⲏ ⲧⲏⲣⲥ, Z 266 S sim, C 43 200 B ⲉⲓⲥ. ⲉⲃ. ϫⲉⲛⲧⲁⲙⲉⲧⲟⲩⲣⲟ ⲧⲏⲣⲥ, Ryl 361 S let thy paternity ⲥ. ⲟⲩⲉⲡⲓⲥⲧⲟⲗⲏ ⲉⲃ. ⲛⲁⲩ, Ep 182 S ⲛϭ̅ⲥ. ⲉⲃ. ⲡⲁⲡϩⲣⲱⲙⲁⲓⲟⲥ, ib 287, ST 227 S sim. On 'outward' cf ? Ep 1 183.

—— ⲉϩⲟⲩⲛ, ⲉϩ. SBF, *write in* (to palace): P 129¹³ 14 S ⲁϥⲥ. ⲉϩ. ⲛ̅ⲧⲣ̅ⲣⲱ ⲉⲧⲣⲉⲥ-; *inscribe, register*: Nu 11 26 B(var + ⲉϫ., S om ⲉϩ.) καταγρ.; CMSS 36 F him have I sent ⲛ̅ⲃⲥⲉⲧ ⲡⲁϩⲣⲡ ⲉϩ.

—— nn m SAA²B, f S v below, *writing, letter* (epistle or alphabetical): Lev 19 28 SB, Jo 5 47 SA²B, Gal 6 11 SB, BMis 560 S ϩⲉⲛⲡⲗⲁϫ...ⲉⲩ̅ ⲙⲉϩ ⲛⲥ., Z 277 S ⲟⲩⲥ. ⲡⲉ̅ⲛϩⲣⲟⲛⲟⲥ γράμμα, Dan 1 17 SB γραμματικὴ (τέχνη), Si 44 6 S γραφή, Z 278 S ϩⲛ̅ⲟⲩⲥ. ἐγγραφῶς, Mt 22 20 B(S = Gk) ἐπιγραφή, Job 31 35 SB συγγρ.; Est 8 17 S πρόσταγμα; Ap 19 20 S(B ⲧⲉⲃ̅ⲥ) χάραγμα; Deu 15 2 S ⲥ. ⲛ̅ⲣⲟ ⲙ̅ⲛⲧ(B diff)χρέος; BMis 231 S ⲟⲩⲥ. ⲛ̅ⲧⲉ ⲡⲣ̅ⲣⲟ, MG 25 271 B saint wrote ⲟⲩⲕⲟⲩϫⲓ ⲛⲥ., BMar 2 S ⲁϥ̅ⲧⲱϭⲉ ⲡⲟⲩⲥ. ⲉⲃⲟⲗ ϩⲓⲣⲙ̅ⲡⲣⲟ, Ep 140 S I salute you ϩⲓⲧⲛⲡⲁⲥ. ⲡⲉⲗⲁⲭⲓⲥⲧⲟⲥ, ST 301 S sim ⲡⲁⲥ. ⲉⲧⲥⲟ ⲭⲃ̅, Ep 434 S send word ϩⲉⲧⲛⲟⲩⲥ., Till Oster 30 A ϩⲉⲛⲥ. ⲡⲉⲓⲣⲏⲛⲓⲕⲟⲛ, ShWess 18 127 S is good to tear up ⲡⲉⲥ. ⲡⲟⲩϩⲏⲕⲉ who cannot pay, ShR 2 3 58 S ϩⲉⲛⲥ. ⲉⲡⲁϩⲟⲩ ⲉⲅⲉⲣⲟϥ ⲛ̅ⲡϩⲏⲕⲉ unable to pay, J 94 5 S writing ϩⲛ̅ⲡⲉⲩⲥ. ⲙ̅ⲙⲓⲛⲉ ⲙ̅ⲙⲟⲟⲩ, BMar 29 S knowest thy father's ϭⲓϫ ⲛⲥ.? (cf Miss 4 210 B blot out ⲡⲓⲥϫⲁⲓ ⲛ̅ϫⲓϫ *record*), ROC 23 156 B written ϫⲉⲛϩⲁⲛⲥ. ⲡ̅ⲣⲱⲙⲁⲓⲕⲏ, DeV 2 164 B sim, My 16 S ⲡⲉⲥ. ⲙ̅ⲡⲁⲗⲫⲁⲃⲏⲧⲁ, Mor 41 48 S ⲁⲗⲫⲁ ⲡ̅ϣⲟⲣⲡ ⲛⲥ., BM 219 S ⲡ̅ⲧⲟⲩ ⲛⲥ. in name Maria, Kropp E 40 S ⲡⲓⲍ ⲛⲥⲧⲓⲭ(ⲟⲥ) ⲛⲥ. on Father's forehead; v also ⲕⲁⲡ *string*: f S, *letter* (epistle): PStras 49 ⲧⲁⲓⲧⲉ ⲧⲁⲙⲉⲣϣⲟⲙⲧⲉ ⲛⲥ., PRain 4703 messenger brought ϩⲛ̅ⲥ. ⲟⲩⲉⲓ ⲙⲉⲛ...ⲁϩⲓⲡⲟⲟⲩⲥ, Ryl 348 ⲧⲉⲕⲥ....ⲡⲉⲧⲡϩⲏⲧⲥ.

ϫⲓ, ϭⲓ ⲥ. SBF, *receive letter*: Ac 28 21 S(B diff) γρ. δέχεσθαι; ShC 42 13 S ⲡⲧⲉⲣⲓϫⲓ ⲛⲡⲉⲥ. of thy paternity, C 43 53 B ⲉⲧⲁⲩϭⲓ ⲛⲛⲥ., ST 174 S worthy to ϫⲓ ⲥ. ⲡⲧⲉⲕⲙ̅ⲛⲧϫⲟⲉⲓⲥ, CO 393 S ⲁⲕϣⲓⲛⲉ ⲛⲥⲁⲭⲓ ⲥ. ⲛ̅ⲧⲱⲧⲛ *didst seek to get written deed of us*, BP 5547 F ⲙ̅ϣⲁⲕϫⲓ ⲛⲁⲥ.

ⲙⲛⲧ-, ⲙⲉⲧⲥ. SB, *writing*: Dif 2 82 B upon wall (Dan 5), Tri 493 S ⲁⲩⲥⲡⲟⲩⲇⲁⲍⲉ ϩⲓⲧⲙ.

ⲁⲧⲥ. SB, *without letters, illiterate*: HL 92 B Pamô was ⲟⲩⲁ., My 45 S figure ⲛⲁⲧⲥ. *uninscribed*.

ⲉⲓⲉⲡⲥ. S, *script*: PS 16 ⲉϥⲥ. ϩⲛ̅ⲧ̅ⲏⲡⲥ. ⲛⲧⲉ ⲡⲁⲡϫⲓⲥⲉ.

ϩⲛⲁⲁⲩ ⲛⲥ. S, *tool for writing, stile*: Ez 23 14 (B ⲥⲕⲉⲟⲥ ⲛⲥ.) γραφίς.

ⲣⲉϥⲥ. S, *writer, scribe*: J 69 15 ⲟⲩⲣ. ⲉⲧⲣⲉϥⲥ. ϩⲁⲣⲟⲟⲩ (sc witnesses, cf ὑπογραφεύς); ⲣⲉϥⲥϩⲁⲓ ϩⲉⲓⲃⲉⲥ: Sa 15 4 σκιαγράφος; ⲣⲉϥⲥϩϥ ϩⲩⲙⲛⲟⲥ (sc David): Mich 550 34; ⲣⲉϥⲥⲉⲕ ⲥ. B: BMOr 8775 88 ⲃⲉⲣⲉⲧⲁⲣⲓⲟⲥ صاحب الرسالة *courier*.

ϭⲓⲛ-, ϫⲓⲛⲥ. SB, *act, form of writing*: Ez 43 12 B(var ⲡⲟⲙⲟⲥ) διαγραφή; ShC 42 13 S ⲧⲉⲕϭ. ϣⲁⲡⲁⲉⲃⲓⲏⲛ, My 22 S ⲧⲉⲩϭ. *form of letters*, PBu 94 S ⲧϭⲓⲛϣⲁϫⲉ ⲙ̅ⲛⲧϭ. of documents, ib 279 ⲧϭ. ⲛ̅ⲡⲟⲙⲓⲕⲟⲥ ⲡⲟⲛⲃⲁⲓⲥ.

ⲥϫⲓ B nn m, *written copy, diploma*: K 141 تعليق, تنزيل; ⲥ. ⲡⲟⲩⲉⲓ, *writing of separation*: Deu 24 1 (S ϫⲱⲱⲙⲉ ⲛⲧⲟⲅⲉⲓⲟ), Mt 19 7 (S do) βιβλίον ἀποστασίου; ⲥ. ⲛ̅ϫⲓϫ *hand-copy, record*: Col 2 14 (S = Gk) χειρόγραφον.

ⲥⲁϩ SA²O, -ϩ A, -ϣ B, ⲥⲉϩ F, pl ⲥⲃⲟⲩⲓ B & sg as pl, nn m f, *writer, teacher, master*: Ex 5 6 B pl, Jos 23 2 B, Jer 8 8 B pl, Mt 13 52 BF(all S = Gk) γραμματεύς, Deu 1 15 SB γραμματο(εἰσαγωγεύς), 1 Chr 28 21 B(reading ? γραμματεία); Jo 3 10 SA² BF, Mk 9 38 SF(B ⲣⲉϥϯ ⲥⲃⲱ) διδάσκαλος; Ex 1 11 A(B = Gk), Lu 8 24 S(B ⲣ.) ἐπιστάτης, Ac 24 5 S(B ϩⲟⲩⲓⲧ) πρωτοστάτης; Mt 23 10 B(S ⲣ.) καθηγητής; ShR 2 3 34 S ⲥ., ⲡⲣⲟⲛⲟⲏⲧⲏⲥ, ⲣⲉϥϫⲓ ⲉⲓⲱⲣ (village-) *scribe*, ib 9 S learning to write ϩⲓⲧⲙ̅ⲡⲥ., ShC 73 xi S ⲡⲉⲡⲥ. ⲁⲩⲱ ⲡⲉⲡⲣⲉϥϯ ⲥⲃⲱ, BMis 374 S = BSM 32 B ⲡⲥ. ⲡⲁⲩⲗⲟⲥ (apostle), DeV 1 122 B Josephus ⲡⲓⲥ. ⲛⲁⲡⲟϩⲉⲃⲣⲉⲟⲥ, Rec 4 154 S George ⲡⲥ. (ⲡ)ⲛⲓⲁⲩⲅⲥⲧⲏⲣⲓⲟⲛ of Galileans (cf C 86 308 B ⲡⲛⲓϣϯ), Bodl(P) a 3 21 S alchem teacher ⲡⲥⲟⲫⲟⲥ ⲉⲧⲉⲡⲥ. ⲡⲉ, Kr 3 F apprentices ⲛ̅ⲧⲁⲩⲧⲉⲓⲧⲟⲩ (ⲡ)ⲛⲉⲥ. to learn τέχνη, Osir pl 37 S ⲡⲁⲥ....ⲡⲉϥⲥⲃⲟⲓ; *title of respect* S: Ep 244 ⲡⲥ. ⲙ̅ⲏⲛⲁ, BKU 1 154 ⲡⲥ. ⲡⲉⲧⲣⲟⲥ, Kr 230 ⲡⲥ. ⲓⲥⲁⲕ ⲡⲃⲟⲏⲑⲟⲥ, but Hall 22 ⲁⲡⲟⲕ ⲇⲓⲟⲥⲕⲟⲣⲟⲥ ⲡⲥ.; *women*: BM 1128 ⲧⲥ. ⲓⲟⲩⲥⲧⲓⲛⲉ, MR 5 27 ϣⲓⲛⲉ ⲉⲧⲥ. ab-bess; *master of a craft* (cf معلّم Lane Mod Eg¹ 2 336 n): Mor 17 15 S ⲁⲛⲧⲟⲩⲥ. ϩⲁⲙ̅ⲡϩⲱⲃ τεχνίτης, Hall 64 S ⲟⲩⲥ. ⲡⲉ...ϥ]ⲛⲟⲓ ⲙ̅ⲡϩⲱⲃ, BM 1109 S, sim, BMar 59 S ⲡⲥ. ϩⲛ̅ⲧⲉⲩⲧⲉⲭⲛⲏ, BM 1037 S ⲯ. ⲓⲱⲁⲛⲛⲏⲥ ⲫⲁⲙ̅ϣⲉ, WS 82 S ⲯ. ⲡⲉⲕⲱⲧ, Saq 16 S ⲯ. ⲡⲣⲁⲅⲧ, Baouit 159 S ⲯ. ⲡⲉϩⲛⲥⲛⲏⲧⲉ, BM 1051 S ⲯ. ⲡⲣⲟⲛⲟⲏⲧⲏⲥ, Ryl 212 S ⲯ. ⲡⲕⲁⲣⲡⲱⲡⲉⲥ; *with gen* ⲛ-: Z 549 S ⲡⲥ. ⲛⲁⲡϩⲏⲃⲉ, Imp Russ Ar S 026 S ⲛ̅ⲕⲁⲗⲗⲓⲅⲣⲁⲫⲟⲥ, Ming 328 S ⲡⲛⲉⲉ̅, BMar 187 S ⲡⲣⲁⲅⲛⲟⲩⲃ, DeV 2 176 B ⲙⲙⲉⲣⲕⲁⲥ, C 89 17 B ⲡⲥⲏⲓⲛⲓ = MG 17 357 طبيب معلّم, Va 172 12 ماهر ظ̄, 'ظ,

SHel 35 *S* ⲙⲙⲁⲅⲟⲥ, R 1 3 28 *S* ⲡⲣⲉϥⲙⲟⲩⲧⲉ, Mor 17 77 *S* ⲙⲫⲓⲗⲟⲥⲟⲫⲟⲥ; here ? belongs PGM 1 48 *O* ⲙⲁⲣⲓⲟⲩⲱϣⲧ ⲛⲡⲥⲁϩ (ⲡ)ⲛⲟⲩⲧⲉ; as adj: Mor 36 62 *S* Pythagoras ⲟⲩⲣⲱⲙⲉ ⲛⲥ., ROC 23 279 *B* ζωγραφος ⲛⲥ., P 44 31 *S* ϫⲱⲱⲙⲉ ⲛⲥ. ˊϫ, PChass 1 23 *S* ⲕⲁϩ ⲛⲥ. (*cf* ⲕ. ⲛⲥⲟⲫⲟⲥ, *v* ⲟⲙⲉ); ecclesiastical title *S*: P 129[20] 164 ⲡⲁⲡⲁⲅⲛⲱⲥⲧⲏⲥ ⲉⲧⲙⲙⲡⲥⲁⲡⲥ. reads λόγος, *ib* reads ἐξήγησις, *ib* ⲡⲁϥⲯⲁⲗⲗⲉⲓ, *ib* dismisses congregation ⲛϩⲉⲗⲗⲏⲛⲓⲕⲟⲛ *in Greek*, Wess 18 4 ⲡⲁⲧⲁⲅⲉ ⲧⲉⲓϩⲉⲣⲙ(ⲏⲛⲓⲁ), Leyd 150, BM 144 sim, *cf* TEuch 1 112, 137 *B* ⲟⲩⲥ. ⲛⲇⲓⲁⲕⲱⲛ reads Greek portions of service; ⲥ. ⲛⲧⲙⲉ, *village scribe*, *notary S*: BM 1079 with ⲡⲁⲡⲉ makes tax-return, Kr 5 writes for witnesses (*cf ib* 138 ⲛⲟⲙⲓⲕⲟⲥ ⲛⲧ.), BM 461 sim. *Cf* Wess 19 66 (Steinwenter) & ⲥⲁϫⲟ.

ⲙⲛⲧ-, ⲙⲉⲧⲥⲁϩ *SB*, *skill*: ShA 2 145 *S* example to others by ϩⲉⲛϩⲓⲥⲉ ⲙⲛϩⲉⲛⲙ., ShIF 183 *S* ⲁϣⲏ ⲛϩⲱⲃ ⲙⲙ. of wood, iron, Gu 99 am come to see ⲧⲉⲧⲛⲙ. in fishing, C 86 114 *B* ⲧⲉϥⲙ. ⲛϩⲁⲗⲓϣⲉ, Miss 4 168 *B* of singers.

ⲣ ⲥ. *SA*, *become*, *be teacher*, *skilled*: He 5 12 (*B* ⲉⲣ ⲣⲉϥϯ ⲥⲃⲱ) διδ. εἶναι, Bor 170 85 ⲛϥⲉⲣ ⲥ. ⲛⲟⲩⲙⲏⲏϣⲉ διδ. γίνεσθαι; ShIF 195 ⲛⲉⲛⲧⲁⲩⲣ ⲥ. ϩⲙⲡⲡⲟⲗⲉⲙⲟⲥ, RNC 50 ⲛⲉⲛⲁⲣ ⲥ. ⲁⲛ beyond other physicians, TU 43 19 *A* ⲙⲡⲣ ⲥ.

ⲥⲁϫⲟ[1], -ⲱ[2] *S*, -ⲁ *FO* nn m f, lit *great scribe* (*v* ⲟ *great* & PSBA 21 249), *village scribe*: CO 36 deed by priest, ⲥ.[2] & lector of village, ST 273 ⲡⲥ.[1] ⲛⲧⲙⲛϭ ⲡⲁϫⲏⲙⲉ (village, Ep 1 119), ST 343 ⲡⲥ.[2] ⲙⲛⲧ[ⲙⲉ ?, Ryl 392 send ⲡⲉⲕⲥ.[1] & I will do thy behest; *craftsman*, *official* (*cf* ⲥⲁϩ): CMSS 33 *F* ⲥ. ⲡⲉⲕⲱⲧ, PMich 3593 a *F* ⲥ. ⲛⲗⲉⲃⲗⲁⲉⲓⲥ, Osir 41 ⲧⲥ.[1], abbess & ⲧⲣⲙⲛⲏ; alone as title: TurO 7 David ⲡⲥ.[1] Jern 4 ⲫⲓⲃ ⲡⲥ.[1], BM 627 *F* ⲡⲁⲥ.[1], *ib* 1135 ⲡⲓⲕⲟⲩⲓ ζⲁϫⲟ, *ib* 609 *F* ⲕⲁⲡζⲁϫⲁ, MR 5 52 *F* ⲡⲕⲁⲡⲥ., BM 706 *F* expenses ⲡⲉⲃⲥ.; meaning doubtful: Mor 51 40 rebellious monks ⲱ ⲛⲁⲑⲏⲡⲁⲓⲟⲥ ⲛⲥ.[1] ⲁⲩⲱ ⲛⲁⲧⲁⲕⲧⲟⲥ, BMOr 9525 (12) monk undertakes ⲡⲛⲉⲓⲟⲩⲟⲣ(ϩ) ⲗⲁⲁⲩ ⲛⲥ.[2] ⲉϩⲟⲩⲛ ⲉϫⲱⲓ if ye disapprove, Ep 103 ⲧⲟⲡⲟⲥ...ⲉϥⲕⲟⲥⲙⲉⲓ ...ⲉⲛⲥ.[1], RE 9 164 ϣⲧⲏⲛ ⲛⲥ.[1] opp ϣ. ⲛⲕⲟⲥⲙⲓⲕⲟⲛ, BP 4977 ϩⲟⲓⲧⲉ ⲛⲥ.[2] Ryl 243 ⲫⲁϭⲁⲣⲉ (φακιάλιον) ⲛϩⲱⲃⲉⲥ ⲕⲟⲩⲓ ⲥ.[1], PGM 2 111 *O* προμ σαχα; ⲣ ⲥ.: Miss 4 696 to nuns ⲣ ⲥ.[1] ⲕⲁⲗⲱⲥ & do honour to God (*cf* ? ⲣ ⲥⲁϩ), BMEA 44768 letter ϯⲛⲁⲟⲩⲱⲙ (ⲡ)ⲛⲕⲁ ⲧⲏⲣⲟⲩ ⲙⲡⲉⲙⲁ ⲁⲗⲗⲁ ϯⲛⲁⲣ ⲥ.[2] ⲉⲣⲟϥ ⲁⲛ.

In names: Καλασάϩ (BM 1076), ⲡⲥⲁϫⲟ (Ryl 129), Ψαχό, -ῶ (Preisigke), ⲧⲥⲁϫⲟ (J 27, ST 153), Τσαχό, -ῶ, Πατσαχό (Pr).

In place-names: ⲡⲙⲁ ⲙⲡⲥⲁϩ (Kr 113), ⲡⲥⲁϩⲣϣⲏϥⲉ (? PRain 4799, HT *W*), Ψⲁϩⲓⲱϩⲁⲛⲛⲏⲥ (Ryl 134), ⲧⲙⲟⲩⲓⲉ ⲛⲡⲥⲁϫⲟ (CO 227 *sic l*, *cf* p 160), ⲑⲉⲡⲏⲧⲉ ⲛⲉⲡⲥⲁϫⲱ (Imp Russ Ar S 032), Πιαϩ σαχω (Pr).

V Spg 132 n.

ⲥϩⲟ *S*, ⲥϧⲟ *B* nn m, *plough-handle*: Glos 389 *S* ἐχέτλη · ⲡⲥ., AZ 13 144 (MS not found) *B* agricult tools made by smith ⲡⲓⲥ., ⲡⲓⲧⲏⲃ, ⲡⲓⲥⲟⲃϯ ⲙⲡⲓϩⲉⲃⲓ.

ⲥϩⲃⲏⲏⲧⲉ[1], ⲥⲃ.[2], ⲥⲃⲏⲧⲉ[3], ⲥⲃⲉⲉⲧⲉ[4], ⲥⲃⲏⲓⲧⲉ[5], ϩⲃⲏⲏⲧⲉ[6], ϩⲃⲏⲧⲉ[7] *S*, ⲥⲫⲏⲓϯ *B* nn m, *foam* of waves, mouth: Va 58 152 *B* ⲡⲓⲥ. on seashore, ShZ 595 *S* ϣⲟⲉⲓϣ, ϫⲓϩ, ϩ.[7], Mich 136 3 *S* for teething child ϯ ⲥ.[1] ⲡⲙⲟⲩⲗⲁϩ ⲉⲛⲉϥⲛⲩⲧⲉ; ⲧⲁⲩⲉ ⲥ. ⲉⲃⲟⲗ *S*, *emit foam*: Lu 9 39[2] (varr[5 7]), Z 302[3] ἀφρίζειν, Mor 17 8 waves ⲧ. ⲥ.[4] ⲉⲃ. (var KKS 166[7]) ἀπαφ.; BHom 138 mouth ⲧ. ϩ.[6] ⲉⲃ.; ϩⲓ ⲥ. *B*: Jude 13 (*S* om) ἐπαφ., HL 83; ϫⲉϣ ⲥ. ⲉⲃ. *B*: Lu *l c*, C 43 244; among maladies: K 160 *B* ⲥ. زبد.

ⲥⲱϩⲙ *S*, -ϧⲉⲙ *B*, ⲥⲁϩⲙ⸗ *S*, -ϧⲙ⸗ *B*, ⲥⲁϩⲙ†, ⲥⲟ.† *S*, ⲥⲁϧⲉⲙ†, -ϩⲉⲙ† (? same) *B* vb **I** intr, *sink*, *fall down*: ShC 42 200 *S* ⲁⲑⲓⲗⲏⲙ ⲥⲱϩⲡ ⲏ ⲁⲥⲉ. (bibl ?), ShP 130[5] 49 *S* ⲁⲛⲉⲩⲥⲧⲏⲙⲱⲛ ⲥ. ⲉⲃⲟⲗ ϩⲙⲡⲉⲩⲕⲣⲟⲕⲓⲟⲛ (*cf* in ⲥⲱϩⲉ), Va 61 105 *B* pit to catch lions ϣⲁⲣⲉⲛⲓⲣⲟⲕϩ ⲥ. & they fall in, MG 25 258 *B* ⲡⲓⲕⲁϩⲓ ⲛⲁⲥ. through much rain, Am 8 9 *S* (apocr Z 217) mountains ⲥⲟ. (*l* ⲥⲱ.); *be pressed down*, *pounded*: Ex 27 20† *B* κόπτεσθαι (but *ib* 29 40 Va Lag, 30 24 HCons ⲥⲁϩⲉⲙ, *cf* Lev 24 2 ⲧⲉⲛⲛⲏⲟⲩⲧ), Ep 309 *S* ⲥⲟⲩⲟ ⲉϥⲥ.†, Bodl 325 151 *B* ⲛⲟⲩⲟⲕⲓ ⲛⲥⲁϩⲉⲛ (*l* -ϩⲉⲙ) طحينة (*cf* K 200 ⲛⲟⲩⲕⲓⲁ ˊط); ⲥ ⲉϫⲛ- *S*: Mor 22 127 caused house to ⲥ. ⲉϫⲱⲟⲩ = BSM 117 *B* ϩⲏⲓ ⲉϧⲣ. ⲉϫ., BMar 136 Jesus touched tomb door ⲁϥⲥ. ⲉϫⲙⲡⲥⲱⲙⲁ (*cf* Synax 2 216 صخرة كبيرة سدّت باب); ⲥ ⲛⲥⲁ- *S*: Mor 46 5 noise of rocks ⲉⲩⲥ. ⲛⲥⲁⲛⲉⲩⲉⲣⲏⲩ; ⲥ ⲛⲧⲛ- *S*: P 129[16] 51 ⲛⲧⲉⲡⲉⲓⲕⲉⲟⲩⲁ ⲥ. ⲛⲧⲟⲟⲧ *lest this one* (*eye*) *also fall out*; ⲥ ⲉⲃⲟⲗ *S*: Eccl 10 10 ἐκπίπτειν; ⲥ ⲉϧⲣⲏⲓ *B*: TSBA 9 381 earthquake ⲉⲣⲉⲡⲓⲕⲁϩⲓ ⲛⲁⲥ. ⲉϧ.

II tr, *cause to fall*, *overwhelm*, *press down S*: ShC 73 111 time when ⲉⲩⲥ. ⲙⲡϫⲓⲉⲓⲣⲉ, Mor 43 26 angels ⲟⲩⲱϣ ⲉⲥ. ⲙⲡⲕⲁϩ (var *ib* 42 25 + ϩⲁⲣⲟⲟⲩ), Sph 10 4 ⲟⲩⲕⲟⲩⲓ ⲛϫⲁⲉⲓⲧ...ⲥⲁϩⲙⲉⲥ ⲛⲁⲕ *press* olives, Win 5 corn ⲁⲛⲥ. ⲟⲩⲁⲓⲛⲉ; refl *B*: ⲥ ⲉϧⲟⲩⲛ Jude 4 (*S* ⲱϣ) παρεισδύεσθαι.

ⲥⲁϩⲙⲉⲥ *SA*, -ⲙⲥ (BAp 168) *S* nn, *pestle*: Pro 23 31 ὕπερος.

V also ⲥⲱϣⲙ & *cf* ⲥⲱϩⲡ.

ⲥⲱϩⲙ *S*, -ϧⲉⲙ, -ϧⲙ⸗ *B* (distinct ? from last) vb tr *B*, *pluck*, *draw*: Am 3 12 (*S* ⲧⲱⲕⲙ), Zech 3 2 (*SA* do), Hab 2 9 (*A* ⲛⲟⲩϩⲙⲉ) ἐκσπᾶν; intr *S* ⲥ ϩⲁ-, *be withdrawn*, *recede from*: Mor 18 153 house ⲥ. ⲉⲛⲉⲥⲏⲧ ϩⲁⲣⲟⲛ κατασπᾶν; BMar 133 hill ⲛⲁⲥ. ϩⲁⲣⲟⲛ, Mor 43 39 ⲉϥⲙⲁϩⲧⲉ ⲙⲡⲕⲁϩ ⲉⲧⲙⲧⲣⲉϥⲥ. ϩⲁⲣⲟⲟⲩ.

ϩⲓⲙⲉ *SAA²*, -ⲙⲓ *BF*, ⲥⲓⲙⲓ -ⲉⲓ (Cant) *F*, ⲥⲓⲙⲉ, *O*, ⲥⲉⲓⲙⲉ (Ryl 361), ⲥϥⲉ *S* (Kr 149), ϩⲓⲙⲉ *SAA²O*, ϩⲓⲙ *S*, ϩⲏⲙⲓ *F*, pl ϩⲓⲟⲙⲉ *S*, -ⲁⲙⲉ *AA²*, -ⲁⲁⲙⲉ, ϩⲓⲁⲙⲉ *A*, ϩⲓⲟⲙⲓ *B*, -ⲁⲙⲓ *F* & sg as pl, nn f, *woman* (ⲥⲁ + ϩⲓⲙⲉ, *v* ⲥⲁ *man*): Ge 2 22 *SB*, Is 13 8 *SB*, Jo 4 9 *SA²BF* γυνή; Lev 27 4 *SB*, Mk 10 6 *SBF*, Gal 3 28 *SB* θῆλυς; PS 28 *S* blessed ⲡⲁⲣⲁ ⲥ. ⲛⲓⲙ, ShA 2 284 *S* ⲡⲱⲣϫ ϩⲣⲟⲟⲩⲧ ⲉⲃⲟⲗ ϩⲓⲥ., Hor 82 *O* ⲥ. ⲛⲣ[ⲱⲙⲉ?], BSM 124 *B* ϩⲁⲛϩⲣⲱⲙⲓ ⲓⲉ ⲥ.; *wife*: Ge 28 9 *SB*, Jud 21 7 *S* (ib ϩ.), 1 Cor 7 2 *SBF* γ.; Aeg 264 *S* ⲟⲩⲉⲡⲧⲕ ⲥ. ⲙⲙⲁⲩ, AM 182 *B* bed of ⲧⲉϥⲥ.; *female of animals*: Ge 7 16 *SB*, Pro 24 66 *S*(*A* pl) θ.; LMär 8 *S* calf ⲟⲩϩⲟⲟⲩⲧ ⲟⲩⲥ.; ϩⲓⲙⲉ &c, *wife*: Lev 18 5 *S*(var & *B* ⲥ.), Mt 14 3 *S*(*BF* ⲥ.), Cl 11 2 *A* γ.; Mt 1 6 *S*(*B* ⲑⲁ-) ἡ τοῦ; ShC 73 76 *S* ⲑ. ⲛⲗⲱⲧ, AP 41 *A²* ⲑ. ⲡⲁⲡⲟⲗⲗⲟⲫⲁⲛⲏⲥ, Hor 79 *O* ⲧϩϥ., BM 1147 *S* ⲧⲉⲃϩ., ib ⲧⲉϥⲥ., BM 689 *S* ⲧⲣⲓⲙ ⳓⲁⲣⲁⲥ, AZ 23 34 *F* ⲑⲏⲗ ⲛϣⲱⲥ, Kr 248 *S* ⲑⲓⲙ ⲛⲗⲁⲧⲟⲓ, J 67 113 *S* ϩ. ⲛⲥⲟⲡ, POxy 2036 θιμε ⲛⲥ-; pl forms: Ge 31 35 *SB*, Is 32 9 *SBF*, Zech 12 12 *SAB*, Ac 16 13 *SBF*; Cl 6 2 *A* ⲡⲕⲱϩ ⲛϩ. (var ⲛⲥϩⲓⲁⲙⲉ) γ.; Br 106 *S* ⲛⲉϩ., El 48 *A* ⲛϩⲓⲁⲙⲉ, Mani 1 *A²* ⲛϩⲁⲩⲧ, ⲛϩ.; *wives*: Nu 14 3 *SB*, Eph 5 22 *SB* γ.; CA 89 *S* ⲛⲉϥϩ., Miss 8 251 *S* ⲛⲉϩ. ⲛⲡⲟϥⲟⲩ ⲁⲛ, N&E 39 333 *B* ⲛⲓϩ. ⲛⲟⲩⲣⲱ *queens*; as adj: Joel 3 3 *B* ⲁⲗⲱⲟⲩⲓ ⲛⲥ. (*A* ϣⲉⲉⲣⲉ ϩⲓⲙ) κοράσιον; 1 Tim 5 2 *B* do (*S* ϣ. ϣ.) νεωτέρα; Aeg 277 *S* ϫⲓⲁⲕⲟⲡⲟⲥ ⲛⲥ. διακόνισσα; Mt 13 56 *SB* ⲥⲱⲛⲉ ⲛⲥ. *F* ⲥⲡⲏⲩ ⲛⲥ. (cf J 76 28) ἀδελφή, ShC 42 94 *S*, C 43 136 *B* sim; Is 32 9 *F* ϣⲉⲣⲥ. (*SB* om ⲥ.), Cant 1 5 *F* ϣⲏⲗⲓ ⲛⲥ. (*S* ϣⲉⲉⲣⲉ) θυγάτηρ, J 66 31 *S* ϣⲉⲉⲣⲉ ⲛⲥ.; Is 14 2 *S* ϩⲙϩⲁⲗ ⲛⲥ. (*B* ⲃⲱⲕⲓ) δούλη; C 43 200 *B* ⲛⲟⲩϯ ⲛⲥ., *S* v ⲛⲟⲩⲧⲉ pl forms, AZ 21 100 *O* ⲧⲁⲣⲉⲓ ⲉⲛⲥ., KroppJ 37 *S* ⲧⲉⲙⲟⲛ (δαίμων)ⲛⲥ., Leyd 446 *S* ϩⲉⲃⲣⲁⲓⲟⲥ ⲛⲥ., C 43 160 *B* ⳝⲏⲣⲁ ⲛⲥ., BMis 446 *S* ϩⲗⲗⲱ ⲛⲥ.; *animals* Nu 15 27 *S* ⲃⲁⲁⲙⲡⲉ ⲛⲥ. ⲁⲓⳟ; Job 1 14 *SB* ⲉⲓⲁ ⲥ. ⲑ., MR 2 46 *S* ϩⲓⲁⲃⲉ ⲛⲥ., Hall 121 *S* ⲙⲁⲥ ⲛⲥ.; *things*: PGen *S* ⲛⲉϩ ⲛⲥ., CR '87 376 *S* ⲉⲗⲟⲟⲗⲉ ⲛⲥ., Ryl 102 *S* ⲛⲉⲡⲓⲡⲉ ⲛⲥ. *V* also ⲛⲟⲩ, ⲗⲓⲃⲉ, ⲥⲙⲟⲧ, ⲥⲁⲉⲓⲛ, ⲥⲱⲡⲧ *custom*.

ⲛⲟϭ ⲛⲥ. *v* ⲛⲟϭ **I b**.

ⲁⲧⲥ. *B*, *wifeless*: Job 24 21 (*S* vbal) ἀγύναιος; ⲙⲛⲧⲁⲧⲥ. *S*: BM 256 222 ⲧⲙ. in this world.

ⲙⲁ ⲛⲥ. *B*, *women's place*: MG 25 41 monk may not go to ⲫⲙ.; ⲙⲁ ⲛⲛⲉϩⲓⲟⲙⲉ *S*, *harem* Est 2 3 γυναικῶν.

ⲙⲛⲧⲥ. *S*, *womanhood*: Jth 12 15 γυναικεῖος; Br 100 sell them not for food nor drink nor ϩⲁⲙ., ShLeyd 305 ⲧⲉϥⲫⲩⲥⲓⲥ ⲛⲧⲙ.

ⲣ ⲥ. *SB*, *become, be wife* ⲛ ⲛ-: Deu 22 19 *SB*, Mk 12 23 *S* (Lu 20 33 ⲣ ϩ.) *B* γ. εἶναι, 2 Kg 14 27 *S* γ. γίνεσθαι; *deflower*: Si 20 2 *S* ἀποπαρθενοῦν.

ϫⲓ, ⳓⲓ ⲥ. *SB*, *take wife*: Lev 21 13 *SB*, Su 2 *SB* γ. λαμβάνειν; Mt 19 10 *S* (var ϩ.) *B* γαμεῖν, ib 22 24 *SB* ἐπιγαμβρεύειν; ShC 73 22 *S* ⲥⲉϫⲓ ⲥ. (var ϩ.) ⲛⲡⲉϥϣⲏⲣⲉ, AM 179 *B* ⲁⲛϣⲁⲛϭⲓ ⲥ. ⲛⲏⲓ, BM 1135 *S* ⲕⲟⲩⲱϣ ϫⲓ ϩ. ⲛⲡⲉⲕⲕⲟⲩⲓ ϣⲏⲣⲉ; as nn, *marriage S*: 1 Tim 4 3 (*B* ⲅⲁⲙⲟⲥ) γαμεῖν; ShC 73 39 ⲉϥⲥⲱϣ ⲛϫ.

ⲥⲁϩⲙⲉⲥ *SA v* ⲥⲱϩⲙ *sf*.

ⲥⲁϩⲛⲉ *S*(vb once)*AA²*, -ⲛⲓ *B*, ⲥⲉϩⲛⲓ *F*, ⲥⲉϩⲛⲉ-, ⲥⲁϩⲛⲏⲧ†*B*, ⲥⲣϩⲛⲩⲧ†*A²*, ⲥⲉϩⲛⲏⲟⲩⲧ†, ⲥⲉϩⲛ.†*B*(?same) vb intr, *provide, supply*, mostly c dat: Jth 12 2 *S* χορηγεῖσθαι; Col 4 6† *B*(*S* ϫⲱⲕⲣ) ἀρτύεσθαι (in AZ 13 145 ممیز, بائن، واضم, Montp 203, P 54 160 ⲥⲉϩ. do), Mani 1, 2 *A²* ⲡⲉⲧ.† ⲁϣⲱⲡⲉ, ib ⲧⲁⲓⲣⲉⲗⲡⲓⲥ ⲥ. ⲡⲉⲥ ⲁⲧⲣⲉⲥⲃⲱⲕ; tr: Is 55 4 *F*(CBeatty gloss on Gk) ⲉⲃⲥⲉϩ̄ⲛⲓ (*S* ⲟⲩⲉϩⲥ., *B* ⲣⲉϥⲟⲩⲁϩⲥ.) προστάσσειν, Ep Jer 1 *B*(*S* do) ⲉⲡⲓⲧ., ib 62 *B*(*F* ⲧⲱϣ) ⲥⲩⲛⲧ.; 2 Cor 9 10 *B* ⲥⲉϩⲛⲉ ⲡⲓⲕⲉⲱⲓⲕ (*S* ϯ) χορ., Gal 3 5 *B*(*S* = Gk), Mart Ign 870 *B* ⲉⲧⲥ. ⲛⲏⲓ ⲛϯϫⲟⲙ = R 1 4 59 *S* χορ. ἐπιχ.; MG 25 154 *B* ⲥ. ⲛⲏⲓ ⲛⲁⲧⲣⲟⲫⲓ, DeV 1 176 *B* wealth ⲉⲧⲟⲩⲥ. ⲙⲙⲟⲥ ⲛⲕⲁⲗⲱⲥ *well managed*, Worr 323 *F* invocation ⲛⲩ (*l* ⲡⲉⲓ) ⲉⲧⲥ. ⲛⲡⲓⲙⲉⲗ[ⲟⲥ; c ⲛⲥⲁ- *B*, *provide for*: Jer 52 34 σύνταξιν διδόναι; Col 2 19 (*S* ϫⲓ ⲉⲃⲟⲗ ϩⲛ-) ἐπιχ.; Va 68 170 ⲛⲏ ⲉⲧⲥ. ⲛⲥⲁⲡⲉϥⲟⲩⲁϩⲥⲁϩⲛⲓ λειτουργός gen.

—— nn m *SBF*, *provision, supply*: Eph 4 16 *B* (*S* ϯ), Phil 1 19 *BF*(*S* ⳓⲟⲣ.) ἐπιχορηγία; *kind of, lit provision of bread* (?) *S*: ShC 73 145 ⲕⲉϣⲛⲓ ⲛⲥ. to be added to loaves baked, BP 402 ϩⲁⲧⲥ ⲛⲥ., ⲑⲁⲗⲓⲥ ⲛⲕⲁⲕⲉ, Win 55 ϯ ⲟⲩϣⲱϥⲧ ⲛⲕⲟⲩϫ ⲛⲧⲁⲕⲱϫ ⲟⲩⲕⲟⲩⲓ ⲛⲥ.; *agreement, contract* (?) *S*: CO 133 ⲉⲓⲟⲩⲱϣ ⲛⲥ. ⲙⲡⲛⲓ ⲁⲓⲧⲁⲡⲟ ⲛⲥ., J 44 49 ⲧⲁⲁⲥ (share of house) ⲉⲡⲉϣⲕⲁⲁⲣ...ⲧⲁⲁⲥ ⲉⲛⲥ.; ⲣ ⲥ. *S*, *make agreement*: ST 359 ⲁⲓⲣ ⲥ. ⲛⲁⲕ ⲉⲩⲙⲏⲣⲟⲥ (μέρος), Hall 106 ϯⲣ ⲥ. ⲛⲏ ⲉⲡⲟⲩⲁⲛ (sic) ⲉⲛⲓⲡⲉ in thy house ...ϯ ⲥⲧⲟⲓⳓⲉⲓ ⲉⲡⲓⲥ. *Cf* Ryl Dem 3 389.

ⲣⲉϥⲥ. *B*, *manager, orderer*: Tit 2 5 (*S* ⲣⲉϥⲧⲉⲩ ⲙⲁ) οἰκουργός, CaiEuch 463 χορηγός, TEuch 2 131 ⲛⲓⲣ. ⲛⲧⲉ ϯⲥⲟⲫⲓⲁ, رازق, BM 1247 161 مراهب.

ⲟⲩⲉϩ ⲥ. *S*, -ⲁϩ ⲥ. *ABF*, -ⲱϩ ⲥ. *A²*, *lay a command, bid* **I** intr: Is 13 3 *B*(*S* ϩⲱⲛ) συντάσσειν, 1 Cor 7 17 *B*(*SF* ⲧⲱϣ) διατ.; ib 7 *SB*, He 6 3 *B*(*S* ϯ ⲧⲉϩⲓⲏ) ἐπιτρέπειν; C 43 104 *B* ⲁϥⲟⲩ. ⲁϥⲓⲛⲓ, AM 166 *B* ⲁϥⲟⲩ. ⲡⲥⲉϫⲱⲧ, C 43 90 *B* ⲡⲉⲛⲕⲣⲁⲧⲟⲥ ⲟⲩ. ϫⲉϩⲓⲛⲁ; c ⲉ- vbal: Lev 7 36 *S*(*B* ϩⲟⲛϩⲉⲛ) ἐντέλλεσθαι, Is 36 21 *SBF* προστάσ., Jth 7 16 *S* ⲥⲩⲛⲧⲁⲥ.; Mt 14 9 *SBF*, Va 57 8 *B* ⲉϥⲟⲩ. ⲉⲣⲱⲗⲉⲙ κελεύειν; Dan 1 18 *B*(*S* ϫⲱ) εἰπεῖν; AM 232 *B* ⲁϥⲟⲩ. ⲉⲥⲓⲧϥ, Mani 1 *A²* ⲛⲓⲙ ⲡⲉⲧⲁϥ[ⲟⲩⲱϩ] ⲥ.ⲡⲉⲕ ⲁⲣ ⲡⲉⲓ?; c ⲉⲧⲛ-: Mt 11 1 *SB* ⲇⲓⲁⲧⲁⲥ. dat; c ⲉⲧⲣⲉ-: Dan 6 9 *SB* ἐπιτάσ., Aeg 216 *S* ⲧⲉⲡⲟⲩ. ⲉⲧ-

ⲣⲉⲅⲕⲁⲑⲁⲓⲣⲟⲩ προστάσ.; AP 11 *A²* ⲁϥⲟⲩ. ⲁⲧⲣⲟⲩ·
ⲉⲓ[ⲡⲉ] ⲕⲉⲗ.; c ⲛ- dat: Is 13 4 *B(S* ϩⲱⲛ) ἐντέλ.;
Mt 11 1 *SB* διατάσ., Lev 10 1 *SB* προστάσ., Mk
9 25 *SB* ἐπιτάσ.; Pro 9 16 *SAB* παρακελ.; Ac 21
39 *B(S* ⲕⲱ) ἐπιτρέπειν; Br 238 *S* ⲉⲧⲟⲩ. ⲙⲡⲧⲏⲣϥ,
TU 24 1 6 *S* ⲁϥⲟⲩ. ⲡⲛⲉϥⲣⲱⲙⲉ ⲉⲧⲣⲉϥ-, AM 244 *B*
ⲡⲁⲥ̄ⲥ̄ ⲡⲉⲧⲟⲩ. ⲡⲁⲕ, *ib* 126 *B* ⲉϥⲟⲩ. ⲡⲁϥ ⲉⲟⲟϩⲓ. II
tr : Nu 15 23 *SB*, Is 27 4 *B(S* ⲧⲱϣ) συντάσ., Ac 23
31 *S(B* ⲑⲱϣ), Aeg 283 *S* ⲑⲉ ⲛⲧⲁⲡⲟⲩ. ⲙⲙⲟⲥ ⲛⲏⲧⲛ
διατάσ., *ib* 244 *S* sim ⲕⲉⲗ.; BHom 62 *S* ⲁⲅⲟⲩ. ⲡ-
ⲡⲁⲓ ⲡⲡⲉⲧⲣⲙⲡⲟⲙⲟⲥ, AM 278 *B* ⲫⲏ ⲉⲧⲁⲅⲟⲩ. ⲙ-
ⲙⲟⲩ ⲡⲱⲧⲉⲛ.   As nn *SBF*, command : Ex 18 16
SB, Is 56 4 *B(S* = Gk) πρόσταγμα, ViSitz 172 4
17 *S* ⲡⲟⲩ. ⲡⲡⲉⲡⲣⲉⲥⲃⲩⲧⲉⲣⲟⲥ διατ.; Deu 6 17 *S(B*
= Gk) ἐντολή, Job 23 11 *S(B* ϩⲟⲛϩ·) ἔνταλμα, 1
Cor 7 25 *SBF* ἐπιταγή; Aeg 239 *S* κέλευσις; PS
64 *S* ⲡⲉⲕⲟⲩ. ⲙⲡⲉⲕⲧⲱϣ, Br 41 *S* ⲙⲡⲉϥⲣⲉ ⲉⲗⲁⲁⲩ
ⲡⲟⲩ. ⲡⲧⲁϥ in me (*cf* Jo 14 30), C 89 89 *B* ⲕⲁⲧⲁ
ⲡⲟⲩ. ⲓⲧⲉ ⲡⲟⲥ̄ = Miss 4 550 *S* ⲧⲱϣ, Mor 40 50 *S*
spake to none ϩⲛ(ⲟⲩ)ⲟⲩ. = MG 25 276 *B* ⲉⲣϣⲓϣⲓ.
   ⲣⲙⲡⲟⲩ. *S, commander* : ShC 73 101.
   ⲣⲉϥⲟⲩ. *B,* sim : Is 55 4 (*S* vb) προστάσσων; ⲙⲉⲧ-
ⲣⲉϥⲟⲩ., *commandment* : DeV 2 14 speaking ⲍⲉⲛⲟⲩ
ⲟⲩⲥⲭⲏⲙⲁ ⲙⲛ.

   cⲱϩⲛⲉ (?), **ⲥⲁϩⲛ- *S*** vb tr, *bring near* (? causat of
ϩⲱⲛ *approach*), c ⲉ- : Ex 19 15 ⲥⲁϩⲛⲧⲏⲩⲧⲛ ⲉⲡⲉ-
ⲧⲡⲣⲓⲟⲙⲉ (*B* ⲧⲱⲙ ⲉ-) προσέρχεσθαι dat ; ⲉϩⲟⲩⲛ ⲉ- :
ib 19 4 sim ⲉϥ. ⲉⲣⲟⲓ (var cⲱⲟⲩϩ, *B* ⲥⲱⲕ ⲉ-) προσάγειν πρός ;   intr(?) : WS 133 workman's contract
ⲙⲡⲉϥⲉϣⲥⲱϩⲛⲉ ⲉⲣⲟⲟⲩ [(same ?).

   cⲱϩⲡ *SA²*, -ϩⲡ *A*, ⲥⲉϩⲡ-, ⲥⲁϩⲡ⸗ *S*, -ϩⲡ⸗ *A* vb
I intr, *sink in, be swallowed* : ShA 2 86 *S* filth ⲉⲁϩⲥ.
ⲛϩⲏⲧⲩ like cattle, *ib* fell in ⲡⲧⲁϩⲥ. ϣⲁⲡⲉϥⲙⲏⲣⲟⲥ,
ShC 42 200 *S* ⲁⲑⲓⲗⲙⲛ c. ⲛ ⲁⲥⲥⲱϩⲛ (bibl ?);   c
ⲉϩⲟⲩⲛ ⲉ- *S* : ShIF 149 snakes flee ⲛⲥⲉⲥ. ⲉϩ. ⲉⲡⲉ-
ϣⲕⲟⲗ ; ⲉϩ. ϩⲛ- *S* : ShA 2 138 ⲉⲁϩⲥ. ⲉϩ. ⲙⲛⲧⲟ-
ⲡⲟⲥ ⲡⲕⲁⲕⲉ ; c ⲉϩⲣⲁⲓ ⲉ- *S* : Tob 14 10 ἐμπίπτειν εἰς ; ShMun 141 filth ⲉⲁϥⲥ. ⲉϩ. ⲉⲣⲟϥ paral
ⲧⲟϭⲣ.   **II** tr : *suck in, drink* : Ez 34 3 *S(B* ⲥⲱ)
κατεσθίειν ; Zech 9 15 *A(B* do) ἐκπίνειν ; ShA 1 239
S ϥⲥⲱ ⲁⲩⲱ ϥⲥ. ⲙⲡⲉϥⲥⲛⲟϥ, ShIF 245 *S* ⲥⲉⲡⲁⲥⲁϩⲡϥ
like milk, Mani 1 *A²* ⲉⲧ]ⲥ. ⲉⲧⲱⲱⲕ ⲡⲓⲯⲩⲭⲁⲅⲉ,
R 1 4 9 *S* ⲟⲩ]ϭⲱϫ ⲡⲥⲁϩⲡϥ (*sic* MS) comminuto
olere, KroppK 45 title of charm ⲉⲧⲃⲉⲟⲩϣⲁⲓ (46
ϣⲏⲓ) ⲉⲥⲁϩⲡϥ ;   ⲣⲉϥⲥⲉϩⲡ ⲥⲛⲟϥ *S, bloodsucker* :
ShA 2 338.   V Dévaud *Ét* 14.   Cf cⲱⲣⲙ *sink*.

   ⲥⲓϩⲡⲉ *S* nn, *drop* : P 131³ 84 Dives in hell crav-
ing ⲟⲩⲕⲟⲩⲓ ⲛⲥ. ⲛⲟⲩⲱⲧ ⲙⲙⲟⲟⲩ = Mor 25 12 *S*,
Va 61 95 *B* ⲧⲗ⳨ⲧⲗⲉ.

   **cⲱϩⲣ *S*, -ϩⲣⲉ *A²*, -ⲣϩ *B*, ⲥⲉϩⲣ- *S*, ⲥⲁϩⲣ- *B*,
ⲥⲁϩⲣ⸗,co. *S*,ⲥⲉϩⲗ *F*, ⲥⲁϩⲣⳁ *SB*, ⲥⲁⲣϩⳁ, ⲥⲣⲁϩⳁ,*B*,** vb
intr, *sweep* : Mt 12 44⁺ *SB* (var cⲣ.) σαροῦν ; Mus

---

42 225 *S* bridal chamber ⲉϥⲥ.⁺ ⲉⲃⲟⲗ ϩⲙⲙⲉⲉⲩⲉ ⲛⲙ
ⲉϥⲥⲟⲟⲩ, Mor 37 190 *S* ⲡⲁⲓ ⲉⲧⲥ.⁺ ϩⲁⲧⲛ ⲧⲡⲩⲗⲏ ;
often with ⲛⲟⲩϫⲕ ϥⲩ.   tr : Lu 15 8 *SB* ⲥⲁ., Is
30 14 *S(B* ⲱϣⲧ, *F* ϣⲱϣ) ἀποσυρίζειν (reading
? ἀποσαροῦν) ; *ib* 22 *SF(B* ϣⲱϣ) ὠθεῖν ; ShWess
9 145 *S* ⲁϥⲥⲁϩⲣⲟⲩ (var P 131⁶ 29 co.) ⲁⲩⲱ ⲡⲟϩ-
ϭⲟⲩ, ShC 73 192 *S* house c. ⲛⲡⲉϥⲧⲱⲗⲙ صبر, BMis
206 *S* ⲥⲉϩⲣ ⲉⲓⲧⲛ from house, Mani 2 *A²* ⲉϥⲥ. ⲁⲃⲁⲗ
...ⲙⲙⲁϥ ⲙⲡⲭⲱⲣⲙⲉ, R 1 3 34 *S* ⲡⲉⲧⲟⲩⲡⲁⲥⲁϩⲣⲟⲩ
ⲉⲃⲟⲗ ϩⲛ ⲡⲉⲡⲗⲁⲧⲓⲁ, BMOr 8811 216 *S* ⲥⲉϩⲣ ⲡⲉⲧ-
ϩⲓⲃⲟⲩⲣ ⲉϩⲣⲁⲓ ⲉⲁⲙⲛⲧⲉ (Mt 25 41);   as nn m,
sweeping SB : Cat 157 *B* ⲡⲓⲥ. (Lu 15 8) is baptism,
J 80 38 *S* oblate to do ⲡⲥ. ⲙⲛⲡⲟⲩϫⲕ.   V Rec
34 205.

   ⲥⲁϩⲣⲉⲥ *S* nn, *sweeping* (?) : Cai 42573 2 title of
recipe ⲟⲩⲥ., mixture to be poured ⲉⲡⲣⲱ ⲙⲡⲏⲓ.
In name (?) ⲡⲥⲁϩⲣϥ (MG 17 309 = *Vita Pach*
§ 79 Ψαρφεῖν, -φιος).

   ⲥⲁϩⲣⲉ v ϩⲣⲁⲓ(ϩⲣⲉ *upper part*).

   ⲥⲁϩⲥ *B*, ⲥⲉϩⲥ- *S*, ⲥⲁϩⲥ⸗ *B*, ⲥⲁϩⲥ⳨ *A²* vb tr, *rub
down, pound* : Lu 6 1 *B* (var ⲥⲁϩⲥ, *S* ⲥⲁϩⲥ ϩ) ψώχειν ; CA 103 *S* ⲉⲧⲣⲉⲩⲥⲉϩⲥ ϩⲙⲥ, Dif 1 67 *B* ⲁϥ-
ⲥⲁϩⲥⲟⲩ ϫⲉⲛϩⲉⲣⲟⲧ دس, Mani 2 *A²* ⲛϥⲥ.⁺ ⲁⲡⲉϥ-
ⲉⲣⲏⲩ.   Cf ⲥⲁϩⲥϩ.

   ⲥⲁϩⲥ *B* nn v ⲥⲁⲁⲥⲉ.

   **(ⲥⲁϩⲥϩ) *S*, ⲥⲁϩⲥⲉϩ *B*(Lu 6), ⲥⲉϩⲥⲱϩ-, ⲥⲉϩⲥⲱϩ⸗
S ⲥⲁϩⲥⲱϩ⸗ *B*, ⲥⲉϩⲥⲱϩ⁺ *S*, ⲥⲁϩⲥⲉϩ⁺ *B*** vb tr, *roll
round, rub down, plane* : Lev 6 21⁺ (*B* ⲟⲩⲱϣⲙ),
4 Kg 2 8, Job 18 8 (*B* ϭⲗⲟⲙⲗⲉⲙ), Ps 101 26 (*B*
ⲕⲱⲗ), He 1 12 (*B* do, *F* ⲕⲱϩϥ ?) ἐλίσσειν, Ez 2 10
(*B* ⲕⲟⲅⲗⲱⲗ) ἀνειλεῖν ; 1 Kg 17 40⁺ (*B* ⲥⲗⲁϫⲗⲉϫ)
λεῖος ; EstC 13⁺ στρεπτός ; Lu 6 1 *B* (var & *S* ⲥⲁϩⲥ)
ψώχειν ; P 54 161 *B* ⲁⲩⲥⲁϩⲥⲱϩϥ يعني مسكو
خرطوا (K 231 sic l), *ib* 118 *B* ⲉⲥⲥⲁ(ϩ)ⲥⲉϩ مسقف
مخروط ; ShMIF 23 25 God will ⲥⲉϩⲥⲱϩⲕ ⲡⲑⲉ ⲛⲟⲩ-
ⲕⲣⲙⲉⲥ, Miss 4 699 ϩⲉⲛⲡⲙⲥ ... ⲥⲉϩⲥⲱϩⲟⲩ & they
turn to ⲕⲉⲣⲙⲥ, *ib* 8 219 ⲁⲩⲥⲉϩⲥⲱϩ ϩⲙⲥ, BAp 62
Jesus took of His flesh ⲁϥⲥⲉϩⲥⲱϩⲥ as food for Adam,
Mor 25 91 tent of skins & sacking ⲉⲩⲥ.⁺ ⲉϥⲧⲁϩⲏⲩ
ⲉⲣⲁⲧⲟⲩ, PSBA 27 168 ⲉⲕⲉⲥⲉϩⲥⲱϩⲥ (*sc* vellum) with
pumice.   Cf ⲥⲁϩⲥ.

   ⲥⲁϩⲧ v cⲱϩⲉ.

   ⲥⲉϩⲧ *S* (once) *B* nn m, *leprosy* : Lev 14 3 (*S*
cⲱⲃϩ), Lu 5 12 (*S* do) λέπρα ; C 86 332 ⲟⲩⲥ. ϫⲏ
ϫⲉⲛⲡⲉϥⲥⲱⲙⲁ ;   with ⲕⲱⲕ, *be barked, coated
with l.* : Miss 4 153 ⲁϥⲕ. ⲡⲥ. = Mor 18 87 *S* cⲱ.,
ROC 23 282 ⲁⲥⲕ. ⲡⲥ. ⲧⲏⲣⲥ, Cat 20 ⲛⲁϥⲕⲏⲕ ⲡⲥ. ;
as nn : C 86 332 ⲡⲁⲓⲕ. ⲡⲥ., EW 92 ⳨ⲛⲁⲓⲛⲓ ⲛⲟⲩⲕ.
ⲡⲥ. ⲉϩⲣⲏⲓ ⲉϫⲱϥ ; ⲕⲁⲕⲥ., *leper* : Nu 5 2 (*S* cⲱ.⁺),
Mt 8 2 (*S* do) λεπρός ; P 44 79 *S* ⲡⲕ.ⲥ. برص.   ⲉⲣ
c., *be leprous* : DeV 2 285 ⲉϥⲟⲓ ⲡⲥ.

ⲥⲱϧⲧ *S* *v* ⲥⲱϣⲧ & ⲥⲱⲣⲉ.

ⲥⲭⲁⲧ[1], -ⲁⲁⲧ[2], -ⲟⲧ[3], ⲥϣⲟⲧ[4], ⲥⲣⲁⲧ[5] *S* nn m, *marriage gift* from bridegroom: ST 48 ⲡⲁⲡ⳿ⲣ…ⲛⲧⲁⲃⲓⲕⲧⲱⲣ ⲡⲉϧⲁⲓ ⲧⲁⲁϥ ⲡⲉ ⲡⲥ.[5], CO 131 mother gave son ⲟⲩⲟⲗⲟⲕ⳿ ⲣⲁⲥ.[1], J 30 9]ϯ ⲡⲏ ⲣⲁⲡⲟⲩⲥ.[1], *ib* 17 25 my father's house ⲛⲧⲁⲓⲧⲁⲁϥ ⲣⲁⲡⲟⲩⲥ.[1], *ib* 37 25 ⲥ.[2], ϣⲉⲗⲉⲉⲧ, ⲣⲟⲙⲡⲉ ⲡⲟⲩⲱⲙ, Ep 98 ⲙⲡⲉϥ ⲗⲁϧⲉ ⲡⲣ̄ⲏⲁⲩ ⲣⲁⲣⲟⲓ ⲣⲙⲡⲉ(ⲥ)ⲥ.[3], *ib* ⲥ.[4], J 76 43 ϣⲱⲧ ⲡⲣ̄ⲏⲧ (*l* ϣⲱⲡ ⲡⲣ̄ⲁⲧ, *cf* 66 39) ⲡⲥ.[1], Ep 546 ⲕⲗⲏⲗ ⲡⲣ̄ⲁⲧ ⲣⲁⲥ.[5], BMOr 9535 ⲉⲧⲃⲉⲡⲥ.[1] since she (wife) bare child by him ⲛⲧⲟⲥ ⲉⲧⲟ ⲙⲡⲉⲩ[ϫⲟⲉⲓⲥ (prob not ⲡⲉϥ-); ⲣⲙⲡⲥ.[1], *partaker in* (?) c.: ShWess 9 121 (about donations to monastery); ϫⲓ ⲥ.[1], *receive* c.: Ep 479 (obscure).

ⲥϧⲏⲧ *SF* *v* ⲥⲣⲁⲓ.

ⲥⲁϧⲧⲉ *S*, -ϯ *B*, ⲥⲉϧϯ *F* vb **I** intr, *kindle fire, heat* thereby: 1 Kg 8 13 *S* μαγείρισσα (γίνεσθαι); BM 915 18 *B* hath broken fast ⲁϥⲥ. ἔψημα ποιεῖν, C 89 25 *B* ⲉ̓ψ. ἕψειν; PO 11 325 *B* ⲡⲛⲟⲟϥ ⲉⲧⲥ. ⲡⲡⲓⲥⲛⲏⲩ, BMar 181 *S* ⲙⲡⲣ̄ⲥ. ⲡⲁⲕ ⲙⲁϧⲁⲁⲕ, C 86 287 *B* ⲡⲏ ⲉⲧⲥ. *stokers*, Mor 28 110 *S* ϣⲉ ⲡⲥ. *firewood*; c e- *B*: AM 290 bade c. ⲉⲟⲩⲧⲁϧⲧ till it boiled; c ⲥⲁⲡⲉⲥⲏⲧ ⲛ- *B*: Am 4 2 (*S* ϧⲁ-) ὑποκαίειν; c ϧⲁ-, ϩⲁ- *SBF*, *light fire beneath*: Jer 1 13 *B*, Am *lc S* ὑποκ.; BMar 39 *S* oil ⲁⲩⲥ. ⲣⲁⲣⲟϥ, C 89 12 *B* ⲉϥⲥ. ϩⲁⲟⲩϣⲓⲱ, BKU 1 21 *F* ⲥ. ϩⲁⲣⲁϥ (*sc* water) ϣⲁⲛⲧⲉϥⲣⲙⲁⲙ, C 86 283 *B* ⲥ. ϩⲁⲟⲩⲧⲁϧⲧ till it melt.

II tr *SB*, *kindle, burn*: Lev 6 5 *B*(*S* Mor ⲣⲱⲕϩ), Is 44 15 *B*(*S* do) καί., Ez 24 5 *S*(*B* ϧⲉⲣⲟ) ὑποκ.; Sa 13 12 *S* ἀναλίσκειν; C 86 219 *B* ⲁϥϩⲣⲟⲥ. ⲛϯⲉϧⲉ ⲛϧⲟⲙⲧ (*cf* TT 76).

—— nn m *SB*, *fire*: Nu 4 16 *S* (P 44 106, *B* ⲟⲩⲱⲓⲛⲓ) φώς; Is 40 16 *B*(*S* p. vb) καῦσις; Mor 31 117 *S* will not eat ⲗⲁⲁⲩ ⲡⲥ., *ib* ⲟⲩⲉⲙ c. *cooked food*, Ryl 106 19 *S* ⲁⲗⲟⲥ ⲉⲡⲥ. ϣⲁⲡⲧⲉⲥⲣⲙⲟⲙ, AZ 23 114 *S* ⲧⲁⲁϥ ⲉⲡⲕⲱϧⲧ…ⲣⲡⲟⲩⲥ. ⲛⲥⲁⲧ.

ϩⲓ c. *B*, *put fire, set alight*: Pro 6 19 (*SA* ⲧⲙⲣⲟ) ἐκκ.; Is 3 14 (*S* p.) ἐμπυρίζειν.

ⲁⲧⲥ. *S*, *unheated, uncooked*: Ryl 106 22 ⲉⲣⲱⲧⲉ ⲡⲁ.

ⲙⲁ ⲡⲥ. *SB*, *cooking place, kitchen*: Wess 15 22 *S* bishop ⲉϫⲉⲛⲙⲙ. μαγειρεῖον; K 155 *B* مطبخ; MG 25 150 *B* ⲡⲓⲙ. ⲡⲧⲉ ⲡⲓⲥⲛⲏⲩ.

ⲣⲉϥⲥ. *B*, *fire lighter, cook*: BMOr 8775 103 ⲙⲉⲓⲅⲉⲓⲣⲟⲩ· ⲡⲓⲣ. نارزن.

ⲥϩⲁⲩ *S* nn m, *a title* (?): BM 1165 ⲡⲥ. ⲁⲑⲁⲛⲁⲥⲉ ⲡⲗⲉⲙⲁⲥ.

ⲥⲁϩⲟⲩ, -ⲟⲩⲉ *SAA*[2], -ⲟⲅⲓ *B*, ⲥⲉϧⲟⲓ *F*, ⲥϩⲟⲩⲣ- *S*, ⲥϩⲟⲩⲉⲣ- *SB*, ⲥϩⲟⲩⲱⲣ- *A*, ⲥⲟⲩⲱⲣ- *Sᶠ*, ⲥϩⲟⲩⲱⲣ⳿ *SAA*[2]*B*, ⲥϩⲟⲩⲟⲣⲧ† *SB*, -ⲱⲣⲧ† *S*(ShMich), -ⲁⲣⲧ† *AA*[2], ⲥⲟⲩⲁⲣⲧ† *Sᶠ F* vb **I** intr, *curse*: Ps 61 5 *SB*, Ro 12 14 *BF*(*S* tr) καταρᾶσθαι; Nu 20 13 *S*(*B* ϩⲱⲟⲩϣ) λοιδορεῖσθαι; Br 270 *S* ⲉϣϣⲉ ⲁⲛ ⲉⲥ. ⲉϣϣⲉ ⲉⲥⲙⲟⲩ. Qual: Job 3 5 *SB*, Mt 25 41 *SB*, Cl 30 8 *A* ⲕⲁ., Ge 3 14 *SB*, Pro 24 39 *SA*, Jer 17 5 *SB* ἐπικα.; ShC 73 119 *S* ϥⲥ.…ⲉϥⲡⲁⲟⲩⲉⲙ ⲗⲁⲁⲩ ⲛⲡⲕⲁ ⲡϫⲓⲟⲩⲉ, ShMich 550 16 *S* ⲉⲓϣⲁⲡⲥ. ⲙⲁⲅⲁⲁⲧ, AM 217 *B* ⲕⲥ(ϩ)ⲟⲩⲟⲣⲧ ⲛⲑⲟⲕ, Mor 39 44 *Sᶠ* idols ⲥⲉⲥ., Pcod 39 *SF* ⲟⲩⲙⲉⲉⲩⲉ ⲉϩⲥ. c e-: Ge 12 3 *B*(*SA* tr), Lu 6 28 *B*(*S* do) ⲕⲁ. acc, Ps 151 6 *B*(*S* do) ἐπικα.; Mor 30 55 *F* ⲡⲡⲉⲕⲥ. ⲉⲡⲁⲣⲭⲱⲛ (Ex 22 28, *S* BMis 276 do), C 89 46 *B* ⲉⲧⲁⲓⲥ. ⲉⲣⲟⲕ=Miss 4 527 *S* ⲛⲧⲁⲓⲥ. ⲙⲙⲟⲕ.

II tr: Nu 22 6 *S*(*B* c e-) ⲁ̓ρᾶσθαι, Ge 12 3 *SA*(Cl)*B*, Ps 36 22 *S*(*B* do) καταρ.; Ex 17 2 *S*(*B* ϧⲱ.), Jo 9 28 *S*(*A*[2]*B* do) λοιδ.; ShP 130[1] 1 *S* God ⲥϩⲟⲩⲣ ⲡⲣⲱⲙⲉ ⲉϩⲣⲁⲓ ⲉⲡⲉϥⲉⲡⲓⲑⲩⲙⲓⲁ, *ib* 2 ϥⲛⲁⲥϩⲟⲩⲱⲣⲟⲩ ⲉϩⲣⲁⲓ ⲉⲁⲙⲛⲧⲉ, *ib* 3 ⲡⲧⲁϥⲥϩⲟⲩⲣ ⲕⲁⲓⲛ ⲉⲃⲟⲗ ϩⲙ ⲡⲕⲁϩ (*cf* Mor 54 30 *Sᶠ* ⲥⲟⲩⲱⲣ ⲕⲁⲓⲛ), Bor 239 53 *S* ⲙⲡⲣ̄ⲥϩⲟⲩⲉⲣ ⲗⲁⲁⲩ ⲉⲃ. ϩⲡⲣⲱⲕ, BM 1224 *A*[2] ⲡⲉⲧⲥ. ⲙⲙⲁⲓ, Mani 1 *A*[2] ⲁϥⲥϩⲟⲩⲱⲣⲥ.

—— nn m *SAA*[2]*BF*, *curse*: Ps 9 28 *S*(var -ⲟⲩⲉ) *B*, Hos 4 2 *SA*-ⲟⲩⲉ *B*, Zech 5 3 *AB* ἀρά, Pro 3 33 *SAB*, He 6 8 *SBF* κατάρα; Pro 10 18 *SAB* λοιδορία; Is 37 3 *B*(*SF* ϫⲡⲓⲟ) ἐλεγμός; ShRec 7 143 *S* ⲁⲡⲡⲛ̄ⲉ ⲓⲥ ϣⲱⲡⲉ ⲡⲥ. ϩⲁⲣⲟⲡ, PGol 47 *A*[2] ⲡⲥ. ⲡⲥⲟⲗⲟⲙⲁ, DeV 2 22 *B* free me from ⲡⲥⲛⲁϩ ⲙⲡⲥ., BM 511(3) *F* free them ϩⲁⲃⲁⲗ ⲡⲥ. ⲡⲓⲃⲓ; ⲉⲡⲥ., *under curse*: Is 64 10 *SB* εἰς κατάραν; ϧⲁⲡⲥ. *SA*[2]*B*, sim: Jo 7 49 *SA*[2]*B* ϣⲱⲡⲉ ϩ. ἐπάρατος, Gal 3 10 *S* do (*B* ϫⲱ ϧⲁ-) ὑπὸ κατάραν; ShIF 285 *S* sinners ⲉⲧϩ., J 78 66 *S* ⲡϣⲱⲡⲉ ϩⲁⲡⲛⲟϭ ⲡⲥ. in Deuteron; ϫⲓ, ϭⲓ c. *SB*, *receive curse, be cursed*: 3 Kg 8 31 *B* ἀρὰν λαμβάνειν; J 87 34 *S* ⲡϥϫⲓ ⲡⲥ. in Deuteronomy.

ⲣⲉϥⲥ. *SAB*, *curser*: Pro 26 21 *SA*, 1 Cor 5 11 *S* (*B* ⲣⲉϥϩⲟⲟⲩϣ) λοιδ., Pro 21 19 *S*(var & *A* ⲣⲉϥϭⲱⲡⲧ) ὀργίλος (reading ? ὀρκίλος by confusion); TstAb 259 *B*, Bor 254 179 *S* God of blessings ⲡⲧⲁⲓⲁⲁϥ ⲡⲣ.

ⲥⲁϧϥ *v* ⲥⲁϧ *awl*.

ⲥⲁϩⲟⲩϥ (1 var -ⲱϥ) *B* vb intr (qual), *having harelip*: K 72 ⲫⲏ ⲉⲧⲥ. أعلم. *V* AZ 13 145 & *cf* ⲫⲉⲣⲕ (ⲡⲱⲣⲕ **I**).

ⲥⲏϫ *B* *v* ⲥⲏϭ.

ⲥⲟϫ *B* *v* ⲥⲟϭ.

ⲥⲁϫⲓ *B*, ⲥⲉϫⲉ *A* *v* ϣⲁϫⲉ.

ⲥⲱϫⲉ *v* ϣⲱϫⲉ.

ⲥϫⲉ *A* *v* ϣϫⲉ.

ⲥⲁϫⲉⲛ *F*, ⲥⲟϫⲉⲛ *B* *v* ⲥⲟϭⲛ.

ⲥⲁϫⲛⲉ *A* *v* ϣⲟϫⲛⲉ.

сωⲭⲡ B v ϣⲱⲭⲡ & ϣⲱⲙⲭ.

сⲭⲣⲉϩⲧ B v сϭⲣⲁϩⲧ.

сⲏϭ SF, сιϭ, сιⲉιϭ A, сⲏⲭ B nn m, f сⲉⲉϭ S, foal of ass, horse: Ge 32 15 SB, Pro 5 19 SA -ⲉιϭ B, Zech 9 9 SAB, Mt 21 2 SBF, Jo 12 15 SB πῶλος; BMis 59 S ⲡсⲟⲉιϣ ⲡс. in chariot, BM 529 S с. ⲡⲕⲁⲙⲏ, BMOr 6201 B 136 S ⲧⲉϩⲧⲟⲟⲣⲉ ⲙⲡⲧⲉсⲉⲉϭⲉ.

сⲟϭ[1] SB(C 86 83, 202), сⲏϭⲉ[2], сⲉϭⲏ[3], сιϭⲏ[4] S, сⲉⲉϭⲉ[5] AA[2] -ι[6] A, сⲟⲭ B, сⲁϭ S/F, pl сⲉϭⲉⲟⲩⲅⲉ A & sg as pl, nn m, *fool*: Ps 93 8 S[1]B, Is 32 5 S[1]BF, Mt 5 22 S[1]B μωρός; Ps 70 7 S[1](PS, var ϩⲡⲉ, B ϣⲫⲏⲣι) τέρας; ShC 42 137 S ⲡс.[1] ⲡⲁⲧсⲃⲱ, ShA 2 326 S there is a saying ⲁⲩϯ ⲡⲟⲩϣⲏⲣⲉ ⲡⲟⲩс.[2] (so divided in MS) & he killed him with much kissing, Mor 56 39 S ⲟⲩс.[1] (var Gu Dorm 345 ⲉϥⲡⲟⲩϣс ⲏ ⲟⲩⲙⲱⲣⲟс), Cat 9 B ⲡιс. ⲡⲉ ⲡιⲁⲧϩⲏⲧ ιⲉ ⲡιⲁⲧⲕⲁϯ, TU 43 21 A ϯⲉ ⲡс.[6] (Mt 25 2), *ib* ⲡсⲉϭⲉⲟⲩⲅⲉ, BIF 15 244 S/ ⲕⲟⲩⲱϣ ⲉϣⲱⲡⲉ ⲡс.;   as adj, *foolish*: Deu 32 6 S[1]B, Si 22 19 S[1]A[5]B, 2 Tim 2 23 S[1](B ⲙⲉⲧс.)μ.; Mor 18 155 S ϩιⲁιⲱⲧⲏс ⲡс.[1], CO 434 S glossary ⲙⲱⲣⲟсⲧⲉ ⲡⲣⲱⲙⲉ ⲡс., BG 16 S ⲧⲗⲙⲧсⲁⲃⲏ ⲡс.[3], C 43 232 B ⲡⲉⲕⲁⲡⲟⲗⲗⲱⲛ ⲡс., Mani 2 A[2] ⲧⲉϥϭⲟⲙιⲗιⲁ ⲡс.;   ϣⲭ с.[1] S, *foolish talk*: Eph 5 4 (var ϣⲁⲭⲉ ⲡс., B сⲁⲭι ⲙⲙⲉⲧс.) μωρολογία, cit ShWess 18 138, Leyd 404;   ⲙⲛⲧ-, ⲙⲉⲧс., *folly*: Is 32 6 SBF μ., 1 Cor 2 14 SBF μωρία; 2 Kg 13 12 S ἀφροσύνη; ShC 42 32 S ⲙⲡⲟⲩⲭⲱ ⲡⲡⲉιⲙ., paral ⲙⲡⲧⲁϩⲏⲧ, C 86 202 B ⲉⲑⲣⲓсⲟϭι ⲡⲧⲉⲡⲙ., J 65 25 S who live ϩⲛⲟⲩⲙ., ShC 42 110 S ⲟⲩϩⲛⲁⲁⲩ ⲉⲣ ⲡⲉιⲙ. ⲡⲟⲩⲱⲧ ⲡⲣⲏⲧϥ (*sc* break it in pieces), CO 300 S ⲙⲁ (v AZ 65 124) ⲁⲡⲁ ⲃιⲕⲧⲱⲣ ⲣ ⲙⲛⲧс. ⲛϭⲉсⲟⲡ...ⲧⲏⲟ ⲡⲁⲡⲟⲕⲗⲏⲣⲟс;   ⲣ, ⲉⲣ с., *be made fool, be f.*, intr: Jer 10 14 SB, Ro 1 22 SB μωραίνειν, Is 19 11 S μωρὸς εἶναι; BMar 38 S ⲁⲡⲟⲩсⲁⲃⲉ...ⲁⲗⲗⲁ ⲧⲉⲡⲟⲩ ⲁⲕⲣ с., AM 61 B sim, CMSS 19 S/ ⲙⲡⲁϯⲉⲣ с. ⲧⲁⲕⲣιⲡⲉ ⲡⲟⲩϩⲱⲃ ere I know facts;   tr: Job 16 7 SB μωρὸν ποιεῖν, Is 44 25 SB μωρεύειν, 1 Cor 1 20 SB μωραίν.; PS 81 S ⲁⲅⲁⲁⲧ ⲡс.

сⲱϭ, сⲉϭ-, сⲟϭ⳽ S, сⲏϭ† SA[2]F, сⲛϣ† S(RNC) vb I intr, *become, be rigid, paralysed*: TU 24 1 3 S ⲁⲡⲟⲩⲁ сⲁ (of body) с.; qual: Mt 4 24 S(B ϣⲏⲗ ⲉⲃⲟⲗ) παραλυτικός, Ac 9 33 SF(B do), BM 320 151 S ⲡⲉсс. ϩⲙⲡⲉссⲱⲙⲁ παραλύεσθαι; Is 35 3 S(B ϯ ⲟⲅⲱ ⲉⲃⲟⲗ, F ⲕⲏ) ἀνειμένος, Ep 592 B 16 S παρειμ.; 3 Kg 21 11 S gloss ⲡⲉⲧс....ⲡⲉⲧⲙⲏⲣ; ShHT K 2 S ⲉⲧⲉⲡс. from head to foot, ShA 2 282 S ⲧⲉⲧс. opp ⲧⲉⲧⲟⲩⲛ ϭⲟⲙ ⲙⲙⲟс ⲉⲭⲉⲛ ⲟⲩϩⲱⲃ ⲉⲃⲟⲗ, BHom 127 S ⲁⲩⲃⲱⲗ ⲉⲃⲟⲗ ⲡⲡⲉⲧс., BMis 314 S ⲉϥс. ⲉⲡⲉϥⲟⲩⲣⲏⲏⲧⲉ, Mor 41 18 ⲉϥс. = Va 59 41

B ⲉϥⲟι ⲙⲡⲟⲧⲁⲕⲣⲟс, AP 55 A[2] healed ⲡⲉⲧс., RNC 54 S ⲉϥсⲛϣ lying in street, ib 55 сⲛϭ.   **II** tr S, *stiffen, paralyse*: Jos 11 20 сⲉϭ ⲡⲉⲩϩⲏⲧ κατισχύειν *indurare*; BIF 14 124 ⲁⲩⲡⲛⲁ сⲟϭϥ, *cf ib* ⲁⲁϥ ⲛ[ϭⲁ]ⲗⲉ.   As nn S: ShC 73 113 ⲉⲣⲉⲡсⲱⲙⲁ ⲟⲅⲟⲭ ⲉс.

сιϭⲉ S vb intr, meaning as last: R 1 4 15 ⲁⲩс. so that could not move hands *obrigare*, *ib* ⲁⲩⲣ παραλυτικος ⲁⲩс., Mor 48 72 demon ⲧⲣⲉсс. ϩⲙⲡⲉссⲱⲙⲁ = C 43 136 B ⲁϥсⲱⲧⲉⲣ ⲙⲡⲉссⲱⲙⲁ.

сⲉϭⲉ AA[2], сⲏϭⲉ S v сⲟϭ.

сⲉⲉιϭⲉ S nn m, meaning unknown, with ⲣ: COAd 19 ⲣ ⲡс. [ⲡ- ?]ⲟⲗ ⲡⲣⲟ ⲡⲁι, *ib* ⲣ ⲧⲁⲅⲁⲡⲏ ⲣ ⲡс. ⲡсⲡⲧⲉ ⲡⲗιⲧⲣⲉ ⲡсιⲡⲡⲉ ⲡⲁι. *Cf* сιϭⲉ nn, so ? *assign to, award* or sim.

сιϭⲉ S nn, *judgement, cause* at law: 2 Kg 15 2 (var ⲇιⲕⲏ) κρίσις, *ib* 4 ἀντιλογία (or ? κρ.). ? l ⲇιⲕⲏ.

сιϭⲉ vb v сⲱϭ.

сϭⲉⲗϭιⲗ v ϣⲕⲗⲕιⲗ.

сⲟϭⲛ S, сⲁⲕⲡⲉ S[a], сⲁϭⲡⲉ A, сⲁϭⲡ A[2]F, сⲟⲭⲉⲡ B, -ⲭιⲡ, -ⲭⲉⲡ, сⲁϭⲉⲡ F, сⲕⲉⲡ- S nn m, *ointment*: Ps 132 2 S(var с. ⲙⲙⲉ GMir 185)B, Cant 1 3 SF-ⲭιⲡ, Am 6 6 AB, Mt 26 7 SBF-ⲉⲡ, Jo 11 2 SA[2]B μύρον, BHom 48 S ⲡс. ⲙⲡⲛϣⲟⲩⲛϩⲛⲉ μύρισμα; Eccl 10 1 S(ShC 42 47) ἥδυσμα; Is 61 3 S(B ⲑⲱⲣⲉс) ἄλειμμα; *ib* 43 24 B (Lakân 147, var сⲉⲟιⲡⲟⲩϭι, S ϣⲟⲩϩⲏⲛⲉ) θυσίασμα; Ex 30 23 B (var сⲟ. ⲡ.) εὐώδης; P 44 65 S с. · ⲡⲁⲣⲧⲟсⲧⲁⲭⲩⲟс (ναρδόσταχυς); ShZ 589 S ⲡⲉϩⲧ с. ⲉⲭⲡⲧⲉсⲁⲡⲉ, ShA 2 65 S ⲡс. ⲁⲅⲱ ⲡⲡⲉϩ, TU 43 2 A с. poured over body, Mor 30 17 F ⲟⲩс. ⲉϥⲧⲁιⲏⲩ = BMis 243 S ϭⲏⲡⲉ, GPar 2 2 S fruit of olive ⲉⲧⲉⲡⲉιс. ⲡⲉ = *ib* sim ⲡⲉιⲡⲉϩ, BMis 543 S adorning selves with ϩⲉⲛс., C 43 230 B ⲟⲩс. ⲡсⲟⲩⲛⲟⲩϭι, ST 257 S[a] ⲡⲕⲟⲣⲕ (l ϭⲱⲣϭ) ⲡⲟⲩс.   ⲙⲛⲧс. S, *anointing, adornment*: Is 3 18 (Tri 523) κόσμος.

ⲡⲉс с. S, *boil ointment*, so *make perfumes*: 1 Kg 8 13 μυρεψός; Tri 660 ϩιⲟⲙⲉ ⲙⲡⲉс с. (Ar misunderst); ⲡⲁс- S, ⲫⲁсс. B, *perfumer*: Ex 37 29 B, Si 38 8 S μυρεψός; ⲣⲉϥ-, ⲗⲉϥⲡⲉс с. SF: Si 49 1, Cant 3 6 -ⲭⲉⲡ μ.

сⲕⲉⲡⲉⲡсⲉ S nn f, *cooking grease*: Hall 103 ⲟⲩⲡⲧⲏⲕ с....ⲡⲧⲁⲃⲁⲕс ⲉⲧⲉⲕⲧⲉ ⲙⲡⲏι, CO 211 ⲟⲩⲗιⲯⲉ ⲡс., ib 466 ⲕⲉⲗⲗⲟⲅⲣⲉ ⲉϥⲡⲱсⲉ с., BM 1041 vo σκενοπισε κε(λλαρια ζ⳽.

сⲟϭⲛι B v ϣⲟⲭⲡⲉ.

сϭⲏⲣ SA, сⲕ., ϣϭⲏⲣ (Aeg), ϣⲕⲉⲣ S, ϣϭⲏⲣ SB vb intr, *sail* on river or sea: Ac 27 24 S(B ⲉⲣ ϩⲱⲧ), Va 66 308 B ⲉⲕϣ. ⲡⲕⲁⲗⲱс πλεῖν, Mor 17 44 S ϣϭ., 47 сϭ. διαπ., Va 57 263 B ⲡⲏ ⲉⲧϣ. ⲡⲉⲙⲱⲟⲩ ⲉⲙⲡ.; ShC 73 38 S ⲉⲣⲉⲡⲉϩⲏⲧ с. heeding not bid-

ding, BMar 188 *S* when cargo aboard ⲧⲏⲡⲁⲥ., Miss 4 103 *B* ⲁⲡⲉⲣ ⲟⲩⲉⲣⲟⲟⲩ ...ⲡϣ., BM 346 *S* ⲥ. opp ⲙⲟⲟⲛⲉ ;   tr : Is 42 10 (*B* ⲉⲣ ⲅ. ϫⲉⲛ-) π. acc.

With following preposition.   ⲥ ⲉ- *SAB, to, to-ward* : RNC 43 *S* ⲉⲛϣⲁⲛⲥ. ⲉⲕⲱⲥⲧⲁⲡⲧⲁ ἀποπ. ἐπί ; Jon 1 3 *SA*(*B* ϣⲉ)βαδίζειν εἰς ; Ac 16 11 *S*(*B* do) εὐθυδρομεῖν εἰς ; MG 17 316 *S* ⲁⲅⲥ. ⲉⲡⲥⲁ ⲙⲡⲉⲙ-ⲣⲓⲧ = C 89 4 *B*, BM 346 *S* ⲁⲅⲣ ⲣⲱⲧ ⲉⲣⲏⲥ *wind hindering* ec. ⲉⲣⲏⲧ, C 43 225 *B* ⲡⲁⲅϣ. ⲉⲣⲏⲥ, *ib* 133 *B* ⲁⲅϣ. ⲉⲃⲏⲧ, RE 9 155 *S* ⲟⲅⲁⲓϣⲕⲉⲣ...ⲉⲡⲙⲁ ; AM 185 *B* when ⲉⲧⲁⲅϣ. ⲉⲡⲓϫⲟⲓ *set sail on board* ; ⲉⲅⲣⲁⲓ ⲉ- : Mor 17 7 *S* ⲉⲛⲉϣϫ. ⲉⲅⲣⲁⲓ ⲉⲧⲁⲥⲓⲁ π. πρός, Ac 13 4 *S*(*B* ⲉⲣ ⲅ.) ἀποπ. εἰς, Lu 8 26 *S*(*B* do) καταπ. εἰς ;   ⲥ ⲡⲥⲁ- *S, along*? : BIF 13 106 ⲥ. ⲛⲥⲁⲡⲉ-ⲥⲡⲟⲧⲟⲩ ⲡⲣⲏⲥ *of sea* = MG 25 290 *B* ⲥⲁ- ;   ⲥ ⲅⲓϫⲛ- *S, upon* : Miss 4 563 ⲉⲅⲥ. ⲅⲓⲡⲉⲛϫⲟⲓ ; ⲅⲓϫⲣⲁⲝ ⲛ-, *on surface of* : RNC 57 stone ⲥ. ⲅⲓϫⲣⲁϥ ⲛⲡⲙⲟⲟⲩ *like leaf* ;   ⲥ ⲅⲛ- *SB, in, upon* : Ap 18 17 (*B* ⲉⲣ ⲅ.) π. ἐπί ; Ps 103 26 (*B* ⲥⲓⲛⲓ) διαπορεύεσθαι ; Sa 5 10 διέρχεσθαι ; Miss 8 16 *no ship should* ⲥ. ⲅⲛⲑⲁⲗⲁⲥⲥⲁ, AM 30 *B* ⲉⲅϣ. ϫⲉⲛⲫⲓⲟⲙ ;   ⲥ ⲉⲃⲟⲗ ⲅⲛ- *S, away from* : Wess 18 94 ⲁⲓⲥ....ⲉⲃ. ⲅⲛⲧⲣⲱⲁⲥ π. ἀπό, Ac 20 6 (*B* ⲉⲣ ⲅ.) ἐκπ. ἀπό ; *ib* 13 13 (*B* ⲓ ⲉⲃ.) ἀνάγεσθαι ἀπό ;   ⲥ ⲅⲓⲧⲛ- *S, through, across* : Sa 14 1 διο-δεύειν.

ⲙⲁ ⲛⲥ. *S, sailing course* : Miss 8 48 ⲙⲙ. ⲛⲑⲁ-ⲗⲁⲥⲥⲁ opp ⲡⲉⲧⲣⲟⲙⲟⲥ (δρ.).

ϣⲉ ⲛⲥⲕ., *S, meaning uncertain* : BMEA ostr 33010 ⲁⲓⲕⲱ ⲡϣⲏ ⲛⲥ. ⲅⲁⲛⲅⲏⲧ ⲉⲩⲛⲁϣⲓⲧⲉ ⲉⲛⲟⲏⲥⲓⲁ-ⲥⲧⲏⲣⲓⲟⲛ ⲙⲙⲟϥ.

—— nn m *SB, sailing, voyage* : Ac 27 9 (*B* diff), BMar 121 ⲛⲉⲥ. ⲛⲑⲁⲗ. ⲅⲓⲛϫⲟⲓ πλοῦς, BHom 8 *ready* ⲉⲡⲓⲥ. ἀποπλ., Ac 27 7 ⲱⲥⲕ ⲅⲙⲡⲉⲥ. (*B* ⲉⲣ ⲅ.) βρα-δυπλοεῖν ; Mk 6 48 (*B* ϫⲓⲛⲥⲱⲕ) ἐλαύνειν ; ShA 1 405 ⲉⲡⲉⲡⲉⲅⲥ. ⲥⲟⲩⲧⲱⲛ, ShC 73 172 *ship* ⲉⲛⲡⲁϣ ⲛⲅⲉⲧ ⲛⲉⲅⲥ. ⲁⲛ, Aeg 261 ⲉϥⲅⲙⲡⲉϣⲥϣⲏⲣ, PSBA 32 30 *distant* ⲛⲉⲥ. ⲛⲟⲩϫⲟ(ⲓ) ⲛⲟⲩⲅⲟⲟⲩ *a day's sail*, C 89 167 *B* *were together* ϫⲉⲛⲛⲓϣ.

ⲥϭⲣⲁϫⲧ, -ⲉⲣⲧ, ϣϭⲣⲁϫⲧ, ⲥϣϭ. *S*, ⲥϭⲣⲏⲣ *A*, *B v* nn, vb **I** intr (qual), *rest, pause, be quiet* : Jud 3 30 -ⲉⲣⲧ, Zech 1 11 *A*(*B* ⲅⲉⲣⲓ), 1 Thes 4 11 (*B* ⲉⲣ ⲣⲉⲙⲣⲁⲅϣ), Z 310 ⲉⲅⲥ. ⲅⲛⲧⲉϥⲣⲓ, Miss 4 526 ⲁⲣⲏⲅ ϭⲛⲁⲥ. = C 89 45 *B* do ἡσυχάζειν, *ib* 524 ⲟⲩⲙⲁ ⲉϭⲥ. = *ib* 43 *B* ⲉϥⲟⲣϭ ἥσυχος ; Lam 2 18 *S*(*BF* ⲕⲁ ⲣⲟ) σιωπᾶσθαι ; 1 Tim 2 2 (*B* ⲣ.) ἤρεμος ; Miss 8 85 ϭⲥ. ⲅⲛⲟⲩⲙⲁ alone ἰδιάζειν κ. ἀναπαύεσθαι ; *ib* 4 568 *each went forth* ⲛⲥⲉⲥ. ⲉⲣⲟⲟⲩ κατὰ μόνας ἀσκεῖσθαι ; Est E 8 ἀτάραχος ; ShC 73 50 *endea-vour* ⲉⲧⲣⲉⲅⲥ. ⲅⲓⲡⲉⲛⲏⲓ, BAp 125 ⲉⲓⲥ. ⲅⲛⲧⲁⲣⲓ *as monk* = MIE 2 418 *B* ϣⲟⲡ ϫⲉⲛ-, Ep App 1 147 ⲟⲩⲁⲅⲉ ⲉϭⲥ. ⲁⲩⲱ ⲉϥϥⲣⲟⲕ, GMir 262 ⲛⲧⲉⲣⲉϭⲥ. ⲡⲟⲩ-ⲕⲟⲩⲓ = Va 59 19 *B* ϣⲱⲡⲓ ϫⲉⲛⲟⲩⲱⲣϥ, Pcod 17 ⲟⲩ-ⲁⲏⲣ ⲉϭⲥ. opp *cold & heat*, BIF 1 113 ⲟⲩⲗⲓⲙⲛⲉ ⲉϥϣ.

II tr (refl) *S, rest oneself* : Gu 67 -ⲉⲣⲧ (ⲙ)ⲙⲱ-ⲧⲉⲛ *in your houses* ἡσ. ; LMär 1 ⲁⲅⲥ. ⲙⲙⲟⲟⲩ 6 *months* = C 43 40 *B* ⲉⲣ ⲅⲥⲏⲭⲁⲍⲓⲛ, Miss 8 23 ⲙⲁⲣⲉⲙⲙⲁⲧⲟⲓ ⲥ. ⲙⲙⲟⲟⲩ.

—— nn m *SA²B* ⲥϭⲣⲁϭ, (ⲥ)ϭⲣⲉϫⲧ, *quiet, rest* : Si 28 17 *S*, Wess 15 134 *S* ⲉⲣⲉⲟⲩⲛⲟϭ ⲛⲥ. ϣⲱⲡⲉ ἡσυχία ; 3 Kg 19 12 *S* (ⲥ)ϭⲣⲉϫⲧ Gk om ; Ac 21 40 *S*(*B* ϫⲁ ⲣⲱϥ) σιγή ; Bor 239 61 *S* ⲧⲥⲁⲃⲟ ⲉⲡⲉⲥ. σιωπη(τι)κός ; P 54 171 *B* ⲛⲓⲥϫ. ... ; ShIF 255 *S* ⲅⲉⲛⲥ....ⲁⲩⲱ ⲟⲩⲥⲣϥⲉ ere I die, Mani 1 *A²* ⲁⲅⲥ. ⲉⲓ ⲁⲡⲓⲧⲛ, Mor 31 61 *S* *being in* ⲟⲩⲛⲟϭ ⲛⲉϣϭⲣⲁϥⲧ *& untroubled*, Miss 4 559 *S* *died* ⲅⲛⲟⲩⲛⲟϭ ⲛⲥ. = C 89 209 *B* ⲱⲣϥ, ViK 9563 *S* *vigils*, ἄσκησις, ⲥ., PO 14 325 *B* ⲡⲓ(ⲥ)ϭ. ⲛⲧⲉ ⲡⲁⲓⲃⲓⲟⲥ *ease of life & deceits of flesh* ; ⲅⲛⲟⲩⲥ. *as advb S, quietly, at rest* : Is 8 6 (*B* = Gk) ἡσυχῇ, 2 Thes 3 12 (*B* ⲙⲉⲧ-ⲣⲉⲙⲣⲁⲅϣ) μετὰ ἡσυχίας ; 1 Tim 2 9 (*B* ⲱⲣϥ) ἐν καταστολῇ ; Bor 170 84 *stood* ⲅ. ἀτρέμας ; ShC 42 79 *I carried off thy gods* ⲅ. *unhindered*(?), MG 17 306 *visiting brethren* ⲅ. = C 89 179 *B* ⲱⲣϥ, BP 12498 ⲛⲡⲧⲁⲁϥ ⲅⲛⲟⲩⲥ. *letting no man know*.

ϫⲓ ⲥ. *S, be quieted, silenced* : Gu 71 ⲁⲅϫⲓ ⲛⲟⲩ(ⲥ)-ϭⲣⲉϫⲧ ἡσυχίαν παρέχειν.

ⲧ

ⲧ, 19th letter of alphabet, called ⲧⲁⲩ (My 92) *S*, (K 1, Stern p 418) *B*, ظا (P 44 124), طاو (*ib* 137), طو (Stern *l c*). As numeral *BF*, rarely *S* (Br 129) = 300 (ϣⲟⲙⲛⲧ ⲛϣⲉ, ϣⲙⲧϣⲉ). Derived from hierogl *t*, as ⲧⲟⲩⲱⲧ, ⲣⲧⲟ, ⲉⲓⲉⲃⲧ ; or *ṭ*, as ⲧⲟⲟⲅⲉ, ⲥⲧⲟⲓ, ⲉⲣⲱⲧⲉ ; or *d*, as ⲧⲱⲃⲉ, ⲙⲟⲩⲧⲉ, ⲕⲱⲧ ; or *ḏ*, as ⲧⲛⲅ, ⲙⲟⲥⲧⲉ, ⲥⲱⲧⲙ. Replaced in *B* in certain positions by ⲑ (*q v*). Varies with ⲇ (*q v*), with ⲑ (*q v*), with ⲕ, ϭ, as ⲕⲕⲁⲥ ⲧⲕⲁⲥ, ⲗⲱϫⲧ -ϫⲕ, ⲙⲟⲩϫϭ

-ϫⲧ, ⲛⲟϭ ⲛⲟⲧ (BP 8095), ⲛⲧⲉⲡⲧⲱⲣⲉ ⲛⲓⲕⲉⲛ-, ⲛϣ-ⲧⲉⲣⲱⲟⲩ (Rec 6 66) -ϭⲣⲱⲟⲩ (Miss 4 761), ⲡⲁⲧⲥⲉ -ϭⲥⲉ, ⲥⲟⲃⲧ -ⲃⲕ (Job 8 7 *S*), ⲧⲁⲗⲓⲧⲥⲛⲡⲉ ⲕⲁⲗⲓⲥⲑⲛⲡⲉ (J 79), ⲧⲗⲟⲟϭⲉ (Ge 28 12 sic MS, ShA 1 306) ⲥⲗ., ⲧⲣⲁ ϭⲣⲁ (Lev 4 11 *S*), ⲧⲁⲧⲥⲓ *B* -ϭⲥⲉ, ⲧⲟⲧⲉ ⲕⲟ. *B* (Pro 9 14), ⲧⲱⲧⲥ -ϭⲥ, ϣⲗⲓⲧ *B* ϣⲗⲓϭ, ϣⲓⲧⲉ *A* (Zech 3 9) -ⲕⲉ, ϥⲱϣⲉ *A* -ⲧⲉ (Mic 3 9), ⲅⲁⲡⲟⲣⲕ -ⲣⲧ (P 44 103), ⲣⲱϫⲧ -ⲝϭ *A*, ϭⲗⲟⲧ *B* (Jon 4 6) ϭⲗⲟϭ, ϭⲱⲡⲧ -ⲛϭ (Pro 24 72), cf also ⲉⲑⲱϣ ⲉϭ., ⲑⲟⲕⲧⲉⲕ ϫⲟⲕϫⲉⲕ

& v Z. f. Semit 5 1, JEA 2 18.   ⲧ for ϫ: ⲁⲣⲏⲧⲥ, ⲛⲟⲧⲉ (v ZDMG 66 783); converse: ⲉⲗⲉⲕⲟϫⲓⲡⲟⲥ (ὁλοκόττινος PMich 1526).   Combined with ⲥ, ϣ = ϫ (q v).   Dropped after ⲥ, as ⲥⲁⲧⲉⲉⲣⲉ (στατήρ), ⲥⲁⲧⲏⲧⲟⲥ (στρα.), ⲥⲓⲡⲡⲓⲛ (στύππιον).   Not written as f termination, as ⲁⲙⲛⲧⲉ imnt·t, ⲡⲟⲩϩⲣⲉ nḥ·t, ⲥⲱϣⲉ sḥ·t, except where construct, as ϩⲁⲑⲱⲣ, ⲛⲉⲃⲑⲱ.   ⲧ-, ⲧⲁ- (from vb ϯ) forms causatives, as ⲧⲥⲟ, ⲧⲁⲕⲧⲟ, ⲧϣⲟⲩⲟ & ? ⲧⲁⲛϩⲟⲩⲧ; dropped, as ⲕⲧⲟ, ⲥⲧⲟ.   Transcribes Ar ت (final), as ⲕⲟⲙⲧ قمت, ϫⲟⲡⲧ كنت (EW 234 ff, otherwise ت = ⲑ); or د, as ⲧⲉⲣⲣⲁⲙ درهم, ϩⲁⲧⲓⲧ حديد (AZ 23 115), ⲥⲁⲓⲧ صعيد (MR 5 24); or ط, as ϩⲁⲧⲓⲉϩ خطيب, ⲁⲣⲧⲁⲕ اعطاك (EW), ⲕⲁⲛⲧⲁⲣⲉ قنطرة (MR 5 45); or (rarely) ض, as ⲁⲡⲓⲁⲧ ابيض (AZ 23 109); transcribed by ت, as بوت ⲕⲱⲧ, رخت ⲣⲁϭⲧ (BIF 5 92 ff) شيهات ϣⲓⲏⲧ; تطون ⲧⲟⲩⲧⲱⲛ; or د, as نودي ⲡⲟⲩϯ, ادفو ⲁⲧⲃⲱ, داك ⲧⲉⲕ-; or ط, as طحا ⲧⲟⲩϩⲟ, اسيوط ⲥⲓⲟⲟⲩⲧ; or ض, as ضور ⲧⲟⲩϩⲟ (BIF lc).

ⲧ-, ⲧⲉ-, ϯ-, ⲑ- defin art f v ⲡ-.   Before certain foreign place-names (esp S), as ϯⲁⲣⲙⲓⲛⲓⲁ, ⲧⲃⲁⲃⲩⲗⲱⲛ (B Jer 27 13, not Bab.-Fostât), ⲑⲓⲗⲏⲙ (not B), ⲧⲉⲡϫⲓⲕⲏ, ⲧⲕⲉⲥⲁⲣⲓⲁ, ⲧⲡⲁⲡⲟⲥ (Achmîm P 129¹⁴ 138) & women's names, as ⲧⲁⲅⲁⲡⲏ, ⲧⲁⲡⲟⲗⲗⲱⲛ, ⲧⲉⲥⲟⲩⲥⲓⲁ, ⲧⲥⲓⲃⲗⲁ, ⲧⲥⲟⲫⲓⲁ, besides many native, as ⲧⲁⲗⲟⲩ, ⲧⲁⲣⲱⲙ, ⲧⲣⲁϣⲉ, ⲧⲥⲱⲛⲉ, ⲧϫⲟⲓ, ⲧⲉϭⲣⲟⲙⲡⲉ.

ⲧⲁ- S (Theban) pref to nn of direction, place (above, below, within, south, north & sim) meaning on...side of, toward (cf ? ⲧⲟⲉ part): Ep 562 ⲡⲏⲓ ⲧⲁⲣⲏⲥ, ib 102 ⲡⲁⲛϩ do, Imp Russ Arch S 026 ⲡⲧⲟⲟⲩ do, TurM 16 ⲧϫⲟⲉⲓ do, Lant 112 ⲧⲡⲉϫⲓⲁⲥ do, ib 111 ⲧⲁϩⲣⲏⲧ, J 93 16 ⲡⲧⲟϣ ⲧⲁⲡϩⲣⲏⲧ, Tur lc ⲧϫⲟⲉ do, Ep 102 (ⲧ)ⲧⲁⲉ do, Tur lc ⲡϭⲓⲣ ⲧⲁϩⲣⲏ, Ep 102 sim -ϩⲣⲁⲓ, CO 204 ⲫⲟⲓ do, (cf BKU 1 41 ⲡⲏⲓ ⲉⲧϩⲣⲁⲓ), CO 151 ⲧⲉϫⲉⲁⲣⲁ ⲧⲁⲡⲉⲓⲧⲓ, ST 109 ⲡⲙⲉⲣⲟⲥ ⲧⲁⲃⲟⲗ, ib sim ⲧⲁⲧⲁⲙⲛⲧⲉ, J 51 16 ⲧϫⲟⲓ ⲧⲁⲃⲁⲗ = ib 6 ⲙⲡⲃⲁⲗ, 8 ⲉⲧⲥⲁⲃⲉ, J 42 15 ⲧⲙⲉⲣⲓⲥ ⲧⲁⲣⲟⲩⲛ, ib 43 28 ⲧⲭⲏⲣⲉ ⲧⲁⲑⲏ.   Cf ? CO 156 ⲡⲣⲙⲟⲩⲅⲁⲓ ⲛⲧⲁϫⲉⲗⲙⲏ.   V ⲣⲏⲥ prepositional phrases s f.

ⲧⲁ- possess pron & possess art f   v ⲡⲁ-.

ⲧⲁⲓ SB DM advb, here (cf ⲧⲏ): Pro 7 19 B ϥⲧ. (SA om) παρεῖναι; Ac 2 10 S ⲉⲧⲧ. (B ⲉⲧϣⲟⲟⲡ ⲛϩⲏⲧⲉⲛ), 2 Cor 5 6 B ⲉⲛϣⲟⲟⲡ ⲧ. (S om) ἐπιδημεῖν; Mt 24 23 B(S ⲙⲡⲉⲓⲙⲁ) ὧδε; P 44 64 S ⲉⲧⲧ., ⲉⲧⲣⲙⲡⲉⲓⲙⲁ هاهنا الدين, Tri 272 S ⲡⲣⲱⲙⲉ ⲉⲧⲧ. الدخلا; PS 37 S ⲛⲥⲉⲣ ⲟⲩⲛⲟϭ ⲡⲟⲩⲟⲉⲓϣ ⲛⲃⲟⲗ ⲧ., BM 626 B ϫⲁ ⲡⲓⲥⲙⲟⲩ ⲡⲏⲓ ϣⲁⲧ., DM 17 20 ⲁⲱⲛ ⲧⲁⲓ open here;   hence: Lu 13 31 B ⲣⲱⲗ ⲧ. (varr ⲛⲧ., ⲉⲃⲟⲗ ⲧ., S ⲡⲉⲓⲙⲁ), Jo 14 31 B ⲙⲁⲣⲟⲛ (ⲛ)ⲧ. (var ⲉⲃ. ⲧ., SA² do), Deu 9 12 B ϣⲉ ⲉⲃⲟⲗ ⲧ. (S do) ἐντεῦθεν; Cat 93 B ere they come ⲉⲟⲗⲧⲉⲛ ⲉⲃ. ⲧ.   Cf ⲧⲉⲓ O

in ⲧⲉⲓ ⲛⲡⲟⲟⲩ here to-day (v DM Index 984).   V AZ 50 99.

ⲧⲁⲓ demonstr pron absol f, ⲧⲁⲓ-, ⲧⲉⲓ- constr   v ⲡⲁⲓ.

ⲧⲁⲓⲉ SA, ⲧⲁⲉⲓ, ⲧⲁⲁⲓ F   v ⲧⲟⲉ part.

ⲧⲁⲁⲓ Sᶠ, ⲧⲁⲓⲉ A   v ⲧⲟⲉ spot.

ⲧⲁⲉⲓⲟ (ⲉⲓ var ı pass) SAA²B, -ⲓⲁ F, ⲧⲁⲉⲓⲉ- SBF, ⲧⲁⲉⲓⲁ- A², ⲧⲁⲉⲓⲟ⸗ SB, ⲧⲁⲉⲓⲁ⸗ AA², ⲧⲁⲉⲓⲏⲧ†, ⲧⲁⲏⲧ† S, ⲧⲁⲉⲓⲏⲟⲩ† A, ⲧⲁⲓⲁⲉⲓⲧ AA², ⲧⲁⲉⲓⲁⲏⲧ †A², ⲧⲁⲓⲏⲟⲩⲧ† BF, ⲧⲁⲏⲟⲩⲧ† F vb I tr, honour, pay respect to, adorn: Ex 20 12 SB, Pro 3 9 SA(B = Gk), Jo 5 23 SA²(B do) τιμᾶν, ClPr 54 36 S ⲁϥⲧⲁⲓⲟⲟⲩ thanked with kind words ἀντιτ., GFr 358 S ⲡϣⲟⲩⲧⲁⲉⲓⲉ ⲡⲡⲉ θεοτίμητος; Si 21 16 S αἰνεῖν, Ps 9 23 S (B ϣⲟⲩϣⲟⲩ ⲉϫⲉⲛ-), Z 298 S ⲁⲩⲧⲁⲓⲟⲩ (cf ib ϯ ⲉⲟⲟⲩ) ἐπαι.; ShMIF 23 100 S ⲧⲁⲉⲓⲉ ⲡⲡⲉ in body (cf 1 Cor 6 20 ϯ ⲉ. δοξάζειν; Si 37 30 S μακαρίζειν; Ep Jer 43 B(F ⲙⲡϣⲉ) ἀξιοῦσθαι; Is 5 23 S (var BF ⲧⲙⲁⲓⲟ), Lu 7 29 S(B do) δικαιοῦν; Pro 29 46 S(var ⲧⲙ.)A beatissimam praedicare; Lu 6 26 S (B diff) καλῶς εἰπεῖν; Ac 23 3 S(B diff) ἀποδέχεσθαι; Miss 8 56 S ⲡⲉⲧⲟⲩⲧ. ⲙⲙⲟⲟⲩ ⲡⲟⲩⲟⲉⲓϣ ⲛⲓⲙ ἀεισέβαστος; Ps 143 12 B(S ⲧⲥⲁⲛⲟ) καλλωπίζειν; BG 32 S ⲡⲉⲛⲧⲁϥⲧⲁⲓⲟϥ ϩⲓⲟⲩⲛⲟϭ ⲛⲧ., Mani 1 A² ⲁⲩⲧⲁⲓⲁϥ ⲁⲩϯ ⲉⲁⲩ ⲡⲉϥ, R 1 3 52 S ⲁⲥⲧⲁⲉⲓⲟϥ (sc Christ's birthplace) adorned it, Wess 11 166 S ϣⲧⲏⲡ...ⲛⲧⲉⲧⲙⲗⲁⲁⲩ ⲧⲁⲓⲟⲥ ⲉϥⲓⲧⲉ deem worth taking, PO 14 368 B ⲁⲓⲡⲁⲧⲁⲓⲟⲕ ϧⲉⲛⲟⲩ?   ⲧⲁⲓⲉ ⲙⲟⲩϯ, salute v ⲙⲟⲩⲧⲉ II s f.

II intr B: Ps 138 17 ⲁⲩⲧ. ⲛⲧⲟⲧ (S ⲁⲓⲁⲓ), Pro 6 8 ⲉⲧⲁϯⲥⲟⲫⲓⲁ ⲧ. ⲛⲧⲟⲧϥ τιμᾶν.   v also Qual ⲥ ⲛⲧⲛ-.

Qual, honoured, excellent, precious: Ps 116 5 SB, Pro 3 15 SA-ⲉⲓⲧ B, ib 20 6 SA-ⲏⲟⲩ, Hos 11 7 B (A ⲧⲙⲁⲓⲏⲩ) τίμιος, Jo 4 44 SA²BF τιμὴν ἔχειν, Deu 28 58 SB, Is 16 14 SB ἔντιμος; Ps 149 8 B (S ϩⲁⲉⲟⲟⲩ), Is 32 2 B(SF do), ib 5 14 SBF ἔνδοξος, Pro 6 8 SAB ἐπίδ.; Deu 26 18 S(B diff) περιούσιος; Sa 3 15 S, Cl 7 2 A-ⲓⲧ εὐκλεής; BMar 127 S ⲟⲩⲙⲁ ⲉϥⲧ. ἐπίσημος; 3 Kg 5 11 S purissimus; Eccl 7 8 F(S = Gk) εὐγένεια; Ps 44 8 S(B ϩⲟⲣϣ) βαρύς for βᾶρις; PS 212 S ⲛⲱⲛⲉ ⲉⲧⲧ., ShC 42 23 S money & ⲡⲉⲡⲉⲭⲣⲟⲡ ⲉⲧⲧ., P 131⁷ 75 S wine ⲉϥⲧ. opp ⲧⲥⲧⲏⲩ ⲉⲃⲟⲗ, J 37 65 S ⲟⲩⲉⲓⲁⲟⲥ ⲉϥⲧ. opp ⲉⲧⲥⲟⲃⲕ, PO 11 374 B basket of ϧⲉⲛⲓ ⲉϥⲧ., DeV 2 240 B lamp's light ⲧ. ϧⲉⲛⲡⲓⲉⲭⲱⲣϩ, BMis 508 S ⲛⲓⲙ ⲧ. ⲡⲧⲉⲕϭⲉ?;   epithet of officials & clerics S: J 4 3, 13 60, 35 8 ⲧⲓⲙⲓⲱⲧⲁⲧⲟⲥ ⲉⲧⲧ., CO 90 ⲉⲧⲧ. ⲕⲁⲧⲁ ⲥⲙⲟⲧ ⲛⲓⲙ, ib 262 -ⲧⲁⲉⲩ, ib 329 -ⲧⲁⲏⲩ, abbrev ib 339 ⲉ͞ⲧ͞ⲧ̄, 341 ⲉ͞ⲧ̄/ⲧ̄; rarely B: PO 11 303 patriarch;   c ⲉ-, more honoured than, precious than: Pro 3 15 SA(B ⲉϩⲟⲧⲉ) τιμιώτερος, Nu

22 15 *S*(*B* do) ἐντιμότερος; C 43 125 *B* ⲙⲙⲟⲛ
ⲡⲉⲧⲧ. ⲉⲡⲁⲓⲣⲁⲛ; ⲥ ⲉⲣⲟⲅⲟ, ⲛⲣ. ⲉ-, ⲉⲣⲟⲧⲉ sim:
Ge 34 19 *SB*, Su 4 *SB* εὐδοξότ.; Mor 48 17 *S* ⲧ.
ⲛⲣⲟⲅⲉ ⲉⲣⲱⲧⲛ (var BMar 211 ⲥⲟⲧⲡ), C 43 115 *B*
ⲥⲉⲧ. ⲉⲣⲟⲧⲉⲣⲟⲕ, Bor 222* 4 *S* thy god ⲧ. ⲛⲣ.
ⲉⲡⲱⲛ; ⲥ ⲡⲧⲛ-, *honoured by, with*: Lu 7 2 *SB*
ἔντιμος dat, Ac 20 24 *B*(*S* ⲧⲙⲁⲓⲟ) τίμιος dat; Mor
37 21 *S* servants ⲉⲩⲧ. ⲛⲧⲟⲟⲧⲥ, WTh 163 *B* ⲕⲧ. ⲛ-
ⲧⲟⲧ ⲉⲙⲁϣⲱ.

—— nn m *SAA²BF*, **a** *honour*: Ge 20 16 *SB*, Ps
61 5 *B*(*S* = Gk), Pro 6 26 *SAB*, Is 35 2 *SBF*, Ro
2 7 *SBF* τιμή; Ps 34 28 *S*(*B* ϣⲟⲩϣⲟⲩ), Phil 1 11
SBF ἔπαινος; Ps 28 1 *S*(*B* ⲱⲟⲩ?), He 3 3 *B*(*S*
ⲉⲟⲟⲩ) δόξα; Ps 118 70 *S*(*B* = Gk), Wess 15 136
S estranged from ⲡⲧ. ⲛⲧⲙⲛⲧⲉⲡⲓⲥⲕⲟⲡⲟⲥ ἀξίωμα;
CaiEuch 474 *B* they send up to Thee ⲡⲓⲧ. εὐφημία; ib 482 *B* ⲛⲓⲣⲛⲏⲟⲅⲓ ⲛⲧⲉ ⲡⲉⲕⲧ. φιλανθρωπία;
1 Tim 4 9 *S*(*B* diff) ἀποδοχή; Pcod 4 *S* receiveth
him ⲣⲛⲟⲩⲛⲟϭ ⲛⲧ., Miss 4 658 *S* began to say ⲣⲛⲧ.
compliments, DeV 2 106 *B* bore with Him ϫⲉⲛⲛⲓ-
ϫⲓⲥⲓ ⲛⲉⲙⲛⲓⲧ., C 43 241 *B* built church ⲕⲁⲧⲁ ⲡⲉϥⲧ.,
CMSS 23 *F* found not clean papyrus ⲕⲁⲧⲁ ⲡⲉⲕⲧ.,
BM 547 *S* greet each ⲕⲁⲧⲁ ⲡⲧ. ⲙⲡⲉⲅⲣⲁ[ⲛ, ST 197
S sim ⲉⲡⲧ. ⲡⲧⲉⲕⲙⲛⲧⲟⲅⲁⲁⲃ. **b** *complimentary
gift*: Ge 32 13 *B*(*S* = Gk), Is 45 13 *S*(*B* = Gk),
Eph 2 8 *SB* δῶρον, Ro 5 16 *B*(*S* ⲧⲙⲁⲓⲟ) δώρημα,
Ge 25 6 *S*(*B* ⲧⲟⲓ), Nu 3 9 *B*(*S* ⲧⲟ), Pro 18 16 *SA*,
Hos 9 1 *ABF* (JEA 11 245), Phil 4 17 *B*(*S* ✝) δόμα,
1 Kg 1 11 *S* δοτός; Nu 18 8 *SB* γέρας; 2 Kg 8 6
S, Hos 10 6 *AB* ξένιον; Lev 3 3 *S*(*B* ⲟⲩⲧⲁⲣ ⲉϥ-
ϣⲏⲡ) κάρπωμα; Mt 6 1 *B*(*S* om) ἐλεημοσύνη; Sh
BM 194 2 *S* many ⲉⲣⲏⲧ ⲛⲣⲉⲛⲧ., ShWess 9 138 *S*
surgeon's fee in money ⲙⲛⲣⲉⲛⲕⲉⲧ., FR 10 *S* ⲡⲉⲩⲧ.
at child's birth, MG 25 416 *S* bringing ⲣⲉⲛⲧ. for
archbishop, PSBA 34 174 *S* bridegroom's additional
gift, R 1 3 46 *S* sent by wedding guest, AM 58 *B*
ⲟⲩⲱⲣⲡ ⲛⲣⲁⲓⲧ. ϫⲁϫⲱⲕ, Cat 169 *B* ⲛⲓⲧ. for temple
named ἀνάθεμα, BMis 418 *S* accept ⲡⲁⲕⲟⲩⲓ ⲛⲧ. =
BSM 59 *B*, Kr 242 *S* list of those that brought
ⲧ. *V* LAl 57.

ⲙⲁⲓⲧ. *B*, *honour-loving*: 2 Cor 5 9 (*S* ⲣⲟⲟⲩⲧ)
φιλοτιμεῖσθαι. Cf 1 Thes 4 11.

ⲉⲓⲣⲉ ⲛⲟⲩⲧ. *A²*, *pay respect*: Mani 2 ⲉⲅⲉⲓⲣⲉ ⲛⲟⲩⲧ.
ⲛⲛⲉⲩⲉⲣⲏⲩ.

ⲣⲉϥⲧ. *S*, *honorable person, thing*: R 1 3 66 ⲛⲣⲟ-
ⲙⲛⲧⲏⲥ (δημότης) ⲛⲛⲡⲟⲗⲓⲥ ⲛⲣ.

✝ ⲧ. *SA²BF*, *give honour, gift*: Est 8 1 *S* δωρί-
ζειν, Ge 47 22 *B* δόσιν διδόναι; Si 29 28 *S* ξενίζειν; 1 Tim 5 4 *B*(*S* ⲧⲱⲱⲃⲉ ⲛⲟⲩⲧⲟⲅⲉⲓⲟ) ἀμοιβὰς
ἀποδιδ.; Va 68 164 *B* ⲙⲡⲉϥⲡⲣⲟⲉⲣⲉⲥⲓⲥ ⲉⲣ ⲡⲕⲉϯ
ⲧ. ⲙⲫⲏ ⲉⲧⲁϥⲑⲁⲙⲓⲟⲥ τιμᾶν; Br 239 *S* ⲁⲩϯ ⲧ. ⲛ-
ⲛⲁⲓⲱⲛ, ShC 73 3 *S* worthy ⲛⲧⲁⲁⲩ ⲛⲧ., TT 17 *S*
ⲁϥϯ ⲛⲁϥ ⲛⲣⲉⲛⲧ....ⲙⲡⲛⲣⲉⲛϫⲱⲣⲟⲛ, AM 194 *B* ad-

vanced to greet him ⲉϥϯ ⲧ. ⲛⲁϥ, Mani 2 *A²* ⲉϥϯ
ⲛⲉϥ ⲛⲟⲩⲧ., AZ 33 54 *F* ⲉⲅϯ (ⲙ)ⲙⲁϥ (ⲉ)ⲧ. (ⲛ)ⲛⲓⲣ-
ⲣⲟⲟⲩ, BM 595 *F* since day when God ⲧⲓ ⲛⲓⲧ. ⲛⲉ[ⲓ]
(so to do) I long to see thy face (again).

ϫⲓ, ϭⲓ ⲧ. *SB*, *receive honour, gift*: Deu 10 17 *S*
(*B* = Gk), Ps 14 5 *B*(*S* = Gk) δῶ. λαμβάνειν; ib
62 11 *S*(*B* ϣⲟⲩϣⲟⲩ) ἐπαινεῖν; ShC 42 129 *S* God
ⲛⲁϫⲓ ⲧ. ⲁⲛ ⲛⲧⲛⲗⲁⲁⲩ, C 43 62 *B* those that obey
shall ϭⲓ ⲛⲣⲁⲛⲛⲓϣϯ ⲛⲧ.

-ⲧⲉ f enclitic *v* ⲛⲏ (-ⲡⲉ). Often with m subject (sg & pl): Ex 15 2 *F*(BM 493) ⲡⲉⲓⲧⲉ ⲡⲁⲛⲟⲩϯ
(*B* ⲫⲁⲓⲡⲉ), Ep 338 *S* ⲡⲱⲓⲧⲉ ⲡⲓⲣⲡ, Mor 30 12 *Sᶠ*
Philopator ⲉⲧⲉⲡⲉϥⲟⲩⲱϣⲙⲧⲉ 'loving his parents'
(var BMis 238 -ⲡⲉ), Z 539 *S* ⲟⲩⲡⲉⲧϣⲟⲩⲉⲓⲧ ⲡⲁⲩⲧⲉ,
LAp 566 *F* ⲡⲛⲉⲉϥ...ⲉⲧⲉ]ⲓⲥ̄ⲧⲉ, Lant 18 17 *F* ⲁⲛⲁⲕⲧⲉ
ⲡⲓⲉⲗⲁⲭ(ⲓⲥⲧⲟⲥ), CMSS 55 *F*, BM 614 *F* sim, Mor
50 34 *S* ⲛⲛⲓⲧⲉ ⲫⲓⲃⲁⲙⲱⲛ?, BMar 154 *S* ⲟⲩⲧⲉ ⲡⲉⲧ-
ⲕⲟⲩⲉϣ ⲧⲣ(ⲁ)ⲁⲁϥ?, Leyd 434 *S* ⲛⲧⲉ ⲡⲙⲉⲣϥⲧⲱⲟⲩ
(letter in name ⲓⲱⲁⲛⲛⲏⲥ), CO 434 *S* glossary ⲫⲣⲟ-
ⲛⲓⲙⲟⲥⲧⲉ ⲡⲣⲱⲙⲉ ⲛⲥⲁⲃⲉ, PcodMor 17 *Sᶠ* ⲡⲁⲓⲧⲉ ⲡⲁϣⲏⲣⲉ (Mt 3 17 -ⲡⲉ), J 14 45, 47 34 *S* ⲛⲧⲟϣⲧⲉ
ⲡⲁⲓ. Peculiar: R 2 1 22 *S* ⲉⲓⲉⲧⲉ ⲙⲛ ϣϭⲟⲙ...
ⲙⲏ ⲙⲛ ϣϭⲟⲙ?

ⲧⲉ *A*, particle pref to ⲣⲱϩⲉ *suffice* in Ob 5 ⲛⲉⲧ-
ⲡⲁⲧⲉⲣⲱϩⲧⲟⲩ (*B* ⲛⲏ ⲉⲧⲣ.). Nah 2 12 (*B* ⲫⲣ.) τὰ
ἱκανά.

ⲧⲉ- *AF* *v* ⲧⲣⲟ.

ⲧⲉ- *v* ⲣⲟⲙⲡⲉ *sf*.

ⲧⲏ *S*, ⲧⲉ (oftenest) *SAA²* nn m, *time, season*:
Job 19 4 (*B* ⲥⲛⲟⲩ) καιρός; ib 24 6 (*B* ⲣⲟϯ) ὥρα;
Mk 4 29 ⲡⲧⲉ ⲙⲡⲱϩⲥ (*B* om) θερισμός; ShR 2 3
58 ⲙⲙⲛ ⲧⲉ ⲛⲕⲟⲧⲟⲩ, Mor 32 32 ⲉⲡⲉϥⲧⲉⲡⲉ ⲡⲁⲓ
ⲉⲙⲉⲣⲉⲓ ⲡⲕⲟⲥⲙⲟⲥ, Mani 2 *A²* to repulse him ⲡⲁⲣⲁ
ⲡⲉϥⲧⲉ; ⲙⲡⲉϥⲧⲉ, *at his (its) time, right time*:
Deu 11 14 (*B* ⲥ.) καθ' ὥραν; Pro 27 25 *SA*(reading ? ὥριμος Lemm), Si 29 2 εἰς τὸν κ.; Gal 1 23
ⲛⲛⲓⲧⲉ (no var, *B* ⲛⲟⲩⲥⲛⲟⲩ) πότε; ShZ 603 ⲡⲉⲭⲡⲟ
ⲙⲡⲉϥⲧⲉ ⲁⲩⲱ ⲡⲉⲧⲉ ⲛⲟⲩⲣⲟⲣϩⲉ ⲁⲛⲛⲉ; ϩⲛ- sim: Job
5 26 *SA*(Cl, *B* ⲟⲩⲛⲟⲩ) ὥριμος; ⲉⲛⲧⲉ, *at, in
time*: Hos 2 9 *A*(*B* ⲟⲩ.) καθ' ὥ.; CO 304 ⲛⲧⲁϯ
ⲡⲉⲧ(ⲉ)ⲙⲟ[ⲥⲓⲟⲛ] ⲉⲛⲉⲩⲧⲉ, BM 487 ϫⲓⲛⲉⲡⲧⲛ (ⲉ)ⲛⲉ-
ⲡⲁⲗⲁⲙⲏⲣ ⲛ (*l* ⲉⲓ) ϩⲛⲧ; ⲉⲓ ⲉⲛⲧⲉ, *reach time, age*:
P 131² 145 ϣⲁⲛⲧⲉⲓ ⲉⲛ. ⲛⲟⲏⲗⲓⲕⲓⲁ, Aeg 12 nursed
me ϣⲁⲛⲧⲉⲓⲉⲓ ⲉⲛ., J 79 22 when child ⲉⲓ ⲉⲛ., BMar
149 ⲁⲅⲉⲓ ⲉⲛⲧⲉⲓ of baptism; ⲣ ⲧⲉ, *be of age*: Jo
9 21 *SA²*(*B* ⲙⲁⲓⲏ) ἡλικίαν ἔχειν (cf 23 ⲣ ⲡⲟϭ), He
11 15 (*B* ⲥ.) καιρὸν ἔχ.; ShC 73 212 ⲙⲡⲁⲧ ⲣ. ⲛⲟⲩ-
ⲉⲙ ⲟⲩϣⲓⲛⲟⲩⲱⲙ, ShA 1 464 ⲡⲉⲁⲩⲣ. ⲣⲱⲡⲉ ⲡϣ
ϩⲓⲥⲉ, BM 1102 ⲁⲕⲣ. ϩⲣⲓ ⲟⲩⲕⲟⲧ ϣⲁⲣⲟⲛ *high time
thou didst visit us*.

V LMis 323.

ΤΗ *O*, ΤΗΙ *DM* nn, *underworld*: AZ 21 94 (*v* 38 86) Osiris περο πτη, DM 17 20 *awn* τηι *open, under-world* (*cf* ται).

ΤΗ *B* advb, *there* (*cf* ται): Mt 24 23 ϥτη (*S* παι-μα) ὧδε; mostly εττη: Ge 24 65 (*S* πειμα), Deu 13 5 (*S* μμαγ), Mt 27 19 (*S* πει-) ἐκεῖνος, Is 44 9 (*S* om), 2 Pet 3 6 (*S* πει-) τότε; MG 25 312 πιμα εττη ετακκοτϥ = MIF 13 118 *S* πκεμα, C 89 129 μπισηογ εττη, AM 148 παιαπομος εττη;   сабол τη, *outside there*: ROC 25 244 ογοπ ογρωμι с. τη.

ΤΕΙ *O* v ται.

✝ *SAA²BF*, τι *SF*, ✝ι, ✝ει, τει, τη (*v* **II**) *S*, τε *A* (c dat), ✝- *SBF*, τε- *AF*, τα- *F*, τα(α)ϩ, ✝ϩ *S*, τεεϩ *AA²F*, τεετϩ *AA²*, τεϩ *A*, τεειτϩ *A²F*, τηιϩ, τηιτϩ *B*, τειϩ, τειειϩ, τειτϩ, ταιτϩ *F* & other irregular *SS"F* forms, τοᵗ, τωᵗ *S*, ταᵗ *Sf* (ViK 9545), τειεᵗ, τεᵗ *A* (Joel), τοειεᵗ *A²*, τοιᵗ *B*, τα(α)ιᵗ, τααιεᵗ *F*, p c ται- *SA²F*, imperat v below   **A** vb **I** intr, *give, pay* & related meanings: Ps 50 16 *SA*(Cl)*B* διδόναι, Lu 7 42 *S*(*B* τωβ) ἀποδ., Va 57 13 *B* μεταδ.; Ps 36 26 *S*(*B* ✝ εθμιϲι)δανίζειν, Kr 3 *F* πεττι εп, Aeg 276 *S* ερεπεπισκοπος ✝ *while giving* (sacrament); c dat: Ps 19 4 *SB*, Cl 13 2 *A* τϩε ετογπατε πητπε δ., Mt 27 26 *S* (var & *B* tr) παραδ.; TU 43 13 *A* ✝-πατε πεϥ; paral with ϫι *sell...buy*: Aeg 243 *S* δ.; ShClPr 22 357 *S* ετμϫι εταμ✝ without leave, Gu Dorm 4 *S* ενϫι εγ✝ ϩππειϩομπτ, J 65 62 *S* he is owner πϥϫι πϥ✝ ϩпπτοπος τηρϥ, *cf* ib 76 63, TRit 457 *B* μπεϥϭι ογϫε μπεϥ✝ whilst he lived; *cf* **D** s f ϫι✝;   *fight*: 1 Cor 9 26 *B*(*S* = Gk) πυκτεύειν; Va 61 218 *B* αϥ✝ αϥϭρο παλαίειν; ShA 1 276 *S* πετ✝...πετερ πολαμος;   v also tr, c εϫп-, μп-, ογϩε-, ϩι-, εβολ ϩιϫп-, εϩογп εϩρп-.

B II tr, mostly c dat: Job 1 21 *SB*, Is 33 16 *SBF*, Si 13 25 *S* τμτπ παϥ μα, Jo 14 16 *S*(ShRyl 70 254) τη πητп п- (*cf* PB 11349 below), ib 3 16 *A²* τεεϥ *F* τειϥ, 1 Cor 7 25 *SBF*, AP 11 *A²* αстε-ειτογ δ., Ps 49 15 *SA*(Cl)*B*, Ap 22 12 *SB* ἀποδ., Ro 1 11 *SB* μεταδ., Pro 27 23 *SA*, Is 33 6 *SBF*, Jo 19 30 *SA²B* παραδ.; Ex 21 19 *SB*, Pro 6 31 *SA* τεϥε (*B* κωβ, var τωβ) ἀποτίνειν; Sa 14 21 *S*, 1 Cor 12 23 *B*(*S* diff) περιτιθέναι; Ps 15 5 *S*(*B* ταϲεθ) ἀποκαθιστάναι; Mt 27 50 *S*(var κω)*B* ἀφιέναι, Va 57 8 *B* ✝ μμογ ппετερ ϩαε προϊέναι; Lu 13 8 *SB* βάλλειν, Ac 18 27 *S*(*B* diff) συμβ.; PS 126 *S* names ε✝πατααγ, Mun 22 *S* αγ✝ παϥ πισααк (var BMis 55 χαριϩε), Miss 4 720 *S* пⲭⲥ πατααϥ μμοι (var παι), BMis 77 *S* μπεϥ✝ μπεϩρο μπβολ μ-προ, C 86 100 *B* αγ✝ πτογαϥε πτепϥι, DeV 2 109 *B* ✝ πογϣε πλογϫη παϥ, ib 162 *B* παρεπισηογ ✝ μμοϥ απпε *suffered* (sufficed) *him not*, J 1 15 *S*

επ✝ ποⲩⲅⲩποⲅⲣⲁⲫⲉⲩⲥ to subscribe (*cf* PMon 105 ὑπογρ. παρέχειν), Mor 51 38 *S* αϥ✝ ппат αϥ✝ τ-κλλε (explained as) *abandoned* patience & silence, Mani 2 *A²* τεεϲ μпϣαρп πρωμε, Win 21 *S* τιϲ πιωϩαппηϲ, Tor 4 *S* ακτιϥ, ib 12 *S* ακ✝ειϥ, J 16 39 *S'* пϯτιαϥ, Hall 117 *S* ϥπατειογαϥ (other *SSᵃ* forms v Ep 1 246), BM 597 *F* τι παϣιπι, Kr 226 *F* τε τεκτιμηп, BM 625 *F* κτε παϣα εφιλ, ib 528 § 1 *F* ϣακτα сипте ϩιχεпεⲩεⲣⲏⲩ (but § 2 sim τα-λα), ib § 64 *F* τειβ, Mor 30 21 *F* τειειϲ πεϥ, BM 583 *F* ✝εειϲ, CMSS 39 *F* τεειτϲ, ib 44 *F* τειτοⲩ;   refl: Jos 8 16 *S* αγτααⲩ εⲩпητ καταδιώκειν (*cf* c e-);   *pay*: Mt 5 26 *SB*, ib 18 25 *S*(*B* τωβ)ἀποδ.; ShA 1 456 *S* ϣαπτϥ ппετεροⲩ, J 63 7 *S* ακτι οⲩпϣϫε προλοκ/, ипι, ib 55 22 *S* εϥпα✝ a pound of gold, Kr 3 *F* птетпети 100 *solidi* as fine, PB 11349 *S* μπεϥτп(п)αι λααⲩ, *cf* ib μπεϥτпαϥ;   *sell S* (*cf* ✝ εβολ): Pcod 20 ϣωп ογειϩος п εταаⲩ, ST 437 τεϩε πταιτααϲ...ϣομпт προλοκ/, J 21 31 ειτι пак half my house, Ep 336 μпιϭп ρωμε ε✝ϥ;   *smite* (*cf* Sophocles δίδωμι 3): Ex 2 11 *A*(*B* μιϣι пеμ-), 13 *A*(*SB* ϩιογε), Pro 23 35 *A*(*S* do) τύπτειν; Sh BMOr 8810 372 *S* reviling them ϩωϲτε ετρετп✝ μμοογ even taking staves & beating (ϩιογε) them.

Imperat μα *SAA²*, μοι *B*, μαι *F*, μα- *SBF*, ματϩ, μηειϩ *S*, μηιϩ, μηιτϩ, μοιτϩ *B*, μαιϩ *F* intr: Ps 27 4 *B*(*S* ✝), Ez 43 19 *B*, Mk 10 37 *SB* δ.; tr: Ge 30 1 *SB*, Mt 6 11 *BF*(*S* ✝), Lu 12 58 *S* ματϥ (var -τεϥ, *B* μοι), Jo 4 15 *SA²BF* δ., Ps 27 4 *B*(*S* ✝) ἀποδ.; CaiEuch 593 *B* μα πογποϭ εὐφραίνειν; PS 293 *S* μα θοτε μπαθοτε, J&C 98 *F* μαιοοⲩ пεк (*sic* l), C 43 195 *B* μηιϥ μпιογηβ, Miss 4 100 *B* μηιτοⲩ пⲇιοσκορος, Bodl(P) f 69 *S* μηειϲ μпαπαιπⲟⲩ[τε п-, RicciL 260 *F* μαι ипι ппетепψⲩⲭⲏ;   with ✝: AP 16 *A²* μα✝ пеϲ δ.; Ps 21 1 *S* μα✝ ϩτηκ (*B* μα ϩθηκ), Lu 17 3 *F* (Mor 30 1) sim (*S* ✝ ϩ., *B* do) προσέχειν; Br 113 *S* μα✝ παι πογμαειπ, BMis 507 *S* μα✝ θε παι (*cf* Lu 12 above);   not as imperat *B* in Ez: 11 15 αⲅμ. пап, 45 6 ερετεпμ. п-, 16 34 пϫιп-θρεμ. (*S* ✝), 18 7 εϥεμπιϲ, 16 33 αρεμ. пωοⲩ (*S* αρ✝); *S* in Tri 697 αϥμα παⲩ; ϫιπμ. *B*: Ez 46 5 (*S* ✝ nn) δόμα.

Qual, *given, being upon*: Job 7 3 *SB*, Ro 12 3 *BF* ται (RylSuppl, *SF* MR ✝), 1 Cor 3 10 *BF* τααι (*S* do) δ., Nu 18 29 *S*(*B* ταιο) δόμα; 1 Cor 7 37 *B* ἔχειν; Joel 2 3 *A* τε (*B* om) εἶναι dat; Tob 6 13 *S* καθήκειν; Jer 45 5 *B* no Gk; PS 32 *S* τεϩογϲια το пак, BIF 22 106 *F* sim τααι, ROC 25 248 *B* пεκραп т. μϥ✝, Dif 2 25 *B* αϥτ. пεμпη εθογαβ *in heaven*; то μπεпιпε, *enchained*: Ps 67 6 *S*(*B* ϩⲱⲟ̄ⲅⲓ п-) πεδᾶν, C 86 106 *B* εϥτ. пβεпιпι;   impersonal use сто, *it fits, befits*: c ε- *S*: Ac 16 21

(B сѱе), 2 Cor 12 4 (B do) ἐξεῖναι; Lu 13 33 (B ϫн) ἐνδέχεσθαι; ShA 2 103 c. ετρεπαι...ϥι, *ib* 258 c. ап етреоуа таϣе пехҏрооу, BMis 39 пс. ап етрепкω; c dat & e-: Est 4 2 S, Jo 5 10 SA^2 (B сѱе), Mor 17 35 S пс. ап пнтп еωтп еҏоүп = EW 33 B ἐξ., Dan 3 32 S(B ѱ) εἶναι (*l* ? ἐξ.), 1 Cor 14 34 SF(B diff) ἐπιτρέπεσθαι; Mt 13 11 BF (S ✝ vb) δ.; BG 82 S петс. пнтп есооүп ппет-мпϣа псооүп, BHom 61 S c. пак ап етале ϩωρоп, BSM 11 B апок етес. пни еѳрι- ; (естω in Mor 33 14 естω акϩрaι = *ib* 34 8 еѱхе акϩ.= BMis 79 опс хеакϩ., BHom 75, BMar 140, Ep 59 sim is prob ἔστω *granted that*).

c With following preposition.

—— e- SAA^2BF **a** intr : Lu 6 34 S ✝ емнсе (B = Gk) δανίζειν; PMéd 103 S ✝ еплнϭн пια *apply to*, Saq 103 S in recipe ✝ι ероoч, ShC 73 98 S none shall ✝ ерωме ϩноүϭерωϧ *strike*, P 131[1] 28 S he who twists rope еϥϣапωск еϥ✝ ероϥ it will become too long (meaning ?); vbal : Mk 5 43 S ✝ пас еоүωμ (B ✝ поүωμ пас), Ap 3 21 SB ✝ паϥ етреϥ- δ. inf; BM 185 S Lord ✝ пак еϩе еүпа; еп-, *tend toward* SF : Lev 13 19 ✝ е-поүϧаϣ (B оүϧ.) λευκαίνειν; Jos 8 29 ✝ епϩωтп ἐπιδύνειν; Jo 4 52 F ✝ епелтап (SA^2 лтоп, B асιaι) κομψότερον ἔχειν; ShCai 8007 2 ϩепаϥ еү✝ еп-λωμc, Wess 15 22 wine еϥ✝ епϩμх, ✝ епапаι *v* апаι пп. **b** tr, *give to* : Ps 4 7 S(B еϩрни е-), Pro 23 31 SA, Ap 17 17 S(B еϩp. e-, var еϩ. e-) δ. εἰς, Ez 23 42 B лоι (S ✝) δ. ἐπί, Is 32 3 SBF δ. inf, Job 16 11 S(B еϩp. e-), Is 33 23 SBF παραδ. εἰς; Jth 10 4 S λαμβάνειν (reading ? βάλλειν) εἰς, Is 37 29 B(S поүхе) ἐμβάλ. εἰς, Pro 2 2 SB(A п-) παραβάλ. εἰς; Ez 16 10 SB ✝ ерат = ὑποδεῖν; Ps 53 1 F (Pcod Mor) λια ϩеп ероι κρίνειν; ShA 2 322 S ✝ пϩепеιϥт епеϥϭιх, BIF 14 17 S ✝ апофасιс ероoү, BMis 472 S parents таат етапснѣе, Miss 4 115 B аγ✝ лпιро ерωη = Mor 19 29 S ϣтам, Z 628 S recipe пϥ✝ пеϩ ероϥ, BIF 13 106 S аγтааγ еγсооk = MG 25 289 B еϩp. e-, Ryl 158 45 S witness to deed аιϥ✝ стаγрос ероc, BIF 13 112 S camel ✝ рωϥ епкаϩ = MG 25 302 B тем-, BM 528 §1 F arithm екетеι-тоγ епеүерпγ *multiply together*; refl : Ac 19 31 B(S diff) δ. εἰς; 1 Kg 28 22 S таак еγϩιн πορεύεσθαι ἐν ὁδῷ; 2 Kg 13 16 S таαϥ епϣωпе ἀρρωστεῖν; R 2 3 37 S ϣаϥтааϥ епϩιсе in all things, DeV 2 238 B sim, *ib* 107 B аγтнιϥ ллаγатϥ е-пϣеп ελкаϩ, BMis 246 S аϥтааϥ етперсιс (var Z 263 ϧωк); rarely sim c dat : ROC 27 143 B ас-тнιс лпιлωιт ελοϣι; refl as auxil S : Jud 10 18 пιл...патааγ ελιϣе ἄρχεσθαι; Jos 14 8 αιтаат етраоүарт προστίθεσθαι; Ru 3 4 тааγ епкотк ἐν

τῷ κοιμηθῆναι. **c** qual : Pro 25 12 SA δ. εἰς; Deu 28 10 B(S таϩо) ἐπικαλεῖσθαι dat; PS 284 S spirit еϥто ероc (*sc* soul) еϥсооϩе ελλος, BMis 167 S soldiers етто ероϥ, El 110 S angels еγтω ероc *set over, in charge of*, MG 25 37 B house's door & windows т. ероϥ, opp сеоүнп (*cf* Miss 4 115 above), *ih* 91 B chain етт. епеϥсоүт (var етϩι-), Mor 31 70 S hand то епнепипе, Aeg 52 B face т. епса пϥа-патоλн, C 41 12 B ллоп нпι т. ерωоγ.

—— ерн- S, *go toward* : Jud 20 37 refl ἐκτείνειν ἐπί; еϩоγп ерн- : BM 190 158 пϥ✝ еϩ. ерн-тϭιпϣахе (PO 8 253 ◌◌ ◌◌◌).

—— етп- (етоотϥ п-) SA^2B, intr *lay upon, command* : Ac 16 4 SB παραδ. dat; Jo 14 31 A^2(S ϩωп, B ϩопϩеп) ἐντέλλεσθαι dat; Aeg 256 S еϥ✝ ето-отγ етреϥ-, ShIF 297 S епто етоотγ ллпѣ through life; tr, *give into hands, entrust* : Job 2 6 S(B еϩp. епекхιх), Mt 5 25 S(B e-), 1 Cor 11 23 B (var птеп-, S п-) παραδ. dat; Jo 15 17 A^2(S ϩωп, B ϩопϩеп) ἐντ. dat; Ac 14 23 S(B ϫω ϩатеп-) παρατιθέναι dat; RE 9 146 S ак✝ оγεπтоλн ето-от, C 43 105 B лнιт етотc птспϥι, J 75 28 S seeking monk пϥ✝ пιλ етоотϥ. *Cf* **c** птп-.

—— ехп- SB, *put upon, add to, on behalf of* intr : Z 628 S recipe ✝ ехωс *apply* (mixture) *to it*, WS 52 S ✝ι, ✝еι ехωϥ; tr : Lev 4 25 S(B таλо) ἐπιτιθ. ἐπί; C 89 65 B аϥпатнιϥ (*sc* stone) е. тафе of Theodore = Wess 11 159 S рaϩтϥ ехп- δ. κατά; Ryl 107 S recipe ✝ оγпеϩ ехωс, PO 11 318 B аϥ✝ ехωϥ пϯϩеѣсω, TEuch 1 1 B those presenting candidate ✝ ελетапоιа ехωϥ ic; *pay for* : Nu 5 7 S(B п-) ἀποδ. acc; ST 94 S will repay it κата ѳе етоγтι е.соγо in winter; *fight for* : Jth 5 21 S ὑπέρ no vb, Ro 8 31 B(S ллϣе) do; ShC 73 100 S еγ✝ е.петкω псωоγ ппептоλн, ShIF 217 S ✝ оγϩепсооγтп...✝ е.пс., DeV 2 269 B crowd ✝ е.поγерноγ = Mor 41 19 S ϩе ехп-; еϩp. ех. intr B : Is 37 35 (S р паϣте) ὑπερασπίζειν ὑπέρ; Jo 18 36 B(SA^2 ли.) ἀγωνίζεσθαι; C 86 108 angels ✝ еϩ.(? еϩ.) ехωк; tr : Jer 12 8 SB δ. ἐπί, Ro 8 32 B(S ϩа-) παραδ. ὑπέρ; Ez 16 10 SB ✝ ϩоιте еϩ. ех. ἐνδύειν acc; Mor 48 73 S ✝пατааγ (money) еϩ. ехωк = C 43 137 B ϩа-. V also реϥ✝.

—— лп-, пел- SB, *fight with* : Ps 108 3 S(B ϧωтc e-) πολεμεῖν acc, MG 25 233 B thoughts еγ✝ пελаϥ п. dat, Jud 2 18 S πολιορκοῦν acc; Deu 28 7 S(B оγϧе-) ἀντιστάναι dat; Si 38 33 S διαμάχεσθαι ἐν; Nu 21 23 B(S ллϣе лп-) παρατάσσεσθαι dat; Mk 9 40 S(B оγϧе- no vb) εἶναι κατά, opp ✝ ехп-; BHom 23 S ἀντίδικος, Jos 5 13 S ὑπεναντίος; ShC 73 17 S sin ✝ плаγ, Mor 33 53 S ететп✝ ллпѣе (varr *ib* 34 25 ✝ оγϧе-, BMis 99 ✝ тωп лп-), C 41 61 B аγ✝ пелλιϧαрϧарос,

JLeip l 34 *S* ⲡ̄ⲧⲏⲧⲓ ⲙ̄ⲡⲉⲛⲉⲣⲏⲩ ϣⲁⲛⲧⲛⲡⲉⲗⲉⲩⲑⲉⲣⲟⲩ ⲙ̄ⲙⲟⲩ *make common effort till we free him* (from conscription).

—— ⲛⲥⲁ- *SA²B*, intr *go after, pursue*: Aeg 27 *S* ⲉⲣⲉⲡⲣⲁϫ ✝ ⲛⲥⲱϥ *like gale*; tr, *give to, upon, pursue*: Si 25 24 *S* ✝ ⲡⲧⲟⲟⲧⲉ ⲛⲥⲁ- (var ⲉⲧⲟⲟⲧⲉ ⲛ-) ἐπιχορηγεῖν dat; Deu 28 25 *S* ✝ ⲛⲡⲉⲕϫⲓϫⲉⲉⲩ ⲛ-ⲥⲱⲕ (*B* as Gk) δ. σε ἐπισκοπὴν ἐναντίον τ. ἐχθρῶν; 2 Kg 2 24 *S* καταδιώκειν ὀπίσω, cf ib 11 23; ShA 1 256 *S* plants ⲉⲧ✝ ⲙ̄ⲡⲉⲅⲕⲁⲣⲡⲟⲥ ⲛⲥⲁⲧⲡⲉ *send up*, BAp 155 *S* ⲉⲕ✝ ϩⲣⲟⲟⲩ ⲛⲥⲁⲥⲟⲟⲩ *add to*, ShA 1 420 *S* ⲁⲩ✝ ⲙⲟⲟⲩ ⲛⲥⲁⲡⲉⲩϭⲉⲣⲏⲧⲉ, R 1 5 31 *S* ⲉⲩ✝ ⲗⲁⲙⲭⲁⲧⲛ ⲛⲥⲱϥ (*sc* martyr's body), FR 106 *B* ⲙⲁ ⲡⲉϥ ⲛⲥⲁⲡⲉⲧⲉⲛⲗⲁⲙⲡⲁⲥ, Mani 1 *A²* sim, Pcod 35 *S* ⲛ̄ⲧⲁⲩ✝ ⲟⲩⲥⲟⲉⲓⲧ ⲉϥϩⲣⲟⲟⲩ ⲛⲥⲱϥ *spread ill report about*.

—— ⲛⲧⲛ- *SA²B*, *entrust to*: 1 Cor 15 3 *B* (var ⲉⲧⲉⲛ-, *S* ⲛ-) παραδ. dat, Miss 1 405 *S* ⲉⲩ✝ ⲙ̄ⲡϣⲁ-ϫⲉ ⲛⲧⲟⲟⲧⲩ ⲛ̄ⲡⲉⲅⲉⲣⲏⲩ *as those that throw dice*; *support*: ShC 42 59 *S* ⲉⲣⲉⲡⲡⲉ ✝ ⲛⲧⲟⲟⲧⲥ, MG 25 270 *B* devil to saint ⲉⲕ✝ ⲛⲧⲟⲧⲕ ⲡⲉⲙⲡⲁⲓⲣⲱⲙⲉⲟⲥ = Mor 40 44 *S* ⲉⲧⲟⲟⲧⲕ, Mani 1 *A²* ⲥⲱⲟⲩϩ ⲡⲉ ⲁ-ϩⲟⲩⲛ ϩⲱⲥ ⲉⲣⲉⲡⲟⲩⲁⲓϣ ✝ ⲛⲧⲟⲟⲧⲉ; *give in, decrease*: Ge 8 3 *B*(*S* ⲥⲃⲟⲕ) ἐνδ.; BM 217 28 *S* if thou see one growing rich cleave to him ϫⲉⲧⲉϥⲥⲁϭ ⲧⲉⲧ✝ ⲛⲧⲟⲟⲧⲩ (meaning?). ✝ ⲧⲟⲟⲧ⸗ *v* ⲧⲱⲣⲉ *hand*.

—— ⲟⲩⲃⲉ- *SAA²BF* (ⲡⲟⲩⲉ), *fight against*: Job 11 19 *S*(*B* ϩⲟⲧⲥ ⲉ-) πολ. acc, Sa 2 18 *S*(*B* ⲁⲛⲧⲓⲕⲓ-ⲙⲉⲛⲟⲥ) ἀνθιστ., Zech 3 1 *SAB*, Phil 1 28 *SBF* ἀντι-κεῖσθαι dat; Jo 6 52 *B*(*SA²* ⲙⲓϣⲉ ⲙⲛ-) μάχ. πρός; 1 Pet 2 11 *S*(*B* ϫⲱⲕ) στρατεύεσθαι κατά; Pro 3 15 *SA*(*B* ⲉϩⲟⲩⲛ ⲉϩⲣⲉⲛ-) ἀντιτάσσεσθαι; ib 20 8 *S*(var ⲉⲓ ⲛ̄ⲡⲁϩⲣⲛ-) ἐναντιοῦν, Mt 14 24 *SB*(*F* ⲉⲣ. ⲉⲣⲗⲏⲓ) ἐναντίος εἶναι; Ps 2 2 *SB* κατά no vb; PS 100 *S* ϣⲁⲩ✝ ⲟⲩⲃⲏⲓ, ShMun 138 *S* ⲉⲓ✝ ⲟⲩ. ⲉⲧⲉⲧⲛ̄ⲙⲛ̄ⲧⲁⲧ-ⲡⲁⲣⲧⲉ, Bor 305 98 *S* these words ✝ ⲟⲩ. ⲉϩⲁⲓⲣⲉⲥⲓⲥ ⲛⲓⲙ, BMis 341 *S* ⲡⲉⲧ✝ ⲟⲩⲃⲉⲡⲉⲕⲭ̄ⲥ̄ (var ⲉⲡⲉⲕ.) = Mor 27 15 *F* ⲡⲟⲩⲉ ⲉⲡⲉⲕ., AP 27 *A²* ⲡⲉⲧ✝ ⲟⲩⲃⲏⲛ, DeV 2 15 *B* ⲡⲁⲧϣ ✝ ⲟⲩⲃⲏⲥ; ⲁⲧ✝ ⲟⲩ. *S*, *not to be opposed*: Bor 254 174 ⲛⲣⲱϩ...ⲟⲩⲁⲧ✝ ⲟⲩⲃⲏⲩ-ⲡⲉ; ⲣⲉϥ✝ ⲟⲩ. *B*, *opponent*: Ez 3 7 (*S* ⲣⲉϥ✝ ⲧⲱⲛ) φιλόνεικος; ⲙⲉⲧⲣⲉϥ✝ ⲟⲩ. *B*, *opposition*: MG 25 38 ✝ⲙ̄. ⲡⲙⲉⲩⲓ.

—— ϩⲁ-, ϩⲁ- *SBF*, *give, sell for*: Mk 10 45 *S* (*B* ⲡ̄ϣⲉⲃⲓⲱ ⲛ-) δ. ἀντί, Ps 137 8 *S*(*B* ✝ ϣ. ⲉϩⲣⲏⲓ ⲉϫ.) ἀνταπόδ. ὑπέρ; Job 2 4 *S*(*B* ⲉϫ.) ἐκτίνειν ὑπ; ShBM 253 56 *S* ⲉⲧⲣⲉⲡⲣⲱⲙⲉ ✝ ϩⲁⲡⲉϥⲛⲟⲃⲉ, ShC 73 43 *S* price ⲉⲧⲟⲩⲛⲁⲧⲁⲁⲥ ϩⲁⲥⲟⲩⲟ, BSM 33 *B* ⲁϥ-ⲧⲏⲓϥ (*sc* robe) ϩⲁⲡⲓⲥⲟⲩⲟ = BMis 376 *S* ⲁϥⲧⲁⲁⲥ ⲁϥ-ϫⲓ, BP 3248 *F* ⲁⲓⲧⲉⲃ ⲡⲉⲕ ϩⲁⲕⲉⲥ ⲃ̄, BMis 33 *S* ⲁⲩϯ ⲙ̄ⲡⲉⲯⲏⲫⲟⲥ ϩⲁⲣⲟⲩ; *as nn* *S*: Si 7 33 ⲛ̄✝ ϩⲁⲡⲛⲟⲃⲉ (δόσις) περί.

—— ϩⲓ- *SAB*, ⲉϩⲓ- *SᶠF*, *lay upon, clothe*: intr *S* Mt 25 36 (*B* ϩⲱⲃⲥ) περιβάλλειν; ib 6 30 (*B* ✝

ϩⲉⲃⲥⲱ ϩⲓ-) ἀμφιεννύναι; ShA 1 456 bade ✝ ϩⲓⲱⲱϥ & feed him; tr: Ge 3 21 *SB*, Ps 108 18 *S*(*B* ϫⲱ-ⲗϫ), Zeph 1 8 *AB*, Mk 15 17 *SBF* ✝ ⲉϩⲓ., Ro 13 12 *Sᶠ* ✝ ⲉϩⲓ. (Mor 54 127)*B*, 1 Cor 15 53 *SBF* ✝ ⲉϩⲓ. ἐνδύειν; Deu 22 12 *S*(*B* ϫ.), Ap 3 18 *SB* περιβ.; Mt 27 28 *SB* περιτίθ.; MG 25 241 *B* ⲁϥ✝ ⲡⲟⲩ-ⲥⲭⲏⲙⲁ...ϩⲓⲱⲧϥ ἀναλαμβάνειν; PS 106 *S* ⲁϥ✝ ⲡ-ⲕⲁⲕⲉ ϩⲓⲱⲱϥ, BMis 473 *S* ✝ ϩⲓⲱⲱⲧ ⲙ̄ⲡⲉⲥⲭⲏⲙⲁ (cf ib ✝ ⲉϫⲱⲓ), Mor 54 81 *Sᶠ* ⲁϥⲧⲁⲁⲧⲉ (f) ⲉϩⲓⲱⲧϥ, C 43 110 *B* ⲙⲟⲓ ϩⲓⲱⲧⲕ ⲡⲡⲉⲕⲃⲱⲥ; *fight for*: Lu 9 50 *B*(*S* ⲉϫⲛ-) ὑπὲρ εἶναι; qual: Zech 3 4 *SAB* ⲉⲛⲇ.; Lu 7 25 *SB* ἀμφι.; BHom 24 *S* ⲥⲁⲣⲝ ⲧⲟ ϩⲓⲱⲱⲛ περικεῖσθαι; Mor 39 9 *F* ⲟⲩⲡⲟⲣⲫⲩⲣⲁ ⲧⲁⲁⲓ ⲉϩⲓⲱⲧϥ = C 43 36 *B*, BSM 8 *B* honour ⲧ ϩⲓⲱⲧϥ, BIF 13 108 *S* ϩⲉⲃⲥⲱ...ⲧⲱ ⲉϩⲓⲱⲛ, BKU 1 182 43 *Sᶠ* sim ⲧⲟ ⲉϩⲓ. (var Gu 45 ⲧⲱ ϩⲓ.).

—— ϩⲁⲧⲛ- *S*: CA 99 ⲛ̄ⲡⲉ(ⲧ)✝ ϩⲁⲧⲟⲟ[ⲧ ?

—— ϩⲓϫⲛ- *SBF*, intr *give for, on behalf of* (?): Lant 43 *F* may he that readeth ✝ ϩ. ⲡⲁⲛⲟⲃⲓ that God may forgive me; tr, *put upon*: Bar 4 20 *B* ⲉⲛⲇ. acc; Sa 2 8 *S* στέφειν dat; AZ 30 41 *S* ⲁⲛ✝ ⲧⲉϥ-ⲃⲟⲗⲗⲁ ϩⲓϫⲱϥ (*sc* letter), C 41 11 *B* ⲥⲭⲏⲙⲁ...ⲙⲛⲓϥ ϩ. this youth (cf ib ⲧⲛⲓϥ ⲉϫ.).

D With following adverb.

—— ⲉⲃⲟⲗ *SAA²BF* intr, *give forth, away, sell*: Ge 41 56 *B*, Is 24 2 *SB*, Ez 7 13 *SB* opp ϣⲱⲡ (var ShA 2 336 ⲧⲟⲟⲩ), Mt 21 12 *SB* opp ϣ. πω-λεῖν; Lev 25 14 *SB* opp ϫⲓ ἀποδ.; Ro 7 14† *SB* πιπράσκειν, Si 27 2 *S* opp ϣ. πρᾶσις; ShR 2 3 27 *S* learning ⲉϥ✝ ⲉⲃⲟⲗ ⲛⲡⲉⲧⲟⲩⲱϣ ⲉϣⲱⲡ; tr: Lev 25 23 *SB*, Mt 13 46 *SBF* πιπ.; Jo 2 14 *SA²B* πω.; Pro 29 42 *SA* ἀποδ.; Cant 3 6 *S*(ShC 42 53) θυμιά-ζειν; TU 24 1 6 *S* ⲁⲉⲓ✝ ⲙ̄ⲡⲱⲙ ⲉⲃ., C 86 347 *B* ⲙⲛⲓⲥ ⲉⲃ. ϫⲉⲛⲡⲓⲑⲉⲣⲙⲛⲥⲓ *for a tremis*, J 1 88 *S* hast the right ⲉⲧⲁⲁϥ ⲉⲃ., Lant 59 *S* ⲁϥϯⲟⲩ ⲉⲃ., Kr 46 *F* ⲁ]ⲛⲧⲉⲓⲧⲟⲩ ⲉⲃ. ⲛⲉⲕ & got their price, BM 580 *F* ⲁⲕⲓ ⲛ̄ⲧⲉⲓⲃ ⲃⲁⲗ, Mor 47 192 *S* dog ⲉϥ✝ ϩⲣⲟⲟⲩ ⲉⲃⲟⲗ; ⲉⲃ. ⲉ-, *sell for, as*: Est 7 4 *S*, Ps 104 17 *S*(*B* ϫⲁ-) ⲡⲓ. εἰς (cf Ex 21 7 *S* sim ⲛ-, *B* do); *to*: ShC 73 122 *S* ⲡⲉⲧⲛⲁϯ ϩⲛⲗⲁⲩ ⲉⲃ. ⲉⲡϩⲗⲗⲟ, Bor 304 55 *S* ✝ ⲥⲟⲩⲟ ⲉⲃ. ⲉⲛⲉⲡⲣⲙⲛⲕⲏⲙⲉ, Mor 34 41 = 35 4 *S* ⲛ̄ϩⲣⲓⲥⲉ ⲉⲧⲟⲩⲧⲟ ⲉⲃ. ⲉⲣⲟⲟⲩ *to which they are given over*; ⲉϩⲣⲁⲓ, ⲉϫ. ⲉ-: Jth 7 25 *S* ⲡⲓ. εἰς, DeV 1 116 *B* brethren ⲧⲏⲓϥ ⲉⲃ. ⲉϫ. ⲉϫⲛⲙⲁⲓ; *set, put forth upon*: 1 Kg 21 5 *S* ⲉⲃ. ⲉ- (var ⲉ-) ἐξέρχεσθαι εἰς; BMis 324 *S* fear ⲉϥ✝ ⲛⲁϧⲟⲓ ⲉⲃ. ⲉⲡⲡⲉⲗⲁⲅⲟⲥ; ⲉⲃ. ϩⲁ-, ϫⲁ-*for, against*: Is 48 10 *S*(*B* om ⲉⲃ.) ⲡⲓ. ἕνεκεν, Jo 12 5 *SA²B* ⲡⲓ. gen; Joel 3 3 *SAB* πω. ἀντί, Mt 10 29 *SB* πω. gen; Pro 28 21 *S* (var & *A* om ⲉⲃ.) ἀποδ. gen; ⲉⲃ. ϩⲓϫⲛ-, *fight on behalf of*: SHel 38 *S* his god ✝ ⲉⲃ. ϩⲓϫⲱϥ; cf ⲣⲉϥ✝; *as nn, sale*: Lev 25 14 *S*(*B* om) πρᾶσις; Jer 39 11 *S* (*B* ϣⲱⲡ) κτῆσις; ⲣⲉϥ✝ ⲉⲃ., *seller*: 1 Tim 1 10

B ρεϥϯ ρμϩε εϭ. (*S* diff) ἀνδραποδιστής; R 2 2 28 *S* ρεϥϯ cογο εϭ. σιτοδότης.

—— επεcητ *SB*, *put, send downward*: Ez 32 12 *B* καταβάλλειν; *ib* 32 18 *B*(*S* ταγο) καταβιβάζειν, FR 6 *S* ϣαϥϯ μπεϥρο επεcητ ετεϥϣτηн & weep.

—— επϣωι *B*, *raise up*: Rec 6 181 ϯ...cθοι ноγϫι επ.=BMar 216 *S* ϯ εϩραι, C 86 114 acϯ εϩραc επ.

—— επαϩογ *SA*, *go backward*: Jer 15 6 (*B* μοϣι ϩιϕ.) πορεύεσθαι ὀπίσω; Pro 10 30 *SA*(*B* χα τοτϥ) ἐνδιδόναι; ShC 42 212 restraining them ετρεγϯ επ. εθη ан, BMis 275 lovesick youth ϯ εп. until nigh death.

—— εθη *S*, *go forward, progress*: 2 Kg 3 1 (var пηγ εθη) πορ.; BMis 309 poor man growing rich ϯ εθη коγι коγι.

—— εϩογн *SAA²BF*, *give, hand in*: Miss 8 73 *S* letters εμπογταaγ εϩ. ἀποδ.; Lu 2 5 *S*(*B* cϭαι) ἀπογράφειν; ShC 73 157 *S* птаϯ паранaγ εϩ. (to community), BSM 79 *B* αϥϯ ннаι нηι εϭ. *delivered over*, Pcod 47 *S* woman ϯ μπεcραн εϩ. for baptism; εϩ. ε-, *into*: tr Is 59 21 *SB* δ. εἰς; ShA 2 114 *S* moving stones нϥϯ нтεϥμαϩϭ εϩ. εροογ, *ib* 130 *S* vineyards нтаγϯ тεγμιтонκε εϩ. εрооγ ϣaнтογ χооγ *in planting which they had spent their poor means*, RNC 90 *S* αϥϯ ноγϭроте εϩ. επεγϩоор, Aeg 31 *B* offering нcεтнιc εϭ. επεκτοποc, Lant 26 *S* book αϥтаaϥ εϩ. ετεκκληcιа, C 41 18 *B* αϥϯ нοϩ εϭ. επιωни; *refl S betake self to, make for*: Jos 8 7 πορ. εἰς; 19 εἰσέρχεσθαι εἰς; 2 Kg 11 23 γίνεσθαι ἐπί; BMar 220 антаан εϩ. επтооγ; *intr S*: ShP 78 44 burning fever εϥϭωλ μμοι εϭολ for my head & feet нετϯ εϩ. επаcωμа тηрϥ, HT *Y* 8 hand εcϯ εϩ. εттапро of child; εϩ. нcа-: 2 Kg 11 23 *S*(var пωт нcа- ϣαϩογн) γίν. ἐπί; εϩ. наϩрн-, *respond to*: P 131¹ 21 if only Eve had not ϯ εϩ. н.паcпаcμоc (of serpent); εϩ. ϩа-, *place beneath*: Wess 18 56 *S* αϥϯ χωϥ εϩ. ϩаппаϩϭ; εϩ. ϩн- *S*, ϩан- *A*, ϩεn- *B*, *strike into, upon*: Hos 11 4 *A*(*B* ϩιογι ϩεn-) ῥαπίζειν ἐπί; ShA 1 202 *S* нcεϯ εϩ. ϩμπεнϩο, TU 24 1 5 *S* εϥϯ εϩ. ϩμπεϥϩητ grieving, SHel 4 *S* аκϯ εϩ. ϩεμ- (*l* εϩμ)паоγεϩcаϩнε *oppose* (cf εϩ. εϩрн-), DeV 1 117 *B* ϯ нтcнϥι εϭ. ϭεнпоγϩнт *thrust into*; εϩ. εϩрн-, *strike against, oppose*: Nu 22 31 *B*(*S* аϩε ратϥ) ῥαπίζειν ἐπί; Ro 9 19 *B*(*S* do ογϭε-) ἀνθισ. dat; Mt 14 24 *F*(*SB* ϯ ογϭε-) ἔναντ. εἶναι; Ac 17 7 *B*(*S* do) ἀπέναντι πράσσειν gen; Pro 3 15 *B*(*SA* do) ἀντιτάσ. dat; Gal 5 17 *B*(*S* do) ἀντικεῖσθαι dat; AM 265 *B* εθнаϯ εϭ. εϩраγ ἀντιλέγειν; Mt 26 67 *S*(*B* ϩιογι ε-) ῥαπ. acc; Ac 4 14 *B*(*S* diff) ἀντειπεῖν; Sh(Besa)Z 515 *S* εнϯ εϩ. εϩрнмϣαϩε, MG 25 417 *S* water ϯ εϩ. εϩраϥ (sc river bank), ROC 25

—— 248 *B* кϯ εϭ. εϩреппιωϣ; ρεϥϯ εϭ. εϩр. *B*, *opposer*: Ac 5 39 (*S* ϯ ογϭε)-μάχος; μετρεϥ-: 1 Tim 6 20 (*S* ογωϩм) ἀντίθεσις.

—— εϩраι *SAA²BF*, εϭ. *B*, *give, send up, in, lay down*, intr *S*: ShC 73 73 εγϯ εϩ. кακωc *stoking* (oven) *badly*; εϩ. ε- Ac 11 29 (*B* Gk om); εϩ. μп- Ap 8 3 (*B* ϯ нcа-) δ. dat; *tr*: Nu 16 47 *S*(*B* ϩιογι εϩ.) ἐπιβάλλειν; Ac 3 13 *S*(*B* om εϭ.) παραδ.; Hos 2 13 *A* ϯ ϩнηε аϩр. (*B* diff) ἐπιθύειν; ShA 1 379 *S* εγϯ ϣооγε εϩ., R 1 3 43 *S* cleansed house & αγϯ εϩ. ноγcϯноγϭε, Cai 42573 2 *S* recipe таaγ εϩ. ϩнϩεнϫεϭc, Bodl(P) d 20 *S* money тарпιтаaγ εϩ. нϫнμоcιон, PRain 4704 *S* пεнтаιтаaγ εϩ. επcооγ ноϩокⁱ *expenses being* (?) 6 *solidi* received from Shenoute; *lift up*: Bor 290 144 *S* maladies ϯ χωογ εϩ. пcεχате; εϩ. ε-, *lift up, commit to*: 2 Kg 10 10 *S* δ. ἐν, Jer 21 7 *SB* δ. εἰς, Joel 3 8 *SAB* ἀποδ. εἰς, Ex 23 31 *SB*, Dan 3 31 *SB* παραδ. εἰς; Ps 36 33 *S*(*B* diff) ἐγκαταλείπειν εἰς; ShA 1 431 *S* ceased not εϯ нтε(c)cмн εϩ. επεccх̅, C 86 279 *B* тнιтоγ εϭ. εϕноγн, ROC 25 252 *B* мнιc (sc soul) εϭ. επεccωμа, Pcod 15 *S* αγϯ кнμε εϩ. ετоотϥ; *refl S*: Jud 10 17 παραβάλλειν ἐν, 1 Kg 4 1 п. ἐπί; *ib* 9 14 ἀναβαίνειν acc; ShA 2 279 аγтаaγ μμιн μμооγ εϩ. епχωρμ, BKU 1 31(7) will ye ετрептаaι εϩ. εрооγ & smite them?, Mani 1 *A²* αϥϯ μμаϥ аϩ. а[; εϩ. ϩа-: ShR 2 3 47 пετоγϯ εϩ. ϩапεϥϩоιте нϩεнϣооγ.

P c, *giver*: He 11 6 *S* таι ϭεкε (*B* ρεϥϯ ϭ.) μισθαποδότης, Si 30 6 *S* т. кϭа ἔκδικος, *ib* т. χарιc χ. ἀνταπоδ.; Mani 1 *A²* ϣнι нт. ογταϩ, *ib* *A²* нт. ειρннн, Ep 311 *S* т. cογо (not a person) н τροφη, CMSS 77 *F* Severus нт. μаγ.

χι-, ϭιϯ *as one vb SB*, *buy & sell, trade*: P 43 75 = 44 91 *S* тϭιϫ ετχιϯ кακωc нпεϣате μпкаϩ (Ar misunderstands), C 86 346 *B* εϥϭιϯ ϭεнϩанμετϣωт, Z 350 *S* αϥχιϯ ϩноγλεϫιc *hesitated, was uncertain as to* (meaning of) *a verse*. *V* also nn below.

E —— nn m *SA*(*B* mostly таιо), *gift, bounty*: Nu 18 7 *S*(*B* таιо), Pro 19 14 *SA* δόμα, *ib* 21 14 *SA*, Ja 1 17 *S*(*B* do) δόσις; ShBM 194 3 *S* пна μιнϯ, AM 211 *B* αϥερ пкεϯ пωтεн; *sale*: Lev 25 14 *S*(*B* om) πρᾶσις; *fight B*: Nu 1 45 (*S* μλаϩ) παρατάσσεσθαι; Job 38 23 (*S* μιϣε) μάχη; Eph 6 12 (*S* do) πάλη; Jer 21 4 ϩοплон нтε пϯ (*S* do) πολεμικός; paral χι, ϭι, *exchange, trading*: Si 41 21 *S*, Phil 4 15 *SB* δόσ. к. λῆψις, Bor 226 162 *S* ογϫι μпоγϯ δοσοληψία; BHom 99 *S* пϣа μεϩ εϭол пϯ ϩιχι (= ALR '96 193 Ib̲ᵃ̲ᵈ̲li̲), MélOr 6 509 *B* trader famed ϭεнпεϥϭι пεμпεϥϯ, Ryl 139 *S* will celebrate marriage jointly ϩεнχι μнпτι, BM 1117 *S* hast not sent пεкχι пεктι to thy wife; *as one*

word SF(once): BMOr 8802 6 пхіϯ ммкосмос *worldly exchange* & intercourse (συνάλλαγμα), BM 1119 таπрасіаті(*l* те) итоущωп хіті ап, Kr 125 yearly rent щмте пкер(атіоп) епхіті, *ib* 126 sim иихіти, *ib* 140 F agreed wage ῡ ϵ хіті етрампі.

ма пϯ B, *fighting place*: 2 Tim 2 5 (S diff) ἀ-θλεῖν; WHatch 761 went like athlete to пима пϯ.

реϥϯ SB, *giver*: 2 Cor 9 7 SB δότης, CaiEuch 463 B фр. пиіатафоп δοτήρ; Ps 111 5 S(B ϯ епоущап) κιχρᾶν; ShC 42 80 S р. ипрнке, Va 61 104 B р. рωми ефмоу; *fighter*: Jer 26 12 B (S реϥмище), Joel 3 11 B(SA do) μαχητής; Nu 31 27 B(S = Gk) πολεμιστής; Bor 253 120 S р. миппе θεομάχος; Va 58 178 B оур. ехепϯργ-ѧоип *striving for pleasure* of belly rather than careful for soul, C 86 189 B р. ехепϯметеусевнс, Va 57 84 B ѧупармахос (ὑπέρμ.) паϥ пемр. евоλ еѧрні ехωϥ; мпт-, метреϥϯ, *generosity, charity*: Si 37 13 S εὐχαριστία; ShMIF 23 100 S ѧепм. ѧппетеоуоу, C 41 63 B, BAp 167 S; р, ер реϥϯ, *be giver*: 1 Tim 6 18 S(B реϥсωоутеп) εὐμετάδοτος εἶναι; Va 63 104 B реϥѧωλем opp р.

ϭιп-, хіпϯ, *giving, selling*: Mor 17 17 S теуϭ. ὠνή of slaves; Va 57 155 B ϯпараѧосіс пте пи-хіптнк (*sc* Jesus), LAl 18 S тϭ. мпфарматоп to Alexander; *fighting B*: Va 61 216 μάχη; *ib* 57 123 πάλαισμα.

Combined with nn to translate Gk vb (*v* Stern p 315), as аіаі αὐξάνειν, κωϣ ζηλοῦν, мтоп ἀναπαύειν, поміϯ παρακαλεῖν, осе ζημιοῦν, пеі καταφιλεῖν, рап ὀνομάζειν, со φείδεσθαι, тоот ἀντιλαμβάνειν, оуω ἀνατέλλειν, ωмс βαπτίζειν, щіпе καταισχύνειν, ѧнг ὠφελεῖν, ѧнт προσέχειν, ϭωπт παροξύνειν; or with Gk nn as архн, каппос, λοгос, ппеума.

On prob ellipse of ϯ *v* Ep 532 n.

V also тто, тооу vb.

то SA²O, ѳо BO, тω, ѳω DM, те-(place-names), pl тооу DM nn m, *land, earth*: Ap 3 10 B пиѳо тнрϥ (S = Gk) οἰκουμένη; MG 25 5 B паіѳо κόσμος; Mani 1 A² пархωп мпто, AZ 21 104 O пто тнрϥ; кмто, комфѳо *earthquake* (*v* кім *s f*), PGM 1 60 680 O птк кмпто; DM 1 28 оуаптω *earth-opener*, *ib* 9 6 nb тооу *lord of lands*.

In place-names (*v* ZDMG 77 2 189): птепетω (var таπатω Amélineau *Géog* 386), птепоуѧар (Lant 15 48), птесеррѧ (*ib* 121). *V* рнс с та-.

то AA² *v* тωп interrogative.

тое¹, тоіе², та(е)³, то⁴ S, таіе⁵ S^a AA², таеіе⁶ A, тоі, тωі⁷ B, таеі⁸ F, тааі⁹ S^f F nn f, *part, share*: Ge 33 19 S¹ (var⁴) B, Ps 49 18 S⁴BF⁸(Pcod Mor), *ib* 62 10 S⁴A⁵(TillOster 21)B, Pro 29 24 S¹ (var⁴)A⁶, Jer 10 16 B(S = Gk) μερίς, He 2 4 B(SF пωрх) μερισμός, Pro 17 2 S⁴A⁶, Lu 12 46 S⁴B, Ap 16 19 B(S оуωп) μέρος; Ps 135 13 S⁴(B фωрх), 1 Cor 12 4 B(S пω.) διαίρεσις; Nu 31 41 S⁴(B = Gk) ἀφαίρεμα; Lev 24 6 B(S соп) ἔνθεμα; Nu 3 9 S⁴(B таіо) δόμα, *ib* 8 11 S⁴(B do) ἀπόδ. (*cf* 13 ϯ); ShMich 550 16 S take тто мпетѧрітоуωϥ, Aeg 259 S ϥі птект¹. (var⁴), Mani 2 A² reckoned тт. пиксоус, AM 43 B аϥер т. споуϯ, C 86 277 B птоу-(*l* пте)щтемоут.⁷ сωк еоут.⁷, J 24 125 S еупатаѧω (т)т.² тарнс, COAd 4 S т[т]о етпиеіти, J 35 44 S тт.³ таѧрнт, *ib* 73 23 S^a тат.⁵ ѧітпоуѧе, Kr 31 S тато пϣωм, Ryl 159 S тато ѧме, CO 352 S тато мпросфора, Kr 218 F акті ткт.⁸

хі, ϭі т. SB, *receive share, be partaker*: ShC 73 58 S ѧпаау пім етоухі птеѧто therein, ShBerl Or 1611 7 370 S eating remnants of пеѧто етоухі ммооу, ShWess 9 143 S as if Satan хі то миппе in ruling world, ROC 23 282 B ареϭі ѧепϯт. пте каіп, Mich 550 25 S хі то ѧітапастасіс; реϥ-хі то S, *partaker*: Mich *lc* епеер р. мппетоуаав.

маіт. проѧо SBF, *loving greater share, covetous*: 1 Cor 5 10 S(B реϥϭі пхопс) πλεονέκτης; SHel 87 S^f маіта пр., TstAb 259 B маіт. пр.; мпт-м., *covetousness*: Mk 7 22 S(B метϭі пх.), 1 Thes 2 5 SF(B do) πλεονεξία, Hab 2 9 A мптмаітаі еϥѧоуω (? corrupt, B ϭі пх. еϥѧωоу) πλ. κακή.

тое, то то S, таді S^f, таіе A, ѳоі B nn f m (K), *spot*: Ge 30 37 S то егоуовϣ (B кнкс) λέπισμα; Lev 13 28 S тто sim (B diff) αὐγάζον; Jer 13 23 S тое (var то, B аѧі аѧаі) ποίκιλμα; K 76 B піѳ. (*sic* all) اَلْش; El 120 S оутое псѧім = *ib* 90 A; R 1 3 49 S white mules емп лаау пто ѧнтоу; *iterated*: Ge 30 33 B піѳ. ѳ. (S diff) διάλευκος, 37 S(B аоуі аоуап) ποίκιλος, Mor 54 99 S^f sheep паупп пт. т.; р то, о пто, *be spotted*: Ge 30 35 S(B do) ῥαντός; Va 61 19 B етоі пѳ. in souls, Mor 16 87 S giraffe о пто то паѧеі аѧап (varr *ib* 15 62 тоте тоте, BMis 227 мпе мпе), BMar 66 S body р тое т. like pard. *Cf* ѳоуѳоу. *V* Spg *Kopt Etym* no 20.

тω етω S(Sh only) preposit phrase as interj (?), meaning doubtful, indicates when followed by п-...мп- comparison (in time or quality), contrast, parallellism: C 42 37 т. поуѧнтемωп standing before Christ...мпоуѧнтемωп before whom God is standing, MIF 23 193 т. мпептаухоос ероϥ thy soul shall be taken (Lu 12 20) мптептасмоу & been raised (Ac 9 40), also *ib* 86, 123, Ryl 70 251 т. птпопнріа п-...мптмптаѧаѳос п-, A 2 71 т. пхоос хе-...мпхоос хе-; without мп-: A 2 192 т. птвлвіле етѧапесит мпкаѧ хеесер ѧітпе,

IF 155 are there not sores that profit by vinegar & salt? алла т. мпсоп етемещще е† ехωоу (cf A 1 282 т. мпсоп), P 131² 114 doth not scripture testify against wicked? т. мпентаq† пeап ероωq (Job 29 14); other uses: P 130⁴ 135 monks may not wander т. тепоу проепрωме...еткωте еппепма ерепма, ib 105 we have transgressed т. тепоу хппхе ме ехι сол, A 1 62 н т. ерепаре епщахе тωп...н еqпатωωме еро пащ пре?, C 73 158 what is the sense if those walking ahead reach place whither they go аγω т. щаппау етеренетоγηγ ммооγ паеі? Τωετω, Τοετω Preisigke W.buch 3 335 is a place.

тнв B v тннве.

тωв B v тωωве seal & repay.

таιве¹, **тннве**², **тн.**³ SSᵃSᶠ, теві S(BKU), тееве A, таιві⁴, тωві (Si), өнві⁵, өе.⁶ B, теве⁷ F nn f m(once B), chest, coffin (cf θήβη חבה IgR), pouch: MG 25 376 B ө.⁵ in which man shuts wives πίθος (ROC 18 289 لاحمـه of wood); K 133 B †т.⁴ قبرة, ib 135, P 55 13 B пιө.⁶ do (var تابوت); ShC 42 63 S snake curled up in тт.³ н тпıра, BKU 1 68 S ттеві прoγп мптаві̯р, CO 450 S оγт.² оγ large box; for clothes: Is 3 25 S²(B = Gk)θήκη; R 2 2 39 S¹ κιβώτιον, ShR 2 3 58 S², JA '75 5 263 S¹ (var R 1 2 44²), BMis 387 S² = Va 63 14 B, BSM 41 B καψ, ib 148 صندوق, PMich 494 F ϩаι† ϩппеγт.⁷, ST 116 S т.¹ пϭриме; for grain, bread: Si 1 16 B ἀποδοχεῖον; Ep 532 S тт.³ еттнк апоеικ; coffin: Ge 50 26 S¹(B слн) σορός; Ex 2 3 ABˢ(varˢ) θῖβις (gloss κιβ. παπύρου); ShA 1 208 S digging they find ϩепсмот пт.³, R 1 3 51 S т.², ib¹, Bor 256 152 S оγт.¹ пωпе, MG 25 405 B оγө.⁵...аγϭιтq епесн† ерос (cf 404 т.⁴), Mor 18 98 S¹ reliquary in martyrium = Miss 4 158 B⁴, Mor 30 22 Sᶠ тт.³ for Julian, BMar 33 S bought теqкаιсе мптеγт.¹; pouch: C 41 16 B put it in †ө.⁵ пте пеqщар = P 129¹⁴ 124 S тωωме = Miss 4 324 اسكيـم (cf Ep 1 150 pockets in monkish aprons), ShZ 506 S моγс, тооγе, т.² (same? or v теві strip).

теві B nn f m(K), obole coin: Nu 3 47 (S = Gk), Ez 45 12 ὀβολός; Mt 5 26 (S do, var λγптоп) κοδράντης; ib 10 29 (S ϩoвол.) ἀσσάριον; Mk 12 42 †т. (SF=Gk)λεπτόν; K 68, 146 пıт. فلس. Cf? тннве seal.

теві, -пι, -пе B, тнві F? nn m, strip, bandage of linen: P 55 1 пιтепı, Bodl 325 158 -пе كتان, C 43 80 body wrapped in ϩапт. пмаϩі, cf paral AM 319 оγпоϭ пспппеп, BM 581 F пıлωмı птаві̯ха т. flax (?) planter (cf ib тепϫа кап(ı)ωϩı елас). Cf? тннве measure BM 1114.

тево A · v таϩо.

тннве SF, **тн.** SA², **теве** S (Kropp), **†ве** S (PMéd)A, **†еіве** A, **тнв** B, **тееве** F nn m, finger: Ex 31 18 SB, Pro 6 13 SA †еі. B, Is 17 8 S (var тннв) B, ib 31 7 SBF, Jo 20 27 SA²B δάκτυλος; ShZ 599 S пеϩвнγе ппеqтнве, Bor 248 58 S щапра пϭтнγ ппат., BSM 111 B аqтале пеqт. ϩιхеппеqщаı & snorted = Mor 22 122 S, P 129¹⁴ 123 S аqтекс т. епепресвγтерос = DeV 1 78 B pointed finger at, Z 630 S recipe for пт. етϩωке, BMar 208 S ерепеqт. талнγ ехппеϩернγ like knife blade = Rec 6 172 B, TU 43 3 A пект̄ве, KroppK 28 S charm written with оγт. пкос, Bor 134 6 (Vita Sin) S stretched out пеqт. поγпам, C 43 6 B sim, PMéd 292 S grip tooth with †. & мпе, KroppR 14 4 S ппоϭ пт. of right hand, AZ 33 133 S sim тн., Cai 42573 2 S blood of поϭ пт. in recipe, TEuch 1 11 B sign forehead with пекпıщ† пт. اصبع (HCons 451 الكبير), Glos 297 S σφάκελος т. птмпте, ib 301 παραντίχειρ пт. птпе, ShIF 102 S faultless щаϩраι епеqт. щнм; Z 629, PMéd 314 S recipes т. prob finger but uncertain: toe: 2 Kg 21 20 S т. пıϭoϩернте, BM 363 S sim δακ. ποδῶν, ShA 1 379 S, MIE 2 403 B sim; ще пт. B, blow of finger, finger-mark: MG 25 177 пıтоиq пте пıщ. of teacher's hand.

As measure SBF, finger's breadth, digit (cf δακт.): Kr 1 S river's rise η етн. ϩı ıа емаϩе, BM 1114 S sim 4 ells щат есооγ етепе (or ? v теві strip), BM 528 F т.,щап, мерı measures of land, CO 473 S size of garment спаγ оγϭас пт., Hall 121 S sim тн., щооп, MMA 23 3 710 S ostr оγпаще птн. пϭωлх (no context), Va 61 28 B splinter еоγоп т. в̄ ероq (cf Gk σπιθαμῶν δύο), PMéd 219 S hung above it пх̄ п†ве, Bodl(P) a 2 61 S sim пϥтооγ птн., CO 450 S оγт. оγ (l o); small quantity: Wess 18 82 S Dives asks оγт. ммооγ (cf Lu 16 24), MG 25 144 B оγт. ппеϩ † ероϩот мпро (sic, cf Ps 103 15); ϭιст.: ShA 2 236 S none can add оγϭ. ехптеqщıп.

An implement, of wood: J 66 41 = 76 44 S щомпте птн. пщп; of metal: AZ 13 144 B сϫо, т., оϩс made by smith.

In name (?) Παπτῆβε (Preisigke).

тннве, тнве, теве chest v таіве.

†ве S vb intr, meaning unknown: BMar 197 апесϩпт †, and she vomited because of the corruption of his body. Cf? ов, which? l ов(е).

тωве (oftenest), тωω. (WTh 196, Miss 4 634, CO 175) S, тωві BF nn, name of 5th month, Gk Τῦβι, Ar طوبة.

ⲧⲱⲱⲃⲉ¹ S, ⲧⲱ.² SA, ⲧⲱⲱⲃⲓ³ Sᶠ, ⲧⲱ.⁴ SᶠB nn f
m, *brick* (cf طوب , *adobe*): Ex 24 10 S²B, Is 24 23 S¹
m B f, Ez 4 1 S²B f, Nah 3 14 AB, Z 301 S ⲟⲩⲧ.¹ f
ⲛⲟⲙⲉ dissolves but ⲧⲉⲣⲡⲟⲥⲉ remains πλίνθος; ShP
130² 6 S ⲉⲗ ⲟⲙⲉ, ⲡⲓⲡ ⲧ.¹ v ⲡⲱⲱⲡⲕ II, Ryl 252 S
ⲛⲧ.² ⲛⲧⲁⲓⲡⲟⲡⲕⲟⲩ ⲉⲓⲛⲥⲧⲁⲃⲗⲟⲛ, BMis 263 S ⲛⲧ.²=
Mor 30 38 Sᶠ ⲛⲉⲧ.⁴, JKP 2 52 Sᶠ³, BMis 121 S
city built of ⲧ.² ⲉⲓⲟⲙⲉ, FR 104 B sim ⲕⲁⲣⲓ ⲛⲉⲗⲧ.,
BM 1089 S ⲟⲩⲕⲟⲧ ⲛⲧ.², Miss 4 539 S tears caused
ⲧⲧ.¹ (sic) whereon he stood to ⲣ ⲟⲙⲉ (cf ib 334),
AJSL 46 245 S charm said over ⲟⲩⲙⲟⲟⲩ ⲛⲧ.²,
KroppH 106 S² sim, El 80 A ⲁⲓⲣⲙⲉⲥ ⲁⲧ. to bear
children (v Z Assyr 14 269), Mich 136 3 S ⲛⲧ.² ⲉ-
ⲙⲓⲥⲉ; ⲡⲁⲡⲉ, ⲫⲁⲫⲉ ⲧ. SBF, *knead, make bricks*
v ⲡⲱⲱⲡⲉ. (On brick making Ep 1 160).

ⲧⲱⲱⲃⲉ S, ⲧⲟⲩⲃⲉ A, ⲧⲱⲃ, -ⲡ B, ⲧⲱⲃⲓ F (v ⲣⲉϥⲧ.),
ⲧⲉⲃ- B, ⲧⲟⲟⲃⲉ S, ⲧⲁⲃⲉ Sᵃ AAᶜF, ⲧⲟⲃ, -ⲡ B, ⲧⲁⲁⲃⲉ
F, ⲧⲟⲟⲃⲉ†, ⲧⲟ.† S, ⲧⲁⲃⲉ† SᵃF, ⲧⲏⲃ, -ⲡ†, ⲧⲟⲃ, -ⲡ† B,
ⲧⲁⲁⲃⲉ† F vb I intr, *seal* B: Ap 20 3 ⲧ. ⲥⲁⲡϣⲱⲓ ⲛ-
(S ⲧ. ⲉⲣⲛ-) σφραγίζειν ἐπάνω; qual: Is 29 11 S
(var ⲧⲟ.)B ⲟⲃ.; Dan 12 9 B ⲧⲟⲡ ἐμφράσσειν (confusion as in Cant 7 3 SF); ShZ 597 S ⲉⲛⲁⲡⲟⲑⲏⲕⲏ
...ⲉⲩⲧ., JKP 2 92 S ⲟⲩⲁⲣⲟ ⲉϥⲧ., Cat 127 B ⲡⲁⲣⲑⲉⲛⲓⲁ ⲉⲥⲧⲏ, AM 190 B ⲡⲓⲗⲁⲕⲕⲟⲥ...ⲧⲟⲡ, DeV 2
111 B on rising He left ⲛⲓⲥⲫⲣⲁⲅⲓⲥ ⲛⲧⲉ ⲡⲓⲉⲙϩⲁⲩ
ⲉⲩⲧⲏⲃ, BMis 392 S bag (παννίον) of coins ⲉⲥⲧ. =
Va 63 10 & BSM 44 B ⲧⲏⲃ, BM 1137 S sim, ib
1122 S ⲁⲥⲫⲁⲗⲓⲁ...ⲉⲥⲧ., Sph 10 1 S ⲥⲟⲟⲩⲛⲉ ⲉⲥ-
ⲥⲟⲗⲉⲥ ⲉⲥⲧ. *smeared* (with clay &) *sealed*, Ep 253 S
sim, ib 304 Sᵃ ⲛⲑⲁⲗⲗⲓⲥ...ⲉⲩⲧ., Kr 3 F ϣⲁⲛⲧⲓ ⲛⲃⲃⲓ
ⲉⲧⲧ. *acacias with* (government) *stamp*, Bor 289 4 S
marks of blows ⲉⲛⲓⲉϥⲟⲩⲟⲥⲉ ⲉⲧⲧ. (meaning?).

II tr: Is 8 16 S(B ϩⲓ ⲧⲉⲃⲥ), Mt 27 66 B(S =
Gk), Ap 7 3 SB ⲧⲉⲃ-, Cl 43 3 A ⲁϥⲧ. ⲡⲓⲣⲟⲟⲩ ⲟⲃ.;
COAd 58 Sᵃ ⲟⲩⲧⲱⲃⲉ ⲛϥⲣⲣⲉ ⲡⲉⲛⲧⲁⲧⲁⲃⲉϥ *a new
seal* (stamp) *has been stamped*, Mani 1 Aᶜ ⲉⲁⲩⲧⲁⲃⲟⲩ
ϩⲙⲡⲭⲓⲥⲉ, C 41 30 B ⲁⲩⲧ. ⲛϥⲉⲡⲓⲥⲧⲟⲗⲏ, AM 286 B
ⲁⲩⲧ. ⲙⲡⲉϥⲁⲗⲟⲕ (q v), C 86 313 B ⲁⲩⲧⲟⲃⲉϥ ⲁⲩϯ
ⲛϩⲁⲛⲥⲫⲣⲁⲅⲓⲥ ⲉⲣⲟϥ.

With following preposition. ⲉ ⲉ-, *set seal
upon*: Sa 2 5 S κατασφ.; Ap 14 9 B(S as Gk)
χάραγμα λαμβάνειν ἐπί, ib 16 2† B(S do) χ. ἔχειν;
ClPr 19 156 S tomb ⲉⲣⲉⲛⲉⲥⲫⲣⲁⲅⲓⲥ ⲧ.† ⲉⲣⲟϥ, C 43
101 B ⲁϥⲫⲟⲣⲧ. ⲉⲣⲟⲥ (sc oven, but var ⲉⲣⲱⲥ), MG
25 118 B ⲉⲧⲁϥⲧⲉⲃ ⲧⲉϥϭⲓϫ ⲉⲧⲉϥⲙⲉⲥⲧⲉⲛϩⲏⲧ *impress
upon*; ⲉ ⲉⲣⲛ-, meaning same: Job 14 17 SB,
Ap 10 4 S(B ⲧ. only) ⲟⲃ.; ShA 2 225 S ⲧ. ⲉⲣⲛ-
ⲛⲉⲧⲕⲁⲕⲓⲁ, AM 240 B ⲟⲩⲕⲁⲙⲓⲛⲟⲥ ⲛⲥⲉⲧ. ⲉⲣⲱⲥ (cf
C 86 102 B ⲡⲣⲱⲥ): ⲉ ⲛ-, *seal
with, by means of*: Cl 43 2 A ⲧⲁⲃⲟⲩ ⲡⲓϩⲟⲩⲣ ⲟⲃ.
dat, Ap 5 1† SB ⲕⲁ ⲁⲥⲟⲃ. dat; Mor 22 131 S ⲛⲥⲉⲧ.†

ⲁⲡ ⲛⲧⲉⲥⲫⲣⲁⲅⲓⲥ (cf 132 ϩⲛ-) = BSM 122 B ⲥⲉⲧⲏⲃ
(sic l) ⲁⲡ ⲉϥⲥⲫ., EW 176 B ⲁϥⲧ. ⲡⲣⲱⲥ ⲙⲡⲉϥϣ-
ⲥⲟⲩⲣ, MR 5 37 F ⲧⲁⲃⲟⲩ ⲛⲧⲉⲕⲃⲟⲩⲗⲗⲁ, Mor 27
36 F ⲉⲥⲧ.† ⲛⲍ̄ ⲛⲥⲫⲣⲁⲅⲓⲥ, Z 285 S Virgin ⲉⲥⲧ.†
ⲛⲧⲉⲥⲡⲁⲣⲑⲉⲛⲓⲁ (? l ϩⲛ- as Aeg 17); *upon* (?): BM
1126 S ⲁⲓⲧⲟⲟⲃⲉ (ⲙ)ⲡⲁⲥⲓⲕⲉⲗⲗⲓⲛ ⲡⲭⲱⲭⲟⲙⲧⲉ ⲡⲗⲁ-
ⲕⲟⲡ; ⲉ ϩⲛ-, ⲍⲉⲛ-, *with*: R 1 1 39 S door ⲉϥⲧ.†
ϩⲛⲧⲉⲩⲧⲏⲃⲉ ⲟⲃ.; ShA 2 163 S ⲉⲩⲧ.† ϩⲙⲡⲧⲃⲃⲟ, C
41 33 B ⲁϥⲧⲟⲃⲥ ⲍⲉⲛⲡⲉϥϣⲥⲟⲩⲣ, Kr 3 F wrote it
& ⲁⲓⲧⲁⲁⲃⲉϩ ϩⲛⲧⲁⲃⲟⲩⲗⲗⲁ.

ⲣⲉϥⲧⲱⲃⲓ F, *sealer*: BM 711 (or ? *brick seller*, cf
ⲣⲉϥⲧⲱⲥ *straw seller*).

—— nn m S, *seal*: BM 187 129 ⲧⲉⲥⲕⲣⲁⲧⲓⲁ ⲛ-
ⲧⲉⲥⲫⲣⲁⲅⲓⲥ (prob l ⲧⲉⲥ. ⲛⲧⲉⲥ.) ⲁⲩⲱ ⲛⲧ. ⲙⲡⲁⲛⲕⲓⲟⲛ
(ἀγγεῖον) ⲛⲥⲡⲉⲣⲙⲁⲧⲓⲕⲟⲛ, BMis 5 cannot restrain
ⲛⲧ. ⲛⲡⲁⲥⲡⲟⲧⲟⲩ (? l ⲧⲱⲱⲃⲉ), COAd 58 *stamp* (v
above).

ⲧⲟⲟⲃⲉⲥ S (once), ⲧⲉⲃⲥ, ⲧⲟⲃⲥ, -ⲡⲥ B nn f (once),
seal's impress: Bel 17, Ap 6 1 (S = Gk) σφραγίς;
K 129 ⲡⲓⲧ. طوب silversmith's *stamp*; Mor 56 34 S
when they saw ⲧⲧ. ⲙⲡⲣⲁⲧ, DeV 2 43 ⲛⲉⲡⲧ. ⲙⲡⲓⲣⲟⲭ-
ⲣⲉⲝ paral ⲛⲉⲛⲭⲣⲱⲙ ⲙⲡⲓⲕⲩⲡⲁⲏⲛⲟⲥ, ib 105 Christ
at birth ⲁϥⲁⲣⲉϩ ⲉⲧⲧⲟⲡⲥ ⲡⲧⲉϥⲙⲁⲩ ⲉⲥⲧⲏⲡ as before,
AM 12 he knew ϯⲧ. of ring, C 43 50 book ⲉϥⲧⲟⲃ
ⲛⲧ. ⲛⲥⲫⲣⲁⲅⲓⲥ; ϩⲓ ⲧ., *set seal*: Job 24 16, Is 8 16
(S ⲧ. vb) ⲟⲃ.; O'LearyH 24]ⲉⲧϩⲱⲟⲩⲅⲓ ⲛⲧ.

ⲧⲟⲟⲃϥ, -ⲉϥ S, ⲧⲁⲃⲉϥ Aᶜ²F, ⲧⲟⲃϥ, -ⲡϥ B nn m, as
last: Cant 8 6 F σφρ.; Mor 55 64 S ⲟⲩⲧ. ⲉⲕϣⲁⲛ-
ⲧⲱⲱⲃⲉ ⲛⲟⲩϩⲟⲗⲟⲕ, ⲡⲣⲛⲧϥ, ib 56 39 S ⲛⲉⲓⲧ. ⲉⲧϩⲓⲱⲟⲩ
(coin), Mani 1 Aᶜ ⲡⲧ. ⲙⲡⲉⲛⲉ ⲛⲟⲓⲕⲱⲛ, MG 25
177 B ⲛⲓⲧⲟⲡϥ ⲛⲧⲉ ⲛⲓϣⲉ ⲛⲧⲏⲃ, Kr 228 vo S ⲟⲩⲧⲱ-
ⲃⲉϥ ⲉⲧϣⲱⲓ (sic) ϩⲛⲛⲁⲓⲣⲏⲡ; Ryl 282 S ⲧⲓ ⲧⲟⲟⲃⲉϩ
ⲉⲭⲱⲡⲣⲟ; MG 25 148 B ⲛⲧⲟⲩϭⲓ ⲧⲟⲃϥ ⲉⲛⲉⲡⲣⲱⲟⲩ.

ⲧⲉⲃⲉ S nn f, *seal*: R 1 1 52 ϯ ϣⲟϣⲧ ⲉⲛⲣⲟ ⲙⲡ-
ϩⲉⲛⲕⲉⲧ. σφραγίς; Tor 29 ⲡϣⲟϣⲧ...ⲧⲧ. ⲙⲏⲣ ⲉⲡⲟⲩ[ⲁ, ROC 23 101 ⲧ. ⲥⲓⲧⲉ one silver, other lead.
Cf ? ⲧⲉⲃⲓ *obole*.

ⲧⲱⲱⲃⲉ SF, ⲧⲟⲩⲟⲩⲃⲉ, ⲧⲟⲩⲃⲉ A, ⲧⲱⲃⲉ SAᶜ², ⲧⲱⲃ,
-ⲡ, ⲧⲟⲃ B, ⲧⲱⲱⲃⲓ F, ⲧⲉⲃⲉ- S, ⲧⲟⲟⲃ SA, ⲧⲏⲃⲟ S
(J bis), ⲧⲱⲃ A, ⲧⲟⲃ, ⲧⲟⲡ B, ⲧⲁⲁⲃ F vb I intr,
repay, requite: Ro 12 19 S(B ϯ ϣⲉⲃⲓⲱ) ἀνταποδιδόναι; Philem 19 B(S ⲧⲟⲩⲉⲓⲱ) ἀποτίνειν; Va 61 91
B ⲡⲓⲥⲛⲟⲩ ⲛⲧ. = P 131³ 81 S ⲛⲧⲁⲁⲩ; **II** tr: Ps
68 5 B(S diff), Is 9 5 B(S ⲣ ϣ.) ἀποτ.; Ro 12 17
SF-ⲃⲓ (B ϯ ⲛϣ.) ἀποδ., Is 35 4 SB(var ϯ)F ἀντα-
ποδ.; Pro 16 33 SA ἐπέρχεσθαι; AP 3 Aᶜ cannot
ⲧ. ⲛⲟⲩⲡⲉⲑⲁⲩ for evil, AZ 21 141 S ⲥⲉⲛⲁⲧ. ⲙⲡⲉϯ-
ⲉⲙⲡϣⲁ ⲙⲙⲟϥ, BSM 40 B ⲧⲉⲛⲛⲁⲧⲱⲡ ⲛⲛⲏ ⲉⲧⲁⲩ-
ϣⲧⲱⲣⲓ ⲙⲙⲟⲛ ⲉⲣⲱⲟⲩ = BMis 385 S ϯ, Miss 4 192
B debt ⲙⲡⲉⲕϭⲓⲙⲉ ⲉⲧⲟⲡⲟⲩ, CRRussAcad '24 99 S
ⲁⲓⲧⲱⲃⲉ ⲧⲁⲓⲟⲩ ⲛⲡⲣⲟⲣⲟⲕⲟⲧ[ⲧⲛ, Mor 33 97 S ⲧⲉⲛⲛⲁⲉϣ
ⲧⲉⲃⲉ ⲟⲩⲕⲟⲩⲓ (var BMis 50 ⲧⲟⲩⲓⲱ).

With following preposition. ⲥ ⲉ- (ⲉⲡⲙⲁ ⲛ-)*S*,
in place of : 1 Thes 5 15 (*B* ϯ ϣ.) ἀποδ. ἀντί; ⲥ ⲉ-
ⲉϩⲣⲁⲓ ⲉ- *S into* : Is 65 6 (*B* do ⲉ-) ἀποδ. εἰς ; ⲥ ⲉϫⲛ-
S, *upon* : Deu 5 9 (var ⲉϩⲣⲁⲓ ⲉϫ., *B* do ⲉϫ.)
ἀποδ. ἐπί ; ⲥ ⲙⲛ- *S*, *with, to* : Nu 31 3 (*B* ⲟⲓ
ⲙⲛϣⲏϣ) ἀποδ. dat ; ⲥ ⲛ- dat (or sometimes
? acc), *to* : Ps 27 4 *S*(*B* ϯ) διδ. dat, Deu 7 10 *S*(*B*
ϯ ϣ.), Ps 93 23 *SB*, Mt 6 4 *SF*(*B* ϯ) ἀποδ. dat, Ps
115 12 *S*(*B* ϯ ϣ.), cit J 89 21 *S* ⲧⲃⲃⲟⲩ, or ? as *consecrate*), Hos 4 9 *SA* ⲧⲱⲃⲟⲩ (*B* ϯ ϣ.), Lu 14 14 *S*
(*B* do) ἀνταπόδ. dat ; Pro 20 22 *SA* ⲧⲓⲛ. acc, Ru 2
12 *S* ἀποτ. acc ; Est 6 13 *S*, BM 177 18 *S* ⲉⲕϣⲁⲛⲧ.
ⲙⲡⲉⲕϫⲁϫⲉ ἀμύνεσθαι ; P 131² 117 *S* if drunken
before Fast art like ⲡⲉⲧⲧ. ⲙⲡⲡⲟⲙⲟⲑⲉⲧⲏⲥ = Va 58
192 *B* ⲉⲕϯ ϣ. ⲛ- κατασοφίζεσθαι acc ; PS 147 *S*
ⲡⲉⲩⲧⲟⲅⲓⲟ...ⲁⲩⲧⲟⲟⲃⲉϥ ⲛⲁⲩ, ShC 42 115 *S* ϥⲛⲁⲧ.
ⲛⲁⲩ a thousandfold, C 89 14 *B* debts ⲉⲧⲟϩⲟⲩ ⲙ-
ⲡⲟⲩⲡⲛⲏ, BMis 396 *S* your gifts ⲛϥⲧⲟⲟⲃⲟⲩ ⲛⲏⲧⲛ
= Va 63 17 *B* ⲧⲟⲡⲟⲩ = Mor 27 22 *F* ⲧⲁⲁⲃⲟⲩ =
BSM 47 *B* ⲧⲏⲓⲧⲟⲩ.

—— nn m *SA*, *requital* : Ps 90 8 *S*(*B* ϯ ϣ.), Is
59 18 *S*(*B* ϣⲱϣ), Hos 9 7 *A*(*B* ϯ ϣ.) ἀνταπόδοσις,
Si 48 8 *S* ἀνταπόδομα ; Ps 118 112 *S*(*B* do) ἄμει-
ψις ; Pro 6 34 *SA*(*B* ϧⲁⲡ) κρίσις *vindicta* ; ShC 42
43 *S* ϥⲛⲁϯ ⲙⲡⲧ. ⲉϫⲛⲧⲉⲅⲁⲡⲉ, ShA 2 6 *S* sim, Mor
25 8 *S* ⲡⲕⲁⲓⲣⲟⲥ ⲙⲡⲧ. (var P 131³ 82 ⲡⲕ. ⲛⲧⲁⲁⲩ)
= Va 61 91 *B* ⲡⲓⲥⲏⲟⲩ ⲛⲧ.

ⲧⲟⲡⲟⲩ *B* nn m, as last : K 95 ‏أبيج‎.

ⲣⲉϥⲧ. *S*, *requiter* : Si 32 10 ἀποδιδούς ; P 44 48
ⲁⲙⲟⲓⲃⲉⲩⲥ (-βός) ‏مكافأ‎.

ⲡⲉⲧⲧⲃⲉ *S*, -ⲃⲏ *F*, *Requiter* name of a god : ShA 1
384 (Z 458) *S* ⲕⲣⲟⲛⲟⲥ ⲉⲧⲉⲡ., KroppK 74 *S* same ?,
GriffStu 162 *F* ⲡ. equivalent to *thunder*. *V* AZ
33 47, PSBA 22 162.

ⲧⲃⲁ *SAA²*, ⲑⲃⲁ *B*, ⲧⲃⲉ *F* nn m, *ten thousand* :
Lev 26 8 *S*(*B* ⲁⲡⲟ.), Ps 90 7 *S* ⲟⲩⲧ. (*B* do), Jon 4
11 *SAB*, Lu 12 1 *SB* ⲟⲩⲧ. μυριάς, Jud 20 10 *S*, 1
Cor 4 15 *SB* ⲟⲩⲧ. μυρίος ; Si 46 12 *S* ⲥⲉ ⲛⲧ. (6 ×
10,000) ἑξακοσ. χιλιάδων, Is 37 36 *S* ⲙⲛⲧϣⲙⲏⲛⲧ.
ⲟⲩⲟⲥⲟⲥ (18 × 10,000 + ½, *B* ⲣ̅ⲡ̅ⲉ̅ ⲛϣⲟ) ἑκατὸν ὀγδοήκ.
πέντε χιλ., Ez 48 8 *B* ⲑ. ⲁ̅ ⲡⲉⲙⲟⲩ̅ⲫⲁ̅ϣ̅ⲓ̅ (10,000 ×
2 + ½) πέντε κ. εἴκ. χιλ.; ShC 42 223 *S* ϧⲉⲡⲧ. ⲡⲣⲏⲃⲥ,
KroppD 66 *S* ⲡⲉⲧ. ⲥⲛⲁⲩ, BMis 207 *S* ϣⲟⲙⲛⲧⲃⲁ,
BM 511 4 *F* ⲧ. ⲛⲁⲡⲧⲉⲗⲟⲥ, BM 1224 19 *A²* sim, C
43 123 *B* ⲧ̅ ⲛⲑ., AM 73 *B* ⲑ. ⲃ̅, PMich 1289 d *S*
ϧⲏϣⲟ ϣⲟ ⲙⲡⲣⲛⲧ. ⲧ. (var BMis 504 ⲧ. ⲛⲧ.), PJkôw
S ⲉϣⲁⲣⲉⲡⲧ. ⲡⲣⲱⲙⲉ ⲉⲓ ⲉⲣⲏⲥ send us your news,
ST 74 *S* as coin ⲟⲩⲧ. ϣⲁϫⲉ (ϣⲙⲧϫⲉ) ⲛⲛⲁⲡⲣⲁ-
ⲗⲱⲙⲁ, ib 163 *S* price of book ⲟⲩⲧ. ⲙⲛⲧ (cf Ryl
310). ⲁⲡ-, ⲁⲡⲁⲛⲑ. *B*, collective pref. : Ps 90 *B*
ut sup, 1 Kg 18 7 ⲁⲡⲁⲛⲑ. (*S* ⲡⲉⲧ.) μυριάς, Cai-
Euch 634 ⲛⲓⲁⲡⲁⲛⲑ. ⲛⲑ. μύριαι μυριάδες (cf Dan 7 10 ϧⲁⲑ.
ⲛⲑ.); Cat 210 ⲛⲓϧⲁⲡⲁⲛⲑ. ⲛⲁⲛⲑ. ;   ⲟ̅ⲓⲥⲧ. *SF*,

half ten th. : Mk 6 44 *S*(*B* ⲉ̅ ⲛϣⲟ) πεντακισχίλ. (*cf*
Ez 45 6 *B* ⲫⲁϣⲓ ⲛⲑ.) ; LAp 570 *F* ⲋ. ⲛϧⲏⲙⲙⲓ, BM
340 *S* ⲟⲅⲋ. ⲡⲣⲟⲗⲟⲕⲟⲧⲧⲓⲛⲟⲥ.

ⲧⲃⲁⲓ- *O* in Anubis's title ⲧⲃⲁⲓⲧⲱⲟⲩ, *upon* (*his*)
mountain (AZ 21 95, *ib* 53 139 n). *Cf* DM 6 24.

ⲧⲃⲉ *F* *v* ⲧⲃⲁ.

ⲧⲃⲃⲉ nn *v* ⲧⲱⲱⲃⲉ *seal*.

ⲧⲃⲃⲟ *S*, -ⲟⲩⲟ *A*, ⲧⲟⲩⲃⲟ *A²B*, ⲧⲉⲃ(ⲃ)ⲟ, ⲧⲉⲃ(ⲃ)ⲁ,
ⲧⲩⲃ. *F*, ⲧⲃⲃⲉ- *S*, ⲧⲟⲩⲃⲉ- *B*, ⲧⲩⲃⲃⲁ- *F*, ⲧⲃⲃⲟ⸗ *S*,
-ⲟⲩⲁ⸗ *A*, ⲧⲟⲩⲃⲁ⸗ *A²*, ⲧⲟⲩⲃⲟ⸗ *B*, ⲧⲃⲃⲏⲩⲧ† *S*, ⲧⲃⲃⲟⲩ-
ⲁⲉⲓⲧ† *A*, ⲧⲟⲩⲃⲁ(ⲉ)ⲓⲧ† (Jo, Mani), ⲧⲟⲩⲃⲏⲩⲧ† (AP) *A²*,
ⲧⲟⲩⲃⲏⲟⲩⲧ† *B*, ⲧⲉⲃⲏⲟⲩⲧⲧ†, ⲧⲩⲃⲃ.†, ⲧⲉⲃⲏⲩⲧ† *F* (Phil 1
10) vb **I** intr, *become, be pure* (causat of ⲟⲩⲟⲡ) : Job
4 17 *S*(*B*†) καθαρὸς εἶναι, Is 47 11 *S*(*B*†) κ. γίνεσθαι, Mt 11 5 *S*(*B*†), Mor 17 70 *S* my son ⲙⲁⲣⲉϥⲧ.
καθαρίζεσθαι, Job 7 9 *B*(*S* tr) ἀποκ., Aeg 267 *S*
καθαίρεσθαι ; Deu 22 9 *B* neg (*S* ϫⲱϩⲙ), Mt 6 9
BF(*S* ⲟⲩⲟⲡ) ἁγιάζεσθαι ; Ps 17 26 *B*(*S* do) ὁσιοῦσθαι ; He 9 18 *SB*(*F* diff) ἐγκαινίζεσθαι ; ShBor 246
82 *S* ⲁϥⲧ. ϣⲁⲃⲟⲗ *utterly cleansed*, Br 118 *S* ⲛⲉϥⲓⲟ-
ⲟⲩⲉ ⲧ., Aeg 252 *S* one possessed ϣⲁⲡⲧϥⲧ., MG 25
399 *B* his field ⲁⲥⲧ. ;   qual : Lev 6 4 *SB*, Job
11 15 *B*(*S* ⲥⲟⲧϥ), ib 35 8 *SBF*, Jo 13 10 *SA²*(*B*
ⲟⲩⲁⲃ) καθαρός ; 3 Kg 8 8 *B*, 2 Tim 2 21 *SB* ἁγιάζ.,
Pro 21 8 *SA*, AP 9 *A²* ἁγνός ; He 9 14 *B*(*SF* ⲟⲩⲁ-
ⲃ) ἄμωμος ; Ex 21 28 *B*(*S* ⲟⲩⲟϫ), Nah 1 3 *SA*
(*B* ⲁⲑⲛⲟⲃⲓ) ἀθῶος ; Ps 42 1 *B* neg (*S* ϫⲁ.) ὅσιος ;
Pro 8 10 *SA*(*B* = Gk) δοκιμάζεσθαι ; Phil 1 10 *SBF*
εἰλικρινής ; Ap 21 21 *S*(*B* diff) διαυγής ; Sa 17 19
S λαμπρός ; Aeg 264 *S* water ⲉϥⲧ., Mani 2 *A²*
ⲡⲥⲛⲏⲩ ⲉⲧⲟⲩⲁⲃⲉ, ⲡⲥⲱⲡⲉ ⲉⲧⲧ., DeV 2 25 *B* hands
ⲉⲩⲧ., P 131² 158 *S* whilst air ⲧ. & calm, ib 156 *S*
ship with good wind ⲉⲣⲉⲧⲉⲥⲗⲁⲅⲟ ⲧ. ⲁⲩⲱ ⲉⲥⲡⲣⲓⲱ-
ⲟⲩ, BMis 217 *S* loaves ⲉⲩⲧ. ; *v* also ⲥⲟⲩⲟ.

II tr, *make pure, purify* : Deu 19 13 *S*(*B* ⲱⲗⲓ),
Ac 10 15 *SB* καθαρίζειν, Job 25 4 *SB* ἀποκ., Lu 3
17 *SB* διακ., Jos 17 15 *S* ἐκκ., Is 6 7 *SB* περικ.,
ib 1 16 *SBF* καθ. γίν., Jo 15 2 *SA²B* καθαίρειν ;
Ex 31 13 *SB*, Joel 1 14 *SAB*, Jo 10 36 *SAA²B*,
He 2 11 *SBF* ἁγιάζειν ; Is 66 17 *SB* refl, Ac 21 24
SB ἁγνίζεσθαι ; Ez 45 20 *B* ἐξιλάσκεσθαι ; Pro 24
35 *SA* ἀπονίπτειν ; Lev 21 10 *S*(*B* om) τελειοῦσθαι ;
Jud 17 12 *S* πληροῦν ; Ez 43 26 *B* πιμπλάναι ; PS
117 *S* body ⲉⲛⲧⲁⲓⲧⲃⲃⲟϥ, ShC 73 178 *S* ⲣ ⲡⲁⲣⲑⲉⲛⲟⲥ paral ⲧ. ⲙⲡⲉⲅⲙⲁ ⲛⲛⲕⲟⲧⲕ, BHom 126 *S* ⲁϥ-
ⲧⲃⲃⲉ ⲡⲉⲧⲥⲟⲃ̄, MG 25 176 *B* ⲟⲩⲣⲟⲓ ⲉⲁⲩⲧⲟⲩⲃⲟⲥ,
Mor 24 26 *F* ⲁⲓⲧⲩⲃⲃⲁⲧⲏⲛⲟⲩ, Cai 42573 2 *S* ingredients ⲧⲃⲃⲟⲟⲩ ϧⲓ ⲉϥⲓⲱ, JKP 2 140 *S^f* one man
ⲉⲣ ⲟⲩⲛⲁⲃⲓ another ⲧⲉⲃⲁⲃ.

With following preposition.
—— ⲉ- *SB*, *pure from* intr : Si 23 10 *SB* καθαρίζ.
ἀπό ; 1 Kg 21 4 *S* φυλάσσεσθαι ἀπό, MG 17 315 *S*

field ⲧ.† ⲉⲉⲡⲧⲏⲥ = C 89 4 B, Mor 51 28 S woman
ⲉⲥⲧ.† ⲉⲣⲟⲟⲩⲧ ;   tr : Ps 18 12 S(B ⲉⲃⲟⲗ ⲣⲁ-) ⲕⲁⲑ.
ἐκ ; Job 10 14 S(B do) ἀθῷον ποιεῖν ;   for : Jer 12
3 SB ἁγιάζ. εἰς, He 9 13 B(SF ⲙⲁⲡⲣⲏ-) ἁγ. πρός ;
Miss 4 108 B ⲙⲡⲟⲩⲧⲟⲩⲃⲱⲟⲩ ⲉⲑⲣⲟⲩⲥⲓ.

—— ⲛ- SB, cleanse, be pure for : Jos 6 19† S
ἅγιος dat ; 2 Cor 11 2† B(S ⲟⲩⲁⲁⲃ) ἁγνός dat ; by
agent F : Is 30 24 (S vb† only, B ϣⲏϣ) λικμᾶσθαι.

—— ⲣⲁ- from B : Ps 18 14 (S ⲟⲛ·), Ez 36 25 (var
=Gk, S ⲉⲃ. ⲣⲛ-), καθαρίζ. ἀπό ; on behalf of S.A²B :
Jo 17 19 ἁγιάζ. ὑπέρ ; ⲉⲃⲟⲗ ⲣⲁ- : 1 Jo 1 9 B(var ⲥⲁⲃⲟⲗ ⲛ-, S ⲉⲃ. ⲣⲛ-) ⲕⲁⲑ. ἀπό, Job 10 14 B(S ⲉ-) ἀθῷον
ⲡⲟⲓ., Rec 6 187 B ϣⲁϥⲧ. ⲉⲃⲟⲗ ⲣⲁⲛⲟⲃⲓ= BAp 221 S
ⲉⲃ. ⲣⲛ-, C 86 308 ⲧⲉⲡⲧ.† ⲉⲃ. ⲣⲁⲡⲉϥⲥⲛⲟϥ.

—— ⲣⲛ-, ⲥⲉⲛ- SABF, by agent intr : 1 Cor 7
14 SBF ἁγιάζ. ἐν ; ShBM 197 37 S ⲁⲡⲧ. ⲧⲏⲣⲡ
ⲣⲙⲡⲉϥⲥⲛⲟϥ, Pcod 39 F impure ⲧⲩⲃⲃⲁ ⲣⲙⲡⲉⲕⲗⲱⲙ
= S ⲁⲡⲣⲁⲗⲓⲥⲕⲉ, BSM 56 B flesh ⲧ.† ⲥⲉⲛⲟⲩⲙⲱⲟⲩ ;
pure, free from : ShIF 100 S sickness spreads to ⲙ-
ⲙⲉⲗⲟⲥ ⲉⲧⲧ.† ⲡⲣⲏⲧϥ ; tr : Is 10 17 SB, Ro 15 16 S(B†)
ἁγιάζ. ἐν ;   ⲉⲃⲟⲗ ⲣⲛ- be pure from : intr Ps 18 13
S(B ⲉⲃ. ⲣⲁ-), Aeg 242 S ⲉⲕⲧ.† ⲉⲃ. ⲣⲙⲡⲉⲑⲟⲟⲩ ⲕⲁⲑ.
ἀπό ; ShC 42 191 S eyes ⲧ. ⲉⲃ. ⲣⲙⲡⲥⲟⲗ ; tr, make
pure from : Is 53 10 SA(Cl)B ⲕⲁⲑ. ἀπό, 1 Cor 5 7
B(S ϥⲓ ⲉⲃ. ⲣⲛ-) ἐκκαθαίρειν ; P 131¹ 25 S ⲉϥⲧ. ⲏⲡ-
ϣⲟⲡⲧⲉ ⲉⲃ. ⲣⲛⲡⲉⲓⲱⲣⲉ, ClPr 39 37 S ϣⲁⲥⲧⲃⲃⲟⲩ ⲉⲃ.
ⲣⲛⲛⲟⲃⲓ (var Mor 54 84 ⲣⲁⲃ. ⲛ-), AM 255 B ⲧⲟⲩ-
ⲃⲟⲕ ⲉⲃ. ⲥⲉⲡⲁϣ ⲡⲛⲟⲃⲓ ; ⲣⲣⲁⲓ ⲣⲛ-, ⲉⲥⲣ. ⲥ. : Jo
17 17 SA²(B ⲛⲥ. ⲥ.), Ez 28 25 B ⲉⲃ. ⲥ. ἁγι. ἐν.

With following adverb. c ⲉⲃⲟⲗ S, emphatic of
ⲧ. : Ap 7 14 (var om ⲉⲃ., B ϥⲓⲣⲓ†) λευκαίνειν ; BP
10588 letter ⲁⲓⲟⲩⲗⲓⲁⲛⲉ ⲧⲃⲃⲟϥ ⲉⲃ. (context obscure).

—— nn m SAA²BF, purity, purification : Ps 17
20·SB καθαριότης, He 9 13 SBF καθαρότης, Pro
14 9 SAB -ισμός ; Ps 23 3 S(B ⲟⲩⲁⲃ), Is 8 14 SB
ἁγίασμα, Ro 6 19 SB -μός, Ps 95 6 B(S ⲟⲩⲟⲡ), 2
Cor 7 1 SB ἁγιωσύνη ; Nu 6 5 SB ἁγνισμός, AP
6 A², Va 66 290 B ἁγνεία ; Deu 9 5 SB ὁσιότης ;
1 Cor 5 8 SB εἰλικρινία ; BG 24 S ⲡⲓⲧ. ⲉⲧⲟⲩⲁⲁⲃ ⲡⲕⲁⲑⲁⲣⲟⲛ, ShBor 246 37 S ϥⲁⲥⲕⲉ ⲁⲡⲧ., AM
254 B ⲡⲧ. ⲙⲡⲉϥⲥⲱⲙⲁ, Bor 240* 7 S ⲡⲧ. sexual
purity ;   adverbial ⲣⲛⲟⲩⲧ. : Phil 1 17 SBF ἁγ-
νῶς, 3 Kg 8 61 B ὁσίως.

ⲁⲧⲧ. B, impure : 2 Tim 3 2 (S ϫⲁϩⲙ) ἀνόσιος.

ⲙⲁ ⲡⲧ. SA²BF, place of purifying : Ps 113 2 B(S
ⲧ. nn), Lam 1 10 F(B ⲙⲁ ⲉⲑⲟⲩⲁⲃ) ἁγίασμα, Lev 12
4 B(S ⲙⲁ ⲉⲧⲟⲩⲁⲁⲃ) ἁγιαστήριον, CaiEuch 467 B art
ⲙ. ⲙⲡⲓⲕⲟⲥⲙⲟⲥ καθαρισμός ; ShA 1 202 S ⲡⲉⲡⲧⲟ-
ⲡⲟⲥ ⲣⲉⲡⲙⲁ ⲡⲧⲃⲃⲉⲧⲏⲩⲧⲛⲏⲉ, Mani 1 A² ⲉϥⲟ ⲙⲙ.

ⲙⲉⲧⲧ. B, purity : Phil 4 8 (S ⲟⲩⲁⲁⲃ) ἁγνός.

ⲥⲓⲛ-, ϫⲓⲛⲧ. SB, purification : Lev 13 7 B(S =
Gk) καθαρίζεσθαι ; P 44 50 S καθαρότης.

тооⲃⲉⲃ v тооⲃⲉϥ.

(ⲧⲃⲕⲟ), ⲧⲃⲕⲉ-, -ⲕⲟⲥ S, vb tr, send (caus of ⲃⲱⲕ) :
Job 14 20 (sic l, B ⲟⲩⲱⲣⲡ), Ps 143 6 (var ⲧⲓⲡⲟⲟⲩ,
B ⲧⲁⲅⲟ) ἐξαποστέλλειν.

ⲧⲃⲛⲗ S, ⲑ. B nn m, fold(?) for sheep : Ricci Acta
Colluthi 115 S charms buried ⲉⲡⲉⲧ. ⲙⲡⲉⲩⲟϩⲉ ⲛⲉⲥⲟⲟⲩ, MG 25 199 B came to ⲟⲩⲑ. of sheep, ib sheep
ⲥⲁⲃⲟⲗ ⲙⲡⲓⲱ.= Gött Ar 114 37 قطيع, BM 390 265
B ⲑ., Ryl 453 336 B ⲑⲃⲁⲗ الخراف ;   hardly
same : PLond 4 515 S among metal (?) objects
ⲡⲉⲥϫⲉⲣⲏⲧ, ⲡⲉⲥⲧⲃⲛⲗ (sic), ⲡⲉⲥⲕⲛⲗ ⲡⲃⲉⲡⲓⲡⲉ.

ⲧⲉⲃⲗⲉ S nn f, a plant : P 44 81 ⲡⲏⲣ · ⲙⲉⲣⲓⲟⲡ · ⲣⲓ-
ⲧⲓⲛⲏ · (ῥητίνη) ⲧⲧ. نارديون, نارمريون (l ?) (نارديون,
Munier) =43 56 ⲩⲃ[ϫ, so ? l ⲧⲉⲃⲡⲉ δάφνη (cf K 199 ⲑⲁⲣⲙⲓⲣⲁ
ⲃⲓϫ).   V Keimer Gartenpfl 1 92, Rec 15 102.

ⲧⲃⲛⲏ SA², -ⲛⲓ A, ⲧⲉⲃⲛⲏ BF, ⲧⲩⲃ. F, pl ⲧⲃⲛⲟ-
ⲟⲩⲉ¹, ⲧⲉⲃⲛⲏⲟⲩ², ⲧⲏⲡⲏⲩ³, ⲧⲃⲛⲉⲩ⁴ S, ⲧⲃⲛⲉⲩⲉ⁵ SᵃA,
-ⲡⲏⲅⲉ⁵ᵃ, -ⲛⲉⲟⲩⲉ⁷A, ⲧⲃⲛⲁⲅⲉ A², -ⲛⲱⲟⲅⲓ B, -ⲛⲁⲅⲓ·,
-ⲛⲁⲟⲅⲉⁱ⁹, ⲧⲉϥⲛⲁⲅⲉⁱ⁰ F & sg as pl, nn m, beast,
domestic animal : Ex 20 10 SB, Pro 24 65 SA, Jer 27
3 BF κτῆνος ; Job 18 3 SB, Ro 1 23 SB τετράπους ;
Sa 13 14 ζῷον ; 2 Pet 2 16 S(B ⲉⲱ) ὑποζύγιον ; Ge
43 18 S(B do), 1 Kg 10 2 S ὄνος ; Tri 353 S ϥⲁⲓ-
ⲡⲁⲣⲃ, ⲧ. دابّ ; PS 35 S ⲧ. ϩⲁⲧⲃⲉ ⲑⲏⲣⲓⲟⲛ, Va
63 99 B sim, ShA 1 239 S ⲑⲏⲣⲓⲟⲛ devouring ⲟⲩⲧ.,
ShMIF 23 21 S ox, ass, camel ⲣⲓⲧ. ⲛⲙ, TstAb 161
B ⲧ. ⲛⲓⲃⲉⲛ whether sheep, goat or ox, BHom 98 S
Balaam's ass, BMis 270 S mule, MG 25 357 B
camel, P 132¹ 31 S 3 days (journeying) ⲡⲧⲃⲛⲏ (ⲛ)
ⲡⲥⲛⲏⲣ, MR 5 50 S ⲉⲕⲱⲡ ⲙⲙⲟⲓ ⲣⲱⲥ ⲧ., Mani 1 A²
ⲛⲑⲉ ⲛⲟⲩⲧ., PMich 4553 S I greet thee ⲙⲡⲉⲛⲧ. ;
ⲟϥⲉ ⲡⲧ. : 3 Kg 22 17 S, Zeph 2 14 A(B ⲟ. ⲛⲉⲥⲱⲟⲩ)
ποίμνιον ;   pl forms : S¹ Ge 2 20, Job 1 3, Ac 23
24, S² Vi ostr ⲛⲏϥⲧ., S³ PTurin A 4 ⲧⲛⲟⲟⲩ ⲡⲁ(l
ⲡⲁ)ⲧ., S⁴ CO 263, Sᵃ⁵ ST 260, Sᵃ⁶ Ep 165 ; A⁵
Pro 12 10, A⁷ Zeph 1 3, A² Jo 4 12 ; F⁸ Is 30 23,
Kr 22, F⁹ PMich 577 ϣⲁⲗⲉⲛⲁⲧ. ⲙⲁⲛⲓ, F¹⁰ CMSS
33, ib -ⲛⲟⲟⲩⲉ ; B C 43 5 ;   ⲡⲁⲡⲧ. S¹, cattle-man,
ploughing with oxen : Gu 17 ⲡⲣⲱⲙⲉ ⲡ.

ⲙⲁⲛⲧⲉⲃⲛⲏ B, cattle-herd : Va 57 60 ⲟⲛⲟⲗⲁⲧⲏⲥ
(l ὀνηλ.) ⲙⲙ.

ⲙⲛⲧⲧ. S, bestiality : ShC 73 95 ⲧⲉⲕⲙ. ere thou
didst enter these τόποι, ib 42 206 ⲟⲩⲙ. ⲛⲕⲟⲥⲙⲓⲕⲟⲛ.

ⲣ ⲧ. S, become, be beast : ShA 1 118 who breaketh
oath save he that will ⲣ ⲧ. ?, P 130⁵ 17 v ⲁⲕⲱ.

ⲣⲉϥⲥⲁⲛϣ ⲧ. SB, cattle-breeder : Ge 46 32 κτηνο-
τρόφος.

ⲧⲁⲃⲓⲣ SB nn m, sanctuary, דביר δαβείρ دبير تفير
(IgR) : Mor 25 193 S ascended to θυσιαστήριον &
entered door of ⲡⲧ. ⲉⲧⲉⲡϣⲓⲉⲣⲁⲧⲓⲟⲡⲡⲉ (cf ROC 23
279), BMis 104 S ⲡⲧ. ⲛⲧⲕⲏⲣⲉ ⲙⲡⲙⲁ ⲉⲧⲟⲩⲁⲁⲃ, cf
ⲕⲏⲣⲉ, also 3 Kg 8 8 B, BKU 1 68 S, K 225 B
ايوان, Tri 717 S ⲥ. CO 481 S.

тѣнр *SA*, ѳрнѣ (*sic*) *B* nn m, *blow with foot,
kick*: Mor 37 131 *S* пет. пшшаспорк λάκτι-
σμα; пех т. еѣολ *S*, *give kick*: Deu 32 15 (*A*
Cl ϯ т., *B* ϩι ѳ. еѣ.) ἀπολακτίζειν, cit Mus 40 278 тек
т. еѣ.; BM 185 horse етп. т. еѣ., R 2 1 47 drunkards
п. т. еѣ.; ϯ т. *SA* sim: Tri 717 ϩпнеϥоγерите
еγϯ т. رقص (*l* ' رز, *cf* P 44 120); с еϩоγп ϩп:
Ac 26 14 (*B* ще пϥат) λα. πρός; ShBMOr 8810
367 horses еγϯ т. еϩ. ϩппеϩерпϩ; еϩ. е-: PStras
54 мпрϯ т. еϩ. еϩраϥ; реϥϯ т. еѣολ *S*, *kicker*:
Mor 29 31 calf пр. = BMis 262 *S* етϯ оγѣе =
Mor 30 37 *F* пλеϥкопс. ϩι ѳ. еѣ. *B* v above Deu.

теѣс *B* v тωωѣе *seal*.

ϯѣс *SAA²*, ти. *SO*, т(е)ѣс *S*, ѳιѣс, ѳе. (Ez)*B*,
тιѣес *F* nn m, *heel*: Ge 3 15 *SB*, Jud 5 22 *S* of
horse, Jo 13 18 *SA²B*, cit JKP 2 142 *F* πτέρνα,
Ps 40 10 *SB* πτερνισμός; Ez 47 3 *B*(*S* келе) ἀστράγαλος *talus*; Ac 3 7 *S*(*B* ? ϭοп пте рат/) σφυρόν;
Ryl 94 *S* bend backward until теϥапе ϭωλx е-
пеϥϯ., AZ 21 100 *O* папιт. пѣепιпе, C 43 151 *B*
шшоϯ пте пеϥѳ., *ib* 79 *B* bade xωтϩ ппеϥѳ.,
WTh 192 *S* тѣс, AM 166 *B* sim, BAp 135 *S* птѣс
of right foot, K 139 *B* пιѳ. كعب *die* (*talus*); xι
ϯ., ϭι ѳ., *take by heel, trip up*: Ge 27 36 *SB*, Hos
12 3 *AB* πτερνίζειν; ShP 130² 44 *S* пететпоγωщ
ех. шшоϥ, Va 68 187 *B* аϥϭ. шшωоγ пxе паι-
ωпϭ; шптxι ϯ.: Jer 9 4 *S*(ShBMOr 8810 463, *B*
ϭι ѳ. nn) πτέρνα.

шетѳ. *B*, among currier's (اﻟﺠﻠﺪ) tools (?): K 138
ϯ̄.ṉ تكبس (*l* ? шешѳ. though f).

V also шешϯѣс.

тооѣес v тωωѣе *seal*.

тωѣс *SA*, тѣс-, те., тоѣсϩ *S* vb I intr, *be pricked,
incited*: ShA 2 74 птатетпт. ϩппетпршеιоγе re-
calling sins, TT 156 be patient щаптϥт. ϩптеϥ-
проϩаιресις = C 89 85 *B* ѳоксϥ, P 130⁴ 87 God
трепекϩнт т., *ib* 131⁴ 148 прωше етпат. пѣрре
pricked anew (by conscience).

II tr, *goad, incite*: Job 6 4 (*B* ѳоγϩ) κεντεῖν;
Pro 24 23 *SA* ὀξύνειν, *ib* 20 2 *SA* παρόξ.; Si 22
20 *SA*, Z 345 апποϭ (псоп) тѣс пкоγι = MG 25
210 *B* кιш νύσσειν; Ac 12 7 (*B* do) πατάσσειν; Cl
Pr 54 41 woman т. шпетпапощоγ (*cf* 3 Kg 3 26)
ἐπείγειν; Ac 13 50 (*B* щопщеп) παροτρύνειν; Mor
37 113 птаγт. шшоϥ ὑπομιμνήσκειν; Job 6 9 (*B*
ϭоϩ) τιτρώσκειν; 2 Cor 9 2 (*B* ϯ xоϩ) ἐρεθίζειν;
ShIF 231 еγт. н еγϯ поγϭс шпλоϭос шппѣ, ShZ
637 петт. шпϩто ϩптеϥшастιϩϩ, AZ 16 15 send
пϩтоѣсϥ шареϥϭепп. с xе-: PS 283 щаϥт.
ппλειтоγрϭос xееϩер шптре, ShMIF 23 23 тоѣсϥ
xешпрр поѣе, TT 102 тоѣсϥ xешпеιрωѣ па-
поγϥ ап.

With following preposition. с е- obj: R 2 1 8
spirit т. епетϩнте (*sc* in Elizabeth's womb), BM
Or 8811 66 петт. ептѣпп, BP 9446 пϩт. епсоп
пϥташιо &c; vbal: Sa 16 11 ἐγκεντρίζειν εἰς; Jud
1 14 ἐπισείειν gen; ShA 1 465 whoso shall т. пϩеп-
рωше еоγωш, BMis 246 аγтоѣсоγ еxιтоγ екпн-
ше, ShMIF 23 144 етоγт. шшоп етрепсι, Miss
8 7 т. пιѣнλшос етреγтωϩп, P 131² 124 щаре-
пλаос т....етреγ-; еϩоγп е-: Z 295 аγтоϥсϥ
еϩ. ероϥ κεντεῖσθαι *punctus invidiæ*; ShA 2 288
петт. шшоϥ еϩ. етептоλн шппѣ, Till Oster 14 *A*
аγшат. оγе аϩ. апϥсап; с ϩιxп-, *by, owing
to*: BM 216 110 аϥт. ϩιxшпщаxе κατανύσσειν ἐπί.

—— nn m *S*, *pricking* of conscience, *compunction, admonition*: Z 289 аγт. щωпе паϥ, BHom 42
κατάνυξις; BMis 235 аϥщωпе ϩπογпоϭ пт. =
Mor 30 8 *Sᶠ* поϭ пекстасις, R 2 4 40 = Mor 22
44 spake also concerning пт. птеψγхн, Z 552,
BMar 46, BMis pl 21 sim, ShC 73 136 пт. ппоι-
копошλос, P 131⁴ 110 птакιш птакепера (κινύρα)
ϩпϩепоγеλλе пт., BMar 91 пщаxе пт.

Cf ? ѳωѣщ.

таѣт (*sic*) *S* nn, meaning unknown: PRain 4812
тпооγ оγкоγпт. паι.

тѣт *SAA²*, ти., тнϥт (PMéd) *S*, теѣт *B*, тγ.,
тιнѣет *F* nn m, *fish*: Ps 8 9 *SB* of sea, Ez 29 4 *SB*
of river, Hos 4 3 *SAB*, Mt 14 17 *SBF* тγ., Glos
406 *S* поϭ пт. ἰχθύς, Mk 8 7 *SB* ἰχθύδιον; Nu 11
22 *SB* ὄψος, Jo 6 11 *SA²BF*, Z 299 *S* ὀψάριον; Sa
19 10 *S* ἔνυδρος; ShC 73 119 *S* xιр пт., т. еϥпосе, тарιхιоп, ShP 130² 25 *S* fish еγтωкс аγω
епаще пеγщпϥе, Mor 25 13 *S* rich man's food т.
пιш λатнс (λάτος) ϩιт. of sea = Va 61 95 *B* т. ш-
шιпе пιѣеп, Mani 1 *A²* spread upon them like nets
аxпϩрнт., DeV 2 206 *B* коγxι пт. foreteller of
storms, Ep 533 *S* тн. паѣпϥ, Ryl 106 63 *S* шперо-
γеш тн., CMSS 78 *F* account еϩоγп тн. (п)пе-
спноγ, BM 529 *Sᶠ* к̄ѣ пλааш птн.; *catch fish*:
Jo 21 3 *S* ϭеп т. *B* таϩе т., KroppF 9 *S* аϥщωпе
поγтн.; *fish-catcher*: P 44 54 *S* оϩιарос (= P 45
161 -рас, *l* оϯарас *i e* ὀψαρᾶς) реϥϭп т., Mor 18
29 *S* do = Miss 4 122 *B* реϥϭаϩе т.; *fish-
monger*: BMOr 6201 A 5 *S* Severus ψа пт., BSM
45 *B* са пт. = Va 63 16 *B* & BMis 393 *S* оγωϩе.

тоѣтѣ *S*, таѣтѣе *A*, таѣтеѣ *B*(once)*F*, тѣт(е)ѣ-,
тѣтωѣ *S*, теѣ. *F* vb tr (intr *B*), *from, compound,
invent*: 2 Pet 1 16 (*B* шетсеѣ) σοφίζειν; EpJer 10
F(*B* соλсеλ) κοσμεῖν; P 44 91 пλастоп · птаγтѣ-
тωѣоγ, ShP 130² 104 things too fragile for hammer
craftsman тѣтωѣоγ като теγшιпе, ShBM 194 1
оγпааγ еаγтѣтωѣϥ, Cai 8010 1 heretic аϥϯтѣтеѣ
ϩепxωωλе, JTS 4 395 ппепт. шпщаxе = Va 61

115 *B* ⲉⲛⲧⲁⲃⲧⲉⲃ intr, PBu 93 words ⲉⲁⲩⲧⲃⲧⲱⲃⲟⲩ ⲙⲙⲉ *fabricated (as if) true*, ShA 2 274 made fast with nails & other ϩⲱⲃ ⲛⲧ., ShP 131⁴ 158 ϣⲁⲭⲉ ⲛⲧ. ϩⲓⲙⲏⲃⲱ; as nn: Nah 3 17 *A* ⲡⲙⲓⲉⲓϣⲉ ⲛⲧ.(*B* ⲙⲟⲩⲝⲧ)συμμικτός; ShIF 267 ⳁⲟⲗ, ⲧ., ⲗⲁ; ⲙⲁⲓⲧ. *F, loving ornament*: EpJer 8 (*B* ⲙⲁⲓⲥⲟⲗⲥⲉⲗ) φιλό-κοσμος.

ⲧⲃⲧⲃ *S* nn, *mixed (?) food*: BMar 5 ate not food ⲉϥϫⲏⲙ ⲟⲩⲇⲉ ⲧ.

ⲧⲟⲟⲃⲉⳅ, ⲧⲟⲃⲥ̄ *v* ⲧⲱⲱⲃⲉ *seal*.

ⲧⲟⲟⲃⲉⳅ *S* nn m, *foliage*: ROC 10 430 trees ⲕⲁ ⲡⲉⲛⲧ. τὰ φύλλα; BM 1127 ⲁⲕϭⲣⲁⲓ ⲉⲧⲃⲉ ⲡⲧⲟⲟⲃⲉⲃ ⲡⲣⲓⲗⲁⲣⲓⲁ, *ib* ⲥⲉ ⲛ̄ⲕⲟⲗⲗⲁⲟ/ ...ⲁⲅⲉⲓ ⲉⲣⲟⲩⲛ ⲉⲡⲧ. (same? or ⲧ. *seal*). *Cf?* ⳁⲱⲱⲃⲉ (ⲧ for ⳁ).

ⲧⲱⲃϩ *SAA²BF*, -ⲃⲁϩ *SF*, ⲧⲃϩ- *SAA²*, ⲧⲉ. *S*, ⲧⲱⲃϩ- *SᵃA* (Zech 8 21), ⲧⲟⲃⲉϩ *SB*, ⲧⲁⲣϩ *Sᶠ*, -ⲃⲁϩ *F* vb **I** intr, *pray, entreat*: Ps 75 12 *B*(*S* ⲉⲣⲏⲧ) εὔχεσθαι, Is 16 12 *B*(*S* ϣⲗⲏⲗ), Mt 6 5 *BF*(*S* ⲇⲟ) προσεύ.; Deu 9 25 *S*(*B* ✝ ϩⲟ) δεῖσθαι; Lu 18 35 *S*(*B* ϣⲁⲧ ⲙⲉⲑⲛⲁⲓ) ἐπαιτεῖν, Job 27 14 *S*(*B* ⲇⲟ) προσαι.; ShR 2 3 17 *S* ⲧⲉⲧⲛⲥⲟⲡⲥ ⲧⲉⲧ̄ⲛ̄ⲧ., BMis 55 *S* ⲉϥⲧ. (var Mun 22 ⲉϥⲥⲟⲡⲥ), C 43 225 *B* ⲉϥϣⲗⲏⲗ ⲉϥⲧ.

II tr, *entreat, console*: MG 25 209 *B* ⲁⲓⲧ. ⲙⲫ✝ ⲉⲩ́. dat, Jer 39 16 *B*(*S* ϣ. ⲉϩⲣⲁⲓ ⲉ-) προσεύ. πρός, 1 Cor 11 13 *B*(*S* ϣ. ⲉ-) ⲡⲣ. dat; Ge 4 26 *B*(*S* = Gk), Ac 22 16 *B*(*S* ⲇⲟ) ἐπικαλεῖσθαι, Ps 131 14 *B* (*S* ⲥⲟⲗⲥⲗ), Lam 1 2 *F*(*B* ✝ ⲛⲟⲙⲧ̄), Z 314 *S* ⲁⲩⲧ. ⲙ̄ⲡⲡⲉ̄ παρακ.; Deu 3 23 *S*(*B* ✝ ϩⲟ), Job 34 20 *SB*, Hos 12 4 *AB* δεῖ. gen; Job 19 17 *B*(*S* ⲕⲱⲣϣ) ἱκετεύειν; Jo 4 10 *A²*(*SBF* = Gk), ViSitz 172 4 36 *S* ⲧⲉⲃϩ ⲟⲩϭⲟⲙ ⲡⲁⲓ αἰτεῖν; Zech 8 22 *SAB* ἐξιλά-σκεσθαι; PS 353 *S* ⲁⲩⲧ. ⲙⲙⲟⲩ saying, Z 304 *S* ⲧⲱⲃⲁϩ ⲙ̄ⲡⲡⲉ̄ ϣⲁⲛⲧⲉϥ-, Mor 43 235 *Sᶠ* ⲁⲩⲧⲁϩⲃⲉⳁ, Mani 2 *A²* ⲛⲥⲧ. ⲡⲛⲟⲩⲥ ⲡⲟⲩⲕⲁ ⲡⲁⲃⲉ ⲁⲃⲁⲗ, Pcod 39 *F* ✝ⲧ. ⲙⲙⲁⲧⲉⲛ (*S* παρακαλεῖ), BSM 42 *B* ⲁⲩⲧ. ⲙⲫ✝ = BMis 388 *S* ⲥⲟⲡⲛ; c ϫⲉⲕⲁⲥ: Wess 15 2 *S* ⲁⲓⲧ. ⲙⲙⲟⲕ ϫ. ⲉⲕⲉ-; c ϩⲓⲛⲁ: Jo 4 47 *F*(*SA²* ⲥⲟⲡⲛ, *B* ✝ ϩⲟ) ἐρωτᾶν ἵνα, Is 30 2 *F* ⲧⲁ-ⲃⲁϩⲧ ϩ. (*S* ⲭⲛⲟⲩ, *B* ϣⲓⲛⲓ) ἐπερ. gen; c ⲧⲁⲣⲉ-: ROC 20 51 *S* ⲧⲉⲃϩ ⲡⲭ̄ⲥ̄ ⲧⲁⲣⲉϥⲥⲟⲟⲩⲧⲛ.

With following preposition.

—— ⲉ-: Dan 6 11 *B* δεῖ. gen; BSM 107 *B* ϥⲛⲁⲧ. ⲉⲡⲉϥⲣⲁⲛ *in his name*, *ib* 100 *B* ⲧ. ⲙⲙⲟⲕ ⲉⲩⲃⲟⲏⲑⲓⲁ *for help*; vbal: Dan 9 13 *B*(*S* ⲥⲟⲡⲥ) δεῖ. inf, Ro 9 3 *B*(*S* ϣ.) ⲉⲩ́. inf; ⲉⲧⲣⲉ-: Si prol *S* παρακ. inf, Lu 8 38 *S*(*B* ✝ ϩⲟ) δεῖ. inf; WTh 180 *S* ⲉϥⲧⲃϩ ⲡⲉϥⲡⲉ̄ ⲉⲧⲣⲉϥ-, RE 9 136 *S* ⲧⲓⲧ....ⲉⲧⲣⲉⲧⲉⲡⲥⲱⲧⲙ, AM 215 *B* ⲛⲁϥⲧ. ⲙⲙⲟϥⲡⲉ ⲉⲑⲣⲉϥϣⲗⲏⲗ.

—— ⲉⲧⲃⲉ-, *for, concerning*: Ps 71 15 *B*(*S* ϣ.) προσεύ. περ́.; 3 Kg 8 52 *B* ἐπικαλ.; Is 55 5 *B*(*S*

= Gk) ἐπ. ἕνεκεν; Mt 6 8 *BF*(*S* = Gk) αἰτ.; CA 98 *S* ⲛ̄ⲧⲉⲟⲩⲁ ⲧⲟⲃϩϥ ⲉⲧⲃⲉ ⲟⲩⲥⲟⲥ.

—— ⲉϫⲛ-, *upon, for* intr: Ez 43 26 *B*(var ⲥⲉⲥ-ⲃⲟϩ) ⲉⲝⲓⲗ. acc, Lev 4 20 *S*(*B* ⲉϩⲣⲏⲓ ⲉⲥ-) ⲉⲝⲓⲗ. περί; MG 25 232 *B* ⲧ. ⲉϫⲱⲓ ✝ⲉⲣ ϣⲁⲩ = Z 317 *S* ϩⲓⲧ̄ⲛ̄ⲡⲉⲕϣⲗⲏⲗ εὐχαῖς σου, *ib* 240 *B* ⲉⲧⲁ ⲩⲧ. ⲉ. ⲟⲩⲡⲉϩ ἐπεύ. dat; Deu 9 18 *S*(*B* ✝ ϩⲟ ⲉⲑⲃⲉ-) δεῖ περί; BM 825 *B* ⲧ. ⲉ. ✝ϩⲓⲣⲏⲛⲏ, BSM 135 *B* ⲉϥⲉⲧ. ⲉϫⲱⲛ ⲛⲁϩⲣⲉⲛⲫ✝; tr: 2 Cor 12 8 *B*(*S* ⲥⲟⲡⲥ ⲉⲑⲃⲉ-) παρακ. ὑπέρ; Ep 201 *Sᵃ* ⲧ. ⲡⲉⲭⲥ̄ ⲁⲕⲛϣⲉⲡⲟⲩⲧⲉ; ⲉϩⲣⲁⲓ, -ⲛⲓ ⲉϫ. intr: Lev 9 7 *S*(*B* ⲉⲑⲃⲉ-) ⲉⲝⲓⲗ. περί; Jer 14 11 *B*(*S* ϣ. ϩⲁ-) προσεύ. περί; Jo 17 9 *B*(*SA²* ⲥⲟⲡⲥ ⲉⲑⲃⲉ-) ⲉⲣ. περί; Miss 4 175 *B* ⲧ. ⲉϩ. ⲉϫⲱⲓ (*cf* 178 ϣ. ⲉϩⲣ. ⲉϫ.); tr *B*: Jer 44 3 προσεύ. πρός...περί; Va 63 5 ⲧ. ⲙⲫ✝ ⲉϩ. ⲉϫⲱⲛ = BMis 371 *S* παρακ., TEuch 1 301 ⲧ. ⲙⲡⲉⲕⲣⲁⲛ ⲉϩ. ⲉϫⲱϥ.

—— ⲛ- dat *S*: COAd 55 ⲛ̄ⲧⲧ. ⲛⲁⲩ ⲛⲥⲉⲟⲩⲱⲙ.

—— ⲛⲥⲁ-, *for B*: Pro 2 3 (*S* ⲙⲟⲩⲧⲉ ⲟⲩⲃⲉ-, *A* ⲙ. ⲁ-) ἐπικαλ. acc; CaiThe 339 ⲛⲁϥⲧ. ⲡⲥⲁⲡⲟⲩⲟⲩ-ϫⲁⲓ(*sc* of his murderers).

—— ⲟⲩⲧⲉ- *B*: Va 57 182 ⲫⲏ ⲉⲧⲧ. ⲟⲩⲧⲱϥ ⲙⲙⲁⲩ-ⲁⲧϥ καθ᾽ ἑαυτὸν εὐ.

—— ϩⲁ-, ϫⲁ-, *on behalf of*: Nu 15 28 *S*(*B* ⲉϫ.) ⲉⲝⲓⲗ. περί; Si 51 16 *S* ἀξιοῦν περί, PSBA 32 249 *S* ⲧ. ϩⲁⲧⲁⲩϫⲛⲉⲓⲥ of fruits, Ep 279 *S* ⲧ. [ⲡ]ⲭ̄ⲥ̄ ϩⲁⲣⲟⲛ, BSM 65 *B* sim.

—— ϩⲁ- *B*, *to*: Ac 8 24 (*S* ⲥⲟⲡⲥ acc) δεῖ. πρός; ⲉⲡϣⲱⲓ ϩⲁ-: Ps 31 6 (*S* ϣ. ⲉ-) προσεύ. πρός; ⲉϩⲣⲏⲓ ϩⲁ-: Nu 11 2 (*S* ⲇⲟ) εὐ. πρός.

—— nn m *SBF*, -ⲁϩ *S*(*PS*)*F*, *prayer*: 3 Kg 9 3 *B*, Est C 10 *S*, Is 1 15 *BF*-ⲁϩ (*S* ⲥⲟⲡⲥ) δέησις; Lev 23 27 *SB* ἐξιλασμός; Job 6 8 *S*(*B* ⲉⲣ ⲉⲧⲓⲛ) αἴτη-σις; Is 30 7 *F*(*S* ⲥⲟⲗⲥⲗ, *B* ⲛⲟⲙⲧ̄) παράκλησις; 1 Tim 2 1 *S*(*B* ⲥⲉⲙⲓ) ἔντευξις; CaiEuch 361 *B* πρεσ-βεία; BG 46 *S* ⲡⲧ. ⲡⲧⲉⲥⲙⲉⲧⲁⲛⲟⲓⲁ, AM 214 *B* ✝-ⲡⲣⲟⲥⲉⲩⲭⲏ ⲡⲉⲙⲡⲓⲧ., MG 25 276 *B* ✝ⲉⲩⲭⲏ of gos-pel ⲙⲉⲛⲉⲛⲥⲁⲡⲓⲧ. = BIF 13 98 *S* ϣ., BSM 55 *B* ⲡⲉⲡⲧ. = BMis 409 *S* ⲛⲥⲟⲡⲥⲛ, BM 1247 159 *B* ⲛⲓⲧ. = TEuch 2 308 طلبات (*cf* Ryl 430 ⲣⲙⲑ).

ⲣⲉϥⲧ. *SA²B*, ⲣⲉⲙⲉϥⲧ. *A²*(Jo), *one who prays, suppliant*: Mk 10 46 *B*(*S* ϫⲓ ⲙ̄ⲛⲧⲛⲁ), Jo 9 8 *SA²* (*B* ϣⲁⲧ ⲙⲉⲑⲛⲁⲓ) προσαίτης; Si 40 31 *S* ἐπαίτησις BMar 199 *S* πτωχός; R 1 4 41 *S* mendicus, BSM 49 *B* = BMis 399 *S* προστατης, ShMIF 23 21 *S* ⲣⲙⲙⲁⲟ opp ⲣ.; AP 23 *A²* ✝ⲟⲉⲓ ⲡⲣ.; ⲙ̄ⲛⲧⲣ. *S*, *beggary*: ShC 73 134 ⲡϣⲓⲡⲉ ⲛ̄ⲧⲙ.

ϫⲓⲛⲧ. *B*, *entreaty*: Va 58 132 ⲟⲩϫ. ⲉϧⲟⲩⲛ ⲛⲁ-ϩⲣⲉⲛⲫ✝.

ⲧⲁⲕ *v* ⲧⲱⲕ *be strong sf*.

✝ⲕ *S*, ⲧⲓⲕ *F* nn *v* ⲧⲱⲕ *kindle sf*.

ⲦⲞⲔ, -ⲥ S, ⲧⲁⲕ Sf, ⲑⲟⲕ, ⲑⲱⲕ B nn m, *knife, razor*: Nu 6 5 SB, Is 7 20 SB, Ez 5 1 SB ξυρόν; 1 Kg 1 11 Sf σίδηρος; P 44 59 S ⲛⲧ., K 135 B ⲡⲓⲑ. (var ⲑⲱⲕ) موس; scribe's *knife*: Jer 43 23 S(C 42 80)B ξ.; surgeon's: Va 58 173 B σιδήριον; ib 63 103 B need of ⲑ. ⲉϥⲟⲏⲙ τομή; ShWess 9 138 S ⲡⲥⲁⲉⲓⲛ ...ϣⲱⲧ...ϩⲙⲡⲧ., Miss 8 263 Sf ϯⲛⲁⲟⲩⲁϫⲉ(f) ϧⲙⲡⲓⲧ., DeV 1 148 B sore opened with ⲡⲓⲑ., C 43 129 B ⲑ. ⲛⲕⲟⲣⲉⲅⲥ to cut out tongue, BMis 541 S ⲧⲟⲥ for same, ib 556 S ⲧ. ⲙⲡⲉⲛⲡⲉ...ⲉⲅⲓⲧⲉ ⲙⲡⲥⲱⲙⲁ, C 43 176 B body gashed with ϩⲁⲛⲟ. ⲙⲉⲛⲓⲡⲓ, ib 86 191 B ϩⲁⲛⲟ. with edge like saw.

ⲦⲰⲔ SAA²F, -ⲕⲉ A(once), ⲧⲉⲕ-, ⲧⲟⲕ⸗ S, ⲧⲏⲕ† SAA²F, ⲑⲏⲕ† B(once, but v below ⲧⲁⲕ) vb I intr, *be strong, firm, thick*: Jos 1 6, Mt 9 12†(B ϫⲟⲣ) ἰσχύειν, Si 15 18† ἰσχυρός; Hos 12 4 A(B ⲉⲣ ϫⲱⲣⲓ) δύνασθαι; Nu 8 4†(B ϫⲟⲣ sic l as Deu 32 13), Miss 4 587 ⲡⲉⲟⲩⲉⲣⲣⲉⲡⲉ ⲉⲩⲧ.† στερεός; Ps 26 14(B ⲧⲁϫⲣⲟ) κραταιοῦν; Pro 28 3† SA ἀνδρεῖος; Ps 118 70 (B ⲥⲱⲥ) τυροῦν; ib 143 13† (B ϣⲟⲧ) παχύς; Sa 7 2 πηγνύναι; Lu 5 31† (B ϫ.) ὑγιαίνειν; ShZ 638 ships hauled with ϩⲉⲛⲛⲟⲩⲥ ⲉⲩⲧ.†, WS 97 ⲛⲕⲁⲙ... ⲉⲩⲧ.† *in good condition*, PLond 4 438 sailors ⲉⲩⲧ.† sim, J 66 21 ⲉⲓⲧ.† ϩⲙⲡⲁⲥⲱⲙⲁ, ib 91 20 tended him ϣⲁⲛⲧⲉⲛⲟⲩⲥⲱⲙⲁ ⲧ., Mani 1 A² ⲡϩⲏⲧ ⲧ.† ⲙⲡⲉϥⲕⲓⲙ, Mor 18 101 cripple healed ⲁϥⲧ. ⲛⲟⲉ ⲛⲣⲱⲙⲉ ⲛⲓⲙ, DeV 2 76 B dialogue between 2 philosophers ⲉⲩⲑ.† *well-liking* (?).

II tr, *strengthen, confirm, stiffen*: Job 15 7 (B ⲥⲱⲥ) πηγν.; ib 10 10 (B do) τυρ.; Bor 260 98 ⲧⲉⲕ ⲡⲉⲕϩⲏⲧ & know Christ, Hall 98 send beam ϫⲉ(ⲉ)ⲡⲁⲧⲟⲟⲕ ⲡⲉⲙⲁⲁⲧ *fix loom*; refl: Ex 20 20 (B ϫⲉⲙ ⲛⲟⲙϯ), Mt 9 22 (var ⲧ. ⲛϩⲏⲧ, B do) θαρσεῖν; 2 Kg 10 12 (var not refl) ἀνδρίζεσθαι; Mor 40 29 to martyrs ⲧ. ⲙⲙⲱⲧⲛ =ib 39 39 Sf ϫⲣⲁ ⲙ. = C 43 58 B ⲥⲣⲟ ⲙ.

With prep & advb. c ⲉ- *dat commodi*: LMär 1 ⲁⲡⲉⲩϩⲏⲧ ⲧ. ⲉⲣⲟⲟⲩ = C 43 40 B ⲧⲁϫⲣⲟ; refl: BMis 14 ⲧ. ⲙⲙⲱⲧⲛ ⲉⲡⲓⲣⲱⲙⲉ *stand firm against*, BM 534 ⲧ. ⲙⲙⲟⲕ ⲉⲡⲁⲡⲉⲧⲛⲏⲩ *be firm* (?) *as to the* (men) *of Atfîh*; c ⲁⲣⲉⲧ⸗: Cl 25 4 A phoenix ⲧⲱⲕⲉ ⲁⲣⲉⲧϥ ϩⲓⲧϩⲛⲟⲩⲉ (reading ? ἐπιστάς), Mani 1 A² ⲡⲓⲕⲟⲥⲙⲟⲥ...ⲧ.† ⲁⲣⲉⲧϥ *is established*, ib 2 A² ⲛϥⲧ. ⲁⲣⲉⲧϥ in fire; c ⲉⲣⲟϩⲛ, *persist, be confident*: Lu 22 59 (B ⲧⲁϫ. ⲛⲧⲉⲛ-), Ac 12 15 (B do) διισχυρίζεσθαι, Lu 23 5 (B ϫⲉⲙ ϫⲟⲙ) ἐπισχύειν; Am 2 15 (B ⲟⲣⲓ ⲉⲣⲁⲧ⸗) ὑφιστάναι; Miss 4 653 ⲡⲉϥ(sic)ⲧ†. ⲉϥ. ⲉϥⲁⲣⲡⲁ συνεχῶς; Z 312 ⲁϥⲧ. ⲉϥ. ⲉϥⲥⲱ καρτερεῖν, BMar 105 ⲁϥⲧ. ⲉϥ. ⲉϥⲡⲏⲧ προσκ., ALR '93 524 ⲁⲥⲧ. ⲉϥ. ⲉⲥⲟⲩⲱϣ ⲉⲧⲁⲕⲉ ⲧⲉϥⲯⲩⲭⲏ (Job 2 9 Gk); ⲉϥ. ⲉ-, ⲉϫⲛ-: 1 Kg 20 12 ἀνακρίνειν (var ἐξερευνᾶν); Miss 8 231 unable ⲉⲧ. ⲉϥ. ⲉⲛⲉⲓⲃⲁⲥⲁ-

ⲛⲟⲥ *endure*, Bor 263 21 ⲉϥⲧ.† ⲉϥ. ⲉⲭⲙⲡϣⲁϫⲉ *relying on*; tr (or ? v ⲧⲱϫⲉ): Win 7 if ye have naught against him ⲙⲁⲓⲧ. ϩⲱⲃ ⲉϥ. ⲉⲣⲟϥ, BMis 131 ⲉⲧⲟⲩⲧ. ⲙⲙⲟⲟⲩ ⲉϥ. ⲉⲧⲭⲟ ϩⲓⲧⲛⲡ(ⲉ)ⲛⲕⲱⲧ; as nn: BHom 54 ⲛⲧ. ⲉϥ. of Susanna ἔνστασις; c ⲉϩⲣⲁⲓ ⲉϫⲛ-: Pro 29 29† SA θαρ. ἐπί; ⲉϩⲣ. ϩⲛ-: Mor 17 21 her heart ⲧ. ⲉϥ. ⲛϩⲏⲧⲥ like stone ἀποπηγν.; WTh 149 nails ⲧⲟⲕⲟϥ ⲉϥ. ϩⲙⲡⲉϥⲥⲱⲙⲁ.

† ⲧ., *give strength, fortify*: R 1 1 55 ⲛⲧⲉⲧⲛϯ ⲧ. ⲛⲛⲉⲧⲛⲯⲩⲭⲏ ἐνισχύειν; Job 4 4(B ϯ ⲛⲟⲙϯ)θάρσος περιτιθ.; 2 Macc 6 19 A ὑπομένειν (prob); ϫⲓ ⲧ., *take courage*: Job 17 9 (B ϭⲓ ϫⲟⲙ) θ. ἀναλαμβάνειν; ϣⲥ ⲛⲧ., *blow, slap* (?): Mor 41 186 ⲁϥϯ ⲡⲁϥ ⲛⲟⲩϣ. saying Shut thy mouth, ib 46 18, 26 sim (or ? belongs to ⲧ. *throw*).

ⲧ. ⲛϩⲏⲧ SAA²F, *be strong of heart, take courage* (cf ⲧⲱⲧ ⲛϩ.): Ge 35 17 (B ϫⲉⲙ ⲛ.), Pro 1 21 SA (B ⲙⲟⲩⲛ), Mt 14 27 (B ϫⲉⲙ ⲛ., F ϭⲉⲙ ϭⲁⲙ), Jo 16 33 SA²(B do), Ep 592 B 8 ⲉϥⲧ.† ⲛϩ. θαρ.; Is 14 6†(B ⲑⲱⲧ ⲛϩ.), Zech 14 11 SA(B do) πείθειν; Ac 27 22 (B ⲱⲟⲩ ⲛϩ.) εὐθυμεῖν, Sa 18 6 ἐπευ.; 1 Cor 10 5 (B ϯ ⲙⲁϯ) εὐδοκεῖν, Si 29 26† εὐδοκίαν ἔχειν; Is 22 3 (B ϫⲟⲣⲓ ⲛϩ.) ἰσχ.; Deu 31 23 (B ϭⲣⲟ) ἀνδ.; PS 8 ⲁϥⲧ. ⲛϩ. ⲛϭⲓ ⲙⲙⲁⲑⲏⲧⲏⲥ, AP 55 A² ⲛⲧⲁⲣⲉϥⲧ. ⲛϩ. he said, Miss 4 829 ϯⲧ.† ⲛϩ. ϫⲉ- their left hand (Mt 6 3); c ⲉϫⲛ-, *rely upon, be content with*: Z 315 ⲉϥⲧ.† ⲛϩ. ⲉϫⲛⲧⲉϥⲡⲟⲗⲓⲧⲓⲁ θ. dat; BHom 7 ⲉⲩⲧ.† ⲛϩ. ⲉϫⲛⲑⲉⲗⲡⲓⲥ νευροῦσθαι; Miss 4 710 ⲉϥⲧ.† ⲛϩ. ⲉϫⲙⲡⲉⲛⲧⲁϥϫⲟⲟϥ in Gospel, J 75 40 ⲁⲛⲧ. ⲛϩ. ⲉϫⲱⲕ *satisfied with thee* (cf ib 38 ⲁⲛⲧⲱⲧ ⲛϩ. ⲉϫⲱⲕ); c ⲛ- gen, *rely upon*: Deu 28 52† (B ⲭⲱ ⲛϩⲏⲧ) πειθ. ἐπί, Phil 1 14† SF(B do) π. dat; c ϩⲛ- sim: Phil 1 6† (var ⲛ-, B ⲑⲏⲧ ⲉϫⲛ-, F ⲧ.† ⲛϩ. ⲉϫ.) π. acc; as nn, *confidence*: Pro 22 19 SA ἐλπίς fiducia, Z 282 ⲡⲉϥⲧ. ⲛϩ. ⲛϣⲡⲓⲣⲉ paral παρρησία; ϯ ⲧ. ⲛϩ., *give conf.*: Est C 23 θαρσύνειν; Sa 12 19 εὔελπιν ποιεῖν; PS 219 ⲁϥϯ ⲧ. ⲛϩ. ⲛⲁϥ, BIF 13 102 sim = MG 25 285 B ϯ ⲛⲟⲙϯ, Mor 16 33 sim (var BMis 197 ϯ ⲙⲛⲧϩⲁⲣ-ϩⲏⲧ), R 1 5 26 ⲁϥϯ ⲧ. ⲛϩ. ⲛⲁϥ ⲉⲣⲟⲩⲛ ⲉⲧⲙⲛⲧⲙⲁⲣ-ⲧⲩⲣⲟⲥ; ϫⲓ ⲧ. ⲛϩ., *take courage*: Z 331 ⲉⲛⲉϫⲓ ⲛⲁⲛ ⲛⲟⲩⲧ. θάρσος λαμβάνειν; Miss 4 655.

ⲧⲁⲕ Sᵃ, ⲑⲱⲕ, ⲑⲟⲕ B nn m, *something fixed, mast*: B v ⲑⲱⲕ & add C 43 212 martyr hanged ϩⲓⲭⲉⲛ-ⲡⲓⲑⲟⲕ of ship = P 4893 118 صاري المركب; CO 148 Sᵃ limits of property ⲧⲭⲏⲣⲉ...ϫⲓⲡⲛⲧ. ⲛϫⲟⲓ *pillar, prop* (?) *of wall*.

Confusion possible between this, next words & ⲧⲱⲕⲉ, ⲧⲱϫⲉ. Cf also ⲧⲱϫⲥ.

ⲦⲰⲔ (S)AF, ⲧⲱϫⲉ(BG)S, -ⲕⲉ, ⲧⲟⲕⲉ A, ⲧⲉⲕ- S, ⲧⲱⲕ- A, ⲧⲉⲕⲥ S, ⲧⲏⲕⲥ SA, ⲣ ⲥ ⲧⲁⲕ- S vb tr *throw, cast*: Pro 1 14 A(S ⲛⲟⲩϫⲉ, B ϩⲓⲟⲩⲓ) βάλλειν; BAp

98 *S* face ⲧⲏⲕ (*l* ⲧⲉⲕ) ⲟⲩⲟⲉⲓⲛ, Miss 1 406 *S* ⲉⲧⲧⲉⲕ
ⲃⲟⲗⲟⲥ ⲉⲩϭⲱⲃⲉ *casting dice* ;   c ⲉ-, *throw at, into*:
Si 22 21 *A*(*S* ⲛ.) β. ἐπί, Cl 45 6 *A* ⲁⲩⲧⲱⲕⲉ ⲡⲇⲁ-
ⲛⲓⲏⲗ ⲁⲡϣⲏⲓ β. εἰς, Ex 2 3 *A*(*B* ϩ. ⲉϩⲣⲏⲓ ⲉ-) ⲉⲙⲃ.
εἰς ; Jo 10 33 *A* ⲧⲱⲕ ⲱⲡⲉ (*SB* ϩ., *A²* ⲛ.) λιθάζειν ;
TU 43 3 *A* ⲧⲱⲕⲉ ⲡⲡⲉⲕϯⲃⲉ ⲁⲡⲉⲓϥⲧ (*cf* Jo 20 27 β.),
ShA 2 19 *S* ⲡⲗⲁⲟⲥ ⲧⲉⲕ ⲱⲡⲉ ⲉⲣⲟⲟⲩ (*cf* Jos 7 26),
ShA 1 9 *S* ⲧⲥⲟⲟⲩϩⲉ...ⲧⲉⲕⲥ ⲉⲩⲟⲩⲟⲟⲧⲉ, ShC 73
161 *S* shall carry corpse's head & feet ⲡⲥⲉⲧⲧⲟⲕϥ
ⲉⲣⲟⲟⲩ, *ib* C 42 78 *S* ⲁⲩⲧⲉⲕϥ ⲉⲡⲧⲟⲡ of Abraham,
ib 25 *S* ⲡⲁⲣⲟⲟⲩϣ ⲧ.† ⲉⲡⲏⲧⲉ (*cf* 1 Pet 5 7 ⲛ.);   c
ⲉⲃⲟⲗ, ⲁⲃ. *SAF*, *cast out, put forth*: Pro 24 58 *A*
(*S* ⲛ.) ἐκβ., *ib* 17 27 *A*(*S* do) προϊέναι ; 2 Macc 6
4 *A* ϭⲓⲁⲙⲉ ⲉⲧⲧ.† ⲁⲃ. ἑταῖραι (?, *cf* ⲡⲏϫ ⲉⲃ.); Nu
17 8 *S*(*B* ⲫⲉⲣ ⲉⲃ.) ἐξανθεῖν ; Is 27 6 *S*(*B* ⲣⲱⲧ ⲉⲃ.)
βλαστεῖν ; Deu 32 15 *S* (cit Mus 40 278, var ⲛ., *A*
Cl ϯ, *B* ϩ.) ἀπολακτίζειν ; 1 Kg 17 20 *S*(*B* ⲱϣ)
ἀλαλάζειν ; BG 38 *S* ⲁϥⲧⲱϭⲉ ⲡⲡⲟⲩϭⲟⲙ ⲉⲃ. ϩⲛⲧ-
ⲙⲁⲁⲩ (*cf ib* 42 ⲧⲱⲕⲙ), ShLouvre 1666 *S* ⲧⲉⲕⲟⲩ
ⲉⲃ. if they repent not, FR 164 *S* ⲧⲉⲕ ⲉⲃⲣⲏϭⲉ ⲉⲃ., Z
611 *S* onyx ⲧⲉⲕ ⲉⲓⲁⲗ ⲉⲃ., BMis 4 *S* pillars ⲧⲉⲕ ⲉⲃⲓⲱ
ⲉⲃ.;   refl : Lam 2 6 *F*(*B* ⲫⲱⲣϣ) διαπετάζειν ; JKP
2 180 *S* ⲁϥⲧⲟⲕϥ ⲉⲃ. ϩⲓⲡⲉϥϩⲁⲣⲙⲁ, PLond 4 507 *S*
woman ⲡⲧⲁⲥⲧⲟⲕⲥ ⲉⲃ. ⲁⲥⲡⲱⲧ (obscure) ;   intr : BG
37 *S* ⲉⲥⲧⲱϭⲉ ⲉⲃ. *swelling out* (?)because of the Πρού-
νεικος within her ;   c ⲁϩⲟⲩⲛ *A*, *cast in, interject* ;
Pro 26 18 (*S* ⲛ.) προβ.; Ex 6 7 ⲧⲟⲕⲉ ⲁϩ. ϩⲁ-(*B* ϩ.
ⲉϩ.) εἰσφέρειν εἰς ;   c ⲁϩⲣⲏⲓ ⲁϫⲛ- *A*, *cast down* :
Ex 4 3 (*B* ⲃⲟⲣⲃⲉⲣ ϩⲓϫ.) ῥίπτειν ἐπί ;   ⲣⲉϥⲧⲕ- *S*,
thrower : Ge 21 20 ⲣ. ⲥⲟⲧⲉ (*B* ϩ.) τοξότης .

p c *S*: ShP 130² 104 congregations filled with ⲁⲩ
ⲁϩⲟⲙ ϩⲓⲧⲁⲕⲟⲩⲱ ϩⲓϩⲉⲡⲡⲁⲣⲁⲃⲟⲗⲏ *answer-throwing,
retort.*

ϯⲕⲉ, ϯⲕ-, ⲧⲉⲕϥ, ⲧⲉⲕⲧ (once) *A* vb tr, meanings
as last : Jon 1 7 ϯⲕ ⲕⲗⲏⲣⲟⲥ (*S* ⲛ., *B* ϩ.) β., Hab 1
17 (*B* diff) ἀμφίβ.   c ⲁ- : Cl 24 5 ϯ. ⲁⲡⲕⲁϩ (var
ⲥⲓⲧⲉ) β. εἰς ; Ex 1 22 ⲧⲉⲕⲧ[ⲟⲩ ῥίπτειν εἰς ; TU 43
3 ⲧⲉⲕϥ ⲁⲡϣⲧⲉⲕⲟ ; ⲁϩⲟⲩⲛ ⲁ- : Zech 5 8 (*S* ⲛ., *B*
ⲃⲟⲣ.) ῥ. εἰς ;   c ⲁϫⲛ- : Ob 11 (*S* ⲛ., *B* ϩ.) β. ἐπί,
Pro 16 5 (*S* ϯ) ἐμβ.;   c ⲙⲛ- : TU 43 21 ⲁⲩⲧⲉⲕⲟⲩ
ⲛⲉⲙⲉⲓ at table ;   c ⲁⲃⲁⲗ : Pro 22 10 (*S* ⲛ. ⲉⲃ.) ἐκβ.,
Cl 44 3 ϯⲕ ⲡⲉⲓ ⲁⲃ. ἀποβ., *ib* 57 2 ϯⲕⲧⲏⲡⲉ ⲁⲃ. ἐκρ.;
Hab 3 17 (*B* ⲙⲟⲩⲛⲕ) ἐκλείπειν ; Hos 7 14 ⲁⲩϯⲕ
ⲗⲓⲗⲱⲓ ⲁⲃ. (*S* ⲛ., *B* ⲉϣ-) ὀλολύζειν ; Zeph 3 19 (*B*
ϩ. ⲉⲃ.) ἀπωθεῖν ; El 46 ϯⲕ ⲥⲉⲉⲧⲉ ⲁⲃ. ;   c ⲁϩⲣⲏⲓ :
Jon 2 11 (*S* ⲛ., *B* ϩ.) ἐκβ.; Zech 11 13 (*SB* do)
κατατίθεναι, Joel 2 20 (*SB* do) ἐξωθ. ;   ⲣⲉϥϯⲕ
ⲥⲁⲧⲉ : Am 2 15 (*B* ⲣⲉϥϩⲓ ⲥ.) τοξότης.

V AZ 63 147.

ⲧⲱⲕ *SF*, ⲑ. *B*, ⲧⲱϭ *SAF*, -ϫ *S* (Saq), ⲧⲟϫⲓ *B*
(Ez), -ϭⲉ *F* (ⲣⲉϥⲧ.), ⲧⲱⲕ- *S*, ⲧⲁϭ- *F*, ⲧⲟⲕϥ, ⲧⲁⲕϥ,
ⲧⲟϭϥ *S* vb **A I** intr, *kindle* fire, *stoke, heat* oven &c,
c ⲉ- obj: Dan 3 46 *SB*, Hos 7 4 *B*(*A* diff) καίειν, Dan

3 22 *B*(*S* ⲧⲙϩⲟ) ἐκκ.; Bor 264 39 *S* ⲉⲩⲧ. ⲉⲧⲉϩⲣⲱ ⲛ
ⲥⲁϭⲉ, DeV 2 82 *B* sim ⲛⲑⲏⲛ, C 43 70 *B* ⲑ. ⲉⲩⲑⲣⲓⲣ
ϩⲉⲛϩⲣⲁⲛϣⲉ, BMar 37 *S* ⲃⲁⲇⲉ ⲧ. ....ⲉⲧⲉⲧⲣⲓⲣ ⲛⲥⲉⲥⲁϩⲧⲉ
ϩⲁⲣⲟⲥ, Worr 237 *S* sim of baker's oven, EW 28 *B*
knew not ⲛⲑ. ⲉϥⲥⲓⲱⲟⲩⲛⲓ, BIF 14 117 *S* ⲁⲩⲧ. ⲉⲧⲁ-
ϩⲛ ⲛⲣⲟⲙⲡⲧ, P 129¹⁶ 51 *S* ⲣⲁϩⲧⲉ...ⲧ. ⲉⲣⲟⲥ ;   c
ⲉϫⲛ- *kindle fire at, above* (or *? against* with hostile
intent): Ann '17 146 *S* cast martyrs into bath-oven
ⲛⲥⲉⲧ. ⲉϫⲱⲟⲩ, AM 49 *B* ⲁⲩⲑ. ⲉϫⲱϥ (*sc* oven) ⲛϩⲁⲛ-
ϣⲉ ;   c ϩⲁ-, ϩⲁ-, *k. below* : WTh 175 *S* cast him
into ⲟⲩⲣⲓ. ϯ ⲕⲱϩⲧ ⲛⲁϥ, ⲧⲱϭ ϩⲁⲣⲟϥ 3 days, DeV 1
88 *B* ⲭⲁⲗⲕⲓⲟⲛ...ⲑ. ϩⲁⲣⲟϥ, Eccl 7 7 *F* thorns ⲉⲩⲧ.
ϩⲁⲗⲁϭⲟⲩ (*S* ⲙⲟⲩϩ, Gk om), BKU 1 1 ⲣⲟ *S* ⲉⲥⲧ. ϩⲁ-
ⲟⲩϩⲣⲱ.

II tr *SB*, *stoke, heat* : Dan 3 19 *B* ἐκκαι.; AM
219 *B* ⲑ. ⲡⲟⲩⲛⲓϣϯ ⲛϩⲣⲱ, BM 1186 *S* ⲧ. ⲛⲉⲧⲣⲓⲣ.

—— *B* nn m, *fuel* : K 132 ⲡⲓⲑ. ⲯⲁ.

ⲙⲁ ⲛⲧ., ⲑ. *SB*, *stoke-hole* of bath : C 89 10 *B*
ὑποκαύστρα ; GMar 181 *S*, Mor 46 15 *S*, AM 44
B, C 43 143 *B*.

ⲛⲧ.¹, ⲉⲛⲧ.², (ⲉ)ⲙⲧ.³ *S* nn m, *oven* of bath : Mor
17 13¹, *ib* 15² κάμινος ; Miss 8 188¹, *ib* 251², BMar
14³ (var AZ 25 115¹), KroppK 25 *Sᵃ* ⲡⲉⲛⲧⲱⲕⲉ.

ⲣⲉϥⲧ., ⲑ., ⲗⲉⲙⲧⲟϭⲉ *SBF*, *stoker* : Mor 17 17 *S*
ἐκκαυστής ; MG 25 195 *B*, CMSS 49 *F*.

B vb *bake*, **I** intr (ⲧⲱϭ *SF*, -ϭⲉ *S*, ⲧⲱⲕ *SF*, ⲑ.
B): 1 Kg 8 13 *S* πέσσειν ; ShC 73 54 *S* ⲉⲩϩⲱⲧⲉ ⲛ
ⲉⲩⲧ. at time of bread-making, Leyd 206 *S* if Pentecost go by ⲙⲡⲁⲧⲟⲩⲧ., ST 363 *S* ⲛⲥⲛⲁⲩ ⲛⲣⲟⲟⲩ ⲛ-
ⲧⲱⲛ, Cai 8010 *S* bakers ⲉⲧⲣⲉⲩⲧ.   **II** tr : Ge 19
3 *S*(*B* ⲫⲓⲥⲓ), Ex 16 23 *S*(*B* ϫⲟϫⲓ) ; Lev 26 26 *SF*
(BM 1221 ϭⲁⲧ, *B* ϫⲱϫ), Ez 46 20 *B* ⲡ.; BMis 503
S ⲁⲕⲧⲟϭⲧ like egg ⲉϣⲁⲥⲡⲓⲥⲉ (var PMich 1289 c
ⲧⲟⲕⲧ), Mor 27 23 *F* ⲧ. ⲛⲣⲛⲁⲓⲕ, Hall 107 *S* ⲛⲟⲉⲓⲕ
ⲛⲧⲉⲛⲧⲁⲕϥ, Ep 309 *S* corn ⲁⲩⲧⲟⲕϥ ⲛⲕⲁⲕⲉ, PRain
4711 *S* ⲉⲓⲧⲱⲕ ⲉⲩϣ(ⲏ)ⲙ ⲛⲕⲟⲩϥⲟⲛ, BM 695 *Sᶠ* ⲡⲉ-
ⲕⲟⲩϥⲟⲛ ⲉⲛⲧⲱⲕ ⲙⲙⲁⲩ ϩⲉⲛⲧⲥⲉⲕⲱⲧ, *ib* 1179 *S* ϩⲣⲱ
ⲛⲧⲱⲕ ⲕⲟⲩϥⲟⲛ ;   as nn m, *baking* : Hos 7 4 *A*(*B*
ⲑ. vb) πέψις (?) ; ShC 73 93 *S* ⲡⲥⲛⲏ ⲙⲛⲧ., Wess
18 16 *S* rubric ⲡⲥⲁⲃⲃⲁⲧⲟⲛ ⲉϫⲙⲛⲧ., Leyd 206 *S* sim.

ⲙⲁ ⲛⲧ., ⲑ. *SB*, *bakery* : Miss 4 584 *S* ⲁⲣⲧⲟⲕⲟ-
ⲡⲉⲓⲟⲛ, ST 167 *S* ⲁⲣⲧⲟⲕⲟⲗⲗⲓⲟⲛ · ⲡⲙ.; Ez 46 23 *B*
μαγειρεῖον ; ShC 73 143 *S* rules for ⲡⲙ., Ep 466
S ⲛⲣⲓ ⲙⲡⲙ., J 106 130 *S* 4th part in ⲙ. bequeathed,
Saq '09 p 101 *S* ⲡⲓⲱⲧ (ⲙ)ⲡⲙⲁ ⲡⲧⲱⲝ.

ⲧⲁⲕⲉ *S* nn, related to ⲧ. *bake* : Ryl 280 send the
watchman & ass ⲛϥⲟⲩⲁϩ ⲧ. ⲡⲁⲓ ⲛⲥⲟⲩⲧⲱϭ the loaves.

ϯⲕ *S*, ⲑⲓⲕ *B*, ⲧⲓⲕ *F* nn m, *spark* : Si 11 34, Is 1
31 (*B* ϭⲱⲣ), Ez 1 7 (*B* ϣⲁϩ, var ϫⲉⲃⲥ), C 89 25 *B*
ⲟⲩϩ. ⲡϫⲣⲱⲙ cast into threshing floor, BHom 42
ϯⲕ in ὕλη will burn it σπινθήρ ; Br 227 ⲟⲩϯⲕ ⲡⲟⲩⲟⲉⲓⲛ, ShA 1 151 small ϯⲕ or ϫⲃⲃⲉⲥ ⲧⲣⲉⲟⲩⲛⲟϭ
ⲛϣⲁϩ ϣⲱⲡⲉ, Mor 24 18 *F* ⲧ. ⲛⲕⲱϩⲧ.

ⲦⲀⲔⲞ *SB*, ⲧⲉ. *S*ᵃ *AA*², ⲧⲁⲕⲁ *F*, ⲧⲁⲕⲉ- *SBF*, ⲧⲉⲕⲉ-, ⲧⲉⲕⲁ- *A*², ⲧⲁⲕⲟⲊ *SB*, ⲧⲉⲕⲁⲊ *AA*², ⲧⲁⲕⲁⲊ *F*, ⲧⲁⲕⲏⲩ(ⲧ)† *S*, -ⲏⲟⲩⲧ† *B* vb **I** tr, *destroy, lose* & many related meanings : Ps 142 12 *SB*, Jo 18 9 *SA*²*BF*(P 129¹⁸ 124), MG 25 19 *B* ship ⲁϥⲧ. ⲙⲡⲓⲁⲟⲩⲓⲏ, AP 9 *A*² ἀπολλύναι, Pro 11 17 *SAB* ἐξολ.; Jer 13 9 *SB* φθεί-ρειν, Is 36 10 *SBF* διαφθ.,Ge 6 12 *S*(*B* ⲥⲱϥ) καταφθ.; Job 5 2 *SB* ἀναιρεῖσθαι, Pro 1 19 *SA*(*B* ⲱⲗⲓ) ἀφαι., Ps 39 14 *S*(*B* ϥⲱⲧⲉ ⲉⲃ.) ἐξαι. ; Jer 29 4 *SB*, Mt 6 16 *SB* ἀφανίζειν; Ex 23 8 *SB* λυμαίνειν; Deu 28 24 *SB* ἐκτρίβειν; Ge 31 39 *S*(*B* ⲟⲩⲱⲙ) -άλωτος; Jo 8 40 *F* (PMich 3521, *SA*² ⲙⲟⲩⲟⲩⲧ, *B* ϣⲟⲩⲧⲉⲃ) ἀποκτείνειν; Ap 7 3 *S*(*B* = Gk) ἀδικεῖν; Deu 24 17 *S*(*B* ⲕⲱⲗⲝ) ἐκκλίνειν; Lev 26 16 *S*(*B* ⲃⲱⲗ ⲉⲃⲟⲗ) ἐκτήκειν; Job 20 19 *S*(*B* ⲣⲱⲗⲉⲙ) θλᾶν; PS 158 *S* ⲁⲧⲉⲕⲟⲩⲡⲁⲙ ⲧⲁⲕⲉ ⲧⲙⲁⲧⲟⲩ (OdSolom 22 7 ‏ܠܡܚ‎), ShA 1 59 *S* ⲁⲩⲧⲁⲕⲉ ⲣⲁⲣ ⲙⲡⲁⲣⲑⲉⲛⲟⲥ, Mani 1 *A*² (ⲛ)ⲡⲓⲧⲉⲕⲁⲕ, BMis 149 *S* ⲛϥⲧⲁⲕⲉ ⲧⲙⲉ ⲛⲩϭⲉⲉⲗⲉ ⲛⲣⲁⲛ, HL 120 *B* inquired ⲁⲛⲁⲟⲩⲟⲛ ⲧⲁⲕⲉ ⲁⲥⲟⲩⲓ, J 70 57 *S* ⲛϥ-ⲕⲱⲧⲉ ⲛⲥⲁⲧ. ⲗⲁⲁⲩ ⲛⲛ̄ϣⲁϫⲉ herein written, Hall 88 *S* ⲙⲡⲣⲧ. ⲧⲉⲕⲡⲣⲟⲟⲉⲣⲉⲥⲓⲥ ⲙⲡⲧⲟⲡⲟⲥ (*good*) *intention toward the* τόπος, BodlCopt insc 341 *S*ᵃ ⲛ]ⲥⲓⲙ ⲧⲉⲕⲟ ⲙ[; ⲧ. ⲙⲡⲣⲏⲧ, *destroy, corrupt mind*: Is 46 12 *B*(*S* ⲥⲱⲣⲙ), Eccl 7 8 *SF* ἀπολ. καρδίαν; 1 Cor 15 33 *SB* φθ. ; BMis 15 *S* devil's lies ⲧⲁⲕⲉ ⲡⲣ. ⲛ̄-ⲡⲉⲓⲕⲟⲟⲩⲉ, C 43 211 *B* ⲉⲧⲁϥⲧ. ⲙ̄ⲡⲣ. ⲛⲛⲁⲓ ; ⲥ ⲉ-, *against* : Jer 50 3 *B* συμβάλλειν πρός ; ⲉⲣⲟⲩⲛ ⲉ-: ShA 2 159 *S* ⲙⲉⲩⲧⲁⲕⲉ ⲡⲣ. ⲡⲗⲁⲁⲩ ⲉ. ⲉⲡⲉϥⲉⲣⲏⲩ; ⲉ- *dat commodi* : 1 Tim 6 5 †*S*(*B* om ⲉ-) διαφθ. νοῦν ; ShP 129¹² 17 *S* ⲡⲉⲩⲣⲏⲧ ⲧ-ⲧ ⲉⲣⲟⲟⲩ, C 89 60 *B* ⲛⲉⲁ-ⲡⲉⲱⲣ. ⲧ. ⲉⲣⲟϥⲛⲉ *so that he* = Va Ar 172 38 ‏رج‎ (TT 112 *S* = MG 17 409 diff) ; vbal : ShP 131² 136 *S* could not ⲧⲁⲕⲉ ⲡⲉⲱⲣ. ⲉⲉⲓ ϣⲁⲣⲟⲛ *dissuade from.* *V* also ⲣⲉϥⲧⲁⲕⲟ.

II intr, *perish, be lost, destroy*: Job 17 1 *S*(*B* ϭⲓ ⲙⲕⲁⲣ), Jer 29 11 *SB* ὀλ., Nu 21 29 *SB*, Is 34 16 *B*(*SF* ⲥⲱⲣⲙ), Jo 6 27 *SA*²*B*, 1 Cor 15 18 *BF*(*S* ⲣⲉ ⲉⲃⲟⲗ) ἀπολ.; Ez 5 12 *B*(*S* ϥⲱⲧⲉ ⲉⲃⲟⲗ) ἀναλίσκε-σθαι ; Deu 34 7 *SB*, Ep 4 22 *SB* φθ., Jer 13 7 *SB* διαφθ., Ge 6 12 *S*(*B*†) καταφθ., Ro 1 23 *SB* φθαρ-τός ; Ex 22 10 *S*(*B* ⲕⲱϣ) συντρίβειν ; Job 4 9 *SB*, Zeph 3 6 *AB*, Mt 6 19 *S*(*B* tr) ἀφαν. ; Ps 87 6 *S* (*B* ⲣⲓⲟⲩⲓ) ἀπωθεῖν ; Is 51 6 *S*(*B* ⲙⲟⲩ) ἀποθνήσκειν ; ib 34 10 *B*(*SF* ϣⲟϥ) ἐρημοῦσθαι ; ib 26 19 *B*(*S* ⲣⲉ) πίπτειν ; Si 14 19 *S* σήπειν ; Ac 27 22 *B*(*S* ⲣⲉ ⲉⲃ.) ἀποβολὴ εἶναι ; PS 107 *S* ⲁⲧⲁϭⲟⲙ ⲧ., ShC 73 166 *S* determined ⲉⲧⲙⲧ. ⲣⲛ̄ⲟⲩⲡⲟⲕⲣⲓⲥⲓⲥ, BIF 13 117 *S* pleasures ⲉⲧⲛⲁⲧ. = MG 25 309 *B* ⲕⲱⲣϥ, BSM 32 *B* lest our gift ⲧ. = Va 63 7 *B* ⲕ. = BMis 374 *S* ϫⲉⲛⲁ, Ep 282 *S* come & meet us lest ⲛⲣⲱⲃ ⲧ. *end badly*, CA 107 *S* wine ⲛϥⲧⲙⲧ. nor turn sour, ROC 25 246 *B* ⲁⲣⲉϣⲁⲛⲣⲱⲃ ⲛⲓⲃⲉⲛ...ⲧ. he told where to find it.

Qual : Bar 3 3 *B*, 2 Cor 4 9 *B*(*S* ⲧ.) ἀπολ. ; Jude 10 *B*(*S* ⲧ.) φθ., Ez 20 44 *S*-ⲧ *B* διαφθ.; Lam 3 11 *S*-ⲧ *B* ἀφαν.; ShZ 601 *S* honey wherein ⲟⲩⲡⲁⲣⲣⲉ ⲉϥⲧ. *destructive*, Bor 253 153 *S* if metal not polished ⲁϥ-ϣⲱⲡⲉ ⲉϥⲧ-ⲧ, MG 25 276 *B* ⲛⲁϥⲧ. ⲛⲉⲙⲟⲩϭⲣⲓⲙⲓ = MIF 13 98 *S* ⲡⲟⲣⲡⲉⲩⲉ ⲙⲛ-, Va 61 203 *B* we can-not find Thee & ⲛⲁⲣⲉⲛⲙⲁ ⲡⲙⲟϣⲓ ⲧ. ⲛⲧⲟⲧⲡⲉ *have lost road* (?), Mor 19 35 *S* ⲣⲟⲓⲧⲉ ⲉⲩⲧ. = Miss 4 120 *B* ⲗⲁⲙ.

With following preposition. ⲥ ⲉⲣⲏⲓ ⲉⲭⲉⲛ- *B*, *upon, for*: C 43 222 ⲁϥⲧ. ⲛ̄ϯⲡⲟⲗⲓⲥ ⲉⲣ. ⲉⲭⲱⲛ ; ⲥ ⲛⲧⲛ-, *away from* : Jer 29 8 *S*(*B* ⲉⲃⲟⲗ ⲣⲁ-) ἀπολ. ἐκ; BSM 29 *B* lest our hope ⲧ. ⲛⲧⲟⲧⲉⲛ = Va 63 5 *B* ϥⲱϫⲓ = BMis 370 *S* ⲱϫⲛ, MG 25 181 *B* let naught ⲧⲁⲕⲉ ⲟⲩⲉⲣⲟⲟⲩ ⲛⲧⲟⲧⲕ, CMSS 44 *F* ⲛⲡⲉⲗⲧⲁⲕⲁⲩ ⲛⲧⲁⲁⲧ[; *v* also qual (Va 61); ⲥ ⲣⲓϫⲛ- *S*, as last : Is 13 9 (*B* ⲉⲃ. ⲣⲁ-) ἀπολ. ἐκ ; Job 2 9 (*B* ⲉⲃ. ⲣⲓϫ.) ἀφαν. ἀπό.

With following adverb. ⲥ ⲉⲃⲟⲗ : Ez 29 8 *SB* ἀπολ. ἀπό ; ⲉⲃ. ⲣⲁ- : Jos 23 13 *B*(*S* ⲉⲃ. ⲣⲓϫⲛ-) do ; ⲉⲃ. ⲣⲓ- : Is 10 27 *SB* καταφθ. ἀπό ; ⲉⲃ. ⲣⲛ-, ϫⲉⲛ- : Ps 20 10 *S*(*B* ⲉⲃ. ⲣⲁ-) ἀπ. ἀπό, Jo 6 39 *SA*²*B* ἀπ. ἐκ ; Deu 13 5 *SB* ἀφαν. ἐκ ; ib 4 3 *S*(*B* ϥⲱϯ ⲉⲃ.) ἐκ-τρίβ. ἐκ ; ⲉⲃ. ⲣⲓϫⲛ- : Jer 10 11 *S*(*B* ⲉⲃ. ⲣⲁ-) ἀπ. ἐκ.

—— nn m *SAA*²*BF*, *perdition*: Is 33 2 *SBF*, Ac 8 20 *SB* ἀπώλεια ; Ps 102 4 *SB*, 1 Cor 15 42 *SBF*, AP 10 *A*² φθορά, Zeph 3 6 *AB* διαφθ., Ps 48 10 *SB* καταφθ.; Jer 27 46 *B* ἅλωσις ; ib 3 *BF* (Louvre 10052), Joel 3 19 *SAB* ἀφανισμός ; Am 6 6 *A*(*B* ϫⲟⲙϫⲉⲙ) συντριβή ; Pro 1 27 *SAB*, 1 Cor 5 5 *SB* ὄλεθρος ; Job 8 16 *S*(*B* ⲧⲣⲟ) σαπρία ; Va 66 297 *B* ⲛⲧ. of bodies λώβη ; BG 58 *S* ⲧⲉⲡⲓⲟⲩⲙⲁ ⲙⲡⲥⲱϣϥ ⲙⲛⲧ., ShC 73 95 *S* see ye not ⲛⲧ. ⲙⲡⲉⲧⲛⲣⲏⲧ ?, BMis 240 *S* body whole ⲉⲙⲛ ⲗⲁⲁⲩ ⲛ̄ⲧ. ⲣⲓⲱⲱϥ, AM 28 *B* words ⲉⲧϭⲓ ⲉⲛⲧ., Cai 42573 1 *S* title of recipe ⲟⲩⲧ. ϣⲁⲗⲟⲟⲩ *for spoiling water-wheel* (?) (ⲙⲉⲥϯ ⲙⲟⲟⲩ), ib ⲟⲩⲧ. ⲃⲁⲛⲧⲉ sim *gourd-garden*.

ⲁⲧⲧ. *SA*²*BF*, *imperishable*: 1 Cor 9 25 *SB* ἄφθαρ-τος ; Bor 100 41 *S* ⲛⲉⲓⲁ. instead of perishable, JEA 13 19 *S* ⲛⲓⲁ. opp ⲛⲉⲧϣⲁ̄ϥⲧ., C 43 229 *B* ⲟⲩⲁⲧⲙⲟⲩ ⲟⲩⲁ. ; as adj : Sa 12 1 *S* ἄφθ. ; BG 66 *S* ⲡⲱⲛⲣ ϣⲁⲉⲛⲉⲣ ⲛⲁ., Mani 1 *A*² ⲡⲙⲁⲩ ⲉⲧⲟⲩⲁⲃⲉ ⲛⲁ., AM 308 *B* ⲡⲓⲭⲗⲟⲙ ⲛⲁ. ; ⲙⲛⲧ-, ⲙⲉⲧⲁⲧⲧ., *incorrup-tion*: Sa 2 23 *S*, Ro 2 7 *SBF* ἀφθαρσία ; DeV 2 21 *B* hast trained us ⲉⲟⲩⲙ. ; ⲟ, ⲟⲓ ⲛⲁⲧⲧ. : 1 Cor 15 52 *SB* ἄφθαρτος ; DeV 2 105 *B* Virgin's womb remained ⲉⲥⲟⲓ ⲛⲁ.

ⲣⲉϥⲧ. *SB*, *destroyer, as adj perishable*: Ex 12 23 *B*, He 11 18 *BF*(*S* ⲛⲉⲧⲧ.) ὀλοθρεύων, 1 Cor 10 10 *B*(*S* ⲛⲉⲩϣⲁϥⲧ.) -θρευτής ; Sa 9 15 *S* φθαρτός ; Zeph 2 15 *B*(*A* ⲣⲉϥϣⲱⲥ) φαυλίστρια ; ShC 42 196 *S* ⲡⲣ. (sc devil), R 1 4 72 *S* this life ⲡⲣⲉϥⲧ. ἐπίκηρος = AM 130 *B* ; Ep 592 A 6 *S* ⲡⲉⲑⲁⲃ ⲡⲣ. ; ⲣⲉϥⲧⲁⲕⲉ- :

Tit 1 10 S ϩ. ϧⲏⲧ (B ⲣⲉϥⲉⲣ ϧⲁⲗ ⲛ̄ϧ.) φρεναπάτης; Mor 17 105 S do κακογνώμων; ROC 19 72 S ⲧⲙⲁ-ⲡⲓⲁ ⲡⲣ. ⲯⲩⲭⲏ of Nestorius, Mor 50 27 S ϩ. ϣⲏⲣⲉ ⲕⲟⲩⲓ (cf C 86 150 B ⲣⲉϥⲧⲁⲕⲟ ⲛ̄ⲡⲓϣ. ϣⲏⲙ); ⲙ̄ⲛⲧ-ⲣⲉϥⲧⲁⲕⲉ ϧⲏⲧ: ShC 42 182 S envy, m., ⲙⲛⲧⲣⲉϥ-ⲙⲓϣⲉ; ⲙⲉⲧⲣⲉϥⲧⲁⲕⲟ ⲛ̄ⲡⲓⲡⲁⲑⲟⲥ Cat 85 B.

ⲭⲓⲛⲧ. B nn m, *destruction*: Is 34 2 (SF ⲧ. vb) ἀπόλ.; Dan 11 44 (S do) ἀφαν. *Cf* ⲁⲕⲱ.

ⲧⲕⲁ F *v* ⲑⲱⲕⲟ *sf.*

†ⲕⲉ, ⲧⲱⲕⲉ *v* ⲧⲱⲕ *throw.*

ⲧⲕⲃⲟ B *v* ⲕⲃⲟ *sf.*

ⲧⲱⲕⲉⲗ Sᶠ *v* ⲧⲱⲗⲕ.

ⲧⲱⲕⲙ S, -ⲙⲉ A, -ⲉⲙ F, ⲑⲱⲕⲉⲙ B, ⲧ(ⲉ)ⲕⲙ-S, ⲑⲉⲕⲉⲙ- B, ⲧⲟⲕⲙⲉ S, ⲧⲁⲕⲙ⸗ SA, ⲧⲟⲕⲙ† S, ⲧⲁⲕⲙ† SSᶠA²F, -ⲙⲉ† A, ⲑⲟⲕⲉⲙ† B vb tr, *pluck, draw, drag*: Ps 36 14 SB, Mk 14 47 SB σπᾶν, Mt 26 51 S(B ϣⲱⲗⲉⲙ) ἀποσ., Ps 128 6 S(B ϥⲱϫⲓ) ἐκσ., Jo 18 10 SB(A² ⲱⲧϩ) ἕλκειν; Mt 13 29 F(S ⲡⲱⲣⲕ, B ϥ.) ἐκρίζειν; Ac 27 40 S(B ϥⲓ) περιαιρεῖν; Mor 17 19 S ⲁⲥⲧⲉⲕⲙ ⲡⲱ of head ἐπιλαμβάνειν; Nah 3 2 A(B † ⲙⲟϥⲉ) στίλβειν (l ⲧⲁⲁⲧⲉ); ShBor 205 366 S they shall ⲧ. ⲛ̄ⲧⲉⲯⲩⲭⲏ ⲙ̄ⲡⲟⲩⲁ ⲡⲟⲩⲁ, BHom 128 S sword ⲧ.† ϧⲛ̄ⲧⲉϥϭⲓⲝ, AP 22† A², C 86 194† B, Mor 30† 5 F, Mor 31 46† Sᶠ all sim, Mor 48 57 S ⲧ. ⲙⲡⲉⲕⲗⲁⲥ = C 43 129 B ⲥⲱⲗⲡ ⲉⲃⲟⲗ, PMéd 299 S eyelashes ⲉⲕϣⲁⲛⲧⲁⲕⲙⲟⲩ; intr: Bor 134 2 S (Vita Sin) ⲡⲧⲉϥⲛⲟⲩ ⲛ̄ⲧⲁϥⲧ. ϧⲣⲁⲓ ϧⲙ̄-ⲭⲟⲓ = C 41 27 B ⲓ ⲉⲡϣⲱⲓ ϧⲉⲛ- = Miss 4 359 طلع.

With following preposition. ⲉ ⲉ-, *draw upon, against*: ShMIF 23 57 S ϣⲁ ⲩⲧ. ⲛ̄ⲧⲡⲁⲣⲁⲙⲏⲣⲁ (παραμήριον) ⲉⲣⲟϥ; ⲉ ⲉϫⲛ- sim: Si 22 22 SA σπ. ἐπί; KroppR S ⲧ. ⲛⲧⲉⲕⲥⲛⲟ⳿ϥ ⲉϫⲙ̄ⲡⲁⲣⲭⲏ-ⲛ̄ⲡⲗⲁⲥⲙⲁ; ⲉϧⲣⲁⲓ, ⲉϧ. ⲉϫ.: Jud 8 20 S σπ.; Ez 28 7 SB ἐκκενοῦν ἐπί; ⲉ ⲛⲥⲁ-, *pluck at*: Mt 12 1 F ⲧ[ⲱⲕⲉ]ⲙ ⲛⲥⲁⲛⲓ ϩⲉ[ⲙⲥ (CMSS 1, S ⲧⲱⲗⲕ, B ⲥⲱⲗⲡ ⲛⲥⲁ-) τίλλειν; ⲉ ⲛ̄ⲧⲛ-, *seize from*: Ps 151 7 S(B diff) σπ., Miss 4 526 S ⲉⲛⲛⲁⲧ. ⲛ̄ⲧⲉⲯⲩⲭⲏ ⲛ̄ⲧⲟⲟⲧϥ ⲙ̄ⲡ⳿ϩⲁϫⲉ = C 89 45 B ⲑ. ⲉⲃⲟⲗ ϧⲉⲛ- ⲉⲕⲥ. ἀπό; ⲉ ⲉⲃⲟⲗ ϧⲛ-, ϧⲉⲛ-, *draw forth, root out from*: Jer 12 14 S(B ⲥⲱⲕ ⲉⲃ. ϧⲁ-) ἀποσπ. ἀπό, 1 Kg 17 35 B(S ϥⲓ ⲉⲃ. ϧⲛ-), Zech 3 2 SA(B ⲥⲱϧⲉⲙ ⲉⲃ. ϧⲉⲛ-) ἐκοπ. ἐκ, Jude 22 S(B ϧⲱⲗⲉⲙ ⲉⲃ. ϧⲓⲧⲉⲛ-) ἁρπάζειν ἐκ; PS 130 S ⲁⲥⲧ. ⲉⲃ. ⲛ̄ϩⲏⲧⲟⲩ ⲛ̄ⲥⲟⲙ ⲛⲓⲙ, BG 42 S light ⲛ̄ⲧⲁϥⲧⲁⲕⲙⲉϥ ⲉⲃ. ϧⲛ̄ⲧⲙⲁⲁⲩ, ShC 42 191 S ⲁⲩⲧ. ⲡⲣⲉⲙⲡϣ ⲉⲃ. ϧⲙ̄ⲡⲕⲱⲧ, ShA 2 302 S ⲧⲟⲕⲙⲉⲛ ⲉⲃ. ϩⲛ̄ⲡⲃⲁⲣⲟⲥ that oppresseth us, C 86 34 B ⲁⲩⲑⲉⲕⲙ ⲡⲓⲕⲁϣ ⲉⲃ. ϧⲉⲛⲡⲉϥⲥⲱⲙⲁ, Mor 37 139 S ⲉⲁϥⲧⲟⲕⲙⲉϥ ⲉⲃ. ϧⲛⲥⲟⲩϩⲉ of heretics; ⲉ ⲉϧⲣⲁⲓ ϧⲛ- S, meaning as last: Am 9 2 (A ⲉⲓⲡⲉ ⲁϧⲣ., B ⲓⲛⲓ ⲉⲡϣⲱⲓ) ἀνασπ. ἐκεῖθεν, 1 Kg

17 51 (var ⲉⲃ. ϧⲛ-, B ⲱⲗⲓ), Ez 21 3 (B ϫⲉⲛ-) ⲉⲕⲥ. ἐκ; ShA 2 76 ⲧⲟⲕⲙⲉⲕ ⲉϥ. ϧⲛⲧⲗⲟⲓϧⲉ; also above intr.

With following adverb. ⲉ ⲉⲃⲟⲗ, *draw forth*: Lev 22 24 B(S ϣⲁⲁⲧ?) ἀποσπ.; ⲉ ⲉϧⲣⲁⲓ, *draw up*: Hab 1 15 S(Wess 9 106) A(B ⲥⲱⲕ ⲉⲡϣⲱⲓ) ἀνασπ.

ⲧ. ⲡϩⲏⲧ S, *be troubled at heart*: Mt 26 37, Mk 14 33 (B ⲉⲣ ⲙⲕⲁϩ ⲛ̄ϩ.) ἀδημονεῖν.

ⲧⲱⲕⲣ *v* ⲧⲱϧⲣ.

ⲧⲕⲟⲩⲣ F nn, *speed*: Jo 13 27 ⲉⲣⲓϥ ϧⲓⲧⲕ. (PMich 3521, S ϧⲛ̄ⲟⲩϭⲉⲡⲏ, A² ϧⲛⲟⲩϭⲗⲁⲙ, B ⲡ̄ⲭⲱⲗⲉⲙ) τάχιον. *Cf* dem *n* tkr.

ⲧⲁⲕⲥ A *v* ⲧⲱⲕⲥ (ⲧⲟ⳿ⲥ).

ⲧⲱⲕⲥ¹ SA, -ϭⲥ² S, -ⲧⲥ³ SB, ⲑⲟⲩϧ, -ⲕⲥ B, ⲧⲱⲥⲥ F, ⲧⲉⲕⲥ- SB, ⲧⲟⲕⲥ⸗⁴, -ϭⲥ⸗⁵ S, ⲑⲟⲕⲥ⸗ B, ⲧⲟⲕⲥ†⁶ SB, -ϭⲥ†⁷ S, ⲑⲟⲕⲥ†⁸ B, ⲧⲟⲧⲥ†⁹ SB, ⲧⲁⲕⲥ†¹⁰, -ⲧⲥ†¹¹ Sᶠ, ⲑⲟⲧⲥ†¹² B, ⲣⲥ ⲧⲁⲕⲥ- S (ⲕⲥ & ϧ vary pass), vb I intr, *pierce, bite, be pierced, be studded* with nails &c: Jer 9 8 B(S ⲭⲓ) τιτρώσκειν; Va 57 226 B ⲉⲩⲑ. ⲉⲩ-ⲭⲱⲧϩ κεντεῖν τιτ.; R 1 3 71 S coarse raiment ⲧ.¹ ⲁⲩⲱ ⲥⲭⲱⲕⲉ (sic), ShC 73 23 S ⲧⲏⲕⲁⲥⲕⲉ ⲧⲓⲧ.¹, ShIF 101 S malady ⲉϥⲧ.¹ ⲏ ⲉϥϫⲱⲕⲉ like scorpion, Mor 51 33 S ⲉⲧⲭⲡⲓⲟ ⲏ ⲉⲧⲧ.¹ ⲛ̄ⲑⲉ (ⲛ)ϩⲉⲛϭⲉⲃⲟⲟⲩ (? *shilbah* fish), EW 12 B Jesus ⲑ.⁸ ϫⲉⲛⲟⲙⲛⲧ ⲛ̄ⲡⲓⲥⲟⲛⲓ; *be fixed, settled* S: Mor 43 115 after funeral his house ⲧ.⁷ ⲭⲱⲣⲓⲥ ϧⲏⲃⲉ, COAd 67 I learn that ⲁⲡⲡⲉ ⲥⲟⲃⲧⲉ ⲁⲕⲧ.²

II tr, *pierce, goad*: Job 6 4 B(S ⲧⲱⲃⲥ) κεν., Jo 19 37 B(S ⲕⲱⲛⲥ) ἐκκ., Va 66 289 B ⲑ. ⲙ̄ⲡⲓⲣⲱⲙⲓ συγκ.; Si 27 2 ¹S πηγνύναι, Hos 5 2 B(S ⲥⲙⲛⲉ) καταπ.; Pro 19 4 ¹S(A intr) ἐρεθίζειν; Is 58 3 B (S ⲙⲟⲩⲕϩ) ὑπονύσσειν; Va 61 218 B ⲁⲩⲑⲟϧϥ τιτ.; C 89 37 B ⲡⲉϥϩⲏⲧ ⲡⲁⲑ. ⲙ̄ⲙⲟϥ = MG 17 404 نخز, Va Ar 172 23 لذع; Mor 52 38 S Mark to Anianus ⲛ̄ⲧⲧ.¹ ⲛ̄ⲧⲁⲡⲟϩⲉ ⲛ̄ⲧⲟⲟϥⲉ, R 1 3 48 S bone ⲁϥⲧ.² ⲛ̄ⲧⲁⲟⲩϭⲉⲣⲏⲧⲉ, C 89 85 B till Lord ⲑⲟⲕⲥϥ ϫⲉⲛ-ⲧⲉϥⲡⲣⲟϩⲁⲓⲣⲉⲥⲓⲥ = TT 156 S ⲧⲱⲃⲥ.

With following preposition. ⲉ ⲉ- intr, *be driven, smitten into, be firm*: 1 Kg 19 10¹ S πατάσσειν εἰς; ShIF 162 S ⲛⲉⲡⲗⲁⲝ ⲉⲧⲧ.⁶ ⲉⲡⲉⲑⲩⲥⲓⲁⲥⲧⲏⲣⲓⲟⲛ, C 86 219 B martyr ⲧ.⁹ ⲉⲡⲓϭⲗⲟⲝ, O'Leary H 26 B embroidery ⲉϥⲧ.⁹ ⲉⲛϣⲩⲧⲁϯ of robe, P 129¹⁷ 43 S Noah's dove ⲟⲩϭⲱⲃⲉ ⲧ.⁶ ⲉⲧⲉⲥⲧⲁⲡⲣⲟ, Mor 19 11 S book ⲧ.⁶ ⲉⲣⲱϥ = Miss 4 99 B ⲗⲟϧ, BMis 271 S thy spear ⲧ.⁵ ⲉⲣⲟⲓ = Mor 30 47 S ϩⲏⲧ ⲛ̄ϩⲏⲧ, BMis 140 S child walking ⲉϥⲧ.⁷ ⲉⲛⲉϥⲕⲟⲩⲓ ⲛ̄ⲥⲟⲡ, J 65 61 S ⲟⲩϩⲁⲙⲉⲧⲱⲛ ⲉϥⲧ.⁶ ⲉϫⲟⲉ, ST 352 S ⲡⲧⲉⲧⲧ.² ⲉⲡⲉⲧⲡⲏⲓ; tr, *drive in, point*: P 131⁵ 96 S ⲡⲙⲁ ⲉⲧⲟⲩⲛⲁⲧ.¹ ⲉⲣⲟϥ ⲛⲡⲉⲓⲃⲧ πηγ., C 86 278 B ⲑ. ⲛⲟⲩ-ⲙⲏϣ ⲛ̄ⲓϥⲧ ⲉⲣⲟϥ ἐμπηγ.; Mt 27 48 B ⲑⲟⲕⲥⲥ (S ⲙⲟⲩⲣ) περιτιθέναι; Mor 41 146 S nails ⲧⲟⲕⲥⲟⲩ ⲉⲛⲉϥⲥⲱⲙⲁ (varr ib 39 42 Sᶠ ⲧⲁϫⲟⲩ, 40 31 S ⲧⲣⲧⲱⲣ-ⲟⲩ), P 131¹ 22 S Mary ⲉⲧⲉⲣⲉⲛⲥⲁⲓⲁⲥ ⲧⲉⲕⲥ ⲧⲏⲛⲃⲉ

ⲉⲣⲟⲥ (Is 7 14) *point finger*, P 129¹⁴ 123 *S* ⲁϥⲧⲉⲕⲥ
ⲧⲏⲏⲃⲉ ⲡⲁⲩ ⲉⲡⲡⲣⲉⲥⲃⲩⲧⲉⲣⲟⲥ = DeV 1 78 *B*, Va 61
205 *B* words that Isaac ⲑ. ⲙⲙⲟⲩ ⲉⲁⲃⲣⲁⲁⲙ (Ge
22 7);   ⲉⲣⲟⲩⲡ, ⲉⲋ. ⲉ-: C 86 283 *B* ⲧ.³ ⲡⲧⲁⲡⲓϥⲧ
ⲉⲋ. ⲉⲣⲟϥ (var ⲧⲱⲥ) = Mun 38 *S* ⲱϥⲧ ⲉⲣ. ⲉ-, C 86
232 *B* sim ⲉⲡⲉⲩⲥⲱⲙⲁ ⲉⲋ. ⲉϯϥⲟϫⲓ ⲛⲱⲉ, Leyd 289
S ⲧⲉϫⲥ ⲉⲓⲃⲧ ⲉⲣ. ⲉⲡⲉϥⲥⲱⲙⲁ;   ⲥ ⲉⲡⲉⲥⲏⲧ ⲉ- AM
308 *B* ⲑ. ⲙⲙⲟⲩ ⲉⲡ. ⲉⲡⲕⲁⲣⲓ;   ⲥ ⲉϩⲗⲏⲓ ⲉϫⲉⲛ- *F*:
Lam 2 9 (v below);   ⲥ ⲛ-, *inlaid with*: Tob 13
17 ⁵*S* ψηφολογεῖν; Cant 3 10 *S* ⲧ.⁷ ⲛⲱⲡⲉ, λιθόστρωτον; BMis 271 *S* ⲧⲟⲕⲥⲩ (*sc* picture) ⲉⲛⲱⲡⲉ (var Mor
30 47 *Sʄ* ⲧⲁⲋⲩ) Mor 28 156 *Sʄ* streets ⲧ.¹¹ ⲛⲱⲡⲛ ⲙ-
ⲙⲏ, EW 118 ⁹*B* sim, AZ 14 13 *S* crown ⲧ.⁷ ⲛⲱⲡⲉ;
pierce with: Jo 19 34 *B* (var ϫⲉⲛ-, *SA²* ⲕⲱⲡⲥ) νύσσειν dat;   ⲥ ϩⲛ-, ϫⲉⲛ-, *pierce with*: ShP 130²
25 *S* ⲉⲧⲧ.¹ ϩⲛⲡⲉⲩⲗⲁⲥ, Va 61 20 *B* ⲑ. ⲛⲡⲟⲩϩⲛⲧ
ϫⲉⲛⲡⲓⲥⲟⲣⲓ, C 43 197 *B* ⲑ. ⲡⲧⲁⲫⲉ ϫⲉⲛⲧⲉϥⲗⲟⲩϫⲏ;
stick, be fixed in: Ps 31 4 ⁹*B* (*S* ⲧⲱⲗⲥ), ib 37 3 ⁹*B* (*S*
ⲧⲟⲣⲧⲣ) ἐμπήγ.;   FR 180 *S* cross ⲧ.⁶ ϩⲓⲡⲙⲁ ⲛⲧⲁⲩ-
ⲟⲃⲧⲩ ⲛⲣⲏⲧⲩ, MélOr 6 517 *B* cross ⲉⲩⲟ.⁸ (*sic* MS)
ϫⲉⲛⲟⲙⲛ̄ϯ, Mor 39 35 *Sʄ* spear ⲧ.¹⁰ ⲛⲣⲏⲧⲩ, Mor
41 81 *S* babes' mouths ⲧ.¹⁰ ϩⲛⲧⲉⲕⲓⲃⲉ of mothers;
ⲉϩⲣⲏⲓ ϫⲉⲛ- *B*: Lam 2 9³ (*F* ⲉϩⲗⲏⲓ ⲉϫ.) ἐμπηγ. εἰς;
C 86 356 splinter ⲑⲟⲩⲍ ⲉⲋ. ϫⲉⲛⲧⲉⲩϫⲁⲫⲉ.

ⲣ ⲥ *S*, meaning uncertain: COAd 50 tell me ϫⲉ-
ϣⲁⲓ[ⲟⲩ]ⲱⲙ ⲡⲱ (= ⲟⲩ) ϫⲉⲁⲡⲟⲕ ⲟⲩⲧⲁⲕⲥⲣⲏⲧ ϫⲉⲡⲧ-
ⲉⲡⲟⲓ (ⲛ̄ϯⲛⲟⲉⲓ) ⲙⲛ[[*l*? ⲁⲛ).

ⲧⲱⲕⲥ, -ⲉⲥ *S*, ⲑⲟⲩⲍ *B* nn m, *piercing*: Job 16 10
B (*S* diff) ἀκίς; Mus 34 206 *B* ⲛⲑ. ⲛϯϣⲉ ⲡⲗⲟⲩϫⲏ;
fixture, settlement: ShIF 290 *S* ⲛⲧ. ⲣⲱ ⲁⲛ ⲛⲡⲉⲧ-
ⲡⲉⲣⲏⲅⲡⲉ ⲡⲁⲓ ⲁⲩⲱ ⲡⲟⲩⲱⲙⲉ ⲛⲱϫⲛ ⲣⲱ ⲁⲡⲡⲉ ⲡⲁⲓ
ⲉⲃⲟⲗ ϩⲓⲧⲛⲡⲉⲧⲡⲉⲣⲏⲩⲧ, MMA 23 3 709 *S* come &
reconcile us for ⲙⲡⲓϣⲡ ⲧⲱⲥⲥ ϣⲁⲧⲉⲛⲟⲩ; *pricking,
admonition*: C 41 47 *B* reciting ϫⲉⲛⲟⲩⲟ. = Miss 4
404 رنشاط وبقظ, C 89 97 *B* disobeyed ⲡⲓⲟ. of heart
= MG 17 473 نغزل.

ⲧⲟⲋⲥ *S*, ⲧⲁ. *Sʄ*, ⲧⲁⲕⲥ *A*, ⲧⲟⲟⲧⲉ *S*, ⲧⲟⲧⲥ, ⲕⲟⲧⲥ,
ⲧⲟϫⲥ *B* nn m, *a thing firmly fixed, seat*: 1 Kg 4 13 *S*
(var P 44 109 -ⲧⲥ), 18 ⲧⲁ., Job 29 7 *SB*, Pro 9 14
SA (*B* ⲕⲟ., var ⲧⲟ.) δίφρος; Ez 45 4 *B* ⲧⲟϫⲥ Gk
om; K 107 *B* ⲛⲓⲧ. كرسي, ib 217 القائم ⲥ̄, ib 151
B كذا, but ib 260 ترصيع تسمير *a thing studded, in-
crusted*: AZ 14 13 *S* Victor ⲡⲉϥⲧⲁⲙⲓⲉ ⲧ. (var BMar
30 ⲧⲟⲟⲧⲥ, cf Synax 2 93 كراسي), MG 25 243 *B* ⲟⲩⲧ.
ⲛⲕⲩⲣⲓⲕⲟⲛ ⲉⲩϭⲟⲥⲓ = Gött Ar 114 100 عالية مصطبة,
R 1 3 47 *S* ⲧ. & ⲧⲣⲁⲡⲉⲍⲁ for προσφορά, BMAdd
39583 *B* seated ϩⲓⲡⲉⲩⲧ.   *V* LMis 406.

ⲧⲁϫ *S* nn m, *molar tooth*: P 44 69 (ⲟ)ⲧⲟⲡⲧⲁⲣⲓⲥ
ⲛⲧ....ⲛⲱⲟⲗ ضرس, ib ⲅⲟⲙⲫⲓⲧⲏⲣⲓⲟⲛ · ⲧⲛⲟⲩⲛⲉ ⲛ-
ⲛⲉⲧ. For ? ὀδάξ.

Cf ⲧⲱⲕ *be strong* & ⲗⲱⲕⲥ *sf*.

ⲧⲏⲃⲁⲥ, ⲕⲁⲥ *SB*, ⲕⲕⲁⲥ (PMéd) *S*, ⲧⲕⲉⲥ *AA²*, ⲛⲕⲉⲥ

F nn m, *pain* (cf ? ⲧⲱⲕⲥ): Job 15 2 *S* (*B* ⲉⲙⲕⲁϧ),
Is 1 5 *SF* (*B* do) πόνος; ib 30 26 *SB* (var ⲉⲙ., *F*
ϣⲉ ⲛⲣⲏⲧ), BMar 157 *S* ⲡⲉⲧ. ⲙⲡⲁϩⲣⲏⲧ ὀδύνη; Eccl
2 23 *S* ⲁⲗⲅⲏⲙⲁ; Mt 4 24 *S* (*B* ⲉⲙ.) βάσανος; ShA
2 322 *S* ⲡⲉⲓϣⲱⲡⲉ ⲉⲧⲟ ⲛⲣⲁϭ ⲛⲥⲙⲟⲧ ⲛⲧ., ShMIF
23 12 *S* ⲟⲩⲟϩ ⲉϣⲱⲡⲉ ϩⲓⲧ., Ryl 94 103 *S* ⲡⲉⲧ. ⲙ-
ⲡⲱϭⲃ, R 1 2 72 *S* ⲡⲉⲧ. ⲛⲛⲡⲗⲁⲕⲉ;   ϯ ⲧ., *give,
have pain*: Is 1 6 *SF* (*B* ϯⲙⲕⲁϩ), Nah 3 19 *A* ⲧⲕⲉⲥ
(*sic*, *B* do) φλεγμαίνειν; Bor 253 163 *S* ϯϯ ⲧ. when
thinking of thy troubles ἀλγεῖν; BAp 116 *S* ⲁϥⲃⲁ-
ⲥⲁⲛⲓⲍⲉ ⲉⲩϯ ⲧ., TillOster 18 *A* ⲣⲏⲧ ⲉⲩϯ ⲧ., Miss 8
195 *S* mind shall not weary nor lips ϯⲓ ⲧ., Mani 1
A² ⲡⲉϣϭⲁ ⲉⲧϯ ⲧ., MG 25 394 *B* boils ⲉⲩϯ ⲧ. ⲙ-
ⲙⲁϣⲱ, Ryl 107 *S* ⲟⲩⲁⲡⲕⲉⲫⲁⲗⲟⲥ (ἐγκ.) ⲉⲩϯ ⲕ.,
PMéd 305 *S* ⲙⲁ ⲛⲓⲙ ⲉⲩⲧⲓ ⲕ., ib 237 *S* ⲙⲁⲭⲉ ⲉⲩⲧⲓ
ⲕⲕ.;   ⲥ ⲉ- of person pained: BMar 63 *S* his inwards ϯ ⲕ. ⲉⲣⲟϥ, C 86 357 *B* head ϯ ⲕ. ⲉⲣⲟϥ; of
painful part: BMis 315 *S* ⲉⲩⲧⲓ ⲧ. ⲉⲡⲉϥⲟⲩⲣⲏⲧⲉ,
MIF 2 245 *B* ⲉⲥϯ ⲧ. ⲉⲡⲟⲩⲁⲓ ⲛⲥⲫⲓⲣ of face; vbal:
Ap 12 2 *S* (*B* ⲙⲟⲕϩ) βασανίζειν inf;   ϯⲧ. as nn:
Ap 9 5 *S* (*B* ⲉⲙⲕⲁϩ) βασανισμός, cf ib ⲧⲕ.; P 44 79
S ϩⲩⲙⲓⲕⲣⲁⲛⲓⲟⲛ · ⲡⲁⲓ ⲧ., ShBor 247 104 *S* ⲟⲩϯⲧ.,
ib ϩⲉⲛⲧⲕ., Pcod 25 *S* ϣⲱⲡⲉ...ⲟⲩⲇⲉ ϯⲧ. (var ⲧⲕ.),
R 1 5 29 *S* ⲡⲉⲕϯⲧ. ⲧⲏⲣⲟⲩ, ib ⲧⲕ., PMéd 204 *S*
ⲛⲧⲕⲕ. ⲛⲛⲗⲉⲣⲟⲥ, Ryl 102 *S* ⲟⲩϯⲕ. ⲛⲃⲁⲗ, Mor 30
55 *F* ⲛⲛⲗⲁϭ ⲛϯⲛⲕ. = BMis 277 *S* ⲧⲕ., C 89 123 *B*
ⲛⲓϯⲧ. of scorpion's bite.

ⲧⲁⲕⲧⲟ *B*, ⲧⲕⲁⲧⲟ *A²*, ⲧⲁⲕⲧⲉ-, -ⲧⲟⲟ *B*, -ⲧⲏⲟⲩⲧ⁺
B vb tr, *put, go around* (caus of ⲕⲱⲧⲉ): Deu 23
9 (*S* no vb), Lu 19 43 (*S* ⲕⲧⲟ) παρεμβάλλειν; Job
26 10 γυροῦν; Mani 1 *A²* ⲁⲓⲙⲟⲩ]ϣⲧ ⲟⲩⲏⲣ ⲙⲙⲁ
ⲁⲓⲧ. ⲟⲩⲏⲣ ⲛⲑⲁ[λασσα, ib do;   ⲥ ⲉ- intr: Ps 117
11 (*S* ⲕⲱⲧⲉ), Jo 10 24 (*SA²* do) κυκλοῦν; Ps 47 13
(*S* ϩⲱⲗϭ) περιβάλ.; Jer 21 9 (*S* ⲱⲣⲃ ⲉⲣⲟⲩⲛ) συγκλείειν; Is 58 8 (*S* ⲱⲗ) περιστέλλειν; Jer 39 2 χαρακοῦν ἐπί; C 43 94 ⲑⲣⲉⲟⲩⲥⲏⲛⲓ ⲧ. ⲉⲣⲟϥ;   tr: Is
29 3 (*S* ⲕⲧⲟ) βάλ. περί; Mt 21 33 (*S* do) περιτιθέναι
dat; Is 37 33 (*S* do) κυκ. ἐπί; ROC 17 405 ⲉⲥⲧ. ⲉⲣⲟⲩ
ⲛⲡⲉⲥⲛⲁⲩϩ ἐμπλέκειν dat; TSBA 9 363 altar ⲁϥⲧ.
ⲉⲣⲟⲩ ⲛⲟⲩⲓⲟⲙ (cf 3 Kg 18 32), DeV 2 15 to Simeon
ⲙⲁⲧⲁⲕⲧⲉ ⲧⲟⲧⲕ ⲉϯⲙⲉⲧⲛⲓϣϯ, PO 14 356 brethren ⲧ.
ⲛⲅⲁⲡⲱⲡⲓ ⲉⲣⲟϥ;   qual: Jer 26 5 περιέχεσθαι κυκλόθεν; C 86 271 wheels ⲉⲣⲉϩⲁⲛⲥⲛⲩⲓ ⲧ. ⲉⲣⲱⲟⲩ *set
around them*.   ⲥ ϫⲉⲛ-: Ex 28 20⁺ περικαλύπτειν
dat;   ⲥ ⲛ-: Lev 25 29⁺ (*S* ⲕⲧⲟ), Hos 8 14⁺ (*SA* do)
τειχίζειν; DeV 2 16⁺ mount ⲉϥⲧ. ⲛⲭⲣⲱⲙ.

—— nn m, *circumference*: Ez 43 17 (HCons,
Tatt diff) κύκλωμα; Zech 12 2 (*A* ϭⲱ vb) περιοχή.

ⲧⲁⲕⲟⲩⲱ v ⲧⲱⲕ *throw* ⲣ ⲥ.

(ⲧⲱⲕϣ), ⲧⲟⲕϣⲋ *S* vb tr, *meaning unknown*:
BM 1191 ⲙⲉⲓⲟⲩⲱϣ ϩⲁⲧⲇⲟⲥⲓⲥ ⲛⲥⲁⲩ̄ ⲓⲃ ϫⲉⲁⲕⲧⲟⲕ-
ϣⲟⲩ ⲉⲃⲟⲗ.

(ⲧⲱⲕϩ), ⲧⲟⲕϩ[†] *S* vb, meaning unknown: Kropp H 13 *sharp 2-edged sword* ⲧ. ϩ[ⲛ]ⲧⲉϭⲧⲁⲡⲣⲟ (*cf* Ap 1 16 ἐκπορεύειν).   But prob *l* ⲧⲟⲕⲙ.

ⲧⲁⲗ, ⲧⲟⲗ (ViK 9795) *S*, ⲑ. *B* nn m, *heap, hillock, cf* תֵל, تَل (IgR): Ge 31 46 *SB*, Ex 17 10 *S*(*B* ⲧⲱⲟⲩ), Jer 4 24 *S*(*B* ⲕⲁⲗⲁⲙⲫⲟ), Hos 10 8 *B*(*SA* = Gk), Lu 3 5 *B*(*S* ⲥⲓⲃⲧ) βουνός ; P 44 54 *S* ⲡⲧ. اجبال, EnPeterson (on Claudius martyr) *S* ⲉϥⲧⲁⲗⲏⲩ ⲉⲭⲉⲛⲟⲩⲧ. ⲉϥϩⲟⲥⲉ = P 4776 136 جبل ; ShP 130[5] 82 *S* ⲟⲩⲧ. ⲡⲕⲁϩ ⲉϥϩⲟⲥⲉ, C 41 63 *B* ⲟⲩⲛⲓϣϯ ⲛⲑ. ⲛⲱⲓⲕ *filling pantry*, DeV 2 229 *B* neither ⲑ. nor ⲁϥⲉ ⲙⲡⲉⲧⲣⲁ *appeared* (above waters), C 86 177 *B* *cast stones* ϣⲁⲛⲧⲉϥⲉⲣ ⲑ. *below gallows*.   *Cf* ? place Ⲡⲧⲉⲗ POxy 042.

ⲧⲁⲗⲁⲧⲏⲗ *F*, same : Is 30 17 (*S* ⲥⲓ., *B* ⲕ.).

ⲧⲁⲗ *S*, ⲧⲉⲗ *F*   *v* ⲧⲁⲣ.

ⲧⲏⲗ⸗ *F*   *v* ⲧⲏⲣ⸗.

ⲧⲁⲗⲟ *SAB*, -ⲗⲉ, -ⲣⲟ *S*, ⲧ(ⲉ)ⲗⲟ *S*[a], ⲧⲉⲗⲟ *AA*[2], ⲧⲁⲗⲁ *F*, ⲧⲁⲗⲉ- *SAB*, ⲧⲉⲗⲉ- *A*[2], ⲧⲁⲗⲁ- *F*, ⲧⲁⲗⲟ⸗ *SB*, ⲧⲗⲟ⸗ *S*[a], ⲧⲉⲗⲁ⸗ *AA*[2], ⲧⲁ. *AF*, ⲧⲁⲗⲏⲩ[†], -ⲗⲉ[†] (?) *S*, ⲧⲁⲗⲁ(ⲉ)ⲓⲧ[†], ⲧⲁⲗⲏⲟⲩ[†] *A*, ⲧⲉⲗⲁⲉⲓⲧ[†] *A*[2], ⲧⲁⲗⲏⲟⲩⲧ[†] *B*, ⲧⲁⲗⲏ(ⲟ)ⲩ[†], ⲧⲁⲗⲏ[†] *F* vb. **I** tr, **a** *lift, offer up, set on beast, ship* (caus of ⲱⲗ): Ac 20 14 *SB* ἀναλαμβάνειν ; *ib* 23 24 *SB* ἐπιβιβάζειν ; PS 282 *S* ⲡⲥⲱⲙⲁ ...ⲧⲁⲗⲉ ϭⲟⲙ ⲉⲃⲟⲗ ϩⲓⲧⲟⲩⲧⲗⲏ, WTh 196 *S* ⲁⲩⲧⲁⲗⲟⲟⲩ (ship), BMar 150 *S* ⲧⲉⲧⲡⲉϣ ⲧⲁⲗⲟⲓ ⲡⲙⲙⲏⲧⲓ ?, BMis 57 *S* ⲁϥⲧⲁⲗⲟⲟⲩ (*sc* victuals) ⲁϥⲙⲟⲟϣⲉ, CO Ad 22 *S* ⲛⲧⲁⲧⲛⲛⲟⲟⲩ ⲛⲧⲁⲧⲁⲗⲟⲟⲩ (sh.?), MIE 2 393 *B* ⲁϥⲧⲁⲗⲟⲥ (sh.) = BAp 120 *S* + ⲉⲡϫⲟⲓ, BM 1119 *S* ⲧⲁⲣⲟ (ⲛ)ⲟⲩϣⲟ ⲛⲕⲁⲣⲁⲑⲉ, ST 63 *S* ⲉⲩϣⲁⲛⲧⲁⲗⲟⲕ ⲡⲡⲉⲉϥ, Mor 30 36 *F* ⲁⲩⲧ. ⲙⲡⲙⲉⲥⲓ ⲁⲛϫⲓⲧϥ ⲉⲩⲙⲉ, *ib* 31 90 *S* ⲡⲉⲧⲧ. ⲙⲡⲣⲱⲃ ⲛϭⲓⲝ ⲡⲛⲉⲥⲡⲏⲩ...ⲉⲕⲛⲙⲉ, EW 44 *B* *come* ⲛⲧⲁⲧⲁⲗⲟⲕ (beast) & *bring thee into city*, BM 592 *F* *give them him* ⲉⲃⲧⲁⲗⲟⲟⲩ ; *refl* : AZ 21 143 *S* *arise* ⲛⲥⲧⲁⲗⲟⲕ ⲛⲙⲙⲁⲛ (sh.), BSM 71 *B* ⲁⲩⲧⲁⲗⲱⲟⲩ *& came to city* = BMis 162 *S* ⲁⲗⲉ ⲉⲡϫⲟⲓ, DeV 1 95 *B* ⲁⲓⲧⲁⲗⲟⲓ ⲡⲉⲙⲁϥ (sh.)

b *set up* (on loom), *weave SB* : Is 59 5 ⲧ. ⲡⲟⲩⲡⲁⲧ (*B* ⲥⲱϭⲓ ⲉⲟⲩⲛ.) ἱστὸν ὑφαίνειν, MG 17 327 ⲁϥⲧⲁⲗⲉ ⲧⲉϥⲧⲁⲛⲏ = C 89 74 *B* ψίαθον ὑφ. ; C 89 156 *B* ⲉⲩⲧⲁⲗⲉ ⲑⲟⲙ, ShP 130[1] 140 ⲧⲣⲟⲉⲓⲧⲉ ⲉⲡⲧⲁⲥⲧⲁⲗⲟⲥ ⲡⲁⲥ, BM 343 2 *monk's occupations* ϥⲓ ⲕⲁⲙ, ⲧⲁⲗⲟ ⲧⲙⲏ, Miss 4 232 ⲟⲩⲡⲁⲧ ⲛⲧⲁⲗⲉ ϩⲃⲟⲟⲥ, Ryl 238 38 ⲉⲙⲡⲱⲧ ⲛⲧⲁⲗⲟ ⲕⲁⲙⲁⲥ(ⲓ)ⲟⲛ, Bodl(P) d 36 ⲡⲧⲉⲙⲟⲥⲉ (δημόσιον)ⲛⲧⲁⲗⲉ ϣⲧⲏⲛ(*cf* Ep 1 157) ; qual, *woven* : Lev 19 19 ⲉⲥⲧ. ⲛⲁⲅⲁⲛ ⲥⲛⲁⲩ (*B* ⲥⲛⲃ) ὑφ., Jth 10 21 ⲧ. ⲉⲃⲟⲗ ϩⲛⲟⲩⲛⲟⲩⲃ καθυφ., Is 3 23 ⲧ. ϩⲓⲛⲟⲩⲃ(*B* do) συνκαθυφ. ; Ep 351 ϩⲉⲛⲕⲁⲓⲣⲉⲁ (κειρία) ⲧ. ⲉⲡϩⲁⲧ *set up on loom*.

II intr, *go up, mount* (beast), *go aboard* : Nah 3 3 *A*(*B* ⲁⲗⲏⲓ) ἀναβαίνειν ; Mich 550 46 *S* ⲁⲩⲧ. (beasts)

ⲡⲧⲉⲩϣⲏ, Bor 143 39 *S* ⲛⲧⲁⲡⲧ. (ship) ⲉⲧⲃⲉⲡⲉⲓϣⲱⲃ, BMOr 9525 89 *S* ⲁⲛⲧ. (sh.) ⲙⲡⲁⲡⲁ ⲃⲓⲕⲧⲱⲣ, MG 25 257 *B* ⲁⲙⲁⲕⲁⲣⲓ ⲧ. ϩⲉⲛϯⲙⲉⲧⲙⲓⲙⲟⲥ *hath progressed in miming* ;   qual : Nu 6 20 *B*(*S* ⲕⲱ ⲉϩⲣⲁⲓ) ἐπίθεμα ; Zech 12 4 *A*(*B* ⲥ ⲉ-) ἀναβάτης ; Glos 77 *S* ἱππεύς, ἱπποβάτης ; Miss 4 739 *S* ϩⲛⲕⲟⲟⲩⲉ ⲉⲩⲧ. (be.), C 43 226 *B* *soldiers* ⲉⲧⲧ. (sh.) ⲛⲉⲙⲁⲡⲁ (ⲁ)ⲡⲟⲩⲃ.

ⲧⲁⲗⲉ *S* : Ac 21 2 (var & *B* ⲁⲗⲉ) ἐπιβαίνειν ; Ryl 144 *have agreed* ⲡⲧ. ⲡⲉⲙⲁⲕ ϩⲱⲥ ⲡⲉⲉⲃ, *ib* 335 ⲡⲧⲁϥⲧ. ⲡ-ⲡⲉⲉⲩ ϩⲁⲣⲟⲕ.   *V* also ⲥ ⲉ-, ⲉⲭⲛ-, ⲉϩⲣⲁⲓ.
With following preposition.

—— ⲉ- *SAA*[2]*BF*, *go up to, be mounted on* intr : Est 6 8 *S*, Hab 3 8 *A*(*S* ⲉⲭⲛ-, *B* ⲁⲗⲏⲓ ⲉⲭ.) ⲉⲡⲓⲃ. ἐπί ; Jo 6 17 *A*[2](*SB* ⲁ. ⲉ.) ⲉⲙⲃ. εἰς ; *ib* 12 14 *A*[2](*SB* ⲁ. ⲉ-) καθίζειν ἐπί ; Nah 2 3 *A* ⲡⲉⲧϩⲁⲣⲟⲩⲧ. ⲁⲡϩⲧⲱⲣ (*B* ϭⲁⲥⲓϩⲑⲟ) ἱππεύς ; ShA 1 400 *S* ⲡⲉⲕⲣⲧⲟ...ⲧ. ⲉⲣⲟϥ, Worr 230 *S* ⲁϥⲧ. ⲉⲧⲉⲧⲣⲓⲣ *to fill it with bread* ; *go aboard* : Jon 1 3 *SA*(*B* ⲁ. ⲉ-) ⲁⲛⲁⲃ. εἰς, Lu 8 22 *S* (*B* do) ⲉⲙⲃ. εἰς ; JSch 6 32 *S* ⲧⲁⲣⲉϥⲧ. ⲉⲧⲕⲟⲩⲣⲥⲟⲛ, BP 9447 *S* ⲉϥⲛⲁⲧ. ⲉⲡϩⲏ[ⲧ *take ship for north* ;   ⲧⲁⲗⲉ *S*, -ⲗⲏ *F* : Nu 22 22[†] (var -ⲏⲩ, *B* do) ⲉⲡⲓⲃ. ἐπί ; Ap 19 14[†] (var do, *B* Gk om), BHom 88 *come* ⲛⲧ. ⲉⲡϫⲟⲓ, Ryl 98 ⲁⲓϥ ⲛⲧ. ⲉⲣⲟϥ (be.), P 131[5] 94 ϩⲙⲡⲧⲣⲉⲩⲧ. ⲉⲑⲁⲗⲁⲥⲥⲁ, BM 1088 ⲡⲓⲥⲕⲉϥ ⲡⲧⲁⲩⲧ. ⲉⲡϫⲟⲓ, Mor 24 22 *F tree* ⲛⲧⲁⲡⲥⲱⲧⲏⲣ ⲧ. ⲉⲗⲁⲥ ; *tr, set, take upon* : Ex 22 25 *B* ⲧ. ⲙⲛⲥⲉ (*S* ⲧⲧⲟ) ἐπιτιθέναι dat, Si 8 19 *S* ⲁⲛⲁⲫⲉⲣⲉⲓⲛ dat ; Lu 10 34 *SB* ⲉⲡⲓⲃ. ἐπί ; Ge 31 17 *SB*, Jo 6 21 *SA*[2]*B* λαμβάνειν ἐπί, Mk 4 36 *S*(*B* ⲱⲗⲓ) παραλ. ἐν ; HL 110 *B* ⲧ. ⲙⲡⲁⲣϩⲱⲥ ⲉⲡ-ϫⲟⲓ ἐμβάλλειν εἰς ; MIE 2 373 *B* ⲁⲩⲧⲁⲗⲟϥ ⲉⲟⲩⲓⲱ, El 56 *A* ⲁⲩⲧⲁⲗⲉⲓ ⲁⲡϫⲁⲉⲓ, BM 1146 *S* *ships* ⲁⲛⲧ. ⲛ-ⲛⲏⲣⲡ ⲉⲣⲟⲟⲩ, AZ 23 105 *S* ⲧⲁⲗⲟⲟⲩ ⲉⲡⲕⲱⲧ, PLond 4 471 *S* ⲙⲡⲉⲛⲧ. ⲗⲁⲁⲩ (*sc* tax) ⲁⲣⲱⲙⲉ ⲡⲁⲣⲁ ⲧⲉϥϭⲟⲙ, J 4 85 *S* ⲁⲓⲧⲁⲗⲉ ⲙⲁⲣⲧⲉⲣⲟⲥ ⲉⲣⲟⲥ (*sc* deed), CDan 94 *B* ⲁⲓⲧ. ⲡⲉϥⲣⲁⲛ ⲉⲣⲟⲓ, BKU 1 30 *F* ⲙⲡⲉⲗⲧⲁⲗⲁⲃ ⲉⲛϣⲓ (*l* ϣⲉ), AM 194 *B boy* ⲉⲡⲧⲁⲓⲧⲁⲗⲟϥ ⲉⲣⲟⲕ *sent* (? riding) *to thee* ;   qual : Is 21 9 *B*(*S* ⲁ. ⲉϩⲣⲁⲓ ⲉⲭⲛ-), Hag 2 23 *SAB* ἀναβάτης, AP 15 *A*[2] *lioness* ⲉⲣⲉⲑⲉⲕⲗⲁ ⲧ. ⲉⲣⲟⲥ καθίζειν ἐπάνω ; ShMich 550 14 *S beast* ⲉⲧⲉⲕϩⲙⲟⲟⲥ ⲉⲭⲱϥ ⲏ ⲉⲕⲧ. ⲉⲣⲟϥ, BAp 12 *S* ⲉϥⲧ. ⲉⲛⲛⲟϭ ⲛϩⲁⲣⲙⲁ, Mor 25 134 *S staggering as those* ⲉⲧⲧ. ⲉⲡⲡⲉⲗⲁⲧⲟⲥ, AM 185 *B cargo* ⲉⲧⲧ. ⲉⲣⲟϥ (*sc* ship), Mor 16 47 *S* ⲉⲣⲉⲟⲩϭⲣϭⲥ ⲧ. ⲉⲣⲟϥ = BMis 205 *S* ⲉϥⲧⲱⲟⲩⲛ ϩⲁⲟⲩϭⲣ., C 86 329 *B* ⲟⲩⲡⲉ ⲫⲁⲓ ⲉⲧⲧ. ⲉⲣⲟⲕ ?, CO 459 *S Book of Job* ⲉⲣⲉⲡⲡⲁⲣϩⲟⲓⲙⲓⲁ ⲧ. ⲉⲣⲟϥ *added to it*.

—— ⲉⲭⲛ- *SABF*, intr, *be raised upon* : ShA 2 253 *S* ⲡⲉⲧⲛⲁⲧ. ⲉⲭⲱϥ *tread on* asp ; ⲧⲁⲗⲉ *S* : Lu 19 4 ⲧ. ⲉⲭⲛⲟⲩϩⲱ (*B* ϣⲉ ⲉⲭ.) ⲁⲛⲁⲃ. ἐπί, ViK 9463 ⲛⲧⲁϥⲧ. ⲉⲭⲛ- = C 89 14 *B* ⲉⲧⲁϥⲁⲗⲏⲓ ⲉⲭ. ; tr, *raise, lay upon* : Ge 48 17 *B*(*S* ⲟⲩⲱϩ) τιθέναι ἐπί, Lev 1 4 *S*(*B* ⲉϩ. ⲉⲭ.), Lam 3 53 *S*(ShA 2 95, *B*

ⲧⲁⲣⲟ) ἐπιτ. ἐπί, Mt 19 13 *S*(*B* ⳉⲱ) ἐπιτ. dat, Is 61
10 *S*(*B* ✝) περιτ. dat, Mt 6 27 *B*(*S* ⲟⲩⲱⲣ) προστ.
ἐπί; Est 6 9 *S* ἀναβιβάζειν ἐπί, Hab 3 19 *B*(*SA*
ⲧⲁⲣⲟ ⲉⲣⲁⲧ⸗) ἐπιβιβ. ἐπί; Ap 2 24 *S*(*B* ⲣⲓⲟⲅⲓ) βάλλειν ἐπί, Nu 19 2 *S*(*B* ⲉ-), Lu 9 62 *S* ⲧ. ⲧⲟⲟⲧ⸗ (*B*
ⲣⲓ ⲧⲟⲧ⸗) ἐπιβ. ἐπί; Jos 3 14 *SB* αἴρειν; Deu 32 11
S(*B* ϥⲓ), Hos 11 3 *B*(*A* ⲁⲣⲣ. ⲁ×ⲛ-) ἀναλαμβάνειν
ἐπί; Ac 21 35 *S*(*B* ⲧⲱⲟⲩⲛ) βαστάζεσθαι ὑπό; Job
2 12 *B*(*S* ϣⲱϣ) καταπάσσειν; Br 255 *S* crown ⲧⲁⲗⲟϥ ⲉ×ⲛⲧⲁⲡⲉ, ShLouvre 10600 *S* ⲉⲧⲙⲧⲁⲗⲉ ⲣⲁⲧⲛ
ⲉ×ⲛⲧⲉⲥⲣⲓⲛ, Aeg 249 *S* bishop ⲛⲁⲧⲁⲗⲉ ⲛⲉϥϭⲓ×
ⲉ×ⲛⲡⲇⲓⲁⲕⲟⲛⲟⲥ, ViK 9450 *S* agreed to ⲧ. ⲙ̄ⲡ̄ⲡⲁⲣⲁ-
ⲡⲧⲱⲙⲁ ⲉ×ⲛ̄ⲙⲁⲣⲓⲛⲟⲥ, Lant 22 *F* ⲡⲣⲁⲛ ⲛ̄ⲧⲁⲩ-
ⲧⲁⲗⲁϥ ⲉ×ⲱⲓ, Cat 146 *B* wishing to ⲧⲁⲗⲉ ⲙⲉⲧⲣⲁⲙⲁⲟ
ⲉ×ⲉⲛⲧⲉϥⲙⲉⲧⲣⲁⲙⲁⲟ *add*;   qual : Ex 15 19 *F*
(BM 493, *B* ϭⲁⲥⲓ) ἀναβάτης, Jer 22 4 *S*(*B* ⲁⲗⲏⲓ)
ἐπιβαί. ἐπί; R 1 3 58 *S* Baptist's head ⲧ. ⲉ×ⲛⲟⲩ-
ⲡⲟⲣⲛⲏ, AM 54 *B* ⲉϥⲧⲁⲗⲏⲟⲩⲧ ⲉ×ⲉⲛⲟⲩⲥⲗⲟⳉ, Ryl
320 *S* portion of tax ⲧ. ⲉ×ⲱⲟⲩ (*cf ib* 323).

—— ⲛ- dat *SBF* : Ge 22 9 *S*(*B* ⲉϩⲣ. ⲉ×.) ἐπι-
ⲧⲓⲑ. ἐπί; C 86 355 *B* ⲧⲁⲗⲱⲟⲩ ⲛ̄ⲣⲁⲡⲉ×ⲛⲟⲩ (var ⲉ-),
ib 264 *B* ⲛⲁϥⲧ.† ⲛ̄ⲡⲟⲩⲣⲟⲟ, AM 315 *B* ⲧⲁⲗⲉ ⲑⲩⲥⲓⲁ
ⲙⲡⲉⲕⲛⲟⲩ†, Ryl 321 *S* didst write ×ⲉⲧⲁⲗⲟⲟⲩ ⲛⲁⲓ
ⲉⲣⲏⲥ (*cf ib* ⲧⲛⲟⲟⲩ), Ep 338 *S* ⲛ̄ϥⲧⲗⲟⲟⲩ ⲛⲁⲕ;   *with:*
CO 227 *S* ⲧ. ⲡⲓϭⲁⲙⲟⲩⲗ ⲛ̄ϣⲉ; *cf* c ⲣⲛ-.

—— ⲣⲓ- *S*, *put upon, add to* : Ryl 338 ⲡⲕⲁⲧⲁⲧⲓⲙⲉ ⲛ̄ⲧⲁⲩⲧⲁⲗⲟⲟⲩ ⲣⲓⲱⲟⲩ *list of villages where*
(ships) *loaded*, *ib* 106 6 ⲧ. ⲡⲉⲧϣⲁϥⲉⲓ ⲉⲡⲉⲥⲏⲧ ⲣⲓⲡ-
ⲥⲟⲗϥ, Z 628 ⲧⲁⲗⲟⲟⲩ (nitre &c) ⲣⲓⲣⲙⲁ×.

—— ⲣⲛ- *SF*, *load with* : BMis 264 *S* ⲁϥⲁⲣ(ⳉⲉⲓ)
ⲛ̄ⲧ. ⲛϭⲁⲙⲟⲩⲗ ⲣⲛ̄ⲡ̄ⲧⲱⲃⲉ = Mor 30 39 *F*; *in,*
at (?) : WS 118 *S* ⲛ̄ⲏⲣⲡ ⲛ̄ⲧⲁⲡⲧⲁⲗⲟⲟⲩ ⲣⲛ̄ⲧⲟⲩⲣⲱ,
PRain 4712 *S* ⲡⲟⲥⲟⲛ ⲛ̄ⲃⲉⲛⲛ ⲛ̄ⲧⲁⲡⲧⲁⲗⲟϥ ⲣⲛ̄ⲡⲉⲧⲙⲉ
collected in villages as διανομή, Kr 22 *F* ⲧ[ⲉⲓ]ⲛⲓ ⲡⲉ-
ⲧⲉⲃⲛⲁⲩⲓ ⲧⲉⲧⲁⲗⲁⲩ ⲣⲉ(ⲛ)ⲡⲉⲛⲓ & *transport* (?) *them to*
thy house.

—— ⲣⲓ×ⲛ- *SB* (mostly), *lay upon* : Lam 2 10 *B*
(*F* ⲉⲗⲏⲓ ⲉ×.) ἀναβιβ. ἐπί; ALR '06 473 *Sᶠ* name ⲛ̄-
ⲧⲁⲩⲧⲁⲗⲁϥ ⲣⲓ×ⲱⲓ, C 43 228 *B* ⲁⲩⲧⲁⲗⲟϥ ⲣ. ⲟⲩⲥ̄ⲧⲟⲥ,
Va 63 23 *B* ⲁϥⲧ. ⲛ̄ⲕⲉⲓ̄ ⲛ̄ⲣⲟⲙⲡⲓ ⲣ. ⲡⲓⲉⲱⲟⲩ of his
life (4 Kg 20 6) = BMis 409 *S* ⲟⲩⲱⲣ, MR 5 54 *F*
ⲧ. ⲧⲉⲕⲯⲩⳉⲏ ⲣⲓ×ⲟⲓ ϣⲁϣⲟⲣⲡ ⲉⲗⲉⲥⲧⲓ ⲧⲁⲉⲓ ⲛⲉⲕ, C
43 215 *B* ⲉϥⲧ.† ⲣ. ⲟⲩⲅⲁⲣⲙⲁ.
With following adverb.

—— ⲉⲃⲟⲗ *S*, *bring, send out* : Tor 43 jars ⲛ̄ⲧⲁ-
ⲧⲁⲗⲟⲟⲩ ⲉⲃ. to sell, ST 351 send wine & I will ⲧ.
ⲥⲟⲩⲛ[ⲧⲟⲩ ⲉⲃⲟ]ⲗ ⲛⲁⲕ, PMich 3539 ⲧⲁⲗⲟⲟⲩ (*sc* jars)
ⲉⲃ. ⲛ̄ⲁ ϭⲁⲙⲟⲩⲗ ⲣⲓⲧⲟⲟⲧⲩ ⲛ-.

—— ⲉⲡϣⲱⲓ *B*, *raise, rise up* : Ez 6 13 *S* ⲉⲣⲣⲁⲓ
διδόναι; C 41 45 chanter ⲁϥⲧⲁⲗⲟϥ ⲉ. ⲁϥⲉⲣ ⲙⲉⲗⲉⲧⲏ
= Miss 4 400 ⲗⲉⲟ; c ⲛ- dat : Ez 20 28 (*S* do) θύειν
dat, AM 307 ⲛ̄ⲧⲁⲧ. ⲑⲩⲥⲓⲁ ⲉ. ⲙⲡⲉⲕⲛⲟⲩ†.

—— ⲉⲣⲟⲩⲛ *S*, *bring, send in* : ST 128 ⲛ̄ⲥⲟⲩⲟ

ⲛ̄ⲧⲁⲡⲧⲁⲗⲟⲟⲩ ⲉⲣ., Ep 353 ⲕⲟⲩⲱϣ ⲉⲧⲁⲗⲟⲟⲩ ⲉⲣ. opp
ⲉⲧⲣⲁⲕⲁⲁⲩ ⲙⲡⲓⲙⲁ, Mor 31 101 ⲁϥⲧⲁⲗⲟⲟⲩ ⲉⲣ. ⲉⲧⲣⲓ,
BM 1103 grain ⲧⲁⲣⲟⲟⲩ ⲉⲣ. ⲉⲧⲁⲡⲟⲑⲏⲕⲉ, CO 244
14 ⲛ̄ⲧⲁⲧⲗⲟϥ (*sic l*) ⲉⲣ. ⲛⲁⲕ.

—— ⲉⲣⲣⲁⲓ, -ⲛⲓ, -ⲗⲏⲓ *SAA²BF*, *rise, raise up*,
intr : Mk 1 44 *S*(*B* ⲓⲛⲓ ⲉⲥⲟⲩⲛ) προσφέρειν; BMis
567 *S* ⲉⲓⲧ. ⲉⲣ. ⲙⲡⲡⲉ̄, ShC 73 156 *S* ⲉⲓ ⲉⲡⲉⲥⲛⲧ opp
ⲧ. ⲉ. to reading-desk, BAp 91 *S* ⲁ⳿ⲧ. ⲉ. & looked
over wall = MIE 2 361 *B* ⲧⲱⲟⲩⲛ, P 129²⁰ 156 *S*
ⲉⲩⳉⲏ ⲛ̄ⲧ. ⲉ., Z 321 *S* ⲁϥⲧⲁⲗⲉ ⲉ. ⲣⲓ×ⲛⲟⲩⲧⲱⲣⲧⲣ,
ViK 9775 *S* ⲃ̄ⲱⲕ ⲛ̄ⲧ. ⲉ. ⲣⲁⲡⲉⲕⲛⲟⲃⲉ *i e* give thanks
to him that healed thee;   tr : Lev 21 6 *S*(*B* do),
Pro 21 27 *SA*, He 9 9 *SF*(*B* do) προσφ., Ge 8 20
S(*B* ⲓⲛⲓ ⲉⲣⲣⲏⲓ) ἀναφ.; Aeg 287 *S* (var om ⲉⲣ.)
προσάγειν; Lu 1 9 *S*(*B* ⲓⲛⲓ ⲉⲣ.) θυμιᾶν; PS 369 *S*
ⲁ⳿ⲧ. ⲉ. ⲛ̄ⲧⲉⲡⲣⲟⲥⲫⲟⲣⲁ, ShA 2 150 *S* ⲧⲁⲗⲉ ⲙⲁⲥⲉ ⲉ.,
AM 286 *B* ⲁϥⲧⲁⲗⲉ ⲗⲩⲃⲁⲛⲟⲥ ⲉ., Mor 30 44 *F* ⲁ⳿-
ⲧⲁⲗⲁϥ ⲉⲣⲗⲏⲓ (*sc* canopy) = *ib* 29 38 *S* ⲧⲁⲣⲟϥ ⲉⲣⲁⲧϥ,
BKU 1 21 ro *Sᶠ* recipe ⲕⲧ. ⲉ. ⲛⲙⲙⲁⲩ *add water*,
PLond 4 482 *S* ⲙⲡⲉⲛⲧ]ⲁⲗⲟ ⲗⲁⲁⲩ (of taxes) ⲉ.
ⲡⲁⲣⲁ ⲡⲉⲛⲧⲁⲡⲧⲁⲁⲩ, Kr 64 *F*]ⲧⲁⲗⲟⲟⲩ ⲉⲣⲗ. ⲣⲉⲡ-
ⲙⲉⲣⲓⲥⲙⲱⲥ *make return*, *add* (?) in tax-register,
Ryl 311 *S* ⲁϥⲧⲁⲗⲉ ⲣⲱϥ ⲉ. ×ⲉⲁ⳿ⲉⲓⲥ;   ⲉⲣ. ⲉ- :
Nu 21 33 *S* ⲧⲁⲗⲉ ⲉ. ⲉ- (*B* ⲓ ⲉ-) ἀναβαί. εἰς, Mani
1 *A²* ⲁϥⲧ. ⲁ. ⲁⲕⲧⲛⲥⲓⲫⲱⲛ;   ⲉⲣ. ⲉ×ⲛ- : Ge 22 9
SB, Mt 9 18 *S*(*B* ⳉⲱ ⲣⲓ×.) ἐπιτιθ. ἐπί; Joel 2 7
A(*B* ϣⲉ ⲉ×.) ἀναβαί. ἐπί, Ex 4 20 *A*(*B* ⲉ-) ἀναβιβ.
ἐπί; Mt 5 23 *S*(*B* ⲓⲛⲓ ⲉⲣ. ⲉ×.) προσφ. ἐπί; Hos 11
3 *A*(*B* om ⲉⲣ.) ἀναλαμ. ἐπί; Si 8 4 *S* ἐπιστοιβάζειν ἐπί; Br 236 *S* ⲛⲉⲓⲁⲩⲛⲁⲙⲓⲥ...ⲉⲣⲉⲡⲙⲟⲛⲟⲅⲉⲛⲏⲥ
ⲧ.† ⲉ. ⲉ×ⲱⲟⲩ, ShC 73 59 *S* ⲧⲁⲗⲉ ⲧⲟⲩⲅⲉⲣⲛⲧⲉ ⲉ. ⲉ×ⲛ-
ⲧⲉⲩⲕⲉⲟⲩⲉⲓ, ShA 2 284 *S* ⳉⲧ.† ⲁⲛ ⲉ. ⲉ×ⲙⲡⲉⲧⲛⲡⲡⲁ
is not borne in upon your minds (*cf* ⲁⲗⲉ 1 Cor 2 9 *S*),
AP 25 *A²* ⲁ⳿ⲧⲉⲗⲉ ⲧⲟⲟⲧⲩ ⲁ. ⲁ×ⲱⲉⲓ, C 41 37 *B* ⲁ⳿ⲧ-
ⲧⲁⲗⲟ ⲧⲉϥⲫⲁⲧ ⲉⳅ. (*l* ⲉⲣ.) ⲉ×ⲱϥ, Miss 4 712 *S* ⲁ⳿ⲧ.
ⲛⲧⲉϥⲉⲣⲃ̄ⲱⲧ ⲉ. ⲉ×ⲱⲥ, *ib* 4 560 *S* at death ⲁ⳿ⲧ. ⲉ.
ⲉ×ⲱϥ ⲛ̄ⲧⲉⲡⲣⲟⲥⲫⲟⲣⲁ = Wess 11 156 *S* ⲁⲩⲥⲩⲛⲁⲡⲉ
ⲛ̄ⲧⲉⲡⲣⲟⲥⲫ. ⲉ×ⲱϥ = C 89 209 *B* ⲓⲛⲓ ⲉ. ⲉ×ⲱϥ, *ib*
43 200 *B* ⲑⲣⲉ-...ⲧ. ⲑⲩⲥⲓⲁ ⲡⲱⲟⲩ ⲉⲣ.;   ⲧⲁⲗⲉ *S* :
Ps 90 13 (*B* ⲣⲱⲙⲓ) ἐπιβαί. ἐπί; Miss 4 685 ⲁ⳿ⲧ. ⲉⲣ.
ⲉ×ⲛⲧⲥⲓⲃ̄ⲧ;   as nn : Lev 7 34 *S*(*B* = Gk) ἐπίθεμα.

—— nn m *S*, *raising up, offering* : Lev 3 5 (*B*
diff) κάρπωμα, Job 42 8 (*B* ϣⲟⲩϣⲱⲟⲩϣⲓ) κάρπωσις,
Ge 22 3 (*B* ϭⲗⲓⲗ) ὁλοκάρπ.; Ps 50 19 (*B* = Gk)
ἀναφορά; BM 304 sheep [ⲉ]ⲡⲧ.; He 6 2 ⲟⲩⲧ. ⲛϭⲓ×,
F ⲧ. ϭⲓ×, *B* ⳉⲁ ×ⲓ× ἐπίθεσις.

ⲙⲁ ⲛ̄ⲧ., *place of rising, whereon to mount* : Mani
2 *A²* fourteen ⲙⲁ ⲛ̄ⲧ. ⲉⲧⲁⲓⲛⲥⲟⲩⲥ ⲧ. ⲁⲣⲁⲩ, Miss 8
212 *S* ⲙⲁ ⲛ̄ⲧ. ⲉⲣⲣⲁⲓ (*cf* Dan 3 38).

×ⲓⲛⲧ. *B*, *raising* : Lev 24 6 (*S* diff) ⲧⲁⲗⲱⲟⲩ ⲉⲡϣⲱⲓ ⲛ×. ⳉ̄ θέμα. *Cf* ⲥⲟⲛ measure.

ⲧⲓⲗⲓ, ⲧⲉ. *B* nn m, *fenugreek* = τῆλις (BIF 28 84) :

BMOr 8775 133, P 55 8 ⲡⲓⲧ. ظلّ, Montp 151 ⲧⲉ
Cf ⲁⲗⲓ & ⳉⲱϥⲓ.

ⲧⲟⲓⲗⲉ *SO*, ⲧⲁⲓ. *A²*, vb intr *rise up* : PS 6 ⲁⲓⲧ ⲧ.
ⲏ ⲁϥⲣⲱⲗ ⲉⲡϫⲓⲥⲉ, Mani 1 *A²* ⲁϥⲉⲓ ⲁⲃⲁⲗ ⲁϥⲧ ⲁⲡⳉ[ⲓ-
ⲥ]ⲉ, AZ 21 94 *O* spirits ⲙⲁⲣⲟⲩⲧ. ⲛⲥⲉⲓ ⲉⲣⲟⲩⲛ. *Cf*
? ⲧⲁⲗⲟ(-ⲗⲉ).

ⲧⲱⲓⲗⲓ *F* nn m, meaning unknown : BM 618 in
account ⲣⲁⲡⲧ. (no context).

ⲧⲱⲗⲓ, ⲧⲟ. *F* *v* ⲧⲱⲣⲉ *hand*.

ⲧⲗⲏ *S* (as nn), ⲑⲗⲏ *B* vb intr, *drip, let drop*,
ⲥ ⲉⲃⲟⲗ ϩⲁ- : Ps 67 9 (*S* ϩⲱⲟⲩ) στάζειν ἀπό; ⲥ
ⲉⲡⲉⲥⲏⲧ : Jer 51 6 σ., Am 9 13 (*SA* ϣⲟⲩⲟ ⲉⲃⲟⲗ)
ἀποσταλάζειν; ⲥ ⲉⳉⲛ- : C 41 46 ⲡⲁⲓⲧⲉⲗⲧⲓⲗⲓ
ⲉⲧⲟ. ⲉⳉⲱⲕ; ⲥ ϩⲓϫⲉⲛ- : Ex 9 33, Ps 71 6 (var
ⲑⲗⲏⲗⲓ, *S* ϩ.) σ. ἐπί; tr : Pro 10 32 (var ⲇⲟ, *SA*
diff) ἀποστάξ., Mic 2 11 (*SA* ⲧⲗⲧⲗ) σταλάζ.; MG
25 235 udders ⲑ. ⲉⲣⲱϯ ⲉϩⲣⲏⲓ; as nn : Nu 6 4
S ⲏⲣⲡ ⲛⲧ. (var ⲧⲗⲧⲗ, *B*=Gk) *strained, filtered* ἀπὸ
στεμφύλλων (cf ⲅⲗ Rec 25 149 n); MG 25 255
mended cup ⳉⲱ ⲛⲟⲩⲑ. ⲉⲃⲟⲗ ⲁⲛ. *Cf* ⲧⲗⲧⲗ.

ⲧⲗⲱ (?) *S* nn, meaning unknown : Kr 92 flax
contract ⲧⲁⲑⲓⲟ ⲡⲣⲏⲃ ⲡⲡⲉⲧⲗⲱ (*sic*) ⲛⲁⲙⲁ ⲧ[.

ⲧⲱⲗⲉⲃ *F* *v* ⲧⲱⲗⲙ.

ⲧⲱⲗⲕ *SA²*, ⲗ𝔠 (once) *S*, -ⲕⲉⲗ *Sᶠ*, ⲧⲟⲗⲕ⸗ *S* vb
tr, *pluck out* : Is 18 7 (*B* ⲱⲗⲓ ⲉⲃⲟⲗ), Mt 12 1 (*B*
ⲥⲱⲗⲡ, *F* ⲧ[ⲱⲕⲉ]ⲙ), Lu 6 1 (*B* ϥⲱϫⲓ) τίλλειν, Ps 51
5 (PS 103, var & *B* ⲇⲟ) ἐκτ.; Mor 18 157 ⲕⲧ. ⲛ-
ⲡⲉⲕⲥⲁⲣϩ σπαράσσειν; P 129¹⁶ 18 ⲁϥⲧ. ⲙⲡⲃⲱ ⲛ-
ⲧⲉϥⲁⲡⲉ, Miss 4 699 ϥⲉⲣϩⲙⲓⲥ ... ⲉⲩϣⲁⲛⲧⲟⲗⲕⲟⲩ,
Mani 1 *A²*]ⲃⲟⲧⲁⲡⲏ...ⲉⲓⲧ. [ⲙⲙⲁⲥ; intr ⲥ ⲛⲥⲁ-
emphatic : BMar 112 ⲁϥⲧⲱⲗ𝔠 ⲛⲥⲁⲡϥⲱ of head ⲧ.
acc, Mor 41 165 ⲛⲥⲉⲧ. ⲛⲥⲱϥ (sc martyr's tongue)
ϣⲏⲙ ϣⲏⲙ; ⲥ ⲉⲃⲟⲗ : BMis 21 ⲁⲥⲧ. ⲉⲃ. ⲙⲡⲉⲥⲃⲱ,
Mor 39 37 *Sᶠ* ⲁⲩⲧ. ⲉⲃ. ⲛⲥⲁⲡⲃⲱ (*B* C 43 56 diff).

ⲧⲁⲗⲕⲁ *F* *v* ⲧⲁⲣⲕⲟ.

ⲧⲗⲟⲕⲗⲉⲕ *S* vb tr, meaning uncertain : R 1 4
22 mad girl ⲁⲥⲧ. ⲛⲧⲉⲥⲁⲡⲉ ⲙⲡⲉⲥϥⲱ *rotare crinem*
(λύειν τ. κόμην PKerameus Ἀνάλ. Ἱερ. 5 98). *Cf*
? ⲧⲱⲗⲕ.

ⲧⲉⲗⲏⲗ *SAA²F*, ⲧⲗⲁ *S* (once), ⲧⲁⲗⲏⲗ *A²* (Mani),
ⲑⲉⲗⲏⲗ *B*, vb intr, *rejoice* : 2 Kg 1 20 *SB*, Ps 50 8
SA(Cl)*B*, Is 5 14 *F* (*SB* om), Jo 8 56 *SA²B*, AP
12 *A²* ἀγαλλιᾶσθαι; Lu 6 23 *SB* σκιρτᾶν; PS 81
S ϯⲧ. ⲉⲙⲁϣⲟ ϩⲉⲁⲕⲥⲱⲗⲡ ⲡⲁⲛ, Mani 1 *A²* ⲣⲉⲩⲉ
ⲧⲁ., DeV 2 14 *B* ⲉϥⲑ. when he saw; ⲥ ⲉϫⲛ-,
rejoice at : Ps 9 14 *S* (*B* refl), Is 65 19 *SB* ἀγ. ἐπί,
ib 19 5 *S* (*B* ⲟⲩⲱⲛϩ ⲉⲃⲟⲗ) ἀγ. ἐν; TU 24 1 4 *S*
crowd ⲧ. ⲉϫⲙⲡⲉⲛⲧⲁϥϣⲱⲡⲉ, Cl 33 2 *A* ⲁϥⲧ. ⲁⳉⲡ-
ⲡⲉϥϩⲃⲏⲟⲩⲉ, DeV 2 51 *B* ⲙⲡⲉⲣⲣⲁϣⲓ ⲉⳉ....ⲁⲗⲗⲁ ⲑ.

ⲉⳉ. ⲡⲟⲩϫⲛⲧⲁⲥⲑⲟ; ⲉϩⲣⲁⲓ ⲉⳉⲛ- : BG 30 *S* ⲁϥⲧ....
ⲉϩ. ⲉⳉⲙⲡⲟⲅⲟⲓⲛ, El 38 *A* ⲉⲩⲧ. ⲁϥ. ⲁⳉⲱⲟⲩ; ⲥ
ϩⲓϫⲛ- : Ps 12 6 *F* (MR 5 34, *S* ⲉ ⳉⲛ-, *B* ⲉϩⲣⲏⲓ ⲉⳉ.)
ἀγ. ἐπί; ⲥ ⲛ- sim : Ps 32 1 *S* (var ⲉ-, *B* refl) ἀγ.
ἐν, ib 94 1 *S* (*B* ⲉϣ ⲗⲏⲗⲟⲅⲓ) ἀγ. dat; refl : Ps
149 5 *B*, Jo 5 35 *SA²B*, AP 13 *A²*, ROC 27 165 *B*
ἀγ.; Br 254 *S* ⲁϥⲧ. ⲙⲙⲟϥ ⲡⲓⲙⲁⲩ, BM 176 *S*
ⲡⲉϥⲧⲗⲗ ⲙⲙⲟⲟⲩ.

— nn m *SABF*, *joy* : Ps 31 7 *SB*, Is 51 3 *SB*
ἀγαλλίαμα, Ps 50 12 *SA*(Cl)*B*, Lu 1 14 *SB* ἀγαλ-
λίασις; 2 Kg 6 12 *B* (*S*=Gk), Is 35 10 *SF* (*B* ⲟⲩⲡⲟϥ) εὐφροσύνη; BMis 90 *S* ⲁⲓⲱϩⲁⲡⲏⲥ ⲕⲓⲙ ϩⲛⲟⲩⲧ.
in her womb, ib 185 *S* ⲉⲩⳉⲱ ⲛⲟⲩⲧ., DeV 2 161 *B*
ⲟⲩⲣⲁϣⲓ ⲛⲉⲙⲟⲩⲑ.; ⲡⲉϥ ⲛⲧ., ⲡⲑ., *v* ⲡⲉϥ & *cf*
Ps 44 7, TEuch 1 286 ἀγαλλιέλαιον الليليون, ⲉⲧⲉⲡⲓ-
ⲡⲉϥ ⲡⲡⲓⲕⲁⲧⲏⲭⲟⲩⲙⲉⲛⲟⲥ.

ⲧⲗⲓⲗ *F* *v* ⲧⲣⲓⲣ.

ⲧⲗⲟⲗ *F* nn m, meaning unknown : Kr 134 lease
regarding ⲡⲉⲛⲧ. ⲥⲡⲉⲟⲩ (ⲟⲩ)ⲓⲱⲣⲓ[(but might be
otherwise divided).

ⲧⲗⲟⲩⲗⲉ, ⲧⲗ[ⲟ]ⲗⲗⲉ *S* nn, meaning unknown :
BP 9421 among ⲓⲧⲉⲥ (εἶδος) of bronze, ⲟⲩⲕⲁⲗⲁϥⲧ,
ⲟⲩⲧ., ⲟⲩⲃⲁⳉ ⲡⲣ ⲡⲉϥ, ST 116 sim list ⲟⲩⲧⲗⲟ. ⲙ-
ⲡⲁⲧϣⲉⲗⲉ[ⲧ] *bridegroom's*... *Cf* ? ⲕⲗⲟⲟⲗⲉ *S* nn.

ⲧⲱⲗⲙ *SA²*, -ⲙⲉ *AA²*, ⲑⲱⲗⲉⲃ *B*, ⲧⲱⲗⲉⲃ *F*,
ⲧⲟⲗⲙ⸗ *S*, ⲑⲟⲗⲙ⸗ (once), ⲑⲟⲗⲃ⸗ *B*, ⲧⲟⲗⲙ† *S*, ⲧⲁ.†
Sᶠ, ⲑⲟⲗⲉⲃ† *B*, ⲧⲁⲗⲉϥ† *F* vb intr, *be defiled, be-*
smirched : Si 13 1 *SB*, Is 65 4† *S* (*B* 𝔠ⲱⳉⲉⲙ), 1 Cor
8 7† *SF* (*B* ⲇⲟ) μολύνεσθαι; 2 Cor 6 3 *B* (*S* ⲥⲱⲱϥ)
μωμεῖσθαι, 2 Pet 2 13 *B* (*S* ⳉⲱⲣⲙ) μῶμος; BHom
4 *S* ⲙⲏⲡⲟⲧⲉ ⲛⲥⲧ. ῥυπᾶσθαι; Mk 7 5† *S* (var ⳉ.) *B*
κοινός; ViK 9349 *Sᶠ* ⲉⲩⲧ.† ⲁⲩⲱ ⲉⲩⳉⲁϩⲙ; tr,
defile, pollute : Tob 3 13 *S*, Cant 5 3 *S* (*F* ⲱⲗⲉⲃ),
AP 8 *A²* ⲡⲧⲉⲧⲛⲧⲱⲗⲙ. ⲛⲧⲥⲁⲣϩ ⲙⲟⲗ.; Mani 2 *A²* ⲁϥ-
ⲧⲱⲗⲙⲉ ⲛⲧⲡⲣⲟ[ⲥⲫⲟⲣⲁ, BM 267 190 *S* mire could
not ⲧ. ⲡⲓⲉⲣⲏⲙⲓⲁⲥ, Va 58 125 *B* Thine image ⲁⲓⲑⲟⲗ-
ⲃⲉⲥ, ib 57 247 *B* ⲧⲉϥϫⲓϫ...ⲉⲧⲁϥⲑⲟⲗⲙⲉⲥ.

With following preposition. ⲥ ⲉ- *S* obj : ShA
2 4 man whom ⲁⲕⲁⲑⲁⲣⲥⲓⲁ ⲧ. ⲉⲣⲟϥ; *with* : Ryl 407
ⲡⲛⲧ. ϩⲁⲧⲕ ⲉϣⲟⲉⲓϣ; ⲥ ⲙⲛ- : Ap 14 4 *SB* μολ.
μετά; BAp 56 *S* ⲙⲡⲉⲓⲧ. ⲙⲡⲥϩⲓⲙⲉ ἀμιγής; ⲥ ⲛ-,
with, by : Is 59 3† *S* (*B* ϭⲉⲛ-) μολ. dat; ib 14 19†
S (*B* ϩⲱⲣⲡ) φύρεσθαι dat; BMis 541 *S* hands ⲧ.†
ⲡⲥⲛⲟϥ ὁλαίματος; ShMIF 23 158 *S* fingertip ⲧ.†
ⲙⲙⲟⲟⲩ, C 86 214 *B* ⲙⲡⲉϥϭⲁⲗⲁϫ ⲑ. ⲙⲙⲟⲟⲩ
(cf Mt 14 25); ⲉⲃⲟⲗ ⲛ- : ShWess 9 108 *S* fingers ⲧ.†
ⲉⲃ. ⲙⲙⲟⲟⲩ, BMis 357 *S* lest they ⲧ. ⲉⲃ. ⲙⲙⲟⲛ⸗
BSM 20 *B* ⲡϣⲏⲧⲉⲡ; ⲥ ϩⲛ-, ϭⲉⲛ-, as last : Ge
37 31 *B* μολ. dat, ClPr 54 36 *S* ⲉⲧⲧ.† ϩⲛⲧⲕⲁⲕⲓⲁ=
EW 153 *B* μολ. ἐν; 2 Kg 20 12 *S* φύρ. ἐν; Pro 20
1† *S* (*A* ⲧⲱ.) συμπλέκειν dat; Z 322 *S* ϩⲙⲡϩⲟⲃⲉ

βορβοροῦσθαι ἐν; BHom 17 S ϩⲛⲟⲩⲗⲟⲓϩⲉ σπίλος γίνεσθαι; Mor 30 60 S spear ⲧ.† ϩⲙⲡⲉϥⲥⲛⲟϥ.

—— nn m SAA²B, stain, pollution: Jer 23 15 B, 2 Macc 5 27 A, 2 Cor 7 1 SB μολυσμός; Job 11 15 S(B ϭⲱ.) ῥύπος, Ja 1 21 SB ῥυπαρία, Eph 5 27 SB ῥυτίς (misread); Si 47 25 S μῶμος, 2 Cor 8 20 S ⲧⲉϭ ⲧ. (B ϣⲱϣ) μωμεῖσθαι; ShWess 9 145 S heretics ϫⲉ ϩⲉⲛⲧ. ⲛⲥⲁⲡⲉϥⲭⲡⲟ, Pcod 24 S ⲛⲉϫ ⲧ. ⲛⲥⲁⲧⲙⲛⲧⲛⲟⲩⲧⲉ, Wess 18 33 S ⲙⲡⲥ(Virgin)ⲟⲩⲱⲙ ⲟⲩⲧ., MIE 2 379 B ⲁϫⲙⲟⲩϫⲧ ⲡⲉⲙⲡⲟ. of women, AP 26 A²]ⲧ. ⲡⲓⲙ; † ⲧ., give stain: Si 30 32 S ⲙⲱ. διδόναι; FR 8 S ⲉⲧ† ⲡⲟⲩⲧ. ⲉⲧⲡⲁⲣⲑⲉⲛⲟⲥ, Miss 4 123 B ⲉⲣⲉⲍⲓⲟⲥⲕⲟⲣⲟⲥ † ⲟⲩⲑ. ⲙⲡⲛⲁϩⲧ†.

ⲁⲧⲧ., ⲑ. SAB, stainless, unpolluted: Sa 7 22 S ἀμόλυντος; Eph 1 4 SB, Cl 1 3 A, CaiEuch 640 B ἄμωμος; Est 2 2 S ἄφθορος; 1 Pet 1 4 S(B ⲁⲧ ⲗⲱⲙ)ἀμίαντος; CaiEuch 531 B, Leyd 442 S = Kropp 2 169 ἄχραντος; Z 278 S take heed ⲉⲧⲉⲧⲛⲟ ⲛⲁ. ἄσπιλος; DeV 2 15 B ϯⲁⲗ ⲛⲁ. of Incarnation.

ⲧⲗⲟⲙ S vb intr, meaning unknown: ShC 73 162 delay not ⲙⲡⲁⲣⲁ ⲡⲛϣⲓ to give rest to those bearing corpse to burial, ⲙⲡⲉⲣⲧ. ⲟⲛ ⲡⲁⲣⲁ ⲡⲛϣⲓ, ⲉⲧⲱⲛ ϩⲱϭϣⲡⲉ ⲡⲟⲩⲉ ⲙⲙⲟⲛ.

ⲧⲗⲟⲙ S, ⲑ. B, pl (?) ⲧⲗⲟⲟⲙ S(Si 7), ⲑⲗⲱⲙ B, nn m, furrow (cf חלם Lacr): Nu 22 24 S(P 44 107, var ϫⲏ)B, Job 39 10 SB pl, Ps 64 10 SB pl, Si 7 2 S pl, C 89 117 B ⲟⲩⲑⲗⲱⲙ αὖλαξ; Si 24 31 S πρασιά; BM 1247 162 B ⲡⲉϥⲑⲗⲱⲙ ...; BMar 47 S ⲡⲱϩ ⲙⲡⲉⲧ. ⲛⲧⲉⲥϣⲙⲉ ϩⲙⲡϩⲉⲉⲃⲉ, BMis 533 S husbandman ϭⲱϫⲉ ⲙⲡⲙⲟⲟⲩ ⲉⲡⲉⲧ.; ⲧⲓⲟⲙ S, ⲧⲓⲁⲙ S^a(cf HOLange Amenope 49): Glos 398 S^a ⲡⲧ. · ⲁⲩ ⲗⲁⲝ; ShA 2 25 S ploughman looks (to see) ⲛⲧⲉⲡⲉϥⲧ. ⲥⲟⲟⲩⲧⲛ, ShP 130⁴ 104 S ⲛⲧⲟϣ ⲛⲧ. ⲡⲟⲩⲕⲁϩ ⲛ ϩⲉⲛ ⲉⲓⲱⲣⲉⲛⲉ ϩⲉⲛⲱⲛⲉ ⲙⲡⲣⲉⲛⲕⲉⲗⲁⲉⲓⲛ.

ⲧⲱⲗⲡ F v ⲧⲱⲣⲡ sew.

ⲧⲱⲗⲥ S, ⲑ. B, ⲧⲟⲗⲥ† S, ⲑ.† B vb intr, be fixed, sunk: Ps 31 4 S(B ⲧⲱⲧⲥ)πηγνύναι; P 130⁴ 89 S save me from ⲗⲟⲓϩⲉ ϫⲉⲕⲁⲥ ⲛⲛⲉⲓⲧ.; c ⲉ-, in; Ps 68 2 S(PS 53 ⲁⲓⲧ. ⲏ ⲁⲓⲱⲙ, B & cit ShZ 638 S ϩⲛ-) π. εἰς; c ϩⲛ-, ϫⲉⲛ-: Ps 9 15 SB π. ἐν; ShA 1 439 S mire ⲉⲧⲉⲛⲧ.† ⲏ ⲉⲛⲗⲁⲗⲱ ⲛϩⲏⲧⲥ, R 2 1 53 S body ϫⲁ ϩⲙ...ϥⲧ.† ϩⲛⲟⲩⲕⲁ[ⲑⲁⲣⲥⲓⲁ, Ryl 94 103 S freezing lake ⲉⲁⲩⲧ. ⲛϩⲏⲧⲥ, MG 25 119 B ⲉⲅⲑ.† ϫⲉⲛⲑⲗⲱ(ⲓ)ϩⲓ.

ⲧⲁⲗⲁⲧⲏⲗ F v ⲧⲁⲗ.

ⲧⲗⲧⲗ S, -ⲗⲉ A, ⲧⲉⲗⲧⲉⲗ B vb intr, drip, let drop: Lev 15 19 B ῥέειν, ib 33 B(S ϣⲟⲅⲟ) -ροεῖν; Z 319 S ⲉϥⲧ. ⲉⲡⲉⲥⲏⲧ ⲉϫⲱϥ(sc stone)στάζειν, Pro 5 3 SAB ἀποσ.; ShA 2 49 S evil ⲉⲧⲧ. ⲛⲁϥ(sc heart), ShP 130² 12 S blood ⲉⲩⲧ. ⲉⲡⲉⲥⲏⲧ ϩⲓⲛⲉⲩⲥⲁⲣⲝ, ShViK 9345 S ⲧ. opp ⲥⲱⲕ, C 43 55 B blood ⲉϥⲧ. ϩⲓⲭⲉⲛ ⲡⲓⲕⲁϩⲓ; Nu 6 4 S ⲏⲣⲡ ⲛⲧ. (var ⲧⲗⲏ q v); tr:

Mic 2 11 SA(B ⲑⲗⲏ)σταλάζειν, Joel 3 18 B(S.A ϣ. ⲉⲃⲟⲗ)ἀποσταλ.; Lev 15 3 B ῥ., ib 22 4 B(S=Gk) -ρυής; ib 1 15 B(S ⲭⲗⲭⲗ, cf 5 9)στραγγίζειν; ShC 73 154 S ⲉⲧ. ⲁⲅⲱ ⲛⲥⲥⲣⲟⲙⲣⲙ (sic Mich 550 18) ⲛⲡⲉⲛⲧⲁⲛⲧϫⲣⲉ, Ryl 67 400 S ⲉϥⲧ. ⲛⲁⲡ...ⲡⲟⲩⲏⲣⲛ, R 1 3 76 S rocks ⲉⲩⲧ. ⲉⲡⲉⲥⲏⲧ ⲡⲟⲩⲙⲟⲟⲩ, DeV 2 13 B let clouds ⲧ. ⲡⲟⲩⲇⲓⲕⲁⲓⲟⲥⲩⲛⲏ (cf Is 45 8); c ⲉⲃⲟⲗ S: Bor 251 293 sponge ⲉⲥϣⲟⲩⲟ ϩⲙϫ ⲉⲡⲉⲥⲏⲧ ⲉⲥⲧ. ⲉⲃ.; as nn m B, dripping: Lev 20 18 (S ϣ. vb), ib 15 25 (S = Gk)ῥύσις.

ⲧⲁⲗϯⲗⲉ SA, ⲧⲉⲗⲧⲓⲗⲉ S, ⲧⲉⲗϯⲗⲓ, -ⲧⲓⲗⲓ B nn f m (Tri), drop: Job 36 27 SB, Mic 2 11 SAB σταγών; Sa 11 23 S ⲟⲩⲧ. ⲉⲁⲥⲉⲓ ῥανίς; BG 103 S ⲟⲩⲧ. ⲉⲃⲟⲗ ϩⲙⲡⲟⲩⲟⲓⲛ, Aeg 265 S ⲛⲧⲉ. of water of baptism, BSG 185 S ⲛⲧ. that leapt from boiling cauldron, Mus 34 197 B ϯⲧ....ⲉⲥⲉⲣ ⲉⲧⲏⲛ...ⲉϯ ⲛⲁⲥ, Tri 514 S ⲧⲥⲓⲉ ⲡⲕⲁϩ ϩⲙⲡⲉⲛⲧ., Va 61 95 B=P 131³ 84 S ⲥⲓϩⲛⲉ.

ⲧⲁⲗⲧⲉⲗ F nn, prob a kind of wine: CO 504 ⲟⲩ ⲕⲁⲧⲟⲥ ⲉⲧ. ⲟⲩⲁⲧⲉⲃ ⲛⲉⲛ, ib 496 on neck of jar ⲉⲛⲕ ⲕⲗⲏⲥⲓⲁⲥ ⲧ.

ⲧⲱⲗⲧⲉⲗ F v ⲧⲱⲣⲧ (ⲧⲱⲣⲧⲣ).

ⲧⲁⲗⲉϥ F v ⲧⲱⲗⲙ.

ⲧⲉⲗϭⲓ B nn f, kind of lizard: Bodl 325 154 ϯⲧ. ⲁⲝ͢ϫ, which in K 172 = ⲧⲉⲗⲙⲟⲛⲓⲁ. Cf ϫⲉⲛϫⲉⲛ.

ⲧⲗⲟϭ v ϫⲗⲟϭ.

ⲧⲁⲗϭⲟ SA²B, ⲧⲗϭⲟ AA²(Mani), ⲧⲉⲗϫⲁ, ϯⲗⲭⲁ F, ⲧⲁⲗϫⲉ- SAB, -ϭⲟ⸗ SB, ⲧ(ⲉ)ⲗⲕⲟ⸗ S^a, ⲧⲗϫⲁ⸗ AA², ⲧⲁⲗϫⲁ⸗ A², ⲧⲁⲗϫⲏ ⲩⲧ† S vb I tr, make to cease, heal (caus of ⲗⲁϭⲉ): Ex 15 26 SB (var ⲧⲟⲩϫⲟ), Hos 6 1 SAB, Mt 13 15 SF(B ⲧⲟⲩ.)ἰᾶσθαι; Mk 6 5 S(B ⲉⲣ φⲁϩⲣⲓ), MG 25 240 B ⲁⲩⲧ. ⲛϩⲁⲙⲙⲏϣ θεραπεύειν; Jo 5 11 SA²(B ⲟⲩϫⲁⲓ) ὑγιῆ ποιεῖν; Ez 34 4 SB σωματοποιεῖν; Job 6 26 S(B ⲕⲏⲛ)παύειν, Ps 84 3 S(B ϩⲱⲗ ⲉⲃⲟⲗ), Si 38 15 S καταπ.; ib 48 10 S κοπάζειν; Sa 18 21 S πέρας τιθέναι; Job 3 10 S (B ⲱⲗⲓ), He 2 15 B(S ⲡⲱⲗϭ)ἀπαλλάσσειν; ShC 73 16 S places where sword smiteth ⲁⲩⲱ ⲉⲧⲥⲧ. ⲙⲙⲟ ⲟⲩ, Mani 1 A² ⲉⲅⲟⲩⲱϣ ⲧⲗϫⲁϥ, ib ⲉϥⲁⲧⲗϭⲟ ⲛⲛⲉⲧ ϣⲁϣⲉ, El 88 A ϥⲛⲁⲧⲗϫⲁϥ = ib 120 S^a ⲧⲗⲕⲟⲟⲩ, BM 239 6 S ⲧⲙⲉⲣⲟⲅⲟⲥⲉ...ⲧⲁⲗϫⲉ ⲡⲉϥⲉⲓⲃⲉ (Jud 15 19), JKP 2 160 S ⲡⲉⲧⲧ. ⲙⲡⲟⲩⲟⲉⲓⲛ in skies, AM 252 B ⲙⲁⲧⲁⲗϭⲉ ⲧⲁⲓⲥⲣⲓⲙⲓ, CO 381 S^a let him make peace ⲛⲧⲉⲡⲁⲣⲓⲕⲉ ⲧⲉⲗⲕⲟϥ ϩⲓⲱⲉⲓ & blame cease from me(?).

II intr: Deu 32 39 S(B ⲧⲟⲩϫⲟ), Job 5 18 SA(Cl) B, Miss 4 525 S forthwith ⲁⲥⲧ. = C 89 44 B ἰᾶσ.; Ez 47 8 B(S ⲧⲁⲛϩⲟ) ὑγιάζειν; RNC 54 S ⲡⲉⲧⲥⲛϣ ⲛⲁⲧ., C 43 213 B not possible ⲛⲧⲉⲕⲧ., Mor 25 28 S ⲛϣⲱⲡⲉ...ⲧ.†, ib 28 165 S beheld saints ⲉⲩⲧ.†

With following preposition. c ϩⲛ-, ϫⲉⲛ-, heal from, of: Lu 8 2 S (varr ⲛ-, ⲉⲃⲟⲗ ϩⲛ-, B ⲉⲣ φ. ⲉⲃ. ϫⲉⲛ-)θερ. ἀπό; Is 1 16 A(Cl, var ⲗⲁϭⲉ, S ⲗⲟ, B ⲧ.

ⲉⲃ. ϫⲉⲛ-) παύ. ἀπό; Ryl 12 S ⲡⲉⲛⲧⲁⲅⲧ. ⲟⲏⲅⲉⲡϣⲱⲡⲉ, AM 205 B ⲁϥⲧⲁⲗϭⲟϥ ϫⲉⲛⲡⲓⲃⲁⲥⲁⲛⲟⲥ, BM 511 F ⲥⲉⲧ. ⲟⲏϣⲱⲡⲓ ⲛⲓⲃⲓ; ⲉⲃⲟⲗ ⲟⲏ-: Lu 7 21 S(B ⲉⲣ. ϥ.) θ. ἀπό; C 89 18 B ⲡⲧⲉϥⲧⲁⲗϭⲟϥ ⲉⲃ. ϫⲉⲛⲡⲉϥϣⲱⲡⲓ;   ⲥ ⲉⲃⲟⲗ ϧⲁ- B, desist from: Ps 33 14 (S ⲉⲃ. ϧⲛ-). Jer 33 3 (S ⲉⲓⲣⲉ neg) παύ. ἀπό;   ⲥ ⲉⲃ. ϧⲓϫⲉⲛ- B, make cease from off: Ps 73 8 (S ϥⲓ ϧⲓϫⲛ-) καταπ. ἀπό.

—— nn m SABF, healing: Ps 37 7 S(B ⲟⲩϫⲁⲓ), Pro 3 8 SAB, Jer 8 22 S(BHom 12)B ἴασις, ib 26 11 S(B ⲫⲁϩⲣⲓ) ἴαμα, Eccl 3 3 SF ⲧⲓⲗϫⲁ ἰάσασθαι; Ez 47 12 B ὑγίεια; ShWess 18 98 S ⲙⲁⲣⲉⲡ. ⲡⲡⲉⲡϣⲱⲱϣⲉ ⲉⲓ ⲉϧⲣⲁⲓ, PSBA 10 197 S till God ⲭⲁⲣⲓⳅⲉ ⲡⲁⲥ ⲙⲡⲧ., BM 511 F ⲟⲩⲧ. ⲡⲛⲟⲩⲁⲛ ⲛⲓⲃⲓ, CO 379 S God hath sent ⲡⲧ. ⲙⲡⲁⲃⲁⲗ, Hall 86 S ⲁⲡⲡⲉ ⲧ ⲡⲧ. ⲡⲁⲕ, AM 241 B ⲁϥⲧ ⲛⲟⲩⲧ. ⲛⲧⲁⲥⲁⲣⳁ, Z 231 S ⲕⲟⲩⲱϣ ⲉⲉⲓⲣⲉ ⲛϥⲉⲛⲕⲟⲩⲓ ⲛⲧ., BHom 32 S ⲉⲅⲉϫⲓ ⲛⲟⲩⲧ., AM 216 B ⲡⲁⲩϭⲓ ⲙⲡⲓⲧ. ⲉⲃⲟⲗ ϧⲓⲧⲟⲧϥ, Va 57 59 B ⲟⲩⲁⲧⲉⲣ ⲡⲕⲉⲧ.

ⲁⲧⲧ. SAB, not to be healed: Deu 32 33 B(S ⲗⲟ neg), Is 13 9 SB ἀνίατος; Till Oster 13 A ⲟⲩⲁ. ⲡⲉ ⲡⲉⲥⲥⲁϧ, AZ 21 151 S ⲡⲗⲏⲅⲏ ⲛⲁ.

ⲣⲉϥⲧ. SB, healer: Job 13 4 SB ἰατής, CaiEuch 397 B ⲛⲓⲣ. of souls ἰώμενος; as adj: BMis 530 S ⲥⲁⲉⲓⲛ ⲛⲣ., DeV 2 24 B ⲫⲁϩⲣⲓ ⲛⲣ.; ⲣⲉϥⲧ ⲧ. S: BM 330 137 ⲁⲩⲛⲁⲙⲓⲥ ⲛⲣ.; ⲙⲛⲧⲣⲉϥⲧ., healing power: Bor 253 140 S ⲧⲙ. ⲡⲧⲉⲕⲭⲁⲣⲓⲥ.

ϭⲓⲛ-, ϫⲓⲛⲧ., healing: Lu 5 17 B ⲡⲭ. (S ⲧ. vb) ἰᾶσθαι; Bor 226 212 S ϧⲉⲛⲥ.

ⲧⲗⲱϭⲉ   v ϭⲗⲟⲟϭⲉ.

ⲧⲁⲙ S nn f, meaning unknown: JAOS 48 155 ostr ϧⲁⲧⲧ.ⲡⲏⲩ(ⲗ̄ⲛⲁϥ) ⲛⲥⲟⲩⲟ ϧⲁⲡⲗⲁⲕⲓⲛⲉ ⲡⲏϥ ⲛⲥⲟⲩⲟ.

ⲧⲁⲉⲓⲙ, -ⲙⲉ F vb intr, help: ZNTW 24 90 if one come ⲧⲁⲉⲓⲙ ⲉⲗⲁϥ βοηθεῖν; as nn: Eccl 7 20 ⲉⲗ ⲧⲁⲓⲙⲉ (altered from -ⲓ) ⲉⲡⲓⲥⲃⲁ (S = Gk) β., Lam 1 7 sim. V Sitz Bayr Ak '25 4 15.

ⲧ(ⲉ)ⲙ-   v ⲧⲱⲙ & ⲧⲱⲱⲙⲉ.

ⲧⲙ- SAA², ⲧⲓⲙ- F(Eccl 5 4), ⲧⲁⲡ- A, ϣⲧ(ⲉ)ⲙ- BF negation of inf, conjunct, caus, condit, temporal, sometimes prefixed to nom subj. V Stern 452, Sdff 464, Till 206, Mallon 256.   Inf: Ps 33 13 SB, Hos 2 9 AB, 1 Cor 9 6 SBF, Br 102 S ϭⲱⲙ ⲉⲧⲟⲟⲧⲩ ⲉⲧⲁⲱⲣⲕ, Bor 226 158 S ⲡⲧⲙⲙⲉⲥⲧⲉ ⲗⲁⲁⲩ, J 79 68 S ⲛⲥⲉⲕⲱⲗⲉⲓ (l -ⲗϥⲉ) ⲙⲙⲟϥ ⲉⲧⲙⲃⲟⲕ ⲉϧⲣⲏⲡ, ShC 73 162 S ⲙⲡⲣⲱⲥⲕ ⲉⲧⲙⲧ ⲙⲧⲟⲛ, ViK 9751 S ⲙⲡⲉϥⲥⲙⲓⲛⲉ ⲉⲧⲙⲕⲁⲁϥ. conjunct: Pro 14 6 SA(B ⲛⲡⲉ-), Jth 10 13 S ⲛⲧⲉⲧⲙⲟⲩⲥⲁⲣⳁ ⲧ ⲉⲣⲟⲟⲩ, Mt 17 20 S(B do), PS 50 S let them stay in darkness ⲛⲥⲉⲧⲙⲛⲁⲩ ⲉⲃⲟⲗ, C 43 121 B if disobedient ⲛⲥⲉϣⲧⲉⲙⲟⲩⲱϣⲧ ⲛⲛⲓⲡⲟⲩⲧ, AP 27 A² ϭⲱϣⲧ ... ⲛⲧⲙⲧ ⲛⲟⲩⲥⲗⲁⲁⲧⲉ ⲛⲉⲛ;   caus: Ps 103 35 S(B conj), Lam 4 14 S ϧⲁ-

ⲡⲧⲣⲉϥⲧⲙϭⲙ ϭⲟⲙ, ShA 2 271 S ⲛⲑⲉ ⲉϥⲟⲩⲁϣⲥ ⲁⲡ ⲉⲧⲙⲧⲣⲉⲥϣⲱⲡⲉ, Cl 21 4 A it is right ⲁⲧⲏⲧⲙⲛⲡⲱⲧ ⲁⲃⲁⲗ; elliptic: ShC 73 144 S ⲁⲅⲱ ⲉⲧⲙⲧⲣⲉⲟⲩⲁ... ⲥⲱⲃⲉ, BMis 277 S ⲉⲧⲙⲡⲣⲱⲙⲉ ⲉⲧⲙⲙⲁⲩ ⲉⲓ; condit: Ex 4 8 AB, Jo 3 3 SA²B, Ac 27 31 SB, Aeg 225 S ⲉⲣϣⲁⲛⲟⲩⲉⲡⲓⲥⲕⲟⲡⲟⲥ ... ⲧⲙⲟⲩⲱϣ ⲉϫⲓ, CO 53 S ⲉⲕⲧⲙⲃⲱⲕ ⲕⲣⲓⲃⲟⲗ ⲙⲡϣⲁ, MG 25 219 B ⲉϣⲱⲡ ⲁⲣⲉϣⲧⲉⲙⲟⲩⲁⲓ ⳅⲟⲗϥ ⲉⲃⲟⲗ;   temp: PS 146 S ⲡⲧⲉⲣⲟⲩⲧⲙⲉϣ ϭⲙϭⲟⲙ ⲉⲧⲟⲩⲡ.

ⲧⲟⲙ S, ⲧⲁⲙ S^a, ⲑⲟⲙ B nn m, mat of reeds (cf ⲧⲙⲏ): MG 25 246 B ⲡⲓⲕⲉⲑ. whereon I stood, ib 210 B sleeping mat = Z 344 S ⲧⲙⲏ, C 89 26 B working at ⲡⲓⲑ. ψιάθιον, Mus 40 36 S two together shall not ϧⲙⲟⲟⲥ ⲉⲧ....ⲟⲩⲧⲉ ⲟⲩⲧⲙⲏ (cf BMar 181) psiathium, K 251 B ⲡⲓⲑ. حصر, K. al-Tagnîz 170 B in commemorative ritual on 3rd day after funeral ⲡϫⲓⲛⲱⲗⲓ ⲙⲡⲓⲑ. ر̇ذ ذ, whereon food been placed (Sobhy, cf TRit 514), C 89 74 B ⲉⲣ ϧⲱⲃ ⲉⲡⲓⲑ. (cf ib ⲧⲁⲗⲉ ⲑⲙⲏ) ὑφαίνειν, ShC 73 124 S ⲡⲕⲟⲧⲕ ϧⲓⲟⲩⲧⲙ, ib 168 none may sleep in cell except ⲛⲥⲉⲥⲱⲕ ⲡⲧ. (as curtain) ⲉϧⲣⲁⲓ, ib 133 ⲛϥⲕⲱⲗϧ ⲉⲡⲧ.(on outside) that sleeper may arise, C 89 123 B window covered by ⲟⲩⲑ., Z 351 S when sleeping ⲙⲉϥⲧ ⲧ. ϧⲁⲣⲟϥ ⲟⲩⲇⲉ ⲃⲟⲗⲁⲧ (l ⲃⲁⲗⲟⲧ), C 89 156 B ⲉⲅⲧⲁⲗⲉ ⲑ. = MG 17 331 S ⲧⲙⲏ, ST 235 S^c ⲧ. ϧⲓⲧⲏⲛ ϧⲓⲛⲱϥ.

ⲧⲱⲙ SAA², ⲑ. B, ⲧ(ⲉ)ⲙ- S, ⲑⲉⲙ- B, ⲧⲟⲙⲉ S, ⲑⲟⲙⲉ B, ⲧⲱⲙⲉ O (?), ⲧⲏⲙⲧ S, ⲑ.ⲧ B, ⲣ ⲥ ⲧⲁⲙ- S, ⲑⲁⲙ- B vb shut a mouth, door, intr: Ro 3 19 SB φράσσειν, Job 5 16 SB ἐμφρ.; Mt 22 12 SB φιμοῦν; ShA 2 78 S how shall ⲣⲱⲟⲩ ⲛⲁⲧ. ⲁⲛ?, Pcod 32 S ⲧⲉϥⲧⲁⲡⲣⲟ ⲛⲁⲧ., TstAb 173 B ⲁⲣⲱⲥ ⲑ., Mus 40 272 S ⲉⲣⲉⲧⲉⲕⲧⲁⲡⲣⲟ ⲧ.†; tr: He 11 33 SB φρ., Ps 106 42 SB ἐμφρ.; Lu 4 35 SB ⲑⲱⲙ ⲣ., Mor 17 77 S ⲛⲧⲙ ⲣⲱⲕ φιμ.; ShWess 9 128 S ⲙⲁⲣϥⲧⲙ ⲣⲱϥ, AZ 23 114 S ⲧⲟⲙ ⲛϥⲣⲟϥ, BMis 107 S ⲧⲁⲡⲣⲟ ⲛ ϣⲟⲩⲧⲟⲙⲥ, Aeg 41 B ⲣⲱϥ ⲛϣⲟⲩⲑⲟⲩⲟⲙϥ, WTh 176 S ⲧⲱⲙ ⲣⲱⲕ, TillOster 13 A ⲧⲱⲙ ⲣⲱⲥ.   ⲃ eyes: Jo 12 40 SA²B τυφλοῦν, Deu 16 19 S(B ϣⲑⲁⲙ) ἀποτ., Ex 23 8 S(B do) ἐκτ.; Job 17 7 S(B ⲧⲱⲙⲧ) πωροῦσθαι; ShA 2 176 S wickedness of Manes ⲧⲙ ⲛⲉϥⲃⲁⲗ, Z 284 S ⲁⲧⲉⲡⲓⲑⲩⲙⲓⲁ ⲧ. ⲛⲛⲉϥⲃⲁⲗ.   ⲥ ϧⲏⲧ, shut the heart: Sa 2 21 SB ἐπιτυφ.; Mk 6 52† B(S diff), Jo 12 40 SA²B πωρ.; BG 75 S ⲁϥⲧ. ⲛⲛⲉϥϧ., EW 176 B sim;   ⲥ ⲉ- dat commodi: Miss 8 177 S why ⲡⲉⲕϧ. ⲧ.† ⲉⲣⲟⲕ?, AM 62 B ⲉⲣⲉⲟⲩϧ. ⲑ.† ⲉⲣⲱⲟⲩ; MélOr 6 501 B devil ⲑⲉⲙ ⲡⲉⲛϧ. ⲉⲃⲟⲩⲛ ⲉⲡⲓⲉⲣⳅⲟⲡⲓ;   as nn m, shutting, hardening of heart: Ro 11 25 SBF πώρωσις; ShC 42 138 S among vices, ib 184 S ⲡⲧ. ⲛϧ. ⲙⲡⲛⲑϣⲉ.   V also p c.   ⲇ otherwise: Pro 25 26 SA, Lam 3 9 B(S ϣⲧⲁⲙ) φρ., 2 Cor 3 14 SB, Miss 4 526 S ⲉⲣⲉⲡⲉⲕⲟⲅⲟⲉⲓⲛ ⲧ.† = C 89 45† B πωρ.; BHom 138 S ⲧⲡⲏⲥⲛ ⲧ.† κλείειν; Is 43 8 S

(*B* ⲟⲓ ⲡⲕⲟⲩⲣ) κωφός; ShC 42 84 *S* т. ⲥⲉ ⲉⲣ ⲁⲡⲟⲙⲓⲁ *cease*, Mor 55 51 *S* ⲟⲩⲗⲉⲍⲓⲥ ⲉⲥⲧ.† ⲡⲧϣⲓⲡⲉ ⲡⲥⲁⲡⲉⲥⲃⲱⲗ; refl AZ 21 94 *O* ⲡⲉⲧⲣⲉⲡⲧⲏ ⲙⲁⲣⲉϥⲧⲱⲙϥ (if this word); Kr 247 *S* ϥⲁⲥⲓⲗⲉ (φάσηλος) ϥⲧ.†, ϥⲁⲥ. ϥⲡⲟⲣⲝ, ST 189 *S* ⲣϣⲓⲡ ⲉⲩⲧ.†, ⲣ. ⲉϥⲣⲉⲭⲣⲱⲝ, BMOr 6201 A 74 *S*]ⲡⲕⲁϣ ... ⲧⲡⲁϣⲉ ⲉⲥⲧ.† *closed* opp open (meaning?).

т. ⲉⲣⲛ-: Tit 1 11 *B*(*S* ϣⲱⲧⲙ) ἐπιστομίζειν; ShZ 593 *S* ⲙⲁ ⲡⲓⲙ ⲡⲁⲧ. ⲉⲣⲱϥ (*sic*), ShBM 253 56 *S* ⲁⲩⲧ. ⲉⲣⲱϥ ⲡⲥⲁⲁ ⲡⲓⲙ, ShA 1 241 *S* flood waters ⲉⲧ. ⲉⲣⲛⲡⲉⲅⲙⲁ ⲡⲉⲓ ⲉⲃⲟⲗ.

т. ⲉϩⲣⲁⲓ *S*, *close up* (?): J 71 58 ⲉⲣⲉⲡⲣⲟ ⲉⲧⲟⲩⲉⲛ ⲉⲣⲏⲥ ⲉⲡⲏⲓ ⲧⲁⲣⲏⲥ ⲡⲡⲁⲧⲟⲙ (*l* ⲡⲁⲧⲱⲙ) ⲉϩⲣⲁⲓ.

—— nn m *B*, *that which shuts, fence*: Eph 2 14 (*S* ⲭⲟⲗⲭⲗ) φραγμός جدار (K 366).

р с: Louvre E 14251 *S* ⲟⲩϣⲧⲟⲩ ⲙⲡⲕⲁⲣⲱϥ ⲙⲡⲧⲁⲙⲣⲱϥ ⲙⲡⲛⲧⲁⲡⲟ, Va 58 128 *B* ⲡⲓⲁⲧⲛⲱⲙⲟⲥ ⲡⲓⲑⲁⲙⲣⲏⲧ; ShC 73 140 *S* ⲟⲩⲙⲛ̄ⲧⲁⲙⲣⲏⲧ.

тⲱⲙ *S*, таам✗ *A*, тⲏⲙ† *SB*, ⲑ.† *B* vb intr, *be sharp*: Ez 21 9 *S*(*B* ϣⲟⲃ̄ϣⲉⲃ̄) ὀξύνειν; tr, *sharpen*: Pro 27 17 (*A* ⲭⲱⲣ), Is 44 12 (*B* do), Zech 1 21 *A*(*B* do) ὀξ.; Ps 63 3 (*B* do) ἀκονᾶν; qual, *be sharp*: Job 41 21 (*B* do), Ps 56 4 (*B* ϩⲓⲟⲧⲓ), Ez 5 1 *SB* т. ὀξύς, ib 21 9 (*B* ϣ.) ὀξύν.; Ps 44 5 (*B* do), Pro 5 4 (*A* ϣⲱⲗⳬ, *B* do) ἀκ.; LCyp 7 ϩⲛⲗⲁⲥ ... ⲉⲩⲧ. ⲛⲥⲁⲡⲉⲅⲉⲣⲏⲩ, Va 63 103 *B* ⲟⲩⲟⲡ ⲭⲣⲓⲁ ⲛⲥⲟⲕ ⲉϥⲑ., ib 59 6 *B* beat him with ϩⲁⲛⲕⲟⲡⲧⲟⲃⲁⲕⲗⲟⲛ ⲉⲩⲑ., KroppD 58 ⲡⲉⲩⲥⲛⲃⲉ ⲭ(ⲏ)ⲣ ⲉⲩⲧ(ⲏ)ⲙ.

тамⲓⲟ *SA*, -ⲓⲁ *F*, ⲑⲁⲙⲓⲟ *B*, ⲧⲁⲙⲓⲉ-, ⲧⲁⲙⲓⲟ- *S*, ⲑⲁⲙⲓⲉ-, ⲑⲁⲙⲓⲟ- *B*, ⲧⲁⲙⲓⲟ✗ *S*, -ⲓⲁ✗ *Sᵃ F*, ⲑⲁⲙⲓⲟ✗ *B*, ⲧⲁⲙⲓⲏⲩ† *S*, ⲑⲁⲙⲓⲏⲟⲩⲧ† *B*, ⲧⲁⲙⲓⲏⲩⲧ *F* vb **I** tr, *make, create*: Ge 1 27 *SB*(*A* ⲧⲁⲡⲟ), Is 31 7 *SBF*, Jon 1 9 *SAB*, Mk 10 6 *SF*(*B* ⲥⲱⲡⲧ), Jo 14 23 *SB*(*A²* ⲧⲉⲡⲟ), He 1 7 *SBF* ποιεῖν; Ge 14 19 *B*(*S* ⲥⲱⲡⲧ), Jer 13 1 *B* κτίζειν; Ez 40 21 *SB* γίνεσθαι; Ps 7 15 *S*(*B* ⲉⲣ ϩⲱⲃ) ἐργάζεσθαι; EpJer 9 *B*(*F* ⲙⲟⲩⲛⲕ) κατασκευάζειν; ib 33 *B*(*F* ⲧⲁϩⲁ ⲉⲗⲉⲧ✗) καθιστάναι; Job 38 12 *B*(*S* ⲥⲙⲓⲛⲉ) συντάσσειν; Sa 15 13 *S* δημιουργεῖν; ib 9 *S* πλάσσειν; ib 15 6 *S* δρᾶν; Ez 4 3 *B*(*S* ⲕⲱ) τιθέναι; Si 29 29 *S* κοσμεῖν; Jth 10 4 *S* καλλωπίζειν; Ru 2 14 *S* βουνίζειν; PS 98 *S* ⲛϣⲟⲣⲡ ⲉⲡⲧⲁⲩⲧⲁⲙⲓⲟⲟⲩ, ShC 73 145 *S* ⲧⲁⲙⲓⲉ...ⲟⲉⲓⲕ, KroppK 47 *Sᵃ* cast charm into well ⲉⲕⲉⲧⲁⲙⲉⲓⲁϥ on 14th of month, C 43 228 *B* ⲁϥⲑⲁⲙⲓⲟ ⲧⲫⲉ, MG 25 306 *B* ⲡⲧⲁⲑⲁⲙⲓⲟ ⲡⲓⲥⲛⲏⲃ ⲛ̄ⲕⲁⲗⲱⲥ = BIF 13 115 *S* ⲭⲉⲣⲟ, ST 302 *S* ⲉⲧⲣⲉϥⲧⲁⲙⲓⲟ ϩⲉⲡⲉⲓϥⲧ, Ep 299 *S* ⲧⲁⲙⲓⲟ ⲡⲉⲥⲛⲉϥⲉ, C 86 269 *B* this book ⲁϥⲑⲁⲙⲓⲟϥ ⲉⲃⲟⲗ ϩⲉⲛⲡⲉϥϭⲓϫⲓ, J&C 92 *S* ⲟⲩⲗⲉⲃⲓⲧⲱⲛ...ⲧⲁⲙⲓⲟⲥ, *cf ib* ⲧⲁⲡⲟⲥ.

II intr (*B* only): 3 Kg 17 15 ποι.; Is 46 11 (*S* tr) κτ.; qual: Job 41 24 *SB*, Eccl 1 9 *F*(Mich) ποι.; Ac 21 2 *S*(*B* ⲥⲟⲗⲥⲉⲗ) κοσμ., Ps 143 12 *S*(*B* do) περικ.; He 9 6 *SB* (var & *F* ⲑⲙⲁⲓⲟ) κατασκευάζειν; Va 66

298 *B* ϩⲁⲛϥ̄ⲣⲏϣ ⲉⲩⲑ. περιττὰ καὶ ἄψαυστα; CDan 88 *B* ask not more for him ϥⲑ. ⲅⲁⲣ ⲕⲁⲗⲱⲥ ⲕ. ἐστίν; 1 Kg 25 18 *S* ⲧⲁϥ ⲛⲃⲛⲛⲉ ⲉⲩⲧ. (var ⲧⲁⲓⲏⲩ) Gk om; Mor 41 180 *S* broken idol mended ⲉϥⲧ. ⲡⲧⲉϥϩⲉ, ib 37 165 *S* eyes ⲉⲩⲧⲙⲁⲉⲓⲏⲩ (*l* ⲧⲁⲙ.) ϩⲛ̄ⲣⲉⲛⲭⲓⲧⲱⲛ.

With prepositions.　ⲥ ⲛ- dat: Ge 18 6 *SB*, Lev 24 5 *SB*, Nu 6 17 *S*(*B* ⲓⲣⲓ) ποι. acc; BIF 13 111 *S* sold baskets ⲛϥⲧⲁⲙⲓⲉ ⲛⲕⲟⲩⲓ ⲛⲟⲉⲓⲕ ⲛⲁⲩ *obtained* (in exchange) = MG 25 301 *B*, Cat 186 *B* Lord ⲑⲁⲙⲓⲉ ⲟⲩⲙⲏϣ ⲙⲙⲁⲑⲏⲧⲏⲥ ⲛⲁϥ;　ⲥ ϩⲓ-, *made, mixed with*: Lev 6 40† *S*(var & *B* ⲟⲩⲱϣⲙ) ἀναποι. ἐν; Ap 21 19† *S*(*B* diff) κοσμ. dat;　ⲥ ϩⲛ- sim: Nu 28 5 *B*(*S* ⲟⲩ. ⲛ-); ⲉⲃⲟⲗ ϩⲛ-: Ez 27 6 *SB*, Jo 2 15 *SB*(*A²* ⲧⲉⲛⲟ) ποι. ἐκ; Nu 6 3 *S*(*B* no vb) κατεργάζεσθαι ἐκ; Sa 15 8 *S* γένεσθαι ἐκ; DeV 2 44 *B* cloak ⲉⲥⲟ.† ⲉⲃ. ϩⲉⲛⲣⲁⲛϥⲱⲓ, Pcod 19 *S* ⲧⲁⲙⲓⲉ ⲕⲉⲓⲙⲏⲗⲓⲟⲛ ⲉⲃ. ϩⲛ̄ⲟⲩⲛⲟⲩⲃ.

—— nn m *SBF*, *thing made, creation*: Ps 63 10 *SB*, Eccl 7 14 *SF*, Eph 2 10 *SB* ποίημα, Ps 18 2 *SB* ποίησις; Ge 2 4 *B* γένεσις; Ps 102 14 *B*(*S* = Gk)πλάσμα; PS 77 *S* ⲛⲧ. ⲛ̄ⲣⲣⲱⲙⲉ, ShA 1 380 *S* ϩⲉⲛⲧ. ϩⲛ̄ⲛⲥⲓⲝ ⲙⲡⲡⲉ, R 1 3 71 *S* hair-cloth ⲉⲡⲧ. ⲛ̄ⲧⲉⲥⲕⲏⲛⲏ, BSM 4 *B* ⲟⲩⲑ. ⲉⲃⲟⲗ ϩⲉⲛⲡⲓⲟⲙⲓ.

ⲣⲉϥⲧ., ⲑ. *SB*, *maker, creator*: R 1 2 62 *S* ⲡⲣ. ⲛ̄ⲡⲉⲧⲛⲛⲁⲩ ⲉⲣⲟⲟⲩ, Cai Euch 473 *B* ⲡⲓⲣ. ⲛⲧⲉ ⲡⲧⲏⲣϥ ποιητής; BSM 9 *B* God ⲛⲉⲡⲣ.;　ⲣⲉϥⲧⲁⲙⲓⲉ-: Ac 18 3 *SB* σκηνοποιός; Va 57 191 *B* ⲣ. ϣⲫⲏⲣⲓ ⲑⲁⲩⲙⲁⲧⲟⲡ.; Aeg 252 *S* ⲣ. ⲧⲟⲩⲱⲧ, Bor 248 53 *S* ⲡⲉⲑⲁⲃ ⲡⲣ. ⲟⲉⲓⲕ;　ⲙⲉⲧⲣⲉϥⲑⲁⲙⲓⲉ- *B*, *act of making*: Va 57 191 ⲙ. ϣⲉⲣϣⲓ ⲡⲉⲛⲥⲱⲃⲓ ⲅⲉⲗⲱⲧⲟⲡ.

ϭⲓⲛⲧ., ϫⲓⲛⲑ. *SBF*, *making, creation*: Dan 11 6 *B* τὸ ποιῆσαι; My 38 *S* ⲡϭ. (*l* ⲧϭ.) ⲙ̄ⲡⲕⲟⲥⲙⲟⲥ, C 86 241 *B* ⲡⲁⲓⲭ. ⲛⲧⲉ ⲡⲁⲓϩⲃⲏⲟⲩⲓ, Mor 24 3 *F* ⲧϭ. ⲙ̄ⲡⲗⲱⲙⲓ.

ⲧⲁⲙⲟ *SAB*, -ⲁ *F*, ⲧⲁⲙⲉ- *SA² BF*, ⲧⲁⲙⲟ- *A*, ⲧⲁⲙⲁ- *F*, ⲧⲁⲙⲟ✗ *SB*, -ⲙⲁ✗ *AA² F* vb tr, *tell, inform* (caus of ⲉⲓⲙⲉ): Ge 9 22 *B*(*S* ϫⲱ), 2 Kg 1 20 *B*(*S* ⲧⲁϭⲟ), Is 30 10 *SBF* ἀναγγέλλειν, Job 1 15 *SB*, Mk 16 10 *S*(*B* ϫⲱ), Jo 4 51 *SA² F*(*B* do) ἀπαγ.; Ps 89 12 *B*(*S* ⲟⲩⲱⲛ̄ϩ ⲉⲃⲟⲗ), Pro 9 9 *SAB* γνωρίζειν; Mt 2 22 *B*(*S* ⲧⲟϭⲡ ⲉⲓⲁⲧ✗), He 8 5 *B*(*SF* ϣⲁϫⲉ ⲙⲛ-) χρηματίζεσθαι; 1 Cor 10 28 *B*(*S* ϫⲱ) μηνύειν; EpJer 3 *B*(*F* ⲟⲩ. ⲉⲃ., *S* diff) δεικνύναι; Aeg 262 *S* ⲙⲁⲣⲟⲩⲧⲁⲙⲉ ⲡⲉⲧⲛⲧⲉⲕⲕⲗⲏⲥⲓⲁ, BMar 190 *S* ⲛⲉⲡⲧⲁⲕⲧⲁⲙⲟⲓ *what didst tell me* (was the fare) I will pay, C 89 180 *B* ⲉϥⲉⲧⲁⲙⲟⲟⲩ from Scriptures = Mun 62 *S* ⲧⲥⲁⲃⲟ, El 68 *A* ⲙ̄ⲡⲛ̄ⲧⲁⲙⲉ ⲁⲛⲅⲉⲗⲟⲥ, Hall 77 *S* †ⲧⲁⲙⲟ ⲙⲙⲟⲕ ⲁⲣⲓ ⲧⲁⲅⲁⲡⲏ ⲛ̄ⲅⲉⲣⲁⲓ.

With ϫⲉ-: Jo 20 18 *SA² B* ἀγγέλ., Ge 3 11 *B*(*S* ϫⲱ) ἀναγ., Is 30 7 *B*(*SF* do) Lu 8 47 *S*(*B* ⲟⲩ. ⲉⲃ.) ἀπαγ.; Eccl 3 18 *S*, Mt 16 21 *SB* δεικ.; Lu 2 26 *SB* χρ.; AP 8 *A²* ⲙⲁⲧⲁⲙⲁⲉⲓ ϫⲉ- εἰπεῖν; ShC 42 137 *S*

ⲉⲩϣⲁⲛⲧⲁⲙⲟⲓ...ⲭⲉⲁⲡⲟⲕ,BHom73 S ⲁϥⲧⲁⲙⲉ ⲟⲩⲟⲡ ⲛⲓⲙ ⲭⲉ-, BSM 120 B ⲙⲁⲧⲁⲙⲟⲓ ⲭⲉⲡⲟⲩ ⲛⲓⲙ, BM 528 F arithm problems begin ⲙⲁⲩⲧⲁⲙⲁⲕ ⲭⲉ- (cf AZ 65 125); in letters after introd greeting (cf διδάσκω...ώς, Ep 188 n, cf Hall above): RE 9 163 S ⲧⲓⲧ. ⲙⲙⲟⲕ ⲭⲉⲁⲣⲓ ⲧⲁⲅⲁⲡⲏ, Sph 10 143 S ⲧⲓⲧ. ⲙⲟⲕ ⲭⲉⲕⲛⲁⲣ ⲛⲓⲙ, Ryl 390 S ⲧⲓⲧ. ⲙⲙⲟⲕ ⲭⲉⲡϣⲁ ⲡⲟⲟⲩ, CMSS 51 F ⲧⲓⲧ. ⲙⲁⲕ ⲭⲉ-.

With ⲉ- of thing told, shown (mostly Gk acc) SAA²BF: Ex 19 3 B(S ⲟⲩ. ⲉⲃ.), 1 Kg 19 3 S (but var ⲧⲁⲅⲟϥ ⲉⲣⲟⲕ), Ps 43 1 S(B ⲥⲁϫⲓ ϩⲁⲧⲉⲛ-), Is 30 10 B(SF ϫⲱ), Jo 4 25 SBF ἀναγ., 1 Kg 24 19 SB, Lu 8 36 SB ἀπαγ., 1 Cor 2 1 B(S ϫⲱ) καταγ.; Ps 24 4 S(B ⲟⲩ.), Jo 15 15 SA²B, 1 Cor 15 1 SBF γνωρ.; Lev 4 23 S(B ⲟⲩ. ⲉⲃ.), Mk 5 43 S sim(B ⲉⲙⲓ)γιγνώσκειν; Ge 12 1 B(S ⲧⲟⲅⲟ, A Cl ⲧⲥⲉⲃⲟ), Ps 59 5 B(S ⲧⲥⲁⲃⲟ), Is 11 11 B(S ⲟⲩ. ⲉⲃ.) δεικ., He 6 17 SBF ἐπιδ., Ac 9 16 SB ὑποδ.; Ps 24 14 S(B ⲟⲩ.), Is 42 9 SB δηλοῦν; Ex 18 20 SB σημαίνειν; 1 Kg 16 3 S (var ⲧⲉ., B ϫⲱ), Mt 17 9 B(S ϫⲱ) εἰπ.; Mk 5 16 S (B ⲥ. ϩⲁ.), Ac 12 17 S(B ⲇⲟ) διηγεῖσθαι; ib 18 26 SB ἐκτιθέναι, ib 17 3 S(B ⲭⲱ ϩⲁⲧⲉⲛ-) παρατ.; Sa 18 18 S, AP 11 A² ⲁϥⲧⲁⲙⲉ ⲫⲏⲧⲉⲙⲙⲟⲛ [ⲁⲡ]ⲉⲛⲧⲁϫϣⲱⲡⲉ ἐμφανίζειν; ib 9 A² διδάσκειν; Mic 7 15 A(S ⲧⲁⲅⲟ, B as Gk) ὁρᾶν; Is 48 6 S(B as Gk) ἀκουστὸν ποιεῖν; BG 83 S ⲙⲁⲧⲁⲙⲟⲛ ⲉⲧⲙⲉ, BMis 263 S ⲧⲁⲙⲟⲓ ⲉⲛⲧⲟϣ= Mor 29 33 S ⲧⲥⲁⲃⲟⲓ, BSM 104 B ⲁϥⲧⲁⲙⲟⲥ ⲉⲟⲩⲙⲏϣ ⲛⲡⲟⲩⲃ, ZNTW 24 84 F perfume ⲉⲧⲉⲣⲁⲕⲧⲁⲙⲁⲛ ⲉⲗⲁϥ, Bodl(P) a 1 ⲉ ⲡⲉⲛⲙⲁ ⲛⲥⲟⲫⲟⲥ ⲛⲧⲁⲛⲧⲁⲙ ⲧⲁⲙⲟⲓ ⲉⲣⲟϥ, CO 387 S ⲙⲡⲉⲛⲁ̣ϩⲏⲧ ⲉⲓϫⲓ ⲕⲱ ⲛⲁⲧⲧⲁⲙⲟⲕ [ⲉⲣ]ⲁⲟⲩ; vbal: Lu 2 26 B(S ⲥ ϫⲉ-), Ac 10 22 B(S ⲧⲥⲁⲃⲉ ⲉⲓⲁⲧ?) χρηματ.; BMis 56 S ⲉⲅⲧ. ⲙⲙⲟⲥ ⲉⲣ ϩⲱⲃ, BSM 112 B ⲁⲓⲧⲁⲙⲉ ⲡⲓⲣⲉⲙⲥⲟϫⲟⲙⲁ ...ⲉⲑⲟⲩϭⲓⲣⲓ, Hall 80 S ⲧⲧ. ⲙⲙⲟⲕ ⲉⲧⲣⲉⲕϫⲟⲟⲥ; show to (rare): Cat 108 B ⲛⲧⲉϥⲧⲁⲙⲉ ⲡⲉϥϫⲓϫ ⲉⲡⲉϥϣⲏⲣⲓ.

With ⲉⲧⲃⲉ- SA²B, tell about, of: Deu 13 9 SB ἀναγ. περί, Lu 7 18 SB ἀπαγ. περί; Mk 9 9 SF(B ⲥ. ϩⲁ.) διηγ. acc, 1 Cor 1 11 SB δηλ. περί; AP 8 A² εἰπ. περί; BMis 459 S ⲁϥⲧⲁⲙⲟⲟⲩ ⲉ. ⲡⲕⲁⲛⲱⲛ, BSM 79 B ⲁϥⲧⲁⲙⲟϥ ⲉ. ⲡⲓϩⲱⲃ, CO 291 S ⲧⲧ. ⲛⲧⲉⲕⲁⲅⲁⲡⲏ ⲉ. ⲡϫⲓⲁⲕⲱⲛ.

—— nn B, thing told: ROC 25 246 ⲛⲓⲧ. ⲉⲧⲉⲡⲓⲡⲛ̅ⲁ̅ ϯ ⲙⲙⲱⲟⲩ.

ⲣⲉϥⲧ., teller: Hos 3 4 AB δῆλος.

ⲧⲁⲙⲙⲉ F v ⲧⲁⲉⲓⲙ.

ⲧⲉⲙⲙⲟ B v ⲧⲙⲙⲟ.

ϯⲙⲉ SAA², ⲧⲓⲙⲉ S, ϯⲙⲓ, ⲧⲓ. BF, pl ⲧⲙⲉ S(v Rec 28 212) & sg as pl, nn m, village: Nu 21 32 B(S pl), Is 32 14 SBF, Jo 11 1 SAA²B, C 89 51 B ⲡⲁⲓϯ. ⲡⲏⲣⲉⲙⲟⲥ (S Miss 4 533 = Gk), Z 294 S κώμη; Mt 13 54 S(B ⲃⲁⲕⲓ, F = Gk), Jo 4 44 SA²(B ⲇⲟ, F ⲡⲟⲗⲓⲥ) πατρίς; Mor 42 5 S=ib 43 3 S χωρίον, BMis 219 S

ⲟⲩϯ. ⲏ ⲟⲩϭⲱⲣⲓⲟⲛ; CDan 86 B = ib 30 κτῆμα; Mus 40 36 S (Reg Pach) shall not wander in & out ϩⲙⲡϯ. in monasterio; Miss 4 737 S ⲟⲩⲛⲟϭ ⲛϯ., BM 331 16 S ⲛϩⲓⲣ ⲙⲡⲁⲧⲱⲣⲁ ⲙⲛϯ., J 68 49 S ϩⲙⲡⲧ. ⲉⲛⲧⲕⲟⲓⲉ, PLond 4 459 S ⲧⲡⲉϫⲓⲁⲥ ⲛⲡⲧ., BMOr 6201 B 188 S ⲧⲥⲱϣⲉ ⲛⲡⲁⲧ., MG 25 205 B ⲡⲓϯ. ⲧⲏⲣϥ ⲥⲉⲟⲩⲱϣ ⲉⲓ, J 105 24 S ⲁⲛⲟⲛ ⲡⲧ. ⲧⲏⲣϥ, BKU 1 318 S ⲛⲛⲟϭ ⲛⲣⲱⲙⲉ [ⲙⲡⲗ]ⲁⲟⲥ ⲧⲏⲣϥ ⲙⲡⲧ., Ryl 466 S ⲡⲕⲟⲓⲛⲱⲛ ⲉⲡⲧ., Kr 134 F sim, Ryl 278 S ⲛⲁⲡⲏⲅⲉ ⲛⲡⲉⲧ., ib 173 S ⲛⲁⲡⲉ ⲛⲡⲉⲛⲧ., PLond 4 467 S ⲡⲁⲅⲁⲣⲭ(ⲟⲥ) ⲛⲡⲧ., J 67 126 S ⲗⲁϣⲁⲛⲉ ⲛⲧ., Bodl(P) c 13 S ⲛⲉⲧⲟⲡⲟⲥ ⲛⲡⲧ., Lant 45 S ⲧⲉⲕⲕⲗⲏⲥⲓⲁ ⲙⲡⲉⲥϯ., CO 61 S ⲛⲧ. ⲧⲏⲣϥ excommunicated, Kr 5 S ⲥⲁϩ ⲛⲧ., cf ib 138 S ⲡⲟⲗⲓⲕⲟⲥ ⲛⲧ., BM 1079 S ⲥⲁϩ & ⲁⲡⲉ ⲛⲧ. make tax return, Ryl 324 S ⲡⲉϫⲏⲙⲟⲥⲓⲟⲛ ⲛⲡⲛⲧ., BM 605 F (ⲧⲉⲡ)ⲡⲟⲩⲗ(ⲏ ἐμβολή) ⲛⲡⲉⲛⲧ., Mani 1 A² ⲛϯ. ⲛⲁⲧⲡⲉ; opp ⲡⲟⲗⲓⲥ S, ⲃⲁⲕⲓ B: Mt 9 35 SB, HL 91 B ⲕ.; ROC 25 250 B ⲟⲩⲃ. ⲛⲉⲙⲡⲉⲥϯ., Mor 16 72 S ⲧⲉⲓⲛ. ⲙⲡⲛⲉⲥϯ. ⲙⲛⲡⲉⲡⲟⲓⲕⲓⲟⲛ ⲉⲧⲣⲏⲓ ⲉⲣⲟⲥ, ClPr 56 7 S ⲡ. ⲕⲱⲙⲏ ϯ. ⲉⲡⲟⲓⲕ., J 65 71 S ⲡ. ⲧ. ϩⲓⲕⲁⲥⲧⲣⲟⲛ; opp ⲥⲩⲛⲁⲅⲱⲅⲏ (of monks, nuns) S: ShC 73 159, ShA 1 11 (cf ShBM 200 1 ⲧⲥⲩⲛ. ⲉⲧϩⲙⲡϯ.) opp ⲥⲱϣⲉ: Mk 6 36 SB ⲕ.; ShC 73 151 S ϩⲙⲡϯ. ϩⲓⲧⲥ., BM 651 F all thou hast ⲛⲁⲡⲧ. ⲙⲛⲡⲁⲧϣⲱ[ϣⲓ]; pl form S: Jos 10 39, 15 44 ⲕ., Jud 1 27 ⲡⲟⲗⲓⲥ...ⲛⲉⲥⲧ. θυγατέρες; Lu 2 1 (B Gk om), Miss 4 644 ⲛⲓⲧ. ⲙⲛⲛⲓⲧⲱϣ.

ⲣⲙ-, ⲣⲉⲙ-, ⲗⲉⲙⲛϯ. SAA²BF, villager, citizen: Pro 11 9 SA(B ⲣ. ⲛⲃⲁⲕⲓ), Zech 13 7 SA(B ⲇⲟ), He 8 11 SF(B ⲇⲟ) πολίτης, Eph 2 19 S(B ⲣ. ⲛⲃⲁⲕⲓ) συμπολίτης; 1 Thes 2 14 SF(B as Gk) συμφυλέτης; Lev 16 29 SB, Nu 15 30 B(S ⲣⲱⲙⲉ ⲙⲡⲕⲁϩ) αὐτόχθων (opp προσήλυτος); ShBM 202 178 S ⲣ. weepeth ⲉϫⲛ ⲟⲩϣⲙⲙⲟ, Z 327 S ⲛⲉⲥⲣⲱⲙⲉ ⲙⲛⲛⲉⲥⲣ.; ⲡⲣⲱⲙⲡⲧ. ⲛⲧⲁⲕⲱⲟⲩ S PLond 4 447, ⲣⲱⲙⲡⲉⲛⲧ. S BM 115.

With place-names: PLond 4 465 ⲛⲧ. ϫⲕⲱⲟⲩ (= κώμη Ἀφροδιτώ), C 41 41 ⲡⲓϯ. ⲡⲗⲉϭⲓⲧ, ib 14 ⲟⲩϯ. ϫⲉⲥⲉⲛϩⲱⲟⲩⲧ, Miss 4 771 ⲟⲩϯ. ϫⲉⲧⲕⲅⲗⲗⲱ, Ryl 211 ⲛⲧ. ϫⲟⲩϣⲟⲣ, HL 94 ⲛⲧ. ⲛϫⲱⲣ جُنَيْن, BM 1134 ⲛⲧ. ϫⲱⲣϭ (cf Πτιμινκῆρκις Wess 10, Πτεμεγκύρκις Athanas Apol. c. Ar. 67), J 88 ϯ. ϣⲟⲣ, Wess 20 232 Χερμετιμι.

ⲧⲟⲟⲙⲉ S nn f, meaning unknown: P 132¹ 29 Alexander & priest Antonius's daughter went till reached ⲉϫⲛⲡⲉⲑⲁⲙⲓⲁ (quid?) ⲉⲧⲉⲧⲧ. ⲧⲉ & there lay down.

ⲧⲱⲙⲙⲉ S (rare), ⲧⲱⲙⲉ, ⲧⲟⲩ. A, ⲧⲱⲙⲓ B, ⲧⲟⲙ-, ⲧⲉⲙ-, ⲧⲟⲙ⸗ B, ⲧⲟ(ⲟ)ⲙⲉ⸋ S, ⲧⲁⲁⲙⲉ⸋ Sᵃ(Sh), ⲧⲁⲙⲉ⸋ A², ⲧⲟⲙⲓ⸋ B vb I intr, join: Ex 26 3 B ἔχεσθαι; Job 14 12 B(S ⲉⲓ ⲉⲧⲟⲩⲛ-) συρράπτειν; Ez 40 16 SʲB κρυπτός; MG 25 255 B broken cup ⲛⲉⲁⲡⲓⲁϥⲟⲧ ⲧ. ⲡⲉ, AM 85 B sim ⲁϥⲧ.; qual, be fitting, appropriate: R 1 5 10 S ⲡⲟⲩϩⲱⲃ ⲁⲛ ⲉϥⲧ. = JA '75 5 233

S ϣϣⲉ ⲁⲛ ἀπρεπές ἐστί; BSM 58 B ⲡⲉⲡⲧⲁⲓⲟ ⲉⲅⲧ.
=BMis 416 S ⲉⲧⲡⲣⲉⲡⲉ; ClPr 30 6 S ⲉⲣⲉⲧⲙⲡⲣⲉϥ-
ⲥⲙⲛ ⲡⲟⲙⲟⲥ ⲧ. ⲙⲡⲕⲁⲓⲣⲟⲥ ⲉⲧⲙⲙⲁⲩ ἁρμόζειν; Κ
245 B ⲡⲓϣⲟⲏⲓ ⲉⲧⲧ. next body, called الشعار; ShBor
246 83 S ⲡⲣⲱ̄ ⲧ. ⲁⲛ, Ζ 281 S ⲛⲧⲁⲡⲭⲡⲓⲟ ϣⲱⲡⲉ ⲉϥⲧ.,
FR 114 B ϯⲣⲱⲛ ⲉⲧⲧ., Leyd 150 S ⲧⲁⲣⲟ ⲡⲉⲧⲥⲛⲉ...
ⲥⲉⲧ.   II tr, *join* B: Ex 26 6 συνάπτειν; Mt 19 6
(S ϣⲱⲡⲛ) συζευγνύναι; Is 44 13 (S ⲧⲱϣⲉ) ῥυθμίζειν.
With following preposition.

—— ⲉ-, *join, cleave to,* intr: Ps 101 6 B(S ⲧ.) κολλᾶσθαι dat, Lu 10 11 B(S ⲇⲟ) κ. εἰς, Deu 13 17 (S
ⲗⲱⲭⲕ) προσκ. ἐν; Ex 19 15 B(S ⲥⲱⲣⲛⲉ) προσέρχεσθαι dat; Is 3 26 B(S ⲣⲱⲣⲧ) ἐδαφίζειν εἰς; Deu 11
30† B(S ⲣⲱⲡ ⲉⲣⲟⲩⲡ ⲉ-) ἔχεσθαι gen; Ac 18 7 B(S
ⲇⲟ) συνομορεῖν dat; R 2 2 22 S eyebrows ⲧ.† ⲉⲛⲉⲩⲉⲣⲏⲩ ⲥⲩⲍ. dat; TU 43 3 A feet ⲥⲉⲧ. ⲉⲡ ⲁⲡⲕⲁⲣ, C 86
229 B παρεπεψοι ⲧ.† ⲉⲟⲩⲥⲧⲩⲗⲟⲥⲛⲉ, ROC 25 253
B mind occupied with God ⲉϥⲧ.† ⲉⲣⲟϥ ⲡⲛⲟⲩ ⲛⲓⲃⲉⲛ;   qual, *be fitting*: BM 247 8 S ⲡⲉⲓϣⲁϫⲉ ⲧ.
ⲉⲛⲉⲡⲧⲁⲅⲉⲙⲡϣⲁ εἶναι dat; Aeg 288 S ⲡⲉⲧⲧ. ⲉⲧⲉϥ-
ⲗⲉⲓⲧⲟⲩⲣⲅⲓⲁ ἀνήκειν dat; Bor 253 171 S ⲡⲉⲧⲧ. ⲉⲡⲉⲧⲓ-
ⲉⲣⲏⲧ τὸ πρέπον; ShA 2 333 S evil said of ear or
eye ⲉⲧ. ⲉⲣⲟⲟⲩ, ShA 1 63 S ⲡⲥⲉⲧⲁⲁⲙⲉ ⲁⲛ ⲉⲭⲟⲟⲩ,
LDi 271 S words ⲡⲥⲉⲧⲱⲙⲉ (? lt) ⲁⲛ ⲉⲧⲥⲟⲫⲓⲁ, Mani
2 A² ⲡⲙⲁ ⲉⲧⲧ. ⲁⲣⲁϥ, BMis 22 S youth ⲉϥⲧ. ⲉⲧⲙⲛⲧ-
ⲣⲣⲟ, BMis 113 S deeds ⲉⲩⲧ. ⲉⲡⲉⲓⲛⲟϭ ⲡϣⲁ, BSM
15 B ⲉϥⲧ. ⲉⲟⲣⲓⲣⲁϣⲓ = BMis 349 S ϯⲙⲡϣⲁ ⲡⲣ.,
BSM 45 B ⲙⲏ ⲥⲧ. ⲁⲛ ⲉⲣⲱⲙⲓ ⲡⲓⲃⲉⲛ ⲉⲟⲣⲟⲩ-= BMis
394 S ⲙⲏ ⲟⲩⲭⲣⲉⲱⲥ ⲁⲡⲡⲉ;   tr B: Deu 6 13 (S
ⲇⲟ) κ. πρός, Ps 100 3 (S ⲇⲟ), Ro 12 9 (SF ⲇⲟ) κ. dat,
Jos 23 8 SB προσκ. dat; Is 5 8 (S ⲇⲟ) συνάπ.; C 43
219 ⲁϥⲧ. ⲛⲛⲓⲙⲉⲗⲟⲥ...ⲉⲛⲟⲩⲉⲣⲛⲟⲩ, MG 25 302 ⲁϥ-
ⲧⲉⲙ ⲣⲱϥ ⲉⲡⲓⲕⲁⲣ as if doing obeisance = BIF 13 112
S ϯ ⲣⲱϥ ⲉⲡⲕ., HL 106 ⲁϥⲧⲟⲙϥ ⲉⲩⲣⲏⲅⲟⲣⲓⲟⲥ; ⲉ-
ϩⲟⲩⲛ ⲉ-: Jer 13 11 (S ⲧⲱϣⲉ ⲉ-) κολ. περί;   DeV
2 285 ⲁϥⲧ. ⲙⲡⲉϥϩⲟ ⲉⲋ. ⲉϯⲣⲓⲕⲱⲡ.

—— ⲛ- dat S, *be fit for*: Bor 290 143 drugs ⲉⲧⲧ.†
ⲙⲡϣⲱⲡⲉ.

—— ⲡⲉⲙ- B, *join with*: AM 304 limbs ⲧ. ⲡⲉⲙⲡⲟⲩⲉⲣⲛⲟⲩ.

—— ϩⲓϫⲛ- A, *join to, be fixed upon*: TU 43 3 ⲙⲁ-
ⲣⲉⲣⲉⲧϥ ⲧⲟⲩⲙⲉ ϩⲓϫⲛⲡⲕⲁⲣ.

—— nn m B, *joint, joining*: Ex 26 4 συμβολή;
BM 889 8 bless this ⲧ. (sc marriage, cf ϫⲓⲛⲧ.), Va 58
66 ⲡⲁⲣⲉⲟⲩⲙⲟⲡⲏ...ⲥⲁⲃⲟⲗ ⲛ†ⲃⲁⲕⲓ ⲉⲡⲧ. *adjoining*(?).
ⲣⲁⲧ. B, *joint*: Va 61 111 bones, ⲣ. & ⲙⲟⲩⲧ of
limbs, C 86 35 ⲡⲥⲉⲥⲉⲧϭⲱⲧϥ ⲕⲁⲧⲁ ⲡⲉϥⲣ. ⲧⲏⲣⲟⲩ. *Cf*
ⲣⲁ(ⲣⲁⲧⲱϭⲉ).
ϫⲓⲛⲧ. B; *joining*: TRit 278 ⲡⲁⲓϫ. ⲫⲁⲓ زواج; *marriage*.

ⲧⲱⲱⲙⲉ, ⲧⲟⲟⲙⲉ S, ⲧⲱⲙⲉ SA, ⲧⲱⲙⲉⲥ A nn f,
purse, wallet: Deu 25 13, Pro 1 14 SA, Mic 6 11 A
μάρσιππος, -πιον; Job 14 17, Lu 10 4 βαλάντιον; Pro

7 20 SA ἔνδεσμος (all B ⲁⲥⲟⲩⲓ); P 129¹⁴ 124 ⲧⲧ. ⲙ-
ⲡⲉϥϣⲁⲁⲣ (v ⲧⲁⲓⲃⲉ s f), ShC 42 29 ⲉⲓⲕⲱⲧϥ ⲭⲗⲉ ⲉⲓ-
ⲡⲟⲩⲭ ⲉⲧⲧ., ShIF 268 ⲟⲩⲧ. ⲉⲥϭⲟⲧⲣ, Mor 56 18 ⲡⲣⲁⲧ
...ϩⲛⲡⲉⲩⲧ., Mich 550 40 monk's ⲣⲁⲅⲧⲟⲩ ⲉⲣⲉⲛⲉⲩⲧⲟ.
ⲡⲁⲁⲩ, BMOr 6201 A 88]ⲛⲥⲟⲩⲟ ⲡⲁⲛ ϩⲛⲧⲧⲟ.

ⲧⲙⲁ(ⲉ)ⲓⲟ, SAA², ⲧⲙⲁⲓⲁ F, ⲑⲙⲁⲓⲟ, ⲙⲁⲓⲟ, ⲙⲁⲓ
B, ⲧⲙⲁ(ⲉ)ⲓⲉ- SA, ⲧⲉⲙⲁⲓⲁ- A (Mic 7), ⲑⲙⲁⲓⲉ- B, ⲧ-
ⲙⲁ(ⲉ)ⲓⲟ⸗ S, ⲧⲙⲁⲓⲁ⸗ A (Ja), ⲑⲙⲁⲓⲟ⸗, ⲙ.⸗ B, ⲧⲙⲁ-
(ⲉ)ⲓⲏⲩ† SA, ⲧⲙⲁⲓⲁⲓⲧ† A(Cl), ⲑⲙⲁⲓⲛⲟⲩⲧ† B, ⲧⲙⲁⲓⲏ-
ⲟⲩⲧ† F vb I tr, *justify, praise*: Ex 23 7 SB, Is 5 23
SBF, Mic 7 9 SAB, Ja 2 21 SAB, Cl 8 4 A ⲙⲁ-
ⲧⲙⲁⲓⲉ ⲧⲭⲏⲣⲁ δικαιοῦν; Cant 6 8 S αἰνεῖν, 1 Cor 11
17 B(S = Gk)ἐπαι.; Mk 7 10 S(var ⲧⲁⲓⲟ, B = Gk)τι-
μᾶν, Ac 20 24 S(var & B ⲧⲁⲓⲟ) τιμίαν ποιεῖν; Is 3 12
S(B = Gk) μακαρίζειν; Aeg 243 S ⲧⲙⲁⲓⲉ ⲁⲍⲓⲱⲙⲁ
προκρίνειν; Sa 1 6 SB ἀθῳοῦν: Mk 6 20 S(B ⲁⲣⲉϩ)
συντηρεῖν; ShBor 300 74 S ⲉⲡⲡⲁⲧⲙⲁⲉⲓⲉ ⲡⲗⲟⲟⲥ
opp ⲥⲟϣϥ, R 2 1 17 S ⲛⲥⲁⲓⲁⲥ ⲧ. ⲙⲙⲟ (sc Virgin),
BSM 52 B ⲙⲡⲉϥϯ ⲑⲙⲁⲓⲱⲟⲩ.

II intr, *be justified*: Ps 50 4 SB ⲙⲁⲓ, ib 142 2 SB
ⲇⲟ, Mic 6 11 SAB, Mt 12 37 B ⲙⲁⲓ (S tr), Tit 3 7
SB ⲇⲟ δικαιοῦν; PS 152 S ⲁⲓⲧ. ϩⲛⲧⲉⲕⲙⲛⲧⲭⲣⲏⲥⲧⲟⲥ
(Od Solom 25 12 ⲗⲟⲩⲧⲓ), AP 32 A² ⲡⲣⲱⲙⲉ ⲛⲁⲧ.
ⲉⲡ..., ϥⲛⲁⲧ., Wess 18 29 S ⲛⲛⲁⲧ. ϩⲛⲟⲩ?;   qual:
Lu 18 14 SB, Cl 30 3 A ⲧ. ϩⲛϩⲉⲛϩⲃⲏⲟⲩⲉ ⲇⲓⲕ.; Hos
13 15 A (ⲧ)ⲙⲁⲓⲏⲩ (B ⲥⲱⲧⲡ) ἐπιθυμητός; Joel 3 5
SA ⲇⲟ (B ⲛⲁⲛⲉⲩ) καλός; He 9 6 B (var & S ⲑⲁⲙⲓⲛ-
ⲟⲩⲧ) F κατεσκευασμένος; ShA 2 283 S ⲉⲓⲧⲉ ⲉⲓⲥⲛϣ
ⲉⲓⲧⲉ ⲉⲓⲧ., BAp 31 S forgive me ⲛ†ⲧ. ⲁⲛ (expression
of modesty), PBu 207 S ⲁⲡⲉⲥϩⲁⲡ ⲉⲓ ⲉⲃⲟⲗ ⲉϥⲧ.

—— SB nn m, *justification*: 3 Kg 8 45 B, Jer 11
20 SB ⲙⲁⲓ δικαίωμα, Lev 24 22 B(S ⲇⲓⲕⲓⲁⲱⲙⲁ),
Ro 4 25 SB δικαίωσις, Is 5 23 B(SF ⲙⲛⲧⲙⲉ) δίκαιον;
Ps 21 25 S(var ⲧⲁⲉⲓⲟ, B ϣⲟⲩϣⲟⲩ), 1 Pet 1 7 S(B ⲇⲟ)
ἔπαινος; Va 63 80 B ⲡⲁⲓⲡⲉ ⲡⲁⲑ. ἐγκώμιον; BMar
89 S ⲉⲣⲉⲡⲁⲧ. ϩⲙⲡⲛⲏⲅⲉ, Miss 4 168 B ⲙⲙⲟⲛ ⲑ....
ϩⲉⲡⲁⲙⲉⲛ†; Tob 14 12 S ϩⲛⲟⲩⲧ. (l ⲧⲁⲉⲓⲟ) ἐνδόξως.

ⲧⲙⲏ S, ⲧⲙⲉⲓ A, ⲑⲙⲏ B nn f, *mat of reeds*:
Mor 37 44 S ⲧ. whereon he slept, BM 216 109 S
ⲉϥⲫⲟⲣⲉⲓ ⲛⲧⲉⲧ., Miss 4 530 S ϩⲟⲃⲥⲧ ⲛⲟⲩⲧ. opp
ⲡⲣⲏϣ = C 89 49 B = MG 17 552 مبدأة = Va ar 172
30 حلفا ﻧﺞ ψίαθος, Z 345 S whereon 2 slept = MG
25 210 B ⲑⲟⲙ, MG 17 327 S ⲁϥⲧⲁⲗⲉ ⲧⲉϥⲧ. = C 89
74 B ψιάθιον; P 44 91 S ϩⲛⲧⲙⲉ ⲙⲡⲣⲏⲥⲱ للحصر والحلفا;
ST 235 Sᵃ ⲧⲁⲙ ϩⲓⲧ., BKU 1 8 35 S ⲉⲕⲛⲕⲟⲧ[ⲕ] ϩⲓ-
ⲟⲩⲧ. ⲛⲕⲁⲙ (sic l), ShP 130⁴ 157 S ⲛⲁⲧ ⲛⲟⲩⲉϫ ⲧ.,
C 89 140 B monks sell ⲕⲟⲩϫⲓ ⲛⲑ. in Rakote, El 60
A clothed in ϩⲉⲛⲧ. ⲛⲕⲱⲧ, BM 1088 S ⲧ. ⲛϫⲓⲉⲓⲗⲉ
(? = -ⲣⲉ);   ⲥⲁϥⲧ(ⲧ)ⲙⲏ S, *mat-weaver*: PMich
3553 place ⲛⲙⲁ (ⲛ)ⲡⲉⲥ. V also ⲧⲟⲙ.

ⲧⲙⲟ B v ⲧⲙⲣⲟ.

ⲧⲉⲙⲑⲁⲙ *B* nn, *mule*: Ge 12 16, Ps 31 9, Is 66 20 (*S* all ⲙⲁⲥⲡⲟⲣⲕ) ἡμίονος.

ⲧⲉⲙⲑⲱⲙ *B* v ⲧⲏⲧⲙ & ϩⲧⲟⲙⲧⲙ.

ⲧⲉⲙⲕⲁ *F* v ⲧϭⲙⲕⲟ.

ⲧⲉⲙⲙⲟ, ⲧⲙⲟ (Mor 41) *S*, ⲧⲉⲙⲙⲟ, ⲧⲉⲙⲟ *B*, ⲧⲙ-(ⲙ)ⲉ- *S*, ⲧⲙⲁ- (Mor 41) *Sᶠ*, ⲧⲙ(ⲙ)ⲟⲋ, ⲧⲙ(ⲙ)ⲉⲋ *S*, ⲧⲙⲙⲁⲋ *A*, ⲧⲉⲙⲙⲟⲋ *B*, ⲧⲙⲙⲏⲩ† *SA²* vb tr, *feed, nourish* (caus of ⲟⲩⲱⲙ): 2 Kg 13 5 *S*, Pro 25 21 *SA*, Ro 12 20 *S*(var ⲧⲙⲟϥ)*B* ψωμίζειν; Mt 25 35 *SB* φαγεῖν διδόναι, ib 37 *SB* τρέφειν; ShC 73 91 *S* ⲉⲧ. ⲡⲉⲧⲛⲁϭⲟⲓⲗⲉ ⲉⲡⲣⲟ, Mor 16 71 *S* ⲡⲥⲉⲧⲙⲟϥ ⲡⲥⲉⲧⲥⲟϥ, MG 17 320 *S* ⲡⲧⲥⲟϩⲧⲉ ⲛⲡⲧⲙⲙⲉ ⲛⲥⲟⲡ = C 89 68 *B* ⲡⲧⲉⲕⲧⲉⲙⲟ, Mor 41 13 *Sᶠ* victuals wherewith ⲉϥⲉⲧⲙⲁ ⲡⲉⲉⲣⲅⲁⲧⲏⲥ = DeV 2 262 *B* ⲧⲉⲙⲙⲟ ⲛ-, CO 379 *S* be so good ⲛⲧⲉⲧⲛⲧⲙⲙⲟ ⲛⲃⲁⲣⲱϣ, Mani 2 *A²* ⲡⲁⲡⲁⲓ [ⲉ]ϥⲧ.†; With 2nd acc (v AZ 53 135): Si 15 3 *S* ⲥⲡⲁⲧⲙⲉϥ ⲟⲉⲓⲕ ψ.; 3 Kg 22 27 *S* ⲧⲙⲙⲉϥ ⲟ. ἐσθίειν; ShC 42 106 *S* sim.; + ⲛ-: Nu 11 4 *S*(*B* † dat), Ps 79 5 *SB*, 1 Cor 13 3 *S*(*B* ⲑⲣⲉⲟⲩⲱⲙ) ψ.; 2 Kg 3 35 *S* περιδειπνίζειν dat; ShA 1 34 *S* ⲧⲙⲙⲟⲟⲩ ⲡⲟⲩⲟⲉⲓⲕ ⲙⲙⲏⲛⲉ, BHom 126 *S* ⲁⲩⲧⲙⲟϥ ⲡⲟⲩϭⲓϣⲉ, C 43 174 *B* ⲁⲕⲧⲉⲙⲙⲟⲩ ⲡⲟⲩϩⲁⲣⲓⲥⲧⲟⲛ, C 86 347 *S* ⲡⲧⲉⲕⲧ. ⲡⲧⲉⲕⲭⲣⲓⲁ *that thou provide for thy needs*; c ⲛ-dat: WS 134 *S* ⲡⲧⲉⲛⲧⲙⲙⲟⲟⲩ (sc wages) ⲛⲁϥ; c ϩⲛ-, ϩⲉⲛ- *SB*, *feed with*: Sa 16 20 ψ. acc, WTh 175 *S* ⲧⲙⲙⲟⲓ ϩⲛⲧⲉⲧⲣⲟⲫⲏ, C 43 168 *B* †ⲛⲁⲧⲉⲙⲙⲟⲩ ϩⲉⲛⲡⲓⲕⲁⲣⲡⲟⲥ; ⲉⲃⲟⲗ ϩⲛ-: Ps 80 16 *SB* ψ. ἐκ; BMis 431 *S* ⲡϥⲧⲙⲙⲟⲟⲩ ⲉⲃ. ϩⲙⲡϣⲛⲏ.

ⲧ. ⲉⲃⲟⲗ *SB*, as ⲧ.: 3 Kg 4 23 (P 44 110) *S* ⲡⲁⲡⲟⲓ ⲉⲅⲧ.† ⲉⲃ. σιτευτός; PasH 108 *B* ⲉⲧⲁⲩⲧⲉⲙⲙⲟⲕ ⲉⲃ. ϩⲉⲛⲡⲉⲕϩⲕⲟ.

ⲧⲉⲙⲙⲟϥ *B* Deu 9 21 (varr ⲗⲟⲡⲕϥ, ⲡⲟⲧϥ, *S* ⲁⲁϥ ⲡϣⲛⲙ ϣⲏⲙ) καταλεᾶν *l* ⲧⲉⲡⲟϥ; do Is 38 21 (*S* ⲧⲛⲡⲟϥ) θρέψον? for τρῖψον.

ⲧⲉⲙⲙⲟ *B* blaze v ⲧⲙϩⲟ.

ⲧⲟⲩⲙⲧ *S* nn, a utensil of bronze: Vi ostr 237 ⲟⲩⲧ. ϩⲁⲣⲱⲧ ⲛϥⲧⲟⲉ ⲡⲗⲓⲧⲣⲁ.

ⲧⲱⲙⲛⲧ v ⲧⲱⲙⲧ *meet & be amazed*.

ⲧⲱⲙⲥ *S*, ⲑⲱ., ⲑⲟ.*B*, ⲧ(ⲉ)ⲙⲥ- *S*, ⲑⲉⲙⲥ- *B*, ⲧⲟⲙⲥⲋ, ⲧⲟⲙⲉⲥⲋ *S*, ⲧⲁⲙⲥⲋ *Sᶠ*(PChass) *AF*, ⲑⲟⲙⲥⲋ *B*, ⲧⲁⲙⲉⲥⲋ *F*, ⲧⲟⲙⲥ† *S*, ⲧⲁⲙⲥ *Sᶠ*, ⲑⲟⲙⲥ† *B*, ⲧⲁⲙⲉⲥ† *F* vb tr, *bury*: Nu 20 1 *SB*, Tob 14 12 *S* ⲧⲟⲙⲥϥ, Ps 78 3 *S* (*B* ⲕⲱⲥ), Hos 9 6 *AB*, Mt 14 12 *SBF*, 1 Cor 15 4 *SF* ⲧⲁⲙⲉⲥϥ (*B* ⲕ.) θάπτειν; Jer 13 7 *SB* κατορύσσειν; Mt 25 18 *S*(*B* ⲭⲱⲡ) ἀποκρύπτειν; BHom 121 *S* sorrowing whilst ⲉⲅⲧ. ⲙⲙⲟϥ, DeV 2 168 *B* were careful to ⲕⲱⲥ ⲙⲡⲟⲩⲥⲱⲙⲁ ⲡⲧⲟⲅⲑⲟⲙⲥⲟϥ, BM 604 *F* ϣⲁⲡⲧⲁⲙⲟⲩ ⲕⲧⲁⲙⲥⲧ; qual: Jos 7 21 *S* ϥⲧ. ϩⲁⲣⲟⲟϥ κρύπτειν; AZ 21 156 *S* water jars ⲉⲅⲧ., Mor 30 23 *Sᶠ* body ⲉⲅⲧ.

With preposition or adverb. c ⲉ- *SSᶠ*, *bury in*: Leip Ber '02 150 ⲧⲉⲙⲥ ⲡⲁⲓ ⲉⲡⲕⲁϩ ⲕⲁⲧⲟⲣ. ἐν; Cai 42573 2 ⲧ. ⲙⲙⲁⲥ ⲉⲧⲙⲉⲧⲉ ⲡⲧⲉⲣⲥⲱ, PChass 1 *Sᶠ* ⲧⲁⲙⲥⲋϥ ⲉⲡⲕⲱⲧ ⲡⲥⲟⲧ, AZ 23 111 ⲧⲟⲙⲉⲥϥ ⲉⲡⲥⲟⲧ; intr: Z 580 Abel ⲛⲧⲁϥⲧ. ⲉⲡⲕⲁϩ; qual: BHom 116 man decays ⲉϥⲧ. ⲉⲡⲕⲁϩ; c ⲛ-: ROC 17 406 *B* ⲙⲁⲣⲟⲩⲑⲟⲙⲥⲧ ⲙⲡⲕⲁϩ; c ϩⲛ-, ϩⲉⲛ- *SB*: Ge 25 10 *S* ⲧⲟⲙⲉⲥϥ *B* ⲑ. εἰς, 2 Kg 3 32 *S* ⲑ. ἐν; Ap 11 9 *S*(*B* ⲭⲱ ϩⲉⲛ-) τιθέναι ἐκεῖ, TU 43 1 *A* ⲁⲩⲧⲁⲙⲥϥ ϩⲛⲟⲩⲧⲟⲡⲟⲥ, AM 137 *B* ⲑⲟⲙⲥϥ ϩⲉⲛⲡⲉⲛⲏⲓ; qual: ShA 2 13 *S* ⲉⲅⲧ. ϩⲙⲡⲁⲣⲁⲫⲩⲥⲓⲥ, Z 260 *S* ⲡⲉϥⲧ. ϩⲙⲡⲧⲣⲉϥϫⲓ ⲟⲩⲁ ⲛⲓⲙ, AM 75 *B* ⲡⲓⲙⲁ ⲉⲡⲁⲅⲑ. ⲛϩⲏⲧϥ; ϩⲡⲣⲏ ϩⲉⲛ-: Jer 7 32 *B* ⲑ. ἐν; c ϩⲁⲧⲛ-: 1 Kg 31 13 *S* (var ϩⲁ-) ⲑ. ὑπό; c ⲉⲃⲟⲗ, as ⲧ.: ROC 17 404 *B* †ⲉⲣ ϩⲉⲗⲡⲓⲥ ⲉⲑⲣⲟⲩⲑⲟⲙⲥⲧ ⲉⲃ. ⲑ.

ⲙⲁ ⲡⲧ., ⲑ. *SB*, *burial place*: Mt 27 7 *SB* ταφή; R 2 486 *S* they build ϩⲉⲛⲧⲁⲫⲟⲥ ϩⲛⲙⲙⲁ ⲡⲧ.

ⲧⲱⲙⲉⲥ *A* v ⲧⲱⲱⲙⲉ *purse*.

ⲧⲙⲁⲥⲉⲓⲟ *A* v ⲙⲓⲥⲉ (ⲙⲉⲥⲓⲟ).

ⲧⲱⲙⲧ *SAA²B*(once), -ⲙⲛⲧ *S*(mostly) *A²*, -ⲙⲉⲧ *F*, ⲧⲟⲙⲛⲧ† *S* vb intr, *meet, befall* c ⲉ-: Ge 28 11 *S*(*B* ⲓ ⲉⲃⲟⲗ ⲉϩⲣⲉⲛ-), Job 4 12 *S*(*B* ϣⲱⲡⲓ ⲙⲙⲟϥ) ἀπαντᾶν, Mt 25 6 *S*(*B* ⲉϩⲣⲉⲛ- no vb) ἀπάντησις, Job 41 17 *S*(*B* ⲑⲟⲡⲧⲉⲛ ⲉ-), Pro 17 20 *SA*, Is 34 14 *SF*(*B* ⲓ ⲉϩⲟⲩⲛ ⲉϩ.), συναντᾶν, Ge 14 17 *S*(*B* ⲉϩ. no vb), Zech 2 3 *A* (*B* ⲉⲣ ⲁⲡⲁⲛⲧⲁⲛ), Aeg 282 *S* avoideth ⲉⲧ. ⲉⲃⲗⲗⲉ συνάντησις, Sa 6 17 *S* ὑπαντᾶν, Jo 12 13 *S*(*A* ϩⲛⲧⲋ, *A²* ϩⲁⲣⲁⲧⲋ, *B* ⲉϩⲣⲁⲋ) ὑπάντησις; Pro 13 17 *A*(*S* ϩⲉ ⲉⲡⲣⲁⲓ, *B* ⲣⲁⲟⲅⲱ), ib 28 14 *A*(*S* do) ἐμπίπτειν, Sa 7 25 *S*(*B* ϩⲱⲡⲧ) ⲡⲁⲣⲉⲙⲡ., ib 17 15 *S* ⲕⲁⲧⲁⲡ., Ac 27 41 *S* (*B* ϩⲉⲓ) περιπ.; Lu 8 29 *S*(*B* † ⲙⲁ†) συντυγχάνειν; Pro 29 13 *SA* συνέρχεσθαι; ShC 73 x *S* ⲡⲉⲓⲣⲓⲥⲉ ⲡⲁⲧ. ⲉⲣⲟⲛ, APBerl Sitz '09 218 *A²* lion ⲧ. ⲁⲣⲁⲥ, BMis 12 *S* ⲁⲡⲉⲕⲗⲏⲣⲟⲥ ⲡⲑⲉⲟⲇⲱⲣⲟⲥ ⲧ. ⲉⲙⲓⲭⲁⲏⲗ *lot fell on M.* (*to care*) *for Th.*, Aeg 14 *S* fear ⲧ. ⲉⲣⲟⲓ = ib *B* ⲧⲁϩⲟⲓ, C 41 53 *B* ⲟⲩ ⲉⲑⲛⲁⲧ. ⲉⲣⲟⲓ?, Mor 31 114 *S* Lent ⲧ. ⲉⲣⲟϥ ⲙⲡⲥⲟⲡ ⲉⲧⲙⲙⲁⲩ; ⲉϩⲟⲩⲛ ⲉ-: Ac 27 26 *S*(*B* ⲓ ⲉϫⲉⲛ-) ⲉⲧⲣⲉⲡⲧ. ⲉϩ. ⲉⲩⲛⲏⲥⲟⲥ ἐκπίπ. εἰς. Qual (same?): ST 221 *S* ϩⲛⲧⲉⲓⲃⲏⲥⲉ ⲉⲧⲧ.†

—— nn m *S*, *meeting, event*: Eccl 2 14, 9 2 (*F* ϫⲓⲛⲕⲱⲗϫ) συνάντημα.

ϭⲓⲛⲧ. *S*, *meeting*: ShC 73 133 ⲧϭ. ⲉⲡⲡⲉ, ALR '93 523 was not pleasant ϩⲛⲧⲉϥϭ. ⲉⲣⲟϥ.

ⲧⲱⲙⲧ *B*, -ⲙⲛⲧ *S* (rare), ⲧⲟⲙⲧ† *B* vb intr, *be amazed, stupefied*: Ex 23 27 (*S* ⲡⲱϣⲥ), Is 33 3 (*S* do, *F* ⲡ. ⲉⲃⲁⲗ), ib 41 2 (*S* ⲣ ϣⲡⲏⲣⲉ), Ez 26 (*S* ϣⲧⲟⲣⲧⲣ), Hos 5 8 (*SA* do) ἐξιστάναι; Ge 34 7 (*S* om), Is 6 5 (*S* ⲙⲕⲁϩ ⲡϩⲏⲧ) κατανύσσεσθαι; Ps 87 16 (*S* diff), Job 17 7 (*S* ⲧⲱⲙ) πωροῦσθαι; BIF 13 114 *S* ⲉⲓⲧ.... ⲉⲓⲣ ϣⲡⲏⲣⲉ = MG 25 308 *B*, DeV 2 78 if drunken his heart ⲧ. ⲙⲫⲣⲏ† ⲙⲡⲓⲉⲱ; tr: Ez 14

5 ⲉϥⲉⲧ. ⲙⲡⲏⲓ πλαγιάζειν; Va 58 191 ⲡⲓϫⲟϩ...ⲉϥⲧ. ⲙⲡⲓϩⲏⲧ; qual: Mt 12 23 (*S* ⲣ ϣ.) ἐξισ.; Is 47 5 (*S* ⲙⲟⲕϩ ⲛϩⲏⲧ) καταν.; Va 61 221 ⲉϥⲧ. ἀπορεῖν; Lev 26 16 (*S* diff) σφακελίζειν; C 89 45 ⲉϥⲧ. & sad = Miss 4 525 *S* ⲟ ⲛϩⲃⲁ μετὰ φόβου; Va 58 191 drunkard ϥⲧ. ϥⲟⲛϣ ⲉⲃⲟⲗ.

With preposition or adverb. c ⲉⲑⲃⲉ-: Ac 25 20 (*S* = Gk) ἀπορεῖν; c ⲉϫⲉⲛ-: Jer 2 12, Mic 7 17 (*S* ⲣ ϣ., *A* ⲣ ⲙⲁⲓϩⲉ) ἐξισ. ἐπί; ROC 23 273 ⲉⲛⲧ.† ⲉ. ⲧⲁⲓϣⲫⲏⲣⲓ; ⲉϩⲣⲏⲓ ⲉϫ.: Is 52 14 (*S* ⲣ ϣ.) ἐξισ. ἐπί; EW 150 ⲡⲏ ⲉⲧⲥⲱⲧⲉⲙ ⲧ. ⲉϩ. ⲉ. ⲫⲏ ⲉⲧⲁϥϣⲱⲡⲓ ἔκπληξις; ⲉϧⲣⲏⲓ ⲉϫ.: AM 234 ⲉⲩⲧ.† ⲉϧ. ⲉ. ⲡⲓϣⲫⲏⲣⲓ; c ⲉⲃⲟⲗ *SB*, as ⲧ.: DeV 2 274 ⲁϥⲉⲣ ϣⲫⲏⲣⲓ ⲉϥⲧ.† ⲉⲃ. = Mun 69 *S* ⲣ ϩⲃⲁ, ⲁϫⲱⲡⲉⲓ, Va 58 69 ⲉϥⲧ.† ⲉⲃ. ϧⲉⲛⲡⲉϥϩⲏⲧ, Mor 51 34 *S* ⲁⲛⲧ. ⲉⲃ. ⲉⲧ(ⲙ)ⲙⲉⲗⲉⲧⲁ ⲙⲡϣⲁϫⲉ *were diverted from*, *cf* Ez 13 22 tr ⲁⲣⲉⲧⲉⲛⲧⲟⲙⲧ ⲉⲃ. ⲙⲡϩⲏⲧ διαστρέφειν.

—— nn m *SB*, *amazement*, *stupefaction*: Ge 15 12 (*S*=Gk), Ps 30 tit (*S* ⲡⲱϣⲥ), Mk 16 8 (*S* ϣⲧ.) ἔκστασις; Ps 59 5 (*S* ⲙⲕⲁϩ ⲛϩⲏⲧ), Ro 11 8 (*S* do) κατάνυξις; HL 91 ἀκηδία; Lam 3 47 ἔπαρσις; Va 61 14 ⲁϥϣⲱⲡⲓ ϧⲉⲛⲟⲩⲧ. ἔκθαμβος γίνεσθαι; ShA 2 258 *S* if one disturb neighbour ϣⲁⲣⲉⲟⲩⲧ. ϣ[ⲟⲟ]ⲡ ⲉⲃⲟⲗ ⲛϩⲏⲧϥ ⲏ ⲟⲩϭⲱⲛⲧ, C 89 94 ⲁⲟⲩⲧ. ⲓ ⲉϧⲣⲏⲓ ⲉϫⲱϥ as he prayed = ViK 9467 *S* ⲉⲕⲥⲧⲁⲥⲓⲥ, Va 58 76 ⲟⲩⲛⲓϣϯ ⲛⲧ. ⲛϩⲏⲧ ⲁⲙⲟⲛⲓ ⲉϫⲱⲟⲩ, *ib* 189 ⲡⲓⲧ. ⲛϩⲏⲧ ⲛⲧⲉ ⲡⲓϩⲩⲇⲟⲛⲏ.

ⲧⲙⲧⲙ *SA*[2], ⲑⲟⲙⲧⲉⲙ, ⲧ. *B*, ⲧⲙⲧⲙ-, ⲧⲉⲙⲧⲱⲙ† *S*, ⲧⲉⲙⲑⲱⲙ† *B* vb intr, *be heavy*, *oppressed*: Job 29 4 *S*(*B* ⲟⲩⲟⲥⲑⲉⲛ) ἐπιβρίθειν; Va 57 199 *B* melt ϯⲡⲁϫⲛⲏ ⲉⲧⲧ.† (or ? *v* ϩⲧⲟⲙⲧⲙ), PMéd 176 *S* stomach ⲉϥⲧ.† ⲛⲧⲏⲩ, EW 193 *B* bindweed ϣⲁⲥⲧ. ⲉⲟⲩⲓⲁϩⲁⲗⲟⲗⲓ destroying its fruit; *strike upon*, *resound*: tr Si 38 34 (28) *S* καινίζειν; intr ShA 2 158 *S* sim? ⲉⲩⲧ. ϩⲛⲛⲉⲩⲉⲣⲏⲧⲉ in midst of assembly, Mani 1 *A*[2] boiling cauldron ⲁϥⲱϣ ⲁⲃⲁⲗ ⲉϥⲧ.; as adj: C 89 131 *B* ϫⲁⲕⲓ ⲛⲑ.; ⲧ. ⲉⲃⲟⲗ *S*, *reverberate*, *resound*: Mor 52 16 Thomas was hard-natured ⲉϥⲧ. ⲉⲃ. ϩⲛⲛⲉϥϣⲁϫⲉ, *ib* 37 84 Antony's words ⲉⲧⲧ. ⲉⲃ., R 2 2 41 her voice ⲉⲥⲧ. [ⲉⲃ. ? ϩ]ⲛⲧⲉⲕⲯⲩⲭⲏ ἔναυλος. In name (?): Πτάμτεμ (Preisigke).

ⲧⲁⲙⲧⲙⲉ *A*, ⲧⲟⲙⲧⲉⲙ *B* *v* ϩⲧⲟⲙⲧⲙ.

ⲧⲙϩⲟ *SA*, ⲧⲉⲙϩⲟ[1], ⲧⲉⲙⲙϩⲟ[2], ⲧϩⲉⲙⲙⲟ[3], ⲧⲉⲙⲙⲟ[4], ⲧⲙⲟ[5] *B*, ⲧⲙϩⲉ- *SAB*, ⲧⲙϩⲟ≈ *S*, ⲧⲉⲙⲙⲟ≈ *B* vb **I** tr, *set on fire*, *kindle SAB* (caus of ⲙⲟⲩϩ): Lev 24 2 *B*[2](var[4], *S* ϯ ⲉ-) καίειν, Job 3 17 *SB*[4], Pro 14 25 *SA* ⲧⲙϩⲟ-(*B* ϩⲓ ⲥⲁϩϯ), Dan 3 22 *S*(*B* ⲑⲱⲕ) ἐκκ., Ps 82 16 *B*[5](*S* ⲣⲱⲕϩ) κατακ., Is 5 11 *S*(*BF* ⲣⲱⲕϩ) συγκ.; Deu 32 22 *B*[3](*S* diff) φλέγειν, Ps 105 18 *B*[1] (varr[3,4], *S* ⲣ.) καταφ., Ja 3 6 *SA*(*B* ⲣ.) φλογίζειν; Job 20 10 *SB* (prob[3]), Pro 16 28 *SA* πυρσεύειν; Ex 22 6 *B*[3](*S* ⲣ.) προσεμπιπράναι; ShC 73 13 *S* ⲛⲧⲁⲧⲙϩⲉ ⲟⲩⲥⲁⲧⲉ ⲉϩⲣⲁⲓ ⲉϫⲱ, ShA 1 425 *S* ⲧⲉϩⲣⲱ...ⲧⲙϩⲟⲥ, DeV 2 41 *B* ⲛⲧⲉϥⲧ.[4] ⲙⲡϣⲁϩ. **II** intr, *blaze*, *burn S*: Nu 11 1 (var & *B* ⲙⲟⲩϩ) ἐκκ.; ShC 73 137 not to let fuel burn till ⲉⲩ(ⲟⲩ)ⲱ ⲉⲩⲧ., R 1 5 41 cloud ⲙⲡⲥⲕⲁ ⲡⲕⲱϩⲧ ⲉⲧ.; c ⲉ-: Miss 4 654 ⲁⲩⲧ. ⲉⲣⲟⲥ (*sc* bath).

—— nn m *SB*, *burning*, *heat*: 1 Pet 4 12 *S*(*B* ⲣ.) πύρωσις; ShC 73 37 *S* ⲧϩⲙⲙⲉ ⲙⲡⲧ. in baths, DeV 2 46 *B* crying in great ⲧ.[4] ⲛϩⲏⲧ, P 129[20] 147 *S* ⲡⲥⲱϣⲙ ⲙⲡⲧ.[1] ⲙⲡⲥⲱⲙⲁ, Tri 285 *S* ⲁϥϩⲩⲡⲟⲙⲓⲛⲉ ⲉⲩⲛⲟϭ ⲛⲧ. بلوى (var محنة, *l* ? ⲧϩⲙⲕⲟ); R 2 1 42 *S* ⲉϥϯ ⲧ. ⲉⲡⲉⲩϩⲏⲧ.

Cf ⲑⲙⲟ (ⲧϩⲙⲟ).

ⲧⲛ- in ⲧⲛⲣⲟⲙⲡⲉ, ⲧⲣⲡ. *v* ⲣⲟⲙⲡⲉ.

ⲧⲛ- *A* prep *v* ⲧⲱⲣⲉ *hand* (ⲛⲧⲛ-).

ⲧⲛ- vb *v* ϯ **II**.

ⲧⲱⲛ *SF*, ⲧⲟ *AA*[2](Jo), ⲧⲱ *AS*f, ⲧⲟⲛ *S*f*A*[2](AP)*F*, ⲑⲱⲛ *B* interrog advb, *where?*: Ge 3 9 *SB*, Is 33 18 *SBF*, Hos 13 10 *A* ⲧⲱ *B*, *ib* 14 *A* ⲧⲟ *B*, Jo 11 34 *SA A*[2]*B*, BHom 29 *S* ⲉⲛⲁϩⲟⲛⲛ ⲧ. (*cf* Ryl 94 n ⲉⲕⲛⲁϩⲟⲛⲕ ⲉⲧ.), MG 25 208 *B* ⲁⲥⲑ. ⲧⲣⲓ, AP 7 *A*[2] ⲉⲥⲧ. ⲑⲉⲕⲗⲁ ποῦ; PS 121 *S* ⲉϥⲧ. ⲓ̅ⲥ̅, Br 236 *S* ⲡⲙⲁ...ϫⲉⲧ. ⲡⲉ, ShBM 195 3 *S* ⲁⲕϩⲁⲣⲉϩ ⲧ. ⲉⲡⲉⲛⲧⲁⲕϫⲟⲟϥ, Mor 30 41 *S*f ⲁⲩⲧ. ⲛⲉⲡⲱⲗϩ = BMis 265 *S*, BHom 71 *S* ⲉⲛⲁϩⲉ ⲉⲣⲟⲟⲩ ⲧ.; *whence*, *how?*: Nu 11 13 *SB*, Job 1 7 *S*(*B* ⲉⲃⲟⲗ ⲑ.), Nah 3 7 *A* ⲧⲱ (*B* ⲛⲑ.), Mt 13 54 *SBF* πόθεν; 2 Kg 1 5 *S* ⲉⲕⲥⲟⲟⲩⲛ ⲧ. (var ⲛⲁϣ ⲛϩⲉ), Aeg 248 *S* ⲉⲛⲛⲁⲉϣ ϭⲙϭⲟⲙ ⲧ. πῶς; BG 117 *S* ⲛⲧⲁⲩⲉⲓ ⲧ. ⲏ ⲉⲩⲛⲁⲃⲱⲕ ⲉⲧ., ShWess 9 127 *S* ⲁⲛⲓⲛⲧⲏϭ ⲉⲓ ⲧ. ⲉϩⲟⲩⲛ ⲉⲛⲕⲁϩ, BMis 473 *S* ⲉⲕⲛⲏⲩ ⲧ., AM 96 *B* ⲁⲕⲥⲱⲟⲩⲛ ⲙⲙⲟⲓ ⲑ., MIE 2 337 *B* if man work not in youth ⲉϥⲛⲁϣ ⲉⲣ ϩⲱⲃ ⲑ. in age?, GuDorm 4 *S* ⲛⲧⲁⲡⲉⲓⲡⲓⲣⲁⲥⲙⲟⲥ ⲧⲁϩⲟⲓ ⲧ., ROC 23 281 *B* ⲁⲛⲛⲁϣ ϥⲁⲓ ⲑ. ⲡⲉ ⲛⲧⲁⲓⲥⲧⲩⲗⲏ *how shall we lift?*

ⲉⲧ., ⲁⲧⲟ, ⲉⲑ., *whither?*: Ge 32 17 *SB*, Ps 138 7 *SA* (Cl)*B*, He 11 8 *SB*, MG 25 212 *B* ⲁⲕϭⲟϫⲓ ⲉⲑ. ποῦ; BG 68 *S* ⲉⲩⲛⲁⲃⲱⲕ ⲉⲧ., C 43 64 *B* ⲛⲧⲁⲱⲗⲓ ⲛⲛⲓϭⲁⲙⲟⲩⲗ ⲉⲑ.; but also *whence?*: 2 Kg 1 3 *S*(var ⲛⲧ.), Is 39 3 *S*(*B* ⲉⲃⲟⲗ ⲑ.) πόθ.; PS 348 *S* ⲉⲩⲛⲁⲉⲓⲙⲉ ⲉⲧ. ϫⲉ-, Mor 27 33 *F* ⲁⲛⲛⲉϭⲛ ⲟⲉⲓⲕ ⲉⲧ. = BMis 386 *S*, BSM 40 *B* ⲛⲧ.

ⲛⲧ., ⲛⲑ., *where?*: Pro 23 30 *S* (Aeg 286, var & *A* ⲧ.), Is 10 3 *B*(*S* ⲧ.), *ib* 30 18 *SF*(*B* ⲑ.), MG 25 216 *B* ⲉⲧⲁⲕϫⲁ ϯⲡⲁⲣⲁⲑⲏⲕⲏ ⲛⲑ. = Z 339 *S* ϩⲛⲁϣ ⲙⲙⲁ ποῦ; MG 25 4 *B* ⲁⲣⲉⲡⲓⲣⲱⲙⲓ ϣⲟⲡ ⲛⲑ. ἐν ποίῳ μέρει; MIF 9 61 *S* ⲛⲧⲁϥϭⲓⲛⲉ ⲛⲧ. ⲛⲧⲉⲓⲙⲛⲧⲛⲟϭ, DeV 2 173 *B* ⲁⲕⲛⲑ.; *whence*, *how?*: ROC 27 154 *B* ⲁⲕⲛⲁϫⲉⲙ ⲱⲓⲕ ⲛⲑ. πόθ.; Mor 31 11 *S* ⲛⲧⲁⲕⲓ ⲛⲧ., ⲉⲕⲛⲁ ⲉⲧ., TstAb 165 *B* ⲉⲣⲉⲥⲱⲟⲩⲛ ⲛⲑ. ϫⲉ-.

ⲉⲃⲟⲗ ⲧ., ⲑ., *whence?*: Ge 29 4 *SB*, Is 41 28 *SB*, Jo 3 8 *BF*(*SA*[2] ⲧ.) πόθ.; Mk 6 2 *S*(*B* ⲟⲩ), AP 8 *A*[2]

ⲛⲧⲛϭⲛ[ⲧϥ ⲁ]ⲃⲁⲗ ⲧ. ⲉⲡⲡⲉ *τίς*; ShA 1 281 *S* ⲉⲣⲉⲡⲉⲓ-
ⲣⲱⲙⲉ ⲙⲉⲉⲩⲉ ⲉⲡⲉⲓⲁⲡⲟⲙⲓⲁ ⲉⲃ. ⲧ., C 86 273 *B* ⲛⲑⲟⲕ
ⲟⲩⲉⲃ. ⲑ., *ib* 246 *B* ⲁⲕⲟⲩⲡⲟⲥϥ...ⲉⲃ. ⲛⲑ., JKP 2 134
Sf ⲟⲩⲁ ⲉⲃ. ⲧⲟⲡ ⲡⲓⲣⲱⲙⲉ.

ϣⲁⲧ. *S, whither?*: Wess 18 37 ⲉⲕⲃⲏⲕ ϣ.

ⲟⲛⲧ. *S where?*: 2 Kg 13 13 (var ⲧ.), *ib* 9 4 (var
ⲛⲧ.) *ποῦ.*

ϫⲓⲛⲧ. *S, from whence?*: BG 16 ⲃⲏⲕ ⲉⲧ....ⲡⲏⲩ ϫ.,
BMis 99 ϫ. ⲉⲧ. ?(= Mor 34 24 *Sf* ⲧⲱ) ϫⲓⲛⲉⲧⲉⲧⲛ-
ⲧⲱⲟⲩⲛ...ϣⲁⲡⲧⲉⲧⲛⲉⲓ, *ib* 124 (on Mt 1 1) ϫ. ⲉⲧ. ?
From Abraham to David, Mun 151 our life shorter
than our fathers', ϫ. ⲉⲧ. *by how much?* From 909
years to 125.

ⲡⲁⲧ., ⲫⲁⲑ., *one from whence?*: BMar 185 *S* ⲛⲧⲟⲕ
ⲡ., Va 61 11 *B* ⲡⲛⲟⲕ ⲫ. ⲙⲙⲁ *πόθ.*;

ⲣⲙⲛⲧ.[1], -ⲛⲑ.[2], ⲣⲙⲧ.[3], -ⲑ.[4], as last: Bor 256 149 *S*
ⲛⲧⲉⲧⲛⲣⲉⲓⲣ.[1], SHel 29 *S* ⲡⲗⲁϣ ⲛⲭⲱⲣⲁ ⲏ ⲟⲩⲣ.[1], C
43 230 *B* ⲟⲩⲣ.[2], BMar 31 *S* ⲛⲧⲕⲟⲩⲣ.[3], C 43 65 *B* ⲁ-
ⲛⲟⲛ ⲟⲁⲡⲣ.[4]

ⲧⲱⲛ *SAA²B*(rare)*F*, ⲧⲟⲛ *S*(BMar 81)*F* nn,
meaning unknown, always with vb ϯ, ⲧⲓ, *dispute,
quarrel*, intr *S*: Mt 12 19 (*B* ϣϭⲛⲏⲛ) *ἐρίζειν*; 2 Tim
2 14 (*B* ⲙⲗⲁϣ) *λογομαχεῖν*; Mk 9 14 (*B* ⲕⲱϯ ⲡⲉⲙ-)
συζητεῖν; Z 273 *φιλονεικεῖν*; BMis 461 ⲟⲩⲣⲓⲥⲉⲡⲉ ϯ
ⲧ. ⲟⲛⲛⲉⲩⲅⲣⲁⲫⲏ;   c ⲉⲧⲃⲉ- *S*: BM 247 11 ⲙⲉϥϯ
ⲧ. ⲉ. ⲡⲉⲧⲉⲛⲟⲩϭⲛⲉ *φιλον.*;   c ⲉⲣⲟⲩⲛ ⲉⲟⲣⲡ- *S*:
ShC 42 167 ⲉⲡϯ ⲧ. ⲉⲟ. ⲉⲟⲣⲁⲩ, *ib* 73 121 sim;   c
ⲉϫⲛ- *S*: ShBor 246 78 ⲁⲟⲩⲁ ϯ ⲧ. ⲡⲙⲙⲁⲓ ⲉϫⲱϥ,
ClPr 54 41 ⲉⲩϯ ⲧ. ⲉ. ⲟⲩⲗⲙⲛⲏ;   c ⲡⲁⲟⲣⲛ- *S*: R 2
1 46 ϣⲁⲩϯ ϯ ⲟⲩⲁ ⲛⲛ. ⲟⲩⲁ;   c ⲙⲛ-, ⲡⲉⲙ-: Mk
8 11 *S*(*B* diff) ⲥⲩⲍ. dat, Ac 9 29 *S*(*B* diff) ⲥⲩⲍ. *πρός*;
ib 17 18 *S*(*B* ϯ ⲟⲩⲃⲉ-) *συμβάλλειν* dat; AP 8 *A²* ⲙⲁ-
χεσθαι εἰς; Sa 15 9 *S* *ἀντερείδειν* dat; C 89 4 *B* ⲁⲩ-
ⲧⲩⲣⲁⲡⲡⲟⲥ ϯ ⲧ. ⲡⲉⲙⲁⲩ = MG 17 316 *S* ⲡⲟⲗⲩⲙⲉⲓ,
BMar 197 *S* ⲁϥϯ ⲧ. ⲡⲙⲙⲁϥ saying Be gone, BMis
99 *S* ϯ ⲧ. ⲙⲛⲡⲏⲡⲉ (var Mor 33 53 ϯ ⲙⲛ-), Mani 1
A² ⲉϥϯ ⲧ. ⲡⲉⲙⲉⲛ, CMSS 39 *F* ⲁⲃϯ ⲧ. ⲙⲉⲛⲏⲃ;   c
ⲟⲩⲃⲉ- *S*: Ac 6 9 (*B* diff) ⲥⲩⲍ. dat; ShA 2 297 ⲁⲩϯ
ⲧ. ⲟⲩⲃⲉⲙⲱⲩⲥⲏⲥ.

——— nn m *SABF*, *dispute, strife*: Si 40 6 *S*, Phil
1 15 *SF*(*B* ϣϭ.), Cl 3 2 *A* *ἔρις*, Ja 3 14 *S*(*B* do) *ἐριθεία*; Pro 10 12 *SA*(*B* do) *νεῖκος*, Lu 22 24 *S*(*B* =
Gk) *φιλονεικία*; Va 66 293 *B* ⲁϥϫⲁ ⲟⲩⲧⲓ ⲧ. ⲡⲉⲙ-
ⲡⲉⲡⲥⲱⲙⲁ *πάλη κ. μάχη*; ShC 42 119 *S* ⲡⲉⲡⲙⲓϣⲉ
ⲙⲡⲛⲉⲡⲧ ⲧ., Aeg 259 *S* opp ⲥϭⲟⲣϭⲧ, Till Oster 12 *A*
ⲡϣⲉϫⲉ ⲙⲛϯ ⲧ.;   ⲙⲁⲓϯ ⲧ., *strife-lover*: 1 Cor 11
16 *S*(*B* ⲣⲉϥⲙⲓϣ.) *φιλόνεικος*; DeV 2 118 *B*.

ⲁⲧϯ ⲧ. *S*, ⲙⲛⲧⲁⲧ-, *without strife*: Tri 484 غيـر عنـاد.

ⲙⲛⲧϯ ⲧ. *A²*, *quarrelling*: Mani 2 ⲡⲙⲗⲟⲟⲟ ⲙⲙⲓϣⲉ ⲙⲛ. ⲡⲕⲓⲛ[ⲁⲩⲛⲟⲥ].

ⲣⲉϥϯ ⲧ., *quarreller*: Aeg 241 *S* *ἐριστικός*, BAp
174 *S* churches filled with ⲛⲣ., Mor 24 10 *F* ⲛⲗⲉϥϯⲓ

ⲧ. ⲙⲛⲡⲉⲃϭⲟ;   ⲙⲛⲧⲣ. *S*: Gal 5 20 (*B* ϫⲉⲣϫⲉⲣ)
ἐριθεία; ViK 9748 *discrepancy* in narrative.

ⲧⲱⲛ, ⲧⲱⲱⲛ *SAA²BFO* v ⲧⲱⲟⲩⲛ.

ⲧⲁⲛⲟ *SA*, ⲧⲉ. *A²*, ⲧⲁⲡⲟ- *SA*, ⲧⲉⲡⲉ- (2 pl) *A*,
ⲧ(ⲉ)ⲡⲁ- *SA²*, ⲧⲁⲡⲟ/ *S*, ⲧⲁⲡⲁ/ *A*, ⲧⲉ. *A²* vb tr, *make*
(*SB* bibl always ⲧⲁⲙⲓⲟ): Ge 1 26 *A*, Pro 8 23 *A*, Cl
14 3 *A* ⲡⲉⲧⲁⲣⲧⲁⲡⲁⲛ, Jo 9 6 *A²* ⲧⲉⲡⲁ ⲟⲩⲁⲙⲉ, AP 13
A² ⲁϥⲧ. ⲡⲛⲉ *ποιεῖν*, El 66 *A* ⲉⲧⲁⲣⲧⲉⲡⲧⲏⲡⲉ; ShC
42 78 *S* ⲧ. opp ⲧⲁⲕⲟ, ShA 1 210 *S* ⲡⲉⲧ(ⲧ)ⲁⲡⲟ ⲡⲛⲭⲏ-
ⲣⲉ, J & C 92 *S* ⲙⲡⲉⲟⲉ ϣⲱⲡⲉ [ⲛⲧ]ⲁⲧⲁⲛⲟⲟⲩ (*sc* sandals), Pap R G Gayer Anderson *S* ⲧⲣⲁϭⲡⲉ ... ⲧⲁⲧⲁⲁⲥ (ⲛ)ⲥⲟⲩⲧⲁⲡⲟⲥ;   *draw up* deed *S*: Rec 6 70
ⲉⲓⲧ. ⲛⲧⲁⲥⲫⲁⲗⲉⲓⲁ ⲉⲓⲥⲣⲁⲓ ⲛ-, *ib* scribe ⲁⲓⲧ. ϯⲁⲥⲫ.
ⲛⲧⲁϭⲓϫ, Ricci pap ⲧⲣⲉⲡⲥⲁϥ...ⲧ. ⲧⲁⲱⲣⲉⲁ ⲉⲡⲣⲁⲛ ⲛ-
ⲡⲧⲟⲡⲟⲥ, Vi ostr 368 *S* have sent thee money ⲟⲩⲱϣⲉ
ⲛⲧⲁⲡⲟϥ ⲉⲣⲟⲩϭⲉⲡⲛ, COAd 46 ⲡⲥⲩⲙⲫⲱⲛⲟⲛ ⲛⲧⲁⲡ-
ⲧⲁⲛⲟⲟⲩ ⲙⲡⲙⲛⲧⲛ, PFrankfurt (Spg's copy) *S* ⲛⲧ-
ⲧⲡⲁ ⲡⲁⲣⲏϥ (ⲁⲣⲏⲃ).   Cf ⲑⲁⲡⲡⲟ.

ⲧⲁⲛⲟ *A²* v ⲧⲛⲡⲟ.

ⲧⲏⲛⲉ *SA* nn m, *dam, dyke*: Dan 12 2 (Mor 43
11, BMar 175, *B* om), Hab 1 10 *SA*(*B* ⲟⲩⲁⲡ), ClPr
54 6 flooded river ⲁⲡⲟⲣϫϥ ⲟⲏⲣⲛⲧ. *χῶμα*, 2 Kg 20 15
πρόσχ.; *ib* 5 20 *διακοπή*; P 43 239 ϭⲉⲣⲏϥⲁ (*γέφυρα*)·
ⲛⲧ. جسر.; ShA 1 194 law & prophets until John (Lu
16 16) ⲁϥϣⲱⲡⲉ ⲡⲁⲩ ⲛⲧⲟϣ ⲁⲩⲱ ⲛⲧ., ShViK 9345
ⲛⲟϭ ⲛⲧ. ⲉⲧϫⲟⲥⲉ ⲉⲧⲟⲩⲟⲙⲧ ⲉⲧⲟⲣϫ ⲙⲡⲛⲉⲧⲣⲟⲉⲓⲥ ⲟⲓ-
ϫⲱⲟⲩ, ShC 73 90 breaches ⲟⲓⲟⲉⲛⲧ., BAp 87 went
forth ⲉϫⲛⲡⲧⲏⲛⲉ to draw water, Kr 127 ⲫⲟⲓ ⲛⲡⲧ.,
ib 1 5 ⲡⲙⲟⲟⲩ ⲁϥⲉⲣ ⲡⲁⲟ (*sic*) ⲟⲣⲁⲓ ⲉⲡⲧ., PMich 3532
ϣⲁϥⲉⲣ ϣⲉ ⲛⲃⲁ ⲛⲧ. *100 lengths of (work on?) dyke*,
Bodl(P) d 39 tax paid ⲡⲁ(ⲧ)ⲧⲏⲛⲉ ⲡⲁⲧⲛⲉϥ (v ⲡⲉⲉϥ
sf).   As place-name: ⲡⲧⲏⲛⲉ (v Ep 300 n), *Πτῆ-
νις* (PLond 3 252), *Τῆνις* (Wess 20 56).   Cf ? الطينة.

ⲧⲟⲛⲟⲩ, ⲧⲟⲡⲁ, ⲧⲟⲡⲱ   v ⲧⲱⲡⲟⲩ.

ⲧⲟⲛⲱ *B* vb intr, *strike*, c ⲉ-: MG 25 119 ⲡⲁϥ-
ⲕⲱϯ ⲛⲥⲁⲧ. ⲉⲣⲟϥ *κρούειν*, *ib* 341 ⲁϥϯ ⲡⲟⲩϣⲉ ⲡⲕⲟⲩⲣ
...ⲉⲧⲁϥⲧ. ⲉⲣⲟϥ, K 234 ⲁϥⲧⲟⲡⲟ بطش. ضرب.

ⲧⲱⲛⲉ *A* v ⲧⲱⲟⲩⲛ.

ⲧⲱⲡⲟⲩ[1] *SB*, -ⲡⲉ[2] -ⲡⲁ[3] *BF*, ⲧⲱⲛⲛⲁ[4] *S*, ⲧⲱⲡⲟ[5]
B, ⲧⲟⲡⲟⲩ[6] *SB*, -ⲡⲱ[7] *SA²B*, -ⲡⲱⲟⲩ[8] *B*, -ⲡⲉ[9], -ⲡⲏ[10],
ⲧⲟⲡⲡⲉ[11] *S*, ⲧⲟⲡⲡⲟⲩ[12] *S*, ⲧⲟⲡⲁ[13] *B* advb, *very, greatly,
certainly* (not in bible, adopted in Egyptian-Gk as
ⲧⲟⲛⲱ, *eg* PG 65 116 A, 201 C, Esaias Scet (1911) 8
ⲧⲱⲛⲱ): Z 336 *S* ϯⲟⲃⲉ ⲧ.[6], Mor 17 66 *S* ⲟⲩⲣⲱⲙⲉ ⲡⲉⲩ-
ⲅⲉⲛⲏⲥ ⲧ.[6], EW 30 *B* ⲟⲩⲥⲁⲓⲉ ⲧ.[7] (ⲟⲟⲡⲱ) *πάνυ*; Z 303
S ϣⲁϥϯ ⲟⲥⲉ ⲧ.[1] *πολύ*, Gu 76 *S* ⲁⲓⲣⲓⲥⲉ ⲧ.[6] *πολλά*;
DeV 1 154 *B* ⲡⲉⲡⲟⲣⲏⲧ...ⲙⲟⲕⲟ ⲧ.[13] (*cf* Lam 5 17 *ὀδύνη
ὀδυνηρά*); PS 374 *S* ⲕⲁⲑⲁⲣⲓⲍⲉ ⲙⲙⲟⲥ ⲧ.[7], ShC 42
25 *S* ⲧⲏϣⲛ ⲟⲙⲟⲧ ⲧ.[2], *ib* 117 *S* ⲧⲉⲧⲛⲙⲟⲕⲙⲉⲕ ⲙ-
ⲙⲱⲧⲛ ⲧ.[1], R 1 5 37 *S* ⲁⲓⲁⲡⲉϫⲉ ⲙⲙⲟ ⲧ.[2], TstAb 159

B ⲙⲓⲟⲕ ⲧ.³, Mani 1 *A*² ⲁⲥϫⲓ ⲉⲁⲩ ⲧ.⁷, C 89 87 *B* ⲁϥⲙⲕⲁϩ ⲧ.⁸= ViK 9466 *S* ⲣⲡⲟⲩϭⲉⲡⲏ, Ep 201 *S* sim¹¹, BMEA 44809 *S*]ⲣⲓⲥⲉ ⲧ.⁴, C 86 338 *B* ⲉϥ†...ϭⲓⲥⲓ ⲛⲁϥ ⲧ.⁵ (var³), Va 58 69 *B* ⲗⲟⲅⲛⲓϣϯ ⲡⲧⲁⲣⲁⲭⲏ ⲁⲙⲟⲛ ⲙⲙⲟϥ ⲧ.¹³, ST 289 *S* (ⲟⲩ)ⲁⲅⲁⲡⲏ ⲉϥ(*sic*)ⲟϣ ⲧ.¹², BMar 44 *S* ϯϣⲓⲡⲉ ⲉⲣⲟⲕ ⲧ.¹, Miss 4 147 *B* sim⁷, Ryl 271 *S* sim⁹, BKU 1 106 *S* sim ⲧ.⁶ ⲉⲙⲁⲧⲉ ⲉⲙⲁⲧⲉ, PMich 4553 *S* ϯϣⲓⲛ ⲉⲁⲡⲟⲗⲗⲱ ⲧ.¹⁰, BAp 122 *S* ⲛϥⲟⲩⲛⲟϥ ⲁⲛ ⲧ.¹, BMOr 7024 (4) children ⲙⲡⲁⲧⲟⲩⲁⲓⲁⲓ ⲧ.⁶, MG 17 328 *S* in weaving take heed ⲉⲧⲙⲣⲓⲥⲉ ⲛⲛⲕⲁⲡ ⲛⲕⲁⲙ ⲧ.⁶ = C 89 74 *B* ⲧ.⁷;   ⲥⲉ ⲧ., *yea verily*: ROC 18 172 *S*¹ ⲛⲁⲓ ⲕ. πάνυ, Mor 17 103 *S*⁶ ⲛⲁⲓ; BMis 381 *S*¹ = Va 63 11 *B*³(BSM 37 *B* ⲁϩⲁ), Mor 27 31 *F*³, AM 33 *B*¹³, C 41 49 *B*⁷.

ⲧⲛⲁ   *v* ⲧⲏⲡⲟ.

ⲧⲛⲟ   *v* ⲑⲛⲟ (ⲧϧⲛⲟ) *bring nigh* & ⲧⲏⲡⲟ.

ⲧⲛⲟⲙ   *v* ⲧⲗⲟⲙ.

ⲧⲏⲡⲟ *S.A*, ⲧⲛⲟ, ⲧⲛⲁ *S*, ⲧⲁⲡⲟ *S*ᵃ*A*², ⲧⲉⲛⲛⲟ *B*, ⲧⲉⲡⲛⲁ *F*, ⲧⲏⲡⲟ⸗, ⲧⲛⲟ⸗, ⲧⲁⲛⲁ⸗ *S*, ⲧⲁⲡⲟ⸗ *S*ᵃ, ⲧⲉⲡⲁ⸗ *S*ʲ*F*, ⲧⲉⲡⲛⲟ⸗, ⲧⲉⲙⲙⲟ⸗ *B*, ⲧⲏⲡⲏⲩ†, ⲑ.† (once) *S*, ⲧⲏⲡⲁⲓⲧ† *A*, ⲧⲉⲡⲛⲏⲟⲩⲧ† *B* vb **I** tr, *pound, tread down*: Nu 11 8 *S*(var ⲑⲛⲟ)*B*(var ⲧⲉⲛⲡⲣⲟ⸗), Is 38 21 *SB* ⲧⲉⲙⲙⲟϥ τρίβειν, Mk 14 3 *F*(*S* ⲧⲱⲣ, *B* ϧⲟⲙϧⲉⲙ), Lu 9 39 *S*(var ⲑⲛ., *B* do), Va 57 197 *B* ⲁⲩⲧ. ⲙⲡⲓⲁⲍⲁⲗⲁⲥ συντρ.; Ex 32 20 *SB*, Deu 9 21 *B* ⲧⲉⲙⲙⲟϥ (varr ⲗⲟⲛⲕϥ, ⲛⲟⲧϥ, *S* ⲁⲁϥ ⲛϣⲛⲁⲙ ϣⲛⲁⲙ) καταλεῖν; ROC 17 403 *B* ⲁϥⲧ. ⲙⲡⲉϥⲥⲡⲗⲁⲭⲛⲟⲛ κεντεῖν; Mich 136 *S* drugs ⲧⲛⲟⲟⲩ ⲙⲡⲛⲉⲩⲉⲣⲏⲩ, *ib* ⲧⲛⲟⲩϥ ϣⲛⲉϩ, KroppK 43 *S* sim ⲧⲁⲛⲁⲩ ⲙⲡⲛⲉⲩⲉⲣⲏⲩ, BKU 1 21 ro *S*ʲ ⲛⲟⲡⲓ ϣⲁⲕⲧⲉⲛⲁϥ, AJSL 46 246 *S* ⲟⲩⲛⲉϩ ⲛⲣⲓⲕ ⲧⲁⲡⲟⲥ ⲉϩⲛⲟⲩⲛⲉϩ ⲛⲥⲡⲁⲛⲟⲛ, BM 1224 *A*² imprecation ⲧⲁⲛⲟ ⲉⲓⲕⲧⲱⲣ...ⲑⲓⲟ ⲙⲙⲁϥ, *ib* ⲁⲕⲁⲑⲓⲟ...ⲧ. ⲁⲣⲁϥ.

II intr, *be beaten, trodden*: EpJer 15 *F*(*B* ϭ.) συντρίβεσθαι; SHel 19 *S* idols fall to ground ⲛⲥⲉⲧⲛⲁ, *ib* ⲁⲩϭⲉ ⲁⲩⲧⲛⲟ; qual, *trodden, contrite*: Lev 24 2 *B*(*S* ⲥⲟⲕⲉ) κόπτεσθαι; Ps 50 19 *A*(Cl)*B*(*S* ⲟⲩⲟϣϥ), Is 57 15 *B*(*S* do) συντρ., *ib* 27 9 *S*(*B* ϣⲟⲙ) λεπτός; Tri 708 *S* ⲏⲧ ⲉϥⲑⲏⲡⲏⲩ ‏مُتَـ‎; P 131⁷ 74 *S* ⲟⲩⲯⲩⲭⲏ ⲉⲥⲧ., BSM 38 *B* send me ⲟⲩⲧⲉⲃⲧ ⲉϥⲧ. (same ?) = BMis 382 *S* ⲉⲛⲁⲡⲟⲩϥ.

—— nn m, *breaking, contrition*: Ps 146 3 *B*(*S* ⲥⲁⲱ), Is 30 14 *F*(*S* ⲟⲩ., *B* ϭ.) σύντριμμα; MG 25 152 *B* ⲟⲩⲧ. ⲛⲧⲉ ⲡϩⲏⲧ.

ⲑⲛⲟ, ⲑⲛⲟ-, ⲑⲛⲟ⸗, ⲑⲛⲱ⸗, ⲑⲉⲛⲟ⸗, ⲑⲁⲛⲟ⸗, ⲑ⸗, ⲑⲛⲏⲩ†, ⲑⲉⲛ.† *S* vb tr, *pound, crush*: Mor 25 24 who cast down Dagon ⲁϥⲑⲛⲟϥ(*l* -ϥ) = Va 61 119 *B* ⲕⲁϣϥ; mostly in recipes PMéd 89 ⲑⲛⲟⲩ ⲕⲁⲗⲱⲥ, AZ 23 111 ⲑⲛⲱϣ ⲛⲍ ⲉⲣⲟⲟⲩ, *ib* 108 ⲑⲛⲱϣ ϩⲓⲧⲙⲕⲁϩⲧ (*cf* Nu 11 8 above), Z 626 ⲑ. ⲟⲩⲕⲟⲩⲓ ϩⲓⲟⲙⲭ, Ryl 104 ⲑⲁⲛⲟϥ ϩⲓⲡⲁϣϣⲟⲩ, Bodl(P) a 2 16 ⲑⲉⲛⲟϥ, *ib* 53 ⲁⲃⲓϭⲉⲉⲓⲛ ⲉϥⲑⲉⲙⲏⲩ(*sic*), PMéd 102 ⲧⲉⲡⲡⲉ ⲉϥⲑ.†, Z 630 κόπρος ⲉϥⲑ.† ϩⲓⲛⲣⲡ, TurM 9 roots ⲑ. (= ⲑⲛⲟⲟⲩ)

ϣⲉⲗϣⲱⲗⲟⲅ, Ryl 106 56 ⲑ, ⲟⲩⲁ ⲟⲩⲁ ϣⲉⲗϣⲱⲗⲟⲅ (*cf* PMéd 158 ⲑⲛⲟⲟⲩ ϣⲗϣ.)

ⲧⲟⲛⲛⲟⲩ, ⲧⲟⲛⲡⲉ   *v* ⲧⲱⲛⲟⲩ.

ⲧⲛⲛⲟⲟⲩ *S*, ⲧⲛⲁⲩ *S*ᵃ, ⲧⲛⲛⲁⲩ *AA*², ⲧⲉⲛ(ⲛ)ⲁⲩ *F*, ⲧⲡ(ⲛ)ⲉⲩ- *S*, ⲧⲛⲁⲩ-, ⲧⲛⲁ(ⲟ)ⲩⲧ- *F*, ⲧⲡ(ⲛ)ⲟⲟⲩ⸗, ⲧⲡⲛⲟⲩⲧ⸗, ⲧⲛⲛⲟⲟⲩⲥ⸗ (Mor 41), ⲧⲛⲟⲩ⸗ *S*, ⲧⲛⲛⲁ(ⲟ)ⲩ⸗ *AA*², ⲧⲛⲁ(ⲟ)ⲩ⸗ *S*ᵃ*F*, ⲧⲛⲛⲁⲟⲩⲥ⸗ *S*ᵃ, ⲧⲛⲛⲁⲩⲧ⸗ *S*ᵃ*S*ʲ, ⲧⲛⲛⲟⲟⲩⲧ⸗, ⲧⲛⲁⲩⲥ⸗ *F* vb tr, *send*: Is 33 7 *F*(*SB* ⲟⲩⲱⲣⲡ), Mt 21 3 *S*(*B* do, *F* ⲧⲁⲩⲁ), Jo 11 42 *SAA*²(*B* ⲧⲁⲟⲩⲟ) ἀποστέλλειν, *ib* 20 21 *SA* ⲧ....ϫⲟⲟⲩ (*B* ⲧⲁ. ...ⲟⲩ.) ἀπ., πέμπειν, Ps 17 14 *S* ⲧⲛⲉⲩ- (*B* ⲟⲩ.), *ib* 56 3 *S*(*B* ⲧⲁ.), *ib* 143 6 *S*(var ⲧⲉⲕⲟ, *B* ⲧⲁ.) ἐξαπ.; Lu 16 24 *S*(*B* ⲟⲩ.), Jo 13 16 *S* (var & *A*²*B* ⲧⲁ.), AP 10 *A*² πέμ.; PS 171 *S* ⲉⲙⲡⲁⲧⲟⲩⲧⲛⲛⲉⲩ ⲡⲁⲉⲡⲁⲅⲙⲁ, *ib* 253 *S* ⲛⲧⲁⲥⲧⲛⲛⲟⲟⲩⲧ, TU 43 4 *A* ⲛⲉⲧⲁⲣⲧⲛⲛⲁⲩⲧ, Mani 1 *A*² ⲉⲧⲁϥⲧⲛⲛⲁⲩⲕ, Kr 3 *F* ⲁⲓⲧⲛⲁⲟⲩⲧ ⲅⲉⲱⲣⲅⲓ, Ryl 414 *F* ⲧⲛⲁⲩⲥⲉⲧ, MR 5 32 *S* ⲁⲓⲧⲛⲟⲩⲥⲟⲩ, Leyd 446 *S* ⲁϥⲧⲛⲉⲩⲧⲏⲩⲧⲛ, J&C 98 *S*ᵃ ⲙⲁⲧⲛⲛⲁⲟⲩⲥⲟⲩ, *ib* ⲙⲁⲧⲛⲛⲁⲩⲧⲟⲩ.

With following preposition.

—— ⲉ-, *send to*: Is 10 16 *S*(*B* ⲟⲩ.), Mt 15 24 *S*(*B* ⲧⲁ. ϧⲁ-), Jo 3 17 *SA*²(*B* ⲟⲩ. *F* ⲧⲁ.) ἀποστ. εἰς; BG 20 *S* ⲁⲩⲧⲛⲛⲟⲟⲩϥ ⲉⲡⲕⲟⲥⲙⲟⲥ, Mani 1 *A*² ⲁⲩⲧⲛⲛⲁⲩϥ ⲁⲣⲁⲥ, Gu 19 *S* first thing ⲛⲧⲁⲩⲧⲛⲛⲟⲟⲩⲕ ⲉⲣⲟϥ *for which wast sent*; vbal *S*: Ge 19 13 (*B* ⲧⲁ.), Ez 30 11 (*B* ⲟⲩ.), Lu 1 19 (*B* ⲧⲁ.) ἀπ. inf; Jo 1 33 (*B* do), Ap 22 16 (*B* do) πέμ. inf; PS 127 ⲉⲁϥⲧⲛⲛⲟⲟⲩⲕ ⲉⲧⲣⲉⲕⲛⲁ.

—— ⲉⲣⲁⲧ⸗ ⲛ-, *to*: Jud 6 8 *S*(var ϫⲟⲟⲩ)ἐξαπ. πρός; BM 1101 *S* ⲧⲛⲛⲟⲟⲩⲥ ⲉⲣⲁⲧϥ (*sic* & PSBA 10 196) ⲛⲧⲉⲧⲛⲙⲛⲧⲡⲉⲧⲟⲩⲁⲁⲃ, Mor 39 34 *F* ⲧⲛⲛⲁⲩⲧϥ ⲉⲣⲁⲧϥ ⲛ-, Mor 39 34 *S*ʲ ⲁⲩⲧⲛⲛⲁⲩⲧϥ ⲉⲣⲁⲧϥ = C 43 54 *B* ⲟⲩ.;

—— ⲉϫⲛ- *S*, *upon*: Sa 16 3 ἐπαπ., BHom 81 judges ⲁϥⲧⲛⲛⲟⲟⲩⲥⲟⲩ ⲉϫⲙⲡⲉϥⲗⲁⲟⲥ; ⲉϩⲣⲁⲓ ⲉϫ.: Lu 24 49 (*B* ⲟⲩ.) ἐξαπ. ἐπί.

—— ⲙⲛ-, *with, by*: Ex 33 12 *S*(*B* do)συναπ. μετά; BM 631 *F* ⲛⲧⲁⲓⲧⲛⲁⲟⲩⲧⲕ ⲙⲉⲛⲛⲉ, Ep 333 *S*ᵃ ⲁⲓⲧⲛⲁⲩⲥⲟⲩ ⲙⲛⲛⲕⲁⲟⲩⲁⲛ ⲁⲩⲱ ⲧⲁⲧⲛⲁⲩ, *ib* 283 ⲧⲛⲛⲟⲟⲩⲥ ⲙⲛⲛⲕⲁⲙⲟⲩⲗ.

—— ⲛ- dat *SAA*²*F*: Lev 25 21 (*B* do), 2 Kg 14 32 ⲁⲓⲧ. ⲛⲁⲕ...ⲧⲁϫⲟⲟⲩⲕ ⲛ- both ἀπ. πρός, Ps 19 2 (*B* do), Joel 2 19 *A* (*B* do)ἐξαπ. dat, Sa 12 25 πέμ. dat, Lu 23 15 (*B* do) ἀναπ. πρός, Pro 17 11 *SA* ἐκπ. dat; Ge 33 8 *S* ⲧⲛⲛⲟⲟⲩⲥⲉ(var -ⲥⲟⲩ, *B* Gk om); PS 118 ⲁⲩⲧ. ⲛⲁⲓ ⲛⲟⲩⲛⲟϭ ⲛϭⲟⲙ, ShA 2 284 hide naught ⲁⲗⲗⲁ ⲧⲛⲛⲟⲟⲩϥ ⲛⲁⲓ, ST 115 ⲧⲛⲛⲟⲟⲩϥ ⲛⲁⲓ ϩⲓⲧⲛ ⲡⲉⲣⲙⲁⲟⲥ, Ryl 277 ⲧⲛⲟⲩⲥⲟⲩ ⲛⲁⲓ, Mani 1 *A*² ⲡⲉⲛⲧⲁⲩⲧ. ⲛⲉ[ⲛ] ⲙⲡⲛⲁ, BM 639 *F* ⲧⲛⲁⲩⲧ ⲧⲁⲓⲛⲓ ⲛⲉⲓ.

—— ⲛⲥⲁ- *S*, *send after, summon*: intr Ge 27 45 (*B* ⲧⲁ.) ἀπ.; Jth 14 12 διαπέμ. ἐπί, Ac 10 5 (*B* ⲟⲩ.) μεταπέμ. acc; BMis 503 ⲛⲧⲧⲛⲧ. ⲛⲥⲁⲧⲯⲩⲭⲏ, Ep

544 ⲙⲏⲡⲁ ⲁⲣϫⲟⲟⲩⲧ ⲡⲥⲱϥ…ⲁⲣⲧⲛⲟⲩⲧ ⲡⲥⲱϥ;   tr
Aeg 231 ἀπ. πρός; Mor 38 10 ⲁϥⲧⲉⲡⲉⲩⲧⲏⲩⲧⲛ ⲡⲥⲱⲓ.

—— ϣⲁ- S, to: Nu 22 10, Jer 33 5 ⲧⲛⲛⲟⲟⲩⲥⲉ, Lu
7 20 (all B ⲟⲩ.) ἀπ. πρός; Ac 15 25 (var ⲧⲁ., B ⲟⲩ.)
πέμ. πρός; BG 74 ⲁⲩⲧ. ⲡⲡⲉⲅⲅⲉⲗⲟⲥ ϣⲁⲡϣⲉⲉⲣⲉ,
Mor 41 87 ⲧⲛⲡⲟⲟⲩⲧⲕ ϣⲁⲣⲟⲟⲩ, ib 89 ⲧⲛⲛⲟⲟⲩⲥⲛ
ϣⲁⲣⲟⲕ.

With following adverb.

—— ⲉⲃⲟⲗ S, send forth: Z 285 ⲁϥⲧ. ⲉⲃ. ϩⲛⲙⲡⲟⲗⲓⲥ, Br 124 ⲉⲕⲉⲧ. ⲉⲃ. ⲡⲧⲉⲓⲛⲟϭ ⲡⲁⲅⲛⲁⲗⲓⲥ, BHom
18 ⲁϥⲧ. ⲙⲡⲉϥϩⲙϩⲁⲗ ⲉⲃ. ⲉⲡⲉⲣⲓⲟⲟⲩⲉ, Ep 329 ⲧ. ⲡ-
ⲣⲟⲙⲡⲧ ⲉⲃ. ⲡⲁⲓ;   ⲁⲃ. ⲡ- A², forth from: Mani 2
ⲁϥⲧ. ⲁⲃ. ⲙⲙⲁϥ ⲡϣⲁⲙⲧⲉ ⲛⲥⲁⲙ;   ⲉⲃ. ϩⲛ-, sim
S: Ps 17 16 (B ⲟⲩ.), Sh 9 17 ἐξαπ. ἐκ;   ϩⲛ- alone:
BHom 115 word ⲉⲧⲟⲩⲧ. ⲙⲙⲟϥ ϩⲛⲙⲙⲏⲅⲉ.

—— ⲉϩⲟⲩⲛ S, in: Lev 26 22 (B ⲟⲩ. ⲉⲭⲉⲛ-) ἀπ.
ἐπί, Aeg 210 ⲧ. ⲡⲧⲉⲅⲁⲡⲁⲣⲭⲏ ⲉⲣ. ⲉⲡⲏⲓ ἀπ. εἰς; ST
217 ⲧ. ⲉϩ. ⲡⲁⲓ ⲛⲧⲟⲧϥ ⲡⲁⲑⲣⲁⲁⲙ.

—— ⲉϩⲣⲁⲓ S, up: BMis 103 ⲁⲓⲧ. ⲡⲁⲕ ⲉϩ. ⲡⲟⲩⲙⲛⲛϣⲉ ⲡⲥⲛⲟϥ, Br 238 ⲁϥⲧ. ⲙⲡⲉⲥⲛⲓⲡⲑⲛⲣ ⲉϩ. ⲉ-
ⲡⲁⲧⲡⲱϣ.

ϭⲓⲛⲧ. S, sending, mission: H SNew Tst iii 381 ⲉⲧⲃⲉⲧϭ. ⲙⲡⲙⲛⲧⲥⲡⲟⲟⲩⲥ.

V Griffith Stories 73, AZ 47 145, but also AJSL
48 53.

ⲦⲞⲎⲦⲎ S, ⲦⲀⲠⲦⲈ A, ⲦⲀⲠⲦⲎ A², ⲐⲞⲚⲦⲈⲚ B, (ⲦⲀⲠ-
ⲦⲈⲚ)F, Ⲧ(ⲉ)ⲚⲦⲚ- S, ⲦⲚⲦⲠⲈ- A, Ⲧⲉⲛⲑⲱⲛ- B, ⲦⲚⲦⲰⲚⲍ
SA, ⲦⲈⲚⲐⲰⲚⲍ B, ⲦⲚⲦⲰⲚ†, ⲦⲚⲦⲞⲚⲦ†(PS)S, ⲦⲚⲦⲀⲠⲦ†
AA², ⲦⲈⲚⲐⲰⲚⲦ, -ⲐⲰⲚ† B(? error), ⲦⲈⲠⲦⲰⲚ F vb tr,
A be like, liken to c ⲉ-: Si 36 19 S, Is 40 25 SB, Hos
4 5 SAB, Mt 11 16 SB, BHom 30 S ⲕⲟⲩⲱϣ ⲉⲧⲛ-
ⲦⲰⲚⲠ ⲉⲡⲉⲭⲥ̅ ὁμοιοῦν dat; Sa 4 2 S, He 13 7 S(B
ⲓⲛⲓ), BHom 141 S ⲦⲚⲦⲰⲚⲠ ⲉⲧⲉⲓⲭⲁⲡⲁⲡⲁⲓⲁ, Va 63
105 B ⲉⲁⲩⲧⲉⲛⲑⲱⲡⲟⲩ ⲉⲡⲓⲅⲅⲉⲗⲟⲥ μιμεῖσθαι acc,
1 Cor 4 16 S(B do), Vi Sitz 172 4 29 S ⲧ. ⲙⲙⲱⲧⲛ
ⲉⲓⲥ̅ ⲡⲟⲉ ϩⲱⲱϥ ⲉϥⲉⲓⲛⲉ ⲙⲡⲉϥⲉⲓⲱⲧ, Cl 17 1 A μιμητὴς γίνεσθαι gen; ib 23 4 A συμβάλλειν dat, Ps 48
20 SB παραβ. dat; Sa 13 13 S ἀπεικάζειν dat; ib 7
29 SB συγκρίνεσθαι dat; Va 57 11 B ⲡⲧⲉϥϣⲧⲉⲙ-
ⲦⲈⲚⲐⲰⲠⲞⲨ ⲉⲣⲱⲟⲩ καθάπτειν gen; PS 186 S ⲉⲉⲓⲛⲁ-
ⲦⲚⲦⲰⲚⲞⲨ ⲉⲟⲩ?, ShC 73 3 S ⲁϥⲧ. ⲡⲡⲣⲱⲙⲉ…ⲉⲡⲧⲁ-
ⲫⲟⲥ (cf Mt 23 27), Till Oster 25 A ⲉⲡⲧ. ⲙⲙⲁⲛ
ⲁⲧⲁⲩⲍⲏⲥⲓⲥ, AM 248 B ⲉⲕⲑⲟⲡⲧⲉⲛ ⲙⲙⲟⲕ ⲉⲣⲟϥ,
BSM 6 B is presumption ⲉⲑⲣⲓⲧⲉⲡⲱⲡⲧ ⲉⲡϣⲏⲣⲓ
(sic l) ⲙⲫϯ = BMis 323 S ⲉⲧⲣⲁϣⲟϣⲧ ⲙⲛ-; intr:
ShC 42 96 S houses ⲉⲡⲛⲡⲁϣⲧ. ⲁⲛ ⲉⲣⲟⲟⲩ ϩⲁⲣⲟⲥ ⲛ-
Ⲧⲡⲉ;   c ⲉⲭⲛ-: Tri 488 S ⲁϥⲧⲛⲧ ⲧⲉϥⲙⲛⲧⲉⲣⲟ
ⲉⲭⲛⲛⲟⲩϭⲣⲉ ش ش;   c ⲙⲛ-, liken with: ShIF
307 S ⲦⲚⲦⲚ ⲡϣⲏⲣⲉ ⲛϯⲣⲏⲛⲏ ⲙⲡⲛϣⲏⲣⲉ ⲡⲦⲀⲠⲦⲀ-
ⲭⲉ, BM 1224 A² ⲁⲕⲁⲧⲛⲧⲟⲛⲟⲩ ⲙⲡⲛⲡⲉⲧⲁⲩⲭⲟⲥ
ⲭⲉ-;   qual: Deu 33 29 S(B ⲓⲛⲓ), Job 1 8 S(B do),
Ez 16 32 SB ὅμοιος dat, Lu 6 47 SB ὅμ. εἶναι dat,
Mt 13 24 S(BF ⲓ.) ὁμοιοῦν dat, He 7 3 SBF ἀφομ.

dat, Mk 7 13 S(B ⲓ.) παρόμοιος; Va 63 85 B ϥⲁⲓ ⲧ.
ⲉⲟⲩⲙⲁⲥⲓ μιμ., Cai Euch 516 B ⲉⲩⲧ. ⲉⲡⲉⲕⲁⲅⲅⲉⲗⲟⲥ
μιμητής gen, Aeg 287 S ⲉⲧⲧ. ⲉⲡⲛⲟϭ ⲡⲁⲣⲭⲓⲉⲣⲉⲩⲥ
μίμησιν περιέχειν gen; He 9 9 B(SF = Gk) παρα-
βολὴ εἰς; BHom 10 S ἐοικέναι; PS 186 S ⲡⲧⲟⲡⲟⲥ
…ⲉⲧⲦⲚⲦⲞⲚⲧ ⲉⲣⲟⲟⲩ, JA '75 5 266 S ⲉϥⲧ. ⲉⲡⲡⲉ̄ (var
R 1 2 49 ⲩⲡⲁⲧⲡⲧⲱⲡϥ), Mani 2 A² ⲉϥⲦⲚⲦⲀⲠⲦ ⲁⲡ-
ⲣⲣⲟⲩⲣⲱⲡⲉ, C 89 173 B ⲁϥⲧ. ⲉⲡⲓⲧⲉⲃⲛⲱⲟⲩⲓ ⲁϥⲟⲡⲓ
ⲙⲙⲟⲟⲩ, C 43 195 B ⲫⲏ ⲉⲧⲦⲈⲚⲐⲰⲠ ⲉⲣⲟϥ, BSM 98
B ⲉⲥⲦⲈⲚⲐⲰⲠ ⲅⲁⲣ ⲉⲟⲩⲥⲱⲙⲁ.

B estimate, speculate, intr S: Si 37 20 ἀπαγγέλλειν; ib 31 5 φαντάζεσθαι; BM 320 physicians ϣⲁⲩⲧ.
ⲡϩⲁⲣ ⲡⲥⲟⲡ στοχάζεσθαι; Is 44 25 (B ⲙⲉⲧⲣⲉϥϣⲉⲡ
ϩⲓⲛ) μαντία; Miss 4 827 since Isidore told you about
me ⲕⲁⲧⲁ ⲑⲉ ⲉⲧⲉⲓⲧ. as I surmise: tr SB: Deu 19
3 B(S ⲦⲰϢ)ⲥⲦⲞ.; Sa 8 8 S, Jer 26 23 B εἰκάζειν; 2
Cor 10 12 B(S ⲕⲣⲓⲛⲉ) ἐγκρίνειν, Sa 15 18 S συγκρ.;
BMis 326 S ⲧⲁⲓ ⲉⲧⲥⲟⲧⲡ ⲡⲁⲣⲁ ⲡϣⲓ ⲉⲧⲉⲣⲉⲡⲣⲱⲙⲉ
ⲡⲁϣⲧ. ⲙⲙⲟⲥ, Cat 25 B (on Lu 8 42, Mt 9 18) when
father went to Jesus, daughter was dying, but when
he reached Him ⲡⲁϥⲑ. ⲙⲙⲟϥⲛⲉ ⲡⲣⲟⲥ ⲡⲓⲣⲏϯ ⲉⲧⲁϥ-
ϫⲁⲥ ⲙⲙⲟϥ ϫⲉⲁⲥⲟⲩⲱ ⲁⲥⲙⲟⲩ, MIE 2 402 B about
3 miles ⲕⲁⲧⲁ ⲡⲓⲣⲏϯ ⲉⲧⲁⲓⲦⲉⲡⲱⲡⲟⲩ ⲙⲙⲟⲥ = PO 22
420 حرت ما حسب;   c ⲉ- S intr: Sa 13 9 ⲥⲦⲞ.;
PS 254 ⲡϣⲁϫⲉ ⲉⲛⲦⲀⲓⲦ. ⲉⲣⲟϥ;   tr: Deu 3 13(B ⲱⲡ)
λογίζειν dat, Is 40 15 (B do) λ. ὡς; R 1 4 30 S ⲡⲧⲉⲣ-
ⲟⲩⲧ. ⲡⲙⲁ ⲡⲉⲗⲟⲟⲗⲉ ⲉϣⲉ ⲡϣⲟϣⲟⲩ aestimari; PMich
601 Sᵃ I adjure thee to-day ⲡⲑⲉ ⲉⲓⲧⲛⲡⲁϣ ⲧ. ⲁⲣⲟⲕ
ⲙⲙⲟⲥ;   qual A²: Mani 2 ⲉⲣⲉⲡⲣⲱⲃ…ⲧ. ⲛϯϩⲉ.

C throw B: Ex 32 24 (S ⲡⲟⲩϫⲉ) ῥίπτειν; 1 Kg 17
49 (S diff) σφενδονίζειν; Ps 75 9 (S diff) ἀκοντίζειν;
C 43 54 ⲁϥⲑ. ⲙⲡⲉϥⲙⲉⲣⲉϥ;   c ⲉ-: Job 41 17 (S
ⲦⲰⲙⲦ) συναντᾶν dat.

—— nn m SAA²B, likeness, oracle: Deu 5 8 S(B
ⲥⲙⲟⲧ) ὁμοίωμα, Ez 28 12 SB ὁμοίωσις; Pro 16 10
SA, Si 31 5 S, Is 16 6 S(B ϣⲓⲛⲓ) μαντία; Nu 12 8 S
(B c.), 1 Cor 13 12 B(S ϩⲣⲃ) αἴνιγμα; Ro 12 6 B(SF
ϣⲓ) ἀναλογία; Cant 5 9 S(ⲉⲃⲟⲗ) ϩⲙⲡⲧ. ⲡⲟⲩⲥⲟⲡ (F
diff) ἀπὸ ἀδελ.; PS 187 S shall see ϩⲛⲟⲩⲁⲗⲏⲑⲓⲁ
ⲁⲭⲓⲧ., ib 254 S ⲡⲁⲣⲁⲇⲓⲅⲙⲁ, ϩⲓⲥⲟⲥ, ⲧ., Aeg 288 S
spake ϩⲓⲧⲙⲡⲉϥⲉⲓⲛⲉ ϩⲓⲧⲛⲟⲩⲧ. ⲁⲛ ἄδηλα, ShBMOr
8810 429 S ⲡⲉⲛⲧ. ⲁⲛⲛⲉ ⲡⲁⲓ for we were not called
unto defilement, Mani 2 A² ⲕⲁⲧⲁ ⲡⲓⲧ. [ⲧⲣⲉ ϩⲱ]ϥ
ⲁⲛⲧⲉ ⲧⲉⲓ ⲉⲧⲉⲣⲉⲡⲁⲓⲕⲁⲓⲟⲥ ϣⲟⲟⲡ ⲙⲙⲁⲥ, Tri 491 S
ate ⲡⲁⲓⲛⲛⲟⲛ ⲙⲛⲡⲧ. similitude (of body & blood).

ϯ ⲧ. S, give likeness, guess: BG 80 their sages ϯ ⲧ.
ⲡⲉⲩⲧ. ϫⲉ ⲙⲡⲉϥⲧⲁⲣⲉ ⲧⲙⲉ.

ⲁⲧⲧ. S, incomparable: Pcod 22 substance ⲡⲁⲧⲉ-
ⲙⲉ ⲉⲣⲟⲥ…ⲡⲁⲧⲧⲛⲧⲱⲡⲥ.

ⲣⲉϥⲧ., ⲑ., guesser, diviner: Is 3 2 SB, Mor 37 76 S
στοχαστής; ROC 20 46 S ⲡⲧⲕⲟⲩⲣⲉϥⲧⲛⲧⲱⲡⲛ ⲉⲡⲉⲧ-
ⲟⲩⲁⲁⲃ.

ⲦⲈⲚⲞⲨ, ϯⲛⲟⲩ   v ⲟⲩⲛⲟⲩ.

ⲧⲛⲁⲩ · v ⲛⲁⲩ *hour* & ⲧⲏⲡⲟⲟⲩ.

(ⲧⲱⲛϣ), ⲧⲟⲛϣⲍ *B* vb tr, *threaten*: Ez 3 17 (*S* BM 268 ⲁⲡⲓⲗⲉⲓ) διαπειλεῖν (var προφυλάσσειν); ROC 25 250 ⲁⲡⲓⲁⲅⲓⲟⲥ ⲧⲟⲛϣⲩ ⲉⲉⲛⲡⲡⲁ ⲉⲑⲃ στύφεσθαι (var δριμύσσειν ἑαυτόν, so ? refl *stiffened self*) ⲟⲩⲟϩ ⲁϥϫⲙⲟⲙ ⲛϫⲉ ⲡⲉϥⲡⲡⲁ. *Cf* ? ⲑⲱⲃϩ (-ⲛϣ).

ⲧⲉⲛϣⲓ nn, *blow*: Bess 7 4 not afraid of ⲡⲓⲉⲃⲓⲁⲓⲕ ⲟⲩⲇⲉ ⲛⲟⲩⲧ.; † ⲧ., *threaten, give blow*: Va 58 191 ἀπειλεῖν; 1 Tim 5 1 (*S* ⲛⲟⲩϣⲥ) ἐπιπλήσσειν; MG 25 250 ⲙⲡⲉϥϯ ⲧ. ⲡⲱⲟⲩ; ⲣⲉϥϯ ⲧ., *striker*: Tit 1 7 (*S* ⲛⲟⲩϣⲥϥ) πλήκτης.

ⲧⲁⲛϣⲟ *B* v ⲧⲁϣⲟ.

ⲧⲏϩⲟ *A*, ⲧⲁⲛϩⲟ *B* v ⲧⲁⲛϩⲟ.

ⲧⲛϩ *SA*, ⲧⲏⲛϩ *SʲF*, ⲧⲉ. *B*, ⲧ(ⲉ)ⲛⲁϩ *S*(KroppR) *F*, ⲧⲉϩⲉⲛ *F* nn m, *wing* of birds, angels &c: Ex 19 4 *SB*, Ps 16 8 *SBF*, Pro 23 5 *SA*, Mt 23 37 *SB* πτέρυξ, Dan 7 6 *SB* πτερόν; Sa 5 11 *S* ταρσός; El 98 *A*, C 43 212 *B*, BKU 1 26 (8116 b) *F*, ib (8117) of cock ⲡⲉϥⲧⲉϩ., ViK 9507 *S* ⲁϥⲣⲱϩⲧ ⲡⲡⲉϥⲧ. ⲉϩⲣⲏ ϩⲁⲙⲡⲉϥϩⲟ; of fish (fin): Lev 11 9 *SB* πτερύγιον; metaph of ship: Is 18 1 *SB* πτέρυξ; earth: Ez 7 2 *B*(*S* ⲥⲁ) -ⲩξ; building: Mt 4 5 *SB*; garment: Nu 15 38 *B*(*S* diff), 1 Kg 24 5 *B*(*S* ⲧⲁⲡ) all -ⲅⲓⲟⲛ; cross: SHel 61 *S*; ⲣ ⲧ., *grow wing, be winged*: Ps 77 27 *B*(*S* diff) πτερωτός, AM 3 15 *B* περίπτερος; PS 287 *S* ϣⲁⲥⲣ ⲧ. ⲡⲟⲩⲟⲉⲓⲛ ⲧⲏⲣⲥ; ⲣⲉⲧ ⲧ., ⲣⲏⲧ ⲡⲧ. sim: Is 40 31 *SB* πτεροφυεῖν, Deu 4 17 *B*(*S* ⲣⲉϥϩⲱⲗ), Ez 1 7 *SB* πτερωτός; ⲧⲁⲁⲧⲉ ⲛⲧ., *flap* (?) *wings*: Mor 20 5 *S* birds ⲧ. ⲡⲡⲉⲩⲧ.; ϫⲓ, ϭⲓ ⲧ., *take wings*: BHom 25 *S* ⲁⲥϫⲓ ⲧ. ἀναπτεροῦσθαι; Miss 4 761 *Sʲ* ⲛⲡⲧⲁϥϫⲓ ⲧ. let him fly forth, Z 316 *S* ϫⲓ ⲧ. ⲡⲧⲏⲡ & come = MG 25 344 *B* ϭⲓ ⲡⲱⲧⲉⲛ ⲛⲣⲁⲛⲧ., Va 57 151 *B* ⲁⲥϭⲓ ⲧ. ⲉⲡⲭⲓⲛϩⲁⲗⲁⲓ.

(ⲧⲱⲛϩ), ⲧⲟⲛϩⲍ, ⲧⲟⲛϩ† *S*, -ⲁϩ† *Sʲ* vb tr, *entangle, be entangled, in converse with*, c ⲉ-: Gu 99 *Sʲ* some fish ⲉⲩϭⲁⲗ⳿ ⲉⲛⲉⲩⲃⲁⲗ others ⲉⲩⲧ.† ⲉⲛⲉⲩⲙⲁϩⲧ; c ⲙⲛ-: 2 Kg 14 10† λαλεῖν πρός, ib refl ⲧⲟⲛϩⲉϥ ⲛⲁⲓ (var ⲧⲟⲛϩⲉϥ ⲙⲙⲟ) ἅπτεσθαι; BHom 52 saw elders ⲉⲩⲧ.† ⲛⲙⲙⲁⲥ ὁρῶσι μετ᾽ αὐτῆς τοὺς β̄ πρεσβ.; BAp 23 ⲡⲉⲡⲣⲉϥⲧⲱⲛϩ ⲛⲁⲡ (*sic* MS, but prob *l* ϯ ⲱⲛϩ). *V* Rec 26 36.

ⲧⲁⲛϩⲟ *SA²* (Jo), ⲧⲏϩⲟ *A*, -ϩⲟ *A²*(Ma), ⲧⲁⲛϩⲟ *B*, -ϩⲁ *F*, ⲧⲁⲛϩⲉ- *S*, ⲧⲁⲛϩⲁ- *A²*, ⲧⲁⲛϩⲉ- *B*, ⲧⲁⲛϩⲟⲍ *S*, ⲧⲏϩⲁⲍ *A*, ⲧⲁⲛϩⲁⲍ *A²F*, ⲧⲁⲛϩⲟⲍ *B*, ⲧⲁⲛϩⲏⲧ† *S*(once) vb **I** tr, *make, keep alive* (caus of ⲱⲛϩ): Nu 31 15 *SB* ζωγρεῖν, Ac 7 19 *SB* ζωογονεῖν, Eccl 7 13 *SF*, Jo 5 21 *SA²B*, Ro 4 17 *SBF*(JEA 13 26) ζωοποιεῖν, Ps 118 37 *SB* ζῆν, ib 79 18 *SB* ζωοῦν; Ge 47 25 *S*(*B* ⲡⲟϩⲉⲙ), Ps 68 2 *B*(*S* ⲧⲟⲩϫⲟ), Is 33 22 *SF*(*B* ⲡ.), Lu 9 24 *S*(*B* do) σῴζειν, Job 36 12 *S*(*B* do) διασ.; Ex 1 16 *AB*, Lu 17 33 *S*(*B* do) περιποι.; PS 131 *S* ⲁⲩⲧⲁⲛϩⲉ ⲡⲥⲱ-

ⲙⲁ, TU 43 12 *A* ⲕⲧ. ⲛⲙⲁⲛ, Mani 1 *A²* ⲁⲩⲧ. ⲛⲕⲱ[, Mor 29 3 *S* God ⲉⲧⲧ. ⲛⲧⲙⲛⲧⲉⲣⲟ = BMis 231 *S* = Mor 30 3 *F* ⲧⲁϩⲟ ⲉⲣⲁⲧⲍ, BSM 12 *B* pardon sinners ⲡⲧⲉϥⲧⲁⲛϩⲱⲟⲩ ϣⲁⲉⲡⲉϩ.

II intr, *make, be alive*: Lev 11 47 *SB*, 1 Kg 2 6 *SB* ζωογο., Jo 6 63 *SA²B*, 1 Cor 15 45 *SB* ζωοπ., Deu 32 39 *SB*, Cl 59 3 *A* ζῆν ποιεῖν; Job 40 9 *S*(*B* ⲡ.), Is 31 5 *SF*(*B* do), Zech 9 9 *SAB*, Ja 4 12 *S*(*B* ⲧⲟⲩ.) σώ.; Ge 12 12 *SB* περιπ.; Mani 2 *A²* ⲁⲩⲧ. ⲁϥⲥⲱⲧⲉ; qual *S*: Bor 234 4 ϣⲱⲡⲉ ⲉⲕⲧ.

—— nn m *SB*, *keeping alive, saving*: Ps 67 21 *S* (*B* ⲡ. vb) σῴζειν; GFr 362 *S* Lord's help & ⲡⲉϥⲧ. (*sic*) ἀντίληψις; Eph 1 14 *B*(*S* ⲟⲩϫⲁⲓ) περιποίησις; Cai Euch 543 *B* hast granted us ⲡⲓⲧ. ἀπολύτρωσις; PS 209 *S* ⲡⲧ. ⲛⲛⲉⲯⲩⲭⲟⲟⲩⲉ.

ⲣⲉϥⲧ. *SBF*, *life giver, saviour*: Ryl 64 *S* Christ's flesh ⲟⲩⲣ. ⲧⲉ, Z 264 *S* Holy Spirit ⲛⲣ., Cai Euch 650 *B* sim ζωοποιός; DeV 2 23 *B* ⲥⲛⲟϥ ⲡⲣ., BM 511 (4) *F*, LAp 515 *F* Spirit ⲗⲉϥⲧ., ShMich 550 13 *S* ⲣⲉϥⲧⲁⲛϩⲉ ⲯⲩⲭⲏ, Aeg 256 *S* ⲣ. ⲙⲡⲧⲏⲣϥ; ⲙⲛⲧⲣ. *S*: Bor 241 211 ⲟⲩⲣ⳿ϩⲟⲡⲏ ⲙⲙⲛⲧⲣ.

ⲧⲁⲛϩⲟⲩⲧ *S*, ⲧⲉⲛϩⲟⲩⲧ *B*, ⲧⲁⲛϩⲉⲧ- *S*, ⲧⲉⲡ., ⲧⲉⲡϩⲟⲩⲧ- *B*, ⲧⲁⲛϩⲟⲩⲧⲍ *S*, ⲧⲉⲛϩⲟⲩⲧⲍ *BF*, ⲧⲁⲛϩⲏⲩⲧ† *S*, ⲧⲉⲡϩⲟⲩⲧ† *B* vb tr, *trust, believe* (cf ⲛⲁϩⲧⲉ): Ex 19 9 *S* (var = Gk, *B* ⲛⲁϩϯ), Pro 14 15 *SB*(*A* = Gk), Mt 24 23 *B*(*S* = Gk), Va 66 300 *B* chooseth ⲉⲧⲉⲛϩⲟⲩⲧ ⲡⲉⲛϩⲏⲧ πιστεύειν, Jud 11 20 *S* ἐμπ., BMis 236 *S* sight ϣⲁⲩⲧⲁⲛϩⲟⲩⲧϥ more than hearing ἀξιοπιστότερος; Bor 226 164 *S* ⲛϥⲛⲁϣⲧⲁⲛϩⲟⲩⲧϥ ⲁⲛ ⲙⲙⲓⲛ ⲙⲙⲟϥ πείθεσθαι; ShC 73 84 *S* ⲡⲣⲱⲙⲉ ⲛⲧⲁⲩⲧⲁⲛϩⲟⲩⲧⲟϥ, ShA 1 48 *S* ⲙⲡⲣⲧⲁⲛϩⲉⲧ ⲡϣⲁϫⲉ, C 89 65 *B* ⲓⲥϫⲉ ⲕⲧ. ⲙⲙⲟⲓ ⲁⲛ = Wess 11 159 *S* ⲡⲓⲥⲧⲉⲩⲉ, ib 166 *B* we beg ⲉⲑⲣⲉⲕⲧⲁⲛϩⲉⲧ ⲛ̄ ⲡⲣⲱⲙⲓ ⲛϩⲏⲧⲉⲛ; c ϫⲉ-: Job 9 16 *SB*, Jo 19 18 *B*(*SA²* = Gk) πισ.; ShC 73 20 *S* ⲛⲓⲙ ⲡⲉⲧⲉϣϣⲉ ⲉⲧⲁⲛϩⲟⲩⲧϥ ϫⲉ-, Bor 258 6 *S* ϯⲛⲁⲧⲁⲛϩⲉⲧ ⲡⲉⲛⲧⲁⲩϫⲟⲟⲥ ⲡⲁⲓ ϫⲉ-, ViK 9463 *S* ⲧⲁⲛϩⲟⲩⲧ(ⲧ)…ϫⲉ- = C 89 14 *B* ⲙⲁⲧ. ϫⲉ-.

Qual: Va 58 192 *B* overload not belly for ϥⲧ. ⲁⲛ ϣⲁⲡⲉϥⲣⲁⲥⲧ ἄπιστον ἐστί; ShC 42 100 *S* ⲛⲧⲧ. ⲁⲛ ⲛⲧⲛⲟⲩⲙⲏⲏϣⲉ *art not trusted by many* for they know thee not, CA 91 *S* ⲉϥⲧ. ⲉⲃⲱⲕ ⲉϩⲟⲩⲛ ϣⲁⲙⲙⲟⲡⲁⲭⲏ, Ostr G Jéquier *S* ⲉϣⲱⲡⲉ ⲟⲩⲡⲧⲁⲓ ⲟⲩⲕⲟⲩⲓ ⲡⲥⲕⲉⲅⲟⲥ ⲡⲣⲟϩⲩⲛ ⲙⲡⲃⲏⲃ ⲟⲛ ⲥⲉⲧ. ⲉⲣⲟϥ (obscure), JKP 2 218 *F* ⲡⲉⲟⲩⲁⲛⲅⲉⲗⲓⲟⲛ ⲧⲁⲡⲟⲩⲧ (*l* ? ⲉⲧⲧⲁⲛϩⲏⲟⲩⲧ).

With following preposition. c ⲉ-, *entrust with*: Lu 16 11 *SB*, 1 Thes 2 4 *SBF*, BM 181 *S* ⲉⲧⲣⲉⲩⲧⲁⲛϩⲟⲩⲧⲟⲩ ⲉⲡⲥⲱⲗⲡ ⲉⲃⲟⲗ πισ. acc; CaiEuch 459 *B* ⲙⲡⲉⲕⲧⲉⲛϩⲟⲩⲧⲟⲩ (sc angels) ⲉⲛⲉⲟⲩϫⲁⲓ ἐγχειρεῖν acc (cf Lu 12 48); PS 228 *S* ⲁⲩⲧⲁⲛϩⲉⲧⲧⲏⲩⲧⲛ ⲉⲙⲩⲥⲧⲏⲣⲓⲟⲛ ⲛⲓⲙ, ShIF 236 *S* ⲕⲛⲁⲧⲁⲛϩⲉⲧ ⲟⲩⲥϩⲓⲙⲉ ⲛϩⲁⲓⲧⲉⲣⲁ (ἑταίρα) ⲉⲛⲉⲥⲟⲩϫⲁⲓ, FR 36 *S* ⲁⲡⲉⲡⲭ̄ⲥ̄ ⲧⲁⲛϩⲟⲩⲧⲕ ⲉⲛϣⲟϣⲧ, Pcod 27 *S* potter labours ϣⲁⲛⲧϥ-

ⲧⲁⲡⲣⲟⲩⲧⲟⲩ (sc pots) ⲉⲡⲏⲣⲡ, AM 163 B ϯϫⲓⲁⲕⲟⲡⲓⲁ ⲉⲧⲁⲩⲧⲉⲡⲣⲟⲩⲧⲕ ⲉⲣⲟⲥ; *entrust to*: Jer 12 6 B(S acc) ⲡ. ⲉⲛ; Si 19 23 S(Gk diff); refl: Jo 2 24 B(S ⲙⲙ-) ⲡ. dat, Ro 3 2 SB πιστεύεσθαι (pass) acc, Va 57 173 B each ſears ⲉⲧⲉⲡⲣⲟⲩⲧϥ ⲉⲡⲉϥⲥⲟⲡ; vbal: ShMun 112 S ⲣⲁⲡⲣⲟⲉⲧ ⲥⲁⲉⲓⲙ ⲛⲓⲙ ⲉⲑⲉⲣⲁⲡⲉⲩⲉ, PO 11 304 B ⲧⲉⲡⲣⲟⲩⲧϥ ⲉⲁⲙⲟⲓⲛ ⲛⲓϩⲓⲣⲏⲃ, Mun 49 S ⲧⲁⲡⲣⲟⲩⲧϥ ⲉⲧⲣⲉϥϣⲱⲡⲉ ⲙⲡⲣⲟⲫⲏⲧⲏⲥ; v also qual; ⲥ ⲉϫⲛ-: 2 Thes 1 10 SB ⲡ. ⲉⲡⲓ; ⲥ ⲙⲙ-, *trust to, confide in*: Job 4 18 SB ⲡ. κατά, Ps 77 8 S(B ⲡ.), Si 1 15 SB ⲡ. μετά, ib 36 34 S ⲡ. dat, Mic 7 5 S(B ϩⲉⲡ-, A ⲡⲁⲣⲧⲉ) κατ⸗π. ⲉⲛ; Si 30 30 S ἀλλάσσειν dat; BM 979 S ⲙⲡⲣⲧⲁⲡⲣⲟⲩⲧⲕ ⲙⲡⲗⲁⲁⲩ ⲛϣⲏⲣⲉ, C 89 146 B sim ⲛⲉⲙⲁϥ; ⲥ ⲡ-, *as*: DeV 2 222 B ⲉⲧⲁⲩⲧⲉⲡⲣⲟⲩⲧϥ ⲙⲙⲁⲡⲉⲥⲟⲟⲩ; ⲥ ⲛⲧⲉ-, v qual; ⲥ ϩⲉⲡ- B v Mic above.

ⲧ. ⲉⲃⲟⲗ B: TThe 217 ⲉⲧⲁⲩⲧⲉⲡⲣⲟⲩⲧϥ ⲉⲃ. ⲉⲡⲓⲙⲩⲥⲧⲏⲣⲓⲟⲛ.

ϭⲓⲛⲧⲁⲡⲣⲟⲩⲧ⸗ S, *trust*: ShA 2 234 ⲧⲉⲛϭⲓⲛⲧⲁⲡⲣⲟⲩⲧϥ ϫⲉⲛⲡⲁⲧⲛⲃⲟ through his drugs.

ⲧⲁⲛⲁϩⲓⲧ (or ? ⲧⲁ-ⲡ.) A² nn: Mani 2 (BerlSitz '33 28) χωρα ⲛⲧ. ⲁⲝⲟⲩⲣⲃⲁϫⲁⲅⲁⲡ (Azerbaijan). Coptic?

ⲧⲁⲡ SB, ⲧⲉⲡ SᶠAA²F, ⲧⲏⲡ F nn m, *horn*: 1 Kg 16 1 SB, Ps 68 31 SB, Hab 3 4 SAB, Ap 5 6 SB κέρας; Mani 1 A² ⲛⲧ. ⲉⲧⲟⲩⲟϩⲁⲣⲉ ⲙⲙⲁ[ⲩ]; ⲡⲁⲡⲧ. ⲛⲟⲩⲱⲧ, *unicorn*: Deu 33 17 B(S = Gk), Ps 77 69 SB μονόκερως; KroppJ 17 S ⲡ. lying on golden meadow; ϩⲁϥ ⲛⲧ., *horned snake*: Pro 23 32 A(S = Gk) κεράστης; ShIF 267 S ϩⲉⲛⲧ. ⲛⲕⲉⲣⲁⲥⲧⲏⲥ, Z 570 S sim, Deu 33 17 B ϯ ϣⲉ ⲛⲧ. (S ⲕⲱⲛⲥ) κερατίζειν; in recipes S: Z 628, Mich 136 1 sheep's burnt, PMéd 120 goat's, ib 54 sim, KroppK 52 (these prob horns, not plants الإيّل قرن, قرن الغزال &c, but cf DM V 4 10); metaphor: Lev 4 7 SB, Ps 17 3 SB, Lam 2 17 SBF ⲕⲉ.; Mor 48 83 S martyr seared with iron ⲧ., PMich 3552 Sᶠ ⲟⲩⲧ. ⲛⲡⲉⲩⲕⲧ, (ψυκτήρ), CO 472 S utensils ϥⲧⲟⲟⲩ ⲛⲧ.; *trumpet*: ShA 1 200 S ϩⲣⲟⲟⲩ ⲛⲛⲧ., C 86 281 B ⲉⲣ ⲥⲁⲗⲡⲓⲍⲓⲛ ϩⲉⲛⲧ.; ⲥⲁⲗⲡⲓⲅⲝ ⲛⲧ.: 2 Kg 20 22 S, Ps 97 6 SB (σάλπ.) κερατίνη; ⲁϣ, ⲉϣⲧ., *sound trumpet*: Mt 6 2 B(S Mor om ⲧ.) σαλπίζειν; as nn m ⲁϣ ⲧ. S: Jud 3 27 κερατίνη; R 1 3 49 ⲥⲁⲗⲡⲓⲍⲉ ϩⲁⲙ.; adj: 2 Kg 20 22 κερατ.; Si 11 32 S κάρταλλος; ⲧⲁⲡⲟⲩ Ez 34 21 B prob l ⲧⲁⲡ ⲟⲩ(ⲟϩ).

ⲧⲁⲡ A   v ⲧⲟⲡ & ⲧⲱ(ⲱ)ⲡ s f.

ⲧⲟⲡ, ⲧⲱⲡ S, ⲧⲁⲡ SᶠA, ⲧⲟⲃ B(C 89), nn m **a** *edge, end, border of garment*: Nu 15 38 (B ϣⲧⲁϯ), Zech 8 23 A(B do), Mt 14 36 (B do, F ⲗⲁⲩ ⲙⲙⲉϯ) κράσπεδον; Ru 3 9, 1 Kg 24 5 Sᶠ(B ⲧⲉⲡϩ) πτερύγιον; Ac 11 5 (B = Gk) ἀρχή; Hag 2 12 SA(B ⲗⲁⲕϩ), Ez 5 3 (B ϣ.) ἄκρον; Tri 615 S ⲛⲧⲱⲡ اذيال; ShA 1 107

ⲛⲧ. ⲛ ⲛⲥⲱⲃⲉ of veil, *ib* 108 ⲧⲉϥⲙⲛⲧⲉ ⲙⲡⲉϥⲧ. ⲥⲛⲁⲩ, Mor 51 36 ⲁⲧⲉⲥⲙⲛⲧⲉ ⲉⲣ ⲑⲉ ⲛⲛⲉⲥⲧ., Miss 4 550 ⲛⲧ. ⲥⲛⲁⲩ before & behind = C 89 88 B, Mor 18 17 Sᶠ ⲛⲧ. ⲥⲛⲁⲩ of robe = Miss 4 111 B ⲥⲁ, FR 78 ⲛⲧⲱⲡ ⲥⲛⲁⲩ, ShA 2 117 drawing back ⲛⲧ. ⲛⲡⲣⲟⲓⲧⲉ & so baring arms, Aeg 252 who clippeth ⲛⲧ. ⲛⲓⲉϣⲧⲏⲛ (*viz* ψαλιστής *sic* l), BKU 1 21 Sᶠ ⲛⲧ. of thing (εἶδος) to be dyed, ShIF 188 garments ⲉⲁⲩ ⲛⲧ. ⲧ. ⲛ ⲡⲟϭⲉ ⲡⲟϭⲉ; ship's *keel* S: Sa 5 10 τρόπις. **b**, *fold, bosom* SA: Hos 8 1 A(B ⲕⲉⲛϥ) κόλπος; ShBor 246 54 ⲛⲧ. ⲛⲁⲃⲣⲁϩⲁⲙ (Lu 16 23 ⲕⲟⲩⲛϥ), ShMun 109 put money ⲉⲛⲧ. ⲛⲧⲉⲕϣⲧⲏⲛ, ShA 2 62 ⲛⲧⲉⲛⲁϫⲧⲉ ϩⲉⲛϣⲏⲣⲉ ⲁⲛ ϩⲙⲡⲟⲩⲧ., ShMIE 23 73 sheep ϣⲟⲟⲡ ϩⲁⲡⲧ. ⲙⲡϣⲱⲥ, ShR 2 3 15 ϫⲓⲧⲟⲩ ⲉⲡⲧ. ⲛ[ⲑⲓⲗⲏⲙ] ⲛⲧⲏⲉ (= BM 285 1 *a*]ⲡⲓⲟⲛ (? l κόλπον) τοῦ ἐπουρ. ιλημ), BHom 74 ϫⲓⲧⲛ ⲉⲡⲧ. ⲛⲡⲉⲧⲟⲩⲁⲃ (cf LMis 265).

ⲧⲱⲡ S, ⲧⲟⲡ⸗ SB, p c (?) ⲧⲁⲡ- S vb tr, *stitch, stop, caulk*: Mor 25 41 ϣⲧⲏⲡ with hole ⲉⲕϣⲁⲛⲧⲁⲧⲟⲡⲥ will become great rent, MG 25 189 B mariner examines ship's joints (ἁρμός) ϣⲁⲧⲉϥⲧⲟⲡⲟⲩ ⲧⲏⲣⲟⲩ, Hall 117 ϩⲉⲛⲛⲱϩ ⲛⲧ. ⲛϣⲃⲃⲓⲛⲉ; ⲧⲁⲡⲟⲩⲱϣ of stone: Si 27 2 ἁρ. (Dévaud *Études* 17).

ⲙⲉⲣⲧ. S nn, *needle, peg* (cf mh n tp DM 8 17): Miss 8 263 small holes in her body like ϩ(ⲉ)ⲛⲥⲉ ⲙⲙ.; correct the reference p 212 *b* 7.

ϩⲁⲙ ⲛⲧ. S nn m, as last: Mt 19 24 (B ⲙⲁ ⲛⲱⲣⲡ, F ⲙⲉⲣⲧⲱⲗⲡ), P 44 62 ⲧϩ. (error?) ابرة برسم الخياطة ῥαφίς; ShP 130ᵇ 19 garment ⲡⲉⲓⲉⲡⲣ ϩⲱⲃ ϩⲁⲡϩ., J 36 26 down to the least potsherd & ⲟⲩϩⲁⲙⲉⲛⲧ., *ib* 65 61 sim ϩⲁⲙⲉⲧ. sticking in wall.

ⲧⲱⲡ O nn, meaning unknown: AZ 21 98 ⲛⲁⲡⲙⲉⲭϩ ⲛϣⲉ ⲛⲁⲫⲟ ⲛⲧ.   Cf ? ⲧⲱⲱⲃⲉ *brick*.

ⲧⲱ(ⲱ)ⲡ S, ⲧⲱⲡ F (nn), ⲧⲉⲡ- S, ⲧⲁⲁⲡ- Sᶠ, ⲧⲟⲡ⸗, ⲧⲏ(ⲏ)ⲡ†, ⲧⲁⲡⲏⲩ† (Si, or l ⲧⲥⲁⲃⲏⲩ?) S vb **I** intr, *be accustomed, familiar*, ⲥ ⲉ-: JA '75 5 231 ⲙⲡⲣⲧ. ⲉϭⲣⲙⲉ = R 1 59 ⲧⲓⲕⲁ ⲥϩ. ⲉⲉⲓ ⲉϩⲟⲩⲛ ϣⲁⲣⲟⲕ γυναῖκα συνείσακτον ἔχειν; ShC 42 220 ⲙⲡⲟⲩⲧ. ⲉⲡⲉⲩⲉⲣⲏⲩ, *ib* 73 50 ⲟⲩⲙⲛⲧⲣⲉϥ ⲛϣⲁϫⲉ ⲉⲁⲥⲧ. ⲉⲣⲟⲟⲩ, Mor 28 221 wine ⲛⲧⲁⲕⲧⲱⲟⲡ ⲉⲣⲟϥ, Mus 42 216 ascetic virgin ⲉⲧⲣⲉⲥⲧ. ⲉⲟⲩϩⲟⲙⲁⲗ ⲛⲣⲟⲟⲩⲧ, Ep 238 ⲛⲧⲁⲓⲧ. ⲉⲣⲱⲧⲛ O my father; vbal: ShIF 279 demons ⲧ. ⲉϭⲟⲉⲓⲗⲉ ⲉⲣⲟⲟⲩ, ShA 1 245 passions ⲛⲧⲁⲕⲧ. ⲉϣⲉⲉⲓ ⲛⲣⲏⲧⲟⲩ; qual: 1 Kg 17 39 (var ⲧⲏⲛⲡ, B ⲕⲉϩ) πειρᾶσθαι; Si 23 15 ⲧⲁⲡⲏⲩ συνεθίζειν; ShR 2 3 44 ⲉϣϫⲉ ⲟⲩⲛ ϩⲟⲓⲛⲉ ⲧ. ⲉⲣⲟϥ *familiar with him*, ShMIF 23 200 shepherd ⲛⲉϥⲧ. ⲁⲛ ⲉⲡⲱⲣϫ ⲉⲡⲉϥⲟϩⲉ, BMis 158 ⲛϥⲧ. ⲁⲛ ⲉϩⲱⲃ ⲛⲧⲉⲙⲓⲛⲉ.

II tr, *accustom*: R 1 2 58 ⲙⲡⲣⲧⲉⲡ ⲣⲱⲕ ⲉⲱⲣⲕ, Lammayer 50 Sᶠ ⲧⲁⲁⲡ ⲡⲉⲕϣⲏⲣⲉ ⲉⲧⲉⲕⲕⲗⲏⲥⲓⲁ; refl: Bor 253 151 ⲙⲁⲣⲉⲛⲧⲟⲡⲛ... ⲉϣⲱⲡⲉ ϩⲣⲟⲉⲛⲥⲙⲟⲩ ἐθίζειν, Si 23 9 συνεθ.; BAp 152 ⲙⲡⲣⲧⲟⲡⲕ ⲉⲥⲟϣ.

—— nn m *SF*, *usage, custom*: 1 Cor 8 7 *SF(B* ⲕⲁⲣⲥ), Mor 37 39 they have ⲡⲧ. ⲉⲣⲟⲟⲩ ⲉⲣⲟⲟⲩ συνή- θεια; ShIF 286 ⲡⲧ. ⲉⲡⲉⲡⲉⲣⲏⲩ; ⲧⲁⲡ (?)*A* : 2 Macc 6 2 ⲕⲁⲧⲁ ⲡⲧ. ⲡⲛⲉⲧⲟⲩⲏⲣ καθὼς ἐτύγχανον.

ⲧⲟⲡⲥ, ⲧⲁ., ⲧⲁⲁ. *S*, ⲧⲁⲡⲥ *B* nn f, *custom, habit*: Si 23 17 *SB* ἐθισμός; Z 307 ⲙⲡⲉⲣⲕⲁ ⲧⲁ. ⲡⲁⲕ ⲙⲡⲟⲩⲣⲏ- ⲧⲉⲙⲱⲡ γνῶσις (var φιλία), *ib* 293 ⲉⲣϣⲁⲛⲟⲩⲧⲁⲁ. ⲱⲡ (*sic* MS) ⲡⲙⲙⲁϥ a long while.

ⲧⲉⲡⲓ, -ⲡⲉ *B* v ⲧⲉⲃⲓ strip.

ϯⲡⲉ *taste* v ⲧⲱⲡⲉ.

ϯⲡⲉ *SAA²*, **ϯⲡⲓ** *BF* nn f, *loins* (sg, only pl where pl persons): Ge 35 11 *SB*, Pro 31 17 *SAB*, Is 32 11 pl *SBF*, Lu 12 35 pl *SB* ὀσφύς; Lev 3 9 *B(S* = Gk) ψόα; BMis 341 *S* girdle ⲙⲟⲣϥ ⲉⲭⲡⲧⲉⲕϯ., GriffStu 163 *F* sim.

ⲧⲱⲡⲉ, ⲧⲱⲡ-, ⲧⲉⲡ-, ⲧⲟⲡ⸗, ⲧⲱⲡ⸗ *S* vb intr, *taste*: ShR 2 3 32 will give thee ⲉⲟⲩ[ⲱⲙ] ⲏ ⲉⲧ.; ⲥ ⲉⲃⲟⲗ ⲅⲛ-: ShC 73 119 ⲉⲧⲣⲉⲡⲧ. ⲉⲃ. ⲅⲡⲡⲁⲓ, ShP 130⁵ 59 ⲧⲉⲧⲛⲧ. ⲉⲃ. ⲡⲣⲏⲧⲟⲩ (fruits); tr: 1 Kg 14 24, Job 12 11 (*B* ⲭⲉⲙ ϯⲡⲓ), Si 36 27, Jo 2 9 (var ⲧⲱⲡ, *B* do), JA '75 5 240 drink not wine ⲉⲓⲙⲡⲧⲉⲓ ⲉⲧⲟⲡϥ (var R 1 5 13 ⲧⲱⲡϥ) γεύειν; ShA 1 249 ⲡⲉⲧⲛⲁⲧⲟⲡϥ (wine), *ib* 2 158 ⲅⲉⲛϣⲟⲩϣⲧ ⲁⲩⲧ. ⲡⲁⲃⲟⲕⲉ ⲉⲣⲟⲟⲩ *cause to taste therefrom*, ROC 20 52 ⲉⲧⲙⲧⲱⲡ ⲗⲁⲁⲩ ⲡⲉⲡⲕⲁ, P 129¹⁸ 20 ⲁϥⲧ. ⲡⲡⲉϥⲏⲣⲡ.

ϯⲡⲉ *SAA²*, **ϯⲡⲓ** *BF* nn f, *taste*: Nu 11 8 *SB*, Job 6 6 *S(B* ⲅⲗⲏⲭⲓ) γεῦμα; ShA 2 238 *S* knew ⲧⲉϥϯ., Mani 2 *A²* ⲧϯ. ⲉⲧⲣⲁⲗϭ; ⲭⲓ, ϭⲓ ϯ. *SAA²B*(once)*F*, *take taste*, intr: Ps 33 8 *S(B* ⲭⲉⲙ ϯ.), Pro 31 18 *SB*, Col 2 21 *SB* γεύειν; BG 57 *S* ⲉⲧⲙⲭ. ⲉⲧⲉⲡⲁⲓⲡⲉ (ⲉ)- ⲧⲙⲥⲱⲧⲙ; tr: Mk 9 1 *SF(B* do), Jo 8 52 *SA²(B* do). BHom 3 *S* ⲁϥⲭ. ⲡⲟⲩⲥⲓϣⲉ γ., Sa 16 3 *S* γεύσεως μετέχεσθαι; Aeg 258 *S* ϥⲛⲁⲭ. ⲙⲡⲟⲉⲓⲕ, Ryl 94 *S* tortures terrible to behold ⲙⲁⲗⲓⲥⲧⲁ ⲉⲭ. ⲙⲙⲟⲟⲩ, ROC *lc S* ⲉⲧⲙⲧⲱⲡ ⲗⲁⲁⲩ…ⲏ ⲉⲭ. ⲡⲗⲁⲁⲩ, Mani 1 *A²* ⲭ. ⲙⲡⲓⲣⲓⲙⲏⲃ, TillOster 25 *A* ⲉⲡⲭ. ⲙⲡⲉⲧⲧⲁⲭⲣⲁ- ⲉⲓⲧ (?); as nn m: BHom 48 *S* ⲡⲥⲱⲧⲙ, ⲡϣⲱⲗⲙ, ⲡⲭ. γεῦσις; ϭⲓⲛⲭⲓ, ⲭⲓⲛϭⲓ ϯ., *act of tasting*: ClPr 30 15 *S* ⲧϭ. ⲙⲡⲉⲕⲃⲟ when fan moves air, Va 66 288 *B* ⲡⲓⲭⲓⲛϭⲱⲗⲉⲙ (*l* ϣⲱ.), ⲡⲓⲭ.; ⲭⲉⲙ ϯ. *B* v above ⲭⲓ ϯ.; ⲥ ⲉⲃⲟⲗ ⲭⲉⲛ-: C 43 16 ⲭ. ⲉⲃ. ⲭⲉⲛⲡⲓⲁϭⲟⲩⲓ; as nn: Dan 5 2 γεῦσις; ⲙⲉⲧⲣⲉϥⲭⲉⲙ ϯ.: MG 25 139; ⲭⲓⲛⲭⲉⲙ ϯ. m: Mus 35 32.

ⲧⲡⲉ, ⲧⲫⲉ *upper part* v ⲡⲉ heaven.

ⲧⲁⲡⲗⲁ *F* v ⲧⲁⲡⲣⲟ.

ⲧⲁⲡ(ⲉ)ⲛ, ⲧⲉⲡⲛ, -ⲡⲉ *S*, **ⲑⲁⲡⲉⲛ** *B* nn, *cumin*: Is 28 25 *SB*, Mt 23 23 *SB* κύμινον, P 44 83 *S* ⲧ. ⲅⲟⲟⲩⲧ ἄγριον ⲕ.; K 193 *B* ⲡⲓⲑ. الابيض كون (*cf ib* ⲑⲁⲓⲙⲟⲩⲅ); ⲓⲧ. recipes *S*: Z 628, Ryl 104 -ⲉⲡ, PMéd 184 ⲧⲉ. ⲉϥ- ⲥⲏⲭ *roasted c.*, *ib* 133 -ⲡⲉ ⲉϥⲟⲡⲏⲩ *pounded*; RE 9

176 in account ⲧⲉϭⲙⲉ ⲡⲧ., Mor 51 34 parable ⲁⲡ- ⲥⲱⲟⲩ ⲉⲃⲟⲗ ⲅⲙⲡϣ(ⲉ) ⲡⲣⲱⲧ ⲡϣⲉ ⲡⲧⲁⲡⲉⲡ, expl ⲁⲡ- ⲧⲉⲩϣ ⲙⲉⲣⲥⲡⲁⲩ…ⲡϭⲱⲃ; σαντεπεν *c.* seller (Prei- sigke 482).

ⲧⲁⲡⲣⲟ *SAA²B*(twice), **ⲧⲁⲡⲣⲁ, -ⲗⲁ** *F* nn f, *mouth, lit*: Nu 12 8 *S*, Ps 16 10 *S(F* ⲗⲁ), *ib* 50 15 *S(A* Cl ⲡⲁⲓϭⲉ), Mic 3 5 *SA*, Jo 19 29 *SA²*, Ap 10 9 *SF* -ⲗⲁ (all *B* ⲣⲟ) στόμα; PS 36 *S* ⲡⲛⲓϣⲉ ⲡⲧⲉⲩⲧ., ShRE 10 160 *S* ⲟⲩⲧ. ⲡⲣⲱⲙⲉ, Bor 143 39 *S* ϯ ⲡⲉⲓ ⲉⲣⲱⲥ ⲙⲡ- ⲧⲉⲥⲧ., Mani 1 *A²* ⲟⲩⲉⲡ ⲡⲧⲟⲩⲧ., BSM 59 *B* ⲁϣ ⲡⲧ. ⲓⲉ ⲁϣ ⲡⲗⲁⲥ, BMOr 8775 137 *B* ϯⲧ. درزز, حرّجك (but these K 76 ϣⲃⲱⲃⲓ), Mor 41 182 *S* said ⲅⲛⲟⲩⲧ. ⲡⲟⲩⲱⲧ, Ep 277 *S* ⲡⲉⲭⲁϥ ⲡⲁⲓ ⲡⲧⲉⲩⲧ., Mor 24 29 *F* -ⲗⲁ, BM 512 *F*; ⲧ. ⲅⲓⲧ., *mouth to mouth S*: 2 Jo 12 (*B* ⲣⲟ ⲟⲩⲅⲉⲣⲟ) ⲥⲧ. πρὸς στ.; Ex 33 11 (var ⲅⲟ ⲅⲓⲣⲟ, *B* ⲣⲟ ⲟⲩⲅⲉⲣⲟ) ἐνώπιος ἐνωπίῳ; Ep 281 tell you all ⲡⲧ. ⲅⲓⲧ.; *metaphor S*: of well Ge 29 2 (*B* ⲣⲟ) ⲥⲧ., BAp 89 (*cf* 88 ⲣⲟ), BSG 180 (*B* *ib* 11 ⲥϥⲟⲧⲟⲩ); of tomb Jos 10 18 ⲥⲧ.; of sword He 11 34 ⲥⲧ. (*B* do); *tip* of tail PS 320 ⲧⲧ. ⲙⲡⲥⲁⲧ of dragon.

ⲧⲟⲡⲥ v ⲧⲱⲱⲡ.

ⲧⲁⲡⲧ *S* vb intr, meaning uncertain, ?*chew*: Si 34 17 ⲧⲁⲡⲧ ⲡⲣⲱⲕ (*sic* both MSS) διαμασᾶσθαι. *Cf* ? ⲧⲟⲃⲧⲃ. *V* Spg *Kopt Etym* §30.

ⲧⲁⲡⲓⲧ *S* nn, meaning unknown: Ryl 282 ⲥⲁⲣⲥⲓⲕⲓ (? σαλοίκιον) ⲅⲓⲧ. ⲅⲓⲫⲁϭⲓⲡⲁ (? φάκινος). A herb?

ⲧⲁⲡⲟⲩⲟⲩϣ v ⲧⲱⲡ stitch.

ⲧⲣ- *A²* prefixed to ⲟⲩⲁⲓⲡⲉ, v ⲟⲩⲟⲉⲓⲡ.

ⲧⲣ-, ⲧⲉⲣ- in ⲧⲣⲣⲟⲙⲡⲉ &c v ⲣⲟⲙⲡⲉ.

ⲧⲁⲣ *SB*, **ⲧⲁⲗ** *Sf*, **ⲧⲉⲣ** *A²*, **ⲧⲉⲗ** *F* nn m, f once, *branch, point*: Ex 25 30 *S*(P 44 104, *B* = Gk) σφαι- ρωτήρ (?) قائمة; Jud 9 48 *S* (var ⲧⲁⲗ), Mt 13 32 *F* (*S* = Gk, *B* ⲭⲁⲗ) κλάδος; Job 40 17 *S(B* do) ῥάδα- μνος; Jo 15 5 *A²*(*S* ϣⲗⲣ, *B* = Gk) κλῆμα; Ge 40 10 *S(B* ⲭⲁϥ) πυθμήν (var κληματίς); Is 17 6 *SB* ἄκρον; Ez 17 4 *SB frons*; Glos 31 *S* ⲗⲱⲃⲟⲥ (*l* ⲗⲟ.) ὠτίου · ⲧⲁⲣ ⲱ[ⲧ(or ϣ[ ); Jos 8 29 *S* ϣⲉ ⲡⲧ. ⲥⲡⲁⲩ δίδυμος; 1 Kg 2 13 *S*, Z 334 *S* ϣⲟⲙⲡⲧ ⲡⲧ. τριόδους; K 133 *B* ⲡⲓⲧ. (of ship), مدرا, قمير *boat-pole, -hook* (Lane 866, AZ 13 180, BIF 20 71); ShA 1 465 *S* ⲡϣⲏⲡ…ⲡⲉϥⲧ. de- stroyed by tempest, *ib* 448 *S* ⲡϣⲉ, ⲡⲕⲗⲁⲇⲟⲥ, ⲡⲧ., Sh(Besa)Z 506 *S* ⲟⲩⲧ. ⲡⲕⲁⲗⲗⲏⲣⲉ, PMéd 247 *S* ⲛⲧ. *sprigs* of herbs, Mor 23 29 *S* ⲅⲧⲏⲩ ⲡⲡⲉⲥⲧ. (*sc* tree's), EW 101 *B* ⲡⲧ. ⲡⲧⲉ ⲡⲓϣϣⲏⲡ, Mani 1 *A²* ϣⲱⲧ ⲡⲡⲧ. ⲙⲡⲡⲕⲗⲁⲍⲟⲥ, DeV 2 234 *B* dove brought ⲟⲩⲧ. ⲡⲭⲱⲓⲧ, Mor 37 165 *S* feathers ⲉⲩⲥⲟⲣϭ ⲅⲡⲧⲧ. ⲡⲧ- ⲥⲁⲣⲝ (of wings); ⲟ, ⲟⲓ ⲡⲧ., *have points*: Mor 38 23 *S* ϣⲗⲓϭ…ⲉⲩⲟ ⲡϣⲟⲙⲡⲧ ⲡⲧ., TstAb 160 *B* tree ⲟⲓ ⲡⲧ ⲡⲧ., MIE 2 408 *B* prongs ⲟⲓ ⲡⲧ. ⲧ. ⲙⲫⲣⲏϯ

ⲛⲣⲁⲡⲗⲟⲩⲭⲏ;   ⲣⲁⲧ ⲧ. ⲉⲃⲟⲗ *B*, *put forth branches*: Is 27 6 (*S* ⲧⲉⲕ ϯⲟⲩⲱ ⲉⲃ.) βλαστάνειν. *Cf* ? ⲧⲣⲁ.

ⲧⲉⲣ- *B* vb tr, meaning unknown: DeV 2 33 we are expecting God's wrath & I see ⲭⲉⲧⲉⲛⲧⲉⲣ ϩⲏⲧ ⲡⲧⲟⲧϥ ⲡⲉⲙⲕⲁϩ ⲛϩⲏⲧ so that we incline to despair. *Cf* ? ⲧⲣⲣⲉ.

ⲧⲏⲣ⸗ *SAA²BFO*, ⲧⲏⲗ⸗ *F*, ⲧⲉⲣ⸗ *O* adj with suff, *all, whole, every*: Ge 1 25 *SAB* ⲛϫⲁⲧϥⲉ ⲧⲏⲣⲟⲩ, Lev 24 17 *B* ⲟⲩⲯⲩⲭⲏ ⲧⲏⲣⲥ (*S* ⲛⲓⲙ), Ps 44 13 *SB* ⲡⲉⲟⲟⲩ ⲧⲏⲣϥ, Si 49 2 *S* ϩⲛⲧⲧⲁⲡⲣⲟ ⲧⲏⲣⲥ (ShC 42 134 sim), Ro 4 16 *SB* ⲡⲉⲡⲉⲓⲱⲧ ⲧⲏⲣⲛ, Ps 31 10 *S* ⲛⲧⲉⲧⲛϣⲟⲩϣⲟⲩ ⲙⲙⲱⲧⲛ ⲧⲏⲣⲧⲛ (*B* ⲟⲩⲟⲛ ⲛⲓⲃⲉⲛ), Joel 1 5 *A* ⲧⲉⲧⲛⲧⲁⲉⲓⲧ ⲧⲏⲣⲧⲛⲉ (*B* ⲧⲏⲣⲟⲩ *v below*), Job 27 12 *S* ⲧⲏⲣⲧⲛ ⲧⲉⲧⲛⲥⲟⲟⲩⲛ (*B* do), Jo 17 21 *SA²* ϫⲉⲕⲁⲥ ⲧⲏⲣⲟⲩ ⲉⲩⲉϣⲱⲡⲉ (*B diff*), *ib* 3 26 *F* ⲥⲉⲛⲏⲟⲩ ⲧⲏⲗⲟⲩ (*S* ⲟⲩⲟⲛ ⲛⲓⲙ), Ac 2 1 *S* ⲡⲉⲩϣⲟⲟⲡ ⲧⲏⲣⲟⲩⲡⲉ, Ja 3 2 *S* ⲧⲛⲣⲏⲩ ⲧⲏⲣⲛ (*A* ⲁⲩϭⲉ) πᾶς, Ge 19 4 *SB*, Ps 21 23 *SB*, Mk 11 32 *B*(*S* ⲟⲩ. ⲛ.) ἅπας; Ps 36 26 *SB* ⲡⲉϩⲟⲟⲩ ⲧⲏⲣϥ, Zech 4 2 *SAB* ⲗⲩⲭⲛⲓⲁ ⲛⲡⲟⲩⲃ ⲧⲏⲣⲥ, Cant 4 7 *S* ⲛⲁⲡⲟⲩ ⲧⲏⲣⲉ, Jo 9 34 *SA²* ⲡⲁⲅⲭⲡⲟⲕ ⲧⲏⲣⲕ, Ac 28 30 *SB* ⲣⲙⲡⲉ ⲥⲛⲧⲉ ⲧⲏⲣⲟⲩ, R 1 4 72 *S* ⲁⲛⲡⲛⲱϣ ⲧⲏⲣⲧ ὅλος; PS 227 *S* ⲛⲧⲟϣⲡⲉ ⲡⲉⲅⲉⲓ ⲉⲃⲟⲗ ⲧⲏⲣⲟⲩ, *ib* 35 ⲧⲉⲧⲅⲩⲗⲏ ⲧⲏⲣⲟⲩ, PGM 1 60 *O* ⲛ]ⲧⲟ ⲧⲏⲣϥ, Hor 84 *O* ⲛⲁⲉⲓ ⲧⲉⲣⲟⲩ, ShA 2 252 *S* Satan ⲛϫⲁϫⲉ ⲧⲏⲣϥ, ShC 42 109 *S* ⲉⲣⲉⲃⲉⲗⲥⲉϩⲟⲩⲗ ⲧⲏⲣϥ ⲡⲓⲙⲁⲩ, *ib* 73 57 *S* one or 2 or ϣⲁϣⲟⲙⲧ ⲧⲏⲣⲟⲩ, *ib* 42 153 *S* ⲛⲟⲩϣⲛⲣⲉ ⲁⲛⲧⲉ…ⲁⲗⲗⲁ ⲧⲉϣⲛⲣⲉ ⲧⲏⲣⲥⲧⲉ ⲉⲣϣⲁⲛ-, *ib* 118 *S* ⲛϣⲁϫⲉ ⲧⲏⲣⲟⲩ ⲛⲭⲡⲓⲟ, DeV 2 26 *B* ⲡⲉⲡⲅⲉⲡⲟⲥ ⲧⲏⲣϥ ⲛⲉⲃⲓⲏⲛ, BKU 31 7 20 *S* ⲕⲏⲙⲉ ⲧⲏⲣϥ ⲥⲉⲛⲁⲥⲱⲧⲙ, MG 25 205 *B* ⲡⲓϯⲙⲓ ⲧⲏⲣϥ ⲥⲉⲟⲩⲱϣ, BIF 22 105 *F* ⲡⲉⲭⲉⲩ ⲧⲏⲗⲟⲩ, Pcod 10 *S* ⲡⲉⲧⲏⲛⲏⲩ ⲧⲏⲣϥ ⲉⲣⲁⲧⲕ, J 627 *S* ⲡⲉⲧⲏⲛⲏⲩ ⲧⲏⲣϥ ⲙⲛⲡⲥⲱⲕ, BMis 390 *S* crowds that I see ⲛⲧⲉⲓϩⲉ ⲧⲏⲣⲥ, C 43 112 *B* art impious ⲛⲧⲁⲓϭⲉ ⲧⲏⲣⲥ?   ⲧⲏⲣⲟⲩ in place of other pl persons *B*: Mt 26 27 ⲥⲱ ⲉⲃⲟⲗ ϧⲉⲛⲫⲁⲓ ⲧ. (*S* ⲧⲏⲣⲧⲛ) πίετε πάντες; DeV 2 45 ⲙⲁⲣⲉⲛⲓⲱⲥ ⲧ., C 86 228 ⲙⲟⲓ ⲛⲁⲛ ⲧ., BM 590 (2) ϣⲁⲡⲱⲗ ⲉⲣⲏⲥ ⲧ.

    ⲡⲧⲏⲣϥ *SABF*, *the whole, all (creation)*: Job 8 3 *S* (*B* ϩⲱⲃ ⲛⲓⲃⲉⲛ), Sa 1 7 *SB*, Ro 11 36 *SF* ⲡ. ϩⲉⲛⲉⲃⲟⲗ ⲙⲙⲟϥⲛⲉ (*B* om), 1 Cor 8 6 *SF*(*B* ⲉⲛⲭⲁⲓ ⲛ.), Cl 34 2 *A* τὰ πάντα, 2 Cor 5 14 *S*(*B* ⲟⲩ. ⲛ.) οἱ πάντες, Job 25 2 *S*(*B* ⲉⲛ. ⲛ.) ἡ σύμπασα, Ge 49 25 *S*(*B* ϩ. ⲛ.), Sa 16 17 *S*, Jo 1 3 *S*(*BF* ϩ. ⲛ,) πάντα, Sa 11 24 *S* πάντες, Mk 5 40 *B*(*S* ⲧⲏⲣⲟⲩ) ἅπαντες; Ps 9 18 *S* ϣⲁⲡ. (*B* ϣⲁⲉⲃⲟⲗ) εἰς τ. αἰῶνα; Sa 16 5 *S* ϣⲁⲡ. μέχρι τέλους; PS 261 *S* renounce ⲡ. world, Pcod 43 *S* died ϩⲁⲡ., Worr 323 *F* ⲡⲓⲱⲧ ⲙⲡⲛⲏⲗⲉϥ, Br 238 *S* biddeth ⲡ. ⲉⲧⲣⲉⲩ ϩⲱⲃ, ShA 1 434 *S* ⲟⲩⲛⲧⲁⲥ ⲡ. ⲙⲙⲁⲩ *hath all*;   ⲛⲓⲡⲧ. *S*, *the wholenesses*, Gnostic, *cf* Hippolytus *Philos* τὰ ὅλα (C Baynes): PS 4 mystery ⲉⲧⲕⲱⲧⲉ ⲉⲛ., Br 266 ⲡ. ⲉⲧⲁⲡⲁⲓⲡⲉ ⲡⲉⲓⲁⲩⲛⲁⲙⲓⲥ ⲧⲏⲣⲟⲩ, *ib* 226 ⲛⲃⲁⲑⲟⲥ ⲛⲡ., BG 51 ⲡⲉⲓⲱⲧ ⲛⲡ., *ib* 87 ⲧⲡⲏⲅⲏ

ⲛⲡ.;   ⲉⲡⲧ. *SAB*, *wholly, at all*: Ez 20 9 *SB*, Zeph 3 6 *AB* τὸ παράπαν, Aeg 216 *S* παντάπασι; Jos 3 16 *SB* εἰς τὸ τέλος, Ps 9 6 *S*(*B* ϣⲁⲉⲃⲟⲗ) εἰς τ., Lu 13 11 *SB* εἰς τὸ παντελές, Lev 23 22 *S*(*B* diff) συντελεῖν; Ac 4 18 *B*(*S* ⲗⲁⲁⲩ) τὸ καθόλου; Ps 118 43 *S*(*B* ϣⲁⲃⲟⲗ) ἕως σφόδρα; 4 Kg 11 18 *S* ἀγαθῶς; PS 218 *S* ⲁⲩⲕⲁ ⲧⲟⲟⲧⲟⲩ ⲉⲃⲟⲗ ⲉ., ShBor 246 37 *S* ⲉⲧⲃⲉⲟⲩ ⲉϥⲛⲁⲣ ⲡⲓⲥⲧⲟⲥ ⲉ. ?, ShA 2 271 *S* ⲉϣϣⲉ ⲁⲛ ⲉⲣⲟⲓ ⲉ. ⲉⲧⲣⲁⲁⲁⲩ, Cat 108 *B* ⲙⲙⲟⲛ ϣϫⲟⲙ ⲉ. ⲉⲑⲣⲉϩⲗⲓ ϧⲱⲛ, BSM 122 *B* ⲁⲧϭⲛⲉϩⲛ ⲧ b̄ ⲉ., BMar 208 *S* clothes ⲁⲩⲧⲁⲕⲟ ⲉ., *ib* 147 *S* those in hell ⲟⲩⲉϣ ⲟⲩⲟⲛ ⲡⲣⲱⲟⲩ ⲉ. & cannot, Miss 8 42 *S* ⲉϥϥⲓ ⲙⲙⲁⲩ ⲉ. ⲛⲧⲙⲛⲧⲣⲱⲙⲉ (of Christ), J 74 78 *S* ⲗⲁⲁⲩ ⲣⲱⲙⲉ ⲉ. (cf *ib* 70 47 ϩⲟⲗⲱⲥ, 61 10 ⲛⲓⲙ);   ⲡⲓⲉⲡⲧ. *B*, *the whole*: HL 74 ⲫϯ ⲛⲧⲉ ⲡ. τῶν ὅλων; Va 57 276 ⲁⲣⲉⲧⲉⲛⲟⲩⲁϩ ⲡ. ⲉⲣⲟⲛ πάντα, *ib* 33 ϣⲁⲡⲱⲥ ⲉϩⲣⲏⲓ ⲛⲡ. πανταχοῦ; Mus 34 202 ϭⲁⲙⲟⲛⲓ ⲛⲡ. (cf 207 ⲉⲧϭⲁⲓ ϭⲁⲡⲧⲏⲣϥ), Aeg 20 die ϭⲁⲛ. = *ib S* ϩⲁⲡⲧⲏⲣϥ, Va 57 269 ⲡ. ⲙⲡⲉⲧϩⲱⲟⲩ.

ⲧⲱⲣ *S* vb intr, *be joined with* (?): Tri 596 ⲛⲧⲁⲣϩⲉ ⲉⲡⲉⲥⲏⲧ ⲡⲧⲁⲣⲧ. ⲙⲡⲛⲕⲁϩ التصق مع.

ⲧⲁⲣⲉ- *SAF*, ⲛⲧⲁⲣⲉ- *S*, ⲧⲁⲗⲉ-, ⲛⲧ. *F* vbal pref in final clause, often = Gk fut.   *V* Stern 450, Sdff 308, Till 131: Ps 68 32 ϣⲛⲉ…ⲧⲁⲣⲉⲧⲉⲧⲙⲯⲩⲭⲏ ⲱⲛϩ (*B* ⲟⲩⲟϩ ⲉⲥⲉⲱⲛϧ), Pro 22 10 *SA* ⲧⲁⲣⲉⲛϯ ⲧⲱⲛ ⲃⲱⲕ ⲉⲃⲟⲗ, Lu 11 9 ⲧⲱⲣⲙ ⲧⲁⲣⲟⲩⲟⲩⲱⲛ ⲛⲏⲧⲛ (var Mor 53 78 ⲛⲧⲁⲣⲟⲩ-, *B* ⲟⲩⲟϩ ⲥⲉⲛⲁ-), Pcod 39 *F* ⲧⲁⲗⲟⲩϯ ⲛⲛⲏⲧⲉⲛ, CMSS 20 *F* ⲧⲁⲗⲉⲅⲓ ϩⲁⲃⲁⲗ, *ib* ⲧⲁⲣⲉϥⲧⲁⲗⲁϥ, LAp 534 *F* ⲁⲗⲓⲧϥ ⲛⲧⲁⲗⲉⲧⲉⲛⲱⲛⲁϩ, Ro 6 15 ⲁϩⲣⲟϥ ⲧⲁⲣⲡⲣ ⲛⲟⲃⲉ (*B* ⲛⲧⲉⲛ-), PS 94 ⲛⲁⲣⲙⲉⲧ ⲧⲁⲣⲓⲣⲁϣⲉ, Till Oster 13 *A* be patient ⲧⲁⲣⲉⲛϭⲱⲡⲧ ϫⲓ ϣⲓⲡⲉ, WTh 196 gladden me ⲛⲧⲁⲣⲓⲟⲩⲙⲡⲉⲩⲉ, Ep 275 ⲛⲧⲁⲣⲉⲛⲡ‾ⲭ‾ⲥ‾ ⲥⲙⲟⲩ ⲉⲣⲟⲕ, BM 1102 shouldest have visited us ⲛⲧⲁⲣⲛⲛⲁⲩ ⲉⲡⲉⲛⲥⲕⲟⲡⲟⲥ; elliptic: Mor 22 116 (I wish) ⲧⲁⲣⲉⲉⲓⲙⲉ ⲡⲉ ϫⲉ- = BSM 104 *B* ϩⲓⲛⲁ ⲛⲧⲉⲉⲙⲓ, BM 1156 (Permit) ⲧⲁⲣⲓⲧⲁⲙⲟ ⲧⲉⲧⲛⲉⲉⲩⲕⲗⲉⲉⲓⲁ ϫⲉ-, Ep 314 sim.   *V* AZ 59 161.

ⲧⲁⲣⲉⲓ *S* nn (?), meaning unknown: Ryl 238 18 ⲟⲩϩⲣⲉⲕⲉ (?? ῥέκος) ⲛⲧ. among church properties.

ⲧⲁⲣⲟ *v* ⲧⲁⲗⲟ.

ⲧⲟⲩⲣⲉ *A²* nn as pl, meaning unknown: Mani 2 archons of the ζώνη ϩⲛⲧ. ⲡⲉ ⲡⲧⲉ ⲧⲗⲛⲉ.

ⲧⲱⲣⲉ *S*, ⲑⲱⲣⲓ *B* nn, *willow*: Ps 136 2 *SB*, Is 44 4 *SB*, ⲃⲱ ⲛⲧ., Lev 23 40 *S* do *B* ⲑ. ἰτέα, P 44 81 *S* ⲧⲃⲱ ⲛⲧ. · ⲧⲣⲩⲥⲧⲣⲓ شجر المصاف = 43 56 *S* ⲧⲣⲓⲥⲧⲓ (quid ?), K 175 *B* ⲛⲓⲑ. ‘ص; MélOr 6 514 *B* crown of ϣⲉ ⲛⲑ., PMéd 286 *S* ϩⲛⲧϥ ⲛⲧ. *sprigs of w.*, Cai 42573 2 *S* ϫⲉⲃⲃ̅ⲥ̅ ⲛϣⲉ ⲛⲧ., WS 141 *S* ⲕⲁⲛⲓⲥⲕⲉ ⲛⲧ. *wicker basket*.   *V* BIF 31 222. In place-names(?): ⲧⲕⲁⲗⲉⲓⲧⲱⲣⲉ (PLond 4 244, but cf 108 *a* 2 above), ⲧⲱⲣⲉⲓ (*ib* 3 203).

ⲧⲱⲣⲉ SA, -ⲣⲓ S⸍BF, -ⲣⲉⲓ S⸍F, ⲧⲟⲣⲉ S, -ⲗⲉ S⸍, ⲧⲱⲗⲓ, -ⲟⲗⲓ, -ⲟⲣⲓ F (on ⲧⲟⲟⲧ⸗ v below) nn f, *hand* (B, rest only in derived meanings & compounds): Dan 5 5 B ϯⲧ. ⲛⲧⲉ ϯϫⲓⲝ الـ ἀστράγαλος τ. χειρός, 5 24 sim; *handle* of tool, weapon: Deu 19 5 S (B ϣⲉ) ξύλον; Jud 3 22 S λαβή; ShC 73 16 S sword's τ. ⲏ ⲡⲉⲥⲙⲁ ⲡⲁⲙⲁⲣⲧⲉ, ViK 9519 S ⲛⲧ. whence axe-blades had melted, C 86 95 B ⲧⲧⲱⲣⲓⲛ (*sic*) of spear: axle of cart: Glos 206 S ἄξων; Hall 108 S, BMOr 6230 (44) S⸍ -ⲗⲉ ⲡⲁⲥⲟ[ⲗⲧⲉ; *spade, pick*: Z 362 S ⲟⲅⲁⲕⲉⲥ (ἀκίς) ⲉⲧⲉⲟⲩⲧ. ⲧⲉ δίκελλα, BAp 54 S ϧⲉⲛⲃⲓⲣ ⲙⲡⲣⲉⲡⲧ. σκαφεῖον; K 124 B ازبط; Sh(Besa)Z 506 S ⲉⲓϧⲧ, ⲟⲣⲥ, ⲧ., MG 25 208 B(Z 344 S Gk om), BM 334 96 S took ⲧⲁⲱⲣⲉ & dug=C 86 320 B, BM 1231 F to each workman ⲟⲩⲧⲱⲣⲓ & ⲟⲩϭⲓⲗ(ⲫⲓⲣ), *ib* 598 6 F workman with ⲧⲉⲓⲕⲟⲩⲧ., Hall 57 S total (ϫⲱⲕ) of reeds 600 ϣⲉ ⲛⲧ. & 37 ⲧ. *spade-handles & spades*; cf Rec 39 157 n; *oar*: Bor 143 40 S angels in stern ⲙⲡⲟⲩϭⲓ ⲟⲩⲧ. back or forward, yet ship sailed on, P 44 54 S ⲛ(ⲟⲩ)ⲟⲥⲣ ⲛⲧ. مقادیف (*cf* K 133), Tri 428 S ⲛⲁ. ١جـ, DeV 2 229 B sailors ⲕⲱϯ ⲙⲡⲓϣⲓⲉ, ⲁⲙⲟⲛⲓ ⲙⲡⲓⲧ.; *doubtful*: Turin ostr St Symeon 651 S if sailor come (as carrier) give him ⲥⲟⲟⲩ ⲛⲧ. ⲛϭⲱ, *ib* 699 sim (cf CO 330 S ϣⲙⲟⲩⲡⲉ ⲛⲧ. ⲛⲉⲱ l ? ϭⲱ), AZ 23 37 F ⲉⲡⲙⲉ (ⲧ)ⲧⲟⲣⲓ (ⲛ)ⲧⲉⲕⲗⲏⲥⲓⲁ.

ⲣ ⲧ. SA, *use hand, clap hands*: Jud 5 11, 2 Kg 6 14 (B ⲕⲱⲗϩ), Ez 23 42 (B l ? ⲕⲉϥ ⲑⲱⲣⲓ cf above ⲣ 131 b inf) ἀνακρούεσθαι; Nah 3 19 A(B ⲕⲱ.) κροτεῖν; Am 6 5 A(B do, var Va 66 306 ϩⲓ ⲧⲉⲣⲧⲱⲣⲓ, l ϩⲓ ⲧⲱ.) ἐπικρότ.; hence *stamp* with feet: ShC 73 81 let us not ⲣ ⲧ. ⲛⲡⲉⲡⲟⲩⲣⲏⲧⲉ ⲛⲟⲩ ϫⲁⲁϫⲉ ϩⲛⲡⲉⲛϭⲓϫ, ShIF 277 sim ϩⲛⲡⲉⲧⲛⲟⲩⲅⲉⲣⲏⲧⲉ; ⲧⲱⲣⲉ S (l ? ⲣ ⲧ.) vb intr, *strike* instrument, make music: Tri 469 ⲉϥⲧ. ϩⲛⲡⲉⲥⲕⲉϩⲏ ⲙⲙⲟⲩⲥⲓⲕⲟⲛ ضر, *ib* 534 ⲧ. ϩⲛⲣⲉⲡⲥⲁⲗⲡⲓⲅϫ & bells ٌ.

ϣ(ⲉ)ⲡ ⲧ. SAF(metath ⲛϣⲡ. ⲧ.) vb intr, *grasp hand*, so *be surety, undertake* (cf ϣⲧⲱⲣⲉ below): Si 8 16 ἐγγυᾶν; RE 10 37 ⲁϥϣ. ϫⲉ ϣⲁϥⲥⲙⲛⲧϥ, Ep 256 ⲣⲱⲙⲉ ⲡⲉϥⲡⲟⲣⲟⲥ ⲛϣ. ⲉⲧⲟⲧ... ϩⲁⲡϣⲱⲃ, CO 33 ϯϣ. ⲉⲧⲟⲟⲧϥ ⲙⲡⲉⲡⲉⲓⲱⲧ ⲉⲧⲣⲁ- *I undertake to our father*; c dat: Miss 8 31 these writings ϣ. ⲛⲧⲉⲧⲛⲙⲡⲣⲧⲣⲉϥϣⲙϣⲉ ⲡⲉ ϫⲉⲕⲁⲥ ⲡⲁⲣⲉϥ., Ep 61 ⲁⲓϣ. ⲛⲁⲡⲟⲥⲧⲟⲗⲟⲥ ⲉϣⲱⲗⲡ ⲛⲁⲩ; *tr* (oftener), *be surety for*: Ge 43 9 (B ⲉⲣ ⲡϣⲧⲱⲣⲓ), Pro 6 1 SA(B do), Z 319 S⸍ ϯⲡⲁϣ ⲡ ⲧⲱⲣⲓ ⲙⲙⲱⲧⲛ ϩⲁⲣⲧⲙⲡⲉ ϫⲉ- *ἐγ.*; WTh 141 ⲡⲧⲁϣϣ. ⲙⲡⲉ ϧⲣⲉⲱⲥ, Pcod 17 ⲉⲧϣ. ⲙⲙⲟⲟⲩ ⲛⲏⲧⲛ, Bor 251 296 ⲡⲧⲁⲕϣ. ⲙⲙⲟϥ ϩⲛⲡⲁϭⲓϫ, Sph 10 2 F ⲁⲕⲛϣⲧⲱⲣⲉⲓ ⲛⲗⲟⲡ ϩⲁⲧⲏⲡⲉⲛⲭ︤ⲥ︥, Mor 44 45 ⲁⲓϣ. ⲙⲙⲟⲕ ⲛⲧⲟⲟⲧⲟⲩ ⲛⲡⲓⲟⲩⲍⲁⲓ, COAd 9 ϯϣ. ⲁⲧⲱⲧⲕ ⲙⲡⲁⲥⲡⲁⲩ ⲡϣⲏⲣⲉ; as nn SB(ⲛϣ ⲧ.)F, *surety*: Si 29 18, He 7 22 SBF ⲧⲱⲗⲓ ἔγγυος, Si 29 20 ἐγγύη; Mor 37 234 ⲡⲉⲡ[ⲉⲡ]ⲕⲓⲛⲏⲧⲏⲥ ⲡⲉⲛϣⲛⲧⲱⲣⲓⲥⲧⲏⲥ; ⲉⲣ ⲡϣ ⲧ. B, *be*

surety: Pro 6 1 (SA ϣⲡ ⲧ.), CDan 88 ⲁⲣⲓ ⲡ. ⲡⲧⲉϥⲯⲩⲭⲏ ἐγγυᾶν; Ge 43 9 (S do) ἐκδέχεσθαι; AM 150 ⲁϥⲉⲣ ⲡ. ⲡⲡⲏ ⲉⲑ︤ⲃ︥ ⲡⲧⲟⲧⲟⲩ, DeV 2 272 ⲁϥⲉⲣ ⲡ. ⲉⲣⲟⲓ; ϯ ϣ. SB, *give surety*: Z 296 ϣⲁⲛⲧϥϯ ϣ. ⲉⲣⲟϥ *for himself* = MG 25 204 B ἐγγυητὴν διδόναι; ShC 42 92 ⲛⲥⲉϯ ϣ. ⲉⲣⲟⲟⲩ (as last?) ⲉⲧⲙ-, Va 61 93 B ϯϯ ⲙ.ⲡ. ⲡⲁⲕ =P 131³ 83 S ϯ λόγος ϩⲁⲣⲟⲕ; ϫⲓ ϣ. S, *take as s.*: Aeg 214 ϫⲓ ⲣⲱⲙⲉ ⲛϣ. ἐγγύας δ., Ac 17 9 ϫⲓ ϣ. ⲛⲧⲏ (B diff)ἱκανὸν λαμβάνειν παρά, ShA 1 90 ⲛⲧⲁⲩϫⲓⲧⲉ ⲛϣ. ⲉⲃⲟⲗ ϩⲛⲡⲉϥϭⲓⲝ, JTS 8 248 ϫⲓⲧ ⲛϣ. ⲡⲧⲟⲟⲧϥ, Gu 87 sim; ⲣⲉϥϣ.S, *guarantor*: MIF 9 87 -ⲧⲱⲣⲉⲓ; ⲙⲛⲧⲣⲉϥϣ., *surety*: Si 29 22 ἐγγύη. *Cf* ϣⲡ ⲧⲟⲟⲧ⸗ below.

ϣⲧⲱⲣⲉ (for ϣⲡ ⲧ.), ϣⲧⲱⲟⲣⲉ¹, ϣⲧⲟⲣⲉ², -ⲣⲓ³ SBF, ϣⲑⲱⲣⲓ⁴ B, ϣⲧⲟⲗⲓ⁵ F vb, as ϣⲡ ⲧ., mostly tr: CDan 88 B ⲫⲏ ⲉⲧϣ. ⲡⲉⲩⲗⲟⲅⲓⲟⲥ ἐγγυᾶν acc; Mor 27 31 S ⲉⲓϣⲁⲛϣ. ⲙⲡⲉⲥⲟⲟⲩ (var BMis 381 ϣⲡ ⲧ.) = BSM 37 B.⁴ ⲙⲙⲟⲕ =Va 63 11 B ⲉⲣ ⲡϣ ⲧ. ⲙⲙⲟⲕ, MG 25 69 B ⲁϥϣ. ⲙⲙⲟϥ =Z 296 S³, AZ 23 148 S ⲉⲛϣ.³ ⲡⲁⲕ ⲡⲓⲛⲱⲭ (Enoch), BM 582 (2) F ϣⲁⲓϣ.³ ⲡⲓⲁⲃ ⲛⲉⲕ, Kr 11 S ⲉⲓϣ.³ ⲙⲁⲟⲩ (ⲡ)ⲧⲟⲩⲙⲉϩⲕ, PLond 4 435 S ⲧⲛϣ.¹ ⲧⲛⲟ ⲡⲉⲧⲧⲩⲏ...ⲙⲡⲉⲡⲣⲟⲥⲱⲡⲟⲛ ⲛ-, ST 245 S ⲁⲓϣ. ⲙⲡⲁⲃⲉⲕⲉ ⲡⲁⲥ, Rec 6 65 S ⲛϣ. ⲙⲡⲩⲧⲉⲙⲟⲥⲓⲟⲛ, OLZ '03 68 S ⲁⲓⲥⲁⲕ ϣ. ⲉⲧⲟⲟⲧϥ ⲙϥⲉⲩ ⲛ-ⲟⲩⲧⲣⲉⲙⲛⲥⲡⲉ, COAd 41 S ⲧⲛϣ. ⲉⲧⲟⲟⲧϥ ⲙⲡⲉⲡⲓⲥⲕ-(ⲟⲡⲟⲥ) ⲡⲧⲛⲡⲱⲗⲏ ⲛ-, ST 290 S ⲁⲓϣ. ⲙⲙⲟ[ⲕ] ⲉ-ⲧⲟⲟⲧϥ ⲙⲡⲉⲃⲱ, AZ 23 148 S ⲉⲛϣ. ⲡⲧⲟⲧⲕ ⲛϩⲁⲙⲁ-ⲡⲉ; *intr* S: BKU 1 70 ϯ ϣ. ⲉⲧⲱⲧⲛ...ϫⲉ-, Bodl(P) d 28 ⲁⲕϣ. ⲉⲧⲣⲉ-, ST 369 ϯ ϣ. ⲁⲡ; *as nn*: He 7 22 SF ϣⲧⲟⲗⲓ (B ⲡϣ ⲧ.) ἔγγυος; PMich 525 F after arrest ⲉϩⲁⲅⲕⲉⲧ ⲉⲃⲁⲗ ⲛϣ.² *on bail* (?), AZ 23 152 S ⲧⲛⲧⲱⲣ(ⲉ) ⲁⲃⲓⲥⲁⲗⲱⲙ; ⲃⲱⲗ ϣ. ⲉⲃⲟⲗ S, *dissolve guaranty*: CO 133 ⲡⲥⲁϩⲡⲉ ⲙⲡⲉϥϫⲓⲧϥ, ⲙⲡⲉϥⲃ. ⲡϣ. ⲉⲃ.; ϯ ϣ. S: CO 42 ⲉⲓϯ ϣ. ⲉⲣⲟⲓ ⲉⲧⲟⲟⲧϥ ⲛ-, BP 5178 ⲁⲓϯ ⲡⲉϥϣ. ⲡⲁϥ ⲡⲧⲉⲓ; ϫⲓ ϣ. S: BM 1211 ⲥϩⲁⲓ...ⲡⲧⲁϫⲓ ⲡⲉϥϣ.; ⲙⲉϣ. B, *guaranty*: CDan 90 ἐγγύη; ⲣⲙ-, ⲗⲉⲙϣ.SF, *guarantor*: Mor 41 22 faithful witness & ⲡ., BM 663 ⲡⲗⲉⲙϣⲧⲟⲗⲓ ⲓⲱⲥⲏϥ.

V Sethe *Dem Bürgsch* 496 ff, 524.

ⲧⲟⲟⲧ-, ⲧⲉⲧ- (ⲧⲉ-) S, ⲧⲟⲧ-, ⲧⲉⲡ- B with 2 pl suff & in preps ⲉⲧⲛ-, ⲡⲧⲛ- &c, ⲧⲟⲟⲧ⸗ SAA²O, ⲧⲟⲧ⸗ SAA² BO, ⲧⲁⲁⲧ⸗, ⲧⲁⲧ⸗ F, where = χείρ (lit or fig): Lev 1 4 S(B ϫⲓⲝ), Deu 3 8 S(B do), 2 Kg 3 12 S, Job 15 22 SB, Ps 122 2 S paral ϭⲓⲝ (B ϫ. both), Si 30 34 S, Ez 46 7 SB, Mic 7 16 SA(B ϫ.), Mt 22 13 B(S ϭⲓⲝ), Ac 11 30 SB; *auxil uses*: ⲕⲁ ⲧ. ⲉ ϫⲛ-S Mk 10 13 (B ϭⲓ ⲡⲉⲙ-) ἅπτεσθαι; ϫⲉⲕ ⲧ. ⲉⲃⲟⲗ B Deu 31 24 (S ⲟⲩⲱ) συντελεῖν; ⲙⲉϩ ⲧ. S Nu 5 26 (B ϭⲓ) δράσσεσθαι; ⲧ. ⲧⲁⲭⲣⲏⲟⲩⲧ B Ge 34 25 ἀσφαλῶς; ⲧ. ϯⲙⲁϯ B Ac 26 7 (S ⲧⲁⲣⲟ) καταντᾶν; ⲧ. ⲙⲡⲉⲡⲟⲩⲣⲟⲧ ⲟⲩⲏ S BHom 46 προθυμία δαψιλής; ShC 73 20 S ⲡⲏⲩ ⲉϩⲣⲁⲓ ⲉⲧⲟⲟⲧⲟⲩ (var ϭⲓⲝ), ShA 2 51 S ⲧⲟⲟⲧⲕ ϩⲛⲧⲏ (cf Mt 26 23 ϭ.), FR 72 S sword ⲛⲧⲟⲟⲧϥ (var

ⲣⲏⲧⲉϥⲥ̅.), BMis 408 *S* saved ⲉⲡⲥ̅. ⲡⲛϥⲥⲡⲏϥ, ⲉⲧⲟⲟⲧⲥ
ⲡⲧⲣⲙⲡⲕⲏⲙⲉ, ViK 9467 *S* angel ⲥⲉⲕ ⲧ. ⲉⲣⲟϥ = C 89
94 *B* ⲝ., AP 20 *A²* sim, Bor 260 105 *S* ⲁϥⲁⲙⲁⲣⲧⲉ ⲛ̅-
ⲧⲟⲟⲧϥ, KroppE 20 *S* ⲡⲧⲉⲧⲛⲥⲱⲧⲙ ⲡⲥⲁⲡⲁⲣⲱ ⲡⲧⲉ-
ⲧⲛⲉⲓⲣⲉ (ⲡ)ⲥⲁⲛⲁⲧⲟⲟⲧ, GriffStu 163 *F* sim ⲛⲁⲧⲁⲧ, El
58 *A* ⲉⲅⲥⲁⲡⲉ ⲛⲧⲟⲟⲧⲟⲩ ⲙⲡⲣⲁⲧⲟⲩ, C 43 26 *B* sim, C
86 329 *B* scourge ⲛⲧⲟⲧϥ (*cf ib* whip ϩⲉⲡⲧⲉϥⲝ̅.), AZ
23 100 *O* ⲡⲉⲧⲉⲛⲧⲟⲟⲧⲥ, Va 62 269 *B* Herod & Innocents ⲁⲣⲏⲟⲩ ⲡⲧⲉⲧⲟⲧ ⲓ ⲉⲭⲉⲡⲡⲁⲓⲟⲩⲣⲟ, PGM 1 60 668
O ⲧⲟⲧϥⲡⲉ ⲡⲁⲣⲁⲡ, K 77 *B* ⲡⲓⲧⲟⲧ ⎝ى̄⎞. emphatic
(refl) use *B*(Stern p 96): He 11 35 ⲛⲧⲉⲧⲟⲧⲟⲩ ϭⲓ =
S ⲉⲅⲉⲝⲓ, Gal 6 1 ⲧⲟⲧϥ ⲛⲟⲩⲣⲱⲙⲓ = *S* ⲟⲩⲣ.; ellipse (?) of vb *S*: Lev 25 26, 49 ⲟⲩⲟⲛ ⲉⲣⲉⲧⲟⲟⲧϥ ⲉⲩ-
ⲡⲟⲣⲉⲓ̂ⲥⲑⲁⲓ ⲧⲏ̂ χ., *ib* 25 35 ⲙⲛ ⲡⲉⲧⲉⲣⲉⲧⲟⲟⲧϥ ⲁⲇⲩⲛⲁⲧⲉⲓ̂ⲛ
ⲧⲁⲓ̂ⲥ χ., 1 Kg 21 3 ⲟⲩⲛ ⲟⲉⲓⲕ ⲉⲣⲉⲧⲟⲟⲧⲕ (var ⲉⲣⲁ-),
ib 4 sim (var ⲛⲧⲟⲟⲧ) ⲩ̔ⲡⲟ̀ ⲧⲏ̀ⲛ χ.

ⲉⲓⲣⲉ ⲛⲧⲟⲟⲧ⸗[1], ⲣ ⲁⲧ.²*SA*, ⲉⲓⲣⲉ ⲛⲁⲡⲁⲧ.³ *S*, ⲣ ⲁ-
ⲡⲁⲧ.⁴ *SAA²*, ⲓⲣⲓ ⲛⲁⲅⲧⲟⲧ⸗⁵, ⲉⲣ ⲁⲅⲧ.⁶ *B*, ⲉⲗ ⲛⲁⲧⲁⲁⲧ⸗
F, *do to extent of hand*('s capacity), *endeavour*: 2
Tim 4 9 *S*⁴(*B* ⲓⲏⲥ ⲛⲧⲟⲧ⸗), Mor 37 98 *S*⁴ ⲥⲡⲟⲩⲇⲁⲍⲉⲓⲛ,
Jude 3 *S*³(*B* = Gk) ⲡⲁ̂ⲥⲁⲛ ⲥⲡⲟⲩⲇⲏ̀ⲛ ⲡⲟⲓⲉⲓ̂ⲛ; Cl 33 1 *A*⁴
ⲥⲡⲉⲩⲇⲉⲓⲛ; Am 6 10 *A* ⲣ ⲁⲧ.² *B*⁶, Jon 1 13 *S*³*A*¹(*B* ϭⲓ
ⲛⲭⲟⲛⲥ) ⲡⲁⲣⲁⲃⲓⲁⲍⲉⲥⲑⲁⲓ; Ro 12 18 *S*¹*B*⁶ ⲁⲅⲧⲉⲡⲉ-
ⲟⲩ *F* ⲧⲟ̀ ⲉ̓ⲝ ⲩ̔ⲙⲱ̂ⲛ (ⲡⲟⲓⲉⲓ̂ⲛ), ViSitz 172 4 29 *S*³ ⲧⲟ̀ ⲓ̓́ⲇⲓⲟⲛ
ⲡⲟⲓ.; Mk 14 8 *S*²(var⁴, *B* ϭⲓ) ⲉ̓́χⲉⲓⲛ; ShHT *B* 68 *S*
ⲛϭⲣ ⲁⲡⲁⲧⲟⲟⲧⲕ ⲉⲧⲙⲧⲣⲉ-, AP 41 *A*² ⲉⲣⲓ ⲁⲡⲁⲧⲟⲟⲧⲕ
ⲁⲧⲣⲉⲕ-, BAp 144 *S* ⲁⲣⲓ ⲁⲡⲁⲧⲟⲟⲧⲧⲏⲩⲧⲛ ⲉϯ, C 43
178 *B* each one ⲓⲣⲓ ⲛⲁⲅⲧⲟⲧⲟⲩ ⲉϭⲟⲩ, ROC 23 283 *B*
ⲁⲣⲓ ⲁⲅⲧⲟⲧⲏⲛⲟⲩ ⲝⲉⲣⲓⲛⲁ.

ⲉⲓⲱ ⲛⲧⲟⲟⲧ⸗, ⲉⲓⲁ ⲧ., *wash hands* v ⲉⲓⲱ, adding
Mani 1 *A*² ⲙⲡⲣⲓⲁ ⲧⲟⲧⲕ ⲛⲥⲱⲓ.

ⲉⲓⲛⲉ ⲛⲧⲟⲟⲧ⸗, ⲛ ⲧ., *bring, place hand* v ⲉⲓⲛⲉ (ⲥ ⲉ-,
ⲉⲭⲛ-), adding ⲥ ⲛ- *B*: Va 68 180 ⲁⲅⲉⲛ ⲧⲟⲧⲟⲩ ⲛⲱⲟⲩ
ⲉⲩϣⲧⲉⲙ-; ⲥ ⲟⲓⲭⲛ- *S*: P 129¹⁸ 130 ⲛⲧⲉⲣⲟⲩⲉⲛ ⲧⲟⲟⲧⲟⲩ ⲉ. ⲓⲱϩⲁⲛⲛⲏⲥ to insult him.

ⲕⲱ ⲛⲧⲟⲟⲧ⸗ ⲉⲃⲟⲗ, ⲕⲁ ⲧ. ⲉⲃ. *SAA²BF*, *loosen
hand, cease, despair*: Is 57 10 *S*(*B* ⲕⲏⲡ), Ac 5 42 *B*
(*S* ⲕⲓⲙ), Z 338 *S* = MG 25 215 *B* ⲡⲁⲩⲉⲓⲛ, Ap 4 8 *S*
(*B* ⲙⲧⲟⲛ) ⲁ̓ⲛⲁ́ⲡⲁⲩⲥⲓⲛ ⲉ̓́χⲉⲓⲛ, Ex 34 21 *S*(*B* do) ⲕⲁⲧⲁ́-
ⲡⲁⲩⲥⲓⲥ, 2 Pet 2 14 neg *S*(*B* ⲁⲧⲕⲏⲡ) ⲁ̓ⲕⲁⲧⲁ́ⲡⲁⲩⲥⲧⲟⲥ;
Ge 25 8 *S*(*B* ⲙⲟⲩⲛⲕ), Aeg 243 *S* ⲙⲡⲣⲕⲁ ⲧⲟⲟⲧⲧⲏⲩⲧⲛ ⲉⲃ. ⲟⲛⲗⲁⲁⲩ ⲛⲡⲛⲁⲩ ⲉ̓ⲕⲗⲉⲓ́ⲡⲉⲓⲛ, Is 5 14 *F*(*S* ⲕⲁ
ⲗⲁⲁⲩ, *B* χⲱ ⲛⲥⲁ-), Lu 7 45 *B*(*S* ⲗⲟ) ⲇⲓⲁⲗ., Ro 1 9
neg *B*(*S* ⲱⲝⲛ ⲛⲛ) ⲁ̓ⲇⲓⲁⲗⲉⲓ́ⲡⲧⲱⲥ, Jer 14 5 *S*(*B* ⲥⲱⲝⲡ)
ⲉ̓ⲅⲕⲁⲧⲁⲗⲉⲓ́ⲡⲉⲓⲛ; Is 37 27 *S*(*B* ⲧⲁⲣⲛⲟ) χⲉⲓ̂ⲣⲁⲥ ⲁ̓ⲛⲓⲉ́ⲛⲁⲓ,
Deu 32 36 *S*(*B* diff) ⲡⲁⲣⲓⲉ́ⲛⲁⲓ, Jer 4 31 *S*(*B* χⲱ ⲝ.),
Zeph 3 16 *S*(P 131⁶ 99)*A*(*B* ⲃⲱⲗ ⲉⲃⲟⲗ) ⲡⲁⲣ. χ.; Mal
3 11 *A*(*B* diff) ⲁ̓ⲥⲑⲉⲛⲉⲓ̂ⲛ; Pro 10 30 *B*(*S* ⲉⲓ ⲉⲡⲁⲣⲟⲩ,
A ϯ ⲉⲡ.) ⲉ̓ⲛⲇⲓⲇⲟ́ⲛⲁⲓ; Mt 24 10 *B*(*S* Gk diff); Eccl 12
3 *S* ⲁ̓ⲣⲅⲉⲓ̂ⲛ; Lu 21 26 *S*(*B* as Gk) ⲁ̓ⲡⲟⲯⲩ́χⲉⲓⲛ; 1 Pet
3 7 *S*(*B* ⲧⲁⲣⲛⲟ) ⲉ̓ⲅⲕⲟ́ⲡⲧⲉⲥⲑⲁⲓ; Is 8 22 *S*(*B* ϭⲣⲟϩ)
ⲁ̓ⲡⲟⲣⲉⲓ̂ⲥⲑⲁⲓ; Si 47 28 *S* ⲇⲓⲁⲫⲑⲉⲓ́ⲣⲉⲥⲑⲁⲓ; BMar 105 *S*
ⲙⲡⲉϥⲕⲁ ⲧⲟⲟⲧϥ ⲉⲃ. ⲁ̓ⲧⲟⲛⲉⲓ̂ⲛ; Va 58 183 *B* χⲁ ⲧⲟⲧⲟⲩ

ⲉⲃ. ⲡⲥⲁϯⲙⲉⲧⲧⲉⲗⲓⲟⲥ ⲁ̓ⲡⲟⲅⲓⲅⲛⲱ́ⲥⲕⲉⲓⲛ; PS 256 *S* ⲙ-
ⲡⲣⲕⲁ ⲧⲟⲟⲧⲧⲏⲩⲧⲛ ⲉⲃ. ⲉⲧⲉⲧⲛϣⲓⲡⲉ = 251 ⲧⲉⲧⲏⲅⲧⲛ,
ShA 1 240 *S* what beasts ⲕⲁ ⲧⲟⲟⲧⲟⲩ ⲉⲃ. ⲉⲩϫⲡⲟ ?,
Mani 2 *A*² ⲁⲧⲉϥⲧⲙⲕⲁ ⲧⲟⲟⲧϥ ⲉⲃ. ⲉϥⲧⲁϣⲉⲁⲓϣ, Tst
Ab 229 *B* ⲁⲅⲣⲓⲙⲓ ϣⲁⲡⲧⲟⲩχⲁ ⲧⲟⲧⲟⲩ ⲉⲃ., BMar 22
S ⲁⲅⲣⲓⲥⲉ ⲁⲅⲕⲁ ⲧ. ⲉⲃ., MG 25 97 *B* ⲁⲡⲭⲁ ⲧⲟⲧⲉⲛ ⲉⲃ.
ⲡⲉⲙⲁⲕ *we despair of thee*, C 41 79 *B* ⲁⲓⲭⲁ ⲧⲟⲧ ⲉⲃ.
ⲉⲩⲥⲁⲭⲓ (var Miss 4 181 ⲁⲓⲇⲓⲥⲓ ⲉⲓⲟⲣⲓ ⲉⲣⲁⲧ); c ⲉ-:
TT 151 *S* depressed ϩⲱⲥⲧⲉ ⲉⲧ[ⲣⲉϥ]ⲕⲁ ⲧⲟⲟⲧϥ ⲉⲃ.
ⲉⲡⲙⲟⲩ = C 89 77 *B*, AM 13 *B* ⲙⲡⲉϥⲭⲁ ⲧⲟⲧϥ ⲉⲃ.
ⲉⲡϣⲗⲏⲗ, Miss 8 152 *S* ϣⲁⲅⲕⲁ ⲧⲟⲟⲧϥ ⲉⲃ. ⲉⲧⲙⲉⲓⲣⲉ *renounced doing*: c ϩⲛ-, ϩⲉⲛ-: ShR 2 3
51 *S* ⲁⲅ]ⲕⲁ ⲧⲟⲟⲧϥ ⲉⲃ. ϩⲛⲡⲉⲅⲡⲓⲥⲧⲓⲁ, TT 154 *S*
ⲡϥⲕⲁ ⲧⲟⲟⲧϥ ⲉⲃ. ϩⲛⲡⲕⲁⲣⲡⲟⲥ ⲙⲡⲉⲡⲛ̅ⲁ̅, BSM 120 *B*
ϯⲛⲁⲭⲁ ⲧⲟⲧ ⲉⲃ. ⲁⲛ ϩⲉⲛⲛⲁⲡⲣⲟⲥⲫⲟⲣⲁ; ⲁⲧⲕⲁ ⲧ.
ⲉⲃ., *unceasing*: OrChr 3 7 112 *S* lips ⲛⲁⲧⲕⲁ ⲧⲟⲟⲧⲟⲩ
ⲉⲃ. = CaiEuch 576 *B* ⲁ̓ⲕⲁⲧⲁ́ⲡⲁⲩⲥⲧⲟⲥ, BIF 13 117 *S*
hold fast ϩⲛⲟⲩⲙⲛ̅ⲧⲁⲧⲕⲁ ⲧⲟⲟⲧⲕ ⲉⲃ. = MG 25 310
B ⲙⲉⲧⲁⲑⲙⲟⲩⲛⲕ; without ⲉⲃ. *B*: MG 25 259
rain ceased ⲁⲥⲭⲁ ⲧⲟⲧⲥ ⲛϫⲉ ⲧⲫⲉ *sky held her hand*,
desisted.

ⲙⲉϩ ⲧ. v ⲙⲟⲩϩ *fill* **I** s f.

ⲥⲙⲛ ⲧ. v ⲥⲙⲓⲛⲉ **II** s f.

ϯ ⲛⲧⲟⲟⲧ⸗, ϯ ⲧ. *SAA²BF*, *give hand, help* **a** suff
= obj: Lam 5 6 *BF*, Ac 9 41 *SB*, Va 66 308 *B* ⲙⲁ
ⲧⲟⲧϥ ⲙⲫⲏ ⲉⲧⲁϥϣⲉ ⲡⲉⲥⲓⲉ χⲉⲓ̂ⲣⲁ ⲇⲓⲇⲟ́ⲛⲁⲓ; Ps 36 24
S(*B* ⲧⲁⲭⲣⲟ ⲛⲧ.) χ. ⲁ̓ⲛⲧⲓⲥⲧⲏⲣⲓ́ⲍⲉⲓⲛ; *ib* 47 3 *S*(*B* ϣⲟⲡ
ⲉ-), *ib* 88 44 *B*(*S* ϣⲟⲡ ⲉ-) ⲁ̓ⲛⲧⲓⲗⲁⲙⲃⲁ́ⲛⲉⲓⲛ gen, Ro 8
26 *S* ϯ ⲡⲧⲟⲟⲧⲛ ϩⲛⲧⲉⲛⲙⲛ̅ⲧϭ̅ⲱⲃ *B* ϯ ⲧⲟⲧⲥ ⲛⲧⲉⲛⲙ.
ⲥⲩⲛⲁⲛⲧⲓⲗ. dat, R 1 1 53 *S* ⲁϥϯ ⲧⲟⲟⲧ ⲉ̓ⲡⲓⲗ. ⲧ. χⲉⲓⲣⲟ́ⲥ;
Ro 16 2 *B*(*S* ⲁⲣⲉ ⲣⲁⲧ⸗ ⲙⲛ-) ⲡⲁⲣⲓⲥⲧⲁ́ⲛⲁⲓ dat; Mk 16
20 *S*(*B* ⲉⲣ ⲣⲱⲃ ⲡⲉⲙ-) ⲥⲩⲛⲉⲣⲅⲉⲓ̂ⲛ; PS 151 *S* ⲟⲩϭⲟⲙ
...ⲉⲥϯ ⲛⲧⲟⲟⲧ, BG 130 *S* ⲙⲡⲉⲗⲁⲁⲩ ϯ ⲧⲟⲟⲧⲉ, ShC
42 59 *S* ⲉⲣⲉⲡⲡⲛ̅ⲁ̅ ϯ ⲛⲧⲟⲟⲧⲥ, El 56 *A* ⲁⲩϯ ⲧⲟⲟⲧ & set
me on ship, BM 660 *F* ϣⲁⲡⲧⲉⲡⲟⲩ̅ ϯ ⲧⲁⲧⲉⲛ. **b**
suff = subj; Ac 27 15 *S*(*B* ⲕⲱ ⲉⲃⲟⲗ) ⲉ̓ⲡⲓⲇⲓⲇ.; DeV
2 167 *B* crowd gathered ⲉⲑⲣⲟⲩϯ ⲧⲟⲧⲟⲩ (var ⲉⲣ
ⲣⲱⲃ); c ⲛ- dat, as **a** above: PS 62 *S* ⲁⲓⲥ̅ ϯ ⲧⲟⲟⲧⲥ
ⲙⲙⲁⲣⲑⲁ, P 131¹ 46 *S* ⲁϥϯ ⲧⲟⲟⲧⲟⲩ ⲛⲡⲉⲧⲟⲩⲁⲁⲃ, MR
5 28 *S* may Lord ϯ ⲛⲧⲟⲟⲧⲉ ⲉ(ⲗ ⲛ-) ⲣⲱϥ ⲛⲓⲙ; as
b above: Pro 6 1 *SA*(*B* ϯ ϫⲓⲝ ⲉⲧ.) χ. ⲡⲁⲣⲁⲇ.; Ps 67
32 *B*(*S* ϯ ϭⲓⲝ) χ. ⲡⲣⲟⲫⲑⲁ́ⲛⲉⲓⲛ; Lu 1 54 *SB* ⲁ̓ⲛⲧⲓⲗⲁⲙ.
gen, Ps 88 22 *B* ⲧⲁⲭⲓⲝ ⲉⲥⲉϯ ⲧⲟⲧⲥ ⲛⲁϥ (*S* ⲧⲉⲧⲛⲁϯ
ⲧⲟⲟⲧϥ), Lu 10 40 *B*(*S* ⲛⲟⲱⲛ) ⲥⲩⲛⲁⲛⲧⲓⲗ. dat; 1 Kg 2
8 *S*(*B* ⲧⲁⲣⲟ ⲉⲣⲁⲧ⸗) ⲁ̓ⲛⲓⲥⲧⲁ́ⲛⲁⲓ acc; ClPr 54 38 *S* eyes
ϯ ⲛⲧⲟⲟⲧⲟⲩ ⲡⲉⲙⲙⲁⲁⲭⲉ ⲥⲩⲙⲃⲁⲓ́ⲛⲉⲓⲛ dat; Miss 8 16 *S*
ⲉϥϯ ⲡⲧⲟⲟⲧϥ ⲛⲡⲉⲥⲧⲟⲣⲓⲟⲥ, Mani 1 *A*² ⲁϥϯ ⲧⲟⲟⲧⲩ ⲙ-
ⲡⲉϥⲥⲁⲡ, ROC 25 242 *B* when he saw ϫⲉⲙⲡⲉⲥϯ
ⲧⲟⲧⲥ ⲛⲁϥ; *lay hands on, seize*: Job 30 18 *F*(WS,
S ⲁⲙⲁⲣⲧⲉ, *B* ⲁⲙⲟⲛⲓ) ⲉ̓ⲡⲓⲗⲁⲙⲃ. gen; R 2 66 *S* ⲁϥϯ
ⲧⲟⲟⲧϥ ⲙⲡⲉϥⲣⲁⲃⲇⲟⲥ ⲉⲧⲣⲡⲧⲉϥⲥⲓⲝ, AM 307 *B* ⲁϥϯ
ⲧⲟⲧⲩ ⲙⲡⲓⲭⲱⲙ; c ⲙⲙⲟ⸗: 2 Kg 13 19 *S* ⲁⲥϯ ⲧⲟⲟⲧⲥ
ⲙⲙⲟⲥ (*sc* ϣⲧⲏⲛ) ⲁⲥⲡⲁⲣⲥ Gk om; *thrust off* (*cf* ϯ

ⲧ. ⲉⲃⲟⲗ), Ps 117 13 *B* ⲁⲩϯ ⲧⲟⲧⲟⲩ ⲙⲙⲟⲓ (*S* ⲧⲱϭⲡ) ὠθεῖσθαι, C 86 298 *B* ⲁϥϯ ⲧⲟⲧϥ ⲙⲙⲟϥ = BSG 192 *S* ⲡⲟϫϥ ⲡⲥⲁⲃⲟⲗ ⲙ. ἀπωθ.;   c ⲉ-, *seize*: 2 Kg 1 11 *S* κρατεῖν gen; Mor 40 27 *S* ⲁϥϯ ⲧⲟⲟⲧϥ ⲉⲧⲉϥⲡⲟⲣ-ⲫⲩⲣⲁ= C 43 56 *B* ⲁⲙⲟⲛⲓ, BIF 22 107 *F* sim, Mani 1 *A²* ϥⲁϯ ⲧⲟⲟⲧϥ ⲁⲡⲟⲩⲁⲓⲛⲉ;   vbal *B*: Job 33 24 (*S* ϣⲱⲡ ⲉ-)ἀντέχεσθαι, C 89 183 ⲙⲡⲟⲩ(ⲟⲩ)ⲱϣ ⲉϥ ⲧⲟⲧϥ ⲉⲑⲣⲟⲩ-;   c ⲉⲣⲛ- *S*: Job 31 27 (*B* ϭⲁ ⲁ. ϩⲓⲣⲉⲛ-) ⲭ. ἐπιτιθ.ἐπί; Ac 7 57 (*B* ⲃⲁⲗⲣⲓ) συνέχειν acc, ViK 9800 118 *S* ϯ ⲧⲟⲟⲧⲟⲩ ⲉⲣⲉⲛⲡⲉⲩⲙⲁⲁϫⲉ;   c ⲙⲛ- *SBF*, *give aid to*: Deu 20 4 *S*(*B* ⲃⲱⲧⲉ ⲡⲉⲙ-) συνεκπολε-μεῖν; Jos 1 14 *S* συμμαχεῖν dat; Lu 5 7 *SB* συλλα-βέσθαι dat; Aeg 248 *S* ⲉⲧⲣⲉϥϯ ⲧⲟⲟⲧⲟⲩ ⲛⲁⲩ ⲛⲙⲙⲁⲩ συνι-στάναι dat; Ps 82 8 *SB* εἰς ἀντίληψιν γίνεσθαι dat, Cai Euch 425 *B* ⲙⲁⲧⲟⲧⲕ ⲡⲉⲙⲱⲟⲩ βοηθεῖν dat; ShBor 233 248 *S* ⲉⲧⲣⲉⲟⲩⲁ ϯ ⲧⲟⲟⲧϥ ⲙⲡⲟⲩⲁ, Mun 26 *S* ⲙⲁ-ⲣⲉⲡⲉⲧⲣⲟⲥ ϯ ⲡⲧⲟⲟⲧϥ ⲡⲁⲙⲁⲓ, C 86 102 *B* ϯ ⲧⲟⲧⲑ-ⲛⲟⲩ ⲡⲉⲙⲏⲓ, CMSS 39 *F* ⲥⲧⲓ ⲧⲁⲁⲧⲉ ⲙⲉⲛⲏⲓ;   c ⲉⲃⲟⲗ *SB*, *expel* (cf ϯ ⲧ. ⲙⲙⲟⲋ): Lev 16 8 *B*(*S* ⲟⲩⲱ-ⲧⲃ ⲉⲃ.) ἀποπομπαῖος, Job 22 9 *B*(*S* ϫⲟⲟⲩ) ἐξαπο-στέλλειν; P 129¹⁴ 96 *S* ⲁϥϯ ⲧⲟⲟⲧϥ ⲉⲃ. ⲉⲣⲧⲡⲟⲗⲓⲥ = PO 1 202 رلى;   ϯ ⲧⲟⲟⲧⲋ nn m: Ps 88 19 *B*(*S* ⲣⲉϥϣⲱⲡ ⲉ-), 1 Cor 12 28 *S* ⲟⲩϯ ⲧⲟⲟⲧⲟⲩ (*B* ⲙⲉⲧⲣⲉϥϯ ⲧ.) ἀντίληψις; PSBA 34 174 *S* ⲉⲧⲛϫⲱⲣⲏⲥⲓⲥ ⲛⲧⲉ ⲡⲛⲉ ⲙⲡⲛϯ ⲧⲟⲟⲧϥ, HCons 428 *B* pray for weal & ϯ ⲧⲟⲧϥ ⲛⲡⲉⲛⲓⲟϯ دعاء;   K 77 *B* ⲡⲓϯ ⲧⲟⲧϥ دعا *upper arm*.   ⲣⲉϥϯ ⲧⲟⲟⲧⲋ *SB*, *helper*: Ps 108 12 *B*(*S* ⲡⲉⲧⲛⲁϣⲟⲡϥ ⲉ-) ἀντιλήπτωρ; BSM 59 *B* = B Mis 417 *S*;   ⲙⲉⲧⲣⲉϥϯ ⲧ. *B*, *help*: 1 Cor 12 28 ut sup, MG 25 398 ⲑⲙⲉⲧⲣⲉϥϯ ⲧⲟⲧⲥ ⲙⲡⲓⲱⲙⲟⲧ (ROC 19 414 ⲧⲟⲧ misunderstood).

ⲟⲩⲉϩ ⲧ. *v* ⲟⲩⲱϩ.

ϣ(ⲉ)ⲡ ⲧ. *SAA²B*, *grasp hand* in greeting: Ex 18 7 *B*, Mt 5 47 *B*(*S* Mor *F*=Gk), AM 271 *B* ⲁⲩϣⲉⲡ ⲧⲟⲧϥ ἀσπάζειν; Ps 84 11 *B*(*S* ϯ ⲡⲉⲓ) καταφιλεῖν; Bor 263 37 *S* ⲙⲁⲣⲉⲛϣⲉⲡ ⲧⲟⲟⲧⲟⲩ ⲛⲛⲉⲛⲉⲣⲏⲩ in holy kiss (cf Ro 16 16 &c *SB* ⲁⲥⲡⲁⲍⲉ), PO 14 335 *B* ⲁϥϣⲉⲡ ⲧⲟⲧⲥ & left her;   in promising: Ps 88 50 *S*(*B* ⲱϣ) ὑπέχειν; Pro 11 21 *SA*(*B* as Gk) ⲭ. χειρὶ ἐμβάλλειν;   in betrothing: Deu 22 23 *S*(*B* ⲱⲡ ⲛⲥⲁ-), Lu 2 5† *S*(*B* ⲇⲟ) μνηστεύειν; R 1 1 19 *S* ⲁⲩϣⲡ ⲧ. ⲙⲡⲉⲥϩⲁⲓ ⲟⲣⲙⲁⲥⲧⲁ γίνεσθαι, AP 9 *A²* ⲧⲉⲡⲧⲁⲩϣⲉⲡ ⲧⲟⲟⲧⲥ [ⲡⲏⲉⲓ] ἡρμοσμένη; BMar 9 *S* ⲁⲓϣⲡ ⲧⲟⲟⲧⲥ ⲡⲧϣⲉⲉⲣⲉ ... ⲡⲁⲕ ⲡⲥⲣⲓⲙⲉ, Va 57 39 *B* ⲁⲩⲥⲉⲃⲧⲱⲧⲥ ⲉⲟⲩⲣⲱⲙⲓ named Joseph (*l* ϣⲉⲡ ⲧⲟⲧⲥ, cf 2 Cor 11 2 *S*);   as nn m *S*, *betrothal gift*: WTh 139 ⲁⲩϯ ⲙⲡϣⲡ ⲧⲟⲟⲧⲥ ⲙⲡⲧⲟⲣⲙⲥⲉ ⲡⲧϣⲉⲉⲣⲉ ϩⲁⲣⲟϥ since he was poor (cf ? ϣⲁⲛ *bridal gift*).

V also ϭⲓ, ϭⲓⲟⲩⲉ.

ⲡⲥⲁⲧⲟⲟⲧⲋ *SF*, ⲥⲁⲧ. *B*, *out of hand, forthwith*: Ge 15 4 *B*(*S* ⲡⲧⲉⲩⲛⲟⲩ), Job 3 11 *B*(*S* ⲇⲟ), Mt 13 20 *BF* (*S* ⲇⲟ) εὐθύς, Mk 5 30 *S*(var ⲡⲧ.)*B*, 3 Jo 14 *B*(*S* ϩⲛ-ⲟⲩⲅⲉⲡⲏ) εὐθέως; Ac 23 30 *B*(*S* ⲡⲧ.)ἐξαυτῆς; *ib* 28

---

6 *B*(*S* ϩⲛⲟⲩϣⲥⲡⲉ) ἄφνω; Mor 31 144 *S* ⲁⲅⲁⲙⲁϩⲧⲉ ⲙⲙⲟϥ ⲡⲥⲁⲧⲟⲟⲧϥ & stripped him, Z 287 *S* did not Paul say (2 Cor 11 2)? ⲁⲗⲗⲁ ⲁⲡⲁⲩⲗⲟⲥ ⲟⲩⲉϩ ⲧⲗⲉϫⲓⲥ ⲡⲥⲁⲧⲟⲟⲧϥ ϫⲉ- (*ib* 3), PO 11 384 *B* had they not van-ished ⲛⲁⲓⲡⲁⲙⲟⲩ ⲥⲁⲧⲟⲧⲡⲉ, Mor 28 74 *S* ⲡⲧⲉⲩⲛⲟⲩ ⲁⲥⲧⲡⲡⲟⲟⲩ ⲙⲡⲣⲱⲙⲁⲗ ⲥⲡⲁⲩ ⲡⲥⲁⲧⲟⲟⲧⲟⲩ;   other meanings: Ge 33 14 *S*(*B* as Gk) ἐναντίον, Su 18 *B* κατὰ τ. πλαγίας θύρας, 26 sim.

Prepositions formed with ⲧⲉ-, ⲧⲟⲟⲧⲋ.

ⲉⲧⲛ- *S*, ⲁ. *AA²*, ⲉⲧⲉⲛ- *B*, ⲉⲧⲟⲟⲧⲋ *S*, ⲁ. *AA²*, ⲉⲧⲟⲧⲋ *B*, ⲉⲧⲁ(ⲁ)ⲧⲋ *F*, with 2 pl ⲉⲧⲛⲧⲏⲩⲧⲛ, ⲉⲧⲉ(ⲧ)ⲧⲏⲩⲧⲛ, ⲉⲧⲟ(ⲟ)ⲧⲧⲏⲩⲧⲛ *S*, ⲁⲧⲟⲟⲧⲛⲉ, ⲁⲧⲉⲧⲏⲛⲉ *A*, ⲉⲧⲉⲛⲑⲏⲛⲟⲩ *B*, prep, *to hand of*, *to* (but *S* often varies with ⲛⲧⲛ- *from*): Ge 2 16 *SB*, Deu 11 32 *S* ⲉⲧⲛⲧⲏⲩⲧⲛ (varr ⲉⲧⲟ-ⲟⲧⲧ., ⲡⲧⲉⲧ.), Job 40 24 *S*(*B* ⲛⲧⲉⲛ-), Ps 117 18 *SA*(Cl) *B*, Is 34 16 *SF*(*B* ⲛ-), Mt 28 20 *S* ⲉⲧⲉⲧⲏⲩⲧⲛ (var ⲛ-ⲧⲉⲧ., *B* diff), Mk 10 3 *S*(*B* ϩⲓⲧⲉⲛ-, *F* ⲛⲧⲉⲛ-), Jo 18 30 *SA²*(*B* ⲛ-), Aeg 273 *S* ⲧⲉⲡⲧⲟⲗⲏ ⲡⲧⲁⲛⲧⲁⲁⲥ ⲉⲧⲟ-ⲟⲧⲛ dat; Ps 26 12 *SB*, Ez 21 15 *S*(*B* ⲉⲧⲭⲓϫ) εἰς; Jer 46 14 *B* πρός; PS 271 *S* ⲟⲩⲟⲱϩ ⲉⲧⲟⲧⲛⲏⲩⲧⲛ, *ib* sim ⲉⲧⲉⲧⲏⲩⲧⲛ, *ib* 87 *S* ⲡⲁⲣⲙⲉⲧ ⲉⲧⲟⲟⲧⲟⲩ, TU 43 15 *A* deliver them ⲁ. ⲡⲙⲟⲩ, BMis 222 *S* ⲁⲓϯ ⲙⲙⲟϥ ⲉ. ⲡⲭⲥ, Mani 2 *A²* ϣⲁⲛⲧⲉⲉϥ ⲁ. ⲡⲁⲅⲅⲉⲗⲟⲥ, Mor 33 142 *S* ϣⲡ ϩⲙⲟⲧ ⲉ. ⲡⲉⲕⲛⲛⲁ (var BMis 69 ⲛⲧⲟⲟⲧⲩ ⲛⲧⲉ), ShC 42 189 *S* ⲣ ϩⲱⲃ ⲉⲧⲟⲟⲧϥ ⲙⲡⲧⲁⲕⲟ, P 131³ 52 *S* ϩⲉ ⲉⲧⲟⲟⲧϥ ⲡⲟⲩϣⲱⲛⲉ, PLond 4 453 *S* when ye re-quire ⲡⲉⲩⲡⲣⲟⲥⲱⲡⲟⲛ ⲉⲧⲟⲟⲧⲛ (cf 454 sim ⲛⲧⲟⲟⲧⲛ), Kr 112 *S* ⲡⲁϣⲉ ⲡⲣⲟⲗⲟⲕⲋ ⲁⲓⲭⲓⲧⲋ ⲉⲧⲟⲟⲧⲏⲩⲧⲛ, *ib* 194 *F* ⲉⲛⲡⲁⲧⲟⲩⲉⲓ ⲉⲧⲁⲁ(ⲧ)ⲛ, *ib* 72 *F* ⲁⲩⲓ (ⲉ)ⲧⲁ(ⲧ)ⲛ, C 89 191 *B* ⲁⲩⲥϧⲏⲧⲟⲩ ⲉⲧⲟⲧⲟⲩ *wrote them down*, BKU 1 70 *S* ⲉϥⲥϩⲁⲓ ⲉⲧⲟⲟⲧϥ ⲛ-, COAd 7 *S* gospel learnt by heart ⲡⲧⲁⲧⲁϥⲟϥ ⲉⲧⲟⲟⲧⲕ, Miss 4 621 *S* this com-mand ϥⲉⲣⲟⲛ ⲉⲧⲟⲟⲧϥ ⲙⲡⲭⲥ ⲉⲁⲁϥ, AM 213 *B* taken hither & thither ⲉ. ⲑⲟⲩⲓ ⲑⲟⲩⲓ ⲛⲛⲓⲧⲓⲙⲱⲣⲓⲁ; for ? ⲛⲧⲛ-: Z 282 *S* ⲡⲏⲧ ⲉ. ⲡⲉⲧⲁⲓⲱⲕⲉⲓ, BIF 13 103 *S* ⲉⲩⲧⲁⲉⲓⲏ ⲉⲧⲟⲟⲧϥ, Z 234 *S* when they heard ⲉⲧⲟⲟⲧϥ ⲙⲡⲣⲁⲗⲏⲧ.   *V* ⲉⲓ, ϯ, ⲧⲁϭⲟ, ⲟⲩⲱϩ, ϩⲱⲛ, ϩⲟⲣϣⲉⲛ & many other verbs.

ⲛⲧⲛ- *SAA²*, ⲧⲛ- *A*, ⲛⲧⲉⲛ- *BFO*, ⲛⲧⲉ- *SB*, other forms as ⲉⲧⲛ-, also ⲛⲧⲟⲧⲛⲏⲟⲩ (KroppM 55) *S*, prep *in, by hand of, by, with, beside, from*,: Ge 39 15, Deu 22 3, Pʳio 14 22 *S* ⲛⲧⲟⲟⲧⲟⲩ ⲛ- *A* ⲧⲛ-, Mt 6 1 *B*(*F* ϩⲁⲧⲉⲛ-), 2 Tim 4 13 *S*(*B* ϩⲁⲧⲉⲛ-), R 1 1 32 *S* heard ⲛⲧⲟⲟⲧⲟⲩ ⲛⲛⲓⲟⲩⲁⲓ παρά; Ps 54 4 *B*(*S* ⲉⲃⲟⲗ ϩⲛ-), EpJer 35 *BF*, Mt 13 12 *SBF*, Jo 16 22 *S* ⲛⲧⲉⲧⲏⲩⲧⲛ *A²* ⲛⲧⲟⲟⲧⲧⲏⲛⲉ *B* ⲛⲧⲉⲛⲑⲏⲛⲟⲩ, Cl 28 4 *A* whither shall go ⲧⲁⲙⲉϩⲣⲟ ⲙⲡⲧⲏⲣϥ?, MG 25 2ʳ6 *B* fell at his feet ⲛ. ϯⲣⲟϯ (var ⲉⲃ. ϧⲉⲛ-), *ib* 119 *B* ⲱ ⲃⲓⲁ ⲛⲧⲟⲧⲕ ἀπό (cf *ib* 97 sim ⲉϫⲱⲕ, DeV 2 191 ⲡⲉⲙⲱⲧⲉⲛ); Is 1 7 *B* ⲛⲧⲉ- (*S* ϩⲓⲧⲛ-), *ib* 30 33 *B*(*SF* ⲇⲟ), Mt 5 26 *SB*, Ac 5 16 *B*(*S* ⲉⲃ. ϩⲓⲧⲛ-), BM 216 109 *S* ⲉⲩⲙⲏⲣ ⲛⲧⲟ-ⲟⲧⲟⲩ ⲛⲛⲉⲧⲟⲩⲁⲁⲃ ὑπό; 2 Kg 2 15 *S* (var ⲉⲃ. ϩⲛ-), Ps 17 20 *B*(*S* ⲉⲃ. ϩⲛ-), Jer 29 8 *S*(*B* ⲉⲃ. ϩⲁ-) ἐκ, Nu

5 25 *B*(*S* ⲉⲃ. ϩⲛ̄ⲧⲥ̄ⲓⲝ ⲛ-) ἐκ χειρός, Va 57 14 *B* ⲛ.
ⲡⲁⲓⲙⲁ ἐκεῖθεν; Ps 108 24 *B*(*S* ⲉⲧⲃⲉ-) διά; 1 Kg 9
7 *S* μετά; Ex 16 3 *B*(*S* ϩⲛ-), Mt 8 10 *SB* παρά; Ex
17 3 *B*(*S* ϩⲁ-), Lev 11 29 *S* ⲛⲧⲉⲧⲏⲩⲧⲛ (var ⲛⲧⲟⲟⲧ,
B ⲛ-), Deu 12 11 *S* (var ⲉⲧⲛ-)*B*, 2 Kg 1 26 *SB*, Pro
12 22 *B*(*SA* ⲛⲁϩⲣⲛ-), Jo 11 41 *SA²B*, 1 Cor 14 11 *B*
(*S* ⲛ-), Philem 19 *S*(*S* ⲉ-) dat; Ge 31 16 *S*(*B* ⲛⲧⲉ)
Jth 14 12 *S*, Pro 27 10 *A*(*S* ⲛⲧⲉ), Is 54 13 *SB*, Lu 19
8 *S*(var do, *B* diff), Cl 55 1 *A*, RNC 23 *S* ⲡⲉⲧⲛϩⲣⲟⲧ
ⲛⲧⲟⲟⲧϥ gen; stands for vb: Deu 4 38 *B*(*S* ⲟϥⲛ̄ⲧϥ̄),
Is 62 11 *SB*, EpJer 13 *BF*, Jo 4 11 *SA²BF*, Phil 1 23
B(*SF* ⲟⲩⲛⲧ·), Mor 17 79 *S* ⲡⲉϥⲛⲧⲟⲟⲧⲟⲩ ϩⲱⲥ ⲡ̄ⲉ̄,
MG 25 204 *B* ⲛⲏ ⲉⲧⲉⲛⲧⲟⲧ ⲙ̄ⲃⲓⲣ, Va 63 103 *B* ⲙⲙⲟⲛ
ϩⲉⲡⲓⲡⲓ ⲛ̄ⲧⲟⲧ ἔχειν, Aeg 276 *S* ⲉⲣⲉⲉⲡⲥⲁⲧⲱ ⲛ̄ⲧⲟⲟⲧⲟⲩ,
Va 57 45 *B* ⲛⲏ ⲉⲧⲉⲛ̄ⲧⲟⲧⲟⲩ κατέχ.; Sa 18 16 *S*, Lu 24
1 *S*(*B* diff) φέρειν; Z 341 *S* son ⲙⲟⲩ ⲛ̄ⲧⲟⲟⲧϥ συνέβη
ἀποθανεῖν; not in Gk (*cf* ethic dat): Ge 24 18 *B* ⲁⲥ-
ⲓⲛⲉ ⲛ̄ⲧⲟⲧⲉ (*ib* 46 om), Tob 4 14 *S* ⲙ̄ⲡⲣ̄ⲧ̄ⲣ̄ϭⲱϣⲕ ⲛ̄ⲧⲟ-
ⲟⲧⲕ, Sa 2 15 *S* ⲥⲉ̄ϣⲟϥⲉ ⲛ̄ⲧⲟⲟⲧⲛ (var om)*B*, Ac 12 15
B ⲁⲥⲧⲁϫⲣⲟ ⲛ̄ⲧⲟⲧⲉ (*S* diff), Z 343 *S* ⲁⲧⲉϥⲙⲟⲣⲧ ⲁⲣⲭⲉⲓ ⲛ̄ⲧⲟⲟⲧϥ;   *with, for*: ShA 1 257 *S* ⲉϣⲱⲡ
ⲛ̄ⲧⲟⲟⲧϥ ⲙ̄ⲡⲉⲭ̄ⲥ̄, ShMIF 23 187 *S* ⲙⲛ ϩⲏⲃⲥ ⲛ̄ⲧⲟ-
ⲟⲧϥ...ⲡϩⲏⲃⲥ ϩ̄ⲡⲉϥϭ̄ⲓⲝ, AZ 21 144 *S* ϩⲁⲣⲡⲁⲍⲉ ⲙ̄-
ⲡⲉⲛⲧ̄ⲛⲧⲟⲟⲧϥ, CO 107 *S* ⲉⲓⲥ ⲡⲗⲟⲅⲟⲥ ⲙ̄ⲡ̄ⲛ̄ⲉ̄ ⲛ̄ⲧⲟⲟⲧⲕ,
Va 57 70 *B* ⲉⲧⲓ ⲉⲣⲉⲡⲓⲥⲛⲟⲩ ⲛ̄ⲧⲟⲧⲉⲛ, BMis 379 *S* ϣ-
ⲧⲏⲛ...ⲕⲁⲁⲥ ⲛⲁⲕ ⲛ̄ⲧⲟⲟⲧⲕ (var ϩⲁⲣⲧⲏⲕ) = BSM 35
B ⲥ̄ⲁⲧⲟⲧⲕ, ViK 9460 125 *S* ⲁⲓⲥϩⲁⲓ [ⲙ̄]ⲡⲉϩⲟⲟⲩ ⲛ̄-
ⲧⲟⲟⲧ (*cf* ϩ̄ⲣⲁⲓ ⲉⲧⲛ-);   *through, because of*: PS 281
S believe every word ⲛⲧⲉⲧⲏⲩⲧⲛ, ShBMOr 8810 371
S ⲛⲧⲁⲗⲩⲡⲉⲓ ⲛ̄ⲧⲟⲟⲧⲟⲩ ⲛ̄ⲛⲉⲧⲉϣϣⲉ ⲉⲧⲣⲁⲣⲁϣⲉ ⲉⲃⲟⲗ
ϩⲓⲧⲟⲟⲧⲟⲩ, CO 252 *S* sent it ⲛⲧⲟⲟⲧϥ ⲛⲁⲡⲁ ⲯⲁⲧⲏⲥ,
BM 531 *S* send ⲛ̄ⲧⲉ(ⲙ)ⲡⲓⲥⲅ[ⲙⲙⲁⲭⲟⲥ, BMis 194
S ⲙⲟⲕϩ ⲛ̄ⲧⲉ(ⲙ)ⲡⲓⲃⲉ, MG 25 224 *B* body swelled ⲛ.
ⲛⲓϣⲟⲗⲙⲉⲥ, C 43 27 *B* ⲁⲓⲣ̄ⲱϣ ⲛ̄ⲧⲟⲟⲧϥ ⲙ̄ⲡⲁⲓⲁⲡⲟⲥⲓⲟ-
ⲟⲥ;   *from, away from*: PS 333 *S* ϥⲓⲧϥ ⲛⲧⲉ(ⲛ)-
ⲡⲁⲣⲭ̄ⲱⲛ, ShViK 9343 78 *S* thing he had made ⲁϥϩⲉ ⲛ̄ⲧⲟⲟⲧϥ, R 1 5 30 *S* sim, Mor 19 80 *S* ⲙ̄ⲡⲣ̄ⲥ̄ⲩⲡⲁⲍⲉ
ⲛ̄ⲧⲉⲡⲗⲁⲁⲩ (var 18 72 & Miss 4 144 *B* ⲛ̄ⲧⲟⲟⲧϥ ⲛ-),
AM 271 *B* ⲁ̄ϥϣ̄ⲉⲡ...ϭⲓⲥⲓ ⲛ̄ⲧⲟⲧϥ, Kr 75 *S* ⲁⲓⲡⲗⲏⲣⲱ
ⲛ̄ⲧⲟⲟⲧⲕ (Ryl 122, 125 sim ⲧⲟⲟⲧⲕ), BMar 17 *S* ⲁϣ̄ⲉ-
ⲗⲉⲉⲧ ⲟⲩⲉⲓⲛⲉ ⲉⲣⲟⲓ ⲁⲙ̄ⲡⲧⲣⲙⲙⲁⲟ ⲟⲩⲉⲓⲛⲉ ⲛ̄ⲧⲟⲟⲧ, *ib*
94 *S* ⲁⲡⲉϥⲟⲩⲥⲓⲁ ϯ ⲉⲡⲁϩⲟⲩ ⲛ̄ⲧⲟⲟⲧϥ, Mor 28 66 *S* lo
time ⲡⲣⲟⲕⲟⲡⲧⲉⲓ ⲛ̄ⲧⲟⲟⲧⲛ, BSM 29 *B* lest hope ⲧⲁⲕⲟ
ⲛ̄ⲧⲟⲧⲉⲛ;   *to*: Ryl 310 *S* ⲁϥⲧⲁⲁϥ ⲛ. ⲟⲩⲁⲣⲭ̄ⲱⲛ,
C 43 118 *B* ⲉ̄ⲩ̄ϯ ⲙ̄ⲙⲱⲟⲩ ⲛ̄ⲧⲉⲛⲡⲟⲩⲅⲉⲣⲛⲟⲩ;   *quasi-*
refl: Miss 8 174 *S* ⲁⲡⲉϥϩⲏⲧ ϫⲓⲥⲉ ⲛ̄ⲧⲟⲟⲧϥ, BAp 149
S ⲁⲡⲁϩⲏⲧ ⲣ̄ ϩⲃⲁ ⲛ̄ⲧⲟⲟⲧ, DeV 2 53 *B* let not hearts
ⲥ̄ⲟⲙⲥ̄ⲉⲙ ⲛ̄ⲧⲟⲧⲉⲛ; here ?belongs BAp 9 *S* ⲁⲥϥⲁⲗⲓⲍⲉ
ⲛ̄ⲧⲟⲟⲧⲕ ⲕⲁⲗⲱⲥ & shut gates;   obscure : Ep 339
S ⲕⲥⲟⲟⲩⲛ ϫⲉ ϯ̄ⲙⲉ ⲙ̄[ⲙⲟⲕ ... ⲡⲉ]ⲕϩⲏⲧ ϩⲓⲥⲉ ⲛ̄ⲧⲟ-
ⲟⲧ;   *with passive*: Lu 2 26 *B*(*S* ⲉⲃⲟⲗ ϩⲓⲧⲛ-) ὑπό; PS
132 *S* ⲛⲧⲉⲣⲟⲩϯ ⲛⲁⲩ ⲙ̄ⲡⲥⲱ ⲛⲧⲟⲟⲧϥ ⲙ̄ⲡⲉⲧϫⲟⲥⲉ (Od
Solom 6 12 �ⲥⲟ), BAp 93 *S* ⲧⲧⲁⲍⲓⲥ ⲛ̄ⲧⲁⲩⲧⲁϩⲟⲟⲩⲧⲛ.

ⲉⲣⲟⲥ ⲛ̄.ⲡⲁⲛϫⲱϩ, DeV 2 25 *B* hands ⲉⲁⲩⲓⲁⲩ ⲉⲃⲟⲗ
ⲁⲛ ⲛ̄. ⲟⲩⲙⲱⲟⲩ.

ⲉⲃⲟⲗ ⲛ̄ⲧⲛ- *SB*, *from*: Ge 31 39 *S* (var ⲉⲧⲛ-, *B* ⲉⲃ.
ϩⲓⲧⲉⲛ-), Ps 16 13 *B*(*S* ⲉⲧⲛ-, *F* ϩⲁⲃⲁⲗ ⲛ-), Ro 9 3 *S*(*B*
ⲉⲃ. ϩⲁ-) ἀπό; Ps 7 2 *B*(*S* ⲉ-), *ib* 68 15 *B*(*S* ⲉⲃ. ϩⲛ-)
ἐκ.

V ⲁⲙⲟⲛⲓ, ⲁⲙⲁϩⲧⲉ, ⲃⲱⲕ, ⲕⲏⲡ, ⲕⲱⲧⲉ, ⲙⲟⲩ, ⲛⲟⲩϩⲙ, ⲡⲱⲧ, ⲥⲱⲣⲙ, ⲥⲱⲧⲙ, ⲧⲁⲉⲓⲟ, ⲧⲁⲕⲟ, ⲧⲱⲣⲡ *seize*,
ⲟⲩⲱ *cease*, ⲟⲩⲱϩ, ⲟⲩϫⲁⲓ, ⲱⲗ, ⲱⲡ, ⲱϭⲛ, ϣⲓⲡⲉ, ϣⲱⲡ,
ϭⲓ, ϩⲙⲟⲧ(ϣⲡ-), ϫⲓ &c.

ϩⲁⲧⲛ- *SA²*, **ϩⲁⲧⲉⲛ-**-*F*, **ⲥ̄ⲁⲧⲉⲛ-**, ϩ.(?error)*B*, other
forms as ⲉⲧⲛ-, prep, lit *under the hand of*, so *beside*,
with (form ϩⲁⲧⲛ- varies constantly with ϩⲁⲣⲧⲛ-, but
pronom forms are distinct: Ge 22 17 *SB*, Lev 3 2
S(*B* ϩⲓⲣⲉⲛ-), Nu 20 19 *S* (var ϩⲁⲣⲁⲧ·, *B* ⲉⲥⲕⲉⲛ-),
ib 24 6 *S*(var ϩⲓϫⲛ-)*B*, Job 40 16 *S*(*B* ⲥ̄ⲁⲣⲁⲧ·), Ps
36 39 *B*(*S* ⲛⲧⲛ-), *ib* 75 13 *B*(*S* ⲛⲁϩⲣⲛ-), Pro 2 18 *SB*
(*A* ϩⲁⲣⲧⲉ-), Lu 1 37 *B*(*S* ⲛⲁϩ., *A* Cl 27 1 ϩ.), Jo 14
17 *SA²*(*B* ⲛⲉⲙ-), Ro 2 11 *SBF*, AP 15 *A²* παρά, Cai
Euch 498 *B* ⲉⲧⲭⲏ ⲥ̄ⲁⲧⲟⲧⲉⲛ παρεῖναι (*cf* Phil 1 27
SBF neg ἀπεῖναι); Lev 20 16 *B*(*S* ⲉ-), Is 73 *S*(*B* ϩⲁ-),
Mk 11 1 *S*(var ϩⲁⲣ.)*B*, Ro 5 1 *B*(*S* ⲉϩⲟⲩⲛ ⲉ-) πρός,
Va 61 29 *B* ⲁϥⲓ ⲥ̄.ⲡⲓⲥⲧⲩⲗⲟⲥ ἔμπροσθεν; Ex 21 6 *SB*,
1 Kg 17 28 *B*(*S* ⲛⲧⲛ-), Ez 21 15 *B*(*S* ϩⲓⲣⲛ-), *ib* 40 16
B(*S* ϩⲁϩ.) ἐπί; *ib* 40 17 *B*(*S* ϩⲁⲧⲉ-), Ep Jer 44 *F*(*B*
ⲥ̄ⲉⲛ-) ἐν; Jer 50 6 *B* μετά; Si 38 32 *S*, Jo 3 23 *S*(var
ϩⲁⲧ.)*B*(*F* ϩⲁⲧⲉ-), *ib* 6 23 *SA²BF*(PMich 3521) ἐγγύς;
Ex 34 3 *SB* πλησίον; Ro 3 20 *B*(*S* diff) ἐνώπιον; 1 Kg
19 3 *S*(var ϩⲁⲣ.), Ps 140 6 *SB*, Dan 10 4 *SB* ἐχόμενος; Jos 11 2 *S*, Mt 8 32 *B*(*S* ⲉϫⲛ-) κατά, Est 4 5 *S*
κατὰ πρόσωπον; 1 Kg 31 13 *S*(var ϩⲁ-), Su 54 *B*,
AM 272 *B* ⲥ̄. ϯϫⲟⲓ ὑπό, Jos 9 31 *S* ὑποχείριος; Ge
40 8 *B*(*S* ⲉ-), 1 Kg 17 20 *B*(*S* ⲛⲧⲛ-), Pro 8 21 *B*(*SA*
ⲛ-), Si 4 28 *SB*, Ac 10 8 *B*(*S* ⲉ-), Gal 2 2 *B*(*S* ⲛ-) dat;
PS 171 *S* ⲉⲓⲣ̄ⲙⲟⲟⲥ ϩⲁⲧⲛⲧⲏⲩⲧⲛ, ShBor 246 53 *S* ⲉⲩ-
ⲙⲧⲟⲛ ⲙⲙⲟⲟⲩ ϩ. ⲡⲛ̄ⲭ̄ⲥ̄, BHom 116 *S* ⲁϥϣⲱⲡⲉ ϩⲁⲧⲟⲟⲧϥ ⲙ̄ⲡⲙⲟⲩ *subject to*, CA 99 *S* ϯⲛⲁⲣⲱⲡ ϩⲁⲧⲟⲟⲧ
ⲡⲣⲉⲛⲭⲣⲏⲙⲁ, J 58 9 *S* ⲉⲓⲕⲱ ϩⲁⲧⲟⲟⲧⲕ ⲙ̄ⲡⲁⲛⲓ, Aeg
6 *B* inscribed ϩⲁⲧⲉⲛⲡⲓⲅⲣⲁⲙⲙⲁⲧⲉⲥ, C 43 64 *B* ⲉϥ-
ϩⲉⲙⲥⲓ ⲥ̄ⲁⲧⲟⲧⲩ, *ib* 89 22 *B* we would ⲉⲣ ⲙⲟⲛⲁⲭⲟⲥ
ⲥ̄ⲁⲧⲟⲧⲕ = Miss 4 543 *S* ϩⲁⲣⲧⲏⲕ, *ib* 89 210 *B* buried
ⲥ̄. ⲡⲉⲛⲕⲁⲥ ⲛⲡⲉⲛⲓⲱⲧ = Wess 11 156 *S* ϩⲓⲧⲟⲩⲛ-,
BSM 22 *B* is there deceit ⲥ̄. ⲫ̄ϯ? = BMis 360 *S*
ϩⲁϩ., Pcod 39 ult *F* ϩ. ⲫ̄ϯ (*S* ϩⲁϩ.), Wess 15 125 *S*
ⲡⲉϣϣⲟⲡ ⲛⲁϥⲛⲉ ⲡⲥⲟⲗⲥ̄ⲗ ϩⲁⲧⲟⲟⲧϥ;   **ⲉⲃⲟⲗ ⲥ̄.** *B*:
Is 51 23 (*S* diff) ἔξω;   further varr with ϩⲁⲣⲧⲛ- *S*,
as Lev 19 21, 1 Kg 21 8 ϩⲁⲧⲟⲟⲧⲕ–ϩⲁⲣⲧⲏⲕ, Mt 13 1,
Jo 19 25, 1 Cor 16 10 ϩⲁⲧⲛⲧⲏⲩⲧⲛ–ϩⲁⲣⲧⲏⲧ., Mor 30
51 *Sᶠ* ⲡⲣⲁⲧⲙⲡⲉⲩⲥⲁϩ = BMis 275 *S* ϩⲁϩ.   **ϩⲁⲧⲉ-,**
ϩⲁⲧⲛ- *v* ϩⲁⲣⲧⲛ.

ϩⲓⲧⲛ- *SAA²*, **ϩⲉ.** *S*(Theban), **ϩⲓⲧⲉⲛ-** *BF*, **ⲓⲧⲉ-** *F*
(BMOr 6948), other forms as ⲉⲧⲛ-, 2 pl *S* ϩⲓⲧⲟⲟⲧ-
ⲧⲏⲩⲧⲛ, ϩⲓⲧⲟⲧ. (ST 212), ϩⲓⲧⲛ. (1 Cor 4 3), ϩⲓⲧⲉⲧ.

(PS 249), *A* ⲣⲓⲧⲉⲧⲛⲡⲉ (TU 43 16), *A²* ⲅⲓ-?]ⲧⲟⲟⲧⲧⲏⲛⲉ, *F* ⲅⲓⲧⲉⲡⲧⲏⲛⲟⲩ (Pcod 28), prep, lit *by the hand of*, so *through, by, from*: Lev 24 12 *S*, Ps 65 12 *S*, Mk 10 25 *S*, Jo 10 9 *SAA²*(all *B* ⲉⲃ. ⲅ.)ⲇⲓⲁ, Sa 5 7 *S* ⲇⲓⲟⲇⲉⲩⲉⲓⲛ; Job 27 13 *SB*, Pro 8 35 *SA*(*B* ⲉⲃ. ⲅ.), Jo 5 34 *SA²*(*B* ⲡⲧⲉ (ⲡ-?)), 1 Pet 2 4 *SB*(var ⲛⲧⲉⲡ-) ⲡⲁⲣⲁ, Is 10 29 *S* (*B* ϩⲉⲡ-) ⲡⲁⲣⲉⲣⲭⲉⲥⲑⲁⲓ; Job 8 16 *S*(*B* ⲉⲃ. ⲅ.), Is 30 2 *S*(*B* do, *F* ⲛⲧⲛ-), MG 25 246 *B* head ⲟⲓ ⲛⲅⲟⲗⲓ ⲅ. ⲡⲓϣⲱⲡⲓ ⲩⲡⲟ; Ps 7 4 *S*(*B* ⲛⲧⲉⲡ-), ib 138 7 *A*(Cl, *S* ⲉⲃ. ⲡ-, *B* ⲉⲃ. ⲅⲁ-), Lu 2 15 *S*(*B* ⲉⲃ. ⲅⲁ-), Ac 1 22 *S* (*B* do), Ja 1 17 *SA*(*B* ⲉⲃ. ⲅ.), BM 189 *S* knowledge ⲅ. ⲧϭⲓⲛϫⲓ ⲡⲉⲓⲣⲁ ⲁⲡⲟ; Sa 13 1 *S*, Ez 7 26 *B*(*S* ⲛⲧⲡ-), Ap 11 11 *S*(*B* diff), CaiEuch 327 *B* ⲡⲓⲗⲓⲭⲓ ... ⲅ. ⲟⲩⲙⲟⲟⲩ ⲉⲕ; Ps 41 4 *S*(*B* ϩⲉⲡ-), ROC 17 398 *B* ⲅ. ⲅⲁⲡⲕⲟⲩϫⲓ ⲉⲛ; Ez 33 27 *B*(*S* ⲅⲓⲅⲣⲁⲍ) ⲉⲡⲓ ⲡⲣⲟⲥⲱⲡⲟⲩ; ib 47 2 *S*(*B* ϩⲁⲧⲉⲛ-)ⲡⲣⲟⲥ; Jud 3 23 *S*, Sa 18 21 *S* acc; Si 26 14 *S*, Cl 55 4 *A* ⲡⲱⲗⲁϧⲥ ⲅ. ⲧⲡⲟⲗⲓⲥ(?) gen; Sa 13 13 *S*, Is 8 11 *S*(*B* ϩⲉⲡ-), Ap 22 14 *S*(*B* ⲉⲃ. ϩⲉⲡ-, var ⲉⲃ. ⲅ.) dat; PS 15 *S* ⲡⲕⲟⲥⲙⲟⲥ ⲡⲁⲡⲟⲩϫⲙ ⲅⲓⲧⲡⲧⲏⲛⲧⲛ, ShC 42 29 *S* knowledge ⲅ. ⲡⲧⲁϣⲉⲟⲉⲓϣ of gospel, *ib* 24 *S* ⲡⲉϫⲁⲕ ⲅ. ⲡⲉⲕⲥⲅⲁⲓ, DeV 2 9 *B* he leapt ⲅ. ⲡⲓⲣⲁϣⲓ, BSM 81 *B* grace ⲁϥⲧⲁϩⲟⲡ ⲅ. ⲫϯ, El 52 *A* sins ⲥⲉⲥⲏϫ ⲅⲓⲧⲟⲟⲧϥ, PSBA 10 198 *S* wrote to king ⲅⲓⲧⲟⲟⲧⲉ ⲛⲧⲉϥϣⲉⲉⲣⲉ, CO 116 *S* ⲉⲁⲡⲱϣⲡⲉ ⲅ. ⲅⲏⲗⲓⲁⲥ ⲁⲡⲣⲉ, J 36 45 *S* sought to ϫⲓ ⲅⲓⲧⲟⲟⲧⲛ ⲛⲡⲉⲓⲉⲩⲅⲣⲁⲫⲟⲛ *to get from us*, Kr 6 *S* I write to John ⲅ. ⲃⲓⲕⲧⲱⲣ ⲡⲉⲧⲣⲁⲙⲙⲁⲧ(ⲉⲩⲥ), Ep 348 *S* ⲉⲁⲕⲥϩⲁⲓ ⲅⲉⲧⲁⲡⲟⲗⲱ, CMSS 26 *B* ⲧⲓ]ⲣⲏⲛⲏ ⲡⲱⲧⲉⲛ ⲅ. ⲡⲓⲥϩⲁⲓ, BM 651 *F* ⲉⲧⲧⲁ(ⲓⲏⲟⲩⲧ)ⲅ. ⲡⲡⲉ ⲙⲡⲓⲡⲉⲣⲱⲙⲓ, CO 55 *S* address of letter ⲧⲁⲁⲥ ⲛ-...ⲅ. ⲁⲃⲣⲁϩⲁⲙ (often om: *ib* 243 ⲡⲱⲁⲓⲡⲉ ⲛⲥⲟⲡ ⲡⲁⲩⲗⲟⲥ ⲓⲥⲁⲁⲕ), BMOr 6948 *F* ⲡⲁⲙⲉⲗⲓⲧ ⲉⲡⲓⲟⲧ ⲙⲛⲁ ⲓⲧⲉⲥⲉⲣⲧⲓ, CO 410 *S* money ⲁϥⲉⲓ ⲉⲧⲟⲟⲧ ⲅⲓⲧⲟⲟⲧⲕ, *ib* 166 *S* will defend thy freedom (from debt ⲁϫⲏⲙⲓⲟⲛ) ⲅ. ⲣⲱⲙⲉ ⲛⲓⲙ that shall sue thee (*cf* ?PLond 5 23 ⲫⲩⲗⲁⲝⲁⲓ ⲁⲡⲟ ⲡⲁⲛⲧⲟⲥ ⲡⲣⲟⲥ[); go forth, depart *from S* (*cf* ⲉⲃⲟⲗ ⲅ.): BMis 89 ⲁⲡⲁⲅⲅⲉⲗⲟⲥ ⲃⲱⲕ ⲅⲓⲧⲟⲟⲧⲥ, Hall 106 ⲁⲣⲃⲱⲕ ⲉⲅⲣⲁⲓ ⲅⲓⲧⲟⲟⲧ, ST 231 ⲕⲁⲧⲁⲑⲉ ⲡⲧⲁⲓⲱⲁⲅⲉ ⲅⲉⲧⲟⲟⲧⲕ, J 74 19 ⲟⲩⲟⲡ ⲛⲓⲙ ⲉⲧⲡⲁⲣⲁⲅⲉ ⲅⲓⲧⲟⲟⲧ, R 1 3 78 came down ⲅ. ⲡⲉⲥϯⲟⲧ (*cf* Lu 1 52 *B*); of time, *during, after*: Deu 15 1 *S* (var ⲅⲓϫⲛ-, *B* ⲕⲁⲧⲁ), Pro 7 20 *SAB*, Is 30 27 *SBF*, Mk 14 58 *S*(*B* ⲉⲃ. ⲅ., *cf* Mt 26 61 *S* ⲛ- *B* ϩⲉⲡ-) ⲇⲓⲁ; Ep 81 *S* ⲅⲉⲧⲛⲡⲁⲓ ⲁϥⲱϣ ⲛⲡⲕⲉⲗⲟⲩⲟⲥ (PO 2 216 ﻟﺪﺧﺪ ﻣﻦ); Aeg 251 *S* examined ⲅ. ⲡⲉⲭⲣⲟⲛⲟⲥ (var ⲅⲛ-), BMis 242 *S* ⲅ. ⲅⲉⲛⲕⲟⲩⲓ ⲛⲅⲟⲟⲩ they reached city, Cat 150 *B* who repent ⲅ. ⲟⲩⲥⲛⲟⲩ ⲉϥ-ⲟⲛⲏϣ; with 3 pl of vb ⲅ. expresses passive(Stern 479): Pro 24 69 *SA* ⲛⲧⲁⲩϫⲉ ⲡⲁϣⲁϫⲉ ⲅ. ⲡⲡⲉ (*B* act), Mt 14 24 *S* ⲉⲩⲙⲟⲩⲅⲅ ⲙⲙⲟϥ ⲅ. ⲡϩⲓⲙⲏ(var ⲅⲓⲧⲟⲟⲧⲟⲩ ⲛ-, *B* do), Cai Euch 486 *B* ⲉⲧⲟⲩⲁⲙⲁϩⲓ ⲉϫⲱⲟⲩ ⲅ. ⲁⲙⲉⲛϯ, R 2 2 22 *S* ⲁⲩⲙⲉⲣⲓⲧϥ ⲅ. ⲡⲉϥⲓⲱⲧ ⲩⲡⲟ; Mt 28 14 *S* ⲉⲩϣⲁⲡⲥⲉⲧⲙ ⲡⲁⲓ ⲅ. ⲡⲅⲏⲅⲉⲙⲱⲛ(*B* act)ⲉⲡⲓ(var ⲩⲡⲟ); Is 32 2 *SF* ⲉⲧⲟⲩⲥⲱⲕ ⲙⲙⲟϥ ⲅ. ⲟⲩⲙⲟⲟⲩ (*B*

do)ⲁⲡⲟ; Ap 2 11 *S* ⲉⲩϫⲓⲧϥ ⲡϭⲟⲡⲥ ⲅ. ⲡⲙⲟⲩ(*B* ϩⲉⲡ-) ⲉⲕ; Sa 17 3 *S* ⲉⲩϣⲧⲟⲣⲧⲣ ⲙⲙⲟⲟⲩ ⲅ. ⲅ(ⲉ)ⲛⲅⲣⲃ dat; PS 127 *S* ⲁⲩⲧⲡⲡⲟⲟⲩⲕ ⲅ. ⲡⲉⲕⲉⲓⲱⲧ, DeV 2 9 *B* ⲁⲩⲧⲁⲙⲟϥ ⲅ. ⲡⲓⲡⲛⲁ.

ⲉⲃⲟⲗ ⲅ., meaning as ⲅ.: Is 30 1 *SBF*, Ro 3 30 *SB*, 1 Cor 6 14 *B*(*S* ⲅ.), Cl 9 4 *A* ⲇⲓⲁ; Job 13 11 *SB*, Mt 18 19 *S*(*B* ⲛⲧⲉⲡ-), Cl 12 4 *A* ⲡⲁⲣⲁ; Jos 22 32 *S*, Ps 17 48 *S*(*B* ⲉⲃ. ⲅⲁ-), Mt 6 13 *S*(*B* do, *F* ⲅⲁⲃⲁⲗ ⲛ-) ⲁⲡⲟ; Ps 2 6 *SB*, Mt 17 12 *S*(*B* ⲛⲧⲉⲡ-) ⲩⲡⲟ; Jo 3 27 *BF*(*S* ⲅⲁ-), Ro 13 3 *S*(*B* ⲉⲃ. ⲛ-) ⲉⲕ; ROC 18 37 *B* ⲉⲃ. ⲅ. ⲫϯ ⲑⲉⲟⲑⲉⲛ; Jer 14 22 *B*, Cai Euch 344 *B* gotten ⲉⲃ. ⲅ. ⲡⲓⲥⲛⲟϥ ⲉⲛ; Is 51 7 *S*(*B* ϩⲉⲡ-), Cai Euch 361 *B* ⲉⲃ. ⲅ. ⲡⲟⲩϯⲣⲟ dat; PS 249 *S* ⲉⲃ. ⲅⲓⲧⲉⲛⲏⲩⲧⲛ ⲁⲧⲉⲧⲛⲁⲱⲡϩⲓⲍⲉ, ShA 2 274 ⲥ̅ struck down ⲉⲃ. ⲅⲓⲧⲟⲟⲧⲟⲩ ⲛⲡⲁⲓⲙⲱⲛ, ShC 42 24 *S* ⲧⲁⲗϭⲡⲓ ⲉⲃ. ⲅⲓⲧⲟⲟⲧⲕ, El 48 *A* saved Israel ⲉⲃ. ⲅⲓⲧⲟⲟⲧϥ ⲙⲫⲁⲣⲁⲱ (*cf ib* ⲉⲃ. ⲅⲛⲧϭⲓⲝ ⲛ-), AP 40 *A²* heard such words ⲉⲃ. ⲅⲓⲧⲟⲟⲧⲕ, BMis 364 *S* ϫⲓ ⲅⲙⲟⲧ ⲉⲃ. ⲅⲓⲧⲟⲟⲧϥ = BSM 24 *B*, CMSS 44 *F* I greet thee ⲉⲃ. ⲅ. ⲡⲡⲉ; depart, send *from* (*cf* above ⲅ.): Mt 2 12 *SB* ⲉⲃ. ⲅ. ⲕⲉⲅⲓⲏ ⲁⲅⲁⲛⲁⲭⲱⲣⲉⲓ ⲇⲓⲁ, Ac 15 41 *B*(var ⲉⲃ. ϩⲉⲡ-, *S* ⲉⲃ. ⲉ-) ⲇⲓⲉⲣⲭⲉⲥⲑⲁⲓ acc, Ap 20 9 *S* fire ⲉⲓ ⲉⲃ. ⲅⲛⲧⲡⲉ ⲉⲃ. ⲅ. ⲡⲡⲉ ⲁⲡⲟ; Nu 11 31 *SB* ⲡⲁⲣⲁ; Ps 36 40 *S*(*B* ⲉⲃ. ϩⲉⲡ-) ⲉⲕ; PS 113 *S* ⲁⲕⲧⲡⲡⲟⲟⲩ ⲡⲁⲓ ⲛⲡⲉⲕⲟⲩⲟⲓⲛ ⲉⲃ. ⲅⲓⲧⲟⲟⲧⲕ, ShC 42 30 *S* ⲁϥⲃⲱⲕ ⲉⲃ. ⲅⲓⲧⲟⲟⲧⲛ, EW 23 *B* went up to heaven ⲉⲃ. ⲅⲓⲧⲟⲧⲉⲛ, BM 184 *S* ϭⲓⲛⲉⲓ ⲉ-ⲅⲟⲩⲡ ϣⲁⲣⲟⲛ, ϭⲓⲛⲃⲱⲕ ⲉⲃ. ⲅⲓⲟⲟⲧⲉⲛ, TU 43 4 *A* ⲉⲉⲓⲡⲏⲩ ⲁⲃ. ⲅ. ⲡⲉⲓⲱⲧ; of time (*cf* ⲅ.) *B*: Ac 1 3 (*S* ⲛ-), *ib* 24 17 (*S* ⲙⲡⲛⲥⲁ-) ⲇⲓⲁ; MG 25 240 ⲉⲃ. ⲅ. ⲕ̅ ⲛⲉⲅⲟⲟⲩ ⲉⲡⲓ; expresses passive (*cf* ⲅ.): Ep Jer 17 *F* ⲛⲥⲉϣⲧⲉⲙⲃⲓⲧⲟⲩ ⲉⲃ. ⲅ. ⲡⲉⲥⲁⲁⲡⲓ (*B* act), Mt 2 16 *S* ⲁⲩⲥⲱⲃⲉ ⲙⲙⲟϥ ⲉⲃ. ⲅ. ⲛⲙⲁⲅⲟⲥ(*B* do)ⲩⲡⲟ; CaiEuch 508 *B* ⲡⲏ ⲉⲧⲁⲩⲓⲛⲓ...ⲛⲉⲙⲛⲏ ⲉⲧⲁⲩⲉⲡⲟⲩ ⲉⲃ. ⲅⲓⲧⲟⲧⲟⲩ *those* (gifts) *brought by them* ⲇⲓⲁ; KroppD 82 *S* ϣⲁⲛⲧⲟⲩϫⲡⲟ ⲛⲁⲛ ⲛⲛⲟⲩⲣⲱⲙⲉ ⲉⲃ. ⲅ. ⲛⲉⲁⲅⲅⲉⲗⲟⲥ.

ⲧⲣⲁ, ϭⲣⲁ *S* nn f, *extremity* of limbs (*cf* ?ⲧⲁⲣ): Lev 4 11 (var ϭ., *B* = Gk)ⲁⲕⲣⲱⲧⲏⲣⲓⲟⲛ(in Tri 521 ϭ. ﻛﺮﻯ); P 44 71 ⲙⲏⲣⲟⲥ · ⲧⲉϭ. ﺟﺬ = 43 42 ﻭﺭﻙ; ⲧ., *joint* (same?): Eph 4 16, Col 2 19 (*B* ⲙⲟⲩⲧ, ⲙⲟϯ) ⲁⲫⲏ.

ⲧⲣⲉ, -ⲏ *S*, ⲟⲣⲉ *B*, pl ⲟⲣⲉⲩ *B* nn m f, *kite*: Lev 11 13 *SB* m, Deu 14 13 *SB* ⲓⲕⲧⲓⲛ ﺣﺪﺍ, P 44 56 *S* ⲥⲉⲗⲓⲗⲉⲛ (43 22 -ⲗⲓⲛ) · ⲧⲁⲓⲁ · ⲧⲉⲧⲣⲉ ﺟﺪﺍ, K 167 *B* ϯⲟ. ʼ ﺩ, Tri 395 *S* ⲡⲁⲃⲟⲕ ⲙⲡ(ⲧ)ⲧ. ﻟﺪ, BMOr 8781 46 *B* ⲡⲓⲟⲣⲉⲩ ﺣﺪﻳﺎﻥ; PMéd 56 *S* ⲥⲓϣⲉ ⲛⲧ. & of raven, Mor 43 279 *S* ⲁⲕⲡⲱⲧ ⲛⲟⲉ ⲡⲟⲩⲧⲣⲏ, DeV 2 228 *B* ⲡⲓⲟ. enemy of dove; Bodl 325 159 *B* among fish ⲛⲟ. ﺍﺭﻯ (error?). *V* GriffStu 251.

ⲧⲣⲉ, -ⲏ *S* nn m, an implement or part of mechanism (wheel?): BKU 1 94 ⲡϥⲧⲟⲟⲩ ⲛⲧⲣⲏ ⲙⲡⲕⲁⲧ ⲛⲧⲡⲉ, BMOr 6201 *A* 90 list ⲁϫⲟⲛ, ⲃⲗϣⲁⲧⲉ, ⲧ. ⲡⲩϣⲁⲗⲟⲟⲩ, *ib* *A* 157 ⲡⲥⲟⲩϫⲉ ⲧϣⲁⲗⲟⲟⲩ...ⲡⲥⲟⲩⲧⲁⲁⲩ

епт. пϣа[λοογ, PLond 4 516 agricult properties ογт. ппогο[.

тре- S, тере- B part v ро (p 289 b).

тро SA² (both rare), ө. B, тре- SAA², те- AF, өре- B, тλе- F, тре⳥ SAA², те⳥ AF, өре⳥ B, vb tr, cause to do (caus of еіре), с е-: Mt 5 32 B ө. ссос еⲝфе ποιεῖν, Nu 14 11 B ө....есбоп (S ϯ) no Gk, Mt 23 5 B ө....есϣαι (S κω) no Gk; MG 25 265 B паϫө. ссωογ еер = Mor 40 39 S do, ShBMOr 8810 480 S devils т. ппепрнт еⲣλοⲡλеⲡ, Mani 2 A² ϣ]αϥт. ссас атресϫωрп; without е-: Is 29 21 B ө....ер поби, Ac 15 17 B ө....огоⲛϩ евоλ ποι.; Mt 5 45 B ө....ϣαι (S тре-) no Gk.

Mostly as pref to vb (Stern 461ff, Sdff 306, 345, Till 145, Mallon 255): Ge 30 36 S аϥтрегоге B аϥор-огⳓа фссωιт, Ps 16 15 S ⲣссптрепекеоог огωⲛϩ евоλ B ⳅеппхіпоре- (F птеλе-), Pro 7 25 S сспр-трепекрнт ріке, A сспте- B сспепоре-, Eccl 6 11 F ϣαγτλеⳅепⲡιхееі аϣеі, Jo 4 46 F пссе етагте-ссаг еλ ⲛλп, Mk 13 22 F епⲧⲟⲩⲥⲱ[ⲣⲉⲙ, 2 Cor 7 11 S пеіⲧⲣⲉⲧⲉⲧⲛⲗⲩⲡⲉⲓ τοῦτο τὸ λυπ. ὑμᾶς, El 42 A suffer not ⲁⲧⲟⲅⲉⲓ, BIF 22 107 F аϥтепссатос пωт, ShMIF 23 182 S огϣаⲭⲉⲛⲉ паі птреϥтωссⲧ ероⲕ, ShA 2 103 S петссⲛⳃⲁ птретегеірⲛⲛ ссⲧοп сс-ссос, ShC 42 189 S ссⲛ огⲛ ⳓеорⳓⲛ псатрепⲡⲉ еⳅогⲣ, v са (сспса- b); elliptic: ShC 73 131 S етатⲣⲉⲗааг ⳅе ⳓⲱϣⲧ ⲉⳅⲟⲩⲛ.

тро⳥ S vb caus, meaning uncertain, upset, transgress (?): J 75 59 ⳅιаө]нⲕⲓ патⲕⲓⲙ агω патⲧⲣⲟ⳥ (l ? троⲥ). Cf ib 65 14 ⳅ. патⲕ. патпараⲃⲁ ссос. V Ep 2 p 345 n 22.

трⲃⲏⲓⲛ[1], тир.[2], тервееⲓⲛ[3], -ⳓⲉⲉⲓⲛ[4], -ⲃⲁⲉⲓⲛ[5] S nn m, papyrus plant: Job 40 16[1] (var[2], B ⲃⲉⳅⲛⲡ), ib 8 11[5] (B do) βούτομον; P 44 20[3], 117[4] (from Job) طرفاء. Cf ерⲃⲏⲛ.

т(е)рⲃⲛⳓ SF v еⲃⲣⲏⳓе.

тωрⲕ v тωⳓⲣ.

тарⲕо SSᵃB, тер.SA², тарⲕⲁ S⁄F, таλ.F, тарⲕе- SB, тⲓⲗⲕⲁ-, теλⲕ- F, тарⲕо⳥ SB, т(е)р. S, терⲕⲁ⳥ S⁄ vb tr, make to swear, adjure, entreat (caus of ωрⲕ): Ge 50 25 SB, 1 Kg 14 27 S (cf 24 p апⲁϣ), Cant 2 7 F ϯ(т)ιλⲕⲁтнпⲟⲩ, ib 3 5 F теλⲕтнпⲟⲩ, R 1 1 52 S агтер. пιωⲥⲛϥ, ib 45 S агтерⲕⲟⲟⲩⲉ ὁρκίζειν acc, BMar 185 S аϥтарⲕⲟϥ прⲉⲡⲁⲡⲁϣ ὅρκοις ἀνακρίνειν; Ac 23 14 B refl (var & S ωрⲕ) ἀναθεμα-τίζειν; R 1 3 13 S аϥтарⲕе пссаⲕⲁⲣⲓⲟⲥ saying, AM 96 B sim, PGol 47 A² ϯт. ппеⲑⲣⲟⲛⲟⲥ ппⲡⲉ, PSBA 19 214 S ϯт. ссоⲕ ϯωрⲕ ссоⲕ, Griff Stu 163 F ϯтаλ. ссаⲕ, BM 604 F ϯтар. ссаⲕ, ib 312 60 S ⳅⲱⲥ еаⲕтарⲕⲟⲓ ϯпⲁϣⲁⳅе, TstAb 256 B пⲓⲁⲡⲁϣ етаϥ-

тарⲕоⲕ, MIE 2 385 B тарⲕⲟⲓ ⳅⲉⲛⳅⲁⲡⲡⲓϣϯ па-паϣ, ViK 9551 S еⲓпатарⲕⲟ сспапаϣ еⲭⲛтⲟⲩ-сарⳅ will lay oath on thee (cf PO 22 439), Kr 62 S will pay debt but еⲓϣапⲟⲩⲟϣϣ етарⲕⲟⲕ татарⲕⲟⲕ та-таⲁⲩ, PBu 32 S тарⲕⲟϥ сспрⳅⲃ сспаⲛⲓ ⳅе- let him swear as to, BP 4906 S пⳅтарⲕⲟⲟⲩ псер пеϥϣар (sc camel's), C 86 108 B ϯт. ссоⲕ...ⳅⲓⲛⲁ; adjure by person or thing: Mk 5 7 B(S ω.) ὁρ. acc acc, Ge 24 3 B ἐξορ. acc acc; RNC 43 S ϯт. ссоⲕ пⲡⲡⲉ διαμαρτύρεσθαι dat acc; Mt 26 63 SB ἐξορ. acc κατά; KroppR 8 9 S ϯт. ссоⲕ ⲕατⲁ ϯⳓⲛⲡⲉ, Gu 49 S ϯт. ссоⲕ сспⲉⲭ̄ⲥ̄ (var BM 312 59 ϯпⲁ-раⲕⲁⲗⲉⲓ), AM 295 B sim, BM 583 F еⲃтар. ссаⲕ сспⲡⲉ, Mor 19 50 S аϥтарⲕе ссссатоⲓ сспⲟⲩⳅаⲓ of king (var ib 18 43 еⲡ.), AZ 33 133 S еⲓт. ссоⲕ па-паϣ сспⲡⲟⳓ птⲛⲃⲉ, Mor 39 34 S⁄ аϥтерⲕаϥ сс-пепⲧαγⲥϯⲟⲩ ссоϥ = C 43 55 B ω. ероϥ; с е-: 1 Thes 5 27 B ϯт. ссωтⲛ епⲥ̄ⲧ̄ (S п-, ⳅп-) ἐνορ. acc acc, C 43 237 B ϯт. ссоⲕ епⲓⳃⲓⲥⲓ, KroppC F тιтаλⲕа ссаⲕ епеⲕλеп (? for п-).

трⲓλ F v трⲓр.

трⲓсс SB, ет. S nn m, trefoil, clover: P 44 83 S оровос · ораⳅ سيرم, трⲓфγⲗⲗоп · т. do (43 59 трγ-феλⲗⲓп حب قرط), K 196 B пⲓт. سيرم قرط; Bodl(P) d 32 S account ⳅает., Mich ostr 9683 S ⳓоогпе пет. λаϣⲓⲛ.

трωсс S nn m, hurricane: P 129[17] 74 there arose огⲛⲟⳓ пт. λаⲓλⲁⲯ, Mor 46 5 пет. сспⲡеⲕрωсс, BM Or 7561 48 еϣϣапⲛⲓⳓе пⳓⲓ пет. огⲕаⲕⲉⲡⲉ; with тнг: Lu 8 23 т. птнг (B пⲓϣϯ пⲑⲛⲟⲩ) λ. ἀνέμου, Ac 27 14 тнг пт.(B ө. еϥⳓⲟⲥⲓ, var өогрⲏⲥ)ἄν. τυφω-νικός.

тωрⲡ SAA²B(Ez)F, т(е)рⲡ- S, тарⲡ-, тλеⲡ- F, торⲡ⳥ S, та. AA²F, таλⲡ⳥ (?) F vb I intr, seize, rob (almost always = B ⳅωλеⲙ), cf טרף (IgR): Lev 19 13, Ps 21 13, Hos 5 14 SA, Ez 18 12 B ἁρπάζειν, Is 42 22 διαρ.; ShA 1 209 пет. агω етⲕⲓогⲉ, AP 27 A² пегт. II tr: Job 24 2, Nah 2 12 A, Mt 13 19 (F ϥⲓ), Jo 6 15 SA² тарⲉⲡϥ ἁρ., Ps 34 10, Is 5 17 SF, Mic 2 2 SA διαρ., Lu 8 29, Ac 27 15 συναρ., Mor 37 123 maiden етагтⲟⲣⲡⲥ ἁρπαγή; Cant 4 9 F атλⲉⲡ пеп[рⲏⲧ (S ϥⲓ) καρδιοῦν; PS 361 ϣαγϥⲓ пеⲯⲩⲭⲟⲟⲩⲉ етог-паϣ торⲡⲟⲩ, ShC 73 102 making excuse ⳅееⲡⲧ. препⲃⲛⳅе псⲱссатⲓⲕⲟⲡ, епт. ссоⲟⲩ ап аλλа еϥт. ссоп еⳅраⲓ ероⲟⲩ, Mani 1 A² еϣϣапⲟⲩⲟϣϣ т. таⲯⲩⲭⲛ, BHom 70 permit none етерⲡ λаⲁⲩ, Mor 53 58 God's mercies пет. ссоⲓ епеⳅогⲟ, ib 21 113 schoolboy пⲧⲉⲣⲉϥⲧ. пⲉⲥⳅаⲓ ⳅⲛⲟⲩⳓⲉⲡⲓ master, acquire, PMich 575 F]таλⲡⲟⲩ (or ? = next word).

With following preposition. с е-, carry off to:

Z 288 ⲉⲩⲧⲟⲣⲡϥ ⲉⲧⲉⲕⲣⲓⲥⲓⲥ ἀρ. εἰς, Mor 16 67 ⲡⲙⲁ
ⲛⲧⲁⲩⲧⲟⲣⲡϥ ⲉⲣⲟϥ, Pcod 38 ⲉϥⲧ. ⲙⲡⲁϩⲏⲧ ⲉⲩⲙⲡⲧⲣⲉϥ-
ϫⲓ ⲟⲩⲁ; ⲉⲣⲟⲩⲡ ⲉ-: Pcod 40 F unbelief ⲧⲁⲣⲡ ⲡⲉⲕ-
(ϩ)ⲏⲧ ⲉⲣ. ⲉ- (S ⲡⲁⲣⲁϫⲓⲥⲙⲁⲧⲓ⸲ⲉ ⲉⲧⲣⲉ-); ⲉϩⲣⲁⲓ ⲉ-:
BIF 13 115 ⲁⲩⲧ. ⲙⲡⲉϥⲛⲟⲩϩ ⲉϩ. ⲉⲧⲡⲉ = MG 25 206
B ϩⲱⲗⲉⲙ ⲉϩ. ⲉ-; c ⲙⲛ-: BG 54 fire, earth, water
ⲁⲩⲧ. ⲙⲙⲟⲟⲩ ⲙⲛⲡⲉϥⲧⲟⲩ ⲧⲏⲩ; c ⲛ- ethic dat:
Aeg 278 ⲉⲣϣⲁⲛ- ... ⲧ. ⲛⲁϥ ⲙⲡⲁⲍⲓⲱⲙⲁ ἀρ. ἑαυτῷ,
Ps 43 10 διαρ. ἑαυ.; BM 232 1 ⲛⲥⲉⲧⲣⲧⲏⲩⲧⲛ ⲡⲁⲩ,
Mor 28 249 schoolboy ⲧ. ⲡⲁϥ ⲛⲡⲙⲁⲑⲏⲙⲁ ϩⲛⲟⲩⲅⲁ-
ⲥⲁⲓ; c ⲛⲧⲛ-, seize from: Deu 28 31 (B ⲱⲗⲓ) ἀρ.
ἀπό; R 1 4 70 ἐξιστάναι gen; PS 355 ⲉⲩⲧ. ⲙⲡⲟⲩⲟⲉⲓⲛ ⲛⲧⲟⲟⲧⲟⲩ, Mani 1 A² found none pitiful ⲁ-
ⲧⲣⲉϥⲧ. ⲛⲧⲟⲟⲧⲟⲩ ⲙⲡⲁⲧⲛⲁⲃⲉ; c ϩⲓ-, from off: Mic
3 2 (A ϩⲓⲭⲛ-, B ϩ. ⲉⲃⲟⲗ ⲛ-) ἀρ. ἀπό, Pro 6 25 SA(B
ϩ. ϫⲉⲛ-) ⲥⲩⲛⲁⲣ. ἀπό; BMis 27 ⲁⲩⲧ. ⲙⲡⲣⲣⲟ
ϩ. ⲡⲉϥⲑⲣⲟⲛⲟⲥ; c ϩⲓⲭⲛ-: BMis 27 ⲁⲩⲧ. ⲙⲡⲣⲣⲟ
ϩ. ⲡⲉϥⲑⲣⲟⲛⲟⲥ; c ϩⲛ-, from: Z 261 ⲁϥⲧⲟⲣⲡϥ
ϩⲛⲧⲉⲩⲙⲛⲧⲉ; ⲉⲃⲟⲗ ϩⲛ-: Job 24 9 ἀρ. ἀπό, Jo 10 28
SAA² ἀρ. ἐκ; Z 350 ⲉϥϣⲁⲛⲧⲣⲡ ⲟⲩⲕⲟⲩⲓ ⲉⲃ. ϩⲙⲡ-
ϩⲓⲛⲏⲃ.

—— nn m SAB(Ez, elsewhere ϩ.), plunder: Si 16
14, Ez 19 3(B ϩ.) ἅρπαγμα, Lu 11 39 ἁρπαγή, Phil 2 6
ἁρπαγμός, Nu 14 31, Ez 23 46 SB διαρπαγή; ShC
73 57 ⲟⲩⲭⲓⲟⲩⲉ ⲙⲡⲟⲩⲧ., El 78 A.
ⲙⲁⲓⲧ. S, plunder-loving: Mor 43 244 ⲙⲁⲓⲥϩⲓⲙⲉ
ⲉⲓⲉ ⲙ.
ⲣⲉϥⲧ. S, plunderer: Ge 49 27 (B ⲣⲉϥϩ.), Mt 7 15
(B do) ἅρπαξ; ShC 42 193 greedy or ⲣ., BHom 110
ϩⲁⲗⲏⲧ ⲡⲣ., Mor 40 37 robbers ⲛⲣ. = MG 25 264 B
do, Mor 36 73 ⲡϩⲁⲗⲏⲧ ⲡⲣⲉϥⲧⲣⲡ ⲙⲁⲥ; ⲙⲛⲧⲣⲉϥⲧ.,
robbery: BHom 8 ἁρπαγή; PS 257 ⲁⲡⲟⲧⲁⲥⲥⲉ ⲛⲡⲙ.
ϭⲓⲛⲧ. S, seizing: Leyd 352 ⲧϭ. ⲛⲡⲉⲩϩⲩⲡⲁⲣ-
ⲭⲟⲛⲧⲁ.

ⲧⲱⲣⲡ S, ⲑ. B, ⲧⲱⲗⲡ F, ⲑⲉⲣⲡ- B, ⲧⲟⲣⲡⲟⲩ, ⲧⲟⲣⲡ†,
ⲧⲁ.† S vb intr, sew, stitch, cf חֵפֶר (Dévaud): Eccl 3 7
S ῥάπτειν, Ex 38 23 B ⲓⲉⲃ ⲡⲱ. ῥαφιδευτός; v also
MG below; qual: Ez 16 16 ⲧ. ⲉⲡⲉⲅⲉⲣⲏⲩ (B ⲛ-
ⲡⲟⲩⲉⲣ.) ῥαπτός, Jo 19 23 neg (var ⲧⲁ., A² ϫⲁⲗⲉϭ, B
ⲁⲧⲟ.) ἄραφος; Racc Lombroso 283 (= TurM tab
xxii 1) sent ϩⲛⲟⲩⲣⲁⲁⲣ ⲉⲥⲧ.; tr: Ge 3 7 B ⲣ́., Mk
2 21 c e- SB(var ϩⲓⲟⲩⲓ) ἐπιρρ. ἐπί, Ez 13 18 B ⲥⲩⲛⲣ.,
Lu 5 36 c e- S(B ϩ.) ἐπιβάλλειν ἐπί; ShIF 153 S
ϩⲉⲛⲣⲟⲓⲧⲉ...ⲉⲩⲧ. ⲛⲣⲉⲛⲧⲟⲉⲓⲥ ⲉⲣⲟⲩⲡ ⲉⲣⲟⲟⲩ, BIF 13
101 S said ⲉⲣⲉⲡⲛⲉⲉⲃ ⲧ. ⲙⲙⲟⲥ = MG 25 282 B ⲑ.
ⲉⲣⲟϥ, P 132¹ 16 S torn garments ⲧⲟⲣⲡⲟⲩ ⲡⲣⲏⲕⲓⲥ
(ἀκίς)ⲡϣⲉⲃⲉⲛⲡⲉ(cf Amélineau Contes 2 109); v also
last word PMich 575.
ⲁⲧⲧ. S(ViK 9779), ⲁⲧⲟ. B, unsewn, v Jo above.
ⲙⲁ ⲡⲱ.B, darning needle: Mt 19 24(S ϩⲁⲙⲛⲧⲱⲡ,
F PMich 538 ⲙⲉϩⲧ.) ῥαφίς.
ⲙⲉϩⲧⲱⲗⲡ v last, also ⲧⲱⲡ stitch.
ⲛⲕⲁ ⲡⲧ. S, sewing thing, needle: WTh 197 caused
stab his fingernails ⲛϩⲉⲛⲡⲓ. ⲡⲧ.

ⲣⲉϥⲧ. SB, sewers, tailors: Ex 27 16 B ῥαφιδευτής;
P 131³ 53 S apostles were poor, ⲟⲩⲟϩⲉ, ⲗⲁⲧⲟⲙⲟⲥ,
ⲥⲁ ⲡⲟⲩⲟⲟⲧⲉ, ⲣ., ⲃⲁⲕϣⲁⲁⲣ.
ⲑⲣⲁⲡⲥ, ⲧⲣ. B nn f (زرد), awl, spike: Ex 21 6 ⲧ.
(S ⲟⲩⲱⲧϥ), Deu 15 17 ⲧ. (var ⲑ., S ⲛⲕⲁ ⲡⲟⲩ.) ὀπήτιον مشقب; K 132 shoemaker's tool ϯⲑ. ʼⲟ, شفا,
WHatch 762 Arianus wounds hand with ϯⲑ. (PO
1 142 ʼⲑ).

ⲧⲣⲁⲡ F nn, among metal utensils: CMSS 76.
Cf ? ⲑⲣⲁⲡⲥ.

ⲧⲣⲟⲡ S(Sh) nn, blow(?): A 1 44 ϯ ⲛⲟⲩⲧ. ⲛ ⲟⲩϣⲥ
ⲛϭⲉⲣⲱⲃ, BMOr 8810 406 who shall raise hand ϩⲛ-
ⲟⲩϭⲉⲣⲱⲃ ⲏ ϩⲛⲟⲩⲧ., Wess 18 137, A 2 84 sim, ViK
9317 104 ⲡⲗⲓⲥⲉ ⲙⲡⲉⲛⲥⲱⲣ ⲡⲉⲧϩⲛⲡⲉⲛϭⲓⲝ ⲉϥϯ ⲧ.
ⲉⲃⲟⲗ ϩⲛⲡⲁⲕⲧⲓⲛ ⲡⲧⲉϥⲙⲛⲧⲡⲉ.

ⲧⲣⲟⲡⲣⲉⲡ S nn, meaning unknown: LCyp 26
ⲟⲩϩⲣⲉ ⲉⲩⲟⲩⲱⲙ ⲙⲙⲟⲥ ϩⲛⲟⲩⲧ. θοίνη ἄτακτος =
Mor 18 174]ϩⲣⲉ ⲉⲩⲟⲩⲱ[ⲙ ⲙⲟⲥ] ϩⲛⲟⲩⲡ[.....]ⲡⲏ.

ⲧⲉⲣⲡⲟⲥⲉ (once), -ⲉⲛ S nn f, baked brick (v ⲡⲓⲥⲉ):
Z 301 ⲧⲱⲱⲃⲉ ⲡⲟⲙⲉ πλίνθος ὠμή opp ⲧⲧⲉⲣⲡⲟⲥⲉ ⲡ.
ὀπτή, ST 124 builder's account]ⲧⲉⲣⲡⲟⲥⲉⲛ φ(οραί)
η, BM 1112 ⲡⲉⲓϣⲕⲟⲩⲗ ⲛⲧⲉⲣⲡⲟⲥⲛ, PLond 4 516
ϣⲟⲙ[ⲛⲧ ⲛϣ]ⲟ ⲛⲧⲉⲣⲡⲟⲥⲉⲛ. V AZ 64 124. In
place-name ⲡⲙⲁ ⲙⲡⲉⲥⲧⲉⲣⲡⲟⲥⲉⲛ the brick-kiln (sic
MS Miss 4 535, parallels om, cf TT 93 n, but improbable).

ⲧⲣⲓⲣ SA, ⲑ. B, ⲧⲣⲓⲗ, ⲧⲗ. F nn f, oven: Ge 15 17
SB, Lev 26 26 SBF(BM 1221) ⲧⲣ., Lam 5 10 SBF
ⲧⲗ., Mal 4 1 S(Ep 56)AB κλίβανος; ShC 73 137 S
cooked ϩⲓⲡⲉϫⲗⲟϥ ⲉⲓⲧⲉ ϩⲓⲧⲉⲧ. (cf ib ⲁϣ), Miss 4 637
S ⲡⲉⲧ. of bakers = C 41 20 B ϭⲣⲱⲡ, Aeg 13 S ⲟⲩⲧ.
ⲡⲕⲱϩⲧ = ib B ϩⲣⲱ, BM 1186 S ⲧⲱⲕ ⲡⲉⲧ., C 43 70 B
ⲑⲱⲕ ⲉⲟϩⲉ., ib 101 B martyr cast into ⲟⲩⲑ., MIF 9
46 S ⲧ. ⲡⲣⲟⲙⲡⲧ, JAOS 48 154 S(to baker) come ⲡ-
ⲧⲛⲃⲱⲕ (ⲧ)ⲧ. ⲉⲣⲟⲩⲡ, AZ 23 111 S ⲟⲩⲁⲡⲟⲧ...ⲧⲟⲙⲥⲉϥ
ϩⲛⲧⲉⲧ.; Gu 60 S ⲧⲉⲧ....ⲡⲉⲥⲣⲱϥ; BM 1069 S ⲡⲉⲧ.
same?.

ⲧⲣⲣⲉ, ⲧⲣⲉⲓⲱⲟⲩ† S, ⲧⲣⲓ.† A² vb intr, be afraid:
Mk 10 32†(B ⲉϩ ϩⲟϯ) φοβεῖσθαι; ShC 42 79 if fox
bark ⲉⲣⲉⲡⲙⲟⲩⲓ ⲧ., Ryl 68 262 sim, Mani 1 A² ϥⲧ.†
ϩⲙⲡⲉϥϩⲣⲁⲩ ϭⲟⲓ ⲛϩⲣⲧⲉ; ⲧ. ϩⲏⲧϥ ⲛ-: Is 57 11
(var ⲣ ϩⲟⲧⲉ, B ϭⲱⲧⲡ), ShA 1 395 ⲉϥⲛⲁⲟⲩⲱⲱⲙⲉ
ⲛϩⲧ. ϩⲏⲧⲥ ⲛ- (cf ? ⲧⲉⲣ-). V Rec 37 20.

ⲧⲱⲣⲧ S(Theban)A²(once) nn m (hierogl ṯꜣrd),
staircase: J 26 9 ⲡⲥⲓⲡⲡⲟⲥⲓⲟⲛ ⲉⲧϩⲓⲡⲧ. ⲉⲧⲛⲡⲓⲧⲛ ⲡⲧⲉϩ-
ⲉϩⲣⲁ, ib 35 48 ⲡⲧⲉⲣⲃⲱⲕ ⲡⲧ. ϩⲓⲣⲟⲩⲡ ⲙⲡⲣⲟ ⲡⲧⲉⲭⲏⲣⲉ
ϣⲁⲁⲣⲁⲧⲏⲩ, ib 42 23 ⲡⲧ. ⲉϩⲣⲁⲓ, ib 35 27 ⲧⲣⲓ ⲉⲥϩⲁⲡⲧ.,
JSch 7 19 ⲧⲣⲓ ⲉⲧⲙⲡⲉⲥⲛⲧ ϩⲓⲡⲧ., CO 149 ⲣⲟ ⲡⲁⲩⲑⲉⲛⲧⲏⲥ (cf J 35 33 ⲣⲟ ⲙⲃⲁⲗ), ⲃⲁⲓⲙⲟⲟⲩ, ⲧ. ϣⲱⲡⲉ ⲛⲕⲟⲓⲛⲟⲛ, J 24 127 sim, ST 109 ⲡⲧⲁⲥⲙ ⲡⲁⲧ.

омокλγрос; v also кωλϫ (каλаϫт.); Mani 1 A²
аꙑн птеꙑаϩе ϩнпіапет. етоγа[ꙉе (cf ?(ϩ)аꙑ-).

тωртр, тωтр (Mor 31) S, -тер B, тωλтеλ F nn
m, *ladder, step, stair, degree* of sundial : 1 Tim 3
13 B(S ϣі), Z 321 S he climbed ϥіхноγт. βαθμός,
Ex 20 26 SB ἀναβαθμίς, Is 38 8 SB, Ac 21 35 SB
-μός, Cant 3 10 S ἐπίβασις ; Ez 40 22 SB κλιμακτήρ;
P 44 31 S пт. птеϭλооϭе درج السلم ; ShHT E 343 S
building ϩепт. еꙉωк еϩраі етпе ϩіωογ, BMOr
6201 A S пт. пкоγ ϩраі етϫепепωр, BMis 79 S еі
епеснт ꙑпт. (var Mor 33 14 ϩꙑпт.), AM 191 B ер
саϭрні ꙑпіт., C 43 47 B fixed on ground ꙑϥрнϯ
поγт. = Mor 39 24 F Mor 41 318 S пет. of St Mark
at Alexandria, ib 31 234 S петωтр(bis) of sanctuary,
TEuch 1 7 B sim. аптωтер B nn m, *threshold* :
BM 920 265 піа. اسكفة معقة (v Kremer *Beitr*, in K
157 ' = кері, in P 55 12 ' = кефаλіс), BMOr
8775 141, Montp 169 do.

тортр S, -тер B, тртр-, тртωр-, тртωр⁄ S, тер.
SB, тртωр† S vb tr, *thrust in, pierce* : Ps 37 2 S(B
тωтс), MG 17 319 S thorns т. ꙑꙑооγ ἐμπηγνύναι;
Eccl 12 11† S φυτεύειν ; Mor 18 182 S sword аϥтер-
тωрϭ ꙑꙑін ꙑꙑоϥ περιεπαίρειν (*Acta SS* Sept vii
223); Tri 596 S nails in wood еγт.† مضروب, ShC
73 123 S thorn т. птоϭернте, R 2 1 63 S nail ϣаϥт-
тртр ϩрнт, Mus 42 235 S псепатртр соте ап ꙑꙑ
ꙑо ; c е- S : Jud 5 26 (Gk diff), Leyd 287 nails
т.† епеϥсωꙑа, Mor 43 157 еγтртωр еіꙉт епеϥ-
ϭіх ; еϩоγп е- intr : 2 Kg 2 16 ἐμπ. εἰς ; Mor 21 122
prickly plants т. еϩ. епеϥсωꙑа ; c ϩп-, ϫеп- :
Jud 4 21 S πηγν. ἐν, 1 Kg 26 7† S ἐμπ. εἰς ; Va 59 8
B sharp reeds аϥϩроγтертωроγ ϫеппеϥсωꙑа,
Mor 40 31 S sim (var ib 39 42 таϫоγ) = C 43 60 B
ϭωоγ, C 43 229 B sim еϫоγп ϫеп- ; intr : C 43 175
B nails аγт. ϫепϥꙑоγт ꙑпіоϩнꙑеꙑоп.

тертωрі B v тωре *hand* (ϩ т.).

троγан S, -еп Sᵃ nn, *cheese*(?) : ShC 73 119
сооγϭе, ϩаλωꙑ, т., ерωте, Ep 264 present of]тр-
оγеп ꙑпϩепоеік ꙑпϩ[еп-. Cf ? τυρός(όν).

ѳероγωϭе S nn, *metal*(?) melted with bronze
& silver in alchem recipe : AZ 23 111. Coptic ?

тωрϣ SA, ѳ. B vb intr, *be red* : Mun 134 S to
Peter аксеϣ пептаϥтаꙑіок актωрϣ (l тω.) ꙑпе-
птаϥϯ еооγ [па]к didst blush for Him, or ? make
blush ; as adj : Nu 19 2 S то. (P 44 107 терϣ, l
тω., B ѳрωϣреϣ) πυρρός ; Joel 2 25 A ϩϩ т. (S
пнрϣ, B етнⲓϣⲓ) ἐρυσίβη ; K 266 B піω. انش, اشقر انش ;
KroppM 15 S оγсаіеⲓⲛ пт. пкаꙑꙉаλ. V троϣ-
реϣ.

троϣ S, тορϣ† SB, тарϣ† S⁄F vb intr, as last : 1
Kg 17 42† B(16 12 ѳрωϣ prob l тορϣ, S о ꙑꙑнрϣ)

πυρράκης, Z 331 S еγт.† πυροειδής ; PChass 1 30 S
bring it forth from fire ϥпат., JTS 10 398 S каλι-
кіоп еγт.†, AZ 23 114 S ϩосꙑ еγт.†, PGen S стγ-
раϩ еϥт.†, BKU 1 21 ro S⁄ хнϭе еϥт.†, PMich 4946
F]коγпріа (cf ? коγпр) етт.†

In names : птнрϣ(ST50), Πταρϣβαλ(Preisigke).
троϣр(е)ϣ S, ѳ. B, треϣреϣ F, тр(е)ϣрωϣ†,
-раϣ† S, -раϣт† A, ѳреϣрωϣ†, т.†(once)B, тλеϣ-
λаϣт† F vb intr, as last : Nu 19 2 † B(S тωрϣ),
Cant 5 10† S(var ꙑорϣ)F, Ap 12 3† S(B аоγап п-
хрωꙑ), Cl 8 3† A πυρρός, Ge 25 25† B πυρράκης,
Lev 13 19† S(var -раϣ, B ϯ ѳ.), R 1 3 60 S cheeks
т.† πυρρίζειν, P 131² 89† S(Epiph *De Gem*) jacynth
ὑπόπυρ.; Is 63 2 SB ἐρυθρός, Sa 13 14 S ἐρυθαίνειν ;
ib 11 7† S αἵματι λυθρώδης ; BMar 120 S еϥт.† ϩꙑпеϥϣω ξανθός ; Job 32 22† S(B as Gk) χρυσαυγεῖν ;
Lam 5 10 BF(S кꙑоꙑ)πελιοῦσθαι ; C 89 95 B ϩωпн
...ест.† = Va ar 172 56 اشقر, MG 17 469 بهي ; ShC
73 202 S пеϥϩо...т.†, BMis 237 S еϥт.† ϩꙑпеϥаγ-
еⲓⲛ еϥо ꙑꙑерϣ ϩꙑпеϥϣω, C 43 27 B body ѳ.† like·
rose (cf ib 81 B sim оі пкоккос), R 2 1 71 S finger
nails еγт.† аγω оⲛ еγоγоꙉϣ, DeV 2 146 B cave
еϥо.† пеλеϥаптіоп ϩіϩопатіоп (τοπάζιον); as
nn, *redness* : Is 63 1 SB ἐρύθημα ; Mt 16 3 πυρρά-
ζειν, Lev 13 19 B v above πυρρίζ.; C 86 206 B пѳорϣ-
реϣ (sic) ꙑпеϥсωꙑа, Dif 2 81 B пѳреϣрωϣ (sic
l) пте пеϥϩꙉωс حمرت (cf Is 63 1). Cf بشروش
(? from пт(р)ϣ.) *flamingo* in Nile Delta.

тϣре(sic)S vb intr, *grow red*(?): Hall 148(v KKS
520) прн ꙑпрт. пооϩ ꙑпрϣа.

тарϣо, -ϣо⁄, тарϣноγт† B vb tr, *increase,
multiply* : Job 19 3†(P 104 68, var арϣнт, S ϩіхн-)
عنف ἐπικεῖσθαι dat ; K 233 еγт. اكثروا, اشرهوا =P 54
169 ⁄, Va 61 91 lender ϣаϥт. ϯꙑнсі=P 131³ 81 S
таϣо, Cat 150 еϥϣаптарϣоγ ϫеппіоγϩсарϩі
beyond measure, Va 57 119 аϥт. ꙑпсωтꙑ of ears
with wondrous words (Mt 3 11). Should ? be
таϣо, or cf тϩрϣо.

терωϩт A v рωϣе.

тωрϭ S (sic) vb tr, meaning unknown, *smear,
anoint*(?): PChass 1 19 alchem recipe ѳпооγ т. п-
ϩат аϩꙑі ꙑꙑоϥ, it will become white. Cf ib 2 2
ѳпооγ λарωϥ (l λаλ.) аϩꙑі ꙑꙑоϥ, 2 33 ѳп]ооγ
тωрϭ ппепіпе аϩ. ꙑ.

тωрϩ, -ϩр (nn), -ϩр⁄, торϩ†, та.†, таϩр† S vb, *be
keen, alert, sober, upright* : qual Sa 7 22, 8 11 ὀξύς ;
1 Tim 3 2(B рнс)νηφάλιος ; P 44 52 атпос· еϥт. مفيق,
ib 92 ϥт.· ϩорк ', متثقف (sic 43 78), ib 121 перепа-
λотоп етꙑꙑаγ т. مفيق ; ShMIF 23 162 етт. аγω
етрокϩ орр ϣтртωр аγω о патріоп, ShViK 9757
194 grieving & sad еϥт. псꙑот(sic l)піꙑ епаꙑоγϥ,

BM 981 say ϧⲛⲟⲩϧⲏⲧ ⲉϥⲧⲁⲣϧ ϫⲉ-, J 104 2 ⲟⲩⲡⲟⲩⲥ
ⲉϧⲧ., Ming 334 ⲉⲕⲃⲏⲗ ⲉⲃⲟⲗ ϧⲙⲡⲉⲕϩⲏⲧ ⲟⲣⲣ ⲉⲕⲧ.,
Mor 37 155 horse ⲉϥⲧⲁⲣⲣ ⲉⲁⲩ(ⲧ)ⲥⲁⲃⲟϥ ⲉⲡⲱⲧ;   tr:
CA 103 if they attain to Christ's humility ⲛⲥⲉⲧ. ⲙ-
ⲙⲟⲟⲩ ⲉⲡⲉϩⲟⲩⲟ, Kr 228 11 if thou (f) need aught
ⲧⲁⲧⲱϧⲣⲉϥ ⲡⲉ;   as nn: Z 624 n withstanding enmity ϧⲛⲟⲩⲧⲱϧⲣ μετὰ νήψεως.

ⲧⲣⲁϧ S, ⲧⲁⲣⲁϧ SB nn, meaning uncertain, *confusion* (?): Si 4 32 S ⲉⲕⲉⲧ. (corrupt?, in P 44 118
ⲟ ⲡⲁⲧⲁⲣⲁϧ = 43 125 ⲁⲧⲣⲁϧ قاس)B ⲟⲓ ⲛⲧ. 'ϳ φαντα-
σιοκοπεῖν *evertens et opprimens*: P 131 1 44 B Satan
attempting to seduce angels ⲉϥϣ ⲡⲧⲉⲣⲧⲉⲓϧ ⲉϥϯ ⲧ.
ⲡⲧⲗⲏⲧⲉ ⲛⲛⲁⲅⲅⲉⲗⲟⲥ.

ⲧⲣⲁϧⲣⲉϧ S vb, meaning unknown: CO 469
men compared to evil beasts & called ⲛⲉⲣⲱⲙⲉ ⲛⲧ.
Cf ? last word.

ⲧⲉⲣϧⲏⲧ B *v* ⲧⲉⲣ-.

ⲧⲣⲟϭ, ⲧⲱⲣϭ *v* ⲧⲱϭⲣ.

ⲧⲉⲣϭⲓϫ S nn m, meaning uncertain, *bench* or
sim: ViK 9458 56 ⲛⲕⲟⲩⲓ ⲛⲧ. ⲉⲓⲣⲙⲟⲟⲥ ϩⲓϫⲱϥ ⲉⲓⲉⲓⲣⲉ
ⲙⲡⲁⲕⲟⲩⲓ ⲛⲣⲱⲃ ⲛϭⲓϫ. *Cf* ? ⲧ- in ⲧⲣⲃⲏⲉⲓⲙ, ⲧⲉⲣⲃⲏϭ,
ⲧⲉⲣⲡⲟⲥⲉ, ⲧⲟⲧⲉ (Dévaud).

ⲧⲁⲥ- *v* ⲧⲱⲥ.

ⲧⲥ S adj (?) abbreviated, meaning unknown: Ep
106 ⲛⲃⲉⲓ ⲉϧⲣⲁⲓ ⲛⲛⲉⲕϭⲓϫ ⲧⲥ ⲉⲧϣⲏⲡ, *ib* ⲉⲧⲏⲕⲩ ⲉϧⲣⲁⲓ
ⲛⲛϭⲓϫ ⲧⲥ ⲉⲧϩⲁⲣⲟⲧⲉ, *ib* ⲛ]ϭⲓϫ ⲧⲥ ⲛⲛⲡⲉ ⲉⲧⲱⲡ,
ST 388 ⲡⲉⲛⲥⲟⲡ ⲧⲥ (or name?). *Cf* ? J 85 38 ⲗⲁϭⲉ
ⲡⲣⲱⲙⲉ ⲡⲓⲙ ⲛⲧⲉⲥ ⲡϫⲛⲁⲗⲉ. In ShEp 56 36 ⲧⲉⲕⲟⲩ-
ⲙⲗⲏⲛ ⲧⲥ = ViK 9068 ⲧⲏⲣⲥ.

ⲧⲓⲥ- F vb tr, *give, pay, send* (?): BM 633 ⲁⲓⲧⲓⲥ ·`·
ⲥⲡ: ⲥⲕⲉⲅⲉⲓ ⲛⲏⲣⲡ ⲉⲛ(ⲁ)ⲓⲁⲕⲟⲩ.

ⲧⲟ(ⲉ)ⲓⲥ, -ⲥⲉ S, ⲧⲁⲉⲓⲥ S/A, ⲧⲱⲓⲥ, -ⲥⲓ B nn f, *piece,
rag* of cloth, linen: EstC 27 S, Is 64 6 S(B ⲫⲉⲗϫⲓ),
Mt 9 16 SB ῥάκος, MG 25 376 B ⲟⲩⲗⲛⲏϣ ⲛⲧⲱⲓⲥⲓ
παλαιά ῥ., Pro 23 21 SA διερρηγμένα κ. ῥακώδη; Sa
7 4 S, Ez 16 4 S(*sic* l)B σπάργανον, Lu 2 7 S ⲥⲱⲱⲗⲉ
ⲛⲣⲉⲛⲧ. B ⲕⲟⲩⲗⲱⲗ ⲛϩ. σπαργανοῦν; *ib* 5 36 SB ἐπίβλημα; Wess 11 165 S old clothes ⲉⲩϧⲛⲏⲧ. πολύρ-
ραφος; ShZ 594 S naught ϣⲁϩⲣⲁⲓ ⲉⲟⲩⲧ. or 5th of
obole, ShIF 153 S garments ⲉⲩⲧⲱⲣⲡ ⲛϧⲉⲛⲧ. ⲉϧⲣⲁⲓ
ⲉⲣⲟⲟⲩ, ShA 2 329 S ⲉⲥϣⲟⲟⲡ ϧⲛⲏⲧ. *swaddling-clothes*,
Mor 51 38 S find ⲧ. ⲉⲡⲉⲧⲉⲛⲡⲗⲅⲩⲏ, BIF 14 152 S ⲧ.
bound on his face like ⲟⲩⲧ. ⲙⲡⲁϩⲣⲉ, PMéd 259 S
ⲧ. ⲛϣⲓⲗ upon wound, Rec 6 172 B ⲟⲩⲧⲱⲓⲥⲓ, C 86 205
B ⲛⲓⲧⲱⲓⲥⲓ ⲛϧⲱⲓ, MG 25 132 B if robe torn ϣⲁϥϯ ⲧ.
ⲛⲁⲥ, ShIF 154 S ⲛⲕⲉⲥⲗⲡⲉ...ⲉⲧϫⲓ ⲧ., ViK 9182 S
ⲟⲩϣⲧⲏⲛ ⲉⲥⲗⲏϧ ⲛⲧ.;   used as *bag, purse*: Miss
4 722 S ⲧⲕⲟⲩⲓ ⲛⲧ. wherein money was, Va 134 3 S
(Vita Sin) ⲟⲩⲧ. ⲛⲡⲟⲩⲃ = C 41 28 B = Miss 4 360

صرّ ذهب, AZ 23 108 S ⲧⲁⲁϥ ⲉⲩⲧ. ⲉⲥⲕⲟⲗϧ (*v* ⲕⲱⲗϧ
I), Bodl(P) a 2 56 S ⲡⲉϩⲙⲟⲩ ϧⲛⲟⲩⲧⲟⲓⲥⲉ, Z 628 S tie
it ⲛⲟⲩⲧ. ⲛϧⲣⲟⲟⲥ, MR 5 37 S/ ⲧⲁⲁⲩ ⲉⲩⲧ. & seal them,
Cai 42573 2 S/ ⲛⲁϧⲧϥ ⲉϧⲣⲟⲩⲛ ⲉⲩⲧ. ⲛϩⲱⲣⲱ;   ⲡⲗϭⲉ,
ⲫⲉⲗϫⲓ ⲛⲧ., *bit of rag v* ⲡⲗϭⲉ, adding MG 25 251 B
ⲟⲩⲫ. ⲛⲧ. *bound about loins*, RChamp 541 S ⲟⲩⲧ.
ⲛⲛ. *on dunghill*, sim Wess 15 2 S ⲗⲁⲕⲙ ⲛⲧ., Z 351
S ⲗⲁϩⲉ ⲛⲧ.

ⲧⲱⲥ SB, ⲧⲉⲥ- S, ⲧⲟⲥ- B, ⲧⲟⲥⲟ SB, ⲧⲁⲥ⳽ S/, ⲧⲏⲥ†,
ⲧⲉⲥ† SB, p c (?) ⲧⲁⲥ- S vb I intr, *become, be hard,
stiff, dry*: HL 116 B flesh ⲧ. ⲙⲫⲣⲏϯ ⲛⲟⲩⲱⲛⲉ πηγνύναι; Mk 9 18 S(B ϣⲟⲟⲩⲓ) ξηραίνειν; 1 Kg 25 37
S gloss on ὡς λίθος γίνεσθαι; ShA 2 253 S devil ⲧ.
ϧⲓⲧⲙⲡⲉⲥϥⲟⲥ, ShRE 10 164 S dying dragon ⲛϥⲧ. &
fell, C 41 44 B hands ⲧ. ⲁⲩϣⲱⲟⲩⲓ, *ib* 43 212 B ⲛⲓⲁ-
ϧⲟⲧ ... ⲁϥⲧ. & petrified;   qual: Lev 26 16 B(S
diff) σφακελίζειν; Mor 51 41 S ⲉⲧⲧ. *stubborn* like
wood, PO 11 345 B ⲉϥⲧ. *like corpse*, LMis 468 S
ⲟⲩⲗⲟⲥϭⲏ ⲉⲥⲧⲉⲥ ⲡⲧⲟⲟⲧⲩ, Mor 52 15 S anthrax ⲟⲩⲱⲡⲉ ⲉϥⲧ., Bodl(P) a 2 36 S ⲃⲁⲣⲱⲧ...ⲟⲩⲥⲱⲙⲁ ⲉⲩⲧ.,
PChass 1 1 S ⲟⲩϩⲁⲧ ⲉⲩⲧ. ⲉϥⲕⲏⲙ (cf *ib* 19 ϥⲛⲁⲟⲩⲃⲁϣ ⲛϥⲗⲟⲕⲗⲉⲕ);   *be firm, implanted, fixed*: C 43
11 B martyr ⲧ. ⲉⲡⲓⲥⲅⲩⲛⲅⲉⲗⲓⲟⲛ.

II tr, *fix*: EW 173 B ⲁⲩⲧⲟⲥ ⲓϥⲧ ⲉϯⲥⲁⲣϩ, C 86
283 B ⲉⲧ. (var ⲧⲱⲧⲥ) ⲛⲣⲁⲡⲓϥⲧ ⲉⲃⲟⲩⲛ ⲉⲣⲟϥ = Mun
38 S ⲱϥⲧ ⲉϧ. ⲉ-, *ib* 153 B ⲛⲥⲉⲧⲟⲥ ⲡⲉϥⲥⲱⲙⲁ ⲛⲓϥⲧ
ⲉⲃⲟⲩⲛ ⲉⲛⲓϣⲉ, Va 59 10 B bade ⲉⲫⲣⲟⲩⲧⲟⲥⲩ ⲛⲛⲉϥϭⲓϫ; Lu 6 30 S ⲛⲛⲧⲉⲥ ⲡⲉⲧϥⲓ (varr ⲧⲙⲙⲉⲥⲧⲉ-, BM
Or 7561 111 ⲧⲙⲧ[ⲉⲥ-, B ϣⲓϯ neg) ἀπαιτεῖν (same?).

—— ⲉⲃⲟⲗ SB, *stretch out, stiffen*: DeV 2 255 B
corpse ⲧ. ⲉⲃ. *like stone* = Mor 41 9 S ⲧ.†, BMis 239 S
bade ⲧⲟⲥϥ ⲉⲃ. ⲉϥⲧⲟⲉ ⲛϣⲙⲟⲩⲓ (varr Mor 29 11 ⲧⲁⲥϥ,
ib 30 12 ϫⲁⲗⲉⲕϥ ⲉⲃ.), Mor 31 24 S sim ⲛⲣⲉⲛϣⲙⲟⲩⲣ.

—— ⲉⲡϣⲱⲓ B, *stand up stiffly*: BSM 110 hair
ⲧⲉⲥ ⲉⲡ. = Mor 22 110 S ⲛⲟⲣⲥ ⲉϧⲣⲁⲓ.

ⲁⲧⲧ. S, *unstiff, limp*: RChamp 541 bind fast flesh
(*sc* penis) of NN ⲛⲛⲁ(ⲧ)ⲧⲱϧⲣⲓ ⲉⲡⲁ(ⲧ)ⲧ. ⲉⲡⲁ(ⲧ)ϯ
ⲥⲡⲉⲣⲙⲁ (*l* -ⲙⲁ), BM 1103 18 ⲡⲧⲉⲛⲉⲙⲁ ⲉⲡⲁⲡⲟⲩϥ
...ⲡⲁⲧⲥⲱ ⲛⲁⲧⲧ. (obscure).

ⲙⲉⲧⲧⲱⲥⲓ B, *dryness*: K 58 ϯⲙ. يبوسة (opp ϯⲙⲉⲧ-
ⲗⲏⲕ), Tri 531 S ⲙⲛⲧⲱⲥⲛ أر same?

ⲧⲁⲥ- S p c, *who hardens* (if same): BAp 161 ⲙⲡⲣⲣ
ⲧ.ⲃⲁⲗ ⲉϧⲣⲡ ⲉⲑⲓⲕⲱⲡ ⲙⲛⲡⲉ متعظم العين ك' القديس
118 أنبا باخوميوس (*v* TT 174) *proud-eyed*;   ⲙⲛⲧⲧ.-
ⲃⲁⲗ, *hardening* (?) *of eyes, impudence*: Si 23 5 (A
ϫ[ⲉⲓⲥⲉ?] ⲃⲉⲗ) μετεωρισμὸς ὀφθ. (cf *ib* 26 9 ⲙⲛⲧϫⲁ-
ⲥⲓⲃⲁⲗ do), BAp 165 = Mus 40 273, ROC 20 49 not
to walk ϧⲛⲟⲩⲙ.

ⲧⲁⲥⲉ (ⲁⲥⲉ) *v* ⲥⲟⲟⲩ.

ⲧⲁⲥⲟ(?) S vb intr, *make light* (caus of ⲁⲥⲁⲓ): Mor
18 159 ⲛⲧⲉⲡⲉⲕϩⲏⲧ ⲧⲁⲥⲓ (*l* ? -ⲥⲟ or -ⲥⲓⲟ) ⲉϧⲣⲡ ⲉⲧ-
ⲙⲛⲧⲉⲩⲥⲉⲃⲏⲥ ἐπικουφισθῇ ἀνανεύσασα πρὸς τὴν εὐ.

ⲧⲥⲁ(ⲉ)ⲓⲟ, ⲧⲥⲁⲓⲉ-, ⲧⲥⲁⲉⲓⲟ⸗ *S*, ⲧⲥⲁⲓⲁ⸗ *A²*, ⲧⲥⲁⲓⲏⲩ† *S*, ⲧⲥⲁⲓⲁⲓⲧ† *A²*, (ⲧ)ⲥⲁⲓⲱⲟⲩ† *B* vb tr, *make beautiful* (caus of ⲥⲁⲉⲓⲉ, *cf* Sdff 264): ShA 2 259 no need ⲉⲧⲣⲉⲟⲩⲁ ⲧⲥⲁⲉⲓⲟϥ ⲏⲣⲧⲉϥ[ϭⲃ]ⲥⲱ, CMSS 7 ⲉⲣϣⲁⲛⲧⲥⲁⲓⲉ ϣⲁϫⲉ he will not hearken, R 1 5 14 sandals ⲉϥⲧ.† ⲁⲛ (var ⲧⲥⲁⲡⲏⲩ)ψιλός, Mani 1 *A²* ⲡⲕⲟⲥⲙⲟⲥ ⲡⲧⲁⲩⲧⲥⲁⲓⲁϥ, *ib* 2 *A²* ϯⲟⲩⲡⲉⲙ … [ⲉⲧ]ⲧ.†, HL 110 *B* ϩⲱⲥ ⲉⲧⲥ.†, C 86 198 *B* ⲉϥⲥ.† ϫⲉⲛⲡⲉϥϩⲣⲟ. *V* also ⲥⲁ vb, as ⲥⲁⲉⲓⲟⲩ, ⲥⲁⲓⲱⲟⲩ belong ? here.

ⲧⲥ(ⲉ)ⲓⲟ *SAA²B*, ⲧⲥⲓⲉ- *SA²*, ⲧⲥⲉⲓⲁ- *Sᶠ*, ⲧⲥⲓⲟ- *B*, ⲧⲥⲓⲟ⸗ *SB*, ⲧⲥⲓⲁ⸗ *SᶠA*, (ⲧ)ⲥⲓⲏⲩ† *S*, ⲧⲥⲛⲟⲩ† (*l* ⲧⲥⲓⲛⲟⲩ) *A*, ⲧⲥⲛⲟⲩⲧ† *B* vb tr, *make satisfied, sate* (caus of ⲥⲉⲓ, confused with ⲧⲥⲟ): Job 38 39 *SB*, Ps 90 16 *B*(*S* ⲧⲁϣⲟ), Pro 13 25 *SA*(*B* ⲧⲥⲟ) ἐμπιμπλάναι, *ib* 26 16† *SA* ἐν πλησμονῇ; Jer 5 7 *SB*, Mt 15 33 *SB* χορτάζειν; Is 55 10 *S*(*B* ⲑⲓⲥⲓ) μεθύειν; Sa 19 12 *S* εἰς παραμυθίαν; BMis 86 *S* bread ⲉⲧ. ⲛⲡⲉⲧϩⲕⲟⲉⲓⲧ, AP 55 *A²* ⲁⲉⲓⲧⲥⲓⲉ ⲟⲩⲙⲏϣⲉ, MG 25 365 *B* fountain ⲉⲧⲧ. ⲙⲙⲱⲟⲩ, Mich 550 44 *Sᶠ* ⲁϥⲧ. ⲙⲏⲧ ⲡϣⲛ; ⲥ ⲛ-, *with*: Ps 102 5 *S*(*B* ϫⲉⲛ-)ἐμπ. ἐν, Hos 7 6 *A*(*B* ⲥⲓ), Ac 14 17 *SB* ἐ. gen; Ps 80 17 *SB* χορ. acc, Lam 3 15 *S* (*B* ⲧⲥⲟ)χ. gen; Sa 2 6 *S* ἀπολαύειν gen; ShC 42 204 *S* ϣⲁⲣⲉⲧⲥⲓⲟ (2 f) ⲙⲡⲟⲉⲓⲕ, DeV 2 15 *B* ⲧⲥⲓⲟⲕ ⲙϥⲏ ⲉⲧⲉⲡⲁⲕϭⲓ ϣϣⲱⲟⲩ ⲙⲙⲟϥ, ViK 9478 *Sᶠ* ⲁⲓⲧⲥⲓⲁⲧⲉⲡ ⲡⲟⲉⲓⲕ, ShIF 254 *S* Lord shall ⲧⲥⲓⲱⲧⲛ ⲛⲡⲉⲧⲛϩⲓⲥⲉ *appease you from troubles*; ⲥ ϩⲛ-, ϫⲉⲛ-, *with*: ShRE 10 164 *S* ⲉϥⲧ. ⲙⲙⲟϥ ⲡϩⲏⲧⲟⲩ, C 41 74 *B* ⲧⲥⲓⲟⲛ ϫⲉⲛ-ϯⲧⲣⲟⲫⲏ; ⲉⲃⲟⲗ ϩⲛ-: Ps 35 9 *B*(*S* ⲧⲥⲟ) μεθ. ἀπό; Bor 240 113 *S* ⲧⲥⲓⲟⲛ ⲉⲃ. ϩⲙⲡⲟⲅⲟⲉⲓⲡ.

ⲣⲉϥⲧ. *B*: Va 57 200, *l* ⲧⲥⲟ ϥ *v*.

ϭⲓⲛ-, ϫⲓⲛⲧ-, *satisfaction, repletion*: Job 38 26 *B* χορτάσαι; P 129¹⁴ 53 *S* ⲧϭ. ⲡⲧⲟⲩ ⲡϣⲟ.

ⲧⲥⲟ *SAB*, ⲧⲥⲁ *F*, ⲧⲥⲉ- *SAA²B*, ⲧⲥⲁ- *F*, ⲧⲥⲟ⸗ *SB*, ⲧⲥⲉ⸗ *S*, ⲧⲥⲁ⸗ *SᶠAA²F*, ⲧⲥⲏⲩ† *S* vb **I** tr, *give to drink, slake* (caus of ⲥⲱ, confused with ⲧⲥⲓⲟ): Ge 2 10 *SB*, Ps 103 13 *S*(*B* ⲧⲥⲓⲟ), Pro 25 21 *SA*, Hab 2 15 *AB*, Mk 15 36 *SBF*, AP 9 *A²* ποτίζειν; Si 39 29 *S* (var ⲧⲥⲓⲟ, *cf* 24 31) μεθύειν; ShC 73 152 *S* ⲡⲉⲓⲱϣⲉ ⲉⲧⲟⲩⲛⲁⲧⲥⲟϥ, Pcod 35 *S* ⲁϥⲧⲥⲉ ⲟⲩⲣⲓⲁⲥ (2 Kg 11 13), AM 256 *B* vineyard ⲉⲑⲣⲉϥⲧⲥⲟϥ, BKU 1 26 (8116) *F* ⲧ. ⲟⲩⲣⲱⲙⲓ, ManiH 2 *A²* ⲉⲩⲧ. ⲙⲙⲁⲓ; ⲥ 2d acc (thing drunk): Ge 19 32 *SB*, Ps 59 3 *SB*, Mk 9 41 *SBF* (Mor 21 142) ⲡⲟ. acc; Mor 23 96 *S* ⲡⲥⲉⲧⲥⲉ ⲟⲩⲁ ⲡⲟⲩⲁⲡⲟⲧ, *ib* 27 39 *F* sim ⲧⲥⲁ ⲟⲩⲁ = Va 63 21 *B* ⲧⲥⲓⲟ ⲡⲟⲩⲁⲓ, BHom 76 *S* ⲁⲩⲣ ⲡⲕⲉ(ⲧ)ⲥⲟϥ ⲡⲟⲩϭⲙⲭ, MG 25 249 *B* ⲉⲁϥⲧⲥⲟϥ ⲡⲟⲩⲕⲟⲩϫⲓ of oil; without ⲡ- (*v* AZ 53 135): Ps 68 21 *S* ⲧⲥⲉⲓ ⲟⲩϭⲙⲭ *B* ⲧⲥⲟⲓ ⲡ-, Si 15 3 *S* ⲧⲥⲉϥ ⲟⲩⲙⲟⲟⲩ ⲡⲟ. acc; ShC 42 106 *S* ⲧⲥⲉϥ ⲙⲟⲟⲩ.

II intr: Ge 13 10† *S*(*B* ⲥⲱ), 1 Cor 3 6 *SBF* ⲡⲟⲧ.; Is 58 11† *S*(*B* ⲑⲓⲥⲓ) μεθ.

With following preposition. ⲥ ⲉ- (for ⲡ-) *S*:

AZ 23 108 ⲧⲥⲟⲟϥ ⲉϩⲙⲭ;   ⲥ ⲉⲃⲟⲗ ⲡ-: Eccl 2 6 *S* (*F* om ⲉⲃ.) ⲡⲟ. ἀπό.;   ⲥ ϩⲓ- *S*: P 129²⁰ 178 wine ⲧⲥⲟⲟⲥ ϩⲓⲱⲥ *let her drink thereof*, Ryl 104 §3 pounded cumin ⲧⲥⲟϥ ϩⲓⲏⲣ(ⲡ) *let him drink it with wine*;   ⲥ ϩⲛ-, ϫⲉⲛ-, *from*: Bodl(P)a l ⲥ ⲧⲥⲱ ⲙⲙⲟⲟⲩ ϩⲙⲡⲥⲱⲡ, MIE 2 391 *B* ⲡⲧⲉⲕ(ⲧ)ⲥⲟϥ ϫⲉⲛⲡⲁⲙⲱⲟⲩ = BAp 114 *S* ⲉⲃⲟⲗ ϩⲛ-; ⲉⲃ. ϩⲛ-: Ge 29 2 *SB* ⲡⲟ. ἐκ, Cant 8 2 *S* ⲡⲟ. ἀπό; Mor 44 5 *Sᶠ* ⲙⲁⲧⲥⲁⲡ ⲉⲃ. ϩⲛⲧⲡⲩⲥⲏ.

—— nn m, *watering*: ShC 73 152 *S* ⲉⲧⲙⲕⲁ ⲡⲙⲟⲟⲩ ⲉⲃⲱⲕ ⲉϫⲙⲡⲉⲧ. land already *drenched* (or ? *l* ⲥⲱ), O'LearyTh 10 *B* flourished ⲁϥⲡⲉϭⲟ ⲡⲉⲗⲧ., Dan vis 14 60 *B* ϩⲁⲛⲧ. *draughts* of magic potions. ⲙⲁ ⲡⲧ., *drinking-place*: Ge 30 38 *SB* ποτιστήριον. ⲣⲉϥⲧ., *drink-giver*: P 44 62 *S* ⲣ. · γαροφόρος سقاء, Va 57 200 (-ⲧⲥⲓⲟ) πότιμος, AM 256 *B* ⲡⲓⲣ. ⲡⲧⲉ ⲡⲓⲕⲏⲡⲟⲥ; ⲙⲡⲧⲣ., *act of watering*: Miss 4 818 *S* (*cf* 1 Cor 3 6).

ⲧⲥⲁⲃⲟ *SB*, ⲧⲥ(ⲉ)ⲃⲟ *SᵃA*, ⲧⲥⲁⲃⲉ- *SB*, ⲧⲥⲁⲙⲃⲉ- (Lu 3 7), ⲧⲥⲉⲃⲉ- (BG) *S*, ⲧⲥⲉⲃⲟ- *A*, ⲧⲥⲉⲃⲁ- *A²*, ⲧⲥⲉⲃ- *F*, ⲥⲉⲃ- *Sᶠ*, ⲧⲥⲁⲃⲟ⸗ *SB*, -ⲙⲟ⸗, ⲧⲥⲃⲟ⸗ *S*, ⲧⲥⲉⲃⲁ⸗ *AA²*, ⲧⲥⲁⲃⲁ *SᶠF*, -ⲙⲁ⸗ *F*, ⲧⲥⲁⲃⲏⲩ†, -ⲏⲩⲧ†, -ⲟⲉⲓⲧ† *S*, ⲧⲥⲉ-ⲃⲁⲉⲓⲧ† *AA²*, ⲧⲥⲁⲃⲛⲟⲩⲧ† *B* (ⲥⲃⲟ, ⲥⲃⲱ, ⲥⲁⲃⲟ *v* below) vb tr, *make wise, teach, show* (caus of ⲥⲁⲃⲉ): Deu 31 19 *SB*, Job 8 10 *S*(*B* ϯ ⲥⲃⲱ), Mk 9 31 *S* (var ⲧⲁⲙⲟ, *B* do), Jo 8 28 *SA²B* διδάσκειν; Nu 24 17 *S* (var ⲧⲁϯⲟ, *B* ⲧⲁⲙⲟ), Am 8 1 *A*(*S* ⲧⲟϯⲟ, *B* do), Ap 22 8 *S* (*B* do) δεικνύναι; Ps 140 5 *B*(*S*=Gk), Pro 10 5† *SA* (*B* ϯ ⲥⲃⲱ), Ac 7 22 *BF*(*S* = Gk) παιδεύειν; Ps 104 22 *SB* σοφίζειν; *ib* 15 7 *S*(*B* ϯ ⲕⲁϯ) συνετίζειν; Is 40 13 *B*(*S* ⲧⲥⲁⲃⲉ ⲉⲓⲁⲧ⸗) συμβιβάζειν, Mt 14 8 *B*(*S* do, *F* ϯ ⲥⲃⲱ)προβ.; Jo 7 15 *SB*(var ⲥⲁⲃⲟ) μανθάνειν; Phil 4 12† *B*(*S* ϫⲱⲡⲧ) μύεσθαι; Col 1 28 *B* ⲧ. … ϯ ⲥⲃⲱ *S* ϯ ⲥⲃⲱ … ⲧ. νουθετεῖν … διδ.; BMar 184 *S* ⲁϥⲧ. ⲡⲡⲉϩⲃⲏⲅⲉ ⲙⲡⲡⲉ(*cf ib* ϫⲓ ⲥⲃⲱ ⲉⲡⲉϩⲃ.), AM 125 *B* ⲁⲩⲧⲥⲁⲃⲟⲛ ϩⲓⲧⲉⲛⲡⲭ̅ⲥ̅.

With following preposition. ⲥ ⲉ- of thing learnt: Ps 105 35 *B*(*S* ϫⲓ ⲥⲃⲱ), HT *S* 1 *S* ⲁϥⲧ. ⲉⲧⲧⲉⲭⲛⲏ ⲡⲧⲙⲡⲧⲣⲁⲙϣⲉ (*v* Hist Laus §35) μανθ.; ShA 1 72 *S* ⲧⲉⲧⲥⲁⲃⲟⲉⲓⲧ ⲉⲡⲡⲟⲗⲉⲙⲟⲥ, AM 225 *B* ϯⲧ.† ⲁⲛ ⲉϩⲁⲛ-ⲅⲩⲙⲡⲁⲥⲓⲁ, BIF 13 109 *S* taught them to weave for ⲡⲉⲩⲧⲥⲁⲃⲏⲩⲧ ⲁⲡⲡⲉ ⲉⲃⲓⲣ; vbal: Jer 13 23 *S*(*B* ⲥⲁⲃⲟ), Ez 19 3 *S*(*B* ϭⲓ ⲥⲃⲱ) μανθ., APBerl Sitzb '09 218 *A²* lion ⲉϥⲧ.† ⲁϥⲱ[ϣⲉ](?), ShBM 206 83 *S* ⲙⲡⲡⲧ. ⲉⲧⲃ-ⲃⲟⲛ, BMis 89 *S* ⲧ.† ⲉⲃⲱⲕ ⲉϩⲣⲟⲩⲡ; ⲥ acc of person, ⲉ- of thing taught, shown: Deu 5 31 *S*(var ⲧⲥⲃ.)*B*, 2 Kg 1 18 *SB*, Ps 50 13 *SB*(ACl ⲧⲉⲃⲟ), Jo 14 26 *SA²B* διδ., Sa 8 7 *S* ἐκδιδ.; Nu 8 4 *S*(*B* ⲧⲁⲙⲟ), Hab 1 3 *SA*(*B* do), Jo 10 32 *SAA²*(*B* do), Ac 7 3 *S* ⲧⲥⲁⲃⲟϥ ⲉⲣⲟⲕ (var -ⲟⲕ ⲉⲣⲟϥ, *B* do), Z 344 *S* ⲁϥⲧⲥⲁⲃⲟⲟⲩ ⲉⲩⲡⲉⲧⲣⲁ = MG 25 208 *B* do δεικ., BHom 38 *S* ⲡ-ⲧⲁⲩⲧⲥⲁⲃⲉ ⲙⲱⲩⲥⲏⲥ ⲉⲅⲥⲧⲓⲗⲟⲥ ⲕⲁⲧⲁⲃ., Si 14 12 *S*, CaiEuch 327 *B* ⲁϥⲧⲥⲁⲃⲟⲛ ⲉϩⲁⲛⲙⲱⲓⲧ ὑπόδ.; Ex 4 12 *SB*, Dan 9 22 *SB* συμβιβ., Deu 6 7 *SB* προβ.; Ro

16 17 B(S ⲝⲓ ⲥⲃⲱ); Ps 89 12 S(B ⳟⲓ ⲥ.) παιδ.; Ge 22 2 S(B ⲧⲁⲙⲟ), 1 Kg 16 3 S (var ⲧⲁⲙⲟ) εἰπεῖν; BMar 109 S ⲧⲥⲁⲃⲟⲓ ⲉⲡⲉⲛⲧⲁⲕⲭⲟⲟⲩ γνωρίζειν; LCyp 2 S ⲁϥⲧⲥⲁⲃⲟⲓ ⲉⲥⲉ μύεσθαι; MG 25 14 B ⲁϥⲧⲥⲁⲃⲱⲟⲩ ⲉⲧⲁⲕⲟⲗⲟⲩⲑⲉⲓⲁ δηλοῦν; PS 375 S ⲉⲩⲧ. ⲙⲙⲟⲥ ⲉⲡⲥⲱⲡⲧ, BG 124 S ⲁⲓⲧⲥⲉⲃⲉⲧⲏⲩⲧⲛ ⲉⲡⲣⲁⲛ, ShC 73 198 S ⲁⲩⲧⲥⲁⲃⲟⲓ ⲉⲣⲟϥ *showed him to me*, P 129¹⁴ 99 S Helena & envoys ⲁⲥⲧⲥⲁⲃⲟⲟⲩ ⲉⲧⲡⲟⲣⲫⲩⲣⲁ, Mor 41 322 S Hilaria ⲧⲥⲁⲃⲟⲥ (refl) ⲉⲧⲙⲛⲧⲣⲙⲛⲕⲏⲙⲉ, Mani 1 A² ⲁϥⲧⲥⲉⲃⲁⲩ ⲁⲧⲉϥⲡⲁⲣⲑⲉⲛⲟⲥ, PLond 4 519 S ϣⲁⲓⲧⲥⲁⲙⲱⲧⲛ ⲉⲧⲕⲁⲧⲁⲅⲣⲁⲫⲏ, Kr 3 F *apprentices* ⲧⲥⲁ·ⲙⲁⲩ (ⲉ)ⲡⲉⲧⲉⲭⲛⲓ; c acc of thing shown, ⲉ- of person to whom: Lev 13 49 S(B ⲧⲁⲙⲟ) δεικ. dat; ShA 2 310 S not your custom ⲉⲧⲥⲁⲃⲉ ⲡⲉⲧϩⲣⲟ ⲉⲣⲟⲟⲩⲧ, ShC 73 54 S kitchen herbs ⲉⲩⲧⲥⲁⲃⲟⲟⲩ ⲉⲡⲏⲗⲟ, Miss 8 261 Sf ⲧⲉϥⲟⲩⲉⲣⲏⲧⲉ...ⲁϥⲧⲥⲁⲃⲁⲥ ⲉⲣⲟϥ, Pcod 39 SF *wound* ⲉⲡϯⲛⲁϣ ⲧⲥⲁⲃⲟⲥ ⲁⲛ ⲉⲗⲁⲁⲩ, Bor 253 159 S ⲁⲓⲧⲥⲁⲃⲉ ⲧⲉϥϣⲏⲛ ⲉⲣⲟⲕ, CO 325 S ⲙⲡⲣⲧ. ⲡⲉⲓⲡⲗⲁϩ ⲉⲣⲱⲙⲉ; ⲉ- vbal: Job 10 2 S(B ϯⲥⲃⲱ), Pro 22 21 SA, Lu 11 1 SB δίδ.; Ac 10 28 S(B ⲧⲁⲙⲟ) δεικ., Mt 3 7 S(B do) ὑπόδ.; Mun 125 Sf ⲁⲧⲁϣⲉⲉⲣⲉ ⲧⲥⲁⲃⲁⲥ (refl) ⲉⲧⲁⲩⲣⲟⲥ on her feet, AM 238 B ⲙⲁⲧⲥⲁⲃⲟⲓ ⲉⲉⲣ ⲙⲁⲧⲟⲥ, RNC 8 S ⲧⲥⲁⲃⲟϥ ⲉⲥⲅⲁⲓ; c ⲉⲃⲟⲗ ⲛ-: ShA 1 134 S ⲁⲅⲁⲣ ⲧ. ⲉⲃ. ⲙⲙⲟⲛ; c ⲉⲃ. ϩⲉⲛ-: DeV 2 53 B ϫⲉⲛⲡϫⲓⲙⲟⲣⲉⲛⲧ. ⲉⲃ. ⲡϧⲏⲧⲟⲩ ⲉⲟⲛⲓϣϯ ⲙⲙⲉⲧⲁⲅⲁⲑⲟⲥ; c ϩⲁⲣⲧⲛ-: RNC 50 S teacher ⲛⲧⲁⲓⲧ. ϩⲁⲣⲧⲏϥ.

—— nn m SF, *teaching, instruction*: Si 39 12 S διδασκαλία, He 6 2 SF(B ⲥⲃⲱ) διδαχή; Eph 6 4 S(B ⲕⲁϯ) νουθεσία; Sh(Besa)BMOr 8810 449 S nourish them ϩⲛⲧⲉⲥⲃⲱ ⲙⲛⲡⲧ. ⲙⲡⲭ̅ⲥ̅.

ⲙⲛⲧⲣⲉϥⲧ. S, *teaching*: My 41 ⲙⲛⲧⲣⲉϥⲧⲥⲁⲃⲉ ϣⲏⲣⲉ ϣⲏⲙ.

ϫⲓⲛⲧ. B, sim: MG 35 333 ⲡϫⲓⲛⲧⲥⲁⲃⲟϥ ⲉϯⲙⲉⲧⲉⲩⲥⲉⲃⲏⲥ.

ⲥⲃⲟ, -ⲱ S, ⲥⲁⲃⲟ S(rare)B, ⲥⲉⲃ- Sf F, ⲥⲁⲃⲟⲉ, ⲥⲁⲃⲏⲟⲩⲧ† B, mostly *learn* intr: Sa 7 13 S, Is 8 16 B(S ⲝⲓ ⲥⲃⲱ), Jo 7 15 B(var&S ⲧⲥ.)μανθ.; Nu 5 7 S -ⲱ ϩⲙⲡⲛⲟⲃⲉ (var ⲉⲓⲙⲉ, B ⲟⲩⲱⲛϩ ⲉⲃⲟⲗ) ἐξαγορεύειν; tr: Mt 28 15 B(S ϯ ⲥⲃⲱ) δίδ.; C 86 115 B wherefore sent I thee to school ⲓⲉ ⲉⲥⲁⲃⲟⲕ ⲉⲥⲃⲁⲓ?, PSBA 29 192 S ⲙⲉⲛⲡⲥⲁⲧⲣⲉϥⲥ. ⲡⲉⲙⲏⲏϣⲉ *teach*; c ⲉ- of thing learnt: Deu 5 1 SB, Si 8 9 S (var ⲥⲁ.), Eph 4 20 S(varr -ⲱ, ⲧⲥ., B ⲧⲥ.), He 5 8 S(B ⲉⲙⲓ, F ⲝⲓ ⲥⲃⲱ) μανθ.; Pro 16 17 S(A ⲧⲉⲃⲟ)δέχεσθαι; Sa 9 18 S δίδ.; HL 93 B ⲙⲡⲁϯⲥⲁⲃⲟ(sic)ⲉⲡⲓϩⲟⲩⲓⲧ ⲛⲥⲧⲩⲭⲟⲥ; vbal: Deu 17 19 SB(var ⲧⲥ.), Is 28 20 B(S ⲝⲓ ⲥ.), 29 24 SB (F ⲧⲥ.), Tit 3 14 SB μανθ.; 1 Thes 4 4 S(varr ⲥⲁ., -ⲱ, B ⲉⲙⲓ) εἰδέναι; ShA 1 366 S ⲉⲁⲧⲉⲧⲛⲥ. ⲉϣⲙϣⲉ, DeV 1 138 B ⲕⲥ.† ⲉⲉⲣ ⲥⲕⲁⲛⲇⲁⲗⲓⲍⲉⲓⲛ paral ⲧⲉⲕⲥⲩⲛⲏⲑⲓⲁⲧⲉ, v also tr; ⲣⲉϥϭⲓ ⲥ. B: Va 57 275 ⲟⲓ ⲡⲣ. μανθ.; ϫⲓⲛⲥ. B: Va 58 123 ⲡⲓϫ. ⲉⲡⲓϩⲃⲏⲟⲩⲓ.

V also ⲉⲓⲁ *eye* (ⲧⲥⲁⲃⲟ ⲡⲉⲓⲁⲧⲉ).

ⲧⲥⲃⲕⲟ SA, ⲧⲥⲃⲕⲉ-, ⲧⲥⲃⲕⲟⲉ S, (ⲧ)ⲥⲛⲃⲕⲁⲉ F, ⲧⲥⲃⲕⲏⲩⲧ† S vb tr, *make small, diminish* (caus of ⲥⲃⲟⲕ): Lev 25 16 (B ⲑⲣⲉ-ⲥⲃⲟⲕ), Nu 33 54 (B ⲉⲣ ⲕⲟⲩϫⲓ), Ps 8 6 SF(PcodMor, B ⲑⲉⲃⲓⲟ), Pro 14 34 SA ἐλαττονεῖν; Ps 88 45 (B ⲉⲣ ⲕ.), Si 17 20 σμικρύνειν; ib 48 2 ὀλιγοποιεῖν; Mk 13 20(BF ⲉⲣ ⲕ., cf Mt 24 22 S ⲥⲃⲟⲕ) κολοβοῦν; P 129¹⁴ 61 bishop may ⲧ. ⲡⲉⲭⲣⲟⲡⲟⲥ ϩⲛⲟⲩⲙⲛⲧⲙⲁⲓⲣⲱⲙⲉ φιλανθρωπεύεσθαι; PS 39 ⲁⲓⲧ. ⲡⲡⲉⲅⲕⲩⲕⲗⲟⲥ, ib 345 ⲉϥⲧ.† ϩⲣⲏⲧϥ, Mor 25 217 ⲁϥⲧⲥⲉⲃⲕⲉ ⲧⲉϥϭⲟⲙ.

ⲧⲁⲥⲑⲟ B   v ⲧⲥⲧⲟ.

ⲧⲥⲁⲙⲟⲉ, ⲧⲥⲁⲙⲃⲉ-   v ⲧⲥⲁⲃⲟ.

ⲧⲥⲁⲛⲟ, ⲧⲥⲛⲟ S, ⲧⲥⲉ. A, ⲧⲥⲁⲛⲁ F (nn), ⲧⲥⲁⲛⲉ-, ⲥⲉⲛⲟ- Sᵃ, -ⲛⲟ S, ⲥⲉⲛⲟⲉ Sᵃ, ⲧⲥⲁⲛⲏⲩⲧ†, -ⲏⲩⲧ† S, -ⲛⲟⲩ†, -ⲛⲟⲩⲧ† F, -ⲙⲓⲏⲩ† S (Mt 12 44) vb tr, *adorn, set in order, provide*: Si 38 35, Mt 25 7 (var ⲧⲥⲛⲟ, B ⲥⲟⲗⲥⲉⲗ), Lu 11 25† (B do) κοσμεῖν; Ps 143 12†(B ⲧⲁⲓⲟ), BMar 158 garments ⲉⲩⲧⲁⲉⲓⲏⲩ ⲉⲩⲧ.† καλλωπίζειν; Si 49 1†σκευάζεσθαι; 1 Thes 4 12†(var -ⲏⲩⲧ, B ⲥⲟⲩⲃⲏⲧ)εὐσχημόνως, LCyp 26 ⲟⲩⲙⲟⲥⲧⲉ ⲡϥⲧ.† ⲁⲛ ἀσχήμων, JA '75 5 241 sandals ⲉϥⲧ.† ⲁⲛ (var ⲧⲥⲁⲓⲏⲩ) ψιλός; ShC 73 142 let all we do ϣⲱⲡⲉ ⲉⲩⲧ.† ⲉⲙⲁⲧⲉ, Z 266 bride ⲉⲩⲛⲁⲧⲥⲁⲛⲟⲥ for bridegroom, Mor 25 209 ⲁϥⲧ. ⲙⲡⲙⲁ for feast, R 1 3 43 house ⲉⲁⲩⲥⲁϩⲣⲉϥ ⲁⲩⲧⲥⲁⲛⲟϥ, TU 43 4 A ⲁⲓⲧ. ⲛⲛⲁⲣⲭⲁⲅⲅⲉⲗⲟⲥ ϩⲛⲟⲩⲉⲣⲁⲩ ⲛⲙⲁⲓⲣⲉ = PO 9 197 ⲍⲏ̅ⲣ̅, Mor 29 54 let all behave well ⲉⲩⲧ.† ⲧⲏⲣⲟⲩ = ib 30 62 F -ⲛⲟⲩ, ib 50 34 sick healed & rose up ⲉϥⲧ.†, Ep 255 ⲡϥⲧ. ⲧⲁⲙⲓⲥⲑⲱⲥⲓⲥ ⲡⲁⲓ for 2 years, COAd 54 Sᵃ ⲛⲧⲁⲥ. ⲡⲗⲟⲧⲟⲥ ⲛⲙⲙⲁⲕ, Ep 371 Sᵃ this shoe ⲛϭⲥⲉⲛⲟϥ ⲡⲁⲡⲁ ⲃⲓⲕⲧⲱⲣ, P 130¹ 88 those flee from vain glory whilst I ⲛⲉⲓⲧ. ⲙⲙⲟⲓⲡⲉ; as nn, *propriety*: Si 26 16 κόσμος, ib 45 12 εὐκοσμία, R 2 2 22 ⲡⲧ. ⲡⲧⲉϥⲥⲱⲫⲣⲟⲥⲩⲛⲏ κοσμιότης; Aeg 285 eat ϩⲛⲟⲩⲧ. (var ⲉⲡⲓⲥⲧⲏⲙⲏ) εὐταξία; 1 Cor 14 40 SF(B ⲕⲱⲧ); ShC 73 19 limbs healed ⲡⲉⲩⲥⲙⲓⲛⲉ ⲏ ⲡⲉⲩⲧ. ⲛⲁⲟⲩⲱⲛϩ ⲉⲃⲟⲗ, ShLeyd 296 renounce evil & ϣⲱⲡⲉ ϩⲛⲟⲩⲧ., Mich 550 46 ⲡⲉⲧ. ⲡⲛⲉϥⲗⲉⲝⲓⲥ ⲉⲧⲉϥⲙⲉⲗⲉⲧⲁ ⲙⲙⲟⲟⲩ.

ⲙⲁⲓⲧ. S, *adornment-loving*: ShHT K 1 among sinners ⲙⲙⲁⲓⲧⲥⲁⲛⲟⲟⲩ ⲉⲧⲉⲛⲟⲩⲱϣ ⲉⲧⲣⲉⲡⲉⲧϩⲣⲟ ⲥⲁ, Bor 240 84 beautiful garments of ϩⲣⲱⲙⲉ ⲙⲙⲁⲓⲧⲥⲁⲛⲟⲟⲩ.

ⲧⲥ(ⲉ)ⲛⲕⲟ, ⲥⲛ., ⲧⲥⲙ. S, ⲧⲥⲉⲛⲕⲁ Sf F, ⲧⲥⲛⲕⲉ-, ⲧⲥⲛⲕⲟ- A² , -ⲕⲟⲉ S vb tr, *give suck* (caus of ⲥⲱⲛⲕ): Ge 21 7 (B ϯ ⲥⲓ), ib 32 15(B ⲥⲓ ⲙⲛⲟⲧ), Lam 4 3 SF(B ϯ ⲥⲓ) θηλάζειν; Mor 34 51 breasts ⲛⲧⲁⲥ. ⲙⲙⲟⲓ (var FR 76 & B Aeg 57 ⲥⲁⲁⲛϣ), BIF 14 148 Sf ⲉⲥⲧ. ⲙⲙⲟϥ ϩⲛⲧⲉⲥⲉⲣⲱⲧⲉ, R 2 4 59 sim ϩⲛⲧⲟⲩⲉⲕⲓⲃⲉ, BMis 345 no milk ⲉⲧⲥⲕⲟ ⲙⲙⲟⲓ = BSM 12 B ϣ, ManiH 10 A² ⲡⲉ(ⲧ)ⲧ. ϣⲏⲣⲉ. intr: Mt 24 19 (B ϯ ⲥⲓ), Lu 23 29 (B ϣⲁⲛϣ) θ.; P 43 239 ⲅⲁⲗⲟⲩⲭⲓⲁ·

тетсупкω ـمرـ; P 44 73 λοχεγολεпα · петс.
'ـ ; Aeg 12 breasts птаιт. пρитογ = *ib* B σι ερωϯ.

атт., *not suckling*: Ryl 73 Elizabeth's breasts п-
татωск патт.

тасρ S nn, meaning unknown: Mor 37 165 ере-
ρепвογρε ϫλϫωλ ρппερнвс пθε погт. псогре
ρпογχο εϥθλο εвολ ппетвλαпτει пθε пρепсатω.

(т)сто SA, ста S*f*F, сθο S, тасθο B, (т)сте- S,
тсто- S(PSBA 10)A, тасθе-, тасθо- B (Ez), ста-
F, (т)стоμ S, тстаμ A, тасθομ, сθομ B, стаμ S*a*S*f*F,
(т)стиγϯ S, тасθηογтϯ B(qual *v* т. евол), vb I tr,
bring, pay back, repeat (caus of сωт): Ex 23 4 B(S
кто), Is 43 13 B(S т. евол) ἀποστρέφειν, Lam 3 3 B
(S кто) ἐπιστ., Jer 21 4 B(S do) μεταστ.; Is 42 22
B(S кω εϥραι) ἀποδιδόναι; Ez 16 55 B(S кто), Hos
2 3 B(A do) ἀποκαθιστάναι; Ez 39 2 B συνάγειν;
Wess 15 135 S evil dogmas етρептстоог ἀποδοκιμά-
ζεσθαι; Is 32 10 SF(B ϫε); Ez 36 12 B тасθθн-
ноγ ἔτι (cf сωт), P 129[19] 30 S с. лпетптааϥ (*l* -таϥ)
лптопос *give back what belongeth to* т., Mor 21 129
S they set corpse on camel етρεγстоϥ плллαγ,
Va 63 13 B robe еактасθос оп лпесρηϯ = BMis
385 S ктос, C 86 158 B αϥтасθе пρατ εϥκнв,
CMSS 44 F лекста пεγпογϣ[, K 231 B αγсθос
ـسترـ لوـ (? same);   refl: Ez 46 9 B ἀναστ., Hos 11 8
S(LCyp 21, A кто)B μεταστ., Ez 41 24 B(S кто)
στροφωτός; Job 14 10 S(B diff) οὐκέτι εἶναι; Mor
30 22 S*f* αϥпωт лпγстаϥ, DeV 2 72 B ετаφαραω
тасθοϥ, BSM 108 B ϯпатасθοι ап ϫε еθρε-, BP
12495 S лпρϭω погεϣ птωт плллαϥ лптγстоϥ
(cf Ep 1 251).

II intr BF, *make to return, turn, bring back*: Ge
8 7 (S кто) ἀναστ., *ib* 18 10 (S кωτε) ἐπαν., Is 9 12
(S кто), Mic 2 4 (S do, A λαϭе) ἀποστ., Jer 27 9
(S do), Hos 11 5 (A do) ἐπιστ., Lu 23 48 (S кω.)
ὑποστ.; Ex 32 27 (S ϯ огкотс), Su 14(S кω.)ἀνα-
κάμπτειν; Lev 13 16 (S сλлпе) ἀποκαθ.; Lu 10 35
(S кто), MG 25 231 ϣατεϥт. ἐπανέρχεσθαι; ϥη етт.,
B weaver's tool (?) *for turning*: K 125 ـمرـ, PCol 2 F
I wrote to George евελ пεвαλραρес(? الخالص) Ryl 106
18) евста пαρα сηϥ епни.

With following preposition.

—— е-, *return to*: Su 49 B ἀναστ. εἰς, Ge 3 19 B
(S кто) ἀποστ. εἰς, Ps 53 7 B(S do), Is 37 29 B(S do)
ἀπ. dat, Mt 26 52 B(S diff) ἀπ. εἰς, 2 Kg 12 23 S(var
кто)ἐπιστ., 3 Kg 8 34 B ἐπ. εἰς, Lam 5 21 B(SF кто)
ἐπ. πρός, Dan 10 8 B(S do)μεταστ. εἰς, Ac 13 34 SB
ὑποστ. εἰς; He 11 15 B(S кω.)ἀνακάμ.; Is 23 17 B
(S таρο ератμ), Jer 29 6 B(S кωτε е-) ἀποκαθ. εἰς,
P 129[14] 84 S εγεстоϥ етεккλнсια птаγпоϣпεϥ
ерос ἀπ. dat; Ex 22 26 B(S ϯ), Ez 46 17 B ἀποδιδ.
dat; *ib* 47 2 B(S кто)περιάγ. πρός, Mt 21 18 B(S do)

ἐπανάγ. εἰς; Ez 26 8 B κύκλῳ ποιεῖν ἐπί; Job 7 9 S
(B ϫе), Ps 102 16 S(B om), Ez 13 23 B тасθθηноγ
(S кто), Ro 6 9 S(var сωт, B ϫе) ἔτι; Jer 41 16 B(S
оп) Gk om; PS 264 S сεпатстоϥ епкослос, ClPr
26 76 S етлτρεптстоп есωтл, TstAb 252 B тас-
θθετηноγ епкαρι, Va 63 8 B αϥтасθοϥ епεϥни =
BMis 376 S кτоϥ = BSM 34 B коτϥ, JKP 2 142 F
евстаϥ етεϥαρχη, AZ 16 15 S тρоιте птакптс...
аιтстос ερнс, RE 14 26 S с. петптаϥ ероϥ, PMéd
219 S take mixture out of vinegar стоϥ етεлϫαθ
пкесоп, AZ 23 113 S sim, DeV 1 142 B ϥпатасθοϥ
ап есωρελ пкесоп, C 86 339 B лпεϥтасθо (var
-оϥ) ероϥ ϫе;   еϩογп е- B: Jer 35 6 ἐπιστ. εἰς.

—— еϫп-, *turn upon, toward*: Ge 37 29 B ἀναστ.
ἐπί, Bar 3 6 B ἀποστ. ἐπί, Ps 118 59 B(S ρικε)ἐπιστ.
εἰς; Ez 18 3 B γίνεσθαι ἔτι; C 89 29 B αпϣαптас-
θοп еϫωк = MG 17 296 S кτоп еϫ., Va 58 183 B
лαρεптасθе пιсαϫι еϫепϯιстоρια, JKP 2 32 S
ερεп̄ϭ̄ пасток [е]ϫωι;   еϩρнι еϫ. B: Is 38 8
(S кто п-) ἀποστ. acc.

—— ϣα- B, *return, turn to*: C 89 62 ϣαптектас-
θοϥ ϣαρоп = Miss 4 546 S кτоϥ ϣα-, *ib* 43 46 ϥт.
ппн еθογαв ϣαроϥ.

—— ϩα- B, *as last*: Ex 24 14(S кωτε ϣα-)ἀναστ.
πρός, Is 7 6 (S кто) ἀποστ. π., Su 47 ἐπιστ. π., MIE
2 395 αϥтасθοϥ ϩαροι & said = BAp 122 S коотϥ
еϫωι.

—— ϩιϫп- BF, *turn upon, to*: Leip 24 50 лαρ-
ептасθоп ϩ. ϯιстоρια (cf еϫп-), BM 635 (2)F каλв
естωλ (*sc* his claim) ϩιϫωι.

With following adverb.

—— евол SABF, *turn out, reject, return*, tr: Jth
1 11 S ἀναστ., 3 Kg 8 57 B, Mt 5 42 B(S кто псαв.),
ROC 17 404 B т. ппεϥλλαϣϫ ев. еϣтελсωτελ
ἀποστ.; Ps 117 22 S(B ϣωϣ), Mk 8 31 S(BF do)
ἀποδοκιμάζειν; Ps 50 17 SA(Cl, B do), Ac 4 11 S(B
do) ἐξουθενεῖν; Mk 6 26 S(B ϥωϫι) ἀθετεῖν; *ib* 7 13
S(B кωρϥ) ἀκυροῦν, Pro 5 7 SA(B diff) ἄκυρον ποιεῖν; Lu 6 22 S(B ϩιογι ев.) ἐκβάλλειν; Pro 26 16
SA ἀποκομίζειν; Si 41 4 S ἀπαναίνεσθαι; Is 51 20 B
(S om) ἀπορεῖσθαι; Ez 5 6 S(B ϩ. ев.) ἀπωθεῖν;
Wess 15 22 S*f* sour wine ϣαιстаϥ ев. ἀφορίζειν; Jer
22 30 S(B do) ἐκκήρυκτος; JA '75 5 217 S атсγп-
ϩογαс сте пειρωв ев. ἀπαγορεύειν; ShC 42 106 S
αϥтс. ев. пϣαϫε лле, *ib* 152 S петс. ев. ппεп-
тоλн, PSBA 10 196 S пп̄е патстотнγтп ев. ап лл-
петпаιтнлα, Bor 239 50 S тпс. ев. whoso confes-
seth not (var R 1 2 67 απαθελατιζε), C 43 56 B т.
ев. ппнпоγϯ = Mor 39 37 S*f* ста ев., BodlCopt
inscr 433 S*a* ϯсоогн ϫекпастаι ев. ап;   qual:
Jer 6 30 S(Wess 18 140, B ϣωϣϥ) ἀποδοκ., Is 1 22
S(B = Gk) ἀδόκιμος; 1 Tim 4 4 S(B ϩ. ев.) ἀπόβλητος; Jth 11 11 S ἔκβολος; Gal 4 20 S(B ϣωλϩ

ⲡⲣⲏⲧ) ἀπορεῖσθαι; ShWess 9 143 *S* apocr gospels ceⲥ. ⲉⲃ., ShC 42 39 *S* ⲡⲉⲧⲥⲟⲟϥ ⲁⲩⲱ ⲉⲧⲧⲥ. ⲉⲃ., P 131[7] 75 *S* of wine opp ⲧⲁⲉⲓⲏⲧ, R 1 3 74 *S* locust ⲧⲥ. ⲉⲃ. ⲁⲛ ⲉⲟⲩⲟⲙϥ, Va 57 269 *B* ⲃⲓⲟⲥ ⲛⲁⲡⲟⲃⲗⲏⲧⲟⲛ ⲟⲩⲟϩ ⲉⲧⲧ. ⲉⲃ., MIF 9 55 *S υ* ⲛⲟⲩϫⲉ ⲉⲃ. qual; ⲉⲃ. ϩⲁ- *B*, *away from*: Is 8 17 (*S* ⲕⲧⲟ ⲉⲃ. ⲛ-) ἀποστ. ἀπό, Jer 42 15 (*S* ⲕⲧⲟ ⲉⲃ. ϩⲛ-) ἀπ. ἐκ; Ez 16 27 (*S* ⲣⲓⲕⲉ ⲉⲃ. ϩⲓ-) ἐκκλίνειν ἐκ; DeV 2 46 each ⲧⲁⲥⲟⲟϥ ⲉⲃ. ϩⲁⲡⲉϥ ⲙⲱⲓⲧ; ⲉⲃ. ϩⲓ- *B*, sim: Is 30 11 (*S* ⲕⲧⲟ ⲉⲃ. ⲛ-, *F* ⲕⲱϯ ϩⲁⲃ. ⲛ-) ἀποστ. ἀπό; ⲉⲃ. ⲝⲉⲛ- *B*, sim: Ez 33 12 (*S* ⲕⲧⲟ ⲉⲃ. ϩⲛ-) ἀποστ. ἀπό, Ja 5 20 (var ⲉⲃ. ϩⲁ-, *S* do) ἐπιστ. ἐκ, Mart Ign 866 (*S* R 1 4 53 do) μεθιστάναι ἀπό; PO 11 357 ⲁϥⲧ. ⲡⲟⲩϩⲏϣ ⲉⲃ. ⲝⲉⲛ- ⲛⲟⲩϩⲉⲣⲉⲥⲓⲥ; ⲉⲃ. ϩⲓϫⲉⲛ- *B*, sim: Ez 23 48 (*S* ⲕⲧⲟ ⲉⲃ. ϩ.) ἀποστ. ἐκ; ⲉϩⲟⲩⲛ ϩⲁ- *B*, *in to*: Ge 8 9 (*S* ⲕⲱⲧⲉ ⲉⲣ. ϣⲁ-) ἀναστ. πρός; as nn m *SB*, *rejection*: Jer 6 19 *B* ἀποστροφή; Ro 11 15 *S* (*B* ϩⲓⲟⲩⲓ ⲉⲃ.) ἀποβολή; Mus 40 267 *S* testifying of ⲛⲉⲧⲥ. ⲉⲃ. ⲡⲟⲩⲕⲟⲗⲁⲥⲓⲥ of Gehenna, BAp 161 *S* ⲭⲣⲱ ⲙⲡⲉⲓ- ⲕⲟⲥⲙⲟⲥ ϩⲛⲟⲩⲧⲥ. ⲉⲃ.; ⲧⲥⲧⲉ ⲉⲃ.[1], ⲥⲧⲉ ⲉⲃ.[2], ⲥⲧⲉⲃ.[3] as nn *S, what is rejected*: Ro 9 3[1] (var[2], *B* = Gk) ἀνά- θεμα; ShC 42 82 (= MIF 23 45) ox ⲉϥϣⲁⲛⲣ ⲥ.[3], Mun 88 hunger & misery ⲙⲡⲟⲩⲥ.[2]

—— ⲥⲁⲃ. ⲛ- *B, turn away from*: Is 57 17 (*S* ⲕⲧⲟ ⲉⲃ. ⲛ-), Ez 33 9 (*S* ⲥⲟⲟϩⲉ ⲉⲃ. ⲛ-) ἀποστ. ἀπό; Va 66 308 ⲙⲡⲉⲣⲧ. ⲙⲡⲉⲕϩⲟ ⲥ. ⲙⲙⲟϥ.

—— ⲉⲡⲁϩⲟⲩ *SBF, turn backward*: 2 Kg 1 22 *B* (*S* ⲕⲱⲧⲉ ⲉⲡ.), Ps 43 11 *B* (*S* ⲕⲧⲟ ⲉⲡ.) ἀποστ. εἰς τὰ ὀπίσω, Ez 1 9 *B* (var ⲧ.†, *S* ⲕⲱⲧⲉ ⲉⲡ.) ἐπιστ.; Miss 4 746 *S* ⲡⲉϥⲛⲁⲧⲥⲧⲟϥ ⲁⲛ ⲉⲡ. from what he purposed, DeV 2 232 *B* ⲧ. ⲙⲡⲉϥϫⲱⲡⲧ ⲉϥ., Va 61 118 *B* ⲧ. ⲉϥ. ⲙⲡⲉϥϫⲱⲡⲧ, Ep 167 *S* ⲙⲡⲣⲥⲧⲟ ⲡⲱⲃ ⲉⲡ., C 86 350 *B* ⲥⲟⲟⲩ ⲡⲏⲓ ⲉϥ. *set me him aside*, BKU 1 26 (8116a) *F* ⲥⲧⲁⲥ ⲉⲡⲉϩⲟⲩ (sic prob) ⲛϩⲁⲡⲙⲁⲩ (*v* ⲙⲟⲟⲩ *inundation s f*).

—— nn *SB, sending back*: Ac 15 3 *B* (*S* ⲕⲧⲟ) ἐπι- στροφή; K 134 *B* ⲡⲓⲧ., *sheet* of sail القلع (*cf* BIF 20 68, Almk 2 103 = شاغول الق); PS 268 *S* ⲙⲙⲛⲧⲟⲩ ⲧⲥ. ⲛⲧⲉϥⲯⲩⲭⲏ ⲉⲛⲕⲟⲥⲙⲟⲥ (*cf* 271 ⲙⲛⲧⲟⲩ ⲥⲱⲧⲉ).

ⲥⲉⲟ *S*, -ⲁ *Sf* in ⲙⲁ ⲛⲥ., *retreat, lodging*: 1 Kg 7 17 ⲙⲁ ⲡⲉⲥⲟⲁ (var ⲙⲁ ⲡⲥⲱⲟⲩϩ) ἀποστροφή; BMis 458 bade bring us to a ⲙⲁ ⲛⲥ., Miss 8 28 said fare- well & departed to ⲡⲉϥⲙⲁ ⲛⲥ. *Cf* Aeg 6 *B* Jesus born in ⲡⲓⲙⲱⲓⲧ ⲛⲧⲁⲥⲉⲟ = *ib* 148 *S* ⲙⲁ ⲡϭⲟⲓⲗⲉ.

ϫⲓⲛⲧ. *B, return*: Ge 3 16 (*S* ⲕⲧⲟ vb), Is 1 27 (*S* do nn) ἀποστροφή; Ez 47 7 (var ϫⲓⲛϥⲉⲣⲧ., *S* ⲕⲧⲟ vb) ἐπιστ.; Va 68 178 ⲙⲙⲟⲛ ⲙⲉⲧⲁⲛⲟⲓⲁ ⲟⲩϫⲉ ϫ.; ϫ. ⲉⲃⲟⲗ: Jer 18 12 ἀποστ.; ϫ. ⲉϥϩⲟⲩⲟ: TRit 15 ⲟⲩϫ. of all things evil; ϫ. ⲉϩⲣⲏⲓ: Cat 149 ⲡϫ. ⲙⲡⲟⲥ from the marriage (Lu 12 36); ϫ. ⲉϩⲟⲩⲛ ⲉ-: CaiEuch 510 ἀποκατάστασις εἰς.

ⲧⲟⲥⲧⲥ *S* vb intr, *be sprinkled* ? or *grow hard* (*cf*

ⲧⲱⲥ) ?: Pap *olim penes* GHorner 5 (ⲉ) Jezebel (?) ⲧ- ⲡⲟⲣⲛⲏ ⲛⲧⲁⲥⲙⲟⲩ ⲡⲁϣ ⲡⲣⲉ ⲙⲛ ⲙⲡⲉⲡⲉⲥ[ⲥⲁⲣⲝ ?] ⲡⲉⲥⲥⲛⲟϥ ⲧ. ⲉϩⲟⲩⲛ ⲉⲧⲟ ? (4 Kg 9 33 ῥαντίζε- σθαι πρός). *Cf* ⲥⲟⲱϣϣ.

ⲧⲥⲟⲩⲧⲥⲟⲩ *S* nn, meaning unknown: ShP 130[2] 104 congregations full of murmurings, gossip ⲁⲛⲧⲓ- ⲗⲟⲅⲓⲁ, ⲧ., ⲥⲱⲃⲉ, ⲗⲗⲏⲃ.

ⲧⲟⲉⲓⲧ *S*, ⲧⲁ. *SfA*, ⲧⲁⲉⲓⲧⲉ *A*[2], ⲧⲱⲓⲧ *B* vb intr, *mourn*: Tob 10 4 *S*, Ez 7 12 *S* (*B* ⲛⲉⲣϩⲓ ⲉⲃⲟⲗ), Joel 1 13 *SA* (*B* ⲉⲣ ϩⲏⲃⲓ), Mt 11 17 *S* (*B* ⲣⲓⲙⲓ), Jo 16 20 *SA*[2] (*B* ⲉⲣ ϩ.) θρηνεῖν; 2 Kg 1 12 *S*, BHom 3 *S* κό- πτεσθαι; BMar 112 *S* ⲉϥⲣⲓⲙⲉ ⲉϥⲧ. ὀδύρεσθαι, Sa 19 3 *S* ⲡⲣⲟⲥⲟⲇ.; Va 63 99 *B* ⲛⲁϥⲧ. πενθεῖν; Sa 11 13 *S* τρύχεσθαι; ShP 130[2] 92 *S* worldlings that chant & ⲉⲧⲧ. ϩⲛⲟⲩⲣⲉⲡϣⲁϫⲉ ⲉⲩϣⲟⲩⲉⲓⲧ, *ib* 130[4] 88 *Sf* ⲡⲉⲓⲧ. ⲥⲉ- ⲉⲩϥⲣⲁⲛⲉ, Va 59 165 *B* ⲉⲩⲧ. ⲉⲩⲉⲣ ϩ. ⲉⲩⲣⲓⲙⲓ; ⲥ ⲉ-, *mourn for*: Jer 28 8 *S* (*B* ⲛⲉⲣϩⲓ), Ez 8 14 *S* (P 44 114, *B* ⲛⲉ.) θρ. acc; Lu 23 27 *S* ⲛⲉ. ⲧ. *B* ⲧ. ⲛⲉ. κόπ. θρ. acc, Sa 18 10 *S* θρ. gen, 2 Kg 3 33 *S* θρ. ἐπί; 1 Kg 25 1 *S* (var ⲉϫⲛ-) κόπ. acc; ShA 1 204 *S* ⲧ. ⲉⲣⲟ ⲙⲙⲓⲛ ⲙⲙⲟ, Mor 25 115 *S* ⲟⲩϣⲟⲩⲧ. ⲉⲣⲟϥ, AP 24 *A*[2] ⲁⲩⲧ. ⲁ[ⲟⲩ]ⲁⲛ ⲛⲓⲙ *to every one*; ⲥ ⲉϫⲛ-, sim: Ez 32 18 *S* (*B* ⲛⲉ. ⲉϫ.) θρ. ἐπί; R 2 165 *S* ⲉⲩⲧ. ⲉϫⲛⲕⲱⲛⲥ, Ryl 62 5 *S* ⲧ. ⲉϩⲣⲁⲓ ⲉϫⲛⲡⲉⲧⲟ ⲡϣⲙⲙⲟ, MG 25 110 *B* ⲉⲩⲧ. ⲉⲩⲉⲣ ϩ. ⲉϩⲣⲏⲓ ⲉϫⲛ-.

—— nn m *SB* (rare), *lament, dirge*: Is 14 4 (*B* ⲛⲉ.), Am 8 10 (*B* do) θρῆνος, Z 330 cried out ϩⲛⲟⲩⲧ. καταθρηνεῖν; Mt 2 18 (*B* do) ὀδυρμός; R 1 145 κο- πετός; Sh(Besa)Mun 165 ⲥⲉⲛⲁϫⲱ ⲙⲡⲉⲓⲧ. ⲉϩⲣⲁⲓ ⲉϫⲱ (*cf* Am 5 1), ROC 20 51 ⲡϣⲁϫⲉ ⲡϣⲃⲱ that women tell (? sing) ϫⲉⲧ., Mor 36 31 ⲡⲉⲓⲧ. ⲉⲣⲉⲡⲉⲧ- ⲟⲩⲁⲁⲃ ⲉⲓⲣⲉ ⲙⲙⲟⲟⲩ ϩⲓⲭⲱⲓ (var P 131[1] 57 ϫⲱ ⲙ- ⲙⲟⲟⲩ ⲉϫⲱⲛ), Hall 4 ϫⲱ ⲛⲟⲩⲧ. ⲉϥϩⲟⲟⲩⲧⲉ for my luckless youth, MG 25 158 *B* ⲉϥϥⲓ ⲧ. ⲉⲃⲟⲗ.

ⲣⲉϥⲧ. *S, mourner*: Jer 9 17 (TT 137, *B* ⲣⲉϥⲛⲉ.) θρηνοῦν.

ⲧⲟⲟⲧ⸗ *v* ⲧⲱⲣⲉ *hand*.

ⲧⲱⲧ *SA*[2]*F*, ⲑ. *B*, ⲧⲉⲧ- *S*, ⲑ. *B*, ⲧⲁⲧ- *SfBF*, ⲧⲟⲧ⸗ *S*, ⲧⲁⲧ⸗ *SaSf*, ⲧⲏⲧ⸗ *SAF*, ⲑ.† *B*, ⲣ ⲥ ⲑⲁⲧ- *B*, ⲧⲁⲧ- *F* (in ⲙⲉⲧⲑ.) vb I intr, *be joined, persuaded, agree- able*: Ex 35 22 *B* δοκεῖν, Si 37 34† *S* εὐδ.; ShViK 9315 180 *S* tilled land ⲉⲧⲧ.† ⲉⲧⲙⲟⲧⲛ ⲉ(ⲧ)ⲧⲥⲟϥ, Mani 2 *A*[2] ⲧⲣⲉ ⲉⲧⲁⲩⲧ. ⲙⲛⲧⲣⲉ ⲉ[ⲧⲟⲩⲛⲁ]ⲡⲱⲣϫ ⲁⲃⲁⲗ, HL 115 *B* wished to make him bishop but ⲙⲡⲉϥⲑ., ALR '06 473 *Sf* ⲛⲧⲁⲡⲟϭ ⲧⲱⲧ ⲁ(ⲓ)ⲉⲓ, AZ 55 70 *S* marriage settlement ⲁⲓⲧϩⲱⲧ (= ⲑⲱⲧ, *l* ⲧ.) ϩⲁⲑⲉ (*l* ⲑⲏ) ⲙⲡⲁⲑⲃⲟⲕ ϣⲁⲣⲟ, BM 849 35 *B* ⲟⲩϭⲣⲉ ⲉⲥⲑ.†, Va 59 15 *B* lose not life & ⲡⲁⲓⲁⲏⲣ ⲉⲧⲉ.† ⲡⲕⲁ- ⲗⲱⲥ (Assemani *AcMar* 2 251 ܟ̣ܠ ܫ̈ܦܝܪ̈ܐ), EW 110 *B* sim (*cf* AM 121 ⲁⲏⲣ ⲉⲑⲛⲁⲡⲉϥ); ⲥ ⲉ-, *agree to*: BMis 281 *S* ⲁⲩⲧ. ⲉⲡⲉⲩⲉⲣⲏⲩ, J 35 37 *S* ⲡⲣⲟⲥ ⲑⲉ

ⲛⲧⲁⲡⲧ. ⲉⲣⲟⲥ ⲙⲡⲡⲉⲡⲉⲣⲏϭ, BKU 1 318 *S* (ⲉ)ⲧⲡⲉⲧ.†
ⲉ†ⲣⲏⲛⲏ, COAd 57 *S* ⲉϣⲱⲡⲉ ⲕⲧ.† ⲉⲧⲧⲁⲗⲓⲥ (*v* ? WS
21, Ep 1 9) †ⲡⲁⲟⲅⲟⲭⲉⲥ ⲡⲁⲕ; vbal: EW 147 *B* ⲙ-
ⲡⲉϥⲟ. ⲉⲣⲓ ⲱⲓϣ ἐπιθαρρεῖν, LAl 7 *S* ⲙⲡⲉⲕⲧ. ⲉⲥⲱⲧⲉⲙ ⲡⲥⲱⲓ, Ep 279 *S* ⲛⲧⲏⲧ. ⲉⲧⲡⲡⲟⲟⲩ; *make equal,
level*: 2 Kg 11 25 *S* (var ⲧⲁⲅⲟ) καταστᾶν;   c
ⲉ×ⲡ-, *agree upon*: JSch 2 7 *S* ⲡⲧⲉⲣⲉⲓⲧ. ⲉ×ⲡⲡ̄ⲣⲱϭ,
EW 130 *B* ⲥⲉⲑ.† ⲁⲡ ⲉ×ⲡⲡⲣⲗⲓ = PO 1 514 تزى ᵞᵞ
ᵞᵞ, BM 1116 7 *S* ⲁϥⲧ. ⲉ×ⲟⲟⲩ (or ? ×. vb);   c
ⲙⲡ-, ⲡⲉⲙ-, *agree with*: Ac 28 24† *B*(*S* = Gk),
ROC 25 248 *B* ⲁⲕϣⲁⲡⲟ. ⲡⲉⲙⲁⲡ πείθειν; J 92 21
S ⲉⲧⲉⲧⲡⲁⲧ. ⲡⲙⲙⲁϥ, BP 12495 *S* ⲙⲡⲣϭⲱ ⲡⲟⲩⲉϣ
ⲛⲧ. ⲡⲙⲙⲁϥ, MG 25 252 *B* ⲥⲉⲑ.† ⲡⲉⲙⲡⲣⲉⲙⲡⲭⲏ-
ⲙⲓ *as to beliefs*, CMSS 56 *F* ⲧⲁⲓⲧ. ⲙⲉ[ⲡ-, *v* also
tr & c ⲉⲃⲟⲗ.   **II** tr, *conjoin, mingle*: Ps 101 10
B(*S* = Gk), Is 5 22 *F* (*sic, S* ⲇⲟ, *B* ⲥⲱ) κεραννύναι, 1 Cor 12 24 *B*(*S* ⲇⲟ) συγκ., Is 65 11 *B* ⲁϥⲟⲧ
ⲉⲧⲉⲑ.† (*S* ⲟⲩⲱⲧⲛ ⲉⲃⲟⲗ) κέρασμα; P 129¹⁶ 51 *S.ᶠ* water
ⲉϥⲕⲉⲣⲁ...ⲉϣϫⲉ ⲁⲩⲧⲁⲧϥ, Mani 1 *A*² place of Mani's
execution ⲉⲧⲁⲩⲧ. ⲙⲡⲉⲡⲁⲧ ⲡⲡⲁⲡⲟ[.....] ⲣⲏⲧϥ,
CO 129 *Sⁿ* ⲁⲓⲧⲁⲧⲟⲩ ⲙⲡⲡⲉϭⲉⲣⲏϭ, CaiTh 36 *B*
laments & tears ⲧⲉⲧⲉⲛⲟ. ⲙⲙⲱⲟⲩ ⲡⲉⲙⲡⲟⲩⲅⲉⲣⲛⲟⲩ;
make even, smooth B: Lev 14 42 (var ⳃⲟⳃ) ἀποξύειν;
GPar 2 12 ⲁϥⲟ. ⲡⲡⲓⲛⲃ of his hands ὀνυχοκόπτειν;
AZ 13 134 *B* †ⲙⲉⲧⲣⲁⲙϣⲉ ⲑ. ⲡⲁⲥ ⲡⲣⲁⲡⲣⲉⲃⲓ *con-
trive*; 1 Chr 29 2 ⲉⲅⲟ.† ⲥⲟⲁⲙ *lapis onychinus.*

—— ⲉⲃⲟⲗ *S, be even, level*: Mor 44 33 corners of
house ⲡⲁⲧ. ⲉⲃ. ⲙⲡⲡⲕⲁⲣ, BMis 262 ox's horns fell
off ⲁⲩⲧ. ⲉⲃ. ⲙⲡⲧⲉϥⲁⲡⲉ = ib 30 37 *F* ϣⲱϣ ⲉⲃ. ⲙⲡ-;
tr: Mor 51 13 burnt temple ⲁⲓⲧⲟⲩ ⲉⲃ. ⲙⲡⲡⲕⲁⲣ.

——ⲛⲛⲙ *SAA²B, agreement, mingling*: Cl(Strassb)
9 4 *A* ⲟⲩⲧ. ⲡⲱⲣ× (var & Gk ὁμόνοια); Ez 22 19 *B*
(var ⲙⲟⲩ×ⲧ) σύγκρασις; CaiEuch 512 *B* ⲟⲅⲟ. ⲉⲡⲁ-
ⲡⲉϥ ⲙⲡⲓⲁⲏⲣ (*cf* GFr 361 *S* ⲡⲉⳅⲙⲡⲉ (*sic*) ⲛ̄ⲡⲁⲏⲣ,
Renau. *Lit* 1 102 εὐκρασία): Va 134 4 *S* (Vita Sin) if
thou come not ⲣⲙⲡⲉⲕⲧ. = C 41 34 *B* ⲡⲉⲕⲟⲩⲱϣ,
Mani 2 *A*² ⲉⲧⲁϭⲉ ⲁⲣⲉⲧⲟⲩ ⲣⲡⲟⲩⲧ., *ib* 1 *A*² ⲡⲧ. ⲉⲧⲁϥ-
ϣⲱⲡⲉ ⲙⲡⲟⲩⲁⲓⲡⲉ ⲣⲛⲡⲕⲉⲕⲉ (not ⲙⲡ̄ⲡ).

With ⲣⲏⲧ (*cf* ⲧⲱⲕ ⲛⲣ.), **a** as obj, *content heart,
persuade, satisfy*: 1 Kg 24 8 *B*(*S* = Gk), Mt 27 20
B(*S* ⲇⲟ), 1 Jo 3 19 *BF*(Cai Copt Mus, *S* = Gk),
C 89 61 *B* †ⲡⲁⲟ. ⲙⲡⲉⲣ. = Miss 4 545 *S* ⲇⲟ πείθ.,
Jer 36 8 *B* ἀναπ.; Z 346 *S* ⲉⲧⲣⲉϥⲧⲉⲧ ⲡⲉⲩⲣ. ×ⲉⲁϣ-
ⲡⲉ ⲡⲱⲓ, *ib* 306 *S* ⲁϥⲧⲉⲧ ⲡⲉϥⲣ. ⲉⲧⲃⲉⲡϣⲁ×ⲉ, AM
268 *B* ⲁⲓⲑ. ⲙⲡⲉⲧⲉⲡⲣ. πληροφορεῖν; Lu 16 25 *B*(*S*
ⲥⲟⲗⲥⲗ), 2 Cor 1 6 *B*(*S* ⲥⲟⲡⲥ), *ib* 7 13 *B*(*S* ⲣ. ⲙⲧⲟⲡ),
2 Tim 4 2 *B*(*S* ⲥⲟⲡⲥⲡ) παρακαλεῖν; Jo 11 31 *B*(*S.A²*
ⲥⲟⲗ.) παραμύθεσθαι; Ac 2 40 *B* (var ⲉⲣ ⲙⲉⲟⲣⲉ, *S*
ⲥⲟⲡⲥ) διαμαρτύρεσθαι; Job 7 11 *B* ⲧⲁⲧ ⲣ. (*S* om)
συνέχεσθαι; Va 57 253 *B* ⲉⲅⲟ. ⲙⲡⲣ. with music
γοητεύειν; EW 150 *B* ⲉⲥⲡⲁϣ ⲑ. ⲙⲡⲁⲣ. ⲉⲟⲣⲓ- προσάγειν; ShBMOr 8810 462 *S* ⲙⲡⲣⲧⲉⲧ ⲡⲉⲕⲣ. ⲉⲣⲟⲕ
ⲡⲧⲉⲓⲣⲉ, BMis 395 *S* ⲧⲉⲧⲡⲟⲩⲱϣ ⲉⲧⲉⲧ ⲡⲉⲧⲣ. (var

ⲡⲉⲧⲛⲣ. ⲙⲧⲟⲛ) = BSM 46 *B* ⲉⲙⲓ, Mor 27 9 *Sᶠ* ⲁⲡⲟⲕ
ⲡⲉⲧⲡⲁⲧⲁⲧ ⲡⲉⲕⲣ., BM 548 *Sᶠ* ⲧ]ⲁⲧ ⲡⲉⲧⲛⲣ. ⲉⲣⲟϥ,
CMSS 44 *F*]ⲧⲁⲧ ⲡⲉⲩⲣⲏⲧ, Mani 1 *A*² ⲡϥ̄ⲧ. ⲙⲡⲣ. ⲡ-
ⲡⲙⲁⲅⲟⲅⲥⲁⲓⲟⲥ, AM 167 *B* ⲙⲡⲟⲩⲱϣ ⲑ. ⲙⲡⲉⲡⲣ. ⲉⲉⲣ
ⲫⲁⲓ.   **b** as subj: Ac 5 36† *B*(*S* ⲥⲱⲧⲙ ⲡⲥⲁ-), 2 Cor
2 3† *B*(*S* ⲕⲱ ⲡⲣ. ⲉ-), Phil 1 6† *B*(*SF* ⲧⲏⲕ ⲡⲣ.), 2 Thes
3 4† *B*(*S* ⲡⲁⲣⲧⲉ), Miss 4 524 *S* = C 89 43 *B*, HL 74
B ⲡⲟⲩⲣ. ⲑ.† ⲁⲡ ⲡⲉⲙⲡⲏ πείθ.; Eccl 8 11 *S*, Ro 4 21†
B(*S* ⲧ. ⲡⲣ.), Z 307 *S* ⲙⲡⲉⲡⲉⲩⲣ. ⲧ. ⲉⲟⲅⲱⲡ πληρ.;
1 Thes 3 7 *B*(*S* ⲙⲧⲟⲡ ⲉ×ⲡ-) παρακαλεῖσθαι; He 4
2† *B*(*S* = Gk) συγκεραν.; Ex 35 21 *B* φέρειν ἡ καρδία; BG 130 *S* ⲁⲡⲉⲧⲛⲣ. ⲧ. ×ⲉ-, ShC 73 149 *S* ⲉⲣⲉⲡⲉϥⲣ. ⲧ.† ⲉⲣⲟϥ before God, Mor 23 86 *S* ⲁⲣⲁ ⲁⲡⲉⲧⲛⲣ.
ⲧ. ⲉⲣⲱⲧ ? ⲁϭⲉ ⲁⲕⲡⲓⲑⲉ ⲙⲙⲟⲛ, TU 43 9 *A* ⲧⲉⲧⲛⲁϭⲓ
ⲁⲩⲱ ⲡⲉⲧⲛⲣ. ⲧ.†, AM 306 *B* ⲙⲡⲁⲧⲉⲡⲉⲕⲣ. ⲑ. ⲛ̄ⲧⲉⲕⲉⲣ
ⲑⲩⲥⲓⲁ?, C 43 76 *B* sim ⲉⲉⲣ ⲑⲩⲥⲓⲁ, Kr 129 *F* ⲁⲡⲁⲣ.
ⲧ. ⲡⲉⲙⲉⲕ, BM 586 *F* come & see us (ⲛ)ⲧⲉⲡⲉⲣ. ⲧ.,
Mor 40 46 *S* ⲁⲡⲁⲣ. ⲧ. ⲉⲉⲣ ⲙⲟⲛⲁⲭⲟⲥ = MG 25 273
B, AM 58 *B* ⲁⲡⲉⲕⲣ. ⲑ. ⲉⲧⲁⲡⲁⲓ ⲙⲟⲩ ⲉⲑⲃⲏⲧⲕ?   **c**
ⲧ. ⲛⲣ., *consent, agree*: Is 32 17 *B*(*SF* ⲡⲁⲣ.), Ro 2 8†
BF(*S* = Gk), Aeg 272 *S* ⲉϥⲧ.† ⲛⲣ. ⲉ×ⲡⲟⲩⲙⲛⲧⲁⲧⲥⲟ-
ⲟⲩⲛ, MG 25 234 *B* ϥⲟ.† ⲛⲣ. ⲡⲉⲙⲛⲓ πείθ.; Lu 1 1 *S*
(*B* ×ⲱⲕ ⲉⲃⲟⲗ), Ro 14 5 *SB*, Cl 42 3 *A* ⲁⲩⲧ. ⲛⲣ. ⲣⲓⲧ-
ⲧⲁⲡⲁⲥⲧⲁⲥⲓⲥ, Z 343 *S* ⲙⲡⲥⲟⲡ ⲧ.† ⲛⲣ. ⲁⲡ ⲉϣⲁ×ⲉ
πληρ.; Ps 50 16 *A*(Cl, *S* ⲟⲩⲱϣ, *B* † ⲙⲁ†), 2 Cor 12
10 *S*(*B* † ⲙ., *F* ⲧⲏⲕ ⲛⲣ.) εὐδοκ.; Jer 14 10 *S*(*B* †
ⲙ.) εὐδοθῦν; R 1 4 73 *S* things endured ⲉⲧⲃⲉⲡⲉⲧϥⲧ.†
ⲛⲣ. ⲉ×ⲱⲟⲩ πιστεύειν; C 89 27 *B* ⲁⲥⲟ. ⲛⲣ. ⲉ×ⲡ-
ⲡ̄ⲣⲱϭ καρδίαν διδόναι πρός; Ac 28 25† *S* neg (*B* ⲇⲟ)
ἀσύμφωνος; Br 94 *S* ⲁⲕⲧ. ⲛⲣ. ⲉⲣⲣⲁⲓ ⲉ×ⲱⲓ, ShC 73
126 *S* ⲉⲣⲉⲡⲡ̄ⲉ ⲡⲁⲧ. ⲛⲣ. ⲉⲃⲟⲗ ⲣⲓⲧⲟⲟⲧⲟⲩ (*cf ib* ⲡⲧⲟⲟⲧⲟⲩ), ROC 7 141 *S* ⲉⲡⲉⲩⲧ.† ⲛⲣ. ⲉ×ⲡⲧⲉϥ×ⲡⲱⲡⲣ
content with, J 75 38 *S* ⲉⲁ×ⲧ. ⲛⲣ. ⲉ×ⲱⲕ (*cf ib* 40 ⲁⲡ-
ⲧⲱⲕ ⲛⲣ. ⲉ×.), C 89 148 *B* sin ⲉⲧⲁϭⲟ. ⲛⲣ. ⲉⲁⲓϥ, AM
207 *B* ⲙⲡⲁⲧⲉⲕⲟ. ⲛⲣ. ⲉⲉⲣ ⲑⲩⲥⲓⲁ? (*cf* **b**);   as nn
m: 2 Cor 1 15 *B*(*S* ⲡⲁⲣ.) πεποίθησις, Is 14 7 *B*(*S*
ⲧⲏⲕ ⲛⲣ.), Jer 23 6 *B*(*S* ⲧⲁⲭⲣⲟ) πείθειν; Col 2 2 *S*(*B*
ⲙⲟⲩⲣ), He 6 11 *S*(*B* ×ⲱⲕ), AM 272 *B* πληροφορία;
Is 57 18 *B*(*S* ⲥⲟⲗⲥⲗ), Ac 9 31 *B*(*S* ⲥⲟⲡⲥ) παράκλησις;
Bor 253 114 *S* οἰκοδομή; 1 Cor 14 3 *B*(*S* ⲥⲟⲗ.) παρα-
μυθία; Eph 1 5 *SF*(*B* † ⲙ.) εὐδοκία; Cl 51 2 *A* ὁμο-
φωνία; Mk 12 37 *SF* (Mor 46 63, *B* = Gk) ἡδέως;
ShA 2 88 *S* ⲙ̄ⲕⲁⲣ ⲛⲣ. opp ⲧ. ⲛⲣ., ShMich 550 13 *S*
to patriarch ⲡⲁⲉⲓⲱⲧ...ⲉⲧⲙⲡϣⲁ ⲛⲧ. ⲛⲣ. ⲛⲓⲙ, BMOr
9536 *S* ⲣⲛⲟⲩⲅⲧⲟⲣ ⲁⲡ ⲁⲗⲗⲁ ⲣⲙⲡⲁⲧ. ⲛⲣ. ⲙⲙⲓⲛ ⲙ-
ⲙⲟⲓ, Va 58 72 *B* daughter sinned ⳃⲉⲛⲟⲩⲅ. ⲛⲣ. ⲛⲧⲉ
ⲡⲉⲥⲣⲏⲧ without compulsion;   adj ⲧⲉⲧ ⲣ. *S, trustworthy*: BM 1 *c* ⲣⲉⲛⲡⲟϭ ⲛⲥⲟⲡ ⲡⲧ. besought you.

ⲙⲉⲧⲟⲁⲧ-, ⲙⲉⲧⲧⲁⲧⲣ. *BF, confirmation*: Ac 20 12
B(var ×ⲁⲣⲣ., *S* ⲥⲟⲡⲥⲡ) παρακαλ., *ib* 9 31 *F*(*S* ⲥⲟⲛⲥ,
B ⲑ. ⲛⲣ.), Ro 12 8 *B*(*SF* ⲇⲟ) παράκλησις.

ⲁⲧⲧ., ⲁⲧⲟ. ⲛⲣ. *SB, unconvinced, disagreeing*: Jer
5 23 ⲣ. ⲛⲁⲧⲟ. *B*(*S* ⲁⲧⲛⲁⲣ.) ἀπειθής; *ib* 3 7 *B* ἀσύν-

ⲉⲧⲟⲥ; ROC 23 286 *B* ⲡⲓⲁⲧⲟ....ⲟⲓ ⲡⲁⲑⲡⲁⲣϯ, AM
209 *B* ⲥⲡⲱⲙⲛ ⲡⲁⲧⲟ. ⲛⲉⲙⲡⲓⲡⲣⲟⲥⲧⲁⲅⲙⲁ, My 73 *S*
ⲡⲉⲓⲁⲧⲧ.; ⲉⲣ, ⲟⲓ ⲡⲁⲧⲟ. *B*: Ex 23 21 (*S* ⲁⲧⲥⲱⲧⲙ),
Ps 67 19 (*S* do), Jo 3 36 (*SF* ⲡⲓⲥⲧⲉⲩⲉ neg) ἀπείθειν,
Tit 1 16 (Va 57 267, var ⲁⲧϯ ⲙⲁϯ, *S* ⲁⲧⲥ.) ἀπειθής;
ⲙⲉⲧⲁⲧ., *refusal*: Eph 2 2 (*S* ⲙⲛⲧⲁⲧⲡⲁϩ.) ἀπείθεια;
Ex 22 17 (*S* ⲣ ϩⲛⲁⲥ neg) ἀνανεύειν.

ⲭⲓⲛⲟ. ⲛϩ. *B*, *agreement, union*: Va 57 15 ⲡⲓⲭ. ⲉ-
ⲭⲉⲛⲏ ⲉⲧⲟⲩⲭⲱ ⲙⲙⲟⲩ ⲡⲉⲓⲑⲱ́, TRit 30 ⲟⲩⲙⲉⲧⲟⲩ-
ⲁⲓ ⲛⲉⲙⲟⲩⲭ. ἔνωσις.

V Dévaud *Études* 20, who separates *join, agree*
from *mingle*.

ⲧⲁⲁⲧⲉ, ⲧⲟⲟ., ⲧⲁⲁⲧⲉ†, ⲧⲟⲟ.† *S* vb **I** intr, *shine*:
Ez 1 7† (ⲧ ϯ ⲙⲟⲅⲉ) ἐξαστράπτειν; Dan 10 6† (*B* diff)
στίλβειν; Ez 21 10 (*B* om) εἰς στίλβωσιν γίνεσθαι;
Mt 17 2 (*B* ⲉⲣ ⲟⲩⲱⲓⲛⲓ) λάμπειν; PS 293 coin ⲁⲥⲧ.
ⲛⲧⲉⲣⲉⲕⲛⲁⲩ ⲉⲣⲟⲥ, ShA 2 94 ⲧⲥⲛⲏⲉ...ⲉⲥⲧ. ϩⲛⲛⲟⳟⲓⲝ,
ShC 73 11 sword ⲑⲉ ⲉⲧⲥⲧ. ⲙⲙⲟⲥ (var ⲧⲟⲟ.), Miss 4
641 God's sword (lightning?) ⲧ. & wrath came forth
from heaven, Pcod 24 face ⲁϥⲧ. (var ⲣ ⲟⲩⲟⲉⲓⲛ), Mus
42 235 star ⲉϥⲣ ⲟⲩⲟⲉⲓⲛ ⲉϥⲧ., PSBA 32 287 sim ⲧⲟⲟ.†,
Miss 4 231 sun ⲙⲡⲉϥⲧ. ⲡⲟⲉ ⲡⲧⲉⲃⲣⲏⳟⲉ, Blake 304
beryl ⲉⲥⲧⲟⲟ.† like snake's eye.　　c ⲛ-, *with*: Si
43 4 sun ⲉϥⲧ. ⲛⲛⲉϥⲁⲕⲧⲓⲛ ἀκτῖνας ἐκλάμπειν; c
ⲉⲃⲟⲗ, *shine forth, glow*: Bor 145 52 paenula in fire
ⲣ ϩⲟⲩⲉ ⲧ. ⲉⲃ. ⲉⲙⲁⲧⲉ, P 131⁴ 96 Stephen's face ⲧ. ⲉⲃ.
ϩⲙⲡⲟⲩⲟⲉⲓⲛ; c ⲉϩⲟⲩⲛ, *shine into*: BAp 37 light
ⲧ. ⲉϩ. ϩⲙⲡⲉϩⲣⲟ.

ⲧⲁⲁⲧⲉ, ⲥⲧⲁⲁⲧⲉ, *clap* hands, *shake, spread*, intr: Is
55 12 (var ⲥⲧ., *B* ϭⲁⲕ, var P 70 268 ⲕⲱⲗϩ) ἐπικροτεῖν dat, cit P 131⁴ 116 ⲥⲉⲥⲧ., Mor 36 1 sim ⲁⲩⲧ.;
Tri 716 dancers ⲥⲧ. ϩⲛⲛⲉⲩϭⲓⳮ ﺻﻔﻖ; PSBA 27 168
white lead ⲛⲧ. ⲉⲣⲟⲥ (sc vellum) ⲛⲧⲉⲡⲉϥϣⲟⲉⲓϣ ⲧⲁⲣⲟⲥ; tr, *spread*: Mor 20 5 birds ⲧ. ⲛⲛⲉⲩⲧⲛⲏ,
Gu 34 rejoice Paradise ⲛⲧ. ⲛⲛⲉⲕⲥϯ ⲛⲟⲩϥⲉ, Miss
8 251 dog shows teeth ⲛⲉϥⲧ. ⲛⲛⲉϥⲙⲉⲗⲟⲥ *stretcheth*
(?) *limbs* & raiseth tail, BMis 284 ⲁϥⲧ. ⲛⲧⲥⲛϥⲉ ⲛⲁϥ
stretched forth (var Mor 30 18 & 29 16 ⲛⲉϥϭⲓⲟⲩⲉ ⲛ-
ⲧⲉϥⲥ.); nn m: BMis 142 ⲛⲧ. ⲛⲛⲉⲩⲧⲛⲏ.

ⲧⲁⲉⲓⲧⲉ ² *v* ⲧⲟⲉⲓⲧ.

ϯϯ *B* vb, *tread* (?) as fuller (*cf* ⲧⲓⲧⲓ Dévaud), as
nn: K 139 = P 54 175 ⲡⲓϯϯ حجر قصّارين *fuller's stone*
whereon clothes are beaten (AZ 14 12); *ib* 113 ⲣⲉϥ-
ϯϯ قصّار *walker, fuller*, *ib* 139 ϣⲃⲱⲧ ⲛⲧⲉ ⲡⲓⲣ. عود القصّ
fuller's club.

ⲧⲟⲟⲧⲉ, ⲧⲁⲁⲧⲉ, *turn back*, intr: Si 46 6, 48 27 ⲧⲟⲟ.
ⲉⲡⲁϩⲟⲩ ἀναποδίζειν (P 44 119 رجع الى وراء); tr: Ep
49 ⲉϣⲁⲣⲉⲡⲡⲉ ⲧⲁ. ⲙⲡⲣⲱⲙⲉ ⲉϩⲟⲩⲛ to idolatry &
bringeth him forth thence.　　But *cf* ? ⲕⲱⲧⲉ.

ⲧⲟⲧⲉ *v* ⲟⲟⲧⲉ.

ⲧⲱⲧⲉ, ⲧⲱⲱ., ⲧⲟⲧⲉ *S*, ⲑⲱϯ *B* (once) nn f, *border,
fringe* of garment: Nu 15 38 (*cf* ⲕⲁⲡ), Deu 22 12 *SB*
(confusion in *B*), Mt 23 5, Lu 8 44 (both *B* ϣⲧⲁϯ)
κράσπεδον; Si 21 22 (var ⲧⲱⲱ.), Is 3 20 (*B* = Gk)
χλιδών; Tri 523 دملج, *ib* 716 ⲧϣⲟⲟⲙⲉ ⲛⲧ. رفيع الثياب;
ShA 2 157 rings on girdles (ζωνάριον) ⲉⲣⲉϩⲛⲧ.
ⲛⲏⲩ ⲉϩⲣⲁⲓ ϩⲓⲡⲁϩⲟⲩ ⲉⲝⲛⲧⲉⲩⲙⲣⲣⲉ, Mor 43 252
ⲛⲟϭ ⲛⲧ. ⲡⲗⲟⲟⲩ on heads, ShIF 65 ⲛⲉϥⲧⲱⲟ. ⲛ ⲛⲉϥ-
ⲗⲁⲁⲩ; ⳯ⲓ ⲧ., *have border, fringe*: Gu 44 = BAp
55 ϣⲧⲏⲛ...ⲉⲥⳳⲓ ⲧⲟ. ⲙⲡⲥⲁ ⲥⲛⲁⲩ (var BKU 1 182
ⲧⲱ.) δικρόσσιος.

(ⲧⲧⲟ), (ⲧ)ⲧⲉ- (& + suff), (ⲧ)ⲧⲟⲥ *S* vb tr, *make
give, require* (caus of ϯ, *v* GöttN '19 139, but ? for
ⲕⲧⲟ): Ex 22 25 ⲛⲡⲉⲕⲧⲉϥ ⲙⲛⲥⲉ (*B* ⲧⲁⲗⲉ ⲙ. ⲉ-) ἐπιτιθέναι dat; Si 20 14 ϥⲛⲁϯ ⲡⲁⲕⲥⲉ opp ⲛϥⲧⲟⲕⲥⲉ
ἀπαιτεῖν; Deu 23 19, 20 ⲛⲡⲉⲕⲧⲧⲉ (var ⲕⲧⲉ) ⲡⲉⲕⲥⲟⲛ
ⲟⲩⲙⲛⲥⲉ, ⲡϣⲙⲙⲟ ⲉⲕⲉ(ⲧ)ⲧⲉϥ ⲙ., ⲡⲉⲕⲥⲟⲛ ⲛⲡⲉⲕⲧ-
ⲧⲟⲩϥ (*B* ϣⲟⲡ) ἐκτοκίζειν; Lu 3 14 ⲙⲡⲣⲧⲧⲉ ⲗⲁⲁⲩ ⲟⲥⲉ
(var ϯ ⲟⲥⲉ ⲉⲗ., *B* ⲗⲱⲉⳳ), cit JA '75 5 250, ShMIF
23 56 διασείειν; He 7 5 ⲧⲧⲉ ⲡⲗⲁⲟⲥ ⲣⲉⲙⲛⲧ (*B* ϭⲓ ⲣ.)
ἀποδεκατοῦν.

ⲧⲱⲧⲣ *S*, -ⲧⲉⲣ *B* *v* ⲧⲱⲣⲧ (ⲧⲱⲣⲧⲣ).

ⲧⲟⲟⲧⲥ, ⲧⲟⲧⲥ *v* ⲧⲱⲕⲥ (ⲧⲟϭⲥ).

ⲧⲱⲧⲥ vb *v* ⲧⲱⲕⲥ & ⲧⲱϭⲥ *bleach*.

ⲧⲁⲧⲥⲓ *B*, ⲧⲉⲧⲥⲓ *F* *v* ⲧⲁⳳⲥⲉ.

ⲑⲏⲧϥ *S* nn, meaning unknown, an object made
or sold: Ryl 222 ⲓⲱϩⲁⲛⲛⲉ ⲯⲁⲛⲧ. (*v* ⲥⲁ man).　*Cf*
? Berl *Wörterb* 5 413 ṭṭf.

ⲧⲁⲧⲟ *B* *v* ⲧⲁⲣⲧ.

ⲧⲁⲧϩⲟ (nn), ⲧⲁⲧϩⲛⲟⲩⲧ† *B* vb intr, *impede, restrain*: Job 7 11† (*S* diff) συνέχεσθαι; Va 57 130
feet ⲧ.† ⲉⲡϣⲉ προσδιδόναι ἐν; P 54 116 ⲧⲁⲣⲧⲛⲟⲩⲧ
مستحم; as nn m, *restraint*: Job 30 3 (*S* ⲧⲁⲕⲟ
sic MS for ? ⲧⲁⲧϩⲟ) συνοχή; *ib* 28 15, Mic 7 17 (*SA*
? ⲱⲣⲃ ⲉϩⲟⲩⲛ) συγκλεισμός; Is 37 29 (*S* ϣⲧⲟϥ) φιμός;
Ob 1 (*A* ⲙⲉⲓϣⲉ) περιοχή; Ro 8 35 (*S* ⲗⲱϫϩ) στενοχωρία.

ⲧⲁⲩ *AA²F* *v* ⲧⲟⲟⲩ nn & *AA²* vb.

ⲑⲏⲩ *SA²*, ⲑⲏⲟⲩ *B*, ⲑⲛⲟⲩ *SAFO*, ⲧⲉⲩ, ⲑⲉⲩ *DM*
(7 28), ⲧⲟⲩ- *SAF*, ⲑⲟⲩ- *B* nn m, *wind*: Pro 8 27
SAB, Mt 14 24 *SBF*, Jo 6 18 *SA²B* ἄνεμος; Job 13
25 *SB*, Ps 47 7 *S*(*B* = Gk), Ez 5 2 *SB* πνεῦμα, Ac 2
2 *B*(*S* = Gk) πνοή; Jer 10 13 *S*(*B* = Gk) *ventus*;
Dan 3 64 *B*(var & *S* ⲛⲓϥ) Gk om; ClPr 30 15 *S* ⲡⲕⲓⲙ
ⲙⲡⲁⲏⲣⲡⲉ ⲛⲧ., BM 227 *S* ⲟⲩⲧ. ⲡⲉⲓⲱⲧⲉ (*cf* Dan 3 50),
AP 55 *A²* ⲁⲉⲓⲟⲩⲱϩ ⲥⲁϩⲛⲉ ⲛⲏⲧ., BM 174 1 *S* ⲟⲩⲧ.
ⲉϥϣⲟⲟⲙⲉ, DeV 2 35 *B* ⲡⲓⲑⲏⲟⲩ ⲃⲱⲛ of iniquity, C
43 213 *B* ⲁⲡⲓⲑ. ⲡⲓϥⲓ ⲉⲡⲓⲗⲁⲃⲟ, Va 58 155 *B* neigh-
bours complain ⳳⲉⲁϥⲱⲗⲓ ⲛⲡⲓⲑ. ⲛⲧⲉ ⲡⲉϥⲛⲓ (*cf* below

ра т.);   *south wind* тоүрнс, ѳоүр., ѳнοΥ р.: Ex 10 13 *B*, Ps 77 26 *SB*, Cant 4 16 *SF*, Ac 27 13 *SB* νότος; PS 214 *S*, C 86 122 *B* пιѳноΥ р., Mor 51 33 *S* птнΥ paral пт., Cai 42573 1 *S* in recipe тааʒ епкωʒт ʒ(ı)пт.; Ez 29 14 *B* паπιтοΥр. Φαθωρῆς (prob *l* патоΥр.);   *north wind* ʋ мʒιт s *f*; ϥтοΥ т., *four winds*: Ez 37 9 *SB*, Zech 2 6 *AB*, Mt 24 31 *SBF*;   *breath*: Ge 7 22 *B*(*S* пιϩⲉ) πνοή; Eccl 5 15 *S* ἄν., cit ShBor 246 49 *S*, cf ShBMOr 8800 202 *S* Origen spends days & nights eϥʒοce епт.; Mani *A²* gavest her пт. етаⲓⲣ, Mor 46 60 *S* they fled мπпеϥт. ммате, PMéd 176 *S* stomach eϥтeлтωм пт., MR 5 121 *S* charm against тıткас & т. пıм, AZ 21 106 *O* will enchant her heart & пст., Miss 4 548 *S* dying man ϯ мпеϥт. = C 89 87 *B* пеϥпⲡⲁ.

ма пт. *S*, *place of breath, life*, vital spot: Pro 7 23 (*A* = Gk, *B* diff) ψυχή, cit Bor 258 104 Holophernes welcoming Judith.

ка пт. *S*, *leave breath, expire*: Jud 4 21 ἐκψύχειν; Lu 23 46 (*B* ϯ мпıпⲡⲁ) ἐκπνεύειν; Miss 1 404 аϥка пт. аϥмоΥ, J 104 15 I gasped & groaned ʒωс ϫ(е)ıпакω пт. епмοΥ.

пеϫ т. еⲃⲟⲗ *S*, *cast out breath, expire*: ST 250 bishop did п. т. еⲃ. мпοοΥ; *v* also p 247 *b*.

ʒı пⲫ. *B*, *gasp, expire*: Ac 5 5 ʒı пеϥⲫ. (*S* моΥ) ἐκψ.; ROC 23 278 аϥʒı пеϥⲫ. аϥмοΥ.

апш, ап(а)ʒ т. *S*, *take breath* (*v* DM 1 3 n): Job 9 18 (*B* пıϥı), Mor 37 49 птереϥапаʒ т. ἀναπνεύειν; Mor 17 48 remove irons пϥапш т. поΥкоϯ ἐν ἀνέσει ποιεῖν; ShC 73 110 еϥшапıтоп ммоοΥ н псеапʒ т., BIF 13 111 аϥка пϭамоΥл еϥапш т.

сек т. *SB*, *draw breath*: Jer 14 6 ἄν. ἕλκειν.

р т. *S*, *make, raise wind, be windy*: ClPr 30 15 eϥшапкıм епанр шаϥер т., P 129²⁰ 159 rubric пеʒооΥ ешаср т. аΥω псʒωοΥ.

пеϣп ѳ. *B* nn *f*, *fan* *v* поΥϣп I.

ра т. *S* nn, *open-air space* on roof, *v* ра & cf Preisigke *W.buch* 1 27 ἀήρ.

ϫа ѳ. *B* nn *m*, *window*: C 89 132 θυρίς; *ib* 133 light етсапϣωı мпıϫ. = MSCai Copt Mus *S* пак (*v* above addendum to p 261) = Va 172 97 منور, *ib* 123 ϫ. above door shaded by ѳол, *ib* ϫ. opened to admit light.

сараѳ. (? сар аѳ., cf ʒат.) *B* nn *f* (Ps 82 16, Is 28 15) = *S* ʒат., ʒн пт. *q v*.

ʒн пт. *S* nn *m*, *breeze*: Ps 106 29 (*B* сараѳ.) αῦρα, cit P 44 53 пʒе пт. السلس ريح.

ʒат. *SF*, ʒат., ʒет. *A* nn *f*, *whirlwind* (*B* always сараѳ.): Ps 106 29, Pro 1 27 (*A* Cl ʒе.), *ib* 10 25 (*A* ʒа.), Lam 5 10 *SF* καταιγίς; Job 21 18, Mk 4 37 (var т.), BHom 48 ѳ. пенʒопн λαῖλαψ; Deu 4 11, He 12 18 θύελλα; Job 1 19 (*B* = Gk) πνεῦ.; Sa 5 15 ἄν.;

3 Kg 19 12 (cit ViK 9492, var т.) αῦρα; Hos 4 19 *S* (ShViK 911, *A* сωк аʒоΥн, *B* diff) συστροφή; P 44 53 ʒали тʒ. عاصف; Ez 13 11 *procella*; ShA 2 163 ʒ. пϭосм, Mor 26 12 ʒ. птпоϥос, BMis 156 мп ʒ. рωʒт ʒıϫωп, Mor 24 23 *F* devil vanished like оΥʒ., P 129¹⁴ 105 ѳло еⲃⲟⲗ ппеʒ. мпперашнт from their dark abodes.

ϫнпт. *S* nn, *blight* from parching wind: 2 Chr 6 28 (P 44 112 мнϫнпт. جرب, *B* ϫıмϥеʒ) ἀνεμοφθορία, Is 19 7 (*B* ер ϫ.), -φθορος; р ϫ., *be blighted*: Ge 41 6 (*B* do), -φθορος; P 44 96 root еаср ϫ. ضرب المسموم; ShBM 192 1 gloss on Cant 5 8 апеϥме аат пϫ., P 131⁵ 27 tree eϥо пϫ. in thirsty land, J 104 14 аıр ϫ. аıϫωм еⲃⲟⲗ.

In names (magical) кептеΥ, копт. (DM 7 28). т. птрωм *v* трωм; т. пϣарⲃа *v* ϣарⲃа. *V* also соοΥʒе.

ϯοΥ *SAA²F*, тıοΥ *B* (K 67, TEuch 1 527), теıοΥ DM, f ϯе *SAA²F*, ϯ *SA* nn, *five* (*BF* mostly ε): Nu 7 23, Jos 10 5, Jo 10 13 *A²*, Ap 9 5 πέντε; PS 3 пϯоΥ пϣнп, Mani 1 *A²* пϯоΥ ппоϥп, Miss 4 760 *Sf* ϯоΥ псап, BM 660 *F* кеϯоΥ, DM 2 26 поΥер теıοΥ (*v* RylDem 3 283, cf Mich 136 3 порϯоΥ); *5th day* пϯоΥ: Ps 80 tit п. мпсаⲃⲃатоп, Aeg 254, *ib* 37 еʒооΥ мптıοΥ, Zech 8 19 *A*, CO 455, *ib* 170 тıϥе пртоΥⲃ; f 1 Kg 25 42 ϯ прмʒал, Sa 10 6 ϯ мпολıс, Zech 8 21 *A* ϯ sim, BHom 48 ϯе паıсѳнсıс, TU 43 21 *A* ϯе прмпʒнт, Jo 5 2 ϯе (var ϯ) *A²* ϯе, BM 527 *F* ϯе птерʒам, R 2 1 38 ϯ птепеа, ShC 73 110 ппаΥ пϫпϯ.   тн in *fifteen*: мптн *SA²*, -те *S*, -тееıе *A²*, -ϯ *A*: Ge 7 20 -те, 4 Kg 14 17 -тн, Ac 27 28 -тн, Hos 3 2 *A*, Jo 11 18 *A²*, J & C 95 *A²* мптееıе, PS 6 пмптн мпоо ʒ; *twenty-five &c*: Nu 8 24 ϫоΥтн, Ge 18 28 ʒметн, *ib* 5 21, AZ 21 106 *O* сетн, Ge 12 4 ϣⲃетн, Ex 1 5 *A* сⲃеϯ, Jos 14 10 ϥтоΥϫоϥωте мпϯ (var ϯе), Ge 5 17 п(с)таıоΥтн; *fifty* та(е)ıοΥ *SA²B* (*ut sup*), теıοΥе *A*, теⲃı *B*: Ge 6 15, Ex 30 23 *B* (TEuch, var Lakân 138 теⲃı), Hag 2 16 *SA*, Lu 7 41, Jo 8 57 *A²*, Leyd 155 пт. пʒооΥ Pentecost, CO 29 sim, PLond 4 497 таıοΥмаϥ *eighty*, *v* also апprefix; *five hundred*: Job 1 3, 1 Cor 15 6 ϯοΥ пϣе; *five thousand*: Mt 14 21 ϯοΥ пϣо, Jud 20 45 ϭıстⲃа.

мерϯοΥ, -ϯе, *fifth*: Jos 19 24, Ez 1 2, Zech 7 3 *A* маʒ-, Br 79, BG 16 мерϯе ммΟрϥн, *ib* 29 мерϯ проΥтсϥıме, PS 192 маʒϯ мϥωпн, Mani 2 *A²* пмаʒϯοΥ (псϫнма); *fiftieth*: Lev 25 10, PS 111 мертаıοΥ.   In place-name: ттıе пкоıе Πέντε πεδιάδες (PLond 4 492). *V* AZ 62 60.

тооΥ *SO*, -οΥе *S* (Blake 246, error?), таΥ *AA²SfF*, тωοΥ *B*, pl forms *v* below & sg as pl, nn *m*, *mountain*:

Ge 22 2 *SA*(Cl)*B*, Ps 82 14 *SB*, Cant 8 14 *SF*, Is 5 25
SBF, Jo 4 20 *SA²B* ὄρος, Mor 37 140 *S* ⲡⲧ. ⲉⲧⲉⲣⲟⲩⲡ
τὸ ἔνδον ὅ., Miss 4 566 *S* ⲡⲧ. ⲉⲧⲣⲓⲃⲟⲗ τὸ ὅ. τὸ ἔξω(*cf Z.
f. Kirchengesch.* 42 28 n), Is 10 18 *S* ⲧ.... ⲥⲓⲃⲧ, *B* ⲧ....
ⲕⲁⲗⲁⲙⲫⲟ ὅ., βουνός, Jos 9 1 *S* ὀρεινός; Ex 17 10 *B*
(*S* ⲧⲁⲗ)βου., ib 19 1 *S*(var ⲝⲁⲉⲓⲉ, *B* ϣⲁϥⲉ), Nu 1 19
B(*S* = Gk, *cf* ib 28 6 ὅ.)ἐρῆμος; Job 15 7 *B*(*S* ⲕⲣⲟ)
θίς; ib 37 9 *SB* ἀκρωτήριον; BMar 105 *S* πέτρα;
ShC 73 18 *S* city, village, ⲕⲁⲓⲉ (var ⲥⲱϣⲉ), ⲧ., J 65
44 *S* ⲧ., ⲕⲏⲙⲉ, ⲥⲱϣⲉ, PNolot 72 *S* ⲣⲏ†ⲙⲉ ⲣⲓⲧ.,
Miss 4 682 *S* house ⲣⲓⲧⲟⲩϣ ⲙⲡⲧ. ⲡⲣⲣⲁⲥ ⲡⲧⲥⲱϣⲉ,
ShMIF 23 21 *S* ⲧ. opp ⲕⲁⲝ, KroppH 98 *S* ⲡⲕⲁⲝ
ⲙⲡⲧ., Miss 4 570 *S* ⲡⲧⲁⲁⲡⲁⲭⲱⲣⲉⲓ ⲡⲁⲓ ⲉⲣⲟⲩⲡ
ⲉⲡⲧ.,BMis 476 *S* ⲉⲓ ⲉⲃⲟⲗ ⲡⲙⲡⲧ.,MG 25 56 *B* barbarians ⲉⲧⲥⲁⲝⲟⲩⲡ ⲙⲡⲧ., Rec 6 173 *B* walked ⲉⲝⲟⲩⲡ
ⲉⲡⲧ. ⲉⲧⲥⲁⲝⲟⲩⲡ, BMis 475 *S* ⲟⲩⲕⲟⲟϥ ⲡⲧ. (*cf* 472 ⲕ.
ⲙⲡⲉⲧⲣⲁ & Job 40 15 *S* ⲧ. ⲡⲕ.),BSM 88 *B* ⲡⲓⲁⲥⲕⲓⲧⲏⲥ
ⲉⲧϨⲉⲡⲡⲓⲧ., AZ 21 100 *O* ⲡⲉⲧⲡⲏⲟⲩ ⲡⲡⲧ.; *community of hermits, monastery* (*v* PLond 4 xvii n, CO
371 n, Ep 1 107 n): MG 25 18 *B* ⲙⲁⲣⲉⲡⲧⲁϥⲉ ⲡⲓⲧ.
ⲕⲉⲗⲗⲓⲟⲛ; ShBM 194 2 *S* God's τόποι & ⲡⲕⲉⲧ. ⲉⲧⲟⲩⲁⲁⲃ, CO 407 *S* ⲁⲡⲟⲛ ⲧⲕⲏⲡⲟⲧⲏⲥ (κοινότ.) ⲧⲏⲣⲥ
ⲙⲡⲧ., P 129¹⁶ 96 *S* ⲡⲧ. ⲙⲡⲛⲙⲟⲛⲏ of Egypt, P 68
65 *S* ⲡⲁⲣⲭⲓⲙⲁⲡ⳹ ⲙⲡⲧ. ⲡⲁⲧⲣⲓⲡⲉ, ST 435 *S* ⲡⲁⲡⲏ
ⲙⲡⲧ. ⲡⲧⲥⲛⲧⲉ, RE 9 168 *S* ⲡⲥⲡⲏⲟⲩ ⲙⲡⲧ. ⲡⲧⲱⲣⲉ, Ep
85 *S* ⲡⲙⲟⲛⲁⲭⲟⲥ ⲙⲡⲧ. ⲡⲭⲏⲙⲉ, N&E 39 334 *B* ⲡⲓⲟ†
ⲡⲧⲉ ⲡⲁⲓⲧ., DeV 2 130 *B* ⲡⲕⲟⲓⲡⲟⲃⲓⲟⲛ ⲡⲧⲉ ⲡⲓⲧ. ⲡⲥⲓⲱ-
ⲟⲩⲧ, on monkish epitaphs †ⲣⲏⲡⲏ ⲙⲡⲓⲧ. ⲉⲧⲟⲩⲁⲁⲃ
Hall 8 *S*, TurM 53 *S*; *cf* Preisigke *W.buch* 3 404
ὄρος, جبل (Synax 1 362 13, 363 10) & Ⲗ·ⲠⲤ; *cemetery* in desert: Gu 92 *S* ⲡⲧ. ⲡⲃⲉⲟⲩⲡⲓⲁ where Lazarus buried, ShC 73 62 *S* ⲃⲱⲕ ⲉⲡⲧ. ⲉⲧⲟⲙⲥⲟⲩ, C
89 93 *B* bore corpse to ⲡⲓⲧ. ⲁⲩⲑⲟⲙⲥϥ, BAp 126 *S*
bore him to ⲡⲧ. ⲡⲧⲁϥⲧⲣⲉⲡϣⲁⲕⲧϥ (*cf* PO 22 477),
LMis 66 *S* ⲁⲩⲧⲱⲙⲥ ⲙⲙⲟⲥ ⲣⲓⲡⲧ. ⲡⲧⲉⲥⲡⲟⲗⲓⲥ,
BHom 117 *S* body ϩⲏⲗ ⲉⲃⲟⲗ ⲣⲓⲡⲧ.; as adj, *of
the hill, desert, so wild*: ⲉⲓⲁ ⲡⲧ. *v* ⲉⲓⲱ *ass*; ⲣⲓⲣ ⲡⲧ.
v ⲣⲓⲣ; ⲉⲣⲉ ⲡⲧ. *v* ⲉⲣⲉ adding BM 527 24 *F*; ⲙⲥⲁⲝ
ⲡⲧ. *v* ⲙⲥⲁⲝ; ⲣⲁⲕⲉⲗϥ ⲉⲧ. Cai 42573 2 *S*; ⲥⲟⲟⲓ ⲡⲧ.
scented wild flowers PO 11 330 *B*; ⲡⲁϣⲟⲩϣ ⲧ. *v* ϩⲁ-
ϣⲟⲩϣ (*l* سذاب بري); ⲙⲱⲟⲩ ⲡⲧ. *B* Ex 7 19 (var om)
συνεστηκώς; ⲣⲙⲟⲩ ⲡⲧ. *S* PMéd 273; ϩⲁⲓⲣⲓ ⲡⲧ. *v* ϩⲓⲣ.

Pl forms (*v* Rec 24 206): *S* ⲧⲟⲩ(ⲉ)ⲓⲏ Ge 7 1 (var
ⲡⲧⲟⲟⲩ), Ps 103 8 (*cf* 11 ⲡⲧⲟⲟⲩ), BMar 48 went to
ⲡⲧ. & became monks, Pcod 20 ⲣⲓⲡⲓⲧ. opp ⲣⲙⲡⲕⲟⲥ-
ⲙⲟⲥ; ⲧⲟⲟⲩⲉ (?, var Ep 9 -ⲟⲩ)Job 29 6; *A* ⲧⲟⲩⲓⲉⲓ
Joel 2 5, Am 9 13, ⲧⲟⲩⲉⲓ Hos 4 13, Nah 3 18, ⲧⲟⲩⲉⲓⲉ
Mic 5 14, -ⲉⲉⲓⲉ Jon 2 7, ⲧⲟⲩⲓⲉⲩⲉ El 102 (*cf* AZ 62
124); *A²* ⲧⲟⲩⲓⲉⲩⲉ Mani 2; *F* ⲧⲟⲩⲉⲓ[BM 1225.

ⲣⲙ-, ⲣⲉⲙⲡⲧ., *mountain man*: MG 25 96 *B* =
GöttAr 114 24 سكان البرية, Rec 6 174 *B* = BMar 210
S ⲉⲓⲁ ⲡⲧ. (prob *l* ⲣⲙ- as ib infra); ⲣⲙⲡⲧ. *S*: ST
437 ⲡⲣ. ⲡⲣⲙⲟⲡⲧ.

ϩⲁⲡⲧ., *S*, ⲁⲡⲧ., ϩⲟ ⲡⲧ., *B* nn m, *mountainous country*: Deu 2 37 *B*, Zech 7 7 *B*(*A* = Gk), Lu 1 39 *B*
ⲁⲡⲧ., Jer 40 13 *B* ϩⲟ ⲡⲧ. (all *S* = Gk) ὀρεινή (*cf* Jos 10
40 ⲧⲟⲣ. ⲡⲕⲁϩ ⲉⲧϩⲟⲥⲉ): Ryl 108 *S* tree growing
ϩⲓⲡⲡⲁⲡⲧ.; with place-names: Pcod 47 *S* ⲡⲣ. ⲡⲉⲣⲏ-
ϩⲉ (Rifah), Lant 21 *Sf* ⲡⲣⲁⲡⲧⲁⲩ ⲡⲥⲱⲡⲉⲣⲉⲥ (var 23
ⲫⲁⲡⲧ.); alone: *ib* 7 monastery of St Michael ⲙⲡϥⲁ.
(var ⲉⲡϩ.), *ib* 18, 38 &c sim. *Cf* Φαντῶ, -ταῦ (Preisigke). *V* AZ 51 123, WS 7 n & ROC 23 94 n (on
حاجر), Lant 1 n.

In many place-names: ⲡⲧ. ⲡϣⲓⲛⲧ (BMis 472),
ⲡⲓⲧ. ⲉⲑⲟⲩⲁⲃ ⲡⲧⲉ ϣ. (EW 128), ⲡⲧⲡⲓⲧⲣⲓⲁ (HT *S* 2),
ⲙⲡⲣⲟⲥⲙ(PSBA 10 198, MG 25 56), ⲙⲡⲉⲣⲡⲟⲩⲝ (*ib*
239), ⲙⲙⲉϥⲉ (RAC 105), ⲡⲥⲓⲟⲟⲩⲧ (Miss 4 761, *cf*
767 ⲧⲡⲉⲧⲣⲁ ⲡⲥ.), ⲡⲧⲥⲉⲡ† (BAp 75), ⲡⲁⲧⲣⲏⲡⲉ (Lant
53), ⲡⲧϩⲱ (*ib* 113), ⲧ. (var ⲧⲟⲩⲱ) ⲡⲉⲁⲡⲓⲥⲕⲱⲡ (WS
199), Τόου (BGU 1221), Πκομπτόου, Πιαϩτόου
(Preisigke), Μουνπτόου(PCai 1),Σιντώου(Wess 20),
Τκοιτόου(PEleph 16), ⲕⲣⲟ ⲡⲧⲟⲟⲩ Ἐποίκιον Βουνῶν
(PLond 4 p vii 497). In name: Θιννεβδοοῦς
(Preisigke).

ⲧⲟⲟⲩ *S*, ⲧⲁⲩ *AA²*, ⲧⲉⲩ-, ⲧⲟⲩⲉ-(once)*S*, ⲧⲁⲩⲉ-*A*,
ⲧⲁⲩ-*A²*, ⲧⲟⲟⲩ⳹ *S*, ⲧⲁⲩ⳹ *S*(ClPr 24)*A* vb intr, *buy* (*B*
always ϣⲱⲡ): Ez 7 13 (ShA 2 336, var ϣ.) κτᾶσθαι;
ShBMOr 8810 417 ϫⲓ †, † ⲉⲃⲟⲗ ⲧ., El 78 *A* ⲡⲉⲧ†
ⲁϩⲁⲗ ⲡⲉⲧⲧ., ShZ 501 find not money ⲉⲧ. ⲡⲧⲉⲓⲙⲟϭ
ⲡⲁⲥⲟⲩ; tr: Lev 25 28, Jos 24 32 (var ϣ.) ⲕⲧ.;
Pro 23 20 *A* ⲧⲁⲩⲉ-(*S* ϣ.), Lu 22 36 ⲧⲉⲩ- (var ⲧⲟⲩⲉ-),
Jo 4 8 *A²* ⲧⲁⲩ-(*SBF* ϣ.)ἀγοράζειν, Pro 29 34 *A* ⲧⲁⲩⲥ
(*S* ϣ.) πρίασθαι; ShMIF 23 83 ⲁϥⲧⲟⲟⲩⲥⲟⲩ ϩⲙ-
ⲡⲉϥⲥⲡⲟϥ,ShViK 9099 ⲁⲓⲧⲟⲟⲩⲕ ⲡϩⲙϩⲁⲗ,ShA 1 127
ⲉⲩⲡⲁⲧⲟⲟⲩⲥⲉ ⲡⲧⲟⲟⲧⲟⲩ, ShClPr 24 353 ⲁϥⲧⲁⲩⲥⲟⲩ
ⲡⲧⲟⲟⲧⲟⲩ, ShP 131⁶ 44 ⲡⲧⲁⲕⲧⲟⲟⲩϥ ⲅⲁⲟⲩⲁⲥⲟⲩ, BP
4929 ⲡϣⲱⲙ ⲡⲧⲁⲡⲧⲟⲟⲩϥ. *V* GöttN '19 142.

ⲧⲁⲩⲉ *S*, nn or name?: J 44 74 ⲡⲏⲓ ϣⲏⲙ ⲡⲧ. ⲙⲡⲓⲡⲉⲣⲡⲉϩ, *ib* 64 sim ϣⲏⲙ ⲧ.

ⲧⲁ(ⲟ)ⲩⲟ, -ⲱ, ⲧⲁⲟⲩⲟ, ⲧⲁⲃⲟ *S*, ⲧⲉ(ⲟ)ⲩⲟ *Sᵃ*(ST
280) *AA²*, ⲧⲁⲟⲩⲟ *B*, -ⲁ *F*, ⲧⲁ(ⲟ)ⲩⲉ-, ⲧⲁⲩⲟ- *S*, ⲧⲉⲩⲟ-
A, ⲧⲁⲟⲩⲉ- *B*, ⲧⲁⲟⲩⲁ- *F*, ⲧⲁ(ⲟ)ⲩⲟ⳹, ⲧⲁⲩⲟⲩⲟ⳹ *S*,
ⲧⲉ(ⲟ)ⲩⲁ⳹ *AA²*, ⲧⲁⲟⲩⲟ⳹ *B*, ⲧⲁ(ⲟ)ⲩⲁ⳹ *F*, ⲧⲁⲅⲱⲟⲩⲟ⳹ *O*,
ⲧⲁⲟⲩⲛⲟⲩⲧ† *B* vb tr, *a send*: Jo 4 34 *SA²BF*, *ib* 13 16
S(var ⲧⲏⲡⲟⲟⲩ)*A²B* πέμπειν; Ps 106 20 *B*(*S* ϫⲟⲟⲩ),
Mt 21 3 *F*(*S* ⲧⲏ., *B* ⲟⲩⲱⲣⲡ), Jo 6 29 *BF*(*SA²* ⲧⲏ.)
ἀποστέλλειν, Ps 143 6 *B*(*S* ⲧϩⲕⲟ), Gal 4 6 *B*(var ⲟⲩ.,
S ⲧⲏ.) ἐξαπ.; Mt 9 38 *B*(*S* ⲡⲟⲩϫⲉ) ἐκβάλλειν; PS 9
S ⲝⲓⲁⲕⲟⲡⲓⲁ ⲉⲡⲧⲁⲩⲧⲁⲅⲟⲉⲓ ⲉⲧⲃⲏⲏⲧⲥ, TU 43 4 *A* ⲡⲉⲧ-
ⲁⲣⲧⲉⲟⲩⲁⲉⲓ, AP 56 *A²* sim, EW 141 *B* ⲁϥⲧ. ⲡⲁⲡ...
ⲁⲃⲃⲁ ⲁⲡⲧⲱⲡⲓ, Mor 24 11 *F* ϣⲁⲗⲉⲡⲁⲓⲱⲧ ⲧ. ⲙⲙⲓⲭⲁⲏⲗ, Ep 278 *S* ⲡⲣⲱⲙⲉ ⲁⲓⲧⲁⲟⲩⲟⲩ ⲡⲏⲕ, ViK 7033
F ⲧⲁⲟⲩⲁ ⲥⲡⲱⲥⲓⲥ ⲧⲁⲓⲙⲓ. **ⲃ** *put forth, produce*:
Ps 106 37 *S*(*B* ⲓⲣⲓ), Is 5 2 *S*(*B* do) ποιεῖν; Lev 26
40 *S*(*B* ⲟⲩⲱⲛϩ ⲉⲃⲟⲗ) ἐξαγορεύειν; Ps 144 7 *S*(*B* ϩⲉ-

ⲫ̅ⲓ) ἐξερεύγεσθαι; *ib* 7 12 *B*(*S* ⲉⲓⲡⲉ) ἐπάγειν, Job 15 13 *S*(*B* ⲉⲓⲡⲉ ⲉⲃⲟⲗ) ἐξάγειν; Nu 24 17 *S*(var ⲧⲥⲁⲃⲟ, *B* ⲇⲟ) δεικνύναι; CO 14 *S* ⲁϥⲧⲁⲅⲉ ⲧⲗⲟⲓⲥ̄ⲉ ⲝⲉ-, Ryl 99 *S* ⲡⲗⲟⲓⲟⲥ ⲡⲧⲁϥⲧⲁⲅⲟⲩ (PO 2 248 ﺣﺪ).   **c** *utter, proclaim, recount*: Is 53 8 *A*(Cl, *S* ϣⲁϫⲉ, *B* ϥⲓⲣⲓ), Ac 8 33 *S*(*B* ⲥⲁϫⲓ) διηγεῖσθαι; Nu 24 13 *S*(*B* ⲝⲱ), Mk 14 39 *S*(*B* ⲇⲟ) εἰπεῖν, Z 277 *S* writings ⲛ̄-ⲧⲁⲡϣⲣⲡ ⲛ̄ⲧⲁⲅⲟⲟⲩ ⲡⲣⲟⲉⲓ.; Mk 14 71 *S*(*B* ⲇⲟ), RNC 21 *S* ⲉⲣⲉⲟⲩⲙⲓⲛ̄ϣⲉ ⲧ. ⲙ̄ⲡⲣⲁⲙⲏⲡ λέγειν, Aeg 271 *S* ϣⲣⲡ ⲧ. ⲡⲣⲟⲗ.; Deu 3 26 *S*(*B* ⲥⲁ.), Ps 39 5 *S*(*B* ⲇⲟ) λαλεῖν; *ib* 118 172 *S*(*B* ⲉⲣ ⲟⲩⲱ) φθέγγεσθαι; Ac 21 19 *S*(*B* ⲥⲁ.) ἐξηγεῖσθαι; Jud 5 1 *S* ᾄδειν; Ez 13 23 *B* ⲧ. ⲛ̄ⲣⲁⲛϣⲓⲛⲓ (*S* ⲝⲱ) μαντεύεσθαι; PS 32 *S* ⲧⲁⲅⲉ ⲡϣⲁϫⲉ ⲉⲧⲉⲣⲛⲁⲕ, ShWess 9 144 *S* ⲙ̄ⲡⲟⲩⲧⲁⲅⲉ ⲏⲡⲉ *named not number* (of years), ShA 2 345 *S* ⲉⲧⲣⲉⲡⲧⲁⲅⲉ ⲡⲣⲟϥ ⲛ̄ⲕⲉⲥⲟⲡ *mention the serpent* (Ex 4 3), J 75 98 *S* ⲡⲉⲛⲧⲁⲡⲧⲁⲟⲅⲟⲩ ⲛ̄ⲅⲁⲣ ⲛ̄ⲥⲟⲡ, Mor 43 30 *S* ⲙ̄ⲡⲣⲧⲁⲅⲉ ⲗⲁⲁⲩ ⲛ̄ϣⲁϫⲉ (var *ib* 42 28 ⲙ̄ⲡⲣϫⲉ-); OstrMoscow Mus *S* ⲡϣⲁϫⲉ ⲛ̄ⲧⲁⲧⲉⲥϭⲓⲙⲉ ⲧⲁⲃⲟϥ, ST 300 *S* ⲁϥ-ⲧⲁⲅⲟ ⲛ̄ⲉⲛⲥⲟⲗ, JA '75 5 211 *S* ⲡⲉⲧⲧ. ⲛ̄ϣⲟⲙⲛ̄ⲧ ⲛ̄ⲡ̄ⲉ̄, AM 128 *B* ⲉⲅⲧ. ⲛ̄ⲣⲁⲛⲙⲏϣ ⲛ̄ⲡⲟⲩϯ, Pcod 20 *S* ⲡⲉⲧ-ⲛⲁⲧⲁⲅⲉ ⲟⲩϭⲱⲃ ⲕⲁⲧⲁ ⲟⲩⲁ of Trinity, Mani 1 *A²* ⲡⲉⲧ-ⲉⲣⲉⲡⲉⲛ̄ⲙⲓⲗⲁ ⲧ. ⲙ̄ⲙⲁϥ;   *recite, repeat*: ShC 73 133 *S* ⲧⲁⲅⲟ ⲙⲏⲧ ⲛ̄ⲯⲁⲗⲙⲟⲥ, MIE 2 335 *B* ⲧ. ⲙ̄ⲡⲓⲯⲁⲗ-ⲧⲏⲣⲓⲟⲛ by heart, Aeg 39 *B* harpers ⲧ. ⲛ̄ⲣⲁⲛⲝⲱ, FR 70 *S* ⲁⲥⲧⲁⲅⲟⲅⲟ ⲛ̄ⲟⲩⲡⲣⲟⲥⲉⲩⲭⲏ, ViK 9463 *S* ⲧⲁⲅⲟ ⲡⲉϣⲗⲏⲗ = C 89 13 *B* ⲝⲱ, AM 247 *B* ⲟⲩⲉⲧⲕⲱⲙⲓⲟⲛ ⲉⲁϥⲧⲁⲟⲅⲟϥ.   **d** *give, say name*: Lev 23 35 *S*(*B* ⲙⲟⲩϯ ⲉ-) καλεῖν, Deu 28 10 *S*(*B* ⲧⲟⲓ) ἐπικ.; Is 26 13 *S*(*B* ⲝⲱ), Ac 19 13 *S*(*B* ⲇⲟ) ὀνομάζειν, Ex 20 24 *S*(*B* ⲙ.) ἔπον.; Br 127 *S* ⲧⲁⲅⲉ ⲡⲉⲥⲣⲁⲛ, Mor 48 57 *S* ⲙ̄ⲡⲁⲧⲉⲕⲧ. ⲙ̄ⲡⲉⲓⲣ. = C 43 129 *B* ϥⲓⲣⲓ ⲉ-, BSM 119 *B* ⲉⲧⲁⲕⲧⲁⲟⲅⲉ ⲡⲉϥⲣ.   **e** *overthrow*: Z 268 *S* ⲉⲁⲓⲡ̄ⲉ̄ ⲧⲁⲅⲟⲅⲟⲕ (*sc* Julian) ⲉⲩⲙⲡⲟⲗⲩⲙⲟⲥ (*cf* ⲧ. ⲉ-, ⲉⲡⲉⲥⲏⲧ).

Intr (rare), *recite*: Mor 18 32 *S* ⲡⲉϥⲧ. ⲉⲣⲱⲱϥ ⲛ̄ⲙ-ⲙⲁⲩ (var *ib* 19 41 ⲝⲱ, Miss 4 125 *B* diff), Mani 2 *A²* let apostle ⲣ ϣⲁⲣⲡ ⲛ̄ⲧ. ⲕⲁⲧⲁ ⲟⲩⲡⲣⲟⲫⲏⲧⲓⲁ.

With following preposition.

—— ⲉ- tr, a *send to, cast upon*: Ps 147 4 *B*(*S* ⲝⲟ.) ἀποστ. dat, Jo 3 17 *F*(*SA²* ⲧⲛ., *B* ⲟⲩ.) ἀπ. εἰς; Mor 17 46 *S* ⲛ̄ⲧⲁⲥⲧⲁⲅⲟⲟⲩ ⲉⲡⲁⲧⲙⲟⲥ παραπέμ. ἐν; Mic 1 6 *SA*(*B* ⲟⲩⲱϣⲡ) κατασπᾶν εἰς; 2 Kg 18 11 *S* ⲧⲁⲅⲟϥ ⲉⲡⲕⲁϩ (var ⲛ̄ⲧϥ) Gk om; PS 263 *S* ⲛ̄ⲥⲉⲧⲁⲅⲟⲥ ⲉⲡⲉ-ⲕⲣⲓⲥⲓⲥ; vbal: Ge 19 13 *B*(*S* ⲧⲛ.), Ac 16 36 *S*(*B* ⲟⲩ.) ἀποστ.   **b** *tell to*: Deu 17 10 *S*(*B* ⲧⲁⲙⲟ) ἀνάγ. dat, 1 Kg 3 18 *S* ἀπάγ. dat; Jud 7 13 *S*, MG 17 315 *S* ⲁϥⲧⲁⲅⲉ ⲡⲁⲓ ⲉⲡⲉⲥⲏⲏⲩ = C 89 3 *B* ⲇⲟ ἐξηγ., Est 1 17 *S*, Joel 1 3 *A*(*B* ⲥⲁ.) διηγ. dat, Hab 1 5 *SA*(*B* ⲇⲟ)ἐκδ. dat; Deu 4 45 *S*(*B* ⲇⲟ), Aeg 242 *S* λαλεῖν dat; 1 Kg 8 10 *S* εἰπ. πρός; Jud 14 12 *S* προβάλ. dat; Jos 22 32 *S* ἀποκρίνεσθαι; Bor 239 77 *S* could not ⲧⲁⲅⲉ ⲗⲁⲁⲩ ⲛ̄ϣⲁϫⲉ ⲉⲣⲟⲥ (varr R 1 2 41 ⲡⲁⲥ, Lammeyer

44 ⲝⲱ), PSBA 10 194 *S* ⲧⲁⲅⲟⲩⲟⲟⲩ ⲉⲣⲟⲥ ⲙⲏⲡⲟⲧⲉ-ⲡⲓⲡ, Ep 431 *S* ⲧ. ⲧⲁⲡⲟⲕⲣⲓⲥⲓⲥ ⲉⲣⲟϥ ⲛ̄ⲣⲱⲕ, Mani 1 *A²* ⲉⲅⲧ. ⲁⲣⲁϥ ⲛ̄ⲣⲥⲉⲝⲉ, Mor 30 55 *F* ⲧ. ⲙ̄ⲡⲁⲡⲁϩ̄ⲣ ⲉⲗⲁⲓ = *ib* 29 47 *S* ⲝⲱ = BMis 277 *S* ⲧⲁⲙⲟⲓ ⲉ-, BM 1151 *S* ⲛ̄ⲛⲉⲡⲁⲝ̄ⲥ̄ ⲧ. ⲣⲱϥ ⲉⲣⲟⲓ ⲣⲁⲣⲟⲥ; *relate concerning, address to*: BMis 74 *S* sermon ⲉⲁϥⲧⲁⲅⲟⲩ ⲉⲡⲉ-ⲭⲡⲟ...ⲁⲅⲱ ⲉⲧⲃⲉⲙⲁⲣⲓⲁ, Va 58 24*B* sim ⲉ-...ⲛⲉⲙ-ⲉⲱ̄ⲃⲉ-, RNC 70 *S* let him ⲧⲁⲅⲉ ⲟⲩ (*sic*) ⲝⲱ ⲉⲡⲓ-ⲭⲣⲓⲥⲧⲓⲁⲛⲟⲥ, Mor 31 22 *S* ⲙ̄ⲡⲉⲧⲛ̄ⲧ. ⲟⲩⲥⲙⲟⲩ ⲉⲣⲟⲛ saying Welcome, Miss 4 574 *S*, ST 266 *S* sim.   **c** *show*: Deu 33 10 *S* δηλοῦν; Nu 22 41 *S*, Jo 20 20 *A²*(*S* ⲧⲥⲁⲃⲟ, all *B* ⲧⲁⲙⲟ) δεικνύναι; Deu 1 5 *S*(*B* ⲥⲁ.) διασαφεῖν; Ac 11 4 *S*(*B* ⲇⲟ) ἐκτιθέναι;   intr: BMis 148 *S* ceased not to ⲧ. ⲉⲣⲟⲓ ⲛ̄ⲧⲁⲡⲩⲝⲓⲟⲛ (πύ-ξινον) *recite to me* until I knew all letters (? scriptures) by heart; ⲉⲣⲟϥⲡ, ⲉϭ. ⲉ-, *send to,*: Jer 16 16 *B*(*S* BMis 194 ⲝⲟ. ⲛ̄ⲥⲁ-) ἀποστ., Ps 77 49 *B*(*S* ⲝⲟ. ⲉϩⲣⲁⲓ ⲉϫⲛ̄-) ἐξαπ.; AP 42 *A²* ⲁϥⲧ. ⲁⲣ. ⲁⲡⲉⲡⲣⲟ-ⲫⲏⲧⲏⲥ, Mor 16 26 *S* ⲧⲁⲅⲉ ϣⲁϫⲉ ⲡⲟⲩⲁ ⲉⲣ. ⲉⲡⲉⲥ-ⲫⲟⲥ (var BMis 194 ⲛ̄ⲥⲁ-), PSBA 28 138 *S* ⲁⲥⲧⲁⲅⲉ ⲫⲩⲥⲓⲥ ⲥⲛ̄ⲧⲉ ⲉⲣ. ⲉⲡⲓⲟⲩⲁ ⲛ̄ⲟⲩⲱⲧ *ascribe to* (*cf* ⲉϫⲛ̄-).

—— ⲉⲧⲛ̄- *SA, tell to*: El 40 *A* recording angels ⲧ. ⲁⲧⲟⲟⲧϥ *recite* (sins) to accuser, COAd 7 *S* gospel learnt ⲛ̄ⲧⲁⲅⲟϥ ⲉⲧⲟⲟⲧⲕ (*cf* CO 39 om ⲉⲧ-).

—— ⲉϫⲛ̄- *SA, say, pronounce upon, about*: 1 Kg 3 12 λαλ. εἰς; Is 18 7 (*B* ⲙⲟⲩϯ) ἐπικαλ. οὗ; Hab 2 1 *A*(*B* ⲉⲣ ⲟⲩⲱ) ἀποκρ. ἐπί; Ryl 62 2 ⲧⲁⲅⲉ ⲛ̄ⲣⲁⲡ... ⲉϫⲛⲣⲉⲡⲛ̄ⲃⲏⲅⲉ, Leyd 136 rubric ⲧ. ⲡⲕⲉⲥⲉⲉⲡⲉ ⲉϫⲛ̄-ⲡⲉⲧⲟⲅⲁⲃ, Bor 248 ⲧⲁⲅⲉ ⲫⲩⲥⲓⲥ ⲥⲛ̄ⲧⲉ ⲉϫⲛ̄ⲡⲉⲓⲟⲩⲁ, Mor 43 3 curses ⲛ̄ⲧⲁϥⲧⲁⲟⲅⲟⲩ ⲉϫⲛ̄- (var *ib* 42 5 ⲝⲱ);   *send upon B*: Ps 105 15 (*S* ⲝⲟ.) ἐξαποστ. εἰς;   ⲉϩⲣⲁⲓ ⲉϫⲛ̄-*SF*: Is 4 1 (*B* diff) καλ. ἐπί, Deu 28 10 (*B* diff) ἐπικ. dat, Ja 2 7 (*B* ⲙ.) ἐπικ. ἐπί; BM 330 ⲧⲟⲡⲟⲥ ⲉⲧⲟⲩⲛⲁⲧ. ⲙ̄ⲡⲉⲕⲣⲁⲡ ⲉⲣ. ⲉϫⲱϥ, Mor 24 11 *F* ⲁⲡⲧ. ⲡⲕⲁⲧⲁⲕⲗⲩⲥⲙⲟⲥ ⲉⲣ. ⲉϫⲱⲟⲩ.

—— ⲛ̄- *SBF, send to*: Ac 19 31 *S*(*B* ⲟⲩ.) πέμ. πρός; Ps 110 9 *B*(*S* ⲝⲟ.), Jer 35 9 *B* ἀποστ. dat; AZ 23 34 *F* ⲑⲟⲗⲟⲕ(ⲟⲧⲥⲓ) ⲁⲓⲧⲁⲟⲅⲁⲥ ⲡⲉⲕ, BM 647 *F* ⲧⲁ-ⲟⲩⲁⲩ ⲡⲉⲓ;   *tell to*: PBu 17 *S* ⲓⲧⲉⲧ. ⲡⲟⲩϣⲁϫⲉ ⲛⲁⲩ, CO 254 *S* ⲁⲓⲧⲁⲟⲅⲱ ⲡⲁⲣⲓⲥⲉ ⲡⲉⲕ, Mani 1 *A²* ⲡⲓⲙ ⲡⲉⲧⲁⲧ. ⲛⲏⲓ ⲉⲧⲃⲉ-?

—— ⲛ̄ⲥⲁ- *SB, send after*: Ge 27 45 *B*(*S* ⲧⲛ.) ἀποστ. μεταπέμ. acc; Ac 24 25 *S*(*B* ⲟⲩ.) μετακαλ. acc; TillOster 23 *A* (?);   *speak, repeat against S*: Lev 19 14 (*B* ⲝⲱ ⲛ̄ⲥⲁ-) εἰπεῖν acc, Bor 226 163 ⲧⲁⲅⲉ ⲟⲩϣⲁϫⲉ ⲛ̄ⲥⲱⲕ λόγον εἰπ. κατά; R 2 2 29 ⲧ. ⲣⲉⲛⲡⲉⲧ-ⲣⲟⲟⲩ ⲛ̄ⲥⲱⲕ αἴσχος ἐπιφάναι dat; Miss 8 28 ⲉⲅⲧ. ⲛ̄ⲣⲏⲛⲟϭ ⲛ̄ⲁⲓⲧⲓⲁ ⲛ̄ⲥⲁⲡⲉⲥⲧⲱⲣⲓⲟⲥ.

—— ϣⲁ- *SBF, send to*: Ac 15 25 *S*(var ⲧⲛ.), Eph 6 22 *F*(*S* ⲧⲛ.) πέμ. πρός; Mt 23 37 *S*(var ⲧⲛ.), 2 Cor 12 17 *F*(*S* ⲧⲛ., all *B* ⲟⲩ.) ἀποστ. πρός; R 1 5 49 *S* ⲁϥⲧⲁⲟⲅⲟⲓ ϣⲁⲣⲟⲕ ⲉⲡⲉⲓⲙⲁ, DeV 2 129 *B* ⲁϥⲧⲁⲟⲩⲟⲛ ϣⲁⲣⲟⲕ.

—— ⲣⲁ- B, as last: Mt 15 24 (S ⲧⲏ.) ἀποστ. εἰς.

—— ϩⲁⲭⲉⲛ- B, send before: Ge 45 5 B ἀποστ. ἔμπροσθεν.

With following adverb.

—— ⲉⲃⲟⲗ SAB, send forth: Mt 15 17 S(B ⲣⲓⲟⲩⲅ) ἐκβάλλειν, Z 311 S ⲧⲁⲅⲉ ⲣⲱⲟⲩ ⲉⲃ. ἐκβ. ⲡⲩⲟⲛ, He 11 11 B(S = Gk) καταβ.; Ge 1 20 S(B ⲓⲛⲓ ⲉⲃ., cf 21 S ⲧ. ⲉⲡⲣⲁⲓ) ἐξάγειν; Hag 2 19 SA(B do) φέρειν, Nu 17 8 S(var ϯ ⲟⲩⲱ ⲉⲡⲣⲁⲓ, B ϥⲓ. ⲉⲃ.), Ps 68 32 B(S ⲡⲟⲩ-ϫⲉ ⲉⲃ., A Cl ϫⲟ ⲁⲃ.) ἐκφ., Lu 6 45 S(B ⲓⲛⲓ ⲉⲃ.) προφ., Col 1 10 B ⲧ. ⲟⲩⲧⲁⲅ (S ϯ) καρποφ.; Si 50 10 S ἀναβάλλειν; Is 5 2 S(B ⲓⲣⲓ), Mt 7 17 S(B ⲓⲛⲓ ⲉⲃ.) ποι.; Jer 27 33 B ἐξαποστ.; Lev 25 19 S(B ϯ) διδό-ναι; ib 11 10 S(B do) ἐρεύγ., Ps 44 1 S(B ⲃⲉⲃⲓ)ἐξερ.; Joel 3 18 SA(B ϩⲁ ϯ) ῥεῖσθαι; Mk 9 18 S(B ⲭⲱϣ ⲉⲃ.) ἀφρίζειν, Jude 13 S(B ϩⲓ ⲥϥⲏⲓϯ) ἐπαφ.; Pro 10 31 SA(B diff) ἀποστάζειν; Is 57 4 SB χαλᾶν; Mic 2 6 B ⲧ. ⲉⲣⲙⲏ ⲉⲃ. (SA ⲣⲓⲙⲉ) δακρύειν; Lev 11 3 S ⲧ. ⲉⲓⲃ ⲉⲃ. (B ⲱⲗⲓ) ὀνυχίζειν; PS 106 S ⲧⲁⲡⲟⲗⲓⲁ ⲉⲡⲧⲁⲥⲧⲁⲅⲟⲩ ⲉⲃ., ShA 2 341 S heresy ⲧ. ⲉⲃ. ⲛⲓⲡⲟⲛⲏ-ⲣⲟⲛ, Miss 4 137 B anus ⲧⲁⲅⲉ ϭⲉⲡⲧ ⲉⲃ. = MR 4 72 S ϣⲟⲅⲟ ⲉⲃ., Miss 8 243 S mouth ⲉⲧⲧⲁⲅⲉ ⲟⲗⲟϭ ⲉⲃ., TillOster 24 A ⲧⲭⲁⲣⲓⲥ ⲧ. ⲟⲣⲏⲣⲉ ⲁⲃ., BMis 312 S ⲧⲁⲃⲉ ⲣⲃⲉⲧⲉ ⲉⲃ. ⲟⲣⲡⲱⲟⲩ;   as nn S, product: Nu 13 21 (B diff) ϣⲣⲡ ⲧ. ⲉⲃ. πρόδρομος.

—— ⲉⲡⲉⲥⲏⲧ SB, send, cast down: 2 Kg 20 15 S, Si 1 39 B, 2 Cor 4 9 S(B ⲣⲱϭⲧ ⲉϩⲣⲏⲓ), Va 61 215 B sin depicted now ⲉⲅⲧϣⲭⲓ (l ⲉϥ-) ⲉϫⲉⲛϩⲁⲡⲟⲩⲟⲛ, now ⲉϥⲧ.† ⲉⲡ. καταβάλ., Nu 22 22 S(B diff) διαβ. (cf 32 ⲧ. ⲉϩⲣⲁⲓ); Jth 9 8 S, Am 3 11 S(B ⲓⲛⲓ ⲉⲡ.) κατάγ.; Ez 32 18 S(B ϯ ⲉⲡ.) καταβιβάζειν; Zech 9 6 S(A ⲧ. ⲁϩⲣⲏⲓ, B ⲑⲉⲃⲓⲟ) καθαιρεῖν; Hag 2 22 S (A do, B ⲫⲱⲛⲭ), Mk 11 15 S(B ⲥⲱⲥ) καταστρέφειν; BHom 16 S devil ϣⲣⲡ ⲧⲁⲅⲟⲛ ⲉⲡ. σκελίζειν; Ps 17 39 S(B diff) συμποδίζειν; Cant 5 5 B(ParisInstCath, S ϣⲟⲅⲟ, F ⲟⲅⲱⲧϩ ⲉⲃ.) στάζειν; PS 138 S ⲁⲅⲧⲁⲅⲉ ⲧⲡⲓⲥⲧⲓⲥ ⲉⲡ., ShC 73 17 S ⲧ. ⲉⲡ. ⲛⲡⲉⲧϯ ⲟⲩⲃⲏⲩ, Bor 248 52 S ⲧ. ⲉⲡ. ⲛⲡⲉⲥⲕⲁⲣⲡⲟⲥ.

—— ⲉⲡϣⲱⲓ B, ⲉϣⲱⲓ O, cast up: MIE 2 415 B fountain ⲧⲁⲟⲅⲉ ⲙⲱⲟⲩ ⲉⲡ., AZ 21 104 O ⲧⲁⲧⲁⲅⲱⲅⲟⲥ ⲉϣ.

—— ⲉϩⲣⲁⲓ, ⲁϩ., ⲉϭ. SABF, a send, cast down: 2 Kg 1 15 (var om ⲉϩ.) βάλ., Nu 22 32 S(B diff) διαβολή, Job 16 14 SB, Ps 72 19 S(B ⲣⲱϭⲧ ⲉϭ.), Pro 7 26 SA(B do) καταβάλ.; Ps 10 3 S(B ⲭⲱ ⲉϭ.) καθ-αιρ.; ib 55 7 S(B ⲓⲛⲓ ⲉⲡⲉⲥⲏⲧ), Hab 3 12 A(S ⲉⲓⲛⲉ ⲉⲡ., B ⲃⲱⲗ ⲉⲃ.), Si 22 20 A(S ⲑⲉⲓⲟ) κατάγ.; Job 11 10 S(B ⲟⲩⲱϭⲡ ⲉϭ. sic l), Si 28 15 S καταστρ.; Ps 16 13 SB(F ⲥⲗⲉϭⲗⲉϭ) ὑποσκελ.; ib 73 6 S(B ⲣⲱ. ⲉϭ.) καταρρηγνύναι; Pro 24 46 SA κατασκάπτειν; Ps 77 31 S(B diff) συμποδ.; Jer 32 27 B ἀποστέλλειν; Br 96 S moved her ⲉⲧⲣⲉⲥⲧⲁⲅⲉ ⲥϥⲣⲁⲅⲓⲥ ⲉϩ., ShA 2 135 S ⲁⲅⲧ. ⲉϩ. ⲛⲛⲉⲧⲡⲉⲓϩⲱⲗⲟⲛ, C 41 41 B sim.   ♭

send, bring up: Ge 3 18 S(B ⲣⲱⲧ) ἀνατέλλειν; ib 1 21 S(B ⲓⲛⲓ ⲉⲃ.) ἐξάγ.; Is 32 13 SF(B do) ἀναβαίνειν; Sa 19 10 S ἐξερεύγ.; Ps 104 30 S(B ⲃⲉⲃⲓ) ἐξέρπειν; Ja 3 11 SA(B do) βρύειν; Si 36 13 S ἀναστρ.; Mich 550 24 = TT 19 S earth ⲧ. ⲉⲣ. ⲡⲟⲩⲃⲟⲧⲁⲡⲏ, BMar 139 S ⲛⲧⲁ ϯⲥⲱϣⲉ ⲧⲁⲅⲟⲟⲩ ⲉⲣ., BSG 178 S earth opened ⲁϥⲧ. ⲉⲣ. ⲡⲟⲩⲙⲟⲟⲩ.

—— ⲛⲛ S, sending mission: Ps 77 49 (B ⲧ. vb) ἀποστολή.

ⲁⲧⲧ. SF, indescribable, inexplicable: P 44 48 ⲡⲁⲧⲧ-ⲁⲅⲟⲩ· ἄφραστος وصف Y, ib ⲡⲓⲁⲧϣ ⲧⲁⲅⲟⲩ· ⲁⲛⲉⲣⲙⲉⲛⲉⲩⲧⲏⲥ يترجم Y; EpApp 1 39 ⲟⲩⲁⲧⲧⲁⲅⲟⲥⲧⲉ ⲧⲉⲩ-ⲕⲟⲓⲛⲱⲛⲓⲁ, Mus 40 275 ⲙⲛⲧⲉⲓⲱⲧ ⲡⲁⲧⲧⲁⲅⲉ ⲣⲓⲛⲥ, BM 583 10 F ⲙⲡⲉⲣϫⲟ ⲡⲁⲧⲧ. ⲧⲗⲟⲩⲕⲟⲧⲥⲓ ⲛⲉⲓ without sending. Cf ViK 9783 10 ⲡϣⲟⲩⲧⲙⲧⲁⲅⲉ ⲡⲉϥⲣⲁⲛ = Aeg 45 B.

ϭⲓⲛ-, ϫⲓⲛⲧ., explanation, recital: My 17 S ⲡϭ. ⲙⲡⲉⲓⲙⲩⲥⲧⲏⲣⲓⲟⲛ, C 41 45 B ⲧⲉϥϫⲓⲛⲧⲁⲟⲩⲉ ⲗⲉⲝⲓⲥ.

ⲧⲟⲩⲁ S, ⲑⲟⲅⲁⲓ, ⲑⲉⲁⲓ B nn m f, door-post or lin-tel: Ex 12 7 S ⲡⲉⲧ. B ⲡⲓⲑ. (cf ⲙⲟⲩⲛⲉ 1ᵒ), ib 23 B ⲡⲓⲑ. قائمتين, Deu 6 9 S ⲡⲉⲧ. (var ⲡⲉⲧ., B ⲟⲩⲅⲉⲭⲣⲱⲟⲩ) فليا; Is 6 4 S(B ⲣⲟ ⲡⲣⲟ) ὑπέρθυρον; Kg 157 B ϯⲑⲉⲃ. 'ⲥ; BMOr 8775 123 B ⲡⲟⲩⲑⲉⲃ. رهوى; Mor 16 38 S smear blood ⲉⲛⲉⲧ. ⲙⲛⲛⲉⲟⲩⲉϩⲣⲟ (var BMis 199 om ⲡⲉⲧ.), Miss 8 39 S decree affixed ϩⲓⲛⲉⲧ. ⲙⲡⲣⲟ, DeV 2 164 B ⲡⲓⲑ. ⲛⲧⲉ ⲡⲓⲣⲟ whereon 3 thetas carved (cf PO 1 430 أبلى), MG 25 186 B ⲟⲩⲥⲕⲉⲡ-ⲗⲁⲣⲓ (sic, l ? σκεπτώριον or σπεκλάριον) ⲉϫⲉⲛⲡⲓⲑ. ⲛⲧⲉ ϯⲡⲉⲧⲣⲁ & thereon fiery pillar (cf AZ 54 133).

ⲧⲟⲟⲩⲉ SA, ⲑⲱⲟⲅⲓ B nn m, shoe, pair of shoes, as sg: Deu 25 10 SB, 3 Kg 2 5 S, Ps 107 10 SB, Ez 24 17 SB(Gk pl), Lu 15 22 SB(Gk do), C 86 275 B ⲟⲩⲑ. ⲙⲃⲉⲛⲓⲡⲓ ὑπόδημα; ShIF 89 S ϩⲟⲩⲟⲩ ϩⲓⲡⲉϥⲧ., KKS 458 S beheld ⲡⲧ. ⲙⲡⲉⲓⲱⲧ ϩⲓⲡⲉϥⲟⲩⲉⲣⲏⲧⲉ, C 43 16 B ⲡⲓⲑ. ⲉⲧⲧⲟⲓ ⲉⲣⲁⲧϥ, ib 219 B sim ⲉⲡⲉϥⲑⲁⲗⲁϫ, Mich 136 4 S ϩⲏⲧϥ ⲙⲡⲉⲩⲧⲟⲟⲩⲉ ⲉϥⲧⲓϭ ⲡⲗⲁϭⲙⲉϥ ⲡⲕⲉⲙ (var ib ⲗⲁⲥ ⲡⲕⲁⲙ), Ep 370 S fetch ⲡⲁⲧ. ⲙⲙⲟⲛ ⲁⲓⲣ ⲡⲉϥⲱⲃϣ;   as pl: Ex 12 11 SB, Is 11 15 SB, Am 8 6 SAB; ShA 1 300 S ϩⲉⲛⲧ. ⲙⲡⲉⲛⲓⲡⲉ, ib 2 158 S ϩⲉⲛⲧ. ⲉⲅⲡⲟⲕ, J&C 92 S ⲡⲧ., Ep 371 S ⲡϥϫⲓ ⲡⲓⲧ. ⲡϥ(ⲧ)ⲥⲉⲡⲟϥ (sic);   ⲙⲟⲩⲥ ⲡⲧ., shoe thong: Ge 14 23 SB, Is 5 27 SB, Jo 1 27 SB (cf ⲙⲟⲩⲥ, where v also EncyclBibl 4492 n on مسح);   ⲡⲟϣⲉ ⲡⲧ. v ⲡⲱϣⲉ (ⲡⲟϣⲉ);   ϭⲟⲛ ⲡⲧ., sole of shoe S: Jos 9 11 κοῖλα τῶν ὑποδ.;   ⲁⲧⲑ. B, shoeless: Mic 1 8 (SA diff) ἀνυπόδετος; cf Is 20 2 S ⲙⲛ ⲧ. ⲡⲣⲁⲧⲕ, B ⲙⲙⲟⲛ ⲑ. ⲧⲟⲓ ⲉⲣ., BMar 161 S ⲡⲟⲩⲉϣ ⲡⲧ. ἀνυπόδ., JA '75 5 241 S sim ἀνυπόλυτος (l ? -υπόδ.).   V AZ 53 138.

ⲧⲟⲟⲩⲓ B v ϩⲧⲟⲟⲩⲉ.

ⲧⲟⲩⲟ S, ⲧⲉⲃⲟ A, ⲧⲟⲩⲃⲟ B(once), ⲧⲟⲩⲟⲍ S, ⲧⲉⲃⲁⲍ,

ⲧⲁⲃ. (once) *A*, ⲧⲟⲩⲁⲉⲓⲧ† *O* (*v s f*) vb **I** tr **a**, *show, teach* (mostly = *B* ⲧⲁⲙⲟ) c acc of person, ⲉ- of thing shown: Ge 12 1 (var P 44 102 ⲧⲁⲟⲩⲟ *l* ⲧⲟⲩ., *A* Cl ⲧⲥⲉⲃⲟ), ib 48 11 (var ⲧⲁⲙ.), Is 53 11 *SA*, Zech 3 1 (*A* ⲧⲥ.), Lu 4 5, He 8 5 (*F* = *B*), ROC 11 305 ⲁϥⲧⲟⲩⲟⲓ ⲉⲅⲛⲟϭ ⲡϣⲱⲥ (*cf* 307 †ⲡⲁⲧⲁⲅⲟⲕ ⲉⲡⲕⲉϣⲱⲕⲡ) δεικνύναι, Mt 22 19, Lu 20 24 (var ⲧⲥ.) ἐπιδ., Hos 13 4 *A* παραδ., Si 17 6 ὑποδ., Ro 2 15 (*B* ⲟⲩⲱⲛϩ ⲉⲃⲟⲗ) ἐνδ.; Ps 33 11 *A* (Cl, var ⲧⲥ., *SB* † ⲥⲃⲱ) διδάσκειν; Bor 304 52 ⲁⲡⲛⲧⲉ ⲧⲟⲩⲟⲕ ⲉⲡⲁⲓ;   ⲉ-+vb: Cl 1 3 *A* ⲉⲧⲉⲧⲛⲧ. ⲛⲛⲓⲗⲁⲩⲉ ϩⲛⲛ ⲁⲙⲉⲅⲉ ἐπιτρέπειν; Hos 10 11 *A* ⲧⲁⲃⲁⲥ ⲇⲓⲇⲁⲥ.; El 80 *A* ⲧⲉⲃⲁⲩ ⲉ†ⲕ ⲥⲁⲧⲉ;   c acc & ⲉⲃⲟⲗ ϩⲛ-: Si 45 5 δεικ. dat & gen;   c acc of thing shown, ⲉ- to whom: Est 4 8, Mk 1 44 δεικ., Lu 17 14 ἐπιδ., Si 49 9 ὑποδ.; BIF 14 153 ⲙⲁⲧⲟⲩⲟⲕ ⲉⲣⲟϥ.   **b** *send*: Jo 6 44 (1 var & BHom 82, rest & *A²B* ⲧⲁⲩⲟ) πέμπειν;   hence ? *send forth rays, light SO*: Mk 9 3 (var ⲙⲟⲩ, *B* ϥⲟⲣⲓ var ⲉⲣ ⲟⲩⲱⲓⲛⲓ, *F* ⲥ†ⲏⲗⲗⲓ) στίλβων γίνεσθαι, cit BM 258; Lu 9 29 (*B* diff) ἐξαστράπτειν; Hor 81 *O* sun ϥⲧ.† ⲛⲛⲁⲟⲩ.

II intr, *learn*: Pro 16 17 *A* (*S* ⲥⲃⲟ) δέχεσθαι; Jo 7 15 *B* (error?, var ⲥⲁⲃⲟ, *S* ⲧⲥⲁⲃⲟ), Cl 57 2 *A* ⲧ. ⲁⲣ ⲉⲩϩⲟⲧⲁⲥⲥⲉ μανθάνειν;   *Cf* ⲧⲟⲩⲃⲟ *S* & ⲧⲟⲟⲩⲧⲉ (ⲧⲟⲩⲏⲧ†).

ⲧⲟⲩ(ⲉ)ⲓⲟ *SB*, ⲧⲟⲩⲓⲁ *F*, ⲧⲟⲩⲓⲉ- *B*, ⲧⲟⲩⲓⲟ⸗ *SB*, -ⲓⲁ⸗ *A²* vb tr, *remove, wean B* (caus of ⲟⲩⲉ): Ge 21 8 ⲉⲧⲁⲩⲧⲟⲩⲓⲉ ⲓⲥⲁⲁⲕ, Hos 1 8 (*A* ⲱⲙⲥ) ἀπογαλακτί-ζειν; ⲧ. ⲡⲧⲉⲣⲱ†: Ps 130 2, Ge *lc*, Is 28 9 ἀπογ. (all *S* ⲱⲙⲥ); K 71 ϥⲏ ⲉⲧⲁⲩⲧⲟⲩⲓⲟϥ فطيم;   tr. *repay, return SA²F*: Deu 32 6 (*B* † ϣⲉⲃⲓⲱ), Eccl 5 4 *F* (*S* †) ἀποδιδόναι, 1 Thes 3 9 (*B* do) ἀνταποδ.; BHom 4 ⲡⲉⲧⲕⲛⲁϣ ⲧⲟⲩⲉⲓⲟϥ ⲙⲡⲉⲛⲧⲁϥ- διαπράσσεσθαι; Sh (Besa)Z 504 ⲡⲉⲧⲉⲧⲛ(ⲛ)ⲁⲧⲟⲩⲉⲓⲟⲟⲩ ⲙⲡⲭ̅ⲥ̅, R 2 2 46 ϥⲛⲁϣ ⲧ. ⲗⲁⲁⲩ ⲛⲁϥ ⲁⲛ, BMis 50 debt we owe ⲧⲏⲛⲁϣ ⲧⲟⲩⲓⲱ ⲟⲩⲕⲟⲩⲓ ⲡⲣⲏⲧϥ, Mani 2 *A²* ⲡⲉⲧⲥⲁⲙⲉ ⲁⲛ[ⲁⲣⲁϥ ?]ⲁⲧⲟⲩⲓⲁⲩ ⲁⲛⲟⲩⲙⲁ;   intr, c dat: Ps 54 20 (*B* † ϣ.), Eccl 5 3 *F* (*S* †) ἀποδ., Ps 17 24 (*B* †), Ro 11 35 *SF* (*B* † ϣ.) ἀνταποδ.; PS 50 ⲛⲛⲧ. ⲛⲁⲩ, Pcod 16 ⲧ. ⲛⲁϥ ⲡⲟⲩⲁϣⲏ ⲡⲕⲱⲃ, Mor 24 31 *F* ⲧ. ⲛⲏϥ ⲕⲁⲧⲁ ⲡⲉϥⲉⲙⲡϣⲏ, PRain 4725 *S* unable ⲉⲧ. ⲛⲁⲕ ϩⲁⲣⲟⲥ. *V* also ⲟⲩⲱ *cease* († ⲟⲩⲱ ⲉⲃ. intr).

—— nn m *S*, *repayment*: Ps 18 11 (*B* ϭⲓ ϣ.), ib 90 8 (var PS 147 ⲧⲱⲱⲃⲉ, *B* † ϣ.), Is 61 2 (*B* do), Col 3 24 (*B* ϣ. nn) ἀνταπόδοσις, Ob 15 (*A* ⲧⲟⲩⲟⲩⲃⲉ, *B* do), Lu 14 12 (*B* do) ἀνταπόδομα, He 10 35 ⲧ. ⲡⲃⲉⲕⲉ (*B* ϣⲉⲃⲓ ⲃ.) μισθαποδοσία; 1 Tim 5 4 (*B* † ϣ.) ἀμοιβή; Tri 525 جزاء; *ib* 528 قصاص; ShZ 638 ⲡⲧ. ⲛⲁϥ ⲙⲡⲉϥⲃⲉⲕⲉ, BHom 126 ⲡⲧ....ⲉⲡⲧⲁⲅⲁⲁⲩ ⲙⲡⲉⲛ-ⲭ̅ⲥ̅, Bor 292 16 ϫⲓⲧϥ ⲉⲡⲧ. ⲛⲡⲁⲓ; ϫⲱⲱⲙⲉ ⲡⲧ., *book of sending back*, deed of divorce: Deu 24 1 (*B* ϫ. ⲛ-ⲥϭⲓ ⲡⲟⲩⲉⲓ), Is 50 1 (*B* do), Mt 19 7 *SF* (*B* ⲥ. ⲡⲟⲩ.) βιβλίον ἀποστασίου; Tri 394 كتاب الطلاق.

ϫⲁⲉⲓⲧ.(?) *S*, *wage-taker, hireling*: CO 304 ⲛϫⲁⲉⲓ-ⲧⲟⲩⲉ[ⲓⲟ.

ⲧⲟⲩⲱ⸗ *SAA²F*, ⲑⲟⲩⲱ⸗ *B* nn, *bosom*: Ex 4 6 *B* ⲑⲟⲩⲱ⸗ (*A* ⲕⲟⲡ⸗) κόλπος; Jos 13 28 *F* (PMich 3521) ⲡⲉⲧⲛⲁⲩⲣⲡⲧⲟⲩⲱⲟⲩ (*SA²* ⲡⲉⲧⲛⲏⲭ, *B* ⲉⲑⲣⲟⲧⲉⲃ) ἀνα-κείμενος.

ⲉⲧⲟⲩⲛ-, ⲉⲧⲟⲩⲉⲛ-, ⲉⲧⲟⲩⲱ⸗ *S*, *beside, at, with*: Nu 33 49 ⲉⲧⲟⲩⲉⲛ (var & *B* ϩⲁⲧⲛ-) παρά; *ib* 2 20 ⲉⲧⲟⲩⲛ (var ϩⲓⲧ., *B* ϩⲁⲟ.) ἐχόμενος; Ex 21 6 do (*B* ϩⲓⲧⲉⲛ-), 1 Cor 7 5 do (var ⲉⲧⲟⲩⲉⲛ, BF diff) ἐπί; Sa 13 15 do ⲉⲛ; Ap 3 21 do (var ϩⲓⲧ., *B* ⲛⲉⲙ-) μετά; Ac 27 4 (*B* ϩⲓⲧⲉⲛ-) ὑπο-; PS 129 ⲁϥⲉⲓ ⲉⲧⲟⲩⲛⲡⲉⲩⲉⲣⲏⲩ, J 50 40 *Sa* ⲡⲭⲱⲣⲏⲙⲁ ⲉⲧⲁⲧⲟⲩⲛⲡⲁⲛⲓ (*cf ib* 16 ⲉⲧϩⲁ-); Ap *lc* ⲉⲧⲟⲩⲱⲉⲓ (var ϩⲓⲧ., *B* ⲛⲉⲙ-) μ.; ShBMOr 8810 434 hopeth ⲉⲁϥⲉ ⲣⲁⲧϥ -ⲱϥ, ShC 73 137 ⲡⲱⲡⲉ ⲛ-ⲡϫⲁⲗⲁϩⲧ -ⲱⲟⲩ *side by side* (on flames).

ϩⲁⲑⲟⲩⲉⲛ-, ϩⲁⲑⲟⲩⲱ⸗ *B*, ϩⲁⲧⲟⲩⲱ⸗ *S* (once), as last: Va 58 142 kingdom is ϩⲁⲑⲟⲩⲉⲛⲡⲏⲛⲛ̄ within you (*cf* Lu 17 21); Nu 2 5 ϩⲁⲑⲟⲩⲱⲟⲩ (*S* ϩⲓⲧ.), Ez 43 8 -ⲱϥ ἐχόμ.; *ib* do ἐν juxta; Nu 13 29 do (*S* ⲙⲡⲉⲙⲧⲟ ⲉⲃⲟⲗ ⲛ-) παρά; Deu 1 1 do (*S* do) πλησίον gen; He 1 9 -ⲱⲕ (*SF* ϩⲓⲧ.) μέτοχος; MG 25 111 cave -ⲱⲥ ⲡϥⲉⲕⲕⲗⲏⲥⲓⲁ, AM 80 ⲁⲙⲟⲩ -ⲱⲓ, WS 89 *S* send so & so ⲡⲥⲟⲩⲉⲣ ϩⲁⲧⲟⲩⲱⲛ ϩⲓⲡ[.

ϩⲓⲧⲟⲩⲛ-, ϩⲓⲧⲟⲩⲉ(ⲛ)- *S*, ϩⲓⲧⲟⲩⲱ⸗ *SAA²F*, ϩⲓⲑⲟⲩⲱ⸗ *B* (rare), *beside, next*: Nu 2 34 *S* ϩⲓⲧⲟⲩⲛ (var ϩⲓⲧⲟⲩ-ⲉⲛ, ⲉⲧⲟⲩⲛ, *B* ⲉⲧϩⲉⲡⲧ), *ib* 34 3 *S* do (*B* ⲉϧⲣⲏⲓ ⲉ-) ἐχόμ.; *ib* 33 37 *S* do (*B* ϩⲁⲧⲉⲛ-) πλησ.; Deu 34 6 *S* do (var ϩⲓⲧⲟⲩⲉⲛ, *B* do), Jer 42 4 *S* ϩⲓⲧⲟⲩⲉ(ⲛ)ⲡⲏⲓ (*B* diff), Wess 11 156 *S* buried ϩⲉⲓⲧⲟⲩⲛⲕⲉⲉⲥ = C 89 210 *B* ϩⲁⲧⲉⲛ- ἐγγύς; ShA 2 52 *S* standing ϩⲓⲧⲟⲩⲛ-ⲧⲉⲧⲣⲁⲡⲉⲍⲁ, Miss 8 13 *S* sailed ϩⲓⲧⲟⲩⲡⲟⲩⲛⲏⲥⲟⲥ, Mor 41 194 *S* general sitting ϩⲓⲧⲟⲩⲛⲇⲓⲟⲕⲗⲏⲧⲓⲁⲛⲟⲥ = BIF 22 108 *F* ϩⲓⲧⲟⲩⲱϥ ⲛ-; Ps 11 2 *S* ϩⲓⲧⲟⲩⲱϥ (*B* ⲡⲉϥϣⲫⲏⲣ), Jon 1 7 *SA* do (*B* do), Cant 2 13 *S* -ⲱⲓ (ShC 42 52, *F* ⲁⲗⲏⲟⲩ), Mt 5 43 *S* -ⲱⲕ (*B* do) πλησ.; Ps 30 11 *S* -ⲱⲓ (*B* ⲑⲉϣⲉ), *ib* 43 13 *S* -ⲱⲛ (*B* ⲉⲧⲕⲱ†), Jo 9 8 *SA²* -ⲱϥ (*B* ⲑ.) γείτων; Nu 22 5 *S* -ⲱⲓ (*B* ϩⲁⲟ.), Am 2 8 *A* -ⲱϥ (*B* ϩⲁⲧⲉⲛ-) ἐχόμ.; Sa 14 24 *S* -ⲱϥ (var ⲉⲣⲏⲩ), Aeg 247 *S* -ⲱϥ ἔτερος; Ac 8 31 *S* -ⲱϥ (*B* ⲛⲉⲙ-) σύν; ShC 73 120 *S* all that ⲟⲩ-ⲱϩ ϩⲓⲧⲟⲩⲱⲛ, ShBor 247 124 *S* Moses wrote Exodus ⲡⲧⲉⲩⲡⲟⲩ ϩⲓⲧⲟⲩⲱⲟⲥ ⲛⲧⲛⲉⲛⲉⲥⲓⲥ, PSBA 32 30 *S* Berenike ϩⲓⲧⲟⲩⲱϥ (sic) ⲡⲉⲗⲉϥⲁⲛⲧⲓⲛⲏ, C 41 48 *B* stand-ing ϩⲓⲑⲟⲩⲱϥ, Miss 4 99 *B* ⲕⲉⲟⲩⲁⲓ ⲉϥϩⲓⲑⲟⲩⲱϥ.

ⲧⲟⲩⲃⲟ, ⲧⲟⲩⲃⲟ⸗ *S* vb tr, meaning unknown: PLond 4 443 contract with sailor (?)] ⲉϩⲛⲧ ⲧⲁⲧ. ⲡⲁ-ⲇⲁⲍ[ⲓⲧⲱⲡ(ταξίδιον), PMich 4577 letter] ⲏ ϣⲙⲙⲟ ⲉⲧⲛⲡⲁⲕⲗⲏⲣⲟⲩ ⲡⲥⲉⲧⲟⲩⲃⲟⲟⲩ ⲉ[.

ⲧⲟⲩⲃⲟ *A²B* *v* ⲧⲃⲃⲟ, *B* *v* ⲧⲟⲩⲟ.

ⲧⲟⲩⲗⲟ *B* *v* ⲑⲟⲩⲉⲗⲟ.

ⲧⲱⲟⲩⲛ *SA*²(AP 26)*BF*, ⲧⲱⲱⲛ *SA*², ⲧⲱⲛ *Sᵃ AA*², -ⲉ *AA*², ⲧⲱⲟⲩⲛⲟⲩ (ⲧ-ⲟⲩ)*B*, ⲧⲟⲩⲛ-*S*, ⲧⲉⲛ-*B*, ⲧⲱⲟⲩⲛⲍ *SO*, ⲧⲱⲛⲍ *SBF*, ⲧⲱⲱⲛⲍ *F*(Ps 16) vb **I** intr, *arise*: Ge 31 35 *SB*, Ps 11 5 *SA*(Cl)*B*, ib 16 13 *SBF*, Si 25 1 *S* ⲧⲱⲱⲛ, Is 32 9 *SF*(*B* refl), Mk 10 34 *S*(*B* do), AP 9 *A*² ⲧⲱⲱⲛ ἀνιστάναι, Ez 7 10 *SB* ἐξαν., Deu 11 19 *SB* διαν.; Is 5 11 *SB*, Mt 11 5 *SB* ⲧ-ⲟⲩ, Jo 14 31 *A*² ⲧⲱⲱⲛ (*SB* refl) ἐγείρειν, Ge 28 16 *SB*, Ps 72 20 *SB* ἐξεγ.; Mt 21 21 *S*(*B* ϥⲓ) αἴρειν; Jud 20 26 *S* (var refl) ἀναβαίνειν; Z 297 *S* ⲛ̄ϯⲡⲁϣ ⲧ. ⲁⲛ βαστάζειν; PS 64 *S* ⲧ. ⲛ̄ⲧⲉϣⲓⲛⲉ, BM 311 103 *S according as we* ⲡⲁϣ ⲥⲙ ϭⲟⲙ ⲉⲧ., AM 136 *B* ⲁⲩⲧ. ⲁⲅⲣⲱⲗ, Ep 227 *Sᵘ* ⲛ̄ⲧ. ⲛ̄ⲧⲁϩⲟⲓ, Mani 1 *A*² ⲧⲱⲛ ⲧⲉⲗⲟ ⲉⲣⲉⲛⲕⲁⲧⲉ, Mor 24 34 *F* ⲉⲕⲉⲧ. ⲛ̄ⲕⲗⲁⲁϣⲉ, DeV 2 106 *B leaven left* ϣⲁⲧⲉϥⲧ.;   ⲧⲱⲟⲩⲛⲟⲩ *B*: C 43 210 ⲡⲁⲥⲛⲏⲟⲩ ⲧ., Aeg 47 ⲁⲛⲧ. ⲧⲏⲣⲟⲩ, MG 25 249 ⲡⲁⲥϣ ϫⲉⲛ ϫⲟⲗ ⲛⲧ.; *where 3d pl ?refl*: Ps 1 4 ⲛ̄ⲛⲉⲡⲓⲁⲥⲉⲃⲏⲥ ⲧ., 1 Cor 15 29 ⲡⲓⲣⲉϥⲙⲱⲟⲩⲧ ⲛⲁⲧ., AM 99 ⲁⲩⲧ., *but cf tr refl.*

II tr, *raise, carry*: Ru 2 16 *S*, Bel 36 *B*, Ac 21 35 *B*(*S* ⲧⲁⲗⲟ), Z 297 *S* ⲉϥⲧ. ⲡⲣⲉⲃⲏⲧ βαστ., EpJer 3 *F* (*S* ⲧⲁ., *B* ϥⲁⲓ), MG 25 212 *B* ⲧ. ⲛ̄ⲛⲓϣⲉ αἴρ., Ps 72 52 *B*(*S* diff) ἀπαίρ., Ge 7 17 *B*(*S* ⲧ. ⲉϩⲣⲁⲓ), 2 Cor 10 5 *B*(*S* do) ἐπαίρ.; Job 15 25 *B*(*S* diff) τραχηλιᾶν; R 1 4 15 *S* ⲛ̄ϥⲧ....ⲙ̄ⲙⲛⲧⲛ ⲙ̄ⲙⲟ ϫⲟⲓⲛ *portare*; PS 148 *S* ⲛ̄ⲥⲉⲧ. ⲙⲙⲟⲥ ϩ̄ⲛⲡⲉⲩϭⲓϫ, BIF 13 98 *S* ⲁ̄ⲩⲧ. ⲙ̄ⲙⲟϥ = MG 25 277 *B* ϥⲁⲓ, C 73 209 *S* ϣⲁϥⲧ. ⲛ̄ⲛⲉⲥⲛ̄ⲏⲩ ⲉⲧⲁⲗⲉ ⲧⲱⲃⲉ ⲛⲁϥ, Cat 78 *B* ⲁϥⲧ. ⲛ̄ⲟⲩⲕⲁϣ *in hand*, PO 11 345 *B* ⲁⲩⲧ-ⲟⲩ ⲙ̄ⲙⲟϥ, C 43 214 *B sim* ⲁϥⲧ-ⲟⲩ, ib 79 *B* ⲉⲩⲧ-ⲟⲩ ⲡⲟⲩⲣⲉϥⲙⲱⲟⲩⲧ, DeV 1 82 *B sin* ⲉⲧⲁⲡ̄ⲧ. ⲙ̄ⲙⲟϥ, ib 2 219 *B* ⲉϥⲧ-ⲟⲩ ⲙ̄ⲙⲟⲟⲩ *bore with them*, Mor 41 192 *S idol* ⲧ. ⲙⲡⲙⲁⲕϩ ⲙ̄ⲡⲟⲩⲛⲏⲃ *clasped & threw him*, ib 18 97 *S* ⲁ̄ⲩⲧ. ⲙⲙⲟϥ & *bore him* = ib 19 99 *S* ⲧⲁ[ⲗⲟϥ] = Miss 4 158 *B* ϥⲁⲓ, PBu 78 *S such paltry deeds* (σχεδάριον) *are not worth that one* ⲧ. ⲙⲙⲟⲟⲩ *or hand them you* (*judges*);   refl: Nu 22 13 *SB*, 1 Kg 16 12 *B*(*S* not), Ps 16 13 *BF* ⲧⲱⲟⲩⲛⲕ (*S* do), Is 32 9 *B* ⲧⲉⲛ̄ⲑⲏ-ⲛⲟⲩ (*SF* do), Ac 9 39 *BF* ⲧⲱⲡϥ (*S* do) ἀνιστ., Jth 12 15 *S* ⲧⲱⲛ̄ⲥ διαν., Si 8 14 *S* ⲧⲱⲛⲕ (var not), Ac 15 5 *S* (var & *B* do) ἐξαν.; Jos 10 4 *S* ⲧⲟⲩⲛ̄ⲧⲏⲩⲧⲛ̄ ἀναβαίν.; Is 5 11 *F* ⲧ. ⲙ̄ⲙⲁⲩ (*SB* do), Mk 3 3 *S*(var do)*B*, Jo 14 31 *SA*² ⲧⲱⲱⲛ *B* ἐγ., Ge 41 21 *B*(*S* ⲛⲉⲣⲥⲉ), Is 51 9 *S*(cf 17 not)*B* ἐξεγ.; AM 293 *B* ϯⲡⲁⲧⲱⲡⲧ ⲛ̄ⲧⲁϣⲉ ⲡⲏⲓ, Mor 24 23 *F* ⲁⲩⲧⲱⲡⲟⲩ ⲁⲩϣⲗⲏⲗ, DeV 2 95 *B* ⲁⲥⲧⲱⲡⲥ ⲁⲥⲓ, AZ 21 100 *O* ⲧⲱⲟⲩⲛⲓ ⲧⲁϣⲉⲣⲓ.

With following preposition.

—— ⲉ-, *rise against S*: Job 30 5 (*B* ⲉϩⲣⲏⲓ ⲉϫⲉⲛ-), Ps 26 12 (*B* do) ἐπανιστ. dat, Si 45 30 ἐπισυνιστ. dat; ShA 1 205 ⲧ. ⲉⲡⲉⲅⲉⲣⲏ̄ⲩ ⲙⲡⲁⲣⲁⲃⲏⲕⲏ (in Mor 18 20 ⲁⲣⲃⲏⲕⲏ = ib 19 28 ϭⲉⲣⲱϥ = Miss 4 114 *B* ϩⲟⲡⲗⲟⲛ); *rise to SB*: Nu 2 9 (*B* ⲧ-ⲟⲩ) ἐξαίρ.; Ps 131 8 *SB*, Jer 29 15 *B* ἀνιστ. εἰς; BHom 14 *S* ⲧⲱⲡⲕ ⲉⲡⲥⲓⲟⲩ, Leyd 313 *S* ⲁⲩⲛⲕⲟⲧⲕ ⲉⲡⲣⲓⲙⲉ ⲁⲩⲧ. ⲉⲡⲁϣⲁϩⲟⲙ *arose to*

—— ⲉϫⲛ- *SBF, rise upon, against*: Ge 4 8 *B*(*A* Cl ⲁϩⲣ. ⲁϫⲛ-), Ps 93 16 *SB* ἀν. ἐπί, Deu 19 11 *SB*, Job 17 8 *SB*, Is 31 2 *SBF* ἐπαν. ἐπί, Job 20 27 *S* (*B* ⲉϩⲣ. ⲉϫ.), Ps 43 5 *S*(*B* do) ἐπαν. dat, Jer 28 29 *B* ἐξαν. ἐπί, Ac 18 12 *S*(*B* ι ⲉϩⲣ. ⲉϫ.) κατεφιστ. dat; Mk 13 8 *SB* ἐγ. ἐπί, Is 19 2 *SB* ἐπεγ. ἐπί, Dan 11 25 *B* ἐξεγ. ἐπί; Ge 43 18 *S*(*B* diff) ἐπιτιθέναι dat, 1 Kg 23 27 *S*(*B* ⲟⲩⲟϩ ϩⲓϫ.) ἐ. ἐπί; Job 6 27 *S*(*B* ⲉϩⲣ. ⲉϫ.) ἐπιπίπτειν ἐπί; ib 16 5 *B*(*S* ϥⲱϭⲉ ⲉϫⲛ-) ἐνάλλεσθαι dat; ib 19 5 *B*(*S* ϭⲓⲥⲓ ⲉϩⲣ. ⲉϫ.) μεγαλύνειν ἐπί; ib 21 27 *S*(*B* diff) ἐπικεῖσθαι dat; MG 25 243 *B* στασιάζειν κατά; ShBM 194 2 *S* ⲁⲙⲡⲉⲣⲉ ⲧ. ⲉϫⲛ-ⲡⲉⲛⲉⲣⲏⲩ, Ryl 72 351 *S* ⲟⲩⲛⲟϭ ⲛ̄ⲧⲏⲧ ⲧ. ⲉϫⲛ̄ⲟⲩ-ⲕⲟⲩⲓ, Aeg 27 *S* ⲁⲧϥⲉⲗϭⲓⲗⲉ ⲧ. ⲉϫⲱϥ *when dying*, MG 25 355 *B said they* ⲧ. ⲛⲁⲛ...ⲁ̄ϥⲧ. ⲉϫⲱⲟⲩ *he lifted* (*the loads*) *upon them* (ROC 18 57 [Arabic]), C 86 349 *B* ⲁⲓⲧⲱⲡⲧ ⲉϫ. ⲡⲁϣⲫⲏⲣ & *slew him*; ⲉ-ϩⲣⲁⲓ, -ⲛⲓ, ⲁϩⲣⲏⲓ ⲉϫⲛ- *SAB*: Su 61 *B*, Mk 3 26 *S*(*B* om ⲉϩ.) ἀνιστ. ἐπί, Jth 16 17 *S*, Ps 108 28 *SB* ἐπαν. dat, ib 17 39 *SB*, Is 9 11 *S*(*B* om ⲉϩ.) ἐπαν. ἐπί, Ob 1 *B*(*A* ⲃ̄ⲱⲕ ⲁϩⲣ.) ἐξαν. ἐπί, Ac 4 1 *B*(*S* ⲉⲓ ⲉϩ. ⲉϫⲛ-) ἐφιστ. dat, Ex 32 1 *S*(*B* ⲑⲱⲟⲩϯ ⲉϫ.) συνιστ. ἐπί; Ac 18 10 *B*(*S* diff) ἐπιτιθ. dat; Job 6 21 *SB* ἐπιβαίν. dat; 2 Cor 10 5 *SB* refl ἐπαίρ. κατά, Cl 16 1 *A* ⲛⲉⲧⲧ. ⲁϩⲣ. ⲁϫⲛ̄ⲡⲉϥϣⲫⲉⲣ ⲉⲡ. ἐπί; BM 216 80 *S trial* ⲧ. ⲉϩ. ⲉϫⲱϥ ἔρχεσθαι ἐπί; Ps 26 3 *B*(*S* om ⲉϩ.) παρατάσσεσθαι ἐπί; Is 29 7 *S*(*B* ϩⲱⲕ ⲉⲥ.); Ps 40 10 *B*(*S* ϥⲓ ⲉϩ. ⲉϫⲛ-) μεγαλ. ἐπί; Ex 18 11 *S*(*B* diff) ὑπερηφανεύεσθαι ἐπί; Jer 29 7 *B*(*S* om ⲉϩ.) Gk om; BM 342 96 *S* ⲛⲛⲉϥⲧ. ⲉϩ. ⲉϫⲱⲟⲩ *as liars*, C 43 148 *B* ⲡⲓⲙⲏϣ ⲛⲁⲧ-ⲟⲩ ⲉϩ. ⲉϫⲱⲓ.

—— ⲛ- *SB, from* (cf ϩⲛ-): TU 24 4 *S* ⲧ. ⲙⲡⲉⲙⲁ, C 41 57 *B* ⲉⲧⲁ...ⲛⲁⲡⲟⲥⲧⲟⲗⲟⲥ ⲧ. ϯⲛⲟⲩ ⲙⲡⲁⲓⲙⲁ; ⲉⲃⲟⲗ ⲛ- *ABF*: 1 Kg 24 1 (*S* ⲉⲓ ⲉϩⲣⲁⲓ ϩⲛ-) ⲁⲛⲓⲥⲧ. ἐκ; Cl 25 3 *A* ϥⲧⲱⲡⲉ ⲁⲃ. ⲡ̄ⲧⲭⲱⲣⲁ, AZ 23 39 *F* ⲟⲩϩⲁⲛ (*l* ?ⲁϩⲛ)...ⲁⲥⲉⲧⲟⲩⲛⲟⲩⲓ ⲉ̄ⲃ. ⲉⲡⲉϩⲕⲁ.

—— ϩⲁ-, ϩⲁ, ϣⲁ- *SAA*²*B, rise from beneath, from*: Pro 6 9 *SA*(*B* ⲉⲃⲟⲗ ϣⲉⲛ-) ἐγείρ. ἐκ, Zech 4 1 *SA*(*B* ⲛⲉⲣⲥⲓ ⲉⲃ. ϩⲁ-) ἐξεγ. ἐκ; Lev 19 32 *S*(*B* ϣⲁ-ϫⲉⲛ-) ἐξαν. ἀπό; ⲉⲃⲟⲗ ϩⲁ-: Jer 28 64 *B*(*S* ⲛⲉⲣ. ⲉⲃ. ϩⲛ-) ἀν. ἀπό; BHom 12 *S* ἐξυπνίζειν; RNC 48 *S* ⲧ. ⲉⲃ. ϩⲁⲛϩⲓⲛⲏⲃ, AM 275 *B* ⲁϥⲧⲱⲛϥ ⲉⲃ. ϩⲁⲛⲙⲁ-ϩⲁⲩ; *rise under, lift up, bear*: Nu 1 50 *S*(*B* ϥⲁⲓ acc), Jos 4 9 *S*(*B* ϥ. ϩⲁ-) αἴρ.; Ac 9 15 *B*(*S* ϥⲓ ϩⲁ-), Ro 11 18 *B*(*SF* do), BMis 537 *S ocean* ⲉⲧⲧ. ϩⲁⲧⲡⲉ βαστ. (cf BAp 70 *S* ⲛⲉⲧⲧ. ⲉϩⲣⲁⲓ ϩⲁⲧⲡⲉ); Est E 12 *S* φέρειν; PS 24 *S could not* ⲧ. ϩⲁⲛⲟⲩⲟⲉⲓⲛ, El 94 *A* ⲧ. ϩⲁⲛ-ⲃⲁⲥⲁⲛⲟⲥ = ib 130 *S* ϥⲓ ϩⲁ-, C 43 5 *B* ⲛⲁⲧ-ⲟⲩ ϩⲁ-ⲛⲁⲓⲃⲁⲥ., PGol 47 *A*² *Virgin* ⲧⲱⲛ ϩⲁⲣⲁⲕ, ManiH 4 *A*² *neck* ⲧⲱⲡⲉ ϩⲁⲡⲉⲕⲉⲧⲁϩ, Worr 292 *S caused one* ⲧ. ϩⲁⲛϩⲓⲣ (var Mor 16 111 ⲛ-), DeV 1 79 *B sin not lest angel* ⲧ-ⲟⲩ ϣⲁⲣⲱⲧⲉⲛ *bear you off*, BMEA 10579

S but for your kindness ⲉⲧⲃⲉⲧ. ⲅⲁⲣⲟⲛ ⲛⲧⲡⲉϣ ⲡⲟⲗϭ ⲁⲛ, PRain 4764 *S* if he default ϣⲁⲓⲧ. ⲅⲁⲣⲟϥ; ⲉⲅⲣⲁⲓ ⲅⲁ-, -ⲛⲓ ϩⲁ-: BMis 144 *S* thy womb ⲧ. ⲉⲅ. ⲅⲁ- Him whose throne is heaven, MIE 2 402 *B* pillars ⲧ. ⲉⲅ. ϩⲁϯⲡⲉⲧⲣⲁ, BAp *l c.*   *V* ⲣⲉϥⲧⲱⲡϥ.

—— ⲅⲓ- *S*, rise from: 1 Kg 28 23 ἀνίστ. ἀπό; ShC 73 144 ⲙⲡⲛⲥⲁⲧⲣⲉⲡⲧ. ⲅⲓⲧⲉⲧⲣⲁⲡⲉⲍⲁ, Leyd 418 ⲁⲡⲟⲥ ⲧ. ⲅⲓⲡⲉⲧⲙⲟⲟⲩⲧ (*cf* ⲅⲛ-), JTS 8 242 ⲁϥⲧ....ⲅⲓⲡⲉϥⲑⲣⲟⲛⲟⲥ; ⲉⲃⲟⲗ ⲅⲓ- *B*: C 86 85 ⲁϥⲧⲱⲡϥ ⲉⲃ. ⲅⲓⲡⲓⲃⲏⲙⲁ (var ⲉⲃ. ⲅⲓϫⲉⲛ-).

—— ⲅⲛ-, ϩⲉⲛ- *SB*, as last: Jo 13 4 *S* refl (*B* ⲉⲃ. ϩ.) ⲉⲅ. ⲉⲕ; R 1 1 32 *S* ⲁϥⲧ....ⲅⲓⲡⲃⲏⲙⲁ ἀνίστ. ἀπό; PS 69 *S* ⲉⲅⲛⲁⲧ. ⲅⲓⲡⲕⲁⲕⲉ, ShC 73 57 *S* ⲧ. ⲅⲓⲡⲙⲁ ⲡⲟⲩⲱⲙ, DeV 2 111 *B* ⲉⲧⲁⲡⲟⲥ ⲧⲱⲡϥ ϩⲉⲛⲛ ⲉⲑⲙⲱⲟⲩⲧ; ⲉⲃⲟⲗ ⲅⲛ-, ϩⲉⲛ- *SA²BF*: Ge 12 8 *S*(*B* ϣⲉ ⲉⲃ. ⲛ-), Is 38 9 *B*(*S* ⲅⲛ-) ἀνίστ. ἐκ, Lu 4 38 *SB* ἀν. ἀπό, Ac 15 5 *SB* ⲉϫⲁⲛ. ἀπό; Is 14 9 *S*(*B* ⲧⲟⲩⲛⲟⲥ), Jo 7 52 *SA²B* ⲉⲅ. ⲉⲕ, Mt 14 2 *SBF*, AP 7 *A²* ⲧⲱⲡ ⲁⲃ. ⲅⲓⲡϣⲟⲩϣⲧ ⲉⲅ. ἀπό; Ac 27 13 *S*(*B* ϫⲱⲟⲩⲛ) αἴρ. acc, Nu 20 22 *S*(*B* ⲟⲅⲱⲧⲉⲃ) ἀπαίρ. ἐκ, Ge 35 5 *S*(*B* do) ἐξαίρ. ἐκ; BG 122 *S* ⲁⲅⲧ. ⲉⲃ. ⲅⲛⲧⲉⲩϩⲏϣⲉ, AM 156 *B* ⲁⲅⲧ-ⲟⲩ ⲉⲃ. ϩⲉⲛⲟⲅⲁⲣⲓⲥⲧⲟⲛ; ⲉⲅⲣⲏⲓ ϩ.: AM 324 *B* ⲁϥⲧⲱⲡϥ ⲉⲅ. ϩⲉⲛⲡⲓϥⲧⲟⲛ.

—— ⲅⲁ(ⲅ)ⲧⲛ- *S*, stand beside, stay with: 1 Kg 19 3 ἐχόμενος ἰστάναι τοῦ; ShA 2 7 wife ⲉⲁⲥⲧ. ⲅⲁⲧⲙⲡⲉⲥⲅⲁⲓ ϫⲉⲉⲥⲛⲁⲃⲱⲕ ⲉⲣ ⲅⲉⲛⲁⲅⲁⲑⲟⲛ, BMOr 8811 238 harlot rejoiceth ⲙⲛⲛⲥⲁⲧⲣⲉⲡⲁⲓ ⲧ. ⲅⲁⲧⲏⲥ fornicating with her.

—— ⲅⲁϫⲛ- *S*, rise before: BMar 19 ϣⲁⲓⲧ. ⲅⲁϫⲱϥ ⲡⲟⲩⲥⲧⲣⲁⲧⲏⲗⲁⲧⲏⲥ, even so ϣⲁⲓⲧ. ⲅⲁϫⲱϥ ⲡⲟⲩⲅⲏⲕⲉ, BMis 37 ⲁϥⲧ. ⲅⲁϫⲱϥ saying Be seated.

—— ⲅⲓϫⲛ- *SBF*, arise upon: Dan 7 17 *B* ἀναστ. ἐπί; *against*: C 86 270 *B* persecution ⲉⲧⲁϥⲧⲱⲡϥ ⲅ. ϯⲉⲕⲕⲗⲏⲥⲓⲁ, BIF 22 106 *F* let each ⲧ. ⲅ. ⲡⲉϥⲟⲩⲏⲃ & slay him = Mor 41 192 *S* ⲉϫⲛ-; tr: Bor 256 145 *S* ⲧ. ⲙⲡⲉⲥⲥⲱⲙⲁ ⲅ. ⲟⲩϭⲗⲟϭ; *rise from*: Mor 48 85 *S* ⲁⲅⲧ. ⲅ. ⲡⲉϥⲑⲣⲟⲛⲟⲥ; ⲉⲃⲟⲗ ⲅ., *from off*: Tob 8 4 *S* ἀνίστ. ἀπό; Ex 10 22 *B* ⲉϫⲁⲛ. ἐκ; Ez 1 9 *S*(BP 11965, *B* ϥⲁⲓ ⲉⲃ. ⲅⲁ-) ἐξαιρ. ἀπό, Ac 9 8 *SB* ⲉⲅ. ἀπό; Miss 4 636 *S* ⲧ. ⲉⲃ. ⲅ. ⲡⲉϥⲑⲣⲟⲛⲟⲥ, Aeg 56 *B* ⲁⲅⲧⲱⲡϥ ⲉⲃ. ⲅ. ⲡⲓⲱⲛⲓ. With following adverb.

—— ⲉⲃⲟⲗ *SABF*, arise: Ps 58 5 *B*(*S* ⲧ.), Jer 27 41 *B* ⲉϫⲉⲅ.; Cl 25 4 *A* ϥⲧⲱⲡⲉ ⲁⲃ. ϥⲃⲱⲕ (Gk diff), Bor 248 55 *S* I carry dwelling with me ⲅⲓⲡⲧⲣⲁⲧ. ⲉⲃ. it followeth me, AM 160 *B* ⲁⲅⲧⲱⲡϥ ⲉⲃ. ⲉⲅⲣⲁⲅ, CO 386 *S* ⲉⲓⲉⲧⲱⲡ ⲉⲃ. ⲛⲧⲁⲃⲱⲕ; as nn *S*, *resurrection*: ShA 2 122 title ⲉϫⲛⲡⲧ. ⲉⲃ. (var P 130³ 18 ⲡϣⲁ ⲛⲧⲁⲛⲁⲥⲧⲁⲥⲓⲥ), Vict&AlbMus 434⁸ 1888 rubric ⲙⲙⲁ ⲛϣⲱⲡⲉ ⲛⲏⲧ. ⲉⲃ. ⲅⲛⲡⲉⲧⲙⲟⲟⲩⲧ ⲉⲧⲉⲛⲡⲉⲅⲁⲅⲅⲉⲗⲓⲟⲛ. ⲙⲁ ⲡⲧ. ⲉⲃ. *v* ⲟⲅⲱⲧⲃ, ϭⲓⲛ-.

—— ⲉⲡϣⲱⲓ *B*, raise up: Nu 20 11 (*S* ϥⲓ ⲉⲅⲣⲁⲓ), Is 6 4 (*S* ⲧ. ⲉⲅ.), Jer 29 6 (*S* ϣⲟⲩϣⲟⲩ ⲙⲙⲟϥ) ἐπαίρ.;

CaiThe 27 ⲧⲉⲡⲉⲛⲏⲟⲩ (var ⲧ-ⲟⲩ) ⲉⲡ. ye sons of light, AM 50 ⲁⲙⲓⲭⲁⲏⲗ ⲧ. ⲉⲡ. ⲛϥⲛⲡⲗⲁⲍ (*cf* BMar 25 *S* ⲧ. ⲉⲅ.); as nn: Ps 140 2 ⲡⲧⲱⲡϥ ⲉⲡ. (*S* ϥⲓ ⲉⲅ.) ἔπαρσις; ϫⲓⲛⲧⲱⲡϥ ⲉⲡ.: Va 57 177 ἐπανιστ.

—— ⲉⲅⲣⲁⲓ, -ⲛⲓ, ⲁⲅⲣ., ⲉⲅⲗ. *SABF*, rise up: Jud 5 12 *S* ἀνίστ.; Nu 10 35 *SB*, Ps 56 8 *SB* ⲉϫⲉⲅ., Jo 6 18 *SA²* ⲧⲱⲡ (*B* ⲡⲉⲣϭⲓ) διεγ.; Ps 36 35 *SA*(Cl, *B* ϥⲁⲓ ⲉⲡϣⲱⲓ)*F*(Pcod 40), Is *l c* ἐπαίρ., BMis 160 *S* waves ⲗⲟ ⲉⲅⲧ. ⲉⲅ., CO 116 *S* ϣⲁⲡⲧⲉⲣⲏⲗⲓⲁⲥ ⲧ. ⲉⲅ. from sickness;   *raise up*: Ge 7 17 *S*(*B* ⲧ.) ἐπαίρ., 4 Kg 2 13 *S*(PMich 607) ὑψοῦν; Zech 5 9 *SA*(*B* ⲱⲗⲓ) ἀναλαμβάνειν; BM 310 67 *S* ⲧ. ⲙⲙⲱⲧⲛ ⲉⲅ. = LAp 528 *F* om ⲉⲅ., Bor 248 59 *S* ⲡⲉⲧⲧ. ⲉⲅ. ⲛⲧⲙⲛⲧⲁⲥⲉⲃⲏⲥ *upholders of iniquity*.

—— nn m *SAA²B*, rising, resurrection, what has arisen: Ge 7 4 *S*(P 44 102, P 131³ 25, R 2 1 36, var & *B* ⲥⲱⲡⲧ) ἀνάστημα, Zeph 3 8 *A*(*B* = Gk), Lu 2 34 *SB* (ⲧⲱⲡϥ), 1 Pet 1 3 *SB* (do) ἀνάστασις; Aeg 258 *S* ⲡⲧ. ⲛⲧⲥⲁⲣⲍ, AP 24 *A²* rejoicing at ⲡⲧⲱⲡ ⲛⲁⲓⲱⲡ, Mani 1 *A²* ⲡⲧⲱⲡ of dead, R 2 1 36 *S* deluge destroyed ⲡⲧ. ⲧⲏⲣϥ that God had created.

ⲧⲱⲡϥ nn m *B*, as last: Mk 9 10 (*S* ⲧ. vb, *F* ⲧ. refl) ἀνάστασις; Nu 26 9 (*S* do) ἐπισύστασις; *v* c ⲉⲡϣⲱⲓ.

ⲣⲉϥⲧⲱⲡϥ *B*, who raises, incites: K 44 ﻌﺐ; ⲙⲛⲧⲣⲉϥⲧⲱⲡϥ *S*, act of raising, supporting: Mus 42 234 ⲧⲙ. ⲅⲁⲡⲉⲑⲗⲓⲯⲓⲥ, Mor 33 34 mother's ⲙ. ⲅⲁⲡϣⲏⲣⲉ ϣⲏⲙ.

ϭⲓⲛ-, ϫⲓⲛⲧ. *SB*, rising, resurrection: Nu 10 6 *SB* ἔξαρσις; Ps 138 2 *SB* ἔγερσις; Lam 3 63 *B* ⲧϫ., Cai Euch 486 *B* ⲡϫ. ⲛⲧⲉ ⲡⲁⲣⲉⲓ ἀνάστασις; ClPr 41 4 *S* ⲥⲱⲙⲁ...ⲧⲉϥϭ., TDiurn 254 *B* quell ⲡⲓϫ. ⲛⲧⲉ ϯⲥⲁⲣⲍ, TEuch 1 184 *B* sim ⲧⲉϥϭ., DeV 1 125 *B* ⲡⲉϥϫⲓⲛⲧⲱⲡϥ from dead, Blake 258 second ϭ. ⲛⲧⲁⲅⲧⲱϣ ⲡⲅⲣⲟⲩⲃⲏⲛ &c, *ib* ⲅⲛⲟⲩϭ. ⲡⲟⲩⲱⲧ *metatio* (*cf* Nu 2 10).

(ⲧⲟⲩⲛⲟ), ⲧⲟⲩⲛ-, ⲧⲟⲩⲡⲉ-, ⲧⲟⲩⲡⲟ- *S*, ⲧⲟⲩⲡⲟⲩ- *SA*, ⲧⲟⲩⲡ- *BF* vb tr, *make to open* (caus of ⲟⲩⲱⲡ, *v* ⲉⲓⲁ eye, but also AZ 47 146 & p 74 *a* 2 above, where for *raise l open*). Whence the following.

ⲧⲟⲩⲛⲟⲥ *SB*, -ⲟⲩⲥ *SA*, ⲧⲟⲩⲡⲥ *A* (Zech 11 16), ⲧⲟⲩⲡⲉⲥ- *SAB*, ⲧⲟⲩⲡⲟⲩⲥ- *SA*, ⲧⲟⲩⲡⲁⲥ- *A²F*, ⲧⲟⲩⲡⲟⲥ- *B*, -ⲟⲥ⸰ *SB*, -ⲁⲥ⸰ *SᶠAA²F* vb tr, *wake, raise, set up*: Pro 10 12 *SA* ⲧⲟⲩⲡⲟⲩⲥ- *B*, Mt 8 25 *S*(*B* ⲡⲉⲣϭⲓ), Jo 2 19 *SA²*(*B* ⲧⲁⲣⲟ ⲉⲣⲁⲧϥ), Phil 1 17 *SBF*, AP 48 *A²* ⲉⲧⲡⲁⲧⲟⲩⲡⲁⲥⲧ ἐγείρειν, Lu 8 24 *S*(*B* ⲛ.) διεγ., Is 42 13 *SB* ἐπεγ., Ps 79 2 *SA* ⲧⲟⲩⲡⲟⲩⲥ- (TillOster 21) *B*, Zech 4 1 *SA*(*B* ⲛ.), Ro 9 17 *SB* ἐξεγ.; Ge 9 9 *B* (*S* ⲥⲙⲓⲛⲉ), Deu 22 4 *S* (var -ⲟⲟⲩⲥⲉ, *B* ⲧⲁⲣⲟ ⲉ.), Job 19 26 *SA*(Cl)*B*, Jer 23 5 *B*(*S* ϯ ⲟⲩⲱ), Ac 13 32 *S*(var -ⲟⲩⲥ)*B*, C 86 287 *B* ⲡⲧⲟⲩⲧⲟⲩⲡⲟⲥ ⲟⲩⲙⲁⲣⲧⲩⲣⲓⲟⲛ ⲡⲁϥ ἀνιστάναι, Ge 4 25 *SB*, Mk 12 19 *SB* ⲉϫⲁⲛ.; Ps 131 17 *B*(*S* ϯ ⲟⲩⲱ) ἐξανατέλλειν; Si 37 7 *S* ἐξαίρειν; 1 Chr 28 7 *B* κατορθοῦν; Jo 11 11 *SA²B* ἐξυπνίζειν;

BG 55 *S* ⲉⲥⲧ. ⲙⲡⲉϥⲙⲉⲉⲩⲉ, ShLeyd 393 *S* ⲉϥⲧⲟⲩⲡⲟⲩⲥ ⲡⲡⲉⲧⲙⲟⲟⲩⲧ, RNC 53 *S* sim ⲡⲉⲧⲙ., P 129¹⁴
115 *S* ⲡⲉⲧⲧⲟⲩⲡⲉⲥ ⲥⲧⲁⲥⲓⲥ, MG 17 304 *S* ⲧⲟⲩⲡⲟⲩⲥ
ⲡⲁⲩ ⲡⲟⲩⲕⲣⲓⲧⲏⲥ, Gu 91 *S^f* ⲧⲟⲩⲡⲁⲥⲟⲩ, AP 23 *A²*
ⲧⲟⲩⲡⲁⲥ ⲡⲁⲥⲁⲡ, Mor 30 15 *F* ⲧⲟⲩⲡⲁⲥⲧ, Aeg 32 *B*
death ⲧⲟⲩⲡⲟⲥ ⲡⲣⲁⲡⲣⲓⲙⲓ, AM 55 *B* ⲧⲟⲩⲡⲟⲥ ⲡⲁⲓⲣⲉϥ-
ⲙⲟⲟⲩⲧ.

With following preposition. ⲉ ⲉϫⲛ-, *raise upon,
incite against*: Jud 2 16 *S* ἐγ. dat, Mic 3 5 *SAB* ἐγ.
ἐπί, Is 13 17 *SB* ἐπεγ. dat, Hab 1 6 *SB* ἐξεγ. ἐπί; 1
Kg 26 19 *S*(var ⲉϩⲣⲁⲓ ⲉϫⲛ-) ἐπισείειν; ShA 1 367 *S*
ⲧⲟⲩⲡⲟⲩⲥ ⲉϫⲛⲧⲏⲩⲧⲛ ⲙⲡⲥⲁϩⲟⲩ, BMis 38 *S* ⲧⲟⲩⲡⲉⲥ
ⲡⲉⲙⲗⲁϩ ⲉϫⲱⲓ, ViK 9781 21 *S* ⲧⲟⲩⲡⲟⲩⲥ ⲟⲩⲡⲟϭ ⲙ-
ⲡⲓⲣⲁⲥⲙⲟⲥ ⲉϫⲛⲧⲏⲩⲧⲛ, C 89 84 *B* ⲧⲟⲩⲡⲟⲥ ⲡⲟⲗⲉⲙⲟⲥ
ⲉ. †ⲯⲩⲭⲏ; ⲉϩⲣⲁⲓ,-ⲏⲓ ⲉϫ.: Jer 279 *B*(*S* ⲉⲓⲛⲉ ⲉϫⲛ-)
ἐγ. ἐπί, AM 271 *B* ⲧⲟⲩⲡⲟⲥ ⲡⲓϣⲑⲟⲣⲧⲉⲣ ⲉϩ. ⲉϫⲱⲡ
ἐπεγ. dat, Ez 23 22 *SB* ἐξεγ. ἐπί; C 86 281 *B* lest
they find relics ⲛⲧⲟⲩⲧⲟⲩⲡⲟⲥ ⲡⲉϥⲥⲡⲟϥ ⲉϩ. ⲉϫⲱⲡ =
BSG 180 *S* ⲉⲓⲛⲉ ⲉϩ. ⲉϫ. ἐπάγειν ἐπί; Mor 22 119 *S*
ⲧⲟⲩⲡⲟⲩⲥ ⲉϩ. ⲉϫⲱ ⲡⲟⲩⲛⲟϭ ⲡⲟⲣⲅⲏ = BSM 109 *B*,
BMis 34 *S* ⲧⲟⲩⲡⲉⲥ ⲡⲣⲣⲟ ⲉϩ. ⲉϫⲙⲡⲉϥⲑⲣⲟⲡⲟⲥ, DeV
2 35 *B* ⲧⲟⲩⲡⲟⲥ ⲭⲛⲏⲙⲱⲡ ⲉϩ. ⲉϫⲱⲟⲩ; ⲉ ⲉⲃⲟⲗ ϩⲁ-
B, *from off*: Ps 112 7 (*S* ϩⲓϫⲛ-) ⲉⲅ. ἀπό; CaiEuch
425 ⲧⲟⲩⲡⲟⲥ ⲡⲟⲩϩⲣⲏⲧ ⲉⲃ. ϩⲁⲙⲉⲅⲓ ἀνιστ. ἀπό; ⲉ
ϩⲛ-, *from out*: J 85 16 *S* ⲧⲟⲩⲡⲱⲥϥ ϩⲙⲡⲛⲟϭ ⲛϣⲱⲡⲉ; ⲉⲃⲟⲗ ϩⲛ-, ϫⲉⲛ-: Jer 23 20 *B* ἀνιστ. ἀπό;
CaiEuch 487 *B* ⲧⲟⲩⲡⲟⲥ ⲡⲓⲣⲉϥⲙⲟⲟⲩⲧ ⲉⲃ. ϫⲉⲛⲡⲓ-
ⲙⲣⲁ ἀν. ἐκ; 1 Kg 2 8 *S*(*B* ⲉⲃ. ϩⲁ-) ⲉⲅ. ἀπό, He
11 19 *SB* ⲉⲅ. ἐκ, Is 41 2 *SB* ἐξεγ. ἀπό; Ps 77 26 *SB*
ἐπαίρ. ἐκ· BG 74 *S* ⲧⲟⲩⲡⲉⲥ ⲟⲩⲥⲡⲉⲣⲙⲁ ⲉⲃ. ⲡⲣⲏⲧⲟⲩ,
AP 42 *A²* ⲧⲟⲩⲡⲁⲥ ⲧⲉⲡⲥⲁⲣⲝ ⲁⲃ. ϩⲡⲡⲉⲧⲙⲟⲟⲩⲧ; ⲉϩⲣⲁⲓ
ϩⲛ-: 2 Pet 3 1 *SB* διεγ. ἐν; ShA 2 303 *S* ⲉⲧⲧ. ⲛⲡⲓⲡⲓ-
ⲣⲁⲥⲙⲟⲥ ϩ. ⲡⲣⲏⲧⲛ; ⲉ ϩⲓϫⲛ-, *upon*: Dan 10 10 *B*(*S*
ⲉϩⲣ. ⲉϫⲛ-) ⲉⲅ. ἐπί; TstAb 178 *B* plagues that God
ⲧⲟⲩⲡⲟⲥⲟⲩ ϩ. ⲡⲓⲭⲱⲣⲁ, AM 286 *B* God pleased to ⲧ.
ⲡⲓⲭⲣⲏⲥⲧⲓⲁⲛⲟⲥ ϩ. ⲡⲓⲕⲁⲣⲓ (cf C 43 124 *B* ϣⲓⲛⲓ ⲛⲥⲁ-);
from off: BMis 555 *S* ⲡϥⲧⲟⲩⲡⲟⲥⲧ ϩ. ⲡⲕⲁϩ *elevare
de*, *ib* 42 *S* sim ϩ. ⲡⲉⲑⲣⲟⲛⲟⲥ; ⲉⲃⲟⲗ ϩⲓϫ.: Is 14 9
B(*S* ⲧⲱⲟⲩⲡ ⲉⲃ. ϩⲛ-) ⲉⲅ. ἐκ; ⲉϩⲣⲁⲓ ϩⲓϫ.: BMis 30
S; ⲉ ⲉⲡϣⲱⲓ *B*, *up*: Va 57 39 ἀνιστ.; *ib* 15 διεγ.;
AM 225 ⲉϥⲧ. ⲙⲡⲁⲡⲟⲩⲥ ⲉⲡ.; ⲉ ⲉϩⲣⲁⲓ, -ⲏⲓ, as last:
2 Pet 1 13 *B*(*S* om ⲉϩ.) διεγ., BHom 37 *S* ⲧ. ⲉϩ. ⲙ-
ⲡⲉⲡⲟⲩϩⲣⲟⲧ διανιστ.; PO 11 303 *B* sim, BM 190 158
S ⲡⲉϥⲡⲁⲧ. ⲉϩ. ⲡⲉ (= PO 8 253 ⲣⲓⲟ); Miss 4 785 *S*
ⲉϥⲧⲟⲩⲡⲟⲩⲥ ⲉϩ. ⲙⲡⲉⲅⲗⲟⲧⲓⲥⲙⲟⲥ.

——nn m *S*, *raising*: PS 279 ⲡⲧⲟⲩⲡⲉⲥ ⲣⲉϥⲙⲟⲟⲩⲧ.

ⲣⲉϥⲧ. *S*, *raiser*: Mus 40 275 ⲣⲉϥⲧⲟⲩⲡⲉⲥ ⲯⲩⲭⲏ
from death.

ϫⲓⲛⲧ. *B*, *raising*: Cat 204 ⲧϫⲓⲛⲧⲟⲩⲡⲉⲥ †ⲙⲉⲧ-
ⲣⲱⲙⲓ.

ⲧⲟⲩⲏⲧ *v* ⲧⲟⲟⲩⲧⲉ.

ⲧⲟⲩⲱⲧ *SF*, ⲑ. *B* nn m f(once), ⲧⲟⲩⲟⲟⲧⲉ *S*, ⲑⲟⲩ-
ⲟ† *B* f, *idol, pillar*: Is 19 3 *S*(*B*=Gk), *ib* 21 9 *S*(*B*
ϥⲱⲧ⳿) ἄγαλμα; ROC 9 331 *B* ⲧⲁⲣⲉ ⲑ. ⲉⲣⲁⲧϥ ἀν-
δριάς; Ge 19 26 *B* -ⲟ†(*S* ⲟⲩⲟⲉⲓⲧ)ⲥⲧⲏⲗⲏ; *shrine*: Ac
19 24 *S*(*B* ⲉⲣⲫⲉ) ναός; LMär 34 *S* ⲧ. of bronze with
staff in hand named ⲫⲩⲗⲁⲕⲗⲏⲥ (ʿΗρακλῆς), *ib* 38 *S*
ⲡⲉⲧ. upon pillar, Mor 39 20 *S* ⲧ. ⲡⲡⲟⲩⲅ = C 43 44
B ⲥⲧⲩⲗⲏ, AM 213 *B* ⲑ. ⲛϣⲉ, C 86 303 *B* ⲡⲓⲑ. of
Apollo, *ib* 292 *B* ϥⲁⲡⲓⲍⲱⲗⲟⲡ ⲡⲉⲙϩⲁⲛⲑ., BIF 14 130
S sim, *ib* 22 106 *F* ⲡⲓⲟ̄ ⲛⲧ., C 43 200 *B* ⲟ̄ ⲡⲡⲟⲩ† ⲛⲑ.,
R 1 5 36 *S* ⲧⲉⲧⲟⲩⲱⲧ...ⲁⲥϩⲉ, JTS 10 399 *S* Potiphar's
wife like ⲡⲉⲓⲧⲟⲩⲟⲟⲧⲉ ⲡⲱⲡⲉ, Mor 31 213, 224 *S* ⲧⲉⲓ-
ⲧⲟⲩⲟⲟⲧⲉ of Astarte, C 86 204 *B* ⲧⲁⲓⲑⲟⲩⲱⲧ of Apollo,
Aeg 252 *S* ⲣⲉϥⲧⲁⲙⲓⲉ ⲧ.

In names (?): Πανετουῶτις, Ψενετουῶτις (Preisigke).

ⲧⲉⲩⲧⲉ *S* (*sic l*?) nn, meaning unknown: ShC 73
73 physician shall treat only visible, outward organs
ⲟⲩⲡⲉϣⲉ, ⲟⲩⲍⲉⲩⲧⲉ, ⲟⲩⲡⲁϫⲉ, ⲟⲩⲃⲁⲗ.   Coptic?

ⲧⲟⲟⲩⲧⲉ *S* (rare), ⲑⲱⲟⲩ† *B*, ⲧⲁⲩ† *F*, ⲑⲟⲩⲉⲧ- *B*,
ⲧ.- *F*, ⲧⲟⲩⲏⲧ⳿ *SF*, ⲑⲟⲩⲱⲧ⳿ *B*, ⲧⲟⲩⲏⲧ† *S*, ⲑⲟⲩⲏⲧ† *B*
vb I intr, *be gathered, collected*: Ps 47 5 *B*(*S* ⲥⲱⲟⲩϩ
ⲉϩⲣⲟⲩⲛ), Is 35 10 *B*(*SF* ⲥⲱⲟⲩϩ), Mt 13 47 *BF*(*S* ⲥ.
ⲉϩ.) συνάγειν, Ez 40 12 ⲧⲟⲩⲃⲏⲟⲩⲧ *B* (*l* ⲑⲟⲩⲏⲧ, *S*
ⲕⲱⲧⲉ ⲡⲥⲁ-) ἐπισυν.; Job 41 8 *B* συνέχειν; Nu 20 26†
B(*S* ⲟⲩⲱϩ tr) προστιθέναι; Ac 12 12 *B*(*S* ⲥ.) συναθροίζειν; *ib* 2 6 *B*(*S* do) συνέρχεσθαι; Nu 24 2 *S* (P
44 107, var ⲙⲟⲟϣⲉ) *B* στρατοπεδεύειν; Ex 19 5† *S*
(var ⲑⲟⲩⲏⲧ *sic*, *B* ⲥⲟⲩⲃⲏⲧ), *ib* 23 22† *S*(*B* ⲥⲟⲧⲡ), Deu
7 6† *S* (var ⲧⲁⲉⲓⲏⲩ, *B* ⲥⲉⲃⲧⲱⲧ), Tit 2 14† *S*(*B* ⲥⲙⲟⲛⲧ), cit ROC 20 56 *S*, CaiEuch 327 خاص περιούσιος (but these ? qual of ⲧⲟⲩⲟ); BSM 84 *B* ⲁ†ⲡⲟⲗⲓⲥ
ⲧⲏⲣⲥ ⲑ., AM 155 *B* ⲡⲓⲙⲏϣ ⲉⲑ.†

II tr (*S* once), *gather, collect*: Jer 38 8 (*S* ⲉⲓⲛⲉ)
ἄγειν, Lev 25 3 (*S* ⲱⲗ ⲉϩⲣⲟⲡ), 2 Kg 6 1 (*S* ⲥ. ⲉϩ:),
Pro 10 10 (*SA* do), Eccl 2 8 *F*(*S* ⲥ.), Is 33 4 (*SF* ⲥ.
ⲉϩ.), Mic 4 12 (*A* ⲥ. ⲁϩ.), Mt 22 10 (*S* ϫⲓ ⲉϩⲣⲟⲡ), Jo
15 6 (*SA²* ⲥ.) συνάγ., Ps 146 2 (*S* ⲥ. ⲉϩ.), Mt 23 37
(*S* do) ἐπισυν.; Lev 8 3 (*S* ⲥ.) ἐκκλησιάζειν, 3 Kg 8 1
ἐξεκ.; Ac 19 25 (*S* ⲥ.) συναθροίζειν; Mt 13 30 *F*(*S*
ⲥ. ⲉϩ., *B* ⲥⲱⲕⲓ) συλλέγειν; Ac 5 21 (*S* ⲥ.) συγκαλεῖν;
ib 17 5 (*S* do) ὀχλοποιεῖν; Ro 12 20 (*S* ⲡⲱⲣϣ ⲉϫⲛ-)
σωρεύειν; Ps 77 50 *S*(*B* ⲙⲁϣⲑⲁⲙ) συγκλείειν; MG
25 352 ⲁϥⲑⲟⲩⲉⲧ ⲡⲓⲥⲡⲟⲩ, C 41 61 ϥⲡⲁⲩ ⲡⲑ. ⲛ†-
ⲉⲕⲕⲗⲏⲥⲓⲁ, BSM 125 ⲁϥⲑ. ⲛ†ⲥⲩⲛⲁⲅⲝⲓⲥ.

Hence *strike* wooden boards ϣⲉⲛ. (PO 5 797
بالودين *to assemble* congregation, *knock* on door: intr
C 89 203 ⲁϥⲑⲣⲉ-...ⲑ. ⲉⲡⲓⲥⲡⲟⲩ κρούειν ⲧ. ἀδελφοῖς,
ib 13 ⲁϥⲑ. ⲉⲡⲓⲣⲟ, HCons 469 ⲛⲧⲉϥⲑ. ⲉϫⲱϥ (*sc* gong)
دق ب; tr CDan 86 ⲑ. ⲙⲡⲓϣⲉ κρ. τὸ κροῦσμα, MIE
2 417 ⲑ. ⲙⲡⲓϣⲉ ⲛⲑ. = BAp 123 *S* ⲣ ⲧⲕⲁⲗⲉⲗⲉ (*q v*),
PO 11 363 ⲁⲩⲑ. ⲙⲡⲓϣⲉ in Rakote (*cf* Synax 1 106

8), AM 194 caused ⲑ. ⲛ̄ϯⲥⲁⲗⲡⲓⲅⲅⲟⲥ (cf ⲕⲱⲗϩ **II**). *V* Rec 27 155, 28 211.

With following preposition (no *S*). c ⲉ-, *gather to, for*: Jer 26 3 ⲡⲣⲟⲥⲁⲅ. ⲉⲓⲥ, Ge 1 9, Dan 3 3 ⲥⲩⲛⲁⲅ. ⲉⲓⲥ, Ge 34 30, C 89 109 ⲁⲅⲑ. ⲉⲑⲉⲟⲇⲱⲣⲟⲥ ⲟ̄. ⲉⲡⲓ, MG 25 218 people ⲑ. ⲉⲣⲟϥ ⲟ̄. ⲡⲣⲟⲥ; 1 Cor 11 17 (*S* c. ⲉ-) ⲥⲩⲛⲉⲣⲭ. ⲉⲓⲥ; Ez 16 57† (*S* do) ⲡⲉⲣⲓⲉⲭⲉⲓⲛ; Jer 3 18 (*S* ⲉⲓ) ⲏⲕⲉⲓⲛ ⲉⲡⲓ; 1 Kg 23 26 (*S* diff) ⲡⲁⲣⲁⲃⲁⲗ. ⲉⲡⲓ; C 43 182 ⲉⲣⲉⲡⲓⲗⲏϣ ⲑ. ⲉⲙⲁⲅ, *ib* 30 ⲁⲥⲱ. ⲉⲡϩⲓⲡⲉⲣ ⲑⲉⲱ-ⲣⲓⲛ, MG 25 319 ⲁϯⲁϩⲱ...ⲑⲟⲅⲩⲧⲟⲩ ⲉⲣⲟⲛ; ⲉϩⲟⲩⲛ ⲉ-: Ez 39 28 ⲥⲩⲛⲁⲅ. ⲉⲡⲓ; Mt 13 30 *BF* (*S* c. ⲉϩ.) ⲟ̄. ⲉⲓⲥ; MG 25 170 ⲡⲧⲉϥⲟ. ⲉϩ. ⲉⲣⲟϥ ⲙ̄ⲡⲉϥⲕⲁϯ, Miss 4 125 ⲡⲁⲅⲑ.† ⲉϩ. ⲉϯⲉⲕⲕⲗⲏⲥⲓⲁ; c ⲉϫⲛ-, *gather upon, to*: Is 56 8 (*S* c. ⲉϫⲛ-) ⲥⲩⲛⲁⲅ. ⲉⲡⲓ; Jer 33 9 (*S* do) ⲉⲝⲉⲕⲕⲗ. ⲉⲡⲓ; Ex 32 1 (*S* ⲧⲱⲟⲩⲛ ⲉϩⲣⲁⲓ ⲉϫⲛ-) ⲥⲩⲛⲓ-ⲥⲧⲁⲛⲁⲓ ⲉⲡⲓ; MG 25 375 crowd ⲑ. ⲉϫⲛⲧⲑⲉⲱⲣⲓⲁ ROC 18 288 ابسر واحدة); ⲉϩⲣⲏⲓ ⲉϫ-: Is 18 6 (*S* c. ⲉϫⲛ-), Dan 11 40 (*S* c. ⲉϩⲣ. ⲉϫⲛ-) ⲥⲩⲛⲁⲅ. ⲉⲡⲓ; ⲉ-ϩⲣⲏⲓ ⲉϫ-: Deu 32 23 (var ⲛ̄ϩ., *S* c. ⲉϩⲟⲩⲛ ⲉ-) ⲟ̄. ⲉⲓⲥ; c ⲡⲉⲙ-, *foregather with*: Ps 46 10 (*S* c. ⲉϩⲟⲩⲛ ⲙ̄ⲛ-) ⲟ̄. ⲙⲉⲧⲁ; Aeg 59 apostles ⲑ.† ⲡⲉⲙⲛⲟⲅⲉⲣⲛⲟⲩ, Miss 4 131 ⲡⲧⲉϥⲟ. ⲡⲉⲙⲛⲱⲁⲡⲛⲏⲥ; c ϣⲉⲛ-, *gather in*: PO 11 380 found saint ⲉϥⲑ.† ϣⲉⲛϯⲉⲕⲕⲗⲏⲥⲓⲁ *holding service* (cf ⲥⲩⲛⲁⲅ.), BSM 129 ⲧⲟⲡⲟⲥ ... ⲛⲑ.† ⲛ̄ϩⲏⲧϥ; ⲉⲃⲟⲗ ϩ., *from*: ZNTW 24 84 *F* ⲧⲟⲩⲏⲧⲥ ⲉⲃ. ϩⲙ- ⲟ̄. ⲁⲡⲟ, Ps 105 47 (*S* c. ⲉϩ. ϩⲛ-), Mt 24 31 *BF* (*S* c. ⲉϩ. ⲉⲃ. ϩⲛ-) ⲉⲡⲓⲥ. ⲉⲕ; c ϩⲁ-, *gather to*: Ge 6 21, Is 49 5 (*S* c. ⲉϩ. ⲉⲣⲁⲧϥ) ⲥⲩⲛⲁⲅ. ⲡⲣⲟⲥ, CDan 86 ⲑ. ϩⲁⲣⲟⲛ ⲉⲡϣⲱⲓ ⲛⲛⲉⲡⲓⲟϯ ⲟ̄. acc; 2 Chr 5 3 ⲉⲝⲉⲕⲕⲗ. ⲡⲣⲟⲥ; Su 6 (*S* ⲡⲏⲩ ⲉⲣⲁⲧϥ) ⲉⲣⲭ. ⲡⲣⲟⲥ; TstAb 249 ⲁⲅⲑ. ϩⲁⲣⲟϥ (cf 252 ⲉⲣⲟϥ); c ϩⲓ-, *gather at*: Ac 17 17 (var ⲉ-, *S* diff) ⲡⲁⲣⲁⲧⲩⲅⲭⲁⲛⲉⲓⲛ ⲉⲛ; 1 Cor 11 20 (*S* c. ⲉϩ.) ⲟ̄. ⲉⲡⲓ ⲧⲟ ⲁⲩⲧⲟ; Ac 2 1 (*S* ϣⲱⲡⲉ) ⲟⲙⲟⲩ ⲉⲓⲛⲁⲓ; AM 280 ⲡⲗⲁⲟⲥ ⲧⲏⲣϥ ⲑ.† ϩⲓⲟⲩⲙⲁ.

With following adverb (no *S*). c ⲉϩⲟⲩⲛ, *gather in, collect together*: Ez 13 5 (*S* c. ⲉϩ.), Jo 6 12 *BF* (PMich 3521, *SA*² do), C 89 6 dew ⲑ. ⲉϩ. & became as honey (cf TT 140 *S* c.), Va 57 12 ⲑ. ⲉϩ. ⲡⲟⲩⲧⲣⲟ-ⲫⲏ ⲥⲩⲛⲁⲅ., Ge 6 16† (*S* ⲉⲓⲛⲉ ⲉϩ.) جمع ⲉⲡⲓⲥ.; Is 23 3 (*S* ⲱⲗ ⲉϩ.) ⲉⲓⲥⲫⲉⲣⲉⲓⲛ; Ez 33 30 (*S* c. ⲉϩ.) ⲥⲩⲛⲉⲣⲭ.; *ib* 36 24 ⲁⲑⲣⲟⲓⲍⲉⲓⲛ; Va 66 299 ⲁⲓⲑⲟⲅⲱⲧⲟⲩ ⲉϩ. ⲑⲏⲥⲁⲩⲣⲓⲍⲉⲓⲛ; AM 34 ⲁϥⲑ. ⲉϩ. ⲛⲛⲓⲙⲉⲗⲟⲥ, Va 61 101 ⲉⲕⲑⲟⲅⲉⲧ ⲭⲣⲏⲙⲁ ⲉϩ. = Mor 25 19 *S* ⲥⲱⲟⲩϩ, C 89 190 nuns ⲉⲧⲑ.† ⲉϩ. ⲉⲑⲃⲉϥϯ, DeV 1 123 ⲁⲩϣⲁⲡⲟ. ⲉϩ. & come to one place; as nn, *congregation*: Ex 34 22 *B* (*S* c. ⲉϩ.) ⲥⲩⲛⲁⲅⲱⲅⲏ; Pro 6 8 *B* (*S* ⲕⲱ ⲉϩⲣⲁⲓ) ⲡⲁⲣⲁⲑⲉⲥⲓⲥ; BSM 88 ⲛⲑ. ⲉϩ. of monks = BMis 179 *S* ⲥⲟⲟⲩϩⲥ, PO 14 354 ⲛⲑ. ⲉϩ. ⲛ̄ⲧⲉ ⲧⲁⲓⲑⲱⲟⲩⲧⲉ.

—— nn m *gathering, congregation*: Ez 27 27 (*S* ⲥⲟⲟⲩϩⲥ) ⲥⲩⲛⲁⲅⲱⲅⲏ, 2 Thes 2 1 (*S* ⲥⲱⲟⲩϩ) ⲉⲡⲓⲥ.; C 89 183 from morn till ϥⲛⲁⲩ ⲙ̄ⲡⲓⲑ., C 41 54 ⲕⲱⲗϩ ⲉⲡⲓⲑ. at even.

ⲙⲁ ⲛⲑ., *place of meeting*: Ge 1 9 ⲥⲩⲛⲁⲅⲱⲅⲏ; *ib* 10,

Jer 28 32 ⲥⲩⲥⲧⲏⲙⲁ; C 89 75 (*S* ViK 9465 ⲥⲱⲟⲩϩ) ⲥⲩ-ⲛⲁⲝⲓⲥ; Nu 31 10 ⲙ. of flocks (*S* ⲡⲣⲱ) ⲉⲡⲁⲩⲗⲓⲥ; C 86 172 ϥⲙ. ⲛ̄ⲡⲓⲧⲉⲭⲛⲓⲧⲏⲥ place in Fostât (*v* BIF 1 159* دار الصناعة, but ʾⲥ does not = ⲙⲁ ⲛⲑ.).

ϫⲓⲛⲑ., *assemblage*: Ex 23 16 m (*S* c. ⲉϩ.) ⲥⲩⲛⲁⲅⲱⲅⲏ, Is 49 5 m (*S* do vb) ⲥⲩⲛⲁⲅⲉⲓⲛ; TEuch 2 91 prayer for ⲛⲉⲡϫ.; ⲙⲁ ⲛϫ. ⲡⲛⲉⲭⲣⲉⲥⲧⲓⲁⲛⲟⲥ منشية النصارى place near Achmîm PSBA 20 272.

ⲑⲱⲟⲩⲧⲉ nn f, *collection, assembly*: Ge 35 11 (*S* = Gk), Job 8 17 (*S* ⲥⲟⲟⲩϩⲥ) ⲥⲩⲛⲁⲅⲱⲅⲏ; Pro 11 13 (*SA* do), Jo 11 47 (*SAA*² = Gk) ⲥⲩⲛⲉⲇⲣⲓⲟⲛ; Nu 32 14 (*S* ⲥⲟ.) ⲥⲩⲥⲧⲣⲉⲙⲙⲁ; Jer 9 2 ⲥⲩⲛⲟⲇⲟⲥ; *ib* 28 30 ⲡⲉⲣⲓⲟⲭⲏ; 1 Kg 17 47 (*S* do) ⲉⲕⲕⲗⲏⲥⲓⲁ; *ib* 45 (*S* ⲙⲏⲛⲏϣⲉ) ⲡⲁⲣⲁ-ⲧⲁⲝⲓⲥ; C 89 52 = Miss 4 534 *S* ⲥⲟ. ⲙⲟⲛⲁⲥⲧⲏⲣⲓⲟⲛ, *ib* 45 = *ib* 526 *S* do ⲙⲟⲛⲏ; K 79 ϯⲑ. بعض الملة وهي نحلة *religious group, sect*; Miss 4 223 ⲑ. *council* at Ephe-sus, C 43 50 ⲑ. of Romans = Mor 39 28 *S* ⲥⲱⲟⲩϩ ⲉⲣⲟⲩⲛ, C 89 83 withdrew to ⲟⲩⲙⲁ ϣⲉⲛϯⲑ., *ib* 156 visiting ⲡⲓⲙⲟⲛⲱⲟⲩⲓ ⲧⲏⲣⲟⲩ ⲕⲁⲧⲁ ⲑ. = MG 17 331 *S* ⲥⲟ.

ⲧⲟⲩⳇⲟ, ⲧⲟⲩⳇⲉ-, ⲧⲟⲩⳇⲟ- (once), -ⳇⲟ﹖ *B* vb tr, *add* (caus of ⲟⲩⱳ): Cat 46 Luke ⲧ. ⲛ̄ⲡⲁⲓⲕⲉⲣⲟⲟⲩ ⲏ̄ (on Lu 9 28), Va 57 269 ⲉϥⲧ. ⲛ̄ⲡⲓⲡⲉⲧⲏⲣϥ ⲛ̄ⲡⲉⲧϩⲱⲟⲩ, *ib* 61 98 ⲛ̄ⲡⲉⲛⲧⲟⲩⳇⲟ ⲡⲣⲟⲥⲉⲩⲭⲏ.

With following preposition. c ⲉ-, *add to*: Va 57 7 ⲁϥⲧ. ⲉⲣⲟⲥ ⲛ̄ⲡⲁⲓϫⲉⲧ ⲧⲓⲑⲉⲛⲁⲓ, Ap 22 18 (*S* ⲟⲩⱳ ⲉϩⲣⲁⲓ ⲉϫⲛ-) ⲉⲡⲓⲧ. ⲉⲡⲓ, Lev 26 21 (*S* ⲟⲩ. ⲉϫ.) ⲡⲣⲟⲥⲧ. dat, Deu 4 2 (*S* do) ⲡⲣ. ⲡⲣⲟⲥ, Lu 3 20 (*S* do) ⲡⲣ. ⲉⲡⲓ; Va 57 15 ⲁϥⲧ. ⲉⲣⲱⲟⲩ ⲉⲡⲁⲅⲉⲓⲛ; AM 198 ⲙ̄ⲡⲓⲧ. ⲉⲣⲱ-ⲟⲩ ⲛ̄ⲡⲓⲱⲗⲓ ⲉⲃⲟⲗ ⲛ̄ϩⲏⲧⲟⲩ; ⲉϩⲣⲏⲓ ⲉ-: C 89 45 ⲁϥⲧ. ⲁⲡⲟⲩⲙⲁ ⲉⲣ. ⲉⲡⲉϥⲡⲉⲧϩⲱⲟⲩ = Miss 4 526 *S* ⲟⲩ. ⲉⲣ. ⲉϫⲛ-ⲡⲣ. dat; c ⲉϫⲛ-, *as last*: Lev 27 13 (*S* ⲟⲩ. ⲉϫ.), Is 38 5 (*S* ⲟⲩ. ⲉ-) ⲡⲣ. ⲡⲣⲟⲥ, Job 29 22 (*S* do) ⲡⲣ. ⲉⲡⲓ; Lev 26 16 (*S* ⲉⲓⲛⲉ ⲉϫ.) ⲉⲡⲓⲥⲩⲛⲓⲥⲧⲁⲛⲁⲓ ⲉⲡⲓ; Va 57 35 ⲧ. ⲉϫ. ⲛ̄ⲡⲓⲡⲣⲟⲑⲩⲣⲟⲛ ⲉⲡⲓⲃⲁⲓⲛⲉⲓⲛ gen; *ib* 61 18 ⲁϥⲧ. ⲉ. ϯⲁⲥⲕⲏⲥⲓⲥ, C 43 155 ⲧ. ⲉ. opp ⲱⲗⲓ ⲉⲃ. ϣⲉⲛ- = Mor 48 114 *S* ⲟⲩ. ⲉϫⲛ-; ⲉϩⲣⲏⲓ ⲉϫ-: Lev 5 16 (*S* ϯ ⲉϥⲕⲏⲃ) ⲡⲣ. ⲉⲡⲓ, Va 68 167 ⲁϥⲧ. ⲉⲣ. ⲉ.ⲛⲓⲥⲟⲡⲛⲓ ⲡⲣ. dat; c ϩⲓϫⲛ-, *as last*: MG 25 351 ⲡⲁϥⲧ. ϩ. ⲡⲉϥ-ⲁⲥⲕⲏⲥⲓⲥ (ROC 18 54 زاد على); c ⲡ̄- as last: Mk 4 24 (*S* ⲟⲩ. ⲉ-) ⲡⲣ. dat; c ⲡⲉⲙ-, *join with*: Ex 23 2 (*S* ϣⲱⲡⲉ ⲙ̄ⲛ-) ⲡⲣ. ⲙⲉⲧⲁ.

—— nn m, *addition*: Lev 19 25 (*S* ⲟⲩ. ⲉ-) ⲡⲣⲟⲥ-ⲑⲉⲙⲁ; Is 3 21 (*S* ϯ ϩⲓ-) ⲉⲡⲓⲃⲗⲏⲙⲁ; P ar 203 153 only-begotten ⲕⲁⲧⲁ ⲟⲩϩⲙⲟⲧ ⲁⲡ ⲓⲉ ⲟⲩⲧ. اضافة.

ⲧⲟⲩⳉⲟ *SAA*²*B*, -ϫⲁ﹖ *S/F*, ⲧⲟⲩϫⲉ- *SAB*, ⲧⲟⲩϫⲟ-*A*, -ϫⲟ﹖ *SB*, -ϫⲁ﹖ *AA*²*F*, -ϫⲉ﹖ *F* (? Mt 14 30 Rev Bibl 7), -ϫⲏⲩ† *S*, -ϫⲏⲟⲩⲧ† *B* vb **I** tr, *make whole, save* (caus of ⲟⲩϫⲁⲓ): Ps 21 8 *SA* (Cl) *B*, *ib* 56 3 *S* (*B* ⲡⲟϩⲉⲙ), Is 34 15 *SBF*, Zech 12 7 *A* (*B* do), BHom 56 *S* God ⲧ. ⲡⲟϫⲟⲡ ⲡⲓⲙ (var R 2 2 37 ⲡⲟⲩϫⲙ) ⲥⲱⳅⲉⲓⲛ, Lu 7 3 *SB* ⲇⲓⲁⲥ.; Ps 17 19 *SB*, Pro 14 25 *SA* ⲧⲟⲩϫⲟ-

(B п.); Ps 40 5 B(S ⲧⲁⲗϭⲟ), Is 30 26 B(SF do) ἰᾶσθαι; Ps 78 11 S(B ⲭϥⲟ) περιποιεῖν; AM 269 B ϣⲁ-
ⲧⲉϥⲧⲟⲩϫⲟⲥ(var ⲭϥⲟⲥ) λυτροῦν; Ez 33 9 SB ῥύεσθαι
(var ἐξαιρεῖν); ShA 2 168 S able to ⲧ. ⲡⲧⲉⲩⲯⲩⲭⲏ,
AM 218 B ⲡⲁⲣⲙⲉⲧ ⲙⲁⲧⲟⲩϫⲟⲓ, Pcod 33 S ⲡⲭ̅ⲥ̅ ⲧⲟⲩϫⲟϥ (var п.), Mor 30 55 F ⲧⲟⲩϫⲁⲕ ⲡⲧⲁⲕ = ib 29
48 S.

II intr, *be safe, saved*: Si 2 12 S σῴ., Va 57 180 B
ⲡⲧⲉⲥⲧ. ⲛϫⲉ ⲧⲟⲩⲁϥⲉ διασ.; Is 7 4 B(S ⲧⲁ.) ἰᾶ.; ib
31 5 SF(B diff) περιποιεῖν; ib 50 2 B(S п.) ἐξαι.;
ShA 2 66 S ⲙⲛ ϭⲟⲙ ⲙⲙⲟϥ ⲉⲧ.;   qual, *safe,
preserved*: Is 66 19 S(B п.), Eph 2 5 S(B do), Miss
8 97 S ⲉⲣⲉⲧⲣⲏⲛⲏ ϣⲱⲡⲉ ⲉⲥⲧ. σ.; Pcod 15 S Egypt
ⲧ. ⲣⲓⲧⲡⲡⲉⲕϣⲗⲏⲗ, SHel 70 S martyrs with Lord in
glory ⲉⲣⲉⲡⲕⲉⲕⲗⲟⲥ(κύκλος)ⲡⲡⲉⲩϭⲓⲥⲉ ⲧ. ⲡⲁⲩ is com-
plete(?),C 43 187 B she escaped ⲉⲥⲧ.,J 75 46 S having
ⲡⲉⲡⲙⲉⲉⲩⲉ ⲉϥⲧ., ViK 4912 S λογισμος ⲧⲁⲭⲣⲏⲩ,
ⲇⲓⲁⲡⲟⲓⲁ ⲧ. (cf ἐρρωμένην ἔχων ⲧ. διάνοιαν PLond 1
232), P 131 5 70 S physical difference in His flesh remained ⲉⲧ., Va 57 82 B ⲉⲩⲧ. ϫⲉⲛⲡⲟⲩⲙⲉⲗⲟⲥ.

With following preposition.

—— ⲉ- SB, *save from* intr: Bor 222* 3 S ⲁϥⲧ. ⲉⲡⲕⲱϩⲧ; tr: Job 6 33 S(B п.) σ. ἐκ, Ps 68 14 S(B do)
σ. ἀπό, Job 29 12 S(B do) διασ. ἐκ; BMis 85 S ⲧⲟⲩϫⲉ ⲡⲕⲟⲥⲙⲟⲥ ⲉⲡⲧⲁⲕⲟ (cf 87 ϩⲙⲡⲧⲁ.), TT 27 S ⲧ.†
ⲉⲧϭⲓⲛϣⲱϥⲧ ⲉⲧⲙⲟⲩⲉⲓⲧ, Va 63 2 B ⲧⲟⲩϫⲟϥ ⲉⲣⲁⲡ-
ⲙⲏϣ ⲡⲕⲓⲡⲁⲩⲛⲟⲥ = BMis 364 S ⲧ. ϩⲛ-(var п.), BAp
98 S body ⲧ.† ⲉϣⲱⲡⲉ (sic);   vbal: Ez 34 22 SB σ.;
Ps 30 15 S, Pro 14 25 SA ῥύ. ἐκ; Gal 1 4 S (all B
п.) ἐξαιρ. ἐκ; *bring safe to* S: Ge 19 17 (B п.) σ. εἰς;
BMis 324 would I could swim ⲧⲁⲧ. ⲡⲧⲁ ⲯⲩⲭ ⲉⲡⲉⲕ-
ⲕⲣⲟ, Miss 8 217 sim;   ⲉϩⲟⲩⲛ ⲉ- S, as last: 2 Tim
4 18 (B п.) σ. εἰς, cit Mus 40 255 no name can ⲧ. ⲉϩ.
ⲉⲧⲙⲡⲧⲉⲣⲟ, Leyd 382 ⲧⲟⲩϫⲉⲧⲏⲩⲧⲛ ⲉϩ. ⲉⲧⲉϥⲙ.; Ac
27 39 (B п.) ἐκσῴζειν εἰς.

—— ⲉⲧⲃⲉ- SB, *for, through*: Ps 105 8 S(B п.) σ.
ἕνεκεν, CaiEuch 361 B ⲙⲁⲧⲟⲩϫⲟп ⲉ. ⲡⲉⲕⲣⲁⲛ σ. διά.

—— ⲉⲧⲛ- S, *from*: 1 Kg 9 16 σ. ἐκ; Job 5 20 (B
п.) λύειν ἐκ.

—— п- S, as last: Si 51 9 (l ⲛⲛϭⲓϫ) σ. ἐκ.

—— ⲡⲧⲉⲛ- B, as last: AM 327 ⲁⲕⲧ. ⲡⲇⲁⲡⲓⲏⲗ п-
ⲧⲟⲧⲟⲩ п-; ⲉⲃⲟⲗ п.: Ps 7 2 (S ⲉ-), Dan 3 88 (var ⲉⲃ.
ϫⲉп-) σ. ἐκ.

—— ⲉⲃⲟⲗ ϩⲁ- B, as last: Ps 139 2 (S ⲉ-) ῥύ. ἀπό;
BSM 67 ⲧⲟⲩϫⲟп ⲉⲃ. ϩⲁⲡⲉⲧϩⲱⲟⲩ.

—— ϩⲛ-, ϫⲉⲛ- SB, *in, from*: Ps 33 17 S(A Cl B
п.) ῥύ. ἐκ; Si 36 1 S ἐξαιρ. ἐν; Jer 3 22 B(S BMOr
8811 214, BHom 13 ⲧⲁⲗϭⲟ) ἰᾶ. acc; PSBA 30 234 S
ⲧⲟⲩϫⲟϥ ϩⲙⲡⲕⲱϩⲧ (cf 235 ⲉ-); *by, through* S: Ps
53 1 σ. ἐν, ib 107 6 σ. dat, ib 30 1 (all B п.) ἐξαιρ.
ἐν; Ep 198 ⲉⲡⲧ.† ϩⲡⲡⲉⲧⲛϣⲗⲏⲗ;   ⲉⲃⲟⲗ ϩⲛ- SAB,
intr: Sa 16 8 S ῥύ. ἐκ;   tr: Zech 8 7 A, Mt 1
21 S σ. ἀπό, Nu 24 19† S (var ⲟⲩϫⲁⲓ, B Va ⲡⲁⲣ-

ⲉⲓⲥⲓ l ⲡⲁⲣⲙⲉϥ شريد var انجر), Jo 12 27 SA² σ. ἐκ;
Job 33 30 S, Ps 50 14 SA (Cl, all B п.) ῥύ. ἐκ, ib
38 8 S(B diff) ῥύ. ἀπό; Ge 32 11 S(B п.), Ps 36 40 B
(S ⲉⲃ. ϩⲓⲧⲛ-) ἐξαιρ. ἐκ; PS 86 S ⲧⲟⲩϫⲉ ⲧⲁϫⲟⲙ ⲉⲃ.
ϩⲙⲡⲉⲭⲁⲟⲥ, ShBor 247 123 S ⲉⲧⲧ.† ⲉⲃ. ϩⲛⲧⲉⲃⲗⲁⲃⲏ,
ViK 9621 Sʃ ⲁϥⲧⲟⲩϫⲁ ⲡⲓⲉⲣⲉⲙⲓⲁⲥ ⲉⲃ. ϩⲙⲡϣⲛⲓ,
BSM 55 B ⲧⲟⲩϫⲟп ⲉⲃ. ϫⲉⲛⲁⲙⲉⲛϯ = BMis 410 S
ⲥⲟⲧⲛ ⲛⲧⲛ-.

—— ϩⲓⲧⲛ- S, *from*: P 129¹³ 72 prayed God ⲛϥⲧ.
ⲙⲡⲉⲩϫⲟⲓ ϩ.ⲡⲉⲭⲓⲙⲱⲛ;   ⲉⲃ. ϩ. SB: 2 Kg 3 18 S
(var ⲛⲧⲛ-), Ps 43 7 S(Bп.) σ. ἐκ; ib 118 B(S ⲉⲃ. ϩп-)
διατηρεῖν ἀπό; BSM 95 B ⲧⲟⲩϫⲟп ⲉⲃ. ϩⲓⲧⲟⲧⲩ.

—— nn SB, *safety, salvation*: CaiEuch 589 B
prayer for voyagers ϫⲉⲛⲟⲩⲧ. ⲉⲩⲧ.† ὑγιαίνειν; BP
4949 S camels are come ⲧⲁⲗⲟ ⲛⲏⲣⲡ ⲛⲁⲩ ϩⲛⲟⲩⲧ.
securely.

ⲣⲉϥⲧ. SB, *health-giver, saver*: Ps 143 2 B(S п.)
ῥύστης; C 89 132 B p. opp ⲣⲉϥⲥⲱⲣⲉⲙ; as adj: R 2
1 76 S ⲡⲁϩⲣⲉ ⲛⲣ., C 43 90 B ⲛⲟⲩϯ ⲛⲣ., Leyd 431 S
ⲙⲁ ⲡⲣⲉϥⲧⲟⲩϫⲉ ⲯⲩⲭⲏ, Cat 85 B sim;   ⲟⲓ ⲛⲣ.
B, v ⲥⲱⲧⲉ (ⲉⲓⲣⲉ п-).

ⲧⲫⲟ B   v ⲧⲣⲡⲟ.

ⲧⲫⲉⲣⲓⲟ B vb tr, *meaning uncertain*: Jer 5 17 (3
MSS) ⲉⲩⲉⲧⲫⲉⲣⲓⲉ ⲡⲉⲧⲉⲡⲃⲁⲕⲓ ϫⲉⲡⲧⲥⲛϥⲓ ἀλοᾶν (Bor
108 27 استأصل).

ⲧⲁϣ, ⲧⲉϣ S (Theban) nn, *meaning unknown,
grain, herb?*: CO 467 ⲟⲩⲁⲓⲡⲉ ⲛⲧⲁϣ, ib 239 ⲟⲩⲙⲁ-
ⲁⲭⲉ ⲙⲡⲟⲩⲅⲣⲁⲧⲙⲉ (sic) ⲛⲧⲉϣ, ST 354 ⲥⲡⲧⲉ ⲙⲙⲁⲭⲉ
ⲛⲧⲉϣ.

ⲧⲟϣ S, **ⲧⲁϣ** AF   v ⲧⲱϣ s f.

ⲧⲱϣ SA²F, -ϣⲉ A, ⲑⲱϣ B, ⲧⲉϣ-, ⲧⲟϣ- (Wess
15 152)S, ⲧⲁϣⲉ- A, ⲑⲉϣ-, ⲑⲁϣ-B, ⲧⲁϣ- SʃF, ⲧⲟϣ⸍
S, ⲧⲁϣ⸍ SªSʃAA²F, ⲑⲁϣ⸍ B, ⲧⲏϣ† SAA², ⲑ.† B vb
I intr, *be boundary, be fixed, be moderate*: Nu 34 6 B
(S ⲧⲟϣ), ὁρίζειν; Ez 44 5 B(HCons 308, var ⲧⲁⲭⲣⲟ),
Zeph 1 14 S(ShA 2 249, var ⲧⲱϫⲉ)AB, Ro 13 1† SB
τάσσειν, Nu 32 27 SB ⲉⲕⲧ., Zech 8 15 AB (var diff)
παρατάσ., Job 12 5† SB τακτός, 1 Cor 14 40† B(SF
= Gk) κατὰ τάξιν; Ac 20 32 B(S ⲕⲱⲧ tr) οἰκοδομεῖν;
ViSitz 172 4 35 S ⲧ.† καλῶς εὐοικονόμητος, BMis
365 S sim = BSM 26 B ⲟⲩⲉⲥⲱп = Mor 27 23 S
ⲟⲩⲁⲁⲗⲉ; EstC 24† S εὔρυθμος; Va 58 182 B ⲟⲩϫⲣⲉ
ⲉⲥⲟ.† εὐσταλής; Si 26 17† S στάσιμος; Wess 11 166
S ⲛⲧⲟⲕ ⲉⲧⲧ. ἐν σοί ἐστιν; J 35 32 S if he would build
ⲛⲧⲟϥ ⲉⲧⲧ., BM 582 F sim, PS 20 S ⲡⲉⲟⲩⲟⲉⲓϣ ...
ⲉⲧⲧ.†, AP 21 A² sim, ShBMOr 8810 370 S ⲉⲣϣⲁп-
ⲡⲡⲉ̅ ⲧ. ϯⲡⲁⲉⲓ, ShC 73 83 S chant ⲕⲁⲧⲁ ⲡϣⲓ ⲉⲧⲧ.†,
Ann 1 118 S ⲡⲉⲝⲟⲩⲥⲓⲁ ⲉⲧⲧ.† *ruling powers*, TstAb
229 B ϯⲑ. ⲁⲛ *I may not decide*, Ep 145 S if thou
know ϫⲉⲡⲣⲱϣ ⲡⲁⲧ., BM 342 55 S ⲡⲁⲛⲣ...ⲧ.† = Va
arab 172 90 مقتدر, DeV 1 89 B ⲉⲩⲑ.† ϫⲉⲛϩⲗⲓ ⲛⲛⲟⲃⲓ

inured, MG 25 266 *B* ογρооγ εϥ.† = Mor 40 40 *S*
πεγκερια, BMis 386† *S v* ⲙⲁⲡⲕ.

II tr, *limit, determine, appoint*: Nu 30 3 *S*(*B* ιρι
ποⲅ.), Ac 17 26 *SB* ὁρ., Eph 1 11 *BF*(*S* ⲛⲱⲣⲝ) προορ., Ez 20 40 *B*(*S* do) ἀφορ.; Dan 9 26 *B*(*S*†), Mic 5
1 *AB*, Aeg 247 *S* ⲁⲡⲉⲣ ϣⲟⲣⲡ ⲉⲧⲉϣ ⲡⲁⲓ τάσ., Sa 11
21 *S*, Gal 3 19 *SB* διατ., Job 35 10 *SB* κατατ., Is 27
4 *S*(*B* ⲟⲩⲁⲣⲥⲁⲣⲏⲓ) συντ., Ac 12 21 *S*(*B*†) τακτός; Si
44 28 *S* διαστέλλειν; Cl 27 5 *A* ⲡⲉⲧϥⲧⲁϣⲟⲩ δογματίζειν; Ac 3 20 *SB* προχειρίζειν; Sa 8 14 *S* διοικεῖν; Bor
235 58 *S* ⲧⲟϣⲕ ⲣⲏⲧϭⲙⲟⲩⲱⲙ τυποῦν; Aeg 239 *S* τ.
ⲡⲡⲁⲍⲓⲱⲙⲁ καταλογίζεσθαι; Jer 47 5 *B* καθιστάναι;
1 Cor 7 17 *SBF* μερίζειν; 2 Kg 6 5 *S*(*B* ⲣⲱⲧⲡ), Ps
151 2 *S*(*B* do), Nah 3 8 *A*(*B* do) ἁρμόζειν; PS 69 *S*
ⲣⲱⲃ ⲡⲓⲙ ⲉⲡⲧⲁⲕⲧⲟϣⲟⲩ, ShC 73 123 *S* ⲁⲝⲡⲣⲉⲅ-
ⲧⲟϣⲩ ⲉⲃⲟⲗ ⲅⲓⲧⲙⲡⲉⲗⲗⲟ, Mani 2 *A²* ⲁⲅⲧⲁϣⲩ ⲅⲓⲧⲙ-
ⲡⲥⲱⲧⲏⲣ, P 130³ 66 *S* hard words of ⲡⲉⲧⲧ. ⲙⲙⲟⲛ,
Blake 270 *S* ⲣⲟⲓⲛⲉ ⲅⲣⲡⲉⲧⲧ. ⲡⲧⲉⲩⲅⲣⲁφⲏ *criticize*(?),
Mor 41 320 *S* ⲁⲅⲧ. ⲡⲣⲉⲡⲧⲁ̄ⲡⲟⲟⲅⲉ & set forth (Synax
1 382 6 ǀ, تشكل ǀ), AM 5 *B* ⲡⲓⲥⲛⲟⲩ ⲉⲧⲁⲓⲑⲁϣⲩ, DeV 2
56 *B* ⲑ. ⲡⲟⲅⲡⲟⲙⲟⲥ ⲡⲡⲓⲥⲧⲓⲁ, PO 11 350 *B* ⲡⲓⲙ ⲡⲉⲧ-
ⲟⲅⲡⲁⲑⲁϣⲩϥ as archbishop, CMSS 20 *Sf* constrain
them ⲡⲥⲉⲧⲁϣ ⲣⲱⲙ[ⲉ], BMis 456 *S* talked long but
ⲙⲡⲟⲩⲧⲉϣ ⲗⲁⲁⲩ ⲡⲣⲱⲕ, BAp 78 *S* ⲁⲅⲧⲉϣ ⲧⲉⲅⲁⲡⲟ-
ⲕⲣⲓⲥⲓⲥ, Z 351 *S* so that God might ⲧⲉϣ ⲡⲥⲟⲡ *moderate* (?, *cf* AZ 45 81), Wess 15 152 *S* ⲁⲡⲝ̄ⲥ ⲧⲟϣ ⲟⲩⲥⲣⲓⲙⲉ *provided*, Mor 25 8 *S* ⲡⲱⲧ ⲡⲧⲉⲡⲝ̄ⲥ ⲧⲟϣⲕ =
P 131³ 82 *S* ⲡⲝ̄ⲥ ⲥⲟⲃⲧⲉ, Hall 28 *S* ⲉⲡⲡ̄ⲉ̄ ⲧⲟϣⲧ ⲕⲁⲧⲁ
ϣⲟⲣⲡ *if God provide for me as formerly*, *cf* CO 90,
BP 9445 *S* be so kind ⲛⲧⲧⲟϣⲕ & bring the *solidus*.

With following preposition.

—— ⲉ- *SAA²BF*, *decide for, ordain to*, intr: Ac
11 29 *B*(*S* tr) ὁρ. εἰς; 1 Chr 16 7 *B* τάσ. gen; Jud 17
11 ʹ*S* ἄρχειν inf; Tit 3 12 *B*(*S* = Gk) κρίνειν; R 2 2
27 *S* ⲡⲧⲁⲣⲧ. ⲉⲉⲡⲓⲃⲟⲩⲗⲉⲅⲉ προαιρεῖσθαι; Jos 22 33
S ⲧⲙⲧ. ⲉⲃⲱⲕ μηκέτι ἀναβῆναι, 1 Kg 20 5 *S* τ. ⲉⲣⲙⲟⲟⲥ καθίσας καθῆσθαι; ShA 1 387 *S* ⲁⲓⲧ. ⲉⲥⲣⲁⲓ
ⲛⲏⲧⲛ, Pcod 15 *S* ⲉⲩⲧ. ⲉⲧⲁⲙϣⲏⲗ, MR 4 72 *S* ⲁⲧⲟⲩ-
ⲙⲁⲁⲩ ⲧ. ⲉⲧⲙⲡⲧⲉⲣⲟ, Kr 200 *F* ⲡⲕⲧ. ⲉⲕⲉⲩ (ⲉ)ⲃⲁⲗ,
CMSS 20 *Sf* ⲡⲥⲉⲧ. ⲉⲡⲱⲣⲥ ⲓⲉ ⲡⲉⲣⲣⲓ; qual, *des-
tined to, about to*: Nu 32 27 *SB* ἐντάσ. εἰς; Ge 19 31
B καθήκειν dat; Gu 36 *S* ⲉⲩⲧ. ⲉⲙⲟⲩ, Va 57 6 *B* ⲧⲉⲡⲑ.
ⲉⲣⲉⲓ μέλλειν; *ib* 11 *B* ⲉϥⲑ. ⲉⲓⲡⲓ ἔχειν; ShC 73 107
S ⲉⲧⲧ. ⲉⲡⲙⲁ ⲙⲡⲣⲟ, Aeg 255 *S* time ⲉⲧⲟⲩⲧ. ⲉⲃⲁⲡ-
ⲧⲓⲍⲉ, BHom 36 *S* ⲡⲉⲧⲧ. ⲉϣⲱⲡⲉ, ROC 25 246 *B* none
ⲉϥⲑ. ⲉⲥⲣⲏⲓ shall enter kingdom; C 86 14 *B* ⲉⲕⲟ.
ⲉⲑⲣⲟⲩϯ ⲣⲁⲡ ⲉⲣⲟⲕ; tr, *appoint, destine to*: Aeg
248 *S* ⲧⲉϣ ⲣⲓⲟⲙⲉ ⲉⲅⲑⲓⲁⲕⲟⲛⲓⲁ ὁρ. acc, Ro 1 2 *B*(*S*
ⲡⲱⲣⲝ ⲉⲃⲟⲗ) ἀφορ. εἰς; Jer 3 19 *SB*, 1 Cor 15 16 *B*
(*S* ⲕⲱ ⲉⲣⲣⲁⲓ) τάσ. εἰς, Ac 15 2 *SB* τάσ. inf, 1 Cor 9
14 *SB* διατ. inf; Job 7 18 *B*(*S* = Gk) κρ. εἰς; *ib* 14
5 *S*(*B* χⲱ ⲉ-) τιθ. εἰς; Si 41 9 *S* μερίζειν εἰς; Bor
253 153 *S* τ. ⲉⲣⲟϥ ⲡⲟⲅⲁⲡⲟφⲁⲥⲓⲥ ἀποφαίνεσθαι acc;

ShC 73 136 *S* ⲡⲣⲱⲃ ⲡⲧⲁⲅⲧⲟϣⲩ ⲉⲣⲟϥ, *ib* 147 ⲡⲥⲉⲧⲉϣ
ⲡⲡⲟⲉⲓⲧ ⲉⲧⲙⲕⲁ ⲗⲁⲁⲩ at bottom, BMar 212 *S* ⲡⲙⲁ
ⲉⲧⲉⲣⲉⲡⲝ̄ⲥ ⲡⲁⲧⲟϣⲧ ⲉⲣⲟϥ, BIF 13 100 *S* ⲁϥⲧⲟϣⲛ ⲉ-
ⲡⲉⲓⲣⲱⲙⲉ & he led us, Va 63 9 *B* φϯ ⲡⲁⲑⲁϣⲧ ⲉⲡⲓⲉⲥⲱⲟⲩ = BSM 35 *B* ⲉⲣⲉϥϯ ⲑⲉϣ ⲟⲩⲉⲥ. ⲉⲣⲟⲛ, C 86
348 *B* ⲁϥϯ ⲑⲁϣⲕ ⲉⲡⲓⲑⲉⲣⲙⲉⲥⲓ?, BM 706 *F* ⲉⲧⲁⲃ-
ⲧⲁϣⲟⲩ (ⲉ)ⲗⲁⲓ ⲣⲱⲭⲱⲡⲓⲁⲙ *assigned me (to spend) on
the wine-vat*, Mani 1 *A²* ⲁⲩⲧ. ⲙⲙⲁⲩ ⲁϣⲁⲙⲧⲉ ⲡ-
ⲥⲁⲙ; ⲉⲣⲟⲩⲡ ⲉ- *S*: Ac 2 22 (*B* diff) ἀποδείκνυ-
σθαι εἰς; ⲁⲣⲣⲏⲓ ⲁ- *A²*: Mani 1 ⲉⲩⲧ.† ⲁⲣ. ⲁϯⲉ
ⲡⲥⲁⲙ.

—— ⲉⲝⲛ- *SABF*, *be appointed over, for*, intr:
Dan 9 27 *B* τάσ. ἐπί; BSM 107 *B* φⲏ ⲉⲑⲡⲁⲑ.
ⲉⲭⲱϥ *his destiny* = Mor 22 118 *S* ⲡⲉⲧⲛⲁⲡⲣⲟⲣⲓⲥⲧⲁ
ⲉⲭⲱϥ; qual: P 44 63 *S* ⲕⲟⲓⲛⲟⲃⲓⲁⲣⲭⲏⲥ · ⲡⲉⲧⲧ.
ⲉ.ⲧⲕⲟⲓⲛⲟⲩⲱⲛⲓⲁ, MR 5 44 *S* angel ⲧ. ⲉ.ⲧⲉⲭⲱⲣⲁ,
BSM 45 *B* ⲉⲧⲟ. ⲉ.ⲡⲉⲡⲥⲱⲙⲁ = BMis 394 *S* ο ⲡ̄ⲝ̄ⲥ̄
ⲉ-; tr, *ordain for, set over*: Mic 5 1 *AB* τάσ. ἐπί;
Dan 9 24 *S*(*B* ϣⲱⲧ ⲉⲃⲟⲗ) συντέμνειν ἐπί; JKP 2 92
S poor man ⲉⲅϣⲁⲛⲧⲟϣⲩϥ ⲉ.ⲟⲩⲅⲏⲕⲉ (*cf* Pro 28 15);
Z 611 *S* ⲁⲩⲧⲟϣⲩ ⲡⲣⲣⲟ ⲉ.ⲡⲓⲏⲗ, WTh 43 *B* ⲁϥⲑⲁ-
ϣⲟⲩ ⲉ.ⲡⲓⲱϣ = *ib S* ⲕⲁⲑⲓⲥⲧⲁ; ⲉⲣⲣⲁⲓ, -ⲏⲓ ⲉⲝ.:
Job 7 12 *B*(*S* diff) κατατάσ. ἐπί; Ps 67 15 *B*(*S* ⲡⲱⲣⲝ
ⲉⲣ. ⲉ.) διαστέλ. ἐπί; OrChr ’32 120 *S* let not schisms
ⲧ. ⲉⲣ. ⲉⲭⲱⲡ, BM 512 *F* ⲧⲁϣ ⲟⲩⲙⲉⲧⲉⲣⲁ…ⲉⲣ. ⲉ.ⲡⲕⲟ-
ⲥⲙⲟⲥ, TstAb 173 *B* ⲁⲡⲟⲕ ⲉⲧⲟ.† ⲉⲣ. ⲉ.ϯⲉⲩⲭⲁⲣⲓⲥⲧⲓⲁ.

—— ⲙⲛ-, ⲡⲉⲙ- *SBF*, *appoint, decide with*: Va
68 166 *B* ⲡⲁⲑⲟ.† ⲡⲉⲙ.ϥϯ τάσ. μετά, Ac 20 13 *S*(*B*
ⲣⲟⲩⲣⲉⲣ) διατάσ.; Ez 48 21 *B* ἐχόμενος gen; ShC
73 58 *S* ⲡⲉⲓⲱⲧ…ⲡⲉⲧⲧ.† ⲡⲙⲙⲁϥ, CO 49 *S* ⲡⲉⲡⲧⲁⲕ-
ⲧⲁϣϥ ⲙⲛⲡⲗⲁϣⲁⲛⲉ, C 41 70 *B* ϯⲑ.† ⲉⲣⲟⲥ ⲡⲉⲙⲁⲕ
own it with thee, DeV 2 283 *B* ⲁϥⲑⲁϣⲥ ⲡⲉⲙⲁϥ ⲉ-
ⲑⲣⲉϥϯ, MIF 59 228 *F* may God ⲧⲁϣⲧ ⲙⲉ(ⲡ)ⲡⲁⲥ-
ⲡⲕⲟⲩ.

—— ⲛ- dat *SABF*: Lu 22 22† *S*(*B* Gk om dat)
ὁρ.; Bor 239 54 *S* fast ⲉⲧⲧ.† (Gk do), Ac 22 10 *SB*
τάσ. dat, Ez 21 19 *SB*, Lu 3 13 *SB*†, Cl 43 1 *A* διατ.
dat, Job 15 23 *SB* κατατ. dat, Nu 2 34 *S*(*B* ⲟⲩⲁⲣⲥ.),
Pro 24 31 *SA* συντ. dat; Ro 12 3 *SF*(*B* φⲱϣ) μερ.
dat, Deu 19 3 *S*(*B* do) κατατⲙ. dat; Ac 3 20 *S*(*B* om
dat) προχειρ. dat; Hos 2 5† *B*(*A* diff), καθήκειν dat;
Deu 29 26 *S*(*B* ϯ) διανέμειν; Aeg 286 *S* ⲧⲉⲭⲣⲓⲁ ⲡ-
ⲧⲁϥⲧⲟϣⲥ ⲡⲁⲩ (var ⲉ-) διατυποῦν; PS 345 *S* ⲡⲉⲅ-
ⲣⲃⲏⲩⲉ ⲉⲧⲧ.† ⲡⲁⲩ, ShR 2 3 21 *S* ⲁⲕⲥⲙⲛⲉ ⲏ ⲁⲕⲧ. ⲡⲁⲕ
…ⲡⲣⲉⲡⲣⲓⲟⲟⲅⲉ, Pcod 40 *SF* ⲡⲉⲥⲙⲟⲩ…ⲡⲡ̄ⲉ̄ ⲡⲁⲧⲟϣϥ
ⲡⲁⲕ, Miss 4 764 *S* single loaf ⲡⲉⲧⲧ.† ⲡⲁⲓ, OstrCai
47400 *S* ⲙⲡⲣⲧ. ⲣⲱⲃ ⲡⲁⲥ hast (f) *not decided aught
for her*, Baouit 1 138 *F* ⲡⲟⲉ̄…ⲧⲁϣ ⲧⲉⲡⲣⲓⲛ ⲡⲥⲁⲃⲧⲓ
ⲡⲏⲡ; + 2d acc: Ro 1 4 *S*(*B* ϯ) ὁρ., *ib* 8 29 *B*(*S* ⲡⲱ.
ⲉⲃ.) προορ.; Aeg 273 *S* ⲁⲩⲧⲟϣⲟⲩ ⲡⲉⲡⲓⲥⲕⲟⲡⲟⲥ τάσ.;
Ac 26 16 *S*(*B* ⲥⲱⲧⲡ) προχ.; BIF 13 118 *S* vineyard
ⲁⲩⲧⲟϣⲕ ⲡⲟⲅⲟⲉⲓⲉ ⲉⲣⲟϥ, BSM 9 *B* ⲁϥϯ ⲑⲁϣⲩ ⲡⲁⲣⲭⲱⲛ; *v* also ⲥ ⲉⲝⲛ-, ⲣⲓⲝⲛ-.

— ⲡⲧⲏ- S: Lev 17 5 (B Gk om) ⲉⲧⲟⲩⲡⲁⲧ. ⲡⲧⲟⲟⲧⲟⲩ (var ⲉⲧ.) ⲉϣⲁⲁⲧⲟⲩ.

— ϩⲓⲭⲡ-: JKP 2 50 S¹ king ϣⲁⲩⲧⲁϣϥ ϩⲓⲭⲟⲡ, Va 57 39 B ⲑⲁϣϥ ⲡϭⲏⲧⲟⲩⲙⲉⲡⲟⲥ ϩ.ⲡⲓⲏⲗ, MIF 9 88 S ⲡⲉⲭⲱⲣⲁ...ⲉϥⲧ.† ϩⲓⲭⲱⲟⲩ.

— ⲛⲛ m SABF, pl ⲧⲱⲱϣ A, ordinance, destiny, affair, fashion: Deu 33 13 S(B diff), MG 25 206 B ὅρος, EstC 20 S, Dan 6 7 S(B = Gk) ὁρισμός; Ps 118 91 S(B ⲟⲩⲁϩⲥ.) διάταξις, Ac 7 53 B(S = Gk) διαταγή, Nu 9 14 S(B do) σύνταξις, Job 15 8 S(B do) σύνταγμα; Sa 7 17 S σύστασις; Nu 18 4 S(B ⲫⲱϣⲉⲡ)λειτουργία; Pro 6 20 B(SA ⲁⲡⲥⲙⲙⲉ), Miss 4 533 S = C 89 51 B θεσμός, Eph 1 11 SF(B ⲥⲉⲙⲡⲓ) πρόθεσις; Jud 13 12 S, Cl 20 5 A pl κρίμα, Si 16 26 S κρίσις; 1 Chr 28 11 B παράδειγμα; 1 Kg 20 26 S (var ϩⲱⲃ) σύμπτωμα; Cant 7 2 S(F ⲙⲉⲗⲟⲥ) ῥυθμός; Mic 2 4 SA(B ϩⲱⲥ) μέλος suavitas; EW 148 B ⲡⲑ. of raiment καταστολή; Cl 20 1 A διοίκησις; Lev 12 8 S(B ⲣⲱϣⲓ) ἱκανός; Aeg 273 S διατύπωσις; 4 Kg 12 9 S σταθμός (var πρόθυρον, l? ⲧⲟϣⲩ); Z 329 S ⲛⲧ. ⲡⲧⲁⲓⲧⲟϣⲟⲩ δεδογμένα μοι; Mus 40 44 S(RegPach) ⲕⲁⲧⲁ ⲡⲧ. ⲡⲛⲣⲉⲑⲛⲟⲥ imitans morem; Gk om: Lev 25 34 S, 1 Kg 25 19 S, 2 Kg 12 21 S, Ps 143 1 B(S om); PS 64 S ⲁⲡⲉⲕⲧ. ⲛⲧ ⲉⲡⲉⲥⲏⲧ, ShC 73 151 S ⲛⲧ. ⲛ†ⲉⲡ ⲟⲩⲟⲉⲓⲉ, ib 42 71 S ⲛⲧ. ⲙⲡⲣⲟ, ShA 1 45 S did naught ⲁⲭⲏⲧ., Miss 4 550 S ⲛⲧ. ⲙⲡⲭ̅ⲥ̅ = C 89 89 B ⲟⲩⲁϩⲥ., TillOster 24 A obeying ⲛⲧ., BMis 175 S ⲛⲧ. of baptismal rite (lit of font) = BSM 85 B ⲛⲧ., BKU 1 126 S be so kind ⲛⲕⲛⲁⲩ ⲉⲩⲧ. ⲡⲉⲙⲁⲓ, ShA 1 460 S ⲛⲧ. ⲛⲧⲉ ⲡⲉϥϩⲏⲧ ⲙⲡⲡϣⲟⲝⲛⲉ ⲛⲧⲉ ⲧⲉϥⲯⲩⲭ ⲏ, Va 58 74 B how long since babe born? ⲓⲥ ⲓ̅ⲃ̅ ⲛⲁⲃⲟⲧ ⲉⲡⲑ. at the utmost(?); destiny, condition: BAp 61 S ⲡⲉⲓⲧ. ⲡⲟⲩⲱⲧ befalleth both, BMar 191 S ⲙⲡⲉⲓⲣⲉ ⲉⲡⲧ. that befell thee, C 86 113 B will tell thee ⲡⲑ. ⲙⲡⲉⲕⲓⲱⲧ, Z 619 S hope to see ⲛⲧ. ⲙⲡⲉϥⲥⲱⲙⲁ & shrine; matter, thing: ShA 1 307 S ⲟⲩϩⲱⲃ ⲏ ⲟⲩⲧ., ShC 42 34 S ⲉⲧⲃⲉⲡⲉⲓⲧ. ϫⲉⲣ ⲉⲡⲓⲥⲕⲟⲡⲟⲥ, ib 73 98 S ⲡⲱⲓ ⲁⲡⲡⲉ ⲡⲉⲓⲧ. no affair of mine, ib 51 S sickness or feebleness ⲏ ⲡⲧⲟⲩ ⲕⲉⲧ., Sh(Besa)Mich 550 22 S I need not visit you ⲉⲓⲙⲏⲧⲓ ϩⲡⲟⲩⲛⲟϭ ⲛⲧ. ⲉϥⲡⲁϣⲧ, R 1 4 36 S ⲁⲩⲡⲟϭ ⲛⲧ. ϣⲱⲡⲉ (sc drought), Mor 26 9 S ⲟⲩⲡⲉ ⲡⲉⲓⲧ.? = ib 22 76 S ϩⲱⲃ, BSM 15 B ⲟⲩⲡⲉ ⲡⲉⲧⲉⲛⲑ.? (cf ib sim ϩⲱⲃ) = BMis 349 S ⲁϩⲣⲱⲧⲛ?, Mor 30 25 F ⲁϥⲓ ⲉⲧⲁⲙⲁⲕ ⲉⲡⲧ., Viostr 468 S will send things, ⲡⲁⲥⲫⲁⲗⲉⲥ ϫⲉ ⲙⲡⲉⲓⲙⲉ ⲉⲡⲉϥⲧ.; fashion, manner S: ShMun 138 ϩⲉⲛⲕⲉⲧ. ⲏ ϩⲉⲛⲕⲉⲧⲩⲡⲟⲥ of risen dead, ShA 1 155 length, breadth, colour ⲙⲛⲡⲧ. ⲧⲏⲣϥ of garments, ShP 78 43 cannot tell ⲛⲧ. ⲙⲡⲡϣⲱⲡⲉ, R 2 1 12 sang hymn ϩⲛⲟⲩⲧ. ⲛⲧⲉⲓⲣⲉ (Lu 1 46), BKU 1 314 this place ⲛⲧⲁϭⲡ ⲛⲧ. ⲛⲧⲁⲁϥ ⲉⲃⲟⲗ; supplementary, explanatory: Ex 29 1 S ⲡⲁⲓⲡⲉ ⲛⲧ. ταῦτα, 1 Kg 4 7 S ⲧ. ⲛⲧⲉⲓⲣⲉ τοιοῦτος, ib 6 4 S ⲛⲧ. ⲛⲧⲃⲁⲥⲁⲛⲟⲥ τὸ τῆς β., ib 23 17 S ⲡⲉⲓⲧ. οὕτως, ib 1 5 S ⲛⲧ. ⲛ-

ⲧⲉⲥⲙⲏⲧⲣⲁ τὰ περί, Eccl 12 13 S ⲛⲧ. ⲡⲣⲱⲙⲉ ⲡⲓⲙ ⲧⲟⲩⲧⲟ πᾶς ὁ ἄνθρ., Ez 40 2 SB ⲟⲩⲧ. ⲡⲕⲱⲧ ὡσεὶ οἰκοδ., 1 Kg 9 6 S ⲛⲧ. ⲛⲧⲉϩⲓⲏ ἡ ὁδός, ib 1 4 S ⲛⲧ. ⲙⲡⲉϩⲟⲟⲩ ⲛⲧⲉⲣⲉϥϣⲱⲡⲉ ἐγενήθη ἡμέρα, 2 Kg 14 26 S(Mor)ⲛⲧ. ⲛϩⲏ ⲡⲛⲉϩⲟⲟⲩ ἀρχὴ ἡμ., Lev 2 5 S ⲉⲃⲟⲗ ϩⲛⲟⲩⲧ. ⲡⲗⲁⲕⲏⲧ ἀπὸ τηγάνου, 3 Kg 10 5 S ⲛⲧ. ⲡⲡⲉϥϩⲟⲓⲧⲉ ἱματισμός.

ⲁⲧⲧ., SB, unlimited, immoderate: MG 25 26 B ⲥⲱⲙⲁ ⲡⲁⲧⲑ. when overfed; ⲙⲛⲧ-, ⲙⲉⲧⲁⲧ.: Va 57 275 B ⲟⲩⲙ. ⲡⲧⲉ ϩⲁⲛⲥⲏⲟⲩ infinity, ShC 42 18 S ⲙ. ⲏ ⲙⲛⲧⲁⲧϣⲟϫⲛⲉ indecision.

ⲉⲓⲣⲉ, ⲣ ⲧ. SB, set in order, prepare: Nu 30 3 B(S ⲧ.) ὁρ. περί, Is 38 1 SB τάσ. περί; 4 Kg 12 11 S ἐπισκοπή; ShC 73 60 S youths may not ⲣ ⲛⲧ. ⲙⲡⲉⲥⲱⲟⲩϩ, RNC 78 S delay till I ⲣ ⲛⲧ. ⲙⲡⲁⲏⲓ, C 89 183 B ⲡⲥⲉⲉⲣ ⲡⲟⲩϣ. according to canons, BMis 453 S ⲁⲣⲓ ⲡⲧ. ⲡⲟⲩⲙⲟⲟⲩ for font, ib 105 S ⲁⲩⲣ ⲡⲉⲥⲧ. ⲉⲧⲁⲁⲥ ⲡⲟⲩⲣⲱⲙⲉ (var Mor 33 64 S ⲁⲩϣⲡ ⲧⲟⲟⲧⲥ ⲉ-), C 43 195 B tell me ⲡⲓⲑ. ⲉ†ⲡⲁⲁⲓϥ to be saved.

† ⲧ., ⲡⲧ. SBF, give orders, take decision, provide: Pcod 11 S befits elder ⲉⲧⲣⲉϥ† ⲛⲧ., Mor 31 112 S God will † ⲙⲡⲉⲛⲧ. in famine, ib 43 47 S ⲁⲩ† ⲡⲟⲩⲧ. saying Let us &c, MG 25 73 B ⲙⲁ ⲡⲉⲕⲑ. & neglect not, MIE 2 394 B fetch money & † ⲙⲡⲟⲩⲧ. = BAp 121 S ⲡⲁⲩ ϫⲉⲕⲡⲁⲣ ⲟⲩ ⲡⲁⲩ; c ⲉ-, give orders to, provide for: Br 263 S ⲛϥ† ⲧ. ⲉⲡⲉⲡⲣⲱⲃ...ⲁⲩⲱ ⲛⲧⲟϣⲡ, BAp 71 S God †ⲧ. ⲉⲡⲣⲱⲙⲉ from birth, Mor 48 95 S shalt not eat ere thou † ⲧ. ⲉⲣⲟⲓ = C 43 146 B † ⲁⲡⲟⲫⲁⲥⲓⲥ, MIE 2 370 B ⲁⲡ† ⲑ. ⲉⲡⲓⲡⲣⲉⲥⲃ/ ϫⲉⲡⲧⲉϥⲣⲓ, FPetrie MS Athribis '08 F ⲟⲩⲱϣ† † ⲧ. ⲉⲧⲁⲁⲓ ⲙⲁⲡ ⲡϣⲁⲥϭⲉⲉⲓ; c ⲛ-: FR 36 S call virgins ⲧⲁ† ⲡⲧ. ⲡⲁⲩ, BM 1121 S † ⲛⲧ. ⲡⲁϥ as it please you, Va 63 13 B † ⲡⲑ. ⲡⲟⲩⲣⲱⲙⲓ ⲛⲧⲉϥ ϣⲱⲧ, MIE 2 416 B † ⲙⲡⲑ. ⲛⲧⲉⲕⲕⲗⲏⲥⲓⲁ & come to heaven; c ⲛ- & ⲉ-: Miss 4 585 S ⲁϥ† ⲧ. ⲡⲁⲡ... ⲉⲙⲡⲏⲛⲥⲏ = C89 176 B, Mor 18 60 S † ⲧ. ⲡⲁⲡ ⲉⲡⲓⲥ ⲧⲓⲥ = Miss 4 135 B, PO 14 352 B ⲁϥ† ⲑ. ⲡⲱⲟⲩ ⲉⲟⲩⲕⲟⲓⲡⲱⲡⲓⲁ; ⲁⲧ† ⲧ. S, unlimited: BG 23 ⲟⲩⲁⲧ † ⲧ. ⲉⲣⲟϥ, for none was before him to limit him.

ⲣⲉϥⲧ., -ⲑ. SB, commander: Dan 6 4 B(S = Gk) τακτικός; K 137 B رئيس, draughtsman; BM 290 S Gabriel ⲡⲁⲓⲟⲓⲕⲏⲧⲏⲥ...ⲡⲣ. ⲕⲁⲗⲱⲥ; ⲣⲉϥⲧⲉϣ ⲙⲁ: Tit 2 5 S(B ⲣⲉϥⲥⲉⲣ) οἰκουργός.

ϫⲓⲛⲑ. B, order, disposition: Ez 42 15 (HCons 295, var & S om) διάταξις; Miss 4 218 ϫ. ⲛⲡⲁⲣ† ὅρος πίστεως.

ⲧⲟϣ SO, ⲧⲱϣ S, ⲧⲁϣ S¹AF, ⲑⲟϣ, ⲑⲱϣ B, ⲧⲉϣ- S (v b), pl forms v below, oftener sg as pl, nn m a border, limit: Ex 23 31 SB, Nu 20 16 S(B ϭⲓⲏ), Jer 15 13 S(B do), Joel 3 6 SAB, Mt 15 39 S(B do) ὅριον, Mk 7 24 S(B ⲥⲁ) μεθόρ., Z 299 S ϩⲛⲟⲩⲧ. ⲡⲟⲩⲱⲧ ἐνορία, Ac 17 26 SB ⲑⲱϣ ὁροθεσία; Is 19 2 SBF(BM 1221) νομός; Deu 32 9 S(B ⲡⲟϩ ⲡⲣⲱϣ), Zeph 2 5

SA(B ϣⲉ ⲛⲛⲟϭ) σχοίνισμα; Deu 3 11 S(B = Gk) ἄκρα; Va 57 13 B ⲡⲓⲟ. ⲡⲧⲉ ϯⲁⲣⲉⲧⲏ ⲕⲟⲣⲩⲫⲏ; Jud 1 18 S περισπόριον; Ez 44 16 S ⲧⲱϣ (CA 91, B ϭ.) φύλαξ; Zeph 1 16 A(SB diff, cf 3 6) γωνία; Hab 1 6 S(AB ⲟⲩⲱⲥϧ) πλάτος; Z 297 S μέρος; MG 25 9 B περίχωρος; ROC 25 246 B γειτονία (var χώρα); Va 57 263 B ⲡⲓⲟ. ⲉⲧⲉⲙⲡⲕⲱϯ τὰ ὑπό; ShLeyd 304 S foods ⲉⲧⲉⲙⲡ ⲧ. ⲡⲣⲏⲧⲟⲩ, ShA 1 194 S was for them ⲛⲧ. ⲁⲩⲱ ⲡⲧⲏⲡⲉ, P 131² 117 S ⲣ ⲡⲛⲃⲟⲗ ⲙⲡⲧ. = Va 58 192 B ϣⲓ, DeV 2 15 B ϯⲙⲉⲧⲡⲓϣϯ ⲉⲧⲉⲙⲟⲛⲧⲉⲥ ⲑ., Br 261 S ⲁϥⲡ ⲣⲉⲡⲧ. ⲟⲩⲧⲱⲟⲩ, ViK 9794 S ⲉⲥⲕⲁ ⲧ. ⲉⲣⲣⲁⲓ ⲛⲡⲕⲁⲙⲟⲥ (γάμ.), BMis 263 S show me ⲡⲧ. ⲡⲡⲁⲧⲱⲃⲉ ⲛⲛⲟⲩⲕ = Mor 30 38 F, ib F ⲧ. = S 264 ⲛⲡⲉ, J 110 13 S ⲉ(ⲉ)ⲥⲟⲩⲧⲱⲛ ⲡⲉⲩⲧ. ⲛⲡⲉϥⲥⲟⲛ, ib 65 55 S ⲡⲉⲩⲧⲟⲟⲩ ⲛⲧ. ⲡⲡⲧⲟⲡⲟⲥ (cf γείτων), Kr 140 F ⲡⲧ. ⲉⲧⲉⲃⲗⲁⲙⲡⲓ of hire.   b nome (νομός, v Tatt 123 inf, Amélineau Géog xxxiv, Ep 1 104, PLond 4 xxii, Wess 19 10): ShC 73 18 S πόλις, ⲕⲱⲙⲏ, ⲕⲁⲓⲉ, ⲧⲟⲟⲩ, ⲧ., χώρα, ib 42 67 S ⲧ., πόλις, ϯⲙⲉ, ShA 2 47 S barbarians ⲉⲓ ⲉⲭⲡⲟⲩⲕⲁϩ ⲛ ⲟⲩⲧ., EW 114 B ⲧⲓⲙⲓ opp ⲑ., AM 180 B ⲃⲁⲕⲓ opp ⲑ., C 43 226 B sim, Mor 51 30 S ⲡⲧ. ⲁⲩⲱ ⲡⲥⲱϣⲉ, C 86 130 B eparchs set over ⲡⲓⲟ. ⲧⲏⲣϥ, ib 43 133 B ⲉϥⲟⲓ ⲡⲁⲫⲉ ⲉⲡⲉϥⲑ., J 12 39 S ϧⲏⲡⲟⲗⲓⲥ ϧⲛⲧ. ⲛⲡⲃⲟⲗ ⲡⲧ., ib 19 60 S ϧⲛⲧ. ⲏ ⲛⲡⲃⲟⲗ (ⲡ)ⲡⲉⲡⲟⲙⲟⲥ(νό.) ⲡⲉⲡⲧ.;   with place-name: C 86 73 B ⲡⲟ. ⲡⲁⲛⲁⲩ(var ⲙⲡⲁ.), Z 551 S ⲡⲧ. ⲛⲡⲥⲟⲓ, Mor 41 119 S ⲡⲧⲉϣ ⲡⲥⲟⲓ = C 43 37 B, BMOr 6201 B 267 S ⲡⲧⲉϣ ⲡⲁⲡⲟⲩⲃⲉ, AM 214 B ⲡⲁⲓⲟⲟⲩϣ ⲛϣⲁϯ, Kr 11 F ⲡⲧ. ϧⲏⲥ, AZ 21 94 O ⲡⲧ. ⲡⲣⲁⲡⲉⲓⲛⲉ (sic), Miss 4 763 Sᶠ ⲡⲧ. ⲧⲟⲩϧⲱ, Lant 29 F ⲡⲧ. ⲡⲓⲁⲙ.   c province, district, suburb: MG 25 423 S ⲡⲧ. ⲡⲕⲏⲙⲉ, BMis 29 S ⲡⲧ. ⲡⲡⲉϧⲣⲱⲙⲁⲓⲟⲥ, Ryl 72 357 S ⲡⲧ. ⲧⲏⲣⲟⲩ ⲡⲃⲛⲑⲗⲉⲉⲙ ⲛⲛⲡⲉⲥⲕⲱⲧⲉ, C 86 193 B Palestine ⲡⲉⲙⲡⲉⲥⲑ., ib 167 ⲭⲏⲙⲓ ⲧⲏⲣⲥ ⲡⲉⲙⲡⲉⲥⲑ., P 129¹⁸ 105 S ⲧⲡⲟⲗⲓⲥ ⲛⲛⲡⲉⲥⲧ. ⲧⲏⲣϥ, Ryl 115 S sim, AZ 3039, MR 5 33 S sim ⲛⲛⲡⲉⲥⲧⲟⲟⲩ ⲧⲏⲣϥ, Ryl 364 n S ⲛ ⲡⲧ. ⲡⲉⲙⲣⲓⲧ of city, Tri 310 S ⲡⲧ. ⲛⲧⲡⲟⲗⲓⲥ تخوم, AM 274 B ⲡⲓⲟ. ⲉⲧⲕⲱϯ ⲉⲧⲁⲓⲃⲁⲕⲓ πέριξ ἐνορίαι.   d bishopric: Aeg 212 S bishop's ⲧ. παροικία; Wess 11 157 S bishops ⲙⲡⲧ. = C 89 56 B sg = MG 17 575 تخوم (Va 172 35 بلد), Bor 134 5 (Vita Sin) bp of ⲡⲉⲓⲧⲱϣ = C 41 35 B πόλις = Miss 4 374 '·, AM 214 B bp of ⲡⲁⲓⲟ. ⲡϣⲁϯ (cf 225 πολ. ⲡϣ.), Tor 31 S ⲡⲣⲱⲥⲓⲱⲧⲁⲧⲟⲥ ⲛ[ⲉⲡⲓⲥⲕ/] ⲙⲡⲧ. ⲡⲕⲏⲃⲧ, CA 104 S clergy ⲉⲧⲟⲩⲙⲡⲧ. = ib ⲣⲩ القرى من اعمال المدينة, CO 40 S priest admits ⲁⲓⲕⲱ ⲡⲁⲧ. ⲡⲥⲱⲓ ⲁⲓⲃⲱⲕ ⲉⲕⲉⲧ., AZ 23 68 S ⲡⲁⲧⲁ ⲍⲓⲥ ϧⲙⲡⲧ. regarding holy mysteries.   e pl (?) forms: Nu 20 17 S ⲧⲟⲟⲩϣ (var ⲧ., cf sg Is 9 7 S ⲧⲟⲟⲩϣ & MR 5 above), Zech 9 2 A ⲧⲟⲟⲩϣ (S ⲧ.), Cl 20 3 A do, ib 29 2 A, Am 1 13 A ⲧⲱϣ; doubtful Ez 40 21 S, J 3 24, ib 71 25 S ⲧⲱϣ (cf ⲧⲱϣ sg ib 92 33, PLond 4 463, CO 167); Mani 1 A² ⲡⲧⲟⲩϣⲉⲩⲉ ⲛⲛⲟⲩⲁⲓⲛⲉ (bis).

ⲣⲙⲡⲧ. S, man of the nome, dweller in same n.: J 74 94 aimed at upsetting (ἀναλύειν) affairs of ⲡⲣⲙⲡⲧⲟ[ϣ]; ⲣⲙⲡⲧ.: Ep 323 ⲣ. ⲡⲕⲉⲃⲧ.

ⲣ ⲧ., ⲉⲣ ⲑ., be limit, adjacent: Jos 13 7 S ὅρ. dat; Nu 21 25 B(S om) συγκυρεῖν gen (cf 35 4 B ⲉⲧⲕⲱϯ); Br 276 S ⲉϥⲟ ⲛⲧ. ⲛⲁⲩ.

ϯ ⲧ., ⲑ., adjoin, set bounds: Jos 23 4 S(B ⲉⲣ ⲑ.) ὅρ.; Deu 2 37 B(S ⲏⲡ) συγκ. gen; Br 261 S ⲁϥϯ ⲧ. ⲉⲧⲉⲭⲱⲣⲁ ⲧⲉⲭⲱⲣⲁ, Miss 4 629 S better not to ϯ ⲧ. ⲉⲁⲥⲕⲏⲥⲓⲥ, BIF 13 111 S will relate a few ⲧⲁϯ ⲧ. ⲉⲡϣⲁϫⲉ = MG 25 300 B.

ϫⲓ ⲧ., ϭⲓ ⲑ., adjoin: Leip 24 12 B ⲡⲗⲓⲙⲉⲧⲟⲡ ⲉⲧϭⲓ ⲑ. ⲡⲉⲙⲡⲉⲑⲛⲟⲥ of Saracens πλησιόχωρος εἶναι; Sh Bor 247 124 S death ϫⲓ ⲧ. ⲛⲛⲡⲙⲓⲥⲉ, J 67 74 S wall ϫⲓ ⲧ. ⲉⲡⲛⲓ ⲛⲛⲃⲗⲗⲉ.

ⲧⲉϣⲉ S, ⲑⲉϣⲉ, -ⲏ (once) B, pl ⲧⲉϣⲉⲉⲩ S, ⲑⲉϣⲉⲩ B nn m f, borderer, neighbour, that which adjoins: Ex 12 4 SB m, ib 3 22 B (var -ⲏ) f, Job 19 15 B(S ⲣⲙⲣⲁⲅⲉ), Jer 29 10 B m(S ⲉⲧϧⲏⲡ) γείτων; Ez 27 13 S ⲡⲧ. (var ⲧⲟϣ, B ⲉⲧⲉⲡϣⲟⲧ for ? ⲉⲧⲟ ⲡⲧⲟϣ) παρατείνειν; P 55 12 B f جارية;   pl forms: Ps 43 14 B (S ⲉⲧϧⲓⲧⲟⲩϩⲟ∙), Jer 12 14 SB, Jo 9 8 B(SA² do) γ.; Ps 37 12 B(S do) οἱ πλήσιον; ib 14 3 B(S ϧⲏⲡ) ἐγγίστος; Jth 14 4 S ὅριον;   ⲟ ⲡⲧ.: Ez 16 26 S(B ⲑⲉϣⲉⲩ) ὁμορεῖν; ROC 25 257 B women ⲉⲧⲟⲓ ⲡⲟⲉϣⲉⲩ ⲉⲣⲱⲧⲉⲛ.

In place-name: ⲧⲁϣⲉ ⲡⲧⲟϣ (MG 25 256).

ⲧⲁϣⲟ SAB, ⲧⲁϣⲟ B, ⲧⲁϣⲁ F, ⲧⲁϣⲉ- SAA²BF, ⲧⲁϣⲉ- B, ⲧⲁϣⲟ∙ SB, -ϣⲁ∙ A, ⲧⲁϣⲟⲩ∙ B vb tr, increase (caus of ⲁϣⲁⲓ): Ge 22 17 S(B ⲑⲣⲉ- ⲁϣⲁⲓ), Ps 17 15 SB ⲧⲁⲛ., ib 64 13 S(B ⲁϣ. ⲛ-), Pro 28 8 SA, Eccl 10 14 S(F ⲁϣ.), Is 1 15 SF(B ⲑⲣⲉ- ⲁϣ.), Ez 16 25 SB, Hos 8 14 AF(JEA 11 245, B ⲑ. ⲁ.) πληθύνειν, Ps 90 15 S(B ⲧⲥⲓⲟ) ἐμπιμπλάναι, Nu 26 54 SB πλεονάζειν, Pro 5 20 SA(B ⲁϣ.) πολὺς εἶναι, Job 1 10 S (B ⲑ. ⲁ.), Pro 22 16 SA π. ποιεῖν, BHom 93 S ⲉⲓⲧ. ⲛⲛϣⲁϫⲉ πολλὰ λέγειν, Ps 11 8 S(B diff) πολυωρεῖν; Lev 26 9 S(B ⲑ. ⲁ.), Job 42 10 S(B diff) αὐξάνειν; Si 9 4 S ἐνδελεχίζειν; Lu 1 58 S(B ⲉⲣ ⲡⲓϣϯ) μεγαλύνειν; Is 22 4 S(B diff) κατισχύειν; Job 1 10 SB ⲧⲁⲛ. كثر Gk diff; PS 365 S ⲉϥⲧ. ⲛⲧⲏϣⲉ in their souls, ShBMOr 8810 393 S ⲁⲧⲉⲡⲧⲁϣⲉ ⲣⲉϥⲙⲟⲟⲩⲧ ϧⲛⲧⲉ ⲡⲓⲕⲁⲧⲁⲫⲣⲟⲛⲏⲥⲓⲥ, ShA 2 258 S not fitting that any ⲧⲁϣⲉ ⲡⲉϥϧⲣⲟⲟⲩ, BMar 96 S ⲁⲓⲧⲁϣⲟϥ ϧⲙⲡⲉⲥⲟϩⲟ, El 88 A ϭⲡⲁⲧⲁϣⲟ ⲡⲡⲉϥⲙⲉⲉⲓⲛⲉ = ib 120 S, C 89 174 B ⲙⲁⲧⲁϣⲟⲕ ⲉⲟⲩⲙⲉⲧⲙⲁⲓⲡⲟⲩϯ, Va 61 7 B ⲉϥⲧ. ⲙⲙⲟϥ ϫⲉⲛⲡⲓϣⲗⲏⲗ, ib 58 134 B didst create & ⲁⲕⲧⲁϣⲟⲛ, Mor 44 12 S ⲛⲡⲉⲡⲧⲁϣⲉ ⲡϣⲁϫⲉ ⲉⲡⲉϩⲟⲩⲟ;   ⲧ. ⲟⲉⲓϣ v ⲟⲉⲓϣ, adding Mani 2 A² ⲉϥⲧ. ⲁⲓϣ ⲡⲉϥ, ib ϧⲣⲁⲥⲉ ϧⲙⲡⲉϥ[ⲧⲁ]ϣⲉ ⲁ.;   ⲧⲁϣⲉ- before vb: Ps 77 38 S ⲧ. ⲕⲧⲟ ⲉⲃⲟⲗ(B ⲁϣⲁⲓ ⲉⲑⲣⲉϥⲧⲁⲥⲑⲟ)ⲡⲗⲏⲑ. ⲧ. ἀποστρέφαι; ib 125 2 SB ⲧ. ⲉⲓⲣⲉ ⲙⲉⲅ. ⲧ. ποιῆσαι; Lev

13 24 *B* ⲧ. (var ⲧⲁⲡ.) ⲟⲩⲟⲛϩ (*S* diff) αὐγάζειν; Pro 25 17 *SA* ⲙⲡⲣⲧ. ⲃⲱⲕ ⲉϩⲟⲩⲛ σπάνιον εἰσάγειν; ι Thes 2 8 *B* ⲧ. (var ⲧⲁⲡ.) ⲙⲉⲓ ὁμείρεσθαι; Mor 37 98 *S* ϩⲙⲡⲧⲣⲉϥⲧ. ⲡⲱⲧ ὑπὸ τῆς ὀξύτητος; Aeg 14 *S* ⲁϥⲧ. ⲟⲩⲱϣⲃ = *ib B* ⲉⲣ ⲟⲩⲱ, Wess 18 37 *S* sim, Mor 47 137 *S* ⲁϥⲧ. ϩⲓⲟⲩⲉ ⲉⲡⲟⲓⲕⲟⲡⲟⲙⲟⲥ = Par 4793 43 ضرب ضربا كثيرا; ⲣⲉϥⲧⲁϣⲉ ⲱⲣⲕ *S*, *much-swearer*: Si 27 14 πολύορκος. Cf ? ⲧⲁⲣϣⲟ.

ⲧⲉϣⲉ *S*, **ⲑⲉϣⲉ** *B* v ⲧⲱϣ *sf*.

(**ⲧϣⲁ**), **ⲧϣⲉ-** *F* vb tr, *send* (caus of ϣⲉ?, cf ⲭⲟⲟⲩ): Ac 9 38 ⲁⲩⲧ. ⲗⲱⲙⲓ ⲃ̄ (*S* ⲭⲟⲟⲩ, *B* ⲟⲩⲱⲣⲡ) ἀποστέλλειν.

ⲧϣⲙⲟ, **ϣⲧⲙⲟ**, **ⲧϣⲙⲟ⸗**, **ϣⲧⲙⲟ⸗** *B* vb tr, *make small* (caus of ϣⲙⲁ): Is 30 22 (*S* ⲣ ϣⲏⲙ ϣⲏⲙ, *F* ⲉⲣ ⲕⲟⲩⲓ ⲕⲟⲩⲓ) λεπτὸν ποιεῖν, ib 41 15 (*S* ϩⲓⲧⲉ ⲉⲃⲟⲗ), Dan 2 45 ϣ. λεπτύνειν; intr: Dan 2 40 ϣ., 7 7 ϣ. λεπτύ.

ⲧⲁϣⲣ, **-ⲉⲣ** *S* nn m, meaning unknown: Ryl 368 ⲡⲉϣⲁⲡⲟⲧ̄ ⲉⲣ ⲁⲕⲁⲡⲏ ⲙⲙⲟϥ ϩⲓⲡⲁⲧⲁϣⲉⲣ ⲧⲁⲁϥ ⲉⲡⲉⲧⲣⲟⲥ, ib ϯⲁϭⲉ ⲙⲡⲓⲧ., PHeidelb 497 in list ⲭⲟⲩⲱⲧ ⲡⲉⲣⲧⲟϥ ⲡⲧⲁϣⲣ (same?).

ⲧϣⲣⲉ v ⲧⲱⲣϣ *sf*.

ⲧϣⲟⲩⲓⲟ *B*, **ⲭⲟⲩⲓⲁ-** *F*, **ⲧϣⲟⲩⲓⲉ-**, **-ⲓⲟ⸗** *B* vb tr, *make dry, parch* (caus of ϣⲟⲟⲩⲉ): Job 12 15 (*S* ⲧⲣⲉⲯⲟⲟⲩⲉ), Am 2 9 *BF* (JEA 11 246 om acc, *A* diff), Nah 1 4 (*SA* ⲧ. ϣ.), Ja 1 11 (*S* ⲇⲟ) ξηραίνειν; intr: Va 57 225 ⲡⲓⲣⲏ ϣⲁϥ(ⲧ)ϣ. & rain maketh fruitful ξ.

ⲧⲁϥ *S*, **ⲑ.** *B*, **ⲧⲉϥ**, **ⲧⲏϥ** *Sf*, **ⲑⲏϥ** *B* nn m, *spittle*: Job 7 19 *B* ⲡⲁⲑ. (*S* ⲡⲁⲥⲥⲉ) πτύελος, Is 50 6 *B* (*S* ⲇⲟ) ἔμπτυσμα; Is 40 15 *B* (*S* ⲭⲓϩ) σίελος; MG 25 133 *B* μαστίχη sucked to sweeten ⲡⲓⲑ. & odours of mouth, Mor 37 295 *Sf* sick man swallows ⲟⲩⲧⲉϥ (var ⲧⲉⲃ) ⲉϥⲟⲩⲁⲁⲃ ⲉⲭⲉⲁ ⲟⲛ expectorated by saint (cf ZDMG 65 782).; *spit*: ⲛⲉϫ ⲧ. *S* Mk 7 33 (*B* ϩⲓ ⲑ.) πτύειν, Deu 25 9 (*B* ⲇⲟ) ἐμπ.; Mor 18 8 ⲡⲉϥⲧⲓ. ⲧ. ⲉϩⲟⲩⲛ ⲉ ϩⲣⲁϥ = ib 19 16 ⲡ.; ϩⲓ ⲑ. *B*: Jo 9 6 (*SA²* ⲛⲉⲭ ⲡ.) πτύειν, Gal 4 14 (*S* diff) ἐκπ., Nu 12 14 (*S* ⲡ. ⲡ.), Mt 27 30 (*S* ⲇⲟ) ἐμπ., Job 30 10 (var ⲑⲏϥ, *S* ⲇⲟ) πτύελος; AM 300 ⲁϥϩⲓⲟⲩⲓ ⲡⲟⲩⲑ. ⲉⲃⲟⲗ ϩⲙⲡⲣⲱϥ; **ⲥⲉⲧ**, **ⲥⲁⲧ** ⲧ., ⲑ.: MG 25 236 *B* ⲁϥⲥⲓϯ ⲡⲟⲩⲑ. ⲉϩⲟⲩⲛ ϩⲙ ⲡⲉϥϩⲟ ἐπιπτ.; ib 201 *B* ⲟⲩⲑ. ⲡⲥⲁⲧϥ ⲉⲃⲟⲗ, Sh(?) Mor 54 94 *Sf* ⲡⲡⲉϥⲥⲉⲧ ⲧⲏϥ ⲉⲃⲟⲗ save when sick, Pmag Heidelb (Kropp) *S* ⲡϥⲥⲁⲧ ⲧ. ⲡⲥⲟϥ, BM 917 *B* ⲥⲁⲧ ⲑ. ⲛⲥⲱϥ. Sim ? Lev 15 8 *B* ⲉⲗ ⲧⲟϥ προσσιελίζειν.

ⲧⲁϥⲉ† *A²* vb, meaning unknown: Mani 1 ⲙ- ⲡⲓⲡⲉⲩ ⲁⲑⲏⲣⲓⲟⲛ ⲉϥⲧ. ⲛⲑⲉ ⲡⲛⲉⲓ, ib ⲛⲟⲩⲱⲡϣ ⲉⲧⲧ. (*foaming* at mouth ? cf ⲧⲁϥ HT).

ⲧⲏϥⲧ v ⲧⲃ̄ⲧ.

ⲧⲁϥⲧⲉ v ϥⲧⲟⲟⲩ.

ⲧⲱϩ *A* v ⲧⲱϩ vb.

ϯϩⲉ *A* v ϯϩⲉ.

ⲧϩⲛⲟ *A* v ⲑⲛⲟ (ⲧϩ.) *bring near*.

ⲧϩⲛⲟ *A* v ⲭⲛⲟ.

ⲧⲓϭⲓ *B* nn m, *crane*: K 168 ⲡⲓⲧ. كركي . *V* ⲉⲧⲏϣⲓ.

ⲧϭⲙⲟ *B* v ⲑⲛⲟ (ⲧϩ.).

ⲧⲁϩ *S* nn, meaning unknown: Ryl 253 in account ϩⲁⲡⲧ. ⲡⲁⲣϣⲓⲛ (each entry begins with ϩⲁ-).

ⲧⲱϩ *SAF*, **ⲧⲱⲁϩ** *S* (Ryl), **ⲧⲟϩ**, **ⲑ.** (rare) *B* nn m, *chaff*: Ge 24 25 *S* (ShA 2 167) *B*, Job 21 18 *SB* ⲟⲩⲧ. (*S* var ϩⲉⲛⲧ.), Is 30 24 *SBF*, Nah 3 14 *AB* ϩⲁⲡⲧ., BHom 134 *S* ⲟⲩⲧ. ⲉⲁⲩⲡⲉϥⲧϥ ⲉⲃⲟⲗ, Va 61 24 *B* ⲁⲩⲙⲟⲥ ⲙⲡϣⲁⲣ...ⲡⲧ. ἄχυρον; Si 30 33 *S* χόρτασμα; ShR 2 3 31 *S* dividing ⲛⲧ. from ⲥⲟⲩⲟ, ShA 2 130 *S* ϩⲣⲉ & ⲧ. for cattle, ShC 42 63 *S* ⲧ. & ⲣⲟⲟϥⲉ for burning, Cat 193 *B* ⲡⲛⲟⲩ ⲙⲡⲁⲓⲑ. ⲡⲉⲥⲟⲧ ⲡⲣⲁⲥⲟⲩⲓ (sc worldly ambition), Miss 4 699 *S* ⲙⲉⲕⲥⲛ ⲗⲁⲁⲩ ⲡϩⲏⲧⲟⲩ (sc corn ears) ⲛⲥⲁⲧ., BM 1175 *S* camels ⲧⲁⲁⲩ ⲉⲡⲧ., CO 222 *S* will not neglect ⲭⲓ ϩⲣⲉ, ⲭⲓ ⲧ., ⲭⲓ ⲉⲓⲱⲧ for cattle, ST 185 *S* calves died [for] ⲙⲛⲧⲁⲛ ⲧⲟϩ ⲙⲛⲧⲁⲛ ⲧⲣⲓⲙ, DeV 2 82 *B* ⲭⲁⲭⲓⲑⲱⲗ is ⲧ. ⲉⲑⲛⲟⲩϥ ⲉⲃⲟⲗ ϧⲉⲛⲡⲓⲙⲁϩⲓ, Ryl 319 *S* ⲙⲟⲓⲁϩⲣ ⲛⲧⲱⲁϩ, C 86 180 *B* ϭⲛⲟⲩ ⲛⲧ., Ep 353 *S* 11½ carats paid for ⲧ., BKU 1 9 *S* ⲧ. ⲛⲡⲥⲟⲩⲟ as fuel (cf Wilcken *Ostr* 1 163); ⲧ. spread on foundations of church (Lab 2 156 still customary): Mor 29 34 *S* ⲛⲧ. ⲉⲧⲟⲩⲛⲁⲥⲟⲣϥ ⲉⲃⲟⲗ ⲉⲧⲥⲛⲧⲉ = ib 30 40 *F*, C 86 317 *B* ⲁϥⲑⲣⲟⲩⲥⲟⲣ ⲧ. ⲕⲁⲧⲁ ⲑⲙⲁⲓⲏ of τόπος, يُعلَّم بالتبن (cf places ⲛⲥⲁⲣ ⲧ. Wess 20 15, Πσαρσωρτωϩ & varr PLond 4 597), KKS 31 *SF* ⲟⲩϩⲓⲣ ⲛⲧ. to mark foundations = EW 38 *B*; K 50 *B* ⲡⲓⲙⲱⲓⲧ ⲛⲧⲉ ⲡⲓⲧ. مجرّة, طريق التبن *Milky Way*; ⲁⲙⲧ. *S* nn, *clay* (v ⲟⲙⲉ) *mixed with chaff*(?), used for stopping leaks in canal bank: ShC 73 152.

ⲣⲉϥⲧ. *S*, *chaff-seller*: PSBA 29 193 Barsôma ⲡϣⲏ ⲣⲉ (ⲙ) ⲛⲣ. تبّان.

ⲧⲱϩ *SA*, **-ϩ** *A*, **ⲑⲱⲃ̄**, **ⲑⲟϩ** *B* (-ⲃ̄ & -ϩ forms originally ? distinct, cf Dévaud Ét 22), **ⲧⲟϩ** *F*, **ⲧⲉϩ-**, **ⲧⲁϩ-**, **ⲧⲱϩ-** *S*, **ⲑⲉⲃ̄-** *B*, **ⲧⲁϩ⸗** *SF*, **ⲑⲁⲃ̄⸗** *B*, **ⲧⲉϩ⸗** *F*, **ⲧⲏϩ†** *SA²F*, **-ϩ†** *A*, **ⲑⲉϩ†** *B*, **ⲧⲉϩ†** *F* vb **I** intr, *be mixed, disturbed, clouded*: Ps 6 8 *B* ⲑⲟϩ (*S* ϣⲧⲟⲣⲧⲣ), Lam 1 20 *F* (*B* ϣⲑⲟⲣ.), Jo 5 7 *SA²B* ⲑⲟϩ ταράσσεσθαι; Ac 19 32 *S* (*B* ⲇⲟ) συγχεῖν; Z 328 *S* ⲁⲡⲁⲏⲣ ⲧ. συγκινεῖσθαι; ShA 1 53 *S* blind woman ⲁⲡⲉⲥⲟⲩⲟⲉⲓⲛ ⲉⲧⲟⲙⲧⲙ ⲏ ⲁϥⲧ., Leyd 313 *S* stars displaced, waters ⲁⲩⲧ., Win 16 *S* letter ends ⲙⲡⲣⲕⲱ (*l* ⲥⲱ)...ⲙⲡⲉⲕϩⲏⲧ ⲧ. (cf ib 21 sim ⲡⲧⲉⲡⲉⲕϩⲏⲧ ⲣⲓⲥⲉ & **II** *sf*), BP 12498 *S* ⲉⲕⲧⲙⲃⲱⲕ ⲡⲉⲕϩⲏⲧ ⲛⲁⲧ., Ep 286 *S* ye said ⲭⲉⲛⲣⲟⲙⲡⲧ ⲟⲩⲁϩ ⲉⲓⲥ ϩⲏⲧⲉ ⲁⲉⲓⲧ., CO 321 *S* hath he gone south on business ⲭⲛ ⲙⲙⲟⲛ ⲡⲧⲁϥⲧ.

(obscure);   qual: Jer 2 18 *S* ⲙⲟⲟⲩ ⲉⲧⲧ. (ShBM Or 8810 462, BAp 99)*B* ⲑⲉϩ ⲧⲁⲣ. (Coisl 191) *turbidus*; *Z lc S* ⲡⲁⲏⲣ ⲧ. συνελαύνειν; PS 282 *S* ⲡⲧⲟⲡⲟⲥ …ⲉⲧⲧ. which is ⲡⲧ. ⲡⲧⲥⲩⲕⲣⲁⲥⲓⲥ, Mun 83 *S* drunkard ϣⲱⲡⲉ ⲉϥⲧ. ⲁⲩⲱ ⲉϥⲧⲁⲕⲏⲩ, MG 25 36 *B* ⲙⲙⲟⲩ ⲉϥⲟ.

II tr, *mix, stir*: Hab 3 15 *S*(ClPr 25 2)*AB*-ϩ ⲧⲁⲣ., Is 5 22 *B* -ⲝ (var ⲥⲱ, *S* = Gk) κεραννύειν; Mk 14 3 *S* ⲧⲁϩ- (var ⲧⲉϩⲥ *l* ⲧⲉϩ-, *B* ⲑⲟⲙϩⲉⲙ, *F* ⲧⲉⲡⲡⲁ) συντρίβειν; Aeg 287 *S* ⲥⲩⲅⲭ.; ShA 1 461 *S* persist not ⲉⲧ. ⲙⲡⲙⲟⲟⲩ ⲉⲧⲥⲟⲧϥ, ShC 73 137 *S* ⲡⲉⲧⲟⲩⲡⲓⲥⲉ ⲙⲙⲟⲩ…ⲉⲩⲧ. ⲙⲙⲟϥ, *ib* 138 *S* scullion shall ⲧⲉϩ ⲡ-ϩⲟⲟⲙⲉⲥ & empty them daily, DeV 2 190 *B* demon ⲑⲱϣ ⲡⲧⲉⲥⲡⲉϫⲓ like anvil, SHel 41 *S* poisons ⲁⲩⲧⲁϩⲟⲩ, BKU 1 27 *S* mixture ⲡⲧⲧ. ⲙⲙⲟϥ, MMA 14 1 116 *S* ⲡⲧⲉ(ϥ)ⲧⲁⲗⲟ ⲡⲥⲟⲩⲟ ⲉϩⲣⲁ[ⲓ …] ⲁⲣⲧ. ⲡⲁϩⲏⲧ. With following preposition.

—— ⲉ- *SA²B*(once), *mix with*: Si 12 15[†] *SA²B* (var ⲑⲁⲝϥ)συμφύρειν ἐν; ShMich 550 19 ⲉⲧⲣⲉⲩⲧⲁϩϥ (victuals) ⲉⲑⲉⲗⲁⲁⲩ ⲡⲣⲓⲁⲁⲩ, ShC 73 144 ⲙⲡ ⲗⲁⲁⲩ ⲧ.[†] ⲉⲣⲟϥ, P 129[14] 115 Julian ⲁϥⲧⲉϩ ⲟⲩϩⲗⲟϭ ⲉⲧⲉϥⲙⲡⲧⲣⲉϥϫⲓ ⲡⲥⲟⲛⲥ, Ryl 106 68 ⲧⲁϩⲥ ⲉⲟⲩⲡⲕⲏⲡ (ἀγγεῖον) ⲉⲡⲉⲣⲱⲧⲉ, BSG 177 water ⲁϥⲧⲉϩ ϩⲛⲡⲉⲁϩⲣⲉ ⲉⲣⲟϥ, AZ 23 105 mixture ⲧⲟϩ ⲉⲣⲱⲟⲩ (*l* -ⲟϥ) till it become one, ManiH 39 *A²* ⲉⲩⲧ.[†] ⲉⲅⲕⲟⲓⲡⲱⲛⲉ ⲁⲡⲉⲁⲩ.

—— ⲙⲛ-, ⲡⲉⲙ- *SABF*, *mix with*: Ge 30 41 *S* μιγνύναι εἰς, Ps 105 35 *S* μ. ἐν, Lu 13 1 *S* μ. μετά, Is 36 8 *SF* (all *B* ⲙⲟⲩϫⲧ), R 2 2 28 *S* dove will not ⲧ. ⲙⲛⲑⲉ μ. dat, Pro 14 10 *SA*(*B* do) ἐπιμ. dat, Nu 11 4[†] *S* (var ⲧⲉϩⲧⲱϩ) ἐπίμικτος, Pro 11 15 *SA* συμμ. dat, Jer 32 24[†] *S* (all *B* ⲙ.) σύμμικτος, 4 Kg 14 14 *S* σύμμιξις, 1 Cor 5 9 *S*(*B* do) συναναμιγνύναι dat, Jos 23 12 *S* συγκαταμ. dat; Hos 4 14 *A*(*B* do) συμφύρειν μετά; Jo 4 9 *S*(var & *A²* ϫⲱϩ, *B* do)*F* συγχρᾶσθαι dat; Deu 7 3 *S*(*B* ⲉⲣ ϣⲟⲙ)γαμβρεύειν πρός, 1 Kg 18 23 *S* ἐπιγ. dat; 2 Tim 2 4 *S*(*B* ϭⲗⲟⲙⲗⲉⲙ) ἐμπλέκεσθαι dat; R 1 4 58 *S* ⲧⲉϩ ⲧⲙⲉ ⲙⲡⲡϭⲟⲗ = MartIgn 870 *B* ϩⲱⲧⲡ συγκρίνειν; Mor 37 68 *S* ⲉⲧⲙⲡⲣⲟⲥⲉⲭⲉ ⲉⲧⲁϩⲥ ⲙⲛⲡⲁⲓ προσέχειν dat; Aeg 211 *S* ⲧⲁϩϥ ⲙⲛⲡⲣⲟⲟⲩϣ ἀναλαμβάνειν acc; *ib* 281 *S* ⲙⲛⲟⲩⲧ. ⲙⲛⲧⲁⲙⲟⲥ ἄγαμος εἶναι; ShC 42 52 *S* water ⲉⲩϣⲁⲛⲧⲁϩϥ ⲙⲛⲡⲏⲣⲡ, ShBerl 1611 5 40 *S* man upsetting loaves in bakery ⲉϥⲧ.[†] ⲡⲙⲙⲁⲩ ϩⲛⲡⲉⲓϣⲟⲣϣⲣ ⲡⲟⲩⲱⲧ, CA 90 *S* ϥⲧ. ⲙⲙⲟⲟⲩ ⲙⲛⲡⲕⲁϩ (*cf* Ge 35 4), C 43 194 *B* ⲁϥⲑⲁⲝϥ ⲡⲉⲙⲡⲙⲏⲛϣ, TstAb 232 *B* ⲙⲡⲉⲣⲑⲉϣ ⲡⲓⲙⲉⲅⲓ of world with God's, BM 351 34 *S* ⲧⲁⲕⲧⲏⲥⲓⲥ ⲧ.[†] ⲙⲛⲧⲱⲥ = Miss 4 321 ⲕⲗⲥ, PMéd 230 *S* water ⲧ. ⲙⲛⲡⲡⲁϩⲣⲉ, BKU 1 26 (8116)*F* ⲧⲉϩ ⲙⲉ-ⲟⲩⲛϩ.   *V* also with adverb.

—— ⲡ- *SF*, *mix in, with*: BMis 150 layman ⲉϥ-ⲡⲁⲧⲁϩϥ ⲡⲗⲁⲁⲩ ⲡⲣⲱⲃ of church, Mor 18 151 ⲡⲉⲧ-ⲟⲩⲱϣ ⲉⲧ. ⲡⲙⲙⲁⲩ ⲡⲣⲉⲡⲙⲛⲧⲡⲟⲉⲓⲕ, PS 292 stater ⲥⲧ.[†] ⲡⲣⲁⲧ ϩⲓⲣⲟⲙⲡⲧ, Mich 136 1 ⲧ. ⲙⲙⲟⲟⲩ ⲡⲣⲉⲛ-

ⲃⲁ, BKU 1 21 ro *F* ⲡⲕⲧⲁϩⲩ ⲡⲟⲩⲕⲉϣ *stir with reed* (*cf* c ϩⲛ-).

—— ⲛⲥⲁ- *S*, *stir diligently*: Bodl(P) a 2 16 knead, pound, put in water, ⲧ. ⲡⲥⲟϥ, Ryl 106 49 *Sᶠ* ⲧ. ⲉⲥⲱⲟⲩ ϣⲁⲡⲧⲟⲩⲃⲱⲗ ⲉⲃⲟⲗ.

—— ϩⲓ- *SAF*, *mix with*: Mt 27 34[†] *S*(*B* ⲙ.)ⲙ. μετά; Is 30 24[†] *SF*(*B* do) ἀναποιεῖν ἐν; Bor 283 76 *S* assemblies ⲉⲩⲧ.[†] ϩⲓⲥⲱⲃⲉ, El 42 *A* eyes ⲧ.[†] ϩⲓⲥⲡⲁϥ, AZ 21 144 *S* eyes filled with blood ⲉⲩⲧ.[†](*l*? ⲉϥ·) ϩⲓ-ⲣⲉⲙⲉⲓⲏ, BM 527 *F* raven's blood ⲉⲕⲁⲡⲉⲧⲉϥ (was -ⲡⲉⲧϥ, *l*? ⲉⲕⲡⲉⲧϥ) ϩⲓⲣⲉⲙⲭ.

—— ϩⲛ-, ϩⲉⲛ- *SBF*, *mix with* (agent): PMéd 320 *S* ⲧⲁϩϥ (*sc* ointment) ϩⲛⲟⲩⲃⲟⲓ (*v* ⲃⲁ), C 89 60 *B* ⲁϥⲑⲁϣϥ ϩⲉⲛⲧⲉϥϭⲓϫ;   *mix, be concerned in*: BMis 539 *S* ⲡⲥⲉⲧⲁϩⲟⲩ ϩⲛϩⲉⲡⲃⲏⲩⲉ ⲙⲡⲡⲱⲟⲩ ⲁⲛ *se inmittere in*; ShBMOr 8810 372 *S* ⲙⲡⲣⲧⲉϩ ⲧⲥⲩⲡⲁⲧⲱⲥⲓ ϩⲛϩⲉⲡϣⲁϫⲉ ⲡⲥⲕⲁⲡⲇⲁⲗⲟⲡ, P 130³ 64 *S* ⲧⲉⲡⲧ.[†] ϩⲛ-ⲡⲣⲟⲟⲩϣ, Pcod 38 *F* faith ⲧⲉϩ ϩⲛϩⲉⲡⲣⲏⲇⲟⲡⲏ = *S* ⲙⲟⲭⲥ, Mor 24 26 *F* sinners ⲧ.[†] ϩⲛⲡⲉⲥⲱⲟⲃ, AZ 21 108 *S* mixture ⲧⲁϩϥ ϩⲓⲙⲡⲉϥϩⲉⲣⲏⲩ (*cf* 110 ϩⲓⲡⲉⲩ-).

With following adverb.   ⲉ ⲃⲟⲗ: AM 154 *B* ingredients, ⲁϥϩⲣⲟⲩⲑⲁϩⲟⲩ ⲉⲃ ⲡⲉⲙⲡⲟⲩϩⲉⲣⲏⲟⲩ;   ⲉ ϩⲟⲩⲛ *SA²*: PS 282 *S* ⲡⲥⲧ.[†] ⲁⲛ ⲉϩ. ⲡⲙⲙⲁⲩ, Mani 2 *A²* ⲁⲩⲧ. [ⲁⲣⲟⲩ]ⲡ ⲡⲉⲙⲉⲥ ⲡⲣⲡϫⲱⲣⲙⲉ, Miss 8 57 *S* may not ⲧⲁϩϥ ⲉϩ. ⲙⲡⲡⲉϩⲃⲏⲩⲉ.

—— ⲛⲛ m *SB*, *mixture, disturbance*: ShMIF 23 84 *S* would that these ⲡⲁⲣ ⲡⲓⲧ. ⲡⲟⲩⲱⲧ ⲛⲙⲙⲁⲛ *unite with us*, ShC 73 159 *S* lest ⲧ. ϣⲱⲡⲉ ϩⲛⲡⲉⲥⲡⲏⲩ, ShA 2 349 *S* craftsmen not to sell in monastery ϩⲉⲛⲧ. ⲧⲁⲣⲡⲉ *meddlers, busybodies*, EpApp 1 12 *S* ⲙⲙⲛ ⲧ]ⲱϩ ϣⲟⲟⲡ ⲡⲓⲅⲛⲟⲥ[ⲧⲁⲥⲓⲥ, C 89 181 *B* ⲡⲓϯ ⲧⲱⲡ ⲡⲉⲙ-ⲡⲓⲱ., Va 61 114 *B* winter ⲙⲉϩ ⲡⲟⲱϣ ⲡⲁⲏⲣ, *ib* 96 *B* ⲛϭⲓ ⲣⲱⲟⲩϣ ⲡⲉ. = P 131³ 85 *S* ⲉⲡⲟⲃϣ ⲉⲩⲙⲏⲛϣⲉ ⲡⲣⲱⲃ.

ⲁⲧⲧ. *SBF*, *unmixed, not confused*: BM 217 137 *S* Father & Son ⲟⲩⲁ. ϩⲛⲧⲏⲡⲉ (context lost), Kr 69 *F* acknowledgement of loan(?)]ⲗⲟⲕⲱϫⲓ ⲡⲁ(ⲧ)ⲧⲱϩ ⲡ-ⲁⲧⲑⲙⲓⲥ (*v* ? ⲑⲙⲓⲥ); CaiEuch 407 *B* united with Godhead in ⲟⲩⲙⲉⲧⲁⲧⲑⲱϣ φυρμός.

ⲙⲁⲓⲧ. *S*, *loving to meddle*: Miss 8 250 among sinners ϩⲛⲕⲟⲟⲩⲉ ⲙⲙ.

ⲣⲉϥⲧ. *S*, *mixer, meddler*: 2 Thes 3 11 (*B* = Gk) περιεργάζειν, 1 Tim 5 13 (*B* do) περίεργος; ShWess 9 135 Athanasius reproved ⲡⲣ. (*sc* heretics), ShC 42 42 ⲣ. who question causes of death, BMar 180 be not friend of ⲣⲱⲙⲉ ⲡⲣ. that mayest stay peaceful; ⲣⲉϥⲧⲁϩ ⲙⲁ: PS 362 ⲣⲱⲙⲉ ⲡⲣ.;   ⲙⲛⲧⲣⲉϥⲧ., *confusion, disturbance* esp of doctrine: ShWess 9 133 Origen ⲧⲱϣⲉ ⲡⲕⲉⲙ. ⲉⲡⲉⲭ̅ⲥ̅ saying, ShA 1 404 inquiring not in ⲟⲩⲙ. ⲁⲗⲗⲁ ϩⲛⲟⲩⲥⲟⲟⲩⲧⲛ, Mus 42 228 sim; PS 256 ⲙⲛⲧⲣⲉϥⲧⲁϩ ⲙⲁ;   ⲙⲉⲧⲣⲉϥϯ ⲑⲱϣ *B*: 1 Tim 6 5 (var om ϯ, *S* diff) διαπαρατριβή.

Cf ⲧⲁϩⲧϩ.

ⲧⲁϩⲟ *SB*, ⲧⲉ. *Sᵃ AA²*, ⲧⲁϩⲁ *F*, ⲧⲁϩⲉ- *SBF*, ⲧⲉϩⲉ-, ⲧⲉϩⲟ *A*, ⲧⲉϩⲁ- *A²*, ⲧⲁϩⲁ- *F*, ⲧⲁϩⲟⲩ *SB*, ⲧⲁϩⲁⲩ *SᵃSⳝF*, ⲧⲉϩⲟⲩ *Sᵃ*, ⲧⲉϩⲁ *AA²*, ⲧⲁϩⲏⲧ† *S*(ⲩ ⲧ. ⲉⲣⲁⲧⳝ), ⲧⲉϩⲟⲉⲓⲧ† *Sᵃ*(ⲩ Ep 1 247), ⲧⲁϩⲛⲟⲩⲧ† *B*(ⲩ ⲧ. ⲉⲣⲁⲧⳝ)*F*(ⲥ ⲉⲱⲡ-) vb **I** tr, *make to stand, set up* (caus of ⲱϩⲉ): Ge 33 19 *B*(*S* ⲧ. ⲉⲣⲁⲧⳝ), Ps 118 38 *S*(*B* ⲥⲉⲙⲛⲓ) ἱστάναι, Pro 9 18 *B* (*SA* ⲥⲙⲓⲛⲉ) ἐφισ., Ps 9 21 *B*(*S* ⲇⲟ) καθισ., *ib* 5 4 *B*(*S* diff), Ro 12 1 *F*(*S* = Gk, *B* ⲧ. ⲉⲣ.) παρισ., *ib* 16 1 *B* (*S* = Gk) συνισ.; Jer 28 12 *B* ἐγείρειν; Dan 3 97 *B* κατευθύνειν; Mor 40 25 *S* ⲧⲁϩⲟⲕ = *ib* 39 34 *S* ⲁϩⲉⲣⲁⲧⲕ, BSM 58 *B* ⲛⲧⲉϥⲧⲁϩⲟⲛ ⲛⲁϥ before Him = Va 63 24 *B* ⲧ. ⲉⲣⲁⲧⲉⲛ = BMis 413 *S* ⲡⲣⲟⲥⲉⲡⲉⲩⲕⲉⲓ, JTS 10 403 *S* no need to ⲧⲁϩⲉ ϣⲟ̅ϣⲧ̅ in heaven, BM 260 *S* ⲁⲡⲁⲥⲱⲙⲁ ⲧⲁϩⲉ ⲥⲓⲕ, EW 100 *B* bade ⲧ. ⲙ̅ⲡⲓⲁⲅⲓⲟⲥ for tortures; DeV 1 105 *B* sim?, BM 545 (1) *B* if you need letter from him ⲧⲁⲧ. ⲡⲉϥⲥϩⲁⲓ ⲛⲁⲕ; *reach, befall, touch*: Ep Jer 4 *B*(*SF* ϫⲓ), Lu 9 39 *S*(*B* ⲛⲛⲟⲩ ⲉϫⲛ-), AP 14 *A²* λαμβάνειν, Ps 47 6 *S*(*B* ϭⲓ), Jer 51 23 *B*(*S* ⲉⲓ ⲉϩⲣⲁⲓ ⲉϫⲛ-) ἐπιλ., Is 35 10 *SBF*, Am 9 13 *SAB*, Jo 12 35 *SA²* ⲧⲉⲣⲁⲧⲏⲡⲉ *B*, C 86 279 *B* = BSG 179 *S* ⲕⲗⲏⲣⲟⲥ ⲉⲧⲁϥⲧⲁϩⲟⲕ καταλ., Sa 17 16 *S* ⲡⲣⲟⲗ., 1 Kg 23 26 *B*(*S* ϭⲱⲡⲉ), Mk 14 48 *B*(*S* ⲇⲟ) συλλ.; Leyd 414 *S* ἐπιτυγχάνειν; Ru 2 22 *S* ἀπαντᾶν, Ac 27 12 *S*(*B* = Gk) καταν.; Eccl 12 1 *SF*, Ro 9 31 *S*(*B* ϥⲟϩ) φθάνειν; BMis 556 *S* ⲛⲧⲁⲥⲧⲁϩⲉ ⲧⲉϩⲟⲩⲥⲓⲁ *pervenire ad*; Deu 24 7 *SB*, Is 22 3 *B*(*Sϭ*.) ἁλίσκειν, Jo 21 3 *B*(*S* ⲇⲟ) ἁλιεύειν; Ex 22 2 *S*(*B* ϫⲓⲙⲓ), Pro 21 21 *SA* εὑρίσκειν; Ez 46 7 *SB* ἐκποιεῖν *invenire*; Lu 15 12 *S*(*B* diff) ἐπιβάλλειν; Ez 17 10 *B* ἅπτειν, 2 Kg 16 *S* συνάπ.; Ge 42 4 *SB*, Si 22 28 *S*(var ϣⲱⲡⲉ ⲛ-) *A* συμβαίνειν, Jth 7 31 *S*, Zeph 2 2 *B*(*SA* ⲉⲓ ⲉϫⲛ-) ἔρχεσθαι ἐπί, Ps 34 8 *B*(*S* ⲉⲓ ⲛ-) ἐρ. dat, Sa 14 30 *S* μετέρ. acc; Lu 1 44 *S*(*B* ϣⲱⲡⲓ ϧⲉⲛ-) γίνεσθαι εἰς; Ap 19 20 *B*(*Sϭ*.) πιάζειν; Job 11 7 *S*(*B* ϣⲉ ϣⲁ-) ἀφικνεῖσθαι; Ac 27 13 *B*(*S* diff) κρατεῖν, Sa 8 21 *S* ἐγκρατὴς εἶναι; Lev 17 13 *B*(*S* ϭⲱⲣϭ) θηρεύειν, Job 18 14 *SB*, Is 13 8 *S*(*B* ϭⲓ) ἔχειν, Am 264 *B* ⲁⲩⲧⲁϩⲉ ⲡⲉⲧⲣⲟⲥ κατέχ., Lu 5 9 *SB* περιέχ.; approx transl: Ac 5 15 *S* ἐπισκιάζειν; Si 11 26 *S* κακωθεῖν; Ez 32 13 *B* ταράσσειν; 1 Tim 1 18 *S* προάγειν ἐπί; Sa 16 11 *S* ἐμπίπτειν; Is 5 2 *B* χαρακοῦν; Jud 16 9 *S* ὀσφραίνεσθαι; Cl 2 14 *A* ὑποφέρειν; *ib* 20 5 *A* neg -ἐκδιήγητος; Gk om: Jud 13 12 *S* ⲡⲧⲱϣ ⲉⲧⲁⲧⲁϩⲉ ⲡϣⲏⲣⲉ, 1 Kg 15 14 *S* voice ⲉⲧⲧ. ⲡⲛⲁⲙⲁⲁϫⲉ, He 7 28 *B* ϥⲧ. ⲡⲟⲩϣⲏⲣⲓ; PS 91 *S* ⲙⲁⲣⲉⲟⲩⲕⲁⲕⲉ ⲧⲁϩⲟⲟⲩ, ShC 42 69 *S* number ⲧⲁϩⲉ ⲧⲁⲓⲟⲩ ⲛⲧⲃⲁ, BM 288 *S* ⲁⲡⲉⲕⲗⲏⲣⲟⲥ ⲧⲁϩⲟⲩ, BMis 242 *S* ⲁⲩⲧⲁϩⲉ ⲧⲡⲟⲗⲓⲥ (var 299 ⲡⲱϩ ⲉ-), *ib* 387 *S* ϩⲙⲟⲧ ⲛⲧⲁϥⲧⲁϩⲟⲟⲩ (var *ib* ϣⲱⲡⲉ ⲛ-), El 46 *A* ⲁⲡⲁⲅⲕⲏ ⲁⲥⲧⲉϩⲁⲓ, BKU 1 280 *Sᵃ* ⲁϩⲉⲛⲡⲓⲣⲁⲥⲙⲟⲥ ⲧⲁϩⲁⲓ, Mani 2 *A²* ϣⲁⲣⲉⲡⲉⲓ ⲧⲉϩⲁⲩ ⲕⲁⲧⲁ ⲧⲁⲙⲟⲓⲉⲓⲏ, C 86 15 *B* stones cast but ⲡⲉⲙⲡⲁⲣⲉⲱⲡⲓ ⲧⲁϩⲟϥ, AM 181 *B* ⲉⲧⲁⲧⲉϥϭⲓϫ ⲧⲁϩⲉ ⲡⲣⲟ of boy, PMéd 219 *S* mixture ⲙ̅ⲡⲣⲕⲁⲁϥ ⲉⲧ. ⲡⲣⲏⲙⲁ̅,

AZ 21 149 *S* share ⲉⲕⲧ. ⲙⲙⲟϥ ϩⲛⲧⲟⲩⲥⲓⲁ, CO 147 *S* ⲡⲉⲧⲡⲁⲧ. ⲧⲉϩⲉϩⲣⲁ, Ryl 117 *S* tax demand ⲛⲁⲓ ⲡⲉⲛⲧⲁⲥⲧⲁϩⲟⲕ ⲙⲙⲟⲟⲩ, 118, 119 sim, BM 528 18 *F* arithm ϣⲁⲣⲉ ⲩ̅ ⲁ ⲧ. ⲟⲩϩⲣ ? *amount to*, BP 9543 *S* 10 litres ⲧ. ⲡⲟⲩϭⲱⲗⲟⲕⳝ, Ann 21 74 *S* ⲡⲉⲧⲉϣⲁϥⲧⲁϩⲟϥ I will pay, CO 94 *Sᵃ* ⲙⲉⲥⲧⲁϩⲟⲓ ⲁⲃⲱⲗ ⲉⲕⲕⲗⲏⲥⲓⲁ ⲁⲃⲟⲗ *is not my duty*, BKU 1 1 col 2 *S* ⲃⲱⲕ ⲙⲉⲕⲧⲁϩⲟⲓ *thou satisfiest (?) me not*, BM 601 *F* ⲛ̅ⲧⲉⲡⲉϩⲃⲏⲉⲉⲓ ⲧⲁϩⲁⲓ, Mor 24 9 *F* ⲟⲩⲛ ⲡⲉⲛⲧⲁϥⲧⲁϩⲁⲕ?, *ib* 31 71 *S* beggar ⲙⲁⲣⲉⲡⲉⲕⲛⲁ ⲧⲁϩⲟⲓ ⲡⲟⲩⲉⲓⲁⲟⲥ, reply ⲙⲛ ⲉⲓⲁⲟⲥ ⲛ̅ⲧⲟⲟⲧ, Louvre E 14251 *S* I invoke you ⲧⲁⲧ. ⲡϩⲏⲧ ⲡⲁ ϩⲱⲥⲉⲉⲓⲛ *that he may serve*; *meet*: ShA 1 70 *S* ⲙⲏ ⲁⲣⲧⲁϩⲟⲥ ⲉⲥⲡⲁⲣⲁⲃⲁ?, JA '05 1 438 *S* ⲙⲁⲧⲁϩⲟⲓ ⲉⲓⲙⲏⲩ, Miss 4 241 *S* testified ⲛϭⲓ ⲡⲉⲛⲧⲁϥⲧⲁϩⲟϥ ϩⲙⲡⲥⲱⲙⲁ, Bor 134 5 *S*(VitaSin) arise ⲛⲧⲁϩⲉ ⲡⲉ ⲡⲓⲥⲕⲟⲡⲟⲥ = C 41 36 *B* ϩⲱⲗ ⲉⲃⲟⲗ ϣⲁ-, C 89 81 *B* ⲧⲁϩⲟⲓ ⲡ̅ϫⲱⲗⲉⲙ ⲉⲡⲓⲙⲁ ⲡⲟϩⲟⲩϯ, AZ 23 28 *F* ⲧⲁϩⲁ ⲡⲉⲓⲕⲁⲛϣⲏⲗⲓ whom I sent thee; *catch, arrest*: PS 220 *S* ⲥⲛⲁϭⲱⲗ...ⲛⲥⲉⲡⲁϣ ⲧⲁϩⲟⲥ ⲁⲛ, ShC 73 160 *S* ⲟⲩϭⲣⲟⲡ ⲧⲁϩⲉ ϩⲟⲓⲛⲉ, CA 96 *S* ⲁⲩⲧⲁϩⲟϥ using 2 measures, Miss 4 139 *B* ⲁⲓⲧⲁϩⲉⲑⲏⲛⲟⲩ ϧⲉⲛⲣⲱⲧⲉⲛ, R 1 2 68 *S* ⲁⲩⲧⲁϩⲟϥ (sc Jesus) on 10th Parmoute, C 43 36 *B* ⲧⲁϩⲟϥ ϩⲱⲥ ⲧⲩⲣⲱⲛ (τίρων) = Mor 40 5 *S* ϭⲟⲡϥ, C 41 18 *B* ⲧ. ⲡⲓⲛⲟϩ (ship's cable) ⲛⲁⲕ = Miss 4 328 خذ, EW 217 n *B* rubric ⲧⲁϩⲟⲥ ϧⲉⲛⲥⲟⲩⲁ̅ ⲛⲟⲟⲩⲱⲧ *find it* (sc hymn).

II intr, *attain, be able*: 1 Cor 9 24 *SB*, Phil 3 12 *SB* καταλαμβ.; CO 330 *S* ⲁⲓ?]ϫⲟⲟⲥ ϫⲉϩⲛⲏⲩ ⲉϩⲟⲩ[ⲛ] ⲙ̅ⲡⲉ(ⲓ)ⲧ.; DeV 2 119 *B* ⲁϥⲧ. ⲓⲥϫⲉⲛⲙⲙⲱⲩⲥⲏⲥ *set to & interpreted scriptures* (cf Lu 24 27 *B* ⲉⲣ ϩⲏⲧⲥ), *ib* 226 *B* when birds & beasts ⲧ. ⲛⲥⲉⲃⲱⲗ ⲉϩⲟⲩⲛ into ark, CO 90 *S* if Lord ordain ⲛⲧⲁⲧ. ⲡⲧⲁϩⲏⲩ, Hall 71 *S* ⲙ̅ⲡⲉⲓⲧ. ⲉⲧⲉⲓ ⲡⲧⲁⲁⲡⲁⲛⲧⲁ ⲉⲣⲱⲧⲛ.

With following preposition. ⲉ ⲉ- (ⲩ also ⲧ. ⲉⲣⲁⲧⳝ below) *SBF*, *assign to, decide for*: Deu 23 4 *B* ⲁⲩⲧ. ⲉⲣⲟⲕ ⲙⲫⲃⲉⲭⲉ (*S* ⲑⲏⲡⲟ) μισθοῦσθαι ἐπί استأجرعلى (cf Mt 20 1 *B*); Ryl 335 *S* ⲉⲩⲧ. ⲛⲥⲡⲁⲩ ⲛ̅ ϩⲟⲗⲟⲕⳝ ⲉⲣⲟⲕ as his wage, Ep 400 *S* I will pay ⲡⲉⲧ ⲕⲛⲁⲧⲁϩⲟϥ (sic) ⲉⲣⲟⲓ, J 70 44 *S* ⲉⲓⲧ. ⲛϣⲟⲙⲛⲧⲉ ⲡⲕⲉⲣⲁⲧⲓⲛ ⲉϩⲁⲙⲓⲁⲛⲟⲥ, PMich 1193 *F* ⲁⲛⲛⲟⲩⲁⲓⲉⲙ ⲩⲓ(ⲟⲥ) ϫⲁⲉⲣ (نعيم بن خير) ⲧⲁϩⲏ ⲩ̅ ⲕⲉ ⲉⲗⲁⲓ, PRain 4768 *S* ϣⲁⲣⲉⲡⲉ ⲧ. ⲡϥⲣⲱϩ ⲉⲣⲱⲧⲛ, Ryl 331 *S* I sent to thee (ⲛ)ⲧⲉⲡⲉⲕⲛⲁ ⲧⲁϩⲟⲛ ⲉⲡⲧⲓⲟⲩ ϩⲟⲗⲟⲕⳝ; *meet at*: ShC 42 35 *S* ⲁϥⲧⲁϩⲟⲛ ⲧⲁϩⲏ (sic) ⲉⲧⲉⲓⲡⲟⲗⲓⲥ, Mor 41 190 *S* fetch idols ⲛⲧⲁϩⲟⲓ ⲉⲡⲉⲓⲙⲁ; *verbal, attain to, befall*: 1 Kg 10 7 *S* εὑρίσκειν; Ru 1 16 *S* ἀπαντ. dat; ShA 2 336 *S* if buyer do not ⲧⲁϩⲟ (sic MS) ⲉⲕⲧⲟ ⲉ ⲣⲁⲧϥ of seller, Kr 232 *S* ⲡⲉ(ⲧⲉ)ⲙⲡⲟⲩⲧⲁϩⲟⲟⲩ ⲉϩⲓⲧϥ, EW 35 *B* ⲁⲥⲧⲁϩⲉ ⲡⲓⲁⲅⲓⲟⲥ...ⲉϩⲣⲓ ⲛⲓϣⲓ *fell to lot of*, Mor 16 26 *S* ⲁⲧⲁⲡⲁⲅⲕⲏ ⲧⲁϩⲟϥ ⲉⲧⲣⲉϥⲡⲱⲧ, ShZ 597 *S* ⲉⲙⲡⲟⲩⲧ. ⲉϫⲓ ϩⲁⲡⲧⲓⲥⲙⲁ, ShR 2 4 49 *S* ⲛϯⲛⲁϣ ⲧ. ⲁⲛ ⲉⲡⲁⲩ ⲉⲣⲟϥ, AZ 21 145 *S* ⲙ̅ⲡⲉⲕⲧ. ⲉⲥⲉⲓ ⲙ̅ⲙⲟⲥ, Ep 245 *S* ⲙⲡⲓⲧ. ⲉ(ⲉ)ⲓ ⲉⲡϩⲏⲧ, Win 36 *Sᵃ* ϥⲧⲉϩⲟⲉⲓⲧ

ⲁⲡ ⲉⲙ[; ⲉϩⲣⲁⲓ, -ⲛⲓ ⲉ- sim: Va 66 304 B ϭⲛⲡⲁⲧ. ⲁⲡ ⲉ. ⲉⲡⲓⲡⲱϣϯ ⲛⲁⲱⲣⲉⲁ ⲛⲓⲕⲁⲛ; PS 70 S ⲧⲁⲙⲉⲧⲁⲡⲟⲓⲁ ⲡⲁⲧⲁⲣⲟⲕ ⲉ. ⲉⲡⲭⲓⲥⲉ; c ⲉⲭⲉⲛ- BF, set up on: Nu 1 50 B(S ⲧ. ⲉⲣⲁⲧ⸗ ⲉϩⲣ. ⲉⲝ.) ἐπιτιθέναι ἐπί; EpJer 58† F(B Gk om), DeV 2 85 B ⲁϧⲧ. ⲡⲥⲉⲟⲣⲁⲕ ...ⲉϩⲣⲏⲓ ⲉ.ⲡⲃⲏⲟⲩⲓ; c ⲛ- S, attain to: Mor 17 20 S ⲙⲡⲁϯⲧ. ⲡⲟⲩⲱϣ̄ϩ φθάνειν; BMis 187 ⲙⲡⲁⲧⲟⲩⲧ. ⲛ̄ⲃⲱⲕ, BM 228 59 what each ⲡⲁϣ ⲧ. ⲛⲁⲁϥ (sic l), Mor 23 50 ⲙⲡⲁⲧϥⲧ. ⲡⲉⲱⲧⲉ his pledge, ST 241 ⲙⲁⲓⲧ. ⲡⲉⲓ ⲉϩⲣⲁⲓ.

With following adverb. c ⲉⲃⲟⲗ S: Pap HT (Antinoe) account ⲡⲉⲧⲥⲁⲓ(ⲗ ⲧⲁⲓ)ⲧⲁⲣⲟⲟⲩ ⲉⲃ.; c ⲉϩⲟⲩⲛ S, meet within (i e ? in inner desert, cf Ep 1 183): CO 377 when this reacheth thee ⲧⲁⲣⲟⲓ ⲉϩ. ⲛ̄ⲣⲁⲥⲧⲉ, Aegyptus 3 278 sim ⲧⲁⲣⲟⲓ ⲉϩ. ⲙ̄ⲡⲛⲁⲩ; c ⲉϩⲣⲁⲓ S: BMar 99 is time ⲛ̄ⲧⲛⲧ. ⲉ. ⲛ̄ⲧⲉⲡⲣⲟⲥⲫⲟⲣⲁ, COAd 40 interdicted ϣⲁⲛⲧϥⲧⲁⲣⲟⲓ ⲉϩ. ⲛⲣⲁⲥⲧⲉ (cf ⲧ. ⲉϩⲟⲩⲛ).

—— nn m B, setting up, laying hold: Jer 7 5 διορθοῦν; ib 41 3 σύλληψις; K 69 ⲡⲓⲧ. (ادرال); MG 25 139 among ascetic virtues ⲟⲩⲧ. ⲛ̄ⲧⲉ ⲡⲉⲕⲙϩⲁⲩ realization(?) of thy tomb as if wert already laid therein.

ⲁⲧⲧⲁϩⲟ⸗ SB(ⲙⲉⲧ-), unattainable, incomprehensible S: P 44 47 ⲡⲁⲧⲧⲁϩⲟⲩ · ⲁⲕⲁⲧⲁⲗⲏⲙⲡⲧⲟⲥ, ib 48 ⲁⲡⲉⲣⲓⲗⲏⲡⲥⲓⲥ (-ληπ.), ib 52 ⲁⲡⲉⲣⲣⲉⲧⲟⲛ (ἀπέραντος?) all لا يدرك, الخ; BM 248 115 ⲡⲓⲁⲧⲡⲁⲩ ⲉⲣⲟϥ, ⲡⲓⲁⲧⲧⲁϩⲟϥ, Or Chr iii 7 112 sim, Ep 1 p 340 ⲧⲥⲟⲫⲓⲁ ⲟⲩⲁⲧⲧⲁϩⲟⲥⲧⲉ; as adj: JA '75 5 226 ⲡⲉⲓⲱⲧ ⲛⲁⲧⲧⲁϩⲟϥ ἀκατάλ.; Bor 251 298 Word entered Virgin ϩⲛ̄ⲟⲩⲥⲙⲟⲧ ⲛⲁⲧⲧⲁϩⲟⲥ; ⲁⲧ(ⲉ)ϣ ⲧⲁϩⲟ⸗ S(once)B sim: Cai The 203 B ⲡⲓⲁⲧϣ ⲧ. (sc Jesus) ⲁⲩϫⲉⲙⲕⲱϥ غير مدرك; ViK 9833 53 S God ⲟⲩⲁⲧⲉϣ ⲧ., CaiEuch 530 B ⲡⲉⲕⲭⲓⲛϭⲓ ⲥⲁⲣⲝ ⲛⲁⲧϣ ⲧ.; ⲙⲛⲧ-, ⲙⲉⲧⲁⲧⲧⲁϩⲟ⸗, incomprehensibility: JA '75 5 227 S we believe ϩⲛⲟⲩⲙ-ⲟϥ τὸ ἀκατάλ.; DeV 2 11 B ⲟⲩⲙⲉⲧⲁⲧϥⲱⲣⲝ ⲡⲉⲙⲟⲩⲙ-ⲟⲥ; ⲙⲉⲧⲁⲧϣ ⲧⲁϩⲟⲥ B sim: DeV 2 19.

ⲣⲉϥⲧⲁϩⲉ- SB, catcher: BSM 38 B ⲣ. ⲧⲉⲃⲧ̄ =BMis 382 S ⲟⲩⲱϩⲉ; as adj: Mt 4 19 B(S do)ἁλιεύς; My 41 S ⲓⲟϩⲉ (l ⲟⲩⲟϩⲉ) ⲡⲣ. ⲧⲃⲧ̄; ⲙⲛⲧⲣⲉϥⲧⲁϩⲟ⸗ S: P 131³ 24 Christ's nature ⲉⲧⲉϣⲁⲩⲧⲁϩⲟⲥ...ⲁⲩϭⲉ ⲉⲣⲟⲥ ⲉⲃⲟⲗ ϩⲓⲧⲛ-ⲟϥ tangibility & thus was He seized & smitten.

ⲧ. ⲉⲣⲁⲧ⸗ SABF, set on feet, make to stand, establish: Nu 30 14 S(B ⲥⲉⲙⲛⲓ), Ps 30 8 SB, Zech 11 12 SA(B c.), Mk 9 36 SBF, Aeg 270 S ⲛ̄ⲧⲉⲣⲉϥⲧⲁϩⲉ ⲡⲣⲏ ⲉⲣⲁⲧϥ (Jos 10 13) ἱστάναι, Ps 77 5 SB, Ac 9 41 B(S ⲧⲟⲩⲡⲟⲥ) ἀνισ., Lev 17 10 S(B c.) ἐφισ., Ge 41 43 S(B ⲭⲱ ϩⲓϫⲉⲛ-), Va 57 102 B ⲁⲩⲧⲁϩⲉ ⲡⲟⲩϩⲩⲓⲟⲥ ⲉⲣⲁⲧϥ in Nazareth καθισ., Ps 34 17 S(B ⲧⲁⲥⲑⲟ ⲉⲃⲟⲗ ϩⲁ-) ἀποκαθισ., Ro 12 1 BF(S&F var = Gk), Miss 4 526 S ⲧ. ⲉⲣⲁⲧϥ ⲉⲣⲟⲓ ⲙ̄ⲡⲁⲡⲟⲃⲉ = C 89 45 B, BHom 27 S ⲧⲁϩⲟⲟⲩ ⲉⲣⲁⲧⲟⲩ ⲉⲡⲃⲏⲙⲁ παρισ., Job 28 23 S(B = Gk), 2 Cor 3 1 B(S = Gk) συνισ.; Ps 145 8 B(S ⲥⲟⲟϭⲉ), He 12 12 SB ἀνορθοῦν, Is 62 7 B(S ⲥⲟⲟⲩⲧⲛ) διορ., Ps 95 10 SB, Va 57 13 B ⲁⲩⲧⲁϩⲉ ⲡⲁⲓⲣⲱⲃ ⲉ-ⲣⲁⲧϥ κατορ.; Is 22 23 SB στηλοῦν; Jo 2 19 BF(S ⲧⲟⲩ.) ἐγείρειν; Zech 7 12 SA(B ⲧⲱϣ) τάσσειν; Sa 13 15 S τιθέναι; 4 Kg 12 8 S ἐνισχύειν; Job 8 15 S (B ⲧⲁϩⲣⲟ) ὑπερείδειν; Ac 25 7 SB ἀποδεικνύαι; PS 131 S ⲁⲩⲧⲁϩⲟ ⲉⲣⲁⲧⲟⲩ ⲡⲡⲉⲥϭⲟⲙ, ShLeyd 296 S schemes ⲛ̄ⲧⲉⲧⲛ(ⲛ)ⲁϣ ⲧⲁϩⲟⲟⲩ ⲉⲣⲁⲧⲟⲩ ⲁⲛ, HSt 459 S bishop ⲉⲧⲟⲩⲛⲁⲧⲁϩⲟϥ ⲉⲣⲁⲧϥ (var ⲕⲁⲑⲓⲥⲧⲁ), DeV 2 96 B ⲁϥⲧⲁϩⲟϥ ⲉⲣⲁⲧϥ ⲙ̄ⲡⲉϥⲙⲑⲟ, P 129¹⁴ 135 S Mark healing Anianus ⲁⲧⲡⲁϭⲥⲉ ⲧ. ⲡⲉⲥⲡⲟϥ ⲉⲣⲁⲧϥ brought to standstill, P 131⁶ 104 S carpenter chooseth ⲟⲩϣⲉ ⲁⲩⲧⲁϩⲟⲥ ⲉⲣⲁⲧⲥ ϩⲛ̄ⲟⲩϣⲓ; qual: Lev 15 3 B(S ?) συνισ. قوام, Va 57 250 B ⲡⲁⲥⲧ. ⲉⲣⲁⲧⲥ ⲛ̄ϣⲟⲣⲡ ⲛ̄ϫⲉ ⲧⲉⲛⲫⲩⲥⲓⲥ προισ.; Z 270 S quietude not ἀναχώρησις of body but ⲡⲉⲥⲙⲟⲧ ⲉⲧⲧ. ⲉⲣⲁⲧϥ, Mor 25 91 S skins & sackcloth ⲉⲩⲥⲉⲣϭⲱ ⲉⲩⲧ. ⲉⲣⲁⲧⲟⲩ erected(?), put together(?), ROC 27 165 B dead ⲥⲁⲣⲝ ⲧ. ⲉⲣⲁⲧⲥ in good condition without ill odour, J 106 34 S ⲧⲁⲇⲓⲁ-ⲛⲟⲓⲁ ⲧ. ⲉⲣⲁⲧⲥ (cf PMon 105 ὀρθῇ διανοίᾳ); as nn m SB, establishment, right order: Dan 10 11 B(S ⲟⲩⲉⲣⲏⲧⲉ), Nah 3 11 B(A om) στάσις, Aeg 271 S ⲡⲧ. ⲉⲣⲁⲧϥ of congregation, Leyd 128 S sim σύστ.; He 9 10 B(S vb), Miss 8 76 S ⲟⲩⲧ. ⲉⲣⲁⲧϥ of things distorted διόρθωσις, Ac 24 2 B(S diff) -θωμα, Va 63 80 B renowned for ⲡⲟⲩⲧ. ⲉⲣⲁⲧϥ κατόρθωμα; ShC 73 102 S ⲡⲧ. ⲉ. ⲙ̄ⲡⲏⲣϥ of mankind, PSBA 29 195 S prayer for life & ⲧ. ⲉ. of patriarch, RE 9 140 S ⲡⲧ. ⲉ. ⲛⲡⲁⲏⲙⲟⲥⲓⲟⲛ, Lant 77 2 ro S he provided for ⲡ̄ⲧ. ⲉ. ⲙ̄ⲡⲉⲓⲭⲱⲙⲉ, Rec 6 179 B food for ⲡ̄ⲧ. ⲉ. of body = BMar 214 S vb, C 86 283 B tortures loosened ⲛ̄ⲓⲧ. ⲉⲣⲁⲧⲟⲩ ⲛ̄ⲧⲉ ⲡⲉϥⲕⲁⲥ, Ryl 90 S festivals of Michael's ⲧ. ⲉ. & of consecrating τόπος, ROC 23 275 B furniture & ⲡⲧ. ⲉⲣⲁⲧϥ of church, My 66 S ⲡⲓⲧ. ⲉⲣⲁⲧϥ ⲥⲛⲁⲩ upright (limbs) of letter ⲗ.

ϭⲓⲛ-, ⲭⲓⲛⲧ. ⲉ., establishment: Is 49 6 B m (S ⲥⲙⲓⲛⲉ vb)ἰστ.; ShA 2 135 S ⲧϭ. ⲉⲣⲁⲧⲟⲩ ⲡⲡⲉⲧⲛ̄ⲡⲉ.

ϯϩⲉ S, ϯϩⲉ A, ⲑⲓϧⲓ B, ϯϩⲓ F, ⲧⲁϩⲉ† S, -ϩⲉ† A, ⲑⲁϧⲓ† B vb intr, become, be drunken: Ge 9 21 SB, Job 12 25† SB, Is 34 5 SBF, Jo 2 10 SB μεθύειν, Ps 22 5 SB, Lu 12 45 SB μεθύσκειν; Aeg 286 S drink ⲛ̄ⲥⲉϯ. παροινεῖν; ShIF 77 S ⲧⲉⲧⲛ̄ⲥⲟⲩⲱⲛϥ ϫⲉ ϥⲧ.† ⲏ ⲁϥϯ., BSM 95 B wine ⲉϣⲁⲛⲥⲱ ⲛ̄ϧⲏⲧϥ ⲛ̄ⲧⲉⲛϥ.

With following preposition. c ⲛ-, drunk with: Pro 23 31 A(S ϩⲛ-)μεθύσκ. ἐν; Jer 23 9 S(ShA 2 98) B συνέχεσθαι ἀπό; SHel 44 S ⲉϥⲧ.† ⲙ̄ⲡⲏⲣⲡ; c ϩⲁ- sim: Ps 77 65 S (var Mor 16 40 ⲧ.† ⲙ-, B ⲉⲃⲟⲗ ϧⲉⲛ-)κραιπαλᾶν ἐκ; c ϩⲛ-, ϧⲉⲛ- sim: Pro 4 17 SAB, Eph 5 18 SB μεθύσκ. dat; Deu 21 20 B(S ⲉⲃ. ϩⲛ-)οἰνοφλυγεῖν; ShC 73 194 S ⲡⲉⲧⲧ.† ϩⲛⲟⲩⲏⲣⲡ, C 43 114 B ⲡⲉϥⲥⲱⲙⲁ ⲑ. ϧⲉⲛⲡⲓⲥⲡⲟϥ; ⲉⲃⲟⲗ ϧⲛ-,

ⲍⲉⲡ-: Deu 32 42 S(B ⲍⲉⲡ-), Is 34 7 B(SF ϩⲡ-)μεθύ. ἀπό, Ap 17 2 SB μ. ἐκ; Is 34 6 B(SF ⲟⲩⲙⲟⲧ)παχύ-νειν ἀπό; DeV 2 78 B ϣⲁϩⲟ. ⲉϩ. ⲍⲉⲡⲡⲥⲡⲟϥ; c ⲉⲃⲟⲗ ϩⲓⲧⲉⲡ- B sim: Is 29 9 (S ϯ ⲋⲗⲟ) κραιπ. ἀπό; AM 135 world ⲑ. ⲉϩ. ϩ.ⲡⲓⲑⲩⲥⲓⲁ.

—— nn m SAB, drunkenness: Pro 24 74 SAB, Ez 23 32 SB, BHom 48 S ⲟⲩϩⲧⲟⲙⲧⲙ ⲙⲡⲟⲩϯ. μέθη, Mic 2 11 SAB μέθυσμα, Va 57 9 B ϣⲱⲡⲓ ⲍⲉⲡⲟⲩ. μεθύειν; CA 97 S drink ⲁϫⲡϯ., R 1 2 51 S who ap-proacheth Lord's body ϩⲛⲟⲩϯ., C 89 112 B ⲁⲓⲙⲟⲣ ⲡⲑ. ⲍⲉⲡⲡⲏⲣⲡ.

ⲣⲉϥϯ., ⲑ. SAB, drunkard: Pro 26 9 SAB (DeV 1 75), 1 Cor 6 10 SB μέθυσος; Tit 1 7 S(B ⲥⲉ ⲏⲣⲡ) πάροινος; R 1 2 55 S consortest with ⲏⲣ.; as adj: Si 19 1, 26 8 S μέθυσος; p p.: Pro 23 20 SA οἰνοπό-της εἶναι; ⲙⲉⲧⲣ. B: Cat 149.

ϫⲓⲛϣⲧⲉⲙⲑ. B, state of not being drunken: Va 57 176.

ϯϩⲟ v ϩⲟ.

ⲧϩⲓⲟ SA, ⲑⲓⲟ SA², ⲑⲓⲉ- S, ⲑⲓⲟ- SA², ⲑⲓⲟⲥ SA², ⲧⲣⲓⲁⲥ, ⲑ. AA², ⲧⲣⲓⲏⲩⲧ, ⲑ.ⲧ S vb tr, make fall, bring down (caus of ϩⲉ): Si 22 20 S(A ⲧⲉⲟϥⲟ ⲁϩⲣⲏⲓ)κατά-γειν; Lam 3 16 S(B ϩⲓⲟⲩⲓ)ἐκβάλλειν; Pro 27 25 SA κείρειν; Si 42 5 S ⲧⲣⲓⲉ ⲥⲡⲟϥ αἱμάσσειν; ShBMOr 8800 51 S ⲁⲕⲟⲓⲉ ϩⲏⲧϥ (sic) ⲡⲡⲉⲣⲓⲟⲙⲉ ⲉⲧⲉⲉⲧ, ShP 130¹ 149 S ⲡⲟⲃ̄ϩⲉ ⲁⲩϩⲓⲟⲟⲩ (cf Lam l c), ShC 73 101 S ⲉⲩⲟⲑ.ⲧ ⲉⲩⲣⲁϩⲧ ⲉϩⲣⲁⲓ, BM 212 S ⲡϭⲟⲩⲟϣ ⲁⲛ ⲉϩⲉ ...ⲕⲱ. ⲙⲙⲟⲕ ⲙⲁⲅⲁⲁⲕ, TU 43 15 A ⲁⲩϣⲁⲧ]ϩⲓⲟ ⲙ̄-ⲙⲁⲩ, BM 1224 A² ⲑ. ⲙⲙⲁϥ, ib ⲁⲕⲁⲑ. ⲡⲁⲡⲡⲟⲩⲧⲉ ...ⲁⲕⲁⲑⲓⲟϥ, Mich 550 31 S world ⲑ.ⲧ ϩⲁⲛϣⲱⲡⲉ = Va 63 99 B ⲥⲁϯ ⲉⲃⲟⲗ ⲍⲁ-, Kr 92 S sowing con-tract ⲧⲁⲑ. ⲡⲣⲏⲃ.

With following preposition & adverb. c ⲉϫⲡ- S, fall upon: Gu 63 fleeing ⲉⲩⲑ.ⲧ ⲉϫⲡⲡⲉⲩ-ⲉⲣⲏⲩ; c ⲉⲃⲟⲗ: Pro 7 21 S(A om, B ⲫⲱⲛϫ ⲉⲃ.) ἐξοκέλλειν; c ⲉⲡⲉⲥⲛⲧ S, make fall down: Aeg 240 ⲑⲓⲉ ϩⲏⲧⲥ ⲡⲟⲩⲥϩⲓⲙⲉ ⲉⲡ., Miss 4 718 devil ⲑⲓⲉ ⲡϣⲏⲣⲉ ⲕⲟⲩⲓ ⲉⲡ. ⲉⲡϣⲏⲓ, ShP 130² 8 ⲉⲥⲟ.ⲧ ⲉⲡ. ϩⲙⲡⲉⲓϩⲉ ⲡⲟⲩⲱⲧ; c ⲁⲡⲓⲧⲛ A² sim: Mani 1 ⲁⲥⲑⲓⲁⲩ ⲁⲡ.; c ⲉϩⲣⲁⲓ S sim: ShA 2 118 ⲡⲉⲛⲧⲁⲩϩⲉ ⲏ ⲡⲉⲛⲧⲁⲩϩⲓⲟⲟⲩ ⲙⲁⲅⲁⲁⲩ ⲉϩ. ⲉⲡϩⲓⲉⲓⲧ; as nn m S: BM 1089 account of brick-making ⲁⲩⲡ ⲟⲩⲕⲟⲧ ⲡⲧⲱⲃⲉ ⲁⲩⲃⲱⲕ ⲉⲡⲉⲑ., ib ⲟⲩⲕⲟⲧ ⲡⲧⲱⲃⲉ (ⲉ)ⲡⲉⲑ. V KKS 119, LMis 375.

ⲧϩⲟ SAB, ⲑⲟ S, ⲑⲟϩ B (q v) vb intr, make, be bad (caus of ϩⲟⲟⲩ): Pro 9 12 SA(B ⲟⲓ ⲡⲥⲁ ⲙⲡⲉⲧϩⲱⲟⲩ) κακῶς ἀποβαίνειν; 2 Kg 11 25 S πονηρὸς εἶναι; Mk 5 26 SB εἰς χεῖρον ἔρχεσθαι; R 1 4 53 S ϣⲁϩⲟ ⲡ-ϩⲟⲩⲟ = Mart Ign 866 B χ. γίνεσθαι; R 2 2 38 S ⲡⲉⲩ-ⲥⲁϣ ⲑⲟ ⲉⲡⲉϩⲟⲩⲟ μεῖζον (γίν.); Va 57 189 B ⲉϥ-ⲡⲏⲟⲩ ⲡϩⲟⲟϩ ⲡϩⲟⲩⲟ λυμαίνεσθαι; Tri 653 S ⲡⲏⲩ ⲡⲉⲟ ‏ڏَأْبَ‎; ShWess 9 105 S grapes ϣⲁⲩϩⲟ ϣⲁⲩⲣ

ϭⲡⲧ, ShA 1 276 S ⲁⲩϩⲟ ϩⲓⲧⲉⲩⲡⲣⲟϩⲁⲓⲣⲉⲥⲓⲥ, Miss 8 255 S not healed but ⲡⲧⲁϥⲉⲓ ⲡϩⲟ ⲉⲡⲉϩⲟⲩⲟ, MG 25 213 B the good ϣⲁϥϩⲉⲣⲟⲩⲧ.

With following preposition. c ⲉ-, be worse than: Mt 27 64 SB, 2 Pet 2 20 B(S ϩⲟⲟⲩ ⲉ-) χ. gen; ShP 130⁵ 49 S end of malady ⲡⲁϩⲟ...ⲉⲧⲉϥⲁⲣⲭⲏ, ShA 2 101 S sim ⲑⲟ ⲉⲧⲉϥϩⲟⲩⲉⲓⲧⲉ; c ⲡ- ethic dat: 2 Kg 19 7 S κακός dat; Mor 23 42 S ⲧⲉⲩⲡⲟⲩ ⲉⲧⲙⲙⲁⲩ ⲑⲟ ⲡⲁϥ beyond all = ib 24 30 F ϯ ϩⲓⲥⲓ, BM 912 4 B ⲡⲓⲉⲙⲕⲁϩ...ⲡⲁⲧ. ⲡⲁϥ παρὰ ϯⲕⲟⲗⲁⲥⲓⲥ; c ⲙⲡ- S: Mor 25 47 ⲡⲁⲓ ⲡⲁϩⲟ ⲡⲙⲙⲁⲩ ⲁⲡ ⲡⲑⲉ ⲙⲡⲙⲁⲩ when they shall knock in vain, Z 266 S ⲡⲥⲉⲑⲟ ⲡⲙⲙⲁϥ ⲉⲡⲇⲓⲟⲅⲙⲟⲥ treat him worse than (in) persecution(?).

—— nn m SB, badness: Jer 24 2 SB πονηρία; Job 8 16 B(S ⲧⲁⲕⲟ)σαπρία; ShViK 9315 180 S herbs ⲡⲁⲧⲣⲓⲟⲡ ⲁⲩⲱ ⲉⲡⲁϣⲉ ⲡⲉⲩϩⲟ, ShIF 252 S ⲡⲉⲓϩⲟ ⲉⲓ...ϩⲙⲡⲉⲩϩⲏⲧ ⲡⲕⲣⲟϥ, Z 269 S ϣⲁⲡⲣⲏⲧⲉ ⲡⲉⲡϣⲁ-ϫⲉ (l ⲡⲡ-) ⲁⲡⲡⲉ ⲡⲉϩⲟⲟ. V Rec 25 148 n.

ⲧⲱϩⲃ, ⲧⲁϩⲃⲥ, ⲧⲁϩⲃⲧ S vb tr, moisten, soak: Miss 4 636 collect fragments (of bread) ⲧⲁϩⲃⲟⲩ ⲙⲡⲁⲛ-ⲏϣⲉ = C 41 20 B ϩⲟⲣⲡⲟⲩ ⲙⲛⲓⲧⲟⲩ = Miss 4 352 ‏فرقوهم‎ only, Sh ib 285 remains (of bread) ⲉⲩⲧ.ⲧ ⲕⲁⲡ ⲉⲩϣⲁⲡⲣ ϭⲡⲧ, 284 things cooked ϣⲁⲣⲣⲁⲓ ⲉⲡⲟⲉⲓⲕ ⲉⲧⲁϩⲃⲉϥ, 286 ϩⲉⲡⲗⲁⲕⲙ ⲡⲟⲉⲓⲕ ⲉⲩⲧ.ⲧ, ShC 73 212 ϣⲁⲅⲕⲁ ⲡⲉⲩⲟⲉⲓⲕ ⲉⲧⲧ.ⲧ ⲉⲡⲁϩⲟⲩ, ViK 9596 186 eat-ing no salt nor ⲉϩⲣⲁ ⲉⲩⲧ.ⲧ ⲙⲡⲉⲩⲟⲉⲓⲕ, PMich 3590 recipe ⲧⲁϩⲃⲟⲩ ϩⲓϩⲙϫ ⲡⲑⲡⲟⲟⲩ, Ostr penes NdeG Davies ⲟⲩⲗⲁϭⲙⲉ ⲡⲧ.

ⲑⲁⲃ S nn m, leaven (B ϣⲉⲙⲏⲣ): Ex 34 25, Mt 13 33 (F ⲥⲉⲓⲗ), 1 Cor 5 6 (var ⲑⲁϥ) ζύμη, Lev 2 11 ⲧⲁ-ⲙⲓⲟ ϩⲓⲑ. ζυμωτὸν ποιεῖν; Ro 11 16 (B = Gk) ἀπαρ-χή; BHom 102 ⲡⲉⲑ. ⲙⲡⲟⲩⲱϣⲙ; ⲣ ⲑ., be leavened: BM 256 189 Sarah ⲁⲥⲣ ⲑ. ϩⲙⲡⲧⲣⲉⲥⲣ ⲣⲙⲅⲉ ⲉⲃⲟⲗ ϩⲓⲧⲙⲡⲁⲧⲁⲥ; ϫⲓ ⲑ., sim: Lev 6 10(B ϭⲓ ϣ.), Lu 13 21 (B ϫⲟ) ζυμοῦσθαι; Ryl 62 2 world ϫⲓ ⲑ. ⲉⲃⲟⲗ ϩⲓⲧⲟⲟⲧⲛ; ⲁⲧⲑ., ⲁⲑ., without leaven: Ge 19 3 (B ⲁⲧϣ.), Lev 2 4 (B ϫⲟ), ib 23 6 ⲛϣⲁ ⲛⲡⲁⲑ. (B ⲡⲓⲁⲧⲕⲱⲃ), ib ⲟⲩⲉⲙ ⲁⲑ. (B ⲁⲧϣ.), Nu 6 15 ⲟⲉⲓⲕ ⲡⲁⲑ. (B ⲁⲧⲕ.), Ac 20 6(B ⲁⲧϣ.) ἄζυμος; 3 Kg 19 6 ⲁⲧⲑ. Gk om.

ⲑϩⲃⲉ- Sⁿ vb tr, for ? ⲑⲃⲃⲓⲉ-: BM 522 (gnostic) ⲁⲥⲑ. ⲛⲁⲣ[.

ⲑⲃⲃⲓⲟ SA, ⲑⲃ(ⲉ)ⲓⲟ A², ⲑⲉⲃⲓⲟ B, ⲑⲉⲃⲓⲁ, -ⲃⲃⲓⲁ F, ⲑⲃⲃⲓⲉ- SA, ⲑⲃⲓⲟ- A², ⲑⲉⲃⲓⲉ- (2d pl), ⲑⲃⲃⲓⲟⲥ, ⲧϩ. (Si 18 19 RylSuppl 7) S, ⲑⲃⲃⲓⲁⲥ A, ⲑⲃⲓⲁⲥ A², ⲑⲉⲃⲓⲟⲥ B, ⲑⲉⲃⲓⲁⲥ, ⲟⲩ. F, ⲑⲃⲃⲓⲏⲩⲧ, -ⲏⲩⲧ (1 Pet) S, -ⲏⲟⲩⲧ, -ⲁ(ⲉ)ⲓⲧ A, ⲑⲃⲓⲁⲓⲧ A², ⲑⲉⲃⲓⲏⲟⲩⲧ BF vb I tr, humiliate (caus of ϭⲃⲃⲉ): Ge 34 2 S(var ⲑⲙⲕⲟ)B, Job 22 12 SB, Pro 29 23 SA, Lam 1 5 BF, 2 Cor 12 21 SBF ταπεινοῦν, Cl 16 17 A ταπεινοφρονεῖν; Jos 10 10 S συντρίβειν; Ps 46 2 S(B ϭⲛⲉ ϫⲱⲥ), Ro 8 20 S(B ϫⲟ) ὑποτάσσειν; Ez 28 8 SB καταβιβάζειν; Aeg

229 *S* virgin ⲛⲧⲁϥⲑⲃⲃⲓⲟⲥ (= PO 8 685 افتزع, var افتذل) αἱρετίζειν; C 86 273 *B* gods ⲉⲧⲁⲕⲟⲑⲃⲓⲱⲟⲩ μικροποιεῖν; BMis 565 *S* trees ⲑⲃⲃⲓⲟⲟⲩ ⲉⲡⲉⲥⲏⲧ συγκύπτειν (h)umiliare se; PS 50 *S* ⲡⲧⲉⲣⲉⲕⲑⲃⲃⲓⲟⲓ, Mor 41 134 *S* ⲁϥⲑⲃⲃⲓⲉ ⲧⲉϥⲁⲡⲉ ⲡⲁⲓ ⲉⲡⲉⲥⲏⲧ, *ib* 24 22 *F* ⲉϥⲑⲉⲃⲓⲁ ⲙⲙⲁⲓ ⲉⲗⲁⲩ *beyond them*, Mani 1 *A²* ⲉⲅⲁⲑ. ⲡϫⲁϫⲉ, *ib* ⲥⲉⲡⲁⲑⲃⲓⲁϥ, BSM 119 *B* ⲑⲉⲃⲓⲟϥ ...ϩⲁⲣⲁⲧϥ ⲙⲡⲓⲉⲩⲥⲉⲃⲏⲥ, BM 586 *F* ⲧⲉⲧⲁⲥⲑⲉϥⲓⲁⲓ.

II intr, *be humble, humbled*: Ps 37 8 *SB*, *ib* 87 15 *S(B* refl), Is 5 15 *SBF*, Hos 2 15 *AB* ταπεινοῦσθαι; Is 13 15 *S(B* diff) ἡττᾶσθαι; Jo 3 30 *SBF* ἐλαττοῦσθαι; 2 Kg 7 19 *S* κατασμικρύνεσθαι; Jud 3 30 *S* ἐντρέπεσθαι; Ez 30 6 *SB*, Mt 11 22 *B(S* ϩⲱⲕ ⲉⲡⲉⲥⲏⲧ) καταβαίνειν; Zech 11 12 *A(SB* ⲁⲡⲟⲧⲁⲥⲥⲉ) ἀπειπεῖν *quiescere*; Ez 3 11 *B* ἐνδιδόναι *quies.*; qual, *humble*: Ps 50 8 *SA* (Cl -ⲁⲉⲓⲧ, var -ⲏⲩ) *B*, Lam 2 5 *B(F* nn) ⲧⲁⲡ., Eccl 10 19 *F* ⲑⲩⲃ. ταπείνωσις, Lev 13 3 *SB*, Ps 101 17 *S(B* ϩⲏⲕⲓ), *ib* 112 6 *S(B* ϫⲁⲡⲉ), Pro 3 34 *SA* -ⲏⲟⲩ *B*, Is 22 7 *SBF*, 1 Pet 5 5 *S(*var -ⲏⲩⲧ)*B* ταπεινός, Cl 13 3 *A* ταπεινοφρ.; Job 20 10 *S(B* ⲕⲟⲩϫⲓ ⲉ-), 1 Cor 11 17 *B(S* ϩⲕⲃⲉ) ἥσσων; Is 10 2 *B(S* ⲉⲃⲓⲏⲛ), Am 8 6 *B(S* ϩⲏⲕⲉ) πένης; Is 58 3 *S(B* ⲉⲧⲭⲏ ϩⲁ-) ὑποχείριος; PS 92 *S* ⲧⲁⲯⲩⲭⲏ ⲑ. ϩⲓⲟⲩⲣⲏⲃⲉ, BMis 5 *S* ⲧⲟⲩⲛⲟⲥ ⲙⲡⲉⲧⲟ., DeV 1 201 *B* ⲙⲡⲁⲥϣⲱⲡⲓ ⲉⲥⲑ. ⲡϩⲗⲓ, Mani 1 *A²* turned swords ⲁⲭⲛⲡⲉⲧⲟ.

ⲑ. ⲉⲃⲟⲗ *B*, *humiliate*: GPar 3 22 enemies ⲙⲁⲑ. ⲉⲃ. ⲡⲉⲙⲡⲟⲩⲥⲟϭⲛⲓ (*l?* ⲑⲉⲃⲓⲟⲩ).

—— nn m *SAA²BF*, *humility*: Deu 26 7 *SB*, Lam 1 3 *BF*, Lu 1 48 *SB* ταπείνωσις, Ac 20 19 *S(B* ⲑ. ⲡϩⲏⲧ), Z 307 *S* ⲑ. ⲡϩⲏⲧ, Cl 21 8 *A* ⲡⲑ. (var ⲡⲧⲃ.) ταπεινοφροσύνη, Lam 2 5 *F(B* vb†) ⲧ. vb; 1 Cor 6 7 *B(S* ϣⲱⲱⲧ)ἥττημα; Job 40 22 *S(B* ϭⲛⲟⲡ)μαλακῶς; PS 61 *S* wept ϩⲛⲟⲩⲑ., Pcod 28 *SF* ϫⲓⲥⲉ ⲏ ⲑ., MR 5 24 n *F*ⲥⲱⲧⲙ (sic) ⲉⲡⲉⲡⲉⲑⲃⲓⲁ, AP 23 *A²* ϣⲱⲡⲉ ϩⲛⲟⲩⲑⲉⲃⲓⲟ, BSM 22 *B* sim = BMis 360 *S* ϫⲓ ⲥⲱϣ.

ⲑⲉⲃⲓⲉ nn *B*, *humble person*: Va 61 15 ⲟⲩⲑ.ⲡⲉ ⲡⲣⲉⲙⲣⲁϣ, HL 117 ⲁⲣⲓ ⲡⲁⲛⲧ ⲡⲑ.

ⲁⲧⲑ. *A²*, *undiminished*: Mani 1 ⲡⲟⲩⲁⲓⲡⲉ ⲡⲁⲧⲑⲃⲓⲁϥ.

ⲣⲉϥⲑ. *A²*, *he who humbles*: Mani 1 ⲡⲣ. ⲡⲛϣⲏⲣ[ⲉ]ⲡⲡⲟⲩⲡ.

ϫⲓⲛⲑ. *B*: Va 58 67 he came to her ⲉⲡϫⲓⲛⲑⲉⲃⲓⲟⲥ *for her humiliation*.

ⲑⲗⲟ, ⲑⲗⲟⲟ *S*, ⲑⲗⲁ⳿ *F* vb tr, *make to fly, drive away, scatter* (caus of ϩⲱⲗ), with ⲉⲃⲟⲗ: Ps 1 4 (*B* ⲡⲟϥ ⲉⲃ.) ἐκρίπτειν; Is 41 16 (*B* ϫⲱⲣ ⲉⲃ.) διασπείρειν; Aeg 276 ⲡⲥⲉϥ. ⲉⲃ. flies with fans ἀποσοβεῖν; Is 29 5 (*B* ⲓⲡⲓ) φέρειν, *ib* 57 13 (*B* ϭⲓ) ἀποφ.; Sa 5 15 διώκειν; Mt 23 24 (*B* ⲥⲱϥ) διϋλίζειν; Tri 723 of flies on altar زَرْ; Sh(Besa)Z 504 ⲡϥⲑⲗⲟⲟⲩ ⲉⲃ. ⲡⲑⲉ ⲡϩⲉⲛⲥⲗⲙ, ViK 9523 Peter ⲉⲁϥⲑ. ⲉⲃ. ⲡⲁⲣⲓⲟⲥ, KKS 576 archer's arrows ⲑ. ⲉⲃ. ⲙⲡⲟⲩⲱⲡϣ, ALR '93 518

Mark's mother ⲑⲗⲟϥ ⲉⲃ. ϩⲙⲡⲕⲁϩ to exercise him like bird in flying; as nn: Cai 42573 2 ⲟⲩⲑ. ⲉⲃⲁⲗ title of recipe ('his face' to be smeared with concoction of lizard's & bat's intestines); Ryl 374 ϣⲁⲡⲧⲟⲩⲑ. ⲡⲡⲟⲩϥ for which we are detaining them, Cai 8075 *F* harvest contract]ⲕⲟⲗⲁⲩ ⲉⲕⲉⲉⲗ ϫⲁⲓⲥ ⲉⲙⲉⲃ[(meaning?).

ⲑⲙ† *S* vb, meaning unknown: Hall 69 ϣⲏⲧ ⲡⲁⲡⲟⲧ ⲉⲩⲥⲏⲕ [ⲁⲩ]ⲱ ϫⲉⲙϫⲉ (= ϣⲙⲧϣⲉ) ⲉⲅⲑ. (or ? *v* ⲧⲱⲙ *shut*).

ⲧⲱⲣⲙ *S*, -ⲙⲉ *AA²*, ⲑⲱⲣⲉⲙ *B*, ⲧⲱⲣⲉⲙ *F*, ⲧⲉⲣⲙ-, ⲧⲁ.(Ryl 282)*S*, ⲑⲁⲣⲉⲙ- *B*, ⲧⲁⲣⲉⲙ- *F*, ⲧⲁⲣⲙ⳿ *SAA²F*, ⲑⲁⲣⲙ⳿ *B*, ⲧⲁⲣⲙ† *S*, -ⲙⲉⲧ *A*, ⲑⲁⲣⲉⲙ† *B*, ⲧⲁⲣⲉⲙ† *F* vb **I** intr, *knock* (on door): Mt 7 7 *S(B* ⲕⲱⲗϩ), Ac 12 16 *S(B* do) κρούειν; hence *summon, invite*: Ro 9 12 *SB*, He 9 15† *SBF* καλεῖν; 1 Cor 1 2† *SAB* κλητός, Nu 1 16† *S(B* ϯ ⲣⲁⲡ) ἐπικλ.; FR 164 *S* ⲡⲉⲧⲧ.†

II tr, *summon*: 1 Kg 16 3 *SB*, Is 41 4 *B(S* ⲙⲟⲩⲧⲉ), *ib* 48 1 *S(B* ⲙ.), Lu 14 8 *SBF*, 1 Cor 7 15 *SBF* ⲕⲁ., Joel 2 32 *SAB*, Ac 2 39 *SB* προσκ., Zeph 1 7 *A(B*†) ⲕⲗ.; BM 216 80 *S* προτρέπεσθαι; TEuch 1 7 *B* ⲉⲩⲡⲁⲑ. ⲡⲟⲩⲅⲩⲡⲟϫⲓⲁⲕⲱⲛ for ordination ⲱⲥ; PS 37 *S* ⲧⲁⲓⲁⲕⲟⲡⲓⲁ ⲉⲡⲧⲁⲩⲧⲁⲣⲙⲉⲧ ⲉⲧⲃⲏⲏⲧⲥ, ShBor 246 74 *S* ⲉⲩⲧ. ⲡⲛⲉⲩⲉⲣⲏⲩ (*cf* Jo 1 41), Mor 40 42 *S* are come ⲡⲧⲉⲣⲙ ⲡⲉⲕϣⲏⲣⲉ = MG 25 269 *B*, MIE 2 416 *B* sent to ⲑⲁⲣⲙⲉⲕ ϩⲁⲣⲟⲛ, Mani 2 *A²* ⲁⲩⲧ. ⲟⲩⲉ ⲁⲃⲁⲗ ⲡⲟⲩⲉ, *ib* ⲉⲧⲁϥⲧⲁⲣⲙⲉⲥ.

With following preposition. ⲥ ⲉ-, *knock upon*: Lu 13 25 *S(B* ⲕⲱ.), Ac 12 13 *S* (var ⲉⲣⲓⲛ-, *B* do) ⲕⲣ. acc, Jud 19 22 *S* ⲕⲣ. ἐπί; BMis 384 *S* ⲁⲩⲧ. ⲉⲡⲣⲟ (var ⲉϩⲟⲩⲛ ϩⲙ-) = BSM 39 *B* ⲕⲱ. = Va 63 12 *B* ⲙⲟⲩⲧ ⲉϩⲟⲩⲛ; *summon*: BHom 69 *S* ⲉⲥⲧ. ⲉⲣⲟⲟⲩ; *summon to*: 1 Kg 16 5 *SB*, Jo 2 2 *SB(F* ⲉϩⲟⲩⲛ ⲉ-)ⲕⲁ. *εἰς*, Gal 5 13 *SB* ⲕⲁ. ἐπί, Aeg 266 *S* ⲧ. ⲡⲡⲓⲟⲩⲁⲓ ⲉⲧⲣⲉⲩ- προσκα. *εἰς*, Ac 16 10 *SB* ⲡ. inf; ShC 42 206 *S* ⲧⲉⲩϩⲁⲣⲓⲥ ⲉⲡⲧⲁⲩⲧⲁⲣⲙⲉ ⲉⲣⲟⲥ, BM 343 75 *S* ⲧⲁⲣ ⲙⲟⲩ ⲉⲡⲓϣⲗⲏⲗ, ViK 9783 10 *S* Judas ⲧ.† ⲉⲡⲉⲕⲗⲏⲣⲟⲥ = Aeg 45 *B* ⲏⲡ ϫⲉⲛ-, PO 14 323 *B* ⲑⲁⲣⲉⲙⲑⲏⲡⲟⲩ ⲉⲟⲩⲁⲣⲓⲥⲧⲟⲡ, C 43 46 *B* ⲑⲁⲣⲙⲟⲩ ⲉⲑⲣⲟⲩϫⲱⲕ ⲉⲃⲟⲗ, TEuch 1 12 *B* ⲉⲡⲑ. ⲙⲙⲟⲕ as subdeacon ⲉⲡⲓⲙ ⲡⲉⲕⲕⲗⲏⲥⲓⲁ; ⲥ ⲉϫⲛ- *S*, *summon on to*: Ann 4 163 ⲁⲩⲧ. ⲙⲙⲟⲩ ⲉ.ⲡⲉⲑⲣⲟⲡⲟⲥ; ⲉϩⲣⲁⲓ ⲉϫⲛ-: Nu 25 2 (*B* ⲙ. ⲉ-) ⲕⲁ. ἐπί; ⲥ ⲡⲉⲙ- (?)*B*: C 86 115 my father ⲁϥⲑⲁⲣ ⲙⲉⲧ ⲡⲉⲙⲡⲉⲕⲓⲱⲧ *betrothed me* (?).

With following adverb. ⲥ ⲉⲃⲁⲗ *F*: BMEA 10585 ⲡⲙⲉ ⲡϣⲁⲗⲉⲡϩⲟⲩⲧⲓ...ⲧⲁⲣⲙⲉⲧ ⲉⲃ. ϣⲁⲓⲡⲱⲧ; ⲥ ⲉ ϩⲟⲩⲛ *SA*, *knock inward* on outside of door: PS 184 *S* every one ⲉⲧⲧ. ⲉϩ. (*cf* Mt 7 8), TU 43 22 *A* virgins at door ⲁⲩⲧ. ⲁϩ., BAp 116 *S* on paying visit ⲁⲩⲧ. ⲉϩ. = PO 22 401 قرعوا الباب; ⲉϩ. ⲉ- *SBF*: Z 304 *S* ⲁϥⲧ. ⲉϩ. ⲉⲡⲙⲟⲛⲁⲭⲟⲥ ⲕⲣ. dat, BM 294 141 *S* ⲧ. ⲉϩ. ⲉⲡⲣⲟ ⲕⲣ. acc, *ib* 247 *ult S* ⲧⲙⲉⲧⲁⲡⲟⲓⲁ ⲧ. ⲉϩ. ⲉⲣⲟϥ

κρ. πρός; PS 316 S ϲⲉⲡⲁⲧ. ⲉϧ. ⲉⲙⲡⲩⲗⲏ (cf Lu 13 25 τ. ⲉ-), Miss 4 539 S ⲁϲⲧ. ⲉϧ. ⲉⲣⲟϥ; summon to: 1 Kg 16 3 B(S Mor ⲉ-), Jo 2 2 F ut sup ⲕⲁ. εἰς, Cai Euch 516 B ⲁⲑⲟⲁϧⲙⲟⲩ...ⲉⲋ. ⲉⲧⲉⲕⲇⲓⲁⲕⲟⲛⲓⲁ ⲕⲁ. πρός; Miss 4 666 S God ⲧⲁϧⲙⲉϥ ⲉϧ. ⲉⲡⲃⲓⲟⲥ ⲉⲧⲟⲩⲁⲁⲃ, ib 193 B God ⲑⲁϧⲙⲉⲕ ⲉⲋ. ⲉⲡⲓⲁⲧⲱⲡ; c ⲉϧ. ϧⲛ-, as c ⲉ-: Mor 41 3 S when began ⲉⲧ. ⲉϧ. ϧⲙⲡⲣⲟ = DeV 2 248 B ⲕⲱ. ⲉ-; c ⲉϧⲣⲏⲓ B, call up: AM 254 ⲁϥⲑⲟⲁϧⲙⲉϥ ⲉϧ. ⲋⲉⲡⲡⲓⲃⲁⲑⲟⲗⲟⲥ.

—— nn m SA²BF, calling, convocation: Ro 11 29 SBF, He 3 1 SBF κλῆσις, Lev 23 21 S(B ⲡⲉⲧⲟⲩⲙ. ⲉⲣⲟϥ) κλητός, Nu 28 18 S(B do) ἐπικλ.; ShC 73 142 S ⲡⲉⲡⲧ. (sc husbandry), BG 66 S life eternal & ⲡⲧ., R 1 3 17 S estranged from ⲡⲧ. ⲧⲏⲣϥ of Christians, Mich 550 29 S Andrew ⲡⲙⲉϧⲥⲛⲁⲩ ⲡⲧ. of apostles, TEuch 1 59 B ⲡⲓⲱ. ⲙⲃⲉⲣⲓ = ib 57 ϥⲟⲩⲛⲉϥ ⲙⲃ. newly ordained (bishop), C 86 158 B martyr is ⲡⲓⲱ. ⲉⲧⲁϥⲉⲣ ϣⲟⲣⲡ ⲛϯϧⲉⲃⲥⲱ ⲡⲟⲩⲱⲓⲛⲓ, Mani 2 A² ⲡⲧ. ⲉⲧⲁϥⲣ ϣⲟⲣⲉ ⲙⲙⲟϥ ⲁϫⲙⲡⲉϥⲥⲱⲙⲁ, ib ϯⲣⲏⲛⲏ ⲉⲧⲁⲡⲧ. ⲧⲉⲥ ⲡⲉϥ (v BerlSitz '33 65).

ⲣⲉϥⲧ. SB, summoner, inviter: Mor 43 134 S apostle Simon ⲟⲩⲣ. ⲉⲡⲙⲁ ⲛϣⲉⲗⲉⲉⲧ (cf ἀριστοκλήτωρ εἰς τ. γάμους at Cana, Schermann ProphetVitae 204), AM 131 B ⲡⲓⲣ. ⲡⲧⲉ ⲡⲓⲱⲙⲓ into kingdom, ShC 42 61 S ⲟⲩⲣⲉϥⲧⲉϧⲙ ⲣⲱⲙⲉ to walk worthily.

ϫⲓⲛϧ. B, act, occasion of calling: TEuch 1 51 ⲡⲉϥϫ. (sc bishop's) shall be on Lord's Day ﺪﻴﻋ, BSM 38 whom hast welcomed ϧⲉⲛⲡⲉⲕϫⲓⲛⲑⲁϧⲙⲉϥ ⲙⲫⲟⲟⲩ = BMis 382 S ⲕⲁⲗⲉⲓ vb.

ⲧⲱϧⲙ, ⲧⲁϧⲙ⸗ S vb intr, chase, urge, pursue: Mor 29 49 ⲁϥⲧ. ϧⲓⲟⲩⲡⲟϭ ⲛϭⲟⲙ till reached shrine (var BMis 278 ϫⲱⲣⲙ, Mor 30 56 Sᶠ ⲕⲱⲗⲙ); c ⲛⲥⲁ- Mor 48 91 stood by workmen ⲉϥⲧ. ⲡⲥⲱⲟⲩ = C 43 144 B ϭⲱⲣⲙ, Mor 31 208 ⲡⲕⲧ. ⲡⲥⲁⲡⲉϧⲧⲟⲟⲣ in mill = BMOr 3599 89 ﻦﺣﺎﻄﻟﺍ ﻞﺤﺒﻣﻊ ﺩﺮﻄﺗ, ViK 9512 stone floats ⲉⲣⲉⲡⲧⲏⲩ ⲧ. ⲡⲥⲱϥ; tr c ⲉ-: Z 614 ship floats in as if ⲡⲧⲁⲩⲧⲁϧⲙⲉϥ ⲉϯⲉⲙⲣⲱ ϧⲓⲧⲙ ⲡⲁⲅⲕⲗⲏⲣⲟⲥ.

ϯϧⲙⲉ. ⲧⲉϧⲙⲉ², ⲧⲉϧⲙ³ S nn m, a receptacle for water, grain, meal &c: ShC 73 138 care of water-vessels ⲛϯ. ⲛϧⲉⲓⲁⲁϥ once a week (paral ϧⲟⲟⲙⲉⲥ), Ep 532 corn in ⲡⲧ.², RE 10 38 ⲧ.² ⲛⲧⲁⲡⲛ, ST 189 ⲧ.³ ⲡⲟⲟϭ ⲡⲕⲁⲕⲟ.ⲏⲩ (l? ⲕⲁⲕⲉ ⲟⲩ) ϯⲟⲩ ⲡⲧ.³ ϣⲏⲙ ⲡⲕⲁⲕⲟ ϣⲏⲙ, Ep 549 ⲟⲩⲧ.² among metal vessels, BP 5131 ⲕⲟⲩⲓ ⲛⲧ.² sim.

ϯϧⲙⲉϥ, ⲧⲓ. S nn m, box, basket (?), bee-hive: 1 Kg 14 25 ⲙⲁ ⲡϣⲏⲡ ⲛϯ. ⲡⲉⲃⲓⲱ δρυμὸς μελισσῶνος; Z 351 ⲛϯ. ⲛⲟⲉⲓⲕ of hermit (cf ib 356 ⲙⲁ ⲡⲟⲩⲉϧ ⲟⲉⲓⲕ), ib 617 bee takes honey-dew ⲛϧⲉⲡⲉϧⲁⲣⲧⲁⲍⲉ ⲙⲙⲟⲥ ϧⲙⲡⲧ., AZ 21 158 bee brings from many flowers ⲉⲩⲧ. ⲛⲟⲩⲱⲧ.

ⲑⲙⲟ S, ⲧϧⲙⲙⲟ A², ⲧϧⲙⲟ, -ⲙⲟⲙ, ⲑⲉⲙⲙⲟ, ⲧϧ., ⲉϧⲙⲟ-, ⲉϧⲙⲟ⸗ B vb tr, warm (caus of ϧⲙⲟⲙ): Is 1 6 B(var ϧⲙⲟⲙ, S diff) φλεγμαίνειν; Nah 3 19 B -ⲙⲟⲙ (A ϯ ⲧⲕⲉⲥ sic) φλεγμαίνειν; Jo 18 18 SA²B (var -ⲙⲟⲙ) θερμαίνεσθαι, Va 57 94 B ⲁϥϭⲑⲙⲱⲟⲩ (sic) ἐκθ.; Ex 22 6 B ⲧϧ. (S ⲣⲱⲕϧ) προσεμπιπράναι; ShC 73 73 S ⲡⲉⲧⲟ. ⲡⲡⲉϥϭⲓϫ, PMéd 311 S ointment ⲉⲕϧ. ⲙⲙⲟϥ ⲕⲁⲧⲁ ⲥⲟⲡ ⲉⲕⲧⲱⲣⲥ, Ep 574 S ⲑ. ⲟⲩⲕⲟⲩⲓ ⲛⲡⲉϧ, Z 628 S opium ⲑⲙⲟϥ ⲙⲡⲟⲩⲙⲟⲩⲗⲁϧ, MIE 2 337 B demon ⲧ. ⲙⲙⲟϥ ⲉϧⲟⲩⲛ ⲉϯⲡⲟⲣⲛⲓⲁ; intr: Va 57 190 B ⲡⲉⲕϧⲏⲧ ϧⲙⲟⲙ ⲟⲩⲟϧ ⲛⲧⲉϥⲑⲉⲙ. διαθ.; as nn B: Jer 28 39 θερμασία. Cf ⲧⲙϧⲟ.

ⲑⲙⲕⲟ S A A², ⲧϧ.(Ez 5 17) S, ⲧϧⲉⲙⲕⲟ B, ⲧⲉⲙⲕⲁ F, ⲑⲙⲕⲉ- S A, ⲧⲉⲙⲕⲉ- F, ⲑⲙⲕⲟ⸗ S, -ⲕⲁ⸗ A, ⲧϧⲉⲙⲕⲟ⸗ B, ⲑⲙⲕⲏϥ† S, ⲧϧⲉⲙⲕⲏⲟⲩⲧ† B vb I tr, ill use, afflict, humiliate (caus of ⲙⲟⲩⲕϧ): Ge 16 6 B(S ⲙⲟⲩⲕϧ), Nu 29 7 S(B ϧⲟⲝϧⲉⲝ), Ps 43 2 S(B ϯ ⲙⲕⲁϧ), ib 88 23 S(B ⲉⲣ ⲡⲉⲧϧⲱⲟⲩ), Is 50 9 SB, Hos 9 7 AB, Ac 7 19 BF ⲧⲉⲙⲕⲉ- (S ⲙ.) κακοῦν, Ge 31 7 S(B ⲉⲣ ⲡⲉⲧ.) κακοποιεῖν; Ac 7 24 BF(S ⲙ.) καταπονεῖν; Ez 22 7 SB καταδυναστεύειν; ib 5 17 SB τιμωρεῖν; Sa 11 9 S κολάζειν; MG 25 206 B βασανίζειν; Ge 34 2 S (var & B ⲑⲃⲃⲓⲟ) ταπεινοῦν; Deu 28 27 S(B ϣⲁⲣⲓ) πατάσσειν; 1 Kg 12 4 S θλᾶν; Sa 14 24 S ὀδυνᾶν; Jud 1 34 S ἐκθλίβειν; Jos 6 18 S ἐκτρίβειν, Ez 27 26 SB συντ.; Lev 25 46 B(S ⲕⲱⲗϫ (ⲙ)ⲡⲙⲁⲕϧ) κατατείνειν; Lam 1 22 S (ViK 9685, BF diff) ἐπιφυλλίζειν; 1 Kg 6 6 S ἐμπαίζειν; Job 5 4 B(S ϧⲓⲟϧⲉ) κολαβρίζειν; BAp 94 S lest barbarians ⲑⲙⲕⲉⲧⲏⲧⲛ = MIE 2 378 B lest God ⲧϧⲉⲙⲕⲟⲛ, AP 35 A²]ϥⲟ. ⲡⲧ[, BMis 507 S prayer ⲡⲧϧ. ⲡⲧⲥⲁⲁⲧⲉ ⲙⲡⲁⲧϣⲓⲡⲉ.

II intr: Ps 106 39 B(S ⲙⲕⲁϧ), Is 41 23 B(S ⲣ ⲡⲉⲑⲟⲟⲩ), Zeph 1 12 A(B ϯ ⲙ.) κακ.; Pcod 35 S brethren ⲑ. (var ⲑⲃⲃⲓⲟ) ϧⲁⲡⲉϥϭⲓϫ; qual: Mt 4 24 B (S ⲙⲟⲕϧ) κακῶς ἔχειν; ib 8 6 B(S = Gk) βασ.; Deu 28 29 S(B ⲟⲓ ⲛϭⲓ ⲛϫⲟⲛⲥ) ἀδικεῖσθαι; CaiEuch 584 B ⲉⲧⲧ. by unclean spirits ἐνοχλεῖσθαι; TRit 193 B ⲡⲏ ⲉ(ⲧ)ⲧ. νοσεῖν; BMar 83 S ⲉⲥⲑ. ϧⲁⲡϧⲓⲥⲉ, Cat 44 B ⲉⲧⲧ. ⲛⲧⲟⲧϥ ⲙⲡⲇⲓⲁⲃⲟⲗⲟⲥ.

—— nn m SB, ill treatment, affliction: Nu 11 15 SB, Ps 17 19 B(S ⲙⲕⲁϧ) Is 53 4 B(S ⲙⲟⲕϧⲥ) κάκωσις; Jer 38 21 B, He 10 29 B(S = Gk) τιμωρία; Ap 9 5 B(S ⲧⲕⲁⲥ) βασανισμός; Deu 32 36 S(B ⲕⲱϯ), Si 23 11 B(S ⲙⲟⲭⲥ) ἐπαγωγή; Bar 3 7 S(ViK 9755, B ⲥⲣⲁϧ) ὄφλησις; Lam 5 20 F ⲧ(ⲙ)ⲕⲁ (B diff) OL contemptus; ShR 2 3 69 S ⲉⲕϣⲟⲟⲡ ϧⲛⲟⲩⲑⲙⲕⲟ (sic MS) opp ϧⲉⲛ]ⲁⲅⲁⲑⲟⲛ, BIF 13 107 S suffered on road from ⲡⲉⲑ. ⲡⲡⲉⲩⲟⲩⲉⲣⲏⲧⲉ = MG 25 291 B, HL 81 B ⲡⲓⲧ. ⲡⲧⲉ ⲡⲓⲥⲱⲙⲁ & labour of journey.

ⲣⲉϥⲧ. B, punisher: Mt 18 34(S = Gk) βασανιστής.

ⲧϧⲉⲙⲙⲟ A² v ⲑⲙⲟ.

ⲧϧⲉⲙⲕⲟ B v ⲧⲙϧⲟ.

ⲑⲙⲥⲟ *S*, ⲧⲣⲉⲙ. *B*, ⲑⲙⲥⲉ- *SA*, ⲧⲣ. *A²*, ⲧⲣⲉⲙⲥⲉ-
B, ⲑⲙⲥⲟⲋ *S*, -ⲥⲁⲋ *A*, ⲧⲣⲉⲙⲥⲟⲋ *B*, ⲧⲣⲉⲙⲥⲁⲋ *F*, ⲑⲙⲥⲟ-
ⲉⲓⲧ† *S*, ⲧⲣⲉⲙⲥⲛⲟⲩⲧ† *B* vb tr, *make to sit, seat* (caus
of ϩⲙⲟⲟⲥ): 1 Cor 6 4 *SB* καθίζειν; Dan 2 21 *B*
καθιστάναι: K 85 *B* ⲫⲏ ⲉ(ⲧ)ⲧ.† جليس *assessor.*

With following preposition. c ⲉ-, *seat in place
of*: Si 10 15 *S* καθίζ. ἀντί; AM 228 *B* ⲁⲩⲧ. ⲙⲡⲁⲓ
ⲉⲡⲉϥⲙⲁ; c ⲉϫⲛ-, *upon*: Job 12 18 *SB*, Ac 2 30
S(*B* ⲑⲣⲉ- ϩⲉⲙⲥⲓ)καθίζ. ἐπί; 3 Kg 1 38 *S* ⲉⲡⲓⲕ. ἐπί;
Ps 131 11 *S*(*B* ⲭⲱ ϩⲓⲭⲉⲛ-)τιθέναι ἐπί; Aeg 274 *S*
ⲑⲉⲙⲥⲟϥ ⲉ.ⲡⲉⲑⲣⲟⲛⲟⲥ ἐνθρονίζειν; BMis 335 *S* sim
(var ϩⲓⲭⲛ-), C 43 37 *B* sim; ⲉϩⲣⲁⲓ, -ⲛⲓ ⲉϫⲛ-: ShP
130¹ 141 *S* nuns ⲉⲩⲑ.† ⲉⲣ. ⲉ.ⲡⲕⲁϩ, MIE 2 368 *B* ⲁⲩ-
ⲧⲣⲉⲙⲥⲟϥ ⲉⲣ. ⲉ.ⲡⲉⲑⲣⲟⲛⲟⲥ; c ⲙⲛ-, ⲛⲉⲙ-, *with*:
1 Kg 2 8 *S*(*B* ⲑⲣⲉ- ϩ.)καθίζ. μετά, Eph 2 6 *SB*
συγκ.; c ϩⲓ-, *at, on*: Mt 19 28 *B*(*S* ϩⲙⲟⲟⲥ)κ.
ἐπί; R 1 3 36 *S* ⲑⲙⲥⲟⲥ ϩⲓⲟⲩⲛⲁⲙ; c ⲥⲁ-, *at side*:
Eph 1 20 *BF*(*S* ϩⲓ-)κ. ἐν; Mani 2 *A²* ⲧⲣⲙⲥ[ⲉ] ⲡⲁϣⲏⲣⲉ ⲥⲁⲟⲩⲛⲉⲙ; c ϩⲛ-, ϩⲉⲛ-, *in*: Lam 3 6 *B* κ.
ἐν, Pro 18 16 *A*(*S* ⲥⲩⲛϭⲣⲓⲥⲧⲁ)καθιζάνειν παρά; Cl 44
5 *A* ⲁⲩⲑⲙⲥⲁⲩ ⲡϩⲏⲧϥ ἱδρύεσθαι; Jth 6 7 *S* ⲧⲓⲑ. ἐν;
LIb 5 *B* ⲧ. ⲡⲡⲁⲕⲁⲥ ϩⲉⲡⲡⲙⲁ; c ϩⲁⲧⲛ-, *beside
S*: R 1 2 35 ⲁⲧⲉⲡⲣⲟϩⲁⲓⲣⲉⲥⲓⲥ ⲡⲣⲟⲉⲓⲡⲉ ⲑⲙⲥⲟⲟⲩ ϩ.
ⲡⲉϫⲥ̅, BMis 204 ⲁⲩⲑⲙⲥⲉ ⲡⲉϥⲉⲓⲱⲧ ϩ.ⲡⲧⲁⲫⲟⲥ; c
ϩⲓϫⲛ-, *upon*: AM 282 *B* ⲁⲩⲧ. ⲙⲡⲓⲁⲣⲭⲏⲉⲡⲓⲥⲕ· ϩ.
ⲡⲉϥⲑⲣⲟⲛⲟⲥ ⲕ. ⲉⲛ; Tri 583 *S* ⲑⲙⲥⲟⲡ ϩ.ⲛⲉⲑⲣ. جلس
لى; C 43 11 *B* bade ⲧ. ⲙⲡⲓⲙⲁⲕⲁⲣⲓⲟⲥ ϩⲓⲭⲱϥ.

With following adverb. c ⲉϩⲣⲁⲓ *S*, *set down*:
Deu 25 2 (*B* om ⲉϩ.), Lam 3 6 (*B* do)καθίζ.; Ryl 94
108 God shall ⲑⲙⲥⲟⲥ (sc martyr's mother) ⲉϩ. at
Judgment.

†ϩⲙⲉϥ v †ϩⲙⲉ.

ⲧⲁϩⲛⲟ *B*(*S* once) vb tr, *hinder*: Nu 11 28 (*S* =
Gk), Ps 39 10 (*S* do), Mk 9 38 (*SF* do)κωλύειν; Ac
24 4 (*S* †ϩⲓⲥⲉ), 1 Thes 2 18 (*S* †ϫⲣⲟⲡ, *F* κωλυ)
ἐγκόπτειν; Ex 32 12 (*S* ⲗⲟ)παύειν; Pro 3 27 ⲧ. ⲛ-
ⲧⲟⲧⲋ (*S* do, *A* ⲟⲩⲁϩⲣⲉ)ἀπέχ.; 4 Kg 4 24 ἐπέχ·, Ge
22 13 *B*(*S* ⲙⲟⲩⲣ), 2 Kg 6 6 (*S* ⲁⲙⲁϩⲧⲉ)κατέχ., Ps
76 10 (*S* do)συνέχ.; Jo 20 23 (*SA²* do)κρατεῖν; Nu
10 21 (*S* ⲧⲁϩⲟ ⲉⲣⲁⲧⲋ), Ac 8 38 (*S* ⲁϩⲉ ⲣⲁⲧⲋ)ἱστάναι;
Jer 44 13 ⲧ. (l ? ⲧⲁϩⲟ), ⲁⲙⲟⲛⲓ συλλαμβάνειν; Deu
24 14 (*S* diff)ἀποστερεῖν; PO 14 362 who may ⲧ.
ⲡⲡⲓⲑⲛⲟⲩ?, C 43 152 ⲡⲉϥⲙⲁϩⲧⲁ ⲧ. ⲙⲙⲟⲛ, Tri 382
S ⲧ. ⲛϣⲡⲙⲟⲟϣⲉ ⲙⲡⲣⲏ خمد; intr, *be hindered*:
Is 43 6 (*S* ⲁⲙ.)κω.; Ge 8 2 (*S* ϭⲱ)συνέχεσθαι; 1
Pet 3 7 (*S* ⲕⲁ ⲧⲟⲟⲧⲋ ⲉⲃⲟⲗ)ἐγκόπτεσθαι; Nu 17 15
(*S* ϩⲣⲟⲕ)κοπᾶν; C 86 266 ⲁⲓⲧ. ⲛⲛⲓⲉⲣ ⲡⲣⲟⲥⲕⲩⲛⲏ,
BSM 32 ⲙⲡⲉⲥⲧ. ⲛϫⲉ ⲟⲩⲙⲟⲩⲅⲓ=BMis 374 *S* ⲗⲟ.

With preposition or adverb. c ⲉ-, *hinder from*:
2 Chr 7 13 συνέχ.; Va 57 131 none can ⲧ. ⲙⲙⲟⲛ ⲉ-
ⲡⲁⲓⲣⲱⲃ ⲉⲙⲡⲟⲇίζειν; vbal: Mt 19 14 (*S* = Gk), Ac
16 6 (*S* do, *F* ϣⲱϣⲧ)κω. inf; C 43 54 ⲧ. ⲙⲙⲟⲕ ⲉ-

ⲑⲣⲓϣⲉⲡⲕ, Cat 46 ⲧ. ⲡⲧⲣⲟⲣⲙⲏ ⲉϣⲧⲉⲙⲧⲱⲟⲩⲛ; intr:
Is 28 6 (*S* = Gk), 1 Cor 14 39 (*S* do, *F* ϣ.) κω.
inf; c ⲉⲃⲟⲗ ϩⲁ-, sim: Ge 23 6 κω. ἀπό; Ps 118
101 (*S* diff) κω. ἐκ; Am 4 7 ἀνέχ. ἐκ; AM 229 ⲧ.
ⲡⲟⲩⲟⲛ ⲛⲓⲃⲉⲛ ⲉⲃ. ϩⲁⲛϣⲉⲙϣⲓ; c ⲉϥϩⲁⲣⲟⲩ, *set
back, repel*: Va 57 190 ⲉⲩⲁⲙⲟⲛⲓ ⲉϫⲱⲟⲩ (sc beggars)
ⲉⲩⲧ. ⲙⲙⲟⲟⲩ ⲉⲫ.

——— nn, with ⲁⲧϩⲛⲉ-, *without hindrance*: MG
25 367 gave self ⲁⲧ. ⲧ. ⲉⲡⲧⲏⲣϥ to further rigours,
PO 14 340 bent knee ⲁⲧ. ⲧ. ⲙⲫⲣⲏϯ ⲛⲟⲩⲕⲣⲓⲕⲟⲥ (cf
Is 58 5).

ⲁⲧⲧ.,*unhindered*: TEuch 1 353 grant them us ⲛⲁⲧⲉⲣ ⲕⲱⲗⲩⲛ ⲛⲁⲧⲧ.

ϫⲓⲛⲧ., *hindering, obstructing*: 3 Kg 8 35 ⲛϫ. ⲛⲧⲫⲉ
συνέχεσθαι.

ⲧⲉϩⲛⲉ *SA*, -ⲛⲓ *BF* nn f, *forehead*: 1 Kg 17 49 *SB*,
Is 48 4 *SB*, Ap 7 3 *SBF*, P 44 68 *S* اﺟﺒﺔ μέτωπον;
K 51 11th lunar station 'ⲋ; PS 344 *S* ⲥⲫⲣⲁϯϫⲉ ⲙ-
ⲙⲟⲟⲩ ⲉⲧⲧ., ShA 2 64 *S* ornament ⲉⲧⲕⲱⲧⲉ ⲉⲧⲟⲩⲧ., El·
98 *A* name written on ⲧⲟⲩⲧ., Z 610 *S* ⲕⲗⲟⲙ ϩⲓϫⲛ-
ⲧⲉⲥⲧ., MIE 2 347 *B* woman with migraine puts sand
ⲉϫⲉⲛⲧⲉⲥⲧ. & is healed (cf under ⲧⲁϭⲥⲉ).   As
place-name: ⲧϫⲉϩⲛⲉ (Hall 132 = Synax 2 184 14
دﻩ), ⲧⲉϩⲛⲉ (BMOr 6201 A 28). *Cf* Ryl Dem 3 40.

ⲑⲛⲟ *pound* v ⲧⲏⲛⲟ sf.

ⲧϦⲛⲟ, ⲑ. *S*, ⲧϦⲛⲟ *A*, ⲧϦⲛⲉ-, ⲑ., ⲑⲛⲛⲉ-, ⲑⲛⲟ- *S*,
ⲧϦⲛⲟ- *A*, ⲧϦⲛⲟⲋ, ⲑ. *S*, ⲑⲛⲁⲋ *Sᵃ*, ⲧϦⲛⲁⲋ *A²*, ⲑⲛⲏⲩ† *S*,
ⲧϦⲛⲁⲓⲧ† *A²* vb tr, a *make to approach* (caus of ϩⲱⲛ),
mostly c ⲉ-: ShC 73 161 ⲉⲩⲛⲁⲑⲛⲉ ⲡⲉⲅⲗⲟϭ ⲉⲡⲥⲱⲙⲁ
ⲉⲧⲙⲟⲟⲩⲧ, Mani 1 *A²* ⲡⲉⲧⲟⲩϩⲛ ⲛⲉⲧⲧ.†; refl, *approach*: ShBM 211 ⲧϦⲛⲟⲕ ⲉⲡⲉⲓⲙⲁ, ShA 2 256 none
may ⲧϦⲛⲟϥ (sic l) ⲉⲟⲩⲁ to speak with him, Mani 2
A² ⲉ]ⲩⲁⲧϦⲛⲁⲩ ⲁⲡⲉⲅⲉⲣⲏⲩ; c ⲉϩⲟⲩⲛ, ⲁϩ., as last:
LCyp 27 ⲑⲛⲟⲕ ⲉϩ. ϩⲛⲟⲩⲡⲁⲣⲣⲏⲥⲓⲁ προσπελάζειν;
ⲉϩ. ⲉ-: Pro 24 15 *A*(*S* ϩⲱⲡⲧ)προσάγειν dat; ShA 1
115 ⲁⲩⲧϦⲛⲉ ⲡⲁⲓ ⲉϩ. ⲉⲣⲟ, ib 2 103 ⲛⲡⲉ ⲑⲛⲟⲟⲩ ⲉϩ.
ⲉⲣⲟϥ, Mor 51 22 ⲁϥⲑ. ⲙⲡⲟⲩⲉⲛⲉⲥⲟⲟⲩ of wine ⲉϩ.
ⲉⲡⲧⲟⲡⲟⲥ; refl: ShC 73 124 ⲛⲥⲉⲧϦⲛⲟⲟⲩ ⲉϩ. ⲉⲙⲙⲁ,
ib 35 worthy ⲑⲛⲟⲡ ⲉϩ. ⲉⲣⲟϥ, Aeg 216 dare ⲉⲑⲛⲟϥ
ⲉϩ.....ⲉⲛϣⲱⲙⲉ.   b *hire*: Deu 23 4 (var ⲑⲛⲛⲉ-,
B ⲧⲁϩⲟ ϥⲃⲉϫⲉ), Is 46 6 (*B* ϭⲓ), Hos 3 2 *A* (prob
l ⲧϦ., *B* = Gk), Mt 20 1 (*B* ⲧⲁϩⲟ)μισθοῦσθαι; R 1
4 39 ⲁϥϩⲛⲉ ⲟⲩⲁⲙⲟⲩⲅⲗ *conducere*; ShC 42 83
many ⲧϦⲛⲉ ⲣⲱⲙⲉ ϩⲁⲡⲉⲩⲃⲉⲕⲉ *with their own wages*
to serve in their stead, ShViK 929 128 sim paral
ⲧⲟⲟⲩ, ShR 2 3 23 ⲉⲁⲕⲧϦⲛⲉ (sic) ϩⲣⲧⲱⲣ ⲙⲡⲟⲛⲏⲣⲟⲥ, P 129¹⁴ 129 Zeus & Athena gone ϫⲉⲕⲁⲥ ⲉⲩ-
(ⲉ)ⲑ. [ⲛ]ⲉⲛⲡⲉ̄ ⲛⲓⲣⲉⲑⲛⲟⲥ to aid us, ViK 9519 workmen ⲉⲩⲑ.† ⲉⲣⲟϥ, BHom 82 could not ⲑⲛⲟⲟⲩ ⲉⲧⲙ-
ⲡⲧⲣⲉⲩϣⲙϣⲉ ⲉⲓⲇⲱⲗⲟⲛ, CO 218 ⲁⲕⲑⲛⲟⲓ ⲉⲧⲣⲁⲣ
ϩⲱⲃ, ib 185 *Sᵃ* hirelings ⲛⲧⲁⲑⲛⲁⲁⲩⲟⲩ, J 68 40 *Sᵃ*
ⲁⲓⲑⲛⲱ ⲟⲩⲃⲏⲥⲡⲛⲧ ϩⲁⲣⲁϥ *for him*, PLond 4 445 ⲁⲛⲟ.

ⲡⲓⲉⲣⲅⲁⲧⲏⲥ, Rec 6 65 ϣⲁⲕⲟⲩⲱϣ ⲑⲡⲓ ⲣⲱⲙⲉ, Wess 15 152 ⲁϥⲑ. ⲡⲉⲥⲃ[ⲩ]ⲕⲏ ⲛ[ⲁⲥ *settled her wage*; as nn: Deu 23 18 (*B* ⲃⲉϫⲉ) *μίσθωμα*.

ⲧϩⲡⲟ *SA*², ⲑ. *S*, ⲧϩⲫⲟ, ⲧⲫⲟ, ⲧⲫⲉ- *B*, ⲡϩⲉ- *F*, ⲧϩⲡⲟ⸗, ⲑ. *S*, ⲑⲡⲁ⸗, (ⲧ)ⲫⲁ⸗ *S^f*, ⲧⲫⲟ⸗ *B* vb tr, *cause to reach, bring back, accompany* (caus of ⲡⲱϩ): Jth 10 15 *S*, Ac 20 38 *B*(*S* + ⲉⲃⲟⲗ), 1 Cor 16 6 *S*(var *S^f*)*B* *προπέμπειν*, Ge 24 54 *B* *ἐκπ.*, *ib* 12 20 *S*(*B* + ⲉⲃ.) *συμπροπ.*; Nu 35 25 *B*(*S* = Gk), Hos 11 11 *B*(*A* ⲕⲧⲟ ⲁϩⲣⲏⲓ), Mk 9 12 *B*(*S* ϫⲱⲕ ⲉⲃ.)*F* ⲡϩⲉ-, Ac 1 6 *B* (*S* ϯ) *ἀποκαθιστάναι*; R 1 4 35 *S* ⲉϥⲉⲑ. ⲛⲛⲉⲧⲟⲩⲱϣ ⲉⲃⲱⲕ *ducere*; TRit 500 *B* funeral hymn (deceased *loq*) ϯⲡⲁⲧ. ⲙⲙⲱⲧⲉⲛ ⲱ ⲡⲁⲓⲟϯ اودعكم *bid farewell*; Gu 21 *S* go with me ϣⲁⲛⲧⲉⲕⲑⲡⲟⲓ ⲉⲡⲁⲙⲁ, DeV 2 163*B* ⲧⲫⲟϥ ⲉⲡⲓⲧⲁⲫⲟⲥ, ManiH 86*A*² ⲛ]ⲉⲩⲧ. ⲙⲙⲁϥⲡⲉ ...ϣⲁⲛⲧⲉϥⲡⲱϩ, BM 288 78 *S* ⲑ. ⲙⲙⲟⲓ ⲉϩⲟⲩⲛ ⲉⲧⲡⲟⲗⲓⲥ, CaiEuch 588 *B* ⲧⲫⲱⲟⲩ ⲉϧⲟⲩⲛ ⲉⲟⲩⲗⲩⲙⲏⲛ; c ⲉⲃⲟⲗ, *lead forth*: Ac 15 3 *SB*, Z 326 *S* all city ⲑⲡⲟϥ ⲉⲃ. *προπ.*, Ac 17 10 *B*(*S* ϫⲟⲟⲩ) *ἐκπ.*, *ib* 15 *B*(*S* = Gk) *καθισ.*, R 1 1 45 *S* ⲉⲧⲣⲉⲩⲑⲡⲟⲟⲩ ⲉⲃ. ⲛⲧⲅⲁⲗⲓⲗⲁⲓⲁ *ἀποκ. ἕως*, *ib* 49 *S* ⲁⲩⲑⲡⲟⲟⲩ ⲉⲃ. *ἀπολύειν*; Mor 40 48 *S* ⲁϥⲑⲡⲟϥ ⲉⲃ. = MG 25 275 *B* om ⲉⲃ., BMis 163 *S* ⲉⲣⲉⲡⲁⲣⲭⲱⲛ ⲑ. ⲙⲙⲟⲟⲩ ⲉⲃ. = BSM 72 *B* passive, BMis 187 *S* ⲉⲩⲑ. ⲙⲙⲟϥ (corpse) ⲉⲃ., PSBA 29 194 *S* sim (ⲧⲡⲟ), Mor 27 24 *S^f* ⲛⲥⲉⲫⲁⲩ ⲉⲃ. = BMis 367 *S* = Va 63 3 *B*, Mani 2 *A*² ⲧ. ⲙⲙⲁϥ ⲁⲃ., Gu 98 *S* ⲁϥⲑⲫⲟⲟⲩ (*sic*) ⲉⲃ. ⲉⲣⲁⲧϥ, Miss 4 833 *S* ⲑⲡⲟϥ ⲉⲃ. ϣⲁⲡⲣⲟ, C 89 197 *B* ⲧ. ⲙⲙⲟϥ ϣⲁⲡⲓϫⲟⲓ.

In MG 25 359 rope weaver (walks backward) ϣⲁⲛⲧⲉϥϫⲫⲟ (*sic* MS) ⲉϯϫⲟⲓ *προσεγγίζειν* dat, for which *l* ? ⲧϩⲫⲟ.

ⲧⲱϩⲣ *v* ⲧⲱⲣϩ.

(ⲑⲣⲕⲟ), ⲑⲣⲕⲉ- *A*² vb tr, *make mild*, *assuage* (caus of ϩⲣⲁⲕ): Mani H 76 ⲛⲧⲁⲩⲑ. ⲧⲟⲩⲃⲗ[ⲕⲉ].

ⲑⲉⲣⲟⲩⲱϭⲉ *S* *v* above p 432.

ⲧϩⲣϣⲟ, ⲑ., ⲑⲁⲣ. (once) *S*, ⲑⲉⲣϣⲁ *S^f*, -ϣⲟ *B*, ⲑ(ⲉ)ⲣϣⲉ- *S*, -ϣⲟ⸗ *SB*, -ϣⲁ⸗ *S^fA* vb tr, *make heavy*, so (mostly) *terrify* (caus of ϩⲣⲟϣ, *cf* ⲧⲁⲣϣⲟ): BHom 95 footsteps ⲑ. ⲛⲧⲁϫⲓⲥⲉ (sea *loq*) *βαρεῖν*; Sa 17 21 (var ϩⲣⲟϣ) *ἐπικεῖσθαι*; Lev 26 6 (*B* ⲛⲟⲩϣⲡ), Job 7 14 (*B* ϯ ϩⲟϯ), Mic 4 4 *SA*(*B* do), 2 Cor 10 9 (*B* ϯ ϩⲉⲗⲓ) *ἐκφοβεῖν*; 2 Kg 22 5 (var ⲑⲣϣⲁ⸗), Sa 17 3 *θαμβεῖν*; *ib* 4 *ἐκταράσσειν*; *ib* 6 *ἐκδειματοῦν*; Hab 2 17 *A*)*B* ⲛ.) *πτοεῖν*; 2 Kg 17 2 *ἐξιστάναι*; K 233 *B* ⲁϥⲑⲉⲣϣⲱϥ (*l* -ⲟϥ) وبّخ، وتب, *reprove*; BG 58 Adam asleep ⲁϥⲑⲣϣⲟϥ ϩⲛⲧⲁⲡⲁⲓⲥⲑⲏⲥⲓⲁ, ShP 130⁵ 34 ⲡⲉⲧⲛⲁⲑⲉⲣϣⲉ ⲡⲉⲩⲧⲃⲛⲏ ϩⲛⲟⲩⲉⲧⲡⲱ, ClPr 43 13 ⲉⲕⲑ. ⲙⲡϩⲓⲥⲉ ⲉϫⲙⲡⲉⲃⲓⲛⲏ, Mart Ign 882 *B* ⲡⲏ ⲉⲧⲉⲣ ⲉⲡⲟϫⲗⲓⲛ ⲟⲩⲟϩ ⲉⲧⲑ. ⲙⲡⲉⲕϫⲟⲓ, J 66 8 lest suddenly ⲡⲙⲟⲩ ⲑⲣϣⲟⲓ, BM 1161 letter ⲁⲓⲑⲁⲣ. ⲡⲥⲁϫⲟ ⲕⲁⲗⲱⲥ, Ryl 94 99 martyrs ⲛⲧⲁⲩⲑⲉⲣϣⲟⲟⲩ ϩⲛⲧⲡⲓⲣⲁ (*πεῖρα*) ⲛⲛⲃⲁⲥⲁⲛⲟⲥ, Pcod 38 if this thought come ⲛϥⲑⲣϣⲟⲕ = *F* + ϩⲓⲥⲓ, OratCyp 47 *S^f* ⲁⲓⲑ. ⲛⲛⲁϭⲱⲛⲧ *repress*; intr: Mor 40 22 when he heard ⲁϥⲑ. = *ib* 39 30 ⲁϩⲉ ⲣⲁⲧϥ = C 43 52 *B* ϣⲱⲡⲓ ϧⲉⲛⲟⲩⲧⲱⲙⲛⲧ; as nn m: P 44 87 ⲡⲃⲁⲣⲉⲓ (*βαρύ*) · ⲡⲑ. ثقلة.

ⲧⲱϩⲥ *SAA*²*F*, ⲑ.*B*, ⲧⲉϩⲥ- *S* ⲧ, ⲁ. *SA*², ⲑⲁ. *B*, ⲧⲉϩⲥⲉ- *F*, ⲧⲁϩⲥ⸗ *SS^fA*, ⲧⲟϩⲥ⸗ *S*, ⲑⲁϩⲥ⸗ *B*, ⲧⲉϩⲥ⸗ *F*, ⲧⲁϩⲥ† *S*, ⲑ.† *B* vb **I** tr, *anoint*: Lev 4 3 *S*(*B*†), Ps 26 1 *SB*, Ez 43 3 *B*(HCons *l* ⲑⲉϩⲥ), Hos 8 10 *S*(*B* ϫⲓⲛⲑ.), 2 Cor 1 21 *SBF*(P 132² 88) *χρίειν*; Nu 3 3 *SB*, Ez 13 10 *B*(*S* ϫⲱϩ), Mt 6 17 *SBF*, Jo 12 3 *SA*²*B* *ἀλείφειν*; Ps 140 5 *S*(*B* ϯ ⲕⲉⲛⲓ) *λιπαίνειν*; ShClPr 24 360 *S* ⲉⲣⲉⲡⲉϥⲛⲉϩ ⲧ. ⲙⲙⲟⲟⲩ, Ryl 109 *S* ⲧⲁϩⲥ ⲡⲉⲕϩⲟ, Mani 1 *A*² ⲧ. ⲙⲙⲁϥ ϩⲛⲧⲉϥϭⲁⲙ, C 43 103 *B* ⲑ. ⲛϯⲁⲗⲟⲩ, BKU 1 26 (8116 b)*F* ⲧⲉϩⲥⲉ ⲧⲁⲡⲉ (*sic*) ⲙⲡⲉ(ⲧ)ϯ ⲕⲁⲥ, AJSL 46 246 *S* ⲛⲅⲧⲟϩⲥϥ (*ter*).

With following preposition. c ⲉ-, *pour*, *smear upon*: Mor 37 44 *S* ⲧⲉϩⲥ ⲛⲉϩ ⲉⲣⲟϥ *ἀλ.* dat; Miss 4 122 *S* ⲉⲩⲧⲉϩⲥ ⲛⲉϩ ⲉⲣⲟϥ ϩⲛⲛⲉⲩϭⲓϫ = C 89 88 *B*, TurM 9 *S* ⲧⲁϩⲥ ⲉⲣⲱⲧⲉ ⲉⲣⲟⲥ, ROC 27 151 *B* oil ⲑ. ⲙⲙⲟϥ ⲉⲡⲉⲥⲥⲱⲙⲁ, Z 628 *S* ⲧ. ⲉⲛⲉⲧⲱ ⲛⲯⲱⲣⲁ (*cf ib* ·ⲛⲛⲉⲧⲟ); c ⲛ-, *anoint with*: Nu 6 15 *S*(*B* ϧⲉⲛ-), Ps 88 20 *SA*(Cl)*B* *χ. ἐν*, Jth 10 3 *S* *χ.* dat, Ps 44 8 *SB*, AM 6 6 *AB*, He 1 9 *SBF* *χ.* acc, Lev 2 4 *S*(*B* ⲟⲩⲱϣⲉⲙ ϧⲉⲛ-) *διαχ. ἐν*; 2 Kg 14 2 *S* *ἀλ.* acc, Jo 11 2 *SA*²*B* *ἀλ.* dat; Ps 22 5 *SB* *λιπ. ἐν*; Mk 14 8 *SB* ⲧ. ⲡⲥⲱϭⲛ *μυρίζειν*; ShR 2 3 8 *S* ⲧⲁϩⲥϥ ⲛⲟⲩⲛⲉϩ, AM 21 *B* ⲁϥⲑⲁϩⲥⲧⲉⲛ ⲙⲡⲓⲛⲉϩ, Miss 4 528 *S* oil ⲉⲥⲧⲁϩⲥ (*l* -ⲥⲉ) ⲙⲙⲟϥ = C 89 47 *B*, Mor 50 61 *S^f* sim ⲧⲁϩⲥⲉⲥ ⲙⲙⲁϥ, PMich 4932 *S* oil that Isis ⲧⲁϩⲥϥ (ⲛ)ⲛⲕⲉⲉⲥ ⲡⲉⲩⲥⲓⲣ (Osiris); *as, for*: Jud 9 15 *S*, 1 Kg 9 16 *S* (var ⲉ-) *χ. εἰς*, Ann 18 68 *S* ⲧⲁϩⲥⲕ ... ⲛⲟⲩϣⲱⲥ, Va 63 22 *B* ⲁϥⲑⲁϩⲥⲉϥ ⲛⲟⲩⲣⲟ; c ϩⲓ- *S*, *with*: TurM 9 ⲧ. ⲉⲣⲟⲃ ϩⲓⲱⲱϥ, Cai 42573 1 ⲧⲁϩⲥ ⲡⲉϥϩⲟ ϩⲓⲛⲉϩ; c ϩⲛ-, ϧⲉⲛ-, sim: Ex 29 2 *B*(*S* ⲟⲩⲱϣⲙ ϩⲓ-), Ps 151 4 *B*(*S* ⲛ-) *χ. ἐν*, Ac 10 38 *SB* *χ.* dat; ShR 2 3 47 *S* ⲡⲉⲧⲧⲱϩⲥ (*sic l*) ⲙⲙⲟϥ ϩⲛⲛⲥⲟϭⲛ, AM 5 *B* ⲑⲁϩⲥⲟⲩ ϧⲉⲛⲛⲓⲥⲟϫⲉⲛ; ⲉⲃⲟⲗ ϩⲛ-: Deu 28 40 *S*(*B* diff) *χ.* acc.

—— nn m *SA*²*B*, ⲧⲁϩⲥ f *S*(Si), *anointing*: Si 38 39 *S* ⲧⲧ., Dan 9 26 *SB* *χρίσμα*; Is 61 3 *B*(*S* ⲥⲟϭⲛ) *ἄλιμμα*; PS 197 *S* ⲡⲧ. ⲙⲡⲛⲉⲩⲙⲁⲧⲓⲕⲟⲛ, BSM 32 *B* ⲡⲑ. ⲛⲧⲁⲫⲉ; ⲛⲉϩ ⲙⲡⲧ.: Lev 21 12 *S*(var ⲛⲧ., *B* om ⲛⲉϩ) *ἔλαιον τ. χρίσματος*; ShCaiCoptMus *S* ⲡⲛ ⲙⲡⲧ.; ϫⲓ ⲧ. *SA*², *get anointment*: 1 Jo 2 20 *S*(*B* diff) *χ. ἔχειν*; BG 30 *S* ⲁϥϫⲓ ⲙⲡⲧ. ϩⲓⲧⲛ-, Mani 2 *A*² ⲡⲁⲛⲣ...ⲁϥϫⲓ ⲧ. ⲡϩⲏⲧϥ.

ⲣⲉϥⲧ., *anointer*: Bor 248 56 *S* ϩⲉⲛⲣ. ⲡϩⲉⲛⲕⲟⲟⲩⲉ for this fight (*cf ἀλείπτης*), Dif 1 30 *B* Samuel ⲣⲉϥⲑ. ⲛϩⲁⲛⲟⲩⲣⲱⲟⲩ.

ϫⲓⲛⲑ. *B*, *anointing*: Dan 9 24 (*S* vb), Hos 8 10 (*A* vb) *χ.* vb; TEuch 1 312 ⲙⲩⲣⲟⲛ...ⲟⲩϫ. ⲛⲧⲉ ⲟⲩⲥⲫⲣⲁⲅⲓⲥ.

ⲧⲁϧⲧ[1] *S.AA²B*, ⲧⲁϧⲧⲉ, ⲧⲁϩ²*S*, ⲧⲁⲧϧ³*B*, ⲧⲉϧⲧ*F* nn m, *lead*: Si 22 15 *S*¹ (var ⲧⲁϧⲧϧ), Zech 5 7 *S*¹*AB*¹, C 86 283 *B*³(var¹) μόλυβδος, Nu 31 22 *S*¹*B*³ (do), Ez 22 18 *B*³(do) μόλιβος, P 44 66 *S* ⲙⲟⲗⲓⲃⲍⲟⲍⲉⲥ · ⲡⲁⲅⲁⲡ ⲁⲏⲧ.¹ رصاص; PS 151 *S* ⲁⲓⲣ ⲑⲉ ⲡⲟⲩⲧ.¹, EW 83 *B* ⲧ.¹ ⲉϥϩⲉⲣⲃⲉⲣ, Mani 2 *A*² ⲡⲟⲩⲥⲱⲙⲁⲡⲉ ⲡⲧ., BMis 224 *S* ϧⲁⲧ, ϧⲟⲙⲡⲧ, ⲧ.¹, Mor 30 33 *F* ⲟⲩⲧ., DeV 2 196 *B* ⲟⲩⲧ.³ (var¹) ⲉϥϫⲗⲓϫⲓ (γλύφειν) *leaden casket*, C 43 141 *B* ⲡϩⲟⲟⲥ ⲡⲧ., ib 86 102 *B* ⲥⲕⲉⲩⲟⲥ ⲡⲧ.,³ Va 57 47 *B* ⲡⲟⲧⲏⲣⲓⲟⲛ ⲡⲧ.,³ Ryl 238 *S* ⲉϩⲁⲥⲕⲉⲗⲟⲡ ⲡⲧ.¹, AZ 23 115 *S* ⲧ.¹ ⲡⲁⲗⲁⲅ, ⲧ.¹ ⲡⲕⲁⲙⲏ, P 43 241 *S* ⲧ.¹ ⲉϥⲣⲱⲕϩ (*l* ⲣⲟ.) رصاص مخروق, PMéd 293 *S*² sim, Z 630 *S* ⲥⲕⲟⲣⲉⲁ ⲡⲧ.¹; ⲧⲁϧⲧϧ *S*: R 1 4 57 ⲕⲟⲅⲙϥⲟⲥ ⲡⲧ. μολυβίς; Ryl 94 102 *water froze like* ⲟⲩⲧ., ViK 9497 ⲁϥⲧⲣⲉⲡⲧ. ⲱϧⲣ, P 129¹⁶ 64 ⲡⲧ. ⲃⲱⲗ ⲉⲃⲟⲗ, BMis 259 ϩⲣⲟϣ ⲡⲑⲉ ⲡⲟⲩⲧ., PChass 1 26 ⲟⲩⲧ. ⲣⲱⲕϧϥ, AZ 23 109 ⲧ. ⲡⲉⲡⲉϩ[ⲟⲟ]ϣ *Ethiopian lead*, Mor 56 43 ⲧⲩⲡⲧⲩⲭⲟⲡ ⲡⲧ. = GuDorm 348 ϧⲟⲙⲡⲧ; ⲟ, ⲟⲓ ⲡⲧⲁϧⲧ, *be leaden*: P 131³ 135 *S* ⲡⲉϥⲟ ⲡⲧ.¹ & *afterwards of gold*, MG 25 197 *B* soul ⲟⲓ ⲡⲧ.³

ⲧⲁϧⲧⲏⲟⲩⲧ *B*　v ⲧⲁⲧϧⲟ.

ⲧⲁϧⲧϧ, ⲧⲟϧⲧⲉϧ (nn), ⲧⲁϧⲧ *S*, ⲑⲟϩⲧⲉϩ *B*, ⲧⲉϧ-ⲧⲱϧ *S*, ⲑⲉϩⲟⲩϩ *B*, ⲧⲁϧⲧϧ *O*, ⲧⲉϧⲧⲱϧ† *S*, ⲑⲉϩⲑⲱϩ† *B* vb tr, *mix, confuse* (cf ⲧⲱϧ): Nu 11 4† *S*(*B* ⲙⲟⲩϫⲧ nn) ἐπίμικτος; Lev 13 4† *S* gloss on ⲕⲣⲙ-ⲣⲱⲙ (*B* ⲟⲓ ⲛϧⲗⲟⲗ) ἀμαυρός; Ez 7 23 *SB* φυρμὸν ποιεῖν; ShA 1 451 *S* ⲉϧⲧ.† ϧⲛⲡⲉϥⲙⲉⲉⲩⲉ, ShC 73 98 *S* ϩⲉⲛⲗⲟⲅⲓⲥⲙⲟⲥ ⲉϧⲧ.†, Mun 88 *S* ⲉⲕⲥϧⲣⲁϧⲧ ⲛⲧⲧ.† ⲁⲡ, Cat 18 *B* ϣⲁϩⲉⲣ ⲡⲕⲉⲑⲉϩⲑⲱϩⲟⲩ (*sc* words) ϩⲉⲡⲡⲟⲩϩⲏⲧ, Bor 240 90 *S* ⲉⲧϣⲧⲟⲣⲧⲣ ⲁⲩⲱ ⲉⲧⲧⲁϧⲧ ⲛⲡⲁ ⲡⲟⲩⲱϩ, Mor 56 24 *S* heretics ⲧ. ⲡⲧⲙⲛⲧϩⲁⲡ-ⲗⲟⲥ of faith, HL 121 *B* soul ⲑ.† ⲁⲡ ⲁⲗⲗⲁ ⲉⲥϫⲏ ϩⲉⲡ-ⲟⲩⲥⲉⲙⲛⲏ, Z 269 *S* not perfect gentleman (ἐλεύθερος) but ⲉϧⲧ.† like mule, AZ 23 116 *S* ingredients ⲧⲉϧⲧⲟϧⲟ[ⲩ], Hor 83 *O* ⲧⲁϧⲧϧϥ (context?); intr *S*: ViK 9179 ⲁⲡⲁⲥⲡⲉ ⲧ. at Babel, Z 570 consort not with juniors ⲛⲛⲉⲕⲧⲁϧⲧ & go backward.

── nn m *SB*, *mixture, confusion*: Ryl 113 *S* ϩⲁⲗⲏ · ⲡⲧⲟⲣⲧⲉϧ, P 44 95 *S* ⲟⲩⲧ. خلطة opp ⲙⲛⲧⲁⲧⲧ. انزال, BMOr 8775 123 *B* ⲡⲓⲱ. اختلاط تخليط; Mor 25 23 *S* ⲡⲟϧ ⲡⲧ. ϩⲓⲙⲁ ⲛⲓⲙ = Va 61 118 *B*, Va 58 183 *B* ϫⲓⲡⲉⲣ ⲛⲥⲓϫⲁϧⲓⲡ opp ⲡⲓⲱ. ϩⲉⲡⲡⲓϩⲓⲣ, P 131⁵ 70 *S* ⲙⲟⲩϫⲧ ⲡⲓⲙ ϩⲓⲧⲁϧⲉⲧ ⲡⲓⲙ.

ⲙⲉⲧⲟ. *B*, *intercourse, society*: K 93 عشر (*sic l*).

ⲑⲟⲟⲩⲧ (oftenest), ⲑⲱ. (BMis 183, JA '05 450). ⲑⲱⲱ (BMar 102), ⲑⲟⲟⲧ (ST 123), ⲑⲟⲉ (Leyd 208) *S*, ⲑⲁⲩⲧ (CO 39, BKU 1 48), ⲑⲁⲟⲩⲧ (Hall 113) *Sᵃ*, ⲑⲱⲟⲩⲧ *B*, ⲑⲁⲟⲅⲉ (Mor 24 20), ⲑⲁⲅⲁ (Ny Karlsberg Æ 1 1544) *F*, name of 1st month, Gk Θωύθ &c (Preisigke *W.buch* 3 46, in Græco-Copt always ⲑⲱⲟ), Ar توت. Thôth (god ⲑⲟⲟⲩⲧ R 1 3 67), in names: Πα-θώτης, -θώντης, Ταθ., Ψενθ. (Preisigke), ⲡⲁⲡⲁ ⲑⲟ-

ⲟⲩⲧ(AZ 21 100); in place-names: Τεκερκεθώθ(BGU 557), ⲡⲉⲣⲕⲓⲑⲟⲟⲩⲧ (Lant 11), Περκεθαύτ (Wess 20), Κερτοῦτ (PLond 4).

ⲧϫ　v ⲧⲁϩ.

ⲧⲱϫ　v ⲧⲱⲕ *kindle* **B**.

ⲧⲁϫⲟ *SA*², ⲧⲁϫⲉ- *A*, ⲧⲁϫⲟϥ *S* (?), -ϫⲁϥ *AA*², -ϫⲁⲓⲧ† *A*² vb tr, *judge, condemn* (cf ⲱϫ): Jo 16 11 *A*² ⲧⲁϫⲁϥ (*S* ⲧϫⲁⲉⲓⲟ, *B* ϯϩⲁⲡ), Cl 11 1 *A* ⲁⲩⲧⲁϫⲉ ⲧϫⲱⲣⲁ κρίνειν; ib 17 4 *A* ϥⲧ. ⲙⲙⲁϥ κατηγορεῖν; ib 51 2 *A* ⲧⲁϫⲁϥ κατάγνωσιν φέρειν; Mani 1 *A*² ⲉⲩⲁⲧⲁϫⲁϥ ⲧϩⲉ ⲡⲡⲓⲁⲥⲉⲃⲏⲥ, ib 2 *A*² ⲡϥⲧ. ⲡⲡⲉⲧⲧ.† ⲕⲁⲧⲁ ⲡⲟⲩϩⲏⲧ ⲉⲧⲃⲁⲃⲥ, BM 1118 5 *S*]ϫⲓ ⲧⲕⲁ ⲉⲡⲧⲱϥ (*ie* ⲡⲧⲟϥ, ? ⲡⲧⲟⲟⲧϥ) ⲧⲉⲕⲧⲁϫⲟⲩ, ib 7 ⲃⲱⲕ ϣⲁⲡⲧⲉⲕ ⲧⲁ-ϫⲟⲩ (obscure); as nn, *judgement*: Mani 1 *A*² ⲡⲧ. ⲙⲛⲧⲕⲣⲓⲥⲓⲥ of sinners, BG 119 *S* to reveal a πλάσμα ...ⲉⲩⲧ. ⲡⲁⲡⲉ, ib 121 *S* garments ⲉϥⲉϩⲟⲣⲙⲁϩⲉ ⲙⲙⲟⲟⲩ...ⲉⲩⲧ. ⲡⲁⲩ ⲡⲡⲓⲥⲟ(ⲟ)ⲛⲉ.　*V* Sethe *Dem Urk* 357.

ⲧⲱϫⲓ *B*, ⲧⲱϫⲉ *F*　v ⲧⲱϭⲉ.

ⲧϫⲁ(ⲉ)ⲓⲟ (once), ϫ., ϭ.(once) *S*, ϫⲁⲓⲁ *F*, ϫⲁⲉⲓⲟϥ *S* vb intr, *make to rise*(?), *appear*, hence *triumph*(caus of ϣⲁ?): KroppC 107 *F* ⲏⲗⲓⲟⲥ ⲡⲉⲧϫ. ϩⲉⲡⲡⲕⲉⲣⲓ ⲧⲏⲣⲉϥ; c ⲉⲃⲟⲗ *S* tr, *show forth, display*: 2 Cor 2 14 (*B* ⲟⲩⲱⲛϩ ⲉⲃ.), Col 2 15 ⲧϫ. (var ϫ., *B* ⲓⲣⲓ ⲛⲥⲣⲁϩ), BHom 91 ⲙⲡⲟⲩϭ. ⲉⲃ. ⲙⲡⲛⲧⲣⲁⲡⲟⲥ (τύρ.) ϫⲉⲟⲩⲁⲧⲉⲓⲱⲧⲡⲉ (as we claim for Christ)θριαμβεύειν; Balestri xli ⲉϥϫ. ⲉⲃ. ⲙⲡⲉϥⲛⲟⲃⲉ & after confessing it &c, P 131² 160 ⲡⲥⲉϫⲁⲉⲓⲟⲟⲩ (*sc* sins) ⲉⲃ. ⲡⲡⲁϧⲣⲡⲟ⳿ⲅⲟ⳿ⲡ ⲡⲓⲙ; intr: Ming 310 ⲁⲡⲉⲩϩⲏⲧ ϫ. ⲉⲃ. ⲡⲧⲉⲡⲣⲟⲥ-ⲍⲟⲕⲓⲁ καταδαπανᾶσθαι ἐπὶ τῇ προσδ. (Mor 17 110 om); as nn: Tri 296 ⲡⲁⲧⲙⲁⲉⲓⲟ ⲙⲡⲛⲁϫ. زكي.

ϫⲁⲉⲓⲟ *A*²　v ⲧϫⲁⲉⲓⲟ.

ⲧϫⲟ *B*　v ϫⲕⲟ.

ⲧⲁϫⲣⲟ *SAA²B*, -ⲣⲁ *F*, ⲧⲁϫⲣⲉ- *SB*, -ⲣⲟϥ *SB*, -ⲣⲁϥ *AA²F*, -ⲣⲏⲧ† *SA*, -ⲣⲁⲉⲓⲧ† *SA*, -ⲣⲏⲟⲩ† *A*, -ⲣⲁⲓⲧ† *A*², -ⲣⲏⲟⲩⲧ† *BF* vb **I** tr, *make strong, firm, fast* (caus of ϫⲣⲟ): Ps 50 12 *SA*(Cl)*B*, Jer 5 3 *SB*, Ro 16 25 *SB* στηρίζειν, Ac 14 22 *SB* ἐπιστ., Ps 36 17 *SB* ὑποστ.; ib 147 1 *S*(*B* ϯ ϫⲟⲙ), Ez 27 9 *SB* ἐνισχύειν; Deu 3 28 *S*(*B* ϯ ⲛⲟⲙϯ), Hos 7 15 *AB*(*S* diff) κατισ., Deu 8 18 *S*(*B* ϯ ⲡ.) ἰσχὺν διδόναι, Pro 8 29 *B*(*SA* ⲱⲣϫ) ἰσ. ποιεῖν; Ge 31 25 *B*(*S* = Gk), He 8 2 *B* (*SF* do) πηγνύναι; Mk 16 20 *SBF* βεβαιοῦν; Mt 27 64 *B*(*S* ⲱ.), ViSitz 172 4 26 *S* ⲉⲓⲧ. ⲙⲙⲱⲧⲛ ἀσφαλίζειν; Pro 3 26 *SAB* ἐρείδειν, Job 8 15 *B*(*S* ⲧⲁ-ϫⲣⲟ ⲉⲣⲁⲧϥ) ὑπερ.; 2 Kg 11 25 *S* κραταιοῦν; Ps 89 2 *S*(*B* diff) ἐδράζειν; Jud 6 34 *S* ἐνδυναμοῦν; Ez 44 5 *B*(var ⲑⲱϣ) τάσσειν εἰς; PS 281 *S* ϣⲁⲡⲧⲉⲧⲛ. ⲡⲧ-ⲡⲓⲥⲧⲓⲥ in world, ShA 1 429 *S* bread ⲧ. ⲙⲡϩⲏⲧ, BIF 14 123 *S* ⲡⲧⲉⲣⲉⲡⲧ. ⲙⲡⲣⲟ of prison, RChamp 541 *S* ⲙⲟⲩⲣ ⲧ. ⲡⲧⲥⲁⲣϧ *fasten, close up flesh* (*sc* penis) of

NN., Va 62 133 *B* ⲙⲁⲧⲁϫⲣⲟϥ (*sc* prisoner) ⲡⲕⲁⲗⲱⲥ, C 86 140 *B* ⲁ̄ⲧ. ⲙ̄ⲡⲓⲡⲟⲗⲉⲙⲟⲥ ⲁⲩⲙⲓϣⲓ, DeV 2 7 *B* ⲁϥⲧⲁⲭⲣⲉ ⲡⲓⲣⲱ̄ϥ ϫⲉⲛⲑⲟϥⲡⲉ ϥ̄ϯ.

II intr, *be strengthened, decided:* Ps 32 6 *SB,* Ac 3 7 *SB* ⲥⲧⲏⲣ., Ps 87 7 *ⲉ*ⲡⲓⲟⲧ., Job 20 7 *SB* ⲕⲁⲧⲁⲟⲧ.; Deu 31 6 *S*(*B* ϫⲉⲙ ⲡⲟⲗ̄ϯ) ⲓⲟⲭ., Ac 12 15 *B*(*S* ⲧⲱⲕ ⲉⲣⲟϥⲡ) ⲇⲓⲱ.; Ps 88 13 *S*(*B* ⲁⲙⲁϩⲓ) ⲕⲣⲁⲧ.; 1 Cor 1 6 *SB* ⲃⲉⲃ.; Ac 27 41 *B*(*S* ⲥⲱ) ⲉⲣ.; BMis 233 *S* ⲡⲡⲟ-ⲗⲩⲙⲟⲥ ⲁϥⲧ. *ⲉ*ⲡⲁⲛⲓⲥⲧⲁ́ⲛⲁⲓ; BG 52 *S* his wisdom ⲧ. ⲡⲣⲟⲅⲟ ⲉⲣⲟⲟⲩ, Mor 22 111 *S* consent thou ϫⲉⲉⲣⲉ-ⲡⲁϩⲏⲧ ⲛⲁⲧ. = BSM 99 *B* ϫⲱ ⲉⲃⲟⲗ; qual: Ex 17 12 *SB,* Lu 16 26 *SB* ⲟⲧ., Z 337 *S* river bed was ⲧ.† ⲥⲧⲉⲣⲉⲟ́ⲥ; Jos 23 9 *S,* Is 33 16 *SF,* Joel 2 2 *SA* -ⲛⲟⲩ, *ib* 11 *A* -ⲏⲩ (all *B* ϫⲟⲣ) ⲓ̓ⲥⲭⲩⲣⲟ́ⲥ; Deu 11 2 *S* (*B* ⲁⲙⲁϩⲓ), Ps 58 3 *S*(*B* do), Hab 3 4 *SB*(*A* diff) ⲕⲣⲁⲧⲁⲓⲟ́ⲥ; Lev 25 18 *S*(*B* ⲧ. ⲛⲛ), Is 32 19 *SF*(*B* ϫⲱⲣ ⲡϧⲏⲧ) ⲡⲉⲓ́ⲑⲉⲓⲛ; Pro 18 11 *SA,* Is 30 13 *B*(*SF* ϫⲟⲥⲉ) ⲟ̓ⲭⲩⲣⲟ́ⲥ, Ps 30 21 *SB* ⲡⲉⲣⲓⲟⲭⲏ́; 2 Cor 5 8 *B*(*S* ⲧⲏⲕ) ⲑⲁⲣⲣⲉⲓ̃ⲛ; Deu 11 18 *S*(*B* ⲁⲧⲕⲓⲙ) ⲁ̓ⲥⲁ́ⲗⲉⲩⲧⲟⲥ; Ge 34 25 *B* ⲉⲣⲉⲧⲟⲧⲟⲩ ⲧ. ⲁ̓ⲥⲫⲁⲗⲱ̃ⲥ; He 2 2 *SBF* ⲃⲉ́ⲃⲁⲓⲟⲥ; 1 Cor 7 37 *SBF* ⲉ̔ⲇⲣⲁⲓ̃ⲟⲥ; Mt 7 25 *SB* ⲑⲉⲙⲉⲗⲓⲟⲩ̃ⲛ; Pro 1 33 *SA*-ⲗⲉⲓⲧ (*B* Gk diff); Is 5 29 *B*(*S* ⲁⲙⲁⲣⲧⲉ)Gk om; Mor 34 36 *S* ⲛ̄ⲥⲉⲣⲱ̄ϥ ⲉⲧⲧ. (var BMis 112 ϫⲟⲟⲣ), Wor 320 *S* ϣⲱⲡⲉ ⲉⲧⲉⲛⲧⲁⲭⲣⲟⲉⲓⲧ (var Mor 16 126 -ⲏⲩ), El 72 *A* ⲡⲓⲥⲧⲓⲥ ⲉ(ⲧ)ⲧⲁⲭⲣⲁⲉⲓⲧ, Mor 23 42 *S* where ⲡ̄ⲕⲱⲣⲧ ⲧ. ⲡ̄ϩⲏⲧ̄ϥ like great river, Mani 1 *A*² ⲡⲉⲧⲧ. ⲉⲧⲟⲩⲏⲣ ⲁⲭⲛ̄ⲡⲁϩ̄, HL 121 *B* ⲡⲓⲣⲟ ⲉϥⲧ., Kr 3 *F* ⲟⲩϩⲟⲙⲟⲗⲟⲅⲓⲁ ⲉⲥⲧ., J 67 9 *S* ⲉⲣⲉⲡⲁⲗⲟⲅⲓⲥⲙⲟⲥ ⲧ. With following preposition.

—— ⲉ-, *set firmly on, toward:* Si 42 31 *S* ⲟⲧ. ⲉ̓ⲛ; Pro 29 35 *SAB* ⲉ̓ⲣⲉⲓ̓ⲇ. ⲉⲓ̓ⲥ; Ac 16 24 *B* (var ⲛ-, *S* ϧⲛ-) ⲁ̓ⲥⲫⲁⲗⲓ́ⲍⲉⲓⲛ ⲉⲓ̓ⲥ (var ⲉ̓ⲛ); C 43 40 *B* ⲁⲡⲟⲩϩⲏⲧ ⲧ. ⲉⲣⲱ-ⲟⲩ = Mor 39 14 *S* ⲥⲁⲗⲥⲉⲗ; vbal: Lu 9 51 *S*(*B* ⲥⲉⲙ-ⲡⲓ) ⲟⲧ. gen; Ru 1 18 *S* ⲕⲣⲁⲧ. gen; Jer 51 11 *B*(*S* ⲕⲱ) ⲉ̓ⲫⲓⲥⲧⲁ́ⲛⲁⲓ gen; C 86 185 *B* ⲉϥⲧ.† ⲉⲡⲉϥϫⲁϫⲓ *steadfast against;* ⲉϩⲟⲩⲛ ⲉ-: 2 Cor 1 21 *SBF* ⲃⲉⲃ. ⲉⲓ̓ⲥ, *ib* 2 8 *SB* ⲕⲩⲣⲟⲩ̃ⲛ; BHom 128 *S* His feet ⲧ.† ⲉϩ. ⲉⲣⲟϥ (*sc* cross).

—— ⲉϫⲛ-, *set, be set, rely upon:* Ez 13 17 *SB* ⲟⲧ. ⲉ̓ⲡⲓ́, Is 36 6 *SF*(*B* ⲟⲩⲱϩ ⲉϫ.) ⲉ̓ⲡⲓⲟⲧ. ⲉ̓ⲡⲓ́, *ib* 50 10 *SB* ⲁ̓ⲛⲧⲓⲟⲧ. ⲉ̓ⲡⲓ́; Jud 3 12 *S* ⲉ̓ⲛⲓⲥⲭ. ⲉ̓ⲡⲓ́; Lev 20 3 *S*(*B* ⲥⲉ.) ⲉ̓ⲫⲓⲟⲧ. ⲉ̓ⲡⲓ́; Pro 24 63† *SA* ⲉ̓ⲣ. dat; Ez 4 7 *SB* ⲉ̓ⲧⲟⲓⲙⲁ́ⲍⲉⲓⲛ ⲉⲓ̓ⲥ; Job 38 6 *SB* ⲡⲏⲅ. ⲉ̓ⲡⲓ́; EW 148 *B* ⲁϥⲧ. ⲡϩⲏⲧ ⲉ. ⲡⲓⲥⲁϫⲓ ⲑⲁⲣ. ⲡⲣⲟ́ⲥ; R 1 2 32 *S* ⲉϥⲧ.† ⲉ.ⲧⲉϥϣⲉⲣⲃ̄ⲱⲧ, Pcod 7 *S* sky ⲧ.† ⲉϫⲟⲩ?, AM 193 *B* ⲧ. ⲙ̄ⲡⲓⲡⲟⲗⲉⲙⲟⲥ ⲉϫⲱϥ *prepare, declare* (?) *against,* ManiH28*A*² new birth cometh ⲛ̄ⲥⲧⲁⲭⲣⲁⲥ ⲁϫⲛ̄ⲡϥ[ⲁ]-ⲅⲁⲑⲟⲛ, P 131³ 41 *S* Jesus ⲧ.† ⲉ.ⲡϣⲉ; ⲉϩⲣⲁⲓ, -ⲏⲓ ⲉϫ.: Jer 24 6 *SB* ⲟⲧ. ⲉ̓ⲡⲓ́, Ge 28 12 *S*(*B* ϫⲉⲛ-) ⲟⲧ. ⲉ̓ⲛ (var ⲉ̓ⲡⲓ́), Ps 31 8 *SB* ⲉ̓ⲡⲓⲟⲧ. ⲉ̓ⲡⲓ́; Ps 102 11 *B*(*S* om ⲉϩ.) ⲕⲣⲁⲧ. ⲉ̓ⲡⲓ́; 2 Cor 1 7 *B*(*S* ϩⲁ-) ⲃⲉ́ⲃⲁⲓⲟⲥ ⲩ̔ⲡⲉ́ⲣ; Ez 4 3 *SB* ⲉ̓ⲧⲟⲓⲙ. ⲉ̓ⲡⲓ́; Ryl 316 *S* ⲉⲓⲧ.† ⲉϩ. ⲉ.ⲡ̄ϯ ⲡⲛⲁ̄ⲛⲧⲡ, TstAb 248 *B* ⲉϥⲧ.† ⲉϩ. (*sic* ?) ⲉ.ⲧⲉⲥⲁϥⲉ (*sc* ladder's).

—— ϩⲓϫⲛ-, *set firmly upon:* PS 161 *S* ⲁⲕⲧⲁⲭⲣⲉ ⲡⲟⲩⲟⲉⲓⲡ...ϩⲓϫⲱⲓ.

—— ⲛ- *dat, confirm for:* Ps 15 6 *SB* ⲕⲣⲁⲧ.; 2 Kg 6 17 *B*(*S* = Gk) ⲡⲏⲅ.; Ro 4 16 *SB*(*F* ϫⲁⲣⲛⲟⲩⲧ) ⲃⲉ́-ⲃⲁⲓⲟⲥ ⲉⲓ̃ⲛⲁⲓ; Bor 248 53 *S* ϯⲧ. ⲡⲏⲧⲡ ⲙ̄ⲡϣⲁϫⲉ, MR 5 33 *F* ⲡⲟ̄ⲧ̄ ⲧ. ⲡⲉⲣⲁⲟⲩ ⲙ̄ⲡⲉⲕⲱⲡⲁⲣ ⲡⲏⲡ; *fasten, confirm with SB:* Col 1 23 *B*(*S* diff) ⲑⲉⲙ.; EW 34 *B* ⲁⲩⲧⲁⲭⲣⲟⲡ ⲙⲡⲉϫⲏⲥ = ViK 9474 *S* ϩⲛ-(Gu 69 *S* diff) ⲁ̓ⲥⲫⲁⲗ. dat, C 43 211 *B* ⲉϥⲧ.† ⲡ̄ϩⲉⲛⲓⲡⲓ, *ib* 86 355 *B* ⲉⲣⲉⲧⲟⲧⲟⲩ ⲧ.† ⲡ̄ⲧⲥⲛϳⲓ (var ϫⲉⲛϩⲁⲡⲥ.), J 5 61 *S* ⲁⲡ-ⲧⲁϫⲣⲟⲥ (*sc* deed) ⲡ̄ⲅⲩⲡⲟⲅⲣⲁⲫⲉⲩⲥ ϩⲓⲙⲁⲣⲧⲩⲣⲟⲥ.

—— ϩⲛ-, ϫⲉⲛ-, *make firm in, with:* 1 Kg 2 1 *SB,* Is 22 25† *SB* ⲟⲧ. ⲉ̓ⲛ, Ac 16 5 *SB* ⲟⲧ. dat, AM 268 *B* ⲩ̔ⲡⲟⲟⲧ. ⲉ̓ⲛ; Is 41 7 *SB* ⲓ̓ⲟ. ⲉ̓ⲛ; Ps 73 13 *SB* ⲕⲣⲁⲧ. ⲉ̓ⲛ, Z 314 *S* ⲙ̄ⲡⲣⲧⲁⲭⲣⲟⲕ ϩⲙ̄ⲡⲁⲓ ⲟⲩ̔ⲧⲱⲥ ⲕⲣ.; Col 3 15 *S* (*B* ⲛ̄ϧⲣⲏⲓ ϫⲉⲛ-) ⲃⲣⲁⲃⲉⲩ́ⲉⲓⲛ ⲉ̓ⲛ; R 1 4 71 *S* ⲧ. ⲡ̄ⲡⲉϥ-ⲟⲩⲉϩⲛ̄ⲧⲉ ϩⲙ̄ⲡϣⲉ ⲁ̓ⲥⲫ. ⲉⲓ̓ⲥ; Ps 118 28 *SB* ⲃⲉⲃ. ⲉ̓ⲛ; Col 2 2 *S*(*B* diff) ⲥⲩⲙⲃⲓⲃⲁ́ⲍⲉⲓⲛ; Ps 143 12† *B*(*S* ⲧⲱⲕ) ⲉ̔ⲇⲣ. ⲉ̓ⲛ; EpJer 17 *B*(*F* ⲡ-) ⲟ̓ⲭⲩⲣⲟⲩ̃ⲛ dat; Jer 22 14† *B* ϫⲉⲛⲡϣⲉ ⲝⲩⲗⲟⲩ̃ⲥⲑⲁⲓ ⲉ̓ⲛ; Br 261 *S* ⲧⲁⲭⲣⲱⲧ̄ⲡ ϩⲛ̄ⲣⲉⲛ-ⲡ̄ⲡⲁ̄, ShA 2 274 *S* idols ⲉϥⲧ.† ϩⲛⲣⲉⲡⲉⲓϩⲧ, BMar 59 *S* ⲧⲁⲭⲣⲉ ⲑⲁⲯⲓⲥ of shrine ϩⲛⲟⲩⲡⲟⲩϩ̄, LIb 4 *B* bodies ⲁⲩⲧⲁⲭⲣⲱⲟⲩ ϫⲉⲛϩⲁⲡⲥⲟⲕ, N&E 39 340*B* ⲧⲟⲧ-ⲟⲩ ⲧ.† ϫⲉⲛϩⲁⲡⲗ̄ⲅⲧⲁⲡⲓⲁ (*l* ⲗⲩⲭ̄ⲛⲓⲁ) *grasped,* Ryl 72 358 *S* untimely babe ⲡⲉⲙⲡⲁⲧϥⲧ. ⲡⲉ ϩ̄ⲣⲉ̄ⲏⲧⲥ.

—— ϩⲓⲧⲛ- *S, confirm through, by:* Z 301 ⲧ.† ϩ. ⲧⲡⲓⲥⲧⲓⲥ ⲉ̔ⲇⲣⲁⲓ̃ⲟⲥ dat, BMis 312 ⲧ. ⲙ̄ⲡⲥⲟⲗ ϩ.ⲡⲁⲡⲁϣ, AZ 21 148 ⲧⲁⲭⲣⲉ ⲡϫⲟⲓ ϩ.ⲡ̄ⲣⲁⲅϫⲁⲗ; ⲉⲃⲟⲗ ϩ.: BG 34 ⲁⲩⲧⲁⲭⲣⲉ ⲡ̄ⲕⲁ ⲡⲓⲙ ⲉⲃ̄. ϩⲓⲧⲟⲧϥ, P 131 '98 sky ⲁϥ-ⲧⲁⲭⲣⲟⲥ ⲉⲃ̄. ϩ.ⲟⲩⲙⲟⲟⲩ (99 sim ⲉⲃ̄. ϩⲛ-).

—— nn m *SABF, firmness, strength, solidity:* Ge 1 7 *B,* Ps 17 2 *SB* ⲥⲧⲉⲣⲉ́ⲱⲙⲁ, *ib* 71 16 *SB,* Ez 5 16 *SB* ⲥⲧⲏ́ⲣⲓⲅⲙⲁ; Jer 10 17 *B*(*S* = Gk), He 11 1 *SB* ⲩ̔ⲡⲟ́-ⲟⲧⲁⲥⲓⲥ; Deu 8 17 *S*(*B* ⲁⲙⲁϩⲓ), Ps 58 9 *S*(*B* do) ⲕⲣⲁ́-ⲧⲟⲥ; Lam 3 18 *SB* ⲛⲓ̃ⲕⲟⲥ; *ib* 2 2 *B*(*F* ⲡⲉⲧⲭⲁⲣ), Nah 3 14 *B*(*A* ⲙⲁ ⲉⲧⲁⲣϫ) ⲟ̓ⲭⲩ́ⲣⲱⲙⲁ; Is 18 4 *B*(*S* ⲱⲣϫ) ⲁ̓ⲥⲫⲁ́ⲗⲉⲓⲁ; Phil 1 7 *SBF* ⲃⲉⲃⲁⲓ́ⲱⲥⲓⲥ; Dan 7 16 *B* ⲁ̓ⲕⲣⲓ́ⲃⲉⲓⲁ; Cant 2 7 *F* ⲇⲩ́ⲛⲁⲙⲓⲥ; MG 25 31 *B* ⲑⲁ́ⲣⲥⲟⲥ; R 1 4 10 *S* wondering at his ⲧ. *constantia;* BIF 13 112 *S* knew not ⲡ̄ⲧ. ⲙ̄ⲡϣⲁϫⲉ *truth of matter* = MG 25 302*B,* Ryl 72 356 *S* ⲡⲧ. ⲡ̄ⲟⲩⲉϩⲛ̄ⲧⲉ of lame, BM 331 15 *S* phantom gifts ⲙ̄ⲛⲧⲁⲩ ⲧ. ⲙ̄ⲙⲁⲩ, Miss 4 120 *B* ⲛⲓⲧ. of faith, PasH 123 *B* foolish virgins ⲙ̄ⲡⲟⲩⲕⲁϯ ⲙⲛ̄ⲧ. of their lamps, J 74 31 *S* oath by ⲡⲧ. ⲙ̄ⲛⲧⲁⲓⲁ-ⲙⲟⲛⲏ of rulers (*cf* PMon 82 ⲛⲓ́ⲕⲏⲛ ⲕ. ⲇⲓⲁⲙ.); ϩⲛ-, ϫⲉⲛⲟⲩⲧ. as advb, *firmly, certainly:* Bar 5 7 *B* ⲁ̓ⲥⲫⲁ-ⲗⲱ̃ⲥ, Is 34 15 *BF*(*S* ϩⲛⲟⲩⲱⲣϫ) ⲙⲉⲧⲁ̀ ⲁ̓ⲥⲫⲁⲗⲉⲓ́ⲁⲥ; Deu 19 18 *B*(*S* do), Lu 1 3 *B*(*S* do) ⲁ̓ⲕⲣⲓⲃⲱ̃ⲥ; Pro 14 16 *SA,* Is 32 18 *SF*(*B* ϫⲟⲣ) ⲡⲉⲡⲟⲓⲑⲱ́ⲥ; Bor 253 157 *S* ϩⲁⲣⲉϩ ⲉⲣⲟⲟⲩ ϩ., BIF 13 106 *S* bade seek them ϩ., C 43 126 *B* sim, DeV 2 6 God became man ϫ̄.

ⲁⲧⲧ. *B, unstable, infirm:* Va 57 274 things human ϩⲁⲡⲁⲧⲧ.ⲡⲉ.

ᴧᴧ пт. *B, firm place*: Is 34 13 (*SF* ετхосе) ὀχύρωμα.

ⲣ т. *S, be strength, security*: Bor 226 177 ереп-
ⲁⲣⲁⲕⲱⲡ о пᴧⲩ пт.

ϯ т. *SB, give strength, confirm*: Miss 8 32 *S* оⲩⲱϣ
еϯ т. ⲡⲧᴧⲏⲧеⲅсеⲃⲏс βεβαιοῦν; ROC 17 408 *B* ϯ
т. ⲡⲣⲏⲧ ᴧⲙⲡⲓ̅ᴧοⲩ παραθαρρύνειν; C 89 11 *B* ϣᴧⲩϯ
т. ⲡⲣⲏⲧ ⲡᴧⲩ = Miss 4 538 *S* тⲱⲕ ⲡⲣⲏⲧ.

хⲓ т. *S, get confirmation*: Miss 4 579 many хⲓ т.
ⲣⲓⲧᴧⲙⲡоⲅⲱⲡ ⲡⲣⲱⲩ.

хⲓⲡт. *B* m, *confirmation*: Ro 1 11 (*S* т. vb) στηρί-
ζεσθαι.

тохс *B*   *v* тⲱⲕс (тоϭс).

тⲱхс *F*   *v* тⲱⲕс.

тᴧϭ, -ⲕ, тх *S*, теϭ *A*, тах *B*(rare)nn m f (once)
lump, piece, cake: 1 Kg 25 18 т. of dates, Is 38 21(*B*
= Gk) of figs παλάθη, cit BAp 69 тᴧⲕ, Jth 10 5 т.
ⲡепⲕᴧ поⲩⲱᴧ κλάσμα π.; Si 22 16 *SB* of iron βῶ-
λος; K 131 *B* ⲡⲓⲧ. قرب butcher's *block*; ShZ 599
Isis тт. ⲡⲱⲡе, ShC 73 19 limbs ⲡⲟⲧⲡет епⲕᴧ т. т.,
BMis 546 pit threw up т. т. ⲡⲕⲱⲣⲧ *massae igneae*,
Mor 41 179 golden idol burnt ᴧⲩϣⲱⲡе поⲩⲡоϭ ⲡⲧ.,
BMis 538 boiling cauldron ереⲡеⲩⲧ. ϭⲱϣе еⲣⲣᴧⲓ,
Kr 242 ⲕⲗе сⲡᴧⲩ ⲡеⲃⲓⲱ ⲡⲧ. *caked honey*, PSBA 27
168 rub vellum with оⲩⲧ. ⲡоⲭⲣⲅ (? ὤχρα), Ep 549
оⲩⲡоϭ ⲡⲧх ⲡⲣоᴧⲓⲧ. ⲣ т.: Mic 3 3 *A*(*S* ⲣ ϣⲁⲩ,
B ϥⲱϣ vb) μελίζειν; TT 140 *S* dew асⲣ оⲩⲧ. of
honey (MG 17 434 قرص).

тᴧϭ *Sⁱ*, ⲑᴧх *F* nn (?) in dating epitaphs, meaning unknown: Stern p 438 соⲩ сооⲩ ⲡᴧⲩⲟⲧ ⲡᴧⲱⲡⲓ
т. ⲙⲏⲧⲓ ⲣоᴧⲡⲓ ⲡⲕⲓⲕⲗос, Ann 8 92 *F* соⲩ ⲓ̅ⲃ̅ ⲡᴧⲱϣⲓⲣ
ⲡⲑ. ᴧⲙⲉⲧ ⲓ̅ⲃ̅ ⲡⲥⲓⲧⲗⲏс ⲣⲓ.

тоϭ   *v* тоⲕ.

тⲱϭ *bake*   *v* тⲱⲕ *kindle.*

ϯϭе, тⲓ. *S*, хⲓхⲓ *B* nn f, *gourd*, or *vegetables* generally: P 44 82 сⲓⲕⲓᴧⲓоⲡ (-ύδιον)· сⲓⲕеⲗⲗⲁⲧоⲩ (сⲓ-
ⲕⲩⲏⲗⲁⲧⲟⲛ)· тⲑоⲡⲧе · тϯ. قثا; Jer 47 12 *B* ὀπώρα;
ib 36 28 *B* καρπός; ShC 73 87 *S* оⲩϭоⲟⲧе salted or
boiled or ⲣⲉⲡⲧⲓ.; ᴧⲁ ⲣⲁⲣеⲣ ⲡϯ., *gourd-bed*:
Ps 78 1 *S*(var om ⲡϯ.)*B*, Is 1 8 *B*(*SF* ⲡⲑⲟⲡте), Mic
1 6 *B*(*SA* om ⲡϯ.), ib 3 12 *B*(*SA* ⲡⲃ̅.) ὀπωροφυλάκιον.   *V* LMis 67, Dévaud *Études* 24.

ϯϭе *S* nn as pl, meaning unknown: PS 257 ᴧⲡⲟ-
тассе ⲡⲡⲓϯ. еⲧⲣоⲟⲩ that ye be worthy of mystery,
paral ᴧⲙⲡⲣⲁⲣ ⲡϣⲁхе, ᴧⲙⲡᴧⲁⲓⲧо ⲡⲣоⲅо &c.

тоϭе *F*   *v* тⲱⲕ *kindle* **A II.**

тⲱϭе   *v* тⲱⲕ *throw.*

тⲱⲱϭе *SA*, тⲱ. *SA²*, тⲱⲕе (El)*S*, тⲱхⲓ *BF*,
-хе, -ϭⲓ *F*, теϭ-, теⲕ-, тоoⲕ- *S*, тᴧϭ- *Sⁱ*, тⲱϭ- *A*,

тᴧх- *F*, тооϭⲍ, тоϭⲍ, тооⲕⲍ, тоⲕⲍ *S*, тᴧϭⲍ *SAF*,
тохⲍ *B*, тооϭеⁱ (once) тⲏϭеⁱ (once) *S*, тⲏϭⁱ, -ⲕⁱ *SF*,
vb **A I** intr, *be fixed, joined SF*: 2 Kg 2 23 ϣᴧⲩⲧ.
(var тⲱϭеⲣ) ⲡⲩⲁⲣеⲣᴧⲧⲩ ὑφιστάναι; Sa 5 12 тⲱ. εἰς
ἑαυτὸν ἀνέρχεσθαι; BIF 14 168 ᴧⲩⲧ. with amazement, BMis 452 broken leg асⲧ. as if never maimed,
BSG 184 each throne т.ⁱ ⲣⲡеⲡⲡоϭе ⲡϣе *compact-
ed of* (*cf* C 86 285 *B*), Mich 136 4 *v* тооⲅе, GriffStu
163 *F* whose head т.ⁱ ⲣⲏⲧⲡⲏ, feet т.ⁱ ⲣᴧⲡⲕеⲣⲓ. **II**
tr, *join, attain S*: Job 38 38 тасϭ (*B* тⲱᴧⲓ) κολλᾶν;
Is 44 13 (*B* do) ἐν κόλλῃ ῥυθμίζειν; ib 15 8 (*B* ϥоⲣ
ϣᴧ-) συνάπτειν; Zeph 1 14 (var ShA 2 249 & *AB*
тⲱϣ) τάσσειν; Job 15 7 тооⲕⲕ (*B* ϭⲱс) πηγνύναι;
BMis 192 Thy providence did тоϭоⲩ (*sc* waters, Ge
1 9), Mor 28 44 wounded them & ⲡеᴧⲡ ⲡеттⲱ. ᴧ-
ᴧⲟⲟⲩ.

With following preposition.

—— e-, *be joined, cleave to, ascribe to*: Deu 6 13
S(*B* тⲱᴧⲓ) ⲕⲟⲗ. πρός, Lu 10 11 *S*(*B* do) ⲕ. εἰς, Ps 21
15 *S*(var & *B* ϭⲱⲗх), Ro 12 9 *SF*(*B* тⲱᴧⲓ), Cl 15 1·
A ᴧⲁⲣⲏⲧасⲡе апете ⲡеⲓⲣⲏⲡⲏ, Wess 11 168 *S* тⲡе
т. епⲕⲁⲣ ⲕ. dat, Mk 10 7 *SF*(*B* do) ⲡⲣосⲕ. πρός, Jos
23 8 *S* ⲡⲣ. dat, Si 22 7 *S* теϭ- (var Miss 8 164 *Sⁱ*
тᴧϭ-) сⲩⲅⲕ. no dat; Is 6 7 *S*(*B* ϭⲓ ⲡеᴧⲙ-) ἅπτειν gen,
ib 5 8 *S*(*B* тⲱᴧⲓ)сⲩⲛⲁⲡ. πρός, Wess 15 137 *S* Christ's
nature т.ⁱ епⲡ̅е̅ ⲣⲡоⲩⲅⲱⲃ еⲩϭоⲭⲃ̅ с. dat, Mor 37
120 *S* етⲣеⲡт. ⲡⲣеⲡⲙⲡⲧⲟⲉⲓⲕ e- προσάπ. dat; Lam
4 8 *SF* -хе (*B* хⲱⲗх) πηγνύναι ἐπί; Jo 19 19 *SA²*
(*B* ⲭⲱ ϭⲓхеⲡ-) τιθέναι ἐπί, Job 13 9 *S*(*B* оⲩⲱⲣ e-)
ⲡⲣост. dat; Ez 18 6 *B* προσεγγίζειν πρός, Lev 21 2ⁱ
S(*B* ⲑⲉⲡⲧ e-) ἔγγιστα; Eph 1 5 *F* тасϭеⲓⲡ [ео]ⲅᴧет-
ϣⲏⲗⲓ (*B* ⲑⲱϣ, *S* diff) προορίζειν εἰς; Si 11 6 *S*
ᴧⲡоⲩтоϭс (*sc* ⲑⲣⲏⲡе) e- ἀνυπονόητος; 2 Cor 8 20
S теϭ оⲩⲧⲱⲗⲙ e-(*B* ϣⲱϣ) μωμᾶσθαι, Mor 17
35 *S* еⲩⲧасⲩ епеⲡⲣⲱⲃ = EW 34 *B* ⲑⲁϣⲩ ἐντασσ.
ἐν; 1 Kg 14 7ⁱ *S* Gk diff; Tri 699 ᴧⲩтоϭⲩ епⲡ̅е̅
لجأ; PS 128 *S* ϯϭоᴧ...астоϭс ероⲕ, ManiH 22*A¹*
sim, El 126 *S* тⲱⲕе ᴧⲙоⲕ e- (*cf* ib 124 еⲕтⲱ.
ᴧⲙоⲕ ⲡеⲡетоⲩᴧᴧⲃ), ShA 2 50 *S* ⲡⲓⲙ ⲡетⲡᴧтоϭс
ероⲡ хе- *who would credit us with*?, ib 5 *S* ⲡⲣᴧⲡ
тⲏⲕ ероⲕ, ib 1 151 *S* ⲕеᴧᴧ ... еттⲏϭе ероⲟⲩ, P
129¹⁴ 53 *S* Tome of Leo т. епⲡ̅е̅ ⲡⲡеϣⲏⲡⲣе...е-
ⲡⲣⲱᴧⲉ ⲡⲡⲣⲓсе, P 132¹ 4 *S* еᴧⲩтⲱ. ᴧⲙⲉⲩⲣо еⲑⲓ-
ⲕⲱⲡ, BMar 131 *S* ᴧⲩтоϭⲩ (*sc* stone) епⲣо (*cf* BIF
14 143 *S* stone еⲩтооϭе еⲣᴧⲡⲣо), Pcod 39 *F*
brethren e(т)тⲏϭ еϥϯ = *S* ϭⲟⲗх, Mor 18 55 *S*
ⲡеⲩт.ⁱ еⲡⲣⲣо = Miss 4 131 *B* ᴧⲏⲡ, BAp 125 *S*
ᴧⲙⲡеⲓⲕⲁ ⲗᴧⲁⲩ ... етⲱϭ ероⲓ = MIE 2 418 *B* ⲭⲁ
ⲣⲗⲓ ⲡтⲟⲧ, Gu 92 *S* bones т.ⁱ епеⲩеⲣⲏⲩ, ViK
9535 *S* ⲡсᴧⲣх ᴧⲩт. епеⲩеⲣⲏⲩ, P 129¹⁶ 105 *S* ᴧⲩ-
тоϭоⲩ епⲓстеⲅе;   еⲣⲣⲏ e-: Nu 36 7 *S*(*B* тⲱᴧⲓ
ⲥⲉⲡ-) προσⲕⲟⲗ. ἐν; Ex 29 5 *S*(*B* do), Ez 37 17 *B*
сⲩⲛⲁⲡ. πρός; Z 273 *S* еⲩт.ⁱ еⲣ. етсᴧⲣх συμβαίνειν

dat; Mich 550 39 *S* ⲡⲥⲉⲧⲙⲧ. ⲡⲧⲉⲩϫⲓⲥⲉ ⲉϧ. ⲉⲗⲁⲁⲩ ⲡϫⲟⲉ κλίνειν πρός (*cf* ⲟⲩⲱⲗⲥ ⲉϧⲟⲩⲛ); PS 298 *S* sins ⲡϧⲧⲟϭⲟⲩ ⲉϧ. ⲉⲧⲉⲯⲩⲭⲏ, ShRE 11 16 *S* ⲡⲧ.† ⲉϧ. ⲉⲡⲏⲧ, BMis 289 *S* hand ⲧⲱ. ⲉϧ. ⲉⲧⲥⲛϭ̄ϥ from much blood (*cf* in ⲧⲱϧⲣ), Mor 52 52 *S* blood ⲧⲱ.ⲉϧ. ⲉⲡⲉϥ ⲱⲡⲉ (*sc* of street), Mor 30 31 *F* foot ⲧ. ⲉϧ. ⲉⲧⲁⲡⲉ ⲡⲧⲥⲉⲗⲗⲁ = BMis 257 *S* ⲉ(ⲓ)ϣⲉ ⲉϧⲣⲁⲓ ϧⲏⲧⲥ.

—— ⲉϫⲛ- *S, join to, fix upon* : BMar 209 ⲁϥⲧⲱ. ⲙⲡⲙⲁ … ⲉϫⲛⲡϥⲉⲣⲏⲩ = Rec 6 173 *B* ⲥⲱⲗⲕ (*sic*) ⲉⲡⲉϥⲉⲣⲏⲟⲩ, Mor 18 21 hastened & ⲁⲩⲧⲟⲕⲟⲩ ⲉϫⲱⲛ = *ib* 19 29 ϧⲟϭⲟⲩ ⲉϫ. (Miss 4 115 *B* diff), Tri 345 ⲧⲱ. ⲙⲡⲉϥⲥⲱⲙⲁ ⲉϫⲛ- cross لصق على.

—— ⲛⲥⲁ- *S, attribute to* : ShA 2 157 ⲙⲡⲣⲧⲉϭ ⲡⲉⲕϧⲉ ⲡⲥⲱϥ.

With following adverb.

—— ⲉⲃⲟⲗ *SBF, fix outwardly, set forth, publish* : Mart Ign 880 *B* ⲁϥⲧ. ⲡⲟⲩⲍⲟⲅⲙⲁ ⲉⲃ. ⲧⲓⲑ., Est 4 3 *S*, Dan 6 8 *S*(*B* ⲧⲁⲭⲣⲟ)ⲉⲕⲧ., LAp 360 *S* ⲁϥⲧⲉϥ ⲟⲩ ⲍⲓⲁⲧⲁⲅⲙⲁ ⲉⲃ. = EW 225 *B* ⲥⲉⲙⲛⲓ προτ.; Jude 4 *S*(*B* as Gk), Gal 3 1 *S*(var ⲧⲱⲙ, *B* do) προγράφειν; Est 3 9 *S* δογματίζειν; ShWess 9 159 *S* ⲍⲓⲁⲧⲁⲅⲙⲁ ⲉⲡⲧⲁⲓⲧⲟϥⲥ ⲉⲃ., Ryl 94 (33 1) *S* ⲁⲩⲧⲉϥ ⲡⲉⲡⲣⲟⲥⲧⲁ ⲅⲙⲁ ⲉⲃ. ⲍⲏⲙⲟⲥⲓⲁ, C 43 210 *B* προστ. ⲉⲧⲁⲓⲧⲟϥ ⲉⲃ., Mor 19 75 *S* ⲙⲡⲉϣ ⲧⲱ. ⲉⲃ. ⲙⲡⲧⲟⲗⲟⲥ = *ib* 18 66 *S* ⲉⲙⲫⲁⲛⲓⲥⲟⲁⲓ = Miss 4 140 *B* ⲟⲩⲱⲛϩ ⲉⲃ., Miss 8 39 *S* ⲕⲁⲑⲁⲓⲣⲉⲥⲓⲥ…ⲧⲟϥⲥ ⲉⲃ. ϧⲓⲡⲉⲧⲟⲩⲁ of door, BMar 2 *S* ⲧⲱ. ⲡⲟⲩⲅϧⲁⲓ ⲉⲃ. ϧⲓⲣⲙⲡⲣⲟ, Mor 48 45 *S* ⲡⲉⲥϧϧⲁⲓ ⲧⲏϭ ⲉⲃ. ϧⲓⲙⲡⲁⲗⲗⲁⲧⲓⲟⲛ, *ib* 30 3 *Sⁱ* ⲧⲁϭϥ ⲉⲃ. ϧⲓⲙ ⲡⲁ ⲛ† ϧⲁⲡ.

—— ⲁϧⲟⲩⲛ *A, join up with* : Zech 14 5 ⲧ. ⲁϧ. ϣⲁ- (*B* ⲧⲱⲙⲓ) ἐγκολ. ἕως.

—— ⲉϧⲣⲁⲓ *S, meaning uncertain* : BM 1014 lease (ἐμφύτευμα) ⲉⲡϣⲁⲡⲧⲟⲕⲛ ⲉϧ. ⲁⲡⲟⲛ ⲧⲉⲡⲧⲓ ϩⲱⲍⲉⲕⲁ[ⲓ Cf ⲧⲱϧⲣ.

B *plant S*(mostly ⲧⲱϣⲉ)*AA²BF*, intr: Lu 17 6 *S* (*B* ⲣⲱⲧ)ⲫⲩⲧⲉⲩⲉⲓⲛ, Jer 1 10 *S*(*B* ⲧϭⲟ)ⲕⲁⲧⲁⲫ.; ShMIF 23 74 *S* beware of evil seed ⲡⲡⲉⲥⲧ., Mor 23 30 *S* to tree ⲧ. ϧⲓⲡⲙⲁ ⲉⲧⲙⲙⲁⲩ = *ib* 24 21 *F* ⲧⲱϭ ⲉⲡⲉ ⲙⲁ; tr: Ge 9 20 *S*(*B* ϭⲟ), Ps 91 13† *S*(*B* ⲣⲏⲧ), *ib* 93 9 *SB*, Pro 27 18 *SA*, Eccl 2 5 *SF* ⲧⲁⲭ-, 1 Cor 9 7 *SF*(*B* ϭⲟ)ⲫ., Lev 19 23 *S*(*B* do), Jer 24 6 *S*(*B* ⲧϭⲟ), Am 9 15 *SAB* ⲕⲁⲧⲁⲫ.; Ro 11 17 *SF*(*B* = Gk) ἐγ κεντρίζειν; TEuch 1 674 *B* Paradise ⲁⲩⲉⲣ ϣⲟⲣⲡ ⲡⲧ. ⲙⲙⲟϥ ⲙⲡⲓϣⲉ of cross في غرس; ShC 73 152 *S* ⲉⲩⲧ. ⲙⲡⲉⲓⲱⲣⲉ, ShZ 599 *S* ⲟⲩϧⲱ…ⲉⲁϥⲧⲟϭⲥ ⲉⲩϧⲱ *grafted upon*, Mor 18 49 *S* ⲁⲓⲧⲟϭⲟⲩ…ⲁⲅⲡⲟⲣⲕⲟⲩ, Mani 1 *A²* ⲡⲕⲏ]ⲡⲟⲩⲣⲟⲥ ⲡⲉⲧⲧ. ⲡϣⲏⲛ, Va 61 25 *B* ⲧ. ⲡⲃⲏ ⲧⲟⲩ ⲛ†ϧⲟϥ, Bor 100 22 *S* ϭⲓⲛⲕⲓⲙ ⲡⲓⲙ ⲉⲧⲧⲏϭ ϧⲣⲁⲓ ⲡϧⲏⲧⲛ; as nn m: Si 3 27 *S*, CaiEuch 483 *B* φυτόν, Ro 6 5 *SB* ϣⲃⲣⲧ. συμφ., Ez 17 7 *B*, Mic 1 6 *S*(*AB* ⲙⲁ ⲡⲭⲟ), Mt 15 3 *SF*(*B* ϣϣⲏⲛ) φυτεία, Is 17 10 *S* (*B* ϭⲟ) φύτευμα, Jer 38 22 *B* καταφύτευσις; Sa 4 3 *S* μόσχευμα; BMis 554 *S* ⲡⲁⲧ. ⲡⲧⲁⲓⲧⲟϭⲟⲩ, JSch 5

105 *S* your successors & ⲡⲉⲧⲡⲧⲱ. ⲉⲧⲙⲏⲡ ⲉⲃⲟⲗ; ⲧ. ⲙⲙⲣⲣⲉ : Ps 143 12 *SB* νεόφυτος; TT 110 *S* ⲟⲩⲧ. ⲛⲃ̄. Va 61 13 *B* do neophyte; ⲣⲉϥⲧ. *S, planter* : P 44 80 φοιτευτης · πρ. غارس. ⲣⲁ ⲧ. *v* ⲣⲁ.

Cf ? ⲡⲧⲏϭ.

ⲧϭⲁ *S* nn (or ? name): Saq 272 ⲁⲃⲣⲁⲅⲁⲙ ⲧ. ⲡϥ ⲣⲟⲉⲓϭ (ⲙ)ⲡⲣⲟ ⲡⲉⲙⲉⲛⲧ (or ⲧ. may be after ⲣⲟⲉⲓϭ).

ⲧϭⲁ(ⲉ)ⲓⲟ *SA*, ϭⲁⲓⲟ *S*, ϫⲁⲉⲓⲟ *A²*, ϭⲁⲓⲁ *F* (nn), ⲧϭⲁ(ⲉ)ⲓⲉ-, ϭ.*S*, ϫⲁⲓⲉ-*B*, ⲧϭⲁ(ⲉ)ⲓⲟⲋ, ϭ.*S*, ⲧϭⲁⲉⲓⲁⲋ*A²*, ϫⲁⲓⲟⲋ *B*, ⲧϭⲁ(ⲉ)ⲓⲏⲩ†, ϭ.† *S*, ϫⲁⲓⲱⲟⲩ† *B* vb **I** tr, *make ugly, hence disgrace, condemn*(caus of ϭⲁⲓⲉ): Jo 16 11 *S* ⲧ.(*A²* ⲧⲁⲭⲟ, *B* ⳨ ϧⲁⲡ ⲉ-), BHom 36 *S* ⲉⲩϭ. ⲙⲙⲟϥ κρίνειν, Mt 12 41 *S* ⲧ. (*B* do), Mk 14 64 *S* ⲧ. (*B* = Gk), Mor 37 100 *S* ϭⲁⲓⲉ ⲡⲉⲧϧⲓⲧⲟⲩⲱϥ κατακρ.; Ps 36 33 *S*(*B* ϧⲓⲟⲩⲓ ⲉⲡϧⲁⲡ), Mt 12 7 *S*(*B* ⳨ ϧ., *F* ϧⲓ. ⲉⲛϧ.) καταδικάζειν; R 1 4 65 *S* why dost ⲧ. ⲙⲡⲉⲛ ϣⲙϣⲉ? = AM 125 *B* ϧⲓ. ⲉⲛϧ. καταγινώσκειν; Sa 12 15 *S* κολάζεσθαι; Aeg 244 *S* ἐλέγχειν; Mor 18 146 *S* ⳨ⲧ. ⲙⲙⲟⲓ αἰτίαν ἐπιγράφειν; Gu 66 *S* ⲙⲡⲟⲩ ⲧϭⲁⲉⲓⲟⲟⲩ = EW 33 *B* -ϣⲟϣⲟⲩ ἀναίτιος; ShC 73 3 *S* ⲥⲉⲛⲁⲧϭⲁⲓⲟⲛ opp -ⲧϭⲁⲓⲟⲛ, ShA 1 377 *S* ⲡϭⲱϣ ⲉⲧϥⲛⲁⲧϭⲁⲉⲓⲉ ⲡⲉⲓⲕⲟⲟⲩⲉ ⲡϧⲏⲧϥ, *ib* 2 255 *S* ⲍⲓⲁⲃⲁⲗ ⲗⲉ ⲡⲟⲩϭⲟⲡ…ⲏ ⲧϭⲁⲓⲟϥ, ViK 9319 43 *S* ⳨ⲧ. ⲙⲙⲟⲓ ϧⲱⲥ ⲣⲉϥⲣ ⲡⲟⲃⲉ, AP 3 *A²* ⲉⲩϫ. ⲙⲙⲁϥ & stoned him, DeV 1 150 *B* ⲁϥϫⲁⲓⲟϥ sim, Mor 25 7 *S* ⲁⲩⲧ. ⲡⲁⲓ (var P 131³ 81 ϭⲡ ⲁⲣⲓⲕⲉ) = Va 61 90 *B* ϫϥⲓⲟ, BAp 149 *S* ⲡϥⲧⲙϭⲁⲓⲉ ⲗⲁⲁⲩ, TillOster 15 *A* sim, Mor 31 35 *S* ⲉϥϭ. ⲙⲙⲟⲟⲩ (var Miss 4 774 ⲧϭ.), AZ 14 81 *B* ⲁⲕϫⲁⲓⲉ ⲫⲏ ⲉⲧⲟϧⲓ ⲉⲣⲁⲧϥ ⲉⲣⲟⲕ, Cai 8087 *S* bribes ϣⲁⲡϯⲧ. ⲡⲡϧⲁⲡ ⲙⲙⲉ.

II intr, *be disgraced, condemned*: Est 2 1 *S* ϭ. κατα κρίνεσθαι; Lu 6 37 *S* ⲧ. (*B* ⳨ ϧⲁⲡ), Ja 5 6 *S* ⲧ. *A*(*B* do) καταδικ., Tri 268 *S* ⲧ. شجب; qual, *ugly B S*(once): Ge 41 3 αἰσχρός; Va 57 226 δυσειδής; *ib* 244 μιαρώτερος; 1 Cor 12 23 (*S* ϣⲓⲡⲉ) ἀσχήμων; Dan 1 10 σκυθρωπός; MartIgn 876 = R 1 4 69 *S* ϭ.† χεί ρων; BSM 20 garments ⲉⲩϫ. = BMis 357 *S* ⲗⲁⲁⲙ, MG 25 156 vessels ⲉⲩⲧⲁⲓⲏⲟⲩⲧ & ⲉⲩϫ.; *disgraced, condemned SB*(once): Tit 3 11 ⲧ. (*B* ϧⲓ. ⲉⲛϧⲁⲡ) κατάκριτος; Ps 108 7 (*B* do) καταδικ., R 1 4 69 ὑπό δικος; Job 36 17 *B*(*S* diff) ὑστερεῖν; Sa 17 2 φυγάς, P 44 73 ⲉⲕⲍⲟⲧⲟⲥ · ⲡⲉⲧ. خصم; ShA 2 276 ϯⲧⲥⲱϣϥ ⲁⲅⲱ ϯϭ., ShC 73 28 if one renounce duties shall be ⲧ. ⲡⲟⲩⲏⲣ? Miss 4 614 Christ on cross ϧⲛⲟⲩ ⲥⲭⲏⲙⲁ ⲉϥⲧ., Mor 36 22 ⳨ϭ. ⲉⲧⲃⲉⲡⲁⲡⲟⲃⲉ.

With following preposition & adverb. ⲉ- *SA²*, *condemn to*: Miss 8 173 ⲧϭⲁⲉⲓⲟϥ ⲉⲡⲙⲟⲩ, Mor 43 165 ⲁⲩϭⲁⲓⲟϥ ⲉⲟⲩϧⲁⲡ of death, R 1 4 74 *S* ⲧϭⲁⲉⲓⲟⲩ ⲉⲧⲁⲁⲩ to beasts = MartIgn 880 *B* ϧⲓⲟⲩⲓ ⲉⲛϧⲁⲡ, AP 15 *A²* sim; ⲥ ⲉⲃⲟⲗ *S*, as ⲧ.: Bor 252 56 ⲡⲉϥⲧ. ⲙⲙⲟϥ ⲉⲃ. ⲙⲙⲓⲛ ⲙⲙⲟϥ, *ib* 282 173 ⲉϥⲧ. ⲙⲙⲟⲛ ⲉⲃ. ⲉϫⲛⲡⲉⲛⲧⲁⲛⲁⲁⲩ.

—— nn m *SA²F*, *disgrace, condemnation*: Ro 8 1 (*B* ϧⲁⲡ)κατάκριμα, P 44 59 ⲟⲩϭ· ⲕⲁⲧⲁⲕⲣⲓⲧⲟⲥ احضام, ClPr 54 42 ⲟⲩϭ. ϣⲁⲉⲡⲉϥ as to disputed property κατάκρισις; Mor 17 77 ⲡⲉⲓⲡⲟϭ ⲡⲧ. καταδίκη; Aeg 217 found no ⲧ. καταγινώσκειν; Si 8 6 ⲧ. (var ϭ.) ἐπιτίμιον; ShA 1 277 ϧⲉⲡⲧ. ⲙⲡⲣⲉⲡⲥⲱϣ, P 131⁴ 137 prisoners ϭⲏⲡ ϧⲛϭ. ⲛⲓⲙ, BM 242 129 ⲡϭ. ⲙⲡⲥⲟⲟⲣⲉ ⲡⲁϫⲁⲙ, AP 22 *A²* am small ϧⲓϫ. ⲡⲡϧⲉⲑⲛⲟⲥ, Mor 30 11 *F* ⲡϭ.

ϭⲁ(ⲉ)ⲓⲉ¹, -(ⲉ)ⲓⲏ², ϭⲁⲏ³ *S*, ϭⲁⲓⲉ *A²*, ϫⲁⲓⲉ⁴, -ⲓⲏ⁵ (sometimes f) *B*, ϭⲁⲓⲏ *F* nn, *ugly one, ugliness, disgrace*: Ge 29 17 *B⁵*(*S* diff) ἀσθενής; ClPr 29 248 *S* ⲟⲩϭ.¹ ϧⲙⲡⲉϥⲉⲓⲛⲉ, *ib* ⲡϭ.¹ ⲙⲡⲛⲥⲁⲓⲉ, Mani 2 *A²* ⲡⲉϥⲗⲱⲙⲥ ⲡⲉϥ., Miss 4 180 *B* ⲟⲩϫ.⁴ ϫⲉⲡⲧⲉϥⲙⲟⲣⲫⲏ, Miss 8 175 *S* ⲡⲥⲁⲛ ⲙⲡⲡϭ.³, DeV 1 173 *B* ⲡⲓⲙⲡⲉ ⲡⲥⲁⲓⲉ…ⲡϫ.⁴, Mor 22 65 *S* ⲡϭⲱⲃ ⲁⲩⲱ ⲡϭ.², *ib* 66 *S* woman ⲉⲧϭ.², Pap *olim penes* G Horner *S* evil women ϧⲉⲡϭ.² ⲡⲉ; as adj: Mor 37 112 *S* beheld one ⲡϭ.¹ ἀειδής; BG 37 *S* ⲡϭ.¹ ϧⲙⲡⲉϥⲉⲓⲛⲉ, ShWess 9 110 *S* ⲡⲱⲛⲉ ⲡϭ.¹ ⲏ ⲉⲧⲛⲉϭⲱϥ, Mani H 30 *A²* ⲥⲁϫⲉ ⲡϭⲁⲗ…ⲡϭ., CMSS 44 *F* ⲡϣⲁⲕⲧⲉ[.] ⲡⲁⲓ ⲡϭⲁⲓⲏ.

ⲙⲛⲧϭⲁⲉⲓⲉ *S*, -ⲓⲟ *A*, ⲙⲉⲧϫ.⁵ *B*, *ugliness, disgrace*: Va 57 244 *B* woman ϫⲉⲡⲙ. ⲡⲓⲃⲉⲛ ἀτερπής; ShA 2 67 *S* ⲧⲙ. ⲡⲡⲉⲩϧⲃⲏⲅⲉ, BMar 147 *S* of bodies in graves, Cat 15 *B* of passions, Leyd 449 *S* ϧⲉⲡⲙ. ϧⲣⲁϥ.

ⲣ ⲧϭ., ϭ., ⲉⲣ ϫ. *SB*, *be ugly, disgraceful*: ShC 42 36 *S* blindness or ⲕⲉϧⲱⲃ ⲉϥⲟ ⲡϭ., ClPr 29 259 *S* ⲉϥⲟ ⲡⲧϭ. ϧⲛⲧⲉϥⲯⲩⲭⲏ, LCyp 7 *S* o ⲡϭ. like beast, C 86 153 *B* ⲟⲩⲉϣⲱϣ ⲉϥⲟⲓ ⲡϫ., Pap Horner *ut sup*]ⲉⲩⲟ ⲡϭⲁⲓⲏ (*sc* women).

V ϭⲁ, ϫⲁⲓ.

ⲧϭⲟ, ⲧϭⲉ- (2 pl), ⲧϭⲟ⸗ *B* vb tr, *plant* (caus of ϭⲟ), in Jer only: 51 31 ⲧϭⲱⲟⲩ (*S* ⲧⲱϭⲉ), 49 10 ⲧϭⲉⲑⲏⲡⲟⲩ φυτεύειν, 24 6 (*S* do) κατάφ.; 38 27 σπείρειν.

ⲧⲏϭⲙⲉⲥ, ⲧⲉϭ. *S*, ϫⲓϭⲙⲓⲥ *B* nn, *castor-oil plant*: P 44 83 *S* ⲕⲣⲟϫⲟⲡⲓⲛ (κροτώνιον Langkavel) · ⲧⲏ. حشيش = 43 59 *S* ⲧⲉϭ. حشايش; K 178 *B* ϫ. خروع; Ep 534 *S* ⲙⲡⲧⲁⲥⲉ ⲙⲙ(ⲁϫⲉ) ⲡⲧⲏⲕⲙⲥ (or l? -ⲙⲉ).

ⲧⲱϭⲛ *S*, -ⲡⲉ *A²*, ⲧⲉϭⲛ-, ⲧⲁϭⲛ- *S*, ⲧⲟϭⲛ⸗ *S*, ⲧⲁϭⲛ⸗ *SF* vb tr, *push, repel*: Nu 35 20 (*B* ⲣⲱϧⲛ), Ps 117 13 (*B* ϯ ⲧⲟⲧ⸗ ⲙⲙⲟ⸗) ὠθεῖν, Ac 7 27 *SF* (ⲧ. ⲉⲃⲁⲗ, *B* ϫⲱⲗ ⲉⲃ.) ἀπω.; Si 12 11 ⲧⲁϭⲡⲉⲕ, *ib* 17 ⲧⲟϭ. ἀνατρέπειν, *ib* 13 23 (P 44 119) προσανατ.; ShA 1 450 ⲁϥⲧⲟϭⲡⲉϥ ⲁϥϧⲃⲃⲱⲣⲃ ⲉϧⲣⲁⲓ, Mor 37 232 ⲁϥⲧⲁϭⲛ ⲡⲡⲟϭ ⲙⲡⲣⲟⲫⲏⲧⲏⲥ (*cf* Ac 7 27), Miss 4 242 ⲁϥⲧⲉϭⲡ ⲟⲩⲣⲟ & entered = C 41 39 *B* ϭⲟϧ ⲉⲟⲩⲣⲟ, Mani H 12 *A²* ⲁⲥⲧ. ⲡⲡϫⲁⲓⲙⲗⲁϧ, R 1 5 36 ⲁⲥⲧⲉϭⲡⲉ ⲧⲉⲧⲟⲩⲱⲧ ⲁⲥϧⲉ; c ⲉ-, *push toward*: BAp 65 ⲁϥⲧⲟϭⲡⲉϥ ⲉⲡⲟϧⲉ, ViK 9512 ⲁⲡⲁⲛⲅⲉⲗⲟⲥ ⲧⲟϭⲛⲉϥ (*sc* floating stone) ⲉⲡⲉⲕⲣⲟ; ⲉϧⲣⲁⲓ ⲉ-: ShA 1 453 ⲡⲧⲁⲡⲣⲱⲙⲉ ⲧⲟϭⲛⲉϥ ⲉϧ.

ⲉⲡϣⲏⲓ; c ⲡⲥⲁ- emphatic, intr: Gu 60 ⲉⲣⲉⲙⲙⲓⲛϣⲉ ⲧ. ⲡⲥⲱⲟⲩ maltreating them, P 131¹ 58 ⲡⲧⲛⲃⲱⲱⲣⲉ ⲁⲛ ⲟⲩⲧⲉ ⲡⲧⲛⲧ. ⲁⲛ ⲡⲥⲁⲡⲉⲡⲉⲣⲏⲩ; c ⲉⲃⲟⲗ, *forth*: Job 14 20 (*B* ϯ ⲧⲟⲧ⸗ ⲙⲙⲟ⸗) ⲱⲑ.; AZ 26 122 ϣⲁⲥⲧ. ⲙⲙⲟⲟⲩ ⲉⲃ.; Ac 7 27 *F ut sup*; c ⲉⲡⲁϧⲟⲩ, *back*: BMis 46 ⲁϥⲧ.…ⲡⲣⲱⲙⲉ ⲉⲡ.

ⲧⲱϭⲡⲉϥ *S* nn m, *urgency* (?): Scala *olim penes* JGWilkinson 168 ⲡⲧ. الو (P 44 87 vo om).

V Dévaud *Études* 26.

ⲧⲱϭ(ⲉ)ⲣ¹, -ⲕⲣ², ⲧⲱⲣϭ³, -ⲣⲕ⁴ *S*, ⲧⲟϭⲣ†⁵, -ⲣⲕ†⁶, ⲧⲁⲕⲣ†⁷, -ⲣⲕ†⁸ *S* ⲧⲁⲣϭ *A†²*, vb intr, *be fixed, joined*: 2 Kg 2 23 ϣⲁϥⲧ.¹ (var ⲧⲱϭⲥⲉ) ⲡϥⲁϧⲉ ⲣⲁⲧϥ Gk om, ShA 1 461 shalt not disturb ⲡⲙⲟⲟⲩ ⲉⲧⲥⲟⲧϥ ⲏ ⲉⲧⲧ.⁷ *clear & calm*, CO 379 of damaged eye ⲥⲱⲙⲡⲧ … ϣⲁⲡⲧϥⲧ.² καλως; c ⲉ-, *be joined to*: BMar 42 trees bound together ϣⲁⲡⲧⲉⲣⲉⲧⲟⲩ (*l* ϧⲧⲏⲩ) ⲧ.⁴ ⲉ- ⲡⲉⲡⲉⲩⲉⲣⲏⲩ (*v* ⲙⲁⲡⲓⲛ), Mor 28 263 snake drags self as if ⲡⲧⲁϥⲧ.¹ ⲉⲡⲟⲙⲉ, J 107 14 land ⲉⲧⲧ.⁶ ⲉⲡⲉⲓⲱⲣⲉ of NN, CO 145 yard ⲉⲧⲧ.⁸ ⲉⲡⲱⲡⲉ ⲡⲡⲟⲩⲧ; ⲉϧⲟⲩⲛ ⲉ-: BMis 233 hand ⲧ.³ ⲉϧ. ⲉⲧⲧⲱⲣⲉ through much blood (varr Mor 29 6 ⲱϧⲣ ⲉϧ. ⲉ-, *ib* 30 6 *S⸍* ⲗⲱϫ ⲉ-)κολλᾶν (*cf* ⲧⲱϭⲥⲉ ⲉϧ. ⲉ-); c ⲁϫⲛ- *A²*: BM 1224 whoso ⲉϥⲧ. ⲁϫⲱⲓ ⲁⲡⲡⲉⲑⲁⲩ; c ϧⲛ-, *be fixed in*: ShMun 141 mud ⲁϥⲥⲱⲣⲡ ⲉϧⲣⲁⲓ ⲉⲣⲟϥ ⲏ ⲁϥⲧ.⁵ ⲡϧⲏⲧϥ, Mor 51 33 ⲁⲛⲧ.¹ ϧⲛⲧⲉⲣⲱⲧⲉ *sunk, engulfed*.

ⲧⲣⲟϭ nn as pl, *bandage* (?): ShIF 104 ⲥⲙⲓⲛⲉ ⲡⲁⲓ ⲡϧⲉⲡⲧ. ⲙⲙⲟⲩⲣ ⲙⲡⲡⲁⲣⲣⲉ in my sickness.

ⲧⲟϭⲥ nn, ⲧⲱϭⲥ nn v ⲧⲱⲕⲥ *s f*.

ⲧⲱϭⲥ *pierce* v ⲧⲱⲕⲥ.

ⲧⲱϭⲥ, -ⲧⲥ, ⲧⲟϭⲥ⸗, ⲧⲁϭⲥ⸗, ⲧⲟϭⲥ† *S* vb intr, *bleach, dye* (*cf* στιβεῖν, στιβεύς, ⲧⲁϭⲥⲉ): Is 7 3 (P 44 112) ⲣⲁϧⲧ ⲡ ⲧⲱϭⲥ = 43 111 ⲧⲟ. (var & *B* om ⲡⲧ.), Mk 9 3 do (var -ⲧⲥ) γναφεύς, P 131⁶ 37 ϧⲉⲛϣⲧⲏⲛ…ⲉⲩⲧⲟϭⲥ ϧⲓⲧⲙⲡⲣⲁϧⲧ; tr: Pap *penes* RGGayerAnderson ϫⲟⲟⲩ ⲧⲉϣⲧ(ⲛ)ⲡ ⲙⲡⲫⲁϭⲁⲣⲉⲡ… ⲉⲓⲁⲧⲁⲁϥ (ⲡ)ⲥⲟⲩ ⲧⲟϭⲥⲟⲩ, Hall 81 ⲙⲙⲁⲡⲁ…ⲙⲁⲣⲉϥϣⲁⲙⲟⲩ ⲡⲩⲧⲁϭⲥⲟⲩ. *Cf*? PMéd 185 ⲃⲏⲡⲡⲉ ⲉϥⲧⲁⲕⲥ (? φοῖνιξ πατητός Chassinat).

ⲧⲁϭⲥⲉ *SS⸍*, -ⲕⲥⲉ (once), -ⲧⲥⲉ *S*, ⲧⲉϭⲥⲉ *Sᵃ A²*, -ⲥⲛ *S⸍*, -ϫⲉ *A*, ⲧⲁⲧⲥⲓ *B*, ⲧⲉϭⲥⲓ, -ⲧⲥⲓ *F* nn f, *foot-sole, foot-print*: Deu 11 24 *S*(*B* ϣⲉ ⲡⲧ.), Jos 1 3 *S* (var -ⲧⲥⲉ), Ps 17 36 (1°) *SBF* ⲧⲏⲧⲥⲓ (PcodMor), 2 Cor 12 18 *B*(*S* ϧⲓⲛ), BHom 92 *S* ⲉⲙⲡⲉⲧ. ⲡⲣⲱⲙⲉ ⲙⲟⲟϣⲉ ϧⲓϫⲱⲥ ἴχνος; Deu 2 5 *S*(*B* ϣⲉ ⲡⲧ.), Ac 7 5 *S*(*B* do) βῆμα (*cf* Rec 35 84 n), Ps 16 5 *SB*(*F* ϣⲉ ⲡⲧⲉϭⲥⲓ), *ib* 17 36 *S*(*B* ⲡⲁⲅϧⲉⲡ), Cant 7 2 *S*(*F* ϫⲁⲗⲁϫ) διαβ.; Ps 43 19 *B*(*S* ϧ.), Bar 3 28 (31) *B* τρίβος; ShA 2 271 *S* distant only ϣⲁⲡϣⲁ ⲡⲟⲩⲧ. ⲡⲟⲩⲉⲣⲏⲧⲉ, ShBor 246 63 *S* ⲟⲩϣⲟⲡ ⲙⲡⲉ ⲙⲡⲟⲩⲧ. ⲡⲕⲁϧ, Ming 341 *S* ⲁⲡⲁⲩ ⲉⲡⲁⲧ. ϧⲓϫⲙⲡⲕⲁϧ, Miss 4 603 *S* earth from beneath saint's ⲧ., El 140 *Sᵃ* (ⲧ)ⲧ. ⲡⲟⲩϫⲓⲕⲁⲓⲟⲥ = BerlSitz

'25 321 *A* ⲧⲧ., Mani 1 *A*²]ⲧ. (context ?), RE 9 157 *S* ⲡⲣⲟⲥⲕⲩⲛⲉⲓ ⲛⲛⲧ. ⲉⲧⲟⲩⲁⲁⲃ of thy paternity (*cf* Preisigke *W.buch* ἴχνος 3), Bal *F* walked ⲛⲥⲁⲡⲉⲧⲉϭ[ⲥⲓ] of saint, MIE 3 578, 585 *S* ⲛⲧⲁⲧⲥⲉ [ⲛⲧⲉⲣⲟ]ⲙⲡⲉ ⲧⲏⲣⲥ measure of shadow on sundial (*cf* ϣⲥ ⲛⲧ.), Cai 67324 *S*^f^ in list of σκεύη ⲟⲩⲧⲉϭⲥⲏ ⲛⲥⲓⲙⲏ *sandals* (?); iterated: P 131⁵ 105 *S* ⲉⲥⲙⲟⲟϣⲉ ⲉⲥϥⲉⲓ ⲧ. ⲧ. ϣⲥ, ϣⲉ ⲛⲧ. *SB* f, *blow, stroke of foot, footprint*: Ez 32 13 *SB*, *ib* 43 7 *B* ϯϣ. (HCons), Ro 4 12 *B*(*S* ϩⲓⲏ), Z 301 *S* where was no ϣⲥ ⲛⲧ. of man ἴχ.; Deu 2 5, Ac 7 5 as above βῆμα; BMar 128 *S* unworthy of ⲟⲩⲥϣ ⲛⲧ. of his feet, MIE 2 347 *B* sand from beneath ϯϣ. ⲛⲟⲩⲛⲁⲙ, BM 512 *S*^f^ ⲟⲩⲥⲉ ⲛⲧ., Inscr (copy J G Wilkinson) with list of months & numbers opposite each, as ⲙⲛⲧⲉ ⲛⲥⲛⲧⲁⲕⲥⲉ, ⲯⲓⲧⲉ ⲛⲥ. (*cf* MIE 3 above).

ϥⲓ ⲧ., *v* iterated above.

ϫⲓ, ϭⲓ ⲧ. *SBF* ⲥ ⲛⲥⲁ-, *take step after, follow*: ShC 42 173 *S* ϫⲓ ⲧ. ⲛⲥⲁⲡⲉⲥⲙⲟⲧ of fathers, P 130⁵ 35 *S* who may ϫⲓ ⲧ. ⲛⲥⲁⲡⲓⲟⲩⲁ ⲙⲁⲩⲁⲁⲧϥ ⲡⲛ̅ⲉ̅?, MG 25 76 *B* ⲁⲩϭⲓ ⲧ. ⲛⲥⲁⲡⲓⲙⲁ ⲛϣⲁϥⲉ, Va 68 181 *B* ϭⲓ ϣⲉ ⲛⲧ. ⲛⲥⲱϥ; ⲁⲧϫⲓ, ϭⲓ ⲧ., *not to be tracked*: Ro 11 33 *BF* (Ryl Suppl 1, var MR 2 70 ϭⲉⲛ ⲗⲉⲧ⸗, *S* ⲛ ⲣⲁⲧ⸗), P 44 47 *S*, DeV 1 185 *B* ἀνεξιχνίαστος; BG 86 *S* ⲟⲩⲁ. ⲛⲥⲱϥ; om ⲛⲥⲁ- *B*: O'Leary Th 53 ⲟⲩϩⲁⲛ ⲛⲁ.; ⲙⲛⲧⲁⲧϫⲓ ⲧ. *S*: BG 118 ⲧⲉϥⲙ. ⲛⲥⲱⲥ.

In names: ⲡⲁⲧⲁⲧⲥⲓ (or ? ⲡⲁⲧⲁ- ⲧⲥⲓ Cai 8594).

(ⲧⲟϭⲧϭ), ⲧⲉϭⲧⲱϭ† *S* vb tr, *press firmly*: Lu 6 38 (*B* ⲙⲉϩ, *cf* ⲛⲟϭ in cit BMis 411 *inf*) πιέζειν. *Cf* ⲧⲱⲱϭⲉ.

Ⲩ (ⲞⲨ)

Ⲩ, 20th letter of alphabet, called ϩⲉ (My 123) *S*, ϩⲉ, ⲩⲉ (K 1), ⲩⲁ (Stern p 418) *B*, ا و (P 44 125). As numeral *BF*=400 (ϥⲧⲟⲟⲩ ⲛϣⲉ, ϥⲧⲉⲩϣⲉ). Vowel ⲩ replaces ⲁⲓ, as ⲕⲩⲡⲏ (Gu 83); or ⲉ, as ⲃⲉⲕⲩ (Kr 141), ⲇⲣⲁⲡⲩⲍⲁ (BMis 7), ⲕⲩⲃⲏⲧ (Keft ST 42), ϫⲩⲡⲟ (BM 1224), ⲥⲕⲩⲡⲁⲍⲉ (Z 282), ϩⲩ (Kr 11); or ⲏ (oftenest), as ⲁⲥⲕⲩⲧⲏⲥ (Z 265), ⲕⲩⲣⲓⲝ (BMis 302), ⲛⲗⲩⲅⲏ (MG 25 331), ⲍⲱⲩ (AZ 33 132), ⲥⲙⲩ (CO 282), ϩⲩⲙⲁⲓ (J 66 26); or ⲓ, ⲉⲓ, as ⲁⲃⲩⲥⲁ ('Αβεισά J 11 24), ⲇⲩⲁⲓⲙⲟⲥ (AM 287), ⲇⲩⲁⲑⲩⲕⲏ (BMis 520), ϩⲩⲛⲓⲙ (C 86 318); or ⲟⲓ, as ϩⲉⲇⲩⲙⲟⲥ (Kr 11), ⲥⲧⲩⲭⲉ (CO 300).

ⲟⲩ as consonant derived from hierogl *w*, as ⲟⲩⲁ, ⲟⲩⲱⲧⲛ, ⲥⲟⲟⲩϩⲉ, ⲧⲱⲟⲩⲛ, ⲉⲟⲟⲩ, ⲛⲁⲩ; rarely from *b*, as ⲥⲓⲟⲩ; replaced by ⲃ, as ⲃⲏⲣ, ⲃⲱϩⲙ, ⲃⲁⲕⲃⲉⲕ, ⲁⲃⲏⲧ, ⲙⲁϩⲃⲁⲗ, ⲣⲁⲃⲛⲟⲩⲧ, ϣⲃⲉ; or (rarely) replaces it, as ⲉⲩⲉⲓⲏⲛ (J 73 3), ⲟⲩⲏⲏⲃ (ⲃⲏⲃ BAp 79), ⲃⲟⲩϩⲉ (ⲟⲩⲱϩⲉ BMis 486), ⲉⲣⲧⲁⲩ (*ib* 494); or has assimilated it, as ⲟⲩϣⲏⲙ (ⲃⲟⲩϣⲏⲙ), ⲟⲩⲉ- (ⲟⲩⲃⲉ-), ⲟⲩⲁϣ (ⲟⲩⲃⲁϣ); or supplemented by it, as ⲟⲩⲃⲗⲗⲉ (BMis 301), ⲟⲩⲃⲟⲛ (Cai *Kopt Kunst* 118), ⲟⲩⲃⲉⲧ (C 86 218), ⲟⲩⲃⲱⲛϣ (MG 25 153); conversely ⲟⲩⲃⲏⲙⲁ (Worr 283). For Latin *v* in ⲟⲩⲏⲗⲟⲛ (R 1 1 33, Ryl 238, but ⲃⲏⲗⲗⲟⲛ DeV 2 149). As vowel for ⲟ, as ⲁⲡⲟⲩⲗⲟⲅⲓⲍⲉ (J 122 32), ⲕⲣⲟⲩϥ *ib* 12 16), ⲙⲟⲩⲛⲁⲭⲟⲥ (Rec 37 57, JSch 1 118), ⲥⲙⲟⲩⲧ (J 7 42); or ⲱ, as ⲟⲩⲣϫ (J 111 19), ⲟⲩⲗⲁⲣⲓⲟⲛ (ὠράριον Miss 4 69), ⲟⲩⲫⲩⲗⲓⲁ (JSch 1 19); regularly in *A*, as ⲟⲩⲟⲩ (*S* ⲟⲩⲱ), ϫⲟⲩ, ϣⲟⲩⲟⲩⲧ, ϩⲟⲩⲟⲩ⸗, ⲛⲟⲩⲟⲩⲛⲉ, ⲧⲟⲩⲟⲩⲃⲉ & after ⲙ, ⲛ, as ⲁⲙⲟⲩⲛ, ⲙⲟⲩⲧⲉ, ϣⲙⲟⲩⲛ, ⲙⲛⲟⲩⲧ, ⲛⲟⲩⲧⲉ; ⲟⲩ- often prefixed to init ⲱ, esp in Edfu MSS, as ⲟⲩⲱϣ (BMis 160), ⲟⲩⲱⲣϫ (*ib* 236), ⲟⲩⲱⲃϣ (*ib* 510), ⲟⲩⲱϫⲛ (BAp 170), ⲟⲩⲱⲣⲕ (J 67 62); conversely om, as ⲱⲛϩ (BMis 193), ⲱϣ (BMar 51), ⲟϣⲉⲙ (C 86 205). *Cf* in general Sethe *Verbum* 1 162, Ep 1 240 ff. ⲟⲩ transcribes Ar و, as ⲉⲑⲗⲟⲡⲟⲩ اطلبو, ⲓⲉⲭⲟⲩⲛ يكوب, ϩⲟⲩ هو (EW 234 ff, initial و is ⲃⲉ-); or ـُ, as ⲛⲟⲩⲣⲁⲧⲉ بُرادة, ⲙⲟⲩⲥⲁⲁⲧ مُسعَد (AZ 23 118), ϭⲟⲩⲡⲡⲉ جُبّة (MR 5 55); transcribed by و, as اوب ⲟⲩⲁⲃ, نودي ⲛⲟⲩϯ, اووه ⲟⲩⲟϩ (BIF 5 92 ff), اشمون ϣⲙⲟⲩⲛ, مرقوريوس ⲙⲉⲣⲕⲟⲩⲣⲓⲟⲥ.

ⲟⲩ- indef art *v* ⲟⲩⲁ *one sf*.

ⲟⲩ *v* ⲟ *great*.

ⲟⲩ for ⲟ *v* Ep 1 241.

ⲟⲩ *AO* *v* ⲱⲱ.

ⲟⲩ *SBO*, ⲟⲩⲱ *S*^a^, ⲱ *S*^a^*A*, ⲟ *A*, ⲉⲩ *A*², ⲟⲩⲛ *S*^f^*F* interrog pron m f, sg pl, *what, who*?: Job 15 12 *SB*, Ps 8 5 *S*(*B* ⲛⲓⲙ), Eccl 3 19 *SF* ⲟⲩⲙⲡⲉ, Mic 6 3 *A* ⲱ & ⲟ *B*, Mt 20 32 *SBF*, *ib* 24 3 *S*(*B* ⲁϣ), Jo 2 18 *SA*²*B*, 1 Cor 7 16 *SF*(*B* diff) τί, 1 Kg 26 18 *S* ⲁϣ... ⲟⲩ τί...τί, Nu 13 19 *S*(*B* ⲁϣ ⲡⲣⲏϯ), 2 Kg 9 8 *S*, Sa 8 6 *S*, Cl 16 17 *A* ⲟⲡⲉ ⲡⲓⲥⲙⲁⲧ, BHom 55 *S* ⲟⲩⲡⲉ ⲡⲉⲓϣⲁϫⲉ τίς; PS 119 *S* ⲉⲕϫⲉ ⲟⲩ, Br 93 *S* ⲟⲩϭⲉ ⲡⲉⲕⲟⲩⲱϣ, ShRyl 68 259 *S* ⲉⲓⲡⲁⲣ ϩⲟⲧⲉ ϫⲉⲟⲩ ⲉϩⲛⲧⲟⲩ, BAp 91 *S* ⲉⲣⲉⲡⲉⲥⲩⲛⲑⲓⲟⲥ ϫⲉⲣⲉ ⲕⲱϩⲧ ⲉⲟⲩ, C 41 53 *B* ⲟⲩ ⲉⲑⲛⲁⲧⲱⲙⲧ ⲉⲣⲟⲓ, Pcod 11 *S* ⲡϩⲟⲩⲛ ⲙⲡⲕⲁⲧⲁⲡⲉⲧⲁⲥⲙⲁ ⲟⲩⲡⲉ, ST 262 *S* ⲥϩⲁⲓ ⲛϫⲱⲕ ⲛⲁⲓ ϫⲉⲟⲩⲡⲉ, C 41 30 *B* ⲟⲩⲡⲉ ⲡϩⲱⲃ of king with me, LAp 534 *F* ⲁⲧⲉⲧⲛϣⲙϣⲓ [ⲡⲛ]ⲟⲩⲛ (*S* ⲛⲓⲙ), Mor 54 133 *S*^f^ others' bread ϩⲗⲟϭ ⲛⲟⲩⲛ beyond our own, ST 318 *S*^a^ ⲉϥⲙⲛϣⲁ ⲛⲱ, *ib* 253 *S*^a^ ⲱⲡⲉ, MMA 24 6 13

S^a ⲟⲩⲱ ⲉⲧϣⲟⲟⲡ, Aeg 47 *B* ⲟⲩ ϩⲁⲣⲁⲡⲉ ⲡⲁⲓⲥⲁϫⲓ, Kr 236 9 *F* ϩⲉⲛϣⲉϫⲓ ⲡⲟⲩⲛⲧⲉ ⲡⲉⲓ, KroppM 22 *S^a* ⲉⲕⲛⲧⲉ (αἰτεῖν) ⲙⲙⲟⲓ ⲡⲱ, RNC 70 *S* ⲟⲩⲡⲉ ⲡⲁⲓ *who is this*; HL 122 *B* ⲛⲑⲟⲕ ⲟⲩ ⲛⲑⲟⲕ;   *aught S*: ShC 73 82 swear not (saying) ⲛϯⲛⲁⲕⲁ ⲟⲩ ⲁⲛ ϩⲁⲣⲟⲓ ⲛ ⲡⲉⲓⲣⲱⲃⲥⲧ ⲡⲟⲩ;   *as f*: Job 6 11 *SB*, Sa 15 7 *S*, Lu 7 39 *SB*, Eph 1 19 *SBF* τίς, τί; PS 8 *S* ⲟⲩⲧⲉ ⲧⲉⲕⲇⲓⲁⲕⲟⲛⲓⲁ, BMis 324 *S* ⲟⲩⲧⲉ ⲧϭⲓⲛⲛⲏⲃⲉ;   as pl: Ge 33 8 *SB*, Job 13 23 *SB*, Zech 1 19 *SAB*, Ap 2 7 *S* (var & *B* sg) τίς, τί; PS 272 *S* ⲡⲣⲱⲙⲉ…ϫⲉⲟⲩⲡⲉ, BMis 360 *S* ⲟⲩⲡⲉ ⲡⲉⲓϩⲣⲟⲓⲧⲉ (var & BSM 21 *B* ⲁϣ), C 86 224 *B* ⲟⲩⲡⲉ ⲡⲁⲓⲱϣ ⲉⲃⲟⲗ.

—— ⲉ- *SB what* (profit) *to me, thee &c* ?: Ge 48 8 *S* (*B* ⲡⲓⲙ) τίς dat; ShWess 9 147 *S* ⲟⲩ ⲉⲣⲟⲕⲡⲉ ϣⲓⲡⲉ ⲡⲥⲁⲡⲉⲧϣⲟⲟⲡ, ShRE 10 159 *S* ⲟⲩ ⲉⲣⲟⲡ…ⲡⲓⲅⲁⲙⲟⲥ ⲉⲧⲥⲟⲩⲟⲣⲧ (var BM 253 ⲟⲩⲱ, cf Ep 1 241 penult), Va 63 15 *B* ⲟⲩ ⲉⲣⲱⲧⲉⲛ(ⲛ)ⲉ ⲡⲁⲓⲙⲏϣ = BSM 43 *B* ⲟⲩ ⲧⲉⲧⲉⲛϫⲣⲓⲁ ⲉⲡⲁⲓⲙⲏϣ, PBu 89 *S* ⲟⲩ ⲉⲣⲟⲕⲡⲉ ⲡⲏⲓ ⲡⲁⲓ, BMis 36 *S* ⲟⲩ ⲉⲣⲟⲓ ⲁⲛⲟⲕⲡⲉ ⲕⲱⲗⲅ, C 86 115 *B* ⲟⲩ ⲉⲣⲟⲓⲡⲉ ⲉⲧⲛⲓⲕ ⲉϯⲁⲛⲍⲏⲇ.

—— ⲛ- *SBF*, partit gen: Jer 2 5 *SB*, Jo 2 18 *SA²BF* τί acc, R 1 4 54 *S* ⲟⲩ ⲙⲙⲓⲛⲉ ὅστις; ShC 73 194 *S* ⲁϣ ⲛ ⲡⲭⲱⲣⲙ ⲛ ⲟⲩ ⲙⲡⲗⲁⲛⲏ, Ann 17 149 *S* ⲟⲩ ⲡⲣⲱϭⲡⲉ ⲥⲟ[ϥⲓⲁ; cf below ⲉⲧⲃⲉⲟⲩ.

—— ϭ indef art *SAA²B* (rare): Zech 1 9 *A* ⲟⲩⲟⲛⲉ (*B* om art) τί, AP 8 *A²* ⲟⲩϭⲉⲡⲉ τίς; ShViK 9291 *S* ⲟⲩⲟⲩⲧⲉ ⲛ ⲭⲉⲣⲉⲙⲡⲓⲛⲉ ⲡⲟⲩⲛⲉ, R 1 5 25 *S* ⲡⲧⲕⲟⲩⲟⲩ, ClPr 38 105 *S* ⲙⲁⲣⲓⲁ ϫⲉ ⲟⲩⲟⲩⲧⲉ; Jos 4 6 *S* ϩⲉⲛⲟⲩ ⲡⲏⲧⲛⲉ (*B* ⲟⲩⲡⲉ) τί dat, AP 8 *A²* ⲛ-ⲧⲱⲧⲛ ϩⲛⲉⲩ τίνες; ShRyl 68 268 *S* ⲡⲧⲉⲧⲛⲣⲉⲡⲟⲩ, ShWess 9 171 *S* many know ϫⲉⲁⲡⲟⲡ ϩⲉⲛⲟⲩ, PS 357 *S* ϩⲉⲛⲟⲩⲡⲉ ⲡⲉⲓϩⲣⲓⲟⲟⲩⲉ, EW 176 *B* ϩⲁⲛⲟⲩⲛⲉ (*sc this money*).

ⲣ ⲟⲩ *SA²BFO, do what*?: Job 9 12 *S* ⲡⲧⲁⲕⲣ ⲟⲩ *B* ⲟⲩ ⲡⲉⲧⲁⲕⲁⲓϥ, Ps 10 3 *SB*, Mt 21 40 *SB*, Jo 6 9 *SA²* (*B diff*), Eph 6 21 *SF* (*B* ⲟⲩ ⲡⲉ ⲡⲉⲧⲣⲁ ⲙⲙⲟϥ) τί; Ge 43 27 *SB*, Ac 15 36 *S* (*B diff*) πῶς ἔχειν; BSM 32 *B* ⲕⲛⲁⲉⲣ ⲟⲩ = BMis 374 *S* ⲟⲩ ⲡⲉⲧⲛⲁⲁⲁϥ, Mor 47 213 *S* ⲉⲥⲣ ⲟⲩ ⲡⲛⲉⲓⲟⲩⲃ, PCol *F* ⲉⲓⲙⲓ ϫ(ⲉ)ⲁⲕⲗ ⲟⲩⲡ, AZ 21 106 *O* ϣⲁⲥⲣ ⲟⲩ;   ⲉⲣ ⲟⲩ ϭ dat *SB, what to me &c*?: Ge 25 32 *B* ⲉ. ⲡⲏⲓ, Nu 11 20 ⲉ. ⲛⲁⲛ *B* (*S* ⲟⲩ ⲉⲣⲟⲛ) ἵνα τί dat, Hos 14 9 *B* ⲉ. ⲡⲁϥ (*A* ⲁϥⲡⲁⲣ ⲟ) τί dat, Z 343 *S* ⲉⲧⲉⲧⲛⲡⲁⲣ ⲟⲩ ⲡⲁϥ = MG 25 208 *B* τί θέλετε αὐτόν.

ⲉⲧⲃⲉⲟⲩ *SAA²BF, because of what? why*: Ge 3 13 *SB*, Ps 8 19 *B* (*S* ⲁϩⲣⲟϩ) τί, Job 3 11 *S* (*B* ⲁϩⲟϩ), Mt 15 2 *SBF*, Jo 7 45 *SA²B* διὰ τί, Ge 4 6 *A* (Cl) *B*, Is 36 11 *SBF*, Ac 7 26 *SBF* ἵνα τί, Sa 4 17 *S*, Mt 26 8 *S* (*B* ⲟⲩⲡⲉ) εἰς τί, Ge 3 1 *B* τί ὅτι; Sa 13 9 *S* πῶς; Pcod 40 *SF* ⲉ.ⲟⲩ ⲡⲉⲧⲣ ⲡⲟⲃⲉ ⲣ ϩⲟⲩⲟ, DeV 1 59 *B* ⲉⲥⲙⲙⲁⲩ ⲉ.ⲟⲩ;   ⲉⲧⲃⲉⲟⲩ ⲡⲣⲱⲃ: Jud 13 18 *S* ἵνα τί (var εἰς τί); Dan 2 15 *B* περὶ τίνος; Lu 8 47 *SB* δι' ἣν αἰτίαν; Va 57 7 *B* δι' ὧν; R 1 1 21 *S*

ποίῳ λόγῳ; BMar 120 *S* I know not ⲉ. πῶς; PS 233 *S* ⲉ. ⲁⲡⲧⲏⲣϥ ϣⲱⲡⲉ, MIE 2 412 *B*.

ϩⲁⲱ ⲡϩⲱⲃ *S^a* sim: BKU 1 144.

ⲡⲥⲁⲟⲩ *S*, as last: KroppB 15 ⲡ. ⲡⲧⲉⲟⲩⲱϣ ⲧⲁⲣⲓⲙⲉ ⲁⲛ, ViK 9495 ⲉⲕⲛⲁⲃⲱⲕ ⲉϭⲉⲡ ⲧⲃⲧ ⲛ.

ϣⲁⲡⲧⲉⲟⲩ ϣⲱⲡⲉ *SA, until what befall? till when?*: Nu 14 11 *S* (*B* ϣⲁⲑⲛⲁⲩ), Hab 1 2 *SA* (*B* ⲇⲟ) ἕως τίνος, BMar 111 *S* μέχρι τ., 1 Kg 1 14 *S*, Jo 10 24 *A²* (*SB* ⲇⲟ) ἕως πότε.

ⲟⲩ ⲙⲛⲟⲩ *SB, this & that*: ShClPr 22 363 *S* ⲙⲡⲉϥⲡⲓⲥⲉ ⲡⲁⲓ ⲡⲟⲩ ⲙⲛⲟⲩ, Va 61 106 *B* physicians to sick ⲙⲡⲉⲣⲟⲩⲉⲙ ⲟⲩ ⲡⲉⲙⲟⲩ, My 39 *S* ⲙⲁⲣⲉⲟⲩ ⲙⲛⲟⲩ ϣⲱⲡⲉ.

V AZ 47 4.

ⲟⲩⲁ *SAB*, ⲟⲩⲉⲉ *A²*, ⲟⲩⲉ *S/F* nn m, *blasphemy*: Mt 15 19 *S* (var & *B* ϫⲓ, ϫⲉⲟⲩⲁ), Jo 10 33 *A²* (*SB* ϫⲓ ⲟⲩⲁ, *A* ϫ. vb) βλασφημία; ShC 42 81 *S* ⲛϭⲟⲗ ⲡϫⲓ ⲡϭⲟⲛⲥ ⲡⲟⲩⲁ, ShBMOr 8800 203 *S* Origen's ⲡⲟϭ ⲡⲟⲩⲁ, R 1 2 18 *S* denial ⲉⲧⲙⲉϩ ⲡⲟⲩⲁ;   as adj *S*: Ac 6 11 (*B* ⲇⲟ), 2 Pet 2 11 (*B* ⲇⲟ) βλάσφημος; Mor 16 26 ϣⲁϫⲉ ⲡⲟⲩⲁ.

ϫⲓ, ϫⲉ ⲟⲩⲁ *SS/AA²BF, speak blasphemy*: Mt 9 3 *SB*, Jo 10 36 *SAA²B*, Gu 73 *Sf* βλασφημεῖν; AM 254 *B* shut mouths ⲉϣⲧⲉⲙⲭ., CO 81 *S* surety for monk ⲉⲧⲙⲧⲣⲉϥϫ. ⲡⲕⲉⲥⲟⲡ;   ϭ ⲉ- *against*: Is 52 5 *SB*, Mk 15 29 *SB* β. acc, ib 3 29 *SB* β. εἰς, Dan 3 96 (29) *B* βλασφημίαν εἰπεῖν κατά, Mt 12 32 *F* (*S* ϫⲉ ϣⲁϫⲉ ⲉ-, *B* sim ⲡⲥⲁ-) λόγον εἰπ. κ., Cl 47 7 *A* βλ. ἐπιφέρεσθαι dat, 1 Cor 4 13 *SB* δυσφημεῖν; Ac 19 9 *S* (*B* ⲥⲁϫⲓ ⲉϥϩⲱⲟⲩ) κακολογεῖν acc; BG 70 *S* ϫ. ⲉⲡⲉⲡⲛⲁ, ShC 73 9 *S* sim, Pcod 40 *F* ϫⲉϫⲉ ⲉϥϯ, C 43 117 *B* judge to martyrs ⲁⲣⲉⲧⲉⲛϫ. ⲉⲡⲉⲧⲉⲡⲱⲡⲭ *despise, make light of* (?), JA' 75 5 250 *S* soldier ⲉϫ. ⲉⲣⲟϥ by those he hath maltreated;   ⲉϩⲟⲩⲛ ⲉ- *S*: Z 277 ⲉϥϫ. ⲉϩ. ⲉⲧⲡⲓⲥⲧⲓⲥ δυσσεβεῖν περί; ShIF 85 ⲉϥϫ. ⲉϩ. ⲉⲧⲙⲉ;   as nn *SB*: Eph 4 31 *SB* βλασφημία, Sa 1 6 *S* (*B* vb) -μος, C 86 339 *B* ϩⲁⲡⲡⲓϣϯ ⲛϫ.; as adj *B*: v ⲟⲩⲁ adj.

ⲙⲛⲧⲣⲉϥϫⲓ ⲟⲩⲁ *SF, act of blaspheming*: Mk 7 22 (*B* ϫ. nn), Ap 2 9 (*B diff*), Aeg 242 βλασφημία, BMar 110 ⲗⲟⲅⲓⲥⲙⲟⲥ ⲙⲙ. δυσφημία; Pcod 38 *SF*.

ϫⲁⲧⲟⲩⲁ *S, speaker of blasphemy*: Si 3 16, 1 Tim 1 13 (*B* ⲣⲉϥϫⲉ ⲟⲩⲁ) βλάσφημος, Bor 253 151 ϣⲱⲡⲉ ⲛϫ. δύσφ.; ShC 73 202 ⲛϩⲁ]ⲃⲉ ⲣⲱⲙⲉ, ⲛϫ.; ⲙⲛⲧϫ. *S* BMis 154.

ⲣⲉϥϫⲓ, ϫⲉ ⲟⲩⲁ *SB*, as last: Is 66 3 *B* (*S* ⲉⲧϫ.), 1 Tim *B* ut sup βλάσφ.; PS 379 *S* ϫⲉ., Ep App 1 132 *S* John Grammarian ⲡⲉⲓⲣⲉϥϫⲓ., AM 219 *B*.

ⲟⲩⲁ *B* nn, *meaning unce ain*: AM 47 bade stretch martyr with thongs (λῶρος) ⲛⲥⲉϯ ⲡⲁϥ ⲛⲡ ⲡⲟⲩⲁ. Prob corrupt.

ⲟⲩⲁ *S* nn, *meaning uncertain, child* (?): Glos 335 νήπιος · ⲟⲩⲁ (not in ϣⲉⲡⲟⲩⲁ, v ϣⲏⲣⲉ).

ογα S, ογε S′AA²FO, ογεε (Jo), ογει A²(Jo 7 28)F, ογεει A²(AP)F, ογαι BO, ογαιει F(Eccl), ογαε DM, ϥ ογ(ε)ι SBF, ογεια S, ογ(ε)ιε SAA², ογι B nn, **one, someone**: Ge 2 11 B(S ⲛ-), Ps 26 4 B (S ογωτ), Eccl 10 11 F(reading ἕν, S diff), Is 30 17 SBF -εει, Mt 19 16 SB, Ro 5 15 B(S ογα ⲡογωτ) εἰς, Aeg 270 S neg (var ογοⲛ) μηδείς, Nu 16 15 B neg (S ⲗααγ) οὐδείς; Ex 21 12 SB, Is 33 4 SBF -εει, Mt 21 3 SBF -ει, Z 338 S ⲡⲉογοⲡ ογα ⲉⲡⲕⲏⲙⲉ τις; Nu 14 4 SB ἕτερος; BHom 37 S ογα ⲡⲡⲁι ὁπότερος; no Gk: Ge 31 39 B ογ. ⲉⲁⲡⲑⲏⲣιⲟⲛ ογⲟⲙϥ S ⲡⲉⲡⲧⲁ- θηριάλωτος, Pro 6 11 SA ογα εϥⲙⲟⲟⲩⲉ B ογⲣⲉϥⲙ. ὁδοιπόρος, Sa 14 18 S ογα εϥⲣⲁⲧⲏⲅ παρών, Mt 8 2 S ογα εϥⲥⲟⲃ̣ϩ̣ (B diff) λεπρός, Ap 4 3 S ⲉⲣⲉογα ϩⲙⲟⲟⲥ B ⲫⲏ ετ϶. ὁ καθήμενος, 1 Cor 9 2 S ⲁⲛⲧογα ⲛⲏⲧⲛ (B diff) ὑμῖν εἰμί; PS 329 S ογα ⲡⲡⲉγⲣⲁⲛ, ShMIF 23 91 S we &...ⲁⲛⲟⲛ ογα, Aeg 275 S ογα ⲡⲡⲁⲡⲓⲥⲧⲟⲥ (cf ib ογⲟⲛ ϩⲏⲡ-), ib 253 S εϣⲱⲡⲉ ογⲥⲡⲟⲩⲇⲁⲓⲟⲥⲡⲉ ογα, Bodl(P) a 1 a S recipe ϫⲓ ογα ⲡⲁⲗⲙⲁⲣⲕ(ⲁϣⲓⲟⲉ marcasite), AZ 23 109 S sim ⲡⲁⲗϫ ⲓⲛ̄ⲣⲓⲧ (كبريت) ογα, BMis 328 S like an angel but ⲉⲡⲉογα ⲁⲡⲛⲉ, LDi 272 S ⲉⲧⲙⲧⲣⲉογα ⲥⲱⲧⲙ, MIE 2 360 B ϫⲉⲡογ. ⲡⲡⲓⲉⲭⲱⲣ϶, C 89 13 B ογ. εϥϣⲱⲡⲓ, BSM 107 B thought enters ⲡϩⲏⲧ ⲡογ., BMis 261 S let them fight ϣⲁⲛⲧⲉογα ⲡⲗⲩⲅⲏ (πλήσσειν) ⲡογα, El 78 A ογⲉⲡⲉ ⲡⲣⲉⲛ = ib 118 S, AP 36 A² ογⲉⲉⲓⲡⲉ ⲡⲛ̄ⲉ, DM 9 1 εογⲁⲉⲡⲉ, PGM 1 60 O ⲁⲛⲕογⲁⲓ; as adj: Nu 15 5 B ϩⲓⲏⲃ̄ ⲡογ. S ογα ⲛϩ. (var ογα ϩ.), 1 Cor 10 17 B ογ. ⲛⲱⲓⲕ (S ⲡογωⲧ) εἰς; Mus 45 43 B ογ. ⲙⲫⲩⲥⲓⲥ, ViK 9518 S ογϩⲣⲟογ ογα; f forms: Job 2 10 SB, Is 34 16 B(SF m), Zech 4 3 SAB, Gal 4 24 SB μία; Is 1 c ἑτέρα; no Gk: ib 30 22 B(SF ογⲥⲉⲓⲙⲉ) ἀποκαθημένη; PS 7 S ογ. ογοτ̄ⲃ̄ ⲉογ., TU 43 2 A ογ. ϩⲡⲧⲏⲛⲉ, Mani 2 Berl Sitz ’33 85 A² ογⲓⲉ ⲡογⲱⲧ, CO 348 S ογⲉⲓⲉ (sc ϩⲟⲧⲉ), Ryl 361 S ογⲉⲓⲁ (sc ⲉⲡⲓⲥⲧⲟⲗⲏ).

Eleven: ⲙⲛⲧογⲉ S m Nu 29 20, Lu 24 9, BMar 43, f Jos 15 51, PS 1; -ογⲉⲓ m Ge 32 22, Deu 1 2; *twenty-one* &c: ϫογⲧογⲉ S m KroppJ 36, ϩⲙⲉ ογⲉ f 4 Kg 14 23, ⲙⲛⲧογⲉ ⲛϣⲉ m Jud 17 3, sim -ογⲉⲓⲉ Ryl 72 352; for *first* v ϣⲟⲣⲡ(ϣⲟⲣⲡ), ϩⲟⲩⲓⲧ; *eleventh*: ⲙⲉϩⲙⲛⲧογⲉ S m Ez 29 1, -ογⲛⲉ BG 40, -ογⲓⲉ A Zech 1 7; f -ογⲉ S Jer 52 5, Ap 21 20, -ογⲛⲉ BHom 81, -ογⲉⲓⲉ Bor 43 28; *twenty-first* &c: ⲙⲉϩϫογⲧογⲉ S f Jer 52 1, ⲙⲉϩⲙⲁⲓογ ⲙⲡογα S m PS 102, ⲙⲉϩϣⲉ ογα S m ib 66.

ογα ογα S, ⲡογ. ογ. B, **one by one, one after another**: Is 27 12 S(B ⲕⲁⲧⲁ ογ. ογ.) κατὰ ἕνα, Mk 14 19 SB εἷς καθ᾽ εἷς; Lu 1 3 S(B diff) καθεξῆς; Mt 26 22 S(B ⲫογ. ⲫογ.) εἷς ἕκασ.; He 9 5 SF -εει (B = Gk) κατὰ μέρος; PS 243 S relate all ⲕⲁⲧⲁ ογα ογα, ShMIF 23 34 S no need ⲛ̄ϫⲟογ ογα ογα, El

94 A ⲡογⲓⲉⲉⲃ̣ⲉ ογⲉ ογⲉ, BMis 392 S found other 3 *tremis* ογα ογα = Va 63 10 B ⲡογ. ογ., Mich 550 39 S fasted ογα ογα *one day at a time* (cf ⲥⲛⲁγ I), AZ 23 114 S recipe ⲑⲛⲟⲟ(γ) ογα ογα, C 43 118 B εγϭⲓ ⲡⲡⲓⲯⲩⲭⲏ ⲡογⲓ ογⲓ; with connecting prep: JKP 2 92 ογα εϥⲑⲉⲃⲓⲏγ εογα, AZ 23 108 S recipe ⲧⲁⲗⲟ ογα ⲉⲝⲛογα, Deu 2 34 B ογ. ⲡⲥⲁογ. (S om) ἑξῆς, MG 25 336 B set them down ογ. ⲡⲥⲁογ. ⲙⲙⲟογ, Ac 2 12 S speaking ογα ⲡⲡⲁⲣⲛογα B ⲉϯⲟγⲛ ⲉϩⲣⲉⲡ-, Is 6 3 S do B ογⲃ̣ⲉ-; ϩⲉⲡογα ογα SB, **some ones, a few**: BMis 565 S ϩ. ⲛⲣⲱⲙⲉ ὀλίγοι ἄνδρες; ShA 2 26 S ⲡⲧⲉϩ. ⲣ ⲃⲟⲗ, R 2 1 74 S none but ϩ., C 89 6 B there were but ϩⲁⲛογ. ογ.; ⲛⲟγα ογα S sim: ViK 9736 98 rubric ⲧⲁγⲟ ϩⲛ̄ⲡ. ⲉⲧⲧⲟⲟⲙⲉ *such as befit*.

With def art SA²BF: Ex 26 28 S ⲡογα ⲥⲡⲓⲣ B ⲡⲓογ. ⲛⲥ., Lev 24 5 S ⲡογα ⲡⲟⲉⲓⲕ B ⲫογ. ⲫογ. ⲡⲡⲓⲱ., Is 6 2 SB ὁ εἷς; Ryl 94 104 S ⲡογα ⲡⲏⲛⲧογ, DeV 1 79 B sim, Mani 2 A² ⲡογⲉ...ⲡⲙⲁϩⲥⲛⲉγ ShLouvre 10600 S ⲧογⲉⲓ (sc gate) ⲉⲥⲙ̄ⲡⲃⲟⲗ ⲛⲧογⲉⲓ, CO 14 S ⲡογⲁ ⲙⲁⲅⲁⲁϥ ⲡⲣⲣⲟ, C 86 272 B sim, BMOr 6201 B 65 S ⲡογⲁ ⲕⲟⲓⲧⲱⲛ, CO 473 S ⲧογⲁ (sic) ⲥⲕⲉⲡⲉ (σκέπη?), J 2 26 S ⲡογⲁ ⲡⲕⲁϩ...ⲡⲕⲉ-, R 1 2 27 S ⲡϣⲟⲙⲛ̄ⲧογⲁ *Trinity*; or demonstr: BMis 263 S ⲡⲉⲓογⲁ ϫⲉⲙⲉⲣⲕⲟγⲣⲓⲟⲥ *this fellow*; or possess: TU 24 3 S ⲡⲉⲥογⲁ ⲥⲁ, J 67 74 S ⲧⲉϥογⲉⲓ ⲛ̄ⲭⲟⲉ; ⲉⲡ., ⲉⲫ., *to each*: Mt 20 9 SB ἀνά; Z 292 S give it ⲉⲡ. dat; Gu 84 S ⲁⲩϫⲓ ⲡογⲥⲛϥⲉ ⲉⲡ. *each took*, BMis 263 = Mor 29 32 S sending a workman ⲉⲡ. *each*, BM 706 F ⲁγⲙⲉϩ ογⲙⲉⲧⲣⲟγ ⲉⲡογⲉ, PMéd 159 S ογϣⲓ ⲉⲡ., ib 91 S ογⲁ ⲉⲡογⲁ, BSM 77 B exacted of them ⲣ ⲡⲗογⲕⲟϫⲓ ⲉⲫ., BMis 375 S ογϣⲧⲏⲛ...ϣⲱⲭⲡ ⲛⲁⲛ ⲉⲡ. = Va 63 7 B ⲡⲧⲉ ⲫ. ⲫ. ⲙⲙⲟⲛ.

ⲡογⲁ ⲡογⲁ SAA²BF, **each one**: Lev 10 1 SB ⲫογ., Pro 5 22 SAB ⲡⲓογ., Is 36 18 SBF -εει, Jo 6 7 SA² -εε (B diff), ib 19 23 A² -ε, Ac 2 3 SB, Cl 3 4 A ἕκαστος, Sa 16 21 S, Ac 2 45 SB τις; Sa 18 18 S ⲡ. ⲡ. ⲡⲥⲁογⲥⲁ ἄλλος ἀλλαχῇ; Ap 4 8 SB ἓν καθ᾽ ἕν; PS 21 S ⲁⲡ. ⲡ. ⲗⲟ ϩⲛ̄ⲧⲉϥⲧⲁϫⲓⲥ, TU 43 20 A ⲡ. ⲡ. ⲙⲙⲁⲛ, Mani 2 A² ⲡογⲉ ⲡ. ⲕⲁⲧⲁ ⲡⲉϥⲙⲡϣⲁ, Lant 48 S′ ⲡογⲉ ⲡ. by his name, BSM 86 B ⲁⲡιογ. ⲡ. ⲉⲣ ⲁⲡⲁⲭⲱⲣⲓⲛ, BMis 302 S Christ ⲡιογⲁ ⲡ.ⲡⲉ *is one & same* being God & man; f: Nu 7 85 B(S diff) ἡ μία; 1 Cor 7 2 SBF ἑκάστη; Zech 12 12 S(AB diff) φυλὴ φυλή; Jo 2 6 S(B ⲉⲑογⲓ) ἀνά; Br 226 S ⲧ. ⲧ. (sc ⲁⲩⲛⲁⲙⲓⲥ) ⲉⲃⲟⲗ ϩⲛ̄ⲧογ, ShA 2 282 S blood of ⲧ. ⲧ. ⲙⲙⲱⲧⲛ, AM 213 B ⲑ. ⲑ. ⲛⲛⲓⲧⲓⲙⲱⲣⲓⲁ.

ⲕⲉογⲁ SAA²BFO, **another one**: Ps 108 8 SB, Is 42 8 SB, Mt 6 24 S(B ⲭⲉⲧ) ἕτερος; Ge 19 12 B(S diff), Job 19 27 SB, Jo 5 43 SA²B ἄλλος, Zeph 2 15 (3 1) A(B ογⲟⲛ ⲭⲉ) ἔτι; f: Ro 13 9 B(S diff) ἕτερ.; Ex 21 10 SB, Mt 12 13 S(B ⲭ.) ἀλ.; ShC 73 163

S hear also ⲡⲉⲓⲕ., BHom 19 *S* ⲙⲛ ογα ⲡⲁϣ ⲃⲟⲏⲑⲉⲓ ⲉⲕ., AZ 21 106 *O* ⲉⲥⲡⲕⲱⲟⲧ ⲙⲉⲛⲕⲉογⲉ, Miss 4 218 *B* ⲕ. ⲡⲡⲁϧϯ, CMSS 61 *F* ⲕⲉογⲉ, PS 176 *S* ογⲡⲣⲟⲃⲟⲗⲏ...ⲕⲉογⲉⲓ, Aeg 246 *S* ⲧⲕⲉογⲉⲓⲉ, AM 99 *B* ⲫⲣⲁⲡ ⲛογ....ϯⲕⲉογⲓ; iterated: Va 57 123 *B* humility ⲡⲉⲙⲕⲉογⲓ ⲕ. ⲡⲡⲓⲁⲣⲉⲧⲏ ἄλλος ἅπας; ⲣ ⲕⲉογⲁ *S*, be other: Lu 9 29 (*B* ϣⲱⲃⲧ intr) ἔτ. γίνεσθαι.

ⲙⲛⲧ-, ⲙⲉⲧογ. *SB*, unity: Jo 11 52 *B*(*SA* ⲙⲁ ⲛογⲱⲧ) εἷς, Eph 4 3 *SB*, LCyp 2 *S* ⲧⲙ. ⲙⲡⲁⲛⲣ ⲙⲡⲡⲉⲑⲏⲣ ἑνότης; Miss 4 217 *B* in peace & ογⲙ. ὁμόνοια; ShLeyd 371 *S* ογⲙ. ϧⲙⲡⲉϣⲗⲏⲗ, Ep 59 *S* wouldst dissolve ⲧⲙ. ⲡⲡⲉⲕⲕⲗⲏⲥⲓⲁ, Z 623 *S* 2 natures joined ⲕⲁⲧⲁ ογⲙ., MG 25 155 *B* ϫⲉⲛογⲙ. ⲛⲉⲙⲡⲉⲛⲉⲣⲛογ.

ⲣ ογⲁ *SA²B*, be, make one: P 44 99 *S* ⲡⲉⲧⲟ ⲛογⲁ· ⲡⲣⲁⲡⲗογⲛ (ἁπλοῦς), Z 270 *S* ⲧⲣⲉⲡⲓⲥⲛⲁγ ⲣ ογⲁ, PS 122 *S* ⲁⲧⲉⲧⲛⲣ ογⲁ ⲛογⲱⲧ; ⲥ ⲙⲛ-, ⲛⲉⲙ-, unite with: Bor 248 7 *S* ⲟ ⲛογⲁ ⲙⲡⲡⲉⲓⲱⲧ, Va 57 261 *B* ⲁⲓⲉⲣ ογ. ⲡⲉⲙⲁⲕ ἑνοῦν; Tri 630 *S* divinity ⲣ ογⲁ ⲙⲛⲧⲉϥⲙⲛⲧⲣⲱⲙⲉ ‫ اجل‬; ManiH 10 *A²* ⲛϥⲣ ογⲉ ⲛⲉⲙⲉϥ, Aeg 45 *B* Rufus ⲟⲓ ⲛογ. ⲡⲉⲙⲁⲛ, EW 14 *B* sim.

ⲗⲁογⲁ　*v* ⲗⲁ-.

ⲥⲟγⲁ　*v* ⲥⲛⲅ *sf.*

ϣ(ⲉ)ⲛογⲁ　*v* ϣⲏⲣⲉ.

V also ογⲱⲧ.

ογ- *SAA²BFO* (AZ 21 100), ⲟ- *Sª*(Ep 1 240) indefinite art, constr of ογⲁ *one*; pl ϧⲉⲛ- *SAA²F*, ϧⲁⲛ- *B*. *V* Stern 231, 305, Sdff 152, Till 52, Mallon 45. With prefixed ⲉ- (vbal or prep) is often written ⲉγ-.

ογⲁ-, ογⲁ⸗ *SSª*(Theban only) verbal prefix indicating future: ST 270 ογⲁ ⲡⲛⲟϭ ⲡⲣⲱⲙⲉ [, Ep 217 if thou come not ογⲁⲓⲣⲱϣ, CO 122 if God ordain ογⲁⲓⲉⲓ ⲉϩⲣⲁⲓ, ST 389 ⲉϣⲱⲡⲉ ογⲁⲕⲉϣ ϫⲓ, CO 198 ογⲁϥⲧⲁⲗⲁγ, BP 4935 ογⲁϥογⲱϣⲉ ⲡⲓ[ⲟⲥ, Ep 531 ⲟ]γⲁⲥⲉⲓⲛⲉ ογⲁ(ⲉ) ⲉϩⲣⲁⲓ, CO 234 ογⲁⲡⲃⲱⲕ, Ep 214 ογⲁⲛⲓⲉⲉⲓ, COAd 38 ογⲁⲛⲉϯ, ST 280 demons ογⲁγϣⲁⲣⲕ, Win 46 ογⲁⲛⲡ ⲛⲣⲡ; ϩⲁⲓ-(?same): J 73 5 ϩⲁⲓⲭⲉⲡ(ⲓ) ⲃⲱⲕ, 6 ϩⲁⲓⲭⲡⲓ.

Cf PSBA 23 243.

ογⲁ⸗, ογⲁⲓ⸗ *S* (Theban) vb tr, *permit, grant* (?): ST 360 St Pesenthius (?) begged to inquire of God ϫⲉⲛⲉϥογⲁⲧ ⲧⲁⲱⲗ ⲡⲁⲃⲁⲗ ⲉϩⲣⲁⲓ for it is injured, *ib* ⲉⲡⲡⲉ ογⲁⲧ ⲉⲕϫⲟⲟγ ⲉⲃⲟⲗ ⲡⲁⲓ, *ib* 93 money ⲉⲧⲁ(ⲓ)ογⲁⲓογ ⲛⲧⲟⲟⲧⲕ, *ib* ογⲕⲉⲣⲁⲧⲥⲉ ⲉⲟγⲁⲓⲥ ⲛⲧⲟⲟⲧⲕ. CO 244 ογⲁⲕ prob not this, *v* Ep 532 n.

ογⲁⲁ⸗¹, ογⲁⲁⲧ⸗², ογⲟⲟⲧ⸗³ *S*, ογⲁⲧ⸗⁴ *S*(2d pl)*B* (rare), ογⲁⲉ(ⲉ)ⲧ⸗⁵ *SªAA²F*, ογⲁϩⲉ(ⲉ)⸗⁶ *A²*, ογⲁϩⲉⲉⲧ⸗⁷ *AA²*, ογⲁϩⲉⲧ⸗⁸ *AA²* adj, *alone, self*: 1 Kg 7 4 *S¹*, Ps 50 4 *Aⁱ*(Cl, *SB* ⲙⲁγⲁⲁ⸗), Pro 9 12 *S¹A⁷*(*B* do), Mk 9 2 *F*(*SB* do), Jo 12 9 *AⁱA²⁵*(*SB* do), 1 Cor 15 19 *F*(var ⲙⲙⲉϯ, *SB* do) μόνος; Job 33 27 *S¹*(*B* do), Pro 3 7 *S¹A⁷*(*B* do), *ib* 5 17 *A⁵*, *ib* 14 14 *S¹*(Ep 64, var ⲙⲁγ.)*A⁷*, *ib* 26 5 *A⁵*(*S* ⲙ.), Hos 8 9 *A⁵*(*B* ϩⲁⲣⲓ ϩⲁⲣⲟ⸗), Lu 18 9 *S²*(*B* om), Ro 12 16 *S²F*(*B* ⲙ.), He 5 5 *S¹F*(*B* do) ἑαυτοῦ, Z 315 *S* preaching ϩⲓⲧⲟⲟⲧϥ ογⲁⲁϥ δι᾽ ἑαυτοῦ, Bor 226 159 *S* ⲙⲡⲣⲧⲁϩⲣⲟⲩⲧⲕ ογⲁⲁⲕ σεαυτῷ, Pro 26 12 *S¹* παρ᾽ αὐτῷ; *ib* 5 18 *S¹A⁷*(*B* do) ἴδιος; PS 185 *S* ⲛⲧⲟⲕ ογⲁⲁⲕ, *ib* 330 *S* ⲡⲥⲁογⲥⲁ ογⲁⲁⲧογ, ShC 42 35 *S* ⲣⲁⲕⲟⲧⲉ ⲁⲡ ογⲁⲁⲧϥ ⲁⲗⲗⲁ ⲡⲕⲉ-, *ib* 73 145 *S* none shall eat ογⲁⲁϥ (var ⲙ.), ShBMOr 8800 57 *S* ⲧⲁⲕⲉⲧⲏⲩⲧⲛ ογⲁⲧⲧⲏⲩⲧⲛ, BMis 150 *S* ογⲁⲧⲧⲏⲩⲧⲛ, El 128 *S* shall draw out ⲛογⲉⲓⲃ ογⲁⲁⲩ (prob *l* ογⲁ ογⲁ, *cf ib* 94 *A*), TillOster 15 *A* accusest self ογⲁϩⲉⲉⲧⲕ, AP 22 *A²* ⲉⲉⲓϣⲟⲟⲡ ογⲁⲉⲉⲧ, ManiH 13 *A²* ⲉⲓ ⲁⲃⲁⲗ ογⲁϩⲉⲉϥ (*ib* ογⲁϩⲉⲧϥ), Mani 1 *A²* ⲙⲙⲟ ογⲁⲉⲧⲉ, *ib* ⲧⲉϥⲯγⲭⲏ ογⲁϩⲉⲧϥ, Mor 30 33 *F* ⲁⲛⲥⲱⲙⲁ ⲕⲓⲙ ογⲁⲉⲧϥ = BMis 258 *S* ⲙ., J 66 37 *Sª* given to me ογⲁⲛⲧ, ST 227 *Sª* ογⲁⲉⲧ, BM 980 302 *S* pitched his tent ογⲁⲁϥ *apart*; with ⲛ-: Deu 6 13 *S* ⲛⲁϥ ⲛογⲁⲁϥ (var ογ., *B* ⲙ.), Est C 14 *S* ⲧⲉⲥϩⲓⲙⲉ ⲛογⲟⲟⲧⲥ, Su 36 *B* ⲉⲛⲟγⲁⲧⲉⲛ (var ⲙ.) μόν., Jud 11 34 *S* ογϣⲉⲉⲣⲉ ⲛογⲟⲟⲧⲥ, Tob 3 14 *S³* sim μονογενής; Pro 29 21 *S* ⲥⲁⲃⲉ ⲛογⲁⲁⲕ (var ογ.) παρὰ σεαυτῷ, Ac 12 10 *B* ⲁⲥογⲱⲡ ⲛογⲁⲧⲥ (*S* ⲙ.) αὐτόματος.

ⲣ ογⲁⲁ⸗ *S*, be alone: BM 980 304 Jacob departed ⲁϥⲣ ογⲁⲁϥ.

Cf ογⲱⲧ adj, ⲙⲁγⲁⲁ⸗.

ογⲉ *S*, -ⲏ *S⁄*, ογⲉⲓⲉ *AA²*, -ⲓⲉ *A²*, -ⲉⲓ *B*, -ⲏ(ⲏ)ⲓ *F*, ογⲏ(ⲏ)γ† *SA²*, -ⲏογ† *ABF* vb intr, *be distant, far-reaching*: Ps 119 5 *S*(*B* ⲥ ⲡ-) μακρύνειν, Si 27 20 *S* μακρὰν ποιεῖν; MG 25 176 *B* ⲉⲧⲁϥογ. ⲉϥⲙⲟϣⲓ; qual: 3 Kg 8 46 *SB* opp ϩⲏⲡ ⲉϩⲟγⲛ, ϫⲉⲡⲧ, Pro 7 19 *SAB*, Mk 12 40 *BF*(*S* ⲱⲥⲕ) μακρός, Ac 2 39 *B*(*S* ⲙⲡⲟγⲉ) μακράν, Deu 28 49 *S*(*B* ογ. ⲛⲛ) μακρόθεν, Ps 22 6 *SB* μακρότης; Is 66 19 *SB* πόρρω, *ib* 43 6 *SB* πόρρωθεν; Ez 12 27 *SB* πολύς; BMis 416 *S* ⲡⲉⲗⲁⲅⲟⲥ ⲉϥογ. = BSM 58 *B*, DeV 2 145 *B* ⲙⲱⲓⲧ ⲙⲙⲟϣⲓ ⲉϩογ. ⲉⲧⲁⲕⲓ ⲡϧⲏⲧϥ, Mani 1 *A²* ⲡⲉⲧογ. ⲡⲉⲧⲧⲛⲛⲁⲓⲧ, Ep 152 *S* ⲡⲥⲁⲃ(ⲛ)ⲗ ϫⲉⲡⲉⲥⲕγⲗⲟⲥ ογⲏγ.

With following preposition.

—— ⲉ- *SA²B*, *be far from*: 2 Cor 1 8 *S*(*B* diff)ἐξαπορεῖσθαιgen; PS 286 *S* ⲉⲙⲡⲁⲧⲟγⲉ ⲉⲡⲭⲓⲥⲉ; qual: ShA 2 271 *S* ⲉⲓογ. ⲉⲣⲱⲧⲛ, Mani 1 *A²* seat ⲉⲧογ. ⲁⲧⲡγⲗⲏ, C 43 225 *B* ⲭⲱⲣⲁ ⲉⲥογ. ⲉⲡⲁϯⲙⲓ, CO 403 *S* ⲡⲥⲕγⲗⲟⲥ ογ. ⲉⲡϩⲏⲧ; ⲉⲃⲟⲗ ⲉ-: PO 14 327 *B* ογ. ⲉⲃ. ⲉⲛϩⲟⲗϫ, BMis 317 *S* ⲉϥογ.† ⲉⲃ. ⲉⲧⲡⲟⲗⲓⲥ.

—— ⲛ- *SAA²B*, as last: Ps 87 8 *S*(*B* ⲥⲁⲃⲟⲗ ⲛ-), Is 49 19 *SB*, Lam 1 16 *B*(*F* ϧⲁⲃ. ⲛ.) μακρύν. ἀπό; Job 11 14 *SB* πόρρω ποι. ἀ., Lu 24 28 *S*(*B* om ⲛ-) πορρωτέρω πορεύεσθαι; Philem 5 (*S*(*B* ⲫⲱⲣϫ)χωρίζειν; Pro

4 16 SA(B diff)ἀφαιρεῖσθαι ἀ.; Lu 22 41 S(B ογω+
εϧ.), Ac 21 1 S(B ϧ.) ἀποσπᾶσθαι ἀ.; Ps 21 11 S(B
caϧ. π-) ἀφιστάναι ἀ.; Job 6 13 SB ἀπεῖναι ἀ.; Sh
MIF 23 9 S God's help ππεcογε ммок, Mani 2
A² πceογ. ππεγερηγ, Va 61 205 B anoγ. мпімωιτ;   qual : Deu 30 11 S(B eϧ. π-), Zech 6 15
AB, Mt 8 30 SB μακρὰν ἀ., Nu 9 10 SB μ. dat;
Pro 15 29 SA, Is 55 9 B(S diff) ἀπέχειν ἀ.; Lu 7 6
B(S diff) ἀπέχ. μ. ἀ.; Job 22 18 SB πόρρω ἀ.; 3 Kg
19 7 S πολὺς ἀ.; Hos 5 3 B(A diff) ἀφιστ. ἀ.; PS
342 S ceογ. ππεγερηγ, ShC 73 111 S πна ογ. м-
мοογ, Mani 2 A² πετογ. ммаq, BSM 48 B паιογ.
ммωтεπ, Miss 4 562 S ετρηι εροq...ετογ. м-
моq;   π- of how far off S: RNC 8 ογ....π+ογ
мпіліоп ἀπό; Z 337 πρεπаτοπ ... ογ. мψιc м-
міліоп, PS 41 ογ. ммоι πογшнм;   εϧολ π- : Ps
118 150 S(B caϧ. π- μακρύν. ἀ.), Eccl 7 25 S(F ϧаϧ.
π-)μακρὰν ὑπέρ, Pro 2 16 A(S om eϧ., B eϧ. ϧа-)μα-
κρὰν ποι. ἀ.; Mt 14 24 B(S†, F diff) ἀπέχ. ἀ.; Jer 9
2 S(ShC 73 125, B шε eϧ. ϧа-) ἀπέρχ. ἀ.; Jud 20 31
S ἐκκενοῦν ἐκ; PS 152 S аγογε εϧ. ммοι, ShBM
199 362 S ετραογε εϧ. ππετπτοπος, P 131⁴ 138 S
prisoners ογ. εϧ. ппεγρіcε & go free, C 43 67 B
ship ογ. εϧ. мпіχρο;   qual : Ex 33 7 S(B χн caϧ.)
μακρὰν ἀ.; Jer 12 2 B(S eϧ. ϧπ-) πόρ. ἀ.; Ps 102
12 B(S ογε π-) ἀπέχ. ἀ.; Mor 56 11 S ογηηγ εϧ.
ммок, C 41 9 B εqογ. εϧ. мп+ліι πογκογχι,
AZ 21 154 S тпογ. εϧ. мπειρωϧ far from (doing)
this;   caϧολ π- B, пcaϧ. π- S sim : Ps 34 22 B,
72 27 SB, Mt 15 8 SB; PS 150 S аγογε пc. ммοι,
MG 25 30 B ϥογ.† c. мпімωιτ;   ϧаϧολ π- S/F
sim : Eccl 7 25 F μακρὰν ὑπέρ, Lam 1 16 F μακρύν.
ἀ.; Mor 39 44 S/ caused them to ογη ϧ. [πтπολιc]
= C 43 61 B ϧρι caϧ. π-.

—— εϧολ ϧа- B, as last : Ep Jer 72† (F† ϧаϧ. π-)
μακρὰν ἀπό; Is 59 9 (S cοορε εϧ. π-) ἀφιστ. ἀ.; C
86 184 ογ.† εϧ. ϧапіχіппаγ πεϧλіογ, BSM 36
паϧογ.† εϧ. ϧапіαρχωп (Ar ib 144 17 om)=BMis
380 S diff.

—— eϧ. ϧπ-, ϧεπ- SB, as last : Ps 55 tit S(B
caϧ. π-)μακρὰν ἀ.; Ez 11 15 B μак. ἀπέχ. ἀ.; Nu
21 13 S(B diff) ἐξέχ. ἀ.

With following adverb.   c εϧολ SAB, be far off :
Lam 3 11 B(S diff)ἀφιστ.; Jer 3 22 S(BAp 144, B
κω+)ἐπιστρέφειν; Ge 44 4 B μакρὰν ἀπέχ.; Mun
33 S мпεϥογε εϧ. εімητεі ογμіліоп, C 89 89 B
ϧωπт εϧογπ πεмογεі εϧ.; qual : Joel 3 8 SA(B +
ϧіϧογει)μакρὰν; Jer 32 26 S(ViK 9782, B om εϧ.)
πόρ.; ShA 1 300 S ετογ. εϧ. ετρнι εроγπ, EpApp
1 25 S εпογ. εϧ. εта[γε] ϧаϧ πογcіа; as nn : Ex 33
7 B(var caϧολ);   c επεcнт S, be far down : BMis
217 pit ογ.† επ. ϧмпіκаϧ; as nn : ShA 1 150 fire
springeth up мпіксапеіпоϭ πογε επ.;   c επа-

ϧογ S, be far behind : ViK 9752 150 times εγογ.†
επ.;   c εϧογπ S, be far, deep in : Sh lc ма ετ-
шокϧ ετϧнγ ετογ.† εϧ., BMis 448 ϥογε εϧ. ϧіπ-
тοογ about a mile.

—— nn m SAB, distance : Ps 20 5 B(S аϣн),
Dan 7 12 B(S diff)μακρότης, Si 1 12 B(S а.) μακρο-
(ημέρευσις); Is 50 1 B(S тογεіο) ἀποστάσιον; ROC
17 399 B χρονία παράτασις; PS 187 S ппоϭ πογ.
ετϥογ.† ммоq, ShC 42 210 S мпϥϣϧωκ εογε
ммооγ, ib ϧωκ εϧεппоϭ (var πρεп-)πογε, ib 73
162 S ετωπ ρωшπε πογε ммоп, Ryl 94 (33 3)
coals scattered шаογпоϭ πογε, C 89 32 B шапϥі
εϧнт εпογпіϣ+ πογεі a long way northward.

επογε SABF, to a distance : Is 59 14 B(S vb),
BMis 546 S caϧωк ε. μακράν; Pro 9 18 SA πωτ ε.
ἀποπηδᾶν; BAp 65 S тоϥпϥ ε., Mor 39 40 F cакϥ
ε.; επ. π-, away from : Gu 84 S πωτ ε. ппіπε пϣε.

мпογε SAF, at a distance (B ϧіϧογει) : Ex 20 18,
Hab 1 8 A(S επ.) μακρόθεν, Mk 15 40 (F ϧіπ.), Ap
18 15 ἀπό μ., Ge 21 16 μακρότερον; Is 33 17 SF
-ннι, Lu 17 12 πόρρωθεν; ShMich 550 15 ετρεππε
паϧмογ м. εϧολ ϧπммεεγε, ShC 42 204 аϥει м.
to visit him, BAp 134 πεтcωтм м., Miss 8 8 εкм.
ммоп, ViK 9469 S м. εϧ. мπεικаϧ = C 89 97 B
ϧіϧ. π-;   ετм.: Is 5 26 (B vb†) μακράν, Ac 2 39
(B do) εἰς μ.; BM 180 376 ετρнп...ετм. ALR '93
518 S ετρнι εроγп, ετм. εϧολ.

ϧіπογε SF, ϧіϧ. B (mostly, v last) : Mk 15 40 BF
(v above); Miss 4 193 B departed ϧ. εϧολ ϧапεϥ-
шϧнρ, C 89 95 B аϥχογшт ϧ. аϥπаγ;   ϧ. π- :
BMar 105 S was ϧ. мпεϥcтратεγма μακράν gen;
Va 61 94 B repelling poor ϧ. ммοογ = P 131³ 83 S
ϧωоρε caϧολ π-, Z 571 S поχc (sc spittle) ϧ. м-
моογ; іcχεπ. B, from afar : Ps 137 6 (S мπ.)
ἀπό μακρόθεν; C 89 198 saw them і. ϧ.;   εϧολ ϧ.
B as last : Pro 31 14 (SA мπ.) μακρόθεν.

ϧмп. SBF, at a distance : Ez 23 40 B(S мп.)
μακρόθεν; Is 33 13 SF(B vb†) πόρρωθεν; PSBA 30
236 S drew aside ϧ., PMéd 195 S causing eyes to
πаγ εϧολ ϧ., Pcod 20 F poverty cometh ϧ. (S мп.)
from afar.

V тογεіο.

ογε- SF v ογϧε-.

ογΗι B advb, indeed, verily with preceding χε-
for : 1 Kg 17 47 (S χε-), Is 33 23 (SF do), Jo 6 38
(SA² do), Jer 50 7 (S ετϧεχε-) ὅτι, Ac 22 18 (S χε-)
Hab 3 17 (A аϧал χε-), Is 50 2 (S diff) διότι, Dan
3 96, Lu 1 7 (S eϧ. χε-) καθότι; BSM 32 χ. аπ-
cωтεм επcаϧ = BMis 374 S επειϧн, ib 45 χ. π-
θωтεπ ϧапрεмраϣ = ib 393 S оптωc χε-, MIE
2 355 χ. ϥεмпϣа = BAp 80 S паптωc, Aeg 23 χ.
а+ογπογ ϧоϧ = ib S χε-, C 43 162 χ. аϥχос, ib

223 ⲭ. ⲡⲡⲉϥⲧⲁⲕⲟ;   +ⲅⲁⲣ: Nu 22 12 (S = Gk), Is 5 24 (SF do) γάρ; Rec 6 179 ⲭ. ⲅⲁⲣ (ⲥ)ⲥⲃⲏⲟⲩⲧ = BMar 214 S ϭⲥⲛϩ ⲅⲁⲣ, C 43 68 ⲭ. ⲅⲁⲣ ⲉⲓⲛⲁϣⲉ ⲡⲛⲓ, DeV 1 165 let us flee ⲭ. ⲅⲁⲣ ⲡⲛⲉⲥⲓ ⲉϩⲣⲏⲓ ⲉⲭⲱⲛ lest.

ογοι S advb showing consent: JTS 10 394 bowed his head saying ⲭⲉⲟⲩ. ⲡⲁⲭⲥ̅ +ⲛⲁⲣ ⲁⲡⲁⲕ.

ογο(ε)ι S, -ⲟⲓ B, -ⲁ(ε)ι A, -ⲁⲉⲓⲉ A², -ⲁⲓ F, ⲡⲟⲩ. SAB (v below) nn m, *rush, course*, swift movement: Pro 3 25 SAB, Jer 29 2 B(S=Gk) ὁρμή, Ps 45 ·5 B (S reading ὁρμος), Am 1 11 B(A ϭⲁⲙ) ὁρμημα; Sa 5 11 S ῥοῖζος; Job 39 25 B (no S) ἅλμα; Hab 2 5 B ⲉⲛⲁϣⲉ ⲡⲉϥⲟⲩ. (A ϣⲁϣⲟ?) ἀλαζών; ib 3 8 B ⲟⲩ. ⲙϥⲱⲧ of horse ἱππασία (A ⲟⲩ.); Mor 31 197 S ⲡⲟⲩ. ⲡⲟⲩⲙⲟⲩ ⲡⲣⲱⲟⲩ, DeV 2 57 B ⲥⲱⲛϩ ⲙⲡⲁⲣⲟⲙⲟⲥ ⲙⲡⲉϥⲟⲩ.; ϭⲉⲡⲟⲩⲟⲩ. B, *with a rush, violently*: Mt 8 32 (S + ⲡⲟⲩ. ⲉϩⲣⲁⲓ), Ac 7 57 (S do) ὁρμᾶν; 2 Pet 3 10 (S ϩⲛⲟⲩϭⲉⲡⲏ) ῥοιζηδόν; Va 61 28 snake ⲱⲛϥ+ ϭ. σύρεσθαι only; MG 25 404 ϭⲉⲡⲟⲩⲛⲓϣϯ ⲡⲟⲩ. (ROC 19 45 ϫⲁⲁ only).

A + ⲟⲩ., *go about seeking*, seek S: Deu 12 5 (B ⲕⲱϯ) ζητεῖν; Z 337 ⲡⲉⲥϯ. ⲉⲥϣⲓⲡⲉ ἐπιζ.; Jud 5 14 ἐξερευνᾶν; Eccl 7 26 κυκλοῦν; Mor 37 43 ⲡⲉϥϯ. like lion περιέρχεσθαι; (Is 5 29 B l? ⲡⲉϥⲟⲩ. as S); ShA 1 55 ⲉϥϯ....ⲉϥⲙⲟⲩϣⲧ.

With following preposition.   ⲥ ⲉ- S: BAp 151 ⲙⲡⲣϯ. ⲉⲑⲏ;   ⲥ ⲉϩⲟⲩⲛ, ⲉϭ. ⲉ- SB: Ryl 94 (33 1) S +. ⲉϩ. (ⲉ)ⲡⲃⲁⲣⲃⲁⲣⲟⲥ, C 89 43 B ⲉⲩϯ. ⲉϩ. ⲉϯⲙⲟ-ⲡⲏ = Miss 4 524 S +. ϩⲛ- = ib 557 يبطلوا, Va ar 172 27 في;   ⲥ ⲙⲛ- S: PS 375 spent 3 days ⲉⲩϯ. ⲙⲙⲁⲥ;   ⲥ ⲡⲥⲁ- SA, *seek, pursue after*: 1 Kg 23 25, Nah 3 7 A(B ⲕⲱ. ⲡⲥⲁ-) ζ.; Am 9 3 (A ⲕⲱ. ⲡⲥⲁ-, B ϩⲟⲧϭⲉⲧ ⲡⲥⲁ-) ἐξερευνᾶν; Jos 2 16 κατα-διώκειν ὀπίσω; PS 34 ⲧⲉϯ. ⲡⲥⲁⲣⲱϩ ⲛⲓⲙ, Ann 19 236 ⲁⲥϯ. ⲡⲥⲱϥ = C 89 34 B ⲕⲱ. ⲡⲥ., Mor 22 25 ⲁϥϯ. ⲡⲥⲁⲁⲗⲁⲙ ⲉⲃⲟⲗ ϩⲙⲡⲁⲣⲁⲇⲓⲥⲟⲥ;   ⲥ ϩⲛ- S: 1 Kg 26 20 καταδιώ.; Cant 3 3 S(F ⲕⲱ.) κυκ.; Mk 6 6 (B ⲙⲟⲩϣⲧ) περιάγειν; Aeg 247 ἐπέρχ.; Eccl 1 13 (F ⲭⲓⲓⲓ) κατασκέπτεσθαι; Pcod 23 let us +. ϩⲛ-ⲧⲉⲅⲣⲁⲫⲏ, BMis 446 ⲉϥϯ. ϩⲛⲧⲡⲟⲗⲓⲥ ⲡⲥⲁⲡⲉϥϣⲏ-ⲣⲉ;   ⲥ ϩⲓ- B: C 89 18 ⲉϥϯ. ϩⲓⲡⲓϣⲁϥⲉ ὁδεύειν acc.

—— nn m B, *progress, impetuosity*: Va 57 202 ⲡϯ. ⲡⲧⲉ ⲡⲓϭⲩⲡⲉⲣⲉⲧⲏⲥ ἐξάγειν; ib 180 ϩⲁⲡϯ. ⲡⲧⲉ ϩⲁⲡⲱϭⲡⲏⲛⲓ.

ⲭⲓⲛϯ ⲟⲩ. B, *onrush, attack*: Va 57 242 ⲡⲓⲭ. ⲉⲣⲟϥ of fire ῥύμη; MG 25 97 +ⲭ. (var ⲛⲓ-) of demons.

B + ⲡⲟⲩ., ⲙⲡⲟⲩ., ⲡⲉⲕⲟⲩ. &c SAA²BF, *go forward*: Nu 25 6 S(B om) ἔρχ., Ps 63 7 S(B ι) προσ-ἐρ.; Ac 8 30 S(B ϭⲟⲭⲓ) προστρέχειν; ib 21 33 S (B ϭⲱⲡⲧ ⲉϩⲟⲩⲛ) ἐγγίζειν; BMis 18 S ⲁϥϯ ⲡⲉϥ-ⲟⲩ. ϫⲉⲉϥⲛⲁⲃⲱⲕ, CA 109 S ⲡⲉⲧⲛⲁϯ ⲡⲉϥⲟⲩ. ⲛϩⲣⲣⲉ as catechumens, Va 59 7 B ⲙⲁ ⲡⲉⲕⲟⲩ. ⲡⲧⲉⲕⲟⲩ-

ⲱϣⲧ;   ⲥ ⲉϩⲟⲩⲛ: Joel 3 9 SA(B do) προσάγ.; R 1 1 37 S παραπηδᾶν; Aeg 281 S προσιέναι; Ryl 40 S people ⲧⲓ ⲡⲉⲩⲟⲩ. ⲉⲣ. ⲡⲥⲉⲁⲥⲡⲁⲍⲉ.

With following preposition.   ⲥ ⲉ-, *advance to-ward*: Mk 11 27 S(B ⲓ ϩⲁ-) ἔρχ. πρός, Va 63 105 B ϣⲁⲩϯ ⲙⲡⲟⲩⲟⲩ. ⲉϯⲧⲣⲁⲡⲉⲍⲁ εἰσέρ. εἰς, Ge 43 19 S (B do) προσέρ. πρός, Deu 22 14 S(B ϣⲉ ⲉϩⲟⲩⲛ ϩⲁ-), Cl 23 1 A, Jo 12 21 SA²(B ⲓ ϩⲁ-) πρ. dat; Mk 10 35 S(B do) προσπορεύεσθαι dat; Jos 4 18 S Gk no prep, Ac 19 29 S(B ϭⲟⲭⲓ ϭⲉⲡⲟⲩⲟⲩ.) ὁρμᾶν εἰς; PS 141 S ⲁⲓϯ ⲡⲁⲟⲩ. ⲉϯϭⲟⲙ, Aeg 261 S + ⲙⲡⲉϥⲟⲩ. ⲉⲧⲡⲓⲥⲧⲓⲁ, C 43 145 B ⲁⲩϯ ⲙⲡⲟⲩⲟⲩ. ⲉⲡⲓⲇⲟⲅⲍ, Pcod 39 SF + ⲡⲉⲩⲟⲩ. ⲉⲣⲟϥ;   vbal: Si 2 1 B προσέρ. inf; Aeg 280 S προσιέναι dat; BMar 122 S ⲁⲕϯ ⲡⲉⲕⲟⲩ. ⲉⲃⲱⲕ ἐξορ. ἐπί, Ac 14 5 S(B ϭ.) ὁρμή γίνεσθαι;   ⲉϩⲟⲩⲛ ⲉ-, *in to*: Ru 2 12 S ἔρ. πρός, Lev 19 33 S(B ⲓ ϩⲁ-), Cl 63 1 A προσέρ. dat; Aeg 288 S προσι. dat; Ez 37 7 SB προσάγ. πρός; Mk 8 32 S(BF diff) προσλαμβάνειν; Bor 263 29 S babes + ⲡⲉⲩⲟⲩ. ⲉⲣ. ⲉⲧⲉⲕⲓⲃⲉ, J 84 7 S ⲁⲛϯ ⲡⲉⲛⲟⲩ. ⲉⲣ. ⲉⲧⲉ(ⲓ)ⲡⲣⲁⲫⲟⲛ (cf PLond 1 232 ὁρ. εἰς), AM 45 B ⲁϥϯ ⲙⲡⲉϥⲟⲩ. ⲉϭ. ⲉⲡⲉϥⲏⲓ;   vbal S: Lev 21 17 (B ⲓ ⲉϭ., var MIE 2 366 ϭⲱⲡⲧ ⲉϭ.), Est A 5, Ac 7 31 (B ⲓ) προσέρ. inf;   ⲉϩⲣⲁⲓ ⲉ-, *up to, on to*: Ge 31 21 S(B ⲓ ⲉϩ. ⲉ-) ὁρ. εἰς; J 18 9 S ⲉⲓⲧⲓ ⲙⲡⲁⲟⲩ. ⲉϩ. ⲉⲧⲉ(ⲓ)ⲡⲣⲁⲥⲓⲥ;   ⲥ ⲉϫⲛ-, *as last*: Jer 4 28 S(B ϭ.) ὁρ., Mk 5 13 S(B ϭⲉⲓ ⲉϩⲣ.) ὁρ. κατά; BIF 14 150 S ⲁⲩϯ ⲙⲡⲉⲩⲟⲩ. ⲉⲡⲃⲏⲙⲁ, AM 223 B ⲁϥϯ ⲙⲡⲉϥⲟⲩ. ⲉⲭⲱϥ;   ⲉϩⲣⲁⲓ ⲉϫⲛ- S: Ac 7 57 (B ϭ. ⲉϩ. ⲉⲭ.) ὁρ. ἐπί, Mt 8 32 (B ϣⲉ ϭⲉⲡⲟⲩⲟⲩ.) ὁρ. κατά; PO 14 364 B ⲁⲩϯ ⲙⲡⲟⲩⲟⲩ. ⲉⲣ. ⲉⲭⲱⲟⲩ to devour them;   ⲥ ϩⲓϫⲉⲛ- B, *as last*: AM 289 ⲁϥϯ ⲙⲡⲉϥⲟⲩ. ϩ. ⲡⲓ-ⲃⲏⲙⲁ;   ⲥ ⲛ- locative: Jos 3 9 SB προσάγ. ὧδε; ⲥ ⲉⲃⲟⲗ ϩⲛ-, ϭⲉⲛ-, *forth from*: Deu 33 2 S(B ⲓ ⲉϭ. ϭⲉⲛ-) κατασπεύδειν ἐκ; AM 16 B ⲁⲩϯ ⲙⲡⲟⲩⲟⲩ. ⲉϭ. ϭⲉⲛⲡⲓⲡⲁⲗⲁⲧⲓⲟⲛ;   ⲥ ⲉϩⲟⲩⲛ ϩⲛ- S, *in to*: Mor 31 42 ⲁϥϯ ⲙⲡⲉϥⲟⲩ. ⲉϩ. ϩⲙⲡⲧⲟⲟⲩ;   ⲥ ϩⲓⲑⲏ ⲛ-, *before*: Jos 4 5 SB προσάγ. ἔμπροσθεν.

ϭⲓⲛϯ ⲡⲟⲩ. S, *act of going*: Mor 53 57 +ϭⲓⲛϯ ⲡⲉⲥⲟⲩ. ⲉⲡⲏⲓ̅.

ⲭⲓ ⲟⲩ. A², *take way, go*: Mani 1 ⲉⲥⲁⲭ. ϣⲁⲡⲉⲕⲡⲁⲉ.

ⲡⲟⲩⲟⲉⲓ S, -ⲁ(ε)ⲓ A, ⲉⲛⲟⲩⲟⲓ B nn m: Nu 11 17 B(S = Gk), Pro 21 1 A(S ⲟⲩ.), Dan 8 6 B(Bardelli) ὁρμή, Ps 67 18 B (as if ὁρ., S Gk ἅρμα), Deu 28 49 B(S ⲟⲩ.) ὁρμημα; C 43 49 B ϭⲉⲛⲡⲉⲛ. ⲙⲡⲁⲓ̅ⲡⲁ̅;   BHom 55 S + ⲙⲡⲉϥ(ⲟⲩ)ⲟⲉⲓ ὁρμᾶν; Mal 3 5 A + ⲙⲡⲁⲛ.(B ϭⲱⲡⲧ ⲉ-) προσάγ. πρός; BHom 136 S + ⲙⲡⲉⲥⲛ. (cf Mk 7 25), ib 138 S + ⲙⲡⲉⲅⲛ. (cf Mt 15 23 ⲡⲉⲩⲟⲩ.).

In place-names (?): ⲡⲟⲩⲟⲓ, ⲡⲉⲟⲩⲟⲓ (Ryl 147 n).

ογο(ε)ι S, -ⲁ(ε)ⲓ AA²F, -ⲟⲓ B interj, *woe!*: BMis 150 S ⲟⲩ. ϩⲛ(ⲟⲩ)ⲟⲩ. ⲉϥⲕⲏⲃ;   ⲥ ⲛ- dat:

Eccl 10 16 *SF*, Is 1 4 *SBF*(not -ⲁⲉ), Mic 7 1 *AB*, Mt 18 7 *SA*(Cl)*B*, MG 25 5 *B* ⲟⲩ. ⲡⲁⲥ ⲣⲁⲕⲟϯ οὐαί; Job 10 15 *SB*, Jer 4 31 *SB* οἴμοι; Jud 11 35 *SB* ⲁ̄ ⲁ̄ (var οἴμ.); CDan 89 *B* ⲟⲩ. ⲏⲏⲓ ἀβάλα ἐμοί; Bar 4 31 *B* δείλαιος *peribunt*; PS 100 *S* ⲟⲩ. ⲡⲁⲓ ⲁⲡⲟⲕ, ShC 42 121 *S* ⲟⲩ. ⲙ̄ⲡⲁⲓ ⲉⲧⲙ̄ⲙⲁⲩ, ShA 2 117 *S* ⲟⲩ-ⲟⲓⲡⲉ ⲡⲡⲉⲧⲛⲁⲁⲡⲓⲭⲉ, ShWess 9 175 *S* ⲉϣϫⲉ ⲟⲩ. ⲡⲁⲡ ⲉⲣϣⲁⲛ-, ShC 73 94 *S* ⲡⲕⲁⲓⲣⲟⲥ ⲉⲧⲉⲡⲁⲓⲁⲧⲟⲩ ⲡⲉ̄ⲛⲧ̄ϥ...ⲉⲧⲉⲟⲩ. ⲡⲁⲩ ⲡⲉ̄ⲛⲧϥ, *ib* 4 *S* ⲡⲉⲧⲡⲁⲁⲙⲉⲗⲉⲓ ...ⲡⲁϣⲱⲡⲉ ⲉⲟⲩ. ⲡⲁⲩ ⲙ̄ⲙⲁⲩ, ShP 130ᵗ 149 *S* cometh ⲉⲗ̄ⲡⲉⲓ ⲙ̄ⲙⲱⲧⲛ ⲁⲩⲱ ⲉⲟⲩ. ⲡ̄ⲣⲱⲙⲉ among you, ShR 2 3 37 *S* ⲡⲟⲉ ⲉⲧⲉⲟⲩ. ⲡⲡⲉⲣⲣⲱⲟⲩ, MIE 2 407 *B* ⲟⲩ. ⲡⲏⲓ ϫⲉⲁⲅ̄ⲭⲫⲟⲓ; as nn m: Pro 23 29 *SA*, Ez 2 10 *SB*, Ap 11 14 *SB* οὐ.; ShA 1 188 *S* ⲗⲩⲡⲏ, ⲡⲉⲉⲡⲉ, ⲟⲩ., ManiH 11 *A²* ⲁϥϣⲣ̄ϣⲱⲣⲉ ⲁϥⲱϣ ⲟⲩ. ⲁⲭⲱⲥ, BMar 8 *S* ⲟⲩ. ⲙ̄ⲡⲉϣⲧⲟⲣⲧⲣ̄ ⲡⲏⲩ ⲉ̄ϩⲣⲁⲓ ⲉϫⲱⲕ. *Cf* Hist Laus § 22 οὐαὶ ποιεῖν dat.

ⲟⲩⲟⲓ *S* interj   *v* ⲟⲩⲏⲓ *s f.*

ⲟⲩⲟⲉⲓⲉ nn m, *husbandman, cultivator* of fields or vines (*v* Wess 19 47 n), forms *v* below: Ge 9 20 *SB*, Jo 15 1 *SA²B*, Ja 5 7 *SB* γεωργός, Jer 52 16 *B* ⲟⲩ. ⲛ̄ⲕⲟⲓ, BHom 7 *S* γηπόνος; Lu 13 7 *B*(*S* ϭⲙⲉ), Is 61 5 *B* ⲟⲩ. ⲛⲁⲗⲟⲗⲓ (*S* do) ἀμπελουργός; K 110 *B* ⲡⲓⲟⲩ. ـٍٟ; Kr 112 *S* tends vines, *ib* 91 *S* sows flax, Ryl 159 *S* ⲁⲛⲟⲕ ⲡⲟⲩ. ⲁⲅⲱ ⲡⲉϭⲙⲉ, CMSS 63 *Sᶠ* ⲉⲩⲕⲁⲣⲉ ⲥⲓⲙ, RE 9 159 *S* ⲃⲉⲕⲉ ⲡⲟⲩ.; Ryl 162 *S* ⲟⲓⲡⲉ ⲡⲟⲩ. ⲡⲁⲓⲕⲁⲓⲟⲡ, GMir 181 *S* (ⲟⲩ)ⲟⲩ. ⲧⲏⲣϥⲡⲉ ⲡⲁϥⲙⲉ *is all peasants*, Lant 110, 111 *S* ⲡⲟⲩ. ⲙ̄-ⲙⲟⲩⲓ *island peasant* (?, ⲟⲩⲁⲓⲉ ⲙⲟⲩⲟⲩ Ryl 165 prob diff), WS 137 *S* ⲟⲩⲁⲓ ⲱ.

Forms: *S* ⲟⲩⲟⲉⲓⲉ R 2 1 76, CA 96, BHom 62, TT 18 (var Mich 550 24 -ⲉⲓⲏ), Kr 60, BM 1130, -ⲟⲓⲉ Ryl 341, BM 1019; ⲟⲩⲟⲓⲉⲓⲉ BMar 167, -ⲟⲓⲓⲉ BMOr 6201 A 110; ⲟⲩⲟⲟⲉⲓⲉ Mor 32 12, -ⲟⲟⲓⲉ Ryl 120, Kr 85, BM 1115, -ⲟⲟⲉ Kr 51, ⲟⲩⲟ(ⲉ)ⲓⲏ Ge *l c*, Si 7 15, ShZ 602, ShC 42 59; ⲟⲩⲉⲓⲏ (*cf* pl) Bor 306 257; ⲟⲩⲟ(ⲉ)ⲓ BHom 26, Z 549, Tor 28, BM 1022, -ⲟⲟⲉⲓ Ryl 127;   Theban (ⲟⲩ)ⲁⲉⲓⲉ CO 293, *ib* Ad 38, ⲟⲩⲁⲉ Ep 356, CO 181 (also PBu), ⲟⲩⲉ Ep 165, ⲟⲩⲁ-ⲉⲓ RE 5 plate 21, -ⲁⲓ CO 156, ⲟⲩⲁ Ep 227;   *Sᶠ* ⲟⲩⲁⲓⲉ CMSS 20, 64 as pl;   *A* ⲟⲩⲁⲓⲉ Joel 1 11 as pl;   *A²* ⲟⲩⲁⲉⲓⲉ Jo *l c*;   *B* ⲟⲩⲱⲓ;   *F* ⲟⲩⲁⲁⲓⲉ 1 Cor 3 9;   pl forms (*v* Rec 31 78): *S* ⲟⲩⲉⲉⲓⲏ Mt 12 1, ShC 73 152, ⲟⲩⲉⲓⲏ Mor 37 76; *Sᶠ* ⲟⲩⲓⲉ CMSS 63; *A²* ⲟⲩⲁⲓⲏ ManiH 12; *B* ⲟⲩⲓⲏ Jer 52 16, C 41 42.

ⲉⲓⲉⲡ ⲟⲩ.   *v* ⲉⲓⲟⲡⲉ.

ⲙ̄ⲛ̄ⲧⲟⲩ. *S, husbandry:* Si 7 15, Z 362 γεωργία; ShBor 247 120 ⲧⲙ. & other crafts, Ryl 159 tenant shall ⲣ̄ ⲧⲉⲩ̄ⲡⲟⲩⲣⲅⲓⲁ ⲛ̄ⲧⲙ., J 59 9 will sow without ⲕⲁⲧⲁⲫⲣⲟⲡⲏⲥⲓⲥ ⲛⲙ.

ⲙⲁ ⲡⲟⲩ. *S:* 1 Cor 3 9 (*BF* ⲓⲉⲫ ⲟⲩ.) γεώργιον; ShR 2 4 45 God gave it ⲉⲩⲙ. opp ⲭⲉⲣⲥⲟⲥ.

ⲣ(ⲉ)ⲙⲟⲩ. *SB, husbandman:* Pro 6 8 *B*(*S* ⲣⲱⲙⲉ), ἰδιώτης; MG 25 241 *B* ⲥⲭⲏⲙⲁ ⲡⲣ. κοσμικός; *ib* 28 *B* ϩⲉⲗⲗⲟ ⲡⲣ., PBu 81 *S* ⲡ. opp ⲡⲟⲗⲓⲧⲏⲥ, Mor 32 25 *S* am not p., father was tribune, Ep 165 *S* ⲡⲏⲕⲉ ⲡⲣⲙⲟⲩⲉ (*ib* -ⲟⲩⲁ), COAd 60 *S* ϣⲏⲣ ⲣⲙⲟⲩⲁⲉ, Hall 91 *S* ⲡ̄ⲕⲣⲙⲟⲅⲟⲉⲓⲉ.

ⲣ ⲟⲩ: *S, do husbandry:* Z 362 ⲁϥⲉⲣ ⲟⲩ. ⲉⲣⲟϥ (*sc* land) γεωργεῖν; Ryl 206 ϭⲱ]ⲙ ⲉⲓⲟ ⲡⲟⲩ. ⲉⲣⲟⲥ.

In name (?): Σενπαπωειε (PSBA 30 11).

ⲟⲩⲟⲩ *A*   *v* ⲟⲩⲱ (all) & ⲱⲱ.

ⲟⲩⲱ *SA²BFO*(+ ϯ), ⲟⲩⲟⲩ *A*, ⲁⲟⲩⲱ *B*(mostly + ϭⲓ), ⲟⲩⲛⲟⲩⲧᵗ *B*(? *v* ϯ ⲟⲩⲱ ⲉⲃⲟⲗ) vb **I** intr, *cease, stay:* Is 24 8 *B*(*S* ⲗⲟ), *ib* 32 10 (*SF* ⲟⲩⲉⲓⲡⲉ), Lu 11 1 *S*(*B* ⲕⲏⲛ), Z 362 *S* ⲡⲧⲉⲣⲉⲡϫⲓⲱⲧⲙⲟⲥ ⲟⲩⲱ παύ-εσθαι; Deu 32 36 *B* ⲁⲟⲩ. (var ⲙⲟⲩ⳪ⲕ, *S* ⲱϫⲛ), 1 Kg 16 11 (*B* diff) ἐκλείπειν; Is 18 5 *S*(*B* ϫⲱⲕ ⲉⲃⲟⲗ) συντελεῖν; Am 8 5 *S*(*B* ⲥⲓⲛⲓ) διέρχεσθαι, Jer 8 20 *S* (Mun 140, *B* ⲕ.) παρέρχ.; Z 352 *S* ⲁⲡⲟⲉⲓⲕ ⲟⲩⲱ, SHel 41 *S* thinkest thou ϫⲉⲁⲡⲁⲧⲉⲭⲡⲏ ⲟⲩⲱ?, N&E 39 337 *B* ⲉⲧⲁⲅ̄ⲟⲩⲱ ... ϫⲉⲛⲡⲓⲉⲅⲕⲧⲏⲣⲓⲟⲡ, Pcod 40 *SF* ⲉⲣⲉⲛⲁⲓ ⲟⲩⲱ where wilt find (others)?;   c 2d pres (Gk inf or part), *cease happening*, have *already* happened: Ge 27 30 *SB*, Lu 5 4 *SB* παύ., Ex 31 18 *S*(*B* ⲕ.) καταπ.; Mt 13 53 *BF*(*S* tr) τελεῖν, Deu 31 24 *S*(*B* ϫⲉⲕ ⲧⲟⲧⲥ ⲉⲃⲟⲗ), Hos 13 2 *A*(*B* ⲕ.), Jo 9 22 *SA²*(*B* om) συντ.; Job 15 22 *S*(*B* = Gk), Eccl 1 10 *S*(*F* Mich = Gk), Lu 11 7 *SB*, Jo 19 33 *SA²*(*B* ϩⲏⲁⲏ + ⲟⲩⲱ), C 89 170 *B* ⲁϥϣⲁⲛⲟⲩⲱ ⲁϥⲧⲁⲕⲟ ἤδη; C 86 307 *B* ⲉⲧⲁⲥ̄ⲟⲩⲱ ⲁⲥ̄ϫⲱ ⲡⲛⲁⲓ ταῦτα εἰπούσης; Aeg 274 *S* ⲉϥϣⲁⲛⲟⲩⲱ ⲉϥϣⲗⲏⲗ μετά; Mk 15 20 *S*(*B* = Gk) ὅτε; no Gk: Mt 6 5 *SF*(*B* ⲕ.), Jo 16 11 *B*(*SA²* om); PS 15 *S* ⲡⲧⲉⲣⲉϥ̄ ⲟⲩⲱ ⲉϥϫⲱ ⲛⲛⲉⲓϣⲁϫⲉ, ShA 1 80 *S* ⲁⲡⲓⲁⲛⲁϣ ⲟⲩⲱ ⲉϥϣⲱⲡⲉ ϩⲓϫⲱⲓ for months past, ShC 73 137 *S* let not sticks burn ϣⲁⲛⲧⲟⲩⲣⲱⲕϩ ⲉⲣⲟⲩⲡ ⲉϫⲱ ⲉⲩⲧⲁⲕⲟ, Miss 8 47 *S* ⲡⲧⲉⲣⲟⲩⲟⲩⲱ ⲉⲩ-ⲙⲏⲛ ⲉⲃⲟⲗ ⲉⲩϫⲓ ϣⲕⲁⲕ (*cf* 49 ϭⲱ ⲉϥⲙⲏⲛ), Mani 1 *A²* ⲛ̄ⲧⲁⲣⲟⲩⲟⲩⲱ ⲉⲩⲃⲏⲓ ⲡⲧⲉϥϭⲁⲡⲉ, C 43 117 *B* ⲁⲅ̄ⲟⲩⲱ ⲉⲅⲥϧⲁⲓ, *ib* 61 *B* ϩⲏⲛ ⲛⲉⲁϥⲟⲩⲱ ⲁϥϫⲱⲕ ⲉⲃⲟⲗ, BIF 22 106 *F* ⲁⲡⲟⲩⲱ ⲉⲡⲭⲱ ⲉⲗⲁⲕ;   c conjunctive (rare): ShBMOr 8810 462 *S* ⲛ̄ⲡⲉⲕⲟⲩⲱ ⲛⲅ̄ⲣ̄ ϩⲧⲏⲕ ⲛⲅ̄ⲧⲉⲕⲣ̄ⲁⲛ.   c ⲉ-: Ryl 94 99 *S* ⲁⲡⲟⲩⲱ ⲉⲧⲁϫⲣⲟⲡ on rock, SHel 11 *S* ⲁⲓⲟⲩⲱ ⲉⲥϩⲣⲁⲓ (*l*? ⲉⲓ-) ⲙ̄ⲡⲉⲕⲣ̄ ⲙ̄, AM 76 *B* ⲁϥϯ ⲟⲩⲱ ⲉⲥⲟⲩϯ, C 86 321 *B* ⲁⲡⲟⲩⲱ ⲉ-ϫⲟⲥ (var ⲉⲡϫⲱ);   c ⲛ̄- (or ? for ⲉⲛ-) *S:* Miss 8 34 ⲛ(ⲉ)ⲛⲧⲁⲡⲟⲩⲱ ⲙ̄ⲡⲣⲁⲥⲥⲉ ⲙ̄ⲙⲟⲟⲩ πεπραγμένα; Bor 264 38 ⲁⲡⲟⲩⲱ ⲛ̄ϫⲱ ⲙ̄ⲙⲟⲥ;   c ⲛ̄ⲧⲛ- *S, cease for, from:* Bor 226 158 ⲡⲧⲉⲡⲉϩⲟⲉⲓϣ ⲟⲩⲱ ⲡⲧⲟⲟⲧⲛ ἀπέχειν dat; Mor 37 98 ⲡⲧⲉⲣⲉⲡⲙⲟⲟⲩ ⲟⲩⲱ ⲡⲧⲟⲟ-ⲧⲟⲩ λείπειν; Mus 45·49 let not Pascha ⲟⲩⲱ ⲡⲧⲟ-ⲧⲉⲡ;   c ϩⲛ- *S, from:* ShBor 281 102 ⲙ̄ⲡⲁⲧⲉⲛ-ⲉϣϫⲁⲥⲉ ⲟⲩⲱ ϩⲡⲣⲱϥ, BMOr 7561 62 sim (var BAp 109 ⲥⲱⲗⲡ ϩⲛ-); ⲉⲃⲟⲗ ϩⲛ-: 1 Kg 9 7 ἐκλείπ. ἐκ.

II tr *S, finish*: Nu 16 31 (*B* c 2d pres) παύ. part,
Job 38 1 (*B* κ.) π. gen; Mt 13 53 (*B*+ϫωκ εβολ,
F+ϫω) τελεῖν; Ru 2 23, Mt 7 28 (*B* do) συντ.; R 1
3 50 πτερεϥογω ⲙⲡⲣϥⲙⲟⲥ, ViK 9465 ⲙ̄ⲡⲓⲥⲁ-
ⲧⲣⲉϥⲟⲅⲱ ⲙⲡⲉϥⲣⲱⲃ ⲛ̄ϭⲓϫ = C 89 75 *B* κηⲛ, ST
217 ⲉⲓϣⲱⲡⲉ ⲁⲕⲟⲅⲱ ⲙⲡ̄ⲭⲱⲙⲉ send it me; Tri 399
ϣⲁⲛⲧⲟⲅⲟⲅⲱ ⲙ̄ⲙⲟⲕ ⲙⲡⲣⲁⲉ ⲡⲕⲟⲡ̄ⲁⲣⲟⲓⲧⲏⲥ من فرغ
(same?, *cf* Mt 5 26).

ⲁⲧⲟⲅⲱ *S, ceaseless*: BHom 11 ⲁⲓⲱⲛ ⲛⲁ. ἀτελεύτη-
τος; Wess 11 166 ⲟⲅⲁ. ⲡⲉ ⲡⲁⲧⲟⲛ ἀπέραντος; ShC
73 129 κολⲁⲥⲓⲥ ⲛⲁ., BKU 1 4 love me ⲉⲛⲟⲟⲅⲟⲅⲱϣ
ⲛⲁ.

ϫⲓⲛⲟⲅⲱ *B, ceasing, end*: TThe 328 ⲡϫ. ⲛ̄ⲧⲁⲛⲁ-
ⲫⲟⲣⲁ فراغ.

✝ ογω *SABO, make cease, release, loose*, intr:
Mk 7 35 *B*(*S* ⲃⲱⲗ εβολ) λύειν, Zeph 2 7 *SA*(*B* κωρϥ)
καταλ.; ShC 73 110 *S* εⲅⲡⲁ✝. ⲙⲡⲡⲁⲅ ⲛ̄ⲭⲡⲥⲟ, Ep
240 *S* will come forthwith ⲉⲓϣⲁⲛ✝., AZ 21 98 *O*
ⲉⲧⲥⲱⲛⲟ ⲉⲧⲧⲓ ογω, Miss 4 543 *S* ⲁⲅ✝. ⲉⲅⲣ ⲣⲱⲃ, BM
590 *B* come ϣⲁⲡⲧⲉⲛ✝ ⲃⲱ ⲉⲡⲕⲱⲧ;   tr *BS* (rare):
Ge 42 27, Jo 1 27 (*S* ⲃⲱⲗ εβολ) λύ., Is 58 6 διαλ.,
Jer 12 5 ἐκλ., Deu 25 9 (all *S* do) ὑπολ.; Mich 550
39 *S* ⲛⲥⲉ✝. ⲙⲡⲣⲱⲃ whereat they worked = MG
17 361 من فرغ, C 43 162 ⲁϥ✝. ⲙⲡⲉϥϭⲱⲕ, Miss 4
199 wished not ⲉ✝. ⲙⲙⲟⲥ (*sc* letter), *ib* 201 ⲙⲁ✝.
ⲙⲡⲓⲥⲛⲁⲟ;   c ⲟⲛ-, ϩⲉⲛ-, *loose from*: ShMich 550
15 *S* ✝. ⲙⲙⲟϥ ⲉⲛⲡⲉϥⲟⲱϣ, P 129¹⁴ 122 *S* ✝. ⲙⲙⲟⲛ
ⲟⲛⲡⲉⲛϭⲓⲥⲉ = DeV 1 76 *B* εⲃ. ϩⲉⲛ-; εⲃⲟⲗ ⲟⲛ-, ϩⲉⲛ-:
AM 266 *B* λύ. ἐκ., Ps 88 45 *B*(*S* ⲃ. εⲃ. ⲟⲛ-) καταλύ.
ἀπό, Jud 19 16 *S* Gk om.

—— εⲃⲟⲗ *B*, as ✝ ογω, intr: 2 Kg 1 23 (*S* ⲡⲱⲣϫ) διαχωρίζειν; Is 40 2, 2 Pet 3 12 λύεσθαι, Is 13
7 ἐκλ. (all *S* ⲃ. εⲃ.), Jer 27 43 παραλ.; *ib* 6 29 τήκε-
σθαι; Is 35 3 (*S* ⲥⲛ̄ϭ, *F* κⲏ) ἀνειμένος; Cat 51 ⲥⲱⲛⲟ
...✝. εⲃ. (*cf* Mt 16 19 ⲃ. εⲃ.);   qual: Lam 2 19
(*S* ϣⲱⲥⲙ) ἐκλ.; Lev 14 46 ⲑⲓⲟⲅⲛⲟⲅⲧ (var Wilkins
ⲫⲱⲣϫ εⲃ., *S* ShIF 133 ⲡⲏⲟ εⲃ.) ἀφορίζεσθαι (but
l? ⲑⲟⲅⲓ- as from ⲧⲟⲅⲓⲟ);   tr: Lu 13 15 (*S* ⲃ. εⲃ.),
C 86 276 ✝. εⲃ. ⲛ̄ⲛⲓⲙⲁⲧⲓⲁ λύ.; Mus 34 205 ϥ✝. εⲃ.
ⲙⲡⲉⲙⲕⲁⲟ ⲡⲣⲏⲧ.

ⲁⲧ✝ ογω, *unending*: Ex 39 23 *B* ἀδιάλυτος; Dan
7 14 *S*(*B* ⲥⲓⲛⲓ neg) παρέρχεσθαι neg; TstAb 249 *B*
ⲁⲛⲁⲡⲁⲅⲥⲓⲥ ⲡⲁ. ⲙⲧⲟⲛ ⲡⲁⲧⲕⲏⲛ.

ϫⲓⲛ✝ ογω *B*: Ps 8 3 (*S* ⲃ. εⲃ.) καταλύ.

ⲁⲟⲅⲱ *B* nn with ϭⲓ, *bring to an end*, so *delay* intr:
EW 150 ⲙⲡⲉϥϭⲓ ⲁ. ἀναβάλλειν;   c ⲉ- Miss 4 211
ⲙⲡⲉⲣϭⲓ ⲁ. ⲉϣⲧⲉⲙϣⲟⲡⲧⲉⲛ, TstAb 166 ϭⲓ ⲁ. ⲉⲑ-
ⲣⲓⲱⲗⲓ;   c ⲛ- *wait for*: Va 61 29 ϭⲓ ⲁ. ⲡⲏⲓ ἐκδέχεσθαι; C 86 68 ⲟⲅ ⲡⲉⲧⲉⲕϭⲓ ⲁ. ⲡⲁϥ? βραδύνειν,
Aeg 55 ϭⲓ ⲁ. ⲡⲁⲛ = ViK 9248 154 *S* κατεχε, Va
59 165 hasten ϫⲉⲁⲣⲉⲛⲁⲓ ϭⲓ ⲁ. ⲡⲁⲕ;   tr: Jud 11
35 (*S* diff) ἐμποδοστατεῖν; Va 57 248 ⲥⲉⲙⲡϣⲁ ⲛϭⲓ
ⲁ. ⲙⲙⲱⲟⲅ κατέχειν; Va 68 167 ϭⲓ ⲁ. ⲡⲧⲉϥⲙⲉⲧⲁ-

ⲡⲟⲓⲁ περιμένειν; 1 Pet 3 16 (*S* ⲥⲱϣϥ) ἐπηρεάζειν,
Va 57 116 ϥϭⲓ ⲁⲃⲱ ⲙⲙⲟⲕ & stoppeth thy tongue.
V AZ 52 113.

ογω *SBFO*, ογⲟⲅ *A* nn m, *news, report*: 1 Kg
4 19 *S*, Pro 26 16 *SA*, Is 37 7 *S*(*B* ϣⲓⲛⲓ) ἀγγελία;
Ob 1 *A*(*B* do), Tob 10 11 *S* ἀκοή; Eph 6 21 *SF*(*B*
εⲑⲃⲉ-) τὰ κατά, Phil 1 27 *SF*(*B* do) τὰ περί; Ac 21
31 *S*(*B* ϣ.) φάσις; ShP 130¹ 142 *S* ⲉⲧⲣⲉⲅⲥⲱⲧⲙ ⲉ-
ⲡⲉⲧⲛⲟⲅⲱ, R 1 2 41 *S* tell no ογω ⲉⲡⲁⲡⲓⲕⲟⲥⲙⲟⲥ
(var Lammayer 44 ⲣⲱⲃ), MR 5 46 *F* ⲙ̄ⲡⲛⲕⲟⲅⲁⲣⲏⲡ
ογω ⲛⲏⲓ, BM 531 *S* ⲧⲛⲛⲟⲟⲅ ⲡⲟⲅⲱ (*sc* answer to
questions), ST 367 *S* ⲡⲟⲅⲱ of sick man, Mor 18 92
S ⲁⲓϫⲛⲟⲅϥ ⲉⲡⲉⲧⲛⲟⲅⲱ = Miss 4 155 *B* ογϫⲁⲓ, Mor
41 169 *S* ⲡⲧⲉⲡⲉⲕⲟⲅⲱ ⲃⲱⲕ ϣⲁⲡⲣⲣⲟ.

ⲛ ⲡⲟⲅⲱ, *bring news S*: Ge 37 14 (Bor 243 157, *B*
ⲧⲁⲙⲟ) ἀναγγέλλειν, 2 Kg 4 4 ἀγγελία ἔρχεσθαι; 1 Kg
17 18 (*B* ϫⲉⲙ ⲡϣ.) ἐπισκέπτειν;   Ryl 94 110 messenger ⲡⲧⲁϥⲙ ⲡⲉⲓⲟⲅⲱ ⲡⲁϥ.

ⲣ, ⲉⲣ, ⲉⲗ ογω *SABF*, *make reply* or merely *speak*,
intr: Ge 18 27 *B*(*S* ⲟⲅⲱϣⲃ), Mic 3 11 *SAB*, Mt 15
3 *F*(*S* do, *B* om) Jo 3 9 *B*(*SA*² do) ἀποκρίνεσθαι;
Jer 38 6 *B* ἀπολογεῖσθαι, Ps 118 172 *B*(*S* ⲧⲁⲟⲅ), Lam
1 12 *B* ⲣ ⲁⲟⲅⲱ (*l*? ⲉⲣ ογω) φθέγγεσθαι; Z 295 *S*
when he knocked ⲁⲥⲣ ογω ὑπακούειν (*cf* Ac 12 13
S ⲟⲅⲱϣⲃ) · R 1 1 20 *S* ⲁⲅⲣ. saying, Rec 6 188 *B*
ⲁⲡⲉⲣ. ϫⲉⲁⲙⲏⲛ = BMar 222 *S* ⲟⲅⲱϣⲃ;   tr: Is
14 2 *B*(*S* ϫⲱ), Zeph 2 3 *B*(*SA* diff) ἀποκρ.; TEuch
2 144 *B* ⲉⲣ. ⲙⲡⲓⲉⲅⲁⲅⲅⲉⲗⲓⲟⲛ ϫⲉⲟⲅⲃⲱⲣⲉⲙ ردّ بلبخ.

With preposition.   c ⲛ-, *reply, speak to*: Nu 13
26 *B*(*S* ⲟⲅⲱϣⲃ) ἀποκρ., Is 36 21 *B*(*S* do, *F* ⲟⲅⲱ-
ⲣⲉⲙ), Mk 14 40 *BF*(*S* ϫⲱ) ἀπ. dat, Job 33 5 *B*(*S*
ⲟⲅⲱϣⲃ) ἀπόκρισιν διδόναι dat; 2 Cor 12 19 *B*(*SF*
=Gk) ἀπολογ. dat; Is 65 12 *B*(*S* ⲥⲱⲧⲙ) ὑπακ.; Jos
4 7 *B*(*S* ⲧⲟⲅⲛ ⲉⲓⲁⲧ⸱ εⲃⲟⲗ) δηλοῦν dat; 1 Kg 14 16 *S*
ⲡⲉⲧⲣ. σκοπός (*cf* ϫⲓ ογω *sf*); Mor 40 28 *S* ⲁϥⲣ. ⲡⲁ-
ⲙⲛⲏϣⲉ ϫⲉ- (var *ib* 39 38 *S* ϣⲁϫⲉ ⲙⲛ-), BAp 110 *S*
he cried to me ⲁⲓⲣ. ⲡⲁϥ ϫⲉⲥⲙⲟⲅ ⲉⲣⲟⲓ, Va 61 29 *B*
throwing cloak on mare ⲁϥⲉⲣ. ⲡⲁⲥ saying, C 41 44
B went toward him ⲁϥⲉⲣ. ⲡⲁϥ ϫⲉⲟⲅⲛⲓϣϯ ⲛ✝-
ⲙⲏ;   c ⲉϧⲟⲩⲛ ⲉϩⲣⲉⲛ- *B*, as last: Rom 9 20 (*S*
ⲟⲅⲱϣⲃ ⲟⲅⲃⲉ-) ⲁⲛⲧⲁⲡⲟⲕⲣ. dat;   c ⲉϩⲣⲏⲓ ⲉϫⲉⲛ-
B, *reply about, respecting*: Ac 24 10 (*S* ϣⲁϫⲉ ϩⲁ-)
ἀπολ. περί; Jer 28 14 ϥⲑ. ἐπί;   c ⲛⲁϩⲣⲉⲛ- *B*,
reply, speak before: Jer 12 1 (*S* diff) ἀπολ. πρός; PO
11 308 ⲁϥⲉⲣ. ⲡⲁϩⲣⲁϥ saying;   c ⲟⲅⲃⲉ- *B*, *reply
to*: Va 61 205 ⲁϥⲉⲣ. ⲟⲅⲃⲉⲓⲥⲁⲁⲕ ϫⲉ-;   c ϩⲁⲣⲡ- *S*,
as last: Deu 20 11 (*B* ⲛ-) ἀποκρ. dat, Mk 12 34 (var
ⲟⲅⲱϣⲃ ⲛ-) ἀπ.; BIF 13 100 ⲁⲡⲣⲁⲅⲓⲟⲥ ⲣ. ϩⲁⲣⲱⲟⲅ
= MG 25 279 *B* ⲛ-, KKS 486 if reproved ⲧⲉⲡⲉⲣ.
ϩⲁⲣⲱⲟⲅ κακως.   As nn m, *reply, verdict B*: Job
15 2 (*S* ⲟⲅⲱϣⲃ) ἀπόκρισις, 2 Cor 1 9 (*S* diff) ἀπό-
κριμα; TEuch 1 167 ϫⲱ ⲡⲟⲅⲉⲣ. رد; ⲁⲧⲉⲣ ογω *B*,
without reply: Rom 1 20 (*S* ⲉⲙⲛ ϣⲁϫⲉ ⲉϫⲱ) ἀνα-

πολόγητος. ϫιπερ ογω *B*, *act of replying*: Lu 2 47 (*S* ϭιιιογωϣ ⲃ) ἀπόκρισις; Va 57 37 wont to reply ϣⲉⲛⲧⲁⲓϫ. ⲙⲡⲁⲓⲣⲏϯ, *ib* 61 5 ⲧⲁⲡⲟⲣⲓⲁ ⲡⲧⲁϫ., TThe 322 ⲡⲓϫ. ⲛϯⲁⲡⲁⲫⲟⲣⲁ ⳉⲣ.

ϯ ογω *S*, *give news*: P 131¹ 31 Gabriel ⲡⲣⲉϥϯ ογω. ⲧⲁⲕⲟⲩω   *v* ⲧⲱⲕ *throw* p c.

ϥⲓ ογω, ϥⲁⲓογω *S*, *news bearer, messenger*: 2 Kg 11 8 ἄρσις stator, 4 Kg 11 19 παρατρέχων; Is 63 9 (*B* ⲡⲣⲉⲥⲃⲉⲩⲧⲏⲥ) πρέσβυς.

ϭⲉ ⲡογω *S*, *find news, inquire*: Z 349 ⲛⲉϣⲁⲣⲉⲡⲉⲉⲓⲟⲧⲉ ϭⲉ ⲉⲡⲉϥογω on Sundays, BM 1118 ϭⲉ ⲡ. ⲡⲓⲱⲅⲥⲉⲃ ϩⲁⲣⲟⲓ, Ryl 379 sim.

ϫⲓ (ⲡ)ογω *SAO*, *bring news, announce*: Is 45 21 (*B* om) ἀναγγέλλειν; Pro 22 13 (*A* ϫⲱ) λέγειν; Bor 262 113 ⲡⲁⲅⲅⲉⲗⲟⲥ ⲙⲡⲛⲟϭ ⲛϣⲟϫⲛⲉ ⲡⲉⲧⲁ. ⲙⲡⲛⲟϭ ⲛϣⲟϫⲛⲉ ⲉⲑⲏⲡ with whom he (sc Father) spake at creation(? Ge 1 26), AZ 21 94 *O* Osiris ⲉⲧϫ. ⲛⲉⲃⲱⲧ (*cf ib* 38 87 dem paral *θ wḥ* & *cf*? ογωϣ Ep 170);   c ⲉ- *S*, *announce to*: Lu 8 34 (*B* ⲧⲁⲙⲟ) ἀπαγ. εἰς; ⲉ-ϩⲣⲁⲓ ⲉ-: Is 7 2 (*B* ⲉⲗ ⲡⲓϣⲓⲛⲓ) ἀναγ. εἰς;   c ⲛ-*SAO*, sim: Ge 32 5 (*B* ⲧⲁ.) ἀν. dat, *ib* 29 12 (*B* do), Hos 4 12 *A* (*B* ϯ ϩⲁⲡ), Lu 7 22 (*B* ⲧⲁ.) ἀπ. dat; Pro 22 21 *SA* ἀποκρ. dat; *ib* 25 13 (*A* ϫⲓ ϣⲓⲛⲉ) χρᾶσθαι; ShA 1 53 ⲁⲩϫⲓ ογω ⲡⲟⲩⲣⲱⲙⲉ ϫⲉ-, Win 4 if money is with you ⲛ̄ϫⲓ ⲡογω ⲛⲁⲛ, AZ 21 94 *O* ⲛⲥⲉϫⲓ ογω ⲡⲁⲓ ⲁϥⲱⲃ; ⲉ̇ⲣⲟⲩⲛ ⲛ- *S*, *bring news in to*: BAp 117 ϫⲓ ⲡⲁογω ⲉϩ. ⲙⲡⲛⲟϭ ⲛⲣⲱⲙⲉ = PO 22 402 اوصل خبري الى ⲉϩⲣⲁⲓ ⲛ- *S*: Miss 4 631 ϫⲓ ⲡογω ⲉϩ. ⲙⲡⲉⲗⲗⲟ;   c ϣⲁ- *S*, *to*: JKP 2 46 ϫⲓ ⲡⲁογω ϣⲁⲑⲉⲩⲁⲱⲥⲓⲟⲥ, Gu 63 sim. ⲣⲉϥϫⲓ ογω *S*, *informer*: 2 Kg 13 34 σκοπός (*cf* ⲣ ογω ⲛ-);   ϭⲓⲛϫ. *S*, *Annunciation* (*cf* εὐαγγελισμός): ROC 20 420 Virgin brings us to God by ⲧϭ. ⲉⲧⲟ ⲛϣⲡⲏⲣⲉ.

ϭⲙ ⲡογω *S*, *find news, inquire*: 2 Kg 13 5 ἰδεῖν; R 1 4 29 went ⲉϭ. ⲛⲡⲣⲉⲡⲉⲉⲧⲛ *visendus*, BAp 123 ⲁⲅⲉⲓ ⲉϭⲙⲡⲉⲕογω = MIE 2 415 *B* ϫⲉⲙ ⲡⲉⲕϣⲓⲛⲓ.

ϩⲗ, ϩⲣ ογω *S* as nn, *throwing a reply, dispute*: Deu 17 8 (var ϩⲣ, *B* = Gk) 25 1 (*B* do) ἀντιλογία;   ϯ ϩⲉⲗ ογω *F*, *give reply*: Cant 2 10 (*S* ϣⲁϫⲉ ⲙⲛ-), Mk 8 29 (*S* ογωϣⲃ, *B* ⲉⲣ ογω) ἀποκρ.; LAp 513 ⲁϥϯ. ⲙⲡⲉϫⲉϥ ⲛⲏϥ.

ογω *S* (? *S*') *F* vb tr (same?): Mt 14 12 *F* ⲁⲩογω ⲛ̄ⲓ̄ⲥ̄ (*S* ϫⲓ ογω, *B* ⲧⲁⲙⲟ) ἀπαγ. dat; Z 234 *S* will not suffer you ⲉογω ⲙⲙⲟⲥ *to evangelize it* (sc city).

ογω in rubric (BM 144, Leyd 146) *v* ογωϩⲙ.

ογω *SB* (rare) *F*, ογ(ογ) *A* nn, *bud, blossom*, with ϯ vb **I** intr, *blossom, sprout*: Nu 17 8 *S* (*B* ⲫⲓⲣⲓ ⲉⲃⲟⲗ), Mt 13 26 *S* (*BF* ⲣⲱⲧ), Cl 43 5 *A* βλαστεῖν, Job 5 6 *S* (*B* ⲣ.) ἀναβ., Is 55 10 *S* (*B* ⲫ. ⲉⲃ.) ἐκβ., Mk 4 27 *S* (*B* ⲑⲏⲡⲓ) βλαστάνειν; Job 20 21 *S* (*B* do), Is 35 1 *SB* (var do) *F* ἀνθεῖν, Job 14 7 *S* (*B* ⲫ. ⲉⲃ.) ἔπαν., Cant 6 10 *SF* ἐξαν.; Ps 71 7 *SA* (TillOster, *B* ⲁϣⲁⲓ), Hos 10 4 *SA* (*B* ⲫ. ⲉⲃ.) ἀνατέλλειν, Mt 13 5 *S* (*B* ⲣ.) ἐξα-

ⲛⲁⲧ.; Deu 29 18 *S* (*B* do) φύειν, Mk 13 28 *S* (*F* + ⲉⲃⲟⲗ, *B* ϩⲓ ϫⲱⲃⲓ ⲉⲃ.) ἐκφ.; Job 8 11 *S* (*B* ⲫ. ⲉⲃ.) θάλλειν, Ps 27 7 *S* (*B* do) ἀναθ.; Jon 4 6 *SA* (*B* ⲓ ⲉⲡϣⲱⲓ) ἀναβαίνειν; Lu 21 30 *S* (*B* + ⲉⲃ.) προβάλλειν; Hab 3 17 *A* (*B* ϯ ογⲧⲁϩ) καρποφορεῖν; PS 117 *S* ⲡⲉⲕⲕⲗⲁϩⲟⲥ ϯ. ϩⲣⲁⲓ ⲛϩⲏⲧ, ShC 73 157 *S* herb ⲁϥⲁⲣϫⲉⲓ ⲛϯ., Aeg 262 *S* church ⲉⲣⲉⲡⲉⲡⲛⲁ̄ ϯ. ⲛϩⲏⲧⲥ.

II tr, *put forth, bring up*: Ja 5 18 *S* (*B* ⲣ., ϯ ογⲧⲁϩ) βλ.; Si 39 18 *S*, Is 35 1 *SF* (*B* ⲫ. ⲉⲃ.) ἀνθ.; Ge 3 18 *S* (*B* ⲣ.) ἀνατέλ., Ps 103 14 *S* (*B* ⲑⲣⲟ ⲣ.) ἐξαν.; Sa 4 4 *S* ἀναθάλ.; Jer 23 5 (*B* ⲧογⲛⲟⲥ) ἀνιστάναι; Hag 1 11 *S* (ViK 9068 278) *A* (*B* ⲓⲛⲓ ⲉⲃ.) ἐκφέρειν; Miss 8 104 *S* ointment ⲉϥϯ. ⲙⲡⲉⲥϯⲟⲩϭⲉ ἀνανεοῦσθαι; ShMIF 23 183 *S* ϯ. ⲛⲣⲉⲡϯ ογω ⲛⲁⲅⲁⲑⲟⲛ, C 86 156 *B* ⲁϥϯ. (ⲙ)ⲙⲟⲕ ϫⲉⲡⲧⲉⲕⲙⲉⲧⲟⲣⲫⲁⲛⲟⲥ.

With following adverb.   ⲉ ⲃⲟⲗ *SAA²BF*, *put forth*: He 9 4 *F* (*S* om ⲉⲃ., *B* ⲫ. ⲉⲃ.) βλ., Ez 17 8 *B* βλαστοὺς ποιεῖν; Hos 14 8 *SA* (*B* do) ἐξανθ.; Si 49 11 *S* ἀναθαλ.; Mt 24 32 *BF* (*S* do) ἐκφύ.; Sa 19 7 *S* χλοηφόρος; PS 122 *S* thy body ⲉⲛⲧⲁϥϯ. ⲉⲃ. ⲛϩⲏⲧ, ShC 42 161 *S* vines ⲁⲩϯ. ⲉⲃ., Mor 48 77 *S* her flesh ϯ. ⲉⲃ. like child's, Aeg 48 *B* ⲁϥϯ. ⲉⲃ. ⲡⲟⲩⲕⲁⲣⲡⲟⲥ, Mor 18 101 *S* ⲁⲧⲕⲱⲟϥ (Antaeopolis) ϯ. ⲙⲙⲟⲕ ⲉⲃ. = *ib* 19 102 *S* & Miss 4 160 *B* ⲉϩⲣⲏⲓ; as nn m: ManiH 86 *A²* ⲛϯ. ⲁⲃ. ⲙⲡⲡⲛ̄ⲁ̄;   c ⲉⲡϣⲱⲓ *B*, *grow, bring up*: Ez 17 6 ἀνατέλ.; C 41 19 ⲁϥϯ. ⲉⲡ. ⲛⲣⲁⲛⲃⲁⲓ;   c ⲉ ϩⲣⲁⲓ *SAB*, as last: Joel 2 22 *SA* (*B* ⲫ. ⲉⲃ.) βλ.; Hos 14 6 *SA* (*B* do) ἀνθ.; Lev 13 37 *S* (but var ϩⲣⲁⲓ, *B* ⲣ.) ἀνατέλ., Mk 4 5 *S* (*B* do) ἐξαν.; Ez 47 12 *B* (*l* ⲉϩ.) ἀναβαίν.; Br 257 *S* ϯ. ⲉϩ. ⲛⲟⲉ ⲙⲡⲣⲱⲧ, C 86 96 *B* ϫⲱⲣⲁ ⲉⲧⲁⲕϯ. ⲉϩ. (*l* ⲉϩ.) ⲡϣⲏⲧⲥ, ShC 42 161 *S* earth ϯ. ⲉϩ. ⲙⲡⲉϥϭⲣⲟϭ, BMis 32 *S* ⲡⲥⲟⲓ (Ptolemais) ⲛⲧⲁϥϯ. ⲙⲙⲟⲕ ⲉϩ.; as nn m: Br 227 *S* ⲛϯ. ⲉϩ. ⲙⲡⲉⲥ ϯⲟⲥ.

—— nn m *SAB* (rare), *blossom, sprout*: Ge 49 9 *S* (*B* ⲗⲁϭⲉⲙ), Job 15 30 *S* (*B* ⲫⲏ ⲉⲧⲡⲁⲣⲱⲧ) βλαστός; Zeph 2 2 *A* (*SB* ϩⲣⲏⲣⲉ), Si 24 19 *S* ἄνθος, Nah 1 4 *SA* ϯ ογ (*B* ⲉⲧⲫ. ⲉⲃ.) ἐξανθεῖν; Lev 25 19 *S* (*B* ογⲧⲁϩ) ἐκφόριον; Ps 79 11 *S* (*B* ⲙⲟⲩⲗϫ), Ez 31 8 *S* (*B* ⲕⲗⲏⲙⲁ) παραφυάς; *ib* 17 10 *B* ἀνατολή; *ib* 17 6 *B* ἀναδενδράς; Blake 236 *S* ⲧⲁⲣϫⲏ ⲙⲡⲧ. ⲉⲁⲣ; Job 14 7 *S* (*B* ϩⲣ.) ῥάδαμνος; ClPr 54 43 *S* ϯ. ⲛⲡⲧⲏϭ λειμών; Br 258 *S* ϯ ⲧⲱϣ ⲛⲡⲁϯ., ShRE 10 161 *S* trees & ⲡⲉⲅϯ., BM 241 193 *S* ϭⲱⲃⲉ, ϯ., ⲕⲁⲣⲡⲟⲥ; ⲧⲉⲕ ϯ. ⲉⲃⲟⲗ *S*: Is 27 6 (*B* ⲉ(ⲣ?) ⲣⲁⲧⲧⲁⲣ ⲉⲃ.) βλαστεῖν.

ϫⲉ, ϫⲓ (mostly) ογω, ϫⲟγω, *S*, *implant germination, conceive*: Ps 50 5 (var ϫⲟγω, *A* Cl ϫⲓ ϩⲛⲟⲟϥ, *B* ϭⲓ ϣϣⲟⲟϥ) κισσᾶν, Ge 30 38 (var & *B* do) ἐγκ.; Mor 37 18 ϩⲙⲡⲧⲣⲉϥⲙⲁⲁⲩ ϫⲉ ογω ⲙⲙⲟϥ, Ming 318 ⲁⲩϫⲓ ογω ⲙⲙⲟⲥ ⲛⲁϣ ⲛϩⲉ; as nn, *conception*: Ming *lc* ⲡⲱ (*l* ⲱⲱ) ⲛ ⲡϫⲓ ογω...ⲉⲧⲁϥϯ ογω ⲉⲃⲟⲗ ⲛϩⲏⲧϥ;   ϭⲓⲛϫ.: ROC 20 420 Mary's ϭ. ⲉⲧⲟ ⲛϣⲡⲏⲣⲉ.

ατογω S, *without conception* (?): BMOr 8802 5 virgins' bodies ⲡⲁ. ⲁⲩⲱ ⲥϫⲉⲧⲱⲡ(ⲥⲭⲉⲇⲟⲛ)ⲛⲁⲧⲡⲡⲟⲛ.

ογααϧ, ογⲏⲏϧ *v* ογⲟⲡ.

ογϧⲉ- SAA²BFO, ογϥⲉ- SA², ογⲉ- SF, ⲉⲟγϧⲉ-
B (C 89), ογϧⲏⲥ SAA²B, -ϧⲉⲥ O, ογⲏⲥ SF prep,
opposite, toward, against: Job 32 4 S (B dat), Ps 75
7 S (B ⲉϧογⲏ ⲉϩⲣⲛ-), Jer 29 20 SB, Ob 7 B (A ⲁ-),
Lu 1 22 S (B ⲉ-), Cl 27 5 A Gk dat (vb often with
ἀντι-); Ge 4 8 B (A Cl dat), Nu 16 15 B (S ⲛⲁϩⲣⲛ-),
1 Kg 16 7 B (S dat), Ps 21 24 S (var ⲉ-)B, Pro 9 18 B
(SA ⲉϧ. ⲉϩⲣⲛ-), Is 32 6 B (SF do), *ib* 52 8 B (S ⲙⲛ-),
Hos 12 2 B (A ⲙⲛ-), 1 Cor 13 12 B (S ϩⲓ-), APBerl
Sitz '09 217 A², MG 25 207 B πρός; Nu 34 15 B (S
ⲙⲡⲉⲙⲧⲟ ⲉⲃⲟⲗ ⲛ-), Ez 20 35 SB, Gal 5 17 SB κατά;
Sa 5 21 S, Jer 41 7 B ἐπί; Eccl 6 10 F (S ⲙⲛ-), BHom
50 S ⲙⲓϣⲉ ογϧⲉⲣⲟⲟγⲧ μετά; Ac 25 16 S (B diff)
περί; 2 Kg 10 9 S ἐξ ἐναντίας, 2 Cor 2 7 B ⲡⲉⲧογ-
ϧⲏⲩ (S ⲡⲧⲟⲥ), Gal 2 7 B do (S do) τοὐναντίον; Pro
18 17 SA ⲉⲧⲟγ., Lu 12 58 S ⲉⲧⲝⲓ ϩⲁⲡ ογ. (B=Gk)
ἀντίδικος; Job 11 3 SB ἀντικρινόμενος, Ps 16 7 S
ⲉⲧⲁϧⲉ ⲣⲁⲧ⸗ ογ. (B ⲉϧ. ⲉϧ.) ἀνθεστηκώς, Ro 7 23 B
ϧⲏⲕ ογ. (S ϯ ογ.) ἀντιστρατευόμενος, Job 7 20 S
ⲕⲱ ογ. (B diff) κατεντευκτής, *ib* 13 24 S do (B ⲓⲧⲉⲛ-)
ὑπεναντίος; PS 354 S ϯⲛⲁⲱϣ ⲉϩⲣⲁⲓ ογϧⲏⲕ (*ib* 93
sim ογⲏⲕ), AP 37 A² sim ογϥⲉⲛⲝⲥ̅, C 89 164 B ⲱϣ
ⲉⲃⲟⲗ ⲉογ. ⲙⲱγⲥⲏⲥ, ShBor 247 117 S ⲁϥⲧⲁϩⲟ ⲉⲣⲁⲧⲥ ογϧⲏⲩ, C 43 39 B ⲁϧⲟⲣⲓ ⲉⲣⲁⲧⲟγ ογ. ⲙⲡⲉⲣⲥⲏⲥ,
ib 89 33 B ⲉϥⲙⲟⲟϣⲓ ογϧⲏⲛ = MG 17 392 قبالته
alongside, J 67 16 S lest I die ⲉⲙⲛ ⲣⲱⲙⲉ ογϧⲏⲓ, Sh
Bor 246 78 S ⲁⲧⲱⲡⲓⲝⲉ ογ. ⲙⲡⲉⲑⲟⲟγ, SHel 82 S
ⲙⲓϣⲉ ογϥⲉⲛⲝⲁⲝⲉ, ShC 42 159 S ογⲱⲣⲙ ογ. ⲛⲉⲓ-
ϣⲁϫⲉ, Pcod 27 S sim, Va 61 205 B ⲁϥⲉⲣ ογⲱ ογ.
ⲓⲥⲁⲁⲕ, Cat 200 B ογⲡⲉ ⲉⲧⲁⲩⲝⲟϥ ογ. ⲫⲁⲓ?, BMis
550 S ⲁⲡⲁⲅⲅⲉⲗⲟⲥ ϫⲱⲣⲙ ογϧⲏⲓ, C 89 160 B ϭⲱⲣⲉⲙ ⲉογϧⲏⲟγ (*ib* 82 sim ογϧⲏϧ), PS 121 S ⲉⲓⲥⲉⲉⲧ
ογϧⲏⲩ, *ib* 7 S ⲉϥϣⲏϣ ογϧⲏⲩ *equal to him*, ShC 42
53 S ϩⲉⲗⲡⲓⲍⲉ...ογ.ⲡⲥⲱⲧⲏⲣ, *ib* 73 94 S ϩⲟⲉⲓⲥ ογ. ⲡⲉⲧ-
ϧⲏⲡⲉⲓⲧⲟⲡⲟⲥ, Mani 2 A² ⲁϥⲉⲓ ⲁϧⲣⲏ ογ. ⲡⲙγⲥⲧⲏ-
ⲣⲓⲟⲛ, C 43 41 B ⲡⲣⲟ ογ. ϧⲟ, Hor 81 O ϥⲧογⲁⲉⲓⲧ
ογ. ϩⲁⲣⲡϣⲱⲧ.   AZ 21 98 O ⲕⲣ ογϧⲉⲓ, AP 35 A²
ϥⲣ ογ.

ογⲏⲥ SF: PS 110 S ⲱϣ ⲉϩⲣⲁⲓ ογⲏⲓ, BKU 1 23
F ⲱϣ ⲉ(ϩ)ⲗⲏⲓ ογⲏⲕ; ⲡ(ⲡ)ογⲉ- SF, -ⲏⲥ S, -ⲉⲥ F:
PS 151 ϥⲧⲙⲡⲉϥⲉ ⲙⲙⲟϥ ϩⲣⲁⲓ ⲡογⲏⲓ, *ib* 283 ⲉϥⲧⲟ
ⲡογⲉⲧⲉⲯγⲭⲏ, Mor 30 5 F ⲱⲣⲓ ⲉⲗⲉⲧογ ⲡ]ογⲉⲉⲓ
ⲡⲉϥⲉⲣⲏγ = BMis 233 S ογϧⲉ-, Pcod 38 F ογⲟγⲣⲉⲙ
ⲡⲡογⲉⲡⲗⲉⲙⲱⲛ (S diff), Worr 325 F ⲱϣ ⲉⲣⲗⲏⲓ ⲛ-
ⲡογ(ⲉ)ⲕ.

V also ⲙⲟγⲧⲉ, ⲙⲓϣⲉ, ϯ, ογⲱϣϧ, ογⲱⲣⲙ, ⲱϣ,
ⲱϩⲉ ⲉⲣⲁⲧ⸗, ϣⲁϫⲉ, ϫⲱⲣⲙ & many other verbs.

ογⲁⲓϧⲉ A² nn, *meaning unknown*: Mani 1 they

took evil counsel against him ϫⲉⲉⲅⲁϯ ογ. ⲁⲣⲁϥ
ⲙⲙⲏⲛⲉ.   For ? ογϧⲉ.

ογⲓⲉⲓϧⲉ A *v* ογⲟⲡ (ογⲏⲏϧ).

ογϧⲁϣ SA²B, -ϧⲁϧ A, ογⲁϣ B, ογⲃⲉϣ F, ογⲟ-
ϧⲁϣ† SB, ογⲁϧⲓϣ† SᶠF vb intr, *become, be white*: Ps
50 7 SA (Cl)B (var ογⲁϣ), Joel 1 7 B (A ⲕⲱⲕ), Mk
9 3 BF (S ⲡⲓⲣⲉ), R 2 2 23 S ⲧⲣⲉⲥογ. ϩⲛογⲯⲓⲙⲓ-
ⲑⲓⲟⲡ λευκαίνειν, Dan 12 10 B ἐκλ., Jo 4 35 SA²B
λευκός εἶναι, Mt 17 2 SB λ. γίνεσθαι, *ib* 5 36 S (B ⲉⲣ
ογⲱϧϣ) λ. ποιεῖν; Ps 67 15 SB (var ογⲁϣ) χιονοῦ-
σθαι; Lam 4 7 SBF λάμπειν; ShBor 246 80 S *baptism* ⲧⲣⲉογ., Mor 41 55 S ⲧⲣⲉογ. ⲛⲥⲕⲓⲙ, PChass
1 19 S ⲇⲁⲧ ⲉϥⲕⲏⲙ...ⲡⲁογ., MG 25 399 B ⲁϥογ.
like light, AZ 33 56 F ⲉϥⲱϣϥ (*l* ογⲱϧϣ) παρα χ[ⲓ-
ⲱⲡ;   qual: Cant 8 5 SF λευκανθίζειν, Lev 13 4
SB λ. εἶναι, Mt 28 3 SBF, Ap 2 17 S (B ⲡογⲱ.) λ.;
Lu 23 11 S (B ⲫⲉⲣⲓⲱογ), Ap 19 8 S (B ⲫⲟⲣⲓ) λαμπρός; Cant 5 15 F (S=Gk) μαρμάρινος; SHel 55 S
ⲕⲁϩ ογ. *like silver*, DeV 2 86 B sim, C 43 82 B λγ-
ϧⲁⲓⲟⲥ ⲉϥογ., KroppR 15 S ⲥⲧⲟⲗⲏ ⲉⲥογⲟϥϣ, Mor
30 29 F ογⲁϣ *like snow*, *ib* 5 F ογⲁϧⲉϣ = BMis
233 S ⲡⲉⲣⲉⲓⲱογ, PMéd 293 Sᶠ ⲙⲡⲗⲁⲥⲧⲣⲟⲡ ⲉⲥογ.

—— nn m, *whiteness*: Lev 13 3 B (S vb) λευκός,
Si 43 19 S, λευκότης; Bor 252 188 S ⲡογ. ⲙⲡⲕⲟⲛ-
ⲓⲁ, Mor 18 70 S=*ib* 19 78 ⲡⲥⲱϧⲁϧ;   ϯ ογ. SB,
grow white: Lev 13 19 (S var ϯ ⲉⲡογ.) λευκαίνειν.

ογⲱϧϣ (often wrongly ογⲟ.) SAB, -ϧϧ A adj,
white, with pref ⲛ-: Ge 30 32 S (B as nn), Mk 16 5
S (B vb†), Ap 1 14 S (B do) λευκός; Lev 13 28 S (B
ϯ ⲙⲱⲟγⲓ) αὐγάζειν; WTh 185 S ⲙⲟγⲗⲗⲟⲛ ⲡογ.,
C 43 140 B ϭⲣⲱⲙⲡⲓ ⲡογ.;   without ⲛ- SA: Zech
6 3 A ϩⲧⲉ ογⲱϧϣ (B ⲛ-), Ap 19 11 S ϩⲧⲟ ογ. (var
ⲛ-, B vb†), *ib* 3 18 S ϩⲟⲓⲧⲉ ογ. (var do, B ⲫⲟⲣⲓ) λ.;
Kropp E 58 S ⲉⲗⲁⲗ ογ.;   as nn B: Ge 30 37 (S
vb†) λ.; BSM 13 ⲡⲉⲕογ. *white* (*hair*) = BMis 346
S vb;   ⲣ ογ. SB, *be white*: Mt 5 36 B (S vb) λ.
ποιεῖν; Mor 44 26 S ⲟ ⲙⲙⲉⲣϣ, ⲟ ⲡογ.

ογⲟϧⲱϣ B adj: TstAb 168 ϩⲁⲡⲥⲧⲟⲗⲏ ⲡογ.

ογϧⲓϧ, ογϧⲉϧ adj, *white, shining* (?): *v* ϭⲁⲗογϧⲓϧ.
In name (?): *Ταεουόβοις bright spot* (Preisigke).

ογⲁⲑⲓ B *v* ⲱⲧϩ (ογⲁⲧϧⲉ).

ογⲁⲑⲛⲓ B *v* ογⲁⲧϧ (ογⲁⲧϧⲉ).

ογⲁⲕⲥ S vb tr, *meaning unknown*: Ryl 306
1]ογⲥⲧⲉ ⲁϥογⲁⲕⲛϥ ⲉⲙⲟϥ ⲧⲉϧⲓ ⲉϣ[, *ib*]ογⲁⲕⲏ ⲉ-
ⲙⲟⲕ ⲉϣⲙⲟγⲡ ⲉϩⲟⲗⲟⲕ/, Ep 280]ογⲁⲕⲩ ⲉⲣⲟⲥ (*no
context*). *Cf* ? next.

ογⲉⲓⲕⲉ S vb intr, *meaning unknown*: Ep 261
ⲡⲧⲉⲧⲛⲡⲟⲗⲓ ⲙⲡⲗⲁⲑⲓⲁⲥ ⲛⲑⲉ ⲉⲧⲉⲧⲛογⲱϣ ϯⲡⲓⲑⲉ
ⲙⲙⲟⲛ ⲉϥογ. ϯⲡⲁⲣⲓⲥⲉ *ye arrange with Matthias as
ye will, I agree; for if he..., I shall have trouble*, BP
1065 ⲉⲡⲁⲉⲓⲟⲧⲉ ογ. ⲉⲧⲣⲁⲧⲁϫⲱⲕ.

ⲟⲩⲟⲕⲓ B nn m, *dregs of sesame* in oil-press (so Ar): Bodl 325 151 ⲡⲓⲟⲩ. ⲛⲥⲁⲣⲉⲛ (sic, l -ⲉⲙ) طـبـق. Cf K 200 'ⲃ = ⲡⲟⲩⲕⲓⲁ.

ⲟⲩⲟⲩⲕⲉ S vb tr, *break, nip*: Am 7 14 (A ⲡⲟⲩ-ⲟⲩⲭⲉ, B ⲡⲟⲩⲕⲉⲣ q v).

ⲟⲩⲁⲗ, ⲟⲩⲏⲗ v ⲙⲁⲣ nest.

ⲟⲩⲉⲗ S nn m, *mucus of nose* (?): P 46 245 ⲧⲕⲟⲩ-ⲕⲉ, ⲡⲟⲩ. خاض (l ? مخاط P 44 69, K 160), ⲡⲟⲩⲟⲟϭⲉ.

ⲟⲩⲏⲗ F v ⲟⲩⲏⲣ.

ⲟⲩⲱⲱⲗⲉ, ⲟⲩⲱⲗⲉ SF, **ⲟⲩⲟⲩⲗⲉ** A, -ⲟⲟⲗⲉ†, -ⲟⲗⲉ† S, **ⲟⲩⲁⲁⲗⲉ†** AF, -ⲁⲗⲉ† SfF vb intr, *be well off, flourish*: Job 21 9† S (B ⲟⲓ ⲛϭⲉ ⲡⲟⲩϭⲓ), Jer 12 1 S (B = Gk), Zech 7 7† A (B do) εὐθηνεῖν, BMar 113 S ⲡⲉⲧⲟⲩ.† ⲙⲡⲉⲟ‌ⲩⲟⲉⲓϣ am now captive ἐν εὐθηνίᾳ διάγειν; Lu 12 16 S (B ⲉⲣ ϣⲁⲩ), Mor 37 36 S fields ⲉⲟⲩ.† εὐφορεῖν; BHom 40 S ⲧⲣⲁⲡⲉⲍⲁ ⲉⲥⲟⲩ.† πο-λυτελής; Blake 270 city ⲉⲥⲟⲩ.† opulentissima; BMis 201 S soweth ⲉⲛⲟⲩϭⲓⲝ ⲉⲥⲟⲩ.†, P 131⁴ 105 S ⲉⲛ-ϭⲓⲛⲟⲩⲱⲙ ⲉⲟⲩ.†, Mor 27 23 F ⲧⲉⲟⲩⲥⲓⲁ ⲟⲩⲁⲁⲗⲉ = BSM 26 B ⲟⲩⲉⲥⲱⲡ, ALR '96 474 Sf after inun-dation all victuals ⲟⲩⲁⲗⲉ, BM 581(2) F ⲙⲡⲉⲧϣⲱϣⲓ ⲟⲩⲱⲗⲉ ⲧⲣⲁⲙⲡⲓ.

With following preposition. ⲉ ⲛ-: Zech 1 17 S (A ϩⲁ-, B ϥⲱⲛ ⲉⲃⲟⲗ ϩⲁ-) διαχεῖσθαι ἐν; BMis 115 S tables ⲟⲩ.† ⲡⲁⲅⲁⲑⲟⲛ; ⲉ ϩⲛ-: Zech 1 17 S (A ϩⲁ-, B ϥⲱⲛ ⲉⲃⲟⲗ) διαχεῖν ἐν; ShViK 9315 179 S ⲉⲕⲟⲩ.† ϩⲙⲡⲧⲱⲧ ⲛϩⲏⲧ & ease & pride, ShA 1 440 S ⲉⲟⲩ.† ϩⲛⲡⲁⲅⲁⲑⲟⲛ, AZ 38 59 S house ⲟⲩⲟⲗⲉ ϩⲛ-ⲧⲁⲡⲟⲗⲉϭⲓⲥ (sic) ⲛⲡⲓⲕⲟⲥⲙⲟⲥ, TU 43 24 A ⲥⲉⲃⲗⲁⲗⲉ (l ? ⲃⲁⲁⲗⲉ for ⲟⲩⲁ., but cf DM 21 23 wlʿlʿ) ϩⲛⲧⲟⲩ-ⲙⲛⲧⲣⲙⲙⲁⲟ; ⲉ ϩⲁ-: Zech 1 17 A v above; ShP 130² 65 S tree ⲟⲩ.† ϩⲁⲡⲉϥⲟⲩⲧⲁϩ.

—— nn m S, *prosperity, plenty*: Ps 29 6 (B ϩⲉ ⲡⲟⲩϭⲓ) εὐθηνία; Bor 253 265 ϯ ⲥⲟⲩⲟ ⲛⲁⲩ ϩⲛ(ⲟⲩ)-ⲟⲩⲟⲟⲗⲉ πλησμονή; Mor 17 114 ⲉⲛⲕⲟⲥⲙⲉⲓ ϩⲛⲟⲩ.ⲛⲓⲙ πλοῦτος; ib 17 42 ⲟⲩⲛⲟϭ ⲡⲟⲩ. πολυτέλεια; GFr 304 ⲟⲩⲟⲩ. of earth's fruits, Mor 31 137 give me ⲧⲉⲭⲁⲣⲓⲥ ϩⲛ(ⲟⲩ)ⲟⲩ., ViK 9527 opp ⲟⲩⲙϣⲱⲱⲧ.

ⲟⲩⲟⲟⲗ(ⲉ)ⲥ S nn, *bounty*: Bor 253 159 corn sold ϩⲛⲟⲩⲛⲟϭ ⲡⲟⲩ. δαψίλεια, Mor 31 184 sim ϩⲛ(ⲟⲩ)ⲟⲩ. ⲁⲝⲛϯⲙⲏⲛ.

V ⲑⲟⲩⲉⲗⲟ.

ⲟⲩⲗⲁⲓ B, *polium*, a plant: K 181 جعدة رومية. Also ? **ⲟⲩⲗⲁⲓ** S جعد P 44 68 = 43 38 *curly-haired* (cf ? οὖλος, -η Pey).

ⲟⲩⲗⲗⲉ SA², **ⲟⲩⲉⲗ**. S, -ⲉⲗⲗⲓ, -ⲏⲗⲗⲓ Sf nn f, *melody, music*: Si 35 6, 40 23 μέλος; Ps 91 3 (B = Gk) ᾠδή; BHom 47 ⲧⲟⲩ. ⲡⲭⲱ ⲃⲥⲙⲁ; Sa 19 17 ⲟⲩ. ⲡⲕⲱϩⲃ ψαλτήριον; Si 22 6 μουσικά; ShA 2 136 ⲉ‌ⲩⲉⲓⲡⲉ ⲉ-ϩⲣⲁⲓ ⲛϩⲉⲛⲟⲩⲉ. like those that ⲭⲱ ϩⲛⲟⲩⲕⲓⲑⲁⲣⲁ, ShA

1 397 ⲕⲓⲑⲁⲣⲁ ... ⲛⲉⲥⲟⲩⲉ., Mor 34 41 ⲕⲓⲑⲁⲣⲓⲍⲉ ϩⲛ-ϩ(ⲉ)ⲡⲟⲩⲉⲗⲗⲏ ⲉ‌ϥⲛⲟⲧⲙ = Aeg 39 B ⲭⲱ, ib 40 7 ⲡⲟⲩ. ⲡⲟⲩⲟⲣ‌ⲧⲁⲡⲟⲡ ⲡⲟⲛⲃⲁⲓⲟⲥ = Mor 39 10 Sf = C 43 37 B ⲣⲱ‌ⲃⲛ ⲡⲟⲣ. ⲡⲟⲁⲃⲁⲓⲥ (Θηβαίς), JA '05 1 450 ⲭⲱ ⲡⲣⲉⲡ-ⲟⲩⲏⲗⲗⲉ ⲙⲙⲟⲩⲥⲓⲕⲟⲡ, Mani H 12 A² ⲧⲟⲩ. ⲡⲁⲯⲁⲗ-ⲙⲟⲥ, ROC 20 50 ϩⲉⲡⲭⲱ ⲡⲁⲣⲧⲟⲡ ... ϩⲉⲡⲟⲩⲉ. ⲉ‌ⲩⲟⲩⲉⲣ (l ⲉⲓⲉⲣ) ⲃⲟⲟⲡⲉ, FR 12 Sf ⲁⲓⲧⲥⲁⲃⲟ ⲉⲥⲉⲕ ⲟⲩⲉ., R 1 2 73 ⲁⲧⲟⲩ. ⲥⲱⲕ ϩⲙⲡⲏⲓ, BKU 1 1 (II) ⲁ‌ϥⲥⲓⲧⲉ ⲡⲉ‌ϥ-ⲟⲩⲉ.; ⲣⲉ‌ϥⲥⲉϩϩ, ⲥⲉϩ ⲟⲩ. v above p 373 b. (BM 703 ⲟⲩⲉⲗⲗⲉ = velum.)

ⲟⲩⲏⲗⲙ[.] S nn m, object belonging to a washer-man or dyer: ST 122 (sic l).

ⲟⲩⲗⲱⲙ v ⲙⲣⲱⲙ.

ⲟⲩⲁⲗⲙⲉ, -ⲟⲗⲙⲉ S nn f, meaning unknown, something for which rent or hire paid: ST 70 ⲡⲡⲁⲕ-ⲧⲟⲡ ⲡⲧⲟⲩⲁⲗⲙⲉ (collated), BP 8725 ϯⲉⲡⲓⲧⲣⲉⲡⲉ ⲛⲁⲕ ⲉⲧⲣⲉⲕⲟⲩⲱϩ ⲉⲡⲟⲩⲟⲗⲙⲉ ⲉⲡⲧⲁ‌ⲅⲓ ⲉⲭⲱⲓ ϩⲁⲡⲁⲉⲓⲱⲧ ⲡⲣⲟⲥ ⲧⲣⲟⲙⲡⲉ.

ⲟⲩⲱⲗⲡ, ⲟⲩⲟⲗⲡ‌ S vb, meaning uncertain, im-plies damaging action, intr: ShP 130² 104 brittle things ⲉ‌ϥϣⲁⲡ‌ⲣⲁϭⲧⲟⲩ ⲉ‌ϥⲛⲁⲡ[ ] ⲛⲥⲉⲟⲩ. ⲛⲥⲉ-ϩⲱⲣⲃ ⲛⲥⲉϣⲱⲡⲉ ⲉ‌ⲩⲣⲟⲟⲩ; tr: PMich 1190 silver thou shalt slay (sic), ⲡⲗⲁⲓⲛ ⲭⲉⲕⲉⲟⲩⲟⲗⲡ‌ϥ, iron shalt melt, stone break.

ⲟⲩⲗⲡⲉ S nn, *hollow place* (?): Lev 14 37 (ShIF 132, B ⲭⲁⲡⲉ) κοιλάς; ShA 2 26 father's leprosy ⲣ ⲟⲩ. ⲟⲩ. ϩⲓⲱⲟⲩ.

ⲟⲩⲟⲟⲗⲥ v ⲟⲩⲱⲱⲗⲉ.

ⲟⲩⲱⲗⲥ SAB (rare), **ⲟⲩⲉⲗⲥ-, ⲟⲩⲟⲗⲥ‌, ⲟⲩⲟⲗⲥ†** S, **ⲃⲟⲗⲥ†** B vb intr, *lean, be bent, be confounded*: Ps 61 3 (B ⲭⲱⲟⲩⲛ) ὠθεῖσθαι; Mor 17 11 ⲟⲩⲟⲉⲓⲛ ⲉⲟⲩ.† κυρτοῦσθαι; Ps 34 4 (B ϭⲓ ϣⲱⲙ), ib 39 14 2° (B ϭⲓ ϣⲓⲡⲓ), Is 45 17 (B ϭⲓ ϣⲓⲡⲧ) ἐντρέπειν; Tri 654 ⲡⲁ‌ϩⲧ ⲟⲩ. اكتأب; P 130³ 68 ⲡⲉⲡϩⲏⲧ ⲟⲩ.† by great humiliation; tr, *bend, humiliate* (? not same Dévaud, cf Ryl Dem 3 342 wls): Ps 88 23 (B ⲓⲣⲓ ⲛ-ⲥⲣⲁϩ) τροποῦν; Pro 10 3 SA (-ⲗⲉ l -ⲗⲥ, B ϥⲟⲩ‌ϯ ⲉⲃⲟⲗ) ἀνατρέπειν; BHom 134 sloth ⲟⲩⲉⲗⲥ ⲧⲉ‌ⲯⲩⲭⲏ, KroppD 59 angels with swords ⲛⲥ(ⲉ)ⲟⲩⲱⲗⲥ ⲛⲡⲛⲁ ⲛⲓⲙ ⲛⲁⲕⲁⲑⲁⲣⲧⲟⲡ.

With following preposition & adverb. ⲉ ⲉ- *dat commodi*: 1 Kg 17 32 (B ⲱⲕⲉⲙ ⲉⲭⲉⲛ-) συμπίπτειν ἐπί; R 1 1 45 ⲧⲉⲧⲛ‌ⲯⲩⲭⲏ ⲟⲩ.† ⲉⲣⲱⲧⲛ περίλυπος εἶναι; Miss 4 688 sim; ⲉ ⲉⲭⲛ-, *bend upon*: Si 26 5 (uncertain) δεῖσθαι ἐπί; ShA 1 53 she followed him ⲉⲥⲟⲩ.† ⲉ. ⲡⲉ‌ϥⲛⲁ‌ϩⲃ, P 129¹³ 61 staff ⲉ‌ϥⲟⲩ.† ⲉ-ⲭⲱ‌ϥ; ⲉ ϩⲓⲭⲛ-: P 129¹³ 51 ⲥⲟⲃⲧ ⲉⲧⲣⲉⲕⲟⲩⲟⲗⲥⲕ ϩⲓⲭⲱ‌ϥ, Z 349 ⲁ‌ϥⲟⲩⲟⲗⲥ‌ϥ ⲉⲭⲡⲧⲉ‌ϥⲙⲉⲥⲧ ⲡϩⲏⲧ ϩ. ⲧⲭⲟ; ⲉ ⲛⲥⲁ-: ShA 2 114 setteth shoulder to them (sc stones) ⲛ‌ϥⲟⲩ. ⲡⲥⲱⲟⲩ *bendeth (back) against*

them; ⲥ ⲉⲃⲟⲗ *v* next; ⲥ ⲉⲣⲟⲩⲛ, ⲉⲃ., *lean upon*: BIF 13 116 sitting ⲉϥⲟⲩ.† ⲉⲣ. ⲉⲧⲭⲟ = MG 25 308 *B* ⲟⲩⲉⲣ ⲉⲃ., C 89 84 *B* ⲁϥⲟⲩ. ⲙⲡⲉϥⲥⲟⲓ ⲉⲃ. ⲉϯⲭⲟⲓ, PO 14 342 *B* sim ⲉϥⲃⲟⲗⲥ, BMis 387 one jar only ⲉϥⲟⲩ.† ⲉⲣ. (var om ⲉⲣ.) *leaning against* (wall) = Va 63 14 *B* ⲉϥⲃⲟⲗⲥ ⲉⲃⲟⲗ = Mor 27 34 *S* ⲣ ⲡⲱⲧⲛⲥ; ⲥ ⲉⲑⲏ: Sh(prob)ViK 909 *S* proud man ⲟⲩ. ⲛⲧⲉϥⲙⲉⲥⲧⲣⲏⲧ ⲉ. & raiseth eyes.

—— nn m *S, humiliation*: Ps 34 26 (*B* ϣⲱϣ), ib 68 19 (*B* ϣϥⲓⲧ) ἐντροπή.

—— ⲛϩⲏⲧ *S, be bowed down in mind, disheartened*: 1 Kg 15 11, Col 3 21 (*B* ⲉⲣ ⲙⲕⲁϩ ⲛ.) ἀθυμεῖν; Ru 1 13 πικραίνεσθαι dat; 1 Kg 30 6 κατώδυνος; ShA 1 74 ⲡⲉⲧⲗⲟⲕϩ ⲛϩⲏⲧ ⲛ ⲡⲉⲛⲧⲁϥⲟⲩ. ⲛϩ., BMis 219 ⲁϥⲟⲅⲟ. (*l* ⲟⲩⲱ.) ⲛϩ. = Mor 16 74 ⲟⲡⲱ ϩⲙⲡⲉϥϩ., Miss 4 633 ⲉϥⲟⲩ. ⲛϩ.= ib 305 كئيب القلب; ⲥ ⲉϫⲛ, *about, for*: 1 Kg 20 34 θραύεσθαι ἐπί; FR 86 ⲉⲛⲟⲩ. (var†) ⲛϩ. ⲉϫⲛⲡⲥⲱⲕ ⲉⲃⲟⲗ ⲛⲧⲉⲕⲙⲁⲁⲩ; ⲥ ⲛⲥⲁ- sim: Mor 56 61 ⲁⲛⲟⲩ. ⲛϩ. ⲛⲥⲱϥ in great grief; as nn m: Deu 28 65 (*B* ϩ. ⲉϥⲙⲟⲕϩ) καρδία ἀθυμοῦσα, 1 Kg 1 6 ἀθυμία; WTh 136 ⲙⲕⲁϩ ⲛϩ. ⲙⲛ(ⲟⲩ)ⲟⲩ. ⲛϩ.

ⲟⲩⲉⲗⲟⲩⲉⲗⲉ *S* vb intr, *yelp, howl* (*cf* الول, Dévaud) ⲥ ⲉⲃⲟⲗ: R 1 4 22 demon ⲟⲩ. ⲉⲃ. ϭⲓⲱⲱⲥ, ib 24 ⲧⲣⲉⲡⲣⲱⲙⲉ ⲟⲩ. ⲉⲃ. *ululare*.

ⲟⲩⲱⲙ *SAA²BF*, ⲟⲩⲟⲟⲙ *S*, ⲟⲩⲟⲓⲙ *O*, ⲟⲩ(ⲉ)ⲙ- *SB*, ⲟⲩⲱⲙ- *SAB*, ⲟⲩⲁⲙ- *F*, ⲟⲩⲟⲙⲝ *SB*, ⲟⲩⲟⲟⲙⲝ *S*, ⲟⲩⲁⲙⲝ *SᵃAA²F* DM, ⲡ ⲥ ⲟⲩⲁⲙ- *SBF* vb I intr, *eat, bite*: Ge 18 8 *SB*, Is 30 27 *SBF*, Jo 4 31 *SA²BF* ἐσθίειν, Is 30 30 *SBF*, Gal 5 15 *SB* κατεσ., Ps 100 5 *SB* συνεσ.; Ez 18 15 *B* βιβρώσκειν; Mt 24 38 *SB* τρώγειν, Mic 7 4 *SAB* ἐκτ.; Ap 3 20 *SB* δειπνεῖν; Lu 11 37 *SB* ἀριστᾶν; Ac 1 4 *SB* συναλίζεσθαι; ShC 42 195 *S* drug ⲉⲧⲣⲟⲧⲣⲧ ⲛ ⲉⲧⲟⲩ. opp ⲉⲧⲕⲃⲟ, Ryl 106 13 *S* after recipe ⲉⲕⲁⲗⲱ (*l* ⲗⲟ) ⲉⲕⲟⲩ., R 2 1 68 *S* worm ⲉϥⲟⲩ. ϩⲓⲣⲟⲩⲛ ⲡⲟⲩϣⲉ, AZ 21 106 *O* ⲉⲥⲥⲟ ⲉⲥⲟⲩ., C 43 115 *S* ⲁϣϣⲉ ⲛⲁϥ ⲉⲟⲩ., PMéd 204 *S* ϩⲙⲟⲩ ⲡⲟⲩ. (*cf* ملح الطعام Chassinat), DeV 2 182 *B* ⲟⲩⲟϯ ⲡⲟⲩ., BM 1117 *S* ⲁⲕⲉⲓⲣ ⲥⲡⲟⲩϭ ⲉⲕⲟⲩ. ⲙⲡⲧⲉ(ⲕ)ⲥϩⲓⲙⲉ *i e keeping house with*.

II tr: Ge 9 4 *S* ⲟⲩⲟⲟⲙⲝ *B*, Is 30 24 *SBF* ⲟⲩⲁⲙ-, Ap 2 20 *S* ⲟⲩⲱⲙ- (var ⲟⲩⲉⲙ-) *B* ⲉⲥ., Job 1 16 *S* *B*, Is 1 20 *SA*(Cl)ⲟⲩⲱⲙ- *B*, ib 33 11 *SBF* ⲟⲩⲁⲙ-, Mic 3 3 *SAB*, Jo 2 17 *SA²BF* κατεσ.; Job 6 6 *SB* βιβ., Ps 43 11 *SB* βρῶσις, Mt 14 15 *S*(*BF* ϭⲣⲉ) βρῶμα; Jo 6 56 *SA²B* τρ.; Nu 21 9 *S* (var ⲗⲱⲕⲥ, *B* ϭⲓ ⲗⲁⲡⲥⲓ), Jer 8 17 *B* δάκνειν; Deu 32 13 *S*(*B* ϭⲓ ⲙⲡⲟⲧ), Is 60 16 *B*(*S* ⲥⲱⲛⲕ) θηλάζειν; Bel 21 *B* δαπανᾶν; ib 13 *B* fire ἀναλίσκειν, Zech 9 15 *A*(*B* ⲙⲟⲩⲛⲕ ⲉⲃⲟⲗ), He 12 29 *B*(*S* ⲟⲩⲱⲱϣⲉ) καταν.; 2 Macc 5 27 *A* (ⲟⲩ)ⲱⲙ χόρτος χορτώδης τροφή; Dan 4 29 *B*, 1 Cor 13 3 *B* ⲑⲣⲉⲟⲩ. (*S* ⲧⲙⲙⲟ) ψωμίζειν; PS 37 *S* ⲉⲩⲟⲩ. ⲙⲡⲥⲟⲣⲙ, ShZ 603 *S* ⲟⲩⲱⲙ ⲉⲣⲱⲧⲉ, JKP

2 50 *Sf* do, Miss 8 224 *S* ⲟⲩⲱⲙ ⲥⲛⲟϥ, BHom 30 *S* ⲉϥϣⲁⲡⲟⲩⲉⲙ ϩⲁⲣ, ShViK 933 *S* snakes ⲟⲩⲉⲙ ϩⲁⲣ paral ⲡⲱⲣⲥ, BSM 38 *B* ⲟⲩⲉⲙ ⲉⲥⲱⲟⲩ, RNC 89 *S* ⲁⲧⲟⲅⲟⲟⲣⲉ ⲟⲩⲟⲙϥ (*cf* 87 ⲗⲟⲕⲥⲝ), KroppK 68 *Sᵃ* ϩⲉⲛⲃⲛⲛⲉ ... ⲟⲩⲁⲙⲟⲩ, TU 43 22 *A* wolves ⲛⲁⲟⲩⲁⲙϥ, Ryl 324 *S* ⲁⲛ(ⲉ)ϭⲁⲡⲉ (headman) ⲟⲩ. ⲡⲉϩⲛⲙⲟⲥⲓⲱⲡ ⲛⲡ(ⲉ)ϥⲧⲓⲙⲉ, AM 49 *B* fire ⲛⲁⲟⲩ. ⲛⲡⲉϥⲥⲁⲣⲝ, ib 62 *B* ⲁϥⲟⲩⲉⲙ ⲟⲩϣⲉ ⲛⲥⲉⲣⲃⲉⲛⲓ *absorbed thorn* into foot, DM 24 5 ⲛⲧⲉⲟⲩⲁⲙϥ; *swallow, submit to S*: Mor 19 48 ⲙⲡⲁⲧⲉⲕⲟⲩ. ⲛⲟⲩϣⲉⲥ ⲛⲁⲁⲥ for faith, Turin *Atti* 30 806 sim, ViK 4719 ⲉⲓⲁⲟⲩ. ϩⲁⲕⲗⲁ, J 18 5 ⲛϭⲓⲥⲉ ⲛⲧⲁⲡⲙⲁⲣ(ⲧⲩⲣⲟⲥ) ⲟⲩⲁⲙⲟⲩ, *cf* Ep 573; ShA 1 464 send them ⲛⲥⲉⲟⲩ. ϩⲁⲡϭⲉⲣⲱⲃ.

With following preposition. ⲥ ⲉ- *dat commodi B*: Job 2 9 (*S* ϭⲱ) ἀναμένειν, ib 17 13 (sic prob, *S* = Gk) ὑπομ.; ⲥ ⲉϫⲛ- C 41 50 *B* ⲉⲓⲟⲩⲉⲙ ⲁⲡⲁⲗⲱⲙⲁ ⲉⲭⲱⲧⲛ *living at your charges*, AJSL 46 244 *Sᵃ* fry egg ⲛⲧⲟⲩⲁⲙⲥ ⲉⲭⲙⲡⲉϩⲓⲱ: ⲥ ⲛⲥⲁ- emphatic, *gnaw at*: Deu 28 53 *S*(*B* tr), He 10 27 *S*(*B* do) ἐσ., Jud 9 15 *S*, Ez 28 18 *SB*, Va 61 13 *B* girdle ⲟⲩ. ⲛⲥⲁⲡⲉϥⲥⲁⲣⲝ κατεσ.; Deu 31 17 *S*Mor(*B* ϭⲣⲉ) κατάβρωμα εἶναι; Wess 18 88 *S* pain ⲟⲩ. ⲛⲥⲱϥ (*sc* eye) = Miss 4 101 *B*, BMis 374 *S* fire ⲟⲩ. ⲛⲥⲁⲡⲁⲥⲁ ⲛⲣⲟⲩⲛ = BSM 32 *B* ϭⲉⲛ-, Miss 4 774 *S* ⲁϥⲟⲩ. ⲛⲥⲁⲡⲉϥⲥⲡⲟⲧⲟⲩ; ⲉⲣⲟⲩⲛ ⲛⲥⲁ- *S*: PS 374 fire ⲟⲩ. ⲉⲣ. ⲛⲥⲱⲥ (*sc* soul), ib 77 sim; ⲥ ⲛⲧⲉⲛ- *F*: EpJer 71 βιβ. ἀπό (*B* ⲉⲃⲟⲗ ϩⲓⲧⲉⲛ- ἐκ); ⲥ ⲉⲃⲟⲗ ⲛ- *B, from, of*: Ge 2 17 (*S* ⲉⲃ. ϩⲛ-) ἐσ. ἀπό; ⲥ ⲉⲃ. ϩⲓ- *B*, as last: BSM 11 ⲟⲩ. ⲉⲃ. ϩⲓⲟⲩⲧⲁϩ; ⲥ ϩⲛ-, ϭⲉⲛ-, as last: Si 11 19 *S* ⲉⲥ. ἐκ; Job 20 18 *S*(*B* ϫⲉⲙ ϯⲡⲓ) γεύ. ἐκ; Pcod 3 *S* ⲟⲩ. ϩⲛⲛⲉⲛⲕⲁ of poor, Mor 43 73 *S* ⲧⲛⲟⲩⲣⲉ ⲉⲧⲟⲩ. ϩⲛⲧⲡⲁⲣⲥ, DeV 2 196 *B* ⲟⲩ. ⲛⲁⲕ ϭⲉⲛⲛⲁⲓ (*sc* money) till we return; ⲉⲃ. ϩⲛ-, ϭⲉⲛ-: Pro 9 5 *SAB* ⲉⲥ. gen, Is 36 16 *B*(*SF* tr) ⲉⲥ. acc, Jo 6 26 *SA²B* ⲉⲥ. ἐκ; Aeg 223 *S* τρέφεσθαι ἐκ (*cf* 1 Cor 9 13); El 100 *A* ⲟⲩ. ⲁⲃ. ϩⲙⲡϣⲏⲛ = ib 136 *S*, DeV 2 74 *B* ⲛⲓⲧⲁⲡⲁⲡⲏ...ⲟⲩ. ⲉⲃ. ⲡϩⲏⲧⲟⲩ, J 108 24 *S* ⲉϥⲛⲁⲟⲩ. ⲉⲃ. ϩⲛ(ⲧ)ⲇⲓⲁⲕⲱⲡⲓⲁ.

ⲥ ⲉⲏⲧ *SB, repent*, as subj (rare): 2 Kg 24 10 *S* ⲛϩ. ⲁϥⲟⲩ. ⲙⲙⲟϥ ἐπάταξε καρδία Δ. αὐτόν; BHom 136 *S* ⲡⲉⲕϩ. ⲟⲩ. ⲛⲥⲱⲕ κατηφὴς γίνεσθαι; MG 25 168 *B* ⲛⲟⲩϩ. ⲟⲩ. ⲉⲣⲱⲟⲩ; as obj *B*(*SAF* ⲡ ϩⲏⲧ): Ps 105 45, Pro 5 11, He 7 21 μεταμέλεσθαι, Ps 33 23(*S* diff), Jer 2 3 πλημμελεῖσθαι; ib 4 28 μετανοεῖν, Ro 2 5 ⲁⲧⲟⲩⲉⲙ ϩⲟⲏϥ (*S* = Gk) ἀμετανόητος; DeV 2 51 ⲉⲧⲁⲟⲩ. ⲛϩⲟⲏⲩ ⲟⲩⲟϩ ⲛⲥⲉⲉⲣ ⲙⲉⲧⲁⲛⲟⲓ, AM 121 sacrifice or ⲧⲉⲧⲉⲛⲛⲁⲟⲩ. ⲛϩⲟⲏⲧⲉⲛ; *S* Bor 226 164 grief ⲟⲩ. ⲛⲥⲁⲡ. κατατρώγ.; ⲥ ⲉϫⲛ- *B, repent of*: Ez 14 22, HL 98 ⲁⲓⲟⲩ. ⲙⲡⲁϩ. ⲉ. ⲟⲩⲥⲁϩⲓ μεταμ. ἐπί; Jon 3 10 μεταν. ἐπί; MG 25 212 ⲁⲓⲟⲩⲉⲙ ϩⲟⲏⲓ ⲉ.ⲡⲓⲁⲥⲡⲁⲥⲙⲟⲥ κατανύσσειν ἐπί; DeV 1 143 ⲛⲧⲉⲛⲟⲩ. ⲛϩⲟⲏⲛ ⲉ.ⲡⲏ; ⲥ ϩⲓϫⲛ- *B*: AM 210 ⲟⲩ. ⲡⲉϩⲑⲏⲕ ϩ.ϯⲙⲉⲧⲧⲟⲗⲙⲏⲣⲟⲥ; as nn m *B, repentance*: Pro

14 15 ογ. πρнτ(*SA* ρ ρнτ)μετάνοια; Hos 11 8 do(*A* diff)μεταμέλεια; Va 58 70 ⲁ(ⲟⲩ)ⲟⲩⲉⲙ ⲣⲟⲏⲥ ⳋⲱⲡⲓ ⲡⲏⲓ; ⲙⲉⲧⲣⲉϥⲟⲩⲉⲙ ⲣ. *B*, as last: DeV 2 34 ⲧⲉϥⲙ. ⲣⲟⲏⲥ ⲉⲭⲉⲡⲡⲉⲛⲕⲁⲕⲓⲁ; ⲁⲑⲟⲩ. ⲛⲣ. *B*, unrepentant: Ro 11 29 (*SF* ⲁⲧⲣ ⲣ.); ⲙⲉⲧⲁⲧⲟⲩ. ⲛⲣ.; TEuch 2 353 πλημμέλημα.

ⲟⲩⲉⲙⳓⲣⲉ *B*, *belly* nn f: Va 63 10 ⲧⲉϥⲟⲩ. (*sc* fish's) = BMis 391 *S* κοιλία = BSM 44 *B* ⲕⲁⲣⲓ.

ⲟⲩⲁⲙ- p c *SBF*, *eater*: BHom 94 *S* ⲟⲩ. ⲣⲱⲙⲉ ἀνθρωποβόρος, R 1 4 64 *S* ⲟⲩ.ⲥⲛⲟϥ αἱμοβ., Si 46 22 *S* ⲟⲩ.ⲉⲣⲱⲧⲉ γαλαθηνός; C 43 30 *B* ⲑⲏⲣⲓⲟⲛ ⲡⲟⲩⲁⲙⲥⲁⲣⳅ, ROC 25 258 *B* babes ⲡⲟⲩ.ⳃⲓ (*cf* Va 58 75 ⲟⲩⲉⲙ ⳃⲓ), Mor 41 150 *S* ⲙⲁⲥⲉ ⲡⲟⲩ.ⲭⲟⲣⲧⲟⲥ (var TT 69 ⲡⲁⲙ-), BM 1113 *S* ⲡⳉⲁⲗⲟⲟⲡ ⳋⲱⲱⲡ ⲡⲟⲩ.ⲕⲟⲩⲧⲧⲁ (γοῦττα, *cf* PLond 4 347 ⲕⲟⲩⲧⲇⲁ), ViK 9796 *S* ⲡⲣⲗⲗⲟ ⲡⲟⲩ.ⲡⲉϥⲥⲕⲓⲙ, BMis 149 *S* sim ⲡⲡⲉϥⲥ.; ⲟⲩ. ⲉϯ, ⲙⲁⲙⲉϯ *B* nn f, *gangrene, cancer*: 2 Tim 2 17 (*S* = Gk) γάγγραινα; MG 25 246 disease called ϯⲟⲩ. καρκίνος; *ib* 277 = MIF 13 98 *S* ⲟⲩⲁⲙⲟⲙⲉ, Va 57 76 drugs ⲟⲩⲱⲙ ⲡⲡⲓⲟⲩ., FR 96 gnawing ⲉⲣⲟⲧⲉ ⲙⲁⲙⲉϯ ⲛⲓⲃⲉⲛ; ⲉⲣ ⲙ.: Va 61 25 bone ⲉⲣ ⲙⲁⲙ. συσσήπειν, *ib* 68 189 wounds ⲉⲣ ⲟⲩⲁⲙⲙ. *V* AZ 63 73. *V* also ⲉⲣⲱⲧⲉ, ⲕⲁⲥ, ⲟⲙⲉ, ⲥⲓⲣ *hair*, ⲥⲟⲧ, ⳋⲁⲁⲣ *skin*, ⲣⲙⲟⲩ, ⲣⲣⲏⲣⲉ, ⳍⲓⲣ, ⳓⲓ *breast*.

—— nn m *SBF*, pl *SA* v ⳃⲓⲡⲟⲩ., *eating, food*: Ge 9 3 *S*(*B* ⳓⲣⲉ), 1 Cor 8 4 *SF*(*B* do), Col 2 16 *SB* βρῶσις; Ex 22 31 *B*(*S* diff) ⲡⲓⲟⲩ. ⲡⲟⲏⲣⲓⲟⲛ θηριάλωτος; Sh(Besa)Z 507 *S* ⲙⲡⲛⲥⲁⲧⲣⲉϥⲉⲓ ⲉⲃⲟⲗ ⲙⲡⲟⲩ.; J 5 R 19 *S* expenses for ⲗⲁⲩⲉ ⲉⲡⲟⲩ.; PO 11 373 *B* platter & ⲡⲓⲟⲩ. ⲉⲧⲉⲡⳉⲏⲧϥ, Rec 6 176 *B* ⲟⲩⲉⲓⳅⲟⲥ ⲉϥⲟⲩⲟⲙϥ = BMar 210 *S* ⲉⲟⲩⲟⲙϥ.

ⲁⲧ-, ⲁⲑⲟⲩ., *not eating, foodless*: MG 25 242 *B* ⲉϥⲭⲏ ⲡⲁ. νῆστις; BKU 1 8 34 *S* ⲉⲕⲡⲏⲥⲧⲉⲩⲉ ⲡⲁ. (*sic* l, *cf* Ryl 106 32), AM 64 *B* ⲟⲓ ⲡⲁⲧⲟⲩ.; ⲙⲡⲧ-, ⲙⲉⲧⲁ., *foodlessness*: Ac 27 21 *B*(*S* diff), Mor 17 21 *S* ἀσιτία; DeV 2 207 *B* lips parched ⳍⲓⲧⲉⲡϯⲙ.

ⲙⲁⲓⲟⲩ. *S*, *fond of eating*, ⲙⲡⲧⲙ.: R 2 1 73 ⲧ-ⲙⲡⲧⲙ. ⲣⲓⲥⲱ.

ⲙⲡⲧⲟⲩ. *S*, *act, habit of eating*: BHom 8 ⲙⲡⲧⲟⲩⲉⲙ ⲅⲁⲣ γαστριμαργία.

ⲙⲁ ⲡⲟⲩ. *SB*, *eating place*: BM 1130 *S* wine for ⲡⲙ., paral τόπ(ος) φακ, (φαγείου?), BM 185 ⲡⲉϥⲙ. that is called ἀκούβιτον; *refectory*: ShC 73 44 *S*, Miss 4 673 *S*, CA 92 *S*, C 43 42 *B* ⲡⲓⲙ. = Mor 39 16 *S* ⲧⲣⲓⲕⲗⲓⲡⲟⲛ; Saq 192 *S* ⲡⲓⲱⲧ ⲙⲡⲙ.

ⲡⲕⲁ, ⲡⲭⲁⲓ ⲡⲟⲩ. v ⲡⲕⲁ b & *cf* ⲭⲟⲩⲱⲙ below.

ⲣⲟⲙⲡⲉ ⲡⲟⲩ. *S*, *year of food, alimony*: J 37 25, 57 everything involved in paternal inheritance: money, clothing ⲣⲁⲥⲭⲁⲁⲧ, ⳋⲉⲗⲉⲉⲧ, ⲣ. ⲡⲟⲩ., ⲡⲟⲩⳍⲣ ⲉⲃⲟⲗ *forming marriage gift, dowry (?), year of alimony, outfit*, Ep 541 ⲧⲣ. ⲡⲁⲅⲁⲙⲉ same? (*v* HT's n there, Mitteis *Grundz* 1 ii 202, ASchiller *Krit Viertelj f Gesetzg*. 1932 264).

ⲣⲉϥⲟⲩ. *S.A²B*, *eater, glutton*: Mt 11 19 φάγος; ManiH 76 *A²* ⲧⲥⲉⲧⲉ ⲡⲣ., AM 219 *B* ⲣ. ⲡⲡⲉϥⲥⲭⲓⲙ (*cf* p c), ShA 2 338 *S* ⲣⲉϥⲟⲩⲉⲙ ⲣⲱⲙⲉ, AM 141 *B* dog ⲡⲣⲉϥⲟⲩⲉⲙ ⲡⲉϥⳋⲓϯ, BSM 10 *B* ⲡⲟ ⲥⲱⲙⲁ ⲡⲣ. may behold him; ⲙⲡⲧⲣ. *S, gluttony*: BM 228 30 Ninive condemned for ⲙ. ⲙⲁⲅⲁⲁϥ *selfish gl.*, Miss 8 259 ⲙ. ⲡⲁⲧⳋⲁⲩ.

ⲭⲟⲩ ⲡⲟⲩ., ⲭⲟⲩⲱⲙ *B* nn, *food*: Ge 25 29 ⲟⲩⳓⲣⲉ ⲉⲟⲩⲭⲟⲩ. (Va 1) ἕψημα; *ib* 27 9 ⲣⲁⲡⲭⲟⲩ ⲡⲟⲩ. (Va 1, var ⲭⲟⲩ.) ἔδεσμα, 14 ⲡⲓⲭⲟⲩ.; Hag 2 12 (*A* ⳃⲡⲟⲩ.) βρῶμα.

ⳃⲓⲛ-, ⲭⲓⲡⲟⲩ.[1] *SABF*, pl (mostly) -ⲟⲩⲟⲟⲙ[2] *S*, -ⲟⲩⲟⲟⲙⲉ,[3] -ⲱⲙⲉ[4] *A* & sg as pl, *food*, sg m; Lev 11 34 *S*[1](*B* ⳓⲣⲉ-) βρῶμα; ShC 73 54 *S*[1], BMar 5 *S*[1], DeV 2 37 *B*; sg f: BMis 143 *S*[1], TT 159 *S*[2], Va 63 14 *B*; gender? : Lu 24 41 *S*[1] (*B* ⲡⲭⲁⲓ ⲡⲟⲩ.) βρώσιμος, He 12 16 *S*[1](*B* ⳅ.) βρῶσις; ShC 42 70 *S*[1], Sh(Besa)Z 513 *S* ⲁⲑⲩⲣⲁⲥ (ἀθήρα), ⳃ.[1], ⳃⲣⲟⲟⲙⲡⲉ &c, ShColumb Univ invent 25 *S* ⳃ.[1] ⲏ ⳃⲉⲗⲁⲁⲩ ⲉ-ⳋⲁⲅⲟⲅⲟⲙϥ ⳍⲡⲓⲭⲟⲡ, MG 25 82 *B* ⲉⲓⳅⲟⲥ ⲡⲓⲃⲉⲛ ⲡⲭ., Ryl 110 *S* ⲟⲩⳃ.[1] title of recipe, Mor 22 49 *S* ⲟⲩⳃ.[2]; pl: Ps 54 14 *S*[1](*B* ⳅ.), Pro 23 3 *S*[1]*A*[3], Si 29 25 *S*[2] (var[1]) ἔδεσμα; Ps 77 18 *S*[2](*B* do), Pro 23 6 *S*[1]*A*[4], Hab 1 16 *A*[4](*B* do), Hag 2 12 *S*[1]*A*[1](*B* ⲭⲟⲩ.), Mk 7 19 *S*[1] (var[2], *B* do), He 9 10 *S*[1]*F*(*B* ⲟⲩ.) βρῶμα; Jth 12 1 *S*[2] ὀψοποίημα; BM 174 *S* τράπεζα ⲛⳃ.[2], Va 57 125 *B* sim τράπ.; ShR 2 3 63 *S* ⲛⳃ.[2] ⲧⲏⲣⲟⲩ, DeV 2 161 *B*, Pcod 35 *S*[1], Mor 37 13 *S* ⲡⲟⲉⲓⲕ...ⲙⲡⲛⲉⳃⲡⲟⲩⲟⲙ; Ez 47 12 *B* ⲡⲭⲓⲡⲟⲩⲟⲙϥ βρῶσις.

In names: Πουαμκήλ (Preisigke), ⲧⲟⲩⲁⲙⲣⲱⲙⲉ (ST 337).

V ⲧⲓⲙⲟ.

ⲟⲩⲱ(ⲱ)ⲙⲉ, ⲟⲩⲱⲙ, ⲟⲩⲟⲟⲙⲉ, -ⲟⲙ⳽ *S* vb intr, *be loosed, dissolved* by emotion: ShA 1 395 on Job 41 17 ⲉϥⲡⲁⲟⲩ. ⲡϭⲧⲣⲣⲉ ⳍⲏⲧⲥ, ClPr 43 13 ⲙⲉⲕⲟⲩ. ⳍⲏⲧϥ ⲙⲡⲣⲓⲥⲉ, Z 578 body ⲉⲧⲉⲙⲉϥⲟⲩ. ⲟⲩⲇⲉ ⲙⲉϥⲥⲉⳋⲃⲉ; tr, *reduce*(?): P 131[6] 47 of camel ⲁⲩⲗⲩⲡⲧⲁⲡⲉ (λεπτύνειν) ⲙⲡⲉϥⲟⲩⲙⲟⲧ ⲁϥ(?ⲁⲩ)ⲟⲩⲱⲙⲉ ⲡ-ⲧⲉϥⳋⲓⲛ that he may pass needle's eye; refl, *accommodate, restrain self*: Mt 5 25 c ⲉ- (var ⲙⲡ-, cit BHom 23 ⲟⲩⲱⲙ = PS 295 ⲃⲏⲗ ⲉⲃⲟⲗ ⲙⲡ-, *B* ⲕⲁϯ ⲉ-) εὐνοεῖν dat; Tri 399 ⲉⲕⲟⲩ. ⲙⲙⲟⲕ ⲉⲃⲟⲗ ⳍⲡⲡⲉⲕⲕⲁⲧⲏⲅⲟⲣⲟⲥ حذ.ار من, ShMIF 23 197 right that each ⲟⲩⲟⲟⲙϥ ⲙⲡⲉⲧⲭⲓ ⲣⲁⲡ ⲟⲩⲃⲏϥ, ShP 131[6] 44 ⲙⲡ-ⲕⲟⲩⲟⲙⲕ ⲛⲁϥ (*sc* adversary), ShZ 592 ϥⲟⲩ. ⲙⲙⲟϥ ⲙⲡⲉⲧⲣⲓⲧⲟⲩⲟϥ, Mus 40 271 sim.

ⲟⲩⲟⲟⲙⲡⲉ v next (ⲟⲩⲟⲙⲧⲉ).

ⲟⲩⲙⲟⲧ *SB*, -ⲁⲧⲉ, *S*[f] -ⲁⲧ*F*, ⲟⲩⲟⲙⲧ⁺ *SB*, -ⲙⲡⲧ⁺ *S*, vb intr, *become, be thick*: Is 34 6 *SF*(*B* ⲟⲓⳅⲓ, l ⳅⲟⲓ), Mt 13 15 *B*(*S* ⲡⳋⲟⲧ, *F* ⳍⲧⲉⲓ) παχύνειν, Is 28 1⁺ *SB* παχύς; Va 58 188 *B* cloud ⲉⲥⲟⲩ.⁺ πυκνός; ShP 131[4] 89 *S* ⲡⲉⲓⲗⲱⲟⲙⲉ ... ⲡⲧⲁⲩⲟⲩ. ⲣⲓⲱⲡ, ShIF 152

S bandages ⲟⲩ.† opp ⲡⲟⲕ, P 131⁴ 100 S ⳁϭⲓⲛⳁⲡⲉ ⲟⲩⲟⲙⲧ & at distance knoweth not sweet & bitter, PMéd 219 S eyelids ⲟⲩ.†, Va 59 6 B beaten till flesh ⲟⲩ.†, Mor 29 58 S sky ⲟⲩ. ⲡⲓⲗⲟⲟⲗⲉ, ClPr 30 14 Sᶠ sky ⲁⲥⲟⲩⲙⲁⲧⲉ ⲉⲃ. ⳍⲡⲡⲉⲕⲗ. (cf 3 Kg 18 45); as nn m, thickness: Nu 24 8 S (ⲟⲩ)ⲟⲙⲧⲉ (var ⳍⲧⲁⲓ, B ⲱⲧ), Ps 140 6 SB πάχος; Ez 41 25 SB σπουδαῖος grossior; ShP 131⁴ 111 S ϣⲓⲛ, ⲟⲩⲱⳍⲥ, ⲟⲩ. of garments, BAp 68 S sim of man, Cat 140 B ⲡⲟⲩ. ⲙ-ⲡⳉⲁⲕⲓ of clouds, Va 61 20 B ⲡⲟⲩ. ⲡⲉⲙⲡϣⲁⲓ of heart.

ⲟⲩⲟⲙⲧⲉ¹, -ⲟⲟⲙⲧⲉ², ⲟⲩⲟⲙⲡⲧⲉ³, -ⲟⲙⲡⲉ⁴, -ⲟⲟⲙⲡⲉ⁵ S nn f, tower heavily built: Ps 47 13¹ (varr²³, B = Gk) πύργος, ib 121 7¹ (B ⲡⲅⲣ. ⲉⲧⲑⲟⲣⳕ) πυργόβαρις (as if βαρύς); P 44 58 ⲡⲉⲣⲓⳅⲱ(ⲥ)ⲙⲉⲛⲟⲥ · ⲙⲉⳉⲧⲟⲗ · ⲟⲩ.¹ ج رِ; J 41 64 ⲡⲁⲡⳍ...ⲉⲧⳉⲓⳉⲓⲡⲧⲟⲩ.⁵ (sic), ⲡⲱⲡⲉ, Mor 31 238 laid them ⲉⳉⲟⲩⲡ ⲉⲧⲟⲩ.⁴ of temple = BMOr 3599 118 عتبة الباب threshold, ib¹.

In names (?): Πατουάμτις, -ῶμπτις (Preisigke).

ⲟⲩⲱⲙⲧ B vb intr, be swollen (?): MG 25 94 ⲉ-ⲁⲡⲟⲩϣⲁⲣ ⲟⲩ. ⲟⲩⲟⳍ ⲁϥⲟⲩⲙⲟⲧ = Gött Ar 114 24 مُتَّفِخ. Cf last.

ⲟⲩⲁⲙⲉⳁ, ⲙⲁⲙⲉⳁ v ⲟⲩⲱⲙ p c.

ⲟⲩⲟⲙϥ S, -ⲁⲙϥ AF, -ⲁⲡϥ A, ⲟⲩⲟⲡⳉ B, ⲟⲩ-ⲁⲙⲁⳉⳉ Sᶠ nn m, manger: Pro 14 4 SA-ⲁⲡϥ B, Is 1 3 SBF, Hab 3 17 SAB, Lu 2 7 SB φάτνη; R 1 4 31 S ⲡⲟⲩ. ⲡⲡⲉⳉⲟⲟⲩ, MG 25 39 B of camel, PcodMor 14 Sᶠ laid Him ⳍⲡ(ⲟⲩ)ⲟⲩ.

ⲟⲩⲛ Sᶠ/F interrog v ⲟⲩ.

ⲟⲩⲁⲛ B nn m, dyke: Ex 8 12, Hab 1 10 (SA ⲧⲏ-ⲛⲉ) χῶμα; LIb 8 chapel built ⳍⲓⳉⲉⲛⲡⲓⲟⲩ.

ⲟⲩⲁⲛ S same?: Hall 106 ⲡⲟⲩ. ⲉⲡⲓⲧⲡⲉ ⲉⲧⳉⲡ-ⲟⲩⲛ... ⲡⲉϥϣⲟⲣ, ViK 4714 ⲡⲗⲁⲥ ⲡϭⲱⲕ ⲉⲧⳉⲡ-ⲟⲩⲁⲡ. As place-name: ⲡⲟⲩⲁⲛ (Ryl 281), ⲡⲟⲩⲁⲡ ⲡⲡⲉ[ϣⲟⲟⲥ (Kr 79, 6, BM 1071).

ⲟⲩⲁⲡ A v ⲁⲩⲱ VI.

ⲟⲩⲉⲓⲛ, ⲟⲩⲓⲛ S nn m, water-channel (?): P 131¹ 61 rivers going forth from Paradise ⳍⲓⲧⲡⲡⲉⲩⲉⲓⲛ ⳍⲁ-ⲡⲉⲥⲏⲧ ⲙⲡⲕⲁⳉ, BMEA 10577 ⲡⲥⲁⲙⲉⲧ ⲡⲧⲁⲓⲥⲙⲡⲧⲟⲩ ⲙⲡⲡⲉⲩⲉⲉⲅⲓⲛ...ⲉⲩⲧⲓ ⲙⲟⲟⲩ ⲉⳉⲟⲩⲛ ⲉⲣⲟⲟⲩ, ib ⲡⲉⲟⲩⲛ ⲥⲡⲁⲩ.

ⲟⲩⲟⲉⲓⲛ S, ⲟⲩⲁ(ⲉ)ⲓⲛⲉ AA² (Ma), ⲟⲩⲁⲉⲓⲛ Sᵃ A² (Jo AP)F, ⲟⲩⲱⲓⲛⲓ B, ⲟⲩⲟⲓⲛ O nn m, light: Job 3 16 SB, Pro 4 18 SAB, Is 5 20 SBF, Mt 4 16 SB, AP 19 A² φῶς, Ps 26 1 SB, 2 Cor 4 4 SB φωτισμός, Ps 73 17 S (B diff) φαῦσις; Job 10 21 SB, Mk 13 24 SB φέγ-γος; Ps 89 17 SB λαμπρότης; ib 17 12 S (B ⲙⲟⳏⲉ) τηλαύγησις; Ap 4 3 S (B = Gk) ἶρις; PS 3 S ⲡⲉ-ⲑⲏⲥⲁⲩⲣⲟⲥ ⲙⲡⲟⲩ., ShC 73 51 S ⳍⲉⲡⲟⲩ.ⲡⲉ ⳉⲉⲥⲉⲟⲩⲟⲡⳉ ⲉⲃⲟⲗ, Bor 254 175 S ⲡⲟⲩ. ⲉⲧⲙⲟⳉ of lamps,

AJSL 46 242 n Sᵃ, Mani 1 A² ⲡⲟⲩ. ... ⲡⲕⲉⲕⲉ, AM 153 B ⲁⲕⲧⲓⲛ ⲡⲟⲩ., AZ 21 105 O ⲡⲉⳅⲥⲓ ⲡⲡⲣⲏ ⲡⲥⲁ-ⲡⲟⲩ., BAp 146 S humble as Jacob ϣⲁⲡⲧⲉϥϣⲱⲡⲉ ⲡⲟⲩ. & beheld Father, Mor 32 5 S as epithet ⲁⲟ-ⲣⲟⲑⲉ ⲡⲟⲩ. (= Synax 1 326 11 النور), P 129¹⁴ 136 S Mark sim, Saq 27, 226 S Apollo sim, Mor 18 96 S will not subscribe tome (of Leo) ⲉⲙⲡⲓⲱϣ ⲙ-ⲡⲉϥⲟⲩ.(var ib 19 98 S ⲱϣ ⲙⲡⲉϥⳕ-ⲅⲫⲓⲥⲙⲁ); dawn: Lu 1 78 S (B = Gk) ἀνατολή; KKS 25 S ⳉⲁⲑⲏ ⲙ-ⲡⲟⲩ.; ⲡⲡⲁⲩ ⲙⲡⲟⲩ.: ClPr 54 42 S ὄρθρος; RNC 30 S ἕωθεν; Mor 22 125 S = BSM 115 B ⲡⲡ. ⲡ-ϣⲱⲣⲡ, DeV 1 114 B; light arises, shines forth: Jud 19 25 S ⲡⲟⲩ. ⲉⲓ ⲉ⳰ⳍⲣⲁⲓ ἀναβαίνειν πρωί, ib 26 S ⲥⲱⲣ διαφαύσκειν; CO 377 S ⲉⲓ ⲉⲃⲟⲗ, AM 139 B sim, C 43 206 B ϣⲁⲓ; light of eyes: Miss 8 257 S have given thee back ⲡⲉⲕⲟⲩ., Mor 31 124 S ⲙⲡⲉⲡⲉϥⲟⲩ. ⲕⲟⲩϥⲓⳅⲉ nor reason disturbed, PO 11 343 B ⲉⲣ ⳉⲱⳉ ⲡⲟⲩ., MG 25 60 B ⳉⲁ ⲟⲩ. like Isaac (Ge 27 1); as adj: Mt 17 5 SB φωτεινός; PS 10 S ⲉⲡⲁⲩⲙⲁ ⲡⲟⲩ., ib 384 S ⲥⲓⲟⲩ ⲡⲟⲩ., AM 296 B ϭⲏⲡⲓ ⲡⲟⲩ., BM 524 F ⳉⲣⲁϭⲧⲟⲥ (ῥάβδος) ⲡⲟⲩ., Mani 2 A² ⳉⲁⲓ ⲡⲟⲩ. ⲁⲧ-, ⲁⲑⲟⲩ., without light: P 131² 144 S ⲟⲩⲁ. ⲡⲉ ⲕⲁⲧⲁ ⲧⲉϥⳕⲩⲥⲓⲥ, PS 92 S ⲁⳏⲣ ⲧⲁϭⲟⲙ ⲡⲁ., Aeg 7 B eyes ⲉⲣ ⲁ.; ⲙⲉⲧⲁ.: Is 59 9 B (S ⲕⲣⲙⲧⲥ) ἀωρία.

ⲣⲙⲡⲟⲩ. SA², man of, dweller in light: PS 52 S ⲟⲩⲡ ⲙⲁⲁϫⲉ ⲙⲡⲁⲣ. (v Sph 11 139), Mani 2 A² ⲡⲁⳉⲉ ⲡⲣ. (sc Mani, elsewhere ⲡⳕⲱⲥⲧⲏⲣ) ⲁⲧⲥⲁⳉⳏ[ⲥ.

ⲣ, ⲉⲣ, ⲉⲗ ⲟⲩ. SABF, make, be light, shine: Nu 4 9 SB, Eph 1 18 B (S ϫⲓ ⲟⲩ.) φωτίζειν, Ge 1 15 B εἰς φαῦσιν εἶναι; Mt 24 27 S (B ⲟⲩⲱⳍ) φαίνεσθαι; Jo 5 35 SA²B, Pro 4 18 SA (B ϥⲓⲣⲓ ⲉⲃⲟⲗ), Ep Jer 67 B (F ⲥϯⲉⲗⲗⲓ) λάμπειν, Is 42 3 SB ἀναλ., Mt 13 43 SBF ⲉⲕⲗ., Ap 22 16 S (B ϣⲁⲓ) λαμπρός; Ep Jer 60 B (F ⲟⲩⲱⳍ ⲉⲃ.) εὔοπτος εἶναι; Lu 24 4 S (B ϩⲓ ⲥⲉⲧⲉⲃⲣⲏϫ ⲉⲃ.) ἀστράπτειν; PS 4 S ⲟⲩⲛⲟϭ ⲡⲁⳏⲡⲁⲙⲓⲥ ⲉⲥⲣ., ShViK 9100 229 S ⲡⲉⲧⲟ ⲡⲟⲩ....ⲁⳏⲣ ⲕⲁⲕⲉ, Pcod 24 S face ⲣ. (var ⲧⲁⲁⲧⲉ), C 89 123 B curtain drawn ⲡⲧⲉ-ⲡⲓⲙⲁ ⲉⲣ., ib 43 125 B lamp ⲉϥⲉⲣ., PMéd 89 S ⲃⲁⲗ ⲉⲧⲱ ⲡⲕⲁⲕⲉ ϣⲁⲣ. ⲕⲁⲗⲱⲥ. With prep or advb. ⲥ ⲉ-: Ps 17 28 S (B ϯ ⲟⲩ.), Lu 11 36 S (B ⲡⲛ) φωτ. acc, Mic 7 8 SAB φ. dat; Ps 96 4 SB φαίν. dat, Lu 1 79 SB ἐπιφ. dat; Mt 5 15 SB λά. dat; Ryl 89 S ⲙⲡⲁⲧⲉⲡⲥⲟⲟⲩⲡ ⲣ. ⲉⲣⲟⲓ, C 86 320 B ⲉⲣ. ⲉⲣⲟϥ ⲙⲡⲓ-ⳍⲏⲃⲥ; ⲥ ⲉϫⲡ-: Is 9 2 B (S ϣⲁ) λά. ἐπί, Lu 17 24 S (B diff) λά. εἰς; ⲉⳍⲣⲁⲓ, -ⲛⲓ ⲉϫ-.: Nu 6 25 B (S ⲟⲩⲱⳍ ⲉⲃ.), Dan 9 17 B (S ⲇⲟ) ἐπιφαίν. ἐπί; ⲥ ⳍⲓ-ϫⲉⲡ- B: Ge 1 17 φαίν. ἐπί; ⲥ ⲡ-: Ps 76 19 B (S ⲉ-) φαίν. dat, Ap 8 12 SB φ. acc; Is 42 16 B (S ⲉ-) εἰς φῶς ποιεῖν dat; ⲥ ⲉⲃⲟⲗ S: J 106 41 martyr ⲉⲧⲣ. ⲉⲃ. ⲁⲩⲱ ⲉⲧⳍⲟⲩⲃⲟⲩ; ⲣⲉϥⲣ ⲟⲩ., one who lights, illuminator: Ge 1 14 B, Si 43 7 S φωστήρ, Ps 135 7 SB φῶς; Pro 6 23 SA (B ⲟⲩ.) λύχνος; ShC 42 88 S Cyril p. of church, DeV 2 161 B ⲡⲓⲣ. of those

in darkness, BAp 76 S ⲟ ⲡⲣ. ⲉⲡⲕⲟⲥⲙⲟⲥ; Va 66 298 B rich ϩⲉⲛⲟⲩⲙⲉⲧⲣ.λαμπρῶς opp indigent; ϭⲓⲡⲣ-, ϫⲓⲡⲉⲣ ⲟⲩ., shining, illumination: My 96 S ⲧⲉϥϭ. ⲙⲡⲕⲟⲥⲙⲟⲥ, Cat 198 B prophets inspired only ⲕⲁⲧⲁ ⲟⲩϫ. of prophetic words, apostles by Paraclete.

ϯ ⲟⲩ. B, give light : Ps 18 9 (S ⲣ ⲟⲩ.), Ep Jer 66 φωτίζειν.

ϫⲓ, ϭⲓ ⲟⲩ., take, get light : Is 60 1 SB, Hos 10 12 A(B ⲉⲣ ⲟⲩ.), He 6 4 SB ϫⲓ ⲙⲫⲟⲩ. φωτίζ.; ShClPr 44 1 S ⲁ ϫⲓ ⲙⲡⲟⲩ. by baptism, P 129²⁰ 121 S ⲡⲉⲛ-ⲧⲁϫⲓ ⲟⲩ. ⲛⲃⲣⲣⲉ newly baptized, BMar 214 S ⲡⲟⲩϩⲏⲧ ϫ. = Rec 6 180 B, TEuch 1 637 B ϭⲓ ⲟⲩ. ϭⲓ ⲟⲩ. O church of God !;   c e- dat commodi S: ShC 73 25 ⲡⲉϥϩⲏⲧ ⲛⲁϫ. ⲉⲣⲟϥ, BSG 196 ⲁϥⲧⲣⲉⲁⲡⲟⲩⲥ ϫ. ⲉⲣⲟⲓ.

ⲧⲣⲟⲩ. A², shine, intr: Mani 2 ⲡⲟⲩ. ⲉⲧⲧ., ib 1]ⲣⲏⲃⲉ ⲉⲧⲧ., 2 ⲛϥⲧⲟⲩⲃⲁⲥ ⲛϥⲧ. ⲁⲣⲁⲥ;   tr: ib 1 ⲁϥⲧ. ⲙⲡⲉϥ-ⲟⲩ. ⲁⲡⲡⲗⲁⲙⲡⲁⲥ, ib 1 ⲁϥⲧ. ⲛⲧⲉϥⲁⲅⲁⲡⲏ ϩⲓⲡⲡⲡⲟⲩϭ. Cf ⲃⲟⲓⲛⲉ.

ⲟⲩⲟⲛ B, -ⲁⲛ F, ⲟⲩⲛ- SAA²O, ⲟⲩⲛⲧⲉ- SA²(Jo), ⲟⲩⲟⲛⲧⲉ- S(rare)B, ⲟⲩⲁⲛⲧⲉ- F, ⲟⲩⲛⲧⲁ∕ S, ⲟⲩⲛ-ⲧ(ⲉ)∕ SAA², -ⲧⲏ∕ A², ⲟⲩⲟⲛⲧⲁ∕ B, ⲟⲩⲁⲛⲧⲏ∕ F vb, be (cf ⲙⲙⲛ- not be), I without other vb: Ge 16 1 SB, Job 1 3 B(S ⲉⲓⲣⲉ), Is 31 9 SBF, Jo 3 1 SA²B, AP 13 A² εἶναι; PS 1 S ⲟⲩⲛ ⲗⲁⲁⲩ ⲙⲫⲟⲩⲛ, Br 231 S ⲟⲩⲛ ⲕⲉⲧⲟⲡⲟⲥ ⲟⲛ, Miss 8 174 S ⲟⲩⲛ ⲟⲩⲙⲉ ⲡⲉϯϫⲱ ⲙ-ⲙⲁⲩ, C 43 7 B ⲟⲩⲟⲛ ⲟⲩϫⲉⲙⲱⲛ ⲡⲉⲙⲁⲥ, Hor 80 O ⲁϥϣⲱⲡⲉ ⲉⲟⲩⲛ ⲥⲟⲩⲃⲱⲛ;   have : Nu 27 18 SB, Pro 26 12 SA, Ep Jer 14 B(F ⲕⲏ), Jo 5 26 SA²B, He 9 1 SBF ⲟⲩⲁⲛⲧⲉ-, Ap 12 12 S(B ⲛⲧⲉ- no vb), Cl 49 1 A ἔχειν; Pro 1 20 SA(B ϣⲱⲡⲓ ϩⲉⲛ-)ἄγειν; Ex 24 14 S(B ϣ. ⲛ-)συμβαίνειν; Ac 11 29 S(B diff) εὐπορεῖν; Jud 18 3 S, Jer 52 22 B dat; BG 84 S ⲟⲩⲛⲧⲁϥ ⲁⲣⲭⲏ, ib 97 S ⲟⲩⲛⲧⲉϥ ⲧⲉϩⲟⲩⲥⲓⲁ, ShC 73 66 S ⲉϣⲱⲡⲉ ⲟⲩⲛⲧⲁⲛ, ViK 9616 S ⲁϣ ⲧⲉⲧⲉⲟⲩⲛⲧⲁⲥ ⲁϣ ⲧⲉⲧⲉⲙⲛⲧⲁⲥ, Mani H 82 A² ⲟⲩⲛⲧⲏ ⲡⲉⲧⲟⲩⲁϣⲉ, Mor 27 23 F ⲡⲉϥⲁⲛⲧⲓⲩ ⲡⲟⲩⲥⲩⲛⲏⲑⲓⲁ = BSM 26 B ⲟⲩⲟⲛ ⲛⲧⲱⲟⲩ = BMis 365 S & Va 63 3 B + ⲙⲙⲁⲩ, J 37 35 S ⲟⲩⲟⲛⲧⲏ ⲗⲁⲁⲩ ⲙⲡⲣⲟⲫⲁⲥⲓⲥ, C 43 103 B ⲟⲩⲟⲛⲧⲏ ⲡⲟⲩϣⲏⲣⲓ (var ⲟⲩⲟⲛ ⲡⲧⲏⲓ).

Double suff SAA² (as with ⲙⲙⲛ-): Ps 72 25 ⲟⲩⲛ-ⲧⲁⲉⲓϥ, P 130³ 10 -ⲧⲉⲉϥ (2d f), Z 303 -ⲧⲁⲕⲥϥ, ib 310 -ⲧⲁⲓⲥⲟⲩ, Cl 49 6 A -ⲧⲉϥⲥ, Job 42 10 -ⲧⲁϥⲥⲟⲩ (var -ⲥⲉ), AP 9 A² -ⲧⲉⲡⲥⲉ, Aeg 243 -ⲧⲓⲧⲡⲉϥ, BM 287 -ⲧⲁⲩⲥ; with intervening ⲥ: 2 Cor 8 12 ⲟⲩⲛⲧⲁⲓⲥϥ, Job 2 4 -ⲧⲁϥⲥϥ (sic l), P 129¹⁷ 73 -ⲧⲁⲡⲥⲕ.

With following ⲛⲧⲉ- B: Su 4 (S + ⲙⲙⲁⲩ) ⲉⲕ. dat; Is 31 9 (SF om ⲡ.), Mt 3 9 (S do) ἔχ.; Ez 18 7 ⲫⲏ ⲉⲧⲉⲟⲩ. ⲛⲧⲁϥ ἐνεχυρασμὸν ὀφείλων; MG 25 2 ⲟⲩ. ⲟⲩⲣⲱⲙⲓ ⲛⲧⲁⲥ ὕπανδρος οὖσα; AM 150 ⲟⲩ. ⲛⲧⲏⲓ ⲡⲟⲩϣⲏⲣⲓ; S rare: Mt 15 34 (B ⲟⲩⲟⲛ∕ ⲙⲙⲁⲩ) ἔχ.

With ⲙⲙⲟ∕ of person or thing having SAB: Ps 114 2 S(B om), Pro 7 10 B(SA diff), Ap 21 12 S(B

ⲟⲩ. ⲛⲧⲉ-) ἔχ.; Dan 7 19 B ⲉⲓ.; Ps 57 4 S(B diff) dat; Br 230 S ⲟⲩⲛ ϣⲟⲙⲛⲧ ⲛⲣⲟ ⲙⲙⲟϥ, TstAb 178 B ⲟⲩ. ⲟⲩⲙⲛϣ ⲡⲁⲫⲉ ⲙⲙⲟϥ.

With ⲛ- dat SAB: Cl 12 7 A ⲉⲓ. dat, Ps 118 165 S(B ϣⲱⲡⲓ), Ez 1 6 B(var ⲉ-, S ϩⲓ-) dat; PS 150 S ⲟⲩⲛ ⲙⲁⲁϫⲉ ⲙⲡⲁⲣⲁⲙⲡⲟⲅⲟⲉⲓⲛ, BMis 280 S yet 3 months ⲟⲩⲛⲧⲁϥⲥⲟⲩ ⲙⲡⲉⲓⲱⲧ.

With ⲙⲙⲁⲩ SAA²BF: 4 Kg 4 13 B, Job 11 18 S (B ϣ. ⲡ-) ⲉⲓ. dat, MG 25 231 B ⲟⲩ. ⲕⲉϣⲁϫⲉ ⲙⲙⲁⲩ ⲉⲓ.; Sa 8 19 S λαγχάνειν; Bodl(P) 1 d S ⲟⲩⲛ ⲟⲩ-ⲙⲏⲭⲁⲛⲏ ⲡⲥⲟⲫⲟⲥ ⲙ.;   c suff: Job 27 10 S(B diff), Mt 13 43 S(BF ⲟⲩ. ⲙⲙⲟ∕), Ac 2 47 SB, Cl 23 1 A, BHom 33 S ⲟⲩⲛⲧⲉ ⲧⲏⲡⲡⲉ ϩⲉⲛⲥⲟⲩⲣⲉ ⲙ. ἔχ.; Lev 25 10 S(B diff), Jer 44 13 B, Nah 3 4 AB no vb; BG 44 S ⲟⲩⲛⲧⲁⲩ ⲙ., ib 40 -ⲧⲟⲩ....ⲙ., ShViK 9027 254 S ⲟⲩⲛⲧⲉ ⲧⲙⲛⲧⲡⲁⲣⲑⲉⲛⲟⲥ ⲟⲩϫⲁⲣⲓⲥ ⲙ., AM 240 B ⲟⲩ. ⲡⲧⲏⲓ ⲙ. ⲙⲫϯ, C 43 175 B ⲟⲩⲟⲛⲧⲏ ⲙ. ⲙⲡⲁⲥⲧ, AP 7 A² ⲟⲩⲟⲛⲧⲏⲉⲓ ⲙ. ⲡⲟⲩϣⲉϫⲉ, Mor 30 26 F ⲟⲩⲁⲛⲧⲏⲥ ⲙ. wealth;   v also ⲙⲁⲩ c.

II Auxil to other vb (often = Gk fut or part): Eccl 7 16 SF, Mk 2 6 SB ⲉⲓ., Ps 93 20 S(B ϣⲱⲡⲓ) συμπροσεῖ.; no Gk: Deu 1 35 S(B ⲉϣ), Ps 138 11 S (B do), Mt 7 22 SBF(PMich 612), Jo 4 21 SA²(B om), Cl 14 2 A, MG 25 231 B ⲟⲩⲛ ⲟⲩⲕⲛⲃⲏ ⲁϣⲓ (Z 317 S om); PS 280 S ⲟⲩⲛ ⲟⲩⲙⲛϣⲉ ⲛⲏⲩ, C 86 275 B ⲟⲩ. ϩⲁⲛϫⲟⲗ ⲟⲩⲟⲧⲉⲛ ⲉⲣⲟϥ;   with ϣⲱⲡⲉ : Job 31 21 B(S om ϣ.), Ps 36 37 SA(Cl)B, Ac 19 2 B(S diff); PS 254 S ⲟⲩⲛ ϣⲁϫⲉ ϣⲟⲟⲛ, Imp Russ Ar S 18 029 Sᵃ ⲟⲩⲛⲛ ⲛⲓϭⲉ ⲛⲓⲙ ϣⲟⲡ ϩⲁⲡⲉϥϫⲓⲝ.

III With ⲉ-, verbal: Ge 18 31 SB, Pro 3 27 SAB, Lu 14 28 SB, Ap 11 6 SB ἔχ. + inf; ShBor 246 83 S ⲟⲩⲛⲧⲉ ϩⲁⲣ ⲟⲩϣⲁϫⲉ ⲉⲭⲟⲟⲩ;   e- against (debtor): Deu 15 2 S ⲡⲉⲧⲉⲟⲩⲛⲧⲁⲕ ⲉ- (B diff) χρέος; Lev 20 11 SB ἔνοχος εἶναι; Job 31 35 S(B diff), Mt 5 23 S(B ⲟⲩⲟⲛ ⲁⲣⲓⲕⲓ ⲟⲩⲧⲉ-) ἔχ. κατά; Is 24 2 SB ᾧ ὀφίλει, Mt 18 28 SB ὃς ὀφ., ib 6 12 S(B om ⲟⲩ.) ὀφειλέτης, Lu 16 5 SB χρεοφειλ.; J 67 38 S ⲟⲩⲛ ⲥⲡⲁⲩ ⲛϩⲟ-ⲗⲟⲕ/ ⲉⲣⲟϥ, COAd 38 S ⲟⲩⲛⲧⲁϥ ⲉⲣⲟⲓ hath claim against me;   ⲟⲩⲛ ⲟⲩⲟⲛ ⲉ- sim S(v also ⲟⲩⲟⲛ pro): Is 1 c (B om vb) ὁ ὀφίλων, Mt 23 16 (B do) ὀφείλειν; ShC 42 149 ⲉⲧⲣⲉⲡⲉⲧⲉⲟⲩⲛ ⲟⲩ. ⲉⲣⲟϥ to forgive neighbour, ShP 130¹ 141 forgive ⲟⲩⲟⲛ ⲛⲓⲙ ⲉⲧⲉⲟⲩⲛ ⲟⲩ. ⲉⲣⲟⲟⲩ, ShRyl 68 260 ⲟⲩⲛ (sic l) ⲟⲩ. ⲉⲣⲟⲓ ⲛⲧⲟⲟⲧⲟⲩ ⲁⲩⲱ ⲟⲩⲉⲛⲧⲁⲩ ⲉⲣⲟⲓ, ShRE 10 159 if I should have said more ϯⲛⲁϣⲱⲡⲉ ⲉⲩⲛ ⲟⲩ. ⲉⲣⲟⲓ ⲛⲧⲉⲧⲏⲩⲧⲛ, if not ⲉⲓⲉ ⲟⲩⲛⲧⲁⲓ ⲉⲣⲱⲧⲛ, ShMIF 23 95 world's tribunal hath no concern with me ⲛⲃⲏⲙⲁ ⲙⲡⲉⲭ̅ⲥ̅ ⲡⲉ-ⲧⲉⲟⲩⲛ ⲟⲩ. ⲉⲣⲟⲓ ⲛⲧⲟⲟⲧϥ (cf PSBA 32 199).   Cf e-prep I f(b);   ⲉϩⲟⲩⲛ ⲉ-, toward: Ac 25 19 S(B diff), Cl 49 6 A ⲧⲁⲅⲁⲡⲏ ⲉⲧⲉⲟⲩⲛⲧⲉⲥ ⲁϩ. ⲁⲣⲁⲛ ἔχ. πρός; Aeg 274 S piety ⲟⲩⲛⲧⲁϥⲥ ⲉϩ. ⲉⲡⲡⲉ αὐτῷ εἰς θεόν; C 43 231 B ⲟⲩⲟⲛⲧⲉⲕ ⲉϩⲟⲩⲥⲓⲁ ⲉϩ. ⲉⲣⲟϥ.   V also ⲣⲏⲧⲉ, ϭⲟⲙ.

ⲟⲩⲟⲛ *SB*, -ⲁⲛ *AA²F* pron, *some one, -thing, some*:
Jer 39 27 *B*, Jo 9 32 *S*(var & *A²* ⲗⲁⲁⲩ, *B* ⲟⲩⲁⲓ), Ac
19 2 *S*(*B* diff) τις; Lev 11 35 *S*(*B* om) πᾶς; Ex 16
25 *S*(*B* do) αὐτός; Dan 9 12 *B*(*S* om), Mt 24 21 *SB*
οἷος; Job 8 18 *SB* τοιοῦτος; Aeg 270 *S* neg (var
ⲟⲩⲁ); MG 25 243 *B* neg μηδείς; no Gk: Ex 16 27
S(*B* om), Deu 33 26 *SB*, Si 25 5 *S*(var om), Ro 6 13
B(*S* om); PS 58 *S* ⲙⲡⲥⲕⲁ ⲟⲩ. ⲙⲙⲟⲛ ⲉϣⲁⲭⲉ, Sh
BMOr 8810 448 *S* suffer them not ⲉϣⲃ ⲟⲩ. ⲉⲟⲩ.,
ShC 73 55 *S* leave them not ⲉⲩϣⲁⲁⲧ ⲛⲟⲩ., DeV 2
219 *B* fear ϩⲉⲛⲡⲟⲛⲧ ⲛⲟⲩ. ⲙⲙⲱⲟⲩ, Mor 38 90 *S*
ⲙⲡⲉⲟⲩ. ⲡⲣⲏⲧⲟⲩ ϫⲓ ⲣⲉⲕⲣⲓⲕⲉ, BMis 535 *S* ⲟⲩⲛ ⲙⲁ
...ⲟⲩⲟⲧⲃ ⲡⲁⲣⲁ ⲟⲩ. (cf *ib* 568), PLond 4 476 *S* ⲙ-
ⲡⲉⲛⲕⲟⲩ]ϥⲓϫⲉ ⲛⲟⲩ. (cf 473 sim ⲛⲟⲩⲁ), BAp 65 *S* ⲛ-
ⲧⲁϥϭⲉ ⲉⲟⲩ. (sc fruit) ⲧⲱⲛ?, BSM 127 *B* ⲙⲡⲉⲛϣⲱ-
ⲗⲉⲙ ⲉⲟⲩ. (sc perfume) ⲙⲡⲉϥⲣⲏϯ, Miss 4 129 *S*
ⲙⲡⲟⲩⲛⲁⲩ ⲉⲟⲩ. ... ϩⲉⲛⲡⲓⲥⲱⲙⲁ *saw not aught of
body*; as pl *BS*(rare): Va 66 292 ⲡⲁⲓⲟⲩ. ⲙⲡⲁⲓⲣⲏϯ πᾶς; *ib* 57 174 sim οὗτος, 1 Cor 16 18 (*SF*
om) τοιοῦτος; Cat 189 ⲡⲓⲟⲩ....ⲁⲩϣⲁⲡⲓ, PO 11 340
ⲙⲡⲟⲩϫⲉⲙ ⲟⲩ. ⲉⲁⲩⲱⲗⲓ (bread) ⲡⲁϥ, MG 25 41
ⲉⲃⲏⲗ ⲉⲟⲩ. ⲉⲁⲩϭⲓ ⲛϯϭⲟⲙ from God, ShA 1 44 *S*
he punished ⲛⲟⲩ. ϣⲁⲡⲧⲟⲩⲥⲕⲣⲕⲱⲣⲟⲩ;   ϩⲁⲡ-
ϩⲉⲡⲟⲩ.: Is 60 8 (*S* om), Ep Jer 31 (*F* ϩⲁⲓⲛⲓ), Ro 3 3
(*S* ϩⲟⲓ.) τις; Ac 14 4 ὁ μέν; MG 25 242 ϩ....ϩⲁⲡ-
ⲕⲉⲟⲩ. ὁ μέν....ὁ δέ, Gk om Ez 6 8 *B*(*S* ϩⲟⲉⲓⲛⲉ), 1 Jo
3 1 *S*; C 89 176 wells ⲉⲧⲁϩ. ϣⲟⲕⲟⲩ, TEuch 2 226
ⲕⲉ ⲅⲁⲣ ⲁⲛⲟⲛ ϩ. *for such we are*, BIF 13 102 *S* ⲛⲧⲉ-
ϩ(ⲉ)ⲛⲟⲩ. ϫⲟⲟⲥ.

ⲕⲉⲟⲩ. *B* pl, *other ones*: C 89 54 like ⲛⲓⲕ. ⲙⲙⲟⲛ-
ⲡⲱⲟⲅⲓ, ROC 23 280 jewels ⲡⲉⲙⲡⲓⲕ. ⲙⲙⲁⲣⲅⲁⲣⲓⲧⲏⲥ, C 86 348 ϩⲁⲡⲕ. ⲙⲡⲁⲓⲣⲏϯ (var ⲕⲉⲭⲱⲟⲩⲡⲓ); *S*
sg: TT 168 ⲟⲩⲛ ⲕ. ⲙⲡⲥⲁⲣⲓⲥ ⲙⲙⲟⲛ.

ⲗⲁⲁⲩ ⲛⲟⲩ. *S, any one*: J 106 178 ⲗ. ⲉϥⲛⲁⲉⲥⲕⲁ-
ⲗⲉⲓ, *ib* 183 sim.

ⲟⲩ. ⲛⲓⲙ, ⲛⲓⲃⲉⲛ, ⲛⲓⲃⲓ *SAA²BF, every one*, as sg:
Nu 5 2 *SB*, Pro 3 18 *SA*(*B* ⲛⲛⲓ), Jo 3 8 *SA²BF*, 1 Cor
2 15 *S*(*BF* ⲛⲭⲁⲓ ⲛⲓⲃ.) πᾶς; Sa 17 15 *S* ὃς δήποτε;
J 105 6 *S* ⲟⲩ. ⲡ. ⲉϥⲛⲁⲙⲟϣⲉ, C 43 79 *B* ⲟⲩ. ⲡ. ϣⲁϥ-
ⲟⲩϫⲁⲓ;   as pl: Ge 7 22 *B*(*S* ⲣⲱⲙⲉ ⲛⲓⲙ), Ez 28
19 *S*(*B* ⲁϣⲉ), Hos 9 4 *AB*, Ro 9 6 *SB* πᾶς; Mt 14
36 *BF*(*S* rel) ὅσος; ShC 73 79 *S* ⲥⲉⲥⲟⲟⲩϣ ⲛϭⲓ ⲟⲩ.
ⲡ., El 68 *A* ⲟⲩ. ⲡ....ⲥⲉⲛⲁϩⲓ, J 89 8 *S* ⲟⲩ. ⲡ. ⲡⲧⲁⲅ-
ⲡⲁⲩ, AM 217 *B* ⲟⲩ. ⲡ....ⲛⲛⲟⲩϭⲓ ϣⲓⲡⲓ;   no concord shown: Job 5 8 *SB*, Pro 1 7 *SAB*, Ro 11 32
SBF; BG 38 *S* ⲧⲙⲁⲩ ⲛⲟⲩ. ⲡ., AP 12 *A²* ⲙⲡⲙⲧⲟ
ⲁⲃⲁⲗ ⲛⲟⲩ. ⲡ., Mor 30 3 *Sᶠ* ⲟⲩ. ⲛⲓⲃⲓ ⲉⲧⲣⲙⲙⲁ ⲛⲓⲙ.

ⲟⲩⲛ ⲟⲩ. *SA²*(*B* rare), *there is one, are some*: Si 44
9 pl εἰσιν οἵ, *ib* sg ὦν, Lu 24 39 (*B* Gk om), Z 355
ⲟⲩⲛ ⲟⲩ. ⲉϥⲉⲓⲣⲉ *est quidem faciens*, ShA 1 258 ⲉⲙⲛ
ⲟⲉⲓⲕ ⲡⲧⲟⲟⲧⲟⲩ...ⲉⲧⲉⲟⲩⲛ ⲟⲩ. ⲡⲧⲟⲟⲧⲟⲩ, ShMIF 23
31 ⲉϣϫⲉ ⲟⲩⲛ ⲟⲩ. (sc swords) ϣⲟⲟⲡ ⲡⲁⲕ ⲡⲟⲩⲕ ⲁⲡⲡⲉ, ManiH 69 *A²* ⲟⲩⲛ. ⲟⲩ. ⲁⲩϭⲱⲕⲉ ⲙⲙⲁϥ ⲟⲩⲛ ⲟⲩ.

ⲁⲩⲡⲱⲣⲕ [, Pcod 10 ⲟⲩⲛ ⲟⲩ. ⲉϥϣⲁⲁⲧ ⲉⲃⲟⲗ, BMar
129 is there any farther in (desert) than thou? ⲟⲩⲛ
ⲟⲩ., MG 25 8 *B* ⲟⲩⲛ ⲟⲩ. ⲟⲩⲣⲟ on earth;   *v* ⲟⲩⲟⲛ
vb *s f.*   ⲟⲩⲟⲛ ϩⲁⲛⲟⲩ. *B*: Ro 3 8 (*S* ϩⲟⲉⲓⲛⲉ) τις;
MG 25 239 ⲡⲉⲟⲩⲟⲛ ϩ. ⲡⲉ ⲛϩⲏⲧⲟⲩ *without doors*
ὁ μέν; Ac 2 5 (*S* Gk om);   ⲙ(ⲙ)ⲛ ⲟⲩ. *S*(*B* rare),
there is not one, any: Z 356 ⲙⲛ ⲟⲩ. (sc loaf) ϣⲟⲟⲡ
εἷς; 3 Kg 8 23 *B*(Gk om), Ro 3 12 (*B* Gk do), PS 6
ⲙⲛ ⲟⲩ. ⲙⲙⲟⲟⲩ ϣⲁϫⲉ, ShMIF 23 149 ⲁϥⲧⲣⲉⲱⲡⲉ
ϣⲱⲡⲉ ⲙⲙⲛ ⲟⲩ. *when there was none*, P 131⁵ 57 ⲙⲛ
ⲟⲩ. ⲧⲛⲧⲱⲛ ⲉⲣⲟϥ, Tor 28 ⲙⲛⲧⲉ ⲟⲩ. ⲙⲙⲟⲟⲩ ⲣϣⲱⲛ
none of them hath cloak.

ⲟⲩ. ⲛⲥⲁⲟⲩ. *B, one after another*: Va 57 127 trials
come ⲟⲩ. ἐπαλλήλους; Ex 10 1 ἑξῆς, HL 74 ⲡⲁⲓⲣⲏϯ
ⲟⲩ. καθεξῆς; MG 25 86 they gathered about him
ⲟⲩ.

V AZ 47 3.

ⲟⲩⲱⲛ *SBF*, -ⲏⲛ *SSᵃA²* (AP), -ⲉⲛ *AA²*, ⲉⲟⲩⲉⲛ
A(TU 43), ⲁ(ⲟ)ⲩⲱⲛ *SBF*, ⲟⲩⲛ- *S*(imperat), ⲁⲟⲩⲛ-
A(do), ⲟⲩⲏⲡ† *SBF*, -ⲉⲛ† *A²*, p c ⲟⲩⲁⲡ- *O* vb **I** intr,
open, be open: Ps 105 17 *S*(*B* tr), Is 35 5 *SBF*, Nah
3 3 *AB* ⲁⲟⲩ., Jo 9 10 *SA²B*, Ap 3 8† *SB* ἀνοίγειν, Ez
24 27 *B*, Ac 7 56† *SB* διαν., Pro 3 20 *SA*(*B* ϥⲱϭ)
ῥηγνύναι; PS 21 *S* gates ⲟⲩ. ⲙⲁⲅⲁⲁⲩ, DeV 2 164 *B*
ⲁϥⲟⲩ. ⲡϫⲉ ⲫⲣⲟ, Mani 2 *A²* ⲡⲉϥⲃⲉⲗ ⲟⲩ.†, BHom 46
S ⲧⲟⲟⲧⲩ ⲙⲡⲉⲛⲟⲩⲣⲟⲧ ⲟⲩ.† *in giving*, PMéd 297 *S*
sore ⲉⲧⲣⲉϥϫⲱⲣⲉ ⲉⲃⲟⲗ ⲉⲓⲉ (ⲛ)ⲧⲉϥⲟⲩ., BIF 13 101
S one ⲟⲩⲣⲱⲙⲉ ⲉϥⲟⲩ.† *broad* (?), other ⲉϥϣⲏⲧ =
MG 25 284 *B* (cf C 86 112 *B* ⲟⲩⲉⲥⲟⲱⲡ).

II tr: Ex 4 12 *SAB*, Ps 50 15 *SA*(Cl)*B*, Mt 13
35 *SBF*, CDan 90 *B* ⲙⲡⲓϣ ⲁⲟⲩ. ⲡⲣⲱⲓ (*ib* ϣ ⲟⲩ.)
ἀν., Is 5 14 *SBF*, Ez 21 22 *B* ⲁⲟⲩ. διαν.; Ge 4 11 *S*
(ShA 2 112)*B* χαίνειν; Br 123 *S* ⲉⲣϣⲁⲡⲡⲉϥⲗⲁⲥ
ⲁⲟⲩ. ⲡⲁⲡⲩⲗⲏ, Mani 1 *A²* ⲁⲅⲟⲩ. ⲡⲧⲟⲩⲧⲁⲡⲣⲟ, C 43
17 *B* bade ⲉϥⲟⲣⲟⲩⲁⲟⲩ. ⲡⲣⲱϥ, *ib* 38 *B* ⲁⲡⲓⲉⲙⲡⲟⲩⲧ
ⲁⲟⲩ. ⲙⲫⲣⲟ, *ib* 41 63 *B* not able ⲛⲁⲟⲩ. ⲙⲙⲟϥ, BIF
22 107 *F* ⲁⲡⲕⲉⲣⲓ ⲁⲟⲩ. ⲡⲗⲱϥ, Mor 27 36 *F* ⲁϥⲁⲩ.
ⲙⲙⲟⲥ, Ostr *penes* WCHall *S* ⲙⲉⲓⲟⲩⲓⲛ ⲛⲡⲉϥⲣⲱ.

Imperat ⲁⲟⲩⲱⲛ *SBFO*, ⲟⲩⲛ- *S*, ⲉⲅⲉⲛ, ⲁⲟⲩⲛ- *A*:
Ps 118 18 *S*(*B* diff) ἀποκαλύπτειν; Pro 24 76 *SA* ⲉⲩ.,
Is 26 2 *SBF* ἀνοίγ., Zech 11 1 *A* ⲁⲟⲩⲛ (ⲛ)ⲕⲣⲱⲟⲩ
διαν.; Ez 28 8 *SB* χ.; BMis 391 *S* ⲁ. ⲡⲣⲏⲧϥ = BSM
44 *B*, POslo 1 312 *O* ⲁⲟⲩⲱⲛ ⲛⲏⲓ;   Ps 80 10 *S* ⲟⲩⲱⲛ
(*B* diff) πλατύνειν; BMar 200 *S* ⲟⲩⲛ ⲡⲁⲓ ⲡⲁⲕ.   *V*
Griff Stu 66.

With following preposition or adverb.   c ⲉ- acc:
Ex 21 33 *S*(*B* ⲛ-), Jud 11 36 *B*(*S* ⲛ-), Is 42 7 *S* (var
& *B* ⲛ-), Jo 9 17 *A²*(*SB* ⲛ-), Cl 43 5 *A* ἀν., Nu 3 12
S(var & *B* ⲛ-), Lu 2 23 *SB*(var both ⲛ-) διαν.; ShA
2 115 *S* must ⲟⲩ. ⲉⲡⲓϣⲱⲡⲉ & cut out flesh, J 106 51
S ⲁⲡⲡⲉ...ⲟⲩ. ⲉⲡⲁϩⲛⲧ, BKU 1 299 *S* ⲡⲛⲉϩⲟⲩⲣ ⲟⲩ-
ⲏⲛ ⲉⲣⲟⲥ *save its own*;   *toward, upon*: Ps 108 2 *B*

(S ерраι ехп-), Si 34 13 S -нп (var -ωп) ἀν. ἐπί, 2
Cor 6 11 S(B ογбε) ἀν. πρός, Dan 6 10 SB ἀν. dat;
Ez 8 14[†] B βλέπειν πρός; PS 169 S етоγ.[†] ёп....
пαιωπ, Br 231 S ереоγα оγ.[†] ёптопос, J 45 32 S
про...оγ.[†]ёпрнт, Kr 36 F песλα оγ.[†]ёрнс; ёроγп
е- S: PS 93 аγоγ. прωоγ ер. ероι, ShA 1 151 п-
кеμα етоγ. ер. ерооγ н еттнёе ерооγ; с ерп-
S: PS 328 key етаоγ. ерμптнрч; с ехп- S: Si
20 13 S -нп ἀν.; PS 23 пеγпγλн оγ. е. пеγернγ,
BMis 247 orchard оγ.[†] е. ρепкопріа (var Z 263
еболλ ехп-); ерраι, -нι ех.: Lam 2 16 SBF διαν.
ἐπί; Ps 34 21 S(B оγωщс) πλατ. ἐπί; с п- dat:
Job 31 32 SB, Cant 5 2 SF, Mt 7 7 SB, AP 11 A[2]
адоγнп пес μпро ἀν. dat; PS 42 S curtains
аγоγ. παι, TU 43 22 A ппоγеоγеп пеγ, Ep 247 S[a]
μпетпоγнп паι μпро, Mor 24 30 F песμпоγт
аоγ. пнб; с пса- S, toward, upon: BAp 65 heavens
оγ. псапеιса μппаι, ib 59 аγоγ. псапеγернγ,
MIF 9 62 sim; с оγбе- B: 2 Cor 6 11 (S е-) ἀν.
πρός; Va 57 263 sim.; с еболλ S: Ac 12 10 (B
ппоγ еб.) φέρειν εἰς; Mk 5 38 S оγп ро еб. (var ꝷ
рооγ еб., B щ λнλογι) ἀλαλάζειν; J 79 68 тμптт-
еро ... оγ.[†] еб., Mor 25 41 wound in tree щадоγ.
еб. & will destroy it; v also с ехп-.

оγαп- p c O: DM 1 28 оγαптω *earth-opener*.

—— nn m SAB, *opening*: Nah 3 13 AB ἀν.;
Miss 4 579 S поγ. прωч; *riddle* B: Ps 48 5 (S =
Gk) πρόβλημα; Deu 28 37 оγ. псахι (S сμот) αἴνιγμα (reading ? ἄνοιγμα); Ez 43 17 B κύκλωμα,
ib 14 B(Gk?) or vb?

оγп ро *v po mouth* I *sf.*
щтаμоγωп *v щωтμ.*
хιπογ. B, *act of opening*: MG 25 377 течхιпаоγ.
пап μфро, TEuch 1 308 пепхιпоγ. прωп.

оγωп SAA[2]B(Ez)F, оγп- SA, оγеп- SB(do)
nn m, *part*, **a** alone: Lev 19 6 S(B = Gk), Jo 19 23
SA[2](B тоι), Z 355 S паоγ. ρппоеιп μέρος; ib 310
S пекоγ. ρμпбγке μισθός; Ez 43 14 B(Gk diff);
ShIF 212 S оγоγ. поγωт ρμпоγоеιп can dispel
darkness, PMéd 304 S (оγ)оγ. пеγфорбιογ, BM
Or 6201 A 27 S поγ. ёпнι пιоγста. **b** numeral
preceding SF: 2 Kg 23 8 щомπт поγ. τρίτον;
Ap 16 19 щµтоγ. (B т.) μέ.; LAp 520 F ιб поγ.,
ShP 78 44 μптоγе поγ. ечщщаат поγпαще поγ.
in my body are sick чтооγ поγ. μπογпα. поγ.
are hale. **c** numeral following SA: Zech 13 8
SA: оγ. спαγ(B тере-)μέ.; BM 1072 S поγ. бтоо-
оγ; оγωп п-: Ez 5 12(B оγеп-)τέταρτον, BHom
5 τρ.; PS 26 поγ. пщомπт πτε теγбολ, ShZ 594
поγ. пꝷоγ, TU 43 6 A поγ. пще; оγωп е- (for п-)
S: Lev 27 27 (var оγеп п-, B ре-)ἐπίπεμπτον, ib 14
21 (var оγп е-, B do) δέκατον; оγ(е)п-: Nu 5 7 S
(var оγеп е-, B тере-) ἐπίπ., Ez 5 12 B оγепꙇ (S

оγ. п-)τέτ., Zech 13 8 A(S var оγп е-, B do) τρί.;
Gu 5 S поγптба ппекаретн, BSG 180 S поγп-
щомπт птпе; оγ(е)п п- S: Ex 16 36 (B ре-) δέκ.,
Ap 6 8 (var оγп-, B do) τέτ.; ShA 2 295 поγп μι-
μнт; оγ(е)п е- (for п-): Lev 5 16 (var оγ. п-, B
do) ἐπίπ., Nu 28 5 (var ра-, B do) τέτ.; Mor 44 48
поγепещомπт поγоγпоγ.

V AZ 47 1.

оγеιпе SAA[2], оγιпι F vb intr, *pass by*: Ge 41
53 (B сιпι), Cant 2 11 SA(Till Oster, F c.?), Mt 14
15 (BF do), Ap 21 1 (B ще п-), Cl 50 3 A, BMar 107
теγщн птасоγ. παρέρχεσθαι, 2 Kg 11 27 διέρ., Ap
21 4 (B с.) ἀπέρ., Is 48 3 (B ι) ἐπέρ.; Ps 143 4 (B с.)
παράγειν; Is 24 13 S(B кнп) ib 32 10 SF(B оγω)
παύεσθαι; Lu 9 12 (B рιкι) κλίνειν; ib 22 59 (B diff)
διιστάναι; Ac 14 16 (B с.) παροίχεσθαι; ib 25 13 (B
do) διαγίνεσθαι; Job 20 8 (B ρωλ) ἐκπετάζειν; Sh
ViK 940 219 птерегтооγе оγ., JTS 4 389 пебот
птаγоγ., Mani 1 A[2] асоγ. пхι тпрω; approx
transl: Mk 6 35 ппаγ ρωп еоγ. (B do) ὥρας πολλῆς
γεν., Lu 15 13 ρας προоγ оγ. (B diff) μετὰ πολ. ἡμέρας, ShR 2 3 18 течθλιψιc етпаоγ. πρόσκαιρος(BM
285 iv), Sa 8 8 пептаγоγ. τὰ ἀρχαῖα; ShViK 94
219 птерегтооγе оγ. we returned.

With following prepositions: BMar 17 ащеλеет
оγ. ероι амптрмμαо оγ. птоот (cf Miss 8 182
парасе пагραι); SHel 94 аппаγ оγ. птоотп;
Orat Cyp 1 ароωб пιμ оγ. пагραι; Ann 19 232
атарелпιс оγ. ρμпеинι = C 86 112 B ще пас еболλ
ꙛеп-.

атоγ., *not passing by, away*: Pcod 31 оγапо-
λαγсιс па., BM 172 39 пιαιωπ епа.

оγωιпι B *harp v* боιпе, *light v* оγоеιп.
оγепπ *v* епπ.

оγωпπ, баκ⳽ S[f] vb tr, *chew* (?): Tebtunis (v
p 150 a), monster with head of human figure in
jaws птекапос (δεκανός) едоγ. течυγχн, ib птек.
ечщιпι псатеуγ. пꝷбакc (l оγаꙛс). Prob for
оγωꙛ, cf оγоꙛоγеꙛ.

оγпαμ SF[1], оγ(е)п.[2], ιογп.[3], оγпоμ[4], ιογп.[5]
S, оγпеμ AA[2], оγιπαμ B, -пеμ[6], -епнμ[7], ιογ-
пеμ[8], -епнμ[9], ιωпαμ[10], -пнμ[11] F nn f, *right hand*:
Job 40 9 SB, Is 30 21 SBF[8], Mt 6 3 SBF[6] δεξιά;
BMis 552 S ꝷорк птоγ. μпащнре, DeV 1 115 B
knowing not т(оγ)оγ. оγꙛе тоγхаꙛн, AM 318 B
(е)пе(оγ)оγ. пе пекпоγꝷ птечхιх споγꝷ yet
could he not save thee, Mor 48 83 S sim о поγ. пт-
бιх сπте (cf C 43 141), Pcod 12 S veil (of temple)
оγоγ.пе μιса спαγ, Mani 2 A[2] тщарп поγ., BP
11347 S stretch forth теγι.[5]; m (rare): BKU 1
26 (8116 b)F[1] μареч ριхепоγ. (sc сμαγ); паоγ.,

those on right: ZNTW 24 90 *F*[6] δ.; PS 188 *S* птопос пп.[2], *ib* 189 *S* sim пατογ., Br 102 *S* пπигстнріоп
пп.;   as adj, ϭιχ, х. пογ.: Ps 72 24 *SB*, Ap 10
5 *S*(*B* om х.) χείρ δ.; Griff Stu 163 *F*[7], KroppC 5
F[10], BMOr 6948(2) *F* ϭιϭ пι.[9];   other limbs:
Ez 4 6 *B* сϥιρ, Mt 5 29 *SB* ϧαλ, Ap 10 2 *F*[6] ϭαλαχ
δεξιός; C 43 151 *B* мαшχ, *ib* 146 *B* αλλογ, *ib* 6 *B*
тнϧ, *ib* 136 *B* ϥατ, Mor 39 14 *F* χпεϧ пι.[11]

With preceding preposition.   c є-, *to, on right*:
Ge 13 9 *SB*, Jos 23 6 *SB* εἰς δ.; PS 30 *S* кнт εογ.,
ib 27 *S* ϭωшт εογ., C 43 40 *B* set seats ετεογ.;
c п- sim: PS 354 *S* порχογ εϧολ погγ.;   c пса-
SF, са- *S*(rare)*A*[2]*B*: Deu 33 2 *SB*, Ps 109 1 *F*[6]*B*
(*S* ϧι-), Mk 10 40 *SBF*[8], R 1 2 66 *S*(var JA '75 5 225
ϧιτογ.) ἐκ. δ.; He 10 12 *SBF*[10], Eph 1 20 *BF*[6](*S*
ϧι-) ἐν δ.; PS 151 *S* lamp псαογ. ммоι (OdSolom
25 7 ـلـمـ مـ), LCyp 32 *S* εптс псαι.[3] ммоϥ,
KroppK 5 *S* петсαογ.[4], ManiH 38 *A*[2] sim, Mor 24
12 *F* псαι.[10] ммаϧ, ROC 25 249 *B* ϧεмιс сαϧογ. of
Father;   c ϧι-, *on, at*: Ps 44 9 *S*(*B* са-) ϧ. ммок,
Mt 20 21 *S* do (*B* сατεκογ.) ἐκ δεξιῶν, Pro 3 16 *A*
(*SB* ϧп-), AP 6 *A*[2] ἐν(τῇ)δ.; PS 105 *S* ϭω ϧ. ммоϥ,
ShA 1 107 *S* αϥпωϧпε мпεισα...ϧ. ммоϥ;   c
ϧп-, ϧεп-, *by, with*: Ps 59 5 *SB*, Is 63 12 *SB* dat;
in, at: Ge 48 13 *S*(*B* са-), Is 44 20 *S*(var[2])*B*, He 8 1
F[1](*B* са-), Ap 1 16 *S*(ϧ χιχ погγ.) ἐν (τῇ) δ.; BAp
138 *S* ϩαχαριας ϧптεϥογ., C 43 47 *B* around throne
ϧεптεϥογ., BM 511 (4) *F* ϧμαас ϧιтϥογ.[8]

ογεειєпιп[1], ογεει-[2], ογαιε-[3], ογοειε-[4] *S*, ογ-
ειε-[5], ογε-[6] *SF*, ογα(ε)ιαпιп[7] *AA*[2], ογαι-[8] *A*, ογει-
пιп *B*, ογιεпιп[9] *F* nn, *Ionian, Greek*: Dan 8 21 *B*(*S*
= Gk), Zech 9 13 *S*[2]*A*[x]*B*, Jo 7 35 *S*[1](varr[26])*A*[2]*B*,
Ac 16 1 *S*[1](varr[24])*B*, Ro 2 9 *S*[2](varr[56])*BF*[9], Gal 3 28
B(*S* = Gk) Ἕλλην, 2 Macc 6 8 *A*[7], Mk 7 26 *B*(*S* =
Gk) Ἕλληνες, Jer 27 16 *S*[5]*F*[5](Louvre 10052)*B* ἑλληνικός; ViK 9774 64 *S* тασпє пиογ.[2] (var P 131[6]
9[1]), EW 106 *B* learnt εсϭαι погγ., CMSS 61 *F* ψαλ-
тнр[ιοп] погγ.[6];   мит-, мετογ-, *Greek* (language):
Jo 19 20 *S*[1](varr[235])*B*, Ac 21 37 *S*[1](var[5])*B*, Z 319 *S*[1]
ἑλληνιστί; PSBA 10 194 *S* тαгογοογ ερος ммп-
тογ.[6], C 89 104 *B* he knew †м.

As name: ογ.[4] (saint RNC 3) = ογεειєпιп(P 129[21]
6), ογ.[6] (Leyd 185), Miss 4 422 ونالو, Οὐενεῖν,
Οὐαινίνις, Τουαειαναεῖνε, Τουαανενῖν &c (Preisigke).
Cf Ἕλλην, ϧнλλнп (Miss 4 759).

V GöttN '16 131.

ογ(ε)нт[1] *S*, огопт[2], -тог[3] *S*, огεпт *AB*, pl
огεптε *A* nn m, *deep, hollow place, hold* of ship: Jon
1 5 *S*[1]*AB*, RNC 41 *S*[1] κοίλη; C 89 58 *B* slept in ϥογ.
мпιχοι σηκός; Am 9 3 *A* pl (*S* пετшнк, *B* пιшωк)
βάθος; Ge 6 14 *S*[3](*B* мοϧ) νοσσιά; *ib* 16 *S*[2](*B* ϩε)
καтάγαιος; P 44 54 *S*[1], K 134 *B* خ (Almk 2 103,

BIF 20 60); Mus 40 40 *S*(Reg Pach) none may sleep
мпεснт ϧαпογ.[1] of ship *locus sentinae*; BMar 26 *S*
αгεпε п-. ... ερραι ϧαпογ.[1] мпχοι, C 43 133 *B*
ϧιтγ εϧрн επιογ., *ib* 86 80 *B* ογωп мпιογ., Mor
46 21 *S* ϭωλп εϧολ мпогнпт; ογ.[2] мпωпϲ of ship,
v пωпк I a.

ογнογ *SAA*[2]*BFO*, pl ογпоογε *S*, -пαγε *A*[2],
-пωογι *B* nn f, *hour* (cf χп- with numerals only):
Ex 18 21 *B*(*S* пαγ), Job 5 26 *SB*, Jo 4 21 *SA*[2]*B*,
ib 52 *BF*(*S* п.) ὥρα, Job 1 c *B* ϧεптεϥογ. (*S* тε)
ὥριμος; Si 40 7 *S* καιρός; Sa 12 18 *S* тεγ. ὅταν;
PS 26 *S* gazing мппαγ погγ., Z 334 *S* пα(ογ)-
ογ. (cf 1 Thes 2 17), ShC 42 87 *S* погγ. εϧολ ϧп-
ογ. *hour after h.*, Mani 2 *A*[2] тамптεпαγсε погγ.,
Aeg 265 *S* ϧптεγ. ετммαγ ... мппαγ ετммαγ,
AP 20 *A*[2] ϧптогγ. ετммεγ, El 46 *A* тогγ. тε тει ет-
мммо *in that same h.*, C 43 53 *B* шα εϧογп εταιογ.,
Miss 4 131 *B* ceased not погγ. сногγ† *during 2 h.*,
AZ 23 111 *S* пαстогγ. пϯ̅ погγ., *ib* 21 106 *O* тιογ.
тιογ. *each h.* (cf *ib* 100 εχεптιογ.), Leyd 459 *S* be
fulfilled мпατεογ. шωпε;   pl: Ge 18 10 *B*(*S*
diff), Job 24 1 *B*(*S* ογοειш) ὥ.; ShC 73 111 *S*, BAp
91 *S* why fire lit пиειογ. *at this time?*, Miss 8 251 *S*
fasting шαптεпεγ. χωк, Mani H 83 *A*[2] crucified at
9th hour, on [-th] day, [...]пπογ., TT 60 *S* ερε[ϧε]-
погγ. птоотγ εϥр ϧωϧ пϧптогγ *spells*(?).

ϭιс ογ. *S, half-hour*: Ap 8 1 (*B* diff) ἡμιώριον;
ShMiss 4 280 пεϧοογ тнрϥ орр ткεϭ. шнм, Mor
39 35 огϭ. мпогсогсог = C 43 55 *B* ογсногγ (cf
Dan 12 7); cf ShC 73 153 ογпαшε погγ.

пτε(o)γ. *SF*, пτογ. *A*[2], пϯογ. *B, on the instant,
forthwith*: Nu 12 4 *SB*, Is 30 13 *SBF* παραχρῆμα;
Ps 69 3 *S*(*B* om) παραυτίκα; Job 5 3 *S*(*B* сατοτγ),
Mk 5 30 *S*(var & *B* do) εὐθέως; Deu 7 22 *S*(*B* пχω-
λεм) τὸ τάχος, *ib* 9 3 (var ϧпογϭεпн, *B* do) ἐν τάχει; Sa 16 11 *S* ὀξέως; AP 6 *A*[2] ϧωс εϥпαχιтε п.
ἤδη; Jo 4 27 *SA*[2](*BF* ϧεпϥαι) ἐπὶ τούτῳ; PS 239
S шαкει εϧολ...п., ShBor 247 124 *S* wrote Exodus
п. ϧιтогγωс птпепεισ *immediately after*, BIF 13
112 *S* п. απϭαμογλ оппϥ εϧραι = MG 25 302 *B*
ϧεпογϧαϩαпιпα, BSM 132 *B* αϥογχαι п., Pcod 39
F(*S* ϧпогϭ.).

ϧпτε(o)γ. *S*, ϧпτογ. *A*, ϧ. *A*[2], ϧεпϯογ. *B*, ε-
χεптιογ. *O, as last*: Hos 11 8 *A*(*B* пϯϧоϯ ϧεпϯϧ.)
ἐν τῷ αὐτῷ; Mk 1 10 *S*(*B* сατοτϥ) εὐθ.; BIF 13 111
S ϧ. αϥпωωпε = MG 25 300 *B* сат., KroppM 18 *S*
ϧ. мпατεсχωк, AP 30 *A*[2] ϧ....αγпωт, AM 63 *B* αϥ-
тωпϥ ϧ., AZ 21 100 *O* εχεпт. т.(cf above *ib* 21 106).

прос тεογ. *S*, п. тογ. *A*, п. огγογ. *B, for an hour*:
2 Cor 7 8 *S*(*B* пр. огκογι), Gal 2 5 *B*(*S* погγ.) п.
ὥραν; Pro 5 3 *SA*(*B* сногγ) п. καιρόν; Ep 592 A 11 *S*
παραχρῆμα; *ib* 151 *S* is not here п. т. *at present*
(cf ST 246 п. †погγ).

ρεϥκα SA², -ϫα ογ. B, astrologer, caster of horo-
scopes: Is 47 13 S(B αϣεγ), Aeg 281 S ἀστρολόγος;
ib 242 S μαθηματικός(?); PS 30 S πρ. ϻπρεϥϣι-
πε, ShMun 102 S ρεϥρ ϧικ, ρεϥρ παϧρε, ρ., ρεϥωπ
ππϲιογ, Mani 2 A² ϻαπτις, ρ., TT 42 S ρεϥϻογτε,
ρ., TstAb 253 B; ϻπτ-, ϻετρ., diviner's art:
Mor 36 20 S, ROC 23 277 B. Cf ShViK 919 S as
if prophets κα ογ. παπ εϧραι or interpreted dreams.

τεπογ SF, ϯπογ SAA²BF, now: Ge 2 23 SA
(Cl)B, Deu 26 10 S ϯ. B, Ps 16 11 SBF ϯ., Hos 10
2 SAB, Mk 15 32 SBF ϯ., Va 57 10 B ογϫε πκεϯ.
οπ νῦν, Job 36 14 B ϯ. ογπ (S πτοογπ), He 13 13
B do (S -ϭε), BHom 47 S αγειϲϭε τ. τοίνυν; Jo 5
17 SA²B, Ap 12 10 SB, BM 320 153 S αϥϻογ τ.
ἄρτι; Eccl 7 11 F παϯ. (S παι) ταῦτα; Va 57 33 B
ϥαι πτε ϯ. παρών; ShR 2 3 16 S ϧϻπεϥϣπϧ τ.
= BM 285 II a ἐντεῦθεν; PS 44 S αιογω ειϲω ϻ-
ϻος πητι τ., BMar 36 S ϧωϲ τ. thou hast chosen
death (cf Miss 8 226 ειϲ ϧπτε), Mani H 30 A² πϧε
πϯ.επ, BSM 37 = Va 63 11 B εταϥϲιπι ϧιϧωκ ϯ. =
BMis 381 S πϲοογτπ, Cat 27 B ππιϲτος πτε ϯ., J
5 55 S τεϧογϲια ετϣοοπ τ., DeV 2 196 B rest here
ϣατεπταϲϧο ϧαροκ ϯ. shortly, CO 342 S ϻπερω-
ϻε ει ερπϲ τ. so far, J & C 92 S ϯ. εϣϫε ογπ ϣ-
ϭοϻ; τ., ϯ. ϭε SAA²F, so now: Ps 2 10 S(B ϯ.
only) καὶ νῦν, Pro 7 24 SA(B ϯ. ογπ) v. οὖν, Is 5 13
SF(B ϯ. ϫε) τοίνυν; PS 81 S τ.ϭε πογϧϻ ππαϭοϻ,
J&C 95 A² ϯ.ϭε ϫειτιπαγ, Ryl 271 S ϯ.ϭε εειϲϧαι,
PMich 1526 S ϯ. ϫε (bis). V also on s f.

ετ., πτ. S, as τ.: BM 1061 ετι. ογπ τιϧοϻολογει,
BMEA 10582 εϯ. ϧοπθι ϻαρεϥϯ, BP 10589 ϻπογ-
ϲρϥε πει ετππογ, Mor 41 145 πτ.ϭε κτετηγτπ (var
ib 40 30 τ.), CO 385 πτ. ειϲϧπητε, BM 1153 ειπηγ
πτι.

ϣατ. SF, ϣαϯ. B, till now, at present: Ge 44 28
B ἄχρι ν., Ro 1 13 S(B ϣαεϧογπ) ἄ. τοῦ δεῦρο; Deu
12 9 SB ἕως τοῦ ν., Ps 70 17 SB μέχρι ν.; MG 25 220
B ϻπαϥερ ϻοπαχος ϣ. οὔπω; PS 81 S ειαπεχε
...ϣ., Pcod 39 SF ϻπε-...ϣ., PBu 135 S ϻπεπϧογτ-
ϧτ πϲαπαππϻολος ϣ., Louvre 7462 S have not answered ϣ.; ϣαεϧογπ ετ.,εϯ. εϯ.: Ge 47 3 B (var
εταιογ.) ἕως τοῦ ν., 1 Cor 8 7 SBF ἕως ἄρτι; ϣα-
εϧρη εϯ. B: Ez 28 15 (S Gk om).

ϫιπ-, πϫ. S, ϫπτ. A, ϫππϯ. A², ιϲϫεπϯ. B, from
now: Job 23 10 S(B = Gk), Lu 3 9 S(B do) ἤδη; Is
54 9 S(B ϫε), Mk 14 63 S(B om) ἔτι, Is 17 3 S(B ϫε)
οὐκέτι, Mt 21 19 S(B om) μηκέτι; Ps 112 2 SB, Mic
4 7 AB, Lu 1 48 SB ἀπὸ τοῦ ν.; Mt 23 39 SB ἀπ᾽
ἄρ.; BM 183 89 S if I beseech you ϫ. παρών; Z 310
S those that labour πϫ. at present receive not grace
as of old, ManiH 15 A² ϫ. ϲαθη, J 1 47 S ϫ. ϣαεπεϧ.

V also αγ II, ρω b.

ογπωογϯ B v πωογϯ.

ογωπϣ SAA²B, ωπϣ S(BMar 113), ογαπϣ A
(TU), ογωω. A²(Jo), nn m, wolf: Ge 49 27 SB, Pro
28 15 SA, Jo 10 12 SAA²B λύκος; Bor 134 2 S(Vita
Sin) απογ. πλγϲη ϻϻογ = C 41 25 B θηριον =
Miss 4 358 ذئب; Miss 4 768 S ογθηρ. επεϥϧαππε
πογ. worshipped at Siut, En Peterson ογ. ϧιθηρ.
πιϻ fill desert, TU 43 22 A πογ. πιαογϧαλϥ, Mani
1 A² πογ. ϻϻογι, MG 25 153 B ογογ....εϣ ογ-
πιϣϯ πϧρωογ εϧολ, ShWess 9 96 S of evil doer
πειογ.; οϧϧε πογ. S, wolf's tooth: PMéd 316
(οϧϧε l οϧ.) in recipe; ϣαρ πογ. S, w.'s skin
wherein tooth wrapped: ib; ϧαϲ πογ. S, w.'s
dung in recipe: ib 281; ελο(ο)λε πογ. S v ελοολε I.

In names: Οὐῶνεζ,Οὐῶνσιος(Preisigke),πογωπϣ
(PLond 4 494),Πουῶνστ,Πουῶνσις,Τουάνσις,Τουῶν-
σις, Σενπουῶνσις (Pr.), Ψονθουῶνσι (Wess 22 11)
&c. In place-name: προγωπϣ (Ryl Suppl 43).

ογπος SB, -αϥ SᶠAF vb I intr (mostly B), rejoice: Deu 16 15 B(var refl, S = Gk), Eccl 10 19 B
(S do), Joel 2 21 SAB, Ap 11 10 SB εὐφραίνεσθαι;
Ps 64 9 B(S ϯ ογ.), Pro 27 9 SA τέρπεσθαι; Is 66
11 B(S = Gk) τρυφᾶν, ib 55 2 B(S ϲααπϣ), 2 Pet 2
13 B(S τργ.) ἐντρ.; Pro 12 11 SA(B ϧηαγπεϲϧε)
ἡδὺς εἶναι; ib 7 18 B(SA ϻτοπ ϻϻοϲ) ἀπολαύειν;
Ru 3 7 S ἀγαθύνεσθαι; Ac 27 25 B ογ. πϧητ (S ογρωτ) εὐθυμεῖν; BMis 181 S εϥροογτ εϧογ., MIE
2 356 B αιογ. as one risen from feast = BAp 81 S
εγϥϧαπε, C 43 27 B πη ετογ. ϫεππιρπ; c e-
dat commodi: Jud 19 22 S, 2 Kg 13 28 S(var ογρωτ
ε-) ἀγαθ.; PO 14 341 B απαϧρητ ογ. εροι, BMar
192 S sim; c εϫπ-, rejoice over, at: 2 Kg 1 20 S
εὐφ., Ps 69 4 S(B εϧρηι εϫ.), Is 25 9 SB εὐφ. ἐπί;
εϧρηι εϫ. B: Ps 39 17 (S = Gk), Lam 2 17 (S do,
F ϫι ογ.) εὐ. ἐπί; Miss 4 220 ϥϯ ογ. εϧ. εϫωπ;
v also tr; c ϧιϫεπ-, sim B: C 86 94 ειογ. ϧ.ϻαρ-
τγρος ҃в, Va 61 94 εϥογ. ϧ.πιαγαθοπ.

II tr (refl): 1 Kg 16 5 B(S = Gk), Ps 44 9 B(S do),
Ps 35 1 B(SF do) εὐφ.; Is 57 4 B(S τργ.) ἐντρ., Ps
36 11 B(S ϲα.)κατατρ.; PS 169 S ειεογ. ϻϻοι πτα-
ραϣε, BM 228 60 Sᶠ εϥογ. ϻϻοϥ ϧεππαγαθοπ,
TstAb 161 B prepare meat πταογ. ϻϻοι πελπαι-
ϣεϻϻο; c εϫπ-: Is 62 5 B(S = Gk) εὐ. ἐπί;
P 129¹⁸ 103 S εϧογ. ϻϻοογ ε.τπιϲτις; εϧρ. εϫ.:
Ps 29 2 B(S = Gk) εὐ. ἐπί; Mor 18 105 S πετογ.
ϻϻοογ εϧ. ε.πεϲϻοτ ππϧαιϻοπιοπ ἐπιτέρπ.; Sh
BM 192 S αϥογ. ϻϻοϥ εϧ. εϫωογ.

—— nn m SAA²BF, joy, gladness: Ge 31 27 SB,
Ps 50 8 SB(A Cl ογρατ), Is 35 10 B(SF τελη̄λ), Ac
2 28 SB εὐφροσύνη; Sa 8 16 S ραϣε...ογ. εὐ., χαρά;
Ez 28 13 B(S = Gk), Lu 7 25 B(S do) τρυφή; Ps 64

8 *SB* τέρψις, ib 26 4 *SB* τερπνότης; Bar 4 34 *B* ἀγαλλίαμα; Eccl 6 6 *S*(*F* πετπαιιογϥ)ἀγαθωσύνη; Ac 24 10 *B* ϩεπογογ. πϧητ(*S* ιιτοπ πϧ.)εὐθύμως; ShC 42 120 *S* ογ., ςολςλ, εγϥροςγπη, ραϣε, ViK 9621 *Sʲ* God is πογ. тнрϥ, Miss 4 162 *B* paradise πτε πογ. (Ge 3 23), AP 44 *A²* ϣωпе ϩпогογ., Br 250 *S* day of his ογ. пϧнт. ιια πογ. *F*: Is 32 14 (*SB* ογ. only) εὐφροσύνη; ιιαιογ. *B*, *pleasure-loving*: Va 57 259 τρυφηλός; ερ ογ. *B*, *make joy, rejoice*: Dan 6 23 ἀγαθύνειν; † ογ., *give joy*: Ps 42 4 *B*(*S* = Gk), ib 93 19 *F*(Pcod 39, *S* do, *B* diff) εὐ.; Eccl 11 9 *SF* ἀγ.; Hos 9 4 *B*(*A* ρ επ⸱)ἡδύνειν; C 89 105 *B* αϣψαп-†. παϥ ϩεпϧапϭιпογωιι, Dif 1 42 *B* †. ппеπϧнт επϫιπερ ϧωϥ ⸗|; ϫι ογ. *F*, *take joy, rejoice*: c εϫεп-, Lam 2 17 (*v* ογ. εϫп-).

ογωης *SAA²BF*, -пεϧ *A²* (Jo), -паϧ *SF*, огεпϧ-*S*, огапεϧ- *A²*, огопϧ⸗ *SB*, -апϧ⸗ *AA²F*, -апεϧ⸗ *A²*, огопϧ† *SB*, -апϧ *SᵃAA²*(Ma), -ап(а)ϧ *F*, огппҳ† *A²*(BM 1224) vb **I** intr (mostly *B*), *reveal, be revealed, appear*: Mt 2 7 (*S* c εϧολ), MG 25 231 φαίνειν, Ac 27 20 (*S* diff) ἐπιφ., Ro 2 28† (*S* c εϧ.) ἐν τῷ φανερῷ, Ep Jer 68 *BF* φανερὸς εἶναι, Mk 1 45 пογ.(*S* do) φανερῶς; Ex 34 3 (*S* do) ὀρᾶν; Ep Jer 14 *BF* -паϧ γνώριμος εἰ.; Lev 13 4 (*S* diff) τηλαυγὴς εἰ.; PS 48 *S* ϥογ.† ιιπεκιιτο εϧολ, ShClPr 24 359 *S* εγϣαпϫпогκ....ιιпрог., Mor 18 18 *S* αγογ. without torture = ib 19 27 *S* ϩοιιολογει = Miss 4 112 *B* ογ., BM 1224 *A²* ετϧнп етог.†, PO 11 345 sim.

II tr, *show, make clear*: Is 32 2 *B*(*SF* c εϧ.), Mt 24 27 *B*(*S* ρ огоειп) φ.; Ge 9 14 *B*(*S* c εϧ.) ὀρ.; Jo 17 26 *SA²*(*B* таιιο) γνωρίζειν; Su 14 *B*(*S* = Gk) ὁμολογεῖν; Ac 9 27 *B*(*S* do) παρρησιάζειν; ib 25 15 *B*(var & *S* ςιιιιε) ἐμφανίζειν; Sa 10 14 *S* δεικνύναι; Miss 8 30 *S* ογ. ιιпιιосте προιпε δῆλος εἶναι; BG 42 *S* пϥογопϧϥ ϩηϧο пιιι, Mun 35 *S* beat him ϣαптεϥογ. пϫιογε пιιι, BSM 30 *B* τεпογ. пτεпιιεтатϫоιι.

—— nn m *B*, *revelation, declaration*: AmerSchool Or Research 6 109 ϥαιпε пαογ. пеιιτаоιιологια, Cat 161 τςαϧоп ϩεпогογ.

аϑог. *B*, *unshown*, with ερ, *be invisible*: Job 24 20 (*S* diff) ἀφανὴς γίνεσθαι; C 89 3 аϥερ а. = MG 17 314 *S* ϧωп.

ϭιп-, ϫιпог., *appearance*: Dan 10 16 *B* ὀπτασία; P 129¹⁶ 97 *S* healed him ϧитϭ. εрοϥ ιιιιате, Va 61 22 *B* тϫ. еρоι ιιпεκϧо, BM 2906 *S* тεкϭιпогопϧк ерос. With following preposition.

—— ε-, *appear to*, intr: Mk 16 9 *S*(*B* п-)φ. dat, Ps 117 27 *S*(*B* ερ огωιпι) ἐπιφ. dat, Pro 16 5† *SA* φανερὸς παρά, Ac 23 15 *B*(*S* diff) ἐμφανίζειν dat; ib 16 9 *BF*(*S* ϭωλп εϧ. п-), Z 320 *S* аϥогωпαϧ ероϥ ὀρ. dat, Nu 14 14 *B*(*S* c εϧ.) ὀπτάζειν; Eph 3 5 *B*(*S*

c εϧ. п-) γνωρ. dat, Ac 4 10 *B*(*S* do) γνωστὸς εἰ.; Z 306 *S* ιιпεппϣ ог. ероϥ ἀποκαλύπτειν dat; ShA 1 208 *S* аϧεппιιαρτγρος ог. ероп, LAp 520 *F* аϥогωпαϧ ελаг, HT Z 392 *S* етог.† ερωтπ...етепсеог.† εϧολ ап; tr, *show to*: Ps 102 7 *SB*, Lu 2 15 *S*(*B* таιιο) γν. dat; Jud 16 17 *S* ἀναγγέλλειν dat; Ps 36 5 *S*(*B* ϭωрп εϧ.) ἀποκαλ. dat; Pcod 14 *S* аιогεпϧ пϣаϫε επεκληρος, C 43 65 *B* ог. ιιпрωιι εροι; refl: Ge 12 7 *B*(*S* intr εϧ.), Ac 7 26 *BF*(*S* intr εϧ. п-) ὀρ. dat; Mt 1 20 *B*(*S* do) φ. dat, Jer 36 14 *B* ἐπιφ. dat, Ex 33 13 *B*(*S* do) ἐμφαν. dat; Nu 12 6 *SB* γινώσκειν dat; FR 72 *S* пςεογопϧογ εϧаϧ (var εϧ. п-), Mus 34 208 *B* аϥогопϧϥ επιρωιιι; *v* also ϭιп-above.

—— εϫεп- *B*, *for, on behalf of*: BSM 49 †ог. ιιιιωог εϫωтεп ϩатεпϥ†. = BMis 399 *S* ϧа-; εϧрнι εϫ., *upon*: Ps 66 2 (*S* ρ огоειп) ἐπιφ. ἐπί.

—— ϩιϫεп- *B*, *upon*: Bar 3 35 ὀρ. ἐπί.; DeV 2 9 аϥогопϧϥ...ϧ.пικαϧι.

—— п-, *to*: Ep Jer 50 *BF* φανερὸς εἰ. dat; Mt 17 3 *S*(var c εϧ., *B* tr ε-) ὀρ. dat; refl: Mk 14 64 *S*(var ϫокει, *B*†) φ. dat, Is 65 1 *B*(*S* intr εϧ. п-) ἐμφανὴς γίν. dat; J 14 56 *S* птωϣ птаιогопϧог пак.

—— паϧрп- *SB*, *in presence of*: Ez 20 9 *SB* γινώσ. πρός; Am 221 *B* огопϧϥ паϧраϥ ιιпικοιιнс. With following adverb.

—— εϧολ *SAA²BF*, *show forth, appear* intr: Pro 11 31 *SA*(*B* ог.), Is 32 2 *SF*(*B* do refl), Mt 13 26 *SBF*, Aeg 234 *S* if servant ог. εϧ. εϥειιпϣа п- φ., Job 13 18 *SB* ἀναφ., Ez 17 6 *B* ἐπιφ., Jo 3 21 *SA²B*, Ap 3 18 *SB* φανεροῦν, Ro 1 19 *SB* φανερὸς εἶναι, 1 Cor 3 13 *SBF* φ. γίν.; Ge 8 5 *SB*, Ps 16 15 *SBF* ὀρ.; Pro 13 20 *SAB*, Mt 10 26 *S*(*B* ϭωрп εϧ.) γινώσ.; Ro 10 9 *B*(*S* = Gk) ὁμολ., Ps 117 19 *SB*(*A* Cl = Gk), Phil 2 11 *SB* ἐξομ.; Pro 29 24 *S*(var&*A* ог.) ἀναγγ., 1 Cor 14 25 *B*(*S* diff) ἀπαγγ.; Va 57 7 *B* птεϥог. εϧ. ϫεςιιотεп δεικ.; Lu 17 30 *S*(*B* ϭω. εϧ.)ἀποκαλ.; He 7 14 *B*(*S*†) προδηλοῦν, Cl 51 3 *A* πρόδηλος γίν.; Sa 19 7 *S* θεωρεῖσθαι; BHom 93 *S* God паог. εϧ. ἐπιλάμπειν; PS 126 *S* sons of God паог. εϧ., ShHT *B* 67 *S* аϥог. εϧ. пρεϥтаке ψγχη *showed self as*, DeV 2 39 *B* sim пρεϥϫε ςаϫι, El 86 *A* ϥпаог. аϧ. ϭε пϣнре, Mani 1 *A²* εраог. аϧ. ερεϭραιт, CA 88 *S* if his repentance ог. εϧ. птειρωιιпε, ST 432 *S* (to fugitive) mayest return home пτ ог. εϧ. & *appear in public*; qual: Sa 7 21 *S*, Mic 4 1 *SA*(*B* tr) ἐμφανής, Is 3 22 *B*(*S* прιиιог) διαφ., Hab 1 7 *B*(*SA* ρ ςοειт) ἐπιφ., R 1 5 9 *S* пϧоог етог. εϧ. τὰ Ἐπιφάνια, Si 41 14 *S* neg ἀφ., Aeg 216 *S* ϩεпεςληιιа εгог. εϧ. φαν., Is 8 16 *B*(*S* огω. εϧ.) φαν. εἰ., Phil 1 13 *B*(*SF* do) φαν. γίν., He 11 14 *B*(*S* tr) ἐμφανίζ.; 1 Cor 15 27 *B*(*SF* diff), Aeg 271 *S* пϧωϧ ог. εϧ. δῆλος, Jth 8 29 *S* πρόδ., Ps 50 6 neg *SA*(Cl, *B* огω. εϧ.)

ἄδηλος; Ps 9 16 S(B ϭωογπ tr) γινώσ., ib 75 1 SB γνωσ., Ep Jer 14 F -παϩ (B ογω.) γνώρ. εἰ.; Pro 12 17 SAB ἐπιδεικ.; Ps 80 3 S(B ᴧᴧнιπι) εὔσημος; Si 37 24 S ἀνατέλλειν; Br 237 S εθнπ...ετογ. εϐ., Pcod 8 S is bishop answerable for people? Yea, but (only) ϩαπετογ. εϐ., P 129¹⁴ 127 S ποϭ πρωᴧε ετογ. εϐ. opp εγϭοχϐ, ROC 23 283 B πιϣϯ πεϩοογ εθογ. εϐ. J 76 29 Sᵃ ϣα ετογ. εϐ., Mani 1 A² ϩнᴧᴧ ετογ. αϐ., Mor 18 11 S at Nicaea 318 bishops ϩᴧπετογ. εϐ. as it seemed, DeV 2 16 B fire all around κατα πεθογ. εϐ.;   tr, show forth, confess: Sa 8 15 S ϕ., Si 22 20 SA ἐκϕ., Jer 40 6 SB, He 9 26 B(SF intr) ϕανεροῦν, Mt 12 16 SB ϕανερὸν ποιεῖν, Is 3 9 SB ἐμϕανίζ.; Ps 101 16 S(B ογ.) ὁρ.; Sa 12 17 S, Ep Jer 3 F(S ϯ, B ταᴧο), Hos 5 9 AB δεικ., CaiEuch 481 B ακογ. εϐ. πτϕγϲιϲ ἀναδ., Job 33 21 S(B intr) ἀποδ., Ro 2 15 B(S τογο), ib 9 17 SB ἐνδ., Ep Jer 58 BF ἐπιδ., Is 41 20 SB καταδ., Est 2 20 S ὑποδ.; 1 Jo 2 23 B(S = Gk) ὁμολ., Ps 53 6 SB ἐξομ.; Pro 3 6 SAB γνωρ.; 1 Cor 3 13 SBF(Mor 38 103) δηλ., Mt 26 73 S(B ογ.) δηλ. ποι.; Su 11 B(S ϫω) ἀναγγ.; Ac 19 8 B(S = Gk) παρρησιάζειν; Dan 9 20 B(S ταγο) ἐξαγορεύειν; 2 Cor 2 14 B(S τϫαιο) θριαμβεύειν; Aeg 247 S ογεπϩ πρωϐ εϐ. μηνεύειν; ib 227 S ογεπϩ ϩεπϫωᴧε εϐ. δημοσιεύειν; PS 65 S αϙογ. εϐ. ᴧπεϙᴧγϲτηριον, R 1 4 67 S stars & moon to ογ. εϐ. ππικαρπος = AM 126 B ερ ϲγᴧεπιπ, El 92 A απατϣιπε ογαπϩϙ αϐ., C 86 183 B εϙογ. εϐ. πτεϙϲγπτεπια set forth, Pcod 38 F απογαπϩογ εϐ.

ογ. εϐ. ε-, show, display to: Nu 17 4 SB γινώσ. dat, 1 Thes 2 2 B(S = Gk) παρρησιάζειν inf; εϩογπ ε-: Sa 16 21 S ἐμϕαν. πρός; Va 57 12 B ογαπϩρογ εϐ. εϲ̄., επεπϲ̄; εϩραι ε- Nu 6 26 S(B ερ ογωιπι) ἐπιϕ. ἐπί;   ογ. εϐ. εϫπ-, show upon: Ps 30 16 S (B do) ἐπιϕ. ἐπί; ib 4 6 S(B ερ ᴧнιπι) σημειοῦν ἐπί;   ογ. εϐ. π- dat (all Gk dat) intr: Mt 6 5 SB ϕ., Job 11 18 S(B diff) ἀναϕ., Sa 17 6 S διαϕ.; Ge 35 9 S(B ογ. refl), Ps 16 15 SF(B do), Z 303 S απпε̄ ογ. παϙ εϐ. ὁρ.; Ez 20 5 S(B do) γνωρ.; Deu 26 3 SB ἀναγγ.; Mt 11 27 S(F refl, B ϭω.) ἀποκαλ.; Mt 7 23 B(S = Gk) ὁμολ., Ps 78 13 SB ἀνθομ., ib 117 19 SB(A Cl = Gk), Ro 14 11 B(S = Gk) ἐξομ.; Cl 11 2 A γνωσ. εἰ.; Est C 10 S ἱλάσκεσθαι; AP 16 A² αϲογ. πεϲ αϐ., TstAb 159 B αᴧιχαнλ ογ. παϙ εϐ.; tr: Jo 17 6 SA²B ϕανεροῦν; Ps 77 5 S(B ταᴧο), Ac 2 28 SB (var do) γνωρ.; Cai Euch 482 B ακογ. πнι εϐ. ᴧπιϣϣнπ δεικ. acc; Ps 15 3 S(B ε-) θαυμαστοῦν; BG 48 S ογ. πεϙειπε παϙ εϐ., PS 114 S ϯπαογοπϩτ πακ εϐ. (Od Solom 5 1 ܠ/ ܝܨܘܐ), Griff Stu 163 F come ппκογαπαϩκ πει εϐ., Kr 121 F αιογαπαϩϲ εϐ. πнτεπ, BSM 51 B πϐοϙ εθογ. ᴧᴧωογ εϐ. ᴧϙϯ, J 2 35 S πιᴧερος πταιογοπϩογ εϐ. πακ (cf ib 13 39 ϫнλογ, 48 42 ϲαϕнιϫε).

ογ. εϐ. nn m, showing forth, declaration: He 3 1 B(SF = Gk) ὁμολογία, Ps 99 tit SB ἐξομολόγησις; 1 Cor 12 7 SB ϕανέρωσις, 1 Tim 6 14 SB ἐπιϕάνεια; Nu 31 6 S(B diff) σημασία; 2 Cor 12 1 S(B ϫιππαγ) ὀπτασία; Ps 118 130 SB δήλωσις; Phil 1 28 B (SF ᴧαειπ) ἔνδειξις; He 10 19 B(SF = Gk) παρρησία; Br 227 S πογ. εϐ. of Cross, Leyd 187 S rubric πογ. εϐ. παπα ϲτεϕαπος invention, BSM 32 B πεϩοογ πογ. εϐ. of Lord = BMis 374 S παρογϲια (cf Phil 1 6 S), LMis 467 S ϩογ πογ. εϐ. (cf ογ. εϐ. qual);   ϩπ-, ϩεπ(ογ)ογ. εϐ., in openness, openly: Mk 1 45 S(B om εϐ.), Z 305 S beheld demons ϩ. ϕανερῶς, Pro 9 14 B(SA vbϯ) ἐμϕανῶς; Ac 2 29 B (S = Gk) μετὰ παρρησίας; 1 Tim 3 16 B(S = Gk) ὁμολογουμένως; Miss 8 44 S said it ϩ. σαϕῶς; PS 158 S will say it ϩ., ShC 73 125 S ϩιογϩωπ н ϩ., AP 25 A² saw all ϩ., DeV 2 7 B testified ϩ.

ατ-, αθογ. εϐ., unshown, invisible: BG 90 S ϫιππια. ϣαπϫωκ ππετογ.ϯ εϐ., J 65 3 S departure from world is ογα.;   ρ, ερ α. εϐ., be invisible, inconspicuous: Z 306 S ρ α. ἀϕανὴς γίν.; Ac 21 39 B neg (S ο πϲοειτ) ἄσημος; BMis 289 S, C 86 292 B, ROC 27 142 B αϙερ α. ϩαροϙ, PO 11 311 B fearing lest he ερ α. ϩαρωογ.

ϫιπογ. εϐ., display: Cat 174 B Jesus did not miracles κατα ογϫ. before π.επ.

ογοπϩρϙ B v ογοᴧϙ.

ογοπϫϙ B v ογοοϭε.

ογοπ S, -απ A(nn), ογααϐϯ SA²(JoAP)F, -ααϐεϯ A, -αϐεϯ AA²(Ma), -αϐϯ B, -ε(ε)ϐϯ, -εϙϯ, -нкϐϯ F vb intr, be pure, innocent S: Ps 17 25 (B τογϐο) ὁσιοῦσθαι; Mt 6 9 (BF do) ἁγιάζεσθαι; Ps 118 79 (B do) ἄμωμος; Si 7 8 ἀθῷος; Job 11 15 (B ερ ογωιπι) absque macula; P 131⁵ 41 πειογοπ ετερεπϩнτ παογ. ϩнτϙ;   as nn m, purity: Pro 14 32 SA πογ., Eph 4 24 (B τ.) ὁσιότης; He 12 10 (B ᴧεττ.) ἁγιότης, Ps 29 4 (B ᴧετατιος) ἁγιωσύνη, ib 92 5 (B τ.) ἁγίασμα, Bor 248 6 ϕορει ᴧπογ. ἁγιοϕορεῖν, ViSitz 172 4 34 ᴧπϣα ᴧπογ. ἀξιόαγνος; Ex 24 10 (B ϕιρι) καθαριότης; 2 Thes 2 4(B ϣεᴧϣι vb) σέβασμα; ROC 19 74 τϐϐο...ϩιογ. πιᴧ, BAp 135 ακϲεκ .ογ. πιᴧ ϣαροκ, Mor 40 23 ϫι ϐαπτιϲᴧα επεϙογ. = C 43 53 B πεϙϩραπ;   ϩπογογ., purely: Sa 6 11, 1 Thes 2 10 (B τ.) ὁσίως; Aeg 289 καθαρῶς; BAp 57 σεμνῶς, ib 211 ὑγιῶς;   ϫι ογ., acquire purity, be hallowed: Is 66 17 (B τ. refl) ἁγνίζεσθαι, Mor 47 155 woman (pagan priestess) εϲϫι ογωπ (Par 4776 107 merely الرأى).

Qual, pure, holy: Nu 5 17 S(B τ.ϯ), Ps 50 10 SA (Cl)B, Mt 27 59 B(S ϩαϙε) καθαρός; Ps 31 6 SB ὅσιος; ib 17 23 S(B αταϭπι) ἄμω.; Job 9 28 S(B ατποϐι)ἀθ.; Sa 8 20 S ἀμίαντος; Lev 19 2 SB, Is 6 3

ⲟⲩⲟⲡ

S(B = Gk), Joel 2 1 *AB*, Jo 6 69 *SA²B*, 1 Cor 7 14 *SBF* ἅγιος, Ps 11 6 *SB*, AP 15 *A²* ἁγνός; PS 161 *S* ⲟⲩⲙⲁ ⲡϣⲱⲡⲉ ⲉϥⲟⲩ., AM 85 *B* ⲙⲱⲓⲧ ⲉϥⲟⲩ., ShC 42 216 *S* ⲡⲥⲉϣⲱⲡⲉ ⲉⲧⲟⲩ., *ib* 73 28 *S* ⲡⲉⲣⲓⲟⲙⲉ ⲉⲧⲟⲩ., El 72 *A* ⲟⲩⲣⲏⲧ ⲟⲩ., *ib* 74 *A* ⲟⲩⲡⲣⲟⲥⲉⲩⲭⲏ ⲉⲥⲟⲩ., Mani 1 *A²* ⲡⲣⲱⲥ ⲉⲩⲟⲩ., Pap *olim* B P Grenfell *F* ⲡⲟⲩⲁⲃⲏ ⲡⲡⲕⲉ[ⲣⲓ], BM 511 (2) *F* ⲡϣⲱⲥ ⲉⲧⲟⲩⲉⲉⲃ, *ib* 1221 *F* ⲡⲙⲉ ⲉⲧⲟⲩⲉϥ, BG 117 *S* ⲡⲉⲭⲥ̄ ⲉⲧⲟⲩ. (voc), Baouit 84 *S* ⲫⲁⲣⲓⲟⲥ ⲉⲧⲟⲩ. Apollo; с ⲉ- *SB*, *pure from, innocent of*: Jos 2 17 *S* ἀθ. dat, Mt 27 24 *S(B* ⲁⲧⲡⲟⲃⲓ ⲉⲃⲟⲗ ϩⲁ-) ἀθ. ἀπό, Pro 20 9 *SA* -ⲁⲃⲉ ⲕⲁⲑ. ἀπό; *ib* 11 21 *SA* -ⲁⲁⲃⲉ (*B* as Gk) ⲉⲣⲓⲥⲉ ἀτιμώρητος; BMis 534 *S* ⲟⲩ. ⲉⲗⲁⲁⲩ ⲡⲭⲱⲣⲙ, *ib* 171 *S* ⲥⲉⲟⲩ. ⲉⲣⲟⲓ *as regards me*, C 43 193 *B* ⲟⲩ. ⲉⲡⲁⲓϣⲱⲧⲉⲃ, *ib* 174 *B* ⲟⲩ. ⲡⲛⲟⲃⲓ (*l* ⲉ-); с ⲉⲃⲟⲗ ϩⲛ- *S*, ⲉⲃ. ϩⲁ- *B*, as last: Ac 20 26 *SB* ⲕⲁⲑ. ἀπό; ShA 2 268 *S* ⲟⲩ. ⲉⲃ. ϩⲙⲡⲉⲧⲡⲕⲣⲓⲙⲁ, C 43 184 *B* ⲟⲩ. ⲉⲃ. ϩⲁⲧⲕⲟⲗⲁⲥⲓⲥ; с ϩⲁⲃⲟⲗ ⲛ- *S*: Mor 54 125 *S* ⲟⲩ. ϩ. ⲡⲭⲱⲣⲙ.

As nn *S*: Jer 3 16 ⲡⲟⲩ. ⲙⲡⲓⲏⲗ̄ (*B* ⲡⲉⲑⲟⲩ.) ἅγιος. ⲡⲉⲧⲟⲩⲁⲁⲃ *SAA²F*, ⲡⲉⲑ., ⲫⲏ ⲉⲑ. *B*(often + ⲡⲧⲁϥ), pl ⲡⲉⲧ., ⲡⲏ ⲉⲑ., *who, what is pure, saint*: Ps 4 3 *SB* ⲡⲉⲑ. ⲡⲧⲁϥ, *ib* 116 5 *S* ⲡⲉⲧ. *B* ⲡⲏ ⲉⲑ. ⲡⲧⲁϥ ὅσ.; *ib* 19 2 *SB*, *ib* 55 tit *S* ⲡⲉⲧ. (*B* = Gk) ἅγ.; *ib* 25 6 *SB* ⲡⲏ ⲉⲑ. ἀθ.; *ib* 63 4 *S(B* ⲁⲧⲁϭ.) ἄμω.; Mt 5 8 *SB* ⲕⲁⲑ.; BG 102 *S* ⲡⲉⲝⲁⲩ ⲛϭⲓ ⲡ. (*l* ? ⲡⲡ.), ShC 42 57 *S* ⲟⲩⲁⲡⲟⲥⲧⲟⲗⲟⲥ ⲁⲩⲱ ⲟⲩⲡ., *ib* 135 *S* ⲡⲟϭ ⲙⲙⲏⲏϣⲉ ⲙⲡ., MR 5 33 *F* ⲡⲭⲟⲣⲟⲥ (ⲡ)ⲛⲉⲧⲟⲩⲉⲃ (same MS -ⲉⲉⲃ), BM 468 *S* ⲡⲉⲡⲉⲓⲱⲧ ⲉⲧⲟⲣⲡⲡ. (cf ὁ ἐν ἁγίοις Ep 140 n); с def art or poss: Ps 15 10 *S* ⲡⲉⲕⲡ. (*B* ⲡⲉⲑ. ⲡⲧⲁⲕ) ὅσ.; Lant 119 *S* ⲡⲡ. ⲁⲡⲁ NN, BMis 1 ⲡⲡ. ⲡⲭⲱⲣⲉ ⲡⲣⲁⲅⲓⲟⲥ NN, RNC 69 ⲡⲡ. ⲙⲙⲁⲣⲧⲩⲣⲟⲥ, C 43 5 *B* ⲫⲏ ⲉⲑ. ⲙⲙⲁⲣ., ST 299 *S* greet ⲡⲡ. ⲁⲡⲁ NN, J 89 5 *S* God & ⲡⲉϥⲡ. ⲁⲡⲁ NN, BHom 66 *S* ⲡⲉⲡⲡ. ⲡⲉⲓⲱⲧ; pl *SF*: FR 34 ⲡⲁⲡ. ⲧⲏⲣⲟⲩ, Sa 18 5 ⲡⲉⲕⲡ., Nu 16 5 ⲡⲉϥⲡ. (*B* = Gk), BM 511 *F* ⲡⲉⲕⲡⲉⲧⲟⲩⲉⲉⲃ, Lant 118 ⲫⲁⲣⲓⲟⲥ NN ⲙⲡⲏⲕⲉⲡ.

ⲙⲛⲧ-, ⲙⲉⲧⲡⲉⲧ. *SF*, *purity, holiness* (in addressing revered person or dignitary): Miss 8 31 ⲧⲉⲧⲡⲙ. ἁγιότης; PSBA 10 196, Pcod 12, Ep 198, BM 588 *F*.

ⲟⲩⲏⲏⲃ *SA²F*, ⲟⲩⲓⲉⲓⲃⲉ, ⲟⲩ(ⲉ)ⲓⲃⲉ *A*, ⲟⲩⲏⲃ *BF*, ⲟⲩ(ⲏ)ⲉⲃ, ⲟⲩⲉϥ *F* nn m, *priest* Christian or pagan: Ex 2 6 *A* -ⲓⲉⲓⲃⲉ, Nu 5 16 *SBF*-ⲉϥ, Mic 3 11 *SAB*, He 5 6 *SBF*-ⲏⲏⲃ, Aeg 279 *S* deacon ⲇⲓⲁⲕⲟⲡⲉⲓ ⲉⲡⲟⲩ. ἱερεύς (cf ϩⲓⲉⲣⲉⲩⲥ Ryl 177, 354); ShC 73 22 *S* we Christians ϫⲓⲡⲣⲣⲟ ϣⲁⲟⲩ., El 78 *A* ϩⲉⲡⲟⲩⲓⲉⲓ., J 106 177 *S* ⲟⲩ., ⲗⲁⲉⲓⲕⲟⲥ, ⲙⲟⲛⲟⲭⲟⲥ, DeV 2 72 *B* ⲡⲓⲟⲩ. of idols, AP 26 *A²*, BIF 22 106 *F* ⲡⲉⲟⲩⲛⲉⲃ; ⲡⲟϭ ⲡⲟⲩ.: Hag 1 1 *AB* i. μέγας; R 1 5 31 *S*; as adj *S*: Lev 21 9 ⲣⲱⲙⲉ ⲡⲟⲩ. (*B* nn), Z 586 ⲥϩⲓⲙⲉ ⲡⲟⲩ.

ⲣ ⲟⲩ. *SBF*, *be priest*: Nu 3 3 *SB*, Si 45 26 (15) *S*, Z 278 *S* ἱερατεύειν; He 7 23 *SF*-ⲏⲏⲃ (*B* ϣⲱⲡⲓ ⲛ-) i. γίνεσθαι, Ge 14 18 *S*(*B* om vb) i. εἶναι.

ⲙⲛⲧ-, ⲙⲉⲧⲟⲩ. *SABF*, *priesthood*: Nu 18 1 *SB*,

ⲟⲩⲏⲣ

He 7 5 *SBF*-ⲏⲏⲃ ἱερατεία, *ib* 7 11 *SB*, Cl 43 2 *A* ἱερωσύνη, Ro 15 16 *B* ⲉⲣ ϩⲱⲃ ⲛⲉⲡⲟⲩⲙ. (*S* ϣⲙϣⲉ) ἱερουργεῖν; Nu 16 10 *S* ⲉⲓⲣⲉ ⲡⲧⲙ. *B* ⲉⲣ ⲟⲩ. ἱερατεύειν; Am 2 11 *A*(*S* ⲟⲩⲏⲏⲃ, *B* ⲧⲟⲩⲃⲟ) ἁγιασμός; ShC 42 218 *S* ⲧⲙ., ⲧⲙⲡⲧⲙⲟⲡⲁⲭⲟⲥ, PO 14 335 *B* ⲡϫⲱⲕ ⲡⲧⲙ., CO 33 *S* ⲡⲉⲡⲧⲟⲗⲓ ⲡⲧⲙ., J 67 122 *S* ⲧⲧⲁϫⲓⲥ ⲡⲧⲙ. bishop, priest or deacon.

As name: Οὐῆβις (Preisigke), Πουήηβ (BM 1075). *V* ⲧⲃⲃⲟ.

ⲟⲩⲣ- *S* nn f, in Glos 113 among harness ζυγοδέσμιον· ⲧⲟⲩⲣ ⲡⲁⲣⲃⲉ *neck* or *yoke strap* (?).

(ⲟⲩⲏⲣ) ⲟⲩⲏⲣⲉ *O* adj f, *great*, only in name ⲉⲥⲟⲩⲏⲣⲉ-’Εσουῆρις (AZ 28 50). In many pre-Coptic names, as Οὐῆρις, Πουῆρις, ’Οσορουῆρις (Preisigke), Σουῆρι (PGM 2 23), Οὐρουῆρ (PLeyd 2 163) & ⲡⲟⲩⲉⲣⲧⲉⲓⲟⲩ (v ϯⲟⲩ). Also ? in σεμουερ = λυχνὶς ἀγρία (Dioscorides).

ⲟⲩⲏⲣ *SAA²BFO*, -ⲏⲏⲣ *S*, ⲉⲏⲣ*B*(*sic*, not*F*), ⲟⲩⲏⲗ *F*, f -ⲏⲣⲉ *S*, -ⲏⲗⲓ *F* interrog pron, *how great, many, much?* independent: Lu 16 5 *SB*, BMis 539 *S* ⲉⲣⲉⲡϣⲓⲕⲉ ⲣ ⲟⲩ. πόσος; MG 25 358 *B* ⲟⲩ. ϩⲁⲡⲁⲓϩⲓⲣ (ROC 18 60 ⲗⲙⲁ), BMar 77 *S* knowest not ϫⲉⲕⲡⲁⲣ ⲕⲉⲟⲩ.(*sc* years), Mani 2 *A²* ⲉϥⲁⲣ ⲟⲩ., BM 528 §55 *F* ϣⲁⲣⲉ ⲣ ⲡⲉⲣⲧⲁⲃ ⲧⲁⲣⲁ ⲟⲩ., Mani H 25 *A²* ⲉⲣⲉⲟⲩ. ⲡⲁⲥⲱⲣⲙⲉ; sg: Job 38 18 *SB*, Mt 6 23 *SB* ⲁⲩ. πόσ.; Zech 2 2 *A*(*B* ⲁϣ ⲙⲙⲁⲓⲏ)πηλίκος; Ps 38 4 *S*(*B* ⲁϣ) τίς; BMis 564 *S* ⲟⲩ. ⲡⲉ ⲡⲉⲥⲝⲁⲝⲓⲟⲡ quanto; *ib* 350 *S* ⲟⲩ. ⲡⲉ ⲡⲉⲧⲓⲣⲁϣⲉ, CMSS 52 *B* ⲉⲏⲣⲡⲉ ⲡⲉⲥⲣⲟⲙⲧ, LMis 196 *S* ⲟⲩ. -ⲧⲉ ⲧⲉϥⲧⲉⲭⲡⲏ, AM 185 *B* ⲟⲩ. ⲧⲉ ϯⲧⲓⲙⲏ; pl: Ge 47 8 *B*, Job 13 23 *SB* πόσ.; BG 106 *S* ⲟⲩ. ⲡⲉ ⲡⲓⲁⲓⲱⲡ, BSM 130 *B* ⲟⲩ. ⲡⲉ ⲡⲓϭⲣⲱⲟⲩ; с preceding ⲛ-, *by how much?*: Sa 13 3 *S*, Mt 12 12 *S*(*B* ⲡⲁⲩ.)πόσῳ, BHom 15 *S* ⲉⲡⲁϣⲱⲡⲉ ⲙⲙⲁⲕⲁⲣⲓⲟⲥ ⲛ. ποταπός; ShC 42 170 *S* ⲉⲩⲡⲁⲣ ⲕⲁⲕⲉ ⲛ., ShViK 9868 *S* ⲉⲩⲡⲁⲣ ⲃⲟⲗ ⲛ. ⲉⲧⲟⲣϭⲛ, ShA 1 414 *S* ⲉⲩϣⲉ ⲛ. ⲉⲙⲉⲣⲉ ⲛϩⲁⲡ, Mun 47 *S* ⲉⲓⲡⲁϭⲙ ϭⲟⲙ ⲛ. ⲡⲣⲟϩⲟ, C 43 235 *B* waves ⲁⲩϭⲓⲥⲓ ⲉⲧⲁϥⲫⲉ ⲛ.; sim without ⲛ-: ShA 1 48 *S* ⲉϥⲛⲁϣ ϯ ⲟⲩⲃⲉ ⲟⲩ.; с ⲛ-gen: Ez 27 33 *S*(*B* diff), Mt 15 34 *SB*, Cl 56 16 *A* ⲟⲩ. ⲡⲡⲁⲣⲧⲉ, MG 25 214 *B* ⲟⲩ. ⲡⲣⲱⲟⲩϣ πόσ., Mt 18 21 *S* ⲡⲟⲩ. ⲡⲥⲟⲡ *B* ϣⲁⲟⲩ. ποσάκις; MG 25 244 *B* ⲓⲥ ⲟⲩ. ⲡⲥⲛⲟⲩ ἐκ πολλῶν ἐτῶν; PS 243 *S* ⲟⲩⲡ ⲟⲩ. ⲙⲙⲉⲗⲟⲥ ϣⲟⲟⲡ, ShA 1 190 *S* ⲙⲡⲡⲥⲁⲟⲩ. ⲙⲡⲟⲩ. ⲡⲣⲟⲙⲡⲉ, BMar 42 *S* ⲧⲉⲣⲡⲟⲩⲏⲣ ⲡⲣⲟⲙⲡⲉ, Mani H 31 *A²* ϣⲁⲕⲉⲟⲩ. ⲡⲟⲩⲁⲓϣ, AZ 23 28 *F* ⲁⲅⲉⲗ ⲟⲩ. ⲡⲗⲓⲧⲣⲁ, Bess 7 7 *B* ⲁⲣⲉⲧⲁⲣⲕⲟⲓ ⲡⲟⲩ. ⲡⲥⲟⲡ; f: Mor 23 28 *S* ⲡⲉϥⲣⲉⲡⲟⲩⲏⲣⲉ ⲡⲣⲟⲙⲡⲉ = *ib* 24 20 *F* ⲟⲩⲏⲗⲓ ⲡⲗ.; without ⲛ- *SA²*: BHom 20 ⲡⲣⲟⲥⲉⲭⲉ ϩⲛⲟⲩ. ϯⲧⲏⲩ, *ib* 51 ⲁⲟⲩ. ϩⲱⲃ ⲕⲱⲧⲉ (var R 2 2 35 ⲟⲩ. ⲛ-) πόσ.; *ib* 76 ⲁϥϣⲡ ⲟⲩ. ϩⲓⲥⲉ, Mani H 91 *A²* ⲟⲩ. ⲭⲱⲣⲁ (but *ib* ⲟⲩ. ⲙⲙⲁ); с ⲁ- *SB*, *about (circa)*: Mk 9 21 *S*(*B* ⲓⲥ ⲟⲩ.), Mt 7 11 *B*(*S* = Gk), He 9 14 *B*

(SF do) πόσ.; BAp 78 S ετετηει…εις λογ. нпαγ, Cat 20 B if I can … ιε αγ. маλλоп пθок; п(п)а-: HL 81 B огот ероι паογ. πολλῷ κρείττων; PS 202 S огнγ нпаογ. поге, BM 912 4 B grief паогωм псωϥ паογ.; επαгнр, -авнр B, to what extent? so in vain: Job (only) 2 9 εἰς τὸ κενόν, 6 5 διὰ κενῆς, 22 6 Პепоγметепаḃ.(all S епхінхн) διὰ κ.; ις ογ. v εις а. щаογ. v Mt 18 21 above.

соγоγ. S, such & such a day in dating: ShIF 232 Პнсоγ(.) пащ певот, BAp 106 shall begin Lent псоγ(оγ)ннр.

мегоγ. S, how-many-eth: Br 83 тм. птазис, BP 11943 εις пм. псоп have I requested thee, cf CO 257.

ог. as nn m S: LDi 275 day, hour & поγ. м-поог what (quarter) of moon.

ογωρ S vb (?), meaning unknown: BMOr 6201 A 124]аιка паны паογ. нвоλ аιḃωк ерогп ᲞА-теп[.

ογειρε S nn f, meaning unknown. V λегλωге.

ογоре S vb intr, meaning unknown: Ryl 370 нтакᲞоп пеᲞаᲞе ᲞАртик акоγ. паγ еоготϥ еḃоλ.

ογρо B v рро.

ογρω SBF, арω SF nn m, bean: P 44 83 S е-реḃінωп есас (v пас below) · парω فول = 43 58 поγрωп (l -рω), ib аракип · аракос · па. 'ᵌ = 43 ib (om па.) دسل, 'ᵌ, ib кγамос · па. 'ᵌ, P 46 159 S паро 'ᵌ, K 193 B фаḃа, аλι, феλ, пιоγ. all 'ᵌ; Jern 15 F ог. θармоγс, BMis 462 S соγо, еιωт, арщιп, ог., Ryl 347 S ог. аλаγ, WS 124 S do, ib 126 S ог. пас, Bodl(P) d 47 S ог. еϥсорщ, ib b 7 S ог. еϥᲞнᲞ (prob), Kr 8 S арт(аḃаι) of ог., BKU 1 140 S ог., PMich 562 F а.; Jern lc F ψапоγ.

ογρωм v мрωм.

ογωрп S(rare)B, -реп SBF, ḃωрп B, ογωреп-S/F, оγорп-, огерп- B, огарнп- F, огорп⳽ SBF, -арп⳽ S/F vb I intr, send: Jer 50 10 (S хооγ), Mt 14 35 (SF do), Ac 9 38 (S do, F тᲞе-) ἀποστέλλειν; DeV 2 96 аϥог. & brought Daniel, ib 165 ог. птек-† θωщ.

II tr: Ge 20 2 (S x.), Pro 9 3 (SA do), Is 33 7 (SF тппооγ) ἀπ., Ps 143 7 (S do), Gal 4 4 (S do), ἐξαπ.; Jo 20 21 (SA² do) πέμπειν; Bar 4 23 ἐκπ.; C 86 80 огорпϥ пемнι, BM 549 огωреп пιω, ib 1182 меγ-ḃорпḃ, CMSS 41 Sf огарпоγ[.

With following preposition. c е- send to: Nu 13 27 (S x.), Is 10 16 (S т.) ἀπ. εἰς, Ep Jer 59 ἀπ. ἐπί; Mt 2 8 (S x.), C 89 110 ог. ммоι епиморωγι п. εἰς; BM 532 S огорпс епмопастнрιоп, AM 216 огорпоγ емпаι, PO 11 371 ог….еιпι, Bor 304 55 S апп̅е̅ огорпϥ ехιоικει; еᲞоγп е-: Am 1 4 (A x.), Mt 8 31 (S x.) ἀπ. εἰς; еᲞрнι, ег. е-: Ac 9 30 ег. (S x.) ἐξαπ. εἰς; C 43 90 огорпϥ еᲞ. ехнмι пармепιос, ib 137 sim ег.; c ератϥ п-, to: Ez 3 5 ἐξαπ. πρός; C 43 54 огорпϥ…ератγ мпеϥ-ιωт; c ехеп-, upon: Is 9 8 (S x.), Ez 7 3 (S т.) ἀπ. ἐπί; еᲞрнι, ег. ех.: CaiEuch 428 ог. еᲞ. ехωп мпιᲞмот ἐξαπ. dat; AM 146 ог. мпекᲞмот ег. ехωп, Jer 9 16 ег. епап. ἐπί, Ex 8 17 ег. еᲞап. ἐπί; c п- dat: Ps 77 25 (S x.) ἀπ. εἰς, Is 19 20 (S do) ἀπ. dat, 2 Thes 2 11 (S т.) π. dat; Va 63 11 щаϯогорпϥ пак=BMis 381 S т., Ryl 348 S акоγ. папа λога паι, MR 5 46 F мппкоγарп огω пнι, ib 42 Პорпϥ пекемтоп пᲞнт пнι, BM 545 ḃωрп пнι, AZ 23 27 S/ ог. сιḃе паι; c пса-, after: 1 Kg 16 12 (S x.) ἀπ., Jer 14 3 (S do), Su 29 ἀπ. ἐπί; Ac 10 32 (var ᲞА-, S т.) π. πρός; C 89 52 аϥог. пса-пепιωт = Miss 4 534 S x., C 43 111 аϥогорпоγ псωϥ; c щА-, to: Ez 2 3 ἐξαπ. πρός; C 43 77 ог. щароι мміханλ, ib 223 огорпϥ еракоϯ щаар-мепιос (cf c е-); c ᲞАхеп-, toward, to: Ps 104 17 (S x.) ἀπ. ἔμπροσθεν; AM 58 ог. ппаι ᲞА-хωι; c ᲞА-, to: Ge 37 13, Is 37 2 (SF x.), 2 Cor 12 17 (S т., F таога) ἀπ. πρός; DeV 1 123 птаог. ᲞАрωтеп, AM 277 огерпθнпоγ ᲞАроι; еḃоλ ᲞА-, from: Su 21 (S x.) ἐξαπ. ἀπό; c Პιхеп-, down upon: AM 133 ог. ᲞᎿ.таιтаιḃι птекхом.

With following adverb. c еḃоλ, send forth: Ge 8 7 (S x.), Is 16 1 (S do) ἀπ. Deu 15 13 (S кω еḃ.) ἐξαπ.; 1 Kg 24 20 (S огωωте) ἐκπ.; C 89 39 bade ог. пас еḃ. ппесщнрι ἀποδοθῆναι dat; Ex 21 2 (S Gk diff); AM 7 огорпеп еḃ. епιполемос, ib 59 аϥог. еḃ. Პеппаι пιḃеп, R 1 4 22 S есоγ. еḃ. мп-поᲞ погωщ proclaiming; as nn: Bar 2 27 ἀπο-στολή; c епеснт, down: Cai Euch 650 ог. е. еḃоλ Პеппексιсι ἐξαπ.; c епщωι, up: Ez 17 15 ἐξαπ. εἰς; Cai Euch 544 ог. пак е. мпιщоγ ἀναπ. dat; AM 133 аϥог. е. мпιамнп; c еᲞоγп, in: C 89 46 аϥог. паϥ еᲞ. = Miss 4 528 S x., BSM 102 асоγ. птесḃωκ пас еᲞ.

ремпḃωрп, man sent, messenger: MG 25 103 (var ремпᲞωḃ, GöttAr 114 44 diff).

реϥоγ., as last: Dif 1 93 Gabriel пιр. of Lord رسول.

Ᏽιп-, хιпоγ., sending: My 31 S тᏽ. of Gabriel, DeV 2 133 B текх. пнι.

ογрас S nn, staff, crutch: 2 Kg 3 29 σκυτάλη; PSBA 25 270 lame man аϥамᲞте погоγ. (but JA '03 1 95 حرق…مو⟩ bandages), Mun 65 sim еϥ-мооще ᲞᎿᲞепоγ. & feet bound with Პепщаар.

ογрıс B nn m, plant κόστος: K 186 пιоγ. قسط مر

ογρτ 490 ογροτ

(cf P 43 34 ˙ₐ ˙ӡ ⲕⲉⲥⲧⲉⲡϩⲉ i e? ⟨Arabic⟩ ˙ӡ though this differs from ˙ₐ ˙ӡ, v Dozy 2 344, AIssa 58).

ⲟⲩⲣⲧ¹ S A², -ⲏⲣⲧ², -ⲁⲣⲧ³, -ⲁⲣⲏⲧ⁴ S, -ⲉⲣⲧ⁵ S B F, -ⲏⲗⲧ⁶ F, ϩⲉⲣⲧ B nn m f (once, cf in name), rose (cf ⟨Arabic⟩ &c, v LöwF 3 194): Sa 2 8¹ S, Si 39 17⁵ S ῥόδον; P 44 23² S ⲡⲟⲩ., K 179⁵ B do ⟨Arabic⟩; ShR 2 3 44 S ϩⲉⲣⲟⲩ.¹ offered in temple, BM 331 16 S ϩⲉⲛⲡⲁϩⲣⲉ ⲙⲡⲟⲛⲟⲩ.¹ whereof idols' robes made (var Mor 18 124 ⲡⲟⲩ.² ⲙⲡⲡⲉϩⲣⲏⲣⲉ ⲙⲡⲁⲓⲣ(ⲉ̆αρ)), R 1 5 50 S body ⲧⲣⲉϣⲣⲱϣ ⲛⲑⲉ ⲡⲡⲉⲓⲟⲩ.², C 43 72 B sim⁵, PO 14 322 B scent of ⲡⲓϭ. in Pharmouthi, KroppR 3 S ⲕⲗⲟⲙ ⲡⲟⲩ.⁵, JKP 2 218 F ⲡⲉⲟⲩ.⁶ (ⲡ)ⲧⲁⲓⲕⲱ(ⲧ)ϩ (ⲙ)ⲙⲁⲩ, Mani 1 A² ϩⲣⲏⲣⲉ ⲡⲟⲩ.¹, PMéd 297 S³, 157 S⁴; rose colour: P 44 66 S ⲣⲟϫⲓⲟⲡ · ⲡⲁⲅⲁⲡ ⲙⲡⲟⲩ.⁵ ⟨Arabic⟩, Blake 254 S ⲡⲁⲅ. ⲡⲧⲟⲩ.², PLond 4 507 S ϣⲧⲏⲡ ⲡⲟⲩ.²; rose water: BMOr 8775 135 B ⲙⲟⲩϩ. ⟨Arabic⟩; in recipes: Z 627 S ⲡⲉϩ ⲡⲟⲩ.², PMéd 240 S do, CR '87 376 S do, BKU 1 26 (8116 b) F ⲡϩ-ⲉⲩⲉⲣⲧ, PMéd 262 S ⲟⲩ.² ⲉϥⲗⲏⲕ fresh, ib 122 S ⲟⲩ.² ⲉϥϩⲟⲕⲙ withered, Ryl 106 53 S ⲟⲩ.² ⲉϥϣⲟⲟⲩ(ⲉ) dried.

In name (?): Τουέρτις, -όρτις (Preisigke); cf Twrt-Mn 'rose of Min' (HT).

ⲟⲩⲣⲓⲧ B v ϩⲟⲩⲣⲓⲧ.

ⲟⲩⲣⲟⲧ S, -ⲣⲁⲧ S f A A² F, ⲉⲣⲟⲩⲟⲧ B, (ⲉ)ⲗⲟⲩⲁⲧ F, ⲣⲱⲟⲩⲧⲍ B, ⲣⲟⲟⲩⲧ† S, ⲣⲁⲩⲧ† A, ⲣⲱⲟⲩⲧ† B F vb I intr, be glad, eager, ready: 1 Chr 29 17 B προθυμεῖσθαι; Ps 67 3 S(B ⲟⲩⲛⲟϥ) τέρπειν; ib 103 15 S(B ⲣⲁϣⲓ) ἱλαρύνειν; ib 64 12 S(B ⲕⲉⲡⲓ) πιαίνειν; Cl 27 2 A ἀναζωπυρεῖν; Wess 11 170 S ⲁⲅⲟⲩ. ⲡⲛⲙⲁϥ χαριεντίζεσθαι; PS 61 S ⲙⲁⲣⲟⲩⲣⲁϣⲉ ⲡⲥⲉⲟⲩ., Ming 341 S ⲁⲓⲟⲩ. ⲁⲓⲣⲱⲛ ⲉⲣⲟⲩⲡ = BMar 206 S & Rec 6 169 B ⲁⲡⲁϩⲏⲧ ⲉⲓ ⲉⲣⲟⲓ, AM 318 B ⲁⲡⲉϥⲥⲱⲙⲁ ⲉⲣ. as if had drunk wine; ϭ ϩⲏⲧ: 1 Chr 29 6 B ⲉⲣ. ⲡϩ. προθ., Ac 27 36 S sim (B ⲟⲩⲛ.) εὔθυμος γίνεσθαι; ϭ ⲉ- dat commodi S: 2 Kg 13 28 (var ⲟⲩⲛ.) ἀγαθύνειν; GMir 189 ⲁⲡⲉϥⲥⲱⲙⲁ ⲟⲩ. ⲉⲣⲟϥ as if had suffered naught, Ep 168 ⲡⲉⲧⲉⲣⲉⲧⲉⲕⲡⲣⲟϩⲁⲓⲣⲉⲥⲓⲥ ⲡⲁⲟⲩ. ⲉⲣⲟϥ; vbal S A B: Phil 4 10 S(B ⲫⲓⲣⲓ ⲉⲃⲟⲗ) ἀναθάλλειν; 1 Thes 4 11 S(B diff) φιλοτιμεῖσθαι; Cl 34 2 A ⲟⲩ. ⲁⲣ ⲡⲉⲧⲛⲁⲡⲟⲩϥ πρόθυμος εἶναι; BMOr 9532 ro S ⲡϭⲟⲩ. ⲉⲣ ϩⲙϩⲁⲗ, Va 63 79 B ϣⲁϥⲉⲣ. ⲉⲥⲓϯ ⲙⲡⲉϥϫⲣⲟϫ.

Qual, glad, fresh, flourishing: Hab 1 8 A(SB ϭⲃⲧⲱⲧ), Mk 14 38 S B F, Mor 37 143 S ⲉϥⲣ. ϩⲛⲧⲉϥϭⲟⲙ πρόθυμος, Ja 5 13 S(B ⲟⲩⲛ. ⲡϩⲏⲧ) εὐθυμεῖν; Pro 22 8 S A, 2 Cor 9 7 S(B ⲣⲁϣⲓ), C 89 54 B ⲉϥⲣ. in spirit ἱλαρός; Ps 127 3 S(B ⲫⲟⲣⲓ ⲉⲃⲟⲗ) εὐθηνεῖν; Pro 24 66 S A(B diff) εὔψυχος; ib 11 25 S A(B = Gk) ἁπλοῦς; Si 34 26 S λαμπρός; Ro 15 20 S(B ⲙⲉⲓ) φιλοτιμ.; BMar 113 S ⲉⲧⲣ. like tree θάλλειν; Si 14 18 S δασύς; Va 58 178 B φαιδρῶς opp ⲟⲕⲉⲙ; 1 Kg 21 6 S(Mor) ⲉϥⲣ. gloss on ⲉϥϩⲛⲙ θερμός (but cf BMar

218 ⲉⲩϩⲛⲙ ⲁⲩⲱ ⲉⲩⲣ.), CA 101 S sim opp ⲥⲕⲁⲡ, BHom 57 S ⲟⲩⲕⲁⲣⲡⲟⲥ ⲉϥⲣ. opp ⲣⲱϩⲃ, PS 94 S ϯⲣ. ⲉⲧⲁⲅⲉ ⲡⲉⲩⲃⲱⲗ, ClPr 47 80 S ϯⲣ. ⲉⲣ ⲧⲉⲟⲩⲥⲓⲁ, Sh Bor 246 87 S risen body ⲉϥⲣ. lacking naught, ManiH 30 A² ⲟⲩϩⲟ ⲉϥⲣ., Mani 1 A² crown ⲉⲧⲣ. ⲉⲧⲡⲣⲓⲱⲟⲩ, Cat 15 B ⲥⲧⲟⲗⲏ ⲉⲥⲥⲉⲗⲥⲱⲗ ⲉⲥⲣ. like lilies, FR 110 B ϩⲁⲓϩⲏⲧ ⲉⲩⲣ., Aegyptus 11 444 S our sister ⲉⲧⲣ. ϩⲙ-ⲡⲉⲥⲥⲁ, Ryl 72 353 S face ⲉϥⲣ. like lightning; ϭ ⲣⲏⲧ: BIF 13 102 S ⲉⲩⲣ. ⲡϩ. ⲉⲧⲏⲏⲧⲟⲩ; ϭ ⲉ-: Gu 40 S ⲡⲉϥⲣ. ⲉϫⲓⲧⲩ; ⲉⲣⲟⲩⲡ ⲉ-: ClPr 54 36 S ⲉⲧⲣ. ⲉⲣ. ⲉⲧⲉⲓⲥⲡⲟⲩϩⲏ ⲡⲣⲟⲑ. περί; P 131² 153 S ϯⲣ. ⲉⲣ. ⲉⲡⲉⲑⲗⲓⲯⲓⲥ, EW 48 B ⲣ. ⲉϭ. ⲉⲡϣⲉⲙϣⲓ; ϭ ⲉⲣⲟⲩⲡ ⲉϫⲡ-: BM 166 S ⲣ. ⲉⲣ. ⲁϫⲡ ϩⲣⲱϩ (var Aeg 282 ⲉϭ. ⲉ-) εὔνοιαν ἔχειν περί; ϭ ⲉⲃⲟⲗ: Va 58 179 B ⲉⲣ. ⲉϭ. ⲉⲩϯ ⲡⲁⲕ ⲡⲟⲩϥⲁϭⲣⲓ εὐθυμεῖν.

II tr (refl): Mus 12 14 S ⲡⲁⲣⲧⲟⲥ ⲉϥⲉⲣ ϩⲱⲃ ⲡⲁⲙⲉⲗⲏⲥ ⲉϥⲉⲟⲩ. ⲙⲙⲟϥ, R 1 1 81 S ⲟⲩ. ⲙⲙⲱⲧⲛ, BSM 90 B ⲫϯ ⲉⲧⲣⲱⲟⲩⲧϥ ⲙⲙⲁⲅⲁⲧϥ.

—— nn m S A A² B F, gladness, abundance, zeal: Si 45 37 (23) S, Ac 17 11 S(B ⲣⲱⲟⲩⲧϥ ⲡϩⲏⲧ) προθυμία; Eccl 6 9 F λ. (S ⲟⲩⲱϣ), ib 1 14 F ⲉⲓⲗ. (S do) προαίρεσις; Mor 37 32 S πρόθεσις; Ps 121 7 S(B = Gk) εὐθηνία; ib 15 11 B(S ⲟⲩⲛ.) εὐφροσύνη; BMar 124 S ⲁϥⲧⲁϣⲟ ⲙⲡⲉϥⲟⲩ. εὐωχία; Ps 15 11 B(S ⲙⲧⲟⲡ) τερπνότης; ShC 73 91 S eateth not ϩⲙⲡⲉϥⲟⲩ. in his zeal, Ryl 94 102 S ⲧⲉⲧⲛⲅⲩⲡⲟⲑⲉⲥⲓⲥ ⲉⲧⲉⲡⲁⲓⲡⲉ ⲡⲉⲧⲡⲟⲩ., BMOr 8811 242 S wine ⲟⲩⲟⲩ. ⲡⲡⲉⲧⲛⲁⲥⲟⲟⲩ, BM 337 98 S husbandmen watch ⲡⲟⲩ. ⲙ-ⲡ-ⲁⲓⲣ & dew & warmth, C 86 108 B ⲡⲉⲣ. ⲡⲧⲉⲕⲕⲟⲓⲡⲉ ⲧⲉⲡⲧⲣⲟⲫⲏ, DeV 2 215 B ⲡⲉⲣ. ⲡⲓϣⲏⲛ, AM 225 B ϩⲟⲗⲙⲉⲧ ϩⲓⲧⲉⲡⲡⲉⲧⲉⲣ. am carried away by your zeal; ϭ ϩⲏⲧ S: PS 132 ⲁⲛϫⲓ ⲡⲟⲩⲟⲩ. ⲡϩ., BIF 13 107 ⲡⲟⲩ. ⲙⲡⲉϩ. = MG 25 291 B ⲣⲱⲟⲩⲧϥ ⲡϩ., PSBA 32 200 S ⲡⲟⲩ. ⲙⲡⲁϩ. ⲥⲱⲕ ⲙⲙⲟⲓ; ϭ ⲉⲣⲟⲩⲡ ⲉ- SB: Miss 4 692 S ⲡⲉⲩⲟⲩ. ⲉⲣ. ⲉⲧⲁⲣⲉⲧⲏ, DeV 2 145 B ⲟⲩⲉⲣ. ⲉϭ. ⲉⲣⲟⲓ assiduity toward me; adverbial ϩⲛⲟⲩⲟⲩ., ϭⲉⲛⲟⲩⲉⲣ., gladly, eagerly: 1 Pet 5 2 S(B ⲣⲱⲟⲩⲧϥ ⲡϩ.), Aeg 274 S προθύμως; Job 22 26 S(B ⲣⲁϣⲓ) ἱλαρῶς; Ro 12 8 S F(B do) ἐν ἱλαρότητι; Pro 9 17 S A(B = Gk) ἡδέως; RNC 31 S ϯ-ⲡⲁⲁⲁϥ ⲛⲁⲕ ϩ. ἐν προαιρέσει; R 1 3 46 S awaiteth him ϩ., Gu 73 S f hearing ϩ., AP 37 A² ϩⲛⲟⲩⲡⲁϭ ⲡⲟⲩ., PO 11 369 B sim; ⲣⲱⲟⲩⲧ, -ⲧϥ B, ⲣⲁⲩⲧϥ A²: Cat 175 B ϥⲣ. ⲙⲡⲓⲫⲓⲣⲓ ⲉⲃⲟⲗ of fruit, ManiH 9 A² ⲣⲱ]ⲙⲉ ⲡⲣ. ⲡⲥⲡⲁⲧⲁⲗⲟⲥ; ϭ ϩⲏⲧ B: C 86 188 endured ϭⲉⲛⲟⲩⲡⲓϣϯ ⲡⲣ. ⲡϩ., AM 208 ϭⲉⲛⲟⲩ-ⲣⲱⲟⲩⲧϥ ⲡϩ.

ϯ ⲟⲩ., ⲉⲣ., give gladness, gladden, incite: Si 32 8 S ἱλαροῦν, ib 36 30 S ἱλαρύνειν; ib 1 12 SB τέρπειν; Ac 18 27 B(S = Gk), AM 278 B ⲡⲓⲟⲩⲁⲓ ϯ. ⲙⲡⲓⲟⲩⲁⲓ προτρέπειν; Pro 15 13 S A θάλλειν; ib 16 2 S A πιαίνειν; 2 Tim 1 6 S(B ⲟⲩⲁϩⲉⲙ ⲱⲡϭ) ἀναζωπυρεῖν; C 89 200 B ⲉϥϯ. ⲡⲱⲟⲩ with God's word ὠφελεῖν;

ib 35 *B* ϯ. πωοⲩ ⲉϩⲟⲣⲟⲩϣⲉ = MG 17 407 نشذ =
Va ar 172 23 حرض; Br 259 *S* ⲛⲁϯ ⲟⲩⲱ ⲛⲧⲁϯ. ⲛⲁⲩ
ϩⲙⲡⲉⲕⲣⲁⲛ, ShBMOr 8810 481 *S* thoughts ϯ. ⲛⲁⲛ
ⲉⲡⲉⲣϩⲏⲩⲉ, SHel 54 *S* greeting martyr ⲉⲩϯ. ⲛϧⲏⲧ
ⲛⲁϥ; *c* ⲉ-: Va 61 21 *B* ⲛⲁϥϯ. ⲡⲱⲟⲩ ⲉϥⲁⲓ; ⲉ-
ϧⲟⲩⲛ ⲉ-: FR 28 *S* ⲉⲥϯ. ⲛⲁⲩ ⲉϩ. ⲉⲡⲁⲅⲱⲛ, AM 21 *B*
ⲉϥϯ. ⲛⲁⲛ ⲉϩ. ⲉ̄ϯⲙⲉⲧⲙⲁⲣⲧⲩⲣⲟⲥ.

As name: ⲡⲟⲩⲣⲟⲧ (Lant 108), Πευρότ (BM 1075).

ογερητε, ⲟⲩⲣⲏⲧⲉ *S*, ⲟⲩⲣⲏⲧⲉ *SAA²*(Ma)*B*
(BM 608), -ⲓⲧⲉ *A²*(JoAP), -ⲏⲧⲓ *F* nn f, *foot*, pl (dual):
Ex 12 9 (*B* ϭⲁⲗⲟⲝ), Job 29 15 (*B* ⲫⲁⲧ), Is 1 6 *SF*(*B*
ϭ.), Lam 1 9 (ShA 2 106, *B* ⲣⲁⲧ, *F* ϫⲁⲗ.), Hab 3 19
SA(*B* ϭ.), Jo 11 2 *SAA²*(*B* do), AP 15 *A²* πούς; Pro
26 7 *SA*, Ez 1 7 (*B* ϭ.) σκέλος; Dan 10 11 (*B* ⲧⲁϩⲟ
ⲉⲣⲁⲧⲩ) στάσις; Aeg 226 βάσις; Lev 11 42 ϥⲧⲟ ⲛⲟⲩ.
(*B* ϥ. only) τέσσαρα; PS 33 ⲛⲁϩⲧⲉ ⲉϫⲛⲛⲟⲩ., ShC 42
104 ⲛⲉϥⲟⲩ., BIF 13 107 walked on hands & ⲛⲉϥⲟⲩ.
= MG 25 291*B* ϭ.,KroppR 13 10 ⲡⲉϥⲉⲣⲏⲧⲉ ⲙⲡⲓⲱⲧ,
Z 551 ⲙⲟⲟϣⲉ ⲛⲡⲉϥⲟⲩ. (*cf* J 66 66 ϩⲛⲡⲉϥⲟⲩ.), Mani
2 *A²* stool ϩⲁⲡⲉϥⲟⲩ., CO 90 ⲡⲉⲓϫⲡⲟⲥ ⲙⲡⲉⲕⲩⲛⲟ-
ⲡⲟϫⲓⲟⲛ ⲛⲛⲟⲩ. of thy holiness, Cai 8038 *F* ⲛⲛⲟ-
ⲡⲟⲧⲓ ⲉⲧϩⲁⲡⲉⲕⲟⲩ., Hall 71 ϣⲟⲉⲓϣ ⲉⲧϩⲁⲣⲏⲧⲟⲩ ⲛⲛⲟⲩ.
ⲡ-; as sg: Deu 25 9 (*B* ϥ.), Ps 9 15 (*B* ϭ.), Eccl
4 17 (*F* ϫ.) ⲡ.; Aeg 232 σκ.; BAp 135 heel of ⲧϥⲟⲩ.,
BMis 452 camel broke ⲧⲉϥⲟⲩⲣⲏⲧⲉ, BIF 13 111 sim
ⲧⲉϥⲟⲩ. ⲥⲛⲧⲉ = MG 25 301*B* ⲫ.; *foot* of bed: Z 339
ⲡ.; PS 121; *leg*: Ez 24 4 (*B* ⲫ.), Dan 10 6 (*B*
ⲕⲉⲗⲓ), Jo 19 31 *SA²*(*B* do) σκ.; ShMIF 23 18 ϣⲱⲱⲧ
ⲛⲡⲉϥⲟⲩ. ϣⲁⲡⲉϥϭⲓⲣⲟⲥ, Miss 8 259 ⲡⲕⲁⲥ ⲛⲧⲉϥⲟⲩ.
ϫⲓⲛⲡⲉϥⲡⲁⲧ ⲉⲡⲉⲥⲛⲧ, LMis 467 brake ⲛⲟⲩ. of thieves
(*cf ib* ⲥⲛϭⲉ ⲛⲣⲁⲧⲟⲩ, ⲕⲁϣ ⲛⲣ.), JSch 5 94 laid Gospels (to swear upon) ⲉϫⲛⲛⲉⲧⲛⲟⲩ.

ⲡⲁϫ ⲟⲩ. *v* ⲡⲱϫϭ.

ϣⲁⲙ ⲟⲩ. *A v* ϣⲙⲁ.

V also ⲉⲓⲛⲉ *thumb* ⲃ, ⲧⲏⲛⲃⲉ.

ογ(ε)ρϣε *SA²*, ⲟⲩⲏⲣ. *S*, ⲟⲩⲉⲣϣⲓ *B* nn f, *watch*,
watch tower: Nu 3 25 *S*(var ⲟⲩⲏⲣ.)*B*, Ps 129 6 *S*(*B*
ⲁⲣⲉϩ), *ib* 89 4 *S*(*B* ⲛⲁⲩ ⲛⲁ.), Lam 2 19 *S*(*BF* ⲙⲁ
ⲛⲁ.), Mt 14 25 *SB*(*F* ϭⲓⲛⲁ.), Mk 6 48 *S*(var ϣⲱⲡ)*B*,
Lu 2 8 *S*(*B* ⲣⲱⲓⲥ) φυλακή, Nu 32 17 *S*(*B* diff)προφ.;
Tri 367 *S* حرس, K 55 *B* حرس, ثقذ; ManiH 78 *A²*
ⲟⲩ]ⲱϭⲡ ⲛⲡⲉⲥⲟⲩ. (*cf* Lam *B*); ⲁⲛⲟⲩ. *S*, *watchman, guard* (*v* Rec 21 21): Ge 4 9 (P 44, *B* ⲟⲩⲣⲓⲧ),
Ac 12 6, 19 (both var ⲁⲩⲣϣⲉ, *B* ⲣⲉϥⲁⲣⲉϩ) φύλαξ; *ib*
16 38 (var do, *B* = Gk) ῥαβδοῦχος; BMis 167 soldiers & ⲁ. guarding him, Kr 232 George ⲡⲉϥⲁ., BM
1134, Ryl 284 (*cf* غفير).

In name: ⲟⲩⲉⲣϣⲉⲛⲟⲩⲃⲉ, Οὐερσενούφιος (PLond
4), ⲃⲉⲣϣⲉⲛⲟⲩϥⲓ (AM 287), شنوفة (Synax 2 160),
Βαρσανούφιος; abbrev? ϣⲉⲡⲟⲩϥⲉ. *Cf* Ryl Dem
3 440.

ογορϣϥ *SB* nn m, meaning unknown (*cf*?last):
EW 170 *B* in desert ⲁⲓⲧⲁϩⲟ [ⲡ]ⲟⲩⲡⲓϣϯ ⲡⲟⲩ. ⲉϥⲥⲏⲣ
ⲉⲃⲟⲗ ⲛⲱⲛⲓ *spread, paved with stones*, BMOr 6206 A
S boundaries ⲡⲉϫⲉⲙϫⲓⲧ ⲡⲟⲩ.

ογωρϩ *SA²*, ⲟⲩ(ⲉ)ⲣϩ-, ⲟⲩⲟⲣⲉϩ-, ⲟⲩⲱⲣϩ-, ⲟⲩⲟⲣ-,
ⲟⲩⲁⲣ-, ⲟⲩⲱⲣ-, ⲟⲩⲟⲣϩ⸗, -ⲟⲣϩ⸗, -ⲁⲣϩ⸗, -ⲁⲣϩ⸗ *S*, ⲟⲩⲱⲣϩ⸗
A²,ⲟⲩⲟⲣϩ⸗†, -ⲁⲣϩ† *S* vb(mostly Theban)intr, *be open,
free*: J 65 59 he shall inherit all ⲕⲁⲡ ϩⲓⲣⲟⲓ ⲕⲁⲡ ϩⲓⲱϩⲥ
ⲕⲟⲩ. *that art free* i e what thou wilt, Hall 107 send
him for camel ⲛϥⲟⲩ. ⲉⲧⲃⲉⲛⲕⲟⲩⲓ ⲡⲟⲉⲓⲕ that we may
bake it, ST 238]ⲛⲁⲟⲩ. ⲛⲥⲉⲃⲱⲕ, BMis 265 dismissed servants ⲉⲩⲱⲣϥ (*l*? ⲟⲩⲱⲣϩ, *cf ib* ⲉⲩⲟ ⲛⲣⲙϩⲉ); tr, *set free, open, renounce*: Ep 182 ⲟⲩⲁ-
ⲉⲓⲟⲩⲱⲣϩ ⲡⲧⲙⲉ ⲛⲧⲁⲃⲱⲕ, ST 379 sim, Vi ostr 434
+344 ⲁⲓ]ⲟⲩⲱⲣϩ ⲛϭⲁⲙⲟⲩⲗ ⲁⲓⲃⲱⲕ, J 42 22 ⲛⲧⲟⲩ-
ⲱⲣϩ ⲡⲉⲕⲣⲟ (*sic*, *l*? ⲣⲟ) ⲁⲛϩⲏⲧ, *ib* 48 6 ⲛ[ⲡⲉ]ϥⲟⲩ. ⲡⲣⲟ
(*sic l*), ST 170 ⲧⲉϥⲥϩⲓⲙⲉ ⲁⲓⲟⲅⲟⲣϩ & delivered her
to him, CO 325 come that I may meet thee ⲛⲧⲁⲟⲩ-
ⲟⲣϩⲕ ϩⲛⲟⲩϭⲉⲛⲓ, Turin ostr 15 ⲟⲩ]ⲟⲣϩ ϣⲁⲛⲧⲉⲧ[.

With following preposition. *c* ⲉ-, meaning uncertain: CO 194 will repay ϩⲛⲥⲟⲩⲁ ⲉⲕⲟⲩ.† ⲉⲡⲁ-
ϣⲟⲡⲥ, BP 12486 I will get part of book by heart
ϩⲛⲥⲟⲩϫ[ⲟⲩⲱⲧ ⲉⲕ]ⲟⲩ.† ⲉⲡⲁⲡⲉ, Ep 537 ⲛ]ⲃⲓⲣ ⲧⲁⲓ-
ⲡⲧⲟⲩ ⲁⲃⲟⲗ ϩⲛⲁⲕⲓⲛ ⲉⲕⲟⲩⲁⲣϩ ⲉⲡⲁⲣⲙⲓϩⲁⲧⲛ *if thou
give freedom, forbear till*, ST 358 benefits ⲡⲉⲧⲉⲕⲟⲩ-
ⲁⲣϩ ⲉⲁⲁⲩ ⲛⲁⲓ, CO 189 to debtor ⲛⲧⲁⲟⲩⲱⲣϩ ⲣⲱⲙⲉ
ⲉⲣⲟⲕ & he mulct thee, Mani H 77 *A²* faithful thrown
to lions ⲁⲩⲟⲩ. ⲡϭⲧⲟⲣⲛⲓ ⲁϩ[, *ib* 68 *A²* ⲟⲩⲱⲣⲟⲩ ⲁⲡⲓⲧⲛⲉ,
CO 81 besought bishop ⲁϥⲟⲩⲁⲣϩⲧ [ⲉ]ⲡϣⲁ (*cf c* ⲉ-
ϩⲟⲩⲛ); *c* ⲛ-, *remit to*: Ep 534 ⲁⲓⲟⲩ. ϥⲧⲟⲉ (ⲙ)-
ⲙ(ⲁϫⲉ) ⲛⲁⲩ, *ib* 349 ⲟⲩⲱⲣ ϣⲏⲧ ⲡⲕⲱⲣ ⲡⲁⲥ, *ib* 277
ⲟⲩ. ⲡⲙⲁϩⲉ ⲡⲁⲓ & I will give thee seed-corn, BM
1143 ⲟⲩⲟⲣⲉϩ ⲁⲣθ(*l*? ⲁⲣⲧ)ⲁ ⲛⲥⲟⲩⲟ ⲛⲁⲛ, Ep 286 if thou
pay forthwith ⲧⲕⲟⲩⲥⲉⲡⲧⲉ ⲡⲕⲉⲣⲁⲧⲥⲉ ⲟⲩⲁⲣϩ ⲛⲁⲕ, ST
448 ⲁⲁⲍⲁⲣⲓⲁⲥ ⲟⲩ. ⲧⲡⲁϣⲉ ⲛϩⲟⲗⲟⲕ ⲡⲁⲙⲱⲩⲥⲏⲥ, *ib*
378 ⲙⲁϥⲟⲅⲟⲣⲥ [ⲛ]ⲁⲓ; *c* ⲛⲧⲛ-: CO 170 ϯⲟⲩⲁⲣ
ⲟⲩϩⲟⲗⲟⲕ/ ⲛⲧⲟⲧⲕ ⲙⲛⲧⲉϥϩⲛⲥⲉ (*l*? ⲙⲛ-).

With following adverb. *c* ⲉⲃⲟⲗ, *set free, dismiss*: CO 343 if he hath ⲟⲩ. ⲛⲣⲱⲙ ⲉⲃ. send them,
ib 481 ⲛⲧⲉⲣⲉⲩⲱⲣϩ ⲛϣⲁ ⲉⲃ., RE 9 152 girl in durance
ⲛⲥⲉⲟⲩⲁⲣϩ (*sic l*)ⲉⲃ. ⲛⲁⲩ, ST 199 ⲛⲥⲟⲩⲱⲣ ⲡⲏⲓ ⲉⲃ.
ⲡⲁϥ, PBu 10 ⲛⲧⲉⲣⲟⲩⲟⲩⲟⲩ. ⲧⲡⲟⲗⲓⲥ ⲉⲃ. ⲉⲑⲉⲕⲗⲁ i e made
her free of or ? expelled from the town; *c* ⲉϩⲟⲩⲛ,
allow in, admit: BAp 106 ⲁϥⲟⲩⲉⲣϩ ⲡⲉⲓⲡⲁⲣⲁⲃⲁⲧⲏⲥ
ⲉϩ. ⲉⲡⲉⲓⲙⲁ = MIE 2 382 *B* ⲑⲣⲉ...ⲓ ⲉϩⲟⲩⲛ = PO 22
388 ترك يدخل, *ib* 125 ⲛϭⲱⲙ ⲁⲩⲟⲅⲟⲣϩϥ ⲉϩ. = PO
22 476 نفخج قد *opened wide*, BP 9446 carpenter to
make ⲣⲁⲙⲟⲩⲛⲉ of door ϫⲉⲡⲙⲁ ⲟⲩⲟⲣϩ ⲉϩ., ST 280
ⲉⲕⲟⲩⲣϩ ⲡⲧⲉⲙⲱⲡ(δαίμων)ⲁϩ. ⲁⲣⲟⲕ,COAd 41 bishop
ⲁϥⲟⲩⲟⲣϩⲧ ⲉϩ. ⲉⲡϣⲁ, BMOr 9536 ⲡⲡⲉⲓⲟⲩⲟⲣ ⲗⲁⲁⲩ
ⲛⲥⲁϫⲱ ⲉϩ. ⲉϫⲱⲓ (*sc* into monastery), MMA 24 6 4
ⲁⲣⲓ ⲡⲡⲁ ⲡⲧⲟⲩⲁⲣⲧ ⲉϩ. *Cf* DM 13 14.

ατογ. *unallowed, unremitted* (?): Ryl 373 ππεϭω πατογορηϩ.

ογρεϩ nn m, *free space*: Z 580 πκογι πογ. ετεπωρεq εϩογιιπε πτμεχαπη, Ryl 165 μπται ογρηϩ πμαγ on north of wall, *ib* -ρεϩ.

In place-name (?): πογαρ πμογι (Ep 163).

ογωϩρ *S*, ογαϩρε *A*, ογαχηρ *F*(?), ογοϩρ⸗ *S* vb, same?: Pro 3 27 *A*(*S* λο, *B* ταϩπο πτοτ⸗), 23 13 *A* sim ἀπέχειν; PStras 409 πταπαρχωπ ογ. ϩαπεπισκοπος, Ryl 344 πεπτακογοϩρεq παιπε ϯογ παρκατες (ἐργάτης), *ib* 368 εις πετρος αιογοϩρεq πακ, CMSS 30 *F* εις ϯμιταπι πϣακογ. μμαγ (*sc* wine asked for).

ογς *S* nn m, *bald person*: Lev 13 40 (*B* κερϩε) φαλακρός; μπτογς, *baldness*: *ib* 42 (*B* μετκ.), Jer 29 5 (*B* do) φαλάκρωμα; Tri 531 μπτογςη كَيّة *cauterized wound*, *ib* 530 μετωςη اثر *cicatrized wound* (For -η *cf*? Lev 13 42 ϩιτμπτογς η ϩιτμπτϭαλογβιϩ Dévaud *Ét* 31); Mor 51 31 harvest μπϭελβοογ μππςιμογς same? *Cf* αпογς.

ογως *S* nn m, part of a snake (δράκων), *v* ςλεπλιπ.

ογειςε, βιςε *S*, ογιειςε *A*, ογιςε *A*², ογιςι, βι. *B*, ογαςτ⸗ *S*, ογας⸗, β. *B*, ογεςτ⸗ *F* vb intr (rare), *saw*: Nu 5 21 *B*(reading πρίζειν for πρήθειν, *S* ρωκϩ reading πιμπράναι); BM 223 *S* qπαϯςο ετμογ. η πωϩ, Va 57 164 *B* μα ππετρα ετβ. ογοϩ ετςωλπ εβολ; tr: Su 59 *B*, He 11 37 *SB*, BHom 95 *S* πρίζειν; Ex 20 25 *B*(*S* ϣωωτ) τέμνειν; Is 36 6 *F* (reading ? πρίζ. *SB* om) τετραίνειν; R 2 2 37 *S* qπαογαςτκ ϩιτεκμητε (var BHom 56 πωϩ) σχίζειν; C 86 286 *B* αγβ. μμοq ϧεπτεqμηϯ διχοτομεῖν; Tri 688 *S* αγβ. μμοq نشر; ShZ 637 *S* βαϣογρ ετβεϣωωτ, λεπτηπ ετβεογ. πϩεππoϭ πϣε, BMar 159 *S* prophets αγογαςτογ, Ryl 447 *B* βαςq ϧεπτεqμηϯ, C 43 15 *B* ογαςq, Mani H 77 *A*² αγογ. πϩαιπε.

With following preposition. ς π- (agent): He *l c* *B*(*S* Gk om), AM 309 *B* ογαςq πογβαϣογρ; ς ϩπ-, ϧεπ-: Am 1 3 *AB* πρ. dat, 2 Kg 12 31 *S* (var ογοςτογ) διαπρ. ἐν; Bor 267 104 *S* ογαςτq ϩπογβαϣ., BMis 351 *S* sim ϩπογλεπθηπ (var π-); ς πςα- emphatic: Mor 32 20 *S* πτερ(ογ)ογ. πςωq, Miss 4 170 *B* βαϣ. εςβ. πςαφη ετεπκοτ.

ρεqογειςε *S*, *sawyer*: Gu 61 ρεp. brought saws.

ογςε or πογςε *q v*.

ογαςβε *v* ογωςq (ογαςqε).

ογςαβιπ *B* nn m, *fennel*: K 198 πιογ. شمار (Lab بقدونس whence ?). Coptic?

ογοςρ *S*, ογα. *S*ᶠ, ογοςερ, βο. *B* nn m, *oar*: Ez 27 6 *SB*, C 89 58 *B* κώπη; BHom 88 *S* πογ. ςπαγ εγϩιπε μμοq, Gu 101 *S*ᶠ ϩιπε μπογ., R 2 1 55 *S* λαγο, ϩαε, ογ., BAp 143 πειογ.; ρεqςεκ ογ., *puller of oar, rower*: Ez 27 26 *SB*, *ib* 27 8 *SB* ρεqςωκ ππογ. κωπηλάτης.

ογοςτπ, ογας. *S*(nn), ογοςθεπ *B*, -τεπ *F*, ογεςθεπ-, -θωπ⸗ *B*, ογεςτωπ† *S*, -ταπτ *A*², -θωπ†, β.† *B* vb **I** intr, *become, make broad* mostly *B*: Ge 26 22 (*S* ογωϣς εβολ) πλατύνειν, Deu 33 20 (*S* do) ἐμπ.; Is 33 21 *SBF* εὐρύχωρος; MIE 2 403 απιμα ογ.; qual: Ps 118 96 (*S* ογοϣς), Ez 23 32 *SB* πλατύς; Is 30 23 (*SF* κιωογ), Hos 4 16 (*A* ογαςϩ αβ.), Mt 7 13 *SB* εὐρ.; Ps 47 1 *SB* εὔριζος; EW 146 ςογ. παμφόρος; ShZ 593 *S* ϩιη ετογωϣς, ετογ. opp ϭηγ, Mani K 13 *A*² sim, C 86 112 εqογ. ϧεππεqςωμα, ROC 23 281 ϯςτγλη...ογ. εμαϣω & heavy to carry, BSM 26 inheritance εςογ. ϧεπογμετραμαο = BMis 365 *S* τηϣ καλως.

II tr *B*, *broaden*: Ge 9 27, Ps 4 2 (*S* ογω. εβ.) π., Am 1 13 (*A* ογω. αβ.) ἐμπ.; FR 100 αqογεςθεπ πισλ̄.

—— nn m *SB*, *breadth*: Ge 13 17 (*S* ογω.), Ez 40 13 (var ογηϣςι, *S* do) πλάτος, Ps 17 19 *S* (var ογας. TT 12) *B* πλατυσμός; Job 11 9 (*S* πωϫϭ), Ez 42 20 (var ογη., *S* do) εὖρος, Ps 30 8 *S*(*B* vb†) εὐρύχωρος; MG 25 166 ογ. opp ϩοϫϩεϫ, *ib* 371 ογ. opp ϣιη, BSM 58 φογ. μπαιεςκωμιοπ (var Va 63 25 ογ. εβολ), AM 71 shall be tended ϧεπογογ.

—— εβολ *B*, *be broad, well provided* intr: Ez 41 7† (*S* ογω. εβ.) διαπ., MG 25 240 cell ογ.† εβ. πλατύς; Va 57 122 sails spread ϧεππιπληρωμα εθογ.† εβ. πτε παηρ, C 43 204 parents παγβ.† εβ., Va 66 298 table ογ.† εβ. ϧεπϩαπϫιπογωμ; tr, *enlarge*: Hab 2 5 (*A* ογω. αβ.) π., Deu 19 8 (*S* do) ἐμπ.; MG 25 54 αqογεςθωπογ εβ. with cattle & crops; as nn m: TstAb 227 from prison επιογ. εβ., Cat 19 πιογ. εβ. πτε ογμηϣ πχρια.

ογωςq *SAA*²*F*, ογεςq-, -οςq⸗, ογοςq† *S*, -αςq† *S*ᵃ*S*ᶠ, p ς ογαςq- *S* vb **I** intr, *be idle, brought to naught*: Si 30 37, Cl 33 1 *A* αππαογ. ϩμϥωβ ετπαπογq ἀργεῖν, Ro 4 14 (*B* κωρq), 1 Cor 15 26 *SF* (*B* do), Mor 18 130 magic arts ογ. καταρ.; Z 341 αικτοι ειογ.† ἄπρακτος; ShA 2 336 αγογ. πϭι πετειρε μμος (*sc* iniquity), ShZ 595 Jews αγογ. ϩιτμπεςϯοc, Mor 23 31 ατειτεχπη ογ. αςερ ατϣαγ, WS 98 come, delay not ϫεπεγογ., Ryl 413 *F* μπελκεογ εγωςq; qual: Mt 20 3 (*B* κορq), Tit 1 12 (var *S*ᶠ) ἀργός; ShP 130⁵ 82 ground tilled ϫεππεqκααq εqογ., ShC 42 110 ετογ. ϩππεϩβηγε μπογϫαι, BHom 82 sim εβολ ϩππεϩβ. πταπομια, JKP 2 50 *S*ᶠ επογαςβ μμαϯ *very idle*, ST 302 *S*ᵃ bid him make nails (for water-wheel) for πϩοι ογαςq τηρq.

II tr, *leave idle, barren, annul*: Lu 13 7 (*B* κ.),

He 2 14 *SF*(*B* do), Mor 37 76 ᴀϥογ. ⲡⲡⲉⲍⲁⲓⲙⲱⲡ
ⲕⲁⲧⲁⲣ.; Si 33 6 ἐκτρίβειν (or ? *l* ογωϣϥ), *ib* 47 9
συντρ.; He 9 26 *SF*(*B* ϣⲱϣ ⲉⲃⲟⲗ) ἀθέτησις; BG
16 ⲡⲉⲧⲕⲧⲟ ⲙⲙⲟⲓ ⲁⲅⲟⲩⲟⲥ̇ϥ(ϥ *sic l*?), ShMIF 23 80
ογ. ⲙⲡⲟⲩⲱϣ ⲙⲡⲟⲛⲏⲣⲟⲛ, Mor 28 148 ⲉⲡⲡⲁⲟⲅⲉⲥϥ
ⲧⲕⲉⲗⲉⲅⲥⲓⲥ ⲙⲡⲣⲣⲟ, Mani 2 *A*² ᴀⲅⲟⲩ. ⲙⲡⲉϥϫⲱⲕ ⲡϩⲏⲧ,
Mor 51 39 ⲛ̇ϯⲡⲁⲟⲅⲉⲥϥ ⲧⲁⲉⲓⲟⲡⲉ ⲁⲛ *will not neglect
my craft*, CO 324 ⲙⲡⲡϣ ογⲱⲥϥ ⲡⲕⲁⲙⲟⲩⲗ ⲡⲧⲓⲧⲏ̇-
ⲡⲟⲟⲩϥ, Kr 153 contract ⲡⲡⲓϣ ογⲟⲥϥ̇ⲕ ⲡⲟⲩϩⲟⲟⲩ
save for sickness, *ib* 184 *prob sim*.

With following preposition. c ⲉ-, *wait upon*: Sh
(Besa)Z 513 ⲁⲡⲉⲥⲡⲏⲩ ογ. ⲉⲣⲟⲟⲩ (*sc* sick) & tended
them, WTh 179 obey & sacrifice ϫⲉⲉⲣⲉⲡⲁⲓⲕⲁⲥⲧⲏ̇-
ⲣⲓⲟⲛ ογ.† ⲉⲣⲟⲕ, Mor 50 55 *sim*, Mor 43 246 servants ⲉⲕⲟⲩ. ⲙⲙⲟⲟⲩ ⲉⲡⲉⲕⲣⲅⲍⲟⲡⲏ *keepest idle*; c
ⲛⲧⲛ-: ClPr 29 244 ϣⲁⲥⲁⲣⲭⲉⲓ ⲡⲟⲩ. ⲡⲧⲟⲟⲧϥ ⲡϭⲓ
ⲧⲙⲡⲧⲣⲉϥϯ ϩⲁⲡ ⲡⲧⲁⲍⲓⲕⲓⲁ.

p c, *deserter, destroyer* (?): BG 16 ⲉⲣⲉⲡⲏⲩ ⲉⲧⲱⲡ
ⲧⲣⲁ[ⲧ]ⲃ̇ⲣⲱⲙⲉ ⲉⲣⲉⲃⲱⲕ ⲉⲧⲱⲡ ⲧⲟⲩ. ⲙⲁ?

—— nn m *SAF*, *idleness, ceasing*: Is 1 13 *SF*(*B*
ⲕ.) ἀργεία, BM 247 9 baptized ⲉⲩⲟⲩ. ⲙⲡⲡⲟⲃⲉ ⲕⲁⲧ-
άργησις (*cf* Ro 6 6); He 7 18 *SF*(*B* ϣⲱϣ) ἀθέτησις;
Pro 28 19 *SA* σχολή; Gal 5 19 (cit ShA 1 287, but
l ? as *B* ⲥⲱⲱϥ) ἀσέλγεια; ShBor 247 8 ⲡⲟⲩ. opp ⲧⲉ̇-
ⲥⲡⲟⲩϫⲏ, Mor 22 23 ⲛⲧⲉⲟⲅⲟⲩ. ϣⲱⲡⲉ ⲡⲧⲙⲡⲧⲭⲁⲥⲓ̇-
ϩⲏⲧ of devil, Mus 42 213 ⲡⲥⲉⲍⲓⲥⲧⲁⲍⲉ...ⲛⲧⲉⲟⲅⲟⲩ.
ϣⲱⲡⲉ ⲛⲧⲡⲓⲥⲧⲓⲥ.

ογⲁⲥϭⲉ *S*, ογⲉⲥⲟⲅⲓ *F* nn f, *idleness*: Ex 21 19 (*B*
ⲕ.), Eccl 10 18 *SF* ἀργεία; Sh(?)ViK 9317 Christ's
birth dispelled ⲡⲁⲥϩⲉⲥ ⲙⲡⲟⲩ. ⲙⲡϣⲁϥ, BM 1089
ⲡⲉϩⲟⲟⲩ ⲡⲟⲩⲁⲥⲃⲉ.

ογⲁⲥϩ *S*, -ⲥϩ, ογⲱⲥϩ *A* *v* ογⲱϣⲥ.

ογⲁⲁⲧ̇ *S*, ογⲁⲧ̇ *B*, ογⲁⲉⲧ̇, -ⲉⲉⲧ̇ *AF* *v* ογⲁⲁ̇.

ογⲁⲓⲧ, ογⲟⲉⲓⲧ *v* ⲁⲩⲏⲧ *s f*.

ογⲉⲧ *v* ογⲱⲱⲧⲉ (ογⲱⲧ) & ογⲏⲧⲉ.

ογⲏⲧ nn *v* ογⲏⲧⲉ vb.

ογⲉⲓⲧ *S* nn m, place or machine where ass works:
BMis 485 man had ass ⲉϥⲣ ϩⲱⲃ ⲛϩⲏⲧϥ ϩⲁⲡⲟⲩ., *ib*
ⲁⲡⲉⲓⲱ ϩⲉ ϩⲁⲣⲁⲧϥ ⲙⲡⲟⲩ. ⲁϥⲙⲟⲩ.

ογⲟⲉⲓⲧ *S* nn m, *pillar*: Ge 19 26 (*B* ⲑⲟⲩⲟϯ), Nu
33 52 (var & *B* = Gk) στήλη; ShP 131⁴ 154 corpse
is as ογⲟⲩ. ⲡⲕⲁϩ. In name(?): Παπουάειτ (Preisigke); in place-name ⲡⲟⲩⲟⲉⲓⲧ, ⲫⲟⲩⲱⲓⲧ, ⲡⲟⲩⲁⲓⲧ,
but *cf* above ⲁⲩⲏⲧ *s f*.

ογⲱⲧ *SB* (rare) DM, ογⲉⲧ-, ογⲉⲧ̇ *S* vb intr,
a *be raw, fresh* (opp dried), *green*: Ex 12 9 *SB*, Z 314
ⲁⲃ ⲉϥⲟⲩ. ὠμός; Lu 23 31 (*B* ⲗⲏⲕ), GMir 119 ox-
hide ⲉⲧⲟⲩ. ὑγρός, Glos 235 ⲗⲁⲙϫⲁⲧⲏ ⲉⲃⲟⲩ. ὑγρόπισσα; Ge 30 37 *B* χλωρός; R 1 4 31 ⲉⲣⲉⲃⲓⲛⲑⲟⲓⲛⲟⲛ

ⲉⲟⲩ. *virens*; ShC 73 173 ϩⲁⲗⲱⲙ ⲉϥⲟⲩ. opp ⲉϥϣⲟⲟⲩⲉ, ⲉϥⲙⲟⲗϩ, ShP 130² 27 ⲃⲱ ⲡⲟⲩϩⲟⲟⲧⲉ ⲉⲥⲟⲩ.,
ShCai 8007 ⲁϥ ⲉⲅⲟⲩ. ⲉⲩϯ ⲉⲡⲗⲱⲙⲥ, Cat 178 *B* ⲧⲉⲃⲧ
ⲉϥⲟⲩ., MG 25 236*B* ϣⲁⲣ...ⲉϥⲟⲩ. (*cf* ϣⲁⲁⲣ), PMéd
131 ⲁⲡⲓⲕⲁⲙ ⲉϥⲟⲩ., *ib* 278 ⲑⲏⲡ ⲉϥⲟⲩ., DM 9 2 *p k*
ⲟⲩ. *fresh, strong bull*. **b** *be, make soft* (same?): C 89
183 *B* brethren ⲟⲩ. ⲉⲑⲃⲉⲧⲟⲩⲙⲉⲧⲁⲙⲉⲗⲉⲥ *so that he
could not re-establish them* ⲉⲟⲃⲉⲛⲃⲱⲗ ⲉⲃⲟⲗ *wherein they were*; tr: Job 23 16 ογⲉⲧ- (*B* diff) μα-
λακύνειν; ShA 2 340 hearts ογⲉⲧⲟⲩ ϩⲛⲟⲩⲙⲉⲧⲁ̇-
ⲛⲟⲓⲁ.

ογⲟ(ⲟ)ⲧⲉ *S*, ογⲁⲧⲉ *SᵃA*, ογⲟϯ, ⲃⲟ. *B*, ογⲁⲁϯ *F*
nn m, *greens, herbs*: Ge 9 3 *SB*, Pro 15 17 *SA*, Mt
13 32 *SBF*, JA '75 5 241 *S* eat ϩⲉⲡⲟⲩ. λάχανον, Z
354 *S* ογ. ⲡⲟⲩⲱⲙ λεπτολ.; Va 61 27 *B* ογ....ⲡⲁⲅⲥⲟ
ⲙⲙⲱⲟⲩ βοτάνη; Deu 28 33 *B* (prob *l* as var ϩⲱϯ,
S ϩⲱⲧ) ἐκφόριον; R 1 4 36 *S* ογⲉⲧⲟⲩⲱⲧ ⲉⲃⲟⲗ
ϩⲛⲡⲉⲓⲟ. *oleribus virens*; P 44 82 *S* ⲡⲟⲩ. بقل = 43
57 خضراوات; K 194 *B* ⲡⲓⲟⲩ. ʼ ﻩﻨﺪﺑﺎ; ShP 129¹² 10
S ϩⲉⲡⲟⲩ. ϩⲱⲥ ⲉⲡⲧⲁϭ ⲉⲅⲡⲟⲥⲉ, Miss 4 533 *S* sim =
Va ar 172 31 خضر المطبخ = MG 17 567 ﺻﻠﻴﻖ (*l* ʼ س.),
RE 9 150 (15 10) *S* ογ. ⲡⲛⲓⲥⲉ, CO 153 *S* am sending ⲡⲓⲕⲟⲩⲓ ⲡⲟⲩ., *ib* 371 *Sᵃ* sim ογⲁⲧⲉ, ShC 73 212
S ϩⲉⲡⲟⲩ. ⲡⲟⲩⲱⲙ *edible herbs*, C 41 13 *B*, DeV 2 182
B & Rec 6 179 *B* ⲃⲟ. = BMar 214 *S* ⲃⲟⲧⲁⲡⲏ, sim
ShBerlOr 1611 7 370 *S* ϩ(ⲉ)ⲛⲣⲟⲟⲩ ⲡⲟⲩⲱⲙ ογ.,
ShP 130² 27 *S* ⲃⲱ ⲡⲟⲩ., PMich 3593 *S* sim, Ostr
penes GJéquier *S* ⲙⲁⲓⲣⲉ ⲡⲟⲩ., TurM 5 *S* ϣⲟⲗ ⲡⲗⲁ̇-
ϫⲁⲡⲟⲛ ϣⲟⲗ ⲡⲟⲩ., BAp 11 *S* ϣⲏⲛ ⲡⲟⲩ., C 41 63 *B*
sim, Miss 4 591 *S* sim ⲙⲡⲟⲩ., ShHT *E* 342 *S* ⲡⲣⲱ̇-
ⲙⲉ ⲙⲡⲟⲩ., DeV *l c* ⲣⲱⲙⲓ ⲛϭⲙⲉ ⲡⲟⲩ., WS 181 *S*
ⲡⲁⲡⲟⲩ.; ⲙⲁ ⲡⲟⲩ. *S*, *herb-garden*: Si 24 31 κῆπος; Is 1 30 (*B*=Gk) παράδεισος; ShC 73 98 ⲡⲙⲁ
ⲙⲡⲟⲩ., *ib* 211 (not Sh) in refectory ⲙⲁ ⲛⲭⲟⲡ ⲛ ⲙⲁ
ⲡⲟⲩ.; ⲥⲁ ⲡⲟⲩ., *herb-seller, gardener*: Mor 44 8
S ⲟⲩⲕⲟⲙⲁⲣⲓⲧⲏⲥ (*v* KKS 212) ⲛⲥ., DeV 1 61 *B* sim
ⲉϥϯ ⲟⲩ. ⲉⲃⲟⲗ. In place-name: ⲡⲧⲟⲟⲩ ⲛϭⲓⲡⲟⲩⲟ̇-
ⲟⲧⲉ (var ϭⲓⲟⲩ. Mor 48 51) = ⲡⲭⲉⲗⲃⲁϩ (C 43 154).
Cf ? شنوﻩ (Amél *Géog* 455). *Cf* ⲡⲟⲃ̇ⲗⲉ.

ογⲟⲧⲟⲩⲉⲧ*SB*, ογⲁⲧ.*A* (nn), ⲃⲟⲃⲉⲧ*B*(nn), ογⲉⲧ-
ογⲱⲧ† *SSʃ*(nn)*B*(nn)vb intr *S*, *become, be green, pal-
lid*: ViK 9551 ⲁⲡⲉϥϩⲟ ογ. ⲁϥⲣ ⲑⲉ ⲡⲟⲩⲛⲏⲅⲍⲓⲟⲛ from
fear; BMar 78 sim of dying man, BHom 123 sim
ϣⲁϥⲟⲩⲟⲧⲟⲩⲉⲓⲧ, P 43 32 ⲱⲡⲉ ⲡⲟⲩ. حجر المس; qual
(oftenest): Ge 30 37 *SB*, Is 27 11 *SB*, Ap 6 8 *SB*
χλωρός, Lev 13 49 *SB* χλωρίζειν, Ps 36 2 *SB* χλόη,
P 131¹ 32 *S* ⲡⲧⲏϭ ⲉϥⲟⲩ. χλοερός; Zech 14 12 *S*
(ROC 20 55, var & *A* ογⲉⲓⲧⲉ, *B* ⲃⲱⲗ ⲉⲃⲟⲗ) τήκειν,
2 Kg 13 4 *S* ἀσθενής (var συντήκ.); R 1 4 37 *S* ⲡⲉϥϩⲟ
[ⲟ]ⲩⲉ[ⲧⲟⲩⲱⲧ] *luridus*; Ming 315 *S* bodies turned to
gold ⲉϥⲟⲩ., Blake 236 *S* sardius's colour ⲥⲛⲕ ⲉⲡⲉⲧⲟ-
ⲟⲩ., ViK 9549 29 *S* vomits poisons ⲉⲅⲟⲩ. ⲛⲟⲉ ⲛ̇-
ⲟⲩϫⲡⲏ, Mor 44 26 *S*◁ⲉϥⲟⲩ. ⲛⲟⲉ ⲛⲡⲉⲧⲁⲥⲕⲉⲓ, Va 57

167 B ⲕⲗⲁⲟⲥ... ⲣⲱⲟⲩⲧ ⲟⲩⲟⲅ ⲉϥⲃⲉⲧⲟⲩⲱⲧ; as nn m *SS/AB, greenness, herbs, pallor*: Ps 67 14 *SB* χλω-ρότης, Nu 22 4 *S*(*B* vb), Pro 27 25 *SA* χλωρός, Job 38 27 *B* ⲃⲟⲧⲃⲉⲧ, Ps 89 5 *SS/*ⲟⲩⲉⲧ(ⲟⲩ)ⲱⲧ (Cai Copt Mus, *B* = Gk) χλόη; Deu 28 22 *SB* ὤχρα; BAp 53 *S* ⲡⲉⲓⲟⲩ. ἄνθος: Bodl Hunt 365 118 *B* ⲟⲩ. نصر صفرة; ShViK 9298 *S* ⲡⲓⲟⲩ. ⲉⲧⲟⲩ.†, ShIF 102 خضرة اليوناني; *S* signs of sickness ⲡⲗⲏⲧⲛ, ⲉⲗⲉⲗⲕⲏⲙⲉ, ⲟⲩ., ⲍⲃⲓⲛ, Miss 4 762 *S* ⲛⲓⲉⲡⲧⲏⲅ ⲙ̅ⲡⲉⲓⲟⲩ., ViK 9736 *S* ϯⲟⲩⲅⲱ, ⲟⲩ., ϣⲏⲡ, MG 25 146 *B* ⲡⲓⲟⲩ. ⲡⲉⲙⲡⲓϥⲣⲏⲣⲓ, *ib* 236 *B* sheep eat ⲟⲩ., BMis 435 *S* ⲡⲟⲩ. ⲡⲁⲥⲕⲏⲥⲓⲥ, R 2 4 58 *S* ⲡⲟⲩ. ⲡⲉⲧⲉⲉⲧ (*cf ib* 2 1 10).

ⲟⲩⲱⲧ *SAA²BF*, f -ⲧⲉ(rare)*SA²* adj, *single, alone, any, one & same*: Ps 26 4 *S*(*B* ⲟⲩⲁⲓ), Ez 23 2 *SB*, Am 6 9 *AB*, Jo 18 14 *SA²B*, Ro 12 4 *SBF*, Z 317 *S* ⲟⲩⲥⲟⲡ ⲡⲟⲩ.(*v* ⲗⲁ-)εἷς, Sa 19 15 *S*, Ro 9 21 *S*(*B* ⲣⲱ), 2 Cor 13 11 *SBF*, Cl 7 1 *A* ὁ αὐτός; Sa 18 11 *S* ὅμοιος, Ps 82 5 *S* ϣⲟⲭⲛⲉ ⲡⲟⲩ. *B* ⲅⲏⲧ ⲡⲟⲩ. ὁμόνοια, Ez 1 16 *B* ⲓⲛⲓ ⲡⲟⲩ. ὁμοίωμα; Mt 8 14 *S*(*B* ⲙⲙⲁⲩⲁⲧⲥ) μό-νος, Ps 24 16 *S*(*B* do), Jo 3 16 *SB* ϣⲏⲣⲉ ⲡⲟⲩ. (*F* = Gk) μονογενής, Ps 21 21 *SB* μονόκερως, Mk 9 47 *SF* (*B* ⲙ.) μονόφθαλμος; Pro 1 14 *SAB*, ROC 17 406 *B* ⲟⲩϣⲱ ⲡⲟⲩ. κοινός; Va 57 15 *B* ⲟⲩⲥⲟⲡ ⲡⲟⲩ. ἅπαξ; Cai Euch 467 *B* ⲍⲉⲛⲟⲩⲥⲙⲏ ⲡⲟⲩ. συμφώνως; PS 86 *S* cried out ⲅⲛⲧⲉⲓⲙⲉⲧⲁⲡⲟⲓⲁ ⲡⲟⲩ. saying, ShRE 11 16 *S* ⲟⲩⲉⲓⲙⲉ ⲡⲟⲩ. opp ⲟⲩⲁϣⲏⲛ ⲡⲥⲙⲟⲧ, ShA 1 7 *S* if I dwell ⲅⲛⲣⲉⲡⲧⲟⲡⲟⲥ ⲡⲟⲩ. with men, CA 89 *S* ⲡⲡⲟⲙⲟⲥ ⲡⲟⲩ., Aeg 244 *S* ⲟⲩⲥⲣⲓⲙⲉ ⲡⲟⲩ., Leyd 423 *S* ⲉⲓⲥⲁⲕ ⲁⲛ ⲡⲟⲩ. but much folk, BMis 257 *S* ⲧⲉϥⲟⲩⲉⲣⲏⲧⲉ ⲡⲟⲩ. *one of his feet* hung in stirrup = Mor 30 31 *F*, AP 38 *A²* ⲟⲩⲥⲙⲏ ⲡⲟⲩ., AM 326 *B* ⲕⲉⲅⲱⲃ ⲡⲟⲩ. *another like thing* shall befall, *ib* 135 *B* born of ⲟⲩⲓⲱⲧ ⲡⲉⲙⲟⲩⲙⲁⲩ ⲡⲟⲩ., *ib* 248 *B* ⲫⲁⲡⲓⲣⲁⲛ ⲡⲟⲩ. ⲡⲉⲙⲁⲕ *namesake*; f *SA²*: Br 93 ⲟⲩⲡⲣⲟⲃⲟⲗⲏ ⲡⲟⲩ., J 6 11, 85 8 ⲟⲩⲁⲡⲁ.ⲕⲏ ⲡⲟⲩ., CO 36 ϯⲕⲱⲗⲏ ⲡⲟⲩ. (*bis*), ST 268 ⲟⲩϭⲓⲝ ⲡⲛⲟⲩ.; without ⲡ- *S* (archaic): Ps 24 16 ϣⲏⲣⲉ ⲟⲩ., Sa 5 15 ⲅⲟⲟⲩ ⲟⲩ., *ib* 17 13 ⲟⲩϣⲏ ⲟⲩ., Ap 18 16 ⲟⲩⲛⲟⲩ ⲟⲩ. (all var ⲡ-), Ryl 127 ⲡⲓⲧⲙⲉ ⲟⲩ.

ⲟⲩⲁ ⲡⲟⲩ. *SB, single one, each one*: Ez 37 19 *B*, Ro 5 15 *S*(*B* om ⲡⲟⲩ.) εἷς, Jos 8 17 *S* neg οὐδείς; Phil 4 2 *S*(*B* ⲣⲱ) ὁ αὐ.; PS 17 *S* ⲁⲡⲟⲛ ⲟⲩⲁ ⲡ., ShC 42 136 *S* no love among them ⲉⲅⲟⲩⲛ ⲉⲟⲩⲁ ⲡ., AM 7 *B* ⲙⲡⲟⲩⲥⲉϫⲡ ⲟⲩⲁⲓ ⲡ.; ⲙⲡⲧⲟⲩⲁ ⲡ. *S*: BMis 130 bound together ⲅⲛⲟⲩⲙ.; ⲣ ⲟⲩⲁ ⲡ., *make one*: Br 248 *S* ⲁⲩⲣ. ⲧⲏⲣⲟⲩ, Aeg 237 *S* ⲉϥⲛⲁⲣⲧⲏⲣⲧⲛ ⲡⲟⲩⲁ ⲡ.; ⲥ ⲙⲛ-, ⲡⲉⲙ-: BM 174 2 *S* ϥⲟ ⲡ[ⲟⲩ]ⲁ [ⲡ]ⲟⲩ. [ⲙⲡⲡⲉⲓⲱⲧ] συνάπτεσθαι dat; ShRyl 71 94 *S* ⲁⲧⲉⲧⲛⲣ. ⲙ̅ⲡⲡⲍⲓⲁⲃⲟⲗⲟⲥ, Pcod 43 *S* divinity ⲟ ⲡⲟⲩⲁ ⲡ. ⲙⲡⲧⲙⲡⲧⲣⲱⲙⲉ, DeV 2 115 *B* ⲁⲓⲥ ⲡⲟⲩⲁⲓ ⲡ. ⲡⲉⲙⲁϥ.

V AZ 47 7.

ⲟⲩⲱⲧ, *it is different v* ⲟⲩⲱⲱⲧⲉ.

ⲟⲩⲱⲧ, *fat v* ⲱⲧ.

ⲟⲩⲧⲉ- (ⲟⲩⲍⲉ- *SF*), ⲟⲩⲧⲱⲍ *SAA²BFO* prep, *between, among*: Lev 23 5 *S*(*B* ⲍⲉⲛⲑⲙⲏϯ ⲡⲧⲉ), Is 22 11 *B*(*S* ⲡⲧⲙⲏⲧⲉ ⲡ-), 1 Cor 6 5 *B*(*S* do) ἀνὰ μέσον; Ac 12 6 *B*(*S* do) μεταξύ; Deu 29 21 *S*(*B* ⲉⲃⲟⲗ ⲍⲉⲛ-), Eph 5 14 *S*(*B* do) ἐκ; Ge 3 14 *SB* ἀπό; Nu 22 24 *S*(*B* ⲍⲉⲛ-) ἐν; Est 3 1 *S*, 1 Cor 15 9 *F*(*S* ⲉⲃⲟⲗ ⲟⲩ., *B* ⲡ-) gen; Va 57 278 *B* even in market place canst ⲫⲟⲡⲅⲕ ⲟⲩⲧⲱⲕ ⲙⲙⲁⲅⲁⲧⲕ συστρέφειν σεαυτόν; BMis 537 *S* David ψάλλει ⲟⲩ. ⲡⲁⲓⲕⲁⲓⲟⲥ ⲧⲏⲣⲟⲩ *prae*; BG 89 *S* ⲟⲩⲁⲓⲁⲫⲟⲣⲁ... ⲟⲩⲧⲱⲟⲩ, Mani 1 *A²*, ⲉⲅⲉⲓϣⲉ ⲙⲙⲁⲥ (*sc* head) ⲟⲩ. ⲡⲗⲏⲛϣⲉ, MIF 9 56 *S* ⲙⲡ ⲡⲱⲣϫ ⲟⲩⲧⲟⲟⲩ ⲅⲓⲟⲩⲥⲟⲡ, BMar 231 *S* chosen ⲟⲩ. ⲡⲕⲟⲥⲙⲟⲥ ⲧⲏⲣϥ, Mor 663 *A* 140 *S* face ⲙⲡⲉⲥⲏⲧ ⲟⲩ. ⲡⲉϥⲡⲁⲧ, C 86 328 *B* ⲁⲡⲓⲣⲱⲃ ⲑⲱϣ ⲟⲩⲧⲱⲟⲩ; c suff & ⲡ-: Ex 26 28 *S*(*B* ⲉⲃ. ⲍⲉⲛⲑⲙ.), Job 9 33 *B*(*S* ⲡⲧⲙ.) ἀνὰ μ., Ez 10 6 *B* ἐκ μ.; Am 3 2 *S*(*B* ⲉⲃ. ⲍ.) ἐκ; Sa 5 3 *B*(*S* ⲅⲣⲁⲓ ⲅⲡ-) ἑαυτοῖς; PS 356 *S* ⲟⲩⲧⲱ-ⲟⲩ ⲡⲏⲧⲟⲡⲟⲥ, Mani 2 *A²* ⲁⲩⲥⲁⲧⲙⲉⲥ ⲟⲩⲧⲱ(ⲟ)ⲩ ⲡ-ⲡϣⲁⲙ, AZ 21 94 *O* Anubis ⲉⲧⲃⲁⲓⲧⲱⲣ ⲟⲩⲧⲱⲟⲩ (ⲡ)-ⲡⲧⲉⲣ ⲣⲥⲓⲙⲉ; c ⲧⲙⲛⲧⲉ, ⲑⲙ. *SAB*: Lev 20 25 *B* (*S* ⲉⲃ. ⲅⲡⲧⲙ.), Is 57 5 *B*(*S* ⲡⲧⲙ.), Zech 5 9 *SAB* ἀνὰ μ., Ge 1 6 *B* ἐν μ.; c ⲙⲡ-, ⲡⲉⲙ- *SBF, between...and*: Ge 9 13 *B*(*S* ⲅⲡⲧⲙ. ⲙⲡⲧⲙ.), 1 Kg 24 13 *S*(*B* ⲟⲩ. ⲟⲩ.), Ez 8 3 *B* ἀνὰ μ....καί; Mt 18 15 *B* (*S* ⲟⲩ. ⲟⲩ.), Jo 4 31 *BF*(*SA²* om) μετ.; Mk 9 2 *F*(*S* ⲙⲁⲩⲁⲁⲥ, *B* ⲥⲁⲡⲥⲁ ⲙⲙⲁⲩⲁⲧⲥ) κατ᾽ ἰδίαν, Va 57 187 *B* ⲟⲩⲧⲱϣ ⲡⲉⲙⲁϥ ⲡⲉⲙⲡⲉϥϣⲫⲏⲣ ἰδίᾳ ἑκάστῳ; Ac 27 5 *B*(*S* ⲡ- ⲙⲡ-) κατὰ...καί; 2 Kg 21 15 *S* dat μετά, Jo 3 25 *F*(*SB* ⲉⲃⲟⲗ ⲅⲡ-) ἐκ...μετά; 1 Cor 14 28 *B*(*S* ⲙⲡ- ⲙⲡ-) dat dat, 1 Tim 2 5 *B*(*S* ⲡ- ⲙⲡ-) gen gen; Lev 5 21 *B*, Col 3 13 (*S* Gk om) πρός; PS 268 *S* ⲥⲟⲟⲅⲉ ⲙⲙⲟⲕ ⲟⲩⲧⲱⲕ ⲡⲉⲙⲁϥ, Mun 70 *S* hanged ⲟⲩϫⲉⲧⲡⲉ ⲙⲡⲡⲕⲁⲅ, Miss 4 553 *S* ⲉⲩⲅⲟⲭⲅⲝ ⲙⲙⲟⲩ ⲟⲩⲧⲱϣ ⲙ̅ⲡ̅ⲡⲭⲟ ⲥⲛⲧⲉ = C 89 75 *B* ⲟⲩ[ⲧⲉ]ϫⲟⲓ ⲃ̄, Mani H 60 *A²* ⲟⲩⲧⲱϣ ⲡⲡⲁⲍⲓⲙⲱⲡ ⲙⲡ[, MG 25 179 *B* covenant ⲟⲩⲧⲱⲡ ⲡⲉⲙⲫϯ ⲡⲉⲙⲡⲉⲡⲉⲣⲛⲟⲩ, C 86 139 *B* if he let him go ⲟⲩⲧⲱϥ ⲡⲉⲙⲁϥ *privately*, BAp 173 *S* ⲣⲓⲙⲉ ⲟⲩⲧⲱⲕ ⲙⲡⲡⲉⲭ̅ⲥ̅; ⲟⲩ...ⲙⲡⲟⲩ. or ⲁⲩⲱ ⲟⲩ. *SABF*, as last: Ge 3 15 *B*(*S* ⲅⲡⲧⲙ. ⲙⲡ-), Ex 26 33 *SB*, Ez 4 3 *S*(*B* ⲍⲉⲡⲧⲉⲕⲙ. ⲡⲉⲙⲑⲙ.), Zech 5 9 ⲟⲩ. ⲧⲙ. ⲡ- ⲁⲩⲱ ⲟⲩ. ⲧⲙ. ⲡ- *SAB* ἀνὰ μ. κ. ἀνὰ μ.; ⲟⲩ....ⲟⲩ.; BMis 295 *S* ⲟⲩ.ⲧⲡⲉ ⲟⲩ.ⲡⲕⲁⲅ (var 239 ⲟⲩ. ⲙⲡ-), Mor 30 31 *F* sim ⲟⲩⲍⲉ, Mich 136 3 *S* ⲉⲓⲛⲏⲩ...ⲟⲩ. ⲕⲁϣ ⲟⲩ. ⲕⲁⲙ; ⲟⲩⲧⲱⲍ...ⲟⲩⲧⲱⲍ: 1 Kg 24 13 *S* ⲟⲩⲧⲱⲕ ⲟⲩⲧⲱⲓ(*B* ⲟⲩ. ⲡⲉⲙ-)ἀνὰ μ. καί; Mt 18 15 *S*(*B* do) μετ. κ.; Ez 43 8 *S*(ShA 1 235) *B* συνεχόμενος...κ. inter...et; TU 43 25 *A* ⲟⲩ]ⲧⲱⲕ ⲟⲩⲧⲱⲍ, BAp 93 *S* ϫⲡⲟⲩϥ ⲟⲩⲧⲱⲕ ⲟⲩⲧⲱϥ *between yourselves*.

ⲉⲃⲟⲗ ⲟⲩ. *SA²BF, from among, between*: Ps 30 12

B, Dan 3 32 B, Lu 13 2 B (all S = Gk) παρά; Job 37
9 S(B eß. ϩεη-), Mk 7 33 S(B eß. ϩα-) ἀπό; Ez 38
8 B ἐκ, ib 28 16 S(B ϩεпоⲙ. п-) ἐκ μέσου; Mt 13
32 BF(S e-) gen; ShA 2 4 S sinner eß. оγ. ⲣⲱⲙⲉ
ⲛⲓⲙ eϥoγaaß, ManiH 15 A² cut them down like
ⲡⲧⲏϭ aß. оγ. ⲛⲥⲟⲩ, BM 215 90 S if souls sinless
how shall they p ⲛⲟⲃⲉ eß. оγ. ⲛⲁⲓ ⲉⲙⲡⲁⲧⲟⲩⲉⲓ ⲉⲛ-
ⲥⲱⲙⲁ?, MG 25 328 B blessed eß. оγ. ⲡⲕⲁϩⲓ ⲧⲏⲣϥ
(ROC 17 359 ﻣﺪ ﻟﻜﻞ).

ϩⲣⲁⲓ оγ. S: ShMIF 23 156 is there none among
you ⲉⲣⲉⲡⲉϥⲏⲓ ϩ. оγ. ⲧⲉⲕⲕⲗⲏⲥⲓⲁ?, ShIF 163 ⲡⲝⲓⲟⲩⲉ ... ϩⲣⲁⲓ оγⲧⲱϥ ⲛⲡⲉⲧⲛⲙⲉⲥⲟⲏⲧ, ib have sinned
ϩⲣⲁⲓ оγⲧⲱϥ ⲙⲡⲣⲟ.

ογⲏⲧⲉ S nn f, lightning (?), calamity : Is 30 30
п оγоγ. ⲉⲝⲡ-(P 44 113 ﺻﺎﻋﻘﺔ, F ϣⲱⲗ, B ⲕⲉⲣⲁⲅⲛⲟⲥ) κεραυνοῦν; ShP 130⁴ 100 ⲡⲥⲁϩⲟⲩ ⲙⲡⲧⲟⲩ.
upon false prophets, ShWess 9 87 ⲛⲧⲁⲧⲉⲓⲛⲟϭ ⲡⲟⲩ.
ⲉⲓ upon house of Eli.

ογⲏⲧⲉ, -ⲉⲧⲉ, -ⲉⲧ S vb tr, remit, abandon : Sh
Wess 18 127 on forgiving poor debtor ⲉⲓⲕⲱ ⲙⲙⲟⲟⲩ
ⲛⲁϥ ⲉⲃⲟⲗ ⲏ ⲉⲓⲛⲟⲩ. ⲡⲁⲣⲛⲁⲁϥ ⲝⲉⲙⲡⲧⲁϥ ⲉϯ, ViK
4701 ⲧⲣⲉⲛⲕⲁ ϥⲟⲓ ⲉⲃⲟⲗ...ⲧⲛⲟⲩⲏⲧⲉ ⲛⲕⲁⲣⲡⲟⲥ ⲉⲧϣⲓ-
ⲱϥ; intr c e-: Hall 115 ϯⲟⲩⲉⲧⲉ ⲉⲣⲟⲟⲩ ⲛⲁⲕ (sic),
ib 113 ⲉⲓⲟⲩⲉⲧ (sic) ⲛⲁⲕ ⲉⲡϣⲱⲛ ⲛⲣⲁⲧ & may not sue
thee for it; as nn -ⲏⲧ, remission (?): MG 17 313
twice yearly ϩⲙⲡⲁⲥⲭⲁ ⲙⲡⲛⲟϭ ⲡⲟⲩ. (п)ⲡⲗⲟⲅⲟⲥ
μεγάλη ἄφεσις τῶν λόγων = ib 661 ﻓﺼﻞ ﻟﻠﺨﺮﻳﻒ autumn,
ib 333 days at year's end called ⲡⲉϩⲟⲟⲩ ⲙⲡⲟⲩ. when
accounts rendered (referring to ib 327 ⲡⲡⲁⲥⲭⲁ &
ⲕⲁⲓⲣⲟⲥ ⲡⲡⲧⲉⲡⲛⲏⲙⲁ = ib 639 ﻋﻴﺪ ﻟﺼﻠﻴﺐ). Cf ?
ογⲱⲱⲧⲉ.

ογⲉⲓⲧⲉ, -ⲉⲉⲧⲉ S, -ⲓⲧⲉ SA, ⲃⲓⲧⲉ S, -ϯ B, ογⲉⲓⲧⲓ
F vb intr, waste away, dry up : Zech 14 12 S(P 44
116, var ROC 20 55 ογⲟⲧⲟⲩⲉⲧ)A(B ⲃⲱⲗ ⲉⲃⲟⲗ) τήκειν ﺟﻒ, cit ShC 73 138 S -ⲉⲉⲧⲉ & ShIF 186 S, Gu
92 S tongue ⲛⲧⲁϥⲟⲩ. ⲉⲧ[ⲃⲉ]ϯⲧⲁⲓⲃⲉ(l ⲓⲁ.), Tri 587 S
ⲕⲗⲁⲇⲟⲥ...ⲛⲥⲉⲧⲙⲡⲟⲩ. ﺟﺒﻲ; tr: ShRyl 68 261 S
ⲙⲡⲉϥⲟⲩ. ⲙⲡⲗⲁⲥ of blasphemers; c ⲉⲃⲟⲗ sim,
intr: Job 7 5 B(S diff) φύρεσθαι, Lag ﺷﺘﻞ, Baudissin ﻧﻤﺮ; Kr 1 6 S ⲁⲛⲧⲙⲉ ⲥⲱⲣⲙ ϩⲁⲡⲙⲟⲟⲩ (п)-
ⲧⲁϥⲃⲓⲧⲉ ⲉⲃⲟⲗ (sic), BKU 1 26 (8116 b)F recipe ⲗⲉϩ-
ⲙⲉⲥ[ϣ]ⲁⲡⲧⲉⲥⲟⲩ. ⲉⲃⲁⲗ[; tr S (Sh): C 42 162
ⲁⲩⲟⲩ. ⲉⲃ. ⲛⲥⲁⲣⲝ, P 130² 132 God ⲛⲁⲟⲩ. ⲉⲃ. ⲛⲧⲉ-
ⲧⲛⲯⲩⲭⲏ in fire.

ογⲟⲟⲧⲉ nn v ογⲱⲧ be raw.

ογ(ω)ⲱⲧⲉ SA²(?), ογⲱϯBF, ογⲱⲱϯF, ογⲁⲁⲧⲉ-
SF, ογⲁⲧⲉ-, ογⲁⲧ- F, ⲃⲱⲧ- S, ογⲉⲧ- B, ογⲟ(ⲟ)ⲧ⸗ S,
ογⲁ(ⲁ)ⲧ⸗ SF, ογⲟⲧ⸗, ⲃⲟⲧ⸗ B, ογⲉⲧ⸗ F, ογⲟⲟⲧⲉ† S,
ογⲟⲧ† B vb, send intr: PMich 577 F ογⲱⲧⲓ ⲧⲁⲃⲁⲩ,
Pap penes FlPetrie(1908)F ⲧⲉⲣⲟⲩⲉϣ ⲧⲁⲧⲁⲁϥ ογⲱ-

ωϯ ⲛⲉⲓ, BM 594 S ογⲱⲧⲉ ϩⲁⲧⲥⲛⲧⲉ ⲛⲣⲟⲩⲗⲟⲅ-
ⲕⲟⲧⲥⲉ : tr : Jud 6 14S(var ⲝⲟⲟⲩ) ἐξαποστέλλειν;
Nu 22 13 S (var & B ⲕⲱ) ἀφιέναι; RE 11 44 S
ογⲁⲁⲧⲉ ⲡⲉⲕϣⲁⲝⲉ ⲛⲁⲓ, ViK 4745 S ογⲁⲁⲧ(ⲧ) ϣⲁⲓ-
ⲧⲁⲗⲟϥ, BM 706 F ογⲱϯ ⲙⲡⲗⲱⲙⲓ ⲛⲏⲓ, ib 585 12 F
ⲛⲕⲟⲩⲁⲧⲉ ⲑⲁⲡⲏⲗ, CMSS 41 F ⲁⲓⲟⲩⲁⲁⲧⲉ v̅ ⲉ, Sph
10 4 F ογⲁⲧⲉ ⲛⲥϩⲉⲓ ⲛⲏⲓ, BM 592 12 F ογⲁⲧ ⲛⲉ-
ⲛⲟⲩⲅ, Kr 3 F ογⲁⲁⲧⲥ ⲛⲏⲓ, BM 591 F ογⲁⲧⲟⲩ ϩⲟⲩⲛ
ⲛⲉⲓ, ib 659 F ογⲉⲧⲥ ⲛⲉⲃ; qual S, separated, choice :
Hall 4 ογⲧⲟⲉⲓⲧ ⲉϥⲟⲩ.† ⲉⲝⲡⲧⲙⲛⲧⲉⲃⲓⲏⲛ of my youth.

With following preposition. c e- (all qual),
different from, surpassing : Mt 12 12 B(S ϣⲟⲃⲉ),
1 Cor 15 41 B(S do, F ογⲁⲧⲉϥ) διαφέρειν; Mt 6 25
S(var ογⲟⲧⲃ)B πλεῖον εἶναι; ib 10 24 B(S o ⲛⲛⲟϭ
e-), Philem 16 B(S ⲛⲁⲁ⸗ e-) ὑπέρ; AM 59 B ογⲙⲁ-
ⲧⲟⲥ ⲉϥⲟⲩ. ⲉⲣⲟⲕ (cf ογⲱⲧⲃ), C 43 36 B v ⲗⲁϩ-
ⲗϩ; c ⲉⲣⲟⲧⲉ- B sim : ib 113 tortures ογ.† ⲁⲛ ⲉϩ.
ⲛⲓϭⲓⲥⲓ; c ογⲧⲉ- B, separate between : Hos 13 15
(A ϯ ⲡⲱⲣⲝ) διαστέλλειν ἀνὰ μέσον; Is 59 2 (S ⲁϩⲉ
ⲣⲁⲧ⸗) διαστάναι ἀν.; ⲝⲓⲛⲟⲩ. ογⲧⲉ-: Ez 42 20 m
(HCons, Tatt & S ⲡⲱⲣⲝ) διαστ. ἀν.

With following adverb. c ⲉⲃⲟⲗ SB, separate
out : Ex 19 23 B ογⲉⲧ-, Lu 6 22 B(S п.) ἀφορίζειν,
Is 45 18 B ⲃⲟⲧ⸗ (S do) διορ.; Lev 18 19 B(S o ⲛⲕⲉⲥⲁ) ἐν χωρισμῷ; Deu 10 8B(S ⲡⲟⲩϩⲉ ⲉⲃⲟⲗ) διαστέλλειν; send forth : 1 Kg 20 21 S (var ⲝⲟⲟⲩ) ἀποστ.;
ib 24 20 S ἐκπέμπειν, Lev 16 10 S ⲙⲁ ⲡⲟⲩⲟⲱⲧⲉ ⲉⲃ.
(var ογⲱⲧϥ, B ⲡⲓϭⲓⲟⲩ ⲉⲃ.) ἀποπομπή, ib 8 S(B ϯ
ⲧⲟⲧ⸗ ⲉⲃ.) ἀποπομπαῖος; ShA 2 6 = HT C 1 S stone
falling on them ⲛⲁⲟⲩⲧⲟⲩ ⲉⲃ.; ⲉⲃ. п-: Lev 20
24 B(S п.) διορ. ἀπό; Lu 22 41 B(S ογⲉ) ἀποσπᾶν
ἀπό; Deu 15 13 S(B ογⲱⲣⲡ ⲉⲃ.) ἐξαποστ. ἀπό; ⲉⲃ.
ογⲧⲉ- B : Ex 26 33 (S ϯ ογⲱϣ ογⲧⲉ-) διορ. ἀνὰ μ.,
Lev 20 25 (S ⲡⲱⲣⲝ ⲉⲃ.) ἀφορ. ἀν.; ⲉⲃ. ϩⲁ- B : Is 45
25 (S do) διορ. ἀπό; ⲉⲃ. ϩⲉп- B : ib 29 22 (S do)
ἀφορ. ἐκ; ⲉⲃ. ϩⲓⲝⲛ-: Pro 8 27 B(SA ⲡⲱⲣϣ ⲉⲃ.)
ἀφορ. ἐπί; Kr 228 S let him come ⲧⲁⲃⲱⲧ ⲧⲁⲡⲟⲩ-
ⲑⲏⲕⲉ ⲉⲃ. ϩⲓⲝⲱϥ; as nn m B, separation : Lev
10 14 (S = Gk) ἀφαίρεμα; ⲝⲓⲛⲟⲩ. ⲉⲃ. B sim :
Job 37 16 (S ⲙⲡⲉ) διάκρισις; Ez 20 31 m(PascLect,
Tatt S diff) ἀφορισμός; ib 43 21 f (HCons) ἀποχωρί-
ζεσθαι; ⲙⲉⲧⲁⲧⲟⲩ. ⲉⲃ. B, not being separate : Cat
186 ⲁⲓⲇⲓⲟⲥ ⲉⲧⲉϥⲁⲓⲡⲉ ϩⲉⲛⲟⲩⲙ.

ⲣⲙⲡⲟⲩ. A² messenger (?): Mani H 92.
Cf ? ογⲏⲧⲉ remit.

ογⲱⲧ S(rare)A², -ⲟⲧ B, -ⲉⲧ SB, -ⲁⲧ F impers vb,
it is different (rarely bibl) : Ez 3 6 S(B diff) ογⲉⲧ
ⲧⲉⲩⲁⲥⲡⲉ ἀλλόγλωσσος; ib 19 2 B ογⲟⲧⲡⲉ ⲡⲥⲙⲟⲧ
ⲛⲡⲉⲙⲗⲁⲥ (S Gk diff); Br 87 S ⲉⲟⲩⲱⲧ ⲛⲣⲁⲛ ⲙⲡⲟⲩⲁ
ⲡⲟⲩⲁ, PS 238 S ογⲉⲧ ⲡⲧⲩⲡⲟⲥ ⲙⲡⲟⲩⲁ ⲡⲟⲩⲁ, Tst
Ab 253 B ογⲉⲧ ⲡⲓⲡⲓ ⲙⲡⲟⲩⲁⲓ ⲡⲟⲩⲁⲓ, BMis 154 S
оγ. ⲛⲛⲟⲃⲉ ⲛⲛⲟⲃⲉ, Gu 91 S оγ. ⲧⲉϣⲡⲏⲣⲉ ⲙⲡⲛⲁⲩ
ⲉⲧⲉⲙⲙⲁⲩ, Miss 8 27 S оγ. ⲛⲛⲟⲙⲟⲥ ⲡⲧⲉⲕⲕⲗⲏⲥⲓⲁ

(from that of realm); ⲟⲩ....ⲟⲩ., *one* (thing) *is…
another is:* Jo 4 37 *SA²F*(*B* ⲕⲉⲟⲩⲁⲓ), 1 Cor 15 39 *SB*
ἄλλος … ἄλλος; PS 31 *S* ⲟⲩⲉⲧ ⲉⲅⲕⲏⲧ ⲉⲣⲃⲟⲩⲣ ⲟⲩ.
ⲉⲅⲕⲏⲧ ⲉⲟⲩⲡⲁⲙ, ShA 2 4 *S* ⲟⲩⲉⲧ ⲡⲡⲁⲩ ⲡⲉⲡⲓⲧⲓⲙⲁ
ⲟⲩ. ⲡⲡⲁⲩ ⲡⲥⲟⲡⲉ, ShBMOr 8810 453 *S* ⲟⲩⲉⲧ ⲡⲓⲣⲟⲟ-
ⲟⲩ (*sc* Lent) ⲟⲩ. ⲡⲕⲉⲣⲟⲟⲩ ⲧⲏⲣⲟⲩ, Ryl 361 *S* ⲟⲩⲱⲧ
ⲡⲉⲕⲱϫⲉ ⲟⲩⲱⲧ ⲡⲁⲣⲱⲙⲉ ⲛⲓⲙ, Bor 257 36 *S* ⲟⲩⲉⲧ
ⲡⲉⲡⲧⲁⲩⲥⲧⲟⲩ ⲙⲙⲟⲩ ⲟⲩ. ⲡⲉⲧⲛⲏⲩ ⲉⲕⲣⲓⲛⲉ (*cf* BMis
199), MIE 2 342 *B* ⲟⲩⲟⲧ ⲡⲓⲣⲁⲡ of God ⲟⲩ. ⲡⲓⲣ. of
men, Cat 209 *B* ⲟⲩⲉⲧ ⲣⲟ ⲑⲁⲓ ⲟⲩ. ⲣⲟ ⲡⲏ, *ib* 141 ⲟⲩⲟⲧ
ⲣⲟ ⲡⲓ-…ⲟⲩ. ⲣⲟ ⲫⲁⲓ, BMOr 8775 117 = P 54 116 *B*
ⲟⲩⲟϩ ⲣⲟ الخَتَال.

V AZ 63 99 & *cf* ? ⲟⲩⲧⲉ-.

ⲟⲩⲱⲧⲃ̄ (& ⲫ for ⲃ̄ throughout) *SA²FO*, -ⲧⲃⲉ *A*,
-ⲧⲉⲃ *BF*, ⲟⲩⲉⲧⲃ- *S*, ⲟⲩⲉⲧⲉⲃ-, ⲟⲩⲁⲧ. *B*, ⲟⲩⲟⲧⲃⲉ *SB*,
-ⲟⲃⲉ,-ⲧⲡⲉ *B*, ⲟⲩⲁⲧⲃⲉ *SF*, ⲟⲩⲟⲧⲃ̄⁺ *S*, -ⲧⲉⲃ⁺ *SB*, -ⲁⲧ(ⲉ)ⲃ⁺
SSᵃSᶠ, ⲟⲩⲁⲧⲃⲉ⁺ *SᵃA²*, ⲟⲩⲁⲧⲉⲩ⁺ *F* vb **A I** intr, *change
(place), be changed,* mostly *B*: Ex 7 17, Hab 1 11(*SA*
ⲕⲧⲟ)μεταβάλλειν, 2 Cor 3 10 (*S diff*)ὑπερβ.; Ps 61 7
(*S* ⲕⲓⲙ)μεταναστεύειν; Is 54 10(*S* ⲡⲱⲱⲡⲉ)μεθιστά-
ναι; *ib* 29 17 (*S* ⲡⲱ. ⲉⲃⲟⲗ)μετατιθέναι; Ex 14 2 ἀποστρέφειν; Lev 13 5(*S* ϣⲓⲃⲉ)μεταπίπτειν; Nu 2 34(*S*
ⲙⲟⲟϣⲉ)ἐξαίρειν opp ϥⲓ ⲕⲟⲧ, Is 7 23(*S* Gk om); C 41
42 ⲁϯⲙⲟⲅⲓ…ⲟⲩ. & went into midst of stream, Cat
178 fish ⲉϥⲟⲩⲱⲧⲉⲩ ⳧ⲉⲙⲡⲓⲡⲉⲗⲁⲅⲟⲥ, HCons 441 we
pray ϩⲓⲡⲁ ⲉⲕⲟⲩ. ⲉⲕⲟⲩⲱⲡⲉ ⲉⲃⲟⲗ, Va 58 137 ⲟⲩϣⲁⲓ-
ⲡⲉ ⲡⲁϑⲓⲟⲥ…ⲉϥ ⲟⲥⲟⲡ ⲁⲡⲓⲥⲧⲁϫⲓⲟⲛ ⲟⲩ. (meaning?),
H B N Test I cxlvi ϯⲛⲁϫⲁϥ (*sc* my writing) ⲡⲧⲁⲟⲩ.
i e die, El 142 *S* like dust ⲉⲩϣⲁⲩⲟⲩ., BM 580 14 *F*
ϣⲁⲡⲧⲉⲧⲉⲓⳓⲏⲡⲓ ⲟⲩ.; Lu 3 17 ⳣⲁⲓ ⲡⲟⲩ. (*S* ϩⲁ only)
πτύον; imperat: Mich 136 3 *S* incantation ⲁⲅⲟⲩⲱ-
ⲧϥ(*l* ⲁⲟⲩ-) ⲑⲟⲟⲩⲧ, AZ 21 94 *O* sim ⲉⲟⲩⲱⲧϥ ⲟⲩⲥⲓⲣⲓ,
ⲉⲅⲱⲧϥ ⲁⲡⲟⲩⲡ; qual, *surpassing:* 2 Cor 12 11 *B*
(*SF* ⲡⲟϣ) ὑπερλίαν; EW 147 *B* ⲟⲩⲅⲟⲣⲙⲏ ⲉⲥⲟⲩ.
ⲡⲧⲉ ⲫϯ θειότερος; ⲥ ⲡⲁⲣⲁ: PS 304 *S* ⲧⲉϥⲕⲣⲓⲥⲓⲥ
ⲟⲩ. ⲡ. ⲕⲣⲓⲥⲓⲥ ⲛⲓⲙ, Mani 2 *A²* ⲧⲁⲉⲕⲕⲗⲏⲥⲓⲁ ⲟⲩ. ⲡ.
ⲡϣⲁⲣⲡ ⲡⲉⲕⲕⲗ. Mor 41 98 *S* ⲕⲟⲩⲟⲧϥ ⲡⲁⲣⲁⲣⲟϥ;
cf ⲥ ⲉ- qual.

II tr, *pass through, remove:* Job 9 11 *B*(*S* ⲥⲓⲛⲉ),
Ps 17 29 *SB*, Pro 9 18 *SAB* ὑπερβαίνειν; Z 336 *S*
ⲁⲟⲩ. ⲙⲡⲓⲉⲣⲟ διαβ.; Dan 7 12 *B*(*S diff*) μεθιστ.;
Am 5 8 *B* μετασκευάζειν; Nu 21 22 *S*(*B* ⲥⲓⲛⲉ) παρέρχεσθαι; R 1 4 29 *S* ⳓⲟⲓⲗⲉ ⲉⲣⲟⲟⲩ … ⲟⲩⲟⲧⲃⲟⲩ *in
transitu visitare;* PS 236 *S* ⲡⲧⲟⲡⲟⲥ…ⲥⲡⲁⲟⲩⲟⲧⲃⲟⲩ,
ShA 2 114 *S* ⲉⲧⲛⲡⲱⲣⲕ ⲏ ⲉⲧϥ(ⲟⲩ)ⲱⲧⲃ̄ ⲡⲡⲱⲛⲉ; Sh
Bor 205 359 *S* ⲟⲩⲟⲧⲃⲟⲩ ⲙⲡⲃⲟⲗ ⲙⲡⲥⲟⲃⲧ, Aeg 26 *S*
ϣⲁⲡⲧⲉⲥⲟⲩ. ⲙⲡⲥⲁϣϥ ⲛⲁⲓⲱⲛ = *ib B* ⲥⲓⲛⲓ, Bor 245
62 *S* virginity ⲟⲩⲉⲧⲃ̄ ⲧⲉϥϥⲩⲥⲓⲥ of mankind, Mor 24
30 *F* after had ⲟⲩ. ⲙⲡⲓⲉⲉⲓ (*l* ⲡⲓⲁⲓⲱⲛ) ⲡⲕⲉⲕⲓ, BSM
133 *B* ⲁⲟⲩ. ⲡⲡⲉⲕⲗⲟⲅⲟⲥ *translate* = Mor 22 143 *S*
ⲉϩⲣⲁⲓ, GöttN '99 42 *B* let him not ⲟⲩⲁⲧⲉⲃ̄ ⲥⲁϫⲓ ⳧ⲉⲛ-
ϩⲗⲓ ⲡⲥⲁϫⲓ ⲡⲁⲣⲅⲟⲛ *exchange, bandy idle words,* but
restrict self to good.

With following preposition.

—— ⲉ- *SA²BF*, *change to, into, surpass* intr: Lev
13 3 *B*(*S* ϣ.) μεταβάλ. acc, Is 60 5 *B*(*S* ⲕⲱⲧⲉ), Mart
Ign 868 *B* ϣⲁⲅⲟⲩ. ⲉⲟⲩⲁⲉⲧⲟⲥ = R 1 4 56 *S* ⲡ. μ. εἰς;
Lam 5 15 *B*(*S* ⲕⲧⲟ)στρέφ. εἰς, *ib* 5 2 *B*(*F* ⲕⲱ.) μεταστ.
dat; EW 150 *B* stone ⲉⲁϥⲟⲩ. ⲉⲕⲉⲙⲁ μετατίθ. πρός;
1 Kg 26 13 *S* διαβαίν. εἰς; Jos 16 6 *S* περιέρχ. εἰς;
Mor 18 90 *S* ⲙⲡⲁⲧⲉⲡⲟⲩ. ⲉⲣⲏⲧ (var 19 94 ⲃⲱⲕ), C 41
35 *B* sim = Miss 4 639 *S* ⲃⲱⲕ, BMis 346 *S* my age
ⲟⲩ. ⲉⲡⲉⲡⲉⲓⲱⲧ = BSM 13 *B* ⲉⲣ ϩⲟⲩⲟ ⲉ-, C 89 10 *B*
if weary ϣⲁⲅⲟⲩ. ⲉⲕⲉⲣⲱⲃ ⲛ⳨ⲓⲝ = Miss 4 537 *S* ⲡ.,
JKP 2 84 *S* ⲙⲡⲉⲣⲟⲩ. ⲉⲡⲣⲟ (*cf* Pro 5 8 ἐγγίζειν πρός),
Mani H 20 *A²* ⲡⲉⲧⲁϥⲟⲩ. ⲉϣⲉ (years old); qual,
surpassing: Mt 6 25 *S*(var & *B* ⲟⲩⲟⲟⲧⲉ) πλεῖον εἶναι
gen; 1 Cor 15 41 *F*(*S* ϣ., *B* do) διαφέρειν gen; Phil
2 3 *S*(*B* ϫⲓⲥⲉ tr) ὑπερέχειν gen; BMar 103 *S* ⲉϥⲟⲩ.
ⲉⲡⲛⲟϭ ὑπερβάλ. acc; BMis 563 *S* ⲉⲧⲟⲩ. ⲉⲡⲁⲓ *maior*
abl; Br 270 *S* ⲡⲁⲡⲉⲣⲁ(ⲛ)ⲧⲟⲥ ⲉⲧⲟⲩ. ⲉⲁⲡⲉⲣ. ⲛⲓⲙ (*cf*
271 ⲉⲧⲣⲓⲧⲡⲉ ⲡ-), ShP 130⁴ 123 *S* Origen's words ⲟⲩ.
ⲉⲡⲉⲡⲧⲁⲡⲉⲧⲟⲩⲁⲃ ϫⲟⲟⲩ, BMar 37 *S* ⲟⲩⲙⲁⲧⲟⲥ ⲉϥ-
ⲟⲩⲟⲟⲧⲃ̄ ⲉⲣⲟⲕ (*cf* ⲟⲩⲱⲱⲧⲉ), J 106 115 *Sᵃ* God ⲟⲩⲁⲧⲃ̄
ⲉⲟⲩⲟⲛ ⲛⲓⲙ, AJSL 46 244 n *Sᵃ* -ⲃⲉ ⲉⲧⲁⲓ, BM 228 59
Sᶠ ⲡⲁⲧⲁⲑⲟⲛ…ⲟⲩⲁⲧⲉϥ ⲉⲡⲉⲡⲧⲁⲡⲁⲁϥ, PO 11 340 *B*
ⲧⲁⲓϣⲫⲏⲣⲓ ⲟⲩ. ⲉⲑⲁⲡⲓⲡⲣⲟⲫⲏⲧⲏⲥ, Br 235 *S* ⲡⲉⲧⲟⲩ.
ⲉϣⲁϫⲉ ⲉⲣⲟⲟⲩ *those more able to say them;* tr *S*
(once)*BF*, *change to:* Ac 7 16 *BF*(*S* ⲡ.) μετατίθ. εἰς;
3 Kg 8 47 (*S* do) μετάγεσθαι ἐκεῖ; Joel 2 31 (*S* ⲕⲱⲧⲉ,
A ⲕⲧⲟ)μεταστρέφ. εἰς; Jer 36 7 ἀποικίζειν ἐκεῖ; Is 59
15 (*S* ⲡ. ⲉⲃ.) μεθιστάναι gen; TRit 109 ⲟⲩ. ⲙⲡⲁⲓ-
ⲙⲱⲟⲩ ϣⲁⲓ ⲉⲧⲉϥⲫⲩⲥⲓⲥ ⲡϣⲟⲣⲡ, DeV 2 167 ⲁϥⲟⲩ.
ⲡⲡⲓ⳨ⲣⲏⲙⲁ ⲉⲡⲓⲁϩⲱⲣ, Sh(Besa?)ViK 923 267 *S* re-
proaching nun for favouritism ⲡⲧⲟ…ⲙⲡⲧⲁⲓ ⲡⲧⲁⲣⲟⲩ
ⲧⲟⲟⲧⲉ ⲉⲣⲟⲥ shall (both) be miserable at Judgment.

—— ϩⲛ-, ⳧ⲉⲛ-, *change from:* Nu 9 17 *B*(*S diff*)
ἀπαίρειν; Mor 23 42 *S* ϥⲛⲁⲟⲩ. ϩⲙⲡⲁⲓⲱⲡ.

With following adverb.

—— ⲉⲃⲟⲗ *SA²BF*, intr, *cross over* & as ⲟⲩ.: Mt
17 20 *B*(*S* ⲡ. ⲉⲃ.) μεταβαίν., Jo 10 1 *SA²*(*B* ⲡⲏⲩ
ⲉⲡϣⲱⲓ) ἀναβ., MG 17 319 *S* = C 89 67 *B* ὑπερβ.;
Ps 108 10 *B*(*S* do) μετανιστάναι; 2 Kg 3 22 *S*(var
ⲃⲱⲕ) ἀπέρχ.; ShA 2 54 *S* Judas ⲁⲟⲩ. ⲉⲃ. ϩⲓⲕⲉⲥⲁ
& became devil, Ét Leem 90 *S* they go up to roof
ⲡⲥⲉⲟⲩ. ⲉⲃ. ⲡⲥⲉⲡⲱⲧ = P ar 4793 46 ونطّروا وبوا, Ryl
449 *B* ⲫⲙⲟⲩ ⲙⲏⲛ ⲡⲁⲓⲕⲟⲥⲙⲟⲥ ⲟⲩ. ⲉⲃ.; tr,
transport BF: Jer 13 19 (*S* ⲡ. ⲉⲃ.), Lam 4 22 *BF*
(var ⲡⲁⲡⲓ) ἀποικ., *ib* 1 3 μετοικ. (*S* ShViK 919 do);
Deu 27 17 (*S* do), He 7 12 (*SF* do) μετατίθ.; Jo
7 3 (*SA²* do) μεταβαίν.; Su 56 μεθιστ., Ac 8 9 (*S*
ⲡⲱϣⲥ)ἐξίστ.; C 89 10 ⲡⲥⲉⲟⲩ. ⲉⲃ. ⲙⲡⲓϣⲱ from
place to place = Miss 4 537 *S* ⲡⲱⲡⲉ μεταφέρειν;
Eph 4 14 (*S* ϣⲉⲉⲓ) περιφ.; C 43 44 *B* God ⲟⲩⲟⲑⲃⲉϥ
ⲉⲃ. & he died; *surpass S*: ShMIF 23 26 ⲕⲟⲩ. ⲙⲙⲟⲥ
ⲉⲃ. ⲕⲣ ϩⲟⲩⲟ ⲉⲣⲟⲥ, ShA 1 156 ill-fitting clothes ce-

ογοϣc н сеоγ. εв. ппапарϩε, PS 21 паϣ пϥε аϥ-
оγотвн εв. *passed through us?*; εв. е- *B, remove
to*: 3 Kg 8 53 διαστέλλειν εἰς; Jer 47 7 ἀποικ. εἰς, Ac
7 4 (*S* п. εϩραι) μετοικ. εἰς; TstAb 227 оγоввεк
εв. епεмтоп; εв. εϩоγп е-: Col 1 13 (*S* п. εϩоγп)
μεθιστ. εἰς; εв. ммаγ *BF, thence*: Mt 12 9 *BF*
(*S* п. εв. ϩп-) μεταβαιν. ἐκεῖθεν; ib 14 13 *F* (*S* =
Gk, *B* ϣе εв.) ἀναχωρεῖν ἐκ.; Ge 13 18 (*S* do) ἀπο-
σκηνοῦν; εв. ϩа- *B, from*: Hos 10 5 (*SA* п. εв.
п-) μετοικ. ἀπό; BSM 25 аγϣапоγ. εв. ϩапаι-
εωп; εв. ϩп-, ϩеп- sim intr*BF*: Jo 13 1 *BF* (P Mich
3521, *SA*² п. εв. ϩп-) μεταβαιν. ἐκ; Va 66 303 оγ.
εв. ϩеппаιма μετατιθ. ἐκ; TEuch 1 17 птεϥоγ.
εв. ϩеппатма...εϩоγп е-, Pap. Liverpool Mus
F ϣаγоγ. εв. ϩмпεϥ-(*l* пεϥ-)вιос; tr *SB*: Ex 10
19 *B* μεταβάλ. ἀπό; Ps 51 6 *B*(*S* п. εв. ϩп-) μετανα-
στεύ. ἀπό; Jer 34 20 *B* ἀποικ. ἐκ; 1 Kg 19 12 *S*
κατάγειν διά; BMis 127 *S* асоγотвоγ εв. ϩрнтϥ
(*sc* window, Jos 2 15), C 89 145 *B* zealous to оγоθ-
воγ εв. ϩеппоγпраζιс ετρωоγ; εв. ϩιхп- *S,
spread over*: ClPr 54 46 *S* torrent оγ. εв. ϩ.тεстω
ὑπερχέειν gen; ShA 1 153 *S* sim, ib 456 *S* may thy
wrath оγ. εв. ϩιхωϥ *over from*; as nn *B*: Jer
30 3 (*S* п. εв.) ἀποικία, ib 26 19 (*S* do) -κισμός, 3 Kg
8 47 (*S* п. εϩраι) μετοικία, Ob 20 (*A* diff) -κεσία, Ps
64 tit (*S* ма пϭоειλε) παροικία; He 7 12 (*SF* п.)
μετάθεσις; Ez 1 2 (*S* п. εв.) αἰχμαλωσία; FR 106
паоγ. εв. *death*; хмоγ. εв. *B, migration, death*:
Is 47 15 m (*S* = Gk) μεταβολή; Lam 1 7 m κατοι-
κεσία; EW 35 †апапаγсιс оγоϩ †х. of St John,
ib pt iii 194 пх., C 86 193 weeping for пх. of father.

—— cавоλ *B, overstep*: Va 57 234 ммоп ϣхом
εоγ. с. птεϥρωпн (*р̇о.*).

—— епϣωι *B, pass upward*: Lu 14 10 refl (*F* оγ.
псарλнι, *S* ωλ εϩраι) προσαναβαιν. ἀνώτερον; Va
57 14 птεпоγ. ε. to limits of virtue, FR 108 пта-
оγоθвεс ε. епιфноγι.

—— εϩоγп, εв. *SB, pass within*, intr: Br 99 *S*
оγ. εϩ. мфоγп пπεϥфλаζ, ShRE 10 164 *S* roads
barred хеппεкоγ. εϩ., Mor 22 51 *S* пεтпаоγ. εϩ.
ϩμпсовт is thief; εϩ. е-, *pass, intrude into*: Va
57 161 *B* μεταβάλ. εἰς; ShA 1 228 *S* εϩоγ. εϩ. епнι,
AM 123 *B* soul оγ. εв. επιτεвнωоγι, C 43 122 *B*
on 1st Pharmouthi εϥпаоγ. εв. εϥρомпι пвερι
= Mor 48 44 *S* пωт е-, PS 267 *S* оγотвεϥ εϩ. εм-
мγстнριоп, Va 57 77 *B* птεϥоγотпоγ εв. епεт-
сотп; хмоγ. εв. *B*: Va 57 161 пх. ετχρнсιс
of wine τρέπειν εἰς.

—— εϩраι, аϩрнι *SA, pass beyond*: El 70 *A* се-
па(оγ)отве пθропос еп аϩ. but thrones shall detain them, ShA 2 86 *S* reached or аγоγотвоγ ρω
εϩ., Miss 4 576 *S* пερεθεоϩωρос оγотϥ εϩ. ϩι-
тпολιс *was distant in town*.

—— псарλнι *F* *v* с епϣωι.

—— nn m *B, passing over, death*: H B NTst I
cxLvi forget not пιоγ. праст, Dif 2 45 пιоγ. *transport* into captivity سبى.

ат-, аθоγ. *B, immutable*: HL 81 προϥερεсιс
паθ.; метат.: He 6 17 (*SF* п. vb) τὸ ἀμετάθετον.

ϭιп-, хιпоγ., *migration, changeableness*: Nu 33
2 *B*(*S* ма птωоγп εвоλ) ἄπαρσις; P 129²⁰ 133 *S*
ϭ., ϣιве, пωωпε, P 44 122 *S* тϭ. мпаιонр خاصل,
Dif 2 36 *B* пιх. of relics to church.

B *transfer SS.fAB from one vessel to another*, so
pour, intr: Zech 4 12 *SA*(*B* хωϣ) ἐπιχέειν; tr:
2 Kg 13 9 *S* κατακενοῦν; 2 Chr 4 17 *B* χωνεύειν.

With following preposition or adverb. c е- *S,
into*: 4 Kg 4 4 (Miss 4 782) ἀποχ. εἰς; Hall 65 птоγат-
воγ епϩпа[γ (*sic*); ShC 73 55 оγотв пεϥ εϩраι
εрооγ, Hall 64 recipe оγатвεϥ εϩ. εγм[; c εхп-
S, upon: Ex 29 7 (*B* х.) επιχ. επί; ShA 2 302 оγотв
мооγ εхмпаι (*cf* 299 sim пεϩт), P 131⁶ 100 jars
аϥоγотвоγ εхмпεθγсιастнριоп; εϩраι εхп-:
Ge 35 14 (*B* оγωтεп) σπένδειν ἐπί; Bor 292 36 аγ-
оγετϥ мооγ εϩ. εхωϥ; c епεснт ϩι- *S, down
upon*: AZ 23 111 оγп(е)ϩ воτϥ е. ϩιтмхаρт; c
εвоλ *S.fB, out*: Dan 2 46 *B* (var оγωтεп), 2 Tim 4 6
B(var do, *S* diff), ROC 17 404 *B* птаоγ. пак εв.
мпιспоϥ σπέ.; Mor 30 3 *S.f* псεоγ. паγ (*sc* gods)
εв. = BMis 231 *S* оγωтп εв.

C *traverse, pierce S*: Tri 657 оγ., ϣохт ϩнтхε-
пεпωρ نفذ; Ex 21 6 (*B* оγωтεп), Job 40 21 (*B* do)
τρυπᾶν; Deu 15 17 *S* пка поγωтϥ (*B* diff) ὀπήτιον.

—— nn *B, meaning uncertain, part of ox-yoke*:
AZ 13 134 carpenter's craft makes ploughs & ϩапоγ.
птε пιзιтос (ζυγός) wherewith beasts may plough.

оγатве, -ϭε *S*, -ετвι *F* nn f, *pierced place, hole*:
Mt 19 24 *S*(var -ϭε)*F*(*B* оγаθнι) τρύπημα, Mk 10
25 *S*(*B* оγωтεп) τρυμαλιά.

оγатвεс *S* nn f, *meaning as last ?* : Win 44 meas-
urements(?)ϣомптε пϣλοп поγ. епоγа, спте поγ.
ϩнтмнте.

Confused ? with оγωтп.

оγωтп *S*, -тпе *AA*²(nn), -теп *B*, оγотп⳽ *SB*,
оγоθп⳽, оγотεп† *B* vb tr a, *pour* (once, *cf* оγωтв)
c εхп- *S*, εϩрнι εх. *B*: Phil 2 17 σπένδειν επί; as
nn m, *libation*: Ge 35 14 *SB*, Jer 51 17 *S*(*B* оγ.
εвоλ) σπονδή; Tri 374 *S* سكب; ϭιп-, хιпоγ.,
pouring of libations: 2 Chr 4 3 *B* χώνευσις(so *l* ? оγωτ-
τϥ) سكب; ROC 20 418 = Mun 130 *S* making of idols
& тϭ.

—— εвоλ *SAA*²*B, pour forth*, intr: Nu 4 7 *SB*
σπέ., Est C 28 *S* σπο.; TT 143 *S* аϥоγ. εв.; εв.
п- dat: Jer 7 18 *B* σπονδὰς σπέ., BMis 231 *S* sacrifice & оγ. паγ εв. σπέ.; Is 57 6 *B*(*S* пωωпε εв.)
ἐκχέειν σπο.; ShR 2 3 44 *S* εϥоγ. паϥ (*sc* Satan)

eⲃ., C 89 2 *B* wine ⲉⲧⲁⲟⲩ. eⲃ. ⲛϭⲏⲧϥ ⲛⲡⲁⲓⲁⲱⲡ;   tr: Nu 28 7 *SB*, Ez 20 28 *S*(*B* ϣⲱⲧ eⲃ.), Hos 9 4 *AB* ⲥⲡⲉ́.; BIF 14 126 *S* ⲁϥⲟⲩ. eⲃ. ⲡⲟⲩⲟⲩⲥⲓⲁ, C 43 45 *B* ⲟⲩ. eⲃ. ⲡⲣⲁⲛϣⲟⲩϣⲱⲟⲩϣⲓ ⲡⲉⲙⲟⲣⲁⲡⲥⲡⲟⲡⲁⲛ;   eⲃ. ⲉⲭⲛ-: Ge 35 14 *B*(*S* ⲡⲱⲣⲧ) ⲉⲡⲓⲭ. ⲉⲡⲓ́; Nu 15 5 *S*(*B* eⲃ. ϩⲓⲭⲉⲛ-) ⲉⲓⲥ ⲥⲡⲟ. ⲡⲟⲓⲉⲓⲛ ⲉⲡⲓ́; Wess 18 60 *S* ⲟⲩ. eⲃ. ⲙⲡⲁⲥⲡⲟϥ ⲉⲭⲛⲡⲣⲟⲓⲧⲉ;   as nn m: Lev 23 13 *S*(*B* = Gk), Deu 32 38 *SB*, Joel 1 9 *AB* ⲥⲡⲟ.; Is 65 11 *S*(*B* diff) ⲕⲉ́ⲣⲁⲥⲙⲁ; Si 50 15 *S* ⲡⲕⲁ ⲡⲟⲩ. eⲃ. ⲥⲡⲟⲛⲇⲉⲓⲛ; Mani 1 *A²* ⲡⲟⲩ. ⲁⲃ. ⲙⲛⲡⲟⲩⲥⲓⲁ;   ⲥⲓⲡⲟⲩ. eⲃ: Bor 253 121 *S* ⲧⲉⲥⲡⲟⲡⲁⲛ ⲉⲧⲉⲧⲥ. ⲧⲉ.

b, *be pierced B* intr: C 41 18 rock ⲁϥⲟⲩ. like wax before fire (*Rev sémit* 8 163 ﺳﺎﺏ, Miss 4 328 اخرق), *ib* ⲁϥⲟⲩ.† until this day (ﻟﯩﻮﻢ ﻩﺩ, ﺨﺮﻮﻖ), C 86 275 ⲉⲟⲅⲟⲡ ⲅⲁⲡϫⲟⲗ ⲟⲩ.† ⲉⲣⲟϥ(*sc* ironboot); tr *pierce*: Ex 21 6 (*S* ⲟⲩⲱⲧⲃ), Job 40 21 (*S* do) ⲧⲣⲩⲡⲁ̃ⲛ; *ib* 41 7 *B*(*S* ⲥⲓⲛⲉ) ⲇⲓⲉⲣⲭⲉⲥⲑⲁⲓ; Va 57 65 burglars ⲟⲩ. ⲡⲣⲁⲛⲥⲟⲃⲧ;   as nn m, *place pierced, hole*: Mk 10 25 (*S* ⲟⲩⲁⲧⲃⲉ) ⲧⲣⲩⲙⲁⲗⲓⲁ́; Ja 3 11 (*SA* ⲙⲟⲩⲙⲉ) ⲟⲡⲏ́; MG 25 248 sending forth water like ⲅⲁⲡⲟⲩ. ⲙⲃⲁⲗⲕⲟⲩ, C 86 212 (ⲟⲩ)ⲱⲧⲉⲡ, *v* ⲗⲁⲥⲟⲩ.

Confused ? with ⲟⲩⲱⲧⲃ.

ⲟⲩⲁⲑⲛⲓ *B v* ⲟⲩⲱⲧⲃ (ⲟⲩⲁⲧⲃⲉ).

ⲟⲩⲟⲧⲡϲ *S* nn, meaning unknown, ? *claim*: PLond 4 439 I undertake]ⲭⲉⲛⲓⲉⲛ ⲗⲁⲁⲩ ⲡⲟⲩ. ⲛⲏⲧⲛ as to payment here acknowledged.

ⲟⲩⲱⲧϥ *v* ⲟⲩⲱⲧⲃ.

ⲟⲩⲧⲁϩ *S*(rare)*A²B*, ⲉⲧⲁϩ *AA²*, ⲟⲩⲧⲉϩ *F*, pl -ⲧⲁⲩϩ *B*, -ⲧⲉⲩϩ *F* & sg as pl, nn m, *fruit*: Ge 4 3 *B*(*SA* Cl = Gk), Cant 8 11 *F*(*S* do), 1 Cor 9 7 *BF*(*S* do) ⲕⲁⲣⲡⲟ́ⲥ, Ps 51 8 *SB*, Hos 14 7 *SAB* ⲕⲁⲧⲁⲕ., Lev 22 27 *B* (*S* ⲥⲗⲓⲗ) ⲕⲁⲣⲡⲱⲙⲁ; Pro 14 4 *B*(*SA* do), Is 30 23 *B* (*SF* ⲥⲣⲟⲥ) ⲅⲉ́ⲛⲛⲏⲙⲁ, Lev 23 17 *B* ϣⲟⲣⲡ ⲡⲟⲩ. (*S* ⲣⲱⲧ ⲛϣ.) ⲡⲣⲱⲧⲟⲩ.; Is 61 11 *B*(*S* = Gk) ⲥⲡⲉ́ⲣⲙⲁ; Lev 25 19 *B*(*S* †ⲟⲅⲱ) ⲉⲕⲫⲟ́ⲣⲓⲟⲛ; Miss 4 695 *S* ⲟⲩⲛⲟⲥ ⲡⲟⲩ. of date palm, Mani H 4 *A²* carrying ⲧⲉⲕⲉⲧⲡⲱ…ⲡⲉⲕⲉⲧ., C 41 70 *B* ⲡⲟⲩ. ⲛⲧⲃⲟⲛⲧ, AM 251 *B* ⲡⲟⲩ. ⲡⲧⲉ ⲧⲁⲡⲉⲭⲓ, WS 94 *S* ⲡⲓⲟⲩ. ⲛϣⲉϣⲟⲧⲉ (obscure);   pl forms: Deu 28 42, 30 9 *B*(var), Cant 8 12 *F*, C 89 73 *B*, Va 57 76 *B*.   *V* also ⲃⲛⲛⲉ **II**.

ⲁⲧⲟⲩ. *B*, *fruitless*: Eph 5 11 (*S* ⲙⲛ ⲕⲁⲣ.) ⲁ́ⲕⲁⲣⲡⲟⲥ; Rec 7 89 ϣϣⲏⲛ ⲛⲁ.; ⲙⲉⲧⲁ.: Va 57 79; ⲉⲣ, ⲉⲗ ⲁ.: Mt 13 22 *BF*(*S* ϣⲱⲡⲉ ⲁⲭⲛⲕ.) ⲁ́ⲕ. ⲅⲓⲛⲉⲥⲑⲁⲓ, 1 Cor 14 14 (*S* ⲁⲧⲕ.) ⲁ́ⲕ. ⲉⲓⲛⲁⲓ.

ⲉⲣ ⲟⲩ. *BF*, *bear fruit*: Ps 106 37 (*S* ⲧⲁⲩⲉ ⲕ.), Mt 13 26 *F*(*B* † ⲟⲩ., *S* ⲉⲓⲣⲉ ⲡⲟⲩⲕ.) ⲕ. ⲡⲟⲓⲉⲓⲛ.

ⲉⲛ ⲟⲩ. ⲉⲃⲟⲗ *B*, *bring forth fruit*: AM 178 tree ⲉⲟⲑⲁⲉⲡ ⲟⲩ. eⲃ.;   ⲉⲛ ⲟⲩ. ⲉⲅⲣⲏⲓ *B*, sim: Dan 3 38 ⲕⲁⲣⲡⲟⲩⲥⲑⲁⲓ.

ⲙⲁⲥ ⲟⲩ. *B*, *fruit-bearer*: Ge 1 12 ϣϣⲏⲛ ⲙⲙ.

ⲕⲁⲣⲡⲓⲙⲟⲥ, Jer 2 21 (*S* ShIF 253 ϥⲁⲓⲟⲩ.) ⲕⲁⲣⲡⲟⲫⲟ́ⲣⲟⲥ; Lev 19 23 (*S* ⲉⲟⲅⲱⲙ) ⲃⲣⲱ́ⲥⲓⲙⲟⲥ.

† ⲟⲩ. *BF*, *give fruit*: Ps 66 7 (*S* † ⲕ.) ⲕ. ⲇⲓⲇⲟ́ⲛⲁⲓ, Mt 13 23 *BF*(*S* do) ⲕⲁⲣⲡⲟⲫⲟⲣⲉⲓⲛ, Ez 19 10 (*S* † ⲟⲩⲱ ⲙⲡⲉⲥⲕ.)ⲕ. ⲅⲓⲛ.; MG 25 347 ⲕ. ⲡⲟⲓ.; ⲧⲁⲓⲟⲩ. *A²* Mani 1 ϣⲏⲛ ⲡⲧ.;   ⲣⲉϥⲧ ⲟⲩ.: Deu 20 20 (*S* diff) ⲕⲁⲣⲡⲟ́ⲃⲣⲱⲧⲟⲥ; C 86 285 ϣϣⲏⲛ ⲡⲣ. = *S* Mun 39 ⲣⲉϥⲧ ⲕ. ⲉ́ⲅⲕⲁⲣⲡⲟⲥ opp ⲁⲧⲟⲩ.; ⲙⲉⲧⲣ.: DeV 2 56 ⲟⲙ. ⲡⲓⲁⲣⲉⲧⲏ;   ϫⲓⲛⲧ ⲟⲩ., *condition of fruit-bearing*: Va 61 27 herbs ⲣⲱⲧ ⲉⲡⲭ.

ϥⲁⲓⲟⲩ. *SBF*, *fruit-carrier*: Ps 148 9 *B*(*S* † ⲕ.) ⲕⲁⲣⲡⲟⲫⲟ́ⲣⲟⲥ, Eccl 2 5 *F*(*S* ⲣⲉϥⲧ ⲕ.) ⲕⲁⲣⲡⲟⲩ̃; BM 348 *S* ⲁⲥⲟⲗⲧⲉ ⲡⲃⲁⲓⲟⲩ.

ⲟⲩⲧⲁϩ *S* nn m, meaning unknown: WS 94 ⲡⲓⲟⲩ. ⲛϣⲉϣⲟⲧⲉ. *Cf* ? ⲱⲧⲉ.

ⲟⲩⲱⲧϩ *S*(-ⲑ)*AA²BF*(-ϩⲑ), ⲱⲧϩ *SBF* (ⲱⲉϩ), ⲟⲩⲉⲧϩ- *SB*, ⲟⲩⲟⲧϩⲥ, ⲟⲧϩⲥ *S*, ⲟⲩⲁⲧϩⲥ *SA²*, ⲁⲧϩⲥ *A²* (Jo), ⲟⲩⲱⲧϩⲥ *B*(once), ⲟⲩⲱⲑ† (*l* ⲟⲩⲟⲑ) *S*, vb **I** intr, *pour* liquid, *cast in mould*, *draw* water &c: Mal 3 3 *S*(R 2 1 49)*B* ⲭⲱⲛⲉⲩⲉⲓⲛ; Jo 2 8 *SB* ⲁ́ⲛⲧⲗⲉⲓⲛ; ShIF 147 *S* ⲡⲧⲉⲡⲟⲩ. in oven, Bodl(P)a 2 35 *S* recipe ⲟⲩⲱϣⲙⲉϥ…ϣⲁϥⲟⲩ. ⲕⲁⲗⲱⲥ, *ib* 42 *S* ⲡⲉⲡⲓⲡⲉ ⲉϥⲟⲩ.†, AJSL 46 249 *S* recipe ⲙⲉⲣⲉⲧⲉⲥⲉⲣⲱⲧⲉ ⲟⲩ. *is not fluid*.

II tr: Is 40 19 *S*(var c ϩⲛ-)*B*, Ep Jer 23 *BF* ⲭ., Lev 19 4 *S*(*B* ⲫⲱⲧϩ) ⲭⲱⲛⲉⲩⲧⲟ́ⲥ, 4 Kg 17 16 *S*(Bodl(P) d 12) ⲭⲱⲛⲉⲩⲙⲁ ⲡⲟⲓⲉⲓⲛ; 1 Kg 13 20 *S* ⲱ. ⲭⲁⲗⲕⲉⲩ́ⲉⲓⲛ; Cant 5 5 *F* ⲱⲉϩ (*S* ϣⲟⲅⲟ) ⲥⲧⲁ́ⲍⲉⲓⲛ; Lam 1 16 *F* ⲱ. (*B* ⲏⲓ ⲉⲡⲉⲥⲏⲧ) ⲕⲁⲧⲁⲅⲉⲓⲛ; Job 28 1 *S*(var ⲟⲧ.)*B* ⲇⲓⲏⲑⲉⲓⲛ; *ib* 19 26 *S* ⲱ. *B*, Is 12 3 *S*(var ⲱ., *B* ⲙⲟϩ) ⲁⲛⲧ.; Jo 18 10 *A²*(*SB* ⲧⲱⲕⲙ) ⲉⲗⲕⲩ́ⲉⲓⲛ; ShA 1 211 *S* ⲡⲙⲟⲩⲡⲡ ⲡϭⲓⲝ … ⲟⲩⲟⲧϩⲟⲩ, TT 45 *S* worn out vessels ϣⲁⲟⲩⲟⲧϩⲟⲩ ⲛⲕⲉⲥⲟⲡ, C 43 44 *B* bade ⲟⲩ. ⲙⲡⲓⲟⲩⲃ (*cf* below), Bodl(P) a 3 38 *S* ⲡⲣⲟⲓⲧⲉ to be dyed ⲟⲩⲱϥ ⲛⲧ ⲛⲥⲟⲡ, PChass 1 ⲛⲃⲁⲣⲱⲧ…ⲟⲩⲁⲑϥ.

With following preposition or adverb.   c ⲉ-, *pour, melt for* intr: TT 144 *S* ⲙⲟⲣⲕ ⲛⲧⲟⲩ. ⲉⲣⲟⲡ, DeV 1 163 *B* drew water ⲛⲥⲉⲟⲩ. ⲉⲣⲱⲟⲩ, BSM 27 *B* of pouring wine ⲉⲧⲟⲩⲱ. ⲉⲣⲱⲟⲩ, KroppA *S* ⲉⲓⲟⲩⲱ ⲉⲥⲁϣϥⲉ (ⲛ)ⲡⲟⲩⲥⲉ; tr: Mic 4 3 *SA*(*B* ϩⲱⲙⲓ) ⲕⲁⲧⲁⲕⲟ́ⲡⲧⲉⲓⲛ ⲉⲓⲥ, Joel 3 10 *SA*(*B* do) ⲥⲩⲅⲕ. ⲉⲓⲥ; R 2 1 56 *S* iron anchors ⲁⲅⲟⲩⲟⲧⲟⲩ ⲉⲣⲉⲡⲉⲓϥⲧ, AZ 23 109 *S* ⲡⲧⲁⲣⲧ ⲛⲧⲁⲕⲟⲩⲁⲣⲧⲩ (sic) ⲉⲧⲧⲟⲉⲓⲥ;   c ⲉϫⲉⲛ- *B*, *for*: DeV 1 60 ⲟⲩ. ⲉϫ.ⲣⲱⲙⲓ ⲛⲓⲃⲉⲛ ϭⲉⲡⲓⲥⲡⲟϥ;   c ⲛ- *S*, *in*: Mich 136 7 ⲟⲩ.† ⲛ[ⲡ]ⲉϩ ⲡⲥⲓⲙ;   c ϩⲛ- *S*, *in*: PMéd 174 ⲟⲩⲱ ⲡⲁⲓ ϩⲛⲡⲕⲱϩⲧ; ⲉⲃⲟⲗ ϭⲉⲛ- *B*, *from*: TEuch 2 275 all that ⲟⲩ. ⲡⲱⲟⲩ eⲃ. ⲡϭⲏⲧϥ (water) ⲁ́ⲣⲩⲉⲥⲑⲁⲓ;   c ϩⲓ- *S*, *with*: PMéd 229 ⲟⲩⲟⲥⲟⲩ ϩⲓⲡⲉϩ;   c ⲉⲃⲟⲗ *SA²B*, as ⲟⲩ., intr: ShRyl 70 250 *S* bodies ⲟⲩ. eⲃ. ϩⲙⲡⲕⲱⲣⲧ, P 131⁴ 92 *S* ϩⲁⲁⲧⲉ (He 2 1) means ⲃⲱⲗ eⲃ. ϩⲙⲡⲡⲟⲃⲉ ⲁⲩⲱ ⲟⲩ. eⲃ. ϩⲙⲛϫⲓ ⲛϭⲟⲛⲥ like wax, Mani 2 *A²* ⲉⲣⲱⲧⲉ ⲉϥ-

ϩⲏⲙ ⲡⲥⲟⲩ. [ⲁⲃⲁ]ⲗ; tr: Ez 22 21 B(var ⲙⲟⲩⲡⲕ ⲉϩ.) ⲭ.; Mor 40 14 S ⲟⲩ. ⲉϩ. ⲙⲡⲟⲩϩ (var ib 39 19 & B C 43 44 om ⲉϩ.), PMéd 260 S ⲟⲩ. ⲡⲕⲏⲡⲉ ⲉϩ. ⲙⲡⲟⲩ-ⲙⲟⲩⲗⲁϩ, Mani 2 A² ⲉⲩⲛⲁⲟⲩⲁⲧϥϩ ⲁϩ. ⲣⲛⲧⲥⲉⲧⲉ; as nn m A²: Mani 2 ⲑⲛⲟⲩⲱϩ. ⲙⲡⲡⲙⲟⲩⲡⲕ of all things; ϫⲓⲡⲟⲩ. ⲉϩ. B: Ez 22 20 ⲭ.; ⲥ ⲉⲡⲉⲥⲏⲧ S, down: Mor 31 239 ⲉϥⲱ. ⲉⲡ. ϩⲓϫⲉⲛⲡⲉⲥⲱⲡⲉ (cf Ps 132 2 ⲡⲏⲩ ⲉⲡ.).

—— nn SAB, thing molten: Deu 9 12 B(S ⲡⲟⲩ.), Hos 13 2 B(A = Gk) χώνευμα, Is 42 17 B(S vb)χω-νευτός; as adj: Ex 32 4 SB-τός, Cl 53 2 A ϩⲓⲉ ⲡⲟⲩ.-μα; Job 40 13 S(B ϫⲏϣ) χυτός.

ⲙⲁ ⲡⲟⲩ. SAB, melting pot: Zech 11 13 SAB, BHom 54 S gold in ⲟⲩⲙ. χωνευτήριον, MG 25 401 B sim.

ⲣⲉϥ-, ⲗⲉϥⲟⲩ. SBF, he that pours, cup-bearer: Eccl 2 8 SF-ϩⲟ οἰνοχόος, Ge 40 1 S(var ⲣⲉϥⲟⲩ)B (ἀρχι)οι.; Jo 2 9 S(B=Gk)διάκονος, cit DeV 1 69 B ⲡⲓⲣ. ⲉⲧⲁⲩⲙⲁϩ ⲡⲓⲙⲟⲩ that drew water; K 142 B ⲣⲉϥϫⲓ وزان, p. كيّال; ShR 2 3 47 S; ⲙⲛⲧ-, ⲙⲉⲧⲣ.: Ge 40 13 SB(ἀρχι)οινοχοία.

ϣⲉ ⲡⲟⲩⲱ(ⲧ)ϩ (sic l?)S nn m, ladle: Glos 210 ρη-στηρ (l ἀρυστήρ)· ⲡϣⲉ ⲡⲟⲩⲱϩ.

ⲟⲩⲟⲧϩ¹, -ⲟⲑ², -ⲁⲧϩ³, -ⲁⲑ⁴ S nn m, pouring thing, cup: Nu 4 7¹ (B ϣⲡⲗⲟⲕ) κύαθος; Mor 17 42¹ ⲟⲩ. ⲛⲣⲙϫ κοτύλη; PMich 136 7 ⲟⲩ.¹ (ⲡ)ⲡⲉϩ, PMéd 287 ⲟⲩ.⁴ ⲡⲏⲣⲡ, CO 459 ⲥⲡⲁⲩ ⲡⲟⲩ.³, ib 472 ϩⲗⲟⲡ ⲡⲟⲩ.³, PLond 4 517, WS 123 ⲟⲩ.²

ⲟⲩⲟⲧϩⲉ, -ⲁⲧϩⲉ S nn, as last: Ex 25 29 (P 44 104, B ϣⲡ.) κύ.; ib 27 3 (P 44 104, B = Gk) κρεάγρα; AZ 16 17 -ⲟⲑⲉ.

Cf? ⲱϣⲧ.

ⲟⲟⲉ S nn f, footprint, outlet of water: 1 Kg 8 5 ὁδός, Ps 106 33 (B ⲙⲁ ⲙⲙⲟϣⲓ) ἔξοδος, ib 118 136 (B ⲙⲱⲓⲧ ⲉⲃⲟⲗ) διέξ.; Ge 37 17 (P 44 104) ⲡⲥⲁⲧⲟ. (B ⲥⲁⲙⲉⲡϩⲏ) κατόπισθε; BAp 89 ϩⲉⲡⲟ. ⲙⲙⲟⲟⲩ from rock, JTS 10 396 brought up son ϩⲛⲧⲉϥⲟ., R 1 3 19 ⲟⲩⲁϩⲟⲩ ⲡⲥⲁⲧⲉϥⲟ. V ⲟⲃⲉ nn.

ⲟⲩⲱⲧϩ tie v ⲱⲧϩ.

ⲟⲩⲁⲧϩⲉ, -ϩⲓ v ⲱⲧϩ.

ⲟⲩⲟⲩ A v ⲱⲱ.

ⲟⲩⲛⲟⲩⲧ B v ⲟⲩⲱ cease.

ⲟⲩϥⲁϫⲓ B nn m, liver: K 77 ⲡⲓⲟⲩ. نجاع ونجي الكبد, Bodl 325 156 ⲡⲉϥⲟⲩ. كبد.

ⲟⲩⲁϫⲏⲣ F v ⲟⲩⲱϩⲣ (ⲟⲩⲱϩⲣ).

ⲟⲩⲉϣ, ⲛ- v ⲟⲩⲱϣ gap.

ⲟⲩⲛⲏϣ S nn m, meaning unknown, an office or occupation: BMOr 6204 B ⲥⲉⲩⲣⲟⲥ ⲡϣⲉ ⲡⲡ-ⲙⲁⲕ/ ⲁⲙⲱⲡⲉ ⲡⲟⲩ. Cf? name ⲟⲩⲛⲉⲓϣ (Ryl 127).

ⲟⲩⲟⲉⲓϣ S, ⲟⲩⲁⲉⲓϣ AA²F, -ⲁⲓϣ A²F nn m, time, occasion: Lev 23 4 S, Eccl 3 3 SF, Is 30 8 SF, Jo 7 8 SA² (all B ⲥⲛⲟⲩ) καιρός, Ps 9 9 S(B = Gk), Mt 26 16 S(B do) εὐκαιρία; Deu 12 19 S(B c.), Job 14 13 S(B ⲡⲉⲓ), Jo 12 35 SA²(B c.), 1 Cor 7 39 SF (B = Gk) χρόνος; Sa 2 5 S βίος; Ps 89 8 S(B ⲉⲡⲉϩ) αἰών; Job 24 1 S(B ⲟⲩⲛⲟⲩ) ὥρα; ZNTW 24 90 F prophets ⲛⲧⲉ ⲡⲓⲟⲩ. ἀρχαῖος; Jo 13 33 A² ⲉⲧⲓ ⲕⲁⲓⲟⲩ. ϣⲏⲙ (SB om ⲟⲩ.) ἔτι μικρόν; Mt 13 30 SF(B c.) Gk om; PS 17 S ϣⲁⲛⲧⲉⲡⲉⲟⲩ. ϫⲱⲕ ⲉⲃⲟⲗ, BG 25 S (ⲟⲩ)ⲟⲩ. ⲡⲉ ⲉⲙⲡⲟⲩϯ ⲧⲱϣ ⲉⲣⲟϥ, ShBor 246 80 S ⲡⲟⲩ. ϣⲟⲟⲡ ⲡⲁⲩ, Z 282 S ⲡⲉⲟⲩ. ⲙⲡⲉϭⲓⲙⲱⲡ, ib 641 S ⲡⲟⲩ. ⲡⲣⲉϥϯ ⲕⲁⲣⲡⲟⲥ = C 89 127 B c., AP 39 A² ⲉ]ⲙⲡⲉⲟⲩ. ⲉⲡⲡⲉ, Ep 253 S ϩⲁϩ ⲡⲟⲩ. ϩⲁϩ ⲡϣⲁ (cf πολυχρονίζειν), BMis 77 S ϣⲁⲉⲡϩ ⲡⲟⲩ., JA '75 5 258 S ⲡⲉⲟⲩ. on earth (var R 1 2 37 ⲁϩⲉ); ⲡⲉⲟⲩ. ⲉⲧⲙⲙⲁⲩ SF, at that time: Ge 12 6, Mt 4 17 τότε; ib 14 1 SF (all B c.) ἐκείνῳ τῷ κ.; J 4 77 ⲉⲧⲁⲣⲭⲉⲓ ⲙⲡ. (cf ib 12 43 καί.); iterated, from time to time: Mani Berl Sitz '33 85 A² wrote them to you κατα ⲟⲩ. ⲟⲩ., J 65 65 S προς ⲧⲉⲩⲛⲑⲉⲓⲁ ⲁⲩⲱ ⲧϭⲟⲙ ⲡⲡⲟⲩ. ⲡⲟⲩ.

With preceding preposition. ⲥ ⲉ-S, at a (certain) time: ShIF 198 ⲡϣⲁϫⲉ ⲉⲧⲥⲏϩ ⲡⲉ ⲉⲩⲟⲩ.; ⲥ ⲉⲓⲥ S, since: Bor 134 4 (VitaSin) ⲉⲓⲥ (ⲟⲩ)ⲟⲩ. ⲉϥⲟ ⲡⲣⲱⲟⲩϣ ⲉⲣⲟⲛ = Miss 4 373 لنا زمان كبير; ⲥ ⲙⲛ-ⲡⲥⲁ- S, after: BMis 562 ⲕⲁϩ ⲡⲁⲟⲩⲱⲡ ⲉⲃⲟⲗ ⲙ. (ⲟⲩ)ⲟⲩ. manifestabitur ante tempus; ⲥ ⲛ-SSfAA²F, in, during: ViK 9670 81 ⲙⲡⲉⲭⲡⲟ...ⲙⲡⲉⲓⲛⲟϭ ⲡⲟⲩ. all this while, Lant 42 Sf let him reign ⲡⲟⲩⲙⲛⲏϣⲉ ⲡⲟⲩ., MR 5 33 F sim, BKU 1 26 (8116 b) F he will love thee ⲡⲟⲩⲛⲁϭ ⲉⲡⲟⲩ.; ⲡⲟⲩ. ⲡⲓⲙ, everytime, always: Lev 24 8, Ps 34 27 (var om ⲡ-) διὰ παντός, Mt 26 11, Phil 1 20 SF πάντοτε; Ps 9 25 παντὶ καιρῷ; Pro 1 22 SA(all B ⲡⲥ. ⲡ.) ὅσον ἂν χρ.; Sa 17 10 ἀεί; PS 80 ⲁⲡⲓⲥⲧⲉⲩⲉ ⲡⲟⲩ. ⲡ.; ⲙⲡⲓⲟⲩ., at this time, now: Sa 14 15 νῦν; at that time, formerly: ib 5 3 (B ϧⲉⲛⲫⲏ ⲉⲧⲁϥϭⲓⲡⲓ), Philem 11 (var ⲙⲡ., B c.) ποτέ; PS 43 ⲁⲓⲥⲱⲧⲙ ⲉⲣⲟⲕ ⲙ., ShBor 246 65 ⲡⲉⲡⲧⲁⲅⲍⲓⲟⲩ ⲙⲡⲃⲁⲣⲁⲗ ⲙ. (3 Kg 18 26), AP 42 A² ϩⲁⲧⲁⲉⲣϩ ⲙ., Blake 314 (ⲙ)ⲡ. ⲙⲉⲡ ⲥⲁⲟⲩⲗ ⲧⲉⲡⲟⲩ ϫⲉ ⲡⲁⲩⲗⲟⲥ; ⲙⲡⲉ(ⲟ)ⲩ., as last: BMar 113 ⲡⲉⲧⲟⲩⲟⲗⲉ ⲙⲡⲉ. ποτέ; Sa 11 15 πάλαι; PS 24 ⲡⲟⲉ ⲁⲡ ⲙⲡⲉⲟⲩ., ShC 73 40 ⲡⲓⲁⲧⲡⲉ ⲙⲡⲉ. at Deluge, BAp 94 Pharaoh's plagues ⲙⲡⲉⲟⲩ.; or in time to come: J 67 125 ⲡⲁⲣⲭⲱⲡ ⲉⲧⲁⲣⲭⲉⲓ ⲙⲡⲉ.; ⲡⲟⲩⲟⲩ.¹, ⲡⲟⲩ.², on a time (past): Sa 18 20², BHom 3 ⲁⲩϭⲱⲣⲡ ⲉⲣⲟⲕ ⲡ.² ϩⲓⲧⲡⲡⲉⲕⲃⲁⲗ, ClPr 54 43 ⲉⲥⲟ ⲡⲗⲓⲙⲡ ⲡ.², Z 339 walking ⲡ.² ϩⲛⲧⲉⲣⲛⲁⲟⲥ ποτέ; ShC 73 186 ⲡⲁⲧⲕⲁⲣ-ⲡⲟⲥ ⲡ.² ⲧⲉⲡⲟⲩ ϫⲉ (cf ib ⲡⲟⲩⲥ.), ib 42 187 stolen ⲡ.² ⲏ ⲙⲡⲡⲥⲁϩⲉⲛⲣⲟⲙⲡⲉ (cf ⲥ ⲙⲛⲡⲥⲁ- above), RChamp 371 who was a priest ⲡ.¹, BMis 16 ⲡ.² ⲙⲉⲛ king's son ⲙⲡⲟⲟⲩ ϫⲉ slave, BM 215 soul created ⲡ.², body

ⲡⲕⲉⲟⲩ.; sim (future): Job 14 11² (B ϩⲉⲛⲟⲩⲥ.)
χρόνῳ; Aeg 260 if one should wish ⲛ.¹, Bor 154 109
if one find ⲛ.², Mus 42 224 ⲉⲧⲣⲉⲩⲥⲣϥⲉ ⲟⲛ ⲛ.¹ ⲉⲡⲉϣⲗⲏⲗ at times;   ϣⲁⲟⲩ. S, until, during, later on
(v KKS 233): Si 1 22 ϣⲁ ⲉ- (B c.), Dan 7 12 (B diff)
ἕως κ.; Ac 13 11 (B c.) ἄχρι κ., Gött N '01 328 words
of scripture ⲉⲧⲉⲧⲛⲁⲥⲱⲧⲙ ϣ. ϫⲉ- (Mt 25 21), BMis
566 ⲛⲥⲉϫⲓⲧⲟⲩ ⲉϩⲟⲩⲛ ϣ. tunc, J 106 193 whoso shall
dare ⲧⲁⲛ (ⲕ.) ⲧⲉⲛⲟⲩ ⲧⲁⲛ ϣ.;   ϩⲁⲑⲏ S, before:
TT 66 ϩ. ⲛⲡⲉⲓⲟⲩ., PBu 53 do;   ϩⲙⲡ(ⲉ)ⲟⲩ. S, in:
Sa 14 16 ἐν χρ.; ShA 2 255 reprove ⲡⲉⲧϫⲓ ⲛϭⲟⲛⲥ
ϩ., Miss 8 132 faith declared ϩⲙⲡⲉⲓ- πάλαι (cf 130
sim ⲙ-), Ryl 62 2 is long-suffering (but) ϣⲁϥⲧⲱⲱⲃⲉ
ϩ., BG 36 had not hastened but ⲁⲩⲥⲱ ϩⲛ(ⲟⲩ)ⲟⲩ. for
a time;   ϫⲓⲛ- S, since, from: ShA 2 113 have heard
ϫ.ⲛⲓⲟⲩ. ⲉⲛⲓⲟⲩ. (cf ib ϫ.ⲛⲓⲥ. ⲉⲛⲓⲥ.), J 76 55 ϫⲉⲛⲟⲩ.
ⲛⲓⲙ ⲉϩⲣⲏⲩ;   ⲕⲁⲧⲁ S, from time to time: Nu 9 3
(B c.) κατὰ κ.; TT 49 yearly gifts ⲟⲩⲁ ⲕ. ⲟⲩ.;   ⲡⲁⲣⲁ ⲡⲟⲩ. S, beyond: 2 Tim 4 2 (B = Gk) ἀκαίρως;
ClPr 47 80 ⲁⲥⲥⲱⲃⲉ ⲡ. (v Ge 18 12);   ⲡⲣⲟⲥ ⲟⲩ. (for
ⲡ. ⲟⲩⲟⲩ.?) SA²F, for, during: Sa 4 4, 1 Cor 7 5 SF
(B c.) πρ. κ., Aeg 243 ⲟⲩⲡⲣⲟⲥⲟⲩ. πρόσκαιρος; BG
17 ⲉⲧϣⲟⲟⲡ ⲡ. ⲟⲩ., AP 56 A² ⲟⲩⲟⲩϫⲭⲉⲉⲓ ⲡ.ⲟⲩ., BMis
138 ⲡⲉⲓϣⲁⲉⲛⲉϩ, ⲡⲉⲓⲡ. ⲟⲩ., Pcod 4 ⲡⲉⲓⲡ. ⲟⲩⲟⲩ.

ⲁⲧⲟⲩ. S, without time, ill-timed: ShP 130² 33 ⲟⲩϯ
ⲧⲱⲛ ⲡⲁ. (on 1 Cor 1 12), ShLeyd 354 ⲧϭⲓⲛϣⲁϫⲉ
ⲡⲁ.;   ⲙⲡⲧⲁ.: Si 35 4 ϩⲛⲟⲩⲙ. ἀκαίρως.

ⲣ ⲟⲩ. SA²F, spend time: Job 29 18 (B as Gk) χρ.
βιοῦν, Ac 14 3 (B = Gk) χ. διατρίβειν, 1 Cor 16 7 SF
(B do) χ. ἐπιμένειν; Pcod 22 ⲁϥⲣ ⲡⲉϥⲟⲩ. ⲧⲏⲣϥ (var
ⲁϩⲉ), PS 33 ⲣ ⲟⲩⲛⲟϭ ⲙⲙⲏⲛϣⲉ ⲡⲟⲩ. ⲛⲃⲟⲗ ⲧⲁⲓ,
Mani H 14 A² ⲁⲅⲣ ⲡⲟⲩⲟⲩ. ⲡⲣⲏⲧϥ (sc world), J 75
24 ⲡⲉϥⲟⲩ. ⲉⲧϥⲛⲁⲁⲁϥ ⲉϩⲟⲛⲣ.

ϩⲉ ⲉⲡⲟⲩ. S, find time: 1 Cor 16 12 (B = Gk) εὐκαιρεῖν.

ϭⲙ ⲡⲟⲩ. S, as last: Ps 74 2 (B ϭⲓ ⲡⲟⲩⲥ.) κ. λαμβάνειν; Phil 4 10 neg (B diff) ἀκαιρεῖν; BMis 247
ⲉⲓϣⲁⲛϩⲉ. ϯⲛⲁⲕⲁⲑⲁⲣⲓⲍⲉ.

ⲟⲩⲱϣ SA²BFO, -ϣⲉ SA², -ϩⲉ A, ⲟⲩϣⲉ Sⁿ(nn),
ⲟⲩⲉϣ F (nn), ⲟⲩⲉϣ- SB(2 pl)F, ⲟⲩϣ- A²F, ⲟⲩⲱϣ-
SA²B, ⲟⲩⲱϩ- A, ⲟⲩⲁϣ- BF, ⲟⲩⲉϣⲉ- S/F, ⲟⲩⲁϣⲍ
SA²BFO, ⲟⲩⲟϣⲍ S, ⲟⲩⲁϩⲍ A, ⲟⲩⲉϣⲍ F vb **I** intr,
desire, love: Ge 39 8 SB, Is 1 19 SA(Cl)B, Lu 5 13
SB θέλειν; Ex 4 23 AB, Pro 1 10 SAB(var ⲣⲁⲟⲩ)
βούλεσθαι; Mt 12 18 S(B ϯ ⲙⲁϯ), He 10 6 F(S ⲣ
ϩⲛⲁⲍ, B do) εὐδοκεῖν; Ro 8 20 B(S ϩⲛⲁⲍ) ἑκών; J 1
30 S I had recourse to this deed ⲉⲓⲟⲩⲱϣ ⲁⲩⲱ ⲉⲓ-
ⲡⲓⲑⲉ (cf PLond 1 232 ἐκ. κ. πεπεισμένος), Aeg 258
S ⲙⲡⲛⲁⲩ ⲉⲧⲉⲟⲩ., HL 107 B ⲧⲁⲓϭⲃⲱ ϫⲟⲩ. ϯⲙⲉⲧ-
ϭⲁⲥⲓϩⲏⲧ (or) if thou wilt, C 43 140 B ⲁⲕϣⲁⲡⲟⲩ. ϯ-
ⲡⲁⲥⲃⲁⲓ, BM 1112 S ϭⲟⲩ. ϭⲙⲟⲥⲧⲉ nolens volens, EW
194 B ϩⲉⲙⲥⲓ ϩⲉⲛⲧⲉⲕⲣⲓ…ⲉⲕⲟⲩ. ⲡⲧⲉⲕⲟⲩⲱⲙ ⲙⲡⲉⲕ-
ⲱⲓⲕ (Gk Esaias Abbas 21 5 om);   as imperat, be

pleased to S (cf θέλησον, v CO 511 n): 1 Kg 18 22 ⲟⲩ.
ⲉⲣⲙⲟⲟⲥ ⲙⲡ- ἐπιγάμβρευσον; Mor 17 61 ⲟⲩ. ϫⲉⲉⲣⲉ-
ⲡⲉⲛⲏⲓ ⲛⲁϣⲱⲡⲉ ϩⲡⲟⲩⲥⲙⲟⲩ θέλησον κ. αὐτὸς πιστεῦ-
σαι; CO 257 ⲟⲩ. ⲛⲡⲧⲛⲛⲟⲟⲩ ⲡⲉⲕϣⲏⲣⲉ, BM 1167
ⲟⲩ.…ⲛⲡⲧⲓ, Ep 354 ⲟⲩ. ⲧⲡⲛⲟⲟⲩϥ, Ryl Suppl 25 ⲟⲩ.
ⲟⲩⲛ ⲧⲁⲁϥ, WS 99 ⲟⲩ. ⲛⲡⲉⲣⲡⲁⲣⲁⲅⲉ, ST 260 ⲟⲩⲱϣⲉ ⲙⲁⲣⲉⲧⲉⲕⲙ(ⲧ)ⲉⲓⲱⲧ ⲧⲡⲛⲁⲩ, cf Ryl 361 ⲕⲟⲩ.
ⲟⲩⲛ ⲙⲁⲣⲉ-;   c ϫⲉ-, ϫⲉⲕⲁⲥ, ϩⲓⲛⲁ: Mani 2 A¹
ⲉϥⲟⲩ(ⲱ)ϣⲉ ϫⲉⲉϥⲁⲃⲱⲕ, Miss 8 231 S ϯⲟⲩ. ϫⲉⲕ.
ⲉⲣⲉⲧⲁⲡⲣⲟ, AM 23 B ⲉⲓⲟⲩ. ϩ. ⲡⲧⲉⲕⲥϩⲁⲓ;   c conj:
Mt 13 28 B(S ⲉⲧⲣⲉⲛ-), MG 25 211 B ϫⲟⲩ. ⲡⲧⲉⲛ-
ϫⲱ θ.; AM 190 B ⲉⲓⲟⲩ. ⲡⲧⲉⲕϣⲗⲏⲗ, J 92 43 S ⲡⲉⲧⲟⲩ. ⲙⲉⲛ (ⲛ)ϥⲡⲁⲣⲁⲃⲁ, Kr 233 F ⲧⲓⲟⲩ. ⲉⲕϣⲁⲡ, Ep
241 S ⲙⲁⲣⲉⲧⲉⲕⲙⲛⲧⲉⲓⲱⲧ ⲟⲩⲱϣⲉ ⲡϭϫⲟⲟⲩ (cf ST
above);   c ⲧⲁⲣⲉ-: BM 1104 S ⲧⲛⲟⲩ. ⲧⲁⲣⲛ-
ⲡⲁⲩ;   c ⲉ-, wish, be ready to: Ps 77 10 SB, 1 Cor
14 35 SBF, BHom 54 S ⲙⲡⲉⲥⲟⲩ. ⲉⲭⲟⲟϥ, Z 294 S
ⲕⲟⲩ. ⲉⲃⲱⲕ?, MG 25 217 B ϯⲟⲩ. ⲉⲱⲣϥ θ.; 2 Kg 6
10 B(S ⲣ ϩⲛⲁⲍ), Is 30 15 SBF, BHom 49 S ⲉⲩⲟⲩ.
ⲉⲉⲓⲣⲉ β.; Ps 67 17 S(B ϯ ⲙ.) εὐδ.; Ro 1 11 B(S
ⲟⲩⲉϣ-) ἐπιποθεῖν; Ex 4 24 B(A ϣⲓⲛⲉ ⲥⲉ-) ζητεῖν;
1 Kg 23 26 B ⲟⲩ. ⲉⲧⲁϩⲱⲟⲩ (S Gk om), BHom 13 S
ⲉⲩⲟⲩ. ⲉⲧⲱⲣⲡ (Gk om); PS 49 S ⲉϣϫⲉ ⲕⲟⲩ. ⲉⲉⲓ,
ST 315 S ϯ(ⲟⲩ)ⲱϣ ⲉⲡⲁⲩ, BMis 317 S ⲉϥ(ⲟⲩ)ⲱϣ
ⲉϩⲟⲡϥ, El 68 A ⲉϥⲟⲩ. ⲁⲁⲙⲕⲟⲩ, ShC 42 39 S in
wrestling ⲡⲉⲧⲟⲩ. ⲉⲧⲁⲅⲟⲓ ⲉϩⲣⲁⲓ, Mor 23 34 S such
heat that skin ⲟⲩ. ⲉϭⲱⲗ ⲉⲃⲟⲗ, Worr 297 S ⲡⲟⲩ.
ⲉⲉⲓⲣⲉ ⲙⲡϣⲁ about to, J 67 117 S ⲁⲩⲟⲩ. ⲉϣⲱⲡⲉ ⲉ-
ⲃⲱⲗ ⲉⲃⲟⲗ, AM 86 B ⲉⲓⲃⲟⲩϣ ⲉⲉⲣ ⲁⲥⲡⲁⲥⲁⲥⲑⲉ, Va 63
8 B ⲉⲣⲉⲟⲩ. ⲉϭⲓ ⲥⲙⲟⲩ ⲡⲁϣ ⲡⲣⲏϯ? = BMis 377 S
ⲉⲣⲡⲁⲥⲩⲡⲁⲅⲉ?, Mor 27 17 F ⲉϥⲟⲩ. ⲉⲕⲁⲡⲥⲧ = BMis
348 S ⲉϥⲛⲁⲕ., AP 20 A² ⲉⲉⲓⲟⲩⲱϣⲉ ⲁⲟⲩⲱⲙ, Bodl(P)
e 47 S ϣⲁⲣⲉⲡⲣⲃⲛⲟⲅⲉ ⲙⲡⲙⲁ ⲟⲩ. ⲉⲁⲁϥ require to be
done, PGM 1 60 673 O ⲁⲡⲕ ⲓⲉϩⲟⲣ (cf ? Ryl Dem 3
207 n) ⲉⲧⲟⲩ. ⲉⲡⲓ[;   BM 247 8 S ⲛⲡⲉ ⲟⲩ. ⲉⲧⲣⲉⲡϭⲱ
θ.; ShC 42 164 S ⲉⲩⲟⲩⲱϣⲉ ⲉⲧⲣⲉϥⲉⲛⲕⲟⲟⲩⲉ ⲙⲉⲧⲁ-
ⲡⲟⲉⲓ, P 129¹⁴ 123 S ⲉⲓⲟⲩ. ⲉⲧⲣⲁⲃⲱⲕ = DeV 1 78 B
(l ⲉⲓⲟⲩ.) was about to, Ep 134 S ϥⲟⲩ. ⲧⲣⲁⲉⲓ, C 43 60
B ϫⲟⲩ. ⲉⲑⲣⲓϯ ⲙⲧⲟⲛ ⲡⲁⲕ; PMéd 216 S ⲉⲕⲟⲩ.
ⲧⲣⲉⲩⲣⲱⲧ;   c ⲡ-, as last: Mor 24 34 F ⲛⲧⲉⲗⲉⲡⲉ-
ⲧⲣⲱⲥ ⲟⲩ. ⲡⲧⲟⲩⲛⲁⲥϥ ⲁϥⲭⲁⲁⲥ (var ib 23 46 S om ⲟⲩ.
ⲛ-), BM 1013 21 S ⲉⲩϣⲁⲡⲟⲩ. ⲡⲣ ⲡⲁⲓ, AM 158 B
ⲡⲁϥⲟⲩ. ⲡⲉⲣ ⲃⲁⲥⲁⲛⲓⲍⲓⲛ ⲙⲙⲟⲟⲩ;   c ⲛⲥⲁ-, after,
toward: Tri 453 S God ⲟⲩ. ⲛⲥⲁϩⲟⲓⲛⲉ that cry unto Him يريد قوما.

II tr: Ps 21 8 SA(Cl)B, ib 39 14 S(B ⲕⲱϯ ⲛⲥⲁ-),
Mt 12 7 SBF, Jo 3 8 SA²(B ϩⲛⲁⲍ), MG 25 216 B ⲫϯ
ⲟⲩⲁϣ ϯⲯⲩⲭⲏ, BHom 17 S ⲡⲉⲧⲕⲟⲩⲟϣϥ θ.; Job
30 14 S(B intr), Is 1 11 SBF, Aeg 222 S give to ⲡⲉⲧ-
ⲉϥⲟⲩⲁϣϥ β.; Ge 22 2 S(B ⲙⲏⲓ), Jo 11 5 A²(SB do)
ἀγαπᾶν; Sa 8 2 S, Ge 29 11 S(var ⲕⲁⲧⲁϥ., B ⲙⲉⲓ)
φιλεῖν; Jos 9 31 S δοκεῖν, Ps 50 16 S(ACl ⲧⲱⲧ ⲡ-
ϩⲏⲧ, B ϯ ⲙⲁϯ) εὐδ.; Mal 3 17 A(B ⲥⲱⲧⲡ) αἱρετί-

ζειν; Deu 7 7 *SB* ἐκλέγειν; Job 3 21 *S(B м.)* ὁμείρεσθαι; Pro 7 15 *SA(B* do) ποθ., Ps 83 2 *S(B ϭι ϣ-*
ϣϣωογ) ἐπιπ.; *ib* 118 40 *SSᶠ*ογεωϣ- (Pcod Mor, *B*
= Gk) ἐπιθυμεῖν; Mt 8 29 *S* εκογεϣ ογ пимаи
(*B* diff) τί ἡμῖν καὶ σοί?, Z 338 *S* ερογεϣ ογ мн-
τί θέλεις αὐτόν?; PS 267 *S* εϥογεϣ ппє, BG 18 *S*
аϥογοϣϲ, ShA 1 419 *S* сеογаϣϥ ... семе ммоϥ,
Gu 44 *S* ϭε птаϥογарϥ ммос (*ib* ογаϣϥ), TU 43.
11 *A* пететпоγарϥ, C 43 57 *B* εθογаϣ ϥϯ, *ib* 68 *B*
εθογωϣ ϥϯ, AP 20 *A²* κογаϣϥ, C 89 53 *B* ειογεϣ
петепιωτ to speak with him = MG 17 570 نزر,
BM 527 *F* potion тса[с] паϯии ϣасογаϣ[ϥ], Kr
91 *S* ϫ(εε)ιογωϣ ϭελαγ ϥарос, Gu 87 *S* ογ пет-
когаϣϥ птоотп?, PGM 1 60 *O* аϥ (*S* аϣ) пет-
когаϣϥ? ϣογογаϣϥ *S, worthy to be loved*:
Dan 9 23 (*B* as Gk) ἐπιθυμῶν; RChamp 371 па-
мерιτ аγω пϣογογаϣϥ, BMOr 7561 85 calf-god
called пϣ. & пϣογмериτϥ (*cf* TT 68); ογεϣ-
before vb *SA²F*: Jud 13 23 (var ογωϣ ε-) θ.; Job
9 3 (*B* ογωϣ ε-), Sa 14 19 (var do) β.; Si 25 18 εὐδ.;
Jo 4 9 *SA²*(*BF* = Gk) αἰτεῖν; Jud 11 17 ειογ. ει
εβολ ϧμпεккаϥ δή; PS 113 аιογ. ει ератк, ShMIF
23 135 ϯογ. εиие ϫε-, Mor 30 52 *F* птпоγ. тωογп
= *ib* 29 45 *S* εκпатωογп, Kr 35 *F* ειογ. ϭапϧ, MR
5 55 *F* аϧογϣ пот пεϧ; Mt 20 32 ετпоγ. траααϥ
(*BF* ογаϣϥ пта-) θ.; Mor 41 189 εκογ. траогω-
ϣт, *ib* 28 81 ειογ. (п)тетамоι, JKP 2 20 sim, BM
661 *F* тιογ. (п)тектала; ογωϣ- sim *SA²F*:
RNC 40 пϯογ. ап ϭω β. εἶναι; Mani H 83 *A²* εγογ.
тλϭаϥ, J 35 31 петογ. кωт, BMEA 10577 damaged
water-conduit соγ. сαптε *needeth repair*; BM 664
F тιογ. тамак, but *ib* 581 *F* тιογ. ετα.), BM 1135
коγ. ϫι ϥіие; ογεϣ (ε)ϧαλ *F* sim ?(elliptic):
BM 619 when thou hast my letter ογεϣ ϫαιι(апι)
...ϧαλ εса[, *ib* 621 ογεϣ пειλομι...ϧαλ εпϣн п-
...пεϧι пεϧανιιло(сιон), *ib* 622 sim.

—— nn m *SAA²BF, desire, love*: Ps 1 2 *SB*, Ro
12 2 *SBF*, Ap 4 11 *S*-ϣε (*B* ϥпа϶), Cl 20 4 *A*, AP 16
A²-ϣε θέλημα; Ps 105 4 *S*(*B* ϯ м.), Si 9 15 *S* εὐδοκία; Ez 16 36 *SB* ἐνθύμημα, Ps 9 37 *S*(*B* = Gk)
ἐπιθυμία; Nu 29 39 *S*(*B* diff) ἑκούσιος, Ps 53 8 *B*
ϫεппаογ. (*S* εϧпаι)-σίως; Ro 1 27 *B*(*S* ме) ὄρεξις;
Lev 22 18 *S*(*B* ογ. п϶нт) αἵρεσις, Eccl 1 17 *S*(*F*
λογат) προαί.; Ap 17 17 *S*(*B* = Gk) γνώμη; BG
124 *S* поγωϣε тнрϥ ппаггелос, ShViK 923 *S*
loving her ϧипетпоγ. псаркικοп, DeV 2 114 *B*
ϥογ. мпесϧнт, ShC 42 172 *S* поγ. εϧογп επεϥ-
ειοτε, Mor 39 33 *S* пεϥογ. εϧογп епεϥϣнре = C
43 53 *B* мει п϶нт, ShA 2 281 *S* огоγ. мпоγсωϧε
мпоγ мптартос *whim*, ShIF 108 *S* scratching itch
ϧипоγ. мпεϥϧωϥ (or *?* ιογωωϣε), TurO 7 *S* пεκ-
огωϣε аριϥ, J 68 57 *S* паι(ε)итϭрафоп поγωϣε
паιαθнкн, *ib* 71 16 *S* sim, C 89 208 *B* паоγ. аппе

to do this, Bodl(P) d 54 *S* εκεϥερμннеγε паι ϧип-
пекоγ. ετϧε- *if it please thee*, PLond 4 435 *S* Basil
ϧиπογ. пппє ... паτарϫ(ος), MR 5 48 *F* ϥεпоγ.
εппоγтι, Kr 19 *F* ϥεпоγεϣ п[п., AM 116 *B* ϥογ.
ипϭε мареϥϣωпι, *ib* 248 *B* begotten ката оγ.
(*bis*), *ib* 180 *B* ordained пара пεϥογ., RE 9 142 *S*
аγϫρω паι прос пεγογ., Va 61 214 *B* ϫεппаογ.
аγαϣт on cross, Cai 42573 2 *S* title of recipe (оγ)оγ.
паλмоϭаррап (جرب, *cf* δόκιμος), *ib* (оγ)оγ. п-
пас϶ ending масογϣ кеоγа ϣарак.

ειρε мпоγ., р поγ. &c *SA²B, do will*: Ps 144 19
SB, Jo 4 34 *SA²B*(*F* петεрпε϶) θέλημα ποιεῖν; Ge
33 10 *S*(*B* ϯ маϯ пεм-) εὐδ. acc; R 2 4 85 *S* let
none р пεϥογ. ϧиоγпаθος пепιθγиιа, C 43 84 *B*
акер паоγ., PMich 601 *Sa* птар паογϣε пεμас,
ShA 1 42 *S* пεϧο поγ. паι н прооϣϣ *desirable*.

оγ. п϶нт *SB, heart's desire*: Is 58 3 *B*(*S* оγ.)
θέλημα; Ez 20 16 *SB* ἐνθύμημα, Ps 18 11 *B*(*S* оγ.)
ἐπιθυμητός, Ro 1 24 *S*(*B* птε поγϥ.) ἐπιθυμία; ShC
42 126 *S* εγειρε пепιθγоγ. п϶., J 6 12 *S* па(оγ)-
ωϣε п϶. мптапроϥγресιс (*cf* PLond 3 280 ἑκουσία
.γνώμη).

—— εϧολ *S* nn, *as* оγ.: BMis 278 п϶оγ. εϧ. ε-
ϧогп εрос = Mor 29 50 om εϧ., *cf* 279 пεϥογ. εϥ. ε.
ϭипоγ. *S, desire, intention*: Ming 295 ара ϣаρε-
τϭ. рωϣε ετρεκτсаϧο ερος (*sc* τεϫпн)?
оγаϣϥ *S* nn m, *desire*: Sh(?)Mor 54 105 heaven
ετεϥп϶нтϥ пϭι петпоγ. (or *? him that we love*).

As name?: поγωϣ (BM 689), BP 10589 поγ.
(п)ϣипоγтε.

оγωϣ *SAB*, ᵇ. *B* nn m, *a cleft, gap*(*B* rare): Ex
33 22 (*B* ϫολ), Eccl 12 3, Cant 5 4 ὀπή; Jud 15 11,
Jer 29 16 (*B* ϧнϧ) τρυμαλιά; 2 Kg 18 17 χάσμα;
Jon 2 6 *SA*(*B* ϥωϫι) σχισμή; Zeph 2 14 *A*(*B* ϣатϭ)
διόρυγμα; Cant 2 14 (misunderst, *F* пεϣϯ) σκέπη;
Ez 13 11 *SB* ἔνδεσμος *joint*; ShC 73 63 peeping in
ϧиπоγ. мпро, ShMun 177 ϧиπογ. пιτооγ н ϧип-
ϣκολ, Bor 134 1 (Vita Sin) поγ. птпетра = C 41
25 *B* ϧωϣ, ShA 2 332 teeth filed ϣапτоγр ϣиа
псер оγ.; таπογ. *v* тωп *stitch*. ᵇ space, *distance B*(*S* rare): Ge 32 16 (*S* ωрϫ) διάστημα, Ac 27
28 (*S* diff), Lu 22 59 (*S* om) διστάναι; MG 25 251
distant поγкоγϫι поγ., C 86 290 prayed ϣафоγ.
(var паγ) поγогпоγ.; with pref аγ- *about (circa)*
B: Lu 22 41 (*S* поγϫε) βολή; Ge 21 16 (*S* Gk om),
Jon 3 3 (*SA* Gk do); ROC 25 256 distant паγфоγ.
поγρεϯ птε огстаϫιоп, AM 239 sim; ка оγ.
S, set an interval: BMis 246 = Z 263 *S* аϥка оγ.
паγ εϧраι that they should come; ϯ оγ. *S, set
a distance*: Ex 26 33 (*B* огωϯ εϧολ) διορίζειν. ᶜ
interval, pause, holiday S (*v* Ep 284 n): Saq 226
пϣа меппоγ. меп(п)кγрιакн, BMis 472 пεпоγ.
пε пεϧооγ ετιιаγ, Ep 457 пϣорп п϶ооγ поγ.,

Tor 27 sim, Ep 284 on 14th Paϣne ϩⲛⲡⲙⲉϩⲥⲛⲁⲩ ⲛ-
ϩⲟⲟⲩ ⲡⲟⲩ., Win 61 1st Pashans ⲡⲟⲩ. ⲛⲧⲙⲛⲧⲉ, *ib* 46
ϩⲙⲡⲟⲩ. ⲛⲧⲙⲛⲧⲉ ⲕⲁⲡ ⲡⲧⲛⲏⲥⲧⲓⲁ ⲟⲩ, Turin ostr
5889 come & fetch it ⲛⲡⲟⲩ. ⲛⲧⲙⲛⲧⲉ, PStras 226
list ⲧⲕⲟⲩⲡⲏⲥⲧⲓⲁ, ⲡⲟⲩ. ⲣ ⲟⲩ., *make pause, wait
for* : BP 9419 ⲉⲓⲥ ϩⲏⲧⲉ ϯⲣ ⲟⲩ. ⲉⲣⲟⲕ & we will go &
work, CO 372 sim (ⲟⲩ)ⲱ., *ib* Ad 47 send & tell us
ⲛⲧⲣ ⲟⲩ. ⲉⲣⲟⲓ, RChamp 495 ⲉⲓⲉⲣ (ⲟⲩ)ⲱϣ ⲁⲡⲣⲉⲩ
(for ⲉⲡⲣⲏⲩ) ⲙⲡⲉϥⲉⲓ, Win 48 ⲁⲓⲣⲓⲥⲉ ⲉⲓⲣ ⲟⲩ. ⲙⲡⲕ-
ⲧⲏⲡⲟⲟⲩⲅ.   Or ? *l* ⲱϣ (*v* ⲱϣ **C b**).

ⲡⲟⲩⲉϣ *SF*, -ⲱϣ *S*(twice)*A²*, -ⲉϣⲉⲛ *B* (*v* below
Aeg 50), ⲟⲩϣ *A* prep c gen ⲛ- (in *B* mostly ⲛ̄-), *with
lack, absence of*, so *without*, followed by nn : Ex 21
11 *S*(*B* ⲁⲧ-), Job 8 11 *B*(*S* ⲁⲭⲛ-) ἄνευ; Ro 3 28 *S*(*B*
ⲁⲧϭⲛⲉ-), He 7 20 *S*(*BF* do) χωρίς; Mt 5 32 *B*(*S* do)
παρεκτός; He 7 24 *B*(*S* do), BMar 161 *S* ⲛ. ⲡⲧⲟⲟⲩⲉ, Aeg 290 *S* ⲛ. ⲓⲥⲡⲟⲩ ἀ-, ἀν-; Ps 80 14 *S* ⲛ.
ⲡⲗⲁⲁⲩ (*B* ⲛϩⲣⲏⲓ ϩⲉⲛⲡⲗⲓ) ἐν τῷ μηδενί; ST 172 *S*
(ⲛ)ⲡⲓⲕⲁⲁⲩ ⲉⲃⲟⲗ ⲛ. ⲡⲗⲁⲩ, KKS 580 *S* slay me ⲛ.
ⲛⲃⲁⲥⲁⲛⲟⲥ, BMis 105 *S* ⲁⲥⲙⲓⲥⲉ ⲛ. ⲡⲣⲟⲟⲩⲧ, Mani H
78 *A²* ⲉ]ⲅϭⲏⲡ ⲛ. ⲡⲣⲏ, C 43 34 *B* throne left ⲛ. ⲟⲩⲣⲟ
= Mor 39 5 *S* ⲛ. ⲉⲣⲟ (cf 40 3 *S* ⲟⲩ. ⲡⲣⲣⲟ), Pcod 18
S ⲉⲟⲩⲱϣ ⲉⲙⲛⲥⲉ(doubtful);   followed by vb : Ps 9
27 *B*(*S* ⲁⲭⲛ-)ἄνευ; Ro 10 14 *S*(*B* ⲁⲧϭ.) χ.; Ac 20 20
B(*S* ⲉⲧⲙ-) τοῦ μή; Mt 15 20 *B*(*S* ⲙⲡⲉ-), Ac 14 17
B(*S* ⲁⲧ-), He 2 8 *B*(*SF* ⲛ- ⲁⲛ), BAp 52 *S* ⲛ. ⲡⲗⲩⲡⲉⲓ
ⲙⲙⲟϥ ἀ-, ἀν-; Mk 8 3 *S* ⲛ. ⲛⲟⲩⲱⲙ (*B* ⲁⲧ-) νῆστις;
Z 338 *S* died ⲛ. ⲛϣⲁϫⲉ *non loquens* (*B* MG 25 215
Gk PG 65 265 om); ShBM 206 84 *S* ⲙⲡⲟⲩϭⲱ ⲛ.
ⲡⲧⲁⲙⲓⲟ, CO 328 *S* ⲙⲡⲣϭⲱ ⲛ. ⲡⲉⲓ, PMich 4553 *S*
ⲙⲡⲣϭⲱ ⲡⲟⲩⲱϣ ⲉϩⲟⲟⲩ, C 43 189 *B* ⲁϥⲟⲣⲓ ⲛ. ⲟⲩⲱⲙ
ⲟⲩⲇⲉ ⲉϣⲧⲉⲙⲥⲱ, Miss 4 93 *B* ⲙⲡⲉϥϩⲉⲙⲥⲓ ⲛ. ⲓ, Aeg
50 *B* ϯⲛⲁⲭⲁⲥ ⲁⲛ ⲡⲟⲩⲉϣⲉⲛ ⲉⲑⲣⲉⲥⲟⲩⲟⲛϩⲥ (cf FR
108), Bor 240 58 *S* ⲡⲟⲩⲉϣ ⲉⲧⲣⲉⲡⲉⲩⲥⲱⲙⲁ ϩⲉ;   om
pref ⲛ-*SA*: Lu 6 49(var ⲛ-,*B* = Gk)χ.; Cl 62 2 *A* ⲟⲩϣ
ⲡⲙⲁⲕⲙⲓⲕ ἀ-; Sh(Besa)Bor 204 245 ⲛⲧⲉⲭⲓ...ⲟⲩ. ⲛ-
ϣⲓⲡⲉ, Mor 40 3 *v* C 43 34 above, R 2 4 75 ⲁⲣⲭⲛⲟ
ⲟⲩ. ⲛⲕⲟⲓⲛⲱⲛⲓⲁ, TU 43 20 *A* ⲁⲧⲉⲧⲛϯ ... ⲟⲩϣ ⲡⲣ
ⲫⲑⲟⲛⲉⲓ, Mus 40 36 (Reg Pach) none may go ⲟⲩ. ⲛ-
ϫⲟⲟⲩ ⲥⲟⲡ ⲛⲙⲙⲁϥ (but *ib* 41 ⲛ. ⲡⲟⲩⲱϣⲙ), *ib* 42
215 she left naught ⲟⲩ. ⲛⲣⲟⲃⲉϥ;   om ⲛ- gen *SF*:
1 Cor 15 27 *F*(Mor 38, *S* ⲛⲃⲟⲗ ⲛ-, *B* ϣⲁⲧⲉⲛ-) ἐκτός;
1 Kg 7 8 ⲡⲟⲩ. ⲱϣ ⲉϩⲣⲁⲓ (var ⲛ-) παρασιωπᾶν; ShC
73 91 ⲛ. ⲟⲩⲱⲙ, Miss 4 242 heat will slay us ⲛ. ⲟⲩⲕⲟⲩⲓ ⲙⲙⲟⲟⲩ = C 41 38 *B* misunderst, Aeg 18 ⲛ.
ⲣⲓⲙⲉ = *ib* *B* ⲁϭⲛⲉϯ ⲉⲣⲙⲏ.   V ϣⲟⲩ, ⲛ-.

ογϣΗ *SA²F*, ⲟⲩϩⲓ *A*, -ϣⲓ *F*, pl ⲟⲩϣⲟⲟⲩⲉ *S*, ⲟⲩⲁ-
ϣⲟⲩⲉ *A²* & sg as pl, nn f, *night*, always = *B* ⲉϫⲱⲣϩ:
Job 7 3, Is 34 10 *SF*, Mic 3 6 *SA*, Jo 9 4 *SA²* νύξ; PS
146, ShC 42 107, BMar 133, Mani 2 *A²* ϥⲧⲟⲉ ⲡⲟⲩ.,
JKP 2 144 *F* -ϣⲓ; ⲧⲡⲁϣⲉ ⲛⲧⲉⲩ., *midnight* : Is 59
10, Mk 13 35 *SF* μεσονύκτιον; ⲡⲟⲩⲟⲩ. *S*, *during a
night* : Bodl(P)a 2 27 ⲉⲓϣⲟⲩⲉⲓ ⲙⲙⲟϥ ⲛ(ⲟⲩ)ⲟⲩ.;   ⲛ-

ⲧⲉⲩϣⲏ, *by night* : Ps 41 8, Ob 5 *A*, Jo 3 2 *SA²* νυκτός,
Ps 104 39, Mk 4 27 νύκτα; ϩⲛⲧ. sim; Ps 21 2 νυκτός,
Hos 7 6 *A* -ⲧⲁ, Mt 26 31 -ⲧⲓ́; AP 22 *A²*;   pl forms:
Ps 133 2, Tob 10 6, ShRE 10 161, R 1 1 70, Mor 23
53 ⲡⲟⲩ. ⲛⲓⲉⲧⲟⲩⲁⲁⲃ *vigils*, Mani 1 *A²*.

ⲁⲧⲟⲩ. *S*, *without night* (sleep): PMich 601 charm
ⲁ(ⲁ)ⲥ ⲡⲁⲧⲛⲕⲟⲧⲉ ⲁ(ⲁ)ⲥ ⲛⲁ., Bodl(P) a *l a* boil it ⲛⲍ̄
ⲡⲣⲟⲟⲩ ⲛⲁ. *not during night*.

ⲣ ⲟⲩ. *S*, *pass night* : BM 217 ϣⲁⲥⲉⲣ ⲧⲉⲩ. undo-
ing her work.

ⲟⲩ. ⲡⲣⲟⲉⲓⲥ *v* ⲣⲟⲉⲓⲥ.

ⲟⲩⲉϣⲉ *S* nn, meaning unknown : ShMIF 23
156 ⲛϣⲟⲉⲓϣ ⲙⲛⲟⲩ. on face and body of runners.
Cf ? ⲟⲩⲱⲱϣⲉ.

ⲟⲩⲟⲉⲓϣⲉ *S* nn f, meaning unknown : Ep 38 ⲙ-
ⲡⲣⲛⲉϫ ϩⲟⲟⲩ ⲛⲥⲁϩⲟⲟⲩ ⲉϣⲱⲡⲉ ⲉⲕϣⲁⲛϭⲛ ⲧⲟⲩ. ⲉⲓ-
ⲙⲛ[.

ⲟⲩⲱϣϣⲉ *SA²* *v* ⲟⲩⲱϣϣ vb.

ⲟⲩⲱ(ⲱ)ϣⲉ *S*, ⲟⲩⲁϣϣ⸗ *S'F* vb intr, *consume by
burning* : Deu 9 3 = He 12 29 (*B* ⲟⲩⲱⲙ) καταναλί-
σκειν; ShA 1 449 flame reached tree & ⲁϥⲟⲩ. ⲉⲙⲁⲧⲉ, *ib* branches ⲁⲩⲣⲱⲕϩ others ⲁⲩⲟⲩ., ShP 130² 3
trees ⲁⲩⲟⲩ. ⲁⲩⲱ ⲁⲩⲣⲱⲕϩ, ShIF 102 diseased limbs
ⲉⲩⲟⲩ. ⲏ ⲉⲩⲗⲟϭⲗⲉϭ ⲉⲃⲟⲗ through fever, Mor 41 221
when coals thrown in his face ⲁⲡⲉϥϩⲟ ⲟⲩ.   tr:
BKU 1 26 (8116 b) *F* ⲟⲩⲁϣϣⲟⲩ (sc parts already
boiled)ϩⲓⲡⲕⲱϩⲧ, CO 335 *Sª* ⲟⲩϭⲗⲱ ⲡⲉⲯⲡⲉⲥⲧⲉⲡⲟⲩ-
ϭⲉ (*l* ? ⲛⲡⲉⲥ ⲥⲧⲉ-)...ⲙⲛⲧⲏⲡ ⲧⲏⲡⲟⲥ ⲡⲉⲟⲩⲁϣϣ.

ⲟⲩⲱϣϩ *SA²*, -ϥ *S*, -ⲃⲉ *A*, ⲟⲩⲉϣϩ- *S*, ⲟⲩⲁϣϩ-
A², ⲟⲩⲟϣⲃ⸗ *S*, -ⲁϣⲃ⸗ *A²* vb intr, *answer* : Ge 31 14
(*B* ⲉⲣ ⲟⲩⲱ), Mt 28 5 (*B* do, *F* ⲟⲩⲱⲣⲙ), Jo 3 9 *SA²*
(*BF* do) ἀποκρίνεσθαι; Job 15 2 (*B* ϯ ⲉ.) ἀπόκρισιν
διδόναι; *ib* 4 1 (*B* ⲉ.) ὑπολαμβάνειν; Ac 12 13 (*B* do)
ὑπακούειν; PS 30 ⲁϥⲟⲩ. ϫⲉ ⲡⲉϫⲁϥ ϫⲉ-, CO 244
ⲁⲓⲟⲩ. ⲁⲓⲭⲟⲟⲩ, Aeg 276 let communicant ⲟⲩ. ϫⲉ-
ϩⲁⲙⲏⲛ;   tr: Is 41 28 (*B* do), Jo 18 22 *A²* ⲟⲩⲁϣϩ-
(*S* dat, *B* do)ἀπ. dat, Job 35 4 (*B* ⲟⲩⲱⲣⲉⲙ) ἀπόκρισιν
δ. dat, ShR 2 3 16 ⲙⲡϣⲁ ⲡⲟⲩⲟϣⲃⲟⲩ ἀξίους ἀποκρί-
σεως (BM 285 ii *a*);   Job 14 15 (*B* ⲉ.) ὑπακ. dat;
Lu 12 11 (*B* do) ἀπολογεῖσθαι; ShC 42 131 ⲁⲛⲡ︦ⲭ︦ⲥ︦
ⲟⲩⲟϣⲃⲉϥ...ϫⲉ-, Ep 455 33 ⲙⲡⲉϥⲟⲩⲟϣⲃⲉⲧ, ManiH
54 *A²* ⲟⲩⲁϣⲃⲉⲧ (imperat).

With following preposition.   ⲥ ⲉ-, *respond to* :
Miss 4 695 ⲉϥⲟⲩ. ⲉϥⲯⲁⲗⲗⲉⲓ (cf C 73 65); ϩⲣⲏⲧ⸗ Ac
25 8 (*B* = Gk) ἀπολογίζειν only;   ⲥ ⲉϫⲛ-, *for* : Ep
176 no man to ⲟⲩ. ⲉϫⲱⲓ;   ⲥ ⲙⲛ-, *converse with* :
ShR 2 3 24 ⲉⲕⲟⲩ. ⲛⲙⲙⲁⲩ ⲏ ⲉⲕϣⲁϫⲉ ⲛⲙⲙⲁⲩ,
BHom 78 ⲉϥⲟⲩ. ⲛⲙⲙⲁⲩ ... ϫⲉⲁⲗⲏⲗⲟⲅⲓⲁ *respond
with*;   ⲥ ⲛ- dat: Nu 22 8, Zech 1 13 *SA*, Mk 12 28
(all *B* ⲉ.) ἀπ. dat; PS 13 ⲁⲓⲟⲩ. ⲛⲏⲧⲛ, ShC 73 2 ⲟⲩ.
ⲛⲡⲉⲧⲛⲁϫⲟⲟⲥ, Pcod 39 ⲡⲗⲉⲝⲓⲥ ⲉⲧⲕⲛⲁⲟⲩ. ⲛⲧⲙⲛⲧ-

Left column

ⲁⲧⲡⲁⲣⲧⲉ ⲡⲣⲏⲧⲟⲩ (*F* ⲟⲩⲱⲣⲉⲙ), Aeg 14 ⲁϥⲧⲁϣⲉ ⲟⲩ.
ⲡⲁⲓ (*B* do), WZKM '02 261 receipt ⲡⲧⲣⲓⲙⲛⲥⲓⲟⲡ…
ⲁ]ⲕⲟⲩ. ⲙⲙⲟϥ ⲡⲁⲓ; c ⲡⲥⲁ-, *respond after, to*: Br
92 ⲟⲩ. ⲡⲥⲱⲓ ⲡⲧⲉⲧⲛϯ ⲉⲟⲟⲩ ⲡⲓⲙⲁⲓ (cf 93 ⲟⲩⲱⲣⲙ
ⲡⲥⲱⲓ), ROC 20 51 ⲟⲩ. ⲡⲥⲁⲡⲉⲧⲯⲁⲗⲗⲉⲓ, R 1 3 50 he
sang hymn ⲉⲣⲉⲡⲣⲣⲟ ⲟⲩ. ⲡⲥⲱϣ; c ⲡⲁⲣⲣⲛ-, *before*: R 1 5 27 ⲁϥⲟⲩ. ⲡⲛ.ⲡⲣⲏⲧⲉⲙⲱⲡ; c ⲟⲩⲃⲉ-,
against: Ro 9 20 (*B* ⲉ. ⲉϩⲟⲩⲛ ⲉⲣⲣⲉⲡ-) ἀνταπ. dat,
Job 32 4 (*B* ⲟⲩⲱⲣⲉⲙ ⲟⲩⲃⲉ-) ἀπόκρισιν δ. dat; Ac
25 16 (*B* as Gk) ἀπολογίας λαμβάνειν περί; R 1 5
39 ⲟⲩ. ⲟⲩⲃⲉⲡⲉⲕϣⲁϫⲉ.

—— nn m *S*, *answer*: Job 6 26 -ϣϥ (*B* ⲥⲙⲏ)
φθέγμα.

ϭⲓⲛⲟⲩ. *S*, *answering*: Lu 2 47 (*B* ϫⲓⲛⲉ.) ἀπόκρι
σις; Sh(?)ViK 9344 60 ⲧϭⲓⲛⲟⲩⲟϣⲃⲟϥ … ⲧϭⲓⲛϣⲁ
ϫⲉ, Bor 258 4 ⲡⲉⲣⲗⲟϭ ⲛⲧⲟⲩϭ. (Lu 1 38), Wess 15
149 his beauty & his ϭ. *affability*.

ⲟⲩⲱϣⲙ *S*, -ⲙⲉ *A* (nn), -ⲉⲙ *B*, ⲟⲩⲉϣⲙ- *S*,
-ⲟϣⲙⲉ *SB*, -ⲁϣⲙⲉ *Sf*, -ⲟϣⲙⲉϯ *S*, -ⲁϣⲙ ϯ *Sf*, -ⲟϣⲉⲙ ϯ
B vb tr, *knead, bruise*: Ge 18 6 *SB*, 2 Kg 13 8 *S*, Va
63 89 *B* ⲁⲥⲟⲩ. ⲡⲥ ⲡϣⲓ φυρᾶν, ib 66 292 *B* ⲁⲩⲟⲩⲟϣ
ⲙⲉⲧ ⲡⲉⲙⲡⲁⲓⲟⲙ συμφ.; Ez 46 14 *B* ἀναμιγνύναι;
Sa 15 7 *S* θλίβειν; Jer 7 18 *B* τρίβειν; Tri 670 *S* μάγ
γανον wherewith to ⲟⲩ. ⲡⲡⲉϥⲁϥ ⲁⲣ; PS 334 *S* ⲟⲩ.
ⲙⲡⲥⲟⲣⲙ ⲣⲓⲡⲉϥⲉⲣⲏⲩ, ib 343 *S* ⲁⲩⲟⲩⲉϣⲙ ⲙⲙⲉⲗⲟⲥ,
ST 282 *S* ⲟⲩ. ⲡⲕⲟⲩⲓ ⲡⲡⲟⲉⲓⲧ, ib ⲟⲩⲁϣⲙⲟⲩ, PMéd
285 *S* ⲟⲩⲟϣⲙⲟⲩ ⲣⲓⲉⲃⲓⲱ, Mor 41 150 *S* ⲟⲩ. ⲙⲙⲟⲟⲩ
ⲡⲡⲉⲣ ⲣⲓⲉⲃⲓⲱ, Bodl(P)a 3 48 *S* ⲟⲩ. ϩⲣⲙⲉⲥ (var ib
1 ⲉ ⲱϣⲙ ϩⲉⲗⲙⲏ) ⲡⲣⲏⲧϥ (sc hot vinegar); qual,
kneaded, compounded: Ex 29 2 *S* ⲟⲩ. ⲣⲓⲡⲉⲣ *B* ϩⲉⲡⲟ
ⲟⲩⲡ., Lev 6 21 *B*(*S* ⲥⲉⲣⲥⲱⲣ), Job 7 5 *S*(*B* diff), Va
57 250 *B* ⲡⲉⲥⲟⲩϫⲟⲡⲏ ⲉⲡⲁⲥⲟⲩ. ⲡϩⲏⲧⲟⲩ φ.; Nu 7
19 *S*(var & *B* ⲧⲁⲙⲓⲏⲩ) ἀναποιεῖν; Lev 23 14 *S*(*B*
ⲫⲟⲣϫ) φρύγειν; ShA 2 50 *S* ⲟⲩⲁⲅⲁⲡⲏ ⲉⲥⲟⲩ. ⲣⲓⲕⲱϩ,
ShIF 68 *S* malady ⲉⲣⲉⲡⲁⲥⲱⲙⲁ ⲟⲩ. ⲡⲣⲏⲧϥ, C 86
205 *B* after tortures ⲡⲉⲥⲥⲱⲙⲁ (ⲟⲩ)ⲟ. ϩⲉⲡⲟⲩⲥⲡⲟϥ
soaked, ShP 131⁴ 156 *S* ⲉⲣⲉⲡⲡⲟⲃⲉ ⲟⲩ. ϩⲣⲁⲓ ⲡⲣⲏⲧⲟⲩ,
ShBor 246 70 *S* ⲉⲛⲟⲩ. ϩⲓⲡⲉⲓⲡⲁⲣⲁⲫⲩⲥⲓⲥ, Va 57 144
B ⲉⲥⲟⲩ. ϩⲉⲛϩⲁⲡⲡⲟⲣⲡⲓⲁ, C 43 106 *B* after flaying
ⲉⲧⲓ ⲉϥⲟⲩ. ϩⲉⲡⲡⲉϥⲥⲛⲟϥ, ViK 9508 *Sf* ⲥⲁⲙⲓⲧ ⲉϥⲟⲩ.

—— nn m *SABF*, *what is kneaded, dough*: Ex 12
34 *B*, Ro 9 21 *SB* φύραμα, Hos 7 4 *AB* φύρασις; ib
7 8 *B* ⲟⲩ. ⲉϥⲣⲏⲡ (*A* = Gk) ἐγκρυφίας; Mt 13 33 *F*
(*B* ϣⲱϯ, *S* Gk om); PS 249 *S* ye are of ⲡⲓⲟⲩ. ⲡⲟⲩⲱⲧ
ⲙⲡⲧⲣ̄ⲅⲗⲏ ⲡⲟⲩⲱⲧ, CaiThe 220 *B* Virgin gave to
God ⲡⲓⲟⲩ. ⲧⲏⲣϥ ⲡⲧⲉ ϯⲙⲉⲧⲣⲱⲙⲓ ᵃᵐˢ.

ⲙⲁ ⲡⲟⲩ. *SB*, *kneading place*: C 89 78 *B* ἀρτοκο
πεῖον; ShViK 9764 95 *S* ⲡⲙⲁ ⲡⲟⲩ. ⲏ ⲡⲧⲱϭ.

ⲟⲩϣⲁⲡ *SB*, -ⲉⲡ *F* nn m, *loan*, always c preceding ⲉ-: ROC 18 176 *S* ⲣⲱⲥ ⲟⲩ(ⲉ)ⲡⲉⲩ. ἐν χρήσει; BM
596 *F* ϫⲟⲩⲧⲉ ⲡⲗⲓⲧⲣⲉ…ⲉⲡⲟⲩ., CMSS 78 *F* account
ⲁⲡⲟⲩ[ⲡ] … ⲉⲡ. ⁹ γ́, PStras 133 *S* ⲡⲗⲟⲧⲟⲥ ⲡ(ⲡ)ϩⲁⲧ

Right column

ⲉⲡ(ⲟⲩ)ϣⲁⲡ; ϯ ⲉⲡⲟⲩ., *give on loan*: Deu 15 8 *B*,
Is 24 2 *B* δανίζειν, Deu 23 19 *B* ἐκδ. (all *S* ϯ ⲉⲙⲏⲥⲉ);
Lu 11 5 *SB*, AM 278 *B* ⲁϥϯ ⲙⲡⲟⲩ. (for ? ⲉⲡ.) χρᾶν,
Pro 13 11 *B*(*SA* om), BM 216 80 *S* ⲙⲉⲣⲉⲗⲁⲁⲩ ϯ
ⲛⲁϥ ⲉⲡⲟⲩ. κιχρᾶν; BMis 490 *S* ϯ ⲙⲏⲧ ⲡϩⲟⲗⲟⲕ/
ⲡⲟⲩⲣⲱⲙⲉ ⲉⲡⲉⲩ.; ⲁⲓⲧⲉⲓ ⲉⲡⲟⲩ., *ask loan*: R 1 5
12 *S* ⲡⲉⲧⲁⲓ. ⲙⲙⲟⲕ ⲉⲡⲉⲩ.; ϫⲓ ⲉⲡⲟⲩ., ϭⲓ ⲉⲡⲟⲩ.,
take, get on loan: 4 Kg 6 5 *S* χρ.; Blake 308 *S* Saul
means ⲡⲉⲭ̅ⲥ̅ ⲏ ⲡⲉⲡⲧⲁϫⲭⲓⲧϥ ⲉⲡⲉⲩ. *received on loan*
(cf K 224 & Lagarde *Onom Sacr* 198 αἰτητὸς ἢ κε
χρημένος), DeV 2 270 *B* ⲉⲑⲣⲉϥϫⲓ ⲡⲣ̄ ⲡⲗⲟⲅⲕⲟϫⲓ ⲡ
ⲧⲟⲧϥ ⲙⲡⲟⲩ., Ryl 193 *S* sim, Bodl(P) b 10 *S* ⲁϥϫⲓ
ⲡⲟⲩϣⲧⲏⲡ ⲉⲡⲉⲩ. (cf Riedel *Kirchenr* 256), PMich
777 *F* ⲁⲕϫⲓ ⲟⲩⲡⲉϣⲓ ⲡⲣⲱⲗⲟⲕ/ ⲡⲉⲓ ⲉⲡⲟⲩ.

ⲟⲩⲱϣⲡ v ⲟⲩⲱϣⲡ.

ⲟⲩⲁϣⲉⲣ *S* nn f (?), *meaning unknown*: GMaspero *Musée Ég*. 2 pl xvi commemorative inscr ⲡⲉⲓⲟ
ⲧⲉ ⲡⲧⲟⲩ. ⲙⲡⲡⲉⲥⲡⲏⲩ ⲧⲏⲣⲟⲩ ⲡⲧⲟⲩ.

ⲟⲩⲱϣⲥ *SBF*, -ⲥ ϩ *A*, ⲟⲩⲉϣⲥ- *SB*, ⲟⲩⲟϣⲥⲉ *S*,
ⲟⲩⲁⲥϩⲉ *A*, ⲟⲩⲟϣⲥϯ *SB*, ⲟⲩⲁ.ϯ *SfF*, ⲟⲩⲁⲥϣϯ *S*, -ⲥϩϯ
Sf, -ⲥϩϯ *A* vb intr, *become, be broad, at ease*: Deu
32 15 *A*(Cl, *SB* ⲥ ⲉϩⲟⲗ), 2 Cor 6 11ϯ *S*(*B* do) πλατύ
νειν, Cl 2 8ϯ *A*(cf Pro 7 3 ⲡⲱϩ) πλάτος, Ps 118 96ϯ
S(*B* ⲟⲩⲉⲥⲟⲩⲛ), Is 33 21 *S*(*BF* ⲥ ⲉϩ.), Mt 7 13ϯ *SB*
πλατύς; Ps 47 3 *B*(*S* ⲟⲩⲉⲥⲧⲱⲡ) εὔριζος; Is 30 23 *SF*
(*B* ⲟⲩⲉⲥ.) εὐρύχωρος; Lu 6 17ϯ *S*(*B* diff) πεδινός; PS
132 *S* ⲟⲩⲡⲟϭ ⲡⲓⲉⲣⲟ ⲉϥⲟⲩ.ϯ (= Od Solom 6 8 ᵃⁿᵈ);
ShZ 593 *S* ϩⲓⲛ ⲉⲧⲟⲩⲟϣⲥ (sic) ⲉⲧⲟⲩⲉⲥⲧⲱⲛ (opp ⲉⲧ
ⲥⲏⲩ), ShViK 9298 *S* sim ⲉⲧⲟⲩⲟⲥⲥ, ib -ⲏⲥ, ShC
42 203 *S* ⲉⲣϣⲁⲛⲣⲙⲟⲟⲥ ⲉϩⲣⲁⲓ ϣⲁⲣⲉ(ⲟⲩ)ⲱϣⲥ, Sh
P 130⁴ 141 *S* ⲡⲗⲏⲛ ⲉⲥⲟⲩ.ϯ ⲉⲥϣⲟⲕϩ (var ShIF 96
ⲟϣⲥ); tr, *make broad*: Ps 34 21 *B*(*S* ⲟⲩⲟϣⲡ), Pro
24 43 *S* refl *A*, Mt 23 5 *B*(*S* ⲥ ⲉϩ.) πλατύνειν.

—— nn m *SAB*, *breadth*: Ge 13 17 *S*(var ⲟⲩⲉϣ
ϣ, *B* ⲟⲩⲟⲥⲟⲉⲛ), Ez 40 5 *S*(*B* ⲟⲩⲏϣⲥⲓ), Zech 5 2
SA(*B* ⲟⲩⲟⲥ.) πλάτος, Cl 3 1 *A* πλατυσμός; Ex 30 2
B(var ⲟⲩⲛ.), Deu 3 11 *S*(*B* do) εὖρος, Ge 26 22 *B*(*S*
ⲟⲩ.ϯ ⲉϩ.) εὐρυχωρία; Ps 64 7 *S*(*B* ⲟⲩⲛ.) κύτος; Tri
453 *S* ⲓ̄ⲱ opp ϩⲟⲩϣ; ShC 42 112 *S* ϫⲓⲥⲉ, ⲟⲩ., BMis
513 *S* ⲡⲉϫϣⲓⲕ ⲙⲡⲡⲉϥⲟⲩ.; ⲟⲩⲉϣⲥ f v ⲟⲩⲁϣⲥⲉ.

—— ⲉⲃⲟⲗ *SABF*, *spread forth* intr: Deu 11 16 *S*
(*B* ⲥⲱⲣⲉⲙ), Ps 24 17 *S*(*B* diff), Hab 2 5 *A*(*B* ⲟⲩⲟⲥ.)
πλατύν., Is 33 21 *BF*(*S* om ⲉϩ.) πλατύς; Hos 4 16ϯ
A(*B* ⲟⲩⲉⲥ.) εὐρύχ.; Jer 21 13 *S*(*B* ⲟⲓ ⲙⲙⲉϣϣⲱⲧ)
πεδ.; BHom 46 *S* offerings ⲉⲧⲟⲩ.ϯ ⲉϩ. δαψιλής; ShC
42 160 *S* ϩⲉⲡⲙⲁ ⲉϥϣⲟⲕϩ ⲉϥⲟⲩ.ϯ ⲉϩ., BAp 136 *S*
ⲙⲁ ⲉϥⲟⲩⲁⲥϣ ⲉϩ., JKP 2 48 *Sf* ⲟⲩⲟⲩⲱϣⲉ ⲉⲥⲟⲩ.ϯ ⲉϩ.,
BMar 93 *S* grew rich ⲁϥⲟⲩ. ⲉϩ., PBu 176 *S* ⲁⲧⲉ
ⲭⲣⲉⲓⲁ ϣⲱⲡⲉ ⲡⲧⲟⲩ. ⲉϩ. ⲡⲧⲏϯ ϩⲓⲥⲉ ⲡⲏⲧⲛ *expatiate*,
PO 14 350 *B* if I told all ⲡⲓⲥⲁϫⲓ ⲡⲁⲟⲩ. ⲉϩ. ⲡⲣⲟⲅⲟ,
C 89 54 *B* his work ⲟⲩ. ⲉϩ. ϣⲁⲁⲩⲣⲓⲭϥ ⲙⲡⲓⲕⲁϩ;
tr *SAB*(rare)*F*: Ex 34 24 (*B* ⲟⲩⲟⲥ.), Is 5 14

SBF, Mt 23 5 (*B* om εϧ.) πλατύν., Pro 18 16 *SA* ἐμπλ., Mich 550 39 began πογ. εϧ. ϻπεγϻⲁ πϣωⲡⲉ πλατύτερον οἰκοδομεῖν; Z 309 ⲁϥογ. εϧ. πⲧⲁⲥⲕⲏⲥⲓⲥ τῇ ἀσ. σχολάζειν; R 2 2 30 πⲧⲉⲧⲛογϣⲥογ εϧ. *expand them* (*sc* our poor words); PBu 146 we are timid ϻⲡⲁⲧⲛογ. πϣⲁϫⲉ ⲅⲁⲣ εϧ. ϣⲁⲧⲉⲡογ, P 131⁴ 99 smoke rising εϥογ. εϧ. ππεϥⲉⲣⲏⲩ εϥϧⲧⲁⲧⲱⲙ.

ογ. εϧ. with following prepositions. ⲥ ⲉϩογⲛ ⲉ- *S*: R 1 4 57 ⲁⲕογ. εϧ. ϻπⲁⲙⲉⲉγⲉ ⲉϩ. ⲉⲡⲉⲭⲥ̄ ἐπιτείνειν εἰς RE 9 142 your love ⲉⲧογ.† εϧ. ⲉϩ. ⲉⲣⲟⲛ; ⲥ ⲉϫⲛ- *S*: Ge 28 14 (*B* ⲉⲡⲥⲁ ⲛ-) πλατύν. ἐπί; ⲥ ⲛ- dat *S*: Ps 4 1 (*B* ογⲟⲥ. tr) π. dat; ShZ 592 ⲑⲁⲓⲃⲉⲥ ϻⲡⲁⲅⲁⲑⲟⲛ...ⲡⲉⲡⲧⲁⲥογ. ⲡⲁγ εϧ. *spread before them*, R 1 3 20 the ill-used εϥογ. ⲡⲁγ εϧ. ⲛ-ⲧⲙⲛⲧⲉⲣⲟ ⲛϻⲡⲏγⲉ; ⲥ ⲛⲧⲛ- *S*: BMar 99 πϣⲁϫⲉ ογ.† εϧ. ⲛⲧⲟⲟⲧⲛ ⲉⲡⲉⲣογ, Miss 8 173 sim; ⲥ ϧⲛ- *SF*, in: PS 133 ⲁϥⲁⲡⲟϧⲣⲟⲓⲁ ογ. εϧ. ϧⲙⲡⲉⲭⲁⲟⲥ, ShA 2 163 virginity ογ. εϧ. ϧⲙⲡⲧⲁⲧⲥⲱⲧⲙ ⲛⲓⲙ, ShBM 198 30 ⲉⲡογ.† εϧ. ϧⲛϩⲉⲛⲕⲱⲧ *dissipating energies in building &c*, Pcod F 23 sinners ογ.† εϧ. ϧⲙⲡⲕⲟⲥⲙⲟⲥ.

ογ. εϧ. nn m *SB*, *breadth, extent, ease*: Ps 17 19 *S*(FR 10, var & *B* ογⲟⲥ.), *ib* 118 45 *SB* πλατυσμός; Wess 15 134 *S* ⲡογ. εϧ. ⲡⲧⲁⲣⲏⲗⲓⲕⲓⲁ μῆκος; R 1 1 71 *S* seeing thee ϧⲙⲡογ. εϧ. ϻⲡⲧⲉϥⲫⲣⲟⲥγⲛⲏ, Ryl 62 4 *S* ⲙⲧⲟⲛ, ογ. εϧ., ϧⲉⲡογϭⲉ, C 89 139 *B* (ογ)-ογ. εϧ. ⲡⲁϣⲱⲡⲓ for righteous through idolater's absence = MG 17 509 واحة واسأع, Ep 168 *S* ⲣ ογⲛⲟϭ ⲡογ. εϧ. ⲡⲓⲙⲁϥ (*sc* sick man).

—— ⲉϩⲣⲁⲓ *S*: ShC 73 11 of avenging sword ⲡⲣⲱⲙⲉ ⲉⲡⲧⲁⲥ(ογ)ⲟϣⲥ ⲉϩ. ⲡⲓⲙⲁϥ ⲏ ϩⲓⲧⲟγⲱϣ.

ογⲁϣⲥⲉ¹, ογⲟ.², ογⲉϣⲥⲉ³, -ⲉϣⲥ⁴ *S*, ογⲏϣⲥⲓ *B*, ογⲉ. *BF* nn f, *breadth*: Ge 13 17 *S*ⁱ(*B* ογⲟⲥ.), Pro 7 3 *B*(*SA* ⲡⲱⲝϭ), Ez 40 5 (*S* ογⲱϣⲥ) πλάτος; Job 38 18 *B*(*S* π.), Ez 41 14 *S*ⁱ*B* εὖρος; *ib* 43 16 *B* μῆ.; PS 202 *S* ϧⲁⲑⲟⲥ, ϣⲓⲏ, ογ.¹, ShA 2 116 *S* ογ.¹, ϣⲓⲏ, ShIF 102 *S*³, Mor 31 211 *S* ⲧογ.² ⲡ(ογ)ογⲉⲣⲏⲧⲉ, Mor 30 40 *F* ϣⲓⲛⲉⲓ, ογ. = *ib* 29 34 *S* ογ.¹, TEuch 2 355 *B* ⲡⲓογ. ⲡⲧⲉ ⲡⲓⲉϩⲟⲟγ.

ογωϣⲧ *SAA²BF*, ογⲁϣⲧ⳽ *A²*(Ma) vb intr, *worship, greet, kiss*: Deu 11 16 *SB*, Ps 21 29 *SB*, Ac 24 11 *SB* προσκυνεῖν; PS 21 *S* ⲁγⲡⲁⲣⲟγ...ⲁγογ., AM 287 *B* ⲁγⲑⲣⲟγ.; tr (but nom obj often indistinguishable from ⲛ- dat) c Gk acc: Is 2 8 *SB*, EpJer 5 *BF*, Ap 9 20 *SB*, CaiEuch 339 *B* ⲧⲉⲡογ. ϻⲙⲟⲕ πρ.; Sa 15 18 *S* σέβεσθαι; *ib* 14 16 *S* θρησκεύειν; Ge 32 20 *B*(*S* ⲥⲟⲡⲥ) ἐξιλάσκειν; c Gk dat: Ps 28 2 *SB*, Mic 5 13 *AB*(prob), Jo 4 23 *SA²BF* πρ.; Ro 1 25 *SB* σέβ.; Cai Euch 498 *B* ογ. ⲙϥ⳨ κλίνειν; PS 29 *S* ⲁⲥογ. ⲡⲡⲉϥογⲉⲣⲏⲧⲉ, Pcod 12 *S* desired ⲉογ. ⲡⲡⲉⲥⲡⲏγ, JKP 2 102 *S* find mercy ⲉⲡⲛⲁγ ⲉ-

ϣⲁογ. ⲉⲡⲉⲕⲣⲓⲧⲏⲥ (for ⲙⲡ.), MIE 2 356 *B* ⲡⲉϥ-ϫⲓϫ ⲁⲓογ. ϻⲙⲱⲟγ = BAp 81 *S* ⳨ ⲡⲉⲓ ⲉ-, C 43 191 *B* ⲁϥογ. ϻⲡϥⲥ̄ⲧ̄, *ib* 83 *B* ογ. ⲡⲡⲉϥⲥⲁⲗⲁⲩϫ, Ep 113 *S* ⳨ογ. ϻⲡⲉⲓⲭⲛⲟⲥ of your feet, Mani H 22 *A²* ⲁϥⲧⲣⲁογⲁϣⲧⲕ.

With following preposition. ⲥ ⲉ- *S*, *upon, at*: Job 31 27 (*B* ⳨ ϥⲓ) φιλεῖν; PS 32 ⲁϥογ. ⲉⲡογⲉⲣⲏⲧⲉ ⲡⲓⲥ̄, Miss 4 529 when given loaf ⲁϥογ. ⲉⲣⲟϥ thrice = C 89 47 *B* ϧⲓϫⲱϥ, Pcod 13 on receiving letters ⲁϥογ. ⲉⲣⲟογ (*cf* DeV 2 165 *B* sim ϻⲙⲱⲟγ); ⲥ ⲉϫⲛ- *SB*, *do obeisance upon*: Ge 19 1 *S*(*B* ϧⲓϫ.), He 11 21 *B*(*S* ⲉ- var ⲛ-, *F* ⲉϧⲏⲓ ⲉϫ.) πρ. ἐπί; BMis 223 *S* ⲁϥογ. ⲉ.ⲡⲕⲁϩ, Worr 290 *S* ⲁγογ. ⲉ. ⲡⲉⲥϭⲓϫ ϻⲡⲓⲥογⲣⲏⲧⲉ, AM 172 *B* ογ. ⲉ.ⲡⲟγⲅⲙ̄ⲯⲁⲡⲟⲡ (λείψ.); ⲉϧⲣⲏⲓ ⲉϫ. *BF*: He *F* above, Miss 4 205 *B* ⲙⲁⲣⲟγⲟγ. ⲉϩ. ⲉ.ⲑⲏⲛογ & beseech for you; ⲥ ϧⲓϫⲛ- *SAA²B*, as last: Zeph 1 5 *AB* πρ. ἐπί, Jo 4 20 *SA²B* (var ⲉϫ.) πρ. ἐν; C 43 222 *B* ογ. ϧ.ⲡⲉⲕⲱⲙⲁ (*cf* AM 112 *B* ⲉϫ. ⲡⲉⲕⲥ.); ⲥ ⲛ- dat *SA²B*(rare): Ge 27 29 *B* πρ. dat (var acc), *ib* *S*(*B* acc) πρ. acc (var dat); Ps 71 11 (*B* acc), Mt 14 33 (*BF* do), He 1 6 *SF*(*B* do) πρ. dat, R 1 1 49 they beheld & ⲁγογ. ⲡⲁϥ πρ. acc; Ac 17 23 (*B* = Gk) εὐσεβ. acc; PS 8 ⲁγⲡⲁⲣ-ⲧογ...ⲁγογ. ⲡⲁϥ, BMis 335 ⲁγογ. ⲡⲁⲓ (var προσ-κγⲡⲏ), Wess 15 151 ⲁϥογ. ⲡⲁγ ⲉϫⲙⲡⲕⲁϩ, BMar 213 ⲁⲓογ. ⲡⲁϥ but he raised me up, J 106 191 ⲗⲁⲁγ ⲡⲧγⲡⲟⲥ ⲉϥϩⲁⲉⲟογ ⲉογ. ⲡⲁϥ, El 50 *A* ⲁⲓογ. ⲡⲉϥ, Mani 1 *A²* ⲉⲓογ. ⲡⲉϥ, Tst Ab 239 *B* ογ. ⲡⲁϥ (*cf* 238 ϻⲙⲟϥ), BSM 83 *B* do; ⲥ ⲡⲁϩⲣⲛ-, *before, in presence of*: Ps 5 8 *SB* πρ. πρός; ⲥ ϻⲡⲉⲙⲧⲟ ⲉⲃⲟⲗ ⲛ- *SBF*, as last: Ps 85 9 *SB*, Lu 4 7 *SB* πρ. ἐνώπιον; Is 36 7 *SBF* πρ. κατὰ πρόσωπον; Ap 22 8 *S*(*B* om) πρ. ἔμπροσθεν; BSM 42 *B* ⲁγογ. ⲙⲡⲉⲙ. ϻⲡⲓⲉⲣⲁ-ϫⲓⲟⲛ = BMis 388 *S* ⲡⲁϩⲧογ ϧⲓⲑⲏ; ⲥ ϧⲁ-, ϧⲁ- *SB*, *below, at*: Mor 41 126 *S* ⲁγογ...ϧⲁⲡⲉϥογⲉⲣⲏ-ⲧⲉ (varr *ib* 40 12 ⲉ-, *ib* 39 16 ϧⲓϫⲛ-) = C 43 42 *B* ⲛ-, AM 182 *B* ογ. ϧⲁⲡⲉⲛⲥⲁⲗⲁⲩϫ.

ϣογογ. *S*, *reverend*; Z 277 ⲧⲉⲓⲥγⲡⲣⲟϩⲟⲥ ⲡϣ. πας προσκυνητής.

—— nn m *A²*, *salutation, obeisance*: Mani 2 ⲡⲓⲙⲁⲣϭⲡⲉϥ ⲡογ.

ⲣⲉϥογ. *SA²B*, *worshipper*: Jo 4 23 *SA²B*, cit BM 247 8 *S* προσκυνητής; ⲙⲛⲧⲣ.: Wess 15 144 *S*, Cat 180 *B*.

ϫⲓⲡογ. *B*, *worship*: Cat 180 ϫⲝ. ⲡ⳨ⲙⲉⲧⲡογ⳨.

ογⲁϣⲧⲉ *S*, -ⲉϣⲧⲉ *A²* nn f, as last: ShA 1 379 *S* ⲧογ. ϻⲡϣⲁⲓ ⲏ ⲡϣⲁⲓ ⲙ̄ⲡ⳨ⲙ̄ⲉ, Mani H 6 *A²* ⳨⳨ ⲉⲡ ⲡⲧⲕογ., *ib* 22 ⲧογ. ϻⲡⲡ̄ⲉ̄.

ογϣογⲉϣ *SB*, ογⲉϣ., -ογⲱϣ *S*, ϧⲟϣϧⲉϣ *B*, ογⲉϣογⲱϣ⳽ *SB*, -ογⲱϣ† *B* vb intr, *strike, thresh*: Mus 34 187 *B* they smote anvil, but ⲡϩⲱⲟγⲡⲉ ⲉⲧ-ⲁγ. κατακλᾶσθαι; ShA 1 210 *S* ⲡϫⲏⲣⲉ ⲏ ⲙⲙⲁ ⲡογⲟϣ., Va 58 129 *B* ⲁγογ. ⲡϫⲉ ⲡⲓⲕⲁⲥ, *ib* ⲉⲣⲉⲡⲉϥ-

κας ογ.† (on Ps 6 2);   tr: Jud 6 11 S ογεϣ. (var
-ογωϣ), Ru 2 17 S ογεϣογωϣϥ, 2 Cor 11 25 B(S
ϧιογε) ῥαβδίζειν; He 11 35 B(S ϧιτε) τυμπανίζειν;
C 86 18 B αγογεϣογωϣκ ᴫπϣⲃⲱⲧ, C 43 165 B ⲃ.
ⲡⲛⲉϥⲕⲁⲥ.   Cf ? ογⲟϭογεϭ.

ογαϣϥ v ογωϣ desire s f.

ογωϣϥ SAA²B (rare) F, -ϣⲃ S, ογεϣϥ-, S,
ογαϣϥ- A², -ⲟϣϥ⳽ SB, -aϣϥ⳽ S, -aϣⲃ⳽ F, -ⲟϣϥ†
SB vb **I** intr, be worn down, crushed, perish: Nah 1
6 SA(B ᴫⲟⲛᴫⲉⲛ), Hab 3 6 SA(B ϭⲟᴫϭⲉᴫ) δια-
θρύπτειν (reading ?διατρίβ.), Z 328 ογ.† ϧⲙⲧϥⲣⲉ διατρίβειν, Nu 32 21 (B ϥⲱϯ εⲃⲟλ) ἐκτρ., Job 31 22 -ϣⲃ
(B ϭ.), Ps 33 18† (B ⲧⲉⲡⲡⲟ), ib 20 (B λⲟϥλⲉϥ), ib 50
17†(ACIογⲱϭⲛ, B ⲧ.), Pro 6 16 (A ϧⲱϣϥ, B ϭ., var
Mus 45 28 ογⲱxⲡ), Jo 19 36 SA²(B κⲱϣ), Mor 17 8
ship εϥⲟγ. by waves συντρ.; Ez 21 7 (B ϭ.) θραύειν;
ib 29 7 SB θλᾶν; Job 41 18† (B aⲧⲛⲟᴫϯ) σαθρός; He
6 12 (B ϣⲱⲡⲓ) νωθρὸς γίνεσθαι; Sa 13 19 ἀδρανής;
R 1 4 56 ϭαλε ετογ.† ⲉⲡⲉϥογⲉⲣⲏⲧⲉ = MartIgn
868 B ᴫaϣⲓ πεδᾶσθαι; ShA 2 136 idols aγογ. ⲏ
aγογⲱϭⲛ, ShC 73 175 fall & ⲡⲧⲟγ. ⲧⲏⲣⲕ, Mun 78
ᴫⲉϥⲟγ. ϧⲛⲟγⲑλⲓⲯⲓⲥ, R 2 1 47 of drunkard ⲣⲱϥ
ογⲏⲛ εϥⲟγ.† ⲡⲉϥλⲁⲥ ϭλⲓᴫλⲱⲙ, Z 217 rocks εγⲟγ.
εxⲛⲡⲉϥⲉⲣⲏⲧ, Ep 162 lo 2 years αⲓⲟγ. ⲉⲓⲛⲕⲟⲧⲕ ϧⲓ-
ⲡⲉϭλⲟϭ, MS Golenischef 17 60 ⲡⲛⲉⲟγⲃⲱ ⲛⲟγⲱⲧ
ογ. εⲃⲟλ ϧⲣⲏⲧⲧⲏγⲧⲛ.

II tr SA²B: Nu 14 15 (B ϥ. εⲃ.), Job 30 23 (B
ᴫⲟγⲛⲕ) ἐκτρ., Ex 23 24 (B ογⲱxⲛ), 3 Kg 19 11 -ϣⲃ,
Lam 3 4 (B ϭ., F ⲧⲉⲡⲡⲁ), Ez 29 7 SB, Mic 4 6 (A
ϧⲱϣϥ, B do) συντρ.; Nu 24 17 (B do), Deu 28 33
(B ⲉⲣ ϭⲱϥⲧ) θραύ.; Ps 28 7 (B ϣⲱⲧ) διακόπτειν; Jo
19 32 A²(S ογⲱϭⲛ, B κ.) καταγνύναι; Nu 33 52 (B
ⲣⲱϭⲧ εϧⲣⲏⲓ) ἐξαιρεῖν; Ac 21 13 (B ϯ ᴫⲕαϧ) συνθρύπ.; ShBMOr 8810 452 εϥⲟγ. ᴫⲡⲥαⲧⲁⲡⲁⲥ beneath feet, RNC 51 idols aϥⲟγⲁϣϥⲟγ, MR 4 68
fire ογ. ⲡⲛⲁⲕⲉⲉⲥ, ib 5 117 F ⲡⲛⲉⲗⲁⲁγ ᴫⲡⲓⲣαⲥ-
ᴫⲟⲥ ογⲁϣⲃⲉϥ (paral texts om), Mich 166 10 God
ογⲉϣϥ ⲧⲉϥϭⲟᴫ.

— nn m SF, breakage, destruction: Pro 20 30
(A ϧ.), Is 30 26 SF(B ϭ.) σύντριμμα, ib 13 6 (B do)
συντριβή, Deu 4 26 (B ⲧⲁⲕⲟ) ἐκτρ.; Lev 13 30 (B
ϭ.) θραῦσμα, Ps 105 30 (B do) θραῦσις; ShIF 91
breaking pots ⲉⲕⲡⲁⲥⲱⲧ ⲉⲡⲉⲟγ. ᴫⲡⲟγⲉ, ShR 2
3 49 ⲡⲟγ. ᴫⲡⲉⲕⲡⲛⲁ, Miss 4 530 ⲡⲟγ. ⲡⲛⲉⲛⲧⲟλⲏ=
C 89 49 B ⲕⲱⲣϥ, ViK 9773 61 πλⲏⲅⲏ treated with
εᴫⲡⲗⲁⲥⲧⲣⲟⲛ, ογ. with ᴫⲁⲗⲁⲅᴫⲁ;   ογ. ⲡϧⲏⲧ:
ShA 2 280 ᴫⲕⲁϧ ⲛϧⲏⲧ, ογ. ⲡϧ.

Cf ογⲱϭⲡ.

ογⲱϣx B v ⲱⲥϭ (ⲱϣx).

ογϥ v ⲱϥ.

ογⲟϥ, -ⲱϥ (P 44) S, -aϥ S^a, ⲃⲟϥ B nn m, lung:

3 Kg 22 34 S(as gloss), Glos 54 S^a πνεύμων, P 44 70
S ⲡⲡⲉγᴫⲱⲛ · ⲡⲟγ. ⲓⲩ = 43 41 S do قصب الرِ, ROC
23 282 B her inward parts & ⲛⲉⲥⲃ. diseased.

ογϧⲓ A   v ογϣⲏ.

ογⲱϧⲉ A   v ογⲱϣ vb.

ογⲁϧⲣⲉ A   v ογⲱⲣϧ (ογⲱϧⲣ).

ογϭⲉ B   v ϧⲟγϧⲉ.

ογⲁϧ S nn   v ογⲁϧ s f.

ογⲁϧ B   v ογⲁϧⲉ.

ογⲟϧ B and   v aγⲱ.

ογⲱϧ SAA²B (rare) F, ογϧⲱ A (Hos 9 15), -ⲟϧ,
-aϧ B, ογⲉϧ- SB, ογⲱϧ- SAF, ογⲁϧ- ABFO, ⲃⲁϧ-
B, ογⲁϧ⳽ SAA²BF, ογⲁϧ⳽ A(Hos 13 4), ογⲉϧ⳽ F,
ογⲏϧ⳽ SAA², -ⲏⲏϧ† S, ογⲧⲏ A(Hos 4 1), -εϧ† BF
(v also aϧ-, aϣ-), pc ογⲁϧ- S vb **A**, put, set, be
(there) intr SB(rare)F: Nah 3 16 B(A ϥⲱϭⲉ) ὁρμᾶν
expandi; Wess 18 70 birds came aγⲟγ. before him,
JKP 2 24, KroppD 25 ογ. of birds opp ϧⲱλ, BM
586 8 F ᴫⲉ(ⲡ) λⲱⲙⲓ ογ. ᴫⲡⲁⲗⲉⲗⲁⲕ, AZ 30 42 ⲉ-
ϣⲱⲡⲉ ⲡϧⲃⲟⲟⲥ...ογ.† please send them, Ep 471 have
searched ᴫⲡⲉⲓⲣⲉ ⲉⲟγⲟⲛ (sic prob) εϥⲟγ.†, Miss 4
733 thrones ογ.† on this side & that, Sh(?)Mor 54 60
ⲡⲉϥⲃⲱⲱⲓ ογ.† (cf 1 Cor 11 14), Bodl(P) a 1 c recipe
ⲕⲁⲁϥ ⲧⲉⲟγ. let it be or settle, ST 391 ⲡⲉⲥⲕⲉγⲉ ⲉⲧⲟγ.†
ⲡⲉγⲱ lie at pledge (v εγⲱ);   tr: Deu 14 1 S(B diff)
ἐπιτιθέναι, Ps 61 11 B(S κα ϧⲏⲧ), ZNTW 24 86 F
προστ.; Mal 3 17 A(B ⲥⲱⲧⲡ) αἱρετίζειν; R 1 5 13 S
ᴫⲡⲣⲟγⲉϧ ϥⲱ τριχὰς τρέφειν; AZ 21 153 S ᴫaⲣⲡ-
ογⲉϧ xⲱⲡ & sleep (cf Lu 9 58 B), BMis 177 S aϥ-
ογⲉϧ ⲧⲉⲡⲧⲉ (var Ryl 90 S ⲥⲱⲣ εⲃⲟλ) = BSM 86 B
ϧⲓⲟγⲓ, TurM 16 S v ⲡⲓxⲉ, BM 527 F ογaϧⲣϥ ⲧⲉϥ-
ϣaγⲉⲓ, Hall 93 S xⲓ ⲡⲉⲧⲥⲟγ.† (sic) ᴫⲙⲟϥ (ref ? to
pledge), AZ 21 100 O ⲉⲧⲙⲟγaϧ(for ⲉⲧⲥ-)ϣⲟⲓϣ ⲉⲓ-
aⲧⲥ;   imperat: aγⲱ S, aⲟγ A (for aⲟγaϧ), ογⲟϧ
B, v aγⲱ.

With following prepositions.

— e- SABF., set on, add to intr: Deu 1 11 B
(S ⲉxⲛ-) προστ. dat, Ps 114 11 SB, Si 21 16 S π. ἐπί,
Is 14 1 SB π. πρός, Ac 2 41 SB π. no prep; Nu 15
15 B(S ⲱⲡ e-) προσκεῖσθαι ἐν; Su 35 B ϧⲏⲧ ογ.† ⲉ-
πείθεσθαι ἐπί; Lu 9 53 B(S diff) ϧⲟ ογ.† e- πορεύεσθαι εἰς; Mk 16 17 S(B ᴫⲟϣⲓ ⲡⲥa-) παρακολου-
θεῖν; ShC 73 212 S ογ ⲡⲉⲧⲟγ.† ⲉⲧⲉⲧⲣaⲡⲓⲍa ?, Miss
4 571 S power from Lord ογ. ⲉⲣⲟⲓ, C 43 94 B sim,
ViK 9574 S soul left body aⲥⲟγ. ⲉⲡⲉϭⲓx ᴫⲙⲓ-
xaⲏλ, C 89 186 B ⲧⲉⲡϧⲉλⲡⲓⲥ ογ.† ⲉⲟγⲣⲱⲙⲓ;   tr:
Pro 3 2 SAB, Is 26 15 S(B ⲧⲟγϧⲟ), Gött N '98 175
S ⲥⲉⲟγⲉϧ xⲣⲟⲛⲟⲥ ⲉⲣⲟⲟγ attribute to, Va 66 310 B
ᴫⲡⲉⲣⲟγaϧ ⲡⲉⲕϧⲏⲧ ⲉⲟγᴫⲉⲧⲣaᴫaⲟ προστ. dat, Gal

1 16 S(B ⲛⲥⲁ-) προσανατ. dat, Mk 3 16 S(B ϯ) ἐπιτ.
dat, Nu 12 11 S(var ⲉϫⲛ-, B ⲓ̈ⲛⲓ ⲉϩⲣⲏⲓ ⲉⲝ.) συνεπιτ.
dat; Mk 14 6 S(B ϯ) παρέχειν dat; 1 Pet 5 7 B(S
ⲡⲟⲩϫⲉ) ἐπιρίπτειν ἐπί; Vi Sitz 172 4 30 S ⲁⲩⲟⲩⲁϩⲩ
ⲉⲣⲟϥ προκεῖσθαι (reading ? προσκ.); refl: Deu 13
4 S(B ⲧ.), Job 13 9 B(S ⲧⲱⲥⲉ), Ac 5 14 B(S not refl)
προστ. dat, Jer 43 25 B ὑποτ. dat; ShMIF 23 154 S
ⲉⲩϣⲁⲛⲟⲩⲉϩ ⲙⲁⲧⲟⲓ ⲉⲣⲟⲛ bring soldiers against us,
R 1 5 35 S pray gods ⲛⲥⲉⲟⲩⲉϩ ⲁϩⲉ ⲉⲣⲟⲟⲩ, P 131[3]
81 S ⲉⲩⲟⲩⲉϩ ⲥⲱⲃⲉ making sport before thee, CO 137
S she did ⲟⲩ. ⲡⲣⲱϩ ⲉⲣⲟⲓ ⲍⲁⲡⲏⲓ, Ep 275 S sim, Va
59 12 B ⲟⲩ. ⲉⲣⲟⲓ ⲡⲟⲩⲃⲉⲭⲉ ⲡⲣⲟⲅⲟ, AZ 23 108 S
recipe ⲟⲩⲁⲣϥ ⲉⲅⲁⲗϫⲉⲡⲟⲅⲏ (كاكل), BM 596 12 F
ⲟⲩⲉⲣⲟⲩ ⲉⲡⲉⲅⲙⲏ;   ⲉϩⲟⲩⲛ ⲉ-: MG 25 308 B·
ⲉⲩⲟⲩ.† ⲉϩ. (ⲉ)ϯϫⲟⲓ = BIF 13 116 S ⲟⲩⲟⲗⲥ ⲉϩ. ⲉ-.

—— ⲉⲣⲛ- S, upon, at: Lu 23 53 (B diff) ἐπιτ. dat.

—— (ⲉⲧⲛ-), ⲉⲧⲟⲟⲧⲟ SAF intr = ⲟⲩⲁϩ ⲧⲟⲧⲟ B, set
hand, add, repeat: Job 34 32 B, Eccl 2 9 SF, Hos 1 6
AB προστ.; PS 271 S ⲟⲩ. ⲉⲧⲟⲧⲧⲏⲩⲧⲛ again; + 2d
vb: Ge 4 2 B(S ⲥ ⲉ-), 2 Kg 2 22 S(var ⲇⲟ), Job 27 1
SB πρ.; Lu 23 23 B(S ⲙⲟⲩⲛ ⲉⲃⲟⲗ) ἐπικεῖσθαι; Va
57 9 B ⲁⲩⲟⲩⲁϩ ⲧⲟⲧⲟ ⲟⲛ ⲉϥϫⲱ ἐπάγειν; Miss 4 526
S ⲁⲩⲟⲩ. ⲟⲛ ⲉⲧⲟⲟⲧⲟ ⲡⲉϫⲁϥ = C 89 45 B ἔτι λέγειν;
PS 30 S sim, BMis 271 S ϯⲛⲁⲟⲩ. ⲁⲛ ⲉⲧⲟⲟⲧ ϣⲁⲉⲡⲉϩ
ⲉⲓⲥⲕⲟⲡⲧⲉⲓ, ib 128 S not content ⲁϥⲟⲩ. ⲟⲛ ⲉⲧⲟⲟⲧϥ
ⲛⲥⲁϩⲛ ⲉϥϫⲱ, AM 45 B ⲧⲉⲣⲁⲟⲩ. ⲧⲟ† ⲁⲛ ϫⲉ ⲡⲧⲉⲡⲁϥ,
C 43 151 B ⲁϥⲟⲩ. ⲧⲟⲧϥ ⲟⲛ ⲁϥϩⲣⲟⲩϩⲓⲛⲓ, Kropp A S
ⲁⲩⲟⲩ. ⲉⲧⲟⲟⲧⲟⲩ ⲁⲩ[ⲛ ⲡⲣⲓ]ⲡⲏⲕ;   + ⲉ-: Ge 8 21
SB, Ps 40 8 S(B ϫⲉ again), Lam 4 22 BF, Hos 9 15
AB πρ.; Tob 14 10 S neg, Jo 8 11 B(var ⲧⲁⲥⲟ) neg
μηκέτι, Zech 9 8 S(ShA 2 339)A(B om ⲧⲟⲧⲟ) οὐκέτι;
ShA 2 338 S ⲛⲥⲉⲡⲁⲟⲩ. ⲁⲛ ⲉⲧⲟⲟⲧⲟⲩ ⲉϩⲛⲧⲟⲩ, RNC
64 S ⲙⲡⲟⲩⲟⲩ. ⲉⲧⲟⲟⲧⲟⲩ ⲉⲕⲟⲧⲟⲩ, AM 24 B ⲙⲡⲉϥ
ⲟⲩⲁϩ ⲧⲟⲧϥ ϫⲉ ⲉϩⲱⲗ;   + ⲉϫⲛ- S: Eccl 1 18 πρ.
acc;   + ϩⲛ- S: Mor 37 89 ⲉϥⲟⲩ. ⲉⲧⲟⲟⲧϥ ϩⲛⲧⲁⲥ
ⲕⲏⲥⲓⲥ ἐπιτείνειν acc; Br 108 ⲁ̅ⲥ̅ ⲟⲩ. ⲉⲧⲟⲟⲧϥ ϩⲙⲡ
ϣⲁϫⲉ;   tr S: Deu 19 9 (B ⲧⲟⲩϩⲟ ⲉⲧⲟⲟ) προστ.
dat, Eccl 1 16 (F ϯ) πρ. ἐπί.

—— ⲉϫⲛ- SAA[2]BF, set upon, add to intr: Deu 4
2 S(B ⲧ. ⲉ-) προστ. πρός, Job 34 37 S(B ⲉϩⲣⲏⲓ ⲉⲝ.)
πρ. ἐπί, Tob 12 1 S πρ. dat, Is 1 5 SF(B ⲧ.) πρ. acc;
Job 21 27 B(S ⲧⲱⲟⲩⲛ ⲉϫⲛ-) ἐπικεῖσθαι dat; Ex 21
19 B(S Gk om vb); Si 44 26 S καταπαύ. ἐπί; Sh
Mich 550 14 S may God ⲟⲩ. ⲉϫⲛⲧⲉϥϩⲉⲓⲣⲏⲛⲏ ⲛⲙ
ⲙⲁⲛ, Z 293 S devil ⲟⲩ. ⲉϫⲛⲡϣⲱⲧ ⲙⲡⲙⲟⲛⲁⲭⲟⲥ
multiplieth needs, Mani 2 A[2] ⲟⲩⲙⲁⲩ ⲉⲁⲩⲟⲩ. ⲁϩⲛ
ⲟⲩⲙⲁⲩ, RNC 90 S crown descending ⲉϥⲛⲁ(ⲟⲩ)ⲱϩ
ⲉϫⲱϥ, DeV 2 198 B staff ⲉϥⲟⲩ.† ⲉϫⲱϥ (cf Ex above),
BMis 541 S ⲉⲣⲉⲟⲩⲣⲁⲡ ⲟⲩ.† ⲉϫⲱϥ;   tr: Ge 48 17
S(B ⲧⲁⲗⲟ ⲉϫ.) τιθ. ἐπί, Lev 26 21 S(B ⲧⲟⲩ. ⲉ-), Is
30 1 SA(El 66)B(F ⲉϩⲗⲏⲓ ⲉϫ.), Lu 3 20 S(B ⲇⲟ)
προστ. ἐπί, Aeg 271 S ⲟⲩⲁϥϥ ⲉϫⲙⲡϣⲁϫⲉ πρ. dat,
Ex 18 11 B اشكل, Ac 15 28 S(B ⲧⲁⲗⲟ ⲉϫ.) ἐπιτ.

dat, Ps 61 4 B refl (S ⲧⲱⲟⲩⲛ ⲉϫⲛ-), R 1 1 29 S
ⲁϥⲟⲩⲉϩ ⲡⲉϥϭⲓϫ ⲉϫⲙⲡⲁⲃⲁⲗ ⲉ̀. ἐπί; Is 36 6 B refl(S
ⲧⲁⲭⲣⲟ ⲉϫⲛ-) ἐπιστηρίζειν ἐπί; 4 Kg 13 16 S (var
ⲕⲱ) ἐπιβιβάζειν ἐπί; 2 Cor 12 16 B(SF=Gk) κατα
βαρεῖν acc; PS 172 S ⲟⲩⲉϩ ⲥⲱⲡⲧ ⲉϫⲛⲥⲱⲡⲧ, MG 25
67 B var ⲉⲁⲩϩⲁϩ ⲕⲉ…ⲛⲟⲃⲓ ⲉϫⲉⲛ-, Miss 8 256 S ⲁϥ
ⲟⲩⲉϩ ⲡⲉϫⲧⲏⲛⲃⲉ ⲉϫⲙⲡⲉϥⲃⲁⲗ, PLond 4 469 S ⲙⲡⲉⲛ
ⲟⲩ. ⲗⲁⲁⲩ ⲉϫⲛⲡⲣⲱⲙⲉ beyond his strength (cf ib 471
ⲧⲁⲗⲟ ⲉ-), Tur O 14 S ϥⲟⲩ. ⲙⲙⲟⲕ ⲉϫⲛⲡⲁⲡⲁ ⲡⲁⲧⲁⲡⲏ
set in charge of;   ⲉϩⲣⲁⲓ ⲉϫⲛ- SB: Deu 12 32 S(B
ⲧⲟⲩ. ⲉ-), Is 30 1 F πρ. ἐπί, Ap 22 18 S(B ⲇⲟ) ἐπιτ.
ἐπί; Sa 2 14 B ⲉϩ. (S ϩⲟⲣϣ) βαρὺς εἶναι dat; ShP
130[1] 141 S if he will ⲟⲩ. ⲉϩ. ⲉϫⲛⲡⲉⲓⲥⲛⲏϫⲉ, C 43
175 B power of God ⲟⲩⲟⲅ ⲉϩ. ⲉϫ.ⲡⲓⲁⲅⲓⲟⲥ.

—— ⲛ- SB, add to: Lu 12 25 S(B ⲧⲁⲗⲟ ⲉϫ.) προστ.
ἐπί; Ac 15 19 B ⲟⲩⲁϩ ϯⲥⲓ ⲛ- (var ⲉ-, S ϯ) παρενο
χλεῖν dat; Tri 294 S ⲁⲕⲟⲩⲉϩ ⲧⲓⲙⲏ ⲡⲁϥ زد, ib 692
S ⲁⲩⲟⲩⲁⲅⲟⲩ ⲙⲡⲉⲛⲧⲁϥⲙⲟⲩ followed رحمة;   ethic
dat, set down, make pause: Ge 27 40 S (BMOr 6954)
B καθαιρεῖν; ClPr 54 35 S unencumbered like ⲡⲉⲧ
ⲟⲩ. ⲡⲁϥ ⲡⲟⲩⲉⲧⲡⲱ ἐλευθεροῦν; ShIF 256 S ⲉⲧⲡⲱ
…ⲉⲙⲁϥⲟⲩ. ⲡⲁϥ ⲙⲙⲟⲥ, P 129[17] 7 S ⲁⲛⲟⲩ. ⲛⲁⲛ to
feed beasts (Ge 43 21);   sim ⲟⲩⲉϩ- S (diff ex
planation AZ 65 127): Ge 33 18 (B ϩⲓ ⲕⲟⲧ), Ex 15
27 (B ⲟⲩ. ⲟⲓ.ⲗⲩ) παρεμβάλλειν; Ge 43 21 (ViK 9378,
B ⲙⲧⲟ ⲉ-), Aeg 225 on journey ⲉⲧⲣⲉⲩⲟⲩ. ⲡⲁⲩ in
inn καταλύεσθαι; Job 13 13 (B ⲙⲧⲟⲛ ⲙⲙⲟⲟⲩ) ἀνα
παύεσθαι; P 129[20] 138 Christ ⲁϥⲟⲩ. ⲡⲁϥ ϩⲁⲣⲟⲛ &
was buried, ib 131[2] 140 burdened with sins ⲉⲧⲣⲉⲡ
ⲟⲩ. ⲡⲁⲛ ⲙⲙⲟⲟⲩ;   ⲙⲁ ⲡⲟⲩⲁϩ ⲡⲉⲩ A(B ⲙⲁ ⲉⲧ
ⲁϥⲧⲁⲥⲟ ⲙⲙⲟϥ) Ex 4 24 κατάλυμα.

—— ⲛⲁϩⲣⲛ- SB, set before: Nu 27 13 S(B ⲭⲱ
ϫⲁⲧⲉⲛ-), Ac 13 36 S(B ⲇⲟ) προστ. πρός; DeV 2 56
B ⲁⲛϣⲁⲛⲟⲩⲟϩⲧⲉⲛ ⲛ. ⲛⲟ̅ⲧ̅ in church.

—— ⲛⲥⲁ- SAA[2]BF, put after, follow, mostly
refl: Ez 29 16 SB, Mk 8 34 SF(B ⲓ ⲥⲁⲙⲉⲛⲑⲏ), Jo
8 12 SA[2](B ⲙⲟϣⲓ ⲛⲥⲁ-), Ap 6 8† S(B ⲥⲱⲕ ⲛⲥⲁ-),
ἀκολουθεῖν, Lev 20 6 S(B ⲇⲟ), AP 15 A[2] ⲉⲡⲁⲕ., Mk
5 37 S(B ⲙ. ⲛⲥⲁ-) συνακ., Lu 1 3 S(B ⲇⲟ) παρακ.; Ge
32 19 S(B ⲇⲟ), Hos 13 4 A(B ⲙ. ⲥⲁⲙ.) πορεύεσθαι
ὀπίσω; Jos 8 17 S not refl καταδιώκειν ὀπ.; Is 56
3† B(S ϭⲏⲛ ⲉϩⲣⲛ ⲉ-) προσκεῖσ. πρός; Ez 23 5 SB
ἐπιτιθ. ἐπί; 1 Cor 9 5 SF(B ⲙ. ⲛⲥⲁ-) περιάγειν; Mt
4 19 S(B ⲇⲟ) no Gk; Br 235 S everything ϣⲁⲣⲉϥ
ⲟⲩ. ⲛⲥⲁⲧⲉϥⲟⲩⲛⲉ, Miss 8 249 S wealth ⲉⲧⲉⲙⲛ ϩⲁⲛ
ⲟⲩ.† ⲛⲥⲱⲥ, J 82 24 S ⲉⲡⲟⲩ.† ⲛⲥⲁⲧϭⲟⲙ ⲛⲡⲡⲟⲗⲟⲥ,
AM 87 B ⲧⲉⲣⲁⲟⲩⲁϩⲧ ⲛⲥⲱⲓ, MG 25 131 B all its
hope ⲟⲩ. †ⲛⲥⲁⲡⲉϥϭⲓⲛⲃ, BP 4949 S ⲉⲓⲥ ϩⲏⲧⲉ ⲧⲛⲟⲩ.†
ⲛⲥⲁⲧⲉⲓⲉⲡⲓⲥⲧⲟⲗⲏ, Leyd 485 S sim;   ϭⲓⲛⲟⲩ. ⲛⲥⲁ
S: SHel 74 ⲧⲉⲕϭⲓⲛⲟⲩⲁϩⲕ ⲛⲥⲁⲡⲉⲭ̅ⲥ̅.

—— ⲛⲧⲛ- S, place with, pledge to: MMA 12 180
193 he shall bring (?) pledges ⲛϥϥⲓ ⲛⲥⲟⲩⲟ ⲡⲣⲟⲥ ⲑⲉ

ⲡⲧⲁϥⲟⲩ. ⲡⲧⲟⲟⲧⲕ, TurM 24 pledges ⲟⲩ.† ⲡⲧⲟⲟⲧⲛ, PSBA 33 pl 50 ⲉⲓⲟⲩ. ⲡⲧⲟⲟⲧⲉ ⲙⲡⲁⲙⲉⲣⲟⲥ ⲡⲉⲓⲱⲣⲉ, TurO 5 ⲁⲓⲟⲩ. ⲟⲩⲕⲗⲁⲗ ⲡⲧⲟⲧⲕ ϥⲁⲟⲩϧⲟⲗⲟⲕ/.

—— ϧⲁ- S, *lie by, in return for*: ST 439 ⲟⲩ.† ϧⲁⲡⲛⲟⲩⲃ *lie* (pledged) *for money* opp ⲟⲩ.† [ⲡ]ⲁⲧⲙⲏⲥⲉ, Paris Cabinet d. Méd. 1896 ⲡⲭⲱⲱⲙⲉ ... ⲟⲩ.† ϧⲁⲣⲟⲓ; *set, place*: BHom 134 ⲁⲡⲁⲅⲗⲟⲥ ⲟⲩⲉϩ ⲧⲉϥⲧⲣⲁⲡⲉⲍⲁ ϧⲁⲣⲱⲛ (sic), PBu 73 ⲟⲩ. ⲡⲉⲓⲛⲓ ⲛⲉⲡⲉⲭⲩⲣⲟⲛ ϧⲁⲟⲩϧⲟⲗⲟⲕ/.

—— ϧⲛ-, ϩⲉⲛ- SAB, *be set, lie in*: Pro 10 27 SA (Bⲛ-)ⲡⲣⲟⲟⲧ. acc, Mich 550 44 S loaves from heaven ⲁⲟⲩ. ϧⲛⲧⲉⲡⲙⲛⲧⲉ; *set, lay in*: Ac 20 18 S ⲟⲩⲉϩ ⲣⲁⲧ ϧⲛ- (B ⲓ ⲉ-) ἐπιβαίνειν εἰς (cf ⲣⲁⲧ); MG 25 149 B if Lord ⲟⲩ. ⲙⲙⲟⲓ ϩⲉⲛⲡⲁⲙⲟⲛⲁⲥⲧⲏⲣⲓⲟⲛ, Kr 228 S ⲡⲡⲏⲣⲟⲩ. ⲡⲁⲥϧⲁⲓ ϧⲛⲡⲕϭⲓⲝ (= ⲉⲃⲟⲗ ϧⲛ-) ϣⲁⲡⲧⲏⲕⲓ, Ryl 322 S sim.

—— ϧⲓⲡⲁϩⲟⲩ ⲛ- S, *set after, follow*: Is 59 13 (B ϧⲉⲛ ⲉⲃⲟⲗ ⲥⲁⲙⲉⲛϧⲏ), ἀφιστ. ὄπισθεν; 1 Tim 5 15 (B ⲣⲓⲕⲓ ⲥⲁⲃⲟⲗ) ἐκτρέπεσθαι ὀπίσω.

—— ϧⲓⲣⲉⲛ- B, *set before*: MG 25 235 ⲁⲥⲟⲩ. ⲙⲙⲟϥ ϧ. ⲡⲉϥⲣⲟ.

—— ϧⲁ(ϧ)ⲧⲛ- SF, as last: Deu 32 50 (B ⲭⲱ ϩⲁⲧⲉⲛ-) ⲡⲣⲟⲟⲧ. πρός; Ryl 368 ⲡⲁⲥϧⲁⲓ ⲟⲩⲁϧϥ ϧⲁⲧⲛⲕ, Ann 22 270 ⲁⲓⲟⲩ. ⲟⲩϧⲁⲧⲏⲣ ϧⲁⲣⲧⲛⲕ ⲡⲉϥ(ⲱ), CMSS 23 F ⲟⲩⲉϧⲟⲩ ϧⲁϧⲏⲓ (l ϧⲁⲣⲧⲏⲓ)ⲁⲡⲁ ⲓⲁⲕⲱⲃ; Mor 19 77 body shall ⲟⲩ. ϧ. ⲡⲱⲛ (var ib 18 68 ϭⲱ) = Miss 4 141 B ϣⲱⲡⲓ.

—— ϧⲓⲧⲟⲩⲛ- S, ϩⲁⲟⲩⲱ/ B, *beside*: Si 14 24 S ⲕⲁⲧⲁⲗⲩ. συνεγγύς; Nu 22 5 B(S ⲟⲩⲉϧ ⲛ-) ἐγκαθ. ἐχόμενος.

—— ϧⲓⲭⲛ- SAB, *rest, alight upon* intr: 1 Kg 23 27 B(S ⲧⲱⲟⲩⲛ ⲉⲭⲛ-) ⲉⲡⲓⲧ. ἐπί; Ep Jer 70 B(F ϧⲙⲁⲁⲥ ϧ.) ἐπικαθ. ἐπί; Nah 3 17 AB ἐπιβαίν. ἐπί; FR 6 S dove ⲟⲩ.† ϧ.ⲟⲩⲛⲏⲧⲛ, Miss 4 675 S feet ⲟⲩ. ϧⲓⲭⲱϥ (sc sand), PO 2 182 S ⲙⲡⲉⲛⲟⲩ. ϧⲓⲭⲱⲟⲩ *add to* opp ϥⲓ ϧⲛ- (cf c ⲉⲭⲛ-), EW 159 B staff ⲉϥⲟⲩ.† ϧⲓⲭⲱϥ; tr: Ge 44 11 B ⲕⲁⲑⲁⲓⲣⲉⲓⲛ ἐπί; Miss 8 175 S ⲉⲱ ⲟⲩⲉϧ ⲟⲩⲣⲟⲟⲩ ϧ.ⲡⲉϥϧⲁⲣⲉ.

With following adverb.

—— ⲉⲃⲟⲗ SBF, intr SF, *set down, pause*: BM 112 rubric for lesson ⲟⲩ. ⲉⲃ. ⲙⲡⲉⲓⲙⲁ ϭⲱⲡⲉ ⲟⲛ ⲉⲧⲉⲭⲡⲥⲟ (cf ib ⲟⲩ. ⲙⲡⲓⲙⲁ), J 48 37 ⲡⲉⲧⲛⲁⲉⲓ ⲉⲃⲟⲗ ⲉⲣⲱⲧⲛ... ⲛϥⲟⲩ. ⲉⲃ. ... ⲉϥⲉⲡⲁⲧⲉ ⲛⲏⲧⲛ, ViK 9450 monks on journey ⲟⲩ.† ⲉⲃ. ϧⲙⲡⲉϥⲙⲁ ⲡϣⲱⲡⲉ (var ROC 7 140 om ⲉⲃ.), C 41 43 B ⲁ‌ⲟⲩ. ⲉⲃ. ϩⲉⲛⲡⲟⲟⲩϣ ⲯⲟⲓ (Miss 4 396 نزلوا wrongly); P Aberdeen Univ frag letter F ⲡⲛⲁⲧⲓⲟⲩ. (ⲉ)ⲃⲁⲗ [; tr S, *let, bring down*: Nu 1 51 (B ⲭⲱ ⲉϧⲣⲏⲓ), ib 4 5 (B ⲓⲛⲓ ⲉϧⲟⲩⲛ) ⲕⲁⲑⲁⲓⲣ.; Gu 22 ⲁϥⲟⲩⲁϧϥ ⲉⲃ. from off pillar = BM 310 68 S = LAp 532 F ⲓ ⲉⲡⲉⲥⲓⲧ, ViK 9572 17 wait ϣⲁⲡⲧⲁⲟⲩⲁϩⲧ ⲉⲃ. *let myself down*(?), Griff St 149 floods ⲟⲩ. ⲉⲃ. ⲡⲡⲏϥⲕⲁϣ (reed fence), J 68 92 hath right ⲉⲕⲁⲧⲟⲩ ⲏ ⲁϧⲟⲩ (l ⲏ ⲉⲟⲩϧⲟⲩ) ⲉⲃ., AZ 23 113 when

boiled ⲟⲩⲁϧϥ ⲉⲃ. *to cool*. With prepositions. ⲛ-dat SB: BIF 13 112 S ⲡⲧⲉⲣⲉϥⲟⲩ. ⲛⲛⲓⲕⲟⲩⲓ ⲛⲟⲉⲓⲕ ⲉⲃ. ⲛⲁⲩ he departed = MG 25 303 B, Kr 104 S wines ⲁⲓⲟⲩⲁϧⲟⲩ ⲛⲁⲕ ⲉⲃ.; ϧⲓ-, *from off*: Mor 28 255 S ⲁϥⲟⲩⲁϧϥ ⲉⲃ. ϧⲓⲡⲉϧⲧⲟ = RAl 98 B, Ryl 252 S ⲧⲭⲟ ⲛⲧⲁⲓⲟⲩⲁϧⲥ ⲉⲃ. ϧⲓⲭⲛⲡⲉⲡⲱⲣ, ib 382 S ⲉⲓⲟⲩ.† ⲉⲃ. ϧⲓⲡⲏⲓ[(obscure); ϧⲛ-, as last: BMis 490 S ⲁ‌ⲟⲩⲟⲁϧϥ ⲉⲃ. ϧⲓⲡⲉⲓⲱ; ϧⲓⲭⲛ-, as last: C 89 60 B ⲟⲩ. ⲛϥⲉⲧⲛⲱ ⲉⲃ. ϧⲓⲭⲱϥ ἀποτιθ. ἀπό; Va 66 309 B ⲟⲩ. ⲉⲃ. ϧⲓⲭⲱϥ ⲙⲡⲓⲙⲕⲁϩ κουφίζειν gen; BHom 27 S sim.

—— ⲉⲡⲉⲥⲛⲧ SBF *descend, alight* intr: Sa 17 18 S birds ⲉⲩⲟⲩ. ⲉ. (var ⲡⲏⲩ ⲉϧⲣⲁⲓ) Gk om, AM 310 B ⲁϥⲟⲩ. ⲉ. ϧⲓⲭⲉⲛⲡⲓϣⲉ; tr, *set down*: Jos 8 29 S ⲕⲁⲑⲁⲓⲣ.; Miss 4 783 S ⲁⲟⲩⲟⲁϧϥ ⲉ. & laid him in hut, BKU 1 26 (8116 b)F after cooking ⲟⲩⲉϥ ⲉ. (cf ⲟⲩ. ⲉⲃⲟⲗ), BMis 223 S ⲁϥⲟⲩⲟⲁϧϥ ⲉ. ϧⲓⲛϥϧⲁⲣⲙⲁ (var Mor 16 80 ⲃⲟϣϥ ⲉ.), ib 1193 S ⲡⲧⲉⲣϥⲟⲩⲟⲁϧϥ ⲉ. ϧⲓⲭⲱϥ ⲛϭⲓ ⲡⲓⲟⲩⲅⲓ whereon he rode.

—— ⲉϧⲟⲩⲛ S, *put, bring in*: Mun 154 ⲉⲩϣⲁⲛⲟⲩⲉϥ ⲧⲉⲓⲗⲉⲝⲓⲥ ⲉⲣ. ⲙⲛ ⲗⲁⲁⲩ ⲛⲗⲟⲓϭⲉ(sic)ϣⲟⲟⲡ ⲛⲁⲕ.

· —— ⲉϧⲣⲁⲓ SF, *set down*: Lev 24 8 (B ⲭⲱ ⲉϧⲣ.) ⲡⲣⲟⲟⲧ.; Mk 15 36 F(S ⲉⲓⲛⲉ ⲉⲡⲉⲥⲛⲧ, B ⲓⲛⲓ ⲉϧⲣ.) ⲕⲁⲑⲁⲓⲣ.; R 1 5 47 bade ⲟⲩⲁϧϥ ⲉϧⲣⲁⲓ from rock, BP 5561 F if contested ⲧⲁⲟⲩⲉϧ ⲡⲉⲓⲧⲓⲕⲉⲱⲛ (δίκαιον) ⲉϧⲏⲓ ⲝⲉⲁϥⲓ ⲉⲧⲁⲁⲧ; ⲉϧ. ϧⲓ- S, *down from off*: Ac 13 29 (var ⲉϧ. ϧⲛ-, B ⲭⲱ ⲉⲡⲉⲥⲛⲧ ⲉⲃ. ϧⲓⲭⲛ-) ⲕⲁⲑ. ἀπό.

p c S: MSMoscow Mus, scorpion charm ⲧⲟⲩϧⲁⲣ ⲕⲱϧⲧ ⲧⲟⲩϧⲁⲣ ⲝⲁϥ *putting* (causing) *heat, cold*, ST 116 among utensils (ⲟⲩ)ⲟⲩⲁϧⲣⲏⲡ (prob sic l) vessel in which to *put wine*(?). Cf? ⲟⲩⲁϧⲣⲉ.

ⲙⲁ ⲛⲟⲩ. SF, *place for putting*: Lam 2 1 F ⲙⲉ ⲛⲟⲩⲁϧ ⲗⲉⲧϥ (B ⲙⲁ ⲛⲥⲉⲙⲛⲓ, S ShC 73 77 = Gk) ὑποπόδιον; Z 356 S ⲙⲁ ⲛⲟⲩⲉϧ ⲟⲉⲓⲕ ἀρτοθέσιον.

B intr *be placed, dwell* SAA²B(rare)F: Ge 13 6, Ez 16 46†, Ap 2 13† (all B ϣⲱⲡⲓ) κατοικεῖν; Job 29 25† B(S diff), Ps 36 27 (B do) κατασκηνοῦν; Si 43 18 καταλύειν; Jo 1 38† (B do) μένειν; ShR 2 3 32 ⲕⲁ[ⲙ]ⲁ ⲡⲁϥ ⲉⲧⲣⲉϥⲟⲩ., BKU 1 92 I know not ⲝⲉ ⲉⲕⲟⲩ.† ⲧⲱⲛ.

With following preposition.

—— ⲉ- S(rare)BF, *dwell by, with*: Lev 16 29† (S ϣⲟⲟⲡ ϧⲉⲛ-), Nu 15 15 (S ⲱⲛ ⲉ-), ib 19 10 SB προσκεῖσθαι ἐν, Is 56 6 (S ϧⲏⲛ ⲉϧⲟⲩⲛ ⲉ-) ⲡⲣ. dat; Ac 28 30 ⲟⲩ.† ⲉⲡⲉϥϣⲝⲟⲣ (varr ϭⲓ ⲉ-, ϩⲉⲛ-, ϩⲁ-, S = Gk) μέν.; Kr 22 F ⲉⲥⲟⲩ.† ⲉ(ⲧ)ⲡⲟⲗⲓⲥ ⲡⲓⲁⲙ (for ?ⲛ-).

—— ⲉⲭⲛ- SA²B, *upon*: Mt 13 32 B(S ϧⲛ-, F ϧⲓ-ⲝⲉⲛ-) κατασκην. ἐν; Mani H 8 A² ⲡⲕⲁϩ ⲉⲧⲟⲩⲟⲩ.† ⲁⲭⲱϥ; ⲉϧⲣⲁⲓ ⲉⲭⲛ-: Ap 3 10 S(B om vb) κατοικ. ἐπί; 2 Cor 12 9 S(B ϣ. ϧⲓⲭ.) ἐπισκ. ἐπί; Jo 1 32 S (B ⲟϩⲓ ϧⲓⲭ.) μέν. ἐπί.

—— ⲙⲛ- *SA²B* (rare), *with*: Ps 139 13 (*B* ⳝ.) κατοικ. σύν, Ge 32 4 (*B* do) πάροικ. μετά, Deu 22 22 (*B* ϧⲉⲗⳝⲓ ⲡⲉⲙ-) συνοικ. dat; Jo 1 14 (*B* ⳝ.) σκην. ἐν; ShViK 9598 368 bringing others ⲉⲟⲩ. ⲛⲙⲙⲁⲩ, BHom 30 ⲕⲟⲩ.† ⲙⲡⲟⲩϭⲣⲓⲙⲉ, Mani 2 *A²* ⲡⲣⲙⲡⲉⲥ ⲟⲩ.† ⲡⲉⲙⲁϥ, BSM 37 *B* angels ⲉⲧⲟⲩ.† ⲡⲉⲙⲁϥ = BMis 381 *S* ⲗⲟⲟϣⲉ ⲙⲛ-.

—— ⲛ- *S*, *in*: Ap 13 6 (var ϧⲛ-, *B* ⲛ⳥ⲣⲏⲓ Ⳟⲉⲛ-) σκ. ἐν.

—— ϧⲁ-, Ⳟⲁ-, *beneath*: Mk 4 32 *SB* κατασκ. ὑπό; ShA 1 466 *S* soul like ἀήρ wherein demons fly ⲏ ⲉⲧⲟⲩ.† ϧⲁⲣⲟⲥ, Kr 125 *S* as long as ⲉⲓⲟ[ⲩ]ⲏϧ ϧⲁⲣⲟ *in thy house*.

—— ϧⲓ- *S*, *on, in*: Ep 87 ⲡⲧⲟⲟⲩ ⲉⲧⲟⲩ.† ϧⲓⲱⲱϥ, BMOr 6204 A dwelling ⲉⲣⲉ-...ⲟⲩ. ϧⲓⲱⲱϥ; ⲛ⳥ⲣⲏⲓ ϧⲓ- *B*: Ge 12 9 (*S* diff) στρατοπεδεύειν ἐν.

—— ϧⲛ- *S.AA²F*, *in*: Is 30 19 *SF* οἰκ. ἐν, Lev 23 42, Pro 24 63 *SA* κατοικ. ἐν, Is 5 9 (*F* ⳝ.) ἔνοικ. ἐν, Ps 93 17 πάροικ. dat; Ap 12 12† σκ. ἐν, Ps 64 4 κατασκ. ἐν; Job 15 28 αὐλίζεσθαι acc; Lu 8 27 μέν. ἐν; Jo 8 37 *SA²* χωρεῖν ἐν (all *B* ⳝ.); PS 52 ⲥⲉⲡⲁⲟⲩ. ϧⲛⲧⲡⲟⲗⲓⲥ, Aeg 278 ⲡⲉⲡ⳯ⲃ̄ ⲟⲩ. ϧⲙⲡⲣⲱⲙⲉ, AP 13 *A²* ⲟⲩⲁⲛ ⲛⲓⲙ ⲉⲧⲟⲩ.† ϧⲛⲁⲅⲟⲣⲁ, BHom 6 ϧⲛϫⲟⲉⲓⲛ ⲉⲧⲟⲩ.† ϧⲣⲁⲓ ⲡϧⲏⲧⲩ.

—— ϧⲓϫⲛ- *SABF*, *upon*: Ge 12 6† *S*(*B* ⳝ.), Hos 4 1† *SA*(*B* do) κατοικ. acc. Dan 4 9† *B* κ. ἐν, Ap 6 10 *S*(*B* ⳝ.) κ. ἐπί; Ps 36 29 *S*(*B* do) κατασκ. ἐπί, Pro 2 21 *SA*(*B* do) κ. acc, Mt 13 32 *F*(*S* ϧⲛ-, *B* ⲉϫⲉⲛ-) κ. ἐν; PS 6 *S* earth & ⲡⲉⲧⲟⲩ.† ϧⲓϫⲱϥ.

—— nn m, *standing-, dwelling-place* & obscure meanings *SB*: TThe 263 *B* ⲡⲓⲟⲩ. of Holy Spirit مَسْكَن; P 129[16] 20 *S* = Mor 28 176 *S* sheep pasturing ϧⲙⲡⲟⲩ. ⲉⲧⲙⲙⲁⲩ, BM 675 *S* wages to workman ϥⲣ ϧⲱϥ ⲉϧⲟⲩⲛ ⲉⲡⲟⲩ., Kr 65 *S* ⲡⲟⲩ., *ib* 64 *S* ⲡⲟⲩϣⲣⲉ (same ?). In place-names: bishop of ⲡⲟⲩ. ⲡⲧ- ⲃⲁⲃⲩⲗⲱⲛ (JA '88 2 372, *v* Amélineau *Géog* 77), ⲡⲟⲩ. ⲡ(ⲛ)ⲁⲙⲏⲩ *v* ⲁⲙⲉ, ⲡⲟⲩ. ⲙⲡⲟⲩⲧⲱ (Saq 369), ⲡⲟⲩ. ⲙⲡⲉϣⲱⲙ (*ib* 372), ⲡⲟⲩ. ϧⲗⲗⲟ (*ib* p 49); as ⲡⲟⲩⲁ: ⲡ. ⲡⲡⲉϣⲟⲟⲥ (Kr 6, *cf* ⲡ. ⲛⲡⲁⲙⲏⲩ above, Πουανποι- μῆνις PSI 304), Πουανπινοῦπις (P Stras Preisigke 74); meanings doubtful: TEuch 2 279 *B* un- spotted by ⲟⲩ. ⲛⲓⲃⲉⲛ ⲛϭⲗⲟϭ (*l* ⳝⲗ.) عيب stain; Ep 170 *S* ⲧⲛⲛⲟⲟⲩ (ⲟⲩ)ⲟⲩ. ⲛⲁⲓ for I am distraught, *ib* ⲡⲟⲩ.; *placing, laying*, so *stroke, blow* in ϥⲓ ⲟⲩⲱϩ *SA*: BHom 137 *S* ⲡⲁⲥⲡⲗⲁⲅⲭⲛⲟⲛ ϥ. κλυδώνιον ἐν τοῖς σπλ.; Nah 3 3 *A* of weapons (*B* ϧⲓ ⲥⲉⲧⲉⲃⲣⲏϫ) ἐξαστράπτειν; Mor 34 43 *S* child learning to walk ⲉϥϥⲓ ⲟⲩ. ⲟⲩ. ϧⲙⲡⲉϥⲕⲟⲩⲓ ⲛϭⲟⲡ...ⲉϥϫⲓ ⲧⲁⲥϭⲉ, BMis 140 *S* ⲉϥⲧⲟⲟⲃⲥ ⲉⲡⲉϥⲕⲟⲩⲓ ⲛϭ. ⲉϥϥⲓ ⲟⲩ. ⲟⲩ. *taking step on step*.

ⲙⲁ ⲡⲟⲩ. *SAB*, *halting-, resting-, dwelling-place*: Jer 32 38 *B*(*S* ⲙⲁ ⲡϣⲱⲡⲉ) κατάλυμα; BM 172 40 *S* οἶκος, Nu 24 21 *S*(*B* ⲙⲁ ⲛϣ.), Ps 131 13 (*B* do)

κατοικία, Nu 15 2 *S*(*B* do) -οἴκησις, Ex 16 35 *S*(*B* do) οἰκουμένη; Mt 8 20 *B*(*S* ⲙⲁϧ) κατασκήνωσις; BHom 1 *S* δοχεῖον; Ge 8 9 *S* (var & *B* ⲙⲁ ⲛⲡⲧⲟⲡ) ἀνάπαυσις; Is 28 17 *S*(*B* ⳝⲓ) σταθμός; Zech 10 4 *A* (*B* Gk diff); ShC 42 208 *S* ⲙ. ⲙⲡⲇⲓⲁⲃⲟⲗⲟⲥ, AM 254 *B* ϧⲉⲙ ⲙ. ϳⲉⲛ⳥ⲣⲏ ⲉⲑⲟⲩⲁⲃ, BMOr 9536 vo *S* ⲙ. monastic *cell*, J 75 64 *S* ⲙⲙ. in monastery (caves, towers &c).

ϭⲓⲛ-, ϫⲓⲛⲟⲩ. *SB*, *act of dwelling, manner of life*: ShIF 285 *S* ⲧⲉⲩϭ. ⲡⲓⲙⲛⲧⲛ, BMis 436 *S* ⲧϭ. ϧⲓ- ⲡϫⲁⲓⲉ, Mor 25 8 *S* ⲧϭ. ⲡⲡⲣⲱⲙⲉ ⲡⲁⲣⲭⲁⲓⲟⲛ = Va 61 91 *B* ϫⲓⲛϣⲱⲡⲓ, DeV 2 16 *B* ⲧϫ. ϳⲉⲛⲧⲁⲡⲉϭⲓ ⲙ- ⲡⲓⲭⲣⲱⲙ; ViK 9760 95 *S* whether He was united with the flesh or ⲉⲁϥⲁⲣⲭⲉⲥⲑⲁⲓ ⲡⲟⲩϭ. ⲉⲣⲟϥ ⲡⲧⲉ ⲧⲥⲁⲣⳉ yet was He still in His divinity ⲙⲡⲉⲗⲁⲁⲩ ⲟⲩⲱϩ ⲉⲣⲟⲥ & *naught was added thereto*.

ⲟⲩⲁϩ *S* nn m, *stave, pole*: Ex 25 14 (P 44 104, *B* = Gk), Nu 4 6 (*B* ϣⲉ ⲛϧⲱ⳥) ἀναφορεύς; ShIF 182 bearing ark ϧⲛϩⲉⲛⲟⲩ. of wood, Mor 31 214 ϧⲛⲟⲩ. ⲛⲣⲁⲧ ⲉⲩⲧⲱⲟⲩⲛ ⲙⲡⲉϩⲁⲣⲁⲗ ⲛⲣⲏⲧⲟⲩ., R 1 5 30 ⲁϥ[ϫⲓ ⲙ]ⲡⲟⲩ. ⲁϥⲣ ⲡⲉⲓϫⲱⲗⲟⲡ ⲛⲗⲁⲕⲙ ⲗⲁⲕⲙ.

ⲟⲩⲁϩϥ *S* nn m, *liturgical functionary, acolyte*(?): Baouit 127 ⲡⲉⲯⲁⲗⲙⲱⲍⲟⲥ, ⲓⲁⲕⲱⲃ ⲙⲡⲁ ⲡⲉϥⲟⲩ., *ib* 111 ⲡⲣⲱϣ & ⲡⲟⲩ., MIF 59 373 sim.

V also ⲣⲁⲧ, ⲥⲟⲓ, ⲥⲁϩⲛⲉ, ϩⲓⲥⲉ, ϫⲱ *head*, ϫⲱⲱⲙⲉ & ⲧⲟⲩϩⲟ.

(ⲟⲩⲱϩ), ⲟⲩⲉϩ- *S* vb tr, *interpret* (*wḥʿ* Dévaud, *v* Berl *Worterb* 1 348): Ge 41 8 ⲣⲉϥⲟⲩⲉϩ ⲣⲁⲥⲟⲩ (*B* ⲥⲫⲣⲁⲛⳝ)ἐξηγητής. But *cf* ? Jer 34 7 *B* ⲟⲩⲟϩⲉⲙ ⲛⲡⲓⲣⲁⲥⲟⲩⲓ.

ⲟⲩⲁϩⲉ *S*, ⲟⲩⲁϩ (K), ⲃⲁϩ (Amélineau *Géog* 573) *B*, ⲟⲩⲉϩⲓ *F* nn, *oasis* "Ὄασις الواح: BM 288 ⲧⲉⲭⲱⲣⲁ ⲡⲟⲩ. where Bartholomew preached, Mich 550 45 where Nestorius exiled, LAp 515 *F* ⲁϥⲉⲓ ⲉ]ⲃⲁⲗ ϧⲓ- ⲡⲟⲩ., HTR 1 ⲉⲩⲛⲁⲭⲓⲧϥ (*sc* N.) ⲉϧⲟⲩⲛ ⲉⲟⲩ., Bor 134 6 (Vita Sin) ⲧⲡⲟⲗⲓⲥ ⲟⲩ. = Miss 4 376 مدينة الواح, R 1 4 37ⲃⲱⲕ ⲉⲟⲩ. ⲉⲧϧⲓϧⲟⲩⲛ, Amél. *lc* 557 ⲟⲩ. الواح, *ib* 559 = K 211 *B*.

ⲟⲩⲁϩⲟ *B* *v* ⲁϩⲟ *B*.

ⲟⲩϩⲓⲉ, -ⲁϩⲉ† *A²*, -ⲟϩⲉ† *S*, p c ⲟⲩϩⲁⲣⲓ- *SAA²* vb intr, *be bitter, sharp*(?): 4 Kg 14 26† *S* πικρός; Mani H 82 *A²* replying to king's threats ⲟⲩⲏⲧⲛⲓ ⲡⲉⲧⲟⲩ.† ⲡⲁⲣⲁⲣⲁⲕ; as nn m, *cruelty*: Mani 1 *A²* ⲁⲓⲉⲓⲣⲉ ⲙ- ⲡⲉⲧⲁⲡⲓⲧ ⲟⲩⲧⲱⲟⲩ ϧⲓⲡⲟⲩϩ. but they crucified me, *ib* H 11 *A²* ⲁⲥⲣ ϫⲟⲗ[ⲏ ⲁⲥ- ? ⲟ]ⲩϩⲓⲉ ⲁϫⲱϥ.

p c ⲟⲩϩⲁⲣⲓⲏⲧ *SA*, ⲟⲩⲁϩ(ⲉ)ⲏⲧ *SA²*, *bitter-hearted, cruel*: 2 Tim 3 3 (*B* diff) ἄσπονδος (or ? ἄστοργος); BHom 74 angels ⲡⲟⲩⲁϩⲉⲓⲏⲧ, Bor 253 124 (ⲟⲩ)ⲟⲩⲁⲓ- ϧⲓⲏⲧ, Ryl 94 (33 3) ⲁⲣⲭⲱⲛ ⲡⲟⲩⲁⲓϧⲓⲏⲧ, Mani 1 *A²* ⲣⲱⲙⲉ ⲡⲟⲩ. that slew my god; ⲙⲛⲧⲟⲩ., *cruelty*: Sa 12 5 -ϧⲓⲏⲧ ἀνελεήμων; ShA 1 398 -ⲟⲩⲁϩⲓϧ.

(var MIF 23 51 -ϩⲓⲏⲧ), Mani 2 *A²* ⲧⲉϥⲙ[ⲛⲧⲟⲩ]ⲁ-
ϩⲓⲏⲧ; ⲣ, ⲟ ⲛⲟⲩ., *be cruel*: Job 19 13 (*B* ⲁⲧⲛⲁⲓ)
ἀνελ.; Ro 1 31 (var -ϩⲓⲏⲧ, *B* ⲁⲧϣⲉⲛϩⲏⲧ) ἄστορ.;
Leip Ber '02 150 -ϩⲓⲏⲧ ἀπηνέστατος; Mor 37 134
ⲟⲩⲁⲓϩ. ὠμός; Bor 265 86 ⲣ ⲟⲩ. ⲉϩⲣⲟⲩⲛ ⲉⲣⲟⲟⲩ, Till
Oster 16 *A* ⲉⲩⲉ ⲛⲟⲩ. ⲁ̅ϩⲟⲩⲛ ⲁ-.

ⲟⲩⲟⲟϩⲉ *SA*, ⲟⲩⲟϩⲉ, -ⲱϩⲉ *S*, -ⲟϩⲓ *B*(once), -ⲁⲁϩⲓ
F nn f, *scorpion*: Deu 8 15, Lu 10 19 *SA* (Till Oster
23), Ap 9 10 -ⲟϩⲉ (var -ⲱϩⲉ, all *B* ϭⲗⲏ) σκορπίος;
ShA 2 272, RNC 89 ⲧⲟⲩ., BMis 557 ⲡⲉⲓⲟⲩⲟϩⲉ, Mor
24 25 *F*, MIE 2 351 *B* ⲟⲩⲟⲩ.; P 43 245 ⲥⲓⲙ ⲛⲟⲩ.
حشيش العقرب *erythraea spicata* (AIssa 78), Hall 65.
As name(?): ⲧⲟⲩⲟϩⲉ (RE 9 149).

ⲟⲩⲟϩⲉ, -ⲟⲟϩⲉ (once), ⲃⲟⲩϩⲉ, ⲟⲩϩⲉ(?) *S*, ⲟⲩⲟϩⲓ,
ⲃⲟϩⲓ *B* nn m, *fisher*: Jer 16 16 *SB*, Mt 4 18 *SB* ἁλιεύς; P 44 54 *S* ⲁⲅⲣⲁⲧⲏⲥ (ἀγρευ.)· ⲛⲟⲩ. صياد (ⲓⲭ-
ⲟⲩⲁⲛⲟⲡ *out of place here*); Va 63 80 *B* ⲟⲩⲟⲩ.
ⲡⲣⲉϥⲧⲁϩⲉ ⲧⲉⲃ̅ⲧ ἰχθυοπώλης; BMis 393 *S* = BSM
45 *B* ⲥⲁ ⲛ̅ⲧ., *ib* 382 *S* = Va 63 12 *B* = BSM 38 *B*
ⲣⲉϥⲧⲁϩⲉ ⲧ., *ib* 477 *S* ⲣⲱⲙⲉ ⲛⲟⲩ. using ϣⲛⲉ & ⲁⲃⲱ,
ib 486 *S* ⲃ̅., CO 436 *S* ϩⲉⲛ(ⲟⲩ)ⲱϩⲉ, Va 57 157 *B*
ⲛⲓⲃ̅. ⲛⲣⲉϥϫⲱⲣⲭ, BMOr 6204 *B S* ⲡⲁⲥⲟⲛ ϣⲉⲛⲟⲩⲧⲉ ⲛⲟⲩ., BKU 1 278 *S* Moses ⲛⲟⲩⲅⲉ, BP 669 *S*
ⲡⲁⲅ[ⲗⲟⲥ] ⲛⲟⲩⲟⲟϩⲉ; ⲙⲛⲧⲟⲩ. *S, fisher's craft*:
Mor 43 133 John, James & Zebedee ⲟ ⲛⲟⲩⲙ.
ⲛⲟⲩⲱⲧ (Mt 4 18), Gu 106 why desirest ⲧⲙ. ⲛⲕⲉⲥⲟⲡ?
ⲙⲛⲧⲣⲉϥⲣ ⲟⲩ., *as last*: Mor 34 64 I taught
thee ⲧⲙ. ϭⲓⲛⲟⲩ. *S, act of, means for fishing*,
so? *fishing outfit, boat*: Mor 44 9 at calling of disciples ⲁⲡⲛⲁⲩ ⲉⲕⲉϭ. ⲉⲣⲉⲟⲩϩⲗⲗⲟ ⲛⲣⲱⲙⲉ (*sc* Zebedee)
ⲧⲁⲗⲏⲩ ⲉⲣⲟϥ (*l* -ⲟⲥ).
As name (here ?): ⲛⲟⲩⲱϩⲉ (J 105̅ 34).

ⲟⲩⲁϩⲃⲉϥ *SB*, -ⲙⲉϥ, ⲟⲩⲟϩⲃⲉϥ *S*, ⲟⲩⲁϩϥ *B* vb
intr, *bark, growl* of dog: Is 56 10 *S*(var -ⲙⲉϥ)*B*
ὑλακτεῖν; Ex 11 7 *B*(var -ϩϥ) γρύζειν; Mor 40 49 *S*
ⲉϥⲟⲩ. like dog = MG 25 275 *B*-ϩϥ. *Cf* ⲃⲉϩⲃⲉϩ
(adding ViK 9336 *S* ⲉϥⲃⲁⲣⲃⲉϩ ⲉⲣⲟⲩⲛ ⲉⲣⲟⲕ).

V Dévaud *Études* 31.

ⲟⲩⲁϩⲕⲱ(?) *v* ⲁϩⲕⲱ.

ⲟⲩⲱϩⲙ *SA²*(Jo)*F*, -ⲙⲉ *AA²*(Ma), -ϩⲉⲙ *BF*,
ⲃⲱϩⲉⲙ, ⲟⲩⲟϩⲉⲙ *B*, ⲟⲩⲉϩⲙ- *S*, ⲟⲩⲁϩⲙⲉ- *A*, ⲟⲩⲉ-
ϩⲙⲉ- *Sᵃ*(J 71 44), ⲟⲩⲁϩⲉⲙ- *B*, ⲟⲩⲟ. *SB*, ⲟⲩⲉϩⲉⲙ-
SBF, ⲟⲩⲁϩⲙⲉ *SA²BF*, ⲟⲩⲟ. *S*, ⲟⲩⲉ. *F*(Ac 9 36),
ⲟⲩⲟϩⲙ† *SF*, -ⲁϩⲙ† *Sᶠ*, ⲟⲩⲟϩⲉⲙ† *B*, ⲣ ⲟ ⲟⲩⲁϩⲉⲙ- *B*
vb **I** intr, *repeat, answer*: Is 50 5 *S*(*B* = Gk), Tit 1
9 *S*(*B* do) ἀντιλέγειν; Mt 28 5 *F*(*S* ⲟⲩⲱϣⲃ, *B* ⲉⲣ
ⲟⲩⲱ), Jo 6 29 *F* (Mich 3521, *SB* do) ἀποκρίνεσθαι;
Ro 2 15 *S*(*B* = Gk) ἀπολογεῖσθαι; 2 Tim 2 25 *S*(*B*
ϯ ⲉⲃⲟⲩⲛ ⲉϩⲣⲉⲛ-) ἀντιδιατίθεναι; PS 200 *S* ⲁϥⲟⲩ.
ⲟⲛ ⲡⲉϫⲁϥ, ShP 130¹ 139 *S* disobedient nun ⲥⲟⲩ.
ⲁⲩⲱ ⲥϯ ⲧⲱⲛ, BMis 537 *S* no blame to sick when
ⲛϥⲟⲩ. ⲁⲛ *compsallere*, HCons 378 *B* ⲡⲓⲗⲁⲟⲥ ⲃ̅. ϫⲉⲁ-

ⲙⲏⲓ, Leyd 175 *Sᶠ* rubric ⲛϩⲉⲣⲙⲏⲛⲓⲁ ⲉⲧⲟⲩ.† *used
as responses*, Mor 22 33 *S* if enemies ⲟⲩ. ⲛ̅ⲥⲉⲉⲓ ⲉ-
ⲣⲟⲟⲩ.

II tr, *repeat, do again, add*: Si 7 14 *S* δευτεροῦν;
Ez 21 14 *SB* διπλασιάζειν; Jth 15 14 *S* ὑπερφωνεῖν;
Va 57 243 *B* ⲁϥⲭⲟⲥ…ⲁϥⲟⲩⲁϩⲉⲙ ⲡⲓⲥⲁϫⲓ ⲉϥϫⲱ ⲙ-
ⲙⲟⲥ ἐπάγειν; Aeg 265 *S*, Cat 16 *B*, Mor 30 19 *F* sim
(but CDan 90 *B* ⲟⲩⲁ. ⲥⲁϫⲓ ἀντιλέγειν), R 1 5 50 *S*
ⲟⲩⲁϩⲙⲉϥ (*sc* martyr) ⲛⲕⲉϣⲉ ⲛⲕⲟⲩⲙⲡⲟⲥ (κόμβος),
Mani 2 *A²* ⲛϥⲟⲩⲁϩⲙⲉ ϩⲟⲟⲩⲉ;   refl *S*: 1 Kg 20
20 τρισσεύειν; Si 19 12 προστιθ.; Mor 19 73 ⲁⲓⲟⲩⲁϩ-
ⲙⲉⲧ ⲟⲛ ⲡⲉϫⲁⲓ = *ib* 18 64 ⲟⲩⲱϩ ⲉⲧⲟⲟⲧ (Miss 4 138
B om), Bor 292 35 Elias ⲁϥⲟⲩⲁϩⲙⲉϥ ⲟⲛ ⲁϥⲛⲱⲟⲣⲧ
thrice (*cf* 3 Kg 18 34), Mor 52 46 sim ⲟⲩⲉϩⲙ̅ⲧⲏⲩⲧⲛ̅
ⲡⲱⲣⲧ, AZ 23 111 recipe ⲧⲟⲙⲥⲟⲩ…ⲟⲩⲁϩⲙⲕ ⲧⲟⲙ-
ⲥⲉⲥϥ, Mor 41 168 curing sick ⲡⲉⲙⲉϥⲟⲩⲁϩⲙⲉϥ ⲟⲙ-
ⲡⲉϥϣⲁϫⲉ ϩⲟⲗⲱⲥ but what he spake befell straightway;   *be interpreted* (3d pl as pass): Jo 9 7 *SÄ²B* ἑρ-
μηνεύεσθαι, Ac 9 36 *SBF* ϣⲁⲩⲟⲩⲉϩⲙ̅ διερ., Mt 1
23 *SB* μεθερ.; BAp 132 *S* John ϣⲁⲩⲟⲩⲁϩⲙⲉϥ ϫⲉ-
ⲧⲉⲭⲁⲣⲓⲥ, C 43 59 *B* name ϣⲁⲟⲩⲟϩⲙⲉϥ ϫⲉⲭⲣ-
ⲓⲱⲙ, Lant 80 vo *S* ⲓⲱϩⲁⲛⲛⲏⲥ ϣⲁⲩⲁϩⲙⲉϥ ϫⲉϭⲟⲩϩⲏ-
ⲡⲉ; ⲟⲩⲉϩⲙ̅-, ⲟⲩⲟ., ⲟⲩⲁ. *before* vb(ἀνα-, ἐπι-) *SBF*:
Lev 1 1 *B*(var ⲟⲩⲟ-, *S* om) ἀνακαλεῖν; Jer 18 9 *B*
ἀνοικοδομεῖν, 1 Cor 3 10 *BF*(*S* om) ἐποικ.; 2 Tim 1
6 *B*(*S* diff) ἀναζωπυρεῖν; Mt 13 25 *F*(*SB* om) ἐπι-
σπείρειν; Gal 3 15 *B*(*S* ⲟⲩⲉϩⲥⲁϩⲛⲉ)ἐπιδιατάσσεσθαι;
LMär 23 *S* day ⲉⲧⲟⲩⲛⲁⲟⲩⲉϩⲙ̅ ⲭⲡⲟⲓ ⲛϩⲏⲧϥ, ROC
19 69 *S* ⲡϣⲟⲣⲡ ⲛⲗⲟⲓⲟⲥ ⲛⲧⲁϥⲧⲁϩⲟϥ…ⲉⲁϥⲟⲩⲟϩⲙ
ⲧⲁϩⲟϥ ⲛⲕⲉⲥⲟⲡ, BM 1113 *S* I summoned thee ⲛ-
ⲡⲉⲕⲟⲩⲁϩⲙ ⲉⲓ, C 41 43 *B* ⲁϥⲟⲩ. ⲉⲣ ⲉⲧⲓⲛ ⲙⲙⲟϥ;
ⲟⲩⲱϩⲙ̅- *S*: J 20 91 ⲉⲕⲕⲱⲧ, ⲉⲕϣⲟⲣϣⲣ, ⲉⲕⲟⲩ. ⲕⲱⲧ,
ib 21 58 ⲛⲧⲉⲧⲛⲟⲩ. ⲕⲟⲧϥ ⲉⲛ̅ⲡϣⲓⲥⲉ(*cf* PMon 142 ἀνοικοδ.
ἐφ' ὕψους), COAd 46 ⲁⲧⲉⲧⲛⲟⲩ. ⲉϩⲣⲁⲓ ⲛⲁⲛ. (*cf* c ⲉ-).

With following preposition.

—— ⲉ- *SB*, *reply to* intr: C 99 93 *S* ⲁϥⲟⲩ. ⲉⲁⲡⲁ
ϩⲟⲣⲥⲓⲏⲥⲓⲟⲥ…ϫⲉ- = MG 17 646 أجاب, TEuch 2
130 *B* rubric ⲡⲁⲓⲃⲱϩⲉⲙ…ⲉⲣⲉⲡⲓⲕⲗⲏⲣⲟⲥ ⲟⲩ.ⲉⲣⲟϥ;
ⲟⲩⲁϩⲉⲙ ⲉ- vbal *B*, *repeat*: Va 57 46 ⲉⲣϣⲁⲛⲡϯ ⲟⲩⲁ.
ⲉⲭⲫⲟ ἀναγεννᾶν, *ib* 10 ⲁϥⲟⲩⲁ. ⲉⲭⲟⲥ ἐπάγειν; DeV
2 9 ⲁⲧⲉϥⲯⲩⲭⲏ ⲟⲩⲁ.ⲉⲱⲛϩ̅;   tr, *do again, repeat*
S: PS 311 a backslider ⲉϩⲉⲥⲧⲓ ⲉⲟⲩⲁϩⲙⲉϥ ⲉⲡⲓⲩ-
ⲥⲧⲏⲣⲓⲟⲛ, Mor 41 50 ⲟⲩⲉϩⲙ ⲡϣⲁϫⲉ ⲉⲣⲟⲛ ⲛⲕⲉⲥⲟⲡ;
refl: Lev 19 10 (*B* ⲕⲱϯ ⲉ-) ἐπανατρυγᾶν; ShC 73
208 ⲟⲩⲁϩⲙⲉⲕ ⲉⲣⲟⲟⲩ ⲉⲕⲱϣ ⲉⲃⲟⲗ they will awake,
ShP 131¹ 90 ⲉⲧⲙⲧⲣⲉϥⲟⲩⲁϩⲙⲉϥ ⲉⲉⲓⲣⲉ; ShC 73 128
ⲉϥ-…ⲟⲩⲁϩⲙⲉϥ ⲉϩⲣⲁⲓ ⲉⲛⲛⲟⲃⲉ.

—— ⲉϫⲛ- *SB*, *reply to*: ShBor 247 103 *S* ϣⲁϥⲟⲩ.
ⲉϫⲛⲛⲁⲓ ϫⲉ-, Va 61 120 *B* ⲁⲛⲟⲩ. ⲉϫ.ⲡⲉⲕⲥⲙⲟⲩ *return thy greetings*; Job 29 22 *S* refl(var ⲟⲩⲱϩ better?,
B ⲧⲟⲩϩⲟ) προστιθ. ἐπί; C 86 156 *B* ⲟⲩⲉϩⲉⲙ ⲕⲉⲥⲁϫⲓ
ⲛⲟⲩⲱⲧ ⲉⲃⲟⲩⲛ ⲉϫⲱⲓ.

—— ⲛ- dat *SBF* intr: Dan 3 16 *B* ἀποκρίν. dat,
Ac 25 16 *B*(*S* ⲟⲩⲱϣⲃ) ἀ. πρός; Job 23 13 *S*(*B* ⲉⲣ
ⲁⲡⲧⲓⲗⲉⲅⲓⲛ) ἀντειπεῖν dat; Br 261 *S* ⲁⲅⲁⲡⲧⲓⲗⲉⲅⲉ
ⲁⲩⲱ ⲁⲅⲟⲩ. ⲡⲁϥ, ShR 2 4 50 *S* ⲁϥⲟⲩ. ⲛⲛⲉⲡⲧⲁⲩⲣ
ϣⲣⲡ ϫⲟⲟⲩ, BMis 450 *S* ⲁⲅ(ⲟⲩ)ⲱϣⲙ ⲛⲛⲡⲉⲧⲟⲩⲁⲁⲃ
Pcod F 18 ⲉⲕⲛⲉⲟⲩ. ⲡⲧⲙⲉⲧⲁⲧⲛⲉϩϯ = *ib S* 39 ⲟⲩⲱϣⲃ, TstAb 167 *B* what sawest thou? ⲟⲩ. ⲛⲁⲛ ϩⲉⲛ
ⲡⲉⲕⲥⲁϫⲓ;   tr: Is 36 21 *F*(*S* ⲟⲩⲱϣⲃ, *B* ⲉⲣ ⲟⲩⲱ)
ἀποκ. dat acc; He 12 19 *S*(*B* ⲡⲉⲙ-) προστιθ. dat;
Jer 34 7 *B* ⲟⲩ. ⲛⲛⲓⲣⲁⲥⲟⲩⲓ ⲛ- ἐνυπνιάζειν dat; ShA
1 454 *S* ⲙⲡⲟⲩⲟⲩⲱϣ ⲉⲧⲣⲁⲟⲩⲉϫⲙ ⲡϣⲁϫⲉ ⲛⲁϥ.

—— ⲛⲥⲁ- *SB*, respond to: BMis 536 *S* these ⲟⲩ.
ⲛⲥⲱϣ ϫⲉⲁⲗⲗⲏⲗⲟⲩⲓⲁ ὑπακούειν dat; Br 93 *S* ⲟⲩ. ⲛ-
ⲥⲱⲓ ϫⲉⲣⲁⲙⲏⲛ (cf 92 ⲟⲩⲱϣⲃ), BMis 572 *S* ⲉϥⲯⲁⲗⲗⲉⲓ...ⲉⲣⲉⲡⲁⲅⲅⲉⲗⲟⲥ ⲟⲩ. ⲛⲥⲱϥ, C 41 46 *B* chorus ⲟⲩ.
ⲛⲥⲱϥ as he chants; Ostr Nicholson (copy BMAdd
31291 106) *S* contract ⲁⲓⲟⲩⲱϣ ⲟⲩⲁϫⲙⲉⲕ ⲛⲥⲁ[ ]ⲁⲓ
ⲉⲡⲕⲁⲙⲟⲩⲗ *put in charge of* (?).

—— ⲡⲁϩⲣⲛ- *SB* in presence of: Cat 12 *B* not to
ⲟⲩⲟ. ⲛ.ⲫⲏ ⲉⲧϯ ϣⲱϣ ⲛⲁⲕ, J 36 33 *S* ⲁⲡⲟⲩⲉϫⲙ ⲛⲧ-
ⲟⲩⲛⲟⲑⲉⲥⲓⲥ (sic) ⲛⲛⲁϩⲣⲁⲡⲛⲧⲓⲙⲓⲱⲧ(ⲁⲧⲟⲥ) ... ⲡⲗⲁϣ-
(ⲛⲏⲩ).

—— ⲟⲩⲃⲉ- *SBF*, contradict, object: Lu 21 15 *SB*
ἀντειπ.; ViK 9788 9 *S* ⲡⲉ[ⲧⲛⲁⲟⲩⲱϣ]ⲙ ⲟⲩⲃⲉⲛϫⲱ-
[ⲣⲟⲛ ἀντιλέγ. dat; Mor 25 198 *S* ⲁⲡⲧⲓⲗⲉⲅⲉ ⲛⲁϥ ⲛ
ⲟⲩ. ⲟⲩⲃⲏϥ, ShA 1 50 *S* ⲉⲣⲉⲛⲁⲟⲩ. ⲟⲩⲃⲏⲕ ⲛ ⲉⲣⲉⲛⲁ-
ⲟⲩⲱϣⲃ, Va 57 113 *B* ⲡϣⲏⲣⲓ ⲉϥⲟⲩ. ⲟⲩ. ⲫⲓⲱⲧ saying,
Pcod 12 *F* ⲟⲩ. ⲛⲛⲟⲩⲅⲉⲡϫⲉⲙⲱⲛ.

—— ϩⲁ- *SA*, as last: Hos 4 4 *SA*(*B* = Gk c ⲛ-)
ἀντιλέγ.; AZ 21 153 *S* ⲡⲉⲙⲉϥⲟⲩ. ϩⲁⲣⲱϥ (l -ⲣⲟϥ)
ⲉⲡⲧⲏⲣϥ.

—— ϩⲓ- *S*, as last: Lu 2 34 (*B* ϯ ⲉϩⲟⲩⲛ ⲉϩⲣⲉⲛ-)
ἀντιλέγ.; ShRyl 70 241 ⲉⲩⲛⲁϣⲁϫⲉ ⲉⲣⲟϥ ⲛ ⲉⲩⲉⲟⲩ.
ϩⲓⲱⲱϥ.

With following adverb.   ⲉ ⲉⲃⲟⲗ *B*, interpret:
OrChr NS 3 38 ⲙⲡⲉⲛⲓⲅⲣⲁⲫⲏ ⲟⲩⲟϩⲙⲉϥ ⲉⲃ. ϩⲉⲛ-
ⲟⲩⲧⲁϩⲣⲟ;   ⲉ ⲉϩⲣⲁⲓ *S*, bring up again, reconstruct:
J 1 89 hast power to destroy it ⲉⲟⲩⲁϩⲙⲉϥ ⲉϩ., *ib* 3
47 ⲉⲕⲁⲧⲟⲩ ⲉⲟⲩⲁϩⲙⲟⲩ ⲉϩ.

ⲡ ⲥ *B*: Mt 19 28 ⲟⲩ. ⲥⲱⲛⲧ (*F* ⲟⲩ. ϫⲡⲁ, *S* ϫⲡⲟ
ⲛⲕⲉⲥⲟⲡ) παλιγγενεσία, Mus 34 193 ⲟⲩ. ⲙⲓⲥⲓ ἀναγέννησις; ⲙⲉⲧⲟⲩ. ⲥⲁϫⲓ *contradictiousness* Cat 49.

—— nn m *SAA²*(Ma)*B*, answer, objection, interpretation: Pro 17 11 *SA*, He 7 7 *S*(*B* = Gk) ἀντιλογία; 1 Tim 6 20 *S*(*B* ϯ ⲉϩⲟⲩⲛ ⲉϩⲣⲉⲛ-) ἀντίθεσις;
Dan 2 5 *B* σύγκρισις, *ib* 5 26 *B* σύγκριμα; 2 Kg 12
25 *S* gloss; P 131³ 23 *S* ⲡⲉϥⲟⲩ. ⲡⲁϩⲏⲧ of heretics,
Mani H 13 *A²* ⲡϧⲱⲣⲉ ⲁⲣⲉϧ ⲁⲡⲟⲩ., Miss 8 232 *S*
ⲥⲧⲉⲫⲁⲛⲟⲩ...ⲡⲉϥⲟⲩ. ⲡⲉ ⲡⲉⲕⲗⲟⲙ, BMis 384 *S* ⲡⲉⲥⲟⲩ. (var ⲃⲱⲗ), Leyd 150 *S* rubric ⲛϭⲉⲣⲙⲏⲛⲓⲁ ⲙⲡⲛⲟⲩ. (abbrev ⲟⲩⲱ, ♀ liturg response, v JKP 1 26), *ib*
164 ⲛⲟⲩ. ⲉϫⲛⲡⲥⲟⲡ ⲛⲱϣ, BM 326 *S* in margin ⲟⲩ.,
C 86 166 *B* his passion read ϩⲉⲛⲡⲁⲛⲃ. ⲡⲉⲙϩⲁⲛⲯⲁ-

ⲗⲓ, K 261 *B* ⲡⲓⲟⲩ. جَوَاب, TEuch 2 297 *B* ⲟⲩⲃ. ⲡⲣⲟⲙⲡⲓ سنوي لَحن, *ib* 358 *B* ⲟⲩⲃ. ⲛⲉⲡⲓⲥⲧⲟⲗⲏ precedes
Pauline lesson, BM 894 *B* sim, BMEA 10453 *S* wine
account ⲥ]ⲉⲡⲏⲑⲓⲁ ϩⲁⲡⲉⲟⲩ. ⲕᵟ β (obscure).

ⲛⲟⲩ. *SABF* adverbial, *again*: Zech 1 16 *SA*(*B* =
Gk), *ib* 13 3 *S*(*AB* ⲕⲉⲥⲟⲡ) ἔτι, Mor 17 56 *S* ⲛⲡⲧⲙϭⲱ
ⲛⲟⲩ., Z 318 *S* will not draw nigh ⲛⲟⲩ. = MG 25 234
B ϫⲉ μηκέτι; Ro 6 9 *S*, cit Bor 226 165 (*B* & other *S*
om) οὐκέτι; Lev 14 43 *B* πάλιν; PS 267 *S* ⲕⲉⲧⲏ-
ⲛⲟⲩ ⲛⲟⲩ., ShA 1 451 *S* ⲙⲡϥⲕⲧⲟϥ ⲛⲟⲩ. ⲉϣϫⲉ, *ib*
74 ⲡⲉϫⲏ (f) ⲛⲟⲩ. ϫⲉ-, PCol 2 *F* ⲙⲉⲉⲓⲧⲏⲥ (ⲉ)ϩⲟⲩⲛ
(ⲉ)ⲡⲏⲓ (ⲛ)ⲟⲩ.

ⲁⲧⲃⲱ. *B*, without response: TEuch 2 300 ϫⲱ ⲙⲡⲓ-
ⲧⲣⲓⲥⲁⲅⲓⲟⲥ ⲛⲁ. دوم *continuously*, without singing (v
Ryl p 197 n).

ⲣⲉϥⲟⲩ. *S*, answerer, contradictor: Aeg 246 ἀντίλο-
γος;   ⲙⲛⲧⲣ., opposition, disobedience: Sh(prob)Ep
66 ⲧⲙ. ⲟⲩⲃⲉⲡⲉⲅⲉⲣⲏⲓ, BMis 154 ⲙ. ϩⲁⲡⲣⲟ ⲛⲛⲓⲛⲟϭ
ⲉⲣⲟϥ, ClPr 53 17 opp ⲥⲧⲙⲏⲧ.

ϭⲓⲛ-, ϫⲓⲛⲟⲩ. *SB*, opposition: ROC 17 409 *B* ϯϫ.
ⲙⲡⲉϥⲓⲱⲧ ἀντιτεῖναι dat; ShBor 247 102 ⲧⲗⲉϫⲓⲥ
ⲛⲧϭ. ⲟⲩⲧⲉⲓϭⲉⲧⲉ (sc Eccl 2 14 b).

ⲟⲩⲁϩⲙⲉϥ *S*, answerer, interpreter: ROC 23 102
Moses ⲟ ⲡⲁⲩ ⲛⲟⲩ. ⲛⲓⲁϩⲣⲁⲡⲛⲉ.

ⲟⲩⲁϩⲙⲉ *S*, -ⲙⲓ, ⲃⲁϩⲙⲓ *B* nn f, *what is added*,
storey of house: Ge 6 16 *S*(sic l as Z 618, P 44 102,
B ϫⲉ) δι-, τριώροφος; DeV 2 234 *B* ϯⲃ. of ark θυρίς
(cf Ge 8 6 *B* ϣⲟⲩϣⲧ, *S* ⲣⲟ); Ac 20 9 *B*(*S* ϩⲉ) -στέγος;
CaiThe 438 *B*(ⲟⲩ)ⲟⲩ. ⲛⲧⲉ ⲥⲓⲱⲛ اعلى (Ac 1 13);
ShC 42 192 *S* ⲧⲙⲉϩϣⲟⲙⲧⲉ ⲡⲉⲛ ⲛ ⲡⲟⲩⲁϩⲙ(ⲉ) ⲙ-
ⲡⲏⲓ, TT 188 *S* house has ⲙⲛⲧⲉ ⲛⲟⲩ., C 86 294 *B*
ϯⲙⲁϩⲣϯ ⲛⲟⲩ. of house; K 75 *B* ⲛⲓⲃ. of eye طبقات
tunic.

ⲟⲩⲟϩⲛ (sic l) *B* v ⲃⲱϩⲛ vb.

ⲟⲩⲱϩⲣ, ⲟⲩⲁϩⲣⲉ v ⲟⲩⲱϩⲣ s f.

ⲟⲩϩⲟⲣ¹ *SB*, -ϩⲁⲣ *Sᵃ*/*A*, f -ϩⲟ(ⲟ)ⲣⲉ² *SA²* -ϩⲱⲣⲉ³
S, -ϩⲁⲁⲣⲓ *S*/, pl -ϩⲟⲟⲣ⁴ *S*(& as sg), -ϩⲱⲣ⁵ *B*(do),
-ϩⲱⲱⲣ *F* nn, dog: 1 Kg 17 43 *S*¹(varⁱ)*B*⁵, Pro 26 11
*S*¹(varⁱ)*A* κύων; PS 256 *S* archon with ϩⲟ ⲛⲟⲩ.¹, BM
286 *S* ⲡⲣⲱⲙⲉ ⲡⲣⲟ ⲛⲟⲩ.¹ (cynocephalus), TstAb 236
B sim, JTS 4 392 *S* ⲟⲩⲟⲩ.⁴ ⲉⲁϥⲕⲡⲟⲟⲥ like heretic, C
43 220 *B* ⲟⲩ.¹ ⲉⲧⲗⲟⲃⲓ, *ib* 89 3 *B* ϩⲁⲛⲃⲁⲗ ⲛⲟⲩ.¹ = Miss
4 315 *S* ⲃ. ⲛⲁⲧϣⲓⲡⲉ, Ep 573 *Sᵃ* sim, AZ 33 132 *Sⁱ*
charm to silence (watch)-dog, CO 469 *Sⁱ*, Z 628 *S*/
ϩⲁⲓⲣⲉ ⲛⲟⲩⲟⲩ., PMéd 293 *S* ⲣⲱϩ (= λⲱⲕⲥ) ⲛⲟⲩ.¹, *ib*
212 *S* ⲟⲩϩⲟⲗ (ⲙ)ⲙⲟⲟⲩ *water-dog* (otter Chassinat),
Bal*S* list of utensils]ϭⲁϭ ⲟⲩ.¹ (cf ?PLond 4 217 place
Πκακουϩⲁⲗ, but v above ⲕⲱⲕ p c), ⲗⲁⲥ ⲛⲟⲩ. v ⲗⲁⲥ
d;   pl: Job 30 1 *SB*, Phil 3 2 *SB* κ., Mt 15 26 *SB*
κυνάριον; ShR 2 3 47 *S* ⲡⲉϥϩ. ⲡⲧⲉϩⲛⲏⲛ (cf ἐκ τῆς
ξένης), C 43 221 *B* ⲡⲓⲟⲩ. ⲛⲧⲉ ϯⲡⲟⲗⲓⲥ, TSBA 9 371

B ⲛⲓⲟⲩ.⁵ (*sic*) ⲡⲉⲙⲛⲓⲉϣⲁⲩ (*cf* 3 Kg 20 19), CMSS 78 *F* in account ⲉⲣⲟⲩⲛ ⲓⲱⲧ (ⲛ)ⲡⲉⲩ.;   f: KroppB *S* may she long for me ⲛⲑⲉ ⲡⲟ(ⲩ)ⲟⲩ.² ϩⲁ(ⲟⲩ)ⲟⲩ.¹ OratCyp 116 *Sʲ* sim, PMich 601 *Sᵃ* ⲟⲩⲱⲣⲱⲣⲉ ⲉⲥⲙⲟⲥⲉ, *ib* ⲟⲩⲟⲩ.³ ⲁⲩⲧⲁⲥ ⲉⲡⲉⲥⲕⲗⲏⲗ, BKU 1 3 *S* ⲟⲩⲟⲩ.² ⲕⲁⲙⲉ...ⲡⲉⲥϣⲏⲣⲉ, Mani H 80 *A²* ⲡⲟⲩϩⲟⲟⲣⲉ, *ib* 92 -ⲟⲣⲉ; as adj: BAp 6 *S* ⲓⲟⲩϫⲁⲓ ⲡⲟⲩϩⲟⲟⲣ.

ⲁϥ ⲡⲟⲩ., *dogfly* *v* ⲁϥ.

In names: ⲡⲟⲩϩⲟⲣ (? ST 282), -ϩⲁⲣ (Hall 131), ⲡⲁⲡⲉⲩϩⲟⲣ (BMOr 6201 A), Πουῶρις, -ᾶρις, Τενῶρις &c, Ψεντουοόρε, Ψεντοουώριος (Preisigke). In place-names: Πατουρόορε (PLond 4 211), -ϩⲟⲟⲗ (*ib* 205), Πιⲁϩ πουϩⲟⲗ (*ib* 225), ⲡⲁⲧⲟⲩⲱⲣ(ⲉ TurO 5), ⲡⲧⲉⲡⲟⲩϩⲁⲣ (Lant 16, *cf* ? طهطب), ⲡⲉⲡⲛϭⲙ ⲙⲡϣⲉⲧⲟⲩϩⲟⲟⲣⲉ (PJkôw; for 1st word *v* Ep 1 118).

ⲟⲩⲁϩⲣⲉ *S* nn f: BKU 1 94 among agricult (?) implements, *l* ? ⲧⲟⲩⲁϩⲣⲉ manger for *holding fodder*, *cf* ⲟⲩⲱϩ **A** p c.

ⲟⲩⲟϩⲥ   *v* ⲱϩⲥ.

ⲟⲩⲉϩⲥⲟⲓ   *v* ⲥⲟⲓ *beam*.

ⲟⲩⲉϩⲥⲁϩⲛⲉ   *v* ⲥⲁϩⲛⲉ.

ⲟⲩⲁϩⲧ⳯   *v* ⲟⲩⲱⲧϩ **II**.

ⲟⲩⲁϩ(ⲉ)ⲉⲧ⳯ *AA²*   *v* ⲟⲩⲁⲁ⳯.

ⲟⲩⲁϩϥ   *v* ⲟⲩⲱϩ vb *s f* & ⲟⲩⲁϩⲃⲉϥ.

ⲟⲩⲟϫ⳯ *B*   *v* ⲱϭⲧ.

ⲟⲩⲁϫⲉ   *v* ⲁϫⲉ.

ⲟⲩⲉⲓϫⲉ   *v* ⲟⲩⲱⲱϫⲉ *s f*.

ⲟⲩⲟϫⲓ *B* vb(?), *bend, twist*: BMOr 8771 79 ⲣⲉϥⲟⲩ. معوج, جرح. *Cf* ϩⲓϫⲓ.

ⲟⲩⲟϫⲓ *B* nn   *v* ⲟⲩⲟⲟϫⲉ.

ⲟⲩⲱ(ⲱ)ϫⲉ *S*, -ⲱϫ, ϩⲱϫ *B*, ⲟⲩⲉⲉϫⲉ- *S*, ⲟⲩⲉϫ- *SB*, ⲟⲩⲱϫⲉ- *Sᵃ*, ⲟⲩⲟ(ⲟ)ϫ⳯ *S*, ⲟⲩⲁϫ⳯ *SⁱSʲ*, ⲟⲩⲟϫ⳯ *B* vb **a**, *cut tr*: Va 58 173 *B* surgeon's knife ⲉϥⲟⲩ. ⲙⲡⲓⲉⲣϭⲟⲧ, *ib* 63 103 *B* ϯⲛⲁϩⲉϥⲑⲏⲛⲟⲩ ⲁⲛ ⲟⲩϫⲉ ⲛϯⲛⲁⲟⲩⲉϫⲑⲏⲛⲟⲩ ⲁⲛ τέμνειν; Mich 550 31 *S* ⲉϥϣⲱⲡⲉ ⲉϥⲣ ⲭⲣⲓⲁ ⲛⲟⲩⲟⲟϫⲉϥ = Va 63 100 *B*, BHom 42 *S* ⲡⲥⲁⲉⲓⲛ ⲉⲩⲟⲩ. ⲛⲡⲣⲱⲙⲉ χειρουργεῖν; K 161 *B* ḅ.گس, ﻃﺐ, ViK 98 28 *S* physicians ϣⲁⲩⲟⲩⲉⲉϫⲉ ⲟⲩⲁ to heal him, Miss 8 263 *Sʲ* ϯⲛⲁⲟⲩⲁϫⲉ (f) ϩⲙⲡⲓⲧⲁⲕ; ϭⲓⲛⲟⲩ. *S*, *cutting*: ViK 9828 enduring ⲡⲉϣⲥ ⲡⲧⲟⲕ ⲛ ⲧϭ. ⲙⲡⲉϥⲥⲁϣ.   **b**, *cut off, out* a woven garment *SB* (rare) intr: Is 38 12(*B* tr)ἐκτέμ.; tr: BM 217 22 desist ϣⲁⲛϯⲟⲩ. ⲙⲡⲉⲓⲣⲃⲟⲟⲥ ⲉϯⲥⲱϭⲉ ⲉⲣⲟϥ, Ryl 238 n they learn ⲡⲥⲱϭⲉ ⲡⲥⲉⲟⲩ. ⲡⲧⲉⲓϣⲧⲏⲛ, DeV 2 102 *B* ϯⲥⲁⲣⳅ...ⲁϥⲟⲩⲟϫⲥ ⲟⲩⲟϩ ⲁϥⲥⲱϩⲓ ⲙⲙⲟⲥ, Mor 37 199 found one making ⲥⲭⲟⲗⲁⲕⲓⲛ (so BIF 13 101 = MG 25 281, PG 65 324 σκολάκιν) ⲉⲁϥⲣⲱⲛ ⲉϩⲟⲩⲛ ⲉⲟⲩⲟⲟϫϥ & bade ϭⲉⲡⲏ ⲉϫⲟⲕϥ ⲉⲃⲟⲗ,

CO 403 ⲟⲩ. ⲟⲩϩⲟⲓⲧⲉ ⲛⲁⲓ, BP 4935 sim, Hall 119 ⲛϩⲃⲟⲥ...ⲉϥⲛ(ⲁ)ⲟⲩⲁϫⲟⲩ, BMOr6201B 77 ⲥⲧⲣⲱⲙⲁ(ⲛ)ⲛ...ⲥⲉⲉⲣ ϩⲱⲃ ⲉⲣⲟⲥ ⲛⲥⲉⲟⲩⲟⲟϫⲉⲥ, RevÉgAnc 1 15 ⲟⲩ. ⲡⲉⲧⲁϩ, *ib* ⲡⲉⲧⲛⲁⲟⲩⲟϫⲉϥ ⲧⲏⲣϥ, ShP 130⁴ 157 ⲟⲩϣⲉ ⲛⲛⲁⲧ ⲡⲟⲩⲉϫ ⲧⲗⲏ, Ryl 238 35 ϣⲙⲟⲩ ⲡⲟⲩⲱ[ϫ]ⲉ (uncertain).

ⲟⲩⲉⲓϫⲉ, ⲃⲛϫⲉ *S* nn, *slash, gash*(?): BMar 23 bade ϯ ⲛϩⲉⲡⲟⲩ. ⲉⲭⲡⲧⲉϥⲁⲡⲉ ⲁⲩⲱ ⲛⲥⲉϯ ⲕⲁⲥⲓⲥ (κάσσις) ⲛⲁϥ, BMOr 6201 A 127 ⲡⲉⲗⲁⲁⲩ ⲉⲃ̄. ⲉⲧⲁⲕϫⲱⲱⲥ ϩⲁⲣⲟⲟ[ⲩ (same ?).

ⲟⲩϫⲁⲓ *SBF*, -ϫⲣⲁⲓ *S*(BP 9105 *pass*), -ϫⲏⲓ -ϫⲓⲉⲓ *Sᵃ*, -ϫⲉⲓ *AF*, -ϫⲉⲉⲓ *AA²F*, -ϫⲉⲓⲧⲉ *A*, ⲟⲅⲟϫ⳯ *SBF* (once), -ⲁϫ⳯ *AA²*(Ma)*F* vb intr, *be whole, safe, sound*: Job 1 15 *S*(*B* ⲛⲟⲣⲙ), Pro 10 25 *SAB*, Is 30 15 *SF* (*B* do), Jo 10 9 *SAA²*(*B* do), Cl 2 4 *A* (var -ϫⲉⲓⲧⲉ) σώζεσθαι, Jer 27 29 *B* ἀνασ., Mt 14 36 *SF*(*B* do) διασ.; Jos 5 8 *S* ὑγιάζειν, Jo 5 6 *SA²B* ὑγιής γίνεσθαι, Is 38 21 *B*(*S* ⲙⲧⲟⲛ) ὑγ. εἶναι, *ib* 53 5 *B*(*S* ⲧⲁⲗϭⲟ), Mt 8 13 *B*(*S* ⲗⲟ) ἰᾶσθαι, *ib* 17 18 *B*(*S* do) θεραπεύειν; Is 51 10 *B*(*S* ⲛⲟⲩϩⲙ) ῥύεσθαι; BG 139 *S* ⲁϥⲡⲓⲥⲧⲉⲩⲉ ⲁϥⲟⲩ., BMis 163 *S* ⲙⲁⲣⲛⲃⲱⲕ...ⲧⲁⲣⲉⲡⲟⲩ., TU 43 18 *A* ⲡⲉⲧⲧⲁϩⲙⲉ ⲁⲩⲡⲁⲟⲩ., *ib* 11 *A* ϭⲟⲩϫⲉⲓⲧⲉ, C 41 53 *B* ⲉⲧⲁϥⲟⲩ. ⲉϥϣⲱⲡⲓ, PBu 10 *S* ⲁⲡⲏⲓ ⲟⲩ. & not yet burnt, AP 24 *A²* begging ϫⲉⲕⲁⲁⲥⲉ ⲉϥⲛⲁⲟⲩϫⲉⲉⲓ;   qual : Ex 4 18 *SA*(*B* nn), Pro 13 13 *SA*(*B* ⲟⲩϫⲁⲓ) ὑγιαίνειν, Lev 13 15 *S*(with gloss ⲏ ⲉⲧⲟⲛϩ)*B*, Ac 4 10 *SB*, BHom 32 *S* ⲡⲓⲥⲧⲓⲥ ⲉⲥⲟⲩ. ὑγιής; Z 274 *S* sim ὀρθός; Ge 43 22 *S*(*B* = Gk), Mt 16 22 *S*(*B* do) ἵλεως dat; Ex 21 28 *S*(*B* ⲧⲟⲩⲃⲏⲟⲩⲧ) ἀθῷος; Deu 27 6 *SB*, 1 Thes 5 23 *SB* ὁλόκληρος; 1 Kg 17 40 *S*(var ⲟⲩⲱϭ)τέλειος; Job 21 23 *B* εὐπαθεῖν; Va 66 307 *B* εὔρωστος opp ⲉⲧϣⲱⲛⲓ; BHom 133 *S* ⲟⲩ. ϩⲙⲡⲉϥⲥⲱⲙⲁ ἀσινής; PS 279 *S* ⲛⲥⲓⲛⲕⲥⲓⲥ (*cf* σίνεσθαι, σίνος) opp ⲛⲥⲱⲙⲁ ⲉⲧⲟⲩ., ShMIF 23 154 *S* ⲉⲧⲣⲉⲡⲉⲛⲣⲓⲥⲉ ϣⲱⲡⲉ ⲛⲁⲛ ⲉϥⲟⲩ., *ib* 167 *S* soul ⲥⲙⲟⲛⲧ ⲛ ⲉⲥⲟⲩ., Mor 34 55 *S* ⲟⲩⲥⲱⲙⲁ ⲉϥⲟⲩ. passed through closed doors (Jo 20 26), SHel 39 *S* found seal ⲉⲥⲟⲩ. (*cf* Leont Neap Gelzer 99 βούλλαν σῷαν), Kr 236 *F* ⲡⲉⲧⲉⲣϩⲁⲙ ⲉⲧⲟⲅⲟϫ, J 67 22 *S* παρθενεια ⲟⲩ. ⲁⲛ, DeV 2 42 *B* Jonah cast ashore ⲉϥⲟⲩ. ⲙⲡⲉϥⲣⲏϯ, COAd 33 *S* ⲉⲧⲉⲧⲛⲟⲩ. body soul & spirit, CMSS 20 *F* sim;   imperat as greeting, ending letter: ⲟⲩ. Ac 15 29 *SB* ἔρρωσθε; Pcod 13 *S*, C 43 53 *B*, Ep 110, 221, 267 *S*;   ⲟⲩ. ϩⲙⲡϫ̄ⲥ̄ *S* ShC 42 14, Miss 4 698, Ep 107, 275, *Sᵃ* BM 1211 -ϫⲏⲓ, CO 276 -ϫⲓⲉⲓ, *A²* AP 41, *F* BM 601 -ϫⲉⲉⲓ, *ib* 582 (2) -ϫⲉⲓ ϩⲉⲡⲟ̄ϭ̄; also as nn *ib* 617 ⲡⲟⲩϫⲉⲓ ⲡϫⲁⲓⲥ, *ib* 1238 ⲡⲟⲩ. ⲡⲟ̄ϭ̄, PMich 524 ⲡⲟⲩ. ϩⲙⲡⲟ̄ϭ̄;   ⲟⲩ. ϫⲉⲡⲧⲭⲟⲙ ⲙⲡⲟ̄ϭ̄ AM 3 *B*; ⲟⲩ. ϩⲛⲧⲉⲧⲣⲓⲁⲥ ⲉⲧⲟⲩⲁⲁⲃ Ep 198 *S*, ⲟⲩ. ϩⲉⲑⲁⲅⲓⲁ ⲧⲣⲓⲁⲥ MR 5 36 *F*.

With following preposition. ⲉ ⲉ- *SAA²BF*, *be saved from*: Ez 6 8 *S* ἀνασώ. ἐκ, Ep Jer 11 *F* διασ. ἀπό; 2 Tim 4 17 *S* (all *B* ⲛ.) ῥύ. ἐκ; Pro 24 23 *SA*

ἐκτὸς εἶναι gen; BM 355 124 S torments ⲁⲥⲟⲩ. ⲉ-
ⲣⲟⲟⲩ, C 43 103 B ⲥⲛⲁⲟⲩ. ⲉϥⲙⲟⲩ;   qual: BHom
48 S ⲟⲩ. ⲉϥⲟⲥⲉ ἀκέραιος; PS 263 S ⲟⲩ. ⲉⲛⲟⲃⲉ,
Mani 1 A² ⲟⲩ. ⲁⲛⲁⲃⲉ, ShZ 599 S ⲛⲃⲁⲗ ⲟⲩ. ⲉⲧⲁⲕⲟ,
BAp 118 S ⲛⲉⲥⲟⲩ. ⲁⲛ ⲉⲡⲉⲕⲣⲓⲙⲁ, C 43 117 B would
ye were ⲟⲩ. ⲉⲙⲁⲧⲓⲁ; come safe to S: Ge 19 22 (B
ⲛ.) σώ. ἐκεῖ; ⲉⲣⲣⲁⲓ ⲉ- S: Jos 10 20 διασ. εἰς; Miss
8 227 ⲉⲧⲣⲉⲥⲟⲩ. ⲉⲣ. ⲉⲥⲛ̄ⲧⲉⲣ;   c ⲛ- dat SA: Joel 2
3 A-ϫⲉⲓⲧⲉ (SB om) ἀνασώ. dat; Ryl 271 S I pray
ⲉⲧⲣⲉ[ⲕ]ⲟⲩ. ⲛⲁⲓ;   c ⲛⲧⲛ- S, from: Nu 10 9 (B ⲛ.)
διασ. ἀπό;   c ⲉⲃⲟⲗ ⲣⲁ- B, from: Mk 5 29 v below,
C 86 333 ⲟⲩ. ⲉⲃ. ⲣⲁⲡⲓⲕⲱⲕ ⲛⲥⲉⲣⲧ;   c ⲣⲓ- S, from
off: SHel 63 use magic ϣⲁⲛⲧⲉⲕⲟⲩ. ⲣⲓⲛⲉⲥⲧⲟⲥ;   c
ⲣⲛ-, ϫⲉⲛ- S.AB, by: Sa 9 18 S σώ. dat; Ryl 291 S
ⲉⲛⲁⲟⲩ. ⲣⲛⲡⲉⲧⲛ̄ϣⲗⲏⲗ; from: Ez 33 21 B (S ⲉⲃⲟⲗ
ⲣⲛ-) ἀνασ. ἀπό; Pro 10 5 SA (B ⲉⲃ. ϫⲉⲛ-) διασ. ἀπό;
Bor 222* 3 A ⲁⲩⲟⲩ. ⲛⲁϣ ⲛⲣⲉ ⲣⲛⲡⲕⲱⲧ; ⲉⲃⲟⲗ ⲣⲛ-,
from S mostly: Ps 17 3 (B ⲛ.) σ. ἐκ, Ac 2 40 (B do)
σ. ἀπό; Nu 5 19 (B ⲧⲟⲩⲃⲟ) ἀθ. εἶναι ἀπό; Mk 5 29
(var ⲗⲟ, B ⲉⲃ. ⲣⲁ-) ἰα. ἀπό; Ps 68 14 (B ⲧⲟⲩϫⲟ) ῥύ.
ἐκ; R 1 2 23 ⲁⲛⲟⲩ. ⲉⲃ. ⲣⲙⲡⲙⲟⲟⲩ, AM 234 B ⲁⲥⲟⲩ.
ⲉⲃ. ϫⲉⲛⲡⲓϣⲱⲛⲓ;   c ⲣⲓⲧⲛ- SB, by: Job 21 20 S
διασ. ἀπό; Br 46 S ⲉⲧⲉⲧⲛⲁⲟⲩ. ⲣ.ⲧⲙ̄ⲧⲣⲓⲥⲉ, BSM
83 B ⲛⲧⲉⲛⲟⲩ. ⲣ.ⲧϩⲟⲙ ⲛⲧⲉ ⲡⲭ̅ⲥ̅; ⲉⲃⲟⲗ ⲣ.: Jo 3 17
S.A² (BF ⲛ.), 1 Cor 15 2 SF (B do) σώ. διά; Pcod 4 S
souls ⲛⲁⲟⲩ. ⲉⲃ. ⲣⲓⲧⲟⲟⲧϥ, AM 172 B ϣⲁⲩⲟⲩ. ⲉⲃ. ⲣ.
ⲡⲉⲡⲛ̅ⲁ̅.

With following adverb: ShC 73 144 S ⲟⲩϣⲏⲙ
ⲛⲣⲙⲟⲩ ⲉϥⲟⲩ.† ⲉⲃⲟⲗ (var om) ⲉⲙⲛ ⲕⲉⲗⲁⲁⲩ ⲧⲏⲥ ⲉ-
ⲣⲟϥ.

—— nn m SAA²BF, health, safety, weal: Ge 28
21 SB, Job 13 16 S (B ⲛ.), Ro 11 11 SB, AP 6 A²
σωτηρία, Lev 3 3 B (S = Gk), Ps 84 7 SB, Is 33 20
SBF σωτήριον; Ps 37 4 B (S ⲧⲁⲗϭⲟ), Ac 4 22 B (S
do) ἴασις, Jer 37 17 B ἴαμα; Is 9 6 SB ὑγίεια; Si
30 15 S εὐεξία; PS 32 S ⲛⲧⲁⲕⲣ ⲡⲁⲓ ⲉⲧⲃⲉⲡⲟⲩ. ⲙⲡⲕⲟⲥⲙⲟⲥ, ShRE 11 17 S He endured ⲉⲧⲃⲉⲡⲉⲛⲟⲩ.,
Lant 20 F book dedicated ⲣⲁⲡⲟⲩ. ⲡⲧⲉϥⲯⲩⲭⲏ, De
V 2 119 B ⲧⲉϥⲁⲡⲟⲗⲏⲙⲓⲁ ⲉⲑⲃⲉ ⲡⲟⲩ., ShA 2 50 S
ϣⲓⲛⲉ ⲛⲥⲁⲡⲟⲩ. ⲛⲛⲉⲡⲉⲣⲏⲩ, Ep 244 S ⲧⲓⲛⲟⲟⲩ ⲡⲉⲕⲟⲩ. ⲛⲁⲓ, Ryl 395 S ⲧⲓⲡⲣⲟⲥⲕⲩⲛⲓ ⲉⲡⲟⲩ. ⲛⲡⲁⲙⲉⲣⲓⲧ
ⲛ̄ⲭ̅ⲥ̅, BM 592 F sim.;   in oath: BMis 25 S ϣⲉ
ⲡⲉⲕⲟⲩ. ⲱ ⲡⲣⲣⲟ, C 43 141 B ϣⲉ ⲡⲟⲩ. ⲛⲡⲉⲛⲇⲓⲥⲉⲩ
= Mor 48 84 S ϣⲉ ⲧⲧⲩⲭⲏ; Mor 41 100 S ⲙⲡⲉⲧⲛ-
ⲟⲩ. ⲙⲡⲉⲣⲕⲁⲁⲧ, ib 28 166 S ⲙⲡⲉⲕⲟⲩ. abandon not,
BMar 16 S ⲡⲟⲩⲟⲩ. ⲱ ⲧⲁⲙⲁⲁⲩ ⲙⲡⲣ-, C 86 85 B
ⲡⲉⲧⲉⲡⲟⲩ. ⲉⲣⲱⲧⲉⲛ have patience, CMSS 23 F ⲡⲁⲟⲩ.
ⲉⲣⲁⲕ if thou need an answer I will give it; BMis 394
S ⲣⲓⲟⲩⲙⲉ ⲛⲧⲉ ⲡⲛ̄ⲧ̅ⲉ̅ ⲙⲡⲡⲟⲩ. ⲙⲡⲁⲝ̅ⲥ̅ = BSM 46 B
ϣⲉ ⲡⲱⲛⲃ ⲙⲡⲁⲝ̅ⲥ̅, J 1 41 S we swear by Trinity &
ⲡⲟⲩ. ⲡⲡⲉⲛϫⲓⲥⲟⲟⲩⲉ ⲡⲉⲣⲟⲟⲩ, PLond 4 436 S sim,
Kr 11 F sim ⲡⲟⲩϫⲉⲉⲓ (ⲛ)ⲡⲉⲣⲱⲟⲩ, BM 1079 S
I swear by...ⲡⲉⲩ. ⲡⲁⲛⲃⲣⲟⲥ ('Amr b. al-'Asi).

As adj, healthgiving: Eph 1 14 S ⲥⲱⲧⲉ ⲡⲟⲩ. (B
ⲧⲁⲛϩⲟ) περιποίησις; Cai Euch 394 B ⲡⲉϥⲙⲕⲁⲩⲣ
ⲡⲟⲩ. σωτηριώδης; DeV 2 100 B sim, BHom 12 S
ⲡⲁⲣⲣⲉ ⲡⲟⲩ.

ⲁⲧⲟⲩ. S, unsound, incurable: P 44 99 ἄσωτος;
ⲙⲛⲧ-, ⲙⲉⲧⲁ. unsoundness: Lam 4 3 B (S ⲁⲧⲛⲁ, F ⲗⲁ
neg) ἀνίατος; Eph 5 18 S (cit Mor 54 141, var ⲙⲛⲧϣⲛⲁ) B ἀσωτία; Va 58 157 B greed breedeth ⲙⲉⲧⲁ.
ⲛⲓⲃⲉⲛ.

In name ϩⲉⲣⲟⲅⲟⲭ, ⲏⲣ. (BM 1028, 1080), Ἁρ-
(ο)υνῶθης, -της, Ψεναρουωτίς (Preisigke).

V ⲧⲟⲩϫⲟ.

ⲟⲩⲱϫⲡ SBF   v ⲟⲩⲱϣⲡ.

ⲟⲩⲉϫⲣⲟ B   v ⲟⲩⲟⲟϭⲉ (ⲟⲩⲉϫⲣⲟ).

ⲟⲩⲟϫⲟⲩⲉϫ B   v ⲟⲩⲟϫⲟⲩⲉϫ.

ⲟⲩⲱϫϥ A   v ⲟⲩⲱϣⲡ.

ⲟⲩⲱϭ S nn, as pl, in Ez where = B ⲟⲩⲟϫⲓ (v
below): 40 16, 49 τὸ αἰλάμ, 26 τὰ αἰλεύ, 37 τὰ αἰλαμ-
μών; 14 θεείμ; 41 16 ostia; 42 5 porticus;   Mor
51 35 v ⲛϣⲓⲧ (l ? ϣⲧⲓⲧ) obscure.   Hence prob
ⲟⲩⲟⲟϭⲉ.

ⲟⲩⲱϭ vb   v ⲟⲩϫⲁⲓ qual (1 Kg 17 40), also
ⲟⲩⲱⲛⲛ.

ⲟⲩⲁϭⲉ, -ⲱϭⲉ S.ʲ, ⲃⲁϫⲓ B nn, blow, same as ⲟⲩⲁϫⲉ (for which wrongly ⲁϫⲉ qv): Mor 46 6 ϣⲥ ⲡⲟⲩⲁ.,
ib 2 sim ⲟⲩⲱ. (cf ib 8 ϣⲥ ⲛⲧⲱⲕ for same), Va 58 73
B ϣⲉ ⲛⲃ.

ⲟⲩⲟ(ⲟ)ϭⲉ, -ⲟⲓϭⲉ S, ⲟⲩⲁϭⲉ A, ⲟⲩⲟϫⲓ B, ⲟⲩⲁ. F
nn f (dual?), jaw, cheek (cf ⲟⲩⲱϭ nn), sg: 3 Kg 22
24 S, Job 21 5 B (S diff), Lam 1 2 F (B pl), Hos 11 4
B (A pl), Mic 5 1 AS (ViK 9004, B pl), Mt 5 39 SB
σιαγών; Mor 41 151 S ⲧⲉϥⲟⲩ. ⲥⲛⲧⲉ like roses;   pl:
Ps 31 9 SB, Cant 1 10 F, Cai Euch 487 B σ., Deu 18
3 B (S ⲙⲁⲣⲟⲩⲟϭⲉ) σιαγόνιον; BHom 5 S παρεία,
Mich 4949 S glossary sim; ShC 42 104 S tears ⲥⲱⲕ
ⲉϫⲛⲛⲉⲕⲟⲩ., MG 25 152 B sheep's ⲟⲩ. ⲉⲩⲙⲉϩ ⲉⲃⲟⲗ
ϫⲉⲛⲡⲟⲗⲟⲭ ⲙⲡⲓⲥⲁⲑⲙⲓ, BMis 77 S ⲥⲧⲏⲙ ⲉⲡⲉⲥⲃⲁⲗ,
ⲕⲣⲟⲕⲟⲥ ⲉⲡⲉⲥⲟⲩⲟϫⲉ (var Mor 33 11 ⲕⲣⲟⲕⲟⲥ ⲉⲡⲉⲥ-
ⲙⲉϫⲉⲛⲣ), Bor 289 4 S ϣⲥⲉ ⲛⲁⲁⲥ ⲉⲧⲣⲛⲛⲉⲩⲟⲩ.

ⲟⲩⲉϫⲣⲟ SA, ⲟⲩⲉϫ. B, pl -ⲣⲱⲟⲩ B nn f, door's
jawbone, door-post: Ex 12 7 SB, Deu 15 17 B (var &
S ⲣⲟ), Pro 8 34 SA (B ⲃⲉⲛⲡⲏ), Is 57 8 S (B = Gk)
σταθμός; Deu 6 9 B pl (S ⲧⲟⲩⲁ), Ez 43 8 B (HCons
299) pl φλιά ⲗⲗ̈ⲗ̇; 2 Chr 3 7 B pl (var -ⲣⲱⲟⲩⲓ) θύρωμα; BSG 196 S ⲧⲟⲩⲉϫⲣⲱ of house = ib 22 B
ⲥⲧⲩⲗⲗⲟⲥ ⲛϣⲉ, C 86 134 B wrote names on ⲛⲓⲟⲩ.
(pl) of city; ⲃⲁⲭⲣⲱⲟⲩ (Bodl 325 156), ⲃⲉⲣⲭⲱⲟⲩ
Ryl 453 337 B ⲁⲃⲁⲝⲗ same?

ⲙⲁⲣⲟⲩⲟϭⲉ (Deu), ⲙ(ⲉ)ⲣⲟⲩⲟ(ⲟ)ϭⲉ S nn f, jaw-
bone: Jud 15 16 σιαγών, Deu 18 3 ut sup; TT 81 ⲛ-

ⲉϥⲙ. ⲙⲡⲛⲉϥⲟⲃϩⲣⲉ, BMis 493 ⲟⲩⲙⲉⲣⲟⲅⲟⲓϭⲉ. Cf ⲕⲁⲥ (ⲕⲁⲥⲣⲟ).

ⲟⲅⲟⲡϫ B (prob for ⲟⲩⲟϫϧ)in ⲕⲉⲗⲟⲅ. v ⲕⲗⲗⲉ sf. Cf ⲟⲩⲟϭⲟⲩⲉϭ.

ⲟⲩⲱϭⲡ SAA², -ϫⲡ SBF, -ϣⲡ S(R 1 5 51), ⲟⲩⲉϣⲡ- S, ⲟⲩⲉϫⲡ- B, ⲟⲩⲁ. F, ⲟⲩⲟϭⲡⲍ S, ⲟⲩⲁ. A, ⲟⲩⲟϫⲡⲍ SB, ⲟⲩⲟϭⲡ† S, ⲟⲩⲁ.† A, ⲟⲩⲟϫⲡ† SB vb I intr, break, be broken: Job 38 11 A(Cl, S ⲟⲩⲱϣϥ, B ϩⲟⲩϭⲉⲙ), Ps 50 17† A(Cl, S do†, B ⲧⲉⲡⲡⲏⲟⲩⲧ), Ez 6 6 B(S do)συντρίβεσθαι; Pro 11 11 B(SA ϣⲟⲣϣⲣ), Joel 1 17 B(A do) κατασκάπτειν; Is 1 7 B(SF do) καταστρέφεσθαι; Mor 17 27 S ⲧⲉⲧⲏⲡⲉ ⲁⲥⲟⲩ. κατα-κλᾶσθαι; Lam 2 17 B(S do, F ⲥⲱⲥ tr) καθαιρεῖν; Bel 33† B ἐνθρύπτειν; Ez 29 7 S(Bor 226 177, var & B ⲟⲩⲱϣϥ)θλᾶν; Sa 15 13 S εὔθραυστος; ShA 2 136 S idols ⲁⲩⲟⲩϣϣϥ ⲏ ⲁⲩⲟⲩ., BIF 13 111 S ⲁⲧⲉϥⲟⲩⲉⲣⲏⲧⲉ ⲟⲩ. = MG 25 301 B ⲕⲱϣ, BMar 85 S ⲁⲧⲧⲁⲡⲣⲟ ⲟⲩ. no longer speaking aright, DeV 1 123 B ⲁϥⲟⲩ. ⲛϫⲉ ⲡⲉϥⲥⲟⲩⲕⲟⲩⲧⲱⲛ (σικύτιον), BMEA 10578 F ⲁⲡⲕⲉⲥ ⲡⲧⲉϥϫⲓⲥⲓ ⲟⲩⲱⲡϫ (sic) = Mor 31 254 S -ϫⲡ.

II tr: Is 59 5 S(B ⲫⲱϫⲓ) ῥηγνύναι; Ex 34 1 S(B ϭ.), Lev 6 28 S(B ⲕⲱϣ), Ez 6 4 B(S -ϣϥ) συντρ.; Job 30 4 B(var & S ⲟⲩⲟϭⲟⲩⲉϭ) μασᾶσθαι; Ro 11 3 B(S ϣ.) κατασκά.; Ge 19 25 B(S ⲧⲁⲕⲟ) καταστρ.; Lam 2 2 B(F ⲥⲱⲥ) καθαιρ.; Mt 12 20 S(B ⲕ.), Jo 19 32 S(A² -ϣϥ, B do) καταγνύναι; Mic 3 3 SA(B ϭ.) συνθλ.; Zeph 3 6 B(A ⲧⲉⲟⲩⲟ ⲁϧⲣⲏⲓ) κατασπᾶν; PS 180 S ⲁⲕⲟⲩ. ⲡⲓⲡⲩⲗⲏ, ShA 1 268 S cat was made ⲉⲧⲃⲉⲟⲩ. ⲛⲣⲉⲡⲡⲉⲓⲛ, ShP 130² 25 S ⲟⲩϥⲓⲧ…ⲟⲩ. ⲛ-ϧⲉⲛⲛⲉⲓ ⲙⲡⲣⲉⲛⲕⲟ, Bor 296 ult S ⲟⲩⲱⲡϫ ⲛⲡⲁⲥⲕⲏⲛ = C 89 136 B ⲣⲱⲡϫ, Z 550 S ⲡⲉⲓⲛⲉ ⲛⲧⲁⲩⲟⲩⲟϫⲡⲟⲩ, Miss 4 244 S ⲡⲉϥⲡⲣⲟⲥⲣⲟⲍⲟⲥ ⲛⲧⲁⲩⲟⲩ. ⲙⲙⲟⲟⲩ wasted, dissipated, Mani H 13 A² ⲛϥⲧⲙⲟⲩ. ⲗⲁⲅⲉ ϩⲙⲡⲉϥⲥϥⲣⲁⲅⲓⲥ, J 106 166 S wishing ⲉⲟⲩⲟⲩⲱⲡ ⲗⲁⲁⲩ …ϩⲙⲡⲁϣⲁϫⲉ, AM 71 B ⲟⲩⲟϫⲡⲟⲩ (sc idols), Mor 30 29 F ⲟⲩⲁϫⲡ ⲡⲓϫⲱⲗⲟⲡ.

With following preposition or adverb. ⲉ- BP 11349 S neglected land ⲁⲡⲉϥϥⲟⲣⲟⲥ ⲟⲩ. ⲉⲣⲟⲓ ⲁⲩ-ⲙⲟⲟⲩⲧ ϩⲁⲣⲟⲟⲩ; ⲉϩⲣⲏⲓ ⲉ-: Mic 1 6 B(SA ⲧⲁⲟ ⲉ-) κατασπᾶν εἰς; ⲉϫⲛ-: BMis 258 S ⲙⲡⲛⲓϣⲉ… ⲟⲩⲟϭⲛⲟⲩ ⲉϫⲛⲡⲉⲅⲉⲣⲏⲩ, C 41 41 B sim; ⲉϩⲣⲁⲓ ⲉ.: ShA 2 304 S ⲉⲓⲟⲩ. ⲉϩ. ⲉϫⲱϥ ⲛⲣⲉⲡⲛⲥⲕⲉⲩⲟⲥ; ⲉⲣⲓϫⲛ-: ShC 42 79 S ⲁⲩⲟⲩ. ⲡⲛⲉⲕⲙⲛ ⲙⲟⲟⲩ…ϩ. ⲙⲡⲛⲏ; ⲛ ⲛⲥⲁ- emphasis: Louvain Bibl Univ 5 90 S came forth ⲉϥⲟⲩⲱⲡ ⲛⲥⲁⲛⲕⲁⲙ wherein had lain hid; ⲛ ⲉⲡⲉⲥⲏⲧ: DeV 2 166 B churches ⲁⲩⲟⲩ. ⲉⲡ. (var ⲣⲱⲡϫ)long since; ⲛ ⲉϩⲣⲏⲓ B: Job 11 10 (S ⲧⲁⲟ ⲉϩ.), Bel 22 καταστρ.

—— nn m S(rare)AB, breakage, collapse: Nah 3 19 A(B ϩⲟⲙ.) συντριβή; Ge 19 29 B(S ⲧⲁⲕⲟ), Pro 1

18 B(SA ϣⲟⲣ.) καταστροφή; Job 15 23 B(S ϩⲧⲟⲡ) πτῶμα, Ps 143 14 B(S ϧⲉ) κατάπ.; ShA 2 149 S ⲡϣⲟⲣϣⲣ…ⲁⲩⲱ ⲡⲉⲩⲟⲩ. ⲉϫⲛⲡⲉⲩⲉⲣⲏⲩ, Cat 105 B ϥⲟⲩ. ⲙⲡⲓⲉⲣϥⲉⲓ.

ⲁⲧⲟⲩ. S, unbroken: My 118 ⲡⲗⲁϧ (ⲛ)ⲁ.

ⲣ ⲟⲩ., be destroyed: ShA 1 302 S walls ⲁⲩⲣ ⲡⲓⲟⲩ. ⲛⲟⲩⲱⲧ.

ϭⲓⲛⲟⲩ. S, breaking: LMis 468 ⲧϭ. ⲛⲛⲥⲛϥⲉ ⲛⲣⲁⲧ-ⲟⲩ (cf Jo 19 33).

ⲟⲩⲁϣⲡⲥ S nn, meaning unknown: Bodl(P) b 4 tax receipt ϩⲁⲡⲛⲟⲩϭ ⲡⲉⲩⲁϣⲡⲥ ⲓⲇ/ ⲓⲉ (15th Indiction).

Cf ⲟⲩⲱϣϥ.

ⲟⲩⲉϩⲣⲟ v ⲟⲩⲟⲟϭⲉ.

ⲟⲩⲱϭⲥ S vb, collect contribution, tr: 4 Kg 15 20 ἐκφέρειν; intr: BMar 43 ⲟⲩⲡ ⲟⲩⲉⲕⲧⲁⲥⲓⲥ (v Prei-sigke W.buch) ⲡⲁϣⲱⲡⲉ ⲛⲧⲉ ⲡⲣⲉⲛϥⲙⲉ ⲟⲩ. (l? ⲡⲧⲉⲣⲉⲡ-); as nn m, contribution, collection: 1 Cor 16 1 (B ⲥⲱⲣ), ib 2 (B ⲱⲡ), Aeg 247 give to poor from ⲡⲟⲩ. λογία.

ⲟⲩⲟϭⲟⲩⲉϭ, ⲟⲩϭⲉϭ(BMis)S, ⲟⲩⲟⲭⲟⲩⲉⲭ, -ϩⲉⲭ B, ϩⲁⲕⲃⲉⲕ F, ⲟⲩⲉϭⲟⲩⲱϭⲍ, ⲟⲩⲉϭⲟⲩϭⲍ (BMis) S, ⲟⲩⲉⲭⲟⲩⲱⲭⲍ, ϩⲉⲭⲉⲕⲱⲭⲍ B vb intr (rare), chew, crush (cf ⲟⲩⲟⲟϭⲉ jaw): Dan vis 14 10 B ⲉϥⲟⲩⲱⲙ ⲉϥⲟⲩ., Miss 4 700 S ϣⲁϥⲟⲩⲱⲙ ⲁⲩⲱ ϣⲁϥⲟⲩ., AM 207 B flogged ϣⲁⲧⲉⲡⲉϥⲕⲁⲥ ⲟⲩ. ⲛⲥⲉⲕⲱⲣϫ (cf? ⲟⲩⲱ-ϫⲡ); tr: Job 30 4 SB(var ⲟⲩⲱϫⲡ), Ap 16 10 SB μασᾶσθαι, Job 20 18 SB neg ἀμάσητος; Ps 41 10 B (S ⲗⲱϧ) καταθλᾶν; BM 320 149 S ⲡⲉϥⲟⲩ. ⲙⲡⲉϥ-ⲗⲁⲥ κατεσθίειν; Miss 8 140 S words ⲉϥⲙⲟⲕϩ ⲛⲟⲩⲉϭ-ⲟⲩⲱϭⲟⲩ δύσπεπτος; Tri 259 S ⲉⲩⲟⲩⲱⲙ ⲉⲩⲟⲩⲉϭ-ⲟⲩⲟϭ (sic) ⲙⲡⲉⲙⲡⲓⲡⲣⲁ ﻛﺄ; ShIF 200 S ⲁϥⲟⲩⲉϭ-ⲟⲩⲱϭⲟⲩ ⲛⲛⲉϥⲛⲁⲁϫⲉ, ShA 1 232 S ⲉⲧⲟⲩ. ⲛⲣⲉⲡ-ⲙⲟⲕⲙⲉⲕ… ⲛϫⲁⲓⲙⲟⲛⲓⲟⲛ, Mor 53 40 S lion ⲟⲩⲉϭ-ⲟⲩⲱϭϥ ⲁϥⲟⲙⲕϥ = TstAb 236 B ϩⲉⲭⲉⲕⲱⲭϥ, BMis 557 S ⲡⲥⲉⲟⲩⲉϭⲟⲩϭⲟⲩ ϩⲡ[ⲧⲉϥ]ⲧⲁⲡⲣⲟ, ib do, Va 58 146 B repentant robber seizes John's hand ⲁϥⲟⲩ-ⲉⲭⲟⲩⲱⲭⲥ (cf Eusebius III 23 19 καταφιλῶν), Orat Cyp 118 Sʹ ⲉⲥⲃⲏⲕϩⲏⲕ ⲛⲑⲉ ⲛⲟⲩϭⲁⲙⲉⲅⲗⲓ gobble(?), paral ϧⲙϧⲙ like mare. Same?

With following preposition. ⲛ ⲉϫⲉⲛ- B: MG 25 133 mastic ⲡⲏ ⲉⲑⲥⲁⲃⲙ ⲟⲩⲟϩ ⲉⲑⲟⲩⲟⲭⲟⲩⲉⲭ ⲉϫⲱϥ; ⲛ ⲛⲥⲁ- emphasis SF: BMis 541 ⲉⲩⲟⲩ. ⲛⲥⲁⲡⲉⲩⲗⲁⲥ κατεσθ. acc; ib 312 ⲁⲩⲟⲩϭⲉϭ ⲛⲥⲁⲡⲛⲗⲁⲥ, Mor 30 24 F ⲙⲡⲉϥⲗⲁ ⲉϥϩ. ⲛⲥⲁⲡⲉⲕⲉⲥ … ϣⲁⲛⲧⲉϥ-ⲙⲟⲩ, MSGolenischef 17 60 ⲁⲩⲟⲩ. ⲛⲥⲁⲡⲛⲕⲁϣ ⲉⲧⲣⲏ-ⲧⲉϥϭⲓⲭ.

—— nn S: PMich 4562 letter ⲛ]ⲥⲁϩⲡⲛⲟϭ ⲛⲟⲩ. (context lost).

Cf ⲟⲩⲱⲡⲧ.

ⲫ

(For most words in ⲫ- *v* ⲡ-.)

ⲫ, 21st letter of alphabet, called ⲫⲓ (My 97) *S*, (K 1, Stern p 418)*B*, ف (P 44 137, Stern *l c*). As numeral *BF*, rarely *S*(Br 128, Lant 8, BIF 5 113)= 500 (ϯⲟⲩ ⲛϣⲉ). Not in *S* except for ⲛϧ (archaic), as ⲫⲱⲃ (PS 105, BG 104), ϣⲫⲙⲙⲁⲧ (J&C 95), ⲫⲛ-ⲕⲉⲙⲱⲛ (Ryl 270); sim *O* ⲫⲟ (AZ 21 98), ⲫⲏⲧ (*ib* 104); converse (rare), as ⲡⲟⲁⲣⲁⲱ (ⲛ ends line Mor 31 174), ⲡⲣⲟⲛⲏ (φωνή Ann 27 63). In *B* = *S* ⲡ (1) before liquids, as ⲫⲙⲟⲅⲓ, ⲛⲁⲫⲣⲓ; (2) before tone vowel, as ⲫⲱⲣϣ, ⲁⲫⲟⲧ; (3) beginning a syllable after consonant, as ⲉⲣⲫⲉⲓ, ϣⲫⲓⲧ, ⲭⲫⲟ; also in ⲁⲫⲉ. Replaces ⲡ, as ⲫⲛⲟⲛ (Mus 34 201), ⲫⲗⲁⲍⲓⲛ (πλάσ-σειν EW 198), ⲫⲓⲥⲕⲓⲛⲁ (C 86 22), ϧⲉⲫ (BM 1223); converse, as ⲡⲗⲉⲭⲙⲁ (φλέγμα Mor 37 147), ⲡⲓⲁⲗⲉ (φιάλη PMich 1190), ⲁⲡⲑⲁⲣⲧⲟⲥ (BMis 270), ⲟⲩⲡⲣⲟ-ⲥⲩⲛⲏ (εὐφ. DeV 1 167). *Cf* LMis 90. Replaces ⲃ, as ⲉⲫⲓⲛⲓ (AZ 40 6), ⲫⲟⲩⲃⲁⲥⲑⲓ (Ez 30 17), ⲫⲗⲁⲥⲫⲏ-ⲙⲓⲁ (BMis 58); converse, as ⲃⲓⲗⲟ- (AZ 40 10), ⲃⲟⲣⲉ (φόρειν Z 632). Replaces ϥ, as ϣⲁⲡⲟⲩϣⲫ (Rec 7 195), ⲡⲁⲛⲛⲫ (Ryl 460), ⲙⲁⲣⲉⲫϣⲱⲡⲉ (J 113 18); converse, as ϥⲱⲱⲡⲉⲓ (BMar 10), ⲕⲗⲓϥⲓ (γλύφειν DeV 2 191). Replaced by ⲑ, as ⲑⲗⲟⲡⲟⲛⲟⲥ (φιλ. BMis 259). Transcribed (in names) by Ar ف, as ابيفانيوس الفيوم, فام (metath for ⲫⲟⲓⲃⲁⲙⲙⲱⲛ), فوقاس.

ⲫⲓ *B* *v* ⲡⲉⲓ.

ⲫⲓⲛ *B* nn f, *sprout, blossom*: Nu 17 23 (*S* ϯ ⲟⲩⲱ) βλαστός; Dan 4 12 (*S* ⲧⲱϭⲉ) φυή. Prob is Gk φυή (but *cf* Rec 31 83).

ⲫⲉⲗ *B* nn m, *bean*: K 193 ⲛⲓⲫ. (no var) فول. *V* AZ 63 142, Dévaud *Études* 33.

ⲫⲗⲏⲟⲩ *B* *v* ⲉⲫⲗⲏⲟⲩ.

ⲫⲟⲗϧ *B* *v* ⲡⲱⲗϧ *s f*.

ⲫⲱⲗϫ *B* *v* ⲡⲱⲗϫ.

ⲫⲉⲗϫⲓ *B* *v* ⲡⲗϭⲉ.

ⲫⲁⲙⲉⲛⲱⲑ *B* *v* ⲡⲁⲣⲙϩⲟⲧⲡ.

ⲫⲟⲛⲃⲉⲛ, -ⲫⲉⲛ, ⲫⲉⲛϥⲱⲛⲧ *B* vb intr, *overflow*, ⲥ ⲛ- *with*: Job 29 6† (*S* ϧⲁⲧⲉ), *ib* (*S* ⲥⲱⲕ)χέειν; ⲥ ϧⲉⲛ-: Pro 3 10 (*SA* ⲙⲟⲩϩ) ἐκβλύζειν; ⲥ ⲉⲃⲟⲗ: Job 21 24† (*S* ⲡⲱⲛ ⲉⲃ.)διαχ., Joel 2 24 (*SA* do)ὑπερχ., Pro 5 16 (*S* do, *A* ⲡⲱϭⲧ ⲉⲃⲟⲗ), Lu 6 38 (*S* do)ὑπερεκ-χύνεσθαι, Ex 1 7 (*A* ⲡⲱⲣϧ ⲁⲃ.) χυδαῖος γίνεσθαι. *Cf* ⲡⲱⲛ.

ⲫⲱⲛϧ, ⲫⲉⲛϧ-, ⲫⲟⲛϧ⸗, ⲫⲟⲛϧ† *B* vb **I** intr, *turn*, *be turned*, *cf* ⲛⲱⲱⲛⲉ (Sethe *Verbum* 1 359): Job 28 5, Dan 10 16 στρέφεσθαι, Jer 8 4† ἀποσ., Deu 32 5† (*S* ϭⲟⲟⲗⲉ), Pro 4 28† (*S* do, *A* ϭⲁⲅϭ), Ac 20 30† (*S* do), MG 25 234 I know not ⲡⲱⲥ ⲁϥⲫ. διασ.; Deu 30 17 (*S* ϣⲓⲃⲉ) μεθιστάναι; Sa 2 15 (*S* do) ἐξαλλάσσε-σθαι; Va 66 301 ⲙⲡⲁⲥϣⲓⲃⲧ ⲙⲡⲁⲥⲫ. μεταπίπτειν; Nu 30 13 (*S* as Gk)περιαιρεῖν; He 12 18† (*S* Gk om), TRit 450 sim; BM 915 17 words ⲉⲧϥ.† opp ⲉⲧⲥⲟⲩ-ⲧⲱⲛ, C 43 188 demon ϥ. *changed shape*, MIE 2 370 ⲁⲡⲉϥϩⲛⲧ ϥ. ϩⲱⲥ ⲣⲱⲙⲓ & he spat =ViK 9629 *S* ⲁ-ⲡⲉϥϩⲛⲧ ϧⲱⲃⲥ = PO 22 412 سهى على قلبى, Va 61 201 ⲁⲡⲉⲕϩⲛⲧ ϥ. *art deranged*.

II tr : Is 38 8 (*S* ⲕⲧⲟ) στρ., Su 9 (*S* do), Mic 3 9 (*SA* ⲛⲟⲩϣⲥ), Ac 13 10 (*S* ϭⲱⲱⲙⲉ) διασ., Gal 1 7 (*S* ⲡⲱⲱⲛⲉ) μετασ., Is 33 18 (*SF* diff) συσ.; Job 5 12 (*S* ϣⲓ.) διαλλάσ.; Deu 1 28 (*S* ⲡⲱⲩϭ) ἀφιστάναι; DeV 2 196 ⲛⲁϥⲫ. ⲙⲙⲟϥ ϧⲉⲛⲡⲉϥϫⲓϫ, MG 25 150 ⲁϥ-ⲫⲉⲛϧ ⲡⲓⲉⲛⲭⲁⲓ ⲡⲟⲩⲱⲙ in cauldron, BSM 71 ⲁϥⲫⲟⲛϧϥ (*sc* name) & called him Matthew; refl: Ge 3 24 (*S* ⲕⲱⲧⲉ), Lam 1 20 (*S* ⲕⲧⲟ, *F* ϣⲧⲁⲗⲧⲉⲗ), Lu 7 9 (*S* ⲕⲱ.) σ., Jos 23 12 (*S* ⲕⲧⲟ) ἀποσ., Ps 17 27 (*S* ϭⲱ., *A* Cl ϭⲟⲟⲩϭ) διασ., Ap 1 12 (*S* do) ἐπισ., Jer 23 19 συσ.; Cai Euch 498 μεταποιεῖν; Cat 113 at turning in road ⲙⲙⲟⲛ ϣϫⲟⲙ ⲙⲙⲟϥ ⲉϥⲟⲛϧϥ ⲡⲉⲙⲡⲓⲥⲧⲟⲥ (on Mk 15 21).

With following preposition. ⲥ ⲉ- *to, toward* : Ps 29 12 (*S* do), Is 34 9 (*SF* ⲕⲱ.) σ. εἰς, Lu 7 44 (*S* ⲕⲧⲟ) σ. πρός, Jer 39 33 ἐπισ. πρός, Ps 65 6 (*S* do), Am 8 10 (*S* ⲡⲱⲱⲛⲉ) μετασ. εἰς, *ib* 6 12 ἐκσ. εἰς; Is 30 32 (*SF* = Gk) μεταβολή; AM 241 ⲁⲕⲫ. ⲙⲡⲓ-ⲭⲣⲱⲙ ⲉⲟⲩⲡⲛⲁ, Aeg 52 ϥ. ⲙⲡⲉⲣⲟ ⲉⲡⲥⲁ ⲛϯⲁⲡⲁ-ⲧⲟⲗⲏ, ROC 25 255 ϣⲁϥⲫⲟⲛϧϥ ⲉⲡⲉϥⲕⲉϩⲱⲓⲣⲓ, AM 155 ⲁϥⲫⲟⲛϧϥ ⲉⲛⲁϯⲧⲁⲅⲓⲥ, Mus 35 28 ⲁϥⲫ. ⲉⲡⲏ ⲉⲧⲥⲟⲡ, C 86 272 ⲁⲡⲉϥϩⲛⲧ ⲫ. ⲉⲭⲱ ⲛⲥⲱϥ ⲛϯⲧⲁⲅⲓⲥ; ⲉϧⲟⲩⲛ ⲉ- Is 38 2 ⲫⲉⲛϧ- (*S* ⲕⲧⲟ ⲉ-) ἀποσ. πρός; Va 63 104 ⲫ. ⲉⲃ. ⲉⲡⲓⲉⲑⲛⲁⲡⲉϥ; ⲉϩⲣⲏⲓ ⲉ-: Cat 6 ⲉⲩⲫ.† ...ⲉⲃ. ⲉⲡⲓⲉⲡⲓⲑⲩⲙⲓⲁ; ⲥ ⲉϫⲉⲛ-, *upon, toward*: Jer 29 3 (*S* ⲕⲱ. ⲡ-) ἐπισ. ἐπί, Hos 12 14 (*A* ⲡⲱϩⲧ ⲁϫⲛ-) ἐκχέειν ἐπί; ⲥ ⲥⲁⲃⲟⲗ ⲛ-, *away from*: 2 Tim 1 15 (*S* diff) ἀποσ. acc, Ps 12 2 (*S* ⲕⲱ. ⲛⲥⲁⲃ.), Is 1 15 (*SF* ⲕⲧⲟ), ἀποσ. ἀπό; ⲥ ϧⲁ-, *from*: Ez 39 23 ἀποσ. ἀπό; ⲥ ϧⲉⲛ-, *in*: Cat 113 ⲟⲩⲙⲱⲓⲧ ⲉϥⲫ.† ϧⲉⲛⲡⲓⲭⲓⲛⲙⲟϣⲓ *where a turning in road*, C 43 197 ⲁϥⲫ. ϧⲉⲛⲡⲉϥⲓⲛⲓ; ⲉⲃⲟⲗ ϧ., *from*: Ac 13 8 (*S* ⲕⲧⲟ ⲉⲃ. ϩⲛ-) διασ. ἀπό; AM 131 ϥ. ⲉⲃ. ϧⲉⲛⲡⲓϣⲉⲙϣⲓ of

idols; ⲛϣⲏⲣⲓ ⲥ., in: BSG 242 ⲗⲟⲅⲓⲥⲙⲟⲥ ϥ.† ⲛⲥ̄. ⲛ̄ⲃⲏⲧϥ; ⲥ ⲉⲃⲟⲗ ϧⲁ-, from: Deu 7 4 (S diff) ἀφιστάναι ἀπό; ⲥ ϧⲓ-, toward: Nu 24 1 (S ⲕⲱ. ⲉ-) ἀποσ. εἰς; ⲥ ϧⲓϫⲉⲛ-, upon: Ez 4 8 (S ⲡ. ⲉⲃⲟⲗ ϧ.) σ. ἐπί;

With following adverb. ⲥ ⲉⲃⲟⲗ, outward, away: Lu 23 2 (S ϣⲧⲟⲣⲧⲣ) διασ., Lev 13 36 (S ⲡⲱⲣϣ) διαχ.; Ex 32 25 (S ϫⲱⲱⲣⲉ ⲉⲃ.) διασκεδάζειν; AM 325 ϥ. ⲛⲛⲓⲡⲣⲟⲥⲧⲁⲅⲙⲁ ⲉⲃ.; ⲥ ⲉϥⲁϩⲟⲩ, backward: Jo 20 14 (S ⲕⲱ.) σ. εἰς τὰ ὀπίσω, Is 42 17 (S ⲕⲧⲟ) ἀποσ. εἰς τὰ ὀ.; Ge 9 23 (S diff) ὀπισθοφανῶς; Miss 4 158 ⲁⲡⲉϥϩⲟ ϥ. ⲉ. = Mor 19 99 S ⲥⲟⲱⲅⲥ ⲛⲥⲁⲡ.; ⲥ ⲉⲃⲟⲩⲛ, in to, toward: 2 Chr 4 4† ἔσω εἶναι.

—— nn m, turning: Pro 1 3 (SA ⲕⲧⲟ) στροφή, Hos 4 19 (A ⲥⲱⲕ ⲁϩⲟⲩⲛ) συσ., Ez 16 34 (S ⲥⲟⲱⲙⲉ) διαστρέφ.; ib 5 (S ϭⲟ) σκολιότης; Ac 27 20 (S = Gk) χειμών (cf 18, but var both ϥⲱⲛ). ⲁⲧϥ., unalterable: Cai Euch 473 ἄτρεπτος; ⲙⲉⲧⲁⲧϥ.; ib 459 incarnate ϫⲉⲛⲟⲩⲙ. -ⲧⲱⲥ (cf ⲙⲛⲧⲁⲧⲡⲱⲱⲛⲉ).

ϫⲓⲛϥ., change, alteration: DeV 2 47 ⲧⲟⲩⲙⲉⲧⲁⲃⲟⲗⲏ ⲛⲉⲙⲧⲟⲩϫ., Miss 4 93 ⲡⲓϫⲓⲛϥⲉⲛϩ ⲡⲓⲥⲁϫⲓ change (in sense) of words.

ϥⲟⲛϩⲥ nn, change: Va 58 193 when drunk seest all things ⲉⲩϭⲓ ϥ. ϩⲁⲣⲟⲕ = P 131² 117 S ϫⲓ ⲡⲱⲱⲛⲉⲥ περιφέρεσθαι; EW 128, 132 (or ? imperat) as rubric, opposite Ps quoted, meaning doubtful, ? translate.

ϥⲱⲛϫ, ϥⲉⲛϫ-, ϥⲟⲛϫ⸗, ϥⲟⲛϫ† B vb tr, overthrow, destroy: Job 28 10 (var ϥⲱⲣϫ, S ⲡⲱϩ) ῥηγνύναι, Ps 88 45 (S ⲣⲱϧⲧ) καταρ.; Jer 29 19 (S ϣⲟⲣϣⲣ), Mt 21 12 (S do) καταστρέφειν; Pro 6 14 (S ϭⲟⲟⲙⲉ, A ϭⲁⲅϭ) διασ.; Ge 19 29 ἐκτρίβεσθαι; Ps 88 40 (S ⲧⲁϧⲟ ⲉϧⲣⲁⲓ) καθαιρεῖν; Lam 2 5 (S ShC 73 78, F ⲱⲙⲥ) καταποντίζειν; AM 324 ⲁϥϥ. ⲙⲡⲉϥⲑⲣⲟⲛⲟⲥ ϩⲁⲣⲟϥ, C 86 10 ⲁϥϥ̄ ϥⲟⲛϫϥ ϫⲉⲛⲟⲩⲏⲥ, EW 42 ⲁϥϥ. ⲙⲡⲣⲏⲧ [ⲛⲛⲓⲣⲱ]ⲙⲓ = Horae Semit 3 57 ﻓﺴﺪ ﻣﺬﻫﺐ; ⲥ ⲉⲃⲟⲗ: Pro 7 21 (S ⲑⲓⲟ ⲉⲃ.) ἐξοκέλλειν; AM 195 ⲁϥϥⲟⲛϫⲥ ⲉⲃ. upset table; as nn m: Pro 2 14 (SA om) διαστροφή, Hos 8 7 (A ⲧⲉⲕⲟ) ⲕⲁⲧⲁⲥ.

ϥⲁⲡⲉ- B v ⲡⲱⲱⲡⲉ.

ϥⲱⲣ B v ⲡⲱⲱⲣⲉ.

ϥⲟⲣⲓ B v ⲃⲱⲣⲉ.

ϥⲱⲣⲕ B nn v ⲡⲟⲣⲕ pallium.

ϥⲟⲣⲡⲉⲣ, ϥⲉⲣϥⲱⲣ⸗, ϥⲉⲣϥⲱⲣ†, ⲣⲥ ϥⲁⲣϥⲉⲣ-, ϥⲁⲣⲡ., ⲡⲁⲣϥ. B vb tr, open, loosen: Ge 44 11 (var ⲟⲩⲱⲛ) ἀνοίγειν; CDan 90 ⲁⲩϥⲉⲣϥⲱⲣⲧ ⲁⲩⲭⲁⲧ ⲉϩⲣⲏⲓ λύειν, Lev 13 45† (S ⲃⲉⲣⲃⲱⲣ) παραλ.; Va 61 18 made dwelling ⲉⲃⲟⲗ ϫⲉⲛϩⲁⲡⲱⲛⲓ ⲛϥ. ξηρόλιθος (or ? κλιβάνιον Anal Boll 46 183); ⲥ ⲉⲃⲟⲗ: Deu 22 17 (S ϭⲱⲗⲡ ⲉⲃ.) ἀναπτύσσειν; intr: N&E 39 343 sack's mouth ϥ. ⲉⲃ.; ⲡ ⲥ v ⲓⲥ̄ (where for ib 144 l 58 144).

ϥⲟⲣⲥ B vb tr, break up (?): C 86 13 earth ⲉⲩϥ. ⲙⲙⲟϥ ⲙⲡⲓϧⲉⲃⲓ (cf PKerameus Συλλογή 165 γῆ τεμνομένη).

ϥⲟⲣϣⲓ B v ⲡⲱⲣϣ sf.

ϥⲉⲣϫ ⲣⲟ B v ⲡⲱⲗϭ II, ⲕⲱⲣϫ.

ϥⲁⲥϥⲉⲥ B nn as pl, wiles: MG 25 317 ⲧⲛⲁⲛⲟⲩⲣⲅⲓⲁ ⲛⲡⲟⲩϥ. ⲛⲭⲣⲟϥ (ROC 17 352 ﺳﺤﻤﺪ ﻟﻮﺣﺪﺓ؟).

ϥⲁⲧⲥⲓ B v ⲡⲱⲧⲥ (ⲡⲁⲧⲥⲉ).

ϥⲟⲧⲥⲓ B v ϥⲱϭⲉ (ϥⲟⲧⲥⲓ).

ϥⲏⲧⲧⲉ, ϥⲉ. B v ⲡⲓⲧⲉ.

ϥⲁϣⲓ v ⲡⲱϣ (ⲡⲁϣⲉ).

(ϥⲱϣⲉⲙ), ϥⲁϣⲙ⸗ B vb tr, meaning unknown: C 86 172 ⲡⲓⲡⲉⲛⲧⲉⲣⲓⲟⲛ (cf K 106 ⲕⲉⲡⲧⲉⲣⲓ ﺟﺎﻧﺪﺍﺭ, BIF 1 130) ⲁⲩϥⲁϣⲙⲉϥ ϫⲉⲛⲛⲓⲡⲗⲁⲧⲓⲁ paraded (?) him in streets among traders.

ϥⲁϣⲛⲓ, ϥⲟϣⲛⲉϥ B v ⲛⲟϣⲛ sf.

ϥⲉϧ B nn m, melon: Bodl 325 152 ⲡⲓϥ. ﺑﻄﯿﺦ. Confused with ϫⲉⲙϥⲉϩ.

ϥⲱϧ, ϥⲏϧⲓ B v ⲡⲱϩ break.

ϥⲱϧⲓ B nn m, shark: Bodl 325 159 ⲡⲓϥ. ﻗﺮﺶ (but K 171 ُﺝ is ⲡⲓⲧⲟ(ⲩ)ⲕⲉⲗⲟⲡⲏ ie ἀσπιδοχελώνη D'Arcy Thompson).

ϥⲱϭⲉⲛ, ϥⲟ. B nn as pl, covering-, roofing-planks: P 54 158 ﻣﺴﻘﻮﻑ ﺗﻄﺒﯿﻖ ﻭﺍﺡ, K 156 ⲛⲓϥ. ﺍﻟﺸﺎﻡ ﺷﻖ ﻭﺍﺡ Syrian planks. Cf ? ⲃⲱϧⲛ.

ϥⲁϧⲉⲣ†, ϥⲁϧⲣⲓ B v p 228 b.

ϥⲱϫⲓ B v ⲡⲱϭⲉ.

ϥⲱϫⲓ B nn as pl, a fish: BMOr 8775 136 ⲛⲓϥ. ﺷﻮﺹ. Cf ? K 170 ⲥⲩⲙⲟⲥ ﺷﻮﺱ (sic) σῖμος (v JEA 14 32).

ϫ

(For most words in ϫ- ν ⲕ-.)

ϫ, 22nd letter of alphabet, called ϫⲓ (My 98)*S*, (K 1, Stern p 418) *B*, چ (Stern *lc*, P 43 249). As numeral *BF*, rarely *S*(Lant 7, 31) = 600 (ⲥⲟⲟⲩ ⲛϣⲉ). Rare in *SAA²F* except for ⲕϩ (archaic), as ⲙⲁϫ (Deu 9 13), ⲙⲁϫ (2 Macc 6 3 *A*), ⲙⲟϫⲥ (Si 25 16), ⲣⲁϫⲏ (Hos 3 1 *A*), ⲣⲁϫϥ (Mani H 19 *A²*), ⲛⲓⲗⲁϫ (LMis 517), ϫⲓϫⲱⲟⲩ (BKU 1 23); converse (rare), as ⲉⲕⲙⲁⲗⲱⲧⲟⲥ (Mor 31 48), ⲕϩⲉⲣⲉ (χαῖρε BIF 27 63 *F*). In *B = S* ⲕ (1) before liquids, as ϫⲗⲁⲗ, ϫⲉⲣ ⲟⲩⲱ (AM 204); (2) before tone vowel, as ⲁϫⲱ, ϫⲱⲡ, ϫⲉϫⲁⲥ; (3) beginning syllable after consonant, as ⲛϫⲁⲓ; also in ⲃⲉϫⲉ. Replaces ⲕ (rare), as ⲉϫⲟⲣⲧⲁ (σκόρδον DeV 1 109), ϫⲟⲛⲕⲏ (κόγχη BSM 129), ⲉϫⲓⲍⲁⲣⲏ (σκυτάλη Ep 391); converse, as ⲑⲉⲕⲛⲓ (τέχνη Va 66 305), ⲕⲁⲗⲕⲓⲟⲛ (Ep 550), ⲕⲗⲁⲙⲓⲥ (χλαμύς C 89 95). Replaces ϣ, as ϫⲧⲏⲓ (BMis 382), ⲥⲁⲛϫ (J 116 4), ϫⲟⲟⲥ (BKU 1 48); converse, as ϣⲓⲗⲓⲁⲣϫⲟⲥ (1 Kg 17 18), *cf* ⲙⲉⲗϫⲓⲥⲉϫⲉⲕ (var He 7 10 *B*). Replaces ϭ, as ⲉϫⲁⲓ (MR 5 42), ϫⲁⲏ (Job 28 3), ϫⲉⲣⲉⲃ, ϫⲓⲥⲓ (BM 1237), ϫⲁⲣⲁⲃⲁⲓ (FR 102), ϫⲉⲛ- (Ryl 460); converse, as ϭⲱⲣⲓⲥ (Va 57 275), ϭⲁⲣⲁⲕⲧⲏⲣ (EW 19). Replaces ϩ (rare), as ϫⲁⲣⲟⲓ (Louvre R 51 vo), ⲉϫⲁⲧ, ⲟⲩⲁϫⲏⲣ (CMSS 30). Replaces ⲧ (rare), as ϫⲗⲓϥⲓ (γλύφειν DeV 2 196); converse, as ⲉⲗⲁⲧⲏⲥⲧⲟⲥ (CO 165). Replaced by ⲝ (archaic), prob mere graphic error (not *B*, Stern 26 *s f* all misprints), as ⲁⲣⲝⲓ (PS 86), ⲁⲓⲝⲙⲁⲗⲱⲧⲟⲥ (Mani 2), ⲁⲛⲧⲓⲟⲝⲓⲁ (AP 14), ⲡⲁⲥⲝⲁ (Jo 6 4 *A²*), ⲯⲩⲝⲏ (Lu 1 46 Lacau), ϣⲓⲝ (Zech 10 11 *A*), ⲝⲓⲱⲛ (Cl 8 4); converse, as ⲉϫⲙ (Lu 1 33), ⲣⲉϫⲛⲁⲩ (Hos 9 2 *F* JEA 11 245), ⲥⲁϫⲛⲉ (*ib* 7 15), ⲧⲁϫⲣⲁⲉⲓⲧ (El 72), ϫⲱⲣⲙⲉ (*ib* 42), ϫⲱⲣⲉ (Ps 46 9 *A*), ϫⲁⲓⲙⲁⲉⲓⲧ (TU 43 21) & prob χ(ρ)ῆⲣⲉ (PMon 131, PLond 5 170), Πϫⲱⲣⲉ (Preisigke), Ϫⲉⲕⲟⲩⲗ (POxy 2037). Transcribes Ar چ, as ⲗⲉϫⲉⲛ لكن, ⲉⲁϫⲟⲣ اذكر, ϫⲉⲛ كان (all EW 234 ff), ϫⲓⲡⲣⲓⲟ كبريت (PMéd 230), ⲙⲓⲥϫ مسك (*ib*), ϩⲁϫⲏⲙ حاكم (ALR '96 473); transcribed by ش, as ϫⲓⲱⲛ شبون (BIF 5 94), ⲁϫⲓⲗⲗⲁⲥ ارشلا (PO 1 401); or خ, as ⲉⲩⲧⲩϫⲏⲥ اوتخس, ⲡⲁϫⲱⲙⲓⲟⲥ باخوميوس; or گ (rare), as ϫⲁ كا (BIF 5 93).

ϫⲃⲟⲃ *B* ν ⲕⲃⲟ.

ϫⲁⲑⲏⲩ *B* ν ⲧⲏⲩ.

ϫⲁⲑⲟⲓ *B* ν ⲕⲁⲕⲧⲉ.

ϫⲁⲕⲛⲁⲙⲁⲩ (mostly), ⲕⲁⲕ. *B* nn f, *small night owl*: K 169 †ⲕ. ام قويق, P 54 140 قوقة. *Cf* PGM 1 12 νυκτίβαυ, so here *l* ? -ⲃⲁⲩ.

ϫⲟⲗ *B* ν ϣⲕⲟⲗ.

ϫⲁⲗⲗⲉ *S*(?) ν ϫⲉⲗϫⲁϫⲱϥ.

ϫⲗⲟⲗ *B* ⲕⲉⲗⲱⲗ *s f*.

ϫⲉⲗⲙⲓ *B* nn f, meaning unknown, something noxious ? : MG 25 132 babe, lying on ground, given something to suck ⲛⲧⲉϥϣⲧⲉⲙϭⲓ ϫ. ⲛⲧⲉϥⲙⲟⲩ (*sic*), *ib* †ϫ. compared to sinful pleasures. *Cf* ? ϩⲁⲗⲙⲓ.

ϫⲗⲟⲙⲗⲉⲙ *B* vb tr, *crown*: Va 57 134 for his deeds ϣⲁⲩⲉⲣ ⲕⲟⲗⲁϫⲓⲛ ⲙⲙⲟϥ ⲟⲩⲟϩ ⲛⲧⲟⲩϫ. ⲙⲙⲟϥ στεφανοῦσθαι. *Cf* ⲕⲗⲟⲙ.

ϫⲗⲟⲙⲗⲉⲙ *B* ν ϭⲗⲟⲙⲗⲉⲙ.

ϫⲉⲗϫⲁϫⲱϥ *B* nn as pl, *abscess, tumour*: BM 920 264, Ryl 453 336 ⲛⲓϫ. دمامل. *Cf* ? P 43 50 *S*(?) ⲡϫⲁⲗⲗⲉ دمل & so *l* ? ϫⲉⲗⲗⲁ-.

ϫⲁⲙⲉ, ϫⲏⲙⲓ *B* ν ⲕⲏⲙⲉ.

ϫⲉⲙⲥ, ϫⲉⲙⲧⲥ *B* ν ⲕⲣⲟⲙⲣⲙ *s f*.

ϫⲱⲛⲥ *B* stink ν ⲕⲛⲟⲥ.

ϫⲁⲛⲉⲣⲱϥ (*sic*, not ϫⲁⲙⲉ-) *B* nn, name of a field pest(?): MG 25 258 ⲟⲩⲙⲛϣ ⲛϫⲉⲛ ⲛⲉⲙⲟⲩϫ. = Gött Ar 114 108 جراد و عطب, *ib* ⲛⲓϫ. ⲛⲉⲙⲛⲓϫ. Ar 'ج only. *Cf* ? ⲕⲛⲟⲥ.

(ϫⲱⲣ), ϫⲉⲣ- *B* vb tr, *destroy*, ⲥ ⲉⲃⲟⲗ: Deu 2 22 (*S* ⲧⲁⲕⲟ) ἐκτρίβειν افني. Or ? *l* ϫⲉⲣ.

ϫⲏⲣⲉ (CO 459), ϫⲉⲣⲉ (BP 9421), ϫⲉⲣⲁ (J 70 40, Ep 340), ϫⲏⲣⲁ (AZ 16 17)*S*, ϫⲉⲣⲁ *B* nn f, *ploughshare*: K 126 †ϫ. سكة; *ib* 129 *gridiron* or *sieve* used by cook مصفاة, مشبكة. In *S* in lists of utensils, tools. Coptic?

ϫⲁⲣⲉⲃ *B* adj or vb†, *lowly, abased*: K 294 مذلولين, منكسين.

ϫⲉⲣⲉⲃ *B* ν ϩⲣⲃ.

ϫⲣⲟⲃⲓ *B* nn m f, *sickle*: MG 25 206 δρέπανον; *ib* 119 sim, *ib* 97 †ϫ. for cutting palm leaves = Gött Ar 114 39 عذق, *ib* سكين, K 127 ⲛⲓϫ. منجل (Schweinf *Ar Pflanz* 232), ⲡⲓϭⲁⲗⲕⲟⲩ مقلم, BMOr

8775 139 ⲡⲓϫ. 'مق, ⲡⲓϧ. منذ. ⲕⲟⲣϩⲓ, ⲕⲣⲱϩⲓ, same?:
K 132 †ⲕ. شفر.   Cf ?? ἅρπη.

ϫⲁⲣⲟⲩϩⲓ B nn m, lizard: K 172 ⲡⲓϧ. ضب.
V AZ 6 55.

ϫⲣⲓⲙ B nn m: Ex 3 1 ϩⲁⲧⲉⲛⲡϣⲁϧⲉ ⲉⲡϧ. Gk
om, Ar var طرف البرية, but Ac 7 30 τοῦ ὄρους Σινᾶ;
or ? cf ⲣⲓⲙ in ϫⲁϫⲣⲓⲙ κρημνός & above Ar var, so
desert edge.

ϫⲣⲉⲙⲣⲱⲙ† B v ⲕⲣⲟⲙⲣⲙ.

ϫⲣⲉⲙⲥ, ϫⲣⲉⲙⲧⲥ B v ⲕⲣⲟⲙⲣⲙ s f.

ϫⲣⲱⲟⲩⲛⲓ, -ⲟⲩⲛ B nn f, tree zizyphus, nabk:
K 174 †ϧ. سدر (1 var نبقة).   Cf ⲁⲡⲉ plant, ⲥⲉⲓ nn.

ϫⲉⲣϫⲉⲙ S (?) nn f, among diseases: P 43 51
ⲧϧ. مكنوية (lues cauteriata AZ 26 122).

ϫⲣⲟϣ, -ⲱϣ B nn m, slap: P 54 177 ⲡⲓϧ. لطمة,
نهرة, K 161 لكم, لطم, لطس; Bess 7 11 ⲥⲉⲛⲁ† ϧ. ⲡⲉ
& spit in thy face.

ϫⲣⲱϣ B nn, wrinkle: K 75 ϭⲓⲛⲉ, ϧ. غضون
(gloss BM 924 وهم تجاعيد للجبهة w. on forehead). Cf
كرش (Dévaud).

ϫⲁⲣⲱϫⲓ B nn f, mallet, among fuller's tools:
K 139 †ϧ. مدقة, مكدة (v AZ 14 18).

ϫⲟⲥ B nn, eructation, vomiting: ROC 25 255
after eating ϣⲁϧⲣⲓ ⲟⲩϧ. & all food (brought up)
dispersed as smoke ἐρεύγεσθαι, ib 273 sim ϩⲓⲟⲩⲓ
ⲛⲟⲩϧ.

ϫⲉⲧ, ϫⲉ† B v ⲕⲉ V.

ϫⲁⲧⲏⲣ B nn m, compass for measuring: P 44
87 ⲡⲉϧ. بيكار = 43 69 ⲡⲓϧ. (Cf K 123 'ب القسمة
ⲧⲣⲁϧⲟⲥ).   Lit ? pair, twin, cf ϩⲁⲧⲏⲣ, ḥtr (HT).

ϫⲟⲩⲱⲙ B v ⲡⲕⲁ b & ⲟⲩⲱⲙ.

ϫⲟⲩⲁⲓⲛ B nn: P 43 32 ⲡⲱⲛⲉ ⲛϫ. حجر الرخام
marble.

ϫⲱⲟⲩⲛⲓ B v ⲕⲉ III.

ϫⲁϥ S nn, meaning unknown: ST 129 account
of barley ⲟⲩⲧⲉⲣⲙⲉⲥⲉⲟⲛ ⲛϧ., ⲙⲁϥ (l ⲙⲁϩ) ⲛⲗⲓⲧⲣ°
ⲛϧ.

ϫⲓϥⲧ B nn m, plant pulicaria: K 197 ⲡⲓϧ.
رعراع.

ϫⲟϩ B nn v ⲕⲟⲟϩ.

ϫⲟϩϫⲉϩ B v ⲕⲱϩ s f.

ϫⲉϩϫⲟϩⲧ B v (ⲕⲱϩ).

ψ

ψ, 23d letter of alphabet, called ψⲓ (My 155) S,
(Stern p 418) B, ابسي (ib l c), but sometimes ignored
(My 159, 172, K 1). As numeral BF, rarely S (Lant
60, 113) = 700 (ⲥⲁϣϥ ⲛϣⲉ). Only used for ⲡⲥ, as ψⲓⲥ,
ψⲱⲧⲏⲣ (BM 1224), ψⲱⲙⲁ (Ryl 273), ψⲁϣϥ (Kropp
D 46) & in names, as ψⲁⲛ, ψⲟⲧⲉ, ψⲙⲱ; converse
(rare), as ⲡⲥⲩϫⲏ (MR 5 49), ⲡⲥⲫⲟⲥ (ψῆφος Z 549,
cf ⲡⲍⲏⲫⲟⲥ Ac 26 10). Note also ⲁⲙψⲓⲁⲥ ('Αμασείας
Am 7 10, 14 A). Strengthened by ⲛ, as ⲑⲗⲓⲡψⲓⲥ (Pcod
Mor 57), ⲛψⲩϫⲏ (Mor 28 261), ⲛψⲓⲥ (CO 144).

ⲱ

ⲱ, 24th letter of alphabet, called ⲱ (Leyd 434,
My 100, P 44 127) S, ⲱ (EW 226), ⲁⲩ (K 1), ⲱⲟⲩ
(Stern p 418) B, او (Stern l c), او (P 44 l c). As numeral BF, rarely S (Br 131) = 800 (ϣⲙⲟⲩⲛ ⲛϣⲉ). On
relation to hierogl half-consonants & to other vowels
v Sethe Verbum 1 42 ff, Sdff 57 ff.   For dialectal
equivalents v under ⲟ, like which it is doubled, esp
in Esne-Edfu texts S, as ⲥⲱⲱⲛⲉ (Ep 268), ⲧⲱⲱϭⲉ
(BMis 452), ⲱⲱⲛⲉ (ib 473), ⲱⲱⲛ (Ryl 72), A² ⲱⲱⲛϣ
(APJo).   Replaced by ⲟⲟ, as ⲟⲩⲟⲟⲙ (Mus 42 224),
ϭⲟⲟϩ (BMis 451), ⲕⲁⲗⲟⲟⲥ (AZ 23 115), ⲣⲟⲟⲙⲉ (Jern

5).   In inaccurate, esp F texts ⲱ for ⲟ & ⲟ for ⲱ
often, as ⲁⲡⲱⲧ (Kr 22), ⲡⲱⲗⲓⲥ (ib 11), ⲃⲱⲏⲑⲟⲥ (ib
15), ⲓⲁⲕⲟⲃ (ib 11), ⲡⲟⲧ (ib 19), ϣⲧⲟⲣⲓ (ib 63), v Asmus
33. S ⲱ replaced in A by ⲟⲩ, v under ⲟ, also in Sᵃ,
where ⲱ for ⲁⲩ, ⲟⲩ is common, v Ep 1 241.   S ⲱ
often preceded by ⲟⲩ, v under ⲟ.

ⲱ SAA²BF interj, O!: Ps 117 25 SB, Pro 2 13
SAB, Ro 11 33 SBF, Hab 2 9 A ⲁⲟⲩ, Zech 11 17 A
do, all Gk ὦ; 1 Kg 26 14 S ⲱ (var ⲛⲓⲙ) ⲡⲉⲧⲙⲟⲩⲧⲉ
ⲟⲩ; ShC 42 96 S ⲱ ⲡⲁⲙⲉⲣⲓⲧ, ib 199 S ⲱ ⲧⲥⲩⲛⲁⲅⲱⲅⲏ,

ib 208 *S* ⲱ ⲉⲧⲃⲉⲡⲉⲧⲛⲁϣⲱⲡⲉ, ShA 1 202 *S* ⲱ ⲉⲛⲉⲣⲉⲡⲙⲁⲣⲧⲩⲣⲟⲥ ⲟⲛ̅ⲅ̅, *ib* 2 105 *S* ⲱ ⲱ ϣⲁⲡⲧⲉⲟⲩ ϣⲱⲡⲉ (*cf* Nu 24 23 *S* ⲱ ⲱ), ShIF 306 *S* ⲟⲩⲡⲉ ⲡⲉⲓⲛⲟϭ ⲡⲧⲱⲣ ⲱ ⲁⲛⲟⲕ?, DeV 1 115 *B* ⲱ ⲡⲁⲓⲁⲣⲟ ⲡⲥⲡⲟϥ, ManiH 32 *A²* ⲱ ⲡⲁⲧⲣⲉⲓⲧⲉ, Mor 22 106 *S* ⲱ ⲭⲉⲡⲓⲙ ⲡⲉⲧⲛⲁ- = BSM 95 *B* ⲱ ⲡⲓⲙ, MG 25 169 *B* ⲱ ⲭⲉⲟⲅⲟⲡ ⲟⲩⲡⲓ̈ϣϯ ⲙⲙⲩⲥⲧⲏⲣⲓⲟⲛ, C 86 322 *B* ⲱ ⲭⲉⲁⲟⲩⲏⲣ ⲡϣⲫⲏⲣⲓ; ⲱ ⲃⲓⲁ (ὦ βία): K 236 *B* غ; ShR 2 3 28 *S*, KKS 583 *S*, BSM 111 *B* = Mor 22 122 *S* om, Wess 15 1 *S* ⲱ ⲃ. ⲱ ⲅⲉⲱⲣⲅⲓⲟⲥ, Miss 4 672 *S* ⲱ ⲃ. ⲉⲣⲟⲕ, BM 920 264 *B* ⲱ ⲃ. ⲡⲧⲟⲧⲕ, BMis 42 *S* ⲟ (*l* ⲱ) ⲛⲃ., BM 217 22 *S* do, *cf* WTh 135 *S* ⲱⲃⲓⲁ (Gk in *Hist Laus* §21, Pomialovski *Paisia* 39; ⲱ ⲛⲃⲓⲁ on amulet, *Arch Religwiss* 21 225); *v* also ⲙⲛ- prep *s f*, ⲧⲱⲣⲉ (ⲡⲧⲛ-). *Cf* ⲱⲣ.

ⲱ *v* ⲟ great.

ⲱ *Sª A* *v* ⲟⲩ interrogative.

ⲫⲱ¹ *S*, **ⲱ²** *SA²*(Ma)*FO*, **ⲟⲩⲟⲩ³** *A*, **ⲟⲩ⁴** *AO*, **ⲉⲉⲧ†** *SAA²*, **ⲉⲧ†** *S*, **ⲛⲏⲧ†** *Sⁱ/F* vb intr, *conceive* child (*B* mostly ⲃⲟⲕⲓ): Ge 16 4¹, Jud 13 3², Hos 1 8 *A⁴*, Ja 1 15 *S²A⁴* συλλαμβάνειν, Ex 2 22², Is 7 14¹(var²) ἐν γαστρὶ λαμβ., Lu 1 31¹(var²) ἐν γ. συλλ.; Mt 1 23¹ ἐν γ. ἔχειν; Is 59 13¹ (*B* ⲙⲓⲥⲓ) κύειν; TT 154 ϣⲁⲥⲟⲩⲱ ⲕⲟⲩⲓ ⲕⲟⲩⲓ & thereafter bringeth forth, Z 285 ϣⲁⲣⲉⲟⲅⲟⲡ ⲱⲱ ⲭⲱⲣⲓⲥ ⲥⲩⲡⲟⲅⲥⲓⲁ?; qual, *be pregnant* (*B* ⲙⲃⲟⲕⲓ): Ex 21 22, Hos 14 1 *A*, Mt 24 19 ἐν γ. ἔχ.; Eccl 11 5 κυοφορεῖν, Lu 2 5 ἔγκυος εἶναι; Mic 5 3 *S*(ViK 9004)*A* τίκτειν; Mich 136 3 ⲉⲓⲧⲙⲁⲥⲓⲟ ⲡⲡⲉⲧⲉ., Mor 31 83 ⲟⲩⲥⲁⲙⲁⲅⲗⲉ ⲉⲥⲉ., ManiH 10 *A²* ⲛ]ⲅⲓⲁⲙⲉ ⲉⲧⲉ.

With following preposition. ⲥ ⲙⲛ-, *with, by* (the father): P 129¹⁴ 99 ⲁϥϣⲱⲡⲉ ⲡⲁⲙⲁⲓ ⲁⲓⲱ ⲡⲓⲙⲙⲁϥ, Miss 4 718 ⲁⲓⲱ ⲙⲡⲡⲟϭ ⲛⲥⲟⲛ; ⲥ ⲛ- gen (ⲙⲙⲟⲥ, *cf* Spg *Krugtexte* A 11 'wr n'm-f HT): Ps 50 5 *Sⁱ* (var²)*A³*(Cl), Lu 1 36² συλλ., Nu 11 12²(Mor) ἐν γ. λ.; Is 59 4 ⲉⲧ (var *Sⁱ*, *B* ⲙ.) κύ.; PS 12 ⲙⲡⲁⲧⲥⲟⲩⲱ ⲙⲙⲟϥ, R 1 3 67 ⲁⲩⲱ ⲙⲙⲟϥ (sc Baptist) 6 months before Christ, *ib* 68 ⲱ ⲙⲙⲟϥ, Mani 2 *A²* ϣⲁⲅⲱ ⲙⲙⲁϥ ⲟⲛⲡⲥⲁⲙ ⲡⲧⲱⲡⲛⲓ, Mor 30 48 *F* ⲁⲥⲱ ⲡϣⲏⲗⲓ ⲥⲡⲉⲩ = BMis 272¹, Br 275 ⲡⲉⲧⲉ.† ⲙⲙⲟⲟⲩ, FR 18 ⲉⲥⲉ.† ⲙⲡϣⲏⲣⲉ, KroppC 29 *F* ⲡⲉⲥϣⲏⲗⲓ ⲉⲥⲛ.† ⲙⲁϥ; ⲥ ⲛ- *for, by*: ShBMOr 8800 51 ⲛⲉⲅⲓⲟⲙⲉ ⲉⲧⲉ. ⲛⲁⲕ, R 2 4 58 ⲡⲓⲙ ⲡⲉⲧⲉⲣⲉ.† ⲡⲁϥ?; ⲥ ⲟⲛ-, *by*: R 2 1 6 Virgin ⲁⲥⲱ ⲟⲛⲡⲥⲱⲧⲙ of ears; ⲉⲃⲟⲗ ⲟⲛ-: Mt 1 18†(*B* ⲙ.) ἐν γ. ἔχ. ἐκ; R 2 1 27 ⲉⲣⲉ.† ⲉⲃ. ⲟⲛⲡⲓⲙ?, Wess 18 33 ⲁⲧⲡⲁⲣⲑⲉⲛⲟⲥ ⲱⲱ ⲉⲃ. ⲟⲛⲡⲟⲅⲛⲏⲃ; ⲥ ⲟⲛⲡⲛ-, sim: Z 586 ⲉⲅⲉⲧ ⲟ.ⲛⲧⲩⲣⲁⲛⲛⲟⲥ (*ib* ⲉⲥⲉⲉⲧ).

—— nn m *SA*, *conception*: Hos 9 11 *A⁴* (?³, *B* ⲙⲃⲟⲕⲓ) σύλληψις; R 2 1 10 signs of ⲡⲱⲟ, Ming 318 ⲡⲱ ⲏ ⲡⲭⲓ ⲟⲩⲱ ⲉⲑⲟⲟⲩ, FR 146 ϣⲟⲙⲡⲧ ⲡⲉⲃⲟⲧ ⲡⲱ.

† **ⲱⲱ** *S*, *be pregnant*: Cant 8 5 (*F* † ⲡⲉⲕⲓ) ὠδίνειν.

ⲙⲉⲡⲧⲱ (gloss ⲟⲩ) *O*, *pregnancy*: AZ 21 100 ⲟⲩⲙ.

ⲥⲓⲡⲱⲱ, -ⲱ *S*, *conception*: ShBor 247 122 ⲡϣⲓ ⲡⲧϭ., BAp 129 Zacharias's tongue gagged ⲟⲓⲡⲧⲉϥϭ. ⲙⲙⲟϥ & opened ⲟⲓⲡⲧⲉϥⲥⲓⲛⲭⲡⲟϥ, My 31 ⲯⲓⲥ ⲡⲉⲃⲟⲧ ⲛⲧⲉⲥϭ.

ⲱⲱ⸗ *back* in ⲟⲓⲱⲱ⸗ *v* ⲟⲓ-.

ⲱⲃ *v* ⲱϥ & ⲱϫⲉ.

ⲱⲃⲉ *v* ⲱϥⲉ.

ⲱⲃⲉⲛ *B* *v* ⲟⲃⲛ.

ⲱⲃⲧ *SA²*, **ⲱϥⲧ** *S*, **ⲱⲃⲉⲧ** *F* nn m, *goose* (or other edible bird, Sethe in *Festschr F C Andreas* 113): BM 528 fol 6 *F* beside picture of bird ⲟⲩⲱ., PMich 601 ⲧϭⲓ(ⲛ)ⲙⲟⲟϣⲉ ⲡⲟⲩⲁⲟⲱⲙ ⲧⲕⲓⲡⲟⲩⲗ ⲡⲟⲩⲱ., Z 630 recipe ⲱⲧ ⲡⲱ., BKU 1 25 ⲕⲉⲡⲛⲉ ⲡⲱ., PMéd 216 sim, Kr 242 among presents ⲱ. ⲥⲛⲁⲩ, Mor 25 13 rich man's diet ⲱ., ⲡⲁⲡⲟⲓ, ⲁϥ ⲡⲣⲓⲣ, BAp 95 sim, Mani 2 *A²* unclean foods ⲱ. ⲟⲓⲡⲁⲡⲁⲓ. In name Πωβέτ; place-name Ψιμανῶβετ, Ψιβ- (Preisigke).

ⲱⲃⲧ vb *v* ⲱϥⲧ.

ⲱⲃⲧ *B* *v* ⲱⲧⲡ *be laden*.

ⲱⲃϣ *SA²BF*, **ⲱⲃⲟ** *A*, -**ⲉϣ** ⲱϥⲉϣ *F*, **ⲉⲃϣ-** *SA²*, ⲟⲃⲉϣ⸗ *SB*, ⲁⲃⲟ⸗ *A*, ⲁⲃϣ⸗, ⲁϥϣ⸗ (once), ⲁⲃⲟ⸗ (do)*A²*, ⲟⲡϣ⸗ *B*, ⲁⲃⲉϣ⸗ *F*, ⲟⲃϣ† *SB*, ⲁⲃⲟ† *A*, ⲁⲃϣ† *A²*(Ma), ⲁⲃⲉϣ† *F* (?) vb *A*, *forget, be forgotten* (this meaning in dem HT) **a** intr *B*: Lev 4 13 (*S* ⲟⲱⲡ), *ib* 5 15 (*S* ⲣ ⲡⲱ.), Mk 7 24 (*S* ⲟ.) λανθάνειν; **c** ⲉ- of obj: Is 40 26 *B*(*S†*) λ.; Lu 9 45 *B*(*S* ⲣ ⲁⲧⲥⲱⲧⲙ), 2 Cor 6 9 *S*(*B* ⲥⲟⲟⲩⲛ ⲁⲛ) ἀγνοεῖν; ShIF 198 *S* ⲡⲟⲩⲟⲏⲧ ⲡⲁⲱ. ⲁⲛ ⲉⲣⲟ, Wess 18 78 *S* ⲱ. ⲉⲡⲉⲧⲣ ϭⲣⲱϥ; qual: Job 28 21 *B*(*S* ⲟⲏⲡ), *ib* 34 21 *S*(*B* ⲟⲏⲡ) λ., Pro 2 17 *SA* (*B* ⲉⲣ ⲡⲱ.) ἐπιλ.; Ro 10 3 *B*(*S* ⲟ ⲡⲁⲧⲥⲟⲟⲩⲛ) ἀγν.; Job 11 11 *B*(*S* refl) παρορᾶν; Mk 6 52 *S*(*B* diff) πωροῦν; ShC 73 37 *S* ⲧⲛⲟ. ⲉⲡⲉⲣⲃⲏⲅⲉ ⲙⲡⲉⲡⲱⲟⲣ, ManiH 4 *A²* ⲥⲉⲁ. ⲉⲧ[, Vat 57 69 *B* ⲁⲛϣⲱⲡⲓ ⲡⲟ. ⲉⲣⲱⲟⲩ; Mor 30 20 *F* ⲙⲡⲉⲡ̅ⲛ̅ ⲁⲃⲉϣ (*l* ? ⲁⲃⲉϣϥ) ⲉⲗⲁϥ, BM 581 18 *F* ⲡϣⲁⲕⲁⲃⲉϣ (? sim) ⲉⲣⲁⲓ. **b** tr, refl: Ps 77 59 *S*(*B* ⲟⲓ ⲡⲣⲟ) ὑπερορ., Va 66 308 *B* παρορ.; Is 65 12 *S*(*B* ⲉⲣ ⲁⲧⲥⲱⲧⲉⲙ) παρακούειν; Si 38 9 *S* παραβλέπειν; ShBor 246 43 *S* knoweth not or ϭⲉⲓⲙⲉ ⲟⲛ ϭⲱ. ⲙⲙⲟϥ, ShA 2 66 *S* ⲡⲧⲉⲣⲉϥⲛⲁⲩ ⲉⲣⲟ ⲁϥⲟⲃϣϥ, CO 58 *S* ⲉⲕϣⲁⲡⲛⲁⲩ...ⲡⲧⲟⲃϣⲕ, J 106 174 *S* I adjure you ⲭⲉⲡⲡⲉⲧⲛⲉⲃϣⲧⲏⲩⲧⲛ; not refl: Ep 174 *S* ⲡⲧⲟⲃϣⲛ (ⲛ)ⲧⲉⲣⲉ ⲧⲏⲣⲥ; **c** ⲉ-, *overlook*: Lev 26 44 *S*(*B* ⲟⲓ ⲡⲣⲟ), Zech 1 12 *SA*(*B* do), Aeg 270 *S* ⲙⲡⲉⲉⲗⲓⲥⲥⲁⲓⲟⲥ ⲟϭⲱⲃ ⲉⲡⲉϥⲕⲟⲩⲓ ὑπερορ., Pro 4 5 *S* (*sic l*) *A* (*B* do), ROC 27 144 *B* ⲙⲡⲉⲣⲟⲃϣⲕ ⲉⲣⲟⲓ παρορ.; Ac 6 1 *S*(*B* ϯ ⲏⲧ ⲁⲛ) παραθεωρεῖν; Nu 30 5 *S*(*B* ⲭⲁ ⲣⲱ)παρασιωπᾶν; Si 29 11 *S* παρέλκειν; Mic 7 18 *SA*(*B* ⲥⲓⲛⲓ) ὑπερβαίνειν; Ps 93 14 *S* (*B* ⲥⲱⲭⲡ) ἐγκαταλείπειν; PS 104 *S* ⲙⲡⲣⲟⲃϣⲕ ⲉⲡⲁ-

ⲅⲩⲙⲡⲟⲥ, ShP 130¹ 142 S ⲙⲉⲧⲉⲧⲡⲉⲃϣⲧⲏⲅⲧⲛ ⲉⲣⲟⲟⲩ, Ep 177 S ⲁⲧⲉⲧⲛⲱⲃϣⲧⲏⲅⲧⲛ ⲉⲣⲟⲛ, ST 196 S sim, BMis 398 S ⲧⲛⲁⲟⲃϣⲧ ⲁⲛ ⲉⲡⲉⲧⲛⲟⲩⲥⲓⲁ (var & Va 63 18 B ⲟ.† ⲉ-) = BSM 48 B ⲉⲣ ⲡⲱ. ⲛ-, Mani 1 A² ⲙⲁⲕⲁⲃⲱⲕ ⲁⲡⲉⲕⲙⲉⲣⲉⲧⲉ, BM 1224 A² ⲙⲡⲱⲣⲁϥⲃⲱⲕ ⲁⲡ[ⲁϣⲗⲏⲗ], ib ⲁⲃⲱⲕ ⲁⲣⲁⲉⲓ, Pcod 39 SF ⲉϥⲱ. ⲙⲙⲟⲩ ⲉⲣⲟⲟⲩ, ROC 23 272 B ϥⲛⲁⲟⲡϣⲙ ⲉⲣⲟⲛ, Ryl 437 B ⲉⲅⲱ. ⲙⲙⲱⲟⲩ ⲉⲛⲟⲩⲥⲡⲛⲟⲩ, Bor 241 217 S ⲁⲥⲟⲃⲱϣ ⲉⲧⲁⲧ†, R 1 5 16 S ⲉϥⲱ. ⲙⲙⲟϥ ⲉⲣⲟⲟⲩ ϩⲓⲧⲉⲣϥⲉ; not refl: MG 25 179 B things ⲉⲧⲁϥ† ⲟⲛϣⲧ ⲉⲣⲱⲟⲩ *wherein God had forgotten me*; ⲥ ⲉⲃⲟⲗ, *be neglectful*: Va 57 236 B ⲧⲉⲧⲛⲟ.† ⲉⲃ. ⲉⲣⲉⲧⲉⲛⲥⲱⲧⲉⲙ ⲉⲡⲁⲓ ναρκᾶν; HL 116 B at first ⲁϥϣⲱⲡⲓ ⲉϥⲟ.† ⲉⲃ. & demon tried him, BMar 182 S attend to thy guest ⲭⲉⲛⲡⲉⲕⲟⲃϣⲕ ⲉⲃ.

—— nn m SF, *forgetfulness*: Sa 16 11 λήθη; Lam 2 18 S(B ⲣⲱⲓⲥ, F ⲡⲏⲣⲉⲓ prob) ἔκνηψις.

ⲣ ⲡⲱ. SAA²BF, *be forgetful, forgotten*: Lev 5 15 S(B ⲱ.) λαν., Job 9 27 SB ἐπιλ.; ROC 17 408 B ⲉⲧⲁⲡⲉϥⲓⲱⲧ ⲉⲣ ⲡⲉϥⲱ. παρορᾶν παρά; Mani 2 A² ⲛϥⲣ ⲡⲱ., CO 271 S ⲙⲡⲱⲣⲣ ⲡⲁⲱ.; ⲥ ⲛ- gen: Deu 4 9 SB, Job 28 4 SB ⲓⲣⲓ ⲙⲡⲱ. ⲛ-, Pro 3 1 SAB, He 6 10 SBF ἐπιλ., ib 12 5 ἐκλ., Job 7 21 SB λήθην ποιεῖν; PS 164 S ⲙⲡⲣⲣ ⲡⲱ. ⲡⲛϩⲟⲙ, Mani 2 A² ⲣ ⲡⲱ. ⲙⲡⲉⲥϯ ⲥⲃⲱ, BSM 49 B ⲛϯⲓⲣⲓ ⲙⲡⲱ. ⲁⲛ ⲛⲟⲗⲓ = BMis 399 S ϯⲟ.† ⲁⲛ ⲉ-, CO 249 S ⲙⲡⲣⲣ ⲡⲱ. ⲛⲭⲟⲟⲩ; ⲥ ⲉ-: Ps 101 4 SB (var ⲛ-), Mk 8 14 B (var & S do), Z 343 S ⲁϥⲣ ⲡⲱ. ⲉⲝⲓ ἐπιλ. inf; as nn m: ROC 18 175 S λήθη; Sa 14 26 S ἀμνησία; ShBor 247 108 S ϣⲁⲭⲡⲉ ⲛⲁϥ ⲛϭⲓ (l ⲛ-) ⲟⲩⲣ. opp ⲣ ⲡⲙⲉⲉⲩⲉ; ⲣⲉϥⲣ ⲡⲱ., *forgetter*: Ja 1 25 A(?)B(S ⲣ ⲡⲱ. vb) ἐπιλησμονή; ⲙⲛⲧⲣⲉϥⲣ ⲡⲱ.: Mor 25 46 S paral ⲥⲉⲣϥⲉ.

B, *sleep*, intr: Ge 2 21 S(B ⲉⲛⲕⲟⲧ), Ps 3 5 S(ACl B ϩⲱⲣⲡ), Pro 3 24 SA(B ⲉⲛ.), Eccl 5 11 S(F ⲛⲕⲁ]ⲧ) ὑπνοῦν; Lu 8 23 S(B do) ἀφυ.; Pro 4 16 SA(B do) κοιμᾶσθαι; 2 Pet 2 3 S(B ϩⲓⲛⲓⲙ) νυστάζειν; Mk 4 38 S(B diff) καθεύδειν; ShR 2 3 68 S having overeaten ⲙⲛ ϭⲟⲙ ⲙⲙⲟϥ ⲉⲱ., RNC 89 S ⲁⲅⲭⲓ ⲣⲉⲕⲣⲓⲕⲉ ⲁⲅⲱ., Miss 8 147 S ⲁϥⲱ. ⲛⲧⲉⲩϣⲏ ⲧⲏⲣⲥ = BMar 65, BKU 1 25 S after drug ϣⲁϥⲱ., C 86 318 B ⲁⲡⲓϩⲣⲏⲓ ⲛⲓⲙ ⲥⲟⲕⲛ ⲁϥⲱ., Mor 24 8 F ⲁϥⲱϣⲉⲙ, PMéd 315 S ointment for eyes ⲧⲉϥⲱ. ⲛⲧⲉϥⲛⲟⲩ *be stilled*; qual S: Pro 6 10 SA(B ⲉⲛ.), Jer 14 9 S(B ϩⲓ.) ὑπ.; Cant 5 2, Mk 14 37(BF ⲉⲛ.)καθ.; Z 345 they deemed ⲭⲉⲧⲟ. = MG 25 210 B ⲉⲓⲉⲛ. ⲕⲟⲓ.; Aeg 263 ⲉⲩϣⲁⲡⲧⲱⲟⲩⲛ ⲛϣⲟⲣⲡ ⲉⲅⲟ. (cf ib 282 sim ⲧⲱⲟⲩⲛ ⲛϣ. ϩⲁⲡ ϩⲓⲛⲏⲃ), BIF 14 118 ⲉϥⲛⲏⲭ ⲉϥⲉⲛⲕⲟⲧ ⲉϥⲟ.

—— nn m SA², *sleep*: Jo 11 13 SA²(AB ϩⲓ.), Nu 24 4 S (var vb, B ⲣⲁⲥⲟⲩⲓ) ὕπνος, Tri 637 S ⲡⲛⲫⲉⲓ ⲉⲃⲟⲗ ϩⲓⲡⲉⲅⲱ. رؤي.

ⲁⲧⲱ. S, *sleepless*: R 2 2 36 ϩⲁⲗ ⲛⲁ. (var BHom 55 ⲁⲧⲛⲕⲟⲧⲕ)ἀκοίμητος; BM 362 ⲟⲩⲁ. ⲧⲉ ⲧⲉⲩⲡⲟⲛⲏⲣⲓⲁ.

ⲥⲓⲡⲱ. S, *state of sleep*: P 129¹⁴ 53 hunger, thirst, ⲧϭ. of Jesus (cf Ep App 1 106 ϩⲣ̄.).

(ⲉ)ⲃϣⲉ SA², ⲉⲃϣⲓ, ⲉⲛ. B nn f, *forgetfulness, carelessness, sleep*: Lev 5 15 B(S ⲱ.)λήθη; He 13 2 B (S ⲥⲟⲟⲩⲛ ⲁⲛ)λανθ.; Nu 5 12 S(var ⲱ., B ϩⲓ ⲡⲣⲟ) παρορ. vb; Lu 24 11 B(S ⲣⲱⲃ ⲛⲥⲱⲃⲉ), Va 57 205 B ⲟⲩⲉ. ⲡⲉⲙⲟⲩϣⲃⲱ λῆρος; Va 57 7 B darkening mind ϫⲉ ⲛⲟⲩϣⲓϣϯ ⲡⲉ. ἐπίστασις; PS 334 S ⲛⲁⲡⲟⲧ ⲡⲧⲃ., Mani 1 A² sim, BG 58 S ⲁϥⲡⲟⲩⲭⲉ ⲛⲟⲩⲉ. ⲉⲝⲡⲁⲝⲁⲙ, SchC 73 139 S ⲡⲉⲣⲥⲉ ⲉⲃⲟⲗ ϩⲓⲧⲃ., ib 42 200 S ⲧⲃ. ⲙⲡⲉⲥⲣⲟⲙⲣ, BAp 153 S ⲧⲉⲃ. ⲧⲗⲁⲁⲩ ⲡⲓϩⲉⲣⲏⲧ ⲧⲏⲣⲟⲩ, AM 10 B ⲁⲓⲑⲣⲉϥϣⲱⲡⲓ ϫⲉⲛⲟⲩⲉ., MG 25 73 B precepts ⲁⲩϣⲱⲡⲓ ⲛⲁⲣⲣⲁⲕ ⲙⲫⲣⲏϯ ⲛⲟⲩⲉ.; ⲉⲣ ⲉ., *be forgetful*: MIE 2 359 B ⲁϥⲉⲣ ⲉ. & took not rope with him = BAp 88 S ⲣ ⲡⲱϣ ⲛ-; ϯ ⲉⲃ., *make forgetful*: MG 25 365 B ϯ ⲛⲁⲛ ⲛⲟⲩⲉ. ⲛⲧⲉ ⲛⲓⲡⲣⲟⲥⲟⲩⲉⲛⲟⲩ, WTh 187 S ⲁⲡⲡⲉ ϯ ⲛⲟⲩⲉ̄. ⲉⲡϩⲣⲏⲧ ⲛ-, ib 162 B sim; ϫⲓ, ϭⲓ ⲉⲃ., *be forgetful*: 2 Pet 1 9 SB λήθην λαμβάνειν; MG 25 341 B ⲉⲁϥϭⲓ ⲛⲟⲩⲉ. ⲛⲧⲱⲟⲩ *hath forgotten them*.

ⲟⲃϣⲉ S, ⲁϥϣⲉ Sf nn f, *forgetfulness*: Sa 16 11 (var ⲟⲃϣⲱ) λήθη; Nu 22 30 -ϣⲧ (sic Hyvernat Alb vi, l -ϣⲥ, var ⲱ., B ϩⲓ ⲡⲣⲟ) ὑπερόρασις; Si 23 3 ἄγνοια; ShMiss 4 282 without (excuse of) ϣⲱⲡⲉ ϩⲓⲟ., ShR 2 3 16 ⲟ. paral ⲥⲟⲣⲙⲉⲥ, Mor 48 114 ⲁϥϯ ⲛⲟⲩⲟ. ⲉ- ⲡϩⲏⲧ ⲛ- = C 43 155 B ⲙⲉⲧⲁⲧⲉⲙⲓ, ViK 9557 Sf ⲧⲁ.

ⲱⲓⲕ B v ⲟⲉⲓⲕ.

ⲱⲕ SA², ⲁⲕ- F, ⲏⲕ† A² vb intr & tr + ϩⲏⲧ, *be content*: Ps 146 10 S ⲱⲕ ⲛϩ. (B ϯ ⲙⲁϯ), 1 Cor 10 5 S sim (var ⲧⲱⲕ, B do) εὐδοκεῖν; Mt 14 6 F ⲁⲕ ϩⲧⲏϥ (SB ⲣ ⲁⲡⲁϩ) ἀρέσκειν, Ro 12 1 F sim (RylSuppl 1, var MR 2 70 & SB do) εὐάρεστος; Mani 1 A² ⲁⲓⲱⲕ ⲛϩ.[, ib ⲧⲛⲏⲕ ⲛϩ. ⲉⲡ ⲁⲧⲣⲉⲕⲉⲓⲣⲉ, Pcod F 21 ϣⲱⲡⲓ ⲉⲕⲁⲣⲕⲧⲛⲟⲩ (sic) ⲛⲛⲓⲗⲉⲙⲁ (S ⲁⲣⲉⲥⲕⲉ); ⲗⲉϥ ⲁⲣⲕⲧⲏⲥ F: Pcod lc (S ⲣⲉϥⲁⲣⲉⲥⲕⲉ); as nn A², *pleasure*: Mani 2 ⲉⲓⲣⲉ ⲙⲡⲱⲕ ⲛϩ. ⲙⲡⲟⲩϫⲁⲓⲥ.

ⲱⲕ B vb intr, *go in, sink (?)* of sun, c ⲉⲝⲉⲛ-: Jer 15 9 (S ϩⲱⲡ) ἐπιδύειν dat. V Spg *Etym* no 2.

ⲱⲕⲙ S, -ⲙⲉ AA², -ⲉⲙ BF, ⲉⲕⲙ- S, ⲟⲕ(ⲉ)ⲙ† SB, ⲁⲕⲙⲉ† A², ⲁⲕⲙ† F vb **I** intr, *be dark, gloomy, changed (for worse)*: Pro 15 13 SA, Jer 27 13 SB σκυθρωπάζειν; Z 324 S ⲁϥⲱ. ⲉⲙⲁⲧⲉ στυγνάζειν; Jth 6 9 S συμπίπτειν; Is 29 22 S(B ϣⲓⲃϯ) μεταβάλλειν erubescere; ShBMOr 8800 1 S seeth them & ⲛϥⲱ., R 1 4 33 S ⲁⲅⲗⲅⲡⲛ (l -ⲉⲓ) ⲁⲅⲱ.; qual: Ge 40 7 SB, BHom 53 S ⲉⲥⲗⲟⲕ ϩⲏⲧ ⲉⲥⲟ. σκυθρωπός, Ps 34 14 SB σκυθρωπάζειν; Is 57 17 SB στυγνός, Va 58 178 B ⲉϥϥⲓ ϩⲟⲙ ⲓⲉ ⲉϥⲟ. στυγνάζειν; Sa 17 4 S ἀμείδητος; Dan 10 15 B (sic l), AM 266 B κατανύσσειν; Z 288 S κατώδυνος; LMär 30 S ⲡⲉⲕ ϩⲏⲧ ⲟ. (var BIF 14 133 ⲛⲃⲟⲗ), BMis 115 S ⲡⲉⲩϩⲟ

о. ⲉⲧⲃⲉ-, Miss 4 107 B о. ⲙ̄ⲫⲣⲏϯ ⲛ̄ⲟⲩⲭⲁⲕⲓ, Mani
1 A² winter ⲉⲧⲁ. & full of trouble, Mor 27 30 F ⲉϥⲙⲟⲟϣⲉ ⲉϥⲁ., Va 58 178 B о. opp ⲣⲱⲟⲩⲧ, BHom
119 S ⲥⲙⲏ ⲉⲥϭⲟϫϥ ⲁⲩⲱ ⲉⲥⲟ. like soundless instrument, PMéd 122 S ⲟⲩⲏⲣⲧ ⲉϥⲟ. withered (cf ib 262
ⲟⲩ. ⲉϥⲗⲏⲕ), PMich 1190 S ⲟⲩⲥⲛⲟϥ ⲉⲃ̄ⲭⲣⲁⲙ (l
ϫⲁⲣⲙ) ⲙ̄ⲛ̄ⲟⲩⲙⲟⲟⲩ ⲉⲃⲟ.

II tr (rare), darken, alter: Mt 6 16 B(S†) σκυθρωπός; Si 12 20 S ⲉⲕⲙ- B ἀλλοιοῦν; Ge 4 5 SA(Cl,
B ϣⲱⲃⲧ) συμπίπ. عبِ ; ROC 20 54 S ⲁⲡⲁϣⲁϫⲉ ⲱ.
ⲡⲣⲟⲓⲛⲉ.

With following preposition.   c ⲉ- dat commodi:
DeV 2 50 B ⲁⲡⲉⲕⲣⲟ ⲱ. ⲉⲣⲟⲕ; toward: Bor 254 179
S God's face о.† ⲉⲣⲟⲓ; ⲉⲣⲟⲩⲛ ⲉ-, toward: Mor
18 15 S ⲡⲣⲟ...ⲉϥⲟ.† ⲉⲣ. ⲉⲣⲟⲓ = Miss 4 109 B; c
ⲉϫⲛ-, as last: Ez 27 35 SB, Mk 10 22 SBF στυγνάζ.
ἐπί; 1 Kg 17 32 B(S ⲟⲩⲱⲗⲥ ⲉ-) συμπίπ. ἐπί; Mor
17 51 S ⲱ. ⲉϫⲛⲣⲱⲃ ⲛⲓⲙ ⲉⲧⲛⲏⲩ ἀθυμεῖν ἐπί; ⲉϩⲣⲏⲓ
ⲉϫ.: Ez 32 10 B στυγ. ἐπί.

——— nn m SAA²B, gloom, sadness: Is 51 11 B(S
= Gk) λύπη; Ja 4 9 SAB κατήφεια; ShR 2 3 78 S
ⲱ. ⲛ̄ ⲙⲕⲁϩ ⲛ̄ϩⲏⲧ, ib 2 4 86 S ⲛ̄ⲣⲓⲥⲉ ⲙ̄ⲛ̄ⲱ. on cross,
Mani 1 A² ⲛ̄ⲛⲟⲡⲟⲥ ⲙ̄ⲛ̄ⲱ., DeV 2 46 B ⲣ̄ⲃⲱⲥ ⲛ̄ⲧⲉ ⲡ̄ⲱ.
ⲁⲧⲱ. B, without gloom: DeV 2 18 ⲡⲓⲣⲁϣⲓ ⲛ̄ⲁ.

ⲱⲗ SAA²F, ⲱⲗⲓ B, ⲟⲗ-, ⲱⲗ- SA², ⲉⲗ- B, ⲟⲗ⸗ SB,
ⲁⲗ⸗ S/AA²F, ⲏⲗ† S, ⲟⲗ† B, imperat ⲁⲗⲓ, ⲁⲗⲓⲧ⸗, ⲁⲗⲓⲟⲅⲓ B, p c ⲁⲗ- S, vb **I** intr (mostly S), hold, contain,
enclose: Mk 2 2 B(S ϣⲱⲡ) χωρεῖν; ShP 130⁴ 99 of
fertilizing date palm ⲟⲩⲛ ⲕⲛⲡⲉ ⲉϣⲁϥϯ ⲡⲓⲗⲟⲥ (εἶδος
tool for purpose) ⲉⲧⲙ̄ⲙⲁⲩ ⲉⲣⲟⲥ ⲡⲟⲩⲥⲟⲡ ⲉⲙⲉϥⲱⲗ
& must be done thrice ϣⲁⲛⲧϥⲱⲗ, Z 629 after ointment ϣⲁⲣⲉ ϣⲁⲁⲣ ⲱⲗ after 3 days, Mich 593 β
wound ⲛⲁⲱⲗ ⲛ̄ⲧⲉⲛⲟⲩ close up (?), ShIF 272 ⲛ̄-
ⲥⲱⲛⲉ (sc nuns) ⲉⲧⲏⲗ recluses;   gather in harvest:
Is 37 30 (B ⲱⲥⲕ̅) ἀμᾶν; ShC 73 39 ⲉⲅⲭⲟ ⲉⲅⲱⲗ,
Bor 260 118 ⲛϥⲥⲕⲁⲓ ⲛϥⲱⲗ, BMOr 8811 233 find
one ⲉⲱⲣⲥ ⲛ̄ ⲉⲱⲗ.

II tr (mostly B), take, lay hold of, gather: Deu 10
8 (var & S ϥⲓ), Is 53 8 (SA Cl do), Mt 14 12 (SF do)
αἴρειν, Ez 3 14 ἐξαί.; Dan 1 16(S do) ἀναιρεῖν, Pro 1
19 (SA ⲧⲁⲕⲟ), Is 36 7 (S om, F ϥⲓ) ἀφαι., Nu 10 17
(S ⲟⲩⲱϩ ⲉⲃⲟⲗ) καθαι., Ep Jer 57 (F ϥⲓ) περιαι.; Ge
16 3 (S ϫⲓ), Is 31 4 (S ⲧⲁϩⲟ, F ϭⲱⲡ), Mt 10 38 (S
ϥⲓ) λαμβάνειν, Zech 5 9 (SA ⲧⲱⲟⲩⲛ ⲉϩⲣⲁⲓ) ἀναλ., Is
5 17 (S ϫⲓ) ἀπολ., Ac 16 33 (S do) παραλ.; Is 46 2 (S
ϥⲓ), Dan 5 13 ἄγειν, Job 24 3 (S do) ἀπάγ., ib 12 17
(S diff) διάγ., Pro 6 22 (SA ⲉⲓⲛⲉ) ἐπάγ., Is 17 5 S
(harvest cf intr, B ⲑⲱⲟⲩϯ), Ez 29 5 (corpse) συνάγ.;
Job 5 26 A(Cl B ⲱ. ⲉϩⲟⲩⲛ, S ϫⲓ ⲉϩ.) συγκομίζειν;
Mt 26 51 (Cat 76, var ϣⲱⲗⲉⲙ) ἀποσπᾶν; Is 64 6 (S
ϥⲓ) φέρειν, Job 15 28 (S ϫⲓ) ἀποφ.; Mk 6 16 (SF ϥⲓ
ⲁⲡⲉ) ἀποκεφαλίζειν; Is 58 8 S(B ⲧⲁⲕⲧⲟ), Tob 12
13 S (corpse) περιστέλλειν, Z 343 S sim; CDan 91

ⲱ. ⲙ̄ⲡⲉⲧⲛ̄ⲧⲱⲟⲩ διαρπάζειν; Deu 20 14 S(B ϣⲱⲗ)
προνομεύειν; Ez 26 12 σκυλεύειν; BKU 1 1 S ⲁϥⲱⲗ
ⲛ̄ⲡⲉϥϣⲛⲏ, Tri 682 S ⲁⲥⲉⲗ ⲡⲁϣⲁϫⲉ as vain, DeV
2 76 wine ⲱ. ⲙ̄ⲫⲛⲟⲩⲥ of drinkers, AM 68 ⲱⲗⲓ ⲛ̄-
ⲧⲉϥⲁⲫⲉ, MG 25 100 ⲁϭⲉⲗ ⲱⲡⲓ = Ryl 95 S ϥⲓ, DeV
1 114 such crowds that ϣⲧⲉⲙⲟⲣⲉⲡⲓⲙⲱⲓⲧ ⲟⲗⲟⲩ ϫⲉ,
C 89 159 water ⲱ. ⲙ̄ⲡⲓⲙⲁ ⲡⲙⲟϣⲓ filled, covered, PO
11 307 ⲁϥⲱ. ⲛ̄ⲛⲓϣⲁⲗⲙⲟⲥ ⲛⲁⲡⲟⲥⲟⲛⲧⲏⲥ (ἀποστῆθος,
cf ϭⲓ C 89 37, ϫⲓ CO 30), Ryl 190 S ⲛ̄ⲣ]ⲟⲥ ⲛ̄ⲟⲗⲥ
reap, BP 11349 S ⲁϥⲟⲗ ⲡⲓⲱⲣⲉ, FR 36 S ⲱⲗ ⲙ̄ⲡⲟⲩ-
ⲗⲓⲯⲁⲛⲟⲛ = BMis 68 S ⲥⲕⲉⲡⲁϫⲉ (prob not l ⲥⲕⲉⲅ-
ⲁϫⲉ as Ep 1 184n), BMis 70 S ⲱⲗ ⲙ̄ⲡⲉⲥⲥⲱⲙⲁ(var FR
40 ⲕⲱⲱⲥ), Mor 24 4 F sim, PMéd 155 S ointment
ⲱⲗϥ set aside & use it, Mor 30 49 F ⲁϥⲁⲗⲥ;   refl
S: Tob 1 19 ἀναχωρεῖν; 1 Cor 7 29 time for thee to
withdraw (B ⲙⲡⲱⲣϥ)συστέλ., cit P 129¹³ 49 ⲛⲉⲟⲩⲟ-
ⲉⲓϣ ⲛⲟⲗⲕⲡⲉ, ϫⲁⲉⲓⲁ ⲅⲁⲣ ⲁϥⲟⲗϥ ⲁϥⲟⲩϫⲁⲓ (1 Kg
19 10 ἀναχ.), ShIF 94 ϯⲛⲁⲟⲗⲧ ⲉⲣⲟⲓ ϩⲙ̄ⲡⲉⲓⲙⲉⲣⲟⲥ,
BAp 149 if art stranger ⲟⲗⲕ ⲉⲣⲟⲕ, visit not others,
Mor 36 22 ⲁⲓⲟⲗⲧ ⲉⲧⲁⲧⲣⲁϫⲙⲟⲟⲥ ϩⲓϫⲙ̄ⲡⲉⲑⲣⲟⲛⲟⲥ
drew back (var P 131¹ 55 ⲟⲗⲧ ⲉϫⲙ̄ⲡⲉⲑ.);   imperat B: ⲁⲗⲓ sg Ac 22 22, Va 57 69 = BM 913 give
me to-day ⲁ. ⲣⲁⲥϯ ⲡⲁⲕ; ⲁⲗⲓⲟⲅⲓ sg Mt 2 13, C 41
44 ⲁ. ⲡⲁⲕ ⲛ̄ϥⲣⲉⲧⲁ (praeda); pl Is 62 10, C 86 197
ⲁ. ⲛ̄ⲱⲧⲉⲛ ⲛ̄ⲧ̄ϯ (ⲛ̄)ⲗⲓⲧⲣⲁ; ⲁⲗⲓⲧ⸗ TstAb 229 ⲁⲗⲓⲧ
ⲡⲉⲙⲁⲕ, Is 46 1 ⲁⲗⲓⲧⲟⲩ, C 86 106 ⲁⲗⲓⲧⲟⲩ...ⲟⲗⲟⲩ.
p c S: PMéd 265 ⲟⲩⲕⲟⲗ(ⲗⲓⲟⲛ) ⲛⲁⲗⲥⲛⲟϥ (but 146
ⲛⲱⲗ c.). Cf ⲥⲛⲟϥ s f.

With following preposition.
——— ⲉ- SA²B (mostly), bring to: Is 49 22 (S ϥⲓ)
ⲁⲓ̈. εἰς; MG 25 211 ⲟⲗⲟⲩ ⲉⲧⲟⲩⲣⲓ λαμβ. εἰς, Ac 1 2
(S = Gk) ἀναλ.; Ez 40 24 (S ϫⲓ) ⲁⲩ. κατά, Va 57
174 ⲟⲗⲥ ⲉⲡⲓϫⲓⲕ ⲁⲩ. ἐπί, Mt 4 1 (S do) ἀνάγ. εἰς, Ge
40 3 ἀπάγ. ἐκεῖ; Dan 11 8 φέρ. εἰς, Ap 17 3 ἀποφ.
εἰς; MIE 2 368 ⲁⲅⲟⲗϥ ⲉⲣⲁⲕⲟϯ, Mani 2 A² ⲱⲗ ⲡⲉ-
ⲧ[ⲛϩ]ⲏⲧ ⲁⲣⲱⲧⲛ, Mor 48 58 S reptiles ⲱⲗ ⲉⲣⲟⲟⲩ ⲛ̄-
ⲧⲉⲩⲙⲟⲧⲟⲩ (l ⲙ̄ⲁ.);   intr S: J 44 33 ⲁⲧⲡⲁϣⲉ ⲙ̄ⲡⲛⲓ
...ⲱⲗ ⲉⲣⲱⲧⲛ devolve on (?) you.

——— ⲉϫⲛ- B, bring upon: Is 13 2 (S ϥⲓ ⲉϫⲛ-) ⲁⲓ̈.
ἐπί; Lev 15 8 ⲉⲗ ⲧⲟⲩ (l ? ⲑⲁⲩ) ⲉ. προσσιελίζειν ἐπί
تفل على, BSM 14 ⲟⲗⲧ ⲉ.ϩⲁⲡⲱⲡⲓ = BMis 348 S ⲧⲁⲗⲟⲓ, v refl Mor 36.

——— ⲛ- B, to: MG 25 231 ⲱ. ⲙ̄ⲙⲟⲟⲩ ⲛ̄ⲛⲓⲥⲛⲏⲟⲩ
ἀποφέρ. dat; DeV 1 110 ⲱ. ⲛⲁϥ ⲛ̄ⲣⲁⲡⲍⲱⲣⲟⲛ, MIE
2 387 ⲟⲗⲥ ⲛⲁϥ ⲛ̄ⲉⲣⲓⲙⲁ = BAp 111 S ϫⲓⲧⲥ.

——— ⲛ̄ⲧⲉⲛ- B, from: Ge 31 31 (S ϥⲓ) ἀφαι. ἀπό;
Ez 24 25 λαμβ. παρά, Va 58 168 ⲁϥⲱ. ⲛ̄ⲧⲉϥⲥⲛϫⲓ ⲛ̄-
ⲧⲟⲧⲩ (cf 1 Kg 17 51) λ.; MIE 2 384 ⲁⲓⲟⲗⲟⲩ ⲛ̄ⲧⲟⲧⲩ
ⲁⲓϭⲓⲧⲟⲩ= BAp 107 S ϫⲓⲧⲟⲩ...ϥⲓⲧⲟⲩ;   as nn: MG
25 356 ⲡⲓⲉⲗ ⲫ̄ϯ ⲛ̄ⲧⲟⲧⲕ (= ROC 18 58 ܠܐܡܝܠܐ
ܠܐ ܡܢ?).

——— ϣⲁ- B, to: C 86 305 ⲱ. ⲙ̄ⲙⲟϥ ϣⲁⲡⲟⲩⲣⲟ

= BSG 199 *S* ⲉⲡⲧϥ ⲉⲣⲁⲧϥ ⲛ- ἀπάγ. πρός, BSM 68 ⲧⲉⲛⲛⲁⲟⲗⲕ ϣⲁⲣⲟϥ.

—— ϩⲁ- *B, hold beneath, support* intr: Ez 34 29 (*S* ϥⲓ) φέρειν acc.

—— ϩⲁⲧⲉⲛ-*B, to, beside*: EW 55 ϯⲡⲁⲟⲗⲧ ϩⲁⲧⲟⲧ.

—— ϩⲁ- *B, to*: Jer 44 14 εἰσάγ. πρός.

—— ϩⲓ- *B, on to*: Mk 4 36 (*S* ⲧⲁⲗⲟ ⲉ-) παραλαμβ. ἐν.

—— ϩⲛ-, ϫⲉⲛ- *SA²B, with, in, by*: Ez 8 3 *B*(*S* ϥⲓ ⲛ-) ἀναλαμβ. gen; Va 63 103 *B* ⲱ. ⲙⲡⲓⲕⲁⲧⲏⲅⲟⲣⲟⲥ ϫⲉⲛⲟⲙⲏϯ παύειν; Mani H 70 *A²* ⲁⲅⲱⲗ ⲡⲉϥⲥⲱⲙⲁ ϩⲛⲡϣⲁⲩ, MIE 2 347 *B* ⲁⲥⲱ. ⲙⲡⲓϣⲱ ϫⲉⲛⲡⲉⲥⲉⲣϣⲱⲛ, Miss 4 637 *S* ⲕⲉⲣⲙⲉⲥ...ⲟⲗⲟⲩ ϩⲓⲧⲙⲛⲧⲉ ⲛⲡⲉⲧⲣⲓⲣ *from* = C 41 21 *B* ⲉⲡⲟⲩ ⲉⲃⲟⲗ ϫⲉⲛ-; intr: O'LearyTh 13 = BM 908 ϥⲛⲁⲩ ⲉϣⲁⲅⲱ. ϫⲉⲛϯⲅⲩⲃⲱⲧⲟⲥ (but *l*? ⲛϯ.).

—— ϩⲓⲭⲉⲛ- *B, upon*: Ez 12 12 (*S* ϥⲓ) αἴ. ἐπί; *ib* 44 20 *take from upon* ψιλοῦν.

With following adverb.

—— ⲉⲃⲟⲗ *SB(mostly), take away*: Va 58 167 ⲉⲗ ⲟⲛⲁⲣϩⲓ ⲙⲡⲓⲁⲗⲗⲟⲫⲩⲗⲟⲥ ⲉⲃ. αἴ.; Ac 5 6 (var ⲓⲓⲓ, *S* ⲭⲓ) ἐκφέρ.; Su 45 ἀπάγ.; Ez 48 20 ἀφορίζειν; Is 18 7 (*S* ⲧⲱⲗⲕ) τίλλειν; Ex 21 27 (*S* ⲡⲟⲩϩⲉ) ἐκκόπτειν; Ac 8 2 (*S* ⲕⲱⲱⲥ) συγκομίζειν (cf ⲱⲗ intr); AM 316 bade ⲟⲗⲟⲩ ⲉⲃ. & behead them, Mor 16 75 *S* ⲡⲉⲡⲉⲓⲟⲧⲉ ⲁⲅⲣⲟⲥⲟⲩ (sc earth) ⲁⲡⲟⲛ ⲧⲏⲛⲁⲟⲗⲟⲩ ⲉⲃ. = BMis 219; intr *S*: Jud 15 7 κοπάζειν; 2 Kg 2 28 ἀφιστάναι (cf *ib* 18 16 refl ἀποστρέφειν); ⲉⲃ. ⲉ- *B, out to*: Aeg 32 ⲟⲗⲩ ⲉⲃ. ⲉⲡⲓⲙⲱⲩ, *ib* 55 sim ⲉⲑⲟⲙⲉϥ; ⲉⲃ. ⲉⲭⲉⲛ- *B, from off*: DeV 1 116 servants ⲱ. ⲙⲙⲱⲟⲩ ⲉⲃ. ⲉ. ⲡⲉⲡⲥⲛⲁⲣ ⲛⲛⲟⲩⲙⲁⲩ; ⲉⲃ. ⲛ- *SB, away from*: Deu 4 2 *B*(*S* ϥⲓ ⲉⲃ. ϩⲛ-) ⲁϥⲁⲓ. ἀπό; Ez 16 42 *B*(*S* do) ἐξαί. ἐκ; Z 332 *S* ⲟⲣⲧⲛ ϣⲁⲅⲟⲗⲥ ⲉⲃ. ⲙⲙⲟⲟⲩ παύειν; C 43 240 *B* ⲱ. ⲛⲟⲛⲁⲣϩⲓ...ⲉⲃ. ⲙⲙⲟϥ; refl: 2 Kg 2 19*S*(var *S.ᶠ* ⲁⲗ⟋)ἐκκλίνειν; ⲉⲃ. ϩⲁ-*B, from off*: Is 57 14 (*S* ϥⲓ ⲉⲃ. ϩⲛ-) αἴ. ἀπό; Pro 4 16 (*SA* ⲟⲩⲉ) ἀφαι.; Ryl 436 ⲁϥⲱ. ⲛⲧⲣⲟϯ ⲉⲃ. ϩⲁⲣⲱⲟⲩ; intr: Is 7 17 (*S* ϥⲓ ⲉⲃ. ϩⲛ-) ἀφαι. ἀπό; ⲉⲃ. ϩⲓ-*B, from off*: Mt 9 16 (*S* ϥⲓ) αἴ. ἀπό; 1 Kg 17 39 ἀφαι. ἀπό; ⲉⲃ. ϩⲛ-, ϫⲉⲛ- *A²B, away from*: 1 Cor 5 2 (*S* ϥⲓ ϩⲛ-) αἴ. ἐκ μέσου; Hos 2 17 (*A* ϥⲓ ⲁⲃ. ϩⲛ-) ἐξαί. ἐκ; Ep Jer 33 ἀφαι.; Is 39 7 (*S* ⲭⲓ ϩⲛ-) λαμβ. ἀπό; Job 7 15 (*S* ⲡⲱⲣϫ ⲉ-) ἀπαλλάσσειν ἀπό; Ac 5 2 (*S* ϥⲓ) νοσφίζειν ἀπό; Ez 11 19 ἐκσπᾶν ἐκ; BSM 82 ⲟⲗⲟⲩ ⲉⲃ. ϫⲉⲛⲡϣⲉⲙϣⲓ of idolatry = BMis 173 *S* ⲡⲧⲟⲩ ⲉⲃ. ϩⲛ-, C 43 60 ⲟⲣⲟⲅⲟⲗⲕ ⲉⲃ. ϫⲉⲛⲡⲁⲓϧⲧ *lift thee off* (for *remove from thee, cf* 61 ⲉⲛϥ ⲉⲃ. ϫⲉⲛ- = Mor 40 33 *S*), Mani 1 *A²* ⲁⲗⲟⲩ ⲉⲃ. ϩⲛⲡϣⲓⲛ; intr: Aeg 62 ⲱ. ⲉⲃ. ϫ.ⲡⲁⲓⲥⲁⲭⲓ opp ⲧⲟⲩϩⲟ ⲉⲭⲉⲛ-, C 86 311 sim; ⲉⲃ. ϩⲓⲭⲉⲛ- *B, from off*: Pro 1 12 (*SA* ϥⲓ) αἴρ. ἐκ, Ez 11 18 (*S* do) ἐξαί. ἐκ; Jer 13 18 (*S* do) καθαι. ἀπό; MG 25 296 ⲱ. ⲉⲃ. ϩⲓⲭⲱⲟⲩ ⲛⲛⲓϩⲃⲱⲥ = BIF 13 109 *S* do.

—— ⲉⲡϣⲱⲓ *B, take upward*: Ez 11 22(*S* ϥⲓ)ⲉⲝⲁⲓ.; Ac 1 11 (*S* do), *ib* 10 16 (*S* ⲭⲓ) ἀναλαμ. εἰς; C 43 61 ⲟⲗⲥ ⲛⲉⲙⲁϥ ⲉⲡ.; ⲉⲡ. ⲉ-: Cai Euch 488 ⲱ. ⲡⲧⲁⲁⲡⲁⲣⲭⲏ ⲉⲡ. ⲉⲧⲫⲉ ἀναβιβάζειν εἰς; ⲉⲡ. ⲉⲭⲉⲛ-: Ez 43 18 ἀναφέρ. ἐπί.

—— ⲉϧⲟⲩⲛ, ⲉⲥ. *SAA²BF, bring in, enclose*: Ac 7 45 *B*(*S* ⲭⲓ) εἰσάγ., Lev 25 3 *S*(*B* ⲑⲱⲟⲩϯ), Zech 9 3 *S*(ShA 2 334)*A*(*B* do) συνάγ.; Deu 28 38 *SB* εἰσφέρ.; Ez 29 5 *B*(*S* ⲕⲱⲥ)περιστέλ.; Mic 1 7 *SA*(*B* ⲧⲁⲥⲑⲟ) συστρέφειν; Cl 45 4 *A* φυλακίζειν; MG 25 242 *B* δέχεσθαι; Z 327 *S* ⲱⲗ ⲉϧ. ⲛⲕⲁⲣⲡⲟⲥ κομίζειν; ShR 2 3 5 *S*(ⲭⲉ?) ⲟⲩⲏⲣ ⲉⲃⲟⲗ, ⲉⲗ ⲟⲩⲏⲣ ⲉϧ., PSBA 32 287 *S* bade ⲟⲗⲩ ⲉϧ. in prison, BSM 124 *B* ⲉⲧⲱ. ⲛⲡⲉⲧⲱϩϩ ⲉϧ. before God, AZ 23 39 *F* ⲟⲩϩⲁⲛ (*l*? ⲁϧⲏ)...ⲁϥϩⲁⲡⲉ ⲁⲃⲁⲗ ⲉϧ.; intr *S*: Mor 51 34 parable ⲁⲡⲉϣϫⲟⲧⲉ ⲱⲗ ⲉϧ. ⲁⲓⲥⲁⲡϭⲁⲗⲓⲧⲁ ⲕⲱⲧⲉ ϩⲙⲡⲧⲓⲙⲉ, *interpret recluses* (ἀποτακτικός) ⲱⲗ ⲉϧ., *Greek monks* (ἑλληνικός) ⲙⲟⲟϣⲉ ⲉⲃⲟⲗ; qual *S, enclosed, confined*: ShC 42 159 those among us ⲉⲩⲏⲗ ⲉϧ. ⲉⲩⲥϭⲣⲁϥⲧ (*cf* ἔγκλειστος, ἡσυχαστής), Ryl 273 have pity on him ⲉⲩⲏⲗ ⲉϧ., Ep 163 redemption of brethren ⲉⲧⲏⲗ ⲉϧ., BP 11349 land neglected whilst ⲓⲱⲥⲏϥ ⲏⲗ ⲉϧ., BMOr 6943 (20) ⲡⲏⲣⲡ ⲉⲧⲏⲗ ⲉϧ. ⲉϧ[. as nn *A, enclosure, siege*: Pro 1 27 (Cl, *S* ⲕⲧⲟ, *B* ϩⲟⲭϩⲉⲭ) πολιορκία; ⲉϧⲟⲩⲛ ⲉ- *SA²B, in to*: Ge 12 15 *B* εἰσάγ. πρός, Ez 40 32 *B* ⲉ. εἰς; 2 Jo 10 *B* λαμβ. εἰς (all *S* ⲭⲓ); ShA 1 192 *S* ⲉⲩⲛⲁⲟⲗⲟⲩ ⲉϧ. ⲉⲁⲙⲛⲧⲉ, Mani 1 *A²* ⲁⲅⲁⲗϥ ⲁϧ. ⲁⲡⲉⲩϣⲧⲉⲕⲱⲟⲩ, ST 389 *Sᵃ* ⲁⲅⲁⲗⲧ ⲉϧ. ⲉⲡⲓⲥⲕⲛⲉ (σίγνον), C 43 247 *B* ⲁϥⲟⲗϥ ⲉⲃ. ⲉⲡⲏⲓ, EW 44 *B* ⲟⲗⲧⲉⲛ ⲉⲃ. ⲉϯⲃⲁⲕⲓ = BM 288 *S* ⲧⲁⲗⲟⲛ ⲉϧ.; intr: BAp 154 *S* ⲱⲗ ⲉϧ. ⲉⲧⲉⲕⲁⲡⲟⲑⲏⲕⲏ, WTh 178 ⲉϥⲏⲗ ⲉϧ. ⲉⲧⲉϥⲫⲩⲗⲁⲕⲏ; ⲉϧ. ϫⲁⲧⲉⲛ- *B, in to, up to*: Ez 8 7 εἰσάγ. ἐπί; ⲉϧ. ϩⲁ- *B, sim*: Jer 33 23 (*S* ⲭⲓ ϣⲁ-) εἰσάγ. πρός; ⲭⲓⲡⲱⲗⲓ ⲉϧ. *B* m: Dan 1 18 (*S* ⲭⲓ ⲉ.) εἰσάγ.

—— ⲉϧⲣⲏⲓ *B, bring down*: ROC 17 406 ⲱ. ⲡⲟⲩⲥⲛϥⲓ ⲉϧ. ⲉⲭⲱϥ φέρ. κατά.

—— ⲉϩⲣⲁⲓ *S, take, lift up, withdraw*: P 129¹³ 37 ⲁϥⲉⲗ ⲡⲉϥϩⲃⲁⲗ ⲉϩ., Mor 41 123 ⲁⲡⲙⲏⲛⲏϣⲉ ... ⲟⲗⲟⲩ ⲉϩ. ⲁⲩⲡⲱⲧ = *ib*. 39 13 ⲕⲁⲧⲟⲩ ⲉⲡⲁϩⲟⲩ, ST 360 will God grant (?) me ⲧⲁⲱⲗ ⲡⲁϩⲁⲗ ⲉϩ. ϫⲉⲁϥⲧⲁⲕⲟ; intr: Si 25 22(20) ⲱⲗ ⲉϩ. ϩⲛ[ⲟⲩⲥⲕⲁⲣⲁⲕⲓⲣ] (but var ⲉϩ. ⲛ-, P 44 119, *cf* ⲁⲗⲉ ⲉϩ.) حمل غرار Gk om; PS 231 ⲛⲃⲱⲗ ⲉⲃⲟⲗ...ⲉⲣϣⲁⲛⲡⲧⲏⲣϥ ⲱⲗ ⲉϩ., R 1 3 58 skirts ⲱⲗ ⲉϩ. *displaying ankles*; as nn m, *withdrawal*: PS 191 end of world & ⲡⲱⲗ ⲉϩ. ⲙⲡⲧⲏⲣϥ, *ib* 321 sim; ⲉϩ. ⲉ- *SB, up to*: Ac 21 34 *B* (var ⲓⲓⲓ, *S* ⲭⲓ) ἄγ. εἰς; DeV 2 57 *B* ⲟⲗϥ ⲉϩ. ⲉⲡⲓⲫⲛⲟⲩⲓ; refl: 1 Kg 14 46 *S* ἀπέρχεσθαι εἰς; Lu 14 10 *S*(*B* ⲟⲩⲱⲧⲉⲃ ⲉⲡϣⲱⲓ, *F* ⲟⲩ. ⲡⲥⲁϩⲣⲏⲓ) προσαναβαίνειν; Mich 550 41 *S* ⲉⲅⲱⲗ ⲙⲙⲟⲟⲩ ⲉϩ. ⲉⲡⲕⲉⲥⲁ *withdraw*; intr: Mor 51 22 *S* ⲁⲡⲉϥⲙⲁϩⲧ ⲱⲗ ⲉϩ. ⲉⲡⲉϥⲙⲁ; ⲉϩ. ⲉⲭⲉⲛ- *S, up upon*:

R 1 1 76 cross which Lamb ⲟⲗϥ ⲉϥ. ⲉⲭⲱϥ, Wess 18 62 bed ⲁⲕⲟⲗⲕ ⲉϥ. ⲉⲭⲱϥ (var Mor 19 53 ⲁⲗⲉ).

—— ⲙⲙⲁⲩ B, *take thence, away*: C 86 66 ⲁⲗⲓⲟϥⲓ ⲙⲙⲁⲩ ⲛⲛⲓⲁⲑⲛⲟⲩϯ ⲁⲓ̈., Ez 16 27 (S ϥⲓ ⲙ.) ἐξᾶι.; *ib* 21 26 ἄφαι., 2 Cor 3 16 (S do) περιαι.; EW 148 ω. ⲙ. ⲙⲡⲓϣⲑⲟⲣⲧⲉⲣ ⲕⲁⲧⲁⲥⲧέλ.; Va 63 84 endeavoured ⲉⲱ. ⲙ. ⲙⲡⲁⲓⲥⲁϫⲓ ἐξαλείφειν.

—— nn m SF, *gathering, harvest*: ShP 131⁴ 149 time of ⲭⲟ, ⲭⲱⲱⲗⲉ, ⲱⲗ, BP 11349 Pashons & Paone time of ⲡⲱⲗ, PCol 2 F ⲡⲱⲗ ⲉⲡⲓⲱⲣⲓ, ShIF 104 prepare ⲙⲡⲁⲣⲣⲉ ⲙⲛⲛⲱⲗ for sickness (*cf prob* ⲱⲗ ⲥⲛⲟϥ, p c above).

ⲣⲉϥⲱ. SB, *gatherer*: ShZ 583 S ⲣⲉϥⲭⲟ, ⲣⲉϥⲱⲗ, Lacr 81 B ⲡⲓⲣ. ⲛⲛⲉⲛϣⲗⲏⲗ.

ϭⲓⲛ-, ϫⲓⲛⲱ. SB, *gathering*: Is 48 14 B(S ϥⲓ) αἲ.; Bor 297 4 S on 1 Cor 7 29 ⲁϣⲧⲉ ⲧϭⲓⲛⲟⲗⲛ ⲛⲛⲁϭⲟⲗⲛ ⲙⲙⲟⲥ…ⲉⲡⲡⲁⲟⲗⲛ ⲉⲟⲩ?, BAp 63 S ⲧϭ. *harvest*, C 86 162 B fig tree ⲡⲉϭⲭⲓⲛⲟⲗⲥ.

ⲟⲗⲥ nn S, *what is collected*: Is 10 6 (B ⲥ̄ⲱⲗⲉⲙ) προνομή.

V also ⲧⲁⲗⲟ, ϣⲓⲡⲉ nn, ϩⲁϥ.

ⲱⲗⲉ *v* ⲁⲗ S nn.

ⲱⲓⲗⲓ B *v* ⲟⲉⲓⲗⲉ (*sic l.*, not ⲟⲗⲉⲓⲉ).

ⲱⲗⲓ B nn, in K 162 ⲡⲓϩⲓⲱⲗⲓ (1 var ⲱⲓⲗⲓ) تقريع, *striking, blow*.

ⲱⲗⲕ SA(+ ϣⲁ)A²B, (ⲉ)ⲗⲕ-, ⲟⲗⲕⲍ, ⲟⲗⲕ† SB vb intr, a *become, be bent*: ROC 17 400 B ⲁϥⲱ. ϩⲁϯⲙⲉⲧϩⲉⲗⲗⲟ κάμπτεσθαι, Ps 37 6 S(B ⲕⲱⲗϫ) κατακ.; Pro 6 10† S(var & A om, B ⲙⲟⲩⲗϫ) ἐναγκαλίζειν; Lu 13 11† S(B ⲕ.) συγκύπτειν; LCyp 4 S sinners ϣⲁⲩⲱ. ⲡⲥⲉⲉⲣ ϭⲁϭⲓϥ σύστασις, ἀνάστασις; P 44 79 S ⲕⲉⲣⲧⲟⲓ · ⲡⲉⲧⲱⲗⲕ (*l* ⲟⲗⲕ) ⲃⲗⲃ = 43 56 S ⲡⲟⲗⲕ ⲥⲟⲕⲟⲛ; ShViK 9346 S smitten by storm ⲥⲉϭⲗⲟⲙⲗⲙ ⲛⲥⲉⲱ., Mor 18 100 S ⲟⲩⲕⲉⲣⲧⲟⲥ ⲉϥⲟ.† (Miss 4 159 B diff), AM 258 B ⲉⲣⲉⲛⲉϥϭⲓϫ ⲟ.†, R 2 1 71 S ϩⲉⲛⲛⲁⲧ ⲉⲩⲱ. ⲉⲩⲥⲟⲩⲧⲱⲛ *which bend & straighten*, PMéd 173 S recipe for ⲡⲉⲛⲧⲁⲡⲉⲩⲙⲉⲣⲟⲥ (μέλος) ω.; tr (rare), *bend* S: Ro 11 10 (B ⲕ.) συγκάμ.; R 1 4 17 ⲁϥⲱⲣⲕ (*sic*) ⲙⲡⲉϥⲙⲁⲕϩ *reflectere*; Z 549 ⲁϥⲱ. ⲙⲙⲟⲟⲩ (wrists) till they broke. b qual S *turned aside, distorted*: ShC 42 63 ⲡⲣⲟϥ ⲟ. ϩⲛⲧⲛⲏⲃⲉ, Berl Or 1611 6 ⲉϥⲟ. ϩⲓⲧⲟⲅⲱϥ ⲡⲟⲩⲥⲧⲩⲗⲗⲟⲥ & was not seen, BAp 2 ⲛⲉⲭⲟ. ϩⲓⲡⲁⲣⲟⲩ ⲙⲡⲉⲓⲣⲁⲁⲩ, My 141 ⲉϥⲟ. ϩⲓⲧⲉⲛⲟⲩⲙⲏⲛϣⲉ ⲛϭⲓ ⲡⲥⲟⲟⲩⲛ; tr (refl): 1 Kg 19 2 ⲟⲗⲉⲕⲕ (var ⲟⲗⲕ, & *cf ib* 19 10) κρύπτεσθαι.

With following preposition or adverb. c ⲉ- SB, *bend toward*: BIF 13 99 S ⲁⲩⲱ. ⲛⲛⲉϥϭⲓϫ ⲉⲣⲟⲟⲩ & *bound them* = MG 25 279 B, Mor 48 72 S ⲁⲡⲉⲥϭⲃⲟⲓ ⲱ. ⲉⲣⲟⲥ = C 43 136 B ϩⲱⲗⲕ, R 1 3 49 S horses' legs ⲱ. ⲉⲣⲟⲟⲩ, Mor 31 74 S sick girl ⲟ.† ⲉⲭⲱⲥ ⲙⲡⲣⲁⲧⲥ *bent as to head & feet*; c ⲉⲃⲟⲗ S as ω.: R 1 1 15 standards ⲟⲗⲕⲟⲩ ⲉⲃ. κάμ.; c ⲉⲡⲉⲥⲏⲧ S,

down: P 44 63 ⲡⲉⲣⲟⲥⲡⲟⲙⲉⲡⲏ (*l* ⲡⲉⲣⲓⲥⲡⲱ.) · ⲉⲥⲱ. ⲉⲡ. ⲃⲗⲃ; c ⲉϩⲣⲁⲓ S, sim (?) Mor 51 40 ⲡⲡⲉⲃⲓⲕⲧⲱⲣ ⲉⲓ ⲉϩⲣⲁⲓ ⲉⲱⲣⲥ…ⲡⲡⲉⲃⲓⲕ. ⲟⲗⲉⲕϥ ⲉϥ. ⲉⲱⲣⲥ *demean self* (?); c ⲡⲥⲁⲡⲁϩⲟⲩ SA², *backward*: Deu 32 24 (B = Gk) ὀπισθότονος; Ryl 94 (33 3) martyr on wheel ⲉϥⲟ.† ⲛ., Mani H 54 A² ⲁϥϯ ⲁⲣⲭⲏ ⲡⲱ. ⲡⲥⲁ[.

ω. ϣⲁ, ϣⲉ SA, (ⲉ)ⲗⲕ ϣⲁ S, ⲉ. ϣⲁⲓ B, *turn up nose, sneer*: Ez 8 17 B μυκτηρίζειν, Lu 23 35 B(S ⲕⲱⲙϣ) ἐκμ.; ShA 1 152 S ⲉⲩⲥⲱⲃⲉ ⲉⲅⲗ. ⲏ ⲉⲅⲕⲱⲙϣ; c ⲛⲥⲁ-, *sneer at*: Job 22 19 B(S ⲕ.), Pro 1 30 SA(Cl)B, *ib* 15 5 AB(S do) μυ., Lu 16 14 B(S do), R 1 1 34 S ⲁⲅⲗ. ⲛⲥⲱϥ ἐκμυ.; Jer 20 7 B εἰς γέλωτα γίνεσθαι; ShMun 165 S ⲁⲣⲉⲱ. ⲛⲥⲁⲡⲉⲭⲡⲓⲟ (*cf* Pro 1 30), Sh C 42 155 S ⲉⲅⲗ. ⲛⲥⲁⲡⲉⲧϯ ⲥⲃⲱ, AM 120 B ⲧⲉⲡⲉⲗ. ⲛⲥⲱⲟⲩ; *as nn* B: Ps 43 14 (S ⲕ.) μυκτηρισμός; BSM 112 beguiling one through envy ⲕⲉⲟⲩⲁⲓ ϩⲉⲛⲟⲩⲉ.

ⲗⲕⲉ S nn, *bend, crease* (?): PSBA 27 187 preparation of parchment ⲉⲓϣⲱⲡⲉ ⲟⲩⲉⲓ (*sc* sheet, leaf) ⲉⲥⲟ ⲛⲗ. ⲗ. ⲏ ⲉⲥϣⲗϣⲱⲗ.

ⲟⲗⲕ 1 Cor 7 29 *v* ⲱⲗ **II** refl.

ⲟⲗⲕⲥ, -ⲉⲕⲥ SS, ⲉⲗⲕⲥ, -ⲍ B nn f, *bend, corner*: Pro 7 8 (SA ⲕⲗⲭⲉ), Su 38 f, Ac 26 26 (S ϩⲱⲡ), MG 25 243 stood in ⲟⲩⲉ. ⲡⲧⲉ ⲧⲉϥⲣⲓ γωνία; 1 Kg 25 20 S (var -ⲉⲕⲥ) σκέπη (var ἀποκρυφή); Va 61 94 ⲟⲩⲉ. wherein to hide = P 131⁵ 83 S ⲕ., C 41 47 sitting ϩⲉⲛⲟⲩⲉ.

ⲱⲗⲉⲕ F *v* ⲱⲣⲕ.

ⲱⲗ(ⲉ)ⲙ SF, ⲱⲗⲙⲉ A², ⲟⲗⲙⲍ S, ⲁⲗⲙⲍ S/, ⲟⲗⲙ† S vb intr, *clasp, embrace, entwine*: Cant 5 11 ϥⲱ ⲉⲧⲟ.† (F ϣⲕⲓⲗ ⲡⲧⲉ ϥⲱⲓ) βόστρυχος ἐλατός; Mor 53 54 ⲃⲱ ⲉⲧⲟ.† ⲉⲧϣⲟⲟⲡ ⲡⲁⲓ ⲉⲅⲥⲁ, *ib* 44 26 ⲡⲉϥⲃⲱ ⲟ.† opp ⲉϥⲟ ⲛⲕⲁⲣⲟⲥ, Bor 258 103 Judith ϩⲱⲗⲕ ⲙⲡⲉⲥⲃⲱ ⲉⲧⲟ.† (Jth 10 3); tr: P 131¹ 10 S/ ⲁϥⲁⲗⲙⲉϥ & kissed him, AZ 55 70 ⲁϥⲟⲗⲙ[ⲥ; *embroider* (?): ShZ 507 n cursed those ⲉⲧⲱ. ⲡⲡⲉⲩⲣⲟⲉⲓⲧⲉ, ShBor 206 572 ⲉⲧϥⲓ ⲣⲟⲟⲩϣ ⲡϩⲉⲛϩⲟⲉⲓⲧⲉ ⲉⲟⲗⲙⲟⲩ; c ⲉ- as obj: Z 329 ⲁϥⲱ. ⲉⲣⲟⲓ & kissed me περιλαμβάνειν, *ib* 292 sim προσλ.; Miss 8 258 saint & falling mason ⲁϥⲱ. ⲉⲡⲉⲕⲱⲧ ere he reached ground (var ? BMar 59 ⲁϥⲁⲙⲁϩⲧⲉ ⲡⲧϭⲓϫ ⲛ-); ⲉϩⲟⲩⲛ ⲉ-: ShC 73 161 none shall bear corpse ⲉⲟⲗⲙⲉϥ ⲉϩ. ⲉⲣⲟϥ ϩⲙⲡⲉϥⲁⲗⲟⲙ (*sic* var ViK 9223), Mor 29 23 woman carrying idol ⲉϥⲟ.† ⲉϩ. ⲉⲣⲟⲥ = *ib* 30 27 F ⲉϥⲧⲁⲗⲏⲩ ⲉⲣⲁⲥ, P 129¹⁷ 81 ⲁϫⲓⲟⲥⲕⲱⲣⲓⲁⲏⲥ ⲟⲗⲙϥ ⲉϩ. ⲉⲣⲟϥ (var Mor 17 30 ⲟⲗⲙⲉϥ ϩⲙⲡⲉϥϭⲓϫ), Mani H 33 A² ⲛⲥⲉⲱ. ⲁϩ. ⲁⲣⲁϥ, Mor 29 26 ⲁϥⲱ. ⲉϩ. ⲉⲡⲥⲱⲙⲁ = *ib* 30 30 F ϩⲙⲡⲥ., BMar 60 ⲉϥϩⲙⲟⲟⲥ ⲉⲣⲉⲛⲉϥϩⲙϩⲁⲗ ⲟ.† ⲉϩ. ⲉⲣⲟϥ.

(ⲱⲗⲝ), ⲉⲗⲝ- B in DeV 2 56 ⲧⲉⲡⲉⲗⲝ ⲕⲁⲥ. But *prob l* ⲧⲉⲡⲕⲉⲗⲝ. *V* ⲕⲱⲣⲝ.

ⲱϣⲙ̅ *B* ⲩ ⲟⲉⲓⲙⲉ.

ⲱⲙⲕ *SAA²B*, ⲉⲙⲕ-, ⲟⲙⲕⲍ *SB*, ⲟⲙⲉⲕⲍ *S*, ⲁⲙⲕⲍ *A* vb tr, *swallow*: Nu 16 30 *SB*, Job 8 18 *S*(*B* intr), Ps 140 6 *S*(*B* do), Pro 1 12 *SA* ⲁⲙⲕⲍ *B*, Mt 23 24 *SB* καταπίνειν; PS 64 *S* ⲁⲓⲱ. ⲡⲧⲱⲧⲉ, *ib* 46 *S* ⲁⲥⲟⲙⲉⲕϥ, *ib* 88 ⲉⲧⲟⲩⲉϣ ⲟⲙⲕⲧ, ShA 2 105 *S* ⲁⲡⲙⲟⲩ ⲉⲙⲕⲧⲏⲩⲧⲛ, Mani 1 *A²* ⲉⲧⲱ. ⲡⲁ ⲯⲩⲭⲁ ⲩⲉ, HL 115 *B* ⲡⲧⲉⲡⲙⲕⲁϩ ⲡ̅ϩⲏⲧ ⲟⲙⲕϥ; intr (rare): Job 8, Ps 140 as above, Is 25 8 *SB* ⲕⲁⲧ.

With following adverb.   ⲥ ⲉⲡⲉⲥⲏⲧ *SB*, *be engulfed*: Gu 60 *S* ⲉⲧⲣⲉⲧⲡⲟⲗⲓⲥ ⲱ. ⲉⲡ. ⲉⲡⲡⲟⲩⲛ = *Horae Semit* 3 17 الى بطوا, Va 61 113 *B* sim ⲱⲕⲙ (*l* ⲱⲙⲕ);   ⲥ ⲉϩⲣⲏⲓ *B*, *swallow down, overwhelm*: Va 68 181 ⲟⲩⲕⲟⲩ ϫⲓ ⲡ̅ⲓ ⲣⲱⲓⲥ ϣⲁ ϥϣⲉⲣⲱⲣⲕ ⲟⲩⲕⲟⲩϫⲓ ⲡⲁⲧⲱⲛ ϣⲁϥⲟⲙⲕ (*l*? ⲟⲙⲕⲕ) ⲉ ϫ̅.

ⲙⲁ ⲛⲱ., *place of swallowing, throat*: P 44 69 *S* ⲅⲁⲧⲁⲡⲟⲧⲏ (*καταπότιον*) · ⲉⲃⲣⲟⲩ ⲭⲟⲥ · ⲙⲁ ⲛⲱ. بلع, K 76 *B* ﺏ لﺍ.

ⲱⲙⲥ *SAA²BF*, ⲉⲙⲥ- *SB*, ⲁⲙⲥ- *S*, ⲟⲙⲥ- *B*, ⲟⲙⲥⲍ *SB*, ⲁⲙⲥⲍ *AA²F*, ⲟⲙⲥ† *S*, ⲁ.† *A* vb **I** intr, *be sunk, submerged*: Ps 106 27 *B*(*S* diff), Lam 3 49 *F*(*B* diff) καταπίνειν; Mt 14 30 *SB*, Z 316 *S* ϣⲁϥⲱ. ⲡ̅ϥⲡⲉⲣⲥⲉ = MG 25 345 *B* ϫⲱⲗⲕ ⲉⲡⲉⲥⲏⲧ καταποντίζειν; Lu 5 7 *SB* βυθίζειν; Jon 2 6 *B*(*SA* diff) δύειν; BHom 14 *S* ⲙⲡⲡⲥⲁⲧⲣⲉⲡ ϫⲟⲓ ⲱ. ναυάγιον; 2 Pet 3 6 *S*(*B* ϫⲱⲗⲕ ⲉϩⲣⲏⲓ) κατακλύζειν; Ap 12 15 *S* ποταμοφόρητον ποιεῖν; Z 330 *S* in furnace ϣⲁⲥⲟ.† ϣⲁⲡⲉⲥⲙⲟⲧⲉ βαπτίζειν; C 89 19 *B* ⲁϥⲱ. ⲛ̅ϫⲉ ⲡⲓⲙⲥⲁϩ = AZ 52 121 *S* ⲱ. ⲛⲁϥ, R 2 1 56 *S* ship struck rocks ⲁⲩⲱ., AM 185 *B* ship ⲁϥⲱ. with cargo.

II tr, *sink, dip*: Ps 68 15 *S*(var ⲟⲙⲉⲥⲧ)*B*, Eccl 10 12 *SF* ⲁⲙⲉⲥϥ καταπον.; Is 21 4 *SB*, Mt 3 11 *SB* βαπ.; Sa 10 4 *S* κατακλ.; Is 43 2 *SB* συγκλ.; Jer 28 64 *S*(*B* intr) καταδύ.; Ez 32 5 *B* ἐμπιμπλάναι; BMis 540 *S* ⲁⲅⲟⲙⲥϥ up to knees χαλᾶν; ShC 73 42 *S* ⲡⲥⲉⲟⲙⲥⲉ ⲡ̅ⲙⲟⲩ, R 2 1 53 *S* ϣⲁϥⲱ. ⲡϫⲟⲓ ⲡⲓⲙ, Aeg 256 *S* baptism ⲟⲙⲥϥ ⲛ̅ϣⲟⲙ̅ⲧ ⲛ̅ⲥⲟⲡ, MG 25 192 *B* ⲟⲙ̅ⲥ ϫⲱⲕ (var ⲉⲙ̅ⲥ, *cf* EW 135 iii).

With following preposition.   ⲥ ⲉ- *SA²BF*, *sink, dive into, dip*: P 131⁴ 107 *S* ⲡⲉⲧⲛⲁⲱ. ⲉϥ ϣⲓⲕ to find pearl, BAp 64 *S* angel's wings ⲟⲙⲥ ⲉ ⲣⲟⲥ (*sc* ⲡ̅ⲧⲏⲛ); *dat commodi* 1 Kg 25 37 *S* ⲁⲡⲉϥϩⲏⲧ ⲱ. ⲉ ⲣⲟϥ ἐναποθνήσκειν ἐν; tr: Ac 2 38 *B*(*S* = Gk) βαπ. ἐν; 1 Tim 6 9 *S*(*B* ⲉϩⲣⲏⲓ ⲛ-) βυθ. εἰς; Mani H 78 *A²* ⲁⲙⲥϥ ⲁⲡⲡⲟⲩⲛ, PChass 2 *S* recipe ⲁⲙⲥϥ ⲉ ⲡⲛⲁϫ, BKU 1 26 (8116 b)*F* sim ;   ⲉ ⲟⲩⲛ, ⲉ ϫ̅. ⲉ-: 2 Tim 3 6 *B*(*S* diff) ἐνδύ. εἰς; LCyp 8 *S* eyes ⲟ.† ⲉ ϩ. ⲉⲧⲉ ϥⲁⲡⲉ;   ⲥ ⲛ- *SB*, *in, with*: R 1 4 59 *S* ⲱ. ⲡⲟⲩ ⲡⲁ ⲡⲩⲣⲟⲛ ⲡⲡⲉ ϩ & burn his sides = Mart Ign 870 *B*, Mich 550 39 *S* hands ⲱ. ⲡⲥ̅ⲛⲟϥ, KKS 585 *S* ⲁϥϣⲱⲡⲉ ⲉ]ϥⲟ.† ⲡ̅ϩⲏⲧ = P ar 4793 37 prob علي خشي (Amélineau *Contes* 2 36 incorrect, *cf* 1 Kg above), Bor 263 26 *S* tongue

ⲟ.† ⲡⲥⲛⲟϥ;   ⲥ ⲡⲥⲁ- *F* emphatic: Lam 2 5 (*S* ShC 73 78 ⲱ. ⲡ-, *B* ⲱ. ⲡ- ⲉϩⲣⲏⲓ) καταπον.;   ⲥ ϩⲁ- *S*, *beneath*: Mor 46 38 ⲡϫⲟⲓ ⲱ. ϩⲁⲣⲟⲟⲩ (*cf* ϩⲱⲕ ϩⲁ-);   ⲥ ϩⲛ-, ϩⲉⲛ- *SABF*, *in, into*: Jos 3 15 *B*(*S* ϩⲱⲣⲡ) βαπ. εἰς; Cl 51 5 *A* βυθ. εἰς; Is 29 4 *SB* δύ. εἰς, Am 9 3 *B*(*SA* ϩⲱⲙ) καταδύ. εἰς; ShA 1 372 *S* Jew ⲉⲧⲟ.† ϩⲛ̅ⲧⲕⲁⲕⲓⲁ, Z 340 *S* ⲁϥⲱ. ϩⲛ̅ⲡⲟⲉⲓⲕ ⲉⲧⲣⲏⲧ, Ryl 89 *S* ⲡⲉⲓⲟ.† ϩⲛ̅ⲙ̅ⲡⲧ ⲣⲉⲗⲗⲏⲛ, PO 11 305 *B* ⲱ. ϩⲉⲛ†ⲕⲱⲗⲩⲙⲃⲏⲑⲣⲁ, Mor 39 42 *S* nails ⲱ. ϩⲉⲙⲡⲉϣⲟ ⲩ ⲛ; tr: Gal 3 27 *B*(*S* = Gk ⲥ ⲉ-) βαπ. εἰς; Mt 18 6 *SA*(Cl) *B* καταπον. ἐν; Jud 3 22 *S* ἐπεισφέρειν; ShRE 10 164 *S* ⲟⲙⲥϥ ϩⲛ̅ⲑⲁⲗⲁⲥⲥⲁ, ShBMOr 8810 394*S* ⲉⲙⲥⲧⲏⲩⲧⲛ ϩⲛ̅ⲧⲉ ⲣⲣⲱ ⲡⲥⲁⲧⲉ, Mor 24 31 *F* ⲁⲙⲥ ϥ ⲡ̅ϩⲏⲧ ϥ (*sc* river); refl: Ryl 62 6 *S* ⲁⲅⲟⲙⲥⲟⲩ ϩⲣⲁⲓ ϩⲙ̅ⲡ ⲡⲉⲗⲁⲅⲟⲥ; ⲉ ϩ ⲟⲩⲛ ϩⲉⲛ-: Jer 4 29 *B*(*S* ϩⲱⲕ ⲉϩ. ⲉ-) εἰσδύ. εἰς.

With following adverb.   ⲥ ⲉⲃⲟⲗ: ShIF 123 *S* ⲡⲉⲧⲛ̅ϩⲏⲧ ϩⲱⲃⲥ ⲉ ⲣⲱⲧⲛ ⲏ ⲱ. ⲉⲃ. ⲡⲧⲉⲧⲛ̅ⲏ ⲩⲧⲛ; as nn m *B*, *weakness of sight*: K 158 ⲡⲓⲱ. ⲉⲃ. عشا (*l* عشا, but AZ 14 19 غشي *faintness*); ⲡϫⲓⲛⲓⲱ. ⲉⲃ. *B*, *immersion*: Abst 17 ⲡⲉϥ ϫ. اماء (Mt 3 16);   ⲥ ⲉⲡⲉⲥⲏⲧ *SB*, *sink down*: Ex 15 10 *B* δύ.;   BM 257 328 *S* church ⲙⲉⲥⲱ ϣⲉ ⲡ ⲣⲁⲥⲓⲉ, ⲙⲉⲥⲱ. ⲉⲡ., Mor 43 226 *S* dead Lazarus's eyes ⲱ. ⲉⲡ. *deep sunken* (*cf* LCyp above), P 131⁴ 131 *S* ⲉ ϥ ⲟ.† ⲉⲡ. in crowd, C 86 259 *B* sea would ⲱ. ⲙⲙⲟⲥ ⲉⲡ.;   ⲥ ⲉ ϩⲣⲁⲓ (once), ⲉ ϫ̅. *SB*, as last: Jer 28 64 (*S* ⲱ. tr) καταδύ., He 11 29 (*S* ⲱ. intr) καταπίν.; Va 57 33 ναυάγια ὑπομένειν; C 89 106 thorn ⲡⲧⲉⲥⲱ. ⲉ ϫ̅. ⲡⲣⲟ ⲩ ⲟ *sunk deeper in* = Va ar 172 62 تدقن في, Va 61 13 cord ⲱ. ⲉ ϫ̅. ϩⲉⲛⲡⲉϥⲥ ⲱ ⲙⲁ, BMis 492 *S* ⲛ̅ϥⲱ. ⲉ ϩ. ϣⲁⲡⲉ ϥ ⲙ ⲁⲕⲉ in river; ⲁ ϩ ⲣ., ⲉ ϫ̅. ⲉ- *AA²B*: Lam 2 2 *B*(*F* ⲱ. tr) καταπον.; Cl 28 3 *A* ⲱ. ⲁ ϩ. ⲁ ⲡ ⲡⲟⲩⲛ καταστρωννύναι εἰς; Ex 15 5 *B* καταδύ. εἰς (*v* CMSS 13 Sᵇ); 1 Tim 6 9 *B*(var ⲛ-, *S* ⲱ. ⲉ-) βυθ. εἰς; Mani 1 *A²* ⲁⲕⲱ. ⲁ ϩ. ⲁ ⲡ ⲡⲟⲩⲛ, AM 56 *B* ⲁⲅⲟⲙⲥⲧ ⲉ ϫ̅. ⲉ ⲣⲟϥ (river); ⲁ., ⲉ. ϩ ⲛ- *AB*: El 58 *A* ⲉⲅⲁ.† ⲁ ϩ. ⲡ̅ϩⲏⲧ ϥ (sea); as nn m *B*, *sinking*: Va 57 74 ⲡ ⲱ. ⲉ ϫ̅. of ships.

—— nn m *SB*, *sinking, dipping, baptism*: Ps 51 4 *SB* καταποντισμός, cit Aeg 13 (*B* ⲉ ϥ ⲃⲛⲟ ⲩ, *cf* AZ 41 148); Mk 7 4 *B*(*S* ϩⲱⲣⲡ vb), Ro 6 4 *B*(*S* = Gk) βάπτισμα; ShA 2 32 *S* ϣⲁϫⲉ ⲙ̅ⲡⲱ. opp ⲙⲡⲱⲣ ϫ, Bor 256 150 *S* lost ship came ⲉ ϥ ⲣ ⲁⲧⲉ ϩⲙ̅ⲡⲱ. ⲡ̅ⲛ ⲉ ⲙⲟⲩ ⲛⲉⲓⲟⲟ ⲩ ⲉ *dripping from depth of waters*, C 43 44 *B* ⲡⲓⲱ. of Christian community, Ryl 447 *B* water from ⲡⲓⲱ. *baptismal tank*.

ⲣⲉ ϥ ⲱ. *S*, *diver*: P 131⁵ 33 brings up pearl, Bor 289 57 ⲛ̅ⲛⲏⲃ among criminals ⲡⲣⲉ ϥ ⲁⲙⲥ ϫⲟⲓ *ship-sinker*.

† ⲱ. *A²B*, *give baptism, baptize*: 1 Cor 1 14 *B*(*S* = Gk) βαπ.; Mani 2 *A²* ⲉ ⲧ† ⲱ. ⲙ̅ⲡ ⲃⲁⲡⲧⲓⲥⲙⲁ, BSM 71 *B* ⲁ ϥ† ⲱ. ⲛ̅ ⲡ ⲱⲟ ⲩ ⲉ ϥ ⲣ ⲁⲛ ⲙ̅ϥⲓ ⲱⲧ = BMis 162 *S* βαπτιζε;   ⲣⲉ ϥ† ⲱ. *B*, *baptist*: Mt 3 1 (*S* = Gk) βαπτιστής.

ϭⲓ ω̄. *B, get baptism, be baptized*: 1 Cor 15 29 (SF = Gk) βαπτίζειν: C 43 19 ϭⲓ ⲙⲡⲓⲱ., BSM 49 ⲡⲓⲱ. ⲉⲧⲁϥϭⲓⲧϥ ⲛⲧⲟⲧϥ = BMis 400 S ⲃⲁⲡ. ⲡⲧⲁϥⲫⲟⲣⲉⲓ ⲙⲙⲟϥ; as nn: He 6 2 (SF = Gk) βαπτισμός; ϫⲓⲛⲓⲱ. m: Va 57 36 βαπτίζεσθαι.

ϫⲓⲛⲓⲱ. *B, baptism*: K 219 ϯⲛⲓⲁ. تعميذ.

(ⲉ)ⲙⲥⲉ SA², ⲉⲙⲥⲓ B, *diving, immersion*: PS 381 S ϫⲓ ⲙ. ⲙⲙⲟⲟⲩ *in rivers*, BIF 13 113 S ⲉϥⲛⲓⲃⲉ ⲉϥϫⲓ ⲉⲙ. ϩⲙⲡⲙⲟⲟⲩ, Mani H 12 A² ⲛϫⲁⲗⲕⲙ. *that bring up pearls*, TRit 107 B *at baptism* ⲕⲁⲧⲁ ⲉ. ⲡⲧⲉϥⲉⲛϥ ⲉⲡϣⲱⲓ ﻏﻤﺲ. *Cf Spg 180 n.*

ωⲙ̄ϫ SA, ⲉⲙϫ-, ⲟⲙϫⲍ S vb tr, *wean*: Ge 21 8 ⲟⲙϫⲍ, *ib* ⲉⲙϫ- (B ⲧⲟⲅⲓⲟ ⲡⲧⲉⲣⲱ̣ϯ), Ps 130 2 (B do), Hos 1 8 A(B ⲧ.) ἀπογαλακτίζειν; ShC 73 22 ω. ⲛⲡⲉϥϣⲏⲣⲉ, Miss 4 720 ω. ⲙⲙⲟϥ ϩⲛⲡⲁⲉⲕⲓⲃⲉ, *ib* ϩⲛⲧⲉⲣⲱⲧⲉ, BMis 55 sim ⲉⲃⲟⲗ ϩⲛⲧⲉⲣⲱⲧⲉ.

ωⲛⲉ SAA²F, ⲱⲛⲓ BF, ⲉⲡⲉ- S, ⲁⲡⲁ- BF nn m f, *stone*: Ex 24 4 SB, Pro 27 3 SA, Mt 27 60 SB λίθος; Sa 17 17 S πέτρα; Ps 113 8 S ω. ⲉⲧⲛⲁϣⲧ (B ⲕⲟϥ ⲡϣⲱⲧ) ἀκρότομος; Ps 101 3 S(B ⲭⲁⲭⲱ) φρύγιον (?); ShA 1 200 n S ⲁⲅⲙⲉⲣ ω. ⲉⲣⲟϥ, ShWess 9 106 S *devil fishing with* ⲧⲟⲉⲓⲙⲉ, ⲡⲱ., ⲧⲁϩⲱ, AM 239 B ϩⲁⲛⲱ. ⲉⲅⲅⲟⲣϣ, BSM 134 B *hard as* ⲡⲓⲱ., KroppM 23 S ⲡⲱ. ϯⲛⲁⲡⲟϥϥ, BKU 1 3 S sim, Ryl 104 §4 S *let all reptiles* ϣⲱⲡⲉ ⲡⲱ., PMéd 173 S *drug* ϣⲁⲥⲡ ⲡⲱ. ⲉⲃⲟⲗ ϩⲛⲡⲕⲁⲫⲓⲥⲙⲁ, Bodl(P) a 1 a S *cook* ϣⲁⲡⲧⲉϥⲣ ⲟⲩⲱ. ⲡⲟⲩⲱⲧ *single mass*; as measure S: ST 445 ⲡⲗⲟϭⲟⲥ ⲡⲛϩⲁⲕ...ⲙⲛⲧⲟⲅⲉ ⲡⲱ. ⲡⲁⲣⲁ ⲥⲡⲧⲉ ⲟⲩϭⲟⲥ ⲡⲗⲓⲧⲣⲁ, Ep 364 (v n) ⲥⲟⲟⲩ ⲡⲱ. ⲡⲭⲁⲕ; as adj: Ge 35 14 SB, Ez 36 26 SB λίθινος, Ex 31 5 B λιθουργικός; C 43 117 B ⲁⲡⲟⲗⲗⲱⲡ ⲡⲱ., KroppB S ⲣⲟ ⲡⲱ., ⲣⲟ ⲡⲡⲉⲡⲓⲡⲉ, J 106 143 S ⲉⲓⲍⲟⲥ ⲙⲡⲉⲡⲓⲡⲉ, ⲉⲓ. ⲡⲱ., *ib* 41 65 S ⲟⲩⲟⲟⲙⲡⲉ (v ⲟⲩⲙⲟⲧ) ⲡⲱ.; c ⲡ-, ⲡⲧⲉ gen, *quality*: Is 54 12 SB ω. ⲡⲕⲣⲩⲥⲧⲁⲗⲗⲟⲥ, Lam 4 7 SBF ⲛⲥⲁⲡⲡⲓⲣⲟⲛ, Ep Jer 39 BF ⲛⲧⲉ ⲡⲧⲱⲟⲩ *all* λ.; Ez 8 2 SB ⲡⲏⲗⲉⲕⲧⲣⲓⲡⲟⲡ εἶδος(?); Va 61 26 B ⲙⲙⲁⲣⲅⲁⲣⲓⲧⲏⲥ, Mor 22 127 S = BSM 115 B sim, Ez 13 13 SB ⲙⲡⲉⲧⲣⲁ πετροβόλος; BAp 138 S ⲡⲁⲅⲁⲁⲗ ⲁⲅⲁⲁⲡ, Mich 136 6 S ⲛⲟⲟⲧⲉ *whereon charm to be written*, ⲡⲁⲗ v ⲁⲗ (2°); ⲡϫⲟⲩⲁⲙ v ϫⲟⲩⲁⲙ; *purpose*: Deu 24 6 S ⲡⲥⲓⲕⲉ (B diff) μύλος, Ap 18 21 S ⲡⲡⲟⲩⲧ (B ⲙⲙⲏⲭⲁⲡⲏ) -ινος λ., Mk 9 42 S(B ⲙⲙⲟⲩⲗⲟⲡ) μυλωνικός λ.; C 41 16 B sim, BKU 1 282 S ⲡⲕⲱⲧ(v ⲣ̄ⲕⲱⲧⲉ I b), ST 117 S ⲡⲣⲓⲟⲅⲉ, P 43 32 S ⲡⲟⲩⲟⲧⲟⲅⲉⲧ حجر المسن, ⲛⲫⲟⲣⲡⲉⲣ v ⲫ., AZ 23 39 F ⲛⲃⲁⲣⲡⲉⲣ; ω., ⲉⲡⲉ ⲙⲙⲉ S, ⲁⲡⲁⲙⲛⲓ BF, *real, precious*, v ⲙⲉ *truth* adj, adding C 86 335 B ω. ⲡⲁⲡ., *ib* 198 B ⲁⲗⲁⲃⲁⲥⲧⲣⲟⲛ ⲡⲁⲡ.; ⲁⲡⲓⲕⲁⲙ, *? black stone*, v p 12; f S: Gloss 164 ῥῶμβος (l ῥό.), ψωλή, ὀρθόδωρον· ⲧⲱ.; MMA 24 6 5 *he made ring (or key) for Matthias* ⲁⲓϫⲁⲣⲓϫⲉ ⲡⲁϥ ⲡⲧⲉϥⲱ., BP 4982 ⲁⲓϯ ⲧⲉⲕⲱ. (context ?); *scarcely* ὠνή.

ⲙⲁ ⲡⲱ. *SB, stony place*: Si 35 20 S λιθώδης; De V 2 184 B ⲡⲓⲙ. ⲉⲧⲁϩⲣ *over which he was dragged*, C 43 94 B sim.

ⲙⲱⲓⲧ ⲡⲱ. *B sim*: Nu 33 52 (S diff) σκοπιά.

ⲣ ω̄., ⲟ ⲡⲱ. *SB, become, be as stone*: Ex 15 16 B ἀπολιθοῦν; ShRyl 70 249 S *dried as wood* ⲛ ⲡⲥⲉⲣ ω., BMar 152 S ⲁⲧⲕⲟⲗϭⲙⲃⲉⲑⲣⲁ ϫⲱⲥ ⲁⲥⲣ ω., AM 310 B *hands* ⲧⲱⲥ ⲁⲅⲉⲣ ω., R 1 2 70 S *heart* ⲟ ⲡⲱ., Bodl(P) a 1 a *amalgam* ⲣ ⲟⲩⲱ. ⲡⲟⲩⲱⲧ.

ϩⲓ ω̄. *SA²B, throw stone* c ⲉ-: Lev 20 2 S(B ⲉⲭⲉⲡ-), Ez 23 47 SB λιθοβολίζειν, Aeg 290 S λίθοις βάλλειν; ViK 9545 S *all town* ⲡⲁⲣⲓ ω. ⲉⲣⲟⲡ, AP 3 A² ⲁⲅⲣⲟⲩ ω. [ⲁⲣ]ⲁϥ; c ⲉⲭⲉⲡ- B: Deu 17 5 (S ⲉ-) λιθο., He 11 37 (S do) λιθάζειν.

ⲥⲉⲧ ω̄. *B, as last* c ⲉ-: Ex 19 13 λιθο., MG 25 126 ⲥⲉⲧ ω. ⲉⲣⲱⲟⲩ λιθά.; c ⲉⲭⲉⲡ-: Ex 21 28 (S ϩⲓⲟⲅⲉ ⲉ-) λιθο.; c ϩⲓ-: AM 308 ⲁⲅⲥⲁⲧ ω. ϩⲓⲧⲣⲓⲕⲱⲛ.

ⲡⲉϫ ω̄.S, *as last* c ⲉⲭⲡ-: Job 38 6 (B ⲭⲱ) λ. βάλ.; ⲣⲉϥⲡⲉϫ ω. BKU 1 31 8.

ⲕⲱⲗϩ ⲡ- AA², *pelt with stones*: Jo 11 8 A²(SB ϩ., A ϯⲕⲉ), Cl 5 6 A (var ⲧⲱⲕ) λιθά.

ϯⲕ ω̄. A, *cast stones*: Cl 45 4 ϯⲕ ω. ⲁⲣⲁⲩ λιθά. *Cf* ⲧⲱⲕ.

ⲃⲁⲕⲱ. S, *stone-thrower*: Job 41 19 (B ⲡⲉⲧⲣⲁ ⲉⲧϩⲓⲟⲅⲓ), Sa 5 23 πετροβόλος; P 44 58 ⲃ. · ⲙⲉⲗⲁⲩⲡⲟⲡ مزارق = P 45 147 حربة لطيفة.

ⲕⲁϩⲕⲉ ω̄. B v ⲕⲱϩ, *make level s f*.

ϣⲁⲧ ω̄. S in ϩⲛ ⲡϣ. Jud 6 2 κρεμαστός (var ὀχύρωμα) *quarry*.

In names (?): Πῶνι, Φανῶνε (Preisigke); place-names: ⲡⲱⲡⲉ (CMSS 63), -ⲡⲓ (BM 546 ?), ϣⲁⲧⲱⲡⲉ (Ep 1 123), ⲡⲙⲁ ⲡⲣⲁⲡⲱⲡⲉ (BM 1024).

ωⲛ̄ⲕ, ⲟⲡⲕⲍ, ⲟⲙⲕⲍ, ⲟⲡⲧⲍ S, ⲁⲡⲧⲍ Sᶠ vb tr (refl), *leap*: Miss 4 553 *after sitting down* ⲁϥⲟⲡⲧϥ; c ⲉⲅⲟⲩⲡ ⲉ-, *at, upon*: ShMich 550 15 *beast & its prey* ϣⲁϥⲟⲙⲕϥ ⲉϩ. ⲉⲣⲟϥ, R 1 4 26 sim ⲟⲙ.; c ⲉϩⲣⲁⲓ, *up*: 1 Kg 25 9(var Sᶠ), Tob 7 6, BMar 117 ⲁⲩⲟⲡⲕⲟⲩ ⲉϩ. *& kissed him* ἀναπηδᾶν; Mor 18 3 ⲁϥⲟⲡⲧϥ ⲉϩ. *from sleep* (var *ib* 19 10 & Miss 4 98 B ϥⲱϭⲉ ⲉϩ.), BMis 205 do = Mor 16 46 ⲃⲟϭϥ ⲉϩ., BIF 13 112 *camel* ⲟⲡⲧϥ ⲉϩ. = MG 25 302 B ϥⲟϭϥ ⲉⲡϣⲱⲓ, Mor 50 42 Sᶠ ⲁⲥⲁ(ⲡ)ϭⲥ ⲉϩ.; ⲉϩ. ⲉϫⲡ-, *upon*: R 1 4 7 ⲁϥⲟⲙⲕϥ ⲉϩ. ⲉϫⲡⲧⲉⲩϫⲓⲥⲉ; ⲉϩ. ϩⲓ-, *up from*: 1 Kg 20 34 (var Sᶠ ⲉϩ. ϩⲓϫⲡ-) ἀν. ἀπό; Mor 18 75 ⲁⲓⲟⲡⲧ ⲉϩ. ϩⲙⲡϭⲟⲣⲟⲙⲁ (var *ib* 19 82 ⲃⲱϭⲉ) = Miss 4 146 B ⲡⲉϩⲣⲓ ⲉⲡϣⲱⲓ ⲉⲃⲟⲗ ϩⲉⲡ-, MR 4 71 ⲁⲓⲟⲡⲧ ⲉϩ. ϩⲙⲡⲥⲩⲛⲕⲗⲓⲧⲟⲛ (var Mor 19 70 ⲃ. ⲉϩ.); ⲉϩ. ϩⲁ-, sim: BMis 276 ⲁϥⲟⲡⲕϥ ⲉϩ. ϩⲁⲡⲣⲓⲛⲏⲃ; ⲉϩ. ϩⲓ- sim: BMar 3 ⲁϥⲟⲡⲕⲩ ⲉϩ. ϩⲓⲡⲉϥⲑⲣⲟⲡⲟⲥ; c ϩⲓϫⲡ-, *from off*: *ib* ⲁϥⲟⲡⲕϥ ϩ. ⲡϫⲙⲁ ⲡⲓⲕⲟⲧⲕ; c ⲉⲃⲟⲗ Sᶠ, *leap out*: 1 Kg 17 35 ⲉⲃ. ⲉⲡⲁϩⲟⲩ ⲡ- (var ϩⲓⲡⲁϩⲟⲩ ⲡ-, B 1 ⲉⲃ. ⲥⲁⲫⲁϩⲟⲩ ⲡ-) ἐκπορεύεσθαι ὀπίσω.

ωнт, ωнϭ S vb intr, *be pinched, contracted*: ClPr 43 14 miser's wine ϣⲁϥω. ⲛϭⲛⲏⲥⲥⲉ ⲉⲩⲡⲟⲩⲃ, ShIF 104 through cold metal ⲱϭⲣ ⲏ ⲉϥⲱⲛϭ ⲉⲣⲟⲩⲛ ⲉⲛⲉϥⲉⲣⲏⲩ; tr (refl): Si 11 18 ⲛⲟⲉ ⲉⲧϥⲱ. ⲙⲙⲟϥ ἀπὸ σφιγγίας αὐτοῦ.

ωнϣ S, ⲱⲟⲛϣ A[2], ⲟⲛϣ[†] SB, ⲟⲟⲛϣ[†] S, ⲁⲛϣ(ⲉ)[†] S[f], ⲁⲛϩ[†] A, ⲁⲁⲛϣ[†] A[2] vb intr, *be astonished, dazed* & so *dumb*: 3 Kg 10 5 S ἐξ ἑαυτοῦ γίνεσθαι; Pro 17 28[†] SA ἐνεὸν ἑαυτὸν ποιεῖν, Is 56 10[†] SB, Ep Jer 40[†] B(F ιⲁⲣⲉⲙ), Ac 9 7 S(B ⲧⲱⲙⲧ) ἐν.; Hos 13 8[†] B (l ? ⲉⲥⲟⲛϣ, A ϩⲁⲣⲕ) ἀπορεῖσθαι; AP 15 A[2] ⲁⲥⲕⲁⲁϥ ⲉϥⲁ.[†] θρίαμβος (as if -βευόμενος Lipsius); JTS 4 389 S which hearing ⲁⲛⲱ., AP 24 A[2]sim, Mor 16 74 S saw king ⲉϥⲟ.[†] ϩⲁⲡⲉϥϩⲏⲧ (var BMis 219 ⲟⲩⲟⲗⲉⲥ ⲛϩⲏⲧ), MG 25 358 B ⲛⲁϥⲟ.[†] ⲉⲧϣⲉⲛⲉ a great while (= ROC 18 60 ⲟⲟⲙⲗ), Mor 16 60 S ⲉϥⲟ.[†] ⲉϥϣⲱϣⲧ ⲉϩⲣⲁⲓ, BMis 137 S ⲕⲟⲕⲙ ⲛϣⲟⲗϩ ⲕⲟⲟ.[†]; ⲥ ⲛⲥⲁ- S, *gape after*: R 1 4 33 ⲁⲩⲱ. ⲛⲥⲁⲛⲉⲩⲉⲣⲏⲩ, ClPr 43 14 gold ⲉⲧⲕⲟ.[†] ⲛⲥⲱϥ is but dream.

—— ⲉⲃⲟⲗ SS[f]B, *gape, muse, be in trance*: Dan 4 16 B ἀπενεοῦσθαι; C 41 75 B silent & ⲁϥⲱ. ⲉⲃ. half an hour = Miss 4 472 ﺧﺐ, BAp 126 S ⲁϥⲟⲩⲱϣⲡ (*sic*) ⲉⲃ. a while = PO 22 476 ﺫ, BMis 534 S sim ⲟⲩⲱⲛ[ϣ] ⲉⲃ., ShA 2 299 S ⲉⲡⲉⲓⲟⲣⲙ ⲏ ⲉⲛⲟ.[†] ⲉⲃ. ⲉⲝⲙⲡⲉⲛⲧⲁⲡⲡⲉ ⲁⲁϥ, Z 578 S ⲡⲉⲛϩⲏⲧ ⲟ.[†] ⲉⲃ. ⲉⲣⲟϥ (*sc* subject of our thoughts), Mor 51 11 S ⲁϥⲱ. ⲉⲃ. ⲉⲧⲃⲉⲡⲉϩⲣⲁⲩⲓⲟⲥ, C 89 66 B ⲉϥⲟ.[†] ⲉⲃ. ⲉⲑⲃⲉⲡⲓϩⲟⲣⲁⲙⲁ = MG 17 318 S ϩⲓⲧⲛ-, Va 58 191 B drunkard ϥⲧⲟⲙⲧ ϥⲟ.[†] ⲉⲃ., Mor 30 6 S[f] ⲁϥϣⲱ ⲉϥⲁⲛϣⲉ ⲉⲃ. = ib 29 6 ⲟ.[†] om ⲉⲃ.

ⲟⲛϣⲥ S, *astonishment, derangement* of mind: Deu 28 28 (B ⲗⲓⲃⲓ) παραπληξία ﻭﺳﻮﺍﺱ; Sh(Besa)BMOr 8810 480 devils cause ⲧⲱⲙ ⲛϩⲏⲧ, ⲟ., ⲙⲕⲁϩ ⲛϩⲏⲧ.

ωнϩ SA[2](Ma)F, -ⲁϩ S[f]F, -ϩ A, ⲱⲱⲛϩ A[2], ⲱⲛϭ BO (as nn), ⲟⲛϭⲍ B (once), ⲟⲛ(ⲁ)ϩ SS[f], ⲁⲛϩ[†] A, -ϩ[†] S[n]A[2], ⲁⲁⲛϩ[†] A[2], ⲟⲛϭ[†] B, ⲁⲛⲁϩ[†], ⲁⲛ(ⲉ)ϩ[†] F vb **I** intr, *live*: Nu 14 38 SB, Job 42 16 SB, Lam 4 20 B (F[†]), 2 Cor 13 4 SBF, AP 48 A[2] ζῆν, Ro 7 9 SB ἀναζ.; I Cor 15 36 SB ζωοποιεῖν; PS 102 S ⲡⲧⲟⲡⲟⲥ ⲛⲛⲉⲧⲛⲁⲱ., ShA 2 253 S poisoned so that ⲛϥⲧⲙⲡⲓⲥⲧⲉⲩⲉ ⲉⲱ., DeV 2 77 B sprinkled vine ϣⲁⲛⲧⲉⲥⲱ., ib 9 B soul ⲟⲩⲁϩⲉⲙ ⲉⲱ., LDi 278 S ⲁⲩⲱ. ⲛⲕⲉⲥⲟⲡ; qual, *living, alive*: Ge 1 24 SAB, Cant 4 15 SF, Jo 4 10 SA[2]B (var & F ⲛⲱ.), I Cor 7 39 SBF-ⲁϩ ζῆν; BG 26 S ⲡⲙⲟⲟⲩ ⲉⲧⲟ. ⲛⲧⲉ ⲡⲟⲩⲟⲓⲛ, ShA 2 36 S ⲟⲩⲱⲙ ⲙⲙⲟϥ ⲉϥⲟ., AP 27 A[2] ⲛⲡⲉ ⲉⲧⲁ., Mani BerlSitz '33 85 A[2] ⲛⲡⲁϭ ⲛⲉⲩⲁⲅⲅⲉⲗⲓⲟⲛ ⲉⲧⲁ., J 68 16 S[a] without constraint ⲉⲓⲁ. ⲉⲓⲙⲁϥⲉ, ib 66 51 S sim, LCyp 13 S[f] ϯⲟⲛⲁϩ, ST 286 S ⲛⲝⲥ ⲟ. ϫⲉ ... ⲙⲡⲛⲛⲁⲩ ⲉϩⲟⲩⲣ, declaration ends ⲉⲓⲥ ⲛⲝⲥ ⲟ., Sph 10 4 F ⲃⲁⲛⲁϩ ⲛⲭⲉ-ⲡⲟⲥ, BMis 380 S ⲁⲣⲁ ⲉⲥⲟⲛϩ? = Va 63 11 B ⲥⲟⲩⲟⲝ, BSM 101 B ⲉⲧⲓ ⲉϥⲟ. ⲙⲡⲁⲧⲉϥⲙⲟⲩ.

II tr (rare): Ge 5 5 SB days ⲛⲧⲁϥⲱ. ⲙⲙⲟⲟⲩ, 3 Kg 8 40 B, Ro 6 10 SB ζ.; ShMiss 4 281 S, ROC 25 253 B all sim, KroppC 76 F ⲧⲟⲅⲱ. ⲣⲁ ⲗⲁⲙⲡⲓ (or ? for ⲉⲣⲁ).

With following preposition. ⲥ ⲉ-, *on, by*: Ge 27 40 B, Mt 4 4 SB ζ. ἐπί; ShA 1 419 S ⲉⲓⲟ.[†] ⲉⲧⲉϩⲣⲉ ⲛⲙⲟⲛⲁⲭⲟⲥ, P 131[1] 63 S ⲉϥⲟ. ⲉⲡⲣⲱⲃ ⲛⲛⲉϥϭⲓⲝ, DeV 2 193 B ⲡⲉϥⲃⲉⲭⲉ...ⲉϥⲟ. ⲉⲣⲟϥ; ⲥ ⲛ-, *during* (of time): Pro 28 16 S(var & A ⲉ-), Jer 42 7 SB, Cl 25 2 A ζ. acc; ShA 2 51 S ⲉϥⲱ. ⲛⲟⲩⲛⲟϭ ⲛⲟⲩⲟⲉⲓϣ, J 67 89 S shalt not expel her ⲉⲥⲟ.[†] *whilst she liveth*; dat: ST 253 S my children ⲙⲡⲉⲟⲩⲟⲛ ⲱ. ⲡⲁⲓ; ⲥ ϩⲛ-, ϧⲉⲛ-, *on. from*: Ming 337 S ⲉⲓⲟ.[†] ϩⲛⲡⲧⲛϭ, Va 58 125 B ⲡⲉⲕⲡⲟⲩⲃ...ⲁⲓⲱ. ⲛϧⲏⲧϥ; ⲉⲃⲟⲗ ϩⲛ-: Hab 2 4 AB = Ro 1 17 SB ζ. ἐκ.

—— nn m SAA[2]BFO, *life*: Ge 7 11 B(S ⲁϩⲉ), Ps 16 14 SBF, Is 53 8 SA(Cl)B, Jo 3 15 SA[2]BF ζωή, 2 Cor 1 8 SB ζῆν; Lu 15 12 B(S diff) βίος; Sa 4 1 S ἀθανασία; PS 291 S ⲧⲛⲡⲩⲗⲏ ⲙⲡⲱ., BG 29 S ⲡⲱ. ϣⲁⲉⲛⲉϩ (*cf* ib 31 ⲛϣⲁⲉ.), ShR 2 3 69 S ⲣ ⲣⲱⲃ ⲉⲡⲉⲕⲱ., Hor 77 O ⲛϥⲱ., TU 43 14 A ⲛϣⲏⲣⲉ ⲙⲡⲱ., ManiH 61 A[2] ⲧⲁϣⲉⲁⲓϣ ⲙⲡⲱ., AP 38 A[2] ⲁϥϯ ⲙⲡⲱⲱ., MR 5 33 F may Lord ⲧⲁⲭⲣⲁ ⲡⲉϩⲟⲩ ⲙⲡⲉⲕⲱ., BSM 46 B ϣⲉ ⲡⲱ. ⲙⲡⲁⲟⲥ = BMis 394 S ⲡⲟⲩϫⲁⲓ; Lant 53 S ⲱ. ⲥⲓ ⲙⲙⲟϥ ϩⲙⲡⲣⲁϣⲉ...ⲛⲧⲉⲕⲕⲗⲏⲥⲓⲁ...ⲡⲁⲉⲓⲟⲧⲉ ⲉⲧⲟⲩⲁⲁⲃ, ib 80 sim, ib 67 ⲱ. ⲥⲓ (ⲙ)ⲙⲟⲟⲩ ϩⲙⲡⲣⲁϣⲉ...ⲙⲡⲉⲭⲥ (here scribe's name), ib 61 ⲱ. ϯ ⲕⲁⲣⲡⲟⲥ ⲙⲡⲛⲉ ⲛϩⲏⲧϥ ϩⲙⲡⲣ....ⲡⲉⲛⲙⲁⲓⲡⲉ ⲛⲕⲗⲏⲣⲓⲕⲟⲥ, where ⲱ.? vocat, ⲥⲓ, ϯ imperat (varr of this ib 2 13, 15 32); as adj: Sa 15 11 S ζωτικός, Ap 7 17 SB ζωῆς; BSM 96 B ⲡⲓⲥⲃⲱⲟⲩⲓ ⲡⲱ.

ⲙⲁ ⲡⲱ. B, *place of life*: Mus 46 209 = 216 n Thou art ⲡⲓⲙ. ﻭﺍﺿﻊ ﻟﻠﺤﻴﺎﺓ.

ϭⲓⲛ-, ϫⲓⲛⲱ. SBF, *way, means of life*: Deu 16 3 B (var & S ⲱ.), Ps 62 3 SB ζωή; Job 10 5 B(S ⲁϩⲉ), Si 38 21 S, MG 25 1 B ⲡⲓϫ. of Abba Paul βίος, ib 14 ἐμβίωσις, Ac 26 4 B(S ⲃⲓⲟⲥ) βίωσις; Mor 38 102 S gave servants ⲧⲉⲩϭ., PO 2 156 S ⲭⲣⲏⲙⲁ...ⲉⲧⲉⲛϭ., Pcod 40 SF ⲧⲉⲕϭ., BIF 13 119 S ϭ. ⲛⲁⲅⲅⲉⲗⲓⲕⲟⲛ, Va 58 65 B ⲡⲓⲃⲓⲟⲥ ⲛⲉⲙϯϫ. of saint.

ⲟ ⲛⲟⲛϩ (*sic*) S: R 1 2 60 fool thinks none knoweth him ⲛϥⲥⲟⲟⲩⲛ ⲁⲛ ϫⲉϥⲟ ⲛⲟ. ⲛⲟⲉ ⲛⲟⲩⲧⲣⲁⲡⲉⲧⲏⲥ (δραπέτης). Prob l ϥⲟⲩⲟⲛϩ.

ⲣⲉϥϯ ⲱ. SB, *life-giver*: BG 25 S[†], GMir 304 S ⲡⲣⲉϥϯ ⲙⲡⲱ. of those in straits; 'adj: R 1 1 79 S ϣⲉ ⲛⲣ., Cat 102 B ⲉⲡⲧⲟⲗⲏ ⲛⲣ.

ϣⲫⲏⲣ ⲛⲱ. B, *who lives with* another: Bel 2 συμβιωτής, Ex 22 18 ⲉⲣ ϣ. (S ⲧⲁⲛϩⲟ) περιβιοῦν.

In name: ⲉⲃⲱⲛϩ(BM 268, C 89 52), -ⲛⲭ(CO 44), ⲁⲃⲱ. (BM 593) Ἐπώνυχος, Ἐφ. (Preisigke).

ⲁⲛϩ-, ⲁⲛϣⲧⲏⲩ (? this word) *v* ⲧⲏⲩ.

V ⲁⲛⲁϩ, ⲧⲁⲛϩⲟ.

ωнϭ *v* ⲱⲛⲧ.

ωπ *SAA²BF*, ωпε *S*(с ε- intr), εп- *SBF*, ϩεп- *A*
(as nn), ∧п-*Sf*, ωп-*A*, оп⸗*SB*, ∧п⸗*SAF*, нп†*SA²BF*,
нпε† *S* vb **I** intr (rare), *count, esteem*: Jer 40 13 *B*(*S*
tr)ἀριθμεῖν; Mani 1 *A²* оγмαϣε (ε)сωп пτε пεϥвн-
γε; qual: Job 36 27 *SB*, Lu 12 7 *SB* ἀρ.; Nu
2 2 *S*(var снп, *B* ⳉεпτ) ἔχεσθαι; BG 121 *S* поγоε-
ειϣ ετнп, ST 163 *S* book's price εмпεϥϣααρ (vellum or ? binding) нп ∧п.

II tr: Ge 15 5 *S*(*B* ϭι нпι), Pro 8 21 *S*(*A* пϭεп- *B*
do), Is 33 18 *SBF* ἀρ., Ps 21 18 *B*(*S* с εвоλ) ἐξαρ.;
Lev 17 4 *B*(*S* с ε-), Lam 4 2 *BF*(*S* топтп), MG 25
214 *B* εκωп ∧п мпϣωϣ λογίζειν, Ro 5 13 *SB* ἐλλο-
γεῖν, R 1 4 72 *S* †ωп ∧п мпειωпε λόγος εἶναι dat,
1 Tim 5 9 *S*(*B* diff) καταλέγειν; Z 298 *S* мпропк
μετρεῖν, Ps 107 7 *S*(*B* ϣι) ἐκμ.; Ac 19 19 *S*(*B* ϭι
ωп) συμψηφίζειν; R 1 5 16 *S* despiseth word пϥωп
ммоϥ ∧п, Mor 31 32 *S* ∧γκ∧∧ϥ εвоλ ετмопϥ, Z
354 *S* птεмопк *not esteeming self*, EW 185 *B* whore
grown old птоγкнп εγωп ммос, BMis 392 *S* ∧ϥωп
нппоγⲃ = BSM 44 *B*.

With ⲝε-: Ps 118 119 *SB*, Is 53 4 *S*(*B* ∧окмεк),
Ro 3 28 *B*(*S* diff) λογ.; Job 30 1 *S*(*B* ⳉω), Phil 3 8
SB ἡγεῖσθαι; Mt 5 17 *S*(*B* мεγι) νομίζειν; 2 Kg 13
5 *S* опс ⲝεεкϣωпε προσποιεῖν ἐνοχλεῖσθαι; BHom
7 *S* ϥωп...ⲝεоγεⲃиннпε ταλανίζειν; ShC 42 209 *S*
∧ιопϥ ⲝεоγпоннроппε, DeV 2 165 *B* ∧ιопс ⲝεоγ-
⳨ⲓⲕⲁⲓⲟⲡⲡⲉ, Mor 53 36 *S* ειопт ⲝεεкнⲗⲟⲅⲱⲣ п∧ι
пкωрт = TstAb 233 *B* ⲝεⳉⲁⲥ εκε-, BM 220 *S* опс
ⲝε∧пεⳉ∧п∧∧ιос...р поⲃε, Mor 50 18 *S* опс ⲝε-
∧сⳉε (sc pillar) *supposing it fell*, Miss 8 183 *Sf* ∧ι∧п
п∧ι тнроγ ⲝεрпосεпε, Wess 15 150 *S* εп тετроϥн
...ⲝεоγ∧∧γтε; with пⲟⲉ, мⲫ⳿ⲣⲏ† п-: Ps 43
22 *SB*, Is 40 15 *B*(*S* топ. ε-) λογ. ὡς; Job 41 22 *S*
(*B* diff) ἡγ. ὥσπερ; PS 189 *S* пк∧ϩ п∧ωп...пⲟⲉ м-
поγоειп, AM 208 *B* ωп ммωоγ мⲫ. прⲁпⲗⲉⲃⳡ
(cf Phil 3 8); with ⳉⲱⲥ (ὡς): Is 40 17 *S*(*B†* ε-)
λογ. εἰς, Dan 4 32 *B* λογ. ὡς; Job 19 11 *S*(*B* ⳉω
птεп-)ἡγ. ὥσπ.; PS 187 *S* εп пεικосмос ⳉⲱⲥ к∧кε,
ShA 2 135 *S* ∧п⳨ⲥ опϥ ⳉⲱⲥ ⳉ∧ϣор, Mor 44 25 *S*
опεп ⳉⲱⲥ εп† оγⲃεппоⲗⲟⲥ.

With following preposition.

—— ε- *SAA²BF*, *count to*, intr: Job 34 37 *SB*
λογ. ἐπί; Deu 24 13 *S*(*B* ϣωпι п-) εἶναι dat, Is
14 23 *S*(*B* ϣ. ε-) εἰ. εἰς; Nu 15 15 *S*(*B* оγωⳉ ε-)
προσκεῖσθαι ἐν, Lev 25 6 *S* п. πρός; Ac 17 4 *B*(*S*
оγ. ε-) προσκληροῦσθαι dat; PS 340 *S* ε∧сωп εп∧-
поγоειп, ShA 2 289 *S* at Last Day пετп∧ωп εп-
тωⳉ...επεсоγп, Mani 2 *A²* εϥп∧ωп ∧тт∧ιε пик-
соγс, AZ 26 123 *S* ∧ϥωпε εп∧ριⲑмос, Worr 308
S ∧ϥωпε ετεпн (l нпε), C 43 227 *B* ∧сωп ετнпι
of martyrs, *ib* 116 v р∧оγϣ с ε-; qual, *belonging, related to*: Sa 15 2 *S* λογ. dat; Ge 32 17 *S*(*B*
ⲫ∧-) εἶναι gen; Z 272 *S* ετнп ετс∧рⲝ ἰδιότης gen;

Aeg 222 *S* ετнп εроϥ διαφέρειν dat; BHom 1 *S*
angel ετнп εпк∧ϩ ἐπίγειος; Ps 118 63 *S*(*B* ϣⲫнр
п-) μέτοχος εἰ.; Ex 16 21 *S*(*B* diff) καθήκειν dat;
Lev 25 25 *S*(*B* ⳉнϥ ε-) ἀγχιστεύειν dat; 1 Kg 14 21
S ὁ μετά, Eccl 7 13 *S*(*F* ϩ∧-) ὁ παρά, Miss 8 127 *S*
letter ετнп...εккριⲗⲗос παρά, Lu 22 37 *S*(*B* diff) ὁ
περί; 2 Kg 2 15 *S*, Ez 41 9 *SB* gen; PS 164 *S* ετнп
επт∧ко, ShA 1 369 *S* each bone joined εпετнп ε-
роϥ, ShC 42 109 *S* εϥнп επоⲗⲓс сιⳉн, Ryl 62 2 *S*
пⳉιос ετнп εпк∧ϩ, Miss 4 668 *S* пεпнп επεпεрнγ
к∧т∧ тεпсγттεпι∧, J 89 30 *S* sick child нп επετ-
мооγт, Kr 152 *S* п∧нрп пⳉωⲗε нп εрооγ (sc to
that due as wage), ManiBerlSitz '33 Taf 1 *A²* пϭ∧м
тнроγ ετнп ∧пкосмос, C 43 163 *B* п∧ϣоⲃι εϥнп
εрок, BIF 22 108 *F* ∧пнп εϥ†; vbal *SA²*, *ought,
be fit to*: Lu 22 7 (*B* сϣε ε-) δεῖ inf, ViSitz 172 4 13
сεнп εⳉ∧рεⳉ εрооγ δέον; Bor 253 154 тнпп εειμε
ὀφείλειν; R 2 2 42 снп εϣωпε χρή; PS 12 εϥнп
εⳉιтϥ (soul) *which it (sc body) should receive*, Mani
2 *A²* εϥнп εп ∧τεπεϥⳉнт мк∧ⳉ, ShWess 18 6 мн
птнпп ∧п εϣωп εроп птεсвω, ShR 2 3 72 птнпε
∧п εⳉι, Pcod 18 εпнп εр оγ?, Bor 311 99 тнпε εр
п∧ι; tr, *ascribe to, reckon as*: Sa 3 2 *S* λογίζεσθαι
nom, Ge 15 6 *S*(*B* п-) λ. dat, Lev 25 31 *SB* λ. πρός,
Ps 31 2 *SA*(Cl)*B* λ. gen (var dat), Is 32 15 *SBF*, Lam
4 2 *B*(*S* топтп ε-) λ. εἰς, Lev 27 18 *SB* προσλ. dat,
Philem 18 *SB* ἐλλογ. dat; Ja 1 2 *S*(*B* diff) ἡγ. acc;
Job 3 6 *S*(*B* l ?ϭι нпι) ἀριθ. εἰς; Ac 7 60 *SB* ἱστάναι
dat; Ex 22 2 *B*(*S* diff) εἶναι dat; PS 302 *S* мεγεп
поⲃε εрос, ShA 2 247 *S* old times ειωп ετεγϣι,
present επεϩооγ, Pcod 21 *S* our good words опоγ
εппε (var похоγ пс∧-), BMis 227 *S* кωп ппεγϣ∧-
ⲝε εрпϣⲃω, Ryl 352 *S* ⳉι...п∧рϣⲓп пт∧поγ εрок
псоγо, C 43 76 *B* εϥεопк επⳉωрос of martyrs,
Stegemann 63 *F* ∧пϥ ετϣειⲗι мпε⳨ⲥ, ST 170 *S*
certain moneys ϣ∧ιопоγ εрок, Kr 136 *F* (п)пεпϣ
εп посει (ппосоп) εⲗ∧ϥ; εⳉоγп ε-, *count in, include*: CaiEuch 504 *B* опτεп εⳃ. εϥмετоγ∧ι συνάπτειν εἰς; Br 108 *S* ∧γωп εⳉ. επεкⲗнрос, PS 371
S мпϣ∧ пωп εⳉ. ετмптεро, AM 330 *B* опк εⳃ.
επⳉорос.

—— ∧рп- *A²*, *ascribe to*: Mani Berl Sitz '33 89
call & obedience ετнп ∧рпоγмнт пс∧п.

—— εⳉп- *S*, meaning?: Ryl 298 сⳉ∧ι пεкпоειμ
(cf BM 1116) п∧ι т∧ωп εⳉоϥ.

—— ∧п- *SAB*, *number with*: Is 53 12 *SA*(Cl)*B*
λογ. ἐν, Lu 22 37 *SB* λ. μετά, 2 Tim 4 16 *B*(*S* ε-) λ.
dat, Is 14 10 *B*(*S* ϩп-) κατ∧λ. ἐν, Ps 87 4 *SB* προσλ.
μ.; Sa 7 8 *S* ἐν συγκρίσει ἡγ.; Cai Euch 516 *B* опоγ
пεмпεкпιстос συναρ. μ.; Ac 1 26 *SB* συγκαταψηφ.
μ.; EstE 13† *S* κοινωνός; ShC 73 6 *S* мппс∧опϥ
мптⲗптоγε, Z 293 *S* εрϣ∧поγτ∧∧пϥ ωп (sic MS)
пмм∧ϥ a long while, AM 241 *B* опт пεмпεк⳪ п∧-

λογ, PS 210 *S* πτμωπ μπρωμε *being of no account with men*; εϥογπ μπ- *S*: Bodl(P) f 12 οπϥ εϥ. μπ ιεсοογ.

—— π- *SSᶠA²B* dat: Ge 31 15 *B*(*S* щωπε παϥρπ-), Ps 105 31 *B*(*S* e-), Ro 4 22 *B*(*SF* e-) λογ. dat; Lev 15 28 *S*(*B* ϭι ιπι) ἐξαρ. dat; WTh 140 *S* οπс πακ ϫe-, C 86 194 *B* αϥωπ πτεϥщερι παϥ πεϥιαι, *ib* 202 sim (*cf* с πса-, щπ ωπ); *as, for*: Ac 26 2 *S*(*B* μεϫι) ἡγ. acc; Is 5 20 *S*(*F* ϫe-, *B* diff) τιθέ- ναι; Nu 35 4† *S*(*B* κωϯ e-) συγκυρεῖν gen; R 1 1 45 *S* words εϥηπ ιιποβε εἶναι; AZ 21 141 *S* οπϥ πταϥε; Mor 30 10 *Sᶠ* απογ ρπιλαογ = *ib* 29 9 *S* εϥλ. vbal: R 1 4 29 *S* щαιηπ πϭοιλε ερооγ (*sc* monasteries) *debere*, Pcod 5 *S* τπηπ πειμε, Mani H 59 *A²* πεϥηπ πιεϥπε. *Cf* с e- vbal.

—— πса- *S*, *count, reckon*: Tob 9 4 ἀριθ. acc; Wess 11 168 ωπ πсαμμιλιоπ μετρεῖν; ViK 9561 εϥωπ πсαπηϥ πταϭϭε of his feet (var BM 363 117 π-) *numerare*; *B*, *be betrothed* с π- of man: Mt 1 18 (*S* do) μνηστεύεσθαι, Ex 22 16(*S* щπ τοοτ϶)neg αμ.; Aeg 3 Joseph εταϥωπ πсαταμαγ παϥ εγϭιμι.

—— πτπ- *SB*, *count with, for*: Is 13 17 *B*(*S* ωπ tr) λογ., Sa 2 16 *SB* λ. dat; Job 14 5 *SB* ἀριθμητὸς παρά; *ib* 41 18 *S*(*B* no vb) ἡγ.; Bor 226 *S* miser επ λααγ πρωμε πτοοτϥ, DeV 2 113 *B* hairs all ηπ π τοτϥ, J 86 28 *S* πταοπϥ πτοот...ϫεαϥμογ.

—— ϩπ-, ϧεπ- *SB*, *in, among*: Si 7 16 *S* πρосλογ. ἐν; Ro 1 6 *S*(*B* no vb) εἶναι ἐν; RNC 78 *S* πταωπ ϩητμητε ππεκсωτπ; ϩραι ϩπ-: Acl 17 *SB* καταρ. ἐν.

—— ϩιϫεπ- *F*, meaning?: BM 653 ακταμαι ετ βηηκεραμμι (κεράμιον) πϩαλωμ αιωπ ϩιϫωβ πεκ (*sic* l). *Cf* с εϫπ-.

—— ϫιπ- *S*, *from*: Lev 23 15 (*B* ϭι π.) ἀρ. ἀπό; Kr 48 ερ]ετμεсε επ ϫιπεсογμπτψιс.

With following adverb.

—— εβολ *S* = ἐξ-: Ps 21 17(*B* om εβ.)ἐξαρ.; BM Add 31290 318 (Paschal Letter) τιπαωπ εβ. πτκε сαϣϥε πρεββολαс (*cf* BM 173 216 τιπαϩωτр, Ryl Suppl 48 επωπ ϫε[, PG 26 1366 *numerantes*, 1376 *adjungentes*, 1403 *supputantes*).

—— nn m *SB*, *reckoning*: Lu 1 9 *B*(*S* diff) λαγ χάνειν; *ib* 16 2 *SB* λόγος, 1 Cor 16 2 *B*(*S* огωϭс) λογία; P 129¹⁴ 97 *S* πϩαιϫεсιс μπωπ ἀριθμητικός; PS 30 *S* πεϥωπ ϫιπμπεογоειϣ επταιπоопог, Br 248 *S* παριθμос π πωπ, ShC 42 71 *S* we redeemed (captives) μπωπ πϥμε πτβα (πϥολπτ) *at rate of*, Ryl 72 352 *S* κατα πωπ μπεϥχροпос, CA 100 *S* πεϥωπ (*sc* of offering) παϥϣωπε ϩπτεκκλнсια, BSM 10 *B* πθоогπε πωπ μπτηрϥ (Mor 27 10 *Sᶠ* diff).

ατωπ *SB*, *unesteemed*: Mor 40 50 *S* πεϥειρε μ μоог πα.= MG 25 276 *B* ατεμπϣα, MG 25 32 *B* οι πατопκ *in all things*; μπτατ.: *ib* 333 *B* ϯ μετ ατопκ & silence, Mor 37 109 *S* μπτατопϥ.

р ωπ *S*, *make reckoning, esteem*: BM 1152 (е)щωπε τεκep ωπ ταταλоϥ...ϫоогϥ παι.

ϯ ωπ *SBF*, *give account*: Dan 6 2 *B* λόγον ἀποδι δόναι; Ac 26 10 *B*(*S* ϯ ψηϕос) ψῆ. καταϕέρειν; R 1 3 18 *S* bishop ϯ ππωπ of church once a year, BIF 14 185 *S* king ϯ μπωπ ππμαρτγрос, Kr 164 *F* απτι πωπ μπχрос (χρέος ?).

щπ ωπ *AA²*, *promise*: Mani 1 *A²* πεταιϣ. μ μ[αϥ]; *as nn A*: Pro 7 14(*S* ερнτ, *B* = Gk)εὐχή, *ib* 20 19 (*S* do) εὔχεσθαι; Mal 3 8 (*B* diff) ἐπιδεκτός.

ϭι ωπ *SA²B*, *take reckoning, calculate*: Mun 131 *S* scribe ϣαϥϭι πωπ for king; с e-: BHom 141 *S* whilst praying πεκϩнт ϭι ωπ επεκκλнсε ἀριθμεῖν, R 1 2 36 *S* sim (var JA '75 5 258 π-), Va 57 106 *B* ϥ. επιαρiθμос of 9 months; с π- gen: Lev 25 27 *B*(*S* ωπ e-) συλλογίζειν, Lu 14 28 *SB* ψηϕίζειν; с μπ-: Lev 25 50 *B*(*S* ωπ μπ-) συλλ. πρός, Job 14 3 *B*(*S* ϭι рооγϣ π-) λόγον ποιεῖν gen, Mt 18 23 *SB* λ. συναίр. μετά; Si prol *S* συγγνώμην ἔχειν; BMis 121 *S* ϭι ωπ μπταμμτϭωβ, Pcod 10 *S* сεπαϫι λоγос πμμαϥ? сεπαϭι ωπ πμμαϥ αι, C 43 31 *B* ϭι ωπ πεμαπ εθβε-, Mani 1 *A²* μπωрϫι ωπ πεμαπ, RE 9 157 *S* ϭι ωπ πμμαι ϩαπαι; μετϥ. *B*, *reckon ing*: K 141 ϯμ. اكياب : рεϥϥ. *B*, *accountant*: *ib* 108 حساب, *v* соксек.

ϩι ωπ *B*, *make reckoning*: DeV 1 100 εγогωϣ εϩ. πεμαι for sins; *cast lot*: Ps 21 19 (*S* επιμ), Mt 27 35 (*S* πεϫ κλнрос) κλ. βάλλειν.

рεϥωπ *S*, *counter*: ShMun 102 wizards, рεϥκα огпог, р. ππсiог *astrologers*.

ϭιπ-, ϫιπωπ *SB*, *reckoning, calculation*: BMar 14 *S* κατα τϭ. of Romans, K 66 *B* ϯϫ. μμετрωμεос ϫμ.

ηπε *SAA²F*, ηπe *SF*, ηπι *BF* nn f, *number*: Deu 28 62 *SB*, Ps 38 5 *SB*, Si 26 1 *S* ηπ., *ib* 42 7 ηπε, Is 34 16 *SBF*, Ap 5 11 *SB* ἀριθμός; Ge 48 16 *S*(*B* α ϣαι) πλῆθος; 4 Kg 12 4 *S* ηπ. συντίμησις; Job 28 25 *S*(*B* θоοϣ) μέτρον, Is 22 18 *S* neg (*B* ατϯ ϣι) ἀμέ τρητος; Nah 2 9 *A*(*B* αγрнϫϥ) πέρας; Mt 15 33 *B* (*S* αϣнι) τοσοῦτος; Ps 16 14 *B* κогϫι ηπ. (*S* om) ὀλίγος, Is 41 14 *B* sim (*S* соβκ) ὀλίγοστός; PS 86 *S* τη. μπаогоειϣ, *ib* 202 *S* огϣι εμπ η. εроϥ, Miss 4 685 *S* πεϥо πϥог ϩπτεγη., C 43 28 *B* sim, Dan Vis 14 47 *B* his name παιрι π[overline: χ̅ϥ̅?] ηπ., BSM 17 *B* тогη. ιρι πρπε, Hall 32 *S* μπ(т)ϣμηπ ηηπε (*sic*) *18 in all*, Z 586 *S* Pallas is virgin κατα τεγη., AP 44 *A²* ατμτреπ. ϣωπε μμаг, DeV 1 124 *B* μμоп η. τοι εрoог.

ατηπε *SAB*, *numberless*: Pro 7 26 *SAB* ἀναρίθ μητος; ShA 2 50 *S* ϩεπα. πε πεπταϥααϥ πϫαϭε, PMich 603 *S* πεϥταμiоп εγα. πε; Br 243 *S* ог μηηϣе πατϯ η. εроог.

ϫι, ϭι η. *SBF*, *take number, count*: Ge 41 49 *B*(*S*

ωπ), Pro 8 21 *B(SA* do), Ap 7 9 *BF(S* do), ἀριθμεῖν, Ps 138 18 *B(S* do) ἐξαρ., Nu 14 29 *SB* καταρ.; Hos 1 10 *B* ἐκμετρεῖν; Jer 22 19 *B* συμψηφίζειν; ShCl Pr 44 18 *S* none can write ογⲁ ⲝ. ⲙⲙⲟⲩ, MG 25 375 *B* eϭ. ⲛⲛⲁⲓ, Ryl 72 358 *S* ⲡⲧⲉⲣⲉϥⲁⲣⲁⲱ ⲭⲓ ⲧⲏ. ⲡⲓϣⲏⲣⲉ ⲙⲡⲓⲏⲗ ⲙⲛⲧⲏⲡⲉ (sic) ⲛⲛⲧⲱϩⲉ; ⲁⲧⲝ., ϭ., *countless*: MG 25 240 *B* ϩⲁⲡⲁ. ⲙⲙⲟⲩ μὴ ἀριθμῷ ὑποβάλλεσθαι; BHom 97 *S* ογⲁ. ⲙⲙⲟϥ, AM 26 *B* ογⲙⲛϣ ⲡⲁ. ⲙⲙⲟⲩ; ⲣⲉϥⲭ. *S, accountant*: C 99 99 Papnoute ⲡⲣ. ⲡⲧⲕⲟⲓⲛⲱⲛⲓⲁ = Va ar 172 98 مدبّر = MG 17 649 خديم (*cf* C 89 73).

ⲁⲡⲥ, ⲏⲡⲥ *v* ⲁⲡⲥ, adding Mani H 22 *A²* ϩⲡⲏ. ⲙⲡⲁⲣⲑⲉⲛⲟⲥ.

ⲟⲡⲥ *S* nn, *reckoning*: RAC 100 = RE 14 31 ⲙⲛ ϩⲱⲃ ⲙⲛ ⲟ. ⲧⲏⲓ ⲛⲉⲙⲁⲕ (*cf* ⲙⲛⲧⲏⲓ ϩⲱⲃ ⲛⲙ-).

ⲱⲓⲡⲓ *B v* ⲟⲉⲓⲛⲉ.

ⲱⲡⲓϣ *F* nn m, *broad river-bed* (so Ar, *v* Quatremère *Rech* 214): Montp 207 among names of rooms هي لفظة بشمورية تفسيرها (اسما قلالي ابو. رغير دلك c&) ⲡⲓⲱ. الفجرة.

ωρ(ε)ϩ *S*, ωⲣϥ *SB*, ωⲣⲃⲉ *Sᵃ A*, ⲉⲣⲃ- *S*, ⲉⲣϥ- *B*, ⲁⲣⲉϥ- *F*, ⲟⲣϩ *S*, ⲟⲣϥ *SB*, ⲁⲣϩ *SfA*, ⲟⲣϩ† *S*, ⲁⲣϩ† *SA²*, ⲟⲣϥ† *SB*, ⲁⲣϩⲉ† *A* vb **I** intr, *be enclosed, apart, quiet*: Is 7 4 *B(S* ⲕⲁ ⲣⲟ), C 89 26 *B* ογⲙⲁ ⲡⲧⲉⲱ. therein, MG 25 217 *B* ϯογⲱϣ ⲉⲱ. ἡσυχάζειν, Cai Euch 597 *B* ⲃⲓⲟⲥ ⲉϥϩⲟⲣⲱⲟⲩ ⲉⲱ. (*l* o.†) ἡσύχιος, C 89 43 *B* ⲙⲁ ⲉϩⲟ.† = Miss 4 524 *S* ⲥϭⲣⲁϩⲧ ἥσυχος, *ib* 111 *B* go to ογⲙⲁ ⲉϩⲟ.† ἀναχωρεῖν σεαυτόν; Zech 11 2† *A(B* diff) σύμφυτος *munitus*; 1 Tim 2 9 *B(S* ⲉϭ.) κόσμιος; Va 66 305 *B* ⲛⲟⲙⲟⲥ ⲉϩⲟ.† βίος ἥμερος; C 89 34 *B* ογⲙⲁ ⲉϩⲟ.† ϩⲉⲛⲡⲉϩⲛⲓ = MG 17 387 منفرد; ROC 27 152 *B* desert place ⲛⲧⲁⲱ. ⲛⲏⲓ ⲙⲙⲁⲩ, JAOS 48 148 *S* ⲙⲡⲣⲓ ⲧⲟⲟⲧⲕ ⲉⲭⲓⲣⲱⲙⲉ ⲉϥⲁ.† ογⲇⲉ ⲉϥⲣⲏϣ, HL 105 *B* ⲡⲟγⲁⲓ ⲡⲟγⲁⲓ ⲟ.† ϩⲁⲣⲓ ϩⲁⲣⲟϥ, Rec 6 170 *B* dwell alone ⲡⲧⲉⲕⲱ. & be anchorite = BMar 207 *S* ⲉⲥⲩⲭⲁⲍⲉ, PO 14 324 *B* ⲉϩⲟ.† ϩⲉⲛⲡⲉϥⲗⲟⲅⲓⲥⲙⲟⲥ.

II tr, *restrict, surround*, refl *B*: PO 14 340 cave ⲉϩⲟ. ⲙⲙⲟϥ ⲡⲃⲏⲛⲧϥ, Va 58 131 my evil thoughts ω. ⲙⲙⲟⲟⲩ ⲁⲛ; not refl *S*: BM 1114 give thy orders ⲙⲡⲁⲧⲉⲡⲙⲟⲟⲩ ⲟⲣⲃⲟϥ (*quid?*), for 6th ell is already completed (? reached).

With following preposition.

—— ⲉ- *SB* (once), *restrict for, as to*: 2 Cor 8 20 *B* (*S* ⲥⲓϭⲉ) στέλλειν; ViK 9798 111 ⲉⲧⲱ. ⲉⲣⲟϥ ⲙⲡⲙⲟⲟⲩ *restricting water for it* & no rain falling shall not tree wither?; as obj: Z 320 demons ⲟⲣⲃ (*l?* ω.) ⲉⲣⲟϥ ⲉⲩⲁⲙⲁϩⲧⲉ ⲙⲙⲟϥ on all sides συνέχειν; ShA 1 240 ω. ⲉⲣⲟⲟⲩ (waters)...ⲁⲙⲁϩⲧⲉ ⲙⲙⲟⲟⲩ, BMOr 8811 110 ω. ⲉⲣⲟⲟⲩ (trees) ⲛⲅⲉⲛⲭⲟ *surround*, cf *ib* ⲙⲁⲩⲱ. ⲛⲅⲉⲛⲭⲟ ⲉⲣⲟⲟⲩ, Mor 46 56 ⲉⲣⲉⲡϩⲓⲣⲁⲗ ω.

ⲉⲣⲟϥ ⲉϥⲛⲟⲩⲭ ⲙⲙⲟϥ ⲉⲃⲟⲗ; ⲉϩⲣⲏⲓ ⲉ- *B, down into*: MartIgn 868 ⲁϥⲱ. ⲉϭ. ⲉογⲡⲓⲑⲟⲥ = R 1 4 56 *S* ⲉϩⲟγⲛ ⲉ-.

—— ⲉⲃⲟⲗ ϩⲁ- *B, be secluded from*: ROC 27 153 ω. ⲉⲃ. ϩⲁⲡⲓⲕⲟⲥⲙⲟⲥ.

—— ⲥⲁⲃⲟⲗ ⲛ- *B, exclude from*: 2 Thes 3 6 (*S* ⲥⲟⲟⲣⲉ ⲉⲃⲟⲗ) στέλ. ἀπό.

With following adverb.

—— ⲉⲡⲁϩⲟⲩ *S, reject*: R 1 3 101 Baptist slain on 1st Thoth, but Encomium on 2d, ⲉϥω. ⲙⲡⲣⲟγⲙⲓⲥⲉ ⲡⲏⲣⲱⲇⲏⲥ ⲉⲡ. (Mt 14 6).

—— ⲉϩⲟγⲛ *SAA²BF, shut in, intr*: Ez 4 3† *SB* ἐν συγκλεισμῷ εἶναι; *ib* 6 12† *SB* περιέχεσθαι; Sh BM 198 1 *S* sheep o.† ⲉϩ. ϩⲛⲧϣⲁⲓⲣⲉ, C 41 55 *B* ⲉⲡⲕⲗⲓⲥⲧⲟⲥ ⲉϥⲟ.† ⲉϭ. ϩⲉⲛⲡϣⲁϩⲉ, Blake 256 *S* valley ⲉϥⲟ.† ⲉϩ....ⲛⲉⲙⲡⲉⲧⲣⲁ *vallari*, Z 583 *S* ϥⲟ.† ⲉϩ. ϩⲱⲥ ⲁⲥⲕⲏⲧⲏⲥ, *ib* ϩⲱⲥ ⲙⲟⲛⲁⲭⲟⲥ, AP 23 *A²* ϥⲁ. [ⲁϩⲟγⲛ; tr: 1 Kg 23 20 *S* κλείειν, 2 Kg 18 28 *S* ἀποκλ., Jer 21 9 *S(B* ⲧⲁⲕⲧⲟ) συγκλ., Mic 7 17 *SA(B* ⲧⲁⲧϩⲟ) συγκλεισμός; *ib* 5 1 *A(B* ϣⲑⲁⲙ ⲉϩⲣⲉⲡ-) ἐμφράσσειν; Lam 3 5 *S(B* ⲕⲱϯ) κυκλοῦν; BHom 95 *S* ω. ⲉϩ. ⲙⲡⲁⲙⲁϩⲧⲉ περιγράφειν; Br 276 *S* ⲉϥⲟ ⲛⲧⲟϣ ⲡⲁⲩ ⲉϥⲟ. ⲙⲙⲟⲟⲩ ⲉϩ., R 1 1 65 *S* city ⲉⲣⲉⲟγⲣⲣⲟ ⲡⲁⲕⲱⲧⲉ ⲉⲣⲟⲥ ⲛϥⲟⲣⲃⲉⲥ ⲉϩ., ShBM 204 77 *S* hunter ω. ⲉϩ. his prey, DeV 2 213 *B* can he not ⲟⲣϥϥ ⲉϭ. *restrict self?*, Mor 30 40 *F* ϣⲁⲡⲧⲉϥⲁⲣⲉϥ ⲧϭⲛⲧϥ (*l* ⲧⲥⲉ.) ⲉϩ. of τόπος = BMis 265 *Sᵃ* ⲱⲃⲣⲉⲓ (*sic, l* ⲱⲣⲃⲉ) ⲉϩ., Ryl 177 *S* cultivator's contract ⲧⲁⲱ. ⲡⲉⲩⲭⲟ ⲉϩ.; ⲉϩ., ⲉϭ. ⲉ- *SB, in to*, qual: Gu 93 *S* Lazarus o. ⲉϩ. ⲉⲩⲧⲁⲫⲟⲥ, DeV 1 90 *B* o. ⲉϭ. ⲉⲧⲉϥⲣⲓ never coming forth; tr: Jer 21 4 *S(B* ϣⲟ. ⲉⲣⲉⲡ-) συγκλ.; Ez 12 13 *B(S* ⲱⲧⲡ ⲉϩ.)περιοχή; EpApp 1 55 *S* ⲙⲉⲩ ⲉϣ ⲟⲣⲃⲉϥ ⲉϩ. ⲉⲩⲙⲁ ⲡⲟϥⲱⲧ, GFr 307 *S* ⲟⲣⲃⲟϥ ⲉϩ. ⲉⲧⲉⲕϣⲁⲓⲣⲉ, C 99 3 *S* ⲡⲙⲁ ⲉⲛⲧⲁϥⲟⲣⲃⲉϥ ⲉϩ. ⲉⲩⲥⲟⲟϩⲥ, Va 61 100 *B* ⲟⲣϥⲉϥ ⲉϭ. ⲉⲡⲟγϣⲡⲏⲟⲩ; as nn m *SB, surrounding, frame, siege*: Ez 4 8 *B(S* ⲱⲧⲡ ⲉϩ.) συγκλεισμός; ClPr 54 1 *S* ⲡⲱ. ⲉϩ. of walls = EW 153 *B* περιβολή; Br 227 *S* ⲡⲱ. ⲉϩ. ⲙⲡⲉϥϩⲟ (cf *ib* ⲛⲕⲱⲧⲉ), ShC 42 196 *S* ⲧⲭⲟ ⲙⲡⲱ. ⲉϩ., Mor 50 48 *S* his inwards gushed forth leaving only ⲡⲱ. ⲉϩ. of bones & skin, Z 580 *S* ⲡⲱ. ⲉϩ. ⲡⲧⲙⲉⲭⲁⲡⲏ *circuit of mill*, ROC 7 140 *S* monk desires ⲡⲱ. ⲉϩ. *seclusion*, K 385 *B* تسمير *nailing in*; ⲙⲁ ⲡⲟⲣϥ (*l* ω.) ⲉϭ. *B*: Ez 27 9 (*S* ⲡⲱⲧⲡ ⲉϩ.) δυσμή (*l? S* ϩⲱⲧⲡ, whence *B*, or reading δεσμά Möhle). *V* also ⲁⲧⲟⲣϩ.

—— nn m *B, seclusion, quietude*: Va 66 290 ⲡϣⲁϥⲉ ⲛⲉⲙⲡⲓⲱ. ἡσυχία; *ib* 63 90 ⲡⲓⲱ. ⲡⲧⲉ ϯϩⲁⲙⲛ γαλήνη; 1 Cor 7 29 (*S* ⲱⲗ vb) συστέλ.; Va 58 193 ογⲥⲉⲙⲛⲓ ⲛⲧⲉ ⲡⲙⲁ ⲛϣⲱⲡⲓ ογⲱ. ⲡⲛⲓϩⲓⲣ εὐστάθεια; K 476 *B* مستور Cat 5 ϩⲉⲛⲡⲓⲱ. & estranged from troubles of world, MIE 3 344 ϣⲗⲏⲗ, ⲡⲓⲥⲧⲓⲁ, ω., Va 59 19 ϣⲱⲡⲓ ϩⲉⲛⲟγ. ⲡⲟγⲕⲟγϫⲓ = GMir 262 *S* ⲥϭⲣⲁϩⲧ *silence*, MG 25 139 monkish virtues ϩⲁⲡⲛ. ⲙⲙⲉⲣⲓ

ⲡⲉⲙⲣⲁⲛϣⲱⲃ ⲛϫⲓⲝ *midday silence*(?), TRit 304 ⲡⲓⲉⲛⲯⲁϣⲓ ⲛⲧⲉ ⲡⲓⲱ. of widower; ⳉⲉⲛⲟⲩⲱ. as advb, *quietly*: C 89 179 inspected cells ⳉ. = MG 17 306 S ϧⲟⲩⲥⲟⲣⲁϧⲧ, ib 210 came ⳉⲉⲛⲟⲩⲛϣⲧⲓ ⲛⲱ. no man knowing, Va 57 171 saying to her ⳉ., Fear not.

ⲁⲧⲟⲣⲃⳉ SS′B, *unlimited, boundless*: P 44 47 S ⲟⲩⲁⲧⲟⲣⲃⲉϥ ϧⲓⲧⲟⲩϭⲣⲁⲓ · ⲁⲡⲉⲣⲓⲅⲣⲁⲡⲧⲟⲥ; ⲁ. ⲉϧⲟⲩⲛ, ⲉⳉ.: ib 49 S ⲁϫⲱⲣⲓⲥⲧⲟⲥ, Mor 53 72 S Trinity ⲛⲁⲧⲟⲣⲃⲉⲥ ⲉϧ., ib 27 10 S′ ⲁⲧⲁⲣⲃⲉϥ ⲉϧ.; Cai Euch 650 B ⲁⲧϣⲟⲣϥϥ ⲉⳉ. ⲉⲕⲉⲛⲁ ⲁⲡⲉⲣⲓⲅⲣⲁⲡⲧⲟⲥ.

ⲟⲣⲉⲃⲥ (*sic*) S nn f, *constraint*(?): BMis 148 ϯⲛⲟϭ ⲛ̄ⲣⲟⲧⲉ ⲙⲛⲧⲛⲟϭ ⲛⲟ. of fiery river.

(ⲉ)ⲣⲃⲉ S, ⲉⲣⲃⲓ B nn f, *enclosure, pen* esp for sheep: Lev 25 31 B(S ⲣⲱ), Nu 32 16 S(B ⲟϧⲓ), Ps 68 26 B (S ⲙⲁ ⲛϣⲱⲡⲉ) ⲉⲡⲁⲩⲗⲓⲥ; K 214 B ϯⲉ. خذ (same?); Mus 40 38 S none but shepherds may ⲃⲱⲕ ⲉϧⲟⲩⲛ ⲉⲣ. *villa*, AJSL 46 248 S charm for ⲡⲉⲕⲏⲓ ⲙⲡⲉⲕⲉ. As place-name: ⲧⲉⲣⲃⲉ (Mor 48 54 = C 43 127, HRanke *Karâra* 32), ⲧⲉⲣⲫⲉ (BM 786 on 19th Bâbeh, *cf* PO 10 256, Abû Ṣâliḥ 74 b اذرب); ⲧⲏⲣⲃⲉ (Z 613) different.

In place-name: ⲛⲱⲣⲃ (Ryl 111), ⲡⲱⲣϥ ⲡⲉⲓⲏⲃⲧ (ib 120).

ⲱⲣⲉⲃ BF, ⲟⲣⲃⳉ B, ⲁⲗⲃⳉ F(?), ⲁⲣϥ† S′, ⲟⲣⲉⲃ† B, ⲟⲣⲡ† O vb tr, *detest, abominate, defile*: Lev 20 23 B (S ⲃⲱⲧⲉ), Job 9 31 B(S do), ⲃⲇⲉⲗⲩⲥⲥⲉⲓⲛ; Ez 36 23 B (var & S ⲥⲱϥ) ⲃⲉⲃⲏⲗⲟⲩⲛ; Cant 5 3 F ⲁⲗⲃⲟⲩ(or *l*? ⲧⲁⲗ., S ⲧⲱⲗⲙ) ⲙⲟⲗⲩⲛⲉⲓⲛ; C 43 97 B ϯⲱ. ⲙⲡⲟⲩⲣⲟ; Ep Jer 43 F ⲡⲙⲉ ⲉⲧⲉϣⲁⲩⲱ. ⲛⲛⲓϣⲁ ⲙⲙⲉⲩ ⲛ ⲉϣⲟ; qual: Lev 18 30 B(S ⲃ.) ⲃⲇ., Pro 11 20 B(SA do) ⲃⲇⲉⲗⲩⲅⲙⲁ, Tit 1 16 B(S do) -ⲕⲧⲟⲥ; Ez 22 26 B ⲃⲉⲃ.; Mor 54 52 S′ ⲛⲁⲓ ⲉⲧⲁ. ⲛⲁϧⲣⲉⲙⲛⲡⲉ (on Is 3 11), AZ 21 100 O′ ⲧⲉϣⲉⲛⲧⲱ ⲟ.; ⲥⲡⲥⲁ- F: Eccl 7 19(S ϫⲱⲣⲙ) ⲙⲓⲁⲓⲛⲉⲓⲛ; as nn B: Ge 46 34 (S ⲃⲱⲧⲉ), Is 1 13 (SF do), DeV 1 188 ⲃⲇⲉⲗⲩⲅⲙⲁ; Lev 18 23 (S ϣⲗⲟϥ) ⲙⲩⲥⲁⲣⲟⲥ; Jer 39 34 ⲙⲓⲁⲥⲙⲁ; Lev 19 19 (Va, S ⲛⲁⲡⲟⲩⲅⲉ ⲁⲛ) ⲕⲓⲃⲇⲏⲗⲟⲥ.

ⲱⲣⲃⲁⲛ (once ⲟⲣ.) B nn m, *box tree*: K 175 ⲡⲓⲱ. قس (AIssa 34 = شمار), which P 44 111 & Tri 505 = ⲁⲣⲕⲉⲩⲑⲟⲥ = (ⲉ)ⲉⲣⲁⲍ *i e* ⲃⲣⲁⲑⲩ, 9th letter of alph, whence ? this).

ⲱⲣⲕ SB, -ⲕⲉ SS′, ⲱⲗ(ⲉ)ⲕ F, ⲱⲣⲕ- SS′, ⲟⲣⲕⳉ S, ⲁⲣⲕⳉ S′ vb **I** intr, *swear*: Ex 22 8 SB, Mt 26 74 SB, MG 25 234 B ⲱ. ⲉϣⲧⲉⲙⲣⲱⲙⲓ ⲟⲙⲛⲩⲉⲓⲛ; Mt 5 33 SB ⲉⲡⲓⲟⲣⲕⲓⲍⲉⲓⲛ; Aeg 252 S ⲙⲡⲣⲧⲣⲉϥⲱ., AM 89 B ⲛⲁⲓⲛⲁⲱ. ⲡⲉ ϫⲉ-, Ep 344 S′ ⲁϥⲱ. ϫⲉ-, BAp 75 S ⲁⲓⲱ. ⲉⲧⲣⲁⲕⲁ ⲣⲱⲓ, ShA 2 341 S ⲁⲩⲱ. ⲉⲧⲙⲟⲩⲱⲣ, J 9 86 S sim.

II tr, *swear* oath, *invoke* person &c: Jos 9 24 S, Ps 88 49 SB, Pro 24 32 S(A ⲣ ⲁⲛⲁϣ) ⲟⲙ. acc, Deu 6 13 SB, Is 48 1 SB ⲟⲙ. dat, Ps 62 11 S(B ⳉⲉⲛ-), Mt 23 16 SB ⲟⲙ. ⲉⲛ, Ge 31 53 SB, Jer 29 13 SB, He 6 16

SF(B ⲛⲁϧⲣⲉⲛ-) ⲟⲙ. ⲕⲁⲧⲁ; Z 574 S ⲡⲣⲁⲡ ⲡⲡⲉⲕⲱ. ⲙⲙⲟϥ ⲉⲡⲓ ⲟⲣⲕⲟⲛ ⲗⲁⲙⲃⲁⲛⲉⲓⲛ; BMar 5 S ⲙⲉϥⲱ. ⲗⲁⲁⲩ ⲛⲁⲛⲁϣ, J 58 36 S′ ⲛⲁⲡⲁϣ ⲛⲧⲁⲡⲉⲧⲣⲟⲥ ⲁⲣⲕϥ ⲛⲥⲉⲛⲟⲩⲑⲓⲟⲥ (*cf* c ⲛⲥⲁ-) CO 219 S ⲛⲧⲁⲱ. ⲟⲩⲡⲓⲥⲧⲓⲥ ⲛⲏⲧⲛ, C 43 22 B ϯⲱ. ⲙⲙⲟⲓ ⲙⲙⲓⲛ ⲙⲙⲟⲓ, Ep 162 S ⲁⲓⲱ. ⲙⲡⲣⲁⲛⲟⲥ ⲓⲱϩⲁⲛⲛⲏⲥ ϫⲉ-, C 43 164 B ϯⲱ. ⲛⲁⲕ ⲙⲡⲓⲁⲡⲟⲗⲗⲱⲛ, Pap Graz Univ Libr F ϯ]ⲱ. ⲛⲏⲕ ⲙⲫϯ, Kr 11 F ⲉⲛⲱ. (ⲙ)ⲡⲛⲟⲩⲧⲓ, Ryl 463 S ⲉⲓⲱ. ⲛⲡⲛⲧⲉ ϫ(ⲉ)ⲛⲛⲓϣ ⲡⲁⲣⲁϥⲁ, *cf* ib 157 S sim ⲉⲡⲛⲧⲉ, ib 198 S ⲉⲓⲱ. ⲛⲡⲛⲧⲉ ⲧⲁ(ⲣⲓ)ⲣⲟⲉⲓⲥ, *cf* ib 196 S sim ⲉⲡⲛⲧⲉ, ST 104 S ⲉⲛⲱ. ⲙⲡⲛⲧⲉ...ⲛⲧⲛ̄ϩⲁⲣⲉϧ, PLond 4 436 S sim ⲉⲧⲣⲛϧ.

With following preposition. ⲥ ⲉ- SBF, person adjured: Is 65 16 B(S ⲛ-) ⲟⲙ. acc, BMar 117 S ⲁⲩⲱ. ⲉⲣⲟϥ ϫⲉ- ⲉϫⲟⲙ. ⲟⲧⲓ; Mk 5 7 S(B ⲧⲁⲣⲕⲟ) ⲟⲣⲕⲓⲍⲉⲓⲛ acc, Mt 14 7 F(S ϧⲟⲩⲁⲛⲁϣ ϧⲟⲙⲟⲗⲟⲅⲉⲓ, B sim) ⲙⲉⲑ′ ⲟⲣⲕⲟⲩ ⲟⲙⲟⲗⲟⲅⲉⲓⲛ; Ac 23 12 S(B ⲧⲁ.) ⲁⲛⲁⲑⲉⲙⲁⲧⲓⲍⲉⲓⲛ acc; BAp 108 S ⲁϥⲱ. ⲉⲣⲟⲓ ⲛϧⲉⲛⲛⲟϭ ⲛⲁⲛⲁϣ = MIE 2 383 B ⲧⲁ., Hall 21 S ϯⲱ. ⲉⲣⲟⲕ ⲙⲡⲛⲧⲉ, MR 5 121 F ϯⲱ. ⲉⲗⲁⲕ ⲛⲡⲉⲕⲛⲁϭ ⲛϫⲁⲙ, but RE 14 26 S ⲧⲓⲱ. ⲛⲁⲕ ⲉⲡⲛⲧⲉ; + vb: ClPr 42 4 S ϯⲱ. ⲉⲣⲟⲕ...ⲉⲧⲣⲉⲕ-, BMar 31 S ϯⲱ. ⲉⲣⲟⲕ ϫⲉⲕⲁⲥ ⲉⲕⲉ-, Stegemann 82 S sim ϯⲱⲣⲕⲉ, AM 191 B ⲁⲓⲱ. ⲉⲣⲟϥ ϣⲁⲡⲧⲉϥ-, BM 1036 S ⲉⲓⲱ. ⲉⲡⲛⲧⲉ...ⲧⲁⲣⲓ-, BMar 232 S ϯⲱ. ⲉⲣⲟⲕ... ⲉϣⲱⲡⲉ ϣⲁⲕϫⲓⲧ (v Jern p 29, 30); ⲥ ⲉⲧⲃⲉ- SBF, *concerning*: Ac 7 17 BF(S = Gk) ⲟⲙ. gen; AM 195 B ⲁϥⲱ. ⲙⲡⲟⲩⲣⲟ ⲉ.ϯⲕⲁⲓⲥⲓ, J 67 62 S ⲟⲩⲱⲣⲕ ⲁⲡⲁϣ ⲛⲁⲛ ⲉ.ⲡⲕⲉⲥⲉⲉⲡⲉ; ⲥ ⲉϧⲣⲉⲛ- B, *upon, by*: Ps 101 9, Am 4 2 ⲟⲙ. ⲕⲁⲧⲁ, Ja 5 12 (all S tr) ⲟⲙ. acc; ⲥ ⲉϫⲛ- SB, *upon, as to*: Lev 19 12 SB, AM 8 14 S (A ⲣ ⲁⲛ. ⲉϫⲛ-, B ⲱ. ⲉϧⲣⲉⲛ-) ⲟⲙ. ⲕⲁⲧⲁ; ShA 1 79 S ⲡⲉⲧⲱ. ⲡⲟⲩⲁⲛⲁϣ ⲉ.ϧⲉⲛⲣⲱⲙⲉ ⲛⲁⲧϧⲏⲧ, AZ 33 133 S ⲉⲓⲱ. ⲁⲛ. ⲉϫⲱⲕ ⲙⲡⲛⲟϭ ⲛⲧⲏⲃⲉ ϫⲉ-, ST 214 S ⲉⲓⲱ. ⲉϫⲱⲕ ⲙⲡⲛⲧⲉ, RE 9 146 S ⲁⲓⲱ. ⲉ.ⲛⲉⲩⲁⲅⲅⲉⲗⲓⲟⲛ, J 67 44 S ⲛⲥⲱ. ⲉ.ⲡⲉⲛⲧⲁⲥⲓⲧϥ ⲉϧⲟⲩⲛ; ⲥ ⲛ- dat SB: 1 Kg 24 23 SB, Ps 23 4 S(B ⲉⲣ ⲁⲛ.), Ac 2 30 SB ⲟⲙ. dat; C 89 166 B they go ϧⲓⲡⲁ ⲛⲧⲟⲩ. ⲛⲁϥ, CO 383 vo S ϯⲱ. ⲛⲁⲕ ϫⲉ-; ⲥ ⲛⲥⲁ- S, *to*: CO 131 oath Susanna ⲟⲣⲕϥ ⲛ.ⲡⲉⲧⲣⲟⲥ (*cf* tr); ⲥ ⲛⲁϧⲣⲉⲛ- B, *before, by*: Ex 32 13 (S ⲛ-) ⲟⲙ. ⲕⲁⲧⲁ; ⲥ ϧⲁ- S, *concerning*: BMOr 6943 (12) ⲛ̄ⲧⲱ. ϧⲁⲡⲁⲥⲫⲁⲗⲉⲥ; ⲥ ϧⲓ- S, *upon*: J 82 42 ⲉⲛⲱ. ϧⲓⲱϥ (*sc* ⲉⲅⲅⲣⲁⲫⲟⲛ) ⲛⲛⲡⲛⲧⲉ ...ⲉⲧⲣⲓ-; ⲥ ϧⲓϫⲛ- S: Mor 31 23 ⲡⲉⲓⲕⲟⲩⲓ ⲛ.ⲣⲱⲃ ⲛⲧⲁⲕⲱ. ϧⲓϫⲱⲓ ⲉⲧⲣ(ⲁ)ⲁⲁϥ *adjured me to do*.

ⲱ. ⲛⲛⲟⲩϫ SB, *swear falsely*: Zech 5 4 S ⲱ. ⲛⲛ., ⲙⲡⲣⲁⲛ (A ⲣ ⲁⲛ. ⲛⲛ., B ⲱ. ⲉϫⲉⲛⲟⲩⲙⲉⲑⲛ.) ⲟⲙ. ⲉⲡⲓ ⲯⲉⲩⲇⲉⲓ; PS 363 S ⲛⲥⲉⲧⲣⲉϥⲱ. ⲛⲛ., C 43 120 B sim; Pcod 33 S ⲱ. ⲙⲡⲣⲁⲛ ⲛⲛ., BM 330 137 S ⲱ. ⲛⲟⲩⲁⲛⲁϣ ⲛⲛ., C 43 242 B sim; Jer 5 2 B ⲱ. ⳉⲉⲛⲟⲩⲙⲉⲑⲛ. ⲟⲙ. ⲉⲛ ⲯⲉⲩⲇⲉⲥⲓⲛ; as nn S, *false swearing*: Sa 14 25 ⲉⲡⲓⲟⲣⲕⲓⲁ; ⲣⲉϥⲱ. ⲛⲛ. SB, *false swearer*: 1 Tim 1 10 SB ⲉⲡⲓⲟⲣⲕⲟⲥ; Mor 18 8 S; ⲙⲛⲧⲣⲉϥⲱ. ⲛⲛ.: Aeg 215 S ⲉⲡⲓⲟⲣⲕⲓⲁ.

—— nn m *SF* (*l* ωλκ), *swearing*: He 7 28 (*B* ⲁⲡⲁϣ) ὁρκωμοσία.

ⲃⲁⲓⲱ. *S, oath-bearer* (?): ST 386 ⲡⲁⲃ.

ⲧⲁϣⲉ ⲱ. *S, much-swearer* Si 27 14 ⲣⲉϥⲧ. πολύορκος; ⲁϣⲁⲓ ⲡⲱ. *SB* sim: *ib* 23 11 do.

ϭⲓⲡⲱ. *S, swearing*: R 1 2 54 ⲡⲓϭ. ⲉⲧⲙⲉⲣ ⲡϣⲗⲟϥ. *V* ⲧⲁⲣⲕⲟ, ϣⲱⲡⲉ (ⲉϣⲱⲡⲉ).

ωρϣ *S*, ϧⲣⲟϣ *B*(*l* ϧⲟⲣϣ), ⲁⲣϣ≠*F*, ⲟⲣϣ†*S*, ϧⲟⲣϣ† *SB* vb intr, **a** *be cold*: Mt 24 12† *B*(*S* ⲱϧ) ψύχεσθαι, Ap 3 15†*SB*, Mt 10 42*S*(*B* ϧⲱⲝ)ψυχρός; MG 25 220 *B* in winter ⲧⲉⲧⲡϧ. = Z 347 *S* ⲱ. ῥιγεῖν; AJSL 46 247 *S* recipe ⲉⲧⲃⲉⲟⲩⲁ ⲉϥϧ.†; ⲉⲣ ϧ.*B, be cold*: AM 313 ⲟⲓ ⲡϧⲣ. opp ⲃⲏⲙ; ⲭⲓⲡϧⲣ. *B, coldness*: Va 57 184 ⲡⲭ. ψυχρότης. **b** *be scorched, inflamed* (?) *S*: Ge 49 12 ⲥⲉⲱ. ⲛϭⲓ ⲡⲉϥⲃⲁⲗ(*B* diff)*cf* glosses θερμός, διάπυρος; Bor 264 43 ⲙⲡⲉⲡⲉⲩⲃⲱ ⲱ. ⲙⲡⲉⲡⲉⲩⲣⲟⲓⲧⲉ ⲣⲱⲕϧ (*cf* Dan 3 94 φλογίζειν, *B* ϣⲱⲣⲡ); tr, *sear*: Mor 24 30 *F* ⲡⲕⲱϧⲧ...ⲁⲣϣⲟⲩ = *ib* 23 42 *S* ϣⲟⲣⲃⲟⲩ. *V* ⲁⲣⲟϣ (where note determ 𝕏 Spg 9).

ωρϥ *v* ωρⲃ, *be enclosed*.

ωρⲝ *SAA²*, -ⲝⲉ (Kr 50, 112, 223), ⲟⲩⲱⲣⲝ *S*, ϧⲱⲣⲝ *A*, ⲱⲣϭ, (ⲉ)ⲣⲝ-, ⲣⲉⲝ-, ⲁⲣⲝ-, ⲱⲣⲏⲝ-, ⲟⲣⲝ≠*S*, ⲟⲣ(ⲉ)ⲝ† *SO*, ⲁⲣⲝ† *AA²* vb **I** intr, *be firm, secure, fastened*: Bor 253 164 ⲡϣⲁⲡⲱ. ⲛⲥⲁϭⲁ ⲡⲓⲙ περιασφαλίζεσθαι; BMar 78 ⲧⲉⲕϣⲟⲩⲱⲃⲉ ⲱ. so that no food may enter, TU 43 22 *A* doors ⲁⲩⲱ. (*cf* Mt 25 10), J 3 58 ⲉⲓⲱ. ⲛⲁⲕ ⲡⲣⲟⲥ ⲱ. ⲡⲓⲙ;   qual (oftenest): Jos 6 1 ὀχυροῦν, Deu 3 5 (*B* ⲧⲁⲭⲣⲏⲟⲩⲧ), *ib* 28 52 (*B* ⲭⲟⲣ),Pro 10 15 *SA*(*B* ⲧⲁ.)-ρός,Lam 2 5 (ShC 73 78, *B* ⲥⲟⲃⲧ,*F* ⲭⲁⲣ),Zech 9 3(ShA 2 334)*A*(*B* ⲭ.)-ρωμα; Ps 107 10(*B* do)περιοχή; Sa 14 3 ἀσφαλής; Si 18 28, Ac 26 5 (*B* ⲧⲁ.) ἀκριβής; ShViK 9343 ⲡⲣⲟ ⲟ. ⲁⲩⲱ ⲡϣⲟⲩϣⲧ, KroppG 30 ⲡⲣⲟ ⲉⲧϣⲟⲧⲙ ⲉⲧⲟ., PMéd 247 ⲙⲏⲧⲣⲁ ⲉⲥⲟ., P 131⁵ 54 ϧⲁⲩϭⲁⲗ ⲉⲥⲟ., Blake 270 some think...ⲡⲥⲉⲱ. ⲭⲉ ⲁⲡ, TillOster 24 *A* ⲉⲧⲁ. ϧⲡⲡⲟⲩⲙⲉⲉⲩⲉ, Mani H 5 *A²* παρεμβολη [ⲉⲧ]ⲁ., J 66 64 ⲭⲓⲁⲑⲏⲕⲏ ⲥⲙⲟⲡⲧ ⲥⲟ. ⲥⲟⲙⲥⲟⲙ (*cf* βέβαιος), AZ 21 100 *O* ⲉϥϣⲟⲟⲙⲉ (or ⲭⲟ.) ⲡⲣⲉⲧⲃ ⲉϥⲟ. (or ⲟⲣϣ) ⲡⲡⲉⲃⲗⲁ[ⲥ], ClPr 47 2 of women opp ⲁⲥⲱⲟⲩ.

II tr, *confirm, fasten, imprison*: Is 41 10 (*B* ⲧⲁⲭⲣⲟ.), Mt 27 64(*B* do),Mor 17 39 ⲁⲅⲟⲣⲝⲡ ϧⲏⲣⲡⲡⲉⲡⲓⲡⲡⲉ ἀσφαλίζεσθαι, Pro 8 28 *SA* ϧ. (*B* do)ἀσφαλὲς τιθέναι; *ib* 29 ⲣⲝ *A* ⲱ. (*B* do)ἰσχυρὸν ποιεῖν; Jth 5 1 τειχίζειν; ShZ 593 ⲉⲩϣⲁⲡϧ ⲡⲱ. ⲙⲡⲣⲟ, ShBM 194 1 ⲡⲉⲧⲡⲁϣ ⲟⲣⲭϥ ⲙⲡⲣⲟϧⲡ ⲛϧⲣⲉⲥⲟⲃⲧ, FR 72 ⲁⲡⲱ. ⲡⲡⲉⲣⲟ, Mor 44 44 bring him to prison ⲛⲧⲓⲟⲣⲭϥ, MIF 9 16 bade ⲱ. ⲛⲁⲙⲙⲁⲧⲟⲓ, R 2 1 76 ⲉⲣⲝ ⲙⲙⲁ ⲉⲧⲟⲩⲟⲭ of body with drugs, Ming 332 ⲉⲣⲝ ⲡⲉⲕⲙⲉⲉⲩⲉ, BHom 8 Paul ⲱ. ⲙⲙⲟⲛ ⲁϥϭⲣⲁⲓ ⲭⲉ-, Mani H 60*A²* ⲁⲩⲱ. ⲡⲧⲉϥⲉⲕⲕⲗⲏⲥⲓⲁ,BMOr6201A 128 ⲱⲣⲏⲝⲧⲏⲩⲧⲡ.

With following preposition.   ⲉ ⲉⲣⲡ-, *upon*,

---

against: BMis 239 shut him in ⲡⲥⲉⲱ. ⲉⲣⲟϥ κατακλείειν; Miss 4 703 ⲁⲩⲱ. ⲙⲡⲣⲟ ⲉⲣⲱⲟⲩ *against them*, BM 220 1 righteous Abel ⲁⲡⲱ. ⲉⲣⲟϥ *shut him out from Paradise*, TU 43 22 *A* ⲁⲩⲱ. ⲁⲣⲱⲟⲩ (*sc* foolish virgins).

—— nn m *SA, firmness, assurance, deed of security, lock*: Pro 8 14 *SA*(*B* ⲧⲁ.), Is 18 4 (*B* do) ἀσφάλεια, Ac 21 34 (*B* do) ἀσφαλής; P 44 60 ⲡⲟⲣⲝ اﻠﻐﻞ (var 43 29 اﻟﺼ); PS 132 ⲁⲙⲁⲣⲧⲉ ⲙⲙⲟⲥ ϧⲏⲣϧⲡⲱ. (Od Solom 6 9 ⲗⲟⲗϧ), ShC 73 159 ⲉⲓⲙⲉ ⲉⲡⲱ. ⲡⲣⲱⲃ ⲡⲓⲙ, TT 101 bolt, chain ϧⲓⲱ. ⲡⲓⲙ, J 18 71 ϯⲥⲧⲉⲭⲉ ⲉⲧⲉⲡⲣⲁⲥⲓⲥ ⲙⲡⲉⲥⲟⲣⲝ, Rec 6 71 deed called ϯⲁⲥⲫⲁⲗⲉⲓⲁ & ⲡⲓⲱ., J 55 23 ⲉⲩⲱ. ⲡⲁⲕ ⲁⲓⲥⲙⲡ ⲡⲉⲓⲉⲅⲅⲣⲁⲫⲟⲡ (*cf* PMon 108 ἀσφάλεια), BMOr 9536 vo ⲉⲩⲟⲩⲱⲣⲝ ⲡⲧⲉⲧⲡⲙⲡⲧⲡⲉⲧⲟⲩⲁⲁⲃ, PLond 4 500 sim ⲉⲧⲃⲉⲡⲉⲧⲡⲱ., Ryl 111 sim ⲉⲡⲉⲕⲱ., Win 57 we beg ⲉⲧⲣⲉⲕⲭⲓ ⲡⲱ. ⲡⲧⲡⲓⲉⲍⲉⲕⲓⲏⲗ;   as adj: MG 17 324 marvelled at ⲡϣⲁⲭⲉ ⲡⲱ. = C 89 71 *B* ⲡⲧⲁ.;   ϧⲡⲟⲩⲱ. as advb, *with assurance, certainty*: Deu 12 10 (*B* ⲭⲉⲡⲟⲩⲧⲁ.),Is 34 15(*BF* do)μετὰ ἀσφαλείας,Mk 14 44 (*B* = Gk) ἀσφαλῶς; Ac 22 3 (*B* ⲉⲡⲧⲁ.) κατὰ ἀκρίβειαν, Si 16 25 ἐν ἀκριβείᾳ, Eph 5 15 (*B*=Gk), Z 291 ⲁⲕⲉⲓⲁⲣϧ ⲡⲁⲓ ϧ. ἀκριβῶς, Aeg 280 ϧⲉⲧϧⲉⲧ...ϧ. ἀκριβοῦν; Pro 13 4 *SA*(*B* ⲭⲱϥ ⲡϧⲏⲧ) ἐν ἐπιμελείᾳ, Lu 15 8(*B* ϭⲓ ⲣⲱⲟⲩϣ)ἐπιμελῶς; Lev 25 30 (*B* ⲭⲉⲡⲟⲩⲧⲁ.) βεβαίως; Pro 6 21 *SA*(*B* diff) διὰ παντός; Ac 12 5 ϧⲁⲣⲉϧ ⲉⲣⲟϥ ϧ. *B*Gk om; PS 270 ⲉⲓⲙⲉ ϧ., *ib* 29 ⲭⲟⲕⲟⲩ ⲉⲃⲟⲗ ⲕⲁⲗⲱⲥ ϧ., BM 257 327 ⲡⲣⲟⲥⲭⲉ (*l* -ⲉⲭⲉ) ϧ. ⲉⲡϣⲁⲭⲉ, TU 43 10 *A* ⲁⲙⲉ...ϧ.

ⲙⲁ ⲡⲱ. &c *SA, place for shutting, strong place*: Job 26 13 (*B* ⲱⲧϧ) κλεῖθρον; ⲙⲁ ⲉⲧⲟ.†: Jud 9 46 ὀχύρωμα; Hos 10 14 *A*(*B* ⲉⲧⲁⲩⲧⲁⲕⲧⲏⲟⲩⲧ ⲛⲥⲟⲃⲧ) περιτετειχισμένος; ⲙⲁ ⲉϥⲟ.†: Mor 41 183 cast into ⲟⲩⲙⲁ ⲉϥⲟ.†

V ⲧⲁⲭⲣⲟ.

ωϲκ *SAA²BF*,ⲟⲥⲕ†*SB*, ⲁⲥⲕ†*Sᶠ* vb intr, *delay, continue, be prolonged*: Deu 4 25 *SB*, Ps 39 17 *SB* χρονίζειν,Jo 5 6 *SA²*(*B* ⲉⲣ ⲟⲩⲙⲏϣ ⲛⲭⲣⲟⲛⲟⲥ)πολ. χρόνον ἔχειν; Ge 43 9*SB*,2 Pet 3 9*SB* βραδύνειν; Is 6 12 *B* ⲑⲣⲉⲱ.(*S* ⲧⲁϣⲟ) μακρύνειν; Ez 12 25 *SB* μηκύνειν; Si 35 11 *S* ῥαθυμεῖν; Lev 13 11 *S*(*B* ⲉⲣ ⲁⲡⲁⲥ) παλαιοῦσθαι; 4 Kg 4 8 *B* ἀφ' ἱκανοῦ γίνεσθαι; PS 37 *S* ⲉⲩⲉⲱ. ⲉⲩⲟ ⲡⲣⲣⲟ, ShA 1 67 *S* dog returning to ⲡⲉⲩⲕⲁⲃⲟⲗ ϧⲡⲟⲩⲥⲉⲡⲏ ⲉⲙⲡⲁⲧⲟⲩⲱ., C 99 162 *S* ⲙⲡⲁⲧⲉⲡⲣⲱϣ ⲱ. = *ib* 89 102 *B* ⲙⲉⲛⲉⲡⲥⲁⲣⲁⲛⲕⲟⲩⲭⲓ ⲡⲉⲣⲟⲟⲩ, Pcod 38 *SF* ⲡⲧⲉⲣⲉⲓⲱ. in waves, C 86 62 *B* ⲁϥⲱ. ⲁϥⲉⲣ ϭⲉⲗⲗⲟ ⲉⲙⲁϣⲱ, MG 25 424*S* grieved ⲭⲉⲁⲕⲱ. = DeV 2 152 *B*, BAp 80 *S* ⲁⲓⲱ. ϧⲓⲣⲙⲡⲣⲟ = MIE 2 355 *B*;   qual: Va 57 210 *B* ϧⲁⲡϣⲱⲡⲓ ⲉⲩⲟ. μακρός; ShA 1 376 *S* ⲉⲩⲟ. ϧⲙⲡⲙⲁ ⲉⲧⲟⲩⲧⲟⲙⲥ ⲡϧⲏⲧϥ, Mor 56 38 *S* this money ⲉⲟ. *long out of date*, BMar 205 *S* ⲁϥⲟⲩⲱ ⲉϥⲙⲟⲩ ⲉⲣⲉⲡⲣⲱϣ ⲟ. = Rec 6 169 *B* ⲁϥⲱ. ⲓⲥⲭⲉⲡⲉⲧⲁϥⲙⲟⲩ, BMis 448 *S* ⲙⲡⲛⲥⲁⲧⲣⲁⲁⲡⲟⲧⲁⲥⲥⲉ ⲉ-

ⲣⲉⲡⲣⲱⲃ o. *having renounced* (*world*) *long since*, Mor 40 26 *S* ⲙⲡⲣⲱⲃ o. ⲁⲛ = *ib* 39 35 *Sᶠ*(C 43 55 *B* imperfect);   preceding 2d pres: Ac 28 6 *B*(*S* ⲡⲟⲩⲟϭ ⲛⲕⲟⲟⲩ), BMar 105 *S* ⲡⲧⲉⲣⲉϥⲱ. ⲉϥⲡⲏⲧ ἐπὶ πολύ, Sa 8 12 *S* ἐπὶ πλεῖον; Z 312 *S* ⲁⲕⲱ. ⲉⲕⲕⲱⲗⲁϩ πολλὴν ὥραν; Ac 20 11 *S*(*B* ⲥⲱⲕ) ἐφ' ἱκανόν; Mk 12 40 *S* (*BF* ⲟⲩⲛⲟⲩ), Cai Euch 584 *B* ⲁⲩⲱ. ⲉⲩϣⲧⲏⲛⲟⲩⲧ μακρός; PS 38 *S* ⲡⲉⲩⲧⲟⲡⲟⲥ ⲱ. ⲉⲩⲙⲏⲏ ⲉⲃⲟⲗ, ShP 130¹ 105 *S* ϯⲛⲁⲱ. ⲉⲓϣⲁϫⲉ, Pcod 39 *SF* ⲁϥⲱ. ⲉϥⲱⲃϣ ⲙⲙⲟϥ, Aeg 53 *B* ⲁⲡⲱ....ⲉⲛⲉⲣ ψαλμ; other tenses: C 86 91 *B* ⲁⲩϣⲁⲡⲱ. ⲛⲧⲟⲩϫⲱⲕ, RE 9 172 *S* ⲙⲡⲉϥⲱ. ⲉⲛⲧⲁϥⲃⲓ(*sic l*), Ac 27 21 *S* ⲛⲧⲉⲣⲟⲩⲱ....ⲙⲡⲟⲩⲟⲩⲱⲙ (*B* ⲛⲓϣϯ ⲙⲙⲉⲧⲁⲑⲟⲩⲱⲙ) πολλῆς ἀσιτίας ὑπάρχων, MIE 2 348 *B* child ⲉⲁϥⲱ. ⲙⲡⲉϥⲙⲟϣⲓ ⲟⲩⲇⲉ ⲙⲡⲉϥⲥϫⲁⲓ = PO 22 364 طال عليه الوقت وهو لم يمشى . With following preposition.   ⲥ ⲉ-, *to* vbal: Ge 34 19 *SB* χρ. gen, Deu 23 21 *S*(*B* ⲱ. ⲙⲡⲁⲧⲉ-) χρ. inf; Lu 24 25 *SB* βρ. gen, Z 294 *S* ⲱ. ⲉⲉⲓ βρ. inf, Is 6 10 *S*(*B* ⲉⲣⲟϣⲓ)βαρέως, Ja 1 19 *SA*(*B* ϩ.)βραδὺς εἰς, HL 108 *B* ⲙⲡⲉϥⲱ....ⲉⲧⲁϩⲟϥ μετ' οὐ πολύ; PS 33 *S* ⲛⲉϥⲛⲁⲱ. ⲡⲉ ⲉϫⲱⲕ, ShA 2 47 *S* ⲙⲡⲟⲩⲱ. ⲉⲉⲓⲙⲉ, CO 383 *S* ⲁⲓⲱ. ⲉⲉⲓ; PS 170 ⲛϯⲛⲁⲱ. ⲁⲛ ⲉⲧⲣⲁ-, BMis 1195 *S* ⲁⲓⲱ. ⲧⲱⲛⲟⲩ ⲉⲧⲣⲁ-; not vbal: Mor 30 12 *Sᶠ* ⲙⲡⲣⲱ. ⲉⲣⲟⲓ (var BMis 239 om ⲉ-);   ⲥ ⲛ- vbal: C 43 242 *B* ⲡⲧⲉϥⲱ. ⲛⲧⲛⲓϥ, Va 61 20 *B* ⲉⲧⲟ.† ⲡⲥⲱⲧⲉⲙ, BM 597 *F* (ⲡ)ⲛⲉⲗⲱ. ⲡⲓ;   ⲥ ⲙⲛ- *v* next;   ⲥ ⲛ-dat, *for*: Pro 10 28 *S*(var & *AB* ⲙⲛ-) ἐγχρ. dat; Deu 7 10 *SB* βρ. dat;   ⲥ ⲛⲧⲛ-, *with*: Tob 4 14 *S* αὐλίζειν παρά; 2 Pet 3 9 *B* βρ. gen; MG 25 86 *B* (*sic* MS) staff ⲉⲁϥⲱ. ⲛⲧⲟⲧϥ = Gött Ar 114 20 الشـبرقـة العتيقة التي كانت عندك ;   ⲥ ϣⲁ-, *till*: Ge 32 4 *SB* χρ. ἕως; Mor 31 114 *S* ⲁϥⲱ. ⲉⲉⲓ...ϣⲁⲉϩⲣⲁⲓ ⲉⲥⲟⲟⲩ ⲡⲉⲃⲟⲧ;   ⲥ ϩⲛ-, ϧⲉⲛ-, *in*: Pro 9 18 *SAB*, Lu 1 21 *S* (*B* ⲛϧⲟⲩⲛ ϧ.) χρ. ἐν, Pro 23 30 *S*(var†) ἐγχρ. ἐν, Ac 20 16 *SB* χρονοτρίβειν ἐν; *ib* 27 7 *S*(*B* ⲛ-)βραδυπλοεῖν ἐν; Ps 48 14 *S*(*B* ⲉⲣ ⲁⲡⲁⲥ), Job 21 7 *S*(*B* do) παλαιοῦσθαι; PS 37 *S* ⲉⲅⲉⲱ. ϩⲛⲧⲉⲩⲙⲛⲧⲉⲣⲟ, ShC 42 42 *S* ⲱ. ϩⲛⲡⲓⲙⲁ, Pcod 4 *S* ⲧⲣⲉⲅⲱ. ϩⲛⲡⲉⲩϩⲣⲟⲟⲩ, DeV 1 130 *B* ⲱ. ϧⲉⲛⲡⲁⲓⲁⲛⲁⲅⲕⲏ;   ⲥ ϩⲓϫⲛ-, *upon*: Nu 9 19 *B*(*S* ϭⲱ) ἐφέλκειν ἐπί;   ⲥ ϫⲓⲛ-, ⲓⲥϫⲉⲛ-, *since*: Wess 11 160 *S* ⲙⲡⲉϥⲱ. ϫⲓⲛⲧⲁϥⲣ ⲙⲟⲛⲁⲭⲟⲥ = C 89 66 *B* ἐλθὼν γίνεσθαι; Mk 15 44 *S* ⲁϥⲱ. ϫⲓⲛⲧⲁϥⲙⲟⲩ (*B* ⲟⲩⲱ) πάλαι (cf qual above); Aeg 278 *S* ⲙⲡⲉⲥⲱ. ϫⲓⲛⲧⲁ- νεωστί; R 1 4 41 *S* ⲙⲡⲁⲧⲉⲡⲣⲱⲃ ⲱ. ϫⲓⲛⲧⲁϥ- *ante paucos dies*.

—— nn m *SB*, *duration, delay*: 4 Esd 13 45 *S*(AZ 41 138) ⲡⲱ. ⲡⲧⲉⲣⲓⲛ *via multa itineris*, PO 11 377 *B* ⲙⲡⲓⲙⲱⲓⲧ, Mor 41 55 *S* ⲙⲡⲉⲭⲣⲟⲛⲟⲥ, C 99 143 *S* ⲙⲡϣⲱⲡⲉ = *ib* 89 50 *B* ⲡⲱ. ⲉⲛⲧⲁϥⲧⲁϩⲟⲓ in sea of unbelief = *ib* 16 *F* ⲁⲙⲉⲗⲓⲁ, Aeg 282 *S* ⲁⲭⲡⲱ., BSM 119 *B* sim, Mor 47 213 *S* will die ⲉⲙⲡⲱ. , BMOr 6954 (53) *S* ⲙⲡⲁⲧⲉⲱ. ϣⲱⲡⲉ ϫⲓⲛⲧⲁⲩϯ ⲉϫⲱⲓ, AM 251 *B* ⲙⲡⲁⲧⲉⲱ. ϣⲱⲡⲓ ⲁⲥⲓⲃⲟⲕⲓ.

ⲁⲥⲕⲉ *S*, ⲉⲥⲕⲓ *B* nn f, *delay*: Ac 5 7 *B*(*S* om) διάστημα; ShViK 9099 *S* ⲙⲡⲁⲧⲉⲁ. ϣⲱⲡⲉ, C 86 282 *B* ⲙⲡⲁⲧⲉⲟⲩϭⲉ. ϣⲱⲡⲓ, BM 1102 *S* ⲁⲕⲣ ⲧⲉⲉⲓⲁ. ⲉⲙⲡⲛⲁⲩ ⲉⲣⲟⲕ.

ⲱⲥϧ *A*, ⲱⲥⲃ *B*, ⲱⲥϩ *SA²* *v* ⲱⲣϧ.

ⲱⲥϭ, -ⲕ, ⲱⲥϭ *S*, ⲟⲩϣϫ *B*, ⲉⲥϭ-, ⲟⲥϭ-, ⲟⲩⲉϭⲥ- (Jo 9 15 var) *S*, ⲟⲩϣϫ- *B*, ⲟⲥϭⲝ, ⲟⲩⲟⲥϭⲝ(Ps 17), ⲁⲙϣϭⲝ(Or 6201) *S*, ⲟⲩϣϫⲝ, ⲟⲥϭ†, ⲟⲩϣϫ† *B* vb I intr, *smear, anoint*, qual c ⲛ- *S* (once)*B*: Mt 23 27 (*S* ϫⲱϩ), Ac 23 3 (*S* do)κονιᾶν; Ps 67 14 (*S* ⲗⲁⲗⲱ)περιαργυροῦν; MG 25 203 pots o. ⲡⲕⲉⲣⲙⲓ ἀσβολοῦν; TEuch 2 12 ark o. ⲛⲛⲟⲩⲃ قار ; MG 25 42 swine o. ⲛⲟⲙⲓ, R 2 1 55 *S* ship o. ⲛⲡⲗⲁⲙϫⲁⲧⲡ. **II** tr: Ez 13 15 *B*(*S* ϫ.) ἀλείφειν, Job 33 24 *B*(*S* do) ἀλοιφή, Lev 14 42 *B* ἐξαλ.; Deu 27 2 *B*(*S* do) κον.; Va 63 96 *B* ⲟⲩϫϩ ⲡⲏⲛⲓ ⲛⲕⲟⲛⲓⲁ λευκαίνειν; 2 Chr 3 7 *B* χρυσοῦν; Ps 17 42 *S*(*B* diff) λεαίνειν (cf 2 Kg 22 43 ϣⲱϣ); BMOr 8811 74 *S* ⲉϥⲱⲥϭ ⲙⲙⲟⲥ ⲛⲁⲙⲣⲏϩⲉ (cf Ge 6 14 ϫⲁϩⲥ), DeV 2 28 *B* ⲁϥⲱ. ⲉⲃⲟⲗ ⲛϩⲏⲧϥ ⲛⲛⲓⲟⲩⲉⲭⲣⲱⲟⲩ, BMOr 6201 *B* 47 *S* ⲟⲩⲛⲟϭ ⲛϣⲟⲉⲓⲥ (l ⲥⲟⲉⲓϣ)...ⲁⲓⲁϣϭⲥ ⲁⲓⲥⲁⲗϭⲟⲩ (*sic*).

With following preposition.   ⲥ ⲉ-, *on*: Jo 9 15 *S* (*A²* ⲥⲱⲗϭ, *B* ⲭⲱ ⲉϫⲉⲛ-) ἐπιτιθέναι ἐπί; WS 48 *S* blood ⲱ. ⲙⲙⲟϥ ⲉⲡⲟⲩⲉϭⲣⲟ, C 43 79 *B* ⲁⲡⲉϥⲥⲛⲟϥ ⲱ. ⲉⲛⲓⲱⲛⲓ;   ⲥ ⲉϩⲣⲁⲓ ⲉϫⲛ-: Ex 12 7 *S*(*B* ⲭⲱ ϩⲓϫⲉⲛ-) ⲧⲓⲑ. ἐπί;   ⲥ ϩⲛ-, *with*: Pcod 27 *S* ⲱ. ⲙⲙⲟⲟⲩ (sc pots) ϩⲛⲟⲩⲗⲁⲙϫⲁⲧⲡ.

—— nn m *B*, *plastering, anointing*: Ez 13 12 (*S* ϫ.), Mic 7 11 (*SA* diff) ἀλοιφή.

ⲱⲧ, ⲛⲧ† *A²* vb intr, *meaning unknown*, c ⲉ-: Mani 2 ⲁⲧⲣⲉⲥⲱⲧ ⲁⲣⲁϥ ⲉϥⲛⲏⲩ ⲁⲃⲁⲗ, *ib* angels with him ⲉⲩⲛⲧ ⲁⲣⲁϥ ⲉⲩϯ ⲡⲉϥ ⲛⲧⲟⲩⲉⲓⲣⲏⲛⲏ.

ⲱⲧ *SBF*, ⲟⲩⲱⲧ *SA* nn m, *fat*: Ge 4 4 *SA*(Cl) ⲟⲩ. *B*, 2 Chr 7 7 *S*(P 44 ⲱⲉ دسـم) *B*, Ps 16 10 *S*(*B* ⲉⲧⲭⲏⲡ, *F* ⲉⲧⲕⲏⲛⲟⲩⲧ), *ib* 62 5 *S* ⲟⲩ. *B*, Is 34 6 *SBF* στέαρ; Ps 65 15 *B* ⲱⲧ ⲡⲁⲧⲕⲁⲥ (*S* ⲕⲓⲱⲟⲩ) μυελοῦν; P 44 68 *S* ⲗⲱⲃⲟⲥ (*l* ⲗⲟ.)· ⲡⲟⲩ. ⲙⲡⲙⲁⲁϫⲉ الأذن ; K 200 *B* ⲡⲓⲱⲧ سـ ; in recipes: Z 627 *S* ⲟⲩ. ⲡⲣⲓⲣ, *ib* 630 *S* ⲱⲧ ⲡⲱⲃⲧ; as fuel: BSG 185 *S* = *ib* 16 *B* ⲱⲧ ⲡⲧⲉⲃⲛⲏ, Mor 38 51 *S*, C 43 100, *ib* 167 *B* paral ⲕⲉⲡⲓ.

ⲱⲧⲡ *SABF*, ϩⲱ. *B*, ⲉⲧⲡ-*S*, ⲱⲧⲡ-*A*, ⲁⲡⲧ-*F*, ⲟⲧⲡ-*S*, ⲁⲧⲡⲝ *A²F*, ⲟⲧⲡ† *SB*, ⲟⲡⲧ† *S*, ⲁⲧⲡ† *A*, ϩⲟⲧⲡ†, -ⲛⲧ† *B* vb tr, *shut, enclose, imprison* c ⲉ- *S*, *in*: Sa 17 15† κατακλείειν εἰς; BM 1156 ⲟⲧⲡⲟⲩ ⲉⲧⲉⲫⲩⲗⲁⲕⲏ;   c ⲉϩⲟⲩⲛ, mostly *S*, *in*: Pro 11 26 *SA*(*B* ⲁⲙⲁϩⲓ ⲉϫⲉⲛ-), Lu 19 43 (*B* ⲣⲟⲭⲣⲉϫ ⲉϧ.) συνέχειν; Z 289 ⲁϥⲟⲧⲡϥ ⲉϩ. ⲙⲁϥⲁⲁϥ κατακλ., Va 57 107 *B* ϩ. ἀποκλ.; Ac 22 19 (*B* ϩⲓⲟⲩⲓ ⲉ-) φυλακίζειν; Mani 1 *A²* ϥⲁⲁⲧⲡϥ ⲁϩ., RNC 83 bade ⲟⲧⲡϥ ⲉϩ., PMich 525 *F* ⲁⲅⲁⲧⲡ(ⲧ) ⲉϩ.;   qual: Cl 55 5 *A* συγκλεισμός; RNC 77 release those ⲉⲧⲟ. ⲉϩ., El 50 *A* souls ⲁ. ⲁϩ. ⲛⲧⲟⲟⲧϥ, AM 31

B saints ⲉⲅϩⲟ. ⲉⲇ., Mus 35 21 *B* ⲉⲧⲥⲟⲡϩ...ⲉⲧⲣⲟⲡⲧ
ⲉⲇ.;   ⲉϩ. ⲉ-: Is 24 22 (*B* ϩⲓ. ⲉ-) ἀποκλ. εἰς, R 1 1
42 ⲟⲧⲡϥ ⲉϩ. ⲉⲅⲙⲁ ⲡⲕⲁⲕⲉ ἐγκλ.; Sa 17 2 κατακλ.
dat, Lu 3 20 (*B* ⲇⲟ) κ. ἐν, Ro 11 32 *SF* ⲁⲡⲧ- (*B* ϣⲑⲁⲙ
ⲉϩⲣⲉⲡ- ⲉⲇ. ϩⲁ-)συγκλ. εἰς; Sa 18 4 ⲫⲩⲗ. dat(var ἐν);
Jude 6 (*B* ⲁⲣⲉϩ ⲉⲇ. ⲉ-) τηρεῖν εἰς; C 99 213 ⲟⲧⲡⲟⲩ
ⲉϩ. ⲉⲡⲉϣⲧⲉⲕⲟ = *ib* 89 4 *B* ϩⲓ. ⲉⲇ. ⲉ-, Mani 1 *A²* ⲁⲧ-
ⲡⲟⲩ ⲁϩ. ⲁⲡⲓⲕⲟⲥⲙⲟⲥ, BP 10589 corn ⲟⲧⲡⲟⲩ ⲉϩ. ⲉⲡⲁ-
ϩⲟ;   qual: R 1 1 53 ⲡⲏⲓ ⲉⲧⲛⲟ. ⲉϩ. ⲉⲣⲟϥ ὅπου κλ.,
BM 216 109 ⲧⲁⲟ. ⲉϩ. ⲉⲅⲣⲓ ἐγκλ. εἰς; Sa 17 4 κατέχ.;
BHom 47 ⲉⲧⲟ. ⲉϩ. ⲉⲡⲉⲥⲕⲟⲓⲧⲱⲛ θαλαμεύειν ἐν; ShA
2 94 ⲁⲙⲛⲧⲉ...ⲉⲅⲟ. ⲉϩ. ⲉⲣⲟϥ ϩⲣⲉⲡⲥⲡⲁϩⲣ, Wess 9 52
ⲡⲉϥⲟⲡⲧ ⲉϩ. ⲉⲡⲙⲁ, TT 55 sim = DeV 1 190 *B*;   ⲉϩ.
ϩⲛ-, ϩⲉⲛ- qual: R 1 2 13 ⲡⲙⲁ ⲉⲧⲛⲟ. ⲉϩ. ⲡϩⲏⲧϥ,
DeV 2 94 *B* ⲡⲓⲁϩⲟ where gold & silver ϩⲟ. ⲉⲇ.
ⲡϩⲏⲧϥ, Ge 39 20 ⲟ. ⲉϩ. ϩⲣⲁⲓ ϩⲛ- (*B* ⲭⲏ ϩⲉⲛ-)
κατέχ. ἐκεῖ;   ⲙⲁ ⲡⲱ. ⲉϩ., *place of confinement*:
Mor 17 55 ⲟⲩⲙ. ⲡⲧⲉ ⲡⲉϣⲧⲉⲕⲟ φυλακή only, Leip 24
12 *B* φρουρά; BM 314 31 τὸ ἐγκλεισθῆναι; Ez 27 9
(*B* ⲙⲁ ⲡⲱⲣϥ ⲉⲇ. *q v*),BMis 245 ⲡⲣⲟϫϩⲧ ⲙⲡⲙ.,ClPr
56 8 churches to be ⲙ. for criminals;   ϭⲓⲡⲱ. ⲉϩ.,
condition of *seclusion S*: ShLeyd 305 cause of women's weakness ⲧϭ. ⲡⲧⲁⲅⲉⲓ ⲉϩⲣⲁⲓ ⲡϩⲏⲧⲥ;   as nn
m, *seclusion, imprisonment S*: Ez 4 8 (*B* ⲱⲣϥ ⲉⲇ.)
συγκλεισμός; 4 Kg 25 29 φυλακή; ShA 2 273 ⲧⲉⲧ-
ⲡⲁⲙⲉⲣⲉ ⲱ. ⲁⲡ ⲉϩ. ⲉⲡⲕⲁⲕⲉ, Z 349 ⲡⲱ. ⲉϩ. of ascete,
BMOr 6203 ⲁⲭⲡⲃⲓⲁ...ϩⲓⲁⲡⲁⲧⲕⲁ ϩⲉ (*l* -ⲕⲏ) ϩⲓⲱ. ⲉϩ.
(no Gk paral in this formula).

ωτπ *SA²*, ⲱⲃⲧ *B* (once), ⲁⲧⲡ-*Sᵃ*, ⲟⲡⲧ-*B*, ⲟⲧⲡⲋ*S*,
ⲁⲧⲡⲋ*Sᵃ*, ⲟⲧⲡ† *SB*, ⲁⲧⲡ† *A²*, ⲟⲡⲧ† *B*, ⲁⲡⲧ† *F* vb **I** intr,
be laden: Miss 4 731 *S* trees ⲡⲉϣⲁϥⲱ. ⲡⲕⲁⲣⲡⲟⲥ, R
NC 64 *S* sim, BMis 269 *S* ⲧⲁϩⲟ ⲕⲁⲣⲡⲟⲥ ⲉϥⲱ. ⲉϣϫⲉ
ⲉϥⲣⲏⲧ (Mor 29 38 *S*, 30 44 *F* om);   qual (mostly):
Mt 11 28 *S*(*B* ϩⲁ-) φορτίζειν; R 1 2 55 *S* ⲡⲁϩⲁⲛ
ⲟ.;   ⲥ ⲛ-, *with*: 3 Kg 10 2 *S* αἴρειν; BMis 562 *S*
trees ⲟ. ⲡⲕⲁⲣⲡⲟⲥ πλήρης; Ps 51 10 *B* sim (*S* diff)
κατάκαρπος; Va 63 100 *B* ⲉϥⲟ. ⲡⲓϣⲁϣ σηπεδών;
Br 236 *S* ship ⲟ. ⲡⲡⲕⲁ ⲡⲓⲙ, C 86 279 *B* clouds ⲟ.
ⲡⲟⲅⲙⲟⲩ ⲡϩⲱⲟⲩ = BSG 179 *S* ⲙⲟⲩϩ, BM 511 §2
F tree ⲁ. ⲡⲕⲁⲣⲡⲟⲥ, Mani H 79 *A²* ⲉ]ⲧⲁ. ⲡⲭⲣⲏⲙⲁ;   ⲥ ϩⲛ-, as last: ShRyl 71 92 *S* ⲟ. ϩⲛⲧⲉⲧⲡⲱ,
Mél Or 6 500 *B* sim, R 1 2 54 *S* ⲟ. ϩⲛⲡⲁϩⲁⲛ of
devil;   ⲥ ϩⲁ-, ϩⲁ-, *burdened under*: Mt 11 28 *B*(*S*
Gk *v* above, *cf* PS 219), R 1 2 55 *S* ⲟ. ϩⲁⲡⲁϩⲁⲛ;   ⲥ
ⲉⲃⲟⲗ: Mor 23 44 *S* ⲉⲅⲟ. ⲉⲃ. ϩⲛⲡⲁⲧⲁϣⲟⲡ ⲛⲓⲙ = *ib*
24 32 *F*.

II tr, *load*: MIF 13 111 *S* ⲁϥⲱ. ⲙⲡϩⲁⲙⲟⲩⲗ =
MG 25 301 *B* ⲁϥⲟⲡⲧ ⲡⲓϭ., BSM 2 *B* ⲡⲧⲁⲱⲃⲧ ⲡⲟⲩⲡⲓϣϯ ⲡⲕⲩⲃⲱⲧⲟⲥ = BMis 323 *S* ⲉⲓ(ⲉ)ⲧⲁⲗⲉ ⲉⲅⲛⲟϥ
ⲡϫⲟⲓ, Ryl 352 *Sᵃ* ⲁⲓⲁⲧⲡ (*sic l*) ⲡϫⲟⲓ, Mor 50 35 *S*
ⲁⲅⲱ. ⲙⲡⲉϥϫⲟⲓ(*l* ⲡⲉϥ.)ⲉⲡⲉϥⲁⲅⲉⲓⲙ, Kr 106 *S* ⲡⲕⲟⲓⲧ-
ⲧⲱⲛ (*cf* BM 1089) ⲡⲧⲁⲧⲡⲉⲱ. ⲡⲉⲙⲁϩⲉ (ⲉ)ⲣⲟϥ;   ⲥ

ⲛ-, *with*: Mor 28 104 *S* ⲡⲉϣϣⲁϥⲱ. ⲡⲓϭⲁⲙⲟⲩⲗ ⲡⲁⲡϩⲟⲗⲟⲙⲁ (ἀνάλωμα), Mani 1 *A²* ⲁⲅⲱ. ⲡⲡⲉϥⲙⲉⲗⲟⲥ
ⲡⲃⲁⲡⲓⲡⲉ.

ⲉⲧⲡⲱ *SA²*, -ⲡⲟⲩ *A* (?), ⲁⲧⲫⲱ *F*, ⲉⲧϥⲱ, ϩⲉⲧ. *B*, pl
ⲉⲧϥⲱⲟⲩⲓ *B* & sg as pl, nn f, *burden*: Ps 37 4 *SB*, Mt
23 4 *SB* pl φορτίον; Ex 23 5 *S*(*B* ⲑⲁⲑ)γόμος; Jer 17
22 *S*(*B* ⲇⲟ) βάσταγμα; Ps 80 6 *SB* ἆρσις; ROC 17
405 *B* ϩⲁⲡⲉ. ⲡⲕⲁⲣⲓ ἄχθος; Mor 23 27 *S* ⲡⲱⲧ ⲉϩⲟⲩⲛ
ϩⲁⲧⲉ. = *ib* 24 19 *F*, TU 43 24 *A* ⲁϥϣⲁⲣⲉⲉⲓⲉ[...ϩⲁ-
ⲟⲩⲉ]ⲧⲡⲟⲩ = PO 9 228 ℛ*C*, Va 58 135 *B* ⲧⲉⲡϩ. ⲉⲧ-
ϩⲟⲣⲱ, JTS 10 396 *S* ⲧⲥⲁⲃⲟϥ ⲉϥⲓ ⲉ., ManiH 4 *A²* ⲧⲁⲁⲡⲉ ϩⲁⲧⲉⲕⲉ.;   ϩⲁⲓⲉ. *SA²*, *weight-carrier, porter*:
3 Kg 5 15 (in BHom 113) αἴρων ἆρσιν; R 1 3 71
camel ⲟ. ⲡϥ., Mani 1*c* ⲡϩⲁϭ ⲡⲃⲁⲓⲉ.;   ⲟ ⲡⲉ.: Job
7 20 *SB* φ. εἶναι.

ωτϩ *SA²B* (nn), ⲟⲩⲱ. *SB*, ⲟⲧϩⲋ, ⲟⲧ† *S* vb intr,
tie, sew, weave: Lu 12 27 *S* (var ⲱⲣⲧ, *B* ⲉⲣ ⲓⲟⲡⲏ)
ὑφαίνειν (var νήθειν); Is 19 10 *B*(*S* tr) διάζεσθαι (*cf*
Jud 16 14 ϣⲱⲛⲧ δ.); P 131⁶ 47 *S* women weaving
wool ⲡⲁⲱϩ ⲡⲥⲉⲣ ⲉⲓⲟⲡⲉ;   tr *S*: Eph 6 15 (var
ⲥ ⲉ-, *B* ϯ ⲉ-) ὑποδεῖσθαι, cit P 129¹⁶ 91, Ryl 62 1 *a*;
Orat Manas 3 *B* (Bodl Hunt 121) ⲉⲧⲱ. ⲙⲫⲓⲟⲙ (var
ib Marsh Or 31, BM 825 ⲧⲁϩⲛⲟ) πεδᾶν; Is 19 10 *ut
sup*; CO 351 ⲁⲓⲟⲩ. ⲑⲁⲗⲓⲥ (*v* Ep 304 n).

With following preposition or adverb.   ⲥ ⲉ- *SB*
(rare), *tie upon*: Mk 6 9†(*B* ⲧⲟⲓ), Eph 1*c*(var tr) ὑποδ.,
cit BAp 101, R 2 1 41, Jos 9 11† ὑπόδημα; 1 Kg 17
6† Gk om, Mor 41 150 ⲁⲅⲟⲩ. ⲉⲡⲉϥⲙⲁⲕϩ ⲡⲟⲩⲙⲁ-
ⲡⲓⲁⲕⲏⲥ, ROC 25 256 *B* ⲡⲧⲟⲅⲱ. ⲉⲣⲱϥ (*sc* prisoner)
ⲉϩⲟⲩⲛ ⲉⲙⲁϥ;   ⲥ ⲙⲛ- *S*, *combine with* (?): ShC
73 109 ⲉⲅⲡⲁⲟⲧϥ (*sc* daily task) ⲙⲡⲡⲕⲉϩⲃⲏⲅⲉ ⲟⲡ
like unto it;   ⲥ ϩⲛ- *S*: Mor 33 11 ⲡⲉⲥⲥⲱⲙⲁ ⲧⲏⲣϥ
ⲟ.†...ϩⲛϩⲟⲧⲉ of God (var *ib* 34 6 ⲧⲁϫⲣⲏⲅ ϩⲛ-);   ⲥ
ⲁϩⲣⲏⲓ *A²*: Mani H 53 ⲱ. ⲙⲡⲁⲡⲡⲁ̄ ⲁϩ. ⲁⲃⲁⲗ ⲙⲡⲭⲓ[
make secure, protect.

—— nn m *B*, *fastened thing* or *place, lock*: Job 26
13 (*S* ⲙⲁ ⲡⲱⲣϫ) κλεῖθρον; P 54 119 ⲡⲓⲱ. ا̊ـ.

ⲁⲧϩⲉ *S*, *woven garment* (?): CO 465 ⲟⲅⲁ.   Or *l*?
(ⲟⲩ)ⲟⲩⲁ.

ⲟⲩⲁⲧϩⲉ *S*, -ϩⲓ, ⲟⲩⲁϩⲓ *B* nn m, *warp on loom*: Lev
13 48 *B*(*S* ϣⲧⲓⲧ) στήμων; BM 920 264 *B* ⲡⲓⲟⲩ. ا̊ـ;
Z 581 *S* ⲡⲟⲩ. ⲙⲡⲡⲃⲏⲕⲏ.

ⲁⲧϩⲥ *S* nn f, meaning uncertain, *woven piece* (?):
COAd 57 ⲟⲩⲁ. ⲉⲕϯ ⲙⲙⲟⲥ ϩⲁⲟⲩⲧⲁⲗⲓⲥ (*cf* above
ⲑⲁⲗⲓⲥ), Hall 99 ⲁⲓⲉⲓⲡⲉ ⲡⲟⲩⲁ....ϩⲁⲧϥⲧⲓⲙⲏ.   Or *l*?
ⲟⲩⲁⲧϩⲥ.

ⲁⲑⲁϩ, pl -ⲁⲧϩ *B* nn m, *what is bound* upon(?) man
or beast, *burden*: Ex 23 5 (*S* ⲉⲧⲡⲱ) γόμος;   pl: Jer
17 22 (*S* ⲇⲟ) βάσταγμα; P 54 168 ⲡⲁ. جـ; ⲣⲉϥϥⲓ
ⲁ., *porter*: K 112 حـّال.

V ⲉⲧⲟϩ, ⲟⲩⲧⲁϩ (2°).

ωτϩ *pour v* ⲟⲩⲱⲧϩ.

ⲱⲧϭ *v* ⲱϭⲧ.

ⲱⲟⲩ *BO* nn *v* ⲉⲟⲟⲩ.

ⲱⲟⲩ *B* vb intr, *be long*, in compounds.

ⲱ. ⲛ̄ϩⲏⲧ, *be long-hearted, patient*: Job 7 16 (*S* ϩⲣⲟϣ ⲛ̄ϩ.), 1 Cor 13 4 (*S* do) μακροθυμεῖν, Ac 27 22 (*S* ⲧⲱⲕ ⲛ̄ϩ.) εὐθ.; 1 Cor 4 12 (*S* = Gk) ἀνέχειν, Ge 8 10 (*S* ϭⲱ) ἐπέχ.; 1 Cor 9 12 (*SF* ϥⲓ ϩⲁ-) στέγειν; BSM 41 ⲱ. ⲛ̄ϩ. ϣⲁⲧⲉⲛⲡⲁⲩ = BMis 387 *S* ϩ. ⲛ̄ϩ., *ib* 77 sim = *ib* 168 *S* ϭⲱ ⲉⲣⲟⲓ, Miss 4 100 ⲙ̄ⲡⲓϣ ⲱ. ⲛ̄ϩ. ...ⲡⲟⲩⲉϣⲉⲛ-. With preposition. ⲥ ⲉ-, *be patient with*: Bar 4 25 μ. acc; ⲥ ⲉⲍⲛ-, sim: Lu 18 7 (*S* ϩ. ⲛ̄ϩ. ⲉϩⲣⲁⲓ ⲉϫⲛ-)μ. ἐπί, Dan 4 24 μακρόθυμος εἶναι dat; AM 141 ⲁⲓϫⲓⲥⲓ ⲉⲓⲱ. ⲛ̄ϩ. ⲉϫⲱⲧⲉⲛ, BSM 39 ⲉϥⲱ. ⲛ̄ϩ. ⲉϫⲱϥ ϣⲁⲛⲧⲉϥⲡⲁⲩ = Va 63 13 ⲡⲉⲙⲁϥ = BMis 384 *S* ϩ. ⲛ̄ϩ.; ⲥ ⲡⲉⲙ-, sim: Mt 18 26 (*S* ϩ. ⲛ̄ϩ. ⲉϩ. ⲉϫⲛ-) μ. ἐπί, 1 Thes 5 14 (*S* ϩ. ⲛ̄ϩ. ⲙ̄ⲛ-) μ. πρός; 2 Cor 11 1 (*S* = Gk) ἀν. gen; C 86 308 ἐκδέχεσθαι acc; C 43 114 tribunal ⲡⲁϣ ⲱ. ⲛ̄ϩ. ⲡⲉⲙⲁⲕ ⲁⲛ; nn, *patience*: Jer 15 15 (*S* ⲱⲥⲕ vb) μακροθυμία; ⲣⲉϥⲱ. ⲛ̄ϩ., *patient person*: Ps 85 15 (*S* ϩⲁⲣϣ̄ϩ.), Joel 2 13 (*A* ϣⲁⲛϩ̄ⲧⲏϥ)μακρόθυμος; Ja 5 11 (*S* ⲡⲁⲛⲧ) οἰκτίρμων; DeV 2 49 ⲁⲓⲉⲣ ϩ. ⲉϩⲣⲏⲓ ⲉϫⲉⲛϯⲫⲩⲥⲓⲥ, *ib* 1 172 ⲁⲣⲓ ϩ. ϣⲁⲛⲧⲉ-; ⲙⲉⲧⲣⲉϥⲱ. ⲛ̄ϩ., *patience*: Is 57 15 (*S* ⲙ̄ⲛⲧϩⲁⲣϣ̄ϩ.), Ro 2 4 (*S* do) μακροθυμία; *ib* 3 25 (*S* = Gk) ἀνοχή.

ⲱ. ⲛ̄ⲃⲁⲗ *v* ⲃⲁⲗ.

—— nn, *length* in ⲱ. ⲛ̄ⲓⲁⲧ⸗, *blessing* (*v* ⲉⲓⲁ *eye*): Ps 31 2 ⲱ. ⲛ̄ⲓⲁⲧϥ̄ ⲙ̄ⲡⲓⲣⲱⲙⲓ (*S* ⲛⲁⲓⲁⲧϥ̄ ⲛ̄-, *A* Cl = Gk), Is 30 18 (*SF* do), Jo 13 17 (*SA²* do) μακάριος; Cat 150 shall be ϩⲉⲛⲟⲩⲱ. ⲛ̄ⲛⲁⲓⲁⲧϥ̄ (*sic, cf* Lu 12 42); ⲱ. alone: Is 35 7 (*SF* ⲟⲩⲛⲟϥ) εὐφροσύνη, or ? ⲱ. *glory*.

ⲱⲟⲩϣ *B* *v* ⲟⲟⲩϣ.

ⲱⲓϣ *B* *v* ⲟⲉⲓϣ.

ⲱϣ *SAA²BF*, ⲉϣ- *SB*, ⲱϣ- *SA²*, ⲁϣ- *SAF*, ϣ- *B*, ⲟϣ⸗ *SB*, ⲁϣ⸗ *SᵃA²*, ⲣ ⲥ ⲁϣ- *B* (?) vb **A** *cry, announce, sound* intr: Ps 45 4 *B*(*S* ⲥ ⲉⲃⲟⲗ), Jer 19 3 *B* (*S* do)ἠχεῖν; Is 5 30 *B*(*S* do) βοᾶν; Jer 31 3 *B* κράζειν; BMis 550 *S* when water floweth ϣⲁⲣⲉⲡⲉⲛⲡⲁ ⲱϣ *flasset*, C 43 79 *B* ⲉⲩⲱϣ ϩⲉⲛⲟⲩⲣⲟ ⲡⲟⲩⲱⲧ, Mani H 8 *A²* ⲧⲥⲁⲗⲡⲓⲛⲍ ⲡⲁⲱ.; tr: Is 40 6 *B* (*S* ⲥ ⲉⲃ.) β.; Va 57 200 *B* ⲙⲁⲣⲉⲡⲱϣ ⲛⲁⲡ ⲙ̄ⲡⲓⲣⲓ καλεῖν, Ac 2 21 *S*(*B* ⲧⲱⲃϩ) ἐπικ.; Aeg 12 *B* ⲉϣ ⲟⲩⲛⲓϣϯ ⲛ̄ϧⲓ ϩⲣⲟⲙ = *ib S* ϣⲟⲡ, Mani 1 *A²* ⲁϥⲱϣ ⲛ̄ⲧⲉϥⲥⲁⲗⲡⲓⲛⲍ.

With following preposition. ⲥ ⲉϧⲟⲩⲛ ⲉ- *S, to*: Br 125 ⲉⲩⲱϣ ⲉϩ. ⲉⲡⲡⲉ̄; ⲥ ⲁϫⲛ- *A²*: Mani H 11 ⲁϥⲱϣ ⲡⲟⲩⲁⲓ ⲁϫⲱⲥ *cried woe upon her*; ⲥ ⲛ̄ⲥⲉ- *A, call after*: Mic 6 16 (*B* ϣⲟⲩϣⲓⲧⲥ) συρισμός; ⲥ ⲟⲩⲃⲉ- *SA²BF, to, across to*: Ps 41 7 *S*(*B* ⲙⲟⲩϯ ⲟⲩ.), Lam 3 55 *F*(*B* ⲧⲱ.), ROC 25 250 *B* ⲉϥⲱϣ ⲟⲩ.ⲛⲓⲭⲉ-

ⲙⲱⲡ ἐπικ. acc; Ps 119 1 *B*(*S* ϫⲓ ϣⲕⲁⲕ) κρ. πρός, MG 25 212 *B* κρ. dat; Is 12 4 *B*(*S* ⲥ ⲉϩ.)β. acc; Tri 148 *S* soul ⲱϣ ⲟⲩ. ⲛ̄ⲡⲉ̄, Mani H 21 *A²* sim, Va 66 293 *B* ⲛ̄ⲧⲉⲡⲱϣ ⲟⲩⲃⲏϧ ⲉⲟⲩⲃⲟⲏⲑⲉⲓⲁ; ϫⲓⲡⲱϣ ⲟⲩ. *B*: Ps 4 4 (*S* ⲱϣ vb) κρ.; ⲥ ϣⲁ- *B, to*: C 86 167 ⲁϥⲉϣ ⲟⲩϭⲣⲱⲟⲩ ϣⲁⲡⲟⲩⲣⲟ saying; ⲥ ϩⲁ- *B, to*: Ps 17 7 (*S* ϫⲓ ϣ.) κρ. πρός.

With following adverb.

—— ⲉⲃⲟⲗ *SAA²BF, cry out*, intr: Ge 29 11 *SB*, Mk 15 34 *SBF*, BHom 50 *S* trumpets ⲱϣ ⲉⲃ. β.; Is 36 13 *SBF* ἀναβ.; Job 19 7 *B*(*S* ϫⲓ ϣ. ⲉⲃ.), Mk 15 13 *S*(var ϫⲓ ϣ.)*BF*, Ac 16 17 *S*(var ⲁϣⲕⲁⲕ ⲉⲃ.)*B* κρ., Ez 21 12 *SB* ἀνακρ.; Mt 12 19 *SB* κραυγάζειν; Is 17 12 *S*(*B* ⲥⲉⲛⲥⲉⲛ) ἠχ.; Am 3 6 *S*(*B* ⲙⲟⲩϯ) φωνεῖν, 1 Chr 16 4 *B* ἀναφ., Lam 2 7 *F*(*B* ϯ ⲥⲙⲏ) φωνὴν διδόναι, AP 16 *A²* φ. ἐπαίρειν; Am 3 4 *S*(*B* ⲉⲗϩⲏⲙ)ἐρεύγεσθαι; 1 Cor 13 1 *S*(*B* ⲉϣ ⲗⲏⲗⲟⲅⲓ)ἀλαλάζειν; 1 Chr 16 32 *B* βόμβειν; Ps 28 3 *S*(*B* ⲉⲣ ϭⲁⲣⲁⲃⲁⲓ) βροντᾶν; PS 41 *S* ⲁⲩⲱϣ ⲉⲃ....ⲉⲩϭⲩⲙⲛⲉⲩⲉ, C 43 166 *B* ⲁⲩⲱϣ ⲉⲃ. ⲉⲩϯ ⲱⲟⲩ, BSM 84 *B* ⲁϥⲟⲣⲉⲡⲓⲕⲩⲣⲓⲍ ⲱϣ ⲉⲃ. = BMis 174 *S* ⲁϥⲕⲏⲣⲩⲥⲥⲉ, BAp 134 *S* of flute, Mani H 69 *A²* boiling water ⲱϣ ⲉⲃ., BMar 181 *S* when drinking let not throat ⲱϣ ⲉⲃ.; tr: Ps 26 7 *S*(*B* intr ϭⲉⲡ-), Is 6 4 *B*(*S* ⲁϣⲕⲁⲕ ⲉⲃ.)κράζ.; C 89 21 *B* cock ⲉϣ ⲟⲩⲥⲙⲏ ⲉⲃ. φω.; COAd 19 *S* ϯⲡⲏⲩ ⲡⲧⲁⲟϣ̄ⲕ ⲉⲃ. *summon*(?), Ep 333 *S* sim, Miss 4 749 *S* let us go to ⲡⲉⲡⲏⲓ ⲛ̄ⲧⲡⲟⲩϣϥ ⲉⲃ. (meaning?); ⲉⲃ. ⲉ-, *to, for*: Jud 12 2 *Sβ*. πρός; Ac 22 24 *S* (var ⲁϣⲕ., *B* + ⲉϩⲣⲏⲓ ⲉϫ.) ἐπιφ. dat; PS 47 *S* ⲁⲓⲱϣ ⲉⲃ. ⲉⲩⲃⲟⲏⲑⲉⲓⲁ, LMär 39 *S* ⲁϥⲱϣ ⲉⲃ. ⲉⲡⲣⲣⲟ ϫⲉ-, AM 143 *B* sim; ⲉⲃ. ⲉϩⲣⲁⲓ ⲉ-: Deu 26 7 *S*(*B* ⲉϩ. ϩⲁ-), Jon 1 5 *SA*(*B* ⲉⲛϣⲱⲓ ϩⲁ-) ἀναβοᾶν πρός; ⲉⲃ. ⲉϫⲛ-: Is 31 4 *S*(*BF* ⲉϩ. ⲉϫ.)β. ἐπί; Ro 9 27 *B*(*S* ϫⲓ ϣ. ⲉⲃ. ϩⲁ-)κρ. ὑπέρ; WTh 46 *S* king ⲱϣ ⲉⲃ. ⲉϫⲱⲟⲩ ϫⲉ- = *ib B* ⲉⲣⲱⲟⲩ (var 158 = *S*); ⲉⲃ. ⲉϩⲣⲏⲓ ⲉϫ.: Is 16 11 *B*(*S* ⲙⲟⲩⲧⲉ ⲉⲃ. ⲉϫⲛ-) ἠχ. ἐπί; ⲉⲃ. ⲉϩ. ϩⲁ-: C 43 93 *B*; ⲉⲃ. ⲉϩⲟⲩⲃⲉ-: Is 34 14 *B*(*SF* ϫⲓ ϣ. ⲉⲃ.)β. πρός; 3 Kg 17 21 *B* ἐπικαλ. acc; Mor 40 13 *S* ⲁϥⲱϣ ⲉⲃ. ⲟⲩⲃⲉⲙⲡⲉⲣⲥⲟⲥ (var *ib* 39 18 ϩⲓϫⲛ-) = C 43 43 *B*; ⲉⲃ. ⲛ̄-: BAp 12 *S* ⲁϥⲱϣ ⲉⲃ. ⲛ̄ⲧⲁⲥⲡⲉ (var MIF 9 51 ϩⲛ-); ⲉⲃ. ϩⲛ-, ϩⲉⲛ-: BSM 119 *B* ⲱϣ ⲉⲃ. ϩⲉⲛⲧⲉⲥⲁⲥⲡⲓ, Mor 18 173 *S* ⲡⲥⲱϣ ⲉⲃ. ⲁⲛ ϩⲛϩⲣⲉⲡⲛⲕⲩⲙⲃⲁⲗⲟⲛ; ⲉⲃ. ⲉϩⲟⲩⲛ ϩⲛ-: R 1 1 14 *S* ⲁⲩⲱϣ ⲉⲃ. ⲉϩ. ϩⲙ̄ⲛⲕⲟⲩⲣⲥⲱⲣ κρ....λέγων πρός: as nn m: He 5 7 *F*(*S* ⲁϣⲕ., *B* ϭⲣⲱⲟⲩ)κραυγή; 1 Kg 4 14 *S* βοή; Va 57 193 *B* ϩⲁⲛⲱϣ ⲉⲃ. ⲡⲉⲙϩⲁⲡⲥⲙⲏ.

—— ⲉⲛϣⲱⲓ *B, up*: Jer 29 2 (*S* ⲉⲃ.) κρ.; Su 24 ἀναβ.; ⲉⲡ. ⲟⲩⲃⲉ-: Ex 14 15 (var ϩⲁ-) β. πρός; Ps 55 10 (*S* ⲉϩⲣⲁⲓ ⲉ-)ἐπικ.; ⲉⲡ. ϩⲁ-: Ps 65 17 (*S* do) κρ. π.; Is 46 7 (*S* do) β. π.; C 41 66 ⲉϥⲱϣ ⲉⲡ. ϩⲁⲡϭⲥ̄, MG 25 34 ⲡⲉⲥϫⲓⲛⲱϣ ⲉⲡ. ϩⲁⲣⲟⲓ.

—— ⲉϩⲣⲁⲓ *SABF, as last*, ⲉϩ. ⲉ-: Nu 12 13 *S*(*B*

ϩⲁ-), Hos 7 14 *S*.*A*(*B* ⲟⲩⲃⲉ-) β. πρός, Jos 24 7 *S* (var ⲉϩ. ⲉϧ.) ἀναβ. π., Sa 14 1 *S* ἐπιβ.; Ps 21 2 *S* (var&*B* ⲟⲩⲃⲉ-), *ib* 140 1 *S*(*B* ⲉⲡ. ϧⲁ-) κρ. π.; Job 5 8 *S*(*B* ⲇⲟ), Ps 19 9 *S*(*B* ⲟⲩ.) ἐπικ.; PS 75 *S* ωϣ ⲉϧ. ⲉⲡⲟⲩⲟⲉⲓⲛ, ShMun 107 *S* ⲉⲣⲟϥ; ⲉϧ. ⲟⲩⲃⲉ-: Ps 101 2 *S*(var ⲉ-, *B* ⲉⲡ. ⲟⲩⲃⲉ-) ἐπικ., Hos 7 7 *B*(*A* ⲁϧ. ⲁ-) ⲉ̀. π.; Ps 30 22 *S*(*B* ⲉϧ. ϧⲁ-) κρ. π.; PS 63 *S* ϯⲛⲁⲱϣ ⲉϧ. ⲟⲩⲏⲕ, BKU 1 23 *F* ϯⲓⲱϣ ⲉⲗⲏⲓ ⲟⲩⲏⲕ; ⲉϧ. ϣⲁ- *F*: Griff Stu 162 ⲉⲓⲱϣ ⲉϧ. ϣⲁⲗⲁⲕ; ⲉϧ. ϧⲁ- *B*: Lam 2 18(*S* ⲉ-)β. π.; Ps 106 6(*S* ⲭⲓ ϣ. ⲉϧ. ⲉ-) κρ. π. ṗ c ? in ⲁϣⲉⲃⲉⲛ *q v*.

ⲣⲉϥⲉϣ- *SB, one who calls, utters*: Deu 18 10 *S* ⲣ. ⲉⲓⲉⲣⲃⲟⲟⲛⲉ (*B* Gk om), C 86 173 *B* ⲣ. ϩⲣⲱⲟⲩ *herald*.
ϧⲓ ωϣ *B*: DeV 2 38 prob *l* ⲓⲱϣ.

V ⲁⲗ (3°), ⲁϧⲟⲙ, ⲥⲟⲗϥ, ⲧⲁⲡ, ϣⲕⲁⲕ, ϣⲙ̅ϣⲏⲥⲉ, ϣⲏⲗ, ϣϭⲁⲡ, also ? ⲟⲉⲓϣ.

B *read SAA²BF* intr: Is 29 11 *B*(*S* tr), Mt 24 15 *SB* ἀναγινώσκειν; ShR 2 3 10 *S those about corpse* ⲉⲅⲱϣ ⲏ ⲉⲅⲕⲱⲟⲥ ⲙⲙⲟϥ, CA 96 *S* ⲉⲣϣⲁⲛⲣⲱⲙⲉ ϣⲁⲭⲉ ⲉⲅⲱϣ *in church*, GFr 432 *S* ⲙⲙⲟⲓ ⲡⲱϣ, Ryl 277 *S* ωϣ ϩⲓⲡⲁϩⲟⲩ, Bodl(P) d 18 *S* sim ϩⲓⲃⲟⲗ *verte* (*cf* POxy 1855 ἀναγίνωσκε ὀπίσω); tr: Deu 31 11 *SB*, Hab 2 2 *AB*, Jo 19 20 *SA²B* ἀν.; BM 775 *B* λέγειν; BAp 37 *S could not* ωϣ ⲙⲡⲉⲥϧⲁⲓ, Pcod 27 *S* ⲁⲓⲉϣ ϯⲟⲩ ⲛⲭⲱⲙⲉ, BSM 82 *B* ⲡⲓⲥϧⲁⲓ...ⲁϥⲟϣⲟⲩ = BMis 172 *S* ωϣ ⲛ̅ϩⲏⲧⲟⲩ, Kr 236 *F* ⲁⲓⲁϣ ⲡⲉⲕⲥϧⲉⲓ, Leyd 154 *S* ⲉⲕⲛⲁⲱϣ ⲡⲉⲓⲗⲟⲅⲟⲥ, Ep 390 *Sᵃ* ωϣ ⲧⲉⲡⲟϭ ⲛⲉⲃⲗϫⲉ, Lant 11 *S.ᶠ* ωϣ ⲡⲓⲥϧⲉⲓ, C 43 217 *B* ⲉⲅⲱϣ ⲛ̅ⲛⲓⲥϧⲁⲓ.

With following preposition. ⲉ ⲉ-, *to, on*: Ex 24 7 *SB* ἀν. εἰς; P 44 64 *S* ⲉⲍⲛ̅ⲛⲉⲓⲥⲟⲁⲓ· ωϣ ⲉ-; Miss 8 49 *S* ⲉⲩⲛⲁⲟϣⲟⲩ (sc *verdicts*) ⲉⲣⲱⲧⲛ, C 100 229 *S* ⲉⲅⲱϣ ⲉⲣⲟϥ (sc *corpse*) ⲉⲩⲯⲁⲗⲗⲉⲓ = *ib* 89 209 *B* ⲉⲣ ⲙⲉⲗⲉⲧⲁⲛ only (*cf* Pachom Vita Tertia 168 ἀναγνώσεσι κ. ψαλμωδίαις), Mor 23 56 *S books* ⲉⲅⲱϣ ⲡⲣ̅ⲏⲧⲟⲩ ⲉⲡⲉⲕⲥⲱⲙⲁ & Thy blood (sc *during communion*), Lant 111 *S* ⲉⲅⲛⲁⲱϣ ⲡⲣ̅ⲏⲧϥ ⲉⲡⲣⲁⲛ ⲛⲁⲃⲕⲁⲧⲱⲡ (subject of book), Ep 389 *S* ⲟϣϥ ⲉⲧⲉⲩ̅ϣⲏ of saint, J 36 63 *S* ⲁⲅⲟⲩ̅ϥ (sc *deed*) ⲉⲣⲟⲛ, *ib* 13 67 *Sᵃ* ⲁϣⲥ, AM 46 *B* ⲡⲓⲥϧⲁⲓ...ⲟϣⲟⲩ ⲉⲣⲟϥ, CO 481 *S undertook* ϫⲉⲙⲁⲓⲱϣ ⲉⲡⲁⲉⲓⲧ ⲡⲁⲣⲁⲙ ⲉⲛⲉϩ (meaning?); ⲉϩⲣⲏ ⲉ- *B*: Jer 43 15 ἀν. εἰς; ⲉ ⲉϫⲛ̅- *S, on, in presence of*: BM 330 138 ωϣ ⲙ̅ⲡϫⲱⲙⲉ ⲉϫⲛ̅ⲡⲣⲱⲙⲉ (cf C 86 315 *B* sim ⲉ-), Wess 18 9 rubric ⲉⲕⲧⲙ̅ⲡⲓⲑⲉ ⲉⲱϣ ⲉϫⲱⲟⲩ (sc *these martyrs*) ⲉⲕⲛⲁⲱϣ ⲡⲁⲓ, Leyd 160 sim (*cf* ⲧⲁⲅⲟ ⲉϫⲛ̅- *ib* 136, 163); ⲉ ⲛ̅- dat: 1 Thes 5 27 *SB* ἀν. dat; *in* (*cf* ϩⲛ̅-): Si prol *S* ⲟϣⲟⲩ ⲛ̅ⲕⲉⲁⲥⲡⲉ μετάγεσθαι εἰς, El 52 *A* ⲁⲓⲱϣ ⲙ̅ⲙⲁϥ ⲡⲧⲁⲉⲥⲡⲉ (*cf* **A** ⲉϩ. ϩⲛ̅-); ⲉ ϩⲓ-, *in*: Ac 8 28 *B* (var ϧⲉⲛ-, *S* tr) ἀν. acc; ShC 73 72 *S may not* ωϣ ϩⲓⲱⲟⲩ, MG 25 425 *S* ⲭⲁⲣⲧⲏⲥ...ωϣ ϩⲓⲱⲱϥ = DeV 2 153 *B* ⲟϣϥ, El 56 *A*; ⲉ ϩⲛ̅-, ϧⲉⲛ-, *in*: BHom 38 *S* ωϣ ϩⲛ̅ⲡⲉⲩⲁⲅⲅⲉⲗⲓⲟⲛ ἀν. acc; ShC 42 218 *S* sim,

Mor 19 23 *S tablets* ⲁⲓⲱϣ ⲡϧⲏⲧⲟⲩ (var *ib* 18 14 & Miss 4 108 *B* ϧⲓ-), Pcod *F* 28 ωϣ ϧⲓⲡⲉϫⲱⲙⲉ = *S* 41 ⲉϣ ⲛⲭ., AM 39 *B* ωϣ ϫⲉⲛⲡⲁⲓⲭⲱⲙ, Vollers *Katal* 421 *B* rubric ωϣ ϫⲉⲛ̅ϯϭⲣⲓⲙⲓ ⲛⲭⲁⲛⲁⲡⲉⲁ.

—— nn m *SB, reading*: Ac 13 15 *SB*, 1 Tim 4 13 *SB* ἀνάγνωσις; Va 57 90 *B hear* ⲡⲱϣ ⲡⲟⲩⲓⲥⲧⲟⲣⲓⲁ πρᾶγμα τῆς ἱσ.; ShC 73 168 *S* ⲡⲡⲁⲩ ⲙⲡⲱϣ, BMOr 8811 227 *S* ⲡⲱϣ ⲡ̅ⲧⲟⲟⲩⲉ...ⲡⲣⲟⲩϭⲉ, CA 97 *S* ⲉⲩⲥⲱⲧⲙ ⲉⲡⲱϣ.

ⲙⲁⲓⲱϣ *S, fond of reading*: Mus 42 229 patriarch Alexander ⲟⲩⲙ.

ⲙⲁ ⲡⲱϣ *A²B, place of, passage for reading*: Va 58 178 ⲡⲓⲙ. ⲉⲧⲁⲟⲩϣⲟⲩ ⲉⲣⲟⲛ ἀνάγνωσμα; MG 25 316 n rubric ⲡⲓϣⲟⲣⲡ ⲙⲙ., Vollers *lc* sim, Mani H 24 *A²* all that chant or ⲧⲉⲩⲟ ⲡⲙ.

ⲣⲉϥ-, ⲣⲉϥⲱϣ *lector, reader, SBF*: RNC 73 *S* Apollonius ⲡⲣ., *ib* *A*. ⲡⲁⲛⲁⲅⲓⲛⲱⲥⲧⲏⲥ, Miss 4 161 *B* ⲯⲁⲗⲙⲱⲧⲟⲥ & ⲣ., C 43 201 *B* ⲓⲧⲉ ⲁⲡⲁⲅⲓⲛⲱⲥⲧⲏⲥ ⲓⲧⲉ ⲣ., AM 285 *B priests, deacons*, ⲣ., Saq 208 *S deacon* ⲡⲣ., *ib* 122 *S* ⲉⲩⲛⲟⲇⲓⲁⲕ⟋ sim, BIF 14 147 *S* ⲕⲁⲑⲏⲅⲉⲓ ⲉⲣⲟⲟⲩ ϩⲱⲥ ⲣ., Mor 31 204 *S Baruch* ⲡⲉϥⲕⲟⲩⲓ ⲡⲣ. (*cf* Jer 43 8), CMSS 78 *F* ⲡⲗ., C 86 89 *B deacon* ⲟⲓ ⲡⲣ. ⲉϫⲉⲛ̅ϯⲕⲁⲑⲉⲇⲣⲁ of St Macarius.

ⲥⲟⲡ ⲡⲱϣ *v* ⲥⲟⲡ **I**.

ϩⲟⲟⲩ ⲡⲱϣ *B, day of reading*: Va 57 141 2d discourse ϫⲉⲛⲡⲉϥϩⲟⲟⲩ ⲡⲱϣ.

ⲭⲱⲙⲉ ⲡⲱϣ *v* ⲭⲱⲙⲉ.

ϭⲓⲡⲱϣ *S, act, art of reading*: Miss 8 33 ⲧϭ. ⲛ̅ⲛⲉⲩⲡⲟⲗⲛ̅ⲏⲙⲁⲧⲁ ἀνάγνωσις; Bor 248 61 ⲧϭ. ⲛⲁⲥϧⲁⲓ, KKS 651 ⲡⲉϧⲗⲟϭ ⲡⲟⲩϫⲟⲡⲓ ⲡⲧⲉϥϭ., Mor 28 228 ⲟⲩⲥⲁϩ ϧⲓⲧⲉϥϭ., GöttN '98 172 ⲧⲧⲁⲍⲓⲥ ⲛⲧϭⲓⲡⲱϣ (sc *scriptures*).

C *a promise, vow B* intr: Nu 6 13 (*S* ⲉⲣⲏⲧ) εὔχεσθαι; Pro 13 12 (*S* ⲇⲟ, *A* ϣⲡ ⲱⲡ), 1 Tim 2 10 (*S* ϫⲱ) ἐπαγγέλλεσθαι; tr: Lev 27 2 (*S* ⲉ.) εὔ.; Ro 4 21 (*S* ⲇⲟ) ἐπαγ.; Jer 51 25 ὁμολογεῖν; C 43 196 ωϣ ⲡⲟⲩⲡⲣⲟⲥⲫⲟⲣⲁ, *ib* 86 336 ⲁϥⲱϣ ⲙⲙⲟϥ ⲙⲡⲁⲓⲣⲏϯ (refl ?). *With following preposition.* ⲉ ⲉ-, *to*: Ac 7 5 (*S* ⲉ.), C 89 169 ωϣ ⲙⲙⲟϥ ⲉϯⲙⲉⲧⲙⲟⲛⲁⲭⲟⲥ ἐπαγ. inf; ⲉ ⲛ̅- dat: Jud 11 30 (*S* ⲇⲟ), Ep Jer 34 (*F* ⲉ.) εὔ.; Gal 3 19 (*S* ⲇⲟ) ἐπαγ.; Lev 19 24 (*S* diff) αἰνετός; AM 239 gifts ωϣ ⲙⲙⲟⲟⲩ ⲡⲱⲟⲩ, DeV 2 217 virgin ωϣ ⲙⲙⲟⲥ ⲙⲡⲭ̅ⲥ̅, C41 44 ωϣ ⲡⲁϥ ⲛϩⲁⲡⲧⲁⲓⲟ; ⲉ ϧⲁ-, *for*: C 86 340 many ωϣ ϫⲁⲛⲟⲩϣⲏⲣⲓ.

—— nn m, *promise, vow*: Lu 24 49 (*S* ⲉ.), Ro 4 16 (*SF* ⲇⲟ) ἐπαγγελία; Lev 23 38 (*S* ⲟⲩⲱϣ) ἑκούσιος; ROC 17 399 ὑπόσχεσις; AM 183 ⲟⲅⲟⲡ ⲟⲩⲱϣ ⲉⲣⲟⲕ ⲡⲧⲟⲧϥ ⲙⲡⲟⲥ̅, BSM 51 ⲁⲩⲥⲟⲩⲧⲱⲡ ⲡⲟⲩⲱϣ ⲡⲉⲙ̅ⲫϯ = Va 63 20 = BMis 403 *S* ⲡⲉⲩϩⲏⲧ (*l* ? ⲡⲉⲩⲉⲣⲏⲧ), BSM 14 Isaac ⲡⲓⲱϣ ⲉⲑⲟⲩⲁⲃ = BMis 348 *S* ⲡⲉ.

ⲙⲉⲧⲱϣ, *promise, threat*: K 97 ϯⲙ. ⲁⲿⲉ⟩.

b expect *S*: Mt 5 17 (1 var ⲱⲡ), 10 34 (*B* ⲙⲉⲅⲓ) ⲛⲟⲙίⲍⲉⲓⲛ. But *cf* ? ⲟⲩⲱϣ *cleft* (ⲣ ⲟⲩ.).

(ⲱϣ), ⲟⲩϣⲍ[1], ⲣⲟⲩϣⲍ, ⲟⲡϣⲍ[2] *S*, ⲁⲛϣⲍ *Sf*, ⲁ̅ⲍ *A* (same ?), ⲁⲙϣⲍ *A*[2] vb tr (refl), *intrude* self, *slip in* c ⲉⲣⲟⲩⲛ: Mk 5 27[1] (var[2], *B* 1 ϫⲉⲛ-) ἔⲣⲭⲉⲥⲑⲁⲓ ἐⲛ, 2 Kg 4 5[2] ⲉⲓⲥέⲣ. ⲉἰⲥ, R 2 2 39 ⲧⲉⲡⲓⲑⲩⲙⲓⲁ ⲣⲟⲩϣ ⲉⲣ. ⲉⲣⲟⲛ stealthly, Mor 17 74 spirit ⲟⲛϣ (*l* ⲟⲛϣⲥ) ⲉⲣ. ⲉⲣⲟϥ ἐⲡⲉⲓⲥέⲣ. ἐⲛ, Gal 2 4[1] (*B* 1 ⲉϫⲟⲩⲛ) ⲡⲁⲣⲉⲓⲥέⲣ., P 129[14] 92 ⲁⲩϭⲟⲙ...ⲟⲛϣ (*l* ⲟⲛϣⲥ) ⲉⲣ. ⲉⲣⲟϥ ⲡⲣⲟέⲣ.; 1 Kg 26 5[2] ⲉⲓⲥⲡⲟⲣⲉⲩⲉⲓⲛ ⲉⲓⲥ; Jude 4[1] (var[2], *B* ⲥⲱϫⲉⲙ ⲉϫ.) ⲡⲁⲣⲉⲓⲥⲇύⲛⲉⲓⲛ; R 1 4 24 demon ⲟⲩϥ ⲉⲣ. ⲉⲣⲟϥ *possessus daemone*; PSBA 10 196 sim (ⲟⲩϥ MS, var LMis 228 *Sf* = Synax 1 387 24 ﺍﻋﺒﺮ), ShIF 197 snake ⲟⲩϥ ⲉⲣ. ⲉⲣⲉⲛϣⲕⲟⲗ, BHom 49 ⲧⲁⲙⲧⲁⲙⲁⲣⲧⲉ ⲣⲟ-ϣⲥ ⲉⲣ. ⲉⲧⲉⲯⲩⲭⲏ like thief, Mani 1 *A*[2] ⲁⲥⲁϣⲥ ⲁⲣ. ⲁⲣⲁⲩ ⲡⲟⲉ ⲡⲟⲩⲃⲏⲛ̅ϣⲉ, KKS 536 ⲁϥⲟⲡⲛϣ ⲉⲣ. ⲉⲙⲡ-ⲙⲏⲛϣⲉ = Mor 47 143; c ⲉϩⲣⲁⲓ: ShA 1 40 snake ⲟⲩϣ ⲉⲣ. ⲉϫⲛⲡⲉϭⲃⲟⲓ, ShC 73 11 man ⲉⲛⲧⲁⲥⲟⲩϣ (*sc* sword) ⲉⲣ. ⲛⲙⲙⲁⲩ ⲛ̅ⲣⲓⲧⲟⲩϥ; TU 43 16 *A* ϥⲁϩⲩ ⲁⲣⲁϥ (obscure).

Cf ? ⲱϣ†.

ⲱϣⲓ *B* nn, in ⲙⲟⲩ ⲛⲱ., *rain*: Lev 26 4 (*S* ϩⲟⲩ-ⲙⲡⲉ), Is 5 6 (*S* ϩⲱⲟⲩ intr) ὑⲉⲧόⲥ; Ps 67 10 (*S* do nn) βⲣⲟⲭή; Bodl Hunt 365 118 gloss ﻣﺎﺀ ﻣﻌﻠﻖ *suspended water*, as if from ⲓϣⲓ; *cf* Spg *Kopt Etym* 10.

ⲱϣⲙ *SF*, ⲟⲩⲱ. *S*, ⲱϭⲙⲉ *A*, ⲱϣⲉⲙ *BF*, ⲟⲩϣ. *B*(?), ⲉϣⲙ- *S*, ⲁϣⲉⲙ- *F*, ⲟⲩϣⲙⲍ *SBO*, ⲁϭⲙⲍ *A*, ⲟⲩϣⲙ† *S*, -ⲉⲙ† *B*, ⲁϣⲉⲙ† *F* vb I intr, *be quenched, dried up*: Job 30 8† *SF*(WS, *B* ϭⲉⲛⲟ), Is 34 9 *SF*(*B* do), *ib* 43 17 *SB*† (var ϭ.), Ez 20 47 *SB* ⲟ. ⲥβⲉⲛⲛύⲛⲁⲓ, Is 10 18 *SB* ἀⲡⲟⲥ., Job 18 5 *S*(*B* 1 ⲉϩⲟⲗ) ἀⲡⲟβⲁίⲛⲉⲓⲛ, Mt 3 12 neg *S*(*B* ⲁⲧϭ.) ἄⲥβⲉⲥⲧⲟⲥ; Jos 3 13 *SB* ἐⲕⲗⲉίⲡⲉⲓⲛ (*cf ib* 16 ⲱϫⲛ); Nah 1 4 *SA*(*B* ϣⲱϥ) ἐⲝⲉⲣⲏⲙⲟῦⲛ; Deu 28 65† *S*(*B* ⲃⲱⲗ ⲉⲃⲟⲗ) ⲧήⲕⲉⲓⲛ; PS 132 *S* ⲁⲡⲉϭⲉⲓϩⲉ ...ⲱ., ShA 1 457 *S* fire ⲉⲙⲉϥⲱ. ⲟⲩⲇⲉ ⲉⲙⲉϥϫⲉⲛⲁ, ShMun 116 *S* ⲙⲡⲉⲡⲉⲧⲛ̅ⲛⲟⲃⲉ ⲱ., El 138 *S* sea ⲛⲁⲱ., Lant 113 (E) *S* ⲁϥⲱ.(*sc* inundation water) ϣⲁⲛⲧⲉϥ-ⲱ. ⲥⲡⲁⲩ ⲙⲙⲁⲣⲉ, PGM 1 60 677 *O*]ⲕⲟⲩϣⲙⲉϥ, Mor 30 13 *F* ⲁϣⲱ. ⲛ̅ϭⲓ ⲡⲕⲱϩⲧ, TstAb 175 *B* ⲡⲁⲓⲓϭⲓ ... ϭⲱⲛⲧ ⲉⲱ.

II tr, *quench*: EstC 20 *S*, Job 30 8† *S*(*B* ϭ.), Cant 8 7 *SF*, Eph 6 16 *SB* ⲥβ., Pro 15 18 *SA* ⲕⲁⲧⲁⲥβ.; *ib* 16 14 *SA* ἐⲝⲓⲗάⲥⲕⲉⲥⲑⲁⲓ; BHom 70 *S* tears ⲱ. ⲛⲛⲁ-ⲡⲓⲗⲏ, BMar 144 *S* ⲁⲅⲟⲩⲱ. ⲙⲡⲛϣⲁϩ, P 129[16] 14 *S* sim ⲟⲩⲱ., PO 14 332 *B* ⲁⲕⲱ. ⲙⲡⲓⲭⲣⲱⲙ, J 65 24 *S* ⲱ. ⲡⲉϭⲉⲓϩⲉ, Mor 56 13 *S* destroy your youth & ⲉⲱ̅ⲙ ⲧⲉⲧⲛ̅ϭⲟⲧ.

ⲁⲧⲱ. *SB*, *unquenched, -able, unslaked*: J 65 23 *S* ⲕⲱϭⲧ ⲛⲁ., AM 154 *B* in tortures ⲕⲟⲡⲓⲁ ⲛⲁ. (*cf* ⲕ. ἄⲥβⲉⲥⲧⲟⲥ), Z 628 *S* in recipes ⲑⲏⲛ ⲛⲁ., AZ 23 114 *S* ⲃⲗ̅ϫⲉ ⲛⲁ.

ⲣⲉϥⲱ. *S*, *quencher*: Sa 19 19 ⲥβⲉⲥⲧⲓⲕόⲥ; Mor 25 64 ⲟⲩⲣ.ⲧⲉ ⲧⲉⲥⲃⲱ.

ⲁϣⲙⲓ *B* nn f, *thing burnt & quenched* (?), soot: Lam 4 8(*S* ⲭⲃⲃⲉⲥ, *F* ⲕⲉⲣⲙⲓ)ⲁⲥⲃόⲗⲏ; *wick*: K 231 †ⲁ. ﺍﻟﺬﺒﺎﻟﺔ; Va 58 152 ϥⲟϣⲉⲙ ⲙⲡⲉⲥⲙⲟⲧ ⲡⲟⲩⲁ.

ⲟϣⲙⲉϥ *S*, nn m, *dipping, tempering*: Si 34 29 βⲁφή. Or *l* ⲟⲩⲟϣⲙⲉϥ.

ⲱϣⲥ v ⲟⲩⲱϣⲥ intr.

ⲱϣ† *B* vb I intr, *drag, crawl, flow*: Is 30 28 (*SF* ⲥⲱⲕ), Va 61 28 snake ⲱ. ϭⲉⲡⲟⲅⲟⲩⲟⲓ ⲥύⲣⲉⲓⲛ; C 86 20 ⲉϥⲱ. ⲟⲓⲡⲉⲥⲏⲧ like snake, Va 61 94 maimed & ⲉϥⲱ.; c ϩⲓϫⲉⲛ-: Deu 32 24 (*S* ⲥⲱϣⲉ), Mic 7 17 (*SA* do) ⲥύ.; Lev 11 42 (*S* ⲙⲟⲟϣⲉ) ἔⲣⲡⲉⲓⲛ; C 86 324 ⲉϥⲱ. ϩ.ⲡⲉϥϫⲓϫ...ⲡⲉϥϭⲁⲗⲁϫ ⲱ. ⲡⲥⲱϥ; c ⲉⲃⲟⲗ: Ac 8 3 (*S* ⲥⲱⲕ ⲉⲃ.) ⲥύ.; *ib* 16 19 (*S* c. ⲉ-) ἔⲗ-ⲕⲉⲓⲛ ⲉⲓⲥ.

II tr: Is 3 16 (*S* ⲥⲱϣⲉ), Ac 14 19 (*S* = Gk), Ap 12 4 (*S* ⲥⲱⲕ) ⲥύ., Is 30 14 (*S* ϩⲱⲣ, *F* ϣⲱϣ) ἀⲡⲟⲥύ., Jer 29 10 (*S* ⲥⲱⲕ ⲉⲡⲉⲥⲏⲧ) ⲕⲁⲧⲁⲥύ.; Hab 1 15 (*A* ⲥⲱⲕ) ἐⲗ.; AM 206 soldiers ⲱ. ⲙⲙⲟϥ, *ib* 317 ⲱ. ⲙ-ⲙⲟϥ ϩⲓϫⲉⲛⲡⲉϩⲣⲟ, C 43 94 ⲱ. ⲙⲙⲟϥ ϭⲉⲛⲣⲁⲙⲁ ⲡⲱⲡⲓ.

—— nn m, *dragging*: C 86 149 clouds of dust ϩⲓⲧ-ⲉⲛⲡⲓⲱ. ⲛ̅ⲧⲉ ⲡⲉϥϫⲓⲛⲙⲟⲟϣⲓ.

ϫⲓⲛⲱ. as last: EW 36 Mark slain ϩⲓⲧⲉⲛⲟⲩϫ. ⲙ-ⲙⲟϥ during 2 days.

Cf ? ⲱϣ, *intrude*.

ⲱϣϫ *B* v ⲱϭϫ.

ⲱϭ *S*, ⲱⲃ *SB*, ⲟⲩϭ *S* nn m, *lettuce*: P 44 82 = 43 57 *S* ⲑⲣⲓⲍⲁϫ· ⲙⲁⲣⲟⲩⲗⲓⲁ· ⲡⲟⲩϭ ﺧﺲ, Tri 497 *S* ⲟⲩϭ ﺧﺲ, P 46 153 *S* ⲡⲓⲱϭ ﺧﺲ, K 196 *B* ⲡⲓⲱⲃ do, PMéd 235 *S* ⲉⲃⲣⲉ ⲱϭ, *ib* 70 ⲉⲣⲱⲧⲉ ⲡⲱⲃ ⲥⲓϣⲉ, Ryl 291 *S* ϣⲟⲗ ⲥⲡⲁⲩ ⲡⲱϭ. *V* AZ 59 142.

ⲱϭⲉ[1], ⲱⲃⲉ[2] *S*, ⲱϭ[3] *SA*, ⲱⲃ[4] *S*, ⲱϭⲓ *B*, ⲉϭ- *SB*, ⲱϭ- *S*, ⲟϭ[5] *SB*, ⲟⲃ[6] *S*, ⲁϭ[7] *SaA* vb intr, a *press*: Nu 6 4 *S* ⲏⲣⲡ ⲡⲱ.[2] (var ⲁⲃⲉ, *B* = Gk) ⲅίⲅⲁⲣⲧⲟⲛ ﺯﺑﻴﺐ; Gu 15 *S* ϣⲉ ⲡⲱ.[1] (var Mor 52 44 *S*[2]) *fuller's club* wherewith St James slain (*cf* Euseb 2 23 ⲝύⲗⲟⲛ ἐⲛ ᾧ ἀⲡⲉⲡίⲉⲍⲉ ⲧὰ ἱⲙάⲧⲓⲁ, Synax 2 230 11), BSM 58 *B* ⲟⲩ-ⲥⲁⲣϫ̅ ⲛⲱ. ﻣﻘﻢ = BMis 416 *S* & Va 63 25 *B* ⲡⲕⲁⲣ (*l* ? ⲡⲕⲁϩ); tr: Mic 6 15 *AB* ⲡⲓέⲍⲉⲓⲛ, Pro 24 68 *S*[5]*A* ⲉⲕⲡ., 1 Cor 9 27 *S*[1](var[4])*B* ὑⲡⲟⲡ.; 2 Kg 3 34 *S*[6] ⲉⲛ ⲡέⲇⲁⲓⲥ; ShC 42 178 *S* ⲧⲁⲙⲉⲓⲟ ⲙⲡⲉⲅⲟⲉⲓⲕ, ⲱ.[1] ⲙ-ⲡⲉⲩⲡⲉⲣ, C 89 52 *B* ϣⲁϥⲉϭ ϫⲱⲧ = MG 17 571 ﻋﺼﺮ, ShP 130[4] 131 *S* if he ⲉϭ ⲡⲉⲕⲓⲃⲉ ⲉⲡⲉϩⲟⲩⲟ he will draw blood, PMéd 315 *S* recipe ⲱϭ ⲡⲉϥⲙⲟⲟⲩ (*cf ib* 247 ⲥⲕ), BKU 1 27 *S*[a] sim ⲛ̅ⲧⲁϥϥ. With following preposition or adverb. c ⲉⲡⲉⲥⲏⲧ ⲉ-: JKP 2 18 *S* leaves ⲧⲉⲕⲟⲃⲟⲩ ⲉⲡ. ⲉⲡⲁⲡⲟⲧ; c ⲉϩⲟⲩⲛ ⲉ-: BMis 139 *S* ⲁϥⲱϭ ⲉϩ. ⲉⲣⲱϥ ⲙⲡⲉⲣⲱⲧⲉ; c ⲉϩⲣⲁⲓ,

ⲱϥⲧ   536   ⲱϩⲉ

eϩ. e-, *down upon*: Ge 40 11 SⁿB ἐκθλίβειν εἰς; c
eϫⲡ-: Tob 11 10 S¹ προσπάσσειν ἐπί; TT 77 S
martyr's hands ϩⲁⲛϭⲗϭⲓⲗ ⲛⲥⲉⲱ.¹ eϫⲱϥ;   c ⲛ-:
AZ 23 115 S recipe ⲟϩ(ϥ) ⲛⲣⲟⲥⲙ;   c eⲃⲟⲗ: AM
311 B when touched by water ⲁⲡⲉϥϣⲁⲣ ⲱ. eϩ. &
became great sore (*meaning?*);   as nn: ST 398 S
ⲧⲁⲟⲃⲕ ⲛϩⲟⲩⲱⲃ.

ᵇ *gather, mop up* B: AM 279 ⲁⲩⲱ. ⲙⲡⲉϥⲥⲛⲟϥ
σπογγίζειν; C 86 290 ⲁⲩⲱ. ⲡⲛⲓⲑⲙⲓⲥ ⲭⲟⲩⲛ συλλέγειν; *ib* 226 ⲁⲩⲱ. ⲡⲛⲓⲕⲁⲥ, C 41 21 ⲕⲉⲣⲙⲓ ⲛⲓⲃⲉⲛ...
ⲟϥⲟⲩ ⲉⲣⲟϥ (*sc* oven) = Miss 4 352 طرف لي.

ⲱϥⲧ *SBF*, ⲱⲃⲧ, ⲉϥⲧ-, eⲃⲧ- *S*, ⲟϥⲧⲥ *SB*, ⲟⲃⲧⲥ *S*,
ϩⲟϥⲧⲥ *B*, ⲟϥⲧ† *SB*, ⲟⲃⲧ† *S* vb tr, *nail, fix S*: Jud 5 26
διηλοῦν; Ps 21 16 (B ϭⲱⲗⲕ) ὀρύσσειν; ShMich 550
20 ⲱ. ⲛⲛⲉϫⲓϫ...ⲁϥⲟϥⲧⲟⲩ, BHom 126 ⲁⲩⲉϥⲧ ⲡⲉⲛⲧⲁϥ-
ⲧⲁϩⲣⲉ ⲡⲕⲟⲥⲙⲟⲥ, P 129¹² 13 his words few ⲛⲉϥⲥⲁⲣⲝ̄
ⲟϥⲧ (*cf* Ps 118 120), BM 1174 about vintage]ⲕⲱⲧⲟⲩ
ⲱϥⲧⲟⲩ ϫⲟⲗϭⲟⲩ (e)ⲃⲟⲗ...ⲧⲟⲟⲃⲟⲩ.

With following preposition.   c e- *SB*(rare)*F*, *to*:
ShC 42 37 eϥⲟ.† ⲉⲡϣⲉ, LAp 320 ⲡⲓϥⲧ eⲧⲱ. ⲉⲡϣⲉ,
BHom 76 eⲓϥⲧ eⲧⲟ.† ⲉⲡⲉϥϭⲓϫ; tr: Nu 16 39 (B ⲧⲁⲕⲧⲟ) περίθεμα προστιθέναι; Col 2 14 (B ϯ ⲓϥⲧ) προσηλ. dat; Leip 24 12 B brought them to town of their
martyrdom ⲡⲥⲉⲟϥⲧⲟⲩ ⲉⲧⲉⲡⲁⲣⲭⲓⲁ ⲡⲁⲛⲧⲟⲩⲅⲟⲥⲧⲟⲥ ἀπάγειν ἐν; ShC 42 104 ⲁⲩⲉϥⲧ ⲡⲉϥⲟⲩⲉⲣⲏⲧⲉ...ⲉⲡϣⲉ,
Mor 30 53 F ⲱ. eⲗⲁⲥ (*sc* bedhead) ⲛⲟⲛⲣⲓⲕⲟⲛ, *ib* 40
32 ϣⲥ ⲡⲉⲓⲃⲧ ⲛⲧⲁⲕⲧⲣⲉⲩⲟⲃⲧϥ ⲉⲡⲁⲥⲱⲙⲁ = *ib* 39 43
Sf ⲧⲁϭⲟⲩ, BSG 182 ⲟϥⲧ (*l* ⲱ.) ⲛⲣⲉⲛⲉⲓⲃⲧ ⲉⲧⲉϥⲁⲡⲉ
= *ib* 13 B ⲑⲟⲩϫ, BMis 202 ⲁϥⲟⲃⲧⲟⲩ ⲉⲡⲥⲱⲙⲁ, HT
M ⲱⲃⲧ ⲙⲙⲟϥ ⲉⲡⲉⲥϥⲟⲥ;   eϩⲟⲩⲛ e- *SB*, *in to, on
to*, intr: ViSitz 172 4 60 ⲉⲧⲉⲧⲛⲟϥⲧ eϩ. ⲉⲡⲉⲥϥⲟⲥ ⲕⲁ-
ⲑⲛⲗ. ἐν; ShIF 182 in ark ϩⲉⲣⲟⲩⲁϩ...ⲟϥⲧ eϩ. ⲉⲣⲉⲛ-
ⲣⲁⲙⲡⲓ, *ib* 149 snakes devouring one another ⲛⲧⲁⲩⲱ.
eϩ. ⲉⲛⲉⲩⲉⲣⲏⲩ, *ib* 251 sorrow ⲟϥⲧ eϩ. ⲉⲛⲣⲏⲧ, Wess
18 113 worldly things ⲉⲛⲟϥⲧ eϩ. ⲉⲣⲟⲟⲩ, C 43 11 B
nails protruded ⲛⲥⲉⲱ. eϩ. ⲉⲡⲓⲥⲩⲛⲯⲉⲗⲓⲟⲛ; tr: Sh
Ryl 70 246 hands eⲟϥⲧⲟⲩ eϩ. ⲉⲣⲟϥ (*sc* cross), Mun
38 ⲱ. eϩ. ⲉⲣⲟⲥ ⲛⲣⲉⲛⲉⲓϥⲧ, C 43 5 B ⲱ. ⲙⲡⲉϥⲥⲱⲙⲁ eϩ.
ⲉⲣⲟⲥ;   as nn m, *nailing; attachment to*: Br 248 S
ⲡⲉⲱ. eϩ. ⲉⲡⲗⲟⲅⲟⲥ, Montp 114 B ⲡⲓⲱ. eϩ.تسمير; c
eϫⲡ- *S*, *upon*: Mor 56 31 cross ⲟϥⲧ eϫⲡⲧⲩⲗⲏ; c
ⲛ- *SB*, *nailed, studded with*: Gu 30 S ⲛⲡⲟⲧⲟⲩ ⲉⲧⲟⲃⲧ
ⲛⲓⲃⲧ προσηλ.; Ex 26 32 B ⲟ.† ⲛⲛⲟⲩⲃ (S ϭⲟⲟⲗⲉ), *ib*
37 2 B ϩⲟϥⲧⲉ χρυσοῦν; *ib* 27 2 B ϩⲟϥⲧⲟⲩ καλύπτειν;
Louvre 10022 S ϩⲁⲗⲕⲟⲥ (? *balteus*) ⲛⲛⲟⲩⲃ eⲟⲃⲧ ⲛ-
ⲡⲥϥⲣⲁⲅⲓⲥ, BMis 549 S ⲁⲟϥⲧⲟⲩ ⲡⲉⲓϥⲧ; c ϩⲛ-,
ϩⲉⲛ- *SB*, *in*: Va 68 173 B ⲟϥⲧϥ ϩⲉⲛⲡⲓϣⲟⲟⲩⲓ περιφράσσειν; ShA 1 86 S nails ⲟϥⲧ ϩⲓⲙⲁϩⲏⲧ, Mor 33
11 S body ⲟⲃⲧ ϩⲛϩⲟⲟⲧⲉ ⲙⲡⲭ̄ⲥ̄ (var BMis 77 ⲧⲁϩⲣⲏⲩ,
cf Ps 118 120), FR 180 S cross ⲧⲟⲕⲥ ϩⲓⲡⲙⲁ ⲛⲧⲁⲅⲟⲃ-
ⲧϥ ⲛϩⲏⲧϥ;   eⲃⲟⲗ ϩⲛ- *S*: Ps 118 120 (B ϯ ⲓϥⲧ) ⲕⲁ-
ⲑⲛⲗ. ἐκ, cit Mus 40 256.

ϭⲓⲛ-, ϫⲓⲛⲱ. *SB, nailing*: BHom 103 ⲧϭ. ⲉⲡⲉⲥϥⲟⲥ
TRit 85 ⲡⲓϫⲓⲛⲓϥⲧ eϩⲟⲩⲛ مسمر.

eⲓϥⲧ *SAA²*, eⲓⲃⲧ *SF*, ⲓϥⲧ *SBF*, ⲓⲃⲧ *SFO* nn m,
nail, spike: Jos 23 13 SB, Jer 10 4 SB, Jo 20 25 SA²B
ἧλος; ShA 2 274 S idols ⲉⲩⲧⲁϫⲣⲏⲩ ϩⲛⲣⲉⲡⲉⲓⲉ., Sh
ViK 9291 S ⲟⲩⲉⲓ. ⲙⲡⲉⲛⲓⲡⲉ, AZ 21 100 O & BKU 1
21 ro F ⲓⲃⲧ sim, PSBA 19 215 S ⲛϯⲟⲩ ⲛⲓⲃⲧ of Cross
(*cf* Faras 3 pl 71 28, Kropp iii 60), C 43 131 B ⲡⲓ.
ⲉⲩϣⲏⲟⲩ ⲉⲩⲗⲟⲡϣ ⲛⲭⲣⲱⲙ, *ib* 60 B ⲡⲓ. each half-ell
long, *ib* 61 B bade lift him eⲃⲟⲗ ϩⲉⲛⲡⲓⲓ., Gött Abh
'17 77 S ϣⲙⲉ ⲛⲓⲃⲧ of water-wheel (*cf* Ryl 340), BM
708 F ⲟⲩⲗⲁⲁⲩ ⲡⲉⲃⲓⲧ for tower, ST 226 S eⲓ. ⲟⲩ (*l*
ⲱ), Ep 320 S eⲓ. ϣⲏⲗ; PMéd 265, 267 S eⲓ., *cf* ἧλος
wart;   ϣⲥ, ϣⲉ ⲡⲉⲓ. *SSfA²B, blow, wound of nail*:
Jo 20 25 SA²(B as Gk) τύπος τ. ἧλ. (*cf* TU 43 3 A
ⲡⲉⲓ. ⲛⲛⲁϭⲓϫ), LMär 5 S ϣ. ⲉⲁⲩⲧⲁⲁϥ ⲉⲡⲁⲥⲱⲙⲁ =
C 43 60 B, Mor 39 42 Sf;   ϯ ⲓ. *B, put, fix nail*: Ps
118 120 (S ⲱ. vb), C 86 69 ⲙⲡⲟⲩϯ ⲓ. ⲡⲁϥ καθηλ.;
Col 2 14 (S do) προσηλ.;

ⲱϥⲧ S vb intr, *be worn, eaten away* (?): R 1 4 33
by much fasting ⲁⲡⲉϥⲥⲱⲙⲁ ⲱ. ⲧⲏⲣϥ & he could no
longer walk *exesus*, *ib* 51 ⲉⲣⲉⲡⲉϥ[ⲥⲱ]ⲙⲁ ⲱ. [ⲉⲙⲁ]-
ⲧⲉ so that naught save bones visible *exesus*.   Same
as last?

ⲱϥⲧ   *v* ⲱⲃⲧ *goose*.

ⲱϩⲙⲉ *A*   *v* ⲱϣⲙ.

ⲱϭⲧ *B*, ⲱϭⲧ *F*, ⲟϭⲧ† *B* vb intr, *drip, trickle*: P 54
118 eⲧⲱ. نقط, قطر, رز; Mor 27 27
F (ⲙ)ⲡⲉⲧⲡⲏⲩⲛ ⲡⲣⲙⲙⲓⲏ ⲗⲁ ⲉⲥⲱϭⲧ ⲉϫⲉⲛⲡⲁⲃⲁⲗ =
BMis 374 S ⲉⲩⲥⲱⲕ = Va 63 7 B c. ϩⲉⲛ-. *Cf?*
ⲟⲩⲱⲧϩ.

(ⲱϩ), ⲟϩⲥ *O* vb tr (refl) as imperat, meaning unknown: AZ 21 99 charm ⲟϩⲕ ⲕⲟⲩⲣ[ⲓ]ⲏⲗ.

ⲱϩ *SA²O*, ⲁϩ *S* interj, *woe!* (?): ShC 73 213 ⲱϩ
ⲱϩ ⲡⲉⲓⲛⲟϭ ⲛϣⲧⲁ ⲛⲧⲁϥϣⲱⲡⲉ, Sh(Besa?)BM 213 38
ⲱϩ ⲱϩ ⲁϩ ⲁϩ ⲙⲡⲉⲛⲣⲱⲙⲉ eⲓⲙⲉ, Sh(?)Leyd 410 who
will weep for him ⲉⲛⲧⲁⲩⲛ ⲡⲉⲓϣⲱⲡⲉ ⲉϩⲣⲁⲓ ⲉϫⲱϥ?
ⲁϩ ⲁϩ, ShC 73 80 ⲁϩ ⲕⲛⲁⲟⲩⲙ ⲡⲉⲓⲕⲟⲟⲩⲉ, Mani H
56 A² ⲱϩ ⲱϩ [   ]e ϫⲉⲙⲡⲓⲛⲣ ⲛⲁⲃⲉ ⲁⲣⲁϥ, PGM 1
60 661 O ⲁⲛⲟⲕ ⲱϩ ⲁⲡⲕ ⲁⲉⲓⲟⲩⲱ (same?);   c e-,
woe to: Mor 50 50 ⲱϩ ⲉⲡⲉϩⲟⲟⲩ that mother bare
me, ⲱϩ ⲉⲧⲉⲩⲛⲟⲩ when I knew the idol!, BMis 32 ⲱϩ
ⲉⲡⲧⲟϣ that nurtured thee!

ⲱϩ *SO*   *v* ⲟⲟϩ, adding prob PMéd 285 S ⲕⲁⲧⲁ
ⲱϩ (*cf ib* 230 ⲕⲁⲧⲁ eⲃⲟⲧ).

ⲱϩⲉ *SA* nn   *v* ⲟϩⲉ.

ⲱϩⲉ *S*(rare)*AA²*, ⲟϩⲉ *S*, ⲟϩⲓ *B*, ⲱϩⲓ *Sf/F*, ⲁϩⲓ *F*, but
mostly qual for absol (except in *A*), ⲁϩⲉ† *SAA²*, ⲟϩⲓ†
BF vb ▲ intr, *stand, stay, wait* (esp *B*): Is 5 11 *SB*

(*F* ϭⲱ), *ib* 66 22 *B*(*S* ϭⲱ), Phil 1 25 *B*(*SF* do), MG
25 219 *B* ⲁⲡⲓⲙⲉⲅⲓ ⲟ. ⲙⲡⲉϥⲣⲏϯ = Z 349 *S* ⲙⲟϭⲡ
ⲉⲃⲟⲗ ⲙⲉⲛⲉⲓⲛ, Va 66 308 *B* ⲟ. ϣⲁⲡⲧⲉⲕⲉⲙ *ἀναμ*., Nu
23 19 *B*(*S* ⲙⲟϭⲡ ⲉⲃ.) *ἐμμ*., Ro 11 23 *B*(*S* ϭⲱ) *ἐπιμ*.,
He 7 23 *B*(*S* ⲙ. ⲉⲃ.) *παραμ*.; Lev 27 14 *B*(*S* ⲧⲁϩⲟ
ⲉⲣⲁⲧϥ), Jer 31 11 *B* ἱστάναι, *ib* 26 14 *B*(*S* ⲁ. ⲣⲁⲧϥ)
ἐφισ.; PS 48 *S* ⲡⲉⲧⲁ.(*sic l*)ϩⲙⲡⲉϥⲙⲩⲥⲧⲏⲣⲓⲟⲛ, C 43
15 *B* ⲁϭⲟ. ϩⲓⲧⲉⲛ ⲙⲡⲓϩⲛⲧⲉⲙⲱⲛ, *ib* 170 *B* ⲛⲧⲉϭⲟ.
ϫⲉⲡⲟⲏ ⲉⲧⲉⲱϣϥ ⲛⲡⲛⲱⲗⲏ, Aeg 31 *B* shroud shall o.
ϫⲉⲡⲡⲉⲕⲥⲱⲙⲁ till last day, Cat 162 *B* ⲉϭⲟ. ⲉϥⲙⲏⲛ
ⲉⲃⲟⲗ, BM 1112 *S* ⲙⲡⲣⲁ. ⲛⲧⲱϣ ⲧⲁⲉⲡⲓⲥⲧⲟⲗⲏ (*cf* c
ⲛ-), TurO 7 *S* I found no camel ϫⲉⲁϥⲃⲱⲕ ⲛⲁϥ ⲉϭⲁ.
had gone after (?) waiting.

With following preposition or adverb.   c ⲉ-
SAB, abide by, wait for: Mor 37 117 *S* ⲁ. ⲉⲣⲟⲓ *μ*. no
prep, Gal 3 10 *SB* ἐμμ. *ἐν*, Hab 2 3 *A* ⲱ. (*B* ϫⲟⲩϣⲧ
ϫⲁⲭⲉⲛ-) ὑπομ. acc; Ac 21 24 *S*(*B* ϯ ⲙⲁϯ) στοιχεῖν;
1 Cor 11 33 *S*(*B* ⲛ-) ἐκδέχεσθαι; Jos 1 18 *S* neg
ἀπείθεσθαι; PS 19 *S* ⲧⲛⲁ. ⲉⲣⲟⲕ to endue thee, ShC
73 158 *S* ⲉϭⲛⲁⲁ. ⲉⲡⲉⲅⲉⲣⲏⲩ till all assembled, ClPr
27 75 *S* ⲉⲧⲉⲧⲛⲁ. ⲁⲡ ⲉⲑⲁⲛ ⲡⲉⲩⲯⲩⲭⲏ, PO 14 355 *B*
ⲡⲁϭⲟ. ⲉⲣⲟϥ, Bor 240 114 *S* ⲁ. ⲉⲡⲣⲱⲃ ⲙⲡⲃⲁⲡⲧⲓⲥⲙⲁ
to do it worthily; vbal: Ge 29 35 *B* ⲟ. ⲉϣⲧⲉⲙ- (*S*
ⲗⲟ) *ισ*.; Is 30 18 *B*(*SF* ϭⲱ) *μ*.;   c ⲙⲛ-, ⲡⲉⲙ- *SB*,
stay with: C 89 61 *B* ⲧⲉⲡⲟ. ⲡⲉⲙⲁϥ *μ*., Si 12 15 *B*
(*S* ϭⲱ) διαμ.; Ez 23 17 *B*(*S* ϣⲱⲡⲉ ⲙⲛ-) καταλύειν;
Lu 8 38 *B*(*S* ⲙⲟⲟϣⲉ ⲙⲛ-) εἶναι σύν; MIE 2 354 *B*
ⲟ. ⲡⲉⲙⲏⲓ ⲡⲕⲉⲟⲩϫⲓ, JAOS 48 149 *S* ⲉϥⲟⲩⲣⲏ ⲛⲁⲙ-
ⲙⲁⲓ;   c ⲛ- *SB*, *wait for, attend to*: Is 8 17 *B*(*S* ϭⲱ)
μ. acc, Deu 27 26 *S*(*B* ⲛⲥⲁ-) ἐμμ. *ἐν* (*cf* Gal 3 10), Ac
1 4 *B*(*S* do) περιμ. acc, Ps 24 5 *B*(*S* = Gk) ὑπομ. acc;
Mor 32 5 *S* found him ⲉϥⲁ. ⲛⲁϥ, Va 57 106 *B* ⲟ. ⲛⲏⲓ
ⲡⲟⲩⲕⲟⲩϫⲓ, Bodl(P) f 30 *S* ⲛⲡⲉⲣⲟϭⲉ ⲛⲟⲱϭ (*sc* letter,
cf intr), Ryl 278 *S* ⲛⲡⲣⲁ. ⲡⲱ[ϣ ⲛⲛ]ⲁⲥϭⲁⲓ ere ye
send;   *as, for*: Ge 44 33 *B* παραμ.; Va 63 100 *B*
poverty ⲉϭⲟ. ⲙⲙⲁⲩ ⲛⲧⲙⲉⲧⲣⲁⲙⲁⲟ;   c ⲟⲩⲃⲉ-
SB, stand before, against: Mt 5 39 *S*(*B* ϯ ⲉϫⲟⲩⲛ ⲉ-
ϩⲣⲉⲛ-) ἀνθισ. dat, Ge 40 4 *B*(var *S* om, gloss ? on ϯ
ⲛϧⲣⲉⲛϥ ⲉ-), Si 51 3 *S* ⲁ. *παρισ*.; Ge 44 21 *B* ἐπι-
μελοῦσθαι dat;   c ϫⲁⲧⲉⲛ- *B, stay with*: Gal 1 18
(*S* ϭⲱ) ἐπιμέν. *πρός*, 1 Cor 16 6 (*S* do) παραμ. *π*.; C 89
201 pray you ϫⲁⲧⲟⲧϥ ⲡⲉⲙⲡⲓϫⲟⲓ (*cf* MG 17 696
مشا امضوا معد (اين), *ib* 41 9 unworthy ⲉⲟⲣⲉϥϭ. ϫⲁ-
ⲧⲟⲧ;   c ϩⲓϫⲉⲛ- *B, upon*: Jo 1 32 (*S* ⲟⲩⲱϩ ⲉϫⲛ-) *μ*.
ἐπί;   c ⲉⲃⲟⲗ *S, stand out, against*: 2 Kg 5 6 ἀνθισ.;
ⲉⲃ. ⲉ-: Jud 9 23 ἀθετεῖν *ἐν*, 1 Kg 24 12 (*B* ϣⲱϣϥ ⲛⲛ)
ἀθέτησις εἶναι εἰς; Pcod 30 ⲁ. ⲉⲃ. ⲉⲣⲟⲕ opp ϩⲩⲡⲟ-
ⲧⲁⲥⲥⲉ ⲛⲁⲕ;   ⲡⲃⲟⲗ ⲉ- *S* sim: Mor 18 47 monastery
ⲉⲧⲛⲁⲁ. ⲡ. ⲉⲣⲟⲕ(var *ib* 19 55 ⲁⲛⲧⲓⲗⲉϭⲉ), *ib* 18 28 ⲁϭⲁ.
ⲡ. ⲉⲡⲉⲅⲉⲡⲓⲥⲕⲟⲡⲟⲥ (var *ib* 19 37 ⲁ. ⲣⲁⲧⲟⲩ ⲉ-), BP
12491 ⲁϭⲁ. ⲡ. ⲉⲣⲟⲓ ⲁⲩⲧⲁⲕ[ⲉ] ⲛⲕⲁⲡⲱⲡ ⲡⲧⲟⲟⲧ;   ⲥⲁⲃⲟⲗ *B, outside, against*: BSM 39 ⲙⲡⲉⲣⲟ. ⲥ. = BMis
384 *S* ⲁ. ⲣⲁⲧⲕ ϩⲓⲡⲥⲁ ⲛⲃ., AM 125 ⲁϩⲗⲓ ⲟ. ⲥ. ⲏ ⲉϥϯ

ⲟⲩⲃⲉⲑⲛⲏⲟⲩ ? (*cf* c ⲉⲃⲟⲗ);   c ⲉⲡⲁϩⲟⲩ *SB, stay behind*: ShBor 300 71 *S* sheep ⲁ. ⲉⲡ. & come not with
flock, LIb 7 *B* ⲁϩⲟ. ⲉⲡ. there;   c ⲉϫⲟⲩⲛ ⲉϩⲣⲉⲡ-
BF, stand against: Lev 26 37 (*S* ϯ ⲙⲡ-), EpJer 55
F(*B* ⲉϫ. ⲉϫⲉⲡ-) ἀνθισ. dat.

ϭⲓⲛⲁ. ⲉϫⲡ- *S, act of remaining on*: Leyd 426
ⲧⲉϥϭ. ⲉϫⲙⲡⲉⲥϯⲟⲥ.

B with ⲣⲁⲧϥ, ⲁ ⲱϭⲉ, ⲁϭⲉ ⲉⲣⲁⲧϥ *S* (rare), *stand on
foot, stand*: BP 11349 ⲁⲓⲱ. ⲉⲣⲁⲧ ϩⲓϫⲱⲟϥ, Eccl 8 3
ⲙⲡⲣⲁ. ϭⲉ ⲉⲣⲁⲧⲕ, Ac 2 14 ϥⲁ. ϫⲉ ⲉⲣⲁⲧϥ (var ⲣⲁⲧϥ),
v also c ⲉ- *s f*.

b ⲱϭⲉ ⲣⲁⲧϥ (archaic), ⲁϭⲉ ⲡ. (for ⲱϭⲉ ⲉⲣ., ⲁϭⲉ ⲉⲣ.)
S, ⲱϭⲓ ⲡ. *S^f*, others not contracted ⲱϭⲉ, ⲁϭⲉ ⲁⲣⲉⲧ
AA², ⲟϭⲓ ⲉⲣⲁⲧ *B*, ⲱϭⲓ, ⲟϭⲓ ⲉⲗⲉⲧ, ⲉⲣ. *F*: Nu 9 15
S(*B* ⲧⲁϩⲟ ⲉⲣ.), Ps 25 12 *SB*, Pro 14 11 *SA* ⲱ. (*B*
ⲥⲉⲙⲛⲓ), Eccl 1 4 *F* ⲟ. (*S* ϣⲟⲟⲡ), Is 36 2 *SBF* ⲱ.,
Zech 2 3 *A* ⲁ. *B*, Mt 6 5 *SBF* ⲟ., Jo 6 22 *SA²* ⲁ. *B*,
Ro 11 20 *SBF* ⲱ., 1 Cor 7 37 *SBF* ⲱ., AP 13 *A²* ⲁⲥⲁ.
ⲁⲣⲉⲧϥ ἱστάναι, Eph 5 14 *B*(*S* ⲧⲱⲟⲩⲛ) ἀνισ., Jer 26 4
B κάθισ., Deu 17 12 *SB*, Dan 7 10 *SB*, Mk 15 39
SBF ⲱ. παρισ., Jo 11 42 *SA²* ⲁ. (*B* ⲕⲱϯ), AM 279 *B*
περισ., Ps 38 1 *SB* συνισ., Jer 20 10 *B* ἐπισυνισ., Ps
129 4 *SB*, Am 2 15 *BF* ⲟ. (JEA 11 246, *S* ⲧⲱⲕ ⲉ-
ϩⲟⲩⲛ) ὑφισ.; Lev 13 5 *B*(*S* ϭⲉⲉⲧ), Jo 9 41 *SA²* ⲁ.(*B*
ϣⲟⲡ), 1 Cor 3 14 *B*(*SF* ϭⲱ) μέν.; EpJer 26 *B* ὀρθοῦσθαι, Is 16 5 *SB* διορ., Aeg 248 *S* praying ⲉϭⲁ. ⲣⲁⲧⲟⲩ ὀρθός, Gal 2 14 *B*(*S* ⲥⲟⲩⲧⲱⲛ) ὀρθοποδεῖν; Jos 3
13 *SB* πόδες καταπαύειν; Cant 6 3 *S*, Ez 30 22 *B*
τάσσειν; El 50 *A* ⲁⲓⲱ. ⲁⲣⲉⲧ... ⲉϥⲁ. ⲁⲣⲉⲉⲧϥ, MG
25 12 *B* ⲁⲧⲉϥⲥⲟⲩⲣⲓ ⲟ. ⲉⲣⲁⲧⲥ ⲛⲁⲣⲕⲁⲛ; Is 14 31 *S*(*B*
ⲟϭⲓ) εἶναι, Sa 9 9 *S* παρεῖ.; *ib* 6 15 *S* πάρεδρος, PS
239 *S* ⲧⲛⲁ. ⲣⲁⲧⲕ ⲛⲧⲭⲟⲕϥ ⲉⲃⲟⲗ *stay & complete it*,
ShA 2 270 *S* ϯⲛⲁⲁ. ⲣⲁⲧ & reprove you, *ib* 281 *S*
ⲉϥⲉⲁ. ⲣⲁⲧϥ ⲛϭⲓ ⲡϫⲁϫⲉ, ShBor 247 109 *S* ⲙⲡⲉⲗⲁⲁ-
ⲗⲁⲁⲩ...ⲁ. ⲣⲁⲧϥ all is upset, Mani 2 *A²* ⲉⲧⲁ. ⲁⲣⲉⲧⲟⲩ
ϩⲛ̄ⲟⲩⲧⲱⲧ, AP 2 *A²* ⲁϥⲁ. ⲛⲁⲉ ⲁⲣⲉⲧϥ, ST 47 *S^a* am
ready ⲛⲧⲁⲱϭ ⲁⲣⲏⲧ ⲛⲧⲁϯ (*ib* var ⲁ. ⲁⲣⲏⲧ), C 42 242
S^f ⲁⲩⲱ. ⲣⲁⲧⲟⲩ in midst, Mor 24 32 *F* ⲉⲧⲱ. ⲉⲗⲉⲧⲃ,
BMis 160 *S* when calm ⲁⲛⲭⲟⲓ ⲁ. ⲣⲁⲧϥ ϩⲛⲟⲩⲥⲙⲓⲛⲉ
= BSM 70 *B*.

With following preposition.

—— ⲉ- *SABF, stand before, against, attend on*:
Ap 7 1 *S*(*B* ϩⲓϫⲉⲡ-) *ισ*. ἐπί, ROC 18 174 *S* unable
ⲉⲁ. ⲣⲁⲧϥ ⲉⲣⲟⲟⲩ *ισ*. κατά, Deu 7 24 *S*(*B* ϯ ⲉϫⲟⲩⲛ
ⲉϩⲣⲉⲡ-) ἀντισ. κ. πρόσωπον, Hos 14 1 *S*(BMOr 8810
505)*A*(*B* ⲟⲩⲃⲉ-) ἀ. πρός, Jer 14 7 *SB* ἀ. dat, Is 59 2
S(*B* diff) διισ., Ge 18 8 *S*(*B* ⲥⲁⲃⲟⲗ ⲛ-), Pro 22 29
SA ⲱ., Ac 9 39 *S*(*B* ⲛⲁϩⲣⲉⲡ-), Va 66 298 *B* servants
ⲟ. ⲉⲣⲁⲧⲟⲩ ⲉⲣⲟⲡ παρισ. dat, Ac 25 7 *SB*(var ϫⲁ-)
περισ., He 12 1 *SB* εὐπερίστατος; Jud 8 1 *S* διαλέγεσθαι πρός; Jos 17 14 *S* ἀντείπειν dat; Nu 5 13 *S*(*B*
ϣⲱⲡⲓ ϫⲁ-) εἶναι μετά; BG 62 *S* virgin ⲉⲧⲱ. ⲣⲁⲧⲥ
ⲉⲁϫⲁⲙ, PS 17 *S* ⲧⲛⲁ. ⲣⲁⲧⲛ ⲉⲣⲟⲕ ⲉⲧⲣⲛ-, El 102 *A*

sins ⲡⲁⲱ. ⲁⲣⲉⲧⲟⲩ ⲁⲣⲁϥ, ShWess 9 171 *S* servant
ⲉⲧⲡⲣⲟϥⲓⲥⲧⲁ ⲡⲡⲉϥⲟⲃⲏⲅⲉ ⲏ ϫⲉϥⲁ. ⲣⲁⲧⲅ ⲉⲣⲟϥ, TurM
1 *S* courtiers ⲁ. ⲣⲁⲧⲟⲩ ⲉⲡⲣⲣⲟ = Miss 4 120 *B*, FR
74 *S* Saviour sat ⲁⲓⲁ. ⲣⲁⲧⲓ ⲉⲣⲟϥ, P 129¹⁴ 122 *S* to
priest ⲁ. ⲣⲁⲧⲕ ⲉⲧⲉⲕⲧⲁϫⲓⲥ = DeV 1 78 *B* ⲕⲁⲧⲁ ⲧⲉⲕⲧ.,
DeV 2 196 *B* we wish ⲉⲑⲣⲉⲕⲟ. ⲉⲣⲁⲧⲕ ⲉⲡⲓⲉⲣⲅⲁⲧⲏⲥ
oversee, BP 12501 *S* ready ⲏⲧⲛⲁ. ⲉⲣⲁⲧⲓ ⲉⲣⲟⲟⲩ, CO
344 *S* let him come ⲛϥⲁ. ⲉⲣⲁⲧϥ ⲉⲡⲉϥϥⲱⲃ *attend to*,
BIF 22 107 *F* soldiers ⲟ. ⲉⲗⲉⲧⲟⲩ ⲉⲗⲁϥ (*sc* king), Kr
36 *F* ⲉⲃⲉⲁϩⲓ ⲣⲉⲧⲃ ⲉⲡⲉⲏⲙⲁ ViK 9126 49 *Sⁱ* ⲁⲥⲟⲣⲉ
ⲣⲁⲧⲥ ⲉⲡⲉⲏⲙⲁ, Kr 228 *S* go ⲛⲕⲁ (*sic*) ⲣⲁⲧⲕ ⲉⲣⲟⲥ, Ryl
380 *S* ⲉⲓⲟⲣⲉ ⲣⲁⲧⲕ ⲉⲡⲁⲃⲉⲗⲱⲛ *at Babylon*;   vbal:
Mk 11 25 *SB* ⲁ. ⲣⲁⲧⲧⲏⲩⲧⲛ ⲉϣⲗⲏⲗ *io.* part; R 1 3
27 *S* ⲁϩⲁ. ⲣⲁⲧⲟⲩ ⲉⲁⲓϣⲉ.

—— ⲉϫⲛ- *SAB, upon, against*: Dan 10 11 *B*(*S*
ϩⲓϫⲛ-), Zech 14 12 *A*(*B* ϩⲓϫ.), Ap 8 3 *S*(*B* ϩⲁⲧⲉⲛ-)
io. ἐπί, Gu 33 *S* ⲁϥⲁ. ⲣⲁⲧϥ ⲉ.ⲙⲁⲣⲕⲉⲗⲗⲟⲥ (var ϩⲓ-
ϫⲛ-), Mt 29 *S*(*B* ⲥⲁⲡϣⲱⲓ) *io. ἐπάνω*, Ac 23 11 *S* (var
ϩ., *B* ⲛⲁϩⲣⲉⲛ-) ⲉϥⲓⲥ. dat, Nu 7 2 *SB* ⲡⲁⲣⲓⲥ. *ἐπί*; MG
25 15 *B* ⲟ. ⲉⲣⲁⲧⲕ ⲉϫ. ⲧⲉⲕⲙⲉⲑⲙⲏⲓ *πείθειν* dat, Ob
13 *S*(*A* ϩⲓϫⲛ-, *B* ⲟⲩⲱϩ ⲉϫ.) *συμπείθ. ἐπί*; Nah 3 14
A(*B* ⲁⲙⲟⲛⲓ) *κατακρατεῖν*; ShA 1 116 *S* ϥⲛⲁⲁ. ⲣⲁⲧϥ
ⲁⲛ ⲉϫⲙⲡⲉⲥⲛⲟϥ *stand in judgment on*, Ryl 94 109 *S*
ⲉⲥⲁ. ⲣⲁⲧⲥ ⲉϫⲙⲡⲕⲱⲣⲧ *at, beside*, BM 1129 *S* I en-
join thee (f) ⲧⲁⲣⲉⲣⲁ. ⲣⲁⲧⲉ ⲉϫⲱⲟⲩ *give heed to*, MIE
2 417 *B* ⲟ. ⲉⲣⲁⲧⲕ ⲉ.ⲡⲓⲥⲛⲏⲟⲩ = BAp 123 *S* ⲡⲣⲟⲥⲉⲭⲉ ⲉϫⲛ-, P 78 14 *S* heretic ⲁ. ⲣⲁⲧϥ ⲉϫⲛ- church, C
43 51 *B* vision ⲟ. ⲉⲣⲁⲧⲥ ⲉϫ. sleepers.

—— ⲙⲛ-, ⲛⲉⲙ- *SBF, with*: Nu 1 5 *SB* ⲡⲁⲣⲓⲥ.
ⲙⲉⲧⲁ, Ps 93 16 *SB* ⲥⲩⲙⲡ. *ἐπί*; 2 Kg 10 9 *S* (var ⲉ-)
γίνεσθαι πρός; 2 Tim 4 16 *S*(*B* diff) *παραγίν.* dat;
Dan 10 21 *S*(BMis 178, *B* ⲁⲙⲁϩⲓ ⲛⲉⲙ-) *ἀντέχεσθαι*
μετά; BG 31 *S* ⲁϥⲱϩⲉ ⲣⲁⲧϥ ⲙⲛⲡⲛⲟⲩⲥ, *ib* ⲁϥⲁ. ⲣⲁⲧϥ
ⲙⲛ-, ShA 1 71 *S* ϯⲛⲁⲁ. ⲣⲁⲧ ⲁⲛ ⲡⲙⲙⲁⲥ, Pcod 11
F ⲟ. ⲉⲗⲉⲧϥ ⲡⲡⲉⲗⲙⲏⲓ, Mor 29 5 *S* armies ⲁ. ⲣⲁⲧⲟⲩ
ⲙⲛⲛⲉⲩⲉⲣⲏⲩ (var BMis 233 ⲟⲩⲃⲉ-).

—— ⲛ- dat *S*: Eccl 2 9 *io.* dat, Ex 34 5 (*B* ⲙⲙⲁⲩ)
ⲡⲁⲣⲓⲥ. dat; Ming 338 ⲁ. ⲣⲁⲧⲕ ⲡⲁⲓ *exspecta me*.

—— ⲛⲁϩⲣⲉⲛ- *B, beside*: Ac 23 11(*S* ⲉϫⲛ-)*io.* dat,
ib 9 39 (*S* ⲉ-) ⲡⲁⲣⲓⲥ. dat; C 43 70 ⲫⲏ ⲉⲧⲟⲅⲟ. ⲉⲣⲁⲧⲟⲩ ⲛⲁϩⲣⲁϥ.

—— ⲟⲩⲃⲉ- *SAB, against*: Ps 75 7 *S*(*B* ϯ ⲉϧⲟⲩⲛ
ⲉϩⲣⲉⲛ-), Is 3 9 *B*(*S* ⲉ-), Cl 27 5 *A*, Bor 235* 131 *S*
ⲁ. ⲣⲁⲧⲕ ⲟⲩ. ⲙⲉⲉⲩⲉ ⲛⲓⲙ *ἄνθισ.* dat, Si 46 11 *S* ⲱ.
ἀν. ἔναντι, Is 43 24 *B*(*S* ⲣ ϩⲓϫⲛ-) *προισ.* gen; Ex 23
22 *B*(*S* ϯ ⲟⲩⲃⲉ) *ἀντικεῖσθαι* dat; BMis 233 *S* ⲁϥⲁ.
ⲣⲁⲧⲟⲩ ⲟⲩⲃⲉⲛⲉⲩⲉⲣⲏⲩ.

—— ϩⲓⲣⲛ- *SA, at*: Si 21 24 ⲱ. ϩⲓⲣⲏⲡⲣⲟ *io. ἔξω*,
Ob 14 *A*(*B* ϩⲓϫ., *S* ϭⲱ ϩⲓⲣⲏ-) *ἐφισ. ἐπί*.

—— ϩⲁⲧⲛ-, ϧⲁⲧⲉⲛ- *SB, at, before*: 4 Kg 4 15 *B*
io. παρά; PS 72 *S* ⲁⲥⲁ. ⲣⲁⲧⲥ ϩ.ⲫⲓⲗⲓⲡⲡⲟⲥ, C 43 242
B ⲉⲅⲟ. ⲉⲣⲁⲧⲟⲩ ϩ. ⲡⲓⲉϧⲟⲩⲥⲓⲁ.

—— ϩⲓϫⲛ- *SBF, upon, at, beside*: Jos 3 17 *SB*,

Jer 14 6 *SB*, Ap 12 18 *SB* *io. ἐπί*, Si 41 24 *S* ⲁ. ⲉϥⲓⲥ.
ἐπί, Lu 4 39 *S*(*B* ⲥⲁⲡϣⲱⲓ) *ἐφ. ἐπάνω*, Ac 14 10 *S*(*B*
ⲉϫ.) *ἀνισ. ὀρθὸς ἐπί*; BMis 237 *S* angel ⲁ. ϩⲓϫⲱϥ
ⲡⲁⲣⲓⲥ.; BG 50 *S* sim ⲱ. ⲣⲁⲧⲟⲩ ϩⲓϫⲱⲟⲩ, Aeg 255 *S*
priest ⲉⲧⲁ. ⲣⲁⲧ ϩ.ⲡⲙⲟⲟⲩ *at baptism*, Miss 8 213 *S*
devil ⲁ. ⲣⲁⲧϥ ϩⲓϫⲱϥ *as accuser*, AM 304 *B* Saviour
ⲟ. ⲉⲣⲁⲧϥ ϩ.ⲡⲓⲙⲉⲗⲟⲥ of martyr, Orat Cyp 214 *Sⁱ*
ⲙⲁⲣⲉⲥⲱⲣⲓ ⲣⲁⲧ(ⲥ) ϩ.ⲡⲡⲉⲥⲡⲁⲧ, MR 5 49 *F* ⲙⲡⲓⲡⲉϣ
ⲟⲩϩ ⲣⲉⲧ ϩⲓϫⲱⲡⲁⲡⲉⲧ.

ⲙⲁ ⲛⲁ., ⲛⲟ. (ⲉ)ⲣⲁⲧϩ, *place of standing*: Si 36 13
S, Dan 8 17 *B* *στάσις*.

ϭⲓⲛⲁ., ϫⲓⲛⲟ. (ⲉ)ⲣⲁⲧϩ, *standing*: 3 Kg 10 5 *S* *στάσις*; PS 278 *S* ⲡⲉϥϭ. ⲣⲁⲧⲟⲩ, Cat 6 *B* ⲟⲩϫ. ⲉⲣⲁⲧϥ
ⲉϩⲁⲡⲟⲅⲟⲛ *in trouble*.

ⲥ ⲁϩⲉ *SA*, ⲟϩⲓ *B* (once), *need* ⲥ ⲛ- dat of thing
needed: Job 17 1 *B* ϯⲟ. ⲛⲁⲥ (*S* ϣⲁⲁⲧ) Aeg 246 ⲡⲉⲧⲟ-
ⲟⲩⲁ. ⲛⲁϥ *δέεσθαι* gen, Pro 24 31 *SA* ⲡⲉϥⲁ. ⲛⲁϥ *τὰ
δέοντα*, Deu 15 8 (*B* ⲉⲣ ϧⲁⲉ) *ἐπιδ.*, Si 42 27 ⲙⲡϥⲁ.
ⲛⲗⲁⲁⲩ *προσδ.* gen; Lu 11 8(*B* ⲉⲣ ⲭⲣⲓⲁ) *χρῄζειν*,
Job 31 16, Si 13 7, 1 Thes 4 12 ⲛⲧⲉⲧⲛⲁ. ⲛⲗⲁⲁⲩ
(*B* do) *χρείαν ἔχειν*; Jud 1 14 ⲁϩⲣⲟ ⲉⲣⲁ. ⲡⲟⲩ? *τί
ἐστί σοι*; Ja 2 16 (*B* ⲭ.) *τὰ ἐπιτήδεια*; Hos 2 5 *A*(*B*
ⲑⲏϣ) *καθ᾽ἕειν*; Br 255 sendeth her ⲡⲉⲧⲥⲁ. ⲛⲁϥ,
ShR 2 3 7 ⲛⲥⲉⲁ. ⲁⲛ ⲙⲡⲣⲁⲧ, Sh(Besa)Z 513 *χρεία*
ⲉⲧⲟⲩⲁ. ⲛⲁⲥ, ShA 2 166 ⲛϥⲁ. ⲛⲁⲥ ⲁⲛ ⲡⲟⲩⲙⲟⲟⲩ
needed not water of her, ShRE 10 162 ⲉⲕⲁ. ⲉⲟⲩ (*l*
ⲡⲟⲩ) ⲛⲧⲟⲟⲧⲛ?, ShMIF 23 101 ⲡⲉⲧⲉⲣⲉϩⲉⲛⲕⲟⲟⲩⲉ
ⲁ. ⲛⲁϥ ⲛⲧⲉⲧⲏⲩⲧⲛ, Mor 29 29 what is in thy hand
ϯⲁ. ⲛⲁϥ (var BMis 260 ⲣ ⲭ. ⲙⲙⲟϥ), *ib* 22 30 ϯ
ⲛⲁⲛ ⲛⲡⲉⲧⲛⲁ. ⲛⲁⲩ, ShA 1 258 ⲡⲣⲱⲙⲉ ⲉⲧⲁ. ⲛⲁⲩ
ϩⲉⲛ(*l* ϩⲛ)ϩⲉⲛⲭⲣⲓⲁ; Si 37 8 ⲉϥⲁ. ⲛⲁⲕ ⲛⲟⲩ *needeth
thee for what* *τίς αὐτοῦ χ.*

V ⲥⲟⲟϭⲉ (2°), ⲧⲁϩⲟ.

ⲱϭⲉ *SA* nn   *v* ⲟϭⲉ.

ⲱϭⲓ   *v* ϭⲟⲓ *bellows*.

ⲱϩⲥ *SSⁱAA²F*, ⲱⲥϩ *A*, ⲟⲥϩ *A²*, ⲱⲥϧ *B*, ⲉϧⲥ-,
ⲱϩⲥ-*S*, ⲟⲥϧ-, ⲱⲥϧ-*B*, ⲁϧⲥ-*Sⁱ/F*, ⲟϧⲥ-, ⲟⲥϧ-*S*, ⲁϧⲥϩ
Sⁱ/A², ⲁⲥϧϩ *A*, ⲁⲥϧϩ *A²*, ⲟⲥϧϩ *B* vb **I** intr, *reap,
mow*: Ps 125 5 *SB*, Jo 4 36 *SA²B* *θερίζειν*; Is 37
30 *B*(*S* ⲱⲗ), Mic 6 15 *AB* *ἀμᾶν*; BM 528 *F* ⲥⲓϯⲱⲣⲓ
ⲡⲱ., CMSS 76 *Sⁱ* ⲉⲗⲕⲟⲩ ⲡⲱ., BMOr 6230 (45) *S*
sim;   ⲥ ⲛⲥⲁ- *A²* emphatic: Mani H 15 ⲡⲁⲓⲱⲕⲧⲏⲥ
…ⲱ. ⲛⲉⲥⲱⲟⲩ.

II tr: Lev 23 10 *SB*, Job 5 26 *SA*(Cl)*B*, Jo 4 38
SA²BF *θ.*, Hos 6 5 *AB* *ἀποθ.*, Lev 25 5 *S*(*B* ⲥⲱⲕ)
ἐκθ.; Deu 24 19 *SB*, Is 17 5 *B*(*S* ⲱⲗ) *ἀμ.*; ShC 73
54 *S* ⲱ. ⲛⲣⲉⲡⲕⲁⲙ, C 89 123 *B* ⲟⲥϧ ⲕⲁⲙ, Mani H 8
A² ⲱ. ⲛⲃⲁⲣⲏⲅⲉ, Va 57 5 *B* ϣⲁⲅⲟϧⲥⲟⲩ (*bis*), Miss 4
178 *Sⁱ* field ⲥⲕⲁⲓ ⲡⲉⲛⲧϥ…ⲁϧⲥ, ManiK 10 *A²* ⲡⲕⲁⲓⲣⲟⲥ ⲛⲁϧⲥϥ, BM 596 11 *F* ⲧⲏⲛⲁϩⲥ ⲡⲓⲱⲣⲉ, ShA 1 108

S garments ϣⲁⲣⲉⲡⲁϩⲟⲩ ϣⲁⲣⲉⲟⲣⲥⲟⲩ(*sic* MS)ⲡⲟϭⲉ ⲡⲟϭⲉ *slash*;   as nn (constr + obj)*SB*, *reaping* : Ex 34 22 *B* ⲡⲱ. ⲥⲟⲩⲟ (*S* tr), Jos 3 15 *S* ⲡⲉϩⲥ ⲥ. (*B* ⲱ. ⲡⲥ.), 2 Kg 21 9 *S* ⲡⲉ. ⲓⲱⲧ θερισμός; C 99 235 *S* ⲡⲱ. ⲕⲁⲙ = *ib* 89 69 *B* tr θερίζ.; Miss 4 782 *Sⸯ* ⲡⲁ. ⲕⲁⲙ;   + suff *B*: Jo 4 35 ⲡⲟⲥϫⲟⲩ (*SA²* tr) θερισ.; MG 25 370 ⲡⲥⲛⲟⲩ ⲙⲡⲟⲥϫϥ.

—— nn m *SAA²BF*, *reaping, harvest* : Ge 8 22 *SB*, Mt 13 30 *SBF*, Jo 4 35 *SA²BF*ⲟϩⲥ θερισ.; Lev 26 5 *S*(*B* ϭⲱⲗ), Pro 6 8 *SAB*, Am 9 13 *SA*(*B* ϩⲓ) ἀμητός; MG 25 362 *B* ϩⲉⲛⲡⲓⲱ. *at harvest-time*, Sh C 73 140 *S* rules for ⲡⲱ., *ib* 42 107 *S* ⲡⲱ., ⲛϭⲣⲏ, CO 455 *S* calendar ⲧⲕⲩⲣⲓⲁⲕⲏ ϩⲛⲡⲟⲩⲟϩⲥ, J 65 59 *S* bequest of ϣⲏⲓ ϩ(ⲓ)ⲓⲱϩⲉ, ϩⲓϩⲟⲓ, ϩⲓⲱ. *reaped crop* (?).

ⲣⲁⲱ. *S*, *act of reaping* : ShC 73 141 let brother be equal with us ϩⲓⲛⲡ.

ⲣⲉϥⲱ. *B*, *reaper* : Va 58 130 ⲡⲁⲣ. ⲓⲏⲥ ⲉϥⲧⲁⲙⲟ ⲙⲙⲟⲓ ⲉⲛⲓⲟϭⲥ.

ⲟϩⲥ, ⲟⲥϩ (once) *S*, ⲁⲥϩ, ⲁⲥⳉ *Sᵃ*, ⲁⲥϩ *A*, ⲟⲥϫ *B*, ⲁϩⲥ *F* nn m, *sickle* : Is 2 4 *SB*, *ib* 18 5 *S*(*B* ⲥⲛϥⲓ ⲛϣⲱⲗ *ϭⲱⲗ*), Mic 4 3 *SAB*, Mk 4 29 *SB*, LCyp 8 *S* tongue long as ⲟⲩⲟ. δρέπανον; 1 Kg 13 20 *S* θέριστρον; Bor 292 4 *S* ⲧⲥⲛϥⲉ ⲉⲧⲉⲡⲟ.ⲡⲉ to prune vine, Mor 51 39 *S* ϩⲉⲡⲟ. ⲉϩⲡⲁ ⲉϩⲡⲏⲩ ⲉⲣⲉⲧⲉⲩⲡⲟⲟⲩϩⲉ ⲕⲱⲧⲉ ⲉⲡⲟⲉⲓⲕ (reeds), Chicago Ostr 855 *S* in list ⲟⲩⲟϩⲥ (*sic*), BKU 1 292 *Sᵃ* ⲟⲩⲁϩⲥ, CO 472 *Sᵃ* ⲟⲩⲁⲥ ϩⳉ; ϫⲓ ⲟ. *S*, ϩⲓ ⲟ. *B*, *wield sickle* : Deu 23 24 *SB* δ. ἐπιβάλλειν; *ib* 16 9 *B*(*S* ⲱ. intr) Gk no vb; ϫⲁⲓ-, ϭⲁⲓⲟ. *SBF*, *sickle-bearer, reaper* : Bel 33 *B*, Mt 13 30 *SBF* θεριστής, Ru 2 3 *S* θεριϛ.; BMar 165 *S* ἀμ.; Bor 258 6 *S* ⲛϫ., AM 183 *B* ⲛⲓϭ., PcodMor 19 *F* ϫⲁⲓⲁ.   *V* ϣⲁⲟⲗ.

ⲟⲥϩϥ, ⲁⲥϩϥ *S*, -ϩϥ *A* nn m, *sickle, knife* : Zech 5 2 *A*(*SB* ⲟϩⲥ) δρ.; BMar 241 *S* fingers like ⲛⲉⲓⲟ. ⲉⲩⲧⲏⲙ, *ib* 235 *S* ⲟⲩⲁ. ⲉϥⲧⲏⲙ to cut paper (χάρτης).

ωϩⲧ *F*   *v* ⲱϩⲧ.

ωϫ *SF* nn, *thief* : Mt 26 55 (var ⲟϫ, *B* ⲥⲟⲛⲓ) λῃστής; ShIF 245 ϩⲉⲛⲥⲟⲟⲩϩⲥ ⲛⲱϫ, ShA 2 16 ⲙⲛⲧ ⲡⲱϫ ⲟⲩϩⲏ ⲡⲁⲙⲁⲩ, Sh(?)Mor 54 74 ⲡⲉⲧⲱ (*lo*) ⲛⲱϫ ϥⲛⲁⲥⲓ ⲛⲧⲙⲡⲧⲣⲏⲕⲉ, *ib* 55 33 ⲟⲩⲣⲱⲙⲉ ⲛⲱϫ... ⲧⲉϥⲙⲛⲧⲱϫ;   ⲙⲛⲧⲱϫ : Eccl 10 18 *F*(*S* ⲙⲛⲧⲣⲉϥϫⲛⲁⲁⲩ) ὀκνηρία, but ? *l* ωϫⲉⲛ; sim in ShIF 300 ⲉⲧⲉⲧⲛϯ ϩⲣⲉⲡⲕⲉⲗⲙ ⲉⲡⲙⲁ ⲡⲧⲉⲧⲛⲱ. *ye lay fuel* (*i e* ? *become active*) *instead of your sloth*.   *Cf* ? ⲧⲁϫⲟ.

ωϫⲉⲃ, ωϫ(ⲉ)ϥ *B*   *v* ⲱϭⲃ.

ωϫⲛ *SF*, -ⲛⲉ *AA²*, ωϫⲉⲛ *F*, ⲉϫⲛ(ⲉ)-, ⲟϫⲛ-, ⲟϫⲛⲍ *S*, ⲁϫⲛⲍ *AF* vb **I** intr, *cease, perish* : Deu 32 36 (*B* ⲟⲩⲱ), Jos 3 16 (*cf* 13 ωϣⲙ), Hos 4 3 *SA*, Lu 16 9 (both *B* ⲙⲟⲩⲛⲕ) ἐκλείπειν, Sa 7 14 ἀνεκλ., Jer 14 17 (*B* ⲙ.) διαλ.; Is 16 10 (*B* ⲕⲏⲛ) παύειν, Lev 2 13 (*B* ⲙ.) διαπ., Ge 8 22 (*B* ⲙⲧⲟⲛ) καταπ.; Nu 14 33 (*B*

ⳉⲱϯ ⲉⲃⲟⲗ) ἀναλίσκειν; *ib* 17 12 ἐξαν. (*B* do), Is 59 14 (*B* ϣⲉ ⲉⲫⲟⲅⲉⲓ) καταν.; *ib* 57 1 (*B* ⲧⲁⲕⲟ) ἀπολλύναι; Ps 7 9 (*B* ⲙⲟⲩⲛⲕ) συντελεῖν; 2 Cor 9 3 (*B* ϣⲟⲩⲓⲧ) κενοῦν; Job 19 10 (*B* ϣⲉ) οἴχεσθαι; *ib* 16 15 (*B* ϭⲉⲡⲟ) σβεννύναι; Si 50 3 ἐλαττοῦν; Ps 57 8 (*B* ⲧⲁ.) ἀνταναιρεῖν; Joel 1 17 *A*(*B* ϣⲟⲩϩⲓ) ξηραίνειν; Job 7 9 (*B* ϣⲱⲡⲓ ⲁⲡ)ⲟⲩⲕ ἔτι εἶναι; PS 86 ⲁⲧⲁϭⲟⲙ ⲁⲣϫⲓ ⲡⲱ., RNC 76 after shooting ⲁⲡⲉⲛⲥⲟⲧⲉ ⲱ., BMis 401 ⲛⲡⲉⲩⲱ. ⲡⲛⲉⲩϣⲱⲧ, LA1 6 ⲁⲥⲱ....ⲁⲥⲥⲱϣⲙ(?ⲱϣⲙ), BHom 128 stars ⲱ. ⲉⲧⲁⲓⲧⲣⲉⲩⲅⲣ ⲟⲩⲟⲉⲓⲛ, CO 361 ⲁⲓⲕⲁⲕⲉ ϣⲏⲙ ⲱ.

II tr, *make cease, destroy* : Job 4 11 (*B* ⲙ.) λείπειν; Pro 24 22 *SA*, Z 355 fire ϣⲁϥⲟϫⲛⲉϥ ἀναλίσκ., Jth 11 13 ἐξαν., Zech 9 4 *SA*(*B* ⲙ.) καταν.; Deu 32 23, Jer 5 3 (Z 515), Zech 5 4 *SA*(all *B* ⲙ.)συντελ.; Si 10 17 ἀπολλ.; Is 14 30 (*B* ϫⲱⲧⲉⲃ) ἀναιρ.; Z 330 ⲉϥⲱ. ⲙⲙⲟⲓ by fire δαπανᾶν; ShMIF 23 163 ⲁⲕⲱ. ⲛⲡⲉϩⲟⲟⲩ ⲙⲡⲉⲕⲱⲡϩ, ShBM 230 158 ⲁⲛⲉϫⲡⲉ ⲡⲉⲡⲁϩⲉ ...ⲉϫⲛ ⲧⲓⲅⲩⲡⲟⲙⲟⲡⲏ, ShBor 246 88 ϣⲁϣⲟⲩ ⲉⲃⲟⲗ ⲛⲥⲉⲟϫⲛⲟⲩ, ShIF 212 light ⲉϥⲟϫⲛⲉϥ (*sc* darkness), R 2 1 68 ⲡⲉϥⲑⲟⲡⲟⲥ ⲱ. ⲛⲧⲉϥⲯⲩⲭⲏ.

With following preposition. ⲥ ⲉ-, *from* (*cf* ⲗⲟ ⲉ-, ⲙⲟⲩⲛⲕ ⲉ-): Job 36 17 (*B* diff) ὑστερεῖν; *to* : Mor 22 20 waters flow away ⲛⲥⲉⲱ. ⲉⲛⲡⲟⲩⲛ, R 2 4 57 sim;   ⲥ ⲛ- dat: Pro 20 20 (10) *SA* σβεν.;   ⲥ ⲉⲃⲟⲗ ⲛ-, *from*: ShWess 9 95 ⲁⲡⲁϩⲏⲧ ⲱ. ⲉⲃ. ⲙⲡⲉⲙⲕⲁϩ;   ⲥ ⲛⲥⲁ-, *for* (*lack of*): Lam 4 17 (*BF* ⲙ.) ἐκλ. εἰς;   ⲥ ⲛⲧⲛ-, *from*: Jth 11 12, Job 21 19 (*B* ⲙ. ⲉ-) ἐκλ. acc; BAp 97 water ⲱ. ⲛⲧⲟⲟⲧⲛ = MIE 2 398 *B* ⲕⲏⲛ ⲡⲧⲉⲛ-;   ⲥ ⲛⲁϩⲣⲛ-, *from before*: Mor 39 15 *Sⸯ* ⲁϩⲛⲟⲩ (*sc* Christians) ⲛⲁϩⲣⲁⲓ = C 43 41 *B* ⲙ. ⲛ.;   ⲥ ϩⲁ-, *through*: ShMun 95 ⲁⲡⲉⲛϩⲏⲧ ⲱ. ϩⲁⲡⲉⲙⲕⲁϩ;   ⲥ ϩⲛ-, *from*: Ge 18 11 (*B* diff) ἐκλ. dat, Ps 54 11 (*B* ⲙ. ⲉⲃ. ϩⲉⲛ-) ἐκλ. ἐκ, Si 16 28 ἐκλ. ἀπό; Jth 13 19 ἀφισ. ἀπό; Job 5 3 *B* Gk diff; ShR 2 3 8 dying ⲡⲉϥⲡⲛⲁ ⲱ. ⲛϩⲏⲧϥ, ShA 1 246 of wine ⲧⲉⲩⲧⲉⲓⲡⲉ ⲉⲧⲛⲁⲡⲟⲩϩⲥ ⲱ. ⲛϩⲏⲧⲟⲩ, BKU 1 8 let magic ⲱ. ⲛϩⲏⲧ, ManiH 53 *A²* ⲱ. ϩⲛⲧⲙⲏⲧⲉ ⲙⲡⲓⲕⲟⲥⲙⲟⲥ;   tr: ShP 131ⁱ 140 lying hath filled earth ⲁⲛⲱ. ⲛⲧⲙⲉ ⲛϩⲏⲧϥ, BMis 368 ⲙⲡⲣⲱ. ⲡⲉⲕⲁⲅⲁⲡⲏ ... ϩⲛⲛⲉⲛϭⲓϫ = Va 63 4 *B* ⲙ. ⲉⲃⲟⲗ ϩⲉⲛ-; ϩⲣⲁⲓ ϩⲛ-: PS 51 ⲁⲧⲁϭⲟⲙ...ⲱ. ϩ. ⲡϩⲏⲧ, Br 116 ⲁⲧⲕⲁⲕⲓⲁ ⲱ. ϩ. ⲡϩⲏⲧⲟⲩ; ⲉⲃⲟⲗ ϩⲛ-: Ge 8 13 (var ⲥⲃⲟⲕ, *B* ⲙ. ⲉⲃ. ϩⲁ-) ἐκλ. ἀπό, *ib* 21 15 (*B* ⲙ. ⲉⲃ. ϩⲉⲛ-) ἐκλ. ἐκ; C 99 16 phantom hand ⲱ. ⲉⲃ. ϩⲛⲧⲉϥϭⲓϫ like smoke, Bor 292 38 Spirit shall ⲱ. ⲙⲡⲙⲉⲉⲩⲉ...ⲉⲃ. ⲛϩⲏⲧⲟⲩ;   ⲥ ϩⲓϫⲛ-, *from off*: Deu 15 11 (*B* ⲙ. ⲉⲃ. ϩⲓⳉ.) ἐκλ. ἀπό; Pro 2 22 *SA*(*B* ⲧⲁⲕⲟ) ὀλλύναι; Jer 10 11 (Miss 8 229, *B* do) ἀπολ. ἀπό; SHel 20 idols broken ⲁⲩⲱ. ϩ. ⲡⲕⲁϩ.

—— nn m *SA*, *ceasing, destruction*: Pro 14 28 *SA*, Is 17 4 (*B* ⲙⲟⲩⲛⲕ vb) ἔκλειψις; Ez 15 6 (*B* do) ἀνάλωσις; 2 Pet 2 12 (*B* ϥⲱϯ ⲉⲃ.) ἅλωσις; ⲁϫⲛⲱ., *without ceasing*: Pro 21 26 *SA* ἀφειδῶς; Ro 1 9 (*B*

ϫⲁ ⲧⲟⲧ ⲉⲃⲟⲗ) ἀδιαλείπτως; Pcod 10 reminding bishop ⲁ.

ⲁⲧⲱ. *S, unceasing*: Lu 12 33 (*B* ⲁⲟⲙ.) ἀνέκλειπτος, Ro 9 2 (*B* ⲙ. neg) ἀδιάλειπτος; ShA 2 277 ⲡⲁⲓⲱⲡ ⲡⲁ., C 99 161 ⲕⲟⲗⲁⲥⲓⲥ ⲡⲁ.=*ib* 89 99 *B* ⲁⲟⲙ., BMis 327 = BSM 10 *B* ⲁⲧⲕⲱⲣϥ.

ⲣ ⲱ. *F, be slothful*: Ro 12 11 ⲁⲓ ⲡⲱ. (*B* ⲟⲓ ⲛϭⲛⲁⲩ, *S* ϫⲛⲁⲩ vb) ὀκνηρός. *Cf* ? ⲙⲛⲧⲱⲝ.

ⲣⲉϥⲱ. *S, who, what makes to cease*: BM 216 79 ⲡⲣⲓⲥⲉ ⲡⲣ. ⲙⲡⲛⲟⲃⲉ ταύτας (*sc* ἡδονὰς) ἀμβλύνειν.

ⲱϫⲉⲣ *B v* ⲱϭⲣ.

ⲱϫⲧ *S,* ⲱⲭϩ *B v* ⲱϭⲧ.

ⲱϭⲃ, ⲣⲱ. *S,* ⲱϭⲃⲉ *A* (ⲛⲛ), ⲱⲭⲉⲃ, -ϥ *B,* ⲉϭⲃ-, ⲣⲟϭⲃ†, ⲟϭϥ† *S,* ⲁⲕⲃ†, -ϥ† *Sª,* ⲟⲭⲉⲃ† *B* vb intr, *become, be cold, frozen*: Mt 24 12 *S*(varr ⲣⲱ., ⲁⲣⲟϣ, *B* ⲉⲣⲟϣ) ψύχειν; Va 66 297 *B* brethren ⲟ.† ϩⲓⲧⲉⲛⲡⲓϫⲁϥ, Z 347 *S* in winter ⲙⲉⲧⲛⲱ. = MG 25 220 *B* ⲣⲟⲣϣ ῥιγεῖν; He 11 12 *B*(*S* diff) νεκροῦν; Va 57 49 *B* ⲉϭⲟ.† ϫⲉⲛⲡⲓϫⲁϥ πηγνῦναι; ShC 42 186 *S* ⲧⲉⲧⲛⲁⲧⲁⲡⲏ ⲉⲧϥ.† (*cf* Mt *l c*), ShBM 263 *S* poison ⲣ ⲟⲩⲉ ϫⲉⲣⲟ ϥⲣ ⲟ.†, BAp 68 *S* ⲱ. ϩⲓⲧⲉⲛⲡⲣⲱ, BSM 90 *B* ⲟ.† = BMis 181 *S* sim, Miss 4 762 *S* ⲱ. ⲡⲧⲉⲡⲣⲱ, KroppM 115 *Sᶜ* like ant ⲉⲥⲁⲕϥ or well ⲉⲥⲁⲕⲃ in winter, Va 61 9 *B* ⲟ.† ϩⲓⲧⲉⲛⲡⲓϫⲁϥ, Cat 61 *B* ⲱ. opp ⲉⲣ ⲕⲁⲩⲥⲱⲛ, Aeg 22 *S* feet ⲱ. ⲁⲅⲕⲃⲟ like ice, Mor 28 128 *S* ⲡⲗⲁϫ ⲉⲥⲟ.†; tr *S*(once), *make cold*: ShP 130² 76 ⲟⲩϣⲛⲉⲓ ⲉⲁϥⲉϭⲃ ⲡⲉϥⲙⲟⲟⲩ.

—— nn m *SAB, cold, frost*: Dan 3 69 *B*(*Sⁱ* ⲁⲣⲁϣ), Zech 14 6 *S* (var ShA 2 249 ⲣ.) *AB,* Ac 28 2 *B* (*S* ϫⲁϥ) ψῦχος; Job 37 10 *B* πάγος, Jer 43 30 *B* παγετός; Ryl 94 103 *S* ⲡⲉⲧⲕⲁⲥ ⲙⲡⲱ. in freezing water, Mor 50 49 *S* ⲡⲱ. ⲙⲡⲉⲕⲗⲟ of snake's bite, DeV 2 210 *B* last sign of death ⲡⲓⲱ., En Peterson 67 *S* ⲡⲱ. ⲙⲡⲙⲟⲩ.

ⲟϭⲃⲥ *S* nn, *cold*: Mor 28 27 ϫⲓ ϩⲙⲙⲉ...ϫⲓ ⲟ. *Cf* ? ⲁϭⲃⲉⲥ.

ⲱϭ(ⲉ)ⲣ *S,* ⲱⲭⲉⲣ *B,* ⲟϭⲣϩ, ⲟϭⲣ† *S* vb intr, *become hard, stiff, freeze*: Ex 15 8 *S*(Ep 3, *B* ϭⲱⲥ), Job 6 16 *S*(*B* do) πηγνῦναι, BHom 27 *S* ⲱ. ϩⲓⲧⲛⲑⲟⲧⲉ ἀποπ.;

Z 347 *S* sim ⲣⲁⲑⲟⲧⲉ = MG 25 219 *B* ⲉⲣ ϧⲟϯ δειλιᾶν; PS 64 *S* ⲁⲧϭⲟⲙ ⲱ. ϧⲣⲁⲓ ⲛϧⲏⲧ, C 86 148 *B* sim, Sh ViK 9346 *S* if frost touch them ϣⲁⲩⲱ., RNC 57 *S* ⲁϥⲱ. ⲛϭⲓ ⲡⲧⲁⲣⲧ, BMis 317 *S* feet ⲱ. ϩⲓⲧⲙⲡⲉⲕⲁⲥ of gout, DeV 2 108 *B* corpse's blood ⲱ. ⲛϧⲏⲧϥ, R 1 3 61 *S* womb ⲱ. ϩⲓⲧⲙⲡⲧⲗⲗⲱ, P 129¹² 16 *S* ⲁⲩⲱ. ϩⲓⲧⲉⲛⲡϣⲱⲣⲁ like sheep, Miss 4 748 *S* ⲉϭⲟ.† ϩⲓⲧⲙⲡϣⲱⲡⲉ; tr *S*: Mor 26 48 ⲡⲱϭⲃ ⲱ. ⲡⲡⲉⲩⲙⲉⲣⲟⲥ ⲉⲡⲉⲩⲉⲣⲏⲩ; c ⲉϧⲟⲩⲛ *S*: ShC 73 162 ⲛⲧⲟⲡ...ⲟϭⲣⲟⲩ ⲉϧ. *tuck in, brace up* (?), *ib* ⲛⲡⲉⲣⲱⲙⲉ ⲱ. ⲛ ⲡϥⲥⲱⲕ ⲉϧⲟⲩⲛ ⲡⲓⲧⲟⲡ ⲛⲡⲉϥϭⲟⲉⲓⲧⲉ; ⲉϧ. ⲉ-: Mor 29 6 blood caused hand to ⲱ. ⲉϧⲟⲩⲛ ⲉⲧⲧⲱⲣⲉ of sword (varr BMis 233 ⲧⲱⲣϭ, Mor 30 6 *Sʄ* ⲗⲱϫ), *ib* 29 26 foot ⲱ. ⲉϧ. ⲉⲧⲁⲡⲉ ⲛⲧⲉⲅⲗⲗⲁ (σέλλα, var *ib* 30 31 *Sʄ* ⲧⲱϭⲓ ⲉϧ. ⲉ-).

ⲱϭⲥ *v* ⲱⲥϭ.

ⲱϭⲧ *SA²F,* ⲱⲧϭ, ⲱϫⲧ *S,* ⲱⲭϩ *B,* ⲉϭⲧ-, ⲟϭⲧϩ, ⲟϫⲧϩ, ⲟⲧϭϩ *S,* ⲁϭⲧϩ *AA²F,* ⲉϭⲧϩ *A²,* ⲟⲭϩⲩ, ⲟⲣϫⲩ *B* vb tr, *choke, throttle*: 1 Kg 16 14 *S*(var ⲱϫⲧ), Mt 18 28 *SB,* Mor 17 19 *S* demon ⲉϭⲧ ⲟⲩϣⲓⲣⲉ πνίγειν, Nah 2 12 *B*(*A* diff), Mart Ign 879 *B* ⲁⲩⲟⲭϥ ἀποπ., Mt 13 22 *SBF* συμπ.; Va 57 190 *B* ἄγχειν, 2 Kg 17 23 *S* ⲟϭⲧϥ (var ⲟⲭ.) ἀπάγχ.; Zech 1 21 *A* ⲁϭⲧⲟⲩ (*B* ⲕⲱⲣϫ) καταγνῦναι (as if κατάγχ.); Va 57 226 *B* of choking thorns ἐμποδίζειν; PS 345 *S* ⲉϥⲛⲁⲱ. ⲙⲙⲟⲩ ⲙⲙⲓⲛ ⲙⲙⲟⲩ, ShIF 266 *S* worms ⲉⲧⲱ. ⲛⲡⲉϭⲣⲟϭ, ShA 2 29 *S* dust & frost ⲟϭⲧⲟⲩ, Mani H 82 *A²* ⲉⲕⲁⲁϭⲧⲕ ⲟⲩⲁϧⲉⲕ?, *ib* 78 *A²* ⲁⲃⲉϭⲧϥ, *ib* 12 *A²* ⲁⲥⲱ. ⲛⲡϫⲁⲗⲕⲙⲥⲉ, Mor 43 186 *F* Judas ⲁϥⲁϭⲧϥ, Va 58 34 *B* sim ⲟϭⲕⲕ, *ib* 61 199 *B* ⲟⲩⲁⲧⲙⲁϭⲧ ⲉⲁⲩⲟϣϫ (*l* ⲉⲁϥⲱϭ) ⲛⲟⲩϩⲣⲱⲙⲓ, TU 24 1 5 *S* had mind to ⲟⲧϭϥ, BMEA 10582 *S* he came & ⲁϥⲟϭⲧ(ⲧ) ϫⲉ ⲉⲓⲟⲩⲱϣ ⲡⲁⲥⲕⲉⲩⲏ (*l* ⲡⲁ-) or my money; intr: BMis 241 *S* hung up with stone about neck ϩⲙⲡⲧⲣⲉϥⲱϭ (var 298 ⲱϫⲧ) & die ἄγχ., Va 57 225 *B* thorns ϣⲁⲩⲱ. ἀποπν.; c ⲉϫⲛ-: Mor 22 132 *S* seized her throat ⲁϥⲱ. ⲉϫⲱⲥ = BSM 123 *B* ⲱ. ⲙⲙⲟⲥ, C 43 188 *B* demon ⲉϥⲱ. ⲉϫⲱⲥ.

—— nn *B, thing strangled*: Ac 15 20 (*S* diff) πνικτός; EW 46 idolaters ⲉⲩϣⲉⲙϣⲓ ⲛⲡⲓⲱ.

ϣ, 25th letter of alphabet, called ϣⲁⲓ, ϣⲉⲓ (K 1, Stern p 418)*B,* شَيْ (Stern *l c*). Derived from hierogl *š,* as ϣⲱⲙ, ϣⲟⲟⲩⲉ, ⲣⲁϣⲉ, ⲟⲩⲱϣⲧ, ⲧⲱϣ; oftener from *ẖ,* as ϣⲓ, ϣⲱⲗⲙ, ⲡϣⲟⲧ, ⲥⲱϣⲉ, ⲡⲱⲣϣ (original sound still in *A,* as ϧⲁⲙⲧ, ⲥⲁⲁⲛϧ, ⲱϧⲉ & in names, as Παμχῆμις, Χεμτονεῦς). Varies with initial ⲥ (*q v*), as *S* ⲥⲱϣ *B* ϣⲟϣ, *S* ⲥⲁϣϥ *B* ϣⲁϣϥ, *S* ⲥϭⲏⲣ *B* ϣϭⲏⲣ, *A* ⲥⲃⲉ *SB* ϣϭⲉ, *S* ⲥⲁϣ *F* ϣⲉϣ, *S* ⲥⲱϣⲉ *F* ϣⲱϣⲓ; rarely in other positions, as *S* ⲱⲥϭ *B* ⲱϣϫ. Replaces ⲥ (abnormal), as *A* ⲛⲧϣ, ϧⲁϣⲉ (RChamp 539). For -ⲏⲥ, as ⲟⲛⲏϣ (Mor 17 74, var ⲟⲛⲏⲥ P 129¹⁴ 92), ⲟϣ (J 3 60, 68 97); added to ⲥ, as ⲥϣϭⲁϧⲧ (Mor 31 61), ϣⲥⲛⲏⲣ (Aeg 261), ⲥϣϭⲏⲣ (Mor 41 25). Doubled as initial *B*: ϣϣⲏⲡ, ϣϣⲱⲟⲩ,

F ϣϣⲉⲛ (Eccl 2 5). Replaces ϫ, as ⲁⲣϣⲛⲙⲁⲛⲑⲣⲓⲧⲏⲥ, ϣⲏⲣⲁ (gloss on ϫⲏⲣⲁ Stern 16). Replaces ϩ (rare), as ⲁϣⲓ (ⲁϩⲉ Pcod Mor 5), ϣⲱⲃⲥ (Eccl 6 4 F), ⲉⲧⲁϣ- relat (ⲉⲧⲁϩ-A); converse (esp Sᵃ, v Ep 1 244), as ϩ- vb, ϩⲟⲗϭ, ϩⲏⲙ, ϩⲱⲡ (ϣⲱⲡⲓ Eccl 2 7 F), ⲥⲟⲉⲓϩ, ⲟⲩⲁϩⲍ (Job 30 14), ⲟⲩⲟϩⲥ† (Sh ViK 9298). Replaces ⲋ, as ϣⲉ (ST 378), ϣⲱ (He 9 20 F), ϣⲱⲛϥ (Miss 8 210), ϣⲟⲩⲧⲏ (Louvre R 49), ϣⲡⲟ (PSBA 19 214), ⲙⲁⲁϣⲉ (Ac 7 57), ϣⲁϣⲉ (Louvre E 14251); esp after ⲧ, as ⲁⲧϣⲃⲓⲛ (B.Mar 163), ⲧϣⲟⲗⲥ (P 44 57); converse B, as ⲭⲱⲗϩ (Cat 8), ⲥⲁⲛⲟⲩϫϥ (Va 75 54), ⲭⲱⲕ (2 Cor 11 25), ϩⲟⲣϫ (ib 10 10) & after ⲧ, as ⲉⲧⲭⲏⲕ (Job 12 22), ⲉⲧⲭⲓⲕⲉⲓ (S ϣⲓⲕⲉ Eccl 10 8 F), ⲙⲉⲧⲭⲏⲛⲓⲉ (Miss 4 763) ⲙⲉⲧⲭⲁⲛⲁϩⲧⲃ (BM 517), ⲧⲭⲓ daughter (Stegemann 67). For ⲧϣ = ϫ v ϫ. Replaces ϭ S, as ⲡⲟⲩϣⲥ (Deu 28 22), ⲛⲟϣ (Mor 38 57), ⲥⲛϣ (RNC 54); converse ϭⲓⲛⲉ corrected to ϣ. (PS 251); often B, as ϣⲓ (C 86 333), ϣⲁⲗⲉ (C 43 79), ⲉϣⲟⲩ tongs (C 86 271), ⲙⲟⲣϣⲡⲁϩ (P 54 170); converse, as ϭⲗⲟϥ (TEuch 2 279), ϭⲱⲣⲡ (1 Cor 14 6), ϭⲁⲧⲥ (Ez 39 17), ϭⲗⲏⲙⲓ (K 194); cf ϣϭⲏⲛⲛ, ϭϣⲛ (Pro 10 12, Mt 12 19), ϭⲛ. Transcribed in Gk by σζ, as σζⲟⲣⲡ (MR 5 41), σζⲧⲱⲣⲓ (ib 2 57), σζⲱⲡⲓ (CMSS 59), μασζⲧζ (EW 86); cf names Ραⲋζⲓδ, Σζεριχ (PLond 4), Ιⲋζεμ (Ryl 346); otherwise = σ, as Σεⲛοⲩθιⲟⲥ, Ψⲉⲛⲡⲛοⲩθηⲥ, Σⲉⲛⲏⲥιⲥ, Ποⲩⲱⲥιⲥ, Ψⲟⲓⲥ, Τⲥⲉⲗⲉⲉⲧ, Τⲥⲉⲉⲣⲉ. Transcribes Ar ش, as ϣⲉⲓϭ شيخ, θⲉⲗⲙϣⲓ تمشى, ϭⲁϣⲉⲛⲉ خشبة (EW 234 ff), ⲡⲟⲩϣⲁⲁⲧⲉⲣ نوشاد (AZ 23 118); transcribed by ش, as شوري ϣⲱⲡⲓ (BIF 5 93), شيري ϣⲏⲣⲓ (ib 95), نشدي ⲛⲓϣϯ (ib 93), اشمون ϣⲙⲟⲩⲛ, ورشنوفة شيهات ϣⲓⲏⲧ, ⲟⲩⲉⲣϣⲉⲡⲟⲩϭⲉ.

ϣ- SA²BF, ⲉϣ- SF, ϩ- Sᵃ, ϩ- A, impers vb, lit *know, so* be able, permitted, a with pronom subj: Deu 12 17 S(B ϣ ϫⲉⲙ ϫⲟⲙ), Job 7 20 SB, Ez 47 5 SB, Am 7 10 A(B ϣ ϫ.), Jo 5 44 SA²(B do) δύνασθαι; Sa 13 1 S, Mt 8 28 S(B do)ἰσχύειν; C 86 66 B ⲙⲡⲟⲩϣ θⲉⲧ ⲡⲉϥϭⲉⲧ ἀποτυγχάνειν gen; Gk om: Nu 24 9 SB, Ps 18 6 SB, ib 70 19 S(B om), Si 10 30 S(var om), Ep Jer 46 B(F om), Ap 3 7 S(B om); c neg pref often = adj in ἀ—τος, unable to: Ex 18 18 S ⲧⲙⲉϣ ϭⲓ (B ϣⲧⲉⲙⲙⲟⲩⲛ ⲉⲃⲟⲗ) ἀνυπομόνητος, Cl 20 5 A ⲙⲁⲩϩ ⲧⲉϩⲁϥ ἀνεκδιήγητος, Job 8 7 S ⲛⲥⲉⲛⲁϣ ϣⲁⲭⲉ ⲉⲣⲟⲟⲩ ⲁⲛ (B diff) ἀμύθητος, ib 31 11 S ⲙⲉⲩⲉϣ ⲁⲙⲁⲣⲧⲉ ⲙⲙⲟϥ ἀκατάσχετος (B diff); sim with ⲁⲧ- B: Ps 123 5 ⲁⲧϣ ⲉⲛ ⲁⲅⲣⲏⲭϥ (S diff) ἀνυπόστατος, Ro 11 33 ⲁⲧϣ ϭⲉⲧϭⲱⲧϥ (S ⲛⲛⲉϣ) ἀνεξⲉ αύνητος, 1 Tim 6 16 ⲁⲧϣ ϭⲱⲛⲧ (S diff) ἀπρόⲥιⲧⲟⲥ, CaiEuch 650 ⲁⲧϣ ⲟⲣϥⲧ ⲉϭⲟⲩⲛ ἀπερίγραπτος; HL 80 ⲛⲁⲧϣ ⲧⲁϩⲟⲥ; PS 8 S ⲧⲁⲣⲡⲉϣ ⲁϩⲉⲣⲁⲧⲛ, ib 200 S ⲛϯⲛⲁϣ ϣⲁⲭⲉ ⲁⲛ, ShC 73 66 S ⲁⲛ ⲗⲁⲁⲩ ⲛⲁϣ ϭⲱ ⲉⲛⲁϩⲟⲩ (cf ib ⲛⲛⲉⲗⲁⲁⲩ ϭⲱ), BHom 30 S

ⲙⲉϥⲉϣ ⲡⲱⲧ, El 104 A ⲙⲁϥϩ ϣⲉϫⲉ, Bor 260 108 S ⲙⲡⲉϥⲛϣ ⲧⲁϩⲟϥ, AM 247 B ⲫⲏ ⲉⲧⲉⲡⲛⲁϣ ⲧⲁϩⲟϥ, Lant 80 34 S finished (writing) book ⲕⲁⲧⲁ ⲡⲛϣ ⲛⲧⲁⲓϣ ⲡⲱⲗϫ, Till Oster 8 A ⲙⲁⲑⲏⲗⲟⲡⲏ ϩ ⲣ ⲕⲁⲧⲉϫⲉ, Mani 1 A² ⲥⲉⲛⲁϣ ⲕⲁⲁϥ ⲉⲛ, C 43 208 B ϫⲛⲁϣ ⲧⲱⲟⲩⲛ ⲁⲛ, ST 56 S (ⲛ)ⲛⲉⲗⲁⲁⲩ...ⲉϣ ϫⲡⲟ⳥ⲕ, ib 395 Sᵃ ⲛⲛⲏϥ ϫⲓ ⲗⲁϥⲉ, J 19 57 Sᵃ ⲛϥϩ ⲉⲛⲁϥⲉ ⲛⲛⲧⲛ, CMSS 20 Sˢ ϣⲁϥϣ ⲉⲣ ϩⲱⲃ, BM 1115 S no man ⲉⲥⲁⲓϣ ⲧⲓ ⲡⲁⲟⲩⲟⲓ ⲉⲣⲟϥ ⲛⲥⲁⲃⲉⲣⲁⲕ (l ⲃⲗⲗⲁⲕ), C 86 271 B ϣⲧⲉⲙⲡⲓⲙⲁ ϣ ⲟⲗⲟⲩ, Va 61 18 B ⲛⲁϫⲉ ϣ ⲫⲏⲧ ⲛⲧⲟⲧⲟⲩ ⲁⲛⲡⲉ *was again unable*, Kr 147 F (ⲛ)ⲡⲉⲛϣ ⲙⲉϩⲓ ⲙⲁⲕ ⲗⲁⲁⲩ, BM 645 F ⲙⲁⲛⲧⲉⲉϣ ⲧⲁⲗⲁ ⲡⲉⲧⲁⲣⲓⲭⲓ, AZ 65 126 F ⲉⲃϣ ⲉⲗ ⲡⲉⲃⲗⲱⲕⲉⲥ (λόγος); without 2nd vb: Kr 228 9 S ⲉϣⲱⲡⲉ ϣⲁⲕⲛⲁϣ ⲛⲛⲏⲣⲟⲩϭⲱ *if thou canst*. ♭ with nom subj: Deu 24 4 S ⲛⲛⲉϣ ⲛϣⲟⲣⲡ ⲛϩⲁⲓ...ⲕⲟⲧϥ, Eccl 1 8 S ⲛⲛⲉϣ ⲡⲣⲱⲙⲉ ϣⲁⲭⲉ, Jo 3 9 S ⲉⲣⲉϣ ⲛⲁⲓ ⲛⲁϣⲱⲡⲉ (A² om ϣ) δύν.; Gk om: Ps 138 11 B ⲉⲣⲉϣ ⲟⲩϫⲁⲕⲓ ϩⲱⲙⲓ (S om ϣ), Ro 9 20 B ⲉⲣⲉϣ ⲡⲓⲙⲟⲩⲛⲕ ϫⲟⲥ (var & S om ϣ), Mk 12 34 S ⲙⲡⲉϣ ⲗⲁⲁⲩ ⲧⲟⲗⲙⲁ; Br 99 S ⲙⲉⲣⲉϣ ⲛⲁⲓⲱⲛ ⲧⲱⲟⲩⲛ, ShC 73 60 S ⲛⲛⲉϣ ⲗⲁⲁⲩ...ⲃⲱⲕ, BM 591 F ⲙⲁⲛ ϣ ⲁⲃⲣⲁϭⲁⲙ ⲗⲉϣⲕ; sim Mk 2 2 S ⲛⲧⲉⲙⲉϣ ϩⲓⲣⲙⲡⲣⲟ ϣⲟⲡⲟⲩ μηκέτι τὰ πρὸς τ. θύραν χωρεῖν.

ⲛⲉϣ- FS(once)B(do)+suff ⲧⲁ-, ⲧⲉⲕ-, ⲧⲉⲃ- &c, neg (? for ⲛⲛⲉϣ), not literary: CMSS 44 ⲛⲉϣⲧⲁⲁⲫⲱⲣⲓϫⲉ ⲙⲙⲁⲕ, BP 3248 contract ⲛⲓϣⲧⲁⲥⲉⲕ ϩⲉⲫⲗ ϩⲉⲗⲉⲃ, CMSS l c ⲁⲛⲉⲩ ⲛⲉϣⲧⲉⲕⲧⲉⲓ, AZ 23 28 ⲛⲉϣⲧⲉⲃⲧⲁⲕⲁ, BM 587(1) ⲛⲉϣⲧⲉⲃⲡⲁⲣⲕⲓ (παράγειν?)ⲛⲉⲡⲧⲓⲙⲓ, Kr 218 ⲛⲉϣⲧⲉⲡⲓ (ⲉ)ⲃⲁⲗ ⲉⲡⲉⲡⲁⲗⲛⲟⲩ, ib 159 ⲛⲉϣⲧⲉⲛⲃⲓⲧⲟⲩ ⲛⲧⲁⲁ(ⲧ)ⲕ; double neg: BKU 1 26 (81 16a)ⲛⲉϣⲧⲉⲥⲛⲉϣ ⲃⲱⲕ ⲉϩⲟⲩⲛ, AZ 23 35 ⲛⲉϣⲧⲟⲩϣⲓ (ⲉ)ⲃⲁⲗ with nom subj: Mor 18 42S ⲛⲛⲉϣⲧⲉⲡⲕⲟⲥⲙⲟⲥ ⲧⲏⲣϥ ⲧⲱⲟⲩⲛ ϩⲁⲣⲟⲟⲩ (var ib 19 50 ⲉⲙⲛ ϣϭⲟⲙ ⲉϥⲓ), P Gol 44 ⲛⲉϣⲧⲉⲡⲕⲉϣⲓⲡⲁⲗⲁⲗⲓ (cf Σεⲛελⲁ̑ⲗⲉ, Ψⲓⲛελⲟ́ⲟⲗⲉ) ⲉⲓ ⲉⲫ[ⲓ]ⲗ ⲉⲗⲁⲉⲓ, HL 87 B ⲙⲙⲟⲛ ⲛⲉϣ(sic) ⲟⲩⲣⲱⲙⲓ ⲱⲛϩ̄...ⲛⲁⲧϣ(sic)ⲟⲩⲉⲙ ϩⲣⲉ; with prefix: BM 544 ⲉϣⲱ[ⲡⲉ] ϣⲁⲕⲛⲉϣ ⲉⲓ, Bodl(P) a 2 37 ϣⲁⲕⲛⲉϣ ⲗⲉⲕⲗⲱⲕϥ, ib a 3 68 ⲙⲁⲅⲛⲉϣ ⲥⲙⲏⲛⲧⲉ, Pcod Mor 5 ⲅⲟ ⲙⲡⲟⲩⲛⲛϣ ⲁϣⲓ ⲣⲁⲧⲟⲩ, MR 5 49 ⲙⲡⲛⲉϣ ⲟⲩϩ(ⲓ) ⲣⲉⲧ.

Forming nn S: Mor 28 223 ⲉⲛⲉⲟⲩⲉϣ ⲗⲟⲡⲉ ϩⲙⲡⲉⲛϣⲱⲛⲉ *if there were possible cure*, I had been healed, ib 241 gift set aside ⲉⲛϣ ⲕⲁ ⲉⲃⲟⲗ ⲉⲧⲉⲡⲣⲟⲥⲫⲟⲣⲁ *eventual cost* (?, BMOr 4723 56 & 63 om both phrases). V also ϭⲟⲙ.

ϣⲁ- SAA²BFO, ϣⲁⲁ- S, ϩⲁ- Sᵃ, ϣⲁⲣⲟⲍ SB, ϣⲁⲁ·S(BHom), ϣⲁⲣⲁⲍ AA²(APMa)F, ϣⲁⲁ·A²(Jo), ϣⲁⲗⲁⲍ F prep a *to, toward* of persons (mostly = B ϩⲁ-): Ge 6 20 S, Is 36 2 SF, Jo 11 46 SAA²(all B ϩⲁ-), Ps 100 2 SB, AP 8 A² πρός, Mt 13 36 F(S ⲉ-, B ϩⲁ-)προσ(έρχεσθαι) dat; Nu 20 18 S(B ⲉϩⲣⲉⲛ-), Is 34 10 SBF, Ac 2 22 B(S ⲉ-)εἰς; Mt 11 13 SB ἕως;

Ac 25 12 *B*(*S* ⲉⲣⲁⲧ⸗ ⲛ-) ἐπί; Sa 8 3 *S* ⲙⲛⲧϣⲃⲏⲣ
ϣⲁⲡⲡ̄ gen; BHom 46 *S* ⲉⲓ ϣⲁⲁⲣⲱⲧⲛ dat; PS 20
S ⲁⲙⲟⲩ ϣⲁⲣⲟⲛ, ShA 2 281 *S* ⲉⲓ ⲛⲏⲧⲛ…ⲉⲓ ϣⲁⲣⲱⲧⲛ,
ShLeyd 354 *S* ⲉϩⲣⲁⲓ ϣⲁⲟⲩⲟⲛ ⲛⲓⲙ, ShC 73 33 *S* doing service ϣⲁⲛⲉⲧϣⲟⲟⲡ ϩⲓⲭⲙⲡⲕⲁϩ, Z 551 *S* ⲟⲩⲉⲡⲓⲥⲧⲟⲗⲏ ϣⲁⲟⲩⲥⲟⲡ, BMis 162 *S* ϫⲓⲧϥ̄ ϣⲁⲡⲉⲡⲓⲥⲕⲟⲡⲟⲥ
= BSM 71 *B*, PO 11 313 *B* ⲓ ϣⲁⲣⲟⲕ (*cf ib* ⲛⲏⲟⲩ
ϩⲁⲣⲟϥ), DeV 2 127 *B* ⲟⲩⲟⲣⲡⲧⲉⲛ ϣⲁⲣⲟⲕ (*cf* 128
ⲟⲩⲱⲣⲡ ϩⲁⲣⲟⲕ), BSM 37 *B* ⲙⲟϣⲓ ϣⲁⲡⲓⲙⲁⲛⲉⲥⲱⲟⲩ
= BMis 381 *S* ϩⲁⲣⲧⲛ-, DeV 2 119 *B* ⲧⲉϥϣⲁⲡⲟϫⲏⲙⲓⲁ
ϣⲁⲣⲟⲛ, Mus 42 226 *S* love ⲉⲧϣⲟⲟⲛ ϣⲁⲣⲟϥ, ManiH
89 *A²* ⲁⲙⲏⲓⲛⲉ ϣⲁⲣⲁⲓ, AZ 21 104 *O* ϣⲟⲓ ϣⲁⲡⲉⲣⲱⲟⲩ;
Ryl 314 *S* ⲡⲱϩ ⲡ̄ϣⲁⲟⲩⲟⲛ ⲛⲓⲙ.   **b** *to, at* of places,
things &c: Ps 50 tit *S*(*B* ϩⲁ-), Ez 2 3 *B*, Dan 11 7 *B*
πρός; Ge 4 8 *A*(Cl)*B*(var Cat 200 ⲉ-), Ps 43 25 *S*(*B*
ϣⲁⲉϩⲣⲏⲓ ⲉ-) εἰς; Deu 1 19 *B*(*S* ⲉ-), Ps 41 4 *SB*,
Lam 5 22 *F* ϣⲁⲉⲙⲁϣⲁ (*SB* om), Ja 5 7 *SA*(Cl)*B*
ἕως; Ro 5 13 *SB*, Miss 8 56 *S* ⲉⲓ ϣⲁⲧⲉⲧⲛⲥⲩⲛϩⲟⲍⲟⲥ
ἄχρι; Ps 49 1 *SB* μέχρι; Ez 1 8 *B*(*S* ϩⲓ-) ἐπί; Si 37
1 *S*(var ⲉ-), Ac 21 31 *S*(var & *B* ⲛ-) dat; Wess 15 22
S am bishop ⲉⲛⲉϭⲁⲗⲁϫⲧ ϣⲁⲡⲥⲓⲟⲩⲁⲙ Gk om; PS
23 *S* ⲡⲱϩ ϣⲁⲛⲧⲟⲡⲟⲥ (*cf ib* 21 ⲡⲱϩ ⲉⲧⲡⲩⲗⲏ), *ib* 242
S ⲕⲗⲏⲣⲟⲡⲟⲗⲓ ϣⲁⲡⲧⲟⲡⲟⲥ, *ib* 287 *S* ⲡⲧⲟⲡⲟⲥ…ⲛⲧⲁⲥ-
ϫⲓ ⲙⲩⲥⲧⲏⲣⲓⲟⲛ ϣⲁⲣⲟϥ, BHom 111 *S* ϣⲣϣⲱⲣϥ ϣⲁⲁ-
ⲡⲉϥⲥⲡⲉ, DeV 1 68 *B* ⲙⲁⲣⲟⲩ ϣⲁⲡϣⲱⲓ (*ib* ϣⲁⲉ-
ⲡϣ.), BSG 192 *S* go in ϣⲁⲡⲡⲁⲗⲗⲁⲧⲓⲟⲛ ϣⲁⲧⲣ̄ⲣⲱ,
BM 185 *S* ⲃⲱⲕ ϣⲁⲡⲧⲟⲟⲩ, Miss 8 29 *S* bring it ⲉ-
ⲉⲫⲉⲥⲟⲥ ϣⲁⲧⲥⲩⲛϩⲟⲍⲟⲥ (*ib* ⲉⲧⲥ.), BSM 15 *B* Joseph
sold ϣⲁⲟⲩⲕⲁϩⲓ ⲡ̄ϣⲉⲙⲙⲟ = BMis 349 *S* ⲉ-(*cf* Ac
7 9 ⲉϩⲣⲁⲓ ⲉ-), J 45 27 *S* ⲧⲕⲁⲙⲁⲣⲉ ϣⲁⲣⲓⲥ, *ib* 46 7 *S*
do ϣⲁⲡϥⲟⲩⲛⲧ, TurM 5 *Sᵃ* send lemons ϩⲁⲧⲡⲟⲗⲓⲥ, ST
199 *Sᵃ* ⲡⲛⲩ ϩⲁⲣⲓⲥ, MMA 24 6 13 *Sᵃ* ϫⲓⲧϥ̄ ϩⲁⲣⲓⲥ,
Va 57 191 *B* ⲁⲙⲟⲓ ϣⲁϥⲁⲓ ⲙⲙⲁⲩⲁⲧⲡⲉ εἴθε τοῦτο
μόνον, C 86 14 *B* sim.   **c** *till, at, by, for* of time: Ps
92 5 *SB*, Dan 11 35 *B*(*S* ⲉ-), Ac 4 3 *SB* εἰς; Dan 1
21 *B*(*S* ϣⲁϩⲣⲁⲓ ⲉ-), Mt 13 30 *SBF* ἕως; Ac 10 16 *B*
(*S* ⲛ-), MG 25 248 *B* prayed ϣⲁⲟⲩⲟⲩⲛⲟⲩ ἐπί; Lu
4 13 *SB* ἄχ.; Ps 70 17 *SB* μέχ.; C 99 238 *S* came
ϣⲁⲥⲟⲩϫⲟⲩⲱⲧ of Mesore = *ib* 89 73 *B* τῷ Μ.; Is 5
11 *SBF* ϣⲁⲣⲟⲩϩⲉ τὸ ὀψέ; C 89 22 *B* said it ϣⲁⲧ̄
ⲛⲥⲟⲛ τρίς; PS 200 *S* as I spake ⲡⲁⲓⲙⲏⲧⲛ ϣⲁⲡⲟⲟⲩ,
ShC 42 25 *S* bade ⲥⲉⲩⲅ ⲟⲩⲥⲩⲛ(ϩ)ⲟⲍⲟⲥ ϣⲁⲡⲥⲁⲃⲃⲁ-
ⲧⲟⲛ, Mor 18 198 *S* cast bodies to dogs ϣⲁϣⲟⲙⲛⲧ
ⲛϩⲟⲟⲩ, C 99 258 *S* ϣⲁⲧⲡⲁϣⲉ ⲙⲡⲟⲟⲩ they shall depart = *ib* 89 130 *B*, BMar 85 *S* ⲉⲩⲡⲁϣⲓⲛⲉ ⲛⲥⲱⲕ
ϣⲁⲁϣ ⲡⲟⲅⲟⲉⲓϣ, Kr 48 *S* will repay ϣⲁⲥⲟⲩⲁ ⲡⲡⲁⲟⲩ-
ⲟⲓⲛⲉ, PBu 162 *S* ϣⲁⲛⲁϣ (*sic*) ⲡⲛⲁⲩ ⲉⲣⲉⲓⲱⲣⲁⲡⲡⲏⲥ
ⲙⲙⲛ ⲉⲃⲟⲗ, PSBA 30 204 *S* ready to pay ϣⲁⲛⲁⲩ
ⲛⲓⲙ, AM 177 *B* ϥⲁⲓ ⲙⲙⲟⲕ ϣⲁϣⲱⲣⲡ, BKU 1 98
S shalt work ϣⲁⲁⲡϣⲁ, Mani H 31 *A²* ϣⲁⲣⲡⲣⲁ-
ⲙⲓⲛⲉ, J 89 16 *S* ϣⲁⲡϫⲱⲕ ⲛⲟⲩϩⲉⲃⲇⲟⲙⲁⲥ *by end of
a week*, C 86 322 *B* built it ϣⲁⲡϫⲱⲕ ⲛⲧ̄ ⲡⲣⲟⲙⲡⲉ, C
41 64 *B* ϣⲁϣⲟⲣⲡ ⲧⲉⲡⲡⲁϣⲉ = Miss 4 451 اذا كان

الصير. **d** *up to, to length of* in reckonings : Ap 21
16 *S*(*B* diff)ἐπί; Pro 6 26 *SA*(*B* om ϣⲁ-)ὅσος; Aeg
244 *S* ϣⲁⲡϣⲓ ⲙⲙⲛⲧⲥⲡⲟⲟⲩⲥ ἐντός; PS 269 *S* ⲙⲛⲧⲣⲉ
ⲥⲛⲁⲩ ϣⲁⲟⲩⲙⲛⲧ(*cf* Mt 18 16 ⲛ), ShC 73 62 *S* ⲟⲩⲏⲩ
…ϣⲁⲟⲩⲛⲟⲩ ⲡϣⲓ, CA 98 *S* hath power (to give)
ϣⲁⲧⲉ ⲡⲟⲉⲓⲛⲉ, DeV 2 283 *B* pay ϣⲁϥⲧ̄ ⲡⲗⲟⲩⲕⲟϫⲓ,
EW 44 *B* price agreed ϣⲁⲗ̄ ⲛⲥⲁⲑⲏⲣⲓ, PLond 4 480
have omitted none ϣⲁⲟⲩⲕⲟⲩⲓ ⲛϣⲏⲣⲉ.   **e** *except*
SB(rare): MG 25 36 *B* in world 3 enemies but in
desert ϣⲁⲟⲩⲅⲏⲧ ⲙⲙⲁⲩⲁⲧϥⲡⲉ πρὸς ἕνα; ShP 130⁵
42 what do ye ϣⲁⲕⲱϣ ϩⲓⲟⲥⲧⲉ?, BMis 369 no garments left ϣⲁⲛⲉⲧⲟⲩⲥⲩⲛⲁⲉ ⲡⲣⲏⲧⲟⲩ = BSM 29
B ⲉⲃⲏⲗ ⲉ-, ViK 9838 62 all did homage ϣⲁⲡⲇⲓⲁ-
ⲃⲟⲗⲟⲥ ⲙⲁⲩⲁⲁϥ, BMis 323 ⲛⲓⲙⲡⲉ ⲡⲁⲓ ϣⲁ…ⲙⲓ-
ⲭⲁⲏⲗ?, Cai 42573 2 if thou do this ⲙⲁⲥⲟⲩⲱϣ ⲕⲉⲟⲩⲁ ϣⲁⲣⲁⲕ, Ep 373 I have no man ϣⲁⲧⲉⲧⲛⲁⲅⲁⲡⲏ,
BKU 1 37 will require naught ϣⲁⲡⲕⲉⲣⲁ ϣⲟⲙⲛⲧ,
PGol 45 ⲙⲓⲕⲓⲛⲉ (*l* ϭ.) ϣⲁⲡϥⲥⲟⲡ, Wess 15 126 ⲙ-
ⲡⲉⲡ̄ϣⲁϫⲉ ϣⲱⲡⲉ ϣⲁⲥⲟⲧⲙⲉϥ ⲙⲙⲁⲧⲉ *not merely heard
but acted upon*.

ϣⲁⲃⲟⲗ, ϣⲁ ⲉⲃⲟⲗ   *v* ⲃⲱⲗ (p 36 *a*).

ϣⲁⲙⲡⲁⲓ *v* ⲙⲡⲁⲓ.

ϣⲁϩⲟⲩⲛ, ϣⲁ ⲉϩⲟⲩⲛ *v* ϩⲟⲩⲛ.

ϣⲁϩⲣⲁⲓ, ϣⲁ ⲉϩⲣⲁⲓ *v* ϩⲣⲁⲓ.

ϣⲁ- in ϣⲁⲛⲧⲉ-, ϣⲁⲣⲉ- verbal preff *q v*.

V also ⲉⲛⲉϩ, ⲙⲁ (p 154 *a*), ⲛⲁⲩ (ⲧⲛⲁⲩ p 235 *b*),
ⲣⲏⲥ, ϫⲓⲛ-.

On derivation of ϣⲁ- from ḫr & šʿ (distinction
lost in Coptic) *v* Rec 31 158, AZ 47 139.

ϣⲁ *SAA²*(Mani 2)*BF* vb, *begin* in nn ϣⲁⲙⲓⲥⲉ
(rather than from ϣⲟⲣⲡ as p 185 *a*, where *S* 1 Kg
6 7, Jer 4 31 are ϣⲁ-), ϣⲁⲥⲱⲡⲧ, ϣⲁ ⲡⲥ. (p 345 *b*);
also ? in condit pref ⲉⲣⲉϣⲁⲛ- (DM 3 29, Sethe;
Sdff, Spg otherwise).

ϣⲁ *S*, ϩⲁⲉ *A*, ϣⲁⲓⲉ *A²*, ϣⲁⲓ *B*, ϣⲉ(ⲉ)ⲓ *F*, ϣⲁⲓⲱ-
ⲟⲩ† *B* vb intr, *rise* of sun &c: Job 3 9 *S*(*B*†), Eccl 1 5
SF ϣⲉⲉⲓ (CSchmidt) ϣⲉⲓ (Mich 3520), Jon 4 8 *S*
AB, Mk 16 2 *SB*, Is 13 10 *B*(*S* ⲛⲃⲟⲗ), ἀνατέλλειν;
ib 58 8 *SB* ῥηγνύναι; Ac 20 11 *S* (var ϩⲉ, *B* ⲓ ⲉⲃⲟⲗ)
αὐγή; ShBerl Sitz '29 430 *S* souls of dead ϣⲁ ⲙⲡ-
ⲡⲣⲏ, BMis 155 *S* ⲁⲡⲣⲏ ⲁⲣⲭⲓ ⲛϣⲁ;   qual *B*: Job
l c, Va 57 229 sun ⲉⲧϣ. ⲙⲙⲏⲛⲓ.

With following preposition or adverb.   **c** ⲉϫⲛ-:
Ex 22 3 *SB*, Is 60 1 *SB* ἀν. ἐπί; *ib* 9 2 *S*(*B* ⲉⲣ ⲟⲩⲱⲓⲛⲓ) λάμπειν ἐπί; Ac 9 3 *S*(*B* do) περιαστράπτειν;
BMis 19 *S* ⲧⲟⲡⲧⲁⲥⲓⲁ…ϣⲁ ⲉϫⲛⲕⲗⲁⲩⲧⲟⲥ; ⲉϩⲣⲁⲓ ⲉ-
ϫⲛ- *S*: Ge 32 31 (*B* ⲉ-) ἀν. dat; FR 14 ⲧⲉⲭⲁⲣⲓⲥ
ⲉⲁⲥϣⲁ ⲉϩ. ⲉϫⲱⲥ;   **c** ϩⲓϫⲉⲛ- *B*: C 89 77 sun ⲉϥϣ.†
ϩ.ⲡⲓⲕⲁϩⲓ;   **c** ⲡ- dat: Ps 96 11 *SB*, CaiEuch 485 *B*
ⲁⲕϣ. ⲡⲡⲉⲧⲥⲱⲣⲉⲙ ἀν. dat; 2 Kg 2 32 *S* διαφαύσκειν;
BM 511 (2) *F* sun ϣⲉⲉⲓ ⲡⲓⲡ, AM 247 *B* thy memory ϣ. ⲡⲁⲛ to-day;   **c** ϩⲛ-, ϧⲉⲛ-: Ps 111 4 *S*(*B*

ⲉⲃⲟⲗ ⳍ.) ἐξαν. ἐν; Ac 12 7 S(B ⲉⲣ ⲟⲩ.) λά. ἐν; PSBA
30 236 S thunder & lightning ϣⲁ ⲟⲛⲧⲡⲉ, DeV 2 7 B
sim of star; ⲉⲃⲟⲗ ⲟⲛ- SA²: Nu 24 17 (B ⳍⲉⲡ-), He
7 14 (B ϥⲓⲣⲓ) ἀν. ἐκ; BMar 155 ⲧⲁⲡⲁⲧⲟⲗⲏ ϣⲁ ⲉⲃ.
ⲟⲩⲡⲏⲓ ⲡⲗⲁⲅⲉⲓⲁ, BMis 113 Word ⲁϥϣⲁ ⲛⲁⲛ ⲉⲃ.
ⲟⲛⲧⲡⲁⲣⲑⲉⲛⲟⲥ, ManiH 60 A² ⲡϣⲓⲥⲙⲉ ϣ. ⲁⲃⲁⲗ ⲟⲛ-
ⲡⲣ[ⲡⲉ; с ⲉⲃⲟⲗ B: C 86 284 ϣⲁⲧⲉⲛⲟⲩⲱⲓⲛⲓ ϣ. ⲉⲃ.
= Mun 38 S ϣⲁⲡⲡⲁⲩ ⲛⲉⲧⲟⲟⲩⲉ.

tr B(once): Va 57 260 ⲁⲓϣ. ⲙⲡⲓⲣⲏ ⲉϫⲉⲛⲡⲓⲥⲁⲙ-
ⲡⲉⲧⲣⲱⲟⲩ ἀν. (cf Mt 5 45).

—— nn S, rising: Sa 16 28 HT ⲡϣⲁ ⲙⲡⲣⲏ, Is
60 19 (B ⲟⲩⲱⲓⲛⲓ) ἀνατολή.

ⲙⲁ ⲛϣ., ⲟ. SABF, place of rising, east: Ge 25 6
SB, ib 29 1 S(B ⲥⲁⲡⲉⲓⲉⲃⲧ), Am 8 12 SAB, Ap 7 2
SBF, Miss 8 43 S bishops from ⲙⲙ. ἀνατολή; PS
16 S sun rose ⲟⲛⲙⲙ., El 64 A ⲙⲙⲁ ⲛⲟ., Mor 24 7
F Paradise near ⲙⲙ. ⲛⲡⲣⲉ.

ϭⲓⲛϣⲁ S, rising: Jud 5 31 ἀνατολή.

ⲣⲁ ϣⲁ S, eastern side: Lev 1 16 (B ⲥⲁⲡ., cf 16 14
ⲣⲁ ⲛϣⲁ), Lu 13 29 (var & B ⲙⲁ ⲛϣ.) ἀνατολή.

ϣⲁ S, ϣⲁⲉ Sᵃ, ϣⲁⲓ SᵃBF, ϣⲉ(ⲉ)ⲓ, ϣⲏⲓ F, ⲟⲁⲉ,
ⲟⲁ (once)A, ϣⲁ(ⲉ)ⲓⲉ A², ϣⲁⲉⲓ O (?) nn m, festival:
Lev 22 21 SB, Lam 1 4 BF, Hos 2 11 AB, 2 Mac 6 6
A ⲟⲁ, Mk 14 2 SBF ϣⲉⲉⲓ, Jo 4 45 SA²BF ἑορτή;
BHom 90 S ⲡϣⲁ ⲙⲡⲉⲛⲥⲱⲧⲏⲣ (sc Easter) πανήγυρις,
Sa 15 12 S -ρισμός; ib 14 23 S τελετή; CA 87 S ⲙⲡⲡⲁⲥⲭⲁ, R 1 5 10 S ⲡⲛⲟϭ ⲛϣⲁ (sc Pascha), Aeg 283
S after Paschal week ⲛϣⲁ (Easter), Ryl 81 S ⲡⲧⲁ-
ⲛⲁⲥⲧⲁⲥⲓⲥ, CO 236 S, Ep 333 Sᵃ ϣⲁⲉ, ST 243 S,
BKU 1 308Sᵃ ϣⲁⲓ all prob Easter, C 99 91 S ⲡⲉϩⲟⲟⲩ
ⲙⲡϣⲁ = Va 172 95 عيد الرب, MG 17 597 يوم القيامة
CA 88 S ⲛⲟⲛ ⲛⲧⲉⲣⲟⲙⲡⲉ =.ib rı السنة راس, Wess 18
84 S ⲛⲧⲱⲃⲉ (Epiphany), R 1 3 44 S, Ep 565 A S
sim, cf Aeg 283 S ⲙⲡϫⲱⲕⲙ τῶν θεοφανίων ἑορτή,
BMis 344 S ⲡⲉⲓϣⲁ ⲉⲧⲉⲡⲁⲣⲓⲥⲧⲟⲛ ⲙⲙⲓⲭⲁⲏⲗ (var
ⲡⲁⲣ. only), Ryl 53 S ⲙⲡⲉⲛⲉⲓⲱⲧ ⲁⲡⲁ ⲡⲁⲛⲛⲟⲩⲧⲉ, J 76
28 Sᵃ ⲛϣⲁⲉ ⲛⲉⲡⲓⲥⲟⲙⲱⲛ (ἐπίσημος, cf MG 25 319)
ⲛϣⲁ ⲙⲡⲧⲟⲡⲟⲥ ⲙⲛⲡⲛⲟϭ ⲛϣⲁ, TU 20 4 b 6 S ⲡⲛⲟϭ
ⲛϣⲁ ⲉⲧⲟⲩⲟⲛϩ ⲉⲃⲟⲗ, Ep 458 S᷍ ϣⲁⲉ ⲛⲁⲏⲙⲟⲥⲓⲟⲛ,
ⲙⲡⲕⲱⲧ q v, Ryl 361 S ⲛϣⲁⲙⲛⲧ ⲛⲛϣⲁⲁ, ClPr 19
155 S ⲡⲉϣⲙⲟⲩⲛ ⲙⲡϣⲁ, BM 591 10 F ⲙⲙⲁϩⲥⲛⲉⲩ
ϣⲏⲓ, ManiH 11A² ⲁⲥⲕⲁ ⲡⲥⲁⲃⲃⲁⲧⲟⲛ ⲛϣ., Ep 53 S as
acclamation ⲟⲁⲣ ⲛϣⲁ; divine, communion(?) service S: ShC 73 152 neglect not ⲡⲥⲱⲟⲩϩ ⲙⲡⲛϣⲁ, Sh
BM 192 273 eyes cast down as they go to ⲛϣⲁ, Leyd
158 rubric ⲡⲉⲧⲥⲱⲣ ⲙⲡⲛϣⲁ ⲉⲃⲟⲗ, ib 145 ⲕⲁ ⲛϣⲁ ⲉⲃⲟⲗ
ⲟⲛⲡⲉⲧⲟⲩⲁⲁⲃ ⲛ ⲛⲡⲗⲁⲓⲁⲧⲩ (sc with verses containing
these words) rubric after ⲛⲛⲁⲩ ⲛⲥⲩⲛⲁⲅⲉ (cf ib ⲕⲁ
ⲡⲥⲱⲟⲩⲟ ⲉⲃ.), CO 481 ⲡⲧⲉⲣⲉⲩⲱⲣⲟ ⲛϣⲁ ⲉⲃⲟⲗ, ib 71
bishop loq ϥⲟⲣⲓⲃⲟⲗ ⲙⲡⲛϣⲁ excommunicated (cf ib 73
ⲉϥⲥⲩⲛⲁⲅⲉ ⲁⲛ,ST 366 ⲟⲓⲃ. ⲛⲡⲙⲏⲥⲧⲏⲣⲓⲟⲛ),BP 12497
ⲉⲓⲥ ⲛϣⲁ ⲥⲟϣⲧ ⲉⲡⲧⲟⲡⲟⲥ, ib 12486 to bishop ⲁⲕⲛⲟϫⲧ

ⲟⲓⲃ. ⲙⲡⲛϣⲁ, ib ⲛⲧ ⲉⲣⲟⲩⲛ ⲉⲛϣⲁ, COAd 41 ⲁϫⲟⲅⲟⲣϥⲧ
ⲉⲟ. ⲉⲛϣⲁ, Win 7 bishop loq ϥⲟⲣⲓⲟⲩⲛ ⲙⲡⲛϣⲁ.

ϣⲁ ⲱ S, ϣⲁⲓ ⲟ B, ϣⲁⲓ ⲁ F (?), great festival: Hos
9 5 B(A ⲛⲁϭ, B ⲛⲓϣϯ) πανήγυρις, CO 60 S opp ϣⲁ
ϣⲏⲙ, BM 585 F ⲁⲃ(ϥ)ⲓⲧⲟⲩ ⲟⲓⲛⲏ.

ⲟⲟⲟⲩ ⲛϣⲁ SA²B, festival day: Lam 2 22 SB
ἡμέρα ἑορ., Aeg 225 S ἡμ. τ. ἑορτῶν; MG 25 375 B
ⲟⲩⲉⲟ. ⲛⲧⲉ ⲟⲩⲧⲟⲡⲟⲥ πανήγ. (ROC 18 289 ل__), ShC
42 111 S, ManiH 72 A² ⲟ. ⲙⲡⲟⲛⲡⲁⲣⲁⲧⲏⲣⲏⲥⲓⲥ, CO
34 S ⲛⲉⲟ. = ib 30 ⲟⲟⲟⲩ ⲛⲥⲩⲛⲁⲅⲉ, C 41 42 B wine
needed for ⲟⲩⲉⲟ., PLond 4 451 S fulfilment promised ⲡⲁⲧⲗⲟⲅⲟⲥ ⲡⲁⲧⲥⲧⲁⲩⲣⲟⲥ ⲡⲁⲧⲟ. (cf Kr 114 S
sim ⲟⲟⲟⲩ ⲡⲕⲏⲣⲁⲕⲛ).

ⲣ ϣⲁ, ⲛϣⲁ SAA²BFO, make, keep festival: Is 30
29 SBF, Nah 1 15 S(Mus 30 12)AB ἑορτάζειν, 3 Kg
8 65 B ἑορτὴν ποιεῖν (cf C 89 24 = ϯ προσφορά); He
12 23 B(S diff) πανηγυρίζειν; BMis 234 S ⲛⲉϥⲣ. in
cities he traversed εὐωχεῖν; ShMIF 23 155 S ⲟⲉⲛ-
ⲟⲣⲟⲟⲩ ⲛⲣ., CA 97 S ⲣ. ⲙⲡⲡⲁⲥⲭⲁ, Aeg 38 B ⲉⲣ.
ⳍⲉⲛⲟⲟⲛ, TillOster 27 A ⲉⲓⲣ. ⲡⲉⲙⲉⲩ, Mani 1 A²
blessed they that ⲣ. ⲟⲛⲡⲓⲉⲟⲟⲩⲉ, BKU 1 313 S ⲉⲓⲣ.
ⲡⲁⲧⲉⲩⲁⲅⲅⲉⲗⲓⲟⲛ, BP 12497 S bishop loq ⲉⲕϣⲁⲛⲣ.
if thou celebrate, art excommunicate, Hor 84 O ⲣ. (?)
ⲛⲙⲁϥ; с ⲉ-, for, at S: CO 290 ⲣ. ⲉⲡⲙⲁ ⲡⲁⲡⲁ ⲡⲁ-
ⲛⲡⲟⲩⲧⲉ, ib 511 ⲉⲑⲁⲅⲓⲁ ⲙⲁⲣⲓⲁ; с ⲛ- dat SB: Lev
23 39 ἑορτάζ. dat; BM 178 88 S Virgin ⲉⲧⲓⲣ. ⲛⲁⲥ
ⲙⲡⲟⲟⲩ, AM 226 B sim, OLZ '03 62 S ⲉⲓⲣ. ⲙⲡⲣⲁⲛ
ⲛⲡⲧⲟⲟⲩ(sic l ?)ⲉⲧⲟⲩⲁⲁⲃ; ⲙⲁ ⲛⲣ ϣⲁ SB, place of
holding f., church: C 99 144 S built ⲕⲟⲩⲓ ⲙⲙ. = ib
89 51 B = Va ar 172 31 بيعة, C 89 27 B take corpse
to ⲡⲟⲩⲙ. = MG 17 382 (sic l) موضع تعيدهن; ⲙⲡⲛ-
ⲣⲉϥⲣ ϣⲁ S, occasion of f., performance of rites: B
Mis 75 at new moon (Ps 80 3), ClPr 26 75 great are
Christian mysteries & wondrous ⲛⲉⲩⲙ.; ϭⲓⲛⲣ
ϣⲁ S, celebration of f.: BM 221 150 ⲧϭ. ⲉⲧϣⲟⲟⲡ
ⲛⲁⲛ in church, Miss 8 238 ⲧϭ. ⲙⲡⲙⲁⲣⲧⲩⲣⲟⲥ mode
of celebrating.

ϯ ϣⲁ S, give communion: CO 61 bishop loq ⲡⲣⲱⲙⲉ ⲉⲧⲛⲁϯ. ⲟⲛⲡⲉⲓϣⲁ is excommunicate, RE 9 162
ⲙⲁϥϯ. ⲉⲡⲧⲟⲡⲟⲥ.

ϫⲓ ⲛϣⲁ S, receive (?) communion: CO 102 come
ⲛⲧⲉⲧⲛϫ., or ? = ϯ ⲛϣⲁ.

As vb S(rare), keep f.: Ex 5 1(ShC 42 84)ⲉⲩⲉϣⲙ-
ϣⲉ ⲡⲁⲓ ⲛ ⲛⲥⲉϣⲁ ⲡⲁⲓ (B ⲉⲣ ϣⲁⲓ) ἑορτάζειν; BKU
1 314 ⲛⲡⲉⲧⲛϣⲁ ⲉⲧⲕⲁⲑⲟⲗⲓⲕⲏ (sc ⲉⲕⲕⲗⲏⲥⲓⲁ, v Ep 1
116), KroppH 86 ϣⲁⲩϣⲁ ⲙⲙⲟϥ in heaven.

As name(?): ⲛϣⲁ (Kr 5, WS 104, Ryl 209), Ψᾶ
(Preisigke).

ϣⲁ S, ϣⲉ SAF, ϣⲁⲡⲧϥ S, ϣⲁⲓ B, ϣⲉⲉ AF,
ϣⲁⲡⲧ⸗ SB, ϣⲁⲁ., ϣⲁ(ⲁ)ⲧ⸗, ϣⲁⲧⲧ⸗, ϣⲏⲡⲧ⸗ S, ϣⲉⲡⲧ⸗
SAF, ϣⲉⲉⲡⲧ⸗AF nn m, nose: Job 40 20S(B om), Ps
134 17 SB, Pro 11 22 SA ϣⲉⲡⲧ⸗B, Cant 7 8 SF ϣⲉ,

Sa 15 15 S ῥίς, P 44 69 S ⲡϣⲁⲁⲛⲧϥ · ⲣⲓⲛ انف, *ib* ⲣⲱⲑⲱⲛ ⲣⲓⲛⲟⲥ· ϧⲏⲧϥ ⲙⲡϣⲁ طرف الأنف (*cf* ⲕⲟⲩⲕⲥ in Addenda to p 102); Job 40 21 *B*(*S* om), Ez 23 25 *S* (Bor 226 174, *B* ϫⲉⲙϣⲁⲓ) μυκτήρ; 1 Cor 12 17 *S*(*B*) ϣⲱⲗⲉⲙ ὄσφρησις; *MélCh Moeller* 228 *S* of Mark ⲡⲉϥϣⲁ ϫⲟⲥⲉ μακρόρρυγχος; Mor 44 39 *S* of Christ ϣⲁⲛⲧϥ ϫⲟⲥⲉ, ShA 2 110 *S* ϣⲧⲁⲙ ⲙⲡⲉⲧⲛϣⲁ, Pcod 23 *S* ϣⲁⲧⲧϥ (var ϣⲁⲁⲛⲧϥ), Z 320 *S* ϣⲁⲧϥ, Mor 28 27 *S* ϣⲁⲁⲧϥ, R 2 2 32 *S* ⲡϣⲉ ⲉⲧϣⲱⲗⲙ, Sh(?)Mor 54 93 *S* ⲛⲁϣⲡ ϣⲉⲡⲧⲟⲩ ⲉⲃⲟⲗ, PMéd 229 *S* ϣⲉⲡⲧϥ, El 94 *A* ϣⲉⲡⲧⲟⲩ, Mor 24 7 *F* ϣⲉⲡⲧⲃ, Miss 4 672 *S* ⲉϥⲥⲉⲕ ϧⲣⲟⲟⲩ ϧⲛϣⲁⲁⲛⲧϥ like wild swine, C 43 56 *B* sim, BP 12491 *S* ⲁⲩⲃⲱⲕ ϧⲣⲟⲟⲩ ⲛϣⲁ ⲉϧⲣⲁⲓ ϧⲓⲱⲓ, Mor 43 230 *S* ⲡϣⲁⲁⲛⲧϥ (of corpse) ⲛⲧⲁϥⲣ ϣⲙⲙⲟ ⲉⲡⲛⲃⲉ, P 131⁵ 44 *S* ϣⲁⲛⲧϥ (*sic*) ⲙⲙⲁⲣⲓⲁ.

ⲥⲱⲃⲉ ⲛϣⲁ (once), ⲥϭⲃϣⲁ, ϫⲉϥϣⲁ, ϭⲃⲙϣⲉ S, ϫⲉⲃϣ., ϫⲉⲙϣ., ϫⲉⲙⲛϣ., ϫⲉϥϣ. *B* nn m f (once each), *nostrils*, lit *leaves of nose*, mostly pl: Job 27 3 *S*(*B* ϣⲁⲓ) ῥίς; Nu 11 20 *S*(*B* do) μυκ. pl, Cant 7 4 *S* μ. sg; BHom 47 *S* ὄσφ.; Z 310 *S* hung up ⲡⲥⲁⲡⲉϥϣ. ῥώθων; K 75 *B* ϫⲉⲙϣ. (varr ϫⲉⲙⲛ., ϫⲉⲃ.) منخر; ShA 1 105 *S* ulcer ϧⲙⲛϣⲁ ⲏ ⲛϭⲱⲃⲉ ⲛϣⲁ, *ib* 78 *S* ⲛϣⲁ ⲏ ⲛϭ., BHom 127 *S* ⲁϥⲉⲓϣⲉ ⲙⲡⲉⲅⲛⲓϥⲉ ϧⲛⲡⲉⲩϭ., Kropp R 14 18 *S* sim ϫⲉϥ., BMEA 10587 *S* ⲡⲉϥϭⲃⲙϣⲉ bird's beak, MG 25 161 *B* devil hooked ⲛⲥⲁⲡⲉϥϫⲉⲃ., DeV 1 164 *B* wizards ϯ ϫⲣⲱⲟⲩ ⲉⲃⲟⲗ ϫⲉⲛⲛⲟⲩϣⲁⲓ & ⲙⲟⲩϯ ϫⲉⲛⲛⲟⲩϫⲉⲃ., BSM 111 *B* snorted ⲉⲃⲟⲗ ϫⲉⲛⲡⲉϥϫⲉⲃ., C 86 219 *B* ⲓ ⲉⲃⲟⲗ ϫⲉⲛⲧⲉϥϫⲉⲃ.

ⲕⲁⲣϣϣⲁⲓ *B*   v ⲕⲱⲣϫ.

ⲛⲁϣⲡ ϣⲁ   v ⲡⲟⲩϣⲡ ⲉⲃⲟⲗ.

ⲱⲗⲕ, ⲉⲗⲕ ϣⲁ   v ⲱⲗⲕ.

ϣⲁⲓⲱⲟⲩ *B*, *hook-nosed*: K 73 ⲉⲧϣ. اقنف. Or *?big-nosed* (pl of ϣⲁⲓⲟ).

ϫⲁϫϣⲁⲓ *B*, *with cut nose*: Lev 21 18 (*S* ϣⲁⲁⲛⲧϥ ⲥⲟⲃⲕ) κολοβόριν.

ϣⲁ *S* nn (?) meaning doubtful: Kropp S 104 angel names ⲏⲗ ⲏⲗ ⲡⲁⲡⲉⲓϣⲁ ⲛⲃⲁⲗ (for ϣⲟ ? or *l* ? ϣⲁⲛⲃ., cf ϣⲁⲛϧⲏⲧ).

ϣⲁ, *festival*   v ϣⲁ, *rise*.

ϣⲁ in swearing   v ϣⲉ, *by*.

ϣⲁ *F*   v ⲉⲙϣⲟ.

ϣⲁ *F*, *thousand*   v ϣⲟ.

ϣⲁ- in ϣⲁⲙⲓⲥⲉ, ϣⲁⲥⲱⲛⲧ   v ϣⲁ, *begin*.

ϣⲁ- *A*   v ⲉⲙϣⲱ.

ϣⲁⲗⲉ *F*   v ϣⲟⲟⲩⲉ.

ϣⲁⲓ *S* nn m, *fortune, fate* (?) c ⲡ- as god's name: ShA 1 379 saluting demons, saying ⲧⲟⲩⲁϣⲧⲉ ⲙⲡϣⲁⲓ ⲙⲡⲟⲟⲩ ⲏ ⲡϣ. ⲙⲡⲧⲙⲉ ⲏ ⲡϣ. ⲙⲡⲏⲓ *to-day is*

worship of Pshai or (that is) *P. of the village or P. of the house* (ϣⲁⲓ for ϣⲁ *festival* not found in Sh). In many names, as ⲡϣⲁⲓ (P 130¹ 139, BP 911), ψⲁⲓ(CO 54), Ψⲁⲓⲁ (J 57 3), Ψάει, Ψάις, Ψαιῶς, Ναβερψάι, Σερεμψάις, Πεμψάις, Μενχεψάις (Preisigke). V Spg *Eigenn.* 57*, DM 2 5 n. Whether ⲡϣⲟⲓ, ⲡϣⲟⲓ, بشاي, ابشاي, Ψόις, Σενψόις, are same or from ϣⲟⲓ† (ϣⲁⲓ) is doubtful, but O ⲡϣⲟⲓ (AZ 21 105), Ψοι(PGM 1 124) prob belong here.

ϣⲁⲓ *S* adj, *new*: Lu 5 36 (cit ShA 2 20, *B* ⲃⲉⲣⲓ), Mor 37 41 sheepskin ⲉϥⲟ ⲛϣ. καινός; Mk 2 21(*B* do) ἄγναφος; Tri 7 22 جلب opp ⲁⲡⲁⲥ; ShIF 153 ⲡⲗϭⲉ ⲡⲧⲟⲉⲓⲥ opp ⲧⲟⲉⲓⲥ ⲛϣ., Ryl 239 ⲟⲩϣⲟⲧ ⲛϣ.   *B*(?) Mus 34 190 ⲟⲩⲁⲅⲁⲑⲉ ⲛⲧⲓⲁ ⲛϣ. (StPaul Girard).

ϣⲁⲓ *A*², meaning unknown: Mani 1 foolish king of the pitiless ⲛⲓⲃⲁⲛϣ. ⲛⲁ[....]ⲃⲟⲟⲡⲉ.   Cf (?) ⲃⲁⲛϧⲟ.

ϣⲁⲓ *B*   v ϣⲁ *rise* & *nose*.

ϣⲉ *S*(rare, mostly = ⲃⲱⲕ) *AA*² (both rare)*B*, ϣⲏ *SS*ᵃ*FO*, ϣⲉⲓ *S*, ϣⲁⲓ *S*ᵃ, imperat ⲙⲁϣⲉ *B* vb intr, *go*, a c ethic dat(*B* mostly so): Jud 11 37, Mt 11 4 πορεύεσθαι; Ps 33 1, Ac 5 26 ἀπέρχεσθαι, Is 47 1 εἰσέρ. (all *S* ⲃⲱⲕ), Ap 21 1(*S* ⲟⲩⲉⲓⲛⲉ)παρέρ.(var ἀπ.); Jer 17 19 βαδίζειν (*S* ⲃⲱⲕ), Ex 2 15 (*S* ⲡⲱⲧ), MG 25 209 ⲁⲓϣⲉ ⲡⲛⲏ ἀναχωρεῖν; ShC 73 156 *S* ⲉⲩⲛⲁϣⲉⲓ ⲛⲁϥ, C 43 217 ⲁⲡⲓⲭⲣⲱⲙ ϣⲉ ⲛⲁϥ, AM 220 ⲙⲁϣⲉ ⲡⲱⲧⲉⲛ, BSM 47 ⲙⲉⲛⲉⲡⲥⲁⲱⲣ ⲓϣⲉ ⲡⲛⲏ = BMis 396 *S* ⲉⲓ, Mani 2 *A*² ⲁⲩⲃⲱⲕ ⲁϧⲣⲏⲓ ⲁⲩϣⲉ ⲡⲉⲩ, CO 363 *S* ⲛⲧⲁϣⲛ ⲡⲛⲏ, Vi ostr 293 *S*ᵃ ⲛϣⲉⲛ ⲡⲉⲕ, Hall 127 *S* ⲛⲧⲁϣⲓ(*sic*)ⲡⲁⲓ.   b without dat: Eccl 1 4 *F*, 1 Cor 16 4 πορ.; Mt 20 4 *F*(*B* c ⲛ-), C 89 50 ⲁϥϣⲉ ⲁϥⲟⲩⲱⲙ ἀπέρ. (all *S* ⲃ.); ShIF 284 *S* ⲙⲁⲣⲉϥϣⲉ ⲛϥⲉⲓ, DeV 2 113 sim, JKP 2 60 *S* ϣⲁⲓϣⲉ ⲧⲁⲕⲁ(ⲁ)ⲥ, MG 25 36 ⲙⲡⲉⲣϣⲉ ⲁⲗⲗⲁ ϧⲟⲗ ⲉ-, AM 6 ⲡⲧⲟⲩϣⲉ ⲡⲧⲟⲩϧⲟⲥ, Hall 73 *S* ⲁϥϣⲉ (*sic l*) ⲁϥϫⲟⲟⲥ, Mor 24 17 *F* ⲧⲁϣⲏ ⲧⲁⲥⲱⲟⲩϧ.   tr refl (?): Va 63 98 ⲉⲩⲉⲣ ⲫⲁϧⲣⲓ ⲉⲣⲱⲟⲩ...ⲙⲡⲉⲡⲟⲩϥⲁϧⲣⲓ ϣⲉ ⲙⲙⲱⲟⲩ οὐκ ὠφελεῖν, *ib* 58 170 moved by her beauty ⲁⲡⲓⲥⲟⲑⲛⲉϥ ϣⲉ ⲙⲙⲟϥ & he loved her βέλος δέχεσθαι.

With following preposition (c ethic dat & without not separated).

—— ⲉ- *SABFO*, *go to*: Ps 138 7 (*SACl* ⲃ.) πορ. ποῦ, Ro 15 25 (*S* do) π. εἰς; 1 Kg 24 23 (*S* ⲃ. ⲉϧⲣⲁⲓ ⲉ-) ἀπέρ. εἰς; Jer 41 3 εἰσέρ. εἰς; Ps 67 19 (*S* ⲁⲗⲉ) ἀναβαίνειν εἰς; Jo 13 36 (*SA*² ⲛⲁ) ὑπάγειν ὅπου; Jon 1 3 (*SA* ⲥϭⲏⲣ ⲉ-) βαδ. εἰς; Mk 13 34 *F*(Mor 21, *S* = Gk, *B* ⲗⲟϣⲓ) ἀπόδημος; MG 25 216 ⲙⲁϣⲉ ⲡⲉ ⲉⲡⲉⲛⲏⲓ ἀναχ. εἰς; Ny Carlsberg ostr 828 *S* ⲉⲓϣⲉⲓ ⲉⲣⲏⲥ, Ep 532 43 *S* ⲁϥϣⲏ ⲁⲡϧⲛⲧ, C 89 51 ⲁϥϣⲉ ⲉϧⲛⲧ = Miss 4 533 *S* ⲉⲓ, El 52 *A* ⲙⲡⲓϣⲉ ⲁϭⲡ ⲡϣⲓⲛⲉ, BSM 22 ϣⲉ ⲡⲁⲕ ⲉⲧⲉⲕⲕⲗⲏⲥⲓⲁ = BMis 360 *S* ⲃ., DeV 2 178 ⲁϥϣⲉ ⲡⲁϥ ⲉⲭⲉⲣⲉⲩ (var ϧⲟⲗ), Hor 78 *O* ⲁϥϣⲏ

ⲁⲕⲧⲁⲣ; ⲉⲙⲁⲩ, *thither*: Ez 20 29 εἰσπορ. ἐκεῖ; Mt 2 22 ἀπέρ. ἐκ. (both S ⸀.); C 89 3 ⲡⲗⲁ ⲉⲧⲁϥϣⲉ ⲉ. = MG 17 315 S ⸀., MG 25 241 walking ϣⲁⲡⲧⲉϥϣⲉ ⲡⲁϥ ⲉ.; ⲉⲣⲁⲧ⸗, *to*: AM 200 ⲁⲩϣⲉ ⲡⲱⲟⲩ ⲉⲣⲁⲧϥ, C 89 203 ϣⲉ ⲉⲣⲁⲧϥ ⲙⲡⲛⲟⲩⲧⲉ; ⲉⲣⲣⲉⲡ-, *toward*: 1 Kg 17 48(S ⲙⲟⲟϣⲉ ⲉϩⲟⲩⲛ ⲉ-), ib 23 28 (S ⸀. ⲉⲣⲁⲧ⸗ ⲛ-) πορ. εἰς.

—— ⲉⲭⲉⲛ-, *on to*: Jer 13 7 (S ⸀. ⲉϫⲛ-) πορ. ἐπί, Ac 17 14 (var ϣⲁ-, S ⸀. ⲉϩⲣⲁⲓ ⲉϫⲛ-) π. ἕως; Ez 38 11 ἀναβ. ἐπί; Jer 13 4 βαδ. ἐπί; Job 40 15 (S ⲁⲗⲉ ⲉϫⲛ-) ἐπέρ. ἐπί; AM 96 ⲁⲩϣⲉ ⲡⲱⲟⲩ ⲉ.ⲡⲓⲃⲏⲙⲁ.

—— ⲛⲥⲁ-, *after*: CDan 85 ⲁϥϣⲉ ⲛⲥⲱϥ & found him.

—— ⲥⲁⲙⲉⲛϩⲉ, *after*: Jer 13 10 (S ⸀. + ⲟⲩⲱϩ ⲛⲥⲁ-) πορ. ὀπίσω; Jo 12 19 (SA² ⸀. ϩⲓⲡⲁϩⲟⲩ) ἀπέρ. ὀπ.

—— ϣⲁ- *BF*, *to*: Ac 25 12 (var ϩⲁ-, S ⸀. ⲉⲣⲁⲧ⸗ ⲛ-) π. ἐπί, Mt 26 14 F(B ϩⲁ-, S ⸀. ϣⲁ-) πορ. πρός; Ps 68 3 (S ⲉⲓ ⲉ-) ἔρχ. εἰς, Jo 4 47 F(B ϩⲁ-, SA² ⸀. ϣⲁ-) ἀπέρ. πρός, Ac 22 26 (S † ⲡⲟⲅⲟⲓ ⲉ-) προσέρ. dat; Ro 16 19 (S ⲡⲱⲣ) ἀφικνεῖσθαι εἰς; C 43 210 ⲛ̄ⲧⲉⲡⲙϣⲉ ϣⲁⲣⲟϥ, ib 145 ⲁϥϣⲉ ⲡⲁϥ ϣⲁⲣⲱⲟⲩ; ϫⲓⲡ- ϣⲉ ϣⲁ-: TstAb 230 ⲡⲁϫ. ϣⲁⲡⲛⲟⲩⲧⲉ.

—— ϩⲁ-, *beneath*: DeV 2 26 ϣⲉ ϩⲁϥⲡⲁⲣⲃⲉϥ.

—— ϩⲁⲧⲉⲛ-, *up to*: Va 61 26 ϣⲉ ϩⲁ. ⲧⲥⲕⲉⲡⲏ εἰσέρ. ἔγγιστα (var ἔμπροσθεν), Lev 20 16 (S diff) προσέρ. πρός; AM 191 ϣⲉ ⲡⲁⲕ ϩⲁ. ⲡⲉⲕⲓⲟ†.

—— ϩⲁ-, *to*: 1 Kg 17 33 (S ⸀. ⲉⲃⲟⲗ ⲉ-), Jer 5 5(S ⸀. ⲛⲁⲣⲣⲏ-) πορ. πρός; Ge 15 15 (S do) ἀπέρ. π., Jer 41 2 βαδ. π.; MG 25 218 ϣⲉ ⲡⲁⲕ ϩⲁⲡⲟⲛ̄ ἐκδημεῖν π.

—— ϩⲓ-, *on*: 3 Kg 2 2 πορ. ἐν; Ez 44 17 ascendere super; Jos 23 14 (S ⸀. ϩⲓ·) ἀποτρέχειν acc.

—— ϩⲛ-, ϩⲉⲛ- *SBF*, *in*: Ps 1 1 BF (Wess 15 90, S ⸀. ϩⲛ-) πορ. ἐν; CaiEuch 588 ϣⲉ ϩⲉⲛⲙⲁⲓ ⲛⲓⲃⲉⲛ ἀποδημεῖν ἐν; Gal 2 13 (S do) συναπάγεσθαι dat; ib 6 1 (S ⲡⲣ ⲡⲣⲉ ϩⲛ-) προλαμβάνεσθαι; PS 333 S ⲡ̄ⲕⲟⲗⲁⲥⲓⲥ ⲛ̄ⲧⲁϣϣⲉ ⲛ̄ϩⲏⲧⲟⲩ paral ⸀. ⲉ-, C 43 170 ⲁϥϣⲉ ⲡⲁϥ ϩⲉⲛⲧϩⲉⲣⲉⲥⲓⲥ, DeV 1 58 ϣⲉ ϩⲉⲛⲡⲉϥⲙⲱⲓⲧ.

—— ϩⲓⲣⲉⲛ-, *to*: AM 314 ⲁⲩϣⲉ ϩ.ⲫⲣⲟ.

With following adverb (c ethic dat & without not separated).

—— ⲉⲃⲟⲗ *SA²B*, *go forth*: Ez 46 10 ἐκπορ., ἐξέρ.; Deu 29 12(S ⲙⲟⲟϣⲉ ϩⲛ-)παρέρ. ἐν; Bel 11 ἀποτρέχ. ἔξω, Ez 43 11 ⲙⲱⲓⲧ ⲛ̄ϣⲉ ⲉⲃ. ἔξοδος; ShC 42 71 S ⲡⲉⲛⲧⲁϣϣⲉ ⲉⲃ. ⲧⲏⲣⲟⲩ *what was expended*, ShViK 9099 S ⲁⲟⲩⲏⲣ ⲛ̄ⲣⲡⲁⲁⲩ ϣⲉ ⲉⲃ. *gone astray*, C 89 23 ⲡⲥⲟⲓⲧ...ϣⲉ ⲉⲃ. *through Egypt*, C 43 162 sim ϣⲉ ⲡⲁϥ ⲉⲃ.; ⲉⲃ. ⲉ- *SB*: Jer 6 25 ἐκπορ. εἰς; 2 Chr 6 34 ἐξέρ. εἰς; C 41 42 ϣⲉ ⲉⲃ. ⲉⲧⲙⲟⲩⲅⲓ, Pap *olim* RevC Campbell S ⲉϥϣⲉ ⲉⲃ. ⲉⲡⲣⲏ[ⲧ; ⲉⲃ. ⲉⲣⲣⲉⲡ-: Is 7 3 (S ⸀. ⲉⲃ. ⲛ̄ⲧⲡⲱⲙⲛⲧ ⲉ-) ἐξέρ. εἰς συνάντησιν; ⲉⲃ. ⲡ-: Ep 465 S ⲁⲓϣⲛ ⲉⲃ. ⲡⲁϥ; ⲉⲃ. ⲧⲁⲓ: 3 Kg 17 3 πορ. ἐντεῦθεν; ⲉⲃ. ϩⲁ-: 1 Kg 23 26 (S diff) πορ.

ἀπό; Ex 10 28 ἀπέρ. ἀ.; Is 57 8 (S ⲟⲅⲉ) ἀφιστάναι ἀ.; C 43 195 ⲁϥϣⲉ ⲡⲁϥ ⲉⲃ. ϩⲁⲣⲟϥ; ⲉⲃ. ϩⲓ-: Ac 19 12(S ⲗⲟ)ἀπαλλάσσεσθαι ἀ.; Va 66 297 voice ϣⲉ ⲡⲁϥ ⲉⲃ. ϩⲓⲱⲧⲟⲩ στερεῖσθαι; ⲉⲃ. ϩⲉⲡ-, ⲁⲃ. ϩⲡ-*BA²*: Jer 28 50 πορ. ἐκ (so B); Ac 14 19 (S ⲉⲓ ⲉⲃ. ϩⲡ-) ἐπέρ. ἀ.; Mani H 76 A² ⲁⲩϣⲉ ⲁⲃ. ⲡϩⲏⲧⲟⲩ, DeV 2 22 ⲉⲑⲣⲓϣⲉ ⲡⲏⲓ ⲉⲃ. ϩⲉⲡⲡⲁⲓⲃⲓⲟⲥ; ϩⲡ- for ⲉⲃ. ϩⲡ- S: COAd 9 ⲧⲡⲱ (ⲡ)ⲛ̄ⲣⲉⲧⲉⲙⲟⲥ ⲛ̄ⲧⲁϣⲉ ⲡⲁⲓ ϩⲡ(ⲡ)ⲧⲱⲡⲟⲥ; ⲉⲃ. ϩⲓϫⲉⲡ-: Mt 9 26 (S ⲉⲓ ⲉⲃ. ϩⲡ-) ἐξέρ. εἰς.

—— ⲥⲁⲃⲟⲗ ⲡ-, *go forth from*: AM 288 ⲁϥϣⲉ ⲡⲁϥ ⲥ. ⲙⲡⲉϥⲏⲓ.

—— ⲉⲡⲉⲥⲏⲧ *BF*, *go down*: Ge 11 7, Is 5 14 BF(S ⸀. ⲉⲡ.) καταβαίνειν; Mus 35 20 ⲉϥⲡⲁϣⲉ ⲉ. & bring up Adam, C 43 138 ⲁϥϣⲉ ⲡⲁϥ ⲉ.; ⲉⲡ. ⲉ-: Ez 32 27 (S ⸀.), Ro 10 7 F(Mor 43 299, S do) κ. εἰς; ϫⲓⲡϣⲉ ⲉⲡ. ⲉ-: BodlOr 32 169 ⲡϫ. ⲉⲡ. ⲉⲣⲱⲟⲩ(sc waters of Jordan).

—— ⲉⲡϣⲱⲓ, *go up*: Deu 1 26 (S ⸀. ⲉϩⲣⲁⲓ), Ps 46 6 (SA do) ἀναβαί.; AM 233 ⲁϥϣⲉ ⲡⲁϥ ⲉ. ⲉⲃⲟⲗ ϩⲓⲧⲟⲧϥ; ⲉⲡ. ⲉ-: Bar 3 29 (S do) ἀν. εἰς; Ps 67 34 (S ⲁⲗⲉ ⲉϩ. ⲉϫⲡ-) ἐπιβαί. ἐπί; ⲉⲡ. ⲉϫⲉⲡ-: Hag 1 8 (A ⸀. ⲁϩ. ⲁ-) ἀν. εἰς; ⲙⲁ ⲡϣⲉ ⲉⲡ.: Ez 40 34 (S ⲡ⸀. ⲉϩ.)ascensus; ϫⲓⲡϣⲉ ⲉⲡ.: CaiEuch 338 ⲡⲉϥϫ. ⲉⲡⲓϥϩⲟⲅⲓ.

—— ⲉϩⲟⲩⲛ, ⲉϩ. *SS^a A²BF*, *go in*: 3 Kg 17 12, Ps 25 4 (S ⸀. ⲉϩ.) εἰσέρ., AM 274 ⲉⲧⲁϥϣⲉ ⲡⲁϥ ⲉϩ. κατέρ.; Ez 10 3 εἰσπορ.; ib 46 19 ⲙⲱⲓⲧ ⲡϣⲉ ⲉϩ. εἴσοδος; MIE 2 386 ⲁⲓϣⲉ ⲉϩ. = BAp 111 S ⸀. ⲉϩ., C 41 19 ⲉⲧⲁⲓϣⲉ ⲉϩ....ⲉⲧⲁⲛ ⲉϩ., Ep 96 S ⲡⲥⲟⲩϣⲉ ⲉϩ. ⲙⲁ ⲡⲡⲁⲡⲁⲥ, ib 531 S^a ⲁⲥⲱϣⲁⲓ ⲁϩ.; ⲉϩ. ⲉ-: 2 Kg 6 19(S ⸀. ⲉϩⲣⲁⲓ ⲉ-), Jo 4 28F(B ⲉ-, SA² ⸀. ⲉϩ. ⲉ-), MG 25 219 ⲁⲓϣⲉ ⲡⲏⲓ ⲉϩ. ⲉⲡϣⲁϥⲉ ἀπέρ. εἰς, Is 30 29 (S ⸀. ⲉϩ., F ⲡⲱⲧ ⲉϩ.), Jo 13 27 BF(SA² ⸀. ⲉϩ. ⲉ-)εἰσέρ. εἰς, 4 Kg 4 11 ⲉ̄. ἐκεῖ, Is 8 3 (S † ⲡⲟⲅⲟⲓ ⲉ-) προσέρ. πρός; Eccl 7 3 F(S ⸀. ⲉϩ. ⲉ-) πορ. εἰς, Ps 95 8 (S do) εἰσπορ. εἰς; He 9 6 F(S do, B ⲡⲁ ⲉϩ. ⲉ-) εἰσιέναι εἰς; Ez 41 6 (S ϫⲱⲧⲉ ⲉϩ. ⲉ-) ingredi per; AM 308 ⲁϥϣⲉ ⲡⲁϥ ⲉϩ. ⲉⲡⲓⲉⲣⲫⲉⲓ, Tri 360 S ⲁϥϣⲉ ⲉϩ. ⲉ-ⲡⲉϥⲉⲟⲟⲩ, CO 185 S ϣⲉ ⲉϩ. ⲉⲙⲁⲩ, Mani 1 A² ⲁⲥϣⲉ ⲁϩ. ⲁⲣⲁⲩ; ⲉϩ. ⲉϫⲉⲡ-: Nu 6 6 (S ⸀. ⲉϩ. ⲉϫⲡ-) εἰσέρ. ἐπί; ⲉϩ. ϣⲁ-: Ps 68 2 (S ⲉⲓ ⲉϩ. ϣⲁ-) εἰσέρ. ἕως, Ac 10 3 (S ⸀. ⲉϩ. ϣⲁ-) ⲉ. πρός; Dan 11 16 εἰσπορ. πρός; TstAb 243 perfume ϣⲉ ⲉϩ. ϣⲁⲡⲓⲕⲁⲧⲁⲡⲉⲧⲁⲥⲙⲁ; ⲉϩ. ϩⲁ-: Lev 18 14 (S ⸀. ⲉϩ. ϣⲁ-) εἰσέρ. πρός, Deu 22 14 (S † ⲙⲡⲟⲅⲟⲓ ⲉ-) προσέρ. dat; C 43 41 ϣⲉ ⲉϩ. ϩⲁⲣⲟⲥ; ⲉϩ. ϩⲉⲡ-: Ps 117 19 (SACl ⲡⲏⲩ ⲉϩ. ϩⲡ-) εἰσέρ. ἐν; Ez 46 2 (S ⸀. ⲉϩ. ϩⲓⲧⲡ-) ⲉ̄. κατὰ τ. ὁδόν.

—— ⲉϩⲣⲏ ⲉ-, *go down to*: Is 30 2 (S ⲙⲟⲟϣⲉ ⲉϩ. ⲉⲡⲉⲥⲏⲧ ⲉ-, F ⲙ. ⲉϩⲗⲏⲓ ⲉ-), Bar 3 19 (S ⸀. ⲉⲡ. ⲉ-) καταβαί. εἰς; MIE 2 348 ⲁϥϣⲉ ⲉϩ. ⲉⲡⲉⲥⲙⲁϩⲧ.

—— ⲉϩⲣⲏⲓ *BF*, *go up*: Ac 20 11 (S ⸀. ⲉϩ.) ἀναβαί.; ⲉϩ. ⲉ-: 1 Kg 2 10(S ⸀. ⲉϩ. ⲉ-), Is 37 1 (S do,

F ⲡⲱⲧ ⲉⲣ. ⲉ-) ἀν. εἰς; Gal 1 17 (*S* ⲃ̄. ⲉ-) ἀνέρ. εἰς; 3
Kg 17 9 ⲡⲟⲣ. εἰς, Eccl 1 6 *F*(*S* ⲙⲟ. ⲉ-)π. πρός; Mk
8 26 *F*(*B* ⲉⲃⲟⲩⲛ ⲉ-, *S* ⲃ̄. ⲉⲣⲟⲩⲛ ⲉ-)εἰσέρ. εἰς; AM
304 ⲙⲁϣⲉ ⲡⲁⲕ ⲉⲣ. ⲉⲧⲃ̄ⲁⲕⲓ; ⲉⲣ. ⲉϫⲉⲛ-: Ps 23 3
(*S* ⲃ̄. ⲉⲣ. ⲉ-) ἀναβ. εἰς, Jer 4 29 (*S* ⲃ̄. ⲉⲣ. ⲉϫⲛ-)ὰ. ἐπί.

     ⲁⲧϣⲉ   *v* ⲣⲁⲥⲓⲉ.

     ⲙⲁ ⲛϣⲉ   *v* ϣⲉ ⲉⲡϣⲱⲓ.

     ϫⲓⲛϣⲉ   *v* ϣⲉ ⲉⲡⲉⲥⲏⲧ & ⲉⲡϣⲱⲓ.

     ϣⲉ ⲛⲣⲁⲥⲓⲉ, ⲉⲥⲓⲉ   *v* ⲣⲁⲥⲓⲉ.

ϣⲉ *SA²*(Ma)*BFO*, ϣⲏ *SF*, ϣⲓ *S* (2 Kg 21 19, *v*
ⲣⲁⲙϣⲉ), ⲅⲉ *A* nn m f (rare), *wood:* Deu 21 23 *SB*,
Job 24 20 *SB*, Ps 50 9 *SA*(Cl, *B* om), Hab 2 19 *AB*
ξύλον, Lev 27 30 *S*(*B* ϣⲏⲛ), Ez 41 22 *SB* ξύλινος;
ib 27 5 *B* ϣⲉ ⲛⲡⲗⲁϩ σανίς; ShA 1 302 *S* walls ⲛϣⲉ,
Kr 242 *S* ⲕⲟⲙⲙⲁ ⲛϣⲉ, *ib* 234 n *S* ϣⲟⲗ ⲛϣⲉ, *ib* 154
S ϫⲉⲛⲟⲃ ⲛϣⲉ, Bodl(P) f 78 *S* ⲋⲟⲣ ⲛϣⲉ, J 66 41 *S*
ⲧⲏⲛⲃⲉ ⲛϣⲏ, ViK 9621 *S* ⲛⲟϭ ⲛϣⲉ ⲉⲧⲙⲡⲓⲫⲟⲣⲟⲥ
beam, ManiH 32 *A²* ⲛϣⲉ ⲛⲁⲟⲩ[ⲉⲛ] ⲡⲣⲱϣ & *tree
shall speak,* J 68 51 *S* ⲣⲏⲗⲉ (ὕλη) ⲛϣⲉ ⲣ. ⲛⲃⲗ̄[ⲭⲉ],
DeV 2 185 *B* ϣⲉ ⲉϥⲥⲟⲧⲡ (cf Si 24 16 Lag), MG 25
112 *B* ϣⲉ ⲛⲁⲡⲁⲧⲕⲉⲟⲛ, ST 118, Ep 159 *S* ϣⲉ ⲛ-
ⲭⲣⲓⲁ (cf ?ShC 73 73 ϣⲉ ⲕⲁⲧⲁ ⲧⲉⲛⲭⲣ. & ?Ryl 139
ϣⲛⲫⲉⲣⲓⲁ), AZ 21 98 *O* ⲙⲉⲣⲭ ⲛϣⲉ;   f *S:* Ryl 252
ⲧϣⲉ ⲛⲧⲁⲓⲧⲁⲁⲥ ⲉⲡⲉⲕⲗⲁⲃⲁⲕⲧ/ (κραβάκτιον), Ep 326
ⲧϣⲉ ⲛⲛⲟⲩⲣⲉ (?ellipse for ⲧⲛⲟϭ ⲛϣⲉ *q v*);   as pl:
2 Chr 3 10 *B*, Eccl 10 9 *SF*, Lu 22 52 *S*(*B* ϣⲏⲱⲧ),
Z 312 *S* ⲡⲱϩ ⲛⲣⲛϣⲉ ξύλα; ShC 73 73 *S* ⲣⲉⲛϣⲏⲙ
ⲛϣⲉ, *ib* 137 *S* ⲛϣⲉ *for oven,* C 86 340 *B* ⲡⲁⲓϣⲉ ⲡⲁ-
ⲧⲯⲩⲭⲏ.

Special uses: *cross* Mt 27 40 *B*(*S*=Gk) σταυρός;
LMär 3 *S* crucify ⲉⲛϣⲉ = C 43 58 *B* ⲉⲭⲉⲛⲟⲩϣⲉ, Bor
143 39 *S* body upon ⲟⲩϣⲉ ⲛⲥⲧ̄ⲟⲥ, Mani 1 *A²* ⲧⲉⲁϣⲉ
ⲁⲛϣⲉ; *gallows* ShIF 294 *S* set up ⲅⲉⲛϣⲉ ⲅⲏⲛⲣⲓⲣ,
AM 308 *B* ⲟⲩϣⲉ 20 ells high, C 43 176 *B* ⲟⲩϣⲉ
ⲉϥⲟⲓ ⲡⲧⲁⲣ ⲃ̄; *stocks, pillory:* Job 33 11 *SB*, Ac 16
24 *SB*, R 1 4 71 *S* = MartIgn 877 *B*, Leip 24 12 *B*
ⲣⲓⲟⲩⲓ ⲛⲛⲟⲩϭⲁⲗⲁⲩϫ ⲉϩⲟⲩⲛ ⲉⲡⲓϣⲉ ξ.; ShZ 596 *S*
cast into prison & ⲣⲁⲛϣⲉ, Mor 25 85 *S* ⲛⲉⲧⲧⲁⲭⲣⲏⲩ
ⲣⲁⲛϣⲉ, C 43 129 *B* sim, ST 30 *S* ⲉϥⲥⲟⲛⲉ ⲣⲛⲟⲩϣⲉ,
BSG 192 *S* ⲁⲥⲫⲁⲗⲓϫⲉ ⲉⲛϣⲉ = C 86 298 *B* ⲣⲓⲟⲩⲓ
ⲉⲛϣⲧⲉⲕⲟ, Mun 37 *S* ⲛⲟϫϥ ⲣⲁⲛϣⲉ = C 86 284 *B*
ⲧⲟⲥϥ ⲉⲛϣⲉ, Mor 32 15 *S* bade ⲧⲁⲁϥ ⲉⲛϣⲏ with
hands tied back, BM 1113 *S* ⲛⲧⲁϥⲟⲧⲛ ⲉⲣⲟⲩⲛ ⲁⲩⲧⲓ
(*sic l*) ⲛϣⲉ ⲥⲛⲁⲩ ⲉⲣⲟϥ, Ep 181 *S* lo 3 days ⲉⲛϣⲉ ⲣⲓ-
ⲛⲁⲟⲩⲣⲏⲧⲉ; *shaft, stave* &c: 2 Kg 21 19, *ib* 23 7 *S*
ξ.; Si 38 27 *S* δόρυ; Ex 30 4 *B* ϣⲉ ⲛⲣⲱⲧ σκυτάλη;
BSG 2 *B* ⲟⲩϣⲉ ⲉϥⲟⲓ ⲛⲁⲧⲣⲉ = *ib* 205 خشب كفون
wooden nippers; MG 25 143 *B* ⲛϣⲉ ⲉϯ ⲙⲙⲟⲟⲩ rising
& falling (*sc shâdûf*);   *v* also ⲛⲁⲧ, ϣⲉ ⲛⲣⲱⲟⲩⲧ
(ⲧⲟⲟⲩⲧⲉ II), ϣⲉ ⲛⲟⲩⲱϩ (ⲟⲩⲟⲧⲣ), ϣⲉ ⲛⲱϥⲉ (ⲱϥⲉ).

Various kinds. ϣⲉ ⲛⲁⲃⲣⲁⲅⲁⲙ *S agnus castus*
شجرة ابراهيم (Löw F 3 493, AIssa 190) KroppJ 51; ⲛⲁ-

ϩⲟⲛ *v* below; ⲛⲁⲡⲁⲥ *S* in recipe Z 628; ⲛⲁⲡⲱⲃⲁⲗ-
ⲥⲁⲙⲱⲛ (ὀποβ.) *S* Mor 31 249; ⲛⲁⲧⲉⲣ ϫⲟⲗⲓ *B* = ⲉ-
ⲙⲉϥⲣ ϫⲟⲟⲗⲉⲥ *S* Deu 10 3, Is 40 20 ἄσηπτος; ⲛⲕⲁ-
ⲣ(ⲟ)ⲓⲁ (καρύϊνος) *SB* Jer 1 11; ⲛⲕⲉϫⲣⲟⲥ *S*(*B* ⲛϣⲓϥ)
Lev 14 4; ⲛⲕⲩⲡⲁⲣⲓⲥⲟⲥ *SB* Ez 27 24; ⲛⲟϫⲛⲟⲛ *B*
AM 311, ⲟϫⲓⲟⲛ *ib* 323, ⲁⲩϫⲟⲛ *C* 43 177, ⲁϫⲟⲛ *S*
Mor 28 113, ⲁϫⲱⲛ GMir 181 (?πύξινος); ⲛⲣⲁⲕⲟⲧⲉ
S Mor 51 37 (*v* ⲕⲁⲗⲉⲗⲉ), Viostr 237 ⲟⲩⲥⲧⲣⲟⲡⲛⲉⲗⲉ
ⲛϣⲉ ⲛⲣ.; ⲛⲥⲱⲟⲓ ⲛⲟⲩϭⲓ *B* Va 61 100; ⲛⲥⲧⲉⲣⲁϩ *S*
Mor 31 249; ⲛⲥⲫⲟⲛϫⲓⲗ(ⲓ)ⲟⲛ *B* AM 49, 311; ⲛⲥⲭⲓ-
ⲛⲟⲛ (?σχίνος)*B* C 43 70; ⲛⲣⲩⲥⲱⲡⲟⲛ *B* Ps 50 9 (*S*
diff);   *v* also ⲉⲗⲟⲟⲗⲉ **II**, ⲉⲙⲓⲥⲉ, ⲉⲓⲁⲩ *s f*, ⲕⲁⲛⲟϣ,
ⲗⲁⲃⲁⲥ, ⲗⲁⲙ, ⲛⲟⲙ, ⲛⲟⲩϭⲉ ⲛⲛ, ⲟⲥⲓ, ⲥⲓϥⲉ, ⲧⲁⲡⲉⲛ, ⲧⲱⲣⲉ
willow, ϣⲟⲩⲉ, ϣⲉⲙⲁⲣ (ⲥⲁⲙⲁⲣⲏⲣ), ϣⲟⲡⲧⲉ, ϫⲟⲉⲓⲧ.
In some of these confusion ? with ϣⲏⲛ.

For compounds *v* ⲉⲓⲟⲡⲉ (ⲉⲓⲉⲡ-), ⲙⲟⲩⲛⲕ *make,*
ⲡⲱϩ *break* (ⲣⲉϥⲡⲉϩ-).

ϣⲉ ⲛⲡⲟϭ *B,* a land measure (100 cubits): Is 54 2
(*S* ⲛⲟⲩϥ only), Zeph 2 5 (*SA* ⲧⲟϣ) σχοίνισμα.   *V*
Spg *Kopt Etym* p 57, JEA 11 152.

ⲣⲁⲙϣⲉ *SB,* -ϣⲓ *S,* -ⲅⲉ *A,* ⲁⲙϣⲉ *B,* ⲣⲁⲙϣⲏ, ⲣⲙ.
F, pl ⲣⲁⲙϣⲏ(ⲟ)ⲩⲉ¹, -ϣⲟⲟⲩⲉ² *S,* -ϣⲏⲟⲩ³, ⲁⲙϣⲏ-
ⲟⲩ(ⲓ)⁴ *B* & sg as pl, nn m, *carpenter:* Sa 13 11 *S,* Ep
Jer 7 *SB* ⲣ. *F,* Hos 8 6 *AB* ⲣ., Mt 13 55 *SB* ⲁ. (var
ⲣ.) *F* τέκτων, P 44 67 *S* ⲣ.· τεκτωπ· λεπτουργος;
ShC 73 72 *S* ⲣ., ⲣⲁⲙⲕⲗ, ⲉⲕⲱⲧ, WS 136 *S* ⲛⲁⲥⲟⲡ
ⲅⲉⲣⲙⲁⲛⲉ ⲫ., CMSS 63 *F* ⲡϩⲓ]ⲁⲕⲱⲛ...ⲫ., BM 1037
S contract with ⲣ., *ib* 1066 *S* ⲯⲁϩ ϣⲉⲛⲟⲩⲧⲉ ⲫ., Ryl
252 *S* ⲫ. at work on door, *ib* 340 on ϣⲁⲗⲟⲟⲩ, CMSS
lc F ⲛⲉⲣ. (ⲉ)ⲛⲙⲟⲩⲛ(ⲁⲥⲧⲏⲣⲓ), Ep 49 14 *S* ⲣⲁⲙϣⲓ,
Lant 107 9 *S* do, *BM Quarterly* 6 pl 15 *F* ⲫⲙϣⲏⲓ; pl
forms: EpJer 45 *B*⁴, ⲧ.; DeV 2 102 *B*⁴, Va 57 1 *B*³,
MIF 59 203 *S*¹, Jern 9 *S*¹, BM 1130 *S*².

ⲉⲣ ⲣ. *B,* be carpenter: C 86 114 ⲉⲧⲁϥⲉⲣ ⲣ. ϣⲁⲧⲉϥ-
ⲑⲁⲙⲓⲟ ⲛⲟⲩⲧⲁⲓⲃⲓ.

ⲙⲛⲧ-, ⲙⲉⲧⲣ., *carpenter's craft:* BMar 30 *S* ⲁϥϫⲓ
ⲥⲃⲱ ⲉⲧⲙ., BM 1064 *S* ⲧⲉⲕⲙ., AZ 13 134 *B* ϯⲙ.
makes ploughs & yokes; C 86 *lc B* ⲙⲉⲧⲥⲁⲃ ⲛⲣ.

In place-names: ⲡⲓⲙⲟⲛⲁⲥⲧⲏⲣⲓⲟⲛ ⲙⲛϣⲉ دير الخشبة
(cf PO 1 675), ⲛⲓⲣⲁϣⲉ (*l* ⲛⲓⲁⲣ., PRoss-Georg 4 82).

ϣⲉ *SAA²B*(rare)*O,* ϣⲏ *S* *F*(*B* & often *F* ⲣ̄) nn,
hundred ἑκατόν: *S* Ge 33 19, 2 Kg 3 14, Mt 18 28, *S*
Mor 39 42, *A* Cl 25 2, *A²* Jo 12 5, ManiH 20, *B* MG
25 242 ⲓ̄ⲁ̄ ⲛϣⲉ, AM 113 ⲉ̄ ⲛϣⲉ, *F* BIF 22 107 ⲃ̄ ⲛϣⲏ,
O AZ 21 106;   as f: ViK 9749 *S* ⲧϣⲉ ⲛⲥⲁⲧⲉⲉⲣⲉ,
Pcod 38 *F* ϯⲣ̄ ⲛϣⲏ ⲛⲣⲁⲟⲩ = *S* m;   *two hundred*
ϣⲏⲧ *SA²B*(once)*F* m: *S* Ge 5 22 ϣ. ⲛⲣⲟⲙⲡⲉ, *ib* 11
19 ϣ. ⲯⲓⲧⲉ, Nu 16 35 ϣⲏ. ⲧⲁⲓⲟⲩ, Cant 8 12 ϣⲏ.,
BM 346 1 ⲛⲉⲓϣ. ⲙⲙⲁⲧⲟⲓ, BMar 4 ϣ. ⲛⲧⲃⲁ, Miss 8
53 ϣ. ⲥⲉⲧⲁϥⲧⲉ, *A²* Jo 6 7, *B* MIE 2 409 ϣ. ⲙⲙⲁⲣⲓ,
F KroppC 30 ϣ. (ⲛ)ⲙⲓⲗⲓⲟⲛ;   *three h.* &c: Jud
8 4 *S* ϣⲙⲛⲧϣⲉ, AZ *lc O* ϣⲟⲙⲧⲉ ⲛϣⲉ, Ge 32 6 *S*

ϥⲧⲟⲟⲩ ⲛϣⲉ (var ϥⲧⲉ̄ϣⲉ), PS 24 S ⲥⲁϣϥ ⲛϣⲉ, Ap 12 6 S ⲙⲛⲧⲥⲛⲟⲟⲩⲥ ⲛϣⲉ; hundredth S: My 88 ⲡⲙⲉⲣϣⲉ, PS 66 ⲡⲙⲉⲣϣⲉ ⲟⲩⲁ, ib 76 ⲡⲙ. ⲝⲟⲩⲧ-ⲯⲓⲥ, ib 107 ⲡⲙ. ⲙⲛϣⲙⲟⲩⲛ, Ge 7 11 ⲡⲙⲉⲣⲥⲟⲟⲩ ⲛϣⲉ. iterated S: 1 Kg 29 2 ϣⲉ ϣⲉ (var ⲉⲡⲉϣⲉ ϣⲉ), 2 Kg 18 4 sim ⲉⲓⲥ ⲉ̔ⲕⲁⲧⲟⲛⲧⲁ́ⲇⲁⲥ. V ⲥⲟⲧⲉ nn. ⲁⲛϣⲉ v ⲁⲛ- (2°).

ϣⲉ (oftenest), ϣⲏ, ϣⲓ S Theban, not literary, nn m, small bronze coin, ? = 1 carat: Ep 286 ⲉⲕϣⲁⲛϯ ϩⲙⲉ ⲛϣⲏ ⲡⲁⲓ ⲡⲥⲁⲧⲡⲓ ⲧⲕⲟⲩⲥⲉⲛⲧⲉ ⲛⲕⲉⲣⲁⲧⲥⲉ (completing solidus) ⲟⲩⲁⲣϩ ⲛⲁⲕ (cf ib 168 n, also Addenda ad loc); highest (& oftenest) figure 40: CO 174, ST 121, TurM 24; ⲡⲣⲟⲙⲡⲧ: CO 186, Vi ostr 87 ⲡⲉⲓ-ⲝⲟⲩⲧⲉⲥⲛⲟⲟⲩⲥ ⲛϣⲉ ⲛϩ., ST 219 ⲡϣⲙⲟⲩⲛ ⲛϣⲏ, Hall 106, BKU 1 292 ϣⲓ, Ep 280; with ⲗⲓⲕⲛⲟⲛ, -ⲛⲁ, -ⲛⲉ (ⲗⲓ́ⲕⲛⲟⲛ?, v ShA 1 256, Ep 313 n, apparently a measure or higher amount than ϣⲉ): COAd 30 24 ϣⲉ, 8 ⲗ., ib 186 20 ϣⲉ & 5 ⲗ. Cf ? TT 143 S ⲟⲩⲁⲡⲥ ⲛϣⲉ ⲛⲥⲟⲩⲟ = MG 17 438 اردب ‎مائة. Same ? as last.

ϣⲉ SBF, ϣⲁ SB, by in swearing (cf ⲁⲛⲁϣ, ⲱⲛϩ): Ge 42 15 B, 1 Cor 15 31 SBF ⲛⲏ́; C 86 285 B ϣⲉ ⲡⲉⲡⲛ̄ⲃ̄ ⲡⲣⲏ ⲙⲁ́; BMar 3 S ϣⲉ ⲡⲟⲩⲝⲁⲓ ⲙⲡⲁⲕⲣⲁⲧⲟⲥ, C 43 27 B ϣⲉ ⲡⲓⲕⲣⲁⲧⲟⲥ of Romans, BAp 113 S ϣⲉ ⲡⲉⲕϣⲏⲗ = MIE 2 390 B ϣⲉ ⲡⲉⲕⲟⲩⲝⲁⲓ, BSM 46 B ⲧⲁⲫⲙⲏⲓ ϣⲉ ⲡⲱⲛϩ̄ ⲙⲡⲁⲥⲟ̄ⲥ̄ = BMis 394 S ϩⲓ-ⲟⲩⲙⲉ ⲡⲧⲉ ⲡⲡ̄ⲉ̄ ⲙⲡⲟⲩⲝⲁⲓ ⲛ-, CO 131 S ϣⲉ ⲡⲉⲓ-ⲧⲟⲡⲟⲥ ⲉⲧⲟⲩⲁⲁⲃ, ST 111 S ϣⲉ ⲧⲁⲅⲩⲛⲁⲙⲓⲥ ⲙⲡⲁⲅⲓⲟⲥ ⲁⲡⲁ ⲫⲟⲓⲃ., Mor 51 41 S ϣⲉ ⲡⲓⲟⲝϥ ⲉⲧⲙⲏⲣ ⲙⲙⲟⲓ (monk), BM 602 F ϣⲉ ⲡⲛⲟⲩϯ, MR 5 49 F ϣⲉ ⲡⲁⲟⲩ ⲛⲧⲁⲡⲛⲟⲩϯ ⲧⲉⲓⲃ ⲛⲧⲉⲛ; ϣⲁ: 1 Cor l c B var; R 1 1 17 S ϣⲁ ⲡⲟⲩⲝⲁⲓ ⲛ- ⲕⲁⲧⲁ́; ib 5 48 S ϣⲁ ⲡⲉⲕⲟⲩⲝⲁⲓ, Bor 143 27 S, LA1 5 S, Tri 263 S, C 86 170 B. V Spg DemGram § 434.

ϣⲉ sow nn v ⲉϣⲱ.

ϣⲉ SBF v ⲥⲱϣ (ϣⲥ-) strike.

ϣⲉ B in ϣⲉ ⲡⲉⲣ ⲫⲙⲉⲩⲓ v ⲙⲉⲉⲩⲉ s f.

ϣⲉ SAF v ϣⲁ nose.

ϣⲉⲓ S vb, meaning unknown: El 130 (ib 96 A diff).

ϣⲉ(ⲉ)ⲓ F v ϣⲁ rise.

ϣⲉⲉⲓ SA vb intr, go & come (ϣⲉ + ⲉⲓ, so Sethe in Spg), be carried to & fro, wander: BMar 175 ⲛⲥⲉⲛⲧⲉ ⲙⲡⲕⲁϩ ⲡⲁϣ. (in Ps 81 5, Is 24 18 ⲕⲓⲙ). With following preposition. c ⲉ-: P 131⁵ 147 monk who ϣ. ⲉⲡⲉⲓⲥⲁ ⲙⲡⲡⲁⲓ; c ⲙⲛ-: Eph 4 14 (B ⲟⲩⲱⲧⲉⲃ ⲉⲃⲟⲗ) ⲡⲉⲣⲓⲫⲉⲣⲉⲥⲑⲁⲓ dat, Pro 11 29 (B ⲝⲉⲙⲙⲟ) ⲥⲩⲙⲡ. dat; Ge 7 17 (var ϩⲓⲝⲛ-, B Gk om), Bor 265 89 ⲉⲕϣ. ⲙⲡⲛⲙⲟⲟⲩ ⲛⲑⲁⲗⲁⲥⲥⲁ, ib 253 153 nature ϣ. ⲙⲛ-ⲙⲡⲁⲑⲟⲥ, AZ 21 142 dead limbs in waves ⲉⲩϣ. ⲛⲙ-ⲙⲁⲩ, C 99 113 Pachom & first disciples ⲉϥϣ. ⲛⲙ-ⲙⲁⲩ ⲕⲁⲧⲁ ⲧⲉⲩⲙⲛⲧϭ̄ⲱⲃ; c ⲛⲥⲁ-: ShIF 267 ⲛⲥⲉϣ.

ⲛⲥⲁ ⲡⲓⲥⲁ ⲙⲡⲛⲁⲓ; c ϩⲛ-: Pro 10 24 (A ϥⲓ ϩⲁ-, B ϭⲓ + ⲓⲓⲓ tr) π. ⲉ̓ⲛ, He 13 9 (B ⲟⲩ. ⲉⲃ.) π. (var ⲡⲁⲣⲁⲫ.) dat; ShA 1 333 ⲛⲉⲧϣ. ϩⲙⲡⲣⲟⲉⲓⲙ, ShMIF 23 29 to devil ⲉⲕϣ. ⲙⲡⲃⲟⲗ ⲡⲛⲉⲩⲥⲱⲙⲁ ϩⲛⲣⲉⲛϣⲱⲡⲉ, Bor 240 93 ⲛϥϣ. ϩⲙⲁⲡⲉⲧϣⲟⲩⲉⲓⲧ; BMOr 7561 97 ⲛⲧⲉ-ⲡⲛⲓϣⲉ ϣ. ϩⲣⲁⲓ ⲛⲣⲏⲧⲕ; c ϩⲓⲝⲛ-: Mor 17 14 ⲉⲓϣ. ϩ.ⲑⲁⲗⲁⲥⲥⲁ π. ⲉ̓ⲛ; Ge l c; as nn, going to & fro, derangement, madness: Eccl 2 12 (F ⲕⲓⲙ) ⲡⲉⲣⲓⲫⲟⲣⲁ́, ib 10 13 (F do) ⲡⲉⲣⲓⲫⲉ́ⲣⲉⲓⲁ; ⲙⲁ ⲛϣ.: ShA 2 253 Judas was for devil ⲙ. place wherein to wander.

ϣⲏ F v ϣⲉ go, ϣⲉ wood.

ϣⲏⲓ SAB(rare)F, ϣⲏⲉⲓ, ϣⲁⲓ S, ϣⲉⲓ F nn m, pit, cistern: Ex 21 33, Ps 87 6, Is 36 16 SF, Dan 6 7, Zech 9 11 SA (all B = Gk), Cl 45 6 A, C 89 20 B = MG 17 363 حفرة, Z 343 ⲛϣ. of drinking-water (cf ib ϣⲱⲧⲉ same), C 99 231 = ib 89 66 B = MG 17 411 بئر ⲗⲁ́ⲕⲕⲟⲥ; Ps 54 23 (B ϣⲱϯ) ⲫⲣⲉ́ⲁⲣ; Eccl 10 8 F ϣⲉ[ⲓ] (S ϩⲓⲉⲓⲧ) ⲃⲟ́ⲑⲣⲟⲥ; C 41 64 B ϣ. for watering garden = Miss 4 452 ٔج; Tri 411 جب (var وحلة); ShA 1 450 ⲧⲟϭⲛⲉϥ ⲉϩⲣⲁⲓ ⲉⲩϣ., ib sim ⲉⲩⲛⲟϭ ⲛϩⲓⲉⲓⲧ, ShZ 595 ϩⲓ. paral ϣ., Miss 4 755 ϣⲓⲕⲉ ⲛⲟⲩϣ., ib ⲥⲙⲓⲛⲉ ⲙⲛϣ., ib 231 ϭⲱⲱⲝⲉ ⲛⲟⲩϣ. to replace ⲕⲟⲩⲓ ⲛϣⲱⲧⲉ, MIE 2 405 B ϩⲁⲛϣ. ⲡⲉⲙϩⲁⲛϣⲱϯ full of fire, C 43 85 B ϣ. (sc ⲗⲟⲩⲧⲏ́ⲣ at martyr's shrine, cf ? AM 314 supra, J 58 10 house ⲛⲧⲡⲉ ⲙⲛϣ., ib 39 ϩⲙⲡϩⲓⲣ ⲙⲛϣ., ib 65 58 v ⲱⲣⲥ nn, KroppK 45 charm ⲉⲧⲃⲉⲟⲩϣⲁⲓ ⲉⲥⲁϩⲡⲥ, write on jar & cast into ϣⲏⲓ. V Spg Demotica 1 29. As name: ϣⲏⲓ (l? ϣⲁⲓ ST 145). In place-names: ⲡϣⲏⲓ ⲙⲟⲟⲩ‧ بئر ما (P 43 52), ϩⲁϩ ϣ. ابيار (ib).

ϣⲏⲓ B nn as pl, temples: BM 920 266 = P 54 168 ⲛϣ. البرابي , هياكل الاوثان. Cf ? last ⲗⲟⲩⲧⲏ́ⲣ.

ϣⲓ SA²(Ma)BF, ϣⲉⲓ S, ϩ(ⲉ)ⲓ A, ϣⲓ-SBF, ϩⲓ-A, ϣⲓⲧ⸗ SB, ϩⲓⲧ⸗ Sᵃ, ϩⲓⲧ⸗ A, ϣⲏⲩⲧ† S, ϣⲏⲟⲩⲧ† B (cf also ϣⲓⲁⲓ) vb I intr (rare), measure, weigh: Ez 40 27 SB ⲇⲓⲁⲙⲉⲧⲣⲉⲓ̄ⲛ; ShC 73 80 S none may urge others to eat ⲕⲁⲛ ⲉϥϣⲓ ⲏ ⲉⲛϣⲓ ⲁⲛ, BMis 411 S ⲙⲁⲣⲛϣⲓ ⲛⲟⲩϣⲓ ⲉⲡⲁⲡⲟⲩϣ; qual: C 99 219 S ϣⲁⲝⲉ ⲉϥϣⲓ. = ib 89 33 B = Va ar 172 21 معتدل ⲉ̓ⲙⲙⲉⲧⲣⲟⲥ; ShP 130³ 2 S ⲟⲩⲱⲙ ⲙⲡⲉⲧϣⲓ., ShA 2 258 S voice ⲉⲥⲙϣⲓ ⲉⲥϣ., Mor 28 228 S ϭⲓⲛϣⲁⲝⲉ ⲉⲧϣⲓ., PMéd 222 S ⲙⲟⲟⲩ ⲛϣⲓ. in measured quantity (?).

II tr: Ex 16 18 SB, Is 40 12 SB, Ap 11 1 SBF, Z 355 S ⲁⲡⲓ ⲟⲩⲟⲓⲡⲉ ⲧⲁϣⲓⲧϥ ⲙⲉⲧⲣⲉⲓⲛ, Ps 59 8 B(S ⲱⲡ), Ez 40 24 SB ⲇⲓⲁⲙ., Mic 2 4 SA (B ⲣⲱϣ) ⲕⲁⲧⲁⲙ.; Job 6 2 SB, Jer 39 10 SB ⲓⲥⲧⲁ́ⲛⲁⲓ, Ez 5 1 SB ⲇⲓⲥ.; BG 93 S ⲡⲧⲉⲗⲏⲗ ⲉⲧⲉⲙⲁⲩϣⲓⲧϥ, ShA 2 88 S ⲛⲏⲓ... ⲁϥϣⲓⲧϥ, CA 96 S ϣⲓ ⲛⲟⲉⲓⲙⲉ ⲛⲥⲡⲧⲉ, Mani 2 A² ⲁϥϣⲓ ⲙⲡⲟⲩⲉ ⲡⲟⲩⲉ (or ?dat), Ryl 439 B ϣⲓ ⲛⲓⲗⲁ̄ ⲛⲝⲉⲥⲧⲏⲥ, J 7 31 Sᵃ coins ⲁⲓϣⲓⲧⲟⲩ; double acc, to amount of: Ap 21 17 S(B diff) ⲙ., Ez 42 18 SB ⲇⲓⲁⲙ.

With following preposition. c ⲉ-, *as to*: Ez 40
20 *SB* διαμ. acc; c ⲛ- dat: Ge 47 12 *B* (σιτο)μ. dat;
ShC 73 55 *S* ϣι ϧⲛⲟ ⲡⲟⲩⲱⲙ ⲛⲓⲙ ⲛⲁⲛ, Kr 132 *S*
ⲛⲉⲫⲟⲣⲟⲥ…ⲧⲁϣⲓⲧϥ ⲛⲁⲕ; ⲛ-, *with* (agent) ⲩ c ϧⲛ-; c
ⲛⲧⲛ-, *for*: ShP 130⁴ 140 *S* ⲛⲉⲛⲭⲣⲉⲓⲁ ϣ.† ⲛⲧⲟⲟⲧⲛ
as with balance (cf Miss 4 617 *S* ⲡⲉⲕϣⲁϫⲉ … ϣ.†
ⲉⲅⲏⲡ ⲡⲧⲟⲟⲧⲕ); c ϣⲁ-, *up to*: Ap 21 16 *S*(*B* diff)
μ. ἐπί; c ϧⲛ-, ⲏⲉⲛ-, *in, with* (agent): Jer 39 10 *SB*
ιστ. ἐν; ShC 73 57 *S* bread ϣ.† ϧⲛⲡⲙⲁϣⲉ, El 56 *A*
ϧⲉⲓ ⲛⲡⲁⲧⲁⲑⲟⲛ…ϧⲛⲟⲩⲙ., MG 25 39 *B* words ϣ.†
ⲏⲉⲛⲟⲩⲙ.; ⲛ- sim: J 1 75 *S* †ⲙⲏ (τιμή) ⲉⲥϣ.† ⲛⲡⲛϣⲓ
ⲛⲡⲕⲁⲥⲧⲣⲟⲛ.

With following adverb. c ⲉϩⲣⲁⲓ, *up by adding*
weight: Ru 3 15 *S* ⲉϧ. ⲉ- μ. ἐπί; Mor 41 127 *S* ⲁϥϣⲓ
ⲡⲟⲩⲃ ⲉϧ. ⲛⲛⲓⲕⲱⲙⲏⲧⲟⲥ (Νικομήδης) *till reached*
his weight in gold (var Wess 15 122 ⲉϧ. ⲟⲩⲃⲉ-) = C
43 43 *B*; Si 8 2 *S* ⲉϧ. ⲟⲩⲃⲉ- ἀντιστ. τ. ὁλκήν.

—— nn m *SABF*, *measure, weight*: Ge 18 6 *S*(*B*
ⲙⲉⲛⲧ), Is 5 10 *S*(*B* do, *F* ⲁⲓⲡⲓ), Lam 2 8 *BF*, Ro 12
3 *SBF* μέτρον, MG 25 366 *B* ⲁϥϣⲟϩ ⲉⲛϣⲓ ⲛⲡⲉⲛⲓⲱⲧ
τὸ μέτρον αὐτοῦ εἶναι (cf *Anal Boll* 7 103 εἰς τοιαῦτα
μέτρα φθάνειν), BHom 29 *S* ⲉⲅⲡⲧⲁϥ ⲙⲙⲁⲩ ⲛⲉⲛϣⲓ
μ. ἔχειν; Ez 42 15 *SB* διαμέτρησις; Lev 26 26 *S*(*B*
ⲙⲁϣⲓ), Job 28 25 *SB* σταθμός, Pro 20 23 *SA* ϧⲓ,
Am 8 5 *S*(*B* do) -θμιον; Pro 11 1 *SA* ϧⲓ (*B* ⲙⲁ.) ζυγόν; 1 Chr 28 15 *B* ὁλκή; 1 Tim 3 13 *S*(*B* ⲧⲱⲧⲉⲣ)
βαθμός; Ps 146 5 *S*(*B* ⲏⲡⲓ) ἀριθμός; *ib* 144 3 *S*(*B*
ⲁⲅⲣⲏⲝ) πέρας; Nu 5 15 *S*(*B* ⲱⲓⲡⲓ), 1 Kg 25 18 *S*
οἰφί; Mt 5 15 *S*(*B* ⲙⲉ.) μόδιος; Nu 15 4 *S*(*B*=Gk)
εἶν; Lev 27 16 *S*(*B* do) κόρος; Hag 2 16 *SA* ϧⲉⲓ (*B*
do), Mt 13 33 *SBF* σάτον; Ez 46 7 *SB* ephi; Lev 24
5 *B* ϣⲓ ⲃ̄ ⲡⲣⲉⲙⲏⲧ δύο δεκάτων; 2 Kg 7 18 *S* ϣⲁϧⲣⲁⲓ
ⲉⲛⲉⲓϣⲓ ἕως τούτων; Job 15 11 *S* ⲡⲁⲣⲁ ⲡϣⲓ (*B* diff)
ὑπερβαλλόντως, MG 25 16 *B* sim ὑπὲρ τὸ μέτ.; Bor
226 159 *S* presume not ϫⲉⲁⲕⲡⲱϣ ⲉⲅⲛⲟϭ ⲛϣⲓ εἰς τὸ
ἄξιον τ. θεοῦ; BHom 22 *S* ⲡⲣⲟⲥ ⲡϣⲓ of sins κατ'
ἀναλογίαν; 2 Kg 16 1 *S* Gk om; PS 202 *S* distance
ⲉⲙⲡ ϣⲓ ⲉⲣⲟϥ, ShC 73 21 *S* ⲙⲡⲧⲉ ⲡⲉⲓϣⲱⲛⲉ ϣⲓ ⲙ-
ⲙⲁⲩ, Aeg 250 *S* ⲧⲁϧⲟ ⲛⲟⲩⲡⲣⲟⲥⲉⲩⲭⲏ ϧⲛⲟⲩϣⲓ =
PO 8 594 قِس, BM 256 190 *S* on Ge 21 2 when Sarah
had attained ⲛⲛⲟϭ ⲛϣⲓ *great age* (?, cf Bor 226
above), Hall 93 *S* praying ⲕⲁⲧⲁ ⲡϣⲓ ⲛⲧⲙⲛⲧⲉⲗⲁ-
ⲭ(ⲓⲥⲧⲟⲥ), Lant 98 *S* ⲡⲣⲟⲥ ⲡϣⲓ ⲛⲧⲁⲙⲛⲧⲥⲃⲟⲓ, MG
25 36 *B* ⲉⲓⲟⲩⲱⲙ ⲡⲟⲩϣⲓ ⲛⲱⲓⲕ, BM 1146 *S* ⲡϣⲓ ⲡⲉⲓⲱⲣⲉ sowed, DeV 2 141 *B* walked ⲛⲡϣⲓ ⲡⲟⲩⲙⲩ-
ⲗⲓⲟⲛ, BMis 282 *S* ⲛⲁⲛⲟⲩ ⲡϣⲓ ϧⲣⲟⲱⲃ ⲛⲓⲙ, AM 184
B ship's cargo ⲡⲁⲣⲁ ⲡⲉϥϣⲓ, BSM 134 *B* ⲁⲡϣⲓ ⲛ-
ⲥⲁϫⲓ ϣⲱⲡⲓ ⲥⲁⲥⲁ ⲛⲓⲃⲉⲛ (due) *limit of speech* (length
of sermon), Miss 8 239 *S* sim;   particular (local)
measures: PAntinoe EES coins ⲛⲡϣⲓ ⲛⲣⲁⲕⲟⲧⲉ =
ib ζυγ(ῷ) Ἀλεξ(ανδρείας), CO 405 sim, J 12 29 ⲛⲡⲕⲁⲥⲧⲣⲟⲛ ϫⲏⲗⲏ (cf *ib* 10 41 κ, μεμνω/), Ryl 189,
BM 1013 ⲛⲧⲡⲟⲗⲓⲥ, *ib* 1033 ⲛⲡⲟⲓⲕⲟ[ⲛⲟⲙⲟⲥ?], *ib*

1040 ⲛⲡⲓⲟⲙ ⲛⲡⲉⲕⲧⲏⲙⲁ ⲛⲁⲡⲁ ⲁⲛⲁⲥⲧⲁⲥⲉ, CO 174
ⲛⲡⲁⲗⲉⲕⲧⲱⲣ (v Ep 138 n).

ⲁⲧϣⲓ *SA²B*, *unmeasured, immeasurable*: 2 Cor 10
13 *B*(*S* ⲛⲃⲟⲗ ⲛⲡϣⲓ) ἄμετρος, Bar 3 25 *B* ⲁ. ⲉⲣⲟϥ (*S*
ⲙⲉⲛⲧⲩ ϣⲓ) ἀμέτρητος; BG 24 *S* ⲡⲟⲩⲟⲓⲛ ⲛⲁⲧϣⲓⲧϥ,
Mani H 14 A² ⲉⲁⲩ sim; ⲙⲛⲧ-, ⲙⲉⲧⲁⲧϣⲓ: 2 Cor 10
15 *B* (as 13 above), Va 58 189 *B* fasting checketh
†ⲙ. ἀμετρία; *ib* 57 125 *B* †ⲙ. τρυφή; ShZ 603 *S*
ⲧⲙ. is not good.

ⲣⲉϥϣⲓ *SB*, *measurer*: P 44 63 *S* ⲣ. ϧⲁⲧ · ϫⲩⲧⲟⲥⲧⲁ-
ⲧⲏⲥ; K 142 *B* زرّاج; ShR 2 3 34 *S* ⲥⲁϧ, ⲡⲣⲟⲡⲟⲏⲧⲏⲥ,
ⲣ. ⲉⲓⲱⲣⲉ; ⲙⲛⲧ-, ⲙⲉⲧⲣ.: K 108 *B* †ⲙ. زراعة; Mor
25 113 *S* among sins ⲧⲙ. ⲕⲁⲕⲱⲥ.

ⲕⲁ ϣⲓ *SB*, *set measure, limit*: Job 38 5 *SB* μ. τιθέναι, Aeg 241 *S* let wrath ⲕⲁ ⲟⲩϣⲓ ⲛⲁϥ μ. ἔχειν; Sh
C 73 52 *S* exhorting to ⲕⲁ ϣⲓ ⲉϩⲣⲁⲓ ⲛⲡⲣⲱⲙⲉ ⲉ-
ⲧⲣⲉϥϣⲗⲏⲗ, Mus 42 218 *S* law ⲕⲁ ϣⲓ ⲉϧ. ⲉⲧⲃⲏⲏⲧϥ
(sc marriage).

ⲣ, ⲟ ⲛϣⲓ *S*, *make, amount to weight*: Ru 2 17 γίνεσθαι ὡς οἰφί; BM 1030 solidi ⲉⲅⲟ ⲛⲛⲉⲅϣⲓ, BMOr
6203 A sim ⲟ ⲛⲛⲉⲅϣⲓ ϩⲛⲡⲉϣⲉⲓ ⲛⲧⲙⲁϣⲉ ⲛⲁⲓⲕⲁ-
ⲓⲟⲛ; ⲉⲣ ϣⲁⲡϣⲓ *B*: C 89 24 ⲉⲣ ϣ. ⲛⲣ̄ ⲡⲣⲱⲙⲓ =
ib 99 134 *S* ⲣ ⲁϣⲉ ⲛ-.

† ϣⲓ *S*(Sh)*B*, *set measure, restrict*: Cai Euch 480
B naught can † ⲉⲡⲓⲡⲉⲗⲁⲧⲟⲥ of thy goodness ἐκμετρεῖν; ShIF 302 ⲁⲓ†. ⲉⲛⲟⲩⲛⲟⲟⲩⲉ ⲡⲟⲩⲱⲙ ⲛⲑⲉ
ⲛⲟⲩⲙⲁϣⲉ, *ib* 126 ⲉⲓ†. ⲉⲛⲉⲓϧⲟⲓⲧⲉ…ⲉⲓⲣⲱⲛ ⲉⲧⲃⲉⲡⲉⲅ-
ⲧⲱϣ, ShC 42 202 knowest ⲛ†. ⲉⲡⲟⲩϣⲗⲏⲗ, BSM
51 *B* † ⲛⲡϣⲓ ⲛⲧⲉⲧⲛⲡϩⲟⲙ in alms-giving (BMis 403
S = Va 63 20 *B* diff);   ⲁⲧ† ϣⲓ, *unmeasured*: Is
22 18 *B*(*S* ⲙⲛ ⲛⲡⲉ) ἀμέτρητος; DeV 1 184 *B*(Orat
Manas 5) Gk diff; PS 5 *S* glory ⲛⲁ. ⲉⲣⲟϥ; ⲙⲛⲧⲁⲧ†
ϣⲓ: Mor 31 176 *S* loved him ϧⲛⲟⲩⲙ. ⲉⲣⲟϥ.

ϫⲓ, ϭⲓ ϣⲓ *SB*, *take measure, estimate*: TEuch 2
353 *B* ϭ. ⲛⲡⲉⲛⲛⲟⲃⲓ ⲉⲡⲉⲛⲕⲙⲉⲧϣⲉⲡⲟⲣⲏⲧ ἐπιμετ. dat;
ShA 2 88 *S* ⲡⲉⲛⲧⲁϭ ϫ. ⲏ ϫⲉⲛⲧⲁϣⲓ ⲟⲩ, *ib* 86 ⲡⲉⲧ†
ϣⲓ ⲉⲣⲟϥ ⲏ ⲡⲉⲧϫⲓ ⲙⲡⲉϥϣⲓ (sc of slough), BM 447
S 17 measures ϧⲁⲛϣⲓ ⲉⲧⲟⲩϫⲓ ⲙⲙⲟϥ.

ϣⲓⲧⲉϥ *S* nn m, meaning doubtful, *measuring, weigh-*
ing (?): Osir pl 37 wine account ϣⲉⲡⲟⲩⲧⲉ ϧⲁⲛϣⲓ.

In place-name (??): ϣⲓⲏⲧ later ϣⲓϧⲣⲧ (v EW *Hist*
MonastNitria 27); cf ? ZNTW 24 84 *F* ϣⲓϧⲣⲧ ἀπόλαυσις.

V also ⲉⲓⲱⲣⲉ *s f*, ⲛⲟⲩϧ, ⲛⲟⲩϧⲃ (ⲛⲁϧⲃ), ⲛⲉⲣϩⲏⲗ &
cf prob ⲙⲁϣⲉ.

ϣⲓ *S* nn m, meaning unknown, in P 44 69 ⲛⲡϣⲓ
ⲡⲣⲱϥ · ⲙⲅⲥⲧⲁϧ الفم (sic MS) مسال.

ϣⲓⲁⲓ *SB*, ϣⲓⲁⲉⲓⲁ(ⲉ)ⲓ, ϣⲓⲁⲓ, ϣⲓⲁⲓⲉ, ϣⲓⲟⲓ†¹, ϣⲁⲓ†²
S, ϣⲉⲓ†³ *F*, ϣⲏⲅⲧ†⁴ *S*, ϣⲓⲏⲟⲩ† *BF* (cf also ϣⲓ) vb intr,
be long B: Dan 4 30, Mt 23 5 *S*(*B* ⲛⲁⲁ) μεγαλύνειν; Is
44 14 (*S* ⲁⲓⲁⲓ) μηκύνειν; *ib* 61 11 (*S*=Gk) αὐξάνειν;
Rec 6 172 ⲁⲛⲁϧⲱⲓ (sic l) ϣ. = BMar 208 *S* ⲁⲩϧ.,

MG 25 95 nails ⲁⲩϣ. (var ⲉⲣ ⲛⲓϣϯ); ⲥ ϧⲓϫⲛ- S, *be long*, so *heavy upon*: 2 Kg 14 26 καταβαρύνειν ἐπί; qual a S¹²BF³: Nu 13 33¹ (B ⲁϥⲱϥ) ὑπερμήκης; Mor 37 83 demon ⲉϥϣ.¹ ὑψηλός (Miss 4 816 sim ⲉϥϣⲱⲓ); ShP 130⁴ 148 garments ⲉⲩⲟⲩⲟⲙⲥ ⲏ ⲉⲩϣ.¹, ShMIF 23 30 rope ⲉϥϣ.¹, ShViK 9346 ⲛⲉⲧϣ.² ⲛⲉⲧϩⲃⲱⲟⲩ (prob), BM 343 2 reeds ⲉⲩϣ.¹ opp ϧⲟⲃⲉ, P 43 44 ⲉϥϣⲓⲁⲓ (*l* ϣ.²) طول, BSG 183 nails ⲉⲩϣ.¹ = *ib* 13 B, Mor 18 100 Elisha ⲉϥϣ.¹ = Miss 4 159 B, Mor 21 102 stream ⲉϥϣ.² ⲡⲟⲩⲙⲓⲗⲓⲟⲛ, P Mich frag F ⲁⲕⲓⲛⲓ (Ἀγένειος, -νῆς) ⲡϣ.³ *the tall*; b S⁶BF: Is 5 18 BF(S¹), C 86 22 B spear ⲉⲥⲱ. μακρός; Is 6 1 B ϣ. ⲉⲡϣⲱⲓ (S ϫⲟⲥⲉ) ἐπαίρεσθαι; 1 Cor 11 14 B ⲉⲣⲉϫⲱϥ ϣ. (S diff) κομᾶν; LCyp 8 S tongue ⲉϥϣ. προφέρειν; BIF 13 101 S ⲟⲩⲣⲱⲙⲉ ⲉϥϣ. = MG 25 284 B, ROC 7 143 S ⲉⲕⲓⲃⲉ ⲉⲣϣ. ⲡⲟⲩⲕⲟⲩⲓ, PLond 4 517 S ⲃⲉⲡⲉϣⲏⲩ (?).

—— nn m SB, *length*: Deu 3 11 S(B ϣⲓⲏ), Ez 40 20 SB(*sic l*), Eph 3 18 S(B ϣⲓⲏ) μῆκος, cit ShA 1 78 S ϣⲓⲁⲉⲓⲁⲉⲓ & EW 222 scala 152 S ϣⲁⲓ; DeV 2 220 B of ark ⲡⲉϣ. (*cf* Ge 6 15 SB), ShIF 180 S ϧⲃⲃⲉ, ϣⲓⲁⲉⲓⲁⲓ, Cat 161 B ⲟⲩⲱⲱϣⲥ ϣ., ⲟⲩ. ϣⲓⲏ, Leip Ber '02 145 S ⲡⲉϣ. ⲛⲧⲉϥⲙⲟⲣⲧ, Lepsius *Denk* 6 102 21 S ⲡⲱϫⲕ & ϣⲁⲓⲉ of garment (*cf* Ep 1 9).

ϣⲓⲏ SB, ϣⲓⲏⲉ, ϣⲓⲉ S, ϧⲓⲏ Sᵃ, ϧⲓⲉ(ⲓ) A, ϣⲓⲏⲉⲓ F nn f, rarely m, *length*: Ge 12 6 SB, Ez 41 13 SB, μῆκος & *v* ϣⲓⲁⲓ nn; 1 Kg 16 7 S(B ⲙⲁⲓⲏ) μέγεθος; *ib* 17 4 S ὕψος; Mt 6 27 S(B do) ἡλικία; Ez 47 15 B m ὅριον; *ib* 45 3 B f διαμέτρησις; 1 Kg 28 20 S ϧⲉ (ϧ)ⲛⲧⲉϥϣ. ἑστηκώς; ShRyl 70 249 S ⲣⲱϧⲧ ⲡⲧⲉϥϣ. ⲉϧⲣⲁⲓ ⲉϫⲙⲡⲕⲁϧ, PS 207 S ⲧⲉϣ. ⲧⲟⲩⲁϣⲥⲉ, ShMun 110 S young tree ⲙⲙⲛ ϣⲓⲏⲉ but later ⲟⲩϫⲓⲥⲉ ⲉⲙⲁⲧⲉ, ShA 1 158 S sic l, Mor 30 40 F sim, *ib* 56 69 S ⲡϧⲱ. ⲛϥⲟⲩⲱϣ, C 41 24 B ⲃⲛⲃ...ⲑⲙⲁⲓⲏ ⲛⲧⲉϥϣ., Bor 264 39 S great beams ⲉⲩⲥⲁ ϧⲙⲡⲉⲩϣⲓⲉ; ⲛϣ., *of, in length*: Ge 6 15 S(B ⲉϯϣ.) τὸ μῆ., Jth 1 2 S ⲉⲓⲥ μῆ., Zech 5 2 SA-ⲉⲓ B μήκους, Ez 42 20 SB ⲡⲏⲭⲱⲛ εὖρος; P 131⁶ 1 S ⲟⲩϭⲟⲧ ⲉⲥⲧⲛϣ. (1 Kg 9 2), MG 25 371 B ⲙⲱⲓⲧ ⲉϥⲟⲓ ⲛⲟⲩⲙⲁϩⲓ ⲛϣ., BMis 556 Sᵃ ⲟⲩϣⲟⲡ ⲡϧⲓⲏ, Bristol Mus Ostr H 1755 A Sᵃ ϫⲟⲩ-ⲧⲁϧⲧⲉ (ⲛϣⲁⲡ) ⲛϣⲓⲉ; c gen ⲛ-, *length, height of*: 1 Kg 10 23 S ϣ. ⲛⲛⲁⲣϧⲉ ὑπερῴα; ViK 9658 7 S ϣ. ⲛⲟⲩⲟⲉⲓϣ, ⲛⲡⲉ ⲛϧⲣⲟⲟⲩ, DeV 2 255 B to depth of ⲟⲩϣ. ⲡⲣⲱⲙⲓ, Mor 31 211 S *v* ⲡⲱⲛⲕ (ⲡⲟⲛⲕϥ); as vb intr, *be long, grow*: Is 54 2 B(S diff) μακρύνειν; Mk 4 27 B(S ⲉⲣ ⲛⲟϭ) μηκύνειν; Mor 31 209 S ⲡϧⲱ ⲡⲧⲉϥⲁⲡⲉ ϣⲓⲉ, Va 58 185 B fasting ⲑⲣⲉϥϣ. (*sc* Samson).

ⲗⲁϣⲓⲏ *v* ⲗⲁ-, adding Mor 39 8 Sᶠ ⲗⲁϣⲓⲏⲛⲓ (var of *ib* 40 5), also ⲥⲁⲗⲁϣⲉⲓⲉ.

As name (?): ϣⲁⲓ (CO 60 &c, or *v* ϣⲁⲓ *fortune*). In place-names (?): ⲛⲓϣⲁⲓ (Lant 47), ⲡⲓⲁ̇ⲣⲓϣⲏⲩ (Mor 51 41), ⲛⲓϣⲁⲉⲓ (Kr 18).

ϣⲓⲱ S(rare)B nn f, *pot* (? ϣⲓ-ⲱ): Nu 11 8 (S ϭⲁ-ⲗⲁϧⲧ), Mic 3 3 (SA do), MG 25 203(= *ib* 68)χύτρα; C 89 3 ϯϣ. ⲡⲁϥ = *ib* 99 210 S ϭ. = MG 17 340 قدر (which Miss 4 353 = *ib* 637 ⲁⲥⲕⲁⲗⲱⲡⲉ, *cf* WS 153), C 89 12 ⲉϥⲥⲁϧϯ ϫⲁⲟⲩϣ. = MG 17 352 'ϫ, *ib* 96 ϯϣ. ... ⲟⲩⲱⲙ ⲉⲃⲟⲗ ⲛϧⲏⲧⲥ = *ib* 472 'ϫ, HCons 474 hands washed ϧⲓⲛϣ. 'ϫ; AM 314 ϯϣ. ⲙⲙⲱⲟⲩ, AZ 39 152 S ⲧⲉⲓϣ. inscr on clay vessel with hole, *funnel, hopper* (so explained HSchäfer). As name (?): ⲥⲁⲙⲟⲩⲏⲗ ⲡϣ. (PGol 53 S), *cf* ? Σίως (Preisigke).

ϣⲟ SA²B, ϧⲟ A, ϣⲁ SᶠF nn, *thousand* χίλιοι: Deu 32 30 SB, Job 33 23 SB, Eccl 6 6 SF, Is 30 17 SBF; χιλιάς: Ex 20 6 S, Mic 5 2 A, Ap 5 11 S (all B ⲁⲛϣⲟ); PS 24 S ϣⲙⲟⲩⲛ ⲛϣⲟ, BMar 4 S ϯⲟⲩ ⲛϣⲟ, C 86 138 B ϥ̄ ⲛϣⲟ, DeV 1 114 B ⲟⲩϣⲟ ⲙⲙⲁⲧⲟⲓ, El 106 A ϧⲟ ⲛⲣⲁⲙⲡⲉ, ManiH 23 A² ϧⲛϣⲟ, LMär 33 S ⲛⲁϩⲛϣⲟⲡ ⲙⲛϣⲟ ⲛⲣⲟⲙⲡⲉ, Aeg 31 B, AM 67 B sim(*v* Lant 51 n 13), KroppS 104 Sᶠ ⲡⲁⲡⲉⲓϣⲁ ⲛ-ⲃⲁⲗ(?); f: Jud 6 15 S ⲧⲁⲙϣⲟ ⲛⲣⲱⲙⲉ ἡ χιλιάς, Ap 20 3 S ⲧϣⲟ ⲛⲣⲟⲙⲡⲉ (B m); ⲙⲏⲧ ⲛϣⲉ for ϣⲟ S: 2 Kg 8 4, Cant 8 11, BMar 5; iterated: Nu 31 4 ·S(B ⲟⲩϣⲟ), 2 Kg 18 4 S. ⲁⲛ-SB, ⲁⲛⲁⲛϣⲟ B *v* ⲁⲛ- (2°).

ϣⲟ S particle, *yea*: Mt 17 25 (B ⲥⲉ) ναί. Cf ? ϣⲉ in swearing.

ϣⲟ B, ϣⲁ F, *bran v* ⲉϣⲟ.

ϣⲟⲓ S nn, meaning unknown: PStras 409 ⲁⲡⲁ-ⲓⲱⲧ ⲗⲱϫⲕ ⲧⲓⲱⲣⲅⲉ ⲉⲣⲟϥ ... ⲙⲡⲟⲩⲗⲟ ⲉⲩϯ ϣ. ⲡⲁⲩ ϫⲓⲛⲉⲕⲁⲗⲁⲛϯⲟⲩⲉⲛ(PLond 5 239 Καλαντίων قلندوذ) ϣⲁⲧⲟⲩⲉⲓ ⲉϣⲙⲟⲩⲛ.

ϣⲟⲓ O vb(?), *arise*(?): AZ 21 104 ϣ. ϣⲁⲛⲉⲣⲱⲟⲩ, 105 ϣ. ⲉⲧⲡⲉ, *ib* ϣ. ⲉⲡⲛⲟⲩⲛ, distinct from ϣⲁⲓ *rise* (*cf ib* 38 92, DM 2 2); *cf* ? ϣⲱⲓ; as nn (adj): *ib* ⲡϣ. *v* ϣⲁⲓ *fortune*.

ϣⲟⲩ *v* ⲉϣⲱ.

ϣⲱ SA(once)BF, ϣⲟⲩ, ϣⲟⲩⲟⲩ(once)A nn m, *sand*: Ge 13 16 SA(Cl)ϣⲟⲩ B, Ex 2 12 A ϣⲟⲩⲟⲩ B, Pro 27 3 SA ϣⲟⲩ, Ac 7 24 F(SB om) ἄμμος, Si 18 10 S ⲃⲗⲃⲓⲗⲉ ⲛϣⲱ ψῆφος ἅ.; Sa 7 9 S, MG 25 252 B ψάμμος, Va 66 300 B children playing ϧⲓⲥⲉⲛⲡⲓϣⲱ ψάμαθος; PS 132 S ⲛϣⲱ ⲉⲧϣⲟⲩⲱⲟⲩ (Od Solom 6 11 ظبي), AZ 21 142 S dragged them to shore ⲉϫⲙⲡϣⲱ, KroppA S (sleep) heavy on eyes like ϭⲟⲟⲩⲛⲉ ⲛϣⲱ, MG 25 252 B ⲙⲉⲡⲧ ⲛϣⲱ, DeV 1 85 B ⲛⲁϥⲣⲓ ⲛϣⲱ, PMéd 173 S ⲛϣⲱ ⲛⲙⲏ *gravel in urine*; ⲕⲏ, ⲭⲏ ⲉⲡϣⲱ, *lying, being in sandy condition*: Jer 2 31 B(S ⲟ ⲛϣⲛⲁ) χερσοῦσθαι, Hos 10 4 SA ϣⲱ (B = Gk), cit ShC 42 160, P 44 116 both ϣⲟ χέρσος ἀγροῦ (*cf* ὑφαμμος). V ⲕⲱ ⲕ & ⲕⲁⲡ-ϣⲱ. As place-names: ⲛⲓϣⲱ (PO 11 304)= ? Πα-

ράλιος برلس (cf Synax 1 97 *ult*, PO 5 23 for شبرا *l* ? بشوا),]ϣϣⲱ (Kr 194).

ϣⲱ (or prob ⲉϣⲱ)*S* nn as pl, a disease: PMéd 105 ⲡⲉϣⲱ ⲙⲛⲥⲁϣ ⲛⲓⲙ ⲉⲙⲛ ⲣⲱϥ ⲛϩⲏⲧϥ, *ib* 265 ⲟⲩⲧⲣⲁⲭⲱⲙⲁ ⲙⲛⲡⲉⲓϭⲧ ⲙⲛⲡⲉϣⲱ. *V* Chassinat *ib* 109.

ϣⲱⲓ *S*(rare)*BF*, -ⲉⲓ, ϣⲟⲓ *F* nn m, *what is high, above* always c def art: Mk 15 38 *B* ⲓⲥϫⲉⲛⲡϣ., *F* ϫⲓⲛⲡϣ. (*S* ϫⲓⲛⲧⲡⲉ) ἄνωθεν; My 47 *S* ⲡϣ. ⲙⲛⲡⲉⲥⲛⲧ, MG 25 145 ⲟⲩⲥⲟϭⲛⲓ ⲛⲧⲉ ⲡⲁⲡϣ. *from on high*.

With preceding prep forms advb. c ⲉ-, motion *upward*: Deu 29 18 (*S* ⲛⲥⲁⲧⲡⲉ), Ac 2 19 (*S* ϩⲣⲛⲧⲡⲉ), Z 343 *S* water ⲉⲓ ⲉⲡ., ἄνω, Lev 27 7 (*S* ⲉⲧⲡⲉ) ἐπά., 1 Kg 2 6 (*S* ⲉϩⲣⲁⲓ), Jer 37 17 ἀν(άγειν), Is 53 12 (*S* do) ἀνα(φέρειν), Ge 19 28 (*S* do), Ez 41 7 (*S* ⲛⲥⲁⲧⲡⲉ) ἀνα(βαίνειν), 2 Kg 6 2 -βασις *v* ⲙⲟⲉⲓⲧ **I** *s f*, Ac 1 22 (*S* ⲉϩ.) ἀνα(λαμβάνειν), Lu 1 42 (*S* diff) ἀνα(φωνεῖν); Nu 20 11 (*S* ⲉϩ.), Ac 1 9 (*S* do) ἐπ(αίρειν), Ps 55 10 (*S* do) ἐπι(καλεῖν); Ez 44 7 προσ(φέρειν); Gk om: Is 17 12 (*S* om) κυμαίνειν, Lam 2 19 (*S* ⲉϩ.) αἴρειν, Z 315 *S* ⲃⲉⲉⲃⲓ ⲉⲡ. βρύειν; Bess 7 5 ⲓⲥϫⲉⲛⲫⲟⲟⲩ ⲉⲡ., Aeg 40 ϫⲉⲛϯⲙⲁϩⲧ̅ ⲙⲫⲉ ⲉⲡ., BSM 4 ⲡⲓⲛⲏⲃ ⲉⲡ. *floating on surface*, *ib* 28 inundation ⲓ ⲉⲡ. = BMis 368 *S* ⲉⲓ, C 43 19 spring ϣⲟⲩⲟ ⲉⲡ., *ib* 41 37 ⲁϥϥⲟⲭϥ ⲉⲡ., AM 176 ⲛⲉϩⲥⲓ ⲉⲡ. from dream, DeV 2 227 beasts that earth ⲙⲁⲥⲟⲩ ⲉⲡ., C 89 68 ⲣⲓⲙ ⲉⲡ. ϩⲁⲡⲥⲉ̅, C 43 50 ⲉⲅⲛⲁ ⲉⲡ. ⲉⲅⲛⲁ ⲉⲡⲉⲥⲛⲧ = Mor 39 27 *S* ⲉⲅⲛⲏⲩ ⲉⲡ., Mor 24 31 *F* wheel ϫⲓ ⲉⲡⲉⲥⲛⲧ ⲉⲥⲓ ⲉⲡ., HT W 80 *S* ϭⲱϣⲧ ⲉⲡ. ⲉⲡⲉⲥⲛⲧ ϩⲓⲱⲱϥ *looked him up & down*, My 86 *S* supports(limbs) ⲉⲧⲥⲟⲩⲧⲱⲛ ⲉⲡ.; ⲉⲡ. ⲉ-: Is 14 14 (*S* ⲉϩ. ⲉϫⲛ-) ἀνα- ἐπάνω gen, Ro 10 6 (var ⲉϩⲣⲏⲓ, *S* ⲉϩ. ⲉ-), Mt 14 19 (*SF* do) ἀνα- εἰς, Ez 8 3 (*S* do) ἄγειν εἰς; C 41 9 hands ⲫⲟⲣϣ ⲉⲃⲟⲗ ⲉⲡ. ⲉⲧⲫⲉ; c ⲛ-, rest *above*: Deu 4 39 (*S* ⲉⲛⲭⲓⲥⲉ), Gal 4 26 (*S* ⲛⲧⲡⲉ) ἄνω, Jer 4 28 (*S* ϩⲓⲧⲡⲉ) ἄνωθεν; ROC 25 254 sun ⲙⲛ. ⲉⲧⲫⲉ, P 131⁵ 102 *S* ⲟⲩⲥⲁ ⲙⲛ. *upper room* (cf Mk 14 15); ⲉⲃⲟⲗ ⲛ-, *from above*: EpJer 62 (*F* ⲉⲃ. ϩⲛϫⲓⲥⲓ), Cai Euch 327 birth ⲡⲓⲉⲃ. ⲙⲛ. ἄνωθεν; DeV 2 86 ϯⲧⲣⲟⲫⲏ ⲉⲃ. ⲙⲛ.; c ⲥⲁ-: Ge 6 16 (*S* ϩⲓⲧⲡⲉ), Ez 1 26, Ac 26 5 ⲓⲥϫⲉⲛⲡⲥ. (*S* ϫⲓⲛⲡϣⲟⲣⲡ) ἄνωθεν, He 10 8 (*S* ⲛⲧⲡⲉ) ἀνώτερος, Ac 19 1 (*S* ϩⲁⲙⲛⲭⲓⲥⲉ) -τερικός, Ex 30 14, Bar 2 5 ἐπάνω, Ez 1 22 -ωθεν, Ge 7 20 (*S* ⲉⲙⲁⲧⲉ), Ps 73 5 (*S* ⲡⲉϥⲉⲧⲡⲉ) ὑπεράνω, Ac 9 37 *BF*(*S* ⲛⲧⲡⲉ) ὑπερῷος; Ez 41 20 ⲙⲁ ⲉⲧⲥ.(*S* do) φατνώμα; BIF 15 246 *S* God ⲉⲧⲥ., P Chass 2 29 *S* recipe ⲧⲓ ⲥⲁⲡⲉⲥⲛⲧ ⲁⲩⲱ ⲥⲁⲡϣⲟⲓ; ⲛⲥⲁ- same: Eph 4 10 *F*(*B* ⲥⲁ-, *S* ⲉⲧⲡⲉ) ὑπερά.; LCyp 6 *S* ⲉⲧⲟⲩⲉⲓϣⲉ ⲙⲙⲟϥ ⲛ. ⲙⲙⲟⲟⲩ (or *l* ⲛⲙⲁⲩ.) ἐπανα- φορά; BSM 51 requireth not ⲛ. ⲛⲧⲉⲛϫⲟⲙ = BMis 404 *S* παρά, Mor 15 3 *S* cross ⲛ. ⲙⲛⲧⲁⲫⲟⲥ = BMis 183 *S* ϩⲁⲡⲉⲧⲡⲉ ⲛ-; ⲥⲁⲡϣ. ⲛ-: Is 36 2 (*S* ϩⲣ. ϩⲛ-) ἄνω, Mt 21 7 (*S* ⲉϩⲣ. ⲉϫⲛ-), 1 Cor 15 6 (*SF* ⲛϩⲟⲩⲟ

ⲉ-) ἐπάνω, Lev 11 21 (*S* ⲛⲧⲡⲉ ⲛ-) ἐπανώτερα, Is 2 2 (*S* ⲉϫⲛ-), Eph 1 21 (*S* ϫⲟⲥⲉ ⲉ-, *F* ⲥⲁⲡϫⲓⲥⲓ ⲛ-), He 9 5 *BF*(*S* ⲛⲧⲡⲉ ⲛ-) ὑπερά., Ez 1 25 ὑπεράνωθεν; Va 57 175 riches c. ⲡⲧⲉⲕⲭⲣⲓⲁ ὑπέρ, *ib* 13 ⲟⲩⲱⲧⲉⲃ c. ⲛ- ὑπερ(βαίνειν); Lev 8 7 † c. ⲛ- (*S* ⲕⲱ ϩⲓϫⲛ-)ἐπιτιθέ- ναι ἐπί; MIE 2 359 fish ⲛⲟⲓⲛⲓ c. ⲛⲛⲙⲟⲟⲩ = BAp 87 *S* ⲡⲟⲥⲱ ϩⲙⲡⲙⲟⲟⲩ ⲉϥϩⲃⲟⲓⲗⲉ = PO 22 346 عام فوق, DeV 2 218 ⲣ̅ ⲡⲣⲟⲙⲡⲓ ⲓⲉ c. ⲙⲙⲟⲟⲩ, C 89 93 ⲁⲅⲓⲥ- ⲛⲓ c. ⲙⲙⲟⲛ = *ib* 99 154 *S* ϩⲓⲧⲡⲉ ⲛ-, CDan 94 ⲫⲟ- ⲣϣ ⲡⲁϥ c. ⲡϯⲙⲟⲡⲏ *in upper part*, Bodl(P) a 2 61 *S* recipe ⲁϣⲉ ⲉϩⲣⲁⲓ ϣⲁⲡϣ. ⲉⲡⲣⲏⲙⲉϫ (prob for ⲥⲁⲡ. ⲙ-); ⲉⲃⲟⲗ ⲥⲁ-: Ex 25 22 (var om ⲉⲃ.) ἄνωθεν; as nn m: Cat 162 ⲛⲓⲥ. ⲛⲧⲉ ⲡⲓⲥ̀ⲣⲟⲥ; ⲉⲣ ⲥⲁ., *overtop*: Dan 3 47 (*S* ⲭⲓⲥⲉ ⲉϩ. ⲉϫⲛ-) διαχεῖν ἐπάνω, C 86 293 ⲉⲣ c. ⲙⲡⲏⲓ διαβαί. ἐπά., Va 58 182 ship ⲉⲣ c. ⲛⲛⲓ- ⲙⲱⲟⲩ ὑψηλότερος γίνεσθαι; Sh(?)Mor 54 42 *S* ⲉⲣ c. ⲙⲡϩⲱⲡⲧ (*l* ⲥⲱ.) ⲧⲏⲣϥ; c ϩⲓ-: Am 2 9 *F*(JEA 11 246, *B* ⲥⲁ., *A* diff) ἐπάνωθεν; c ϩⲛ-, *above*: Kr 25 *F* ⲡⲓⲣⲉⲃ (*v* ⲁⲣⲏⲃ) ϩⲉ(ⲙ)ⲡϣⲱⲉⲓ ϩⲉ(ⲙ)ⲡⲉⲓ- ϫⲱⲙⲉ.

In place-name (?): ⲧⲁϣⲱⲓ (BM 1039).

ϣⲱⲓ *B* nn f, *genital organs* (?): K 78 ϯϣ. إسو (cf P 43 41 *S* '⸻ = ⲙⲁⲗⲏ, θακος). *V* ⲃⲱϣ (ⲃⲉⲙ- ϣⲱⲓ).

ϣⲁⲁⲃ¹, ϣⲁⲁϥ², ϣⲟⲟⲃ³ *S* nn m, *skin*: Lam 5 10³ (*B* ϣⲁⲣ)δέρμα; Mus 40 36(RegPach)ⲛⲛⲉⲗⲁⲁⲩ ⲡⲣϣ ⲉⲓⲁⲟⲥ [ϩⲓ?ⲛ]ⲉϥϣ.² [ⲉⲓ]ⲙⲛⲧⲓ ⲉⲩⲧⲟⲙ [ⲙⲙⲁⲧ]ⲉ(Latin om), C 100 295 sleeping not ϩⲛⲛⲉϥϣ.² according to the ordinance (C 89 179 *B* om), Imp RussArS 026 *l* 23 (*sic*) am coming ⲛⲧⲁⲛ ⲡϣ.¹ ⲙⲛⲡϫⲱⲱⲙⲉ (for writing or binding?).

ϣⲱⲃ¹, -ϥ² *S*, ϣⲱⲡ³, ϭ.⁴, ϣⲟⲡ⁵, ϭ.⁶ *B*, ϣⲃ-, ϣⲉϥ- *S*, ϣⲉⲃ-, ϣⲉⲡ-, ϭ. *B*, ϣⲟⲃ⸗ *SB*, ϣⲟϥ⸗ *S*, ϣⲁⲃ⸗ *F*, ϣⲏⲃ⁺⁷ *SB*, -ϥ⁸ *S*, ϣⲉⲡ⁺⁹ *B* vb **I** intr (rare), *shave, clip*: Jer 30 10⁹ *B* κείρειν, *ib* 32 9 *B*⁵, *ib* 9 26 *S*⁸*B*⁷ περικ.; Mor 19 61 *S* ⲁϥϣ.² ⲛⲥⲁⲡϩⲱ of head (var *ib* 18 53 tr), Ryl 238 *S* church properties ⲥⲡⲁⲗⲓⲥ (*sc* ψάλις) ⲡϣ.², ShC 73 158 *S* ⲥⲛⲃⲉ ⲡϣ.², CO 459 *S* ⲥⲉ ⲡϣ.¹, ShA 2 157 *S* ϩⲣⲁⲩ ϣ.⁷. **II** tr: 2 Kg 14 26 *S*, Job 1 20 *S*²*B*³, Cant 6 5 *F*(*S* ϩⲱⲱⲕⲉ), Jer 7 29 *S*(ShA 2 318, *B* ⲃⲱϣ *l*?ϣⲱⲃ), 1 Cor 11 6 *B*(var ϩⲱⲕⲣ, *S* ϣⲃ ϫⲱ)ⲕ., R 1 5 13 *S* ⲙⲟⲣⲧ...ϣⲟⲃⲥ περικούροις χρῆσθαι, BMar 192 *S* ϣⲃ ⲡϣⲱ ⲡⲧⲉⲅⲁⲡⲉ ἀποκουρεύειν; Lev 10 6 *S*(*B* as Gk) ἀποκιδαροῦν (var -μαδαροῦν); *ib* 19 27 *S* gloss on ⲧⲁⲕⲟ (*B* ⲧⲁ.) φθείρειν; GPar 2 8 *S* ϣ.² ⲙⲡⲉϥϣⲱ ξυρίζειν; Ez 29 18 *S*(*B* diff) μαδᾶν depilari; K 162 *B* ϣⲉⲡ ⲙⲟⲣⲧ حلق as humiliation; ShC 73 113 *S* ϣ.² ⲙⲛⲭⲟⲕ ⲛⲧⲉϥⲁⲡⲉ, *ib* 158 *S* ϣⲃ ⲡⲕⲱⲧⲉ ⲡⲣⲱϥ, *ib* 123 *S* refl ⲡⲉⲧⲛⲁϣⲟⲃϥ, ShViK 9101 7 *S* cursed whoso shall ϣⲃ ⲟⲩϣⲏⲣⲉ ϣⲏⲙ, ROC 11 72 *B* tonsuring ϭⲓ ⲛⲟⲩⲯⲁⲗⲓⲥ ϭ.⁶ ⲙⲛⲓϧⲟⲓ of head in form of cross, ViK 4720 *S* after beating me he began ⲛϣ.¹

ⲧⲁⲁⲡⲉ ϣⲁⲡⲧⲉϥϫⲓ ⲧⲁⲉⲧⲧⲅⲏ (*cf* ? K above), Bor 304 51 *S* ϣ.² ⲛⲡⲉϥⲉⲓⲃ, RE 14 28 *S* ⲧⲥⲟⲩⲣⲉ ⲛϣ.¹...ϣ.¹ ⲡⲉⲓⲙⲟⲅⲥ ⲛⲧⲁⲩⲥⲱⲗⲡ, Aeg 252 *S* ⲡⲉⲧϣ.² ⲛⲡⲧⲟⲡ ⲛⲡⲉϣⲧⲏⲛ ⲉⲧⲉⲙⲯⲉⲗⲗⲓⲥⲧⲛⲥⲡⲉ = PO 8 598 من يشتري الحلصين *who buyeth garments from grave-diggers* (reading ϣⲱⲡ, HSt 118 2 om, *v* Riedel *Kirchenrechtsq* 207 n), Hall 96 *S* ⲁⲓϣⲟⲃϥ...ⲉϥϣ.⁷ (obscure, same?); ϣⲃ ⲭⲱ *SB*, *shave head*: Mic 1 16 *SB(A* ⲣⲟⲣⲟⲩⲕⲉ), Ac 18 18*B(S* ⲣⲱ.)*κ*.; Ez 44 20 *B* ξυρεῖν; *ib* 7 18 *B(S* do) φαλάκρωμα; Bodl Marsh 32 81 *B* rubric ϭⲉⲡ ⲭⲱϥ, Mich 550 44 *S* *day when* ⲁⲩϣⲉϥ ⲭⲱⲓ, PO 11 318 *B* ϣⲉⲡ ⲭⲱϥ ⲙⲡⲓⲁⲗⲟⲩ *& endued him with habit.*

—— nn: P 131⁴ 107 *S* *of Samson* ⲛϣ.¹ ⲙⲡⲉϥⲃⲱ. ⲭⲓⲛϭⲱⲃ *B*: Bess 14 327 ⲛⲭ. ⲙⲛⲓϭⲱⲓ (*l* as var ⲭⲓⲛⲑⲣⲉⲥϭ.).

ϣⲃⲁ *S* vb tr, *change*(?): P 44 96 *physician's drugs* ⲁⲩⲧⲣⲉϣ. ⲧⲉⲭⲣⲏⲥⲓⲥ ⲉⲧⲧⲏϣ (*l* ? علهم يعمون (يتغيّرون) الحميص. *Cf* ϣⲓⲃⲉ.

ϣⲃⲉ, ϣϥⲉ, *seventy* *v* ⲥⲁϣϥ.

ϣⲃⲉ, *persea* *v* ϣⲟⲩⲉ.

ϣⲃⲉ, -ⲏ *O* adj(?), *majestic*: DM 29 6 gloss ϣⲃⲉ ϣⲃⲏ. *V* AZ 38 88 & *cf* ϣⲁϥ *O*.

ϣⲉⲃⲉ, -ϭⲉ *v* ϣⲁϥⲉ, *swell* & ϣⲏⲃⲉ (ϣⲏⲃⲉ).

ϣⲏⲃⲉ *S*, ϣⲓ. *SA*, ϣⲏⲓⲃⲓ *B*, ϣⲓⲃⲓ *F* nn m, *rust*, *verdigris* (*cf* ܕܚܠܐ Dévaud): EpJer 11 *BF*, Ez 24 6 *S* ϣⲏ. & ϣⲓ. (*B* ⲭⲉⲃϭ), *ib* 11 *S(B* ⲭⲣⲉⲙⲧⲥ), Ja 5 3 *S* ϣⲓ.(*BAp* 171)*AB*, C 89 171 *B* *silver* ⲡⲟⲩϣ. ἰός; P 44 87 *S* ϣⲏⲛ. الصد, K 257 *B* 'الصد; Bor 253 151 *S* ⲟⲩϣⲓ. ⲣⲙⲡⲟⲙⲛⲧ οὐλὴ χλωρά; ShIF 271 *S* ⲡϣⲏⲛ. ⲙⲡⲣⲁⲧ. ShMIF 23 196 ⲛⲧⲡⲣⲱⲕⲉ ⲙⲡϣⲏ., ShR 2 3 66 *S* ⲁⲡϣⲏⲛ. ⲧⲁⲕⲟ ⲙⲡⲉⲕⲡⲟⲩⲃ, R 2 1 67 *S* *iron* ⲕⲱ ⲡⲉϣⲱ ⲙⲡⲉϥϣⲓ. ⲣⲓⲧⲛⲧⲁⲕⲟⲡⲏ, Mor 55 21 *S* *silver in fire* ⲛⲡϣⲓ. ⲧⲏⲣⲟⲩ ⲁⲡⲁⲭⲱⲣⲉⲓ ⲛⲁⲩ, P 129¹⁴ 86 *S* ⲛϣⲓ. ⲛⲥⲁⲃⲉⲗⲓⲟⲥ (var ? R 1 5 18 ⲙⲛⲧⲙⲁⲓϣ.), *but prob for* ἰός *poison*); ⲣ ϣ., *become, be rusted*: Si 29 13 *S* ϣⲏⲛ. ἰοῦσθαι, Ja 1 *c* *SA*(*prob*)*B* ⲕⲁⲧⲓ.; ShA 2 112 *S* ⲣⲛⲁⲁⲩ ⲛⲧⲁⲩⲣ ϣ., *here belongs* ? Bodl(P) a 1 *e* *S* *recipe* ⲓ̄ ⲡⲕⲟϭ ⲡⲣⲉⲗⲙⲛ ⲉⲓⲟ ⲛϣⲓ. (var *ib* 3 44 ϣⲉⲓⲃⲉ); *as vb*: GuDor 5 *S* *coins* ⲙⲡⲟⲩϣⲓ. ⲉⲡⲧⲏⲣϥ.

ϣⲃⲉ *SB*, ϣϥⲉ, ϣⲉⲃⲉ *S* nn, *off-scouring, filth*: 1 Cor 4 13 *SB* ⲣ ϣ. περίψημα γίνεσθαι, cit P 44 77 ϣϥⲉ موسوجين, *ib* 15, K 295 مكنوسين, Va 75 60 موكوسين; Phil 3 8 *S* var ⲣⲉⲛⲗⲁⲁⲩ ⲛϣⲉ. (*B* ⲗⲉⲃϣ) σκύβαλον.

ϣⲏⲃⲉ, *scale* *v* ϣⲛϥⲉ.

ϣⲓⲃⲉ *SAA²*, -ⲃⲓ *F*, ϣⲃ-*SA²*, ϣ(ⲉ)ⲃⲧ-, ϣⲉϥⲧ-*S*, ϣⲃⲧⲥ *SA*, ϣⲉⲃⲧⲥ, -ϥⲧⲥ, ϣⲟ(ⲟ)ⲃⲉ†, -ϭⲉ *S*, ϣⲁⲃⲉ† *A*, ϣⲁⲃⲓ† *F*, ⲣ ⲥ ϣⲁⲃⲉ-, ϣⲁϥⲉ-*S*, ϣⲁⲃⲓ-*AA²*, ϣⲉⲃⲓ-*B* (once) vb **I** intr, *change, be changed*: Ps 72 21 (*B*

ϣⲱⲃⲧ), Mal 3 6 *A(B* ϣⲓⲃϯ) ἀλλοιοῦν, Ps 101 26(*B* do), 1 Cor 15 51 (*B* ϣⲱ.), He 1 12 *SF(B* ϣⲓ.) ἀλλάσσειν; Lev 13 3(*B* ⲟⲩⲱⲧⲉⲃ)μεταβάλλειν; Deu 17 17(*B* ⲣⲓⲕⲓ)μεθιστάναι; BHom 93 τρέπειν, Eccl 12 6 ἀνατ.; BG 85 ⲙⲉϥϣ., PSBA 10 197 ⲁϥϣ. ⲛϭⲓ ⲡⲉⲥⲁⲩⲁⲡ, Mani 1 *A²* ϣⲁⲩⲡⲱⲡⲉ ⲛⲥⲉϣ.; qual, *changed* (often pejorat): Ge 45 22 (ShIF 140, *B* ⲥⲟⲧⲛ) ἀλλάσ., Sa 2 15(*B* ⲫⲱⲛⲣ)ⲉϫⲁⲗ., *ib* 15 4 διαλ.; Ro 12 6 *SF(B* ϣⲉⲃⲓⲏⲟⲩⲧ) cit Aeg 269 ϣⲟⲟ. διάφορος; Mk 1 34 (*B* ⲟⲩⲙⲏϣ ⲡⲣⲏϯ), C 99 234(*B* *ib* 89 68 ϣⲉⲃ.) ποικίλος; Sa 18 10 ἀσύμφωνος; *ib* 19 5 ξένος; Mic 4 8 *S*(ShP 130⁵ 43) *A* (*B* ⲣⲗⲟⲗ) αὐχμώδης; PS 241 κρίσις ⲉⲧⲡⲁϣⲧ, ⲕⲱⲣⲧ ⲉϣ., ShViK 9345 16 *sick to eat in place appointed* ⲕⲁⲛ ⲟⲩⲣⲙⲟⲩⲡⲉ ⲉϥϣ., BMis 147 *in world is* ⲟⲩⲁⲧⲱⲛ ⲉϥϣ., R 1 5 37 *sacrifice lest thou die* ⲣⲛⲟⲩⲙⲟⲩ ⲉϥϣ., Mor 22 120 *devil took* ⲟⲩⲙⲟⲣ-ⲫⲏ ⲉⲥϣ. *& terrible* = BSM 110 *B* ϣⲉⲃ., Bor 254 181 *fair faces opp* ⲣⲟ ⲉⲧϣ., J 85 11 ⲛⲟϭ ⲡϣⲱⲡⲉ ⲉϥϣ.

II tr : Ps 33 tit (*B* ϣⲱ.), Cl 6 3 *A* ἀλλοι., Ge 31 7 (*B* do) Is 24 5(*B* ϣⲓ.)ἀλλάσ., Job 5 12(*B* ⲫⲱ.)διαλλάσ.; Mk 9 2 *F*(*SB* refl) μεταμορφοῦσθαι; Aeg 287 *daring to* ϣ. ⲡⲧⲉⲭⲓⲣⲟⲭⲟⲛⲓⲁ παρακινεῖν; PS 140 ⲙⲡⲟⲩϣ. ⲙⲡⲉⲩⲣⲟ, R 2 4 81 ⲙⲁ]ⲣⲉⲥϣ. ⲛⲡⲉⲥϭⲟⲓⲧⲉ, Bor 304 51 ⲁⲩϣⲃⲧ ⲡⲉϥϭⲟⲓⲧⲉ (Ge 37 23), Bodl(P) a 1 *b* *recipe* ⲉⲕϣ. ⲛⲡⲥⲟⲧ (var *ib* a 3 25 ϣⲓϭⲧⲉ), ViK 4721 ⲛⲧⲱϣⲧ ⲧⲉⲓⲉⲣⲉ ⲛⲁⲩ ⲡⲛϯ ⲕⲉⲥ ⲅⲉⲓ, Ep 400 *give him the* tremis ⲛϣⲃⲧϥ ⲛⲁⲡ; refl : Lev 27 27 (*B* ϣⲓ. intr) ἀλλάσ.; Mt 17 2 (*B* ϣⲱ.) μεταμ., 3 Kg 22 30 συγκαλύπτειν; El 90 *A* ϥⲛⲁϣⲃⲧϥ *before them.*

With following preposition.   ⲉ ⲉ-, *SAA²*, *to* : Pro 4 15 *SA*(*B* ϣⲱ.) παραλλάσ.; Sa 16 25 μεταλλεύειν εἰς; Job 15 5 (*B* = Gk) διακρίνειν acc, Ja 2 4 ϣⲃⲧ- (var ϣⲓⲃ, *B* ⲭⲁ ⲟⲩϣⲓ.), cit ShP 130² 63 ϣⲃ- διακ. ἐν; ShC 73 149 ⲛⲡⲉϥϣ. ⲁⲡ ⲙⲙⲟϥ ⲉⲡⲉⲥⲡⲏⲩ *prefer self to*, ShP 130² 62 *accursed whoso* ϣ. ⲛⲣⲉⲛⲕⲁⲧⲁⲥⲁⲣⲝ ⲉⲣⲉⲛϣⲙⲙⲟ, Sh(Besa)Bor 206 574 ϣ. ⲛⲧⲉⲛⲫⲩⲥⲓⲥ ⲉⲩⲡⲁⲣⲁⲧⲉⲛⲫⲩⲥⲓⲥ, Mus 40 274 ⲙⲏ ⲁⲓϣⲉⲃⲧⲕ ⲗⲁⲁⲩ ⲉⲣⲟⲓ (paral BAp 166 ϣⲁⲁⲧⲕ ⲡⲗⲁⲁⲩ), Mani 1 *A²* ⲧⲥⲟⲫⲓⲁ...ⲥϣⲃ ⲥⲭⲏⲙⲁ ⲁⲣⲟ; qual : Pro 20 2 *SA*, 1 Cor 15 41 (*B* ⲟⲩⲱϯ, *F* ⲟⲩⲱⲧⲉⲃ) διαφ. gen, He 1 4 (*B* ⲟⲩⲟⲡ ϣⲓ. ⲉⲣⲟⲧ ⲉ-, *F* do) δ. παρά; PS 317 ⲉⲣⲉⲣⲟ ϣ. ⲉⲡⲉⲩⲉⲣⲏⲩ (*cf* 320 sim ϣⲃⲃⲓ-ⲉⲓⲧ), BHom 10 *things that* ϣ. ⲁⲡ ⲉⲣⲉⲡⲣⲁⲥⲟⲩ, Bor 239 75 ⲉⲕϣ. ⲉⲣⲟⲟⲩ ⲣⲛⲟⲩ ? (var Lammayer 42 ϣⲉⲃ-ⲃⲓⲏⲩ ⲙⲙⲟⲥ);   ⲉ ⲛ-, *as to* : 1 Kg 28 8 ϣⲉⲃⲧϥ ⲛⲥⲙⲟⲧ συγκαλύπτειν, Mor 32 11 sim ϣⲉϥⲧϥ ⲛⲥ. (var P 129¹⁶ 57 ⲣⲙⲡⲉⲥϭ.), *ib* 23 79 *Christ* ϣⲉⲃⲧϥ ⲙ-ⲡⲉⲥⲙⲟⲧ ⲛⲟⲩⲣⲉⲓⲃ, R 1 4 66 *cannot* ϣ. ⲙⲙⲟϥ ⲛⲧⲉϥⲧⲁⲝⲓⲥ; *for*: Ex 34 20 ϣⲁϥⲧⲥ(*B* ⲥⲱϯ ⲥⲁ-) λυτροῦν dat;   ⲉ ⲣⲛ-*SA*, *into* : Ps 105 20 (*B* ϣⲓ.) ἀλλάσ. ἐν, Ro 1 25 (*B* do)μεταλ. ἐν; EstD 7 μεταβάλλειν ἐν; Sa 16 21 μετακρίνεσθαι dat; Z 305 *devil* ϣⲃⲧϥ ⲣⲛ-ⲟⲩⲥⲭⲏⲙⲁ ⲛⲁⲅⲅⲉⲗⲟⲥ μετασχηματίζειν (*cf* 2 Cor 11

14 ϫⲓ ϧⲣⲏ̄); Zech 12 10 *A*(*B* Gk diff); ShBM 203 88 ⲙⲡⲟⲩϣ. ϧⲛⲧⲉϥⲙⲁⲡⲓⲁ, ShA 2 108 ϣ. ⲛⲧⲁⲗⲉ... ϧⲁⲡⲥⲟⲗ, ShWess 9 130 ϧⲉⲧⲉⲣⲟⲩⲥⲓⲟⲥ ⲡⲉⲧϣ.† ϧⲛⲧⲉϥⲟⲩⲥⲓⲁ, J 75 49 ⲛⲧⲡϣ. ϧⲁⲙⲡⲉⲓⲱⲛϧ *from out*, *ib* 61 sim ⲉⲃⲟⲗ ϧⲛ-; c ϧⲓⲧⲛ-, *through*: BMis 217 bodies ϣ. ϧ. ⲡⲱϭⲃ of pit = Mor 16 71.

p c, *changing*, so *strange*, *fearful*: ShC 73 200 *S* air ⲙⲉϧ ⲡϣ.ϧⲟ, BMis 70 *S* ⲡⲉϣ.ϧⲟ = FR 38 *S* ϧⲟ ⲉⲧϣ.†, Mor 41 164 *S* ϫⲉⲕⲁⲡⲟⲥ ⲡϣⲁϥⲉϧⲟ, TillOster 16 *A* ⲡϣ.ϧⲟ ⲡⲁⲕⲱⲧⲉ ⲁⲣⲱⲧⲛⲉ (*cf* BAp 155), Mani 1 *A*[2] ⲧⲣⲉⲓⲧⲉ ⲡⲡⲓϣ.ϧⲟ, DeV 1 104 *B* demons ϧⲁⲛϣ. ϧⲟⲡⲉ, CO 469 *S* hyena ⲟⲩϣ.ⲫⲉⲥⲛⲥ (φύσις).

—— nn m *SF*, *change*, *difference*: Sa 7 18 ἀλλαγή, Z 332 ⲁⲡⲉⲓϣ....ϣⲱⲡⲉ ⲡⲁϥ ⲕⲁⲧⲁⲗ., Ja 1 17 (*B* ϣⲓⲃϯ) παραλ., Lam 5 4 *F*(*B* ϣⲉⲃⲓⲱ) ἄλλαγμα, Ps 76 10 (*B* ϣⲓ.) ἀλλοίωσις; Sa 7 20, C 99 92 when he saw ⲡϣ. ⲙⲡⲉⲡⲣⲏϣ *superiority* διαφορά; 4 Kg 3 7 (BP 10623) ⲙⲡ ϣ. ὅμοιος; ShRE 10 161 beasts ϧⲁⲙⲡⲉⲧϣ., ShA 1 393 ⲙⲙⲛ ϣ. ⲙⲡⲣⲙⲛⲡⲉ̄ ⲙⲛⲡⲁⲧⲡⲉ̄, BG 97 ⲡϣ. ⲡⲟⲩⲉⲓⲱⲧ ⲉⲩϣⲏⲣⲉ, C 99 21 *despicable* ⲛⲁϧⲣⲛⲣⲱⲙⲉϣ. ⲡⲡⲉⲧⲙⲙⲁⲩ, P 132[1] 18 ⲟⲩⲛ ϣ. ⲡⲧⲉⲛⲯⲩⲭⲏ ⲙⲛⲧⲱⲕ, Miss 4 603 ⲙⲛ ϣ. ⲟⲩⲧⲱϥ ⲙⲛ-, P 129[12] 16 *beguile-* ment of ⲡϣ. ⲡⲛⲉⲩⲃⲁⲗ ⲉⲑⲟⲟⲩ ⲙⲛⲡⲉⲓⲱ ⲙⲡⲉϧⲟ.

ⲙⲁⲓϣ. in ⲙⲡⲧⲙ., *loving change*: Si 42 5 διάφορος (*cf* 27 1 ϣⲃϯ); *ib* 41 21 (19) σκορακισμός.

ⲁⲧϣ., *unchanging*, *unaltered*: P 44 48 ⲁ.·ἄτρεπ-τος; Br 259 ⲡⲁ. ⲙⲁⲅⲁⲁϥ, P 131[5] 52 *of risen body* ⲟⲩⲥⲁⲣⲝ ⲡⲁ., J 106 26 ⲗⲟⲅⲓⲥⲙⲟⲛ (*l* -ⲟⲥ) ⲡⲁ. (*cf* ἀμε-τάτρεπτος); ⲙⲡⲧⲁⲧϣ.: Bor 295 ⲧⲙ. ⲡⲧⲟⲩⲥⲓⲁ, P 129[20] 133 *took flesh* ϧⲛⲟⲩⲙ.

ⲣⲉϥϣ., *who changes*: R 1 4 67 water, fire ϧⲉⲛⲣ. (var P 129[16] 81 ⲣⲉϥⲥⲓⲛⲉ) φθαρτός.

ϭⲓⲛϣ., *act of changing*: PS 325 ⲧϭ. ⲡⲧⲉⲯⲩⲭⲏ *migration*, LDi 270 ⲧϭ. ⲡⲡⲉϥⲱⲥⲧⲏⲣ, Br 255 ⲧⲉϥⲧⲟ ⲡϭ. (*cf* CABaynes *Gnostic Treatise* 159).

ϣⲟⲃⲓ *B* nn m, *changed, disguised person, hypocrite*: Mt 7 5 (*S* = Gk), Va 58 179 who in theatre playeth & deceiveth is called ϣ. ⲭⲉⲙϣⲁϥϯ ⲡⲟⲩϧⲟ ⲡϣⲉⲙⲙⲟ ϧⲓⲱⲧϥ ὑποκριτής; as adj: Job 34 30 ὑπ.; ⲉⲣ ϣ.: AM 84 ⲡⲏ ⲉⲧⲟⲓ ⲡϣ.; ⲙⲉⲧϣ., *hypocrisy*: Gal 2 13 (*S* = Gk) ὑπόκρισις; Va 58 70 enticed all ϧⲓ-ⲧⲉⲡⲧⲉϥⲙ., BSM 22 is there ⲙ. ϫⲁⲧⲉⲛϥϯ? = BMis 360 *S* ϫⲓ ϧⲟ; ⲁⲧⲙ.: 2 Cor 6 6 (*S* ⲁⲭⲛϧⲩⲡⲟⲕⲣⲓⲛⲉ) ἀνυπόκριτος.

ϣⲃⲧⲥ *S* nn, *change*: GFr 309 ⲧⲡⲓⲥⲧⲓⲥ ⲉⲭⲛϣ.

(ϣⲉⲃⲓⲟ) *S*, ϣⲓⲃⲓⲱ *S*[a] (once), ϣⲉⲃⲓⲱ *B* (once), ϣⲉⲃ-ⲓⲉ-, -ⲓⲏⲧ✠, ϣⲃⲃⲓⲱⲥ *B*, ϣⲉⲃⲓⲏⲧ†[1], ϣⲃⲃ.†[2], ϣⲃⲉⲓⲁ-ⲉⲓⲧ†[3], ϣⲃⲃⲓⲁⲉⲓⲧ†[4] *S*, ϣⲃⲓⲁⲓⲧ†*A*[2], ϣⲉⲃⲓⲟⲩⲧ† *BF* vb tr, *change* (*cf* ϣⲓⲃⲉ) mostly *B*: Dan 3 95 ϣⲉⲃⲓⲏⲧϥ (var -ⲟⲩⲧϥ) ἀλλοιοῦν, Lev 27 10 ϣⲉⲃⲓⲉ-(*S* ϣⲓⲃⲉ), Ro 1 23 ϣⲉⲃⲓⲉ-(*S* do)ἀλλάσσειν; Jer 28 24 ϯⲡⲁϣⲉⲃⲓⲱ ⲡ- ἀνταποδιδόναι; MG 25 245 ⲡⲧⲟⲩϣⲉⲃⲓⲏⲧⲟⲩ ϫⲉⲛ-ⲟⲩⲙⲛϣ ⲡⲫⲁⲡⲧⲁⲥⲓⲁ, AZ 40 63 ⲫϯ ϣⲃⲃⲓⲱⲟⲩϥ, Br

141 *S*[a] ϣⲁϥϣ. [ⲙⲙ]ⲟⲣⲫⲏ ⲡⲓⲙ; ϣⲉⲃⲓⲉ- + nn *B*: 2 Cor 6 13 ⲡⲁⲓϣ. ⲃⲉⲭⲉ (*S* ϯ ϣⲉⲃⲓⲱ ⲙⲡⲃ.) ἀντιμι-σθία, He 2 2 sim (*SF* ⲃ.) μισθαποδοσία; qual: Ro 12 6 *B*(*SF* ϣⲟⲃⲉ) διάφορος; C 89 68 *B* = *ib* 99 234 *S* do ποικίλος; P 54 161 *B* ⲡⲟⲩϧⲟ ϣⲓⲃⲛⲟⲩⲧ ⲓ̄ⲗ̄ⲙ; ⲓ̄ⲗ̄ⲙ; PS 249 *S* ϧⲉⲛⲣⲱⲙⲁ ⲉⲩϣ.[3], *ib* 318 *S* ⲉⲧϣ.[4], ViK 9511 *S* ⲉⲩϣ.[1], Aeg 260 *S* ⲉⲩϣ.[2], Mani 2 *A*[2] ⲕⲉ-ϧⲱⲃ ⲉϥϣ., C 43 122 *B* tortures ⲉⲩϣ., Mor 24 10 *F* demons ⲉⲩϣ., FR 96 *B* sim ⲡⲟⲩϧⲟ ϣ. ⲉⲙⲁϣⲱ; c ⲉ-, *different from*: LCyp 7 *S* ⲉϥϣ.[1] ⲉⲣⲟϥ, Va 57 164 *B* ⲡⲉⲥϣ. ⲁⲛ ⲉⲟⲩϫⲓⲙⲁⲣⲟⲥ διαφέρειν; C 89 182 *B* ⲁⲛⲡϣ. ⲉⲟⲩ ⲉⲡⲛ?, AM 56 *B* ⲡⲟⲩϧⲟ...ϣ. ⲉⲡⲟⲩⲉϧⲛⲟⲩ, ViK 9616 *S* ⲉⲩϣ.[2] ⲉⲡⲉⲩⲉⲅⲉⲣⲏⲩ; c ϧⲛ-, ϫⲉⲛ-: Blake 254 *S* ⲡϭⲁⲕⲓⲡⲟⲟⲥ ⲉϥϣⲉⲃⲓⲏⲟⲩ(sic prob)ϧⲙ-ⲡⲉϥⲉⲓⲡⲉ διάφ.; DeV 2 256 *B* terrible δύναμις ⲉⲥϣ. ϫⲉⲛⲡⲉⲥⲥⲙⲟⲧ.

ϣⲃ(ⲉ)ⲓⲱ[1], ϣⲉⲃⲃⲓⲱ[2], -ⲓⲟ[3] (twice), ϣⲉⲃⲓⲱ[4], ϣⲉⲃⲃ.[5], ϣⲉϥⲓⲱ[6] *S*, ϣⲃⲃⲓⲟⲩ *A*, ϣⲃⲓⲱ *A*[2], ϣⲉⲃⲓⲱ *BF* nn f, *change, exchange, requital*: Lev 27 10 *S*[2]*B*, Deu 23 18 *B*(*S* ⲁⲥⲟⲩ) ἄλλαγμα, Ps 88 51 *S*[1](var[2])*B*, Si 6 15 *S*[2], *ib* 26 14 *S*[1], Jer 15 13 *S*[5]*B*, Mk 8 37 *S*[1](var[6])*BF* ἀντάλ.; Ge 30 2 *B*(*S* om), Ps 44 17 *B*(*S* ⲉⲡⲙⲁ), Hab 3 7 *B*(*SA* do), Mk 10 45 *B*(*S* ϧⲁ-) ἀντί, Deu 28 62 *B* ⲡⲧϣ. ⲭⲉ-(*S* ⲭⲉ- only) ἀνθ' ὧν; Lu 6 34 (*S* ⲕⲱⲃ), Miss 8 76 *S* ⲉϧⲣⲁⲓ ⲛⲧϣ.[2] ⲡⲡⲉⲓⲥϧⲁⲓ ἴσος; ShC 42 66 *S* ⲧϣ.[1](var[2])ⲡⲡⲉⲛⲧⲁⲕⲧⲁⲁⲩ, *ib* 133 *S* ⲟⲩⲙⲟⲥⲧⲉ ⲡϣ.[2] ⲉⲡⲙⲁ ⲙⲡⲉϥⲙⲉ (*cf* Ps 108 5), ShA 2 334 *S* ⲛⲧⲁⲡ-ϣⲉϣ ⲧⲉⲩϣ.[1] ⲡⲕⲁϧ ⲉϫⲱⲛ *like amount* (on Zech 9 7), Mani H 83 *A*[2] ⲁϥϭⲓⲛⲉ ⲡⲧϣ. ⲙⲡϥϭⲣⲓⲥⲉ, Mani 2 *A*[2] ⲉⲓⲣⲉ ⲡⲉⲩ ⲕⲁⲧⲁ ⲧⲟⲩϣ., Gu 100 *S* to Peter ⲕⲟⲩⲉϣ ⲧϣ.[2] ⲡⲡⲭⲓⲛⲡⲟⲩⲱϧⲉ?, BSM 46 *B* ⲡⲓⲧⲉⲣⲙⲛⲥ ⲡⲧϣ. ⲙ-ⲡⲓⲉⲥⲟⲟⲩ = BMis 394 *S* ⲉⲡⲙⲁ ⲛ-.

ⲉⲓⲣⲉ, ⲣ ϣ. *SB*, *be instead, replace*: ClPr 54 43 *S* ⲧⲣⲉϥⲣⲏⲏⲓ ⲣ ϣ.[1] ⲙⲡⲛϣⲱⲡⲧ διαδέχεσθαι; Is 9 5 *S*[1](*B* ⲧⲱⲃⲓ) καταλλαγή; EW 174 *B* man crucified ⲉⲧⲁϥⲉⲣ ⲧⲉϥϣ.

ϯ ϣ. *AA*[2]*B*, *give the like, requite*: Deu 5 9 (*S* ⲧⲱ-ⲱⲃⲉ), Ps 75 12 (*S* ϯ), Lam 3 65 (*F* ϯ ⲟⲩⲃⲉ) ἀποδιδό-ναι, Lev 18 25 (*S* ⲧⲱ.), Ro 11 35 (*SF* ⲧⲟⲩⲉⲓⲟ) ἀντα-ποδ., Ez 4 15 (*S* ⲉⲡⲙⲁ) διδ. ἀντί, Pro 12 14 *A*(*S* do, *B* nn) ἀνταπόδομα διδ.; Is 43 3 (*S* ⲉⲡⲙⲁ) ἄλλαγμα ποιεῖν ὑπέρ; 1 Kg 24 20(*S* ⲧⲱ.)ἀνταποτίνειν; Cat 156 ⲉⲩϯ. ⲡⲡⲟⲩⲉⲅⲉⲣⲟⲩ ϫⲉⲛⲡⲓⲁⲣⲓⲥⲧⲟⲛ, C 43 244 ϯⲡⲁϯ. ⲡⲁⲕ ⲁⲡ, Mani H 14 *A*[2] ⲁⲡⲕⲟⲥⲙⲟⲥ ϯ. ⲡⲉϥ; ϯ ⲡϣ. *S*: Si 46 18 (12)[1] ἀντικαταλλάσσεσθαι; J 100 36 ⲧⲁⲁϥ ⲡⲁϥ ⲡϣ.[2], *ib* 89 22[3] sim; as nn m *B*: Ps 54 20 (*S* ϣ.[2]) ἀντάλλαγμα; Is 34 8(*S* ⲧⲱ., *F* ϧⲉⲡ)ἀνταπόδοσις; *ib* 1 23 (*S* ⲧⲟⲩⲉⲓⲟ) ἀνταπόδομα; Ps 118 112 (*S* ⲧⲱ.) ἀντάμειψις; Va 57 69 ϭⲓ ⲡⲡⲓϯ. for our crimes; ⲁⲧϯ ϣ. *B* in ⲙⲉⲧⲁⲧ.: MG 25 139; ϫⲓⲡϯ ϣ. *B*: Ps 54 21 (*S* ⲧⲟⲩ.) ἀποδιδόναι.

ϫⲓ, ϭⲓ ϣ., ⲧϣ. *SA*[2]*BF*, *take requital, be repaid*: Col 3 24 *B*(*S* ⲧⲟⲩ.) ἀνταπόδοσις; BM 182 2 *S* ⲁⲛϫⲓ

πⲧϣ.² ⲛⲧⲉⲓⲟⲣϫⲟⲡⲏ ἀντιλαμβάνειν, Jo 1 16 B(S ⲉⲡⲙⲁ)ἀντί; Va 61 15 B ⲛⲧⲁⲥⲓ ϣ. ⲕⲁⲧⲁ ⲛⲁⲡⲟⲃⲓ, ManiH
9 A² ⲛⲁϫⲓ ⲧⲟⲩϣ., AZ 23 38 F ϭⲓ ϫⲉⲃⲓⲱ ⲛ(ⲡ)ⲉⲧⲛⲁ-
ⲛⲟⲩϥ; as nn: Ps 18 12 B(S ⲧⲟⲩ.)ἀνταπόδ.

V ϣⲱⲃⲧ, ϣⲓⲃϯ, ϣⲉⲃϣⲓ, ϣⲃⲁ.

ϣⲓⲃⲉ S, ϣⲓⲛⲓⲃⲓ B, ϣⲓⲃⲓ F, rust ν ϣⲛⲃⲉ.

ϣⲟⲃⲓ B ν ϣⲟⲟⲩⲉ.

ϣⲟⲃⲓ B nn ν ϣⲓⲃⲉ.

ϣⲱⲃⲉ, ϣⲱⲱⲃⲉ ν ϣⲱⲡⲉ gourd.

ϣⲃⲉ B ν ϣⲟⲩⲉ.

ϣⲃⲱ ν ϣϥⲱ tale & measure.

ϣⲃⲓⲃ ν ϣⲟⲩⲉ.

ϣⲃⲱⲃⲓ B ν ϣⲟⲩⲱⲃⲉ.

ϣⲃⲏⲗ F ν ϣⲃⲏⲣ.

ϣⲃⲓⲛ B nn, grain: K 192 ϣ., ⲭⲣⲟⲝ, ⲛⲁⲫⲣⲓ حبوب,
C 41 13 ⲟⲩϣ. ⲉⲧϩⲟⲣⲡ = Miss 4 314 'ﺣ; HL 102
loading ships with ϣ. ⲛⲉⲙⲱⲓⲕ. Cf? ϣⲃⲱⲛ.

ϣⲃⲓⲛ(sic MS)B nn, part of sheep's intestine (?):
MG 25 152 ruminated food ⲉⲣ ⲛⲟⲫⲣⲓ ⲛⲡⲉϣ. ⲛⲉⲙ
ⲛⲉϥⲥⲁϩⲟⲩⲡ ⲧⲏⲣϥ. Or ? = last, grain already
swallowed.

ϣⲃⲱⲛ SA², kind of herb or cereal (?): ShP 130¹
157 S ϩⲉⲛⲥⲓⲙ, ϩⲉⲛϣ. ⲕⲁⲧⲁ ⲥⲙⲟⲧ ⲛⲓⲙ, Mani K 14
A² Parmoute ϣⲁⲣⲉϣ. ⲡⲱϩ ⲡⲣⲏⲧϥ. Cf? ϣⲃⲓⲛ (1°).

ϣⲃⲏⲛⲉ, ϣⲉⲃ. ν ⲃⲏⲡⲉ sf, adding BM 585 F δ̄
ⲛϭⲁⲙⲟⲩⲗ ⲛϣⲃⲏⲡⲓ, ib ϣⲃⲏⲡⲓ.

ϣⲃⲏⲣ SA², ϣⲫⲏⲣ S, ϣⲃⲏⲣ A, ϣⲫⲏⲣ B, ϣⲃⲏⲗ
F, ϣⲃⲏⲣ-SA², f ϣⲃⲉⲉⲣⲉ S, ϣⲫⲉⲣⲓ B, ϣⲃⲏⲛⲗⲓ F, pl
ϣⲃⲉⲉⲣ SA², -ⲣⲉ S, ϣⲃⲉⲣⲉ A², ϩⲃⲉⲉⲣⲉ A, & sg as pl,
friend, comrade (חבר IgR): Ex 33 11 S (Aeg 288)
B, Pro 3 29 SAB, Jo 3 29 SBF, ib 19 12 SA²B, Ja 2
23 SA(Cl)B φίλος, Mor 18 195 S ⲛⲟϭ ⲛϣ. μόνος
φ.; Job 30 29 SB, Mt 20 13 SB ἑταῖρος; Is 5 8 B
(S ϩⲓⲧⲟⲩⲱϩ, F ⲁⲗⲛⲟⲩ), Ro 15 2 B(S do)πλησίον;
Eccl 4 10 S, Hos 4 17 B(A diff)μέτοχος; Ro 13 8 B
(S ϩ.), Gal 6 4 B (S ⲕⲉⲟⲩⲁ) ἕτερος; Ap 1 9 B(S ϣ.
ⲕⲟⲓⲛⲱⲛⲟⲥ)συγκοινωνός; Pcod 15 S ⲛⲉϣ. ⲙⲡⲉⲭⲥ̄,
El 88 A ⲛⲧⲣⲉ ⲡⲟⲩϩ. ⲙⲡⲟⲩϩ., BMis 168 S ⲟⲩϣ. ⲛ-
ⲧⲁϥ=BSM 77 B ⲣⲱⲙⲓ ⲛϣ. ⲛⲧⲁϥ, C 43 166 B ⲛⲉ-
ⲧⲉⲛϣ.; f: Cant 4 7 S(F ⲁⲗ.), Ep Jer 43 BF πλ.;
BG 94 S ⲧⲉϣ. ⲧⲥⲟⲫⲓⲁ, ViK 9126 S ⲧⲉϣ. ⲛⲙⲁⲣ-
ⲧⲩⲣⲟⲥ, DeV 1 176 B ϯⲙⲉⲧⲁⲡⲟⲓⲁ ϯϣ. ⲛⲧⲉ ⲫϯ, Cai
The 170 B ⲧⲁϣ., FR 126 B ⲡⲉⲥⲕⲉϣ....ⲉⲧⲉⲛⲉⲥⲡⲣⲁ-
ⲝⲓⲥ, BMOr 7024 (4) S ⲧⲉϣⲃⲏⲣⲉ; pl: Job 19 21
S, Mic 7 5 S(var -ⲣⲉ)A, Jo 15 13 SA² φ.; Mt 11 16
S ἑταῖ.; Lu 5 7 S μέτ.; HSt 469 S(var ϣⲃⲏⲣ)ὁμό-
φυλος; AP 23 A², Mani H 75 A² ϣⲃⲉⲣⲉ, PS 212 S

ⲛⲁϣ., ShA 1 158 S ϩⲉⲛϣ., ShMIF 23 93 S ⲛϣⲃⲣ...
ⲛⲉϥϣⲃⲉⲉⲣⲉ; as f: Jud 11 37 S συνεταιρίς; R 1 5 32
S ⲡⲉⲥϣ. ⲙⲡⲁⲣⲑⲉⲛⲟⲥ.

ϣⲃⲣ-SA², ϣⲃⲏⲣ-S, ϣ. ⲛ-, ⲡⲧⲉ BF, companion in,
often = σνν + nn, as: Ru 1 15 S -ϣⲉⲗⲉⲉⲧ, Si 9 21 S
-ⲟⲅⲱⲙ, Is 19 11 B-ⲥⲟϭⲛⲓ, Dan 1 10 B-ⲙⲁⲓⲏ, Jo 11
16 SA²B-ⲙⲁⲑⲏⲧⲏⲥ, Ac 13 1 B-ϣⲁⲡϣ, Ro 6 5 SB
-ⲧⲱϭⲉ, 1 Cor 3 9 SBF-ⲣⲱⲃ, -ⲣⲉϥⲉⲣ ϩ.; or=φίλος:
Mt 11 19 SB, ὁμο-: Ac 18 3 B; PS 135 S ϣ.
ⲟⲅⲟⲓⲛ, BG 36 S ϣ.ⲥⲱⲡⲉ, BHom 64 S ϣ.ⲣ ϩⲱⲃ ⲙⲛⲡⲏ, Mor 40 37 S ϣ.ⲣⲉϥϣⲁϫⲉ ⲙⲛⲡⲏ, Mani 2 A²
ϣ.ⲁⲣⲭⲱⲛ, Va 61 210 B ⲟⲩϣ. ⲛⲟⲩϭⲱⲙ ⲛⲉⲙⲁⲕ,
LAp 520 F ϣ.ⲉⲙⲉ[ⲗⲟⲥ] = ib S ϣⲃⲏⲣ ⲙ., ϣ.ⲙⲙⲟ-
ϣⲓ B ν ⲙⲟⲟϣⲉ sf.

ⲙⲛⲧ-, ⲙⲉⲧϣ. SAB, friendship, community: Pro 7
18 SA(B ⲙⲉⲓ), Sa 8 18 S φιλία, ib 3 ⲙ. ϣⲁⲡⲡⲉ συμ-
βίωσις gen; Ac 2 42 B(S = Gk), Phil 1 5 B(SF do)
κοινωνία, Ac 2 44 B ϫⲉⲛⲟⲅⲙ. (S ϩⲓⲟⲩⲥⲟⲡ) κοινός;
ShP 130¹ 140 S hasting to NN ϩⲛⲟⲩⲟⲅⲱϣ. ⲙⲛⲟⲩⲟⲅⲱϣ
ⲛⲥⲁⲣⲕⲓⲕⲟⲛ, Wess 18 101 S not right to ⲕⲁ ⲙ. ⲛⲁⲛ
with wicked, BSM 24 B ⲥⲉⲙⲡⲉ ⲛⲟⲩⲙ. ⲟⲩⲧⲱϥ ⲛⲉⲙ-
ⲟⲩⲁⲓ = BMis 363 S ⲕⲱ ⲛⲟⲩⲙ. ⲙⲛ-.

ⲣ, ⲟ ⲛϣ. SABF, be friend, partner: AM 84 B ⲉⲛⲟⲓ ⲛϣ.; c ⲉ-: Jud 14 20 S φιλιάζειν gen, Sa 7
14 S φιλίαν στέλλειν πρός, Lu 23 12 SB (varr ⲛ-,
ⲛⲉⲙ-) φίλος γίνεσθαι μετά; Pro 8 36 SA(B = Gk)
ἀγαπᾶν; Eccl 9 4 F κοινωνεῖν πρός, Ro 15 27 B(S =
Gk) κ. dat, Is 1 23 B(S do) κοινωνός gen; He 6 4 B
(S do)μέτοχος γίν. gen, Eph 5 7 B(S ϫⲏⲡ)συμμ. gen;
ShC 73 155 S ⲟ ⲛϣⲃⲣ ⲉⲛⲉⲅⲉⲣⲏⲩ, R 1 2 55 S ⲟ ⲛϣ.
ⲉⲛⲣⲉϥϫⲓⲟⲩⲉ, ShP 130¹ 102 S ⲣ ϣⲃⲉⲉⲣⲉ ⲉⲛⲣⲱⲙⲉ
ⲡⲁⲥⲉⲃⲏⲥ, AM 266 B ⲉⲣ ϣ. ⲉⲡⲓⲙⲕⲁϩ; c ⲙⲛ-,
ⲛⲉⲙ-S(rare)B often = σνν-+ vb as: Ge 30 8 -ἀνα-
στρέφειν dat, Ps 100 6 -καθῆσθαι μετά, Bar 3 10
-μιαίνειν dat, Cai Euch 588 -πλους γίν.; PS 245 S ⲣ
ϣⲃⲣⲣⲣⲟ ⲡⲗⲙⲛⲧⲓ, Mor 33 129 S ⲁⲅⲉⲣ ϣ. ⲙⲡⲛⲉⲩⲉⲣⲏⲩ, Va 61 211 ϯⲉⲣ ϣ. ⲡⲣⲁϣⲓ ⲛⲉⲙⲁⲕ; c ⲛ-
dat: Ge 14 13 B συνωμότης εἶναι gen, Ro 11 17 B(S
ϣⲱⲡⲉ ⲛⲕⲟⲓⲛ. ⲛ-)συγκοινωνός γίν. gen; ShC 42 76
S ⲟ ⲛⲁϥ ⲛϣⲃⲏⲣϲⲩⲙ; ⲣⲉϥⲣ ϣ. B: 1 Tim 6 18
(S = Gk) κοινωνικός.

ϣⲓⲃϯ BBᶠ, -ⲧⲉ, ϣⲓϥⲧⲉ S(once each) vb I intr,
change, mostly = S ϣⲓⲃⲉ (here ϣ.): Dan 3 94 ἀλλοιοῦν, Ps 101 26 (S ϣ.) ἀλλάσσειν; Va 66 301 ⲙ-
ⲡⲁⲥϣ. ⲙⲡⲁⲥⲫⲱϩ ὑποχωρεῖν; ib 63 96 harlot ⲉⲁⲥϣ.
ⲁⲥϣⲱⲡⲓ ⲡⲉⲡ(ⲓⲉ)ⲛⲓⲕⲏⲥ σωφρονεῖν; ib 57 71 ϥⲛⲁϣⲓⲡϯ
ⲡϫⲉ ⲡⲁⲓⲥⲛⲟⲩ, ib 61 26 maggot ⲁϥϣ. & became
pearl. II tr: Dan 2 21 ἀλλοι., Is 40 31 (S do), Gal
4 20 (S do), CDan 91 ⲁϥϣ. ⲡⲡⲉϥⲥⲭⲏⲙⲁ ἀλλάσ.; Is
13 8 (S = Vulg diff), ib 29 22 (S ⲱⲕⲙ) μεταβάλλειν;
Phil 3 21 BBᶠ(BodlP f 7, S ϣ.) μετασχηματίζειν;
MG 25 241 ϣ. ⲙⲡⲉϥⲥⲭⲏⲙⲁ μεταμφιάζειν; Va 61

212 ⲁϥϣ. ⲙⲡⲉϥϣⲏⲣⲓ & brought ram (Ge 22 13), De V 2 93 not single punishment but ⲉⲩϣ. ⲙⲙⲟⲟⲩ ⳓⲉⲛⲕⲟⲗⲁⲥⲓⲥ ⲛⲓⲃⲉⲛ, PO 11 354 villages on either bank ϣ. ⲛⲡⲟⲩⲉⲣϩⲟⲩ in greeting him, Bodl(P) a 3 25 S ⲕⲁⲧⲁ ⲍ̄ ⲛⲣⲟⲟⲩ ⲉⲕϣⲓϣⲧⲉ ⲛⲡⲥⲟⲧ (var ib a 1 b ϣ.).

With following preposition or adverb.   c ⲉ-, to: Lev 13 4 (S ϣ. ⲉ-) μεταβάλ. acc, Va 63 95 ⲛⲏ ⲉⲧⲧⲁⲕⲛⲟⲩⲧ ϣ. ⲉⲛⲓⲁⲛⲁⲓ μεταβολή εἰς; ⲉⳓⲟⲩⲛ ⲉ-: Jude 4 (S ⲡⲱⲱⲛⲉ) μετατιθέναι εἰς; ⲉⳓⲟⲩⲛ ⲉϩⲣⲉⲛ-: C 86 280 none can ϣ. ⲉⳓ. ⲉϩ. ⲡⲉⲕⲟⲩⲁϩⲥⲁϩⲛⲓ ἀντείπειν dat;   c ⲉϩⲣⲏⲓ ⲉϫⲉⲛ-, upon: Dan 7 28 ἄλλοι. ἐπί;   c ⲛ-, into: 2 Cor 11 13(S ϫⲓ ϩⲣⲃ ϩⲱⲥ)μετασχ. εἰς; C 43 208 four to beat him ⲛ̄ ⲉⲩϣ. ⲛⲃ̄ (cf ib 77 ⲛ̄ ⳓⲁⲓϩⲛ ⲛⲃ̄);   c ⲛⲧⲉⲛ-, through: Ps 108 24 (S ϣ.) ἄλλοι. διά;   c ⳓⲉⲛ-, in: Ps 105 20 (S do) ἄλλασ. ἐν, Ro 1 25 (S do) μεταλ. ἐν; Cat 97 ⲁϥϣ. ⲁⲛ ⳓⲉⲛⲡⲉϥⲣⲟ; ⲉⲃⲟⲗ ⳓⲉⲛ-, from: Va 57 77 ϣ. ⲉⲃ. ⳓⲉⲛⲛⲓⲡⲁⲑⲟⲥ;   c ⲉⲃⲟⲗ ϩⲁ-, from out: MG 25 314 ϣ. ⲉⲃ. ϩⲁⲡⲓⲥⲩⲛⲏⲑⲓⲁ = BIF 13 119 S ⲡⲱ. ⲉⲃ. ϩⲛ-.

—— nn m, change: Ps 76 11 (S ϣ.) ἀλλοίωσις, Lev 27 33 (S do) ἀλλάσ., Va 66 305 ⲡⲓϣ. ⲛⲛⲓⲟⲩ-ⲛⲱⲟⲩ ι ἀλλαγή, Ja 1 17 (S do) παραλ.; Lev 19 19 (S diff), He 1 4 (S ϣ. vb) διάφορος, Gal 4 1 (S do) διαφέρειν; Ac 15 9 ⳓⲁ ϣ. (S ⲡⲱⲣϫ) διακρίνειν, He 5 14 (SF = Gk) διάκρισις; Ge 2 17 (S Gk om); Va 57 141 how can ⲟⲩϣ. ϣⲱⲡⲓ ⲛⲛⲓⲡⲣⲟⲫⲏⲧⲓⲁ, Cat 185 ⲡⲓϣ. ⲛ-...ⲛⲉⲙ-, AM 124 ⲁϥⲉⲣ ⲣⲱⲙⲓ ⲁⳓⲛⲉϣ.

ⲁⲧϣ., unchangeable: C 86 213 Christ ⲡⲓⲁ., AM 124 ⲁⲅⲁⲡⲏ ⲡⲁ.; ⲙⲉⲧⲁⲧϣ.: Cai Euch 407 ἀλλοίωσις.

ⲣⲉϥϣ., one who changes: AM 127 earth's fruits ϩⲁⲡⲣ. = R 1 4 67 S ⲣⲉϥϣⲓⲃⲉ (var P 129¹⁶ 81 ⲣⲉϥⲥⲓⲛⲉ).

ⳓⲓⲛ- S(once), ϫⲓⲛϣ. B, changeableness, difference: Deu 33 14 (S ⲕⲟⲧⲥ), Job 38 33 (S ⲕⲧⲟ)τροπή; Va 57 111 καταλλαγή; ib 78 ⲟⲩⳓ. ⲓⲉ ⲟⲩϫⲓⲛⲟⲩⲱⲧⲉⲃ ⲉⲃⲟⲗ, My 91 S ⲧⳓ. ⲛⲡⲉϩⲟⲟⲩ.

V ϣⲓⲃⲉ, ϣⲱⲃⲧ, ϣⲃϣⲓ.

ϣⲱⲃⲧ, -ⲡⲧ, ϣⲉⲃⲧ-, ϣⲟⲃⲧⲍ, -ⲡⲧⲍ, B vb I intr, change, be changed: Lam 4 1 (S ShC 42 127 F ϣⲓⲃⲉ), Dan 5 6 ἀλλοιοῦν; Ge 4 5 (SA Gk diff);   c ϩⲁ-, concerning: Dan 6 17 ἀλ. ἐν;   c ⲉⲃⲟⲗ ϩⲁ-, from: Job 37 5 (36 28, S ⲡⲱⲗϫ)διαλλάσσειν ἀπό;   c ϩⲓ-, over: Dan 4 13 ἀλλάσ. ἐπί. II tr: Ps 33 tit (S ϣⲓ.), Dan 7 25 ἄλλοι.; Jer 19 4 (S ⲣ ϣⲙⲙⲟ) ἀπαλλοτριοῦν; Ge 41 14 (S ϣⲓ.), Jer 13 23(S do) ἀλλάσ., Job 12 24 (S do) διαλ., Ge 48 14 (S ⲡⲱⲱⲛⲉ) ἐναλ., Pro 4 15(SA ϣⲓ.)παραλ.; Ro 12 2 (F ϣⲓ. S ϫⲓ ϩⲣⲃ) μεταμορφοῦν; 1 Cor 4 6 ϣⲟⲡⲧⲟⲩ(S ϫⲓ ⲡⲥⲙⲟⲧ)μετασχηματίζειν; Ge 29 25 ϣⲉⲃⲧ ⲥⲁϫⲓ (S ⲣ ϩⲁⲗ)παραλογίζειν; Cat 46 ⲡⲓⲉϩⲟⲟⲩ ⲉⲧⲁϥϣⲟⲡⲧϥ ⲛⳓⲏⲧϥ.

V ϣⲓⲃⲉ, ϣⲓⲃϯ, ϣⲃϣⲓ.

ϣⲃⲱⲧ S(rare)BF, -ⲟⲧ S, pl ϣⲃⲁⲧⲉ S, -ⲟϯ B & sg as pl, nn m rod, staff (שׁבט IgR) mostly = S ⳓⲉⲣⲱⲃ:

Ex 4 4 (SA ⳓ.), Is 36 6 (SF do) ῥάβδος, Ac 16 22 (S do) ῥαβδίζειν; Pro 13 24 (SA do) βακτηρία; Ep Jer 13 BF σκῆπτρον; R 1 5 25 S smote with ⲡⲉϥϣⲃⲟⲧ, Mor 51 38 S ϧⲉⲛϣⲃⲟⲧ ⲙⲛϩⲉⲛⲃⲁ, RE 11 35 S ⲙⲛⲧ ⲛⲥ̄ⲯ ⲡⲓϣ., CO 465 S ⲟⲩϣ., C 41 59 archimandrite invested with ⲟⲩⲗⲁⲣⲓⲟⲛ(ὡράριον) & ϣ., Va 59 5 beaten with ϩⲁⲛϣ. ⲉⲩⲙⲉϩ ⲛⲥⲟⲩⲣⲓ, C 43 100 sim ϩⲁⲛϣ. ⲉⲩⲗⲏⲕ;   ϣ. ⲛⲃⲉⲛⲓⲡⲓ Ps 2 9 ῥ. σιδήρεος, ⲛⲃⲁ, ⲃⲁⲓ ROC 25 250 βαίνῃ ῥ., MG 25 268 = Mor 40 41 S, ⲡⲓⲟⲩⲃ BSM 115, ⲛⲕⲁϣ Ez 29 6 (S ⳓ.) καλαμίνη, ⲕⲁⲙ (of black wood?) CO 467;   pl forms: Ge 30 37, Hos 4 12 ῥ., Mt 26 47 ξύλον; ROC lc monks' ϣ. ⲉⲃⲟⲗ ⳓⲉⲛⲛⲓⲃⲉⲛⲓ, ShBM Or 8810 372 S ϩⲉⲛϣ....ϩⲓⲟⲩⲉ ⲛⲣⲏⲧⲟⲩ; ϥⲁⲓϣ. S, staff-bearer: Ac 16 35 (B = Gk) ῥαβδοῦχος; Mor 26 21 = BMis 166 ⲡⲣⲟⲥⲟⲩⲣⲟⲥ = BSM 75 B ⲁⲣⲭⲏ-ⲣⲉϥⲣⲱⲓⲥ, LMär 11 ϥ. ⲡⲓⲟⲩⲁⲓ crucified Christ.

ϣⲃⲧⲥ v ϣⲓⲃⲉ.

ϣⲉⲃⲟⲓϣ B nn (?), as term of abuse, with privative ⲁⲧ-: MG 25 21 ϩⲉⲙⲥⲓ ⲛⲁⲕ ⲡⲓⳓⲁⲥⲓϩⲏⲧ ⲡⲁⲧϣ. Cf ? Eph 5 16 S, so (from ϣⲉⲡⲟⲩⲟⲉⲓϣ) untimely, inopportune.

ϣⲱⲃϣ v ϣⲱⲡϣ.

ϣⲃϣⲉ, ϣⲉⲃϣⲓ v ⲥⲃϣⲉ.

ϣⲃϣⲓ (sic MS)S nn m, a thing different (?): Si 27 1 διάφορος (var ⲁⲇ.); cf 42 5 ⲙⲡⲧⲙⲁⲓϣⲃⲉ ⲇ. (var do). L ? ϣⲃⲓⲱ.

ϣⲟⲃϣⲉⲃ¹, -ϣⲉⲡ², ϣⲟⲡϣⲉⲃ³, -ϣⲉⲡ⁴, ϣⲉⲃϣⲉⲃ-, -ϣⲱⲃ¹⁵, -ϣⲟⲡ¹⁶, ϣⲉⲡϣⲱⲃ¹⁷, -ϣⲱⲡ¹⁸ B vb tr, sharpen, incite: Ps 63 4¹ (S ⲧⲱⲙ), Va 57 173 ϫⲱⲣ ⲛϯⲥⲛϥⲓ, ϣ.² ⲛⲡⲥⲟⲃⲉϥ ἀκονᾶν; Is 44 12¹ (S do) ὀξύνειν; Pro 6 3 ϣⲉⲃϣⲉⲃ- (so Bsciai, var ⲛⲉϥⲉⲣ-, SA ⲧⲱⲃⲥ) πάροξ.; Ac 13 50¹ (var³, S do) παροτρύνειν; ib 7 54¹ (varr³⁴, S ϫⲱⲛⲧ) διαπρίειν; C 86 63 ⲉϥϣ.³ ⲙⲙⲱⲟⲩ ⲉϧⲟⲩⲛ ⲉⲣⲟϥ that they (beasts) should devour him, ib 220 ϣ.⁴ ⲛⲛⲓⲕⲁϣ with knives;   qual: Ps 119 4⁵ (var⁷, S ⲧⲏⲙ var ϣⲟⲗⳓ) ἀκ., Ez 21 11 (S ⲧ. tr) ἐξακ., Job 41 21⁸(S ⲧⲏⲙ) ὀξύς, Ps 44 2 ϣ.⁸ ⲡⲉⳓⳓⲁⲓ(S ⳓⲉⲡⲏ ⲉⲧⲥ.)ὀξυγράφος; K 85 ⲉⲧϣ.⁸ ﻣﺎﻝ, Cai The 347 ⲙⲉⲅⲓ ⲉⲧϣ.⁵ ﺣﺎﺫﻕ crafty; MG 25 66 ⲙⲉⲣⲉϩ ⲉⲧϣ.⁵ (var⁸), ib 325 ⲕⲁϯ ⲉⲧϣ.⁸ (ROC 17 357 ﺣﺎﺭ ﺣﺎﺩﻩ), Va 57 71 ⲉⲧϣ.⁸ ⳓⲉⲛϯⲕⲁⲕⲓⲁ. Cf ϣⲟⲃⲓ.

ϣⲱⲃϩ SB, ϣⲟⲟϩ S(nn once), ϣⲱⲃϩ A, ϣⲱⲡϩ, -ϩⲉⲃ, -ϩⲡ B, ϣⲟⲃϩⲍ, ϣⲟⲃϩⲧ S vb intr, be scorched, withered (cf ⲱⲣϣ): Dan 3 94 B-ϩⲡ φλέγεσθαι; ShIF 246 S ⲉⲛⲡⲁϣ. as grass, ShC 73 23 S tongue like ⲡⲉⲧ-ϣ.ⲧ, AM 156 B hair of head ⲙⲡⲉϥϣⲱϩⲣ, C 43 71 B sim -ⲃϩ, DeV 2 85 B -ⲡϩ;   With following preposition S: P 132¹ 35 ⲁⲩϣ. ⲛⲟⲩⲛⲟϭ ⲛⲕⲁⲩⲥⲱⲛ, ShP 130² 3 trees ϣ. ⲉⲃⲟⲗ ⲙⲡϣⲁϩ, ShC 73 43 some ⲥⲟϫⲙ

ⲛ ϣ.† ϩⲁⲡϭⲱⲡⲧ, ShR 2 3 10 ⲉⲩϣ.† ϩⲏⲡⲥⲁϭⲟⲩ, ShA 2 29 seed ϣ. ϩⲓⲧⲙⲡⲧⲟⲩⲣⲏⲥ, Mor 43 147 lips ⲣⲱϭϩ ...ⲁⲩϣ. ϩⲓⲧⲡⲛⲟⲙⲙⲉ. tr: Ps 120 6 S(B ⲣⲱⲕϩ) ἐκκαίειν, El 72 A (ⲛ)ⲡⲉϥϣ. ⲙⲙⲱⲧⲛⲉ ⲛϭⲓ ⲡⲡⲟ(ⲡⲏ)ⲣⲟⲥ (cf Budge Bibl Texts 271), C 86 18 B fire ⲙⲡⲉϥϣⲱⲣⲉϩ ⲛⲟⲩϣⲟⲓ ⲛⲧⲁϥ; as nn S: Jer 31 34 -ⲟⲩϩ (Sh A 1 464, B ⲣⲱⲕϩ) κατάκαυμα; ShMIF 23 185 ⲡⲓⲕⲙⲟⲙ ⲛϣ. ϩⲓⲧⲡⲧⲣⲙⲙⲉ.

ϣⲟⲉ, ϣⲟⲉϩ B mast v ϣⲧⲉ.

ϣⲁⲑⲱⲗ, -ⲟⲩⲗ B, ϩⲁⲧⲟⲩⲗ DM nn m, *ichneumon* (חֹלֶד IgR): K 165 ⲡⲓϣ. نمس (cf P 44 55 ⲁⲓⲗⲟ(ⲩ)ⲣⲟⲥ '؞); DeV 2 227 ϣ. at enmity with ϭⲁⲧϥⲓ ⲛⲓϩⲉⲛ, MG 25 363 demon in form of ⲟⲩϣ. (ROC 18 125 ܠܐ), DM vo 30 9. Cf ⲉⲙⲟⲩ.

ϣⲟⲗⲙ, -ⲟⲙ B v ϣⲧⲁⲙ.

ϣⲟⲏⲛ B v ϣⲧⲏⲛ.

ϣⲟⲱⲣⲓ B v ⲧⲱⲣⲉ *hand* (ϣⲧⲱⲣⲉ).

ϣⲟⲟⲣⲧⲉⲣ B v ϣⲧⲟⲣⲧⲣ.

ϣⲟⲱⲧ B nn f, *rope of palm-fibre*: K 126 †ϣ. سلبة, 138 ⲡⲓϣ. '⸗. V BIF 20 51.

ϣⲟⲟⲩⲓⲧ B v ϣⲧⲟⲩⲏⲧ.

ϣⲟⲉϩ B nn m, *street* (حَارَة Lacr): Ge 19 2, Ps 17 43, Mt 6 5, Ap 21 21 (all S = Gk, F Mt do) πλατεῖα طريق; TRit 407 ⲛⲛⲧⲉⲛ ⲛⲧⲉ ⲡⲓϣ. شوارع; Va 57 191 beggars sitting in ⲡⲓⲙⲁ ⲙⲙⲟϣⲓ ⲛⲧⲉ ⲡⲓϣ. As place-name: ⲡⲓϣⲟⲉϩ, where temple of Zeus (AM 74), also ? S in Kr 130 ⲫⲁⲅⲓⲟⲥ ⲫⲟⲓⲃⲁⲙⲙⲱⲛ ⲡϣⲧⲉϩ, Ryl 125, 187 sim.

ϣⲓⲕ v ϣⲓⲕⲉ s f.

ϣⲱⲕ S(nn)BF, ϣⲱⲕⲓ, ϣⲟⲕ, -ⲕⲓ(both Ez)B, ϣⲉⲕ- SB, ϣⲟⲕ⸗ B, ϣⲏⲕ† SA²BF, ϣⲏⲕⲓ† F vb **I** intr, *dig, be deep dug* B: Jer 13 7 (S ϣⲓⲕⲉ), MG 25 12 ὀρύσσειν, Mk 2 4(S ϣⲟⲭⲧ)ἐξορ.; Ps 91 6 (S ⲁϣⲁⲓ)βαρύνειν; MG 25 352 ϣⲉⲕ ⲟⲩϣⲱ† ...ⲉⲣ ⲉ̄ ⲡⲉϩⲟⲟⲩ ⲉⲩϣⲱⲕⲓ; qual, *deep*: Job 12 22 SB, Pro 25 3 S(A ϣⲁⲕϩ), Is 30 33 BF(S ϣⲁⲕϩ), Jo 4 11 A²B(S ϣⲟⲕϩ) βαθύς, Am 9 3 (S ⲟⲩⲉⲡⲧ, B ϣⲟⲕ nn), Lu 5 4 SB βάθος; Deu 6 11 B(S ϭⲛⲝ)λατομεῖν; Cant 7 2 F(S ϣⲉⲧϣⲱⲧ) τορευτός; Eph 4 9 S(B ⲉⲧⲥⲁⲡⲉⲥⲏⲧ), Gu 70 S ⲙⲁ ⲉⲧϣ. κατώτερος; ClPr 54 43 S ⲡⲉⲥⲙⲁ ⲉⲧϣ. (sc lake's) κοιλία; PS 112 S ⲡⲧⲟⲡⲟⲥ ⲉⲧϣ. ⲛⲧⲉ ⲡⲉⲭⲁⲟⲥ, Mor 31 174 S ⲣⲁⲥⲟⲩ ⲉⲧϣ., C 86 241 B ⲍⲏⲧⲓⲙⲁ ⲉⲧϣ. of scriptures, ROC 23 287 B long since ⲡⲁϣ.ⲡⲉ ⲙⲙⲁⲩ. With preposition B: Lacr 128 ⲛⲉϥ(ϩ)ⲃⲛⲟⲩⲓ ϣⲉϣ.† ⲉⲝⲉⲡⲡⲓⲣⲱⲙ, C 41 41 ⲡⲓⲱ... ϣⲱⲕⲓ ⲛⲧⲉϥϥⲁⲧ, Ez 8 8 ϣⲱⲕⲓ ϩⲉⲛ†ⲭⲟⲓ ὀρ. ἐν; DeV 2 167 builder ϣⲱⲕⲓ ϩⲉⲛ†ⲥⲉⲛ†.

II tr S(rare)B: Nu 21 18(S ϣⲓⲕⲉ), Mt 25 18 (S

do) ὀρ., Ez 12 7 ϣⲟⲕ(S ϣⲟⲭⲧ)διορ.; Jer 29 8 βαθύνειν; Ex 21 33 (S ϭⲱⲝⲉ), Mt 27 60 (S ⲕⲁⲣⲕϩ) λατ.; ShIF 235 S ϣⲉⲕ ϣⲛⲓ, RNC 59 S ϣⲟⲕⲓ ⲛⲟⲩⲅⲫⲟⲥⲥⲁ, C 43 9 ϣⲟⲕⲓ ⲛⲟⲩⲅⲫⲟⲥⲥⲁ, ib 27 sim ϣⲱⲕ, C 86 155 ⲁϥϣⲟⲕϥ (sc idol) ϩⲉⲛⲡⲉϥⲙⲉⲣⲉϩ (but ? cf ϣⲱϣⲉ). With adverb. c ⲉⲃⲟⲗ: Dan 2 22† B βαθύς; c ⲉⲡⲛⲥⲧ: Lam 3 55† B κατώτατος; Mor 23 35 S pit ⲉϥϣ.† ⲉⲡ. = ib 24 25 F, C 41 13 B eyes from weeping ϣ. ⲉⲡ. ⲙⲫⲣⲏ† ⲛϩⲁⲡⲭⲟⲗ ⲛⲧⲉ ϩⲁⲛⲝⲟⲓ(Miss 4 315, Rev Sémit 7 159 diff, cf ϣⲱⲕⲣ); c ⲉϩⲟⲩⲛ: Va 59 163 B eyes ϣ. ⲉϩ. from austerities; c ⲉϩⲣⲏⲓ B: Lu 6 48 (S ϣⲓⲕⲉ) βαθύν.; Va 63 92 ϣ. ⲉϩ. ϣⲁⲕϭⲓⲙⲓ διασκάπτειν.

—— nn m S(rare)B ϣⲱⲕ F, *depth*: Job 28 11(S ϣⲓⲕ), Mic 7 19(S do, A ϣⲓⲭϩ), Ro 11 33 BF(S do), Eph 3 18 (S ϣⲓⲕⲉ), ROC 25 248 ⲡϣ. ⲙⲡⲉϧⲣⲏⲧ βάθος, Is 29 15 ϩⲉⲛⲟⲩϣ. (S ⲉϥϧⲏⲡ) βαθέως, 2 Cor 11 25 (S ⲛⲟⲩⲡ) βυθός; Pas H 42 ⲟⲩϣ. ⲡⲕⲁ† فهم رفيع; Mor 22 6 S stray not in ⲡϣ. ⲙⲡⲡⲟⲛⲏⲙⲁ, Cat 182 ⲡϣ. ⲛⲡⲓϩⲟⲧⲙⲁ, C 86 204 ⲡϣ. ⲙⲫⲓⲟⲙ = ib 274 ⲡⲉϣⲓⲕ ⲛⲧⲉ ⲫ., J 65 55 S ⲉⲓⲧⲉ ⲃⲛⲃ ⲉⲓⲧⲉ ϣ. belonging to τόπος (v Ep 1 128).

ⲙⲁ ⲉⲧϣⲓⲕ S v qual.

Cf ϣⲓⲕⲉ, ϣⲟⲕϣⲉⲕ, ϣⲱⲕⲣ.

ϣⲁⲕⲉ v ϣⲁⲣⲕⲉ.

ϣⲓⲕⲉ SA, -ⲧⲉ A, -ⲕⲓ B(rare)F, ϣⲉⲕⲉⲓ F(Eccl), ϣⲉⲕⲧ-S, ϣⲓⲧ-A, ϣⲁⲕⲧ⸗, ϣⲓ., ϣⲟⲕⲉ† S vb intr, *dig*: Lu 6 48 (B ϣⲱⲕⲓ ⲉϩⲣⲏⲓ) βαθύνειν; Aeg 263 wage of ⲉⲣⲅⲁⲧⲏⲥ ⲉⲧϣ. *gravedigger* & price of clay (κέραμος) = PO 8 616 الذي يحفر والفارس; ShC 73 201 ⲧⲟⲡⲟⲥ ⲉϥϣ.†, Mor 30 29 F ϫⲓ ⲛⲟⲩⲥⲕⲉⲟⲥ ⲛⲧϣ., Z 234 ⲁϥϣ. ϩⲁⲣⲁⲧϥ ⲛⲟⲩϫⲟ; Wess 15 133 ⲥⲕⲉⲏⲓ ⲛϣ. ὀρυκτήρ, BIF 13 109 sim = MG 25 296 B, BMis 219 sim (var Mor 16 75 ⲛϭⲱⲝⲉ), ShIF 267 ⲥⲟⲧⲃⲉϥ ⲛϣ. ⲁⲩⲱ ⲛϭⲣⲏ; tr: Ge 26 21 (B ϣⲱ.), Pro 26 27 SA -ⲧⲉ, Eccl 10 8 SF ⲡⲉⲧⲭⲉⲕⲉⲓ, Zech 3 9 A ϣⲓⲧ- ὀρύσσειν; ShA 1 388 ϩⲓⲉⲓⲧ...ϭⲣⲏ ⲙⲙⲟϥ, ϣⲁⲕⲧϥ, BAp 125 ⲡⲙⲁ ⲛⲧⲁⲧⲣⲉⲩϣⲓⲕⲧϥ (sc grave), ib 126 ϣⲁⲕⲧϥ.

With following preposition or adverb. c ⲉ-, *in*: BAp 67 ⲁϥϣ. ⲉⲡⲕⲁϩ & buried them (cf ib ϭⲱ. ⲉⲡⲕ.); c ⲡⲥⲁ-, *after, for*: Job 3 21(B ⲫⲱⲣⲕ)ⲁⲛⲟⲣ.; FR 26 ϣ. ⲛⲥⲁⲟⲩⲙⲟⲟⲩ; c ϩⲛ-, *in*: Mt 25 18 (B ϣⲱ.) ὀρ. ἐν, Job 39 21 B ⲁⲛⲟⲣ. ἐν; BAp 54 ϣ. ϩⲙⲡⲉⲓⲙⲁ σκάπτειν, ib 55 ⲉⲩϭⲱ. ⲙⲡⲧⲟⲡⲟⲥ ⲉⲧⲟⲩϣ. ⲛ. ⲣⲏⲧϥ σκάμμα τελεῖν; ShA 1 212 ⲉⲡϣ. ϩⲙⲡⲕⲁϩ, Mor 48 6 sim (var BMar 206 ϭⲱ.) = Rec 6 169 B ϣⲱ.; *with* (agent): Deu 23 13 (B do tr) ὀρ. ἐν; ϩⲣⲁⲓ ϩⲛ-: Is 5 2 (B ϣⲱⲕ *sic* l) ὀρ. ἐν; ShIF 308 ⲡⲛⲥⲛ...ⲁϥϣⲁⲕⲧⲉ ϩ. ⲛϩⲏⲧⲟⲩ; c ⲉⲡⲉⲥⲏⲧ, *down*: AZ 21 156 ϣ. ⲉ. 3 ells, J 106 152 buildings ϣⲁⲕⲧⲟⲩ ⲉ. ⲕⲱⲧ ⲉⲝⲱⲟⲩ ⲉⲡϫⲓⲥⲉ, cf ib 67 96 ⲙⲛ ⲗⲁⲁⲩ ϣ.† ⲉⲧⲡⲉ ϣⲁⲡⲙⲁ ⲉⲧⲙⲙⲁⲩ.

—— nn m S S[f], *what is dug, depth*: Is 7 11 opp
ϫⲓⲥⲉ (B ϣⲱⲕ), Ro 11 33 (BF do) βάθος; Si 1 3 (B
ϣⲓⲕ) ἄβυσσος; Orat Cyp 34 S[f] ⲡϣ. ⲙⲡⲁϧⲏⲧ (*cf* below Jth & Miss 4).

ⲋⲓⲡϣ. S, *act of digging*: Mor 31 26 at his approaching death ⲡⲉⲩϣⲧⲣⲧⲱⲣ ⲉⲧⲉⲧⲉⲋ. ⲛⲥⲉⲧⲱⲙⲥ ⲙ-
ⲡⲉϥⲥⲱⲙⲁ.

ϣⲓⲕ SBF, ϣⲉⲓⲕ, ϣⲏⲕ S nn m, *what is dug, depth*:
Jth 8 14 S, Ps 68 14 S(B ϣⲱⲕ), Eccl 7 25 S(F ⲡⲉϫⲏⲕ), Mic 7 19 S(A ϣⲓⲭϧ, B do)βάθος; Ps 56 7 B
(S ϧⲓⲉⲓⲧ), Ez 32 18 S(B ⲗⲁⲕⲕⲟⲥ)βόθρος, Mt 15 14 B
(S do)βόθυνος; Ps 7 16 B(S do), Sa 10 14 S ϣⲏⲕ
(but var ϣⲏⲓ) λάκκος; Si 1 3 B(S ϣⲓⲕⲉ) ἄβυσσος;
Job 41 23 S(B = Gk) τάρταρος; Pro 16 25 S(A ϣⲓⲭϧ) πυθμήν; Lu 16 26 B(S = Gk) χάσμα; Ex 7
19 B ⲓⲟⲣ ⲡϣ. διῶρυξ; ShBor 247 118 S if one pay
heed to ⲡϣ. ⲙⲡϣⲁϫⲉ, ShA 1 236 S ⲡϣⲉⲓⲕ of sea,
Mor 48 29 S laid corpse in ⲟⲩϣ. ⲛⲧⲉ ⲧⲡⲉⲧⲣⲁ (var
BMar 217 ⲟⲩⲱϣ)= Rec 6 183 B, Miss 4 788 S pray
ϧⲙⲡϣ. ⲙⲡⲉⲧⲡⲣⲏⲧ, DeV 2 144 B ⲡϣ. ⲡⲡⲓⲙⲟⲅⲓ (*cf*
145 ϣⲏⲓ same), Pcod F 17 (S 39 diff) ⲡϣ. of unbelief, C 89 97 B ϣ. full of fire = *ib* 99 159 S ⲉⲓⲁ.

Cf ϣⲱⲕ, ϣⲟⲕϣⲉⲕ, ϣⲱⲕϧ.

ϣⲱⲕⲉ S nn, meaning unknown: CO 472 list of
varia ⲟⲩϣ. (? incomplete).

ϣⲕⲁⲕ SB(once)F nn m, *cry, shout*: Ex 2 23 S
(B ϩⲣⲟⲟⲩ)βοή;   with preceding vb; ϧⲓ ϣ. B, lit
throw a cry: P 44 190 بنادى يصرخ.

ϫⲓ ϣ. SF c ⲉⲃⲟⲗ, *cry out*: Ex 32 17 (B ⲱϣ ⲉⲃ.),
Ps 16 6 (BF do), *ib* 33 17 (A ⲁϣϭⲁⲡ ⲁⲃ., B do), Mk
15 13 (var & BF do) κράζειν, Jud 7 20, Mk 6 49 (var
& B do), ἀνακρ.; Deu 22 24 (B do), Is 34 14 SF(B
do) βοᾶν, Ge 21 16 (B do) ἀναβ.; Lu 23 21 (B do)
ἐπιφωνεῖν; P 131[1] 32 birds in spring ϫ. κλαγγάζειν;
ShR 2 3 15 ⲡⲉⲧⲣⲓⲙⲉ, ⲛⲉϧⲡⲉ, ϫ., Mor 18 65 ⲡⲉϫ.
(var *ib* 19 74 & Miss 4 139 B ⲱϣ ⲉⲃ.); ⲉⲃ. ⲉ-: Ge
41 55 (B do ϧⲁ-) ⲕⲣ. πρός; BAp 135 ⲉⲩϫ. ⲉⲃ. ⲉⲡⲉ-
ⲭ̅ⲥ̅, Miss 8 231 ϫ. ⲉⲃ. ⲉϧⲟⲩⲛ ⲉⲡⲭ̅ⲥ̅, Lam 3 8 ϫ. ⲉⲃ.
ⲉϩⲣⲁⲓ ⲉ-(B ϯ ϩⲣⲟⲟⲩ)ⲕⲣ. only; ⲉⲃ. ⲉϫⲛ-: LMär
25 crowd ϫ. ⲉⲃ. ⲉϫⲱϥ at martyr tortured; ⲉⲃ. ϧⲁ-:
Ro 9 27 (B ⲱϣ ⲉⲃ. ⲉϫ.) ⲕⲣ. ὑπέρ; c ⲉϩⲣⲁⲓ ⲉ-, *cry
upward*: Job 30 20 (B ⲱϣ ⲉⲡϣⲱⲓ ϧⲁ-), Ps 27 1 (B
ⲱϣ ⲟⲩⲃⲉ-), *ib* 29 8 (B ⲱϣ ⲉϧⲣⲏⲓ ⲟⲩ.) ⲕⲣ. πρός, Hab
1 2 (A ⲁϣϭ. ⲁϧ. ⲁ., B ⲱϣ ⲉⲃ.) ⲕⲣ. only; Ex 15 25
(B ⲱϣ ⲟⲩ.) β. πρός; Ps 5 2 (B ⲧⲱⲃϩ) προσεύχεσθαι
πρός; as nn: Ap 21 4 (var ⲁϣⲕⲁⲕ, B ϩⲣⲟⲟⲩ)
κραυγή.

ⲁϣⲕⲁⲕ(= ⲁϣ ϣ.)SF, as last: Jer 29 2 (B ⲉϣ ⲗⲏⲗⲟⲩⲓ) ἀλαλάζειν; c ⲉⲃⲟⲗ: Nu 11 2 (var & B ⲱϣ
ⲉⲃ.), Ac 16 17 (var & B ⲱϣ ⲉⲃ.) ⲕⲣ., Jo 19 6 (var ϫⲓ
ϣ. ⲉⲃ., A² ⲁϣⲏⲗ ⲁϩ., B do) κραυγάζειν; Ac 17 6
(B do) β.; *ib* 21 34 (B do) ἐπιφω., Lu 17 13 (var ϫⲓ

ϣ. ⲉⲃ., B ⲋⲓⲥⲓ ⲥⲙⲏ) φωνὴν αἴρειν; ShC 42 67 ⲉⲓⲁ.
ⲉⲃ. ⲉⲧⲃⲉⲑⲟⲧⲉ, ShA 2 105 ⲛⲉϧⲡⲉ, ⲣⲓⲙⲉ, ⲁ. ⲉⲃ.; ⲉⲃ.
ⲉ-: BHom 38 ⲉϥⲁ. ⲉⲃ. ⲉⲟⲩⲟⲡ ⲡⲓⲙ β.; Ac 22 24 (var
& B do) ⲉⲡⲓⲫⲱ. dat; ⲉϩⲣⲁⲓ ⲉ-: Job 38 41 (B ⲱϣ ⲉⲡϣⲱⲓ ϧⲁ-)ⲕⲣ. πρός; as nn m: Ge 18 20 (var & B
ϧⲣⲟⲟⲩ), Jer 18 22 (B do) κραυγή; Ja 5 4 (A ⲁϣϭⲁⲡ,
B ⲥⲙⲏ) βοή; 2 Kg 19 4 φωνή; PS 61 ⲁⲥⲣⲓⲙⲉ ϧⲛ-
ⲟⲩⲁ., BAp 124 ⲟⲩⲛⲟϭ ⲛⲁ. ⲡⲣⲓⲙⲉ, PMich 777 F ⲛⲁ.
(ⲛ)ⲛⲁⲣⲗⲁϯ.

V ϣϧⲏⲗ, ϣϭⲁⲡ.

ϣⲕⲓⲗ SF, -ⲏⲗ (once) S nn, *curl* of hair: Cant 5
11 F(S ϭⲱ ⲉⲧⲟⲗⲙ)βόστρυχος ἐλατός; Gloss 10 ϣⲕⲓⲗ
...[πλόκαμος; Mor 43 252 what free woman ⲛⲁⲕⲁ
ⲟⲩⲃⲱ ⲡϣ. on head?, *ib* 251 ϧⲱⲗⲕ, ϣ., ⲕⲟⲥⲙⲏⲥⲓⲥ ⲙ-
ⲡⲉϧⲣⲟ, R 2 1 65 ⲡⲉϣ. ⲛⲧⲉ ⲡ(ϥ)ⲱ ⲛⲁⲓ ⲉⲛⲉϧⲱⲗⲕ ⲙ-
ⲙⲟⲟⲩ, *ib* 1 2 38 ϥⲱ ⲃⲏⲗ ⲉⲃⲟⲗ ⲉⲧⲉⲡⲁⲓⲡⲉ ⲉϥⲟ ⲡϣ. (var
Lammayer 39 ϣⲕⲉⲗⲕⲓⲗ), CA 89 ⲥⲧⲏⲙ, ϣⲕⲏⲗ, ϧⲱⲗⲕ
= *ib* ⲣⲁ خصلة الشعر *anklet*.

ϣⲕ(ⲉ)ⲗⲕⲓⲗ[1], -ⲕⲉⲗ[2], ϣϭⲗϭⲓⲗ[3], ϣⲕⲓⲗ.[4], ϣϭⲓⲗ.[5], ⲥϭⲉⲗ-
ϭⲓⲗ[6]S, ϣⲕⲉⲗⲕⲓⲗ B, nn m, *curl*(once)as above; *bell*:
Ex 28 33 B, Si 45 14 (9) S[3] κώδων; Tri 534 S ⲛⲧⲓⲧ-
ⲧⲱⲣⲉ ϧⲛϩⲉⲛⲥⲁⲗⲡⲓⲅϩ ⲙⲛϩⲉⲛϣ.[4] اجراس; BMis 6 S
ⲡⲉϣ.[2] ⲛⲛⲟⲩⲃ hung on veil, BMar 14 S ⲉϣⲧ ⲟⲩϣ.[5]
ⲉⲡⲉϥⲙⲁⲕϩ, Mor 47 211 S ⲟⲩϧⲩⲡⲏⲣⲉⲧⲏⲥ ⲙⲛⲟⲩϭ.[6]
& led thief through village = P ar 4776 152 misunderst اجناد من انثين Bodl(P) f 78 S ⲛⲟϭ ⲛϣ. ⲙ-
ⲡⲉⲛⲓⲛ[ⲉ, Ryl 238 S church furniture ϣⲟⲙⲧ ⲛϣ.[1]
ⲙⲛⲛⲉⲅⲁⲗⲏⲥⲓⲥ (ἄλυ.), PO 14 368 B ϣ. ... ⲁϥϣⲁⲛϯ
ⲛⲧⲉϥⲥⲙⲏ.

ϣⲕⲟⲗ S, ⲭⲟⲗ B, (ⲕⲗⲟ) pl ⲕⲗⲟⲟⲩⲉ A nn m, *hole*:
Job 30 6 SB, Is 11 8 SB τρώγλη; Jer 16 16 S(B
ⲫⲱϫⲓ), Z 317 S pots hung ⲕⲁⲧⲁ ⲟⲩϣ. *from each hole*
= MG 25 231 B τρυμαλιά; Ex 33 22 B(S ⲟⲩⲱϣ),
Ez 8 7 S(P 131[5] 4, B ϣⲟⲩϣⲧ), Ob 3 SA pl (B ⲫ.),
He 11 38 SB ὀπή; Leip 24 12 B ⲡⲭ. ⲛⲧⲉ ⲡϣⲉ κέν-
τημα; Ap 6 15 B(S Gk diff); EW 222 *v* ⲙⲉϣⲕⲟⲗ;
ShP 131[6] 49 S if ship have ⲟⲩϣ. ⲛⲟⲩⲱⲧ she will
sink, ShA 1 39 S ⲡⲉϣ. ⲏ ⲡⲃⲏⲃ of snake, C 41 13 B
eyes deep sunk like ϧⲁⲛϣ. ⲛⲧⲉ ϧⲁⲛϫⲟⲓ (*cf* ϣⲱⲕ nn),
BAp 143 S ⲥⲁϣϥ ⲛϣ. ⲕⲁⲧⲁ ⲗⲩⲭⲛⲓⲁ *wick-holes*,
BM 1112 S ⲡⲉϣⲕⲟⲅⲗ ⲡⲧⲉⲣⲡⲟⲥⲓ ⲉϥⲙⲡⲉⲙⲛⲧ ⲉⲡϣⲏⲓ; ⲟ ⲛϣ. ϣ. S, οἱ ⲛⲭ. ϫ. B, *be full of holes*:
MG 25 231 B cloak ⲉⲥⲟⲓ ⲛϫ. ϫ. = Z 316 S ⲋⲱⲧϧ
ϭ. τρωγλωτός; P 131[6] 46 S vessel's foot ⲟ ⲛϣ. ϣ.
whereby water might go down, Mor 55 62 S honeycomb sim, C 41 70 B ⲕⲁⲯⲁ (coffin) sim.

ϣⲕⲗⲕⲓⲗ *v* ϣⲕⲓⲗ.

ϣⲕⲗⲕⲉⲗ S, ϣⲕⲏⲗ. SF, ϣϭⲗϭⲉ A nn m, *gnashing, grinding* of teeth: Mt 13 42 F(S ⲋⲁϧⲋϧ B ⲥϧⲉⲣ-
ⲧⲉⲣ)βρυγμός; cit Mor 31 94 S, Till Oster 26 A ⲡϣ.
ⲛⲛⲁⲃ[ϧ]ⲉ, Mor 54 111 S ϯⲛⲁⲙⲁⲥⲧⲓⲅⲟⲩ ⲙⲙⲱⲧⲛ

ⲣⲙⲡⲉϣⲕⲏⲗ. ⲡⲡⲉⲟⲃ̅ⲣⲉ. Here ? belongs BKU 1 28 = AZ 16 20 *S* recipe ϫⲓ ⲡⲥⲟⲟⲩⲣ ⲡϣⲗⲕⲕⲱⲗⲥ (*l* ϣⲕⲗ-)ⲙⲡ[ⲟⲩ]ⲕⲟⲅⲓ ⲡⲥⲓϥⲉ ⲡϥ[ⲧ]ⲥⲁⲥ.

ϣⲕⲁⲡ *B v* ϣϭⲁⲡ.

ϣⲕⲁⲣ *v* ϣϭⲟⲣ.

ϣⲕⲉⲣ, ϣϭⲏⲣ *v* ⲥϭⲏⲣ.

ϣⲓⲕⲣⲉ *F v* next.

ϣⲟⲩⲕⲣⲉ *SSᶠ* nn, a plant: ShZ 596 *S* trifles suffice to estrange us from God ⲣⲉⲛϣⲟⲉⲓϣ ⲣⲉⲛⲣⲟⲟⲩⲉ ⲣⲉⲛϣ. ⲣⲉⲛϭⲱⲃⲉ, CaiCoptMus 1784 *Sᶠ* bishop's letter ψⲩⲭⲏ ⲛⲓⲙ ⲉⲛϣⲁⲩϭⲁⲗ ⲟⲩϣ. (ⲛ)ⲡⲓⲕⲁⲗⲁⲅⲟⲩⲗⲉ (place, *ib* ⲧⲕⲁⲗ.) shall be accursed. *Cf ?* BM 706 *F* ϣⲓⲕⲣⲉ (word or name ?).

ϣⲱⲕⲁⲥ (ⲥ uncertain)*S* nn, a measure: OstrChicago 29 211 ⲟⲩϣ. ⲛⲥⲟⲅⲟ.

ϣⲕⲱϯ *B* nn as pl, among weaver's implements: K 126 ⲛϣ. الطاق (=مواسير) بكر *bobbin, reel* Lab, but *cf* AZ 14 22).

ϣⲟⲕϣⲉⲕ *B*, ϣⲉⲕϣⲱⲕ-*S*, ϣⲉⲕϣⲱⲕ⸗ *SA*, ϣⲉⲕϣⲱⲕ† *B* vb tr, *dig, pick, hollow*: Ez 40 42† *B*(*S* ⲕⲉⲣⲕⲱⲣ) λαξεύειν, *ib* 41 18† *B*(*S* ϣⲉⲧϣⲱⲧ) γλύφειν; Pro 24 52 *SA*(*B* ⲡⲱⲣⲕ ⲉⲃⲟⲗ) ἐκκόπτειν, cit Miss 4 624, Mor 22 83 *S* ϣⲉⲕϣⲱⲕ ⲡⲉϥⲃⲁⲗ, BMor 8775 122 *B* نسول (*l* تشوّك), تخلّل، يعلل Sobhy). *Cf* ϣⲱⲕ, ϣⲓⲕⲉ, ϣⲱⲕⲣ.

ϣⲟⲕϣⲉⲕ *B* vb intr, *hiss*, Jer only: 27 13 (*S* ϭⲓ ϣⲗⲏϣⲛⲥⲉ), 29 17 ϣ. ⲡⲣⲱϥ(*S* do)συρίζειν; as nn: 18 16 (*S* ϣⲗⲙ.) σύριγμα, 32 18 -μός.

ϣⲱⲕⲣ *SB* (prob once), ϣⲟ. *B*, ϣⲉⲕⲣ-*S*, ϣⲟⲕⲣ⸗ *SB*, ϣⲁ. *Sᶠ*, ϣⲟⲕⲣ† *S*, ϣⲁ.† *SA*, ϣⲁⲭⲣ† *A* vb a *dig deep*, tr *S*: Is 51 1(*B* ϣⲟⲩⲕ)ὀρύσσειν; Mor 17 18 ⲉⲩϣ. ⲛⲧⲉⲡⲧⲉ διορ.; ShViK 924 ⲉⲡϣⲉⲕⲣ (*l* -ⲣ) ⲛⲓ ⲡⲡⲓⲁ ⲣⲓϣⲱⲧⲉ; intr *B*: Ez 12 5 (*S* ϣⲱϣⲧ) διορ.; ⲉ ⲡⲉⲥⲏⲧ *S*: PSBA 10 197 ascete's eyes ϣ. ⲉⲡ., Gu 92 sim (*cf* ϣⲱⲕ), Mor 22 50 stone ϣ. ⲉⲡ. ⲣⲓⲧⲁⲙⲙⲟⲟⲩ; qual, *deep*: Pro 18 4 *A*-ⲭⲣ(*S* ϣⲏⲕ), *ib* 25 3 *A*(*S* do), Is 30 33(*BF* ϣⲏⲕ), Jo 4 11(*A²B* do), Mor 17 59 ⲣⲓⲡⲏⲃ ⲉϥϣⲁ. βαθύς; ShP 131⁸ 133 ⲣⲉⲛϣⲏⲓ ⲉⲧϣ., ShP 130⁴ 141 ⲡⲗⲏⲧⲥⲛ ⲉⲥⲟⲩⲟϣⲥ ⲉⲥϣ., ShBor 247 106 ⲁⲟⲏⲧ ⲡⲁⲓ ⲉⲡϣ. ⲁⲡ; as nn m: Ez 43 13 *B* prob *sic l* βάθος; ShIF 106 ⲡⲁϣⲉ ⲡϣ. ⲛ ⲧⲟⲩⲁϣⲥⲉ ⲡⲧⲉⲡⲗⲏⲧⲥⲛ, ShP 131⁴ 143 falling ⲉⲣⲣⲁⲓ ⲉⲡϣ. of devil. *Cf* ϣⲱⲕ, ϣⲓⲕⲉ, ϣⲟⲕϣⲉⲕ.

b *smite B* (*cf ?* ϣⲱⲱϭⲉ): AM 278 ϥⲏ ⲉⲑⲛⲁϣⲟⲕⲣ ϥ κρούειν; *ib* 38 ⲁϥϣⲟⲕⲣ ⲛⲧⲥⲛϥⲓ ⲁϥⲱⲗⲓ ⲛⲧⲉϥⲁϥⲉ, C 41 40 dealt him blow in face, ϭⲉⲛϯⲟⲩⲛⲟⲩ ⲉⲧⲁⲩϣⲟⲕⲣ ϥ.

ϣⲓⲕⲣ *SA*, ϣⲓⲭⲣ, ϣⲓⲭ *A* nn m, *depth*: Pro 14 12

A-ⲕⲣ(*S* ϣⲓⲕ, *B* ϩⲁⲉ)πυθμήν; Mic 7 19 A-ⲭⲣ(*SB* ϣⲓⲕ), Jon 2 4 A-ϫ(*i e* -ⲭ, *S* do, *B* ϣⲟⲕ), BMis 539 *S* ⲡⲉⲓϣ. ϣⲟⲕⲣ ϣⲁⲁⲣⲏϥϥ ⲙⲡⲡⲟⲩⲡ βάθος.

ϣⲁⲗ *SB*, ϣⲟⲗ *S*(?), ϣⲉⲗ *A²F*, ϩⲉⲗ *A*, ϩⲉⲗ *DM* nn m, *myrrh*: Ps 44 8 *S*(*B* = Gk), Cant 5 1 *SF*, Mt 2 11 *SB*, Jo 19 39 *SA²B*, Cl 25 2 *A*, P 44 65 *S* ⲡϣ. ⲙ̄ⲣ̄ σμύρνα, Mk 15 23 *SF*(*B* ϣⲁϣⲓ) σμυρνίζειν; Br 109 *S* ⲁⲣⲕⲏⲛⲥ (-ευθίς), ϣ., ⲗⲓⲃⲁⲛⲟⲥ, Ann 1 118 *S* ⲥϯⲡⲟⲩⲃⲉ ⲉⲧⲉⲡϣ. ⲡⲉ, C 86 177 *B* ⲟⲩⲙⲁⲣⲙⲁⲣ ⲛⲉⲙ ⲟⲩϣ. for wounds, PMéd 274 *S* ϣⲟⲗ in recipe, DM 13 10.

ϣⲁⲗ *v* ϣⲟⲗ 1° & 2°.

ϣⲁⲟⲗ *S* nn m, an implement (?): AZ 16 17 among σκεύη ϣⲟⲙⲛⲧ ⲡϣ. ⲡⲱⲥ (? ϣⲟⲗ ⲡⲱⲣⲥ *sickletooth*).

ϣⲉⲉⲗ *F v* ϣⲁⲁⲣ *skin*.

ϣⲓⲗ *S* nn, meaning unknown: PMéd 259 bind on wound ⲟⲩⲧⲟⲉⲓⲥ ⲡϣ. *Cf ?* ⲥⲓⲣ, ⲥⲉⲓⲗ.

ϣⲟⲗ *SB*, ϣⲓⲱⲗ *S*(once), ϣⲁⲗ *SᶠB*, ϩⲁⲗ *A* nn m, *molar tooth, tusk*, a of man: Job 19 20 *B*(*S* ⲡⲁⲁϫⲉ) ὀδούς; Tri 475 *S* ⲟⲃ̅ⲣⲉ, ϣ. ضرس ; C 43 4 *B* martyr's ⲡⲁⲭⲣⲓ & ϣ. drawn, *ib* 86 271 *B* pincers ⲛϫⲟⲭ ϣⲁⲗ, PMéd 292 *S* ⲟⲩⲡⲁ. ⲉⲉⲓⲉ ⲟⲩϣ., but *ib* 272 ⲡⲁ. & ϣ. same. b of animals: Job 41 5 *B*(*S* ⲟⲃ̅ⲣⲉ), Ez 27 15 *SB* ϣⲁⲗ, Joel 1 6 *B*(*A* ⲁⲃ̅ⲣⲉ)ὀδ.; Br 101 *S* swine-faced ⲡⲉϥϣ. ⲙⲡⲃⲟⲗ ⲡⲣⲱϥ, El 40 *A* leopards ⲛⲟⲩⲣ. ⲙⲡⲃⲗ ⲡⲣⲱⲟⲩ (*cf ib* 48 sim ⲛⲉⲉϫⲉ), ShA 2 104 *S* ⲡⲁ. & ϣ. of swine & ass, MIE 2 409 *B* snake's ϣ. ⲙⲡⲥⲙⲟⲧ ⲡⲣⲁⲡϣⲙⲟⲩ ⲛⲃⲉⲡⲡⲓ =PO 22 426 .أسنان المنشار *S*.

ⲁⲧϣⲁⲗ *Sᶠ*, *toothless*: PMich 4946 aged fleas ⲛⲥⲕⲓⲙ ⲡⲁ.

V KKS 38.

ϣⲟⲗ *SB*, ϣⲁⲗ *SA²F* nn m, *bundle*: Ex 12 22 *B*, Mt 13 30 *SF*(*B* ⲗⲛⲓⲣⲓ) δέσμη, cit ShViK 9624 169 *S* ϣⲁⲗ, R 1 4 31 *S* ϣ. ⲡⲉⲣⲉⲃⲓⲛⲉⲑⲓⲛⲟⲛ *fascis*; Tri 475 *S* حزم ; Miss 4 766 *S* ϣⲁⲗ ⲉⲡⲃⲛⲧ, PO 11 315 *B* ⲛⲥⲓⲙ, TurM 5 *S* ⲛⲟⲩⲟⲟⲧⲉ, ⲛⲥⲧⲟⲓ, MR 5 34 *S* ⲛϣⲉ, BP 11349 *S* crop yields neither rent nor ⲟⲩϣⲁⲗ ⲛⲣⲣⲉ, ManiH 24 *A²* tares ⲙⲁⲣⲟⲩ ⲡϣ.

ϣⲱⲗ *SBF*, ϩ. *A*, ϣⲉⲗ-*SBF*, ϣⲗ-*SA²*, ϣⲁⲗ-*F*, ϣⲟⲗ⸗ *SB*, ϩⲟⲗ⸗ *Sᵃ*, ϣⲁⲗ⸗ *SᵃF*, ⲣ ⲥ ϣⲁⲗ-*S* vb intr, *despoil*: Is 8 3 *SB* σκυλεύειν, *ib* 33 4 *SBF* σκῦλον; ShA 1 330 *S* ⲛⲧⲁⲡⲃⲁⲣ(ⲃⲁ)ⲣⲟⲥ ϣ., C 86 345 *B* thieves ϣ. ⲛⲥⲁⲡⲛⲓ; tr: Sa 10 20 *S*, Hab 2 8 *B* (*A* illegible) σκ.; Deu 20 14 *B*(*S* ⲱⲗ), Is 24 3 *S*(*B* ⲣⲱⲗⲉⲙ) προνομεύειν; Deu 28 29 *S*(*B* do), Zech 14 2 *SA*(*B* do) διαρπάζειν; Lu 10 42 *B*(*S* ϭⲓ) ἀφαιρεῖν; Job 12 6 *S*(*B* do) ἐκπορθεῖν; Is 1 8 *B*(*SF* ϣⲟϥ)πολιορκεῖν; ShMIF 23 165 *S* paral ⲃ̅ⲱϣ, Mor 16 59 *S*

ⲡⲉϥⲭⲣⲏⲙⲁ ⲛⲧⲉⲡϣⲟⲗⲟⲩ ⲛⲁⲛ, BM 337 97 ϯⲡⲛⲏ
ⲧⲁϣ. ⲙⲡⲉⲧⲛϯⲙⲉ, C 100 319 S ⲕϣ. ⲡⲡⲉⲣⲡⲏⲅⲉ,
BSM 74 B ϣⲉⲗ ⲡⲛⲓ=BMis 164 S ⲥⲩⲗⲁ, DeV 1 15
B wealth ⲙⲡⲁϣⲟⲗⲥ, CMSS 39 F ϣⲁⲗ ⲡⲉⲡⲉⲥⲕⲏ
ⲟⲩⲉⲓ of church; v also ⲣⲡⲉ;   ⲥ ⲉⲃⲟⲗ SA, spoil,
destroy tr: Zech 2 8 A(B ϣ. only) σκ.; Col 2 8 S(B
ⲕⲱⲗⲡ)συλαγώγειν; ShP 130⁴ 141 members ⲁⲕϣⲟⲗ
ⲟⲩ ⲉⲃ. ϣⲏⲡⲉⲓⲡⲁⲣⲁϥⲩⲥⲓⲥ, ShC 42 198 whoso shall
dare with own hands ⲉϣⲟⲗ ⲉⲃ. ⲯⲓⲛⲡⲣⲱⲃ ⲉⲧⲥⲟⲟⲩ,
ShA 1 126 ⲯⲉⲡⲣⲡⲁⲁⲩ...ⲉⲧⲙⲧⲁⲕⲟⲟⲩ ⲏ ⲉⲧⲙϣⲟⲗⲟⲩ
ⲉⲃ., J 65 71 not lawful to ϣ. ϯⲇⲓⲁⲑⲏⲕⲏ ⲧⲁⲓ ⲉⲃ., ib
95 26 Sᵃ ⲛϥⲟⲩⲱϣ ⲉⲣⲟⲗϥ ⲉⲃ. (sc deed of gift), ib 87
32 sim ϣⲁⲗϥ ⲉⲃ.; intr: ShViK 9346 ⲡⲥⲱⲡⲏ (l ⲍⲱ.)
ⲉⲧⲗⲟⲟⲙⲉ...ⲁⲩⲗⲱⲕ ⲁⲩϣ. ⲉⲃ. on reaching water,
BM 1059 ⲁⲡⲁⲧⲛⲕⲃⲉ ϣ. ⲉⲃ. opp ⲁⲃⲣⲟ (l ⲗⲟ recover).   ⲁⲧϣ. ⲉⲃ., indestructible or sim: J 12 9
ⲡⲣⲁⲥⲓⲥ ⲡⲁⲧⲁⲑⲉⲧⲉⲓ ⲙⲙⲟⲥ ⲡⲁⲧϣⲟⲗⲥ ⲉⲃ., ib 68 9
ⲡⲁⲧⲡⲁⲣⲁⲥⲁⲗⲉⲅⲉ ⲡⲁⲧϣⲁⲗⲥ ⲉⲃ.

ⲣ ⲥ in ϣⲁⲗⲣⲡⲉ   v ⲣⲡⲉ.

—— nn m SABF, spoil, booty: Pro 1 13 SAB,
Is 33 4 SBF, Zech 14 1 SAB σκῦλον; Pro 12 24
SAB, Is 33 23 SBF προνομή; Jth 15 7 S λάφυρα;
He 7 4 SF(B diff) ἀκροθίνιον; P 44 78 S ⲡϣ. ⲇⲏ
ⲙⲉⲅⲥⲓⲥ; BMis 29 S ⲡϣ. ⲡⲧⲉ ⲙⲡⲉⲣⲥⲟⲥ, C 86 195
B ⲱⲗⲓ ⲡⲡⲟⲩϣ.;   ⲉⲓⲣⲉ ⲡϣ.: Is 10 6 B(S ϥⲓ ⲡ
ϣⲟⲗⲥ) σκύ. ποιεῖν; ib 33 23 SBF πρ. ποι.

ⲣⲉϥϣ. S, spoiler: BHom 91 ⲣ. ⲙⲡⲙⲟⲩ πορθητής.
ϭⲓⲛ-, ϫⲓⲛϣ. SB, spoiling: Is 8 1 B(S ϣⲟⲗⲥ)
πρ.; BHom 103 S ⲧϭ. ⲡⲁⲙⲡⲧⲉ (= ALR '96 197
ⲗⲁⲓⲁⲕⲙⲟ, cf Renaudot Lit² 1 146 τὸν ᾅδην σκυ-
λεύσας).

ϣⲟⲗⲥ S, ϣⲁ. A² nn f, spoil: Deu 3 7 (B ϣⲱⲗ) σκ.;
Ez 34 22 (B ⲣⲱⲗⲉⲙ) πρ.; BIF 14 128 ϥⲓ ⲛⲣⲡϣ. ⲡ
ϫⲓⲟⲅⲉ, Mani H 8 A² ⲧϣ. ⲡⲏⲩ ⲁⲭⲡⲓⲭⲣⲏ[ⲙⲁ].

ϣⲱⲗ SA²B, ⲣⲱⲗ A, ϣⲉⲗ- F, ϣⲟⲗ÷ S, ϣⲏⲗᵗ SB
vb a intr, flow c ⲉ-: Pro 23 32 SA διαχεῖν; ShViK
9101 8 S poison ϣ. ⲉⲡⲣⲟ ⲙⲡⲉⲕⲣⲏⲧ;   ⲥ ⲣⲛ-:
Sh(?)Mor 54 142 S poison ϣ. ⲣⲣⲏⲧϥ;   ⲥ ⲉϫⲛ-(?):
PMéd 98 S ⲃⲁϣⲟⲩϣ (?) ⲉϥⲟⲏⲛⲩ ⲉϥϣ.ᵗ ⲉϫ[(cf ϣⲟⲗ
ϣⲗ Chassinat);   ⲥ ⲉⲃⲟⲗ, flow forth intr: Mani
H 80 A² blood ϣ. ⲁⲃ. ⲣⲓⲭⲙⲡⲕⲁⲣ, ViK 9659 8 S
ⲧⲕⲁⲕⲓⲁ ϣ. ⲉⲃ. ⲉϫⲛⲧⲉⲥⲣⲓⲙⲉ (sc Eve); tr: Pro 1
16 A(S ⲡⲱⲡⲉ, B om) ἐκχέειν, Nu 18 17 S(var ⲡⲱ
ⲣⲧ, B ⲫⲱⲡ) προσχ.; Mani H 75 A² ⲁⲩϣ. ⲁⲃ[ⲁⲗ ⲙ
ⲡⲉϥⲥⲡⲁϥ], PMich 593 S put juice against aching
tooth ⲡⲧϣ. ⲣⲱⲕ ⲉⲃ. rinse (?) mouth.   ⲃ tr, loosen,
dissolve, paralyse: BMis 32 S ⲁϥϫⲓ ⲡⲧⲉϥⲥⲛⲃⲉ ⲁϥ
ϣⲟⲗⲥ drew (?) it & slew sheep, ib 34 ⲁϥϣ. ⲡⲧⲉϥⲥⲛⲃⲉ
ⲁϥⲣⲓⲟⲅⲉ(but cf ϣⲱⲗⲙⲉ), AZ 65 126 F when he goeth
ⲉⲃϣⲉⲗ ⲡⲉⲃⲗⲱⲕⲉⲥ (λόγος); meanings obscure S: Ep
313 ⲡⲣⲟⲙⲡⲧ ... ⲡⲧϣⲟⲗⲟⲩ ⲕⲁⲗⲱⲥ ϫⲉⲡⲡⲉⲡⲗⲓⲕⲛⲟⲡ
ϥⲓⲧⲟⲩ, ST 251 ⲛⲧⲁⲗⲁⲥ[ⲉ] ⲙⲙⲟⲩ (quid ?) ⲡⲁⲩ ϫⲉ-

ⲛϥⲧ[..]ⲁⲓϣⲟⲗⲉϥ[...]ⲛⲣⲟⲙⲡⲧ ⲡⲧⲟⲟⲧϥ, Louvre ostr
R 1780 ⲡⲣⲧⲁⲃ ⲛⲥⲟⲅⲱ ⲛⲣⲃⲁⲕ...ⲕⲁⲛ ϣⲁⲗⲟ (l ? -ⲗϥ)
ⲛⲣⲟⲙⲧ ⲕⲁⲛ ⲁⲗⲗⲓⲥ(ⲉ) ⲙⲙⲟⲩ (both these doubtful),
Ep 260 ⲡⲧⲉⲣⲟⲩϣⲟⲗⲧ ⲉⲁⲓⲭⲟⲟⲩ (sc my share) ⲉⲃⲟⲗ
ⲉⲣⲟⲓ, ST 282 ⲡϣⲱⲡⲉ...ⲧⲥⲁⲃⲟϥ ⲡϥϣⲟⲗⲟⲩ...ⲛⲧⲁⲟⲩ
ⲁϣⲙⲟⲩ;   qual ⲥ ⲉⲃⲟⲗ, loosened, paralysed: Is 35
3 B(var & S ⲃⲏⲗ ⲉⲃ.), Mt 8 6 B(S ⲥⲏϭ), Ac 9 33 B
(SF do) παραλύεσθαι; Mor 26 17 S ⲛⲉⲧϣ. ⲉⲃ. ⲣⲛ
ⲡⲉϥⲥⲱⲙⲁ, ShIF 271 S sullied like ⲣⲉⲛⲣⲁⲁⲩ ⲉⲧϣ.
ⲉⲃ. neglected (?), Bristol Mus ostr H 4124 S if art
neglectful ⲡⲓⲥⲟ[ⲁⲓ ⲡⲁϣⲱⲡⲉ ⲉϥ]ϣ. ⲉⲃ., DeV 2 49 B
ⲧⲉⲕⲯⲩⲭⲏ ϣ. ⲉⲃ. at parched crops;   nn om ⲉⲃ.:
Lacr 128 B ⲡϣ. paralytics;   ⲣⲉϥϣⲟⲗ ⲉⲃⲟⲗ B in
ⲙⲉⲧⲣ., paralysis: Cat 131 leprosy & ϯⲙ. of sin.

ϣⲁⲗⲉ B   v ϭⲁⲗⲉ.

ϣⲁⲗⲉ- F   v ϣⲁⲣⲉ-.

ϣⲁⲗⲓ, ϣⲏⲏⲗⲓ F   v ϣⲁⲁⲣⲉ.

ϣⲏⲗⲓ, ϣⲏⲏⲗⲓ F   v ϣⲏⲣⲉ.

ϣⲉⲓⲗⲓ F   v ϣⲁⲓⲣⲉ.

ϣⲗⲏ SA² vb intr, creep (cf ? ϣⲱⲗ flow): P 44
122 worm ⲉⲧϣ. ⲣⲛⲙⲙⲁⲣⲧ ٤ٯٯ, R 1 2 17 poison
ⲉⲧϣ. ⲣⲛⲧⲉⲯⲩⲭⲏ, ShA 2 113 disease ⲉⲧⲣⲱⲣ ⲁⲩⲱ
ⲉⲧϣ., Mani 1 A² ⲁⲥϣ. ⲙⲡⲉϥⲥⲁ ⲛⲣⲟⲩⲛ, ib ⲉⲣⲉⲡⲟⲩ
ⲥⲁϩⲡⲉ ϣ. ⲛⲣⲏⲧⲟⲩ ⲉϥⲕⲓⲙ ⲁⲣⲁⲩ.   For ϣⲗⲏ R 1 3
25, 35 v ϣⲱⲗⲙ (LMis 423); ϣ. BMar 155 l ? ⲯⲩ
ⲭⲏ (cf ib π͞π͞α).

ϣⲗⲱ F   v ϣⲣⲱ.

ϣⲉⲗⲃⲉ S nn, meaning doubtful, veil or sim ?:
Mor 18 70 ⲁⲡⲟⲩⲃⲁϣ ⲉⲧⲣⲓⲱⲥ (sc leper) ⲕⲱⲕ ⲛⲑⲉ
ⲛⲟⲩϣ. (var ib 19 78 ⲡⲥⲱⲃⲣ ϭⲱⲗ ⲛⲑⲉ ⲛⲟⲩⲣⲏⲃⲥ, Miss
4 143 B diff). L ? ϣⲉⲡⲃⲉ (ϣⲉⲡϥⲉ).

ϣⲱⲗⲕ SB, ϣⲗⲕ-, ϣⲟⲗⲕ-S, ϣⲟⲗⲕ-B, ϣⲁⲗⲕ÷Sᵃ,
ϣⲟⲗⲕ÷ B vb intr, weave, stitch: Z 344 S ⲧⲥⲁⲃⲟⲟⲩ...
ⲉϣ. = MG 25 209 B ῥάπτειν; BM 536 S give me
ⲃⲏⲧ ... ϣⲁⲓϣ. ⲡⲧⲉⲓⲕⲩⲣⲓⲁⲕⲏ; tr: ROC 18 175 S
ϣ. ⲡⲧⲡⲏⲩⲧⲉ ⲛⲃⲓⲣ ⲥⲛⲁⲩ πλέκειν; Mor 37 97 S ϣⲗⲕ
ⲃⲓⲣ, MG 25 359 B ϣⲟⲗⲕⲟⲩ ⲉⲟⲩⲃⲓⲣ ⲛⲟⲩⲱⲧ ῥ., HL
97 B ϣⲟⲗⲕ ⲃⲓⲣ κατάρρ.; Sh(Besa)Z 506 S ⲡⲉⲧϣⲱⲗⲕ
ⲃⲓⲣ, JSch 10 29 S ⲓⲱⲣⲁⲡⲛⲓⲥ ⲡϣⲗⲕ (ⲕ)ⲁⲙ (or ? for
ϣⲗϭ), COAd 50 S' book ⲛϭⲟⲩⲣϥ ⲛⲧϣⲁⲗ[ⲕ]ϥ.

ϣⲗⲁⲕ S nn, among metal utensils: PMich 3552
ϭⲁⲣⲧⲉ, ϣ., ⲉϩⲁⲕⲉⲗⲗⲁⲣ(ⲓⲟⲛ).

ϣⲗⲟⲕ B   v ⲗⲟⲕ.

ϣⲁⲗⲟⲩⲕⲓ, -ⲁⲩⲕⲓ (once) B nn m, wasp: K 173
ⲡϣ. زنبور.

ϣⲗⲟϭ B   v ϣⲱⲗϭ (ϣⲗⲓϭ).

ϣⲗⲕⲏⲧ S nn as pl, meaning unknown (? ϣⲱⲗⲕ

+ ϩⲏⲧ): Lant 71, 72, 73 ⲡⲛⲓ ⲛⲛϣ. to which MSS dedicated.   Prob locality in White Monastery.

ϣⲗⲟⲕϣⲓ *B*   *v* ϣⲟⲗϫ (ϣⲗⲓϫ).

ϣⲗⲏⲗ *SAA²BF*, ϣⲗⲗ *S* vb intr, *pray*: Sa 7 7 *S*, Z 344 *S* εὔχεσθαι, Mt 26 36 *S*(*BF* ⲧⲱⲃϩ), Ro 8 26 *S* (*B* do), AP 49 *A²* προσεύ., MG 25 209 *B* εὐχὴν ποιεῖν; Lu 5 33 *S*(*B* ⲧ. nn) δεήσεις ποι.; ShC 73 63 *S* ⲉⲅⲛⲁϣ. (var ϣⲗⲗ), C 43 225 *B* ⲉϥϣ. ⲉϥⲧⲱⲃϩ, AM 267 *B* ⲉⲓⲟⲣⲓ ⲉⲣⲁⲧ ⲉⲓϣ., COAd 48 *S* ⲛⲉϥ ⲛϣ., ManiH 30 *A²* ⲛⲟ ⲛϣ., Hall 118 *S* invite him to come ⲛϥϣ. ϩⲓⲧⲛⲧⲟⲡⲟⲥ, BP 3274-75 *S* ϯϣ. ... ϫⲉⲕⲁⲥ ⲉⲣⲉⲡⲛ̄ⲛ[ⲁⲥⲙⲟⲩ ⲉⲣⲱ]ⲧⲛ, Cai Euch 222, 275 &c *B* ϣ. as rubric, not otherwise in Anaph Basil.

With following preposition.

—— ⲉ- *SB*(rare)*F*, *to, for*: Job 22 27, 2 Cor 13 7 *SF* εὔ. πρός, Ac 26 29 εὔ. dat, Ps 31 6 προσεύ. πρός, Phil 1 9 *SF*(all *B* ⲧ.)πρ. acc; Sa 8 21 ἐντυγχάνειν dat; ShWess 9 143 ⲡϣⲱϣⲉ ⲁⲛ ⲉϣ. ⲉⲡⲉⲭ̄ⲥ̄, Blake 280 ϣ. ⲉⲡⲓⲏⲃⲧ, BM 978 ϣⲁⲩϣ. ⲉϯⲣⲏⲛⲏ, Miss 8 138 ⲡⲉⲓϩⲱⲃ ⲉⲓϣ. ⲉⲣⲟϥ, J 75 37 ⲉⲛϣ....ⲉⲛⲁⲓ; vbal: Ro 9 3 (*B* ⲧ.), ViSitz 172 4 19 ϯϣ. ⲉⲡⲟⲭⲧ ⲡⲛⲉⲑⲏⲣⲓⲟⲛ εὔ.; ShA 1 186 ϣ. ⲉⲧⲣⲉϥϯ ϭⲟⲙ, *ib* 192 ϣⲗⲗ ⲉⲧⲙⲧⲣⲉ-, ROC 17 404 *B* ϣ. ⲉⲙⲟⲅ; ⲉϩⲣⲁⲓ ⲉ- *S*: Nu 21 7 (var ⲥⲟⲡⲥ, *B* ⲧ.) εὔ. πρός, 1 Kg 7 5 προσεύ. π.; BMis 54 ⲁⲩϣ. ⲉⲣ. ⲉⲡⲭ̄ⲥ̄.

—— ⲉⲧⲃⲉ- *SA*, *for*: Cl 56 1 *A* εὔ. περί, Ps 71 15 (*B* ⲧ.) προσεύ. π.

—— ⲉϫⲛ- *SA²B* (rare), *over, for*: Deu 9 20 (var ⲥⲟⲡⲥ, *B* ⲧ.), Job 42 8 (*B* ⲓⲣⲓ ⲛⲟⲩϣⲟⲩϣⲱⲟⲩϣⲓ) εὔ. περί, AP 16 *A²* ϣ. ⲁϫⲱⲉⲓ εὔ. ὑπέρ, Z 305 ϣ. ⲉϫⲙⲡⲉⲕⲟⲩϫⲁⲓ εὔ. acc, Lu 6 28 (*B* ⲧ.) προσεύ. ὑπέρ; Mt 5 44 (*B* do) εὐλογεῖν; ShC 42 136 ϣ. ⲉϫⲱⲓ, Miss 4 686 ϣ. ⲉϫⲙⲡϣⲟⲣϣⲣ of temple, BMis 175 ϣ. ⲉϫⲛⲧⲗⲓⲙⲛⲏ = BSM 85 *B*, MG 25 384 *B* ⲁϥϣ. ⲉϫⲉⲛⲡⲉⲛⲓⲱⲧ & dismissed him, Ep 244 ⲧⲁϣⲏⲣⲉ...ⲛϣ. ⲉϫⲱⲥ, BAp 79 ϣ. ⲉϫⲱⲓ ⲛⲧⲁⲃⲱⲕ = MIE 2 252 *B* (cf ROC 17 297 εὖξαι περὶ ἐμοῦ, PG 65 177 εὔ. ὑπέρ *farewell*), AM 215 *B* ⲧⲱⲃϩ ⲙⲙⲟϥ ⲉⲑⲣⲉϥϣ. ⲉϫⲱϥ; ⲉϩⲣⲁⲓ ⲉϫⲛ- *S*: Ac 8 15 (*B* ⲧ.) προσεύ. περί; Aeg 249, Baouit 1 140 God bless ⲡⲉⲧϣ. ⲉⲣ. ⲉϫⲱⲟⲩ.

—— ⲙⲛ- *S*, *with*: RE 9 150 ⲁⲡⲉⲛⲥⲙⲟⲩ ϣ. ⲙⲛϩⲭⲓⲗ (confirming agreement), *ib* 149 ⲁⲛϣ. ⲙⲛⲛⲉⲛⲧⲁϥⲉⲓ ϫⲉⲉϥⲛⲁⲧⲟⲣⲡ[, CO 291 ⲁⲛϣ. ⲙⲛⲛⲉⲛⲉⲣⲏⲩ ⲙⲛⲡⲣⲡⲗⲁⲡⲉ ⲙⲛϣ., *v* also nn. Cf nn, Mor 25.

—— ⲛ- dat *S*: Z 622 begged archbishop to ϣ. ⲛⲁϥ, BMOr 6201 A 165 ⲧⲁⲣⲉⲕⲉⲓ ⲛⲕϣ. ⲛⲁⲛ.

—— ϣⲁ- *SB*, *to*: Miss 8 207 ⲧⲛϣ. ϣⲁⲡⲭ̄ⲥ̄, BSM 39 *B* ϣ. ϣⲁϥϯ = BMis 384 *S* ⲥⲟⲡⲛ = Va 63 12 *B* ⲧ.

—— ϩⲁ-, ϩ̇ⲁ-*SAB*, *about, for*: Ge 20 7 (*B* ⲧ.), Jer 14 11 (*B* do), Aeg 241 ϣ. ϩⲁⲣⲟⲉⲓⲛⲉ προσεύ. περί; BMis 25 ϣⲗⲗ ϩⲁⲡⲡⲟⲃⲉ, TU 43 19 *A* ϣ. ϩⲁⲣⲁⲅ, Z 286 epistle ends ⲟⲩϫⲁⲓ...ⲉⲕϣ. ϩⲁⲣⲟⲛ, ST 17 sim

—— ⲉⲡϣⲱⲓ ϩⲁ- *B*, *up to*: C 43 164 ϣ. ⲉ. ϩⲁⲫϯ;   ⲉϩⲣⲏⲓ ϩⲁ- *B*: AM 151 ϣ. ⲉ. ϩⲁⲡⲥ̄ⲧ̄.

—— ϩⲛ- *S*, *in*: Deu 10 8 (*B* ⲥⲙⲟⲩ) ⲉⲡⲉⲩ́. ἐπί.

—— ϩⲓϫⲛ- *SB*, *over*: AM 215 *B* ϣ. ϩ.ⲟⲩⲕⲟⲩϫⲓ ⲙⲙⲱⲟⲩ, Lant 3 vo *S* ϣ. ϩⲓϫⲱⲟⲩ (sc donors of MS), *ib* 15, 58 sim.

—— nn m *SAA²BF*, *prayer*: Job 16 17 *S*(*B* ⲡⲣⲟⲥⲉⲩⲭⲏ), Pro 15 29 *SA* εὐχή, Ps 53 2 *S*(*B* = Gk), Ro 12 12 *SF*(*B* do) προσεύ.; ShC 73 130 *S* ⲕⲱⲗϩ ⲉⲡⲉϣⲗⲗ, *ib* 226 (Cyril) ⲉⲓⲧⲟⲩϫⲏ ϩⲙⲡⲉⲕϣⲗⲗ, BIF 13 119 *S* through ⲛⲉϣ. of fathers = MG 25 315 *B* ⲡⲣⲉⲥⲃⲓⲁ, ROC 27 150 *B* ⲁⲥϭⲓ ⲛⲁⲥ ⲛⲛϣ. of saint, El 54 *A* ⲡⲛⲟ ⲙⲛϣ., ManiH 18 *A²* ⲛϣ. ⲙⲡⲙⲯⲁⲗⲙⲟⲥ, BSM 88 *B* ⲡⲉⲛϣ....ϩⲓϫⲉⲛϯⲧⲣⲁⲡⲏⲍⲁ, AM 190 *B* ⲡϣ. ⲛⲧⲉ ⲡⲓⲉⲩⲁⲅⲅⲉⲗⲓⲟⲛ, BM 511 (2) *F* ⲟⲩϣ. ⲛⲕⲉ ϭⲓϫ, Hall 92 *S* ⲁⲣⲓ ⲡⲁⲙⲉⲉⲩⲉ ϩⲙⲡⲉⲧϣ. ⲉⲧⲟⲩⲁⲁⲃ, Mor 25 200 *S* ⲁϥϣⲱⲡ ϣ. ⲙⲙⲁϥ & promised (cf c ⲙⲛ-);   c ⲉⲓⲣⲉ: Miss 8 182 *S* chamber (κοιτών) ⲛⲧⲁⲕⲉⲓⲣⲉ ⲙⲡⲉⲕϣ. ⲛϩⲏⲧϥ, Lant 113 1 vo *S* ⲡⲉϣⲗⲗ ⲉⲧⲉⲥⲉⲓⲣⲉ ⲙⲙⲟⲟⲩ, AM 59 *B* ⲓⲣⲓ ⲛⲣⲁⲛϣ.;   c ϯ *SA²*: Ps 21 25(*B*=Gk) εὔ. ἀποδιδόναι; Mor 41 169 ⲧⲱⲟⲩⲛ ⲛⲧⲛϯ ⲛⲟⲩϣ., AP 2 *A²* ⲁϥϯ ⲙ[ⲡⲉϥϣⲗ]ⲏⲗ at 9th hour.

ⲁⲧϣ. *B*, *without prayer*: Miss 4 115 ⲉⲕⲛⲁⲣⲉⲙⲥⲓ ⲛ̇ⲁ.= Mor 19 30 *S* ⲁⲝⲛⲛϣ. (var *ib* 18 28 ⲁⲝⲛⲧⲣⲉⲕϣ.).

ϭⲓⲛϣ. *S*, *manner of praying*: BMis 450 ⲧⲉϥϭⲓⲛ ϣⲗⲗ, ϭⲓⲛϩⲙⲟⲟⲥ, ⲕⲁⲧⲁⲥⲧⲁⲥⲓⲥ.

V ⲥⲟⲛ **I**.

ϣⲗⲟⲗ, pl -ⲱⲗ (often confused) *B* nn m, *folk, people*, *SAF* always = Gk: Ex 33 13, Ps 32 12 (var -ⲱⲗ), Pro 24 61 (*SA*), Is 30 28 (*SF*), Ac 8 9 (var -ⲱⲗ) ἔθνος; 2 Cor 11 26 γένος; Ez 22 29 λαός; MG 25 297 ⲡⲉⲛϣ. = BIF 13 110 *S* ⲅⲉⲛⲟⲥ, C 43 238 ⲡⲁⲓϣ. ϫⲉⲭⲣⲏⲥⲧⲓⲁⲛⲟⲥ, *ib* 86 229 ⲡⲓϣ. ⲛⲧⲉ ⲡⲓⲅⲁⲗⲓⲗⲉⲟⲥ, DeV 2 228 ⲡⲁⲓϣ. ⲧⲏⲣⲟⲩ;   pl form: Ge 10 5, *ib* 35 11 (var -ⲟⲗ), Ps 46 4 (var do) ἔθ.

ϣⲗⲗⲟⲣⲉ *v* ⲗⲓⲗⲟⲟⲣⲉ.

ϣⲱⲗⲙ *SSᶠ*, -ⲉⲙ, ϣⲉⲗⲉⲙ- *B*, ϣⲗⲏ- *S*(R) vb intr, *smell*: Ps 114 3 *SB*, Am 5 21 *B* ὀσφραίνεσθαι; Pcod 23 *S* if nose shut ⲙⲉϥϣ., AM 120 *B* ⲡⲥⲉϣ. ⲁⲛ; tr: Ex 30 38 *B* ϣⲉⲗⲉⲙ- ὀσ.; R 1 3 25 *S* day when Lord ϣⲗⲏ ⲟⲩϭ̇ϯⲛⲟⲩϥⲉ (cf Ge 8 21 ϣⲱⲗⲙ), *ib* 35 *S* ⲁⲩϣⲗⲏ ⲟⲩⲥⲧ̇ⲛ. (v LMis 423), BMar 58 *S* ϣ. ⲛⲟⲩⲛⲟϭ ⲛⲥϯⲛ.;   With following preposition or adverb.   c ⲉ-: Lev 26 31 *SB* ὀσ. gen; Bor 226 181 *S* lions ϣ. ⲉⲣⲟϥ (sc Daniel), R 2 2 32 *S* ϣ. ⲉⲡⲉⲥⲧ̇ⲛ. (BHom 47 diff), BMis 279 *S* ϣ. ⲉⲩⲥϯⲛ.= Mor 30 58 *Sᶠ*, AM 5 *B* sim;   c ⲛ- agent *S*: Sa 15 15 (Gk diff);   c ⲉⲃⲟⲗ *B*: Va 61 100 hunters ϣ. ⲉⲃ. ⲛⲥⲁⲡⲉϥⲥⲟⲟⲓ *smell after* (track by smell) = Mor 25

18 S ϣ. ⲙⲡⲉϥϯ ⲛ.;   as nn m, *SB, sense of smell*: 1 Cor 12 17 B(S ϣⲁ), BHom 48 S ⲛϣ. ϩⲣⲁⲁⲡⲉ ⲛⲥⲁⲡⲧⲟⲓ ὄσφρησις.

ⲙⲁ ⲛϣ. *S, place, organ of smell*: P 131⁶ 12 (on Cant 7 4) ⲙⲙ. ⲡⲧⲉⲕⲕⲗⲏⲥⲓⲁ ⲉϣ. ⲉⲩⲧⲃⲃⲟ.

ϭⲓⲛ-, ϫⲓⲛϣ. *SB, sense, power of smell*: Va 66 288 B ⲛⲓϫ. when beholding flowers ὄσφρησις; Z 290 S ϭⲓⲛⲛⲁⲩ, ϭⲓⲛⲥⲱⲧⲙ, ϭ.

ϣⲱⲗⲙ *S nn, meaning unknown*: PMich 1545 list of names, often with following place: ⲕⲟⲗⲗⲟⲩⲑ(ⲟⲥ) ⲡϣⲉ ⲡⲉⲧⲣⲟⲥ ϣ.

ϣⲱⲗⲉⲙ *B vb, meaning unknown*: C 86 173 ⲡⲁϥⲙⲏⲛ ⲉϣ. ⲛⲉⲙⲡⲓⲉⲡⲟⲩⲣⲁⲛⲓⲟⲛ, ib 175 ⲡⲉϥⲛⲟⲩⲥ ϣ. ⲛⲉⲙⲡⲉⲡⲥⲱⲧⲏⲣ, ib 179 ⲙⲡⲉⲕ(l? ⲙⲡⲉⲣ)ϣ. ⲙⲡⲉϥ-(l ⲙⲡⲉⲕ- Amélineau) ⲛⲟⲩⲥ ⲉⲣⲟϥ *concern not (?) thy mind with him*.

ϣⲱⲗⲙⲉ A², ϣⲉⲗⲉⲙ- *B vb tr, draw forth* (cf שׁל‍ל Dévaud Ét 51): Mt 26 51 B(var Cat 76 ⲱⲗⲓ, S ⲧⲱⲕⲙ) ἀποσπᾶν; K 361 B جرّ; Mani H 8 A² ⲉⲩⲁϣ. ⲧⲥⲛϥⲉ. *Cf* ϣⲱⲗ *flow* ϧ.

ϣⲗⲁⲙ *B v* ϭⲗⲙ.

ϣⲗⲏⲓⲙⲓ *B v* ϣⲗⲁⲉⲓⲛ.

ϣⲗⲱⲙⲉⲃⲏϫ *B v* ⲃⲏϭ.

ϣⲗⲉⲙⲗⲉⲙ, -ⲗⲟⲙⲉ *B vb intr, breed*: Va 58 179 worms ⲉⲧϣ. ϩⲉⲛⲡⲓⲙⲁϩⲧ ζῳογονεῖν; ib 63 100 sores ⲉⲣⲉⲡⲓϥⲉⲡⲧ ϣ. ⲛϩⲏⲧⲟⲩ σκώληκες σηπεδόνες no vb; MG 25 155 passions like worms ϣ. ϩⲉⲛⲡⲓϧⲣⲏⲧ; tr: K 472 ⲉ(ϥ)ϣⲗⲉⲙⲗⲟⲙϥ تحبّب, (sic l?).

ϣⲟⲗⲙⲉⲥ SB, ϣⲁⲗ. Sᶠ, ϭⲟⲗ. *B nn f, gnat*: Mt 23 24 SB, Mor 18 125 Sᶠ κώνωψ; BM 491 116 S ⲧϣ. باعوضة (l 'بعـ'); K 173 B ϭ. ناموسة, ShRyl 70 249 S hands ⲧⲟⲗⲙ ⲕⲁⲧⲁ ⲡϣⲓ ⲛⲧϣ. ⲉⲧⲟⲩϩⲟⲗⲟ ⲙⲙⲟⲥ ⲉⲃⲟⲗ, Bor 252 129 S ϩⲉⲛⲁⲃ ⲙⲡⲉⲛϣ., C 99 105 S hands bled from ⲛⲁϣⲁⲓ ⲛϣ. ⲉⲧⲟⲩⲱⲙ ⲙⲙⲟⲟⲩ, MG 25 224 B body swelled ⲛⲧⲉⲛⲛⲓϣ., ViK 9533 S ϣ. ⲛⲁⲧϭⲟⲙ beating wings against rock.

ϣⲗⲁⲉⲓⲛ, ϣⲗⲉⲓⲛ S, ϣⲗⲏⲓⲙⲓ, ϭⲗ. *B nn m, cress, nasturtium*: P 44 83 S ⲕⲉⲣⲁⲙⲱⲛ · ϣ. حبّ الرشاد, K 194 B ⲛⲓϭ. (var ϣ.) ', ; Ryl 106 66 S ϣ. among drugs, PMéd 171 S sim, Ryl 388 S. *V* Löw 396.

ϣⲁⲗⲁⲛⲟⲥ *S nn, among metal implements*: Ep 547 ϣ. ⲡⲉⲓⲱ, for ? χαλινός, or cf ? bédane (bec d'âne) *chisel* (Dévaud).

ϣⲗⲟⲡ *S nn m, ply, strand* of cord (cf DM 8 17 ḥlpe): BMis 241 ⲟⲩⲙⲁⲥⲧⲓϩⲅ...ⲛϥⲧⲟⲟⲩ ⲛϣ. (varr Mor 29 14 ⲕⲱⲃ, ib 30 16 ⲣⲁ), Mun 35 ⲟⲩⲧⲁⲩⲗⲉ (ταυρεία)sim, Louvre R 73 ⲡⲣⲏⲃⲥ ⲛⲧⲗⲩⲭⲛⲓⲁ...ⲡⲏⲩ ⲉϩⲣⲁⲓ ⲛⲟⲩϣ. ⲛⲟⲩⲱⲧ, Win 44 v ⲟⲩⲱⲧⲃ C (ⲟⲩⲁⲧⲃⲥ). *Cf* ϣⲱⲗⲡⲓ, ϣⲗⲟⲡⲗⲡ, ϩⲗⲟⲡ.

ϣⲱⲗⲉⲡ *F v* ϣⲱⲣⲡ.

ϣⲗⲱⲗⲡⲓ *B nn f, warp*: K 257 ϯϣ. سَدِى (= سَدَى as K, but word ambiguous). *Cf?* ϣⲗⲟⲡ.

ϣⲗⲟⲡⲗⲡ *S nn, meaning unknown, thread, cord?*: Louvre 10022 ϩⲁⲗⲟⲥ (? *balteus*) ⲛⲛⲟⲩⲃ ⲉϥϩⲟⲃⲧ ⲛⲥϥⲣⲁⲅⲓⲥ ⲉϥⲁϣⲉ ⲛϣ. ⲛⲕⲁⲕⲟ *studded with jewels* (σφ.) *hung about with scarlet*.... *Cf* prob ϣⲗⲟⲡ, ϣⲱⲗⲡⲓ.

ϣⲟⲗⲥ *v* ϣⲱⲗ *despoil*.

ϣⲉⲗⲉⲉⲧ SA, -ⲏⲧ S, -ⲉⲧ AA²B, -ⲏ(ⲛ)ⲧ, ϣⲏⲗⲏⲧ F *nn f, a bride*: Ge 11 31 SB, Is 61 10 SB, Mic 7 6 SAB, Jo 3 29 SBF νύμφη; Ap 19 7 SB γυνή; ShA 2 153 S ⲟⲣϣⲓⲣⲉ ⲙⲡⲉϥϣ., Mani 1 A² ⲧⲉⲕϣ. ⲡⲁⲧⲭⲱⲙⲉ, Pcod 13 S ⲡⲡⲩⲙⲫⲓⲟⲥ ⲡⲧⲉϥϣ., DeV 2 178 B Sarah ϯϣ. ⲧⲥϩⲓⲙⲓ of Abraham, BMar 8 S father loq ⲧⲉⲕϣ. ϯⲡⲁϩⲓⲧⲉ ⲛⲁⲕ, Miss 8 182 S mother loq ⲁⲓϣⲉⲡ ⲧⲟⲟⲧⲉ ⲛⲧⲉⲕϣ. ⲛⲁⲕ = BMar 17 S ⲉⲓⲛⲁϫⲓ ϩⲱⲛ ⲛⲁⲕ ⲛⲧⲉⲕϣ., PMéd 287 S ⲟⲩⲣⲏⲧ (ⲛ)ⲕⲗⲟⲙ ⲛϣⲉⲗⲗⲉⲧ in recipe (cf ⲡⲁⲧϣ.); *daughter-in-law*: Lev 18 15 SB, Ru 1 6 S, Mt 10 35 SBv.; ⲣ, ⲟ ⲛϣ. *S, be bride*: BHom 29 ⲣ ϣ. ⲛⲓⲥ̄ νυμφεύεσθαι; Mus 42 214 ⲟ ⲛϣⲁⲗ. (sic, l? ϣⲗⲗ.); ϭⲓ ϣ. *B, take bride, marry*: Aeg 38 day of ⲡⲉϥϭⲓ ϣ.

ϧ *marriage SB*(rare)F: Est 9 22, Sa 13 17, Jo 2 1 SF-ⲏⲛⲧ(B ϩⲟⲡ)γάμος, ROC 17 404 B ⲗⲁⲙⲡⲁⲥ ⲛϣ. γαμήλιος; Cant 3 11 SF-ⲏⲛⲧ νύμφευσις; Mor 19 37 bidden to ⲟⲩϣ. = Miss 4 121 B ⲙⲁ ⲛϣ., Bor 143 41 bid to ⲧϣⲉⲗⲉⲉⲧ, WTh 152 ⲕⲁⲓⲣⲟⲥ ⲛⲧⲉⲛϣ., BM 691 F wine (ⲉ)ϩⲟⲩⲛ (ⲛ)ⲧⲉⲃϣⲏ., Aeg 39 B ⲡϣⲁⲓ ⲛⲧϣ. of king's son (cf 38 sim ϩⲟⲡ), J 37 25 inherited share ϩⲁⲥⲭⲁⲁⲧ, ϩⲁϣ. ϩⲁⲣⲟⲙⲡⲉ ⲛⲟⲩⲱⲙ; ⲉⲓⲣⲉ, ⲣ ϣ., *make marriage*: Ge 29 22 (B ϩ.), Tob 8 16 γάμον ποιεῖν; BMis 281 ⲉⲓⲣⲉ ⲛⲧϣ. ϩⲛⲟⲩⲛⲟϭ ⲙⲙⲛⲧⲗⲁⲙⲡⲣⲟⲥ, Mor 30 61 F ⲓⲣⲓ ⲛⲧϣⲉⲗⲛⲏⲧ; ⲥ ⲉ- S, *for*: BMar 185 father ⲟⲩⲱϣ ⲉⲡⲣ ϣ. ⲉⲣⲟⲓ γάμῳ προσομιλεῖν; Mor 34 40 ⲉⲓⲣⲉ ⲛⲟⲩϣ. ⲉⲡⲉϥϣⲏⲣⲉ = Aeg 38 B ϩ., Bor 143 39 Paul ⲉϥⲣ ϣⲉⲗⲗ. ⲉⲩⲣⲱⲙⲉ named Paêse (var Mor 28 140 ⲛⲟⲩⲣⲱⲙⲉ), meaning doubtful, J 68 71 ⲧϣⲉⲗⲏⲧ ⲛⲧⲁⲓⲁⲁⲥ ⲉⲣⲟϥ (mother for son); ⲥ ⲙⲛ- S, *with*: Mor 37 9 parents to son ⲡⲧⲉⲓⲣⲉ ⲛⲧⲉⲕϣ. ⲛⲙⲙⲁⲥ, Ryl 139 ⲧⲁⲣⲛ-(sc parents) ⲣ ⲧϣ. [ⲙⲡⲓⲏ]ⲛⲏⲣⲏⲩ; ⲥ ⲛ- S, *for*: Mt 22 2 (var ⲉ-, B ϩ.) γ. ποι. dat.

ⲙⲛⲧϣ. S: AZ 14 22 ⲙⲉⲧϣ. (sic?, not found).

ⲙⲁ ⲛϣ. *SAB, place of marriage, bridechamber, marriage*: Mt 22 9 S(var ϣ., B ϩ.)γ.; Mk 2 19 S(B ⲡⲓⲡⲁⲧϣ.)νυμφῶν; Ps 18 6 SB, Joel 2 16 AB παστός; ROC 17 404 B ⲕⲟⲓⲧⲱⲛ ⲙⲙ. θάλαμος; TU 43 22 A ⲡⲣⲟ ⲛⲡⲙ., Mor 43 134 S ⲣⲉϥⲧⲱϩⲙ ⲉⲡⲙ. (v ⲧⲱϩⲙ s f), Miss 4 121 B ⲟⲩⲁⲣⲓⲥⲧⲟⲛ ⲓⲉ ⲟⲩⲙ., Va 63 1 B bidden to ⲫⲙ. = BMis 361 S ⲧϣ. = BSM 22 B ⲫⲙⲱⲓⲧ ⲛⲡϩ.

ⲡⲁⲧϣ. *SAA²BF*, *he of the bride*, *bridegroom* mostly + art ⲡⲡ., ⲡⲓⲡ.: Is 61 10 *SB*, Mt 25 1 *S*(var ⲡ.)*B*, Jo 3 29 *S*(var do)*BF* ⲡⲡ. νυμφίος; R 1 3 68 *S* ϣⲏⲣ ⲙⲡⲁ., TU 43 21 *A* ⲡⲡ., ib 22 ⲡ., Mani 1 *A²* ⲡⲡⲁϫⲉⲗⲉⲧ, BM 889 *B* ⲡⲁⲓⲡ., Aeg 40 *B* ⲡⲉⲥⲡ., ST 116 *S* ⲟⲩⲧⲗ[ⲟ]ⲗⲗⲉ ⲙⲡ., GPar 2 4 *S* crowns of ⲡⲉⲓⲡ. *bridal pair*: ⲙⲉⲧⲡ. *B*, *condition of marriage*, *nuptials*: BSM 41 raiment finer than that of their ⲙ.

In names: ⲧϣⲉⲗⲏ[ⲧ(Win 60), *Τσελῆτ*(POxy 2058), *Τσελέτ*, -ⲉⲉⲧ (Preisigke), ϫⲉⲣⲉⲧ (? WZKM 26 339).

ϣⲗⲓⲧ *B* *v* ϣⲗⲓϭ.

ϣⲗⲧ(ⲉ)ⲙ, ϣⲉⲗⲧⲁⲙ *v* ϣⲗϭⲟⲙ.

ϣⲁⲗⲓⲟⲩ, -ⲏⲟⲩ *S*, -ⲓⲅ *SF*, ϣⲁⲣⲓⲟⲩ *S*, *Τσαλιου* (τσ = ϣ) nn m, an administrative (financial?) official: ST 98 no service shall be demanded save ⲡⲉⲧⲁⲣⲟⲕ ⲙⲁ ⲡⲡϣ. (v Studi … A Albertoni 339), Ryl 373 ⲛ ⲧⲓ ⲁⲣ̅ ⲕⲩ…ⲛⲧⲁⲡϣ. ⲉϭⲁⲓ ⲡⲁⲓ ϫⲉⲧⲁⲁϥ, BMOr 6201 A 168 distribution of ⲥⲟⲓ & ϩⲁ to villages ⲛⲡⲉⲣⲕⲁ ⲡϣ. ⲉⲙⲓϣⲉ ⲛⲉⲙⲁⲛ, ST 212 ⲡϣ. ⲁϥⲧⲛⲛⲟⲟⲩϥ (ⲉ)ϩⲣⲁⲓ ⲁϥⲁⲡⲁⲓⲧⲉ ⲁϥϯ ⲡⲣⲱϣⲉ ⲙⲙⲁⲕⲗⲁⲃⲉ (μαγκλάβιον)…ⲡϣ. ϯ ⲁⲡⲁⲛⲕⲏ ⲉⲣⲟⲓ, ViK 4720 am in trouble ϫⲛⲧⲁϣ. ⲉⲓ ⲉⲧⲓⲭⲱⲣⲁ, Bodl(P) d 20 debt repaid to ⲁⲡⲁ (? ابى) ⲁⲙⲣⲟⲩ ⲡϣ., ViK 4707 ⲧⲗⲉϩⲉⲣⲡⲟⲥ (ship) ⲛⲧⲁⲡϣ. ϩⲓⲧⲃ̅, PLichatschov (Jern) ⲡϣⲁⲗⲓⲅ ⲛⲡⲧⲏ-ⲛⲉ, *ArchaiolEphem* '15 31 *F* ⲡϣⲓ ⲡϣⲁⲗⲓⲅ, Cai 42573 1 ⲟⲅⲁⲣⲭⲱⲛ ⲡϣⲁⲗⲓⲅ, PFrankfurt 43 (Spg) ⲡϣⲁⲣ., Ryl 374 ⲡϣⲁⲗⲏⲟⲩ, PCai 3 38 *Παπνούθης τσαλιου.* In place-names: PLond 4 218 *Νιαϩ Τσαλιου*, PRoss-Georg 4 81 *Πιαϩ Τζαλιου*.

ϣⲁⲗⲟⲟⲩ *S*, -ⲗⲁⲩ *Sᶠ* nn f, implement or mechanism which turns, *water-wheel* (?): Gu 94 ⲁⲡⲧⲟⲟⲩ (where Lazarus's tomb) ⲕⲱⲧⲉ ⲛⲑⲉ ⲛⲟⲩϣ. (var MIF 9 84 *Sᶠ*), Mor 51 16 *Sᶠ* cloud like ϣ. ⲉⲥⲕⲱⲧⲉ pours down water (cf ? wheel of *sâḳiah*), Ryl 340 ϣ.…ⲁⲓ-ⲙⲁϩⲥ ⲡⲓⲃⲧ… ϣⲁⲥϯ ⲧⲉⲓϩⲁⲙⲟⲟⲩ…, ⲧϣ.…ⲫⲁⲙϣⲉ ⲛⲏⲩ ⲉⲣⲟϥ (*l* -ⲟⲥ), ib 241 ϣ. ⲥⲡⲧⲉ ⲛⲃⲁⲣ[ⲱⲧ(?), BM Or 6201 A 157 ⲧϣ. ⲛⲃⲁⲣ[ⲣⲉ, ⲉ̄ ⲛⲧⲣⲉ ⲛⲧϣⲁ[ⲗⲟⲟⲩ, ib A 90 ⲧⲣⲉ ⲡϣ., ViK 4741 list ⲡⲁⲣⲃ, ϣ., ϭⲱⲧ, ϣⲟⲧⲉ, Bodl(P) f 44 list ϩⲛϭⲉ, ϩⲁⲙⲉ, ϣ., BM 1063 wages ϩⲁⲧϫⲁⲣⲟⲟⲩ, Cai 42573 *v* ⲧⲁⲕⲟ nn.

ϣⲗⲱⲟⲩϣ *B* *v* ϭⲗⲱⲟⲩϣ.

ϣⲁⲗϣⲉⲗ *F* *v* ϣⲟⲣϣⲣ.

ϣⲁⲗⲁϣⲓⲗ *S* nn m, meaning unknown: Hall 92]ⲡϣ. [no context.

ϣⲗⲙϣⲓⲗ *S*(once), ϣⲉⲗϣⲏⲓⲗⲓ, -ϣⲏⲗⲓ *B* nn m, *unripe*, *sour grapes*: Job 15 33 (*S* ⲉⲗⲉⲗϩⲓϫ), Pro 10 26 (*SA* do), Jer 38 29 (*S* ShA 1 263 do) ὄμφαξ; Glos 246 *S* ⲡϣ. · γιγαρτώνιον; K 178 (var -ϣⲏⲗⲓ) = Bodl 325 157 ⲡⲓϣ. حصرم; DeV 1 100 vine ⲥⲟⲩⲟϫ ⲉϣ. *free from sour grapes.*

ϣⲟⲗϣⲗ *S*, ϣⲉⲗϣⲉⲗ-*B*(once), ϣ(ⲉ)ⲗϣⲱⲗ⸍, ϣ(ⲉ)ⲗϣⲱⲗ⸓, ϣⲣϣⲱⲣ⸓ *S* vb tr, *shake in sieve*, *sift*: Lu 22 31 *B*(*S* ⲥⲱⲕ) σινιάζειν; ShA 2 74 ⲉⲅϣ. ⲡⲣⲉⲡⲉⲥⲏⲧ ϩⲛⲡⲕⲟⲡⲣⲓⲁ seeking gold, PMéd 89 ⲑⲛⲟⲟⲩ ϣⲗϣⲱⲣⲟⲩ ϩⲛⲟⲩⲥⲟⲣϥ (*l* -ⲗϥ), AZ 23 104 sim, PMéd 158 ϣⲗϣⲱⲗⲟⲩ, TurM 9 ⲡⲟⲩⲛⲉ ⲛⲕⲉⲡⲁⲣⲓⲥ (? κάππαρις) ϣⲉⲗϣⲱⲗⲟⲩ, BM 1031 ⲛⲥⲟⲩⲟ…ⲉⲅϣ.⸓, ib 1073 sim ϣⲣϣⲱⲣ⸓ (*cf* κεκοσκινευομένος); PSBA 27 167 ⲉϣⲱ-ⲡⲉ ⲟⲩⲉⲓ (*sc* vellum leaf) ⲉⲥⲟ ⲡⲗⲕⲉ [ⲗ]ⲕⲉ ⲛ ⲉⲥϣ.⸓ meaning?; as nn, *shaking*: Si 27 4 σεῖσμα.

ϣⲗϣⲟⲗ *S* nn m, meaning unknown: ST 108 ⲡϣ., ? place-name.

ϣ(ⲉ)ⲗϥ *v* ϣⲗⲁϩ (ϣⲗϩϥ).

ϣⲟⲗϥ *S* nn, meaning unknown: Ep 533 ⲡⲥⲁⲛϣ. For ? ⲥⲟⲗϥ.

ϣⲗⲟϥ *SB*, -ⲁϥ *AF*, ϭⲗⲟϥ *B* nn m, *shame*, *disgrace*: 1 Cor 14 35 *SF*(*B* ϣⲓⲱϣ), Cl 47 6 *A* αἰσχρός, Eph 5 4 *S*(*B* ϣⲟⲩϣⲧ) αἰσχρότης; Lev 18 23 *S*(*B* ⲱⲣⲉⲃ) μυσαρός; Ac 10 28 *S*(*B* ϩⲟϥ) ἀθέμιτος; ShC 73 59 *S* ϩⲉⲛϣ. ⲡⲉ ⲡⲉⲓⲡⲁⲑⲟⲥ, R 1 4 33 *S* was as if ⲛⲧⲁⲟⲩϣ. ⲧⲁϩⲟⲥ, ROC 20 46 *S* dancers & rest of ϣ. ⲡⲣⲉϥⲁⲡⲁⲧⲁ, Sh(Besa)Bor 205 363 *S* ⲡⲁⲓ ⲉϣ. ⲡⲉ ⲉ-ϫⲟⲟⲩ, ShViK 9346 *S* ⲉϣ. ⲡⲉ ⲡⲁⲩ ⲉⲣⲟⲟⲩ, K 89 *B* ⲫⲁⲛⲓϭ. ذو الاباطيل; as adj, *shameful*: ⲟⲩⲧⲣⲟϥⲏ ⲛϣ. Bor 226 172 *S*; ϣⲁϫⲉ ⲛϣ. Col 3 8 *S*(*B* ϣⲟⲩϣⲧ) αἰσχρολογία; ShC 73 45 *S* ϩⲉⲛϣⲱ. ⲡⲉⲡⲣⲁ ⲛ ⲛϣ., Z 636 ⲛ *S* ϣⲭⲱ. ⲏ ϣϫⲥⲱⲃⲉ, Va 58 190 *B* ⲟⲩⲥ. ⲛϣ.; ϫⲓⲛⲉ ⲛϣ. ib 61 19 *B*; ϩⲏⲅ ⲛϣ. 1 Tim 3 8 *S*(*B* ϣⲛϣ) αἰσχροκερδής; ⲙⲁⲓϩ. ⲛϣ. Pcod 36 *S*, ⲙⲛⲧⲙⲁⲓϩ. ⲛϣ. 1 Pet 5 2 *S*(*B* ⲙⲉⲧⲁϥϭⲓⲣ) -κερδῶς; JA '75 5 250 *S*, Va 61 92 *B*.

ϣⲗϩ *SAA²*, ϣⲉⲗϩ, ϣⲗⲉϩ *S*, ϭⲗⲉϩ *B*(rare) nn m, *twig*, *shoot*: Nu 13 24 (*B* ⲥⲙⲁϩ), Ps 79 11 (*B* = Gk), Ez 19 11 (*B* ⲭⲁⲗ), Nah 2 3 *A*(*B* = Gk), Jo 15 2 *SA²* (*B* do), ib 5 *S*(*A²* ⲧⲉⲣ, *B* do) κλῆμα, Deu 32 32(*B* do) κληματίς, Job 40 17 (*B* ϫ.) κλών; ib 29 18 (*B* ⲭⲁϥ) στέλεχος; Ge 49 11 (*B* = Gk) ἕλιξ كرم; K 256 *B* ⲡⲓϭ. قطب; ShR 2 3 44 *v* ⲣⲡⲱ, ShA 2 24 ⲡϣ. of vine withers if cut off, TT 18 ⲡϣ. ⲉⲧⲉϥⲛⲁϯ ⲕⲁⲣ-ⲡⲟⲥ ⲁⲛ, Mor 31 228 basket of grapes ⲁϥⲥⲟⲩⲗⲱⲗⲟⲩ ⲛϩ(ⲉ)ⲛϣⲉⲗϩ = BMOr 3599 101 عرق, BMis 562 ⲛ-ⲥⲙⲁϩ ϩⲛⲛϣ. of vine; ϣⲗ(ⲉ)ϩ *stave*, *wand*: Ps 22 4 -ⲉϩ (var ϣⲗϩ, *B* ϣⲃⲱⲧ) ῥάβδος; Is 31 9 ϣⲗϩ (*B* ϭⲗⲟ, *F* ϫⲁⲗϭⲉⲗ) χάραξ; PSBA 25 274 ⲕⲟⲩⲓ ⲛϣⲗ-ⲉϩ ⲉϥϩⲛ[ⲧⲉϥ]ϭⲓⲝ.

ϣⲗⲉϩ, -ⲏϩ *S*(Sh only) vb intr, *use twigs*, ? in faggots for strengthening canal banks (*cf* Schnebel *Landwirtschaft* 1 39): C 73 152 ⲡⲉⲧⲡⲣⲟⲥⲉⲭⲉ ⲉϣ. ⲉⲡⲙⲟⲟⲩ ⲉⲧⲓⲕⲁ ⲡⲙⲟⲟⲩ ⲉⲃⲱⲕ ⲉϫⲙⲡⲉ(ⲧ)ⲧⲥⲟ, 153 ⲙⲁ ⲉϥⲙⲟⲕϩ ⲛϣ. ⲙⲙⲟϥ, ib ⲡⲉⲧϣⲗⲏϩ, 152 ⲙⲟⲩϣⲧ ⲙⲡⲣⲁϣ. ⲙⲙⲏⲛⲉ. Otherwise explained AZ 33 68,

Rec 26 37. ⲡⲣⲁϣ (p 269) ? scribal error for ⲡⲣⲁ-
ϣⲗⲉϩ.

ϣⲱⲗϩ SBF, -ⲁϩ(nn) S, -ⲉϩ F, ϣⲱⲗϩ- S, ϣⲟⲗϩⲉ SB,
ϣⲟⲗϩ† SB, vb tr, *make, impress mark, trace line* &c:
Ap 13 16 B(S ϯ ⲉϩⲣⲁⲓ) χάραγμα διδόναι; ShC 73 130
S ϣ. ⲙⲙⲁⲉⲓⲛ ⲙⲡⲉϥϥⲟⲥ ⲉⲧⲧⲉϩⲛⲉ, BMis 476 S ϣ.
ⲡⲟⲩⲥ†ⲟⲥ ⲉⲡⲕⲁϩ, Mor 28 256 S ϣ. ⲉϫⲱϥ ⲡⲟⲩⲥ†ⲟⲥ
= RA199 B, BAp 112 S ⲥϥⲣⲁⲅⲓⲥ ⲡⲧⲁⲡⲡⲉⲧⲟⲩⲁⲁⲃ ϣ.
ⲙⲙⲟⲥ ⲉⲧⲉⲣⲉ = MIE 2 389 B ⲉⲥⲱ.† ⲉ-, BM 334 S
ⲁⲡⲣⲁⲧⲓⲟⲥ ϣⲱⲗϩϥ ϩⲙⲡⲉϥⲧⲏⲃⲉ = C 86 320 B ⲧⲏⲓϥ
ϩⲉⲡ-, R 1 4 29 S ⲁϥϣ. ⲡⲁⲩ ⲡⲧⲉⲕⲕⲗⲏⲥⲓⲁ *lineam
mittere*, LAp 513 F sim by scattering chaff, DeV 2
229 B Noah's ark ϣ.† ⲕⲁⲧⲁ ⲙⲁⲣⲓ, Cat 162 B letter
ⲉⲧϣ.† ⲓⲥϫⲉⲡⲧϥⲉ ⲉⲡⲉⲥⲏⲧ is *iota*, Pcod 24 S forms
that Satan ϣ. ⲙⲙⲟⲟⲩ ϩⲙⲡⲉϥϩⲏⲧ, RE 9 160 S ⲁⲓϣ.
ⲡⲣⲁⲛ ⲙⲡⲕⲉⲁⲙⲣⲏ *mark off, set mark against*; intr:
P 44 96 S ⲙⲡⲟⲩⲉⲧⲕⲁϩⲉⲓ (ἐγκακεῖν) ⲉⲩϣ. ⲗⲁ.

—— SBF nn m, *stake, mark*: Is 37 33 S(B ϭⲗⲟ,
cf 31 9 ϣⲗϩ), Lu 19 43 S(B diff) χάραξ, Ap 14 11 B
(S ⲙⲁⲉⲓⲛ) χάραγμα, Lev 13 28 B(S ⲉⲓⲡⲉ) χαρακτήρ;
Cant 1 11 F, Gal 6 17 BF(S ⲙ.) στίγμα, Is 29 5 B
(S ⲥⲟⲩⲥⲟⲩ) στιγμή; Mt 5 18 SB κεραία ⲗⲁ; Blake
252 S ⲟⲩϣⲱⲗⲁϩ ⲉϥⲟⲩⲉⲧⲟⲩⲱⲧ *punctum*; K 255 B
ϣⲟⲗϩ ⲣⲟ; Br 49 S ⲡⲉⲓϣⲟⲙⲛⲧ ⲛϣ. (*sc* 3 strokes),
Miss 4 647 S surrounded demon with ⲟⲩϣ. ϫⲉⲛ-
ⲡⲉϥⲛⲡⲱⲧ, CO 149 S land measured ϫⲓⲛⲙⲡϣ. ⲉϩⲣⲁⲓ,
JKP 2 174 S Constantine's cross ⲉⲣⲉⲡϣ. ϩⲓⲧⲉϥ-
ⲙⲏ[ⲧⲉ], C 86 212 B ⲡⲉϥϣ. *spokes* (?) of torture
wheel, BM 1114 S ϣ. ⲉⲕⲓⲛϩⲏⲣ, BMOr 6201 B 38
S ϣⲱⲣⲁϩ ⲛⲕ., Ryl 291 S sim; ϯ ϣ., *set mark,
boundary* S: ShBM 210 ⲡⲟⲩ]ϫⲁϩⲉ ⲛ[ⲁϯ ⲡ]ⲟⲩϣ.
[ⲉ]ⲣⲟ & shut thee in, Mor 41 170 ⲁϥϯ ⲡⲟⲩϣ. ⲉⲡⲕⲁϩ…ⲛⲧⲡⲁⲥⲛⲧ ⲡⲉⲓϣ. ⲁⲡ ⲉⲃⲟⲗ, Miss 4 766 ⲁⲛⲁⲓⲱⲧ
ϯ ⲡⲟⲩϣ. ⲉⲣⲟϥ ⲉⲡⲕⲱⲧⲉ so that he could not stir,
BMis 264 ϯ ⲡϣ. ⲉⲡⲁⲙⲁⲣⲧⲩⲣⲓⲟⲛ (var Mor 29 34
ⲟⲩⲱϩ ⲡⲧⲥⲛⲧⲉ).

ϣⲱⲗϩⲥ B nn, *line traced*: K 255 ⲗⲁ.

ϣⲗⲁϩ SAB, ϣⲟⲗϩ† SB vb intr, *be afraid*: Deu
1 21 S(B ϣ. ⲛϩⲏⲧ), Jos 8 1 S δειλιᾶν; Deu 2 4 S(B
do), Hab 2 20 A(*sic* MS, B ⲉⲣ ϩⲟⲧ) εὐλαβεῖσθαι; Z
338 S ϯϣ.† ϩⲛⲧⲟⲩ ⲡⲛⲉϥϣⲗⲏⲗ, ib 319 S ⲁϥϣ. ⲁϥⲃⲱⲕ φοβεῖσθαι; ib 321 S ⲉⲩϣ.† ϩⲉⲙⲏⲛⲟⲧⲉ δεῖδεν;
Deu 20 3 S(B ϩⲏⲧ ϣ.) ἐκλύεσθαι; Jer 8 18 B ϩⲏⲧ
ϣ.† ἀπορεῖσθαι; BM 216 79 S ⲡⲉⲧⲛϣ.† ⲙⲉⲅⲛⲟⲭⲟⲩ
ⲉⲡⲉϣⲧⲉⲕⲟ (Gk om Lat diff), TT 163 S ⲧⲁⲣⲟⲩⲥⲱⲧⲙ
ⲡⲥⲉϣ., P 131⁷ 31 S ⲁⲡⲉϩⲗⲓⲁⲥ ϣ. ϩⲏⲧϥ ⲙⲡϩⲁⲣⲙⲁ
(4 Kg 2 11), BM 326 2 S† sim; + ϩⲏⲧ S(once)
B, *be afraid, grieved at heart*: Ge 32 7 (S ⲣ ϩⲃⲁ)
Mk 6 20 (S ⲣ ϣⲡⲏⲣⲉ) ἀπορ.; Jo 14 27 (SA² ⲣ ϣⲱⲃ)
δειλ., Mt 8 26† (S ⲣ ϩⲟⲧⲉ) δειλὸς εἶναι; Ge 42 1† var
ἀθυμεῖν; G 1 47 S ⲙⲡⲣϣ. ϩⲙⲡⲉⲓϩ[ⲱⲃ], DeV 2
168 ⲡⲉϥϣ.† ⲡϩ. ⲡⲉ ⲉⲑⲃⲉⲡⲓ ⲉⲧⲁⲩϣⲱⲡⲓ; ϣ. ⲛϩ.

nn: Pro 12 8 (S ϭⲁⲃϩ.) νωθροκάρδιος; Jer 8 21 (S
ShA 2 98 ϩⲃⲁ) ἀπορία; Ro 9 2 (S ⲙⲕⲁϩ ⲛϩ.) ὀδύνη;
K 255 ⲅⲙ, حزن; ⲉⲣ ϣ. ⲛϩ., *be afraid*: Is 13 7 (S
ⲣ ϭ.) δειλ., Ap 21 8 (S ϭⲁⲃϩ.) δειλός; Deu 1 29(S
ϣⲧⲟⲣⲧⲣ) πτήσσειν; Lu 9 7 (S ⲁⲡⲟⲣⲉⲓ) διαπορ.; Mt
26 37 (S ⲧⲱⲕⲙ ⲛϩ.) ἀδημονεῖν; Is 25 4(S ⲙⲟⲕϩ ⲛϩ.)
ἀθυμ.; Nu 22 3 (S ϩⲟⲭϩⲭ) προσοχθίζειν; Va 57 128
δυσχεραίνειν; *ib* 63 98 φρόνημα καταβάλλειν; DeV
2 48 ⲁϥⲉⲣ ϣ. ⲛϩ. (cf Jon 4 8 ⲟⲩⲉⲓ ⲡⲧⲉϥⲯⲩⲭⲏ),
MG 25 143 ⲟⲓ ⲡϣ. ⲛϩ. ⲛⲉⲙⲭⲁⲃⲓϩ.; ⲙⲉⲧϣ. ⲛϩ.
B, *anguish of mind*: Sa 5 3 (S ϩⲱⲭ, varr ϩⲟⲭϩⲭ,
ⲗⲱⲭϩ) στενοχωρία; TRit 102 sins of ⲟⲩⲙ. or ⲟⲩ-
ⲙⲉⲧⲕⲟⲩϫⲓ ⲛϩ. جزع القلب; Va 61 9 sleep ϩⲉⲛⲟⲩⲙ.
ⲉⲥⲟϣ; ⲙⲉⲧⲣⲉϥⲉⲣ ϣ. ⲛϩ.: Va 57 154 count joy
ⲉⲟⲩⲥⲩⲙⲫⲟⲣⲁ ⲡⲧⲉ ⲟⲩⲙ.

ϣⲗⲉϩ, ϣⲗϩ (mostly) S, ϣⲉⲗϩ B (rare) nn, *fear*,
with ⲛⲉϩ-, ⲛⲁϩ- (ⲡⲟⲩϩⲉ) vb, *throw out, emit fear*, so
be terrified(cf ⲣⲙⲟⲡⲧ, ⲥⲟϩⲣⲉ): Job 4 15(B ⲥⲑⲉⲣⲧⲉⲣ),
Dan 7 15 (P 44 115, B do) φρίσσειν; 2 Kg 6 8 ⲛ. ϣ.
ⲛⲣⲏⲧ (var ⲟⲩϣⲗⲥ ⲛϩ.) ἀθυμεῖν; ShWess 9 142 ⲁⲡⲁⲥⲱⲙⲁ ⲡ. ϣ., BP 11965 35 ϯⲛ. ϣⲗⲃ ϩⲙⲡⲁⲥⲱⲙⲁ,
P 131¹ 52 ⲧⲡⲓⲁⲥⲧⲱⲧ ⲛⲧⲛⲛⲁϩ ϣⲗϩ, Rec 7 91 B ϯⲛ.
ϣ. (var Mus 45 35 ϣϩⲟⲣⲧⲉⲣ); as nn, *terror*: Job
4 14 (B ⲡϩⲟⲩⲅⲣ) φρίκη, BHom 34 dread day ⲉⲧⲙⲏϩ
ⲛⲛⲁϩ ϣ. φρικτωδέστατος; BM 920 265 B ⲓⲗⲉ; ShB
MOr 8800 197 depth of iniquity ⲉϥⲙⲉϩ ⲛⲛ. ϣ., B
Mis 149 ⲥⲧⲱⲧ ϩⲛⲛ. ϣⲗⲉϩ, Mor 53 40 ϣⲧⲟⲣⲧⲣ ϩⲛⲛ. ϣ.,
P 129¹⁴ 123 ϩⲟⲧⲉ ϩⲙⲛⲁϩ ϣ. ⲡⲉ ⲥⲱⲧⲙ ⲉⲣⲟⲥ; ⲙⲛⲧ-
ⲛ. ϣ. S: Leyd 448 ⲙ., ⲙⲛⲧⲣⲉϥϩⲓⲧⲉ, ⲙⲛⲧⲉⲙⲡⲟ *produced by witchcraft*.

ϣⲗⲉϩ *v* ϣⲗϩ.

ϣⲟⲗϩⲥ B nn f, *corpse*: Ex 22 13 (S ⲡⲁϩⲥ) θήρα;
Job 39 30 τεθνεώς; Mt 14 12 (SF diff) πτῶμα; K
255, *ib* 437 ϭⲟⲗϩⲥ ϫⲏ; BM 915 18 ⲟⲩϣ. ϩⲓⲡⲧⲱⲟⲩ
that stank, Abst 585 ϯϣ. ⲛⲧⲉ ⲡⲙⲁⲣⲧⲩⲣⲟⲥ, C 43 35
lion roaring ⲉⲩϣ. (cf Is 31 4 ϫⲟⲣϫⲉⲥ); ⲉⲣ ϣ.:
Va 58 129 serpent ⲁⲓⲧ ⲛϣ., C 43 221 martyr ⲟⲓ ⲛϣ.
ϩⲉⲛⲛⲓⲃⲁⲥⲁⲛⲟⲥ.

ϣⲱⲗϩⲥ B *v* ϣⲱⲗϩ.

ϣⲗϩⲓⲧ (?) S, a title: PTurin A 7 ⲙⲁⲑⲓⲁⲥ ⲡϣⲗ-
ϩⲓⲧ.[.

ϣⲗϩϥ *v* ϣⲗⲁϩ.

ϣⲁⲗϫ- S, ϣⲗⲓϫ B *v* ϣⲱⲗϭ.

ϣⲗⲱϫ B *v* ϭⲗⲟϭ.

ϣⲱⲗϭ, ϣⲗϭ-, ϣⲁⲗⲕⲉ, ϣⲟⲗϭ† S, ϣⲁⲗϭ† AA²,
p c ϣⲁⲗϫ- S vb tr, *cut* (cf شلق شلخ Dévaud): BMis 239
bade ϣ. ⲙⲡⲉϥⲥⲱⲙⲁ ϩⲛⲣⲉⲡϭⲟⲣⲧⲉ (var Mor 30 13
ⲡⲱⲧⲥ) τέμνειν, Lev 21 5 (B ϣⲱⲧ ⲡⲣⲁⲡϭⲟⲧϭⲉⲧ) κα-
ⲧⲁⲧ.; ShP 130⁴ 157 ⲧⲟⲕ ⲡϣⲗϭ ⲕⲁϣ; qual, *cut-*

ting, sharpened: Ps 119 4 (var ⲧⲏⲙ, B ϣⲉⲃϣⲱⲃ), Pro 5 4 A(S ⲧ., B ⲇⲟ) ἀκόνην; Mor 41 70 horns ⲉⲧϣ., Mani 1 A² ⲡⲉⲕⲧⲏϭ ⲉⲧϣ. ⲛⲃⲣⲏϭⲉ, ib ⲟⲩⲃⲣⲏϭⲉ ⲉⲥϣ.; intr: CO 468 v ⲕⲁⲡ (3°), or ? belongs to ϣⲱⲗⲕ; p c: MR 4 128 ⲟⲍⲅⲕⲉⲫⲁⲗⲟⲥ: ⲡϣⲁⲗⲕ- (sic MS) ⲁⲡⲉ.

ϣⲗⲓϭ SA, -ⲉϭ, ϣϩⲗⲓϭ S, -ⲓⲝ¹, -ⲓⲧ², ϣⲗⲟⲍ³, ϣⲗⲟⲕ- ϣⲓ⁴ B n m, **a sharpened thing, spike**: Jud 5 8 S ϣ. ⲙⲡⲉⲡⲓⲡⲉ σειρομάστης; Z 334 S ϣ. ⲡⲕⲱⲣⲧ ⲡϣⲟⲙⲛⲧ ⲡⲧⲁⲣ τριόδους; BMis 540 S sim σίδηρος; MIE 2 407 B ϩⲁⲡϣ.¹ ⲛⲃⲉⲛⲓⲡⲓ (PO 22 425 خطال) ⲡⲉⲙ- ϩⲁⲛⲕⲉϣ.³ ⲛⲃⲉⲛⲓⲡⲓ ⲉⲅⲟⲓ ⲛⲧⲁⲣ ⲧⲁⲣ (Ar om); K 131 B ⲡϣ.¹ (var ϭⲗⲓⲝ ضم) among butcher's utensils; ShA 2 316 S ϣ. ⲙⲡⲉⲡⲓⲡⲉ driven into ears, El 94 A sim into eyes = ib 128 S ⲥⲁϭ, Ann 17 148 S sim ⲉⲅⲟ ⲛⲕⲱⲣⲧ, Mor 48 113 S ϣⲗⲉϭ ⲛϣⲉ ⲛⲭⲟⲉⲓⲧ for goading beasts = C 43 154 B ϣ.⁴, ib 140 B ϣ.² = Mor 48 81 S τρίβολλος. **b** *pointed, forked flame, ray* S: PS 235 soul shall ⲣ ⲟⲩⲛⲟϭ ⲛϣ. ⲛⲟⲩⲟⲉⲓⲛ, P 129¹⁵ 22 demon leapt forth like ⲟⲩϣϩⲗⲓϭ ⲛⲕⲱⲣⲧ, BSG 135 boiling cauldron ⲛⲛⲁϫ ϣ. ⲉⲃⲟⲗ 15 ells high = ib 16 B ϣⲁϩ.

ϣⲗϭⲟⲙ¹, ⲥⲉⲗϭⲁⲙ², ϣⲗⲧⲁⲙ³, ϣ(ⲉ)ⲗⲧ(ⲉ)ⲙ⁴, ϣⲁⲗⲧⲉⲙ⁵, -ⲧⲏⲙ⁶, ϣⲉⲗⲧⲏⲙ⁷ S, ϣⲁⲗⲧⲁⲙ⁸ SB, ϣⲉⲗ. B, -ⲧⲉⲙ F nn m f, **mustard, rape**: Mt 13 31 S³(var⁴) BF, Mk 4 31 S⁵B, Lu 13 19 S³(varr⁴⁷)B σίναπι all خردل; P 44 82 S ⲃⲉⲣⲛⲓⲕⲟⲛ· ⲥ.² سليم, ib ⲥⲓⲛⲛⲡⲓ· ⲛⲗⲁⲧⲛ(v ⲗⲁⲧⲛ) ’ أ = 43 57 S ⲥⲉⲛⲁⲡⲓ ϣ.⁴ أ, K 194 B ⲡϣ. ’ل, ib 366 أ, P 50 106 B⁸ (not ϫⲁⲗ. Fleischer *De Gloss* 104) ’ل, P 54 146 B ’أ; Mor 41 122 S pepper, salt, ϣ.⁷ into martyr's wounds, Cat 89 B ⲧ ϣ. ⲟⲩⲧⲉⲣⲙⲁⲧⲓⲕⲟⲛ (θερμαν.) ⲧⲉ ⲥⲭⲏϭ, PMéd 171 S⁶, 277 S⁸ in recipes, Mor 51 41 S no bread...nor ϣ.¹ ϩⲛⲧⲁⲡⲕⲟⲩⲗⲁⲅⲭⲉ, interpr as ⲡⲛⲁ ⲉⲧⲟⲩϣⲗ ϭⲟⲙ ϩⲓⲱⲱϥ, CO 348 S ϩⲟⲧⲥ ... ⲛϣ.¹, MIF 9 93 S ⲛ- ⲡⲉⲟⲩϣ.⁷ ⲡϣⲁⲣ ϭⲱⲗ *small particle* (but cf KKS 270). V Alssa 32, 33, 169, LöwF 1 489, PMéd 171 n, Sethe *Dem Urk* 187.

ϣⲁⲙ, ϣⲉⲙ B v ϣⲙⲙⲁ.

ϣⲁⲙ AA² v ϣⲟⲙ.

ϣⲏⲙ SA²B(once)F(rare)O, ϣⲙⲙ S, ϩⲏⲙ, ϩⲙ Sᵃ, ϩⲏⲙ A nn, **small person, thing, quantity**: Pro 5 14 SA(B ⲕⲟⲩϫⲓ), Miss 8 76 S ϩ(ⲉ)ⲡϣ. among bishops ὀλίγος; Is 63 18 S(B ⲇⲟ), Jo 14 19 A²(SB ⲇⲟ)μικρός; ib 6 7 A²(SB ⲇⲟ)βραχύς; ShC 42 109 S ⲁϫⲕⲉ ϩⲉⲡϣ., Mor 18 19 S ⲟⲩϣ. ϩⲙⲡⲉⲅⲕⲣⲙⲉⲥ (var ib 19 27 ⲕⲟⲩϣ) = Miss 4 113 B ⲙⲏϣ(prob from S ϣ.), ROC 25 240 Bϩⲁⲡϣ. ⲡⲧⲉ ⲡⲉϥⲁⲣⲉⲧⲏ, PGM 1 60 650 O ϣ.(no context); ⲛⲟⲩϣ.SA as advb, *a little*: Si 51 18 ὀλίγον; 2 Cor 11 16 (B ⲛⲟⲩⲕ.) μικρόν τι; PS 9 ⲉⲓⲟⲩⲏⲧ ⲙ- ⲙⲱⲧⲛ ⲛⲟⲩϣ., ib 382 ⲡⲉⲗϩⲱⲃ...ⲧⲁϩⲟ ⲙⲙⲟⲥ ⲙⲙⲁⲧⲉ ⲛⲟⲩϣ., El 90 A ⲡⲉⲗⲏϭ ⲛⲟⲩϩ. = ib 120 S ⲛⲟⲩⲕ., HT W 79 drowned ⲛⲁⲁⲡϣⲁⲩ ⲛⲟⲩϩ.; P 131⁴ 113 ϭⲓ ⲙⲡⲉⲕϩⲏⲧ ⲉⲡϫⲓⲥⲉ ⲛⲕⲉϣ. (v ⲕⲉ II g).

As adj, *small, few, young, humble*, **a** before nn SA: Sa 7 9, 2 Macc 6 17 A, Mt 15 34 (B ⲕ.) ὀλ.; Z 299 ϩⲉⲡϣ. ⲡⲣⲟⲟⲩ ⲙⲓ.; 1 Kg 14 29 βραχύς; PS 368 ⲙⲛⲡⲥⲁⲟⲩϣ. ⲡⲟⲩⲟⲉⲓϣ, ShC 73 145 ϯ ⲕⲉϣ. ⲡⲥⲁϩⲛⲉ, Ryl 323 ⲕⲟⲩϥⲓϫⲉ ⲛⲟⲩϣ. ⲡⲁⲛⲙⲟⲥⲓⲟⲛ ⲛⲁϥ, R 1 5 35 ⲡⲉⲓϣ. ⲛⲗⲓⲃⲁⲛⲟⲥ, C 99 110 ⲡⲟⲩϫⲉ ⲛⲟⲩϣ. ⲛⲕⲁⲙ ⲉⲡⲙⲟⲟⲩ, BP 9105 ⲡϣ. ⲡⲭⲓⲣ, ViK 4711 ⲧⲱⲕ ⲉⲧϣⲙ ⲡⲕⲟⲩϥⲟⲛ, C 99 138 ⲕⲟⲩⲓ ⲡⲗⲁⲙⲯⲁⲡⲏ, ϣ. ⲡⲟⲩⲟⲟⲧⲉ (var ib 220 ϣ. ⲡⲗ., ⲕ. ⲛⲟⲩ.), ST 165 books ⲟⲩϣ. (ⲛ)ⲯⲁⲗⲧⲏⲣⲉ, ⲟⲩϣ. ⲡⲉⲅⲁⲅⲅⲉⲗⲓⲟⲛ *small* or ? *part of*. **b** after nn SSᵃAA²: Ps 41 6 (B ⲕ. ⲛ-), Zech 4 10 A(SB ⲇⲟ), Jo 12 35 A²(SB ⲇⲟ) ⲙⲓ.; Cl 30 5 A (S ϣⲁⲣ-)ὀλιγο-; Jo 2 12 A²(S ⲕ., B as Gk) οὐ πολύς; Ex 4 10 A ⲥⲙⲉⲓ ϩ. (S ϩⲁϯϩ, B ϣⲟⲙ) ἰσχνο-; Mal 4 2 A ⲙⲉⲥ ϩ. (B ⲙⲁⲥⲓ) μοσχάριον; ShMich 550 13 ⲧⲛⲧⲛⲧⲏⲕⲉ ϣ. ⲉⲧⲉⲟⲩⲛⲧⲁⲓⲥ, ShMIF 23 14 ⲟⲩϩⲱⲃ ϣ. ⲁⲡⲡⲉ, ShCai 8007 destroy them ⲡⲧⲉⲓⲣⲉ ϣ. ⲁⲛ *not merely* but root up foundations, ShA 2 148 ⲙⲏ ⲡⲱⲛⲉ ϩⲟⲣϣ ⲁⲡ ⲛ ⲧⲉⲓⲣⲉ ϣ. ⲡⲉ ⲥⲟⲕϥ ⲉⲭⲡⲉⲛⲙⲁ ⲉⲅⲭⲟⲥⲉ, PSBA 27 167 ⲉⲕ]ⲛⲁϫⲉ ⲧⲕⲉⲥⲓⲗⲉ(κίσηλις)... ϩⲓⲱⲱⲥ ⲡⲧⲉⲓ[ⲣⲉ] ϣ. ⲛⲛϭⲟⲧⲉ *merely*, ShBor 246 75 Joseph ⲡⲉϥ(sc Jesus')ϩⲙϩⲁⲗ ϣ., TU 43 11 A ⲡⲁⲧ- ⲡⲓⲥⲧⲓⲥ ϩ. (cf ⲡⲁⲧⲕⲟⲩⲓ ⲙⲛ.), J 113 4 Sᵃ ⲕⲁⲧ ϩ. (cf p 127 a), ST 116 ⲕⲉⲣⲓⲧⲥⲱⲛ (χαριστίων?) ϩⲙ, Miss 4 696 hindered by ⲡⲣⲟⲟⲩϣ ϣ. ⲉⲧⲣⲓⲭⲱⲓ, Leyd 150 ⲥⲁⲃⲃⲁⲧ(ⲟⲛ) ϣ. *Saturday before Passion week*, Ep 226 n ⲧⲛⲏⲥⲧⲓⲁ ϣ. (cf ib 1 171), CO 245 ⲧⲓⲃⲗϫⲉ ϣ., Ep 431 ⲡⲗⲉⲗⲟⲩ ϣ., BKU 1 137 ⲧⲗ. ϣ., Ep 359 ⲡ- ⲗⲉⲗⲁⲅⲉ ϣ.; with names (v below): CO 249 ⲓⲁⲕⲱⲃ ϣ., Miss 1 387 ⲉⲗⲓⲥⲁⲃⲏⲧ ϣ., BAp 79 ⲡⲉⲥⲩⲡⲉⲓⲟⲥ ϣ.

ⲕⲟⲩⲓ ϣ. S: Z 328 ϩⲛⲕ. ϣ. ⲡⲧⲉ ⲡϯⲙⲉ *few* ὀλ.; J 79 21 ⲡⲕ. ϣ. *little child*, Rec 11 135 among books ⲟⲩⲕ. ϣ. ⲉⲧⲃⲉⲡⲣⲙⲙⲁⲟ; as adj: ShRyl 71 91 ⲡⲕ. ϣ. ⲡⲣⲟⲟⲩ of life, Ep 328 ⲕ. ϣ. ⲡⲗⲁⲯⲁⲡⲉ, C 99 251 ϩⲉⲡⲕ. ⲡϣ. ⲡⲭⲣⲓⲁ = ib 89 103 B ⲕ. ⲡϫ.; BHom 15 ⲕ. ⲡⲟⲩⲟⲉⲓⲛ ϣ.

Iterated, *little by little SA*: Sa 12 2 κατ' ὀλίγον; Ex 23 30(B ⲕⲁⲧⲁ ⲕ. ⲕ.)ⲕ. μικρόν; Sa 12 8 ⲕ. βραχύ; Pro 29 11 SA ⲕ. μέρος; Ge 33 14 (B ⲕⲁⲧⲁ ⲕ.) ⲕ. σχολήν; Deu 7 22(B ⲕⲁⲧⲁ ⲕ. ⲕ.)ⲕ. ⲙⲓ. ⲙⲓ.; Tri 146 ⲙⲟⲟϣⲉ ϣ. ϣ. ’, ليروأ; Cl 25 4 A ⲕⲁⲧⲁ ϩ. ϩ., R 1 4 45 S sim, PS 5 ⲁⲥⲕⲱⲧⲉ ⲉⲣⲟϥ ϣ. ϣ., ShA 2 140 ⲁ- ⲧⲉⲧⲡⲱϫⲛ ϣ. ϣ., ShA 1 150 ⲕⲁⲧⲁ ϩⲟⲟⲩ ϩⲟⲟⲩ ⲛ ⲟⲩϣ. ⲟⲩϣ.; ⲣ, ⲟ ⲡϣ. ϣ., *make small*: Is 30 14 (B ϣⲟⲙ, F ⲁⲓ ⲡⲕ. ⲕ.) λεπτός, ib 22(B ⲧϣⲙⲟ, F ⲇⲟ)ⲗ. ποιεῖν; Deu 9 21 (B ⲛⲟⲩⲧ, var ⲙⲟⲩⲛⲕ) καταλεῖν; Mic 1 7 (A ⲣ ⲗⲉⲕⲙⲉ ⲗ., B ϩⲟⲙϩⲉⲙ) κατακόπτειν; Mor 25 25 idol fell ⲁϥⲣ ϣ. ϣ. = Va 61 120 B ⲉⲣ ⲙⲉⲣⲟⲥ ⲙ., Mor 41 182 ⲉⲓⲣⲉ ⲛⲡⲉⲕⲥⲁⲣⲍ ⲛϣ. ϣ.

ρ ϣ. *S*: El 122 = *ib* 90 *A* ρ ϣⲏⲣⲉ ϩ.   Prob *l* ϣⲏⲣⲉ ϣ.

ⲙⲛⲧϩ. *A, smallness, childhood*: Pro 29 21 ϫⲛⲡⲧⲉϥⲙ. (*S* ⲙⲛⲧⲕ.) ἐκ παιδός.

In names: Ψέμ, Βησσῆμ (cf Βησκοῦι), Παχομχῆμις (Preisigke), ⲥⲟⲡϣⲏⲙ (Ryl 300), ⲥⲟⲡⲭⲏⲙ, ⲥⲁⲡϩⲏⲙ (J).

V also ϣⲏⲣⲉ, ϣⲏⲧ & *cf* ⲕⲟⲩⲓ, ϣⲙⲁ.

ϣⲏⲙ *SB* nn, *sign, omen* (?), only + ϫⲓ, ϭⲓ, *take omens, divine*: Ge 30 27 *B*(*S* ϫⲓ ⲙⲁⲉⲓⲛ), Deu 18 10 *SB* (var ϫⲉ ⲙⲧⲁⲩ), Bor 253 267 *S* = Mor 31ʹ 188 *S* ⲧⲁⲫⲓⲁⲗⲏ ⲉϯϫⲓ ϣ. ⲡⲏⲣⲧⲥ (cf Ge 44 5) οἰωνίζεσθαι; ShZ 599 ⲧⲉⲧⲛϫⲓ ϣ. ⲉⲡⲡⲟⲩⲃ ⲉⲧⲙϫⲓⲧⲩ ⲉⲡⲉⲡⲛⲉϫ ϫⲉⲧⲉⲧⲛⲙⲁⲁⲣⲉⲥⲕⲉ ⲛⲛⲁⲓⲙⲱⲛ; as nn *B, augury*: Nu 24 1(*S* diff)οἰωνός, *ib* 23 23(*S* ⲣⲉϥϫⲓ ⲙ.)οἰωνισμός, Jer 14 14(*S* ⲙⲛⲧⲣⲉϥϫⲓ ⲙ.)-ισμα; Deu 18 14 (*S* ⲣⲉϥϫⲓ ϣ.) κληδών (var -ισμός) تفأل; ⲣⲉϥϫⲓ, ϭⲓ ϣ., *augur, diviner*: Ex 7 11 *B* الفأل صاحب, Dan 1 20 *B*(*S* ⲣⲉϥⲙⲟⲩⲧⲉ) ἐπαοιδός; Deu 18 14 *S ut sup*; ⲙⲛⲧ-, ⲙⲉⲧⲣ.: LCyp 3 *S* κληδονισμός; ROC 23 277 *B* ⲙ., ⲙⲉⲧⲣⲉϥϫⲁ ⲟⲩⲟⲡ; ρ, ⲉⲣ ρ.: Lev 19 26 *B* ⲉⲣ ρ. ϫⲉⲛⲡⲓϩⲁⲗⲁϯ (*S* ϫⲓ ⲙ.) ὀρνιθοσκοπεῖν; ShHT K 1 *S* παρατηρεῖ ⲉϩⲉⲛϩⲟⲟⲩ ... ⲟ ⲛⲣ. ϩⲓⲣⲉϥϫⲓ ⲙⲁⲉⲓⲛ.

ϣⲟⲉⲓⲙ *S*, ϣⲁⲉⲓⲙ *F* nn m, *row, course*: Ann 17 151 bade set them (martyrs) out ⲡⲥⲉⲙⲁⲩ ⲛϣ. ϣ., Mor 48 93 sim = C 43 145 *B* ⲛⲥⲧⲩⲭⲟⲥ ⲥⲧⲩⲭⲟⲥ, BMis 536 ϩⲉⲛϣ. ⲛϯⲣⲟⲛⲟⲥ, BKU 1 18 *F* ⲥⲉⲙⲩ ⲛⲧⲓⲁ ψⲁⲗⲙⲁ ⲛϣⲁⲙⲛⲧ ⲛϣ.

ϣⲙⲉ, ϣⲏⲕ.(?), ϣⲟⲓⲙⲉ*S*, ϣⲁⲓⲙⲉ*A*², ϣⲙⲏ*B*(once) nn f, *sim*: 3 Kg 7 6 (P 44 111) στίχος مَفّ; Jer 52 4 ϥⲧⲟⲩϣ.(*B* ⲫ. λακϩ)τετράποδος; K 124 *B* ⲛϣ. مداميك *courses* of stones; Mor 13 179 Christ at founding of church ⲁϥϯ ⲟⲩϣ. ⲉⲧⲉⲕⲕⲗⲏⲥⲓⲁ (cf ? Miss 4 354), BMis 570 ⲟⲩϣⲏ. (*l* ? ⲙⲏϣⲉ) ⲛⲥⲧⲣⲟⲃⲓⲗⲟⲥ within each wall, Blake 266 ⲧⲉϥⲧⲟⲩϣ. ⲙⲡⲗⲟⲩⲧⲓⲟⲛ, *ib* 288 ⲧⲙⲉϩϣⲟⲙⲧⲉ ⲛϣ. (in Ex 28 *SB* = Gk), ManiH 36 *A*² gather like sheep ⲙⲛϣⲉ ⲙⲛϣⲉ ⲉⲅⲟ ⲛϣ., Bodl copt inscr 149 ⲛϣⲉ ⲛϣⲟⲓⲙⲉ [.

ϣⲟⲙ*SB*, ϣⲟⲟⲙ *S*, ϣⲙ *AA*², ϣⲱⲙ*B*, f ϣⲱⲙⲉ *SA*², -ⲙⲓ *B*, ϣⲟⲙⲓ *F*, pl ϣⲙⲟⲩⲓ *S*, ϣⲙⲱⲟⲩ *B* nn, *father-, mother-in-law* (ⲟⲛ IgR): Ex 4 18 *SAB*, Nu 10 29 *SB* (var πενθερός), Jud 19 4 *S* γαμβρός; 1 Kg 4 19*S*, Jo 18 13 *SA*²*B* πεν.; Tri 145 *S* حمو, K 82 *B* ϣⲱⲙ صهر, ۻ; J 44 11 *S* deceased Theodore ⲡⲉⲡϣⲟⲟⲙ, WZKM 14 234*S* ⲕⲱⲥⲙⲁ ⲡϣⲱⲟⲙ(or ? son-in-l.); *son-in-law*: Ge 19 12 *SB* γ. ۻ (var ۻ); R 1 4 49 *S* ⲡⲉⲥϣ. & daughters *gener*; f *mother-in-l.*: Ru 1 14 *S*, Mic 7 6 *SAB*, Mt 8 14 *SB*(F cit RChamp 543)πενθερά; BM 1073 *S*; *daughter-in-l.*: Deu 27 23 *B*(*S* diff)νύμφη; pl: Ge 19 14 *SB* γ.; Tob 14 13 *S* π.

ρ ϣ. *SB, be father-in-law* c ⲉ-: Deu 7 3 *B*(*S* ⲧⲱϩ ⲙⲛ-) γαμβρεύειν, Ge 34 9 *SB* ⲉⲡⲓⲅ., Jos 23 12 *B* (sic *l*, *S* ϫⲓ ⲥϩⲓⲙⲉ ⲉⲃⲟⲗ ϩⲛ-) ἐπιγαμίας ποιεῖν.

ϣⲟⲙ *B* adj *v* ϣⲙⲁ (ϣⲱⲙⲉ).

ϣⲱⲙ *SSʲ*, ϣⲟⲙϩ, ϣⲟⲟⲙϩ *S*, ϣⲁⲙϩ *Sᵃ* vb tr, *wash* clothes: Lev 11 25(*B* ⲣⲱϩⲓ), Mor 37 90, Wess 11 167, C 99 141 = *ib* 89 46 *B* do πλύνειν; R 1 4 7 ⲧϭⲟⲟⲩⲛⲉ...ⲙⲡϣⲟⲟⲙϩ (sic prob) ⲉⲡⲉϩ *lavare*; C 99 105 ϣⲟⲟⲙⲟⲩ, CO 368 ⲧⲣⲟⲓⲧⲉ...ϣⲟⲙϩ, Hall 81 *Sᵃ* ⲙⲙⲁⲡⲡⲁ ... ϣⲁⲙⲟⲩ ⲛϥⲧⲁϫⲥⲟⲩ; intr c ⲉ- *Sʲ* (same?): BKU 1 21 6 lay thing to be dyed in water ⲡⲕϣ. ⲉⲣⲁϥ ⲡⲟⲩⲕⲟⲩⲓ, *ib* 31, 43 sim.

ϣⲱⲙ *SAA*²*BFO* nn m, *summer*: Ge 8 22 *SB*, Zech 14 8 *SAB*, Mk 13 28 *SBF*, Z 348 *S* ⲙⲡⲣⲱⲕϩ ⲙⲡϣ. θέρος, Am 3 15 *SB*, Cl 20 9 *A* θερινός; Nu 13 21 *S*(? error, *B* ϩⲛ ⲡϣ.)ἔαρ; Cl *lc A* ⲡⲉⲧⲉⲙⲡⲥⲉⲡϣ. μετοπωρινός; ShBM 194 3 *S* ⲡϣ. ⲙⲡⲡⲉⲡⲣⲱ, Miss 4 762 *S* ⲱϭⲉⲃ ⲡⲧⲉⲡⲣⲱ ⲥⲟⲩϫⲙ ⲙⲡϣ., C 86 283 *B* dust of ⲟⲩϣⲛⲟⲩ ϫⲉⲛⲡϣ., BMOr 6201 A 38 *S* contract ⲧⲁⲣ ϩⲱⲃ ⲉⲣⲟϥ ϣ. ⲡⲣⲱ, Ryl 158 33 *S* will water ⲧⲉⲡⲣⲱ...ⲡϣ., ManiK 10 *A*² ⲧⲡⲣⲱ...ⲡϣ., MIE 2 339 *B* ⲡⲓⲣⲙⲉ ⲡⲧⲉ ⲡϣ. in Paôni, DeV 1 96 *B* sim, AZ 21 100 *O* ⲉⲧⲛⲏⲟⲩ...ⲙⲡⲉⲣⲉ ⲡϣ. *at midday in summer*; ϩ(ⲉ) ⲡϣ. *S*(rare), ϩⲏ ⲡϣ. *B* nn m, *spring*: Ge 8 22 (*S* = Gk), Ps 73 17 (*S* do), Zech 14 8 (*SA* do),ἔαρ; Jude 12 *S* ⲡⲣⲙϣ. خريف P 44 18 (var Va 75 72 ϩⲛ-, bible & *B* diff) φθινοπωρινός, P 46 143 *S* ϩⲉ ⲡϣ., K 365 *B* do ۻ.

ϣⲱⲙ *SAF* nn m, *tribute, tax*: Ro 13 7 (*B* ϩⲱϯ) φόρος, P 44 58 ⲡⲫⲟⲣⲟⲥ · ⲡϣ. خراج; Cai ostr 47400 ⲥⲓⲙⲥⲓⲙ...ⲏⲣⲡ...ⲙⲛⲡⲟⲩϣ., COAd 18 we owe ⲣⲧⲟⲃ ⲛⲥⲟⲩⲟ [ⲙ]ⲡⲛⲉϣ., Chicago ostr 29 211 2420 corn to be paid ⲙⲛⲡⲉϣ., ST 230 corn ϣⲁⲓⲧⲁⲗⲟⲟⲩ...ⲙⲛⲡⲟⲩϣ., CO 230 camel-load of seed ⲙⲛⲡⲉϣ., Kr 129 *F* I sell thee field ⲛⲉⲃϣ. ⲡⲧⲁⲓⲃⲁⲗⲉⲃ ⲡⲉⲙⲉⲕⲡⲉ ⲁⲣⲓ ν̄ β; ϯ ϣ., *pay tribute*: Lu 23 2 (*B* ϯ ϩ.) φ. διδόναι, Ro 13 6 (*B* do) φ. τελεῖν, Deu 20 11 (*B* do) φορολόγητος; P 130³ 62 ⲛⲧⲛϯ...ⲡϣ., ⲡⲧⲉⲗⲟⲥ, ST 449 ⲉⲃⲣⲁ...ϯⲛⲁϯ ⲡⲉϣ. ⲛⲁⲕ; ϫⲓ ϣ., *take tribute* in ⲣⲉϥϫⲓ ϣ.: Job 39 7 (*B* = Gk) φορολόγος, cit R 1 3 66, Zech 9 8 *A* gloss on ⲡⲉⲧϫⲱⲣⲙ (cf ShA 2 340 & *B*) ἐξελαύνων. This word prob BM 1013 17, ? 1117 4. *V* Rec 28 196.

ϣⲓⲙⲉ, ϣⲟⲓⲙⲉ &c *v* ϣⲟⲉⲓⲙ.

ϣⲟⲟⲙⲉ† *SO v* ϣⲙⲁ.

ϣⲱⲙⲉ *S* nn, *meaning unknown*: Cai 42573 2 ingredients ϩⲓⲧⲟⲩ ⲉⲩϣ. ⲧⲁⲁⲩ ⲉⲅⲉⲣⲡ.

ϣⲱⲱⲙⲉ, ϣⲱ. *S*, ϣⲱⲙⲓ *B* nn f, *cliff, precipice*: Mt 8 32 *S*(*B* ϫⲁϫⲣⲓⲙ), C 99 233 *S* = *ib* 89 67 *B* κρημνός, ROC 11 305 *S* ⲙⲁ ⲛϣ. κρημνώδης; P 54

119 B ϯ ϣ. جرف ; ShViK 9345 16 S water ϯ ⲉϩⲟⲩⲛ ⲉϩⲣⲛⲡϣⲱ.,ShA 1 459 S sim ϣϣⲱ.,JTS 8 244 S ⲛϣⲱ. ⲛⲑⲁⲗⲁⲥⲥⲁ, C 99 206 S ⲧϣⲱ. ⲙⲡⲓⲉⲣⲟ, ST 37 S sowing of ⲟⲙⲉ ϩⲁⲣⲁⲧⲉ ⲛⲧϣⲱ.

ϣⲱⲱⲙⲉ adj v ϣⲙⲁ infra.

ϣⲙⲁ SB, ϣⲁⲙ, ϣⲉⲙ B(Dan), ϣⲟⲟⲙⲉ† SO, ϣⲟ.† S, ϣⲟⲙ† B, p c ϣⲁⲙⲁ- S, ϣⲁⲙ- A vb intr, be light, fine, subtle : Ex 32 20 B(S p ϣϭⲓϭ), Deu 9 21 S(Bᵗ) λεπτός, Ps 17 43 B(S ⲡⲁⲕⲉ), ib 28 6 B(S p ϣ.), Dan 2 35 B ϣⲁⲙ (var ϣⲉⲙ) λεπτύνειν, Mor 17 27 S idol stoned ϣⲁⲛⲧϥϣ. ⲉⲡⲧⲏⲣϥ ⲇⲓⲁⲗ.; ShA 2 332 S scraping teeth ϣⲁⲡⲧⲟⲩϣ. ⲛⲥⲉⲣ ⲟⲩⲟϣ, Mor 25 139 S iron subdueth all things ⲛϥⲧⲣⲉⲩϣ., AM 215 B through sickness legs ϣ. like bird's, HL 110 B flesh ϣ. ⲙⲫⲣⲏϯ ⲡⲟⲩⲕⲁⲡ, MG 25 140 B ⲡⲉϥⲛⲟⲩⲥ ϣ. as grain of mustard seed; qual (mostly B): Ge 41 3 (S ϩⲟⲟⲙⲉ), Ex 16 14 (S ⲡⲟⲕ), Lev 16 12 (S ⲥⲟⲧⲡ), Is 27 9 (S ⲧⲡⲏⲛⲩ), ib 30 14 (S ⲟ ⲡϣⲏⲙ ϣⲏⲙ, F ⲁⲓ ⲛⲕⲟⲩⲓ ⲕ.), Va 57 260 ⲁⲏⲣ...ϣ., ib 68 171 ϣⲉⲛⲧⲱ ⲉⲧϣ., BM 174 S ⲧⲏⲩ ⲉⲧϣ., Aeg 276 S ϩⲉⲛⲥⲁⲧⲱ ⲉⲩϣ. λεπτός; Ex 4 10 (S ϩⲁϭⲃ, A ϩⲏⲙ) ἰσχνο-; Is 35 4 ϩⲏⲧ ⲉⲧϣ. (Lakân 143, Tatt om, S ϩ. ϭⲏⲙⲁ, F ⲕⲟⲩⲓ ⲛϩ.) ὀλιγο- عفيف (var ضعيف); Sh(Besa)BMOr 8810 480 S ⲡⲉⲩⲕⲁⲕⲓⲁ ⲉⲧϣ. = PG 40 983 malitia only, RNC 77 S ⲥⲓⲙⲁϩⲱⲡⲓⲟⲛ ⲉⲩϣ., PMéd 89 S ⲥⲟⲣϥ ⲉϥϣⲟ., Ep 297 S ⲡⲟⲉⲓⲧ ⲉϥϣ., Miss 4 759 S heard ⲉⲩⲥ[ⲙⲏ] ⲉⲥϣ., O'LearyTh 14 ⲧⲉⲭⲛⲓⲁ ⲉⲥϣ. of goldsmith, BM 248 115 S how shall they ⲛⲟⲓ ⲉⲡⲣⲱⲃ ⲉⲧϣ.?, DeV 2 53 ϯⲭⲓⲛⲉⲣ ⲛⲟⲓⲛ ⲉⲧϣ. ⲛϯⲑⲉⲟⲣⲓⲁ ⲙⲡⲡⲁⲧⲓⲕⲏ, MG 25 330 ⲙⲉⲅⲓ ⲉⲧϣ. ⲛⲧⲉ ϯⲕⲁⲕⲓⲁ, AZ 21 100 O ⲉϥϣ. ⲛⲣⲉⲧⲃ (cf p c).

—— ⲉⲃⲟⲗ B : BSM 131 sick woman ⲁⲥϣ. ⲉⲃ. ⲉⲡⲧⲏⲣϥ = Mor 22 140 S ϩⲱⲱⲙⲉ ⲉⲃ.

p c SA : El 120 S ⲟⲩⲥⲁⲗⲁϣⲉⲓⲉ ⲛϣⲁⲙⲁⲣⲉⲧϥ = ib 90 A ϣⲁⲙⲟⲩⲣⲏⲧⲉ (cf MR James Cat MSS Corp Chr Coll 2 270 macris pedibus & Apocr Anecd 153 tibiae tenues).

—— nn m SB, fineness, subtlety : Bor 171 57 S ⲡⲉϣ. ⲙⲡϣⲁϫⲉ, My 156 S ⲡⲉϣ. ⲉⲧⲣⲡⲡⲉⲗⲉϩⲓⲥ, MG 25 141 B admiring ⲡⲓϣ. ⲡⲧⲉ ⲡⲉϥⲛⲟⲩⲥ, P 44 92 = 43 77 S ⲟⲩϣ. ⲙⲡⲟⲩⲉⲅⲕⲣⲁⲥⲓⲁ جلا calm, BMOr 8875 118 B رقيق.

ϣⲱⲱⲙⲉ S, ϣⲟⲙ B as adj, light, fine: Ez 16 10 SB τρίχαπτος subtilis; Tri 716 S ⲧϣⲟⲟⲙⲉ ⲛⲧⲱⲧⲉ فيّ الثياب (sic l s v ⲧⲱⲧⲉ), JTS 10 399 S wearing ϩⲃⲥⲱ ⲛϣ. so that nakedness seen through it, BM 1183 S woman came for ⲧⲓϩⲃⲟⲥ ⲛϣ.

V ⲧϣⲙⲟ.

ϣⲙⲁ S/F v ϣⲙⲙⲟ.

ϣⲙⲟⲩ SB, -ⲟⲩⲉ S, -ⲟⲅⲓ SBF, ϣⲙⲉ B(once) nn f, peg, stake: Nu 4 32 S(var -ⲟⲩⲉ) B, Jud 4 21 S, Is 33 20 BF(S ⲡⲁⲉⲓⲱ) πάσσαλος; Ez 27 11 SB -ⲟⲅⲓ ὅρμος;

K 134 B sailor's implements ⲛϣ. رند, اخريطن, rowlock (v BIF 20 71), P 55 13 B wooden things ⲛϣ. رتاج ib 7 ⲛϣⲙⲙⲉ متمّنات pegs joining beams in church roof (Sobhy); ShC 73 165 S everything down to ⲟⲩϩⲱⲥ ⲙⲡⲟⲩⲙⲟⲩⲥ ⲙⲡⲟⲩϣ., ShA 2 304 S bind men ⲉϩⲣⲉⲛⲡϣⲙⲟⲩⲉ, MIE 2 409 B tusks like iron ϣ., C 86 208 B bade stretch martyr ⲛ̄ ⲛϣ. ⲉⲩϭⲟⲥⲓ, BMis 239 = 295 S sim ϥⲧⲟⲉ ⲛϣⲙⲟⲩⲓ, Ryl 238 35 S ϣ. ⲛⲟⲩϣⲙⲟⲩ[ⲝ]ⲉ, J 65 61 S ⲟⲩϣⲙⲟⲩⲉ ⲉⲧⲧⲟϩ ⲉⲝⲟⲉ.

ϣⲙⲟⲩⲗ S nn m, meaning unknown : CO 307 boundaries of land ϫⲓⲛⲡϣ. ⲉⲣⲏⲥ.

ϣⲙⲙⲟ SAA², ϣⲙⲟ (Leyd 484), ϣⲙⲱ (PLond 4) S, ϣⲉⲙⲙⲟ B, ϣⲉⲙ(ⲙ)ⲁ, ϣⲓ. F, ϣⲙⲁ S/F, f ϣⲙⲙⲱ SA², -ⲟⲩ A, pl ϣⲙⲙⲟⲓ S(once), -ⲁⲓ AA², ϣⲉⲙⲙⲱⲟⲩ B, ϣⲓⲙⲙⲁⲁⲩ F & sg as pl, nn, stranger: Ge 31 15 SB-ⲱⲟⲩ, Job 19 13 SB do, Pro 5 17 SAB ἀλλότριος, Jo 10 5 SA²B ἀλλότριος, Nu 3 10 S(B=Gk) ἀλλογενής; Lam 5 2 F ϣⲉ. B-ⲱⲟⲩ, Ro 16 23 B(S ⲡⲉϣⲁⲓϭⲟⲓⲗⲉ ⲉⲣⲟϥ) ξένος; Ex 22 21 SB ϣ. ⲡⲣⲉⲙⲛϫⲱⲓⲗⲓ, Deu 5 14 B(S = Gk), Ez 22 7 B(S do), R 1 1 20 S προσήλυτος; Is 14 1 SB γειώρας; CA 103 S ϣ. ⲉⲃⲟⲗ ϩⲓⲕⲉⲫⲁⲗⲏ, AP 27 A² ⲛϣ. ⲙⲡⲣⲓⲁⲙⲉ, AM 17 B ⲟⲩϣ. ⲡⲣⲉⲙⲛⲭⲏⲙⲓ, J 5 46 S ϣ. opp ⲣⲙⲛⲏⲓ, BM 834 36 B opp ⲣⲉⲙϥⲙⲓⲁ, PLond 4 483 S ⲡϣⲉⲙⲟ dwelling there, ib ϣⲙⲱ (cf Ryl 277); c ⲉ-, stranger to : Sa 12 15 S, R 1 2 64 S ϣ. ⲉⲧⲛⲓⲥⲧⲓⲥ ἀλλοτ. gen; ShMIF 23 22 S garments ϩⲉⲛϣ. ⲉⲣⲟⲕ, Mani 2 A² ⲛϣⲱⲣⲙⲉ ... ⲟⲩϣ. ⲁⲣⲁϣⲡⲉ, BM 511 (2) F ⲕ̄ ϣⲉ. ⲉⲡⲙⲟⲩ, MG 25 171 B ⲟⲩϣ.ⲡⲉ ⲉⲡⲓⲙⲟⲛⲁⲭⲟⲥ ⲉⲑⲣⲉϥϫⲱⲛⲧ, AM 126 B ϩⲁⲛϣ. ⲡⲉ ⲉϯⲫⲩⲥⲓⲥ, PBu 274 S they have no share ⲁⲗⲗⲁ ϩⲉⲛϣ. ⲉⲣⲟⲡⲛⲉ; c ⲡⲁϩⲣⲛ- sim : ShBM 253 58 S ϩⲉⲛϣ. ⲛⲡⲁϩⲣⲁⲩ.

f : Pro 5 20 SA ἀλλότριος; Ru 2 10 S, AP 14 A² ξένη; Mani 2 A² ⲣⲉⲓⲧⲉ ⲛϣ., ShC 73 63 S [ϩⲣⲓ?]ⲙⲉ ⲛϣ., also ST infra.

pl : Deu 32 16 B, Ps 108 11 B, Hos 8 12 AB, Mt 17 26 B ἀλλότ.; Lam 5 2 B, He 11 13 B ξ.; Is 54 15 B προσηλ.; Mani H 17 A², AM 321 B ⲛϣ. ⲛⲉⲙ ⲡⲓⲣⲉⲙⲛϯⲙⲓ, J 93 34 S ⲛϣ. ⲉⲧⲛⲁⲡⲁⲣⲁⲧⲉ.

As adj, strange, before nn (rare) : Eccl 6 2 S(F ϣⲓ. after), CDan 86 B ϣ. ⲛⲣⲱⲙⲓ ξ.; ShC 42 26 S ϩⲉⲛϣ. ⲛⲣⲱⲙⲉ; after nn : Lev 10 1 SB, Ps 43 20 SB, Ro 14 4 B(S ⲛⲟⲕ ⲁⲛ) ἀλλότ., Lev 22 25 S(B=Gk) ἀλλογ.; Ge 29 19 S(B ⲕⲉ-) ἕτερος; ShC 73 172 S ϩⲏⲧ ⲛϣ., Mor 18 33 S ⲙⲡⲣⲁⲁⲧ ⲛϩⲟ ⲛϣ. = Miss 4 126 B ⲁⲓⲧ ⲛϣ., Miss 8 190 S sim, Bor 171 60 S Arius spake ϩⲉⲛϣⲁϫⲉ ⲛϣ. ⲉⲧⲃⲉⲡⲙⲟⲛⲟⲅⲉⲛⲏⲥ, Va 61 204 B ⲟⲩϣⲫⲏⲣⲓ ⲛϣ. to see old man skipping like calf, C 43 225 B ⲭⲱⲣⲁ ⲛϣ., Mun 46 S/ ⲣⲱⲙⲉ ⲛϣ., BM 660 F ⲧⲉⲛⲃⲁϣ ⲡⲉⲣⲛⲏⲃⲓ (l? ϩⲃⲛⲟⲩⲓ) ⲛϣⲙⲁ [ⲉ]ⲃⲁⲗ; without ⲛ- S : ST 222 ⲕⲁⲙⲟⲩⲗ ϣⲉⲙⲙⲱ, Ep 487 ⲉⲓⲱ ϣ.

ⲉⲡϣ. *SB, to strange parts, abroad,* with vb *go*: Mt 25 15 *BF*(*S* = Gk), Cai Euch 587 *B* brethren ⲉⲧⲁⲩϣⲉ ⲉⲡϣ. ἀποδημεῖν; R 1 5 14 *S* ⲃⲱⲕ ⲉⲡϣ., BM 247 8 *S* sim ἐπὶ ξένης ἀπέρχεσθαι; CO 29 *S* ordinands promise ⲙⲁⲛⲃⲱⲕ ⲉⲡϣ. ⲁⲭⲏϣⲓⲡⲉ.

ϩⲓⲡϣ. *SB, in strange parts, abroad*: 2 Cor 5 6 *B* ⲧⲉⲡϩ. (*S* om) ἐκδημεῖν; ShC 73 61 *S* women not admitted ⲉⲓⲧⲉ ϩ. ⲏ ϩⲙⲡⲁⲙⲉ, J 123 8 *S* sim, Miss 8 207 *S* ⲛⲧⲁϥⲉⲓ ϩ. *from abroad,* J 67 78 *S* we were not present ⲉⲛϩ.

ϩⲁⲙⲡϣ. *S,* as last: BMar 16 ⲡϣⲱⲡⲉ ϩ. ϣⲁⲛⲧϥⲙⲟⲩ, Kr 39 ⲉⲛϩ.

ⲡⲁⲣⲁ ⲡϣ. *SF,* meaning doubtful: BM 1122 vo *S* ⲉⲛ ϩⲟⲥⲟⲛ (*sic l*) ⲟⲩⲉⲡⲟⲓⲕⲓⲱⲛ ⲁⲓⲡⲉ ⲡ. ⲡϣ., CMSS 44 *F* ⲡⲛ. ⲡϣ. (context lost).

ⲙⲛⲧ-, ⲙⲉⲧϣ. *SBF, condition of stranger, strangeness*: Jer 13 27 *SB* ἀπαλλοτρίωσις; Z 300 *S* ξενιτεία; Kr 102 *S* tax on ⲙⲏⲧⲭⲉⲙⲟ (*cf* ξένιον PLond 4 284 n); ShC 42 137 *S* quitted us ϩⲛⲟⲩϩⲏⲧ ⲙⲙ., *ib* 73 41 (prob Esaias Abbas) be not boastful ⲝⲉⲡⲉⲥⲧⲁⲕⲟ ⲛⲧⲟⲟⲧⲕ ⲛϭⲓ ⲧϭⲟⲙ ⲛⲧⲙ. (*cf* He 11 13), C 43 235 *B* look upon ⲧⲁⲙ., MR 5 47 *F* ⲡⲁⲉⲙⲕⲉϩ ⲉⲧⲃⲉⲧⲏⲛⲟⲩ ... ⲙⲛⲧⲁⲙⲉⲧϣⲉⲙⲁ; ϩⲛⲟⲩⲙ. Is 28 21 *SB* ἀλλοτρίως.

ⲙⲁⲓϣ., *SABF, loving strangers, hospitable*: 1 Pet 4 9 *SB* φιλόξενος; BMis 535 *S* ⲟ ⲙⲙ., AM 136 *B* ⲍⲉⲗϣⲓⲣⲓ ... ⲙⲙ.; ⲙⲛⲧ-, ⲙⲉⲧⲙⲁⲓϣ., *hospitality*: Ro 12 13 *SBF* φιλοξενία, Pro 15 17 *SA* ξενισμός; R 1 2 59 *S* Abraham's ⲙ. (Ge 18); ⲣ, ⲉⲣ ⲙ.: Ac 28 7 *S*(*B* ⲙⲉⲧϣⲁⲡϣ., var ⲙⲉⲧⲙⲁⲓϣⲉⲙϣⲓ ϣ.) ξενίζειν; Rec 6 170 *B* = BMar 207 *S*; ⲙⲛⲧⲙⲁⲥⲧϣ., *hatred of strangers*: Sa 19 13 *S* μισοξενία.

ⲣ, ⲟ ⲛϣ. *SAA²BF, become, be stranger*: Jer 19 4 *S*(*B* ϣⲱⲃⲧ), Col 1 21 *SB* ἀπαλλοτριοῦν, Jer 2 21 *S* (ShA 1 291, *B* ϣ. adj) ἀλλότριος; Mt 25 35 *SB*, Eph 2 12 *SB* ξένος, ViK 9562 *S* ⲧⲟⲩⲱϣ ⲉⲣ ϣ. ξενιτεύεσθαι; C 43 84 *B* hast left thy town ⲁⲕⲉⲣ ϣ.; ⲥ ⲉ-, *estranged from*: Pro 2 16 *SAB* ἀλλότ. ποιεῖν gen, Aeg 288 *S* ⲁⲁϥ ⲛϣ. ⲉⲧⲙⲛⲧⲉⲣⲟ ἀλ. καθιστάναι gen, Ps 68 8 *SB* ἀπαλλοτ. γίνεσθαι dat; Pro 27 8 *SA* ἀποξενοῦν ἐκ; RNC 38 *S* ⲣ ⲡⲁⲓ ⲛϣ. ⲉⲧⲛⲡⲧⲟⲅⲛⲏⲃ ἐκκήρυκτον ποιεῖν gen; PS 122 *S* ⲁⲁϥ ⲛϣ. ⲉⲡⲛⲟⲃⲉ, ShC 42 198 *S* ⲟ ⲛϣ. ⲉⲧⲕⲟⲓⲛⲱⲛⲓⲁ, Leyd 343 *S* depart & ⲉⲣ ϣ. ⲉⲡⲡⲉⲓⲣⲁⲥⲙⲟⲥ, C 43 218 *B* ⲁϥⲁⲓⲧ ⲛϣ. ⲉⲡⲓⲃⲁⲗ ⲙⲡⲟⲡⲏⲣⲟⲛ, Mani 2 *A²* ⲡⲉⲧⲉ ⲡϣⲙⲙⲁⲓ ⲁⲣⲁϥ, Mor 30 14 *F* ⲁⲓ ⲡϣⲙⲁ ⲣⲟϥ, J 13 55 *S* ⲉϥⲛⲁϣⲱⲡⲉ ⲉϥⲟ ⲛϣ. ⲉⲡⲁⲡⲁϣ ⲉⲧⲟⲩⲁⲁⲃ, CO 9 *S* ϣⲟ ⲛϣ. ⲉⲡⲓⲱⲧ ... ϣⲁⲛⲧϥⲙⲉⲧⲁⲛⲟⲓ; ⲥ ⲛ-, as last: Eph 4 18 *B* (var ⲉ-, *S* = Gk) ἀπαλλοτ. gen; Lant 100 *S* whoso shall ⲉⲓⲣⲉ ⲙⲙⲛⲧⲭⲟⲙⲉ ⲛϣ. ⲙⲡⲓⲙⲟⲛⲁⲥⲧⲏⲣⲓⲟⲛ, *ib* 91 *S* sim ⲁⲁϥ ⲛϣ. ⲉⲧⲙⲧⲣⲉⲩϭⲉ ⲉⲣⲟϥ, Mor 31 35 *S* ⲕⲱ ⲛϣ. ⲡⲥⲛⲏⲡⲁⲥⲉ ⲡⲧⲟⲟⲧⲕ (var Miss 4 774 ⲛⲧⲙⲡϣⲁ ⲁⲛ ⲡⲉ ⲛⲧ.); ethic dat: C 86 169 *B* ⲉⲣ ϣ. ⲡⲁⲕ ⲉⲑⲃⲉ-

ⲡ︤ⲭ︥ⲥ︦; ⲥ ⲉⲃⲟⲗ ϩⲁ- *B, from*: Ge 42 7 ἀλλοτριοῦν ἀπό; Miss 4 208 ⲕⲟⲓ ⲛϣ. ⲉⲃ. ϩⲁ ⲡⲙⲉⲧⲁⲣⲭⲓⲉⲣⲉⲩⲥ.

ϣⲙⲟⲩⲛ *S* nn m: Worr 273 prob *l* ϩⲙⲟⲙ as var Mor 16 102.

ϣⲙⲟⲩⲛ *SA²F,* ϥ. *A,* ϣⲙⲏⲛ *B*(K 67, *cf* Lu 13 11 gloss اشمان), f ϣⲙⲟⲩⲛⲉ *S*, -ⲛⲓ *F,* ϣⲙⲏⲛⲓ *B*(Tatt 608) nn. *eight* (*BF* mostly ⲛ̄ m f): Kropp K 34 ⲡⲉϣ. ⲙⲡⲱϩ *8th day of moon;* as adj: Mic 5 5 *A,* Jo 20 26 *SA²* ὀκτώ; PS 30 ϣ. ⲛⲥⲙⲟⲧ, Mani H 60 *A²* ⲥⲟⲩϣ.; f: Ge 5 26 ϣ. ⲛⲣⲱⲙⲡⲉ ⲥⲛⲧⲉ ⲡⲣ., ShViK 9223 68 ⲭⲡϣ., BM 657 *F* ϣ. ⲛⲕⲟⲗⲗⲁⲑⲓ; *eighteen* &c -ϣⲙⲏⲛ, -ϣⲙⲏⲛⲉ: Jud 20 25 ⲙⲛⲧϣ., Lu 13 11 do f, Miss 4 763 *Sf* ⲙⲉⲧⲭⲙⲏⲛⲉ, Jo 5 5 *SA²* ⲙⲁⲃϣ., PS 364 do f, Tob 14 2 ⲧⲁⲓⲟⲩϣ. ⲛⲣⲟⲙⲡⲉ, Job 42 16 (var ϩⲙⲉϣⲙⲏⲛ); *Ordinals*: Ps 6 tit ⲙⲉϩϣ., Mani 2 *A²* do, PS 52 ⲙⲉϩⲥⲉϣⲙⲏⲛ; f *ib* 85 ⲙⲉϩϣⲙⲟⲩⲛⲉ, BG 123, Lant 87.

ϩⲙⲉⲛⲉ *S,* ϩⲁⲙⲛⲉ *B*(K 67), *eighty*: Ps 89 10 ὀγδοήκοντα; Br 131 ϩⲙⲡⲉϣⲓⲥ, PS 119 ⲙⲉϩϩⲙⲉⲛⲉⲧⲁϥⲧⲉ.

As place-name: ϣⲙⲟⲩⲛ Hermopolis اشمون (rare), اشمونين (BIF 36 18-21, *cf* ϣ. ⲃ̄), ⲧⲉϣⲙⲟⲩⲡⲓ (CMSS 78, Kr 69).

ϣⲟⲙⲛⲧ, ϣ(ⲉ)ⲙⲛⲧ *S,* ϣⲟⲙⲧ *SB* (rare) ϣⲁⲙⲉⲛⲧ *Sf,* ϣⲁⲙⲏⲧ *SᵃA²,* ϩⲁⲙⲧ *A,* ϣⲁⲙⲧ *A²F,* ϣⲙⲧ- *SA²,* ϣ(ⲉ)ⲙⲛⲧ-*S,* ϩⲛⲧ-, ϩⲛⲧⲉ-*A,* f ϣⲟⲙⲧⲉ *SO,* ϣⲟⲙⲡⲧⲉ *S,* ϩⲁⲙⲧⲉ *A,* ϣⲁⲙⲧⲉ, ϩⲟ. *A²,* ϣⲟⲙ︦ϯ *B*(once, mostly ⲅ̄, ⲅ̄ϯ) nn, *three*: 1 Cor 13 13, ROC 25 243 *B* ⲡⲉϣ. *3d day* τρεῖς; Mani H 60 *A²* sim -ⲙⲧ, CO 455 ⲡϣ. ⲡⲧⲕⲩⲣⲓⲁⲕⲏ (*v* Ep 498 n), BKU 1 296 ⲡϣ. ⲙⲡϣⲁ, Kropp K 51 *Sᵃ* ⲡⲭⲟⲩⲧϣ. ⲉⲡⲟⲱϩ, BMar 9 ⲡⲉⲕϣ. ⲛⲧⲁⲩⲭⲡⲟⲕ *3d day after thy birth*; as adj: ⲥ ⲡ-: Ge 18 2, Jo 2 19 *SA²,* Ac 7 20 ⲧⲣ.; PS 30 ϣ. ⲛⲕⲟⲟϩ, Miss 4 763 *Sf* ϣ. ⲛⲥⲟⲡ, BM 527 *F* ϣ. ⲉⲣⲁ[ⲟⲩ]; after nn: Ap 12 4 ⲡⲟⲩⲛ ⲡϣ. τρίτον; PS 26 ⲡⲟⲩⲱⲡ ⲡϣ.; Miss 4 735 ⲥⲟⲩϣⲟⲙⲧ; constr: Nu 1 46 ϣⲙⲧⲯⲟ, Job 1 17 ϣⲙⲛⲧⲧⲁⲅⲙⲁ (BMOr 6807 4, var ϣⲙⲛⲧ ⲛⲧ.), Pro 22 20 *A* ϩⲛⲧⲥⲟⲡ, *ib* 24 56 ϣⲙⲧⲧⲟⲱⲃ (*A* ϩⲁⲙⲧ ⲛⲣ.), Si 25 1 do (var ϣⲟⲙⲧ ⲛⲣ.), Ap 16 19 ϣⲙⲧⲟⲩⲱⲡ, Mani H 68 *A²* ϣⲙⲭⲉ, ST 74 sim, BG 96 ϣⲙⲧⲣⲟⲟⲩⲧ; +f nn: Job 1 4 ϣⲙⲛⲧⲥⲱⲡⲉ, Pro 24 50 ϣⲙⲧϣⲉⲉⲣⲉ (*A* ϩⲁⲙⲧⲉ), Br 231 ϣⲙⲛⲧⲥⲟⲙ; *three in one*: R 1 2 27 ⲡϣⲟⲙⲛⲧ ⲟⲩⲁ, P 129²⁰ 123 sim; ϣⲙ(ⲛ)ⲧ (ⲉ)ⲡⲟⲟⲩ, var ⲙⲛ. *SA, 3 days before to-day, heretofore*: Ru 2 11 (var ϣⲟ.), 2 Kg 3 17 (var ϣ. ⲡⲟⲟⲩ) τρίτης; BMis 158 ϣ. ⲉⲡ.; +ⲡ-ϩⲟⲟⲩ: Ge 31 2 ϣ. ⲉⲡ. ⲛⲣ. (*B* ⲅ̄ ⲙⲫⲟⲟⲩ), 1 Kg 14 21 ϣ. ⲙⲛ. ⲛⲣ. (var ϣ. ⲡ.) τρίτην ἡμ., Ex 4 10 *SA* ϩⲁⲑⲏ ⲛϣ. ⲉⲡ. ⲛⲣ. πρὸ τ. τρίτης ἡμ.; P 44 136 ϣ. ⲥⲁϥ أمس; BMis 505 road I knew not ϩⲁⲑⲏ ⲛⲥⲁϥ اول مس; sim PMich 3571]ⲛⲕⲟⲩϥⲟⲣ ⲉⲣⲟϥ ϩⲁⲥⲛⲟⲩϥ ... ϩⲁϣⲙⲛⲧ ⲉⲧⲣⲟⲙⲡⲉ *year before last,* ϣⲟⲙⲧ ⲥⲁϥ Tuki 23 (whence?); f: Job 1 2, Am 1

3 *A*, Ap 9 18, Mani Berl Sitz '33 85 *A*² ϣ. ⲛⲧⲅⲣⲁⲫⲏ, BM 1224 *A*² ϣ. ⲛⲧⲉⲛⲉⲁ, BG 39 ϣⲟⲙⲛⲧⲉ ⲛϭⲟⲙ, AZ 21 106 *O* ⲧⲉϣ. ⲛϣⲉ ⲥⲉⲧⲏ ⲕⲉⲗⲓ, PS 6 ϣ. ⲡⲟⲩⲡⲟⲩ, *ib* ⲭⲛ ϣ., Ryl 436 *B* ⲑϣ. ⲛϯϫⲓⲡⲉⲣ ⲟⲡⲟⲙⲁⲍⲓⲛ ; elliptic? *ib* 158 share of ⲧϣⲟⲙⲛⲧ ⲉⲣⲏ̄ⲃ, Cai ostr 47400 ⲧⲉⲓϣⲟⲙⲧ ⲛⲓⲣⲡ, Mor 51 41 ⲛⲛⲉⲡⲱϥⲥ ... ⲛ-ⲡⲉ(ⲛ)ϥⲓ ϣⲙⲧⲉ ⲟⲩⲛⲓⲁϥⲓ ϣⲏⲩ ; *thirteen :* Nu 29 13 ⲙⲛⲧϣⲟⲙⲧⲉ ⲛⲙⲁⲥⲉ, Jos 18 28 ⲙ. ⲛⲡⲟⲗⲓⲥ, JSch 1 43 ⲛⲁⲛⲧϣ. ⲛⲣⲟⲗⲟⲕ/ ; *thirty v* ⲙⲁⲁⲃ ; iterated: BAp 98 fasted ϣ. ϣ. ⲛⲣⲟⲟⲩ, ShC 73 103 when fasting ⲉⲩⲣⲱⲧⲣ...ϣ. ϣ., Mani 2 *A*² ⲥⲁⲣⲟⲩ ⲁⲃⲁⲗ ... ϣ. ϣ., PMich 593 a recipe ⲉⲧⲃⲉⲡϣ. ϣ. *tertian fever (cf* C 99 196 ⲕⲁⲧⲁ ϣ. ⲛⲣⲟⲟⲩ).

Ordinals : Nu 2 24, Is 19 24 ; ⲥ ⲛ- : Ge 2 14, Hos 6 2 *SA* τρίτος ; PS 43 ⲡⲙⲉϩⲙⲛⲧϣⲟⲙⲧⲉ ⲛⲁⲓⲱⲛ, Br 82 do, AP 37 *A*² ⲡⲙⲁϩϣⲁⲙⲛⲧ ⲛⲣⲟ[ⲟⲩ] ; Mk 14 41 ⲡⲙⲁϩϣⲙⲧⲥⲱⲱⲡ τὸ τρίτον ; f : Ge 50 23 ⲧⲙⲉϩϣⲟⲙⲧⲉ ⲛⲅⲉⲛⲉⲁ, Nu 10 6 ⲥⲩⲙⲁⲥⲓⲁ ⲙⲙⲉϩϣ. τρί. ; Br 244 ⲧⲙⲉϩϣⲟⲙⲧⲉ ⲙⲙⲛⲧⲉⲓⲱⲧ, ManiH 19 *A*² ⲧⲙⲁϩϣⲁⲙⲧⲉ[.

ⲙⲡϣ., *three together, all three :* Nu 12 4 οἱ τρεῖς ; PS 71 ⲛⲧⲱⲧⲛ ⲙ. ⲛⲉⲧⲛⲁⲥϧⲁⲓ, J 67 19 ⲁⲩⲥⲟⲓⲗⲉ ⲉⲡⲕⲟⲥⲙⲟⲥ ⲙ. (*sc* 3 sons).

In name : ϣⲙⲛⲧⲥⲛⲏⲩ (J *pass, cf* Τριάδελφος).

In place-name : ⲡⲏⲓ ⲙⲡⲓ̄ⲧ̄ (Amélineau *Géog* 263).

ϣⲁⲙⲁⲣ, -ⲙⲉⲣ *v* ⲥⲁⲙⲁϩⲣ.

ϣⲉⲙⲏⲣ *B* nn m, *leaven (cf* ‎خمير‎ IgR, *S* ⲑⲁⲃ) : Deu 16 3, Mt 13 33 (*F* ⲥⲉⲓⲗ), 1 Cor 5 7 ζύμη, Lev 2 11 ζυμωτός, *ib* 7 13 ζυμίτης, *ib* 23 17 ζυμοῦσθαι ; DeV 2 106 ⲡⲓϣⲱϯ ⲁⲕϣⲁⲡϯ ϣ. ⲉⲣⲟϥ ⲉⲧⲉⲡⲓⲕⲱⲃⲡⲉ ; ϭⲓ ϣ., *be leavened :* Lev 6 10 (*S* ϫⲓ ⲑ.), Hos 7 4 (*A* ϭⲓ), Gal 5 9 (*S* ϭⲓ) ζυμοῦσθαι ; MG 25 141 ϭⲓ ⲙⲡⲓϣ. which is grace of Lord ; ⲁⲧϣ., *without leaven (S* ⲁⲑⲁⲃ) : Ex 12 8, Ac 20 6 (var ⲙⲉⲧⲁⲧ.) ἄζυμος ; ⲙⲉⲧⲁⲧϣ. : 1 Cor 5 8 (*S* ⲁⲑ.) ἄζ.

ϣⲟⲩⲙⲁⲣⲉ, ϣⲱ., ϣⲟⲩⲙⲁⲣⲁ (once), ⲣⲟⲩⲙⲁⲣⲉ (twice) *S* nn m, meaning unknown, a locality(?) at Jeme : PSBA 33 256 field ϩⲛⲡϣ., J 13 25 (house of) ϩⲁⲣⲱⲡ ⲙⲡϣⲟⲩⲙⲁⲣⲁ, *ib* 7 27 sim ⲙⲡϣ., *ib* 15 31 ⲡϭⲓⲣ ⲛⲓⲣⲙⲡϣ., 39 ⲛⲕⲗⲏⲣⲟⲛⲟⲙⲟⲥ ⲛⲓⲣⲙⲡϣ., *ib* 6 14 ⲡⲁⲛϩ ⲛ(ⲛ)ⲣⲙⲡϣ. Coptic ?

ϣⲁⲙⲥⲉ *v* ⲙⲥⲉ nn.

ϣⲙϣⲉ *SAA*², ϣⲉⲙϣⲓ *BF*, ϣⲛⲙ. *F*, ϣⲙϣⲉ-*S*, ϣⲉⲙ. *B*, ϣⲙϣⲏⲧ⸗ *S*, ϣⲉⲙ. *B*, ϣⲙϣⲏⲩ† *A*²(?), p c ϣⲁⲙϣⲉ-*B* vb **I** intr, *serve, worship :* Nu 1 50 *S(B* ⲫⲱϣⲉⲛ), Ez 42 14 *SB* λειτουργεῖν ; Est 6 10 *S*, Pro 19 3 *SA* θεραπεύειν ; Ac 26 7 *SB*, Cl 45 7 *A* λατρεύειν ; Jo 12 2 *BF(SA*² = Gk) διακονεῖν ; Ac 17 4 *S(B* = Gk) σέβεσθαι ; Lu 1 8 *S(B* ⲓⲣⲓ ⲛϯⲙⲉⲧⲟⲩⲏⲃ) ἱερατεύειν ; BIF 13 98 *S* priest approached altar ⲉϥⲛⲁϣ. *to celebrate* = MG 25 277 *B*, BMis 450 *S* we wish

tonsure ϫⲉⲕⲁⲥ ⲉⲡⲉϣ. ϩⲁⲣⲁⲧⲕ (*sc* bishop) ;   qual *A*² (this word?) : Mani H 20 ⲧⲥⲛϭⲉ ⲡⲁϣⲉ[ⲡⲟ]ⲩⲥⲱⲙⲁ ⲉⲧϣ. ⲙⲛⲛⲟⲩⲥⲛⲁϥ, Mani 2 birds ? ⲉ]ϥⲧⲙⲏⲩ ϩⲓⲣⲓⲣ ⲉϥϣ. ;   ⲥ ⲛ- dat *SB* : Ex 20 5 *S(B* tr), Deu 28 48 *SB*, Mt 4 10 *S(B* tr), He 9 14 *SF*ϣⲏ.(*B* ⲉⲣ ⲃⲱⲕ ⲛ-) λατ. dat ; Ps 100 6 *S(B* tr), Ez 40 46 *SB* λειτ. dat, Ac 19 27 *S(B* = Gk) σέβ. acc ; Sa 16 24 *S*, Ac 13 36 *SB* ὑπηρετεῖν dat ; Sa 10 9 *S* θερ. acc ; *ib* 11 16 *S* θρησκεύειν acc ; Ex 29 1 *S(B* ⲉⲣ ⲟⲩⲏⲃ ⲛ-) ἱερ. dat ; He 6 10 *B(SF* = Gk), Philem 13 *S(B* tr) διακ. dat ; Pro 29 12 *SA* ⲡⲉⲧϣ. ⲛⲁϥ οἱ ὑπ᾽ αὐτόν ; ShBor 300 70 *S* king's ϩⲙϩⲁⲗ ⲙⲛⲡⲉⲧϣ. ⲛⲁϥ, CA 102 *S* ⲙⲁⲣⲉⲡⲉⲛⲕⲁ ⲧⲏⲣⲟⲩ ... ϣ. ⲛⲧⲉⲣⲣⲉ ⲙⲡⲟⲃⲥⲱ (var ⲣ ϩⲱⲃ ⲉ-), J 13 55 *S* ⲛⲁⲡⲁϣ...ⲉⲧⲟⲩϣ. ⲛⲁϥ (*cf* σεβάσμιος ὅρκος), BSM 103 *B* ⲉⲧϣ. ⲛⲏⲓ ⲛⲛⲓⲭⲣⲓⲁ ⲛⲧⲉ ⲡⲓⲥⲱⲙⲁ, Mor 30 32 *F* idol ⲉⲧⲉⲥϣⲛ(ⲙ)ϣⲓ ⲛⲏϥ = BMis 257 *S*.

II tr ⲥ ⲛ- (where Gk acc), ⲙⲙⲟ⸗, suff : Deu 6 13 *B(S* dat), Ro 1 9 *B(S* do)λατ. dat ; *ib* 15 27 *B(S* do), Dan 7 10 *B(Va* 57 68, var dat)λειτ. dat ; Job 1 9 *SB*, Mt 15 9 *S(B* = Gk)σέβ. acc, 1 Tim 5 4 *S(B* diff)εὐσεβ. Mk 15 41 *BF(S* = Gk), Ro 15 25 *B(S* do) διακ. dat ; acc ; Pro 14 19 *A(S* ϩⲓⲣⲏ-, *B* ⲛⲁϩⲣⲉⲛ-), EpJer 25 *BF* θερ. acc ; Ac 24 23 -ⲧϥ *SB* ὑπηρ. dat ; CDan 87 *B* ϣⲉⲙϣⲓⲧⲟⲩ τρέφειν ; Ac 27 3 *S*-ⲧϥ (*B* ϥⲓ ⲣⲱⲟⲩϣ) ἐπιμελείας τυγχάνειν ; ShBMOr 8664 4 *S* ⲛⲕⲉⲣⲓⲥⲉ ...ⲉⲓⲁⲥϣⲙϣⲏⲧϥ ⲡϩⲏⲧⲟⲩ, ClPr 56 7 *S* temples ⲉⲧⲟⲩϣ. ⲉⲓⲇⲱⲗⲟⲛ ⲡϩⲏⲧⲟⲩ, BSM 70 *B* ⲫⲣⲏ ⲉⲧⲉⲡϣ. ⲙⲙⲟⲩ = BMis 161 *S* dat, *ib* 48 *B* ⲁⲓϣ.ⲑⲏⲛⲟⲩ = *ib* 398 *S* ⲇⲓⲁⲕⲟⲛⲉⲓ, MG 25 331 *B* in form of servant ⲁϥϣⲉⲙϣⲏⲧⲉⲛ.

p c *B*, *worshipper :* Jo 9 31 ϣⲁⲙϣⲉⲛⲟⲩϯ (*SA*² ⲣⲙⲛⲛⲟⲩⲧⲉ) θεοσεβής ; 1 Cor 10 7 ϣ. ⲓⲁⲱⲗⲟⲛ (*S* ⲣⲉϥϣⲙϣⲉ-), Ap 21 8 ϣ. ⲓⲇ̄ (*S* ⲣⲉϥϣ. ⲉⲓⲇⲱⲗⲟⲛ) εἰδωλολάτρης ; C 86 109 ⲛⲉⲟⲩϣ. ⲓⲁⲱⲗⲟⲓⲧⲉ ; ⲙⲉⲧϣ. ⲡⲟⲩϯ Ge 20 11 (*S* ⲙⲛⲧⲣⲉϥϣ. ⲡ̄ⲉ̄) θεοσέβεια ; ⲙⲉⲧϣ. ⲓⲁⲱⲗⲟⲛ 1 Cor 10 14 (*S* ⲙⲛⲧⲣⲉϥϣ.) εἰδωλολατρεία.

—— nn m *SAA*²*BF*, *service, worship :* Nu 18 21 *S(BM* 2 V, var = Gk, *B* ⲫⲱϣⲉⲛ), Ez 29 20 *SB*, He 8 6 *SB*(var ⲫⲁϣⲛⲓ)*F* ϣⲏ., CaiEuch 474 *B* ⲓⲛⲓ ⲛⲁⲕ ⲉϩⲟⲩⲛ ⲙⲡϣ. λειτουργία ; Ex 12 26 *B*, Jo 16 2 *SA*² (*B* diff), Ro 12 1 *SBF* ϣⲏ., CaiEuch 577 *B* ϣ. ⲡⲁⲧⲥⲛⲟϥ λατρεία ; Col 2 18 *SB* θρησκεία ; Ac 6 1 *B(S* = Gk) διακονία ; Joel 1 14 *SAB* θεραπεία ; Sa 15 7 *S* ὑπηρεσία ; *ib* 12 4 *S* τελετή ; Ex 29 9 *S(B* ⲙⲉⲧⲟⲩⲏⲃ) ἱερατία ; Cl 1 2 *A* εὐσέβεια ; Est 2 3 *S* ἐπιμέλεια ; Ez 44 14 *B ministerium* ; BAp 151 *S* fasts & prayers ⲛⲕⲉⲥⲉⲉⲡⲉ ⲡϣ., Bor 254 172 *S* ⲁϥϫⲓ ⲛⲟⲩϣ. ⲙⲡⲟⲩϭⲣⲉ ⲉⲃⲟⲗ ϩⲓⲧⲟⲅⲁⲅⲅⲉⲗⲟⲥ, C 89 209 *B* ⲓⲛⲓ ⲉϩⲣⲏⲓ ⲉϫⲱϥ (*sc* dead) ⲙⲡϣ. ⲉⲑⲟⲩⲁⲃ = *ib* 99 203 *S* ⲡⲣⲟⲥⲫⲟⲣⲁ, BSM 42 *B* ⲡⲓϣ. ⲉⲑⲟⲩⲁⲃ in church = BMis 388 *S* ⲧⲥⲩⲛⲁⲝⲓⲥ, C 86 272 *B* ⲡⲓϣ. ⲛⲧⲉ ϯⲙⲉⲧⲟⲣⲓⲃⲟⲩⲛⲟⲥ *duties* ;   as adj : Lev 23 7 *SB* λατρευ-

τός; 1 Chr 28 20 B λειτουργία; C 43 111 B ϩⲃⲱⲥ ⲛϣ., MG 25 137 B ⲡⲕⲁⲑⲟⲗⲓⲕⲟⲛ ⲛϣ.;   ⲙⲁ ⲛϣ. S: Leyd 448 *place of worship*.

ⲉⲓⲣⲉ, ⲣ ϣ. *SA²B, do service*: Nu 4 24 S(var=Gk, B ϥⲱ.) λειτουργεῖν, Bor 235 118 S go into cell ⲛⲧⲉⲣ ⲡⲉⲕϣ. λειτουργίαν ποιεῖν; MIE 2 417 B brethren ⲉⲣ ⲡⲟⲩϣ. ⲕⲁⲧⲁ ⲟⲩⲛⲟⲩ = BAp 123 S ⲡⲉϥϣⲗⲏⲗ; CA 94 S ⲁⲣⲓ ⲡϣ. ⲙⲡⲉⲑⲩⲥⲓⲁⲥⲧⲏⲣⲓⲟⲛ; c ⲛ- dat: Jo 16 2 SA²(B diff) λατρείαν προσφέρειν dat; Cai Euch 384 B ⲉⲣ ϣ. ⲙⲡⲉϥⲣⲁⲛ λειτουργεῖν dat.

ⲣⲉϥϣ. *SAB, server, worshipper*: 3 Kg 10 5 S, Ps 103 4 B(S = Gk) λειτουργός; Pro 10 4 SAB, Ro 16 subscr διάκων; MG 25 12 B ὑπηρέτης; TEuch 2 187 B ⲡⲓⲟⲩⲏⲃ ⲡⲉⲙⲡⲓⲣ خادم; WTh 182 S Joshua ⲣ. ⲙⲙⲱⲅⲥⲏⲥ, Va 57 163 B ⲇⲓⲁⲕⲱⲛ ⲉⲧⲟⲓ ⲡⲣ.; ⲣ. ⲙⲡⲡⲉ̄: Ex 18 21 S(B = Gk), Job 1 1 S(var ⲣ. ⲡⲉ̄, B do)θεοσεβής, ⲣ. ⲛⲧⲉ ⲫϯ B(S ϣⲙϣⲓⲧ)λειτ. τ. θεοῦ; ⲣ. ⲡⲉ̄ S: Miss 8 30 θ., Z 274 S θεοφιλής; Si 13 19 εὐσεβής; Z 308 εὐλαβής; CO 225 addressed to ⲡⲣⲱⲙⲉ ⲡⲣⲉϥⲣ ϩⲟⲧⲉ ⲁⲅⲱ ⲛⲣ. ⲡⲉ̄; ⲣ. ⲉⲓⲇⲱⲗⲟⲛ: Ap 21 8 (B ⲛ ⲣ ⲥ) εἰδωλολάτρης; ⲛϣⲙⲧ-, ⲙⲉⲧⲣ., *service*: Cai Euch 651 B ⲕⲁⲧⲁ ⲟⲩⲙ. διακονικῶς opp αὐτεξουσίως; Mor 18 157 S ⲛⲉϩⲃⲏⲅⲉ ⲡⲧⲙ. ἔνθεα ἔργα; Job 28 28 S ⲙ. ⲡⲉ̄ (B as Gk), Miss 8 31 S θεοσέβεια; Aeg 266 S εὐσέβεια; AP 42 A², Ep 282 S ⲧⲓⲙϣⲓⲛⲉ ⲉⲧⲉⲧⲛⲙ. ⲡⲉ̄ ⲉⲧⲧⲁⲓⲏⲩ ϫⲓⲛⲡⲕⲟⲅⲓ ϣⲁⲡⲛⲟϭ; BM 189 168 S ⲙ. ⲉⲓⲇⲱⲗⲟⲛ εἰδωλολατρεία.

ϭⲓⲛ-, ϫⲓⲛϣ. *SB, service, religion*: Si 8 10 S λειτουργεῖν; Pcod 14 S made ready ⲧϭ. ⲉⲧⲟⲩⲁⲁⲃ, C 43 47 B ⲧϭ. ⲛⲛⲓⲇⲱⲗⲟⲛ, ib 58 B ⲛϭ. ⲛⲛⲓⲛⲟⲩϯ, ClPr 56 8 S ascertain ⲉⲧⲉⲛϭ.

ϣⲙϣⲓⲧ *SA² nn m, servant*: Jos 1 1, Ps 102 21 (B ⲉⲧϥⲟϣⲉⲛ), Is 61 6 (B ⲣⲉϥϣⲉⲙϣⲓ) λειτουργός; Aeg 280 subdeacons ⲛϣ. ⲛⲛⲓⲇⲓⲁⲕⲟⲛⲟⲥ ὑπηρέτης; ShViK 9325 397 thou ⲡϣⲙϣⲉⲧ(prob)ⲛⲕⲣⲟⲛⲟⲥ, BMis 174 clergy & ⲛⲫⲓⲗⲟⲡⲱⲛⲟⲥ ⲁⲅⲱ ⲛⲣⲕⲉϣ.(BSM 83 B om), ROC 20 51 priests & ⲛϣ. ⲙⲡⲉⲑⲩⲥⲓⲁⲥⲧⲏⲣⲓⲟⲛ, Mani H 93 A² ⲁⲡⲁⲕ ⲛϣ. ⲙⲛ[   ]ⲡⲉⲧⲁⲩⲧⲛⲡⲁⲅⲧ.

ϣⲙϣⲏϭⲉ S, ϣⲉⲙϣⲏϫⲓ (?) B *vb intr, whisper*: Tri 518 ϯⲗⲩⲡⲉⲓ ⲉⲓϣ. ϩⲁⲡⲉⲓⲗⲁⲟⲥ, ib 682 sim تأسّف (*be sad, distressed*); ShIF 248 ⲡⲉϣⲙϣⲏϫⲉ ⲡϣⲟⲩϣϣⲁ ϭⲓⲝ ⲉⲭⲱϥ ⲁⲅⲱ ϣ., BHom 113 sim; as nn: Jer 18 16 (B ϣⲟⲕϣⲉⲕ) σύριγμα; ⲉϣ ϣ.: Si 12 18 S (var P 44 119 ϥⲓ ϣ. أسِّف)B ⲛϣⲧⲉⲙϣ. (var ⲭⲉⲙϣ.) διαψιθυρίζειν; ϥⲓ ϣ.: Jer 29 17 (B ϣⲟⲕ. ⲡⲣⲱϥ), Lam 2 16 (B ⲉⲣ ϣⲟⲩϣⲓⲧⲉ, F ϣⲱϫⲓ) συρίζειν, Si 22 1 (var lc ϣ. vb) ἐκσυρ.

(ϣⲱⲙⲝ) S, ⲥⲱⲭⲡ B, ϣⲙⲝ- S, ϣⲁⲙⲝⲉ S/, ϣⲟ-ⲙⲝ† S, ϣⲁⲙⲝⲉ† S/, ϣⲟⲭⲡ† B *vb tr, pierce*: P 44 88 S ⲉϥϣ.† زرب (v Rec 14 108); Ep 287 S ⲉⲓⲛⲁϣⲙⲝ (?) ⲛⲕⲁⲙⲟⲩⲗ, Mor 40 19 S dragon ⲉϥϣ.† ⲉϥϣⲁⲁⲡⲧϥ ϩⲛⲟⲩϩⲁⲗⲅⲩⲥⲓⲥ = ib 39 27 S/ = C 43 49 B ⲉϥϣ.†

ⲉⲡⲉϣϣⲁⲓ ⲡⲟⲩ-, AM 260 B ⲥ. ⲙⲡⲉⲕϣⲁⲓ ϫⲉⲡⲟⲅⲁ-ⲗⲁⲕ, MIF 9 100 S/ ϣⲁⲙⲝϥ (sc devil) ϩⲛϣⲁⲁⲡⲧϥ.

ϣⲁⲛ- v ϣⲟⲟⲡⲉ, ϣⲱⲡⲉ.

ϣⲁⲛ- vbal pref v ⲉⲣϣⲁⲛ.

ϣⲁⲛ B *conj, or*: Job 10 20, ib 18 4, Mt 20 15 *bis* (all S = Gk), Mk 11 30, Ac 8 34, Gal 1 10 (all S ⲭⲛ-), Ro 2 4 (S ⲙⲙⲟⲛ) ἤ; Va 57 270 ⲙⲛ ⲟⲩⲁⲕⲁⲑⲁⲣⲧⲟⲥⲧⲉ ⲓⲉ ϣ. ⲕⲉⲟⲩⲁⲓ ⲡⲉⲡⲓⲧⲙⲁⲡⲉ εἰ μή; C 89 146 from God ⲓⲉ ϣ. ⲟⲩⲉⲃⲟⲗⲡⲉ ϫⲉⲛⲡⲓⲁⲉⲙⲱⲡⲡⲉ, MG 25 225 ϩⲁⲣⲁ ⲉⲕϣⲟⲡ ϫⲉⲛⲡⲓⲙⲧⲟⲛ ϣ. ⲉⲕϣⲟⲡ ϫⲉⲛⲡⲓϯϭⲓ, Va 61 200 ⲉⲕⲙⲉⲓ ⲙⲙⲟⲓ ϣ. ⲓⲥⲁⲕ; ϣ. ⲙⲙⲟⲛ, *or no* (present): Nu 11 23, Deu 8 2 (both S ⲭ.), Lu 20 22 ἤ οὔ; C 43 65 ⲡⲁⲓⲡⲉ ⲡⲉⲕϣⲏⲣⲓ ϣ. ⲙ.; not neg: ib 238 ⲁⲣⲓⲉⲙⲓ ϫⲉⲡⲓⲗⲁⲟⲥ ⲟⲛϩⲟ̄ ϣ. ⲙ. ⲁϥⲕⲏⲡ ⲉⲃⲟⲗ ⲉⲃⲟⲗ, Va 57 116 ⲟⲩⲥⲱⲡⲧⲡⲉ ϣ. ⲙ. ⲟⲩⲣⲉϥⲥⲱⲡⲧⲡⲉ; ϣ. ⲙⲫⲏ(past): Ge 24 21 ἤ οὔ; C 43 18 ⲁⲡⲁⲅ ϫⲉⲁϥⲙⲟⲩ ϣ. ⲙ., ib 189 ⲁⲛ ⲁϥϯ ⲡⲁⲓ ⲡⲏⲓ ϣ. ⲙ.

ϣⲉⲛ B nn v ϣⲓⲛⲉ s f.

ϣⲉⲛ-, ϣⲛ- v ϣⲉ *wood*, ϣⲓⲛⲉ, ϣⲱⲡⲉ, ϣⲏⲣⲉ.

ϣⲏⲛ *SAA²F*, ϣⲏⲏⲛ B, ϣⲉⲛ, ϣⲏⲉⲛ F *nn m, tree* (cf ϩⲱ): Lev 26 4 SB, Ps 148 9 SB, Eccl 2 5 SF ϣϣ., Ap 2 7 SB, Cl 23 4 A ξύλον; Ge 18 4 SB, Is 2 13 SB, Mt 12 33 SBF δένδρον, Ez 47 7 S ⲟⲩϣ. ⲉⲡⲁϣⲱϥ B ⲉϥⲟⲓϣ δένδρα πολλά; Ge 18 1 SB, Jer 2 34 SB, Zech 11 2 B(A ⲥⲉⲓ) δρῦς; Job 24 18 S(B ⲉⲧⲣⲏⲧ), Sa 10 7 S φυτόν; Nu 24 6 S(B = Gk) παράδεισος; Ge 21 15 S(B diff)ἐλάτη; Is 2 13 B(S = Gk)κέδρος; Jos 17 9 S ϣ. ⲛⲧⲧⲉⲣⲉⲙⲓⲛⲑⲟⲥ τερ.; P 44 83 S ϣ. ⲙⲡⲣⲏ · ⲁⲣⲧⲉⲙⲓⲥⲓⲁⲥ (v ⲁⲡⲁϣ nn); Ez 27 6 SB ϩⲁⲓⲃⲉⲥ ⲛϣ. ἀλσώδης; PS 18 S ⲛϯⲟⲩ ⲛϣ., Mani 2 A² do, ShC 73 ix S ⲕⲁⲣⲡⲟⲥ ϩⲛⲛϣ. ⲏ ⲛⲃⲛⲛⲉ, Miss 4 231 S ϩⲉⲛⲕⲟⲅⲓ ⲛϣ. ⲙⲡⲣⲉⲛⲃⲛⲛⲉ ⲙⲡⲣⲉⲛϫⲟⲉⲓⲧ (cf ⲃⲛⲛⲉ), EnPeterson S ϣ. ⲙⲡⲉⲥϯⲛⲟⲩϥⲉ(sic l p 363b), Mani 1 A² ϣ. ⲛⲧⲁⲓⲟⲩⲧⲁϩ, BSM 11 B ⲡⲟⲩⲧⲁϩ ⲙⲡϣ., P 131⁴ 135 S ⲣⲉϥⲕⲉⲉⲣⲉ ϣ.

ⲉⲓⲁϩ, ⲓⲁϩ ϣ. S(rare)B, *grove*: Deu 16 21 S(B ϣ. only), Mic 5 13 (A ⲙⲁ ⲛϣ.) ἄλσος: Ps 73 5 (S ⲥⲱⲱϣⲉ), Jer 12 8 (S ⲙⲁ ⲛϣ.) δρυμός; Ez 31 12 πεδίον. ⲙⲁ ⲛϣ. S(mostly)ABF, as last: Ps 28 9 (B ⲓⲁϩ ϣ.), Eccl 2 6 (F ϣⲟⲩⲏ), Is 32 15 SF(B do), Zech 11 2 B(A = Gk) δρ.; Jud 3 7, Mic 5 13 A(ut sup) ἀλ.; Jer 14 6 (B diff) νάπη; Va 66 288 B where flowers grow λειμών; ShA 1 448 ⲟⲩϣⲏⲛ ⲉϥⲣⲓⲧⲟⲩⲱϣ ⲛⲟⲩⲙ., BMis 519 ⲧⲉϥⲥⲱϣⲉ, ⲡⲉϫⲙ., LAp 513 F ⲙ[ⲁ ⲛ]ϣⲉⲛ, ⲙⲁ ⲛⲑⲁⲗⲁⲗⲓ, DeV 2 138 B ⲟⲩⲙ. ⲉϥⲟⲓ ⲛϣⲁϥⲉ where-in wild beasts.

In ϣⲉⲛⲥⲓϥⲓ & ?others it is difficult to say whether ϣⲉⲛ- or ϣⲉ ⲛ- *wood* q v.

ϣⲱⲛ S *nn, meaning unknown*: PSBA 33 pl 50 ⲡⲁⲙⲉⲣⲟⲥ ⲡⲉⲓⲱϩⲉ...ⲙⲛⲡϣ. ⲉⲧϩⲣⲏⲧϥ. Prob not for ϣⲱⲙ.

ϣⲏⲛⲉ S nn, among various grains: CO 170 ⲟⲩⲣⲧⲟⲅⲁⲃ (l ⲣⲧⲟⲃ) ⲡϣ.

ϣⲓⲛⲉ SAA², -ⲛⲓ BF, ϣⲓ(ⲛⲓ) F, ϣⲉⲛ- SB, ϣⲉⲛⲧ- SF, ϣⲛ- A², ϣⲓⲛⲧⲕ SAA², ϣⲉⲛⲕ BFO, ϣⲉⲛⲧⲕ F vb **I** intr, *seek, ask*: Ps 9 33 S(B ⲕⲱϯ) ζητεῖν, Mt 7 7 S(B do) ζητεῖν, Am 9 12 SA(B ⲕ. ⲡⲥⲁ-) ἐκζ.; Jer 37 6 B ἐρωτᾶν, Lu 23 6 SB ἐπερ.; ib 18 36 SB πυνθάνεσθαι; Jer 3 16 B(S ⲥⲙ ⲡϣ.)ἐπισκέπτεσθαι; Ez 12 24 SB, Mic 3 11 SA(B ⲉⲣ ϣⲉⲡ ϣⲓⲛ), 1 Kg 28 8 S μαντεύεσθαι, Nu 22 7 B(S ϧⲛⲁⲅ ⲡϣ.)μαντεῖον; ShBMOr 8810 386 S ⲉⲓⲡⲟⲩϣ. ⲁⲩⲱ ⲉⲓⲡⲟⲩⲧⲁⲙⲉ ⲣⲱⲙⲉ, RNC 49 S knocking at door ⲁⲩϣ. saying ' Is NN. here' ?, AM 18 B ⲁϥϣ. ϫⲉⲛⲟⲩⲓⲱⲥ ϫⲉ-.

II tr: Deu 13 14 SB, Is 41 28 B(S ϫⲛⲟⲩ), Jo 16 5 B(SA² do), MG 25 220 B ⲁⲩϣⲉⲛ ⲁⲃⲃⲁ ⲙⲁⲕⲁⲣⲓ ⲉⲣ., Is 19 3 SB, ib 30 2 B(S do, F ⲧⲱⲃϩ), Mk 9 11 BF (S do) ἐπερ., 1 Kg 28 6 S ⲉⲡ. διά, Ez 21 21 B ⲉⲡ. ἐν; Jo 4 52 F(B ⲡⲧⲉⲛ-, SA² do), Ac 23 19 B(S do) πυν.; Si 23 10 B(S do) ἐξετάζειν; PS 237 S ⲙⲡⲣϭⲱⲛⲧ ⲉⲣⲟⲓ ⲉⲓϣ. ⲙⲙⲟⲕ, CA 92 S ⲉϥⲉϣ. ⲙⲡⲉⲡⲣⲉⲥⲃⲩⲧⲉⲣⲟⲥ ⲙⲡⲁⲧⲉϥϫⲱⲕ, TU 43 9 A ⲧⲓⲟⲩⲱϣⲉ ⲁϣⲛⲧⲕ, Mani 2 A² ⲁⲙⲙⲁⲑⲏⲧⲏⲥ ϣⲙ ⲡⲁⲡⲟⲥⲧⲟⲗⲟⲥ, ib 1 A² ⲉⲓϣ. ⲛⲟⲩⲁⲛ ⲛⲓⲙ, C 43 54 B draw nigh ⲉⲑⲣⲓϣⲉⲛⲕ = Mor 39 34 S ϫ., GriffStu 162 F ⲉⲓϣⲱⲕ (ⲙ)ⲙⲁⲕ ⲉϩⲣⲁⲓ ⲡⲥⲁϣⲉⲛⲕ, AZ 21 100 O ϥⲁⲃϣⲉⲛⲥ ϫⲉ-, Ryl 339 S ⲧⲓⲉⲣ χρεια ⲡϣⲉⲛ ⲛⲁ ⲉⲣⲟⲓ *to beg mercy for myself* (or ? v ϣⲟⲟⲡⲉ); *greet* (rare, v c ⲉ-): MR 5 27 S ⲉⲓϣ. ⲛⲡⲁⲙⲉⲣⲓⲧ ⲛⲥⲁϩ (or ? ⲛ- dat).

With following preposition.

—— **ⲉ-** SA²BF, *visit*: Ge 21 1 B(S ⲥⲙ ⲡϣ.), Nu 4 29 B(S do), Lu 1 78 B(S do) ἐπισκ. acc, Jer 11 22 SB ⲉ. ἐπί; *inquire for, greet, bid farewell*: Ro 16 3 SB, 1 Cor 16 19 SBF, Wess 18 95 S ϯϣ. ⲉⲟⲩⲟⲛ ⲛⲓⲙ by name ἀσπάζεσθαι; RNC 45 S dying man ϯϣ. ⲉⲣⲱⲧⲛ σώζεσθαι; BMis 147 S beginning of sermon ϯϣ. ⲉⲣⲱⲧⲛ & greet you, Ryl 272 S ϯϣ. ⲉⲡⲉⲕⲟⲩϫⲁⲓ, BM 658 F ⲉⲓϣⲓⲛ (ⲉ)ⲛⲟⲩϫⲁⲓ ⲡⲁⲙⲉⲗⲓⲧ ⲥⲁⲛ, MR 5 54 F ϯϣ. (ⲉ)ⲧⲉⲕⲙⲉⲧⲥⲁⲛ, BP 5567 F ϯϣ. ⲗⲁⲕ, PLond 4 522 S ⲧⲓϣ. (ⲉ)ⲣⲟⲕ ϩⲓⲧⲛⲡⲉⲓⲥϩⲁⲓ, Ep 382 S ϣ. ⲉⲛⲉⲥⲛⲏⲩ ϩⲙⲡⲁⲣⲁⲛ; tr, *ask*: Mt 21 24 B(S ϫⲛⲟⲩ), MG 25 215 B ⲫⲏ ⲉⲧⲟⲩⲁϣⲙⲉⲛϥ ⲉⲣⲟϥ ⲉⲣ.; PS 39 S ⲡϣⲁϫⲉ ⲉⲧⲉⲣⲉϣ. ⲙⲙⲟⲓ ⲉⲣⲟϥ, ib 184 S sim ϣⲛⲧⲕ ⲉⲣⲟⲟⲩ, Sh(?)Mor 54 100 S ⲉⲧⲛⲁϣⲉⲛⲧⲧⲏⲛⲟⲩ ⲉⲩϣⲁϫⲉ, Mani H 49 A²]ⲛⲥⲉϫⲉ ⲉⲧⲁϥϣⲛⲧⲩ ⲁⲣⲁϥ, AM 140 B ⲁⲕϣⲉⲡⲧⲉⲛ ⲉⲛⲉⲛⲣⲁⲛ.

—— **ⲉⲧⲃⲉ-** SA²BF, *concerning*: Eccl 7 11 SF ⲉⲡⲉⲣ. περί; Mt 2 8 SB ⲉⲝⲉⲧ. π.; Ac 23 20 S(B ⲉⲙⲓ)πυν. π.; BG 106 S ⲧⲉⲧⲛϣ. ⲉⲡⲓⲛⲟϭ ⲛⲁⲓⲱⲛ, ShZ 596 S ⲁⲧⲉⲧⲛϣ. ⲉⲧⲃⲏⲏⲧⲩ, Mani H 82 A² ϣⲓⲛⲧⲩ ⲉ.ϩⲱⲃ ⲛⲓⲙ, C 89 103 B ϣ. (ⲙ)ⲙⲟⲟⲩ ⲉ.ⲡⲟⲩⲓⲱⲧ = ib 99 251 S ϫ.

—— **ⲙⲛ-** F, *in common with*: Ac 9 29 (B acc, S ϯ ⲧⲱⲛ ⲙⲛ-) συνζητεῖν πρός.

—— **ⲛ-** dat SB: Nu 27 21 B(S ϫ. ⲉ-) ⲉⲡⲉⲣ. acc; Jud 20 27 S ⲉ. ⲉⲛ (cf 18 5 ϩⲛ-); BSM 125 B till Lord ϣ. ⲛⲏⲓ ⲡⲧⲁⲣⲱⲗ ϣⲁⲣⲟϥ = Mor 22 134 S ϣ. ⲛⲥⲱⲓ.

—— **ⲛⲥⲁ-** SAA²B(rare)F, *inquire for, seek after*: Ge 43 8, Job 6 5, Ps 36 36 SA(Cl), Is 31 1 SF, Mk 16 6(F = B), Jo 4 23 SA², He 8 7 SF(all B ⲕⲱϯ) ζ., Job 10 6 ἀναζ., Ex 18 15, Ps 77 7 (all B do), Ro 3 11 SB ἐκζ., Mt 6 32 SB, Lu 4 42 (B ⲕ.) ἐπιζ.; Ge 32 29 SB, Ps 121 6 SB ⲉⲣ.; Sa 6 4 ἐξετ.; Mt 2 7 (B ϫⲟⲧϫⲉⲧ) ἀκριβοῦν; Ps 118 69 (B do) ἐξερευνᾶν: PS 45 ⲉⲥϣ. ⲛ. ⲡⲟⲩⲟⲉⲓⲛ, ShC 73 56 ⲡⲧⲉⲟⲩⲁ ϣ. ⲛ. ⲟⲩⲕⲟⲅⲓ ⲛⲏⲣⲡ, BMis 41 ϣ. ⲛⲧⲟⲟⲧϥ ⲛ. ⲡⲉϥⲥⲟⲛ *ask him about his brother*, JA '88 2 370 bishops to ϣ. ⲛ.ⲡⲉⲕⲗⲏⲣⲓⲕⲟⲥ *once a month*, J 68 45 *lest God* ϣ. ⲛⲥⲱⲓ ⲉϫⲁⲡⲓⲛⲁ, AM 140 B ⲉⲕϣ. ⲛ. ⲡⲉⲡⲣⲁⲛ, C 89 202 B *letter begins* ⲉϥϣ. ⲛ. ⲡⲉϥⲙⲉⲣⲓⲧ ⲛⲥⲟⲛ *greeteth*, Miss 4 146 B sim, AZ 23 37 F ⲡⲉϥ ⲛⲓⲃⲓ ϣⲁϣⲓⲛ(ⲡⲓ ⲉ)ⲥⲟⲥ *require it* (cf Kr 116 sim ⲕⲱϯ ⲛⲥⲁ-); vbal: Ex 2 15 SA, Ps 36 32, Mk 12 12(all B ⲕ.) ζ.; Z 282 ⲉⲩϣ. ⲛ. ⲱⲙⲕ ⲙⲙⲟⲛ, AP 21 A² ϣ. ⲛ. ⲡ. ϩⲁⲧⲃⲉϥ; c ⲁⲧ-: PBu 48 ⲕⲛⲁⲕⲱ...ⲧⲁⲡⲣⲟⲥⲫⲟⲣⲁ ϩⲓϫⲱⲕ ⲛⲁⲧϣ. ⲛⲥⲱⲥ.

—— **ⲛⲧⲛ-** SB, *of, from*: Nu 23 3 B(S ϫ.) ⲉⲡⲉⲣ. acc; Mt 2 4 B(S ⲉⲃⲟⲗ ϩⲓⲧⲛ-) πυν. παρά; BIF 13 112 S ϣ. ⲛⲧⲟⲟⲧⲩ ϫⲉ- = MG 25 304 B ϣ. ⲙⲙⲟϥ, Bor 263 19 S ⲉⲩϣ. ⲛⲧⲟⲟⲧⲩ ⲉⲧⲃⲉⲡⲉⲩⲟⲉⲓϣ, Aeg 2 B ⲥⲉⲛⲁϣ. ⲛⲥⲁⲟⲩⲥⲁϫⲓ...ⲛⲧⲉⲛⲑⲛⲏⲟⲩ.

—— **ϩⲁ-** S, *seek for*: Lant 92 22 ⲟⲩⲟⲛ ⲛⲓⲙ ⲉⲧϣ. ϩⲁⲡⲉⲓⲕⲁⲡⲱⲛ.

—— **ϩⲛ-, ϫⲉⲛ-** SB, *in, among*: BM 178 S ⲁⲩϣ. ϩⲙⲡⲓⲛⲁ ⲁⲩϭⲉ, Ryl 316 S ⲕⲛⲁϣ. ϩⲙⲡⲁϩⲱⲃ *into my affair*, EW 74 B ⲁⲩϣⲓⲛⲓ (sic MS) ϫⲉⲛϯⲡⲟⲗⲓⲥ ⲁⲩ-ϫⲓⲙⲓ; ⲛϧⲣⲏⲓ ϫ.: Jer 18 13 B ⲉⲣ. ἐν.

—— **ϩⲓⲧⲛ-** S, *through*: Miss 4 707 ⲁⲓϣ. ϩⲓⲧⲟⲟⲧⲟⲩ ⲛϩⲁϩ ⲛⲥⲟⲡ, PBu 31 ϣ. ϩ. ⲡⲣⲱⲙⲉ ⲉⲧϥ ϣϭⲟⲣ ⲛⲁϥ; ⲉⲃⲟⲗ ϩ. SB: 1 Kg 28 7 S (var ⲛⲧⲛ-) ζ. ἐν; Mt 2 4 v c ⲛⲧⲛ-; BMar 189 S ⲧⲁϣ. ⲉ. ϩⲓⲧⲟⲟⲧⲟⲩ ϫⲉ-, DeV 2 88 B ⲁϥϣ. ⲉ. ϩⲓⲧⲟⲧϥ.

ϣⲉⲛϩⲟ, ϣⲉⲛϩⲓⲛⲓ B v ϩⲟ, ϩⲓⲛ.

—— **nn** m SAA²BF, ϣⲓⲛ-SA², ϣⲉⲛ-BF, *inquiry*: 1 Tim 6 4 S(B = Gk), Tit 3 9 S(B ⲕⲱϯ) ζήτησις, 1 Tim 1 4 S(B ϫⲓⲛⲕ.) ἐκζ., R 1 1 58 S ⲟⲩⲛⲟϭ ⲡϣ. ϩⲙⲡⲥⲩⲛϩⲉⲇⲣⲓⲟⲛ ἐπιζ.; Ge 43 6 SB ἐρωτᾶν; Is 16 6 B(S ⲧⲟⲛⲧⲛ), Ez 13 7 SB, Mic 3 6 SA(B ϣⲉⲛϩⲓⲛ) μαντεία; CO 29 S *will not go* ⲁϫⲛϣ. *without asking (leave)*; *news, report*: Pro 12 25 AB(S ⲟⲩⲱ), Nah 3 19 AB ἀγγελία, Is 7 2 B ⲉⲗ ⲡϣ. (S ϫⲓ ⲛⲟⲩϣ) ἀναγγέλλειν; C 89 23 B ⲁⲩⲥⲱⲧⲉⲙ ⲉⲡϣ., Va 61 18 B ⲁⲡⲉϥϣ. ⲥⲱⲣ ⲉⲃⲟⲗ φήμη, Ac 21 31 B(S ⲟⲩⲱ)φάσις; Is 18 2 B(S do) ὅμηρος; Ob 1 B(A ⲟⲩⲟⲩ)ἀκοή; Phil 2 19 B(S do) τὰ περί; MG 25 233 B ⲡϣ. ⲛⲧⲉ ⲡⲓⲥⲛⲏⲟⲩ ϩⲁⲡⲟⲩⲛⲉ = Z 318 S ⲛⲉⲥⲛⲏⲩ ⲣ ⲟⲩ πῶς οἱ ἀδελφοί?, CDan 92 B sim; BMis 40 S ⲟⲩⲡⲉ ⲡϣ. of youth entrusted to thee?, ViK 9530 S ⲙⲡⲉⲥⲥⲱⲧⲙ

ⲉⲗⲁⲁⲩ ⲡϣ. ⲛⲧⲁϥ, *ib* 9549 28 *S* ϭⲓ ⲙⲡⲁϣ. ⲉⲣⲟⲅⲛ ⲙ- ⲡⲛⲟϭ ⲡⲣⲱⲙⲉ, CO 126 *S* ⲉϩⲣⲁⲓ ⲡⲉⲕϣ. ⲛⲁⲡ, BM 617 *F* ⲥⲉⲧ ⲡⲉⲕϣ. ⲛⲏⲓ, C 41 79 *B* awaiting ⲡϣ. ⲙⲡⲟⲩⲣⲟ, AM 14 *B* ⲁⲡⲓϣ. ⲥⲱⲣ ⲉⲃⲟⲗ ϩⲉⲛⲧⲡⲟⲗⲓⲥ, Kr 1 25 *S* ⲡϣ. ⲙⲡⲙⲟⲩ (*sc* river's rise), Hall 22 *S* found no man ⲛⲧⲁⲭⲁⲩ ⲡⲁϣ. ⲛⲏⲧⲛ, Va 61 98 *B* ⲁⲅⲉⲛ ⲡⲛϣ.... ⲛⲏⲓ, C 89 42 *B* ⲁϥⲁⲡⲣⲟ ⲱⲗⲓ ⲙⲡⲛϣ. ⲉϩⲟⲅⲛ = *ib* 99 137 *S* ϭⲓ ⲡⲟⲩⲱ ⲉⲣ., Ryl 290 *S* ϯ ⲡⲁϣ. ⲙⲡⲁ𝕏ⲥ̄, Gu 96 *S* sim.

ϣⲙⲛⲟⲩϥⲉ *SA²*, ϣⲉⲡⲛⲟⲩϥⲓ *BF*, *good news* (*cf* C 41 66 *B* ⲟⲩϣⲓⲛⲓ ⲛⲟⲩϥⲓ): Ro 1 1 *F*(Mor 43 2, *B* ϩⲓ ϣ., *S* = Gk)ⲉⲩⲁⲅⲅⲉⲗⲓⲟⲛ, AP 18 *A²* ⲉⲩⲁⲅⲅⲉⲗⲓⲍⲉⲓⲛ; Phil 4 8 *B*(*S* ⲥⲙⲟⲩ) εὔφημα; R 2 1 12 *S* when she heard ⲡⲉⲓϣ., BMis 63 *S* archangel went to her ⲙⲡⲛϣ., *ib* 25 *S* to give thee ⲡϣ. ⲙⲡⲉⲕϣⲏⲣⲉ ϫⲉ ⲟⲟⲩϥ, BAp 75 *S* day of his (saint's) ϣ. *commemoration* (?), PO 11 338 *B* ⲟⲩϣⲙϣϯ ⲡϣ. ⲛⲧⲁϥ ϩⲁⲧⲉⲛⲟⲩⲟⲛ ⲛⲓⲃⲉⲛ *good report*, Mani 1 *A²* ⲣⲉϥϯ ϣ.; ϥⲁⲓϣ. *v* below; ϩⲓ ϣ. *B, tell good news*: Is 40 9 (*S* = Gk), Ac 8 4 (*S* ⲧⲁϣⲉ ⲟⲉⲓϣ), 1 Cor 15 2 (*SF* = Gk) ⲉⲩⲁⲅⲅⲉⲗⲓⲍⲉⲓⲛ; BSM 18 ⲉϥϩⲓ ϣ. ⲛⲱⲟⲩ ϫⲉ- = BMis 355 *S* ϯ ⲙⲡϣ.

ⲙⲁ ⲡϣ. *S, place of inquiry, oracle*: Mor 37 76 ⲙⲙ. ⲡϩⲉⲣⲉⲑⲟⲥ μαντεῖον; ShWess 9 139 ⲙⲙ. ⲡⲓ- ⲍⲁⲓⲙⲱⲛ, ShViK 9040 181 ⲉⲅⲡⲉⲣⲉ ⲣⲁⲥⲟⲩ ⲛⲑⲉ ⲛ- ⲡⲉⲧϣⲓⲛⲉ ⲙⲙ., ShA 1 ⲙⲙ. ⲏ ⲛⲉⲥⲧⲁⲥⲧⲣⲓⲙⲅⲟⲟⲥ.

ⲣⲉϥϣ. *SABF, inquirer, wizard*: Jos 13 22 *S*, Mic 3 7 *SA*(*B* ⲣⲉϥϣⲓⲛⲓ ⲛϥ̅ⲏⲣⲓⲛ) μάντις, *cf* KKS 28; Aeg 252 *S* ٵﻷ; PS 30 *S* ⲡⲣⲉϥϣⲁ ⲟⲩⲓⲟⲩ ⲙⲡⲓⲣ. cannot foretell events, CA 88 *S* ⲣⲉϥϣⲁ ⲟⲩⲓⲟⲩ, ⲣⲉϥⲙⲟⲩⲧⲉ, ⲣ., Miss 4 171 *B* sim; *as adj*: Ac 16 16 *SB* πύθων; 1 Kg 28 21 *S* Gk om, Z 585 *S* ⲙⲡⲏⲅⲑⲁⲅⲟⲣⲓⲟⲥ ⲉⲅⲟ ⲛⲟⲩⲏⲛⲃ ⲡⲣ., LAp 524 *F* ⲡⲛ̄ⲁ̄ ⲡⲗⲉϥϣ.; ⲙⲛⲧⲣ. *S, wizardry*: LCyp 3 μαντική; R 1 4 56 ⲧⲙⲁⲛⲧⲓⲕⲏ ⲉⲧⲉⲧⲙ.; ⲉⲣ ⲣ. *B*: Lev 20 27 (*S* ⲣⲉϥⲙⲟⲩⲧⲉ) ἐγ- γαστρίμυθος γίνεσθαι.

ϫⲓ, ϭⲓ ⲙⲡϣ. *AA²B, get, bring news, visit*: Ex 14 5 (*S* = Gk) ἀγγέλλειν; Pro 25 13 *A*(*S* ϫⲓ ⲟⲩⲱ) Gk diff, Su 55 φάσιν λαμβάνειν; Ac 17 15 (*S* = Gk) ἐν- τολὴν λαμ.; C 89 51 ϭⲓ ⲙⲡⲟⲩϣ. = *ib* 99 228 *S* ϭⲓⲛⲉ ⲙⲡⲉϥϣ. ἐπισκέπτεσθαι, Job 7 18 (*S* ϭⲙ ⲡϣ.) ἐπι- σκοπὴν ποιεῖν; AM 288 ϭⲓ ⲙⲡϣ. ⲡⲏⲛ ⲉⲧϣⲱⲡⲓ, *ib* 193 ⲁⲅϭⲓ ⲙⲡϣ. ϣⲁⲇⲓⲟⲕⲗⲏⲧⲓⲁⲛⲟⲥ, Mani 1 *A²* ϥϫⲓ ϣ. ϥⲡ ϣ.

ϭⲓⲛⲉ ⲙⲡϣ., ϭⲙ ⲡϣ. *SAF*, ϫⲓⲙⲓ ⲙⲡϣ., ϫⲉⲙ ⲡϣ. *B, visit*: Ex 18 21 *B*(*S* ⲥⲱⲧⲡ) σκέπτειν, Deu 11 12 *SB*, Jer 9 9 *SB*, Lam 4 22 *BF*, Hos 4 14 *AB*, Ac 7 23 *SBF*, BHom 15 *S* ϭ. ⲛⲡⲉⲧϣⲱⲡⲉ ⲉⲡⲓⲥ., Eccl 1 13 *F* (*S* ϯ ⲟⲩⲟⲓ) ⲕⲁⲧⲁⲥ., Sa 2 20 *S*(*B* diff) ἐπισκοπὴ εἶναι, Pro 29 13 *SA* ⲉⲡ. ποιεῖν; Sa 1 9 *SB* ἐξέτασις εἶναι; Va 61 14 *B* went to ϫ. ⲙⲡⲉϥⲙⲁ ⲡⲉⲡⲕⲟⲧ καταμανθά- νειν; 2 Kg 13 6 *S* ὁρᾶν; PS 64 *S* ϣⲁⲕϭ. ⲡⲡⲉⲧⲣⲏⲭ, BAp 79 *S* ϭ. ⲙⲡⲉⲓⲥⲟⲡ = MIE 2 352 *B*, BMis 55 *S* ⲁⲓⲱⲁⲕⲓⲙ ϭ. ⲛⲁⲡⲡⲁ ⲁⲥⲱ, El 46 *A* God ⲁϥⲉⲓ ⲁϭⲙ

ⲡⲁϣ. *cause me die*, C 99 102 *S* ϣⲁⲛⲧⲉⲡ𝕏ⲥ̄ ϭⲙ ⲡⲉϥ- ϣ. *ie* till he died;   as nn m, *visitation*: Nu 1 21 *S*(*B* = Gk), Job 10 12 *SB* ἐπισκοπή, Nu 4 37 *SB* ἐπί- σκεψις; Sa 4 6 *S* ἐξετασμός; *ib* 3 18 *S* διάγνωσις; BMis 67 *S* time of my ϭ. = Mor 33 136 *S* ⲃⲱⲗ ⲉⲃⲟⲗ, C 89 159 *B* we die ϩⲉⲛⲡⲁϣϫ., AZ 21 141 *S* ⲁⲡϭ. ⲙⲡⲡⲉ̄ ⲧⲁⲣⲟⲓ;   ⲁⲧϭ. *B, unvisited, unrelieved*: BSM 90 poor sick man ⲡⲁⲧϭⲙ ⲡⲉϥϣ. = BMis 181 *S* ⲉⲙⲛ ⲡⲉⲧϭⲓⲛⲉ ⲙⲡⲉϥϣ., EW 97 ⲛⲓⲕⲟⲗⲁⲥⲓⲥ ⲛⲁ. ⲡⲟⲩϣ.

ⲁϫⲛ- *S* = ⲁⲧϣⲛ, *unasked* (Sdff in Sethe *Verbum* 1 63, Spg 13).

ϥⲁⲓϣ. *SABF, news-bearer, messenger*: Ge 32 3 *S*(*B* ⲣⲉⲙⲛϩⲱⲃ), Pro 13 17 *SA*(*B* do), Is 30 4 *SF*(*B* = Gk), Ez 23 16 *S*(*B* ⲡⲣⲉⲥⲃⲉⲅⲥ) ἄγγελος; Hos 5 13 *SA*(*B* = Gk) πρέσβυς, Lu 14 32 *S*(*B* do) πρεσβεία; 4 Kg 11 18 *S* gloss on ⲉⲡⲓⲥⲕⲟⲡⲟⲥ; BAp 132 *S* ⲛϥ. of John (*cf* Mt 11 2), AM 24 *B* ⲡⲓϣ. ⲉⲧⲉϥⲟⲅⲱⲣⲡ ⲙⲙⲟⲟⲩ; ⲟ ⲛϥ.: 2 Cor 5 20 *S*(*B* as Gk) πρεσβεύ- εσθαι; BMis 300 *S* Gabriel ⲡϥⲁⲓϣⲙⲛⲟⲩϥⲉ.

ϭⲓⲛ-, ϫⲓⲛϣ. *SB, inquiry*: Dan 4 14 *B* ἐπερώτημα; PS 34 *S* ⲧⲉϣⲓⲛⲉ ⲕⲁⲗⲱⲥ ⲉⲛⲧϭ., ShRyl 68 268 *S* ⲟⲩϭ. (Ge 3 9), Cat 174 *B* ⲛⲓϫ. ⲡⲉⲙⲡⲓⲉⲍⲉⲧⲁⲥⲓⲥ.

ϣⲉⲛ *B* ⲡⲛ̄?, *v* ⲙⲁⲛⲕ (BSM 40 = *ib* 147 دعني أسأل).

ϣⲟⲟⲛⲉ *S* vb intr, *be merciful*(?): Mor 41 81 to Herod ⲙⲡⲉⲕϣ. ϥⲁⲛⲓⲁⲧⲛⲟⲃⲉ?; *as adj*: Mor 31 189 (on Ge 44 18) when Joseph heard Judah's ϣⲁϫⲉ ⲛϣ. ἐλεεινὰ ῥήματα. *V* ϩⲛⲧ (ϣⲛϩⲏⲧ).

ϣⲱⲛⲉ *SAA²*, -ⲛⲓ *BF*, ϣⲟⲟⲛⲉ† *S*(? He 5) vb intr, *be sick, weak*: Job 4 4 *SB*, Ps 17 37 *B*(*S* ϭⲃⲃⲉ), Is 32 4 *B*(*SF* ϭⲱⲃ), Jo 4 46 *SA²BF*, 2 Cor 13 3 *B*(*SF* ⲟ ⲛⲁⲧϭⲟⲙ), Cl 59 4 *A* ἀσθενεῖν; Sa 17 8 *S*, Cai Euch 515 *B* ⲡⲏ ⲉⲧϣ. νοσεῖν; Mt 14 14 *SBF*, Mk 6 5 *S*(*B* ⲣⲉϥϣ.), ἄρρωστος; Is 39 1 *B*(*S* ⲗⲟϫⲗⲉϫ) μαλακί- ζειν; 1 Cor 12 26 *S*(*B* ϭⲓ ⲙⲕⲁϩ), BHom 12 *S* ⲉⲣ- ϣⲙⲁⲡⲟⲩⲙⲉⲗⲟⲥ ϣ. πάσχειν; Si 11 14 *S*, He 6 12 *B* (*S* ⲟⲩϣⲟⲩϭ) νωθρός (*cf* c ϩⲛ-); Ez 34 4 *SB* κακῶς ἔχειν; ShC 73 137 *S* ⲡⲣⲟⲥⲉⲭⲉ ⲉⲡⲉⲧϣ., *ib* 172 *S* ⲉϣ., ⲉⲅⲙⲟⲧⲛ, ShBM 209 35 *S* ⲡⲉⲧϣ. ⲡⲁⲗⲉ ϩⲁ- ⲧⲏⲛ, C 99 196 *S* ⲉϥϣ. ⲕⲁⲧⲁ ϣⲟⲙⲛⲧ ⲡⲣⲟⲟⲩ, BM 1136 *S* ⲉⲣⲉⲛⲁⲃⲁⲗ ϣ., C 43 214 *B* ⲁϥⲉⲣ ⲙⲁⲕⲓⲁ (*l* ⲙⲁⲓ.) ⲉⲣⲟⲕ ϣⲁⲧⲉⲕϣ., DeV 2 38 *B* ⲉⲥϣ. ⲛϫⲉ ⲧⲟⲩ- ⲣⲓⲛⲱⲙⲛ, Ep 144 *S* pray for my house ⲙⲙⲟⲛ ⲡϣⲏⲣⲉ ϣ., *ib* 359 sim.

With following preposition.   c ⲉ-, *at, in*: Ac 28 8 *S*(*B* c ϩⲉⲛ-) συνέχεσθαι dat; RNC 26 *S* ⲁⲡⲡⲣⲟ ϣ. ⲉⲡⲉϥⲟⲅⲉⲣⲓⲧⲉ ἀλγεῖν acc; C 89 17 *B* ⲁϥϣ. ⲉⲡⲉϥ- ⲥⲡⲗⲏⲛ πάσχειν acc; BMar 208 *S* ⲉⲓϣ. ⲉⲡⲁϩⲏⲡⲁⲣ = Rec 6 172 *B*; *dat commodi*: 1 Cor 8 7 *B*(*S* ϭⲱⲃ) ἀσθενὴς εἶναι; Miss 8 257 *S* ⲙⲡⲟⲩϣ. (*sc* eyes) ⲉ- ⲣⲟϥ;   c ⲛ-, *as to*: ViK 9540 *S* ⲛⲉⲥϣ. ⲁⲡ ⲡⲥⲱⲙⲁ,

Mani H 15 *A²* ⲛⲧⲡϣ. ⲛϩⲏⲧ;   ⲥ ⲛⲧⲉⲛ-, *through*: Ps 108 24 *B*(*S* ⲥⲃⲃⲉ) ἀσθ. ἀπό;   ⲥ ϩⲛ-, ϩⲉⲛ-, *in, as to*: Lam 5 13 *B*(*S* ⲣ ⲥⲱⲃ), Ro 8 3 *B*(*S* ⲥⲃ.) ἀσθ. ἐν; He 5 11 *S⁺*(no var)*B* ⲛⲱⲑ. γί. dat; Z 327 *S* ⲉϥϣ. ϩⲙⲡⲉϥⲥⲱⲙⲁ νοσώδης dat; HL 76 *B* ⲉⲥϣ. ϩⲉⲛⲟⲩⲗⲓϩⲓ, C 43 222 *B* ⲉⲧϣ. ϩⲉⲛϫⲓⲛϣ. ⲛⲓⲃⲉⲛ.

—— nn m *SAA²BF*, ϣⲡ- *SA*, ϣⲉⲡ- *SA²BF*, ϣⲁⲡ- *SAB*, *sickness, disease*: Ps 15 4 *SB*, Jo 5 5 *SA²B*, He 7 28 *B*(*S* ⲙⲛⲧⲁⲧϭⲟⲙ) ἀσθένεια; Deu 29 22 *SB*, Mt 9 35 *SB* νόσος; Ge 42 4 *B*(*S* ⲗⲟⲝⲗⲉⲝ) μαλακία; Pro 25 20 *SA* πάθος; Ge 48 1 *S*(*B* diff), Eccl 5 12 *SF* ἀρρωστία, 2 Kg 12 15 *S* ⲣⲱϧⲧ ⲉⲛϣ. -τεῖν; Mk 6 55 *S* ⲙⲟⲕϩ ϩⲛϣ. (*B* diff) κακῶς ἔχ.; Deu 28 22 *S* ϩⲙⲟⲙ ⲛϣ. (*B* om ϣ.) πυρετός; ShVi K 921 *S* ⲗⲟⲝⲗⲉⲝ, ⲡⲗⲏⲅⲏ, ⲕⲉⲗⲁⲁⲅ ⲛϣ., ShA 1 136 *S* ⲕⲣⲟⲥⲉ ϩⲁⲛϣ., Mor 18 90 *S* ⲉϥⲙⲟⲕϩ ⲛϣ., PSBA 10 197 *S* ⲉⲥϩⲣⲟⲕ ⲉⲃⲟⲗ ϩⲁⲛϣ., AM 49 *B* ⲉⲣ ⲫⲁϩⲣⲓ ⲉⲛϣ., ST 186 *S* ⲉⲓⲛⲁⲣⲙ ⲉⲛϣ., Mani 1 *A²* ⲧⲉⲣⲁϩⲧ ⲁⲛϣ., GPar 2 19 *B* ⲟⲩϣ. ⲥⲁϧⲟⲩⲛ ⲙⲙⲟⲩ, Ep 144 *S* ⲧⲁⲡⲁⲥⲕⲏ ⲙⲛϣ. ⲉⲧϩⲓϫⲱⲓ, *ib* 168 sim ⲉⲧⲛⲙⲙⲁϥ, *ib* App 1 138 *S* ⲛⲧⲏϭ ⲉⲧⲁⲙⲉⲣ ⲛϣ., BM 1223 *A* ⲟⲩϣ. ⲉϥϩⲣⲁⲥⲉ, Stegemann 64 *F* ⲟⲩϣ. ⲉⲧⲣⲁⲟⲩ;   ⲥ ⲛ ϩⲉⲛ: Lev 26 16 *S* ϣ. ⲡⲓⲕⲧⲉⲣⲟⲥ (*B* ⲡⲓⲥⲉⲣⲑⲉⲣ) ἴκτερος, Hag 2 17 *SA* do (*B* ⲭⲓⲙⲫⲉϩ) ἀνεμοφθορία; Sh Wess 9 171 *S* ϣ. ⲙⲯⲱⲣⲁ, Mor 51 18 *S* ϣ. ⲛⲭⲁⲗⲕⲓⲟⲙⲁ (καρκίνωμα, cf BMar 63, P 44 79 vo), En Peterson 67 *S* ϣ. ⲛϣⲧⲟⲣⲧⲣ (cf above), AZ 21 152 *S* ϣ. ⲛϭⲁⲗⲉ, C 99 141 *S* ϣ. ⲛⲝⲁⲓⲙⲱⲛ, ShBM 209 34 *S* ⲛϣ. ⲙⲡⲙⲟⲩ, Miss 4 178 *B* ⲛⲉϥϣ. ⲙⲙⲟⲩ;   as adj: Lu 13 11 *SB* ἀσθένεια; Jer 14 15 *S*(*B* ⲣⲉϥϣ.) νοσερός; Gu 74 *S* ⲡⲁⲑⲟⲥ ⲛϣ. *V* also ⲉⲓⲁⲃⲉ.

Compounds: Z 630 *S* ⲡϣⲛⲉⲓⲕⲧⲉⲣⲟⲥ (ἴκτερος KKS 232, cf Lev 26 above), *ib* 629 *S* ϣⲓⲛⲓⲕ., Ac 28 8 *B* ϣⲉⲛ- (var ϣⲁⲛ-) ⲙⲁⲥⲧ (*S* ϣ. ϩⲏⲧϥ) δυσεντερία; AP 35 *A²* ϩⲉⲛϣⲉⲛ[ϩ]ⲏⲧ *sickness*, C 43 86 *B* ϣⲉⲛ-ⲝⲉⲙⲱⲛ *possession*, PMéd 316 *S* ϣⲉⲡⲉϣⲁⲩ v ⲉⲙⲱ, Kropp K 24 *S* ϣⲛⲓϣⲧ *meaning*? (cf above p vi, 89 a).

ⲁⲧϣ. *B, without sickness*: DeV 2 233 ⲁⲅⲙⲟⲩ ⲛⲁⲙⲁ ⲛⲛⲉⲧϣ. *SB, place of the sick, infirmary*: ShC 73 145, *ib* 44 *S* ⲛⲡⲣⲱⲙⲉ ⲉⲧϣ., Saq 2 *B* ⲡⲓⲱⲧ (ⲛ)ⲡⲙ. ⲣ ϣ. *S, be sick*: CO 252 ⲁⲕⲣ ⲟⲩⲕⲟⲩⲓ ⲛϣⲱ[ⲡⲉ. ⲣⲉϥϣ. *SB*(mostly), *sick man*: 1 Cor 9 22 (*S* ϭⲱⲃ) ἀσθενής; Mk 6 5 (*S* ϣ. vb) ἄρρωστος; adj: Jer 14 15 v nn (adj), R 1 3 11 *S* ⲣⲱⲙⲉ ⲛⲣ. ϭⲓⲛ-, ϫⲓⲛϣ. *SB, state of sickness*: ShR 2 3 11 *S* Lord made him worthy of ⲟⲩϭ., PMéd 84 *S* ⲉⲧϣⲱⲡⲉ ϩⲛϭ. ⲛⲓⲙ, MIE 2 389 *B* sim = BAp 113 *S* ϣ. ⲛⲓⲙ, AM 201 *B* ϩⲁⲛⲙⲛϣ ⲛⲝ.

ϣⲱⲛⲉ *S*, ϣⲱⲡⲁ *F*, ϣⲉ(ⲉ)ⲡⲉ- *SS'*, ϣⲁⲡⲉ- *F*, ϣⲟ(ⲟ)ⲡⲝ, ϣⲟⲟⲡⲉ⁺ *S* vb tr, *exclude, deprive*(?): Lam 1 6 *F* ⲁⲩϣⲁⲡⲉ ⲧⲙⲉⲛⲧ[ⲥⲉⲓ (*B* diff) ἐξαίρειν; JTS 10 392 Noah & Ham ⲙⲡⲉϥⲧⲱⲃⲉ ⲛⲁϥ ⲉϣⲟⲟⲛⲉϥ

but made him equal in inheritance; BMis 302 ⲁⲕϣ. ⲙⲡⲉⲕⲉⲟⲟⲩ & shalt die in exile, Mor 25 7 ⲛⲧⲁϥϣⲟⲟⲡⲉϥ (cf Mt 25 25) ⲁⲛ ⲣⲱ *did not even spend it* (var P 131³ 81 ⲙⲡⲉϥϭⲟⲣⲙⲉϥ) = Va 61 90 *B* ⲙⲡⲉϥⲭⲟⲗϥ ⲉⲃⲟⲗ.   qual, *deprived*: Bor 240 89 ⲉⲛϣ. ⲏ ⲉⲛⲡⲟⲣϫ ⲉⲃⲟⲗ ⲛⲧⲕⲟⲓⲛⲱⲛⲓⲁ, Ryl 62 5 ⲉⲕϣ. ⲉⲧⲉⲭⲁⲣⲓⲥ.

With following preposition. ⲥ ⲉ-, *from, of*: ShA 1 226 child ϣⲁϥϣⲟϥ ⲉⲧⲉⲕⲗⲏⲣⲟⲛⲟⲙⲓⲁ, ShP 130¹ 137 ⲁⲩϣⲉⲛⲉⲧⲏⲩⲧⲛ ⲉⲛⲉⲧⲛⲟⲩⲥⲉ, P 131¹ 4 ⲁⲩϣⲟⲟⲡⲉⲥ ⲉⲡⲣⲁϣⲉ ⲙⲙⲡⲁⲧϣⲉⲗⲉⲉⲧ, BMar 191 ⲁⲩϣⲟⲛⲧ ⲉⲡⲉⲕ-ϩⲟ, BHom 86 ⲁϥϣⲟⲟⲛⲉϥ ⲙⲁⲅⲁϥ ⲉⲧⲉⲕⲕⲗⲏⲣⲟⲛⲟⲙⲓⲁ, Aeg 23 sickness ⲛⲁϣⲉⲛⲉ ⲛⲉⲡⲉⲓⲱⲧ ⲉⲣⲟⲛ; *dat com*: Miss 4 729 ⲉⲣⲓⲛⲁϣⲉⲛⲉ ⲡⲟⲩϫⲟⲓ ⲉⲣⲟ ⲛⲁϣ ⲛⲣⲉ *how wilt thou be in want of, how canst do without*?;   ⲥ ⲉⲃⲟⲗ ϩⲛ- sim: P 129¹⁷ 4 ⲛⲧⲉⲧⲛϣⲉⲛⲉ ⲡⲁⲣⲁⲛ ⲉⲃ. ϩⲛⲡⲣⲱⲙⲉ, Louvre 10060 ⲛϥϣⲟⲟⲛⲟⲩ ⲉⲃ. ϩⲛⲧⲉϥⲉⲕ-ⲕⲗⲏⲥⲓⲁ;   ⲥ ⲛⲥⲁ-: Lam 1 15 *F* ϣ. ⲛⲥⲁⲛⲁⲭⲱⲣⲁ (*B* ϥⲱⲧ ⲉⲃⲟⲗ) ἐξαί.; ViK 9444 *S'* (var of Miss 4 above) ⲉⲣⲓⲛⲁϣⲉⲛⲉ ⲡⲟⲩϫⲁⲓ ⲛⲥⲁⲟⲩⲛ?

Cf ϣⲱⲡⲉ.

ϣⲛⲁ *SA*, ϣⲛⲁⲁ *S*(once)nn m, *profligate, prodigal*: Pro 7 11 *S*(var -ⲁⲁ)*A*(*B* ⲁⲧⲟⲩϫⲁⲓ)ἄσωτος; Mus 40 276 ⲛⲉϣ. ⲉⲧⲉⲣⲟϥⲣⲉϥ ⲛⲉⲛⲧⲁⲣⲛⲟⲥ (ⲛⲛⲓⲕⲁⲣ.) = BAp 168, Aeg 252 ⲟⲩⲛⲟⲣⲛⲓⲛ ⲏ ⲟⲩⲣⲱⲙⲉ ⲛϣ. = PO 8 598 ﺟﻼﺣ ﺑﺎ;   ⲙⲛⲧϣ., *profligacy, intemperance*: Pro 28 7 *SA*, Eph 5 18 (*B* ⲙⲉⲧⲁⲧⲟⲩϫⲁⲓ) ἀσωτία, Lu 15 13 ϩⲛⲟⲩⲙ. (*B* do) ἀσώτως; Sa 2 9 ἀγερωχία; Jth 1 16 ϯ ⲙⲙⲟϥ ⲛⲧⲙ. ῥᾳθυμεῖν; BMar 168 thirst bringeth ⲧⲙ. πολυποσία; Tri 262 ⲡϣⲏⲣⲉ ⲙⲙ. ﺑﺪﯼ; ShR 2 3 71 wealth ⲁⲕⲭⲟⲥ ⲉⲃⲟⲗ ϩⲛⲟⲩⲙ., Mor 22 101 ⲛⲥⲉϯϩⲉ ⲛⲧⲉⲟⲩⲙ. ϣⲱⲡⲉ = BSM 95 *B* ⲙⲉⲧⲁⲧϣⲁⲩ, Miss 8 172 ϫⲓⲟⲩⲉ, ⲡⲟⲣⲛⲓⲁ, ϩⲱⲃ ⲙⲙ.

ϣⲛⲁ *SA* nn m, *waste land* (? same as last): Is 5 6 (*B* ⲕⲁⲛϣϥ) χέρσος, cit (prob) P 44 22 ⲛⲉϣ. ﻻﺻ (v ⲕⲁⲛϣⲁ), Is 7 25 (*B* = Gk) χ.; Tri 423 ⲟⲩⲁⲣⲟⲟⲩⲉ ⲙⲛⲟⲩϣⲛⲟ '—;   ⲣ ϣ., *be waste, dry*: Pro 24 46 *SA*, Jer 2 31 (*B* ⲭⲱ ⲉⲛϣⲟ) χερσοῦⲑ.ⲓ, ClPr 54 43 caused lake to ϣⲟⲟⲩⲉ ⲁⲥⲣ ϣ. ἀποχ.; P 44 91 ⲛⲉⲩⲗⲟⲥ (ἕλος) ⲉⲧⲟ ⲛϣ. = 43 76 ﺟﺎﺏ ﻏﯿﺎﺽ ﺍﻟﻌﻤﺮﺓ (cf AZ 26 128); Blake 272 ⲙⲡⲉⲛⲕⲁϩ ⲉⲣ ϣ. ⲛϥⲧⲁⲕⲟ *luxurians sine cultore*, P 131³ 1 man's nature shipwrecked through ⲃⲓⲟⲥ ⲉⲧⲟ ⲛϣ. (belongs ? to ϣ. *profligate*).

ϣⲛⲁ *A²* nn m, *meaning unknown*: Mani H 89]ⲁϩⲟⲩⲛ ⲁⲃⲁⲗ ϩⲛⲡϣⲛⲁ[& twice in Mani 1.

ϣⲛⲉ *SAA²B*, -ⲏ *SBF*, pl ϣⲛⲏⲩ, -ⲅⲉ *S*, -ⲛⲟⲩ *AB* & sg as pl, nn m, *net*: Job 18 8 *S* -ⲏ *B*, Lam 1 13 *BF*, Ez 12 13 *S*(*B* ⲥⲁϣⲛⲏⲓ), Hos 7 12 *AB* δίκτυον; Ps 140 10 *SB*-ⲏ ἀμφίβληστρον, Mk 1 16 *S* ϩⲓ ϣ. *B* ϣ. ⲛⲥⲓϯ ἀμφιβάλλειν, Is 19 8 *S* ⲉⲧⲛⲉⲝ ϣⲛⲏ *B* ϩⲓ ⲭⲉⲗⲓ ἀμφιβολεύς; PMich 1191 *S* ⲧⲁⲃⲱ ⲡⲟⲣⲉⲩ ⲉⲃⲟⲗ ⲉⲩϩⲣⲟϥⲧ ⲙⲡⲉϣⲛⲏ, Gu 98 *S* ϣⲛⲏ ϩⲓⲁⲃⲱ, Mus

45 52 B ⲥⲱⲕ ⲙⲡϣ. ⲉⲡⲓⲭⲣⲟ, Mani 2 A² ⲡⲉ[ϥ]ϣ.
ⲉⲧϥϣⲱⲣϥ ⲁⲙⲯⲩⲭⲁⲅⲉ ⲡⲟⲏⲧϥ, Va 61 104 B ⲣⲉϥⲣⲓ
ϣ.; ϣ. ⲡⲣⲓⲟⲩⲉ, casting-net: Hab 1 15 S(Wess 9
106)AB ἀμφίβλ. opp ⲁⲃⲱ; ShViK 934 222 S ⲡⲉⲭ
ⲁⲃⲱ ⲉⲃⲟⲗ, ⲡⲉⲭ ϣ. ⲛϥ., Mor 43 255 S ϭⲟⲡⲟⲩ ϩⲙ
ⲡⲉϥϣⲏⲛ ⲛϥ. ⲥⲟⲟⲩⲅ(ⲟⲩ?) ⲉϩⲟⲩⲛ ϩⲛⲧⲉϥⲁⲃⲱ; pl:
Ez 19 8 SB, Mt 4 21 SB δί.; Pro 11 8 SA(B ϥⲁϣ) θήρα; ShZ 595 S ⲛⲁϣ, ⲁⲗⲟⲟⲩⲉ, ϣ., Gu 101 S ⲛⲉϣⲏⲛ
ⲅⲉ ⲉⲧⲉϣⲁⲅⲥⲱ ⲛ̄ⲧⲉⲧ, JTS 4 394 S ⲟⲣⲉϩ [ⲉϩⲟⲩⲛ
ⲉ]ⲡⲟⲩϣⲏⲛⲅⲉ, BKU 1 1 ro S ⲱⲗ ⲡⲉⲧϣ., ib ϣⲏⲛⲅⲉ,
C 86 118 B ⲧⲁⲣⲟⲕ ⲉⲛⲛⲏϣ.; sg as pl S: BAp 40
ⲥⲟⲕⲟⲩ ⲡⲛⲁϣⲏⲛ ⲉⲧⲁⲃⲱ, Mor 31 30 ⲛⲉϣⲏⲛ called
ⲥⲡⲉⲣⲓⲟⲛ (? σπυρίδιον); as adj B: Ex 27 4 ϩⲱⲃ
ⲛϣ., 4 Kg 1 2 (P 44 111 = 43 107) ⲙⲟⲩⲛ̄ ⲛϣ. δικτυωτός; K 156 = P 54 156 ⲛⲛⲉⲃ ⲛϣ. شبابيك net-
work, trellis of window.

ϣⲏⲛ SAA²B(once)F nn f, garden: Deu 11 10
(B ⲥⲱⲙ), Eccl 2 5 F(S = Gk), Cant 8 13 F(S do)
Jo 18 1 (BF ϭ., A² = Gk) κῆπος; Su 4 (B = Gk),
R 2 2 33 (var BHom 49 ⲕⲏⲡⲟⲥ) παράδεισος; Am 9
14 SA (sic l, B ϭ.) ἀμπελών; Deu 6 11 ϣ. ⲛ̄ϫⲟⲉⲓⲧ
(B ⲓⲁϫϣⲟⲓⲧ) ἐλαιῶν; P 44 82 ⲧⲉϣ. ⲥⲉⲩⲧⲗⲟⲛ مقلة
= 43 57 بستان; BAp 11 ⲧⲁϣ. ⲡⲟⲩⲟⲟⲧⲉ, C 41 63 B
sim, MIF 9 17 ⲡϣⲏⲛⲓ ⲙ̄ⲙⲟⲟⲩ ⲡⲧⲉϣ.; ⲡⲁⲧⲉϣ.,
gardener: Jo 20 15 SA²(B ⲡⲓϫⲁⲓ ⲙⲡⲓϭ.) κηπουρός;
Leyd 427 ⲡⲣⲱⲙⲉ ⲡⲁⲧⲉϣ., Saq 81 ⲡⲁⲧⲉϣ., BMOr
6201 B 211 ⲡⲁⲧⲛⲟϭ ⲛϣ. In place-names: ⲧⲉϣⲏⲛ
ⲛⲉⲣⲁϩⲧ (BMOr 6201 B 204), ⲧⲉϣⲏⲛ ⲉⲛ̄ⲡⲉ (l ? ⲟⲩⲛ̄ⲡⲉ
Kr 130), ⲡⲣⲟⲓ ⲉⲧⲉϣⲏⲛ[(Ryl 170), شنا(?). Cf WS
204 n.

ϣⲱⲛⲃ v ϣⲱⲛϥ.

ϣⲏⲛⲃⲉ v ϣⲛϥⲉ.

ϣⲛⲃⲛⲛⲉ, ϣⲉⲛⲡⲛⲉ v ⲃⲛⲛⲉ.

ϣⲁⲛⲑⲙⲁϩⲧ B v ⲙⲁϩⲧ.

ϣⲉⲛⲛⲟⲣ B v ϣⲉ wood s f.

ϣⲛⲥ SA, ϣⲉ. B nn m, linen of fine flax: Ex 26 31
SB, Pro 29 40 SA, Ez 27 7 SB pl, Lu 16 19 SB βύσ-
σος, Is 3 23 pl SB, Ap 19 14 pl SB βύσσινος; P 44
58 S, K 121 B حرير; BMis 10 S ϩⲟⲓⲧⲉ ⲛⲕⲏϥⲉ ϩⲓϣ.,
Mor 43 251 S ⲛϣ. ⲉⲧⲥⲁⲣⲧ ⲉⲛⲛⲟⲩⲃ (cf Is l c B), R 1
3 51 S ϩⲉⲛϣ. ⲙ̄ⲡⲣⲉⲡⲏⲅⲥⲥⲙⲟⲛ as shroud, Aeg 55 B
sim; as adj: Ge 41 42 SB βύσσινος; 2 Kg 13 18
S ⲡⲗⲟⲩⲛ̄ ⲛϣ. καρπωτός (cf 19 ⲛⲓⲉⲡⲥⲁ ⲕ.); BMar
80 S ϩⲟⲓⲧⲉ ⲛϣ., El 92 A ϩⲃⲁⲥ ⲛϣ. = ib 122 S, Mor
44 40 S ⲉⲣϣⲱⲛ ⲛϣ., BSM 83 B ⲗⲁⲡⲡⲁ ⲛϣ. ⲉⲧⲥⲟⲧⲡ = BMis 174 S ⲡⲓⲉⲡⲛⲟⲩⲃ, Aeg 27 B ⲗⲁⲡⲡⲁ
ⲛϣ. ⲛⲟⲗⲟⲥⲓⲣⲓⲕⲟⲛ.

ϣⲟⲩⲛⲓⲥ B nn m, black cumin: Bodl 325 151
ⲛϣ. الكون الاسود. Is Pers شونيز (AIssa 125), σαουνιζ
(Langkavel 4).

ϣⲁⲁⲛⲧ⸗, ϣⲉⲉⲛⲧ⸗ v ϣⲁ nose.

ϣⲉⲛⲏⲧ S nn m, a fish: Gloss 410 κυνίσ(κος)· ϣ.,
425 κέφαλος· ϣ. ⲡⲣⲁⲥ ⲁⲡⲉ. Cf ? names ϣⲉⲛηⲧ,
Ⲡϣⲉⲛⲏⲧ (BM 449, 450).

ϣⲱⲛⲧ SBF, ϣⲱⲱ. S(nn).A², ϣⲛⲧ- S, ϣⲉⲛⲧ-,
ϣⲟⲛⲧ⸗, ϣⲟⲛⲧ† SB vb tr, plait: Is 28 5 SB, Mk 15
17 SBF, Jo 19 2 SA²B, R 2 2 24 S ϣ. ⲡⲣⲉⲡⲕⲗⲟⲙ,
Mor 18 182 S ⲁⲡⲉⲭ̄ⲥ̄ ϣ. ⲣⲓⲧⲛⲓⲟⲩⲥⲧⲓⲛⲁ ⲙⲡⲟⲩϫⲁⲓ
ⲉⲧⲟ ⲛⲥⲛⲁⲩ, πλέκειν; Jud 16 13 S ὑφαίνειν; PS 117
S ⲁⲓϣ. ⲛⲁⲓ ⲙ̄ⲡⲉⲕⲗⲟⲙ (Od Solom 1 2 ⲃⲓ), B
Hom 133 S of Job ⲁⲧⲉϥⲉⲓⲁⲁⲃⲉ ϣⲛ̄ⲧ ⲡⲉⲕⲗⲟⲙ, P 131¹
105 S ⲟⲩϭⲣⲏⲡⲉ ⲉⲙⲉⲩⲉϣ ϣⲟⲛⲧⲉ without jewels,
Mor 37 13 S taught me ⲉϣⲉⲛⲧ ϣⲛ̄, BM 787 B may
we pass night ⲛⲁⲧⲛϣⲱⲛⲧⲉⲛ ⲉⲛⲡⲓⲡⲉⲧϩⲱⲟⲩ; qual:
Ex 28 22 B, ib 39 21 B, LCyp 12 S ⲕⲗⲟⲙ...ⲉϣ.
ⲉⲃⲟⲗ ϩⲣⲉⲡⲱⲡⲉ συμπλ.; O'Leary Th 15 B ϩⲁⲛϩⲁ-
ⲗⲏⲥⲓⲥ ⲉⲩϣ., C 86 258 B ⲡⲁϣ. ⲉⲃ. ⲉⲛⲛⲓϩⲣⲏⲣⲓ, P
131⁶ 37 S ⲥⲧⲣⲱⲙⲁ...ⲉⲩϣ. ⲉⲃ. ⲙⲙⲛⲉ ⲛⲓⲙ ⲛϣⲱⲛⲧ,
ib στολὴ ⲉⲩϣ. ⲛ̄ⲑⲉ ⲛⲛⲉⲓⲙⲁⲣϫⲟⲟϣⲉ, Ryl 244 S
ϩⲃⲟⲥ ⲉⲥϣ. ⲡⲁⲡⲁϩ, PStras 41 S ϩⲃⲟⲥ ⲉⲥϣ. ⲛ̄ⲛⲟϭ
ⲉϣⲱⲛⲧ; as nn m: BAp 53 S wove crown ϩⲙ
ⲡⲉⲕϣ. ⲡⲱⲕ πλοκή, Is 3 20 S(B = Gk) ἐμπλόκιον;
Mor 43 77 S ⲧⲉϣⲧⲛⲏ ... ⲛϣ. ⲉⲧⲣⲓⲱⲱⲥ, Ryl 243 S
ⲕⲁⲗⲗⲁⲥⲉ (قلادة) ⲟⲩϫⲓ (l ⲉⲩ-) ⲁⲗⲁⲣⲏⲣⲉ (الحرير) ...
ⲟⲩϫⲓ (l ⲉⲩ-) ϣⲱⲛⲧ; ib 244 S ⲟⲩⲥⲙⲉⲣⲡⲉⲟⲡ...ⲉϥϫⲓ
ⲕⲟⲅⲓ ϣ. ⲛ̄ⲯⲉⲗⲓⲟⲩ (ψιμύθιον), ViK 4752 S ⲟⲩⲕⲟⲅⲓ
ϣ. ⲛ̄ⲥⲙⲛⲏⲣ(ⲟ)ⲛ (l ⲥⲙⲏⲣⲓ.).

ϣⲟⲛⲧⲉ, ϣⲛ. S, ϣⲉⲛ† B nn f, plaited work: Ge
31 34 B(S ϩⲁⲡⲟⲣⲕ) σάγμα قتب, Lev 15 9 B(S ?)ἐπί-
σαγμα فراش; Is 30 17 S ϣⲟ.(BF ϣⲟⲉ)ἱστός; Jud 16
13 S ϣⲛ. δίασμα; 3 Kg 7 6 S(P 44 111) ϣⲛ. ⲡⲥⲁϣⲉ
(l ? ⲡⲁϣⲉ) ἔργον κρεμαστόν; Ex 25 10 (?) S ϣⲛ. (P
44 104, B diff) στρεπτός; KroppK 72 S cast it (sc
what hast enchanted) ⲉⲩϣⲛ. (meaning?); ⲉⲓⲉⲡ
ϣ. S: 2 Chr 3 5 (? P 44 112) ϩⲁⲗⲩⲥⲓⲥ ⲡⲉⲓⲉⲡ ϣⲛ. مضفور
gloss on χαλαστόν; Tri 660 ⲡ ⲡⲉⲓⲉⲡ ϣⲟ. ⲡⲛⲉϩⲃⲱⲟⲥ
ⲣⲙ, ib 533 needle of ⲉⲓ. ϣⲟ. '⸗.

ϣⲱⲛⲧ (often var ϣⲟ.) SB, ϣⲁ. Sˡ, ϣⲟⲛⲧ† SB
vb intr, quarrel: Deu 25 11, Is 27 8†, Ja 4 2 B (var
ϣϭⲛⲏⲛ, all S ⲙⲓϣⲉ) μάχεσθαι; c ⲙⲛ-, ⲡⲉⲙ-:
Ge 26 20 B μ. μετά, ib 31 36 B(S ⲙ. ⲙⲛ-) μ. dat,
Z 328 S ⲉⲥϣ.† ... ⲙ̄ⲡⲟⲩⲟⲡ ⲛⲓⲙ μάχαι συνάπτεσθαι
πρός; c ⲟⲩⲃⲉ-: Va 57 179 B ⲉⲧϣ.† ⲟⲩⲃⲉⲛⲓⲁⲟⲙⲁ
μ. dat; as nn m: Ge 13 7 B(S ⲙ.), 2 Kg 22 44 Sˡ,
2 Cor 7 5 B(S do) μάχη; 1 Tim 6 4 B(S † ⲧⲱⲛ)ἔρις;
Pro 21 9 S ⲏⲓ ⲛ̄ϩⲣⲣⲉ ϩⲛⲟⲩϣⲱⲛⲧ (A ⲙ.) cf μετὰ γυ-
ναικὸς μαχίμης (but var ⲛϣⲟⲧ, cf next), Ps 59 5 B(S
ϩⲃⲏⲩⲉ ⲉⲩⲡⲁϣⲧ) σκληρός; Pro 3 31 B(SA ⲛⲟϣⲛⲉϣ)
ὄνειδος; PS 258 S ⲡⲓⲙ̄ⲡⲣⲉϥⲙⲓϣⲉ ⲙ̄ⲡⲓϣⲟ.; ⲙⲁ
ⲛϣ. B, place of quarrel: K 438 التجربة موضع ⲙ.

ϣⲁⲛⲧⲉ- SA²F, ⲛϣ.S(rare), ϣⲁⲡⲧⲍ S.A²FO, ϣⲁ-(ⲡ)ⲧⲉ-, ϣⲁ(ⲡ)ⲧⲍ A, ϣⲁⲡⲧⲍ F(rare), ϣⲁⲧⲉ-, ϣⲁⲧ(ⲉ)ⲍ S (archaic)B vbal pref, *until*: Deu 2 14 SB, Jon 4 5 SAB, Mt 13 33 SBF ἕως οὖ, Job 27 5 B(S ⲁⲛⲉ-), 1 Cor 4 5 SB ἕως ἄν, Jo 9 18 SA²B ἕως ὅτου, Ps 6 4 S ϣⲁⲧⲉⲟⲩ (var ϣⲁⲛ.) ϣⲱⲡⲉ? ἕως πότε; Λp 2 25 SB ἄχρις οὖ; PS 166 S ⲁⲓⲕⲁⲁⲥ…ϣⲁⲛⲧⲉⲓ ⲛⲉⲱⲥ, ib 239 S ϩⲉⲱⲥ ϣⲁⲛⲧⲥⲃⲱⲕ, Br 89 S, ManiK 72 A² sim, Sh C 73 70 S ⲉⲧⲣⲉϥⲙⲉⲗⲉⲧⲁ ϣⲁⲡⲧⲟⲩⲅⲉⲓ ⲉϩⲟⲩⲛ, AZ 23 32 F ϣⲁⲛⲕⲓ ⲉⲡⲟⲗⲓⲥ, BP 5558 F ϣⲁⲡⲕⲧⲓ, AZ 21 106 O ϣⲁⲛⲧⲉⲥⲓ ϩⲁⲣⲟⲓ, BIF 15 245 S/ ⲛϣ. ⲡⲕⲁⲡⲛⲟⲥ ⲡⲉϩⲣⲉⲓ ⲉϩⲣⲁⲓ, JEA 20 195 S ⲡϣⲁⲡⲧⲉⲕⲧ ⲛⲁⲥ, Miss 4 183 B I kept naught of his gift ϣⲁⲛⲧ(sic)ⲧⲛⲓϥ ⲡⲓⲡⲧⲣⲁ ϥⲉⲅⲥ *but rather gave it*; *so that*: Gal 1 4 B(v Stern 449, S ⲭⲉⲉϫⲉ-) ὅπως; PS 122 S He baptized man ϣⲁⲡⲧϥⲁⲁϥ ⲡϣⲙⲙⲟ ⲉⲡⲛⲟⲃⲉ, ib 276 S ⲟⲩ ⲡⲉⲧⲛⲁⲁⲁϥ ϣⲁⲡⲧⲟⲩⲡⲟⲟⲛⲉϥ ⲉⲃⲟⲗ?, Br 226 S ⲡⲓϣⲟⲣⲡ ⲛⲉⲡⲉⲡ ϣ. ⲡⲧⲏⲣϥ ⲁⲓⲥⲱⲡⲉ, RNC 56 S to martyr, What is thy magic ϣⲁⲛⲧⲕⲭⲡⲁ ⲡⲛⲁⲗⲁⲗⲛⲁⲥ?, Pcod 12 S Baptist called many ϣⲁⲡⲧϥⲧ ⲡⲁⲩ ⲁⲡⲃⲁⲡⲧⲓⲥⲙⲁ, ROC 20 54 S take wife ϣⲁⲡⲧⲕⲕⲱ ⲉⲕⲡⲟⲣⲛⲉⲩⲉ, P 131⁴ 150 gathering great stores ϣⲁⲡⲧⲟⲩϣⲱϥ *lest*, LMis 508 S they bore Him away ϣⲁⲛⲧⲉⲛϫⲟⲟⲥ (ⲭⲉ)ⲙⲡⲉϥⲧⲱⲟⲩⲛ, Miss 4 113 B they gave money ϣⲁⲧⲟⲩⲛⲟϫⲉⲁ, C 86 242 B He died ϣⲁⲧⲉϥⲥⲱⲧ ⲁⲙⲟⲛ, KKS 508 S queen (Eudoxia) hath expelled me ϣ.ⲛⲁⲓ ⲧⲏⲣⲟⲩ ϣⲱⲡⲉ ⲁⲙⲟⲓ, MG 25 107 B ⲟⲩⲙⲉⲧⲁⲧϫⲟⲙⲧⲉ ϣⲁⲧⲉϥⲁⲓ ϣⲱⲡⲓ ⲁⲙⲟⲛ, BM 1090 S ⲛⲡⲧⲁⲓⲧⲁⲁϥ ϣⲁⲡⲧⲟⲩϫⲓ ⲛⲡϣⲓⲛϣⲱⲧⲉ, DeV 2 127 B who am I ϣⲁⲧ ⲛⲁⲩ ⲉⲟⲩϩⲱⲃ ⲁⲡⲁⲓⲣⲏⲧ?

ϣⲉⲛⲧ B v ϣⲱⲡⲧ *plait*, adding Bodl 325 154 ‏ازر‎.

ϣⲟⲛⲧⲉ S, ϣⲁ. S′AA², ϣⲟⲛⲧ B, ϣⲁ.F nn f, *thorn tree (acacia nilotica)* ‏لصق‎, ‏ا.-‎, ‏لصنا‎ (cf MIF 30 115 n); single tree: Is 33 12 SBF, C 89 173 B ἄκανθα (*Vita III* § 192) = MG 17 683 ‏اشرد‎; Bod 325 158 B ‏لصنا‎, P 43 56 S ⲧϣⲩ., K 266 B ϯϣ. ‏لصنا‎; ShA 2 30 S ⲟⲩϣ. ⲉⲥⲣⲟⲕⲣ, Mor 31 59 S/ ⲟⲩϣ. ⲉⲥⲉⲛⲣⲟⲩⲡ ⲉⲛⲟϩⲉ, BM Or 8811 243 S ⲭⲉⲃⲉⲗ ⲡⲧϣ.; as pl: Ge 3 18 SB, Ps 57 8 S(B ⲥⲟⲩⲣⲓ), Pro 15 19 SA, Eccl 7 7 SF, Hos 10 8 SAB, Jo 19 2 SA²(B c.), Ryl 338 S shiploads of ϣ. ἄκ., Mk 15 17 SF(B do), C 99 232 S ϩⲛⲧⲁⲛⲧⲉ ⲛϣ. = ib 89 67 B ἀκάνθινος; Joel 3 18 SA(B ϣⲉ ⲡⲥⲛϥⲓ) σχοῖνος; ShC 73 73 S went to ⲛϣ. ⲉϥⲱⲗ ⲡⲣⲉⲡϣⲏⲛ ⲛϣⲉ, C 89 7 B ⲡⲣⲟⲕϩ ⲉⲃⲟⲗ ϩⲉⲛⲛϣ. = MG 17 345 ′ـ, TT 142 S came forth from ϩⲉⲛϣ. = MG 17 438 ′ـ, Mus 34 213 B ⲥⲟⲩⲣⲓ ⲉⲃⲟⲗ ϩⲉⲛϣⲁⲡϣ., Kr 3 F ⲧⲓⲕⲁⲧⲁⲅⲣⲁⲫⲓ ⲛϣ. ⲛⲓⲃⲓ ⲉⲧⲧⲁⲁⲃⲉ (cf PLond 4 xlviii), PMéd 292 S ϭⲱⲃⲉ ⲛϣ., ib 156 ϫⲓⲉⲓⲣⲉ ⲛϣ. *acacia pod*, ib 172 ϩⲣⲏⲣⲉ ⲛϣ., ib 196 ⲕⲛⲁⲗⲙⲉ ⲛϣ., ib 305 ϩⲉⲛϣ. *thorns* in hands or feet; m, *thicket* of ϣ.: C 89 16 B ⲡⲛⲛϣⲧ ⲛϣ. in desert ἀκάν-

---

θων πλήρης = MG 17 356 ‏ازر‎, ib 7, 12 B sim, BAp 107 S shepherd ⲉⲓⲙⲟⲟⲛⲉ ϩⲁⲡⲉϣ. = MI E 2 383 B = PO 22 389 ′ـ; ϣⲉ ⲛⲉϣ., *ac. wood*: Is 34 13 SBF ἀκάνθινος; R 1 5 48 S ϩⲉⲛϣⲉ ⲛϣ. as fuel.

In names: Πανσόντε, Τσονεσόντις (Preisigke); as place-name: Πιϣⲟⲛⲧⲉ (PLond 4 597, cf Ep 1 118), ⲡⲓϣⲱⲡⲧⲉ (Lant 44), ⲡⲓϣⲁⲡⲧⲉ (ib 49), ⲧ (BM 624), Πατσῶντις (BGU 1 107, P Goodspeed 17).

ϣⲟⲛⲧⲉ S v ϣⲱⲡⲧ *plait*.

ϣⲛⲧⲱ SO, ϣⲉⲛ. B nn f, *sheet, robe* of linen (cf σινδών Jablonski): Mt 27 59 B(S = Gk) σινδών; Jo 19 40 B ϣ. ⲛⲓⲁⲩ (S ϩⲃⲟⲥ) ὀθόνιον, Va 68 171 B ϣ. ⲉⲧϣⲟⲁ ⲟ. λεπτόν; Si 27 8 S ⲧϣ., Λp 1 13 S(B = Gk) ποδήρης; 1 Kg 2 19, 28 14 S διπλοῖς; Nu 31 50 S(B = Gk) ἐμπλόκιον (cf ϣⲱⲡⲧ 1° nn); P 44 57 S ⲗⲟⲩⲣⲓⲕⲏⲛ (λωρίκιον)· ϣ. ‏ رد ‎; N&E 39 348 B ⲕⲟⲥⲟⲩ ⲭⲉⲛϩⲁⲛϣ. ⲉⲑⲟⲩⲁⲃ, AZ 21 100 O ⲧⲉϣ. ⲟⲣⲛ.

ϣⲉⲛⲧⲱⲗⲓ, ϣⲉⲡ. B nn m, *unbleached, raw cloth*: K 122 ⲛϣ. ‏ خام ‎ (v Almk 1 305, Dozy 2 419).

ϣⲉⲛⲧⲥ v ϣⲛⲧⲥ.

ϣⲉⲛⲧⲏⲥ B nn m, *louse's egg*: BMOr 8775 131 ⲛϣ., P 55 18 ⲡⲓϣⲉⲛⲧⲉⲥ ‏صئبان‎.

ϣⲛⲧⲁⲉⲥⲉ S (Theban) nn, a measure of wine: ST 382, BKU 1 113, CO 463 ϫⲟⲩ[ⲧ ⲛ]ⲯⲉⲡⲧⲁⲉⲥⲉ; vinegar: ib 212; herbs: BP 402 ⲟⲩϣ. ⲡⲗⲁⲯⲁⲡⲏ, ib ⲡⲭⲓⲣⲗⲁⲯ. CO 217, 467 quite uncertain.

ϣⲁⲛⲧϥ v ϣⲁ *nose*.

ϣⲛⲓⲁⲩ B nn m, *market*: MG 25 358 ⲁϥϩⲱⲗ ⲉⲡⲓϣ. to sell baskets (= ROC 18 60 ‏لـ_‎), C 43 126 ⲡⲓϣ. ⲛⲉⲙⲭⲉ where to buy cow = Mor 48 53 S ⲑⲟⲟⲃⲉ ⲁⲡ.

ϣⲁⲛⲓϣ B, ϣⲏⲛⲓϣ F v ⲥⲁⲁⲛϣ.

ϣⲛⲟϣ S, ϩⲛⲁϣ A, ϣⲛ. A², ϣⲟⲡϣ S vb intr, *stink*: Job 6 7 (B ⲁⲣⲟϣⲧ)βρόμος; ShR 2 3 84 [ⲡⲁⲓ] ϣ.ⲧ ⲉϩⲟⲩⲟ ⲉϣ. ⲛ[ⲓⲙ], Mor 56 6 ⲁⲥⲱ. ⲛϭⲓ ⲧⲡⲟⲗⲓⲥ from sacrifices, Pcod 7 goats ⲉⲧϣ.ⲧ; as nn: Job 17 11 (B do), Joel 2 20 SA(B do) β.; ShA 1 128 ⲥⲧ ⲃⲱⲡⲉ ⲛϣ., ib 2 113 ⲛⲉϣ. ⲡⲛⲉⲥⲛⲱⲟϥ, Mor 36 72 ⲡⲉϣⲛⲟ(ϣ) ⲛⲡⲧⲃⲛⲟⲟⲩⲉ, Mani 1 A²]ⲥⲧ ⲛⲟⲩϥⲉ ⲉⲧϩⲗⲁϭ ⲃⲁϣϥ ⲁⲡⲉϣ.

ϣⲛⲉϣⲱⲧⲉ, ϣⲛⲓⲛ.S, ϣⲏⲛⲓϣⲁⲧⲓ Sᵃ nn f, *cushion*(?): ShP 130⁵ 34 rich ⲛⲣϣ ϣ. ϩⲓⲧⲁⲡⲟⲥ(τάπης)ϩⲁⲣⲟⲟⲩ ⲛⲛⲉⲩ(ⲟⲩ)ϩⲟⲟⲣ, ShR 2 3 44 ϩⲉⲛϣ. […] ⲁⲡϩⲉⲛϣⲟⲧ on bed, ShP 130⁵ 65 ⲧϣ. ⲡⲉ ϩⲛⲧⲟ ⲁⲡⲣⲱⲙⲉ ⲁⲩⲱ ⲡⲉⲡⲗⲟⲩⲙⲁⲧⲓⲟⲛ ⲡⲉ that sick may lie thereon, ib ϩⲉⲛϣⲟⲧ ⲛ ⲟⲩⲕⲟⲩⲓ ⲛϣ., BM 1090 price of ⲛϣⲓⲛ. (*bis*), Sph 10 147 Sᵃ ϫⲟⲟⲩ (ⲟⲩ)ϣ. ⲛⲁⲓ. Cf? ϣⲉϣⲟⲧⲉ.

ϣⲱⲛϥ SF (nn), -ⲃ, ϣⲉⲛϥ-, ϣⲉⲛⲃ-, ϣⲟⲛϥⲍ, -ⲃⲍ,

ϣⲟⲛϥ†, -ϥ†, *S* vb **I** intr, *join, come together*: Eccl 11
6 ἐπὶ τὸ αὐτό (no vb), Blake 260 ⲙⲡ ϣϭⲟⲙ ⲉⲧⲣⲉϥ.
ⲛϭⲓ ⲡⲧⲱϣ ⲡⲡⲉⲓⲱⲛⲉ; qual: ViSitz 172 4 34 ⲉϥϣ.
ϩⲣⲁⲓ ϩⲛ(ⲉ)ⲡⲧⲟⲗⲏ ⲛⲓⲙ ἑνοῦσθαι; *ib* 21 ϩⲛⲧ ⲉϥϣ.
ἀμέριστος; Eph 4 16 (*B* ϩⲱⲧⲡ) συναρμολογοῦσθαι;
ShR 2 3 44 [ⲡⲉⲓ]ϣⲁϫⲉ ⲉϥϣ. ⲁⲩⲱ ⲉⲅⲧⲟⲟⲙⲉ ⲉ[ⲣⲁ]-
ⲙ[ⲁⲟ] ⲛⲓⲙ. **II** tr: Mk 10 9 (*B* ⲧⲱⲙⲓ) συνζευγνύ-
ναι; Blake *lc* ⲙⲡⲓⲥϫⲛ ⲑⲉ ⲛϣ. ⲡⲡⲉⲓⲱⲛⲉ. With following preposition. **c ⲉ-**: 1 Cor 2 13 (*B* = Gk, *F*
ϩⲁⲧⲣⲉⲧ) συγκρίνειν; Vi *lc* 20 ⲡⲉⲧϣ. ⲙⲙⲟⲟⲩ ⲉⲟⲩⲁ
ⲉⲛⲱⲥⲓⲛ ἐπαγγέλλειν; Mus 42 233 ⲡⲉⲅⲛⲁϣⲉⲛ̅ⲉⲧⲛ-
ⲧⲓⲡⲉ ⲉⲣⲟϥ, RE 10 37 ⲁⲡⲁⲉⲓⲟⲧⲉ ϣⲟⲃ̅ⲧ (*l* ϣⲟⲛⲃ̅ⲧ)
ⲉⲅⲧⲁⲙⲟ; **c ⲙⲛ-**: Mor 17 77 words ⲙⲛⲟⲩϣ.
ⲙⲛϩⲣⲟⲙⲡⲱⲛ συναινεῖν dat; ShBor 247 106 ⲛⲧⲓϣ.
ⲛⲓⲡⲟⲛⲏⲙⲁ ⲙⲛⲛⲉⲣⲣⲏⲧⲟⲛ, Mor 39 10 ϣ. ⲙⲛⲛⲉⲩⲉⲣⲏⲩ in marriage (var *ib* 40 7 ϩⲱⲧⲣ) = C 43 37 *B*
ϩⲱⲧⲡ, Blake 300 ⲧⲣⲉⲡⲣⲱⲙⲉ ϣ. ⲙⲛⲧⲉⲥϩⲓⲙⲉ ⲉⲧⲉ-
ϩⲛⲁϥ, EpApp 1 83 ⲧⲣⲉⲡⲉⲥⲛⲁⲩ ϫⲱⲛϥ (*sic*) ⲙⲛⲛⲉⲩⲉⲣⲏⲩ, Bor 260 121 ϣ. ⲡⲉⲓⲉⲣⲣⲉ ⲙⲛⲡⲉⲓⲁⲥ; qual: Sh
P 130² 36 deeds ⲉⲧϣ. ⲙⲛⲛⲓϣⲁϫⲉ, Mor 28 22 Trinity
ⲉⲩϣ. ⲙⲛⲛⲉⲩⲉⲣⲏⲩ ϩⲛⲟⲩⲙⲛⲧⲟⲩⲁ; *ib* 17 67 wife ⲉⲧ-
ϫⲟⲛϥ ⲛⲙⲙⲁⲓ ϩⲓⲧⲙⲡⲛⲁⲙⲟⲥ; **c ⲛ- dat**: Pro 19 11
(*A* = Gk) ἁρμόζειν dat, Jth 16 1 ἐναρ. dat; **c ϣⲁ-**:
Z 606 how can I ϣ. ⲡⲡⲉⲥϩⲣⲁⲓ ϣⲁⲁⲗⲩⲡⲓⲟⲥ? *convey
letters to.*

—— nn m, *union, unity*: Ez 23 42 (*B* ⲥⲩⲙⲫⲱ-
ⲛⲓⲁ) ἁρμονία; 2 Cor 6 15 (*B* ϯ ⲙⲓⲁ ϯ) συμφώνησις,
ib 16 (*B* do) συγκατάθεσις; Z 278 ⲉϥϩⲧⲏϭ ϩⲛⲟⲩϣ.
συνάφεια; Miss 8 94 ⲡϣ. ⲛⲧⲡⲗⲏⲧⲟⲅⲁ συνδρομή; R
2 2 31 ⲡϣ. ⲙⲛⲡⲁⲙⲟⲥ (var BHom 47 ϩⲱⲧⲣ) συνζυγία,
Ryl 113 ζεῦγος• ⲛⲥⲟⲉⲓϣ ⲡⲣⲱⲧⲣ ⲡϣ.; Wess 18 95
ⲡϣ. ⲙⲛⲡⲛ̄ ⲙⲛⲡⲉⲡⲓⲥⲕⲟⲡⲟⲥ ἑνότης; Br 247 ⲡϣ. ⲡ-
ⲡⲉⲩⲙⲉⲗⲟⲥ, ShC 42 224 ⲡϣ. ⲙⲛⲡⲉⲓⲕⲟⲥⲙⲟⲥ wherein
are things opposed, ViK 9748 gospels ⲙⲏⲣ ⲉⲩϣ.
ⲡⲟⲩⲱⲧ; ϩⲛⲟⲩϣ. adverbial: Eccl 7 15 (*F* om) συμφώνως; 1 Cor 7 5 SF(*B* ϯ ⲙ.) ἐκ συμφώνου; ROC
19 135 divinity & flesh united not ϩⲛⲟⲩϣ. ⲁⲗⲗⲁ…
ⲕⲁⲧⲁ ⲑⲩⲡⲟⲥⲧⲁⲥⲓⲥ.

ϣⲱⲛϥ *v* ϫⲱⲛϥ.

ϣⲛⲟϥ, ϣⲛⲟⲩϥ *B* *v* ϫⲛⲟϥ.

ϣⲛⲟⲩϥ *B* nn, meaning uncertain: Va 57 95
ⲟⲩϣ. ⲟⲩⲟϩ ⲛⲕⲁⲧⲁϩⲅⲣⲟⲛ(-ξηρος)ⲡⲉ ϥⲛⲟⲃⲓ κνησ-
μώδης (*l* ? κληματώδης E C Owen) ἡ ἁμαρτία, *ib*
fig-leaves called ⲡⲗⲁⲧⲩⲫ(ⲩ)ⲗⲟⲛ ϩⲱⲥ ⲉⲅϫⲟⲧⲉ ⲟⲩⲟϩ
ⲉⲩϣ. ⲉϩⲟⲓ ⲛⲕⲁⲧⲁϩⲅⲣⲟⲛ. Prob not = ϭⲛⲟⲩϥ *heavy.*

ϣ(ⲉ)ⲛϥⲉ¹, -ⲃⲉ², ϣⲛⲏⲡⲉ³, ϣⲛϥⲉ⁴, ϣⲛⲃⲉ⁵, ϣⲓϥⲉ⁶ *S*,
S, ϣⲉⲛϥⲓ⁷, ϣⲛⲓϥⲓ⁸ *B* nn f, *scale of fish*: Lev 11 9 *S*¹
(varr² ⁴)*B*⁷ λεπίς, Ep 571 *S* ⲗ]ⲉⲡⲓⲥ ϣ.⁶ ⲛⲧⲃ̅[ⲧ: Job
40 26 *S*¹(*B* = Gk) βύρσα; 2 Kg 21 16 *S*²(var⁵, Pey
Gr 192 ⲥⲛⲃⲉ prob error) κορύνη (but var παραζώνη,
cf Syr ﺟﻳﺮ؟ ﻟﻳﺤﺎ); ShP 130² 25 *S* fish ⲉⲛⲁϣⲉ

ⲡⲉⲅϣ.¹, MG 25 397 = AZ 14 45 *B* ϩⲁⲡⲕⲏⲕⲥ ⲁⲩⲣⲉⲓ
ⲉⲃⲟⲗ ϫⲉⲛⲡⲉϥⲃⲁⲗ ⲙ̅ⲫⲣⲏϯ ⲡϩⲁⲛϣ.⁸, PMéd 211 *S*
ⲧϣ.³ ⲡⲟⲩϩⲟⲣⲡ (= ϩⲟϥ Chassinat). *Cf* ϣⲉⲗⲃⲉ.

ϣⲁⲛⲟⲩϩ *v* ⲡⲟⲩϩ *sf.*

(ϣⲱⲛϩ), ϣⲟⲛϩⲉ *B* vb tr, *deprive* (*cf* ϣⲱⲱⲛⲉ): Deu
33 9 (*S* ⲕⲱ ⲛⲥⲁ-) ἀπογινώσκειν; Cat 221 ϣⲟⲛϩⲟⲩ
ⲉϣⲧⲉⲙⲛⲁⲩ ⲉⲡⲱⲟⲩ; **c ⲛ-**: Ge 48 11, Ps 20 3 (*S*
ϩⲟⲩⲣⲱⲥ) στερεῖν; 1 Thes 2 17 (*SF* diff) ἀπορφανί-
ζειν; Va 66 295 ϣⲟⲛϩⲟⲩ ⲛⲡⲟⲩⲙⲉⲗⲟⲥ περικόπτε-
σθαι; Cat 92 ⲁϥϣⲟⲛϩⲟⲩ ⲙⲡⲉϩⲙⲟⲧ, C 86 105 ⲉⲅⲛⲁ-
ϣⲟⲛϩⲥ ⲙⲡⲉⲥⲥⲟⲛ;   MG 25 111 ⲡϫⲓⲛϣⲟⲛϩⲟⲩ ⲙ-
ⲫⲣⲉϥϣⲁⲛϣ.

ϣⲉⲛϩⲟ *B* *v* ϩⲟ.

ϣⲁⲛ-, ϣⲛϩⲏⲧ *v* ϩⲏⲧ *heart.*

ϣⲁⲡ *S* nn, prenuptial *marriage gift* (*v* Ryl Dem
3 268 n, AZ 55 74): Bodl(P)b 3 (= Petrie *Gizeh &
Rifeh* 42) marriage contract ⲁⲓⲧⲓ ⲛⲉ ⲡⲟⲩⲡⲁϣⲉ ⲛϩⲟ-
ⲗⲟⲕ/ ⲙⲛⲟⲩⲧⲣⲓⲙⲩⲥⲓⲟⲛ (ⲡ)ⲛⲟⲩϥ ⲛϣ. *Cf* p 427 *a*
ϣ(ⲉ)ⲡ ⲧⲟⲟⲧⲥ *sf.*

ϣⲏⲡ *S* nn m, meaning doubtful: J 58 39 mort-
gage of house ⲛⲓⲥⲁⲕ … ⲙ̅ⲛⲡⲉϥϣ. (? Theban for
ϣⲁⲡ, *v* Ep 1 238).

ϣⲟⲡ *SB* (bibl), ϣⲟⲟⲡ *S*, ϣⲁⲡ *SᵃF*, ϣⲱⲡ *SB* nn
m, a *4-fingerbreadth, palm*: Tri 467 ⲧⲡⲉ…ϩⲓⲡⲉϥϣ.
شبر (*cf* Is 40 12 ⲣⲧⲱ); as measure: 2 Chr 4 5 *B*, Ez
40 5 *SB* παλαιστή;   ShZ 592 ⲟⲩⲧⲁϫⲥⲉ ⲡⲟⲩⲉⲣⲏⲧⲉ
ⲛ ⲟⲩϣ. ⲛⲕⲁϩ, J 65 61 sim (*cf* ? PLond 1 233 πλέθρον γῆς), ShC 73 200 tongue hung out ⲛⲁⲙϣ. ⲥⲛⲁⲩ,
ib 137 ϣ. ⲥⲛⲁⲩ ⲛⲓϣⲉ, Hall 80 *Sᵃ* sim, BMar 241 sim,
Lepsius *Denkm* 6 102 ⲙⲛⲧⲁϥⲧⲉ ⲡϣ. ⲙⲛⲥⲛⲁⲩ ⲛⲧⲛⲃⲉ, Hall 121 sim ϣⲟⲟⲡ, BM 528 § 18 *F* ⲧⲏⲛⲃⲉ, ϣ.,
ⲙⲉⲣⲓ, CO 473 ϣⲙⲟⲩⲛ ⲛϣ. ⲉⲧⲛⲟϭⲉ, Bristol Mus
ostr H 1755 ϥⲧⲟⲟⲩ ⲛϣ. ⲙⲛⲥⲛⲁⲩ ⲙⲛⲟⲣⲕ, Mor 41
176 ϣⲟⲡ ⲥⲛⲁⲩ ⲡⲟⲩⲱϣⲥ, TurM 16 ⲡⲯⲓⲥ ⲛϣ. ⲛϩⲓⲣ
ϣⲱⲡⲉ ⲛⲕⲟⲙⲟⲡ (*cf* CO 144, J 24 126), Bodl copt
inscr 427 ⲟⲩⲥⲧⲓⲱϭⲉ(ⲙ)ⲙⲁϣⲉ ⲙⲛⲟⲩϫ̄ⲟⲡ(ⲗϣⲟⲡ, same
measure?), ShC 42 70 ⲙⲛⲧϣⲏⲙⲛ ⲡϣⲱⲡ of bread
(same?), TurO 15 ⲕⲁⲛⲑⲏⲗⲉ (-θήλιον) ⲛⲥⲟⲟⲩ ⲛϣⲱⲡ
(*sic*), *ib* ⲟⲩⲛ ⲕⲁⲗⲏⲗⲉ (*sic*) ⲙⲙⲁⲩ ⲧⲛⲟⲟⲩ ⲟⲩϣ. ⲛⲁⲡ
(*sic*), Hall 87 ϣⲱⲡ ⲛⲛⲟⲩϩ, ϣ. ⲛⲥⲁⲣⲧⲁⲛⲏ, CO 221
sim. **b** ϣⲱⲡ, *group of four*: Ac 12 4 *B* ⲝ̄ ⲛϣ. (*S*
ⲙ̅ⲛⲧⲁⲥⲉ)δ' τετράδιον(P 44 18, K 16 نون), BM 335 *S*,
AM 205 *B* sim; Mk. 6 48 (var & *B* ⲟⲩⲉⲣϣⲉ) φυλακή;
Leyd 175 rubric ⲡϩⲉⲣⲙⲏⲛⲓⲁ…ⲡⲉⲅϣ. ⲡⲗⲉⲝ̣ⲓⲥ (of 4
versicles in each).

ϣⲟⲡ *B* *sole* of foot *v* ϭⲟⲡ.

ϣⲱⲡ *SAAᵃᵇⁱᵃBF*, ϣⲡ- *SAAᵃᵇⁱB*, ϣⲉⲡ- *SB*, ϣⲁⲡ-
SF, ϣⲱⲡ- *SAᵃ*, ϣⲟⲡ⸗ *SB*, ϣⲁⲡ⸗ *SᵃAAᵃᵇⁱF*, ϣⲏⲡ†

SABF, ⲣ ⲥ ϣⲁⲡ-A²B vb tr, *receive, contain, take, suffer*: Ps 146 6 B(S ϥⲓ ⲉϩⲣⲁⲓ)ἀναλαμβάνειν, Mt 1 20 B(S ϫⲓ)παραλ.; Ge 13 6 SB, Jo 2 6 S(B ⲱⲗⲓ)χωρεῖν; He 2 18 SF(B ϭⲓ), Ap 2 10 S(B do)πάσχειν; Jer 9 20 B, Mt 11 14 B(S ϫⲓ)δέχεσθαι; 1 Cor 7 28 S (B do)ἔχειν, Sa 1 7 S(B diff)συνέ.; Jo 11 39 B(S ϥⲓ, A² ⲗⲁⲑⲉ)αἴρειν; ShC 42 63 S ⲡⲙⲁ...ⲛⲁϣⲟⲡⲟⲩ ⲁⲛ, PS 98 S ⲁⲥϣⲡ ⲛⲉⲓⲛⲟϭ ⲛϭⲓⲥⲉ, Mani H 22 A² ⲛϭⲓⲥⲉ ⲉⲛⲧⲁϥϣⲁⲡⲟⲩ, BMar 16 S ϣⲡ ϩⲏⲙⲟⲕⲣⲥ, *ib* 17 S ⲉϥϣⲡ ⲛⲁ at gate, Mor 25 200 S ⲁϥϣⲱⲡ ϣⲗⲏⲗ ⲛⲙⲙⲁϥ & promised, Mani 1 A² ⲁⲓϣⲱⲡ ⲛⲉⲓ before you, PO 11 317 B ϣⲉⲡ ϩⲁⲡⲟϩⲁ ⲛⲕⲩⲡⲁⲓⲛⲟⲥ; *buy:* Pro 23 20 S(A ⲧⲁⲩ), Jo 4 8 SBF(A² ⲧ.) ἀγοράζειν, Eph 5 16 SB, RNC 23 S ϣⲡ ⲡⲉⲥⲟⲩⲟ ⲉϫⲁⲩ.; Ex 21 2 S(B ⲝϥⲟ), Jos 24 32 S(var ⲧⲟⲟⲩ), Is 1 3 B(SF ϫⲟⲉⲓⲥ)κτᾶσθαι; Pro 29 34 S(A ⲧ.), BMar 116 S ϣ. ⲛⲟⲩⲏⲣⲡ πρίασθαι; BMar 54 S ϣⲡ ϩⲙϩⲁⲗ, J 1 28 S ⲡⲉⲧϣⲟⲟⲡ ⲕⲁⲧⲁ ⲡⲣⲁⲥⲓⲥ, BSM 38 B if God grant ⲛⲧⲁϣⲟⲡⲥ = BMis 382 S ϫⲓ, BM 1233 F ϣⲁⲡ ⲥⲟⲩⲁ; *intr:* Ge 42 5 SB, Is 24 2 SB, 1 Cor 7 30 SBF ⲁⲩ.; Ez 7 13 SB ⲕⲧ.; ShC 73 142 S opp ϯ ⲉⲃⲟⲗ, MG 25 29 B sim, Ryl 346 S ϣ. ⲛϭⲓϫ ⲙⲛϭⲓϫ (cf διὰ χειρὸς εἰς χεῖρας), C 43 75 B ⲣⲱⲙⲓ ⲛϣ. *bought men, slaves.*

qual, *acceptable:* Pro 10 24 B(SA ⲥⲟⲧⲡ), Is 49 8 SB, Lu 4 24 SB δεκτός, 1 Tim 2 3 SB ἀπόδ., Ro 15 16 SB εὐπρόσδ.; *ib* 6 17 SB ⲡⲉϩⲙⲟⲧ ⲙⲡⲛⲟ̅ⲩⲧⲉ ϣ. χάρις τῷ θεῷ; Jer 20 14 S(MIF 23 12)B ἐπευκτός.

With following preposition.

—— ⲉ- SAA²BF dat commodi, *accept, restrain self, take* (mostly B): Job 6 11 (S = Gk), Va 57 10 ⲙⲡⲁⲥϣ. ⲉⲣⲟⲥ ⲉⲑⲣⲉⲥⲟϩⲓ ἀνέχειν; Mt 19 12 (S ϥⲓ) χωρεῖν; MG 25 7 ϣⲁⲥϣ. ⲉⲣⲟⲥ in all things ὑπομένειν (cf 1 Cor 13 7 ⲁⲙⲟⲛⲓ ⲛⲧⲟⲧⲥ); Job 2 9 (S do) καρτερεῖν; *ib* 31 23 (S om) ὑποφέρειν; Lam 4 15 F (S ⲥⲟⲟϩⲉ ⲉⲃⲟⲗ, B ϧⲉⲛ/ ⲉⲃ.) ἀφιστάναι; ShA 1 101 S ⲛϭⲓϫ ⲉⲧⲛⲁϣ. ⲉⲣⲟⲟⲩ ⲏ ⲉⲧⲛⲁϥⲓ ϩⲁ-, Ep 1 19 S ⲁⲓⲟⲩⲱϣ ⲉϣ. ⲉⲣⲟⲓ ; as obj: PS 355 S ⲁϥϣ. ⲉⲣⲟϥ ϩⲓⲧⲉⲥϥⲁⲓⲣⲁ *took him from*(?), BHom 137 S ϣ. ⲉⲣⲟⲓ ϩⲙⲡⲉⲓⲣⲙⲟⲙ, C 86 5 ϣ. ⲉϥⲁⲓ ⲉⲃⲟⲗ ϩⲉⲡⲧⲉⲛⲭⲱⲣⲁ; + ⲛⲉⲙ-: 1 Thes 5 14 (S ϥⲓ ϩⲁ-) ἀντέχειν; C 86 239 ϯⲛⲁϣ. ⲉⲣⲟⲓ ⲛⲉⲙⲁⲕ *be indulgent*; tr, *take to self, contain:* Deu 32 11 SB, Si 2 4 SB, Zeph 3 2 AB, Jo 4 45 SA²BF, 1 Cor 2 14 SBF ϣⲁⲡ-, BHom 16 S ⲛϣϣⲟⲡⲓ ⲉⲣⲟϥ, ZNTW 24 86 F ϣⲁⲛϥ ⲉⲗⲁⲧⲡ δέχ., Ac 2 41 SB ἀπόδ., Ez 20 34 SB εἰσδ., Mic 2 12 SAB ἐκδ., MG 25 203 B not willing ⲉϣⲉⲡ ⲡⲓⲣⲱⲃ ⲉⲣⲟⲓ καταδ., Pro 3 12 SAB παραδ., Lev 26 43 B(S ϫⲓ), Ro 16 2 SB προσδ., Lu 10 38 SB ὑποδ.; Ge 8 9 S(var ⲁⲙⲁϩⲧⲉ, B ϭⲓ) λαμ., Ps 3 5 SB, *ib* 88 43 S(B ϯ ⲧⲟⲧ⸗), *ib* 106 17 S(B ⲁⲙⲟⲛⲓ), Mic 6 6 S(MIF 23 89)AB ἀντιλ., Mt 1 20 B(S ϫⲓ)παραλ., Ps 17 16 SB, Ac 18 26 SB προσλ., *ib* 1 9 B(S do) ὑπολ.; Pro 4 6

SAB ἀντέχ.; 2 Cor 7 2 SB χωρ.; Ps 68 8 B(S ϥⲓ) ὑποφέρ.; Ge 30 8 SB συμβάλλειν; Mt 25 35 SB συνάγειν; Aeg 286 S ϣ. ⲉⲣⲟⲟⲩ ⲙⲡⲧⲱⲣⲡ προιέναι; PS 105 S ⲙⲡⲣⲧⲣⲉⲗⲁⲁⲩ ϣⲟⲡϥ ⲉⲣⲟϥ, FR 166 S each jar ϣ. ⲉⲣⲟⲥ ⲙⲙⲉⲧⲣⲉⲧⲏⲥ ⲥⲛⲁⲩ, El 96 A ⲡⲛⲟ̅ⲥ̅ ⲡⲁϣ. ⲛⲟⲩⲡⲛ̅ⲁ̅ ⲁⲣⲁϥ, Mani 1 A² ϣ. ⲁⲣⲁⲕ ⲡⲁⲯ[ⲩⲭⲁ]ⲅⲉ, BSM 54 B ⲁϥϣ. ⲉⲣⲟϥ ⲡⲧⲉϥⲟⲩⲥⲓⲁ = BMis 407 S ϫⲓ ⲛⲧⲛ-, Lant 7 10 F ⲡⲛⲟ̅ⲥ̅ ϣⲁⲡ ⲧⲉϥⲯⲩⲭⲏ ⲉⲣⲟϥ, ST 72 S tax receipt ⲟⲩⲡⲛ̅ϣⲉ...ϯⲛⲁϣⲟⲡⲉ ⲉⲡⲉⲕⲗⲟⲅⲟⲥ, J 75 86 S shalt not ϣⲉⲡ ⲣⲱⲙⲉ ⲉⲣⲟⲕ (as heir) under 20 years. V also ⲣⲉϥ-, ϭⲓⲛϣⲏ.

—— ⲉϫⲛ-SB, *on behalf of, for:* BM 1105 S ⲧⲉⲧⲛⲉⲛⲟϭ ⲛⲁⲅⲁⲡⲏ ϣ.⁺ ⲉ.ⲧⲙⲛⲧⲙⲁⲓⲣⲱⲙⲉ ⲛⲧⲉⲧⲛⲉⲗⲁⲥ, MG 25 409 prayers ϣ.⁺ ⲉϫⲱⲛ ⲛⲁϩⲣⲉⲛⲡⲛⲟ̅ⲥ̅ (ROC 19 47), C 89 208 B ⲡⲓϩⲙⲟⲧ ⲛⲧⲉ ⲫϯ ϣ.⁺ ⲉϩⲣⲏⲓ ⲉϫⲱⲓ (cf Phil 1 3).

—— ⲛ- a dat SABF: Mt 16 5 B(S ϫⲓ) ⲗⲁⲙ., Jer 39 7 B παραλ. εἰς κτῆσιν; Is 55 1 S(B om ⲛ-), Mt 13 46 S(BF om ⲛ-) ⲁⲅ.; Ge 33 19 S(B do), Ac 1 18 SB κτᾶσθαι; Ep 592 A 24 S ϣ. ⲛⲁⲕ ⲛⲡⲁⲧⲧⲁⲕⲟ ὠνεῖσθαι; MS Antinoe *penes* EES S ϣⲉⲡ ⲡⲱⲛⲉ ⲛⲁⲕ ⲉⲧⲛⲁϣⲉ ⲥⲟⲩⲛⲧϥ, C 43 126 B ⲛⲧⲁϣ. ⲛⲏⲓ ⲛⲟⲩⲉⲣⲉ, Imp Russ Ar S 026 S ϣⲱⲡ ⲟⲩⲧⲉⲣⲙⲛⲥⲓⲟⲛ (a *solidus*-worth) ⲛⲁⲓ, BM 597 F ⲁⲓϣⲁⲡⲟⲩ ⲛⲉⲧⲏ; qual: Lev 22 20 SB, Pro 14 35 SA δεκτός, 1 Pet 2 5 SB εὐπρόσδ.; MG 25 326 B ⲛⲓⲙⲁ ⲉⲧⲉϥϣ. ⲛⲏⲓ ⲙⲙⲟϥ ⲛϫⲉ ⲡⲓⲥⲟⲩⲡⲟⲩϥⲓ (ROC 17 358). b *expend on:* BAp 125 S ϣⲟⲡϥ (sc solidus) ⲛϩⲃⲟⲟⲥ = MIE 2 418 B, BSM 33 B ϣⲟⲡϥ (sc robe) ⲛⲥⲟⲩⲟ = BMis 375 S ⲧⲁⲁⲥ ϩⲁ-, ST 173 S ϣⲟⲡϥ ⲛⲁⲓ ⲛⲥⲟⲩⲟ, Miss 4 183 B ϣⲟⲡϥ ⲛϩⲱⲙ ⲉⲃⲟⲩⲛ ⲉϯⲉⲕⲕⲗⲏⲥⲓⲁ, J 80 42 S ϣⲟⲡϥ ⲛⲡⲉϩ ⲉⲡϩⲏⲃⲥ, Ryl 385 ϣⲟⲡⲃ ⲉϩⲣⲉ.

—— ⲛⲧⲛ-SSªBF, *from:* Deu 2 6 S(B + ϩⲁϧⲁⲧ), Ap 3 18 SB ⲁⲅ. παρά; Lev 25 14 B(S ϫⲓ ⲛⲧⲛ-) ⲕⲧ. π.; Ac 7 16 BF(S ϩⲓⲧⲛ-) ὠν. π.; Deu 33 16 SB⁺ δεκ. dat; Phil 1 3 SBF ϣⲡ ϩⲙⲟⲧ ⲛ. εὐχαριστεῖν dat; Br 106 S ϣ. ⲛⲁⲛⲧⲥⲓⲟⲛ...ⲛⲧⲟⲟⲧⲟⲩ, ShR 2 3 27 S ϣ. ⲛⲧⲛ-ⲡⲉⲧϯ ⲉⲃⲟⲗ, ShA 1 257 S ⲉⲅϣ.⁺ ⲛⲧⲟⲟⲧⲩ ⲙⲡⲉⲭ̅ⲥ̅, C 89 68 B ϣⲉⲡ ⲟⲩϩⲣⲓ...ⲛⲧⲟⲧϥ ⲙⲡⲛⲟ̅ⲥ̅ = *ib* 99 234 S ϩⲓⲧⲛ-, J 2 19 Sª ⲛⲙⲉⲣⲟⲥ...ⲛⲧⲁⲡⲉⲡⲉⲓⲱⲧ ϣⲁⲡⲟⲩ ⲛⲧⲟⲟⲧⲉϥ; meaning doubtful: Mt 16 22 S ⲁϥϣⲟⲡⲉ (impers) ⲛⲧⲟⲟⲧϥ (= Mk 8 32 F, where S ϯ ⲡⲉϥⲟⲩⲟⲓ ⲉϩⲟⲩⲛ ⲉ-, B both ⲁⲙⲟⲛⲓ ⲙⲙⲟϥ) προσλαμβάνεσθαι.

—— ⲛⲁϩⲣⲛ-SA, *before,* with qual: Pro 15 8 S(A om ⲛ.) δ. παρά, *ib* 11 20 SA(B ⲛⲧⲉⲛ-) προσδ. dat; Ep 106 S lifting of your hands ⲉⲧϣ. ⲛⲛⲁϩⲣⲛⲡⲛⲟ̅ⲥ̅.

—— ϩⲁ-, ϧⲁ-SBF, *for* price of: Si 20 10 S, 1 Cor 6 20 SBF ⲁⲅ. gen; Is 43 24 SB ⲕⲧ. gen; BHom 18 S ὠν.; Is 55 2 SB τιμᾶν gen; ROC 20 53 S ⲧⲣⲟⲫⲏ...ϣⲟⲡⲉ ϩⲁⲣⲟⲙⲛⲧ, BM 1147 S ϣ. ⲟⲩⲣⲟϫⲧⲉ ϩⲁ ⲩ̄ ⲁϳ; as adj: Lev 22 11 S ⲯⲩⲭⲏ ⲛϣ. ϩⲁⲣⲟⲙⲛⲧ (B ϣ. vb) ἔγκτητος; J 82 16 S ϭⲁϭⲟⲡ ⲛϣ.

ϩⲁⲣ.; ⲉⲃⲟⲗ ϩⲁ- S, *from out*: Gal 3 13 (B ϩⲁ-, var ⲉⲃⲟⲗ ϩⲉⲛ-) ἐξαγ. ἐκ.

—— ϩⲛ·, ϧⲉⲛ-S, *buy with*: BHom 101 ⲁϥϣ. ⲙ̄ⲡⲕⲟⲥⲙⲟⲥ ϩⲙⲡⲉϥⲥⲛⲟϥ, Lant 102 vo ⲁϥϣ. ⲙ̄ⲡⲓⲭⲱⲙⲉ ϩⲙⲡⲉⲧⲛⲧⲁϥ; in B: TThe 262 to Virgin ⲁⲣⲉϣ. ϧⲉⲛⲧⲉⲛⲉϩⲓ *conceive*.

—— ϩⲓⲧⲛ- S, *from*: BM 447 12 ⲕⲧⲏⲙⲁ...ⲛ̄ⲧⲁⲕϣⲟⲡϥ ϩⲓⲧⲟⲟⲧ, v also ⲉⲃ̄ⲧⲛ-; ⲉⲃⲟⲗ ϩ.: Ge 25 10 (B ⲛ̄ⲧⲉⲛ-) ⲕⲧ. παρά.

With following adverb. ⲥ ⲉⲃⲟⲗ B: Ez 43 27 (H Cons 307, var diff) προσδ.; Dif 2 93 suffering ⲉⲧⲁⲩϣⲟⲡⲟⲩ ⲉⲃⲟⲗ; ⲥ ⲉϧⲟⲩⲛ, ⲉϧ., *accept*: AM 268 B δ.; 1 Kg 25 35 S αἱρετίζειν; Ro 11 15 S ⲡⲉⲩϣⲟⲡⲟⲩ ⲉⲣ. (B ⲙ̄ⲙⲓ ⲉϧ.) πρόσλημψις; ShBM 202 184 S fruit ϣ.† ⲉⲣ. opp ⲧⲥⲧⲏⲩ ⲉⲃⲟⲗ, BMOr 8811 230 S ϩⲉⲗⲡⲓⲥ...ϣ.† ⲉⲣ. ⲙ̄ⲡⲉⲭ̄ⲥ̄; ⲉⲣ. ⲉ-: Lu 16 9 SB δ. εἰς; ⲥ ⲙ̄ⲙⲁⲩ B, *take away*: Jo 11 39 (S ϥⲓ F ⲗⲁ) αἴρειν; C 43 176 ϯⲡⲁϣ. ⲙ̄ϥⲁⲓ ⲙ. (cf ⲙⲁⲩ b).

ⲡ ⲥ A²B, *receiver*: Mani 1 A² ⲛⲓϣⲁⲛϭⲕⲟ, BSM 50 ⲁ·ⲕⲏⲡ ⲡϣⲉⲡⲉⲛⲏⲟⲩ ⲡϣⲁⲛϩⲙⲟⲧ ⲛ̄ⲧⲟⲧϥ ⲙ̄ⲫ̄ϯ = B Mis 400 S ϫⲓⲧⲏⲩⲧⲛ (sic prob, var ⲙ̄ⲙⲱⲧⲛ) ⲡⲉⲙⲟⲧ = Va 63 19 B ϭⲓ ⲙⲡⲉⲧⲉⲛⲣ.; ⲙⲉⲧϣⲁⲡ-: Ac 28 7 ⲙ. ϣⲉⲙⲙⲟ(var ϣⲉⲡ-, S ⲙⲁⲓϣ.)φιλοφρόνως; MG 25 125 ⲙⲉⲧϣⲁⲡϣⲱϣ *suffering contempt*.

—— nn m SB, *acceptance*: 1 Tim 1 15 B(S ⲧⲁⲓⲟ) ἀποδοχή; Ps 107 8 S ⲡϣ. ⲉⲣⲟϥ (B ⲁⲙⲁϩⲓ) ἀντίλημψις; *purchase*: Si 27 2 S ἀγορασμός; Jer 39 11 B (S ϯ ⲉⲃⲟⲗ) κτῆσις; BM 288 S ⲟⲩϣ. ⲙ̄ⲡⲟⲩϯ ⲉⲃⲟⲗ; ϯ ϩⲁ-: Ge 17 12 B ⲡϣ. ϧⲁⲣⲁⲧ, Jth 4 10 S ϣ. ϩⲁ ⲣⲟⲙⲡⲧ ἀργυρώνητος; ST 201 S ϩⲛⲟⲩϣⲱⲡ ϩⲙⲟⲧ.

ⲁⲧϣⲱⲡ, ϣⲟⲡϥ SB, *uncontainable, illimitable*: Cai Euch 485 B ⲁⲧϣⲟⲡϥ ἀχώρητος; BMis 144 S whose womb ϣⲱⲡ ⲉⲣⲟⲥ ⲙ̄ⲡⲉⲓⲁⲧϣⲟⲡϥ, Va 58 127 B benevolence ⲛⲁⲧϣⲟⲡⲥ, AM 239 B ⲛⲁⲧϣ. ⲉⲣⲱⲟⲩ ⲛ̄ⲛⲓϩⲱⲣⲉⲁ *that accept not*.

ⲣⲉϥϣ. SAB, *receiver*, ⲥ ⲉ-: Jth 9 11 S, Ps 41 9 S(B ⲡⲁϣϯ), ib 58 16 SB, ib 88 26 S(B ⲣⲉϥϯ ⲧⲟⲧϥ) ἀντιλήπτωρ; PS 139 S ⲡⲁⲣⲉϥϣⲟⲡ ⲉⲣⲟⲕ, TU 43 8 A sim, Mus 42 233 S body became ⲣⲉϥϣ. ⲉⲣⲟϥ ⲙ̄ⲡⲗⲟⲅⲟⲥ, C 43 205 B ⲣⲉϥϣ. ⲉⲣⲟϥ ⲛ̄ⲛⲓⲣⲉϥⲉⲣ ⲛⲟⲃⲓ; ⲙⲉⲧⲣ. B: CaiEuch 515 ⲟⲩⲙⲉⲧⲣⲉϥϣ. ⲉⲣⲟⲕ ⲛ̄ⲛⲓⲟⲣⲫⲁⲛⲟⲥ βοήθεια.

ϭⲓⲛ-, ϫⲓⲛϣ. SB, *receiving, acceptance*, ⲥ ⲉ-: Ps 21 20 B(S vb) ἀντίλημψις; P 129²⁰ 121 S ⲟⲩϭ. ⲉⲣⲟⲛ ⲙ̄ⲡⲉⲕⲛ̄ⲡⲁ through Jesus, ib 129¹⁴ 74 S ⲧϭ. ⲉⲣⲟϥ ⲡⲉϥⲧⲩⲭⲏⲥ, AM 222 B ⲡϫ. ⲡⲣⲁⲡⲕⲉⲃⲁⲥⲁⲡⲟⲥ ⲉⲣⲟϥ.

ϣⲟⲡⲥ SB, ϣⲁ. F nn f, *reception, entertainment*: Ge 21 8 SB, Lu 5 29 SB δοχή; Va 57 160 B jars ϩⲁⲡϣ. ⲛ̄ⲧⲉ ⲟⲩⲏⲣⲡ δοχεῖον; Ge 19 3 S(B ⲥⲱ) πότος; Tri 434 S ضيافة; BMis 273 S ⲉⲓⲣⲉ ⲛⲟⲩⲛⲟϭ ⲛϣ. ⲉⲣⲟϥ = Mor 30 49 F, TstAb 165 B ⲓⲣⲓ ⲛ̄ϯϣ. ⲉⲣⲱⲟⲩ, PSBA 30 277 S ⲟⲩϣ. ⲉⲩⲛⲁⲁⲁⲥ, P 130⁵ 121 S ϩⲉⲛⲁⲣⲓⲥⲧⲟⲛ ⲙ̄ⲡⲣⲉⲛϣ.

ϣⲱⲡⲉ S nn, *seizing, impressing*: JSch 6 30 (cf ⲡⲉⲉϥ) fine ϩⲁⲙ. ⲙ̄ⲡⲉⲉϥ.

Cf ϣⲟⲡϣⲡ.

V also ⲗⲟⲕ, ⲙⲕⲁϩ, ⲡⲟⲩⲡⲉ, ⲥⲱϣ *be despised* (ϣⲁⲡ ϣⲱϣ), ⲧⲱⲣⲉ *hand*, ⲱⲡ, ϩⲟ (ϩⲣⲁ⸗), ϩⲙⲟⲧ, ϩⲓⲥⲉ, ϩⲏⲧ.

ϣⲱⲡ S nn m, *a metal object, mostly of silver, necklet, bracelet* (Strzygowski *Kopt Kunst* 7022, cf ? šbj Berl *Wörterb* 4 438, also Spg *Petub* 3 23 špe n ḥt): J 34 3 ⲡⲁϣ. ⲛ̄ϩⲁⲧ sold, ib 66 39 ϣⲟⲙⲛⲧ ⲛϣ. ⲛⲏⲣⲧ & 3 chains bequeathed (= ib 76 42), Ep 545 ⲟⲩϣ. ⲛ̄ϩⲁⲧ ⲛⲥⲛⲁⲩ ⲡⲣⲟⲗⲟⲕ, ST 439 ⲡⲟϭ[ⲉ ⲛ]ϣ. ⲛϩ., Ostr Chicago 29 1930 ⲟⲩϣ. ⲛ̄ⲡⲟ(ⲩ)ⲃ, CO 477 among metal objects ⲟⲩϣ. ⲉϥϩ[...]ϥ.

ϣⲱⲡ SB(once), -ⲡⲉ A², -ⲡⲓ F only in ϣ(ⲉ)ⲡ S A²F, ϣⲡⲉ SB ⲛϣⲱⲡ, *moment, instant*, ⲥ ϩⲛⲟⲩ-, *suddenly*: 1 Cor 15 52 ϣⲡⲉ (B ⲥⲟⲩⲥⲟⲩ) ἐν ἀτόμῳ; Sa 18 12 πρὸς μίαν ῥοπήν; Z 341 bring news ϩⲛⲟⲩϣⲡⲉ ⲛϣ. ὀξέως; Wess 11 168 fear ϣⲱⲡⲉ ϩⲛⲟⲩϣ. ἄφνω; Pro 13 23 S (var ⲛ̄ⲧⲉⲩⲛⲟⲩ, A ϩⲛⲟⲩϭⲉⲡⲉ, B ϧⲉⲛⲟⲩϣⲱⲧ ⲉⲃⲟⲗ) συντόμως; R 2 4 61 ϩⲛⲟⲩϣⲥⲡⲉ ...ϩⲛⲟⲩϣ., Miss 8 255 ϩⲛⲟⲩϣ. ⲁⲡⲉϥϩⲁⲗ ⲉⲣ ⲫⲗⲉⲕⲙⲁ, J 66 8 lest ϩⲛⲟⲩϣ. death befall me, Mani H 10 A² ⲡⲏⲩ ϩⲛⲟⲩϣ., Mor 30 44 F ϩⲛⲟⲩϣ. ϫⲉ ⲛϣ. = BMis 269 S ϩⲛⲟⲩϣⲥⲡⲉ, Dif 1 61 B sat up ϧⲉⲛⲟⲩϣ.; as adj: PS 277 ⲟⲩⲙⲟⲩ ⲛϣ.; alone only DM 2 6 ⲡ ⲛⲧⲉ ⲡ-ϣⲱⲡ (this word?).

ϣⲱⲡ B v ϣⲱⲃ B *shave*.

ϣⲓⲡⲁ S nn, *a land measure*: BM 447 8 ⲡⲉⲕⲧⲏⲙⲁ...ⲉⲧⲉⲛⲁⲓⲛⲉ ⲙ̄ⲛ̄ⲧⲥⲁϣϥ ⲛϣⲓⲡ[ⲁ, ib 448 8 ⲡⲉⲓϣⲓⲡⲁ in sale of ⲕⲧⲏⲙⲁ. Nubian?

ϣⲓⲡⲉ SAA²O, -ⲡⲓ BF vb **I** intr, *be ashamed*: Ge 2 25 B, Is 33 9 B(SF ϫⲓ ϣ.) αἰσχύνεσθαι, Lu 13 17 B(S do) καταισ.; 2 Thes 3 14 SB ἐντρέπεσθαι; PS 232 S ⲙ̄ⲡⲓϯ ⲥⲟ ⲟⲩⲇⲉ ⲙⲡⲓϣ., ShA 1 92 S those so doing ϣ. ⲁⲛ, Miss 4 102 B lest he be exposed ⲛ̄ⲧⲉϥϣ., Va 61 119 B ⲉϥϣ. opp ⲉⲩⲣⲁϣⲓ, PBu 91 S ⲧⲛ̄ϣ. ⲉⲛⲡⲁⲩ ⲉⲛϫⲓⲕⲱⲛ talking nonsense, AM 317 B ⲕⲱϣ. ⲁⲛ ϯⲡⲟⲩ ⲉⲕⲉⲣ ϩⲓⲕ?, Hor 83 O ϣ. (context?).

II tr, *shame, make ashamed*: He 2 11 SBF ἐπαισ., 2 Cor 7 14 B(S ϫⲓ ϣ.), BHom 52 S ϯϣ. ⲛ̄ⲡⲁⲉⲓⲟⲧⲉ καταισ.; C 86 302 B ⲉϥϣ. ⲙ̄ⲡⲓⲇⲓⲁⲃⲟⲗⲟⲥ = BSG 196 S ϯ ϣ.

With following preposition. ⲥ ⲉ-vbal: Su 11 SB, Lu 16 3 SB, BHom 49 S ⲁϥϣ. ⲉⲧⲁⲙⲉ- αⲓσ. ⲥ ⲉⲧⲃⲉ-S, *concerning*: R 1 4 65 ⲉⲧⲉⲧⲛϣ. ⲉ.ⲧϣⲉⲉⲣⲉ ϣⲏⲙ; ⲥ ⲉϫⲛ-, sim: 1 Cor 7 36 SF(B ϭⲓ ϣ.) ἀσχημονεῖν ἐπί; Z 288 S ⲁϥϣ. ⲉ.ⲡⲉⲛⲧⲁϥⲥⲟⲧⲙⲟⲩ ⲉⲛⲧ. ἐπί; ⲥ ⲛ-, *of, at*: AP 15 A² ⲡⲉϥϣ. ⲙ̄ⲡⲉⲛⲧⲁϥ[ϣⲱⲡⲉ] αⲓσ. acc, C 86 294 B ϣ. ⲛ̄ⲧⲁⲙⲟⲩ αⲓσ. inf, Ro 1 16 S(B ϧⲉⲛ-) ἐπαισ. acc, 2 Tim 1 12 B(S intr) ἐπ. intr; ⲥ ϩⲁ-S,

sim: ShViK 909 ϯϣ. ϩⲁⲡⲁϣⲁⲓ ⲙⲡⲁⲡⲟⲃⲉ; ⲥ ϩⲓ-
S, sim: Si 41 16 ϣ. ϩⲓⲙⲁϣϫⲉ ⲉⲛⲧ. ἐπί; ⲥ ϩⲏⲧⲍ
ⲛ- SA ⲋⲁⲧϩⲏ ⲛ- B(rare), *be ashamed before, revere*:
Job 32 21 (B ϣϥⲓⲧ ⲋ.), Pro 28 21 SA αἰσ. acc, Si
41 17 αἰσ. ἀπό; Mt 21 37 (B do), Lu 18 2 SB ἐντ.
acc; Cl 21 6 A ϣ. ϩⲏⲧⲟⲩ ⲛⲛⲁ⳪ αἰδ. acc; Sa 18 25
ⲉⲓⲕⲉⲓⲛ; Deu 28 50 (B diff) θαυμάζειν acc; ShBM
253 56 have not feared God nor ϣ. ϩⲏⲧⲍ ⲙⲡⲣⲟⲫⲏⲧⲏⲥ, BMis 149 ϣ. ϩⲏⲧⲍ ⲛⲟⲩⲣⲙⲙⲁⲟ, CO 61 ⲙⲁⲧ-
ⲛⲉϣ. ϩⲏⲧⲍ ⲛⲣⲱⲙⲉ, AM 53 B ⲉⲓ ϣ. ⲋⲁⲧϩⲏ ⲛⲛⲓⲙⲏⲏϣ,
Mor 25 71 ⲛⲣⲟ ⲉⲧⲟⲩϣ. ϩⲏⲧⲍ *revered face*, Bor 240*
7 ⲁⲙⲙⲟⲩⲓ ϣ. ϩⲏⲧⲍ; ⲥ ⲋⲁϫⲉⲛ- B sim: Va 66 311
ⲙⲁⲣⲉⲡϣ. ⲋⲁϫⲱⳤ ⲡⲧⲁⲓⲉⲛⲧⲟⲗⲏ αἰδεῖσθαι acc; AM
33 ϯϣ. ⲋⲁϫⲱⳤ ⲛⲧⲉⲕⲙⲉⲧⲛⲓϣϯ.

—— nn m SABF, *shame*: Job 6 20 S(B ϣϥⲓⲧ),
Pro 9 13 SAB, Is 30 3 SB(F ϣⲡⲓⲧ), *ib* 6 SBF, Lu
14 9 SB αἰσχύνη; Lam 1 8 B(F ϣⲱⳡ), Ap 16 15 SB
ἀσχημοσύνη; Eph 5 12 B(S ϣⲗⲟⳡ) αἰσχρός; Ps 43
15 S(B do) ἐντροπή; *ib* 151 7 B(S ⲛⲟⳡⲛⲉⳡ) ὄνειδος;
Job 40 8 S(B do) ἀτιμία; PS 48 S ⲁⲩϣ. ⲣⲱⳃⳡ ⲉⲃⲟⲗ
ⲉϫⲱⲓ, ShBM 198 20 S ϣ. ⲡⲉ ϫⲉ ⲡⲁⲓ, ShA 1 102 S
ⲟⲩϣ. ⲛⲁⲓⲡⲉ ϫⲉⲁⲓⲡⲁⲣⲁⲃⲁ, AM 186 B ⲟⲩϣ. ⲛⲁϥⲡⲉ,
BSM 34 B ⲙⲙⲟⲛ ϣ. ϩⲓϫⲱⲓ, BKU 1 313 S other
things they said ⲡⲁϣ. ⲡⲁⲧⲁⲅⲟⲟⳟ ⲁⲛ, CO 397 S
ⲛⲁⲣⲟ ⲙⲉϩ ⲛϣ. ϫⲉⲁⲓⳡⲁⲓ ϩⲟⲗⲱⳤ; as adj: Ge 34
7 B(S ⲡⲉⳡⲉ-) ἀσχήμων; ShC 73 160 S ϩⲉⲛⲙⲉⳡⲟⳡ
ⲛϣ. ⲡⲟⲩϩⲟⲟⲩⲧ.

ⲁⲧϣ. SAA²B, *unashamed*, nn: Si 23 6 A(S ⲁⲧ-
ϭⲁⲗ), Is 56 11 B(S do) ἀναιδής; El 122 S = 92 A,
AM 298 B; adj: 1 Kg 2 29 S, Pro 7 13 SAB, Bor
253 114 S ⲋⲣⲁⲕⲱⲡ…ⲛⲁ. ⲁⲛ.; ShC 73 157 S ϩⲟ ⲛⲁ.,
DeV 2 37 B ⳤⲣⲓⲙⲓ ⲛⲁ.; ⲙⲛⲧ-, ⲙⲉⲧⲁⲧϣ., *shame-
lessness*: Jer 30 4 S(prob)B ἰταμία; P 44 78 S ⲧⲙ.·
ⲁⲛⲅϫⳡⲉⲛⲧⲓⲁ (ἀναισχυ.); ManiH 48 A² ⲧⲉϥⲙ., C 43
164 B speakest ⲋⲉⲛⲟⲩⲙ., ST 364 S amazed at your
ⲛⲟⳡ ⲙⲙ.; ⲣ ⲁⲧϣ. S: Eccl 8 1 ἀν.; BM 247 8
ϣⲁⲥⲉⲣ ⲁ., ⲁⲧϩⲟⲧⲉ ἀναίσχυντος; BHom 85 ⲟ ⲛⲁ.
ϩⲓⲡⲉϥⲃⲁⲗ.

ⲣⲉϥϣ. in ⲙⲛⲧⲣ. S, *shyness, modesty*: 1 Tim 2 9
(B ⲙⲉⲧⳡⲫⲓⲛⲧ) αἰδώς; BM 301 art filled with ⲉⲛⲓ-
ⲥⲧⲏⲙⲏ ϩⲓⲛ.

ϯ ϣ. SA²BF, *give, put to shame*: 1 Kg 13 4 S αἰσ.
acc (*sic*), Lu 9 26 S(B ϣ. vb) ἐπαισ., Ru 2 16 S, 1 Cor
11 4 SB(var ϯ ϣⲱϣ)καταισ.; *ib* 15 34 SF(B ⲋⲉⲛⲟⲩ-
ϫⲫⲓⲟ) πρὸς ἐντροπήν (λαλεῖν); Pro 28 7 S (var & A
ⲥⲱϣ) ἀτιμάζειν; R 1 5 40 S ϯ. ⲙⲡⲉⲓⲁⲡⲟⲙⲟⳤ, AM
141 B sim, Blake 298 S ⲁϥϯ. ⲛⲧⲉⳤⳤⲓⲙⲉ ⲙⲡⲉϥⲉⲓⲱⲧ
(Ge 35 21), Mani 1 A² ϯ. ⲛⲉⳤ; ⲣⲉϥϯ ϣ.: Si 22 4
S ⲧⲣ. καταισ.

ϫⲓ, ϭⲓ ϣ. SAA²BF, *take shame, be ashamed*: Ps
69 3 S(B ϣϥⲓⲧ), Pro 1 22 SAB, Is 33 9 SF(B ϣⲓ.)
αἰσ., Ps 118 6 SB ἐπαισ., Jer 27 2 B(F Louvre 10052
ϣⲡⲓⲧ), Mic 3 7 SAB καταισ.; Ps 39 15 B(S ⲟⲩⲱⲗⳤ),

Lev 26 41 S(B ϣϥ.), Is 50 7 SB ἐντ.; Ez 39 26 B
ἀτιμίαν λαμβάνειν; BG 122 S ⲁⲩϫ. ⲧⲏⲣⲟⲩ, Mani 1
A² ⲁϥϫ. ⲛϫⲓ ⲡⲕⲣⲓⲧⲏⲥ, C 43 164 B worship gods lest
ⲛⲧⲉⲕⳡ. ⲋⲉⲛⲡⲓⲙⲁⲗⲁⲧⲓⲟⲛ; ⲥ ⲉ- S: Jud 5 28 αἰσ.
inf; ⲥ ⲉⲧⲃⲉ- S: Ps 68 6 (B ⲉⲩⲣϩⲓ ⲉϫⲉⲛ-) αἰσ.
ἐπί; ⲥ ⲉϫⲛ- : Is 20 5 S(B diff), Zech 9 5 A(B ⲋⲉⲛ-)
αἰσ. ἐπί; 1 Cor 7 36 B(SF ϣ. ⲉϫⲛ-) ἀσχ. ἐπί; Ps 14
3 B(S ⲛⲟⳡⲛⲉⳡ)ὀνειδισμὸν λαμβ. ἐπί; ⲥ ⲛ- Jud 3 25
S (*cf* above ϣ. ⲥ ⲛ-) αἰσ. intr; ethic dat: BM 344
S ϫ. ⲛⲁⲕ, AM 50 B sim; ⲥ ⲛⲛⲁϩⲣⲛ- S: PS 252
archons ⲛⲁϫ. ⲛⲛⲁϩⲣⲏⲧⲛ, ShA 1 410 those contending with sin ⲣⲱϣⲉ ⲉⲧⲣⲉⲛϫ. ⲛⲛⲁϩⲣⲁⳡ; ⲥ ϩⲁ- B:
Jer 3 3 ἀπαναισχυντεῖν πρός; ⲉⲃⲟⲗ ϩⲁ-: Dan 3 44
καταισ. ἀπό; ⲥ ϩⲛ-, ⲋⲉⲛ-: Ex 43 11 B ⲉⲛⲧ. ἀπό;
ShC 42 125 S ⲉⲧⲣⲁϫ. ϩⲙⲡⲉϯϭⲱϣⲧ ⲉⲃⲟⲗ ϩⲏⲧⳡ;
ⲉⲃⲟⲗ ϩⲛ-: Is 1 29 S(B ⲉⳤ.) αⲓⲥ. ἀπό (var ἐπί), Hos
4 19 AB καταισ. ἐκ.

ϣⲡⲓⲛⲧ S, ϣϥⲓⲛϯ B, f ϣⲡⲓⲉⲉⲧⲉ S, *modest person*
(*v* AZ 44 94): Si 35 10 S ⲛⲉϣ. (var ⲛⲉⳡ. = ⲡⲉⲧⳡ.),
ib 41 27 S ϣⲱⲡⲉ ⲛϣ., adj f *ib* 26 15 ⳤⲣⲓⲙⲉ ⲛϣ. all
αἰσχυντηρός; ⲙⲉⲧϣ. B, *modesty*: 1 Tim 2 9 (S
ⲙⲛⲧⲣⲉϥϣⲓⲡⲉ), Va 57 110 αἰδώς; MG 25 356 ⲑⲉⲃⲓⲟ ⲛⲉⲙⲧⲉϥⲙ. (ROC 18 59 ⲗⲁⲁⲙⲗ⳪).

ϣϥⲓⲧ B, ϣⲡⲓⲧ F vb intr (qual), *be ashamed*: Is 24
9 (S ϫⲓ ϣⲓⲡⲉ), Ep Jer 25 F(B ϣⲓ.) αⲓⲥ., MG 25 214
ⲁⲩϣⲉ ⲛⲱⲟⲩ ⲉⲩϣ. καταισ.; *ib* 204 ⲉϥϣ. αⲓⲇ.; Is 16
12 (S do) ⲉⲛⲧ.; C 43 239 ϫⲛⲁϣ. before multitude,
ROC 25 250 ⲉⲧⲁϥϣ. (252 sim ϭⲓ ϣⲓ.); ⲥ ⲉ-: MG
25 232 ⲛⲁϣ.ⲡⲉ ⲉϫⲟⳤ = Z 317 S ϣⲓ. αⲓⲇ. inf; ⲥ
ⲉⲑⲃⲉ-: C 86 357 ⲁϥϣ. ⲉⲑ. ⲛⲓⲙⲏⲏϣ; ⲥ ⲉϫⲉⲛ-: Is
1 29 (S ϫⲓ ϣⲓ.) αⲓⲥ. ἐπί; ⲥ ⲛ-: AM 276 ⲉⲩϣ.
ⲛⲥⲁϫⲓ ὑποστέλλεσθαι inf; ⲥ ⲋⲁⲧϩⲏ-: Bar 4 16 αⲓⲥ.
acc; Ex 10 3, Mt 21 37 (S ϣⲓ. ϩⲏⲧⳟ) ⲉⲛⲧ. acc; ⲥ
ⲋⲁϫⲉⲛ-: Job 19 3 (S do) αⲓⲥ. acc; tr: Mk 8
38 F ⲉⲧⲛⲁϣ. ⲙⲙⲁⲓ (S ϯ ϣⲓ. ⲡⲁⲓ, B diff) ἐπαισ.
acc; nn m, *shame*: Ps 68 20 (S ⲟⲩⲱⲗⳤ), Is 30 3 F
(SB ϣⲓ.) αⲓⲥχύνη; Ps 21 7 (SA Cl ⲛⲟⳡⲛⲉⳡ) ὄνειδος;
ib 108 29 (S ϣⲓ.) ἐντροπή; DeV 2 111 ϯ ⲡⲱⲟⲩ
ⲛⲟⲩϣ. ⲡⲉⲡⲉϩ; ⲁⲧϣ.: Deu 28 50 (S ⲛⲁϣⲧ ϩⲟ)
ἀναιδής; ϯ ϣ.: Ps 68 10 (S ⲛⲟⳡ.) ὀνειδίζειν, *ib* 77
66 (S ϯ ⲛⲟⳡ.) ὄνειδος διδόναι; Mk 1c ἐπαισ.; MG
25 165 ⲉⲩϯ ϣ. ⲛⲁϥ calling him thief; ϭⲓ ϣ.: Ps 39
16 (S ϫⲓ ϣⲓ.) αⲓⲥχύνην κομίζειν; Jer 27 2 F(Louvre
10052, B ϭⲓ ϣⲓ.) καταισ.; Is 45 17 (S ⲟⲩⲱⲗⳤ) ⲉⲛⲧ.
V ϫⲡⲓⲟ.

ϣⲱⲡⲉ SA²O, ϩⲱ.A, ⲓϣⲱⲡⲓ BF, ⲋⲱⲡⲉ(Hor), ⲥⲱⲃⲓ
O, ϣⲟⲟⲛ† SA², ϩⲟ.† A, ϣⲟⲡ† BF(once), ϣⲁⲁⲡ† F vb
intr, *become, befall*: Ge 7 23 S(B ϫⲏ), Ps 68 25 SB,
Is 34 12 SBF, Ap 10 6 SB εἶναι; Ge 1 5 B, Job 1 21
SB, Jer 33 1 SB, Mt 13 22 S(BF diff), MG 25 210
B ⲉⲧⲁⲣⲟⲩϭⲓ ϫⲉ ϣ. γίνεσθαι; Ps 36 10 SB, Hab 3 17
AB, 1 Cor 7 26 BF(S†) ὑπάρχειν; Ge 25 18 B ⲕⲁⲧⲟⲓ-

κεῖν; Cl 4 11 A(sic l), αὐλίζειν; no Gk vb: Ps 6 3 S
ϣⲁⲛⲧⲉⲟⲩ ϣ.? (B ϣⲁⲑⲛⲁⲩ) ἕως πότε, Job 4 17 S
ϣⲁⲣⲉⲟⲩ ϣ. ? (B diff) τί γάρ; ROC 17 400 B ϥⲛ
ⲉⲧⲁⲡϥ. ἀποτέλεσμα; Sa 8 8 S ⲛⲉⲧⲛⲁϣ. μέλλειν;
MG 25 211 B ⲉⲣⲉϣⲱⲣⲡ ⲛⲁϣ. περὶ τ. πρωίαν; PS
27 S ⲣⲱⲃ ⲛⲓⲙ ⲉⲧⲛⲁϣ., Aeg 262 S ⲉⲣϣⲁⲛⲡϣⲁⲭⲉ
ⲡⲧⲕⲁⲑⲏⲥⲓⲥ ϣ., C 43 126 B ⲉⲧⲁ ⲧⲟⲟⲩⲓ ϣ., Ep 156
S ⲁⲡⲉⲛⲧⲁⲕⲭⲟⲟⲩ ⲧⲏⲣⲟⲩ ϣ., BSM 31 S ϥⲟⲩⲱϣ
ⲙϥϯ ⲙⲁⲣⲉϥϣ., CO 376 S ⲉⲣϣⲁⲛⲧⲉⲭⲣⲉⲓⲁ ϣ., El
36 A ϣⲁ]ⲧⲉⲟ ⳋ. ⲉⲕϭⲉⲉⲧ?, AP 27 A² heard ⲡⲉⲛⲧⲁϥϣ., PGM 1 114 O ⲙⲁⲣⲉⲡⲉⲧⲉⲡϭⲟⲙ ⲥⲱⲃⲓ ⲥⲁⲃⲟⲗ
ⲁⲡⲟ ⲧⲟⲩ ⲍ(ⲉⲓⲛⲁ), PLond 4 445 S ⲁⲡⲉⲧⲓⲡⲁ ϣ., Ryl
325 S sim, Tebtunis (v ⲗⲁⲟⲙⲅ) F ⲡⲉⲧⲃⲁⲗ ⲡⲛⲥϯⳋ
ⲉⲃⲟⲗ ⲙⲡⲁⲧⲉϥϣ. *untimely*;   auxil to 2d vb, qual
(mostly): Ge 12 2 SA(Cl)B, Ps 17 23 SB, Is 31 8
SF, Ro 11 25 B(SF diff) ⲉⲓ̈.; Job 22 21 S(B diff),
Eccl 7 18 SF, Is 32 11 SBF γί.; Cai Euch 548 B
ⲁϥϣ. ⲉϥⲟⲓ ⲛⲁⲧⲙⲕⲁⳏ μένειν; Va 57 15 B ϣ. ⲉϥⲭⲟ-
ⲍⲉⳃ ἡττᾶσθαι; Ap 11 8 S ϣ. ⲉⲩⲛⲏⲭ (B ϣ. only)
no Gk; Sh Berl Sitz '29 430 S ϣⲁⲥϣ. ⲉⲥⲟⲏⲗ, BMis
359 S ⲛⲉⲭⲡⲓⲟ ⲡⲧⲁⲛⲁϣ. ⲉⲩϥⲓ ⳋⲁⲣⲟⲟⲩ (var om ϣ.
ⲉⲩ-), BHom 33 S words ϣ. ⲉⲩⲥⲛⲉⳏ, AM 220 B
memory ⲛⲁϣ. ⲉϥⲙⲏⲛ ⲉⲃⲟⲗ;   not qual: Ge 1 6 B,
Is 32 2 B, Mt 5 25 S ⲉⲓ̈.; Lu 7 38 S(var ⲥⲱ) Gk om;
ShA 2 282 S ⲙⲁⲣⲓϣ. ⲉⲧⲉⲧⲛϯ ⳋⲁⲡ ⲉⲣⲟⲓ, Leyd 464
S city ⲛⲁϣ. ⲉⲥϣⲓϣⲉ ⲙⲡⲉⲕⲑⲣⲟⲛⲟⲥ, BM 1035 S
ⲧⲁⲣⲉⲓⲥϣ. (l ⲉⲓϣ.) ⲉⲓⲣⲟⲉⲓⲥ, C 43 126 B ⲁⲩϣ. ⲉⲩⲕⲱϯ
ⲡⲥⲱϥ, El 48 A ⲁⲓⳋ. ⲉⲉⲓⲧⲱⳃⳋ, Mor 30 45 S/ ⲁⲩϣ.
ⲉⲩⲉⲩⲭⲁⲣⲓⲥⲧⲟⲩ.

Impersonal, *befall*, 3d sg f: Ex 4 9 AB, Deu 6
10 SB ⲉⲓ̈.; Nu 5 22 SB, Jer 33 8 SB, Ro 3 4 SB neg
γί.; MG 25 203 B ⲁⲥϣ. συμβαίνειν; PS 13 ⲁⲥϣ. ϭⲉ
ⲙⲡⲛⲥⲁⲡⲁⲓ, ShC 73 69 S ⲉⲥϣⲁⲛϣ. ⳋⲉ ⲡⲧⲉⲡⲉⲥⲏⲛⲩ
&c, Mor 31 179 S ⲡⲡⲉⲥϣ.;   3d sg m: Ps 40 13 S
(B f), Ap 16 17 B(S f) γίν.; Lant 77 (2) S ⳋⲁⲙⲏⲛ
ⲉϥⲉϣ. (mostly here f: ib 4 19, 7 11, or Gk ib 98 29
ⲅⲉⲡⲟⲓⲧⲟ), Hor 81 O ⲁϥϣ. ⲟⲩⲛ ⲥⲟⲩⲛⲟⲩϥⲉ ⲧⲓ ⲡⲉϥ,
ib 84 sim.

Qual, *be, exist*: Ex 3 14 SB, Ps 140 10 S(B ⲭⲏ),
Is 30 13 SF(B diff), ib 31 1 B(SF om), Jo 1 1 S(B
om), *ib* 16 32 A²(S ϭⲉⲉⲧ, B ⲭⲏ), Ap 16 5 SB, Aeg
240 S ⲥⲡⲧⲉ ⲡⳋⲓⲛ ⲉⲧϣ. ⲉⲓ̈.; Jo 10 19 S(B ϣⲱⲡⲓ), Ac
2 43 B(S ϣⲱⲡⲉ) γί.; Ps 103 33 SB ὕπαρ.; Jo 9 41 B
(SA² ⲁⳋⲉ ⲣⲁⲧⳍ) μέν.; 2 Cor 8 12 B(S ⲕⲏ ⲉⳋⲣⲁⲓ)ⲡⲣⲟ-
κεῖσθαι; EstB 6 S, 1 Cor 7 26 SBF ἐνιστάναι; Ro 4
16 B(S Gk om), Ap 22 2 S(B Gk om), BAp 52 S
ⲡⲥⲱϣ ⲉⲧϣ. ⲉⲃⲟⲗ ⳋⲓⲧⲛ- Gk om; PS 9 S ⲛⲉϥϣ. ⳋⲓⲡ-
ⲡϣⲟⲣⲡ, ShC 73 82 S ⲟⲩⲛ ⳋⲉⲛⳋⲃⲏⲩⲉ ϣ. that profit
not, C 100 322 S Adam formed from ⲛⲉⲧⲉⲛⲥⲉϣ. ⲁⲛ,
C 86 20 B sim, Mani 2 A² ϯⲟⲩ ⲡⲓⲱⲧ ⲛⲉⲧϣ.†, J 5 55
S ⲧⲉⳋⲟⲩⲥⲓⲁ ⲉⲧϣ. ⲧⲉⲡⲟⲩ *reigning power*, BSM 67 B
ⲟⲩⲡⲉⲡⲓⲑⲱϣ ⲉⲧϣ. Ⳍⲉⲛⲧⲁⲡⲟⲗⲓⲥ ⲙϥⲟⲟⲩ?
With following preposition.

— ⲉ- SA²BF, *for*: Nu 5 27 S(B diff), Is 4 6 B
(S ⲛ-), Mk 10 8 SB ⲉⲓ̈. ⲉⲓⲥ, Jo 11 4 SA²(B no vb) ⲉⲓ̈.
πρός, Is 40 17 B(S no vb) ⲉⲓ̈. ὡς; Ps 68 22 S(B ⲛ-),
Is 33 2 SBF, Ac 5 36 SB (var ⲛ-) γί. ⲉⲓⲥ, Is 64 10 B
(S ⲉⲓⲣⲉ) γί. no prep; C 43 62 B ⲉⲩⲉϣ. ⲉⲡⲧⲁⲕⲟ, TT
56 S ϣⲁⲣⲉⲟⲩϭⲉ ϣ. ⲉⲣⲟϥ, Mani 2 A² ⲙⲡⲉⲡⲣⲱⳃ ϣ.
ⲁⲡⳋⲧⲉ *at* (right) *time*; vbal: Job 27 5 SB ⲉⲓ̈.; Ac 21
35 SB συμβαί.; ROC 18 37 B ⲉⲥⲉϣ. ⲉⲑⲣⲉⲡⲁⲙⲟⲛⲓ,
Miss 4 703 S ⲁⲡⲧⲱϣ ϣ. ⲉⲧⲣⲉⲛⲣ ⲡⲃⲟⲗ;   ⲉⲣⲟⳋⲛ
ⲉ-: Ap 22 14 S(B ⳋⲓⳋⲉⲛ-) ⲉⲓ̈. ἐπί; Ps 55 5†S(B Ⳍⲁ-)
Gk om, Sh 42 66 S ⲛⲉⲓⲥⲕⲟⲡⲟⲥ...ϣ.† ⲉⲣ. ⲉⲡⲛⲁ, Mus
42 236 S ⲧⲥⲟⲣϭⲥ...ϣ.† ⲉⲣ. ⲉⲣⲟⲛ ⲉⲩⲧⲁⲕⲟ, J 106 113
S donation ϣ. ⲉⲣ. ⲉⲡⲙⲟⲛⲁⲥⲧⲏⲣⲓⲟⲛ, DeV 2 53 B
mercy ⲉⲧϣ.† ⲉⳋ. ⲉⲡⲣⲉⲛⲟⲥ of men.

— ⲉⳋⲛ- SB, *upon*: Ro 2 2 SB ⲉⲓ̈. ἐπί; Ps 32 22
S(B ⳋⲓⳋ.) γί. ἐπί, Lu 19 19 SB γί. ἐπάνω; Ge 15 12
S(B diff) πίπτειν dat; LCyp 20 S God's mercy ϣ.†
ⲉⳋⲛⲥⲁⲣⳍ ⲛⲓⲙ; ⲉⳋⲣⲁⲓ ⲉⳋⲛ-: Ps 89 17 SB ⲉⲓ̈. ἐπί;
Dan 3 97 B ἡγεῖσθαι; BMis 290 S schism ⲛⲧⲁϥϣ.
ⲉⳋ. ⲉⳋⲛⲧⲟⲓⲕⲟⲩⲙⲉⲛⲏ.

— ⲙⲛ-, ⲛⲉⲙ- SABF, *with*: Ps 90 15†S (var
om ϣ., B ⲭⲏ), Mt 12 30 S(B om ϣ.) ⲉⲓ̈. μετά, MG
25 9 B ϣ. ⲛⲉⲙⲡⲭ̅ⲥ̅ ⲉⲓ̈. σύν, Est 6 9 S ⲉⲓ̈. dat; MG
25 2 B ⲛⲁϣ.† ⲡⲉ ⲛⲉⲙⲧⲉϥϣⲱⲡⲓ συνοικεῖν dat; Pro
22 24 SA συναυλίζειν dat; PS 116 S ⲡⲟⲩⲟⲓⲛ ϣ.†
ⲛⲙⲙⲁⲓ, ShC 73 87 S since our first father ϣ.† ⲛⲙⲙⲁⲛ
ⲙⲁⲛ, N&E 39 332 B ⲡⲧⲉⲥⲙⲟⲩ ⲛⲓⲃⲉⲛ ϣ. ⲛⲉⲙⲧⲁⲓ-
ⲭⲱⲣⲁ, CMSS 39 F ⲧⲉⲥϭⲁⲙ ϣⲟⲡ ⲛⲉⲙⲏⲛ;   sexually: Lev 22 12 SB γί. dat, Tob 3 8 S, Su 20 B(S ⲛ-,
cit BHom 51 S ⲙⲛ-)γί. μετά; Deu 21 13 SB, Is 62
5 B(S ⲟⲩⲱⳋ) συνοικ. dat; Ex 22 16 S(B ⲛⲕⲟⲧ) κοιμᾶσθαι μετά; Jud 19 22 S γινώσκειν; Miss 4 245 S
ⲕⲁⲁⲧ ⲧⲁϣ. ⲡⲙⲉ.

— ⲛ- SAB, *a in*: Mt 2 13 S(B ⲙⲙⲁⲩ)ⲉⲓ̈. ἐκεῖ;
MG 25 208 B ϣ. ⲙⲡⲁⲓⲙⲁ μέν. ὧδε; Cai Euch 506
B ⲉⲧϣ.† ⲙⲡⲁⲓⲙⲁ περιεῖναι; Is 23 18†B(S ⲟⲩⲏⳋ)ⲕⲁ-
ⲧⲟⲓⲕ. ἔναντι; BHom 5 S ⲙⲛ ⲙⲉⲧⲁⲡⲟⲓⲁ ϣ.† ⲙⲡⲉⲓⲙⲁ,
El 36 A ⲙⲕⲉⲕⲉ ⳋ.† ⲙⲡⲓⲙⲁ; ⲙⲙⲟⳍ SAA²BF, *to,
in*: Ps 127 2 S(B ⲛ-) ⲉⲓ̈. dat; Eccl 10 14 F(S om ⲙ.)
ⲉⲓ̈.; Ac 12 18 SB γί. nom, Ge 18 12 SB, Deu 5 16 S
(B ⲛ-), Ac 22 6 SB, Cl 1 1 A, R 1 4 70 ⳋⲓⲥⲉ ⲉⲧⲁϣ.
ⲙⲙⲟⲓ γί. dat, Ac 12 11 S(B diff) γί. ἐν, C 89 63 B
ⲥⲱⲓⲧ ⲛⲁϣ. ⲙⲙⲟⲛ γί. κατά (var περί); Si 22 28 S
(var ⲧⲁⳋⲟ), Ac 3 10 SB συμβαί. dat; 1 Kg 20 9 S
ⲡⲛⲉⲡⲁⲓ ϣ. ⲙⲙⲟⲕ μηδαμῶς σοι; PS 48 S ⲁⲛⲁⲓ ϣ.
ⲙⲙⲟⲓ, ShC 42 101 S ⲉⲣϣⲁⲛⲡⲁⲓ ϣ. ⲙⲙⲟⲕ ⲛ ⲡⲁⲙⲁⲕ, ib 73 157 S ⲉⲁⲡⲉⲓϣⲱⲡⲉ ⲧⲁⳋⲟⲟⲩ ⲛ ⲉⲁϥϣ. ⲙ-
ⲙⲟⲟⲩ, BMis 388 S ⲡⲉⳋⲙⲟⲧ ⲛⲧⲁϥϣ. ⲙⲙⲟⲟⲩ (var
ⲧⲁⳋⲟⲟⲩ) = Va 63 14 B ϣ. ⲛⲱⲟⲩ = BSM 41 B 1
ⲛⲱⲟⲩ, J 74 51 S ⲡⲉⲧⲉϣⲁϥϣ. ⲡⲟⲩⲟⲛ ⲛⲓⲙ ϣ. ⲙ-
ⲙⲟⲓ, AP 44 A² ⲁⲧⲙⲧⲣⲉⲛⲛⲉ ϣ. ⲙⲙⲁⲩ, TT 17 S
ⲧⲉⲥⲙⲏ ⲛⲧⲁϥϣ. ⲙⲙⲟⲥ, BAp 107 S ⲁⲥϣ. ⲙⲙⲟⲓ ⲉⲓⲙⲟⲟⲛⲉ = MIE 2 383 B, ROC 7 141 S ⲟⲩ ⲁϥϣ. ⲙ-

ⲙⲟⲕ?; qual: Ge 31 35 *S* (*B* diff) ⲉⲧ. gen, Is 53 2 *A* (Cl, *SB* om ϣ.) ⲉⲧ. dat; Ac 28 9 *B* (var ⲁⲉⲛ-, *S* diff) ἔχ., Job 2 9 *S*(*B* diff) συνέχ. acc; Phil 1 12 *B*(*SF* ⲣ̄ⲛ-) τὰ κατά; PS 20 *S* ⲡⲛⲟϭ ⲛⲟⲩⲟⲉⲓⲛ ⲉⲧϣ. ⲙⲙⲟⲓ, ShViK 9040 172 *S* ⲧⲓⲧⲁⲗⲉ ⲣⲱⲙⲉ ⲝⲉϥϣ. (*sc* sickness) ⲙⲙⲟⲟⲩ, C 86 220 *B* ⲙⲙⲟⲛ ⲣ̄ⲗⲓ ⲛⲧⲁⲕⲟ ϣ. ⲙⲙⲟϥ; ⲙⲙⲟϥ adverbial (*cf c* ⲙⲙⲁⲩ): ShRyl 68 269 *S* questioned them as to ⲡⲉⲛⲧⲁⲩϣ. ⲙⲙⲟϥ (Lu 24 17), BAp 17 *S* things ⲛⲧⲁⲩϣ. ⲙⲙⲟϥ, Tst Ab 253 *B* ⲡⲓⲙⲁ ⲉⲧⲉϥⲣⲓⲙⲓ ϣ. ⲙⲙⲟϥ, ShC 73 99 *S* cannot bear ⲡⲉⲥⲧⲟⲓ ⲙⲡⲉⲧϣ.† ⲙⲙⲟϥ.

b dat *SAA²BFO*: Ge 18 14 *SB*, Is 30 3 *SBF*, Cl 2 4† *A* ⲉⲧ. dat, Sa 11 22 *S* παρεῖ. dat; Ge 32 5 *SB*, Ps 44 16 *SB*, Eccl 2 7 *SF* γί. dat, Ap 11 15 *B* (*S* ⲉⲓⲣⲉ) γί. gen, Su 20 *S*(*B* ⲛⲉⲙ-) γί. μετά sexually; Joel 1 18† *AB*, Ac 3 6† *SB* ὑπάρχ. dat; Jo 8 41 *SA*⁹(*B* diff), MG 25 215 *B* ⲟⲩ ⲡⲉⲧϣ.† ⲛⲧⲁⲓⲁⲉⲗ- ⲗⲱ? ἔχ.; Jud 20 9 *S* ποιεῖσθαι dat; ROC 17 405 *B* ⲡⲡⲉⲣⲱⲃ...ϣ. ⲡⲥⲁⲣⲣⲁ πάσχειν; Ex 2 2 *A* ⲁⲥϣ. ⲡⲉϥ (*B* Gk om) Cant 6 2 *S*(*F* Gk om), Sa 3 9 *S*(Gk om); PS 113 *S* ⲙⲡⲣⲧⲣⲉϥϣ. ⲡⲁⲩ, *ib* 132 *S* ⲡⲁⲓ...ⲁⲩϣ. ⲛ- ⲧⲡⲓⲥⲧⲓⲥ ⲥⲟⲫⲓⲁ, ShC 73 26 *S* ⲉⲧⲣⲉϥⲉⲛϣⲏⲣⲉ ϣ. ⲡⲁϥ, El 82 *A* ⲙⲛ ϣⲏⲣⲉ ⲣ̄.† ⲛⲉⲛ, Hor 80 *O* sim ⲁ. ⲛⲏϥ, BMis 441 *S* ⲧⲣⲟⲫⲏ ϣ.† ⲡⲁⲡ ⲉⲃⲟⲗ ⲟⲛⲡⲉⲓⲃⲛⲛⲉ, DeV 2 193 *B* ⲟⲩⲛⲓϣϯ ⲛⲡⲁⲣϯ ϣ.† ⲡⲁϥ, BM 651 *F* ⲕⲁⲛⲉ ⲡⲓⲙ ⲉⲧϣ.† ⲡⲉⲕ; + ⲉ-, *for, as*: Ge 1 29 *B* ⲉⲧ. dat ⲉⲓⲥ; Ps 30 2 *S*(*B* dat ⲛ-), Sa 2 14 *S*(*B* do) γί. dat ⲉⲓⲥ; Phil 1 19 *SBF* ἀποβαί. dat ⲉⲓⲥ; ShC 73 29 *S* ϣ. ⲡⲁⲩ ⲉϥⲉⲛϣⲏⲣⲉ; + ⲛ- sim: Lev 26 12 *SB* ⲉⲧ. dat, Is 8 13 *S*(*B* dat ⲉ-), Lu 14 27 *S*(*B* om) ⲉⲧ. gen; Ps 17 18 *SB* γί. gen, *ib* 93 22 *S*(*B* dat ⲉ-) γί. dat ⲉⲓⲥ, Is 50 7 *SB* γί. dat; Ps 21 2 *S*(*B* do) Gk om; PS 128 *S* ⲡⲧⲟⲥ ⲧⲉⲧϣ.† ⲡⲁⲕ ⲡⲥⲱⲙⲁ, El 68 *A* ⲉϥϣ., ⲛⲏⲧⲛⲉ ⲡⲓⲱⲧ, AP 15 *A*² ⲡⲉⲥϣ.† ⲡⲉⲥ ⲡⲥⲁⲗⲥⲗ, C 43 84 *B* ⲁⲕϣ. ⲛⲏⲓ ⲙⲙⲉⲡⲣⲓⲧ.

c + predicate (Stern 496): Job 3 7 *S*(*B* diff), Ps 62 10 *SB* ⲉⲧ., Is 35 7 *B*(*SF* ⲉⲓⲣⲉ) ⲉⲧ. ⲉⲓⲥ; Ex 4 4 *A* (*B* ⲓⲣⲓ), Ps 88 41 *SB*, Lu 6 16 *SB*, Cl 5 6 *A* γί.; Ro 5 19 *SB* καθιστάναι; CaiEuch 467 *B* ϣ.† ⲙⲙⲁ ⲡ- ⲧⲟⲩⲃⲟ ὑπάρχ.; PS 84 *S* ⲁⲧⲉⲧⲛ̄ϣ. ⲡⲡⲟⲉⲣⲟⲥ, ShC 73 38 *S* ϣ. ⲛ̄ϫⲱⲱⲣⲉ (*ib* p ϫ.), C 43 4 *B* sim, Kr 50 *S* ⲧⲓϣ.† ⲡⲣⲉⲧ(ⲟⲓ)ⲙⲟⲥ (*ib* 7 ϣ. ⲣⲉⲧ., *cf ib* 20 ⲟ ⲣⲣⲉⲧ.), *ib* 160 *S* ⲡⲉⲛⲧⲁⲩϣ. ⲛ̄ⲇⲓⲁⲕ[ⲟⲛⲟⲥ (*cf* γενόμενος διάκ. Ryl 141 n & ἀποπρεσβύτερος RChamp 372), Hor 79 *O* ⲁϥϣ....ⲛⲥⲟⲩ ⲛ̄ϫⲁⲕⲉ. *V* also + ⲛ- above. Predic without ⲛ-: Jos 19 18 *S* γί.

—— ⲟⲩⲃⲉ- *SB, toward*: Eph 6 12 *SB* ⲉⲧ πρός; Pro 6 6 *B*(*SA* ⲃⲱⲕ ϣⲁ-) ἰέναι πρός; Ez 5 8 *S*(*B* ϯ ⲟⲩ.) ἐπί no vb.

—— ⲟⲩⲧⲉ- *SBA²*, *betwixt*: Ac 23 7 *B*(*S* ⲣ̄ⲛ- ⲙⲡ-) γί. gen καί, 2 Kg 21 15 *S* γί. dat μετά; BG 89 *S* ⲇⲓⲁ- ⲫⲟⲣⲁ ⲥϣ.† ⲟⲩⲧⲱⲟⲩ, Mani 2 *A*³ ⲡⲓⲁⲥⲡⲁⲥⲙⲟⲥ ϣ.† ⲟⲩⲧⲱ[ⲟⲩ ⲙ]ⲡⲣⲣⲱⲙⲉ.

—— ϣⲁ- *SA²BF, to, till*: Ps 80 15 *SB*, Is 30 8 *SBF* ⲉⲧ. ⲉⲓⲥ; Ge 15 1 *S*(*B* ⲣⲁ-) γί. πρός; Ps 88 36 *SB*, Is 14 20 *SB* μέν. ⲉⲓⲥ; Ac 10 15 *S*(*B* do)π. no vb; Miss 8 8 *S* ⲁⲡⲟⲅⲱ (*sic l*) ϣ. ϣⲁⲡⲉⲩⲥⲉⲃⲏⲥ ⲡⲣⲣⲟ, Wess 15 126 *S* ⲙⲡⲉⲡϣⲁϫⲉ ϣ. ϣⲁⲥⲟⲧⲙⲥ ⲙⲙⲁⲧⲉ *scarce was word heard* ere &c (*v* p 542 *b*), ManiH 5 *A*² ϯϣ.† ⲉⲛ ϣⲁⲣⲁⲕ ⲣ̄ⲛⲟⲩⲡⲉⲥⲉ.

—— ⲣⲁ- *SF*, ⲁ- *B, under*: Deu 33 3† *S*(*B* ⲭ̄ⲏ ⲁ-) ⲉⲧ. ὑπό; Ro 3 19 *SB* γί. ὑπό(δικος); Eccl 1 10 *SF* γί. ἀπὸ ἔμπροσθεν; Lu 7 8 *S*(*B* = Gk) τάσ- σεσθαι ὑπό; Job 19 20 *S*(*B* diff) ἔχεσθαι ἐν; PS 350 *S* ⲥⲉϣ.† ⲣⲁⲡⲡⲟⲃⲉ, ViK 9816 *S* if he speak ϣⲁϥϣ. ⲣⲁⲁⲣⲓⲕⲉ, RNC 77 *S* ⲉϥϣ.† ⲣⲁⲃⲁⲥⲁⲛⲟⲥ, De V 2 22 *B* ⲡⲏ ⲉⲑⲛⲁϣ. ⲁⲡⲓⲥⲙⲟⲩ, Ep 200 *S* ϣ. ⲣⲁⲟⲩⲛⲟϭ ⲛ̄- ⲕⲓⲡⲁⲅⲛⲟⲥ, Cai The 203 *B* ⲡⲓⲁⲧⲥⲛⲟⲩ ⲁϥϣ. ⲁⲟⲩ- ⲭⲣⲟⲛⲟⲥ.

—— ⲣⲁ- *B, to*: Ge 3 16 (*S* diff), Jer 25 1 (*S* ϣⲁ-), MG 25 344 ⲁⲥϣ. ⲣⲁⲣⲱⲟⲩ ⲡⲭⲉ ⲟⲩⲥⲙⲏ = Z 316 *S* ϣⲁ- γί. πρός; Ge 4 7 (*ACl* diff) Gk om.

—— ⲣⲓ- *S* (rare) *B, on, in*: Ac 4 22 *B*(*S* ⲉⲣ̄ⲣⲁⲓ ⲉϫⲛ-) γί. ἐπί; Jer 9 12 *B* διοδεύειν; MG 25 2 *B* ϣ. ⲣⲓⲡϣⲁϫⲉ διαγωγὴ ἐν; P 129¹⁴ 110 *S* kings ⲛⲧⲁⲩϣ. ⲣⲓⲱⲱϥ *in his time*, *ib* 131⁵ 85 *S* ⲁⲅⲁϣⲏ ⲡⲣⲙⲙⲁⲟ ϣ. ⲣⲓⲱⲧ sim. *Cf* next.

—— ⲣⲛ-, ⲁⲉⲛ- *SAA²BF*, ⲣⲓ-*F, in*: Jud 18 31† *S*, Ps 62 tit *S*(*B* ⲣ̄ⲓ-), Ro 12 3† *B*(*SF* om), Cl 20 11 *A* ⲉⲧ. ἐν; Deu 17 9 *S*(*B* ⲛ-),γί. ἐν; Is 30 19 *B*(*SF* ⲟⲩⲛ- ⲱⲣ), 1 Cor 3 16† *BF*(*S* do) οἰκ. ἐν, Lev 26 32† *B*(*S* do) ἐνοικ. ἐν; Mk 5 3† *S*(*B* diff) κατοικ. ἐν; Jo 15 10 *A*²⁺*B*(*S* ϭⲉⲉⲧ) μέν. ἐν, 1 Cor 16 8 *B*(*S* do) ἐπιμ. ἐν; Mic 5 4 *AB*, Phil 2 6† *B*(*S* om) ὑπαρχ. ἐν; Ps 7 5 *SB* κατασκηνοῦν εἰς; Lu 21 37 *S*(*B* ⲙⲟⲧⲉⲛ) αὐλίζειν εἰς; Job 3 24† *S*(*B* diff), Mt 4 24† *S*(*B* diff) συνέχεσθαι dat; ROC 17 403 *B* ⲁⲣⲉⲧⲉⲛϣ. ⲁⲉⲛⲁϣ ⲡⲥⲙⲟⲧ? τι πεπόνθατε; Is 36 1 *SBF* gen no vb, Gk om Ps 1 2† *SB*, Mt 5 15† *SB*, Ap 21 8 *SB*; PS 5 *S* ⲁⲩϣ. ⲣ̄ⲛⲟⲩ- ⲡⲟϭ ⲡⲣⲟⲧⲉ, *ib* 11 *S* ⲧϭⲟⲙ ⲉⲧϣ.† ⲣ̄ⲛⲧⲏⲩⲧⲛ, El 36 *A* souls ⲣ̄.† ⲣ̄ⲛϯⲕⲟⲗⲁⲥⲓⲥ, ManiH 3 *A*² ⲡⲉⲧϣ.† ⲣ̄ⲛⲡⲥⲱ- ⲙⲁ, Mor 40 30 *S* ⲧⲉⲧⲛ(ⲡ)ⲁϣ. ⲣ̄ⲛⲡⲧⲁⲕⲟ (var *ib* 39 41 ⲉⲡⲧ.), TstAb 173 *B* ⲉⲣⲉϣ.† ⲁⲉⲛⲟⲅⲟⲩⲙⲁ ⲡⲉⲙⲟⲩ- ⲥⲱ, KroppC 3 *F* places ⲉⲕϣ.† ⲉⲡⲣⲏⲧⲟⲩ, BM 580 *F* ⲉⲓϣ.† ⲣ̄ⲓⲟⲩⲛⲁϫ ⲉⲭⲟⲩⲗⲏ (χολή); ⲣⲣⲁⲓ ⲣ̄ⲛ-: Ps 15 3† *S*(*B* ⲛ̄ⲣ̄ⲏⲓ ⲛ-) Gk om, El 52 *A* no falsehood ⲣ̄.† ⲣ̄ⲣⲏⲓ ⲛⲣ̄ⲏⲧⲟⲩ.

—— ⲣⲁⲣⲛ- *S, under, in*: ShR 2 3 54 ϣ. ⲣⲁⲣⲱϥ ⲙⲡϥⲓⲧ.

—— ⲣⲁⲧⲛ-, ⲁⲁⲧⲉⲛ-*SB, under, with*: Jo 1 39 *SB* μέν. παρά; Is 21 12 *B*(*S* ⲟⲩⲱⲣ) οἰκεῖν π.; Nu 2 18 *S* (*B* ⲥⲁⲡⲥⲁ ⲛ-) π. no vb; Jos 7 2† *S* ⲉⲧ. κατά; 1 Kg 21 8† *S*(var ⲣⲁⲣⲧⲛ-)ὑπὸ τ. χεῖρα; CA 112 *S* church's goods ⲡⲁϣ. ⲣⲁⲧⲟⲟⲩⲧ ⲙⲡⲟⲓⲕⲟⲛⲟⲙⲟⲥ, BHom 116 *S* Adam because of sin ϣ. ⲣⲁⲧⲟⲟⲧϥ ⲙⲡⲙⲟⲩ(*cf c* ⲣⲁ-),

Z 585 *S* many women ϣ. ⲅ. ⲙⲡⲅⲑⲁⲅⲟⲣⲓⲟⲥ, MG 25
10 *B* disciples ⲁⲩϣ. ⲉⲁⲧⲟⲧϥ.

—— ⲅⲓⲧⲛ- *SBF*, *through, by*: 2 Cor 3 11 *S*(*B*
ⲉⲃⲟⲗ ⲅ.) no vb; PS 10 *S* ⲁⲥϣ. ⲅ.ⲧⲕⲉⲗⲉⲩⲥⲓⲥ, Z 282
S ⲛⲧⲁⲩϣ. ⲅ.ⲡⲉⲛⲉⲓⲱⲧ, Leyd 441 *S* ⲉⲛⲉⲣⲅⲓⲁ…ϣⲁⲅⲓϣ.
ⲅ.ⲡⲉⲣⲱⲙⲉ, BSM 66 *B* ϣⲫⲏⲣⲓ ⲉⲧⲁⲥϣ. ⲅ.ⲧⲭⲟⲙ ⲙ-
ⲫϯ, Ryl 157 *S* ⲛⲧⲁⲧⲓⲁⲥⲫⲁⲗⲓⲁ ϣ. ⲅⲓⲧⲟⲟⲧ, ST 48 *S*
sim; ⲉⲃⲟⲗ ⲅ.: Is 8 18 *SB* ⲉⲓ̂. παρά; Ac 2 43 *SB*
ⲅⲓ̂. διά; Ps 117 23 *SB*, Mt 18 19 *S*(*B* ⲡⲧⲉⲛ-)ⲅⲓ̂. π.;
Ep Jer 47 *BF* κατασκευάζειν ὑπό; BMis 160 *S* πα-
ράβασις ϣ. ⲉⲃ̄. ⲅ. ⲧⲉⲥϩⲓⲙⲉ = BSM 69 *B*, MR 1 111
F ⲡⲟⲩϫⲉⲓ…ϣ.† ⲉⲃ̄. ⲅⲓⲧⲁⲁⲧⲕ.

—— ⲅⲓϫⲛ- *SB*, *upon*: Ez 3 14 *B* ⲅⲓ̂. ἐπί; Is 35 10 *B*
(*SFGk* om vb), Ge 43 16† *S*(*B* ⲭ̄ⲏ) Gk do; PS 132
S ⲡⲉⲧϣ.† ⲅ.ⲡϣⲱ, CO 58 *S* ⲡⲉⲩⲕⲣⲓⲙⲁ ⲡⲁϣ. ⲅⲓⲭⲱⲕ.
With following adverb.

—— ⲙⲙⲁⲩ *SAA²BF*, *there*: Is 35 7 *SBF* ⲉⲓ̂.
ἐκεῖ; Ps 86 4 *SB*. ⲅⲓ̂. ἐκ.; Is 13 21 *B*(*S* ⲟⲩⲱⲅ) κατοικ. ἐκ.; Jo 11 54 *SAA²B* μέν. ἐκ.; Ac 12 19 *SB*
διατρίβειν; PS 204 *S* ⲡⲙⲁ ⲉⲧⲙⲙⲁⲩ…ϥⲛⲁϣ. ⲙ.,
ShC 73 4 *S* ⲥⲉⲡⲁϣ. ⲉⲅⲟⲩⲟⲓ ⲡⲁⲩ ⲙ., PO 11 318 *B*
go to desert ϣ. ⲛⲱⲧⲉⲛ ⲙ. *Cf* c ⲛ-, *in s f*.

—— ⲛⲛ m, *being*: Phil 1 24 *B*(*SF* ⲥ̄ⲱ) ἐπιμένειν;
K 258 *B* ⲡⲓϣ. بقي; Br 125 *S* ⲡⲉⲓϣ. ⲙⲁⲅⲁⲁϥ (*sc*
God), ROC 25 241 *B* ⲡⲓϣ. ⲅⲓⲡⲓϣⲁϥⲉ.

ⲁⲧϣ. *SB*, *not being, undwelt in*: Hos 13 5 *B*(*A*
ⲟⲩⲱⲅ), Pro 8 26 *B* ⲙⲁ ⲡⲁ. (*SA* diff) ἀοίκητος; ShC
73 11 *S* ⲟⲩⲁ. ⲡⲉ ⲉⲧⲣⲉϥϫⲓ ⲉⲃⲟⲗ; ⲙⲛⲧⲁ. *S*, *nothingness*: R 1 5 19 ⲁϥϣⲱⲡⲉ ⲁⲛ ⲅ̄ⲛⲟⲩⲁ.

ⲙⲁ ⲛϣ. *SAA²BF*, *dwelling place*: Deu 11 20 *S*
(var ⲙⲁ ⲛⲟⲩⲱⲅ, *B* ⲏⲓ) οἶκος, Nu 31 10 *SB* οἰκία,
Lev 23 3 *SB*, Zeph 2 5 *SA* ⲙⲁ ⲅ. *B*, Ac 17 26 *S*(*B*
ϫⲓⲛⲏϣ.) κατοικία, 3 Kg 8 43 *SB*, Nah 2 12 *AB*, Ap
18 2 *SB* -κτήριον, Jer 30 5 *SB* πάροικος, Ps 54 15 *S*
(*B* ⲙⲁ ⲛϫⲱⲓⲗⲓ)-οικία; Job 5 24 *SA* (Cl, *B* = Gk)
σκηνή, Ps 119 5 *SB*, Hos 9 6 *A* ⲙⲁ ⲅ. *B*, Lam 2 6
BF, Ac 7 46 *SB* σκήνωμα; Nu 1 16 *B*(*S* = Gk), Jer
2 4 *B*(*S* do)πατριά; Je 30 33 (11) *B*(*S* ⲙⲁ ⲛⲟⲩ.) διατριβή; Job 8 6 *SB* δίαιτα; Ez 23 21 *SB* κατάλυμα;
Philem 22 *S*(*B* = Gk) ξενία; Jo 14 2 *SA²*(*B* = Gk)
μονή; Is 33 16 *SF*(*B* ⲉⲏⲃ̄) σπήλαιον; PS 100 *S* ⲙ̄ⲙ.
ⲡⲧⲉ ⲡⲉⲭⲁⲟⲥ, LCyp 4 *S* subterranean ⲙ. ⲛ̄ⲕⲁⲕⲉ,
BSM 39 *B* ⲡⲣⲟ ⲙⲡⲓⲙ. = BMis 384 *S* ⲏⲓ, Mani K
6 *A²* ⲙ̄ⲡⲟⲗⲓⲥ ⲙⲛ̄ⲙ̄.; esp *monk's cell*, or *group
of cells*: Z 290 *S* κελλίον; C 89 20 *B* Pachom's cell
ἀσκητήριον (varr μοναστήριον, οἴκημα), Mor 37 38
S ⲡⲉϫ̄ⲙ. ⲉⲧⲉϥⲁⲥⲕⲉ ⲛ̄ⲅⲏⲧϥ ἀσκητηρίου τόπος, C 99
237 *S* = *ib* 89 71 *B* σκηνή = Va ar 172 44 كسم,
C 89 179 *B* inspected ⲡⲓⲙ. ⲛⲛⲓⲥⲛⲏⲟⲩ = *ib* 100 295
S ⲏⲓ, MIE 2 349 *B* hermit's ⲙ. = PO 22 365 قلاية،
BMar 207 *S* hermit builds ⲙ. in desert = Rec 6 170
B, MG 25 349 *B* ⲟⲩⲙ. ⲉⲛϣⲏⲧ = ROC 17 374
صومعة, J 75 42 *S* ⲙ̄ⲙ. ⲧⲏⲣⲟⲩ in monastery (*cf ib*

64 ⲙⲁ ⲛⲟⲩⲱⲅ), N&E 39 336 *B* ⲡⲁⲓⲛⲓϣϯ ⲙ̄ⲙ. cell
in monastery of Macarius, TSBA 9 110 *B* ϯⲙ. (*sic*
MS) ⲡⲉⲣϣⲱⲧ sim, Ep 92 *S* ⲉⲧⲟⲩⲏⲅ ⲅ̄ⲙⲡⲙ. ⲡⲁⲡⲁ
ⲉⲡⲓⲫⲁⲛⲓⲟⲥ, J de Morgan *Cat* 1 140 *S* ⲙ. ⲡⲁⲡⲁ ⲅⲁⲧⲣⲉ
(*sc* monastery of H at Aswân), WS 93 *S* monastery ?, Saq 319 *S* ⲡⲓⲱⲧ ⲡⲡⲓⲙ. In Ar ديره (*Zeits
f Semit* 9 252), pl مناشيب (PO 10 441). *V* EW
Hist Mon 361, Ep 1 128.

ϭⲓⲛ-, ϫⲓⲛϣ. *SB*, *act, state of being*: Ps 22 6 *B*(*S*
ⲟⲩⲱⲅ vb) κατοικεῖν; ShBor 246 39 *S* ⲧⲉⲓϭ. ⲛⲟⲩⲱⲧ
ⲛⲟⲩⲟⲡ ⲛⲓⲙ, TEuch 1 173 *B* brought us ⲉⲩϫ.
ⲉⲃⲟⲗ ϩⲉⲛϥⲓ ⲉⲛⲁϣ.† ⲁⲛ, Va 61 91 *B* ϯϫ. ⲡⲧⲉ ⲡⲓ-
ⲣⲁⲙⲁⲟⲓ of old, P 129²⁰ 122 *S* didst create spirits ⲉⲛⲧ-
ⲧϭ. ⲛϣⲟⲣⲡ ⲅⲁⲑⲏ ⲙⲡⲥⲱⲛⲧ, ViK 9655 *S* without beginning, time or ϭ.

ⲉϣⲱⲡⲉ *SA²F*, ⲉϥ. *A*, ⲉϣⲱⲡⲓ *S f B*, ⲉϣⲱⲡⲓ *S f F*,
ⲉϣⲟⲡ, ϣⲱⲡ, ϣⲟⲡ *F* conjunction, *if it befall, if, when*:
Ge 4 7 *B*(*A* Cl om), Ex 4 8 *AB*, Job 13 3 *S*(*B* ⲓⲥϫⲉ),
Ps 89 10 *SF* ϣ. (*B* om), Pro 6 11 *SAB*, Cant 1 8 *F*
ⲉϣⲱⲡⲓ, Ep Jer 33 *F*(*B* om), Hos 8 7 *A*(*B* om), Jo 5
31 *SA²B* ἐάν; Ge 40 14 *B*(*S* om), Is 1 15 *B*(*SF* do),
ib 30 15 *BF*(*S* = Gk), Mt 6 5 *B*(*S* om, *F* = Gk)
ὅταν; Lu 11 34 *SB* ἐπάν; Ex 1 10 *AB*, 2 Cor 3 16 *B*
(*S* ⲉⲡⲉⲓ) ἡνίκα ἄν; Ge 12 12 *B*(*S* ⲉⲛⲁϣⲱⲡⲉ) ἔσται;
Nu 5 19 *S*(*B* ⲓⲥϫⲉ), Eccl 6 6 *S*(*F* om), Mt 19 17 *S*(*B*
ⲓⲥ.) εἰ, Ac 8 22 *S*(*B* ⲁⲣⲏⲟⲩ) εἰ ἄρα, R 1 4 58 *S* ⲉ.
ⲟⲩⲡⲉ εἴπερ; PS 31 *S* ⲉ.…ⲉⲅϣⲁⲛⲉⲡⲓⲕⲁⲗⲉⲓ, ShC
42 107 *S* ⲉ. ⲉⲛϣⲁⲛϭⲁⲣⲉⲅ, AM 168 *B* ⲉ. ⲁⲕϣⲁⲛⲥⲱ-
ⲧⲉⲙ, BMis 473 *S* ⲉ. ϯⲛⲁϣ ϫⲟⲕϥ ⲉⲃⲟⲗ, *ib* 347 *S* =
BM 304 *S* ⲉ. ⲣⲱ ϯⲛ̄ⲡϣⲁ ⲁⲓⲟⲩⲱ ϣ *since, because*,
CO 204 *S* ⲉ. ⲕⲁⲕⲡ (*l* ϭⲡ) ⲟⲩⲙⲁ, MR 5 42 *Sf* ⲉϣⲱⲡ
ⲁⲛⲛⲟⲩⲧ ϯ ⲙⲁϯ, CMSS 19 *Sf* ⲉϣⲱⲡⲓ ⲁⲓⲥϫⲁⲓ ⲛⲏⲧⲛ ⲕⲁⲕⲱⲥ, CO 507 *F* ⲉϣⲟⲡ ⲁⲕⲧⲓ ⲛⲉⲕ, BM 586 *F*
ϣⲱⲡ ⲫ[ⲱ]ϥ ⲉⲙⲧⲁ(ⲛ) ⲡⲉⲕ, AZ 23 30 *F* ϣⲟⲡ ⲉⲗⲉ-
ⲧⲉⲕⲙⲛⲧⲥⲁⲡ (ⲉⲗ) ⲭⲣⲓⲁ, C 43 191 *B* ⲉ. ⲭⲟⲩⲱϣ,
Ep 303 *S* ⲉ. ⲓⲱⲅⲁⲡⲏⲥ ⲟⲩⲁϣϥ ⲁⲛ, MR 5 52 *F* ϣⲟⲡ
ⲉ(ⲕ)ⲕⲉⲗⲉⲩⲉⲓ, *ib* 55 *F* ⲉϣⲱⲡⲉ ϣⲁⲕⲉⲗ ⲧⲉⲃⲁⲡⲟⲕⲣⲓⲥ-
(ⲓⲥ), AM 28 *B* ⲉ. ⲛⲧⲟⲩⲅⲁⲩ, AP 40 *A²* ⲉ. ⲟⲩⲛ ϣϭⲟⲙ,
Ep 213 *S* ⲉ. ⲟⲩⲛ ⲑⲉ ⲙⲙⲁⲩ, ShC 73 66 *S* ⲉ. ⲙⲉⲛ
ⲧⲉⲩϣⲛⲧⲉ, Pcod 5 *S* ⲉ. ⲟⲩⲇⲓⲕⲁⲓⲟⲥⲡⲉ; ⲉ. ⲙⲙⲟⲛ *v*
p 168 *a infra*, ⲉ. ⲙⲛⲉ- *v* p 178 *a*; after vb 'adjure':
BMar 232 *S* ϯⲱⲣⲕ ⲉⲣⲟⲕ…ⲉ. ϣⲁⲕϫⲓⲧ ϣⲁⲣⲟϥ *that
thou bring me not*, Berl Ak Abh '97 (Erman) 17 n *S*
ϯⲧⲁⲣⲕⲟ…ⲉ. ⲙⲉⲕⲉⲓ ⲉⲃⲟⲗ *that thou come forth*, J 97
48 *S* ⲛⲧⲁⲣⲕⲟ…ⲉ. ⲙⲁϥⲧⲁⲅⲟϥ ⲉⲣⲁⲧϥ *that he establish
it*, CMSS 39 *F* ⲁⲓⲣⲱϫ ⲗⲁⲕ (ⲉ)ϣⲱⲡⲓ ⲙⲉⲕϣⲗⲏⲗ (*sic l*)
ⲅⲓϫⲱⲓ, BM 535 *F* ⲁⲓⲧⲁⲣⲕⲁⲕ…ⲉ. ⲙⲉⲕⲉⲣ ⲡⲉⲧⲛⲁⲛⲟⲩϥ
(*cf ib* 583 *F* ⲉⲃⲧⲁⲣⲕⲁ ⲙⲁⲕ ⲛϣⲁⲕⲁⲃⲉϣ ⲉⲣⲁⲓ). *V*
Jern p 29 (comparing אֹל אֹם).

For ⲉϣⲱⲡⲉ from ⲉⲥϣⲱⲡⲉ *v* AZ 38 147.
Cf ϫⲡⲟ.

ϣⲱⲡⲉ¹, -ⲃⲉ², ϣⲱⲱⲡⲉ³, ϣϣⲱⲃⲉ⁴, ϣⲟⲟ.⁵, ⲉϣⲱⲡⲉ⁶,
ϣⲱⲡ-⁷ *S*, ϣⲱⲡⲓ⁸, ϣⲟⲡ⁹ *B* nn m f (once), *cucumber,*

gourd, Nu 11 5 $S^{12}B^8$ σίκυς= قثاء, MG 25 206 B ш.[8]
συκίδιον(? σικύδιον), P 44 82 S ϥⲓⲕⲟⲩⲥⲓⲛ · ⲥⲓⲕⲓⲑⲓⲁ ·
ⲁⲕⲟⲩⲣⲓⲁ (ἀγκούριον Langkavel) · ⲛⲉⲱ.[5], ib S ϥⲁ-
ⲕⲟⲩⲥⲓⲟⲛ · ⲛⲉⲱ.[5] قثد =43 58 S ⲛⲱ.[1], ib 235 Se ⲗⲁ-
ⲧⲏⲣⲓⲟⲛ (v Löw 332) · ⲉⲡⲱ.[7] (l ⲛⲱ.) ϩⲣⲅⲧ قرى, Aeg
261 S ⲛⲱ.[4] = PO 8 612 ΄ڏ, Tri 419 S ⲛⲱ.[1] ΄ڏ (var
΄ڏ), K 197 B ⲛⲱ.[8] ΄ڏ, ib 258 B ⲛⲧⲋⲱⲡⲓ, P 44 83 S
ⲃⲟⲩⲕⲉⲣⲟⲥ (l-ας) · ⲧⲏⲗⲓⲥ ⲡⲉⲡⲱⲛⲉⲥ · ⲛⲉⲱ.[2] الاصفر ;
Kr 245 S^6, ShP 130[4] 157 S ⲟⲩⲱ.[1] ⲏ ⲟⲩⲙⲉⲗⲱⲡⲉⲡⲱⲛ,
ShViK 9596 187 S ϩⲉⲛⲱ.[2], R 2 4 21 S swine's food
ⲛⲱ.[1] ⲛⲛⲡⲙⲉⲗ., BM 332 S fingers swelled to ⲡⲉϩⲧⲁⲓ
ⲛⲡⲱ.[1], Z 627 S recipe ⲟⲩⲱ.[2] ⲛⲅⲗⲁϩⲙⲉϥ & use as
poultice, ib ⲟⲩⲱ.[2] ⲉϥϭⲏϭ, BP 11349 25 S neglected
crops ⲛⲏϫ ⲉⲃⲟⲗ ⲛⲱ.[2] ⲟⲛ ⲁϥⲕⲁⲁϥ cucumber field(?),
PLond 4 500 S ⲉⲣⲧⲟϭ ⲡⲛϣⲟϭⲉ, WS 121 S ⲟⲉⲓⲛⲉ ⲡⲉ-
ⲱⲱ[ⲛⲉ], ST 243 S ⲱⲟⲙⲧⲉ ⲛⲱ.[3], C 86 172 B bread,
cheese & ⲟⲩⲱ.[9]; ϩⲣⲁ ⲱ.[1] S, cucumber seed: P 43
34 ΄ڏ زرع; ⲡⲟⲉⲓⲧ ⲛⲱ.[2] S, cucumber meal: PMéd 185;
ⲙⲟⲟⲩ ⲛⲱ.[2] ⲉϥϩⲟⲗⲙ, water of cuc. (wherein cooked):
ib 301.

ⲱⲡⲗⲁⲕ, -ⲗⲟⲕ   v ⲗⲟⲕ.

ⲱⲡⲟⲛⲟⲩ S nn f, girl(?): Mor 31 61 ⲧⲉⲓⲱ. tending
goats, 66 ⲱⲁⲛⲧⲉⲧⲉⲱ. ⲱ ⲛⲥⲟⲛ ⲉⲣⲟⲩⲛ ⲉⲙⲓⲥⲉ, 70 Samuel's hand in fetters ⲙⲛⲧⲁⲟⲩⲱ.   In FMEPereira
Vida do Abba Samuel 100 ff = ⲱⲗⲧ.   Coptic?

ⲱⲡⲱⲡ AA^2 v ⲱⲡ.

ⲱⲡⲏⲣⲉ SA^2, ⲱϥⲏⲣⲓ B, ⲱⲡⲏⲣⲓ F nn f (mostly)
m, wonder, amazement: 2 Cor 11 14 SB θαῦμα, Deu
34 12 SB, Ps 25 7 SB, Mt 21 15 SB, ClPr 27 76 S
ⲛⲉⲱ. ⲁⲃⲃⲁⲕⲟⲩⲙ, C 86 64 B ⲡⲟⲗⲓⲕⲁⲣⲡⲟⲥ ⲡⲛⲱ. θαυμάσιος, Pro 6 30 SB(A ⲙⲁⲓϩⲉ), Dan 9 4 S(B ⲟⲓ ⲛⲱ.),
Jo 9 30 SB(A^2 ⲙ.) θαυμαστός, 2 Kg 1 26 SB ⲱⲱⲡⲉ
ⲉⲅⲱ. θαυμαστοῦν; Ex 7 3 B(A ⲙ.), Ps 70 7 B(S ⲥⲟϭ,
var ϩⲛⲉ), Is 28 29 SB, Jo 4 48 SBF(A^2 ⲙ.) τέρας;
Job 4 12 SB ἐξαίσιος; Lu 5 26 SB παράδοξος; Ac 2
22 SB σημεῖον; Z 312 S ⲉϥϩⲛⲟⲩⲱ. ἔκθαμβος; AZ
21 158 S ⲛϭⲟⲙ ⲙⲛⲱ., ViK 9320 181 S ⲉϩⲉⲛⲱ.
ⲡⲉ ⲉⲛⲁⲩ ⲉⲣⲟⲟⲩ, Cai 42573 1 S ending recipe ⲉⲕ-
ⲛⲁⲡⲁⲩ ⲉⲅⲛⲟϭ ⲛⲱ. (cf PGM 2 165 καὶ θαυμάσεις),
J 84 5 S God ⲛⲁⲡⲛⲟϭ ⲛⲱ., C 89 28 B ⲟⲩⲱ. ⲡⲉ
ϩⲉⲛⲡⲉϥⲥⲙⲟⲧ, ib 43 52 B ⲛⲁϥⲱⲟⲡⲛⲉ ϩⲉⲛⲟⲩⲱ. in
amazement; do wonders c ⲉⲓⲣⲉ, ⲓⲣⲓ: Ps 71 18 SB
θαυμάσια ποιεῖν; Dan 3 99 B τέρ. π., Ps 45 8 S(B
ⲥⲉⲙⲛⲓ) τ. τιθέναι; PS 178 S ⲛⲉⲱ. ⲉⲛⲧⲁⲓⲁⲁⲩ, C 43
95 B ⲛⲁϥⲓⲣⲓ ⲛϩⲁⲛ...ⲱ.; as adj, wonderful: Ps 41
4 SB, Is 3 3 S(B ⲱ. nn) θαυμαστός; Job 18 12 S(B
ⲟⲓ ⲛⲱ.) ἐξαί.; Sa 19 5 S παράδ.; ShA 1 383 S ⲉⲓⲉⲣ
ϩⲱⲃ ⲛⲱ., BM 255 9 S ⲟⲩϫⲱ ⲛⲱ. (Lu 15 4 ff), AM
255 B ⲡⲁⲓϩⲱⲣⲡ ⲉⲃⲟⲗ ⲛⲱ.; ϩⲁⲱ. S, lit under
wonder, wonderful: BHom 86 ⲟⲩⲟⲉⲓⲛ ⲉⲧϩ., PMéd
262 ⲇⲓⲁϩⲣⲟⲧⲟⲛ (διαρρόδιον) ⲉⲥϩ., C 99 122 said

---

angel to him ⲉϥϩ. whilst he marvelled;   ϩⲛⲟⲩⲱ.
as advb, marvellously: Ps 44 4 SB θαυμαστῶς; DeV
2 6 B ⲁⲧⲡⲁⲣⲑⲉⲛⲓⲁ...ⲟϩⲓ...ϩ.

ⲣ, ⲉⲣ ⲱ., ⲟ, ⲟⲓ ⲛⲱ. a intr, be amazed: Job 21 5
SB, Mk 15 44 SBF, MG 25 10 B ⲁϥⲉⲣ ⲱ. ϫⲉ-
θαυμάζ., Job 18 20 SB θαῦμα ἔχειν; 1 Kg 16 4 B(S
ⲉⲓⲱⲣⲙ), Mt 12 23 S(B ⲧⲱⲙⲧ), Lu 24 22 B(S ⲛⲱⲱⲥ)
ἐξιστάναι, Mt 13 54 SBF ἐκπλήσσειν; Is 14 9 B(S
diff) σαλεύειν; Mk 6 20 S(B ⲱⲟⲗϩ ⲛϩⲏⲧ) ἀπορεῖν;
PS 248 S ⲉⲓⲣ. ⲁⲩⲱ ⲉⲓⲱⲁⲩⲙⲁϩⲉ ϫⲉ-, Mor 29 23 S
ⲁϥⲉⲣ. ⲉⲙⲁⲧⲉ (var BMis 264 ⲣ ϩⲃⲁ), AP 42 A^2 ϯⲣ.
ϫⲉⲥⲉⲡⲏⲧ, DeV 2 85 B ⲁϥⲉⲣ. ⲉⲙⲁⲱⲱ ϫⲉ-; Kr 236
F ⲁⲓⲉⲗ. ⲕⲁⲗⲱⲥ;   Mor 18 177 S ϩⲣⲟⲟⲩ ⲉϥⲟ. θαυμάσιος, Dan 9 4 B ut sup -στός; Jth 13 13 S παράδ.;
BMis 390 S like to one ⲉⲧⲟ. = BSM 43 B & Va 63
15 B, DeV 2 87 B will make you ⲉⲣⲉⲧⲉⲛⲟⲓ. admirable before all nations.   b tr, marvel at, admire:
Lev 19 15 S ⲙⲛⲡⲣⲟ (B ϭⲓ ⲱ.), Job 34 19 SB sim πρόσωπον θαυμάζ., Ps 16 7 SBF, Is 61 6 S(B ⲛ- dat),
Lu 7 9 SB, Miss 8 137 S ⲁⲓⲣ. ⲛⲧⲥⲩⲙⲫⲱⲛⲓⲁ θ., Job
42 11 S(B ⲉϫⲉⲛ-), Si 27 23 S ⲉⲕⲑ. ἐπί, Ps 138 14 B(S
diff) θαυμαστοῦσθαι; Br 238 S ⲉⲣⲉⲡⲧⲏⲣϥ ⲣ. ⲙⲙⲟϥ,
ShA 2 319 S ϯⲣ. ⲙⲙⲱⲧⲛ ⲧⲱⲡⲉ, C 99 196 S ⲛⲉⲩⲣ.
ⲙⲙⲟϥ ϩⲙⲡⲉϥⲑⲃⲃⲓⲟ, ST 364 S ⲁⲓⲣ. ⲛⲧⲉⲧⲛⲛⲟϭ ⲙ-
ⲙⲛⲧⲁⲭⲓⲛⲉ, CO 61 S sim, C 43 144 B ⲉⲣⲉⲡⲙⲛⲱ...ⲉⲣ.
ⲙⲙⲟϥ, ViK 9647 S ⲟⲩⲱⲱⲟⲩⲣ. ⲙⲙⲟϥ, Va 61 27 B sim;
Miss 8 212 S ϯⲟ. ⲙⲙⲟⲕ ϫⲉ-, BM 1147 S ϯⲟ. ⲙ-
ⲙⲱⲧⲛ (ⲙ)ⲡⲉⲧⲉⲛⲧⲛ(ⲛ)ⲟ(ⲟ)ⲩ, Aeg 34 B ⲧⲉⲛⲟⲓ.
ⲙⲙⲟⲕ ϫⲉ-, Ryl 398 S ϯⲟ. ⲛⲧⲉⲕⲱ.

With following preposition.   c ⲉ-SB: BM 172
40 S ⲣ. ⲉϩⲉⲛⲣⲟ πρόσωπον θ. (cf above tr & c ⲛⲥⲁ-);
AM 150 B ⲁϥⲉⲣ. ⲉⲧⲟⲩⲙⲉⲧⲥⲁⲓⲉ;   c ⲉⲧⲃⲉ-SB: Mk
6 6 SB θ. διά; Z 286 S ⲡⲉⲓϩⲏⲧⲛⲙⲁ ⲉϥⲟ ⲛⲱ. ⲉⲧⲃⲏⲛⲧϥ, BSM 44 B ⲁϥⲉⲣ. ⲉ.ⲡⲓϩⲱⲃ = Va 63 10 B ⲉⲣ.
ⲛ- = BMis 391 S ⲑⲁⲩⲙⲁϩⲉ ⲉϫⲛ-;   c ⲉϫⲛ-SB:
Lev 26 32 S(B ⲉϩⲣⲏⲓ ⲉϫ.), Ac 3 12 SB θ. ἐπί; Is 52
14 S(var ⲉϩⲣⲁⲓ ⲉ., B ⲧⲱⲙⲧ) ἐξιστ. ἐπί; Mk 11 18
SB ἐκπλ. ἐπί; MélOr 6 502 B ⲉⲣ. ⲉ.ⲡⲓⲥⲁϫⲓ;   ⲉ-
ϩⲣⲁⲓ ⲉϫⲛ-: Eccl 5 7 S(F ⲉⲗ) ⲙⲁⲓϩⲉ) θ. ἐπί; Lu 4 32
S(B do)ἐκπλ. ἐπί; PS 200 S ⲣ. ⲉϩ. ⲉϫⲛⲡⲁⲡⲟⲫⲁⲥⲓⲥ,
C 43 192 B ⲁϥⲉⲣ. ⲉϩ. ⲉ.ⲡⲓⲥⲁϫⲓ;   c ⲛⲥⲁ- S: Jude
16 (B ⲉ-) πρόσωπον θ. (cf tr & c ⲉ-);   c ϩⲛ- S: Job
17 8 (B ⲉϫ.) θαῦμα ἔχ. ἐπί;   c ϩⲓϫⲛ- B: AM 125
ϯⲟⲓ ⲛⲱ. ϩ.ⲡⲉⲕⲛⲓⲱϯ ⲛⲥⲱⲟⲩⲛ.

ⲣⲉϥⲑⲙⲓⲉ ⲱ. B, wonder worker: as adj Va 57 191
θαυματοποιός; ib 61 23 ϯϫⲟⲙ ⲛⲣ. of the holy
Simeon.

ϭⲓ ⲱ. B, be amazed: Lev 19 15 (S ⲣ ⲱ.) πρόσω.
θ., HL 94 ⲟⲩⲣⲱⲙⲓ ⲛϭ. ⲙⲙⲟϥ θαυμαστός; MG 25
347 ⲛⲁϭ. ⲡⲉ (ROC 17 373 تعجّل), Va 58 34 ϯϭ.
ⲙⲙⲟⲕ.

ⲱⲟⲡⲥ, ⲱⲱⲡⲥ   v ⲱⲱⲡ vb s f.

ϣⲱⲡⲧ v ϣⲱⲃⲧ.

ϣⲡⲓⲧ F v ϣⲓⲡⲉ sf.

ϣⲉⲡⲁϣ S, meaning unknown: Bal frag of list
ⲃ̄]ⲓⲣ ⲥⲛⲁⲩ ⲡϭⲁⲡⲓⲭⲟⲩ,]ⲁⲙ ⲡϣ., ⲥⲛ]ⲧⲉ ⲡⲥⲟⲓ.　Prob
from ϣⲱⲡ vb.

ϣⲱⲡϣ SB(rare), ⳝ. A, ϣⲱⲃ̄ϣ B nn m, *arm,
foreleg of animals*: Lev 7 32 B (var -ⲡϣ, S ϭⲃⲟⲓ),
Nu 6 19 S (var ϣⲱⲭⲡ) B (var do), ib 18 18 S (var
ϭⲃⲟⲓ)B, Deu 6 21 B(var ⲭϥⲟⲓ, S ϭ.), Is 53 1.A(Cl)
B(S ϭ.), Hos 7 15 B(A ϭⲃⲁⲓ, S diff), Ac 13 17 B(S
ϭ.) βραχίων; BodlOr 32 173 B stretch forth ⲡⲉϥϣ.
& bless ذ.ـﻳ;　　as constellation name: Job 9 9 SB
'Ἀρκτοῦρος; P 44 52 Sﺭﺪـﺳ; Tri 484 S ى.ﻯﺮ; P
129²⁰ 123 S ⲥⲟⲩⲡⲣⲟⲩⲅⲉ, ϣ., ⲥⲟⲩⲡⲣⲧⲟⲟⲩⲉ, Mor 41
152 S ⲥⲟⲩⲡⲣⲧ., ϣ., ⲥⲙ̄ϩⲟⲩⲧ; on identification v
Brugsch *Aegyptologie* 343; JJHess(by letter) a polar
constellation, cf Ora 4 400;　　*shoulder*: Job 31 22
B(S ⲛⲁⲣⲃ̄), Ez 24 4 S(B ⳝ.), Mal 2 3 S(ViK 920)B,
Va 68 171 B linen stoles ϩⲓⲭⲉⲛⲡϣ. ὦμος; ShC 73
162 S arms bared ϣⲁⲣⲟⲩⲛ ⲉⲡⲉⲛϣ., EW 109 B ⲡⲉϥϣ. ϭⲟⲥⲓ above all soldiers, MG 25 63 B wings growing ϩⲓⲭⲉⲛⲛⲟⲩϣ., TEuch 1 189 B cross ϩⲓⲭⲉⲛⲡⲉⲕϣ.
نﺍﺪﻋﺎﺳ (var نﺍﻋﺍﺮذ);　　*crop, gizzard*: Lev 1 16 S(B
ⲗⲟⲃⲟⲥ) πρόλοβος ةﻭﺰﺣ, Tri 484 S ةﻧﺎـﻗ.

ϣⲁⲡϣⲓ O nn f, *noble, distinguished*: AZ 21 105
(cf ib 38 92, PGM 1 75, comparing Σαῦψις, Σέψις,
epithet of goddess).

(ϣⲟⲡϣⲡ), ϣ(ⲉ)ⲡϣⲡ-, ϣⲡϣⲱⲡ⸗ S vb tr, *take in
the arms, nurse*: Si 30 9 τιθηνεῖν; Mk 10 16 (B ϩⲓ
ⲧⲟⲧ⸗ ⲡⲥⲁ-) ἐναγκαλίζεσθαι; Bar 4 8 S (ShBMOr
8810 411, B ϣⲁⲡϣ) ἐκτρέφειν.　Cf ϣⲱⲡ.

ϣⲟⲡϣⲉⲡ B v ϣⲟⲃϣⲉⲃ.

ϣⲟⲡϣⲟⲡ S, ϣⲁⲡϣⲁⲡ Sᵃ, *a plant* (?): Kropp J
50 S with others in ⲡϭⲱⲣϭ ⲛ̄ⲧϭⲁⲗⲁϩⲧ, ib K 55 Sᵘ
ⲕⲗⲟⲙ ⲡϣ.

ϣⲁⲣ- p c, *being small, short* (Sethe *Verbum* 1 389)
v ⲁϩⲉ sf, ⲉⲓⲱⲧⲉ & cf ϣⲏⲣⲉ, ϣⲓⲣⲉ & ? ϣⲁⲣⲕⲉ.

ϣⲁⲁⲣ S, ϣⲁⲣ SSᴶB, ϩⲁⲣ Sᵃ, ϩⲁⲁⲣⲉ A, ϣⲁⲣⲉ
A², ϣⲉⲉⲗ, ϣⲉ(ⲉ)ⲣ, ϣⲉⲣⲓ F, ϣⲁⲁⲣ- S, ϣⲁⲣ- SB, pl
ϣⲁⲁⲣⲉ S nn m, *skin*: Lev 11 32 SB, Job 10 11 SB,
Lam 4 8 SBFϣⲉⲣ (C Schmidt), ib 5 10 SBFϣⲉⲉⲗ
(Quatr), AM 277 B δέρμα; ib ϣ. ⲛ̄ⲧⲉⲧⲣⲁⲧⲉⲣⲙⲱⲛ
τετράδερμον only; Mic 2 8 sg SAB δορά; ShA 2
349 S ⲡⲉϥⲣ ⲣⲱⲃ ⲉϣ., BMis 452 S bone broken ⲡϣ.
ⲙ̄ⲙⲁⲧⲉ ⲡⲉⲧⲁⲙⲁⲣⲧⲉ, El 94 A ⲡⲟⲩϩ. = ib 128 S
ⲡⲉⲩϣ., ManiH 69 A² ϩ]ⲱⲕ ⲡϣ. ⲙ̄ⲡⲉϥⲡⲉⲗⲙⲁ, Tri
265 S sim, C 43 106 B ϭⲓ⳨ ⲙ̄ⲡⲉϥϣ., ib 140 B ⲡϣ.
ⲛ̄ⲧⲉ ⲡⲉϥⲥⲱⲙⲁ ϫⲱⲗ = Mor 48 81 S ⲕⲟⲩⲕⲉ;　　as
covering, bag, vellum: Ps 103 2 B(S ϩⲃⲱ) δέρρις;

AZ 21 156 S ⲡⲁϣ. glossed ⲡⲙⲟϫϩ ⲡϣ. of Baptist;
of monks: Z 318 S = MG 25 136 B μηλωτάριον (cf
EW *History* 196); P 129¹⁴ 124 S ⲧⲧⲱⲱⲙⲉ ⲙ̄ⲡⲉϥϣ.
= C 41 16 B ﻝﺳﺍ; Z 352 S ϣ. into which ⲡⲣⲓϣ
packed = ib ⲃⲁⲗⲟⲧ, MG 25 251 B bread ϫⲉⲛⲡⲉ-
ⲧⲉⲛϣ., HL 119 B ⲁⲡⲭⲁ ⲡϣ. ⲉϩⲣⲏⲓ wherein to
kneel, Bodl(P) g 17 S ϣ. ⲡⲉⲣⲅ(ⲁⲧⲏⲥ), C 100 273 S
struck ⲡⲉϥϣ. ⲉⲧⲧⲟ ϩⲓⲱⲱϥ, Mun 66 S crippled feet
ⲙⲏⲣ ⲡϭⲉⲛⲡϣ.;　　BM 1102 S ϣ. ⲛ̄ⲃⲁⲃⲩⲗⲱⲛ, CMSS
70 Sᶠ ϣ. (ⲙ̄)ⲙⲏⲛⲣ(ⲁⲛⲟⲛ);　　of animals: He 11 37
SA(Cl)B ⲛ̄ⲃⲁⲙⲡⲉ, BMEA 44808 Sᶜ ⲛ̄ⲃ[ⲁⲙⲡⲉ,
Ex 25 5 B ⲛ̄ⲱⲓⲗⲓ, cit ViK 9754 115 S, Lev 4 11
SB ⲙ̄ⲡⲙⲁⲥⲉ δέρμα, MG 25 236 B ⲡⲉⲥⲱⲟⲩ κώδιον,
CO 459 S ϣ. ⲛⲉ., BKU 1 26 (8116 b)F ϣⲉⲉⲣ ⲡⲟⲩ-
ϭⲁⲗⲁⲛϭⲱϣ, PMéd 316 S ϣⲁⲣ ⲛ̄ⲟⲩⲱⲡϣ, Z 628 S
ⲡⲓⲱ, Hall 86 S ⲟⲩϣ. ⲛ̄ϩⲣⲟⲙⲡⲉ ⲛ̄ⲣⲟⲙⲧ *quid?*; ϣⲁ-
ⲁⲣ-, ϣⲁⲣ-: Nu 31 20 S -ⲃⲁⲙⲡⲉ αἴγειος; GMir
119 S ϣⲁⲁⲣⲙⲁⲥ ⲉⲧⲟⲩⲧ (cf Mor 28 119 ϣⲁⲁⲣ
ⲉⲧⲟⲩ.), P 129¹⁶ 12 S -ⲟⲩⲱϩ, AM 324 B ⲡⲉⲩⲣⲟⲛ
ⲛ̄ϣⲁⲣⲃ̄ⲱⲧ, Mor 48 61 S sim ⲛ̄ϣⲁⲣⲟⲩⲱⲧ, C 43 80 B
ⲧⲁⲩⲣⲉⲁ ⲛ̄ϣⲁⲣⲃ̄., Va 58 73 B λῶρος ⲛ̄ϣⲁⲣⲃ̄., PMich
3552 S -ⲉⲥⲟⲟⲩ;　　as adj: Ge 3 21 SB, Nu 4 8 S(B
as nn), Mt 3 4 SB δερμάτινος, Lev 13 49 SB, Va 57
271 B ϫⲱⲙ ⲡϣ. δέρμα, Jud 4 18 S δέρρις; BG 50 S
ⲯⲩⲭⲏ ⲡϣ., ⲯ. ⲛϥⲱⲉ, PS 151 S ⲡⲉϣⲧⲏⲛ ⲡϣ. (Od
Solom 25 8 |ﺮﻣﺪﺣ ﺍ ﻦﺤﺩ|), Mor 36 38 S sim, Va 57
270 B ⲡⲓⲣⲉⲛⲟⲩⲓ ⲡϣ. ⲉⲑⲙⲱⲟⲩⲧ, BMis 221 S ⲧⲟⲙⲟⲥ
ⲡϣ. (var Mor 16 78 ⲡⲭⲁⲣⲧⲏⲥ), ST 118 S ϣⲟⲧ ⲡϣ.,
JKP 2 134 F ⲙⲁⲭⲃ̄ ϣⲉⲣⲓ.

ⲣⲙ̄ϣ. S, *man of skin*: Mich 550 25 of Herod's
death ⲁⲡⲣ. ⲉⲧϫⲓ ⲉⲟⲟⲩ ⲧⲁⲕⲟ, ib ⲉⲣϣⲁⲛⲡⲣ. ⲣ ⲣ̄ⲣⲟ
ϩⲛ̄ⲧⲥⲁⲣⲝ let reason & understanding flee.

ⲥⲁ ⲛ̄ϣ. B, *skin-seller, -dresser*: K 138 ⲡⲓⲥ. ﺪﻠﺠ.

ⲃⲁⲕⲓϣ. SB, *tanner*: Ac 9 43 S(var -ϣⲁⲣ)B βυρσεύς بﺍﺪﻏ, Mor 17 76 S ⲣⲉϥⲃ̄. βυρσοδεψῶν.　V
ⲃⲱⲕⲉ.

ⲕⲟⲕϣⲁⲣ B *nickname?*: DeV 2 202.　V ⲕⲱⲕ ⲣ ⲥ.

ⲟⲩⲁⲙϣ. S nn f, *skin-eater, ulcer*: PMéd 137
(ⲟⲩ)ⲟⲩ. ⲉⲧⲣⲉⲥⲕⲁϭⲕ, ib 257 ⲧⲟⲩ. (sic l), PSBA 27
128 if (writing-)parchment ⲟ ⲛ̄ⲟⲩ., shalt scrape it
with pumice.

Cf ϣⲁⲁⲃ̄.

ϣⲁⲁⲣ¹, ϣⲁⲣ², ϣⲁⲁⲣⲉ³, ϣⲁⲣⲉ⁴ S, ϣⲉⲉⲣ F nn m,
price: ShA 2 350 ⲙ̄ⲡⲟⲩⲡⲗϭ ⲡⲉⲩϣ.¹ ⲉⲃⲟⲗ, CO 244
ⲙ̄ⲡⲓⲱⲣϫ ϣ.² ⲡⲙ̄ⲙⲁⲕ, Kr 29 ⲡϣ.³ ⲉϣⲁ(ⲣⲉ ?)ⲡⲉ-
ϣⲟⲧⲉ ϫⲓ ⲙ̄ⲙⲟϥ, Ep 253 ⲡϣ.² ⲉⲧⲏⲛⲩ ⲉⲧⲁⲡⲱⲣϫ,
ib 303 ⲧⲁⲗⲟ ⲛ̄ϩⲟⲗⲟⲕ/ (of corn) ⲙ̄ⲡϣ.² ⲡⲓⲕⲟⲟⲩⲉ, BP
11349 shall pay ⲡⲣⲟⲥ ⲡϣ.¹ ⲛ(ⲧ)ϣⲏⲣⲉ, Ryl 201 ⲡⲣⲟⲥ
ⲡϣ.¹ ⲉϥⲁϣⲱ[ⲡⲉ, Vi ostr 192 ⲡⲣⲟⲥ]ⲡϣ.² ⲉⲧⲛⲁϣⲱⲡⲉ,
Kr 41 F ⲡⲣⲟⲥⲉⲛ ⲙ̄ⲡϣ. ⲡϣⲁⲃⲱ̄ϣⲡⲓ, WS ostr unpubl
ⲏ̄ⲣⲡ ⲡϣ.⁴, PMich 604 wine account ϣ.⁴ ⲕⲁⲓ ⲕⲟⲩϥ/
Bodl(P) e 13 ⲡⲣⲟⲥ ⲡϣ.¹ ⲉⲧⲁ(ϥ)ⲥⲱⲗⲡ;　　ⲣ ϣ., *make,*

fix price: Jer *loc apocr*[1] (Balestri lxiv = Tatt *Proph Maj* 1 vi B ϯⲙⲏ, cf Mt 27 9), ShA 1 303 ⲡⲉⲧⲣ ϣ.[1] ⲉⲡⲉⲧⲛⲁⲣ ⲧⲃⲛⲏ, ShR 2 3 26 ⲁⲩⲣ ϣ.[1] ⲉⲣⲟϥ (*sc* Jesus), ShA 1 67 ⲉⲩⲣ ϣ.[3] ⲉⲣⲟⲟⲩ ⲉⲃⲟⲗ ϩⲓⲧⲙⲛⲥⲁⲧⲁⲛⲁⲥ *being bought by Satan*, JSch 4 9 ⲁϥⲁⲁⲥ ⲛϣ.[2], Ep 271 ⲛϭⲓ ⲧⲉⲣⲧⲱⲣⲉ ⲛϥⲁⲁⲥ ⲛϣ.[2] ⲡⲁⲓ, BP 4906 ⲣ ⲡⲉϥϣ.[2] ⲕⲁⲧⲁ ⲡⲇⲓⲕⲁⲓⲟⲛ ⲙⲡⲛⲉ;   ϯ ϣ., as last: Mt 27 9[1] (B ⲉⲣ ϯⲙⲏ) τιμᾶσθαι, WZKM 14 234 ϫⲓ ⲧϥⲧⲓⲙⲏ προς ⲟⲉ ⲛⲧⲁⲩϯ ϣ.[2] ⲉⲣⲟⲥ.

ϣⲏⲣ *S nn m*, reading & meaning uncertain : PMéd 70 ϣ. ⲛⲉⲃⲓⲱ with milk of lettuce and opium. *Cf* شير (Chassinat).

ϣⲱⲣ *SA*²*B*, ϣⲉⲣ-(?)*B*, ϣⲟⲣⲝ *SB*, ϣⲟⲟⲣⲝ, ϣⲏⲣⲧ *S vb tr*, *pile up, make thick*, so *stop up* (of wells &c): Ge 26 15 B, Is 22 7 B(S ⲧⲱⲙ) ἐμφράσσειν; Ez 41 16 S(B ⲧⲁⲭⲣⲟ) δικτυωτός; Ge 21 25 B ἀφαιρεῖν; Hos 13 15 B(A ⲱⲙⲉ) ἐξερημοῦν; Va 57 227 B roots which fire destroyeth ⲛⲧⲉϥϣⲟⲣⲟⲩ ἐξέλκειν; P 54 169 B, Montp 204 B ⲁⲓϣⲉⲣ- سد (K 233 سند wrongly); C 86 214 B ϣⲟⲣϥ ⲛⲓⲧⲉⲛ ϣⲁⲣⲱϥ(*sc* of pit), *ib* 221 B ⲉⲑⲟⲣⲟⲩϣⲟⲣ ⲓⲧⲉⲛ ⲉϫⲱϥ, Hall 108 S wages for mending cart to ϥⲁⲙ ⲛⲧⲁϣϣⲟⲣⲉ, Mani K 85 A² ⲁϥ[ϩ]ⲱⲙ ⲁϥϣ. ⲁϥⲧⲱⲥϭ ⲡⲟⲩⲥⲓⲁ ⲙⲡⲓⲟⲩ; *intr*: MG 25 89 B ϣ. ⲛⲥⲁϯϣⲱϯ till filled to brim, ShC 73 137 S ⲡⲣⲁⲕⲉ ϩⲏⲧⲉⲧⲣⲓⲣ ⲉⲧⲣⲉⲩϣⲱ ⲉϥϣ.[†] ⲉⲛⲉⲩ ⲉⲣⲏⲩ, *Mél Ch Moeller* 1 228 S ⲉⲩⲛⲟϭ ⲙⲙⲟⲣⲧⲡⲉ ⲉⲥϣ.[†] δασυπώγων, Louvre 10013 S of Baptist ⲟ[ⲩ ⲙⲟⲣⲧ] ⲉⲥϣ.[†] ⲕⲁⲗⲱⲥ (var Mor 18 25 ⲉⲥⲣⲏⲧ, *cf* Miss 4 119). V ? ϩⲁⲣ-.

ϣⲁⲣⲉ-, ϣⲁⲝ *SB*, ⲉϣⲁⲣⲉ- *S*, ⲉϣⲁⲣⲉⲝ *S*ᵃ, ⲛϣⲁⲣⲉ-, ⲛϣⲁⲝ *SF*, ϩⲁⲣⲉ- ϩⲁⲣⲉⲝ *A*, ϣⲁⲣⲉ-, ϣⲁⲣⲉⲝ *A*², ϣⲁⲗⲉ-, ϣⲁⲝ *F pref aorist* (habit, continuance), opp ⲙⲉⲣⲉ- : Pro 3 12 *SA* ϣⲁⲣⲉⲡⲛⲉ ϯ ⲥⲃⲱ, Ps 145 3 S ϣⲁⲣⲉ ⲡⲉⲩϩⲏⲧ ⲉⲓ (B ⲉϥⲓ), EpJer 17 F ϣⲁⲗⲉⲡⲉⲩⲟⲩⲉⲉⲃ ⲧⲁⲭⲣⲁ (B ⲥⲉⲧⲁⲭⲣⲟ), Pro 7 13 *SB* ϣⲁⲥϫⲟⲟⲥ *A* ϩⲁⲣⲉⲥ-, Si 35 23 S ϣⲁϥⲧ (var ϥⲛⲁ-), 1 Cor 13 6 *SB* ϣⲁⲥⲣⲁϣⲉ, Jo 9 31 *SB* ϣⲁϥⲥⲱⲧⲙ *A*² ϣⲁⲣⲉϥ-, PS 4 S ⲉⲡⲉⲓⲇⲏ ⲉϣⲁⲣⲉⲧⲥ ϫⲟⲟⲥ, Ep 373 S*ᵃ* ⲕⲁⲓ ⲅⲁⲣ ⲉϣⲁⲣⲉϥϯ; as *fut* S: PS 240 ⲧⲡⲁⲣⲑⲉⲛⲟⲥ ⲛⲁⲛⲁⲩ...ϣⲁⲥⲣ ϣⲡⲏⲣⲉ, ViK 1112 ⲉⲕϣⲁⲛϣⲱⲡ ϭⲁⲙ[ⲟⲩ]ⲗ ϣⲁϥⲙⲟⲩ, J 89 8 S all that saw sick child said ϣⲁϥⲙⲟⲩ (*cf ib* 85 12 ⲉϥⲛⲁ-); esp in recipes: Bodl(P) 1 d ϣⲁϭⲱⲗ ⲉⲃⲟⲗ ⲛⲥⲱⲙⲁ ⲧⲏⲣⲟⲩ, AZ 23 110 ϣⲁϥⲉⲣ ⲟⲟϩ (*sc* silver) ⲛ-ⲥⲁⲛ; + *rel e*-: Eccl 7 16 S ⲉϣⲁϥⲙⲟⲩ (F ⲛⲁ-), Jo 9 7 *SB* ⲉϣⲁⲩⲟⲩⲁϩⲙⲉϥ *A*² ⲉϣⲁⲣⲟⲩ-, 1 Cor 9 7 *SB* ⲉϣⲁϥⲣ ⲙⲁⲧⲟⲓ *F* ϣⲁϥ-, PS 31 S ⲛⲉϩⲃⲏⲩⲉ ⲉϣⲁⲅⲁ-ⲁⲩ; + ⲛ-(mostly *S/F*), as last or = *when, if*: BM 601 F ⲛϣⲁⲕϣⲗⲏⲗ ⲉⲛⲟⲥ remember me, AZ 23 32 F ⲛϣⲁⲕϫⲓ ⲛⲁⲥϥⲉⲓ, BM 658 S*f* ⲛϣⲁϥⲓ ⲛⲁⲕ ⲧⲁⲁⲩ, BP 5561 F ⲛⲉⲩ ⲛⲓϥⲓ ⲛϣⲁⲁⲗⲉϣⲉⲭⲓ ϣⲱⲡⲓ, BM 1124 S ⲛϣⲁⲓⲉⲓ ϩⲏⲧ *I will come north*, Bor 265 87 S ye cannot be saved ⲛϣⲁⲧⲉⲧⲛϫⲟⲟⲩⲥⲟⲩ ⲉⲃⲟⲗ ⲉⲩⲣ ϩⲕⲁⲉⲓⲧ,

---

Z 627 S ϣⲱⲛⲉ ⲛⲓⲙ ⲛϣⲁϥⲉⲓ ⲉϫⲛⲡⲣⲱⲙⲉ, Bodl(P) 2 12 S recipe ⲛϣⲁⲕϣⲟⲩⲉⲓ ⲙⲙⲟϥ; or as ϣⲁⲣⲉ- : BKU 1 21 47 F ⲛϣⲁⲣⲉⲡⲉⲕⲣⲏⲧ ⲉⲙⲧⲁⲛ; + *pe past aor*: Ps 118 62 S ⲛⲉϣⲁⲓⲧⲱⲟⲩⲛ(B ϣⲁⲓ-), Ez 27 7 S ⲡⲉ ϣⲁⲣⲉϩⲟⲟⲗⲉ (B ϣⲁⲣ-), PS 36 S ⲛⲉϣⲁϥⲉⲓ ⲉⲃⲟⲗⲡⲉ, MG 25 371 B ⲛⲉϣⲁϥⲧ ⲡⲟⲩⲕⲟⲩϫⲓ ⲛⲛⲓϥⲓ.

ϣⲁⲁⲣⲉ[1], ϣⲁⲓ.[2], ϣⲁⲁⲣ[3] S, ϣⲁⲣⲓ[4], ϣⲁⲓ.[5] B, ϣⲛⲏⲗⲓ[6] F(v also ⲣⲉϣ.), ϣⲁⲣⲉ- (?), ϣⲁⲣ[7] SA², ϣⲁⲗⲝ F, ϣⲁⲣⲧ S *vb I intr, smite*: 1 Kg 18 7 B⁴(S = Gk), Ps 106 29 B⁴(S do), Is 27 7 S¹(B ϯ ⲉⲣϩⲟⲧ) πατάσσειν; Job 5 18 S³(cit BMar 55¹, B do) παίειν; *ib* 9 12 B⁴(S ⲧⲁⲕⲟ) ἀπαλλάσσειν; ShIF 107 S whoso scratcheth self let him consider ϫⲉⲁϥϣ.[3] ⲡⲟⲩϩⲣ ⲙⲁⲩⲁⲁϥ ϩⲛⲛⲉϥϭⲓϫ ⲛ ⲟⲛⲣⲉⲛϣⲉ, Mor 28 94 S waves ⲛⲟⲉ ⲛⲑⲁⲗⲁⲥⲥⲁ ⲙⲛⲛⲁⲩ ⲛϣⲁϣϥ.[3] (*cf* ⲣⲉϣ.), TstAb 178 B in wrath ϣⲁⲛϣ.[5] & spare none, Va 57 4 B(on Lu 12 18) ere corn laid in his granary ⲁⲡⲉⲧⲉⲙⲙⲁⲩ ⲉⲣ ⲁⲡⲟⲣⲛ ⲉⲟⲣⲉϥϣ.[5] *thresh*;   *qual, smitten* with sickness : Tri 265 ⲧⲁⲗϭⲟ ⲙⲡⲉⲧϣ. علیل.

II *tr*: Ge 8 21 S ϣⲁⲣⲉ- (or ? *l* ϣⲁⲣ ⲉ-)B⁴, Ex 32 35 B⁴(S = Gk), Ps 135 17 B⁴(S do) πατ.; Ex 7 27 B⁴ τύπτειν; *ib* 10 2 B⁴ ἐμπαίζειν *dat*; Ez 6 4 B⁴(S ⲣⲱϩⲧ) καταβάλλειν; Is 30 30 F ϣⲁⲗⲟⲩ (S *diff*, B = Gk) κεραυνοῦν; ST 280 S demons ⲟⲩⲁⲩ(*l* ? ⲁⲩ)ϣⲁⲣⲕ, Mani 1 A² ⲥⲙⲟⲩ ⲁⲡⲉⲧⲣⲁⲩϣⲁⲣⲁⲩ.

With following preposition.   *c e*- as obj : Deu 7 2 S¹(var³)B⁴, 1 Kg 17 49 B⁴(S p.), Ps 3 8 B⁴(S = Gk, A ϣⲟⲩϭⲉ), Is 5 25 B¹F⁶(S = Gk), *ib* 30 31 B¹(SF p.) πατ.; Job 2 7 S³(B ϫⲟⲩϩⲣ), Is 14 29 S¹(var³, B ⲙⲓϣⲓ) παι.; ShMun 179 S ⲁϥϣⲁⲣⲉ ⲉⲣⲟⲟⲩ, ShC 42 115 S ⲉⲩϣ.[3] ⲉⲛⲉⲩⲥⲁⲣϩ...ϩⲛⲣⲉⲡⲁⲕⲁⲑⲁⲣⲥⲓⲁ, ShA 2 168 S sin ϣ.[3] ⲉⲣⲟⲟⲩ ⲉⲅⲟⲧⲉ ϣⲁⲁⲣ ⲛⲓⲙ, Sh(?)Mor 54 60 S ⲉⲩϣ.[2] ⲉⲛⲉⲩⲥⲱⲙⲁ *tattooing them*, Mor 16 38 S ϣ.[1] ⲉⲛⲉⲩϣⲏⲣⲙⲓⲥⲉ (var BMis 199 ⲧⲁⲕⲟ), BIF 13 98 S ϣ.[1] ⲉⲣⲟϥ ϩⲛⲟⲩⲛⲟϭ ⲛϩⲣⲓⲥⲉ = MG 25 277 B⁴, ALR '93 524 S ⲁⲩϣ.[3] ⲟⲛ ⲉⲛⲉϥⲥⲱⲙⲁ, AZ 30 40 S ⲉⲃⲉϣⲁⲣ ⲉⲣⲟⲟⲩ...ϣ.[3] ⲉⲥⲟⲧⲟⲙⲁ, MG 25 91 B ϣ.[4] ⲉⲟⲩⲟⲛ ⲛⲓⲃⲉⲛ (var ϯ ⲉⲣϩⲟⲧ), C 41 52 B ⲁϥϣ.[4] ⲉⲡⲓ-ⲃⲁⲣⲃⲁⲣⲟⲥ ϫⲉⲡⲟⲩϣⲓϣϯ ⲙⲡⲗⲏⲧⲛ, CDan 97 B ⲛⲟⲥ ϣ.[5] ⲉⲛⲓⲥⲁⲑⲏⲛⲥ & he died, BSM 17 B ⲁϥϣ.[5] ⲉⲣⲱⲟⲩ = BMis 352 S ⲛⲁⲧⲁⲥⲥⲉ.

—— *nn m SB, blow, stroke*: Deu 25 2 B(Wilk, var & S ⲥⲏϣⲉ) πληγή; 2 Kg 6 8 S³ διακοπή, cit ShA 1 154 ⲛϣ.[1]; ShC 42 78 ⲛϣ.[3] ⲡⲧⲟⲣⲕ of God, Sh Wess 9 117 ⲉⲣⲉⲛϣ.[3] ⲧⲏⲣϥ ⲛⲛⲓⲣⲃⲏⲩⲉ ⲛⲗⲟⲓⲙⲟⲥ ⲧⲟⲟⲃⲉ ⲉⲣⲟⲟⲩ.

ⲣⲉϥϣ.[1], -ϣ.[3], -ϣⲟⲟⲣ[7] S, -ϣⲱⲣ[8], -ϣ.[4] B, *smiter*: Va 61 120 B Daniel ⲡⲓⲣ.[4] ⲛⲧⲉ ⲛϫⲱⲗⲟⲛ (Mor 25 26 S *diff*);   *demon S*: Tob 6 15[7], Mt 8 31[3] (B ⲓⲥ) δαιμόνιον, Mk 5 15[3](var⁷, B *diff*)δαιμονίζεσθαι; Tri 265 شیطان; PS 107 tossed about like ⲟⲩⲣ.[7] ⲉϥϩⲛⲁⲏⲣ; as *adj*: Mor 17 56 ⲛⲛⲁ ⲛⲣ.[7] πυθωνίος (but *ib*

= ⲡⲛⲁ ⲡⲣⲉϥϣⲱⲡⲉ), Aeg 26 θάλασσα ⲛⲣ.³, R 1 5 40 ⲇⲁⲓⲙⲟⲛⲓⲟⲛ ⲛⲣ.⁷, Mor 18 183 sim p.¹; ⲙⲏⲧⲣ.⁷ S, ⲙⲉⲧⲣ.⁸ B, devilry: Ja 3 15 S(B ⲥⲙⲟⲧ ⲛⲇⲉⲙⲱⲛ) δαιμονιώδης; Ryl 453 336 B شيطانية; ShP 130⁴ 124 σοφια ⲙⲙ. of heretics.

ⲉⲣ ϣ.⁵ B, meaning doubtful: Va 57 174 B would it (wealth) were removed & ⲉⲥⲉⲣ ⲡⲕⲉϣ. ⲟⲩⲟϩ ⲉⲥⲛⲁⲧⲁⲕⲟ ἀναιρεῖν for both.

ϣⲁⲣⲓ B nn or adj in ⲫⲓⲟⲙ ⲛϣ. ἐρυθρὰ θάλασσα Ex 10 19 (بحر الأحمر, 13 18 do (varr سوف, د' القلزم); C 43 125 ⲫ. ⲡϣⲁⲓⲣⲓ. V Pey s v & AZ 66 37 sea of *sunrise* (?). Cf σάρι, Egyptian water plant (Theophrastus in Tatt s v).

ϣⲁⲓⲣⲉ SO, -ⲣⲓ BO, ϣⲉⲉⲓⲣⲉ A, ϣⲉⲓⲣⲉ A², ϣⲉⲓⲗⲓ F nn f, *couch, cohabitation*: Lev 18 22 B(S ⲙⲁ ⲛⲕⲟⲧⲕ), Nu 5 13 B(S ϭⲛⲕ.), Pro 7 17 B(SA ϭⲗⲟϭ), He 13 4 B(S ⲙ.) κοίτη; TEuch 2 506 B ⲁⲣⲉϩ ⲉⲧⲟⲩ ϣ. ⲉⲥⲧⲟⲩⲃⲏⲟⲩⲧ مضّ; MG 25 49 B married pair abstained ⲉⲃⲟⲗ ϩⲁⲧⲟⲩϣ., PGen S let him not quit ⲡⲏⲓ ⲛⲁⲁ ⲧⲉϥϣ. ⲛⲕⲟⲧⲕ; *sheepfold*: Is 17 2 S(B ⲙⲁ ⲡⲉⲛⲕ.), Mic 2 12 SAB ⲕ.; 2 Kg 7 8 S, Zeph 2 6 SAB μάνδρα; GFr 427 S ⲧϣ. where many sheep ποίμνη; Jer 40 12 S(B ⲙⲁ ⲡⲉⲙⲧⲟⲛ) κατάλυμα; Is 7 25 S(B as Gk) καταπάτημα; ShA 2 18 S sheep ϩⲙⲡⲟϭⲉ ⲛ ⲧϣ., R 1 2 72 S sheep gathered ⲉⲧⲉⲩϣ. ⲉⲧⲟⲣϫ, Mani 1 A² bring sheep ⲁⲡϣ. ⲉⲧⲟⲣϫ, GFr 307 S enfold them ⲉⲡⲉⲕⲟϩⲉ...ⲉⲧⲉⲕϣ., Stegemann 63 F ⲁⲡϥ ⲉⲧϣ. ⲙⲡⲉⲭ̅ⲥ̅, MG 25 87 B monks ϫⲉⲛϯϣ. ϩⲁⲧⲉⲛⲡⲓⲥⲡⲏⲗⲁⲓⲟⲛ; Tri 425 S ⲧⲉⲓⲛⲟϭ ⲟⲩϣ. suddenly fallen & whose skin hath need of salting قطيع (same word?).

ⲙⲉⲛⲧ-, ⲙⲉⲧϣ. OB, *concubitus*: AZ 21 100 O ⲟⲩⲙⲉⲛⲧϣⲁⲓⲣⲓ ⲡⲁⲣⲣⲁⲕⲧⲉ, ib -ϣⲁⲓⲣⲉ, K 103 B مضاجعة.

ⲣ ϣ. SB, *lie down*: Cant 1 6 S(F ⲙⲁⲛⲉⲓ) κοιτάζειν; ⲙⲁ ⲛⲣ ϣ.: Jer 29 21 S(prob)B κατάλυσις.

ϭⲓ ϣ. B, *take rest*: P 54 171 استظل, ل' , K 234 ؤ.

As place-name: ϯϣⲁⲓⲣⲓ (K 208) الحلّة. V MIF 36 164.

ϣⲁⲣⲟ, -ⲟⲩ B nn with ϯ, *give command*: HL 95 ⲁϥϯ ϣ. ⲛⲁϥ ϫⲉⲙⲡⲉⲣϯ παραγγέλλειν; ib 120 sim, O'Leary Th 25 ⲁϥϯ ϣ. ⲛⲁϥ ϫⲉϫⲁⲥ ⲡⲧⲉϥⲙⲟϣⲓ, K 232 (var -ⲣⲱ) اوصا, BMOr 8775 117 -ⲣⲟⲩ, P 54 168 sim اوصا أمر.

ϣⲏⲣⲉ SAA², -ⲣⲓ BFO, -ⲗⲓ F, ϣⲣ-SAA², ϣⲏⲣ-A, ϣⲉⲗ-F, ϣⲉ-S, ϣⲓ-SF, ϣⲟⲩ-SB, ϣ(ⲉ)ⲛ- (for ϣⲉ ⲛ-)SBFO, ϣⲏⲛ-SF, f ϣⲉⲉⲣⲉ SAA², ϣⲏⲛⲣⲉ SS', ϣⲉⲣⲉ A²O, ϣⲉⲣⲓ B, ϣⲏⲏⲗⲓ F, pl (Theban) ϣⲣⲏⲩ, -ⲉⲩ S & sg as pl, nn m *son, child*: Ge 25 3 S(B ϣⲏⲣⲟϯ), Pro 1 1 SAB, Is 30 9 SBF-ⲣⲓ, Jo 3 13 SA²BF-ⲗⲓ υἱός; Ge 27 25 SB, Lev 25 41 S(B ϣ.), Deu 28 57 B(S ⲕⲉⲕⲉ), Pro 24 70 SA, Mt 15 26 SB τέκνον; Ge 48 6 S(B ϫⲫⲟ), Pro 24 34 SA ἔκγονος; Jth 4 10 S, Ps 16 14 S(BF ⲕⲟⲩϫⲓ ⲛⲁⲗⲟⲩ) νήπιος, Sa 2 13 SB, Mk 7 28 S ⲁ.) παῖς; Ac 7 19 S(B ⲕ. ⲛⲁ.) βρέφος; Is 23 4 B(S ⲟ ϣⲓⲣⲉ) νεανίσκος; ShA 2 104 S ⲛϣ. ⲙⲡⲥⲁϩⲟⲩ, BMar 4 S ⲟⲩϣ. ⲉϥϩⲏⲙⲡⲧϫⲓⲧⲉ ⲡⲣⲟⲙⲡⲉ, CA 90 S ⲛϥⲕⲁ ϣ. ⲛ̄ⲙⲁⲥ *beget son*, BMar 16 S father ⲙⲙⲁⲥⲧϣ., Mani H 10 A² ⲧⲉⲛⲕⲟ ϣ., C 43 91 B ϫⲫⲟ ⲛϣ. ⲃ̅, ib 172 B ⲡⲓⲁⲥⲉⲃⲏⲥ ⲛϣ., Hor 80 O ⲡⲡⲉϣ. ϫⲱⲡⲉ ⲛⲁϥ, PGM 1 114 O ⲯϣⲏⲣⲓ ⲛⲫⲓⲱϩ, Ep 247 S ⲛⲉⲧϣ. ⲙⲙⲁⲓⲡⲉ *spiritual sons*, Z 21 B ⲛⲉϥϣ. ⲙⲡⲛⲁⲧⲓⲕⲟⲛ, CO 54 S bishop calls archpriest ⲛⲁϣ., ib 49 vo S ⲡⲉϥϣ. ⲡⲉⲗⲁⲭ(ⲓⲥⲧⲟⲥ) addressing bishop; ⲩ̅ⲥ̅, ⲩ̅ⲩ̅ (υἱός) in late S prob to be read ϣ.: JKP 2 146 ⲉⲓⲥ ⲟⲩⲩ̅ⲥ̅ (cf Jo 19 26 ϣ.), ib 182 ⲛⲁⲩ̅ⲥ̅ ⲥⲛⲁⲩ (cf Mt 20 21 ϣ.), Lant 80 vo ⲛⲩ̅ⲥ̅ ⲛⲓⲱⲥⲏⲫ, ib 95 ⲛⲩ̅ⲩ̅ ⲙⲡⲁⲣⲭⲏⲡⲁⲡⲁ, v Orat Cyp below & ϣ. ϣⲏⲙ; *daughter*: Jud 11 34 SB, Cant 2 7 F, Joel 2 28 SAB, Mt 14 6 SBF, AP 15 A² θυγάτηρ; ib 8 A² τέκ.; Jo 19 25 SA²B (B as Gk) ἡ τοῦ; Jud 15 6 S ⲛⲉⲛⲧⲁϥϫⲓ ⲧϣ. ⲛ- γαμβρός (var νυμφίος); BMis 34 S ⲟⲩϣ. ⲛⲣⲣⲟ, LCyp 26 S' ϩⲉⲛϣ., C 43 34 B ϣ. ⲥⲛⲟⲩϯ, Lant 21 S ⲧⲉϥϣⲉⲉⲣⲓ, MR 5 47 F ⲧⲁϣⲏⲗⲓ, Mani H 91 A² ⲧⲁϣⲉⲣⲉ, K 54 B ⲛϣ. ⲛⲧⲉ ⲁⲃⲓⲁ بنات النعش (3 stars in Pleiades), Orat Cyp 127 F ϥ̅ⲩ̅ ⲧⲩ̅ (ⲧϣⲉⲉⲣⲓ) ϥ̅ⲩ̅; pl: ST 143 ⲛϣⲏⲣⲏⲩ ⲛⲕⲱⲙⲉⲥ, Moskow ostr ϫⲟⲟⲩ ⲛⲥⲁⲛⲉⲥϣ., Ep 179 ⲁⲕⲧⲣⲉⲡⲣⲱⲙⲉ ϩⲱⲙ ⲁϫⲛ(ⲛ)ⲁϣⲣⲉϥ; *young* of animals: camel Ge 32 15 S(B ϫ̅.); ox Is 11 7 S(B do) παιδίον; Ez 46 6 S(B diff) μόσχος, 1 Kg 6 7 S τέκ.; ass Mt 21 5 B(S ϣ. as adj) υἱ., Bodl(P) b 8 S; horse LAl 13 S; sheep Ps 28 1 SB υἱ.; eagle Deu 32 11 S(B ⲙⲁⲥ) νοσσιά; dove Ps 83 3 S(B do) ν.; snake Is 30 6 SB (F ⲙⲉⲥ) ἔκγ.

ϣ. ϣⲏⲙ SAA²F, lit *small child*, then *babe, child, youth*: Eccl 4 13, Mt 17 18 (B ⲁⲗⲟⲩ), Aeg 270 ⲡϣⲟⲙⲛⲧ ⲛϣ. παῖς, Pro 1 4 SA(B ⲁ. ⲙⲕⲉⲣⲓ) π. νέος, Ex 2 8 SA(B ⲁ.) babe, Mt 14 21 (B do, F ϣ. ⲕⲟⲩⲓ), Mk 9 36 (B do, F ⲕ. ⲛⲁ.), Jo 21 5 (B do) disciples, He 2 13 SF(B do), C 99 239 = ib 89 74 B do youth, Z 341, ib 340 same child ⲕ. ⲛϣ. παιδίον, Ge 22 12 (B do), 2 Kg 1 6 (var ϩⲉⲣϣⲓⲣⲉ), Joel 3 3 SA(B ⲁ. ⲛϩⲱⲟⲩⲧ), Jo 6 9 SA²(B do) παιδάριον, BHom 55 Daniel π. νεώτερος; Pro 7 10 SA(B do), AP 8 A² νέος, PS 148 12 (B ϫ ⲉⲗϣⲓⲣⲓ), Eccl 10 16 (F ⲁ.) νεώτερος, Pro 20 29 SA opp πρεσβύτερος, Ac 23 17 (B ϫ̅.) νεανίας, Jud 17 7 ν. (var παιδάριον), Is 20 4 (B do) νεανίσκος; Job 3 16 (B ⲁ.), Lu 10 21 (B ⲕ. ⲛⲁ.) νήπ.; ib 1 41 (B ⲙⲁⲥ) babe unborn, 1 Pet 2 2 (B do) βρ.; 2 Kg 5 4 aged 30 υἱ.; P 44 68 ⲙⲓⲣⲁϩ· ϣ. ϣ. صبى, ⲛⲏⲡⲓⲟⲥ ϣ. ⲕⲟⲩⲓ, R 2 2 21 μειράκιον; PS 345 ⲡⲉϫⲡⲟ ⲙⲡϣ. ϣ., ShC 73 98 ϣ. ϣ. (var ⲗⲉⲗⲟⲩ ϣ.), ShWess 9 140 ⲛϣ. ϣ. ⲉϣⲁⲅⲭⲛⲟϥ, Mor 31 214 from 2 years old. BMar 63 of 15 years, Mor 39 24 of 21 years, ib 25

193 of 30 years, JKP 2 12 ⲡⲣ̄ⲥ̄(ϣⲏⲣⲉ) ϣ. ϣⲉⲉⲣⲉ
ϣ. *SAA²*, *female child, maiden*: Deu 22 15 (*B* ⲁ.),
Lu 8 51 (*B* ⲇⲟ) παῖς, Mk 5 39 (*B* ⲇⲟ) παιδίον, Jth 12
13, Ac 12 13 (*B* ⲁ. ⲁⲃⲱⲕⲓ) παιδίσκη; Tit 2 4 (*B* ⲁ.
ⲛ̄ϭⲣⲓⲁⲓ) νέα, BHom 47 νεώτερα, Ps 67 26 (*B* ⲃ̄.)
νεᾶνις; Su 19 (*B* ⲁ.), Joel 3 3 *SA*(*B* ⲁ. ⲛ̄ϭⲣ.), Mt 14
11 (*BF* ⲁ.) κοράσιον; Ge 34 3 (*B* = Gk) παρθένος;
RE 9 151 ⲧϣ. ϣ. ⲛ̄ⲧⲁⲥϫⲡⲟⲥ, BMis 55 of 3 years,
ib 112 ⲧⲉⲓϣ. ϣ. who bare God, R 2 2 21 ϣ. ϣ. ⲉⲧ-
ⲣⲁⲙⲡⲁⲁⲟⲥ, AP 37 *A²*; ϣ. ϣ. ⲡⲣⲟⲟⲩⲧ *S* J 86 23;
ϣ. ϣ. ⲛ̄ϭⲣⲓⲁⲉ *S* BM 247 7 γυνὴ νεᾶνις, Miss 8 229
Sᶠ; ⲙⲛ̄ⲧϣ. ϣ. *SAB*(once): Ps 42 4 (*B* ⲁⲉⲧⲁ.),
Pro 5 18 *SA*(*B* ⲇⲟ), Eccl 11 9 (*F* ⲙⲛ̄ⲧⲁ.), Ez 23 3
(*B* ⲁⲉⲧⲕⲟⲩϫⲓ), Zech 13 5 (*A* ⲙⲛ̄ⲧⲗⲓⲗⲟⲩ, *B* ⲙⲉⲧⲁ.)
νεότης; Jud 11 37 (*B* = Gk) παρθενεία; ShBM 230
158 sins of ⲁⲉ. or ⲙⲛ̄ⲧⲉ̄ⲣⲣⲉ or ⲙⲛ̄ⲧⲣⲗⲗⲟ, BMar 85
ⲙ̄ⲡⲁⲑⲟⲥ ⲛ̄ⲧⲁ., C 86 91 *B* ⲁⲉⲧⲕⲟⲩϫⲓ paral ⲁⲉⲧⲩ.
ϣ.; ⲟ ⲛ̄ϣ. ϣ. *S*: Jo 21 18 (*B* ⲟⲓ ⲛⲁ.) νεώτερος
εἶναι; BMar 39 wilt die ⲉⲕⲟ. (aet 19).

Other combinations. ϣ. ⲛⲟⲩⲱⲧ *S*(var ϣ. ⲟⲩ.),
ϣ. ⲙⲙⲁⲩⲁⲧϥ *B* Ps 24 16 μονογενής; ϣ. ⲛⲥ̄ϣ. 1 Tim
5 4 *SB* ἔκγ.; ϣ. ⲡⲣⲟⲟⲩⲧ, ⲛϭⲱ. Ex 2 2 *B* ἄρσην, P
131¹ 63 *S*, J 81 15 *S*, C 43 34 *B*; ϣ. ⲛ̄ϭⲣⲓⲁⲉ Job
15 14 *S*(*B* diff) γεννητὸς γυναικός, Cant 1 5 *F*(*S* ϣ.
only), Lam 4 3 *F* ϣ. ⲛ̄ϭⲣⲓⲁⲙⲉ (*SB* ⲇⲟ) θν., BMis 76
S, ROC 20 49 *S* ϣⲏⲣⲉ ⲛⲥ., J 66 31 *S*, AM 79 *B*;
ϣ. ⲕⲟⲩⲓ *v* ⲕⲟⲩⲓ II A B; ϣ. ⲟ *v* ⲟ *great*; ⲛⲟϭ
ⲛ̄ϣ. *v* ⲛⲟϭ I *s f*.

Constr forms. ϣ(ⲉ)ⲛⲉⲓⲱⲧ: Ge 20 12 *SB* ἐκ πατρός, Lev 18 11 *SB* ὁμοπάτριος; ϣ(ⲉ)ⲛⲙⲁⲁⲩ:
Deu 27 22 *SB* ἐκ μητρός, Ge 43 16 *SB* ὁμομήτριος,
K 82 *B* ابن الخال (of maternal uncle), AZ 21 100 *O*
ϣⲉ ⲛ̄ⲧⲁⲙⲉⲟⲩ; ϣⲏⲛⲉⲓ. ϭⲓⲛ. Mor 41 85 *S*; ϣⲛ̄-
ⲥⲟⲛ, -ⲛⲥⲟⲛ, -ⲥⲱⲛⲉ: Lev 10 4 *S* ϣⲛ̄ⲡⲉ. (*B* ϣⲏⲣⲓ ⲛ-),
P 44 71 *S* ϣⲉⲛⲛⲥⲟⲛ· ⲑ(ⲉ)ⲓⲟⲥ, K 81 *B* العم, J 18
47 *S*, *ib* 2 41 *S* ϣⲩⲛ-, PBu 46 *S* ϣⲏⲛⲛⲥ. (*cf* AM 177
B ϣ. ⲛ̄ⲧⲉ ⲥ.), J 16 46 *S* ϣⲛ̄ⲥⲱⲛⲉ, PJkôw *S* ⲛ̄ϣⲉⲛ-
ⲧⲉⲕⲥⲟⲛⲉ; ϣⲛ̄ϣⲏⲣⲉ: J 20 79 *S*; ϣ(ⲉ)ⲛⲟⲩⲁ, -ⲟⲩⲁⲓ,
ϣⲟⲩⲟⲩⲁ, *cousin*: Nu 36 11 *S*(*B* ϣⲟⲩⲃ̄), Tob 7 2 *S*,
Col 4 10 *S* ϣⲟⲩⲁ (cit P 129¹⁴ 101 ϣⲉⲛⲟⲩⲁ = *ib* 102
ϣⲏⲣⲉ ⲙ̄ⲛ̄ⲥⲟⲛ, *B* ϣⲟⲩⲃ̄, var -ⲟⲩⲁⲓ, *cf* ALR '93 518
Barnabas Mark's ⲑⲓⲟⲥ ⲕⲁⲧⲁ ⲉⲓⲱⲧ), Mor 17 78 *S*
ϣⲟⲩⲁ ἀνεψιός; AZ 24 62 *B* ϣⲟⲩⲡⲟⲩⲁⲓ ⲃ̄ اي ابن العم من الاثنين
(var P 44 144 ϣⲏⲣⲓ ⲛ̄ⲧⲉ ⲟⲩⲁⲓ ⲃ̄
ابن العم من اثنين ابن الواحد من الاثنين, ابن الو᾿ من اثنين, BMar 145
S ⲧⲁϣ̄ⲛⲟⲩⲁ daughter of father's brother, J 10 52
ϣⲟⲩⲛⲟⲩⲁ, 26 14 ϣⲟⲩⲟⲩⲁ, 11 47 ϣⲟⲩⲁ; this followed by ϣⲛ̄-, ϣⲟⲩⲥⲛⲁⲩ: J 4 68 & *pass* (*cf* PLond
1 234 συγγενής, ἀνεψ.); ϣⲛ̄ⲧⲉⲥϭⲓⲙⲉ *S*, ϣⲉⲣⲥ.,
ϣⲉⲗⲥ. *F*: Lev 24 11 (*B* diff) υἱ. τ. γυν.; Is 32 9 *F*
ϣⲉⲣ. (*SB* ϣ. only) θυ.; Mor 24 11 *F* ϣⲉⲗ.; ϣⲛ̄-
ⲛⲟϭ *S*: R 1 5 50 ⲡ̄ⲧⲕⲟⲩⲛⲟϭ ⲛ̄ϣ. (var Mor 32 26
Sᶠ ϣⲏⲣⲉ ⲛ̄ⲛⲁϭ); ϣⲣ̄ⲛⲟⲩⲧ *SA²*, ϣⲣⲟⲩⲱⲧ *S*,

ϣⲉⲗ ⲛ̄- *F*: Jo 3 18 *S*(var ϣⲣⲟⲩ.)*A²F*(*B* = Gk) μο-
νογ.; ϣⲣϩⲟⲟⲩⲧ *S*: Nu 27 3 (var & *B* ϣ. only)
υἱ., Ap 12 5 (*B* ϣ. ⲛϭ.) υἱ. ἄρσην; Job 3 3 (*B* ϩ. only)
ἄρ.; ϣⲣⲙⲁⲣⲣⲓⲧ *AA²*: Cl 59 3 ἠγαπημένος, Mani
1 -ⲙⲉⲣⲓⲧ; ϣⲣⲃⲱⲱⲛ *S*, ϣⲏⲣⲃⲟⲩⲅⲡⲉ *A*: Pro 24
35 ἔκγονος κακός; K 234 ϣⲉⲛϩⲟⲛ *B* شر; ϣⲏⲣⲱ-
ⲙⲉ *S*, *daughter of man*: Glos 25 κόρη ὀφθαλμοῦ
ϫⲛⲣ. ⲛ̄ⲡⲃⲁⲗ *pupil of eye*; various: BM 659 *Bᶠ*
ⲛϣⲓ παλιμρ (الامير), Journ Soc Or Research '28 27
S ϣⲏⲉ (var ϣⲉⲛ) ⲥⲛⲓⲧⲓϩⲏⲩ, Lant 62 *S* ⲛϣⲏⲛ ⲛ̄ⲡⲁⲡⲁ
ⲃⲓⲕⲧⲱⲣ, ST 175 *S* ⲧϣⲓ ⲛ̄ⲧⲉ ϩ̄ⲛⲕⲉ, Kropp *B* 28 *S* ⲧϣⲏⲛ-
ⲛⲓⲙ, *ib* C 14 *F* ⲧϫⲏⲗⲓ ⲛⲓⲙ, BKU 1 3 *S* ϫⲛⲓⲙ (ⲧϣⲉ
ⲛ̄ⲛⲓⲙ), Ora 4 201 *F* ϫⲏ ⲛ̄ⲕⲁⲣϭⲓⲗⲓⲁ (Gabrilia).

ⲁⲧϣ. *SBF*, *without child*: Cant 6 5 *S* ἀτεκνοῦν,
Is 49 21 *B*(*S* ⲟ ⲛⲁ.), Lu 20 28 *S*(*S* diff) -νος; Job
30 3 *SB* ἄγονος; ⲙⲛ̄ⲧⲁ.: Ps 34 12 *SB*, Is 47 9 *SB*
ἀτεκνία; ⲣ, ⲟ ⲛⲁ.: Ge 15 2 *SB* ἄτεκνος, Jer 15 7
SB, Lam 1 20 *SBF* ⲁⲧϫⲏⲗⲓ -νοῦν, Ge 27 45 *SB* ἀπο-
τεκνοῦσθαι.

ⲙⲛ̄ⲧ-, ⲙⲉⲧϣ. *SBF*: Eph 1 5 *SBF* υἱοθεσία; Br
232 *S* ⲟⲩⲙⲛ̄ⲧϣⲏⲣⲉ, DeV 2 22 *B* ⲟⲩ. ⲛ̄ⲡⲟⲩ†,
BM 217 132 *S* ⲉ̄ⲡⲡⲓⲥⲧⲉⲩⲉ ⲉ̄ⲡϣⲏⲣⲉ ϭⲓ ⲛ̄ⲧⲁϫⲓⲥ ⲛ̄ⲧⲁ.,
CO 53 *S* from bishop †ϣ̄ⲡⲉ ⲉⲧⲉⲕⲙ.; ⲙ. ⲡⲟⲩⲱⲧ
S, ⲙ̄ⲙⲁⲩⲁⲧ⳽ *B*, *only-sonship*: Ps 21 20 *S* (var ⲙⲛ̄ⲧ-
ϣⲣⲛⲟⲩ.) *B* μονογενής; ⲣ ⲧⲁ. *S*, *act as son*: Cai
8068 letter ⲣ ⲧⲁ. ⲛ̄ϭⲡⲁⲣⲁⲩ(ⲧ)ⲉⲓⲗⲉ ⲛⲁⲩ.

ⲣ, ⲟ ⲛ̄ϣ. *SB*, *be child*: Pro 4 3 *SA*(*B* ϣⲱⲡⲓ ⲛ̄ϣ.)
υἱὸς γίνεσθαι, 1 Pet 3 6 *B*(*S* ϣⲱⲡⲉ ⲛ̄-) τέκ. γίν.; JA
'75 5 222 *S* saying ϫⲉⲡⲉⲓⲱⲧⲡⲉ ⲉ̄ϥⲟ ⲛ̄ϣ., C 43 47 *B*
ⲭⲟⲩⲱϣ ⲉⲉⲣ ϣ. ⲛⲏⲓ?, *ib* 208 *B* †ⲛⲁⲁⲓⲕ ⲛ̄ϣ. ⲛⲏⲓ.

In names: ⲙ ⲡϣⲏⲣⲉ (CO ST J), Ψⲏⲣⲉ (J Preisigke), ϣⲉⲡⲧⲁⲛⲥⲓ (C 89 208) = ⲡϣⲉⲡⲧⲁⲛⲥⲉ (C 100
298), Ψⲉⲛⲧⲁ., ϣⲉⲟⲩⲧⲉ, ϣⲛ. (Ryl 222 Kr 83),
Σινούθιος, ⲡϣⲁⲙⲛⲟⲩⲧⲉ (Hall 143), ϣⲉⲡⲉⲧⲱⲙ, Ψⲉ-
ⲛⲉⲧⲩⲙⲓⲥ (Preis), ⲡϣⲉⲛⲧⲣⲃⲱ (C 89 55), ϣⲛ̄ⲧⲃⲁⲣⲥⲉ
(*v* ⲃⲁⲣⲥⲉ), ⲡϣⲉⲙⲡⲙⲁⲓ (Saq 334), many in Ψⲉⲛ-
(Preis); ϥ ⲧϣⲉⲉⲣⲉ (RE 9 164), Τσέερε, Τσέρη
(Preis), often ϫ- for ⲧϣ-: ϫⲓⲛⲟⲩⲧⲉ (Miss 4 680),
ⲧϫⲉⲡⲟⲩⲧⲉ (J), ϫⲉⲛⲡⲁⲣⲁϫ (Cai 8461), ϫⲉⲛϩⲱⲣ (ST
137), ϫⲉⲛϣⲉⲛⲁⲙⲟⲩⲛ (BMQuarterly 6 pl 15), many
in Τσεν-, Σεν-, Σερεν- (Preisigke).

V ϣⲁⲣ-, ϣⲓⲣⲉ.

ϣⲏⲣⲓ *B* var of ⲉⲣⲓ Lev 22 7 ἄρτος (BMOr 8790
102). *V* addition to p 57 *b*, also Spg 205.

ϣⲓⲣⲉ *SAA²*, ϣⲏⲣⲉ *S*, ϣⲓⲣⲓ *B*, ϣⲏⲗⲓ, -ⲣⲓ, ϣⲓⲗⲓ *F*,
f ϣⲉⲉⲣⲉ *S*, ϣⲁⲓⲣⲓ *B* adj, *small*: Ex 4 10 *S* ⲗⲁⲥ ⲛ̄ϣⲓ
(var ϣⲏ. *sic*, *AB* diff) βραδύγλωσσος; Glos 151 *S*
sim κιονίς; ShP 130¹ 16 *S* ⲣⲁⲙⲛ̄ϣⲉⲉ. paral ϩⲉⲛϩⲱⲱⲛ,
Miss 4 748 *S* sim ϣⲓ.; ϩ(ⲉ)ⲣϣⲓⲣⲉ *SA²*, ϩⲣ-*A*,
ϫⲉⲗ-*B*, ϩⲉⲗ-, ϩⲉⲣ-*F*, lit *little*, *young servant* (*v* ϩⲁⲗ),
youth, opp ϩⲗⲗⲟ: Ge 14 24 *SB*, Pro 20 14 *SA*, Eccl
11 9 *S*(*F* ⲁⲗⲟⲩ), Is 31 8 *SBF*-ⲣⲓ (*ib* 5 15 *F*-ⲗⲓ),

Lam 1 18 *BF* ϣⲓ., Am 8 13 *SAB*, Mk 14 51 *SBF*
ϣⲏ. νεανίσκος, 2 Kg 6 1 *SB*, Pro 7 7 *SAB*, Ac 20 9
SB νεανίας, BAp 54 *S* (var Gu 44 ϥⲏⲣ.) νέος, Jer 14
3 *SB* νεώτερος; MG 25 244 *B* ⲋ. ⲓⲥⲡⲏⲟⲩ παιδίον,
2 Kg 1 6 *S*(var ϣⲏⲣⲉ ϣⲏⲙ) παιδάριον, Is 5 15 *SBF*
ἀνήρ; Job 14 10 *S*(*B* ⲣⲱⲙⲓ) βροτός; P 46 161 *S*
ⲁⲗⲟⲩ طفل, ϥ. حدث, K 71 *B* ⲁ. صبي, 'ط, ⲋ. شاب;
ShC 73 160 *S* ϣⲏⲣⲉ ϣⲏⲙ ⲛ ϥ., ShIF 298 *S* ⲛϥ.
ϧⲏⲧⲉⲩⲙⲛⲧⲉⲣⲣⲉ ⲡϣⲏⲣⲉ ϣ. ϧⲓⲧϥⲅⲗⲓⲕⲓⲁ ⲡⲟⲩⲱⲧ,
Mani H 77 *A²* ⲛϥ. paral ⲡⲗⲓⲗⲁⲅⲉ, Va 59 160 *B* ⲋ.,
cf ib 161 same person ⲕⲟⲩⲓ ⲡϣⲏⲣⲓ & ⲁⲗⲟⲩ, DeV 2
10 *B* ⲟⲩⲋ. ⲡⲣⲱⲙⲓ, Miss 4 158 *B* ⲟⲩⲋ. of 12 years,
BM 511 *F* ϧⲉⲣϣⲓⲣⲓ;   f: Deu 22 19 *B*(*S* ϣⲉⲉⲣⲉ
ϣⲏⲙ), Dan 11 6 *B* νεᾶνις; BMis 112 *S* ⲛϥ. ⲙⲛⲛ-
ϣⲏⲣⲉ ϣ., PO 14 325 *B* ⲟⲩⲋ. ⲙⲡⲁⲣⲑⲉⲛⲟⲥ, Va 58 67
B ⲟⲩⲡⲁⲣⲑ. ⲛⲋ.;   ⲙⲛⲧϥ. *S*, *state, time of youth*:
BKU 1 181 ⲛⲧⲉⲣⲉϥⲣ ⲛⲟϥ ⲛϥⲉⲓ ⲉⲧⲉϥⲙ. *V* ϣⲁⲣ-,
ϣⲏⲣⲉ.

ϣⲓⲣⲉ *S* nn, *leaf of plant* سلم (*acacia or mimosa*)
used in tanning: Tri 425 neither salt nor ϣ. ⲉⲧⲣⲉⲩ-
ⲙⲉⲗϧ ⲡⲉⲥϣⲁⲣ قرظ. *V* LöwF 2 388, AIssa 2.

ϣⲣⲁ *S* vb   *v* ϧⲣⲁ.

ϣⲣⲱ *SSf* vb intr & tr, *meaning uncertain*, ? *cast
forth* (cf ϧⲣⲁ): Sh(Besa)Z 505 ϧⲓ ⲡⲉⲓϭⲗⲗⲙ ⲙⲡⲛⲓ-
ϧⲛⲁⲩ ⲡⲥⲉϣ. ⲉⲃⲟⲗ ϧⲓⲧⲙⲏⲧⲉ ⲙⲡⲉⲓⲙⲁ & *purify it*,
PBaden 5 411 *Sf* magical rubric ϫⲁϧ ⲡⲉⲩϧⲁ ϣⲣⲟ
ⲡⲡⲉϧ ⲉⲧϩⲉϥ ⲉⲡϧⲁ;   as nn m (*same?*): ib 402 *Sf* ϭϧⲁⲓ
ⲡϣⲣⲱ (*sc foregoing charm*) ⲉⲡⲃⲓⲧ (ⲛ)ⲟⲩϭⲁⲗⲉϧⲧ.

ϣⲣⲱ, -ⲟ *SB*, ϣⲗⲱ *F* nn f, *menstruation* (cf ? last
word): Lev 12 5 *S*(*B* ϭⲱϭⲉⲙ), ib 15 33 *SB* ἄφεδρος;
EstC 27 *S* καταμήνιος; Is 64 6 *S*(*B* ⲟⲓ ⲡⲕⲉⲙⲁ) ἀποκαθημένη; P 44 73 *S* ⲉⲡⲓⲙⲓⲛⲓⲁ (-μήνια) ⲧⲉϣⲣⲟ
حايظة (*l* حائضة), K 103 *B* ϯϣⲣⲟ حيظ (P 54 162);
Tri 691 *S* ⲥⲩⲛⲏⲑⲓⲁ ⲡϣ. حيض (var طمث); PS 381 *S*
ⲥⲡⲉⲣⲙⲁ ⲡⲡϧⲟⲟⲩⲧ ϣ. ⲡⲧⲉⲥϧⲓⲙⲉ, Br 100 *S* ⲧⲉϣ. ⲡ-
ⲧⲉϥⲁⲕⲁⲑⲁⲣⲥⲓⲁ, MG 25 94 *B* ⲉⲥϭⲟⲗⲉϧ ϧⲉⲡⲧⲉⲥϭⲣⲱ
(*sic* MS) 'ⲃ, Cai 42573 2 *Sf* ⲧⲁⲉⲓⲥ ⲡϣ.;   adj: Ez
18 6 *B* ϭⲉⲓⲙⲓ ⲡϣ. ἐν ἀφ.; Mor 34 46 *S* ⲥϧ. ⲛⲓⲙ ⲡϣ.
= Aeg 43 *B* ⲉⲧⲟⲓ ⲡϣ.;   ⲣ ϣ., ⲟ, ⲟⲓ ⲡϣ., *be menstruous*: Lev 15 20 *B* ἐν ἀφ.; Ep Jer 28 *F*(*B* ⲟⲓ ⲡⲕⲉⲙ-
ⲙⲁ), Ez 36 17 *S*(ShC 73 77)*B* ἀποκ.; BMis 189 *S*
ⲡⲧⲉⲟⲩⲥϧⲓⲙⲉ ⲉⲣ ϣ.

ϣⲁⲣⲃⲁ *SAB*, ϣⲁⲃⲣⲁ, ϣⲁϥⲣⲁ *S*, ϣⲣⲃⲁ *A*(Hab)
nn m, *scorching heat* (cf שרב IgR): Jth 8 3 *S*, Hos 12
1 *S*(*B*=Gk) καύσων, Jer 17 8 *S*(*B* do) καῦμα; ShA
1 465 *S* tree ⲁⲡⲧⲟⲩⲣⲏⲥ ⲛ ⲡϣ. ⲧⲁⲕⲉ ⲡⲉϥⲧⲁⲣ, ShC
42 220 *S* ⲙⲁ ⲡϧⲁⲓⲉ ⲁⲩⲱ ⲡϣ. (var ϣⲁⲃ.), P 131⁵ 13
S vineyard feareth not ⲡϣ. (cf Jer *lc*), MG 25 182
B stay not without lest ⲡⲓϣ. ⲡⲉϭⲓ ⲉⲣⲟⲕ, C 43 141
B ⲟⲩϣ. ⲡⲕⲁⲩⲙⲁ = Mor 48 82 *S* ⲕⲁⲩⲙⲁ ⲉϥϣⲟⲟ-
ⲥⲙ;   ⲧⲏⲩ ⲡϣ., *scorching wind*: Ez 19 12 *S* ϣⲁϥ.

(*B* ⲑ. ⲡⲕⲁⲩⲙⲁ) ἄνεμος καύσ., Jon 4 8 *A*(*S* ⲧⲏⲅ, *B*
ⲕⲁⲩⲥⲱⲡ) πνεῦμα καύσ.;   ⲟ ⲡϣ. *S*, *be parched*: C
99 86 ⲟⲩⲙⲁ ⲉϥⲟ ⲡϣ. = MG 17 548 تشف., Va ar
172 92 مقفر, Wess 15 9 *sim where naught shall grow*,
BMis 538 ⲡⲟϭ ⲡⲥⲱϣⲉ ⲉⲥⲟ ⲡϣ.;   ϯ ϣ., *scorch*:
Hab 1 9 *A*(*SB* diff) ἄν. καύσ. *ventus urens* (*l* ? ⲉⲥϯ)
Mor 53 51 *S* ⲡⲁⲑⲟⲥ ⲉⲧϯ. ⲉϧⲟⲩⲛ ⲉϧⲣⲁⲩ. *Cf* LMis
459.

ϣⲁⲣⲃⲱⲧ *B*   *v* ϣⲁⲁⲣ *skin*.

ϣⲁⲣⲕⲉ *SB*(mostly) nn m, *lack of water, drought*
(cf شراق AZ 14 42): Jer 14 1 (*S* ⲙⲡⲉⲟⲩⲟⲩⲙⲡⲉ ϣⲱⲡⲉ) ἀβροχία; C 41 20 ⲟⲩⲛⲓϣϯ ⲡϣ. = Miss 4 351
غلاء وقحطاء;   adj: Jer 17 8 ⲣⲟⲙⲡⲓ ⲡϣ. ἀβ.; Va 57
33 ⲟⲩⲕⲁϩⲓ ⲙⲡⲉⲧⲣⲁ ⲡϣ. ⲉϥϭⲡⲏⲟⲩⲧ, Mor 55 81 *S*
ⲕⲁϧ ⲡϣⲁⲣⲕⲏ ⲛⲁⲧⲙⲟⲟⲩ;   ⲣ ϣ. *S*, *be dried up*: PS
213 he knoweth why ⲁⲡⲕⲁϧ ⲣ ϣⲁ(ⲣ)ⲕⲉ ⲁⲩⲱ ⲁⲡⲙⲟⲩ ⲉⲓ ⲉϫⲱϥ. *V* AZ 53 133 (as if ϣⲁⲣ- *small, qv*).

ϣⲱⲣⲡ *SA²*(nn)*BF*(nn), ϧⲱ. *A*(nn), ϣⲱⲗ(ⲉ)ⲡ *F*
(nn), ϣ(ⲉ)ⲣ(ⲉ)ⲡ- *S*, ϣⲉⲣⲡ- *B*, ϣⲟⲣⲡϩ *SB*, ϧⲁⲣⲡϩ *A*,
ϣⲟⲣⲡϯ *S*(once)vb **I** intr (rare), *be early S*: R 1 1 39
in morning ⲁⲩϣ. (ὀρίζειν misunderst); ShA 1 2 ⲙ-
ⲡⲣϣ. ⲡⲁⲣⲁ ⲡⲛⲁⲩ, COAd 49 ⲛϥϣⲟⲣⲡ ⲉϧⲣⲁⲓ ⲛⲧⲟⲩ-
ϣⲏ;   qual *S*: Job 29 7 (so Ep 9, *B* ⲛϣⲱⲣⲡ) ὄρ-
θριος.   **II** tr (refl): Ge 19 2 *SB*, 1 Kg 17 20 *SB*
ὀρθρίζειν; ShA 2 232 *S* ⲧϭⲓⲛⲁⲙⲉⲗⲉⲓ ⲉⲧⲛϣⲟⲣⲡⲓ, AZ
21 156 *S* ϣⲣⲡⲧⲏⲩⲧⲛ ⲛⲡⲧⲟⲟⲩ, AM 250 *B* ϣⲟⲣⲡϯ
ⲡⲣⲁⲥⲧ, BMar 5 *S* ϣⲁϥϣⲟⲣⲡϥ ⲉϧⲧⲟⲟⲩⲉ.

With prep.   ⲉ ⲉ-, *be early to, at*: Ps 77 34 *S*
(*B* ϧⲁ-), Si 6 37 *S* ὀρ. πρός; ShC 73 53 *S* ⲉⲩϣⲁⲛϣ.
ⲉⲧⲟⲟⲩϧ, R 1 2 60 *S* ⲛⲡϣ. ⲉⲧⲉⲕⲕⲗⲏⲥⲓⲁ, AM 252
B ⲟⲩⲟⲛ ⲛⲓⲃⲉⲛ ϣⲟⲣⲡⲟⲩ ⲉϯⲉⲕⲕⲗⲏⲥⲓⲁ, Ep 134 *S*
ⲡⲧⲁϣ. ⲉⲧⲡⲟⲗⲓⲥ ⲛⲧⲉⲩϣⲏ, ShC 42 45 *S* ⲉⲧⲉⲧⲛϣ.
ⲙⲙⲱⲧⲛ ⲉⲡⲙ. *on whose account?*;   ⲉⲃⲟⲗ ⲉ-: Cant
7 12 *S* ὀρ. εἰς;   ⲉ ⲉⲣⲁⲧϥ: Hos 6 1 *SA*(*B* ϧⲁ-), Lu
21 38 *S*(*B* do) ὀρ. πρός;   ⲉ ϣⲁ- *S*: Is 26 9 (var ⲉ-,
B ϧⲁ-)ὀρ. πρ.;   ⲉ ϧⲁ- *B*: Ps 62 2 (*S* ⲉ-), Is Hos *llc*.

ϣⲣⲡ- *S* preceding a vb, *first, before, already*: Jth
13 2 ϣ. ⲡⲟϧϥ, Mt 24 25 ϣ. ϫⲟⲟⲩ (*B* ⲉⲣ ϣⲟⲣⲡ ⲛ-),
Ro 1 2 ϣ. ⲉⲣⲏⲧ (*B* do), BHom 35 ϣ. ⲥⲱⲧⲙ, Miss 8
77 ϣ. ⲧⲁϧⲟϥ Gk all προ-; ShA 2 97 prophets ϣ.
ⲡⲁⲩ ⲉⲡⲉⲧⲛⲁϣⲱⲡⲉ, R 1 3 78 ⲡⲉϥϣ. ⲥⲟⲟⲩⲛ ⲙⲡⲁⲓ-
ⲡⲓⲙⲁ, Mor 18 51 fathers ⲡⲧⲁⲩϣ. ⲡⲕⲟⲧⲕ, J 50 28
ⲡⲉⲛⲧⲁϥϣ. ⲥϧⲁⲓ ⲛⲧⲡⲉ (cf προγεγραμμένος & below
ⲣ ϣⲣⲡ-), ib 5 37 ⲁⲓϣ. ϩⲏⲗⲟⲩ ⲙⲙⲟϥ (cf προδηλοῦν);   ϯ ⲛ-: Z 277 ⲛⲧⲁⲡϣ. ⲛⲧⲁϧⲟⲟⲩ ⲡⲣⲟⲉⲓⲣⲏ-
ⲙⲉⲛⲟⲥ; ViK 9753 34 ⲡⲉⲛⲧⲁϥϣ. ⲡϧⲟⲟⲩ, J 47 40 ⲡ-
ⲧⲁⲓϣ. ⲡϫⲏⲗⲟⲩ.

ϣⲱ., ϧⲱ. nn *SABF*, *morning*: Jud 9 35 *S*, Ps 54
18 *B*(*S* ϧⲧⲟⲟⲩⲉ), Mk 13 35 *F*-ⲗⲡ (*S* ⲡⲛⲁⲩ ⲛϩ., *B*
ϧⲁⲡⲁⲧⲟⲟⲩⲓ), Is 5 11 *F* ϧⲓϣ. (*S* ⲉϧ., *B* ⲛⲧⲟⲟⲩⲓ) πρωί,
AM 277 *B* ϣ. ⲡⲉ πρωία ἐστί; Job 7 4 *B*(*S* ϧ.), MG
25 6 *B* ⲉⲧⲁϣ. ϫⲉ ϣⲱⲡⲓ ἡμέρα; Jer 51 4 *B* ⲓⲥϫⲉⲛϣ.

(S ⲛϣⲟ.), ib 7 25 B ϧⲓϣ. ὄρθρου; ShC 73 60 S ⲉϣⲱⲡⲉ ⲙⲉⲛ ⲉϣ. ⲡⲉ, ShC 42 111 S ϣ. ⲛⲧⲕⲩⲣⲓⲁⲕⲏ, Mor
18 50 S ϣ. ⲙⲡⲉϥⲣⲁⲥⲧⲉ (var 19 58 ϧ.), ib 48 32 S
prayed ϣⲁϣ. (var BMar 218 ϣⲁⲣ.) = Rec 6 184 B,
Mor 30 25 F slept ϣⲁϣ., C 41 64 B ϣⲁϣⲟ. ⲧⲉⲡⲛⲁ-
ϣⲉ, Ryl 106 32 S recipe ⲟⲩⲟⲙϥ ϧⲁϣ., PO 11 386 B
ⲉⲧⲁϣ. ϣⲱⲡⲓ; ⲡⲛⲁⲩ ⲛϣ.: Ex 16 13 B(S ϧ.), Is
14 12 B(Sdo) ⲡ., Joel 2 23 A(SB ⲛϣ.) πρώιμος; Ps
56 8 S(B ⲛϧⲁⲡ.) ὄρ., Hos 13 3 A(B ⲛϣ.) ὀρθρινός, Ps
138 8 S(B do) κατ' ὄρθρόν.

ϣⲟⲣⲡ SBF, ϣⲁⲣ(ⲉ)ⲡ A²F, ϧⲁⲣⲡ A, ϣ(ⲉ)ⲣⲡ- SA²B,
ϧⲣⲡ- A, f ϣⲟⲣⲡⲉ S, -ⲡⲓ B, ϣⲁⲣⲡⲓ F & m as f, as nn,
earliest, first: Ge 32 17 S(B ϧⲟⲅⲓⲧ), Job 18 20 SB,
ib 42 14 f S(B do f), Is 44 6 S(B ⲛϣ.), Hag 2 9 SAB,
He 8 7 f SF-ⲣⲡ (B ϧ. f) πρῶτος, Si 41 3 S, Is 65 17
SB πρότερος; ROC 17 408 B ⲭⲱⲭⲉⲃ ⲉⲛϣ. προλαμ-
βάνειν; Job 42 12 S(B ϧ.) τὰ ἔμπροσθεν; Is 41 26 B
(S ϫⲓⲛⲛϣ.) τὰ ἐξ ἀρχῆς, Ro 16 5 S(B ⲁⲣⲭⲏ) ἀπαρ-
χή, Ps 138 4 SB ἀρχαῖος; Sa 12 3 S παλαιός; Sh
Wess 9 108 S ⲛⲉϥϣ. ⲁⲩⲱ ⲛⲉϥϧⲁⲉⲟⲩ, BMis 96
S sinners ⲁⲡⲟⲕⲡⲉ ⲡⲉϥϣ., BM 178 88 S ⲧϣ. ⲧⲉ
ⲙⲁⲣⲓⲁ, Va 59 2 B ⲟⲩϣ. ⲇⲉⲡⲡⲉϥⲁϩⲓⲱⲙⲁ, C 43
175 B tortures ⲉⲩⲇⲟⲥⲓ ⲡⲁⲣⲁ ⲛϣ.; c ⲉ-: Va 65
118 (palimps) B ⲁⲡⲟⲕⲡⲉ ⲛϣ. ⲉⲁϫⲁⲗ take precedence of; ⲉⲡϣ. (for ⲛⲛϣ.) advb F: BM 580 9
ϫⲓ ⲡⲉϥϧⲁⲙⲧ ⲉⲥⲟⲩⲁ ⲉⲡϣ., ib 26 ϣⲁⲓⲟⲅⲁⲧⲉ ⲡⲁϣⲏⲓ
ⲉⲡϣ.; ⲛⲧⲉ ϣ. B: Job 8 8 (S ϣ. ⲛ-) πρῶ., Deu 4
32 (S ⲛϣ.) πρότ.; Ps 88 50 (S = Gk) Lam 1 8 (F
ⲛϣ.) ἀρχ., Va 59 158 soul's ⲥⲱⲙⲁ ⲛⲧⲉ ϣ., MG 25
362 ⲡⲉϥⲁⲟⲅⲁⲡ ⲛⲧⲉ ϣ.

——, as adj, a before nn: Nu 7 12 S(B ϧ.), Sa 7
3 f S, Ap 20 5 f S(B ϧ. f) πρῶ., Mic 6 7 AB πρωτό-,
Jth 10 11 S, Eph 1 11 BF(S diff), P 129¹⁴ 61 S ⲛⲉⲩϣ.
ⲙⲃⲓⲟⲥ, Is 28 4 B(S v ⲥⲉⲧⲏ) προ-; PS 3 S ⲛϣ. ⲛⲧⲱϣ
(cf ib 1 ⲛϣⲣⲡⲧ.), J 18 54 S ⲛϣ. ⲛⲧⲩⲡⲟⲥ (cf πρωτο-
τύπως PLond 1 234), Mor 41 11 S ⲛϣ. ⲛⲥⲧⲩⲗⲗⲟⲥ
= DeV 2 260 B ⲡⲓⲥ. ⲛϩⲟⲩⲓⲧ, ib 2 161 B ⲛϣ. ⲙ-
ⲙⲁⲣⲧⲩⲣⲟⲥ, Mani 2 A² ⲧⲉⲥϥ. ⲡⲟⲩⲥⲓⲁ, ST 378 S
ⲧϣ. ⲡⲣⲟⲙⲡⲉ; f -ⲡⲉ, -ⲡⲓ: Dan 9 1 S(B ϧ. f), Mt
22 38 S(B do) πρῶ., He 7 18 F(S ϣⲟⲣⲡ, B do) προ-;
Ge 32 8 S(B ⲟⲅⲓ) μία; Va 57 188 B ϯϣ. ⲡⲉⲡⲓⲥⲧⲟⲗⲏ,
ROC 27 163 B ⲧⲉⲡϣ. ⲙⲙⲁⲩ, Bor 239 78 S ⲧⲉⲧϣ.
ⲛⲥⲡⲟⲩⲁⲏ (var R 1 2 42 ϣⲟⲣⲡ); ϣⲣⲡ ⲛ- SA:
Ex 4 23 A(B ϣⲟⲣⲡ ⲛ-), Pro 24 70 SA, He 12 23 (B
ϣⲁ-, cit DeV 2 87 ϣⲟⲣⲡ ⲛ-) πρωτο-, Job 15 7 (B
diff) πρῶ., 1 Pet 1 2 (ST 14, var om ⲛ-, B ϣⲟⲣⲡ ⲛ-),
R 1 2 64 ϣ. ⲛⲧⲱϣ προ-; Pro 9 10 SA(B = Gk)
ἀρχή; BG 29 ⲛϣ. ⲛⲥⲟⲟⲩⲛ. b after nn: Dan 8
21 S(B ϧ. ⲛ-) πρῶ., Lev 23 17 S(B ϣ. ⲛ-), Lu 11
43 S(B do) πρωτο-; Ge 40 13 S(B ⲛⲧⲉ ϣ.), Is 1 26
SB πρότ., Nah 2 6 A(B om) προ-; Ps 43 1 S(B ⲛⲧⲉ
ϣ.) ἀρχαῖος, Is 2 6 SB ἀπ' ἀρχῆς, Ez 38 17 B ἔμπρ.;
TT 55 S ⲡⲉϩⲟⲟⲩ ⲛϣ., Miss 4 179 B ⲙⲫⲣⲏϯ ⲛϣ.

ⲛϣⲱ., ⲛϧⲱ. SAA²BF, ⲛϣⲟ. SB(rare) advb, early:
Ge 21 14 B(S ⲉϧ.), Eccl 10 16 F(S ⲙⲡⲛⲁⲩ ⲛϧ.)
πρωί, Joel 2 23 S ⲛϣⲟ. B(A ⲙⲡⲛⲟ ⲛϧⲱ.) πρώιμος;
Jos 6 15 S, Jer 42 14 S ⲛϣⲟ. B, AP 9 A² ὄρθρου,
ROC 10 431 S ⲁⲕⲉⲓ ⲉⲡⲉⲓⲙⲁ ⲛϣ. ὀρθρινός; Pro 29
33 A(S ⲛϭⲱⲣ̅ϧ̅) ἐκ νυκτῶν; Aeg 282 S arise ⲛϣ.
ἑώθεν; ShC 73 60 S ϫⲉⲣⲉ ϧⲏⲃⲥ ⲛϣ., BHom 112 S
ϣⲁϥⲧⲱⲟⲩⲛ ⲛϣ. ⲙⲙⲏⲛⲉ, Miss 4 176 B ⲛϣ. ⲙⲡⲓⲉϩⲟⲟⲩ ⲉⲧⲉⲙⲙⲁⲩ, LAp 566 F ⲁϥⲧ[ⲱⲡϥ] ⲛϣ., C 43
182 B ⲁⲩϣⲁⲡⲧⲱⲟⲩⲛⲟⲩ ⲛϣⲟ., JKP 2 22 Sᶠ sun
riseth ⲉϣ., BM 527 F recipe ⲥⲁⲁϥ ⲡⲁⲕ ⲉϣⲱⲣⲡⲓ;
ⲛϩⲁϣ. S: PMich 590 if wind arise ⲛ. ⲛϣⲟ., ϣⲟ.,
at first, formerly: Is 9 1 SB, Mt 13 30 SBF, Jo 15
18 B(SA² ϧⲁⲧϩⲏ), Ro 1 8 S(var ϣ.) B, Aeg 240 S
ⲉⲧⲣⲉⲓⲱϩⲁⲡⲡⲓⲥ ϣⲁϫⲉ ⲛϣ., Cl 23 4 A ϧ. ⲙⲉⲛ ϩⲁ-
ⲣⲟⲩϫⲁⲗⲟⲥ πρῶτον, Nu 2 3 SB, Is 11 14 SB, ib 44 6
B ⲁⲡⲟⲕ ⲛϣ. ⲡⲉ (S ⲁ. ⲡⲉ ⲛϣ.) πρῶτος, Deu 17 7 SB,
Cai Euch 345 B ⲛϣ. ⲙⲉⲛ ⲁⲣⲓ ⲫⲙⲉⲩⲓ ἐν πρώτοις,
Job 42 11 SB ἐκ πρώτου, Est 3 1 S, Sa 10 1 S πρω-
το-, Ge 13 3 SB, Is 52 4 SB, Jo 6 62 SA²B τὸ πρό-
τερον, Ro 11 35 SF(B ⲉⲣ ϣ. ⲛ-), MG 25 2 B ⲁϥ-
ϫⲉⲙ ⲧⲁⲣⲭⲏ ⲛϣ. προ-; Ez 16 55 SB ἀπ' ἀρχῆς;
Jer 7 12 B ἔμπρ.; Sa 12 27 S πάλαι; BMar 115 S
who went with me ⲛϣ. πότε; PS 131 S ⲑⲉ ⲉⲡⲉϧⲟ
ⲙⲙⲟⲥ ⲛϣ., Br 52 S ⲛϣ. ⲁϥⲧⲣⲉⲥⲃⲟⲩⲃⲟⲩ, Mani H
50 A² ⲛϣ. ⲁϥⲕⲉⲗⲉⲩⲉ, ShC 73 60 S may not go except ⲡⲥⲉⲕⲱⲗϫ ⲛϣ., ib 46 ⲛⲉⲡⲧⲁϥⲉⲓ ⲉϩⲟⲩⲛ ⲛϣ. =
ib ⲛⲃⲉⲣⲣⲉ, Va 61 210 B hath spurned me ⲙⲫⲣⲏϯ
ⲛⲕⲁⲓⲛ ⲛϣ., Cat 122 B ⲉⲃⲏⲗ ⲛϣ. ⲛⲧⲉⲡⲣⲱⲙⲓ ⲡⲟϫⲉⲙ
he cannot serve God; initial phrase in letters: Rec
6 64 S ϧⲙⲡⲣⲁⲛ ⲙⲡⲛⲟⲩⲧⲉ ⲛϣ., Kr 72 F ϧⲉⲡ]ⲗⲉⲛ ⲡⲛⲟⲩ-
ⲧⲓ ϣⲁⲣⲉⲛ, ST 252 S ϣ. ⲙⲉⲛ ϯϣⲓⲡⲉ, CMSS 28 F sim
ⲛϣ.; CA 99 S ϣ. ⲙ. ⲙⲁⲣⲉϥⲣ ⲡⲙⲉⲉⲩⲉ, AM 197
B ϣ. ⲙⲉⲛ ⲡⲉⲡⲣⲁⲡⲡⲉ ⲭⲣⲓⲥⲧⲓⲁⲛⲟⲥ; ⲛϣ., ϣ. ⲛ-,
before: Aeg 273 S ⲛϣ. ⲙⲉⲛ ⲙⲡⲉⲓⲗⲟⲅⲟⲥ τὰ μ. πρῶ-
τα; ShC 42 99 S ⲉϥⲟⲩⲱϣ ⲛϣ. ⲡⲣⲱⲃ ⲛⲓⲙ, DeV 1
59 B Jesus' mother there ⲛϣ. ⲛ̅ⲏ̅ⲥ̅; in letters: MR
5 27 S ⲛϣ. ⲙⲉⲛ ⲡⲣⲱⲃ ⲛⲓⲙ (cf πρὸ μὲν πάντων P
Lond 5 245, POxy 1863 & in Copt προ ⲡⲁⲡⲧⲱⲡ RE
9 136, CO 90, ST 267, also ϧⲁⲑⲏ ⲙⲉⲛ ⲛ-), CO 216
S ⲛϣ. ⲙⲉⲛ ⲙⲡⲛϣⲁϫⲉ; ⲛϣ. ⲉ-, sim: Nu 32 30 S
(B ⲇⲁϫⲉⲛ-) πρότ. gen, Va 57 232 B woman ⲛϣ. ⲉ-
ⲡⲉⲥϩⲁⲓ πρό, Ac 27 34 B(S ϧⲁⲑⲏ ⲛ-) reading πρό;
R 1 3 41 S ⲛϭⲣ ⲡⲁⲓ ⲛϣ. ⲉⲡⲁⲓ, Mor 18 77 S shalt go
ⲛϣ. ⲉⲣⲟⲓ = Miss 4 148 B, Mani 1 A² went ⲛϣ. ⲁ-
ⲣⲁϥ, FR 104 B ϣⲟⲡⲧⲉⲛ ⲉⲣⲟⲕ ⲛϣ. ⲉⲣⲟⲥ.

ⲕⲁⲧⲁ ϣⲟ. S, as formerly: Hall 28 ⲉⲡⲛ̅ⲉ̅ ⲧⲟϣⲧ
ⲕ. ϣ.

ϫⲓⲛ(ⲡ)ϣⲟ. SAA², ϫⲓⲛⲉϣ. SF, ⲛϫⲓⲛ- SᶠF, ⲓⲥⲭⲉⲛ-
ϣ. B, from the beginning: Ac 2 31 B(S ϣⲣⲡ-), ib 4 28
S(B ⲉⲣ ϣ. ⲛ-) προ-, Is 41 4 S(B ϣ. nn) πρῶτος; 1
Kg 9 9 S ϫⲓⲛⲉ- (var ϫⲓⲛⲛ-) ἔμπρ., Eccl 1 10 F ⲛϫ.
(PMich 3520, S & Schmidt's F ϧⲁⲑⲏ) ἀπ' ἔμπρ.; Ps

73 2 *SB*, Mt 19 4 *S*(*B* ⲓⲥϫⲉⲛϩⲏ) ἀπ' ἀρχῆς, He 1 10 *SF* ⲛϫ. (*B* do) κατ' ἀρ., Jo 6 64 *SA²B* ἐξ ἀρ.; Is 37 26 *B*(*S* ⲛϣ.) πάλαι; PS 9 *S* ⲛⲉϥϣⲟⲟⲡ ϫ., ShC 42 126 *S* ϫⲁⲣⲧⲏⲥ ⲉⲧⲥⲏϩ ϫⲓⲛ. (var ϫⲓⲓⲛ.), BMis 160 *S* sin through woman ϫⲓⲛⲉ., Miss 8 258 *Sf* ⲛϫⲓⲛⲉ. till now, MR 2 111 *F* ⲡⲟⲥ̅ ⲉϫⲓⲛⲉ., Mani H 47 *A²* ϫⲛⲡⲧϣ., DeV 2 102 *B* ⲓⲥϫ. ϣ. when He made man.

ⲣ, ⲉⲣ ϣⲟ., ⲟ, ⲟⲓ ⲛϣ. *SAA²BF*, be before, first, hasten: Ex 35 34 *B*, Ac 20 5 *SB*, 2 Jo 9 *S*(*B* ⲙⲟϣⲓ ⲉⲧϩⲏ) προ-, Mt 19 30 *SB* πρῶ. εἶναι; C 99 239 *S* ⲁϥⲣ. ⲁϥⲧⲁⲗⲉ ⲧⲉϥⲧⲁⲛ = *ib* 89 74 *B* ⲁϥϫⲱⲗⲉⲙ ⲁϥⲉⲣ., Z 280 *S* ⲁⲩⲣ. ⲁⲩⲃⲱⲕ ⲉϩⲟⲩⲛ, C 99 197 *S* ⲛⲙⲁ ⲉⲧⲕⲛⲁⲣ. ⲛϯϥⲉ ⲉⲙⲟⲟⲩ ⲛϩⲏⲧϥ, BM 153 53 *S* ⲁⲣⲓ ϣ. ⲛϫⲓ = *ib* 511 (3) *F* ⲁⲗⲓ ϣ. ⲛϫⲓ, BSM 5 *B* what wilt more ⲙⲉⲡⲉⲛⲥⲁⲑⲣⲉⲕⲉⲣ. ⲡⲧⲉⲕϫⲱ after hast already spoken? = BMis 322 *S* ⲟⲩⲱ ⲉϫⲓⲧⲟⲩ, C 43 117 *B* ⲁϥⲉⲣ. ⲁϥⲁⲗⲏⲓ ⲉϫⲉⲡⲡⲓⲃⲏⲙⲁ, Mor 56 6 *S* ⲡⲉⲧⲟ ⲛϣ. ϩⲓⲧⲡⲟⲗⲓⲥ;   c ⲉ-: Jo 1 15 *S*(*B* ϣ. nn) πρῶ. gen, Nu 14 14 *S*(*B* ⲥⲱⲕ ϩⲁϫⲉⲛ-) πρότ. gen, Jo 5 7 *SA²B* πρό, Ps 16 13 *SBF*, Mt 17 25 *SB* προφθάνειν; *ib* 26 32 *SB* προάγειν; Ac 20 5 *SB* προέρχεσθαι; PS 198 *S* ⲥⲉⲛⲁⲣ. ⲉⲛⲁⲧⲟⲡⲟⲥ, ShA 1 407 *S* man sinneth not except his will ⲣ. ⲉⲡⲙⲉⲉⲩⲉ ⲙⲡⲁⲓⲁⲃⲟⲗⲟⲥ go to meet, BMis 454 *S* ⲁⲩⲣ. ⲉⲟⲩⲏⲏⲃ began with priest, then townsfolk, RNC 78 *S* ⲁⲣⲓ ϣ. ⲉⲣⲟⲓ & stand by me, LMis 178 *S* great trials ⲟ ⲛϣ. ⲉⲣⲟⲛ, AM 43 *B* ⲁϥⲣ. ⲉⲡⲓⲙⲁⲧⲟⲓ outstripped;   ⲉⲃⲟⲗ ⲉ-*S*: 3 Kg 21 14 συνάπτειν;   ⲉϩⲟⲩⲛ ⲉ-: PS 97 *S* ⲧⲉⲧⲛⲁⲣ. ⲉϩ. ⲉⲧⲙⲡⲧⲉⲣⲟ;   vbal: Pro 13 12 *SA*(*B* ϯ ⲛⲧⲟⲧϥ) ἐνάρχεσθαι; Ez 33 9 *SB* προ-; Aeg 247 *S* ⲉⲣ. ⲉⲧⲉϣ ⲡⲁⲓ φθάνειν; ShMIF 23 74 *S* ⲣ. ⲉϥⲓ ⲙⲙⲁⲩ, ShBM 253 57 *S* ϥⲣ. ⲉⲉⲓⲙⲉ ⲙⲡⲭⲓⲕⲃⲁ speedily bringeth, BIF 13 109 *S* ⲣ. ⲉⲥⲟⲩⲱⲛⲟⲩ be first to know = MG 25 295 *B*;   c ⲉϫⲛ-*S*: Is 27 2 (*B* = Gk) ἐξάρχειν κατά;   Bor 240 58 let not pleasure ⲁⲣϫⲓ ⲏ ⲡⲥⲉⲣ. ⲉϫⲛⲡⲉⲧ(ⲛ)ⲡⲁⲟⲩⲟⲙⲟⲩ;   c ⲛ- vbal *S*(rare)*AA²BF*: Ex 32 34 (*S* ϩⲁⲧⲉϩⲛ), Ps 15 8 (*S* om), *ib* 67 32 *S* (var ⲉ-)*B*, *ib* 118 148 (*S* ϣⲱⲣⲡ vb), Pro 9 9 *A*(*S* om ⲛ-, Gk misunderst, *B* ⲉⲣ ⲛϣⲟⲣ⳿, Is 41 26 (*S* ⲙⲡⲁⲧⲟⲩϣⲱⲡⲉ), Ac 1 16 (*S* ϫⲓⲛⲛϣ.), 2 Cor 13 2 *BF*(*S* do), Cl 43 1 *A* ⲛⲉⲧⲁⲩⲣ. ⲛϫⲟⲟⲩⲉ, Cai Euch 522 ⲁⲩⲉⲣ. ⲡⲉⲡⲕⲟⲧ, C 89 3 ⲉⲣ. ⲛⲉⲙⲓ = *ib* 99 211 *S* ϣⲣⲡ ⲉⲓⲙⲉ προ-; ShIF 262 *S* tree ⲙⲡϣⲣ. ⲛϣⲟⲟⲩⲉ, Mani K 95 *A²* ⲣ ϣ. ⲛⲉⲉϥ, MIE 2 394 words ⲉⲧⲁⲛⲉⲣ. ⲛϫⲟⲧⲟⲩ = BAp 120 *S* ϣⲣⲡ ϫⲟⲟϥ, AM 32 ⲁⲡⲭⲥ̅ ⲕⲏⲛ (ⲉ)ⲉⲣ. ⲛⲧⲁⲙⲟⲛ, DeV 1 23 ⲁⲛⲉⲣ. ⲛϣⲱⲡⲓ ⲉⲛⲧⲟⲩⲃⲏⲟⲩⲧ, C 43 206 ⲁϥⲉⲣ. ⲛⲟϣ ⲉⲃⲟⲗ began, BIF 13 114 *S* ⲁϥⲣ. ⲛⲉⲡⲕⲟⲧⲕ = MG 25 305 *B* ⲉⲣ ϩⲏⲧⲥ;   ⲣ ϣⲣⲡ ⲛ-*S*: BG 30 ⲡⲧⲁⲣ. ⲛⲟⲩⲱⲛϩ ⲉⲃⲟⲗ; ShWess 9 145 Baptist ⲣ. ⲛⲥⲟⲩⲧⲛ ⲛⲙⲁ ⲙⲙⲟⲟϣⲉ;   without ⲛ-: Mk 14 8 (*B* ⲉⲣ ϣⲟⲣⲡ ⲛ-)προ-; ShA 2 4 who hateth instruction ⲉⲙⲡϥⲣ. ⲙⲉⲥⲧⲉ (or ? ⲗ ⲙⲙⲛ.) ⲡⲉⲧϯ ⲙⲙⲟⲥ, BM 323 ⲕⲁⲧⲁ ⲑⲉ ⲉⲛⲧⲁⲓⲣ. ϫⲟⲟⲥ, CO 159 signatory ⲡⲉⲛ-

---

ⲧⲁϥⲣ. ⲥϩⲁⲓ;   c ϩⲁϫⲉⲛ- *B*: C 43 60 ⲁⲩⲉⲣ. ϩⲁ ϫⲱⲕ in heaven;   ⲣ ϣ. nn, being first, early: ClPr 46 *S* on Ps 118 147 ⲡⲣ.…ⲡⲡⲁⲡⲉ ϩⲁⲑⲏ ⲛⲧⲡⲁϣⲉ ⲡⲧⲉⲩϣⲏ;   ⲙⲁⲓⲣ ϣ. *S*, loving to be first: 3 Jo 9 (*B* ⲙⲁⲓⲉⲣ ϩⲟⲩⲓⲧ) φιλοπρωτεύειν;   ⲣⲉϥⲉⲣ ϣ. *B*: Cat 5 ⲣ. ⲛⲉⲙⲓ foreknowing.

ⲙⲛⲧϣⲣⲡ-*S*: C 100 337 chose apostles ϩⲛⲧⲉϥⲙ. ⲥⲟⲟⲩⲛ.

ϭⲓⲛϣⲱⲣⲡ *S*, state of being early: ShA 2 231 on Ps 62 2 ⲧⲉⲛϭⲓⲛϣⲟⲣⲡ ⲉⲣⲁⲧϥ; BMis 529 ⲧⲉϥϭⲓⲛϣⲉⲣⲡⲥⲟⲟⲩⲛ ⲛⲛⲉⲧⲛⲁϣⲱⲡⲉ (*cf ib* ⲙⲛⲧⲡⲣⲟⲅⲛⲱⲥⲧⲏⲥ.) *V* also ⲙⲓⲥⲉ p 185 *a infra*.

ϣⲣⲱⲓⲥ *B* v ⲣⲟⲉⲓⲥ sf.

ϣⲟⲣⲧ *SSf*, ϣⲟⲟ. *S*, ϣⲁ. *Sf* nn m, awning, veil: Ex 40 19 (P 43 88 = 44 104 ϣⲟⲟ., *B* ⲁⲩⲗⲏ) αὐλαία قلس; ShA 2 157 ⲉⲩⲕⲱ ⲡⲟⲩϣ. ⲉϫⲙⲡⲉⲩϩⲟ ⲉϥⲕⲱⲧⲉ, Miss 4 236 σκηνή of skins & ϩⲉⲛϣ. ⲛⲗⲁ ϭⲟ (*cf* Ex *lc*), Ep 564 ϣⲙⲟⲩⲛ ⲡⲉⲧⲟϩ…ⲛϥⲧⲟⲟⲩ ⲛϣ.…ⲥⲟⲟⲩ ⲛⲙⲁⲣⲉ ⲉⲡϣ.; PMich frag *Sf* ⲥⲁ ⲛϣⲁ., *ib* ⲥⲁ ⲛϣⲟ.

ϣⲱⲣⲧ *SB*, ϣⲟ.† *B*, ϣⲁ.† *A²* vb intr, be demented: C 86 346 *B* ⲁⲟⲩⲁⲓ…ϣ. ⲁϥⲉⲣ ⲁⲉⲙⲱⲛ تَبِّخ, MG 25 68 *B* dragging him this way & that like ⲛⲏ ⲉⲧϣ.† = GöttAr 114 12 تبخ, Mani K 34 *A²* ⲣⲉϥϯ ⲙⲉⲓⲛⲉ ⲉⲧⲣⲏⲧⲩⲡⲟⲥ ⲛⲓⲙ ϩⲛⲛⲉⲧϣ.†;   tr, derange: P 131ᵃ 33 *S* ⲛⲥⲉϣ. ⲙⲡⲉⲛⲡⲁⲓⲟⲣⲁⲧⲓⲕⲟⲛ & blind mind's eyes. *Cf* ϩⲱⲣⲧ.

ϣⲁⲣⲱⲧ, -ⲱⲁ, -ⲟⲁ *F* nn, meaning unknown: PMich 584 list of sheep ⲛⲉⲥⲁⲩ ⲉⲧⲙⲁⲥⲓ, ⲡⲉⲓⲁⲗ, ⲡⲉϣⲁⲣⲱⲁ,…ⲡⲉϣⲁⲣⲟⲁ ⲡ[, ⲡⲉⲡⲁϭ ⲡϣⲁⲣⲁ[ⲁ, CMSS 78 ⲡϣⲏ ⲛⲁⲡⲟⲩ ⲁⲟⲟⲩⲁ ϩ (ⲉϩⲟⲩⲛ ὑπέρ) ⲟⲩϣⲁⲣⲱⲧ. Coptic? Prob not in place-name ⲡⲓϣⲁⲣⲱⲧ (Amélineau *Géog* 349).

ϣⲣⲱⲧ *S* nn m, meaning unknown: Vict & Alb Mus stele 56163 ⲡϣⲃ̅ⲣ ⲉⲡⲛϣⲣⲱⲧ. Place?

ϣⲟⲣⲧϥ *B* v ϣⲟⲧⲣⲉϥ.

ϣⲁⲣⲓⲟⲩ v ϣⲁⲗⲓⲟⲩ.

ϣⲁⲣⲟⲩⲱⲧ v ϣⲁⲁⲣ skin.

(ϣⲱⲣϣ), ϣⲁⲣϣ† *Sᵃ* vb intr, meaning unknown: Louvre ostr R 1780 make effort to pay her it (sc ⲛⲡⲧⲁⲃ ⲛⲥⲟⲩⲱ), for ⲟⲩⲟⲛ ⲟⲩϭⲟⲗⲟⲕ/ ⲡⲓⲟⲩϥ ϣ. ϩⲁⲣⲟϥ.

ϣⲣϣⲉ *S* nn, meaning unknown: CO 220 camel-herd's contract ⲛⲕⲛⲁⲁⲩ ⲉⲧⲉⲓ[…] ⲉⲣⲟϥ ⲉⲓⲧⲉ ϣ. ⲉⲓⲧⲉ ⲡⲣⲁⲥⲟⲩ (? ⲣ ⲁⲥⲟⲩ). *Cf* in next 2 Cor 12 *S* ϫⲟⲕϫⲉⲕ & so ? connect here with branding of camels (v Schnebel 1 334).

ϣⲉⲣϣⲓ *B* nn m, hilarity, mockery: Jer 20 8 χλευασμός; Gal 5 21 (*S* ⲭⲏⲣ) κῶμος; 2 Cor 12 20 (*S* ϫⲟⲕϫⲉⲕ, *F* ϫⲏⲗϫⲉⲗ) ἐριθεία (v ϣⲣϣⲉ); TSBA 9

378 accosting him as man of God ⲣⲱⲥ ϩⲉⲛⲟⲩϣ. (cf 4 Kg 1 9), MG 25 69 despising him ϩⲉⲛⲡⲓϣⲁϣ ⲡⲉⲙⲡⲓϣ., Cat 157 ϣⲱⲡⲓ ⲛϣ. ⲛⲁⲣⲣⲉⲡⲫϯ (cf Lu 14 30 ⲥⲱⲃⲓ); as adj: Va 57 96 ⲣⲁⲓⲥⲱⲃⲓ ⲛϣ. ⲕⲱ.; C 89 136 ⲥⲁϫⲓ ⲛϣⲗⲟϥ ⲓⲉ...ⲛϣ. = ib 100 262 S ϣⲭⲥⲱⲃⲉ; ⲙⲉⲧⲣⲉϥⲑⲁⲙⲓⲉ ϣ.: Va 57 191 γελωτο-ποιός; ⲉⲣ ϣ., make sport, be light-hearted: Ac 2 13 (S ⲛⲟⲃⲛⲉⲍ)διαχλευάζειν; Bar 1 19 σχεδιάζειν; MG 25 257 ⲁⲩⲉⲣ., DeV 2 56 ⲧⲉⲡⲉⲣ. ⲧⲉⲡⲥⲱⲃⲓ; ⲣⲉϥⲉⲣ ϣ.: Va 61 91 ϩⲁⲡⲣ. = P 131³ 81 S ⲟⲩⲉϩ ⲥⲱⲃⲉ, Va 57 116 who is Only-begotten, creator or created, ⲟⲩⲣ. ⲡⲉⲍⲟⲩⲥⲓⲁⲥⲧⲏⲥ or one under authority? (confusion? with ⲉⲣϣⲓϣⲓ); ⲙⲉⲧⲣⲉϥⲉⲣ ϣ.: K 248 ⲉⲩⲥⲧⲣⲁⲡⲉⲗⲟⲥ (ι εὐτρά.), تلاعب, زهي; Va 61 116 ⲟⲩⲙ. paral ⲟⲩⲙⲉⲧⲗⲟⲓⲙⲟⲥ.

ϣⲱⲣϣⲓ B nn m, wrinkle, furrow in skin: K 75 ⲛⲓϣ. (var ⲡⲓ-) (اسارير سرو).

ϣⲟⲣϣⲣ S, ϣⲁⲣ. A², ϩⲁⲣϩⲣⲉ A, ϣⲟⲣϣⲉⲣ B, ϣⲁⲗϣⲉⲗ F, ϣⲣϣⲣ- S, ϩⲣϩⲣⲉ- A, ϣⲣϣⲱⲣ⸗ SA², ϣⲣϣⲟⲣ⸗ Sᵃ, ϩⲣϩⲱⲣ⸗ A, ϣⲉⲣϣⲱⲣ⸗ B, ϣⲉⲗϣⲱⲗ⸗ F, ϣⲣϣⲱⲣⲧ†, -ϣⲟⲣⲧ† S, ϩⲣϩⲁⲣⲧ† A vb I intr, upset, overturn: Job 12 14 S(B ⲥⲱⲥ) καταβάλλειν; Eccl 3 3 S καθαιρεῖν; Pro 10 32 SA(B ⲫⲱⲛϩ ⲉⲃⲟⲗ) ἀπο-στρέφειν; Ac 15 16 S(B c.) καταστ.; PS 101 S ⲛⲥⲱ. ⲛϭⲓ ⲧⲉⲕⲕⲉⲣ̄ⲅⲗⲏ, ShC 73 19 S ⲥⲉⲛⲁϣ. ϣⲁⲡⲉⲩⲥⲡⲧⲉ, DeV 2 137 B tower ⲉⲧⲁ̄ϣ. ϣⲁⲧⲉϥϥⲁϣⲓ, Mor 30 29 F ⲙⲁ ⲛϭⲁⲓⲗⲓ ⲉⲧ̄ϣ. = ib 29 24 S; qual: Pro 25 28 SA καταβ.; ShA 2 272 S ϩⲉⲛⲙⲁ ⲉⲩϣ. ⲉⲩⲕⲏ ⲉⲃⲟⲗ, ShC 42 75 S ⲉⲩϣⲣϣⲟⲣⲧ ⲉϫⲡⲡⲉⲩⲉⲣⲏⲩ.

II tr: Ex 34 13 S(B ⲟⲩⲱϣⲡ), Ps 51 5 S(B ⲣⲱϩⲧ), Eccl 10 8 S(F ⲥⲱⲥ), Lu 12 18 SB καθ.; Pro 15 25 SA κατασπᾶν; Jo 2 15 SA²(B ⲫⲱⲛϫ) ἀναστρέφειν; Job 9 5 S(B ⲟⲩ.), Is 1 7 SF(B do), Cl 27 4 A καταστ.; Tit 1 11 S(B ⲣⲓⲕⲓ ⲉⲃⲟⲗ) ἀνατρέπειν, Sa 5 24 S περι-ριτρ.; Is 10 33 SB συνταράσσειν; Deu 12 3 S(B do), Hos 10 2 SA ϩⲣϩⲣⲉ- κατασκάπτειν; ShC 42 123 S ϣ. ⲛⲛⲡⲁⲣⲁⲇⲟⲥⲓⲥ, BHom 111 S ϣⲣϣⲱⲣϥ ϣⲁⲁⲡⲉϥ-ⲥⲡⲧⲉ, Imp Russ Ar S 18 029 Sᵃ ⲁⲕⲁϣⲣϣⲟⲣⲟⲩ, AP 40 A² ⲛⲧⲁ̄ϣ. ⲛⲧⲡⲓⲥⲧⲓⲥ, ManiH 11 A² ϣⲣϣⲱⲣⲥ, AM 74 B ϣ. ⲛⲛⲓⲉⲣⲫⲛⲟⲩⲓ, J 20 90 S ⲉⲕⲕⲱⲧ ⲙⲙⲟϥ (sc house) ⲉⲕϣ. ⲙⲙⲟϥ (cf below).

With following prep or advb. c ⲉ-: J 9 55 S hast power ⲉⲕⲱⲧ ⲉⲣⲟϥ ⲉϣ. ⲉⲣⲟϥ (cf above); c ⲉϫⲛ-: ShViK 915 S ϥϩⲏⲣ ⲉⲣⲉ ⲁⲩⲱ ⲉϣ. ⲉϫⲡⲡⲉϥ-ⲉⲣⲏⲩ, C 41 18 B devil wished ⲉϣⲉⲣϣⲱⲣⲉ (sc cistern) ⲉϫⲉⲛⲡⲓⲣⲱⲁⲧⲏⲥ; c ⲛⲥⲁ- emphasis: C 86 317 B ⲁϥϣ. ⲛⲥⲁⲛⲓϣⲟⲓ (var ⲛ-); c ⲉⲡⲉⲥⲛⲧ: BMis 28 S ϣ. ⲙⲡⲉⲣⲡⲉ ⲉ. ⲉϫⲱⲟⲩ, My 131 S ϣ. ⲉ. ⲛⲧⲙⲁ-ⲡⲓⲁ, Va 57 42 B ⲛⲧⲁⲕⲟ ⲉⲧ̄ϣ. ⲉ. ⲛⲛⲉⲧⲉⲛⲯⲩⲭⲏ; c ⲉϩⲣⲏⲓ: Ps 9 7 B(S om advb) καθαι.

—— nn m SABF, overthrow, destruction: Pro 1 19 SA(B ⲟⲩ.) καταστροφή; 2 Cor 13 10 SBF καθαί-

ρεσις; BHom 11 S ⲛϣ. ⲙⲡⲣⲡⲉ ⲕⲁⲧⲁⲥⲕ.; Ming 309 S sim πτῶμα; Aeg 234 S ⲉⲓⲣⲉ ⲡⲟⲩϣ. ⲡⲣⲉⲡⲛⲓ ἀνα-τροπή; Sh Cambr Univ Libr Add 1876 2 S ϣⲱⲡⲉ ⲛϣ. ⲛⲧⲉⲧⲣⲩⲡⲟⲙⲟⲛⲏ, MG 25 356 B worldly hon-ours ϩⲁⲛϣ. ⲡⲧⲉ ϯⲁⲣⲉⲧⲛⲉ (ROC 18 59 مذكّر).

ⲣⲉϥϣ., overthrower, destroyer: Sh(Besa)Bor 205 702 S ⲁⲛϣⲱⲡⲉ ⲛⲣ. ⲛⲛⲉⲡⲉⲣⲏⲩ, EW 63 B Elijah p. of altars.

ϭⲓⲛϣ. S, overthrowing, destruction: ShC 73 19 ϭⲓⲛⲕⲱⲧ, ϭ., Mor 56 24 ⲧϭ. ⲛⲛⲉⲓⲡⲉⲑⲟⲟⲩ.

ϣⲱⲣϫ S vb, meaning unknown: ST 189 ⲥⲟⲩⲟ ⲛϣ. (sic, not ⲛⲱⲣϫ), ⲣϣⲓⲛ ⲉⲩⲧⲙⲁ, ⲣϣⲓⲛ ⲉϥϩⲉⲭ-ϩⲱϫ. Cf? ⲥⲱⲣϣ.

ϣⲥ-, ϣⲥⲉ- v ⲥⲱϣ strike (ⲥⲁϣ).

ϣⲁⲉⲓⲥ, ϣⲟ. v ⲥⲟⲉⲓϣ a measure.

ϣⲱⲥ SAA²F, ϣⲱⲱⲥ, ϣⲟⲟⲥ S, ϣⲟⲥ, ϣⲁⲥ- F, pl ϣⲟⲟⲥ, ϣⲱⲱⲥ SA, ϣⲱⲟⲥ S, ϣⲁⲥ A, ϣⲁⲁⲥ F & sg (ϣⲱⲥ) as pl, nn m, herd, shepherd (B mostly ⲙⲁⲛⲉ-ⲥⲱⲟⲩ), cf ⲁⲙⲉ cowherd: Ge 46 32, Mic 5 5 SA, Jo 10 2 SA² ποιμήν; ShA 2 263 ⲧⲉϥⲁⲅⲉⲗⲏ ⲛ ⲛⲏ ⲙⲡϣ., R 1 5 25 ⲟⲩϣ. ⲙⲙⲁⲛⲉⲥⲟⲟⲩ, Ora 4 21 ⲕⲉⲗⲉⲗⲉ ⲛϣ., ⲓ̄ϣⲃⲱⲧ ⲡⲉⲗⲟⲓϩ, ϫⲟⲟⲕⲉϥ ⲡⲉⲙⲉ(ⲁⲙⲉ), BMis 379 ⲣⲱ-ⲙⲉ ⲛϣ. (var ϣ. only), ManiH 24 A², AZ 36 139 F, CMSS 78 F ϣⲟⲥ, MIF 59 151 ⲛϣⲱⲟⲥ, ib 150 ⲥⲱ-ⲱϣ; BM 1160, ST 47 ⲛϣⲟⲟⲥ, BM 226 Christ ⲡⲁⲣ-ⲭⲏϣ. (ἀρχιποι.); pl: Ge 29 3, Ex 2 19 SA, Is 32 14 F(S diff), Jer 23 1 F(S ϣⲟⲥ), Nah 3 18 A ϣⲟⲟⲥ, Lu 2 8 π., Zeph 2 6 A ϣⲱⲱⲥ (B ⲓⲟϩⲓ) ποίμνιον; Sh IF 87 ⲛϣⲱⲥ ⲛ ⲛϣⲟⲟⲥ, Bor 295 109 ⲡⲉⲓϣⲱⲥ, BP 11349 ⲛⲉϥϣⲟⲟⲥ, Ep App 1 136 flock following ⲛⲉϥ-ϣ., Pcod 38 F ϩⲉⲛϣⲁⲁⲥ, El 104 A ⲛϣⲁⲥ; CMSS 77 F ⲛϣⲁⲥⲃⲁⲙⲡⲉ; ⲙⲛⲧϣ. S, function of shep-herd: Z 286 ⲧⲙ. ⲉⲧϩⲓϫⲱⲓ (sc archbishop), PSBA 30 276 ⲧⲉⲕⲙ. ⲙⲙⲁⲛⲉⲥⲟⲟⲩ.

In place-names: ⲡⲟⲩⲁ ⲛⲡⲉϣⲟⲟⲥ (Kr 6, BM 1071, cf Πουανποιμῆνις & ⲡⲟⲩⲱϩ ⲡⲁⲙⲏⲩ), Φαινεϣⲟⲟⲥ (PLond 4 225). Cf? ϣⲟϣ (P 129¹⁴).

ϣⲱⲥ v ⲥⲱϣ be despised.

ϣⲱⲥⲙ SF, -ⲙⲉ A v ⲥⲱϣⲙ.

ϣⲱⲥⲙ O nn m, meaning unknown: PGM 1 50 ⲁⲛⲧ ⲕⲱⲟⲩ ⲃⲱⲟⲩ ⲛϣ.

ϣⲓⲥⲙⲉ A² nn m, statue, idol (cf ϣⲙ Polotsky): Mani 1 we are thy temple ⲛⲧⲁⲕⲡⲉ ⲛⲛϣ., ManiBerl Sitz '33 I Taf 1 ⲙⲙⲁ ⲛⲟⲩϣⲧ ⲛ(ⲛ)ϣ. ⲙⲛϩⲓⲕⲱⲛ, ManiH 60 ⲛϣ. ϣⲁⲓⲉ ⲁⲃⲁⲗ ϩⲁⲙⲡⲣ[ⲉ. Cf ϣⲓϣⲉⲙ.

ϣⲟⲥⲙⲉⲥ S nn f, fatigue (?): Mor 37 75 ⲧϣ. ⲛ ⲧⲃⲱⲧⲉ ⲙⲡⲛϣⲱⲙ, P 131⁶ 5 dust, sweat & ⲧϣ. ⲙⲡⲛ-ⲕⲁⲅⲙⲁ. Cf ⲥⲱϣⲙ.

ϣⲥⲛⲉ SSʲ, ϣⲥⲛ̄ⲛⲉ (once, cf? ⲛⲉⲓ, so stroke of time),

cϣⲡⲉ S, cϧⲛⲉ A nn, always adverbial c ⲣⲛⲟⲩ-, *on a sudden*: Nu 6 9 (B=Gk), Pro 6 15 SA(B do), Mk 9 8 (B do, F=Gk + ⲡⲧⲉⲩⲛⲟⲩ) ἐξάπινα; Pro 1 27 SA(B ⲡⲟⲩϧⲟϥ ϩⲉⲛⲟⲩϧⲟϥ), Jer 18 22 (var cϣ., B do), Ac 28 6 S(B ⲛⲥⲁⲧⲟⲧϥ) ἄφνω; Sa 17 14, Lu 21 34 (B do) αἰφνίδιος, Job 1 19 (var cϣ., B do), Mk 13 36 (B do, F ⲉϩⲁⲫⲓⲛⲁ) ἐξαίφνης; Zech 6 12 A(B om) *subter*; Pro 13 23 A(S ⲡⲧⲉⲩⲛⲟⲩ, var ϩⲛ[ⲟⲩϣⲡ ⲛ]ϣⲱⲛ, B ϩⲉⲛⲟⲩϣⲱⲧ ⲉⲃⲟⲗ) συντόμως; BHom 135 ϩⲛⲟⲩϣⲥⲡⲏ ἀθρόον; RNC 10 εὐθέως, Lu 10 31 (B diff) κατὰ συγκυρίαν; Aeg 283 (var cϣ.) ἀπροσδόκητος; C 99 220 ϩⲛⲟⲩⲥⲏⲡⲓ...ϩ. = ib 89 42 B both ⲛϫⲱⲗⲉⲙ, J 75 48 ⲙⲏⲡⲱⲥ ϩ. ⲡⲧⲏϣⲓⲕⲉ ϩⲙⲡⲉⲓⲱⲛϩ, Mor 30 24 Sſ.

ϢⲤⲞⲞⲨ S nn as pl: Lev 22 25 ϩ(ⲉ)ⲡⲧⲁⲕⲟ ⲏ ϩ(ⲉ)ⲡϣ. (P 44 106 = 43 92 cooⲩ ﻋﻴﺐ, varr om, B ⲁϭⲛⲓ ʿⲉ) μῶμος. Prob *l* ϣⲱϣ.

ϢⲀⲦ SF *v* ϣⲟⲧ.

ϢⲎⲦ *v* ϣⲉ *hundred*.

ϢⲒⲦ *v* ⲛϣⲓⲧ & ϣⲓϥ.

ϢⲒⲦϥ *v* ϣⲓ, ϣⲓⲧⲉ.

ϢⲞⲈⲒⲦ S nn with ⲣ, ⲟ ⲛ-, *be inspired, possessed, frenzied*: Deu 14 1 (B ϧⲉⲕ ϫⲱ) φοιβᾶν; Sa 12 5 θίασος (? as if from θειάζειν); ib 14 23 ἐμμανής. V Griffith *Stories* 172, Spg *Demotica* 1 47 or *cf* ? ϣⲱⲣⲧ.

ϢⲞⲈⲒⲦ *v* ϣⲟⲩⲟ(ϣⲟⲩⲉⲓⲧ).

ϢⲞⲦ, ϣⲱⲧ S, ϣⲁⲧ SᵃSſF, ϣϩⲟⲧ, -ⲱⲧ B, pl ϣϣⲱⲧⲉ S (or for ϣⲛϣⲱⲧⲉ), ϣⲟϥ B & sg as pl, nn m, *pillow, cushion, bag* (?): Ez 13 18 S(P 44 114)B pl, Mk 4 38 SB προσκεφάλαιον; K 251 B ⲛϣ. ﺯ ﺍﺩﺓ, P 55 17 B-ⲱⲧ ʿſ; ShR 2 3 44 S lolling among ϩⲉⲛϣⲛϣⲱ-ⲧⲉ [...] ⲙⲛⲣⲉⲛϣ. (on Am 6 4), ShC 73 84 S ⲟⲩϣⲁ-ⲁⲣ ⲡⲉⲥⲟⲟⲩ ⲏ ⲟⲩϣ. on beds, ShP 130² 62 S ⲟⲩ-ϣ. ⲙⲡⲟⲩ̄ⲡⲣⲏϣ, BAp 124 S ⲛϣ. ⲉⲧϩⲁⲣⲧⲓⲧⲉϭⲁⲡⲉ, Z 351 S ⲟⲩϣ....ⲛϥϩⲙⲟⲟⲥ ϩⲓⲭⲱϥ, R 1 5 42 S loaves, fish &c ⲛⲟϫⲟⲩ ⲉⲩϣⲱⲧ, Bodl(P) f 19 S ϣ. ⲛⲃⲁⲗⲟⲧ, Vi 164 ostr S ϣ. ⲛⲙⲟⲅⲥ, ST 118 S ϣ. ⲛϣⲁⲁⲣ, *ib* 117 S ϣ. ⲛⲥⲟⲣⲧ, Ryl 239 S ⲟⲩϣ. ⲛϣⲁⲓ, *ib* 243 S ⲟⲩⲡⲱⲣϣ ⲁⲩ(ⲱ) ⲡⲉϥϣⲱⲧ, COAd 56 Sᵃ ⲛϣ. ⲙⲡⲓⲱ, PLond 4 517 Sſ ϣⲙⲟⲩⲛ ⲛϣ. = BMOr 6230 (45) ϣⲙ. ⲉϣⲱⲧ, BM 606 F ϥ̄ ⲛϣ., BMOr 6201 B 77 S ⲟⲩⲛⲟϭ ϭⲣⲱⲃ ⲁⲡⲉ ⲡⲉⲓϣⲱⲧⲉ ⲡⲁⲓ, BM 1135 S alum for cleaning ⲡⲓⲕⲟⲩⲓ ⲛϣ. ⲛⲁⲡⲁⲛⲧⲉ (ἀναγκαῖος). V Dévaud *Études* 34.

ϢⲰⲦ S nn m, meaning unknown: Imp Russ Ar S x (1896) 80 one that can write dirges, that knoweth to weep, ⲉϥⲁⲓⲥϩⲁⲓ ⲉⲛϣ. ⲉⲧϥⲁⲡⲉ (*l* ⲛⲧ.) ⲙⲙⲓⲛ ⲙ-ⲙⲟϥ (paral Alex Botti 110 omits). *Cf* ? ϧⲱ *sf*.

ϢⲰⲦ S(in ⲉⲓⲉⲛϣ.)B, ⲉϣⲱⲧ SAA²B(Ez)FO, ⲉ-ϣⲱⲟⲧ (rare) S, f (?) ⲉϣⲱⲧⲉ S, pl ⲉϣⲟⲧⲉ S, ⲉϣⲁ. SA²,

ϢⲞϤ, ⲉϣ. B & sg as pl, nn m, *trader, merchant*: Si 37 13 S, Is 23 8 SB pl, BHom 7 S ⲙⲁⲣⲉⲡⲉ. ⲉⲡⲕⲁ-ϭⲉⲓ but braves storm ἔμπορος, Jo 2 16 B ⲏⲓ ⲛϣ. (SA² ⲙⲁ ⲡⲉ.) ἐμπόριον, Pro 29 32 SA ἐμπορεύεσθαι; PO 2 175 S ⲁⲛϣⲱⲡⲉ ⲡⲉ. buying & selling, Mor 28 233 S ⲙⲉⲣⲉⲉ. ⲉⲣ ⲃⲟⲗ ⲉⲡⲟⲃⲉ, BM 1157 S if hast need of money ⲁϫⲓⲥ ⲉⲁⲡⲁ ⲓⲱϩⲁⲛⲛⲏⲥ ⲡⲉ., BSM 3 B ⲛϣ....ⲉⲑⲣⲟⲩⲉⲣ ϣ., Mani K 11 A²; f: Ep 534 S ϯ ⲡⲕⲉⲓⲥⲁϣϥ ⲡⲥⲟⲉⲓϣ ⲛⲧⲉϣ.; pl: Ge 37 28 B, Ez 27 22 SB, Ap 18 3 B(S=Gk), BMar 165 S ϩⲉⲛⲉ. ⲙ̄ⲡ̄ⲁ̄ⲧⲓⲕⲟⲛ ἔμπορος, Am 4 2 S (as if ἔμπο., cf Field *Hex in loc*, cit R 1 2 72 ⲉϣⲁ., B as Gk); P 44 91 S ⲡⲉϣⲁ. (43 75 & Ar misunderst), Mani 1 A² ⲛϭⲓ-ⲡⲟⲩⲉⲗ ⲡⲧⲉ ⲡⲉϣ., Kr 29 S ⲡϣⲁⲁⲣⲉ ⲉϣⲁⲡ(ⲛ)ⲉ. ϫⲓ ⲙⲙⲟϥ; adj: Mt 13 45 SBF ⲣⲱⲙⲉ ⲡⲉ. ἄνθρ. ἔμ.; C 99 171 S sim = ib 89 136 B, DeV 1 164 B ⲣⲉϥϭⲓ ⲙⲛⲥⲓ ⲛϣ.

ⲙⲁ ⲡⲉ. SA², *place of traders*: Ez 27 3 S(B om), Jo 2 16 ut sup ἐμπόριον.

ⲙⲡⲧⲉϣ., ⲙⲉⲧϣ. SB, *trading, commerce*: Ps 70 15 B(S diff) πραγματεία; Is 23 18 S(B ⲓⲉⲃϣ.) ἐμπορία; R 1 1 46 S πλεονεξία; ShR 2 3 80 S ⲧⲙ. ⲡⲕⲣⲟϥ, BHom 97 S ⲧⲙ. ⲛⲧⲁⲅⲟⲣⲁ (ALR '96 191 ﺟﺎﺭﺓ ﻟﺔ), Pcod 20 S traders ⲉⲩϣⲟⲣ ⲉⲧⲉⲩⲙⲛⲧⲉϣⲱⲧ, Cat 146 B ⲡⲟⲣⲛⲓⲁ, ⲙ., ⲙⲉⲧⲁⲑⲛⲓ, C 86 346 B ϭⲓ ϯ ϩⲉⲛ-ϩⲁⲙⲙ., BMis 158 S ⲧⲧⲉⲭⲛⲏ ⲛⲧⲁⲙⲡⲧⲉϣⲱⲧ.

ⲣ ⲉ. SA, ⲉⲣ ϣ. B, *be trader, traffic*: Ez 27 13 SB, Hos 12 1 A(B ⲉⲣ ⲓⲉⲃϣ.), Ja 4 13 S(B do) ἐμπορεύε-σθαι, Ez 27 15 SB ἔμπορος; R 1 5 11 S πραγμα-τεύειν; Aeg 221 S ⲣ ⲉ. ϩⲛⲡⲉⲣⲡⲁⲁⲩ of church ἀπεμ-πολᾶν; 2 Cor 2 17 S(B do) καπηλεύειν; ShA 1 255 S ⲡⲣⲱⲙⲉ ⲉⲧⲟⲩⲱϣ ⲉⲉⲣ ⲉϣϣⲱⲧ, *ib* ⲉⲣ ⲉ., ViK 9334 S ⲡⲉⲙⲡⲟⲣⲟⲥ ⲉⲧⲉⲡⲉⲧⲟ ⲡⲉ. ⲡⲉ, C 99 94 S whoso builds chapel to martyrs ⲉⲃⲟ ⲡⲉ. ϩⲛⲡⲉⲥⲱⲙⲁ ⲛⲛ-ⲉⲧⲟⲩⲁⲁⲃ = Va ar 172 97 ﺍﺟﺮﺍ ﰲ ﺍﺟﺴﺎﺩ, CO 29 S ordination candidate ⲛⲛⲉⲡⲣ ⲉ. ⲛⲛⲉⲛϫⲓ ⲙⲛⲥⲉ, DeV 1 82 B ϭⲓ ⲛϣ. ϩⲉⲛⲡⲥⲱⲙⲁ ⲙⲡⲛⲟ̄ⲧ̄ being Manichae-ans; ϭⲓⲡⲉⲣ ⲉ. S, *trading, profit* therefrom: Gött N '98 176 ⲟⲩϭ. ⲛⲧⲁⲙⲡⲧⲉⲩⲥⲉⲃⲏⲥ πορισμός (cf 1 Tim 6 5 S ϩⲛⲅ).

ⲉⲓⲉⲛϣ. SAA²O, ⲓⲉⲃϣ. B nn m, *merchandise*, *v* ⲉⲓ-ⲟⲡⲉ, adding Mani 2 A² ⲛϥⲣ ϫⲁⲓⲥ ⲁⲧⲉϥⲙⲛⲧⲓⲉⲡϣ., Mani H 12 A² ⲣ ⲓⲉⲡϣ. ϩⲛⲡⲭⲣⲏⲙⲁ.

ϢⲰⲦ O nn m, in name of planet Jupiter: Hor 85 ϩⲁⲣ ⲡϣⲱ[ⲧ], 79 ϩⲣ ⲡϣ.; *cf ib* 75, PSBA 22 163.

ϢⲰⲰⲦ SA²F, ϣⲱⲧ SA²B, ϣ(ⲱ)ⲱⲧⲉ S(Sh), ϣⲟϥ B (Ez), ϣⲟⲩⲟⲩⲧ, ϣⲟⲩⲧ A, ϣ(ⲉ)ⲧ- SA²BF, ϣⲉⲉⲧ- SF, ϣⲁⲧ- B, ϣⲟⲱⲧ- A², ϣⲁⲁⲧϥ SA², ϣⲁⲧϥ SAB, ϣⲉⲉⲧϥ F, ϣⲁⲁⲧ† SA, ϣⲁⲧ† SB, ϣⲛⲧ† S, rc ϣⲁⲧ- SBF, ϣⲟⲧ-B vb **A** *cut, slay* (cf ϣⲟⲧϣⲧ) **I** intr: Is 10 15 S(B ⲕⲱ-ⲣϫ) κόπτειν, Mic 2 13 SA(B ϫⲱϫⲓ) διακ.; Deu 12

15 SB, Jo 10 10 SA²B θύειν; Lev 17 3 SB σφάζειν;
BHom 23 S τέμνειν, Is 10 23 S(B tr) συντ.; Ez 8 3
B ϥ̄ⲏ ⲉⲧϣⲱϯ εἰκών(?); PS 101 S ⲛⲑⲉ ⲡⲟⲩⲛⲉⲡⲓⲛⲉ
ⲉⲧϣ. (l ⲉϥ-), ShMIF 23 82 S a deed ⲉϥϫⲱⲕ ⲉⲃⲟⲗ
ⲁⲩⲱ ⲉϥϣ., ShZ 637 S ⲃⲁϣⲟⲩⲅ ⲉⲧⲃⲉϣ., Mani 1 A²
didst endure ϣⲁⲡⲧⲕⲱ. ⲡⲕⲥⲱϫⲉ till wast slain, Cai
Th 47 B ⲁϥϣ. (sc Red Sea), BP 10587 S send worm
& wrath ⲉⲧⲣⲉⲩϣⲱⲧ ⲉⲙⲡⲥⲱⲙⲁ of perjurer; qual:
Is 27 9 S(B ⲕⲱ.) ἐκκό., Eccl 1 8 S(F ϩⲁⲥⲓ) ἔγκοπος;
Lev 22 22 B(S ⲟⲅⲟⲩϣ, cit P 131¹ 52 ϣⲏⲧ)-τμητός;
ib 24 S(B ϣ. ⲉⲃⲟⲗ) ἀποσπᾶν; Deu 28 31 S(B ϭⲉⲗϭⲱⲗ) σφ.; He 4 13 S(B diff) τραχηλίζεσθαι; Mt 22
4 SA(Till Oster 25)B θυ.

II tr: Nu 13 25 S(B ϣ. ⲉⲃ.), Mk 11 8 S(B ⲕⲱ.)
κό., Jud 1 6 S ἀποκ., Hab 3 14 S(prob)A ϣⲟⲩⲧ B
διακ., Dan 9 26 S(B ϭⲟⲧϭⲉⲧ), Zech 12 11 A ϣⲟⲩⲧ
(S ⲕⲱⲱⲣⲉ, B ⲕⲱ.), Mt 18 8 S(B ϫⲱ.) ἐκκ., Mk 5 5
B(S ⲡⲱϫ) κατακ., Ps 128 4 S(B ⲥⲱⲗⲡ) συγκ.; Ge
31 54 SB, Ps 14 14 SA(Cl) ϣⲟⲩⲧ B, Jer 11 19 B(S
ⲕⲱⲡⲥ) θύ., 2 Kg 6 13 S(B diff) θύμα; Lev 25 3 B(S
ϫⲱⲱⲗⲉ) τέμ., Hos 7 14 AB κατατ., 2 Tim 2 15 S
(var & B ϣ. ⲉⲃ.) ὀρθοτομεῖν; Ez 16 21 S(B ϭⲟⲗϭⲉⲗ) σφ.; Ro 11 19 SF ϣⲉⲉⲧ-(B ⲕⲱ.) ἐκκλᾶν; Sa
13 11 S ἐκπρίειν; Jo 15 2 A²(S ⲥⲱⲗⲡ, B ⲕⲱ.) αἴρειν;
P 43 37 S ⲡⲉⲧϣⲱⲧ ⲱⲡⲉ ⲉⲃⲗ̄ϫ̄; Tri 373 S ⲁϥϣⲉⲉⲧ
ⲡⲉϥⲥⲱⲙⲁ ⲉⲃϫ̄; ShBor 246 70 ϣⲁⲁⲧⲟⲩ ⲙⲉⲗⲟⲥ ⲙⲉⲗⲟⲥ, ShA 2 240 S ϣ. ⲡⲣⲉⲡⲱⲡⲉ, Ryl 85 22 S ⲁⲩϣⲉⲧ
ⲱⲡⲉ, Mani 1 A² ⲁⲡ]ⲗⲓⲗⲟⲩ ϣⲧ ⲃⲟ ⲁϥⲣⲓⲙⲉ tore hair
(?, cf ϥⲱ), Bor 226 174 S ϣⲉⲉⲧ ⲡⲉϥϣⲁ (nose), RNC 83
S ⲧϣⲱⲧⲉ ⲉⲡⲧⲁⲩϣⲁⲧⲥ, BMar 218 S loaves fresh ϩⲱⲥ
ϫⲉⲛⲧⲁⲩϣⲁⲧⲟⲩ ϩⲓⲧⲉⲧⲣⲓⲣ = Rec 6 184 B ⲉⲧⲁⲩⲉⲛⲟⲩ
ⲉⲡϣⲱⲓ ⲉⲃⲟⲗ ϭⲉⲛ- (cf ? Ep 540 S ⲕⲁⲕ ϣⲱⲧ & below
ϣ. ⲛⲛ), Mani 1 A² ϣⲱⲧ ⲛⲡⲓⲣⲣⲉ, Mani K 84 A²
ⲉⲩϣⲁⲛϣⲱⲧ ⲟⲩⲉ ϩⲛⲙⲙⲉⲗⲟⲥ, BSM 32 B have no
sheep ⲉⲙⲁⲧϥ = BMis 375 S ⲕⲟⲡⲥϥ, BM 511 2 F
sheep ⲁⲩϣⲉⲉⲧϥ, LAp 541 F ϣ. ⲡϥⲣⲡⲉϥ[ⲡⲁϫⲓ], ShR
2 3 46 S ⲉⲡⲉⲡ(l ⲡⲓⲉⲡ)ϣ. ⲏ ϫⲉⲛⲡⲉⲛϫⲱⲣⲉ ⲉⲃⲟⲗ
ⲙⲡϣⲁϫⲉ.

With following preposition. c ⲉ-, *for*: Lu 15 27
SB θύειν dat; 2 Kg 12 4 S(var ⲛ-) ποιεῖν dat; c
ⲉϫⲛ-, *on*: Lev 21 5 B(S ϣⲱⲗϭ) κατατέμ. ἐπί; ⲉϩⲣⲁⲓ
ⲉϫⲛ-: Ex 20 24 S(B ϩⲓϫⲉⲛ-) θύ. ἐπί; c ⲛ- dat:
Ex 34 15 S(B ϣ. ϣⲟⲩϣⲱⲟⲩϣⲓ), Is 66 3 B(S ⲕⲱⲛⲥ),
Jon 1 16 SAB, R 1 4 65 S ϣⲉⲧ ⲣⲱⲙⲉ ⲡⲁⲣⲧⲉⲙⲓⲥ θύ.
dat, Hos 2 13 B(A diff) ἐπιθ. dat; Jer 19 4 B ϣⲉⲧ
ϣⲟⲩϣ. (S diff) θυμιᾶν dat; Nu 11 22 S(B ϭⲟⲗ.)
σφ. dat; ShA 1 368 S ϯⲛⲁϣ. ⲛⲏⲧⲛ ⲡⲉⲧⲛⲃⲟⲧⲉ &
will tell you what ye would not to hear, Miss 4 117
B ⲉⲩⲛⲁϣⲁⲧⲧⲉⲛ ⲙⲡⲉⲕⲡⲟⲩϯ = Mor 18 23 S ⲕⲟⲡ-
ⲥⲛ; c ϩⲛ- S, *with*: Ps 73 5 (B ⲕⲱⲣϫ) ἐκκοπ. ἐν;
ShA 1 243 whom barbarians ϣⲁⲁⲧⲟⲩ ϩⲛⲙⲁϭⲁⲧ,
ShBM Or 8800 49 ⲉϥϣ. ⲙⲙⲟⲟⲩ ϩⲛⲟⲩⲥⲏϥⲉ.

With following adverb. c ⲉⲃⲟⲗ, *cut, cut off,
decide, be severe*: **a** intr: Sa 5 21 S, Va 57 174 B
ⲕⲣⲓⲙⲟⲥ (κρημ.)...ⲉϥϣ. ⲉⲃ. ἀπότομος; Wess 18 94
S ⲙⲡⲧⲣⲙⲙⲁⲟ ⲉⲧϣ. ⲉⲃ. σύντονος (? σύντομ.); ShA
1 84 S ⲡⲉⲕϩⲁⲡ ⲉⲧϣ. ⲉⲃ. in day of wrath, ib 132 S
ⲙⲡϣ. ⲉⲃ. ⲉⲧⲃⲉⲧⲙⲛⲧϣⲁⲡⲟⲧⲏϥ ⲙⲡⲡⲛ̄, ShBor 247
119 S whether they be apt...ⲛϯⲛⲁϣ ϣ. ⲉⲃ. ⲁⲛ, ShZ
602 S ⲁⲟⲩⲁ ϣ. ⲉⲃ. ϫⲉⲡⲁⲟⲩ ⲡϣⲓ ⲉⲧⲧⲛϣ, COAd 47
S ⲁⲓϣ. ⲉⲃ. ϫⲉ- *have decided that* (?), MG 25 151 B
ⲁⲥⲁϭⲟⲩⲛ ⲙⲙⲟⲟⲩ ϣ. ⲉⲃ. because of coarse food,
TSBA 9 379 B tongue ϣ. ⲉⲃ. ⲉⲣⲟⲧⲉ ⲥⲛϫⲓ, Hall 4 S
death ⲡⲉⲧϣ. ⲉⲃ. ⲡⲉⲧⲡⲱⲣϫ; qual: Deu 23 1 SB
ἀποκόπτεσθαι; Is 10 23 SB, Dan 9 26 B(S ⲧⲏϣ)
συντέμνεσθαι; C 89 60 B ⲧⲉϥϫⲓⲛⲥⲁϫⲓ ϣ. ⲉⲃ. ἀπότ.;
Mor 18 178 S sim ἁπλούστατος; Z 625 S ⲟⲩⲡⲟⲛⲏ-
ⲣⲓⲁ ⲉⲥϣ. ⲉⲃ. **b** tr: Ps 76 9 B(S ϭⲱⲧⲃ) ἀποκόπτειν,
Nu 16 14 B(S ⲡⲱⲣⲕ) ἐκκ., C 89 17 B ϣ. ⲉⲃ. ⲛⲛⲟⲩ-
ⲙⲉⲗⲟⲥ κατακ.; Jer 43 23 B ἀποτέμ.; Is 10 23 B(S
om ⲉⲃ.) συντέμ.; Pcod 46 S if one demented ϣⲁⲧϥ
ⲉⲃ. χειρίζειν; Aeg 215 S ⲁϥϣⲁⲁⲧϥ ⲉⲃ. ⲙⲙⲓⲛ ⲙⲙⲟϥ
ἀκρωτηριάζειν; 2 Kg 4 12 S κολοβοῦν; Ez 20 28 B
(S ⲟⲩⲱⲧⲛ ⲉⲃ.) σπένδειν(?); ShA 1 117 S ⲡⲉⲧϣ. ⲉⲃ.
ⲙⲡⲣⲁⲛ, ib 434 S ⲉⲓⲛⲁϣⲉⲧ ⲡϣⲁϫⲉ ⲉⲃ. & desist, Miss
8 15 S ⲉⲅⲟⲩⲱϣ ⲉϣⲉⲧ ⲡⲣⲱⲃ ⲉⲃ., BMis 151 S ϣ.
ⲉⲃ. ⲛⲡⲁⲙⲁⲕ, C 41 36 B go to bishop ϫⲉⲡⲛⲉϥ-
ϣⲁⲧⲕ ⲉⲃ. = Bor 134 39 S(Vita Sin)ⲡⲉϥⲕⲁⲕ ϩⲓⲣⲟⲩⲡ,
OrCyp 237 Sf ⲧⲁϣⲉⲉⲧⲕ ⲉⲃ. ⲧⲁⲁⲡⲁⲑⲉⲙⲁ ⲉⲙⲙⲁⲕ,
BKU 1 21 ro F ϣⲉⲧ ⲧϭⲁⲗⲁϫⲧ ⲉⲃ. (sc from fire)ⲛⲧⲉⲉ-
ϣⲧ (l ⲛⲕ-)ⲉϩⲣⲁⲓ, vo paral ⲡⲧⲩ ⲉϩⲣⲁⲓ *remove from* (cf c
ϩⲓ-, ϩⲛ-); ⲉⲃ. ⲉ-, *for*: Mor 26 14 S ⲁϥϣⲉⲉⲧ ⲡϣⲁϫⲉ
ⲉⲃ. ⲉⲣⲟⲟⲩ ϣⲏⲙ ϣⲏⲙ (var BMis 161 ϫⲉ ⲡϣ. ⲉⲣⲟⲟⲩ); c ⲉϫⲛ-, *decide upon, condemn*: Dan 9 24 B(S
ⲧⲱϣ) συντέμ. ἐπί; P 131⁶ 89 S ⲁⲡⲡⲛ̄ ϣ. ⲉⲃ. ⲉϫⲛⲁ-
ⲇⲁⲙ ϩⲓⲧⲛⲟⲩⲁⲡⲟⲫⲁⲥⲓⲥ (Ge 3 19), TSBA 9 372 B
ⲉϥϣ. ⲉⲃ. ⲉϫⲉⲛⲁϧⲁⲃ ⲡⲓⲥⲁϩⲟⲩⲓ, Cat 196 B ϣ. ⲉⲃ.
ⲉϫⲱⲟⲩ according to their blasphemy, MG 25 33 B
ϣ. ⲉⲃ. ⲉϫⲱⲟⲩ ϭⲉⲛⲁⲡϫⲫⲓⲟ; ⲉⲃ. ⲛ-, *from*: Ez 39
10 B ⲕⲟ́. ἐκ, Mk 9 43 S(B ϫⲱϫⲓ ⲉⲃ.), ViK 9455 S
ⲁⲩϣⲉⲉⲧ ⲡⲧⲛⲃⲉ ⲉⲃ. ⲡⲟⲩⲥⲓⲟⲩⲣ ἀποκ.; ShA 1 134
S ⲡⲉⲧⲣ ⲡⲁⲣϩⲉ ϣⲱⲟⲧⲉ ⲉⲃ. ⲙⲡⲥⲱⲙⲁ ... ⲛⲙⲙⲉⲗⲟⲥ
(cf ib 2 115 sim -ⲧⲉ ⲉⲃ. ϩⲛ-), ib 2 24 S ⲡⲛⲉ̄ ⲛⲁϣⲁ-
ⲁⲧⲡ ⲉⲃ. ⲙⲙⲟϥ, Mani 2 A² worthy ⲛⲓϣⲱⲧ ϩⲛⲙⲙⲉⲗⲟⲥ
ⲁⲃ. ⲙⲙⲁⲩ, JKP 2 140 Sf wife ⲁⲕϣⲁⲁⲧⲥ ⲉⲃ. ⲉⲡⲉⲥϩⲁⲓ; c ⲟⲩⲃⲉ-B, *against*: Cat 72 ⲙⲡⲉϥϣⲁⲧ ⲡⲓⲥⲁϫⲓ
ⲉⲃ. ⲟⲩⲃⲏϥ *pronounced condemnation*; ⲉⲃ. ϩⲓ-, *from,
from out*: Dan 2 45 B τέμ. ἀπό; ib 34 B ἀποσχί-
ζειν ἐκ; ShIF 126 S garments to be made ⲉⲓϣ. ⲉⲃ.
ϩⲓⲱⲟⲩ ⲏ ⲉⲓⲣⲱⲛ ⲉⲧⲃⲉⲡⲅⲧⲱϣ, BKU 1 21 vo F ϣⲉ(ⲧ)
ⲡⲓⲧⲟⲥ (εἶδος) ⲉⲃ. ϩⲓⲧϭⲁⲗⲁⲣⲧ (cf c ϩⲛ-); ⲉⲃ. ϩⲛ-,
ϭⲉⲛ-, as last: Nu 13 24 SB ⲕⲟ́. ἐκεῖθεν, Mic 5 14 A
(B ⲕⲱ.), Ro 11 24 SF(B do) ἐκκ. ἐκ; AM 266 †B
χωρίζειν ἐκ; PS 310 S ϣⲁϣ. ⲉⲃ. ⲡⲡⲉⲯⲩⲭⲏ ϩⲛ-
ⲡⲉⲕⲕⲗⲏⲣⲟⲛⲟⲙⲓⲁ, ib ϣⲁⲁⲧⲥ ⲉⲃ. ϩⲛⲧⲙⲛⲧⲉⲣⲟ, ShC 73

140 *S* ϣⲉⲧ ⲟⲩϣⲗϩ ⲉⲃ. ϩⲏⲧⲃⲱ, ShA 2 115 *S* ⲩ с п-, Mor 37 86 *S* boiling ceased ⲛⲑⲉ ⲛⲟⲩⲭⲁⲗⲕⲓⲟⲛ ⲉⲁⲩϣⲁⲧϥ ⲉⲃ. ϩⲛⲟⲩϩⲣⲱ.   *V* also nn.

p c *SBF, he who, that which cuts, is cut*: Job 15 32 *B* ϣ. ϣⲉ (*S* ⲭⲱⲗϩ), Cant 2 12 *F* ϣⲁⲧⲭⲛ (*sic ? l*, *S* ⲭⲱⲱⲗⲉ) ⲧⲟⲙⲏ; BM 920 264 *B* ⲡϣⲟⲧϣⲉ قليم التَّ; P 129¹⁶ 92 *S* ⲧⲟⲕ ⲛϣ. ⲗⲁⲥ, ST 437 ϣ. ⲃⲁⲙⲡⲉ, Ep 271 ϣ. ⲣⲡⲉ, ϣ. ⲁϥ (*v* ⲁϥ *flesh*), ϣ. ⲃⲁⲡⲧⲉ (*v* ⲃⲟⲡⲧⲉ), ϣ. ⲃⲟⲓ (*v* ϥⲱ), ϣ. ⲙⲉϩⲏⲗ (*v* ⲙⲉϩⲏⲗ), ϣ. ⲱⲡⲉ (*v* ⲱⲡⲉ).

—— nn m *SABF, thing cut*, esp of sacrifice: Ex 34 25 *SB*, Pro 9 2 *SAB* θῦμα; 1 Cor 8 1 *SBF*, Ap 2 14 *SB* ϣ. ⲡⲉⲓⲇⲱⲗⲟⲡ εἰδωλόθυτος; Ez 21 10 *S*(*B* ⲃⲟⲗⲇⲉⲗ) σφάγιον; Phil 3 2 *B*(*S* ϣ. ⲉⲃ.) κατατομή; Lev 19 28 *B* ϣ. ⲛⲥⲟⲧⲥⲉⲧ (*S* diff) ἐντομίς; ShC 42 70 *S* of loaves ⲙⲛⲧϣⲙⲏⲛ ⲛϣⲱⲧ (var ϣⲱⲛ less prob, *cf* above vb tr), ShMiss 4 278 *S* ⲙⲡⲡⲣ ⲃⲟⲗ ⲉⲡⲉϥϣ. *decision, verdict*, Va 57 68 *B* ⲛϣ. ⲡⲉⲛⲡⲓⲁϥ, BSM 54 *B* ⲡⲉϥϣ. *sacrifice* (sc of Isaac), Mus 40 276 *S* ⲡⲓϣⲧⲟⲣⲧⲣ ⲙⲉⲛⲡϣ. ⲉⲧϣⲟⲟⲡ ϩⲙⲡⲏⲣⲡ = BAp 168 ⲡⲟⲥⲉ ⲉⲧⲛⲁϣⲱⲡⲉ ⲉⲧⲃⲉⲡⲏⲣⲡ;   as adj : Ex 20 25 *S* (*B* ⲟⲩⲓϭⲓ) τμητός; Ps 135 16 *B* ⲕⲟϩ ⲛϣ. (*S* ⲡⲁϣⲧ) ἀκρότομος.

—— ⲉⲃⲟⲗ nn m *SBF, cutting out, off, excommunication*: Z 278 *S* ⲛϣ. ⲉⲃ. of diseased part τομή; Phil 3 2 *S*(var ⲥⲃⲃⲉ, *B* ϣ. ⲛⲥ.) κατατ., Ro 11 22 *B* (*SF* ⲙⲛⲧⲣⲉϥϣ.) ἀποτομία, C 89 109 *B* ⲛⲟⲩϣ. ⲉⲃ. ἀπότομον opp ⲙⲉⲧⲭⲣⲏⲥⲧⲟⲥ; 2 Kg 6 8 *S*, Pro 6 15 *B*(*SA* ⲟⲩⲱϣϥ) διακοπή; AM 265 *B* free Arius from ⲛϣ. ⲉⲃ. χωρισμός; R 1 4 54 *S* ϣ. ⲉⲃ. ⲡⲁⲙⲉⲗⲟⲥ ἀφαίρεσις; ShC 42 208 *S* ⲡⲉⲓⲛⲟϭ ⲛϣ. ⲉⲃ. at Judgment, Bor 287 137 *S* ⲛϣ. ⲉⲃ. of fleshly desires, Va 57 78 *B* ⲫⲱⲗϩ, ϣ. ⲉⲃ., ϣⲱⲗ of war;   ϩⲛ-, ϩⲉⲛⲟⲩϣ. ⲉⲃ. adverbial, *sharply, shortly*: 2 Cor 13 10 *SBF* ⲛⲟⲩ ἀποτόμως, Pro 13 23 *B*(*S* ⲛⲧⲉⲩⲛⲟⲩ, var ϩⲛⲟⲩϣⲡ ⲛϣⲱⲡ, *A* ϩⲛⲟⲩϭϩⲡⲉ), Ac 24 4 *SB*, Va 63 95 *B* ⲧⲁⲟⲩⲉ ⲡⲓⲥⲁϫⲓ ⲃ. συντόμως, Miss 8 98 *S* ⲭⲟⲟⲩ ϩ. ἐν συντόμῳ; Z 273 *S* ⲉϩⲣⲁⲓ ϩ. συνελών; *ib* 249 *S* ⲥⲧⲉ ⲡⲉⲓϩⲱⲃ ⲉⲃ. ϩ. καθόλου; ShBMOr 8810 506 *S* death ⲧⲁϩⲟⲟⲩ ϩ., P 129¹⁸ 88 *S* ⲁϥⲙⲗⲏⲗ ϩ. that fire might destroy them, Mor 18 52 *S* tell us truth ϩ. (var *ib* 19 60 ϩⲛ(ⲟⲩ)ⲟⲩⲱⲡϩ ⲉⲃ.), MG 25 264 *B* speak ⲃ. = Mor 40 37 *S* ϩⲛⲟⲩⲥⲩⲛⲧⲟⲙⲓⲁ, Bess 7 17 *B* ⲙⲡⲉϥⲥⲟϫⲓ ⲃ. ⲁⲗⲗⲁ ⲃⲉⲛⲟⲩⲙⲉⲧⲣⲉϥϣⲟⲩ ⲛϩⲏⲧ.

ⲁⲧϣ. *S, uncut*: P 44 73 ⲁⲧⲣⲟⲧⲟⲥ (ἄτρω.)· ⲡⲁⲧ ϣⲟⲧϥ.

ⲙⲉⲧϣ. ⲉⲃⲟⲗ *F, severity*: Ro 11 22 (*S* ⲙⲛⲧⲣⲉϥϣ., *B* ⲙⲉⲧⲣ. ⲉⲃ.) ἀποτομία.   Or *? l* ⲙⲉⲧⲗⲉϥϣ. as *ib*.

ⲣⲉϥϣ. *SABF, cutter*: Pro 24 37 *SA* τομίς; Mus 35 22 *B* Abraham ⲡⲓⲣ. *sacrificer*; ⲙⲛⲧⲣ.: Ro *l c* (*B* ϣ. ⲉⲃ. nn) ἀποτομία; *v* also ⲕⲱⲃϩ;   ⲣⲉϥϣ. ⲉⲃ.

SB sim : Sa 11 11 *S* ἀπότομος; ShMIF 23 90 *S* ⲛⲡⲁ ⲡϣⲁⲡϥⲧⲏϥ ⲁⲅⲱ ⲡⲣ. speaketh in prophets & apostles, ClPr 25 1 *S* ⲟⲩⲣ. (ⲉ)ⲡⲁⲡⲟⲩϥⲡⲉ ⲡⲉⲧⲣⲟⲥ (on Jo 13 8), AM 145 *B* ⲛⲑⲟⲕ ⲟⲩⲣ. ⲕⲭⲟⲣ *determined & brave*; ⲙⲛⲧ-, ⲙⲉⲧⲣⲉϥϣ. ⲉⲃ.: Ro *l c B*; Sh ViK 919 *S* ⲙⲙ. ⲙⲡⲛⲉ ϫⲉ- (Ez 7 9), Gu 53 *S* be patient ⲙⲡⲣϣⲱⲡⲉ ϩⲛⲧⲉⲕⲙ., Cat 150 *B* burdened ϩⲓⲧⲉⲛⲟⲩⲙ. ⲉⲥⲟⲓ ⲙⲡⲁⲣⲁ ⲡϣⲓ.

ϭⲓⲛ-, ϫⲓⲛϣ. ⲉⲃ. *SB, cutting off, slaying*: 1 Kg 16 2 *B*(*S* ⲣ ⲟⲩⲥⲓⲁ) θύειν; Bor 240 84 *S* ⲧϭⲓⲛϣⲁⲧⲟⲩ ⲉⲃ. *excommunicating them*.

B intr, *be cut short, want, lack*: Eccl 10 3 *S*(*F* ⲭⲱⲗⲭ), 1 Cor 8 8 *SF*(*B* ϭⲣⲟϩ), Phil 4 12 *S*(*B* ⲉⲣ ⲃⲁⲉ), Va 57 159 *B* ⲁⲅϣ. ⲟⲩⲟϩ ⲁⲅⲙⲟⲩⲛⲕ ὑστερεῖν; Ex 16 18 *SB* ἐλαττονεῖν, 1 Kg 2 5 *S*(*B* ⲉⲣ ⲃ.) -τοῦν; Lev 25 47 *S*(*B* diff) ἀπορεῖν, Pro 28 27 *SA* ἐν ἀπορίᾳ εἶναι; PS 48 *S* ⲙⲡⲣⲧⲣⲁϣ., BMis 401 *S* ⲛⲡⲉⲅⲱϫⲛ ⲟⲩⲇⲉ ⲛⲡⲉⲅϣ., Mun 89 *S* sim, Mor 29 54 *S* ⲛⲁⲧⲁ ⲑⲟⲛ ⲉⲧⲉⲙⲉⲩϣ., *ib* 50 15 *S* smith's bellows ⲙⲉⲩϣ. ⲉⲛⲉϩ ⲉϥⲛⲓⲃⲉ, DeV 2 194 *B* ⲁⲡⲓⲣⲱⲙ...ϣ. ϩⲓⲧⲉⲡ ⲡⲓϩⲃⲱⲛ;   qual: Dan 5 27 *S* (ShBor 246 56, *B* ⲭⲟⲣϩ), 1 Cor 12 24 *SB* ὑστερεῖν, Eccl 1 15 *S*(*F* ⲭⲁⲗϩ) ὑστέρημα; Aeg 222 *S* ⲡⲉⲧϣ. δεῖσθαι, *ib* 248 *S* ⲡⲉⲧϣ. ἐνδ., Pro 3 27 *A*(*S* ⲣ ϭⲣⲱϩ, *B* ⲉⲣ ⲃ.), *ib* 21 17 *SA*, Ac 4 34 *S*(*B* ⲉⲣ ⲭⲣⲓⲁ) ἐνδεής, Si 4 1 *S* ἐπιδ.; Pro 11 24 *SA*(*B* ⲉⲣ ⲃ.) ἐλαττονοῦν; ClPr 30 15 *S* ⲛⲕⲱⲧ ϣ. ⲉⲧⲣⲉⲛⲟⲩⲟⲛϩϥ ⲉⲃⲟⲗ how it came to be λείπειν, BHom 46 *S* ⲉⲛϣ. ἐλλ.; Si 42 30 *S* ἐκλείπ., Eph 4 28 *S*(*B* do) χρείαν ἔχειν; Pro 22 22 *S*(*B* ⲉⲣ ⲃ.) πτωχὸς εἶναι; PS 358 *S* ⲉⲡⲟ ⲡⲉⲃⲓⲏⲛ ⲉⲛϣ., Sh BerlOr 1611 5 35 *S* ϩⲛⲁⲁⲅ ⲉⲅϭⲟⲭⲃ ⲉⲩϣ., ShMIF 23 30 *S* to devil ⲕϣ. ⲁⲅⲱ ⲕϣⲛϣ ⲉⲃⲟⲗ, AM 174 *B* ⲡⲓϩⲏⲕⲓ ⲡⲉⲗⲡⲏ ⲉⲧϣ., Ep 105 *S* ϯϣ. ⲉⲙⲁⲧⲉ, BM 1110 *S* ⲁⲅϩⲉ ⲛϥϩⲟⲗⲟⲕ/ ⲉϥϣ., Ep 298 *S* sim, Va 58 149 *B* scale (πλάξ) of balance ⲉⲧϣ. *lacking* in weight, Ryl 162 *S* in contract ⲥⲉⲙⲉⲣ ⲥⲉϣ., BM 1021 *S* sim (cf *?* πλέον ἔλασσον);   + conjunct *S*: Sh(Besa)Bor 206 592 ⲧⲛϣ. ⲛⲧⲉⲡⲛⲉ ⲡⲁⲓⲇⲉⲩⲉ ⲙ ⲙⲟⲛ (ShA 1 85 ⲉⲧⲣⲉⲡⲛⲉ), ShBMOr 8810 401 ⲧⲛϣ. ⲡⲧⲟⲩϯ ⲥⲃⲱ ⲛⲁⲛ (*ib* 377 ⲉⲧⲣⲉⲩϯ).

With following preposition or adverb.   c ⲉ-, *lack for*: Ps 33 10 *S*(var ⲛ-, *B* ⲉⲣ ⲃ.) ἐλ. gen; Ja 2 15† *S*(var & *B* ⲛ-) λείπ. gen; R 1 5 43 *S* ϩⲙⲡⲧⲣⲁϣ.† ⲉⲡⲁⲓ ⲛⲧⲛⲛⲓⲟⲩⲇⲁⲓ, Miss 4 226 *B* ⲙⲡⲓⲥⲱⲧⲉⲙ ⲉⲣⲟϥⲟ ⲓⲉ ⲉϣⲱ.† ⲉⲡⲏ *more nor less*, C 89 162 *B* ⲧⲉⲡⲡⲁϣ. ⲉⲣϩⲓ ⲁⲡ, PLond 4 445 *S* moneys ⲉⲩϣ.† ⲁⲛ ⲉⲅⲫⲟⲗⲟⲥ ⲡⲟⲩⲱⲧ, Ryl 326 *S* sim, BM 220 *S* all perished ⲛϣ.† ⲉⲛⲁⲡⲉϩⲛⲓ *excepting*:   c ⲛ-, as last: He 4 1 *S*(*B* ⲉⲣ ⲃ.), Aeg 223 *S* ⲉⲧⲙⲧⲣⲉⲩϣ. ⲡⲗⲁⲁⲩ ὑσ., Ps 22 1 *S*(*B* do), Mt 19 20† *SB*, 2 Cor 12 11 *SF*(*B* ⲃ.) ὑσ. acc, Ro 3 23† *SB*, C 99 137 *S* ⲡⲧⲉⲣⲟⲩϣ. ⲡⲥⲟⲩⲟ = *ib* 89 41 *B* ⲉⲣ ⲃ. ὑσ. gen, Si 11 14† *S* ὑσ. dat, 1 Cor 1 7 *S*(*B* ⲃⲉⲛ-) ὑσ. ἐν; Ge 18 28 *SB* ἐλαττονοῦν,

Si 19 6 *S* ἐλαττοῦν acc, 1 Kg 21 15† *S* -τοῦν gen, Lev 27 8 *S*(*B* om) ἐλάσσων dat, Sa 9 5† *S* ἐλάσ. ἐν; Pro 7 7† *SAB* ἐνδ. gen, Job 17 1† *S*(*B* ⲟⲣⲓ) δεῖ. gen, ib 6 22† *SAB* ep ⲭⲣⲓⲁ) ἐπιδεῖ. gen, Pro 12 9† *AB*(*S* ⲣ ⲋ.) προσδεῖ. gen; Lu 18 22† *SB*, Z 294 *S* ⲁⲡⲉⲗⲗⲟ ϣ. ⲡⲛⲉⲭⲣⲓⲁ λείπ. acc, Ja 1 5† *S*(*B* ⲝ.) λείπ. gen, Miss 8 76 *S* lest churches ϣ. ⲡⲛⲉⲧⲣⲱϣⲉ ⲉⲣⲟⲟⲩ ἐλλείπ.; Eccl 4 8 *S* στερεῖν ἀπό; PS 51 *S* ⲁⲓϣ. ⲙⲡⲁ ⲟⲩⲟⲉⲓⲛ, Br 258 *S* ⲡⲧⲟⲕ ⲡⲉⲧⲟⲩϣ.† ⲙⲙⲟⲕ ⲧⲏⲣⲟⲩ, ShP 131⁴ 142 *S* wherein is Lord changed or ⲛⲧⲁϣϣ. ⲡⲟⲩ?, ShA 1 429 *S* ⲙⲡⲛϣ. ⲡⲧⲉϥϫⲁⲣⲓⲥ, C 100 356 *S* told to each ⲡⲉⲧⲉϥϣ.† ⲙⲙⲟϥ *his shortcomings*, ib 89 96 *B* sim, Mor 36 40 *S* Baptist *loq* ⲉⲓϣ.† ⲡⲕⲉϣⲟ ⲙⲛⲧ ⲛⲉⲃⲟⲧ before birth, RE 11 44 *S* ⲡⲣⲟⲗⲟⲕ/ ϣ.† ⲡⲟⲩⲕⲉⲣⲁⲧⲓⲟⲛ, Kr 111 *S* sim, RAl 88 *B* ⲙⲡⲓⲭⲁ ⲣⲗⲓ ⲉⲓϣ.† ⲙⲙⲟϥ *of all crimes*, BAp 124 *S* by thy death ⲧⲡⲛⲁϣ. ⲡⲟⲩⲉⲓⲱⲧ ⲡⲁⲅⲁⲑⲟⲥ, BSM 27 *B* ⲟⲩⲟⲛ ⲛⲓⲃⲉⲛ ⲉⲧϣ.† ⲛⲇⲣⲉ = BMis 366 *S* ⲉⲧϣ.† only; vbal *S*†(Sh), *have need to, must needs, want to*: A 2 149 house derelict ⲏ ⲉϥϣ. ⲡⲕⲟⲧⲩ, C 73 6 ⲥⲉⲡⲁϣ. ⲁⲛ ⲡⲭⲱⲗⲝ, IF 296 I know that ⲛⲧⲡⲛϣ. ⲁⲛ ⲡ† ⲋⲱⲡⲧ ⲛⲁϥ, Miss 4 286 ⲡ†ϣ. ⲁⲛ ⲡⲟⲩⲉⲙ ⲡⲁⲟⲉⲓⲕ, A 1 58 ⲧⲡϣ. ⲡⲧⲁⲕⲟϥ (*l* ⲧⲁⲕⲟ ⲙ-) ⲡⲉⲡⲣⲓⲥⲉ by such indignities; c ⲣⲁ-*S*, *because of*: Ep 438 †ϣ.† ⲧⲱⲡⲉ ⲣⲁ ⲡⲁⲡⲟⲃⲉ; c ⲣⲛ-, ⲍⲉⲛ-, *be lacking in, in need of*: 1 Cor 1 7 *SB*† ὑσ. ἐν; 2 Cor 7 9 *S*(*B* † ⲟⲥⲓ) ζημιοῦν ἐν; ShMIF 23 99 none knoweth ⲡⲡⲉ†ϣ.† ⲡⲣⲏⲧⲟⲩ; ⲉⲃⲟⲗ ⲣⲛ-, ⲍⲉⲛ-: Ge 8 3 *S*(*B* ⲡⲛⲟⲩ ⲡⲥⲃⲟⲕ) ἐλαττονοῦν; He 12 15 *SB* ὑσ. ἀπό; TEuch 2 353 *B* ⲉⲛϣ.† ⲉⲃ. ⲍⲉⲛⲁⲡⲟⲗⲟⲅⲓⲁ ⲛⲓⲃⲉⲛ στερ. ἀπό; c ⲉⲃⲟⲗ *S* as ϣ.: Pcod 10 ⲉϥϣ.† ⲉⲃ. ⲉⲛⲉⲣⲟⲩⲟ, COAd 47 †ⲭⲣⲓⲁ ⲧⲉ ⲉⲃⲟⲗ ϫⲉⲁⲓϣ. ⲉⲃ.

—— nn m *SAF, need, shortage*: Jud 19 20, 1 Cor 16 17 *SF*(*B* ⲋⲣⲟⲋ), Col 1 24 (Bor 248 58, var ⲥⲉⲉⲡⲉ, *B* do) ὑστέρημα, Mk 12 44 (*BF* ⲉⲣ ⲍⲁⲉ)-ησις; BM 216 110 ⲟⲩϣ. ⲡⲧⲁⲙⲧⲋⲱⲃ ἐλάττωμα, Si 20 7 -τωσις; Pro 10 21 *A*(*S* ⲋⲣⲱⲟ, *B* ⲙⲉⲧⲣⲉϥⲉⲣ ⲋ.) ἔνδεια; Lev 26 16 (*B* diff), Hag 2 17 *A*(*S* ⲋ., *B* diff) ἀφορία; Ps 138 16 (*B* ⲁⲧⲉⲣ ⲣⲱⲃ) ἀκατέργαστος; Sh ViK 941 47 ⲟⲩϣ. ⲛⲏⲧⲡⲉ ϫⲉⲟⲩⲧⲏⲧⲛ ⲣⲁⲡ ⲙⲡ ⲡⲉⲧⲡⲉⲣⲏⲩ, ShC 73 88 ⲡϣ. ⲡⲡⲉⲧⲛⲁⲟⲩⲱⲙ ... ⲡⲁⲉⲓ ⲉⲣⲣⲁⲓ ⲉϫⲡⲡⲉⲧⲇⲓⲁⲕⲟⲡⲉⲓ, P 131³ 63 opp ⲙⲛⲧⲣⲙ ⲙⲁⲟ, C 99 158 tell them ⲡⲉⲩϣ. ⲉⲧⲟⲩⲋⲟⲭⲃ ⲛⲣⲏⲧϥ = ib 89 96 *B* ⲡⲉⲧⲟⲩϣ.† ⲙⲙⲟϥ, PLond 4 443 supplies (?) will be delivered ⲁⲭⲡϣⲱⲧ.

ⲁⲧϣ. *S, without shortage*: BMOr 6201 A 2 *S* will deliver money ⲛⲁ. ⲣⲓⲕⲁⲧⲁⲫⲣⲟⲡⲏⲥⲓⲥ.

ϣⲁⲁⲧⲛ- (ϣⲁⲁⲧ ⲛ-) *S*, ϣⲁⲧⲛ-*S*(mostly)*S*ᶠ*A*, ϣⲁ ⲧⲉ-*SF*, ϣⲁⲧⲉⲛ-*BF* prep, *short of, excepting, minus*: Lev 11 36 *SB*, ib 23 38 *S*(*B* ⲥⲁⲃⲟⲗ ⲛ-), Nu 18 3 *B* (*S* = Gk), Deu 1 36 *S*(*B* ⲉⲃⲏⲗ ⲉ-), Ps 74 8 *S*(*B* = Gk) πλήν; Jth 8 6 *S*, He 4 15 *S*(cit Bor 290 45 ϣⲁ ⲧⲉ-, *B* ⲁⲧⲋⲡⲉ) χωρίς; 2 Cor 11 24 *SB*, RNC 40 *S*

fifteen years ϣⲁⲁⲧⲛϣⲟⲙⲧ ⲛⲉⲃⲟⲧ παρά; 1 Cor 15 27 *B*(*SF* ⲡⲃⲟⲗ ⲛ-, *F* var ⲉⲃⲟⲗ ⲛ-), R 1 1 21 *S* ϣⲁ ⲁⲧⲙⲡⲉⲓⲙⲛⲧⲥⲡⲟⲟⲩⲥ ἐκτός, Ac 26 29 *SB* παρεκ.; Br 267 *S* ϣⲉ ⲛⲧⲃⲁ…ϣ. ϥⲧⲟⲟⲩ ⲛⲧⲃⲁ, ShA 2 349 *S* among crafts ⲣⲉϥⲣ ⲣⲱⲃ ⲉϣⲁⲁⲣ ϣ. ⲃⲱⲕⲉ ⲙⲙⲁⲧⲉ, ShR 2 3 47 *S* serving him ϣⲁⲁⲧⲙⲡⲟⲣⲡⲉⲩⲉ ⲣⲁⲣⲟϥ, Pcod 30 *S* destroyed all ϣ. ⲡⲉⲧⲛⲧⲕⲓⲃⲱⲧⲟⲥ, BSM 29 *B* naught left ϣ. ⲡⲟⲩⲕⲉⲣⲉⲃⲥⲱ = BMis 369 *S* ϣⲁⲣⲣⲁⲓ ⲉ-, AM 9 *B* all assented ϣ. ⲓⲟⲩⲥⲧⲟⲥ ⲙ ⲙⲁⲅⲁⲧⲋ, ib 124 *B* we obey rulers ϣ. ⲡⲣⲃⲏⲟⲩⲓ ⲉⲧ ⲉⲡ† ⲙⲕⲁⲣ ⲙⲫ† ⲛⲃⲏⲧⲟⲩ, C 41 10 *B* drew nigh to τόπος ϣ. ⲟⲩⲙⲅⲗⲗⲓⲟⲛ, WS 118 *S* ⲥⲁⲙⲃⲉ ⲡϣⲉ ϣⲁ ⲧⲉⲟⲩⲉⲓ, BIF 22 107 *F* spare none ϣ. ⲡⲏ ⲉⲧⲉⲣⲱ ⲙⲱⲗⲱⲧⲓ, Mor 24 7*F* every tree ϣⲁⲧⲉⲡϣⲏⲛ ⲡⲥⲟⲩⲱⲡ ⲡⲡⲉⲧⲛⲁⲡⲟⲩⲃ; PLond 5 135 *S* ⲡⲁⲧⲁⲙⲙⲁⲁⲩⲡⲉ ⲡϣⲁ ⲁⲧⲛⲧⲉⲭⲟⲣⲏⲅⲓⲁ, PJkôw *S* ⲥⲁϣⲩ ⲛⲣⲟⲗⲟⲕ/ ⲡϣⲁⲁⲧⲛ ⲡⲟⲩⲧⲣⲓ(ⲙⲏⲥⲓⲟⲛ); ϣ. ⲕⲉⲕⲟⲩϫⲓ *B*, *except a little more, almost*: Ps 72 2 (*S* ⲡⲁⲣⲁ ⲟⲩⲕⲟⲩⲓ), MG 25 204 they beat me ⲉⲑⲣⲓⲙⲟⲩ ϣ. ⲕ. παρὰ μικρόν, Ps 118 87 (*S* do) π. βραχύ, Pro 5 14 (*SA* π. ⲕⲉϣⲏⲙ) π. ὀλίγον; AM 301 ϣ. ⲕ. ⲥⲉⲡⲁⲣⲓ ⲱⲡⲓ ⲉⲭⲱⲡ; ϣ. ⲟⲩⲕⲟⲩⲓ, -ϫⲓ: Va 63 4 *B* all came to an end ϣ. = BSM 28 *B* ⲉⲃⲏⲗ ⲉⲟⲩⲕ. = Mor 27 25 *S*ᶠ ϣⲁⲧⲉⲟⲩⲕ., R 1 4 38 *S* ⲟⲩⲣⲟⲙⲡⲉ ϣⲁⲁⲧⲛⲟⲩⲕ. *plus minus*.

ϣⲁⲁⲧⲉ, -ⲧⲥ *S* nn f, *part cut off, portion*: Lu 24 42 (var -ⲧⲥ, cit Bor 290 150, P 131³ 1, Mor 43 121 all -ⲧⲉ, *B* = Gk) μέρος; Mor 46 35 bade ⲧⲁⲗⲟ ⲡⲟⲩϣ. ⲡⲥⲧⲉⲗⲗⲟⲥ (στῦλος, cf AM 297 ⲫⲁϣⲓ ⲡⲧⲉ ⲟⲩⲥⲧ.) ⲣⲓ ⲭⲡⲣⲏⲧϥ, P 44 91 ⲡⲉϣⲁⲧⲉ ⲙⲡⲕⲁⲣ جدد = 43 75 ⲡⲉ ϣⲓ قياس, Kr 92 about flax crop ⲧϣⲟⲣⲡⲉ ⲡϣ. ⲙⲛⲧ ⲙ[ⲉⲣⲥⲡⲧⲉ. *Cf* ? DM 9 11 *p hry* ϣⲁⲧⲉ *n tpt*.

ϣⲁⲁⲧⲉ *S*, ϣⲁⲧⲉ *SB* nn f, *cutting, ditch*: Ex 8 1 *B* διῶρυξ, AM 279 *B* διορυγή, Ex 22 2 *B*(*S* ⲙⲁ ⲉⲛⲧⲁϥ ⲋⲱⲧⲣ ⲉⲣⲟϥ), Zeph 2 14 *B*(*A* ⲙⲁ ⲉⲧⲉ ⲡⲟⲩⲱϣ)-γμα; ShC 73 152 *S* let water in ⲉⲩϣⲁⲧⲉ ⲏ ⲟⲩⲙⲁ ⲉϥϩⲟⲃⲉ, Ryl 343 *S* ⲧ]ϫⲁⲧⲉ…ⲧⲏⲧⲁⲥⲧⲁⲕⲟ ⲡⲉⲡϫⲱⲙⲁ, ib ⲟⲩⲏⲣ ⲡⲣⲱⲙⲉ ⲣ ⲣⲱϥ ⲉⲧϫⲁⲧⲉ, BMOr 6201 B 72 *S* ⲧϫⲁⲁⲧⲉ …ⲉⲛⲧⲓ ⲣⲱⲙⲉ ⲉⲣⲟⲥ, BMEA ostr 44717 *S* field on north of ⲧϫⲁⲧⲉ; ⲣⲓ ϣ. *B*, *make cutting, breach*: AM 273 ⲁⲩⲣⲓ ϣ. in wall ὀρύσσειν; c ⲉ-: Mt 6 19 (*S* ϣⲟϫⲧ) διορύσ., Job 24 16 ⲍ. acc; PO 14 345 ⲡⲡⲉ ⲣⲗⲓ…ⲣⲓ ϣ. ⲉⲛⲥⲟⲃⲧ, Va 57 70 adversary ⲉⲧⲣⲓ ϣ. ⲉⲡⲉⲓⲯⲩⲭⲏ, C 43 183 ⲣⲓⲟⲩⲓ ⲡⲟⲩϣ. ⲉⲡⲏⲓ; c ⲉϩⲟⲩⲛ: Cat 203 thieves ⲣⲓ ϣ. ⲉϩ.; as nn: Ez 4 2 (*S* ⲧⲏ[ⲡⲉ?]) περιοχή; K 435 شعب (l ⲛⲅⲣ), خندق; ⲁⲧ ⲣⲓ ϣ., *without breach*: Va 57 174 ⲑⲏⲥⲁⲩⲣⲟⲥ ⲡⲁⲧ ⲭⲱⲧⲉ ⲡⲁ. ⲉⲣⲟϥ; ⲣⲉϥⲣⲓ ϣ., *cutter*: AM 272 λατομῶν; Va 57 65 ⲡⲓⲣ. ⲉⲧⲟⲩⲱⲧⲉⲛ ⲡⲣⲁⲡⲥⲟⲃⲧ, Cat 178 ⲟⲩⲣ. ⲉϩⲟⲩⲛ ⲉⲡⲓⲧⲁⲙⲓⲟⲛ; ⲙⲉⲧⲣ.: Va 58 155 thieves ϫⲱⲕ ⲉⲃⲟⲗ ⲛⲣⲁⲡⲛ. As place-name: church of St Michael ⲣⲓ(ⲧ)ϣⲁⲧⲉ = الخندق (Amélineau *Géog* 577).

ϣⲧⲁ *S* vb intr, *be faulty, have need, defect*: BG

23 ⲟⲩⲁⲧϫⲟⲕϣⲡⲉ ϩⲱⲥ ⲉⲙⲡⲉϥϣ. ⲣⲱ ϫⲉⲉⲅⲉϫⲟⲕϥ *is unending as having no need to be ended*, ST 391 ⲡⲉⲥⲟⲩⲟ … ⲁⲩϣ. ⲡⲟⲩϩ[ⲟⲗⲟⲕⲁⲟⲥ; tr: Bodl(P) a l f ⲡⲡⲣⲕⲁϥ (sc mixture) ⲉϣ. ⲥⲱⲡ *lack soaking*; ϣ. ⲉⲃⲟⲗ: PMich 4935]ϣ. ϩⲏⲧ ⲉⲃⲟⲗ ⲁⲩⲱ[.

ϣⲧⲁ SAA², ϣⲧⲟ (?) F nn m, *defect, fault*: Cl 2 6 A ὑστέρημα; Mus 40 43 (RegPach) *if sin be done* ⲛϥⲧⲙⲡⲟⲗⲟϥ, BG 64 ϣⲱⲡⲉ ⲡⲟⲩϫⲱⲕ …ⲉⲙⲡ ϣ. ⲡⲣⲏⲧϥ, ib 47 ⲉⲧⲁϩⲟ ⲡⲡⲉⲥϣ. ⲉⲣⲁⲧⲟⲩ *repair defects*, ib 118 ⲉϥⲉ(ⲟⲩ)ⲱⲛϩ ⲛϭⲓ ⲡⲉϣ. ⲡⲧⲉⲥϭⲓⲙⲉ, C 73 213 ⲡⲉⲓⲛⲟϭ ⲛϣ. ⲛⲧⲁϥϣⲱⲡⲉ (sc his death), ST 122 *list of utensils headed* ⲡϣ. ⲡⲟⲩⲗⲏ [ⲡⲁⲡⲁ ⲁⲡⲁⲡⲓⲁⲥ] *ends* ⲛⲁⲓ ⲧⲏⲣⲟⲩ ⲟⲩⲗⲏ ⲡ(ⲧⲁ)ⲁⲡⲁ ⲁ. ϣⲁⲁⲧ ⲙⲙⲟⲟⲩ (cf? ib 439 1 l ⲡⲡϣⲧⲟ), Mani 2 A² *cannot remain* ⲉϥ[ⲟⲩ]ⲱϣ ⲡⲉⲓⲣⲉ ⲡⲣⲏⲧϥ ⲡⲟⲩϣ. ⲙⲡⲟⲩϭⲱϫⲃⲉ, CO 499 F *give 4 measures* ⲁⲣⲁ ⲡϣⲧⲟ ⲡⲓⲥⲁⲕ (ⲕ)ⲁⲑⲁⲣⲟⲛ; f: PBu 94 ⲧϭⲓⲛϣⲁϫⲉ … ⲡⲧϣⲟⲣⲡ ⲡⲕⲟⲟⲥ ⲡⲉⲥⲭⲓⲧⲁⲣⲓ[ⲡ (σχεδάριον) ⲙⲡⲧ]ϭⲓⲛϣⲁϫⲉ ⲛⲧⲙⲉϩⲥⲛ̄ⲧⲉ ⲡϣ. (same?); ⲣ ϣ., *come short*: Pro 11 16 A(S ⲣ ϭⲣⲱϩ, B ϣⲱⲧ) ἐνδεὴς γίνεσθαι, ib 13 11 A(S do, B ϭⲣⲟϩ) ἐλάσσων γίν.; CO 95 ⲧⲉⲧⲡⲁϭⲛ ⲧⲩⲡⲟⲥ ⲛⲧⲉⲧⲛⲣ ⲡϣⲉ ⲡⲟϭ ⲡϣ.

ϣⲁⲧⲉ- v ϣⲁⲡⲧⲉ- & ϣⲟⲱⲧ (ϣⲁⲁⲧⲛ-).

ϣⲏⲧⲉ S nn f, *palm fibre, ? whence belt, collar* of it : Glos 244 περιτραχήλιον; BMis 478 *man climbing tree* ⲁⲧϣ. ⲥⲟⲗⲡ (l ⲥⲱ.) *& he fell backward* (cf طلب), Mor 41 181 ϣ., ϫⲟⲟⲩϥ ⲙⲡⲣⲉⲡⲕⲉⲃⲟⲧⲁⲡⲏ *as fuel* (cf ⲥⲁⲁϭⲉ, ϣⲉ ⲡⲉⲗⲟⲟⲗⲉ, ϫⲁϫⲓⲑⲱⲗ *thus used*), Ryl 238 ⲟⲩⲕⲁⲙⲡⲁⲡⲟⲥ ⲡⲁⲧⲉϣ. *weighing-machine without…(quid?)*.

ϣⲓⲧⲉ SF, -ϯ B, ϣⲱⲧ SB, ϣⲟⲱⲧ-S(v c ϣⲁ ϩⲁ-, ? confused with ϣⲟⲱⲧ), ϣⲁⲁⲧ- S(once), ϣⲁⲧ-¹ B, ϣⲉⲧ-² ŠBF, ϣⲓⲧ-SA, ϣⲁⲧⲝ³ SB, ϣⲁⲁⲧⲝ⁴, ϣⲓⲧⲝ S, ϣⲉⲧⲝ S/ BF, ϣⲉⲉⲧⲝ F, ⲣ ⲥ ϣⲁⲧ- B vb Ⅰ intr, *demand, extort*: Is 9 4 SB ἀπαιτεῖν; BMis 257 S ⲡⲉⲧϣ. (var Mor 29 27 ϫⲓ ⲙⲡⲧⲛⲁ) = Mor 30 32 S/ *demanding* (alms), Va 66 298 B ⲟⲩϩⲁⲡⲓⲥⲧⲏⲥ ⲉϥϣ. Ⅱ tr: Deu 15 2³ SB, Is 30 33 S⁴B(prob)F, Lu 12 48 S³(B ⲕⲱϯ ⲡⲥⲁ-) ἀπ.; ShC 42 64 S ⲉⲓⲡⲁⲧⲣⲉⲡⲁⲓⲕⲁⲥⲧⲏⲥ…ϣⲁⲧⲟⲩ (sc debt), ShA 2 132 S ϣ. ⲙⲡⲣⲟⲙⲡⲧ, BHom 64 S ⲙⲉϥϣⲉⲧ ⲧⲉⲗⲟⲥ, Va 58 156 B ⲉⲧϣ. ⲡⲡⲓⲣⲉⲙⲁϯ, Z 625 S *wicked to* ϣ. ⲁⲩⲱ ⲉⲥϭⲗⲁ ⲡⲡⲧⲁⲫⲟⲥ *of martyrs* (or ? = ϣⲓⲕⲉ, v JEA 13 24 n); c double acc: Deu 23 19 B²(var ϣⲁⲡ error, S ⲧⲧⲉ-) ἐκτοκίζειν; Aeg 223 S ϣⲉⲧ ⲡⲉⲧⲭⲣⲉⲱⲥⲧⲉⲓ ⲡⲁϥ ⲙⲙⲏⲛⲥⲉ ἀπ.; Va 66 299 B ⲡⲧⲉϥϣⲁⲧ(ⲧ) ⲙⲫⲗⲟⲅⲟⲥ ὑπέχειν; Ps 68 4 S³(B diff) ἀποτιννύειν; ShHT X 3 S ϣⲁⲧϥ ⲡⲣⲉⲡⲁϣⲉ ⲛⲭⲣⲏⲙⲁ, ShC 42 91 S ϣ. ⲙⲙⲟϥ ⲡⲧⲁⲥⲟⲩ *of wine*, KKS 667 S ⲡⲣⲣⲟ ⲡⲁϣⲁⲁⲧⲟⲩ ⲙⲡⲉⲫⲟⲣⲟⲥ, P 130³ 69 S ϥⲡⲁϣⲉⲧ ⲡⲟⲩⲁ ⲡⲟⲩⲁ ⲙⲡⲉϥⲉⲣⲏⲧ, Worr 266 S ⲉⲧϣ. ⲙⲙⲟϥ ⲙⲡⲉϣϭⲟⲣ *of house*, BMis 261 S ⲡϥϫ̄ⲥ ⲡⲁϣⲓⲧⲕ ⲙⲙⲟϥ (sc wounded ox, var Mor 29 31

S ϣⲁⲧⲕ ib 30 36 F ϣⲉⲧⲕ), RE 9 170 S ⲁⲩϣⲓⲧϥ ⲡⲟⲩⲏⲣ ⲡⲣⲟⲗⲟⲕ/, Ryl 361 S/(or A²) ⲉⲓⲁϣϣⲉⲧⲧⲏⲩⲧⲡ ⲙⲡⲕⲉⲥⲉⲉⲡⲉ, ST 91 S ⲕⲱ ⲡϩⲣⲉⲧⲟⲓⲙⲟⲥ ⲉϣⲓⲧ ⲡⲓⲧⲕⲟⲟⲩϥ ⲡⲣⲏⲧϥ, El 60 A ⲉϣⲓⲧ ⲙⲛⲥⲉ ⲡⲙⲛⲥⲉ, BSM 77 B ϣⲁⲧⲟⲩ ⲡⲣ̄ ⲡⲗⲟⲅⲕⲟϫⲓ = BMis 168 S ⲁⲡⲉⲧⲉⲓ, C 41 42 B ϣ. ⲙⲙⲟⲟⲩ ⲙⲫⲏ ⲉⲧⲉⲡⲧⲱⲟⲩ ⲁⲡ, C 86 328 B ϣⲁⲧ ⲫⲏ … ⲡϥⲕⲉ·ϯ ⲡⲗⲟⲅⲕⲟϫⲓ, PJkôw S/ ϣⲁⲡⲧⲟⲩϣⲉⲧⲡ ⲙⲡⲁⲓⲙⲟⲓⲣⲉ; + ⲟⲥⲉ, *exact fine*: Sh Wess 9 123 S ⲟⲩϩⲏⲕⲉ ⲁⲓϣⲁⲁⲧϥ ⲡⲟⲩⲟ., BMis 486 S *if we fail* ⲡⲡⲉϥϩⲟⲣ[ϣ] ⲉϫⲱⲡ ⲡϥϣⲁⲁⲧⲡ ⲡⲟⲩⲟ., DeV 1 74 B *brought to judge, beaten* ⲡⲥⲉϣⲉⲧⲟⲩ ⲡϩⲁⲡⲕⲉⲟ., Ep 162 S ϩⲉⲡⲕⲉⲟ. ⲉⲁⲩϣⲓⲧ(ⲧ) ⲙⲙⲟⲟⲩ ϩⲓⲧⲙⲡⲁⲣⲭⲱⲡ; + ⲙⲡⲧⲛⲁ, ⲙⲉⲑⲡⲁⲓ, *ask charity*: Ac 3 2 S²B¹ ἐλεημοσύνην αἰτεῖν, Lu 16 3 B¹(S ⲧⲱⲃϩ) ⲉⲡⲁⲓ., Jo 9 8 S²B¹(A² ϫⲓ ⲙⲡⲧⲛⲁⲉ) προσαι.; BMis 359 S ⲉⲧϣⲉⲧ ⲙ. ⲉⲣⲙⲡⲣⲟ = BSM 21 B, AZ 21 153 S ⲉⲧϣⲁⲁⲧ ⲙⲙ. (l ⲙ.), Mor 30 23 F ⲁϥϣⲉⲧ ⲙ.; v also p c.

With following preposition. c ⲉ- SBF, *mulct of*: Cat 48 B ⲉⲩⲟⲩⲱϣ ⲉϣⲁⲧⲧ ⲉⲧⲉⲗⲱⲥ (-ⲗⲟⲥ), Va 57 191 B ⲡⲓⲡⲉⲧⲉϣⲱⲟⲩ ⲉⲧⲟⲩϣ. ⲙⲙⲟⲟⲩ ⲉⲣⲟϥ, Ryl 324 S ϣⲁⲧϥ ⲉⲡⲉⲛⲧⲁϥϣⲱⲡ (sic l), BM 597 F ϣⲉⲧ ⲁⲣⲭⲉⲗⲗⲓⲧⲏⲥ ⲉⲧⲃ ⲡⲗⲉⲕⲱⲧⲥⲓ; c ϩⲁ- S, ϣⲁ- B(once), *for, concerning*: Z 289 ⲉⲩⲡⲁϣⲁⲧⲏ ϩⲁⲡⲉⲡⲧⲁⲡⲁⲁⲩ ⲁⲡⲁⲓ. κατά, Aeg 221 ϣⲁⲁⲧⲩ ⲙⲡⲗⲟⲅⲟⲥ ϩⲁⲡⲉⲩⲯⲩⲭⲏ ⲁⲡ. ὑπέρ; Miss 4 644 ϣ. ⲙⲙⲟⲟⲩ ⲡⲟⲩⲛⲟϭ ⲡⲧⲓⲙⲏ ϩⲁⲡⲏⲣⲡ, ib 734 ⲥⲉⲡⲁϣⲁⲁⲧⲕ ⲙⲙⲟⲟⲩ (sc duties neglected) ϩⲁⲣⲟⲕ, Turin ostr 5929 ⲁⲓϣⲓⲧϥ ⲡⲟⲩⲧⲣⲉⲙⲏⲥⲓ ϩⲁⲣⲱⲧⲓ, BMOr 6201 A 21 ⲡⲣⲟⲗⲟⲕ/ ⲡⲧⲁⲕϣⲱⲧ ⲡⲁϭⲙⲉ ⲙⲙⲟϥ ϩⲁⲣⲟⲓ, Va 66 309 B *beasts* ϣⲱⲧ ⲙⲙⲟⲛ ⲡⲟⲩⲙⲉⲧϥⲁⲓⲣⲱⲟⲩϣ ϩⲁⲣⲱⲟⲩ.

ⲣ ⲥ ϣⲁⲧⲙⲉⲑⲡⲁⲓ: Ps 34 10 (S ⲉⲃⲓⲏⲡ) πένης; Ap 3 17 (S do) πτωχός.

ⲣⲉϥϣ. B, *demander, exactor*: Is 14 4 (S ⲡⲉⲧϣ.) ἀπαιτῶν; CDan 86 *sitting here like* ϩⲁⲓⲡ. = ib 30 συνάδελφος = Pereira *Abba Daniel* 8 ⲏⲉⲗⲫⲣ: ⲅ°ⲝⲯϯ.

ϣⲓϯ, ϣⲁⲧ-, ϣⲁⲧⲝ, ϣⲁⲧϯ B vb intr, *leap, gush, vomit*: Lev 11 21 (S ϭⲱϫⲉ)πηδᾶν, Deu 33 22(S do) ἐκπ.; Joel 2 5 (A ϥⲓ ϥⲁϭⲥ), Mic 2 12(SA ⲡⲱⲧ ⲉⲃⲟⲗ) ἐξάλλεσθαι; Is 19 14 (S ⲕⲁ ⲃⲟⲗ) ἐμεῖν; K 159 B ⲥⲡⲟϥ ⲉⲧϣ.ϯ نزيف; tr: Ap 3 16 (S do) ἐμ., Job 20 15 (S do) ἐξέμ.; C 89 25 *spark* ⲁⲩϣⲁⲧϥ ⲉⲟⲩϭⲡⲱⲟⲩ βάλλεσθαι القى; MG 25 189 *proving ship's joints* (to see) *which of them* ⲉⲧϣⲁⲧ ⲙⲱⲟⲩ ⲉⲣⲟϥ, ib 190 ⲡⲁⲑⲟⲥ ⲉⲧϣⲁⲧ ⲙⲱⲟⲩ ϩⲱⲛ ⲡⲡⲟⲩⲯⲩⲭⲏ; as nn m, *vomit*: 2 Pet 2 22 (S ⲕ.) ἐξέρεμα; K 160 ⲡϣ. وقى استفراغ; AM 141 ⲟⲩⲉⲙ ⲡⲉϥϣ.; ϣ. ⲉⲃⲟⲗ: Jer 32 16 (S Cai 8316 ⲕ.) ἐξέμ.; Lu 8 44ϯ(S ϣⲟⲟⲩ) ῥύσις; TRit 184 ⲉⲧⲉⲡⲓⲥⲡⲟϥ ϣ.ϯ ⲉⲃ. ϩⲁⲣⲟⲥ نزفة الدم.

ϣⲓⲧ S: Ora 4 20 ⲉⲓⲧⲙⲁⲥⲓⲟ ⲡⲡⲉⲧⲉⲉⲧ ⲉⲓⲱⲧⲡ ⲡⲡⲉⲧϣ. *Belongs here?*

ϣⲱⲧⲉ *SAA²*, ϣⲱⲱ. *S*, ϣⲱϯ *BF* nn f, *well, cistern, pit*: Ex 2 15 *SAB*, Ps 54 24 *B*(*S* ϣⲏⲓ), Cant 4 15 *SBF*, Jo 4 11 *SA²BF*, Ap 9 1 *SB*, HL 116 *B* standing all night in ϯϣ. φρέαρ; Ge 24 29 *B* πηγή; ShP 130¹ 37 *S* ⲧⲃⲟ ⲛ ⲧϣ. wherein clothes washed, ShIF 300 *S* ⲛϣ. ⲙⲙⲉϩ ⲙⲟⲟⲩ, Miss 4 231 *S* they dug ⲟⲩϣⲏⲓ for till then had only ⲟⲩⲕⲟⲓ ⲛϣ., BAp 88 *S* ϣⲱⲱ. = PO 22 348 بٔر, AM 186 *B* bastard babes abandoned ϩⲉⲛⲛⲓϣ. ⲡⲉⲙⲛⲓϣⲏⲓ, SHel 52 *S* ϣⲓⲕⲉ ⲛⲟⲩϣ. ⲉⲡⲉⲥⲏⲧ, C 41 18 *B* ϯϣ. ⲉⲩϣⲱⲕⲓ ⲙⲙⲟⲥ, Miss 4 813 *S* ⲧϣ. of church, BIF 13 100 *S* = MG 25 280 *B* sim, Tst Ab 238 *B* ϣ. ⲉⲥⲙⲉϩ ⲛϭⲉⲡⲧ = Mor 53 42 *S* ϩⲓⲉⲓⲧ, ROC 23 286 *B* ϣ. ⲙⲙⲱⲟⲩ ⲃⲉⲃⲓ ⲉⲡϣⲱⲓ = 287 ⲙⲟⲩⲙⲓ, Rec 6 185 *B* ϣ. ⲙⲙⲱⲟⲩ = BMar 219 *S* ⲡⲩⲅⲏ, CO 459 *S* among metal objects, ⲃⲛⲧⲉ ⲡⲣⲱⲕ ϣ. (same ?), Kr 125 *S* lease of ⲡⲙⲉⲣⲟⲥ ⲉⲣⲛⲓϣ.; ⲟⲓ ⲛϣ. *B*: Ge 14 10 φ.

ϣⲱⲧⲉ *SAO*, -ϯ *B* nn m, *flour, dough*: 2 Kg 13 8 *S*, Jer 7 18 *B* σταῖς; Hos 7 4 *AB* στέαρ (reading ? σταιτός); Bor 253 164 *S* ⲛϣ. ⲉⲧⲭⲓ ⲑⲁⲃ ἄλευρον; Mt 13 33 *SB*(*F* ⲟⲩⲱϣⲉⲙ) Gk om; P 44 62 *S* ⲛϣ. عجٔن; ShA 2 170 *S* ⲟⲩⲑⲁⲃ ⲡⲟⲭϥ ⲉⲟⲩϣ., ShP 130¹ 8 *S* ⲡⲉⲥⲧⲟⲓ ⲙⲡϣ. ⲡⲡⲉⲧⲛⲟⲉⲓⲕ, ShC 73 146 *S* ⲡⲉⲧⲥⲉⲭ ϣ. ⲉⲃⲟⲗ to make cakes thereof, DeV 2 106 *B* ⲡⲓϣ. ⲁⲕϣⲁⲡϯ ϣⲉⲙⲛⲣ ⲉⲣⲟϥ, DM 13 *O* tnˤ ḥr ϣ.

ϣⲱⲓϯ *B* K 12 ضٔڤ, *l* ϩⲱⲓϯ ضٔڤ (*cf ib* 257).

ϣⲱⲱⲧⲉ *S*, ϣⲱϯ *B* *v* ϣⲱⲱⲧ *A*.

ϣⲧⲁ, ϣⲧⲟ *S* nn m, meaning unknown: BMOr 6203 in boundaries ⲡⲉϫⲉⲙⲡⲧ ⲡⲉϣ. ⲙⲛ̄ⲧⲉⲣⲕⲁⲥⲓⲁ (ἐργ.), 6202, -04 sim ϣⲧⲟ, J 16 31 as boundary ⲛⲣⲙ̄ⲡϣ. *Cf* ? next.

ϣⲧⲁ *F* nn, *thicket, wood*: Cant 2 3 ⲛⲧⲙⲏ̄ϯ [ⲛ̄ⲟⲩ]ⲧⲁ, Ep Jer 62 (*B* = Gk) δρυμός.

ϣⲧⲁ *S* nn f, in place-name: Ep 1 7 (10) ⲙⲙⲁⲣⲧⲉⲣⲱⲥ ⲛⲧⲉϣ. Same ? as last, but reading doubtful.

ϣⲧⲁ *v* ϣⲱⲱⲧ *sf* & ⲭⲧⲟ.

ϣⲧⲉ *SB*(once), -ⲏ *SF*, ϣⲟⲉ, ϣⲟⲉϩ *B* + ⲛⲃⲁⲓ, pl ϣⲧⲏⲩ *S*, -ⲏⲟⲩ *F* & sg as pl, nn m, *ship's mast*: Is 30 17 *S* ϣⲟⲛⲧⲉ(*l* ϣ.)*B* ϣⲟⲉϩ(*sic* 3 MSS)*F*, *ib* 33 23 *S*-ⲏ *BF*, Ez 27 5 *SB*(prob) ἱστός, LAp 572 *F* sat by ⲡⲉϣ. ⲙⲛⲭ[ⲁⲓ] ἱστίον; P 44 54 *S* صٔارٔي (*v* ⲑⲱⲕ); R 2 1 56 *S* ship's ϣ. ⲁϥⲟⲩⲉⲓⲥⲉ ⲙⲙⲟϥ, BHom 88 *S* ship's ϣ. & ϩⲓⲉ, SHel 59 *S* martyr hanged ⲉⲩϣⲧⲏ ⲛⲭⲟⲓ; pl: Nu 4 26 *S*(var ⲗⲁⲅⲟ, *B* diff), Is 33 23 *BF*(*S* ⲗ.) ἱστίον; ϣⲧⲉ *B* m رٔجٔل, *rudder* Bodl 325 148 (but *cf* ϩⲓⲉ).

ϣⲧⲉ *S* nn, *nest*: Tri 714 ⲛⲁⲉⲧⲟⲥ ϩⲛⲛⲉϣ. عٔش̄, Rec 7 27 ʿ, خٔصّ.

ϣⲧⲉ *S* nn as pl, meaning doubtful: ShMIF 23

149 ⲛϣ. ⲛⲉ ⲛⲁⲓ that believe not on Christ as chief corner-stone. *L* ? ⲡⲉⲕⲟⲧⲉ (*cf* Mt 21 42 &c, but there ⲡⲉⲧⲕⲱⲧ, except Ps 117 22 *B*).

ϣⲧⲉ- *v* ⲥⲱϣ, *strike* (ⲥⲁϣ).

ϣⲧⲟ, ϣⲧⲁ *v* ⲭⲧⲟ.

ϣⲱⲧⲃ̄, ϣ(ⲉ)ⲧⲃ- *S* vb tr, *muzzle*: Deu 25 4 (*B* ϯ ⲥⲁⲭⲟⲗ) φιμοῦν; 1 Cor 9 9 (*B* do, *F* ϯ ⲥⲗⲏⲃ) κημοῦν; Mus 30 13 ϣⲱ. (var ϣⲱⲧⲃ̄) ⲡⲛⲁⲥⲡⲟⲣⲉⲕ.

ϣⲧⲟⲃ̄ *S*, ϣⲧⲟϥ *SB*(Ez), ϣⲧⲁϥ *Sf* nn, *muzzle, halter*: Is 37 29 *Sf*(*B* ⲧⲁⲧϥⲟ), Si 20 28 φιμός; Ps 31 9 -ϥ (*B* = Gk), Ez 19 9 *S* -ϥ κημός; Job 40 20(*B* ϩⲁⲗⲁⲕ) φορβέα; RNC 32 ⲟⲩϣ. ϩⲓⲣⲡⲣⲱϣ κατοχή; P 43 61 ⲕⲩⲙⲱ (κημός) حٔكٔمٔة, ϣⲧⲟϥ ⲙⲭⲟⲣⲟ; ShC 42 120 ϩⲉⲛϣ. ⲉϣⲧⲙ ⲣⲱⲟⲩ, ViK 9658 7 ⲟⲩϣⲧⲟϥ ⲉⲡⲉⲥⲡⲟⲧⲟⲩ, Mor 47 69 *Sf* ⲟⲩϣ. ⲉϣⲁⲁⲡⲧϥ.

ϣⲧⲃⲟ *AA²* vb intr, *snort, groan*: Jo 11 33 *A*(*S* ⲟⲟⲧ, *A²* ⲙⲁⲭ ⲡ[ϩⲏⲧ], *B* ⲙⲕⲁϩ)ἐμβριμᾶσθαι(*cf* Rösch 150); ManiH 91 *A²* whale arose from sea, beseeching ⲉϥϣ.; as nn: *ib* 78 *A²* ⲁⲥⲧⲉⲟⲩⲟ ⲡⲓⲣⲓⲙⲉ ⲁⲣⲁϥ [   ]ⲛⲡⲉϣ.

ϣⲁⲧⲃⲟⲓ *B* *v* ϭⲱ.

ϣⲁⲧⲃⲁⲙⲡⲉ *v* ϣⲱⲱⲧ *A* ʀ ⲥ.

ϣⲁⲧⲃⲁⲛⲧⲉ *v* ⲕⲟⲡⲧⲉ.

ϣⲧⲉⲕⲟ *SAA²B*, ⲉϣ. *S*, ϣⲧⲉⲕⲁ *F*, pl ϣⲧⲉⲕⲱⲟⲩ *SA²B* & sg as pl, nn m, *prison*: Ge 40 7 *SB*, Jer 39 8 *SB*, Mt 14 3 *SBF*, 2 Cor 6 5 *S*(var ⲉϣ.)*B* pl, AP 19 *A²*, EW 32 *B* ϩⲓⲧⲟⲩ ⲉⲡϣ., φυλακή; Ge 39 22 *S* (*B* ⲙⲁ ⲛⲥⲱⲛϩ), Mt 11 2 *SB* δεσμωτήριον; Ac 4 3 *S* (*B* ⲁⲣⲉϩ) τήρησις; Sa 17 15 *S* ⲉϣ. εἰρκτή; Ac 16 23 *S* ⲡⲉⲧϩⲓϫⲙⲡⲉϣ. (*B* diff) δεσμοφύλαξ; ShA 1 192 *S* deeming world ⲟⲩⲉϣ., TU 43 5 *A* ⲧⲉⲕϥ ⲁⲡϣ., W Th 150 *S* ϫⲓⲧϥ ⲉⲡⲉϣ., EW 100 *B* ϩⲟⲧⲓ ⲉⲃⲟⲩⲛ ⲉⲡⲓϣ., JKP 2 206 *F* ⲡⲉϣⲧⲉⲕⲁ (*sic* MS), PLond 4 525 *S* ϣⲧⲓⲕⲟ;   pl: Ac 22 4 *S*, He 11 36 *B* φ.; Is 24 22 *S* δ.; ShC 42 103 *S*, BMis 288 *S*, Mani 1 *A²*, Aeg 39 *B*, KroppM 24 *S* ⲡⲉϣϯⲕⲱ;   as adj: Jer 44 15 *B* ⲛⲓ ⲛϣ. φ.

ϣⲧⲟⲩⲗ *S* nn, *hook*: P 44 89 ⲛϥⲁⲓϣ. حٔامٔلٔين (كٔلٔالٔيب) (var 43 72 الخٔطٔاطٔف).

ϣⲁⲧⲓⲗⲁ, ⲭⲁ., ϣⲁⲧⲉⲗⲁ *S* nn m, *bag* or some such receptacle: ST 118 ϣ. ⲛϣⲃⲏⲛⲉ (σεβένιον), ϣ. ⲛⲙⲟⲩⲥ, Bristol Musostr H 1755 measurements of ⲑⲁⲗⲓⲥ & ϣⲁⲧⲉⲗⲁ, CO 366]ⲙⲟϩ ⲡⲓϣ. ⲛⲕⲁⲕⲉ, *ib* 214 ⲕⲁⲡ ⲡⲕⲟⲩⲓ ⲕⲁⲡ ⲡⲛⲟϭ ⲛⲭⲁ. (*sic l*) ⲕⲁⲡ ⲧⲥⲁⲕⲓⲁ, Vi K 4741 ⲟⲩϣ. at ½ a *tremis*, Ep 401 ⲛϣ.

ϣⲧⲟⲗⲓ *F* *v* ⲧⲱⲣⲉ, *hand* (ϣⲧⲱⲣⲉ).

ϣⲧⲁⲗⲧⲉⲗ *F* *v* ϣⲧⲟⲣⲧⲣ.

ϣⲱⲧⲙ, ϩⲱ. (once)*S*, ϩⲱⲧⲙ *A* (once), ϣⲱⲧⲙ

B, ϣ(ⲉ)ⲧⲙ- S, ϣⲁⲧⲙ⸗ A², ϣⲟⲧⲙ⸗ S, ϣⲁ.† S/A², ϣⲟⲧⲉⲙ† B vb **I** intr, *shut, be shut*: Ap 3 7 S(B ϣⲑⲁⲙ) κλείειν, Is 45 1 S(B ⲙⲁϣⲑ.) συγκ.; Ez 33 22 SB συνέχειν; R 1 4 36 S ⲧⲡⲉ...ⲁϭϣ.; qual: Cant 4 12 S, Ez 46 1 SB, Ac 5 23 SB, BHom 138 S ⲧⲡⲗⲏϭⲏ ⲧⲏⲙ ⲁⲩⲱ ⲩϣ. (*l* ϭϣ.) κ., Jos 6 1 S συγκ.; Mor 40 45 S ⲣⲱⲕ ϣ. = MG 25 271 B, MIF 9 102 S/ ⲡⲱⲡⲉ of tomb ϣ., Mani 1 A² ⲡⲩⲗⲏ ⲉⲧϣ.

II tr: Eccl 12 4 S, Si 42 6 S ϣⲧⲙ-, Ap 21 25 S (B ϣⲑ.) κ., Jud 3 23 S ἀποκ., Jth 5 1 S συγκ.; Mt 22 34 S(B ⲑⲱⲙ) φιμοῦν; Tit 1 11 S(B ⲇⲟ).ἐπιστομίζειν; ShA 2 67 S ⲡϣⲟⲩϣⲧⲙ ⲣⲱϥ, ShC 73 141 S *let none* ϣⲉⲧⲙ ⲣⲟ ⲉⲡⲉⲧⲣⲓⲧⲟⲅⲱϥ *so as to leave him behind whilst reaping*, Mani H 59 A² *eyes* ϣⲁⲧⲙⲟⲩ, Sdff 45* S ⲧⲉⲧⲛϩ. ⲡⲧⲡⲩⲗⲏ.

With following ⲉⲡⲛ- *SA*, *shut upon, against*: Jud 9 51 κ. ἐπί, 4 Kg 4 4 (BP 10623) ἀποκ. κατά, Tob 8 4 συγκ.; R 2 4 88 ϣ. ⲉⲣⲱⲛ ⲙⲡⲣⲟ, Till Oster 9 A ⲧ]ⲡⲩⲗⲏ ϩ. ⲁⲣⲱⲟⲩ.

ϩⲱⲧⲙ *A* nn, *closed thing, chain*: Pro 25 11 (*S* = Gk) ὁρμίσκος.

ϣⲧⲙ *SO*, ϣⲧⲟⲙ *S*, ϣⲧⲉⲙ *S/A²F*, ϣⲑⲁⲙ *B*, ϣⲧⲁⲙ-*S*, ϣⲧⲉⲙ-*F*, ϣⲑⲁⲙⲏⲟⲩⲧ† *B* vb **I** intr, *shut*: Is 60 11 S(B ⲙⲁϣⲑ.), Lu 4 25 SB κ., Jer 13 19 B(S tr) συγκ.; Ge 8 2 S(B ϩⲱⲃⲥ) ἐπικαλύπτειν; PS 88 S ⲙⲁⲣⲉϣ. ⲛ ⲧⲧⲁⲡⲣⲟ, BMar 138 S ⲟⲩⲉⲕⲕⲗⲏⲥⲓⲁ ⲧⲏⲧⲁⲥϣ., LMär 37 S ⲡⲉⲣⲉⲡⲉⲣⲟ ϣ., DeV 1 90 B *cannot eat* ⲭⲉϯϣⲃⲱⲃⲓ ϣ., Hor 81 O ⲙⲡⲛⲥⲁϣ. ⲡⲧⲏϥ; qual B: Ez 44 2 (HCons 307, var ϣⲟⲧⲉⲙ *sic l* = S) κ.; K 231 ⲉϥϣ. غلق; MG 25 37 *windows* ⲥⲉϣ. **II** tr: Ap 11 6 B(S ϣⲱⲓⲧ) κ.; Is 33 15 SBF, Mt 13 15 S(B ⲙ.) καμμύειν; Pro 21 13 S(var ϣⲧⲟⲙ, *A* ϩⲱⲭⲧ)φράσσειν, Lam 3 8 B(S ϩⲱⲥ?)ἀποφ., EstC 20 S ⲉⲙⲫ.; Deu 11 17 S(B ⲧⲁϩⲛⲟ), Is 52 15 SB συνέχειν; Ps 57 4 S(B diff) βύειν; Ge 19 6 S(B ⲥⲱⲕ) προσάγειν; PS 24 S ⲙⲡⲟⲩⲉϣ ϣ. ⲛⲛⲉⲩⲧⲟⲡⲟⲥ, R 1 1 80 S ⲁϥϣ. ⲛⲡⲣⲡⲏⲅⲉ, Mor 54 28 S ⲟⲩϣⲟⲩϣⲧⲟⲙ ⲡⲣⲱϥ, AM 15 B ϣ. ⲛ ⲛⲓⲣⲱⲟⲩ; ϣⲧⲉⲙⲃⲉⲗ *F* nn, *eye-closer among diseases* Kropp C 24. ⲙⲁϣⲑ. *B* imperat: Su 17 κ., Ez 3 24 ἐγκ.; *whence also not* imperat: Is 60 11, Mt 25 10 κ., Ge 19 10 (all *S* ϣⲧ.) ἀποκ., Ps 30 9 (S diff) συγκ.; Cai Euch 481 ⲁⲕⲙ. ⲙⲫⲓⲟⲙ χαλινοῦν; DeV 1 86 ⲡⲉϩⲡⲁϣ ⲙ. ⲡⲡⲉϥⲙⲁϣⲭ, MIE 2 346 ⲡⲧⲉϥⲙ. ⲙⲡⲣⲟ (*cf* 348 *sim* ϣⲑ.).

With following preposition (*including* ⲙⲁϣ.). ϭ **ⲉ-** *SA²BF obj*: Mt 23 13 B(var & S tr) κ. acc, 1 Kg 24 19 B(S diff) ἀποκ. acc, Is 45 1 B(S ϣⲱⲧⲙ), Gal 3 23 B(S diff) συγκ.; PS 315 S ϯⲛⲁϣ. ⲉⲙⲡⲩⲗⲏ, ManiH 59 A² ϣ. ⲁⲛⲃⲉⲗ, LAp 562 F *sim*, Miss 4 126 B ϣ. ⲉⲛⲓⲣⲱⲟⲩ; *upon, against*: Mt 6 6 BF(S Gk om prep) κ., Ge 7 16 S(B as Gk)κ. ἔξωθεν, C 86 307 B ⲙⲡⲣϣ. ⲉⲣⲟⲓ ⲙⲫⲣⲟ κ. ἔμπροσθεν, 2 Kg 13 17 S ἀποκ. ὀπίσω, Is 26 20 B(S & Gk om prep)ἀποκ.,

Gal 4 17 *SB* ἐκκ. acc; BM 290 S/ ⲁⲩϣ. ⲙⲡⲣⲟ ⲉⲣⲟϥ, Va 58 128B ⲙⲡⲉⲣϣ. ⲉⲣⲟⲓ ⲙⲫⲣⲟ; ϭ ⲉⲣⲛ-*SA²* *BF*, *upon* intr: Job 12 14 S(B ⲉϩⲣⲉⲛ-) κ. κατά, Ap 20 3 SB κ. ἐπάνω, Jth 13 1 S ἀποκ. acc, Ro 3 27 SB ἐκκ., Ge 16 2 S(B acc) συγκ. acc, Job 3 23 SB συγκ. κατά; ib 38 8 SB φρ. acc; 1 Pet 2 15 S(B ⲉϩⲣ.) φιμοῦν; Z 277 S ἐμποδίζειν; ShC 73 139 S ϣ. ⲉⲣⲱⲟⲩ (Mt 25 10), AP 3 A² ϣ. ⲁⲣⲱϥ, Mor 28 269 S/ ϣ. ⲉⲣⲱⲕ; tr: BHom 22 S ϣ. ⲉⲣⲱⲛ ⲙⲡⲣⲟ ἀποκ.; Va 57 212 B ϣ. ⲉⲣⲱⲟⲩ ⲉⲙⲟⲓⲧ ⲛⲓⲃⲉⲛ ἀποτειχίζειν dat; DeV 1 172 B ϣ. ⲉⲡⲣⲟ ⲙⲡⲓⲁⲅⲁⲩ ⲉⲣⲱϥ, Mor 54 70 S ⲡⲥⲉϣⲧⲟⲙ ⲉⲣⲱⲛ ⲙⲡⲣⲟ, ib 25 37 S/ ϣ. ⲉⲣⲱⲕ ⲙ. ⲡⲙⲁ ⲡϣⲉⲗⲉⲉⲧ, C 43 127 B ⲙⲡⲉⲣⲙⲁϣ. ⲉⲣⲱⲓ ⲛⲡⲓⲡⲩⲗⲏ; ϭ ⲉϩⲣⲉⲛ-*B*, *as last*: Ps 16 10 (S ϩⲱⲭⲡ), Pro 4 12 (S ⲉⲣⲛ-, A ϩⲱⲭⲧ ⲁⲣⲛ-), Ro 11 32 (SF ⲱⲧⲡ ⲉϩⲟⲩⲛ) συγκ. acc; Mic 5 1 (A ⲱⲣⲃⲉ ⲁϩ.) ἐμφ. acc; DeV 2 65 ⲙⲁϣ. ⲉ. ⲛⲓⲡⲩⲗⲏ, ib 43 ϣ. ⲉ. ϩⲩⲗⲏⲕⲓⲁ (ἡλικ.) ⲛⲓⲃⲉⲛ ⲉⲇⲟⲩⲛ ⲇⲉⲡⲟⲩⲛⲁⲓⲥⲓ; ϭ ⲉϫⲛ-*SB*, as last: Tri 591 S ⲡⲣⲟ ϣ. ⲉϫⲱⲓ, Ps 68 16 B ⲙⲁϣ. ⲉⲉϩⲣⲏⲓ ⲉϫ. (S ⲁⲙⲁⲣⲧⲉ) συνέχειν ἐπί; ϭ ⲉⲃⲟⲗ ⲛ-*S*, *against*: ShA 2 110 ϣ. ⲙⲡⲉⲧⲛϣⲁ ⲉⲃ. ⲙⲡⲉⲥϯⲟⲩϭⲉ; ϭ ⲡⲥⲁ- *A²*: Mani K 87 ϣ. ⲡⲥⲱϥ; ϭ ⲡⲁϩⲣⲉⲛ-*B*, *before*: C 86 246 ϣ. ⲡⲧⲫⲉ ⲡⲁϩⲣⲁⲛ; ϭ ⲉⲃⲟⲗ ϩⲁ-*B*, *against*: Va 57 277 ϣ. ⲡⲣⲱⲕ ⲉⲃ. ϩⲁⲣⲱⲟⲩ; ϭ ⲉⲇⲟⲩⲛ ⲇⲁ-*B*, as last: ib 250 ϣ. ⲡⲣⲱⲟⲩ ⲉⲇ. ⲇⲁⲡⲉⲣ ϣⲓϣⲓ *of devil*.

ϫⲓⲛϣⲑ. *B*, *closing*: Am 1 6 (A ⲥⲁⲟⲩϩⲥ ⲁϩⲟⲩⲛ) συγκ.; Va 61 17 *austerities may save from* ⲡⲓϫⲓⲛⲙⲁϣ. ⲉⲣⲱⲓ ⲙⲫⲙⲟⲩ ⲉⲧⲥⲁⲡⲉⲥⲏⲧ; Ps 67 31 ⲡⲭⲓⲛϣⲧⲉⲙⲙⲁϣ. ⲉϩⲣⲉⲛ- (S ⲧⲥⲧⲟ ⲉⲃⲟⲗ) ἀποκ.

ϣⲧⲁⲙ *O* nn: Hor 84 ⲭⲓ ϣ. (*meaning*?).

ϣⲧⲟⲙ *S*, ϣⲑ. *B* nn m, *thing shutting* or *shut, gate*: Ge 43 18 B(S ϩⲁⲉⲓⲧ), Mt 26 71 B(S ⲇⲟ), Ac 12 14 B (var & S ⲣⲟ), Ap 21 15 B(S = Gk) πυλών; ViK 4727 S ⲧⲣⲓ ϩⲁⲡⲉϣ., BMOr 6203 A S *boundaries* ⲡⲉϥⲉⲙⲛⲧ ⲡⲉϣ. ⲡⲧⲉⲣⲅⲁⲥⲓⲁ, J 71 39 S *house* ϩⲓⲡⲉϣⲧⲱⲙ, AJSL 46 251 S ⲡⲉϣ. ⲙⲡⲛⲉϥϣⲟⲩϣⲧ; TurM 16 12 S ⲑⲏⲉ[ⲓⲧ] ϣ., J 39 87 S ⲧϩⲁⲉⲓⲧ ϣⲧⲁⲙ, *v* ϩⲁⲉⲓⲧ.

ϣⲧⲁⲙⲉ *S* nn, *closing*: PBaden 5 405 ⲟⲩⲭⲁⲗⲓⲛⲟⲥ ⲙⲡⲟⲩϣ. ⲉⲧⲧⲁⲡⲣⲟ.

ϣⲧⲙⲟⲩⲱⲛ *S* nn as pl, *joints* (*which shut & open*): BHom 123 ⲡⲕⲉⲥⲉⲉⲡⲉ (*l* ⲡⲕⲉⲉⲥ) ⲉⲛⲧⲁⲩⲃⲱϣ ⲡⲉϣ. ⲉⲛⲧⲁⲩⲃⲱⲗ ⲉⲃⲟⲗ (= *ib* 411 ﺤﻞ), *ib* 124 ⲁϥⲙⲉⲣ ⲧⲥⲁⲣⲝ ϩⲓⲛⲉϣ., BMar 36 (ⲟⲩ)ⲱϭⲡ ⲛⲛⲉϥϣⲧⲙⲛⲟⲩⲛ (*sic* MS) ⲙⲛⲛⲉϥⲕⲉⲗⲓⲛⲕⲉϩ.

ϣⲧⲉⲙ- *BF* *v* ⲧⲙ-.

ϣⲧⲙⲟ *B* *v* ⲧⲙ̇ⲙⲟ.

ϣⲧⲉⲙⲉϩϩ *S* nn, *meaning uncertain, a form of salt*? (ⲙⲗϩ): WS 88 ⲙⲏⲧ ⲛⲃⲏⲣ ⲡϣ.

ϣⲧⲙⲟⲩⲱⲛ *v* ϣⲱⲧⲙ *sf*.

ϣⲁⲧⲙⲉϩⲏⲗ *A* *v* ⲙⲉϩⲏⲗ.

ϣⲁⲧⲛ- *v* ϣⲱⲱⲧ *s f.*

ϣⲧⲏⲛ *SA²*(once)*F*, ϣⲧⲛ *S*, ϣⲑⲏⲛ *B* nn f, *garment, tunic*: Ex 29 8 *B*(*S* ⲣ̄ϩⲥⲱ), Lev 8 7 *SB*, Is 3 16 *S*(*B* ⲣϩⲟⲥ), Jo 19 23 *SB*(*A²* ⲣⲁⲉⲓⲧⲉ), Ac 9 39 *SBF*, AM 267 *B* χιτών; Ge 9 23 *S*(*B* do), Ps 108 18 *S*(var ⲣⲟⲉⲓⲧⲉ, *B* do), Is 33 1 *SF*(*B* do), *ib* 59 17 *S* opp ⲣϣⲱⲛ (*B* do), C 99 141 *S* = C 89 46 *B* ἱμάτιον; Ex 28 31 *B* ὑποδύτης; MG 25 14 *B* στιχάριον; Br 259 *S* ⲣⲟ., ϣ., ⲣϣⲱⲛ, ShA 2 91 *S* ⲡⲱⲣ ⲛⲛⲓϣ., ⲥⲱⲗⲡ ⲛⲛⲁⲛⲥⲱⲛⲏ (ζώνη), BM 239 5 *S* when crucified He had but ⲟⲩϣ. ⲛⲙⲁⲧⲉ ⲙⲡⲟⲩⲣⲟⲓⲧⲉ ⲙⲡⲟⲩⲅⲉ ⲉⲙ̄. ⲥⲓⲧⲉ ⲡⲥⲱϥ, Mor 18 8 *S* found ⲧⲉϣ. ⲣⲓⲭⲡⲡⲉⲣⲟⲉⲓⲧⲉ = Miss 4 103 *B* ϫⲉⲛⲛⲓⲣⲃⲟⲥ, Mani 1 *A²* ϯ ϣ. ⲁⲭⲱⲟⲩ, BM 178 *S* ⲧⲉϣ. ⲛⲙⲁⲣⲓⲁⲧⲉ ⲑⲃⲥⲱ of naked, MG 25 376 *B* ⲁⲥⲑⲁⲗⲓⲟ ⲡⲟⲩϣ. from rags, PStras 41 *S* ϣ. ⲛⲥⲟⲓⲙⲉ, ⲣⲃⲟⲥ ⲡⲥ., TT 135 *S* ⲛⲕⲟⲥⲙⲓⲕⲟⲛ opp monk's, Bodl(P) f 19 *S* ⲗⲉϩⲓⲧⲟⲛ, ϣ., ⲡⲟⲣⲕ, CMSS 70 *Sᶠ* ⲛⲕⲗⲏⲣⲓⲕⲟⲥ, ViK 76 *F* ⲛⲡⲁⲡⲁ, BMis 449 *S* priest ordained with ⲟⲩϣ. & ⲉⲡⲱⲙⲓⲥ, BMis 375 *S* ⲡⲥⲅⲡⲁⲧⲉ = Va 63 7 *B* = BSM 33 *B* ⲣϩ., BM 1103 *S* ⲙⲏⲧ ⲡⲥⲅⲡⲏ (ζυγή) ⲛϣ., Bodl(P) d 36 *S* tax on ⲧⲁⲗⲉ ϣ.; of various materials, forms &c: ⲛϣⲁ ⲁⲣ Ge 3 21 *SB* χ. δέρμ., Mor 37 141 *S* μηλωτή (*cf* Ryl 246 *S* ϣ. ⲉⲙⲁⲗⲗⲱⲧ), PS 151 *S*(Od Solom 25 8 ܠܒܘܫܐ); ⲛϥⲱ Mor 37 142 *S* τρίχινον ἔνδυμα, Va 61 13 στιχάριν τρ., Bor 239 61 *S* σακκίον, PS 11 307 *B*, Mor 31 15 *S*; ⲛⲑⲟⲟⲩⲡⲉ R 1 4 49 *S* tunica saccea, C 99 86 *S* = Va ar 172 92 ثوب خشن, MG 17 547 'ثوب من وبر; ⲡⲉⲓⲁⲁⲩ Lev 6 3 *S*(*B* ⲣϩ.) χ. λινοῦς, C 43 87 *B*; ⲡⲣⲃⲟⲟⲥ BAp 55 *S* δικρόσσιος; ⲛⲥⲁⲣⲧ Ryl 238 n *S*; ⲛⲣⲃⲧ *q v*; ⲉⲃⲟⲗ ϫⲉⲛⲛⲓⲭⲁϥⲁⲧ ⲛⲧⲉ ⲛⲓⲃⲉⲛⲓ MG 25 351 *B*(= ROC 18 54 n ܘܕܠܟܠ ܡܢܐ ܠܒܫܐ); ⲡⲗⲓⲧⲟⲛ (λιτός) Mor 38 70 *S*(*cf* Va 57 119 ⲉϥⲟⲓ ⲡⲗ. ϫⲁⲟⲩϣ. ⲡⲟⲩⲱⲧ); ⲛⲡⲗϫⲥ Mt 9 16*S*(*B* ϥⲉⲗϫⲓ ⲛⲣⲃⲟⲥ)ἱμ. παλαιόν; ⲉⲧⲧⲟⲙ ⲉⲡⲥⲱⲙⲁ σιμικίνθιον K 245 *B*; ⲉⲥϫⲓ ⲭⲉⲣⲓⲥ (χειρίς) RE 9 164 *S*; ⲉⲥϫⲓ ⲕⲟⲧ ⲣⲓⲥⲡⲁⲑⲛ, ⲉⲥ ϣⲟⲡⲧ ⲛⲁⲡⲁⲣ Ryl 244 *S*(*cf ib* ⲣϩⲟⲥ ⲉⲥϣ. ⲛⲁ.); colours: ⲉⲧⲟ ⲛⲁⲅⲉⲓ ⲁϫⲁⲡ Ex 29 5 *S*(*B* & Gk diff); ⲡⲁⲣⲉⲩ (ⲁⲗ.) ViK 76 *F*; ⲡⲟⲩⲱϩⲙ̄ PLond 4 508 *S*, ⲡⲟⲩⲏⲣⲧ *ib* 507, ⲛⲕⲟⲣⲁϫⲉⲛ Ryl 213 n (? κοράκινος, *v* JEA 14 25); ⲛⲧⲱⲕⲧⲟⲥ (κόκκος) CMSS 70 *Sᶠ*, ⲛⲕⲟϫⲟⲥ (do) ViK 76 *F*; ϣ. ⲡⲁⲭⲁⲟⲡ (?) ⲛⲁⲅⲁⲡ ⲡⲉⲗⲟⲟⲗⲉ (of Christ's raiment before Pilate, *cf* ? Is 63 2) Mor 44 40 *S*; ⲡⲟⲡⲓⲭⲉⲟⲛ, ⲛⲭⲱⲗ, ⲛⲯⲉⲙⲓⲑⲛ (ψιμύθιον), ⲛⲁⲅⲁⲡ ⲛⲭⲱⲡⲉⲣ, ⲛⲗⲉⲩⲕⲟⲛ, ⲛⲁⲅⲁⲡ ⲡⲉ ϩⲓⲱ all Ryl 244 *S*.

ϣⲁⲧⲱⲡⲉ *v* ⲱⲡⲉ.

ϣⲁⲧⲟⲟⲛⲧϥ *S* nn f, *kind of ship, freighted with grain*: Saq ostr 370 ⲧϣ. ⲙⲡⲁⲧⲉⲣⲙⲟⲩⲧⲉ (*cf* 368 ⲡ‑ ϫⲟⲓ ⲛⲡⲁⲧⲉⲣⲙ., also ⲣⲁⲗⲗⲏⲣⲉ in paral texts).

ϣⲱⲧⲡ, ϣⲁⲧⲛ‑ *A²* vb tr (refl), *hasten*: Mani 1

ⲙⲡⲱⲣ ⲁⲣ ⲁⲙⲉⲗⲏⲥ ϣⲁⲧⲡⲉ ⲡⲧⲉⲁⲡⲉ ʾⲁⲡⲉⲧⲑⲃⲓⲁⲓⲧ, ManiK 42 ϣⲱⲧⲡⲧⲏⲡⲉ ⲁⲣⲟⲩⲡ ⲁⲡⲓϯⲟⲩ ⲡ[; as nn: ManiK 7]ⲡⲉ ⲣⲓⲟⲩϣ.

ϣⲧⲟⲡ *B* in ⲛϣ., *quickly*: MG 25 194 after miraculous transport I said ⲁⲡⲓ ⲛϣ. = Gött Ar 114 27 ⲁ̄ⲥⲛ̄.

ϣⲧⲱⲣⲉ, -ⲣⲓ *v* ⲧⲱⲣⲉ *hand* p 425 *b*.

ϣⲁⲧⲣⲡⲉ *v* ϣⲱⲱⲧ *cut* p c.

ϣⲧⲟⲣⲧⲣ *S*, ϣⲧⲁⲣ. *A²*, ⲣⲧⲁⲣⲧⲣⲉ, ϣⲧ. (nn) *A*, ϣⲑⲟⲣⲧⲉⲣ*B*, ϣⲧⲁⲗⲧⲉⲗ, ϣⲧⲁⲣⲧⲉⲣ*F*, ϣⲧⲣⲧⲣ‑*S*, ϣⲑⲉⲣⲧⲉⲣ‑*B*, ϣⲧⲣⲧⲱⲣ⸗*S*, ⲣⲧⲣⲧⲱⲣ⸗*A*, ϣⲧⲉⲣⲑⲱⲣ⸗*B*, ϣⲧⲣⲧⲱⲣ† *S*, ϣⲧⲣⲧⲁⲣⲧ† *A²*, ⲣⲧⲉⲣⲧⲁⲣⲧ† *Sᵃ*, ⲣⲧ.† *A*, ϣⲧⲉⲣⲑⲱⲣ† *B* vb **I** intr, *be disturbed, troubled, in haste*: Ge 19 16*SB*, Ps 30 9*S*(*B* ⲑⲟⲣ), *ib* 89 7 *SBF*, Eccl 10 10 *F*(*S* tr), Sa 5 2 *S*(*B* ⲕⲓⲙ), Lam 2 11 *BF*, Mt 14 26 *SBF*, Jo 11 33*SAA²B* ταράσσειν, Hos 118*AB* συντ.; Deu 31 6 *SB*, Job 11 16 *SB*, Ob 9 *S*(ViK 9004).*A* (*B* ⲛⲟⲩϣⲡ), Lu 24 37 *SB* πτοεῖν; Deu 1 29 *S*(*B* ϣⲗⲁⲣ ⲛⲣⲏⲧ)πτήσσειν; *ib* 20 3 *S*(*B* do)ἐκλύειν; Ps 36 24 *SB* καταράσσειν; Job 4 5 *S*(*B* ⲓⲏⲥ) σπουδάζειν (var θορυβεῖσθαι), Is 14 4 *S*(*B* do) ἐπισπουδαστής; Ps 15 4 *S*(*B* ⲭⲱⲗⲉⲙ) ταχύνειν; Mk 13 7 *SB* θροεῖν; Ac 20 10 *SB* θορ.; 1 Kg 14 15 *S*, Dan 2 1 *B* (*S* ⲡⲱⲱⲥ)ἐξιστάναι; Mk 10 26 *S*(*B* ⲉⲣ ϣⲫⲏⲣⲓ) ἐκπλήσσειν; *ib* 9 15 *S*(*B* ⲉⲣ ⲣⲟϯ) ἐκθαμβεῖν; Ps 52 4 *B*(*S* ⲣ ⲁⲧⲙⲁⲩ) ἀχρειοῦν; Ac 2 6 *SB* συγχύνειν; C Dan 90 *B* ⲁⲓⲙ. as leaf in wind τρέμειν; Ex 15 15 *F* (*SB* nn)λαμβάνειν (sc τρόμος); Ps 77 57 *S*(*B* ⲉⲣ ⲁⲧϯ ⲙⲁϯ) ἀσυνθετεῖν; Lu 24 4 *S*(*B* = Gk) ἀπορεῖν; BHom 27 *S* ἰλιγγιᾶν; Job 21 10 *S*(*B* ⲣⲓ ϫⲛⲧ⸗ ⲉⲃⲟⲗ) σφάλλειν; Dan 7 15 *S*(*B* ⲥⲑⲉⲣⲧⲉⲣ) φρίσσειν; PS 24 *S* ⲁⲩϣ. ⲁⲩⲕⲓⲙ, ShC 42 219*S* ⲁⲧⲁⲯⲩⲭⲏ ⲛϣ., PSBA 33 116 *S* ⲡⲉϥⲥⲁ ⲡⲣⲟⲅⲛ ϣ., Mani 1 *A²* ⲙⲛⲡⲱⲣ [ϣⲧ]‑ⲁⲣⲧ ⲉⲧⲃⲉⲟⲅⲉⲁ[ⲩ, AP 21 *A²* ⲁϣⲙ. ⲉϥϫⲟⲩ ⲛⲙⲁⲥ, AM 98 *B* ⲁⲥⲙ. ϫⲉⲛⲡⲉⲥⲣⲏⲧ, Pcod 6 *S* ⲡⲕⲉⲉⲥ ⲙⲡⲣⲱⲙⲉ ϣ., C 86 281 *B* ϥⲓⲟⲗ ϣ. ⲡⲣⲱⲓⲙⲓ; qual: Ge 40 6 *SB*, Ps 29 7 *SB*, Lu 24 38 *SB* ⲧⲁⲣ.; Mt 9 23 *SB* θορ.; Ge 48 1 *B*(*S* ⲙⲟⲕⲣ) ἐνοχλεῖσθαι; Ac 3 11 *S*(*B*ⲉⲩ‑ ϫⲉⲛⲟⲩⲣⲟϯ)ἔκθαμβος; Ja 1 8*S*(*B* ⲁⲧⲥⲉⲙⲛⲓ) ἀκατάστατος; Pro 5 6 *SA*(*B* ϣⲟ̣ϥⲧ) σφαλερός; 2 Thes 3 2 *S*(*B* diff)ἄτοπος; Va 58 191 *B* ⲉⲧϣ. ϫⲉⲛⲡⲓⲭⲁⲕⲓ ἐν νυκτομαχίᾳ; PS 21 *S* were afraid & ⲡⲉϣ. ⲡⲉ, ShR 2 3 8 *S* ϣ. ⲣⲛⲡⲉϥⲙⲉⲉⲩⲉ, Miss 8 225 *S* if one die ⲉⲛϣ. ⲛⲁⲙⲁ̄ϥ hastening to bury him, ROC 20 52 *S* ϣ. ⲣⲛⲧⲉⲛⲧϭⲓⲛⲙⲟⲟϣⲉ opp ⲙⲟⲟϣⲉ ⲣⲛⲟⲩⲧⲥⲁⲛⲟ, ST 335 *Sᵃ* ⲛⲙⲁ ⲣ., ManiH 55*A²* sea ⲉⲧϣ., Tst Ab 163 *B* ⲉϥϣ. ⲉⲃⲟⲗ ϫⲉⲛⲡⲓⲛⲕⲟⲧ, C 43 67 *B* ⲉⲩϣ. ⲉⲑⲃⲏⲧⲥ, *ib* 86 *B* among sick to be healed ⲟⲩⲁⲓ ⲉϥϣ. (*cf* nn Kropp).

II tr, *disturb, cause to hasten*: Job 8 3 *SB*, Eccl 10 10 *S*(*F* intr), Gal 1 7 *SB* ⲧⲁⲣ., Ps 17 14 *SB* συντ.; Sa

18 19 S θορ.; Si 30 9 S ἐκθαμβ.; Ge 19 15 S(B ⲓⲏⲥ
ⲛⲥⲁ-), Job 22 10 S(B do) σπου.; Dan 4 16 B κατασπεύδειν; Ex 22 25 S(B do) κατεπείγειν; Job 13 11
SB στροβεῖν; Ac 9 22 SB συγχύν.; Job 31 16 S(B ✝
ⲉⲙⲕⲁϩ)ἐκτήκειν; Jud 4 15 S ἐξιστάναι; Gal 5 12 SB
ἀναστατοῦν; Lu 23 2 S(B ϥⲱϫ ⲉⲃⲟⲗ) διαστρέφειν;
Job 38 30 S(Bⲑⲃⲣⲉ- ⲧⲱⲙⲧ)πτήσ.; ib 13 21 SB καταπλήσ.; Pro 13 3 SA(B diff), Jer 21 13 S(B diff)
πτοεῖν; Ez 32 27 SB ἐκφοβεῖν; Lu 23 5 SB, AP 7
A² ἀνασείειν; PS 172 S ⲉϥⲉϣⲧⲣⲧⲣ ⲧⲡⲓⲥⲧⲓⲥ ... ⲛⲥⲉ-
ϣⲧⲣⲧⲱⲣⲥ, Aeg 252 S ⲡⲉⲧϣ. ⲛⲣⲉⲙⲙⲏⲛϣⲉ = ⲢⲞ 8
598 مفتّن (? ὀχλαγωγός), Ep 258 S ⲉⲧⲣⲉϥϣⲧⲣⲧⲱⲣⲧ
ϩⲁⲡⲣⲱⲃ, Bor 254 180 S ⲡⲉⲧⲥⲱⲕ ⲙⲙⲟⲓ ⲉⲅϣ. ⲙⲙⲟⲓ
to eternal punishment, Mor 31 241 S ⲛⲉϥϣ. ⲙⲙⲟⲟ-
ⲟⲩ ⲉⲡⲕⲁϩ of Chaldaeans, TstAb 159 B lest beast
ϣⲧⲉⲣⲑⲱⲣⲕ ⲃⲉⲛⲧⲕⲟⲓ.

With following preposition or adverb.   ⲥ ⲉ- B:
Ps 41 7 (S ϩⲛ-)ⲧⲁⲣ. πρός; DeV 2 50 ⲁϥⲑⲣⲉⲧⲉⲕⲯⲩ-
ⲭⲏ ϣ. ⲉⲣⲟⲕ;   ⲥ ⲉϫⲛ- SBF: Is 30 28 SF(B ϫⲓⲛ-
ϣ.) ⲧⲁⲣ. ἐπί, Lu 1 29 SB διατ. ἐπί; Mk 10 24 S(B
ⲉⲣ ϩⲟⲧ) θαμβ. ἐπί; ROC 17 403 B ϣ. ⲉⲭⲉⲡⲡⲁⲓⲥⲁϫⲓ
καταπλήσ. πρός; PS 20 S ⲁⲅϣ. ⲉⲭⲛⲡⲉⲅⲉⲣⲏⲩ ⲛϭⲓ
ⲙⲡⲅⲗⲏ, BMis 378 S ⲁⲧⲉϥⲯⲩⲭⲏ ϣ. ⲉϫⲱⲥ = BSM
35 B ⲉⲑⲃⲏⲧⲥ;   ⲥ ⲛⲥⲁ- S: Cant 5 4 (F ⲉⲧⲃⲉ-) θρο-
εῖσθαι ἐπί; R 1 1 82 angels ϣ. ⲛⲥⲁⲛⲉⲅⲉⲣⲏⲩ ϣⲁⲛ-
ⲧⲟⲩϯ ⲡⲁⲩ ⲙⲡⲉϥϩⲓⲧⲟⲩⲙⲁ incite (or jostle) each his
fellow;   ⲥ ⲉⲃⲟⲗ S: Worr 264 powers of darkness
ⲛⲁϣⲧⲣⲧⲱⲣⲕ ⲉⲃⲟⲗ(var EnPeterson 67 om ⲉⲃ.)hurry
thee away.

—— nn m SABF, disturbance, trouble, haste: Ps
30 20 SB, Lam 3 59 BF, AM 271 B ταραχή, Ac 19
23 SB -χος; Pro 23 29 SA, Mk 14 2 SBF θόρυβος;
Ac 23 7 B(S = Gk)στάσις, Mk 16 8 SF(B ⲧⲱⲙⲧ)
ἔκσ., 1 Cor 14 33 S(B ϥⲱⲣϫ), Cl 3 2 A ἀκαταστασία; ib 1 1 A περιπτῶσις; Aeg 212 S ἀταξία; Deu
16 3 S(B ⲓⲏⲥ), Jer 8 15 B σπουδή formido; Lu 4 36
S(B ϩⲟⲧ) θάμβος; Job 38 25 S(B om) κυδοιμός; PS
24 S ⲧⲛⲟϭ ⲡⲣⲟⲧⲉ ⲓⲧⲉ ⲡⲉⲅϣ., ShC 42 124 S ⲡⲉϣ.
ⲙⲡⲡⲱϣⲥ ⲛϩⲏⲧ, BHom 68 S ⲡⲉϣ. ⲛⲙⲡⲁⲑⲟⲥ, CO
115 S expel him ⲙⲏⲡⲟⲧⲉ ⲛⲧⲉⲟⲩϣ. ϣⲱⲡⲉ, El 76 A
ⲡⲉϥⲡⲟⲗⲉⲙⲟⲥ ⲙⲡⲛⲉϥϣ.=ib 116 S, C 86 286 B fear
& ⲟⲩϣ. (var ⲥⲟⲉⲣ.), ib 103 B fell sick ϩⲓⲧⲉⲛⲡⲓϣ.
ⲃⲉⲛⲡⲓⲡⲟⲗⲉⲙⲟⲥ, KroppC 25 F maladies ⲁⲣⲁϣ, ϩⲏ-
ⲙⲁⲙ, ϣ. (cf above qual);   ϩⲛ-, ⲃⲉⲛⲟⲩϣ. SB adverbial: Is 52 12 SB μετὰ ταραχῆς; Ez 7 11 SB μ.
θορύβου; Pcod 5 S fetch him away ϩ., Mor 31 70 S
ⲉϥϯ ⲟⲅⲟⲓ ϩ., ImpRussAr S 18 029 A thy wrath upon
him ϩⲓⲟⲩϣ.

ⲁⲧϣ. SB, unperturbed: Jer 26 28 B ἀπτόητος;
Miss 8 136 S faith ⲟⲩⲁ. ⲁⲅⲱ ⲟⲩⲁⲧⲣⲓⲕⲉ ἄρραγής; P
129²⁰ 133 S of one substance with us ⲛⲁⲧⲧⲁⲕⲟ ...
ⲡⲁ.;   ⲙⲛⲧ-, ⲙⲉⲧⲁ. SB, tranquillity: Miss 8 75 S τὸ
ἀτάραχον; C 89 209 B ⲟⲩⲛⲓϣϯ ⲡⲱⲣϫ ⲛⲉⲙⲟⲩⲙ.,

Bor 240 53 S ⲧⲙ. ⲁⲅⲱ ⲧϫⲁⲙⲏ;   ⲟ ⲛⲁ. S: CA 88
church ⲟ ⲛⲁ.

ⲉⲓⲣⲉ, ⲓⲣⲓ, ⲣ ϣ. SAB, make disturbance: Pro 6 14
SA(B ⲑⲁⲙⲓⲉ ϣ.) ταραχὰς συνιστάναι; ib 26 28 SA
ἀκαταστασίας ποιεῖν, Ac 21 38 B(S diff) ἀναστατοῦν.

✝ ϣ. S, as last: Is 27 12 (B diff) συνταράσσειν.

ⲣⲉϥϣ. SB, disturber: Ps 90 3 B(S diff) ταραχώδης; Mor 41 332 S women by nature ⲣⲉⲛⲡ.

ϫⲓⲛϣ. B, disturbance: Is 30 28(SF vb)ταράσσειν.

ϣⲧ(ⲉ)ⲣⲧⲓⲣ S, ϩⲧⲣ. A, hasty, rash person: Pro 10
14 SA(B ⲉⲧⲁⲥⲓⲱⲟⲩ) προπετής; Z 570 S be not
friends with ⲟⲩϣ.

ϣⲟⲧⲣⲉϥ, ϣⲟⲃ., ϣⲟⲣⲧϥ B nn m, falcon: K 167
ⲡⲓϣ., Bodl 325 155 ϣⲟⲃ. باز, بازى (var Ryl 453 رخمة,
ايهة); Va 63 96 ⲡⲓϣⲟⲣ. became dove ἱέραξ.

ϣⲁ(ⲁ)ⲧⲉ   v ϣⲱⲱⲧ s f.

ϣⲏⲏⲧⲥ¹, ϣⲉⲏⲧⲥ², ϣⲏⲥ³ S, ϣⲓⲧⲉ B nn m, plant
agnus castus: Lev 23 40¹ S ϩⲁⲣⲙⲟⲥ ⲉⲧⲉⲟⲩϣ. ⲧⲉ (var
P 44 106², 43 92³ صندل quid?)B(Ar om), Job 40 17
ⲡⲓϣ.¹ (B diff) ἄγνος.   Cf ? št,š (Keimer).

ϣⲓⲧⲥ, ϭⲓ.(oftener)B, ϫⲓⲧ A nn as pl, land tortoise
(cf štw, štj Dévaud): Hos 12 11 AB χελώνη.

ϣⲧⲏⲓⲧ O, meaning unknown: AZ 21 98 to be
written as amulet ϣ. ϫⲓⲉⲛ ⲧⲉⲡϩⲁ (so divided in
MS).

ϣϯⲧ S nn m, weaver: P 44 67 ⲅⲡⲁⲡⲧⲏⲥ (ὑφ.)·
ⲡⲉϣ. نسّاج, ib 93 حيّاك;   warp on loom: Lev 13 48
(B ⲟⲩⲁⲧϩⲓ) στήμων سدس; ShEp 56 = ViK 9067 275
ⲡⲃⲛⲕⲉ ⲙⲙⲡⲉϣϯⲧ [ⲛ]ⲧⲣⲟⲓⲧⲉ.   V ⲥⲱϩⲉ, weave
(Sethe Verbum 1 59, AZ 54 132), also ϣⲓⲧ.

ϣⲓⲧⲁϯ, ϣⲟ. B nn m, edge, border of garment:
Ex 28 22 κροσσός, Ps 44 14 (S ⲗⲟⲟⲩ) -ωτός; Nu 15
38 (S ⲧⲱⲧⲉ ⲛⲧⲟⲡ, var ⲕⲁⲡ), Mt 9 20 (S ⲧⲟⲡ = Lu 8
44 ⲧⲱ.), ib 14 36 (S ⲧⲟⲡ, F ⲗⲁⲅ), ib 23 5 (S ⲧⲱ.)κρά-
σπεδον; Ez 5 3 (S ⲧⲟⲡ) ἄκρον; ROC 23 276 Virgin
ⲥⲉⲗⲥⲱⲗ ⲃⲉⲛϩⲁⲛϣ. ⲛⲓⲉⲃ ⲛⲡⲟⲩⲃ, O'Leary H 26 ⲟⲩ-
ⲓⲉⲃ...ⲉϥⲧⲟⲧⲉ ⲉⲡϣ. ⲡⲧⲉⲥⲡⲟⲣⲫⲩⲣⲁ.

ϣⲧⲟⲩⲏⲧ SA², ϣⲟⲟⲅⲓⲧ B nn, accusation, always
with preceding ✝, accuse: Lu 16 1 S ⲧⲁⲁϥ ⲡϣ.(B =
Gk) διαβάλλειν dat; MG 25 7 B ✝ ϣ. κατηγορεῖν;
Mani 1 A² ⲁϥⲧⲉⲉϥ(sc Jesus) ⲁⲧⲟⲟⲧⲟⲩ ⲡϣ.;   ⲥ ⲉ-,
against: Ps 37 20 S(B ϩⲁ-) ἐνδιαβ.; Ac 19 40 S(B
ⲉⲣ ⲕⲁⲧⲏⲅⲟⲣⲓⲛ)ἐγκαλεῖν; Lu 19 8 S(B ϭⲓ ⲡⲭⲟⲛⲥ)
συκοφαντίζειν; C 99 117 S ⲁⲩϯ ϣ. ⲉⲣⲟϥ saying...,
Mor 56 11 S ⲁⲩϯ ϣ. ⲉⲣⲟⲟⲩ ⲡⲛⲁϩⲣⲓⲛⲡⲣⲣⲟ, C 41 64
B ⲁⲩϯ ϣ. ⲉⲣⲟϥ ⲃⲁⲧⲟⲧⲕ;   ⲥ ⲛ-, sim: BMis 290 S
ⲁⲩⲧⲉ ϣ. ⲙⲡⲙⲁⲕⲁⲣⲓⲟⲥ saying..., LMär 20 S sim;   ⲥ
ϩⲁ-, ϩⲁ- sim: Dan 6 24 B διαβ. acc, Nu 22 22 B(S
diff), Ps 108 4 B(S ⲁⲓⲁⲃ.) ἐνδ.; BIF 13 99 S ⲡⲉⲩϯ-
ϯ ϣ. ϩⲁⲣⲟⲟⲩ saying... = MG 25 279 B, C 43 110

B ⲁⲩϯ ϣ. ϩⲁⲣⲟϥ ϩⲁⲧⲉⲡⲁⲣⲓⲁⲡⲟⲥ; ⲙⲉⲧϣ. (*l* ⲙⲉⲧϯ ϣ.) *B, accusation*: Pro 6 24 (*SA* = Gk) διαβολή; ⲣⲉϥϯ ϣ. *S, accuser*: 1 Tim 3 11 *S*(*B*=Gk) διάβολος; BHom 53-4 *S* serpent ⲡⲣ. συκοφάντης; Mani 1 *A*² Judas ⲟⲩⲣⲉϥϯⲡⲟⲩⲧⲉ ⲡϣ.; ⲙⲉⲧⲣⲉϥϯ ϣ. *B, accusation*: HL 84 ⲟⲩⲙ. ⲡⲧⲉ ⲡⲓⲥⲏⲏⲟⲩ, Cat 196 opposition, plottings, **ⲙ.**

ϣⲟⲧϣⲧ¹, ϣⲟⲧⲧ² *S*, ϣⲟⲧϣⲉⲧ *B*, ϣⲉⲧϣⲱⲧⲋ *SB*, -ϣⲱⲋ *F*, ϣⲉⲧϣⲱⲧ† *SB* vb tr, *cut, carve, hollow* (*cf* ϣⲱⲱⲧ): Si 38 30 *S*² (var P 44 119¹), Is 44 10 *S*²(*B* ⲫⲱⲧϩ) γλύφειν; Zeph 1 11 *B* (var ϭⲟⲧϭⲉⲧ, *A* ⲧⲉⲕⲟ) κατακόπτειν; R 1 4 36 *S* cells in rock ⲉⲁⲩϣⲉⲧϣⲱⲧⲟⲩ *excidere*; P 54 174 *B* ⲁⲩϣⲉⲧϣⲱⲧⲉ نقش, جت; ShA 2 112 *S* ⲟⲩⲙⲁ ⲉⲁⲩϣⲉⲧϣⲱⲧϥ, BSG 182 *S* ⲟⲩⲱⲡⲉ...ϣⲧϣⲱⲧϥ = *ib* 13 *B* ⲫⲟⲛⲕ; qual: Ez 41 18 *S* (*B* ϣⲉⲕϣⲱⲕ) γλ.; Ac 17 29 *S*(*B* ⲫⲱ.) χάραγμα; Cant 7 2 *S*(*F* ϣⲏⲕ) τορευτός; R 2 1 71 *S* navel ⲉⲥϣ., *ib* 1 3 52 *S* rock ⲉⲥϣ., MIE 2 402 *B* tomb like ⲟⲩⲱⲡⲓ ⲉϥϣ.(*cf* PO 22 420 تنحت); intr: Mk 2 4 *S*²(*B* ϣⲱⲕⲓ) ἐξορύσσειν.

With following preposition. ⲥ ⲉ- *S*: Mt 6 19² (var ⲥⲱⲧϩ, *B* ϩⲓ ϣⲁⲧⲥ) διορ.; Ming 316 ⲉⲣϣⲁⲡⲟⲩ ϣ.² ⲉⲩⲭⲟ; ⲥ ⲛ-, *with*: BMis 274 *S* couch ϣⲉⲧϣⲱⲧϥ ⲡⲛⲓⲉⲗⲉⲫⲁⲛⲧⲓⲡⲟⲛ = Mor 30 53 *F* ϣⲉⲧϣⲱϣⲟⲩ, BMis 275 *S* ϣⲉⲧϣⲱⲧⲟⲩ ⲙⲡⲉⲧⲁⲗⲟⲡ; ⲥ ϩⲛ- *S, in*: Sa 18 24 γλυφή, Job 19 24 (*B* ⲫ.) ἐγγλύφειν ἐν; Ez 12 7² (*B* ϣⲱⲕ) διορ. acc; Mk 15 46 (*B* do) λατομεῖν; Ex 32 16†(*B* ⲫ.) κολάπτειν ἐν; 2 Cor 3 7† (*B* do) ἐντυποῦν dat; Is 22 16¹(*B* do)γράφειν dat; Tri 657 ⲙⲡⲉϥϣ.² ϩⲛ̄ⲧⲭⲉⲡⲉⲡⲱⲣ نقب; KKS 634 temple ϣ.† ϩⲓⲧⲡⲉⲧⲣⲁ.

——, -ⲧ *S*, ϣⲟϣⲧ *SB*, nn, *thing carved*: Si 45 18 *S* ϣⲟϣⲧ γλύμμα; Ez 40 16 *S*-ⲧ *B*(but var & *ib* 22 &c ϣⲟⲩϣⲧ) φοίνιξ; Ge 6 14 *S* ⲧⲁⲙⲓⲟ ⲛⲧⲕⲩⲃⲱⲧⲟⲥ ⲛⲧⲭⲟⲧⲭⲉⲧ (P 44 102 طبق, var ⲟⲩⲓⲧⲟⲩ, *B* ⲙⲟϩ) νοσσιά same?

ϣⲧⲟϥ, ϣⲧⲟⲃ *v* ϣⲱⲧⲃ.

ϣⲧⲉϩ *v* ϣⲑⲉϩ.

ϣⲁⲩ *SB*, ϣⲁⲟⲩ *S* DM, ϣⲟⲟⲩ *Sᶠ* (JKP 2 26), ϣⲉⲩ *AA*²*F*, ϣⲟⲩ- *SABF* nn m, *use, value*: Si 18 6 *S* χρῆσις, *ib* 10 4 *S* χρήσιμος, Pro 29 31 *SA* εὔχρηστος, Hos 8 8 *B* ⲙⲙⲟⲛⲧ(ϥ) ϣ. (*A* ⲁⲧϣ.) ἄχρ., Jer 31 38 *B* χρεία; 1 Chr 28 2 *B* ἐπιτήδεια; Nu 20 5 *S* ⲟⲩⲡⲉ ⲡϣ. ? (var & *B* ⲉⲧⲃⲉⲟⲩ) ἵνα τί; BMis 549 *S* ⲟⲩⲡⲉ ⲡⲉϣ. ϫⲉⲁⲩϫⲡⲟⲛ ?*opus*; ShR 2 3 90 *S* ⲟⲩϭⲉⲡⲉ ⲡϣ. ⲙⲡⲣⲱⲙⲉ if God reject him ?, ShA 2 346 *S* if we know God ⲟⲩⲡⲉ ⲡⲉⲡϣ. ⲉⲡϯ ϭⲱⲡⲧ ⲡⲁϥ ?, Va 61 200 *B* will cut firewood ⲙⲡϣ. ⲛϯⲣⲁⲕϩⲓ (or ? *v* next word); as adj **a** *useful, fitting*; CO 434 *S* χⲣⲏⲥⲓⲙⲟⲥⲧⲉ ⲡⲣⲱⲙⲉ ⲡϣⲁ[ⲩ, Va 61 100 *B* ⲁⲫϯ ⲭⲁϥ (*sc* this beast) ⲡϣ. ϩⲓϫⲉⲡⲕⲁϩⲓ, DM 8

13 ⲣⲁ ⲙϣ. magical name (*cf* AZ 46 127). **b** *virtuous S*: BMar 158 if ⲡⲟⲣⲛⲟⲥ see them at prayer he will become ϣ. σώφρων; ShP 131⁶ 56 ⲣⲱⲙⲉ ⲛⲡⲟⲉⲓⲕ...ⲥϩⲓⲙⲉ ⲡϣ., ShC 73 185 ⲯⲩⲭⲏ ⲙⲡⲁⲣⲑⲉⲛⲟⲥ ⲁⲩⲱ ⲡϣ. صالح, Tri 322 sheep spotless & ⲡϣ. ʿⲱ, Mus 42 234 ϩⲓⲱⲙⲉ ⲡϣ. opp ⲉⲧϩⲟⲟⲩ.

ⲁⲧϣ. *SAA*²*BF*, *useless, worthless, obscene* as nn: Sa 2 11 *S*, Si 37 25 *S* ἄχρηστος, C 89 20 *B* despised demons ϩⲱⲥ ⲁ. ἀχρεῖος; He 6 8 *B*(*SF* ⲧⲥⲧⲏⲩ ⲉⲃⲟⲗ) ἀδόκιμος; ShMIF 23 172 *S* adulteress ⲟⲩⲁ., Balestri xl *S* sim ⲛⲁ., Mani 1 *A*² sim ⲧⲁ., Ep 128 *S* ⲁⲡⲟⲕ ⲁ-ⲡⲁⲡⲓⲁⲥ ⲡⲉⲓⲁ.; as adj following: Sa 16 29 *S*, Hos 8 8 *A* ut sup ἄχρη., Lu 17 10 *SB* ἀχρεῖος; CaiEuch 392 *B* ϩⲃⲏⲟⲩⲓ ⲡⲁ.ἀπρεπής; RNC 42 *S* gnostics ⲛⲁ. ἀκάθαρτος; ShCl Pr 39 43 *S* ⲗⲁⲟⲥ ⲡⲁ. that made golden calf, ShP 130⁵ 100 *S* ϣⲱⲡⲉ ⲡⲁ. ⲛⲡⲁⲣϩⲙⲡⲉ ...ⲡϣⲁⲩ ⲙⲡⲇⲓⲁⲃⲟⲗⲟⲥ, Sh(?)Mor 54 129 *S* through lust man & woman ϣⲱⲡⲉ ⲡⲁ. before marriage, AM 99 *B* words lewd & ⲡⲁ., Va 61 118 *B* ⲙⲁ ⲡⲥⲱ ⲡⲁ. = Mor 25 23 *S* ⲙⲁ ⲡⲥⲱ only, Mor 30 39 *F* man of blood & ⲡⲁ.; preceding *B*: Mt 25 30(*S* follows)ἀχρεῖος; C 43 106 ⲡⲓⲁ. ⲙⲙⲁⲧⲟⲓ.

ⲣ ϣ., ⲟ ⲡϣ. *SAA*²*BF*, *be useful, prosperous, virtuous*: Sa 4 3 *S* χρησιμεύειν; Jer 51 17 *B*(*S* ⲥⲙⲡⲉ)χρηστὸς γίνεσθαι; Lu 12 16 *B*(*S* ⲟⲩⲱⲱⲗⲉ) εὐφορεῖν; Ac 15 29 *S*(*B* ⲉⲣ ⲣⲱⲃ ⲛⲕⲁⲗⲱⲥ) εὖ πράσσειν; Job 11 2 *A*(Cl, *S* om, *B* diff) εὔλαλος; C 99 147 *S* ⲁⲡⲣⲱⲃ ⲣ. = *ib* 89 61 *B* καλῶς ἔχειν; Z 317 *S* ϯⲣ. = MG 25 232 *B* κα. εἶναι, Klio 13 31 *S* ⲉϥⲉⲣ. ⲁⲕⲉⲓ ⲕⲁ. ἦλθας; Nu 22 32 *S*(*B* ⲥⲟⲟⲩⲧⲡ) ἀστεῖος; P 44 47 *S* ⲡⲉⲧⲣ. ⲁⲧⲁⲑⲟⲥ صالح; PS 269 *S* ⲉϥϣⲁⲡⲧⲓⲣ. ϩⲙⲡϣⲟⲣⲡ ⲙ-ⲙⲩⲥⲧⲏⲣⲓⲟⲛ, ShA 1 247 *S* wine if kept ϣⲁϥⲣ. ⲡϩⲟⲩⲟ, Ora 4 20 *S* ⲉⲓⲧⲣⲉⲥⲟⲟⲩϭⲉ ⲛⲓⲙ ⲣ. ϣⲁⲧⲛⲥⲟ-ⲟⲩϭⲉ ⲛⲁϥⲣⲏⲛ, Sh Berl Or 1611 5 35 *S* apprentices not to sell their wares ϣⲁⲛⲧⲟⲩⲣ. ⲉⲙⲁⲧⲉ *until well finished, ready for use*, ShWess 9 105 *S* ⲡⲉⲩⲣ. ⲁⲩⲱ ⲙⲡⲁⲣⲑⲉⲛⲟⲥ, Bor 251 299 *S* Mary ⲧⲁⲡⲓⲥⲙⲟⲧ ⲉⲧⲣ., Mor 22 137 *S* God grant me to meet Him ϩⲛⲟⲩϩⲟ-ⲡⲟⲩ ⲉⲥⲣ. = BSM 127 *B* ⲉⲡⲁⲛⲉⲥ, BMis 504 *S* sim, P 129¹⁶ 105 *S* Julian dying ⲁⲕⲣⲟ ⲡⲉⲭ̅ⲥ̅...ⲁⲕⲣ. ⲡ-ⲡⲁϫⲱⲣⲁⲓⲟⲥ (*cf* BMis 247 ⲁⲕϭⲓ ⲡⲙⲁ ⲧⲏⲣϥ = PO 1 420), PMéd 230 *S* pound them ϣⲁⲛⲧⲟⲩⲣ., TU 43 20 *A* ⲟⲩϩⲏⲧ ⲉϥⲣ., Mani H 23 *A*² asking pardon ⲛⲥⲉⲣ. ⲡⲕⲉⲥⲁⲡ, MG 25 339 *B* after rain palms ⲛⲁⲉⲣ. (ROC 17 367 محصد), C 41 53 *B* ⲁϥⲉⲣ. ϩⲉⲛⲡⲉϥϣⲱⲡⲓ; ⲟ ⲡϣ.: Ep Jer 58 *F*(*B* ⲉⲣ ⲭⲣⲓⲁ) χρήσιμος; Mor 18 143 *S* women ⲉⲧⲟ ⲡϣ. σεμνός. ⲥ ⲉ-, *for*: Jer 13 7 *B* χρᾶσθαι εἰς, 2 Tim 4 11 *SB* εὔχρη. εἰς; Lu 14 35 *SB*(?) εὔθετος εἰς; Mt 5 13 *S*(*B* ϣϫⲉⲙϫⲟⲙ)ἰσχύειν εἰς; BMis 33 *S* ϭⲉⲣ. ⲉⲡⲡⲟⲗⲉⲙⲟⲥ, BMOr 6201 A 170 *S* thank God ϯⲣ. ⲉⲩⲕⲟⲩⲓ *am a little better, cf* WS 98 *S* sim ⲛⲟⲩⲕⲟⲩⲓ, PMéd 307 *S* ϣⲁϥⲣ. ⲉⲡⲗⲩⲧⲓ ⲛⲓⲙ, DeV 2 38 *B* water ⲉϥⲉⲣ. ⲉⲡⲥⲟϥ; vbal: P 129¹⁸

89 *S* mouth ⲣ. ⲁⲛ ⲉⲟⲩⲱⲛϩ ⲛⲁⲕ ⲉⲃⲟⲗ ἐξαρκεῖν; 1
Kg 16 1 *B* ⲉϥⲉⲣ. ⲡⲏⲓ ⲉⲉⲣ ⲟⲩⲣⲟ (*S* ϥⲛⲁⲣ ⲣⲣⲟ) Gk
om, PS 306 *S* ⲙⲉⲅⲣ....ⲉⲕⲟⲧⲟⲩ, ShC 73 88 *S* ⲛⲉⲧⲣ.
ⲁⲛ ⲉⲟⲩⲟⲙⲟⲩ (var ⲛ-), OrChrNS 3 42 *B* ⲡⲓϧⲱⲃ ⲉⲣ.
ⲁⲛ ⲉⲉⲑⲣⲉⲙⲡⲉⲧⲓ ⲉⲣⲟϥ (PO 14 85 ܠܡܐ ܕ), Miss 4
117 *B* ⲛⲑⲟⲕ ⲉⲣ. ⲁⲛ ⲉⲁⲓⲕ ⲛ̄ⲥⲡⲟⲡⲏⲛ = Mor 18 24
S;   ⲥ ⲉϫⲛ-: BMis 260 *S* if thou hast any kindness ⲁⲣⲓ ϣ. ⲉϫⲙⲡⲉⲕϣⲃⲏⲣ (varr wrong ? Mor 29 30
ⲁⲓⲣ ϣ. ⲉⲓⲣⲓϫⲙ-, *ib* 30 35 *F* ⲁⲓⲉⲗ ϣ. ϩⲓϫⲙ-);   ⲥ
ⲙⲛ-, ⲛⲉⲙ-, *with*: Tob 3 9 *S* ὀνινάναι; MG 25 143
B ⲁⲓⲉⲣ. ⲛⲉⲙⲁⲕ;   ⲥ ⲛ- dat: Ps 32 1 *B*(*S* = Gk)
πρέπειν dat; Pro 17 7 *SA* ἁρμόζειν dat; Si 13 5 *S*
χρησιμεύειν; R 1 1 38 *S* καλῶς πράσσειν κατά; Nu
22 34 *S*(*B* ⲣ ⲁⲛⲁⲋ) ἀρέσκειν dat; Bor 170 90 *S* ⲛⲁ
ⲉϥⲉⲣ. ⲡⲭⲟϥ ἐπιτήδειος; ShA 2 252 *S* holes for snake
ⲉⲅⲣ. ⲛⲁϥ, CA 92 *S* ⲧⲁⲥⲕⲛⲥⲓⲥ ⲣ. ⲛⲁϥ ⲡⲁⲣⲁ ⲟⲩϭⲟⲡ-
ⲗⲟⲛ, ViK 9182 *S* ϣⲧⲏⲛ...ⲉⲥⲣ. ⲛⲧⲁⲁⲥ ϩⲓⲱⲱϥ, PSBA
32 251 *S* ⲡⲉⲕⲥⲙⲟⲧ ⲉⲩⲣ. ⲡⲁⲓ ⲉⲙⲁⲧⲉ *pleaseth me*,
Baouit 1 114 *S* may God ⲛ ⲧⲉⲡⲣⲁⲛ ⲉⲃⲟⲗ ⲉⲥⲣ. ⲙ-
ⲡ̄ⲭ̄ⲥ̄ (oftener ⲉⲥⲣ ⲁⲛⲁϥ), CMSS 45 *F* ⲡⲕⲁⲙⲁⲥⲓ
(-ⲓⲥⲓⲟⲛ) ϣⲁϥⲉⲗ ϣ. ⲛⲏⲕ;   vbal: PS 307 *S* ⲙⲉⲅⲣ. ⲛ.
ⲕⲟⲧⲟⲩ, PBu 83 *S* ⲙⲁⲡⲉⲓϣⲃⲱ ⲡⲁⲓ ⲣ. ⲛⲏⲧⲟⲩ before
your honour, ROC 25 246 *B* ⲟⲩ ⲡⲉⲧⲉⲣ. ⲡⲁⲓϥ;   as
nn m *S*: PS 210 ⲧⲕⲓⲛⲏⲥⲓⲥ ⲙ̄ⲡⲥⲱⲙⲁ paral ⲡⲉⲧⲣ ϣ.

ⲣ ⲁⲧϣ. *SBF*, *be, make useless, vain*: Ps 13 3 *SB*,
Jer 11 16 *S*(ShA 1 291)*B*, Ro 3 12 *SB* ἀχρειοῦν, Ep
Jer 15 *BF* ἄχρηστος γίν., Va 58 184 *B* drunkenness
ⲑⲣⲉⲡⲁⲓⲛ ⲡⲉⲣⲟⲟⲩ...ⲉⲣ. ἀχρ. ἀποδεικνύαι, Is 3 10 *B*
(*S* ⲙⲟⲕϩ ⲛ̄ⲣ ⲭ̄ⲣ.) δυσχρ., Ez 15 4 *B* μὴ χρήσιμος
εἴ.; ShViK 9100 230 *S* ⲁⲁϥ ⲡⲁ. ⲉⲧⲙⲟⲩⲱⲛϩ ⲉⲃⲟⲗ
in Christ's presence, ShMIF 23 149 *S* despised him
& ⲁⲅⲁⲁϥ ⲡⲁ., P 131³ 81 *S* squandering wealth with
those ⲉⲅⲟ ⲡⲁ. = Va 61 91 *B* ⲣⲱⲙⲓ ⲡⲁ., DeV 2 115
B God's image ⲁⲓⲁⲓⲥ ⲡⲁ., *ib* 24 *B* one drug ⲉⲣ. ϩⲓ-
ⲧⲉⲡⲧⲉⲡⲉⲣⲅⲓⲁ ⲡⲕⲉϥⲁϩⲣⲓ, Bor 145 52 *S* robe burnt
& ⲁϥⲣ ⲁ. ⲉⲡⲧⲏⲣϥ, Mor 24 22 *F* ⲁⲅⲉⲗ ⲁⲧϣⲉϥ.

ⲙⲛⲧ-, ⲙⲉⲧϣ. *SB*, *usefulness, propriety, modesty*:
C 100 301 *S* ⲧⲉϥⲙ. ⲉⲧϣⲟⲟⲡ ϣⲁⲣⲱⲧⲛ = *ib* 89 215
B χρήσιμος; Z 329 *S*, BMar 168 *S*, R 1 4 57 *S* σωφροσύνη, Aeg 278 *S* ϩⲛⲟⲩⲙ. σωφρόνως; TEuch 1 6
B ܠܚܝ̈; ShC 73 207 *S* ⲙ̄ⲛⲧⲡⲁⲣⲑⲉⲛⲟⲥ, ⲙ., *ib* 42 68
ⲙ. ⲙ̄ⲡⲛⲁⲩⲥ, ShMich 550 20 *S* ⲙ. ⲙⲡⲉⲅⲙⲁ ⲡ̄-
ⲛⲓⲕⲟⲧⲕ, Miss 4 640 *S* ⲥⲩⲗⲁ ⲡⲧⲙ. ⲡⲧⲉⲥϩⲓⲙⲉ;   ⲙⲛⲧ-
ⲙⲉⲧⲁⲧϣ., *worthlessness*: Tob 4 13 *S* ἀχρειότης;
ShC 42 75 *S* impure children ⲡⲉϩⲙ., R 1 2 39 *S*
whoso painteth eyes ⲧⲁϣⲉⲟⲉⲓϣ ⲡⲧⲉⲥⲗ., BSM 95 *B*
when we are drunken ⲟⲩⲙ. ϣⲱⲡⲓ ⲛ̄ϩⲏⲧⲉⲛ = Mor
22 101 *S* ⲙ̄ⲛⲧϣⲛⲁ;   ⲣ ⲙ̄ⲛⲧⲁⲧϣⲉⲩ *A*, *be worthless*:
2 Macc 6 4 ῥᾳθυμεῖν.

—— vb intr, *be useful, valuable*: Is 41 7 *B* ⲡⲁⲡⲁⲓ
ϣ. (*S* ⲡⲁⲡⲟⲩϋ) καλός εἶναι; BKU 1 26 (8116 b) *F*
recipe ϭⲁⲡ ⲧⲉϣⲉⲩ (for ⲡⲉⲧϣⲉⲩ) ϩⲓⲛⲉⲕⲉⲉⲥ.

ϣⲟⲩ-*SABF*, *worthy of, fit for* with following vb:
-ⲉⲓ (?) Nu 6 3 *S*(*B* ϩⲛ ⲡⲗⲱⲕ) πρόσφατος; -ⲙⲉⲣⲓⲧ Ps
83 1 *B* ἀγαπητός, Cl 1 1 *A* ἀξιαγ., Est D 5 *S* προσφι-
λής; -ⲙⲟⲥⲧⲉ *q v*; -ⲡⲁ Bor 253 124 *S* ἐλάχιστος, Va
66 294 *B* ἐλεεινός; -ⲉⲣ ⲉⲡⲓⲟⲩⲙⲓⲛ Is 32 14 *F* ἐπιθυμητός; -ⲣ ϣⲡⲏⲣⲉ Miss 8 140 *S* θαυμαστός; -ⲥⲱⲃⲉ
Sa 15 12 *S* παίγνιος; -ⲧⲁⲁϥ ⲁⲛ ⲉⲥⲉⲗⲁⲁⲩ *ib* 14 21 *S*
ἀκοινώνητος; -ⲧⲁⲉⲓⲉ ⲡⲡⲉ GFr 358 *S* θεοτίμητος;
-ⲟⲩⲉⲙ ⲡⲉϥⲕⲁⲣⲡⲟⲥ Deu 20 20 *S* καρπόβρωτος;
-ⲟⲩⲱϣⲧ Z 277 *S* προσκυνητός; -ϭⲓ ϣϣⲟⲟⲩ Va 57
6 *B* ποθεινότερος; -ⲡⲟⲩⲱ 2 Kg 18 20 *S* εὐαγγελίας;
ShA 1 269 *S* men ⲡϣ. ⲉⲣⲟⲩϩⲟⲣ, *ib* 259 *S* ⲛϣ. ⲣⲓⲙⲉ ⲡⲁⲩ, ShA 1 440 *S* ⲡⲉⲓϣ. ⲧⲓⲧⲁⲅⲉ ⲡⲉϥⲣⲁⲛ, Aeg
45 *B* sim, ShA 2 68 *S* ⲡϣ. ⲡⲱϩ ⲙ̄ⲡⲉⲥϩⲓⲙⲁ ⲉⲧⲣⲓ-
ⲱⲱϥ, Bor 260 107 *S* ϣⲁϫⲉ ⲡϣ. ϩⲉⲧⲣⲟⲧϥ, *ib* 262 120
S ⲉⲧⲟ ⲡϣ. ϣⲓⲡⲉ ϩⲓⲧⲟⲩ, ViK 9552 *S* ⲡϣ. ⲧⲣⲉϥⲙⲟⲩ,
C 43 29 *B* ⲁⲧⲱⲡ ⲡϣ. ϭⲣⲟ ⲛ̄ϧⲏⲧϥ, *ib* 41 8 *B* ⲟⲩϣ.
ⲥⲁϫⲓ ⲛⲛⲉϥϩⲃⲏⲟⲩⲓ, Mor 25 194 *S* marvel ⲡⲟⲩϣ.
ⲥⲁⲁⲧⲉ ⲁⲡⲉ, DeV 2 108 *B* ⲗⲁⲥ ⲡϣ. ⲥⲟⲗⲡϥ, BM 601
F ϣ. ⲙⲉⲗⲓⲧⲁ, Miss 4 762 *S.f* ⲛⲧⲁⲕ ⲟⲩϣ. ⲙⲟⲧⲉ ⲉ-
ⲣⲟⲕ ϫⲉ-, J 65 34 *S* fathers ⲡϣ. ⲣ ⲡⲉⲩⲙⲉⲉⲩⲉ ⲁⲓ-
way;   with prep -ⲉⲣⲟ⸗ Si 30 37 *S* ϩⲱⲃ ⲡϣⲟⲩⲣⲟϥ
πρέπειν dat.

V ϣⲟⲟⲩ (2°).

ϣⲁⲩ *SB*, ϣⲉⲩ *A²* nn m, *measure, extent* (same ?
as last): ShC 73 51 *S* time of rising ⲡⲁⲕⲟⲟⲩ ⲏ ⲡϣ.
ⲛⲡϣⲟⲙⲧⲉ ⲡⲟⲩⲛⲟⲩ, ShRE 11 161 *S* God's benefits ⲛⲁ-
ⲡⲁⲛⲣ ⲉⲧⲣ ⲡⲟϥⲣⲉ ⲡⲁⲡϣ. ⲉⲧⲁⲩϩⲁⲡⲉ ⲡⲁⲅⲁⲑⲟⲛ ⲛⲓⲙ,
Miss 4 749 *S* ⲡϣ. ⲛ̄ⲭⲛⲁϥ ⲡⲟⲉⲓⲕ.   With preceding
preposition.   ⲥ ⲉ- *S*: Ex 22 17(*B* ⲕⲁⲧⲁ)καθ' ὅσον;
ShC 73 145 ⲧⲁⲙⲓⲟⲟⲩ (sc loaves) ⲉⲡϣ. ⲛⲁϥⲟⲩ ⲛ̄ⲃⲣ
(var ⲙ̄ⲡϣ. ⲛ-);   ⲥ ⲛ-: Mk 6 37 *S* ⲙ̄ⲡϣ. ⲡⲟⲩⲕⲟⲩⲓ
(*B* om)βραχύ (cf Jo 6 37); ROC 23 280 *B* dug ⲙ̄ⲡϣ.
ⲙⲙⲁϩⲓ ⲙ̄ ⲉⲡⲉⲥⲏⲧ, Rec 6 173 *B* provisions ⲙ̄ⲡϣ.
ⲛ̄ϯ ⲛ̄ϩⲟⲟⲩ, ManiK 71 *A²* ⲙ̄ⲡϣ. ⲙ̄ⲡⲕⲁⲓⲣⲟⲥ, Tor
29 *S* ⲙ̄ⲡϣ. ⲛ̄ⲥⲡⲁⲩ ⲡⲁ̄ⲥⲛⲏ, RAl 100 *S* went forth
ⲙ̄ⲡϣ. ⲡⲟⲩⲙⲩⲅⲗⲓⲟⲛ;   ⲥ ⲛⲁ- (*v* ⲁ- advb): Lu 17
6 *S*(*B* ⲙ̄ⲫⲣⲏϯ ⲛ-)ὡς; 3 Kg 19 4 *S*(ViK 9687)ὁδός;
BMar 129 *S* knocked at door ⲛⲁⲡϣ. ⲡⲟⲩϭⲛⲟⲩ,
HT *W* 79 *S* sank ⲛⲁⲁⲡϣ. ⲡⲟⲩϣⲏⲙ, Va 63 7 *B* bread
ⲛⲁⲡϣ. ⲛ̄ϫⲱ ϩⲁⲣⲱⲟⲩ = BMis 374 *S* ⲛⲁⲡϣⲓ = BSM
32 *B* ⲛⲁⲡϣⲁ ⲛ-;   ⲥ ϣⲁ-: Va 57 164 *B* ϣⲁⲡϣ.
ⲡⲟⲩⲉϩⲟⲟⲩ μέχρι; R 1 5 11 *S* ϣⲁⲡϣ. ⲛ̄ⲧⲉⲭⲣⲓⲁ χάριν; ShA 2 271 *S* distant ϣⲁⲡϣ. ⲡⲟⲩⲧⲁϭⲥⲉ, *ib* 1
217 *S* ϣⲁⲡϣ. ⲡⲟⲩⲃⲗⲃⲓⲗⲉ (cf Lu 17 6 above), C 89
10 *B* reeds soaked ϣⲁⲡϣ. ⲙ̄ⲡⲓⲉϫⲱⲣϩ = *ib* 99 214
S, Miss 4 239 *S* raised on high ϣⲁⲡϣ. ⲛ̄ⲧⲉⲡⲣⲱⲙⲉ
ϣⲁϫⲉ ⲡⲥⲉⲥⲱⲧⲙ ⲉⲣⲟϥ = *ib* 387 ܠ ܢܐ ܕ.

ϣⲁⲩ *SB*, ϣⲉⲩ *A*, pl ϣⲏⲩ *S* (Ez 19 11 P 44 115,
var ϣⲁⲩ) nn m, *trunk, stump, piece*: Lev 26 30 *S*(*B*
ⲕⲉⲗⲓ), Is 66 24 *S*(*B* do) κῶλον; Ge 49 21 *S*(*B* ⲗⲁϩⲉⲙ), Jer 17 8 *S*(BMOr 8810 521, *B* ϧⲁⲗ)στέλεχος;
Zech 3 2 *A* ϣ. ⲛϩⲣⲉ(*S* λαμπας, *B* = Gk)δαλός; Is

34 13 S(B ϣⲉ, F ϣⲏⲛ) ξύλον; Ez 27 5 S(B ? ⲡⲗⲁϩ) ταινία; 1 Kg 14 14 S ϣ. ⲡⲱⲛⲉ βολίς; ib 9 24 S gloss on ⲥⲉⲉⲛⲉ ὑπόλιμμα; ShZ 637 S ⲛⲉⲕⲗⲁⲧⲟⲥ ⲛ ⲡϣ. ⲉⲧⲣ ϩⲟⲩⲟ ϩⲏⲡϣⲏⲛ, ShP 131³ 70 S sim, ShIF 145 S ⲛϣ. ⲡϣⲉ on to fire, Mor 41 197 S burnt ⲛϣ. ⲡⲛⲉϥⲥⲁⲣⲝ, ib 150 S his flesh like ⲟⲩϣ. ⲡⲣⲁⲧ; iterated: Ez 24 4 S(B ⲫⲁϫⲓ ⲫ.) διχοτόμημα, ib 6 S(B do)μέλος; Tri 322 S ⲡⲉϣ ⲡⲉⲩⲁϥ ⲛϣ. ϣ. ﺁﺨﻀ; AM 33 B flesh fell ⲛϣ. ϣ., Bor 100 102 S Thy body divided ϣ. ϣ.; ⲉⲓⲣⲉ ⲛϣ. ϣ.: 1 Kg 11 7 S, Mic 3 3 S(A ⲧⲉϭ ⲧ., B ⲫⲱϣ)μελίζειν; Lev 8 20 S(B diff)κρεανομεῖν; Mor 18 157 S ⲉⲓⲣⲉ ⲙⲙⲟⲕ ⲛϣ. ϣ. κόπτειν; C 86 83 B ϯⲛⲁⲓⲣⲓ ⲡⲛⲉⲕⲙⲉⲗⲟⲥ ⲛϣ. ϣ.

ϣⲁⲩ B nn m, *male cat*: K 165, 257 ⲡⲛϣ. ﻄﺐ , ﺭﻢ.

ϣⲁⲩ v ⲉϣⲱ.

ϣⲁⲩ A² v ϣⲟⲟⲩ.

ϣⲁⲓⲱⲟⲩ B v ϣⲁ *rise* & ϣⲁ *nose* s f.

ϣⲉⲩ A² vb intr, meaning uncertain, *know* (?): ManiK 19 ⲙⲡϣ. ϫⲉⲣⲡⲉⲅⲛⲉ.

ϣⲉⲉⲩ S nn as pl, meaning unknown: Hall 102 inquire for ⲛϣ. & send them me. Pl of ϣⲉ, *wood* or ϣⲁⲩ *trunk*? Cf ? Sph 10 147 S ⲡ]ⲉϣⲉⲩⲉ.

ϣⲏⲩ v ϣⲓ, ϣⲓⲁⲓ, ⲃⲏⲡⲉ (ⲃⲉⲡⲉϣ.), ⲃⲣⲉϣⲏⲩ.

ϣⲟⲩ S nn m, meaning unknown: Mor 44 33 ⲛϣ. ⲡⲛⲕⲗⲱ ⲉⲧⲉⲡⲉⲗϭⲟⲓⲡⲉ. V ⲉⲣϭⲟⲓ. Cf ? ϭⲟⲩ B AM 60 ingredient of poison.

ϣⲟⲩ, ⲥⲟⲩ- S with preced ⲛ- (Theban), *without* + nn (adj): COAd 16 ⲛϣ. ⲗⲁⲁⲩ ⲛⲁⲛϯⲗⲟⲅⲓⲁ, ib 230 sim (cf ib Ad 9 ⲛⲁⲧⲗ., ST 85 ⲁϫⲛⲗ., ib 91 ⲭⲱⲣⲓⲥ ⲗ.); + vb after ⲙⲡⲣϭⲱ, *tarry, delay not*: CO 120 ⲙ. ⲛϣⲟⲩⲧⲁⲁϥ, ST 243 ⲙ. ⲛϣⲟⲩⲉⲓ, Ep 199 ⲙ. ⲛϣⲟⲩⲥⲉⲡ ⲡⲡ͞, ib 465 ⲙ. ⲛⲥⲟⲩⲝⲟ[ⲟ]ⲩ, ib 177 ⲙⲡⲣϭⲱ ⲛⲥⲟⲩⲧⲁϩⲟⲛ (cf ST 341 ⲛⲁⲧ-, also ϭⲱ ⲛⲟⲩⲉϣ ⲛ-). Metathesis of ⲛⲟⲩⲉϣ (above p 502 a)according to Sethe *Dem Urk* 504.

ϣⲟⲩ- v ϣⲁⲩ *use*.

ϣⲟⲟⲩ, -ⲟⲩⲉ S(Sh only), ϩⲁⲩ A, ϣⲁⲩ A², ϣⲟⲩ- SAF (v ϩⲏⲡⲉ) nn m, *incense, perfume*: Cl 25 2 A(var ϣⲟⲩϩⲏⲡⲉ[ⲉ] ἄρωμα; ShA 1 128 ⲛϣ. ϩⲓⲝⲏⲛⲝⲃⲃⲉⲥ… ⲛ ⲛϣ. ⲡϣⲟⲩϩⲏⲡⲉ, ib 253 smoke of ⲡϣⲟⲟⲩⲉ ⲙⲡⲛⲉⲣϩⲏⲡⲉ, ib 379 ϯ ϣⲟⲟⲩⲉ ⲉϩⲣⲁⲓ in name of phantoms, ib 201 daughters ϯ ⲡⲉⲩϣ. ⲉⲧⲉⲅⲁⲡⲉ, Z 511 (Besa)ⲁⲣϯ ϣ. ⲁⲩⲱ ⲙⲉⲥⲟⲩⲅⲁⲫⲓ ⲡⲟⲩⲗⲉⲗⲟⲩ (same?), R 2 3 47 laying among raiment ϩⲉⲛϣ. ⲉⲩⲥⲟⲧⲛ, Mani H 70 A² ⲱⲗ ⲡⲉϥⲥⲱⲙⲁ ϩⲓⲛϣ. V also ϩⲏⲡⲉ.

ϣⲟⲟⲩ S nn, meaning uncertain: BG 58 serpent beguiled her toward lust & perdition ϫⲉⲥⲉⲣ ϣ. ⲛⲁϥ, JKP 2 26 a pillar (στῦλος) in my country ϣⲁϥⲉⲣ ϣ. ϩⲓⲛⲉⲕⲡⲁⲗⲗⲁⲧⲓⲟⲛ. Prob = ⲣ ϣⲁⲩ, *be useful, acceptable*, q v, esp c ⲛ-.

ϣⲏⲅⲉ S, ϩ., ϩⲛⲟⲩⲉ A, ϣⲛⲟⲩⲓ BF, ϣⲛⲓⲃⲓ B, pl (?) S ϣⲟⲟⲩⲉ nn f, *altar*: Nu 23 2 SB, Is 16 12 SB, Hos 10 8 SAB, Cl 25 4 A βωμός; Ex 30 10 B, Lam 2 7 F(B ⲙⲁ ⲡⲉⲣ ϣⲟⲩϣⲓ) θυσιαστήριον; BMOr 8800 200 S kindled fire ⲡⲣⲉⲛϣ. ⲛⲃⲟⲧⲉ ara; P 44 60 S ⲧϣⲟⲩⲣⲏ· ⲧϣ. ﺝﻣﺮ , ﻣﺠﻤﺮ = 43 28 but 'ﺝ, 'ﻣ (so ? *censer*); P 55 18 B ⲛⲓϣⲏⲛⲓ (sic) ﻫﻴﺎﻛﻞ ﺍﻻﺩﻳﺎﻥ ; WTh 189 S ϯ ⲗⲓⲃⲁⲛⲟⲥ ⲉⲝⲡϣ., ib 123 B ϭⲉⲣⲟ ⲛϯϣⲛⲓⲃⲓ, El 98 A ϫⲉⲣⲟ ⲛⲣⲉⲛϩ. = ib 134 S, Aegyptus 3 276 S ⲧϣ. ⲡⲣⲁⲧ (cf PGrenf 2 161 βω. χαλκοῦς), ST 125 S metal utensils ⲥⲛⲧⲉ [ⲛ]ϣ.; pl S(?): Is 27 9 ⲛⲉⲩϣⲟⲟⲩⲉ (var ⲛⲉⲩϣⲏⲅⲉ, B ⲛⲟⲩϣ.).

ϣⲟⲅⲉ v ϣⲟⲩⲛⲏⲃ.

ϣⲟⲟⲩⲉ S, ϣⲁ(ⲟ)ⲩⲉ S^f, ϣⲉ(ⲟ)ⲩⲉ S^f A, ϣⲁⲩⲉⲓⲉ A², ϣⲱⲟⲩⲓ B, ϣⲁⲩⲉⲓ F, ϣⲟⲩⲱⲟⲩ† SAA²B -ⲟⲩⲉ† S(Sh), ϣⲱⲟⲩ† B vb intr, *be dry*: Jos 9 18 S, Job 12 15 S ⲧⲣⲉϣ.(B ⲧϣⲟⲩⲓⲟ), Ps 101 4 SS^f(PcodMor)B, Si 40 15 S(var ϣⲟⲩⲟ), Nah 1 4 SA ⲧⲣⲉϣ.(B ⲧϣ.), Jo 15 6 SA²B ξηραίνειν, Hos 13 15 AB ἀναξ., Ps 36 2 SB ἀποξ., Nu 11 6 SB κατάξηρος; Ps 102 15 SB ἐξανθεῖν; PS 132 S lips ⲉⲁⲩϣ.(Od Solom 6 14 ﺣﺐﻝ), ShA 2 140 S wind blew ⲁⲧⲉⲧⲛϣ., ShRE 11 16 S if thou forsake us ⲧⲛⲛⲁϣ., Ryl 94 109 S ϩⲉⲛϣⲉ ⲉⲩⲗⲏⲕ ⲙⲡⲁⲧⲟⲩϣ., BIF 13 99 S wounds ⲁⲩϣ. = MG 25 278 B, Va 59 7 B sea ⲛⲁϣ., PMéd 153 S ⲕⲁⲁϥ ϣⲁⲛⲧⲉϣ., BM 527 F recipe ⲟⲩⲁⲣϩ ⲧⲉϣ., AZ 33 56 F ⲧⲃⲱ…ⲁⲥϣⲁⲉ (?) ⲁⲥⲧⲁⲕⲁ, Ryl 361 S^f ⲫⲱϥ ⲡⲛⲛⲁⲕⲉ (? ἀνάγκη)ⲁⲡⲁⲗⲉϥ ⲙⲡⲁⲧϣ.; as if qual (in recipes) S: PMéd 267 ⲛϭⲉ ⲉϥϣ., CR '87 376 ϫⲏⲛ ⲉⲩϣ., Ryl 106 2 ⲗⲓⲗⲟⲟⲩⲉ (ⲉ)ϥϣ.; cf Tri 496 ⲟⲉⲓⲕ ϣ. ﻳﺎﺑﺲ , Nu 6 3 ⲉⲗⲉⲗⲙ.(var ⲉϥϣ.†, B ⲁⲗϣⲟⲟⲩ)σταφίς; WS 118 ⲃⲛϣ., ST 118 ⲗⲓⲗϣⲟⲟⲩ; qual, *dry, stale*: Joel 1 17 B(A ⲱϣⲛⲉ), Mk 9 18 B(S ⲧⲱⲥ) ξηρ., Jos 3 17 SB(l-ⲱⲟⲩ), Ez 20 47 S(B ⲟⲓ ⲛϣⲱⲟⲩⲓ), Hos 9 14 AB, Jo 5 3 SA²B, He 11 29 SBF, Z 310 S bread ⲉϥϣ. opp ⲛⲃⲣⲣⲉ, MG 25 347 B wood ⲉϥϣ. ξηρός; Z 291 S ⲡⲥⲱⲙⲁ ⲉⲧϣ. of monk *siccatus*; PS 117 S ⲟⲩⲕⲗⲟⲙ ⲉϥϣ.(OdSolom 1 3 'ﺣﺐ), ShA 1 447 S ϩⲉⲛϣⲏⲛ ⲉⲧϣ. (sic), ShZ 598 S body ⲉϥϣ. ⲉϥⲟ ⲛⲕⲱⲟⲥ, Z 261 S bowels having fallen out he (Arius) sat ⲉϥϣ. & lifeless; v also ⲉⲗⲟⲟⲗⲉ I. ⲡⲉⲧϣ.†, *what is dry*: Ps 65 6 SB, Jon 1 9 SAB, R 1 1 31 S sea became as ⲡⲡ. ξηρός; Va 57 122 B ⲟⲩⲡ. ⲛϫⲉ ⲡϭⲓⲥⲓ ἀνόνητος; Job 9 8 S(B ⲕⲁϩⲓ) ἔδαφος; ShA 1 267 S ⲁϥⲙⲟⲟϣⲉ ϩⲉⲓϫⲙⲡⲉⲧϣⲟⲩⲱⲟⲩ ⲁϥⲥⲉϣⲧ ⲧⲡⲉ, BAp 89 S Israelites crossed sea ⲕⲁⲧⲁ ⲡⲡ., Mani K 92 A² opp ⲡⲉⲧⲁϭⲃⲉ. Qual sometimes as if from ϣⲟⲩⲟ q v. With following preposition or adverb. ⲥ ⲉⲃⲟⲗ ⲛ-: Jer 12 4 S(B ⲉⲃ. ϫⲉⲛ-)ξηραίν. ἀπό; ⲥ ⲉϫⲛ-: Ge 8 7 S(B ⲉⲃ. ϩⲁ-)ⲝ. ἀπό; ⲥ ϩⲁ-: BMis 543 S tongues ϣ. ϩⲁⲡⲉⲓⲃⲉ; ⲥ ϩⲛ-: BAp 151 S ⲟⲩⲡⲁϭⲥⲉ ⲉⲁⲥϣ. ϩⲛⲣⲱⲕ, ShBM 212 S ⲡ[ⲉⲛ]ⲧⲏϭ ϣ. ϩⲛⲡⲉϥ-

ⲉⲓⲱⲣⲉ, Bodl(P) a 3 53 *S.f* recipe ⲕⲁ(ⲁ)ϥ ⲧⲉϥϣⲟⲟⲩⲉ ϩⲛⲧⲣⲁⲓⲃⲉⲥ; ϩⲣⲁⲓ ϩⲛ-: ShC 73 23 *S* ⲙⲡⲉⲛⲛⲟϩⲉ... ϣ.(var ⲱϧⲡ)ϩ. ⲡⲉϩⲧⲡ; ⲉⲃⲟⲗ ϩⲛ-, ϩⲉⲛ-: Is 41 17 *B* (*S* ϩⲁ-)ξ. ἀπό; Mor 37 136 *S* ⲙⲡⲉϥϣ. ⲉⲃ. ϩⲛⲓϩⲣ-ϫⲟⲡⲏ ἐξαρνεῖσθαι (as if ξηραίν.); ⲥ ϩⲓϫⲉⲛ-: C 89 159 *B* till water ϣ. ϩ.ⲡⲓⲕⲁⲣⲓ; ⲥ ⲉⲃⲟⲗ: CDan 88 *B* struck rock ⲁϥϫⲉⲙⲥ ⲉⲥϣ.† ⲉⲃ. ὑπόκουφον ψόφον ἀκούειν.

ⲟⲓ ⲡϣ. *B, be dry*: Ez 20 47 (*S* ϣ.†) ξηρός.

ϫⲓⲡϣ. *B, dryness, withering*: DeV 2 49 ⲡϫ. ⲙⲡⲓⲣⲱⲧ (*sc* gourd, Jon 4 10).

ϣⲟⲩⲓⲉ *B* nn m, *dryness, what is dry*: Ge 1 9, ib 7 22 (*S* ⲡⲉⲧ)ϣ.†), Ex 4 9 (*A* ⲡⲉⲧϣ.†), MG 25 18 fish ⲁⲩϣⲁⲡⲱⲥⲕ ϩⲉⲛⲡⲓϣ. ξηρός; as adj: Va 58 73 ⲱⲓⲕ ⲡϣ.

As name (?): MIF 59 27 ⲙⲏⲛⲁ ϣⲟⲩⲱⲟⲩ.

V ⲧϣⲟⲩⲓⲟ.

ϣⲟⲩⲟ *SAA²B*, -ⲁ*F*, ϣⲟⲩⲉ-*SAB*, ϣⲟⲩⲁ-*F*, ϣⲟⲩ-*SB*(?), ϣⲟⲩⲱ⸗*SAB*, ϣⲟⲩⲟ⸗*SB* vb **I** intr, *flow, pour, discharge*: Job 38 30 *SB*, Ps 147 18 *S*(*B* ϩⲁϯ) ῥεῖν, Lu 8 44*S*(*B* ϣⲓϯ ⲉⲃⲟⲗ)ῥύσις; 3 Kg 22 35*S* ἀποχύνειν; Ac 21 3 *S*(*B* ϩⲓⲟⲅⲓ), P 129¹⁷ 74 *S* ship ⲁϥϣ. ϩⲓⲟⲡⲡⲏ ἀποφορτίζειν; BHom 110 *S* ⲁⲩϣ. ⲛϭⲓ ⲛⲕⲁⲧⲁϩⲣⲁⲕⲧⲏⲥ. **II** tr, *pour, empty*: Tri 478 *S* ϣⲟⲩⲉ ⲛⲉⲡⲣⲉⲙⲉⲓⲟⲟⲩⲉ ⌐ٮٯ; ManiH 22 *A²* ⲛⲥⲉϣ. ⲛϩⲓⲥⲉ ⲉⲧⲉⲙⲡⲟⲩϩⲣⲏⲧ, Br 234 4 *S* of freighted ship ⲛⲧϣⲟⲩⲟϥ.

With following preposition. ⲥ ⲉϫⲛ-: Eccl 11 3 *S* ἐκχέειν ἐπί; Deu 28 24 *S*(*B* diff) καταβαίνειν ἐπί; Mk 3 10 *S*(*B* ⲓ ⲉⲝ.) ἐπιπίπτειν dat; Lu 5 1 *S*(*B* ⲑⲟⲩϯ)ἐπικεῖσθαι; ShMiss 4 283 *S* ϣⲟⲩⲉ ⲟⲩⲥⲟⲡⲉ ⲙⲙⲟⲟⲩ ⲉϫⲱϥ, Mor 38 96 *S* ⲡⲙⲛⲏϣⲉ ⲉⲧϣ. ⲉϫⲱϥ (cf Lu above), BMis 106 *S* pains ⲉⲩϣ. ⲉϫⲱⲓ like raindrops, Miss 8 258 *S* ⲛⲉⲡⲕⲟ (ⲗ-ⲁ) ⲛⲁⲙⲉ ⲡϥϣⲟⲩⲟϥ ⲉϫⲛⲧⲝⲟ, Ryl 94 102 *S* lake ⲉⲣⲉⲡⲉⲭⲓⲱⲛ ϣ. ⲉϫⲱⲥ, TU 43 2 *A* ointment ϣⲟⲩⲱϥ [ⲁϫⲛⲡϥ]ⲥⲱⲙⲁ, C 43 55 *B* blood ϣ. ⲉϫ. ⲡⲉϥϩⲟ; ⲥ ⲛ-(-ⲙⲙⲟ⸗), *from*: Lev 20 18 *S* ⲛⲉⲥⲥⲛⲟϥ ⲉⲧϣ. ⲙⲙⲟⲥ (*B* ⲧⲉⲗⲧⲉⲗ) ῥύσις; Worr 271 *S* ⲡⲉⲧⲉⲣⲉⲡⲗⲟⲟⲩ (var EnPeterson 71 ⲟⲩⲥⲡⲉⲣⲙⲁ) ϣ. ⲙⲙⲟⲟⲩ (cf ⲛⲥⲁ- & ⲉⲃⲟⲗ); ⲥ ⲛⲥⲁ-: Nu 5 2 *S*(*B* diff) γονορρυής; ⲥ ϩⲛ-, *into*: P 131⁵ 32 *S* wine ϣⲟⲩⲱϥ ϩⲛⲡϣⲟⲩϩⲟⲣ, C 43 175 *B* jars ⲉⲩϣⲟⲩⲟ ⲥⲉⲙⲁ (ζέμα) ⲛⲃⲏⲧⲟⲩ.

With following adverb. ⲥ ⲉⲃⲟⲗ, intr: Ps 104 41 *S*(*B* ϩⲁϯ ⲉⲃ.) ῥ.; Dan 9 25 *B*(*S* ϣⲟⲩⲉⲓⲧ) ἐκκενοῦν; R 1 3 30 *S* ⲉⲣⲉⲟⲩⲙⲟⲟⲩ ϣ. ⲉⲃ., DeV 2 164 *B* ⲁϥϣ. ⲉⲃ. ⲛϫⲉ ⲟⲩⲛⲟⲩⲃ ⲉϥⲟϣ; tr: Ex 33 3 *S*(*B* ϩ.), Joel 3 18 *SA*(*B* do) ῥύ.; 1 Cor 9 15 *B*(*SF* ϣⲟⲩⲉⲓⲧ), Phil 2 7 *B* ϣⲟⲩⲟ⸗(*S* ⲡⲱⲣ ⲉⲃ.) κενοῦν, Is 51 17 *B*(*S* ⲡⲱ.) ἐκκ.; Am 9 13 *SA*(*B* ⲟⲗⲏ ⲉⲡⲉⲥⲛⲧ) ἀποσταλάζειν; Va 68 164 *B* ϣ. ⲉⲃ. ⲛϯⲙⲉⲧⲣⲁⲙⲁⲟ ἀπολλύναι; BHom 76 *S* His side ϣ. ⲉⲃ. ⲛⲟⲩⲥⲛⲟϥ, C 43 54 *B* ϣⲟⲩⲟ ⲥⲛⲟϥ ⲉⲃ., SHel 29 *S* face ϣⲟⲩⲉ ⲣⲁϣⲉ ⲉⲃ.; ⲉⲃ. ⲛ-:

BM 1223 *A-S* may worms ϣ. ⲉⲃ. ⲙⲙⲟⲥ; ⲉⲃ. ϩⲛ-: Cant 4 15 *S*(*F* ⲡⲛⲟⲩ ⲉⲃ.) ῥ. ἀπό, Zech 14 12 *S*(ROC 20 55).*A*(*B* ϥⲟⲣϥⲉⲣ ⲉⲃ.) ῥ. ἐκ, Jud 6 38 *S* ἀπορ. ἀπό; Ex 17 6 *S*(var & *B* ⲓ ⲉⲃ.)ἐξέρχεσθαι ἐκ; ShMIF 23 195 *S* ⲙⲡⲛϣⲟⲩⲱϣ (sc heart) ⲉⲃ. ϩⲛⲧⲙⲛⲧⲙⲁⲓⲣⲟⲙⲡⲧ, ViK 9534 *S* milk ϣ. ⲉⲃ. ϩⲓⲣⲱⲟⲩ, AM 166 *B* ϣⲁⲧⲉⲡⲟⲅⲁⲡⲡⲉϥⲁⲗⲟⲥ(ἐγκέ.)ϣ. ⲉⲃ. ϩⲉⲛⲡⲟⲩϫⲁⲓ; ⲥ ⲉⲡⲉⲥⲛⲧ: Lam 2 18 *S*(*B* ⲓⲓⲓ ⲉⲡ., *F* ⲓ ⲉⲃ.) κατάγειν; Jud 5 4 *S*, Cant 5 5 *S*(*B* ⲧⲁⲟⲅⲟ, *F* ⲟⲩⲱ ⲉⲃⲁⲗ) στάζειν, Cant 4 11 *S* ἀποστ.; BMar 122 *S* ϣ. ⲉⲡ. ⲡⲣⲉⲙⲣⲙⲉⲓⲟⲟⲩⲉ προχέειν; ShA 2 299 *S* ϣ. ⲉⲡ. ⲉⲃ. ϩⲛⲡⲉϥⲃⲁⲗ ⲡⲣⲉⲡⲣⲙ., AZ 21 142 *S* ⲉⲣⲉⲡⲉϥⲣⲉⲙ. ϣ. ⲉⲡ., MIE 2 348 *B* navel burst ⲁⲥϣ. ⲉⲡ. ⲛⲛⲓⲁⲕⲁⲑⲁⲣⲥⲓⲁ, BMar 84 *S* mouth ϣⲟⲩⲟ ϫⲓⲣ ⲉⲡ., ib 23 *S* ϣⲟⲩⲟ ⲑⲏⲡ ⲉⲡ.; as nn: BHom 109 *S* ⲡⲉϣ. ⲉⲡ. ⲡⲧⲉⲓⲱⲧⲉ; ⲥ ⲉⲡϫⲱⲓ: C 43 19 *B* spring ϣ. ⲉⲡ.; ⲥ ⲉϩⲣⲁⲓ, ⲉϩ.: Pro 3 20 *SA*(*B* ϩ.) ῥ.; Jos 3 13 *SB* καταβαίνειν; Bor 138 142 *S* ⲉⲩϣ. ⲉϩ. ⲡⲣⲉⲛⲁϣⲏ ⲛⲣⲙⲉⲓⲏ ἀποστ.; Is 45 8 *S*(*B* ⲡⲟⲩϫϩ) ῥανίζειν; BM 216 80 *S* sailors ϣ. ⲉϩ. ⲛⲛⲁⲅⲉⲓⲛ ἀποσκευάζειν; ManiK 48 *A²* ⲁⲥⲃⲉⲃⲉ ⲁⲥϣ. ⲁⲣⲏ[ⲓ; ⲉϩ. ⲉ-: Ryl 62 1 *S* lung ⲉⲧϣⲟⲩⲟ ⲡⲓϣⲉ ⲉϩ. ⲉⲡⲣⲏⲧ, ib 94 102 *S* at night ⲡⲭⲁϥ... ϣ. ⲉϩ. ⲉⲣⲟⲥ; ⲉϩ. ⲉϫⲛ-: ShA 2 275 *S* tears ϣ. ⲉϩ. ⲉϫⲛⲡⲗⲟⲅⲟⲥⲉ (var om ⲉϩ.), AM 53 *B* pots (? κρέαγρα) full of pitch ⲁⲩϣ. ⲉϩ. ⲉϫⲱϥ; ⲉϩ. ϩⲛ-: Sh BMOr 8800 1 *S* ⲡⲉⲗϩⲱⲃ ⲉⲧϣ. ⲉϩ. ϩⲛⲧⲉⲕϣⲟⲩⲱⲃⲉ(= R 2 3 6), C 41 50 *B* tears ϣ. ⲉϩ. ϩⲉⲛⲡⲉϥⲃⲁⲗ; ⲉϩ. ϩⲓϫⲉⲛ-: BM 511 *F* ⲉⲧϣ. ⲓⲱϯ...ⲉϩ. ϩ.ⲡⲓⲕⲉⲣⲓ.

ϣⲟⲩⲉⲓⲧ *SS*.f*AA²F*, ϣⲟⲉⲓⲧ (?) *S*, ϣⲟⲩⲓⲧ *A²BF* vb (qual), *empty*: Deu 32 47 *SB*, Job 33 21 *S*(*B* ϣⲟⲩⲱⲟⲩ), Is 32 6 *BF*(*S* ⲡⲱⲣⲧ tr), Jer 14 3 *S*(*B* do), 1 Cor 15 14 *SBF* κενός, LeipBer '02 155 *S* ⲉⲩϣ. ⲉⲃⲟⲗ ϩⲙⲡⲉⲛⲡⲛⲁ ⲉⲧⲟⲩⲁⲁⲃ κοῦφος κ. κε., Mt 5 22 *S*(var ⲡⲱϩ, *B* = Gk) ῥακά (κε., *v* Preuschen-Bauer 1177), Nu 21 5 *S*(*B* ϣⲟⲩⲱⲟⲩ) διάκενος (var ξηρός), MG 25 251 *B* ⲡⲓⲱⲟⲩ ⲉⲧϣ. κενοδοξία, Ro 4 14 *SB* κενοῦν, Dan 9 25 *S*(*B* ϣⲟⲩⲟ ⲉⲃⲟⲗ), Hab 3 13 *SB*(*A* diff)ἐκκ.; Deu 5 11 *S*(*B* ⲉϥϣⲗⲏⲟⲩ), Ja 1 26 *SA*(*B* do)μάταιος, Ps 38 5 *S*(*B* do)ματαιότης; Pro 14 4 *SA*(*B* ⲧⲟⲩⲃⲏⲟⲩⲧ)καθαρός vacuus; Mt 12 36 *B*(*S*= Gk) ἀργός; Jude 12 *S*(*B* ⲁⲑⲙⲟⲟⲩ)ἄνυδρος; BHom 94 *S* the Crucified ⲟⲩⲣⲱⲙⲉ ⲉϥϣ. ψιλός; Jer 28 18 *B* μωκᾶσθαι; Va 63 82 *B* ⲥⲁϫⲓ ϣⲱⲡⲓ ⲉⲩϣ. καταλύεσθαι; Eph 5 4 *B* ⲥⲁϫⲓ ⲉⲧϣ.(*S* ϣⲗⲟϥ)αἰσχρότης; PS 173 *S* ⲕⲁⲁⲧ ⲉⲃⲟⲗ ⲉⲓϣ., ShC 42 189 *S* ⲡⲕⲁⲓⲣⲟⲥ ⲉⲛⲧⲁⲡⲁⲁϥ ⲉⲓϣ., ShMIF 23 196*S* soul ⲉⲥϣ. ⲛⲧⲙⲛⲧⲙⲁⲓⲣⲟⲙⲡⲧ(cf ϣⲟⲩⲟ ⲉⲃ. ϩⲛ-), JTS 8 241 *S* on Mt 11 7 ⲧⲥⲛⲏϥ ⲛϫⲱ ⲉϩⲣⲟⲓ ⲡⲟⲩⲙⲁ ⲉϥϣ. (var BAp 134 ⲉⲣⲉⲡϣⲟⲉⲓⲧ), CA 92 *S* ⲡϩⲓⲥⲉ... ϣⲱⲡⲉ ⲉϥϣ., BP 11349 *S* through bad harvest &c ⲁⲓⲙⲟⲟϣⲉ ⲉⲓϣ., AP 7 *A²* ϩⲛϣⲉϫⲉ...ⲉⲩϣ., Mani 2 *A²* ⲡⲉϥϩⲣⲁϥ ⲉⲧϣⲟⲩⲓⲧ, Orat Cyp 142 *S*.f ⲛⲉⲕϭⲓϫ ϣ., BSM 14 *B* ⲧⲱⲟⲩ ⲉϥϣ.= BMis 348 *S* ⲡⲭⲁⲓⲉ; *flow* (?): R 1 3 74 *S* Baptist's head ⲉⲣⲉϩⲉⲛⲧⲁⲗϭⲟ...ϣⲟⲉⲓⲧ

ⲡⲣⲏⲧⲥ ϧⲏⲡⲥⲁ ⲉⲧⲟⲩⲟϣⲥ ⲉⲃⲟⲗ;   as adj: Col 3 8
B ⲥⲁϫⲓ ⲛϣ. (S ϣⲗⲟϥ) αἰσχρολογία; ϩⲉⲛⲟⲩϣ.
B, in vain: Is 65 23 (S ⲉⲡϫⲓⲛϫⲏ), Jer 18 15 (S ⲉⲡ-
ⲡⲉⲧϣ.), Gal 2 2 (S do) εἰς κενόν; ϩⲉⲛⲟⲩⲙⲉⲧϣ. B:
Is 49 4 (S ⲉⲡϫ.) κενῶς.

ⲡⲉⲧ-, ⲡⲉⲧϣⲟⲩⲉⲓⲧ SABF, what is empty, vain: Pro
12 11 SA(B ⲙⲉⲧⲉⲫ.) μάταιος, Ps 143 11 S (do)
-ότης;   with art ⲡⲡⲉⲧϣ., ⲟⲩⲡ., ϩⲉⲛⲡ.: Ex 20 7 S
(B ⲟⲩⲙⲉⲧⲉⲫ.), Hos 6 8 SA(B do), Ac 14 15 S(B do)
ⲙⲁⲧ., Ro 8 20 S(B do) -ότης; Job 15 31 SB, Is 30 7
SBF κενός; Hos 7 16 v ⲛⲡⲉ; ShWess 9 141 S ⲉϥϫⲱ ⲛⲛⲉⲓ. thinking self wise, Pcod 31 S ⲟⲩⲡ. ⲡⲉ
ⲡⲉϥⲙⲉⲉⲩⲉ, AM 217 B ⲓⲣⲓ ⲛϯⲁⲛⲟⲙⲓⲁ ϩⲉⲛϩⲁⲡⲡ.; ⲥ
ⲉ-: Lev 26 16 B ⲉⲡ. (S ⲉⲡϫ.) διὰ κενῆς, Jer 26 11 S
ⲉⲩⲡ. (B ϩⲉⲛⲟⲩϣ.) εἰς τὸ κε.; Ps 34 7 S ⲉⲡⲡ. (var
ⲉⲡϫ., B do) μάτην; ⲙⲛⲧⲛ. S: Eccl 4 7 ματαιότης;
R 1 4 38 ϩⲓⲟⲩⲙ. sine causa, ShViK 923 ⲉⲥⲥⲟⲩ
ⲉⲣⲱⲧⲛ ϩⲓⲟⲩⲙ.   ⲣ ⲡ., act vainly: Ro 1 21 S(B do)
ⲙⲁⲧⲁⲓⲟⲩⲛ.

ϣⲟⲩ- SB in ϣⲟⲩⲃⲁⲗ (v ⲃⲁⲗ), ϣⲟⲩⲙⲏ (v ⲙⲏ sf)
belong ? here.

ϣⲟⲩⲟ S nn f, a vessel holding corn (? + final -ⲟ
great): BKU 1 259 ⲧⲉⲓⲩϣ. ⲥⲙⲉϩ ⲉⲣⲱⲥ ⲛⲥⲟⲩⲟ.

ϣⲟⲩⲏ(ⲏ)ⲃ[1], ϣⲃⲓⲃ[2], ϣⲟⲩⲉⲃⲉ[3], -ϥⲉ[4], ϣⲏⲃ[5], ϣⲏⲅⲉ[6],
ϣⲟⲩⲏⲛⲟⲩ[7], ϣⲟⲩⲉ[8] S, -ⲏ S[f], ϣⲃⲉ B, ϣⲉⲅⲃ(?) F nn m,
persea tree, lebbakh (LöwF 3 347, AIssa 119): P 44
81 S ⲡⲉⲣⲥⲁⲓⲁ · ⲡⲉⲣⲥⲱⲓⲁⲥ · ⲡⲉϣ.[8] = 43 56 om
ⲡⲉⲣⲥⲱ., K 178 B ⲡϣⲏ. ⲍ; Mor 40 31 S ⲛⲉϣ.[8] whereon Theodore hanged, BMis 3 S[8], Leyd 287 S[8], LMär
4 S[3], 6[4], Mor 39 41 S[f], C 43 59 B all this tree (cf PO
11 581 ⲍ); other martyrs: HT W 80 S[f], BM 357 S[8],
RNC 76 S[3], ViK 9525 S[8]; used for building: BMis
268 ϣⲉ ⲛϣ.[3], 269 S[3] = Mor 30 44 S[f]; planted by
Persians as sign of their supremacy (play ? upon Gk
name): Mor 40 4 S[7] = ib 41 118[6] = ib 39 6 S[f] = C
43 35 B; JTS 8 241 S ⲃⲏⲡⲉ, ⲛⲟⲩϩⲣⲉ, ϣ.[8] (var BAp
134[2]), Cai 42573 1 S leaves of ϣ.[8] in recipe, CMSS
78 F in account ⲉϩⲟ(ⲩ)ⲛ ⲛⲉϣⲏⲅⲉⲃ(?).   In place-
names: ⲡⲧⲟⲟⲩ ⲙⲛϣ.[1] (Ep 78, 132), or ⲙⲛϣ.[5] (ib
522) = جبل شوارو (Synax 1 340), church of Virgin
ⲉⲛϣ.[8] (BM 1100), ⲛⲙⲁ ⲙⲛϣ.[8] (BMOr 6201 B 256,
cf ⲛⲙⲁ ⲙⲛϣ.[8] where Theodore died WTh 134). In
dem t mtn·t n pšⲱb (Rec 35 153).

ϣⲟⲩⲱⲃⲉ, -ⲟⲃⲉ SA, ϣⲃⲱⲃⲓ B, ϣⲟⲩⲱⲃⲓ F nn f,
throat: Job 6 30 SB, Ro 3 13 SB, Bor 235 117 S
when drinking let not ⲧⲉⲕϣ. ⲉⲱⲙ ⲉⲃⲟⲗ like worldlings (cf BMar 181) λάρυγξ; Pro 5 3 SAB, ib 24 13
A ϣⲟⲩⲟ., Cant 5 16 SF φάρυγξ; K 76 B ϯϣ. حُلْبُر;
ShBor 247 114 S ⲉⲣⲉⲟⲩϣ. ϣⲟⲟⲡ ⲛⲁϥ ⲉⲡⲙⲁ ⲛⲣⲉⲛ-
ⲗⲟⲅⲓⲥⲙⲟⲥ, Pcod 48 S ⲧϣ. ϫⲁϫⲉ ϩⲁⲧⲉⲓⲃⲉ, MG 25
133 B mastic sweetens spittle in ⲧⲟⲩϣ., AM 166 B
ⲙⲟⲩϯ ⲡⲟⲩⲥⲙⲛ ⲉⲃⲟⲗ ϩⲉⲛⲧⲟⲩϣ.

ϣⲉⲅⲛⲓ B nn f, barn: PO 11 314 went up to ϯϣ.
ⲁϥⲱⲗⲓ ⲛⲟⲩϣⲟⲗ ⲛⲥⲟⲩⲃⲉⲛ, ib 315 sim ϣⲟⲗ ⲛⲥⲓⲙ.
Cf شونة.

ϣⲟⲩⲣⲏ SBF nn f, censer, brazier, altar: Lev 16
12 SB, Si 50 9 S πυρεῖον; He 9 2 SF, ib 4 B θυμιατήριον; Si 50 12 S βωμός; Ap 8 3 S(B λιβανον)λι-
βανωτός; C 99 136 S = C 89 29 B مجمر; TThe 61
B ϯϣ. ⲛⲡⲟⲩⲃ مجمر; BMar 2 S ⲃⲱⲙⲟⲥ ⲛⲣⲁⲧ ϣ. ⲛ-
ⲡⲟⲩⲃ, Bor 258 41 S ⲧϣ. ⲉⲧⲉⲣⲉⲛϣⲟⲩⲣⲏⲛⲉ ⲛⲣⲏⲧⲥ,
ROC 23 285 B ϩⲁⲛϣ. ⲛⲣⲁⲧ, AM 200 B ϣ. ⲛⲥⲉⲟⲓ-
ⲛⲟⲩϥⲓ, Br 114 S ⲕⲱⲧ ⲛⲟⲩϣ. ϩⲣⲁⲓ ϩⲓϫⲛⲑⲁⲗⲁⲥⲥⲁ (sic
prob).

ϣⲟⲩⲥⲟⲟⲩϣⲉ[1], -ⲥⲱⲟⲩϣⲉ[2], -ⲥⲟⲟⲩⲣⲉ[3], ⲥⲟⲩⲥⲟⲟⲩϣⲉ[4] S, ϣⲟⲩϣⲱⲟⲩϣⲓ, ϣⲱⲟⲩϣⲓ B, ϣⲟⲩϣⲁⲩϣⲓ F nn
m, sacrifice, offering (mostly B): Ge 4 3 (SACl = Gk),
Ps 39 7 (S = Gk), EpJer 27 (F = Gk), Mt 12 7 (SF
= Gk) θυσία, Deu 12 6 (S ⲑⲩⲥⲓⲁ) θυσίασμα, 2 Kg 6
13 (S ϣⲱⲱⲧ vb) θῦμα, Jer 11 13 ϣⲉⲧ ϣ. θυμιᾶν, Ex
32 9 sim θύειν, Is 65 3 ⲉⲡ ϣ. ⲉϩⲣⲏⲓ (S ⲧⲁⲗⲉ ⲑ.) θυσιάζειν; Jo 16 2 ⲛⲛⲓ ⲛⲟⲩϣ. (SA[2] ⲉⲓⲣⲉ ⲛⲟⲩϣⲙϣⲉ)
λατρείαν προσφέρειν; ROC 17 407 ⲛϣ. ἱερουργία;
Ez 46 11 ⲥⲛⲟⲩ ⲛⲧⲉ ⲛϣ. πανήγυρις; Is 1 11 S[1]F(B
ϭⲗⲓⲗ) ὁλοκαύτωμα; BHom 92 S[4] κνίσσα; Tri 513
S[2] ذبح; ShWess 9 176 S ⲛⲉϣ.[3] ⲛⲥⲉϣⲏⲡ ⲁⲛ,
BSM 16 ⲁⲛϥⲁⲓ ⲛⲟⲩϣ. ⲙⲫ‡, Bor 263 36 S ⲧⲉⲡⲣⲟⲥ-
ⲫⲟⲣⲁ ⲛⲧⲉ ⲛϣ.[1]

ⲓⲣⲓ, ⲉⲣ ϣ. B, make sacrifice: Is 19 21 (S ⲟⲩⲥⲓⲁ)
θυσίας ποιεῖν; EpJer 42 (F diff) θυμιᾶν; C 43 78
ⲁⲣⲓ ϣ. ⲛⲛⲓⲛⲟⲩϯ; ⲙⲁ ⲡⲉⲣ ϣⲱⲟⲩϣⲓ, place of
sacr.: Ps 25 6 (S = Gk), Lam 2 7 (F ϣⲛⲟⲩϣⲓ), 1 Cor
9 13 (SF = Gk) θυσιαστήριον; Ez 16 24 ἔκθεμα; K
333 مذبح; C 43 128 ⲡⲓⲥⲕⲉⲩⲟⲥ ⲛⲧⲉ ⲡⲓⲙ.

ϣⲟⲩⲉⲓⲧ v ϣⲟⲩⲟ sf.

ϣⲟⲟⲩⲧ S nn m, meaning unknown: PLond 4
213 place τόπος Παϣϣⲟⲟⲩⲧ, cf ib 244 Παϣⲟⲟⲩⲧ.

ϣⲟⲟⲩⲧⲥ (sic) S nn, meaning unknown, a measure?: BM 1099 in list ⲥⲉ ⲛϣ. ⲛⲧⲱⲣ.

ϣⲱⲟⲩϣⲓ B   v ϣⲟⲩⲥⲟⲟⲩϣⲉ.

ϣⲟⲩϣⲏⲧ B nn, herb eaten by sheep: MG 25
236 sheep came to marsh ⲉⲟⲩⲱⲙ ϣ., whilst cattle
there eat ⲟⲩⲟⲧⲟⲩⲉⲧ = GöttAr 114 97 ... العشب و
الشعارى من النواحى P 54 127 = BMOr 8775 123
حشيش.

ϣⲟⲩϣⲓⲧⲉ B nn m, whistling, hissing: Mic 6 16
(A ⲱϣ ⲛⲥⲁ-) συρισμός; Va 61 208 ⲡⲁⲓϣ. ⲫⲁⲡⲓ-
ϩⲟⲩ; ⲉⲣ ϣ., whistle, hiss: Is 7 18 (S ⲥⲱⲕ as if σύρειν), Lam 2 15 (S ϥⲓ ϣⲙϣⲏⲅⲉ, F ϣⲱϫⲓ), Zeph 2
15 (A ⲁϣ ϭⲁⲡ) συρίζειν; ⲥ ⲛⲥⲁ-: Is 5 26 (S ⲥⲱⲕ
ut sup). Cf ϣⲙϣⲏⲅⲉ.

ϣⲟⲩϣⲟⲩ *SAA²BF*, -ϣⲟ *S* (nn), ϣⲁⲩϣⲟ *A* (nn)
vb **I** intr *B*, *boast*: Jer 9 24 (*S* refl), 1 Cor 13 3 (*S*
do) καυχᾶσθαι; Ps 62 12 (*S* ϫⲓ ⲧⲁⲉⲓⲟ) ἐπαινεῖσθαι.

II tr (refl), *pride oneself*: 1 Kg 2 3 *SB*, Pro 20 9
SA, Gal 6 14 *SBF* ⲕ., Ps 73 4 *SB* ⲉⲅⲕ., Jer 27 11 *SB*
ⲕⲁⲧⲁⲕ.; Ps 105 5 *B*(*S* ϫⲓ ⲧ.) ⲉⲡ.; ib 9 38 *SB*(+ ϩⲉⲛ-
ⲣⲁⲡⲙⲉⲧⲛⲓϣϯ) μεγαλαυχεῖν; Sa 2 16 *SB* ἀλαζονεύ-
ⲉⲓⲛ; C 43 101 *B* ⲛⲡⲟⲩϣ. ⲙⲙⲱⲟⲩ, Mani 1 *A²* ⲉⲣⲉϣ.
ⲙⲙⲟ.

With following preposition. ⲉ ⲉ-, *upon*: Pro 27
1 *SA* ⲕ. εἰς; ⲉ ⲉⲧⲃⲉ-, *about*: 2 Cor 10 8 *S*(*B* ⲉϩⲣⲏⲓ
ⲉϫⲉⲛ-) ⲕ. περί; ⲉ ⲉϫⲛ-, *about, over* intr: Ps 9
23 *B*(*S* ⲧⲁⲉⲓⲟ) ⲉⲡ., Ge 12 15 *SB*, Lu 16 8 *B*(*S* =
Gk), HL 85 *B* ⲉⲧϣ. ⲉϫⲱⲟⲩ opp ϯ ϣⲱϣ ⲉⲡ. acc; tr
(refl): Pro 25 14 *S*(var ϩⲛ-)*A*, Ro 5 2 *S*(*B* ϧⲉⲛ-) ⲕ.
ἐπί, ib 11 18 *SBF* (var ϩⲓϫⲛ-)*B* ⲕⲁⲧⲁⲕ.
gen; Job 3 14 *B*(*S* ϫⲓⲥⲉ) ἀγαυριᾶν ἐπί; Miss 8 127
S ⲉϣϣ. ⲙⲙⲟϥ ⲉϫⲛⲟⲩⲛⲟϭ ⲛⲡⲁⲓϫⲉⲩⲥⲓⲥ αὐχεῖν acc;
Cant 8 5 *S* ἐπιστηρίζειν ἐπί; 1 Cor 4 6 *S*(*B* ϭⲓⲥⲓ)
φυσιοῦν ὑπέρ; R 1 4 15 *S* ⲛⲉϥϣ. ⲙⲙⲟϥ ⲉϫⲛⲧⲉϥ-
ϭⲟⲙ sibi applaudere; ⲉϩⲣⲁⲓ, -ⲏⲓ ⲉϫ.: Jud 7 2 *S* ⲕ.
ⲉⲡⲓ, 2 Cor 5 12 *B*(*S* ϩⲁ-) καύχημα ὑπ.; C 43 10 *B*
wicked ϣ. ⲙⲙⲱⲟⲩ ⲉϩ. ⲉϫⲱⲓ; ⲉ ϩⲓ-, *upon*: Si 30
2 *S* ⲕ. ⲉⲡⲓ; ⲉ ϩⲛ-, ϧⲉⲛ-, *in*: 1 Kg 2 10 *SB*, Jer 9
24 *S*(*B* ⲛϩⲣⲏⲓ ϧⲉⲛ-) ⲕ. ἐν, Ps 5 12 *SB* ⲕ. ⲉⲡⲓ; ib 33
3 *B*(*S* ϫⲓ ⲧⲁⲉⲓⲟ) ⲉⲡ. ⲉⲛ; Jth 9 7 *S* ⲅⲁⲩ. ⲉⲛ; Joel 2 8
A(*B* as Gk) καταβαρύνεσθαι ἐν; BHom 3 *S* εὐφραίνεσθαι; PS 102 *S* ⲉϣ. ⲙⲙⲟⲥ ϩⲙⲡⲁϣⲁⲓ ⲙⲡⲟⲅⲟⲉⲓⲛ,
ShC 73 2 *S* ⲉⲧϣ. ⲙⲙⲟⲟⲩ ϩⲙⲛⲥⲟⲟⲩⲛ, Mani K 23
A² ϣⲟⲩ]ϣⲟⲩ [ⲙ]ⲙⲁⲩ ⲛϩⲏⲧⲟⲩ, C 86 222 *B* ⲧⲉⲛϣ.
ⲙⲙⲟⲛ ⲛϩⲏⲧⲕ; ⲉ ϩⲓⲧⲉⲛ-, *on account of*: PO 11
322 *B* ⲙⲛⲉⲣϣ. ⲙⲙⲱⲧⲉⲛ ϩ.ⲛⲁϣⲁⲓ of possessions.

—— nn m *SAA²BF*, *boast, pride*: Deu 10 21 *SB*,
Pro 11 7 *SAB*, Zeph 3 20 *A* ϣⲁ. *B*, Phil 1 26 *SBF*
καύχημα, Jer 12 13 *SB*-χησις; Ps 21 4 *B*(*S* ⲧⲁⲉⲓⲟ),
Ro 2 29 *B*(*S* do) ἔπαινος; Lev 26 19 *S* gloss on
ϭⲱϣ (*B* & var om), Ez 30 6 *SB* ὕβρις; Job 13 12
γαυρίαμα; 1 Pet 2 20 *B*(*S* ⲉⲟⲟⲩ) κλέος; EstE 12 *S*
ὑπερηφανία; Ez 24 25 *B* ἔπαρσις; Va 63 80 *B* ⲡⲁⲓⲡⲉ ⲡⲁϣ. πλεόνεκτημα; Eccl 2 8 *S* περιουσιασμός;
Va 57 193 *B* τῦφος; 2 Kg 2 26 *S* ϣⲁⲃⲟⲗ ⲉⲅϣ. εἰς
νῖκος; 1 Tim 5 13 *S*-ϣⲟ (*B* = Gk) φλύαρος; Aeg
272 *S*-ϣⲟ ἀλαζονεύειν, ib 281 *S*(varr -ϣⲟ sic *l*, ⲙⲁ-
ⲗⲁⲕⲟⲥ, cf R 1 3 71 below) κίναιδος = PO 8 646
رٔوت; CA 110 *S* ⲛϣ. ⲛⲧⲡⲟⲗⲓⲥ is church, El 66 *A*
ⲛϣ. ⲙⲡⲕⲟⲥⲙⲟⲥ = Budge *Bibl Texts* 270 *S*, Mani 1
A² ⲛϣ. ⲛⲛⲁⲓⲱⲛ, Mor 50 65 *S* ⲙⲡⲉⲡⲉϣϣ.(sc corpse's)
ⲃⲱⲗ ⲉⲃⲟⲗ ⲁⲗⲗⲁ ⲡⲉϥⲧⲙⲁⲉⲓⲏⲩ, DeV 2 37 *B* ⲡⲁⲅϭⲁⲕ
ⲉϩⲣⲏⲓ ⲉϫⲱⲥⲡⲉ ϧⲉⲛⲣⲁⲡϣ., Mich 550 42 *S* Mary
ⲧϣ. ⲙⲡⲉⲛⲅⲉⲛⲟⲥ; as adj, *superb, proud*: Si 45 13
S καύχημα; Hab 2 5 *A* ϣⲁ.(*B* ⲡⲁϣⲉ ⲡⲉϥⲟⲩⲟⲓ) ἀλαζών, Aeg 272 *S* ⲧⲙⲛⲧϫⲁⲥⲓϩⲏⲧ ⲡⲓϣⲟⲩϣⲟ ἀλαζονεύειν; Gal 5 26 *S* -ϣⲟ (*B* diff) κενόδοξος; ShBM

200 288 *S* ϩⲟⲓⲧⲉ ⲛϣ., P 131³ 83 *S* sim -ϣⲟ = Va 61
94 *B*, R 1 3 71 *S* ⲙⲛ ⲭⲁⲣⲓⲥ ⲛϣ. ϩⲓⲧⲉϥϩⲃⲥⲱ (cf Mt
11 8 μαλακός).

ⲙⲁⲓϣ. *S*, *loving adornment*: BMis 143 women
ⲛ.ⲛ.

ⲙⲛⲧϣⲟⲩϣⲟ, -ϣⲟⲩ *S*, -ϣⲁⲓϣⲟ *A*, *pride, impudence*: Phil 2 3 -ϣⲟⲩ (*B* ⲙⲁⲓⲱⲟⲩ ⲉϥϣⲟⲩⲓⲧ), Mor
37 100 κενοδοξία; 1 Jo 2 16 -ϣⲟⲩ(*B* ⲙⲉⲧⲣⲉϥϭⲓ ⲡⲣⲟ)
ἀλαζονεία; Est C 13 ὑπερήφανος; Cl 49 5 *A* βάναυ-
σος; PS 257 ⲙⲛⲧϫⲁⲥⲓϩⲏⲧ, ⲙ., ShC 42 143 who
have left us ϩⲓⲧⲉⲛ ⲙ., ShP 130¹ 37 who deny misdeeds ϩⲛⲟⲩ ⲙ., Pey Gr 163 if art ashamed (to sacrifice)ⲕⲁⲧⲁ ⲟⲩ ⲙ., BHom 61 ϩⲉⲛ ⲙ.(sic)ⲡⲉ ⲡⲉⲓ ϩⲃⲏⲩⲉ.

ⲣ ϣ., *boast*: 2 Cor 7 14 *SB* ⲕⲁⲩ.; ⲟ ⲛϣ.: Zeph
3 20 *B*(*A* ϩⲟⲟⲡ ⲛϣ.) καύχημα; 3 Jo 10 *S* (*B* = Gk)
φλυαρεῖν; ShBMOr 8810 481 *S* ⲟ ⲛϣⲟⲩϣⲟ ⲙⲡⲉⲡⲉⲛⲣⲏⲩ, C 89 160 *B* ⲉϥⲟⲓ ⲛϣ. ⲛϩⲁⲛⲟⲩⲟⲛ *object
of pride*.

ϯ ϣ., *glorify*: BKU 1 31 (5) *S* ⲉⲛϯ. ⲡⲁⲛ ⲉⲛϯ
ⲉⲟⲟⲩ ⲙⲡⲉⲛⲭⲥ ⲫⲁⲣⲁⲱ.

ⲣⲉϥϣ. *S*, *boaster*: BMis 338 ⲣ. (var ⲛϣⲟⲩϣⲟ)
ⲡⲣⲉϥϥⲟⲟⲛⲉⲓ; ⲙⲛⲧⲣⲉϥϣⲟⲩϣⲟ: ShC 73 115.

ϣⲟⲩϣⲟⲩ *v* ϣⲱϣ *scatter & make equal*.

ϣⲟⲩϣⲱⲟⲩⲓ *B*, -ϣⲁⲩϣⲓ *F* *v* ϣⲟⲩⲥⲟⲟⲩϣⲉ.

ϣⲟⲩⲉϥⲉ *v* ϣⲟⲩⲏⲏⲃ.

ϣⲱⲟⲩϩ *v* ϣⲱⲃϩ (where prob vb, not nn).

ϣⲟⲩϩⲏⲛⲉ, -ϩⲏⲡⲓ *v* ϩⲏⲡⲉ.

ϣ ⲫⲏⲣ *B* *v* ϣⲃⲏⲣ.

ϣ ⲫⲏⲣⲓ *B* *v* ϣⲡⲏⲣⲉ.

ϣ ⲫⲓⲧ *B* *v* ϣⲓⲡⲉ *sf*.

ϣⲓϫϥ *A²* nn m, meaning uncertain: Mani 1
ⲧ]ϯⲉ ⲛⲫⲩⲥⲓⲥ ... ⲛⲉⲧⲁⲩⲉⲣϭⲉ ϩⲙⲡⲉⲩⲛⲟⲩⲡ ... they
thought to break bond (of net), ⲉⲩⲟⲩⲱϣⲉ ⲁ[..]
ⲁⲛⲉⲩϣ. Prob for ϣⲓⲕϥ, *v* ϣⲱⲕϩ (ϣⲓⲕϩ).

ϣⲁϣ *B*, ϣⲉϣ *F* *v* ϭⲱϣ *strike* (ϭⲁϣ).

ϣⲁϣ (mostly), ϣⲁϣⲧ, -ϣϥ, -ϣϥⲧ (each twice)*B*
nn as pl: K 156 ⲛϣϣ. among parts of building كُتُب
(*door-posts* or *leaves of door*, but *l* شرافات acc to
Sobhy), دروز (? *projecting parts*, ? *balcony*, but K
latrines). Cf Ryl Dem 3 395 & ? ϣⲉϣⲓ, also Lab
5 44 *sv*.

ϣⲁϣ *Sᵃ* nn m, meaning unknown: CO 350
ⲉϣⲱⲡⲉ ⲟⲩⲟⲛ ϫⲁⲕ ⲙⲙⲁⲩ ϫⲟⲟⲩ ⲟⲩⲕⲟⲩⲓ ⲛⲁⲓ ⲁϥ-
ⲉⲗⲱ (cf ⲧⲉⲗⲗⲱ) ⲛⲧⲁϣⲱⲡ ⲛϣ. ϣⲁⲛϣⲁⲩ ⲛⲡⲭⲟⲩⲧ
ⲛⲉⲧⲟⲡ. Cf ? ϣⲱϣ *twist*.

ϣⲁϣ *Sᵃ*, ϣⲉϣ *F* nn, a vessel or liquid measure:
Cai ostr 47405 ⲥⲛⲁⲩ ⲛⲁⲕⲕⲏⲛ (ἀγγεῖον) ⲙⲡⲟⲩϣ.

ⲧⲉⲗⲁϫ (الص in Fayyûm), BM 697 *F* among wine, vinegar, oil ϣ. ⲧⲗⲁϫ (*bis*), wine of Telaj, *v* Ep 1 162 n. *Cf* ϣⲟϣⲟⲩ (WS 119).

ϣⲁⲓϣ *F*, ϣⲱⲓϣ *B*   *v* ⲥⲟⲉⲓϣ *pair*.

ϣⲓϣ *B*   *v* ⲉⲣϣⲓϣ.

ϣⲟⲉⲓϣ *S*, ϣⲁ. *Sᵃ*, ϣⲟⲓϣ *SO*, ϧⲁⲉⲓϧ *A*, ϣⲱⲓϣ *B*, ϣⲁⲓϣ *F*, nn m, *dust* (*cf* ϣϣⲱϣ *scatter*): Deu 9 21 *S*(var ϣⲟⲩⲉⲓϣ)*B*, Is 10 6 *B*(*S* ϣⲣⲓⲥ), Ep Jer 13 *BF*, Nah 1 3 *SAB* κονιορτός; Ps 77 27 *S*(*B* ⲕⲁϩⲓ), Mk 6 11 *SB* χοῦς; Ps 1 4 *S*(*B* ⲣⲏⲓⲥⲓ), Is 5 24 *S*(*B* do, *F* ⲑⲉⲙⲓⲥ) χνοῦς; Ja 4 14 *B*(*S* ⲗⲟⲟⲩ) ἀτμίς; Ez 27 30 *B*(*S* ⲉⲓⲧⲛ) γῆ; Lam 4 5 *S*(ViK 919, var & *F* ⲉⲓ., *B* = Gk) κοπρία; PS 317 *S* ⲝⲁϥ, ϣ., ⲁⲣⲟϣ coming from dragon's mouth, *ib* 187 *S* distant world as it were ⲟⲩⲛⲁⲡⲡⲉ ⲛϣⲟⲓϣ, ShC 73 147 *S* ⲛϣ. ⲙⲛⲛⲟⲉⲓⲧ, ShA 1 236 *S* keep himself from ⲡⲉⲓϣ. ⲙⲡⲟⲛⲏⲣⲟⲛ, PSBA 10 196 *S* ⲧⲁⲥⲡⲁⲍⲉ ⲙⲡϣ. ⲙⲡⲟⲅⲣⲏⲧⲉ of your holiness, CO 93 *Sᵃ* sim, C 86 215 *B* ⲛⲓⲕⲁⲥ, ⲡⲓⲁϧⲟⲩⲓ, ⲡⲓϣ. of corpse, DeV 2 44 *B* ⲡϣ. ⲙⲡⲓⲕⲉⲣⲙⲓ, PMéd 233 *S* ϧⲉⲛ(ϧⲉⲗ)ⲙⲓⲥ (ἕλμις) called ⲧⲙⲟⲥ ϣ. (*sic l*), AZ 21 100 *O* ⲛⲥⲓ...ⲉⲧϣⲟⲩ (?) ϫⲁϣⲟⲓϣ;   ⲣ ϣ., *become dust*: BHom 119 *S* dead limbs ⲁⲩⲣ.ϧⲛⲡⲧⲁⲫⲟⲥ, Va 61 109 *B* corpse ⲁϥⲗⲟϥⲗⲉϥ ⲉⲃⲟⲗ ⲉⲁϥⲉⲣ., Hall 64 *S* swollen eyes ⲉⲩⲟ ⲛϣⲟ[ⲉ]ⲓϣ (*sic l*) *granulated lids* (?); ϫⲓ ϣ., *become dusty*: El 78 *A* market-places ⲛⲁϫ., Mor 31 232 *S* ark ⲁϭⲝ. ϧⲓϫⲙⲡⲧⲟⲟⲩ = BMOr 3599 104 بالغبار تلف; ⲣⲉϥϣ., *one who is dusty* (?): Tri 527 *S* who neglect judgment & ϣⲱⲡⲉ ⲛⲣ. ϧⲁⲣⲁⲧⲉ ⲛⲁⲡⲩⲗⲏ متربين (var وابين, *l ?* or نو', or *l*-ϣⲱϣ); as title: Osir pl 37 *S* supra ⲙⲱⲥⲛⲉ ⲛϣ.

ϣⲟⲓϣ *B* vb qual, meaning unknown: C 43 188 demon like ⲉⲟⲱϣ ⲛϩⲣⲟ ⲛⲑⲏⲣⲓⲟⲛ ⲉϥϣ. Or. *? l* ϣⲟⲓ (*v* ϣⲓⲁⲓ).

ϣⲟϣ *SB*, ϣⲁϣ *Sᶠ* ϣⲱϣ, ϣⲟϣⲟⲩ *B*, pl ϣⲟⲟϣ(?) *S* nn m f, *kind of antelope, hartebeest* (bubalis buselaphus): Deu 14 5 *SB* βούβαλος ثيتل (3 Kg 4 23 β. var of δορκάς), MG 25 235 *B* ⲧϣ. β. = Gött ar 114 96 بقرة (*ib* بقر وحش); Va 61 24 *B* ⲧϣ. ἔλαφος; BM 298 *S* ⲥⲩⲗⲁ ⲛϣ. ⲉⲡⲙⲁ ⲛⲛⲃⲟⲩⲕⲟⲗⲟⲥ β. = Bargès *Hom s St Marc* 68, Synax 2 97, PO 1 146 (*sic l*) ثيتل = *Horae Sem* 3 129 جاموس, P 54 141 *B* ⲡⲓϣⲟϣⲟⲩ (var K 165 ϣⲟ.) 'ﺝ; K *lc* ϣⲟϣ *B* وبر; P 129¹⁴ 104 *S* church at ⲧⲁ ⲃⲟⲩⲕⲟⲗⲟⲥ ⲉⲧⲉⲡⲙⲁ ⲛⲛϣⲟⲟϣⲛⲉ τοῖς βουκόλοις (but *l* prob ϣⲟⲟⲥ); C 89 2 *B* ⲁϥ ⲛϣ. eaten by labourers = MG 17 340 خ مطبوخ لحم (*cf* ϫⲱϫ, ϭⲱϭ); ShA 2 129 *S* hunted ϧⲏⲧⲟⲟⲩ, R 1 3 5 *S* Aphou dwelt with ⲛϣ. ϧⲛⲧⲉⲣⲏⲙⲟⲥ (*cf* ROC 12 181 § 62), *ib* 16 *S* ⲛϣ. ⲁⲧⲉⲧⲛϭⲟⲡϥ, BIF 13 113 *S* ⲙⲁⲥ ⲛϣⲁϣ, Miss 4 761 *Sᶠ* ϧ(ⲉ)ⲛϣ. ⲙⲡⲉⲥⲛⲧ ⲉⲩⲉⲓⲁ, *ib*

762 *Sᶠ* Apa Aphou ⲛϣ., MIF 59 390 *S* ⲁⲛⲟⲩⲡ ⲛϣ. (*bubalus* = vagrant ascete *Zeits f Kircheng* 1923 35).

ϣⲟϣ *S* nn m, meaning unknown: Mor 46 54 εὐκτήριον of Phoebammon at ⲛϣ. on south of Antinoe.

ϣⲟⲩϣ *F* nn m, meaning unknown: BKU 1 26 (8116 b)]ⲟⲩ ⲛⲁⲣϣϥ ⲉⲃⲟⲗ ⲙⲉ(*l* ⲙ)ⲛⲧϥϣ. (ⲛ)ⲧⲟⲩϣⲁⲩ[ⲉⲓ]. Part of cooked bird (? ⲛⲟⲩⲣⲓ) used in recipe.

ϣⲱϣ *SBF*, ϧⲱϣ *A*, ϣⲟϣⲟⲩ *S*(*Sᶠ* ?), ϣⲉϣ- *SBF*, ϣⲁϣ- *B*, ϣⲁϣ⸗, ϣⲟϣ⸗ *SB*, ϣⲏϣⲧ *SA²BF* vb **I** intr, *scatter, spread* esp of odour & by wind (? same as next word): Is 17 13 *SB* λικμᾶν; C 86 70 *B* ⲟⲩⲗⲓⲃⲁⲛⲟⲥ ⲉϥϣ. πνεῖν; Cant 4 10 *S* καλλιοῦσθαι; Hos 14 7 *A*(*SB* Gk diff, *l* ? ϧⲱⲡⲉ); Tri 309 *S* perfume ϣ. till it filled garden فاح; P 50 87 *B* ⲡⲏ ⲉⲧϣ. (K 115 ⲉⲧϣⲟⲩⲓϣ) مذربين; ShC 42 105 *S* perfume ϣ. ⲉⲟⲩⲟⲉⲣⲏⲡⲉ ⲛⲓⲙ, Mor 50 15 *S* saint ϣⲟⲩϣⲟⲩ ⲉϧⲟⲩⲟ ⲉⲧⲟⲩⲏⲣⲧ ⲙⲡⲛⲕⲁⲥⲓⲁ (*l* prob ⲛⲟⲩ. ⲙⲛⲧⲕ., though *v* p 490 *a* 15); Am 9 9 *B* ⲙⲁⲛⲥⲁⲗⲉ ⲛϣ.(*SA* diff)λικμός; ShP 130⁵ 15 *S* ϧⲛⲗⲁⲁⲩ ⲛϣ. separates corn & chaff; qual: Va 57 33 *B* ⲟⲩⲡⲉⲗⲁⲧⲟⲥ ⲉϥϣ. τεταμένος; Miss 4 695 *S* if impure his prayers & fasts ⲥⲉϣ. ⲧⲏⲣⲟⲩ (or *l* ⲥⲛϣ), JKP 2 134 *F* ϫⲉⲓⲡⲛⲱⲡ ⲉⲧϣ. (do?) **II** tr: Ru 3 2 *S*, Is 30 22 *B*(*SF* ϫⲱⲱⲣⲉ ⲉⲃⲟⲗ) λι.; Ps 143 5 *B* ϣ. χⲣⲉⲙⲧⲥ (*S* ⲧ ⲕⲁⲡⲛⲟⲥ) καπνίζειν; Mic 4 13 *S*(ShA 1 385)*A*(*B* ⲃⲱⲗ ⲉⲃⲟⲗ) λεπτύνειν; 2 Kg 22 43 *S* λεαίνειν; Is 30 14 *F*(*S* ⲥⲱⲣⲡ, *B* ⲱϣⲧ) ἀποσύρειν (var ⲥⲩⲣⲓⲍⲉⲓⲛ, *cf* p 386 *b sup*); Tri 639 *S* ϣⲉϣ ⲛⲉⲡϫⲡⲟⲟⲩ ذرى; *ib* 640 sim درس; *ib* 425 ϣⲉϣ ⲥⲧⲃⲱⲛ 'ﺝ; *ib* 272 *S* ϣ. ⲛⲟⲩⲛⲟϭ ⲛⲥⲧⲟⲓ تأرّج; Mor 55 80 *S* gather corn ⲛⲧϣⲟϣϥ & make bread.

With following preposition. ⲥ ⲉ-*S*: Ez 29 12(*B* ⲫⲱⲛ λι. εἰς; ⲥ ⲉϫⲛ-: Job 2 12 *S*(*B* ⲧⲁⲗⲟ), Mic 1 10 *SA*(*B* ⲉⲃⲟⲗ ϧⲓϫⲉⲛ-)καταπάσσειν acc; Jth 4 11 *S* ϣ.(var ⲕⲱ)ⲕⲣⲙⲉⲥ σποδοῦσθαι acc; Jos 7 6 *S* ἐπιβάλλειν ἐπί; ShA 2 334 *S* ⲛⲧⲁⲛϣⲉϣ...ⲕⲁϩ ⲉϫⲱⲛ, C 86 115 *B* ϣⲉϣ ⲕⲉⲣⲙⲓ ⲉϫⲱϥ; ⲥ ⲙⲛ-, ⲡⲉⲙ-: Si 5 11 *S* λι. ἐν; ShC 42 48 *S* insects ϣⲁϣ. ⲙⲛⲡⲧⲏⲩ, Mun 137 *S* ϣ. ⲛⲛⲉⲧϣⲁϫⲉ ⲙⲛⲡⲧⲏⲩ, C 86 233 *B* ϣⲁϣ ⲧⲉϥⲕⲉⲣⲙⲓ ⲛⲉⲙⲡⲓⲑⲏⲩ; ⲥ ⲛ-*B*: Is 30 24 (*SF* ⲧⲃⲃⲟ)λι. ἐν; ⲥⲁⲃⲟⲗ ⲛ-: Ez 26 4 λι. ἀπό; ⲥ ϧⲓ-*A*: Hos 7 1 (*B* Gk diff, *cf* בשד); ⲥ ϧⲉⲛ- (for ⲉⲃⲟⲗ ϧ.)*B*: TEuch 2 296 ⲁⲩϣⲱϣⲉⲛ ϧⲉⲛⲧⲫⲉ طرد من.

With following adverb. ⲥ ⲉⲃⲟⲗ *SA²BF*, *scatter abroad* intr: BMis 241 *S* perfume ϣ. ⲉⲃ. πνεῖν; Deu 4 49 *B* ⲫⲓⲟⲙ ⲫⲏ ⲉⲧϣ.ⲧ ⲉⲃ. (var ⲛⲧⲉ ⲡϣⲁϥⲉ) Gk om المنتنة; Mun 38 *S* martyr's limbs ϣ. ⲉⲃ. ⲛⲟⲉ ⲛⲟⲩϣⲟⲉⲓϣ = C 86 283 *B* ⲉⲣ ⲙⲫⲣⲏⲧ ⲛⲟⲩϣⲟⲓϣ, Mor 31 131 *S* perfume ϣ. ⲉⲃ. (var Wess 15 4 ϣⲟⲩϣⲟⲩ), BSM 110 *B* stench ϣ. ⲉⲃ., Mor 23

62 *S* your flesh ⲛⲁϣ. ⲉⲃ. ϩⲙⲡⲥⲧⲟⲓ *shall spread perfume*, ShMIF 23 30 *S* to devil ⲕϣⲁⲁⲧ ⲕϣ.† ⲉⲃ. ⲛⲁⲣⲁ ⲡϩⲟϥ(or ? = next word, *cf* Ge 3 14), Bess 7 9 *B* ointment (Mt 26 7) may prevail when sins ϣ. ⲉⲃ. ⲙⲡⲉϥⲙⲑⲟ, Miss 4 727 *S* sim, ManiH 63 *A*²]ⲡⲏϫ ⲉϥϣ.† ⲁⲃ.; tr: Sa 5 24 *S*, Jer 38 10 *S*(ShA 2 339, *B* ϫⲱⲣ ⲉⲃ.), Mt 21 44 *SB* λι.; Cant 5 13 *S* φύειν; BMis 243 *S* ἐκπέμπειν; Mic 1 10 *v* c ⲉϫⲛ-; ShMIF 23 67 *S* ϣⲁϣϥ ⲉⲃ. like dust, Sh(?)ViK 916 359 *S* pagans ϣⲉϣ λιⲃⲉ ⲉⲃ., C 86 258 *B* ϣⲉϣ ⲥⲑⲟⲓ ⲛⲟⲩϥⲓ ⲉⲃ.; ⲉⲃ. ⲉ-*B*, *extend to*: AM 277 ϯϭⲉλλⲟⲧ ⲉⲧϣ.† ⲉⲃ. ⲉⲫⲙⲁ ⲛⲛⲓⲙϩⲁⲩ κοιλὰς ὅπου τὰ μνημεῖα (or ? = next word); ⲉⲃ. ⲙⲛ-, ⲛⲉⲙ-: Jer 30 32 *B*(*S* ϩⲛ-) λι. dat; HM 1 108 *S* ϣⲉϣ ⲡⲉϥⲕⲣⲙⲉⲥ ⲉⲃ. ⲙⲛⲛⲧⲏⲩ; ⲉⲃ. ϩⲁ- *S*: Tob 6 17 ϣⲉϣ ⲥⲧⲟⲓ ⲉⲃ. ϩⲁⲣⲟⲟⲩ καπνίζ. only; ⲉⲃ. ϩⲓ-, *from*: MIE 2 402 *B* odours ϣ. ⲉⲃ. ϩⲓⲛⲓⲥⲱⲙⲁ, AZ 33 55 *S*^f sim ϣ. ⲉⲃ. ϩⲓⲡⲁλλⲱⲛ; ⲉⲃ. ϩⲛ-, ϧⲉⲛ-, *forth from*: Job 27 21 *B* λι. ἐκ; ShViK 913 *S* every place whence ⲥⲧⲟⲉⲓ ϣ. ⲉⲃ. ⲛϩⲏⲧⲟⲩ, DeV 2 129 *B* perfume ϣ. ⲉⲃ. ϧⲉⲛⲡⲓⲙⲁ, BMis 68 *S* perfume ⲛⲁϣⲟⲩϣⲟⲩ ⲉⲃ. ϩⲙⲡⲟⲩⲥⲱⲙⲁ (var FR 34 ϣ. ⲉⲃ.), Mor 50 15 *S* his name ϣⲟⲩϣⲟⲩ ⲉⲃ. ϩⲛⲣⲱϥ ⲛⲟⲩⲟⲛ ⲛⲓⲙ.

ⲣⲉϥϩ. *A*, *winnower*: Pro 20 26 (*S* ⲣⲉϥϩⲓ) λικμήτωρ.

ϣⲱϣ *B* nn f, *fork* or *rake* separating grain from chaff: K 127 ϯϣ. مذراة (next ϭⲁⲓ). *Cf* BIF 20 72 n.

ϣⲱϣ *S*(*A*²)*BF*, ⲥⲱϣⲉ *S*(once), ϣⲟⲩϣⲟⲩ *S*^f (*v* c ⲉⲃⲟλ), ϩⲱϩ *A* (nn), ϣⲉϣ- *SB*, ϣⲁϣ- *S*^f, ϣⲁϣ⸗, ϣⲟϣ⸗ *SB*, ϩⲁϩ⸗ *A*, ϣⲉϣ⸗ *F*, ϣⲏϣ† *SA*²*BF*, ⲥⲏϣ† *S* (Sh), ϩⲏϩ† *A* vb tr, *make equal*, *level*, *straight* (? same as last word): Is 28 25 *SB*(var ⲉⲣ ϩⲓⲥⲟⲛ), *ib* 45 2 *B*(*S* ⲥλⲟϭλⲉϭ) ὁμαλίζειν; JTS 10 392 *S* ⲁϥϣⲁϣϥ ϩⲛⲛⲉⲕλⲏⲣⲟⲥ, Miss 4 93 *B* soldier ϣ. ⲙⲡⲉϥⲥⲟⲑⲛⲉϥ with left hand whilst right ready to draw (bow) = Mor 19 4 *S* ϣ. ⲥⲟⲧⲉ; qual(*B* rare): Si 21 11 ὁμ., Va 63 90 *B* ⲡⲓⲥⲛⲟⲩ ⲉⲧⲉⲛⲥⲉϣ. ⲁⲛ καιρῷ ἀνωμαλίας; Mor 37 54 ⲛⲉϥϣ. as if reason guided him ἴσος εἶναι; Z 313 carry in plank ⲉϥϣ. ἐπ' εὐθείας; Lev 26 21 neg (*B* ⲣⲁⲕⲓ) πλάγιος; PS 238 ⲛⲥⲉϣ. ⲁⲛ ϩⲛⲧⲙⲛⲧⲉⲣⲟ, BG 97 ⲥⲉϣ. opp ⲥⲉϣⲟⲃⲉ, ShBor 233 246 ⲥⲙⲏ ⲉⲥϣ. ⲉⲥϣⲏⲩ, R 2 1 12 ⲁϣ ⲡⲉⲧϣ. ϩⲙⲡⲟⲩϫⲓⲥⲉ O Virgin?, Mor 23 63 ⲟⲩϩⲓⲏ ⲉⲥϣ. καλως, J 99 6 testament ⲉⲧϣ. ⲉⲧⲃⲉⲃⲁⲓⲟⲩ ϩⲛⲟⲩϩⲱⲃ ⲛⲟⲩⲱⲧ (*cf* ? ὁμότυπος Steinwenter), Hall 61 *inf* ⲉϣⲱⲡⲉ ⲡϩⲱⲃ ϣ. ⲧⲛⲛⲟⲟⲩ ⲡϫⲱⲕ ⲛⲁⲓ, DeV 1 57 *B* ⲙⲁϣⲓ ⲉⲧϣ. ⲡⲁⲧⲣⲓⲕⲓ, Kr 129 *F* ἀριθ β...ⲉⲧϣ., BMOr 6203 ϣⲟⲙⲉⲧ ⲡϩⲟλⲟⲕ/ ⲉⲩϣ. ⲉⲩⲟ ⲛⲛⲉⲩϣⲉⲓ, BKU 1 25 *ro* to be done when moon ⲙⲟⲩϩ ⲉϥϣ. *hath grown to full*(?).

With following preposition.

—— ⲉ- *S*: ShViK 9028 ⲡⲉⲧϣⲣϣⲟⲣⲧ ⲁⲩⲱ ⲉⲧⲥⲏϣ ⲉⲡⲕⲁϩ, BMOr 6201 A 38 of vines ⲧⲁⲧⲁⲁⲩ ⲉⲡⲕⲁϣ ⲧⲁϣⲁϣⲟⲩ ⲉⲡⲕⲁ[ϩ, Cai 42573 2 do this ⲉⲣⲉⲡⲣⲉϣ.† ⲉⲧⲙⲉⲧⲉ ⲛⲧⲡⲉ (*cf* BKU above).

—— ⲙⲛ- intr *SF*(*B* once): Ge 30 8 (*B* diff) συναναστρέφεσθαι dat; R 1 4 26 ⲧⲣⲉⲧⲉϥⲁⲡⲉ ϣ. ⲙⲡⲕⲁϩ *coaequare* dat; PS 233 ⲥⲉⲛⲁϣ. ⲡⲙⲙⲏⲧⲛ, SHel 1 perfume of ⲧⲉⲩⲡⲣⲟⲥⲫⲟⲣⲁ ϣ. ⲙⲡⲧⲁⲡⲙⲡⲏⲩⲉ (or ? ϣ. *spread abroad*), DeV 2 84 *B* fire (flames) ϣ. ⲛⲉⲙⲡⲓⲡⲁλⲁⲧⲓⲟⲛ all but a cubit, LAp 526 *F* head of pillar ϣ. ⲙⲡⲕⲉϩⲓ = Gu 21 *S*(*sic l*); qual: Ex 26 24 *SB*, Ez 40 5 *S*(*B* = Gk), Mk 14 56 *S*(*B* do) ἴσος, Phil 2 20 *B*(*S* ⲡⲏⲩ ⲉϩⲛ-), Aeg 211 *S* nights ϣ. ⲙⲛⲛⲉϩⲟⲟⲩ, Va 66 304 *B* ⲡⲓⲧⲁⲓⲟ ⲉⲧϣ. ⲛⲉⲙⲛⲓⲁⲅⲅⲉλⲟⲥ ἰσο-, Zech 4 7 *SA*(*B* do) ἰσότης, Si 9 12 *S* ἔφισος, Ex 37 15 *B* ἐξισοῦν; Ez 40 18 *S*(*B* ⲉⲣ ϩⲓⲥⲟⲥ ⲛⲉⲙ-) κατά; ShC 73 7 *S* their impiety ϣ. (var ⲥⲏϣ) ⲙⲛⲧⲟⲣⲅⲏ (Jo 3 36), ShCai 8007 *S* shall dwell with ⲛⲉⲧϣ. ⲛⲙⲙⲁⲩ, Leyd 175 *S* lections ϣ. ⲙⲛⲛⲉⲩⲉⲣⲏⲩ ⲉⲩⲥⲩⲙⲫⲱⲛⲓ ϩⲓⲟⲩⲥⲟⲡ, C 86 92 *B* ⲥⲉϣ. ⲛⲉⲙⲛⲟⲩⲉⲣⲏⲟⲩ; tr *S*(*B* once): Is 51 23 ⲥⲱϣⲉ (*B*†) ἴσ. τιθέναι dat, Mt 20 12 (*B* ⲉⲣ ϩⲓⲥⲟⲥ) ἴσ. ποι. dat, Phil 2 6 (*B* as Gk) ἴσ. εἶναι (cit BMOr 6807(5) ⲛ-), Si 35 9 ϣⲁϣⲕ (var ϣⲟ.) ἐξισάζειν; Lam 2 2 (ShC 73 77, *B* ϫⲱλⲉϫ) κολλᾶν εἰς; P 131⁵ 100 Joseph burying Jesus ⲁⲕϣ. ⲛⲛⲉϥϭⲓϫ ⲙⲛⲛⲉϥⲥⲡⲓⲣⲟⲟⲩⲉ = Mus 34 203 *B* ϣ. ⲉϧⲣⲏⲓ περιστέλλειν; 2 Cor 10 12 (*B* ϣⲓ), *ib* (*B* ⲑⲟⲛⲧⲉⲛ) συγκρίνειν dat; ShA 1 373 ϯⲛⲁϣⲁϣⲧ ⲙⲛⲛⲡⲉ, BMis 323 ⲉⲧⲣⲁϣⲟϣⲧ ⲙⲛⲛⲉⲛⲧⲁⲡⲡⲉ ϭⲟⲓλⲉ ⲉⲣⲟϥ = Mor 27 4 *F* ϣⲉϣⲧ ⲙⲛ- = BSM 6 *B* ⲧⲉⲛⲑⲱⲛⲧ ⲉ-, Mor 41 53 *S*^f ⲙⲉⲥϣⲁϣ ⲡⲉⲥϣⲁϫⲉ ⲙⲛⲡⲱϥ, Bor 248 52 ϣⲉϣ ⲡⲉϥⲥⲡⲉⲣⲙⲁ ⲙⲛⲧⲙⲛⲧλⲁⲙⲡⲣⲟⲥ of stars.

—— ⲛ- dat *S*: Ryl 344 workmen (ⲙ)ⲡⲉⲟⲩ(ⲁ) ⲉⲣ ⲟⲩϩⲱϥ ⲉϥϣ.† ⲛⲁⲓ *satisfactory to me*(?).

—— ⲟⲩⲃⲉ- *S*: Ps 88 6 (*B* ⲉⲣ ϩⲓ.) ἰσοῦν dat, R 2 2 21 ⲥⲉϣ.† ⲟⲩⲃⲉⲛⲉⲩⲉⲣⲏⲩ ἰσοστάσιος; PS 7 ⲉϥϣ.† ⲟⲩⲃⲏϥ ϩⲙⲡⲉⲓⲟⲩⲟⲉⲓϣ.

With following adverb.

—— ⲉⲃⲟλ *SBF*: BMis 58 *S* hills ϣ.† ⲉⲃ. ϩⲓⲟⲛ ⲙⲙⲟⲟⲩ...ⲉⲩϣ.† ⲉⲃⲟλ ⲉⲛⲉⲩⲟⲩⲉⲣⲏⲧⲉ, Mor 50 19 *S* fallen stele set up again ⲉⲥϣⲟⲩϣⲟⲩ ⲉⲃ., C 86 305 *B* where chasm had gaped earth ϣ. ⲉⲃ. ⲙⲡⲉϥⲣⲏϯ ⲛⲕⲉⲥⲟⲡ, MR 5 48 *F* ϣⲉϣ ⲡⲉⲕϩⲱⲃ ⲉⲃ. ϣⲁⲛⲧⲁⲉⲓ ⲛⲉⲕ *set in order*, Ryl 374 *S* (ⲙ)ⲡⲁⲧⲉⲡϩⲱϥ...ϣ. ⲉⲃ., BM 597 *F* ⲉϣⲱⲡ ⲁⲛ ⲧⲉϣ. ⲉⲃ. bring me the corn; ⲉⲃ. ⲙⲛ-: P 129¹⁶ 58 *S* ⲁⲧⲡⲩλⲏ ϣ. ⲉⲃ. ⲙⲛⲡⲕⲁϩ, Sh(?) Mor 54 69 *S* pray whilst ⲛⲉⲛϭⲓϫ ⲕⲏ ⲉⲃⲟλ ⲙⲡⲁⲧⲟⲩϣⲁϣⲟⲩ ⲉⲃ. ⲛⲙⲙⲁⲛ (var P 131⁵ 58 ϣ. ⲉϩⲣⲁⲓ, *cf* above περιστέλλειν), Mor 30 37 *F* to ox ⲡⲉⲕⲧⲏⲛ ⲉⲩⲉϣ. ⲉⲃ. ⲙⲛⲧⲉⲕⲁⲡⲏ = BMis 262 *S* ⲧⲱⲧ ⲉⲃ. ⲙⲛ-.

—— ⲉϩⲟⲩⲛ, ⲉϧ. *SB*: Mor 37 253 *S* ⲁⲥϣⲉϣ ⲡⲉⲥϩⲟ ⲉϩ. ⲉⲣⲟϥ, *ib* 241 *S* ploughman keeps eye on goal

ϣⲁⲡⲧⲉϥϣ. ⲙⲡⲉϥⲧⲗⲟⲙ ⲉϩ. ⲉϫⲙⲡⲉⲥⲕⲟⲡⲟⲥ, Va 57
37 B ϣ. ⲡⲥⲛⲁⲩ ⲉϭ. ⲉⲡⲟⲩⲉⲣⲛⲟⲩ ⲉⲟⲩⲙⲉⲧⲟⲅⲁⲓ.

—— ⲉϩⲣⲁⲓ, ⲉϭ. *SA²B*: ROC 7 143 *S* ϣ. ⲙⲡⲉϥ
ⲥⲱⲙⲁ ⲉϩ. *lay out corpse*, Mani 1 *A²* ⲡⲣⲱⲙⲉ...ϥϣ.†
ⲁϩ. ⲡⲉⲙⲉ *lying prone*, TstAb 174 *B* ⲁϥϣⲁϣϥ ⲉϭ.
ⲡⲉⲙⲡⲥⲫⲓⲣ ⲡⲁⲑⲣⲁⲁⲙ ⲉϥⲉⲛⲕⲟⲧ.

—— nn m *SAB*, *equality*, *sameness*: Lev 6 40 *S*
(*B* ⲙⲉⲧⲣⲓⲥⲟⲥ) ἴσος, BMOr 6807 (5) *S* ⲡⲉⲓϣ. ⲛⲟⲩⲱⲧ
ἰσότης; Mic 7 12 *SAB* ὁμαλισμός; Si 35 17 *S* σύγ
κριμα; BMar 8 *S* ⲡⲉⲓϣ. ⲛⲟⲩⲱⲧ *shall be to both* (*cf
1 Kg 30 24* μερίς & ShC 73 148), ShA 2 173 *S* others'
sins & own ⲡⲉⲓϣ. ⲛⲟⲩⲱⲧⲡⲉ, *ib 1 405 S all world
seeth sun* ϩⲙⲡⲉⲓϣ. ⲛⲟⲩⲱⲧ, CA 102 *S neglect none*
ⲉⲧⲣⲉⲟⲩϣ. ϣⲱⲡⲉ ϩⲓⲱⲟⲩ, Mor 19 94 *S* ⲛⲧⲉⲣⲉⲛⲡⲱϣ
ⲉⲡϣ. ⲙⲡⲙⲟⲛⲁⲥⲧⲏⲣⲓⲟⲛ *reached level of* = Miss 4
154 *B* ⲙⲡⲉⲙⲑⲟ = Gött ar 114 72 قيل, BMOr 6201
A 168 *S* ⲟⲩⲁϩ ⲛⲓⲥⲟⲓ ⲙⲡⲛⲓϭⲁ ⲉϫⲱⲡϣⲧⲁ ⲡⲡϣ. ⲉⲡⲓ
ⲧⲓⲙⲉ *apportion equally*; adverbial: 3 Kg 22 34 *S*
ⲉⲡϣ. εὐστόχως; Z 273 *S* ϭⲓ ⲣⲟⲟⲩϣ ϩⲛⲟⲩϣ. καλῶς;
Pro 12 13 *A* ϩⲛⲟⲩϭ. (*S* ⲉⲙⲁⲧⲉ, *B* ⲕⲁⲗⲱⲥ) λεῖος (?);
ShC 73 172 *S* ⲡⲉⲧⲣ ϩⲙⲙⲉ ⲙⲙⲟⲟⲩ ϩⲛⲟⲩϣ., Pcod
21 *S pay wage* ϩⲛⲟⲩϣ.; ⲥ ⲉⲃⲟⲗ, *equality*, *level*:
Mor 23 60 *S judgment place* ϩⲁⲡⲡϣ. ⲉϭ. ⲉⲡⲡⲁⲣⲁ
ⲇⲓⲥⲟⲥ ⲉⲡⲉⲙⲛⲧ.

ⲣ ϣ., ⲟⲓ ⲛⲡϣ.: Col 4 1 *S*(*B* ϣ.† ⲡⲉⲙ-) ἰσότητα
παρέχειν, cit ShR 2 3 72 *S*, Ex 26 24 *B* ἐξ ἴσου.

ϣⲟⲱϣ, ϣⲉϣ- *SB*, ϣⲟⲱϣ- *S*, ϣⲛϣⲧ† *SB* vb intr,
twist rope &c: Mus 40 41 *S*(RegPach) ⲛⲛⲉⲩϣ. *funiculum torquere*, *ib* ⲥⲱ ⲉⲩϣ. *juncos ad operandum*;
K 138 *B* فتل, برم; Lev 14 4† *S*(*B* ⲥⲁϯ) κλώθειν; Ez 40
3† *SB*(Gk diff, *cf* OL *resticula tortorum*); tr: RNC
90 *S monk* ⲉϥϣⲱϣ ⲛⲟⲩϩ, BMis 486 *S monk's task*
ⲧⲁⲙⲓⲟ ⲛⲣⲉⲡⲕⲩⲣⲓⲁ (ⲕⲉⲓ.)...ϣⲉϣ ⲛⲟⲩϩ, C 89 37 *B*
ⲉϥϣⲉϣ ⲡⲟϩ, CO 324 *S of rope* ϣⲟⲙⲛⲧ ⲙⲙⲏⲣ...
ϣⲁⲡϣⲟϣ ⲡⲕⲉϣⲟⲙⲛⲧ. *V* also ⲛⲟⲩϩ.

ϣⲁϣϥ *B* nn m, *weaver*: K 110 ⲡⲓϣ. حائك; P 54
157 ⲙⲉⲧϣ. حياكة. *Belongs here* ? or = *ḥsf, spin*
(Dévaud).

ϣⲟⲱϣ *BF* v ⲥⲱϣ *be despised*.

ϣⲁϣⲉ (or ϣⲟ.) *Sᵃ* nn, *meaning unknown*: ST
247 ⲥⲉⲡⲁϯ ⲡⲁⲕ ⲛⲣⲉⲛϣ. ⲕⲁⲧⲁ ϩⲁⲓ (for ϩⲟⲓ). *V* ?
ⲥⲱϣ *strike* (ⲥⲁϣ).

ϣⲁϣⲓ, ϣⲛϣⲓ *B* v ⲥⲱϣ *strike* (ⲥⲁϣ).

ϣⲁϣⲓ *B*, ϣⲓ. *F* v ⲥⲓϣⲉ.

ϣⲁϣⲱ *A* v ϣⲟⲩϣⲟⲩ (ⲙⲡⲧϣ.).

ϣⲉϣⲓ *F* nn f, *meaning unknown*: ViK 11005
ⲁⲓϭⲁⲡ ⲧϣ. ⲛⲡⲉⲣⲱ (*l* ⲛⲡⲣⲟ) ⲛⲧⲁⲁⲧⲃ. *Cf* ? ϣⲁϣ *B*
قبط.

ϣⲟⲱϣⲓ *F* v ⲥⲱϣⲉ nn.

ϣϣⲉ, ⲉϣ. *SAA²*, ϣⲉ *S*, ⲥϣⲉ *S̀AA²B*, ⲥⲛϣϣⲉ *A²*,
(ⲉ)ϣϣⲏⲛ *F*, neg ⲙ(ⲉ)ϣϣⲉ *S*, ⲙⲁ. *A* (also ⲥ ⲡ-...ⲁⲛ)
impers vb, *it is fitting*, *right* (lit ⲥϣⲉ *it goes*): Ac 25
27 *S* ⲛⲟⲩϩⲱⲃ ⲁⲛ ⲉϣ. ⲡⲉ (*B* diff) ἄλογος; PS 381 *S*
ⲟⲩϩⲱⲃ ⲉϣ. ⲡⲉ ⲭⲙⲙⲟⲛ; c conjunc *B*: Ac 15 5
(*S* ⲥ ⲉⲧⲣⲉ-), He 11 6 (*S* ⲉ-) δεῖν; Ac 21 37 (*S* ⲧⲟ ⲉ
ⲧⲣⲉ-) ἔξεστι; EW 166 ⲓⲥϫⲉ ⲥ. ⲡⲧⲉⲛϫⲟⲥ; c rel ⲉⲧ-:
2 Macc 6 20 *A*, Ro 8 26 *S* ϣⲉ *B*, *ib* 12 3 *SF*(*B* ⲡⲉⲧ-)
ⲇ., Si prol 4 *S* δέον; Eccl 10 17 *F* ⲡⲛⲉⲩ ⲉⲧⲉϣ. (*S*
ⲡⲉⲩⲟⲉⲓϣ) πρὸς καιρόν; Lev 9 16 *SB*, Cl 3 4 *A* (var
ⲥⲙⲁⲛⲧ) καθήκειν; ShC 42 183 *S* ⲡⲉⲟⲩⲟⲉⲓϣ ⲉⲧⲉϣ.,
BHom 46 *S* ⲕⲁⲧⲁ ⲑⲉ ⲉⲧⲉϣ. (var R 2 2 30 ⲕ. ⲡⲉⲧⲉϣ.),
Z 261 *S* Arius's dysentery ⲁϥⲃⲱⲕ ⲉⲡⲙⲁ ⲉⲧϣ. (PO
1 413 ارزج, var مرحاض, *cf* ἀναγκαῖος τόπος); ⲡⲉⲧ-,
ⲡⲉⲧ-: Ex 21 10 *S*(*B* ⲙⲡϣⲁ), Mt 26 54 *B*(*S* ϩⲁⲡⲥ),
Va 57 11 *B* ⲟⲩⲡⲉⲧ. ⲁⲡⲡⲉ ⲇ.; Pro 29 37 *SA*(*B* ⲉⲣ
ⲛⲟϥⲣⲓ) συμφέρειν; MG 25 3 *B* ⲛⲉⲡⲉⲧ. ⲡⲉ ⲡⲧⲉⲕⲓⲛⲥ
ὀφείλειν; Lu 2 27 *B*(*S* ⲉⲓⲣⲉ ⲙⲡⲥⲱⲛⲧ) ἐθίζειν; Miss
8 57 *S* ⲥϩⲁⲓ ⲡⲉⲧⲉϣ. εἰκός; Lu 12 57 *S*(*B* ⲙⲉⲑⲙⲏⲓ)
δίκαιος; Jude 3 *S*(*B* = Gk) ἀνάγκην ἔχειν; Miss 8 31 *S*
ⲡⲃⲟⲗ ⲙⲡⲉⲧⲉϣ. ἀνακόλουθος; BHom 11 *S* ⲡⲁⲣⲁ ⲡⲉⲧ
ⲉϣ. σφοδρότερος; P 130⁴ 88 *S* ϩⲟⲩⲟⲡⲉⲧⲉϣ. ⲡⲧⲁⲓϣⲡ
ⲡⲁⲓ, Ep 438 *S* ⲁⲓⲧⲁϥⲉ ⲡⲉⲧⲉϣ. ⲡⲁϥ, BSM 114 *B* ⲕⲁⲧⲁ
ⲡⲉⲧⲥ. = Mor 22 125 *S* ⲡⲉⲧⲡⲣⲉⲡⲉⲓ, AM 325 *B* ⲛⲉ
ⲡⲉⲧⲥ. ⲡⲁⲕⲡⲉ ⲡⲧⲉⲕ-.

With following preposition.

—— ⲉ- *S*: Pcod 15 ⲑⲉ ⲉⲧⲉϣ. ⲉⲡⲙⲟⲛⲁⲭⲟⲥ, BM
Or 8811 210 ⲭⲛⲟⲩⲟⲩ ⲉⲛⲉⲧⲉϣ. ⲉⲣⲟⲟⲩ, TU 24 1 5
ⲡⲉⲥϣⲉ ⲉⲣⲟⲕ...ⲛⲡⲧⲙ-; vbal + infin: Tob 12 1 *S*,
Pro 22 14 *SA*, Mt 23 23 *S*(*B* ⲙⲡϣⲁ), Lu 22 7 *B*(*S*
ⲏⲡ ⲉ-), Jo 4 20 *SA²*(*B* ⲡ-), *ib* 9 4 *A²* ⲥϣϣⲉ, He 9 26
SF(*B* ϩⲱϯ)ⲇ.; Jo 19 7 *SA²*(*B* ⲙ.), Cl 51 1 *A* ⲟ ϥ.;
ib 63 1 *A* θεμιτός; Mt 3 15 *S*(*B* do) πρέπον; Va 57
13 *B* ⲥ. ⲉϯ ⲉⲃⲟⲗ χρή; Ep Jer 39 *B* ⲥ. ⲉⲙⲉⲅⲓ...ϫⲉ
(*F* ⲉϣ.) νομιστέος; Nu 4 31 *S* ⲉϣ. ⲉϥⲓⲧⲟⲩ (*B* om)
αἱρόμενος; PS 30 *S* ⲡⲉⲧⲉϣ. ⲉϣⲱⲡⲉ, ShC 73 25 *S*
ϣ. ⲉⲣⲟⲛ ⲉϣⲱⲡⲉ ⲙⲡⲓⲥⲧⲟⲥ, TT 156 *S* ⲛϣ. ⲁⲛ ⲉⲣⲟϥ
ⲉⲟⲩⲉⲛ-, AM 126 *B* ⲥ. ⲉⲟⲩⲱϣⲧ; +ⲉⲧⲣⲉ- (mostly
S): 2 Kg 4 10, Dan 6 15 *B*, Jo 4 24 (*A²* fut, *B* ⲙ., *F*
dat ⲉ-), Ac 1 21 (*B* ϩⲱϯ), He 2 1 *SF*(*B* ⲛⲧⲉ-)ⲇ., Miss
8 57 ⲡⲉⲧⲉϣ. ⲉⲧⲣⲉⲩⲧⲩⲡⲟⲩ ⲙⲙⲟⲟⲩ ⲟ ϥ.; Ac 2 29 (*B*
ⲉ-)ἐξ.; *ib* 6 2 ⲥϣϣⲉ(var ϣϣⲉ, *B* ⲣ ⲁⲡⲁⲥ)ἀρεστὸν εἶναι;
Aeg 232 ϣ. ⲁⲛ ⲉⲧⲣⲉ- οὐ χρή; Deu 16 8 ϣⲉ(*B* ϣⲁⲣⲉ-)
ποιεῖσθαι fut; Br 117 ϣ. ⲉⲣⲟϥ ⲉⲧⲣⲉϥϫⲓ, ShC 42 154
ⲡⲉⲧⲉϣ. ⲉⲣⲟⲟⲩ ⲉⲧⲣⲉⲩϫⲟⲟⲩ, Mani 2 *A²* ⲥ. ⲁⲡⲇⲓⲕⲁⲓⲟⲥ
ⲁⲧⲉⲧⲙ-; c ⲡⲉⲧ-: Ep Jer 6 (*B* ⲉⲧ-), BHom 43
ⲡ. ⲡⲉ ⲉⲕⲁⲧⲁⲫⲣⲟⲡⲉⲓ, Va 57 12 *B* ⲟⲩⲡ. ⲁⲡⲡⲉ ⲉⲥⲓϯ ⲇ.;
Miss 8 31 ⲡ. ⲡⲉ ⲉⲧⲣⲉϩⲱⲃ ⲡⲓⲙ ... ϣⲱⲡⲉ χρή; Aeg
234 ⲡ. ⲡⲉ ⲉⲕⲁⲑⲁⲓⲣⲟⲩ ⲙⲙⲟϥ καθαιρείσθω; ShA 2
280 ⲛⲉⲡ. [ⲁⲛ] ⲉⲕⲁⲧⲁⲫⲣⲟⲡⲉⲓ, J 104 24 ⲟⲩⲡ. ⲁⲩⲱ
ⲟⲩⲇⲓⲕⲁⲓⲟⲛ ⲉⲧⲣⲁ-, R 1 4 53 ⲛⲟⲩⲡ. ⲁⲡⲡⲉ ⲉϯ.

—— ⲛ- dat, (mostly *B*): Jo 4 24 as above ⲇ.;

Ac 22 25 (var ⲉ-, S ⲧⲟ) ἔξ. dat; Tit 2 1 S (B ⲥⲁⲓⲱⲟⲩ)
πρέπειν, 1 Cor 11 13 (S ⲉ-)πρέπον; Aeg 255 S ⲡⲉⲧⲉϣ. ⲡⲉ ⲙⲡⲉⲛⲧⲁϥⲙⲡϣⲁ; vbal: 4 Kg 4 14, 1 Cor 8
2 (SF ⲉ-) δ. inf; Mk 12 14 BF (PMich 545, S = Gk)
ἔξ. inf; MG 25 220 c. ⲡⲧⲱⲃⲣ ⲟ̇ϥ. inf; Ro 1 28 neg
(S ⲙⲉϣ.) καθήκ.; AM 219 c. ⲡⲉⲣ ⲟⲩⲱ.

ⲙ(ⲉ)ϣϣⲉ S, ⲙⲁϣ. A, not be fitting: Miss 1 404
ϩⲉⲡⲕⲉⲃⲏⲩⲉ ⲉⲩⲙ.; ⲉⲙ.: Job 15 3 (B ⲛ-...ⲁⲡ) ⲟⲩ̇
δ.; ib 27 6 (B diff), Lu 23 41 (B ⲇⲟ) ἄτοπος; Aeg
227 ϩⲱⲃ ⲉⲙ. ἀπαγορεύεσθαι; ib 252 ϩⲱⲃ ⲉⲙ. ⲉϩⲟ-
ⲟϥ; ⲉⲧⲉⲙ.: Mk 13 14 (B ⲁⲡ) ⲟⲩ̇ δ.; Eph 5 4 (B ⲙ.
ⲁⲡ) οὐκ ἀνῆκειν; ShA 1 197 ϩⲃⲏⲅⲉ ⲉⲧⲉⲙ.; ⲡⲉⲧⲉ-,
ⲡⲉⲧⲉⲙ.: Job 4 8 (B = Gk) ἄτοπος; Si 13 24 ἀπόρρη-
τος; 2 Macc 6 4 A μὴ καθήκ.; Mt 12 2 (BF ⲛ-...ⲁⲡ)
οὐκ ἔξ.; ShRE 11 16 turn aside from ⲡⲉⲧⲉⲙ., BAp
174 ϩⲉⲡⲕⲁⲧⲁⲫⲣⲟⲛⲓⲧⲏⲥ ⲟⲩⲡⲉⲧⲉⲙ.

ϣⲉⲙϣ F   v ⲥⲁⲙϣ.

ϣⲓϣⲉⲙ B nn, *phantom, shadow*: Va 57 173 ⲛϥ-
ϣⲟⲡ ⲁⲛ...ⲡⲭⲉ ϥⲟⲩⲱⲛϩ ⲉⲃⲟⲗ...ⲁⲗⲗⲁ ⳽ⲉⲡⲟⲩⲥⲕⲓⲁⲥ-
ⲙⲉⲛⲟⲥ ⲉⲧⲉⲟⲩϣ. ⲙⲙⲉⲧϣⲟⲃⲓⲡⲉ οὔτε δῆλος ἀλλὰ συν-
εσκιασμένος; Cat 208 He became man κατα ⲟⲩϣ.
ⲓⲉ ⲟⲩⲫⲁⲛⲧⲁⲥⲓⲁ, ib 30 John's disciples held Him
ⲟⲩⲣⲱⲙⲓ ⲛϣ. ⲓⲉ ⲉϥϫⲟⲭⲉⲃ. Cf ϣⲓⲥⲙⲉ.

ϣⲱϣⲉⲛ B nn, *lily* (שׁושׁן‎ سوسن‎ IgR): 2 Chr 4 5,
Is 35 1 (SF = Gk), Hos 14 6 (SA = Gk) κρίνον; K
179 خزام‎ (lavandula spica Schweinf Ar Pfl 57. In
Nu 8 4 S, Ex 25 31 B κρ. = ϩⲣⲏⲣⲉ).

ϣϣⲏⲛ B   v ϣⲏⲛ.

ϣⲁϣⲛⲓ B vb intr, *reach, obtain*: Ja 4 2 (S ⲙⲁⲧⲉ)
ἐπιτυγχάνειν; DeV 2 52 ⲙⲡⲉⲧⲟⲧⲕ ϣ. κατα ⲡⲉⲕ-
ⲙⲉⲩⲓ; c ⲉ-, *to*: C 89 1 ⲁϥϣ. ⲉⲟⲩⲛⲓϣⲧ ⲛ̄ⲡⲁⲓ
τυγχ., MG 25 7 ⲁⲓϣⲧⲉⲙϣ. ⲉⲡⲁⲓϩⲱⲃ ἀπο., Ro 11 7
(S ⲙ.) ἐπιτ.; MG 25 212 ⲁϥϣ. ⲉⲣⲟϥ συναντᾶν dat;
C 43 193 ⲁϥϣ. ⲉⲡⲓⲙⲧⲟⲛ, PO 11 332 ⲙⲡⲉϥϣ. ⲉⲡⲉϥⲟⲩⲱϣ, MG 25 185 ⲁⲓϣ. ⲉⲁⲃⲃⲁ ⲡⲟⲓⲙⲏⲛ, ib 127 ϣ.
ⲉⲟⲩⲡⲓⲥⲧⲏ ⲛⲥϩⲓⲙⲓ as wife; c ⲛ-dat (?): AM 201
ⲉⲑⲣⲉⲡϣ. ⲙⲡⲓⲕⲗⲏⲣⲟⲥ; c ⲡⲉⲙ-: MG 25 206 ⲁϥ-
ϣⲁⲡϣ. ⲡⲉⲙⲣⲁⲡⲥⲓⲛⲟⲩ εὐκαιρεῖν μετά.

ⲉⲣ ⲁⲧϣ., *fail to obtain*: DeV 2 47 ⲛⲭⲓⲛⲑⲣⲉϥⲉⲣ.
ⲉⲡⲭⲱ ⲡⲏⲛ.

ⲙⲉⲧⲁⲧϣ., *unattainedness*: Lev 26 16 (S ϣⲱⲱⲧ)
ἀφορία.

ϫⲓⲛϣ., *attainment*: MG 25 314 ϯ̄ϫ. (sic l) ⲉⲛⲓⲁ-
ⲅⲁⲑⲟⲛ.

ϣⲁϣ[ⲡⲉ] A², ϣⲟϣⲛⲓ B nn f, *stomach*: 1 Tim 5
23 (S = Gk) στόμαχος; K 78 ϯⲱ. شاش‎; Mani K 90.
Cf ⲥⲃϣⲉ.

ϣⲁϣⲧ B   v ϣⲁϣ B.

ϣⲉϣⲧ S nn (?), meaning unknown: PLond 4
452]ⲉ ⲡϣ. ϩⲡⲡⲧⲱϣ ⲡⲥⲟⲓ, so ? place-name.

ϣⲟⲩⲧ SB, ϣⲱ. B, ϣⲁ. S" S^f A² F nn m, *hindrance,
impediment* (cf ⲥⲱϣⲧ), so *key*: Jud 3 25 S, Lu 11
52 SB ϣⲱ. (var ϣⲟ.), Ap 9 1 SBF (cit Mor 28 39)
κλείς; P 55 13 B ⲛϣ. مفاتيح‎; PS 328 S ⲛϣ. ⲉⲧⲁⲟⲩ-
ⲱⲛ, ⲉⲧϣⲧⲁⲙ, ShC 73 56 S ⲛϣ. [ⲛⲙ]ⲙⲁ entrusted
to them, ShP 130² 75 S granaries ⲉⲩϩⲏⲕ ⲟⲛϣ.,
ShViK 9815 27 S ϣ. ⲙⲡⲉⲛⲓⲡⲉ, ⲛϣⲉ ⲛ ϩⲟⲩⲣ, BM
1017 S ϣ. ⲛⲡⲉⲛⲓⲡⲉ ⲛⲡⲣⲟ, R 1 5 42 S ϩⲟⲩⲣ ⲛⲡⲟⲩⲃ
ⲉϥⲟ ⲛϣ. (cf ib ⲛⲉϫ. ⲉⲙⲁϥⲟⲩⲱⲡ), BKU 1 299 S ⲥⲛⲁⲩ
ⲛϣⲟⲩⲧ...ⲉⲕⲁϯ ϩⲟⲩⲣ ⲉⲣⲟⲟⲩ, Mor 41 4 S ⲛϣ. ⲛ-
ⲧⲃⲓⲃⲗⲓⲟⲑⲏⲕⲏ = DeV 2 249 B, TT 101 S ϣ. of door
(ⲩ ⲛⲱ), Z 265 S patriarch given ⲛϣ. ⲡⲓⲣⲡⲏⲅⲉ, BMis
215 S sim, Miss 4 648 S^f ⲁⲛⲟⲩⲱⲡ ⲙⲛϣ. ⲙⲡⲉⲛⲉϣ-
ⲟⲩⲱⲡ ⲙⲡⲣⲟ, Va 57 137 B ⲟⲩⲑⲏⲥⲁⲩⲣⲟⲥ ... ⲛⲉϣ.,
PMich 602 S^a ⲛϣ. ⲛⲁⲙⲉⲛⲧⲉ, BMis 448 S staff given
to future bishop ⲉⲣⲉⲟⲩϣ. ⲙⲏⲣ ⲙⲙⲟϥ, JTS 10 403 S
what need to ⲧⲁϣⲉ ϣ. ⲟⲛⲛⲙⲁ ⲉⲧⲙⲙⲁⲩ?, P 129^17 17
S ⲁⲩϩⲙⲁⲣⲧⲉ ⲙⲙⲟⲓ ⲛϭⲓ ⲛϣ. ⲛⲧⲉϥⲫⲩⲥⲓⲥ & hindered
me giving birth, ManiH 5 A² ⲛⲡⲁ]ϭ ⲛϣ. ⲉⲧⲟⲓ ⲛⲉⲁⲩ,
ShA 1 455 ⲛϣ. ⲙⲡⲣⲃⲃⲉ ⲙⲡⲧⲥⲓⲛⲉ (what part of
plough?), BM 594 (2) S ⲛϣ. ⲛⲧⲥⲁⲕⲓ[ⲁ (what?); ϯ
ϣ. S, *impede, fasten with key*: R 1 1 52 ⲁⲛϯ ϣ. ⲉⲡⲣⲟ κ. ἐπιτιθέναι; Mor 41 56 ϯ ϣ. ⲙⲡⲣⲟ; ⲣ ϣ. S,
act as key, shut: Mor 43 83 His hands ⲣ ϣ. ⲁⲩⲱ
ⲁⲩⲟⲩⲱⲡ gates, v above R 1 5 42; ⲁⲧϣ. B, *without key*: Miss 4 116 gate opens ⲛⲁ. = ib 792 S ⲉϫⲛⲛϣ.

As name or title: ⲡⲉⲧ]ⲣⲟⲥ ⲡϣ. (PMich 3553).

ϣⲟϣⲧ   v ϣⲟⲧϣⲧ sf.

ϣⲟⲩϣⲧ SA²B, ϣⲱ. SA nn m, *window*: Ge 8 6
SB, 2 Kg 6 16 SB, Pro 7 6 SAB, Ez 41 26 SB, Joel
2 9 AB, 2 Cor 11 33 SA² (ManiH 69) B, R 1 1 52 S
house ⲉⲧⲉⲙⲛ ϣ. ⲙⲙⲟϥ, Z 312 S ϯ ⲟⲧⲛϥ ⲉⲃⲟⲗ ϩⲛⲟⲩϣ., BHom 3 S ⲟⲩⲱⲛ, ϣⲧⲁⲙ ⲛⲡⲉⲕϣ., AP 6 A²
ⲧⲱⲛ ⲁⲃⲁⲗ ϩⲛⲛϣ. θυρίς; Ez 8 7 B (S ϣⲕⲟⲗ), Z
346 S ϣ. in hermit's cell ⲟⲡⲏ; C 89 8 B ϫⲟⲩϣⲧ ⲉ-
ⲃⲟⲗ ⳽ⲉⲛⲛϣ. ἄνωθεν παρακύπτειν = Va ar 172 6 مه
ذلب ؟ڡ; HCons 386 B ⲛϣ. ⲉⲧ⳽ⲉⲑⲙⲛⲓϯ ⲛ̄ϫⲟⲓ طاق؟;
Ez 40 16 &c B (S ϣⲟⲭⲧ) φοίνιξ (v ϣⲟⲧϣⲧ nn); ShA
1 388 S ⲥⲟⲛⲧ ⲉⲃ. ϩⲛⲛϣ., DeV 2 84 B sim, ShViK
9343 S ⲛⲣⲟ ⲟⲣϫ ⲁⲩⲱ ⲛϣ., HL 95 B to one bringing
gift ⲭⲁϥ ϩⲓϫⲉⲛⲛⲁⲓϣ., Mor 37 98 S ϣⲧⲁⲙ ⲙⲡⲣⲟ
ⲙⲛϣ. (PG 26 920 om), LMär 38 S ⲁϥϭⲱϣⲧ ⲉⲡⲡⲉⲧ-
ⲟⲩⲁⲁⲃ ϩⲛⲛϣ., P 131⁵ 102 S chamber where ⲟⲩϣ.
ⲕⲧⲏⲩ ⲉⲡⲉϥⲥⲁ ⲡⲓⲣⲓⲧ; *niche, alcove* (B rare): Wess
11 167 ⲛϣ. ⲉϥⲙⲉϩ ⲛⲭⲱⲙⲉ θυρίς; Mus 40 37 (Reg
Pach) ⲛϣ. wherein books *in fenestra id est in risco*;
Ryl 94 (33) picture of Christ ϩⲛⲟⲩϣ. ϩⲓⲧⲭⲟ, Mor
25 23 idol ⲧⲁⲗⲏⲩ ⲉϫⲛⲟⲩϣ. ϩⲓϩⲟⲩⲛ ⲙⲡⲉⲩⲣⲟ = Va
61 118 B ϩⲓϫⲉⲛⲟⲩϣ. ⲥⲁϩⲟⲩⲛ ⲙⲫⲣⲟ, Miss 4 112 B
sim, LMär 32 idols ⲁⲥⲉⲣⲁⲧⲟⲩ ϩⲓϫⲛⲟⲛϣⲱϣⲧ, ShA
2 158 ⲁⲩⲧⲁⲙⲓⲟ ⲛ̄ϩⲉⲛϣ. where ravens & vultures

feed, Mor 37 18 mother sat listening ⲉⲓⲭⲡⲟⲩϣ. ⲉⲙⲙⲁ ⲛⲧⲡⲉ, COAd 48 ⲡϣ. ⲙⲡⲡⲉϩ ⲡϣⲗⲏⲗ in sanctuary, Cai 67324 ϣ. ⲙⲃⲏⲧ among σκεύη found in house (or ? l ϣⲟϣⲧ).

ϣⲱϣⲧ S/BF v ⲥⲱϣⲧ.

ϣϣⲟⲧ, -ⲱⲧ B v ϣⲟⲧ.

ϣⲉϣⲟⲧⲉ S nn, meaning unknown unless = ϣⲛϣⲱⲧⲉ qv: WS 94 go into cell & fetch ⲡⲓⲟⲩⲧⲁⲅ ⲡϣ. ⲙⲛⲧⲙⲁⲅⲉ ⲙⲡⲉϩⲟⲩⲣ.

ϣⲟϣⲟⲩ[1] SB, ϣⲁϣⲟⲩ[2] SA[2]F, ϣⲟϣⲟ S nn m, pot, jar: Is 5 10 BF(S ⲛⲣⲡ), Jer 42 5 S[1]B, Mk 14 13 S[1]B, Z 343 S[1] ⲙⲟⲩⲣ ⲡⲁⲛⲥⲓⲟⲡ…ⲙⲟⲩⲣ ⲡⲉϣϣ. κεράμιον, 2 Kg 17 28 S[2](var -ϣⲟ) ⲛⲏⲣⲡ κέραμος; R 1 4 30 S vineyard estimated at ϣⲉ ⲡϣ.[1] lagena; K 130 B ϣ. = ⲙⲁⲩⲣⲏⲥ (μάρις); Tri 343 S[2] ـجُرّ; ShC 73 124 S ⲣ ⲙⲛ ⲉⲩⲃⲁⲅⲕⲁⲗⲓⲟⲛ ⲏ ⲉϣϣ.[1] ib 42 79 S ⲙⲛ ⲙⲟⲟⲩ ⲉⲧⲉⲣϣⲉⲛϣ.[1] ⲣⲱⲥ ⲛⲣⲡ, BMis 387 S ϣ.[2] ⲛⲏⲣⲡ = Va 63 14 B = BSM 41 B ⲕⲉⲗⲗⲁ (cf ? ⲁⲗⲟ), Mani 1 A[2] ϣ. ⲛⲏⲣⲡ, Faras 3 pl 67 7 S ⲟⲩϣ.[2] of honey, ROC 27 157 B bread ϫⲉⲛⲛⲁϣ., WS 119 S ϣ.[1] ⲛⲏⲣⲡ ⲛⲧⲓⲗⲟⲭ (cf ϣⲁϣ vessel), Ep 311 S ⲥⲟⲅⲟ ⲏ ⲧⲣⲟⲫⲏ ⲏ ϣ.[2] (sc of wine), Kr 31 S vintner owes x ⲡϣ.[1], MIE 2 360 B ϣ. ⲙⲙⲟⲟⲩ = BAp 88 S ⲕⲉⲗⲱⲗ = PO 22 348 ٔجر, Ep 101 S ⲁⲓⲭⲓ ϣⲟⲙⲧⲉ ⲛϫⲓⲡⲗⲁ ⲛⲏⲣⲡ ⲅⲁ ⲡϣ.[1], ST 388 S ⲡⲧⲣⲓⲙⲛⲥⲉ ⲡϣ.[2], ib 248 S ⲛⲕⲉϣ.[1] …ⲧⲁϯ ⲥⲟⲩⲛⲧⲟⲩ, Tor 43 S ⲡϣ.[1]…ϫⲓ ⲧⲉⲩⲧⲓⲙⲏ ⲡⲏⲣⲡ (cf PSBA 29 319 will pay thee debt ⲛⲏⲣⲡ), BM 531 S ⲉⲡϣ.[1] … ⲟⲩ(ⲛ)ⲣ ⲉⲁϣⲫⲟⲗⲟⲕⲟⲧⲧⲓ, Ep 404 S ϣⲁⲓϣⲧⲕ ⲛϣⲟⲙⲛⲧ ⲛϣⲉ ⲡϣ.[2], ib 312 S ⲙⲡⲧⲉ ⲡϣ.[1] ⲙⲁ ⲡⲡⲁⲥⲥⲏⲛ, CO 228 S let camel fetch ⲡϣ.[2] ϫⲉⲛ(ⲡ)ⲉⲡⲣⲏ ⲧⲁⲕⲟⲟⲩ, RE 9 156 S ⲃⲓⲧⲟⲩ (sc ⲛⲏⲣⲡ) ϫⲉⲛ(ⲡ)ⲉⲩⲧⲁⲕⲟ ⲉⲡⲉⲓϫⲏ ⲡϣ.[1] ⲛⲧⲣⲟⲙⲡⲉ ⲧⲁⲕⲛⲟⲩ.
ⲕⲁⲧϣ.[1] S, potter: Glos 234 κεραμοπλάστης(cf ⲕⲟⲉⲓⲥ); Pap olim penes Wessely ⲡⲉⲧⲣⲁⲙⲙⲁⲧⲓⲟⲛ ⲙⲡⲕ. relates to purchase of κοῦφα. Cf ϣⲁϣ, a vessel.

ϣⲟϣⲟⲩ, ϣⲱ. B v ϣⲟⲩ.

ϣϣⲏⲟⲩ, ϣ. B nn m, coriander: Bodl 325 151 ⲡⲓϣϣ., BMOr 8775 127 ⲡϣϣ. ؑجُرّ. V ⲉⲣⲉϣⲏⲩⲧ.

ϣϣⲱⲟⲩ B, ϣϣⲁⲩ S/(once) nn, desire with ϭⲓ, yearn for, conceive tr: Ps 118 174 (var ⲛⲥⲁ-, S ⲙⲉ) ἐπιποθεῖν, Va 57 6 ⲡⲉⲡϣⲟⲩϭⲓ ϣ. ⲙⲙⲟϥ ποθεινός; Ps 50 7 (S ϫⲓ ⲟⲩⲱ) κισσᾶν; C 86 353 ⲡⲓⲙⲁ ⲉⲧⲁⲩϭ. ⲙⲙⲟϥ. Bess 7 7 ⲡⲁϩⲏⲧ ⲁϥϭ. ⲙⲙⲟϥ; ⲉ ⲉ-: Ps 118 131 (S ⲉⲡⲓⲑⲩⲙⲉⲓ) ἐπ.; Ge 30 38 (S/ Mor 54 99 ⲉⲃⲟⲗ ⲉⲛ-, S ϫⲓ ⲟⲩⲱ) ἐγκ. εἰς; C 86 184 ϭ. ⲉⲡⲁⲧϥⲉ; vbal: Ps 41 2 (S ⲙⲉ), 2 Cor 5 2 (S ⲟⲩⲱϣ) ἐπ.; AM 13 ϯϭ. ⲉⲡⲁⲩ ⲉⲣⲱⲧⲉⲛ; ⲉ ⲡⲥⲁ-: Ps 118 174 ut sup; ⲉ ⲉⲃⲟⲗ: Ge 30 38 S/ ut sup, Mus 45 51 ⲉⲕⲡⲁϭ. ⲉⲃ. & God will hear thee, Dif 2 82 ⲁⲕϭ. ⲉⲃ. ⲉⲑⲣⲉⲕ-; as nn m, desire, longing: Va 57 128 ⲟⲩϭ. ⲉϥⲣⲟⲕⲉ ⲉⲃⲟⲩⲛ ⲉϥϯ, CaiEuch 533 πόθος, ib 395

ⲡⲓϭ. ἐπιπόθησις; AM 107 ⲟⲩϭ. ⲛⲧⲉ ⲡⲁϩⲏⲧ; ⲣⲉϥϭ., who desireth: Cai Th 271 Jesus ⲫⲣ. ⲡⲧⲉⲟⲩⲟⲡ ⲛⲓⲃⲉⲛ ⲡⲟⲅⲉⲙ مشتاق.

ϣⲁϣϥ B v ⲥⲁϣϥ & ϣⲟϣ twist.

ϣⲁϣϥ, -ϣϥⲧ B v ϣⲁϣ B.

ϣⲱϣϥ B v ⲥⲱϣ be despised (ⲥⲱϣϥ).

ϣⲟⲩϣⲏⲛ S nn, meaning unknown, 8 of them among σκεύη found in house: Cai 67324.

ϣⲁϥ S nn m, meaning doubtful, waste, unwatered land (?): Ryl 158 7 ⲥⲧ]ⲱⲧⲉ ⲙⲉⲛ ⲡⲕⲁϩ ⲕⲁⲓ- (l ⲕⲉ)ⲥⲧⲱⲧⲉ ϫⲉ ⲡϣ., ib 11 ⲥⲉⲧⲓⲱⲣⲉ ⲡϣ. ⲉⲓⲕⲁϩ (cf BM 1073 7), WZKM 16 266 share of ⲛⲉⲙ(ⲟ)ⲟⲩ ⲙⲡⲡⲉϣ., Ryl 298 ⲁⲓⲁⲡⲁⲛⲧ(ⲁ) ⲉⲣⲟ(ⲟ)ⲩ ⲅⲁⲡϣ. Cf? ϣⲟϥ(ϣⲁϥⲉ).

ϣⲁϥ O adj, epithet of Michael, mighty ? (Griffith): AZ 21 94 = 38 88 ⲙ. ⲡⲓϣ. ⲡⲁⲅⲅⲉⲗⲟⲥ. Cf ϣⲃⲉ DM 29 6.

ϣⲁⲁϥ v ϣⲁⲁⲃ.

ϣⲓϥ v ⲥⲓϣϥ.

ϣⲱϥ SA[2]BF, ϥ. A, ϣⲉϥ-S, ϣⲟϥ⸌ SB, ϣⲏϥ† SBF, ⲅⲏϥ† A(-ϥ & -ⲃ vary in S), vb I intr, be desert, laid waste, destroyed: Is 34 10 B(SF ⲣ ϫⲁⲉⲓⲉ), Jer 33 9 SB, Ap 18 17 SB, Z 319 S ⲡⲧⲟⲡⲟⲥ ⲛⲁϣ. ἐρημοῦν, Is 61 4 SB ἐξερ., Lev 26 33 S(B ϣⲱⲡⲓ ⲉⲩ ϣ.†) ἔρημος εἶναι; Nah 1 10 SA(B as Gk) χερσοῦν; Job 8 14 S(B diff) ἀοίκητος; Ez 36 34 B ἀφανίζειν; Am 4 7 S(B ϣⲱⲟⲩϣ) ξηραίνειν; BMis 2 S ⲟⲩⲡⲟⲗⲓⲥ ⲉⲙⲉϣ., MG 25 390 B ⲙⲏ ⲅⲁⲣⲁ ϯⲡⲟⲗⲓⲥ ϣ. (ROC 19 34 ⲥⲛ), P 131[4] 150 S gathering ⲅⲉⲛⲙⲛⲓϣⲉ ⲛ ⲥⲟⲩⲟ ϣⲁⲡⲧⲟⲩϣ. lest they be lacking, Aeg 7 B not one tooth ϣ. ϫⲉⲛⲡⲣⲱϩ, RNC 76 S arrow struck eye [ⲁⲥ]ϣ. ⲡϭⲓ ⲧⲁⲁⲗⲟⲩ (cf Ryl 80 below), DeV 1 123 B dying Herod ⲁⲡⲉϥⲃⲁⲗ ⲃ̄ ϣ., KroppK 47 S charm ⲉⲧⲃⲉⲟⲩⲥⲁⲙⲛⲧ…ⲉⲧⲣⲉⲥϣ.; qual: Is 16 1 B(S ϫⲁⲓⲉ), ib 5 17 F(S do, B ϣⲁϥⲉ), Jer 51 2 SB ἐρ.; Ps 68 26 B(S. ⲣ ϫ.)ἐρημοῦν; Deu 13 16 S(B diff)ἀοίκ.; Sa 10 7 S χέρσος; Jos 9 18 S βιβρώσκειν; Pro 9 12 c SA(B Gk diff); ShRE 10 162 S ⲧⲟⲓⲕⲟⲩⲙⲉⲡⲏ … ϣ. ⲡⲣⲱⲙⲉ, BM 289 S ⲧⲣⲉⲙⲙⲁ ⲡⲉⲗⲟⲟⲗⲉ ⲉⲧϣⲏⲃ ϯ ⲟⲩⲱ = EW 44 B = Horae Sem 3 60 ⲭⲣⲃ, BAp 9 S hell ϣ. ⲉϥⲟ ⲡⲉⲣⲛⲙⲟⲥ, KKS 11 S exiled to ⲟⲩⲕⲁⲥⲧⲣⲟⲛ…ⲉϥϣ. (cf Miss 8 206 ⲉϥⲟ ⲡϫ.), Cat 64 B ⲉϥϣ. ⲉϥⲟⲓ ⲡϣⲁϥⲉ (cf Mt 23 27); ⲉ ⲡⲥⲁ- S: Mor 52 32 ⲡⲉϥϣ. ⲡⲥⲁⲡⲉⲕⲕⲗⲏⲥⲓⲁ (cf 2 Cor 11 8).

II tr: Ps 78 7 B(S ⲣ ϫ.), Is 49 17 B(S do) ἐρημοῦν, Nah 1 4 B(SA ϣⲟϣⲙ)ἐξερ.; Jos 7 3 S, Is 1 8 SF(B ϣⲱⲗ) πολιορκεῖν; Gal 1 13 SB πορθεῖν; Ac 8 3 S(B diff) λυμαίνεσθαι; 1 Kg 24 5 S(B ⲱⲗⲓ) ἀφαιρεῖν; ShMIF 23 145 S ⲟⲩⲡⲟⲗⲓⲥ…ⲁⲩϣⲟϥⲥ, ShA 2 331 S ⲥⲡⲁϣⲉϥ ⲡⲏⲓ, KKS 666 S ⲁⲕϣⲉϥ ⲧⲉⲕⲕⲗⲏⲥⲓⲁ

because of Arius, Z 233 *S* Jesus descended ⲁϥϣ. ⲛⲁⲙⲡⲉ, BIF 13 111 *S* gave thanks ⲋⲉⲁϥϣ. ⲙⲡⲉϥ- ⲃⲁⲗ which had been torn out = MG 25 301 *B*, Ryl 80 *S* gifts ϣ. ⲛⲉⲃⲁⲗ ⲉⲛⲉⲣⲱⲟⲩ(*cf* Deu 16 19),ManiH 11 *A*² ⲁⲩϣ. ⲙⲡⲉⲥⲣⲡⲉ, C 41 25 *B* ⲁⲩϣ. ⲙⲡⲁⲛⲓ = Bor 134 2 *S*(Vita Sin) ⲥⲩⲗⲁ.

—— *SBF* nn m, *devastation, destruction*: Lev 26 35 *SB*, Jer 51 22 *B*(*S* ⲝ.),Mk 13 14 *SB*, Z 318 *S* ⲡϣ. ⲡϣⲓⲛⲧ ἐρήμωσις, Bar 4 33 *B* ἐρημία, Is 5 9 *BF*(*S* ⲝ) ἔρημος; Jer 12 11 *S*(*B* ⲧⲁⲕⲟ) ἀφανισμός; Jud 20 40 *S* συντέλεια; ShA 2 8 *S* ϣⲱⲡⲉ ⲉⲡϣ. ⲁⲩⲱ ⲡⲭⲁⲓⲉ, ShBM 230 157 *S*ⲧⲓⲥⲱⲟⲩⲅ ⲛⲁⲡ ⲉⲅⲟⲩⲛ ⲛⲟⲩϣ., BAp 123 *S* ⲁⲡϣ. ⲙⲡⲧⲟⲟⲩ ⲅⲱⲛ ⲉⲅⲟⲩⲛ, Cai 42573 1 *S* title of charm ⲟⲩϣ. ⲛⲏⲓ (*cf* KroppM 79), PBad 5 410 *S*. ᶠ among evils invoked ϣⲟϥ, ⲙⲟⲥϯ, ⲟⲗⲁ ⲉⲃⲟⲗ.

ⲋⲓⲡϣ. *B* nn m, *desolation*: Dan 9 27 (*S* ϣ. nn) ἐρήμωσις.

In place-name: ⲧⲉⲣⲥⲱ ⲉⲧϣⲏϥ (Lant 36).

ϣⲁϥⲉ *BS* (once), ϣⲁⲃⲏ *S*ᶠ(do), f ϣⲁϥⲏ, pl -ⲉⲩ, -ⲛⲟⲩ(once)*B* nn m, *desert*: Ps 28 8(*S*=Gk), Is 35 1 (*SF* do), ib 62 4(*S*ⲭⲁⲉⲓⲉ), Mt 3 1 (*S* do) ἔρημος, Ps 119 4(*S* do)ἐρημικός; ⲡϣ. ⲉⲧⲥⲁⲃⲟⲗ(*v* Ep 1 183, EW *Hist* 24) MG 25 230 πανέρημος; PO 14 333 ⲡϣ. of Abba Macarius, ALR '06 473 *S*ᶠ ⲡϣ.; as adj: Is 61 4(*S* ⲟ ⲛⲭ.) ἔρ.; ib 41 19(*S* ⲉⲧⲟⲃⲉ)ἄνυδρος; Ryl 158 11 *S* ⲓⲱⲣⲉ ⲛⲧⲁϥ(ⲉ) ⲅⲓⲕⲁⲅ; f: Gal 4 27 (3 MSS & Is 54 1 -ⲉ, *S* diff) ἔρ.; Miss 4 141 ⲟⲩⲡⲟⲗⲓⲥ ⲛϣ.; pl: Is 44 26 (*S* ⲙⲁ ⲛⲭ.) ἔρ., He 11 38 (*S* ⲭ.)ἐρημία; EW 133 ⲛϣ. (sc of Nitria), Va 61 9 ⲛⲓⲁⲟⲩⲏⲧ ⲛⲉⲙⲛⲓϣⲁϥⲛⲟⲩ; ⲙⲁ ⲛϣ.: Mt 15 33 (*S* ⲭ.)ἐρημία, ib 14 13 (*S* do, *F* as Gk) ἔρ. τό- πος, Ez 38 12 ἐρημοῦν; C 43 159 ⲟⲩⲙ. outside city; ⲙⲉⲧϣ.: MG 25 109 ϯⲙ. caused by saint's death; ⲣⲉⲙⲛϣ., *eremite*: Miss 4 217 ⲥⲉⲗⲗⲟⲓ ⲛⲣ. ἐρημίτης; PO 14 367, MG 25 29(*sic*); ⲙⲉⲧⲣⲉⲙⲛϣ.: DeV 1 48 ϯⲙ. of Baptist = R 1 3 64 *S* ⲙⲡⲧⲉⲣⲛⲙⲓ- ⲕⲟⲥ; ⲉⲣ, ⲟⲓ ⲛϣ.: Ge 47 19, Bar 4 12 ἐρημοῦν, Ez 12 20 (*S* ⲡ ⲭ.)ἔξερ.; Va 57 176 ⲉⲣ ϣ. ⲉⲃⲟⲗ ⲅⲁⲛⲓⲕⲉ- ⲕⲟⲩⲭⲓ γυμνοῦν; DeV 2 37 ⲟⲓ ⲛϣ. ⲟⲩⲟⲅ ⲡⲣⲏⲕⲓ ⲅⲉⲛ- ⲛⲏ ⲉⲧⲥⲟⲡ, PO 11 378 lest churches ⲉⲣ ϣ. for lack of clergy; ϣⲱⲡⲓ ⲉⲛϣ.: Is 15 6 (*S* ⲣ ⲭ.) ἔρ. εἶναι; Jer 30 2 εἰς ἄβατον εἶναι.

ϣⲱⲟϥⲉ, -ⲃⲉ *S*, ϣⲟⲩⲟⲩϥⲉ, ϣⲟⲩϥⲉ *A* nn m, *barren- ness, poverty*: Pro 9 12 c *S*(var -ⲃⲉ),*A*, ϣⲟⲩ.(*B* ⲙⲉⲧ- ⲁⲧⲟⲩⲧⲁⲅ)ἀκαρπία, cit ShC 73 51, ShP 131⁶ 57 ϣⲱ- ⲟϥ; Pro 6 11 *A*(*S* ⲋⲣⲱϥ, *B* ⲙⲉⲧⲣⲉϥⲉⲣ ϭⲁⲉ, ⲙⲉⲧ- ⲣⲏⲕⲓ)ἔνδεια.

ϣⲱϥ, *shave* *v* ϣⲱⲃ.

ϣⲁϥⲉ¹, ϣⲁⲁ.², ϣⲁⲃⲉ³, ϣⲉϥⲉ⁴, -ⲃⲉ⁵, -ⲃⲓ⁶, ϣⲏⲛϥⲉ⁷, -ⲃⲉ⁸, ϣⲓϥⲉ⁹, -ⲃⲉ¹⁰ *S*, ϣⲁϥⲓ *B*, ϣⲉϥⲉ DM, ϣⲟⲃⲉ *S*, ϣⲁϥⲓⲟⲩ† *B* vb intr, *swell*: Aeg 241 vices ϣⲁⲩϣ.¹ ⲅⲛⲧⲉⲯⲩⲭⲏ οἰδαίνειν; R 1 4 42 ⲉϥϣ.¹ ⲧⲏⲣϥ *tumere*,

C 99 105 ϣⲁⲩϣ.¹ ⲛϭⲓ ⲡⲉϥⲟⲩⲉⲣⲏⲧⲉ = Va ar 172 14 ترقّل, MG 17 361 ورم; Mor 47 138 ⲁⲡⲉϥⲥⲱⲙⲁ ϣⲟ- ⲃⲉ (*l* ϣⲁ.) ⲅⲓⲧⲛⲡⲥⲁϣ = P ar 4793 ورم, MIE 2 345 *B* was dropsical ⲉⲥϣ.† ⲧⲏⲣⲥ = PO 22 361 هرملة; P 129¹⁵ 24 sim ⲡⲉϣ.³ ⲧⲏⲣⲥ, ShA 1 218 by eating thereof ϣⲁϥϣ.¹ ⲛⲥⲉⲙⲟⲩ, ShP 130² 84 dying Nesto- rius ⲁⲡⲉϥⲗⲁⲥ ϣ.¹ & filled mouth, BM 332 sim, Mor 28 242 ⲁⲩϣ.³ ⲁϥⲙⲟⲩ, BMar 61 sick man ⲁϥⲗⲟ ⲉϥϣ.², PO 14 356 *B* body ϣ. ⲙⲫⲣⲏϯ ⲡⲟⲩⲥⲧⲩⲗⲟⲥ, MG 25 224 *B* body ϣ. ⲛⲧⲉⲛⲛϣⲟⲗⲙⲉⲥ, Blake 236 healeth ⲅⲉⲛⲙⲁ ⲉⲩϣ.† (= ib 103, 197 *tumours, swellings*), Vi K 9549 27 ⲉⲣⲉⲡⲉϥⲥⲱⲙⲁ ϣ.†, PMéd 102 ⲡⲉϥⲥⲱⲙⲁ ϣ.⁴, ib 287 ⲡⲉϥⲭⲟⲉⲓⲧ...ⲉϥϣ.⁴, ib 204 ϣ.⁵, Hall 64 ⲅⲉⲛⲃⲁⲗ ⲉⲩϣ.⁴, DM 13 13 *ntef* ϣ. *ntef* ⲙⲟⲩ, AJSL 46 245 ⲉⲧⲃⲉⲟⲩⲁ ⲉϥϣ.⁷, Mor 38 50 ⲛⲉⲙⲁ ⲛⲧⲁⲩϣ.⁶ ⲅⲉⲙⲡⲉϥⲥⲱⲙⲁ, BMar 56 breasts ⲁⲩϣ.⁹ ⲁⲩⲡⲟⲙⲡⲉⲙ, HM 1 46 sim ⲁⲩϣ.⁸ ⲁⲩⲡⲱⲙⲡⲉⲅⲉ, Wor 273 thy hands enfeebled ⲛⲧⲉⲛⲉⲕⲧⲏⲛⲃⲉ ϣ.¹⁰; as nn : MG 25 248 *B* like wineskin ⲋⲓⲧⲉⲛⲡⲛϣ. ⲛⲧⲉ ⲡⲉϥⲥⲱⲙⲁ ῥυσιπέλαντος γίνεσθαι *intumescere*, PMéd 204 ⲛϣ.⁵ ⲛⲛⲥⲱⲙⲁ, Z 626 recipe ⲉⲧⲃⲉϣ.¹ ⲛⲙ, BKU 1 25 ro sim³.

ϣⲁϥⲉ, *desert* *v* ϣⲱϥ *sf*.

ϣⲏϥⲉ, ϣⲓ. *v* ϣⲛϥⲉ & ϣⲁϥⲉ vb.

ϣⲏϥⲓ *B* vb intr, *be used, consumed* (?): BMOr 8775 123 ⲉϥϣ. دبل.

ϣⲏⲓϥⲓ *B* *v* ϣⲛϥⲉ.

ϣⲓϥⲉ *S* nn m, Egyptian for *cardamum*: Ryl 108 ⲟⲩⲉⲛⲧⲏⲛϭ ⲋⲉⲕⲁⲣⲧⲁⲙⲱⲛ ⲙⲛⲧⲣⲙⲉⲕⲏⲙⲉ ⲋⲉⲛϣ. *Cf* ϣⲗⲁⲉⲓⲛ & ? ⲥⲟϥⲱ Dioscor. (D'Arcy Thompson).

ϣϥⲉ, ϣϥⲃⲉ *S*, ϣϥⲃⲏ *F* *v* ⲥⲁϣϥ, adding ϣϥⲃⲉ *A*² Mani H 68.

ϣϥⲉ *v* ϣⲛⲃⲉ (ϣⲃⲉ).

ϣϥⲱ, ϣϥⲱ (mostly) *SB* nn f, *tale, fable*: 1 Tim 4 7 *SB*, 2 Pet 1 16 *B*(*S* ϣⲁⲭⲉ ⲉⲁⲩⲧⲃⲧⲱⲃⲟⲩ), Va 57 246 *B* ⲋⲁⲛϣ. ⲡⲉ...ⲛⲓⲥⲁⲭⲓ μῦθος, ib 205 *B* ⲟⲩⲉⲃϣⲓ ⲡⲉⲙⲟⲩϣ. λῆρος; Wess 15 137 *S* ⲋⲟⲥⲙⲁ ⲛϣ. ψυ- χρός; P 44 78 *S* ⲧⲙⲁⲛⲁ · ⲡⲉⲛϣ. هذيان ، خرافات; K 89 *B* خزن; ShWess 9 131 *S* Origen's teaching ⲋⲉⲛ- ϣ. ⲙⲡϥⲉⲛⲛⲁⲓⲣ[ⲛ]ⲟⲛ, Mor 36 62 *S* no lawgiver taught them but ⲛⲉϥϣ. ⲙⲙⲓⲛ ⲙⲙⲟⲟⲩ ⲡⲉⲛⲧⲁⲩ- ⲧⲟⲩⲡ ⲉⲓⲁⲧⲟⲩ ⲉⲃⲟⲗ; as adj: Tri 358 *S* ⲛⲉⲣⲃⲏⲛⲉ ⲛϣ. مرذولة; ShA 1 384 *S* Kronos child-devourer ⲕⲁⲧⲁ ⲡⲉⲧϣⲁⲭⲉ ⲛϣ., ROC 20 51 *S* ⲛϣⲁⲭⲉ ⲛϣ. named ⲧⲟⲉⲓⲧ, Va 57 137 *B* ⲙⲩⲑⲟⲗⲟⲅⲓⲁ ⲛⲥⲁⲭⲓ ⲛϣ. of Homer, PBu 69 &c *S* my adversaries ⲥⲭⲟⲗⲁⲍⲉ ⲉⲅⲉⲛϣⲁⲭⲉ ϣ.; ϣ(ⲉ)ⲭ ϣ. *S* nn : Aeg 282 ⲛϣ. of Jews μῦ., Gött N '98 176 ⲅⲉⲛϣ. ⲡⲁⲡⲟⲅⲣⲁⲫⲟⲛ (*l* ⲁⲡⲟ- ⲕⲣⲩ.), R 1 3 67 month named after Thoth ⲕⲁⲧⲁ ⲡϣ.

ⲣⲉϥⲧⲅⲫⲉ ϣ. B: Bar 3 23 μυθολόγος. V Rec 34 157.

ⲣⲉϥϫⲉ ϣ., *tale-tellers*: Va 57 210 B ⲙⲅⲑⲟⲗⲟⲅⲟⲥ ⲛⲣ., ShA 1 391 S ⲣⲉⲗⲗⲏⲛ ⲛⲣ.; ⲣⲉϥϫⲉ ϣⲁϫⲉ ⲛϣ.: Blake 246 S what ⲛⲣ. tell of emerald(= *ib* 110 *qui fabulosa confingunt*).

ϣϥⲱ, ϣⲃⲱ SB nn f, measure of length, *schoenus, parasang*: Ps 138 3 SB, Jer 18 15 SB, cit ShP 130² 10 σχοῖνος; C 99 156 S=C 89 95 B ⲛ̄ ⲛϣ. = Va ar 172 56 اميال. V JEA 11 151.

ϣϥⲱ B nn f, *tomb*: Commentar Philol I Pomialovski 1897 10 Jews cast thee into tomb (ⲙⲣⲁⲩ) & sealed it ⲣⲱⲥ ϫⲉⲉⲅⲣⲱⲓⲥ ⲉϯϣ., Dif 2 16 ⲁⲩⲭⲁϥ (Obadiah)ϫⲉⲛϯϣ. belonging to his fathers(*cf* Synax 1 213 ربعة).

ϣⲁϥⲟⲩⲣ S(once), -ⲣⲓ B nn f, a fish, *tilapia nilotica*: P 46 168 S ⲧϣ., Bodl 325 159 B ϯϣ. ابلط, K 171, P 54 150 B ⲛⲓϣ. بلط. V AZ 30 27, JEA 14 24.

ϣⲁϥⲣⲁ   *v* ϣⲁⲣⲃⲁ.

ϣⲱϥⲧ SA²B, ϣⲉϥⲧ-, ϣⲉⲃⲧⲋ S, ϣⲟϥⲧ† SB(S ϥ & ⲃ vary) vb I intr, *stumble, err*: Deu 32 35 B(S ⲡⲱϫⲥ ⲉⲃⲟⲗ), Job 18 7 B(S ⲡⲱⲣϫ) σφάλλειν; RNC 38 S confessing ϫⲉⲁϥϣ. ἁμαρτάνειν, Jud 20 16 S ⲉϫⲁⲙ.; Lev 5 19 SB πλημμελεῖν; Is 34 16 S(P 131¹ 118, var ⲥⲱⲣⲙ, B ⲧⲁⲕⲟ) ἀπολλύναι (var ἐμποδίζειν); ShZ 604 S ⲉⲛϣⲁⲛⲛⲟⲓ ⲙⲙⲟⲟⲩ ⲛⲧⲛⲛⲁϣ. ⲁⲛ, BIF 13 106 S ⲁⲓϣ. ⲣⲱⲥ ⲣⲱⲙⲉ = MG 25 290 B, GMir 172 S thou seest ⲙⲡⲉⲓϣ. ϫⲉⲁⲓϫⲟⲟⲥ ... ϫⲉ-, BMis 413 S ⲛⲱⲡⲛⲉ ϣ. ⲛⲱⲕⲡⲉ ϫⲓⲟⲣⲟⲟⲩ, ManiH 48 A² (ⲛ)ⲡⲉⲣⲱⲙⲉ ϣ. ⲛϥⲣ ⲛⲁⲃⲉ, PO 11 326 B if I should say...ϯⲛⲁϣ. ⲁⲛ; qual: Z 313 S ⲛⲉϣ. ⲡⲉ ⲉⲧⲃⲉⲧⲙⲛⲧⲅⲓⲁⲓⲱⲧⲏⲥ σφ., Pro 5 6 B prob (S.A ϣⲧⲣⲧⲱⲣ) σφαλερός; Gu 55 S ⲉϣⲱⲡⲉ ⲛϯϣ. ⲁⲛ ⲉⲓⲥ ⲟⲩϭⲟⲓ *if I am not mistaken*, Bor 248 10 S ⲧⲙⲛⲧⲁⲕⲣⲓⲃⲏⲥ ⲉⲧϣ., AM 127 B ⲥϣ. ⲛⲥⲧⲁⲭⲣⲓⲟⲩⲧ ⲁⲛ.

II tr, *commit error, err in anything*: Deu 9 18 B (S ⲣ ⲛⲟⲃⲉ) ἁμ.; 3 Kg 8 50 B ἀθετεῖν; Ming 316 S if one call it...ⲛϥⲛⲁϣ. ⲁⲛ ⲙⲡⲉⲧⲥⲙⲟⲛⲧ, EpApp 1 90 S sim ⲛϥⲛⲁϣ. ⲁⲛ ⲛ[ⲗⲁⲁⲩ, Cai The 121 B sim, Z 579 S ⲛϥⲧⲉⲙⲙϣⲉϥⲧ ⲗⲁⲁⲩ, C 41 48 B ⲁⲩⲥⲟⲛ ϣ. ⲛⲟⲩ-ⲣⲱⲃ = Miss 4 406 اخطل, R 1 3 20 S if chanter ϣ. ⲛⲟⲩⲗⲉϫⲓⲥ ⲛ ⲛϥⲡⲟⲟⲛⲉⲥ, Lant 14 52 S mind distraught ⲁⲛϣ. ⲛⲟⲩⲗ.; refl: RChamp 372 S if he say so ⲛϥⲛⲁϣⲉⲧϥ ⲁⲛ.

With following preposition.   ⲥ ⲉ-, *in, as to*: Mani K 51 A² ⲡⲉⲧⲁⲡⲣⲣⲟ...ⲁϥ ⲁⲣⲁϥ, Va 61 205 B I fear lest ⲁⲛϣ. ⲉⲡⲓⲉⲥⲱⲟⲩ (Ge 22 7); ⲥ ⲁⲃⲁⲗ ⲛ-, *away from*: ManiH 47 A² world ϣ. ⲁⲃ. ⲛⲧⲥⲟ-ⲫⲓⲁ; ⲥ ⲣⲛ-, ϫⲉⲛ-, *in*: Z 571 S ⲉⲕϣⲁⲛϣ. ⲣⲛⲟⲩⲣⲱⲃ σφ. ἐν; ShIF 264 S brethren ϣ. ⲣⲓⲱⲱⲛ ⲣⲛⲟⲩ-ⲣⲱⲃ, MG 25 357 B ⲣⲱⲃ ⲉⲧⲉϥⲛⲁϣ. ⲛϩⲏⲧϥ (ROC 18

59 ⲛⲓⲁ), Mor 37 168 S ⲁⲛϫⲟⲟⲩ ⲕⲁⲗⲱⲥ ⲟⲡⲣ ⲁⲛϣ. ⲛⲣⲏⲧⲟⲩ, Mor 53 93 S ⲥⲉϣ.† ⲣⲛⲧⲡⲓⲥⲧⲓⲥ, TstAb 165 B ϯϣ.† ϫⲉⲛⲡⲁⲣⲏⲧ; ⲥ ϩⲓϫⲉⲛ-: Am 5 2 B(S ⲥⲗⲁ-ⲁⲧⲉ) σφ. ἐπί.

——, ϣⲟ. SB nn m, *error, fault*: Sa 2 12 B ϣⲟ. (S ⲛⲟⲃⲉ) ἁμάρτημα; Lev 5 19 B(S diff) πλημμέλεια; 3 Kg 8 50 B ϣⲟ. ἀθέτημα; R 2 1 49 S ϣ. ϩⲓⲙⲛⲧⲁⲧ-ⲥⲟⲟⲩⲛ, Va 58 27 B in margin beside cancelled lines ϣ., PO 14 369 B forgive ⲡⲁϣ. ⲛⲗⲁⲥ, Mor 18 S *v* below ϣⲟϥⲧⲉ.

ⲁⲧϣ., *unerring*: He 6 19 B(S ⲟⲣϫ)ἀσφαλής; Lant 16 32 S ⲙⲉ(ⲛ) ⲁⲧϣ. except Lord only.

ⲣⲉϥϣ., *erring person*: Va 63 24 B ⲁⲛⲟⲛ ϩⲁⲛⲣ., Lant 6 7 S sim.

ϣⲁϥⲧⲉ S, -ϥⲧ SB¹, ϩⲉϥⲧ, -ϥⲧⲉ (once) A, ϣⲁϥϯ², -ϭⲟ B, ϣⲉϥϯ F nn m, *iniquitous, impious person* or *thing*: Ge 18 23 B¹(S = Gk), Job 10 3 S(B = Gk), Pro 18 22 SA ἀσεβής; K 86 B ⲡⲓϣⲁϥⲑⲟ فاجر; ShC 42 135 S ⲉⲧⲉⲧⲛⲣϣⲏ., *ib* 118 S ϩⲉⲛϣ. ⲡⲉ ⲛϣⲁϫⲉ, ShMich 550 15 S ⲣ ϩⲁⲥ ⲛⲣⲱⲙⲉ ⲛϣ. ⲉⲧⲥ, Mor 44 23 S Judas ⲛⲓϣ.; as adj: Sa 14 16 S-ϥⲧ ἀσ.; ⲙⲛⲧ-ϣ., -ϩ., *iniquity*: Deu 9 4 S(B ⲙⲉⲧⲁⲥⲉⲃⲏⲥ), Pro 1 31 SA(Cl, var -ⲧⲉ, B do), Sa 14 9 S-ϥⲧ, Am 1 6 A (B do), Ro 11 26 SF(B do) ἀσέβεια, Lev 18 17 S(B do), Lam 1 14 B¹(F ⲙⲛⲧⲁⲥ.) ἀσέβημα; Lev 7 1 B¹ (S diff) πλημμέλεια; Pro 10 23 SA(B ⲡⲉⲧⲣⲱⲟⲩ) κα-κός; Miss 8 213 S ⲁⲓⲣ ⲛⲟⲃⲉ ϩⲓⲣⲉⲛⲙⲛⲧϣⲁⲃⲧⲉ, DeV 2 280 B ⲃⲓⲟⲥ ⲙⲙ.²; ⲣ ⲙⲛⲧϣ.: 2 Pet 2 6 S(B diff) ἀσεβεῖν; ShP 130¹ 139 S ⲁⲥⲉⲓⲣⲉ ⲛⲅⲉⲛⲙⲙ.; ⲣ ϣ., *do iniquity*: Deu 17 13 S(B ⲉⲣ ⲁⲥⲉⲃⲏⲥ), Is 59 13 S (B do) ἀσ.; TT 153 S ⲁⲕⲣ., DeV 2 279 B will not again ⲉⲣ.²; ⲥ ⲉ-: Hos 7 13 SA(B ⲉⲣ ⲁⲥ.) ἀσ. εἰς; ShBMOr 8810 499 S to nun ⲁⲣ ϣ. ⲉⲣⲟⲓ.; ⲥ ϩⲛ-S: Jude 15 (B do) ἀσ. gen; Sa 10 8 σφ. ἐν.

ϣⲟϥⲧⲉ, ϣⲟⲃ., ϣⲁϥⲧⲉ S, nn, *error*: Mor 19 75 ⲉⲣ]ⲉⲡⲁⲓ ⲥⲙⲟⲡⲧ ⲛⲛ ⲗⲁⲁⲩ ⲛϣ. ⲛⲣⲏⲧⲟⲩ (var *ib* 18 66 ϣⲟⲃⲧ) = Miss 4 140 B ⲁϫⲛⲓ, Wess 18 77 forgive ⲛⲉⲛϣⲁ., Mor 33 120 ϯϣⲟⲟⲛ ϩⲓⲟⲩⲛⲟϭ ⲛϣⲁ. (varr ViK 9504 ϣ., BMis 61 ϯϣⲟⲃⲧ), Lant 80 81 ϩⲓ ϩⲁ-ⲛⲁϣ., *ib* 70 23 ϭⲓ ⲉⲣⲱⲧⲛ ⲙⲡⲛⲁϣⲁⲃ.

ϣⲱϥⲧ, ϣⲟ. S, ϣⲟϥⲟ B(K) nn m, *hollow of hand, handful*: K 260 B كَفّ, حفنة; BMis 494 ⲁϥⲙⲉϩ ⲡⲉϣ. ⲙⲙⲟⲟⲩ;   as measure: Bodl(P) e 33 in list of *varia* ϣⲟ. γ, Sh Berl Or 1611 5 40 ⲟⲩⲛⲟⲩⲙⲉⲥ (νοῦμμος) ⲡⲟⲩⲱⲧ ⲛ ⲟⲩϣ. ⲛⲉⲃⲣⲁ, ST 303 ϣ. ⲛⲥⲟⲩⲟ, *ib* 259, Viostr 122, CO 204, Ep 324 sim, *ib* 227 ϣⲟ. ⲛⲕⲁⲣⲁϥ, Win 55 ϣ. ⲛⲕⲟⲩϫ, Hall 115 ϣⲱⲧϥ (*sic*) (ⲛ)-ⲃⲛⲛⲉ, BKU 1 73 ⲃⲓ ⲛϣⲟ. ⲉϩⲟⲩⲛ ⲉⲡⲉϥⲏⲓ, WS 93]ⲛϣ.

ϣⲁϥⲧⲉ S, -ϯ B, ϣⲉϥϯ F *v* ϣⲱϥⲧ vb.

ϣⲟϥⲧⲉ, ϣⲁ. *v* ϣⲱϥⲧ vb.

ϣⲟϥϣⲉϥ, ϣⲉϥϣⲱϥ† S, ϣⲉϥϣⲁϥⲧ† A² vb intr, meaning uncertain, *spread, burrow* (?): ShP 130² 25 trees where insect ⲃⲟⲗⲃⲗ ⲁⲅⲱ ⲛ̄ϣ. [ⲉⲣⲉ]ⲛⲉϥⲃⲏⲃ [ϩⲣⲁⲓ ⲛ̄]ϧⲏⲧⲟⲩ & breeds there, ShP 130⁴ 141 disease in body ⲛⲁϣ. ⲉϥⲕⲱⲧⲉ ϩⲣⲁⲓ ⲛ̄ϧⲏⲧϥ ⲛ̄ϣⲱⲡⲉ ϩⲙ̄ⲡⲉϥⲟⲩⲟⲉⲓⲱ (l ? ⲡⲟⲉⲓⲱ), P 44 94 (ⲉ)ⲧϣ.† ⲛ̄ⲑⲉ ⲙ̄ⲡⲁⲓ ϫⲓⲟⲛ مشوى مثل الذاتى (so Munier) =43 79 ⲉϥϣ.† ⲛ̄ⲑⲉ ⲙ̄ⲡⲓⲧⲓⲟⲛ داويدى مثل متتر, Mani 1 A² ⲡⲕⲉϣ ⲉϥⲉⲗⲉϭⲗⲉϭⲧ ⲉⲣⲉⲡⲉϥ . . ⲛ̄ϣⲏⲛ ⲉ'ϣ.†

ϣⲃⲉⲗⲧ, ϭⲃ. (once), ϣⲃⲁⲧ(l ? -ⲗⲧ)B nn m, *what is excessive, exudes, humour, pus*: Va 63 87 Paul did ⲁⲡⲟⲧⲁϫⲓⲓ (ἀποτάσσειν) ⲙ̄ⲛⲓϭ. of this life & its vain glory (Gk om); K 159 ⲛ̄ϣ. خلط; P 54 130, BMOr 8775 125 ϣⲃⲁⲧ قيح (cf ϩⲓϩⲱⲧⲏⲣ), P 54 lc ⲙ̄. خارج, ج, ib 163, but ib ϣⲗⲁϭⲧ corrected to ϣⲃⲁⲗⲧ 'ۥ, 'ۥ. Two words? Cf ? DM V 5 7 *šhʾlt*.

ϣⲁϩ S vb intr, meaning unknown. Perhaps incomplete. V ⲃⲁⲣ.

ϣⲁϩ SAA²B, ϣⲉϩ F nn m, *flame, fire*: Ge 15 17 SB, Is 5 24 SBF, Joel 2 3 SA ϣⲁ B φλόξ; Lu 22 55 S(B ⲭⲣⲱⲙ) πῦρ; ib 11 36 S(B ⲥⲉⲧⲉⲃⲣⲏϭ) ἀστραπή; Jo 18 18 SA²(B ⲣⲁⲕϩⲓ) ἀνθρακιά; Sa 7 25 B(S diff) ἀτμίς; Nu 19 6 S(B ⲣⲱⲕϩ) κατάκαυμα; PS 116 S ⲛⲓϣ. ⲡⲟⲩⲟⲓⲛ, ib 373 S ⲡⲉⲧϣ. ⲙⲟⲩϩ, ShC 42 74 S sickness with ⲧⲉϥϩⲙⲙⲉ ⲁⲩⲱ ⲡⲉϥϣ., ShIF 188 S ϩⲉⲡⲧⲓⲕ...ϭⲱϣⲉ ϩⲓⲧⲛ̄ⲟⲩϣ. ⲉϥϫⲉⲣⲟ, BHom 39 S ⲛⲓϣ. ⲛⲟⲩϫⲟⲡⲛ̄, C 43 238 B ⲡⲓϣ. ⲛ̄ⲧⲉ ⲡⲓϣⲱⲙ, DeV 2 83 B ⲁⲡ̄ϣ. ⲉⲣ ⲥⲁⲡϣⲱ ⲛ̄ⲧ̄ϩⲣⲱ; ϣ. ⲛ̄ⲕⲱϩⲧ SA: Is 29 6 (B ⲛ̄ⲭⲣⲱⲙ), Ac 7 30 (B do) φ. πυρός, Ob 18 SA(B ϣ.) φ.; Hos 7 6 A(B ⲙⲟⲩϩ) φέγγος; BMar 58 demon leapt forth like ⲟⲩϣ. ⲛ̄ⲕ. (cf ϣⲗⲓϭ), Pcod 23 ⲟ ⲡⲟⲩϣ. ⲛ̄ⲕ.; ϣ. ⲛ̄ⲥⲁⲧⲉ SA²: Ps 28 7 (B do) φ. π., Sa 19 20 φ.; JTS 10 404 Andrew ⲟⲩϣ. ⲛ̄ⲥ. ⲡⲉ, Mani 1 A²; ϣ. ⲛ̄ⲭⲣⲱⲙ BF: Ez 1 7 (S ⲧ̄ⲕ ⲛ̄ⲕⲱϩⲧ) σπινθήρ; Mor 24 18 F; ⲟⲓ ⲛ̄ϣ. B: Dan 7 9 (S ⲙⲟⲩϩ) φλέγειν; Cai Euch 464 ⲑⲣⲟⲛⲟⲥ ⲉⲧⲟⲓ ⲛ̄ϣ. φλόγινος; PO 11 358 ⲉⲣⲉⲡⲉϥⲥⲁϭⲟⲩⲛ ⲟⲓ ⲛ̄ϣ.; ϯ ϣ., *burn*: Ex 24 17 S(var ⲙ., B ϩⲓ ϣ.) φλέγ.; Jer 50 12 B(S ⲣⲱⲕϩ) ἐμπυρίζειν; Va 63 103 B surgeon says ⲙ̄ⲡⲁⲓⲣⲱⲕϩ ⲓⲉ ⲁⲓϯ ϣ. καίειν; BG 39 S ⲟⲩⲁⲓⲱⲛ ⲉϥϯ ϣ. ϩⲛ̄ⲟⲩⲕⲱϩⲧ, PMéd 306 S ⲟⲩ ⲡⲁϣⲉ ⲉⲥϯ ϣ. ⲛ̄ⲕⲱϩⲧ, BM 357 S lightnings ϯ ϣ. ϩⲙ̄ⲡⲉⲧϫⲟⲥⲉ, BMis 18 S shining vision so that palace ϯ ϣ. was illumined, MG 25 388 B ϯⲁⲛϥⲁⲙⲓ ⲙⲟ ⲉⲥϯ ϣ. (ROC 19 33 ...ڤور ﺍﻟﻨﺎﺭ, cf DeV 2 155); ϭ ⲉⲃⲟⲗ S: Blake 288 amethyst ϯ ϣ. ⲉⲃ. like fire, Berl Or 1607 3 97 pillar of light ϯ ϣ. ⲉⲃ. ⲉϫⲙ̄ⲡⲥⲱⲙⲁ; ϫⲓⲛϯ ϣ. B: C 89 98 fire was mighty ϧⲉⲛⲡⲉϥϣ.; ϩⲓ ϣ. B: v ϯ ϣ.; ϩⲓ ϣ. ⲉⲃⲟⲗ: Ex 9 24 φλογίζειν.

ϣⲟⲩϩⲉ v ϫⲟⲩϩⲉ.

ϣⲱⲃϩ, ϣⲉϩⲃ-, ϣⲟϩⲃ⸗ S vb intr, *be withered, scorched*: Ac 28 6 (B diff) πίμπρασθαι; tr, *wither*: Si 43 3 ϣⲉϩⲃ- ἀναξηραίνειν; Mor 23 42 fire devours them ⲛ̄ϣⲟⲩⲟⲣⲃⲟⲩ = ib 24 30 F ⲁⲣϣⲟⲩ. V ϣⲱⲃϩ to which this belongs.

ϣⲉϩⲃⲉⲥ S nn as adj: R 1 4 35 ϣⲉ ⲛ̄ϭⲁⲙⲟⲩⲗ ⲛ̄ϣ. ⲉⲧⲉⲛϩⲣⲟⲙⲁⲥⲛⲉ *camelus dromas*.

ϣⲁϩⲗ B nn, something used as fuel: C 86 221 poured over body in cauldron ⲧⲁϩⲧ, ⲁⲥⲫⲁⲗⲧⲟⲛ ⲛⲉⲙⲟⲩϣ. Cf ? ϣⲗϩ.

ϣⲁϩⲙ S nn, ingredient in recipe: PMéd 162. Prob = شحم *fat* (Chassinat).

ϣⲁϩⲟⲩⲛ, -ⲉϩⲟⲩⲛ v ϩⲟⲩⲛ.

ϣⲟϩⲉⲛ B v ϩⲏⲛⲉ (ϣⲟⲩϩⲏⲛⲉ).

ϣⲱϩⲡ B v ϣⲱⲃ ϩ.

ϣⲁϩⲏⲣⲉ S nn, in recipes: PChass 1 to turn iron to gold ϣⲁⲛ[ ]ϣ. ⲛ̄ ⲟⲛⲟⲟⲩ ϩⲓϩⲙ̄ϫ, ib 2 ⲡⲏⲣ̄ϣ, ⲁⲡⲁⲣⲁⲛⲉⲓ, ϣ. ⲓ̄ measure of each, ib vo ⲙⲓⲥⲉⲟⲥ (μίσυ) ⲛ̄ ϣⲁϩⲁⲣⲉ ⲁ̄. Cf شيح (Dozy 1 732).

ϣⲁϩⲣⲁⲓ, -ⲉϩⲣⲏⲓ v ϩⲣⲁⲓ.

ϣⲁϩⲉⲩⲧ A v ⲉϣⲱ.

ϣⲓϩⲏⲧ F v ϣⲓ s f (place-name).

ϣⲁϩϣⲉϩ, ϣⲁϩϣⲱϩ† B vb intr, *be harsh, rough, hardy*: Va 57 226 ⲑⲙⲉⲧⲥⲕⲗⲏⲣⲟⲥ ⲛ̄ⲛⲓⲥⲟⲩⲣⲓ ⲉϥϣ. τραχύς; C 89 8 ⲡⲁⲣⲉⲧⲉϥϫⲓⲛⲥⲁϫⲓ ϣ.† ἀπότομος = MG 17 346 جاف; ib 116 ⲟⲩⲣⲱⲙⲓ ⲉϥϣ. ϧⲉⲛⲧⲉϥϫⲓⲛⲉⲣ ϩⲱⲃ σκληρός = MG 17 580 'ج; ROC 23 278 ⲡⲁⲑⲛⲁⲓ ⲉⲧϣ. ϧⲉⲛⲡⲉϥϩⲃⲏⲟⲩⲓ, Va 58 65 ⲛ̄ⲥⲓⲛⲟⲩ ϣ. ϧⲉⲛⲧⲁⲥⲕⲩⲥⲓⲥ, AM 136 ⲉϥϩⲟⲣ...ⲉϥϣ.; as nn m: K 231 ⲡⲛ̄ϣ. (شظف) = P 54 163 غض, شديد, 'ضۥ; Cat 158 husks if eaten ϣⲱⲡⲓ ϧⲉⲛⲟⲩϣ., MG 25 122 ⲡⲓϣⲓϭⲓ ⲛ̄ⲧⲉ ⲡⲓⲁⲣⲉⲧⲏ ⲛⲉⲙⲡϣ. ⲙ̄ⲡⲓⲃⲓⲟⲥ; ⲙⲉⲧ�-ϣ., *harshness, severity*: C 89 118 = MG 17 582 جفاء = Va ar 172 68 وضوص.

ϣⲓϣ S, -ⲓϣ SB(rare) nn m, *dust* (cf ⲡⲛϣ̄ Dévaud Études 53): Sa 5 15, Is 17 13 (B ⲣⲏⲓⲥⲓ) χνοῦς (var χοῦς); ib 5 24 SB(P 70 23, var & F ϣⲟⲓϣ) κονιορτός; Ex 32 20 -ⲓϣ (B ϣⲙⲁ) λεπτός; P 54 174 B ⲡⲓϣ. هباء; ⲣ, ⲟ ⲛ̄ϣ., *become dust*: Ps 28 6 (B do) λεπτύνειν; Is 10 6 (B ϣⲱ.) εἰς κον. τιθέναι; 1 Tim 6 4 (var ϣⲓϭ, B as Gk) νοσεῖν (this word?); ViK 9754 116 wind shall ⲁⲁⲩ ⲛ̄ϣⲓⲣⲓϣ.

ϣⲟⲉⲓϣ S, ϣⲁⲓϣ A², ϣⲟⲓϣ B v ϣⲱϫⲉ s f.

ϣⲟⲩϫ B v ϭⲟⲩϭ.

ϣⲁϫⲉ S, ϣⲉϫⲉ Sⁿ AA²(AP), ϭⲉ. A²(JoMa), ⲥⲁϫⲓ

B, ϣⲉϫⲓ, ⲥⲉ. F vb **I** intr, *speak*: Job 1 16 *SB*, Eccl
1 8 *SF* (C Schmidt's ϣ., P Mich 3520 c.), He 6 9
SBF λαλεῖν; Pro 12 18 *SA*(*B* ϫⲱ) λέγειν; Mt 26
62 *S*(*B* diff) ἀποκρίνεσθαι; Ps 91 14 *S*(*B* ϫⲱ) ἀναγγέλλειν; Sa 8 12 *S* φθέγγεσθαι; Ps 54 16 *SB* διηγεῖσθαι; PS 6 *S* ⲉⲓⲙⲡ ⲟⲅⲟⲛ ⲙⲙⲟⲟⲩ ϣ., CA 96 *S*
ⲉⲧⲃⲉⲣⲟⲉⲓⲛⲉ ⲉⲩⲛⲁϣ. *during prayers*, El 34 *A* ⲁⲓⲥⲱⲡⲧ
ⲁⲣⲁⲩ ⲉⲩϣ., AP 56 *A*[2] *said to him* ϣ. ⲡⲉⲧⲣⲉ, BSM
64 *B* ⲛⲉⲧⲥ....ⲛⲏ ⲉⲧⲥⲱⲧⲉⲙ.

II tr *AB*, *speak, say*: Ps 40 7 (*S* ϫⲱ), Is 32 6 (*SF*
do) λα.; Is 43 9 (*S* do) ἀναγ., Pro 12 17 (*SA* do)
ἀπαγ.; Mt 13 35 (*S* do, *F* ϣ. ⲉ-) ἐρεύγεσθαι; El 56
A ⲧⲟⲩⲉⲥⲡⲉ ⲛϣ. ⲉⲧⲟⲩϣ. ⲙⲙⲁⲥ; PO 11 303 ⲡⲓⲙ
ⲡⲉⲑⲛⲁϣ ⲥ. ⲙⲡⲧⲁⲓⲟ ?, BSM 105 *every one etc.* ⲛⲧ-
ⲙⲉⲑⲛⲟⲩϫ, DeV 2 39 ⲡⲓⲡⲉⲧϛⲱⲟⲩ ⲉⲧⲁϥⲥ. ⲙⲙⲟⲟⲩ.
With following preposition.

—— ⲉ- *SABF*, *to, into*: Nu 14 28 *S*(*B* ⲉϩⲣⲏⲓ
ⲉ-), Is 36 11 *SBF*, 1 Cor 14 9 *SB* λα. ⲉⲓⲥ; Si 25 12
S διηγ. ⲉⲓⲥ; Ps 26 8 *S*(*B* ϫⲱ ⲛ-) εἰπεῖν dat; ShIF
86 *S* ⲟⲩ ⲡⲉⲧϫⲱ ⲙⲙⲟⲟⲩ ⲏ ⲡⲓⲙ ⲡⲉⲧϣ. ⲉⲣⲟⲟⲩ,
Miss 8 252 *S* ⲉⲓϣ. ⲉⲣⲟⲕ ⲡⲧⲟⲕ ⲱ ⲡϛⲁⲅⲓⲟⲥ (*cf* ⲉⲓϣⲉ-
ⲣⲟⲕ); *concerning, about*: Aeg 242 *S* ϣ. ⲉⲙⲙⲛⲧⲭ̄ⲥ̄
λα. *passive*: Is 53 8 *S*(*B* ϥⲓⲣⲓ ⲉ-) διηγ., Jo 1 18 *S*(*B*
om ⲉ-) ἐξηγ.; Aeg 268 *S* ϣ. ⲉⲛⲉⲭⲁⲣⲓⲥⲙⲁ λέ.; Pro
29 2 *S*(var ⲙⲡ-)*A* ἐγκωμιάζειν; Job 8 7 *S* neg(*B* diff)
ἀμύθητος; PS 7 *S* ⲙⲡ ϣϭⲟⲙ...ⲉϣ. ⲉⲡⲟⲩⲟⲉⲓⲛ, ShA
1 300 *S* ⲛⲥⲉϣ. ⲉⲣⲟϥ ϛⲓⲙⲁ ⲛⲓⲙ, ShMIF 23 134 *S*
ⲉⲓϣ. ⲉⲧⲉϫ ⲟⲩⲥⲓⲁ ϫⲉⲧⲥⲛϥⲉ *by the sword I mean power*,
ShViK 9292 *S* ⲡⲁⲓ ⲉⲧⲟⲩϣ. ⲉⲣⲟⲟⲩ ϛⲓⲧⲛⲡⲉⲅⲣⲁⲫⲏ,
Pcod 11 *S* ⲧⲛⲅⲗⲏ ⲉⲛⲧⲁϫⲁⲅⲉⲓϫ ϣ. ⲉⲣⲟⲥ, Va 61 87 *B*
ⲉⲓⲥ. ⲉⲡⲓⲙ ⲉⲃⲏⲗ ⲉⲡⲓⲥϛⲟϥⲟⲥ ?, DeV 2 213 *B* ⲟⲩϣⲫⲓ-
ⲣⲓⲛⲉ ⲉⲥ. ⲉⲡⲣⲱⲃ ⲙⲡⲟⲩⲁⲓ ⲡⲟⲩⲁⲓ *tell of*, R 1 3 81 *S*
ⲡⲗⲁⲥ ⲉⲧϣ. ⲉⲧⲙⲉ; *against* (*cf* ⲥ ⲛⲥⲁ-) *S*: Ps 108 2
(var & *B* ⲛⲥⲁ-) λα. κατά, Hos 7 13(*AB* do)καταλ. κ.;
ShC 73 96 ϣ. ⲉⲣⲟⲓ ⲛϫⲓⲟⲩⲉ, BMis 188 ϣ. ⲉⲣⲟϥ ⲛ-
ϛⲏⲡⲉⲑⲟⲟⲩ; ⲉⲣⲟ ⲩⲛ ⲉ-, *to*: BMar 237 *serpent to*
Eve ⲉϥϣ. ⲉϛ. ⲉⲣⲟⲥ; ⲉϛⲣⲁⲓ, ⲉϛ. ⲉ-, *to, about*: Nu
14 28 *B*(*S* ⲉ-), Cai Euch 596 *B* λα. ⲉⲓⲥ; Mich 550 45
S ⲡⲉⲛⲧⲁϥϣ. ⲉϛ. ⲉⲡϫ̄ⲥ̄ ⲡⲟⲩ̇ⲙⲗⲁⲡⲏ (*sc* Nestorius),
Ep App 1 146 *S* ⲉϥⲉϣ. ⲉϛ. ⲉⲡⲉϥϛⲏⲧ ϛⲁ†ⲣⲏⲛⲓ.

—— ⲉⲧⲃⲉ-, ⲉⲑ., *concerning, about*: Ac 1 3 *SB* λέ.
περί; ShC 42 108 *S* ⲙⲛϭⲉⲓ ⲛϣ. ⲉⲧⲃⲏⲛⲧⲥ, BSM 1
B ⲁϥⲥ. ⲉⲑⲃⲉⲡⲓ ⲉⲑⲟⲩⲁⲃ.

—— ⲉϫⲛ- *SB*, *for, on behalf of*: Ac 26 1 *B*(*S* ϛⲁ-)
λέ. ὑπέρ; Pey Gr 166 *S* *bribe advocates* ⲛⲥⲉϣ. ⲉ-
ϫⲱⲛ, Tst Ab 255 *B* ⲥ. ⲉϫⲱⲓ ϛⲁⲧⲉⲛⲫⲁⲣⲁⲱ, EW 117
B ⲁⲣⲉⲥ. ⲉϫⲉⲛⲡⲁⲓϥⲁⲣⲙⲁⲕⲟⲥ ?; *concerning*: DeV 2
39 *B* ⲥ. ⲉϫⲱⲟⲩ ⲛϛⲁⲡⲉⲧϛⲱⲟⲩ; *in*: ShC 42 141 *S*
ϣ. ⲉϫⲙⲡⲣⲁⲛ ⲙⲡϫ̄ⲥ̄ *from Scriptures*; ⲉⲡⲉⲥⲛⲧ
ⲉϫⲛ-*S*, *down upon, to*: Mor 28 90 ⲁϥϣ. ⲉⲡ. ⲉϫⲙⲡⲣ-
ⲣⲟ *from cloud*, BMis 171 sim; ⲉϛⲣⲏⲓ ⲉϫ. *B*: Lam
3 20 (*S* diff) καταδολεσχεῖν OL *taediari super*; DeV
2 41 *lest He* ⲥ. ⲛⲟⲩϭⲱϯ ⲉⲃⲟⲗ ⲉϛ. ⲉϫⲱⲟⲩ.

—— ⲙⲛ- *SAA*[2]*BF*, *with*: Ge 12 4 *SB*, Is 30 10
SBF, Jo 4 26 *SA*[2]*B*, AP 7 *A*[2] λα. dat, Deu 5 24 *SB*,
Is 36 11 *SBF*, Ac 28 25 *SB*(var ⲟⲩⲃⲉ-)λα. πρός, Nu
11 17 *SB*, Ps 27 3 *SB*, Jo 4 27 *SA*[2]*BF* λα. μετά; Mt
21 3 *SBF*(Mich 539)εἰπ. dat, Ge 7 1 *S*(*B* ⲡⲉϫⲉ), Ac
2 29 *B*(*S* ϫⲱ dat)εἰπ. πρός; Ex 6 27 *B*(var ⲟⲩⲃⲉ-)
διαλέ. π.; Mk 9 33 *S*(*B* diff)διαλογίζειν; Jer 33 2
SB χρηματίζειν dat; PS 10 *S* ⲉⲧⲣⲁϣ. ⲙⲛⲡⲥⲉⲛⲟⲥ ⲛ-
ⲧⲙⲛⲧⲣⲱⲙⲉ, BG 17 *S* ⲁϥϣ. ⲙⲡⲟⲩⲥϛⲓⲙⲉ, El 58 *A*
ϣ. ⲡⲉⲙⲡⲉⲗⲉⲅ, WZKM 14 234 *S* *none may* ⲉⲓ ⲉⲃⲟⲗ ⲉϥϣ.
ⲡⲉⲙⲙⲁⲕ (*cf* ⲉⲡⲁⲧⲉ ⲙⲛ-), DeV 2 90 *B* ⲁϥⲥ. ⲡⲉⲙⲙⲁϥ
ⲡⲟⲩϛⲁⲡ, C 41 51 *B* ⲁϥⲥ. ⲡⲉⲙⲙⲁⲛ ϫⲉ-.

—— ⲛ-, *in, with*: Ac 2 4 *B*(*S* ϛⲣⲁⲓ ϛⲛ-), 1 Cor 13
1 *S*(*B* ϛⲉⲛ-)λα. dat; ⲉⲃⲟⲗ ⲛϛⲏⲧ⳽: Is 19 3 *S*(*B* ⲙⲟⲩϯ
ⲉⲃ. ϛⲉⲛ-) ἐγγαστρίμυθος.

—— ⲛⲥⲁ- *SAB*, *after, against, malign*: Nu 12 1
SB, Job 19 18 *SB* λα. κατά; Ja 4 11 *B*(*SA* = Gk)
καταλα. gen, Mic 3 7 *SAB* κα. κ.; Ac 19 9 *B*(*S* ϫⲓ
ⲟⲩⲁ ⲉ-) κακολογεῖν acc, Lev 20 9 *S*(*B* ϫⲉ ⲥ. ⲛⲥⲁ-)
κακῶς εἰπ. acc; ShC 73 64 *S* ⲛϭⲉ ⲉⲧⲟⲩϣ. ⲛⲥⲁⲣⲁϛ
ⲛⲥⲩⲛⲁⲅⲱⲅⲏ ⲉⲩⲥⲱϣ ⲙⲙⲟⲟⲩ, ShBor 300 74 *S* ⲙⲛ-
ⲛⲥⲁⲧⲣⲁⲟⲩϛⲟ ⲉⲓϣ. ⲛⲥⲱⲓ ϫⲉ-*retort*, Mor 19
7 *S* ⲥ. ⲛⲥⲁⲡⲁⲓⲕⲁⲓⲟⲥ = Miss 4 96 *B*, Gött ar 114 5
عـ قطن, Va 57 76 *B* ⲥ. ⲛϛⲣⲁⲛⲃⲗⲁⲥⲫⲏⲙⲟⲥ ⲛⲥⲁⲡⲓⲥⲛⲏⲡⲓ.

—— ⲛⲁϛⲣⲛ-, *before*: Nu 34 1 *S*(*B* ⲟⲩⲃⲉ-), Ps 11
2 *S*(*B* ⲡⲉⲙ-) λα. πρός; Ez 13 19 *B* ἀποφθέγ. dat.

—— ⲟⲩⲃⲉ-, *against*: R 2 146 *S* ⲉⲩϣⲁⲛϣ. ⲟⲩⲃⲉ-
ⲡⲉⲩⲉⲣⲏⲩ & *quarrel*; *v also* ⲥ ⲙⲛ-, ⲛⲁϛⲣⲛ-.

—— ϛⲁⲧⲉⲛ- *B*, *before*: Ps 43 2 (*S* ⲧⲁⲙⲟ) ⲁⲛⲁⲅ.
dat; Mk 5 16 (*S* do) διηγ. dat; Ac 21 19 (*S* ⲧⲁⲩⲟ)
ἐξηγ.; PO 11 338 ⲁⲩⲥ. ϛⲁⲧⲟⲧⲟⲩ ⲡⲟⲩⲟⲛ ⲛⲓⲃⲉⲛ
ⲉⲑⲃⲉ-.

—— ϛⲁ-, ϛ̇ⲁ-, *concerning*: Jer 18 20 *SB* λα. ὑπέρ;
Mic 7 3 *S*(Mor 54 19, var & *A* ⲉⲡⲟⲩⲱϣ ⲛ-, *B* diff)
λα. καταθύμιον; Ac 26 1 *S*(*B* ⲉϫⲉⲛ-) λέ. ὑπ.; *ib* 24
10 *S*(*B* ⲉⲣ ⲟⲩⲱ ⲉϛⲣⲏⲓ ⲉϫⲉⲛ-) ἀπολογεῖσθαι περί;
ShC 73 96 *S* ⲉⲧⲉⲧⲛϣ. ϛⲁⲣⲱⲧⲛ ⲙⲁⲅⲁⲁⲧⲧⲏⲅⲧⲛ, BM
260 *S* ϣ. ϛⲁⲡⲉⲧⲣⲓⲧⲟⲩⲱϣ ϛⲛⲟⲩⲕⲣⲟϥ.

—— ϛⲛ-, ϛⲉⲛ- *SA*[2]*B*, *with (agent), in*: Ps 11 2
SB, *ib* 38 3 *SB* λα. ἐν, Mk 16 17 *SB*, 1 Cor 13 1 *B*(*S*
ⲛ-)λα. dat; Sa 8 *SB* φθέγ. acc; Mani K 27 *A*[2] ⲡ-
ⲡ̄ⲛ̄ⲁ̄ ⲛⲕⲉⲕⲉ etc. ϛⲓⲙⲡⲓⲙⲡⲧⲥⲛⲁⲩ[ⲥ ⲙⲡ̄ⲛ̄ⲁ̄].

—— ⲛⲛ m *SAA*[2]*BF*, ϣ(ⲉ)ϫ- *S*, *saying, word,*
affair: Deu 4 9 *SB*, Ps 16 4 *SBF*, Pro 1 2 *SAB*,
Eccl 1 8 *SF* ϣⲉϫⲓ(PMich 3520), Jo 1 1 *SBF*(BP
5569), Cl 3 3 *A*, 1 Cor 14 36 *SBF* λόγος, Ps 118 25
SB, Is 30 11 *SBF*, Ac 7 38 *SB* λόγιον, Ps 103 34 *S*
(*B* ϫⲓⲛⲥ.) διαλογή, Ro 1 20 *S* ⲙⲡⲧⲟⲩϣ. ⲙⲙⲁⲩ (*B*
ⲁⲧⲉⲣ ⲟⲩⲱ)ἀναπολόγητος; Job 4 2 *SB*, Ps 16 6 *SBF*,
He 6 5 *SB*, Cl 10 1 *A* ῥῆμα; 1 Cor 15 33 *SB* ὁμιλία;
Ez 13 19 *B* ἀπόφθεγμα; Job 17 6 *S*(*B* ϣϫⲏⲓ) θρύλη-
μα; Si 22 6 *S* διήγησις; *ib* 44 6 *S* ἔπος; Ro 11 4 *S*
(*B* = Gk) χρηματισμός; *ib* 15 18 *B*(*S* ⲗⲁⲁⲩ ⲛϣ.),

Ac 28 21 *B*(var ϩⲱⲃ, *S* om), 1 Cor 14 35 *SF*(*B* ϩⲱⲃ) ⲧⲓ; Cl 50 1 *A* ⲙⲁⲉⲓⲧ ⲡϣ. ἐξήγησις, 3 Kg 10 1 *S* ⲥⲗⲟⲧ ⲡϣ. αἴνιγμα, Ps 34 20 *SB* ϣ. ⲡⲉⲓⲣⲏⲛⲏ εἰρηνικά, Mt 19 9 *SB* ϣ. ⲙⲡⲟⲣⲛⲓⲁ πορνεία, 1 Cor 1 10 *SB* ϣ. ⲛⲟⲩⲱⲧ τὸ αὐτό, Ac 26 28 *S* ⲕⲟⲩⲓ ⲡϣ. (*B* ⲕⲟⲩϫⲓ only) ὀλίγος; PS 29 *S* hear me ⲧⲁϫⲡⲟⲩⲕ ⲉⲡⲉⲓϣ., *ib* 15 *S* ⲁϥⲟⲩⲱϩ ⲉⲧⲟⲟⲧϥ ϩⲙⲡϣ. saying, *ib* 120 *S* ϫⲱ ⲙⲡⲉⲓϣ. ⲡⲟⲩⲱϩⲙ *retort*, ShC 73 99 *S* ⲉⲕϣⲱⲡⲉ ⲡⲁϥ ⲡϣ. ⲡⲥⲱⲃⲉ, ShMich 550 19 *S* if they wish...ⲉⲩⲡⲁⲙ ⲡⲉⲩϣ. ⲡⲓⲁⲣⲙ⳿ⲡⲡⲉⲗⲗⲟ, BHom 46 *S* ⲡϣ. ⲡⲧⲉⲭⲏⲣⲁ ⲡⲣⲏⲕⲉ *story*, BMis 456 *S* ⲟⲩϣ. ⲉϥⲙⲡϣⲁ ⲡⲁⲁϥ, Mor 50 41 *S* ⲙⲡⲧⲁⲕ⳿ϩⲱⲃ ⲙⲡⲉⲓϣ. ⲡⲁⲓ, BP 4927 *S* said to them ⲟⲩⲡⲉ ⲡϣ.?, Miss 4 639 *S* (ⲛ)ⲧⲁⲁⲡⲁⲡⲧⲁ ⲉⲣⲟⲕ ⲙⲡⲉⲓⲕⲟⲩⲓ ⲡϣ. = C 41 35 *B* ϩⲱⲃ, ST 115 *S* sim, C 86 75 *B* ⲁϫ⳿ⲟⲕ ⲡⲉⲟⲕ ⲡⲉⲙⲡⲁⲓⲥ.?, CO 153 *S* will bring it ⲡⲁⲧⲗⲁⲁⲩ ⲡϣ., J 62 8 *S*ᵃ sim, El 52 *A* ⲉⲥⲡⲉ ⲡϣ., Mani K 38 *A*² ⲡⲓⲧⲟⲩ ⲡⲥ., Fragm *penes* E C Hoskyns *F* ⲡⲥⲉϫⲉ ⲙⲙⲉ, ROC 25 257 *B* ⲁⲛϫⲉ ⲡⲁⲓⲕⲉⲥ. ⲡⲏ ⲟⲡ ϫⲉ- *tale*, J 74 44 *S* is fitting ⲉⲧⲣⲁⲟⲩⲱⲛϩ ⲡⲁϣ. ⲉⲃⲟⲗ ϩⲙⲟⲩⲧⲁϩⲣⲟ, Ep 281 *S* I found ⲉⲁⲣⲉⲛⲕⲉϣ. ϣⲱⲡⲉ; ⲡⲟϭ, ⲡⲓϣⲧ̄ ⲡϣ. *SAB*, *big words* with ϫⲱ, ϫⲉ-: Ps 11 3 *S*(*B* ⲙⲉⲧϩⲉⲣⲟⲩⲱ), *ib* 54 12 *SB*, Ob 12 *SA*(*B* do)μεγαλορρημονεῖν, Ap 13 5 *S*(*B* diff) μεγάλα λα.; with ⲧⲁϫⲟ: 1 Kg 2 3 *S*(*B* c. ⲉⲩϭⲟⲥⲓ) ὑψηλὰ λα.; ⲣⲉϥϫⲉ ⲡⲟϭ ⲡϣ.*S*: ShP 130¹ 139 ⲗⲁⲥ ⲡⲣ., BM 321 sim = AM 204 *B*-ⲙⲉⲧϩⲉⲣ.; ⲙⲛⲏϣ ⲡⲥ. *B*, *multitude of words*: MG 25 220 ϫⲉ ⲟⲩⲙ. ⲡⲥ. βαττολογεῖν; ϩⲁϩ ⲡϣ. *SA* sim: Job 8 2 (*B* ϫⲉ ⲙⲛⲏϣ ⲡⲥ.) πολυρρήμων; Cl Pr 47 80 women ϩⲉⲛⲣ. ⲡⲉ ϩⲛⲧⲉϥⲫⲩⲥⲓⲥ, Ep 373 ⲁⲡⲟⲕ ⲟⲩϩ.; ⲙⲡⲧⲣ.: Pro 10 19 *SA*(*B* ⲙⲛⲏϣ ⲡⲥ.), Mt 6 7 (*B* do) πολυλογία; Miss 8 140 μακρηγορία; 4 Kg 9 11 ἀδολεσχία; ShWess 9 132 ⲡϣⲓⲡⲉ ⲙⲙ. of Origen, ShC 73 144 ϫⲱⲣⲓⲥ ⲙ. (var ⲣ ϩⲁϩ ⲡϣ.); ⲣ ϩⲁϩ ⲡϣ. *S*, ⲉⲣ ⲙⲛⲏϣ ⲡⲥ. *B*: Mt 6 7 *SB* βατ.; BMar 114 *S* ⲟ ⲡⲣ. ⲡϣ. πολυλογ.; Mk 14 31 *S*(*B* c. ϩⲉⲛⲟⲩⲙⲉⲧϩⲟⲩⲟ) ἐκπερισσῶς λα.; ShC 73 70 *S* ⲧⲙⲣ ϩ. ϩⲡⲡⲉⲣⲓⲟⲟⲩⲉ, C 43 163 *B* ⲉⲕⲓⲣⲓ ⲡⲟⲩⲙ. ⲡⲥ.

ⲗⲁ c. *B*, *loquacious* *v* ⲗⲁ-.

ⲡⲉϫ ϣ. *S*, *cast in word, make mention*: BMOr 6203 ⲁⲕⲡ. ϣ. ⲉⲣⲟⲛ ⲉⲧⲃⲉⲡⲉⲓⲙⲁ ⲡϣⲱⲡⲉ & we accepted thy request to sell it.

ⲣ ϣ. *S*, *make agreement*: PO 2 179 ⲁⲩⲉⲣ ⲟⲩϣ. ⲡⲟⲩⲱⲧ ⲙⲡⲛⲉⲩⲉⲣⲏⲩ ϫⲉ-.

ⲧⲁϣⲉ ϣ., *multiply words*: Si 22 12 *S* λόγον πληθύνειν; Tri 238 *S* ⲡⲉⲧⲧ. ϣ., Pcod 23 *S* ⲡⲡⲉⲡⲧ. ⲡϣ., BSM 89 *B* let us not ⲑⲁϣⲉ ⲡⲓⲥ. ⲡϩⲟⲩⲟ; as nn: ShC 73 133 *S* ⲡⲧ. ϣ. ⲙⲡⲗⲁⲁⲩ.

ϫⲓ ϣ., ϭⲓ c., *take, accept word*: LCyp 10 *S* ϫⲓ ⲙⲡⲁϣ. πείθεσθαι dat; AM 270 *B* ⲟⲩϭ. ⲡⲟⲩⲱⲧ ϯϭⲓ ⲙⲙⲟϥ ⲁⲡ λόγον ἔχειν; RE 9 136 *S* ϫⲓ ϣ. ⲡⲧⲏⲣⲙⲉ ⲉϩⲟⲩⲛ ⲉⲣⲟⲛ.

ϭⲛ ϣ., ϫⲉⲙ c. (rare), *find word* of complaint: Ac

4 14 neg(*B* ϯ ⲉϩⲟⲩⲛ ⲉϩⲣⲉⲡ-) οὐδὲν ἔχειν; Su 27 *B* λόγον ῥηθῆναι; ShA 2 281 will bid tend you ϫⲉⲕⲁⲥ ⲡⲓⲉⲧⲡϣⲛ ϣ. ⲉϩⲱ, ShClPr 39 41 no man shall ϭⲉⲡ ⲗⲁⲁⲩ ⲡϣ. ⲉϩⲟⲩⲛ ⲉⲣⲟⲟⲩ (*sc* clergy) in their houses or in church, Pcod 44 lest devil ϭⲛ ϣ. ⲡϫⲭⲟⲟⲥ.

ϣ(ⲉ)ϫ- *S*: Bor 226 170 ϩⲉⲛϣϫⲱⲃⲉ γελωτοποιός λόγος; Wess 18 110 ⲙⲡⲧϣⲓⲛⲁ, ϣϫⲥ., ⲉⲗⲗⲏⲃ, R 2 1 58 ⲡϣϫⲥ. ⲙⲫⲓⲗⲓⲥⲧⲓⲱⲛ, Eph 5 4 ϣϫϫⲟⲥ μωρολογία (*v* ⲥⲟϭ), C 99 170 sim = C 89 135 *B* ⲥ. ⲡⲥⲟϭ, ShWess 18 138 sim, Aeg 282 var ϣⲉϫⲙ⳿ⲃⲱ μῦθος (*v* ϣϥⲱ), ϣϫⲙ⳿ⲗⲟϥ (*v* ϣⲗⲟϥ), BHom 19 ϣⲗⲏϥ (*v* ⲗⲗⲏⲃ), Tit 3 9 ϣϫϫⲱⲙ (*B* ϫⲱⲟⲩ ⲡⲥ.) γενεαλογία.

ⲁⲧϣ., -c. *SBF*, *speechless, unspeakable*: Ps 37 14 *B*(*S* ⲙⲡⲟ) ἄλαλος; Ex 6 12 *B*, Ac 25 27 *B*(*S* diff) ἄλογος; 2 Pet 2 16 *SB* ἄφωνος; LCyp 26 *S* ⲧⲃⲛⲟⲟⲩⲉ ⲡⲁ.; c ⲛ- *B*: Ro 8 26 (*S* diff) ἀλάλητος; 2 Cor 12 4 (*S* diff) ἄρρητος; Cai Euch 464 Thy coming ⲡⲁ. ⲙⲙⲟⲥ ἄφατος; DeV 2 10 ⲟⲩⲑⲉⲗⲏⲗ ⲡⲁ. ⲙⲙⲟϥ; c ⲉ-: He 7 3 *B* ⲁ. ⲉϫⲱⲟⲩ *F* ⲁ. ⲉϫⲱ ⲙⲙⲓⲥⲓ (*S* vb neg) ἀγενεαλόγητος; PS 9 *S* ⲡⲓⲁ. ⲉⲣⲟϥ, ShC 42 102 *S* ϩⲉⲡⲁ. ⲉⲣⲟⲟⲩⲡⲉ ⲡⲉⲥⲧⲟⲗⲏ, Pcod 39 *F* ⲡⲓⲣⲁⲥⲙⲟⲥ ⲡⲁ. ⲉⲗⲁϥ(*S* ⲁⲧⲧⲁϩⲟϥ); ⲙⲛⲧⲁⲧϣ. *S*: Leyd 449 ⲙⲛⲧⲉⲙⲡⲟ, ⲙⲡⲧⲁ., My 48 ⲟⲩⲙⲡⲧⲁ. ⲉⲣⲟⲥ; ⲉⲣ ⲁⲧⲥ. *B*: Ps 30 19 (*S* ⲣ ⲙⲡⲟ) ἄλαλος γίνεσθαι.

ⲙⲁ ⲡϣ., c., *place of talk, gossip*: ROC 17 404 *B* ⲉⲓⲉϣⲱⲡⲓ ⲙⲙ. μῦθος; P 131¹ 73 *S* ϣⲱⲡⲉ...ⲙⲙ. ⲡⲡⲓⲟⲩϫⲁⲓ.

ⲣⲉϥϣ., c. *SA*²*BF*, *speaker, eloquent person*: Ex 4 10 *SA*(*B* diff), Job 11 2 *S*(*B* ⲉⲧϫⲱ ⲡⲟⲩⲙⲛⲏϣ ⲡⲥ.) εὔλαλος, *ib* 38 14 *S*(*B* c. vb) λαλητός; 1 Tim 3 8 *B* (*S* diff) ⲡ. ⲏ̄ δίλογος; ShMIF 23 154 *S* honoured as ϩⲉⲛⲣ., BM 252 2 *S* John evangelist ⲡⲣ. ⲙⲡⲛⲓⲧ̄ⲉ (*cf* θεολόγος), BHom 15 *S* sim ⲉⲧⲃⲉⲡⲡⲉ, ManiH 12 *A*² ⲡⲓⲣⲉϥⲥ. that preach wisdom, Cat 125 *B* dove ⲟⲩⲣ. ⲡⲉ ϩⲉⲡⲧⲉϥⲁⲥⲡⲓ; ⲙⲡⲧⲣ., *eloquence*: Z 273 *S* ⲧⲙ. ⲉⲡⲡⲉ θεολογεῖν; Eccl 10 14 *F* ⲁϣⲉⲓ ϩⲓⲟⲩⲙⲉⲧⲗⲉϣϣ. (*S* ⲧⲁϣⲉ ϣ.) λόγους πληθύνειν.

ⲥⲁ ⲡϣ. *S*, *man of words, babbler*: Ac 17 18 (*B* = Gk) σπερμολόγος.

ϩⲟⲩⲟ c. *B*, *saying too much*: BSM 6 ⲟⲩϩ. c. ⲡⲧⲏⲓ to liken self to God's friend = BMis 323 *S* ⲟⲩϩⲟⲩⲟ ⲉⲣⲟⲓⲡⲉ ⲉⲧⲣⲁ-; ⲙⲉⲧⲣⲉϥⲉⲣϩ. c.: HL 82 φλυαρία.

ϭⲓⲛϣ., ϫⲓⲛⲥ. *SA*²*B*, *speech, saying, tale*: Job 33 1 *S*(*B* c.), Cant 4 3 *SF*, Jo 8 43 *SA*²*B* λαλιά; Ps 103 34 *B*(*S* ⲙ.) διαλογή, Va 57 127 *B* ⲟⲩϫ. ⲡⲉⲙⲫϯ διάλεξις, MG 25 4 *B* διάλεκτος; Deu 28 37 *S*(*B* diff) διήγημα; Ps 54 3 *B*(*S* diff) ἀδολεσχία; Ro 16 18 *SB* χρηστολογία; Ez 3 6 *SB* γλῶσσα; PS 33 *S* ⲉⲧⲡⲉⲥⲱⲥ ϩⲓⲧⲉⲥϭ., R 2 1 68 *S* ⲡϭ. of philosophers, Z 573 *S* ⲟⲩⲡ ⲟⲩϭ. ϣⲟⲟⲡ ϩⲛⲧⲁⲡⲣⲟ ⲡⲡⲣⲱⲙⲉ, *ib* 267 *S* ⲧⲧⲉϫⲏⲛ ⲡⲧⲉϥϭ. (*sc* of Julian's writings), MG 25 294 *B* understood not ⲧⲉⲛϫ. = BIF 13 108 *S* ⲁⲥⲡⲉ, DeV

2 54 B ϫ. ⲡⲁⲣⲅⲟⲡ, Pcod 35 S ⲟⲩⲅⲙⲟⲧ ⲛ̄ϭ. *gift of eloquence.*

ϣⲱⲝⲉ, ϣⲱⲱ.(once)S, -ⲝⲓ F, ⲥⲱⲝⲉ Sᶠ A² vb intr, *contend, wrestle*: R 2 2 27 ϯⲛⲁϣ. as did my father (Jacob) παλαίειν; ShViK 9100 230 ⲁϩⲁϥ ⲡⲣⲱⲙⲉ ϣ. ⲉⲙⲡⲉⲥⲧⲁϫⲓⲟⲛ, ShA 1 392 ⲉⲣϣⲁⲛⲡⲉⲧϥ. ϫⲣⲟ, ib 2 120 fearing lest ⲛ̄ⲧⲛⲁϣⲱⲝⲉ ⲁⲛ, Mani K 30 A² ⲛ̄ϩⲣⲁⲡ ⲙⲙⲓϣⲉ ⲙⲡⲛⲏⲗ (?) ⲛ̄ⲥ., BM 528 fol 5 F picture of lions fighting ⲥⲡⲉⲩ ⲙⲙⲉⲩⲓ ⲉⲩ ϣ.

With following preposition. ⲙⲛ ⲙⲛ-, *with*: R 2 2 26 was able ⲉϣ. ⲙ̄ⲡⲁⲅⲅⲉⲗⲟⲥ ⲡ. μετά; ShC 42 38 ⲁϥϣ. ⲛⲉⲙⲙⲁⲓ so as to escape, ShMich 550 15 ϣ. ⲙⲛ- paral ⲙⲓϣⲉ ⲟⲩⲃⲉ-, Ryl 361 Sᶠ (or A²) ⲁⲛⲥ. ⲛⲉ ⲙⲁϥ ϣⲁⲉϩⲣⲁⲓ ⲉⲡⲗⲟⲩ, ib do; ⲙⲛ ⲟⲩⲃⲉ-, *against*: R 2 2 25 ϯϣ. ⲟⲩⲃⲏ ⲡ. dat; ⲙⲛ ⲉⲛ- sim: Cant 1 6 F(S ⲙⲓϣⲉ) μάχεσθαι ἐν.

—— nnS, *contest*: ShA 1 286 ϩⲉⲛϣ. ⲙⲛⲡⲉⲩⲉⲣⲏⲩ.
ⲙⲁ ⲛ̄ϣ. S, *place of contest, arena*: R 2 2 28 ⲟⲩ ϣⲟⲉⲓϩ...ϩⲙⲡⲙ. σκάμμα, Leyd 313.
ⲣⲉϥϣ. S, *contender*: P 131¹ 36 Paul was ⲟⲩⲣ.
ϣⲟⲉⲓϣ S, ϣⲁⲓϣ A², ϣⲱⲓϣ B nn m f, *athlete, gladiator*: BHom 14 S ϣⲁⲣⲉⲡⲓϣ. ϭⲉ ⲑⲙⲡⲁⲅⲱⲛ ἀθλητής; Z 642 S ⲡϣ. athlete at Olympia, C 43 221 B ϣ. ⲡⲣⲉⲩⲉⲣ ⲁⲅⲱⲛⲓⲍⲉⲥⲑⲉ, AM 1 B ϣ. ⲡⲣⲉϥϫⲣⲟ, Mani 1 A² ⲟⲩⲅⲣⲟ ⲛ̄ⲧⲯⲩⲭⲏ ⲙⲡⲓϣ., P 131⁴ 152 S wastest wealth on ⲛⲉϥⲁⲣⲙⲁⲧⲟⲥ ⲙⲛⲓϣ., BMis 281 = Mor 29 52 S ⲙⲙⲁⲣⲓⲟⲛ, ϣ., ⲕⲓⲡⲛⲕⲟⲛ (κυνηγός) at wedding feast; f S: Mor 18 191 ⲧϣ. ⲛ̄ⲧⲙⲛ̄ⲧⲉⲩⲥⲉⲃⲏⲥ; ⲙⲛ̄ⲧϣ. S: BMis 242 ἄθλησις; BAp 171 ⲧⲙ. of saints; ⲣ ϣ: 2 Tim 2 5 (B ϣⲉ ⲉϥⲙⲁ ⲛ̄ϯ) ἀθλεῖν.

In place-name: ⲡⲙⲁ ⲛ̄ϣ. (Ryl 132).
ϣⲟⲉⲓϣϥ S, ϣⲁ. Sᶠ F nn m, as last: Miss 4 769 S ⲡϣ. ⲉⲡⲉ⳨ⲥ̄, ib 760 Sᶠ, Mor 30 13 F ϣ. ⲡⲣⲉϥϫⲣⲟ = BMis 239 S ϣⲟⲉⲓϣ, BIF 22 107 F ⲛⲉϣ. ⲙ̄ⲡⲉ⳨ⲥ̄.

ϣⲝⲁ v ϫⲁ.

ϣⲝⲉ SAB, ⲥϫⲉ A, pl ϣⲝⲏⲩ S, -ⲛⲟⲩ BF & sg as pl, nn m, *locust*: Lev 11 22 SB, Jud 6 5 S, Pro 24 62 SA ⲥ., Joel 1 4 A ⲥ. B, Nah 3 15 A ϣ. B ἀκρίς; B Hom 126 S ⲛⲟϣⲛ ⲉⲃⲟⲗ ⲛⲟⲉ ⲛⲟⲩϣ., Va 57 116 B Arius like ⲟⲩⲥⲧⲁϭⲟⲩⲗ ⲓⲉ ⲟⲩϣ.; pl: S only Ap 9 7; B Nu 13 33, Ps 108 23, Ap 9 3, MG 25 101 = Ryl 95 S sg ϣϫⲉ; F Is 33 4.

ϣⲝⲉ S nn, *sprig*: Ge 8 11 ϣ. ⲛ̄ϭⲃ̄ⲟⲉⲓⲧ (var om, B ϫⲱⲃⲓ ⲛ̄ⲧⲉ ⲟⲩⲗⲁϫⲉⲙ ⲛ̄ϫⲱⲓⲧ) κάρφος. Cf ? ϫⲏ 2°.

ϣⲝⲏⲓ B nn, *common talk, gossip*: Job 17 6 ϣ. ϫⲉⲛ- (var Gött Copt 8 ϣⲝⲏ ϩⲓϫⲉⲛ-, S ϣⲁϫⲉ) θρύλημα ⟨…⟩; ⲉⲣ, ⲟⲓ ⲛϣ., *be talked of*: Job 31 30 (S ϣⲱⲡⲉ ⲛ̄ϣⲁ.)θρυλεῖν, ib 30 9 ϫⲏⲓ(var Mich Pasc Lect 283, BM 1247 229 ϣⲉⲛⲏⲣ where ϩⲓ error, or ? cf ϩⲓϫⲉⲛ- above, S do) -ⲏⲙⲁ; Va 68 169 ⲡⲓⲣⲃⲛ̄ⲟⲩⲉ ⲥⲉⲓⲣⲓ ⲙⲙⲟⲓ ⲛϣ. στηλιτεύειν. Cf ? ϣⲁϫⲉ.

ϣⲝⲁⲗ S nn m, meaning?: Copt Mus Cai P 4-7 ⲥⲟⲟⲩ ⲛϣ. sent.

ϣⲝⲓⲗ S nn m, meaning unknown: Saq 244 ⲡⲓⲥⲣⲁⲏⲗ [ⲡⲣⲱ]ⲙⲁⲉ ⲙ̄ⲡⲉϣ. As place?

ϣⲝⲏⲛ S, ϣϭ. B, ϩⲝⲁⲛ DM nn m, *garlic*: Nu 11 5 SB σκόρδον; Aeg 261 = PO 8 612 ⟨⟩; R 1 4 68 S ⲡⲉϣ. (sic l) ⲙ̄ⲡⲛⲉⲙϫⲱⲗ = AM 128 B, Z 628 S recipe ⲟⲛⲟ ϣ. ϩⲓⲛⲉϩ, CR '87 376 S ϩⲉⲛ(ϣ)ϫ. ⲉⲩ ϣⲟⲟⲩⲉ, Ryl 106 31 S ⲟⲩⲡⲁⲣⲣ(ⲉ) ⲛϣ., DM 19 8 nt ϩ. hr ⲥⲙⲟⲩ; BMOr 6201 B 234 S ⲯⲁⲡϣ., Cai 8485 S sim (sic l), PLond 4 215 τόπος ψανσχην.

ϣⲟⲝⲛⲉ S, ϣⲁ. SSᶠ AA², ⲥⲁ. A², ⲥⲟϭⲛⲓ B, ϣⲁⲭⲛⲓ F vb I intr, *take counsel, consider*: Is 42 21 B(S ⲝⲓ ϣ.), Ac 27 39 B(S do) βουλεύεσθαι; 1 Cor 13 11 S(B prob), MG 25 3 B ⲁⲓⲥ. ϫⲉⲛⲡⲁϩⲣⲏⲧ λογίζεσθαι; AM 265 B ⲡⲁⲣⲉⲡⲓⲧⲣⲓⲃⲟⲩⲛⲟⲥ ⲥ. ⲡⲉ ϫⲉ- πολλὴ σκέψις εἶναι; ShA 2 263 S no good thought in man except God ϣ. ϩⲣⲁⲓ ⲛ̄ϩⲏⲧϥ ⲛ̄ϣⲟⲣⲡ, TU 43 13 A ⲡⲉⲧⲁⲓϣ. (PO 9 209 ⳑ.ⲫⲥ.), DeV 2 209 B ⲁϥⲥ. ϫⲉⲛⲧⲉϥⲥⲟⲫⲓⲁ, AM 208 B ⲁϥⲥ. ϫⲉⲟⲩⲡⲉ ⲉϥⲛⲁⲁⲓϥ.

II tr BF: Is 32 8 F(B ⲥ ⲉ-, S ⲙⲉⲉⲩ ⲉ-)β.; Ps 139 3 (S do) λογ., ib 20 12 (S do) διαλ.; Va 61 118 ⲡⲓⲟⲣⲅ̄ⲛ ⲉⲧⲁϥⲥ. ⲙ̄ⲙⲟⲩ, AM 168 ⲁϥⲥ. ⲙ(l ? ⲡⲉⲙ) ⲡⲉϥⲥⲩⲛⲕⲁⲑⲉϩⲣⲟⲥ saying What shall we do?

With following preposition.

—— ⲉ- SAA²BF, *concerning*: Pro 12 20 SA(B ⲟⲩⲱϣ), Is 32 8 BF(S ⲙ.), 2 Cor 1 17 B(S do)β.; Jer 43 3 SB λογ., Ps 9 23 B(S do)διαλ.; PS 114 S ⲛⲉⲡⲧⲁⲩϣ. ⲉⲣⲟⲟⲩ, ShR 2 3 21 S ϣ. ϩⲣⲁⲓ ⲛ̄ϩⲏⲧⲕ ⲉⲧⲃⲃⲟ ⲡⲙ; *against*: Ge 50 20 S(B ϫⲁ-)β. κατά, Ps 34 4 B (S ⲙ.)λογ. dat, Hos 7 15 BF(SA do)λ. εἰς, Jer 18 18 S(B ϫⲁ-)λ. ἐπί, EW 33 B ⲉⲟⲩⲣⲉⲧⲉⲡⲥ. ⲉⲣⲱⲟⲩ ⲕⲁⲕⲱⲥ = Gu 66 S ⲉⲡⲓⲃⲟⲩⲗⲉⲩⲉ, Mani 1 A² ⲁⲩⲥ. ⲁⲣⲁϥ in evil designs, Miss 4 686 S ⲑⲉ ⲉⲧⲁⲩϣ. ⲉⲣⲟⲟⲩ (sc to slay them), Gött N '98 170 S ⲉⲩϣ. ⲕⲁⲕⲱⲥ ⲉⲣⲟⲡ ⲉⲧⲙⲉ; *consult with*: BIF 13 104 S went to them ⲉϥϣ. ⲉⲣⲟⲟⲩ, MG 25 266 B ⲉⲧⲁⲩⲥ. ⲉⲡⲟⲩⲓⲱⲧ he gave them leave, Miss 4 725 S wishing ⲉϥϣ. ⲉⲣⲟϥ ⲉⲧⲃⲉⲟⲩϩⲱⲃ, BSM 104 B let me go ⲛ̄ⲧⲁⲥ. ⲉⲡⲁⲕⲟⲩⲗⲁⲧⲱⲣ (curator) = Mor 22 116 S ⲥⲕⲉⲡⲧⲉⲓ ⲙ̄ⲙⲟⲓ ⲙⲛ-, BP 11937 Sᶠ will do naught ⲁ̄ϫⲛ̄ⲧⲁϣ. ⲉⲡⲉⲛⲟϭ ⲛϣⲏⲣⲉ; vbal: Ps 30 14 S(sic)B, Is 51 13 SBβ.; Ps 139 5 B(S ⲙ.) λογ.; AM 272 B ⲁϥⲥ. ⲉⲧⲛⲓϥ σκέπτεσθαι; PS 105 S ⲁⲩϣ. ⲉⲧⲣⲉⲩϭⲓ, J 67 117 S ϣ. ⲉⲃⲟⲗ ⲉⲃⲟⲗ, Aeg 5 B ⲁϥⲥ. ⲉϫⲁⲥ ⲉⲃⲟⲗ = FR 148 S ⲟⲩⲱϣ.

—— ⲉⲑⲃⲉ- B, *concerning*: Ac 10 19 (S ⲙⲟⲕⲙⲉⲕ ⲙ̄ⲙⲟ⳽) διενθυμεῖσθαι περί; C 43 102 bade imprison him ϣⲁⲧⲉϥⲥ. ⲉⲑⲃⲏⲧϥ ϫⲉⲟⲩ ⲡⲉⲧⲉϥⲛⲁⲁⲓϥ.

—— ⲉϫⲛ- S(once)B, *upon, about*: Is 23 8(S ⲙⲉ.), Jer 30 30 SB β. ἐπί; Dan 11 24 λογ. ἐπί.

—— ⲙⲛ-, ⲡⲉⲙ- SA²BF, *with*: EpJer 48 BF β.

πρός, Si 8 22 *S* συμβ. μετά; Lu 20 14 *SB* διαλογ. πρός; Jo 16 19 *A²*(*S* ϣⲓⲡⲉ ⲙⲡ-, *B* ⲕⲱϯ ⲡⲥⲁ-) ζητεῖν μετά; BMis 286 *S* ⲉϥϣ. ⲡⲙⲙⲁϥ about affairs of state, ROC 23 274 *B* ⲡⲏ ⲉⲧⲁϥⲥ. ⲙⲙⲱⲟⲩ ⲡⲉⲙⲏⲓ.

—— ⲛ- *S* dat: ShR 2 3 75 ⲙⲁ ⲡⲓⲙ ⲉⲧⲉⲣⲉⲡⲉⲅⲣⲏⲧ ⲡⲁϣ. ⲡⲁⲩ ⲉⲣⲟϥ, ShViK 937 42 ⲁⲡⲡ̄ⲉ̄ ϣ. ⲡⲁⲩ ⲉⲃⲟⲗ ϩⲓⲧⲟⲟⲧⲟⲩ ⲡⲛⲉⲅⲉⲓⲟⲧⲉ, ShA 1 41 ⲡⲉⲧϣ. ⲡⲁϥ ⲉⲧⲉϥ-.

—— ⲡⲥⲁ- *B*, *after, against*: EW 58 ⲡⲓⲡⲁⲣⲁⲡⲟⲙⲟⲥ ⲁⲅⲥ. ⲡⲥⲱⲡ.

—— ϩⲁ- *B*, *against, about*: Ps 82 4(*S* ⲙⲉ. ⲉϩⲟⲩⲡ ⲉ-)β. κατά; Jer 18 18 *v* ⲥ ⲉ-; AM 270 ⲥⲉⲥ. ϩⲁⲡⲁⲙⲟⲩ θρυλλεῖν περί.

—— ⲛⲛ *m* *SAA²BF*, *counsel, design*: Deu 32 28 *SB*, Job 10 3 *SB*, Pro 2 11 *SAB*, Eccl 2 12 *SF*, Is 32 8 *SBF*, Eph 1 11 *SBF* βουλή, Ac 20 3 *B*(*S* diff)ἐπιβ., ib 27 43 *SB* βούλημα, Sa 1 9 *SB* διαβούλιον, Ro 11 34 *BF* ϣⲫⲏⲣ ⲡⲥ. (*S* & var *F* ⲣⲉϥϫⲓ ϣ.) σύμβουλος, R 1 1 42 *S* ⲥⲙⲓⲛⲉ ⲡⲟⲩϣ. συμβούλιον; Ez 13 6 *B*(*S* ϣⲁϫⲉ), HL 85 *B* ⲥⲉ ⲛⲣⲡ ϩⲉⲡⲟⲩⲥ. λόγος, Pro 15 22 *SA*, Eccl 9 10 *F*(*S* BMar 81 = Gk)λογισμός, Ps 55 6 *B*(*S* ⲙⲉⲉⲩⲉ)διαλ.; Sa 6 17 *S* ἐπίνοια; AM 282 *B* ⲡⲓⲥ. ⲡⲧⲉ ⲡⲁϩⲏⲧ σκόπος; Pro 1 8 *B*(*SA* ⲁⲡⲥⲙⲙⲉ)θεσμός; 4 Kg 14 19 *S* σύστρεμμα; ib 12 20 *S* ⲙⲣⲣⲉ ⲡϣ. σύνδεσμος; BMis 231 *S* ϫⲓⲁⲧⲁⲅⲙⲁ, ϣ. ψῆφος; Ps 34 17 *S* ϣ. ⲉⲑⲟⲟⲩ(*B* ⲙⲉⲧⲥⲁⲙⲡⲉⲧϩⲱⲟⲩ)κακουργία; PS 113 *S* ⲡⲉⲩϣ. ⲉⲡⲧⲁⲅⲙⲉⲉⲩⲉ ⲉⲣⲟϥ, BG 61 *S* ⲡϣ. ⲙⲡϫⲓⲥⲉ ⲉⲧⲟⲩⲁ(ⲁ)ⲃ, ShC 73 27 *S* Isaac blessed Jacob ϩⲙⲡϣ. ⲛⲣⲉⲃⲉⲕⲕⲁ, Z 280 *S* ⲡⲉϥϣ. (*sc* emperor's)ⲡⲁⲗⲁⲟϩⲧⲉ ϩⲡⲧⲟⲓⲕⲟⲩⲙⲉⲛⲏ, PSBA 10 195 *S* ϣⲱⲡ ⲉⲣⲟⲕ ⲙⲡⲉϩϣ., Mor 33 142 *S* ⲡϣⲏⲣⲉ ⲁⲩⲱ ⲡϣ. ⲙⲡⲉⲓⲱⲧ (var BMis 69 ⲡⲗⲟⲅⲟⲥ), MIE 2 383 *B* may not accept them ⲁϥⲡⲉⲥ. ⲡⲧⲉ ⲡⲁⲓⲱⲧ = BAp 107 *S* ⲥⲃⲱ, ib 355 *B* ⲁⲕϯ ⲙⲡⲉⲕⲟⲩⲟⲓ ⲉϩⲟⲩⲡ ⲁⲡⲥⲉⲥ. = ib 80 *S* ⲙⲟⲩⲙϣ = PO 22 341 دستور, C 86 202 *B* ϩⲉⲡⲟⲩⲥ. ⲡⲧⲉ ⲡⲁⲧⲁⲭⲱⲣⲁ *by advice of*, AP 22 *A²* ⲡⲡ̄ⲉ̄ ϭⲟⲩϣⲧ ⲁϩⲣⲏⲉⲓ ⲁϩⲡ(ⲡ)ⲟⲩϣ., Mani 1 *A²* ⲟⲩⲙⲡϩⲁⲣϣϩⲏⲧ ⲙⲡⲡⲥ., ib K 81 *A²* ⲡⲡⲁϭ ⲛⲥ., J 68 8 *S* ⲃⲟⲩⲗⲏⲙⲁ ⲡϫⲓⲁⲑⲏⲕⲏ [ⲡ]ϣ. ⲡϭⲁⲛ, TEuch 1 349 *B* prayer for ⲡⲓⲁⲣⲭⲱⲡ, ⲡⲓⲥ., ⲡⲓⲙⲏϣ مشيرين.

ⲁⲧϣ., ⲙⲛⲧ-, ⲙⲉⲧ- *SB*, *being without counsel, ill-considered*: Bar 3 28 *SB* ἀβουλία; HL 84 *B* ἄλογος; ShC 42 18 *S* ⲙⲛⲧⲁⲧⲟϣ ⲛ ⲙ., ViK 9854 *S* drew nigh ϩⲛⲟⲩⲙ. (*cf* Nu 3 4).

ⲣⲉϥⲥ. *B*, *counsellor, adviser*: Is 1 26 (*S* ⲣⲉϥϫⲓ ϣ.) σύμβουλος; DeV 2 160 ⲡⲓⲣ. ⲡⲉⲙϥϯ, C 86 164 ⲡⲁⲣ. ⲡ‾ⲭ‾ⲥ‾ⲛⲉ in life & death.

ⲉⲓⲣⲉ, ⲣ ϣ., ⲓⲣⲓ, ⲉⲣ ⲥ. *SBF*, *take counsel, make decision*: Is 30 1 *SBF* β. ποιεῖν; Ac 27 12 *B*(*S* ϫⲓ ϣ.) β. τιθέναι, Jer 29 21 *S*(*B* ⲥ.) βουλεύ., Dan 6 7 *B*, Mt 26 4 *B*(*S* do) συμβ., ib 12 14 *B*(*S* ϫⲓ ϣ. ⲉϩⲟⲩⲡ ⲉ-) συμβούλιον λαμβάνειν; AM 278 *B* γνώμην ποι.; BG 73 *S* ⲁϥⲉⲓⲣⲉ ⲡⲟⲩϣ. ⲙⲡⲡⲉϥⲁⲅⲅⲉⲗⲟⲥ, DeV 2 274 *B*

ⲙⲟϣⲧⲕ ⲉⲃⲟⲗ ⲁⲣⲓⲟⲩⲓ ⲙⲡⲉⲕⲥ., C 86 132 *B* ⲁϥⲉⲣ ⲟⲩⲥ. ⲡⲟⲩⲱⲧ ⲡⲉⲙⲡⲟⲩⲅⲉⲣⲟⲩ. *V* also ϫⲓ ϣ.

ϯ ϣ., *c*. *S*(once)*B*, *give counsel*: Is 33 18 (*SF* ϫⲓ ϣ.), C 89 68 ϩⲱⲃ ⲡⲓⲃⲉⲡ ⲉϣⲁⲓϯ ⲥ. ⲙⲙⲱⲟⲩ ⲙⲫⲏ (ib 99 234 *S* = Gk) συμβουλεύ.; BG 53 *S* ⲁⲩϯ ϣ. ⲡⲁϥ ϩⲱⲥⲧⲉ..., Miss 4 205 ⲉⲓϯ ⲥ. ⲡⲱⲧⲉⲡ ⲉⲣⲟⲥ (*sc* God) that He convert you, BSM 103 ϯⲡⲁϯ ⲥ. ⲡⲉ ⲉⲡⲓϩⲱⲃ ⲉⲑⲛⲁⲡⲉϥ, C 43 58 ϯ ⲥ. ⲡⲱⲧⲉⲡ ⲉⲡⲭⲓⲡϣⲉⲙϣⲓ; ⲣⲉϥϯ ⲥ., *counsellor*: Is 3 3 (*S* ⲣⲉϥϫⲓ ϣ.), Va 58 181 take not serpent as ρ. σύμβουλος.

ϫⲓ ϣ., ϭⲓ ⲥ. *SAA²B*(rare)*F*, *take counsel, reflect, advise*: Ps 82 5 (*B* ⲥ.), Jo 11 53 *SA²*(*B* do) βουλεύ., Is 33 18 *SF*(*B* ϯ ⲥ.) συμβ., Mk 15 1 (*B* ⲥ. ⲡⲟⲩⲥ., *F* ⲓⲗⲓ ⲡⲟⲩϣ.) συμβούλιον ποι.; BM 286 123 ϫ. ⲡⲧⲛⲧⲁⲗⲗⲓⲟⲛ *take counsel with*, AM 27 *B* come ⲛⲧⲁϭⲓ ⲥ. ⲉⲃⲟⲗ ϩⲓⲧⲟⲧⲕ; ⲥ ⲉ- *S*: Est 3 6, Ps 61 4 (*B* ⲥ. ⲉ-), Ac 27 39 (*B* ⲥ. ϫⲉ-) βουλεύ., Mk 3 6 (*B* ⲓⲣⲓ ⲡⲟⲩⲥ. ϩⲁ-) συμβούλιον ποι. κατά, Ac 20 3 (*B* ⲥ. ϣⲱⲡⲓ)γνώμης γίνεσθαι; ib 7 19 (*B* ϫⲉⲙ ⲥⲃⲱ ⲉϩⲟⲩⲡ ⲉ-) καταⲥⲟφίζεσθαι; ShP 130⁴ 101 ⲡⲥⲉϫ. ⲉⲣⲟⲕ ⲉⲙⲟⲅⲟⲩⲧⲕ, BM 323 29 ⲁϥϫ. ⲉⲩⲙⲁ ⲡⲉⲣⲛⲙⲟⲥ...saying I long to build chapel there, Bor 248 56 write to me & ϫ. ⲡⲧⲁⲙⲡⲧⲉⲗⲁⲭⲓⲥⲧⲟⲥ ⲉⲡⲉⲧⲣ ⲡⲟⲃⲣⲉ *advise*, BHom 70 enemies ϫ. ⲉⲣⲟⲡ *against*, AP 21 *A²* ϫ. ⲁⲣⲁⲩ [ⲁⲧⲣⲟ]ⲩ̣ⲙ[ⲗⲁⲥ; ⲉϩⲟⲩⲡ ⲉ-: Mt 27 1 (*B* ⲉⲣ ⲟⲩⲥ. ϩⲁ-)συμβ. λαμβ. κατά; Ps 82 3 (*B* ⲓⲣⲓ ⲡⲟⲩⲥ. ⲉϩⲣⲏⲓ ⲉϫⲉⲡ-)καταπανουργεύεσθαι ἐπί; BMOr 8811 78 ⲁⲩϫ. ⲉⲣ. ⲉⲡⲡ‾ⲭ‾ⲥ‾; ⲥ ⲉϫⲉⲡ- *B*: BSM 25 ϥϭⲓ ⲙⲡⲥ. ⲉϫⲱⲟⲩ ϩⲓⲡⲁ = BMis 364 *S* ϫⲓ ⲕⲉⲗⲉⲩⲥⲓⲥ ... ϩⲁⲣⲟⲟⲩ; ⲥ ⲙⲡ-, ⲡⲉⲙ- *SB*: Jos 15 18 *S* συμβουλεύ. dat, Is 40 14 *SB* σ. πρός; Ps 140 5 *S*(*B* ϯ ⲙⲁϯ) συνδοιάζειν μετά; BM 221 150 *S* ⲁⲩϫ. ⲙⲡⲡⲉⲅⲉⲣⲏⲩ ⲉⲧⲣⲉⲩ-, Z 349 *S* ⲉⲡⲉⲡⲧⲁⲁⲗⲁⲙ ϫ. ⲙⲡⲡⲁⲅⲅⲉⲗⲟⲥ they would have told him, AM 79 *B* ⲡⲁϥϭⲓ ⲥ. ⲡⲉⲙⲟⲩϣⲫⲏⲣ; ⲥ ⲛ- dat *SA²*, *counsel*: Ex 18 19 (*B* ϯ ⲥ.), Ap 3 18 (*B* = Gk), Jo 18 14 *SA²*(*B* ⲥ. vb) συμβουλεύ. dat; Ac 27 9 (*B* diff)παραινεῖν; ShA 1 445 ϩⲙⲡⲧⲣⲉϥϫ. ⲡⲉ ⲉⲧⲃⲉⲡⲃⲁⲣⲃⲁⲣⲟⲥ that he fall not upon thee, BM 185 ϫ. ⲡⲁϥ ⲉⲧⲣⲉϥϣⲉⲣϣⲱⲣϥ; ⲣⲉϥϫⲓ ϣ. *SAB*(once)*F*, *adviser*: Si 6 6, Is 1 26 (*B* ⲣⲉϥⲥ.), Ro 11 34 *SF*(var & *B* ϣⲃⲏⲗ, ϣ.ⲫ. ⲡ.) σύμβουλος; BHom 28 shall be for thee ρ. συνόμιλος(ib 327 ܠܒܐ); Sa 8 4 μύστις; Sh MIF 23 83 magnates with their ⲙⲁⲧⲟⲓ & ρ., ShC 42 123 ϣⲱⲡⲉ ⲡⲣ. ⲙⲡⲡϫⲓⲁⲃⲟⲗⲟⲥ, AM 239 *B* ϣϥⲫⲏⲣ ⲡⲉⲙⲣ.; *as adj*: Pro 24 6 *SA* βουλευτικός.

ϣⲟϫⲡ *B* *v* ϣⲱϫⲙ.

ϣⲱϫⲡ *SAF*, ⲥⲱ. *A²BF*, ϣⲉϫⲡ- *S*, ⲥⲁ. *A²*, ⲥⲉ. *B*, ϣⲁ. *F*, ϣⲟϫⲡ⸗ *S*, ⲥⲟ. *B*, ϣⲁ. *F*, ϣⲟϫⲡⲧ *S*(rare), ⲥⲟ.† *B* vb **I** intr, *be over & above, remain over*: Ex 12 10 *SB*, He 10 26 *SB* ἀπολείπειν, Lev 14 18 *B*(*S* ⲥⲉⲉⲡⲉ), Is 30 17 *BF*(*S* diff) καταλ., ib 60 15 *B*(*S* ⲕⲱ ⲡⲥⲁ-) ἐγκαταλ., 1 Thes 4 17 *SB* περιλ., Ge 32 24 *SB*, Zeph

3 3 B(A ⲕⲟⲩ ⲁⲡⲁⲅⲟⲩ) ὑπολ.; Jo 6 13 F(PMich 3521, SB ⲣ ⲅⲟⲅⲟ, A² ⲥⲉ.) περισσεύειν; Ex 23 18 S (B diff) μένειν, Ac 17 14 B(S ⲥⲱ) ὑπομ.; R 1 3 5 S ⲁϥϣ. ⲙⲁⲅⲁⲁϥ, Mani H 29 A² ⲛⲉⲧⲁⲥ., C 86 147 B he slain ⲁⲓⲥ. ⲡⲉⲙⲡⲁϣⲏⲣⲓ, ib 309 B ⲡⲧⲉϣⲧⲉⲙⲟⲅⲁⲓ ...ⲥ., C 89 170 B ⲡⲉⲙⲡⲉⲧⲥ. (cf καὶ τὰ λοιπά); qual B: Is 62 4 (S ⲕⲱ ⲡⲥⲁ-) καταλ., ib 32 14 (SF ⲕⲱ ⲉⲃⲟⲗ) ἐγκ., Ge 45 6, Phil 1 13 (SFⲥⲉ. nn) λοιπός; 1 Tim 5 5 (S ⲥⲱ ⲟⲩⲁⲁⲧⲍ) μονοῦσθαι; C 43 176 ⲡⲓⲕⲁⲥ ⲙⲙⲁⲅⲁⲧⲟⲩ ετc.

II tr, *leave over, behind*: Sa 14 6 S ἀπολ., Nu 21 35 S(var & B intr), Pro 12 11 B(SA ⲕⲱ), Is 30 17 B (SF do), Lam 5 20 B(SF ⲕⲱ ⲡⲥⲁ-), Mk 14 52 B(S ⲕⲱ ⲉⲃⲟⲗ, F ⲕⲱ) καταλ., Ps 93 14 B(S ⲱⲃϣ), Jer 32 38 B(S ⲕⲱ ⲡⲥⲁ-) ἐγκ., Ex 10 24 B ὑπολ.; Jer 31 9 B ἀνάπτεσθαι; Is 5 6 B(S do), He 13 5 B(S ⲃⲱϣ)ἀνιέναι; Ps 138 10 S(B ⲁⲙⲟⲛⲓ) κατέχειν; HM 1 131 S ⲙⲡⲉϥϣ. ⲡⲣⲉⲛⲗⲟⲅⲟⲥ ⲉⲅⲱϥⲉⲗⲉⲓ?, R 1 2 53 S God filleth all ⲉϥϣ. ⲙⲡⲧⲏⲣϥ (cf ? Ps 138), MG 25 75 B ⲉⲧⲁϥⲥ. ⲅⲱⲃ ⲛⲓⲃⲉⲛ (var ⲥⲱϫⲡϥ ⲛⲅ. ⲛ. = Gött ar 114 15 ⲱϫ), FR 104 B ⲉⲛⲁϣ ⲡⲣⲏϯ ϯⲛⲁⲥⲟϫⲡⲓ ⲙⲡⲁⲓⲙⲁ?, Mani 2 A² bidding ⲁⲧⲣⲉϥⲥⲁϫⲡ ⲅⲱⲃ ⲛϯⲅⲉ.

With following preposition.

—— ⲉ- SB, *from, out of*: Jos 13 12 S καταλ. ἀπό, Ps 16 14 B(S ⲥⲉ. nn, F ⲥⲛ. vb) κατάλοιπος; Ez 48 18 B περισσός gen; BMis 216 S ⲁⲣⲉⲛⲕⲟⲅⲓ ϣ. ⲉⲛⲧⲁⲕⲟ (var Mor 16 68 ⲥⲉ. ⲉ-); *for*: Is 17 2 B(S ⲕⲱ ⲉⲃⲟⲗ ⲉ-), ib 65 15 B(S ⲕⲱ ⲡⲥⲁ- ⲉ-) καταλ. εἰς, Jos 13 1 S ὑπολ. εἰς; Is 11 5 S†(B ϫⲱⲗⲅ) εἰλεῖν (reading ? λελειμμένος AMöhle).

—— ⲛ- SABF dat: Ge 33 15 S(B ⲛⲉⲙ-)καταλ. μετά, Lev 19 10 B(S ⲕⲱ ⲛ-), Pro 14 26 B(SA do), Ro 11 4 SB κ. dat, Is 1 9 SBF ἐγκ. dat, Zech 9 7 S (ShA 2 239)AB, 1 Pet 2 21 B(S ⲕⲱ ⲛ-) ὑπολ. dat; BSM 29 B ⲙⲡⲉⲅⲗⲓ ⲥ. ⲡⲱⲟⲩ = BMis 369 S ϣ. ⲛⲁⲅ ⲉⲡⲁⲅⲟⲩ, C 99 103 S of 2 loaves ⲁϥϣ. ⲛⲁϥ ⲙⲡⲟⲅⲁ, J 2 39 S ⲛⲓⲙⲉⲣⲟⲥ ⲙⲙⲁ... ϣⲟⲭⲡⲟⲩ ⲡⲛⲉⲕϣⲏⲣⲉ, Pcod 40 F ϣⲁⲭⲡⲟⲩ ⲡⲛⲕ ⲉⲧⲉⲕⲅⲁⲛ (S l ? ϣⲟⲭⲡⲟⲩ).

—— ⲉⲃⲟⲗ ⲛ- B, *from*: Ex 12 10 (S ⲥⲉ. ⲉⲃ. ⲅⲛ-) καταλ. ἀπό. Cf ⲉⲃⲟⲗ ⲅⲛ-.

—— ⲡⲥⲁ- B, *behind*: TSBA 10 380 ϯⲛⲁⲥ. ⲡⲥⲱⲕ ⲁⲛ (cf 4 Kg 2 4 ἐγκαταλ.), Lu 2 43 (S ⲥⲱ)ὑπομένειν.

—— ⲛⲧⲛ-, *by*: Bar 4 12 B καταλ. ὑπό; *with*:Pcod 3 S money ⲁⲩϣ. ⲛⲧⲟⲟⲧϥ.

—— ⲉⲃⲟⲗ ⲅⲁ- B, *from*: Jer 21 7 (S ⲉ-) καταλ. ἀπό, Lev 26 43 (S ⲕⲱ ⲉⲃ. ⲅⲁ-) ἐγκ. ὑπό.

—— ⲅⲓ- B, *on, in*: Is 17 6 (S ⲅⲣⲁⲓ ⲅⲛ-) καταλ. ἐπί, Pro 2 21 (SA ⲅⲓⲭⲛ-) ὑπολ. ἐν.

—— ⲅⲛ-, ⲥⲉⲛ- SBF, *in*: Ob 18 S(AB diff)καταλ. dat, Ge 39 12B(S ⲕⲱ), Jer 45 22 B, 1 Thes 3 1 SBF κ. ἐν, Ps 15 10 B(S ⲕⲱ ⲡⲥⲁ-) ἐγκ. εἰς, Is 31 9 S(BF diff) περιλ. dat, Jer 24 8 S(B ⲥⲉ.), Dan 10 8 B(S ⲥⲉ.) ὑπολ. ἐν; Va 58 192 B drinking ⲡⲁⲥ. ⲥⲉⲛⲡⲉⲕⲥⲱⲙⲁ

ⲡⲟⲩⲡⲓϣϯ ⲛⲥⲟⲙⲥⲉⲙ ἐναπομέν.; Jos 2 11 S ἔτι εἶναι ἐν; PS 329 S ⲛⲥⲉϣ. ⲅⲛⲡⲕⲟⲗⲁⲥⲓⲥ, Ryl 94 106 S breath ϣ. ⲡⲣⲛⲧⲩ, C 86 217 B sim, EW 37 B ⲉⲧⲁⲡⲥⲟⲭⲡϥ ⲥⲉⲛⲡϣⲓⲕ we departed; ⲉⲃⲟⲗ ⲅⲛ-, ⲥⲉⲛ-, *from*: Lev 25 52 B(S ⲥⲉ.) καταλ. ἀπό, Nu 33 55 SB κ. ἐκ, Jth 10 19 S ὑπολ. ἐκ; DeV 1 123 B ⲙⲡⲉⲣⲥ. ⲁⲛ ⲡⲟⲅⲁⲓ ⲉⲃ. ⲡⲥⲛⲧⲟⲩ, Miss 4 654 S ⲛⲧⲙϣⲉⲭⲡ ⲗⲁⲁⲩ ⲉⲃ. ⲡⲣⲛⲧⲥ; ⲅⲣⲁⲓ ⲅⲛ-, ⲉⲅⲣⲏ ⲥⲉⲛ-, *in*: Nu 21 35 S(Mor, B ⲛ-) καταλ. dat (var gen), Jer 51 12 B (S ϣ. nn)κατάλοιπος ἐν, Ge 50 8 S(B ⲥⲉⲛ-)ὑπολ. ἐν.

—— ⲅⲓϫⲛ- SAB, *upon*: Is 7 22 SB καταλ. ἐπί, Jer 47 6 B κ. ἐν, ib 27 20 B ὑπολ. ἐπί, Pro 2 21 SA(B ⲅⲓ-) ὑ. ἐν; BMis 82 S ϣ. ⲡⲟⲩⲥⲡ(ⲉ)ⲣⲙⲁ ⲅ.ⲡⲕⲁⲅ.

With following adverb. ⲥ ⲉⲃⲟⲗ B: Dif 1 4 ⲙⲡⲉⲩⲥ. ⲡⲁⲅ ⲉⲃ. ⲡⲧⲉ ⲡⲓⲭⲣⲏⲙⲁ; ⲥ ⲉⲡⲁⲅⲟⲩ SA²BF, *behind*: Deu 28 51 S(B om) καταλ., 1 Kg 25 22 S ὑπολ.; Deu 16 4 S(B ⲉⲛⲕⲟⲧ) κοιμᾶσθαι; Br 98 S ⲁⲕϣ. ⲉⲡ. ⲡⲟⲩⲕⲟⲅⲓ, ShR 2 3 72 S ⲧⲙϣⲉⲭⲡ ⲗⲁⲁⲩ ⲉⲡ., CA 104 S ϣ. ⲉⲡ. ⲡⲟⲩⲙⲉⲣⲓⲥ, Mani K 14 A² tree ⲥ. ⲁⲡ. ⲭⲱⲣⲓⲥ ⲕⲁⲣⲡⲟⲥ, Miss 4 95 B allowed them ⲉⲑⲣⲟⲩⲥ. ⲉⲫ., BIF 22 106 F ⲙⲡⲉⲗϣⲁⲭⲡ ⲗⲁⲡϯ ⲉⲡ., PSBA 34 174 S ⲡⲉⲡⲧⲁϣ. ⲉⲡ. of payment; ⲥ ⲅⲓ ⲡⲁⲅⲟⲩ AB sim: Joel 2 14 ὑπολ. ὀπίσω.

—— nn m SAA²BF, *remainder* as sg: Deu 17 14B (var ⲥⲉ., S ⲕⲉ-), Mt 25 11 B(S ⲥⲉ.), 2 Cor 13 2 B(SF do), Cl 25 2 A(var ⲥⲉ.) λοιπός, Mk 4 19 SB τὰ λοιπά, Dan 2 18 B ἐπίλ., Jer 29 4 SB καταλ., Ro 11 5 S(B = Gk) λεῖμμα, Is 10 22 SB κατάλειμ., Ps 36 37 SB ἐγκατάλ., Ro 9 27 SB ὑπολ., Ge 45 7 B κατάλειψις; JTS 8 243 S saints pass over ⲭⲱⲣⲓⲥ ϣ. ⲗⲁⲁⲩ, Aeg 264 S ⲡⲕⲉϣ. ⲙⲡⲉⲅⲟⲟⲩ (var ⲥⲉ.), AM 260 B sim, Mani 1 A² ⲡⲥ. ⲙⲡⲟⲅⲁⲓⲡⲉ, C 43 120 B Apollo ⲛⲉⲙ-ⲡⲥ. ⲛⲛⲓⲡⲟⲩϯ, Cat 4 B ⲓⲏⲥⲟⲩⲥ ϫⲉ (Mt 2 1)...ⲡⲉⲙ-ⲡⲥ. ⲕ.ⲧ.λ.; as pl: Jud 20 47 S, Lu 24 9 B(S ⲡⲕⲉⲥⲉ.) λοι., Dan 7 7 B(S do) ἐπίλ., Jer 32 37 SB, Am 9 12 SAB κατάλ.; Ez 48 23 B περισσός; Deu 24 20 S(B ⲡⲏ ⲉⲧⲣⲓϥⲁⲅⲟⲩ) τὰ ὀπίσω; DeV 2 223 B ⲡⲧⲉⲛⲥⲁϫⲉ ⲉⲑⲃⲉⲡⲓⲕⲉⲥ.

ϫⲓ ϣ. S, *bring, give remainder*: Miss 8 246 of Noah ⲁϥϫ. ⲉⲡⲛⲕⲟⲥⲙⲟⲥ (cf Leyd 288 sim ϯ ⲡⲟⲩϣ.)

ϣϫⲁⲡ B nn, *slap*: K 162 ⲟⲩϣ. كسه (? Kabis AZ 14 45 reads كبل, var + لطمة), P 54 169 لطم.

ϣϫⲟⲥ v ϭⲣⲟⲥ.

ϣⲟϫⲧ v ϣⲟⲧϣⲧ.

ϣϫⲓⲧ, ϣϫⲓϭ (once)S nn m, *dyer* (?): Wess 15 21 John of Lycopolis had ⲟⲩⲥⲟⲛ ⲡϣϫⲓϭ (*Hist Laus* § 35 βαφεύς) = HT S 2 ⲉⲩϣ. ⲡⲉ, ib 1 John's parents ⲅⲉⲛϣ. ⲡⲉ ⲉⲛⲧⲉⲅ ⲉⲓⲟⲡⲉ (but Ethiop Synax 21 Hedar BMOr 667 79 ⲥⲟⲃⲧ⳽ⲃⳬⳡ ⵗⵘⵁⵗ : *glass workers*, confused ? with ϣϯⲧ زجّاج, Ar Synax 1 305 om), Mor 25 218 Athanasius in hiding served ⲡⲉⲓⲣⲱⲙⲉ ⲛϣ.

v PO 1 404), JKP 2 198 same ⲣⲱⲙⲉ ⲡⲉϣ[ϫⲓⲧ] named Arsenius, Lant 54, 55 ⲡⲉϣ.

ϣϫⲱⲧ *SB* nn f, meaning uncertain, *strip, cord*(?): C 43 79 *B* bade pierce heels ⲛⲥⲉϭⲓⲟⲩⲓ ⲛ(ⲣⲁⲛ)ϣ. ⲛ̄ϣⲉϩⲉⲡⲓ ⲉⲙⲏⲣ ⲛ̄ϩⲏⲧⲟⲩ (*cf* AM 166 sim ⲛⲟϭ ⲛ̄ϣⲉϩⲉⲛⲓ), BMOr 6201 A 3 *a S* account ϩⲁⲧⲉ̇ϣ., *ib* 3 *b* ⲙⲟⲩⲣ ⲥⲡⲁⲩ ⲉϣ., *ib* ⲛ̄ⲧⲉⲣⲟⲥ (καιρός) ⲉⲙⲉϣϫⲱⲧ, Bodl(P) e 54 *S* ⲥⲛⲓⲛⲉ(ⲥⲡⲧⲉ) ⲛϣ.;   ⲥⲁ ⲛϣ., maker of ϣ.: CMSS 33 where connected with building cattlefold.

ϣⲟⲉⲓϫϥ *S*, ϣⲁ. *SⁱF v* ϣⲱϫⲉ *s f.*

ϣϫⲓϭ *v* ϣϫⲓⲧ.

ϣⲓϭ *v* ϣⲣⲓϭ.

ϣⲱⲱϭⲉ *S*, ϣⲟⲩ(ⲟⲩ)ϭⲉ *A*, ϣⲱϭⲉ *A²*, ϣⲉ(ⲉ)ϭⲉ *S*, ϣⲁϭⲉ *A²*, ϣⲟ(ⲟ)ϭ⳾ *S*, ϣⲁⲁϭ⳾ *SⁱAF*, ϣⲟⲩϭ⳾ *A*, ϣⲁϭ⳾ *A²*, ϣⲟ(ⲟ)ϭⲉ† *S*, ϣⲁϭⲉ† *A²* vb **I** intr, *smite, wound, be wounded*: Ps 101 4 (*B* ϫⲱϫⲓ), Is 9 13 (*B* ϭⲓ ⲉⲣϩⲟⲧ), Ap 8 12 (*B* ⲙⲓϣⲓ) πλήσσειν; Job 5 18 *A* ϣⲟⲩ. (Cl, *S* ϣⲁⲁⲣⲉ, *B* ϯ ⲉⲣ.) παίειν; Zeph 2 12 *A* ϣⲟⲅⲟⲩ. (*B* ϩⲱⲧⲉⲃ nn) τραυματίας εἶναι, 1 Kg 31 1 ⲧⲣ.; BHom 37 limbs ϣ. ϩⲓⲧⲛⲟⲩϣⲱⲡⲉ βλάπτειν, Z 289 ⲛⲛⲉϥϣ. through much weeping βλάβην ὑπομένειν; Ez 40 1 (*B* ϩⲟⲙϩⲉⲙ) ἁλίσκεσθαι; ShClPr 36 203 ⲁⲩϣ. ⲉⲃⲟⲗ ϩⲓⲧⲟⲟⲧϥ (*sc* snake), ShA 1 105 ⲁⲧⲁⲁⲡⲉ ϣ., Mani H 20 *A²* ϩⲁⲗⲓⲃϣⲉ ⲡⲁϣ. ⲁⲭⲓⲣⲁⲗⲓⲃϣⲉ, Mani 1 *A²* ⲡⲉⲧⲁϣ. ⲡⲧⲟⲟⲧϥ (*sc* lion);   qual : 2 Kg 9 3, Aeg 232 ⲉⲣⲉⲧⲉϥⲟⲩⲉⲣⲏⲧⲉ ϣ. ⲡⲗ.; Lam 2 12 (*BF* prob ϩⲱ.) ⲧⲣ.; Mor 17 75 παράλυτος (74 same man ⲉϥⲥⲏϭ), ShP 78 43 ⲙⲉⲗⲟⲥ ⲉⲧϣ. ⲛ̄ⲣⲏⲧϥ (*sc* malady), ShA 2 97 ⲛⲉⲧϣ. ⲏ ⲛⲉⲧϣⲱⲱϭⲉ ϩⲙ̄ⲡϣⲱⲛⲉ, ShZ 595 ϭⲉ ⲉⲧⲟⲩϩⲁϥⲧ ⲉⲩϣ. ⲉⲩⲟⲩⲟϣϥ, Mani 1 *A²* ⲧⲗϭⲟ ⲛ̄ⲡⲉ̇[ⲧ]ϣ.;   *beaten, wrought* (of metal), so ? *locked, bolted* (*cf* Ep 397 n): Mus 40 38 (Reg Pach) ⲛ̄ⲡⲉⲣⲱⲙⲉ ⲛ̄ⲕⲟⲧⲕ ϩⲙⲣⲓ ⲉⲥϣ. (*sic* MS Lefort) τόπος ἠσφαλισμένος *clausa cella, ib* ⲙⲁ ⲉϣ⳾. *quod claudi possit* (yet *ib* ⲉⲣϣⲁⲛⲟⲩⲥⲟⲡ ϣⲟⲟϭⲉϥ *laesus, percussus*, Lant 73 books not to be taken from ⲧⲣⲓ ⲉⲧϭ̄ϣⲟⲟϭⲉ (*l* ⲉⲧⲙ̄ϣ.), CO 459 ϩⲟⲩⲣ ⲉⲩϣ. *wrought* (iron) *keys*.

II tr: Ex 22 2 (*B* ϯ ⲉⲣϩⲟⲧ), Pro 7 23 *SA*(*B* ⲙⲓϣⲓ), MIF 67 167 ⲙⲡⲉⲣϣⲉⲉϭⲉ ⲡⲉⲕⲉⲓⲱⲧ ⲡⲗ.; 2 Kg 1 22(*B* ϭ.), Lam 4 9(*BF* do), Ez 28 8(*B* ⲣⲱϭⲧ)τραυματίας, Is 53 5 *Sⁱ*(Mor 54 15, *B* ϭⲓ ⲉⲣϭ.)-τίζειν; Ps 3 7 *A* ϣⲟⲅϭⲉ (TU 43 8, *S* = Gk, *B* ϣⲁⲣⲓ), Hos 6 1 *SA*(*B* do) πατάσσειν;   Jo 18 10 *A²*(*S* ⲣⲱϭⲧ, *B* ϩⲓⲟⲩⲓ) παίειν; Is 58 4 (*B* ⲙ.) τύπτειν; Ja 1 6 (*B* ⲓⲛⲓ) ῥιπίζειν, Jo 18 22 *A²* ϣ. ⲛ̄ⲟⲩⲕⲟⲩⲣ (*S* ⲣ. ⲛ̄ⲟⲩⲁⲁⲥ, *B* ϯ ⲛ̄ⲟⲩⲕ.) ῥάπισμα δίδ.; Hos 12 11 *A* ϣⲟⲅϭⲉ (*B* ⲉⲣ ϣⲟⲩϣⲱⲟⲩϣⲓ) θυσιάζειν; BG 132 ⲥⲛⲁϣ. ⲛ̄ⲣⲁϩ ⲙ̄ⲯⲩⲭⲏ, ShIF 123 ⲁϥⲙⲉⲉϭⲉⲧⲏ̄ⲛ̄ⲧⲧ ⲛ̄ⲧⲉⲡⲉⲣⲅⲓⲁ ⲙ̄ⲡⲉⲧⲕⲁⲥ, ShViK 9325 397 fire ϣ. ⲛ̄ⲡⲓϣⲏⲛ, ShMIF 23 28 snake ⲛⲁϣⲉϭⲉ ⲟⲩⲏⲣ?, ShA 2 113 wounds ⲉⲛⲧⲁⲧⲉⲧⲛ̄ϣⲟⲟϭⲟⲩ ⲉⲙⲡⲥⲱⲙⲁ, P 129¹⁶ 105 ⲁⲩϣⲟⲟϭⲥⲉϥ

ϩⲛⲟⲩⲡⲗⲏⲅⲏ, P 129¹⁴ 135 ⲁϥϣⲉϭⲉ ⲧⲉϥϭⲓϫ ϩⲛ̄ⲧⲉϥⲥⲟⲩⲣⲉ, C 100 277 wounds ⲛ̄ⲧⲁⲩϣⲟⲟϭⲟⲩ ϩⲛ̄ⲧⲧⲏⲩⲧⲛ̄, Mani H 26 *A²* ϣ. ⲡⲗⲁⲕⲓⲕⲓ *beat drum*, Mani 1 *A²* ⲁⲛⲡⲓϣⲁϭⲉ ⲣⲱⲙⲉ ⲁⲛⲏϭⲉ, *ib* ⲡⲉϥⲣⲉϥⲣ ⲣⲙⲙⲉ ⲁⲩϣⲁϭⲟⲩ, Mor 30 22 *F* ⲧⲛⲟϭ ⲡⲗⲉϩⲧⲥ ⲛ̄ⲧⲁⲛⲣⲁ̄ⲧⲓⲟⲥ ϣⲁⲁϭϥ ⲛϩⲏⲧⲥ, BKU 1 299 ⲥⲛⲁⲩ ⲛϣⲟⲩϣⲧ...ϯ ϩⲟⲩⲣ ⲉⲣⲟⲟⲩ...ⲁⲩⲱ ⲡⲉⲕⲉⲣⲟ ⲁ[ⲓⲧ]ⲛ̄ⲡⲟⲟⲩⲩ ⲛⲁⲕ ϫⲉⲕⲁⲥ ⲉⲕⲁϣⲁⲕⲟⲩ ⲕⲁⲗⲱⲥ *beat, fashion* (to fit).

With following ⲉ- *SA*, *at, in*: 1 Kg 5 12, Pro 7 23 *SA*(*B* ⲙ. ϩⲉⲛ-) ⲡⲗ. εἰς; Z 311 ⲁϣ. ⲉⲡⲉϥⲙⲉⲉⲩⲉ βλ. acc; Mor 37 248 ⲛⲉⲧϣ.† ⲉⲡⲉⲩⲃⲁⲗ, Ep 397 ⲡⲉ]ϩⲟⲩⲣ...ⲉⲧϣ.† ⲉⲡⲉϥⲣⲟ *wrought to (fit) its door.*

—— nn m *S*, *blow, wound*: Jth 13 18 τραῦμα; Aeg 232 ⲡϣ. ⲙⲡⲥⲱⲙⲁ λώβη; ShC 42 114 ⲡϣ. ⲙ̄ⲡⲗⲁⲥ opp ⲧⲁⲗϭⲟ (*cf* Pro 15 4), ShC 73 49 ⲡⲉϣϭⲁ ⲏ ⲡϣ., R 1 2 56 ϫⲟⲟⲩ ⲛⲟⲩϣ. ⲉϩⲙ̄ⲡⲕⲁⲣⲡⲟⲥ.

ϣϭⲁ *SA²*, ⲥϭⲁ *S* nn m, *blow, wound*: ShA 1 81 ⲡϣ. ⲏ ⲡⲁⲥⲛⲉϣ, *ib* 2 120 ⲡⲉⲓⲥϭⲁ ⲏ ⲧⲉⲓⲡⲗⲩⲧⲏ, ShC 73 49 *v* above, PO 2 168 ⲕⲃⲱⲕ ⲉϩⲟⲩⲛ ⲉⲡⲁϣ. ϩⲓⲧⲛ̄ⲡⲉⲕⲧⲛⲏⲃⲉ (Jo 20 27), Mani 1 *A²* ⲡⲉϣ. ⲉⲧϯ ⲧⲕⲉⲥ;   ⲣ ϣ.: Mor 41 328 ⲡⲉⲧⲟ ⲛ̄ϣ. ϩⲙ̄ⲡⲉϥⲥⲱⲙⲁ, Mani K 78 *A²* ϣⲁϩⲣ ⲟⲩϣ.

—— vb tr *SA* with ϭⲓϫ, *strike, clap hands*: Si 12 18 (P 44 119, *B* ϩⲓⲟⲩⲓ) ἐπικροτεῖν, Nu 24 10 (P 44 107, var ⲣⲱϭⲧ, *B* ⲕⲱⲗϩ) συγκ.; 1 Kg 21 13 τυμπανίζειν; BHom 113 ⲡⲉⲧⲡⲁⲣⲁⲅⲉ ⲣ ϣⲡⲏⲣⲉ ⲛ̄ⲥⲉϣ. ϭ., ShIF 248 ⲡⲉϥϣⲙ̄ϣⲉ ⲛ̄ϣⲟⲩϣ. ϭ. ⲉϫⲱϥ;   as nn: Nah 2 10 *A*(*B* ⲛⲉϥ ⲧⲟⲧ⳾ ⲉⲃⲟⲗ) ἐκτιναγμός.

Cf ϣϭⲁⲥⲉ.

ϣϭⲉ *S* nn m, meaning unknown: in place-name ⲡ(ⲉ)ϣϭⲉⲡⲟϩⲉ (Miss 4 763, Mor 47 174), ⲡⲉⲥϭⲡⲟϩⲉ (WS 83).

ϣϭⲏⲗ *A²* *v* ϭⲏⲗ.

ϣϭⲟⲗ *v* ϣϭⲟⲣ.

ϣϭⲗϭⲗⲉ *A* *v* ϣⲕⲗⲕⲉⲗ, adding prob *A²* Mani H 54]ϣϭⲗϭⲗ ⲙ[.

ϣϭⲏⲛ *B* *v* ϣϫⲏⲛ.

ϣϭⲓⲛ *S* nn m, among metal objects, meaning unknown: ST 125 ϣⲟⲙⲡ(ⲧ) ⲛϣ.   *Cf* Leyd AC 79 in list ⲟⲩϣⲟⲛϭⲓⲛ (*sic*).

ϣϭⲛⲏⲛ, ϭⲛ. *B* vb intr, *strive, contend*: Mt 12 19 (*S* ϯ ⲧⲱⲛ) ἐρίζειν; Is 42 2 (*S* diff) ἀνιέναι; Ja 4 2 (var ϣⲱⲡⲧ, *S* ⲙⲓϣⲉ) μάχεσθαι; Pro 10 12 (*SA* ϫⲓ ⲛ̄ϭⲟⲛⲥ) φιλονεικεῖν; Va 58 190 spendest day ⲉⲕϣ. ⲉⲕϭⲓ ϩⲁⲡ εἰς δικαστήρια; Va 61 204 whilst Abraham hastened on ⲉⲣⲉⲡⲓⲣⲟⲕⲥ ⲛ̄ⲧⲟⲧϥ ⲙ̄ⲡϣⲏⲣⲓ ⲉϥϣ. *rivalling* (his father in zeal, Ge 22 6);   ⲥ ⲡⲉⲙ-: MG 25 8 ⲁⲩϣ. ⲡⲉⲙⲡⲟⲩⲅⲉⲣⲟⲩ φιλ. μετά;   ⲥ ⲟⲩⲃⲉ-: Ge 26 35 (var ϭ.) ⲉⲣ. dat.

—— nn m, *strife, rivalry*: 2 Cor 12 20 (*SF* ϯ ⲧ.) ἔρις, Ro 2 8 (*S* do, *F* ⲙⲉⲧⲉⲣⲓⲥ) ἐριθεία, Deu 28 22

(var ϭ., S ⲛⲟⲩϭⲥ) ἐρεθισμός; Pro 10 12 (SA ϯ ⲧ.) ὀνειδίζειν; Cat 156 ⲉⲩϯ ϣ. ⲉϩⲣⲏⲓ ⲉⲍⲉⲛⲡϣⲟⲣⲡ ⲙ̅ⲙⲁ ⲡⲣⲱⲧⲉⲃ (Lu 14 7); ⲙⲉⲧⲣⲉϥϯϣ.: Deu 31 27 (S ⲙ̅ⲡⲧⲁϣⲧ ⲙⲙⲉ) ἐρεθισμός.

ⲣⲉϥϣ., *quereller*: Deu 21 18 (S ϯ ⲛⲟⲩϭⲥ) ἐρεθιστής; ⲉⲣ ⲣ.: 1 Cor 11 16 (S ⲙⲁⲓϯ ⲧ.) φιλόνεικος εἶναι.

ϣϭⲛϭⲓⲛ *v* ϣϭⲓⲛ.

ϣϭⲁⲡ SS*ᵃ*, ϣϭⲕ. B (each once), ϣϭ. A ⲛⲛ, *cry,* *sound* with vb ⲱϣ (ⲁϣ ϣϭ.): ShMIF 23 22 S ⲉⲕⲁϣϭ. ⲉⲕ̇ϣ̇ⲧⲣⲧⲱⲣ;   ⲥ ⲁⲃⲁⲗ A: Ps 33 17 (Cl, S ϫⲓ ϣⲕⲁⲕ, B ⲱϣ ⲉⲃⲟⲗ), Joel 1 14 (S do, B ⲱϣ ⲉϩⲣⲏⲓ) κράζειν; Jon 2 3 (S do, B ⲱϣ ⲉⲃ.) βοᾶν; ⲥ ⲁϩⲣⲏⲓ ⲁ- A: Hos 8 2 (S do, B ⲱϣ ⲉϩ.) κρ.; Cl 60 4 ἐπικαλεῖν; El 36 ⲁⲓⲁϣϭ. ⲁϩ. ⲁⲡⲭ̅ⲥ̅: as ⲛⲛ: Zeph 1 10 A(B ⲥⲙⲏ ⲛ̅ϩⲣⲱⲟⲩ) κραυγή; Ja 5 4 A(S do, B ⲱϣ ⲉⲃ.)βοή; Ora 4 3 S*ᵃ* ⲟⲩⲛⲁϣ ⲡⲁϣϭ.; without ⲁϣ ϣ B: C 86 324 cripple's feet when pulled ϯ ⲟⲩⲡⲓϣϯ ⲛϣ. *Cf* ϣⲕⲁⲕ.

ϣϭⲏⲣ B *v* ⲥϭⲏⲣ, adding A*²* Mani 1]ⲣ ϩⲱⲧ ⲥⲉϣϭⲏⲣ.

ϣϭⲟⲣ SB (rare), -ⲟⲗ, ⲥϭⲟⲗ S, ϣⲕⲁⲣ S*ᵃ*, ϣϭⲁⲣ F ⲛⲛ m, *rent, hire*: Ac 28 30 B ⲙⲁ ⲉⲧⲁϥϭⲓⲧϥ ⲉⲡⲉϥϣ. (S ⲙⲓⲥⲑⲟⲩ vb) μίσθωμα; Worr 266 tenant of house ⲉⲩϣⲓⲧⲉ ⲙ̅ⲙⲟϥ ⲙ̅ⲡⲉϣ., *ib* ⲉϥⲟⲩⲏⲏϩ ϩⲁⲡⲏⲓ ϩⲁⲡⲉϣ.,

ib 268 ⲉⲣϣⲁⲡⲡⲉϣ. ⲙⲟⲩϩ ⲉⲃⲟⲗ landlord will require it, *ib* 288 ⲁϥⲧⲁⲗⲉ ϣ. ⲉⲡⲣⲱⲙⲉ & expelled him, Gött Abh 16 77 ϣ. of water-wheel paid in corn (*cf* Ryl 165, Kr 77), PMich 3583 ϩⲁⲡⲉϣ. ⲙ̅ⲡⲙⲁ ⲡⲁⲙⲣⲉ ⲛⲧⲁⲓⲭⲓⲧⲟⲩ, ST 273 S*ᵃ* ⲡϣ. ⲙ̅ⲡⲏⲓ, CMSS 78 F ⲉϩⲟ(ⲩ)ⲛ̅ ⲡϣ. ⲙ̅ⲡⲏⲓ, J 5 R 15 S*ᵃ* ϣ. ⲡⲁⲡⲟⲑⲏⲕⲏ, CO Ad 15 S*ᵃ* ⲡⲉⲓⲏⲓ ⲛⲧⲁϯ ⲡⲉϣ. ⲛⲁⲕ, J 10 48 S*ᵃ* ⲉⲧⲁⲁϥ (*sc* piece of ground)ⲉⲡϣ. ⲉⲭⲱⲣⲓⲍⲉ ⲙ̅ⲙⲟϥ, BM 1015 lessee of house ⲛⲫϫⲓ ϣ. ⲙ̅ⲙⲟϥ ⲛϥⲕⲱⲧ ... ⲛϥⲧⲁⲁϥ, *ib* 1017 ϩⲁⲡⲉϣ. ⲛⲟⲩⲧⲣⲓⲙⲏⲥⲓⲛ, Hall 106 ⲛⲧⲁϯ ϣ. ⲡⲏ ⲕⲁⲧⲁ ⲣⲟⲙⲡⲉ, Ryl 171 ⲧⲁⲧⲓ ⲛⲁⲕ ϩⲁⲡⲉϣ. ⲧⲉⲣⲟⲙⲡⲉ, Kr 77 ⲁⲓⲡⲗⲏⲣⲟⲩ ⲛⲧⲟⲟⲧⲕ ϩⲁⲡⲉϣ., J 110 14 ⲡⲉⲧⲛⲏⲩ ⲉϩⲣⲁⲓ ϩⲁⲡⲁⲥⲕⲟⲩⲣ (this word?), BM 1054 ⲡⲉϣ. ⲛ̅ⲡⲏⲓ ϩⲁⲭⲓⲛⲉⲡⲁϣⲟⲡⲉ, C 86 259 B ⲡⲁⲩⲭⲏ ⲛ̅ϩⲏⲧϥ (*sc* house) ⲛ̅ⲡⲓϣ. ⲛⲋ̅ ⲡⲣⲟⲙⲡⲓ, Kr 234 wine & fodder as ϣϭⲟⲗ of house, BMOr 6201 B 273 ⲡⲉ ⲥϭⲟⲗ ⲛⲡⲁϣ ⲛ̅ⲡⲏⲓ, *ib* 277 sim;   ⲁⲧϣ., *rent-free*: PBu 55 may dwell therein ⲛⲁ.;   ⲣⲙ̅ⲡϣ., *tenant*: Si 29 29 πάροικος.

ϣϭⲓⲣ S ⲛⲛ m: CO 306 ϩⲁⲡⲣⲱⲃ ⲙ̅ⲡϣ. I will not require more of thee. Same ? or = ϣϭⲏⲣ *water-transport*.

ϣϭⲟⲩⲣ B *v* ϩⲟⲩⲣ.

ϣϭⲟⲥ *v* ϭⲣⲟⲥ.

ϣϭⲏϭⲓ B *v* ϣⲁϭⲉ (ϣϫⲏⲓ).

ϣϭⲁϫⲉ A*²* vb intr, *be smitten* (Polotsky): Mani H 29 ⲛ̅ⲗⲟⲩⲙⲁ ⲁⲩϣ. ⲁ[ⲩ̅ⲕⲁ]ⲧⲁⲗϭⲉ. *Cf* ϣⲱⲱϭⲉ.

ϥ

ϥ, 26th letter of alphabet, called ϥⲁⲓ, ϥⲉⲓ (K 1, Stern p 418)B, فاي (P 44 129, Stern *l c*). Derived from hierogl *f*, as ϥⲓ, ϥⲧⲟⲟⲩ, ⲡⲟⲩϥⲉ, ϣⲱϥⲧ, ⲧⲁϥ, ϫⲟⲟⲩϥ. Frequently (esp S*ᶠ*/F) replaces ⲃ̅, as ⲁⲣⲧⲟϥ (BM 1161), ⲉⲗⲧⲁϥ(CMSS 75), ⲉϥ̇ⲟⲗ(BMEA 10577), ⲉϥⲓⲏⲡ (LAl 6), ⲡⲓϥⲉⲛ (Kr 116), ⲃⲏϥ (ShA 2 252), ⲡⲟⲩϥ, ϩⲱϥ, ⲥⲟϥⲧⲉ, ϣⲉϥⲓⲱ, ϥⲓⲗ (ⲃⲓⲣ BM 1231), ϥⲓ-ⲥⲁ (ⲃⲏⲥⲁ بيصا Miss 4 636), ϥⲉⲡⲓⲁⲙⲓⲓⲛ (Mor 31 180), ⲁⲕⲣⲏϥⲓⲁ(ἀκρίβ. BMis 51), ⲁϥⲣⲁϩⲁⲙ(Ryl 165), ⲁϥ-ⲃⲁⲕⲟⲩⲙ (ClPr 25 2), ⲅⲁϥⲣⲓⲏⲗ (KroppR 5); converse, as ⲃ̅ⲱ, ⲃ̅ⲱϭⲉ, ⲛⲟⲃⲣⲉ, ⲥⲣⲟⲃⲣⲉϥ, ϩⲏⲣⲃⲱⲣⲃ(ShA 1 450), ϩⲃⲱ(*f* of ϩⲟϥ), ϫⲁⲧⲃⲉ, ⲉⲃⲱⲛϩ('Ἐπώνυχος) & Beatty-Merton O*ᶠ* Isaiah glosses; ϥⲃ, ⲃϥ = ϥ in ϥⲃⲱ (Lev 13 3 S), ⲁϥⲃⲡⲧⲟⲩ (Ryl 403), ⲁⲃϥϫⲉⲙⲧⲟⲡ (Saq 302), ⲉϥⲃⲁⲉⲣ(Ann 10 275), ϭⲟϫϥⲃ(ViK 9182).

Replaces ⲟⲩ rarely: ⲗⲉⲥϥ F (Eccl 5 6, *cf* ⲗⲉⲥⲃⲓ, ⲣⲁ-ⲥⲟⲩⲓ); ϩⲓⲡⲡⲉϥ A f⟨ⲟ⟩ⲣ ἱππεύς(Nah 3 3, Hab 1 8); converse: ⲟⲩⲱ (Lant 111 a), ⲟⲩⲉⲓⲧ (BMis 546); ⲡ rarely: ϥⲣⲏⲧⲱⲛ *praeco* (Mor 32 32); Replaced by φ where Gk alphabet used, as ⲡⲉϥ-, ⲧⲏⲣϥ (CMSS 59), ⲉⲣⲟϥ, ⲉϥⲉ- (EW 86) & elsewhere: ⲟⲩⲛⲱⲫ (LMis 132), ⲡⲁⲡⲛⲏⲫ (Ryl 460), ⲙⲙⲁⲫ (J 113), ⲫⲟⲧⲥⲓ (RAl 89), ⲫⲟϫⲕ (AM 40); converse *v* p 514 a. transcribes Ar ف, as ϥⲓ في, ⲡⲉϥⲥⲁⲕ نفسك, ϣⲉⲣⲓϥⲉ شريفة, ⲓⲁϩⲣⲉϥ يعرف (EW 234 ff), ⲁⲥϥⲁⲣ اصفر (PMéd 169, *cf* ⲁⲥⲃⲁⲣ *ib* 154), ⲕⲁⲗⲁⲡϥⲟⲩⲣ قرنفل (*ib* 155, *cf* ⲕⲁⲣⲁⲡ-ⲃⲟⲩⲗ Ryl 106 51), ⲙⲁⲗⲁϥϧⲉ ملقة (Ryl 243); transcribed by ن, as ⲙⲛⲟⲩϥ منوف ⲡⲁⲡⲟⲩϥ (Amélineau *Géog* 558), دفرى ⲧⲉϥⲣⲉ (BM 865, *cf* ϯϥⲣⲉ), ⲟⲩⲉ-ⲛⲟϥⲣ, ابو نفر ⲙⲁⲣⲉϥ-, اسنوف ⲥⲡⲱϥ (BIF 5 93, 94).

ϥⲁⲓ   *v* ⲃⲁⲓ *night-raven.*

ϥⲓ *SAA²BF,* ϥⲉⲓ *S,* ⲃⲓ *A²*(Ma)*FO,* ϥⲁⲓ *B,* ϥⲓ-
SAA²BF, ϥⲉⲓ-*S,* ϥⲓⲧ⸗*SAA²BF,* ⲃⲓⲧ⸗*A¹*(Ma), ϥⲏ̄ⲧ†*S*
(rare), p c ϥⲁⲓ- *SAB,* ⲃⲁⲓ- *SA²*(Ma)*FO,* ϥⲁⲉⲓ-*AF* (ⲃ
for ϥ esp *F,* not *B,* Mani always ⲃ) vb **I** intr, *bear,
carry, take*: Jer 51 22 *B(S* c ⲉ-) ϕέρειν; Jo 16 12 *SA²*
(*B* c ⲃⲁ-), MG 25 17 *B* ⲥⲉⲱϥ ϥ. ⲁⲡ βαστάζειν; Lu
22 36 *S(B* ⲱⲗⲓ) αἴρειν, Ez 1 4 *B(S* ⲭⲓⲥⲉ) ἐξαί.; *ib* 22
14 *SB* ὑφιστάναι, Z 318 *S* not able ⲉϥⲓ ⲏ ⲉⲥⲱ ϩⲣⲓ
ⲕⲁⲑⲓⲥ.; Ex 18 18 *S* ⲉϣ ϥⲓ (*B* ⲗⲟϭⲛ ⲉⲃⲟⲗ) ὑπομόνητος; Is 8 3 *SB*(sic ⲗ?) προνομεύειν; Job 2 9 *S(B*
ϣⲱⲡ ⲉ-) καρτερεῖν; Mt 19 12 *S(B* do) χωρεῖν; Nu
30 13 *S(B* ϥⲱⲡϥ) περιαιρεῖν; Hos 7 4 *A(B* ϭⲓ ϣⲉ-
ⲗⲏⲣ). Gal 5 9 *S(B* do) ζυμοῦν; ShA 1 453 *S* better
to ϥⲓ ⲡⲣⲟϭⲉ ⲁⲡⲟⲧⲁⲥⲥⲉ, ShP 129¹² 8 *S* ⲟϩⲛ ϭⲟⲙ ⲙ-
ⲙⲟϥ ⲉϥⲓ & to fast whole week, TU 43 9 *A* ⲧⲉⲧⲛⲁϥⲓ
& hearken, Cl Pr 47 81 *S* ⲛⲥⲡⲁϣ ϥⲓ ⲁⲡ ϩⲓⲟⲩⲙⲛⲧ-
ⲭⲱⲣⲉ, Miss 4 204 *B* seeing Christ's sufferings ⲙ-
ⲡⲉϥϣ ϥ., ShIF 68 *S* sickness causeth body to ⲟⲩⲟ-
ϣⲙ...ⲁϥⲧⲣⲉϥϥⲓ as leaven;   *arise B*: DeV 1 109
ⲙⲁⲣⲉⲛϥ. ⲡⲧⲉⲡϣⲉ ⲛⲁⲡ;   qual *S*: Tri 730 ⲡⲉϥⲁ-
ⲡⲁⲥ ⲡⲕⲁⲗⲩⲙⲁ ϥ. ⲉϥⲏⲏϩ ϩⲁⲃⲗ̄; *v* also c ⲉϩⲣⲁⲓ ⲉ-
& c ⲙⲙⲁⲩ.

II tr: Nu 4 25 *S(B* ⲱⲗⲓ), Ps 95 8 *SB,* Is 33 23 *SF*
(*B* do), Mk 6 29 *SF(B* do), Jo 10 24 *SA²(B* do) αἴ-
ρειν, Zech 5 7 *SA(B* ⲓⲛⲓ) ἐξαί., Ps 101 11 *SB* ἐπαί.;
Ac 7 21 *SF(B* ⲱ.) ἀναιρεῖν, Ps 45 9 *S(B* ⲧⲁⲗϭⲟ), *ib*
71 7 *S(B* ⲙⲟⲩⲛⲕ) ἀντανα ι., Ge 31 9 *S(B* ⲱ.), Pro 14
35 *SA,* BMar 119 *S* ϫⲱⲣⲁ ⲛⲧⲁⲡⲉⲃⲃⲁⲣⲃⲁⲣⲟⲥ ϥⲓⲧⲉ
ἀφαι., Pro 27 22 *SA* περιαι., Job 21 18 *S(B* do)ὑφαι.;
Ge 31 34 *S*(var & *B* ϫⲓ), Mt 10 38 *S(B* ⲱ.)λαμβάνειν,
Ge 48 1 *S*(var & *B* ϫⲓ) ἀναλ.; Job 13 25 *S(B* ⲕⲓⲙ),
Is 52 11 *B(S* ⲉⲓⲛⲉ) ϕέ.; Lam 1 4 *SF(B* diff) ἄγειν,
Ge 31 26 *S(B* ⲱ.). Lu 13 15 *S(B* ϭⲓ) ἀπάγ.; Mt 3 11
B(S c ⲃⲁ-), Jo 10 31 *SAA²(B* ⲱ.), Ac 3 2 *S(B* ⲧⲱⲟⲩⲛ)
βασ., Jud 16 3 *S* ἀναβ.; Job 27 5 *S(B* ϫⲱ ⲛⲥⲁ-)
ἀπαλλάσσειν; *ib* 21 30 *B* κουφίζειν; Mt 9 17 *B(S*
ⲟⲩⲟϫ)συντηρεῖν; Jo 18 10 *A²(S* ⲥⲱⲗⲡ, *B* ϫⲱϫⲓ)ἀπο-
κόπτειν; Job 1 15 *S(B* = Gk)αἰχμαλωτεύειν; PS 359
S ϣⲁϥϫⲓ ⲡⲡⲉϥⲯⲩⲭⲏ ⲛⲥⲉⲭⲟⲟⲩ, *ib* 162 *S* ⲙⲡⲕⲧⲣⲉⲩ-
ϫⲓ ⲡⲁⲟⲩⲟⲡ, BG 59 *S* ⲁϥϫⲓ ⲡⲟⲩⲃⲏⲧⲥⲡⲓⲣ (Ge 2 21
ϫⲓ), ShC 42 42 *S* ϣⲁϥϫⲓⲧⲟⲩ (by death) ⲧⲁϫⲏ, Miss
4 776 *S* ⲁⲡⲉⲟⲟⲩ...ϥⲉⲓ ⲡⲉⲕⲡⲟⲩϭ, *ib* 676 *S* bishop
ⲧⲁϭⲟ ⲡⲡⲉⲩϫⲏ ⲁϥϥⲓ ⲡⲧⲁⲡⲁϕⲟⲣⲁ, Z 282 *S* bishops
ⲉⲧⲉⲟⲩⲟϣ ⲉϥⲓⲧⲟⲩ *to take* (with him), Ep 370 *S* go
& ϥⲓ ⲡⲁⲧⲟⲟⲩⲉ *fetch,* Mor 19 81 *S* ϥⲓ ⲡⲡⲁⲭⲣⲏⲙⲁ
(var *ib* 18 73 ϫⲓ) = Miss 4 145 *B* ⲱ., C 99 104 *S* bread-
pan small ⲙⲟⲩⲓⲥ ⲁⲥϥⲓ ϥⲧⲟⲟⲩ ⲡⲟⲉⲓⲕ, Worr 314 *S* ⲉⲕⲛⲁϫⲓ ⲟⲩ when quitting world?, BMis 247 *S* Julian
dying cries ⲁⲕϥⲓ ⲡⲙⲁ ⲧⲏⲣϥ (cf PO 1 420), Mor 52
32 *S* ⲁϥϩⲱⲡ ⲉϥⲉⲓ ⲡⲧⲙⲡⲣⲱⲙⲉ by his teaching,
ib 16 15 *S* went to tank ⲉⲧⲉϥⲓ ⲙⲟⲟⲩ, Miss 4 158
B ⲁⲩϥ. ⲙⲙⲟϥ ⲁϩⲟⲩⲛ to shrine, Ryl 95 *S* ⲁⲩⲃⲓ ⲱⲡⲉ

& smote door = MG 25 100 *B* ⲱ., J 44 148 *S* ⲥⲟϕⲓⲁ
ⲛⲁⲃⲓ ⲧⲡⲁϣⲉ ⲙⲡⲏⲓ, *ib* 66 42 *S* ϥⲓ ⲧⲁⲡⲣⲟⲥϕⲟⲣⲁ ⲡⲣⲟⲥ
ⲟⲩⲣⲟⲙⲡⲉ *offer,* Ep 270 *S* he put away wife ⲁϥϥⲓ ⲧⲉⲣⲏⲧ, BSM 21 *B* ϣⲱϥ ⲉⲧⲁⲓϥ. ⲙⲙⲱⲟⲩ = BMis 359
S ϩⲁ-, Va 61 213 *B* †ⲁⲧϣⲏⲣⲓ ⲉⲥϥ. ⲡⲟⲩϣⲏⲣⲓ, BM
592 *F* ⲃⲓⲧⲁⲩ (ⲉ)ⲗⲉⲣⲱⲡⲓ, AM 152 *B* ϥ. ⲡⲣⲁⲡⲃⲁⲥⲁ-
ⲡⲟⲥ, AZ 21 104 *O* ⲁⲡⲟⲩⲡ ⲉϥⲃⲓ ⲕⲗⲟⲙ, Aeg 18 *S* ⲁⲕϥⲓ ⲗⲟⲧⲟⲥ ⲡⲙⲙⲁⲓ = *B* ϥⲓ ⲱⲡ, Mor 25 50 *S* ⲡⲙⲁ
ⲛϥⲓ ⲗ.;   ϥⲓ ⲡⲧⲁⲡⲉ *SF, behead*: Ps 151 7 (*B* ⲱ.), Mt
14 10 *SF(B* do)ἀποκεϕαλίζειν; Jth 13 8 ἀϕαι.; SHel
7 he stretched forth head ⲁⲩϥⲓⲧⲥ;   ϥⲓ ⲧⲟⲟⲧ⸗ *SAB,
raise hand*: Job 31 21 *SB* ἐπαίρειν; Eccl 2 10 *S(F*
ϣⲱⲡ ⲉ-) ἀϕαιρεῖν; R 1 5 36 *S* ⲁⲥϥⲓ ⲧⲟⲟⲧⲥ ⲡⲉϫⲁⲥ *began,* El 46 *A* ⲁⲩϥⲓ ⲧⲟⲟⲧⲟⲩ ⲁϩⲛⲁⲡ ⲁϩⲟⲩⲡ.

With following preposition.

—— ⲉ- *SB* dat commodi: Is 53 3 *B(S* ϩⲁ-), He
12 20 *S(B* ϩⲁ-), Va 57 273 *B* ϣⲁϥϥ. ⲉⲣⲟϥ in losses,
BMar 160 *S* sun could not ϥⲓ ⲉⲣⲟϥ whilst Lord
maltreated ϕⲉ́., Ps 54 12 *SB* ὑποϕέ.; Job 21 3 *S*
(*B* ⲡ-) αἴρ. (var βασ.); Ap 2 3 *S(B* do)βασ.; Si 2 2
SB, C 89 17 *B* ϣⲁϥϥ. ⲉⲣⲱⲟⲩ till death καρτερεῖν;
BMar 158 *S* ⲉϥϥⲓ ⲉⲣⲟϥ when reviled ὑπομένειν;
ShBMOr 8810 486 *S* ⲁϥϥⲓ ⲉⲣⲟϥ ⲉⲩⲥⲱϣ ⲙⲙⲟϥ,
ShC 73 37 *S* are despondent ⲉⲧⲓϥⲓ ⲉⲣⲟⲛ, Mor 19
13 *S* ⲙⲡⲓⲛⲉϣ (*v* p 541 *b*) ϥⲓ ⲉⲣⲟⲓ...ⲉⲧⲉⲙⲣⲓⲙⲉ (var
ib 18 5 ⲉϣ ϭⲱ) = Miss 4 100 *B* ⲱⲟⲩ ⲡⲣⲏⲧ, C 86 126
B sim ⲁⲗⲗⲁ ⲁϥⲣⲓⲙ, R 2 1 72 *S* ϥⲛⲁϫⲓ ⲁⲡ ⲉⲣⲟϥ ⲉϥ-
ⲡⲁⲩ, *ib* 1 5 29 *S* ϥⲓ ⲉⲣⲟϥ ϩⲁⲡⲉⲣϩⲟ, Va 63 90 *B* ϥ.
ⲉⲣⲱⲟⲩ ϩⲉⲡⲧⲟⲩⲙⲉⲧⲏⲛⲕⲓ, Lant 70 *S* ϥⲓ ⲉⲣⲱⲧⲛ ⲙ-
ⲡⲁϣⲁⲃⲧⲥ;   ⲙⲡⲧⲣⲉϥϥⲓ ⲉ- *S*: Ryl 94 1 10 ⲧⲙ. ⲉⲣⲟϥ
of Job;   *to, upon*: Is 49 22 *B(S* ϩⲓϫⲛ-)αἴ. ἐπί,
Deu 2 1 *B(S* ⲙⲟⲟϣⲉ ⲉϩⲣⲁⲓ ⲉ-) ἀπαί. εἰς; Ac 27 43
B(S diff) ἀπορρίπτειν; ShC 73 38 *S* ϥⲓ ⲡⲧⲉⲕϭⲓⲙⲉ
ⲉⲡϫⲓⲡⲟⲡ, Miss 8 194 *S* ⲁⲩϥⲓⲧⲕ ⲉⲣⲏⲥ (cf 195 ϫⲓⲧϥ
ⲉⲣ.), Mor 18 65 *S* ϥⲓⲧⲛ...ⲉⲡⲧⲁⲕⲟ (var *ib* 19 74 ϫⲓⲧⲛ)
= Miss 4 139 *B* ⲥⲟⲕⲧⲉⲛ, BMis 223 *S* ⲁϥⲃⲓⲧϥ ⲉⲡϥ-
ϩⲁⲙⲏⲣ *pressed it to breast,* J 41 27 *S* ⲡϥϥⲓⲧϥ ⲉⲡϫⲗⲟ-
ⲧⲟⲥ (paral *ib* 39 34 ⲟⲓⲕⲉⲓⲟⲩⲥⲉⲁⲓ ⲉ-);   ⲉⲡⲉⲥⲏⲧ ⲉ-
S: C 99 232 ϥⲓ ⲡϣⲏⲣⲉ ⲉⲡ. ⲉⲡⲉⲓϣⲏⲓ (cf *ib* 54 ϫⲓⲧⲟⲩ
sic ⲗ) = *ib* 89 66 *B* ϭⲓ ⲉϩⲣⲏⲓ ⲗⲁⲙⲃ. κάτω;   ⲉϩⲟⲩⲛ ⲉ-
S: PS 262 ϥⲓⲧϥ ⲉⲣ. ⲉⲧⲙⲡⲧⲉⲣⲟ, FR 32 ϥⲓ ⲡⲧⲟⲩ-
ⲯⲩⲭⲏ ⲉⲣ. ⲉⲧⲁⲡⲟⲗⲓⲥ (var BMis 67 ϫⲓ), ST 331 ⲃⲓ
ⲡⲡⲟⲉⲓⲕ ⲉⲣ. ⲉⲡⲏⲓ.

—— ⲉϫⲛ- *SAB, upon, for*: Ps 90 12 *SB* ⲁⲓ́. ἐπί,
Mic 4 3 *SA(B* ϭⲓ) ἀντ αἰ. ἐπί; ShP 130¹ 11 *S* ⲡⲥⲉϥⲓ
ⲛⲡⲉⲧⲛⲁⲡⲏⲅⲉ ⲉϫⲱⲧⲛ (cf c ϩⲓϫⲛ-), JTS 9 383 *S* ϥⲓⲧⲟⲩ (*sc* children) ⲉϫⲛⲡⲉϥⲡⲁⲧ, C 43 30 *B* ⲁϥϥ. ⲙⲡⲓⲙⲁⲣⲧⲩⲣⲟⲥ ⲉ.ⲡⲉϥⲥⲟⲓ, ViK 9496 *S* ϥⲓ ⲉϫⲱϥ (*sc* deceased) ⲡⲧⲉⲡⲣⲟⲥϕⲟⲣⲁ (cf c ϩⲓϫⲛ-);   ⲉϩⲟⲩⲛ ⲉϫⲛ-:
BMOr 9535 *S* ϥⲓⲧϥ(*sc* legacy)ⲉϩ. ⲉϫⲡⲧϣⲉ ⲙⲙⲁⲣⲑⲁ.

—— ⲙⲛ-, ⲛⲉⲙ- *SAA²B* intr, *agree with*: Ge 14
3 *S(B* = Gk) συμϕωνεῖν ἐπί, Mt 18 19 *S(B* † ⲙⲁ†)
σ. περί, Ac 5 9 *S(B* do)σ. dat; Lev 20 5 *S(B* do)ὁμο-

νοεῖν dat; Ex 1 10 *A*(*B* ϯ ⲧⲟⲧ⸍) προστιθέναι πρός, 1 Kg 22 13 *S* ⲥⲩⲛⲧ. καί, Lu 23 51 *S*(*B* do)συγκατατ. dat; Ps 82 8 *S*(*B* ⲓ ⲛⲉⲙ-)συμπαραγίνεσθαι μετά; Ex 18 22 *S*(*B* ϯ ⲧⲟⲧ⸍) συναντιλαμβ. ˙dat; ViSitz 172 4 23 *S* ⲥⲉϥⲓ ⲙⲡⲡⲉⲡⲓⲥⲕⲟⲡⲟⲥ ἐν ἑνὶ εἶναι σύν; BM 183 89 *S* βοηθεῖν dat; ShWess 9 176 *S* ⲁϥϥⲓ ⲙⲡⲡⲉⲅⲉⲣⲣⲏⲅ ϩⲛⲧⲕⲁϩⲓⲁ, Mani 2 *A²* ⲉϥϫⲕⲱⲧ ⲁⲕⲡⲧⲁⲛⲉ ⲉϥϩⲓ ⲡⲉⲙⲉⲥ, DeV 2 106 *B* godhead ϥ. ⲡⲉⲙⲁϥ (sc manhood)ϫⲉⲛⲛⲓϫⲓⲥⲓ; tr, *take with*: Job 28 16 *B* συμβαστ. dat; Ez 1 20 *B* ἐξᾶϊ. σύν; BM 217 27 *S* coming ϣⲁⲥⲉⲛ ⲁⲅⲁⲑⲟⲛ ⲛⲓⲙ ⲛⲙⲙⲁⲥ, departing ϣⲁⲥϥⲉⲓ ϩⲱⲃ ⲛⲓⲙ ⲛⲙⲙⲁⲥ.

—— ⲛ- *SAA²B* ethic dat: Jer 4 6 *B* ἀναλαμβ.; PS 131 *S* ⲙⲡⲟⲩϥⲓ ⲗⲁⲁⲩ ⲡⲟⲩⲟⲓⲛ ⲛⲁⲩ, ShBor 246 84 *S* ⲡⲉⲧϥⲓ ⲙⲙⲟϥ (sc riches) ⲛⲁⲩ, Mor 28 115 *S* ϥⲓ ⲛⲡⲁⲓ ⲛⲁⲕ (var Wess 15 147 om ⲛⲁⲕ); *by, with*: Ez 8 3 *S*(*B* ⲱ. ϫⲉⲛ-) ἀν. gen; *to*: Ep 408 *S* ϥⲓ ⲛⲣⲡⲗⲁⲩ ⲛⲁⲡⲣⲱⲙⲉ, Rec 6 70 *S* ⲛⲧⲁϥⲓ ⲧⲁϣⲉⲉⲣⲉ ⲛⲁⲕ as wife, BSM 16 *B* ϥ. ⲛⲟⲩϣⲟⲩϣⲟⲩⲟⲩϣⲓ ⲙϥϯ = BMis 350 *S* ⲧⲁⲗⲟ ⲉϩⲣⲁⲓ; ϥⲓ ⲛⲧⲙⲏⲧⲉ (often ϩⲛ-), *from midst, away*: AP 12 *A²* ϥⲓⲧϥ ⲛ. ⲁⲓ., 2 Kg 14 7 *S*, Cl 48 1 *A* ἐξᾶϊ.; ShA 2 336 *S* ϥⲓⲧⲟⲩ ⲛ. ⲛⲡⲉⲅⲟⲩⲃⲉ (cf 337 sim ϩⲛ-),ShMIF 23 71 *S* ⲉⲓϥⲓ ⲙⲡⲁⲕⲁⲑⲁⲣⲧⲟⲥ(sc devil)ⲛ.

—— ⲛⲥⲁ- *Sf*, *upon*: PMich 525 ϩⲁϥϥⲓ ϩⲉⲛⲃⲉⲛⲓⲡⲉ ⲛⲥⲟⲓ ⲙⲡⲗⲁⲧⲓ (? πλάγιον).

—— ⲛⲧⲛ- *SAA²F*, *from*: Cant 5 7, Mt 13 12 *SF* (*B* ⲱ. ⲛ.), Jo 16 22 *SA²*(*B* do)ⲁⲓ. ἀπό, Mk 2 20(*B* do) ⲁⲡⲁⲓ. ἀπό, Hos 5 14 *SA*(*B* ⲥⲱϯ)ἐξᾶϊ.; Ge 31 31 (*B* ⲱ.), Lu 16 3 (*B* do) ⲁϥⲁⲓ. ἀπό, Nu 30 16 (*B* ⲫⲱⲛϩ)περιαι.; Sa 15 8 ἀπαιτεῖν; ib 18 4 στερεῖσθαι; Deu 7 4 (*B* ⲫ.) ἀφιστάναι ἀπό; Mor 37 72 ϥⲉⲓ ⲛⲧⲟⲟⲧϥ his goods φιλοῦσθαι; PS 49 ⲧⲁϫⲟⲙ ⲉⲛⲧⲁⲅϥⲓⲧⲉ ⲛⲧⲟⲟⲧ, ShC 42 93, ViK 9328 107 angel ⲛⲁϥⲓⲧⲕ ⲛⲧⲛⲓⲭⲁϫⲉ, Pcod 9 ϥⲓ ⲙⲡⲛ̄ⲧ̄ ⲛⲧⲟⲟⲧⲟⲩ ⲛⲛⲣⲏⲕⲉ, Kr 159 *F* ⲡⲉϣⲧⲉⲛⲃⲓⲧⲟⲩ ⲛⲧⲁⲁ(ⲧ)ⲕ.

—— ϩⲁ-, ϫⲁ- *SAA²BF*, *bear under, support, tolerate*: Nu 2 17*S*(*B* ⲱ.), Jos 3 15*SB* ⲁⲓ̈.; Ac 9 15*S*(*B* ⲧⲱⲟⲩⲛ), Ro 11 18 *SBF*, Va 66 296 *B* ϭⲓ ⲡⲉⲙⲡⲉⲙϣⲱⲛⲓ... ϥ. ϫⲁⲡⲉⲛⲓⲁⲃⲓ βασ.; Pro 24 56 *SA*, He 1 3 *SBF*, C 99 147 *S* ye ought to ϥⲓ ϩⲁⲡⲉⲧⲛⲉⲓⲱⲧ = C 89 61 *B*, BHom 11 *S* cannot ϥⲓ ϩⲁⲡⲁⲏⲣ of bath φέ., 2 Cor 4 10 *SB* περιφ., Job 2 10 *SB*, MG 25 242 *B* ϥ. ϫⲁⲧⲟⲩϭⲟⲗⲕⲥ ὑποφ.; Ja 1 12 *S*(*B* ⲁⲙⲟⲛⲓ ⲛⲧⲉⲛ-), Z 362 *S* ϥⲓ ϩⲁⲟⲩϭⲣⲓⲥⲉ ὑπομένειν; Lam 5 7 *B*(*F* ϫⲓ)ὑπέχειν; Pro 13 8 *SAB* ὑφιστ.; Ex 17 12 *S*(*B* ⲧⲁϩⲣⲟ)στηρίζειν; 1 Cor 9 12 *SF*(var ⲁⲓ ⲛⲛⲁϭ ⲛ̄ϩⲏⲧ, *B* ⲱⲟⲩ ⲛϩ.) στέγειν; Ac 20 35 *S*(*B* ϯ ⲧⲟⲧ⸍)ἀντιλαμβ.; Mt 19 11 *S*(*B* ϣⲱⲡ)χωρεῖν; Joel 2 11 *S*(*A* = Gk, *B* ϣ ϫⲉⲙ ϫⲟⲙ)ἱκανὸς εἶναι dat; PS 233 *S* ϥⲓ ϩⲁⲣⲟⲓ, Sh BM 230 158 *S* thy victims ϥⲓ ϩⲁⲣⲟⲕ, RNC 54 *S* ϥⲓ ϩⲁⲣⲟϥ ϩⲓⲭⲡⲟⲩϭⲗⲟϭ, Miss 8 48 *S* ⲁϥϥⲓ ϩⲁⲣⲟⲟⲩ *brought them* (sc letters), BMis 173 *S* in letter ⲛⲧⲃⲓ ϩⲁⲟⲩⲕⲟϥⲓ ⲛⲣⲓⲥⲉ ⲛⲧⲃⲱⲕ = BSM 82 *B*(cf sim ϯ ϩⲓⲥⲉ

παⲕ CO 53),AM 294 *B* ⲁⲓϫⲓⲥⲓ ⲉⲓϥ. ϫⲁⲣⲟⲕ, ManiH 91 *A²* ⲉϥϩⲓ ϩⲁⲣⲁϥ ⲉϥⲑⲗⲓⲃⲉ.

—— ϩⲓ- *SB*, *from off*: Ex 33 5 *S*(*B* ϩⲱϣϣ) ⲁϥⲁⲓ.; ShBor 246 84 *S* ϥⲓⲧϥ (sc armour) ϩⲓⲱⲱϥ, Pcod 18 *S* sim, ShViK 9593 *S* ⲛⲛⲉⲡⲉϣ [ⲟⲩⲱϩ] ⲉⲣⲟⲟⲩ ⲟⲩϫⲉ ...ϥⲓ ϩⲓⲱⲟⲩ (cf c ϩⲛ-); ϥⲓϩⲏ sim *S*: Lev 10 4 (*B* ⲱ. ⲉⲃⲟⲗ ⲙⲡⲉⲙⲑⲟ) ⲁⲓ̈. ἐκ προσώπου; *upon B*: Is 46 7 (*S* ⲉϫⲛ-) ⲁⲓ̈. ἐπί; Ep Jer 25 (*F* ⲧⲱⲟⲩⲛ ϩⲓ-) φέ. ἐπί, Mk 6 55 (*S* ⲉⲓⲛⲉ ϩⲓϫⲛ-) περιφ. ἐπί; Aeg 57 ϥ. ⲛⲧⲉⲥⲁϥⲉ ϩⲓⲧⲉⲕⲁⲫⲓ.

—— ϩⲛ-, ϫⲉⲛ- *SABF*, *from in, out of*: Ps 151 4 *S* (*B* ⲱ. ⲉⲃⲟⲗ ϫ.), Mk 13 15 *S*(*B* do)ⲁⲓ̈. ἐκ, Is 30 14 *SF* (*B* ⲱ. ϫ.)ⲁⲓ̈. ἐν; Deu 12 32 *S*(*B* ⲱ. ⲉⲃ. ϫ.)ⲁϥⲁⲓ. ἀπό, Jer 33 2 *S*(*B* ⲱ. only) ⲁϥ.; Cl 31 4 *A* ἐκχωρ. gen; Si 18 4 *S* ἐλαττοῦν; Lu 16 4 (*B* ϩⲓⲟⲅⲓ ⲉⲃ. ϫ.) μετατιθ. ἐκ(var ἀπό); Aeg 221 *S* σφετερίζεσθαι ἐκ; BMis 557 *S* ϥⲓⲧⲉ ϩⲛⲧⲉⲙⲏⲧⲉ *de medio auferre*; PS 120 *S* ⲛⲟⲩⲟⲓⲛ ⲉⲛⲧⲁⲅϥⲓⲧⲟⲩ ϩⲛⲧⲡⲓⲥⲧⲓⲥ, Br 126 *S* ϥⲓ ⲛⲧⲕⲁⲕⲓⲁ ϩⲛⲛⲧⲧⲏⲅⲛ, ShC 42 32 *S* ϥⲓ ⲛⲓⲭⲱⲙⲉ ϩⲁⲣⲡⲏⲓ ⲙⲡⲓⲁⲧ ϩ̄ⲛ̄, ib 73 61 *S* ϥⲓ ϩⲛⲣⲏⲧⲟⲩ opp ⲟⲩⲱϩ ⲉ-(cf c ϩⲓ-), Pcod 30 *S* ⲁϥϥⲓ ⲙⲡⲣⲣⲟ ϩⲙⲡⲉϥⲕⲣⲁⲧⲟⲥ, Mor 24 11 *F* ϥⲓ ⲙⲙⲁⲩ ϩⲛⲧⲥⲓϫ ⲙⲡⲉⲃⲓⲱⲧ; *on, with* (agent): Ep Jer 3 *B*(*S* ⲧⲁⲗⲟ ⲉϫⲛ-, *F* ⲧⲱⲟⲩⲛ ϩⲓ-) ⲁⲓ̈. ἐπί, Mk 16 18 *S*(*B* ⲛϩⲣⲏⲓ ϫⲉⲛ-) ⲁⲓ̈. ἐν; 1 Chr 15 15 *B*(Gk om), DeV 2 7 *B* ϥ. ⲙⲙⲟϥ ϫⲉⲛⲡⲉⲥⲁⲙⲏⲣ; ϩⲣⲁⲓ ϩⲛ-: Br 102 *S* ϥⲓ ⲛⲧⲕⲁⲕⲓⲁ ϩ. ⲛϩⲏⲧⲧⲏⲅⲛ (cf above), DeV 2 58 *B* ⲛϥ. ⲛϩⲣⲏⲓ ⲛϩⲏⲧⲉⲛ *harvest of virtues*; ⲉϩⲟⲩⲛ ϩⲛ- *S*: Mor 43 9 ⲁϥϩⲓ ⲛⲧⲁⲓⲭⲙⲁⲗⲱⲥⲓⲁ ⲉϩ. ⲛϩⲏⲧⲟⲩ (sc gates).

—— ϩⲓϫⲛ-*SB*, *upon, for*: Mt 4 6 *B*(*S* ⲉϩⲣⲁⲓ ⲉϫⲛ-) ⲁⲓ̈. ἐπί; AM 36 *B* ϥ. ⲙⲙⲟϥ ϩ. ⲡⲉϥⲧⲉⲡ, R 1 3 51 *S* ϥⲓ ⲛⲧⲉⲡⲣⲟⲥⲫⲟⲣⲁ ϩⲓϫⲱϥ (cf c ⲉϫⲛ-); *from off*: Job 19 9 *S*(*B* ⲱ. ⲉⲃ. ϩ.) ⲁϥⲁⲓ. ἀπό, Jer 13 18 *S*(*B* do)ⲕⲁⲑⲁⲓ. ἀπό; Ps 73 8 *S*(*B* ⲧⲁⲗϫⲟ ⲉⲃ. ϩ.)καταπαύειν ἀπό; Job 9 34 *S*(*B* ⲱ. ⲉⲃ. ϩⲁ-) ἀπαλλάσσειν ἀπό; Miss 8 191 *S* ⲧⲣⲉⲩϥⲓ ⲛⲧⲉⲕⲁⲡⲉ ϩⲓϫⲱⲕ (cf c ⲉϫⲛ-), El 138 *S* ϥⲓ ϯⲣⲏⲛⲏ ϩ.ⲡⲕⲁϩ, Louvain Univ 5 90 *S* ⲁⲛⲛ̄ ϥⲓ ⲙⲡⲉϥⲉⲓⲙⲉ ϩ.ⲡⲉϥϩⲟ & gave him ⲥⲙⲟⲧ ⲛⲣⲓⲣ. *V* also c ⲉⲃⲟⲗ, ⲙⲙⲁⲩ.

With following adverb.

—— ⲉⲃⲟⲗ *SAA²BF*, *take, take away*: 1 Kg 24 17 *S*(*B* c ⲉϥϣⲱⲓ) ⲁⲓ̈.; Jud 1 20 *S* ἐξᾶϊ., Ac 22 22 *S*(*B* ϭⲓⲥⲓ ⲉϩⲣⲏⲓ)ⲉⲡⲁⲓ.; Mk 14 47*S*(var ⲥⲱⲗⲡ, *B* do)ⲁϥⲁⲓ.; Ac 5 9 *SB* ἐκφέ.; Si 45 37 (23) *S* ἐξιλάσκειν (*l* ? ⲉϩⲣⲁⲓ); 2 Kg 3 31 *S*(of corpse) no Gk; AP 2 *A²* ϥⲓ... ⲡϣⲏⲣⲉ ϣⲏⲙ ⲁⲃ., Ostr *penes* Crum *S* send some water ⲙⲙⲟⲛ ⲟⲩⲛⲟϭ ⲛⲣⲓⲥⲉⲡⲉ ϥⲓ ⲛⲗⲁⲕⲱⲛ ⲉⲃ. *move out, displace*(?); as nn: Nu 6 20 *S*(*B* = Gk) ἀφαίρεμα; c ⲛ-: Z 291 *S* ϥⲓ ⲉⲃ. ⲙⲙⲟⲓ ⲙⲡⲓⲙⲟⲩ ⲁⲓ̈. ἀπό; Ex 33 5 *S*(CA 90, var ϩⲓ-, *B* ϩⲱϣϣ), Nu 21 7 *S* (var ⲉⲃ. ϩⲁ-, *B* ⲱ. ⲉⲃ. ϩⲁ-)ⲁϥⲁⲓ. ἀπό, Ps 118 22 *S* (*B* do) περιαι. ἀπό, Pro 4 24 *SA*(*B*do)ⲛ. gen; Ez 42 5 *SB* ἐξέχειν ἐκ *supportare*; FR 14 *S* ⲁϭϥⲓϥ (heart)

еѣ. ⲙⲡⲥⲁ ⲙⲡⲉⲓⲁⲓⲱⲛ; c ⲅⲁ- B: Ez 1 19 ἐξαί. ἀπό
(ib 21 l ⲙⲙⲱⲟⲩ); c ⲅⲓ- S: Is 25 8 (B do) ἀφαι.
ἀπό; c ⲅⲏ- tr: Ps 151 7 S(B ⲱ. eѣ. ϫⲉⲛ-)αἴ. ἐκ,
Mt 9 16 S(B ⲱ. eѣ. ⲅⲓ-, ⲅⲁ-)αἴ. ἀπό, Nu 18 30 S(var
ⲡⲱⲣϫ eѣ., B ⲱ.) ἀφαί. ἀπό, Deu 17 7 S(B ⲱ. eѣ.
ϫⲉⲛ-) ἐξαί. ἐκ; Jos 7 23 S ἐκφέ. ἐκ; Ap 6 4 S(B ⲱ.
eѣ.ⲅⲓϫⲉⲛ-)λαμβ. ἐκ; Is 28 9 S(B ⲱ.ⲅⲁ-)ἀποσπᾶν ἀπό;
Eccl 11 10 S(F ϣⲱⲡ eѣ. ⲛ-)ἀφιστ. ἀπό, Jud 10 16 S
μεθιστ. ἐκ; ShA 2 334 S by filing teeth ϣⲁⲩϥⲓ ⲡⲡⲟⲃⲉ eѣ. ⲅⲏⲡⲉⲅⲛⲁϫⲅⲉ; intr: Ge 35 21 B ἀπαί. ἐκ
(cf ⲧⲱⲟⲩⲛ eѣ. ⲅⲏ-); PS 333 S ϥⲓ eѣ. ⲅⲏⲧϥⲱⲧⲉ; c
ⲅⲓⲣⲙ- S: Jo 20 1 (B ⲱ. eѣ. ⲅ.)αἴ. ἐκ; c ⲅⲓⲧⲉⲛ- B:
Ac 23 10 (S diff)διασπ. ὑπό; c ⲅⲓϫⲛ-: Pro 1 12 SA
(B ⲱ. eѣ. ⲅ.) αἴ. ἐκ, Is 53 8 S(B do) αἴ. ἀπό; ShMun
94 S ϥⲓ ⲡⲡⲉⲓⲑⲗⲓⲯⲓⲥ eѣ. ⲅⲓϫⲱⲡ; ⲡⲥⲁⲃⲟⲗ ⲛ- S,
out of: Ps 50 11 (B ⲱ. eѣ. e-) ἀντανaι. ἀπό; PS 151
ϥⲓ ⲡϣⲱⲡⲉ ⲡ. ⲙⲙⲟⲓ(OdSolom 25 9 مِنْ أَحَدٍ), BMis
97 ϥⲓ ⲑⲟⲧⲉ ⲡ. ⲙⲙⲟⲟⲩ, SHel 15 ϥⲓ ⲡⲡⲉⲅⲁⲡⲏⲅⲉ ⲡ.
ⲡⲡⲉⲅⲥⲱⲙⲁ; ⲅⲁⲃⲁⲗ ⲛ- F: Is 30 11 (S eѣ. ⲛ-, B
ⲱ. eѣ. ⲅⲁ-) ἀφαι. ἀπό.

—— ⲉⲡϣⲱⲓ B, up: 1 Kg 24 17 (S ⲉⲃⲟⲗ), Ps 23 9
(S ⲉⲅⲣⲁⲓ), Zech 1 18 (SA do) αἴ., Ge 13 10 (S do),
Ac 1 9 (S do) ἐπαί.; Va 57 126 ϥ. ⲡⲟⲩϥⲁⲧ ⲉ. ⲡⲉⲙⲟ-
ⲟⲩⲁⲓ ⲉⲡⲉⲥⲏⲧ, AM 114 ϥ. ⲡⲧⲉϥⲥⲙⲏ ⲉ.; c ⲉ-: Is
51 6 (S ⲉⲅ. e-) αἴ. ⲉἰς; BSM 44 ϥ. ⲡⲡⲉϥⲃⲁⲗ ⲉ. ⲉⲧϥⲉ
= BMis 392 S ⲉⲅⲣⲁⲓ e-; c ⲟⲩⲃⲉ-: Ps 118 48 (S
do) αἴ. πρός; c ϫⲁ-: Miss 4 96 ϥ. ⲉ. ϫⲁⲡⲉϥϫⲓϫ
= Mor 19 8 S [ϥⲓ] ⲉⲅ. support; c ⲅⲁ-: Lam 2 19
(S do, F ⲧⲱⲟⲩⲛ ⲅⲗⲏⲓ ⲟⲩⲃⲉ-) αἴ. πρός; Job 11 13 (S
ϫⲓⲥⲉ ⲉⲅ. e-) ὑπτιάζειν ⲡ.

—— ⲉⲡⲁⲅⲟⲩ S, backward: Lu 23 26 (B ⲧⲱⲟⲩⲛ
ⲅⲓϥⲁⲅⲟⲩ)ϥⲉ. ὄπισθεν; Ps 77 71 (B ϭⲓ eѣ. ⲅⲓϥ.)λαμβ.
ἐξόπ.; HM 1 81 ⲙⲡⲟⲩϥϥⲓ ⲟⲩⲧⲱⲅⲉ ⲉ. ⲟⲩⲇⲉ ⲉⲑⲏ yet
ship floated on.

—— ⲉⲅⲣⲁⲓ SAA²BF, up: Is 8 8 S(B ⲧⲱ. ⲉⲡϣⲱⲓ)
αἴ., Ge 7 17 S(B ⲧ.), Jo 4 35 SA²F(B ⲉⲡϣ.)ἐπαί., Ez
11 22 S(B ⲱ. ⲉⲡϣ.) ἐξαί.; R 1 4 59 S ⲉⲓϥⲓ ⲉ. ⲉⲓⲅⲅ-
ⲡⲟⲙⲡⲉ = Mart Ign 870 B ϥⲉ., BHom 27 S ϥⲓ ⲡⲡⲉϣⲗⲏⲗ ⲉ. ἀναφέ.; Ps 146 6 S(B ϣⲱⲡ)ἀναλαμ.; Job
10 15 S ϥⲓ ϫⲱ ⲉ. (B om ⲉ.)ἀνακύπτειν; ShViK 9223
68 S ⲡⲉϥⲛⲁϥⲓ ⲡⲉϥϭⲓϫ ⲁⲛ ⲉ. ⲙⲡⲉⲅⲟⲟⲩ ⲧⲏⲅϥ to do
work, ShR 2 3 7 S ϥⲓ ⲉ. ⲅⲓⲧⲁⲡⲁⲅⲕⲏ, ViK 9527 S
ϥⲓ ⲉ. ⲅⲓⲟⲩⲙⲡⲧⲱⲱⲣⲉ, BMis 419 S ϥⲓ ⲉ. ϣⲁⲡⲡⲉ
offer up, Mani 1 A² ⲃⲓⲧⲕ ⲁ. ⲱ ⲡϣⲁⲣⲡ ⲡⲣⲱⲙⲉ; as
nn: Ep 254 S remember me ⲅⲓⲡⲛⲃ ⲉ. ⲡⲡⲉⲧⲛϭⲙⲁ ⲉⲧⲟⲩⲁⲁⲃ; down: Ac 22 23 S(B ⲥⲓϯ) ῥίπτειν; c ⲉ-
Ps 24 1 S(B ⲉⲡϣ. ⲅⲁ-) αἴ. ἐπί, Mic 2 1 SA(B ⲧⲱ.
ⲟⲩⲃⲉ-) αἴ. πρός, Jo 11 41 SA²(B ⲉⲡϣ.) αἴ. ⲉἰς, Lu 18
13 S(B do) ἐπαί. ⲉἰς; ShClPr 22 356 S ϥⲓ ⲟⲩϭⲉⲣⲱⲃ
ⲉ. ⲉⲅⲁⲥⲉⲃⲏⲥ, BSM 132 B canst ϥ. ⲉ. ⲉⲡⲓⲕⲁⲧⲁⲡⲉ-
ⲧⲁⲥⲙⲁ unhindered (but = Mor 22 141 S ϥⲓ ⲉ. ⲙ-
ⲡⲕ.); qual: Ps 140 8 S(B ⲟⲩⲃⲉ-) πρός; ShC 73
130 S eyes ϥ. ⲉ. ⲉⲡⲭ̄ⲥ̄; c ⲉϫⲛ-: Ps 120 1 S(B om

ⲉⲅ.) αἴ. ⲉἰς, Mt 4 6 S(B ⲅⲓϫ.)αἴ. ἐπί, Jo 13 18 S(A²
ⲉⲓⲡⲉ, B ⲧⲱ.)ἐπαί. ἐπί; c ⲡⲧⲛ-: Ac 1 22 S(B ⲱ.
ⲉⲡϣ.) ἀναλαμ. ἀπό; c ⲅⲁ-, ϫⲁ-: BHom 7 S ϥⲓ ⲉ.
ϫⲁⲅⲉⲛⲅⲟⲉⲓⲁ, Mart Ign 868 B ⲙⲡⲟⲩϣ ϥ. ⲉⲅ. ϫⲁⲅⲟϥ
= R 1 4 55 S ϥⲓ ⲉⲅⲟϥ ϥⲉ.; C 99 101 S ⲉⲕϥⲓ ⲉ. ϫⲁⲅⲟⲓ =
C 89 18 B om ⲉ. = Va ar 172 13 ﻣﺒﻌﺪ; ShC 73 115 S
ϥⲓ ⲉ. ϫⲁⲅⲱ� ⲛⲓⲙ, ShP 130² 54 S sim ϥⲁⲧⲉⲅⲣⲱ ⲡⲕⲱⲅⲧ,
Mani K 85 A² ѣⲓ ⲁ. ϫⲁⲡⲟⲅⲓϣⲉ, PBu 145 S ϥⲓ ⲉ. ⲡⲟⲩⲕⲟⲩⲓ ϫⲁⲅⲟⲛ have a little patience with us, ROC 20
49 S let her not ϥⲉⲓ ⲡⲡⲉⲥⲃⲁⲗ ⲉ. ϫⲁⲡⲅⲟ of any man.

—— ⲙⲙⲁⲩ SAF, thence, tr: Jo 11 39 (A² ⲗⲁϫⲉ,
B ϣⲱⲡ), 1 Jo 3 5 SF(Cai Copt Mus tablet, B ⲱ.) αἴ.,
Deu 7 1 (B ϥⲱϯ eѣ.), Ob 10 SA(B do) ἐξαί.; Lev 1
16 (B ⲱ.), Pro 26 7 (A om ⲙ.), Ep Jer 33 F(B do)
ἀφαι., Jos 24 14(var om ⲙ.)περιαι.; 2 Kg 12 13 παρα-
βιβάζειν; Aeg 272 ϥⲉⲓ ⲙ. ⲡⲧⲙⲡⲧϫⲁⲥⲓⲅⲏⲧ καταστέλλειν; PS 157 ϥⲓ ⲙ. ⲡⲡⲉⲧⲅⲓⲧⲙⲛⲧⲉ (but Od
Solom 22 2 ⲙⲁⲥⲟ), ShC 42 132 ϥⲓⲧⲟⲩ ⲙ. ⲙⲡⲉϥⲙⲧⲟ
ⲉⲃⲟⲗ, ShMiss 4 282 those neglectful ϥⲓⲧⲟⲩ ⲙ. ⲉⲩ-
ⲧⲛⲏⲩ ⲉⲡⲉⲓⲅⲃⲏⲅⲉ, ShA 2 115 stones ⲉⲧϥϥⲓ ⲙⲙⲟⲟⲩ ⲙ.
ⲅⲓⲧⲉϥⲓⲛ, Miss 8 163 if he in front ϥⲓ ⲡⲧⲉϥⲟⲩⲉⲣⲏ-
ⲧⲉ ⲙ. he that followeth ⲟⲩⲉⲅ ⲧⲱϥ ⲉⲡⲉⲥⲙⲁ; intr,
be carried off, disappear S(Sh): A 1 394 ⲁⲡⲕⲁⲕⲉ ϥⲓ ⲙ.
ⲅⲙⲡⲧⲣⲉⲡⲣⲓ ⲡⲓⲣⲉ, IF 217 flame ⲱϥⲙ ⲛ ϥⲓⲙ., C 73
17 ⲧⲟⲡⲟⲥ ⲡⲓⲙ...ⲃⲱⲗ ⲉⲃⲟⲗ ⲛ ⲥⲉϥⲓ ⲙ.; qual: Ez 41
8(l? ⲟⲩⲏⲩ, B ϣⲉ) διάστημα (?); as nn m: Eccl 7
26 S(P Louvain, var ϣⲉⲉⲓ)περιφορά; c ⲉⲃⲟⲗ ⲅⲓ- S:
BMis 241 ϥⲓ ⲡⲱⲛⲉ ⲙ. eѣ. ⲅⲓⲡⲉϫⲙⲁⲕⲅ (var ib 298 om
eѣ.); c ⲅⲁⲃⲁⲗ F: Is 31 7 (S eѣ. ⲛ-, B ѣⲱⲗ eѣ.)ἀφαι.,
BMOr 6948 (2) ѣⲓ ⲙⲉⲩ ⲡⲉⲅⲉⲙⲁⲙ ⲅ. ⲙⲁⲥ, Kropp C
103 sim; c ⲅⲏ- S, from: Mk 2 21 (B ⲱ. ⲡⲧⲉ-) αἴ. ἀπό;
ShA 2 323 sickness ⲡⲁϥⲓ ⲁⲡ ⲙ. ⲅⲙⲡⲉϥⲥⲱⲙⲁ, ShC
73 56 ϥⲓⲧⲟⲩ ⲙ. ⲅⲓⲙⲙⲁ ⲉⲧⲟⲩⲅⲡⲅⲏⲧⲟⲩ, BMis 2 ϥⲓⲧⲟⲩ
ⲙ. ⲅⲛⲟⲩⲡⲟⲗⲓⲥ where reigneth death; c ⲅⲓⲣⲛ-
S: BIF 14 143 ѣⲓⲧϥ (sc stone) ⲙ. ⲅ. ⲡⲣⲟ; c ⲅⲓϫⲛ-
S, from upon: C 99 142 ϥⲓ ⲙⲡⲉⲓⲡⲣⲏϣ ⲙ. ⲅⲓϫⲱⲓ =
C 89 49 B ⲱ. eѣ. ⲅ. αἴ. ἀπό; Ge 48 17 (var om ⲙ.,
B ⲱ. eѣ. ⲉϫ.) ἀφαι. ἀπό; ShLMis 415 ϥⲓⲧϥ ⲙ. ⲅⲓ-
ϫⲱⲧⲛ, BMis 338 ϥⲓ ⲙ. ⲅⲓϫⲱϥ ⲙⲡⲉϥⲉⲟⲟⲩ (var ib om
ⲙ.), R 1 3 62 ⲁϥϥⲓ ⲙ. ⲙⲡⲉϥϣⲱ ⲅ.ⲡⲉϥⲙⲁⲕⲅ.

ⲣ c SAA²BFO, carrier: v ⲕⲗⲟⲙ (adding Mani 1
A² ѣⲁⲓⲕ.), ⲕⲁⲅ(adding BM 449, 450), ⲙⲉⲣⲉⲅ, ⲙⲟⲟⲩ,
ⲡⲁⲅѣ, ⲣⲟⲟⲩϣ, ⲟⲩⲱ news, ⲟⲩⲧⲁϥ, ⲱⲣⲕ, ⲱⲧⲡ 2° (ⲉⲧⲡⲱ), ϣѣⲱⲧ, ϣⲓⲛⲉ (adding Mani 1 A²), ϣⲧⲟⲩⲗ, ⲅⲏⲧ
heart; further Mt 21 12 B ϥ.ⲕⲉⲣⲙⲁ (var ⲣⲉϥⲉⲣⲕ.),
DeV 2 160 B ϥ. ⲗⲁⲙⲡⲁⲥ(cf λαμπαδηφόρος), Mor 28
36 S ѣⲁⲓⲙⲩⲥⲧⲏⲣⲓⲟⲛ (cf μυσταγωγός), AM 209 B ϥ.-
ⲅⲟⲡⲗⲟⲛ(cf ὁπλοφόρος), Baouit 1 8 S ѣⲁⲓϣⲱⲙ, cf Ryl
339 ѣ. ϫⲏⲙⲟⲥⲓⲟⲛ, AZ 21 94 O ⲛⲥⲉ ⲧѣⲁⲓⲧⲱⲟⲩ(doubtful, v ib 38 89).

ⲁⲧϣ ϥⲁⲓ B, unbearable: Va 68 178 grief ⲛⲁⲧϣ
ϥⲓⲧϥ; ⲙⲉⲧⲁⲧϣ ϥ., impatience: Cat 189 monkish
failings ϫⲱⲛⲧ, ⲙ., ⲙⲉⲧⲣⲉϥⲗⲉⲗⲉ ⲉⲃⲟⲗ.

ⲙⲛⲧϥⲓ S, *patience*; ViK 9754 115 ⲙⲛⲧϩⲁⲣϣ ϩⲏⲧ, ⲙ. ⲉⲣⲟⲛ.

ⲣⲉϥϥⲓ SB, *bearer, despoiler*: Jude 16 B ⲣ. ⲁⲣⲓⲕⲓ(S ⲣⲉϥϭⲛ) ⲙⲉⲙⲯⲓⲙⲟⲓⲣⲟⲥ; ShC 73 21 ⲣ. ⲯⲩⲭⲏ ⲛϣⲏⲣⲉ; C 100 305 ⲣ. ⲉϩⲣⲁⲓ ϩⲁⲣⲓⲥⲉ ⲕⲁⲣⲧⲉⲣⲓⲕⲟⲥ; ⲙⲛⲧⲣ. S: BM 216 79 ⲙ. ⲉⲣⲟⲕ ϩⲓⲡϣⲱⲡⲉ ⲉⲅⲕⲁⲣⲧⲉⲣⲉⲓⲛ, P 131³ 83 ⲧⲙ. ⲉⲣⲟϥ of Lazarus = Va 61 94 B ϩⲩⲡⲟⲙⲟⲛⲏ, R 1 4 71 ⲙ. ϩⲁⲣⲓⲥⲉ ⲕⲁⲣⲧⲉⲣⲓⲁ; Aeg 270 sim ⲁⲛⲉⲝⲓⲕⲁⲕⲓⲁ.

ϭⲓⲛ-, ϫⲓⲛϥ. SB, *bearing*: Nu 1 51 B(S diff) ⲉⲝⲁⲓⲣⲉⲓⲛ; Va 57 115 B at Christ's birth ⲟⲩⲡⲱⲟⲩϯ, ⲟⲩⲥⲡⲏⲗⲉⲟⲛ, ⲡϫ. ⲛⲧⲉ ⲟⲩⲥⲓⲟⲩ *guidance, encouragement* (?), BMis 436 S ⲧϭ. ⲉϩⲣⲁⲓ ϩⲁⲡⲙⲉⲉⲩⲉ ⲛⲛⲇⲁⲓⲙⲟⲛⲓⲟⲛ.

V also ⲁϩⲟⲙ, ⲉⲓⲁ *eye*, ⲡⲏⲓ, ⲣⲟⲟⲩϣ, ⲧⲁϭⲥⲉ, ⲟⲩⲱϩ, ⲱⲡ, ϣⲙϣⲏϭⲉ, ϭⲱϭⲉ (ϭⲟϭⲥ), ϩⲟⲉⲓⲙ, ϩⲣⲟⲟⲩ (ϩⲣⲁ⸗), ϫⲱ *head*.

ϥⲟ¹, ϥⲱ², ϥⲟⲟ³ S, ϥⲟⲓ⁴ B, ϥⲱⲓ⁵ SB nn f, *canal, water conduit*: Ps 1 3 B⁴(S ⲙⲁ ⲛⲣⲁⲧⲉ) ⲇⲓⲉⲝⲟⲇⲟⲥ, cit C 89 216 B⁵; Si 24 30 S¹(var²), Is 36 2 S¹(F ⲙⲁ ⲛϫⲓ ⲙⲁⲩ ⲉϩⲟⲩⲛ, B = Gk), ib 41 18 S²(B ϥ.⁴ ⲙⲙⲱⲟⲩ) ⲩⲇⲣⲁⲅⲱⲅⲟⲥ; K 153 B ⲟⲩϥ.⁵ ﺍﻟﺝ, ib 340 B ⲡⲓϥ.⁴ '.⸗; Tri 715 S tree growing ϩⲓⲧⲙⲏⲧⲉ ⲛⲧⲛⲟϭ ⲛϥⲟ ﺍﻟﺝ (cf ⲁϩⲱ 2°); ShP 130¹ 37 S washing clothes in ⲡⲉⲡⲗⲅ ⲛⲡⲓⲟⲛ ϩⲓⲭⲛⲧⲃⲟ ⲏ ϩⲓϫⲛⲧϣⲱⲧⲉ, ShAZ 13 111 S water ⲥⲱⲕ ⲉϩⲟⲩⲛ ⲉⲩⲥⲱϣⲉ ϩⲣⲁⲓ ⲛⲡⲟⲩϥⲟ ⲉⲥⲟ ⲛϭⲱⲧϩ ϭⲱⲧϩ, ShC 73 152 S root not up ⲛⲟⲉⲓⲕ ϩⲓⲡⲃⲟ ϣⲏⲙ, ib ⲛⲛⲟϭ ⲛⲃⲟ, ib ⲥⲡⲓⲣ ⲛⲧⲃⲟ, ShA 2 286 S cheeks ⲟ ⲛⲃⲟ ⲛⲡⲣⲙⲉⲓⲟⲟⲩⲉ, Ryl 209 S will deliver wine ϩⲓⲡⲁⲕⲧⲛⲙⲁ ϩⲓⲧⲁϥⲟⲓ, BMEA 10577 S ⲧⲃ.³ ⲡⲱⲛⲉ ⲉⲧϯ ⲙⲟⲟⲩ ⲉϥⲟⲗ (l ⲉⲃ.) ⲉⲡⲓⲱϩⲉ, Ep 102 Sᵃ ⲃⲱ (?).

ϥⲱ, ⲃⲱ, ⲟⲩⲱ (once) S, ϥⲱⲉ SSᵃA²B (once), ϥⲟⲩⲉ A, ⲃⲱⲉ, ⲃⲟ (?) A², ϥⲱⲓ BF, ⲃⲱⲉⲓ (?), ⲃⲱⲱⲓ, ϥⲱⲟⲩ, ϥⲟⲩⲱϩ⸗ F nn m, *hair*: Lev 13 3 SB, Ps 39 12 S pl B sg, Is 7 20 S pl B sg, Lu 7 38 SB sg, Jo 11 2 SA²B sg ⲑⲣⲓⲝ, Ez 24 17 SB ⲧⲣⲓⲭⲱⲙⲁ; Job 1 20 SB, Ez 24 33 B ϥⲱⲉ, 1 Cor 11 15 SB ⲕⲟⲙⲏ; Cant 7 5 S(F ϩⲱⲗⲕ) ⲡⲗⲟⲕⲓⲟⲛ; Ez 8 3 SB ϥⲱ ⲛⲧⲁⲡⲉ ⲕⲟⲣⲩⲫⲏ (var ⲙⲁⲗⲗⲟⲥ), Ps 67 22 B ⲥⲱⲟϩϩ ⲙⲛϥ. (S diff) ⲕ. ⲧⲣⲓⲭⲟⲥ; Mt 5 36 B ⲕⲁⲡ ⲙⲛϥ. (S ϥ. only) ⲙⲓⲁ ⲑ. *single hair*, EW 116 B sim, Mor 18 50 S ⲛⲕ. ⲛⲃⲱ of his head as trees of Paradise = Gött ar 114 75 ﺷﻌﺮ; Jud 16 14 S ⲗⲟⲟⲩ ⲛϥⲱ, Cant 5 11 S ϥⲱ ⲉⲧⲟⲗⲙ (v ⲱⲗⲉⲙ, F ϣⲕⲓⲗ ⲡϥⲱⲓ) ⲃⲟⲥⲧⲣⲩⲭⲟⲥ; C 99 235 S ϩⲟⲉⲓⲧⲉ ⲛϥⲱ = C 89 70 B ⲧⲣ. ⲓⲙⲁⲧⲓⲟⲛ; JA '75 5 245 S ϣⲧⲏⲛ ⲛϥⲱ ⲥⲧⲓⲭⲁⲣⲓⲟⲛ...ⲥⲁⲕⲕⲟⲛ, K 125 B ⲕⲁϣ ⲙϥ. ﻗﻠﻢ ﺍﻟﺸﻌﺮ; JKP 2 134 F ϣ. ⲛⲃⲱϩⲓ (illegible), BG 50 S ⲟⲩⲯⲩⲭⲏ ⲛϥⲱⲉ, ⲥⲟⲕ ⲙϥ. v ⲥⲟⲕ, Br 268 S ⲛϥⲱⲉ ⲡⲉⲛⲧϥ, El 112 S ⲡⲉϥϥⲱⲉ ⲃⲏⲗ [ⲉⲃⲟⲗ] as women's, ib 42 A sim ⲛϥ., Mor 41 109 S ⲡⲉϥⲛⲟϭ ⲛⲃⲱ(sc Baptist's), Miss 4 119 B ⲟⲩⲛⲓϣϯ ⲛϥ. ϩⲓⲭⲱϥ, Lant 111 a S ⲡⲟⲩⲱ ⲛⲧⲁⲡⲉ, Mor 24 7 F ⲛⲉⲃⲱⲱⲓ ⲛⲧⲉⲃⲁⲡⲏ, Mani 1 A² ⲡⲁⲃ. ⲃⲏⲗ ⲁⲃⲁⲗ, Miss 4 743 S ⲛϥⲱ ⲛⲃⲁⲙⲡⲉ (cf ϫⲁⲕ), Cai

42573 2 S in recipe ⲛϥⲱ ⲛⲡⲣⲓⲣ, PMéd 288 S sim ⲛ-ⲥ(ϩ)ⲓⲙⲉ ⲉϥⲣⲱϫ, Ora 4 25 S sim ⲃⲱ ⲛⲣⲉⲗ(ⲗ)ⲱ, AM 38 B ⲁⲙⲟⲛⲓ ⲙⲡⲉϥϥ., MIE 2 355 B ⲉⲣⲉⲡⲉϥϥ. ϣⲏⲟⲩ = BAp 81 S ⲣⲁⲧϥⲱ, EW 31 B ⲁⲥⲥⲱⲗⲡ ⲉⲃⲟⲗ ⲛⲥⲁⲡⲓϥ. of head, DeV 2 181 B ϥⲱϫⲓ ⲛⲥⲁⲡⲓϥ. of beard; ⲗⲁϥⲱⲓ B, *hairy*: Miss 4 159; ⲣⲁⲧϥⲱ S sim: ShMing 325 S Isaiah ⲟⲩⲣⲱⲙⲉ ⲛⲣ. (cf 4 Kg 1 8 ⲇⲁⲥⲩⲥ), BAp v sup; ⲣⲏⲧ ⲙϥ.: Ge 27 23 S(B ⲟϣ ⲙϥ.) ⲇⲁ.; MIE 2 356 B; ⲥⲕ ϥⲟⲟⲩ F, *draw, comb out, hair, so make straight, smooth*: Eccl 7 14 ⲙⲁⲛ ϣⲭⲁⲙ ⲡⲧⲉⲗⲁⲡϯ ⲥⲕ ϥ. (S = Gk) ⲕⲟⲥⲙⲉⲓⲛ, ib l 15 ⲡⲉⲧϫⲁⲙⲁⲓ ... ⲥⲕ ϥⲟⲟⲩϣ (S do) ⲕ.; cf Bor 134 2 S (VitaSin) one of them ⲥⲱⲕ ⲛⲥⲁⲡϥⲱ ⲛⲧⲉϥⲁⲡⲉ; ⲟⲩⲉϩ ϥⲱ S, *let hair grow*: Deu 14 1 (B Gk diff); 1 Cor 11 14 (B ⲉⲣⲉϫⲱ ϣⲏⲟⲩ) ⲕⲟⲙⲁⲛ; JA '75 5 239 ⲙⲛⲣⲟⲩ. ⲧⲣⲓⲭⲁⲥ ⲧⲣⲉⲫⲉⲓⲛ; ShA 2 134 ⲉⲧⲟⲩ. like women. ϣⲧ ⲃⲟ A², ϣⲁⲧ ⲃⲟⲓ B, *tear* (?) *hair*: MG 25 134 an animal ⲉⲥϣ. (v ⲃⲟⲓϣⲓ & ⲙⲉϩⲏⲗ) ... ⲉⲥⲣⲓⲙⲓ, Mani 1 ⲁⲡ]ⲗⲓⲟⲩ ϣⲧ ⲃⲟ ⲁϥⲣⲓⲙⲉ.

V also ϣⲃ.

ϥⲱ O, nn m, meaning unknown: Hor 78, 83, 84 (ter) all ⲛϥⲱ, 82 ⲛⲡϥⲱ.

ϥⲱ S nn, meaning unknown, as title or nickname: ST 149 among names ⲡⲁⲁⲙ ⲡⲕϫⲁ, ⲙⲁⲕⲁⲣⲓⲟⲥ ϥⲱ.

ϥⲁⲕⲥ A v ϥⲱϭⲉ sf.

ϥⲟⲩⲕⲁⲥⲓ, ϥⲟⲕ. B nn f, a fish: K 171, P 54 150 ϯϥ. ﺍﻡ ﻋﺒﻴﺪ. Cf ? ⲫⲩⲕⲓⲥ (D'Arcy Thompson).

ϥⲓⲕⲟϥⲓ B nn f, among weaver's tools: K 125 ϯϥ. ﻁﻁﺮ (1) *cylinder* on which stuff rolled, (2) *knife*. V Dozy 2 76, Almk 2 84.

ϥⲓⲗ F v ⲃⲓⲣ.

ϥⲛⲧ SA, ⲃ. S, ϥⲉⲛⲧ SB, ⲟⲩⲉⲛⲧ S, ⲃⲉⲛⲧ S/F, ⲃⲛ. F nn m f, *worm*: Deu 28 39 Sf B, Ps 21 6 SB, Pro 12 4 SAB, Jon 4 7 SA², Mk 9 48 SBF, Va 58 167 B ⲡⲓϥ. ⲉⲧⲧⲁⲕⲟ ⲙⲡⲓⲥⲟⲣⲧ ⲥⲕⲱⲗⲏⲝ; Joel 1 4 B(S ⲕⲟⲟⲙⲥϥ Mor 22 9, A = Gk) ⲕⲁⲙⲡⲏ; BMis 546 S ⲡⲟⲩ. ⲉⲓⲣⲉ ⲛⲟⲩⲙⲁϩⲉ ⲛϣⲓⲛ *vermes*; Tri 305 S ⲛⲃ., K 172 B ϯϥ. ﺟﺮﺫ; ShBM 214 S fire & ⲛϥ. of hell, ShP 130² 128 S unsalted meat ⲉⲣ ⲛⲕⲉⲗⲁⲁⲗⲉ ⲛϥ., R 2 67 S ⲟⲩϥ. ⲉϥⲟⲩⲱⲙ ϩⲓⲣⲟⲟⲩϩ ⲛⲟⲩϣⲉ, Gu 92 Sf ⲛⲉⲃⲉ. devouring corpse, PBad 5 397 F ⲟⲩⲃⲛ. ⲉⲃⲛⲕⲁⲧ, Mor 24 25 F ⲃⲛ. ⲉϥϩⲁⲩ, BM 1223 A]ⲟⲩϥ. ϣⲟⲅⲟ ⲉⲃⲟⲗ ⲙⲙⲟⲥ, DeV 1 122 B sim; ⲣ ϥ., *produce worms, be worm-eaten*: Ex 16 20 SB ⲥⲕ. ⲉⲕⲍⲉⲓⲛ (cf ⲗⲁⲁⲗⲉ); Mor 16 16 S water ⲗⲟⲙⲥ ⲉϥⲟ ⲛⲃ., DeV 1 123 B ⲁⲡⲉϥⲥⲙⲟⲧ ⲛϩⲱⲟⲩⲧ ⲗⲟϥⲗⲉϥ ⲉⲃⲟⲗ ⲁϥⲉⲣ ϥ. (cf Si 19 3); ⲉⲣϭⲓ(ϫⲓ) ϥ. B Ac 12 23 (var ϫⲓ ⲛϥ., S ⲣ ϥ., var ϥⲛⲧϥ) ⲥⲕⲱⲗⲏⲕⲟⲃⲣⲱⲧⲟⲥ ⲅⲓⲛⲉⲥⲑⲁⲓ.

ϥⲛⲧ- v ⲃⲟⲛⲧⲉ.

ϥⲣⲉ B nn m, *seed*: BMOr 8775 134, P 54 146
ⲡⲓϥ. حبّ, زريع. *Cf S* ⲉϩⲣⲁ (ϩⲣⲉ).

ϥⲟⲣⲓ B *v* ϩⲱⲣⲉ.

ϥⲟⲣϥⲉⲣ, ϥⲉⲣϥⲱⲣ≠ B vb intr, *fall, rush down*:
Job 14 2 (S ϭⲣⲟϥⲣⲉϥ), Ja 1 11 (S do, cf 1 Pet 1 24 B
ϩⲉⲓ ⲉⲃⲟⲗ) ἐκπίπτειν; Zech 14 12 (S ROC 20 55, A
ϣⲟⲩⲟ) ῥεῖν, Ps 1 3 (S ϭⲣ.)ἀπορρ., Deu 28 40 B (var
ϩⲟⲣϩⲉⲣ, S ϭⲣⲟϥⲣⲉϥ) ἐκρ., Jer 8 13 καταρρ.; Va 58
180 fruit ϣⲁϥϥ. ϩⲁⲣⲓϩⲁⲣⲟϥ καταστρέφειν; AM
158 beaten till ⲡⲁϧⲣⲓ ϥ. ⲡⲥⲉⲣⲉⲓ ⲉⲡⲉⲥⲏⲧ, ib 55 grave-
clothes ϥ. ⲉⲃⲟⲗ ⲙⲙⲟϥ, Va 57 133 worldly ease &
honour ⲉⲑⲛⲁϥ.; tr, *cast off, down*: Lam 1 2ϩ (S
diff, F ⲥⲗⲓⲧ) ἐπιφυλλίζειν; Ap 6 13 (S ⲛⲟⲩϫⲉ ⲉⲃⲟⲗ)
βάλλειν; ⲥ ⲉⲃⲟⲗ: Ez 47 12 defluere; Lam 1c ⲁⲩϥⲉⲣϥⲱⲣⲧ ⲉϩ. ἐπιφ. *Cf* ϩⲟⲣϩⲉⲣ (ϩⲟⲣϩⲉⲣ).

ϥⲱⲥ B nn m, *chisel, knife*: K 123 ⲡⲓϥ. ازميل (l
ازميل σμίλη). *Cf* BIF 20 53, Almk 2 74.

ϥⲱⲧⲉ SAA², ϩ. SA²(Ma), ϩⲟⲧⲉ SA, ϥⲟϯ BF,
ϥⲟϯ B, ϩⲱϯ F, ϥⲉⲧ-SBF, ϥⲟⲧ-AB, ϥⲱⲧ-A, ϥⲁⲧ-A²,
ϩⲁⲧ-F, ϥⲟⲧ≠ SB, ϥⲁⲧ≠ AF, ϩⲁⲧ≠ A²(Ma), ϥⲏϯ† B(v
ⲥ ⲉⲃⲟⲗ), p c S ϩⲁⲧ-(ϥ & ϩ vary, but A² Ma always ϩ)
vb I intr B(rare)*wipe, wipe off*, so *obliterate*: Jer 4 7,
ἐξαίρειν; ⲥ ⲡⲥⲁ- emphasis: MG 25 303 ⲉϥϥ. ⲡⲥⲁ-
ⲡⲣⲟ ⲙⲡⲓϩⲉⲗⲗⲟ= BIF 13 112 S ⲉⲃⲟⲗ ⲛⲥⲁ-. II tr:
Tob 7 16 S, Lu 10 11 S(B ⲡⲟⲩϩ ⲉⲃⲟⲗ) ἀπομάσσειν,
Si 12 10 S, EpJer 23 B(F ⲉϩ.) ἐκμ.; BHom 23 S ϥ.
ⲡⲧⲉⲡⲓⲟⲩⲙⲓⲁ ἐπαλείφειν; ShBor 246 41 S ϥⲉⲧ ⲡⲉϥⲣⲁⲛ from before God, ShR 2 3 47 S ⲡⲉⲧⲟⲩϥ. ⲙⲙⲟϥ
ϩⲛ(ⲡ)ϩⲁⲗⲁⲡⲓⲟⲛ ϩⲓⲧⲛⲡϩⲙⲣⲁⲗ, PO 11 344 B ⲁϥϥ.
ⲙⲙⲟⲥ (sc ϯⲛⲁⲡⲡⲁ) ⲉϩⲟⲩⲛ ϩⲉⲡⲡⲣⲟ ⲙⲡⲓⲣⲱⲙⲓ,
ShP 130² 104 S ⲙⲉϥⲙⲉⲣⲉϩⲱ ⲉⲣⲟϥ ⲉϥϩ. ⲙⲙⲟⲟⲩ (sc
pots he has made) ⲉϥⲕⲟⲥⲙⲉⲓ ⲙⲙⲟⲟⲩ, GMir 183 S
ϥ. ⲡⲡⲉϥⲥⲛⲟϥ ⲉⲧⲣⲁⲧⲉ ⲉⲡⲉⲥⲏⲧ, C 43 212 B sim, BKU
1 28 (8116 b) F ϩⲁⲧ ⲡⲉⲕⲣⲁ, MG 25 222 B oven having burnt long he waited ϫⲉⲡⲧⲉϥϥⲟⲧ ⲡⲓϣⲣⲱⲙ *to
wipe (scour)* it; ⲥ ⲉ-: PBad 5 410 F ϩⲁⲧ ⲟⲩⲛⲉϩ
ⲉⲡϩⲁ (ⲡ)ⲡⲉⲕⲭⲁϫⲓ; ⲥ ⲡ-, ϩⲛ- agent: Lu 7 38 S
(var ϩⲛ-, B ⲉϩ. ϩⲉⲡ-), Jo 11 2 S(var do)A²B ἐκμ.
dat; AM 31 B ϥ. ⲡⲧⲁⲓϩⲁⲕⲓ ϩⲉⲡⲧⲥⲏϥⲓ.
With following adverb.

—— ⲉⲃⲟⲗ SAA²BF, *be wiped out, destroyed* intr:
Jer 2 30 B ὀλεθρεύειν, Ps 91 8 B(S refl) ἔξο.; Deu 9
14 SA(Cl ϥⲱⲧ-)B, Pro 6 33 SA(B tr) ἐξαλείφ.; Nu
32 13 SB ἐξαναλίσκειν; ib 21 B(S ⲟⲩⲱϣϥ)ἐκτρίβειν;
Jer 49 17 B ἐκλείπειν(as if ἐξαλείφ.); Hos 10 8 B(SA
ϥⲓ ⲙⲙⲁⲩ) ἐξαί.; ShWess 9 87 S not one ⲙⲡϧⲱⲙⲓ
ⲁⲩⲱ ϥ. ⲉϩ., ManiH 24 A² ⲁⲡⲟⲩⲱϣϥ ϩ. ⲁϩ., C 89
125 B ⲡⲕⲁϩⲓ ϭⲱⲡⲧ ⲡϥ. ⲉϩ.; tr: Ex 22 20 SB,
Jer 32 36 B ὀλ., Lev 17 4 S(B intr), 1 Kg 24 22 SB,
Hos 8 4 B(A ⲧⲉⲕⲟ), AM 1 5 AB ἐξόλ.; Ge 6 7 SB,
Is 44 22 S(B ⲥⲱⲗϫ) ἀπαλ., Ex 17 14 SB, Ps 50 1 SA

(Cl, B c.), Ac 3 19 SB ἐξαλ.; Lu 9 54 S(B ⲣⲱⲕϩ)
ἀναλίσκ., Deu 5 25 S(B ⲙⲟⲩⲛⲕ), Ez 20 13 SB ἐξαν.;
Nu 17 12 S(var ⲱϧⲓⲓ, B ⲙ.) παραν.; Deu 28 24 SB,
Sa 18 5 S ἀπολλύναι; Nu 33 52 S(B ⲱⲗⲓ), Is 16 6 B
(S ϥⲓ), Am 9 8 B(SA do), Nah 2 1 A(B ⲱ.) ἐξαί.; Is
1 28 S(B ⲙ.), Jer 14 12 B(S ⲱϧⲡ) συντελεῖν; Ex 12
13 S(B ϩⲟⲙϩⲉⲙ), Job 9 17 B(S ⲟⲩⲱϣϥ)ἐκτρ.; Ac
13 19 B(S ⲣⲱϣⲧ) καθαι.; Pro 10 3 B(SA ⲟⲩⲱⲗⲥ)
ἀνατρέπειν; Ge 6 17 S(B ⲧⲁⲕⲟ) καταφθείρειν; Jer
39 31 B ἀπαλλάσσειν; Ps 5 10 SB ἐξωθεῖν; PS 262
S ϥ. ⲉϩ. ⲛⲛⲟⲃⲉ, ShWess 9 176 S ⲁⲡⲛ̄ⲉ ϥⲉⲧ ⲡⲕⲁϩ
ⲉϩ. ⲉⲧⲃⲏⲛⲧⲟⲩ, C 73 212 S eating & seeing our father
approaching ⲁϥⲙⲟⲟϣⲉ ⲉϥϥ. ⲙⲙⲟϥ ⲉϩ. *wiping*
(mouth), BIF 14 169 S ⲁϥϩⲉⲧ ⲡⲉϥϩⲟ ⲉϩ., Mor 41
158 S ϩ. ⲡⲡⲉϥϩⲁⲗ ⲉϩ. with sponges, El 54 A ϥ. ⲙ-
ⲡⲁⲭⲉⲓⲣⲟⲅⲣⲁⲫⲟⲛ ⲁϩ., Imp RussAr S 029 A ⲁⲕϥⲟⲧ
ⲥⲟⲙⲟⲣⲣⲁ(l ⲅⲟⲙⲟⲣⲣⲁ)ⲁϩ., ManiK 54 A² ⲁϥϩⲁⲧⲟⲩ
ⲁϩ., EW 46 B ϥ. ⲡⲡⲟⲅⲓⲁϣϣⲏⲛⲓ ⲉϩ., Mor 39 18
F ϩⲁⲧⲧⲏⲅⲧⲡ ⲉϩ. = ib 40 13 S & C 43 43 B ϥⲉⲧ-,
Mor 24 24 F didst bring us ⲉϥⲁⲧⲉⲡ ⲉϩ.?; a's
nn: Ob 13 SAB, 1 Tim 6 9 B(S ⲧⲁⲕⲟ) ὄλεθρος; 2
Kg 6 8 B(S ϣⲱⲧ ⲉϩ.) διακοπή; ManiH 7 A² ⲡϩ.
ⲁϩ. of worlds, DeV 2 41 B ⲥⲁϫⲓ ⲡⲟⲩϥ. ⲉϩ. ⲉϩⲣⲏⲓ
ⲉϫⲱⲟⲩ.

ϥ. ⲉⲃⲟⲗ with prepositions (often implying 2d
ⲉϩ.). ⲥ ⲡ-: Lev 22 3 S(B ⲉϩ. ϩⲁ-) ἐξόλ. ἀπό; Jer
51 7 B(S ϩⲱⲧϥ) ἐκκόπ. ἀπό; ⲥ ⲡⲥⲁ- v ϥ. I; ⲥ
ϩⲁ-: Ge 7 4 B(S ϩⲓϫⲛ-) ἐξαλ. ἀπό, Ap 7 17 B(S ϩⲛ-)
ἐξαλ. ἐκ; 4 Kg 9 7 S ἐξολ. ἐκ; Hos 2 2 B(A ϥⲓ ⲁϩ.
ϩⲛ-) ἐξαί. ἐκ; EpJer 12 B(F ⲡⲧⲉⲡ-) ἐκμάσσ. διά;
BM 363 S ⲁⲩⲙⲛⲓϣϩ ϥ. ⲉϩ. ϩⲁⲡⲉⲕⲣⲟ; ⲥ ϩⲓ-B:
Ex 32 32 (S ϩⲛ-), Ps 68 29 (S ⲇⲟ) ἐξαλ. ἐκ; ⲥ ϩⲛ-,
ϩⲉⲡ-, *from out*: Ps 9 36 S(B ⲧⲁ.) ἀπολλ. ἐκ; Ap 21 4
SB ἐξαλ. ἐκ; Ex 31 14 SB, Ps 100 8 SB ἐξόλ. ἐκ;
Lam 1 15 B(F ϣⲱⲡⲁ ⲡⲥⲁ-), Am 6 7 B(A ϥⲓ) ἐξαί.
ἐκ; Jer 11 19 B(S ϥⲓ ⲉϩ. ϩⲓϫⲛ-) ἐκτρίβ. ἀπό; Ps 48
14 S(B om) ἐξωθ. ἐκ, Sh(Besa)Bor 205 366 S ϥ.
ⲡⲧⲣⲙⲉⲓⲛ ⲉϩ. ϩⲡⲡⲉⲡϩⲁⲗ, Lant 87 28 S cursed whoso
shall ϥⲉⲧ ⲡⲣⲁⲛ...ⲉϩ. ⲡⲣⲏⲧϥ (sc book), ManiH 39 A²
ϩⲁⲧⲟⲩ ⲁϩ. ϩⲛⲡⲕⲟⲥⲙⲟⲥ, C 43 189 B sins ⲉϥϥ.† ⲉϩ.
ϩⲉⲡϯⲡⲉⲛⲧⲁⲕⲓⲟⲛ (πιττά.); *by, with*: Lu 7 38 B(S
ϥ. ϩⲛ-, ⲡ-) ἐκμάσσ. dat; ShA 2 324 S ⲡⲙⲟⲩⲡⲉ ⲡϥⲟⲧ-
ⲟⲩ ⲉϩ. ϩⲛⲧⲟⲣⲧⲛ of God, Bor 304 52 S lest land ϩ.
ⲉϩ. ϩⲛⲡⲣⲉϩⲱⲱⲛ, C 43 38 B ϯⲛⲁϥⲟⲧⲟⲩ ⲉϩ. ϩⲉⲡ-
ⲡⲉⲕϫⲓϫ = Mor 39 11 F ⲁⲭⲡⲟⲩ ⲉϩ. ϩⲓⲧⲁⲁⲧⲕ, DeV
1 113 B ϥⲟⲧⲟⲩ ⲉϩ. ϩⲉⲡⲣⲱⲥ ⲡⲧⲥⲏϥ; ⲥ ϩⲓϫⲛ-: Ge
7 23 SB ἐξαλ. ἀπό; Pro 2 22 SA(B ⲧⲁ.) ὀλλύναι ἐκ;
Ps 16 14 S(B om vb, F ⲧⲁⲅⲁ ϩⲁⲃⲁⲗ ⲡ-) ἀπολύειν
ἀπό, Ps 33 16 SB ἐξολεθ. ἐκ; ShBM 253 55 S ϩⲟⲧ-
ⲟⲩ ⲉϩ. ϩ. ⲡⲕⲁϩ.

ⲁⲧϥ. ⲉⲃⲟⲗ S, *ineffaceable*: LMis 507 Christ's
wounds ⲛⲁⲧϩ. ⲉϩ.

ϫⲓⲛϥ. ⲉϩ. B, *wiping out, destruction*: Ps 105 23 (S

vb) ⲉϩⲟⲗ.; Dan 7 26 ἀπολλ.; BSM 13 God wroth with world ⲉⲛϫⲓⲛϭⲟⲛⲧ ⲉⲃ. = BMis 346 S vb.

p c S: PLond 4 507 list of clothing &c ⲟⲩⲃⲁⲧϭⲓⲝ (cf χειρόμακτρον), Bodl(P) e 33 sim list. V also ⲃⲁⲑⲱ.

ϣⲱⲧⲉ, ⲃ. S, ϣⲱϯ B nn f m, *sweat*: Ge 3 19 SB, Ez 44 18 B, Lu 22 44 B m, Aeg 243 S, Z 273 ⲡϥ. ἱδρώς; Jer 8 6 B m κάθιδρος; K 265 B m عرق; PS 333 S ⲧϥ. ⲡϩⲁⲣⲭⲱⲡ, ib 64 S ⲧϥ. ⲡⲧⲁⲣⲅⲗⲏ, R 1 5 49 S body ϫⲟⲕⲙ ⲡⲃ., PO 14 340 B ϯϥ. ϩⲁϯ ⲉⲃⲟⲗ, B Mar 78 S ⲧϥ. ⲕⲱⲧⲉ ⲉⲧⲉⲕⲧⲉⲣⲡⲉ, BMis 319 S body ⲙⲉϩ ⲡⲃ., C 89 12 B ⲡⲁϣⲁⲓ ⲡⲓⲛϣ. of body, J 106 105 S laboured ϩⲓⲛϣ. ⲛⲁⲡⲟⲥⲧⲟⲗⲓⲕⲟⲛ, AM 205 B ⲡⲓϣ. of martyrdom, ROC 25 258 B ⲡⲓϭⲓⲥⲓ ⲡⲉⲙⲡⲓϣ. ⲉⲧ-ⲁϣϣⲟⲡⲟϥ, Wess 18 111 S ⲙⲉⲛϫⲓ...ⲣⲓⲥⲉ ⲟⲩⲧⲉ ⲃⲱϭⲉ (*l* ϣⲱⲧⲉ), Cai 42573 1 S recipe ⲃ. ⲡⲓⲱ ⲕⲁⲙ.; ϯ ϥ., *give, produce sweat*: AM 271 B ⲁⲩϯ ⲡⲟⲩⲏⲣ ⲡϥ. ⲓⲇ. ἀναντλεῖν; ShP 130⁴ 99 S of one in fever ⲙⲏ ⲁⲣⲁ ϥⲛⲁϯ ⲃ. ⲡⲕⲉⲥⲟⲡ ⲁⲩⲱ ⲉⲣϣⲁⲡⲡⲉ̄ ⲣ ϩⲛⲁϥ ⲡϥϯ ⲃ. ⲟⲡ, ib ⲡϥϯ ⲃ. ϣⲁⲟⲩⲙⲏⲛϣⲉ ⲡⲥⲟⲡ, Z 628 S recipe ⲉⲣϣⲁⲡⲡⲣⲱⲙⲉ ϯ ⲃ. in bath.

ϣⲱϯⲁ B nn f, *hind part* of body : K 78 ϯϥ. ردف. Coptic ?

(ϣⲱⲧⲉ), ϣⲟⲧⲥ†B vb, meaning uncertain, *be broad, splayed* (?): Va 57 95 fig leaves called ⲡⲗⲁⲧⲩⲫⲩⲗ-(ⲗ)ⲟⲛ ϩⲱⲥ ⲉⲡⲅ. ⲟⲩⲟϩ ⲉϣϣⲡⲟⲩϥ ⲉⲅⲟⲓ ⲡⲕⲁⲧⲁϩⲅⲩⲣⲟⲡ ⲡⲗⲁⲧⲩⲫ. τὸ φυτὸν (? φύλλον) τ. συκῆς. Cf ?? ⲡⲱⲧⲉ or ⲡⲱϫϭ.

ϣⲟⲧⲥⲓ B *v* ϣⲱϭⲉ sf.

ϣⲧⲱⲧϥ *v* ⲙⲧⲟⲧϥ.

ϣⲧⲟⲟⲩ SB (rare, mostly ⲍ), ⲃⲧ. S, ϣⲧⲁⲩ AA², f ϣⲧⲟⲉ SAA², ϣⲧⲟ SA²B, ⲃⲧⲟ S, ⲃⲧⲁ F, ϣⲧⲟⲩ- SAA²B, ϣⲧⲟⲟⲩ-, ϣⲧⲉⲩ- S, ϣⲧⲉ- B, ϣⲧⲁⲩ- F nn, *four*: Ps 93 tit SB, JA '75 5 232 τετράς, Jo 11 39 SA² τεταρταῖος; ShC 42 2 ⲡⲉϥ. ⲙⲡⲛⲥⲟⲟⲩ *Wednesday & Friday*, BMar 220 ⲁⲛⲧⲱⲟⲩⲛ ⲙⲡϥ., BMis 449 a book ⲉϥⲉⲓⲣⲉ ⲡϥ. *fourfold*: Jo 19 23 SA² ⲥⲁⲣⲧϥ. (*B* Gk diff, *v* ⲥⲱϭⲉ p c); f: Lev 11 21 B(S ϥ. ⲡⲟⲩⲉⲣⲏⲧⲉ); as adj, before nn: Zech 1 18 SA, Ap 4 8 τέσσαρες, Sa 18 24 τετρα-; PS 30 ϥ. ⲡⲕⲟⲟⲩ; f: Ge 2 10 ϥⲧⲟⲉ, Ac 21 9 (var -ⲟ) τέσ.; PS 354 ϥⲧⲟ ⲡⲁⲅⲓⲁⲙⲓⲥ, Br 269 ϥⲧⲟ ⲙⲡⲩⲗⲏ, ManiH 37 A² ϥ. ⲡⲣⲉⲓⲧⲉ, Mani 1 A² ϥⲧⲟ ⲡⲥⲧⲟⲗⲓ, BM 1013 13 B ⲡϩⲓⲥⲉ, BM 528 I tit F ⲃ. ⲡϩⲁⲁⲓ; after nn: Ap 6 8 ⲟⲩⲛ ϥ. (var ⲡϥ.) τέταρτος; constr: Is 30 5 B ϥⲧⲉϥⲁⲧ (SF ⲧⲃⲏⲡ) τετράπους, Lev 11 21 S ϥⲧⲉⲟⲩⲉⲣⲏⲧⲉ (var ϥⲧⲟ ⲡ-, B ϥ. alone), Job 1 19 B ϥⲧⲟⲩⲗⲁⲕⲉ (S ϥ. ⲡⲕⲟⲟϥ), Nu 1 21 S ϥⲧⲉⲩϣⲉ (var ϥⲧⲟⲩ-), Job 42 12 S ϥⲧⲉⲩϣⲟ (var ϥⲧⲟⲟⲩ ⲡ-), Dan 7 2 B ϥⲧⲟⲩⲑⲛⲟⲩ, Zech 2 6 A, Mt 24 31 SF sim, Ac 10 11 S ϥⲧⲟⲩⲧⲟⲡ (var ϥⲧⲟⲟⲩ ⲡ-); PS 78 S ϥⲧⲟⲩϫⲟⲩⲧ (ϥ. ⲡϫ. 2 Kg 19 32, Ryl 158 place-name?, ib 385) *eighty*, CO 459 S ϣⲧⲟⲟⲩⲙⲛⲧ *fourteen* (cf below), Mor 18 73 S ⲧⲉⲩϣⲏ ⲡϥⲧⲉⲩⲡⲟⲟⲩ (var ib 19 81 ⲡⲉϥⲧⲟⲟⲩⲡ., cf ϣⲙⲧⲡⲟⲟⲩ) = Miss 4 145 B ⲡⲓⲙⲁⲣⲍ ⲡⲉⲭⲱⲣⲡ ⲓⲥϫⲉⲡ-; *fourteen*: Ge 31 41 ⲙⲡⲧⲁⲧⲉ ⲡⲣⲟⲙⲡⲉ, Nu 29 13 ⲙ. ⲡⲣⲓⲉⲓⲃ, ManiK 42 A² ⲙⲛⲧⲉϥⲧⲉ ⲡⲛⲁϭ ⲡ[ⲁⲓ]ⲱⲡ; *twenty-four*: Ap 11 16 ϫⲟⲩⲧⲁϥⲧⲉ, Hag 2 1 A -ⲉϥⲧⲉ, AZ 34 87 Sf -ⲉϥⲧⲉ, Pcod Mor 11 F ϫⲟⲩⲧⲏⲃϯ, ib ϫⲟⲩⲧⲁⲃ; *thirty-four*: Ge 11 16 ⲙⲁⲁⲃⲧⲁϥⲧⲉ; *forty-four*: Mani 1 A² ϩⲙⲉⲧⲉϥⲧⲉ. Ordinals: Ge 2 14 ⲡⲙⲉϩϥ. ⲡⲓⲉⲣⲟ, ib 15 16 ⲧⲙⲉϩϥⲧⲟ ⲡⲧⲉⲡⲉⲁ, Zech 7 1 S(Tuki 203) ⲧⲙⲉϩϥⲧⲟⲉ ⲡⲣⲟⲙⲡⲉ, Am 1 3 A ⲧⲙⲁ(ϩ)ϥⲧⲟⲉ ⲡⲣ.; BM 244 ⲡⲉϥⲙⲉϩϥ. (cf Jo 11 39 above), ManiK 36 A² ⲡⲙⲁϩϥ. ⲡⲓⲱⲧ, ib 27 ⲧⲙⲁⲣϥⲧⲟⲉ ⲡⲟⲩϣⲏ, BG 16 ⲧⲙⲉϩϥⲧⲟⲉ ⲡⲉϩⲟⲩⲥⲓⲁ; PS 81 ⲡⲙⲉϩϫⲟⲩⲧⲁϥⲧⲉ ⲙⲯⲁⲗⲙⲟⲥ, ib 94 ⲡⲙⲉϩⲙⲁⲃⲧⲁϥⲧⲉ ⲙⲯ., R 1 4 49 ⲧⲙⲉϩϥⲧⲟⲩ(ϫⲟⲩ)ⲱⲧⲉ ⲡⲣⲟⲙⲡⲉ.

ϣⲁϩ v ⲃⲁϩ.

ϣⲱϭⲉ SAA², ⲃ. SAA²(Ma), ϣⲱⲱϭⲉ (BMAdd 31290 312)S, ϣⲱϫⲓ, ϣⲟ. B, ϣⲉϭ-S, ϣⲉⲭ-, ϣⲟⲭ-B, ⲃⲁϭ-F, ϣⲟϭⲍ S, ⲃⲁϭⲍ Sf A²(Ma)F, ϣⲁϭⲍ AA², ϣⲟⲭⲍ B, ⲃⲁⲭⲍ F, ⲃⲏϭ†S, ϣⲏⲭ†B(ϥ & ⲃ vary S) vb **A**, *leap, move hastily* intr: Nah 3 16 A(B ⲟⲩⲟϩ) ὁρμᾶν; ib 2 5 A(B ϭⲟⲝⲓ) διατρέχειν; Ac 21 38 S(var ⲃⲱϭⲉ, B ⲓⲣⲓ ⲡϭⲁⲡϣⲟⲣⲧⲉⲣ) ἀναστατοῦν; Jos 8 14 S σπεύδειν, Si 35 10 S κατασ.; Job 41 9 S(B ϣⲱⲡⲓ) ἐπιφαύσκειν; Aeg 282 S ⲡⲕⲓⲙ ⲡⲓⲙⲉⲗⲟⲥ ⲉϥϣⲁⲛⲃ. παλμός; ShRyl 68 262 S children ϥ. ⲡⲥⲉⲧⲣⲣⲉ at voice of fox, Br 99 S ⲧⲉⲯⲩⲭⲏ ... ϥ. ⲕⲁⲧⲁ ⲧⲟⲡⲟⲥ ⲧⲟⲡⲟⲥ, BMis 514 S ⲡⲉⲣⲉ...ⲡⲉⲃⲣⲏϭⲉ ϥ., Mani 1 A² ⲁϥⲃ. ⲁϥⲉⲓ ⲁⲃⲁⲗ, C 43 227 B ⲁⲡⲓϫⲉⲙⲱⲡ ϥ. ϭⲉⲡⲟⲙⲏϯ, Va 61 113 B at Judgment trees ⲡⲁϥ. ⲡⲉⲙⲧⲟⲩⲡⲟⲩⲡⲓ, ib 59 13 B limbs cut off ⲉⲅϥ. ⲙⲡⲉⲕⲙⲟⲟ; tr (refl): Ac 14 10 S(B ϭⲓ ϥⲉⲓ) ἄλλεσθαι; Tob 2 5 S ἀναπηδᾶν; 1 Kg 20 36 S τρέχ.; BMis 479 S ⲁⲕⲃⲟϭⲕ ⲁⲕⲁϩⲉⲣⲁⲧⲕ, Till Oster 14 A wrath ϩⲁⲣⲉϭϣⲁϭⲥ[, Mani 1 A² ⲁϥⲃⲁϭϥ ⲁϥϫⲱⲧⲉ ⲁⲡⲓⲧⲡ, BSG 196 S ⲁϩⲉⲣⲁⲧⲕ ⲡⲧϭⲟϭ(ⲕ ⲡ)ⲡⲉⲕⲟⲩϩⲉⲣⲏⲧⲉ.

With following preposition.   c e- intr: Jo 4 14 S (var PS 368 ⲉⲣⲟⲩⲛ ⲉ-, B ϭⲓ ϥⲉⲓ ⲉ-) ⲁⲗ. εἰς; Mk 4 37 S(B ϩⲓⲟⲩⲓ) ἐπιβάλλειν εἰς; Jth 7 15 S στασιάζειν; Z 320 S ⲙⲡⲣⲕⲁⲁϥ ⲉⲃ. ⲉⲡⲗⲁⲥ φυλάττου τὸ μὴ λαλεῖν; Lev 17 15 S(B diff, θηρι) ἁλωτος; Br 118 S ⲃ. ⲉⲧⲡⲉ... ⲡⲧⲉⲧⲡⲃⲱⲕ ⲉϩⲣⲁⲓ, C 89 198 B ⲁϥϥ. ⲉⲡⲓⲭⲣⲟ;   refl: Jo 21 7 S(B ϩⲓ.) βάλ. εἰς; Ac 27 43 S(B diff) ἀπορρίπτειν ἐπί; BMis 70 S ⲁⲥϥⲟϭⲥ...ⲉⲡⲣⲁⲙⲏⲣ of son, Mor 50 56 Sf ⲁⲩⲃⲁϭⲟⲩ ⲉⲡⲉⲙⲟⲩⲡⲉⲓⲟⲟⲩⲉ, ManiH 60 A² ⲁϥⲃⲁϭϥ ⲁⲡϩⲓⲥⲉ, C 43 224 B ⲁⲩϥⲟϭⲟⲩ ⲉϥⲓⲁⲣⲟ; e-ϩⲣⲏⲓ e- B: BSM 85 ϥⲟϭⲟⲩ ⲉⲃ. ⲉⲡⲓⲙⲟⲟⲩ = BMis 175 S ⲃ. ⲉⲡⲉⲥⲏⲧ ⲉ-;   c ⲉϫⲡ- intr: Jud 14 6 S ⲁⲗ. ἐπί (cf 19 ⲉⲓ ⲉϩⲣⲁⲓ ⲉϫⲡ-), Job 16 4 S(B ⲧⲱⲟⲩⲡ ⲉϫ.) ⲉⲛⲁⲗ. dat, Ez 44 31 B(θηρι)ⲁⲗ.; Bor 253 164 S ϣⲁϥϥ. ⲉϫⲱⲛ like bee παρεισπηδᾶν; C 99 157 S angels ϥ. ⲉ.

ⲛⲉⲡⲓⲱⲧ = C 89 128 *B* = Va ar 172 74 علی ونبوا, MG
17 495 بوجقﺗ, Z 261 *S* ⲉϥ̅ⲃ̅. ⲉ.ⲧⲉⲕⲕⲗⲏⲥⲓⲁ علی 'ز;
ShA 2 251 *S* cat watcheth man's face ⲉϥ. ⲉⲁⲟⲱϥ, Va
62 275 *B* evil spirit ϥ. ⲉ. ⲡⲉϥⲣⲱⲙⲓ; refl: 1 Kg 16
13 *B*(*S* intr)ἐφάλ. ἐπί; Gu 70 *Sᶠ* all ⲃ̅ⲁϭⲟⲩ ⲉ.ⲓⲱϩⲁⲛ-
ⲛⲏⲥ ἐπέρχεσθαι dat (var κατά); Mor 19 29 *S* ⲁⲅⲃⲟϭ-
ⲟⲩ ⲉ. ⲡⲁⲉⲓⲱⲧ = Miss 4 155 *B* ⲧⲱⲟⲩⲛ ⲉⲝ., R 1 3 81
S her curls ϭⲟⲃⲟⲩ ⲉ.ⲛⲉⲥⲟⲩⲟⲃⲉ like eggs ⲉⲁⲩϩⲉ ⲉ-
ⲃⲟⲗ from nest, C 43 187 *B* ⲁϥϭⲟϫⲩ ⲉ.ϯϭⲣⲓⲙⲓ; ⲥ
ⲛⲥⲁ- *SSᶠF*: BMar 120 ⲁⲩⲙⲟⲩⲓ ϭⲟⲕϥ ⲛⲥⲱⲓ ἁρπάζειν; ShBM 196 2 bull ϥ. ⲛⲥⲁⲡⲉϥ𝔛𝔠, ShMIF 23 27
ⲡⲉⲧⲕϩⲱⲡ ⲉⲣⲟⲟⲩ…ⲉⲕϥ. ⲛⲥⲱⲟⲩ, C 99 194 crocodile
ϥ. ⲛⲥⲱϥ, AZ 14 46 ⲉϥ̅ⲃ̅.† ⲛⲥⲁⲛⲣⲱⲙⲉ, Miss 4 766 *Sᶠ*
ⲁϥⲃⲁⲥϥ ⲛⲥⲱⲓ, Mor 30 35 *F* one ox ⲃ̅ⲁⲥϥ ⲛⲥⲁⲛⲕⲉ-
ⲟⲩⲉⲉⲓ = *ib* 29 30 *S* ⲉⲝⲛ-; ⲥ ⲡⲧⲛ- *S*: Z 231 ⲁϥ-
ϭⲟϣϥ ⲡⲧⲟⲟⲧⲛ ⲉⲡⲙⲟⲟⲩ; ⲥ ϩⲓⲝⲛ-, upon: Job 41
16 *S*(*B* ϭⲓ ϥ.) ἀλ. ἐπί; Lev 11 21 *S*(*B* ϣⲓϯ) πηδᾶν;
R 1 3 74 *S* locust ϥ. ϩ.ⲡⲕⲁϩ, BMis 221 *S* light ϥ. ϩⲓⲝⲱϥ like lightning, DeV 1 130 *B* waves ϥ. ϩ.ⲡⲓⲝⲟⲓ,
AZ 21 157 *S* Baptist's head ⲁⲥϭⲟϭ ϩ.ⲡⲉⲟⲩⲥⲓⲁⲥⲧⲏ-
ⲣⲓⲟⲛ thrice; *from off*: Miss 4 657 *S* ⲁϥⲃⲟϭϥ ϩ.
ⲡⲉϥⲧⲏⲃⲏ (*cf* ⲥ ⲉⲃⲟⲗ ϩⲓ-, ϩⲛ-).

With following adverb.

—— ⲉⲃⲟⲗ *SAA²BF*, *leap, fall forth*, implying
hasty motion, intr: Eccl 5 1 *S*(*F* ⲕⲱⲗⲟⲙ) σπεύ. (var
προπετὴς γίνεσθαι, cit C 42 101 *S*(Esaias Scet)ⲉⲕⲃ̅.†
ⲉⲃ̅.; Mus 40 39 *S*(Reg Pach) if riding ⲉⲕⲡⲁϥ. ⲉⲃ̅.
desilire; El 80 *A* ϥ. ⲁⲃ̅. (from rocks), ShC 42 215 *S*
of new house ϩⲉⲛⲥⲁ ⲉⲩϥ. ⲉⲃ̅. opp ⲗⲱⲕϣ ⲛⲥⲁϩⲟⲩⲛ,
DeV 2 186 *B* ⲁⲗⲗⲟϥ ⲛⲁϥ. ⲉⲃ̅; refl: Mor 18 110 *S*
limbs ⲃ̅ⲟⲥⲟⲩ ⲉⲃ̅.(var LCyp 3 om ⲉⲃ̅.) παλμός; PS
58 *S* ⲁϥϭⲟϭϥ ⲉⲃ̅. ⲛϭⲓ ⲡⲉⲧⲣⲟⲥ, ShA 1 34 *S* ⲉⲩϣⲁ-
ⲛϯϭⲟⲥⲟⲩ ⲉⲃ̅. ϩⲓⲧⲉⲩⲧⲁⲡⲣⲟ ⲛⲥⲉⲱⲣⲕ (*cf* Eccl 5 1 &
ⲣⲉϥϥ.), Mani H 55 *A²* ⲉϥⲁⲃⲁϭϥ ⲁⲃ̅., Mor 52 8 *S* hast
seen Him teaching fear of Lord & humility, ⲙⲡⲉϥ-
ϭⲟϭϥ ⲉⲃ̅. ⲛⲥⲟⲟⲩⲧⲛ *hastened not* to promise pleasures
& honours but rather afflictions; ⲉⲃ̅. ⲉⲝⲛ-: Mor
41 342 *S* ⲧⲉϥϭⲁⲗⲟⲩ ϭⲟⲥϭ ⲉⲃ̅. ⲉ.ⲡⲕⲁϩ (*cf* R 1 5 51 ϭⲉ
ⲉⲝⲛ-); ⲉⲃ̅. ϩ̅ⲁ-: EtLeem 92 *S* ⲁϥⲃⲟϭϥ ⲉⲃ̅. ϩ̅ⲁ-
ⲡⲉϥⲉⲣⲧⲟ; ⲉⲃ̅. ϩⲓ-: BM 995 102 *S* ⲁⲩϭⲟⲥⲟⲩ ⲉⲃ̅.
ϩⲓⲡⲉϥⲧⲱⲣ, AM 16 *B* sim; ⲉⲃ̅. ϩⲛ-, ϩⲉⲛ-: Sa 5
22 *S* ἀλ. ἀπό; Si 36 34 *S*(var ϭⲱⲥϭ) ἀφάλ. ἐκ; Sa 11
19 *S* ἀστράπτειν ἀπό; Deu 33 22 *S*(*B* ϣⲓϯ)ἐκπηδ.
ἐκ; Pcod 21 *S* words ϭⲟϭⲟⲩ ⲉⲃ̅. ϩⲛⲣⲱϥ, EW 96 *B*
eyes ϥ. ⲉⲃ̅. ϩⲉⲛⲡⲉϥϩⲟ, Mor 30 31 *F* ⲉϥⲛⲁⲃⲁϭϥ ⲉⲃ̅.
ϩⲙⲡⲉϥⲧⲏⲃⲏ = BMis 257 *S* ⲉⲃ̅. ϩⲓⲝⲛ-; ⲉⲃ̅. ϩⲓⲝⲛ-:
Est D 8 *S* ἀναπηδ. ἀπό; C 86 303 *B* idol ϭⲟⲝϥ ⲉⲃ̅.
ϩ.ⲧⲉϥⲃⲁⲥⲓⲥ; ⲛⲥⲁⲛⲃⲟⲗ *S*, *forth*: BM 217 3 when
soul seeth death ϣⲁⲥⲃⲟϭ ⲛ. ϩⲙⲡⲥⲱⲙⲁ.

—— ⲉⲡⲉⲥⲏⲧ *SB*: EW 96 *B* ⲁⲡⲓϩⲁⲗⲟⲡ ϭⲟϭϥ ⲉ.,
C 89 77 *B* ⲁϥⲟϩⲓ ⲉϥϥⲱⲝ[ⲓ] ϥ. ⲉ. (iterated or ?error)
like fish on land = TT 150 *S* ϥ. ϩⲓⲝⲙⲡⲕⲁϩ = Va
ar 172 46 علی ⲛⲧⲉϥⲣ = MG 17 444 تتﺒﺑ; ⲉ. ⲉ- *S*:

Mor 40 28 ⲃ̅ⲉⲥⲧⲏⲅⲧⲛ ⲉ. ⲉⲡⲓⲉⲣⲟ (var *ib* 41 144 ⲃ̅ⲟϭ-)
= C 86 57 *B* ϩⲓⲑⲏⲛⲟⲩ ⲉ. ⲉ-, BAp 57 *S* ⲁϥϭⲟϭϥ ⲉ. ⲉⲡϣⲓⲕ; ⲉ. ϩⲓ- *S*: Mor 16 81 ⲁϥⲃⲟϭϥ ⲉ. ϩⲓⲡⲉϥϩⲁⲣⲙⲁ (var BMis 223 ⲟⲩⲁⲣϩ); ⲉ. ϩⲓⲝⲛ- *S*: Lu 4 9
(var ⲉⲝⲛ-, *B* ϩⲓⲟⲩⲓ ⲉ. ⲉⲃⲟⲗ) βάλλειν ἐντεῦθεν, LMär
36 idol ⲃ̅ⲟϭϥ ⲉ. ϩ.ⲡⲉⲥⲧⲩⲗⲗⲟⲥ(var BIF 14 138 ⲉ.ϩⲛ-).

—— ⲉⲡϣⲱⲓ *B*: Mk 10 50 (*S* ⲧⲱⲟⲩⲛ) ἀναπηδ.;
Va 57 226 ϥ. ⲉ. 𝔛ⲉⲛⲑⲛⲟⲩⲡⲓ ⲛⲛⲓⲥⲟⲩⲣⲓ ἀνασπᾶν; MG
25 352 fountain ⲁⲥϥ. ⲉ. (ROC 18 55 ⲃﺻﻭ), *ib* 302
camel ϥ. ⲉ. = BIF 13 112 *S* ⲟⲛⲧϥ ⲉϩⲣⲁⲓ, AM 158
angel causes knocked out teeth to ϥ. ⲉ. each to its
place, *ib* 86 ⲁⲓϭⲟϫⲧ ⲉ. 𝔛ⲉⲛϯⲣⲁⲥⲟⲩⲓ, PO 11 362
ϭⲟϫϥ ⲉ. ⲉⲃⲟⲗ 𝔛ⲉⲛⲡⲓⲙⲁ ⲡⲉⲛⲕⲟⲧ.

—— ⲉⲑⲏ *SB*: PS 72 *S* ⲁⲥϥ. ⲟϭ ⲉ. ⲛϭⲓ ⲙⲁⲣⲓϩⲁⲙ
(*cf* 98 sim ϭⲟⲥϭ ⲉⲃⲟⲗ, 123 ⲉⲓ ⲉⲑⲏ), C 43 218 *B* ⲁϥϥ.
ⲉⲧϩⲏ = Par 154 25 قزﻓ فى; ϩⲓⲧϩⲏ *B*: Miss 4
125 ⲁϥϭⲟϫϥ ϩ. ⲙⲡⲙⲏϣ = Mor 18 33 *S* ⲃ̅ⲟϭϥ ⲁϥⲉⲓ
ⲉⲑⲏ.

—— ⲉϧⲟⲩⲛ, ⲉϧ. *SA²BF*: ShMich 550 15 *S* spirit
of fornication ϥ. ⲉ. ⲛϥⲁⲙⲁⲣⲧⲉ ⲙⲙⲟⲟⲩ, C 86 350 *B*
sim; ⲉ. ⲉ-: ShWess 18 137 *S* ϥ. ⲉ. ⲉⲡⲉⲧⲡⲉⲣⲏⲩ &
smite one another, ShA 1 227 *S* ϩⲉⲛⲕⲉⲙⲉⲉⲩⲉ ϥ. ⲉ.
ⲉⲣⲟⲟⲩ, BMar 56 *S* demon ϭⲟϭϥ ⲉ. ⲉⲧⲉⲥⲉⲕⲓⲃⲉ,(*ib* 58
later ⲁϥϭⲟϭϥ ⲉⲃ̅. ϩⲓⲡⲉⲥⲉⲕ.), Mani H 87 *A²* ⲁϥⲃⲁϭϥ
ⲁ. ⲁⲡⲣ[, DeV 2 174 *B* ⲁⲥϭⲟϭ ⲉ. ⲉⲣⲟϥ & kissed
him. ⲉ. ⲉⲝⲉⲛ- *B*: C 86 282 finding them seated
ⲁϥϥ. ⲉⲃ̅. ⲉⲝⲱⲟⲩ = BSG 181 *S* ϩ ϩⲓⲑⲏ ⲙⲙⲟⲟⲩ; ⲉ.
ϩⲛ-: HM 1 58 *S* ⲁϥϭⲟϭϥ ⲉ. ϩⲙⲡϣⲏⲣⲉ ϣⲏⲙ, EW
176 *B* ⲁⲡⲓⲕⲟⲩϫⲓ ϭⲟϫϥ ⲉ. 𝔛ⲉⲛⲑⲙⲏϯ, Mor 30 6 *F*
ⲁϥⲃⲁϭϥ ⲉ.ϩⲛⲛⲓⲃⲁⲣⲃⲁⲣⲟⲥ = *ib* 29 5 *S* ⲃ̅. ⲉϩⲣⲁⲓ ⲉⲝⲛ-.

—— ⲉϩⲣⲁⲓ *SAA²BF*: Pro 18 4 *SA* ἀναπηδύειν;
Jo 4 14 *A²*(*S* om ⲉϩ., *BF* ϭⲓ ϥⲉⲓ ⲉ-) ἀλ. εἰς; PS 71 *S*
ⲁϥϭⲟϭϥ ⲉ. ⲁϥⲁϩⲉ ⲣⲁⲧϥ, FR 184 *S* sim (var BMis 205
ⲟⲛⲧϥ ⲉ.), Miss 4 103 *B* ⲁϥϭⲟϫϥ ⲉ. & seized servant,
Mor 30 37 *F* ⲁϥⲃⲁϭϥ ⲉ., HTW 79 *S* ⲁϥⲃⲟϭϥ ⲉ. *leaped
down* (?) from ship & went in; ⲉ. ⲉ- *S*: Sa 18 15 ἀλ.
εἰς; Ez 47 9 (*B* ϭⲓ ϥ. ⲉϧ.) ἐκχεῖν ἐπί; Ac 19 16 (*B* ϩⲓ. ⲉϧ.) ἐφάλ. ἐπί; Ge 31 10 (*B* ⲛⲁ ⲉϩ.)
ἀναβαίν. ἐπί; Mor 29 5 *v* above; ⲉ. ϩ̅ⲁ- *F*: Mor
30 54 ⲃⲁϫϥ ⲉϩⲗ. ϩⲁⲡⲓϩⲓⲣⲏϥ = BMis 276 ⲟⲛⲕϥ
ϩⲓⲝⲛ-; ⲉ. ϩⲛ- *S*: Mor 19 82 ⲁⲓⲃⲟϭⲧ ⲉ. ϩⲙⲡⲣⲟⲣⲟ-
ⲙⲁ (var *ib* 18 75 ⲟⲛⲧ)= Miss 4 146 *B* ⲛⲉϩⲥⲓ ⲉⲡϣⲱⲓ,
BSG 185 drops ⲉⲧϥ. ⲉ. ϩⲙⲡⲉϭⲁⲗⲕⲓⲱⲛ, P 129¹⁶ 69
nails ⲃ̅ⲟϭⲟⲩ ⲉ. ϩⲙⲡⲙⲁⲕ & fell to earth; ⲉ. ϩⲓⲝⲛ-
Sᶠ: Miss 4 760 ⲁϥⲃⲁϭϥ ⲉ. ϩ.ⲡⲉϥⲑⲣⲟⲛⲟⲥ *up from off*.

—— ⲥⲁⲡⲉϩⲟⲩ *F*, *backward*: Mor 30 31 ⲁϥⲃⲁϫϥ ⲥ.

B *pluck, seize, rob* intr: Lu 17 6 *BF*(Mor 30 1, *S*
ⲡⲱⲣⲕ) ἐκριζοῦν; Mk 10 19 *SB*, 1 Cor 6 8 *SB* ἀπο-
στερεῖν; Br 102 *S* ⲛϥⲧⲙ. ⲛϥⲧⲙⲁⲥⲟⲩ, Mich 550
24 *S* ⲛⲡⲁϥ ⲛϥ. ⲛⲛⲉⲥⲟⲟⲡⲉ; tr: Lu 6 1 *B*(*S* ⲧⲱⲗⲕ)
τίλλειν; Job 16 13 *SB* διατ.; Ps 51 5 *SB*, Jer 24 6 *B*
(*S* ⲡⲱ.) ἐκτ.; Zeph 2 4 *B*(*SA* do), Mt 13 29 *B*(*S* do,
F ⲧⲱⲕⲉⲙ) ἐκρ.; 1 Cor 7 5 *SBF*, Bor 226 162 *S* if

thou tradest ⲛⲥⲉϭⲟϭⲕ ἀποστ.; Ps 128 6 *B*(*S* ⲧⲱⲕⲙ) ἐκσπᾶν; *ib* 14 4 *S*(*B* ϫⲱⲗ ⲉⲃⲟⲗ), Mk 6 26 *B*(*S* ⲧⲥⲧⲟ ⲉⲃ.) ἀθετεῖν; 2 Cor 7 2 *SB* πλεονεκτεῖν; Mor 37 258 *S* fraudulent trader ϥⲉϭ ⲡⲉⲧϩⲓⲧⲟⲩⲱϥ, *ib* sim ϥⲁϭ-, C 43 4 *B* ϥ. ⲛⲡⲉϥϫⲁϧⲣⲓ, C 86 271 *B* ⲉϣⲟⲩ ⲛϧⲟϫ ϣⲁⲗ, PO 11 330 *B* ϧⲱ ⲛⲥⲉⲟⲓ ⲉϥⲛⲁϭⲟϫⲥ.

With following preposition.   ⲉ ⲉ-, as obj: PS 116 *S* her light ⲛⲛⲉⲩϩ. ⲉⲣⲟϥ, AM 297 *B* bade ϥ. ⲉⲛⲛⲉⲃ ⲡⲧⲉ ⲡⲉϥϫⲓϫ (*cf ib* 235 ϥⲱⲣⲕ ⲉⲃⲟⲗ, C 43 140 ⲙⲏ ⲉⲃ.); *rob of*: C 89 137 *B* ϥⲛⲁϭⲟϫϧ ⲁⲛ ⲉⲡⲱⲛϧ ⲡⲉⲡⲉϩ = Va ar 172 يجرد للبيا , MG 17 508 للبوز , RE 9 137 *S* ⲉⲕⲣ ⲕⲉϯ ⲉⲡⲣⲟⲙⲡⲉ ⲙⲡⲉⲕϭⲟⲕⲕ ⲉⲡⲉⲡϱⲱⲃ there would not be durable peace;   ⲉ ⲛ- sim: Ge 30 2 *SB*, Job 22 7 *SB* ⲟⲧ. acc, Nu 24 11 *B*(*S* ⲁⲡⲟⲥⲧ. ⲉ-) ⲟⲧ. gen, Si 31 24 *S*(var ϱⲟⲩⲣⲉ-) ⲁⲡⲟⲥⲧ. acc, 1 Tim 6 5 *B*†(*S* do) ἀ. gen; Ps 83 11 *S*(*B* ⲉⲣ ϧⲁⲉ ⲛ-) ὑστερεῖν acc, Cai Euch 511 *B* ϥⲉϫ ⲡⲉⲕⲗⲁⲟⲥ ⲙⲡⲓϩⲙⲟⲧ ὑ. gen; 2 Cor 12 17 *SF*(*B* ϭⲓ ⲛϫⲟⲡⲥ) πλεονεκ. acc; Va 66 304 *B* ϥⲉϫ ϯⲛⲉϫⲓ ⲡⲟⲩⲕⲟⲩϫⲓ ὑφαιρεῖν acc, *ib* 292 *B* ϭⲟϫⲟⲩ ⲡⲡⲟⲩϩⲩⲡⲁⲣⲭⲟⲛⲧⲁ δημεύειν; Sh Wess 9 123 *S* ϥⲉϭ ⲧϫⲟⲉⲓⲥ ⲡⲓⲡⲣⲁⲅⲙⲁ ⲡⲡⲉⲥⲏⲕⲁ, R 1 3 20 *S* ⲉⲩϥ. ⲙⲙⲟⲟⲩ ⲙⲁⲩⲁⲁϥ ⲙⲙⲟⲥ, Bor 260 102 *S* ϧⲉϭ ⲧⲥⲁⲣϫ ⲡⲧⲉⲥⲧⲣⲟⲫⲏ, *ib* 254 175 *S* lamps ⲉⲁⲩϩⲟϭⲟⲩ ⲙⲡⲉⲩϭⲟⲉⲓⲛ for lack of oil, Rec 6 182 *B* ⲫϯ ⲡⲁϭⲟϫⲕ ⲁⲡ ⲙ̇ⲫⲏ ⲉⲧⲁⲕⲉⲣ ⲉⲧⲓⲓ ⲙⲙⲟϥ = BMar 217 *S* ⲗⲩⲡⲉⲓ ⲙⲙⲟⲕ ⲁⲡ ϩⲛ-, MIE 2 359 *B* sim = BAp 87 *S* do;   ⲉ ⲛⲥⲁ- *B* emphasis: MG 25 20 ϥ. ⲡⲥⲁⲡⲉϥ ϭⲱⲓ τίλ.; DeV 2 181 sim, PO 11 330 ϥ. ⲛⲥⲁⲛⲓⲥⲟⲟⲓ ⲛⲧⲱⲟⲩ;   ⲉ ⲡⲧⲉⲛ- *B*: Ja 5 4†(*A* ϩⲱ., *S* ϱ.) ἀφυστ. ἀπό; Va 63 5 ⲡⲛⲉⲥϥ. ⲛⲧⲟⲧⲉⲛ ⲛϫⲉ ⲧⲣⲉⲗⲡⲓⲥ = BMis 370 *S* ⲱϫⲛ ⲛ. = BSM 29 *B* ⲧⲁⲕⲟ ⲛ.;   ⲉ ϩⲛ-, ϧⲉⲛ-: 1 Thes 4 6 *S*(*B* ϭⲓ ⲛϫⲟⲡⲥ ϧⲉⲛ-) πλε. ἐν; *from*: Mor 40 26 *S* ϧⲉϭ ⲡⲙⲉⲣⲉϩ ϩⲛⲧⲉϥⲁⲡⲉ = C 43 55 *B* (*cf* C 86 153 sim ⲉⲡϣⲱⲓ ϧⲉⲛ-), C 43 187 *B* serpent did not ϥⲉϫ ⲣⲱϥ ⲛϧⲏⲧϥ till he expired.

With following adverb.   ⲉ ⲉⲃⲟⲗ *B*, *pull out*: Ez 17 9 ϥⲟϫⲥ (*sic l*) ἐκσπᾶν; ⲉⲃ. ⲛⲥⲁ-: AM 321 ϥ. ⲛⲥⲁⲡⲓϥⲱⲓ of head (*cf* ϥ. ⲛⲥⲁ-); ⲉⲃ. ϱⲁ-: Dan 7 8 ἐκρίζ. ἀπό; Lam 5 10 (*S* ⲥⲱⲕ ⲉⲡⲉⲥⲏⲧ, *F* ⲧⲱⲙⲥ) συσπᾶν ἀπὸ προσώπου; ⲁⲃ. ϩⲛ-*A*², ⲉⲃ. ϧⲉⲛ-: T Euch 2 174 idolatry ϥⲟϫⲥ ⲉⲃ. ϧⲉⲛⲡⲓⲕⲟⲥⲙⲟⲥ نزع من; ManiH 60 *A*² ⲁⲓⲃⲁϭϥ ⲁⲃ. ϩⲓⲧϧⲣⲟ[, Miss 4 211 ϥⲟϫⲧⲉⲡ ⲉⲃ. ϧⲉⲛⲁⲙⲉⲛϯ, MIE 2 410 ⲁⲩϩⲱϫ(ⲓ) ⲉⲃ. ϧⲉⲛⲣⲱⲓ ⲙⲡⲓⲭⲁⲙⲟⲥ = PO 22 427 اقلع من , C 86 216 ϥ. ⲡⲏⲓϥⲧ ⲉⲃ. ϧⲉⲛⲡⲉϥⲥⲱⲙⲁ.

—— nn m *S*, *impetuosity*: Bor 263 16 Christ suffered Peter to fall ⲉⲛⲧϥ ⲉⲃⲟⲗ ϩⲛⲧⲉϥⲙⲛⲧⲁⲅⲑⲁϩⲏⲥ ⲉϥⲓ ⲙⲙⲁⲩ ⲙⲡⲉϥϥ.; *grasping, greed*: Is 28 8 (*B*ⲙⲉⲧ-

ϭⲓ ⲛϫⲟⲡⲥ), Lu 12 15 (*B* ϭⲓ ⲛϫ.) πλεονεξία; PS 258 ⲁⲡⲟⲧⲁⲥⲥⲉ ⲙⲡϫⲓⲟⲩϥⲉ..., ⲁⲡⲟⲧ. ⲡⲡⲓϥ.

ⲣⲉϥϥ. *S, impetuous, violent person*: R 1 1 70 thief ⲡⲣⲉϥⲧⲱⲣⲡ...ⲡⲣ., P 131 6 24 among vices ⲁϣⲕⲁⲕ, ⲣ., ϫⲓ ⲛϭⲟⲡⲥ; Mor 41 62 ⲟⲩⲣⲉϥϩⲉϭ ⲃⲏⲕⲉ; ⲣ. ⲉⲃⲟⲗ: Si 9 23 προπετής; ShC 73 41 be not ⲣ. ⲉⲃ. ϩⲛⲧⲉⲕⲧⲁⲡⲣⲟ (*cf* ⲁ ⲉⲃⲟⲗ);   Mor 25 45 devil comes ϩⲛⲟⲩⲙⲛⲧⲣⲉϥϩⲁϭϥ ⲉⲃ.

ϭⲓⲛ-, ϫⲓⲛϥ., *zeal, violence*: Z 323 *S* ϭ. & devil's wiles ὁρμή; *seizing, privation*: MG 25 111 *B* ⲡϫⲓⲛϭⲟϫⲟⲩ ⲡⲟⲩϭⲓⲱⲧ = Gött ar 114 49 قبض.

ϭⲟϭϥ *S* nn, *seizer, robber*: BHom 134 ⲣⲉϥⲧⲱⲣⲡ ϭⲱ ⲉϥⲟ ⲡϭ. ἅρπαξ;   adj: Si 14 9 πλεονέκτης.

ϭⲱϭⲥ *S*, ϧ. *SA*², ϧⲁϭⲥ† *A*² vb intr, meanings *cf* ϭⲱϭⲉ **A**: Nu 27 3 (var ⲁϧⲉ ⲣⲁⲧ⸗, *B* ⲧⲱⲟⲩⲛ both refl) ἐπισυνιστάναι, Ac 21 38 (varr ϩⲱϭⲉ, ϭⲱϭⲉⲓ, *B* ⲓⲣⲓ ⲡϩⲁⲡϣⲱⲣⲧⲉⲣ) ἀνισ.; Si 36 34 (var -ϭⲉ) ἀφάλλεσθαι; Mani K 58 *A*² ⲁⲡⲁⲣⲭⲱⲡ ϧ. ⲁⲩϭⲉⲣⲱϥ, *ib* 59 *A*² ⲡϧⲉ]ϩⲉⲅⲉ ⲉⲧⲁϧ. ⲙⲡⲥⲁ ⲛⲧⲡⲉ, *ib* 51 *A*² ⲕⲁⲧⲁ ⲡⲟⲩϩⲏⲧ ⲉⲧϧ.†, ⲡⲉϥⲕⲉϫⲁⲗ ⲉⲧϧ.†, Mus 40 268 Esau ⲡⲧⲁϥϧⲟϭⲥ ⲙⲡⲉⲥⲙⲟⲩ *deprived of blessing*.

ϭⲟϭⲥ, ϧ. *S*, ϭⲁⲕⲥ *A*, ϭⲟⲭⲥ *B*(once), ϧⲁϭⲥ *S'A*²*F*, nn, *leap, dance*: 1 Kg 10 2 ἄλλεσθαι;   ϥⲓ ϭ.: Joel 2 5 *A*(*B* ϣⲓ†), Nah 3 17 *A*(*S* P 44 116 ϫⲓ ϭ., *B* ϭⲓ ϥⲉⲓ) ἐξάλ.; Mal 4 2 *A*(*B* do) σκιρτᾶν; Pro 7 10 *A*(*S* do, *B* diff) ἐκπέτεσθαι; *ib* 22 15 *SA* ἐξάπτειν (as if ἐκπέτ.); Mani 1 *A*² ⲡⲏⲥⲏ...ⲉⲧⲃⲓ ϧ. ⲁⲡⲱⲛϥ;   ϫⲓ, ϭⲓ ϭ.: Job 6 10 (*B* ϭⲓ ϥ.), Is 35 6 *S*(var *S'*)*F*(*B* do, *cf* Pey 324 b) ἄλ.; Mich 550 40 dissolute monks ϫ. ⲛⲑⲉ (ⲡ)ⲛⲓϭⲁⲣϭⲉ whilst poor starve, R 1 2 55 feet run after iniquity, mouth ϫ. ϱⲙⲡϫⲓ ⲛϭⲟⲡⲥ, BM 187 130 ⲡⲗⲟϭⲟⲥ ϫ. ⲙⲡⲉⲧⲡⲉ ⲙⲡⲕⲁϩ, P 129 16 2 ⲉϥⲡⲏⲧ ⲉϥϫ. ϱⲙⲡⲕⲁϩ, MIE 2 359 *B* fish in water ⲉϥϭ. (BAp 87 *S* diff);   ⲉ ⲉ-: ShC 42 149 ⲡⲉⲧⲉⲣⲉⲡϩⲏⲧ ϫ. ⲉⲣⲟϥ ϩⲛⲧⲙⲛⲧⲁⲥⲓϩⲏⲧ, BMis 197 his spirit ϫ. ⲉⲣⲟϥ as he hearkened to God's word (var Mor 16 34 = 15 24 om ⲉ-);   ϭⲓⲛϫⲓ ϭ., *exultation*: BHom 103 ⲧϭ. ⲙⲡⲉⲧϣⲱⲡⲉ (ALR '96 197 ⲗ̣ϭⲟϥ);   ⲙⲛⲧⲣⲉϥϩⲟϭⲥ *S, leaping, haste*: P 44 95 ⲧⲙ̇. مقافز; P 131 1 22 lest Mary answer ϩⲛⲟⲩⲙ. ⲉⲃⲟⲗ.

ϧⲉϭⲉ *A*², ϭⲟⲧⲥⲓ, ϥ., ϭⲟⲭⲥⲓ *B* nn, *leap*: BMOr 8775 125 ⲡⲓϥ. قفزات, BM 920 265 ⲡⲓϥ. حركات; Mani K 89 *A*² ⲡⲣⲙⲡⲉⲥ ⲙⲏⲣ... ⲟⲩⲛ ϧ. ϣⲱⲡⲉ ⲛϩⲏⲧϥ ϩⲛⲧⲉϥⲙⲣⲣⲉ;   ϭⲓ ϥ.: Tst Ab 174 ⲁⲧⲉϥⲯⲩⲭⲏ ϭ. within him, C 43 58 ⲁⲩϭⲓ ϭⲟⲭ. ϧⲉⲛⲟⲩⲣⲁϣⲓ, RAl 89 child in womb ⲛⲁϭⲓ ϥ. ϥ.

ϭⲱϭⲉ A v ϧⲱⲧⲉ vb.

Ϩ

Ϩ, 27th letter of alphabet, used in *A* only; no name recorded. Derived from hierogl *ḥ* & *ḫ*, as ϩⲏⲃⲥ, ϩⲛⲙ, ⲙⲓϩⲉ, ⲟⲩϩⲓ, ⲥϩⲉⲓ, ⲡⲱⲥϩ, ⲱⲛϩ. Corresponds to *S* ϩ *B* ⳉ, as ϩⲁⲉ, ϩⲗⲗⲟ, ⲁϩⲱⲙ, ⲣⲱϩⲉ, ⲙⲁⲭϩ; or to *SB* ϣ, as ϩⲓ, ϩⲱⲣⲡ, ϩⲃⲏⲣ, ⲙⲁϩⲉ, ⲥⲁⲉⲓϩ & to *O* ḫ (Hor, *v* below p 629 *a*), as ϩⲟⲩⲡ, ϩⲣⲁⲩ, ⲱⲡϩ. Omitted rarely: ⲗⲟⲩⲡ (Pro 24 15; Nah 1 11).

Ϩ   *v* ϣ- vb.

Ϩⲁ   *v* ϩⲁ- 1° & 3°.

Ϩⲁⲉ   *v* ϣⲁ *rise, feast.*

Ϩⲁⲉ, ϩⲁ(ⲓ)ⲉⲓ, ϩⲁ(ⲉ)ⲓ   *v* ϩⲁⲉ *last thing.*

Ϩⲉ   *v* ⲣϩⲉ, ϣⲉ *wood,* ϩⲉ *manner.*

Ϩⲉⲓ, ϩⲓ   *v* ϩⲏ *belly* & ϣⲓ.

Ϩⲓⲉ(ⲓ)   *v* ϣⲓⲁⲓ (ϣⲓⲏ).

Ϩⲟ, pl ϩⲱⲟⲩ[1], -ⲟⲩⲉ[2], ϩⲟⲟⲩ[3], -ⲟⲩⲉ[4] nn m, *road, path* (*S* ϩⲓⲏ, *B* ⲙⲱⲓⲧ): Ex 4 24, Is 53 6 (Cl), Hos 7 1 ὁδός; ib 2 6 (*S* ShRE 10 164) τρίβος; TU 43 11 ⲛϩⲟ ⲉⲧⲥⲟⲩⲧⲁⲡⲧ; pl: Pro 3 6[2] (?), ib 17[1], Nah 2 5[3], Zech 1 4[1], ib 6[3], ib 9 3[4], Mal 2 9[1] ὁδ.; Cl 60 2 ϩ.[3] ⲙⲙⲁϩⲉ διάβημα. *V* Spg 305.

Ϩⲟ   *v* ϣⲟ *thousand.*

Ϩⲁⲉⲓⲃⲉ   *v* ϩⲁⲉⲓⲃⲉⲥ.

Ϩⲃⲉ   *v* ⲥⲁϣϥ (ϣϥⲉ).

Ϩⲃⲏⲣ   *v* ϣⲃⲏⲣ.

Ϩⲏⲃⲥ   *v* ϩⲏⲃⲥ.

Ϩⲟⲩⲟⲩⲕ   *v* ϩⲱⲱⲕⲉ *scrape.*

Ϩⲱⲕ   *v* ϩⲱⲱⲕ *gird.*

Ϩⲁⲗ   *v* ϣⲟⲗ.

Ϩⲉⲗ   *v* ϣⲁⲗ & ϩⲁⲗ *servant.*

Ϩⲱⲗ   *v* ϣⲱⲗ *despoil* & *flow.*

Ϩⲗⲗⲟ   *v* ϩⲗⲗⲟ.

Ϩⲗⲁⲡ   *v* ϩⲗⲟⲡ.

Ϩⲏⲙ   *v* ϣⲏⲙ.

Ϩⲙⲁⲙ   *v* ϩⲙⲟⲙ.

Ϩⲙⲟⲩⲡ   *v* ϣⲙⲟⲩⲡ.

Ϩⲁⲙⲧ   *v* ϣⲟⲙⲛⲧ.

Ϩⲙϩⲉⲗ   *v* ϩⲁⲗ *servant* (ϩⲙϩⲁⲗ).

Ϩⲛ-   *v* ϩⲛ-.

Ϩⲟⲩⲛ   *v* ϩⲟⲩⲛ.

Ϩⲛⲁⲛ   *v* ϩⲱⲛ *approach.*

Ϩⲱⲛⲧ   *v* ϩⲱⲛⲧ.

Ϩⲛⲧⲉ   *v* ϣⲟⲙⲛⲧ.

Ϩⲛⲁϣ   *v* ϣⲛⲟϣ.

Ϩⲛⲟⲟϥ   nn with ϫⲓ, *conceive*: Ps 50 7 ⲁⲧⲁⲙⲱ ϫⲓ ϩ. ⲙⲙⲁⲓ (Cl, *S* ϫⲓ ⲟⲩⲱ, *B* ⲉⲣ ⲃⲟⲕⲓ) κισσᾶν.

Ϩⲡⲉ   *v* ⲉϣϫⲉ.

Ϩⲱⲡⲉ   *v* ϣⲱⲡⲉ.

Ϩⲱⲡϣ   *v* ϣⲱⲡϣ.

Ϩⲁⲣ- in ϩⲁⲣⲃⲉⲗ, *hard-eyed* (cf ⲧⲁⲥⲃⲁⲗ): Pro 27 20 (*S* ϫⲁⲣⲃⲁⲗ) στηρίζων ὀφθαλμόν (Correct ref. p 32 *a*). *Cf* prob ϣⲱⲣ.

Ϩⲓⲣ   *v* ϩⲓⲣ.

Ϩⲁⲣⲉ-   *v* ϣⲁⲣⲉ-.

Ϩⲁⲁⲣⲉ   *v* ϣⲁⲁⲣ *skin.*

Ϩⲁⲣⲓϩⲁⲣⲟ⸗   *v* ϩⲁ- (ϩⲁⲣⲓϩⲁⲣⲟ⸗).

Ϩⲣⲉ   *v* ϩⲣⲉ *food.*

Ϩⲣⲉ in ⲥⲁϩⲣⲉ   *v* ϩⲣⲉ *upper part.*

Ϩⲣⲏⲓ   *v* ϩⲣⲁⲓ.

Ϩⲣⲃⲉ   *v* ϩⲣⲃ.

Ϩⲣⲃⲟ   *v* ϩⲣⲟⲩⲟ.

Ϩⲱⲣⲃⲉ   *v* ϩⲱⲣⲃ.

Ϩⲱⲣⲡ   *v* ϣⲱⲣⲡ.

Ϩⲣⲏⲁⲣⲓⲧ vb intr, meaning unknown, or ? place-name: El 82 kings of Persia ⲛⲁⲡⲱⲧ...ⲁϩ. ⲙⲡⲣⲣⲁⲓ ⲡⲡⲁⲥⲥⲩⲣⲟⲥ & 4 kings shall fight with 3.

Ϩⲣⲁⲩ   *v* ϩⲣⲟⲟⲩ.

Ϩⲣⲟⲩⲟ   *v* ϩⲣⲟⲩⲟ.

ϩⲣϣⲓⲣⲉ   *v* ϣⲓⲣⲉ (ϩⲉⲣϣⲓⲣⲉ).

ϩⲁⲣϩⲣⲉ   *v* ϣⲟⲣϣⲣ.

ϩⲣϩⲣⲉ   *v* ϩⲣϩⲣ.

ϩⲓⲥⲉ   *v* ϩⲓⲥⲉ.

ϩⲱⲥϥ   *v* ⲥⲱϣ *be despised* (ⲥⲱϣϥ).

ϩⲓⲧ, ϩⲓⲉⲓⲧ nn m, *threshing-floor* (*SB* ϫⲛⲟⲟⲩ):
Hos 9 2, Joel 2 24, Hag 2 19 ϩⲓⲉⲓⲧ ἅλων. ϩ(ⲉ)ⲃⲉϩⲓⲧ
nn f, same: Job 5 26 (Cl, *SB* do), Mic 4 12 (*B* do),
Cl 29 3.

ϩⲁⲧⲉ vb tr, *pluck out* (?) feathers: Cl 25 4 (both
MSS). Cf *ḫtt* (Erman) & Rec 38 200. Or cf ϩⲱⲧⲉ
& ϫⲟⲁ in paral Syr texts (Mus 47 64).

ϩⲁⲉⲓⲧⲉ   *v* ϩⲟⲉⲓⲧⲉ *garment*.

ϩⲓⲧⲉ   *v* ϩⲓⲧⲉ.

ϩⲉⲧⲃⲉ, ϩⲱⲧⲃⲉ, ϩⲁⲧⲃⲉⲥ   *v* ϩⲱⲧⲃ.

ϩⲱⲧⲙⲉ   *v* ϣⲱⲧⲙ.

ϩⲧⲁⲣⲧⲣⲉ, ϩⲧⲣⲧⲓⲣ   *v* ϣⲧⲟⲣⲧⲣ.

ϩⲁⲧⲛⲟⲩ, ϩⲉ.   *v* ⲧⲏⲩ (ϩⲁⲧⲏⲩ).

ϩⲁⲧϩⲧ   *v* ϩⲟⲧϩⲧ.

ϩⲁⲩ   *v* ϣⲟⲟⲩ *incense*.

ϩⲏⲩⲉ   *v* ϣⲏⲩⲉ.

ϩⲱϣϥ, ϩⲁϣϥⲍ, ϩⲁϣϥ† vb intr, *be broken, destroyed* (*S* ⲟⲩⲱϣϥ, *B* ϫⲟⲙϫⲉⲙ): Pro 6 16, Joel 2 6
συντρίβεσθαι; Till Oster 16 ϩⲏⲧ ... ⲉϩ̄ⲣ.† (cf Ps 50
19); tr, *destroy*: Ps 3 7 (TU 43 9), Pro 24 22 ϩⲁϣϥ
(*l* -ϥϥ), Mic 4 6 σ.; as nn m: Pro 10 29, Hos 13
13 συντριβή, Pro 23 29 σύντριμμα.

ϩⲱϣϥ   *v* ⲥⲱϣ *be despised* (ⲥⲱϣϥ).

ϩⲱϥ   *v* ϣⲱϥ.

ϩⲉϥⲧ   *v* ϣⲱϥⲧ (ϣⲁϥⲧⲉ).

ϩⲁⲉⲓϩ   *v* ϣⲟⲉⲓϣ.

ϩⲱϩ   *v* ϣⲱϣ *scatter & make equal*.

ϩϩⲧⲱⲣϣ nn m, *rust, red blight*: Joel 1 4, 2 25
(*S* ⲡⲏⲣϣ, *B* ⲉⲧⲛⲓϣⲓ) ἐρυσίβη. Cf ⲧⲱⲣϣ.

ϩⲁϩⲧⲉ-   *v* ϩⲁϩⲧⲛ-.

ϩϫⲉ   *v* ⲉϣϫⲉ (but cf AZ 57 138, 63 144).

ϩϫⲁⲛ-   *v* ϫⲱ *head* (ϩⲁϫⲛ-).

ϩϫⲁⲛ DM   *v* ϣϫⲏⲛ.

(For most words in ϫ- *v* ϩ-.)

ϫ, 28th letter of alphabet, called ϫⲉⲓ (K 1), ϫⲁⲓ
خاي (Stern p 418). Only in *BO*, om in *S* alphabets
(Hall pll 28, 29, *Class Philol* 16 193); corresponding
regularly to *SA²F* ϩ, *A* ϩ̄. Derived from hierogl *ḫ*,
as ϫⲏⲃⲥ, ϫⲣⲟⲟⲩ, ⲁϫⲱⲙ, ⲱϫⲥ, or *ḥ*, as ϫⲙⲟⲙ, ϫⲱⲧⲉⲃ, ⲙⲁϫⲧ, ϥⲁϫⲣⲓ. Found in *O* (Hor) as ⳍ (made
always thus in 2 strokes) in ⳍⲛ-, ⳍⲣⲱⲧ, ⲱⲛⳍ &c, in
PMich 6131 as ϫ: ϫⲉⲗ. In DM glosses thrice: ⲁϫ,
ϫⲱ, ϫⲭⲉⲓ. Sporadically in non-literary *FBⁱ*, as
CMSS 25, 52, 57, BM 590 (2), 626 (cf *Amer J Philol*
56 105). Rarely replaced by ⲭ, as BM 1237, Ryl
460, except where Gk alphabet employed, as MR 5
41, CMSS 59. In late *S* improperly, as PChass 1
ⲡⲁϫⲣⲉ, ⲧⲱⲣϫ, ⲧⲱϫ (error ? for ϩ); in this & Bodl
(P) a 1 also as ϣ́: ⲡⲁϥⲣⲉ, ⲥⲁϭ, ϩ́ⲛⲧϥ (not so in duplicate (P) a 3), PMéd ⲗⲟϫⲙ, ϥ̄ⲱϥ̄. Transcribes Ar خ,
as ⲭⲁⲗϫ كلخ (P 43 33), ⲁϫⲁⲣ اخر, ⲓⲉϫⲟϫ يأخذ, ϣⲉⲓϫ
شيخ (EW 234 ff); rarely ح, as ϫⲗⲟⲩⲁ حلوا (PChass
2); transcribed by خ, as ϫⲉⲛ- خان, ϫⲏⲧ (BIF
5 106).

ϫⲁ-, ϩⲁ-, ϣⲁ-, ⲭⲉ- *B* (all 3 once), ϩⲁ- *S* (once)

particle of apposition before pronoun or art (Stern
483, Mallon 155), not expressed in *SAF* Gk: Ps 113
26 ⲁⲛⲟⲛ ϫⲁⲡⲏ ⲉⲧⲟⲛϩ, Bar 4 12 ⲙⲙⲟⲓ ϫⲁ†ⲭⲏⲣⲁ,
Dan 1 12 ϭⲟⲡⲧⲉⲛ ⲣⲱ ϫⲁⲡⲉⲕⲁⲗⲱⲟⲩⲓ, Ro 12 5 ⲁⲛⲟⲛ
ϩⲱⲛ ϫⲁⲡⲓⲙⲏⲛϣ, MG 25 233 ⲁⲛⲟⲕ ϫⲁⲡⲓϫⲉⲗⲗⲟ, Hyvernat *Alb* 21 ⲁⲛⲟⲕ ⲭⲉⲡⲓⲁⲗⲁⲭⲓⲥⲧⲟⲥ, *ib* ⲁⲛⲟⲕ ϣⲁ-
ⲡⲓϫⲱⲃ, AZ 23 146 *S* ⲁⲛⲟⲛ ϩⲁ[ⲙⲙⲟⲛⲁⲭⲟⲥ] ⲙⲡⲙⲟⲛⲁⲥⲧⲏⲣⲓⲟⲛ; 2d pers: Su 48 ⲛⲑⲱⲧⲉⲛ ϫⲁⲡⲉⲡϣⲏⲣⲓ
ⲙⲡⲓⲥⲗ, Lu 6 25 ⲟⲩⲟⲓ ⲛⲱⲧⲉⲛ ϫⲁⲛⲏ ⲉⲧⲥⲱⲃⲓ, Ro 2 1
ⲱ ⲫⲣⲱⲙⲓ ϫⲁⲟⲩⲟⲛ ⲛⲓⲃⲉⲛ ⲉⲧ†, ϩⲁⲡ, Ja 4 12 ⲛⲑⲟⲕ
ϫⲁⲫⲏ ⲉⲧ† ϩⲁⲡ, MG 25 244 ⲛⲉⲕⲡⲟⲗⲓⲧⲉⲓⲁ ϫⲁⲡⲓⲣⲱ-
ⲙⲓ, Strzygowski *Kopt Kunst* p 118 ⲧⲓⲧⲓϩⲟ (ⲉ)ⲣⲱⲧⲉⲛ
ϩⲁⲟⲩϩⲟⲛ ⲛⲓⲃⲉⲛ; 3d pers: Jer 50 6 ⲛⲏ ⲉⲧⲁⲩⲕⲟⲧ-
ⲟⲩ...ϫⲁⲡⲓⲣⲱⲙⲓ, Dan 9 8 ⲛⲉⲡⲓⲟ† ϫⲁⲛⲏ ⲉⲧⲁⲩⲉⲣ
ⲛⲟⲃⲓ, Cat 106 ⲕⲁⲧⲁⲇⲓⲕⲁϫⲓⲛ ⲙⲙⲟϥ...ϫⲁⲫⲏ ⲉⲧⲉⲙ-
ⲡⲉϥⲉⲣ ⲛⲟⲃⲓ.

ϫⲁ (or ϫⲁⲓ?) nn m, *heel*, *mark of heel* (?): Synax
2 136 (1 MS only) Jesus when in Egypt set His heel
كعب on rock & place was named ⲡⲓϫⲁ ⲓ̄ⲏ̄ⲥ̄ ايجا ايسوس
اي كعب يسوع. Neither Theophilus (ALR '22) nor
Cyriacus (ROC 15 157) mention it; Timothy Alex

(P 131⁵ 103) tells of His ⲧⲁϭⲥⲉ on rock. *Cf* ? ϩⲁ, *pole, mast* & ϣⲧⲉ.

ϭⲁⲓ nn, *nitre*: Jer 2 22 (*S* Z 511 ϧⲟⲥⲙ), MG 25 215 as camel-driver ⲉⲕⲕⲉⲗⲡ ϭ. νίτρον.

ϭⲁⲓ nn m, *breath of nose* (so Ar): TRit 522 = BM 846 125 of corpse ⲁϥϥⲉⲣⲓ ⲛϫⲉ ⲡⲓϭ. ⲁϥⲕⲱⲣϥ ⲛϫⲉ ⲡⲓⲗⲁⲥ الانف, but *K. al-Tagnîz* (1905) 166 ⲛⲓϥⲓ ⲙⲡⲓϣⲁⲓ, so prob *l* ϣⲁⲓ.

ϭⲁⲓ nn m, *ship's pole, boat-hook*: P 55 13 ⲡⲓϭ. مدراة (Dozy 1 439, Almk 2 103 مدرى). *Cf* ⲧⲁⲣ, with which ? confused, & ? ϩⲁ *pole*.

ϭⲁⲓ *v* ϩⲁ *fan* & ϣⲧⲉ *mast*.

ϭⲉ nn m, *woof*: Lev 13 49 (*S* ⲃ̅ⲏⲕⲉ) κρόκη.

ϭⲏⲓ nn m, *sun*: Jer 15 9 ⲁⲡϭⲏⲓ ⲱⲕ ⲉϩⲱⲥ (*S* ⲣⲏ) ἥλιος, or ? *l* ⲁⲡⲣⲏ ⲥⲱⲕ ⲉ.; *cf* BMOr 8775 123 ⲡⲓϭ. حَرّ.

ϭⲏⲓⲃⲓ *v* ϩⲁⲉⲓⲃⲉⲥ.

ϭⲑⲁⲓ, ϭⲑⲏ *v* ϩⲧⲁⲓ.

ϭⲟⲕ *v* ϩⲱⲕ.

ϭⲱⲕ *v* ϩⲱⲱⲕ, ϩⲱⲱⲕⲉ.

ϭⲱⲕϩ *v* ϩⲱⲱⲕⲉ, *scrape* **B**.

ϭⲉⲗ O nn m, *context lost*: PMich 6131]ⲙⲛϭⲉⲗ.

ϭⲉⲗ DM *v* ϣⲁⲗ.

ϭⲱⲗ *v* ϩⲱⲗ, *be hoarse*.

ϭⲉⲗⲃⲓ *v* ϩⲗⲡⲉ.

ϭⲉⲗⲓⲃϣ *v* ϩⲁⲗⲃϣⲉ.

ϭⲉⲗⲗⲟⲧ, ϭⲉⲗⲟⲧ nn f, *ravine, wady* including water & rocks: Nu 13 23 (var ϭⲉⲗ.), Ps 59 2, Is 30 33 (*SF*), Lu 3 5 (var do) φάραγξ; Ge 14 8, Ps 83 7 (var do), Mic 1 4 (*SA*) κοιλάς (all *SAF* ⲉⲓⲁ); Ez 7 16, 33 28 (*S* ⲧⲟⲟⲩ) ὄρος; *ib* 47 9 (*S* ⲭⲓⲙⲁⲣⲣⲟⲥ) ποτα-μός; K 214 ϭ., ⲙⲟⲩ ⲡⲥⲱⲣⲉⲙ, ⲁⲡⲁⲡⲁⲓ, ⲭⲓⲙ., ϩⲉⲗⲟⲥ all وادي; Ez 39 15 *vallis*; MG 25 89 ϯⲡⲉⲧⲣⲁ ⲉⲧⲥⲁⲡⲣⲏⲥ ⲙⲡⲓϩⲉⲗⲟⲥ ⲥⲁⲡⲉⲙⲉⲛⲧ ⲙⲡⲓϣⲏⲓ ⲥⲁⲡϣⲱⲓ ⲛϯϭ. (var ⲡⲉⲧⲣⲁ); as adj: Ez 47 5 ⲙⲙⲟⲟⲩ ⲛϭ. (*S* = Gk) χείμαρρος. Place in Nitria *v* EW *Hist* 33, Amélineau *Géog* 447.

ϭⲉⲗⲙⲉϩⲓ *v* ϩⲁⲗⲙⲏϩⲉ.

ϭⲉⲗⲡⲓ *v* ϩⲗⲡⲉ.

ϭⲉⲗϣⲓⲣⲓ *v* ϣⲓⲣⲉ.

ϭⲉⲗϭⲉⲗⲧ *v* ϩⲉⲗϩⲓⲗⲉ.

ϭⲗⲓϫ *v* ϩⲣⲟϫⲣϫ.

ϭⲁⲙ- (ϭⲁⲙⲛⲓϥⲓ) *v* ⲛⲓϥⲉ *s f*.

ϭⲉⲙⲓ, ϭⲙⲟⲙ *v* ϧⲙⲟⲙ.

ϭⲁⲙⲛⲉ *v* ϣⲙⲟⲩⲛ (ϧⲙⲉⲛⲉ).

ϭⲁⲙⲛⲓϥⲓ *v* ⲛⲓϥⲉ.

ϭⲉⲙⲥ nn m, *as title*: C 43 248 colophon ⲅⲉⲱⲣⲅⲓ ⲛⲧⲉ ⲓⲱⲁⲛⲛⲏⲥ ⲡⲓϭ.

ϭⲟⲙϭⲉⲙ B, ϧⲁⲙϧⲉⲙ F, ϭⲉⲙϭⲱⲙⲓ, ϭⲉⲙ-ϭⲱⲙ† B vb I intr, *be crushed, broken, destroyed*: Ps 36 15 (*S* ⲟⲩⲱϣϥ), Pro 6 16 (*S* do, *A* ϩⲱϣϥ), Ep Jer 15 (*F* ⲧⲉⲛⲛⲁ), Joel 2 6 (*A* do), Mk 5 4 (*S* ϩⲱⲣⲃ̅), AM 281 ϣⲁⲩϭ. ⲛϫⲉ ⲛⲁⲕⲁⲥ συντρίβεσθαι; 2 Chr 6 24, Ez 21 7 (*S* ⲟⲩ.) θραύειν; Hab 3 6 (*SA* do) δια-θρύπτειν; Ez 40 1 (*S* ϣⲱⲱϥⲉ) ἁλίσκεσθαι; C 86 13 body ϭ. ϩⲓⲧⲉⲛϩⲁⲛϭⲓⲥⲓ, MG 25 115 devil ϭ. ⲛⲁϩⲣⲉⲛ-ⲡⲁⲓⲁⲧⲓⲟⲥ, Cat 183 ⲥⲉⲛⲁϭ. ϭⲉⲛϥⲁⲓ (*sc* this opi-nion); qual: Lev 22 22, Mt 12 20, MG 25 253 ⲉⲣⲉⲡⲉϥⲥⲱⲙⲁ ϭ. συντ.; Is 58 6 (all *S* ⲟⲩ.†) θρ.; *ib* 42 3 (*S* ⲡⲟⲧⲥ) θλᾶν; FR 106 ⲅ̅ϭ. ⲛϫⲉ ⲡⲟⲩϩⲏⲧ.

II tr, *crush, break, destroy*: Ex 15 7 *BF* (CMSS 13), *ib* 34 1 (*S* ⲟⲩⲱϣⲛ), Lev 26 13 (*S* ⲥⲱⲗⲡ), Ps 104 33 (*S* ⲟⲩⲱϣϥ), Lam 3 4 (*S* do, *F* ⲧⲉⲡ.), Am 1 5 (*A* ϩ.), Mk 14 3 (*S* diff, *F* do), Va 58 182 ϭ. ⲙⲡⲉⲕⲥⲱⲙⲁ by over-eating συντ., Hos 8 5 (*A* ⲧⲉⲕⲟ) ἀποτρ., Ez 43 8 (var ⲙⲟⲩⲛⲕ) ἐκτρ.; Ps 109 5 (*S* ⲗⲱϧⲣ) σύνθλ.; Mic 1 7 (*S* ⲉⲓⲣⲉ ⲛϣⲏⲙ ϣⲏⲙ, *A* sim) κατακόπτειν; Ez 38 20 ῥηγνύναι; Ps 74 11 (*S* ⲕⲱⲗϫ) συγκλᾶν; Va 57 197 ϭ. ⲙⲡⲁϩⲏⲧ (*cf* Ac 21 13 † ⲙⲕⲁϩ ⲛ-) συνθρύπ.; Jer 31 12 λεπτύνειν; DeV 2 172 horses ϭⲉⲙϭⲱⲙⲩ like corn, C 43 40 ⲁϥϭ. ⲙⲡⲁⲣⲭⲱⲛ = LMär 2 *S* ⲡⲁⲧⲁⲥⲥⲉ, Miss 4 207 ⲕϭ. ⲡⲧⲁⲯⲩⲭⲏ.

With following preposition or adverb. ⲉ ⲉϫⲛ-: Is 36 6 (*SF* ⲡⲱⲧⲥ) θλ. ἐπί; Va 61 120 ⲁⲡⲓⲉⲣⲫⲉⲓ ϭ. ⲉϫⲱⲟⲩ = Mor 25 25 *S* ϩⲉ ⲉϫⲛ-; ⲥ ⲛⲧⲉⲛ-: DeV 2 53 ⲭⲁ ⲡⲉⲛϩⲏⲧ ⲉϭ. ⲛⲧⲟⲧⲉⲛ; ⲥ ϩⲓϫⲉⲛ-: Is 21 9 (*S* ⲟⲩⲱϣϥ ⲉϩⲣⲁⲓ ⲉϫⲛ-) συντ. εἰς; ⲥ ⲉⲃⲟⲗ: Dif 2 78 ⲁϥϭ. ⲉⲃ. ⲙⲡⲉϥϥⲁϣ (*cf* Ps 123 7); ⲉⲃ. ϩⲁ-: Nah 1 13 (*A* ϩ.) συντ. ἀπό; ⲉⲃ. ϭⲉⲛ-: Jer 35 11 συντ. ἀπό; ⲥ ⲉϧⲟⲩⲛ ϭⲉⲛ-: Ps 57 7 (*S* ⲟⲩ. ϩⲛ-) συντ. ἐν; ⲥ ⲉϧⲣⲏⲓ: Job 38 11 (*S* do) συντ. ἐν; Dif 2 79 enemy's schemes ⲁⲡⲁⲓⲁⲣⲭⲏⲉⲣⲉⲅⲥ ϭⲉⲙϭⲱⲙⲟⲩ ⲉϭ.; ⲥ ⲙⲙⲁⲩ: Ps 75 4 (*S* ⲟⲩ. ⲙ.) συντ. ἐκεῖ.

—— nn m, *crushing, fracture, destruction*; Lev 21 19 (*S* ⲟⲩ.), Is 30 26 (*SF* do), Lam 4 10 (*S* do, *F* ⲧ.) σύντριμμα, Zeph 1 10 (*A* ϩ.) -μός, Pro 6 15 (*S* do, *A* do), Lam 2 13 (*S* do, *F* do) συντριβή, Ex 12 13 (*S* ϥⲱⲧⲉ ⲉⲃⲟⲗ) ἐκτρίβειν; Nu 17 13 (*S* do) θραῦσις, Nah 2 11 (*A* ⲡⲱϣ) θραυσμός; TRit 151 heal ⲛϭ. ⲛⲧⲉ ⲡⲉⲛⲯⲩⲭⲏ انسحاق; ROC 23 285 ⲁϩⲁⲛϭ. ϣⲱⲡⲓ ϩⲁ-ⲣⲁⲧⲟⲩ ⲛⲛⲓⲥⲧⲩⲗⲟⲥ *crack, split*, Va 58 192 wine drunk will leave behind ⲟⲩⲛⲓϣϯ ⲛϭ. ⲡⲉⲙⲟⲩⲭⲟⲗⲏ.

V also ϧⲟⲙϧⲉⲙ B, sometimes written with ϧ.

ϭⲉⲛⲓ vb intr, *quarrel* (*cf* ḫnnw Dévaud): K 234 خاصم، تقابل = P 54 171 + تقايل; as nn: ROC 25 243 ⲁⲡⲓⲥⲛⲏⲟⲩ ⲉⲣ ϭ. ⲡⲉⲙⲡⲓⲣⲱⲙⲓ (var 272 ⲉⲙⲗⲁϭ ⲡⲉⲙ-) μάχεσθαι.

ϩⲁⲓⲟⲣ v ⲉⲓⲟⲟⲣ.

ϩⲱⲣ, ϩⲉⲣ-, ϩⲟⲣⲥ vb tr, *destroy*: C 86 21 idolatry ϩⲟⲣϥ ⲛ̄ϫⲱⲗⲉⲙ; ⲥ ⲉⲃⲟⲗ: Deu 20 19 ϩⲉⲣ ⲛⲉⲥ- ϣϣⲏⲛ ⲉⲃ. (*S* ⲧⲁⲕⲟ) ἐξολοθρεύειν; intr: *ib* 28 63 ϩ. ⲉⲃ. ϩⲓⲭⲉⲛ- (var ϫⲱⲣ, *S* ϭⲱⲧⲉ ⲉⲃ. ϩ.) ἐξαίρειν ἀπό من . Here ? belong AZ 23 111 *S* ϩⲉⲣ ⲛⲡⲟⲩⲃ ⲉⲃ., Lam 3 45 *F* ϩⲁⲣⲉⲛ ϩⲁⲃ. ἀπωθεῖν. *Cf also* ⲭⲱⲣ.

ϩⲁⲓⲣⲓ nn m, *serpent*: BM 920 264, Ryl 453 335 ⲛⲓϩ. تعبان . Prob = ⲁϩⲱⲣⲓ.

ϩⲣⲁ- O v ϩⲟ.

ϩⲣⲏⲓ v ϩⲣⲁⲓ *down*.

ϩⲉⲣⲉⲃ v ϩⲣⲃ.

ϩⲁⲣⲁⲃⲁⲓ v ϩⲣⲟⲩⲃⲃⲁⲓ.

(ϩⲁⲣⲉⲛ-), ϩⲁⲣⲱⲥ v ⲣⲟ (ϩⲁⲣⲡ-).

ϩⲟⲣⲡⲉ nn f, *handful*: Lev 2 2 (*S* ⲧⲟⲟⲧⲥ), 3 Kg 17 12, Is 40 12 (*S* ϫⲁⲙⲏ) δράξ; Mus 34 202 held all creation ϩⲉⲛⲧⲉϥϭ.,EW160 ⲙⲟϩ ⲛ̄ⲧⲉϥϩ.(with dates) ⲫⲏ ⲉⲧⲉⲧⲟⲧϥ ⲡⲁⲟⲗϥ.

ϩⲁⲣⲁⲧⲥ v ⲣⲁⲧ (ϩⲁⲣⲁⲧⲥ).

ϩⲟⲣⲧ (ϩⲱ. AZ 14 47 not found) nn m, *madman*: P 54 162 ⲛⲓϩ. مجنون . Prob = ϣⲱⲣⲧ.

ϩⲣⲟⲧ *B*,ϩⲗⲁⲧ *F*,ϩⲣⲱⲧ *O*,ⲣⲁⲧ DM nn m as pl (sg *B* once DM),*child, young*: Ge 35 5 (*S* ϣⲏⲣⲉ),Jo 4 12 *F*(*SA²B* do) υἱός; Lev 25 41 (*S* do), Is 54 13 (*S* do) τέκνον, 1 Jo 3 18 *F*(Cai Copt Mus tablet, *SB* do) τεκνίον; Ge 32 15 of camel (*S* do), Lam 4 10 *F*(*S* do, *B*

ⲁⲗⲟⲩ) παιδίον; Bodl 325 153 ⲛⲓϩ. جنس الاولاد (collective),Va 57 2 ⲛⲁϩ.,*ib* 68 ⲛⲓϩⲣⲟⲧ (*sic*),PMich 777 *F* ⲛⲁϩ.,Baouit 2 37 *F* ⲛⲉⲃϩ.,Hor 79 *O* ⲛϥϩ.,DM 19 19 ⲛⲣⲁⲧ gloss on *p·ḥrt*. *Cf* Ἁρποχράτης.

ϩⲣⲱϯ nn, *jugular veins* (dual AZ 47 43): K 76 (all MSS) ⲛⲓϩ. وريدان .

ϩⲣⲱⲟⲩ v ϩⲣⲟⲟ.

ϩⲉⲣⲟⲩⲱ v ϩⲣⲟⲩⲟ.

ϩⲓⲣϩⲓⲣ v ϩⲓⲣ s f.

ϩⲣⲓϫ, ϩⲣⲁⲭⲣⲉϫ v ϩⲣⲟⲭⲣⲉϫ.

ϩⲁⲣⲁϭⲱⲟⲩⲧⲥ v ⲥⲁⲣⲁϭⲱⲟⲩϣ.

ϩⲱⲥ nn, *meaning uncertain*: Deu 23 18 (*S* ⲥϩⲓ- ⲙⲉ...ⲉⲥϯ ⲧⲉⲗⲟⲥⲛ ⲉⲥϫⲓ) τελισκόμενος (var ἐνδιηλλαγμένος) مدان .

ϩⲟⲧ v ϩⲧⲁⲓ.

(ϩⲱⲧ), ϩⲏⲧ† ⲉⲃⲟⲗ vb intr, *meaning uncertain*: Jer 18 15 ϩⲁⲡⲙⲱⲓⲧ ⲉⲛⲥⲉϩ. ⲉⲃ. ⲁⲛ (*S* ⲉⲙⲡⲧⲟⲩ ⲙⲁ ⲙ̄ⲙⲟⲟϣⲉ ⲙ̄ⲙⲁⲩ) غير متقومة οὐκ ἔχοντες ὁδὸν εἰς πορείαν (var ἀνόδευτος).

ϩⲱⲧ nn m, *cloth, change of raiment*: BMOr 8775 98 ⲓⲙⲁⲧⲓⲟⲛ · ⲛⲓϩ.,قماش (which P 55 14 = ϩⲃⲱⲥ, ⲉⲡⲁϩⲙⲁ).

ϩⲁⲧⲟⲩⲗ DM v ϣⲁⲑⲟⲩⲗ.

ϩⲁϭ nn m, *neck*: Job 39 19 (no *S*) τράχηλος; K 75 ⲛⲓϩ. قفا , رقبة ; BMOr 8775 119 معرفة .

ϩⲱϭ vb intr, *tighten, strengthen*: K 479 ⲉⲩϩ. شدّ; as nn: *ib* 265 ⲛⲓϩ. (var ϩⲟϭ) شدّ (var سلّ).

ϩⲱϭ, ϩⲁϭⲟⲩ v ϩⲱϩ.

ϩ

ϩ, 29th letter of alphabet, called ϩⲟⲣⲓ (K 1, Stern p 418), هورى (Stern *lc*) *B*, ه،و (P 44 137) *S*. In early *S* MSS written S (*v* JEA 13 19 n). Derived from hierogl *h*, as ϩⲁⲓ, ϩⲁⲡ, ϩⲣⲱⲃ, ⲡⲟⲩϩⲣⲉ, ⲟⲩϩⲟⲣ; or *ḥ* (oftenest), as ϩⲟ, ϩⲣⲱⲧⲡ, ⲁⲙⲣⲏϩⲉ, ⲡⲟⲩϩⲃ, ⲙ̄ⲥⲁϩ, ϭⲱⲣϩ; or *ḫ*, as ϩⲏ *belly*, ϩⲙⲟⲙ, ⲥⲱϩⲛ, ϩⲗⲡⲉ, ⲙⲟⲩϩ *burn*; or *ẖ*, as ϩⲏⲃⲥ, ϩⲣⲟⲟⲩ, ⲁϩⲟⲙ, ⲱϩⲥ, ⲙⲟⲩⲗϩ. Corresponds to *A* ϩ, as ϩⲁⲉ, ϩⲱⲱⲕ, ⲁϩⲱⲙ (Pro 23 5), ⲡⲱϩⲧ, ⲙⲟⲩϩϩ; to *B* ϧ, as ϩⲁ-, ϩⲓⲣ, ϯϩⲉ, ⲗⲱϩⲙ, ⲧⲱϩ. Varies with ϣ *Sᵃ v* Ep 1 244. Initial om often *B*, as ⲁⲓⲟ, ⲁⲛⲣⲟ, ⲁⲣⲟϣ, ⲁⲩϫⲁⲗ, ⲉⲣⲙⲁⲡ, ⲃⲟⲣ- ⲃⲉⲣ, ⲗⲱⲓⲗⲓ, ⲗⲁⲡⲗⲉⲡ, ⲟⲩⲣⲓⲧ, ⲟⲩϭⲉ; *S* (rare), as ⲉⲣⲏⲥ (ϩⲁⲣⲉϩ Nu 3 25), ⲟⲙⲡⲧ (Ap 1 15); *F*, as ⲁⲑⲏ (Eccl 7 19), ⲁⲗⲁⲥ (*ib* 1 13), ⲃⲟⲩⲣ (JKP 2 50), ⲓⲧⲉ-(ϩⲓ- ⲧⲉⲛ- BMOr 6948), ⲱⲃⲓ (MR 5 24); *A* (though often added afterwards), as ⲁⲗⲏⲧ (Pro 6 5), ⲁⲓⲣⲉ (Zeph 1 17), ⲉⲛ (PGol 47), ⲛ̄ⲃⲉ (Hos 9 4), ⲙⲉⲥⲧ (*ib* 3 3), ⲱϣϥ (Pro 10 15); om in other positions: *S* ⲡⲁⲁⲕⲉ, ⲡⲁⲁⲭⲉ, ϣⲉⲗϥ, ⲡⲁⲛⲧ, ⲟⲩⲁϩⲓⲛⲧ, ⲗⲁⲗⲏⲩ (ST 415, *cf* 414), ⲡⲟⲟⲩ; *A* ⲡⲉⲧⲁⲩ (2 Mac 6 9), ⲛⲉⲕⲉ (Hos 9 11), ⲟⲩⲱ (Pro 10 22), ϣⲁ (Joel 2 3), ⲧⲉⲁⲕ (Pro 3 13); *F* ⲥⲓⲉ (BM 584), ⲥⲁⲓ (CMSS 58), ⲥⲓⲙⲓ (BP 5717), ⲧⲉⲙⲕⲁ (Ac 7 24), ⲙⲉⲕ (ⲙⲉϩⲕ Kr 10), ⲉⲗⲛⲓ (AZ 23 42), *cf* ⲉⲣⲓⲛ (*sic* Stegemann 44), ϫⲉ (ϫⲉϩ Mor 30 41), ⲡⲁⲣⲁⲩ (ⲡⲁϩⲣⲁⲩ BM 686); in *O* om: ⲉⲗⲏⲓ *O* (ⲉϩⲗⲏⲓ), ⲏⲧ (ϩⲏⲧ), ⲱ (ϩⲉⲛ-) in Beatty-Merton Isaiah glosses, ⲥⲁⲣⲛⲓ (PGM 1 114); or as *spiritus asper* ⲉⲟⲩⲡ, ⲣⲏⲓ, ⲙ̄ⲓⲧ (AZ 21 107). Added as

initial: S(rare), as ϧⲓⲉ (BM 1102), ϧⲉⲱ (Ora 4 22), ϧⲁⲃⲁϭⲛⲉⲓⲛ (Ap 4 6), ϧⲙⲧⲟⲡ (BM 1123), ϧⲁⲣⲏⲧ (Ep l 245); A, as ϧⲉⲡ (Pro 8 21), ϧⲱⲥϧ (Hos 6 5), ϧⲃⲣⲏϭⲉ (Nah 2 5), ϧⲱϧⲉ (El 48); B, as ϧⲓⲁ (EW 14), ϧⲓⲛⲃ (Ex 25 4), ϧⲟⲃⲓ (Va 57 215), ϧⲟⲙⲥⲕ (Is 43 2), ϧⲱⲙⲙⲓ (MG 25 161), ϧⲱⲗⲕ (C 43 136), ϧⲱⲡ (Is 33 18), ϧⲟⲧⲡⲟⲩ (Miss 4 112), ϧⲁϫ (IgR 27), ϧⲉⲧϥⲱ (Va 58 135), ϧⲱⲟⲩ (ib 57 196); F, as ϧⲉⲥ (Lam 3 4); as final: S ⲙⲟⲩ-ⲗⲁϧ (μοῦλα Mor 51 35); A ϧⲉⲫ (BM 1223); B ⲓⲁϧ (BSM 22); F ϫⲓⲭϧ, ⲭⲁⲗⲁⲅⲭϧ (Lam 1 10, 13), ⲕⲏϧ, ⲧⲓϧ (BKU l 23). Inserted before ⲥ Sᶠ: ⲑⲁⲗⲁϧⲥⲁ, ϧⲏⲡⲱⲧⲁϧⲥⲓ (ὑποτάσσειν), ⲉⲕⲙⲁⲗⲱⲧⲓϧⲥⲓ (αἰχμ.Pcod Mor). Abnormal metathesis S: ⲡϧⲱ (ⲡⲱϧ), ϫϧⲁⲙ (ϫⲁϧⲙ), ⲕϧⲱⲧ (ⲛⲱϧⲧ), ⲙϧⲟⲩ (ⲙⲟⲩϧ Worrell Copt Sounds 146-7). On ϧ added to verbal roots, as ϣⲱⲡϧ, ϣⲱϧⲃ, ϣⲱⲕϧ, v Sethe Verbum 1 359. As syllable-divider: A ⲟⲩϧⲉⲉⲧⲍ (p 470 a), ⲡⲁϧⲱⲣϫ (Pro 8 28), ϧⲓϧⲱⲱϧ (Zech 3 3); S ⲟⲩϧⲱⲓⲏϧ, ⲃⲟⲏⲅⲉⲟⲓⲥ (βοηθός BM 1123), ⲧⲁϧⲉⲓ- (ⲧⲁⲓ- Kr 116), ⲉⲧⲛⲁ-ϧⲉⲡ (PJkôw), ⲡⲁϧⲟⲩⲱϧ (Ps 101 28 Aeg), ⲟⲩϫϧⲁⲓ (BP 9105) & in names: S ⲁⲃϧⲁϧⲁⲙ (cf DM 8 8 'br'hme), ⲁϧⲁⲣⲱⲛ (Bor 106), ⲃⲁⲗϧⲁⲙ, ⲃⲁϧⲁⲗ (not in compounds: ⲓⲉⲣⲟⲃⲁⲁⲗ, ⲃⲉⲉⲗⲫⲉϧⲱⲣ), ϧⲉϧⲉⲡⲡⲁ, ⲓⲱⲁϧⲁⲛ-ⲛⲏⲥ, ⲙⲁϧⲓϧⲁⲙ, ⲡⲱϧⲉ, ⲉⲩϧⲟϧⲓⲟⲥ (Mor 43 57), ⲉⲩ-ϧⲁⲓⲟⲥ (Ge 10 17), ⲫⲁϧⲁϧⲱ (Cl 51 5), ⲡⲓϧⲓⲁⲧⲣⲟⲥ (Ep 223); O ⲓⲁϧⲟ (AZ 21 99); cf ⲙⲩϧϧⲁ Μύρρα (AP 19); Gk spiritus asper mostly by ϧ- SAA²; wrongly in certain common words, as ϧⲉⲑⲛⲟⲥ, ϧⲉⲗⲡⲓⲥ, ϧⲉⲧ-ⲁϫⲉ, ϧⲓϩⲓⲱⲧⲏⲥ, ϧⲓⲕⲱⲛ, ϧⲓⲥⲟⲥ; B often om as ⲁⲧⲓⲟⲥ, ⲉⲃⲇⲟⲙⲁⲥ, ⲉⲣⲙⲏⲛⲉⲩⲓⲛ, ⲛⲥⲩⲭⲓⲁ, ⲟⲙⲟⲗⲟⲅⲓⲛ; some-times wrongly prefixed, as ϧⲁⲣⲁ, ϧⲓⲣⲏⲛⲏ, ϧⲱϩⲛ. In compounds, as S ⲁⲡϧⲏⲕⲉⲓ (J pass), ⲁϧⲟⲣⲁⲧⲟⲥ, ⲁⲡϧⲟ-ⲥⲓⲟⲥ, ⲁⲣⲭⲏϧⲓⲁⲧⲣⲟⲥ (BMar 60), ⲕⲁⲧⲁϧⲣⲁⲕⲧⲏⲥ, ⲡⲁⲣ-ϧⲓⲥⲧⲁ, ⲡⲣⲟϧⲁⲓⲣⲉⲥⲓⲥ; also where no sp asp, as ⲁⲡϧⲁ-ⲗⲓⲥⲕⲉ, ⲡⲣⲟϧⲟⲓⲙⲓⲟⲛ, ⲡⲣⲟⲥϧⲟϫⲟⲥ. Lost in Gk transcripts, as Παϧα (ⲡⲁϧⲁ BM 1130), Βησναυ ητ (ϧⲏⲧ PLond 4 203), Πκαμ ητ (sim PCai l 171), Πια μελ (ⲡⲓⲁϧⲙⲏⲗⲉϧ PLond 4 162), Πια σε (sim PLond 5 108), Πκασο (ⲡⲕⲁⲥϧⲟ PRoss-Georg 3 72), λαϧ (ⲗⲁ-ϧⲏ WS 24). Transcribes Ar ع, as ϧⲁϫⲓⲙ عظيم, ϧⲁⲗⲁ على, ⲓⲁϧⲣⲉϥ يعرف, ⲙⲁⲩϧⲁϧ موضع (EW 234 ff), ϧⲟⲩⲑⲙⲉⲛ عثمان (C 86 161), ⲡⲟⲩϧⲉⲉⲙ نعيم (AZ 55 71); or ح, as ϧⲁⲣⲓⲣⲉ حريرة (Ryl 243), ⲙⲁϧⲗⲟⲩⲗ محلول (AZ 23 109), ⲓⲉⲩϧⲣⲁϧ يفرح (EW); or ه, as ϧⲟⲩ هو, ⲑⲉϧⲗⲉⲕ تهلك, ⲗⲉϧⲱⲡⲉ لاهون; transcribed by ه, as ϧⲣⲟⲧⲉ أمودا, ⲟⲩⲟϧ أورو, ϧⲓϫⲉⲛ هيجان (BIF 5 92 ff), ϧⲙⲁ هما (PO 11 703), ϧⲏⲛⲥ اهناس; by ح hardly ever: ⲡⲣⲉϧⲧ ابرحت (CR 1913 299), ⲧⲟⲩϧⲟ طحا, ⲙⲥⲁϧ امساح (p 187 b).

ϧⲁ- SA²FO, ϧⲁ- A, ϩⲁ- BO, ⲭⲁ- O, ϧⲁⲣⲟⲍ S, ϧⲁⲣⲁⲍ A, ϧⲁⲣⲁⲍ A², ϩⲁⲣⲟⲍ B, ϧⲁⲗⲁⲍ F prep, a under, in, at: Ge 9 2 SB, ib 18 4 S(B ϩⲁⲧⲉⲛ-), Lev 27 32 S

(B ⲥⲁⲡⲉⲥⲏⲧ ⲛ-), Job 41 21 S(B ϩⲁⲧ.), Ps 17 38 S(B ϩⲁⲣⲁⲧⲍ), Mt 5 15 SB ὑπό, Bor 227 159 S ϥⲛⲁϣⲱ ⲉϥϧⲁϧⲟⲧⲉ Esaias Scet 146 ὑπὸ φόβον, Ge 21 15 S(B ϩⲁⲣ.), Is 14 11 SB, Lu 8 16 S(B ⲥⲁⲉϧⲣⲏⲓ ⲛ-) ὑπο-κάτω, Hag 2 17 SA ⲉⲓⲟⲙ ϧⲁϩⲣⲡ ὑπο(λήνιον), Ro 7 2 B ϩⲁⲣⲁⲓ ὑπ(ανδρος), Ge 14 20 SB ϧⲁⲡⲉⲕϭⲓϫ ὑπο-(χείριος), MG 25 213 B ⲭⲁϥ ϩⲁⲧⲉϥⲁϩⲫⲉ ὑπο(τιθέ-ναι); ϧⲁⲣⲟⲍ ⲛ-: Deu 4 17 S(B ⲥⲁⲡ. ⲛ-), Eccl 1 3 SF ὑπό, Jud 1 7 S, 4 Kg 16 4 S ὑποκ., Gloss 23 S ὑπώπια· ϧⲁⲣⲁϥ (sic) ⲛⲛⲃⲁⲗ; PS 359 S ϧⲁⲣⲟⲥ ⲛⲧⲉ-ⲥⲫⲁⲓⲣⲁ, PGol 47 A ϧⲁⲣⲁϥ ⲙⲡⲉⲑⲣⲟⲛⲟⲥ, BSM 126 B sim; Ac 25 7 B stood about him (var & S ⲉ-) περι-(ιστάναι); Aeg 269 S taken up ϧⲁⲡⲉϩⲣⲟ ἐπί (cf Ac 1 9 ἀπό), Pro 25 10 SA ϣⲱⲡⲉ ϧⲁⲛⲟϭⲛⲉϭ ἐπ(ονεί-διστος); Ex 23 19 S(B ϩⲉⲡ-), Deu 5 1 B(S ⲉ-), 2 Kg 13 28 S, 1 Kg 17 39 B(S diff), Ps 56 1 SB, ib 91 11 S (B ϩⲉⲡ-), Cant 8 10 S(F ⲙⲡⲓⲙⲧⲁ ⲛ-), Dan 6 17 B, Zech 1 17 A(S ⲛ-, B ϩⲉⲡ-), Ac 1 7 S(var ϧⲛ-)B, 1 Thes 2 7 B(SF diff) ἐν, Eccl 1 7 SF ⲙⲟⲩϧ ϩⲁ- ἐμ-(πιμπλάναι); Ge 28 11 SB, Mt 3 10 B(S ϧⲁⲧⲛ-), Jo 11 32 SA²(B ϩⲁⲧ.), Ap 1 17 S(B ϩⲁⲣ.) πρός, Jth 14 7 S ⲡⲟϫϥ ϧⲁⲟⲩⲅⲉⲣⲏⲧⲉ προσ(πίπτειν); Hos 14 7 SA ⲃⲱ ϧⲁⲡⲉⲥⲟⲩⲧⲁϧ (B diff) κατά(καρπος); Ps 35 10 B (S ϧⲁⲣⲁⲧⲛ-) παρά, 1 Cor 10 27 S ⲕⲁⲁⲩ ϧⲁ- (B ϩⲁⲧ.-) παρα(τιθέναι); dat: Est D 7 S, Ps 38 tit S (var ⲛ-, B ⲉϫⲉⲛ-); not in Gk: Mt 9 20 S ⲥⲛⲟϥ ϧⲁⲣⲟⲥ αἱμορροεῖν, 1 Kg 7 9 S ϧⲁⲡⲉϥϭⲉⲣⲱⲧⲉ γαλαθηνός, Am 6 4 A sim, Jo 7 49 SA²B ϧⲁⲡⲥⲁϩⲟⲩ ἐπάρατος, Cl 57 3 A ϧⲁⲁⲣⲉⲧⲏ ⲛⲓⲙ πανάρετος, Mor 17 8 S ϧⲁⲣⲟⲉⲓⲙ ῥευματώδης, Lev 7 16 S ϧⲁⲡⲉϥⲟⲩⲱϣ ἑκούσιος, Lu 7 14 S ϥⲓ ϧⲁ- βαστάζειν, ib 8 6 S ⲙⲛ ⲁⲧⲃⲉⲥ ϧⲁⲣⲟⲟⲩ μὴ ἔχειν ἰκμάδα, Ez 24 10 SB ⲙⲟⲟⲩ ⲉⲧϧⲁⲣⲟⲟⲩ ζω-μός; ib 27 25 B ⲉⲧⲥⲉⲕ ⲃⲟⲥⲉⲣ ϩⲁⲣⲟ κωπηλάται σου; 2 Cor 11 25 S ⲡⲭⲟⲓ ⲃⲱⲕ ϧⲁ- ναυαγεῖν; expressing Gk gen: Ex 32 18 S(B ⲛⲧⲉ-), Eccl 1 8 S(F ⲛ-), Is 30 19 F(S ⲛ-, B diff), Ez 30 11 SB; PS 219 S ⲉⲧϧⲟⲥⲉ ϧⲁⲧⲉⲅⲉⲧⲡⲱ, ib 337 S ϫⲱ ϧⲁⲧⲉⲩϧⲩⲡⲟⲧⲁⲅⲏ, Br 103 S ⲡⲁⲣⲧⲟⲩ ϧⲁⲡⲟⲩϧⲉⲣⲏⲧⲉ, LAp 541 F ⲉⲩⲛⲟⲩ[ϫⲏ] ⲡϧⲁ-ⲗⲁⲓ (sic MS), ShC 42 44 S ϫⲱⲟⲡ ⲉϥϧⲁⲡⲁⲏⲣ opp ϩⲓ-ϫⲙⲡⲕⲁϩ, ib 216 S torrents flowing into soul ⲛⲥ-ⲙⲟⲩϧ ⲁⲛ ϧⲁⲣⲟⲟⲩ, ShA 2 129 S by night ϧⲁⲡⲓⲛⲟϭ ⲡϩⲁϥ, ib 1 114 S ϣⲱⲡⲉ ϧⲁⲡϩⲁⲡ, PS 350 S ⲥⲉϣⲟⲟⲡ ϧⲁⲡⲛⲟⲃⲉ, R 1 5 51 S ⲛⲉϥϧⲁⲃⲁⲥⲁⲛⲟⲥ, AZ 21 100 O ⲓⲁⲧⲥ ⲭⲁⲉⲙⲣⲏ full of tears, Mani K 99 A² ⲙⲟⲩϧ ϧⲁ-ⲙⲡⲡⲁ ⲉⲧϧⲁⲩ, R 2 1 34 S the marvel is ϧⲁⲡⲉⲛⲃⲁⲗ, ib 1 4 30 S bade ⲉⲧⲙⲧⲣⲉϥⲉⲓ ϧⲁⲡⲉϧⲣⲟ, ZNTW 24 90 F ⲡⲉϥϧⲉⲡ ϧⲁϥϯ, Ep 110 S ye are ϧⲁⲥϯⲛⲟⲩϥⲉ ⲛⲓⲙ, BHom 68 S ⲟⲩⲟⲉⲓⲛ ⲉⲧϧⲁϣⲡⲏⲣⲉ, PMéd 262 S sim, CaiThe 203 B ⲡⲓⲁⲧⲥⲛⲟϥ ⲁϥϣⲱⲡⲓ ϩⲁⲟⲩ-ⲭⲣⲟⲛⲟⲥ, C 43 235 B cherubs ⲥⲱⲕ ϩⲁⲡⲉϥϩⲁⲣⲙⲁ, PLond 4 435 S ready to ⲥⲱⲕ ϧⲁⲡⲣⲟⲥⲧⲓⲙⲟⲛ ⲛⲓⲙ, J 79 65 S sim ϧⲁⲡⲛⲟϭ ⲡⲥⲁϧⲟⲩ, BMar 21 S ⲕⲁⲁⲩ ϧⲁ-ⲡⲉϩⲕⲟ, BKU 1 26 (8116 b) F ⲧⲁⲁⲩ (sc remedies)

ⲉϩⲣⲁⲓ ϩⲁⲡⲉⲧⲱ ⲛⲧⲉⲙⲙⲱⲛⲓⲱⲡ, Aeg 20 B I sat ϩⲁⲧⲉϥⲁ-ⲫⲉ = *ib S* ϩⲁⲣⲧⲛ-, Stegemann 52 *S* ⲉϥⲧⲟⲩⲉ ϩⲁⲡⲕⲁϩ, El 94 *A* ⲧⲱⲡⲉ ϩⲁⲛⲃⲁⲥⲁⲛⲟⲥ, AP 37 *A²* ϥⲓ ϩⲁⲡⲉⲃⲗⲁϭ, BSM 3 *B* sim ϩⲁⲛⲓϫⲓⲥⲓ, HL 107 *B* ⲟⲩⲥϭⲣⲁⲙ ϩⲁⲣⲁⲓ, R 1 5 50 *S* raise head ϩⲁⲡⲣⲟ ⲙⲡⲉⲧⲟ ⲛⲛⲟϭ ⲉⲣⲟϥ (cf BMar 5 ϩⲓⲑⲏ ⲛⲛⲟϭ ⲉⲣⲟϥ), DeV 2 180 *B* ⲉⲩⲥⲱϩⲓ ⲉⲡ-ϣⲱⲓ ϩⲁⲡⲁϩⲟ, Mor 24 10 *F* ⲉⲩϭⲏⲗ ⲉⲃⲁⲗ ϩⲁⲡⲁⲏⲣ (cf above ShC 42), Hor 84 *O* ⲛϥⲱ ϩⲁⲛϥⲱⲡϭ (meaning?); of time *SF*: Ryl 106 32 recipe ⲟⲩⲟⲙϥ ϩⲁ-ϣⲱⲣⲡ (cf PMéd *pass* ⲛϣ.), BKU 1 26 (8116 a) *F* ϩⲁ-ⲗⲟⲩϭⲓ, PMich 590 wind ⲉⲓ ⲉⲃⲟⲗ ⲛϩⲁϣⲱⲣⲡ, Miss 8 239 ⲁⲙⲏ ⲡⲁⲓ ⲛⲭⲓⲛϩⲁⲣⲟⲩϭⲉ.

b *from* (mostly *S*): 1 Kg 21 10, Ps 77 65 (*B* ⲉⲃ. ϩⲉⲛ-), Pro 6 9 *SA*(*B* do), Ez 18 8 *B*, Am 9 3 *A*(*B* ⲉⲃ. ϩⲁ-) ἐκ; 1 Kg 28 3, Job 7 9 (*B* ⲉⲃ. ϩⲉⲛ-), Ez 39 23 *B*, Jo 3 27 (*BF* ⲉⲃ. ϩⲓⲧⲉⲛ-), BHom 91 redeeming our nature ϩⲁⲛⲥⲁϩⲟⲩ ἀπό; PS 92 ⲁⲩⲡⲱⲧ ⲁⲩⲗⲟ ϩⲁⲣⲟⲓ, BMar 132 ⲁⲩⲡⲱⲧ ϩⲁⲡⲣⲟ ⲛⲛⲥⲁⲩ, Mor 22 52 ⲁⲩϩⲁⲣ-ⲡⲁϫⲉ ⲛⲡⲉϣⲏⲣⲉ ϩⲁⲡⲉⲛⲃⲁⲗ, LAl 10 ⲡⲉⲣⲥⲉ ϩⲁⲡⲉⲣⲉⲛ, BMis 42 theirs is kingdom ϩⲁⲛⲉⲩⲉⲓⲟⲧⲉ, J 3 19 land ⲉⲓ ⲉϫⲱⲛ ϩⲁⲡⲉⲛⲉⲓⲟⲧⲉ, Mor 26 9 had not seen the like ϩⲁⲡⲉϥⲉⲓⲟⲧⲉ, C 86 305 *B* ⲡⲁⲓ ⲉⲧⲁϥⲥⲟⲟⲙⲟⲩ ϩⲁⲣⲟϥ (*sic* all MSS, *l*? ϩ-).

c *by reason of SAA²F*: Job 30 4 (*B* ϩⲓⲧⲉⲛ-) ὑπό; Is 41 17 *S*(*B* ⲉⲃ. ϩⲉⲛ-), Ac 22 11 (*B* ⲛⲧⲉⲛ-, R)1 41 were as dead ϩⲁⲟⲩⲟⲧⲉ ἀπό; Gk dat: Deu 32 24 (*B* ⲛⲧⲉⲛ-), Lu 9 32 (*B* ⲛ-); ShHT *H* 28 enfeebled ϩⲁⲡⲁϣⲁⲓ ⲛⲧⲉⲩⲡⲟⲣⲛⲉⲓⲁ = Mus 45 28 *B* ϩⲓⲧⲉⲛ-, El 84 *A* ⲙⲟⲩ ϩⲁⲡⲡⲗⲓⲅⲏ, *ib* 50 *A* ⲡⲉⲧϩⲏⲕ ⲁⲃⲁⲗ ϩⲁⲡⲉϥϩⲁⲩ, Mani K 93 *A²* world filled ϩⲁⲧⲟⲩⲉⲡⲓⲑⲩⲙⲓⲁ, Mor 24 13 *F* ⲟⲩⲛⲁⲃ ϩⲁⲡⲗⲉϣϫⲓ.

d *for, in respect of, on behalf of*: 4 Kg 14 6 *S*, Job 2 4 *SB*, Ps 7 tit *S*(*B* ⲉⲑⲃⲉ-), *ib* 31 6 *S*(*B* ⲉϩⲣⲏⲓ ⲉϫⲛ-), *ib* 68 tit *S*(*B* ⲉⲭ.), Is 43 4 *S*(*B* ⲛⲧϣⲉⲃⲓⲱ ⲛ-), Mic 6 7 *AB*, Lu 22 19 *S*(*B* ⲉⲭ.), Jo 11 50 *SA²*(*B* ⲉϩ. ⲉⲭ.), BHom 53 *S* ⲁϣ ϩⲁⲟⲙ ϩⲁⲣⲟⲥ ὑπέρ; Lev 8 34 *S*(*B* ⲉⲭ.), Job 42 8 *S*(*B* ⲉϩ. ⲉⲭ.), Jo 1 8 *BF* (BP 5569, *S* ⲉⲧⲃⲉ-), Aeg 241 *S* ϣⲗⲏⲗ ϩⲁⲣⲟⲉⲓⲡⲉ, AM 270 *B* ⲥⲟϭ-ⲛⲓ ϩⲁⲡⲁⲙⲟⲩ περί; Mt 14 14 *BF*(*S* ⲉϩⲣⲁⲓ ⲉϫⲛ-) ἐπί; Cai Euch 328 *B* ⲥⲱϯ ϩⲁⲣⲟⲛ ἀντί(λυτρον); Miss 8 45 *S* had naught to say ϩⲁⲡⲉϥⲙⲛⲧⲣⲉϥϫⲓ ⲟⲩⲁ πρός; Ps 104 17 *B*(*S* ⲉ-), Mt 6 34 *B*(*S* do), Ro 16 6 *B*(*S* do) εἰς; R 1 1 62 *S* ⲣ ⲙⲛⲧⲣⲉ ϩⲁ- παρά, Is 53 6 *SB* ⲧⲁⲁϥ ϩⲁⲡⲟⲃⲉ παρα(διδόναι); *ib* 1 1 *B*(*SF* ⲉⲧⲃⲉ-) κατά; Gk gen: 1 Cor 9 9 *SBF*, BHom 53 *S* ⲙⲛⲧⲣⲉ ϩⲁⲡⲣⲱⲃ, AM 271 *B* ϭⲓ ⲣⲱⲟⲩϣ ϩⲁⲧⲉⲕⲕⲗⲏⲥⲓⲁ, *v* also below of price; not in Gk: Lam 3 32 *B* ϣⲉⲡ ϩⲏⲧ ϩⲁ- οἰκτείρειν, Mt 18 33 *BF* ⲡⲁⲓ ϩⲁ-(Mich 537, *S* ⲛ-) ἐλεεῖν, 3 Kg 22 18 *S* ⲡⲣⲟⲫⲏⲧⲉⲩⲉ ϩⲁⲡⲉⲧⲛⲁⲡⲟⲩϥ ⲡⲣ. ⲕⲁⲗά; Br 245 *S* ⲉⲧϣⲁϫⲉ ϩⲁⲣⲱⲃ ⲛⲓⲙ, PS 326 *S* ⲉⲓⲣⲉ ϩⲁⲣⲟⲟⲩ ⲙⲡⲙⲩⲥⲧⲏⲣⲓⲟⲛ, *ib* 107 *S* ϣⲡ ϩⲧⲏⲕ ϩⲁⲣⲟⲓ, El 98 *A* sim, CA 99 *S* ϯ ⲗⲟⲅⲟⲥ ϩⲁⲣⲟⲟⲩ, TU 26 1 50 *S* commemorations ϩⲁⲡⲉⲛⲧⲁⲩⲉⲛⲕⲟⲧⲕ

(var Aeg 285 ⲉⲧⲃⲉ-), BMis 192 *S* ⲁϥⲙⲟⲩ ϩⲁⲣⲟⲛ, Bor 294 118 *S* speaking ill ϩⲁⲧⲁⲡⲁⲥⲧⲁⲥⲓⲥ, BMis 102 *S* ⲁⲩⲉⲓⲣⲉ ⲙⲡⲥⲱⲛⲧ ⲙⲡⲛⲟⲙⲟⲥ ϩⲁⲣⲟϥ (cf Lu 2 27), BSM 126 *B* give alms ϩⲁⲣⲟⲓ, AM 229 *B* ungrateful ϩⲁⲡⲟⲩϫⲱⲣⲉⲁ, Kr 200 *F* ⲧⲉⲓⲃ ϩⲁⲉⲙⲡⲟⲗⲏ (*l* ⲉⲙⲃ.), CO 407 *S* hast paid *solidus* ϩⲁⲡⲉⲕⲏⲙⲟⲥⲓⲟⲛ, Kr 80 *S* sim ϩⲁⲡⲉⲫⲟⲣⲟⲥ, *ib* 100 payment ϩⲁⲧⲓⲣⲟⲙⲡⲉ ⲧⲁⲓ, BM 1064 *S* will give thee 36 jars ϩⲁⲡⲉⲕⲃⲉⲕⲉ, Ryl 243 *S* ⲕⲟⲩϫⲟⲩ ϩⲁⲡⲏϩ, Ep 548 *S* ⲡⲁⲡⲁⲣⲓ ϩⲁⲭⲁⲣⲧⲓⲥ, CMSS 39 *F* ϭⲏ ⲡϣⲓⲛⲓ ⲛⲁⲡⲁ ⲡⲓⲛⲏⲡ ϩⲁⲗⲁⲓ, J 1 16 *S* ϩⲩⲡⲟⲅⲣⲁⲫⲉ ϩⲁⲣⲟⲛ, ST 171 *S* ⲡⲣⲱⲙⲉ ⲡⲧⲁⲕϩⲁⲓ ⲡⲁⲓ ϩⲁⲣⲟϥ, Miss 8 192 *S* ϣⲗⲏⲗ ϩⲁⲡⲉⲓϩⲱⲃ, Mani 1 *A²* ⲥⲉⲙⲓϣⲉ ϩⲁⲩⲕⲧⲏⲥⲓⲥ, J 4 68 *S* none may sue thee, neither I nor brother ... ⲟⲩⲇⲉ ϩⲁⲡⲁⲉⲓⲱⲧ ⲙⲡⲧⲁ-ⲙⲁⲁⲩ, *ib* 9 66 *S* sim ⲉⲓⲧⲉ ϩⲁⲡⲁⲅⲉⲛⲟⲥ ⲉⲓⲧⲉ ⲙⲡⲃⲟⲗ ⲙⲡⲁⲅⲉⲛⲟⲥ, PLond 5 132 *S* ⲧⲉⲩϭⲱⲡⲉ ϩⲁⲉⲓⲱⲧ *stepsister*; + ⲙⲁⲅⲁⲁⲥ *SB* (rare): Nu 16 28 (*B* ⲉⲃⲟⲗ ϩⲓⲧⲉⲛ-) ἀπ᾽ ἐμαυτοῦ, Jo 18 34 (*A²* ⲁⲃⲁⲗ ⲛ-, *B* do) ἀφ᾽ ἑαυτοῦ; *ib* 12 49 (*A²* ϩⲁⲣⲁⲥ ⲟⲩⲁⲉⲧⲥ, *B* do) ἐξ ἐμ.; Ac 21 23 (*B* do) ἐφ᾽ ἑαυ.; Nu 24 13 (var ⲉⲃ. ⲛⲧⲛ-, *B* do) παρ᾽ ἐμ.; Aeg 285 ⲡⲛϥⲉ ⲙⲙⲱⲧⲛ ϩⲁ-ⲣⲱⲧⲛ ⲙⲁⲅⲁⲁⲧⲧⲏⲛⲩⲧ πρὸς ἑαυ.; ShC 73 96 ⲉⲓⲭⲱ ⲙⲙⲟϥ ⲁⲡ ϩⲁⲣⲟⲓ ⲙⲁⲅⲁⲁⲧ, cf BMis 452 *S* ⲙⲡⲉϥⲟⲩ-ⲱϣ ⲉⲣ ⲡⲣⲱⲃ ϩⲁⲡⲉϥⲧⲟⲣ ⲟⲩⲁⲁϥ, AM 153 *B* ϣⲉⲛ-ϩⲏⲧ ϩⲁⲣⲱⲧⲉⲛ ⲙⲙⲁⲩⲁⲧⲉⲡⲑⲏⲛⲟⲩ; cf below ϩⲁⲣⲓ-ϩⲁⲣⲟ-.

e *for*, of price: Lev 24 18 *SB*, Joel 3 3 *SAB*, Ro 12 17 *SF*(*B* ⲛⲧϣⲉⲃⲓⲱ ⲛ-) ἀντί; Is 52 3 *B* (*S* ϩⲛ-), Mic 3 11 *B*(*SA* diff) μετά; Deu 14 25 *SB* ἐπί; Jer 39 44 *SB* ἐν; Pro 28 21 *SA* ϯ ⲉⲃⲟⲗ ϩⲁ- ἀπο(διδό-ναι); Gk gen: Ge 33 19 *SB*, Is 7 23 *SB*, Jo 12 5 *SA²B*; Bor 307 4 *S* betrayed Lord ϩⲁⲭⲣⲏⲙⲁ, ViK 7592 *S* fixed price ϩⲁⲙⲁⲁⲃ ⲛϩⲁⲧ, BM 1102 *S* ⲁⲧⲉⲣⲙⲁⲛⲉ ϯ ⲟⲩⲏⲣ ϩⲁⲧⲥⲟⲣⲧ, MG 25 358 *B* ⲟⲩⲏⲣ ϩⲁⲡⲁⲓⲃⲓⲣ? (ROC 18 60 ⲥ), BMis 378 *S* ⲕⲟⲩⲱϣ ϩⲁⲟⲩⲏⲣ ⲛϯ-ⲙⲏ = BSM 35 *B* ⲟⲩⲏⲣⲧⲉ ⲧⲉϥϯⲙⲏ? Answer *S* ⲉⲓⲟⲩ-ⲱϣ ϩⲁⲟⲩⲧⲉⲣⲙⲏⲥⲓⲟⲛ = *B* ϥⲣⲱϣⲓ ϩⲁⲟⲩⲧ., ST 292 *S* ⲉⲕⲟⲩⲱϣ ⲉⲧⲣⲁⲧⲓⲅ ϩⲁⲥⲟⲩ, Worr 266 *S* dwelling in house ϩⲁⲡⲉϣϫⲟⲣ, J 70 43 *S* ⲡⲉⲓϩⲟⲗⲟⲕ/ ⲛⲧⲁⲓⲧⲁⲁϥ ...ϩⲁⲏⲣⲡ, *ib* 26 16 *S* ⲁⲓⲙⲟⲩϭ ⲛⲧⲟⲟⲧⲉ ϩⲁⲡⲥⲓⲛⲡⲟ-ⲥⲓⲟⲛ, *ib* 82 16 *S* ϭⲁⲟⲛ ⲡϣⲱⲡ ϩⲁⲣⲟⲙⲛⲧ, MR 5 50 *F* ϯ ⲟⲩⲧⲉ(ⲣ)ⲙⲏⲥⲩ...ϩⲉⲗⲉⲩ.

f *against*: Nu 14 37 *S* (var & *B* ⲛⲥⲁ-), Job 4 18 *B*(*S* ⲙⲛ-), Ps 40 8 *B*(*S* ⲉ-), Dan 6 4 *B*(*S* ⲉϩⲟⲩⲛ ⲉ-), Am 3 1 *B*(*S* ⲉϫⲛ-), Mt 12 32 *B*(*S* ⲉϩ. ⲉ-, *F* ⲉ-), Ac 25 3 *B*(*S* ⲛⲧⲛ-), Aeg 214 *S* punishment ordained ϩⲁⲣⲟⲟⲩ κατά, Mt 26 62 *S*(var ⲉ-)*B* ⲣ ⲙⲛⲧⲣⲉ ϩⲁ- καταμαρ-τυρεῖν; Hos 4 4 *SA*(*B* = Gk) ἀντι(λέγειν); Jer 18 18 *B*(*S* ⲉ-) ἐπί.

ⲉⲃⲟⲗ ϩⲁ-, ϩⲁ- (mostly doubtful if ⲉⲃ. belongs to vb or prep) *SB*, *away from*: Gal 3 13 *S*(*B* ϩⲁ- var ϩⲉⲛ-) ἐκ; ShC 73 101 *S* ⲙ ⲡⲉϥⲙⲁⲕϩ ⲉⲃ. ϩⲁⲡⲡⲁⲣ-ⲃⲉϥ, DeV 2 21 *B* sim (cf *ib* ⲉⲃ. ϩⲉⲛϥ̄ⲡ.), BIF 13

98 S ⲥⲉⲕ ⲏⲡⲧ ⲉϩ. ϩⲁⲣⲟϥ = MG 25 277 B, R 2 1 37 S ⲡⲟⲭⲟⲩ ⲉϩ. ϩⲁⲡⲉϧⲟ, C 86 187 B ⲁⲙⲟⲛⲓ ⲛ̅ⲧⲟⲧⲩ ⲉϩ. ϩⲁⲡⲓϫⲓ ϩⲣⲁϥ. V also ϧⲁ- B(ⲉϩ. ϧⲁ-), confused with this.

ⲉϧⲟⲩⲛ ϧⲁ-, ⲉϩ. ϫⲁ-SB, in beneath: Ge 19 8 SB, Jer 34 11 B ὑπό; ShP 130¹ 141 S blows to be given ⲉϩ. ϩⲁⲡⲉϧⲟⲩϭⲉⲣⲏⲧⲉ, AM 294 B ϫⲁⲩ (sc lamps) ⲉϫ. ϫⲁⲡⲉϫⲙⲁ ⲡ̅ⲣⲉⲙⲥⲓ, DeV 2 43 B ϣⲱⲙ ⲉϧⲣⲉⲛⲉϩⲗⲓⲕⲓⲁ ⲛⲓⲃⲉⲛ ⲉϫ. ϫⲁⲟⲩⲕⲁⲓⲥⲓ, PLond 4 522 S ϭⲱϣ(ⲧ) ⲉϩ. ϩⲁⲡⲁϩⲟ; ⲡⲣⲟϧⲛ ϧⲁ-SA², Jo 1 48 (B ϩⲁⲧⲟⲧ⸗ ⲡ-) ὑπό; ib 5 3 A²(S ϧⲁ-, B ϫⲉⲡ-) ἐν; J 74 56 ⲉϭⲙⲟⲟⲥ ⲛ. ϩⲁⲣⲟⲓ.

ⲉϩⲣⲁⲓ ϧⲁ- S, under, up to: ShBor 247 127 ⲉϥⲧⲱⲟⲩⲛ ⲉ. ϩⲁⲡⲙⲟⲩ ⲛ̅ⲥ̅ in his body, Mor 48 15 lifted eyes ⲉϩ. ϩⲁⲡⲕⲟⲟϩ (var BMar 210 ⲉ. ⲉ-) = Rec 6 174 B ⲉⲡϣⲱⲓ ⲉ-, Aeg 20 sim ⲉ. ϩⲁⲡⲁϩⲟ = ib B ⲉⲡϣⲱⲓ ϧⲁ-, Mun 37 † ⲛⲟⲩⲛⲟϭ ⲛⲕⲁⲡⲛⲟⲥ ⲉ. ϩⲁⲣⲟϥ up beneath.

Forming nn S: Br 226 ⲡⲛⲟϭ ⲛϧⲁⲡⲛⲟⲩⲛ, PMich 4949 glossary ⲁⲛⲑⲏⲣⲓⲟⲡ(ἀνθερεών)· ⲧϧⲁⲙⲟⲣⲧ, Glos 24 ὑποβλέφαρα· ϩⲁⲛⲃⲱϩⲉ.

Also ? in ϩⲁⲙⲟⲟⲩ (p 197 b inf), ϩⲁⲡⲟⲣⲏ q v, ϩⲁⲙⲟⲩⲗⲁϩⲝ (v ⲥⲁⲙⲡⲧ ⲃ), ϩⲁⲧⲏⲩ (p 440 a inf), ϩⲁϫⲱ⸗ (Kr 245).

V also ⲕⲱⲗ (ϩⲁⲃⲟⲗ), ⲉⲥⲏⲧ, ⲉⲟⲟⲩ, ⲉⲓⲁ eye, ⲙⲁ, ⲙⲡⲁⲓ, ⲣⲟ (ϩⲁⲣⲡ-), ⲣⲏⲥ, ⲣⲁⲧ⸗, ⲧⲱⲣⲉ hand (ϩⲁⲧⲛ-), ⲧⲟⲩⲱ⸗, ϧⲏ front, ϩⲏⲧ north, ϩⲏⲧ heart (ϩⲁⲣϩⲧⲛ-), ϫⲱ head (ϩⲁϫⲛ-), ϫⲓⲛ- (ϩⲁϫ.).

ϩⲁⲣⲓϩⲁⲣⲟ⸗ S, ϩⲁⲣⲓϩⲁⲣⲁ⸗ A, ϩⲁⲣⲓϩⲁⲣⲁ⸗ A², ϫⲁⲣⲓϫⲁⲣⲟ⸗ B refl pron, of my-, himself &c, alone, apart: Est 9 30 S, Is 47 15 B(S ⲕⲁⲧⲁⲣⲟ⸗), Hos 8 9 B(A ⲟⲩⲁⲉⲧ⸗), Mic 7 14 SAB, Zech 12 13 AB(S ⲙⲁⲩⲁⲁ⸗) καθ᾽ ἑαυτοῦ, 1 Pet 4 10 B(S ⲛ- ⲉⲣⲏⲩ) εἰς ἑ., Sa 7 27 S ἐν ἑ., ib 19 17 S δι᾽ ἑ., Aeg 284 S let each ψάλλει ϩ.ϩⲁⲣⲟϥ παρ᾽ ἑ., Job 7 13 B(S ⲙ.) πρὸς ἐμαυτόν, Va 57 173 B ⲛⲑⲱⲟⲩ ⲙⲙⲁⲩⲁⲧⲟⲩ ϫ.ϫⲁⲣⲱⲟⲩ κατ᾽ αὐτ., BMOr 6807 5 S words he spake ϩ.ϩⲁⲣⲟϥ παρ᾽ αὐτ-, Mk 4 10 S(B ⲙⲙⲁⲩ.) κατὰ μόνας, R 2 2 32 S ⲧⲉⲯⲩⲭⲏ ϭⲱ ϩ. ϩⲁⲣⲟⲥ ἀκέραιος, Ja 2 26 S(B Gk om); J 65 60 S ⲡⲉⲧⲕⲓⲙ ⲡⲉⲧⲕ. ⲁⲛ ⲡⲉⲧⲕ. ϩ.ϩⲁⲣⲟϥ (cf αὐτοκίνητος), ShA 2 14 S wall falleth not ϩ.ϩⲁⲣⲟⲥ ⲙⲙⲁⲧⲉ but on others, ShC 73 66 S ⲧⲏⲣⲛ ϩⲓⲟⲩⲥⲟⲡ opp ϩ. ϩⲁⲣⲟⲛ, Gu 8 S hands & feet stiffened ⲁⲩⲱ ϩ. ϩⲁⲣⲟⲟⲩ (Horae Semit 3 28 قعدوا على ارجلهم), Mor 18 52 S became as stones ⲁⲩⲱ ϩ. ϩⲁⲣⲟⲟⲩ (ib 19 61 diff), Aeg 253 S stand ϩⲛⲟⲩⲙⲁ ϩ.ϩⲁⲣⲟⲟⲩ ⲙⲙⲓⲛ ⲙⲙⲟⲟⲩ, Bodl(P) b 3 S marriage contract ⲉⲣϣⲁⲡⲟⲩⲱϣ ⲉⲃⲟⲕ ⲡⲉ ϩ. ϩⲁⲣⲟ, Mani K 52 A² ⲉϩⲟⲩⲥⲓⲁⲥⲧⲏⲥ ⲁⲕⲏⲡⲉϧⲉⲣⲏⲩ...ϩ.ϩⲁⲣⲁⲩ, BSM 98 B body without head ϥⲙⲱⲟⲩⲧ ϫ. ϫⲁⲣⲟϥ, MG 25 106 B my conscience ϭⲟϩⲓ ⲙⲙⲟⲓ ϫ.ϫⲁⲣⲟⲓ, Cat 161 B ⲁϥⲙⲟⲩϯ ⲉϧⲟⲩⲁⲓ ϧⲟⲩⲁⲓ ⲡⲛⲟⲩⲣⲁⲛ ϫ.ϫⲁⲣⲟϥ its separate name; strengthened by ⲙⲁⲩⲁⲁ⸗, ⲙⲙⲁⲩⲁⲧ⸗: Va 63 81 B ⲡⲉⲛ ⲥϫⲁⲓ

ⲁⲡ ϫ.ϫⲁⲣⲟϥ ⲙⲙⲁⲩⲁⲧϥ ἀφ᾽ ἑαυτ-; ShIF 95 S ⲡⲉϥⲟⲩⲱϣⲡⲉ ϭⲱ ϩ.ϩⲁⲣⲟϥ ⲙⲁⲅⲁⲁϥ, Pcod 24 S none knoweth godhead ⲛⲥⲁϥ. ϩⲁⲣⲟⲥ ⲙⲁⲅⲁⲁⲥ (var ⲛⲥⲁⲃⲃⲗⲗⲁⲥ ⲙⲁⲅⲁⲁⲥ ϩ.ϩⲁⲣⲟⲥ), Miss 4 698 S ⲉⲣⲱⲧⲛ ⲙⲁⲅⲁⲧⲧⲏⲩⲧⲛ ϩ.ϩⲁⲣⲱⲧⲛ.

ϧⲁ- B scribal error? for ϫⲁ-: Ez 42 13 (S ϧⲁ-) περί, ib 43 25 ὑπέρ, ib 44 27 pro, Is 19 10 (S ϧⲛ-), Jer 5 1 (S do) ἐν, Gal 3 13 (S ⲉⲃⲟⲗ ϧⲁ-) ἐκ; C 86 305 ⲡⲁⲓ ⲉⲧⲁϥⲥⲱⲙⲟϥ ϩⲁⲣⲟϥ (so all MSS) from him.

Doubtful whether ϧⲉⲗⲉϫ F belongs here (cf JKP 2 142 ⲗⲉⲛ = ⲉⲣⲟⲕ, 144 ⲧⲁⲗⲉϩ = ⲧⲁⲗⲟϥ) rather than to ϩⲓⲣⲛ-. Cf besides examples p 290 a, AZ 23 34 ⲁⲡⲉⲟⲩ ϫⲉⲗⲉⲟⲩⲛ ϧⲉⲗⲉϩ (S ⲁⲡⲁⲩ ϫⲉⲉⲣⲉⲟⲩ ϩⲁⲣⲟϥ), Brussels Mus Cinquant E 6346]ⲉϧⲁⲓ ⲡⲛⲓ ϧⲉⲗⲉⲥ, BM 527 6 ⲥⲱ ϫⲉⲗⲉϥ (sc potion, cf Ryl 106 35) ⲉϣⲁⲙⲧ ⲉϧⲁ[ⲩ].

ϧⲁ-, ϧⲁⲣⲟ⸗ BS(rare) prep, to, toward, a of persons (v Rec 31 158): Ge 18 6 (S ϣⲁ-), Deu 2 26 (S ⲉⲣⲁⲧ⸗ ⲛ-), Is 1 15 (SF ⲉ-); ib 30 6 (SF ⲉⲣ. ⲛ-), Lam 1 12 (F ϣⲁ-), Mt 13 56 (S ϩⲁⲧⲛ-, F ϩⲁⲧⲁⲁⲧ⸗), Lu 18 16 S(var ⲉⲣ. ⲛ-)B, MG 25 218 go ϩⲁⲡⲟⲥ̄ πρός, Is 34 1 (SF ⲉ-), προσ(άγειν); Jer 19 2 (S ⲉ-), 2 Cor 13 3 (SF ⲉϧⲟⲩⲛ ⲉ-) εἰς; Lam 3 40, Ac 9 38 (var & S ϣⲁ-) ἕως; Is 2 2 (S ⲉϫⲛ-), Mt 3 16 (S ⲉϩⲣⲁⲓ ⲉϫⲛ-) ἐπί; Su 19 (S do) ἐπί(τρέχειν) dat; Job 15 15 (S ⲙⲛ-), Ap 2 14 (S ⲉ-) κατά; Deu 29 17 (S ⲛ-), Jer 44 13 παρά; Is 7 5 (S ⲉ-) περί; Jer 4 12, ib 36 1 dat, Ez 22 7 ϫⲱ ϧⲁ- (S ⲛⲥⲁ-) acc; 2 Cor 13 10 (SF ϩⲁⲧⲛ-) Gk om; C 41 26 ⲁⲙⲟⲩ ϩⲁⲣⲟⲓ (cf 25 ⲁ. ϣⲁⲣⲟⲓ), C 86 246 ⲁϥⲓ ϩⲁⲡⲓⲱⲙⲓ = ib 303 ϣⲁⲡⲓⲁⲧⲓⲟⲥ, MIE 2 395 ⲁⲩⲧⲁⲥⲟⲟⲩ ϩⲁⲣⲟⲓ = BAp 122 S ⲉϫⲱⲓ, BSM 82 joy ϣⲱⲡⲓ ϩⲁⲣⲟⲛ = BMis 173 S ⲡⲱϩ ϣⲁⲣⲟⲛ, Va 63 11 ϩⲱⲗ...ϩⲁⲡⲓⲙⲁⲛⲉⲥⲱⲟⲩ = BSM 37 & BMis 381 S ϣⲁ- (but ib 12 ϩⲱⲗ ϣⲁ-), PO 11 313 ⲛⲛⲟⲩ ϩⲁⲣⲟϥ, cf ib ϣⲁⲣⲟⲕ, Kr p 14 n S ⲁⲕⲓⲣⲓ ⲙⲁⲣⲕⲟⲥ ⲃⲱⲕ ϩⲁⲡⲡⲣⲱⲙⲉ (sic), JKP 2 238 S ⲁⲡⲉⲣⲟ ϫⲟⲟⲩ ϩⲁⲣⲟⲓ. b not of persons: Nu 11 26 (S ⲉ-), Is 7 3 (S ϩⲁⲧⲛ-), Bar 1 3 πρός; Is 16 12 (S ⲉ-) εἰς; Deu 21 19 (S ⲉⲣⲁⲧ⸗ ⲛ-) ἐπί; Nu 6 13 (S ⲉⲣⲛ-) παρά; ϩⲁⲙⲡⲁⲓ v p 174 b.

ⲉⲃⲟⲗ ϧⲁ-, from: Ge 18 2 (S ⲉϩ. ϧⲛ-), Pro 4 27 (SA ⲉϩ. ϩⲓ-), Is 30 11 (SF ⲉϩ. ϩⲓϫⲛ-), ib 31 8 (S ϧⲏⲧ⸗ ⲛ-, F ϩⲁϫⲉⲛ-), EpJer 9 (F ⲉϩ. ϩⲓ-), ib 11 (F ⲉ-), Mt 10 17 (S ⲉϩ. ϧⲛ-), Ac 1 11 (S ⲛ̅ⲧⲛ-), Gal 2 12 (S ⲉϩ. ϩⲓⲧⲛ-) ἀπό; Ez 16 27 (S ⲉϩ. ϩⲓ-), Jo 12 32 (S ⲉϩ. ϩⲓϫⲛ-) ἐκ; Jer 28 27 ἐπί; Jo 15 26 (var & SA² ⲉϩ. ϩⲓⲧⲛ-) παρά; Va 57 12 ⲃⲏϣ ⲉϩ. ϩⲁϧⲱⲃ ⲛⲓⲃⲉⲛ Gk gen; BSM 98 ⲡⲟϩⲉⲙ ⲙⲙⲟⲓ ⲉϩ. ϩⲁⲙⲉϭⲓ ⲛⲓⲃⲉⲛ = Mor 22 110 S ⲉ-, BSM 40 ϩⲱⲗ ⲉϩ. ϩⲁⲣⲱⲟⲩ = BMis 385 S ⲉϩ. ϩⲓⲧⲛ-, Cat 44 ⲟⲩϫⲁⲓ ⲉϩ. ϩⲁⲧⲛⲗⲁⲡⲛ. V also ϧⲁ- 1° (ⲉⲃⲟⲗ ϫⲁ-).

ⲉϧⲟⲩⲛ ϧⲁ-, into, unto: Ps 77 50 (S diff), Ro 11 32 (var ⲉϩ. ϫⲉⲡ-, S ⲉ-) εἰς; Ge 6 4 ϧⲁ- (Va, var ϫⲁ-) πρός.

ϧⲁ, ϧⲟ S, ϧⲁ A, ϧⲁⲓ B, ϧⲉⲉⲓ F nn m, *winnowing fan*: Is 30 24 BF(S om), Mt 3 12 SB, Lu 3 17 S(var ϧⲟ, B ϧ. ⲡⲟⲅⲱⲧⲉϩ) πτύον; Am 9 9 S (sic prob, Rec 7 27 ϧⲟ) A(B ⲙⲁⲛϫⲁⲗⲉ ⲛϣⲱϣ) λικμός (var κόσκινον); Miss 8 227 S ϧⲟ, Tri 710 S ⲧⲃ̄ⲃⲟ ⲡⲉⲭⲡⲟⲟⲩ ϧⲁⲙⲡⲁ رڡ, P 44 62 S ⲡⲧϭⲟⲡ· ϧⲣⲁ مد, ,ﻥ, K 127 B ⲡⲓϧ. ,ﻥ, ϯ ϣⲟⲱϣ ϧ·; ShViK 9628 ⲙ ⲡⲉⲩϫⲱⲣⲙ ⲉⲃⲟⲗ ⲡⲣⲏⲧⲟⲩ ϧⲁⲙⲡⲁ ⲙⲏⲡⲧⲏⲩ. ⲣⲉϥϧⲁ Pro 20 26 (R 2 2 8) λικμήτωρ, but var ⲣⲉϥϧⲓ, v ϧⲓ *thresh*.

ϧⲁ, ϧⲟ, ϧⲁⲉ S nn m, *pole, mast*, weaver's *beam*: 1 Kg 17 7 (P 43 100 جلال, var Mor ϧⲟ), 2 Kg 21 19 (var do) ἀντίον (varr μέσαν., ἱστός); Is 30 17 (BF ⲙⲛⲓⲡⲓ) σημαία (var ἱστίον); Tri 710 ϣⲟⲡⲉ ⲙⲙⲁⲉⲓⲛ ⲛⲟⲉ ⲙⲡⲣⲁ علم (varr ﺩﺏﺩ, رمح); R 2 1 55 parts of ship ⲡⲉⲕⲡⲁⲅϧ, ⲧⲉⲕⲗⲁⲅⲟ, ⲡⲉⲕϧⲁⲉ, ⲡⲉⲕⲟⲩⲟⲥⲣ (or ? cf ϧⲁⲓ).

ϧⲁ SAA²FO   v ϧⲟ.

ϧⲁ- S in ϧⲁⲡⲧⲟⲟⲩ v p 441 b *supra*.

ϧⲁ-, ϧⲁⲕ-, ϧⲁϥ- &c A²F, pref 1st perf: v references in JEA 13 21 (adding Mani 1, PMich 3520) also AZ 36 140, 42 60, 52 113, Rec 26 43, Spg *Dem Gram* 188. But in WS 29 used both as pres & perf.

ϧⲁⲉ (?, MS now illegible) A vb, *give, bring* upon, c ⲁϩⲣⲏⲓ ⲁϫⲛ-: Jon 1 14 (SB ⲉⲓⲛⲉ ⲉϩⲣⲁⲓ ⲉϫⲛ-) διδόναι ἐπί.

ϧⲁⲉ SA², ϧⲁ(ⲉ)ⲓⲏ S, ϧⲁⲓⲉ SS.f, ϧⲁⲉ A, ϧ., ϧⲁⲓⲉ B, ϧⲁⲏ S f F, f ϧⲁⲏ SA²F, ϧⲁⲉ S, ϧⲁ(ⲉ)ⲓ, ϧⲁⲓⲉⲓ A, ϧⲁⲏ, -ⲓⲏ B, ϧⲁⲓⲏ F, pl ϧⲁ(ⲉ)ⲩ, ϧⲁⲉⲟⲩ S, -(ⲉ)ⲅⲉ SA², -ⲉⲟⲩⲅⲉ A², ϧⲁⲉ(ⲟ)ⲅⲉ A, ϧⲁⲉⲩ B, ϧⲁⲛⲟⲩ, ϧⲁⲓⲏⲩ (Lant 3 52, but not pl) F & sg as pl, **I** nn (properly adj, so Sethe AZ 44 95), *last thing, end*: Jer 23 20 B, Ap 1 17 SB ἔσχατος; Jer 27 17 B(SF ⲉⲧⲙⲡⲡⲥⲁ-), Mt 21 31 SB, ROC 18 173 S ⲧⲉⲣⲟⲩⲉⲓⲧⲉ...ⲡϧ. ὕστερος; Deu 32 17 B(S ⲛⲉϩⲥⲉ) πρόσφατος; Sa 2 16 B(S Gk diff); BM 825 B ⲁⲅⲥⲃⲏⲧϥ ⲡϧ. ⲛϯϣⲉⲙϣⲓ, My 28 S ⲟⲩϧⲟⲩ ⲉⲣⲟⲟⲩ ⲡϧ. (for ? ⲉⲛ-): f: Eccl 7 3 SF, Is 19 15 S(B ϫⲱⲕ), Lu 1 33 SBF ϧⲁⲏ (Pcod Mor 14), 1 Pet 4 7 S(Leyd 226 ϧⲁⲉⲓ, B ϫ.) τέλος, Bar 3 25 B(S ⲁⲣⲏⲭϥ) τελευτή, Pro 14 12 SA ϧⲁⲉⲓ B, ib 20 11 SA ϧⲁⲓⲉⲓ -ταῖος, Ps 58 12 S(B ϫ.ⲉ-ⲃⲟⲗ), Am 9 5 SAB, He 9 26 SF(B do) συντέλεια; Job 8 13 SB, Pro 25 8 SA ϧⲁⲓⲉⲓⲉ, Eccl 10 13 SF, Mt 12 45 S(B pl) ἔσ.; Ps 7 6 S(B ⲁⲅⲣⲏⲭϥ), Ez 7 2 SB πέρας, Eccl 4 8 S περασμός; Aeg 269 S ϧⲏⲟ. ⲛⲛⲉⲓ-ϧⲟⲟⲩ ⲩ̄ⲥ.; Cl 5 7 A(Stras) τέρμα; Sa 2 17 S(B ϫ. ⲉϩ.) ἔκβασις; Joel 2 3 A ϧⲁⲓ (SB ϧⲓⲡⲁϩⲟⲩ) ὄπισθεν; Lev 23 22 S(B ⲥⲱϫⲡ) λοιπόν; PS 268 S ϧ. ⲛⲧⲉϥⲙⲉⲧⲁⲛⲟⲓⲁ, ShBor 246 43 S ⲙⲛ ϧ. ⲛⲁϣⲱⲡⲉ ⲛⲛⲉϥϧⲓⲥⲉ, TU 43 17 A ⲧⲟⲩϧ. ⲛⲉ ⲡⲥⲱⲣⲙⲉ, BHom 65 S ⲛⲥⲧⲁϩⲟⲡ ⲛϭⲓ ⲧⲉⲛϧⲁⲏ, Mor 40 19 S ⲑ. ⲙⲡⲧⲱⲣⲧⲣ

(var ib 39 27 ⲡϧ.) = C 43 49 B, Cat 21 B ⲧϧⲁⲏ ⲛⲛⲓⲉ-ϧⲟⲟⲩ...ⲡϧⲁⲓⲉ ⲛⲧⲉ ⲡⲓⲥⲛⲟⲩ, ib 188 sim, Rec 13 65 S ⲛⲧⲉⲡⲡ̄ⲉ ⲛ ⲧⲉⲡϧ. ⲉⲃⲟⲗ ⲉⲥⲉⲣ ⲁⲡⲁϥ, Ep 164 S, WS 70 S, Lant 24 F sim (cf in Gk BMis 255), Mani K 52 A² ⲡⲥⲏⲩ ⲛⲧⲣⲁ[ϩ, Pcod F 26 ⲧⲉⲕ[ϧ]ⲁⲏ, BM 145 S ⲧϧⲁⲉ *end* of lesson (opp ⲧⲉⲥⲁⲣⲭⲏ), Lant 71 S ⲧⲉⲩϧ-ϧⲁⲉ;   pl: Nu 2 31 S(var -ⲉⲅⲉ, B sg), Job 8 7 S -ⲉⲉⲅⲉ B, Ps 72 17 SB, Eccl 1 11 S-ⲉⲉⲅⲉ F(PMich 3520), Is 37 24 B(S ⲁⲣ.), Mt 12 45 B(S ⲑ.), Cl 28 3 A ϯϧⲥ.; Jer 30 10 S(B diff) πέραν; LAp 304 S ⲡ-ϧⲁⲉⲟⲩ (var -ⲉⲉⲩ) τέλος; ShC 73 193 S ⲛϧ. ⲛⲧϣⲟⲣⲡ ⲛⲉⲡⲓⲥⲧⲟⲗⲏ, P 129¹⁴ 123 S days of life ⲛⲉϥϧⲁⲉⲉⲅⲉ opp ⲛⲉϥϣⲟⲣⲡ, Leyd 154 S ⲡϧⲁⲉⲉⲅⲉ ⲛⲧⲉⲣⲟⲙⲡⲉ, Mani H 5 A² ⲡⲉϥϧⲁⲉⲅⲉ, Mani 2 A² ⲡⲓϧⲁⲉⲟⲅⲉ, Miss 4 210 B ⲡⲓϧ.....ⲛϧⲟⲩⲁϥ, BG 109 S ϣⲁⲡⲓϧⲁⲉ.

II adj, *last* **a** before nn: Mt 5 26 SB, Jo 6 44 S (var ϧⲁⲓⲉ)A²B, 1 Cor 15 26 SBF, BHom 29 S ⲡϧ. ⲡϧⲟⲟⲩ ⲉ̄ⲥ.; Mor 37 138 S ⲡⲁϧ. ⲛⲥⲟⲡ ⲩ̄ⲥ.; PS 17 S ϧ. ⲙⲙⲩⲥⲧⲏⲣⲓⲟⲛ, ShR 2 3 10 S ⲛⲉϥϧ. ⲛⲛⲓϫⲉ, Mor 31 64 S sim ϧⲁⲓⲉ, Miss 4 126 B sim ϧⲁⲓⲉ, Lant 3 52 F sim ϧⲁⲓⲏⲩ, El 96 A ⲡϧ. ⲛϧⲟⲟⲩⲉ, LCyp 22 S sim, Pcod 43 S ⲑ. ⲛⲥⲁⲗⲡⲓⲛⲅⲝ, AM 284 B ϯϧ. ⲙⲡⲟⲗⲓⲥ, Va 57 59 B ϯϧⲁⲏ ⲛⲧⲁⲍⲓⲥ, Mani K 106 A² ⲧϧⲁⲏ ⲃⲟⲡⲉ.   **b** after nn: Ex 4 8 AB, Lev 23 16 SB, Jon 2 6 SA, Ac 2 17 B(S ⲙⲛⲛⲥⲁ-), Cai Euch 428 B ⲛⲓϧ. ⲉ̄ⲥ.; Hos 6 3 SAB ὄψιμος; Pro 24 71 SA ὕστερο-; ShC 42 164 S ⲡⲉϧⲟⲉⲓϣ ⲛϧ., MR 5 28 S ⲛⲓⲃⲉ ⲛϧⲁⲓⲉ, LAl 6 S τροφὴ ⲛϧⲁⲏ, AM 243 B ⲡⲓⲉϩⲟⲟⲩ ⲛϧ., Va 58 157 B ⲡⲓϫⲙⲟⲙ ⲛϧⲁⲓⲉ, El 96 A ϧⲛ ϧ.;   pl: Mic 4 1 SA-ⲉⲟⲅⲉ (B nn), 2 Kg 23 1 S, 2 Pet 3 3 S -ⲉⲉⲅⲉ (B ϧⲁⲉ), Ap 219 S-ⲉⲩ B ⲉ̄ⲥ.; ShMIF 23 161 S ⲛϧ. ⲛϧⲟⲟⲩ, Cl Pr 41 32 S ⲛⲉϥϧⲟⲟⲩ ⲛϧⲁⲓⲏ, C 73 212 S ⲛⲉϥϧⲁⲉⲅⲉ ⲛⲣⲟⲙⲡⲉ.

ⲉⲛϧ., ϧ. SA²BF, *at the end*: Nu 10 25 B(S o ⲛϧ.) ⲉ̄ⲥ., ib 24 14 B(S ϧⲛϧ.), Is 41 23 B(S ϧ. nn) ἐπ' ἔσ., Pro 23 32 S ⲉⲛϧⲁⲉⲓⲏ (A ⲁⲧⲩϥ.), Mk 12 6 SB ἔσχατον; Jer 36 2 B, Mt 4 2 B(S ⲙⲛⲛⲥⲱⲥ) ὕστερον, Ep Jer 71 BF ἐξ ὑστ.; PS 85 S ⲁⲩϧⲱϫ ⲙⲙⲟⲥ ⲉ., Mor 23 90 S f ⲣ ϩⲧⲏⲧⲛ ⲉⲛϧⲁⲏ, FR 80 S they confessed ⲉ. (var ⲙⲛϧ.), C 43 170 B ⲉⲛϧ. ⲉⲕⲉⲣⲟⲕϧⲩ, AM 30 B ⲉⲛϧⲁⲓⲉ ⲛⲧⲉⲕⲱⲗⲓ ⲛⲧⲉϥⲁϥⲉ; f: 2 Kg 2 26 S ⲉϧ. (var m) εἰς τὰ ἔσ.; Mani K 31 A² ⲁⲧϧ.

ⲙⲫⲁⲉ S, *at the last, finally*: 2 Kg 1 c (var ⲉϧ.) εἰς τὰ ἔσ.; PS 145; ⲛϧⲁⲏ sim: Is 41 23 (B ⲉⲡϧ.) ⲉⲡ' ἔσ., Si 22 8 (var ⲑⲁⲏ) ἐπὶ συντελείᾳ; without ⲛ-: Si 1 c, ib 13 9 ⲉⲡ' ἔσ.; ⲛϧ. SA sim: Ge 33 2 (B ⲉⲡϧ.) ἔσ., Lev 27 18 (B do), 1 Cor 15 8 (B do, F ⲛϧ.) ἔσχατον, 1 Kg 29 2 ⲉⲡ' ἔσ.; Zech 10 1 A(B ϧ. adj) ὄψιμον; PS 173 ⲁⲩⲧⲱⲟⲩⲛ ⲉϫⲱⲓ ⲛϧ., ShRE 10 164 ⲉϥⲛⲁⲡⲁⲓⲁϫⲉⲅⲉ ⲙⲙⲟⲛ ⲛϧⲣⲏⲧϥ ⲛϧ.

ⲉⲭⲛϧ. S sim: P 78 58 ⲉⲭⲛϧ. ⲁⲩⲡⲁⲗⲁⲙⲃⲁⲛⲉ ⲙ-ⲙⲟϥ (sc Elijah).

ⲛⲥⲁϧⲁⲏ F, ⲥⲁϧ. B, *at the last*: Ps 37 7 B(S ϣⲁ-

ⲃⲟⲗ) ἕως τέλους; Eccl 1 11 F(CSchmidt, var PMich 3520 ϣⲁⲟ., S ⲉⲟ.) εἰς τὴν ἑσ.

ϣⲁϧ., ⲋ. SB, till, at the last: Ge 46 4 B, Ps 102 9 B(var ϣⲁϧⲁⲓⲉ, S ϣⲁⲃⲟⲗ) εἰς τέλος, 2 Cor 1 13 B (S do) ἕως τ.; PS 313 S ϫⲓⲛⲡϣⲟⲣⲡ ϧⲉⲱⲥ ϣ., BG 94 S ϣ. ⲡⲧⲁⲡⲧⲟⲏⲕⲉ, Va 58 125 B ⲁⲓⲉⲣ ⲧⲁⲗⲉⲡⲱⲣⲓⲛ ⲁⲓⲕⲱⲗϫ ϣ., Cat 55 B those shall be first ⲉⲧⲁⲩϣⲱⲡⲓ ϣ.; ϣⲁⲟⲑⲛ SA²: Sa 4 19 ἕως ⲉⲥ., Si 47 12 μέχρι συντελείας; Mani H 67 A²]ϫⲓ ⲉⲁⲩ ϣ.

ϧⲛⲑ. SA², at the last: Deu 32 20 (B ⲉⲛϧ.), Sa 3 17 ἐπ' ἑσ.; Mor 31 52 what should befall ϧⲛⲑⲁⲓⲉ, Mani K 81 A² ϧ. ⲁⲡ ϥⲁⲥⲁϧϧⲩ.

ⲁⲧϧ. B, without end: DeV 2 26 life everlasting & ⲡⲁ., MG 25 385 ⲡⲁⲧⲁⲣⲭⲏ ⲟⲩⲟϩ ⲡⲁ.

ⲙⲉⲧϧ. B: AmerSchoolOrResearch 6 109 ⲟⲩ ⲙⲙ. ⲉⲧⲉⲡⲓⲡⲁϧϯ ⲉⲧⲥⲟⲩⲧⲱⲛ ⲉⲣ ϧ. ⲙⲙⲟϥ? Prob l ⲙⲉⲧⲉⲣϧ. need.

ⲉⲓⲣⲉ ⲛϧ., ⲣ ϧ., ⲉⲣ ϧ. SA²BF, be last, be in want: Mt 19 30 SB ⲉⲥ. εἶναι; Lu 15 14 B(S ϣⲱⲟⲧ), He 11 37 B(S ⲣ ϭⲣⲱϧ) ὑστερεῖν, Ex 22 29 B(S om) καθνσ.; 1 Kg 2 5 B(S ϣ.), Pro 11 24 B(SA do) ἐλαττοῦν; Is 41 17 B(S ⲣ ϭ.) ἐνδεής, Deu 15 4 B(S do) ἐνδεὴς εἰν.; Eph 4 28 B(S ϣ.) χρείαν ἔχειν; Si 35 11 S οὐραγεῖν; Miss 8 77 S will not suffer ⲉⲧⲣⲉϥⲣ. ἀπολιμπάνεσθαι; ShZ 395 S ⲉⲕϣⲁⲡⲣ. ⲧⲓⲡⲁⲅⲩⲡⲟⲙⲓⲛⲉ ⲉⲣⲟⲕ, CA 89 S shall rank with subdeacons ⲛϥⲣ., Mor 43 89 S ⲁϥⲣ. ⲉⲡⲥⲁ ⲥⲛⲁⲩ in this world & next (var R 2 4 25 ⲣ ϣⲙⲙⲟ), Mani 2 A² ⲧⲣⲉⲡⲣⲱⲃ ⲣ. ⲡⲁⲣⲁ ⲡⲉϥⲥⲛⲟⲩ, Mor 27 26 S ⲁⲛⲣ. (var BMis 372 ⲣ ϧⲛⲕⲉ = Va 63 6 B), AM 220 B charity to ⲛⲏ ⲉⲧⲉⲣ.; ⲥ ⲉ-, be in want of, lose: 2 Cor 11 5 B(S ϣ.) ὑσ. acc; Miss 8 84 S ⲛⲁⲕ ⲛϧ. ⲉⲡⲉⲧⲟⲩⲧⲩⲡⲟⲩ ⲙⲙⲟⲟⲩ ἀπολείπεσθαι gen; Mus 40 40 S(RegPach) ⲣ. ⲉⲟⲩⲥⲟⲡ ⲛϣⲗⲏⲗ tardius venire; ShA 1 124 S ⲣ. ⲉⲡⲙⲁ ⲛⲙⲧⲟⲛ, BM 980 308 S wandered & ⲁⲩⲣ. ⲉⲧⲡⲟⲗⲓⲥ, BMar 181 S ⲉⲕϣⲁⲡⲣ. ⲉⲅⲗⲁⲁⲩ at table, Hall 74 S I thank my God ϫⲉⲕⲉⲓⲣⲉ ⲙⲙⲟⲓ ⲛϧ. ⲉ[hast need of me for [; vbal S: Jud 5 28 χρονίζειν, Nu 9 7 (B ϭⲣⲟϧ) ὑσ.; ShC 42 125 ⲣ. ⲉⲃⲱⲕ; ⲥ ⲛ- (mostly B) as last: Ps 22 1 (S ϣ.), Mk 10 21 (S do) ὑσ. acc, C 89 41 ⲉⲣ. ⲛⲥⲟϥⲟⲩ = C 99 137 S do ὑσ. gen, Mk 12 44 BF(Mor 46, S do) ὑστέρησις, Ps 33 10 (S ϭ.) ὑστέρημα; Bor 253 162 S ⲁⲓⲣ. ⲙⲙⲟⲟⲩ στερεῖσθαι; Deu 8 9 (S do) ἐνδεῖσθαι acc, Job 30 4 (S ⲣ ϭ.) ἐν. gen; Ps 33 11 (S ϣ.) ἐλαττοῦν gen; De V 1 201 not suffer him to ⲉⲣ. ⲛϧⲗⲓ ⲛⲉⲙⲧⲟⲛ ἀπολιμπάνεσθαι acc; Pro 31 11 (S ⲣ ϭ., A ϣ.) ἀπορεῖν gen; Mor 31 167 Sˢ if he die ϯⲛⲁⲉⲣ ϧⲁⲓⲉ ⲛⲛⲁⲩ ⲉⲡⲉⲥⲁ, ib 146 Sˢ ⲁⲁⲧ ⲛϧⲁⲓⲉ ⲙⲡⲁⲉⲓⲱⲧ, DeV 2 217 ⲉⲣ. ⲛϯⲙⲉⲧⲟⲩⲣⲟ ⲡⲧⲉ ⲫϯ; ⲟ ⲛϧ., ⲟⲓ ⲛϧ.: Nu 10 25 S(B ⲉⲛϧ.) ⲉⲥ.; Va 57 50 B ⲟⲓ ⲛϧ. ⲙⲡⲉⲥⲉⲧⲛⲙⲁ ἀτελέστερος; ib 135 B ⲛⲏ ⲉⲧⲟⲓ ⲛϧ. δεῖσθαι; MG 25 196 B ⲉⲩⲟⲓ ⲛϧ. ⲛⲧⲕⲉϩⲛⲓⲃⲓ στερεῖν; Miss 8 83 S ⲧⲉⲓ-

cⲩⲡⲣⲟϧⲟⲥ...ⲉⲕⲟ ⲛⲣ. ⲉⲣⲟⲥ ἀπολείπειν; ⲁⲧⲉⲣ ϧ. B, without want: TRit 275 ϫⲓⲛⲡⲱⲛϧ ⲡⲁ. till old age غير; ⲣⲉϥⲉⲣ ϧ. B: Va 66 307 ⲟⲩⲣ. ⲡⲉⲙⲟⲩϧⲛⲓ; ⲙⲛⲧ-, ⲙⲉⲧⲣ., want: Deu 28 20 (S ϭ.), Job 30 3 SB, Pro 10 21 (S do, A ϣ.), Si 18 25 (Va 57 176, S do) ἔνδεια; Phil 4 11 (S ϣ. vb) ὑστέρησις; Deu 28 48 (S ϭ.) ἔκλειψις; ROC 25 241 ⲟⲩⲙ. ⲡⲧⲉ ⲡⲓⲙⲁ ⲛϣⲱⲡⲓ σπάνις χρειῶν (Budge Paradise 141 ⲓⲕⲟⲟϧϧ); Cat 55 ⲟⲙ. of eternal life.

ϣⲱⲡⲉ ⲛϧⲁⲓⲉ S, be lacking: ViK 9834 54 day, night, stars &c ⲛⲧⲁⲩϣ. when God created world.

ϫⲓ ϧ. S, take last (place), stay behind: Z 280 ⲁϥϫ. ⲉⲧⲙⲃⲱⲕ ⲉϧⲟⲩⲛ ⲟⲣⲡ ⲣ ϣⲟⲣⲡ ⲉⲃⲱⲕ ⲉⲣ., BP 11938 let him act straightway (ⲙ)ⲙⲟⲛ ⲉϥϣⲁⲛϫⲓ ϧⲁⲉⲓⲉ ⲧⲉⲛⲟⲩ ⲙⲩⲗⲟ ϧⲓⲡⲁϧⲟⲩⲉ.

V AZ 27 109.

ϧⲁⲏ F nn f, an animal, ? for ⲁϧⲏ cow: AZ 23 39 ⲟⲩϧ. ⲡⲧⲉⲓ ⲡⲧⲁϥϭⲁⲡⲥ ⲁⲃⲁⲗⲥ ⲉϧⲟⲩⲛ ⲙⲡⲉⲃⲕⲉⲧ ⲧⲁⲧⲓ ϧⲣⲏ ⲡⲉⲥ. Cf Spg Demotica 1 25 n.

ϧⲁⲓ SB, ϧⲉⲓ AF, ϧⲉⲉⲓ A² nn m, husband: Ge 3 16 SB, Pro 31 11 SAB, Jer 51 19 B(S ϧⲟⲟⲩⲧ), Jo 4 16 SA²BF, 1 Cor 7 16 SBF, AP 8 A², Aeg 281 S(var ϧⲟⲟⲩⲧ) ἀνήρ; LCyp 2 S part wives from ⲛⲉϧ., Ep 300 S ⲡⲙⲁϧⲁⲣⲓⲟⲥ ⲡⲁϧ., P 44 71 S ⲛϧ. ⲛⲧϣⲉⲉⲣⲉ · γαμβρός.

ⲁⲧϧ. SB, not being h.: Mus 34 194 B Joseph ⲡⲓⲁ. ⲛϧⲁⲓ of virgin ἄνανδρος ἀνήρ; ⲣ ⲁ.: Ru 1 5 S Gk diff.

ⲣ ϧ. SB, be h.: Tit 1 6 ἀν. no vb.

ϧⲁϧ. B, under, having h.: Nu 5 20 (S diff), Ro 7 2 (S diff) ὕπανδρος; HL 107 ⲟⲩⲥϧⲓⲙⲉ ϧ. ⲧⲉ; Pro 6 24 ϧⲁⲟⲩϧ. (SA diff) ὕπ.

† ϧⲁⲓ (?) B in H B 3 p xxxvii, an obscure version of Ro 1 27.

ϧⲙⲟⲟⲥ ⲙⲛϧ. SB, dwell with h.: Lu 20 34 S(B ϭⲓ) γαμίσκεσθαι, Mt 24 38 S(B ϭⲓ ϧ.) ἐκγαμίζειν; Deu 22 22 B(S ⲟⲩⲱϧ ⲙⲛϧ.) συνοικίζεσθαι ἀνδρί.

ϫⲓ, ϭⲓ ϧ. SA²B, take h.: Mt 1c B ⲉⲕⲩ., 1 Tim 5 11 SB γαμεῖν, AP 8 A² γάμος γίνεσθαι; Si 42 11 S συνοικεῖν; Z 586 S ⲧⲉⲥϧⲓⲙⲉ ⲉⲧⲟⲩⲛⲁϫⲓⲧⲥ ⲛϧ.

ϧⲁ(ⲉ)ⲓⲟ S, ⲁ(ⲉ)ⲓⲟ SO, ϧⲁⲓⲱ, ⲁⲓⲱ S, ϧⲁⲓⲉ A, ⲁ(ⲉ)ⲓⲉ A², ⲁⲓⲟ, ⲁⲓⲁ F, ⲁⲓⲏ O(PGM 285) interj of entreaty, yea, verily, come: Lu 12 5 ϧ. (B ⲁϧⲁ), Phil 4 3 ϧ. (varr ⲁ., ⲉⲓⲟ, B ⲥⲉ), Cl 60 3 A ναί; 1 Kg 23 11 ϧ., 4 Kg 63 ϧ. Gk om; Tri 594 ⲁ. ⲧⲁⲭⲏ أسرعي العجل; PS 328 ⲁ. ⲡⲭⲥ ⲡⲁ ⲡⲡⲉⲯⲩⲭⲟⲟⲩⲉ, ib 357 ϧ. ⲡⲭⲥ ϭⲱⲗⲡ ⲛⲁⲛ, Br 111 ϧ. ⲥⲱⲧⲙ ⲉⲣⲟⲓ, ShR 2 3 57 ϧ. ϯⲥⲟⲡⲥ ⲙⲙⲱⲧⲛ, BM 220 ⲁ. ⲡⲁϣⲏⲣⲉ ⲙⲁⲣⲛⲟⲩⲱⲙ (var Mor 41 57 ⲁ. ⲱ ⲡⲁϣ.), ib 41 111 ϧ. ⲱ ⲡⲉⲡⲉⲓⲱⲧ, Mor 52 47 ⲁ. ⲡⲭⲥ ⲉⲕⲉⲥⲱⲧⲙ, BM 1224 A² ⲁⲉⲓⲉ ⲛⲡⲉ, LMis 100 A² ⲁ. ⲡⲭⲥ, P 130ᵗ 89 ϧ. † ⲡⲉⲕⲟⲩⲟⲓ ⲉⲣⲟϥ, Bor 297 101 ϧ.

ⲛⲉⲥⲡⲏⲩ ϫⲉⲛⲡⲉⲛϫⲓ ϣⲓⲡⲉ, Osir pl 37 2 ⲁ. ⲡⲉⲭ̅ⲥ̅ ⲁ-
ⲙⲏⲡ, PSBA 32 250 ϧ. ⲡⲁϣⲏⲣⲉ ⲉⲓϣⲁⲛⲃⲱⲕ ϣⲁⲓϭⲙ
ϭⲟⲙ ⲛⲧⲱⲃϧ, Ep 167 ϧ. ⲟⲩⲛ ⲙⲡⲣⲥⲧⲟ, RNC 90
prayer ends ϧ. ϭⲉ ⲡⲁⲭ̅ⲥ̅, Worr 264 ⲁ. ϭⲉ ⲧⲓⲥⲟⲡⲥⲛ
(var En Peterson ϧ. ϯ ⲥⲟⲡⲥ), Griff Stu 163 F ⲁ. ⲛ-
ϫⲉϯⲧⲁⲗⲕⲁ; iterated: Jth 9 12 ϧ. ϧ. ⲛⲁⲓ ⲛ.; mostly
in magic: BKU 1 3 ϧ. ϧ. ⲧⲓⲱⲣⲉⲕ ⲉⲣⲟⲕ, ib 9 ϧⲁⲓⲱ
ϧ. ϫⲉⲧⲓⲟⲣⲟ[ⲕ, ib 6 ⲁ. ⲁⲓⲱ, Kropp K 11 Sᵃ ⲉⲓⲉⲓⲁ ⲡⲉⲓⲱⲧ (same?), BKU 1 3 ϧ. ϧ. ⲧⲁⲭⲏ ⲧⲁⲭⲏ (ταχύ),
Kropp C 48 F ⲁⲓⲁ ⲁ. ⲉⲧⲓ ⲉ. (ἤδη) ⲧⲁⲭⲏ ⲧ., BKU 1
24 F sim ⲁⲓⲟ, Sph 10 159 imprecation ends ϧ. ϧ.,
Brit Acad Proc 17 240 O ⲛⲥⲧⲉ ⲁ. (bis).

ϧⲉ, ϧⲉⲉ, ϧⲏⲉ (J 69 7, ST 246) S, ϧⲏⲓⲉ Sᵃ, ϧⲉⲉⲓⲉ A,
ϧⲉⲓⲉ AA²(Ma), ϧⲁⲉⲓⲉ A², ϧⲉⲓ A²B, ϧⲏⲓ (Ez 11 10) B,
ϧ(ⲏ)ⲏⲓ S/F, ϧ(ⲉ)ⲉⲓ F, ϧⲉⲝ S (once v B), ϧⲏⲅⳁ S, ϧⲓⲱ-
ⲟⲩⲧⳁ B vb intr **A** fall: Lev 26 17 SB, Pro 11 14 B(S
ⲥⲣⲟϥⲣⲉϥ), Is 30 13 SBF, Ac 15 16 SB πίπτειν, Ps
5 11 SB ἀποπ., Nu 5 21 S(B diff) διαπ., Eccl 10 10
F ϧⲏⲓ (S ⲥⲱϧⲙ ⲉⲃⲟⲗ) ἐκπ., Ps 144 14 B(Sⳋ), Ac 28 6
B(S ϧⲉ ⲉϧⲣⲁⲓ) καταπ., Sa 12 2 S παραπ., Ez 30 4 SB
συμπ.; Deu 7 25 B(S ⲣ ⲛⲟⲃⲉ) πταίειν; Job 4 9 S(B
ⲧⲁⲕⲟ) ἀπολλύναι; AP 7 A² ἁλίσκεσθαι; Jer 46 2 B
ῥηγνύναι; Ap 17 8 B(S ϣⲱⲡⲉ) παρεῖναι; Dan 11 21
B ἥκειν; Pro 10 8 SA(B ⲥⲗⲁϯ) ὑποσκελίζειν; 2 Kg
1 21 B(S ϧⲉ ⲉⲃⲟⲗ) προσοχθίζειν (var ἀποβάλλειν);
Ac 20 11 S(var ϣⲁ, B ⲓ ⲉⲃⲟⲗ) Gk diff; PS 229 S
ⲥⲉⲡⲁⲥⲱϣⲙ...ⲛⲥⲉϧⲉ, TU 43 12 A ⲡⲉⲧⲁϧϧ., Mani H
68 A² ⲁϥϧ. ⲡϣⲁⲗⲧ ⲛⲥ[ⲁⲡ, Mani 1 A² ⲟⲩⲏⲡⲥ ⲡⲏⲓ
ⲁϥϧⲉⲓ, DeV 2 88 B ⲁϥϧ. ⲛϫⲉ ⲡⲓϫⲱⲗⲟⲡ, Mor 39 13
S/ ⲡⲧⲉⲣⲉϥϧ., F Petrie fragm Athribis F ϯ ⲧⲱϣ ⲉⲧ-
ϫⲁⲁⲓ (ⲙ)ⲙⲁⲡ ⲡϣⲁⲥϧⲉⲉⲓ; qual: Jud 20 29 S π.,
Ps 144 14 S(B ϧⲉⲓ) καταπ.; ib 145 8 S(B ⲣⲱϧⲧ) κα-
ταρρηγ.; Ja 3 2 SB πτ.; Lev 22 24 S(B ϣⲱⲧ ⲉⲃⲟⲗ)
ἐκτομίας; Va 57 12 B ⲡⲓⲣϧⲏⲟⲩⲓ ⲉⲧϧ. τὰ σφόδρα ἀπειρημένα; Tri 357 S ⲧⲉⲕⲗϫⲩⲭⲓⲓⲁ ⲉⲧϧ. ابلي; Mus
42 228 S ⲡⲉⲧϧ. opp ⲡⲉⲧⲥⲟⲩⲧⲱⲛ, AM 223 B ⲡⲁⲥϧ.
ⲡⲉ ⲉⲥⲡⲁⲙⲟⲩ.
With following preposition.
—— ⲉ- SAA²B, upon, into: Lev 11 35 B(S ⲉϧⲣⲁⲓ
ⲉ-) π. ἐπί, Ps 77 28 SB π. εἰς, ib 140 10 B(S ϧⲛ-) π.
ἐν, ib 7 16 B(S ϧⲣ. ⲉ-), Pro 12 13 SAB ἐμπ. εἰς; PS
30 S ⲉⲩϣⲁⲛϧⲉ ⲉⲑⲓⲙⲁⲣⲙⲉⲛⲏ, CA 98 S ⲛϥϧⲉ ⲉⲩ-
ⲑⲗⲓⲯⲓⲥ, Mani K 23 A² ϧⲁϧ. ⲁⲡⲕⲁϧ; qual: ShC
42 82 S ⲡⲣⲱⲙⲉ ⲉⲧϧ. ⲉⲣⲉⲛⲡⲟϭ ⲙⲡⲉⲑⲟⲟⲩ, Bodl
Marsh 32 74 B face ϧ. ⲉⲡⲕⲁϧⲓ.
—— ⲉϫⲛ- SAA²B, upon: Job 1 19 SB, Ps 139 10
S(B ⲉϧⲣⲏⲓ ⲉϫ.), Mk 4 5 SB π. ἐπί, Jo 18 6 S(A²
ⲁϧⲣ. ⲁϫⲛ-, B ⲉⲡⲉⲥⲏⲧ) π. χαμαί; Pro 26 27 SA κυλίειν ἐπί; Mor 25 25 S ⲁϧⲣⲡⲉ ϧⲉ ⲉϫⲱⲟⲩ = Va 61
120 B ϧⲟⲙϫⲉⲙ ⲉϫ., Mani K 87 A² ϧ. ⲁϫⲙⲡⲕⲁϧ,
TstAb 178 B ⲁϥϧ. ⲉ. ⲡⲟⲩϧⲟ, Mor 31 254 S ϧⲉ ⲉ.
(prob l ϧⲓϫⲛ-) ⲡⲉϥϧⲧⲟ = BMEA 10578 F ⲥⲉⲧϥ ⲉⲃⲟⲗ
ϧⲓϫⲛ- = Ryl Bull 11 416 b رجل من; qual: MG 25

5 B tears ϧ. ⲉ.ⲡⲕⲁϧⲓ π. ἐπί, Job 4 13 S(B diff) ἐπιπ.
ἐπί; BMis 514 S ⲉⲩϧ. ⲉ.ⲡⲣϥⲣ ⲛⲟⲃⲉ.
—— ⲛⲥⲁ- SB, from: MG 25 206 B ⲁⲟⲅⲓ ϧ. ⲛ-
ⲥⲱⲟⲩ ἐν ἔπεσεν ἐξ αὐτῶν; ShA 1 431 ⲉϥϧⲉ ⲛⲥⲁⲡⲁϧ-
ⲟⲩ, Va 64 180 B (HL 120 om) purse ⲁⲥϧ. ⲛⲥⲁⲟⲩⲁⲓ
hath dropped from some one.
—— ⲛⲧⲛ- S, away from: Mk 7 28 (var ⲉⲃⲟⲗ ϧⲓⲧⲛ-,
B Gk om, cf Mt 15 27), ShViK 9343 78 thing he had
made ⲁϥϧⲉ ⲛⲧⲟⲟⲧϥ, BIF 13 112 ϧⲙⲡⲧⲣⲉϥϫⲁⲙ-
ⲟⲩⲗ ϧⲉ ⲛⲧⲟⲟⲧϥ when he lost camel.
—— ϧⲁ- S v c ϧⲁⲣⲁⲧ⸗.
—— ϧⲛ-, ϧⲉⲛ-, into: Ps 34 8 B(S ϧⲣⲁⲓ ϧⲛ-), Ez
27 27 SB π. ἐν, Job 24 23 SB π. dat, EpJer 54 BF
ἐμπ. εἰς; PS 141 S ⲁϥϧⲉ ⲙⲡⲉⲭ̇ⲁⲟⲥ, Z 284 S ⲉⲣϣⲁⲛⲡⲣⲱⲙⲉ ϧⲉ ϧⲙⲡⲛⲟⲃⲉ, Cat 13 B lest we ϧ. ϧⲉⲛ-
ϧⲗⲓ ⲙⲡⲁⲑⲟⲥ, BIF 14 153 S ⲡⲣⲣⲟ ϫⲉ ⲁϥϧⲉ ϧⲙ-
ⲡϣⲁϫⲉ fell into the talk, was beguiled; qual: Job 41
10 S(B Gk diff), Cat 27 B ⲉⲩϧ. ϧⲉⲛⲡⲓⲡⲓⲣⲁⲥⲙⲟⲥ; ϧⲣⲁⲓ ϧⲛ-, ⲛϧⲣ. ϧⲉⲛ-: Ps 34 8 S ut sup, Jer 27 30 B
π. ἐν.
—— ϧⲁⲣⲁⲧ⸗, ϧ., below: Ps 17 39 B(S ϧⲁ-) π.
ὑπό, ib 44 5 S(B diff) π. ὑποκάτω, Jud 5 27 S κατα-
κυλίειν ἀνὰ μέσον; BMis 485 S ⲁⲡⲉⲓⲱ ϧⲉ ϧⲁⲣⲁⲧϥ
ⲙⲡⲟϫⲉⲓⲧ.
—— ϧⲁⲧⲛ- S, before: JAOS 48 148 ⲁϥϧⲉ ϧⲁ-
ⲧⲟⲟⲧⲕ ϧⲓⲡⲙⲁ ⲙⲙⲓϣⲉ.
—— ϧⲓϫⲛ- SBF, upon: 1 Kg 17 49 B(S ⲉϧⲣⲁⲓ
ⲉϫⲛ-), Ez 29 5 B(S ⲉϫⲛ-) π. ἐπί; PO 11 336 B ϧ. ϧ.
ⲡⲕⲁϧⲓ, Mor 24 5 F sim ϧⲏⲏⲓ; from upon, off: 1 Kg
4 18 S π. ἀπό; Miss 8 258 S ⲁⲡⲉⲕⲱⲧ ϧⲉ ϧ. ⲧⲭⲟ (cf
ⲉⲃⲟⲗ ϧ.).
With following adverb.
—— ⲉⲃⲟⲗ SA²BF, out, away, perish: Ru 3 18 S
π., Ps 36 2 B(S ⲥⲣⲟϥⲣϥ) ἀποπ., Ro 9 6 SB ἐκπ., Ez
22 4 SB παραπ.; Si 2 8 S(B ⲧⲁⲕⲟ) πτ.; Pro 8 33 B
(SA ⲣ ⲛⲟⲃⲟⲗ) ἀποφράσσειν; Ps 30 22 S(B diff) ἀπορρίπτειν; Job 27 6 S(B diff) προιέναι; R 1 4 63 S ⲙⲛ
ⲁⲗⲁⲁⲩ ϧⲉ ⲉⲃ....ⲟⲩⲃⲉⲧⲙⲡⲉⲣⲟ συμβαίνειν; 2 Kg 1
27 S(B ⲧⲁ.), Jo 3 16 SA²(BF do), 1 Cor 8 11 SF(B
do), AP 6 A² ἀπολλύναι; R 1 4 60 whoso hath turned
from demons ϧⲱⲥ ⲛⲧⲁⲩϧⲉ ⲉⲃ. ϧⲓⲧⲙⲡⲛ̅ⲃ̅ = MartIgn
871 B ἀποστάτης θεοῦ; ShBor 246 61 S ⲡⲃⲉⲕⲉ ⲛⲁϧⲉ
ⲉⲃ. ⲁⲛ, BMis 173 S ⲡⲉⲕⲣⲓⲥⲉ ⲛⲁϧⲉ ⲉⲃ. ⲁⲛ = BSM
82 B, Mani 1 A² sleep not ϫⲉⲛⲉⲕ. ⲁⲃ., TT 163 S
ⲁϥϧⲉ ⲉⲃ. ⲙⲡⲟⲩϭⲙⲓⲉ; nn m: Gu 61 S rising after
ⲡϧⲉ ⲉⲃ.; ⲁⲃ. ⲛ- A²: Mani K 122 ⲁⲥϧ. ⲁⲃ. ⲙⲡⲥⲁ-
ⲛⲧⲡⲉ; ⲉⲃ. ⲛⲧⲛ-: Ps 7 5 B(S ⲉⲃ. ϧⲓⲧⲛ-) ἀποπ. ἀπό,
Est 6 10 S παραπ. gen; Miss 4 683 S not a verse ϧⲉ
ⲉⲃ. ⲡⲧⲟⲟⲧϥ; ⲉⲃ. ϧⲓ-: Mt 15 27 B(S ⲉⲃ. ϧⲛ-) π.
ἀπό; Ps 2 12 S(B ⲧⲁ.) ἀπολ. ἐκ; ShA 1 375 S dead
limbs ⲁⲩϧⲉ ⲉⲃ. ϧⲓⲱⲟⲩ ⲟⲩⲁ ⲟⲩⲁ (cf ib ⲡⲟⲧⲡⲉⲧ ⲉⲡⲉⲥⲏⲧ); ⲉⲃ. ϧⲛ-, ϧⲉⲛ-: Si 14 2 S π. ἀπό, Mk 13 25
SBⳁF, Ap 8 10 S(B ⲉⲡⲉⲥⲏⲧ ⲉⲃ. ϧⲉⲛ-) π. ἐκ, Ac 9 18

SB ⲁⲡⲟⲡ. ⲁⲡⲟ́, Jth 6 9 *S* ⲇⲓⲁⲡ. gen, Is 28 1 *SB* ⲉⲕⲡ. ⲉⲕ; Lu 21 18 *S*(*B* ⲧⲁ.) ⲁⲡⲟⲗ. ⲉⲕ; PS 87 *S* ⲟⲩϭⲟⲙ ⲉⲁⲥϩⲉ ⲉϩ. ϩⲛⲡⲁⲣⲭⲱⲛ, BAp 157 *S* ⲁϥϩⲉ ⲉϩ. ϩⲛⲧⲉⲛⲧⲟⲗⲏ, Mor 56 7 *S* ⲉⲧϩ.† ⲉϩ. ϩⲛⲧⲡⲓⲥⲧⲓⲥ, C 43 176 *B* knives ϩ. ⲉϩ. ϫⲉⲛⲛⲉⲛϫⲓⲝ, BM 311 104 *S* not a tooth ϩⲉ ϩⲛ (for ⲉϩ. ϩⲛ) ⲧⲉϥⲧⲁⲡⲣⲟ; nn m: ShRE 10 159 *S* ⲡϩⲉ ⲉϩ. ϩⲛⲟⲩⲙⲛⲧⲡⲁⲣⲑⲉⲛⲟⲥ; ⲉϩ. ϩⲓϫⲛ-: Deu 22 8 *B*(*S* ⲉϩ. ϩⲛ-), Ac 20 9 *S*(*B* ⲉⲡⲉⲥⲏⲧ ϫⲉⲡ-) ⲡ. ⲁⲡⲟ́; Mor 48 91 *S* ⲁϥϩⲉ ϩ.ⲡⲕⲱⲧ = C 43 144 *B*, BMEA 10578 *F* ϩⲛⲏⲓ...ⲉϩ. ϩ.ⲡⲉϥϩⲁⲣⲙⲁ = Mor 31 254 *S* ⲉⲡⲉⲥⲛⲧ ϩ., AM 297 *B* pillar crushing martyr ⲁϥϩ. ⲉϩ. ϩⲓϫⲱϥ *fell off him.*

—— ⲉⲡⲉⲥⲏⲧ *SA²B, down*: Jer 26 12 *B*(*S* om), Lu 10 18 *S*(*B* om) ⲡ. only; Jo 18 6 *B*(*S* diff, *A²* ⲁϫⲙⲡⲕⲁϩ) ⲡ. χⲁⲙⲁⲓ́; AP 28 *A²* ϩ. ⲁⲡⲉⲥ[ⲏⲧ, AM 145 *B* stones ϩ. ⲉⲡ.; nn m: Mor 34 70 *S* ⲡϩⲉ ⲉⲡ. ⲡⲧⲗⲟⲓϩⲉ; ⲉ. ⲉ-: PS 115 *S* ⲁⲩϩⲉ ⲉ. ⲉⲣⲟⲟⲩ (*cf* OdSolom 5 9); ⲉ. ⲉϫⲡ-: Is 10 4 *B* ⲡ. ⲩⲡⲟⲕⲁⲧⲱ; BHom 86 *S* ϩⲉ ⲉ.ⲉϫⲙⲡⲕⲁϩ, Mor 31 210 *S* ⲉⲧⲉⲧⲛϩ.† ⲉ. ⲉϫⲉⲛⲡⲉⲧⲡⲉⲣⲏⲩ (var Wess 9 51 ⲑⲓⲛⲩ ⲉϫⲡ-); ⲉ. ϩⲣⲁⲓ ϩⲛ-: PS 25 *S* ⲁⲩϩⲉ ⲉ. ϩ. ϩⲛⲡⲁⲓⲱⲛ; ⲉ. ϩⲓϫⲡ-: Dan 8 17 *B* ⲡ. ⲉⲡⲓ́; LMär 25 *S* ϩⲉ ⲉ. ϩ. ⲡⲕⲁϩ, AM 158 *B* sim, C 99 166 *S* ϩⲉ ⲉ. ϩ. ⲟⲩϫⲉⲡⲉⲡⲱⲣ *down from.*

—— ⲉϩⲣⲁⲓ *SAA²BF, down*: Ez 13 11 *S*(*B* om ⲉϩ.), 12 *SB*, Am 9 11 *SA*(*B* do) ⲡ., Ac 28 6 *S*(*B* do) ⲕⲁⲧⲁⲡ.; R 2 40 *S* ϩⲗⲗⲟ ⲉⲧϩ.† ⲉϩ. in street, AP 21 *A²* ⲁϥϩ. ⲁϩ., AM 186 *B* stumble & ϩ. ⲉϩ.; ⲉ. ⲉ-: Lev 11 33 *S*(*B* ⲉϩ. ϫⲉⲡ-), Lam 1 7 (*F* ⲓ ϩⲗⲏⲓ ⲉ-), Dan 3 23 *B*(*S* ⲉ- only), Mt 17 15 *S*(*B* ⲉ- only) ⲡ. ⲉⲓⲥ, Ps 7 15 *S*(*B* do), Pro 13 17 *S*(*A* ⲧⲱⲙⲧ, *B* ⲣⲁⲟⲅⲱ), 1 Tim 6 9 *SB* ⲉⲙⲡ. ⲉⲓⲥ, Va 57 14 *B* ϩ. ⲉϩ. ⲉⲧⲕⲁⲕⲓⲁ ⲕⲁⲧⲁⲡ. ⲡⲣⲟ́ς, Pro 11 5 *SA*(*B* ⲣⲁⲟⲅⲱ ϫⲉⲡ-), Bor 239 58 *S* ϩⲉ ⲉϩ. ⲉϥϣⲱⲡⲉ (var ⲉ- only) ⲡⲉⲣⲓⲡ. dat; J 106 61 *S* sim ϩⲉⲉ, BHom 3 *S* ⲡⲡⲉⲕϩⲉ ⲉϩ. ⲉⲩⲥⲩⲛⲏⲑⲓⲁ, DeV 2 79 *B* ϩ. ⲉϩ. ⲉⲟⲩⲧⲁⲕⲟ, Pcod F 39 ϩ. ⲉϩ. ⲉⲡϣⲓⲕ, ST 393 *Sᵃ* ϩ. ⲁϩⲣⲏ ⲁⲧⲙ[; ⲉ. ⲉϫⲡ-: Nu 14 5 *S*(*B* ϩⲓⲟⲅⲓ ⲉϫ.), Ps 139 11 *B*(*S* ⲉϫⲡ- only), Sa 18 23 *S*†, Mt 13 5 *S*(*B* ⲉϫ. only), Ap 6 16 *SBF*(Lacau), *ib* 7 16 *S*(*B* ⲓ ⲉϫ.) ⲡ. ⲉⲡⲓ́, Jo 12 24 *SA²*(prob, *B* ⲉϫ. only) ⲡ. ⲉⲓⲥ, Jos 2 9 *S*, Ps 68 9 *S*(*B* ⲓ ⲉϩ. ⲉϫ.) ⲉⲡⲓⲡ. ⲉⲡⲓ́, Sa 7 3 *S* ⲕⲁⲧⲁⲡ. ⲉⲡⲓ́; PS 23 *S* fear ϩⲉ ⲉϩ. ⲉϫⲱⲟⲩ, C 43 173 *B* flesh ϩ. ⲉϩ. ⲉ. ⲡⲓⲕⲁⲣⲓ; ⲉ. ⲡⲧⲡ-: Bor 240 58 *S* only strong can bear hardships ⲡⲟⲩϣⲙ ⲉⲧⲣⲉⲡⲉⲩⲥⲱⲙⲁ ϩⲉ ⲉϩ. ⲡⲧⲟⲟⲧⲟⲩ *collapse*; ⲉ. ϩⲓⲣⲛ-: 1 Kg 21 13 *S*† ⲡ. ⲉⲡⲓ́.

—— nn m *SAA²BF, fall, destruction*: EstC 22 *S*, Is 17 1 *SB*, Nah 3 3 *B*(*A* ϩⲁⲧⲃⲉⲥ) ⲡⲧⲱ̂ⲥⲓⲥ, Jer 22 21 *B* ⲡⲁⲣⲁ́ⲡⲧ., Job 31 29 *SB*, Is 30 13 *SBF* ⲡⲧⲱ̂ⲙⲁ, Ps 143 14 *S*(*B* ⲟⲩⲱϫⲡ) ⲕⲁⲧⲁ́ⲡⲧ., Zech 9 5 *S*(ShA 2 334) *AB* ⲡⲁⲣⲁ́ⲡⲧ.; Hab 2 15 *B*(*S* ShClPr 22 364 ⲧⲁⲕⲟ) ⲁⲛⲁⲧⲣⲟⲡⲏ́; Lu 6 49 *SB* ⲣⲏ̂ⲅⲙⲁ; Pro 18 7 *S* (Miss 8 189, var ⲟⲩⲱϣϥ) ⲥⲩⲛⲧⲣⲓⲃⲏ́; ShA 2 49 *S* ⲉⲣⲉ-

ⲡϩⲉ ⲟⲩⲏϩ ⲡⲥⲱⲟⲩ, Sh(?)ViK 911 *S* ϩⲉ ⲡⲓⲙ ⲉⲅⲥⲗⲉϩⲗⲱϭ, Cat 229 *B* if heretics say thus ⲟⲩϩ. ⲡⲱⲟϩⲡⲉ, K 54 *B* ⲡⲓϩ. ⲡⲧⲉ ⲡⲓⲥⲓⲟⲩ ⲯ٭٭ٮ٭٭ *setting.*

ⲁⲧϩ. *SB, without falling, indestructible*: MG 25 347 *B* ⲡⲓⲕⲁⲣⲓ ⲟⲩⲁ. ⲡⲉ(ROC 17 372 ٭٭٭٭,...٭.٭ٮٮ٭ ٭٭),R 1 2 26 *S* ⲡⲓⲥⲧⲓⲥ...ⲡⲁ., BM 151 *S* ⲥⲡⲟⲧⲟⲩ ⲡⲁ.; ⲙⲛⲧⲁ.: BHom 57 *S* ⲧⲙ. ⲡⲧⲁⲣⲉⲧⲏ; ⲟ ⲡⲁ.: BM 982 *S* city ⲉⲥⲟ ⲡⲁ., BodlMarsh 32 115 *B* ϩⲣⲟⲙⲟⲥ ⲉϥⲟⲓ ⲡⲁ.

ϭⲓⲡ-, ϫⲓⲡϩ. *SB, act of falling*: BHom 12 *S* ⲧⲉⲩϭ. ⲡⲓ́ⲡⲧⲉⲓⲛ, *ib* 44 *S* flee from ⲧⲉⲩϭ. ⲡⲧⲱ̂ⲙⲁ; BMis 419 *S* ⲧⲁϭ. ⲙⲛⲧⲁϭⲓⲛⲧⲱⲟⲩⲡ = BSM 60 *B* ⲡⲁϫ., C 86 162 *B* God had patience with ⲡⲉϥϫ.; Va 57 9 *B* ⲡⲓϫ. ⲉϩ. ϫⲉⲛⲡⲓⲁⲧϩⲟⲡ ⲉⲕⲡⲓ́ⲡ. gen.

B *light upon, find* SF(*B* mostly ϫⲓⲙⲓ), ⲥ ⲉ- obj: Ge 2 20, Ps 36 36 (*A* Cl *B* ϭⲓⲛⲉ, ϫ.), Mt 13 44 (*BF* do) ⲉⲩⲣⲓ́ⲥⲕⲉⲓⲛ; Job 7 2 ⲧⲩⲅⲭⲁⲛⲉⲓⲛ, BHom 49 ⲕⲁⲧⲁⲧ.; Lev 25 26 ⲉⲩⲡⲟⲣⲉⲓ̂ⲛ (*cf* 28 ϭ.), Sa 5 13, Mt 13 27 (*BF* do) ⲉ́ⲭⲉⲓⲛ; Nu 11 13 ϩⲉ ⲧⲱⲛ ⲡⲟ́ⲑⲉⲛ; Pro 25 8 (*A* ϭ.) passive ⲡⲣⲟⲥⲡⲓ́ⲡ. ⲉⲓⲥ; PS 42 ⲁⲓϩⲉ ⲉⲧⲡⲓⲥⲧⲓⲥ, BG 83 ⲙⲛ ⲗⲁⲁⲩ ⲡⲁϣ ϩⲉ ⲉⲧⲙⲉ, Pcod 23 ⲥⲉⲡⲁϩⲉ ⲉⲣⲟϥ ⲉⲟⲩⲉⲧ (var ϭⲓⲧⲥ ϫⲉ-), BHom 64 ϣⲁⲩϩⲉ ⲉⲣⲟϥ ⲛϭⲩⲡⲓⲣⲉⲧⲏⲥ, BAp 161 we thought thee sheep ⲁⲛϩⲉ ⲉⲣⲟⲕ ⲡⲟⲩⲱⲡϣ, BM 1128 ⲁⲙⲟⲩ ⲧⲁϩⲉ (ⲉ)ⲡⲉⲕϣⲓⲛⲉ (*cf* ϭⲙ ⲡⲱ. & ⲟⲩⲱ ⲡ 475 a), CO 472 *Sᵃ* ⲡⲥⲕⲉⲅⲉ ⲡⲧⲁϩ. ⲉⲣⲟⲟⲩ, BM 594 (2) *F* ⲉⲓⲡⲁϩⲏ ⲉⲗⲁ[; ⲥ pleonastic ⲉⲣⲟⲥ: Aeg 17 ⲁⲓϩⲉ ⲉⲣⲟⲥ ⲁⲧⲉⲕⲙⲛⲧⲡⲉ ⲧⲁⲣⲟϥ, Hall 108 ⲁⲛϩⲉ ⲉ. ⲉⲁⲧⲉⲕϣⲉⲉⲣⲉ ⲙⲟⲩ, RE 9 137 ⲕⲡⲁϩⲉ ⲉ. ϫⲉⲡⲓⲙ ⲡⲉⲡⲧⲁϥⲣ ϣⲟⲣⲡ, AZ 23 71 ⲕⲡⲁϩⲉⲉ. ⲉⲓⲁⲓ (*l* ⲉⲁⲓⲉⲓ) ⲉⲃⲟⲗ, Kr 228 ⲁⲓϩⲉ (ⲉ)ⲣⲟⲥ ⲡⲡⲟϭⲓⲣ ϩⲱϥ; qual: Is 58 3, Jo 19 6 (*cf* Lu 23 4 ϭⲡ-) ⲉⲩ́.; BMar 211 if thirsty ⲧⲏⲣ. ⲉⲙⲟⲟⲩ = Rec 6 175 *B* ϫⲉⲙ ⲙⲱⲟⲩ, C 100 326 ⲧⲏⲣ. ⲉⲙⲱⲅⲥⲛⲉ ⲁϥⲟⲩϩⲣⲥⲁϩⲛⲉ, Pcod 5 ⲧⲏⲣ. ⲉⲡ‾ⲭ‾ⲥ‾ ⲉϥⲭⲱ ⲙⲙⲟⲥ; ⲥ ⲡⲥⲁ-, *with, in possession of*: Ex 21 17 (*B* ϫ. ϫⲉⲡ-) ⲉⲩ́. ⲉ́ⲛ; ShC 73 134 if one earn not own bread ⲡⲥⲉϩⲉ ⲉⲕⲉⲟⲉⲓⲕ ⲡⲥⲱϥ, Ryl 305 ϣⲁⲡⲧⲉⲡⲉϩⲉ ⲉϩⲟⲗ ⲡⲥⲱⲡ, BM 239 5 ⲙⲡⲟⲩϩⲉ ⲉϣⲧⲏⲛ ⲥⲡⲧⲉ ⲡⲥⲱϥ (*cf* Jo 19 23); ϭⲓⲡϩⲉ: BMar 123 ⲧⲉⲩϩ. ⲉⲡⲉϥⲉⲣⲏⲣⲏ ⲁⲛⲉⲩ́ⲣⲉⲥⲓⲥ.

tr: PMich 4552 *S*(archaic) ⲁⲛϣⲓⲛⲉ ⲁⲛϩⲉⲥ ϫⲏ-.

V ⲧϩⲓⲟ.

ϩⲉ *SA²*, ϩⲓⲏ *S*, ϩⲉ *A*, ϫⲉ *B* (rare, mostly ⲣⲏϯ), ϩⲏ *S*/*F*, ϩⲓ *F* nn f, *manner* (Coptic locution often does not correspond with Gk): Deu 13 10 ⲕⲱⲧⲉ ⲡⲥⲁⲑⲉ ⲡ- *seek how to* (*B* om), Est 2 21 sim ϩⲓⲏ, Ac 11 4 ⲧⲁϩⲉ ⲑⲉ *recount* (*B* diff) ⲉ́ⲕⲧⲓⲑⲉ́ⲛⲁⲓ, R 1 3 16 ⲧⲁⲙⲟϥ ⲉⲑⲉ, BMis 267 sim ⲉⲧⲃⲉⲑⲉ, Jud 18 4 ⲉⲓⲥ ⲑⲉ ⲟⲩ̂ⲧⲱⲥ, Lu 8 36 told them ⲉⲑⲉ ⲉⲡⲧⲁ- ⲡⲱ̂ς, Miss 4 650 ⲑⲉ ⲉϣⲁⲣⲉⲡⲧⲩⲣⲁⲛⲛⲟⲥ ⲧⲱⲟⲩⲡ ⲉϫⲱϥ ⲙⲙⲟⲥ, Mor 28 76 *S*/ ⲑⲏ ⲉⲧⲥⲏⲣ ⲉⲃⲟⲗ ⲙⲡⲡⲓϣⲧⲟⲣⲧⲣ ⲉⲧϣⲟⲟⲡ, BM 1013 8 ⲡϥⲭⲣⲱ ⲡⲁⲩ ⲡϩⲉ ⲡⲓⲙ ϩⲓⲟⲩⲱϣ, *ib* 1116 ⲁⲓⲉⲓⲙⲉ ⲉϩⲉ ⲡⲓⲙ ⲉⲧⲁⲕⲥϩⲁⲓ ⲡⲁⲓ ⲉϫⲱⲥ, DeV 1

96 B ϯϩⲉ ⲉⲧⲉⲕⲟⲩⲁϣⲥ, J&C 92 ⲙⲡⲉϩⲉ ϣⲱⲡⲉ [ⲛⲧ]ⲁⲧⲁⲡⲟⲟⲩ, MG 25 33 B ϩⲁⲣⲁ ⲟⲩⲟⲛ ⲟⲩϩⲉ ϣⲟⲡ *what is meaning of?*, PS 7 ϣⲟⲗⲧⲉ ⲛⲣⲉ ⲡⲟⲩⲟⲉⲓⲛ; ϩⲉ ⲩ ⲙⲁⲛⲕ; ⲧⲁⲓⲧⲉ ⲑⲉ, *this is the way, thus*: Ps 60 8, Is 30 15 SF, Jo 3 8 SA²F ⲟⲩⲧ.; El 86 A ⲧ. ⲉⲧϥⲡⲡⲏⲩ, BIF 13 108 ⲉϣϫⲉ ⲧ. ⲁⲙⲏⲓⲧⲛ = MG 25 295 B ⲡⲁⲓⲣⲏϯⲡⲉ, BM 998 ⲑⲉⲧⲉ ⲧⲁⲓ; Ps 1 4 ⲛⲧⲁⲓ ⲁⲛⲧⲉ ⲑⲉ ⲟⲩⲭ ⲟⲩⲧ., Mani K 50 A² ⲧⲣⲉ ⲣⲱϥ ⲁⲛⲧⲉ ⲧⲉⲓ; ⲧⲉⲓⲣⲉ, ⲧⲁⲓϩ.: Mt 1 18 ⲡⲉϥⲧ. ⲡⲉ ⲟⲩⲧ.; ἦν; ShViK 9346 ⲧ. ⲧⲉ ⲁⲅⲩⲓⲧⲟⲩ ⲧ. ⲧⲉ ⲙⲡⲟⲩϭⲓⲧⲟⲩ; *iterated*: C 89 8 B ⲡⲁⲓⲣⲱⲃ ⲛⲧ. ⲧ. ⲁⲛⲡⲉ ἁπλῶς (*var* μικρόν); ⲟⲩⲛ ⲑⲉ, *there is a way, it is possible*: Si 22 23 ⲟⲩ. ⲡⲣⲱⲧⲛ ἔστι; BHom 10 ⲟⲩ. ⲉⲧⲣⲉⲛⲙⲉⲧⲁⲛⲟⲉⲓ, Ep 233 ⲉ‌ϣⲱⲡⲉ ⲟⲩ. ⲡⲉⲧⲉⲧⲛⲁ, ib 341 *send answer* ⲉϣⲱⲡⲉ ⲟⲩ.; ⲙⲛ ⲑⲉ, *there is not a way*: Eccl 3 14 ⲙ. ⲉⲟⲩⲱϩ, Is 1 6 SF ⲙ. ⲛϯ ⲟⲩⲕ ἔ., Ep 141 ⲙ. ⲛⲥⲣⲁⲓ ϩⲁⲣ, BMis 506 ⲙ. ⲉⲧⲣⲉϥⲟⲩⲱⲙ.

ⲛ‌ⲑⲉ ⲛ-, *in manner of, even as*: Hos 10 7 SA, Mk 13 34 SF ὡς, Ps 37 20 ὡσεί, Job 2 10, Pro 1 12 SA ὥσπερ, Mt 12 4 πῶς, ib 23 37 ὃν τρόπον, Sa 11 15 ὅμοιος, R 1 1 17 ⲛ. ⲛϣⲟⲣⲡ τὸ σχῆμα τὸ πρῶτον, Sa 7 1 ⲛ. ⲡⲟⲩⲟⲡ ⲛⲓⲙ ἴσος, ib 12 24 δίκην; PS 25 ϣⲱⲡⲉ ⲛ. ⲛⲡⲓⲣⲙⲛⲕⲁϩ, ShC 73 22 ⲛ. ⲛⲧⲁⲓⲁⲕⲱⲃ ϫⲟⲟⲥ, AP 24 A² ⲛ. ⲡⲟⲩⲅⲉⲉⲓ ⲛϣⲙⲙⲟ, ViK 9504 *heretics confess not* ⲛ. ⲛⲁⲡⲟⲛ ⲉⲡⲣⲟⲙⲟⲗⲟⲅⲉⲓ, BMar 13 *thou lovest none* ⲛ. ⲛⲁⲛⲟⲕ ⲙⲛⲛⲁⲡⲉ, BM 355 318 ⲟⲩⲡⲉ ⲡⲉϥⲃⲱⲗ ⲛ. ⲉⲧⲕⲙⲉⲉⲩⲉ ⲉⲣⲟⲥ?; *iterated*: ShR 2 365 ⲛ. ⲑⲉ ⲛⲧⲁⲡⲭ̅ⲥ̅ ⲣ ϩⲛⲕⲉ; ⲛⲑⲉ *before prep or advb*: BM 267 ⲛ. ⲉⲝⲟⲟⲥ *so to speak*, Lev 16 24 ⲛ. ⲉϫⲛ- ὡς, Jth 14 5 ⲛ. ⲉϩⲟⲩⲛ ⲉ- ὡς, Sa 5 22 ⲛ. ⲉⲃⲟⲗ ϩⲛ- ὡς, R 2 2 64 *sim*, Ap 2 27 ⲛ. ⲉ‌ϣⲙⲁⲅⲟⲩⲱϣⲡ ὡς; *without preceding* ⲛ-: Job 1 21, Hos 11 11 A ὡς, Cl 56 15 A ὥσπερ; Mani K 29 A² ⲧⲣⲉ ⲉⲧⲁⲓⲟⲩⲱⲛϩ ⲛⲏⲧⲛ ⲁⲃⲁⲗ, Mani 1 A² ⲧⲁϫⲁϥ ⲧ. ⲛⲛⲓⲁⲥⲉⲃⲏⲥ, ST 201 ⲑⲉ ⲉⲧⲉⲣⲡⲁϫⲓⲧϥ.

ⲛⲧⲉⲓϩⲉ, *in this way, thus, of this sort*: Nu 2 34, 3 Kg 22 20, Mk 15 39 F, Cl 12 4 A οὕτως, Sa 13 9 τοσοῦτος, Si 20 14 (*var* ⲁⲓⲡⲉ), Job 8 18, AP 8 A² τοιοῦ., Lu 6 26 κατὰ τὰ αὐτά, Ap 8 12 ὁμοίως; Ep Jer 27 F ὡσαύτως; PS 56 ⲉⲥϫⲱ ⲙⲙⲟⲥ ⲛ. *as follows*, ShC 42 83 ⲡⲉⲡⲣⲟⲟⲩ ⲁⲛⲡⲉ ⲣⲱⲃ ⲛ., CO 481 ⲉⲓⲣⲟⲙⲟⲗⲟⲅⲉⲓ ⲛ....ϫⲉ-, DeV 2 113 B ϥⲃⲱⲗ ⲙⲡⲓⲥⲁϫⲓ ⲉⲧⲁϥϫⲟⲩ ⲛ. ϫⲉ-, BMis 532 ⲛⲧⲕⲛⲓⲙ ⲛ. ⲡⲁ‌ⲭ̅ⲥ̅?; *without* ⲛ-: El 102 A ϯⲅⲉ ⲟⲩⲛ ⲟⲩϩⲙⲁⲧ ⲛⲁⲣⲱⲡⲉ; *cf* Mani K 101 A² ⲧⲣⲉ ϫⲉⲙⲡⲉⲟⲩⲣⲱⲙⲉ ⲡⲟⲩⲱⲧ ϣ ϭⲣⲟ; ϯⲧⲏⲣⲥ SB, *so greatly, so much* (*mostly in question*): Z 303 S *why do demons fight with us* ⲛ. ⲧ. ? οὕτως, BM 174 1 S *fire* ⲉⲧⲟϣ ⲛ. ⲧ. οὗτος λάβρος; ShCai 8007 264 S ⲉϣϫⲉ ⲛⲡⲉ̅ ⲡⲁⲕⲁⲁⲡ ⲡⲥⲱ ⲛ. ⲧ.?, HM 1 1 S ⲉⲓⲉ ϩⲉⲛⲁⲧⲥⲟⲗⲡⲉ ⲡⲉⲕⲡⲉ ⲛ. ⲧ.?, MIE 2 345 B *importuned him* ⲛ. ⲧ. (PO 22 361 ⲓⲟⲁ), C 43 112 B ⲛ‌ⲑⲟⲕ ⲟⲩⲁ‌ϩⲡⲟⲩⲧ ⲛ. ⲧ.?, Ep 174 S *not right* ⲛⲟⲩϩⲱⲛ (ⲛ)ⲧ. ⲧ.; ϯϩⲁⲡⲗⲱⲥ, ⲁⲡ. SB, *merely thus*: C 99

234 S = 89 69 B *not king* ⲛ. ϱ. οὐ μόνον ἀπ., Va 57 7 B ⲟⲩ ⲙⲏⲛ ⲛ. ⲁⲡ ⲁ. ⲁ. ⲟⲩⲧ.; ShC 73 196 S ⲉⲧ‌ⲟ‌ⲩⲱⲙ ⲁⲡ ϱ. ⲁⲗⲗⲁ ⲥⲉⲧⲱⲣⲡ, Cat 5 B ⲟⲩⲥⲓⲟⲩ ⲁⲛⲡⲉ ⲛ. ⲁ.; ϯϣⲏⲙ *v* ϣⲏⲙ *as adj* b.

With poss pron ⲛⲧⲁ‌ϩⲉ, ⲛⲧⲉⲕϩⲉ &c: Lev 19 18 *love neighbour* ⲛⲧⲉⲕϩⲉ, Ac 10 47 *have received* ⲛⲧⲉⲛϩⲉ, Ap 6 11 *slain* ⲛⲧⲉⲩϩⲉ ὡς, Deu 3 20 *your brethren* ⲛⲧⲉⲧⲛϩⲉ ὥσπ., Mt 24 21 *been none* ⲛⲧⲉⲥϩⲉ οἷος, Joel 2 2 SA, Jo 8 55 SA² *liar* ⲛⲧⲉⲧⲛϩⲉ ὅμοιος, He 4 15 (B ⲥⲙⲟⲧ) -ότης, Job 9 32 *man* ⲛⲧⲁϩⲉ κατά, *cf ib* 36 22, BMar 202 *put upon him rags* ⲛⲧⲉⲩϩⲉ *as before* πάλιν: ShBor 246 37 *serpent turned again to rod* ⲛϣⲱⲡⲉ ⲛⲧⲉϥϩⲉ, Mor 24 7 F *he shall* ϣⲱⲡⲓ ⲛⲕⲉⲣⲓ ⲛⲧⲉⲃⲏⲣ, BMis 64 *Elizabeth returned to* ϫⲱⲣⲓⲛ (ὀρεινή) ⲛⲧⲉⲥϩⲉ, P 129¹⁹ 30 ϯⲛⲁⲧⲁⲁⲩ (*sc* loan) ⲛⲧⲉⲩϩⲉ, BMar 12 ⲁⲅⲩⲣⲟ ⲛⲧⲁϩⲉ ϫⲟⲟⲩ ⲡⲟⲩϩⲣⲛⲧⲉⲙⲱⲡ, AZ 21 141 *set him in my house* ⲛⲧⲟ‌ⲡϥ ⲛⲧⲁϩⲉ; *iterated, as heretofore*: Mor 23 10 *will take my spirit from him* (*sc* Adam) ⲛϣⲱⲡⲉ ⲛⲕⲁϩ ⲛⲧⲉϥϩⲉ ⲧⲉϥϩⲉ, Ryl 72 354 *Mary after birth* ⲟ ⲙⲡⲁⲣⲑⲉⲛⲟⲥ ⲛⲧⲉⲥϩⲉ ⲧ., PLond 4 445 *have paid us the money* ⲛⲧⲉϥϩⲉ ⲧ., Mor 51 22 *diseased part* ⲉⲣ ⲧⲉϥϩⲉ ⲧ. ⲛⲑⲉ ⲛϣⲟⲣⲡ.

ⲁϣ ⲛ‌ϩⲉ, *of what sort*: Mk 13 1 ϩⲉⲛⲁ. ⲡⲉ (*var* ϭⲟⲧ) ποταπός; BG 20 ⲟⲩⲁ. ⲡⲉ ⲡⲓⲁⲓⲱⲛ; ⲛⲁϣ ⲛϩⲉ: Job 11 5, Ps 72 11 (B = Gk), Ro 10 14 (BF Mor 43 *do*), Cl 21 8 A, Jo 3 9 SA² (BF *do*) πῶς; PS 21 ⲛ. ⲁϥⲟⲩⲟⲧⲃⲛ ⲉⲃⲟⲗ, ShC 42 91 ϥⲟⲩⲱⲙ ⲛ., *v also* ⲣ ⲑⲉ.

ⲕⲁⲧⲁ ⲑⲉ, *even as, like*: Ps 38 12, Jo 5 30 SA², Cl 16 2 A καθώς, Ps 55 6 καθάπερ, ib 102 12 καθ᾽ ὅσον; PS 36 ⲕ. ⲉϣⲁϥⲁⲁⲥ, ShBor 246 39 ⲕ. ⲉⲧⲧⲱⲙⲛⲧ ⲉⲡϫⲁϫⲉ, El 62 A ⲕ. ⲉⲧⲣⲛⲉϥ, Blake 240 *gave name* ⲕ. ⲛⲧⲁϥϭⲉⲛⲧϥ ⲙⲙⲟⲥ, MIE 2 382 B ⲕ. ⲉⲧⲁϥⲟⲩⲁϩⲥⲁϩⲛⲓ ⲡⲏⲓ, BM 589 7 F ⲕⲁⲧⲁ ⲧⲣⲓ ⲛϣⲟⲣⲡ, CO 128 ⲕ. ⲉⲡⲧⲁⲓⲉⲓ ⲉⲃⲟⲗ ϩⲓⲧⲱⲧⲉ ⲛⲧⲉⲧⲛⲁⲅⲁⲡⲏ, CMSS 45 F ⲕⲁⲧⲁ ⲧⲣⲛ ⲛⲧⲁⲁⲕⲭⲁⲁⲥ; ⲕ. ⲧⲉⲓϩⲉ, *in this way, likewise*: BMar 109 ⲟⲩⲧ., Aeg 223 ὡσαύτως; BAp 141 *odorous plants &* ⲛϩⲩⲛⲡⲱⲣⲁ (ⲟⲡ.) ⲕ., Ep 231 *come in* ⲛⲧⲓⲥⲩⲡⲁⲧⲉ ⲉⲓⲥ ⲛⲡⲟϭ ⲡⲣⲱⲙⲉ ⲟⲛ ⲕ. (*will be there*) *likewise*(?), BMis 462 *lentils, beans & rest of plants* ⲕ.

ⲡⲣⲟⲥ ⲑⲉ, *according as*: BMis 363 ⲡ. ⲉⲧⲉⲕⲙⲉⲉⲩⲉ ⲉⲣⲟⲥ (*var* παρά ⲑⲉ) = BSM 24 B ⲕⲁⲧⲁ ⲡϣⲓ, PLond 4 453 ⲡ. ⲉⲥⲥⲏϩ ⲙⲙⲟⲥ, Kr 41 F ⲡ. ⲙⲡϣⲉⲣ *acc. to price*.

ⲣ ⲑⲉ, *make, be like*: Ps 1 3, Mt 6 5 F (S ϣⲱⲡⲉ ⲛⲑⲉ) εἶναι ὡς, Ps 30 12, ib 87 5 γίνεσθαι ὡς, Job 10 19 γ. ὥσπερ, Hos 4 9 A ⲣ ⲑⲉ ⲡⲗⲁⲟⲥ καθὼς εἰ., AP 7 A² ⲣ. ⲡⲟⲩⲅⲁⲗⲟⲅⲥ ὡς *no vb*; Ps 27 1 ὁμοιοῦσθαι, Lu 12 36 (B ⲓⲛⲓ) ὅμοιος *no vb*, Sa 3 1 δοκεῖν; Ps 72 22 (κτην)ώδης; PS 131 ⲁϥⲣ. ⲉⲛⲉϩⲟ ⲙⲙⲟⲥ ⲛϣⲟⲣⲡ, ShC 73 23 ⲁϥⲣ. ⲙⲡⲉⲧϣⲟⲃϥ, PChas 1 *iron* ⲉⲁⲁϥ ⲛⲑⲉ ⲛⲡⲡⲓⲟⲩϥ; ⲟ ⲛⲑⲉ: Ps 28 6, Ap 13 2 (B ⲓ.) ὡς, Ps 35 6 ὡσεί, Is 44 7 ὥσπ.; BG 96 *had* νοῦς *of own* ⲙⲛⲟⲩⲉⲡⲛⲟⲓⲁ ⲛⲧϩⲉ ⲉⲧϥⲟ ⲙⲙⲟⲥ, ShMun 102 ⲉϥⲟ ⲛⲁϣ

ⲛⲣⲉ, El 50 *A* ⲛϥϩⲱ ⲉ ⲡ. ⲙⲡⲉⲧϫⲏⲕ ⲁⲃⲁⲗ, BMis 485 stood up ⲛⲉϥ ⲉⲧϥⲟ ⲙⲙⲟⲥ *as had been (before)*, Leyd 448 I adjure you all ⲛⲑⲉ ⲉⲧⲉⲧⲛⲟ ⲙⲙⲟⲥ ϩⲓⲟⲩⲥⲟⲡ *howsoever ye be*, Ep 131 shalt find letter enclosed within this one ⲑⲉ ⲉⲧⲥⲟ ⲙⲙⲟⲥ *even as it was*, unaltered (?), PLond 4 516 in list ϣⲙⲟⲩⲛⲉ ⲛⲧⲛϩⲉ ⲑⲉ ⲉⲅⲟ ⲙⲙⲟⲥ sim; with poss: Ps 114 5 (*B* ı.), Pro 26 4 *SA* ⲟ̄ⲙ. γ.; Jth 14 7 ⲛⲧⲉⲣⲉϥ(ⲣ) ⲧⲉϥϩⲉ ὡς ἀνέλαβον αὐτόν *recreatus*, Ryl 72 360 phoenix grows anew ⲛϥⲣ ⲧⲉϥϩⲉ ⲛⲕⲉⲥⲟⲡ, BMis 159 ⲙⲉⲕϣ ⲣ ⲧⲉⲡϩⲉ = BSM 67 *B* ϣⲱⲡⲓ ⲙⲡⲉⲛⲣⲏϯ.

ϯ ⲑⲉ (confused with ϯ ⲧⲉϩⲓⲛ *q v*), *give means*: Nu 20 21 (*B* ϯ ⲉⲑⲣⲉⲩ), 2 Kg 21 10, Lu 1 74 (*B* ⲛ̄ϫⲓⲛ ϯ), Ac 4 29 (*B* ϯ dat) διδόναι inf; 1 Cor 10 13 (*B* diff) ποιεῖν; Wess 15 135 ⲙⲡⲉⲧⲁⲡⲁⲅⲕⲏ ϯ. ⲡⲁⲛ ⲉⲭⲟⲟⲩⲥ συγχωρεῖν; Lu 12 58 ἐργασίαν διδ., Bor 235 57 ϯ. ⲡⲁϥ ⲉⲧⲣⲉϥⲃⲱⲕ τόπον διδ. (*cf* ϯ ⲙⲁ); Jth 11 14 ἄφεσιν μετοικίζειν; Mk 10 4 (*B* ⲟⲩⲁϩⲥⲁϩⲛⲓ, *F* ϯⲡⲥⲉⲙ ⲙⲓ), *cf* Mt 19 8 ϯ ⲧⲉϩⲓⲛ (cit ShC 73 148), He 6 3 do (*B* do), ἐπιτρέπειν; 2 Kg 14 12 ϯ. ⲡⲁⲓ ⲉⲧⲣⲁϣⲁϫⲉ λαλησάτω δή; Z 344 ⲉⲧⲃⲉⲟⲩ ϯⲛⲁ ϯ. ⲡⲁⲩ ⲁⲛ *give them a chance* διώκειν = MG 25 208 *B* ϭⲟϫⲓ ⲛⲥⲱⲟⲩ; ShC 73 x ⲁⲩϯ. ⲛⲏⲧⲛ ⲉⲧⲣⲉⲧⲉⲧⲛⲙⲉⲧⲁⲛⲟⲓ, BAp 79 ⲣϣⲁⲛ ⲡⲭ̅ⲥ̅ ϯ. ⲡⲁⲓ ⲛⲧⲁⲕⲧⲟⲓ = MIE 2 352 *B* ⲉⲣϣⲁⲛ ⲫ ϯ ⲟⲩⲱϣ, *ib* 118 ⲛⲡⲉ ⲉϥⲉ ϯ. ⲡⲁⲕ ⲛⲓⲙⲁⲥ (sc wife) & she will conceive, Ep 105 if God ϯ. ⲡⲁⲓ ⲛⲧⲉⲡⲉⲕϣⲗⲏⲗ ⲧⲁϩⲟⲓ, BM 512 *F* ⲉϥⲉ ϯ. ⲡⲁⲛ (ⲡ)ⲧⲛⲡⲱⲧ.

ϭⲛ ⲑⲉ, *find means*: Ac 4 21 (*B* diff) τὸ πῶς εὑρίσκειν, *ib* 25 16 (*B* ϫⲉⲙ ⲙⲁ) τόπον λαμβάνειν; Ps 141 4 (*B* Gk diff); ShC 42 99 ⲉⲓⲕⲛⲁϭ. ⲛⲥⲱⲧⲙ, ShA 2 276 I wished but ⲙⲡⲓϭ., Ep 198 sim, R 1 2 54 ⲧⲁⲣⲉϥϭ. ⲛⲃⲱⲕ ⲉϩⲟⲩⲛ; *cf* Lu 5 19 ϩⲉ ⲉⲧⲉϩⲓⲛ (*B* ⲣⲏ.) ποῖος, πῶς εὑρ., Mor 31 110 ⲙⲡⲟⲩϭⲉ ⲉⲑⲏ ⲛⲧⲁⲗⲉ ⲡⲟⲉⲓⲕ.

ϫⲓⲛⲑⲉ[1], -ⲉⲑⲉ[2], -ⲉⲑⲏ (once)[3], ϫⲓⲛ(ⲉ)ⲛⲑⲉ[4], *from when (?), since*: Ryl 99 ϫ.[1] ⲛⲧⲁϥⲣ ⲟⲩⲁ ⲛⲟⲩⲱⲧ ⲙⲡⲗⲟⲅⲟⲥ (= PO 2 251 .....), Mor 19 53 ϫ.[1] ⲛⲧⲁⲓⲉⲓ ⲉⲃⲟⲗ (var Wess 18 62 ϫⲓⲛⲧⲁⲓⲉⲓ), Pcod 7 ϫ.[1] ⲉⲡⲧⲁⲩϫⲟⲟⲥ, Ryl 321 7 ϫ.[2] ⲛⲧⲁⲡⲁⲭ̅ⲥ̅ ϭⲣⲁⲓ, BM 1122 ϫ.[2] ⲉⲕⲁⲉⲓ, *ib* 1107 ϫ.[3] ⲛⲧⲁⲓⲉⲓ, Pcod 6 ϫ.[4] ⲉϣⲁⲅϫⲓ, PLond 4 524 ϫ.[4] ⲛⲧⲁⲓϫⲓ. Belongs here? (*cf* ⲕⲁⲧⲁ ⲑⲉ ⲛ- CO 128, Ep 353) or = ? ϩⲛ, ϩⲉ- *season* (Jernstedt) or ϩⲏ *front* (*q v s f* Hyvernat).

ϩⲉ *B* interj, *ho!*: MG 25 212 cried after him saying ϩⲉ ⲡⲑⲟⲕ ⲡⲓϫⲉⲗⲱⲡ αἶ αἶ δαίμων.

ϩⲉ *B*, ϩⲏ *F* nn, *hinder part, back* in ⲥⲁⲙⲉⲛϩⲉ, *v* ⲙⲉⲛϩⲏ, adding ⲛⲥⲁⲡⲉⲛϩ⸗ Mk 8 33 *F*(*S* ⲉⲡⲁϩⲟⲩ, *B* ⲥⲁⲫⲁϩⲟⲩ) ὀπίσω (Spg).

ϩⲉ *S* nn m, *meaning unknown*: *v* PLond 4 in ⲥⲟⲓ 2°.

ϩⲉ *v* ⲉϩⲉ *yea*.

ϩⲉ- in ϩⲉⲃⲱⲱⲛ &c *v* ϩⲛ *season*.

ϩⲉⲓ *BF*, ϩⲉ(ⲉ)ⲓⲉ *AA²* *v* ϩⲉ *fall*.

ϩⲉⲓ *F* *v* ⲉⲓⲥ ⲡ 86 *a* & ϩⲁⲓ.

ϩⲉⲉⲓ *A²F* *v* ϩⲁⲓ & ϩⲁ *winnowing fan*.

ϩⲏ *SBF*, ϩⲓⲏ *S*, ⲉϩⲏ *SA²*, ϩⲓ, ⲉϩⲓ, ⲉϩⲓⲉⲓ *A*, ϩⲓ- *AA²*, ϩⲏⲧ⸗ *SAA²B*, ⲉϩⲏⲧ⸗ *SO*, nn f, *fore part, beginning*, without art: Eccl 10 13 *F*(*S* = Gk), Nah 3 10 *B*, Mt 24 8 *B* = Mk 13 8 (*S* do) ἀρχή; 1 Kg 20 24 *S* ϩⲏ ⲙⲡⲉⲃⲟⲧ νουμηνία, Mor 43 128 *S* sim; Lev 2 14 *B* ϩⲏ ⲛⲧⲉⲡⲉⲕⲟⲩⲧⲁϩ (*S* ⲣⲱⲧ ⲛϣⲟⲣⲡ) πρωτο-, Ora 4 185 *S* ϩⲏ ⲙⲙⲟϥ...ⲡⲁϩⲟⲩ ⲙⲙⲟϥ, *cf* GriffStu 163 *F* ⲧϩⲏ ⲙⲁⲃ, Ostr *penes* Crum *S* bring flax ⲛⲧⲏⲛⲟⲭϥ ⲛϩⲏ ⲉⲛⲕⲉⲣⲉⲁ (κείρ.); as adj: Nu 6 3 *B* ⲁⲗⲟⲗⲓ ⲛϩⲏ ⲛⲗⲱⲕ, Deu 24 5 *B* ϭⲓⲙⲓ ⲛϩⲏ (*S* ϩⲣⲣⲉ) προσφάτως (var καινή); 2 Kg 14 26 *S* ⲡⲧⲱϣ ⲛϩⲏ ⲛⲛⲉϩⲟⲟⲩ ἀρ. ἡμερῶν; CA 88 *S* ⲛϣⲁ ⲛϩⲏ; with art: Ez 27 29 *S* ⲛⲉⲉϥ ⲛϩⲏ (*B* diff) πρωρεύς (*cf* Jon 1 6 *S* ⲉⲧⲟⲣⲓⲏ), Ac 27 41 *S* ⲡⲉϥϩⲏ (*B* ϩⲓⲧⲉ̄ⲛ) πρώρα; J 40 19 *S* ⲡⲥⲓⲡⲡⲟⲥⲓⲟⲛ ⲛϩⲏ; with poss art: Phil 3 13 *SB* ἔμπροσθεν; Is 48 7 *S*(*B* ⲛϣⲟⲣⲡ) πάλαι, JA '88 2 370 *S* ⲛⲁϩⲏ ⲙⲡⲛⲓⲁⲡⲁϩⲟⲩ, J 43 28 *S* ⲧⲭⲏⲣⲉ ⲧⲁϩⲏ.

ϩⲏⲧ⸗ *SAA²*c vb *go, come, look &c forward, fear &c before*: Mt 2 9 (*B* ϩⲁϫⲉⲛ-), Lu 22 47 (var ϩⲁⲑⲏ, *B* do) προ-; Ge 18 2 (var ϩⲁϫⲛ-, *B* ⲉϩⲣⲉⲛ-), Ps 103 27 (*B* ϩⲁⲧϩⲏ), Sa 3 9, Mt 24 50 (*B* ϩⲁϫ.) προσ-, Si 22 28 πρόσωπον; ϫⲓ ⲙⲟⲉⲓⲧ ϩ.: Ps 44 4 (*B* ϭⲓ ⲙ. ⲛ-), Jo 16 13 *SA²*(*B* om) ὁδηγεῖν; ⲉⲓ ⲉⲃⲟⲗ ϩ.: 1 Kg 6 13, Z 317 sim (*B* ϩⲁϫ.) εἰς ἀπάντησιν, Deu 23 4 (*B* ⲉϩ.) συναντᾶν, Jud 11 31 (*B* do) εἰς συνάντησιν; 1 Kg 21 11 ἐξέρχεσθαι dat; ϣⲓⲡⲉ ϩ.: Job 19 3 (*B* ϩⲁϫ.) αἰσχύνεσθαι acc; Lu 20 13 (*B* ϩⲁⲧ.) ἐντρέπεσθαι; ⲣ ϩⲟⲧⲉ ϩ.: Job 5 22 *SA*(Cl) ϩⲓ- (or ? prep) φοβεῖσθαι ἀπό, Ps 21 25 (*B* do), Mt 10 26 (*B* do), AP 7 *A²* φ. acc; ϭⲱⲧⲡ ϩ.: Is 51 7 (*B* diff) ἡττᾶσθαι dat, BHom 34 ὀλιγωρεῖν; ⲥⲧⲱⲧ ϩ.: 2 Pet 2 10 (*B* ⲥⲟⲉⲣⲧⲉⲣ ϩⲁⲧ.) τρέμειν; ϩⲏⲧ⸗ ⲛ-: Ps 3 tit (*B* ϩⲁⲧ.) ἀποτρέχειν ἀπὸ προσώπου; *ib* 54 8 (*B* do) προσδέχεσθαι acc; Mt 11 3 (*B* ϩⲁϫ.) προσδοκᾶν acc; 1 Kg 4 17 φεύγειν ἐκ πρ.; Aeg 284 φρίττειν acc; Pro 7 1 *SA*(*B* ϩⲁⲧ.) φοβεῖσθ. acc; Is 66 2 *SA*(Cl Stras, Cl Berl ϩⲓ-, *B* ϩⲁⲧ.) τρέμειν acc; PS 368 ⲥⲱⲕ ϩⲏⲧⲟⲩ ⲙⲯⲩⲭⲏ ⲛⲓⲙ, BMis 29 ⲃⲱⲕ ϩⲏⲧϥ ⲛⲓⲁⲕⲱⲃ, Mani H 69 *A²* ⲭⲁⲗⲁ ⲙⲙⲁϥ ...ϩⲏⲧϥ (sic) ⲛⲛⲓⲟⲩⲇⲁⲓⲟⲥ; ⲉϩⲏⲧ⸗ *SO*: Ge 32 11 (var ϩ.), Deu 13 6 (var do), Ac 25 8; PS 26 ⲡⲟⲗⲉⲙⲓ ⲉϩⲏⲧϥ ⲙⲡⲟⲅⲟⲉⲓⲛ, C 99 175 ⲣ ϩⲟⲧⲉ ⲉϩⲏⲧϥ ⲡⲗⲁϥ, PMich 1289 h sim, AZ 21 100 *O* ⲁⲡⲁⲓ ⲛⲙⲟϥ ⲉϩⲏⲧ; ⲡⲉϩⲏⲧ⸗ *A*: El 34 ⲉⲛⲣ ⲕⲓⲑⲁⲣⲁ ⲡϩⲏⲧ[ϥ *before him*.

ⲉⲣ ϩⲏⲧⲥ *B*, *make beginning*: Ge 9 20, Ps 76 11, Ac 10 37 ἄρχειν (all *S* = Gk), Phil 1 6 (*SF* do) ἐνάρ.;

Job 8 15 (*S* diff) ἐπιλαμβάνειν, AM 125 ⲡⲓⲉⲣⲟⲟⲩ ⲉ-
ⲧⲁϥⲉⲣ.; ⲥ ⲉ-: 2 Chr 3 1 ⲉⲣ. ⲉⲕⲱⲧ, HL 73 ⲡⲧⲁⲉⲣ.
ⲉϯⲉⲡⲓⲥⲧⲟⲗⲏ ἄρ. gen, MG 25 33 ⲁϥⲉⲣ. ⲉⲡⲓⲙⲱⲓⲧ ⲙ-
ⲙⲟϣⲓ, *ib* 82 ⲁⲩⲉⲣ. ⲉⲣⲟⲓ ⲛϫⲉ ⲡⲓⲙⲉⲩⲓ; ⲥ ϩⲁϫⲉⲛ-:
Ex 15 21 ἐξάρ. gen; ⲥ ⲛ-: Ge 18 27, MG 25 232
ⲁϥⲉⲣ. ⲡⲣⲟⲓ ἄρ. inf, Ez 13 6 ἄρ. gen, Ps 146 7 (*S* ⲣ
ϩⲓⲣⲏ) ἐξάρ. dat: Va 63 4 ⲁⲩⲉⲣ. ⲡⲉⲣ ϩⲁⲉ = BMis
368 *S* ⲁⲣⲭ. ⲡϣⲱⲧ, MIE 2 419 ⲁϥⲉⲣ. ⲡϣⲱⲡⲓ.

ⲉϩⲏ *SBF*, *to the front, forwards*: Pro 6 8 *B*(*SA* ⲉⲓ
ⲉⲃⲟⲗ), Mk 1 19 *SB*, Z 274 *S* ⲡⲧⲉⲣⲉⲡϣⲁϫⲉ (*sc* letter)
ⲙⲟⲟϣⲉ ⲉ. ⲡⲟⲩⲕⲟⲩⲓ προ- ; Lu 19 4 εἰς τὸ ἔμπροσθεν; PS 61 *S* ⲙⲁⲣⲉϥⲉⲓ ⲉ. ⲡϥϫⲱ, ShC 73 95 *S* ⲡ-
ⲡⲉⲩⲡⲧⲟⲩ (*sc* their children) ⲉ. ⲙⲙⲟⲟⲩ to pray &
bow, RNC 88 *S* ⲁϥϭⲟϥϭ ⲉ. ⲙⲡⲣⲣⲟ, FR 20 *S* to
muleteer ϫⲱⲣⲙ ⲉ. ⲡⲕⲉⲕⲟⲩⲓ, BMis 384 *S* ⲁⲙⲓⲭⲁⲏⲗ
ⲧⲱϫⲙ ⲉ. (? ⲧⲱϫⲙ 2°) ⲡϣⲟⲣⲡ = Mor 27 33 *S* ⲡⲱⲧ
ⲉⲣⲟⲩⲛ ⲡϣ. but = Va 63 12 *B* ⲉⲣ ϣⲟⲣⲡ ⲁϥⲙⲟⲩϯ
ⲉϩⲟⲩⲛ, Pcod 4 *S* fruits ⲉⲧⲉϣⲁⲩⲧⲟⲥ[ⲟⲩ] ⲉ. & ripen
untimely, BM 1013 9 *S* ⲡⲧⲟϥ ⲟⲡ ⲉ. ϣⲁⲉⲡⲉϩ &
thenceforth forever, ST 98 *S* ⲉⲛϣⲁⲛⲉⲓ ⲉⲓϩⲏ ⲟⲡ *if we
go on further* (continue to live), DeV 2 208 *B* ϯ ⲡⲟⲩ-
ϫⲁ ⲣⲱϥ ⲙⲡⲓⲥⲁϫⲓ ⲡⲧⲉϥⲙⲟϣⲓ ⲉ., *ib* 195 ϯ ⲡⲏⲓ (ⲡ)-
ⲟⲩⲕⲟⲩϫⲓ ⲛϩⲉϫⲉ ⲉ. *in advance*, BodlMarsh 32 12
B ⲡⲉⲕⲓ ⲉ. ϩⲉⲡⲡⲁⲓⲃⲁⲑⲙⲟⲥ, C 86 337 *B* ⲁⲡⲉϥϥⲁⲧ
ⲓ ⲉ. ⲕⲟⲩϫⲓ ⲕⲟⲩϫⲓ (*sic* prob); ϫⲓⲛⲙⲡⲟⲟⲩ, -ⲉⲡ.
ⲉϩⲏ *S*, *from to-day forward*: BMar 15, 97, BM
1059, JSch 2 11; ⲉϫⲓⲛⲡ. Mor 31 93; ϩⲁϫⲓⲛⲉⲡ. Ryl
144; ⲓⲥϫⲉⲛϯⲛⲟⲩ ⲉ. *B*: Va 61 25; as ⲛⲛ *S*: BM
1137 I wished not to ϫⲓ ⲡⲉⲙⲟⲧ ⲡⲣⲱⲙⲉ ⲉⲕⲉⲛ (*ⲓϭⲛ*)
ⲡⲉⲡⲉ. *so as to get our (payment) in advance*; ⲣ
ⲉ., *be before*: MG 25 211 *B* ⲁⲣⲓ ⲉ. προλαμβ., Ps
76 4 *S* (*sic* 2 MSS, *B* ⲉⲣ ϣⲟⲣⲡ) προκαταλαμβ.,
MartIgn 880 *B* ⲉⲧⲁϥⲉⲣ ⲉ. ⲙⲡⲓⲡⲗⲁϩ πρόμαχος
εἶναι; Va 66 304 *B* none can ⲉⲣ ⲉ. ⲡⲧⲉϥϩⲛⲓⲃⲓ ὑπερβαίνειν; ϯ ⲉ., *advance, progress*: Jud 4 24 *S* (var
ⲉⲣⲏ) πορεύεσθαι; ShMun 91 *S* ⲉⲧⲣⲉⲧⲛϯ ⲉ. ϩⲓⲣⲱⲃ
ⲡⲓⲙ, HM 1 56 *S* child ϯ ⲉ. ⲙⲙⲏⲛⲉ, C 41 70 *B* ϯ-
ⲃⲟⲏϯ...ϯ ⲉ. ⲉⲧⲁⲟⲩⲉ ⲕⲁⲣⲡⲟⲥ ⲉⲃⲟⲗ.

ⲡⲥⲁϩⲏ *SF*, ⲥⲁⲧϩⲏ *B*, *before, formerly*: Dan 7 8 *B*,
Va 57 6 *B* ⲡⲏ ⲉⲧⲁϥϫⲟⲧⲟⲩ ⲥ. ἔμπροσθεν; MG 25
353 *B* as already said ⲥ. (ROC 18 55 ﺣﺪﺙ), My
38 *S* sim ⲡⲥ., Miss 4 106 *B* as we have read to you
ⲥ.; *in front*: Ex 28 14 *B* -θιος, Ac 27 30 *B*(*S* ϩⲓⲑⲏ)
ἐκ πρῴρης; MG 25 402 *B* saw great man ⲥ. ⲙⲙⲱⲟⲩ
(ROC 19 43 ﺣﺼﻦ), Va 61 93 *B* I undertake to
thee ⲥ. ⲙⲡ⳿ⲭ⳿ⲥ⳿, C 99 244 *S* grasped sheet ϩⲓⲡⲁϩⲟⲩ &
ⲡⲥ. = C 89 88 *B* ϩⲓⲧϩⲏ; *afterward, henceforth*:
Va 57 134 *B* ⲉⲑⲛⲟⲩ ⲙⲉⲡⲉⲡⲥⲁⲡⲁⲓ ⲓⲉ ⲥ., C 99 236
S ϩⲁⲣⲉϩ ⲉⲣⲟⲡ ⲡⲥ. = C 89 70 *B* εἰς τὰ ἔμπ., *ib* 141
S sim = *ib* 47 *B* εἰς τὰ μετὰ ταῦτα, Miss 8 30 *S* shall
be established ⲡⲥ. εἰς τὸν ἑξῆς χρόνον; ShC 73 113
S so long as we can ⲙⲟⲟϣⲉ ⲡⲥ., BMis 181 *S* ϯ ⲡⲁⲡ
ⲡⲟⲩⲁⲓⲟⲣⲡⲱⲥⲓⲥ ⲡⲥ., *ib* 128 *S* ⲁϥⲟⲩⲱϩ ⲟⲡ ⲉⲧⲟⲟⲧϥ

ⲡⲥ., AZ 21 144 *S* as word ⲡⲁⲧⲁⲙⲟⲛ ⲡⲥ., ST 429 *S*
will pay interest ϩⲁⲣⲟϥ ⲡⲥ., Pcod *F* 22 ⲁⲕⲛⲁϭⲓⲛⲓ
ⲧⲱⲛ ⲡⲥ. ? (*S* 40 om), BSM 108 *B* help & protection
ⲡⲥ.; ⲉⲣ ⲥ. *B*, *be before, go to meet*: C 43 69 ⲁⲩⲉⲣ.
ⲙⲡⲓϫⲟⲓ, *cf* ⲣ ϩⲓϩⲏ.

ϩⲁϩⲏ *SAA²BF*, *in front of, before*: Job 3 24 *S*(*B*
ϩⲁϫⲉⲛ-), Pro 8 23 *SA*(*B* do), Is 30 33 *SF*(*B* do),
Ez 4 1 *B*(*S* ϩⲓϩⲏ), Jo 11 55 *SAA²*(*B* do) πρό, Ez 23
41 *B*(*S* ϩⲓϩⲏ), Ac 13 24 *S*(*B* do) πρὸ προσώπου, Ps 3
7 *B*(*S* ϩⲏⲧ⳿ ⲛ-), Is 2 19 *B*(*S* ⲉⲃⲟⲗ ϩⲓ-) ἀπό, Jos 7 4
S, Jer 15 17 *SB*, Ac 3 19 *S*(*B* ⲙⲡⲉⲙⲧⲟ ⲉⲃⲟⲗ ⲛ-)ἀπὸ
πρ., Ez 40 47 *B*(*S* ϩⲓϩⲏ) ἀπέναντι, Phil 3 20 *B* ϫⲟⲩϣⲧ ϩ. ⲛ- (*S* ϩⲏⲧ⳿ ⲛ-) ἀποδέχεσθαι; Ez 39 11 *B*, Ac
27 34 *S*(*B* ⲡϣⲟⲣⲡ ⲉ-) πρός, Job 2 9 *B* ϫⲟⲩϣⲧ ⲉϩ. ϩ.
(*S* do) προσδεχ., Jud 4 23 *S*, Jo 3 28 *S*(*BF* ϩⲁϫ.)
ⲉⲙⲡⲣ., Ge 29 26 *S*(*B* ⲙⲡⲁϯ-) πρίν, Job 15 24 *S* ϩ.
ⲡⲟⲩⲙⲗⲁϩ πρωτοστάτης; Mt 22 16 *S*(*B* ϩⲁ-) περί;
Deu 15 20 *B* (var ⲥⲁⲙⲉⲛϩⲏ ⲛ-, *S* ϫⲓⲛ-), 2 Pet 2 8 *B*
ⲡⲉϩⲟⲟⲩ ϩ. ⲡⲉϩⲟⲟⲩ (*S* ⲉϩ. ϩⲛ-) ἐκ; Dan 1 5 *B* sim
κατά; Ps 54 20 *B*(*S* ϩⲏⲧ⳿ ⲛ-), Eccl 7 19 *F*(*S* do) acc;
PS 199 *S* ⲥⲉⲛⲁⲣ ϣⲟⲣⲡ...ϩ. ⲡⲁⲣⲭⲱⲛ, ShA 2 275
S have often wept ϩ. ⲙⲡⲟⲟⲩ, BMis 1190 *S* destroy
me not ϩ. ⲙⲡⲁⲟⲅⲟⲉⲓϣ, C 43 197 *B* sim, Mus 40 43
S(RegPach) if he tell it not ϩ. ⲡϣⲟⲙⲧ ⲛϩⲟⲟⲩ *ante*,
C 99 186 *S* as he said ϩ. ⲙⲡⲛⲁⲩ, Mor 22 115 *S* hath
died ϩ. ⲛⲡⲉϩⲟⲟⲩ = BSM 103 *B*, Hall 94 *S* ϩ. ⲡⲟⲩⲛⲟϭ ⲡⲟⲩⲟⲉⲓϣ, DeV 2 16 *B* fulfilled ϩ. ⲡⲟⲩⲕⲟⲩϫⲓ,
BMar 90 *S* grape sour ϩ. ⲡⲟⲩⲕⲟⲩⲓ, BSM 29 *B* ⲓⲥϫⲉⲛϩ. ⲡⲥⲁϥ = BMis 369 *S* ⲉⲓⲥ ⲕⲉϩⲟⲟⲩ ⲥⲛⲁⲩ, Z 364
S ϩ. ⲡϣⲟⲙⲛⲧ ⲛϩⲟⲟⲩ ⲉⲡⲙⲟⲩ ⲡⲓⲟⲩⲗⲓⲁⲛⲟⲥ = BMis
247 *S*, BM 144 *S* ϩ. ⲡϥⲧⲟ ⲛⲣⲉϥⲃⲱⲗⲙⲁⲥ ⲉⲛⲣⲟⲩⲙⲓⲥⲉ
= Wess 18 11, CO 386 *S* letter begins ϩ. ⲙⲉⲛ ⲡ-
ⲣⲱⲃ ⲡⲓⲙ, Pcod *F* 39 I look ϩ. ⲙⲡⲉϥⲡⲉⲉⲓ (*S* ϩⲏⲧ⳿
ⲛ-), AM 326 *B* 4 torturers ⲃ̄ ϩ. ⲛⲃ̄ *facing one another* (?, *cf* PBaden 5 150 *S* bade them beat her
ⲙⲡⲉⲛⲧⲟ ⲉⲃⲟⲗ ⲛⲛⲉⲩⲉⲣⲏⲩ), C 43 77 *B* sim (*cf ib* 208
ⲃ̄ ⲉⲩϣⲓϣⲓ ⲛⲃ̄), Mor 29 6 *S* ⲁⲩϭⲱⲧⲡ ϩ. ⲛⲡⲉⲣⲣⲱⲙⲁⲓⲟⲥ (var BMis 233 ϩⲓϩⲏ); ϩⲁϩⲏ-*F* = ϩⲁⲣⲧⲓ-
ϥⲩ; ⲡ. ϩ. ⲉⲧⲣⲉ- *SS*^*f*: BMis 334 ϩ. ⲉⲧⲣⲉϥⲕⲁⲁⲧ ...
ⲉⲙⲡⲡⲁⲣⲁⲇⲓⲥⲟⲥ, CMSS 19 *S*^*f* ϩ. ⲉⲧⲣⲁⲥϭⲁⲓ; ShA 2
275 ϩ. ⲡϣⲟⲙⲧⲉ ⲛⲣⲟⲙⲡⲉ ⲉⲧⲣⲉⲡⲉⲡⲉⲓⲱⲧ ⲛⲕⲟⲧⲕ, FR
6 ϩ. ⲛϭⲙⲉ ⲛϩⲟⲟⲩ ⲉⲧⲣⲉⲁⲡⲁ ⲱ; ϩ. (ⲉ)ⲙⲡⲁⲧⲉ-:
PS 12 *S* ϩ. ⲉⲙⲡⲁⲧⲥⲱⲟⲩ, Br 126 *S* ϩ. ⲉⲙⲡⲁϯϯ ⲛⲏⲧⲛ,
BMis 442 *S* ϩ. ⲙⲡⲁⲧⲉϥⲣ ⲙⲟⲛⲟⲭⲟⲥ, ManiK 116
A² ϩⲁⲧⲉϩⲏ ⲉⲙⲡⲁⲧⲟⲩϣⲟⲩⲟ, MIE 2 415 *B* ϩ. ⲙⲡⲁ-
ϯⲥⲁϫⲓ ⲛⲉⲙⲁⲕ = BAp 123 *S* ϩ. ⲉⲧⲣⲁ-, Tst Ab 167
B ϩ. ⲙⲡⲁⲧⲁⲓ ⲉⲃⲟⲗ; ϩⲁⲧⲉϩⲏ *S*: PS 1 ϩ. ⲙⲙⲩⲥⲧⲏⲣⲓⲟⲛ ⲡⲓⲙ, *ib* 124 ⲁϥⲕⲏⲣⲩⲥⲥⲉ ϩⲁⲧⲉϩⲓⲛ ⲛⲧⲙⲉ,
namely ⲁϥⲕ. ϩⲁⲧⲉϩⲛ, BG 26 ϩ. ⲙⲡⲧⲏⲣϥ, *ib* 86 ϩ.
ⲡⲥⲉⲟⲩⲱⲡ ⲗⲁⲁⲩ ⲉⲃⲟⲗ; with poss: Lev 18 28 *S*
(*B* ϩⲁϫ.), Mt 5 12 *S* (var ϩⲓⲛ, *B* do) πρό, Lu 1 17 *S*(*B*
ⲉⲣ ϣⲟⲣⲡ ⲛ-) προ-, Is 43 27 *S*(*B* ⲛϣ.), Jo 15 18 *SA²*
(*B* do) πρῶτος, Si 34 19 *S* πρότερος, Ge 33 3 *S*(*B*

ⲥⲁϩ.), Eccl 1 10 S ϩⲓⲏ F(C Schmidt, var PMich
3520 ϩⲁⲭ.) ⲉⲙⲡⲣ., Jos 8 6 S, Ps 77 55 S(B ϩⲁⲧϩⲏ
ⲙⲡⲟⲩⲣⲟ)ἀπὸ προσώ., Mk 1 2 S (var ϩⲓϩ, B do)πρὸ
προσώ.; Ps 84 13 S(B ⲉⲣ ϣ. ⲛ-)ἐναντίον, 1 Kg 18
6 S εἰς συνάντησιν; Ps 66 8 B(S ϩⲏⲧ⳽), Is 33 7 BF(S
do) acc, Jo 4 51 F(S ⲉϩⲣⲏ-, B ⲉ-)dat; HM 1 77 S
ϫⲟⲟⲩ ⲡϩⲉⲡϩⲱⲣⲟⲡ ϩⲁⲧⲉⲕϩⲓⲏ, Z 281 S ⲡⲣⲣⲟ ⲉⲧⲁ-
ⲧⲉⲕϩⲏ, TstAb 255 B ⲉⲣ ⲅⲩⲙⲡⲟⲥ ϩⲁⲧⲉϥϩⲏ; ⲉϩⲏ
&c : PS 12 S ϩⲁⲧⲡⲉϩⲏ (17 ϩⲁⲧⲉⲡⲉϩⲏ), BG 23, 39 S
ϩⲁⲧⲉϥⲉ.,Am 2 9 A, Jo 10 8 A ⲉϩⲓ, El 44 A ⲉϩⲓⲉⲓ, Jo 10 4
A² ,AP 42 A² ⲉϩⲏ; v also ϩⲓⲟⲏ; as nn m S: ShC
73 53 ⲡⲛⲁⲩ ⲛⲧⲱⲟⲩⲛ ⲛ̄ⲅ. ⲙⲡⲟⲩⲟⲉⲓⲛ; ϩⲁ- ϩⲏⲧ⳽
A : Hag 1 12 ϩⲁϩⲏⲧϥ ⲙⲡⲭ̅ⲥ̅ (B ϩⲁⲧϩⲏ ⲙⲡϩⲟ ⲙ-)
ἀπὸ προσώπου.

ϩⲓⲟⲏ SAA²BF, to, at front, forward: Ge 33 14 S
(var ϩⲁⲟⲏ, B ϩⲁⲭ.), 1 Kg 8 11 S προ-, Jos 3 14 SB
πρότερος; 2 Kg 9 11 S πρός, Jos 4 12 S, Is 41 26 B
(S ϩⲟⲩⲉⲓⲧ), EpJer 5 BF(S ϩⲓⲟⲏ), Mk 2 12 S(B ⲙ-
ⲡⲉⲙⲑⲟ)ⲉⲙⲡⲣ., Ge 33 2 SB ἐν πρώτοις, 1 Kg 18 11
S (var ϩⲁⲡϩⲟ ⲛ-), Joel 2 6 A ϩⲓⲧⲉϩⲓ (B ϩⲁⲧ.) ἀπὸ
προσώ., Hos 7 10 A ϩⲓⲧⲉϩⲓ (B ⲉϫⲉⲛ-) εἰς πρ., Lev 10
4 S(B ⲙⲛ.), 2 Kg 7 15 S(var ϩⲓϩⲏ)ἐκ πρ., 1 Kg 9 12
S κατὰ πρ., Mic 2 13 A ϩⲓⲧⲉϩⲓ (S ϩⲓϩⲏ, B do) πρὸ
πρ., Jon 1 6 A ϩⲓⲟⲓ B(S do) πρωρεύς, Ac 27 30 S(B
ⲥⲁⲧϩⲏ)ἐκ πρῴρης; 1 Kg 6 20 S, Ps 67 7 S(B ⲙⲡ.)
ἐνώπιον, Deu 22 17 S(B do) ἐναντίον; Ap 5 1 S(B
ⲥⲁⲃⲟⲩⲛ)ἔσωθεν; Mic 7 17 A(S ϩⲁⲟⲏ, B ϩⲁⲭ.)ἀπό;
Z 289 S judgment ϩ. ⲙⲡⲉⲭ̅ⲥ̅ ἐπί, Is 51 20 S(B ⲉϥ-
ⲫⲗⲁⲕ)ἐπ᾽ ἄκρου; Jos 7 20 S dat; Br 106 S set them
ϩ. ⲛⲧⲉⲩⲅⲥⲓⲁ, ShC 73 40 S covenant made ϩ. ⲙⲡⲡⲉ;
BAp 138 S went ϩ. ⲙⲙⲟⲛ (var JTS 8 242 ϩⲓⲏ),
BMis 389 S opened door ϩ. ⲛⲡⲉⲧⲛⲏⲩ (var ib ϩⲁϫⲱⲟⲩ) = Va 63 15 B ϩⲁⲧ., MIE 2 355 B ⲁⲓⲱⲥⲕ ϩ.
ⲙⲡⲣⲟ = BAp 80 S ϩⲓⲣⲛ-, Va 63 1 B table ϩ. ⲙⲙⲟⲕ
= BMis 361 S ϩⲁⲣⲱⲕ, Kropp R 3 12 S depart ϩ.
ⲙⲡⲁϩⲟ, El 120 S leprosy ϩⲓⲧⲉϩⲏ ⲛⲛⲉϥϭⲓⲝ = ib 90
A ϩⲓⲧⲉϩⲓ, AM 7 B sat ϩ. ⲙⲡϩⲟ ⲙ-, ManiH 58 A²
ϩⲓⲧⲉϩⲣⲛ ⲙⲙⲁϥ, Pcod 13 S words ⲉⲧⲛⲁϣⲏⲧⲟⲩ ϩ. in
what follows, C 86 334 B ⲉⲧⲁⲩⲙⲟϣⲓ ϩ. ⲛⲟⲩⲕⲟⲩϫⲓ,
J 39 19 S ϩ. ⲛⲧⲉϥⲉⲡⲓⲛ(ⲟⲩϩⲟⲧⲛⲉⲥ) ⲛⲧⲟⲩ ⲕⲟⲗⲉⲥ (cf ϩⲓⲃⲟⲗ); with poss: 2 Macc 6 7 A ⲙⲁϩⲉ ϩⲓⲧϥϩⲓ
dat, Mani 1 A² ⲟⲩⲉⲛ ϩⲓⲧⲁⲉϩⲛ ⲙⲡⲣⲟ, Mani 1 A² ⲁⲡ-
ⲥⲉϫⲉ ⲕⲁⲁⲩ ϩⲓⲧⲉⲉϩⲛ (sc soul's); p ϩ. S, be, go
before: Mor 37 113 ⲣ. ⲙⲙⲟϥ ⲉⲙⲡⲧⲁⲉⲓⲟ προάγειν
gen; BSG 181 ⲁϥⲣ. ⲙⲙⲟⲟⲩ = ib 12 B ϭⲟⲝⲓ ⲉ-
ⲥⲟⲩⲛ ⲉⲣⲱⲟⲩ, BMis 127 ⲡⲧⲉⲣⲉϥⲣ. ⲛⲟⲩⲕⲟⲩϫⲓ, Tor 2
I begged thee ⲁⲕⲣ ϩⲓⲧⲁϩⲏ camest to meet me (with
loan, cf Hall below), Ep 85, CO 160 sim; as nn
in rubric S: Leyd 139 ⲅⲩⲙⲛⲟⲥ...ⲉⲓⲥ ⲧⲉϥϩ. opp ⲉⲓⲥ
ⲧⲉϥϩⲓⲁϩⲟⲩ, Ryl 53 sim.

ϩⲓϩⲏ S, as last: Jth 10 22, Mk 10 32, BHom 22
send ϩ. ⲙⲙⲟⲕ ⲡⲣⲟ-, Nu 32 17 (B ⲥⲱⲕ ϩⲁⲭ.)πρό-
τερος, Jon 1 6 ⲡⲉⲉϥ ⲉⲧⲣ. (AB ⲉⲧϩⲓⲧϩⲓ, -ⲧϩⲏ) πρω-

ρεύς(cf Ez 27 29 ⲡⲟ.); Deu 7 1 (B ϩⲁⲧ. ⲙϥϩⲣⲟ),Eccl 8
3 (var ϩⲓϩⲓⲏ) ἀπὸ προσώ., Jud 6 9 ἐκ πρ., 3 Kg 3 15
κατὰ πρ., Am 9 4 (A ϩⲓⲧⲉϩⲓ, B ⲙⲡⲉⲙ.) πρὸ πρ., Nu
14 43 (var ϩⲓⲏ, B ϩⲁⲭ.), Mk 9 3 (B ⲙⲡⲉⲙ.) ⲉⲙⲡⲣ.;
Lev 6 7 (var & B do) ἔναντι, Jos 9 6 ἀπέν.; Jud 20
39 ἐνώπιον; Ez 40 15 (B do) ἔξωθεν (cf 26 ἔσωθεν);
ib 19 (B do) αἴθριος; Jth 14 2 ⲕⲁ ϩ. ἀρχηγὸν διδόναι;
Br 242 ⲟⲩⲡⲏⲧⲛ ϩ. ⲙⲙⲟϥ, ShBor 300 71 ⲙⲟⲟϣⲉ
ϩⲓϩⲏ ⲙⲙⲟϥ, BMis 379 ϭⲱϣⲧ ϩ. ⲙⲙⲟϥ = Va 63
10 B ϩⲓⲧϩⲏ = BSM 36 B ⲙⲡⲉϥⲉⲙⲑⲟ, Ep 254 ⲁⲥ-
ϯⲟϫⲏ (δοκεῖν) ϩ. ⲛⲧⲉⲧⲛⲙⲁⲕⲁⲣⲓⲟⲧⲏⲥ, BMis 233 ⲁⲩϭⲱⲧⲡ ϩ. ⲛⲡⲉⲣⲣⲱⲙⲁⲓⲟⲥ; p ϩ.: Ps 146 7 (B ⲉⲣ
ϩⲏⲧ⳽ ⲛϣⲟⲣⲡ) ἐξάρχειν; Mor 43 119 ⲁϥⲣ. ⲙⲙⲟϥ
(on Jo 20 4), Hall 119 ⲁⲕⲣ. ⲙⲙⲟⲓ (as Tor 2 above).

ϫⲓⲡⲛ- S (rare), ⲓⲥϫⲉⲛϩⲏ B, from beginning: 2 Cor
13 2 (SF ϫⲓⲛⲛϣⲟⲣⲡ) προ-; 2 Tim 1 3 (S ϫⲓⲛ-) ἀπό,
Ps 92 2 (S do) ἀπὸ τότε, Deu 11 12 S(var ϫⲓⲛϩ.)B,
Bar 3 26 (S ϫⲓⲛⲧⲉⲟⲩⲉⲓⲧⲉ) ἀπ᾽ ἀρχῆς, Jo 6 64 (SA²
ϫ. ⲛϣⲟⲣⲡ) ἐξ ἀ., He 1 10 (SF do) κατ᾽ ἀ., 2 Pet 2 3
(S do) ἔκπαλαι; DeV 2 12 Thou art God ι., ib 1 47
ι. ⲙⲡⲓⲕⲟⲥⲙⲟⲥ.

ϩⲏ SO, ϩⲉⲓ, ϩⲓ A, ϩⲏⲧ⳽ SA², ϩⲏⲧ⳽ A, ϩⲏⲧ⳽ B,
ⲭⲏ O nn f (B mostly ⲛⲉϫⲓ) belly, also womb (cf ⲕⲁⲗⲁϩⲏ): Ge 3 14, Job 1 21, Pro 24 15 SA ϩⲉⲓ, Hos 12 3
A ϩⲉⲓ, Mt 15 17(F ⲕⲁⲗⲁϩⲏ), Jo 3 4 SA² κοιλία; Job 3
10, Ps 16 14 (F do), Tit 1 12 γαστήρ; Deu 18 3 (B
diff) ἤνυστρον; ⲥⲉⲗⲉⲡⲓⲛ ⲡϩⲏⲧϥ 1 Kg 31 3 ὑποχόν-
δριον; ϩⲏ ⲙⲡⲓⲣⲉ Ex 16 13 (B ⲙⲉⲥⲓⲱϯ) ὀρτυγομήτρα; MG 25 203 B ⲓϣⲓ ⲉϩⲏⲧ τράχηλος (cf AM 296
below); PS 106 ⲃⲱⲕ ⲉϩⲟⲩⲛ ⲉϩⲏⲧϥ like water, Sh
BMOr 8810 418 ⲧⲣⲟⲫⲏ ⲡϩⲏ, ShIF 275 ⲗⲓⲃⲉ ⲡϩⲏ
(v ⲗⲁⲃϩ. below), ShA 1 243 ϫⲓⲛⲉⲩϩⲣⲓⲧⲟⲟⲧⲉ...ⲉⲩϩⲣⲏ-
ⲑⲏ, ShP 131⁴ 141 ⲁϥⲧⲣⲉϩⲏ ϣⲏⲙ ⲙⲙⲁⲣⲓⲁ ϣⲟⲡϥ,
El 70 A ⲉⲓⲣⲉ ⲡⲧⲟⲩϩⲉⲓ ⲛⲡⲟⲩⲧⲉ ⲡⲉⲩ (sic l), Aeg 13
ⲙⲙⲁⲟⲧ ⲙⲡϩⲏ = ib B ⲡ., Mor 40 50 ⲁⲟⲏ ⲉⲧⲣⲉⲡ-
ⲧⲉⲥⲕⲁⲗⲁϩⲏ ⲉⲓ ⲉⲡⲉⲥⲏⲧ with babe = Gött ar 114 189
(l᾽ مثل) امعاها مع البشيمة، BM 215 89 body & soul ⲉϥ-
ⲡⲗⲁⲥⲥⲉ ⲙⲙⲟⲟⲩ ϩⲓϩⲏ, Z 261 ⲡⲁϩⲏⲧϥ = PO 1 413
ما كان في بطنه (cf ib ⲡⲉϥⲙⲁⲟⲧ), Pcod 44 Word entered ϩⲏⲧⲥ ⲛⲧⲡⲁⲣⲑⲉⲛⲟⲥ (var ⲕⲁⲗ.), C 43 80 B ϣⲧⲟϥ
ⲉϫⲉⲡϩⲏⲧ, AM 296 B ⲕⲟⲗⲗⲁⲣⲓⲟⲡ ⲛ̄ ⲧⲟⲓ ⲉϩⲏⲧϥ (cf
C 43 171 sim ⲡⲉϥⲙⲟⲙⲧ),Va 66 297 B rags ⲧⲟⲓ ⲉϩⲏⲧ-
ⲟⲩ, PMéd 286 ϩⲏⲧϥ ⲛⲧⲱⲣⲉ pith, AZ 21 100 O ⲑⲉⲗⲡⲓ ⲛⲟϩ (gloss-ⲛⲧⲭⲏ), ib ⲡⲉⲧⲉⲡⲭⲏⲥ ⲉⲭⲏⲧ; ϩⲏⲧ⳽
with vbs: ⲉⲓⲙⲉ ϩ. ⲉⲡⲉⲥⲏⲧ, ⲉϩⲣⲏ, bring down womb,
produce abortion Mor 25 215 ⲡ ϩⲏⲧⲥ ⲡⲟⲩϭⲓⲙⲉ ⲉ.,
ib 18 14 ⲁⲩⲉⲛ ϩⲏⲧⲟⲩ ⲉ. = Miss 4 109 B ⲉϩ.; ⲛⲉϫ
ϩ. ⲉⲃⲟⲗ sim Mor 31 240 pregnant women ⲛⲟϫ (l
ⲛⲉϫ) ϩⲏⲧⲟⲩ ⲉⲃⲟⲗ = RylBull 11 410 طرحوا ما في
بطونهن; ϩⲓ ϩ. sim Job 21 10 (B ⲙⲓⲥⲓ ϩⲁϫⲉⲡ ⲡⲥⲛⲟⲩ) ὠμοτοκεῖν (var ἐκβάλλειν), ib B ϩⲓ ϩ. ⲉⲃⲟⲗ (S
ϣⲧⲟⲣⲧⲣ)σφάλλειν, Aeg 240 ⲑⲓⲉ ϩⲏⲧⲥ سقط ما فيها

...επεϲнт = PO 8 576 قتل جنينا في بطن; лες, лаϩ ς., v лоүϩ, fill I s f; ллιϩ., belly-love, gluttony PS 215 тллнтлаιϩнтϲ, 257 ниλ. -ϩнтϥ; λаϩς., λаϩ. v p 137 a inf; ϣаϫε εϭολ нϩ., ventriloquize Is 8 19 (B лоγϯ εϭ. ϫεπονεϫι) ἐγγαστρίμυθος, cf PS 27 лоϭтε εϭ. нϩнтϥ; пнϭ εϩ., be close to Deu 13 6 (B as Gk) ἴσος τῇ ψυχῇ; оγωϭп аϩ. A, break (? redundant), Joel 1 7 (B diff) συγκλασμός; ϩωϣϥ аϩ. A (sim) Zeph 3 18 (B diff), συντρίβειν; ϣωπε ϩ., suffer in stomach Ac 28 8 (var εϩ., B ϣапллаϭт) δυσεντρία συνέχεσθαι; ϫι ϩ., take belly, occupy mind Bor 260 penult птερεπικωϩ ϫι ϩнтϥ (sc of Cain).

Used also with suff for prep ϩн-, q v.

ϩΗ, ϩε S, ϩε B(once) nn f, storey of house : Ge 6 16 B(S оγаϩлε), ClPr 30 12 house о нϩн ϲнтε (δι-, τρι)ώροφος; Ac 20 9 ϩε (B оγ.) -στεγος; 4 Kg 1 2 (P 44 111) тϩε нтпε ὑπερῷον; ShC 42 192 тлεϩϣоллтε пϩн н поγаϩл(ε) ллпнι, Miss 8 257 diningroom ϩιϫнтлεϩϣоллтε пϩн ллнтопоϲ, Kr 125 εϩεϩ-ϩра εϲϩнтϣорпε пϩε ϩпнн, BMOr 6201 A 35 ϫнтϣорп пϩε пϲо нлла ϲпаγ поγωϩ, ib тлε(ϩ)ϩε ϲнтε.

ϩΗ S nn, quarry (?): Jud 6 2 ϩн пϣаτωпε κρεμαστός (var ὀχύρωμα). V AZ 54 131, Griff Stu 169.

ϩΗ B, ϩε- SAA²BF, ϩι- S⁄A, ϩ- SB nn m, season (?): пιϩн нϣωλλ v ϣωλλ 2°; ллпаλоλι Nu 13 20 B(S ϣрп таϭо εϭоλ) πρόδρομος (σταφυλῆς); ϩεϭωπ SF, ϩϭ. S (rare), ϩεϭоγ[оγпε ?], -ϭоγпε, ϩιϭωпε (sic ?) A, ϩϭωπ B, bad season, famine: Ge 12 10 S(B ϩκο), Job 5 20 SA(Cl) -ϭоγпε B, Is 5 13 F(SB do), ib 14 30 B(S do), Am 8 11 SA ϩι. B λιμός; Leyd 155 S ϩεнϩ. εγпаϣωпε, Mor 27 26 S ϩϭ., Bor 304 51 S sim, C 43 137 B ϩ., λοιллоϲ, El 102 A ϩε.; р ϩ. S: BAp 65 пκаϩ р ϩ.; ϩεпоγϥε SAA², -ι B, good season, plenty : Ge 41 48 SB, Ps 29 7 B(S оγωωλε) εὐθηνία; Va 63 4 B пιϩ. εтϫεпϫнлаι = BMis 368 S пϲει (on Ge 41 30), El 86 A land filled with good things ϩпоγϩ. επаϣωϥ, Mani 1 A² пнι ллпϩ., MG 25 54 B пι пϣϯ пϩ. in house, Mor 31 242 S⁄ robbed us επϩ. ллпκаϩ, Bor 304 51 S⁄ оγϩ. оγϩϭωπ; adj : Z 350 S оγειωτε пϩ.; р-S, оι пϩ. B, be in plenty : Job 21 9 (S оγ.), Va 66 307 ετοι пεпоγϥι(sic) ϫεппιαϲαθон εὐθηνεῖν; BAp 150 апεϲнι р ϩ., DeV 2 166 royal city оι пϩ.

ϩΗ v тнγ s f.

ϩΗ v ϩϩε p 65 a supra.

ϩΗ F v ϩε manner.

ϩΗΗϩ in ϩннпε, -тε v p 85 b.

ϩΗΗι F v ϩε fall.

ϩι SAB(rare)F, ϩιτϩ, ϩаτϩ S vb intr, thresh, beat,

rub : 1 Cor 9 9 SBF ἀλοᾶν; Mor 25 138 нϥϩι нϥ-ϣωϣ, Miss 8 227 ϩι ϩнтεκερϫпаγ; tr: Jud 8 7, Is 41 15 SB, Mic 4 13 S(ShA 1 385) A(B εϫεп-) ἀλ.; Tob 11 7 διατρίβειν, Lev 6 28 (B diff) ἐκτ.; Hab 3 12 A(SB diff) συμπατεῖν conculcare; He 11 35 (B оγоϣоγεϣ) τυμπανίζειν; ShA 1 387 ϩιτоγ поε поγϣоειϣ, Mor 25 138 as corn εϣаϩριтϥ, ib 46 23 ллпεκϩι ппаϫпооγ, BMOr 9532 send tow (ϲιппωп σίππιον) птпааγ пϲεϩριтоγ, RNC 59 ϩι ллоϥ (sc martyr) ϣаптεпεϥϲарϩ ϲωλп εϭоλ, R 2 1 71 пϲεϩриτϥ (sc rusty metal) ϩιϩоγн н пϲепаϲ-тϥ; in recipes : Z 628 ϯ (sc mixture) επεϥϲωлла лареϥϩриτϥ, AZ 23 107 ϩιтϥ ϣаптϥлоγ (v p 159 a inf), ib 110 sim ϩатоγ, ib 106 ϩатϥ κалооϲ, Bodl (P) a 1 a ϩι пεϥϲωп ϣаптεϥр оγωпε поγωт.

With following preposition. c εϫп-: Jer 28 33 B ἀλ. passive, 1 Cor 9 10 (B diff) ἀλ. ἐπί, C 89 118 B ϩι εϫωоγ (sc grain) ϩιπιϭпооγ τὸ ἀλοῆσαι = Va ar 172 68 درس; c ϩι-: Eccl 12 6 συντροχάζειν ἐπί; BAp 162 рллаι поωпε ϩι ϩпλεειп fire is kindled, PMéd 154 ϩι ллоϥ ϩιлооγ rub down with (in) water, ib 204 ϩιтоγ ϩιϩнаϫ; c ϩп-: 2 Kg 1 21 (var п-, B ϭωϩϲ) χρίεσθαι ἐν; R 1 4 57 ϩι ппεϥϲаϣι ϩпоγϩιоγ ἀνατρίβειν dat; Blake 238 ϩι ллоϥ (sc topaz)ϩпоγακωпн; c ϩιϫп-: Mor 32 48 пεϩтωр ϩι ϩιϫωϥ (49 sim εϫωϥ).

—— nn m, threshing : Am 9 13 B(SA ωϩϲ) ἀλοητός (var ἀμητός); BM 1073 S among property пεϥειоор...ллпεϥϩι пϣε.

реϥϩι S, thresher: Pro 20 26 (cit Mis 8 153, var R 2 2 8 -ϩа, A реϥϩωϩ) λικμήτωρ; P 44 62 трι-ϭεγϲ· р.

ϩι- v ϩιоγε.

ϩι- SAA²BFO, εϩι- (v p 394 b sup) S⁄BF, нϩι-AB(v e below), ϩε- S(Theban), ϩιωωϩ (+ ωω back, dorsum) SAA²F, εϩιωωϩ (v l c) S⁄, ϩιооϩ A, ϩιωтϩ B, ϩιωωтϩ F prep a on, at, in: Ge 28 12 S(var ϩιϫп-) B, Ex 21 19 S(B εϫεп-), Lev 25 37 S(B п-, B ε-), 1 Kg 20 27 S(var ε-), Job 40 11 S(var & B ϩп-), Ps 77 7 S(B do), Pro 16 10 S(A ϩιрп-), Si 32 12 S, Is 30 8 B(SF ε-), ib 35 8 B(SF ϩιϫп-), Ep Jer 25 BF, Hag 2 19 SA(B ϩιϫ.), Jo 19 31 SA²(B do), He 9 17 SF(B εϫ.), BHom 37 S апоλоτιϩε ϩιпθнлла ἐπί, Ez 33 27 S ϩιϩраϲ п-(B ϩιтотε п-)ἐπὶ προσώπου; Ex 15 22 S(B пϩρнι ϩι-), Nu 6 15 S(B ϫεп-), Deu 5 4 S(var ϩп-)B, Pro 3 16 A(SB ϩп-), Is 30 21 B(SF εϩραι ϩп-), Lam 4 8 B(S ϩп-, F ϩλнι ϩιп-), Mt 14 13 SBF, Cl 25 1 A, AP 14 A² embraced her ϩιпϩιр, R 1 1 23 S find no fault ϩιωωϥ (cf Lu 23 4 ϩп-) ἐν; Pro 27 24 S(var & A ε-), Is 41 27 B(S ε-), Lu 11 7 S(B ϩιϫ.) εἰς; Nu 2 3 S ϩιпϲа п-(B пϲа-), Ac 2 10 B sim (S no prep), Ps 67 34 S(B ϲа-) κατά; Nu 3 23

S ϩıпса п- (var ϩатп-, *B* сапса) παρά, *ib* 34 4 *S*(*B* са-) πρός; AP 10 *A*² ϩıпвнма πρό; Mk 15 17 *F*(*SB* ϩıхп-), Ap 11 3 *SB* περι-; Pro 15 10 *A*(*S* ϩıтп-) ὑπό; Ex 32 15 *S* ϩıпеıса мппаı (*B* саммаı) ἔνθεν κ. ἐν., Ap 22 2 *S* sim (*B* do) ἐντεῦθεν κ. ἐντ., Jo 10 1 *SA*² ϩıкеса(*B* ϭоүтеп) ἀλλαχόθεν, Jer 6 11 *S* ϩıпса пвол (ShC 42 196, *B* савол) ἔξωθεν; Lu 23 45 *S* ϩıтеϥмпте(var & *B* ϩп-), R 2 2 37 *S* sim (var BHom 56 е-) μέσον; Ge 50 10 *S* ϩıпекро (*B* ϩıмнр) πέραν; Gk dat: 1 Kg 9 20 *S*, Pro 13 3 *SA*(*B* ϫеп-), Si prol *S* τισί, Is 15 5 *SB*, *ib* 53 6 *A*(Cl)*B*(*S* ϩп-), Ap 21 19 *S*(*B* евол ϫеп-), BHom 51 *S* ϩıтеүмпте ἀμφοτέροις; Gk acc: Is 33 21 *SBF*, *ib* 56 10 *B* (*S* п-), Ac 8 28 *B*(var ϫеп-, *S* п-); PS 158 *S* кет текмптрммао ϩıоүт (Od Solom 22 12 ⟍), *ib* 166 *S* аϥкаат ϩıтеϩıн, Br 50 *S* his mark ϩıпеϥϩо, ShC 73 90 *S* ϩепϭωтϩ ϩıϩепшпе, *ib* 61 *S* ϩıпшммо п ϩıп†ме, *ib* 121 *S* ϩıхаеıе opp ϩıтсүпагωгн, ShBor 246 83 *S* children carried ϩıтаϩве, Aeg 57 *B* sim, ShA 1 406 *S* sun riseth ϩıмпеıевт еϥвωк еϩраı ϩıпемпт, J 29 25 *S* ϩıпрнс епткавол. екклнсıа, CA 102 *S* етреоүшωш шωпе ϩıоүоү (var пϩнтоү), *ib* 103 *S* bishop shall come forth ϩıоүоү пϥϫıакопеı паү to (?) them = *ib* ٠٠ ‏وﺧﺪﻣﻦ‎, BAp 11 *S* каıаϥ ϩıоүωϥ (sc tomb, var MIF 9 49 пϩнтϥ), BHom 117 *S* ship мп реϥрϩıмме ϩıоүωϥ (cf *ib* sim пϩнтϥ), BMis 398 *S* теүϭелпıс ϩıппе (var ϩп-), J 18 59 *S* require ϩıтϭıх ппархωп (cf 13 60 ϩп-), COAd 15 *S* house тареıшωпе ϩıоү поүромпе, *ib* 221 *S* етрар ϩωв ϩıпеккамоүл (cf 219 sim пϩнтϥ), MIE 2 398 *B* мошı ϩıпıмωıт = BAp 97 *S* ϩıтеϩıн, Ep 533 *S* ϩепϫоı, BSM 36 *B* аϥкотϥ ϩıпеϥмωıт = BMis 379 *S* етеүϩıн, Ep 87 *S* птооү еϥоүнр ϩıоүωϥ, C 41 67 *B* corpse сıϥ евол ϩıпıтωоү, CO457 *S* пеүаггелıоп...(written) ϩıоүхωме пхартнс, Miss 4 181 *B* пхωм ... еϥсϩноүт ϩıоүтϥ, J 58 16 *S* house етϩıпшнı (cf *ib* 10 птпе м-), Mor 30 5 *F* clothes ϩıоүωтв = BMis 233 *S* ϩıхωϥ, BKU 1 26 (8116 a)*F* lay a cover ϩıпеϭра, PGM 1 114 *O* Satan еϩнıωϩ (ϩıωтϥ); often for ϩп-, in: Kr 132 *S* ϩıпвооү, *ib* 21 *F* ϩı(п)таш поүωт, BM 1042 *S* found one ϩıшмоүп, PBu 214 *S* witness ϩıтепкеϫопıа (γειτνία), JKP 2 26 *S* оүстүллос ϩıтаϫωра, CMSS 47 *F* ϩıпоүωш еппоүтı (v also above where = ἐν); in adjectival & participial phrases: Is 24 6 *B* шоп ϩı- (*S* ϩп-) κατοικῶν, *ib* 59 8 *B* мошı ϩı-(*S* do) διοδεύων, Lu 2 34 *S* оүϩωϭм ϩı-(*B* diff) ἀντιλεγόμενος, Nu 6 14 *S* мп ϫвıп ϩı- (*B* diff) ἄμωμος, Mk 15 23 *S* мохϭ ϩıоүшал (*B* diff) ἐσμυρνισμένος, *ib* 5 15 *S* ϩоеıте ϩı-(*B* тоı ϩı-) ἱματισμένος, 2 Kg 1 2 *S* пнϭ ϩı- διερρωγώς, Sa 10 7 *S* карпос ϩı-καρποφορῶν, Deu 11 11 *S* ϩıпкıсе(*B* diff) ὀρεινός, Jer 3 2 *B* ϩıпшаϥе ἐρημούμενος. **b** con-

cerning: Si 41 17 *S* περί; Ac 11 19 *SB* ἐπί; ShBor 246 83 *S* еүпоϭпеϭ ммоп ϩıппомос мпетхосе, CA 108 *S* кω[те] ϩıϩепхωмме ммагıа = *ib* ٢٠ ‏ﻓﺘﺶ‎, Pcod 20 *S* inquire ϩıшωп оүеıϫос н етааϥ, RE 9 136 *S* lest destitution come ϩıтааформн, Ryl 280 *S* птапескапϫалоп шωпе ϩıпıм, PBu 61 *S* птасепıтрепе паϥ ϩıоүωϥ, J 122 40 *S* agreed together ϩıпкаϩ етммаү, Ep 300 *S* мпоү† лаге паı ϩıωϥ, CO 411 *S* solidus paid ϩıтшорп пкатавол (cf *ib* 427 үпер). **c** *with*: Is 28 27 *B*(*S* мп-), Mic 3 11 *SA*(*B* ϫа-), Mt 27 34 *S*(*B* пем-) μετά; Is 3 23 *SB* σύν; PS 334 *S* оүωшм мпсорм ϩıпеϥернү, Ryl 106 67 *S* оүошмоү ϩıоүоү (cf Nu 7 19), PMéd 287 *S* тсоү ϩıкрп, BKU 1 26 (8117) *F* леϫмеϥ ϩıмаү, Pcod 34 *S* порпıа мохт ϩıмаı (var мп-), Cai 42573 2 *S* тввооү ϩıеϥıω, PBu 158 *S* еıпнү ϩıталласн. **d** *from, out of*: Lev 13 58 *S*(*B* om), Nu 30 9 *S*(*B* do), Job 5 22 *A*(Cl, *S* ϩıтϫ п-), Ps 74 6 *S*(*B* евол ϫеп-), Mic 3 2 *S*(*A* ϩıхп-, *B* ев. п-), Pro 4 24 *A* ϩıса пвал п- (*S* псавол, *B* сав.) ἀπό, 1 Kg 20 38 *S* ϩıпса п- ἐκεῖ ἀπό; Mk 11 20 *B* (*S* хıп-), Ac 20 30 *S*(Ryl 99, var & *B* ев. ϩп-), Z 346 *S* what God shall assign us ϩıоүоү, CDan 90 *B* could not open mouth ϩıтеϥϩо† ἐκ; Mk 15 24 *F* паш...ϩıωωтоү (*SB* еϩрп-) διά-; PS 356 *S* еоүапе ϩıпшомпт, ShC 73 98 *S* петϭе еϩраı ϩıпвнпе, ShBMOr 8810 411 *S* turn back ϩıпıмптреϥ† ϭωпт, Leyd 418 *S* тωоүп ϩıпетмооүт (cf Mt 14 2 &c евол ϩп-), BMar 23 *S* set him down ϩıпϩермета-рıоп, *ib* 133 *S* птаϥеı ϩıпшммо, Miss 8 207 *S* sim, PBu 149 *S* еıпнү ерıс ϩıвавүлωп, ST 199 *S* moneys еүо плнпас (λοιπάς)ϩıттıмн; ShA 2 329 *S* ϭı ϩıоүωϭ мпескосмос, ShR 2 3 51 *S* аүтсаво ϩıоүωк еϥı ерооү, R 1 4 21 *S* cup ешаϥϭе мооү ϩıоүωϥ, BMis 271 *S* пеϩ пеккоүптарıоп ϩıоүωϥ (var Mor 30 47 *Sᶠ* евол ϩп-), Ep 181 *S* пωϭе мпше (stocks) ϩıеıωт, BM 1124 *S* маıтı лаау паϥ ϩıоүоү, AZ 23 108 *S* recipe ϭоп оүϫı ϩıоооү, Ryl 344 *S* of men sent ашомет шωпе ϩıоүоү, PLond 4 435 *S* ерϣапоүа ϩıоүоү (sc conscripts) кам(п)теı, BM Or 6203 *S* оүмерос ϩıоүωϥ (cf J pass мерос птаϥ), Ryl 211 *S* тпаше ϩıоүоү. **e** *under, in time of, presence of*: Deu 17 6 *S* (var ϩıтп-, *B* ев. ϩıт.), Is 54 9 *S*(*B* паϩреп-), Hag 2 10 *SA* пϩı- *B*, Mt 1 11 *SB*, Cl 5 7 *A*, Aeg 272 *S* there were prophets ϩıωωп ἐπί; Deu 9 27 *B* ωрк пϭ(ı)ωтк (var еϩрак) ммıп ммок (v JTS 3 269 *inf*) κατὰ σεαυτοῦ; BHom 114 *S* птако...ϩıсеϫекıас, RNC 65 *S* martyred ϩıарıапос, J 23 65 *S* каас (sc пρасıс) евол ϩıппомıкос, PSBA 33 pl 49 *S* аıсϫаı...ϩıпаүлос плашапе, P 129¹⁴ 110 *S* перωоү птаүшωпе ϩıωωϥ, J 91 5 *S* пıкаıрос паı етϩıωϥ, BM 1026 *S* тıр]омпе епϩıωωс, Kr 7 *S* sim, Mor 28 206 *S* ϩıωωк оүп ϩепр-

ⲣⲱⲟⲩ ⲛⲁⲧⲱⲟⲩⲛ, J 84 17 S ϩⲓⲱⲓ ⲙⲡⲉⲧⲛⲏⲩ ⲙⲡ-
(ⲛ)ⲥⲟⲓ. *f at* time of: Jer 7 25 B ϩⲓϣⲱⲣⲡ ὄρθρου;
ShC 73 103 S ϩⲓⲣⲟⲩϩⲉ (var ⲛ-), Miss 4 634 S ϫⲟⲟⲩϥ
ⲡⲁⲓ ϩⲁⲣⲟⲩϩⲉ…ϯⲛⲁⲧⲛⲛⲟⲟⲩϥ ϩⲓⲣ. *g and:* Lev 25
23 S(B ⲟⲩⲟϩ), Nu 13 28 S(B ⲛⲉⲙ-), Pro 29 31 S
(var & A ⲙⲛ-), Eccl 2 11 S(ShZ 593, var ⲁⲩⲱ, F
ⲁⲣⲁ), Hos 8 10 A(B ⲛ.), Mt 13 17 SF(B do), *ib* 14
21 S(BF do), Jo 2 14 S (var ⲁⲩⲱ, A²B do), Cl 46 5
A ⲡⲟⲩⲕⲥ ϩⲓⲡⲱⲣϫ ⲁⲟⲩ ϩⲧⲁⲣⲧⲣ ϩⲓⲡⲟⲗⲉⲙⲟⲥ καί;
Br 109 S ϯ ⲁⲣⲕⲏⲑⲓⲥ (ἄρκευ.) ⲉϩⲣⲁⲓ ϩⲓⲙⲁⲗ ⲁⲩⲱ ϩⲓⲗⲓⲃⲁⲛⲟⲥ (*cf* p 170 a *inf*), PS 35 S ϫⲁⲧϥⲉ ϩⲓⲧⲃⲛⲏ,
Sh(Besa)Bor 205 365 S ⲣⲉϥϯ ⲧⲱⲛ ϩⲓⲣⲉϥⲕⲣⲙⲣⲙ…
ⲁⲩⲱ ⲣⲉϥⲣ ⲛⲟⲃⲉ ⲛⲓⲙ, Mun 31 S angels ϩⲓⲁⲣⲭ-
ⲁⲅⲅⲉⲗⲟⲥ ⲙⲡⲁⲡⲟⲥⲧⲟⲗⲟⲥ, BMis 302 S ⲉϥⲟ ⲛⲑⲉ ϩⲓ-
ⲣⲱⲙⲉ, ManiK 70 A² ϯ ϣⲓ ϩⲓⲙⲉⲧⲣⲟⲛ, BSM 3 B
world filled with ⲛⲟⲩϩ ϩⲓⲣⲁⲧ, C 41 11 B his sister
ⲛϣⲉⲛⲓⲱⲧ ϩⲓⲙⲁⲩ, Va 61 108 B bishop ⲛⲉⲙⲡⲣⲉⲥⲃⲩ-
ⲧⲉⲣⲟⲥ ϩⲓⲇⲓⲁⲕⲱⲛ, Kr 1 Sϐ̄ ⲉⲧⲛⲃⲉ ϩⲓⲑ̄ ⲉⲙⲁϩⲉ; *or:*
ShC 73 171 S ⲡⲉⲧⲡⲁϣⲃ ϩⲟⲕ (*l* ϩⲁⲕ) ϩⲓⲗⲁⲁⲩ ⲙⲙⲁ-
ⲛⲧⲁϥ, R 2 4 90 S not worthy to be bishop ⲏ ⲡⲣⲉⲥⲃⲩⲧⲉⲣⲟⲥ ϩⲓⲇⲓⲁⲕⲟ[ⲛⲟ]ⲥ, BMis 317 S distant ⲛⲁⲥⲟⲟⲩ
ϩⲓϣⲙⲟⲩⲛ ⲙⲙⲓⲗⲓⲟⲛ, Aeg 43 B χωρις ⲫⲁⲍⲣⲓ ϩⲓ-
ⲃⲟⲧⲁⲛⲏ, J 28 35 S ⲟⲩⲇⲉ ⲁⲛⲟⲕ ⲟⲩⲇⲉ ϣⲏⲣⲉ ϩⲓⲕⲗⲏ-
ⲣⲟⲛⲟⲙⲟⲥ; *с* ⲁⲭⲛ-, ⲁⲧϭⲛⲉ: Job 24 6 S(B ⲁⲧ-…
ⲟⲩⲟϩ) καί; BMis 180 S ⲁⲭⲛϫⲱⲣⲙ ϩⲓⲛⲟⲃⲉ, C 41 57
B ⲁ. ϩⲗⲓ ⲛϫⲟⲓ ϩⲓⲛⲉϥ (*cf ib* χωρίς ϫ. ⲡⲉⲙⲛ.).

ϩⲓⲛⲁⲓ SA²B(Ez), *thus:* Ge 1 20, Job 23 13, Lu 2
48 (all B ⲙⲡⲁⲓⲣⲏϯ), R 1 1 24 ⲙⲡⲉⲓⲣⲉ ϩ. οὕτως, Mt
20 5 (B do) ὡσαύτως; Lu 10 37 (B do) ὁμοίως; 1
Kg 14 41 τάδε; Ez 21 27 B τοιοῦτος; *ib* 12 9 B ⲉⲧⲁⲕⲉⲣ ⲟⲩ ⲡⲟⲟⲕ ϩ. ? (Gk om); AP 21 A² ⲁϩⲣⲁⲥ ϩ.?, PS
191 ⲛⲡⲉⲥⲡⲁϣϣⲱⲡⲉ ⲁⲛ ϩ., ShR 2 3 67 ⲙⲡⲉⲕⲉⲓⲣⲉ
ⲟⲛ ϩ., Mor 26 8 ⲉⲓⲣⲉ ϩ. (var *ib* 22 76 ⲛⲧⲉⲓϩⲉ), ClPr
40 2 ⲉϥϭⲣⲁⲓ ϩ. *as follows* in letter, P 129¹⁴ 116 ϩ. ⲇⲉ
ⲁϥⲛⲕⲟⲧⲕ *thereupon*, Bodl(P) b 3 marriage contract
ⲛⲧⲟ ϩⲱ ⲧⲉⲟ ϩ. *whilst thou* (bride) *hast like* (rights),
BMis 224 ⲛϯϩⲉ ϩ. ⲁϥ…ⲕⲁⲁϥ ⲉϩⲟⲩⲛ.

ⲉⲃⲟⲗ ϩⲓ- SAB, *from off, from:* Deu 11 17 B(S ⲉⲃ.
ϩⲓϫⲛ-), Pro 4 27 S (var ⲉⲃ. ϩⲛ-) A (B ⲉⲃ. ϩⲁ-), Is 30
11 S B(F ϩⲁⲃ. ⲛ-), Jon 3 6 B(SA ⲉⲃ. ϩⲓϫⲛ-), Mt 14
29 B(SF om ⲉⲃ.), C 86 303 B set child down ⲉⲃ. ϩⲓ-
ⲡⲉϫⲓϫ ἀπό, 4 Kg 5 11 S ⲁⲡⲟ-; Ex 32 32 A(Cl)B(S
ⲉⲃ. ϩⲛ-), Job 3 16 S(B ⲉⲃ. ϫⲉⲛ-), Ez 16 27 S(B ⲉⲃ.
ϩⲁ-) ἐκ, Ac 8 7 B(S ⲉⲃ. ϩⲛ-) ἐκ; Mt 8 28 S(B ⲉⲃ.
ϫⲉⲛ-) διά; Is 51 23 S(B ϭⲓⲛⲓ only) παρα-; *ib* 52 2
B(S ⲛ-), Ac 7 33 B(S ⲉⲧⲛ-) gen; Deu 28 49 B ⲉⲃ.
ϩⲓⲫⲟⲩⲉⲓ (S ⲟⲩⲏⲩ) μακρόθεν; Is 49 12 B sim (S do)
πόρρωθεν; PS 285 S ⲛⲧⲥ ⲉⲃ. ϩⲓⲧⲉϩⲓⲏ, ShMun 141
S remove filth ⲉⲃ. ϩⲓⲱϥ, ShA 2 284 S ⲡⲱⲣϫ ϩⲟⲟⲩⲧ
ⲉⲃ. ϩⲓⲥϩⲓⲙⲉ, HM 1 62 ⲉⲓ ⲉⲃ. ϩⲓⲛϫⲁⲉⲓⲉ, C 41 21 B
sim, BMis 241 S take stone ⲉⲃ. ϩⲓⲡⲉϥⲙⲁⲕϩ (var 298
om ⲉⲃ.) = Mor 30 16 F ⲉⲃ. ⲛ-, Cat 121 B ϫⲉⲛϫⲱ-
ⲟⲩ ⲉⲃ. ϩⲓⲛⲟⲩϩⲟⲣⲟⲛⲟⲥ (*cf ib* ⲉⲃ. ϩⲓⲧⲉⲛ- & ⲉⲃ. ϩⲓ-

ϫⲉⲛ-), Va 61 106 B ϭⲓ ⲉⲃ. ϩⲓⲛⲟⲩⲧⲁϩ, Ep 84 S camel-
herd's contract ⲉⲓϣⲁⲛⲛⲟϩⲕ ⲉⲃ. ϩⲓⲡⲕⲁⲙⲟⲩⲗ.

ⲉⲡⲉⲥⲏⲧ ϩⲓ- SBF, *down from off:* Ge 24 64 S(B ⲉⲃ.
ϩⲓ-), Mk 9 9 SF(B ⲉⲃⲣⲏⲓ ⲉⲃ. ϩⲓ-), Mor 17 92 S ⲉⲓ ⲉ.
ϩⲓⲧⲭⲉⲛⲉⲡⲱⲣ (var Gu 71 ⲉⲡ. ⲉϫⲛ-) ἀπό; Nu 20 28
S(B ⲉⲃ. ϩⲓϫ.), Bor 253 265 S took sacks ⲉ. ϩⲓⲛⲉⲩⲧⲃ-
ⲛⲟⲟⲩⲉ ἐκ; C 86 66 B ⲥⲟⲕϥ ⲉ. ϩⲓⲡⲓϩⲁⲣⲙⲁ καθαιρεῖν;
Mun 40 S ⲉⲧϣⲟϫⲟ ⲉ. ϩⲓⲛⲉⲥⲥⲡⲟⲧⲟⲩ.

ⲉϩⲟⲩⲛ ϩⲓ- S, *in toward:* BMis 448 ⲉϥⲟϭⲉ ⲉ. ϩⲓⲡⲧⲟⲟⲩ about 3 miles.

ϩⲣⲁⲓ ϩⲓ- F, *above on:* Is 36 2 (S ϩ. ϩⲛ-, B ⲥⲁⲡϣⲱⲓ ⲛ-) ἄνω ἐν.

ⲉϩⲣⲁⲓ ϩⲓ- SBF, *down from:* Si 36 13 S, Mt 14 29
F(S ⲉⲡⲉⲥⲏⲧ ϩⲓ-, B ⲉⲃⲣ. ⲉⲃ. ϩⲓ-), Ac 13 29 S (var
ϩⲛ-, B ⲉⲃ. ϩⲓϫ.), RNC 46 S ⲉⲓ ⲉ. ϩⲓⲡϫⲟⲓ ἀπό, KKS
254 S sim ἀποβαίνειν gen; PBu 44 S ⲉⲓ ⲉ. ϩⲓⲡⲧⲱⲣ-
ⲧⲣ; *up from:* Cant 3 6 S(F ⲉⲃ. ⲛ-), Lu 5 2 SB
ἀπό; BMar 3 S ⲁϥⲟⲓⲕϥ ⲉ. ϩⲓⲡⲉϥⲑⲣⲟⲛⲟⲥ; *upon:*
Job 4 15 S(B ⲉϫⲉⲛ-), Dan 5 5 B ἐπί; Ac 17 23 B(S
ⲉ-) ἐν; ⲡϩⲣⲏⲓ, ⲛⲃ̄. (rare) ϩⲓ- B, *upon, in:* Deu 1 1
S(S ϩⲛ-), Jer 9 26 (S ϩⲣⲁⲓ ϩⲛ-), Ez 20 15 (S ϩⲓ-) ἐν;
Is 15 5 (S ϩⲣ. ⲛ-) ἐπί; Ge 12 9, Jer 3 21 ⲛⲃ̄. ⲉⲛ.

ϩⲗⲉϥ F st pron of ϩⲓ- (Till, Polotsky OLZ '31 840):
Ep Jer 23 ⲉⲧϩⲗⲉⲩ ⲉⲩⲙⲉⲧⲥⲉⲓ(B ϩⲓϫⲉⲛ-)περικεῖσθαι
εἰς, *ib* 71 ⲉⲗ ϩⲁⲁⲗⲓ ϩⲗⲉⲩ (B ϩⲓ-) ἐπ' αὐτούς; BP 5716
among payments made ⲗⲟⲕϫⲓ ⲛ̄ ⲗⲓⲧⲣⲁ ϩⲗⲉⲩ same?

V also ⲃⲱⲗ (ϩⲓⲃⲟⲗ), ⲉⲣⲏⲩ *sf*, ⲉⲥⲛⲧ, ⲙⲁ, ⲙⲏⲣ, ⲡⲉ,
ⲡⲁϩⲟⲩ, ⲣⲟ (ϩⲓⲣⲛ-), ⲣⲁⲧ⸗, ⲣⲟⲩϩⲉ, ⲥⲟⲡ, ϯ, ⲧⲱⲣⲉ *hand*
(ϩⲓⲧⲛ-), ⲧⲟⲩⲱ⸗ (ϩⲓⲧⲟⲩⲱ⸗, ϩⲓⲧⲟⲩⲛ-), ⲟⲩⲉ, ⲟⲩⲁⲙ,
ϣⲱⲓ, ϩⲏ *front*, ϩⲓⲏ, ϩⲟ, ϩⲃⲟⲩⲣ, ϩⲟⲩⲛ, ϩⲣⲁⲓ, ϫⲱ *head*
(ϩⲓϫⲛ-).

ϩⲓⲉ, -ⲏ SB, ϩⲓⲉⲓ S(once), pl ϩⲓⲏⲩ S, -ⲛⲟⲩ, -ⲉⲩ B
& sg as pl, nn m f (B once), *rudder:* Ja 3 4 SB (both
var -ⲏ) πηδάλιον; K 133 B ϯϩⲓⲛ رجل, سكان, ﻗﺪﺓ,
P 46 164 S ϩ. بصل (*cf* ? وصلة); PS 354 S ship with
two serpents ⲉⲅⲟ ⲛϩ. ⲉⲣⲟϥ, ShIF 85 S man ⲉⲧⲣ
ϩⲓⲙⲙⲉ ⲁⲛ ⲙⲛϩ., Berl Or 1607 4 103 S ⲛϩ. ⲉⲧⲣ ϩⲓⲙⲉ ⲙⲙⲟϥ (*sc* ship), Mus 42 228 S sailors regard
not sinking ships ⲛⲥⲉⲕⲁ ⲛⲉϩ. ⲉⲃⲟⲗ, but steer on
steadily, Cai 8024 S fishes steer with tails ⲛⲑⲉ ⲛⲟⲩ-
ϩⲓⲏ, DeV 2 215 B none sitteth ϩⲁⲧⲉⲛⲛⲉϩⲉϭ., *ib* 229
B ϣⲁⲩⲕⲱϯ ⲙⲡⲓϩ. ϩⲉⲛⲛⲟⲩϫⲓϫ, BMar 91 S ⲁⲓⲕⲧⲉ
ⲡϭⲓⲉⲓ ⲙⲡⲁⲗⲁⲥ to narrate to you, Mor 22 83 S ⲁⲕ-
ⲕⲧⲟ ⲙⲡⲁⲅⲭⲏⲛ ⲛⲧⲉ ⲡϩ. ⲙⲡⲉⲕⲗⲁⲥ ⲉⲕⲉⲙⲁ; pl:
Ac 27 40 SB πηδ.; Va 57 263 B ϩⲓⲉⲩ οἴαξ; ShIF
193 S ⲡⲉⲧⲁⲙⲁϩⲧⲉ ⲛⲓⲉϩ. of ships, AM 257 B sim,
BAp 90 S ⲁⲕⲁⲙⲁϩⲧⲉ ⲛⲛϩ. & wast helmsman.

ⲁⲧϩ. B, *rudderless:* MG 25 123 ϫⲟⲓ ⲛⲁⲧϩ., BSM
98 sim = Mor 22 110 S ⲉⲙⲛ ϩ. ⲛϩⲏⲧϥ.

V Spg *Demotica* 1 37. *Cf* ϩⲓⲙⲉ nn.

ϩⲓⲉ S(once). A² particle = ⲉⲓⲉ *a:* BM 1102 20 S
(ⲉ)ϣⲱⲡⲉ ⲟⲩⲛ ϩⲟⲙⲛⲧ ⲛⲧⲟⲟⲧⲕ ϩ. ϥⲓⲧⲟⲩ ⲛⲁⲕ, ManiK

98 ⲉϣⲱⲡⲉ...ϩ. ϣⲁⲣⲉⲡⲡⲁⲃⲉ ⲁⲛ ⲉⲓ ⲁϩⲣⲏⲓ;   or ⅆ: Jo 10 36 (S ⲉⲓⲉ, B Gk om), AP 27 ϩ. ⲙⲡⲉⲧⲡⲥⲱⲧⲙ?, Mani H 80 ϩ. ⲉⲧⲃⲉⲡⲓⲙ ⲥⲉϩⲣϩⲁⲗⲧ?

ϩⲓⲏ SA²F, ϩⲓⲁ F, pl ϩⲓⲟⲟⲩⲉ, ϩⲓⲏⲩ (once) S, ϩⲓⲁ-(ⲟ)ⲩⲉ SᶠA², ϩⲓⲁⲅⲓ, -ⲁⲩ F & sg as pl (rare), nn f, *road, path* (A mostly ϩⲟ, B ⲙⲱⲓⲧ): Ge 3 24, Is 30 11 SF, Jo 14 4 SA² ὁδός, Sa 5 12 δίοδ.; Nu 33 2 (B ϫⲓⲡⲙⲟϣⲓ), Pro 26 7 πορεία; ib 24 54 ἴχνος; 1 Kg 6 12, Ps 118 35 τρίβος; PS 158 ⲕⲉϩ ⲧⲉϩ. ⲡⲡⲉⲕⲡⲓⲥⲧⲟⲥ, BG 105 ⲧⲉϩ. ⲛⲡϣⲁϫⲉ ⲙⲡⲟⲩⲟⲉⲓⲛ, Mor 52 39 ⲁⲕⲉⲓ ϩⲛⲟⲩϩ. ⲉⲥⲟⲩⲏⲩ, ib 46 26 ⲁϥⲧⲁⲁⲩ ⲉⲧⲉϩ. ⲉⲧⲣⲉϥⲙⲟⲟϣⲉ, Pcod 13 sim, Mani H 5 A² ⲡⲁⲟⲩⲣⲏⲧⲉ ϩⲛⲑⲓⲏ, Baouit 1 138 F may Lord ⲧⲁϣ ⲧⲉϩ. ⲛⲥⲁⲃϯ ⲛⲏⲡ, Lant 101 sim;   pl: Ps 16 4 SF, Pro 3 17, Lam 1 4 F ϩⲓⲁⲩ, Ro 11 33 SF ὁδ., Deu 13 16 δίοδ., Ps 64 8 ἔξοδ., Eccl 6 6 κάθοδ.; Ps 8 9, Pro 2 15 τρ.; Ps 36 23 διάβημα; Jon 2 4 (error?, var & A ϩⲟⲧⲉ, ϩⲛⲱϩⲉ, B ⲣⲱⲟⲩϣ) μετεωρισμός; PS 79 ⲛⲉⲕϩ., AJSL 46 249 charm for weal of house & ⲛⲉϩ. ⲙⲡⲉⲕⲣⲟ, Tri 520 ⲕⲱⲧⲉ ϩⲛϩⲓⲣ ⲙⲡⲛⲉϩ., Mor 32 51 Sᶠ ⲛⲉϩ. ⲙⲡⲱⲛϩ, ib 18 109 ⲛϩⲓⲏⲩ of stars (var LCyp 3 ⲛⲉϩⲓⲏ), Mani K 94 A² ⲥⲁⲩⲧⲛ ⲛϩⲡ.

ϩ. ⲡⲉⲓ ⲉⲃⲟⲗ, *way out*: Ps 76 13, Ez 42 11 ἔξοδ., cf Sa 17 9 ⲙⲛ ϩ. ⲡⲣ ⲃⲟⲗ φευκτός; ⲡⲉⲓ ⲉϩⲟⲩⲛ, *way in*: 4 Kg 14 25, Ps 73 5 εἴσοδ.; BHom 41 ϭⲛ ϩ. ⲡⲉⲓ ⲉ., J 24 126 length of ϩ. ⲉ.; ⲡⲃⲱⲕ, *way of going*: Miss 4 777 ϩ. ⲡⲃ. ⲉⲕⲁⲗⲁⲙⲟⲡ, BMis 148 ϩⲓⲟⲟⲩⲉ ⲛⲃ. ϣⲁⲡⲛ̄;   ⲛⲃ. ⲉϩⲟⲩⲛ 2 Pet 1 11 εἴσοδ.; ShC 73 17 ϩⲓⲟⲟⲩⲉ ⲛⲃ. ⲉ. ⲛϣⲁⲣⲟⲟⲩ; ⲧⲉϩ. ⲉⲧⲉϩⲏⲕ ⲉ. J 75 17; ⲛⲃ. ⲉϩⲣⲁⲓ to heaven BMis 85;   ⲙⲙⲟⲟϣⲉ, as ϩⲓⲏ: 2 Kg 15 2 ὁδ., Lam 2 19 ἔξοδ., 2 Cor 11 26 ὁδοιπορία; Ps 16 5 F ϩⲓⲁ, Is 30 11 F do (S both ⲙⲁ ⲙⲙ.) τρ.; ROC 20 56 ⲛϩⲓⲣ & ⲛⲉϩ. ⲙⲙ., Miss 8 27 ⲡⲉϩⲣⲟⲙⲟⲥ ⲛⲧⲉϩ. ⲙⲙ., Mani 1 A² ⲧϩ. ⲙⲙⲁϩⲉ; ⲣ ϩ. ⲙⲙ.: Deu 2 27 ⲉⲃⲟⲗ ϩⲓⲧⲙⲡⲉⲕⲕⲁϩ παρέρχεσθαι διά; ϩ. ⲛϫⲓⲟⲟⲣ: Is 51 10 (B ⲙⲱⲓⲧ ⲛⲥⲓⲛⲓ) διάβασις; ϩ. ⲛⲡⲣⲣⲟ, ⲙⲡ., *king's road*: Nu 20 17 (var ⲙⲡ.) ὁδ. βασιλική; ShP 130⁵ 28 ⲧⲉϩ. ⲡ., opp ϩ. ⲡϫⲁⲓⲉ, HM 1 117 came south ϩⲛⲧⲉϩ. ⲡ., R 1 3 41 ϩ. ⲙⲡ., Mani 1 A² ⲧϩ. ⲡ.

ϩⲓⲧⲉϩ., *on road*: Ex 18 8 (B ⲛϩⲣⲏⲓ ϩⲓ-), Deu 6 7 (var ϩⲛ-, B ϩⲓ-), Pro 22 13 ϩⲓⲛⲉϩⲓⲟ....ϩⲛⲛⲉⲡⲗⲁⲧⲓⲁ, Mt 5 25 (var ϩⲛ-) ἐν τῇ ὁδ.; Jud 5 10, Ac 8 26 (var ϩⲛ-) ἐπί; Lu 10 4, Ac 25 3 κατά; Deu 28 7 dat, Lam 1 12 F acc; Ps 8 9 ⲙⲟⲟϣⲉ ϩⲓⲧⲉϩ. τρίβους διαπορεύεσθαι; ⲉⲃⲟⲗ ϩⲓⲧⲉϩ.: Ps 2 12 ἐξ ὁδ., ZNTW 24 90 F ⲡⲛⲟⲩ ⲉⲃⲁⲗ ϩ. πάροδιος εἶναι.

ⲣⲙϩ., ⲣⲙⲛϩ., *man of the road, travelling companion*: BMis 530 Raphael ⲟⲩⲣⲙⲛϩ. ⲉϥϩⲣⲟⲧ (cf Tob 5 συμπορεύεσθαι), Miss 4 774 angel was to him ⲣⲙϩ., Pcod 12 sent them to thee as ⲣⲙⲛϩ., BMis 89 ⲉⲥⲟ ⲛⲁⲥ ⲛⲣⲙⲛϩ. (var Mor 33 32 ⲣⲙϩ.).

ϯ ⲧⲉϩ., *give road, means*: Nu 21 23 (B ϯ) διδόναι; PS 80 ϭⲛⲡⲁϯ ⲧⲁϩ. ⲡⲁⲓ ⲉⲧⲣⲁⲡⲟⲩϩⲙ, R 2 1 32 ϯ

ⲡⲧⲉϩ. ⲛⲣⲱⲙⲉ ⲛⲓⲙ ⲉϩⲟⲩⲛ ⲉⲡϣⲏⲡ, ViK 9586 20 ϯ ⲧ. ⲙⲙⲟⲟϣⲉ ⲛⲁⲡ ϣⲁⲡⲛ̄, Mor 50 32 ⲁϥϯ ⲧ. ⲛⲁⲩ ⲁϩⲟⲩⲗ. BMis 65 ϯ ⲧ. ⲛⲁⲡ ⲉⲧⲟⲩⲛⲃⲱⲕ (var FR 28 ϫⲓ ⲙⲟⲉⲓⲧ ϩⲏⲧⲟⲩ ϩⲛⲧⲉϩ.), Ep 382 ⲉⲣϣⲁⲛⲡⲛ̄ ϯ ⲧ. ϯⲛⲏⲩ.   Cf ϩⲉ, *manner* (ϯ ⲑⲉ).

ϩⲓⲏ   v ϩⲏ *front* & ϩⲓⲉ *rudder*.

ϩⲓⲟⲓ B (? ϩⲓ ⲟⲓ) vb intr, *discuss, dispute*: AM 253 heretics came ⲉⲩⲟⲩⲱϣ ϩⲣ.; tr: HL 114 ⲉⲩϩ. ⲛ̄ⲡⲟⲩⲙⲉⲅⲓ ⳃⲁⲧⲟⲩϩ, ROC 25 257 sat & ⲁⲩϩ. ⲡⲟⲩⲙⲉⲅⲓ;   c ⲙⲛ-: MG 25 196 ⲁⲓϩ. ⲡⲉⲙⲁϥ con-cerning virtues λόγους γυμνάζειν; ib 232 began ⲛϩ. ⲡⲉⲙⲁϥ = Z 317 S ϣⲁϫⲉ ⲙⲛ- ἰδιάζειν; HL 122 ϩ. ⲡⲉⲙⲁϥ ⲉⲑⲃⲉⲡⲓⲡⲁϩϯ συνζητεῖν; PO 14 358 ⲙⲡⲉⲣϩ. ⲡⲉⲙϩⲉⲣⲉⲥⲓⲥ (l ? ϩⲉⲣⲉⲧⲓⲕⲟⲥ) οἰκεῖν μετά *habitare cum*; as nn *discussion* leading to *confirmation*: Ro 14 1 (S ϩⲟⲧϩⲧ) διάκρισις; Eph 4 16 ⲉϥϯ ⲙⲁϯ ⳃⲉⲛⲟⲩϩ. (var ϩⲓⲟⲅⲓ, S ⲁⲓⲁⲓ ⲙⲛϯ), Col 2 2 ⲧⲥⲁⲃⲛⲟⲩⲧ ⲉⲃⲟⲗ ϩⲓⲧⲉ-ⲛⲟⲩϩ. (S ⲧⲁϩⲣⲟ) συμβιβάζειν; ⲣⲉϥϩ. (varr -ϩⲓⲟⲓ, -ϩⲓⲟⲅⲓ), *ambitious* (*contentious?*): K 88 [Arabic]; ϫⲓⲡ-ϩ.: Miss 4 218 (in Henotikon) μάθημα, σύμβολον.

ϩⲟ SA(Cl Stras, TU 43)A²BO, ϩⲁ SSᶠA(Pro 27 19)A²(Ma)FO, ϩⲱ SA(Ex Cl Berl, Pro mostly), ϩⲁⲥ S, ϩⲣⲁⲥ SBO, ϩⲣⲉⲥ AA²BF, ϩⲗⲉⲥ F, ⳃⲣⲁⲥ O (Hor) nn m, *face*: Ge 3 19 SB, Ps 16 15 SBF, ib 50 9 SA ϩⲱ (Cl, var ϩⲟ)B, Pro 7 13 SAB, ib 15 A ϩⲱ, Hos 5 15 SAB, 1 Thes 2 17 SBF, Sa 17 4 S ⲥⲙⲟⲧ ⲡⲣⲟ πρόσωπον; Lev 13 3 B(S ⲙⲁⲉⲓⲛ), ib 30 B(S ⲥⲙⲟⲧ), Ap 1 16 SB ὄψις; Dan 5 6 B μορφή; ib 1 13 S(B ⲣⲏϯ) εἰδέα; Jer 26 8 B(S Gk om); ϩⲟ ⲡⲟⲩⲱⲃϣ Ge 30 32 S(B diff) διάλευκος, ϩⲟ ⲫⲟⲡϩ ⲉϥⲁϩⲟⲩ ib 9 23 B(S diff) ὀπισθοφανῶς, ⲉⲓⲁ ⲡϩⲟ Jo 9 15 SA²B νίπτειν, ϩⲉ ⲉϫⲛⲡϩⲟ Ac 1 18 SB πρηνὴς γίνεσθαι; Br 230 S ⲉⲟⲩⲛ ϣⲟⲙⲛⲧ ⲛϩⲟ ⲙⲙⲟϥ, Mani K 112 A² ϩⲓϫⲛⲡϩⲟ ⲙⲡⲕⲁϩ, ShIF 305 S who counselled him ⲉⲁϥⲥⲉⲕ ⲡⲉϩⲟ ⲛⲙⲙⲁϥ?, ShC 73 141 S let none ϣⲉⲧⲙ ϩⲟ ⲉⲡⲉⲧⲉⲩⲣⲓⲧⲟⲩⲟϣ neglecting him, MG 25 247 B have pity & ⲙⲁ ⲡⲉⲕϩⲟ ⲛⲁϥ, Ryl 290 S let us go ⲧⲉⲛⲟⲩⲉϩ ⲡⲉⲛϩⲟ ϩⲓϫⲛⲡⲉⲡⲣⲏ (meaning?), BMis 380 S ⲡⲉϥϩⲟ ⲡⲁⲣⲧ ⲉⲡⲉⲥⲛⲧ = BSM 36 B, AP 27 A² ⲣⲱϩⲉ ⲁϩⲟⲩⲛ ϩⲁ ⲡⲉϩⲟ, MG 25 165 B ⲙⲙⲟⲛ ϩⲗⲓ ϩⲟ ⲙⲙⲟⲓ ⲉϫⲁⲓ ⲡⲟⲩⲃⲁⲓ *I have not the face to*, PGM 1 60 655 O ⲡⲉϥϩⲟ ⲡⲧⲁⲛⲧⲉ;   ϩⲟ ⲛⲣⲱⲙⲉ Ez 1 10 SB προ. ἀνθρ., ⲡϣⲙⲙⲟ Miss 8 190 S, ⲙⲙⲟⲓ PS 45 S, ⲛϩⲓⲣ ib 318 S, ⲛⲕⲁⲡⲣⲉⲥ (κάπρος) Griff Stu 163 F, ϩⲟ ⳃⲣⲟⲙⲡⲉ Mor 51 35 S;   with suff: Is 5 24 B(S diff), ib 44 8 ϩⲣⲉⲡⲉⲑⲏⲡⲟⲩ B, PS 353 S ϩⲣⲁϥ ⲕⲏⲧ ⲉⲡⲉⲓⲃⲧ, TEuch 1 2 B ϩⲣⲁⲕ ⲧⲟⲓ ⲉⲡⲉⲙⲏⲧ, Ge 2 7 S(ShC 73 37, B ⲡⲉϥ-ϩⲟ), Nah 2 2 A(B diff) ⲁϩⲟⲩⲛ ⲁϩⲣⲉⲕ, Mor 24 6 F sim ⲉϩⲗⲉϥ, Mani 1 A² ⲃⲓ ϩⲣⲉⲕ ⲁϩⲣⲏⲓ, PGM 1 60 675 O ϩⲣⲁϥ (prob);   ϩⲁ SA²(O v ϩⲁϩⲣⲟ): Ge 31 12 ⲡⲟⲩⲱⲃϣ (cit Z 583), Si 35 4 ⲡⲥⲁⲃⲉ (or ? l ϩⲁϩ ⲡ-), BP 8503 ϩⲁ ⲡⲕⲟⲩⲣ, PS 138 ⲛϩⲁⲣⲁⲕⲱⲡ, Ora 4 185

ϩⲁ·ⲇⲣⲁⲕⲱⲡ, Mani K 30 *A*² ⲛⲁ·ⲗⲙⲱⲡ, Mor 51 35
ϩⲁⲙⲟⲩⲗⲁϩⲝ, *ib* 32 46 *Sʃ* ⲓⲁ ⲡⲉⲕϩⲁ ; *cf?* here ϩⲁ·ⲡ-
ⲧⲟⲟⲩ p 441 *b*; ⲣ ϩⲟ ⲛ- *S*: Bor 304 56 ⲁϥⲁⲁϥ
ⲛ·ϩⲁ ⲡϣⲏⲗⲟ (Ge 42 7, *B* ⲓⲣⲓ ⲙⲙⲟϥ ⲛϣ.), BMis
552 ⲕⲁⲁϥ ⲉⲣ ϩⲁ ⲛϣ. *tamquam peregrinos*, Mor 18
33 ⲙⲡⲣⲁⲁⲧ ⲛϩⲟ ⲛϣ.

*Side, edge SAA*² : ϩⲟ ⲥⲛⲁⲩ Ps 149 6 (*B* ⲣⲟ ⲃ̄), Pro
5 4 *SA*(*B* ⲇⲟ) δίστομος; Mani 1 *A*² ⲕⲁⲗⲁϩⲏⲓ ⲙⲡϩⲟ
ⲥ.; ϩⲟ ⲛⲡⲣⲟ Is 6 4 *B*(*S* ⲧⲟⲩⲁ) ὑπέρθυρον ; Kr 127
ⲡⲉⲥⲩⲧⲉⲡⲓⲁ ϫⲱⲕ ⲉⲃⲟⲗ ⲛⲡⲉⲥϥⲧⲟⲟⲩ ⲛϩⲟ, Ryl 190 sim,
J 42 22 ⲛⲧⲟⲩⲱⲣϩ ⲡⲉⲕϩⲟ ⲁⲡⲣⲏⲧ, BM 1206 same?

Adverbial uses. ϩⲟ ⲙⲛⲡϩⲟ *S face to face*: Ge 32
30 (cit P 131² 138 v below, *B* ϩⲟ ⲟⲩⲃⲉϩⲟ) πρόσωπον
πρὸς π., Is 52 8 (*B* as Gk) ὀφθαλμοὶ πρὸς ὀ. ; PS 296
will reveal it to thee ⲛϩ. ; ϩⲟ ⲟⲩⲃⲉϩⲟ : Ez 20 35 *SB*
π. κατὰ π., 1 Cor 13 12 *B*(*S* ϩⲓ-) π. πρὸς π. ; PS 248
S reveal it ⲛϩ. ; ϩⲟ ϩⲓϩⲟ *S* : Ge 32 30 v above, Deu
34 10 (*B* ⲇⲟ) π. κατὰ π. ; Ex 33 11 (*B* ⲇⲟ) ἐνώπιος
ἐνωπίῳ ; ShA 2 271 ϯⲛⲁⲥⲟⲟϩⲉ ⲉⲣⲱⲧⲛ ⲛϩ., BMis
236 ⲛⲁⲩ ⲉⲡϩⲱⲃ̄ ⲛϩ. ; Ora 4 23 *S* give power ⲛⲁ-
ϩⲣⲏⲁ ϩⲁ ⲡⲉϩϩⲟ ⲛⲥⲁⲡⲉϩϩⲟ ; ⲛϩⲟ, *by face, by sight*:
Gal 1 22 *S*(*B* ϩⲉⲛⲛϩ.) τῷ πρ. ; ⲙⲡϩⲟ : ShMun 104
S know them not ⲙ. ; ϩⲁⲙⲡϩⲟ : AP 6 *A*² had not
seen him ϩ. τὸν χαρακτῆρα ; BMis 396 *S* know thee
not ϩ., Mor 18 3 *S* knew deacon ϩ. ϩ. = Miss 4 98
B, Ostr Jéquier *S* worthy ⲛⲛⲁⲩ ⲉⲛⲉⲡⲉⲣⲏⲩ ϩⲁⲙⲫⲟⲟ-
ⲟⲩ (*l?* ⲫⲟ) ; ϩⲁ·ⲡϩⲟ, *from face, away from*: Jud 6
2 *S*, Is 31 8 *B*(*S* ϩⲏⲧⲍ ⲛ-, *F* ϩⲁ·ϫⲉⲡ-) ἀπὸ πρ., Lev
26 36 *S*(*B* ⲉⲃⲟⲗ ϩⲉⲛ-) ἀπό (var ἀπὸ πρ.), Aeg 269 *S*
was taken up ϩⲁ·ⲡⲉⲩϩⲟ ; Am 2 9 *B* ϩⲁⲧⲉⲛ ⲙⲡⲟⲩϩⲟ
(*Sʃ* JEA 11 246 ⲛⲡⲉϩϩⲁ) ἐκ πρ., 2 Thes 1 9 *B* ⲉⲃⲟⲗ
ϩ. ⲙ. (*S* diff) ἀπὸ πρ. ; AZ 21 94 *O* Osiris ⲡⲉⲧϩⲁϩ-
ϥⲁ (*l* ϩⲁⲫⲁ or? for ⲡⲉⲧϩⲁ-) ⲛⲛⲟⲩⲃⲥ *over against, beside* (cf DM 21 3).

With various vbs. ⲣ (ⲓⲗ *F*) v ϫⲓ ϩⲟ below ; ⲕⲱ,
give leave, licence, heed(?): ShBor 247 110 *S* ⲕⲁ ϩⲣⲁⲥ
ⲛⲑⲟⲟⲣⲙⲏⲛ...ⲉⲧⲣⲉⲥⲥⲕⲓⲣⲧⲁ, DeV 2 55 *B* ϫⲁ ϩⲣⲁⲩ ⲛ-
ⲡⲉⲡⲗⲟⲩⲥⲓⲙⲟⲥ & not restrain them, Wess 15 151 *S*
ⲕⲁ ⲡⲉⲕϩⲟ ϩⲏⲡⲧⲉⲓⲕⲟⲩ ⲛⲡⲕⲁⲗⲓϩⲉ, PLond 4 524 *S* ⲕⲁ
ϩⲟ ϩⲓϫⲛ- sim ; ⲕⲱⲧⲉ, ⲕⲧⲟ, *turn*: He 12 25 *B*(*S* diff)
ἀποστρέφεσθαι ; PS 353 *S* ⲉⲣⲉϩⲣⲁⲩ ⲕⲏⲧ ⲉⲡⲉⲓⲃ̄ⲧ, Bodl
Marsh 32 152 *B* ⲕⲉⲧ ϩⲣⲁⲕ ⲉⲡⲉⲙⲛⲧ ; ⲧⲁⲥⲑⲟ sim :
DeV 2 52 *B* ; ⲫⲱⲛϩ sim : Ps 9 22 *B*(*S* diff) ὑπερορᾶν.
ⲡⲉⲥⲉϩⲣⲁⲍ v ⲡⲉⲥⲉ- ; ⲡⲉⲧϥ ϩⲟ v ⲛⲟⲩⲧϥ ; ⲛⲁϣⲧϩⲣⲁⲍ
v ⲛϣⲟⲧ.

ϯ, *put, direct* (ϯ ϩⲟ *beseech* v below): 4 Kg 12
17 *S* πρόσωπον τάσσειν ; Mus 34 203 *B* of Joseph Ari-
math ⲁⲕϯ ⲉϩⲣⲁϥ ⲉⲡⲓⲙⲁ ⲛϣⲁⲓ πρὸς ἀνατολὰς κατα-
θάπτειν ; BIF 14 140 *S* ⲁϥϯ ⲙⲡⲉϥϩⲟ ϩⲓⲡⲉⲑⲉⲁϩ-
ⲣⲟⲛ (var LMär 38 ⲁϥϭⲱϣⲧ ϩⲓⲡϣⲟⲩϣⲧ ⲙⲡⲉⲑ.),
BKU 31 9 11 *S* by persuasion mayest conquer, if not
ⲕⲛⲁϯ ⲙⲡⲉⲕϩⲟ ⲁⲛ ⲛⲛⲙⲁⲩ, LAl 7 *S* wilt not hear
me ⲟⲩ·ⲇⲉ ⲙⲡⲉⲕϯ ⲛⲡⲉⲕϩⲟ ⲉϫⲟⲓ, BAp 154 *S* ⲙⲡⲣⲧ ϯ

ϩⲟ ⲉⲃⲟⲗ as hypocrites, but renounce desires (meaning?), Aeg 51 *B* ⲁⲩϯ ⲙⲡⲟⲩϩⲟ ⲉϥⲁϩⲟⲩ & wept, *ib*
49 *B* ⲁⲛϯ ϩⲣⲁⲡ ⲉⲃⲟⲗ & wept = Wess 15 124 *S* ϥⲉⲓ
ϩⲟ ⲉⲃ̄., TT 109 *S* sim, C 43 39 *B* ⲁⲩϯ ϩⲣⲁⲩ ⲉⲃ̄. ⲁⲩ-
ⲫⲱⲧ = Mor 39 13 *S* ⲕⲁⲧⲟⲩ ⲉⲡⲁϩⲟⲩ = *ib* 41 123 *S*
ⲟⲗⲟⲩ ⲉϩⲣⲁⲓ, C 86 114 *B* ⲁⲥϯ ⲉϩⲣⲁⲥ ⲉⲡϣⲱⲓ & wept.

ϣⲱⲡ, *receive, accept*: Ge 32 20 *SB* ⲡⲣ. προσδέχεσθαι ; Mani 1 *A*² ⲁⲓϣ. ϩⲣⲉϥ opp ⲁⲓⲕⲁⲁϥ ⲛⲥⲱⲓ,
BMis 204 *S* may Lord ϣⲉⲛ ϩⲣⲁⲕ ⲉϩⲟⲩⲛ ⲉⲧⲉϥⲙⲛⲧ-
ⲉⲣⲣⲟ, Mor 41 103 *S* ⲙⲡⲉϥϣⲡ ϩⲣⲁⲩ ⲉϩⲟⲩⲛ ⲉⲡⲧⲏⲣϥ,
P 132¹ *S* ⲁϥϣⲉⲛ ϩⲣⲁϥ ⲙⲡⲣⲣⲟ *besought*, BMis 39 *S*
hath released him ⲙⲡⲉϥϣⲉⲛ ϩⲣⲁⲕ *without asking
thee* ; Gu 66 *S* ⲉϥⲟ ⲛⲁⲧϣⲡ ϩⲣⲁϥ *inexorable* = EW
34 *B* ⲛⲁϣⲧ ⲛϩⲣⲣⲁϥ σκληρὸς εἶναι.

ϥⲓ *SB, raise*: Is 23 16 *S* ϥⲓ ϩ. ⲉⲃⲟⲗ (*B* ⲕⲱϯ ⲉϩⲣⲏⲓ)
ῥεμβεύειν ; FR 98 ⲁⲛϥⲓ ⲉϩⲣⲁⲓ ⲉⲡϣⲱⲓ, BSM 127
ⲁⲥϥⲁⲓ ⲙⲡⲉⲥϩⲟ ⲉⲡϣ., *cf* C 86 114 above & LMis 392.

ϩⲓ (ϩⲓ·ⲟⲩⲓ) ⲛϩⲟ *B, overlook, disregard*: Lev 26 40
(*S* ⲕⲱ ⲛⲥⲁ-), Ps 77 62 (*S* ⲱϩϣ ⲉ-) ὑπεριδεῖν, Is 57
11 (*S* ⲇⲟ) παριδ. ; Job 19 18 (*S* ⲕⲱ ⲛⲥⲁ-) ἀποποιεῖσθαι ;
Pro 1 8 (*SA* ⲇⲟ) ἀπωθεῖν ; Lam 1 19 (*F* ϩⲓ ϩⲧⲉ) παραλογίζεσθαι ; Va 61 16 ⲉⲑⲃⲉⲟⲩ ⲁⲕϩⲓ ⲛϩⲟ ⲙⲙⲟⲩ?,
DeV 2 44 ⲁϥϩ. ⲙⲡⲁⲓⲁϫⲓⲱⲙⲁ ; ⲣⲉϥϩ. : Ps 118 21
(*S* ϫⲁⲥⲓϩⲏⲧ) ὑπερήφανος ; Ro 1 30 (*S* ϩⲁ·ⲃⲉⲣⲱⲙⲉ)
ἀλαζών ; ⲙⲉⲧⲣⲉϥϩ. : Deu 17 12 (*S* ⲙⲛⲧϫⲁⲥⲓϩⲏⲧ),
Ps 30 19 (*S* ⲇⲟ) ὑπερηφανία ; 1 Jo 2 16 (*S* ⲙⲛⲧϣⲟⲩ-
ϣⲟⲩ) ἀλαζονεία ; DeV 2 96 ⲁϥϫⲓⲥⲓ ϩⲉⲛϯⲙ. (Dan 5
20) ; ϫⲓϩⲟ. : Va 57 214 ⲡⲓϫ. ⲛⲡⲓϩⲏⲕⲓ ὑπεροψία.

ϫⲓ, ϭⲓ ϩⲟ, ⲛϩⲟ, ⲙⲡϩⲟ, *take face, respect person,
pay heed*: Lev 19 15 *SB*, Si 32 12 *S*, Lam 4 16 *SB*
(*F* ⲓⲗ ϥⲁ), Gal 2 6 *SB* ⲡⲣ. λαμβάνειν ; Job 13 10 *S*
(*B* ϫⲟⲩϣⲧ ⲉ-), *ib* 22 8 *S*(*B* ⲉⲣ ϣⲫⲏⲣⲓ ⲛ-), Pro 18 5
SA ⲡⲣ. θαυμάζειν ; *ib* 24 38 *SA* ⲡⲣ. αἰδεῖσθαι ; Deu
1 17 *S*(*B* ⲥⲱⲟⲩⲛ) ⲡⲣ. ἐπιγινώσκειν ; Ex 23 21 *S*(*B*
diff), Sa 6 8 *S* ὑποστέλλεσθαι ; Nu 9 13 *B*(*S* as Gk)
ὑστερεῖν ﺮﻈﻧ ; Va 68 167 *B* ⲙⲡⲉϥϫⲓ ϩⲟ ⲉⲓ ἀναμένειν ; 1 Pet 3 20 *B*(*S* ⲕⲱ ⲉⲃⲟⲗ) ἀποδέχεσθαι ; Mk 12
14 *F*(PMich 545, *SB* ϭⲱϣⲧ ⲉ-) βλέπειν εἰς ; Bor 252
304 *S* let us not ϫⲓ ⲙⲡϩⲟ ⲛⲟⲩⲟⲛ ⲙⲙⲟⲟⲩ, Mor 48
38 *S* angel comforted me ⲁⲓϫⲓ ϩⲱ ⲛⲧϫⲓ·ⲭ ⲙⲡⲁⲅⲅⲉⲗⲟⲥ (BMar 222 om), Mani K 6 *A*² ⲁⲓϫⲓ ⲛϩⲟ ⲙ-
ⲡⲟⲩⲉ ⲡⲟⲩⲉ ; *cf* ϭⲱϣⲧ ⲛⲥⲁϩⲟ ⲛⲣⲱⲙⲉ PBu 238 *S* ; C
41 51 *B* caused (belated) water to come ⲛⲧⲉϥϭⲓ ⲛϩⲟ
ⲙⲡⲓⲕⲁϩⲓ *cover* = Miss 4 411 ﻦﻛﻮﻜﻳﻭ ; ϫⲓ, ϭⲓ
ϩⲟ *nn* : Ro 2 11 *S*(BF ⲙⲉⲧⲣⲉϥϭ.) προσωποληψία,
Aeg 274 *S* -ληψις ; 1 Tim 5 21 *S*(*B* ⲣⲓⲕⲓ) πρόσκλισις ;
Ac 25 17 *B*(*S* diff) ἀναβολή ; Mor 24 22 *F* ⲛⲉⲓϫ. ⲛ-
ⲧⲁϥⲉⲓⲧⲟⲩ in neglecting us, J 106 91 *S* ⲕⲣⲓⲙⲁ ⲉⲧⲉⲙ-
ϫ. ⲛⲣⲏⲧϥ ; ⲁϫⲛϫ., *without favour*: 1 Pet 1 17 *S*
(*B* ⲁⲧϫⲟⲩϣⲧ ⲉϩⲟ), Cl 1 3 *A* ἀπροσωπολήπτως ; ⲁⲧϫⲓ, ϭⲓ ϩⲟ sim : Va 57 134 *B* ψ·ⲅⲫⲟⲥ... ⲡⲁ. ἀδέκαστος ;
J 75 121 *S* ⲃ̄ⲏⲙⲁ ⲡⲁ. ; ⲙⲛⲧⲁ. among virtues Bor
254 174 *S* ; ⲣⲉϥϫⲓ, ϭⲓ ϩⲟ, *who shows favour*: Ac

10 34 *SB*, C 99 227 *S* = C 89 50 *B* προσωπολήπτης ; PS 365 *S* ⲛ̄ⲣ. who favour sinners ; ⲙⲛ̄ⲧ-, ⲙⲉⲧⲣ.: Ro 2 11 *BF*(*S* ⲝ. ⲛⲛ), Ja 2 1 *S*(*B* ⲙⲉⲧⲣⲉϥϭⲟⲩϣⲧ ⲉ-) -ληψία ; Jo 7 24 *S*(*B* ϩⲟ) ὄψις ; ShViK 9812 *S* accursed thou ⲧ.ⲙ., Sh(?)Mor 54 96 *S* ϭⲱϣⲧ ϩⲓⲭⲏⲡⲉⲙⲩⲥⲧⲏⲣⲓⲟⲛ ϩⲉⲛⲟⲩⲙ. to favour certain ; p p.: Mor 25 62 *S* ⲉⲓϣⲁⲡⲁⲣⲓⲥⲕⲉ ⲛ̄ⲧⲁⲣ ⲣ.

ϫⲓ, ϭⲓ ϩⲣⲁϥ, ⲡϣ. *SAB*, ϫⲓ ϩⲣⲁⲉⲓⲧ† *SA*²(once each), *disport, amuse, occupy self, converse*: Ge 24 63 *S*(*B* ⲥⲛⲏⲛⲓ), Ps 76 3 (*B* ⲉⲣ ⲙⲉⲗⲉⲧⲁⲛ) ἀδολεσχεῖν ; Is 1 18 *A*(Cl, *SB* diff) διελέγχειν (as if ? διαλέγεσθαι C Schmidt) ; C 99 187 *S* ⲉϥϫⲓ ϩⲣⲁϥ ⲏ ⲉϥⲥⲱⲃⲉ πλέον γελᾶν (for both) ; ShC 42 49 *S* children ⲉⲩⲥⲱⲃⲉ ⲉⲩϫⲓ ϩⲣⲁϥ, ShC 73 80 *S* ⲉⲛϫⲱ ⲙⲙⲟⲥ ⲉⲩϫⲓ ϩⲣⲁϥ *even if joking*, BerlOr 1607 1 110 *S* ϩⲟⲥⲟⲛ ⲉⲧⲉⲧⲛ̄ϫⲓ ϩⲣⲏⲧⲛ̄ ⳿ⲓⲛⲁⲃⲱⲕ, BM 363 116 *S* looking from side to side ⲉϥϫⲓ ϩⲣⲁϥ & stumbled, DeV 2 55 *B* suffering not thoughts to ϭⲓ ϩⲣⲁϥ ; Mani H 59 *A*² ⲡⲉϥϫⲓ ϩ.† opp ⲕⲁⲣⲁⲧϥ ; c ⲛ-acc : EW 4 *B* ⲙⲁⲣⲟⲛ ⲉⲧⲕⲟⲓ ⲡⲧⲉⲛϭⲓ ⲉⲩϩⲣⲁϥ (sic) ⲙⲙⲟⲛ ; c ⲉ-, *attend to*: Is 1 23 *S*(*B* ϯ ϩⲏⲧ) προσέχειν acc, 1 Tim 1 4 *S*(*B* do), Mor 37 36 *S* each that desired to ϫⲓ ϩⲣⲁϥ ⲉⲣⲟϥ ⲡ. dat ; *ib S* ⲝ. ⲉⲧⲁⲥⲕⲏⲥⲓⲥ σχολάζειν dat ; 1 Thes 4 11 *S* dat commodi (*B* as Gk) τὰ ἴδια πράσσειν ; ShC 73 111 *S* after resting ⲉⲩⲛⲁϫⲓ ϩⲣⲁϥ ⲉⲡⲉⲩϩⲱⲃ, ShC 42 24 *S* we in our τόποι ⲧⲓϫⲓ ϩ.† ⲉⲣⲟⲛ, BAp 122 *S* ϫⲓ ϩⲣⲁⲕ ⲉⲣⲟⲕ for I found great serpent = PO 22 417 احترس على نفسى ر, واحترز, Bor 258 42 *S* hands ϫⲓ ⲁⲛ ϩⲣⲁϥ ⲉⲧⲁⲙⲛ̄ⲧⲁⲙⲉⲗⲏⲥ, BM 657 *S*ᶠ ϥϫⲓ ϩⲣⲁϥ ⲉⲧⲁⲓⲁⲕⲟⲡⲁ, Till Oster 16 *A* ϫⲓ ϩⲣⲏⲧⲛⲉ ⲁⲡⲉⲧⲛ̄ϣⲱⲡ ; c ⲙⲛ̄-, *sport, converse with*: Lam 3 20 *S*(*B* ⲥⲁϫⲓ ⲉⲝ., *F* ⲱⲃϣ, cf above c ϩⲓ) κατάδολ. ἐπί ; ShR 2 3 50 *S* hast lapdogs with thee in bed ⲉⲧⲣⲉⲕϫⲓ ϩⲣⲁⲕ ⲛⲙ̄ⲙⲁⲩ, BMar 54 *S* ⲉϥϫⲓ ϩⲣⲣⲁϥ ⲙ̄ⲡⲁⲧⲉϥϭⲟⲧ (*sc* children of like age), Gu 56 *S* ⲉⲩϫⲓ ϩⲣⲣⲁϥ ⲙⲛ̄ⲛⲉϥⲉⲣⲏⲩ = *HorSem* 3 ١٣ يكرّروا الخطاب, Bor 248 51 *S* ⲁⲓϫⲓ ϩⲣⲁⲓ ⲙⲛ̄ⲡⲁϩⲏⲧ, BIF 13 101 *S* ⲡⲉϥϫⲓ ϩⲣⲣⲁϥⲡⲉ ⲛⲙ̄ⲙⲁⲩ about ships = MG 25 282 *B*, C 89 148 *B* evil passions ⲛⲁϥϭⲓ ϩⲣⲁϥ ⲛⲉⲙⲱⲟⲩⲡⲉ = Va ar 172 85 بهما المستلذ (MG 17 518 diff) ; c ⲛ̄-: Lu 10 40 *B*(*S* = Gk) περισπᾶν περί ; c ϩⲁ-: ShCl Pr 36 201 *S* heretics ϫⲓ ϩⲣⲣⲁϥ ϩⲁⲡⲉⲧⲟⲩⲁⲁⲃ ; c ϩⲓ- *S*, *reflect upon, talk against*: Ps 68 12 (*B* ⲥⲁϫⲓ ϩⲁ-) ἀδολ. κατά ; ViK 9318 ⲉⲧϫⲓ ϩⲣⲁϥ ϩⲓⲡⲉⲥ⳿ⲧⲟⲥ, Mor 41 3 begged a book ⲛ̄ⲧⲁϫⲓ ϩⲣⲁⲛ ϩⲓⲱⲱϥ = DeV 2 249 *B* ⲡ̄ϩⲏⲧϥ̄ ; c ϩⲛ̄-, *meditate upon, sport with*, *SAA*²: Ps 118 15 (*B* ⲥⲁϫⲓ), *ib* 26 (*B* ⲉⲣ ⲙⲉⲗ.) ἀδολ. ἐν, BM 247 5 hindering us ⲉϫⲓ ϩⲣⲁⲛ ϩⲛ̄ⲛⲉϥϣⲁϫⲉ ἀδ. dat, Mor 17 106 sim ἡδέως δέχεσθαι ; Eccl 1 13 (*F* ⲱⲃϣ) περισπ. ἐν ; Bor 253 119 ⲛⲧϫⲓ ϩⲣⲁⲛ ϩⲛ̄ⲛⲉⲣⲃⲏⲩⲉ ⲛ̄ⲧⲕⲁⲕⲓⲁ στήκειν ἐν ; Hab 1 10 *SA*(*B* ⲥⲱⲃⲓ ⲛⲛ) παίγνια (εἶναι) ; ShA 2 256 ⲛⲉⲧϫⲓ ϩⲣⲁⲩ ϩⲛⲟⲩⲛⲉⲧϣⲟⲩⲉⲓⲧ paral ⲥⲱⲃⲉ, ShZ 601 children ϫⲓ ϩⲣⲁⲩ ϩⲛⲟⲩϣⲱ, Mani 1 *A*² ϫⲓ ϩⲣⲉ ⲁⲣⲟ

ϩⲓⲡⲡⲁϭⲧⲉ ; ϫⲓ, ϭⲓ ϩⲣⲁϥ, ⲡϣ. ⲛⲛ m, *distraction*: Z 292 *S* ⲡⲝ. ⲛ̄ⲛⲃⲁⲗ μετεωρισμός (in Si 26 9 = ⲙⲛ̄ⲧϫⲁⲥⲓⲃⲁⲗ) ; Va 57 126 *B* strayeth ⲥ̄ⲉⲛⲡⲓϭ. ⲉⲧⲥⲁⲃⲟⲗ ἔξω ῥέμβεσθαι ; MG 25 245 *B* ϭⲓ ϩⲗⲓ ⲛϭ. ⲁⲡ ἀπερίσπαστος ; Va 58 183 *B* ⲡⲓϩⲱⲣϥ ἠρεμεῖν opp ⲡⲓϭ. παλαίειν ; ShWess 18 138 *S* whoso despiseth neighbour ϩⲉⲛⲟⲩϭⲱⲛⲧ ⲏ ϩⲉⲛⲟⲩϩ. *in wrath or sport*, Bor 262 121 *S* virgins to avoid ⲝ. ⲡⲓⲙ ⲡϩⲟⲟⲩⲧ(?ⲙⲡϩ.), *ib* 138 *ult* dissolute songs & ⲛⲝ. & ⲥⲡⲁⲧⲁⲗⲁⲓⲁ (as BMar 172, cf BHom 75 sim), C 41 53 *B* ⲟⲩⲝ., ⲟⲩⲃⲱⲗ ⲉⲃⲟⲗ, ⲟⲩϭⲱⲃⲓ ; as adj: TT 27 *S* ⲥⲩⲛⲧⲩϫⲓⲁ ⲛⲝ., Miss 4 617 *S* shalt give account of ϣⲁϫⲉ ⲛⲝ. (cf Mt 12 36), Aeg 2 *B* sim ; ⲉⲓⲣⲉ ⲛ̄ⲣⲉⲡⲝ.: Aeg 271 *S* παιδιὰς ἐπιδείκνυσθαι ; ⲁⲧϭⲓ ϩ. *B*, *without distraction*: MG 25 246 ⲙⲉⲩⲓ ⲛⲁ. ἀπερίσπαστος ; TRit 41 ⲡⲟⲩϭ ⲛⲁ. مستتر غير, ⲙⲉⲧⲁⲧϭ.: 1 Cor 7 35 (*S* ⲁⲝⲣⲟⲟⲩϣ) -σπάστως ; ⲙⲛ̄ⲧϫⲓ ϩ.: Mor 25 29 *S* eating, drinking & ⲙ. ⲉⲩϣⲟⲩⲉⲓⲧ ; ⲣⲉϥϫⲓ ϩ., *light talker, trifler*: ROC 20 47 *S* ⲟⲩⲣ. ϩⲛ̄ⲛϣⲁϫⲉ ⲛ̄ⲣ̄ϭⲱⲃ.

ϫⲉⲙ ϩⲟ *B*, *find face, be sufficient, able*: Ex 4 10 (*SA* diff) ἱκανὸς εἶναι ; MG 25 129 ⲡⲕⲝ. ⲛ̄ⲥⲁϫⲓ ⲁⲡ.

† ϩⲟ *BS*(Tri only), *give face, beseech* (mostly), *encourage*: Is 10 32 (*S* ⲥⲟⲛⲥ) παρακαλεῖν ; c ⲉ-obj : Ge 19 18 (*S* ⲥⲟⲛⲥ), Ps 118 58 (*S* do), MG 25 241 ††. ⲉⲣⲟⲕ ϣⲟⲡⲧ ⲉⲣⲟⲕ δεῖσθαι, Is 57 10 (*S* ⲥⲟⲛⲥⲡ) κατάδ.; Ge 38 12, Deu 3 28 (*S* ⲥⲟⲗⲥⲗ), Is 66 12 (*S* do), MG 25 217 ⲁⲓϯ. ἐπιϭⲉⲗⲗⲟ ϫⲉ-ⲡ., Is 55 6 (*S* = Gk) ἐπικαλ.; Cai Euch 501 δυσωπεῖν ; Job 19 17 (*S* ⲕⲱⲣϣ) κολακεύειν ; Tri 593 *S* ††. ⲉⲣⲟϥ ⲉⲧⲣⲉϥ- ضر, *ib* 688 طلب ; DeV 2 75 ⲧⲉⲡϯ. ⲉⲣⲟⲕ ⲙⲟⲓ ⲡⲁⲛ, BSM 126 ⲁⲥϯ. ⲉⲣⲟϥ ⲉⲑⲣⲉϥ- ; c ⲉϫⲉⲛ-, *on behalf of*: Deu 32 36 (*S* ⲥⲟⲗ.) παρακ. ἐπί ; MIE 2 406 ⲙⲁϯ. ⲉⲡⲟⳑ ⲉⲝⲱⲓ ; ⲉϩⲣⲏⲓ ⲉϫ.: Jer 21 2 ἐπερωτᾶν περί ; TRit 220 αἰτεῖν acc ; BSM 88 ϯ. ⲉⲫϯ ⲉϩ. ⲉϫⲱⲟⲩ ; c ⲡ-dat : Cai Euch 579 ⲧⲉⲡϯ. ⲡⲧⲉⲕⲙⲉⲧⲁⲅⲁⲑⲟⲥ δεῖ.; BSM 29 ⲙⲁϯ. ⲙⲡⲟⳑ ; c ⲡⲥⲁ-: Is 33 7 (*S* ⲧⲱⲃϩ ϩⲛ̄-, *l* ⲛ-, *F* ⲛ̄-) παρακ. acc ; c ϩⲁ-: BSM 65 ϯ. ⲉⲡⲟⳑ ϩⲁⲛⲧⲉⲛⲟⲥ = BMis 157 *S* ⲥⲟⲛⲥ ; as nn m, *supplication*: Ps 6 10 (*S* ⲥ.) δέησις ; Jer 38 9, Ac 4 36 (*S* do) παράκλησις ; TstAb 261 ⲡⲟⲩϯ. ⲡⲉⲙⲡⲟⲩⲧⲱⲃϩ ; ϫⲓⲛϯ.: DeV 2 55 ϯϫ. ⲉϩⲣⲏⲓ ⲉⲣⲟϥ.

Compounds. ⲃⲁϩϩⲟ *q v*; ⲃⲁⲥⲧϩⲟ *v* (ⲃⲱⲥⲧ), adding PBad 5 331 *S* ⲟⲩϣⲓⲡⲉ ⲟⲩϩⲟⲡⲉ ⲟⲩϩ., *ib* 401 *S*ᶠ hatred & strife ϩⲓⲃⲁⲥϩⲁ ⲉⲡϩⲁ (ⲡ)ϩϩ.; ⲕⲁⲕϩⲣⲁϥ *v* ⲕⲱⲕ *p c*, adding = Gött ar 114 27 الشبم طوبى; ⲗⲁⲗϩⲟ *v* ϩⲁⲗϩⲟ *below*; ⲡⲁϣⲧϩⲣⲁ⸗ *v* ⲡϣⲟⲧ *s f*; ⲥⲕⲉⲡϩⲟ *v* ⲥⲕⲉⲡ; ϣⲁⲃϩⲟ *v* ϣⲓⲃⲉ vb *p c*; ϣⲉⲡϩⲟ ⲛⲛ *B* + ϭⲓ, *placate face, be acceptable*: Va 57 232 ⲁϥⲉⲣ ⲉⲩⲇⲟⲕⲓⲙⲓⲛ ⲟⲩⲟϩ ⲁϥϭⲓ ϣ., *ib* 197 ⲁϥϭⲓ ϣ. ⲟⲩⲟϩ ⲁϥ ⲣ ⲁⲡⲁϥ ⲙⲫϯ εὐδοκιμεῖν ; HL 104 of Evagrius ⲡⲉϥ ϩ(ⲃ)ⲛⲟⲩⲓ ⲡϣ. & his progress ; ϩⲁⲗϩⲟ *S*, ⲗⲁⲗϩⲟ *B* nn, *deceiving face*: Mor 40 5 *S* ⲣⲉϥϯ ϩ. ⲡⲁⲡⲧⲓⲙⲁⲧⲟⲥ = *ib* 39 7 *S*ᶠ ⲣⲉϥϭⲗ ϩⲉⲗ(ⲣ ϩⲁⲗ) ⲙⲙⲁⲧⲟⲥ = C

43 36 *B* ⲣⲉϥϯ ⲗ.;   ⲙⲏⲧϩ. *S*: 2 Kg 20 6 ⲕⲱ ⲡⲟⲩⲙ.
σκιάζειν; ViSitz 172 4 19 died ϩⲛⲟⲩⲥⲙⲟⲧ ⲙⲙ. τὸ
δοκεῖν πεπονθέναι, Miss 8 22 ϩⲛⲟⲩⲙ. (sic MS) ⲥⲉϫⲓ
ⲥⲟⲗ;   ϩⲁⲗⲁϩⲟ *S* (same?), *deception, fraud* or ? a
disease: Kropp K 29 no context (*cf* DM 18 10 *h'l'-
ḥr* HT).

ⲣⲉⲙϩⲣⲁϩ, *man of face, of consideration* (?): 1 Kg
17 12 *S* ἀνήρ (only) *grandaevus*; Va 63 87 *B* Paul as
persecutor ⲉⲟⲩⲁⲓⲉ ⲉⲃⲟⲗ ϫⲉⲛⲡⲓⲣⲉⲙϩⲣⲁϩ (*cf* Gal
1 14).

ⲉϩⲣⲛ- *S*, ⲁϩ. *AA²*, ⲉϩⲣⲉⲡ- *B*, ⲉϩⲣⲁϩ *SBO*, ⲁϩⲣⲉϩ
A, ⲉϩⲗⲉϩ, -ⲣⲉϩ *F* prep, *toward face of, to, among*:
Nu 20 6 *B*(*S* ⲉⲣⲛ-), Mk 3 24 *B*(*S* ⲉ-), Ac 10 17 *B*
(var ϩⲓⲣⲉⲡ-, *S* ⲉⲣⲛ-) ἐπί; 1 Kg 17 48 *B*(*S* ⲉϩⲟⲩⲛ ⲉ-)
εἰς συνάντησιν; Ps 34 3 *B*(*S* ⲙⲡⲉⲙⲧⲟ ⲉⲃⲟⲗ) ἐξ ἐναντίας; 1 Kg 20 1 *S* (var ⲉϩⲟⲩⲛ ⲉ.) ἐνώπιον; Deu
9 27 *B*(*S* acc), Mt 12 25 *B*(*S* ⲉϩⲣⲁⲓ ⲉϫⲛ-) κατά,
Ps 47 14 *B*(*S* om) κατα-; Mk 15 24 *SB*(*F* ϩⲓ-) δια-;
R 2 2 20 *S* sailors observe stars ⲛⲥⲉⲥⲟⲟⲩⲧⲛ ⲙⲡ[ⲉⲩ-
ⲥⲕⲁ]ⲫⲟⲥ ⲉϩⲣⲁⲩ πρός; Ge 31 55 *B*(*S* ⲉⲣⲛ-), Ps 67
31 *B*(*S* diff), Ro 11 32 *B*(*SF* diff), 1 Cor 9 9 *B*(*S*
diff, *F* ⲉⲗⲉⲡ-) acc; Pro 8 21 *B*(*SA* ⲉϫⲛ-), Lu 15
12 *B*(*S* do) dat; Is 9 3 *B*(*S* do) Gk om; ShA 1
465 *S* ⲉⲅⲧⲙϫⲟⲟⲩⲧ ⲉϩⲣⲁⲩ (*cf ib* ϫⲟⲟⲩⲕ ⲉⲣⲁⲧⲟⲩ), Z
579 *S* painter looks at picture ⲛⲩⲥⲙⲉⲛ ⲕⲉⲟⲩⲉⲓ ⲉ-
ϩⲣⲁⲥ, ManiK 135 *A²* ⲁⲅⲡⲗⲁⲥⲥⲉ ⲁ. ⲡⲉϥⲉⲓⲛⲉ ⲡⲁϫⲁⲙ,
Mani K 90 *A²* ⲧⲡⲗⲁⲛⲏ...ⲁϥⲥⲙⲛⲧⲉ ⲁ. ⲡⲉⲓⲛⲉ ⲡⲟⲩⲣⲱⲙⲉ, Kropp G 5 *S* Mary ⲧⲉⲧⲉⲟⲩⲣⲉⲙⲡⲡⲉ, AZ 39 152
S ⲁⲓⲥⲙⲓⲛⲉ ⲡⲧⲉⲓϣⲓⲱ ⲉϩⲣⲉⲡⲓⲡⲉ (*l* ⲉϩⲣⲉⲡⲛ.), Mani
1 *A²* ⲡⲧⲱⲙⲉ ⲉⲧⲁϥⲧⲁⲙⲓⲟⲩ ⲁ. ⲧⲉϥⲙⲛⲧⲛⲁϭ, C 86
252 *B* ⲥⲱⲣ ⲙⲡⲁⲥⲱⲙⲁ ⲉϩⲣⲁⲩ, AM 295 *B* cried out
ⲉ. ⲡⲓⲣⲏⲛⲉⲙⲱⲛ;   ⲉⲃⲟⲗ ⲉ. (*B* mostly, often one ⲉϩ.
for two?), *out toward*: Ge 19 1 (*S* ⲉⲧⲱⲙⲛⲧ ⲉ-), Deu
1 44 1 ⲉϩ....ⲉϩ. ⲉ. (*S* diff) εἰς συνάντ., Jud 11 31 (*S*
ⲉϩ. ϩⲏⲧϥ), 1 Kg 9 14 *S* (var om ⲉ.), Jer 48 6 εἰς ἀπάντ., Mt 8 34 (*S* ⲉⲧⲱ. ⲉ-) εἰς ὑπάντ., Ge 28 11 (*S* do)
ἀπαντᾶν dat, Deu 23 4 (*S* ⲉϩ. ϩ.), Ps 84 11 (*S* ⲧⲱ. ⲉ-)
συναντᾶν, Jo 11 20 (*SA* prob *A²* ⲉϩ. ϩ.) ὑπαντᾶν dat;
Is 36 3 (*SF* dat) πρός; Mani H 30 *A²* ⲡⲱⲧ ⲁϩ. ⲁϩ-
ⲣⲉϥ, BIF 14 124 *S* ⲉϥⲡⲏⲩ ⲉϩ. ⲉϩⲣⲁⲥ, C 89 80 ⲁϥⲓ
ⲉϩ. ⲉϩⲣⲁⲩ ⲛⲑⲉⲟⲇⲱⲣⲟⲥ, AM 160 ⲁϥⲧⲱⲛϥ ⲉϩ. ⲉϩⲣⲁⲩ, DeV 2 257 ⲱϣ ⲉϩ. ⲉϩ. ⲡⲓⲣⲱⲙⲓ (*cf* below TT
117);   ⲉϩⲟⲩⲛ, ⲉϩ. ⲉ., *in toward, before*: Mt 27
30 *S*(*B* ⲉϩ. ϫⲉⲛ-), Ac 3 4 *S*(*B* ⲉ-), *ib* 6 15 *SB* εἰς;
Nu 20 18 *B*(*S* ϣⲁ-), 1 Kg 18 6 *B*(*S* ϩⲁⲑⲏ) εἰς συνάντ.;
ib 21 1 *S* τῇ ἀπαντ., Nu 9 7 *S*(var ⲉ-, *B* dat), Pro 9 18
SA(*B* ⲟⲩⲃⲉ-), Ac 2 12 *B*(*S* ⲛⲁϩⲣⲛ-) πρός; *ib* 27 14
SB κατά, Deu 11 25 *B*(*S* ⲉ-) κ. πρόσωπον; 1 Kg
29 8 *S* (var ⲛⲁϩ.) ἐνώπιον; *ib* 9 7 *S* (var ⲉⲣⲁⲧϩ ⲛ-),
Mk 14 65 *S*(*B* ϫⲉⲛϩⲣⲁϩ), *ib* 15 19 *SF*(*B* do), Jo 1
42 *S*(*B* ⲉ-) dat; ShMIF 23 184 *S* ⲡⲱⲧ ⲉⲃⲟⲗ ϩⲏⲧ
opp ⲛ. ⲉϩ. ⲉϩⲣⲁⲥ, Sh BMOr 8810 367 *S* ⲙⲓϣⲉ ⲉϩ.
ⲉ. ⲡⲉⲧⲛⲉⲓⲟⲧⲉ, TT 117 *S* ⲱϣ ⲉⲃⲟⲗ ⲉϩ. ⲉϩⲣⲁⲩ, Mani

1 *A²* ϯ ⲁⲁⲥ ⲁϩ. ⲁϩⲣⲉⲩ, Miss 4 212 *B* ϣⲑⲁⲙ...ⲉϩ.
ⲉ. ⲛⲏ ⲉⲑⲟⲩⲱϣ ⲉⲉⲣ ⲙⲉⲧⲁⲛⲟⲓ, C 86 280 *B* ⲛⲧⲉⲣϩⲓ
ϣⲓⲃϯ ⲉϩ. ⲉ. ⲛⲉⲕⲟⲩⲁⲣⲥⲁⲡⲛ ἀντειπεῖν dat. ⲉⲓ ⲉϩ.,
ⲉϩ. ⲉ.: Jer 13 22 *B*(*S* ⲧⲱ. ⲉ-) ἀπαντᾶν dat, Pro 12
23 *B*(*SA* do), Ac 20 22 *B*(*S* do) συναντ. dat; Mt 5
39 *B*(*S* ⲁϩⲉ ⲣⲁⲧϩ ⲟⲩϩⲉ-) ἀνθιστάναι dat; *ib* 14 24
F(*SB* ϯ ⲟⲩϩⲉ-) ἐναντίος εἶναι; 2 Kg 14 24 *S* Gk
diff; Sh Cambr Univ Add 1876 2 *S* ⲛⲓⲙ ⲡⲉⲧⲛⲁⲉⲓ
ⲉϩ. ⲉϩⲣⲁⲓ & dwell with us?, RNC 76 *S* arrow ⲉⲓ ⲉϩ.
ⲉϩⲣⲁⲡⲉϥϩⲟ, C 86 333 *B* lions ⲓ ⲉϩ. ⲉϩⲣⲁⲩ;   ϯ
ⲧⲱⲛ ⲉϩ. ⲉ., *fight against*: ShC 42 167 *S* ϯ. ⲉϩ. ⲉ-
ϩⲣⲁⲩ ⲛⲡⲉⲧϯ ⲥⲃⲱ ⲛⲁⲛ;   ϩⲓⲟⲩⲉ ⲉϩ. ⲉ., *strike a-
gainst*: Ez 3 13 *B* wings ϩ. ⲉϩ. ⲉ. ⲡⲟⲩⲉⲣⲏⲟⲩ πτερύσσεσθαι; ShA 1 459 *S* water ϩ. ⲉϩ. ⲉϩⲣⲁⲥ ⲡⲧⲓϣⲱⲗⲉ;
ϫⲱ, ⲡⲉϫⲉ ⲉϩ. ⲉ., *say* (forcibly) *to*: RNC 30 *S* ⲛⲧⲉⲣⲉϥϫⲟⲟⲩ ⲉϩ. ⲉ. ὑβρίζων εἰπεῖν; ShMIF 23 20 *S* ⲉⲓϫⲱ ⲙⲡⲁⲓ ⲉϩ. ⲉϩⲣⲁⲕ O foul spirit, TT 98 *S* ⲡⲉϫⲁϥ
ⲉϩ. ⲉϩⲣⲁⲩ, C 43 42 *B* sim, AM 129 *B* ⲛⲏ ⲉⲧⲁⲕϫⲟ-
ⲧⲟⲩ ⲉϩ. ⲉϩⲣⲁⲡ;   ϭⲱϣⲧ ⲉϩ., ϫⲟⲩϣⲧ ⲉϩ. ⲉ., *look
(fixedly) at*: Job 2 10 *S*(*B* ⲉ-), Mk 10 21 *S*(*B* do)
ἐμβλέπειν dat; Ex 25 20 *B* εἰς; ShA 2 284 *S* ϭ. ⲉϩ.
ⲉ. ⲡⲉⲧⲛϣⲏⲣⲉ, AM 153 *B* ϫ. ⲉϩ. ⲉ. ⲡϩⲟ ⲛ-; Br 247
S ⲧⲉϥϭⲓⲛϭ. ⲉϩ. ⲉϩⲣⲁⲩ;   ϯ ⲁⲁⲥ ⲉϩ. ⲉ., *give blow
upon, at*: ShC 73 117 *S* ϯ. ⲉϩ. ⲉϩⲣⲏⲧⲛ, Mani 1 *A²*
ϯ. ⲁϩ. ⲁϩⲣⲁⲩ;   ⲣⲓⲙⲉ ⲉϩ. ⲉ., *weep to, before* v ⲣⲓⲙⲉ;   ⲛⲓϣⲉ ⲉϩ. ⲉ. v ⲛⲓϣⲉ;   ϯ ⲉϩ. ⲉ., *oppose, with-
stand* v ϯ **D**.

ⲛⲁϩⲣⲛ- *SAA²*, ⲛⲛ. *S*(older MSS)*AA²*, ⲛⲁϩⲣⲉⲡ-
BF, ⲛⲁϩⲗ.*F*, ⲛⲁϩⲣⲁϩ *SBO*, ⲛⲛ., ⲛϩⲁⲣⲁϩ *S*(Worrell's
Prov), ⲛⲛⲁϩⲣⲉϩ *A*, ⲛⲁϩⲣⲉϩ *A²*(Ma) ⲛⲁϩⲗⲉϩ *F* prep,
in presence of, before: Ge 15 15 *S*(*B* ϩⲁ-), Ps 119 3 *S*
(*B* ⲟⲩⲃⲉ-), Is 33 6 *SF*(*B* ϩⲁ-), Zech 4 6 *SA*(*B* do),
Mk 14 53 *S*(var ⲉⲣⲁⲧϩ, *B* do), Jo 5 45 *SA²*(*B* ϫⲁ-
ⲧⲉⲡ-) Cl 53 5 *A* ⲣ ⲡⲁⲣⲣⲏⲥⲓⲁⲍⲉ ⲡ. ⲡⲉϥϫⲥ, Mor 17
126 *S* ⲁϥϣⲁϫⲉ ⲛⲁϩⲣⲁⲓ, ROC 11 309 *S* ⲛⲛ. ⲡⲟⲩⲱϣ
ⲡ-, Bor 100 27 *S* crying ⲟⲩⲁ ⲛⲛ.ⲟⲩⲁ = CaiEuch
477 *B* ⲟⲩⲃⲉ- πρός; Ac 17 5 *S*(*B* ϩⲁ-) εἰς; Is 54 9 *B*
(*S* ϩⲓ-), Ac 23 30 *B*(*S* do) ἐπί; Lev 25 35 *S*(*B* ϫⲁ-
ⲧⲉⲡ-), Ps 72 22 *SB*, Pro 21 15 *S*(var ⲛⲧⲛ-, *A* diff),
1 Cor 3 19 *SB* παρά, Ex 19 7 *S*(*B* do), Dan 7 10 *B*
(*S* ⲙⲡⲉⲙⲧⲟ ⲉⲃⲟⲗ), Ac 9 39 *BF*(*S* ⲉ-) παρα- dat;
Jon 1 10 *S*(*A* ϩⲁ-, *B* ϫⲁⲧϩⲛ ⲙⲡⲣⲟ ⲛ-) ἐκ; Deu 17
8 *S*(*B* ⲛⲧⲉⲡ-), Is 64 2 *S*(*B* ⲉϩ. ϩⲁⲡϩⲟ ⲛ-) ἀπό; Ge
4 16 *S*(*B* ϩⲁ-), Ps 30 22 *S*(*B* ⲙⲡⲉⲙ. ⲉϩ.), *ib* 67 2 *S*
(*B* ϩⲁⲡϩⲟ ⲛ-) ἀπὸ προσώπου; He 6 16 *B*(*S* ⲙⲡⲉⲙⲧⲟ, *F* ⲛ-) κατά, Nu 17 8 *B*(*S* om), Ps 17 42 *SB*(*B* ⲙⲡⲉⲙ.
ⲉϩ.) κατὰ πρ.; 1 Kg 18 8 *B*(*S* ⲙⲡⲉⲙ. ⲉϩ.),
Ps 89 4 *SB* ἐν ὀφθαλμοῖς, Gal 3 1 *B*(*S* do) κατ' ὀφ.,
Ps 100 3 *S*(*B* do) πρὸ ὀφ.; Lev 26 8 *S*(*B* do) ἐναντίον, Si 22 19 *S* κατέναντι; 1 Kg 8 6 *S* ⲛ. (var ⲛⲛⲁϩⲣⲁϥ ⲛ-), Is 5 21 *F*(*SB* do) ἐνώπιον; Mt 25 32 *B*(*S*
do) ἔμπροσθεν; Ge 31 15 *S*(*B* ⲛ-), Job 36 27 *S*(*B*
ⲛⲧⲉⲡ-), Ez 16 21 *SB*, Cl 20 8 *A* dat, Lu 10 36 *S*(*B*

diff), Ac 25 27 *S*(*B* diff), ROC 10 429 *S* trees ⲉⲧϣⲟⲩⲟⲩ ⲛⲛⲁϩⲣⲁⲓ δοκεῖν dat; Mk 14 8 *S* ⲡⲉⲧⲛⲁϩⲣⲁⲥ (var ⲡⲉⲛⲧⲁϥⲣ ⲁⲡⲁⲧⲟⲟⲧⲥ, *B* ϕⲏ ⲉⲧⲁⲥϭⲓⲧⲩ) ὃ ἔσχεν; PS 87 *S* ⲁⲡⲧⲟⲩⲗⲁⲁⲩ ⲛⲛⲁϩⲣⲁⲕ, *ib* 247 *S* word ⲡⲁϣⲧ ⲛⲛⲁϩⲣⲁⲓ, ShMun 149 *S* at man's death repentance ⲟⲩⲉⲓⲛⲉ ⲛⲛⲁϩⲣⲁϥ, ShP 131ᵗ 141 *S* earth ⲟⲩⲏϩ ⲛⲧⲡⲉ ⲛⲛⲁϩⲣⲁⲛ, ShC 42 48 *S* ⲉⲩⲙⲉⲉⲩⲉ ⲛⲛⲁϩⲣⲁⲩ ϫⲉ- *in their opinion, ib* 54 *S* ⲡⲉϫⲁϥ ⲛⲛⲁϩⲣⲁⲥ ϫⲉ- *said to her,* ShMIF 23 108 *S* ⲁⲓϫⲱ ⲉⲣⲟⲧⲛ ⲙⲡⲉⲧⲛⲁϩⲣⲁⲓ & hide not that revealed to me, ShC 73 11 *S* of sword ⲁⲥϯ ϭⲟ ⲛⲛ. ⲡⲟⲩⲱϣ of him that wieldeth it, BHom 44 *S* ⲡⲣⲓⲛⲏⲃ ϩⲟⲗϭ ⲛⲁϩⲣⲁⲕ, BAp 62 *S* ⲁϥⲉⲓ ⲉⲃⲟⲗ ⲛⲛ. ⲡⲉϥⲉⲓⲱⲧ, SHel 82 *S* healeth sick ⲛ. ⲧⲧⲉⲭⲛⲏ ⲛⲧⲉϥⲙⲛⲧⲥⲁⲉⲓⲛ, BMis 30 *S* mark of arrow ⲛⲧⲁⲩⲧⲁⲁϥ ⲛ.ⲛⲡⲟⲗⲁⲓⲙⲟⲥ *in war,* BM 256 222 *S* marriage ⲥⲟⲃⲕ ⲛⲛ. ⲧⲡⲁⲣⲑⲉⲛⲓⲁ *as against, compared with,* AM 130 *B* sim ⲛⲓϭⲓⲥⲓ…ⲛ. ⲛⲓⲧⲁⲓⲟ, R 2 4 60 *S* am weary ⲁⲓⲕⲁ ⲧⲟⲟⲧ ⲉⲃⲟⲗ ⲛⲛⲁϩⲣⲁⲕ = Mart Ign 871 *B I give up* (exhorting) *thee,* COAd 42 *S* oath sworn ⲛ. ⲕⲟⲗⲗⲟⲩⲑⲟⲥ magistrate (*cf ib* 131 ⲉⲡⲛ), Cat 170 *B* destruction of Jerusalem ⲛⲁϩⲣⲁϥ ⲛⲕⲗⲁⲩⲍⲓⲟⲥ, Aeg 29 *B* pains ⲕⲏⲛ ⲛⲁϩⲣⲁϥ نزل نزل, AP 25 *A*² brought him in ⲛⲛ. ⲡⲉϫⲛⲏⲣⲁ, ManiK 99 *A*² ⲡⲉⲥⲛⲏⲩ ⲣ ⲙⲉⲥⲧⲟⲩ ⲛⲁϩⲣⲉϥ, AZ 21 100 *O* ⲟⲩⲙⲉⲛⲧϣⲁⲓⲣⲉ ⲛⲁϩⲣⲉⲛⲧⲉ my daughter (*cf ib* ⲡⲁⲣⲁⲕⲧⲉ), Hor 84 *O* ⲛⲁϩⲣⲁϥ (context?).   *V* GriffStu 51.

ϩⲓϩⲣⲁ *SA, on face of*: Eccl 11 1, *ib* 33 27, Hos 10 7 *SA*(*B* ϩⲓⲭⲉⲛⲡⲣⲟ) ἐπὶ πρ., Lev 13 40 (*B* diff) κατὰ πρ.; BMar 113 child ϩⲓϩⲣⲁϥ ⲙⲡⲛⲟϭⲓ βασταζόμενος ὑπό; RNC 57 stone floated ϩⲓϩⲣⲁϥ ⲙⲡⲙⲟⲟⲩ, P 129¹⁶ 68 sim, Miss 4 682 ϩⲓⲧⲟⲩϣ ⲙⲡⲧⲟⲟⲩ ϩⲓϩⲣⲁⲥ ⲛⲧϣⲱϣⲉ;   as nn: Jer 9 26 ⲉⲣⲉϩⲓϩⲣⲁϥ ϣⲏⲩ (*B* ϩⲣⲁϥ) τὰ κατὰ πρόσωπον, Hab 1 9 *A* ϩⲓϩⲣⲁϥ ⲙⲡⲟⲩϩⲟ ἐξ ἐναντίας προσώ.; Ez 40 15 (*B* ϩⲁⲣⲁⲧⲥ) αἴθριον; ShA 2 75 παρὰ ⲧⲣⲉⲡϭⲉⲗⲡ ϩⲓϩⲣⲁϥ ⲉⲃⲟⲗ.

In names: ⲡⲁϩⲣⲟ (*v* p 240 *a*), ⲡⲕⲁϩϩⲣⲟ (PCai 2 179), Πανβάάμπε, Φαναχῶμ (Preisigke). In place-names: ⲧⲁⲣⲁ ⲛϩⲓⲣⲟ (BM 1146, ViK 4792), ⲡⲛϩⲓⲣⲟ (ViK 4708, prob Kr 112), ⲡⲛⲡϩⲓⲣⲟ (PStras 171), ⲯⲉⲛϩⲓⲣⲟ (AM 182, *cf* شنبسير Ibn Duḳmâḳ 5 62), also ? ⲡⲁⲙⲁϩⲣⲟ, ⲡⲁⲡⲁϩⲣⲟ (Amélineau *Géog.* 297, 298).

ϩⲟ, ϩⲱ, ϩⲁ *S* (Theban) nn m, a grain & fodder measure, larger than ⲙⲁⲁϫⲉ: of corn ⲥⲟⲩⲟ BMEA P Hartwell ⲟⲩϩⲟ ⲟⲩϭⲟⲥ, ST 92, *ib* 201 ⲛϩⲁ ⲛⲥ., Ep 531 ⲭⲟ, *ib* 532 ϩⲟ ϣⲙⲟⲩⲛⲉ(*sic, l*? ϣⲙⲟⲩⲛ), WZKM 16 268 ⲟⲩϩⲟ ⲙⲡⲟⲩⲙⲁⲭⲉ ⲛⲡⲥ.;   barley ⲉⲓⲱⲧ BKU 1 45, COAd 16 ϩⲱ;   lentils ⲁⲣϣⲓⲛ Hall 131 ϩⲱ, BP 9420 ⲛϩⲣⲟ ⲛⲁ., Hall *lc* ⲟⲩϩⲱ ⲙⲡϣⲙⲟⲩⲡⲉ ⲛⲙⲁ-ϫⲉ ⲛⲁ.;   sesame ⲥⲓⲙⲥⲓⲙ ST 90, 140; ⲟⲣⲁⲍ (ἄραξ *v* Ep 1 147n), Hall *lc* ϩⲱ, CO 170 ϩⲱ, *ib* 497 ϩⲁ;   unstated BP 13367 ⲙⲡⲱⲣ ⲁⲙⲉⲗⲉ ⲉⲣⲟⲓ ⲉⲧϣⲩⲙ ϩⲣⲟ ⲉⲙ(ⲙ)ⲟⲛ ⲧⲉⲭⲣⲓⲁⲧⲉ, ST 86 ⲟⲩϩⲟⲗⲟⲕⲟⲧⲥⲉ…ⲙⲡⲟⲩϩⲟ ⲛⲙⲉⲥⲉ (? ⲙⲛⲥⲉ).

ϩⲟⲓ *S*, ϩⲁⲓ (Theban), pl (prob) ϩⲓⲉⲉⲩ(ⲉ) nn m **a** field, arable or pasture: BM 1130 ⲁⲡⲁ ⲓⲟⲩⲥⲧⲉ ⲡⲁⲡϩ. corresponds to πατρ(ι) οργ(ανον *sic l,* which sometimes = field, PLond 5 88, 205), ShC 42 82 giving them cattle ⲕⲁⲧⲁ ϩ. ⲉⲧⲣⲉⲩⲥⲁⲡⲟⲩϣⲟⲩ, ShC 73 152 ⲙⲟⲩϣⲧ ⲛⲧⲛⲟϭ ⲛϩⲟ…ϣⲁϩⲟⲩⲛ ⲉⲡϩ., Leyd 445 ⲧⲥⲱϣⲉ, ⲡϩ., ⲛϭ̄ⲟⲟⲙ, BAp 112 ⲧⲉϩⲓⲏ ⲙⲡⲣⲱⲧ ⲉⲃⲟⲗ ⲙⲡϩ. = PO 22 396 سافية, Tri 732 ⲧⲉⲥⲥⲱϣⲉ ⲉⲧⲉⲡⲉⲥϩ. ´⸗, Miss 4 751 ⲟⲩϩ. called ⲡⲕⲁϩ ⲛⲃⲣⲣⲉ…ⲉϥⲟ ⲡⲟⲩⲟⲓⲛ ⲉⲡϩ. ⲉⲧⲙⲙⲁⲩ, J 59 4 will sow flax for thee in ⲡⲁϩ., Ryl 127 ⲟⲩϩ.…ⲉⲕⲁⲭⲟϥ, Kr 251 ⲡⲉⲛⲉⲓⲛⲙⲁ ⲛⲡϩ., PMich 1298 ⲛⲛⲉⲡⲁϩ. ⲕⲁⲧⲉⲭⲉ ⲛⲧⲉⲡⲁⲕⲁⲣⲡⲟⲥ ⲉⲓⲃⲉ, *ib* ⲧ]ⲃⲏⲛ ⲉⲧⲕⲱⲧⲉ ϩⲙⲡⲁϩ., Kr 77 corn as rent of ϩ., J 65 58 tank in (ⲉ)ⲓⲱϩⲉ, ϩ. or ⲱϩⲥ, *ib* 111 5 date-palms in ⲡⲁϩ., *ib* 18 27 share in ⲡϩⲁⲓ, *ib* 67 83 ⲛⲁⲡϩ. in ⲡϩⲁⲓ;   with names: Kr 127 ϕⲟⲓ ⲛⲡⲧⲛⲏⲉ, J 108 7 ⲡⲥⲁⲕⲁⲩ, COAd 18 ⲛⲁⲡⲁ ⲗⲉⲱⲛⲧⲓⲟⲥ, Aegyptus 13 559 ϕⲟⲓ ⲡⲁⲧⲁⲡⲉ, Hall 126 tax receipt for ⲡϩ. ⲕⲁⲙⲟⲩⲗ (*cf* ST 72).   **b** *canal, ditch*: P 44 53 (after ⲡⲓⲧⲛ) ⲁⲧⲱⲧⲟⲥ · ⲁⲭⲉⲧⲟⲥ (ὀχ.) · ⲡϩ. ´⸗.   **c** *waterwheel, sâḳiyah* (on its various meanings *v* Edrisi *ed* Dozy & De Goeje 323, EES *An Report* 1894-5 37, *cf* K 137, 153, HAWinkler *Bauern* 1934 90, depicted Ep 1 pl xvii, *Cathol Encycl* 5 350): Ryl 94 (33 3) iron wheel like ⲛϭⲉⲗϭⲓⲗ ⲙⲡϩ., Miss 4 718 boy ⲧⲁⲗⲏⲩ ⲉⲩϩ. driving cattle…falls into tank ϣⲏⲓ…, crowd ⲉⲧϣⲟⲟⲡ ϩⲙⲡϩ. in field, Gött Abh 16 77 ⲟⲩⲛⲟϭ ⲛϩ. ⲉⲣⲉⲙⲉ ⲛⲓⲃⲧ ϩⲓⲱⲱⲃ ⲙⲛⲛⲟⲩⲁⲛⲧⲗⲉⲁⲥ (ἀντλία), ST 302 let him make new nails (pegs, cogs) ⲙⲙⲟⲛ ⲛϩ. ⲟⲩⲁⲥϥ ⲧⲏⲣϥ, *ib* 226 big nails for ϩ., CO 140 ⲛⲉϩ. ⲙⲡⲉϥⲥⲕⲓⲛⲉ ⲧⲏⲣⲟⲩ…ⲙⲛⲡⲉϥⲱⲧⲉ, Ryl 189 ⲧⲛⲟϭ ⲙⲡⲟϩⲉ ⲛϩ. ⲛϣⲉ, Ep 89 ⲁⲧⲉⲡⲣⲟⲙⲡⲉ ⲛⲃⲱⲕ ϩ. ⲉϥ-[ⲟⲓ] ⲧⲁϩ[ⲟⲛ] *our year hath come round for working the wheel on the field* ⲁⲛⲃⲱⲕ ϕ. ⲁⲛϥⲓ ⲡⲥⲟϥ[ⲟ, Hall 106 prob sim, WS 99 ⲁⲡⲁⲧⲕⲁϫⲉ…ⲉⲡⲟⲩϩⲃ ⲉϕ., Ryl 340 ⲛⲉⲟⲅⲟⲓⲉ… ⲁⲓ(ⲧ)ⲣⲉⲩⲛⲁϩⲃ ϕ.… ⲛⲧⲁⲓⲕⲁ ⲛⲙⲟⲟⲩ ⲉϩⲟⲩⲛ ⲉⲛϭⲟⲟⲙ *yoke* (beast to) *wheel,* BM 341 ⲡⲙⲁ ⲙⲡϩ. where water-jars filled;   doubtful: WS 123 ⲟⲩϩ. ⲉϥϩⲟⲣⲉϩ (*cf* Tri 613 ⲥⲱϣⲉ ⲉⲁⲥϭ.), CO 229 ⲃⲱⲕ ⲡⲓⲱ ⲉϕ. (*cf* ? Schnebel *Landw* 1 337, 359), ST 215 ⲃⲱⲕ ⲛ…(?) ⲉⲛϩ., J 66 30 bequests ⲧⲉⲕⲕⲗⲏⲥⲓⲁ ⲙⲛⲡⲉ(ⲥ)ⲥⲃⲏⲉ, ⲡⲉϩ., ⲡⲉϥϫⲓⲙⲟⲥ(ⲓⲟⲛ), ST 38 ⲧϩⲓⲙⲉ ⲛⲕⲁⲙⲟⲩⲗ (*cf ib* 215) ⲙⲛⲡⲃⲉⲕⲉ ϩⲁⲓ *wage for wheel* (-*worker?*);   pl: PMerton (*olim* Beatty) 1924 letter to ⲛⲉⲟⲅⲟⲉⲓⲉ ⲧⲏⲣⲟⲩ ⲡⲛⲉϩⲓⲉⲉ[ⲩ] ⲛⲙⲙⲟⲛⲁⲥⲧⲏⲣⲓⲟⲛ with lists of ⲛⲉⲟⲅⲟⲉⲓⲉ each beginning with ⲡⲓⲱⲧ ⲛⲡϩ. (*cf* BM 1130 above), BM 1064 carpenter to ϕⲓⲗⲟⲕⲁⲗⲉⲓ ⲡⲛⲉϩⲓⲉⲉⲩⲉ.

ⲣⲉϥϩⲓⲱⲓ (no var) *B, l*? -ϩⲱⲓ: K 137 in parts of سافية ⲡⲓⲣ. سواق (wooden catch over which cogs pass, so Yassa Abd al-Masîḥ).

In place-names: ⲡⲥⲟⲃⲧ [ⲙⲡ]ϩⲟⲓ (EW 92), ⲡⲣ. ⲛ- ⲋⲁⲙⲟⲩⲗ (Miss 4 752), ⲡⲣ. ⲕⲁⲙⲟⲩⲗ (Hall 126 possibly same), ⲡⲥⲟⲟⲩ ⲛⲣⲁⲓ (Lant 74, 75), Φαινεϣόος (PLond 4 225), Σεθρενπάει (PFay 344) & doubtless many more.

ϩⲟⲓ S nn, meaning doubtful, *trouble, zeal* (?): Si 35 8 ⲁⲣⲓ ϩ. ⲉϣⲁϫⲉ ⲡⲟⲩⲁ (var ⲁⲣⲓ ϩⲁϩ ⲛϣ.) κεφα-λαίωσον λόγον, ἐν ὀλίγοις πολλά; PS 280 souls ⲣ ϩ. ⲡⲉⲓ ⲉⲃⲟⲗ ⲛϩⲏⲧⲛ *strive to come forth*; Mk 5 35 ϯ ϩ. ⲙⲡⲥⲁϩ (var & B ϯ ϩⲓⲥⲉ) σκύλλειν; Ryl 311 ⲁⲅⲟⲩⲱ ⲉⲩϯ ϩ. ⲉⲓⲥ ⲥⲁϣϥⲉ [ⲡⲣⲟⲙⲡⲉ (?)]; as vb (same?): ST 178 ⲛⲛⲁϩ. ϫⲉⲉⲓ(ⲟⲩ)ⲱϣ ⲡⲁⲗⲁⲩ ⲛⲥⲟⲟⲩⲛⲉ[.

ϩⲟⲓ B nn f, *heap of grain*: Job 5 26 (S ϫⲁⲧⲙⲉ) θιμωνιά ⲗⲉⲙ⸗, ib 39 12 (S ?, Gk om) انل; Va 57 4 ⲭⲱ ⲙⲡⲓⲥⲟⲩⲟ ϩⲉⲛϯ. ⲛⲧⲉ ⲡⲉϥϭⲛⲱⲟⲩ, MG 25 176 ⲟⲩϩ. ⲉⲁⲩⲧⲟⲩⲃⲟⲥ *on threshing-floor.*

ϩⲟⲓ B nn m, *bellows*: Job 32 19 (S ϩⲱⲧ) φυσητήρ رٰ; ⲱϩⲓ same?: K 125 = P 55 9 *blacksmith's tools* ⲡⲓⲱ. منفخ, 'S (but P 44 67 'S ϩⲣⲱ).

ϩⲱ SAA²BF vb mostly impers, *suffice, be enough*: 3 Kg 19 4 S ἱκανοῦσθαι; Pro 24 51 SA ἀρκεῖν; ShA 1 73 S ϩⲱ ⲡⲧⲉⲓⲣⲉ *let this suffice*, ib 55 S ⲡⲁⲡⲟⲩⲥ ⲉϩⲱ ⲡⲧⲉⲓⲣⲉ, ib 115 S ⲁⲅⲁⲡⲓⲗⲉⲓ ⲛⲁϥ ⲉϩⲱ *admonished him to cease*, ShP 131⁴ 90 S ⲉⲓⲥ ϩⲏⲏⲧⲉ ϯⲛⲁϩⲱ ⲡⲧⲟⲟⲩⲛ, ShViK 9027 255 S ⲛϥⲛⲁϩⲱ ⲁⲛ ⲉϣⲁϫⲉ, R 1 5 46 S ⲙⲡⲉϥϫⲟⲟⲥ ϫⲉϩⲱ, BMis 47 S ⲁⲛϩⲁⲅⲓⲟⲥ ϩⲱ ⲙⲙⲁⲧⲉ (*l* ⲉⲙ.) [ⲉϥ]ϭⲓ ⲡⲉϥⲃⲁⲗ ⲉϩⲣⲁⲓ.

With following preposition. c ⲉ- *dat commodi*: Ge 33 15 S (B ⲕⲏⲛ) ἱκανός (εἶναι); Jo 14 8 SA²F (MS Louvain, B do) ἀρ., Mt 10 25 S (B do), 1 Pet 4 3 S (B do, sim BMis 106 S ult) ἀρκετός; C 99 216 S ϩⲱ ⲉⲣⲟⲕ = C 89 13 B ⲕ. ⲉⲣⲟⲕ παύειν; ShWess 9 132 (Theoph Alex) S ⲙⲁⲣⲟⲩϩⲱ ⲉⲣⲟⲟⲩ *quiescere*; Br 44 S *tell us the end* ⲁⲩⲱ ϩⲱ ⲉⲣⲟⲛ, ShRyl 70 253 S ϩⲱ ⲉⲣⲟⲟⲩ ϫⲉⲁⲩⲙⲡϣⲁ ⲛⲛⲁⲩ, ShA 1 91 S ϩⲱ ⲉⲣⲟⲟⲩ ⲛϭⲉ ⲉⲡⲧⲁⲑⲙⲕⲉ ⲡⲁⲣⲏⲧ, TstAb 173 B ϩⲱ ⲉⲣⲟⲓ ϫⲉ ⲱ ⲡⲓ-ⲕⲣⲓⲧⲏⲥ ⲉⲩⲥⲟϩⲓ ⲙⲙⲟⲓ, ShMiss 4 822 S ϩⲱ ⲁⲛ ⲉⲣⲟⲓ ϫⲉⲁϥⲣ ⲛⲟⲃⲉ ⲁⲗⲗⲁ ⲙⲡϥⲥⲱⲧⲙ ⲟⲛ ϫⲉ-; vbal ShA 2 302 S ⲙⲏ ϩⲱ ⲁⲛ ⲉⲧⲣⲉⲡⲁⲓ ⲣ ⲡⲙⲉⲉⲩⲉ ?, ib 122 ϩⲱ ⲉⲧⲣⲉϥϫⲓ ⲉⲟⲟⲩ…ⲛϩⲟⲩⲟ ⲉⲧⲣⲉⲩϫⲓ ⲟⲩⲁ; with vbal pref: Va 63 83 B *having spoken* ⲁϥϩⲱ ⲉⲣⲟϥ παύ.; 4 Kg 13 18 S ἱστάναι; ShA 2 18 S ⲛⲧⲁϥϩⲱ ⲉⲣⲟϥ ⲙⲁⲩⲁⲁϥ *been self-sufficient* (acted independently?), ShBor 246 114 S ⲡⲉⲓⲕⲉⲟⲩⲁ ⲙⲡⲉⲧⲛϩⲱ ⲉⲣⲟϥ *were not content with*, Miss 8 258 S *will relate a few* ⲛⲧⲁ-ϩⲱ ⲉⲣⲟⲓ.

c 2d ⲉ-, *be satisfied with*: Lu 3 14 S (B ⲣⲱϣⲓ), Va 63 100 B ⲙⲡⲉϥϩⲱ ⲉⲣⲟϥ ⲉϥⲁⲓ ἀρ. dat, Mt 6 34 S (B ⲕ.) ἀρκετός dat; ShC 42 166 S ϩⲱ ⲉⲣⲟⲛ ⲉⲡⲉⲕⲣⲓⲙⲁ *that awaiteth us*, ShA 1 380 S ⲛϩⲱ ⲁⲛ ⲉⲣⲱⲧⲛ ⲉⲡⲟⲩⲟ-ⲉⲓϣ *spent in ignorance?*, P 129¹⁶ 51 S ϩⲱ ⲉⲣⲟⲓ ⲉⲩ-ⲃⲁⲗ (var Mor 32 47 ⲛⲟⲩ.) ⲛⲟⲩⲱⲧ *one eye sufficeth me*,

HT Q 36 S ⲛⲧⲁϥϩⲱ ⲉⲣⲟϥ ⲉϥϩⲱϣⲧ ⲉⲣⲟⲩⲛ, C 43 55 B *adjured him* ⲉⲑⲣⲉϥϩⲱ ⲉⲣⲟϥ ⲉϣⲧⲉⲙ-= Mor 39 34 S ϫⲉⲉϥⲉⲕⲁⲁϥ; with 2d pres: Deu 1 6 S (B ⲕ.) ἱκ. dat & inf, C 99 108 S ϩⲱ ⲉⲣⲟⲕ ⲉⲕⲟ ⲙⲡⲉⲣⲡⲉⲣⲟⲥ = ib 1 ⲁⲗⲟⲕ παύ.; PS 377 S *let women* ϩⲱ ⲉⲣⲟⲟⲩ ⲉⲩ-ϣⲓⲡⲉ, ShA 1 372 S ⲙⲡⲉϥϩⲱ ⲉⲣⲟϥ ⲉϥⲟ ⲛⲥⲕⲁⲛⲇⲁ-ⲗⲟⲛ, C 43 146 B ϩⲱ ⲉⲣⲟⲕ ⲉⲕϭⲱⲡ ⲉⲃⲟⲗ; with ⲉⲧⲣⲉ- S: ShA 1 304 ϩⲱ ⲉⲡϯ ⲧⲱⲛ…ⲉⲧⲣⲉⲡ̄ⲛ̄ ϫⲟⲟⲥ ϫⲉ-, SHel 67 ⲙⲏ ⲛϩⲱ ⲁⲛ ⲉⲣⲟⲛ ⲉⲧⲣⲉⲡ̄ⲛ̄ ⲕⲱ ⲛⲁⲛ ⲉⲃⲟⲗ?, ib 79 ϩⲱ ⲉⲡⲉⲥⲃⲟⲩⲓ ⲉⲧⲣⲉⲥⲣ ⲑⲉ ⲙⲡⲉϥⲥⲁϩ; c ⲉϫⲛ-: Mor 17 106 S ϩⲱ ⲉⲣⲟⲕ ⲉϫⲙⲡϯ ⲟⲩⲱ ⲉⲑⲟⲟⲩ ἀρ. ἐπί; c ⲛ-: Mor 41 168 S ϩⲱ ⲉⲣⲟⲕ ⲛϣⲟⲙⲛⲧ ⲛⲥⲟⲡ (of prayer) ⲙⲙⲏⲛⲉ, Cat 52 B *man should* ϩⲱ ⲉⲣⲟϥ ⲛⲟⲩϭⲣⲱⲙ ⲛⲟⲩϩⲱⲧ, Bor 286 34 S ϩⲱ ⲉⲣⲱⲧⲛ ⲛϣⲁϫⲉ; c ϣⲁ-: Lu 22 51 S ϩⲱ ⲉⲣⲱⲧⲛ (var ϭⲱ ⲧⲉⲛⲟⲩ) ϣⲁⲡⲭⲓ (B ⲕ. ϣⲁⲉⲙⲡⲁⲓ) ἐᾶν ἕως; ShA 1 55 S ϩⲱ ⲡⲧⲉⲓⲣⲉ ⲛ ϣⲁⲡⲉⲓⲙⲁ, BSM 132 B ⲙⲁⲣⲉⲛϩⲱ ⲉⲣⲟⲛ ϣⲁⲡⲁⲓⲙⲁ ⲉⲡⲥⲁϫⲓ, PSBA 19 221 S ϩⲟⲣⲟⲕ (*l* ϩⲱ ⲉⲣⲟⲕ) ϣⲁⲡⲛⲧϫⲟⲟⲥ ⲛⲁⲕ; c ϩⲛ-: RNC 26 S ϩⲱ ⲉⲣⲟⲕ ϩⲛⲛⲓⲁⲧⲁⲍⲓⲁ παύ. gen; Eccl 5 9 S (F = Gk diff); BMis 40 S ⲙⲡⲉⲛⲇⲓⲁⲃⲟⲗⲟⲥ ϩⲱ ⲉⲣⲟϥ ϩⲛⲧⲉϥ-ⲙⲁⲛⲓⲁ, EW 82 B ϩⲱ ⲉⲣⲟⲛ ϩⲉⲛⲡⲁⲓⲥⲁϫⲓ, C 43 25 B sim ⲉⲃⲟⲗ ϩⲉⲛ-.

ϩⲱ O, *house* in ⲛⲉⲃϩⲱ *Nephthys* AZ 21 100, constr ϩⲁⲧ- in ϩⲁⲑⲱⲣ, v GöttN '25 54, ZDMG 77 188.

ϩⲱⲱ⸗ SA²(APMa)F, ϩⲱ⸗ SA²(Ma)BF, ϩⲟ⸗ SO, ϩⲟⲩⲟⲩ⸗, ϩⲟⲩ⸗ A, ϩⲱ(ⲟ)ⲩ⸗ A²(MaJo) pron of emphasis or contrast **A**, *self, also, for my, his part* (Stern 256, Till 48), with personal pron: Ge 4 22 SB, Lev 6 37 S (B ⲟⲛ), Nu 24 25 S (B ⲟⲩⲟϩ), Is 30 33 SBF, Hos 4 6 SAB, Mk 8 38 SBF καί; Mt 7 12 SB οὕ-τως; PS 116 S ⲛⲧⲟ ϩⲱⲱⲧⲉ ⲙⲁⲣⲓⲁ, Br 254 S ⲧⲉϫⲁ-ⲣⲓⲥ ⲉⲛⲧⲁⲡⲉⲓⲱⲧ ⲧⲁⲁⲥ ⲛⲁϥ ⲛⲧⲟϥ ϩⲱⲱϥ ⲡⲉⲡⲣⲟⲡⲁⲧⲱⲣ, ShA 2 282 S *as my fathers* ⲁⲛⲟⲕ ϩⲱ (var ϩⲱⲱⲧ) ϯ-ⲡⲁϯ, ShC 42 24 S ϯⲛⲏⲩ…ⲁⲩⲱ ⲧⲉⲧⲛⲛⲏⲩ ϩⲱⲧⲧⲏⲩⲧⲛ, Louvre E 14250 S ⲁⲛⲟⲕ ⲟⲩⲛⲉ̄ ϩⲟⲟⲧ (*cf* BKU 1 2 S ⲁⲛⲕⲟⲩⲛⲉ̄ ϩⲱ), El 56 A ⲁⲛⲟⲕ ϩⲟⲩⲟⲩⲧⲧ, Mani 1 A² ⲁ-ⲡ]ⲁⲡ ϩⲱⲡⲉ ⲡⲁⲥⲡⲏⲩ, Hor 79 O ⲛⲧⲏϥ ϩⲟⲩϥ; without pers pron: Ge 30 30 SB, Job 6 18 S (B + ⲁⲡⲟⲕ), Pro 1 26 SA (B do), Is 14 10 B (S + ⲛⲧⲟⲕ), Ep Jer 40 F + ⲕⲉ- (B + ⲛⲉⲃⲟⲟⲩ), Mt 19 28 SBF, 1 Cor 7 40 SBF, AP 6 A² καί; Job 23 2 S (B ⲕⲉ ⲅⲁⲣ) κ. δή, 2 Kg 13 36 S, Eccl 2 15 κ. ⲅⲉ; Mk 4 16 S (B ⲟⲛ ⲙⲡⲁⲓⲣⲏϯ), Lu 16 25 SB ὁμοίως; Jos 6 8 S ὡσαύτως; Ro 11 21 SF (B = Gk) κατὰ φύσιν; Lu 16 11 S (B as Gk) τὸ ἀληθι-νόν; Ge 48 19 S ϯⲥⲟⲟⲩⲛ ϩⲱ (B do) οἶδα οἶδα; PS 204 S ⲕⲉⲗⲉⲩⲉ ϩⲱ ⲡⲁⲓ, Miss 8 9 S *God hath established you* ⲉⲃⲟⲗ ϫⲉⲧⲉⲧⲛⲧⲁϫⲣⲟ ϩⲱⲱϥ ⲙⲡⲇⲟⲅⲙⲁ, Leyd 464 S *I pray* ⲉⲧⲣⲉⲕⲣ ⲡⲙⲉⲉⲩⲉ ϩⲱⲱⲥ ⲛⲁⲓϫⲉⲥ-ⲥⲁ, Bor 265 S ⲥⲉⲛⲁ ϫⲟⲟⲥ ⲛⲁϥ ϩⲱⲱϥ ϫⲉ-, Pcod 50 S ϩⲁⲡⲥ ϩⲱⲡⲉ ⲉⲧⲣⲉⲩ[ⲧⲁϩⲟⲓ] ⲉⲣⲁⲧ ⲉⲡⲃⲏⲙⲁ, J 67 70

S ⲉⲓⲥ ϩⲏⲏⲧⲉ ϩⲱ ⲡⲧⲉϥ (l ⲧⲉϥ, cf ib 86) ⲙⲙⲟϥ ⲛⲁⲕ, PLond 4 451 S have written for him & ϩⲁⲣⲟⲓ ϩⲱⲱⲧ, J 2 5 S ⲧϣⲏⲣⲉ ⲛⲧⲁϥⲁⲡⲉ ⲧϣⲏⲣⲉ ϩⲱⲱⲥ ⲛⲥⲟⲗⲟⲙⲟⲛ, TU 43 14 A what I have promised ϯⲛⲁⲧⲉⲟⲅⲉ ⲛⲉϥ ϩⲟⲅⲉ, ib 17 A ⲥⲉⲛⲁϩⲱⲡⲉ ϩⲟⲅⲟⲅⲉ ⲛⲉⲙⲉⲓ, Mani H 91 A² ⲧⲁϩⲉ ϩⲱⲧⲧⲉ ⲧⲉⲓ, Mani 1 A² ⲛⲧⲉⲙⲙϣⲉ ϩⲱⲉ, Aeg 19 B ϩⲱϯ ⲉⲣⲟ ϩⲱ, AM 218 B teach me this magic that I may ϭⲣⲟ ⲉⲡⲓⲭⲣⲱⲙ ϩⲱ, ib 321 B as seest me do ⲁⲣⲓ ⲟⲅⲓ ϩⲱⲕ; + ⲟⲛ: Deu 14 7 S(B om), Sa 14 4 S, Lu 17 8 S(B om ⲟⲛ), Jo 18 17 SA² ϩⲱⲅⲕ (B do), BHom 56 S ⲛⲧⲟⲕ ϩⲱⲱⲕ ⲟⲛ ⲁⲕϫⲓ ϭⲟⲗ καί; Ac 15 27 S(B + ⲣⲱ) κ. αὐτός; TU 43 9 A ⲧⲉⲓⲧⲉ ⲧϩⲉ ϩⲓⲧⲏⲡⲉ (sic) ⲁⲛ, ManiK A² ϩⲁⲧⲏⲓ ϩⲱⲧ ⲁⲛ.

B but, on other hand, a with concord: Job 42 4 S ϩⲱ (var ϩⲱⲱⲧ, B om), Dan 6 22 B, Mt 16 15 S(B om), BHom 51 S serpent worked in elders but ⲧⲡⲓⲥ ⲧⲓⲥ ϩⲱⲱⲥ ϩⲛⲧⲉⲓⲥϭⲓⲙⲉ, ib 29 S ⲡⲉⲧⲙⲙⲁⲅ..., ⲛⲧⲟⲕ ϩⲱⲱⲕ δέ; Job 5 8 S(B = Gk), C 86 292 B ⲁⲛⲟⲕ ϩⲱ ϯⲛⲟⲩ ἀλλά; Sa 13 6 S τάχα; Is 5 9 S(BF = Gk), BMar 121 S ⲁⲛⲟⲕ ϩⲱ ϯⲙⲉⲉⲅⲉ ϫⲉ- γάρ; Gk om: Ps 23 8 B(S om), Jo 1 17 S(B ⲇⲉ); PS 313 S man that hath known divinity ⲁⲩⲱ ⲟⲩⲣⲱⲙⲉ ϩⲱⲱϥ ⲉⲙ ⲡϥϣⲉ ⲉⲧⲙⲛⲧⲡ̄ⲡ̄, BM 217 22 S riches bribe judge ⲁⲩⲱ ⲧⲙⲛⲧⲣⲏⲕⲉ ϩⲱⲱⲥ ϣⲁⲥ ϣⲱⲡⲉ ϩⲁⲡⲣⲁⲛ, C 86 199 B spake to thee as to a son ⲟⲩⲟϩ ⲛⲑⲟⲕ ϩⲱⲕ didst despise us, Br 125 S ⲛⲧⲟϥ ⲇⲉ...ϥⲛⲁⲟⲩϭⲉ ϩⲱⲱϥ ⲛⲟⲩⲁⲅⲡⲁⲙⲓⲥ, TU 24 1 3 S those thou healest are seen ⲧⲉⲕϣⲉⲉⲣⲉ ϩⲱⲕ ⲁⲕⲣ ⲁⲙⲉⲗⲓ ⲉⲣⲟⲥ, ShC 73 3 S what men take to be corn ⲉⲅⲧⲱϥ ϩⲱⲱϥ ⲛϭⲟⲅⲟⲡⲉ, BHom 38 S ⲉⲅϣⲁⲛⲥⲁϩⲟⲩ ⲙⲙⲟⲕ ⲛⲧⲟⲕ ϩⲱⲱⲕ ⲛⲥ ⲥⲙⲟⲩ, ib 44 S sea they crossed unhurt ⲁⲩⲱⲥⲙ ⲇⲉ ϩⲱ ⲱϥ ϩⲓϫⲙⲡⲕⲁϩ, Aeg 258 S bishops shall say..., ⲙⲁ ⲣⲉⲡⲉⲧϫⲓ ϩⲱⲱϥ ⲟⲩⲱϣⲃ ϫⲉ-, TillOster 10 A ⲛⲧⲱⲧ ⲛⲉ ϭⲉ ϩⲟⲩⲧⲏⲡⲉ, Mor 41 68 Sᶠ ⲛⲧⲟ ⲇⲉ ϩⲱⲱⲧⲉ (cf ib ϫⲓ ⲡⲉ ϩⲱⲟⲓ), El 88 A ϥⲛⲁϩⲟⲩ ⲧⲟⲟⲧϥ ϩⲟⲅⲟⲅϥ ⲁⲛ, DeV 1 85 B I eat & drink, ⲡⲥⲱⲙⲁ ϩⲱϥ of Saviour is in sinners' hands, AM 186 B blind..., ⲛⲉⲧⲉϩⲱⲟⲩ ⲉ- ⲣⲉⲡⲟⲩϩⲁⲗ ⲟⲩⲏⲡ, ManiH 75 A² ⲙⲡⲟⲛⲏⲣⲟⲥ ϩⲱⲟⲅⲉ, C 43 29 B ⲁⲛⲟⲛ ϩⲱⲛ do to us what thou wilt; interrogative: Lu 18 26 B(S ⲛⲧⲟⲟⲩⲛ) καί; Cat 9 31 B ⲁϫⲟⲕ ϩⲱⲕ? = ῥακά, K 239 B ⲣⲁⲕⲁ ϫⲉϩⲱⲕ [Arabic] (cf PG 57 248 σύ); PS 215 S knoweth ⲉⲧⲃⲉⲟⲩ ϩⲱⲱϥ ⲁⲡⲕⲱϩ ϣⲱⲡⲉ ⲉⲧⲃⲉⲟⲩ ϩⲱⲱⲥ ... ⲧⲙⲛⲧⲁⲧⲕⲱϩ, ShMich 550 13 S ⲁⲛⲧⲟⲩⲟⲩ ϭⲉ ϩⲱⲱϥ?, BMis 352 S ⲟⲩ ϩⲱⲱⲕⲡⲉ ⲡⲉⲕⲣⲁϣⲉ?, C 43 19 B ⲁⲣⲉⲧⲉⲛⲛⲁⲩ ⲉⲟⲩ ϩⲱⲧⲉⲛ?, AM 316 B ⲁⲧⲉⲧⲉⲛⲥⲉ ⲙⲙⲟⲩ ⲡⲗⲓⲃⲓ ϩⲱⲧⲉⲛ?, JEA 13 24 S ⲛⲓⲙ ϩⲱⲟⲅⲡⲉ ⲛⲧⲁϥϯ ⲡⲉⲓϩⲱⲃ ⲛⲧⲟⲟⲧ ⲟⲩ? + ⲟⲛ: PS 194 S ⲥⲉⲛⲁϭⲱ ϩⲱⲟⲩ ⲟⲛ ϩⲓ ϩⲃⲟⲩⲣ, Br 125 S ⲛⲧⲟϥ ⲇⲉ ϩⲱⲱϥ ⲟⲛ ⲛ̄ⲡ̄ⲉ̄, CA 90 S ⲡⲕⲉⲙⲩⲅⲥⲏⲥ ϭⲉ ϩⲱⲱϥ ⲟⲛ, AP 23 A² ⲟⲩⲛ ϭⲁⲙ ⲙ ⲙⲁϥ ϩⲱⲧ ⲁⲛ ⲁⲧⲣⲉϥⲛⲁϩⲙⲉⲧ. b ϩⲱ(ⲱ)ϥ without concord, expressing contrast, opposition (cf ⲛⲧⲟϥ): Nu 15 15 S(B diff), Deu 11 28 S(B om) καί **PS 119**

S ⲧⲙⲉ ϩ. ⲧⲉ ϯϭⲟⲙ ⲉⲛⲧⲁⲥⲉⲓ ⲉⲃⲟⲗ, ib 299 S ⲧⲉⲯⲩ ⲭⲏ ϩ. ⲙⲛⲧϭⲁⲙ ϣⲁϥⲡⲟⲣϫⲟⲩ ⲉⲕⲉⲙⲉⲣⲟⲥ, Br 112 S have received baptism of water, ⲁⲙⲛⲉⲓ ϩ. ⲛⲧⲁϥ ⲡⲏ ⲧⲛ ⲙⲡⲃⲁⲡ. ⲙⲡⲉⲡ̄ⲛ̄ⲁ̄, BHom 109 S ⲡⲉⲧⲛⲏⲡ ⲁⲛ ⲉϣⲱ ⲡⲉ ... ⲛⲉⲧⲛⲏⲡ ϩ. ⲉϣⲱⲡⲉ, ManiK 26 A² ϥⲧⲁⲩ ϩⲣⲟⲟⲩⲉ ...ϥⲧⲟⲉ ϩ. ⲛⲟⲩϣⲏ, Mani Berl Sitz '33 85 A² ⲡⲉⲡⲓⲥ ⲧⲟⲗⲁⲅⲉ ϩ. ⲧⲏⲣⲟⲩ, C 43 182 B ⲥⲱⲧⲉⲙ ϩ. ϯⲛⲟⲩ ⲉⲓⲏⲡ, ShA 2 326 S ⲡⲧⲉⲡⲉⲓⲑⲉ ϩ. ⲛⲣⲟⲙⲡⲉ, R 1 1 66 S ⲁⲅⲉⲓⲥ ϩ. ⲛⲧⲡⲛⲁⲩ, ShMun 164 S ⲧⲉⲛⲟⲩ ⲇⲉ ϩ. ϯϫⲱ ⲙ ⲙⲟⲥ; concord accidental ?: BMis 16 S ⲛⲟⲩⲟⲉⲓϣ ⲙⲉⲛ...ⲙⲡⲟⲟⲩ ⲇⲉ ϩ., C 43 8 B sim, P 131² 117 S door to incontinence is drunkenness ⲁⲩⲱ ⲡⲣⲟ ϩ. ⲛ ⲧⲙⲛⲧⲁⲧⲁⲡⲉ ⲡⲣⲱϣⲉ = Va 58 192 B.

ϩⲁⲁⲃ S nn m, meaning uncertain, *bottom, sediment?* (Sethe), cf ϩⲓⲃⲉ (ϩⲃⲃⲉ) or cf [Hebrew] (Dévaud): PS 77 will fulfil for you all mysteries ... ϫⲓⲛⲡⲟⲩⲟⲓⲛ ⲛ ⲡⲟⲩⲟⲓⲛ ϣⲁϥⲁⲁⲃ ⲛⲟⲩⲗⲏ; ϩⲁϥⲉ A² nn m, sim ?: ManiK 110 ⲡϩ. ⲙⲙⲛ ⲭⲱⲣⲙⲉ, ib 114 ⲡⲥⲁⲣⲙⲉ ⲡϩ. ⲙ ⲡⲓϣⲉ ⲁⲃⲁⲗ.

ϩⲓⲏⲃ B v ⲉⲓⲟⲡⲉ s f.

ϩⲓⲉⲓⲃ SAA²(AP), eq., ϩⲉⲓⲉⲃ S, ϩⲓⲃ SA, ϩⲓⲏⲃ A² (Ma), ϩⲓⲏⲃ BF, f ϩ(ⲉ)ⲓⲁ(ⲉ)ⲓⲃⲉ¹, ϩⲓⲁⲃⲉ², ϩⲓⲉⲓⲁⲃⲉ³, ϩⲓ ⲉⲉⲃⲉ⁴, ϩⲓⲉⲓⲃⲉ⁵, ϩⲓⲃⲉ⁶, ϩⲓⲏⲃⲉ⁷, ϩⲁ(ⲉ)ⲓⲃⲉ⁸, eq.⁹ S, ϩⲓ ⲉⲃⲓ B nn m f, *lamb*: Lev 9 3 SB, Is 53 7 SA(Cl) ϩⲓⲃ B, Ez 46 4 S eq. B, Zech 10 3 B(A ⲁⲓⲗⲉ) ἀμνός, Ge 31 41 S(B f), Jos 24 32 S ἀμνάς; 1 Kg 7 9 S ⲟⲩⲉϩ. (var ⲟⲩϩ.), 2 Kg 6 13 S (var ϩⲛⲉϩ.) B, Is 5 17 SBF, Mic 6 7 A(S ShA 1 413, B ⲱⲓⲗⲓ), Lu 10 3 SB ἀρήν, Jer 11 19 S ⲟⲩⲉϩ. (var ⲟⲩϩ.) B, Ap 5 6 SB ἀρνίον; Ez 45 15 B πρόβατον *aries*; Am 6 4 A(B ⲙⲁⲥⲓ) μοσχάριον; Z 617 S wool of ⲛⲉⲧⲛⲉϩ., KroppM 35 S sim ϩⲉⲓⲉⲃ (sic), AP 35 A², Mani 1 A², MR 2 46 S in list of cattle ⲉϩⲓⲃ, Hall 121 S ϩⲉⲓⲉⲃ ⲛϩⲣⲟⲟⲩⲧ & ⲛⲥϩⲓ ⲙⲉ; f: Ge 21 29⁴ (Bodl (P) c 20) B, Lev 5 6¹ (var m) B, 2 Kg 12 3⁹ (var¹), ib 6⁸ (var¹), BHom 49¹ (var R 2 2 33²), Glos 104⁵ ἀμνάς, Ge 31 7 B(S m), Nu 28 27 B (S do) -ός; P 44 55¹ = 43 22⁸, Tri 308⁸ [Arabic]; ShA 2 33¹, R 1 4 25 ⲧⲉϩ.⁵ ⲙⲙⲉ, Worr 151⁶ sim, Aeg 17 ⲧⲉⲓ ⲉϩ.⁹, MR l c¹, Mor 18 193⁷. Name ⲫⲓⲃ (P·hb) is written ⲡⲉϩⲓⲉⲓⲃ Leyd 216 (cf under ϩⲓⲃⲱⲓ).

ϩⲟⲩⲃ v ϩⲟⲩϥ.

ϩⲱⲃ SB, ϩⲁⲃ⸗ S vb tr, *send*: 4 Kg 14 19 S ϩⲱⲙ (l ?ϩⲱⲃ) ⲛⲥⲱϥ ἀποστέλλειν ὀπίσω; BKU 1 22 S ⲙ ⲡⲉⲓϩⲁⲃⲕ ⲡⲥⲁⲛⲓⲕⲟⲟⲩⲉ, paral ϫⲟⲟⲩⲕ; ⲣⲉⲙⲛ̄ϩ. B, *man sent, messenger*: Ge 32 3, 1 Kg 23 27 (var ⲣⲉⲙⲛ̄ϩ.), Is 33 7, Lu 7 24 (all S ϥⲁⲓϣⲓⲛⲉ) ἄγγελος; MG 25 103 ⲡ. (var ⲣⲉⲙⲛ̄ϩⲱⲣⲡ, Gött ar 114 44 misunderst [Arabic]), PO 11 377 ⲁⲛⲟⲩⲣⲟ...ⲟⲩⲱⲡ ⲛϩⲁⲡⲣ., C 86 38 man sent by king...ⲡⲓⲣ. ⲓⲧⲉ ⲡⲟⲩⲣⲟ (sc executioner) = Assemani *Ac Sanct Mart* 1 248 [Arabic]. Ep 84 S ϫⲟⲟⲩⲕ ⲛⲟⲩϩⲱⲃ prob next word.

ϩⲱⲃ *SAA²BFO,* -ϥ *SA²F,* ⲱϥ *S,* ϧⲟϥ *SF,* ⲟⲃ, ϧⲱⲃⲓ, ⲟⲃⲓ, ⲟⲃⲃⲓ *F,* ϧⲉⲃ- *B* (ⲩ ⲣⲉϥⲣ ϧ.), pl ϧⲃⲏⲅⲉ *SA²,* -ⲟⲅⲉ *A,* -ⲟⲅⲓ *BF,* ⲉϧ. *B* & sg as pl (rare), nn m

I *thing, work, matter, event:* Ex 24 10 *SB,* Jud 16 11 *S,* Pro 20 6 *SA,* Jer 10 3 *SB,* Ro 2 7 *SBF,* AP 6 *A²* ἔργον, Ge 29 27 *SB,* Pro 6 8 *SA*(*B* ϫⲓⲛⲉⲣ ϧ.), Ac 16 19 *SB,* Z 344 *S* ⲁϣⲡⲉ ⲛϧ. ⲛⲛⲁⲓ? ἐργασία, Ez 46 1 *SB* ἐνεργός; Lev 7 21*SB,*Ps 90 6*SB,*Su 63*BF*(ViK 3771) πρᾶγμα,Job 24 5*S*(*B*=Gk),Lu 23 51*S*(*B* do) πρᾶξις; Eccl 8 14 *S* ποίημα ; Mor 17 26 *S* ὑπηρεσία ; Ge 24 66 *S*(*B* ⲥⲁϫⲓ) ῥῆμα, Ex 22 9 *S*(*B* do) ῥητός; BHom 49 *S* ⲁϧⲣⲟⲙⲟⲗⲟⲅⲉⲓ ⲙⲛϧ., Ac 25 18*S*(*B* ⲗⲱⲓϫⲓ),MG 25 205 *B* ⲛϧ. ⲉⲧⲁⲛ ⲉⲑⲃⲏⲧϥ αἰτία, Ac 19 40 *S*(*B* ⲗ.) αἴτιον; Phil 4 17 *B*(*S* ϣⲁϫⲉ) λόγος; Ac 18 14 *SB* ῥαδιούργημα; Ge 3 13 *S* ⲡⲉⲓϧ. (*B* ϥⲁⲓ), Aeg 277 *S* do, Va 57 11 *B* τοῦτο, Is 66 8 *S* ϧ. ⲛⲧⲉⲓⲙⲓⲛⲉ, *B* ⲙⲡⲁⲓⲣⲏϯ. τοιοῦτο; Sa 11 26 *S,* Is 8 8 *SB,* Mt 20 20 *SB* τι, ROC 17 405 *B* ⲛϧ. ⲛⲡⲓϧⲓⲣⲓⲟⲙⲓ γυναικεῖόν τι; Ac 25 14 *SB* τὰ κατά; not in Gk: 1 Kg 20 39*S,* Jo 15 5 *SA²* ⲗⲁⲁⲩ ⲛϧ. (*B* om) οὐδέν, Ge 28 15 *SB* ϧ. ⲛⲓⲙ, Nu 3 10*B*(*S* ⲛⲕⲁ) sim, Col 1 16*B* sim, (*S* ⲡⲧⲏ-ⲣϥ) πᾶν, πάντα, Aeg 218 *S* ϧⲁϩ ⲛϧ. πολλά, Z 307 *S* ⲛⲟϭ ⲛϧ. μέγα, BHom 14 *S* ⲕⲟⲅⲓ ⲛϧ. ὀλίγα, MG 25 6 *B* ϧ. ⲛⲁⲧϫⲟⲙ ἀδύνατον, Aeg 288 *S* ϧ. ⲛⲥⲱⲃⲉ παι-διά; PS 9 *S* hearken ⲧⲁϫⲱ ⲉⲣⲱⲧⲛ ⲛϧ. ⲛⲓⲙ, ShC 73 45 *S* ϭⲓⲧⲟⲩ ⲙⲙⲁⲩ ϧⲙⲡϧ. ⲉⲧⲟⲩⲡⲣⲏⲧⲩ, *ib* 107 *S* ϫⲟⲟ-ⲟⲩ ⲟⲩϣⲁϫⲉ ⲏ ⲟⲩϧ.,TU 43 7 *A* I am Word ⲁⲓϣⲱⲡⲉ ⲛⲉϥ ⲡⲟⲩϧ. (Ethiop om), R 1 4 41 *S* ⲙⲡⲁⲧⲉⲡϧ. ⲱⲥⲕ *without delay,* BMis 448 *S* ⲉⲣⲉⲡϧ. ⲟⲥⲕ *long since,* CO Ad 17 *S* ⲛⲁⲧⲗⲁⲁⲩ ⲛϧ. *without anything* (of uncertainty, *cf* Ryl 207 sim ϧ. ⲡⲁⲙϥⲓⲃⲟⲗⲉⲓⲁ & Preisigke *Wb* πρᾶγμα 2),LMär 28 *S* if king hear ϫⲉⲁⲩϧ. ϣⲱⲡⲉ ⲛⲧⲉⲕⲙⲛⲧ̄ⲣⲟ he will be grieved, Mor 22 56 *S* ϣⲁ-ⲡⲉⲓϧ. ⲡⲁⲓ ⲙⲙⲁⲧⲉ *thus far only,* Win 7 *S* ⲙⲡⲉⲧⲛϧⲡ ϧ. ⲉϧⲟⲩⲛ ⲉⲣⲟϥ (*cf* III), Ep 219 *S* ϯϧⲛⲏ ϧⲁⲡⲉϧⲕⲟ ⲡⲁⲣⲁ ϧ. ⲛⲓⲙ, CO 229 *S* ϧⲁⲑⲏ ⲙⲉⲛ ⲡϧ. ⲛⲓⲙ, PMich 4552 *S* sim ⲱϧ ⲛⲓⲙ, BP 5717 *F* sim ϧⲟⲃⲓ ⲛⲓⲃⲓ, MR 5 24 *F* sim ⲱⲃⲓ ⲛ., *ib* 27 *F* sim ⲟⲃⲃⲓ ⲛ., BM 1239 *F* sim ⲟⲃ ⲛ., PAntinoe EES *S* ⲛⲛⲟϭ ⲛⲱϧ, DeV 2 50 *B* ⲙⲏ ⲡⲉⲛϧ. ⲥⲟⲧⲡⲉ ⲉϣⲧⲉⲙⲃⲟⲗⲟⲅ ⲉⲃⲟⲗ ? Bor 260 100 *S* He was taken up ⲕⲁⲧⲁ ϧ. ⲛⲣⲱⲙⲉ, *ib* sim ϧⲱⲥ ⲣⲱⲙⲉ, Va 63 88 *B* ⲙⲡⲟⲩⲙⲟⲩ ϭⲉⲛϧϧ. *in fact,* MG 25 407 *B* crying to us ϭⲉⲛϧϧ. *indeed* (?) & saying, BMis 239 *S* he saith I have armour, ⲛϧ. ⲕⲁⲓⲡⲉⲣ ⲉϥ-ⲕⲏⲕ ⲁϧⲏⲩ *though in fact is naked* (var Mor 29 11=30 12 om ⲛϧ.) γυμνὸς ὑπάρχων, BMOr 9532 *S* through sickness ⲙⲡⲟⲩⲣ ⲙⲙⲁϧⲉ ⲛϧ. ⲛⲁⲛ sim?, AZ 21 94 *O* ϥ. ⲉⲧⲓϫⲛⲟⲩ ⲙⲙⲟⲟⲩ ⲉⲣⲟϥ (*l* ⲉⲣⲟⲩ), BHom 83 *S* ⲡ-ⲃⲉⲕⲉ ⲙⲡⲉⲩϧ., MélOr 6 511 *B* ⲟⲩⲣⲟⲙⲡⲓ ⲛϧ., ShA 2 274 *S* nails & other ϧ. ⲡⲧⲟⲃⲧⲃ, ϧ. ⲡⲉⲓⲣⲉ ⲩ ⲉⲓⲣⲉ 2°, P 129¹⁵ 21 *S* ϧ. ⲛϥⲁⲣⲙⲁⲅⲓⲁ *as philtre,* Mor 41 66 *S* ϧ. ⲛⲅⲁⲙⲟⲥ *subject (function) of marriage,* ShR 2 3 26 *S* fulfil ⲛϧ. ⲙⲡⲉⲥϫⲛⲁⲙ, BMis 245(=Z 267)*S* will

rebuild it ⲛϧ. ⲛⲣⲣⲟ *royally,* BG 104 *S* ⲁⲓⲃⲱⲗ ⲙⲡⲉⲱ-ⲛⲧ ⲁⲓⲥⲱⲗⲡ ⲙϧ. ⲙⲡⲁϧⲁⲟⲩ, Pcod 30 *S* ⲛϧ. ⲛⲡⲁⲥⲉ-ⲃⲏⲥ *fate of sinners* befalleth righteous, ROC 20 44 *S* imitate his life each ⲡⲣⲟⲥ ⲡⲉⲩϧ., GuDorm 5 *S* ⲉⲓⲥ ϧⲟⲩⲟ ⲉϣⲉ ⲡⲣⲟⲙⲡⲉ ϧⲙⲡⲉⲩϧ. *over 100 years (have passed) in their matter,* ViK 9065 *S* marvellous ⲛϧ. ⲙⲡϣⲓ (? ϣⲏⲓ) ⲉⲧⲙⲙⲁⲩ (*cf* DeV 2 136), DeV 2 213 *B* marvellous to recount ⲛϧ. ⲙⲡⲟⲩⲁⲓ ⲡⲟⲩⲁⲓ, BSM 37 *B* prepared ⲉⲑⲃⲉⲡϧ. ⲙⲡⲛⲓⲛⲓϣϯ ⲡⲣⲱⲙ = BMis 382 *S* ϫⲣⲓⲁ, J 5 14 *S* deed ⲉⲧⲃⲉⲃⲁⲓⲟⲣ ⲉⲧϣⲛϣ ϧⲛⲟⲩ-ϧ. ⲡⲟⲩⲱⲧ (*cf* above p. 606 *a*), *ib* 54 6 *S* ϧⲁⲛϧ. ⲛⲡ-ⲧⲉⲣⲙⲏⲛⲥⲓⲟⲛ *as regards the t.,* BMis 386 *S* come let us ⲣ ⲛϧ. ⲙⲡⲛⲓ = BSM 40 *B* ⲥⲉⲃⲧⲉ ⲡⲉⲡⲥⲕⲉⲟⲥ ⲙ-, KroppR 10 *S* send Gabriel ⲛϭⲓⲣⲉ ⲙⲡⲁϧ., AZ 23 110 *S* after recipe ⲡⲉⲕϧ. ⲡⲁϫⲟⲕ ⲉⲃⲟⲗ ⲕⲁⲗⲟⲟⲥ, Ryl 360 *S* let thy fraternity ⲉⲣ ⲛϧ. ⲛⲥⲧⲛⲟⲟⲩ, PMich 525 *F* ⲁⲣⲓ ⲟⲩϧⲁϭ ϧⲣⲟϥ ϫⲉⲣⲁϥϫⲓ ϧⲉⲛⲃⲉⲛⲓⲡⲉ ⲛⲥⲟⲓ ; ite-rated *A²,* *each thing* : Mani 1 ⲁϥⲣ ⲕⲉⲗⲉⲅⲉ ⲡⲉⲩ ⲉⲧⲉ-ⲛϧ. ⲛϧ. ; *BF* +ⲕⲉ-, *any other thing* : EpJer 45 *F* ϣⲱ-ⲡⲓ ⲉⲕⲉϧ. ⲕ. (*B* diff) οὐδὲν ἄλλο ; Va 57 265 ⲕⲉϧ. ⲕ. ϫⲉ ⲟⲩϫⲉ ϧⲟⲗⲱⲥ περαιτέρω δὲ μηδέν; HL 99 word of Scripture ⲓⲉ ⲕ. ⲕ., C 43 112 ⲙⲡⲉϥϫⲁ ⲕ. ⲕ. ⲡⲁϥ ⲛ-ⲥⲁⲡϧ. ⲡⲁⲡⲁ ⲡⲁϥⲛⲟⲩϯ ; pl : Ps 16 4 *SBF,* Hos 13 2 *AB* ⲉϧ., Eccl 9 1 *SF* ἐργασία ; Is 25 1 *B*(*S* diff), Cl 1 1 *A* πρᾶγμα, Si 11 11 *S,* Mt 16 27 *SB* πρᾶξις ; Ps 9 11 *SB,* Jer 11 18 *SB* ἐπιτήδευμα ; 1 Kg 20 39 *S* σκεύος; Gal 1 13 *S*(*B* ϫⲓⲛⲙⲟϣⲓ) ἀναστροφή; Ps 55 8 *S*(*B* ⲱⲛϧ) ζωή; Mor 37 78*S* ⲛⲉϧ. ⲡⲧⲉⲉⲓⲥⲉ τὰ κατά, MG 25 208 *B* τὰ περί, Z 267 *S* ⲛⲧⲉⲕⲕⲗⲏⲥⲓⲁ τὰ τῆς ἐκ., Aeg 216 *S* ϧ. ⲛⲧⲉⲓⲙⲓⲛⲉ τοιοῦτος; not in Gk: Deu 1 30 *S* ϧ. ⲧⲏⲣⲟⲩ πάντα, Ps 59 3 *S* ϧ. ⲉⲩⲡⲁϣⲧ σκληρά, Is 12 5 *SB* ϧ. ⲉⲩϫⲟⲥⲉ ὑψηλά, 1 Cor 6 3 *B* ϧ. ⲛⲧⲉ ⲡⲁⲃⲓⲟⲥ (*S* diff) βιωτικά,Va 57 12 *B* ϧ. ⲉⲧⲣⲓⲟⲩⲧ ἀπειρημένα ; BHom 31 *S* ϧ. ⲛⲥⲱⲃⲉ καταγέλαστα ; PS 41 *S* ϫⲟⲕ ⲉⲃⲟⲗ ⲡⲛⲓⲉϧ., ShC 42 134 *S* put on us ϧⲉⲛϧ. ⲡⲁⲣⲁ ⲧⲉⲛϭⲟⲙ, El 38 *A* ⲛϧ. ⲉⲧⲛⲁⲡⲟⲅⲉ, AP 15 *A²* ϧ. ⲉⲩϧⲁⲣⲙ, BSM 59 *B* ϯϫⲱⲃ ϩⲉⲛⲛⲁϧ. = BMis 417 *S* ⲡⲣⲁ̅ⲅ̅ⲓⲥ,DeV 2 78 *B* ϧⲁⲛⲉϧ., Ryl 439 30 *B* ⲛⲉⲩ-ⲉϧ. ; sg as pl *S* : Lu 24 11 ⲛⲉⲓϧ. ⲛⲥⲱⲃⲉ (*B* diff) λῆρος; BMis 343 ϧⲉⲛⲛⲟϭ ⲛϧ. (var pl).

II ⲟⲩⲛⲉ ⲛϧ., *what is the matter?*: R 1 4 32*S,* BMis 121 *S,* ϑT 256 *S* ; c poss pref : Ge 46 33 *SB* τί τὸ ἔρ. ὑμῶν, Jud 11 12 *S* τί σοί; R 1 4 31 *S* he knew ⲟⲩⲛⲉ ⲡⲉⲩϧ., Miss 4 768 *S* ⲟⲩⲛⲉ ⲡⲉⲧⲛϧ. *what of you?,* Mor 18 71 *S* to God the glory, ⲉⲙⲙⲟⲛ ⲟⲩⲛⲉ ⲡⲁϧ.? = Miss 4 144 *B* ⲁⲛⲟⲕ ⲟⲩⲉⲗⲁⲭⲓⲥⲧⲟⲥ, FR 22 *S* ⲟⲩⲛⲉ ⲡⲉⲧⲛϧ. ⲉⲧⲉⲧⲛⲡⲗⲁⲛⲁ ⲛⲡⲣⲱⲙⲉ ?, Va 61 29 *B* ⲟⲩⲛⲉ ⲡⲉⲕϧ. ? ⲟⲩⲛⲉ ⲛϧ. ⲡ-, *what is business, history, use of …?* : ShA 2 45 *S* ⲡⲟⲩϧⲁϣⲛ ⲡⲣⲏⲃϭ ?, Wess 18 52 *S* ⲛⲡⲉⲧⲥⲁⲡⲉⲥⲏⲧ ⲙⲙⲱⲧⲛ *in depths of hell?,* Pcod 8 *S* of one entrusted with stewardship ⲛϥϧⲱϥⲧ ϧⲓⲱⲱⲥ?, MG 25 136 *B* ⲡϣⲓⲛⲧ ? He said As 4 cities of refuge, BSM 9 *B* ⲛⲡⲁⲡⲕⲁϧⲓ ?= BMis 326 *S* ⲁϧⲣⲟⲟⲩ; ⲟⲩ-

ⲡⲉ ⲡⲣ. ⲙⲛ-, ⲛⲉⲙ- sim : R 1 3 16 S ⲟⲩⲡⲉ ⲡⲉⲧⲛϩ. ⲡⲁ
ⲙⲁⲓ ?, BMis 38 S ⲟⲩⲡⲉ ⲡⲁⲣ. ⲁⲛⲟⲕ ⲙⲛⲧⲙⲛⲧⲣⲣⲟ ?, C
41 30 B ⲟⲩⲡⲉ ⲡⲣ. ⲙⲡⲟⲩⲣⲟ ⲡⲉⲙⲛⲓ ?   ⲟⲩ ⲡⲣ. SA²,
what thing, what : Lu 19 15 (B diff), Mor 17 35 ⲉⲛ
ⲡⲁⲣ ⲟⲩ ⲡⲣ. ? τί; ManiK 146 A²; ⲉⲧⲃⲉⲟⲩ ⲡⲣ. *v* p 468
a infra.

III ⲟⲩⲡ ϩ. ⲙⲛ-, *there is a matter with* : Ac 24 19
B(S ⲗⲁⲁⲩ) τι ἔχειν πρός, 1 Cor 6 1 SB πρᾶγμα ἐχ. π.;
ShC 42 89 S ⲡⲉⲧⲉⲟⲩⲛⲧϥ ϩ. ⲡⲁⲙⲁⲁⲛ let him come to
law, C 43 230 B ⲟⲅⲟⲛ ϩ. ⲛⲧⲁⲕ ⲡⲉⲙⲁϥ?;   ⲥ ⲉⲣⲟⲩⲛ
ⲉ-: Mt 5 23 S(B ⲁⲣⲓⲕⲓ) τι ἐχ. κατά, cf Win 7 in **I**.

ⲙⲙⲛ ϩ. SBF, *there is not a matter, is no business* :
Z 300 S ⲙⲛⲧⲁⲓ ϩ., MG 25 205 B ⲙⲙⲟⲛ ϩ. ⲛⲧⲁϥ οὐκ
ἔχειν πρᾶγμα; TT 47 S judge them not ⲙⲛⲧⲁⲕ ϩ. ⲛ
ⲧⲟⲕ;   ⲥ ⲙⲛ- : Z 296 S ⲙⲛⲧⲉ (sic l) ⲛⲁⲛⲁⲭⲱⲣⲓⲧⲏⲥ
ϩ. ⲡⲁⲙⲁⲓ = MG 25 205 B ut sup, Jud 18 28 S λόγος
οὐκ εἶναι dat; ROC 23 278 B ⲙⲙⲟⲛ ϩ. ⲛⲧⲏⲓ ⲡⲉⲙ
ⲁⲅⲁⲡⲏ ⲁⲛ *I have naught to do with alms,* ShA 2
271 S ⲙⲛϯ ⲗⲁⲁⲩ ⲡϩ. ⲡⲁⲙⲛⲧⲛ, CO 157 S ⲙⲛⲧⲁⲓ
ⲕⲉϩ. ⲡⲁⲙⲁⲕ ϩⲁⲗⲁⲅⲉ ⲛⲡⲣⲁⲕⲙⲁ, ViK 7033 F ⲙⲟⲛ
ϩ. ⲛⲧⲉⲓ ⲡⲉⲙⲉⲃ, C 43 117 B ⲙⲙⲟⲛ ϩ. ⲟⲩⲧⲱⲛ ⲡⲉ
ⲙⲁⲕ;   ⲥ ⲉ- S: PS 298 ⲙⲛⲧⲟⲩ ϩ. ⲉⲥⲟⲟⲣⲉ ⲙⲙⲟⲟⲩ
no cause to reprove them, PSBA 32 199 ⲙⲛⲧⲉ ⲡⲁⲓ
ⲕⲁⲥⲧⲏⲣⲓⲟⲛ ϩ. ⲉⲣⲟⲩⲛ ⲉⲣⲟⲓ (paral ShMIF 23 95 ⲙⲛ
ⲧⲉ ⲁ. ϣⲁⲝⲉ ⲙⲙⲁⲩ ⲉⲝⲱ ⲉⲣⲟⲓ), ShBM 253 56 at
Judgment where no escape, refuge, excuse ⲉⲙⲛ ϩ.
ⲉⲥⲱⲧⲉ.

IV ϩ. ⲛϭⲓⳓ, ϫⲓⳓ SB, *handiwork* : Deu 4 28 S(B
ϩⲃⲏⲟⲩⲓ ⲛ-) ἐρ. χειρῶν, Z 294 S, MG 25 203 B, Bor
235 118 S ϫⲓ ⲥⲃⲱ ⲉⲩϩ. ἐργόχειρον; ShC 73 211 S
whoso neglecteth ⲡⲉϥϩ. cannot be monk, BAp 125 S
solidus earned ϩⲙⲡⲁϩ. = MIE 2 418 B, J 68 43 S acquired ϩⲁⲡⲉⲛϩ. (cf ib 89 44 ⲉⲣⲧⲱϫⲉⲓⲣⲱⲛ), CO 16 S
ⲧⲧⲉϫⲛⲏ ⲙⲡⲉⲕϩ. (var R 1 2 36 ⲧⲧ. only), BKU 1 306
S none hath bought ϩ. of me this year, ST 283 S ⲡ
ⲕⲟⲩⲓ ⲡϩ. ⲉⲧⲉ(ⲛ)ⲛⲟⲟⲩϩⲡⲉ.   V Ep 1 155.

ⲁⲧϩ. F, *without work* : BM 580 4 ⲉⲓⲣⲙⲁ(ⲥ) ⲛⲁⲧϩⲟⲃ
ⲛⲁⲧ[ⲓ]ⲁⲡⲓ ⲉⲓⲥⲁⲣⲉⲙ ⲉⲃⲁⲗ.

V ⲣ, ⲉⲣ, ⲉⲗ ϩ. SAA²BF as vb, *do work* : Nu 8 25
SB, Jo 5 17 SA²B, 1 Cor 9 6 SBF ἐργάζεσθαι; Lu
19 13 S(B ⲉⲣ ⲓⲉⲃϣⲱⲧ) πραγματεύεσθαι; Job 34 20
S(B diff) χρᾶσθαι; 1 Cor 16 9 B(S = Gk) ἐνεργής;
Br 238 S bidding all ⲉⲧⲣⲉⲩϩ., ManiK 52 A² ⲁ]ⲩϩ.
ⲕⲁⲗⲱⲥ, CDan 91 B take thy tools ⲁⲣⲓ ϩ., Miss 4 231
S ⲙⲁ ⲛⲟⲩϩⲱⲃ, ⲙⲁ ⲛⲣ. in monastery;   ⲥ ⲉ-, *at, on* :
Ge 3 23 SB, Nu 31 51 B(S ⲙⲟⲛⲧ), Is 30 24 SBF,
Zeph 2 3 SA(B ⲛ-), Jo 6 27 SA²B ἐρ., Ps 7 14 B(S
ⲧⲁⲙⲓⲟ) ἐξερ., Gal 3 5 B(S = Gk) ἐνερ., Deu 28 39
SB, Ro 4 15 SB κατερ.; Ex 15 17 B, Ps 67 29 B(S
ⲥⲟⲃⲧⲉ) καταρτίζειν; R 1 1 38 S ⲙⲡⲛⲁⲩ ⲁⲓⲡⲉ ⲉⲧⲣⲉⲛⲣ.
ⲉⲣⲟⲕ πράσσειν κατά; Bar 3 17 B(S ⲭⲛⲟ) τεκταίνειν;
MG 25 209 B ⲉⲣ. ⲉ·ϯⲡⲉⲃϯ πλέκειν; Pro 29 31 SA
ⲣ. ⲉⲡⲥⲟⲣⲧ μηρύεσθαι; PS 335 S ⲡⲉⲧⲣ. ⲉⲧⲉⲯⲩⲭⲏ,

ShA 1 127 S ⲉⲧⲣ. ⲉⲣⲟⲟⲩ (*sc* clothes) ⲏ ⲉⲧⲧⲁⲙⲓⲟ ⲙ
ⲙⲟⲟⲩ, Bor 263 29 S ⲟⲩϭⲟⲙ ⲙⲙⲛⲧⲣⲱⲙⲉ ⲁⲛ ⲧⲉⲧⲉⲣ.
ⲉⲣⲟⲟⲩ *inspire*, AM 256 B ⲉⲣ. ⲉⲡⲓⲕⲏⲡⲟⲥ, BSM 44 B
bring the fish ⲙⲡⲁⲧⲉⲧⲉⲡⲉⲣ. ⲉⲣⲟϥ, J 556 S ⲛⲡⲣⲁⲅⲙⲁ
ⲧⲉⲓⲁ ⲉⲧⲡⲣ. ⲉⲣⲟⲥ ⲙⲡⲛⲉⲡⲉⲣⲏⲩ, CO 218 S hired me to
ⲣ. ⲉⲡⲉⲕⲕⲁⲙⲟⲩⲗ (cf ⲥ ϩⲓ-), BMOr 11289(14) F ⲁⲅⲉⲗ
ϩⲟⲩ ⲉⲡⲁⲕⲟⲙⲁⲣⲓ (πωμάριον), PSBA 19 215 S ⲉϣⲱ
ⲡⲉ ⲁⲩⲣ. ⲉⲣⲟϥ *if he hath been bewitched* (cf RChamp
below & KroppM 88);   ⲥ ⲛ- dat : Jer 34 6 B, Bar
2 23 B ⲉⲣ. dat; Ps 118 126 S(B ⲓⲣⲓ only), Z 338 S
cannot ⲣ. ⲙⲛⲧⲏ ⲡⲟⲓⲉⲓⲛ dat; DeV 2 195 B find someone ⲛⲧⲁⲉⲣ. ⲛⲁϥ, CA 102 S church's goods ⲣ. (var
ϣⲙϣⲉ) ⲡⲧⲉⲣϥⲣⲉ ⲙⲛⲉⲑⲃⲱ;   dat or acc? B : Ps 14 2
ⲉⲣ. ⲡⲉⲑⲛⲓ (S ⲉ-); ib 73 12 (var & S do), Pro 3 30
(SA ⲣ. only) ἐρ. acc, 1 Cor 12 6 (S = Gk) ἐνερ. acc;
Dan 11 20 πράσ. acc; *in, with* : Ex 20 9 B days ⲉⲕⲉ
ⲉⲣ. ⲙⲙⲟⲟⲩ (S om ⲙ.) ἐρ. acc, 1 Cor 4 12 B(S ϩⲛ-)
ἐρ. dat; RChamp 541 S ⲡⲉϯⲛⲁ ⲉⲣ. ⲉⲣⲟϥ ⲛⲟⲩⲙⲟⲩⲣ
bewitch with a binding-spell (cf PSBA above);   ⲥ
ϩⲁ-, *for* : Kr 148 F ⲉⲗ. ϩⲁⲗⲁⲕ for a year; ϩⲁⲣⲁⲧ⳽: BG
64 S ⲁϥⲣ. ϩⲁⲣⲁⲧϥ ⲙⲡⲉⲥⲡⲉⲣⲙⲁ;   ⲥ ϩⲓ- S sim : CO
221 ⲉⲧⲣⲁⲣ. ϩⲓⲡⲉⲕⲕⲁⲙⲟⲩⲗ (cf ⲥ ⲉ-), Ryl 374 ⲉⲣ. ϩⲓ
ⲧⲉϥⲧⲓⲙⲏ;   ⲥ ϩⲛ-, ⳍⲉⲛ-, *in, with, by* : Si 30 34 S,
Mt 25 16 SB ⲉⲣ. ἐν, Ap 18 17 S(B diff) ⲉⲣ. acc, Ro 7
5 B(S = Gk) ⲉⲛⲉⲣ. ἐν, Eph 1 11 BF(S do) ἐνερ. acc,
C 89 65 B demon ⲉⲧⲉⲣ. ⲛϩⲏⲧⲟⲩ = C 99 231 S ⲉⲡⲉⲣ.
ⲅⲉⲓ ⲙⲙⲟⲟⲩ ἐνέργεια; Ps 30 20 B(S ⲧⲱϩ) ⲉⳓⲉⲣ. dat,
Ez 34 14 SB κατερ. acc, Ps 106 23 S(B ⲓⲣⲓ ⲡⲟⲩϫⲓⲛⲉⲣ.)
ἐργασίαν ποι. ἐν; Pro 3 14 SA(B ⲉⲣ ⲓⲉⲃϣⲱⲧ) ἐμπορεύεσθαι acc; PS 355 S ⲁϥⲣ. ϩⲙⲡⲙⲩⲥⲧⲏⲣⲓⲟⲛ ⲙ
ⲡⲟⲩⲟⲉⲓⲛ, R 2 220 S sailors ⲉⲧⲣ. ϩⲓⲡⲛⲟⳓ ⲙⲡⲉⲗⲁⲅⲟⲥ,
CA 108 S ⲉϥⲣ. ϩⲛⲡⲉϥϭⲓϫ, Bor 263 31 S ϣⲁϥⲣ. (*sc*
Christ) ϩⲛⲧⲓⲟⲩⲅⲓⲁ, C 86 343 B trader ⲉϥⲉⲣ. ⲍⲉⲛⲟⲩ
ⲛⲓϣϯ ⲙⲡⲣⲁⲅⲙⲁⲧⲁ, BMOr 8803 2 B lectionary ⲉϥ
ⲉⲣ. ⳍⲉⲛⲛⲓⲕⲩⲣⲓⲁⲕⲏ ذكرمه, PMéd 239 S ⲟⲩⲛⲟϭ
ⲙⲡⲁϩⲣⲉ ⲉⲓⲣ. ⲛϩⲏⲧⲥ *which I* (physician) *employ*;   as
nn m : Eph 1 19 B(SF = Gk) ⲉⲛⲉⲣⲅⲉⲓⲁ, Ro 7 18 S(B
vb) κατεργάζ.; ShC 42 190 S give selves over ⲉⲡⲣ.
ⲉⲁⲕⲁⲑⲁⲣⲥⲓⲁ ⲛⲓⲙ, R 2 162 S ⲡⲉⲣ. ϩⲡⲟⲩϩⲟⲟⲩ ⲉⲙⲉⲩⲣ.
ⲛϩⲏⲧϥ (on Mt 12 10), AZ 67 102 S ⲣⲟⲙⲡⲉ ⲛⲉⲣ.,
DeV 2 195 B sim, ROC 7 139 S selling ϩⲙⲡⲣ. ⲛ
ⲡⲉⲩϭⲓⳍ, CO 122 S ⲛⲡⲉϥϫⲓ ⲥⲁⲣⲁⲡⲓⲱⲛ ⲉⲡⲣ.;   ⲣⲁ ⲣ
ϩ. *v* ⲣⲁ (on which *Rev. d'Ég* 2 35);   ⲁⲧⲉⲣ ϩ. B: Ps
138 16 (S om) ἀκατέργαστος; Pro 13 4 (SA ⲁⲣⲅⲟⲥ)
ἀεργός;   ⲣⲉϥⲣ ϩ. S: Wess 15 21 ⲉⲣⲅⲁⲧⲏⲥ; Z 313
πρακτικός; Sa 7 22 εὐκίνητος; ShA 2 349 among
trades ⲣ. ⲉⲣⲟⲓⲧⲉ, ib ⲉϣϩⲁⲣ;   ϣⲫⲏⲣ ⲡⲣ. BF:
1 Cor 3 9 (S ϣⲃⲣ ⲣ ϩ.) συνεργός;   ⲙⲛⲧ-, ⲙⲉⲧⲣⲉϥⲣ
ϩ.: Pro 6 8 a SA ⲧⲉϥⲙ. ὡς ⲉⲣⲅⲁⲧⲓⲥ ἐστί; ShA 1 448 S
felling trees ϩⲛⲧϭⲟⲙ ⲛⲧⲉⲙ., DeV 2 232 B Noah's
ⲛⲓϣϯ ⲙⲙ. in building ark;   He 13 16 B(S diff)
ϯⲙⲉⲧⲣⲉⲩⲉⲣ ϩⲉⲃⲛⲟⲩϥⲓ εὐποιία; 1 Tim 6 2 B do
(S ϩ. ⲉⲧⲛⲁⲛⲟⲩϥ) εὐεργεσία;   ϣⲃⲣ ⲣ ϩ. *v* ϣ-

ⲃⲏⲣ; ϭⲓⲡⲣ, ⲭⲓⲙⲉⲣ ϩ.: Ps 106 23 B f(S ⲣ ϩ. vb), Ac 19 25 B f(S=Gk), MG 25 209 B f=Z 344 S ϩ. ἐργασία, Va 57 15 B m ἔργον; DeV 1 96 B f ascete's ϫ. & ⲁⲛⲁⲥⲧⲣⲟⲫⲏ, ShA 2 151 S who writeth ⲧⲉϥϩ. *manner of work* ⲉⲁⲩⲕⲁⲁⲥ ⲡⲛⲉⲩϣⲏⲣⲉ?, Bor 260 118 S fishers know ϭ. ⲉⲛⲑⲁⲗⲁⲥⲥⲁ, AZ 30 43 S let me know so that ⲉⲓⲥⲟⲟⲩⲛ ⲧⲁϭ., BMis 211 S ⲁϥϣⲱⲡⲉ ⲡⲣⲟⲥ ⲧⲉⲩϩ. (*sc* parents' religion, var Mor 16 58 ⲑⲣⲏⲥⲕⲓⲁ), BMar 213 S taught me ⲧϭ. ⲉⲛϫⲁⲓⲉ = Rec 6 178 B ⲡⲓϫ. ⲛⲧⲉ ⲧⲙⲉⲧⲁⲛⲟⲓⲁ in desert, Mor 31 56 S ϩⲛϭ. ⲉⲩ ϩⲟⲥⲉ *hard labour*, KroppM 10 S magical *procedure*, AZ 23 104 S ⲡⲉⲡⲁϩⲣⲉ ⲙ̄ⲡⲉⲩϭ. *employment*.

† ϩ., *give work*, *employment*: Pro 29 33 SA ⲡ ϩ. ἔργον διδόναι; LCyp 2 = Mor 18 108 S priests ⲉⲧ†ϩ. ⲙⲡⲟⲩⲁ ⲡⲟⲩⲁ ⲡⲛⲉϫⲁⲓⲙⲟⲛⲓⲟⲛ, Kr 184 S.

ϩⲱⲃ v ϩⲱⲡ *horn*.

ϩⲁⲁⲃⲓ F nn, meaning unknown: Kr 233 (collated) letter about local tax-official ⲁⲛⲁⲕ ⲉⲧⲥⲉⲧ ϩ. ⲙⲉⲡⲏ̄ϥ ⲉⲡⲉⲓ ⲟⲩϫⲓⲁⲥⲧⲣⲉⲫⲉ ⲡⲁⲡⲉⲕⲏⲓ ⲉⲧⲃⲉⲡⲉⲓϩⲱⲃ̄.

ϩⲁⲓⲃⲉ v ϩⲓⲃⲉ *s* f.

ϩⲉⲃⲓ B v ϩⲏⲃⲉ & ϩⲓⲃⲉ.

ϩⲏⲃⲉ SSᶠAA², ϩⲏⲛ. SSᶠ, ϩⲏⲓ. S, ⲏⲃⲉ A, ϩⲏⲃⲓ, ϩⲏⲃⲓ BF, ϫⲏⲃⲓ, ϫⲏⲓ. B nn m f, *grief*, *mourning*: Ge 50 10 S(B ⲡⲉϩⲡⲓ), Pro 14 13 SAB ϫ., Eccl 7 3 SF, Hos 9 4 Sᶠ(JEA 11 246) A ⲛ̄ⲃⲉ, Ja 4 9 SAB, BerlSitz '09 217 A² πένθος; 2 Kg 1 17 B(S ⲧⲟⲉⲓⲧ), Lam 1 tit B θρῆνος; Jer 9 19 B οἰκτρός; Va 57 172 B ϩⲏⲓ. λυπηρός; Sa 14 21 S συμφορά; PS 92 S soul humbled ϩⲓⲟⲩϩ., Mor 41 105 S Herod's birthday ⲙⲁⲗⲗⲟⲛ ⲇⲉ ⲡⲉϥϩ., BMis 456 S ⲟⲩⲛⲟϭ ⲛ̄ϩ. at bishop's death, Mor 31 134 S 7 days ⲡ̄ϩⲛⲏⲃⲉ, TstAb 179 B ⲡⲓϩ. for Abraham, ManiH 28 A², K. al-Tagnīz 70 B ⲛⲓⲕⲟⲩϫⲓ ⲛ̄ϩ. *abbreviated service* for patriarch مختـ تجنيز; f: BMis 7 S ⲛ̄ⲧⲉⲣⲉϥ. ⲙⲡⲉϥⲉⲓⲱⲧ ⲟⲩⲉⲓⲛⲉ, ManiH 42 A² ⲣⲁⲓⲥ ⲁ†ϩ. ⲙ̄ⲡⲛ̄ⲏⲥⲧⲓⲁ, *ib* 79 A² †ⲡⲟ ⲁϩ. ⲡⲡⲁϣⲏⲣⲉ; as adj: 2 Kg 14 2 S ϩⲟⲓⲧⲉ ⲛⲣ. πενθικός; as vb (error?): Mor 24 19 F ⲉⲡϩⲏⲓ. ⲉⲓⲱⲁ ⲓⲓⲏⲥ = *ib* 23 28 S ⲉⲣ ϩⲏⲛ. ⲛ̄-.

ⲣ, ⲉⲣ ϩ. SAA²BF, *grieve*, *mourn*: Nu 14 39 SB, Job 14 22 SB ϫ. (var ϫⲏⲃⲓ), Is 33 9 SBF ϩⲏⲓ., Hos 4 3 SAB, Mt 5 4 SSᶠ ϩⲏⲛ. (PMich 549) B πενθεῖν, Eccl 7 5 F(S?) ⲡⲉⲧⲉⲓⲗ ϩ. πένθος, Mor 18 106 S ⲁⲓⲣ ⲡⲉϭ. π. ὑπομένειν; Joel 1 5 B(A ⲓⲁⲉⲓⲧ), Jo 16 20 B(SA² ⲧⲟ.) θρηνεῖν, AM 280 B θρῆνον ποιεῖν; Job 29 25 SB παθεινός; Is 13 8 B(S ⲛⲓⲕⲁϩ ⲛ̄ϩⲏⲧ) συμφοράζειν; 2 Kg 3 1 S gloss? on ⲣ ϭⲱⲃ; PS 42 S ⲉⲥⲗⲩⲡⲉⲓ ⲉⲥⲣ., JTS 9 379 S ⲁⲣⲓ ϩⲏⲛ. for your craft is brought to naught, DeV 2 44 B ⲉϥⲟⲕⲉⲙ ⲉϥⲉⲣ., ManiH 15 A² weep & ϩ. With following preposition. ⲛ ⲉ-: Jth 16 24 S, Bel 40 B, 2 Cor 12 21 B(SF ⲛ̄-) πεν. acc; BIF 14 172 S ⲉϥⲉⲣ. ⲉⲡⲉⲓⲱⲧ, DeV 2 168 B ⲉⲣ. ⲉⲡⲏ ⲉⲧⲁⲩⲙⲟⲩ; ⲛ ⲉⲧⲃⲉ-: C 99 20?

S ⲣ. ⲉⲧⲃⲏⲛⲧϥ; ⲛ ⲉϫⲛ-: Is 61 3 S(B ⲛ̄-) π. acc, Cl 2 6 A π. ἐπί; 2 Kg 1 17 B(S ⲧⲟ.) θρ. ἐπί; Bor 226 161 S †ⲣ. ⲉ. ⲛⲁⲡⲟϩⲉ κλαίειν acc; BHom 77 S sim; Lam 3 51 B(F Gk diff, *cf* Hebr); ⲉϩⲣⲁⲓ ⲉϫⲛ-: Hos 10 5 SAB π. ἐπί; ⲛ ⲛ-: Ge 50 3 S(B ⲉ-), Ez 31 15 B ϫ., 2 Cor 12 21 SF(B do), Aeg 285 S ⲁⲡⲗⲁⲟⲥ ⲣ. ⲙ̄ⲙⲱⲅⲥⲏⲥ (var ϩⲏⲓ.) π. acc, RNC 31 S π. περί; ShC 42 213 S ⲉⲧⲣⲉⲡⲣ. ⲛⲁⲡ ⲙⲁⲅⲁⲁⲛ, MIF 9 95 S ⲁⲙ̄ⲡⲧⲉ ⲣ. ⲡⲁⲕ, AP 16 A² ⲛⲉⲥⲣ. ⲡⲉⲥⲡⲉ; ⲛ ϩⲓϫⲛ- S: 2 Kg 14 2 (var ⲉϫⲛ-) π. ἐπί; Sh(?)Mor 54 36 S ⲣ ϩⲛⲓ. ϩ. ⲧⲉϥⲡⲁⲣⲁⲃⲁⲥⲓⲥ; ⲣⲉϥⲣ ϩ. SB: Mus 40 44 S(Reg Pach) ⲟ ⲛⲣ. *lugere*, Sh(?)ViK 9344 59 S ⲛⲓⲙ ⲛⲣ. ⲡⲉⲧⲉⲙⲉⲩⲙⲧⲱⲙ ⲉⲣⲓⲙⲙⲓⲛⲧϩⲁϩ ⲛϣⲁϫⲉ?, P 131¹ 29 S ⲛⲣ. ⲓⲉⲣⲏⲙⲓⲁⲥ; ⲙⲛ̄ⲧ-, ⲙⲉⲧⲣ.: Va 57 175 B -ϩⲏⲓ. κατήφεια; ShA 1 284 S among monastic virtues, DeV 2 44 B summoned them ⲉⲧⲁⲓⲙ., Cat 155 B ⲧⲁⲓⲥⲙⲓ ⲙⲙ. (Lu 13 34); ϭⲓⲡⲣ ϩ. S: Wess 18 90 πένθος.

V ⲉⲃⲏ.

ϩⲏⲃⲉ v ϩⲃ̄ⲃⲉ.

ϩⲏⲃⲓ F nn as pl, meaning unknown: BM 660 ϭⲁⲡ ⲕⲉⲧⲟⲩ (of what?) ⲛ̄ⲧⲟⲟⲧⲩ ⲧⲁⲩⲁⲩ ⲉϥⲓⲣ ⲧⲉⲡⲃⲁϣ ⲡⲉϩ. ⲡϣⲙⲁ (ⲉ)ⲃⲁⲗ[. Prob not same as last.

ϩⲏⲓⲃⲓ BF v ϩⲏⲃⲉ.

ϩⲓⲃⲉ S (once), ϩⲉⲃⲓ B (once), ϩⲟⲃⲉ† S, ϩⲁ.† SA² vb intr, *be low*, *short*: Jer 38 37 B ταπεινοῦσθαι; ShC 73 16 ϣⲁⲥϭⲱⲟⲩ...ϣⲁⲥϩ. (var ϩ̄ⲃⲃⲉ); qual: Ps 103 8 (B ⲡⲏ̄ϥ ⲉⲡⲉⲥⲛⲧ) καταβαίνειν; P 44 63 ⲃⲣⲁⲭⲉⲓⲁ·ⲉϩⲁ. ثـبـت = 43 45 ϩⲁⲓⲃⲉ, C 99 121 reeds ϩⲟⲓⲛⲉ ⲉⲩϫⲟⲓ ϩⲟⲓⲛⲉ ⲉⲩϩ. ᵃ; ShA 1 153 ⲙⲁ ⲉⲧϩ. ⲙⲁ ⲉⲧϩⲟⲥⲉ, ShC 73 152 ⲟⲩϣⲁⲧⲉ ⲏ ⲟⲩⲙⲁ ⲉϥϩ., ShP 130⁴ 148 ill-fitting garments ⲉⲩϭⲏⲩ ⲉⲩϩ. παρα ⲡϣⲓ, paral ⲉⲩⲟⲩⲟϣⲥ ⲉⲩϩ. ⲉⲩϫⲟⲓ, ManiK 38 A² ordination by Exalted of him ⲉⲧϩ. ⲡⲁⲣⲁⲣⲁϥ. (ϩⲟⲃⲓ B AZ 14 59 = ⲟⲃⲓ, v ⲉⲓⲃⲉ).

ϩⲃ̄ⲃⲉ (once), ϩ̄ⲃⲱⲟⲩ †S vb intr, sim: ShC 73 16 *ut sup*; qual: ShIF 180 garments ⲉⲩϭⲏⲩ...ⲉⲩϩ., *ib* ⲉⲩϫⲟⲓ...ⲉⲩϩ. (*cf* P 130⁴ above), ShViK 9346 ⲛⲉⲧϣⲁⲓ ⲡⲉⲧϩ.; **ϩ̄ⲃⲃⲉ** nn m, *low part, place*: Jos 15 19 ἡ κάτω; 1 Cor 11 17(B ⲑⲉⲃⲓⲏⲟⲩⲧ) τὸ ἧσσον; Tri 237 ⲙ̄ⲡⲣⲧⲣⲉⲡϫⲓⲥⲉ ϫⲉⲛⲡⲉⲛⲉⲓ ⲉⲩϩ. بلابـ'ل; PS 179 ⲡϫⲓⲥⲉ ⲙⲛⲡϩ. of Chaos, *ib* 202 ⲡϫⲓⲥⲉ, ⲡⲥⲁϩⲣⲉ, ⲛϩ.; ShViK 9315 180 land ⲉⲧϩⲓⲛϩ. easy to water, ShIF 180 of garments ⲡⲉⲩϩ., ⲡⲉⲩϣⲓⲁⲉⲓⲁⲓ, R 2 172 ⲡϫⲓⲥⲉ, ⲛϩ.

ϩ̄ⲃⲁⲓ S nn, *shortness*: ShIF 181 of garments ⲡⲃϣⲓⲛ ϩ̄ⲃ. ϩⲓⲟⲩⲟϣⲥ ϩⲓⲥⲃⲟⲟⲩ ϩⲓⲟⲩⲙⲟⲧ ϩⲓⲡⲁⲕⲉ.

ϩⲁⲓⲃⲉ S nn f: J 9 35 share in yard ⲡⲁⲓ ⲉⲧⲕⲏ ⲉϩⲣⲁⲓ ϩⲓⲧϩ. Belongs here? or to ϩⲁⲉⲓⲃⲉⲥ. Place-name(?): ϩⲓⲃⲉ (PGoi 45, Hibeh S of Feshn). *Cf* ⲉⲃⲃⲓⲟ.

ϩⲓⲃⲉ Sᶠ v ϩ̄ⲃⲃⲉ.

ϩⲓⲃⲱⲓ¹ SF, ϩⲉ.², ϩⲓⲃⲟⲅⲓ³, ϩ̄ⲃ.⁴, ϩⲁⲃⲓⲟⲅⲓ⁵ S, ϩⲓϥⲟⲅⲓ⁶, ϩⲃⲟⲅⲓ⁷, ϩⲓⲡ⁸ B nn m, *ibis*: Lev 11 17 S¹ (var⁵

P 44 105 misunderst زنبور) B⁸ (misunderst باشق), Deu
14 14 S¹ (var⁸ P 44 108 واق) B⁸ ʼ϶, Is 34 11 S¹B⁴F, R 1
4 57 S¹ = MartIgn 869 B⁷ ἴβις ; ϩ.⁷ Deu 14 17 B Lag
(sc BM 712 336, Va om) is for ἔποψ ; Mor 29 22 S
idol with ϩⲁ ⲛϩ.¹ = ib 30 26 F, Ora 4 26 S smear salve
with ⲙⲏϩⲉ ⲛϩ.¹, PMéd 240 S⁴ sim, ib 276 S ⲕⲟⲡⲣⲟⲥ
ⲛϩ.⁴ in recipe, AJSL 46 247 S ⲥⲡⲟϥ ⲛϩ.² sim, Mor 18
29 = 19 38 S Juvenal reproached ⲁⲕⲃⲱⲕ ⲉⲕⲟ ⲛⲟⲩⲱϩⲉ...ⲁⲕⲕⲟⲧⲕ ⲉⲕⲟ ⲛϩ.¹ ⲡⲣⲉϥϭⲉⲡ ⲧⲃⲧ ⲉⲧϩⲁϭⲙ = Miss
4 122 B (collated) ... ⲛⲟⲩⲱⲓ ... ⲛⲟⲩϩⲓ (prob transposed) = Gött ar 114 30 both صيّاد.　　P 44 56 = 45 140
ⲓⲃⲓⲥ سعد (sic l) طائر يعرف بابي, var 43 23 السعيد (l بغيبة
بغاء Guest).

In names : ᾽Ἰβ, ῎Ἰβις (Preisigke), ⲫⲓⲃ (pass, not
Thebes), ⲫⲓϥ (Mor 56 51 ابيب Synax 1 77), ⲫⲓⲫ
(Rec 6 64) Φῖβις, Φίβιος (Pr), perhaps ⲫ(ⲟ)ⲓⲃⲁⲙ-
ⲙⲱⲛ (v Ep 1 116 & cf P-ḥb-ʼnp RylDem 3 443), فيف
(Archiv Orient 7 450).

ϩⲱⲃⲓ F　v ϩⲱⲃ nn.

ϩⲃⲁ S, ϩⲃⲉ S^fF nn m, straits, embarrassment, misfortune : Is 24 19 (B ϣⲟⲟⲣⲧⲉⲣ), Jer 8 21 (ShA 2 98,
B ϣⲗⲁϩ ⲛϩⲏⲧ) ἀπορία ; Is 24 3 (B ⲧⲁⲕⲟ) φθορά ; 1 Kg
14 20 σύγχυσις ; BMar 115 ϣⲱⲡⲉ ϩⲛⲟⲩⲛⲟϭ ⲛϩ. ἀδη-
μονία ; PS 367 ⲡⲁⲣⲁⲙ ϩⲙⲡⲉⲓⲛⲟϭ ⲛϩ., ShBM 209 36
ⲡⲉⲩϩⲏⲧ ⲉⲧⲟ ⲛⲕⲁⲕⲉ ϩⲛⲟⲩϩ., ShBMOr 8800 60 ⲣ ϩⲟⲃⲉ ϩⲛⲟⲩϩ., Aeg 14 ⲡⲛⲟϭ ⲛϩ. when dying = ib B ϣⲟ.,
BerlOr 1607 3 91 ⲁⲩϣⲱⲡⲉ ϩⲛⲟⲩⲛⲟϭ ⲛϩ., BMis 105
= Mor 33 66 ⲛⲉϩ. ⲉⲧⲉϣⲁϥϣⲱⲡⲉ ⲛⲡϣⲁ ⲛⲥⲉ, Mor 30
28 S^f awoke ϩⲛⲟⲩⲛⲟϭ ⲛϩ. = ib 29 24 S ϣⲧⲟⲣⲧⲣ ; as
adj : BMOr 8811 74 ⲟⲩⲙⲟⲩ ⲛϩ. ϩⲓⲟⲣⲅⲏ, Mor 30 25
S^f sim = ib 29 21 S ⲛⲉⲃⲓⲏⲛ.

ⲣ ϩ., be in straits, distress : Ge 32 7 (B ϣⲗⲁϩ ⲛϩ.)
ἀπορεῖν ; Jer 4 31 (B ϯ ⲟⲅⲱ ⲉⲃⲟⲗ) ἐκλύεσθαι ; Ac 27
9 (B diff) ἐπισφαλὴς εἶναι ; PS 32 ⲧⲣⲉⲩϩ. ϩⲛⲧⲉⲩϭⲓⲛ-
ⲙⲟⲟϣⲉ, Mun 69 ⲁϥⲣ. ⲁϥⲁϩⲟⲡⲉⲓ (ἄτον.) = DeV 2
274 B ⲣ ϣⲫⲏⲣⲓ ⲧⲟⲙⲧ ⲉⲃⲟⲗ, Leyd 312 ϣⲧⲟⲣⲧⲣ, ⲣ.,
ⲥⲧⲱⲧ, BAp 2 ⲁⲙⲁ ⲣ. ⲡⲧⲟⲟⲧ ⲁⲡⲁⲏⲣ ϣⲓⲃⲉ, Mor 16
74 ⲁϥⲣ. ⲙⲡⲉϥϩⲏⲧ = BMis 219 ϩⲟⲭϩⲉϩ, AZ 23 106
ending fragmentary recipe ⲙⲡⲉⲣⲉⲣ ϩ[ⲃⲁ] ⲥⲁⲃⲟⲗ ⲉⲡ-
ⲕⲏⲡⲧⲗⲟⲥ (κύκλος) ... ⲙⲡⲉⲣⲉⲣ. ϫⲉⲟⲩϩ. ⲡ(ⲉ) ⲡⲛⲟⲩϥ
(meaning ?) ;　　ⲟ ⲛϩ. : Z 318 ⲉϩⲟ. θορυβεῖν ; C 99
139 ⲉϩⲟ. wondering what should befall = C 89 45 B
ⲧⲟⲙⲧ, Sh R 2 3 8 dying man ⲟ. ϩⲛⲧⲉϥⲯⲩⲭⲏ ; 　 tr :
PS 31 ⲥⲉⲡⲁⲣ. ⲙⲙⲟⲟⲩ ⲁⲩⲱ ⲥⲉⲛⲁⲁⲡⲉⲓⲗⲓ ⲉⲣⲟⲟⲩ, ShA
1 81 ⲁⲡⲓⲣⲱⲙⲉ ⲁⲁⲧ ⲛϩ., BHom 129 ⲁϥⲣ ⲡϩⲁϫⲉ ⲛϩ.

ϯ ϩ., disturb, distress : BMar 147 smoothness of her
body did not ϯ. ⲙⲡⲉⲕⲗⲟⲅⲓⲥⲙⲟⲥ, Ryl 321 ⲥⲟⲩⲧⲓ. ⲛⲡ-
ⲛⲙⲁⲙⲉⲭ ⲡⲉⲧⲛⲡⲣⲟⲥⲱⲡⲟⲛ ; Giron Légendes 63 ϩⲉⲛ-
ⲣⲉϥϯ. ⲡⲉ ϩⲉⲛⲓⲟⲙⲉ = Mor 41 332 ⲣⲉϥϣⲧⲟⲣⲧⲣ.

ϩⲃⲁⲓ　v ϩⲓⲃⲉ s f.

ϩⲃⲱ S nn f, covering, tent : Ge 33 17, Jth 8 5, Is
1 8, cit ShC 73 185 (= راقود, cf K 155 where l ⲥⲧⲩ-

λος), He 11 9 (all B = Gk) σκηνή ; Ps 103 2 (B ϣⲁⲣ)
δέρρις ; Tri 241 خيم ; BMOr 6201 A 126 ⲉⲣϣⲁⲛⲧⲉ]ⲧⲛ-
ϭⲱ ⲉⲧⲡⲉⲁⲙⲉⲗⲉⲓ ⲛⲧⲓⲣⲉ ϣⲁⲣⲉⲧⲉϩ. ⲡⲁⲓ...ⲃⲱⲗ ⲣ ⲉ-
ⲣⲱⲧⲛ[(obscure), BM 461 wine jars promised ⲧⲉⲓⲟ ⲛ-
ⲣⲉⲧⲉⲙⲟⲥ (ἔτοι.) ⲧⲁⲧⲉⲓ ϩ. ⲉⲣⲟⲟⲩ [ⲛⲡⲁⲟ]ⲡⲉ ⲛⲧⲉⲓⲣⲟ-
ⲡⲉ, ib 1040 sim ⲧⲁⲧⲓ ϩ. ⲡⲁⲕ ⲉⲣⲟ[ⲩ], PMich 4237 d
sim put under cover, protection (?), BP 5183 ⲁⲩϣⲱⲥ
ⲟⲩⲱⲙ ϩⲛⲉⲡⲟⲅⲟⲓⲉ ... ⲧⲛⲟⲟⲩ ϩⲛⲣⲱⲙⲉ ⲛⲥⲉϯ ⲧⲉϥϩ.
ⲛⲥⲧⲛⲟⲟⲩ ⲡϣⲱⲥ ⲉⲧⲙⲙⲁⲩ [ⲕ]ⲁⲓ [ⲅⲁⲣ ⲟⲩ]ϩⲟⲩⲣⲓⲧⲛⲉ.

In place-name : ⲡⲣⲟ ϩⲃⲱ (l ϫⲉⲛⲡⲣⲟ qv), cf شبرا الخيمة
(BIF 1 176).

ϩⲃⲱ SF, **ϩⲃⲟⲩ** A　v ϩⲟϥ.

ϩⲃⲃⲉ, ϩⲉⲃ., ϩⲏⲩⲃⲉ, ϩⲏⲃ(ⲃ̅)ⲉ S, ϩⲓⲃⲉ S^f, ϩⲉⲃⲓ B,
ϩⲏⲃⲃⲓ F nn m, plough : Is 2 4 S(B ⲥⲏⲓⲡⲓ ⲛϩ.), Mic 4
3 B(S ⲥⲓⲛⲉ ⲛⲥⲕⲁⲓ, A ⲉⲙⲉ ⲛⲥ.), Lu 9 62 SB, BerlOr
1607 1 110 S Peter girt self & took ⲛϩ. ἄροτρον ; BMar
47 S ⲡⲱϩ ⲙⲡⲉⲧⲗⲟⲙ ⲛⲧⲥⲱϣⲉ ϩⲙⲡϩ., BMis 261 S
gave him ⲡϩⲛⲩⲃⲉ ⲉⲧⲣⲉϥⲥⲕⲁⲓ = Mor 30 35 S^f, ST
118 S ϩⲛⲃⲉ ⲛⲥⲕⲁⲓ, CO 138 S ⲧⲁⲕⲁⲗⲧⲉ (sic) ⲛⲟϩⲏⲃⲃⲉ,
ib 461 S ⲛϩ. ⲡⲧⲁⲛⲃⲁⲕⲟⲩ ⲉⲡⲓⲱϣ[ⲉ, BM 708 F among
iron utensils ⲙⲟⲩⲅⲗⲱⲗ ⲛϩ. (sic l p 165 a) ;　　yoke of
ploughing beasts B : Job 1 3 (S ⲥⲟⲉⲓϣ), Is 5 10 (SF
do) ζεῦγος ; K 108 ⲛϩ. فدّان ; Ryl 438 ⲉϥⲥϫⲁⲓ ⲛⲓⲃ
ⲛϩ. ⲛⲉϩⲉ (cf 3 Kg 19 19 ζ.), C 43 64 ϩⲁⲛϩ. ⲛⲉϩⲉ.

ϩⲃⲃⲉ vb & nn　v ϩⲓⲃⲉ.

ϩⲃⲃⲓⲏⲛ A　v ⲉⲃⲓⲏⲛ.

ϩⲃⲃⲥ　v ϩⲱⲃⲥ nn.

ϩⲱⲃⲕ S vb intr, prick, incite : ShA 2 130 beasts
ⲡⲥⲉϩ. ⲉⲣⲟⲟⲩ ⲛϭⲉⲛϫⲟⲟⲕⲉϥ that they should turn
(water-wheel) & water vineyards ;　ϩⲃⲟⲕ, -ϭ nn,
prick, stab : PeyGr 167 ϩⲱⲕⲉ ⲙⲙⲟϥ (sc martyr) ⲛⲥⲉϯ
ϩ. ⲛⲁϥ, BMar 36 ⲁϥⲧⲣⲉⲩϯ ϩⲃⲟϭ ⲛⲁϥ.　　V Rec 37
21 & cf ? ϩⲱⲕⲡ.

ϩⲃⲟⲓⲛⲉ S nn f, meaning unknown : PMéd 207
ⲟⲩϩ. to be pounded with ⲭⲏⲗⲗⲟⲥ (χυλός) of purslane, for anointing eyes.

ϩⲉⲃⲱⲱⲛ, ϩⲃⲱⲛ　v ϩⲛ season.

ϩⲃⲟⲩⲣ SF, **ϭⲃⲟⲩⲣ** A², **ϭⲃⲓⲣ** A nn f, left hand (B
always ϫⲁϭⲏ) : Ge 48 14, Pro 3 16 SA, Jon 4 11 SA,
Mt 6 3 (F = B) ἀριστερά ; PS 128 ⲛⲧⲟⲡⲟⲥ ⲛⲡⲁϩ. those
on left ;　m : Mani 1 A² ⲧⲟⲩⲛⲉⲙ, ⲡⲙⲁⲓⲧ ⲡⲧⲙⲏⲧⲉ,
ⲡϭ. (sc ⲙⲁⲓⲧ), BKU 1 26 (8116 b) F ⲛⲉϩ. (sc ⲥⲁⲧⲉⲣ) ;　　as adj : Jud 3 21 ϭⲓⲝ ⲛϩ. χεῖρ ἀρ. ; BMis 264
ⲟⲩⲣⲏⲧⲉ ⲛϩ. = Mor 30 39 S^f, BIF 13 111 ⲃⲁⲗ ⲉϩ. =
MG 25 301 B ;　　c ⲉ-, on left hand : Ge 13 9 (B ⲉⲝ.)
εἰς ἀρ., Pro 4 27 SA(B do) εἰς τὰ ἀρ., Is 30 21 SF (sic
l, B do) ἀρ. ; PS 30 ⲕⲛⲧⲉϩ., Br 117 ⲉⲡⲉⲙⲛⲧ ⲉϩ., ib 104
sim ⲉⲧⲉϩ. ;　　c ⲛⲥⲁ-, ⲥⲁ-, on, to left side : Ge 48 13
(B ⲥⲁϩ.) ἐξ ἀρ., Is 9 20 (B do) ἐκ τῶν ἀρ. ; Jos 13 3,
Zech 4 11 (A ϩⲓⲥⲁϭ., B do) ἐξ εὐωνύμων ; KroppH

45 ⲁϭⲉ ⲣⲁⲧϥ ⲥⲁϩ. ⲙⲙⲟⲓ, ManiH 38 *A²* goats ⲉⲧⲥⲁϭ.; ⲥ ϩⲓ- sim: Mt 20 21 (*B* ⲥⲁⲧⲉⲕⲝ.) ἐξ εὐ.; Ps 90 7 (*B* do) ἐκ τοῦ κλίτους.

ϩⲃⲟⲣⲃⲣ, ϩⲟⲣ. *S*, ϩⲗⲁⲣⲃⲉⲣ *S*ᶠ, ϩⲗⲁⲣⲃⲣⲉ *A*, ϩⲟⲣⲃⲉⲣ *B*, ϩⲉⲣⲃⲉⲣ-, ϩ. *S*, ⲃⲉⲣⲃⲉⲣ- *B*, ϩⲣⲃϩⲱⲣⲥ *SA²*, ⲟⲩⲅⲉⲣⲟⲩⲱⲣⲥ, ϩⲣⲟⲩⲱⲣⲥ *S*, ⲟⲩⲣⲟⲩⲱⲣⲥ *A²* (Ma), ϩⲉⲣⲃⲱⲣⲥ *B*, ⲃⲣϩⲟⲣⲧ†, ⲃⲣϩⲱⲣⲧ† &c (*v* below) *S*, ϩⲣⲃⲣⲁⲣⲧ†, ⲟⲩⲣⲟⲩⲁⲣⲧ† *A²* vb intr (rare), *be loosed, fall to pieces*: Va 63 87 *B* grass that withereth, flowers ⲉⲁϥⲃ. ⲛⲭⲱⲗⲉⲙ, ib 61 105 *B* ϥⲛⲁⲥⲓⲛⲓ ⲛⲧⲉϥⲃ. like flower; tr, *throw down, push*: Dan 9 18 *B* (*S* ⲛⲟⲩϫⲉ) ῥίπτειν, Sa 17 17 *S* ⲕⲁⲧⲁⲣⲣ.; C 86 281 *B* bade ϩⲉⲣϩⲉⲣ (*l* ϩⲟⲣ.) ⲛⲡⲉϥⲕⲁⲥ outside city = BSG 180 *S* do ἀκοντίζειν; Ge 35 16 *S* ϩⲟⲃ. ⲙⲓⲥⲉ (*B* ϣϣⲱⲧ ⲉⲙ.) δυστοκεῖν = P 44 104 الطو (*cf* ⲧⲱⲱⲃⲉ *brick s f*); Wess 18 25 *S* ⲁⲥϩⲟⲣ. ⲙⲓⲥⲉ (on Ge *lc*), CA 109 *S* ⲁⲥϩⲣⲃ. ⲙ[ⲓⲥⲉ (on 1 Kg 4 19), Mor 43 145 *S* ⲛⲉⲣⲉⲡⲁⲅⲙⲟⲥ (δήμιος) ϩⲃ. ⲙⲙⲟϥ on road to Golgotha, BAp 7 *S* angels ϩⲃ. (var MIF 9 44 ϩ.) ⲙⲙⲟϥ (*sc* Judas), BMis 285 *S* dragging & ⲉⲩϩⲱⲣⲃⲣ (*l* ϩϩⲟ.) ⲙⲙⲟⲟⲩ, TSBA 9 380 *B* ⲁϥϩ. ⲡⲧⲉϥⲙⲉⲗⲱⲧⲏ (on 4 Kg 2 8 ⲥⲁⲣϭϩ εἰλεῖν), C 43 91 *B* ϩⲉⲣⲃⲱⲣⲟⲩ (*sc* corpses) ⲛϩⲣⲉ for dogs (*cf* ⲥ ⲉⲃⲟⲗ), PStras 169 *S* mother to son ⲉⲣⲉⲡ︤ⲛ︦ⲁ︦ ⲛⲁⲃⲣⲃⲱⲣⲕ ⲧϥⲧⲓ ⲭⲁⲣⲓⲥ ⲛⲁⲕ & preserve thee (meaning ?).

Qual *SA²*: Lev 13 45 *S*† ⲃⲣϩⲱⲣ (cit ShA 2 116 ⲃⲣϩⲟⲣⲧ, *B* ⲫⲉⲣⲫⲱⲣ) παραλύεσθαι; ManiK 120 ⲛϭⲁⲙ...ⲉⲧⲟⲩ. ⲉⲧⲙⲏⲣ ϩⲛⲛⲕⲁϩ ⲉⲧⲙⲡⲓⲧⲛⲉ; as adj *S*: J 66 81 ⲙⲉⲣⲟⲥ ⲛⲕⲁϩ ⲃⲣϩⲱⲣ, Ryl 158 ⲥⲉⲧⲓⲁϩ ϩⲟⲩⲱⲣ (for ? ϩⲟⲩⲣⲟⲩⲱⲣ, *cf* ib ⲓⲁϩϭⲱⲙ & above p 89 *b* inf) J 1 50 ⲭⲱⲣⲏⲙⲁ...ⲡⲉⲓⲱ ϩⲉⲣⲃⲱⲣⲉⲧ...ϩⲛⲛϩⲓⲣ, *ib* 38 24 ⲛⲓ ⲉϥⲕⲏⲧ, ⲉⲓⲁϩⲟⲩ ⲃⲣϩⲱⲧ, *ib* 68 49 ⲓⲱϩⲉⲣⲃⲱⲧ ϩⲁⲙⲡ︦ⲧ︦ⲙⲉ ϩⲛⲧⲕⲟⲓⲉ, *ib* 7 21 ⲉⲓⲱϩⲃⲣⲣⲟⲧⲉ ϩⲛⲡⲁⲛⲅ, *ib* 69 33 ⲛⲓ...ⲉⲓⲱϩⲉⲣⲃⲱⲧⲉ, JSch 9 1 ⲡⲕⲁϩ ϩⲉⲣⲃⲟⲩⲧⲉ; so ?? *open, unoccupied*. But *cf* ByzZ 34 79 ⲛ ⲕⲁϩ ϩ. = ? γῆ ἐπηντλημένη (Schnebel *Landwirtsch* 1 27).

With following preposition. ⲥ ⲉ-: Ps 70 9 *B* (*S* ⲛ. ⲉⲃⲟⲗ ⲉ-), Mic 7 19 *B* (*S* ⲛ. ⲉϩⲣⲁⲓ ⲉ-, *A* ϯⲕⲉ ⲁϩ. ⲁ-) ἀπορρ. εἰς; Ps 135 15 *S* (ⲣⲱⲧ ⲉ-) ἐκτινάσσειν εἰς; Cl 14 2 *A* (var + ⲁϩⲣⲏⲓ) ἐξακοντίζειν εἰς; 1 Kg 17 49 *S* ϩⲟⲩⲉⲣⲟⲩⲱⲣϥ (sic *l*, var ϩⲣⲟⲩⲱⲣϥ ⲉⲃⲟⲗ ⲉ-) *B* Gk om; ShA 2 71 *S* ⲉⲧⲉϩ. ⲙⲙⲱⲧⲛ ⲉϩⲉⲡⲙ︦ⲧ︦ⲭⲁϫⲉ, Mor 18 33 *S* soldiers ϩ. ⲙⲙⲟϥ ⲉⲡⲥⲁ ⲛⲃⲟⲗ (var 19 42 ϩ. ⲛⲥⲱϥ) = Miss 4 126 *B* ϩⲉⲣⲃⲱⲣϥ ⲉⲃⲟⲗ = Gött ar 114 33 طر, ManiK 109 *A²* ϩⲃⲣϩⲱⲣⲟⲩ ⲁⲡⲥⲁ ⲛⲃⲁⲗ, FR 4 *S*ᶠ ϣⲁⲥϩⲃ. ⲙⲙⲟⲥ ⲉϩⲟⲩⲛ, ManiK 72 *A²* ⲧⲟⲩⲛⲟⲩ ⲉⲧⲁϥϩⲟⲩⲱⲣϥ ⲁⲡⲓⲧⲛⲉ, *ib* 28 ⲁϩⲟⲩϩⲣⲟⲩⲱⲣⲉϥ ⲁⲡⲧⲟⲩ ⲛⲧⲁⲙⲓⲟⲛ, DeV 2 42 *B* ⲁⲩϩⲉⲣⲃⲱⲣϥ ⲉⲡⲓⲡⲉⲗⲁⲅⲟⲥ (*cf* Jon 1 15 *S* ⲛ., *B* ϩⲓⲟⲩⲓ ἐκβάλλειν εἰς); ⲥ ⲉϫⲉⲛ- *B*: Nu 35 20 (*S* ⲛ. ⲉϫⲛ-), Jer 15 8 (*S* ⲛ. ⲉϩⲣⲁⲓ ⲉϫⲛ-), Lu 19 35 (*S* diff) ἐπιρρ. ἐπί; ⲥ ϩⲉⲛ- *B*, Is 14 19 (*S* ⲛ. ϩⲛ-) ῥ. ἐν, Jer 28 63 (*S* ⲛ. ⲉ-) ῥ. εἰς; Ez 34 21 *with* (*S* ϩⲱⲱⲣⲉ ⲉⲃ. ϩⲛ-) διωθεῖν ἐπί; ManiH 63 *A²*]ⲁⲓⲕⲁⲓⲟⲥ ϩⲃⲣⲃⲁⲣⲧ ϩⲛ[; ⲥ ϩⲁⲣⲉⲛ- *B*: Ge 21 15 (*S* ⲛ. ϩⲁ-) ῥ.

ὑποκάτω; ⲥ ϩⲓϩⲁⲣⲟⲩ *B*: Is 38 17 (*S* ⲕⲧⲟ ⲉⲡⲁϩⲟⲩ) ἀπορρ. ὀπίσω; ⲥ ϩⲓϫⲉⲛ- *B*: Ex 4 3 (*A* ⲧⲱⲕ ⲁϩⲣⲏ ⲁϫⲛ-), Dan 8 7 ῥ. ἐπί; MG 25 132 ϩⲉⲣⲃⲱⲣϥ (*sc* babe) ϩ. ⲡⲕⲁϩⲓ.

With following adverb. ⲥ ⲉⲃⲟⲗ *BS* (rare), *cast forth*: Is 34 3 (*S* ⲛ.†, *F* ⲛ.† ⲉⲃ.), Joel 1 7 (*A* ϯⲕⲉ ⲁⲃ.) ῥ., Ps 37 21 (*S* ⲛ. ⲉⲃ.), Jer 16 13 (var BM 1247 ϩⲓⲟⲩⲓ), *ib* 22 26 (*F* ViK 903 ⲥⲓϥ) ἀπορρ., Is 62 10 (*S* do) διαρρ., Pro 5 23 (*S* do, *A* do) ἐκρ.; Lam 2 7 ἀποτιν., Ex 14 27 ἐκτιν.; Job 16 12 (*S* om) παραδιδόναι; 1 Kg 25 29 *S* ⲛϥϭ(ⲣ)ⲟⲩⲱⲣϭ ⲉⲃ. σφενδονᾶν (*cf* above *ib* 17 49); Ac 27 18 (*S* ⲛ. ϩⲛⲁⲁⲩ ⲉⲃ.) ἐκβολὴν ποιεῖσθαι (*cf* Jon 1 5 *S* ⲛ., *B* ϩⲓⲟⲩⲓ); ShA 2 114 *S* ⲛϥϭⲃ. ⲙⲙⲟⲟⲩ (*sc* stones) ⲉⲃ. ϩⲛⲧⲉϥϭⲟⲙ, BM 217 22 *S* by day she wove, by night ⲉⲥϭⲃ. ⲉⲃ. (*cf* ⲃⲟⲗⲃⲗ ⲉⲃ. II), C 43 114 they cut belt ⲁⲩϩⲉⲣⲃⲱⲣⲥ ⲉⲃ., PO 11 330 snake clings to hand ⲁϥϩⲉⲣⲃⲱⲣⲥ ⲉⲃ., AM 43 ϩⲉⲣⲃⲱⲣϥ ⲉⲃ. ⲛϩⲣⲉ for birds, ShC 73 90 *S cf* ⲃⲟⲗⲃⲗ ⲉⲃ.; ⲉⲃ. ⲉ- *S*, *v* 1 Kg 17 above; ⲉⲃ. ⲛ- *S*: Mor 56 68 ⲁⲛⲉⲣϩⲟⲟⲥ ϩ. ⲉⲃ. ⲙⲙⲟϥ, opp ϭⲗⲟⲙⲗⲙ ⲉϩⲟⲩⲛ; ⲉⲃ. ϩⲁ- *B*: Job 30 22 (*S* ⲛ. ⲉⲃ. ⲛ-), Ps 50 13 (*S* do) ἀπορρ. ἀπό; DeV 2 34 ϩ. ⲉⲃ. ϩⲁⲣⲟⲛ ⲙⲡⲉⲣϣⲱⲡ, HL 113 ϩ. ⲙⲡⲓϩⲓⲛⲓⲙ ⲉⲃ. ϩⲁⲣⲟϥ (*cf* ib ⲥⲱⲣ ⲉⲃ.); ⲉⲃ. ϩⲛ- (once), ϩⲉⲛ-: Ex 32 19 (*S* ⲛ. ⲉⲃ. ϩⲛ-) ῥ. ἀπό, Jer 16 13 ἀπορρ. ἀπό, Lam 2 1 (*S* ViK 9685 do) καταρρ. ἐκ; MG 25 340 ⲁϥϩⲉⲣⲃⲱⲣϥ ⲉⲃ. ϩⲉⲛⲧⲉⲕⲕⲗⲏⲥⲓⲁ (ROC 17 367 ⲟⲃⲉⲝⲃ), C 86 304 ϩⲉⲣⲃⲱⲣⲧ ⲉⲃ. ϩⲉⲛⲧⲫⲉ = BSG 197 *S* ϩⲃ.; ⲥ ⲉⲡⲉⲥⲏⲧ: Dan 8 12 *B* ῥ. χαμαί; BSG *lc S* ϩⲃ. ⲉ. ⲉⲡⲡⲟⲩ; ⲥ ⲉⲡϣⲱⲓ *B*: Ex 9 8 πάσσειν εἰς; MG 25 143 nurse & babe ⲛⲧⲉⲥϩⲉⲣⲃⲱⲣϥ ⲉ. ⲉⲝⲉⲡⲧⲉⲥⲙⲉⲥⲧⲉⲛϩⲏⲧ; ⲥ ⲉϩⲟⲩⲛ *B*: Mt 27 5 (*S* ⲛ. ⲉϩ. ⲉ-) ῥ. εἰς; ⲥ ⲉϩⲣⲏⲓ *B*: Jer 33 23 (*S* ⲛ. ⲉϩ. ⲉ-) ῥ. εἰς; Ap 18 21 (*S* do) βάλλειν εἰς; Va 57 207 καταποντίζειν; ⲥ ⲉϩⲣⲁⲓ, -ⲛⲓ, *upon, into*: Job 27 22 *B* ⲉⲡⲓⲣ. ἐπί, Sa 10 19 *S* ϩⲃ. ⲉ. ⲉ- but ἀναβράσσειν ἐκ; ShA 1 150 *S* ⲃⲣϩⲱⲣⲃ ⲉ. ⲉⲩⲧⲟϭ ⲛϭⲓⲉⲓⲧ; ⲣⲉϥϩⲃ. ⲉⲣ.: P 130 97 *S* ⲣⲉϥϩⲃⲣϩⲉⲣ ⲣⲱⲙⲉ ⲉ. ⲉⲡⲡⲟⲛⲏⲣⲟⲛ.

—— nn m *B*, *expulsion*: K 98 ⲡⲓϩ. طرح.

As place-name (?): ⲡⲧⲓⲙⲉ ϩⲟⲩⲱⲣ (Ryl 211, *cf* above qual Ryl 158).

Cf ⲃⲟⲗⲃⲗ, ϥⲟⲣⲡⲉⲣ.

ϩⲃⲣⲏϭⲉ *A*   *v* ⲉϩⲣⲏϭⲉ.

ϩⲁⲃⲥ *A²F* nn   *v* ϩⲱⲃⲥ.

ϩⲁ(ⲉ)ⲓⲃⲉⲥ, ϩⲟⲓⲃⲉⲥ (rare) *S*, ϩⲁⲓⲃⲉ *S*ᵃ (? *v* ϩⲓⲃⲉ *s f*), ϩⲁ(ⲉ)ⲓⲃⲉ *A*, ϩⲁⲓⲃ(ⲉ)ⲥ *A²*, ϧⲏⲓⲃⲓ, ϧⲏⲃⲓ (rare) *B*, ϩⲏⲃⲉⲥ, ϩⲏ(ⲓ)ⲃⲓ, ϩⲓϩⲃⲓ *F* nn f, *shade, shadow*: Job 3 5 *SB*, Eccl 7 1 *S* ϩⲟⲓ. *F* ϩⲏⲃⲓ, He 10 1 *SBF* σκιά, Ja 1 17 *SAB* ἀποσκίασμα; Job 37 8 *S* (*B* = Gk), Ps 16 8 *SBF* ϧⲏⲓⲃⲓ, Hos 14 8 *SAB* σκέπη; Nu 24 5 *B* (*S* = Gk) σκηνή; PS 151 *S* ϩⲁⲃ. ⲙⲡⲉⲕⲛⲁ (OdSolom 25 8] ⲙⲉⲥⲁⲗ), Miss 4 202 *B* ⲧϧⲏⲃⲓ of death, Mus 34 188 *B* do, *ib* 191 ϧⲏⲓ., ManiK 108 *A²* clear away ⲧϥ. ⲧⲏⲣⲥ

ⲛⲧⲉⲕⲟ, Mani 1 *A²* ⲑ. ⲙⲡⲕⲱⲙⲁⲣⲓⲟⲛ, BM 1121 *S* let your pity reach him ⲛϥϭⲱ ϩⲁⲧⲉⲧⲓϩ., BM 625 *F* ⲛⲁⲓⲁϯ … ⲉ(ⲓ)ϣⲁⲁ[ⲡ] ϩⲁⲧⲉϭⲣⲏⲃⲱⲥ, DeV 1 96 *B* dwelt under ✝ⲥ. ⲛⲛⲉϥϣⲗⲏⲗ, PLiverpool Mus *F* ϣⲁⲅⲟⲩⲱⲧⲉⲃ ⲉⲃⲁⲗ ϩⲁⲡⲉϥ (*l* ⲡⲉⲩ)ⲃⲓⲟⲥ ⲛⲧⲡⲏⲛ (*l* ⲛⲧϭⲏ) ⲡⲟⲩϫⲓⲏ., Mor 31 230 *S* empty bed ⲉⲣⲉⲑ. ⲛⲧⲉϥⲥⲁⲣⳅ ⲙⲛⲧⲉϥⲃⲱⲧⲉ ⲛϩⲏⲧϥ *impress.*

ⲁⲧϩ. *S, shadowless:* BG 116 ⲟⲩⲟⲓⲛ ⲛⲁ.

ⲣ ϩ., ⲉⲣ ⲑ. *SABF, make shade, overshadow:* Pro 18 11 *SA* ἐπισκιάζειν, Jer 11 16 *B*(*S* ShA 1 291 ⲟ ⲛϩ.) εὔσκιος, *ib* 2 20† *B* ⲕⲁⲧⲁⲥⲕ.; Deu 12 2† *S*(*B* ⲗⲁϩⲁⲗ) δασύς; Ez 27 6† *SB* ἀλσώδης; Job 15 32 *S*(*B* diff) πυκάζειν; Wess 15 9 *S* tree ⲉϥⲟ ⲛϩ. = Miss 4 117 *B*;   ⲥ ⲉ-: Ps 26 5 *S*(*B* = Gk ⲥ ⲉϫⲉⲛ-), Is 51 16 *S*(*B* = Gk acc) σκεπάζ. acc; Lu 9 34 *S*(*B* ex.) ἐπισκι. acc, *ib* 1 35 *SB* ἐπ. dat, Cant 1 16 *F* ϩⲛⲏⲓ (*S* ⲟ ⲛϩ. ⲉⲃⲟⲗ ⲉϫⲛ-) σύσκιος; Ap 7 15 *S*(*B* ex.) σκηνοῦν; BMis 108 *S* ox & ass ϩ. ⲉⲣⲟϥ, C 86 304 *B* ⲥⲉⲉⲣ. ⲉⲣⲟⲓ;   ⲥ ⲉϫⲛ-: Is 4 5 *B*(*S* om ⲉ.) σκιάζειν acc, Ex 37 9 *B* ⲥⲕ. ἐπί, Mt 17 5 *B*(*S* ⲉϩⲣⲁⲓ ⲉϫⲛ-) ἐπισκι. acc, Ps 139 8 *B*(*S* ⲉ-) ἐπισκ. ἐπί, He 9 5 *BF*(*S* ⲉ-) κατασκ. acc, Job 15 29 *S*(*B* as Gk) σκιὰν βάλλειν ἐπί, Jon 4 6 *SA*(*B* ϣⲱⲡⲓ ⲉⲅⲑ.) σκ. εἶναι ὑπεράνω; Zeph 2 3 *B*(*SA* diff) σκεπάζεσθαι; ⲉⲃⲟⲗ ⲉϫⲛ-: Deu 33 12 *S*(*B* ex. only) σκι. ἐπί; ⲉϩⲣⲁⲓ ⲉϫⲛ-: Mt 17 5 *S*(*B* ex. only) ἐπισκι. acc;   ⲥ ⲛ- dat: 1 Chr 28 18 *B* σκι. ἐπί, Si 6 30 *S* ⲉⲓⲥ σκέπην εἶναι dat;   ⲥ ϩⲓϫⲛ-: Nu 9 18 *S*(*B* ex.) σκι. ἐπί.

ϫⲓϩ., ϭⲓ ⲑ. *SAB, be shaded, take shelter:* MIE 2 345 *B* ⲉⲅϩⲉⲗⲥⲓ ⲉⲅϭ. (PO 22 300 om);   ⲥ ϩⲁ-, ⲑⲁ-: Jon 4 5 *SA*(*B* no vb) ἐν σκιᾷ; Ps 60 5 *SB* σκεπάζεσθαι; BMis 42 *S* they are pride of realm ⲉⲓϫ. ϩⲁⲣⲟⲟⲩ, DeV 1 28 *B* Salome's curls ⲉⲧⲉⲡⲥⲁⲧⲁⲛⲁⲥ ϭ. ϭⲁⲧⲉϥⲛⲟϫⲓ, C 89 *B* ϭ. ϭⲁⲧⲥⲕⲉⲡⲏ of her teaching;   ⲥ ϩⲛ-: Job 40 17 *S*(*B* ⲉⲣ ⲑ. ⲉϫⲛ-) σκιάζεσθαι ἐν; ⲙⲁ ⲛϫ. *S*: ShC 42 220 flocks in ⲡⲉϫⲙ. (var ⲙⲁ ⲛϩ.), P 131⁵ 101 sim beneath tree.

ⲣⲉϥⲥⲉϩ ϩ. *S*: Sa 15 4 σκιαγράφος.

As name (?): Θαῖβις (Preisigke).

ϩⲃⲥ nn   *v* ϩⲱⲃⲥ.

ϩⲏⲃⲥ *SA²F*, ϩ(ⲉ)ⲃⲥ *S*, ϩⲛⲃⲥ *A*, ϭⲏⲃⲥ *B*, ϩⲏⲃⲉⲥ *F* nn m, *lamp:* Lev 24 2 *SB*, Ps 17 28 *SB*, Pro 29 36 *S* (var ϩⲃⲥ) *A*, EpJer 18 *BF*, Zeph 1 12 *AB*, Jo 5 35 *SA²B, Klio* 13 29 *S* ϩⲏⲃⲉⲥ λύχνος; P 44 60 *S* ⲛϩ. ج‍ م‍; with λυχνία: Nu 4 9 *SB*, Zech 4 2 *SAB*, Mt 5 15 *SB* λ., ShIF 178 *S* ⲛϩ. ⲉⲧⲭⲉⲣⲟ ϩⲛⲧⲗⲩⲭⲛⲓⲁ, ShA 2 45 *S* sim ⲉⲅⲕⲏ ϩⲓⲭⲛⲡⲗⲩⲭⲛⲓⲁ; PS 151 *S* ϩⲉⲡ-ϩ. on my right (OdSolom 25 7 ل‍ ‍ ‍), ShP 130⁵ 83 *S* ϩⲉⲡⲗⲁⲙⲡⲁⲥ ⲙⲡⲣⲉⲛϩ., ManiH 60 *A²* ϩ. ⲉⲧⲧⲣⲟⲅⲁⲓⲛⲉ, BMis 168 *S* night-watchman ⲁϥϭⲉⲣⲉ ⲡϩⲃⲥ, MG 25 422 *S* ϩ. ⲉϥⲙⲟⲩϩ = DeV 2 149 *B* ⲫⲁⲡⲟⲥ, Mor 25 40 *S* mice upset ϩ. ⲛⲥⲉⲟⲩⲟϭⲛϥ (so of clay, *cf* ⲥⲟⲗ),

C 43 85 *B* προσφορά, ⲑ., ⲥⲑⲟⲓⲛⲟⲩϥⲓ offered by sick, J 99 17 *S* δημόσιον to pay for προσφ. ⲙⲛⲏϩ. of sanctuary (*cf ib* 92 14 sim ⲗⲏⲭⲛⲓⲕⲱⲛ), ST 354 *S* ϩ. ⲛⲃⲁⲣⲱⲧ, Ryl 242 *S* ⲡⲣⲟⲙⲓⲧ, TurM 18 *S* (collated) ϣⲟⲙⲧ ⲛⲕⲉⲣⲟⲡ (*v* Ep 545 n) ⲡⲟⲩⲁ ⲡⲟⲩⲁ ⲛϥϩⲉⲃⲥ ϩⲓⲛⲓⲱϣ (*l* ϩⲓⲛⲓⲱϣ) ⲡⲛⲁⲕⲟⲧ (?) ⲛⲏⲧⲟⲩ ϥϭⲟⲧⲣ ⲛⲥⲛⲁⲩ ⲛϩ., BP 8095 *F* ⲁⲗⲙⲁⲛⲁⲣⲓ (النار) & ϩ. in list of εἴδη.

ϩⲏⲃⲥ *covering*   *v* ϩⲱⲃⲥ nn.

ϩⲱⲃⲥ *SAA²BF*, -ⲡⲥ *B*, -ϥⲉⲥ *F*, ϩ(ⲉ)ⲃⲥ- *SBF*, ϩⲟⲃⲥ⸗ *SB*, ϩⲟⲡⲥ⸗ *B*, ϩⲁⲃⲥ⸗ *AF*, ϩⲃⲥ⸗ *A²* (Ma), ϩⲟⲃⲥ† *SBF*, ϩⲁ.† *SᶠAF*, ϩⲟⲡⲥ† *B* vb **I** intr, *cover, be covered:* Ge 8 2 *B*(*S* ϣⲧⲁⲙ) ἐπικαλύπτειν; Jer 29 2 *B*(*S* om) κατακλύζειν; Va 58 171 *B* ⲡⲓⲉⲣϭⲟⲧ ⲛⲁϩ. συσκιάζειν; BMis 93 *S* at death ϣⲁⲣⲉⲡⲉⲡⲧⲁⲓⲟ ⲙⲛⲡⲉⲛⲣⲁⲛ ϩ., ViK 9800 118 *S* if they repent ϣⲁⲣⲉⲡⲣⲁⲛ ⲉⲑⲟⲟⲩ ϩ., *ib* 9629 177 & 178 *S* ⲁⲡⲉϥϭⲏⲧ ϩ. ϩⲱⲥ ⲣⲱⲙⲉ ⲁϥⲛⲉϫ ⲫⲗⲉⲅⲙⲁ ⲉⲃⲟⲗ = MIE 2 370 *B* ⲫⲱⲛϩ = PO 22 412 على قلب سو‍, AZ 23 109 *S* pour water upon it ϣⲁⲧϥϩ.

II tr: Ex 16 13 *SB*, Job 21 26 *SB* ϩⲟⲡⲥ⸗, Ps 54 5 *SBF* ϩⲁⲃⲉⲥ⸗, Pro 10 12 *SAB*, Hos 10 8 *SA*(*B* ϩ. ⲉⲃⲟⲗ ⲉϫⲉⲛ-) ⲕⲁⲗ., Ge 7 19 *SB*, Jer 14 4 *SB* ἐπικ., Lev 3 3 *SB*, Jer 26 8 *SBF* (ViK 3271) ⲕⲁⲧⲁⲕ., Mk 14 65 *SB* περικ., Ez 12 6 *SB* συγκ.; Ex 40 3 *B* σκεπάζειν, Lam 3 44 *B*(*F* ϩⲱⲡ) ἐπισ.; Ps 9 16 *B*(*S* ϩⲱⲡ) κρύπτειν; Lev 13 45 *SB*, Mt 25 36 *B*(*S* ϯ ϩⲓ-) περιβάλλειν; Jon 2 6 *B*(*SA* ⲕⲱⲧⲉ) κυκλοῦν; 1 Cor 7 18 *S*(*BF* Mor 38 104 ⲥⲱⲕ dat) ἐπισπᾶσθαι; Ps 104 28 *S*(*B* diff) σκοτάζειν; R 2 2 21 *S* hair & beard ϩ. ⲛⲧⲉϥⲙⲟⲣⲫⲏ πυκάζειν; MG 25 208 *B* bring wood & ϩⲟⲡⲥϥ (*sc* cell) στεγάζειν; Va 66 299 *B* ϩ. ⲙⲡϣⲓⲡⲓ ⲛⲧⲉⲛⲥⲁⲣⳅ περιστέλλειν; PS 332 *S* ⲡⲟⲩⲟⲉⲓⲛ…ϩ. ⲙⲡⲕⲁⲕⲉ, ShC 73 162 *S* ⲡⲉⲩⲧⲟⲛ…ϩ. ⲡⲡⲉⲩϫⲡⲁϩ, Aeg 253 *S* ⲙⲁⲣⲟⲩϩⲉⲃⲥ ϫⲱⲟⲩ, ManiH 1 *A²* ⲁϥϩⲱⲃⲥ ⲡⲉⲧ[, MG 25 190 *B* his fame ϩ. ⲛⲧⲣⲱⲙⲁⲓⲁ ⲧⲏⲣⲥ, Va 58 134 *B* ⲁⲕϭⲟⲡⲥⲧⲉⲛ when naked, BMis 405 *S* ϩⲃⲥ ⲟⲩⲁ ⲉϥⲕⲏⲕ ⲁϩⲏⲩ = BSM 52 *B* ϩ. ⲛⲟⲩⲁⲓ, Mor 24 21 *F* ⲧϭⲏⲡⲓ ϩⲱϩⲉⲥ ⲙⲙⲁⲡ; Ex 29 5 *S* ⲛϩⲃⲥ ⲛⲁϩⲃ (*B*=Gk) ἐπωμίς (*v* LMis 193);   qual: Mt 10 26 *SB* ⲕⲁⲗ., Su 32 *S* (ViK 2604) *B* ⲕⲁⲧⲁⲕ., He 9 4 *B*(*SF* ϭⲟⲟⲗⲉ) περικ., Lu 12 2 *SB* συγκ.; Mk 4 22 *F*(ViK 3272, *SB* ϩⲏⲡ) ἀπόκρυφος; Pro 29 39 *SA* ἐνδύεσθαι; Mor 18 116 *S* ⲙⲛ ⲗⲁⲁⲩ ⲙⲙⲉⲗⲟⲥ ϩ. σκιάζ.; 1 Cor 11 4 *SB* ἔχειν κατά; 2 Kg 7 6 *S* ⲙⲁ ⲉⲧϩ. κατάλυμα; Mor 56 8 *S* ⲙⲁ ⲉⲧϩ. ⲛⲧⲁⲅⲟⲣⲁ στέγη (*AnalBoll* 41 376); ViK 9752 150 *S* ⲡϣⲁϫⲉ ⲉⲧϩ. ϩⲛⲧⲉⲅⲣⲁⲫⲏ, Bodl(P)a 1 *a* ⲕⲁⲁⲥ (*sc* mixture)…ϩⲛⲟⲩⲕⲁⲣⲁⲉⲓⲉ (قراءة) ⲉϥϩ., BKU 1 21 *ro* *F* ⲧⲁⲗⲁⲥ (*l*? -ⲁϥ) ⲉⲡⲕⲱϩⲧ…ⲉϥϩ.

With following preposition.   ⲥ ⲉ-: Lu 24 32 *S*(*B* diff) καλύπτεσθαι ἐν, *ib* 9 45 *S*(*B* ϩⲱⲡ) παρακ. ἀπό; ShWess 9 112 *S* ⲉⲣⲉϥ† ⲉⲡⲟⲅⲟⲉⲓⲛ, ShIF 123 *S* ⲡⲉⲧⲛϩⲏⲧ ϩ. ⲉⲣⲱⲧⲛ, Mor 17 38 *S* sim ϩ.†, C 43 50 *B*

ϩ. ⲉⲡⲉϥϩⲟ in shame;   c ⲉⲣⲛ-: Ps 68 7 *S* (var ⲉⲝⲛ-, *B* tr), Pro 10 11 *SA*(*B* tr) ⲕⲁⲗ. acc :   c ⲉⲝⲛ-: Ps 105 11 *S*(*B* + ⲉϩⲣⲏⲓ) ⲕⲁⲗ., Nu 4 11 *S*(*B* diff) ἐπικ., Lev 3 9 *B*(*S* diff) ⲕⲁⲧⲁⲕ.; Job 36 28 *S*(*B* ⲉⲃⲟⲗ ⲉⲝ.) σκιαζ. ἐπί, Mk 9 7 *S*(*BF* ⲉⲣ ϭⲏⲓⲃⲓ ⲉ-) ἐπισ. dat, Mor 17 118 *S* ⲡⲉⲧϩ.† ⲉⲭⲡⲉⲥⲁⲡⲉ σκέπασμα; C 99 142 *S* ⲟⲩⲡⲣⲏϣ ⲁϥϩⲟⲃⲥϥ ⲉϫⲱϥ = C 89 49 *S* ϩⲟⲡⲥϥ ⲉⲝ. ἐπιβάλλειν dat; Br 255 *S* mystery ⲉⲧϩ. ⲉϫⲛⲛⲁⲓⲱⲛ, C 41 46 *B* ⲉⲣⲉⲡⲉⲩϩⲃⲟⲥ ϩ.† ⲉϫⲱϥ, Rec 6 174 *B* leaves ϩ.† ⲉ. ⲡⲉϥⲙⲁ ⲛⲣⲱⲟⲩⲧ = BMar 210 *S* tr, AZ 23 113 *S* ⲧⲁⲁⲩ ⲉⲅⲁⲗⲕⲁ[ⲧⲁ]ϩ (ـۘل) ϩⲟⲃⲥ ⲛⲉⲟⲩⲁ ⲉϫⲟϥ; ⲉϩⲣⲏⲓ ⲉⲝ.: Ps 105 11 *B*(*S* om ⲉϩ.), Eccl 6 4 *F* ⲓϣⲱⲃⲥ (*S* ϩ. intr) ⲕⲁⲗ.;   c ⲛ- instr : 1 Kg 19 13 *S*, Mal 2 13 *S*(*B* Hom 61) *AB* ⲕⲁⲗ. dat, Jud 4 18 *S* (var ϩⲛ-) ⲥⲩⲅⲕ. ἐν; Is 28 15 *S*(*B* diff) σκεπ. dat; ib 49 2 *S*(*B* diff) ⲕⲣ. ἐν; ShC 73 82 *S* ⲡⲡⲉⲓⲣⲟⲃⲧ ⲛⲟⲩ ?, R 1 3 32 *S* ⲟⲩϩⲟⲉⲓⲧⲉ ... ⲉⲧⲣⲉⲥϩⲟⲃⲥ ⲙⲙⲟϥ, ViK 9805 *S.f* ⲉⲧϩ.† ⲛⲟⲩⲕⲁⲗⲩⲙⲁ = Va 63 92 *B* ϭⲉⲡ-, BMis 361 *S* ⲡⲉⲩⲥⲱⲙⲁ ϩ.† ⲛⲟⲩϩⲃⲥⲱ = Mor 27 22 *F* ϩ.†, C 86 215 *B* sky ϩ. ⲛⲥⲏⲡⲓ = ib 281 ϭⲗⲱⲕ (*l* ϭⲱⲗⲕ);   c ϩⲛ-, ϭⲉⲛ- sim : Ps 146 8 *B*(*S* ϭⲟⲟⲗⲉ) περιβάλ. ἐν; BMar 208 *S* ⲁⲓϩ. ⲙⲙⲁ ... ϩⲛⲡⲁϣⲱ = Rec 6 172 *B*, C 86 255 *B* †ⲛⲁϩⲟⲃⲥϥ ϭⲉⲛⲛⲉⲛⲧⲏⲗⲁ (ἔνδυ.), Mor 27 28 *F* thy garment ⲛⲧⲁⲣⲉⲣϩⲟⲃⲥ ϫⲱ ⲛϩⲏⲧϥ = BSM 33 *B* ⲉⲛϫⲓⲛϩⲱⲃⲥ† ⲛⲧⲉⲕⲉⲁϩⲉ ⲛϩⲏⲧϥ = Va 63 8 *B* ⲉⲣ ⲥⲕⲉⲡⲁⲍⲓⲛ ⲛϩ̄., Mani 1 *A²* ⲡⲟⲓⲥⲉ ⲉⲧⲁⲛⲓⲧ ⲉⲧⲁⲓϩⲃⲥⲧ ⲛϩⲏⲧϥ;   c ϩⲓϫⲛ- *S*: BIF 14 125 ⲉⲣⲉⲟⲩⲡⲣⲏϣ ϩ. ϩⲓϫⲱϥ; ϩⲣⲁⲓ ϩ.: Nu 9 20 (*B* tr) ⲥⲕⲉⲡ. ἐπί.

With following adverb.   c ⲉⲃⲟⲗ: ⲉⲃ. ⲉϫⲛ- intr Lev 13 13 *S*(var ⲛⲱⲣϣ ⲉⲃ., *B* om ⲉⲃ.), Ps 43 15 *S*(*B* ⲉⲃ. ⲉϩⲣⲏⲓ ⲉⲝ.), Hos 10 8 *B*(*SA* tr), Ja 5 20 *SB* ⲕⲁⲗ. acc, Ps 105 17 *B*(*S* tr) ⲕ. ἐπί, Job 16 18 *SB* ἐπικ. ἐπί, Lev 9 19 *SB*(var tr) ⲕⲁⲧⲁⲕ. ἐπί; Ex 12 13 *B*(*S* = Gk), MG 25 220 *B* ⲫ† ϩ. ⲉⲃ. ⲉ. ⲡⲓⲕⲟⲥⲙⲟⲥ σκεπ.; Job 36 28 *B* ϩⲱⲡⲉ (*S* tr ⲉϫⲛ-) ⲥⲕⲓ. ἐπί; Deu 11 4 *S*(*B* ⲉϩⲣ. ⲉⲝ.) ἐπικλύζειν ἐπί, Sa 10 19 *S* ⲕⲁⲧⲁⲕⲗ. acc; 2 Kg 1 9 *S*(var ϩⲓϫⲛ-) κατέχειν; PS 150 *S* ⲁⲕϩ. ⲉⲃ. ⲉϫⲱⲓ, ShC 42 155 *S* ⲉⲧϩ. ⲉⲃ. ⲉ. ⲙⲙⲛⲧϣⲁϥⲧⲉ, AM 300 *B* darkness ϩ. ⲉⲃ. ⲉ. ⲡⲓⲙⲁⲧⲟⲓ, ST 287 *Sᵃ* ⲡⲓⲗⲁⲉⲓⲛ ... ⲉⲧϩ.† ⲉⲃ. ⲉϫⲱⲓ, ib 233 *S* letter ⲁⲡⲁⲅⲗⲟⲥ ⲙⲟⲩ ⲉⲕⲣⲟⲃⲥ ⲉⲃ. ⲉϫⲱϥ ... ⲁϥⲙⲟⲩ ⲁⲛ *hadst thou protected him, he had not died*;   tr : ShA 2 111 *S* ϩ. ⲡⲟⲩⲕⲁϩ ⲉⲃ. ⲉϫⲱⲟⲩ, Miss 4 643 *S* ⲁϥϩ. ⲉⲃ. ⲉϫⲱⲓ ⲛⲧⲉϥⲥⲧⲟⲗⲏ, RO 11 323 *B* ⲉϥϩ. ⲛⲡⲉϥⲧⲉⲛϩ ⲉⲃ. ⲉϫⲱϥ;   ⲉⲃ. ⲥⲁⲡϣⲱⲓ ⲛ-: Ez 1 11 *B*(H Const 280, var ϩ. only) ἐπικαλ. ἐπάνω;   ⲉⲃ. ϩⲓϫⲛ-: Ez 24 7 *SB* ⲕⲁⲗ. ἐπί; PO 2 180 *S* ⲉⲣⲉⲛⲙⲁ ⲡⲁⲣ. ⲉⲃ. ϩⲓϫⲱⲛ *overwhelm*, C 41 42 *B* water ϩ. ⲉⲃ. ϩⲓϫⲱⲟⲩ, Mor 24 23 *F* cloud ϩ. ⲉⲃ. ϩⲓϫⲱⲟⲩ.

——¹ nn m *S* (rare) *BF*, ϩⲟⲃⲥ², ϩⲃⲥ³, ϩⲏⲃⲥ⁴, ϩⲏⲃⲥ⁵, ϩⲁⲡⲥ⁶ (once each) *S*, ϩⲁⲃⲥ *A²F*, *covering, lid*: Nu 4 25 *S²*(var³)*B*, Aeg 269 *S* ⲛϩ. ⲛⲡⲓⲟⲩϩⲁⲓ κάλυμμα, Ex 26 14 *B* ἐπικ., Nu 4 6 *B*(*S* ϩⲃⲥⲱ) ⲕⲁⲧⲁⲕ., Sa 17 3 *S³* ⲡⲁⲣⲁⲕ., Deu 22 30 *S* (ⲛⲣⲏϣ) ⲥⲩⲅⲕ.; 1 Kg 24 5 *B*(*S* =

Gk) διπλοῖς; Ac 9 18 *S³* (varr⁴ ⁵, *B* ⲕⲏⲕⲥ) λεπίς; ib 13 11 *S³* (var⁴, *B* ϩⲗⲟⲗ) ἀχλύς; ShA 1 110 *S* ⲟⲩϩ.³ ⲛⲕⲁⲕⲉ on their eyes, Gu 59 *S* ϭⲱⲗⲛ ⲉⲃⲟⲗ ⲙⲡϩ.² ⲛⲧⲉⲧⲣⲓⲣ, ManiK 105 *A²* ϩ. ⲁϥⲧⲉⲓⲃⲉ, Mor 48 81 *S* martyr scraped until ⲛϩ.⁵ ⲛⲣⲏⲧϥ ϭⲱⲗⲛ ⲉⲃⲟⲗ (*sc* ribs?) = C 43 140 *B* ⲡⲉϥⲕⲁⲥ, ib 19 78 *S* leper healed ⲁⲡⲥⲱⲃϩ ... ϭⲱⲗ ⲛⲑⲉ ⲛⲟⲩϩ.⁵ (var 18 70 ⲕⲱⲕ ⲛⲑⲉ ⲛⲟⲩϣⲉⲗⲃⲉ, Miss 4 143 *B* = Gött ar 114 61 diff), J 68 65 *S* provide ⲛϩ.¹ ⲙⲡⲁⲥⲱⲙⲁ for burial, C 43 68 *B* ⲛⲓϩ. ⲛⲁⲉⲣ ϩⲟⲗⲓ, Ryl 243 *S* list of clothes ⲫⲁϭⲁⲣⲉ (φακιάλιον) ⲛϩ.¹, CMSS 70 *S* sim ⲟⲩϩ.¹ ⲉϥϩⲓ ⲥⲧⲁⲩⲣⲟⲥ, Ryl 238 *S* ⲥⲕⲁⲫⲓⲛ ⲙⲡⲛⲉⲥϩ.², AZ 23 115 *S* ⲥⲁⲧⲟⲩ ⲉⲡϩ.⁶ ⲉⲩⲕⲏⲃ, BKU 1 26 (8116 a) *F* ⲟⲩϩ. ⲛⲁⲃⲓϭⲉⲛⲓ, BP 9446 *S³* as part of door *v* ⲣⲁⲙⲟⲛⲉ.

ⲣⲉϥϩ., *coverer, protector* c ⲉⲃⲟⲗ: Ex 15 2 *B*(*F* BM 493 = Gk), P 44 49 *S* σκεπαστής.

ϫⲓⲛϩ. *B*, *act of covering*: MIE 2 418 ⲡϫⲓⲛϩⲟⲡⲥ ⲡⲁⲥⲱⲙⲁ for burial = BAp 125 *S* vb tr, Va 57 87 ϩⲁⲛⲥⲕⲉⲡⲁⲥⲙⲁ ⲉⲡϫⲓⲛϩⲟⲡⲥϥ, BSM 33 ⲡϫⲓⲛϩⲱⲃⲥ† f.

ϩⲃⲟⲟⲥ¹ *SAA²*, ϩⲃⲟⲥ², ϩⲃⲱⲥ³ *SB*, -ⲁⲥ *SᵃA²F*, pl ϩⲃⲱⲱⲥ⁴ *SAF*, ϩⲃⲱⲥ *BF*, ⲉϩⲃ. *B* & sg as pl &, as *linen*, pl form ? as sg, nn m f *A* *covering, garment* (not *S* bibl): Ge 9 23 (*S* ϣⲧⲏⲛ), Nu 4 6 (*S* ϩⲟⲉⲓⲧⲉ), Ps 101 27 (*S* ⲣⲏϣⲡ), Is 33 1 (*SF* ϣ.), Ac 12 8 (*S* do) ἱμάτιον, Ep Jer 11 (*F* ⲓⲉⲡⲛⲟⲩϩ) ἱματισμός; Nu 31 20 (*S* ϩ.) περίβλημα; 1 Kg 24 12 (*S* ϫⲗⲁⲙⲥ) διπλοῖς; C 89 49 = C 99 142 *S* ⲛⲣⲏϣ στρῶμα, Va 58 169 στρωμνή; Lev 6 3 (var ϩⲃⲥⲱ, *S* ϣ.) χιτών; Ex 26 36 (*S* ϩⲟⲃⲥ) ἐπίσπαστρον; Is 59 17 ϩ. ⲡⲭⲱⲗϩ (*S* ⲣ.), Ex 22 27 ⲡⲭⲟⲗϩ (*S* ϩⲃⲥⲱ) περιβόλαιον; Lev 8 7 ⲛⲧⲉ ⲥⲁϩⲟⲩⲛ (*S* = Gk) ὑποδύτης; C 86 64 ⲉⲧϩⲓϫⲱϥ (*l* ϩ? ϩⲁⲝ.) προσκεφάλαιον; Dan 5 29 ⲡϭⲏϫⲓ πορφύρα; C 99 152 *S* ⲟⲩⲛⲟϭ ⲛϩ.² (var ib 244¹) to receive departing soul = C 89 88 *B* = Va ar 172 52 منديل, MG 17 462 ثوب شبه; ShC 42 71 *S* ϩ.² ⲛⲕⲱⲱⲥ, Sh(Besa)Z 506 *S* ⲥⲁϩⲧϩ.², ShC 73 61 *S* ⲥⲟⲉⲓϣ ⲛϩ.¹, CO 403 *S* sim, El 122 *S* woman's ϩ.² ⲛϣⲛⲥ = ib 92 *A*, BSM 33 *B* ϩ. ⲉⲑⲃⲉⲡⲓⲥⲙⲟⲩ = BMis 375 *S* ϣ. ⲛⲥⲩⲛⲁⲧⲉ, BM 480 *Sᵃ* ϩ. ⲛⲥ(ϩ)ⲓⲙⲉ, ST 118 *S* ⲕⲟⲩⲓ ⲛϩ.² ⲛⲥϩ., Ryl 243 *S* ϩ.², ⲡⲁⲧ†ⲛⲁϭ (الديباج), Va 61 91 *B* ⲡⲉϥⲫⲉⲗϫⲓ ⲛϩ. = P 131³ 82 *S* ⲡⲗϭⲉ ⲛⲣⲟⲓⲧⲉ, PSBA 34 175 *S* marriage contract ⲛⲧⲱ ⲧⲉⲥϩⲓⲙⲉ ⲉⲣⲛϩⲁⲣⲟⲩ ⲙⲡⲉⲓϩ.³: f: Ryl 244 *S* ⲟⲩϩ.² ⲉⲥϩⲓ ⲁⲡⲟⲱⲙⲥ (ἐπωμίς), PStras 41 *S* ϩ.² ⲛⲥϩⲓⲙⲉ ⲉⲥϣⲟⲡⲧ, PMich 3552 *S* ⲥⲛⲧ(ⲉ) ⲛϩ.², Ep 575 *S* recipe ⲧⲁⲁⲩ ⲉⲅϩ.² ⲛⲡⲛⲁϩⲉ ⲉⲣⲟϥ (*sc* liver), Kr 245 *S* ⲧⲁϩ.², also Z 316 below;   pl : Nu 8 7 (*S* ϩⲟⲓⲧⲉ), Is 37 1 (*SF* do), Hos 2 5 (*A* ϩⲁⲉⲓⲧⲉ), Ac 9 39 *BF*(*S* do), HL 110 ⲛⲓϩ. ⲉⲧⲥⲁⲓⲱⲟⲩ ἱμ.; Is 36 22 (*SF* do), EpJer 30 *BF* χι.; Ez 13 18 ἐπιβόλαιον; Lam 4 14 (*S* do, *F* ϩⲩⲃⲥⲱ) ἔνδυμα; Ez 44 19 στολή; Tri 660 *S* 'ϩ, TEuch 2 48 *B* ⲡⲁⲓϩ. wherein elements wrapped 'ϩ; ShP 130² 6 *S* ⲛⲉⲥϩⲟⲓⲧⲉ ⲙⲡⲛⲉⲥϩ., C 43 144 *B* ⲃⲁϣϣ ⲛⲡⲉϥϩ., ib 111 *B* ⲛⲉϥϩ. ⲛϣⲉⲙϣⲓ *liturgical vestments*, TEuch 2 29 *B*

ⲛ̄ϩ. *altar cloths* (var HCons 460 ϩⲉⲃⲥⲱ), P 44 60 *S*
sim لفاف; Gu 51 *S* ⲛⲉϩ. *grave-clothes*, BAp 125 *S*
ϩ.= MIE 2 418 *B* ⲕⲁⲓⲥⲓ, P 129¹⁶ 84 *S* sim ϩ. ⲡⲣⲟⲗⲟ-
ⲥⲧⲣⲓⲕⲟⲛ, MIE 2 403 *B* sim, Va 61 95 *B* ⲛ̄ϩ. ⲡϣⲉⲡⲥ
= P 131³ 95 *S* ⲡϣ., C 89 193 *B* ϩⲁⲛϩ. ⲙ̄ϭⲱⲓ; ⲉ-
ϩⲃ̄ⲱⲥ *B*: C 86 204 ⲛⲉϥⲉ., Mus 34 204 ⲛⲓⲉ. ⲉⲧⲁⲕⲕⲟⲥⲟⲩ
ⲉⲣⲟϥ;   sg as pl: Nu 15 38 *B*(*S* ϩⲟ.) *ἱμ.*; PS 370
S ϩⲉⲛϩ.² ⲛ̄ⲡⲉⲓⲁⲩ, Br 106 *S* sim ϩ.¹, ShA 1 108 *S*
ϩⲉⲛϩⲟⲉⲓⲧⲉ ⲏ ϩⲉⲛϩ.¹, AZ 30 42 *S* ⲛ̄ϩ.¹, Mani H 70 *A*²
ⲛ̄ϩ.;   ⲁⲧϩ.³ *B*, *without clothing*: Job 24 7 (*S* ϩⲟⲉⲓⲧⲉ) *ἄνευ ἱμ.*

  B *linen* *S A A²B*: Z 316 *S* ⲟⲩⲥ†ⲭⲁⲣⲓⲟⲛ ⲉⲅϩ.² ⲧⲉ=
MG 25 231 *B* ⲛⲓⲁⲩ ⲟⲧ. *λίνον*; Ac 10 11 *S*⁴(var²) *B*
ὀθόνη, Hos 2 5 *A*(*B* ϣⲉⲡⲧⲱ), Jo 20 5 *S*⁴(var²) *A*²*B* *ὀθόνιον*;   as adj *S*: Lev 16 4² (var⁴, *B* ⲓⲁⲩ), Jer 13 1²
(P 44 113, *B* do) *λινοῦς*; ShR 2 3 58 ϩⲟⲓⲧⲉ ... ⲛ̄ϩ.¹,
BAp 55 ϣⲧⲏⲛ ⲛ̄ϩ.¹ (var⁴ BKU 1 182), PSBA 27 168
ⲧⲟⲉⲓⲥ ⲛ̄ϩ.², BP 4977 ⲙⲁⲡⲧ]ⲏⲗⲉ ⲛ̄ⲥⲟⲣⲧ, do ⲛ̄ϩ.¹, BMOr
6943(20) ⲕⲁⲙⲛⲥⲉ ⲛ̄ϩ.¹

  ϭⲓϩⲃⲟⲥ, -ϩⲃ̄ⲱⲥ *B*, ϫⲓϩ. *A²F* nn m, *clothing*: Ex 21
10 (*S* ϩⲃ̄ⲱⲥ), EpJer 19 *BF*, Lu 9 29 (*S* do) *ἱματισμός*,
Ap 4 4 (*S* ϩⲟ.) *ἱμάτιον*; Mani 1 *A²* † ⲛⲉϫ. ϩⲓⲱⲉ.

  ϩⲃ̄ⲥⲱ *S A²F*, -ⲥⲟⲩ *A A²*, ϩⲉⲃⲥⲱ *S B*, pl ϩⲃ̄ⲥⲟⲟⲩⲉ *S*,
-ⲥⲁⲩⲉ *A²* & sg as pl nn f, *garment*: Ps 108 19 *S*(var
ϩⲟⲓⲧⲉ, *B* ϩⲃⲟⲥ), Mt 11 8 *S*(*B* do), BHom 4 *S* *ἱμάτιον*,
Ps 21 18 *SB*, Is 3 18 *S*(*B* ϭⲓϩⲃⲱⲥ), Jo 19 24 *S A²* -ⲥⲟⲩ
B *ἱματισμός*; 2 Kg 1 24 *B*(*S* pl), Is 63 2 *SB*, Zeph 1
8 *A*(*B* ϩⲃ̄ⲱⲥ), Mt 28 3 *SBF*, C 89 23 *B*, Z 325 *S* ⲧϩ.
ⲡⲧⲁⲛⲧⲱⲡⲁⲭⲟⲥ *ἔνδυμα*; Ge 41 42 *B*(*S*=Gk), Deu
22 5 *S*(*B*=Gk), Va 58 169 *B* ϩ. ⲙⲙⲉⲧⲟⲩⲣⲟ *στολή*;
Lu 23 11 *SB*, Va 66 297 *B* ϩ. ⲉⲅⲭⲏⲛ *ἐσθής*; Job 22
6 *SB* *ἀμφίασις*; Ex 22 27 *S*(*B* ϩⲃⲟⲥ) *περιβόλαιον*, Si
11 4 *S* ϩ. ⲡⲣⲟⲉⲓⲧⲉ *περιβολὴ ἱματίων* (cit BMis 143);
Ex 29 8 *S*(*B* ϣⲑⲏⲛ) *χιτών*; Nu 4 6 *S*(*B* ϩⲱⲃⲥ) *κατακάλυμμα*; Mor 37 69 *S* corpses swathed in ϩⲉⲛϩ.
ὀθόνιον; P 44 60 *S* ⲛⲉϥⲟⲣⲓⲥⲙⲁ· ⲛ̄ϩ. ملاء; PS 257
S ⲛ̄ϩ. ⲡⲗⲁⲙϫⲁⲡ ϩⲓⲕⲱⲣⲧ, BG 76 *S* ϭⲓⲛⲟⲩⲙ, ⲥⲱ,
ϩ., ShA 1 31 *S* ⲧⲉⲣⲣⲉ ⲙⲛ̄ϩ., ShP 130⁵ 17 *S* ϩ. ⲛⲉⲥⲟⲟⲩ,
El 56 *A* ϩ. ⲛⲁⲅⲅⲉⲗⲟⲥ, Miss 8 216 *S* ϩ. ⲛ̄ⲧⲁⲛⲧⲙⲁⲧⲟⲓ,
C 100 279 *S* ⲧϩ. beneath monk's outer ⲥⲧⲟⲗⲏ, C 89
44 *B* Pachom's ϩ.= C 99 139 *S* ⲛⲉϩⲟⲓ., ib 89 161 *B*
ⲥⲓⲡⲡⲟⲛ (*στύππιον*) ⲉⲑⲃⲉⲧⲟⲩϩ., BIF 13 106 *S* ϩ. ⲙ̄
ⲙⲟⲛⲁⲭⲟⲥ = MG 25 289 *B* ϩⲃ̄ⲱⲥ, Mor 36 18 *S* Baptist's ϩ. ⲛ̄ϭⲁⲙⲟⲩⲗ, Bor 264 33 *S* ϩⲉϥϭⲱ ⲛ̄ⲃⲱ, Miss
4 225 *B* ϩ. ⲛⲓⲁⲩ, P 129¹⁷ 29 *S* ⲧⲉⲥϩ. ⲙ̄ⲡⲉⲥⲣ̄ϣⲱⲛ,
ManiK 69 *A²* ⲧ†ϩ ⲛ̄ϩ., Bodl Marsh 32 93 *B* †ϩ. ⲉⲑⲟⲩⲁⲃ *monkish habit*, TEuch 2 127 *B* ϩⲁⲛϩ. ⲉⲩⲧⲁⲓⲏⲟⲩⲧ *altar cloths*, Va 63 10 *B* ϩ. ⲛ̄ⲥⲟⲣⲧ = BSM 36 *B*
ϩⲁⲛⲥⲟⲣⲧ;   pl: 2 Kg 1 24 *S*(*B* sg) *ἔνδ.*; ShP 131⁴
111 *S*, BAp 64 *S*, BMar 29 *S*, ManiH 6, ib K 4 *A²*.

  ⲣ̄ ϩ., *be clothing*: R 1 2 70 *S* fasting & prayer ⲁⲩⲣ̄.
ⲡⲡⲉⲧⲕⲏⲕ ⲁϩⲏⲩ, Mani 1 *A²* ϣⲁⲥⲣ̄. ⲛ̄ⲛⲁⲓⲕⲁⲓⲟⲥ.

ϩⲟⲃⲥⲧ *S* nn, *storm* (?): Mor 17 44 ⲁⲩⲛⲟϭ ⲛ̄ϩ. ϣⲱⲡⲉ ϩⲙ̄ⲡⲭⲟⲓ *ζάλη* (var *λαῖλαψ*).

ϩⲃ̄ⲏⲛⲧⲉ   *v* ϩⲃ̄ⲏⲛⲧⲉ.

ϩⲉⲃⲉⲧⲱⲣⲉ   *v* ϩⲙ̄ⲡⲧⲱⲣⲉ.

ϩⲁⲃⲓⲟⲩⲓ *ibis* *v* ϩⲓⲃⲱⲓ.

ϩⲁⲃⲟⲩⲉⲓ, -ⲓⲟⲩⲓ *S* nn as pl (?), *wasp*: P 44 56 ⲥϥ̄ⲓ-
ⲡⲓϩ (*σφήξ*) ⲫⲁⲗⲉⲧⲓⲟⲡ (*φαλάγγ.*)· ⲥⲓⲙⲁⲗⲟⲥ (*quid?*)·
ⲛ̄ⲃⲁⲃⲓⲟⲩⲓ زنبور; (cf ϩⲓⲃⲱⲓ Lev 11 17), Tri 424 ⲧⲅⲉⲛⲉⲁ
(of Israelites) ⲁⲩⲟⲩⲉⲙ ⲛⲉⲥⲥⲱⲙⲁ ⲛϭⲓ ⲛϩⲁⲗⲁⲧⲉ ⲙ̄ⲛ̄
ⲛϩⲁⲃⲟⲩⲉⲓ زنابير;   ⲁⲛⲟⲩⲓ m sg same?: Sh(?)Mor
54 104 ⲛ̄ⲙⲁ ⲛ̄ϣⲁⲣⲉⲧϩⲟⲟⲗⲉⲥ ⲙ̄ⲛⲁ. ⲧⲁⲕⲟⲟⲩ.
(ⲁϥ ⲙ̄ⲃⲓⲟⲩ *B*= ⲁⲙⲏ *S* q v).   *Cf* AZ 30 118.

ϩⲩⲃϣ *S* nn m, *meaning unknown*: PMéd 260
ⲕⲏⲛⲉ ⲛ̄ⲗⲓⲗ ⲛ̄ⲧⲁϥϫⲓ ⲛⲉϥ. ⲛ̄ϩⲣⲣⲉ *hog's fat whose* ϩ.
has been newly removed.   Perhaps Arabic (حفش ??
Chassinat, خبث? Guest).

ϩⲉⲃⲉϩⲓⲧ *A*   *v* ϩⲓⲧ.

ϩⲃⲟϭ   *v* ϩⲱⲃⲕ.

ϩⲁⲃⲁϭⲏⲉⲓⲛ   *v* ⲁⲃⲁϭⲏⲉⲓⲛ.

ϩⲑⲏⳇ *B*   *v* ϩⲏⲧ *tip.*

ϩⲟⲟ *B*   *v* ϩⲧⲟ.

ϩⲁⲕ *S A²*, ϩⲓⲕ- *A* adj, *sober, prudent, mild*, as nn:
Sa 12 18 *ἐπιείκεια*, Ps 85 5 (*B*=Gk), 1 Tim 3 3 (*B*
do), Z 327 *ἐπιεικής*; Phil 4 3 (*B* ⲥⲱⲧⲡ) *γνήσιος*; P
44 50 ⲥⲩⲡⲁⲧⲟⲥ (-ⲉⲧⲟⲥ)· ⲟⲩϩ. حليم (*sic*), ib 92 حكيم (=
43 76 ʾاحل), نهيم; Miss 4 245 woman ⲡⲉϩ. ⲧⲉ ⲙ̄
ⲡⲓⲥⲧⲏ, ClPr 47 5 ⲧⲣⲉⲟⲩⲡⲟⲣⲛⲏ ϣⲱⲡⲉ ⲛ̄ϩ.;   adj
after nn: Pro 29 22 (*A*=Gk), Ja 3 17 (*AB* do) *ἐ-
πιει.*; Marucchi *MusEgVat* 299 ⲣⲱⲙⲉ ⲛ̄ϩ., Aeg 244
ⲣⲙ̄ⲛ̄ϩⲏⲧ ⲛ̄ϩ. *σώφρων*; Gött N '98 172 ⲥⲡⲏⲩ ⲛ̄ϩ.
ⲅⲛ.; Z 291 ⲙⲟⲛⲁⲭⲟⲥ ⲛ̄ϩ. *castus*; Mor 22 113 ⲥϩⲓⲙⲉ
ⲛ̄ϩ. = BSM 102 *B* ⲛ̄ⲥⲁⲃⲉ, Wess 15 10 ⲁⲡⲟⲕ ⲡⲉⲕ-
ⲁⲣⲭⲓⲉⲣⲉⲩⲥ ⲛ̄ϩ. = Miss 4 117 *B* misunderst ⲉⲧⲟⲓ
ⲛ̄ⲁⲣⲭ. ⲛ̄ⲁⲕ, ViK 9816 177 ⲛ̄ⲁϣⲃⲉⲉⲣ ϩ.;   before
nn: Tit 1 4 (*B* ⲙⲉⲣⲓⲧ) *γν.*; ShC 42 225 ⲛ̄ϩ. ⲛⲁⲡⲁ-
ⲡⲛ̄ⲱⲥⲧⲏⲥ; ⲙⲛ̄ⲧ., *sobriety, mildness*: Sa 2 19 (*B*
ⲑⲉⲃⲓⲟ), Ac 24 4 (*B* ⲙⲉⲧⲉⲡⲓ.), LCyp 26 *ἐπιείκεια*;
BHom 47 of Joseph *σωφροσύνη*; 2 Cor 8 8 (*B* ⲙⲉⲧ-
ⲥⲱⲧⲡ) *γνήσιος*; Z 294 *ἁγνεία*; ShC 42 32 ϣⲓⲡⲉ ϩⲛ̄-
ⲟⲩⲙ. opp ϫⲱ ⲛ̄ⲡⲉⲓⲙⲛ̄ⲧⲥⲟϥ, Aeg 259 keep silence
ϩⲛ̄ⲟⲩⲙ. = PO 8 610 بصمت; Cl 23 1 *A*(Stras) ⲙⲛ̄ⲧ]-
ϩⲓⲕⲏⲧ (= ϩⲓⲕⲏⲧ Rösch 21 c, var ⲙⲛ̄ⲧⲉⲡⲓⲉⲓⲕⲏⲥ) *ἠ-
πίως*; ⲣ̄ ϩ., ⲟ ⲛ̄ϩ.: BAp 52 ⲟ ⲛ̄ϩ. *σωφρονεῖν*; Si
prol ⲣ̄ ϩ. ⲕⲁⲧⲁ [ⲡⲛⲟⲙⲟⲥ *βιοτεύειν*]; Mich 550 31
ⲛⲟⲣⲛⲏ ⲁⲥⲣ̄ ϩ. = Va 63 96 *B* ϣⲱⲡⲓ ⲛⲉⲡⲓⲕⲏⲥ, BHom
140 ⲕⲉⲓⲣⲉ ⲙⲙⲟⲟⲩ ⲛ̄ϩ.

ϩⲁⲕ, ϩⲁⲁⲕ S nn m, *cobbling tailor* (cf ẖʿ ḳ AZ 51 93): AZ 60 109 among guilds ⲧⲕⲟⲓⲡⲟⲧⲏⲥ ⲛⲛϩ., Mor 51 38 ν p 381 b ⲥⲁϧⲧ, ib ⲛⲣⲟ ⲛⲛϩⲁⲁⲕ, ShC 73 59 among abusive terms ⲃⲗⲗⲉ, ⲥⲱϩ, ... ⲕⲁⲥⲉ, ϩ. (gloss أَقْرَع *bald*, cf ϩⲱⲱⲕⲉ *scrape*, but as joined with ⲕⲁⲥⲉ prob *tailor*),LeydAC 24 ⲛⲣⲁϧⲧ, ⲛϩ.,WS 115 ⲅⲉⲱⲣⲅⲉ ⲫⲁⲁⲕ, Win 5 ⲁⲛⲁⲣⲉⲁⲥ ϩ., J 76 32 ⲛϧⲓⲣ ⲛⲛϩ.

ϩⲁⲕ† S vb, meaning unknown: AZ 23 110 recipe ⲧⲁⲁⲩ ⲉⲩⲁⲗⲕⲁⲣⲟⲟⲣⲉ (الخَرُّوب?) ⲉⲥϩ. ⲙ̄ⲙⲟⲟⲩ ⲛ̄ⲕⲉⲥⲟⲡ.

ϩⲁⲕ A² v ϩⲱⲱⲕ *gird* s f.

ϩⲓⲕ SAA²BF nn m, *magic* (charms, potions &c): Ap 9 21 S v below; Is 54 17 B ⲥⲕⲉⲩⲟⲥ ⲉⲑⲙⲉϩ ⲛϩ. (S c. ⲙⲙⲟⲩ) φθαρτός; Mor 17 72 S ⲧⲉⲩⲙⲛ̄ⲧϩⲁⲕⲟ ⲙ̄ⲛⲉϩ. μαγικὴ κακοτεχνία, Leyd 460 S ϩ. ⲛⲓⲙ ϣⲁ̄ⲧⲉ ⲛⲓⲙ be gone !, Stegemann 70 S Christ's Letter shall dispel sickness ⲉⲓⲧⲉ ϩ. ⲉⲓⲧⲉ ⲙⲁⲅⲓⲁ, Ricci MS (*Colluthus*) 115 S wizard made ⲟⲩⲙⲏⲏϣⲉ ⲛϩ. & buried them, PMéd 319 S who hath drunk φαρμακεία ϥⲛⲁⲕⲁ ⲃⲟⲗ ⲛ̄ⲛϩ., ManiK 107 A² drugs ⲛⲥⲉⲃⲁⲗ ϩ. ⲛⲓⲙ ⲁⲃⲁⲗ, Mani 1 A² ⲟⲩⲥⲉⲓⲛⲉ, ⲟⲩⲃⲁⲗϩ. *counter-actor of potions*, ManiK 31 A² ⲙⲙⲁⲅⲓⲁ ⲙⲛⲛⲉϩ. [ⲙ]-ⲛⲕⲉⲕⲉ ; ⲛⲁϩⲣⲉ, ⲫⲁϩⲣⲓ ⲛϩ.: Ap 9 21 B(S ϩ. only) φαρμακεία, Dan 2 2 B ⲣⲉϥϯ ⲫ. ⲛϩ. (S om ⲛϩ.) φαρμακός; R 1 3 28 S ⲛⲛ. ⲛ̄ⲛϩ. ⲛⲛⲉⲭⲣⲉⲓⲥⲧⲓⲁⲛⲟⲥ, AM 220 B ⲛⲥⲱ ⲛⲣⲁⲛϥ. ⲛϩ., MIE 2 367 B ⲙⲉⲧⲣⲉϥϯ ⲫ. ⲛϩ.,R 1 1 66 S ⲙⲛ̄ⲧⲣⲉϥⲣ ⲡ. ⲛϩ.,PMich 594 a anointed with ⲟⲩⲛⲉϩ ⲛϩ., C 41 41 B ⲛⲓⲥⲕⲉⲩⲟⲥ ⲛϩ. buried to impede progress; ⲙⲉⲧϩ. B: Ac 8 11 (S ⲙⲛ̄ⲧⲙⲁⲅⲟⲥ) μαγεία.

ⲣ ϩ. SBF, *bewitch, enchant*: Bor 239 52 S ⲛⲛⲉⲕⲣ. φαρμακεύειν ; c ⲉ- obj: Mor 17 9 S wizard ⲁϥⲣ. ⲉⲣⲟⲡ μαγεύειν; BMis 542 S ⲙⲁⲅⲟⲥ ⲉⲧⲣ ϩⲓⲥ̂ ⲉⲡⲣⲱⲙⲉ φαρ. κ. γοήτης, C 86 274 B ⲡⲓⲁⲭⲱ ⲁϥⲉⲣ. ⲉⲡⲓⲭⲣⲱⲙ γοητεύειν; ShC 73 199 sick beasts ⲙⲉϣⲁⲕ ⲉⲛⲧⲁⲩⲣ. ⲉⲣⲟⲟⲩ, BIF 14 179 S ⲁϥⲣ. ⲉⲛⲁⲙⲁⲧⲟⲓ, Mor 30 56 F maiden ⲛⲧⲁⲓⲉⲗ. ⲉⲗⲁⲥ = ib 29 49 S ⲙⲁⲅⲉⲅⲉ,C 43 76 B ⲁⲕⲉⲣ. ⲉⲡⲓⲭⲁⲗⲕⲓⲟⲛ not suffering it to boil; c ϩⲓ- S: P 129¹⁶ 83 ⲟⲩϣⲱϣⲧ ⲉϥⲣ. ϩⲓⲱⲱϥ ⲁϥⲧⲁⲁϥ ⲉ-ⲡⲣⲟ ; ⲙⲉⲧⲉⲣ ϩ. B: MartIgn 871 ⲟⲩⲙⲁⲅⲓⲁ ⲙⲙ. = R 1 4 60 S ⲙⲛ̄ⲧⲣⲉϥⲣ ϩ. γοητεία ; ⲣⲉϥⲣ ϩ. SAA²B, *wizard, enchanter*: Deu 18 10 S(B ⲣⲉϥϯ ⲫⲁϩⲣⲓ ⲛ.) φαρμακός; Ac 8 9 S(var ⲣ ϩ., B ⲟⲓ ⲛⲁⲭⲱ) μαγεύειν; Dan 4 4 B ἐπαοιδός; ROC 25 248 B ⲣ. ⲉ-ⲙⲁϣⲱ μάντις; R 1 4 20 S *maleficus*; ShHT K 1 S ⲣⲉϥⲙⲟⲩⲧⲉ, ⲣ., ⲣⲉϥⲣ ⲛⲁϩⲣⲉ, ShC 42 88 S sim, Mani 1 A² ⲛⲓⲣ.; as adj: Mor 40 50 S ⲙⲁⲅⲟⲥ ⲛⲣ., C 86 327 B ⲁⲭⲱ ... ⲛⲣ. (var -ϩⲓⲕⲕ, cf ? AZ 47 17); ⲙⲛ̄ⲧ-ⲣⲉϥⲣ ϩ.: Nah 3 4 A(B ⲫⲁϩⲣⲓ) φαρμακός; C 86 228 B by thy ⲙⲉⲧⲣ. hast called up demons = ib 292 ⲙⲁⲅⲓⲁ, Ming 305 S ⲧⲉⲭⲛⲏ ⲛⲧⲙ. μαγικὴ κακοτεχ. (cf above Mor 17 72 & R 1 4 60 S above),ROC 25 242 B ϯⲧⲉⲭ. ⲛⲧⲉ ϯⲙ. γοητικὴ μαγγανεία, C 86 28 B didst receive

gifts because of thy ⲙ. (SEAssemani *Acta Mart* 1 244 ܠܚܪ̈ܫܐ).

Cf ϩⲁⲕⲟ.

ϩⲱⲱⲕ S (rare), ϩⲱⲕ SSƒA²F, ϩⲱⲕ A, ϭⲱⲕ B, ϩⲉⲕ- S, ϩⲁⲕ- SƒA², ϭⲉⲕ B, ϩ(ⲟ)ⲟⲕ⸗ S, ϩⲁⲕ⸗, ϩⲉⲕ⸗ A(Cl), ϩⲁⲕ⸗ A²F, ϭⲟⲕ⸗ B, ϩⲏⲕ† SA²F, ϭ.† B vb tr, *gird, brace* with harness, armour: Ge 22 3 SB, 2 Kg 17 23 S ἐπισάσσειν; Deu 3 18 S(B as Gk) ἐνοπλίζειν, Lu 11 21 B(S†) καθοπ.; AM 282 B ⲁⲩϭⲟⲕⲟⲩ (*sc* clergy) περιζωννύναι, Jos 1 14 S εὔζωνος; 2 Tim 2 4 B(S diff), EW 225 B darest ⲉϩⲉⲕ ⲙⲁⲧⲟⲓ ⲙ̄ⲡⲉⲕⲟⲩⲣⲟ = Gu 37 S ϩⲉⲕ ⲣⲱⲙⲉ ⲙ̄ⲙⲁⲧⲟⲓ στρατολογεῖν; BHom 140 S ϩ. ⲙⲙⲟⲟⲩ (*sc* paralytics) σφίγγειν; BMis 261 S ⲁϥϩ. ⲛⲛⲉϥϭⲁⲙⲟⲩⲗ, CMSS 20 Sƒ ϩⲁⲕ ⲛⲉⲅ̄ⲧ ⲛⲓⲱ, TSBA 9 365 B ϭ. ⲙ̄ⲡⲉⲕϩⲁⲣⲙⲁ (cf 3 Kg 18 44 ζεῦξον), R 1 3 72 S ⲧϯⲡⲉ...ⲉⲙⲟⲣⲥ ⲁⲩⲱ ⲉⲣ. ⲙⲙⲟⲥ, BMis 276 S ⲁϥϩⲟⲕϥ like soldier = Mor 30 54 F ϩⲁⲕϥ, AM 193 B ⲁϥϩ. ⲙ̄ⲡⲉϥⲥⲧⲣⲁⲧⲉⲩⲙⲁ for war, ManiK 72 A² ⲁϥ-ϩⲁⲕϥ ⲁϥⲙⲁⲣϥ, C 86 221 B ϭⲟⲕϥ (*sc* martyr) ϭⲉⲛ-ⲑⲙⲏϯ ⲛ̄ⲧⲫⲟϫⲓ ⲥⲡⲟⲩϯ, BM 1089 S of labourers ⲙ̄-ⲡⲟⲩϩⲟⲕⲟⲩ ⲛⲧⲁⲡⲟ ϩⲁⲣ ⲧⲭⲟ ⲉⲃⲟⲗ *exert selves* ;   intr (passive): CMSS 20 Sƒ asses ⲛⲥⲉϩ. ⲁⲛ;   qual: 2 Kg 16 1 S ἐπισάσ.; Nu 32 27 SB, Jth 15 13 S ἐνοπ., LCyp 26 S ⲉⲩϩ. as if at war καθοπ.; 2 Cor 10 3 S(B ⲟⲓ ⲙⲙⲁⲧⲟⲓ) στρατεύεσθαι; Lu 12 35 B(S ⲙⲏⲣ) περιζ., Si 36 34 S εὔζωνος; Jos 4 12 S διασκευάζειν.; ShMing 322 S monks ⲙⲏⲣ ⲡⲟⲩⲍⲱⲏ ... ⲉⲩϩ. like asses, ShA 2 289 S arrow ⲉϥϭⲟⲗⲕ ⲏ ⲉϥϩ., BSM 42 B ⲡⲁϩ. -ⲡⲉ = BMis 389 S ⲙⲏⲣ (cf Lu 12 37), HM 1 43 S standest here (before king) ⲛⲣϩ. ⲁⲛ = C 43 123 B, ManiH 14 A² ⲡⲉⲧϩ. ⲙ̄ⲡⲙⲡⲓ[ⲥⲧⲟⲥ, AM 287 B soldier ⲉϥϭ. ϩⲓⲫⲣⲏⲥ *under arms, serving*.

With following preposition: c ⲉ-: Nu 32 29 SB† ἐνοπ. εἰς ; Deu 1 40 B(var ϩⲓ-, S diff) στρατο-πεδεύειν εἰς ; ViK 9562 S ⲁϥϩⲁⲕϥ ⲉⲩϭⲓⲛⲱⲡⲁϩ ⲉⲥ-ϫⲁⲭⲱ σφιγ. εἰς; Cl 45 7 A ⲡⲁⲩϩⲉⲕⲟⲩ (*sic* prob) ⲁⲛ-ⲕⲁⲙⲉⲓⲛⲟⲥ κατείργεσθαι εἰς ܘ ... ل, Mor 16 62 S ⲛⲉϩ.† ⲉⲡⲛⲟⲩⲙⲉⲣⲟⲛ of Constantine, C 43 2 B sim, SHel 6 Sƒ ϩⲁⲕⲧⲏⲩⲧⲛ ⲉⲡⲉⲥⲧⲣⲁⲧⲉⲩⲙⲁ, Mor 48 111 S ϩ. ⲙ̄ⲡⲉⲭⲁⲙⲱⲥ (κημός) ⲉⲣⲱϥ = C 43 154 B ϯ ⲉ-, BKU 1 26 (8116a) F set cover on mouth of hole ϩⲁⲕϥ ⲉⲥⲁⲓⲛ *fasten it well*, Blake 296 S ⲉϩ. ⲛⲧⲭⲟ ⲥⲓⲧⲉ... ⲉϩⲟⲩⲛ ⲉⲧⲙⲡⲧⲟⲅⲁ, BMis 131 S sim (cf Eph 2 14), ManiK 106 A² ϩⲁⲕⲧⲏⲡⲉ ⲁϩⲟⲩⲛ ⲁⲛϩⲃⲏⲅⲉ; c ⲉϫⲛ-: Is 31 4 B(SF ⲥⲱⲣ ⲉⲃⲟⲗ ⲉϫⲛ-) ἐπιστρ. ἐπί; Jer 27 14 B(S ⲥⲣ ⲙⲗⲁϩ ⲉⲃⲟⲗ ⲉϫⲛ-, F Louvre 10086 ⲥⲟⲃⲧⲉ ⲉ.) παρατάσσειν ἐπί; Eph 6 14 B†(S ⲙⲏⲣ ⲉ-), CDan 84 B ⲉϥϭ.† ⲡⲟⲩⲗⲉⲛⲧⲓⲟⲛ ⲉ. ⲧⲉϥϯⲡⲓ περιζ. acc; c ⲛ-, *with, in*: Sa 5 18 S ὁπλοποιεῖν acc, 1 Pet 4 1 B(S ϩⲛ-) ὁπλίζειν, Jer 26 9 SF(ViK 3271, B ϭⲉⲛ-) καθοπ. dat; 1 Tim 1 18 SB στρατ. acc; Lev 8 7 B(S ⲙ.) ζωννύναι acc, Ex 29 9 B(S do), Ez 16 10 B(S do), ζω. dat; ShIF 266 S ϩⲟⲕⲟⲩ ⲛⲛⲓϩⲱⲕ & set upon each other,

El 96 *A* ϩⲁⲕⲟⲩ ⲙⲡϩⲱⲕ ⲙⲡⲛⲉ = *ib* 132 *S* ϩⲛ-, Ryl
62 ı *a S* ⲉⲕϩ.† ⲡⲣⲟⲡⲗⲟⲛ, C 86 204 *B* ϫⲟⲕϥ ⲡⲟⲩⲡⲉ-
ⲣⲓⲥⲱⲙⲁ (*l* -ⲍⲱⲙⲁ); *as, for:* Gu 37 *ut sup* στρατολογεῖν, BHom 135 *S* ϩⲟⲕⲩ ⲙⲙⲁⲧⲟⲓ στρατιώτων
ποιεῖν; C 86 272 *B* ϫⲟⲕϥ ⲡⲕⲟⲙⲓⲥ ζω. ἔπαρχον; Wess
18 34 *S* ⲉⲓ ϩ. ⲙⲙⲟⲓ ⲙⲙⲁⲧⲟⲓ; c ⲟⲩ ⲃ ⲉ-, *against:*
Ro 7 23 *B*†(*S* ϯ ⲟⲩ ⲃ ⲉ-) ἀντιστρατ., ı Pet 2 ıı *B*†(*F*
ViK 8691 ϩ.† ⲉ[, *S* diff) στρατ. κατά; Mor 22 28 *S*
ϩⲟⲕⲩ ⲟⲩ ⲃ ⲉⲡⲟⲗⲉⲙⲟⲥ, C 43 39 *B* ϫ.† ⲟⲩ ⲃ ⲛⲟⲩ ⲉⲡⲡⲟⲗ.; c ϩⲁⲣⲁⲧ=, ϫ. ⲛ-, *under:* RNC 88 *S* ϩ. ϩⲁ-
ⲣⲁⲧⲩ ⲡⲧⲉ ⲡⲣⲣⲟ, SHel 5 *S* sim ⲙⲡⲣⲣⲟ, C 43 163 *B*
ⲉⲓ ϫ.† ⲙⲙⲁⲧⲟⲓ ϫⲁⲣⲁⲧⲩ ⲙⲡⲁⲥⲥ; c ϩⲛ-, ϫⲉⲛ-,
with, in: Pro 5 22 *SA*(*B* ⲥⲱ ϩ ϫⲉⲛ-) σφ. dat; ShP
130² 75 *S* ϩⲉⲡⲁⲡⲟⲑⲏⲕⲏ ... ⲉⲩϩ.† ϩ ⲡⲏ ϣ ⲱ ϣⲧ, BKU 1
31 12 *S* ⲉⲩϩ.† ϩ ⲡⲡⲉⲩⲥⲟⲧ ⲃ ⲉ ϥ, BMis 285 *S* ⲉ ϩ ϥ.† ϩ ⲙ-
ⲡⲁⲣⲑⲉⲙⲟⲥ, BIF 14 152 *S* ⲟⲩⲧⲟⲉⲓⲥ ϩ.† ϩ ⲙⲡ ϩⲟ ⲛ-.

With following adverb. c ⲉ ⲃⲟⲗ *SB*(once): Pro
24 62 *B* (or? ⲉ ⲃ. ϩⲓⲧⲉⲛ-, *SA* ϩ ⲱⲗ ⲉ ⲃ.) ἐκστρατ. ἀπό;
Bor 260 101 ϩⲟⲕⲟⲩ ⲉ ⲃ. ⲉⲡⲡⲟⲗⲩⲙⲟⲥ, Z 633 He ate
(Lu 24 42) as token of our nature ⲛ ⲧⲁ ϥ ⲧ ⲣⲉⲥⲧⲱⲥ ⲁ ⲩ ⲱ
ⲁⲥ ϩ. ⲉ ⲃ. ⲙⲡⲉ ϩ ⲛⲟ ⲛ ⲡⲡⲉ ϩ ⲛ ϩⲟ ⲛ (or ? ⲉ ⲃ. ⲛ-) *which
He stiffened and braced;* as nn m: C 86 305 *B* soldier's *belt* (var *ib* 247 ϫ. only) = BSG 198 *S* ⲙⲟⲩⲥ
ζώνη; c ⲉ ϩ ⲟ ⲩ ⲛ, ⲉ ϫ. *SBF*, emphasis: WTh 191
S ⲁ ϥ ϩ ⲟ ⲕ ϥ ⲉ ϩ. braced self & confessed Christ, DeV 2
55 *B* ⲉ ⲁ ⲛ ϫ ⲉ ⲕ ⲧ ⲉ ⲛ ⲡⲣⲟ ϩⲉⲣⲉⲥⲓⲥ ⲉ ϫ. & devote selves
to goodness, BMis 260 *S* (ⲉ) ϣ ⲱⲡⲉ ⲉ ⲕ ϩ.† ⲉ ϩ. ⲉⲡⲁ ϩ ⲓ
shalt see my power, ViK 7033 *F* letter ϣ ⲁⲓ ϩ ⲁ ⲕ ⲧ ⲉ ϩ.
ⲧ ⲁ ⲉ ⲗ ⲧ ⲉ ⲕ ⲁ ⲡ ⲟ ⲕ ⲣ ⲓ ⲥ ⲓ ⲥ, BMEA 10579 *S* letter ⲧ ⲏ ϩ. ⲉ ϩ.
ⲉ ϫ ⲱ ⲡ ⲥ ⲉ ⲉ ⲡ ⲉ ⲛ ⲧ ⲁ ⲧ ⲛ ⲉ ⲧ ⲁ ⲥ ⲥ ⲉ ⲡⲁ ⲛ ⲙ(ⲙ)ⲟⲟ ⲩ, ManiK
106 *A*¹ ϩ ⲁ ⲕ ⲧ ⲏ ⲡ ⲉ ⲁ ϩ. ⲁ ⲡ ⲉ ϩ ⲛ ⲏ ⲅⲉ ⲛ[ⲧ ⲉ ⲡ ⲱ] ⲛ ϩ; as nn
S: Bor 240 113 ⲙ ⲁ ⲣ ⲉ ⲥ ϣ ⲗ ⲏ ⲗ ϩ ⲛ ⲟ ⲩ ϩ. ⲉ ϩ., ViK 9451
of martyrs ⲛ ϩ. ⲉ ϩ. ⲛ ⲡ ⲉ ⲩ ⲥ ⲱ ⲙ ⲁ ϩ ⲛ ϩ ⲓ ⲙ ⲱ ⲣ ⲓ ⲁ (τιμ.)
ⲛ ⲓ ⲙ; c ⲉ ϩ ⲗ ⲏ ⲓ *F*, *as last: Archaiol Ephem* '15 31
letter ϩ ⲁ ⲕ ⲏ ⲉ ϩ. ⲡ ⲉ ⲗ ⲗ ⲁ ⲡ ⲱ ⲗ ⲓ (ⲙ ⲡ ⲣ ⲁ ⲡ ⲟ ⲣ ⲉ ⲓ).

—— nn m *SABF*, *girdle, breastplate:* MG 25 210
B monk's σχῆμα (?) = Z 345 *S* ⲉ ⲛ ϩ ⲱ ⲛ ⲏ, C 86 247 *B*
v ϩ. ⲉ ⲃ ⲟ ⲗ ζώνη; 2 Kg 21 16 *S* ϩ. ⲡ ϣ ⲛ ϥ ⲉ *q* v; Is 5 18
B(*SF* ⲙ ⲟ ⲩ ⲥ), Ac 22 25 *B*(*S* do) ἱμάς; ı Kg 17 38
S(*B* ⲙ ⲟ ϫ ϫ), Eph 6 14 *S*(*B* ϫ ⲉ ⲗ ⲓ ⲃ ϣ), Ap 9 9 *S* ϩ ⲱ ⲱ ⲕ
(*ib* 17 ϩ ⲱ ⲕ both pl, *B* do) θώραξ; Ez 27 10 *SB* πέλτη;
Lu 11 22 *B*(*S*=Gk) πανοπλία; P 54 154 *B* ϫ ⲟ ⲕ ⲉ ϫ ⲟ;
ShMIF 23 33 *S* ⲟ ⲩ ϩ. ⲡ ⲁ ⲅ ⲅ ⲉ ⲗ ⲟ ⲥ ⲁ ⲅ ⲱ ⲟ ⲩ ϩ ⲱ ⲡ ⲏ, ShZ
598 *S* soldier's ϩ. ⲉ ⲙ ⲡ ⲛ ⲥ ⲟ ⲧ ⲉ ⲡ ⲁ ϣ ϩ ⲟ ⲧ ⲩ, BIF 13
110 *S* Syrian monks' σχῆμα has neither ⲙ ⲟ ⲩ ⲣ ϩ ⲙ ⲁ ϩ
nor ϩ., C 41 61 *B* Shenoute's ϫ. as safeguard in battle,
El 74 *A* to battle ⲉ ⲙ ⲛ ϩ. ϩ ⲓ ⲟ ⲟ ⲩ ϥ, BMis 338 *S* bade
ϩ ⲟ ⲩ ϣ (soldier) ⲙ ⲡ ⲉ ϥ ϩ., C 43 29 *B* soldiers ⲁ ⲩ ⲥ ⲱ ⲗ ⲡ
ⲡ ϩ ⲟ ⲩ ϫ., MIF 9 59 *S* ϩ. ⲙ ⲙ ⲁ ⲣ ⲅ ⲁ ⲣ ⲓ ⲧ ⲏ ⲥ, Aeg 23 *S*
demons ϫ ⲓ ϩ. ⲛ ⲕ ⲱ ϩ ⲧ = *ib* *B* ϩ ⲃ ⲱ ⲥ, ViK 76 *S* among
clothes ϩ. ⲡ ⲁ ⲣ ⲉ ⲩ (*l* ⲁ ⲗ.), ϩ. ⲡ ⲕ ⲁ ⲙ ⲉ, ϩ. ⲡ ϣ ⲉ ⲓ (v p 548
b inf), CMSS 78 *F* payment for ⲡ ϩ. ⲡ ⲁ ⲡ ⲁ ϩ ⲓ (name,
S ⲡ ⲁ ⲡ ⲟ ϩ ⲉ).

ϩ ⲁ ⲕ *A*², *fastening, latch:* Mani 1 ϩ. ϩ ⲓ ⲉ ⲡ ⲱ.

ϩ ⲱ ⲕ, ϩ ⲟ ⲕ ⲉ (?) *S*, ϫ ⲟ ⲕ *B* (once), ϩ ⲉ ⲕ-, ϩ ⲟ ⲕ=, ϩ ⲏ ⲕ†
S vb tr, *smite, crush:* Mor 17 43 ⲉ ϥ ϩ ⲉ ⲕ (ⲡ)ⲡ ⲉ ⲡ ⲓ ⲡ ⲉ
(chains that were on him) διακρούειν; R 1 5 50 ⲁ ϥ-
ϩ ⲟ ⲕ ϥ ⲡ ⲕ ⲉ ϣ ⲥ ⲡ ⲕ ⲟ ⲩ ⲙ ⲡ ⲟ ⲥ (κόμβος, cf Mor 32 23 sim
ϯ ⲡ ⲁ ϥ ⲛ ⲟ ⲩ ϫ ϣ ⲉ), Pcod 18 ⲡ ϩ. ⲡ ⲣ ⲱ ⲙ ⲉ *jostled* as if
to push him forth, PMéd 318 ⲡ ⲟ ⲉ ⲓ ⲧ ⲛ ϭ ⲟ ⲩ ϭ ⲡ ⲣ ⲟ ⲕ ⲉ
pounded (?). With following preposition. c ⲉ-:
Mor 41 192 ⲡ ⲥ ⲉ ϩ ⲟ ⲕ ϥ ⲉ ⲡ ⲕ ⲁ ϩ, HM 1 95 ⲁ ϥ ϩ ⲟ ⲕ ϥ ⲉ ⲧ-
ⲙ ⲏ ⲧ ⲉ ⲙ ⲡ ⲉ ϥ ϫ ⲗ ϩ ⲥ ⲡ ⲁ ⲩ; c ⲉ ϫ ⲛ-: BSG 179 cast
him under wheel ⲁ ⲩ ⲱ ⲡ ⲧ ⲉ ⲣ ⲟ ⲩ ϩ. ⲉ ϫ ⲱ ϥ = C 86 280 *B*
ϫ ⲟ ⲕ ⲉ ϫ ⲱ ϥ πιέζειν, BIF 15 253 sim, Gu 61 sim ϩ.
ⲉ ϩ ⲣ ⲁ ⲓ ⲉ ϫ ⲱ ⲟ ⲩ, HM 1 184 sim ⲉ ϫ ⲱ ϥ, *ib* ϩ ⲓ ϫ., Mor 19
43 rushing forward ⲉ ϩ ⲣ.† ⲉ ϫ ⲛ ⲡ ⲉ ⲅ ⲉ ⲣ ⲏ ⲩ (var *ib* 18
35 ϩ ⲉ ϩ ϩ ⲱ ⲕ ⲉ ϩ ⲟ ⲩ ⲛ), = Miss 4 127 *B* ϭ ⲟ ϫ ⲓ ⲉ-, ViK
9320 172 ⲁ ⲩ ⲕ ⲱ ⲧ ⲉ ⲁ ⲩ ⲱ ⲁ ⲩ ϩ. ⲉ ϫ ⲱ ϥ (*sc* flax) so that
its oil flows forth (or is this ϩ ⲱ ⲱ ⲕ ⲉ *scrape*?); c ⲛ-
agent: BMar 44 ϩ ⲟ ⲕ ϥ ⲛ ⲧ ⲥ ⲛ ϥ ⲉ, BMis 270 sim ⲙ ⲡ ⲉ ϥ-
ⲕ ⲟ ⲩ ⲛ ⲧ ⲁ ⲣ ⲓ ⲟ ⲛ = Mor 29 40 ϩ ⲁ ⲣ ⲧ ϥ.

ϩ ⲁ ⲕ ⲉ *F* v ϩ ⲱ ⲱ ⲕ ⲉ *s f.*

ϩ ⲁ ⲕ ⲓ *F* nn, among iron σκεύη: BM 708 ϩ ⲁ ⲕ ⲓ ⲡ-
ⲭ ⲉ ⲡ ⲏ (or ϫ ⲁ.).

ϩ ⲁ ⲕ ⲟ *SA*², -ⲧⲟ *S*, ⲁ ⲭ ⲱ *B*, ϩ ⲁ ⲕ ⲁ *Sᶠ*, pl ⲁ ⲭ ⲱ ⲟ ⲩ ⲓ
B & sg as pl, nn m, *magician, wizard:* Ac 13 8 *B*(*S*=
Gk) μάγος, C 86 276 *B* ⲁ., ⲙ ⲁ ⲧ ⲟ ⲥ, P 44 78 *S* ϩ ⲁ ⲧ ⲟ·ⲙ ⲁ.
= ساحر = 43 49 *S* ساحر; Gu 24 *S* περίεργος; K 114 *B*
'ـ'; ClPr 56 8 *S* ⲛ ϩ. ⲙ ⲡ ⲓ ⲣ ⲉ ϥ ϩ ⲓ ⲕ, Bor 253 156 *S*
φαρμακος, ϩ., Mor 41 119 *S* ϩ ⲉ ⲛ ϩ. ⲡ ⲣ ⲉ ϥ ϯ ⲙ ⲁ ⲛ-
ⲧ ⲟ ⲟ ⲧ ⲟ ⲩ = *ib* 39 7 *Sᶠ* = C 43 36 *B*, C 43 217 *B* ⲙ ⲁ., ⲁ.,
C 86 17 *B* ⲟ ⲩ ⲛ ⲓ ϣ ϯ ⲛ ⲁ.; pl: Dan 2 2 (*S*=Gk)
μ.; Va 59 121 ⲛ ⲓ ⲁ. ⲙ ⲙ ⲁ.; as adj: BM 314 32
S ⲙ ⲁ. ⲛ ϩ., ROC 23 282 *B* ⲣ ⲱ ⲙ ⲓ ⲛ ⲁ., C 43 218 *B*
ϫ ⲉ ⲗ ϣ ⲓ ⲣ ⲓ ⲉ ⲡ ⲁ. ⲙ ϥ ⲁ ⲣ ⲙ ⲁ ⲧ ⲟ ⲥ; ⲙ ⲛ ⲧ ϩ., ⲙ ⲉ ⲧ ⲁ.,
magic: Mor 17 9 *S* ⲁ ⲧ ⲉ ⲧ ⲛ ⲥ ⲱ ⲙ ⲛ ⲟ ⲩ ⲙ. ϩ ⲛ ⲡ ⲟ ⲓ μαγεία,
ib 111 *S* ⲧ ⲉ ⲭ ⲛ ⲏ ⲙ. (var Ming 313 ⲙ ⲛ ⲧ ⲣ ⲉ ϥ ϩ ⲣ ϩ ⲓ ⲕ)
μαγικὴ κακοτεχνία; P 129¹⁴ 92 *S* γοητεία (cf PSBA
24 75); Mor 47 197 *S* ⲣ ϩ ⲱ ⲃ ϩ ⲛ ϩ ϩ(ⲉ)ⲙ., C 43 13 *B*
sim, Cat 106 *B* Antichrist & ⲡ ⲉ ϥ ⲙ. (Mt 24 24), AM
64 *B* ⲓ ⲣ ⲓ ⲛ ϩ ⲁ ⲛ ⲛ ⲓ ϣ ϯ ⲙ., ManiH 10 *A*²; ⲟ ⲓ ⲛ ⲁ.:
Ac 8 9 *B*(*S* ⲣ ϩ ⲓ ⲕ) μαγεύειν. Cf ϩ ⲓ ⲕ.

ϩ ⲁ ⲕ ⲟ *S* nn m, meaning unknown: BM 1013 13
lease ⲡ ⲣ ⲟ ⲥ ⲑ ⲉ ⲛ ⲧ ⲁ ⲛ ⲥ ϧ ⲁ ⲓ ϩ ⲓ[   ]ⲡ ⲉ ⲙ ϥ ⲩ ⲧ ⲉ ⲩ ⲙ ⲁ
ϩ ⲁ ϥ ⲁ ⲕ ⲟ.

ϩ ⲏ ⲕ ⲉ *S* nn f, a measure of corn: BP 11932 ⲙ ⲛ ⲧ-
ⲟ ⲩ ⲉ ⲛ ϩ. ⲛ ⲥ ⲟ ⲅ ⲟ, *ib* 11349 crop attained not to
ϣ ⲙ ⲟ ⲩ ⲛ ⲉ ⲛ ϩ. ⲛ ⲥ ⲟ ⲅ ⲟ.

ϩ ⲏ ⲕ ⲉ *poor* v ϩ ⲕ ⲟ.

ϩ ⲟ ⲕ ⲉ v ϩ ⲱ ⲕ.

ϩ ⲱ(ⲱ)ⲕ ⲉ ϩ ⲱ(ⲱ)ⲕ *SA*², ϩ ⲱ ⲕ ⲉ *Sᶠ*, ϩ ⲟ ⲩ ⲟ ⲩ ⲕ *A*,

ϩⲱⲕⲓ, ⲋ., ⳪ⲱⲕ B, ϩⲉ(ⲉ)ⲕⲉ-, ϩⲉⲕ- S, ϩⲟⲕ- A, ⳪ⲉⲕ- B, ϩⲁⲕⲉ- F, ϩⲟ(ⲟ)ⲕⲝ S, ⳪ⲟⲕⲝ B, ϩⲟⲟⲕⲉⳁ S, ⳪ⲏⲕⳁ B, ϩⲁⲁⲕⲉⳁ F vb **A**, scrape, scratch (cf حكّ خكّ Dévaud) tr: Job 2 8 S(B ⳪ⲱⳅ) ξύειν; Mor 18 190 S martyr on ϩⲉⲣⲙⲏⲧⲁⲣⲓⲟⲛ ⲡⲥⲉϩ. ⲙⲙⲟϥ, C 86 274 B sim ξέεσθαι (cf *Mélanges de Harlez* 322); R 1 4 70 S ϩ. ⲛⲧⲉϥϫⲓⲥⲉ = MartIgn 876 B, R 1 4 57 S ϩ. ⲡⲡⲉϥⲥⲡⲓⲣⲟⲟⲩⲉ with iron claws, C 43 167 B sim, C 86 62 B ϩ. ⲛ̅ⲛⲟⲩⲥⲁⲣ⳨ ⲉϩⲟⲩⲛ ⲉⲟⲩⲡⲉⲩⲧⲟⲡ καταξαίνειν; Ps 31 9 B(S ⲥⲱⲕ) ἄγχειν ـ S (l ? ⳪ⲱⲕ gird); ShMIF 23 196 S ⲛⲧⲏⲣ. ⲙⲡⲱϣⲛⳃⲉ, ShA 2 332 S ⲉⲩϩ. ⲡⲡⲉⲩⲛⲁϫϩⲉ with iron tool, ShIF 107 S how sweet to ϩⲱϩ ⲛⲟⲩⲯⲱⲣⲁ ...ⲉⲧⲁϣⲉ ϩ. ⲙⲙⲟϥ (sc ⲥⲱⲙⲁ), BMar 209 S ⲡⲉⲡⲗⲩⲅⲏ (ⲡⲗⲏ.) ⲁϥϩⲟⲕⲟⲩ = Rec 6 172 B ⳪ⲁⳃⲟⲩ ⲉⳃⲟⲗ, ViK 9480 S colophon ⲡⲉⲧⲡⲁⲧⲟⲙⲙⲁ...ⲉϥⲉⲛ ⲡⲉⲓⲣ ⲡⲙⲉⲉⲩⲉ erase, BMis 294 S ϩⲱⲕ ⲙⲙⲟϥ on ϩⲉⲣⲙⲏⲧⲁⲣⲓⲟⲛ till bones showed forth, BIF 15 232 Sʄ sim ϩⲱⲕⲉ, Z 596 S ϩⲱⲕ ⲡⲡⲉⲩⲥⲡⲓⲣ, SHel 32 S ϩ. ⲡⲡⲉϥⲥⲡⲓⲣⲟⲟⲩⲉ ϣⲁⲛⲣⲉⲛϭⲟⲙ ⲙⲡⲉⲛⲓⲡⲉ, C 86 235 B brought ⲟⲩⲟⲙ ⲛⲉⲙⲟⲩⲥⲙⲓⲗⲗⲁ (σμίλη) ⲁⲩϩ. ⲙⲡⲓϣⲁⲣ of head, RAl 100 B bade flay him ⲛⲁⲩϩ. ⲙⲙⲟϥⲡⲉ, C 86 155 B ⲁⲩ⳪. ⲙⲡⲉϥϣⲁⲣ (sc serpent's), C 43 171 B ϩ. ⲙⲙⲟϥ, AM 104 B ⳪. ⲙⲙⲟⲟⲩ, same MS ϩ., EW 83 B sim ⳪., MG 25 245 B ⲉⲩ⳪. ⲡⲡⲁⳃⲁⲗⲁ⳨ ⲡⲡⲟⲩⲓⲉⳃ, Mani H 69 A² ⲁⲩϩ. ⲙⲙⲁϥ, CO 459 S metal tools ⲛⲣⲱⲕ ϣⲱⲧⲉ *for scraping* (?) wells, Ryl 211 S ⲗⲁⲥ ⲛⲣⲱⲕⲉ *flax to be scraped*, combed (?), ViK 4714 S ⲗ. ⲛⲣⲱⲕ, BMOr 6201 A 104 ⲗ. ⲉⲩϩ.ⳁ *scraped* (Blümner 1² 192); c ⲉ- obj B: AM 105 ⲉϥϩ. ⲉⲟⲩϣⲉ; c ⲛⲥⲁ- B: Va 57 177 of Job ⲉϥ⳪. ⲡⲥⲁⲡⲓⲉⲣ⳪ⲱⲧ ξέειν, AM 105 ⲉⲩϩ. ⲡⲥⲁⲡⲉⲥⲥⲱⲙⲁ; c ⲉⲃⲟⲗ SA²: Lev 14 41 (ShIF 132, B ⳪ⲱⳅ) ἀποξύειν; BMar 38 like statue (ἀνδριάς) ⲡⲥⲉϩⲟⲕϥ ⲉⳃ. & it is as new, Lant 86 (2) ϩ. ⲉⳃ. prob of *erasure* in MS, ManiK 108 A² ⲥⲱϩⲣⲉ ϩⲱⲕⲉ ⲁⳃ. ⲛⲧⲣⲁⲓⳃⲉⲥ ... ⲙⲡⲟⲩⲗⲱⲙⲥ (cf *ib* H 39 ϩⲱⲕ); as nn B: C 43 114 ⲙⲙⲟⲛ ϩⲗⲓ ⲛϩ. ϩⲓⲡⲉϥⲥⲱⲙⲁ ⲁⲡ; ϣⲉ ⲛϩ.: AM 326 sim, EWʲ83 ⲛϣⲉ ⲛⳃ. ⲉⲧⲁⲩⲧⲛⲓⲧⲟⲩ ⲡⲁϥ; intr (rare), *itch* (?) S: Mor 31 123 after fasting ⲁⲡⲉϥⲙⲁ ⲛⲣⲏⲛ ϩⲱⲕ ϩⲓϩⲟⲩⲛ ⲙⲙⲟϥ, Z 627 recipes ⲡⲉⲧϩⲱⲕⲉ ϩⲙⲡⲉϥⲥⲱⲙⲁ ⲧⲏⲣϥ, *ib* ⲡⲉⲟⲩⲉⲣⲏⲧⲉ ⲉⲧϩ.

ϩⲟⲕⲥ B nn, *scraper*: MartIgn 869 ϩⲱⲕⲓ ⲡⲡⲉϥⲥϥⲓⲣⲱⲟⲩⲓ ⲛϩⲁⲛⲡ. (sic l) ⲛⳃⲉⲛⲓⲛⲓ = R 1 4 57 S ⲉⲓⲉⲓⳃ ὄνυξ; AM 235 sim.

B shave, shear (⳪ⲱⲕ B, ⳪ⲱⲕϩ in variants) tr: Ge 41 14 SB(var ⳪ⲱⲕϩ), Deu 21 12 S(B ⳪ⲉⲕϩ-), Mic 1 16 SAB, 1 Cor 11 6 S(B ⳪ⲟⲕϩϥ) ξυρᾶν; Ge 31 19 SB (var do), Cant 6 5 S(F ϣⲱ⳪), Is 53 7 SA(Cl)B κείρειν; *ib* 3 24 S(B diff) φαλάκρωμα ἔχειν; Deu 14 1 υ ϣⲟⲉⲓⲧ; ShP 130² 92 S ⲛⳃ ϫⲱ...ϩⲉⲕⲉ ϫⲱ, R 1 2 39 S ϩ. (var ϩⲱⲱⲕ) ⲡⲧⲉϥⲙⲟⲣⲧ, MG 25 300 B ⲁϥ⳪ⲉⲕ ϫⲱϥ, C 86 40 B like sheep ⲉⲁⲩⳃⲟⲕⲧ ⲛⲛⲁϫⲓϫ, Mor 19 62 S ϩⲉⲉⲕⲉ ϫⲱⲟⲩ with σπαλίς (var *ib* 18 53 ϣⲱϥ

ⲙⲡϥⲱ), CMSS 63 F ⲡⲉϩⲁⲕⲉ ⲛⲧⲁⲩϩⲁⲕⲉ ⲡⲉⲥⲁⲩ, RAl 88 B ⲥⲛϭⲓ ⲉϣⲁⲩϩϥ. ⲡⲡⲉϥⲉⲥⲟⲟⲩ ⲛ̄ϩⲏⲧⲥ; intr (rare) S: Ps 51 2 ⲧⲟⲕ ⲛⲣⲱⲱⲕ (var & B om ⲛϩ.) ξυρόν; Ez 29 18 (B tr) φαλακρός; P 131⁶ 47 lamb ⲙⲡⲁⲧϥⲣⲱⲧ ⲥⲟⲣⲧ ⲛϥϩ., PMich 4544 ⲡⲉⲥⲟⲟⲩ ⲁⲩⲉⲓ ⲉⲧⲟⲟⲧ ⲉⲩϩ. (or l ? ϩⲟ.); qual: EpJer 30 BF, 1 Cor 11 5 S(B ⳪ⲟⲕϩ) ξυ.; c ⲉⲃⲟⲗ S: Lev 13 33 (B do) ξυ., *ib* 14 41 (ShIF 132, B ⳪ⲱⳅ) ἀποξύειν; BP 10589 ⳪ⲁⲙⲟⲩⲗ ...ϣⲁⲛϩⲟⲕⲟⲩ (ⲉ)ⲃⲟⲗ (or ? ϩ. gird, saddle); as nn, *shaved condition, baldness*: Is 22 12 SB ξύρησις; *ib* 15 2 S(B ⲙⲉⲧⲕⲉⲣϩ) φαλάκρωμα; Mor 22 48 S ⲡⲕⲁⲓⲣⲟⲥ ⲙⲡϩ. of sheep.

ϩⲁⲕⲉ F, *shearer* v CMSS above.

ϩⲱⲱⲕⲉ S, ⳪ⲱⲕ B nn m, *fleece*: Deu 18 4 (var ⳪ⲱⲕϩ, S ⲥⲟⲣⲧ), Mor 25 10 S(var P 131³ 82 c.) = Job 31 20 S ϩⲕⲁ (B Va 61 92 ⲛⳃ.) κουρά; Dif 1 65 B ⳪. ⲡⲥ. حزف جزّ as shroud.

ϩⲕⲁ S v above.

In place-name (?): ⲡⲙⲁ ⲛϩⲱⲕⲉ (WS 129).

ϩⲕⲟ SAA²B, ⲉϩ. SB (nn), ϩⲕⲁ, ϩⲓⲕⲁ F (nn), ϩⲕ-ⲁⲉⲓⲧⳁ¹, ϩⲕⲟⲉⲓⲧⳁ², ϩⲟⲕⲣⳁ³ S, ϩⲕⲉⲉⲧⳁ⁴ AA², ϩⲕⲉⲓⲧⳁ⁵ A², ϩⲟⲕⲉⲣⳁ B, ϩⲁⲕⲉⲗⳁ F vb intr, *be hungry*: Ge 41 55 SB, Pro 18 8 SA, Jo 6 35 SA²B πεινᾶν; Ps 58 6 SB λιμώσσειν; ManiH 73 A² ⲡⲉⲧⲁϩ. ⲉⲧⲃⲉ[, DeV 2 108 B ϣⲁϥϩ. ϣⲁϥϩⲃⲓ; qual: Deu 25 18 S³ (both MSS ϩⲟⲣⲕ) B, Jud 8 4 S¹, Pro 6 30 S¹AB, Is 32 6 S¹(var²) BF, Cl 59 4 A π.; Deu 8 3 S³ (3 MSS, B intr) λιμαγχονεῖν; Mt 15 32 S¹(B diff) νῆστις; Sa 16 25 S¹ δεῖσθαι; Ac 27 33 S¹(B diff) ἄσιτος; ShC 42 114 S ⲡⲉⲧϩ.², BMis 86 S ⲧⲥⲓⲟ ⲛⲡⲉⲧϩ.², *ib* xxxix S ⲉϥϩ.³, BHom 77 S ⲡⲉⲧϩ.¹, ManiH 14 A² ⲉⲩϩ.⁵, Mani 1 A² ⲡⲉⲧϩ.⁴, C 43 168 B ⲟⲩⲁⲓ ⲉϥϩ., Mor 24 27 F ⲧⲙⲁ ⲟⲩⲉⲉⲓ ⲉϥϩ.

With following preposition. c ⲛ-, *hunger for*: Si 24 22 S π.: ShC 73 211 S ⲉϥϩ.ⳁ¹ ⲙⲡⲟⲉⲓⲕ, *ib* 42 91 S sim ⲉϥϩ.¹³, ShRE 10 164 S ⲛⲧⲟⲟⲩ ⲛⲉⲧϩ.ⳁ¹² ⲙⲙⲟⲟⲩ, P 131³ 83 S ⲉⲣⲉⲗⲁⲍⲁⲣⲟⲥ ϩ.ⳁ¹³ ⲙⲙⲟⲟⲩ (on Lu 16 21) = Va 61 93 B ⲉⲣ ⲉⲡⲓⲑⲩⲙⲓⲛ, DeV 2 11 B ⳁϩ.ⳁ ⲙⲙⲟⲕ; c ϩⲁ- S: BMis 154 ⲉϥϩ.¹³ ϩⲁⲡⲉϩⲕⲟ.

—— nn m SAA²BF, *hunger, famine*: Ge 12 10 B, Job 30 4 S(B ϩⲃⲱⲡ), Is 5 13 SB(F ϩⲉⳃⲱⲱⲛ ⲡⲁⲓⲕ), Lam 5 10 F(SB ϩⲉⳃ.), Ro 8 35 SB λιμός, Pro 10 3 SAB λιμο-; Sa 16 4 S ἔνδεια; BM 232 2 S ⲡⲁⲓⲁⲉⲩⲉ ⲙⲙⲟⲟⲩ ϩⲛ ... ⲟⲩϩ., BHom 69 S ⲡⲉⲧϣⲟⲟⲡ ϩⲁⲡⲉϩ., Mor 31 68 S ⲡⲉϩ. ⲛⲧⲁϥϥⲉⲓ ϩⲁⲣⲟⲟⲩ, ManiH 9 A² ⲡϩ. ⲡⲉⲓⳃⲉ, BSM 28 B ⲛⲧⲁⲕⲟ ⲙⲡϩ., CO 209 S ⲉⲡⲙⲟⲟⲩⲧ ϩⲁⲡⲉϩⲕⲟ, Ep 344 S sim, AZ 23 39 F ⲟⲩϩⲁⲛ (l ⲁϩⲛ) ⲛⲧⲉⲓ ... ⲁⲥⲉⲧⲟⲩⲡⲟⲩⲓ ⲉⲃⲟⲗ ⲉⲡϩ. *that should preserve me from hunger*, BM 1221 F ⲟ(ⲩ)ϩⲓⲕⲁ ϩⲛⲡⲉⲕⲡⲟⲗⲓⲥ, Mani 1 A² ⲡⲓϣⲁⲡϩ.; ⲉϩ.: Mor 31 178 S, C 86 238 B, Rec 6 174 B.

ⲁⲧϩ. S, *without (liability to) hunger*: Pcod 44 ⲛⲡⲉⲟⲩⲁ. (var ⲙⲉⲩϩ.).

ϭⲓⲛϩ. *S, state of hunger* : P 129¹⁴ 53 Tome of Leo saith ⲧϭ. ⲙⲛⲧϭⲓⲛⲉⲓϩⲉ ... ⲡⲁⲧⲁⲙⲛⲧⲣⲱⲙⲉⲡⲉ.

ϩⲕⲕⲉ *SAA*², -ⲓ *BF* adj, poor, as nn : Deu 24 19 *SB*, Ps 11 5 *SA*(Cl)*B*, EpJer 27 *BF*, Jo 12 8 *SAA*²*B*, AP 19 *A*² πτωχός ; Ex 23 3 *SB*, Ps 9 19 *B*(*S* ⲉⲃⲓⲏⲛ), Pro 24 77 *SAB*, 2 Cor 9 9 *SB* πένης, Pro 28 15 *SA*, ⸗Aeg 229 *S* πενιχρός ; Sa 18 12 *S* δημότης ; PS 261 *S* ⳉⲓⲁ-ⲕⲟⲡⲉⲓ ⲉⲡϩ., AZ 21 150 *S* ⲁⲡⲟⲕⲡⲉ ⲡϩ., AM 196 *B* ⲡⲓϩ. ⲡⲉⲙⲡⲏ ⲉⲧϣⲁⲧ, BMis 175 *S* ⲁⲣⳉⲱⲡ, ⲣⲙⲙⲁⲟ, ϩ. ⸗ BSM 84 *B*, CO 75 *S* begging letter ⲣ ⲟⲩⲛⲁ ⲙⲡ-ⲡⲉϩ., *ib* 94 *S* sim, ST 175 *S* ⲧⲉϩ., RE 9 141 *S* ⲡⲉⲓϩ. ⲉⲧⲏⲗ ⲉϩⲟⲩⲏ ; as adj, before nn : 2 Kg 12 6 *S*(Gk om), Miss 8 167 *S* ⲟⲩϩ. ⲡⲣⲱⲙⲉ, Ryl 315 *S* ϩⲏⲕⲉ ⲡⲣ., C 43 128 *B* sim, CO 267 *S* ⲟⲩϩ. ⲡⳉⲏⲣⲁ, Ep 167 *S* ⲡⲉϩ. ⲡⲡⲉⳉⲙⲁⲗⲟⲧⲟⲥ (*l* ⲡⲁⲓⳉ.) ; after nn : Ps 108 16 *B*(*S* nn), Pro 14 20 *SAB*, Mk 12 42 *SBF* ⲡⲧ. ; Va 66 288 *B* ϣⲫⲏⲣ ⲡϩ. συμπένης ; BHom 16 *S* ⲣⲱ-ⲙⲉ ⲡϩ. εὐτελέστατος ; Mun 32 *S* ⲡⲁⲗⲁⲥ ⲡϩ., Hyver-nat *Alb* 23 *B* ⳨ⳉⲏⲣⲁ ⲡϩ., BSM 125 *B* ⲥⲡⲛⲟⲩ ⲡϩ., ST 360 *S* ⲁⲡⲟⲕ ⲟⲩϭⲱⲃ ⲡϩ. ; ⲙⲛⲧ-, ⲙⲉⲧϩ., *po-verty* : Ps 30 10 *SB*, Lam 3 19 *SBF*, Ap 29 *SB* πτω-χεία ; Pro 6 11 *SAB* πενία ; Is 24 19 *B*(*S* diff) ἀπορία ; BG 70 *S* ⲡⲁⲅⲅⲉⲗⲟⲥ ⲡⲧⲙ., ShC 42 83 *S* ⲡⲉⲟⲃⲧⲉ ⲡ-ⲧⲉϩⲙ. *poor belongings* loaded on beasts, ShEp 56 9 *S* ⲧ]ϩⲟⲓⲧⲉ ⲡⲧⲉ ⲧⲉϩⲙ., PBu 179 *S* house ⲡⲧⲁⲡϫⲟ ⲧⲉⲡⲙ. ⲧⲏⲣⲥ ⲉⲃⲟⲗ ⲉⲣⲟϥ, Mani 1 *A*² ⲡⲧⲡⲙⲉⲣⲓ ⲧⲙ., ROC 25 241 *B* ⳉⲓⲡⲟⲩⲱⲙ ⲙⲙ., BSM 30 *B* ⳨ⲙ. ⲓⲣⲓ ⲡⲟⲩⲙⲏϣ ⲡⲟⲃⲛⲟⲩⲓ leading to death ; ⲙⲁⲓϩ., *poor-loving* : Miss 4 715 *S* ⲙ. opp ⲟⲩⲁϩⲓϩⲏⲧ, CO 366 *S* ⲡⲙⲁⲓⲡⲉ ⲙⲙ. ; ⲙⲛⲧ-, ⲙⲉⲧⲙ. : Va 66 288 *B* φιλοπτωχία ; Sh(Besa)*S* Z 517 ; ⲙⲛⲧⲙⲁⲥⲧϩ. *S, hatred of poor* : ShA 1 398 among vices ; ⲣ ϩ., *become, be poor* : Ps 33 10 *SB*, 2 Cor 8 9 *SB* πτωχεύειν ; Pcod 39 *S* ⲕⲡⲁⲣ. *F* ⲉⲗ ϩ., DeV 2 10 *B* ⲉⲁⲕⲉⲣ., Mani 1 *A*² ⲁⲩⲣ. ⲉⲧⲃⲏⲧϥ ; Is 24 6 *B* ⲟⲓ ⲡϩ. (*S* ⲣ ϩ.) πτωχός ; *make poor* : 1 Kg 2 7 *B*(*S* ⳨ ⲡⲧⲙⲡⲧϩ.) πτωχίζειν, Jud 14 15 *S* πτωχεύειν ; KKS 302 *S* have our days diminished or ⲡⲧⲁⲡⲡⲉ ⲣ. ⲉϥϥⲓ ⲙⲙⲟⲡ ?

ϩⲁⲕⲗϥ¹ *SA*, -ⲕⲏⲗϥ², -ⲕⲉⲗϥ³, ϩⲁⲡⲕⲗϥ⁴ (P 44 117) *S* nn m, species of *lizard* : Lev 11 30¹ (*B* ⲁⲡⲑⲟⲩⲥ) ⲏⲣⲍⲱⲛ Pro 24 63¹ (varr²⁴) *A*(*B* do) καλαβώτης ; Cai 42573 2 in recipe ⲟⲩϩ.³ ⲉⲧⲟⲟⲩ (*l* ⲡⲧ.).

ϩⲟⲕⲗⲉϥ *B* nn m, *camel-saddle* : K 137 ⲡⲓϩ. ⲫⲟⲅ ; ⲕⲟⲣ ; *wooden palanquin, litter* : P 55 13 ⲡⲓϩ. ⲡϣⲉ ⲕⲟⲟⲟ ⲭⲇⲍ ; ⲁⲗⳉⲉⲃⲧ, BMOr 8775 141 ⲕⲟⲣⲗⲉϥ 'ⲁ (which K 137 ⲗⲁⲙⲡⲁⲡⲏ *ie* -ήνη), but Montp 168 ⲡⲓϩ. ⲭⲟⲣϫ *wooden bolt* (Dozy, but *ib* 165 ⸗ ⲙⲁⲡϭⲁⲗⲉ μάκελλα & HA Winkler *Bauern* 99 ⲭⲟⲣϫ *rake*). Miswritten ? for ϩⲟⲕⲙⲉⲥ.

ϩⲱⲕⲙⲙ *v* ϩⲱϭⲃ.

ϩⲟⲕⲙⲙⲉⲥ *S* nn as pl, *palanquin, litter* : P 44 88 ⲡⲕⲁⲡⲓⲡⲟⲥ· ⲡϩ. ϩⲟⲩⲁⲇⲟⲣ (var 43 70 ϩⲟⲕⲙⲟⲥ· 'ⲁ, ⲙⲕⲥ) Prob = ϩⲟⲕⲡⲟⲥ (ὄκνος) KKS 423. *Cf* ϩⲟⲕⲗⲉϥ.

(ϩⲱⲕⲡ), ϩⲟⲕⲡ⸗ *S* vb tr, meaning doubtful : PS 283 he caused soul to desire things of world, in short ϣⲁϥϩⲟⲕⲡⲥ ⲉⲡⲉϩⲃⲏⲩⲉ ⲧⲏⲣⲟⲩ that had been bidden him. *L* ? ϩⲟⲡⲕⲥ, *v* ϩⲱⲡⲕ.

(ϩⲱⲕⲡ), ϩⲟⲕⲡ⸗ *S* vb tr, meaning unknown : BM 1115 letter ⳨ⲥⲟⲟⲩⲡ ⲅⲁⲣ ⳉⲡⲡⲉⲕⲗⲩⲡⲉⲓ ⲡⲙⲟⲓ ⲉⲡⲉϩ ϫⲉⲡⲉⲃⲉⲥⲱⲕ (*l* ? ⲡⲉⲧϥⲡⲥⲱⲕ) ⲙⲉⲕϩⲟⲕⲡϥ ⲉⲣⲟⲓ. *L* ? ϩⲟⲃⲕϥ (*cf ib* ⲓⲡⲉ for ⲉⲓⲃⲉ).

ϩⲟⲕⲥ *v* ϩⲱⲱⲕⲉ *scrape* **A.**

ϩⲓⲕⲏⲧ *A v* ϩⲁⲕ *sober.*

ϩⲟⲕϩⲕ *S* nn, meaning unknown : Ryl 349 7]ⲡ-ⲧⲁⲩⲡⲧⲟⲩ ⲁⲩⲱ ⲡⲁⲧⲡⲉϩϩ. (*cf* ⲁⲧ- MR 5 42).

ϩⲁⲗ *SB*, ϩⲉⲗ *S*ᶠ*A*²*F*, ϩⲁⲗ- *S* nn, with vb ⲣ, ⲉⲣ, ⲉⲗ, *deceive* : Ge 3 13 *SB*, Ex 22 16 *S*(*B* ⲥⲟⲡⲥⲡ), Is 36 14 *B*(*SF* = Gk), Eph 5 6 *SB* ἀπατᾶν, Su 56 *B*, 1 Cor 3 18 *BF*(Mor 38 4, *S* do) ἐξαπ., Gal 6 3 *SB* φρεναπ. ; Ge 29 25 *S*(*B* diff), Col 2 4 *SB* παραλογί-ζειν, BHom 35 *S* ⲙⲉⲅϣ ⲣ. ⲙⲙⲟϥ ἀπαραλόγιστος ; Sa 12 24 *S* ψεύδειν ; Mor 18 155 *S* ⲁⲓⲣ. ⲙⲙⲟⲟⲩ χλευάζειν ; Ac 8 11 *B*(*S* ⲡⲱϣⲥ) ἐξιστάναι ; Va 66 301 *B* ⲉⲣ. ⲡⲡⲏ ⲉⲧⲁⲩⲛⲁϩ⳨ ⲉⲣⲟⲥ σφάλλειν ; Ez 22 5 *SB* ἐμπαίζειν ; R 1 4 22 *S* ⲣ. ⲡⲟⲩⲙⲏⲛϣⲉ ϩⲡϥⲉⲡⲣⲁⲥⲟⲩ *deludere* ; PS 98 *S* ⲙⲡⲟⲩⲣ. ⲙⲙⲟⲥ ϩⲓⲧⲡⲗⲁⲁⲩ ⲡⲱⲃ, ShC 42 221 *S* ⲙⲡⲣⲧⲣⲉⲗⲁⲁⲩ ⲣ. ⲙⲙⲟϥ ⲟⲩⲁⲁϥ, TT 28 *S* ⲉⲩⲣ. ⲙⲙⲟⲓ ϩⲙⲡⲉⲛⲧⲁⲩϫⲟⲟϥ, BMis 395 *S* ⲙ-ⲡⲣⲣ. ⲙⲙⲟⲡ...ϩⲡⲡⲉⲓϣⲁϫⲉ = Mor 27 37 *F*, = BSM 46 *B* ⲥⲱⳉⲓ, C 43 11 *B* sim ϫⲉⲡⲡⲉⲕⲥⲁϫⲓ, Bor 248 48 *S* ⲥⲉⲟⲩⲱϣ ⲉⲣ. ⲙⲙⲟⲓ ⲉϩⲟⲩⲡ ⲉⲩϩⲱⲃ, BMis 42 *S* ⲡϥⲣ. ⲙⲙⲟⲕ ϫⲉⲁϥⲙⲓⲟ, Mani 1 *A*² pride ⲣ. ⲙⲙⲁϥ, LAp 541 *F* ⲁⲩⲉⲗ] ϩ. ⲡⲡⲓⲙⲏⲛϣ =EW 38 *B* ⲥⲱ., HL 86 *B* she could not ⲉⲣ. ⲙⲙⲟϥ ... ⲉⲡϩⲱⲃⲉⲙ ; as nn : Jer 4 10 *S*(BMOr 6954) *B* ἀπατᾶν ; BKU 1 31 9 *S* consider well ϫⲉⲡⲡⲉⲕϣⲱⲡⲉ ϩⲡⲟⲩⲣ., KroppG 5 *S* power of devil ⲡⲉϫⲉⲡⲉⲣⲅⲓⲁ ⲙⲡⲡⲉϥⲣ. ; ⲙⲡⲧⲣ ϩ. : 4 Kg 12 16 *S* πλημμέλεια ; Jer 10 15 *S*(*B* ⲉϥⲫ-ⲗⲏⲟⲩ) ἐμπαίζειν ; Mani 1 *A*² wept for ⲧⲙ. ⲉⲧⲁⲥ-ϣⲱⲡⲉ ; ⲣⲉϥⲣ ϩ. : Jude 18 *B*(var ⲣⲉϥⲥⲱ., *S* ⲣⲉϥ-ϫⲏⲣ, *A* ⲣⲉϥϫⲣⳉⲣⲉ) ἐμπαίκτης ; Mor 17 15 *S* ἐπι-θέτης ; R 1 4 33 *S* ⲣ ⲡⲁ⳨⳨ ⲡⲣ. *fallax* ; Tit 1 10 *B* ⲣ. ⲡⲣⲏⲧ (*S* ⲣⲉϥⲧⲁⲕⲉ ϩⲏⲧ) φρεναπάτης ; R 2 4 82 *S* ⳉⲩ-ⲣⲟⲥⲧⲁⲧⲏⲥ ⲡⲣ., Va 59 47 *B* devil ⲡⲓⲣ. = Mor 41 27 *S* ⲣⲉϥϩⲁⲡⲁⲧⲁ, Mor 39 7 *S*ᶠ ⲣⲉϥⲉⲗ ϩⲉⲗ ⲙⲙⲁⲧⲟⲥ = *ib* 40 5 *S* ⲣⲉϥ⳨ ϩⲁⲗϩⲟ = C 43 36 *B* ⲣⲉϥ⳨ ⲗⲁⲗϩⲟ (*cf* ϩⲟ, compounds ϩⲁⲗϩⲟ) ; ⲙⲛⲧ-, ⲙⲉⲧⲣⲉϥⲣ ϩ. : Wess 15 129 *S* ⲡⲉⲧⲡⲁⲃⲱⲗ ⲉⲃⲟⲗ ⲡⲡⲉⲕⲙ. =EW 29 *B* ἐπι-θεσία ; Mor 18 106 *S* δραματουργία of demons ; Va 57 85 *B* ⲟⲩⲁⲡⲁⲧⲏ ⲙⲙ.

ϩⲁⲗ S(rare)A², ϩⲉⲗ A, ϩⲉⲗ F, pl(?)ϩⲗⲟϭⲓⲉ S/ nn m f, *servant, slave*: Eccl 10 7 F(S ϩⲙϩⲁⲗ), Mt 13 27 F(S do, B ⲃⲱⲕ), Ap 6 15 F(Lacau, S do, B do) δοῦλος; Ryl 72 359 S Herod ⲙⲡⲉϥϩ. ⲧⲏⲣⲟⲩ, CO 436 S Paul ⲡϩ. ⲙⲡⲓ̄ⲥ̄ ⲡⲉⲭ̄ⲥ̄ (cf Ro 1 1); BM 588 F ⲁⲡⲁⲕ ⲟⲩϩ. ⲁⲡⲁⲕ ⲟⲩϣⲏⲗⲓ, CMSS 45 F ⲡⲉⲕϣⲏⲗⲓ ⲡⲉⲕϩ., ib 63 F ϥⲗ ⲙⲱⲏⲥⲏⲥ, Rec 11 147 A ⲃⲉⲛⲓⲁⲙⲓⲛ ⲡϩ., Mani 1 A² ⲛϩⲁⲗ ⲉⲧⲏⲡ ⲁⲡⲁⲡⲏⲓ; Eccl 2 7 F ϩ. ⲛⲥϩⲓⲙⲓ (S do) παιδίσκη; Mor 30 51 F ϩ. ⲛϩⲁⲟⲩⲧ, ϩ. ⲛⲥϩⲓⲙⲓ = BMis 274 S do; f: Ann 23 54 F ⲧⲉⲕϩ. ⲙⲁⲣⲓⲁ, PGol 44 F ⲧⲉⲥϩ.; pl: JEA 13 19 S-S/ ⲡⲉⲧⲕⲱ ⲉⲃⲟⲗ ⲛⲡⲉⲧⲉⲣⲟⲟⲩ ⲛⲛⲉϩϥ. (but meaning not certain); ⲙⲛⲧϩ. F, *servitude*: Lam 1 3 (S ⲙⲛⲧϩⲙϩ., B ⲙⲉⲧⲃ.) δουλεία; ⲣ ϩ.: Wess 15 129 S art come hither ⲉⲣ. ⲛϩⲣⲱⲙⲁⲛⲡⲁ = EW 29 B ⲥⲱⲃⲓ (misunderstanding S)-εύεσθαι. In name: Ἑλκούϊς (Preisigke).

ϩⲙϩⲁⲗ S, ϩⲉⲙ. S/, ϩⲙϩⲉⲗ, ϩⲏϩ(ⲉ)ⲗ A, ϩⲙϩⲉⲗ SA²F, ⲙϩⲁⲗ S(rare)B(once), ϩⲉⲙϩⲉⲗ F nn m f, *servant, slave*: Deu 32 36 (B ⲃⲱⲕ), Job 40 23 (B do), Ps 89 13 SF(CoptMusCai tablet), Pro 9 3 SA(B do), Jo 4 51 SA²(B do) δοῦλος, Ap 19 10 ϣⲃⲣϩ. (B ϣⲫ. ⲙⲃ.) συνδ.; Nu 32 4 (B ⲁⲗⲟⲩ), Ps 112 1 (B do), Is 36 11 SF(B do), Mt 14 2 (BF do) παῖς; Ge 9 25 (B ⲁ. ⲙⲃ.), Pro 22 7 SA, Ac 10 7 (B ⲃ.) οἰκέτης; Nu 12 7 (B ⲁ.), Job 19 16 (B ⲃ.) θεράπων; ShR 2 3 46 ⲁϥⲙⲁⲥⲧⲓⲅⲟⲩ ⲛϩⲁϥ ⲛϩ., ShA 2 58 shocking that ϩⲉⲛϩ. ⲥⲟⲩⲧⲛ ⲧⲟⲟⲧⲟⲩ ⲉⲃⲟⲗ ⲉⲟⲩⲱⲙ ⲛϣⲟⲣⲡ, BMar 54 ⲉⲩⲣⲱⲙⲉ ⲉϣⲱⲡ ϩ., J 104 33 ϩ. ⲛϣⲱⲡ ϩⲁⲣⲟⲙⲡⲧ, BMis 206 ⲛϩ. ⲁϥⲁⲁⲩ ⲛⲣⲙϩⲉ, ST 239 Paham ⲛϩ. ⲛⲧⲉⲕⲕⲗⲏⲥⲓⲁ, Ann 8 86 priest & ϩ. ⲙⲡⲉⲓⲧⲟⲡⲟⲥ, Lant 3 35 S/ ⲁⲡⲁⲕ ... ϥⲉⲙϩ. ⲡⲡⲟⲩⲧⲓ, ib 56 ⲡⲓⲥϩⲟⲩⲓ ⲛϩ., Rec 11 147 A ⲛⲣⲙϩ(ⲉ)ⲗ (bis), Mor 24 20 F ⲛⲉϩ. ⲓⲱⲁⲛⲛⲏⲥ, C 86 130 B ⲟⲩⲙϩⲁⲗ ⲉϥⲱϣⲡ (var WTh 156 ⲃ.), TurO 7 ⲡⲉϥⲙ.; f: Ex 21 7 (B ⲃⲱⲕⲓ), AP 15 A² δούλη; Ge 16 1, Am 2 7 A, Mk 14 66 (all B ⲃ.), Jo 18 17 SA²(B ⲁⲗ.) παιδίσκη; Lev 19 20 οἰκέτις; Job 31 13 θεράπαινα (all B ⲃ.); Aeg 253 ⲟⲩⲡⲁⲗⲗⲁⲕⲏ ... ⲧⲉϥϩ. ⲧⲉ, BM 469 S ⲧⲉⲧⲛϩⲙϩⲉⲗ, RChamp 495 ⲧⲉϥⲙ.; ϩ. ⲛⲣⲟⲟⲩⲧ, ⲛⲥϩⲓⲙⲉ: Ge 20 14 π. παιδ. (B do), Eccl 2 7 (F ϩⲉⲗ), Cl 60 2 A δου. παιδ.; ⲙⲛⲧϩ.: Deu 5 6 (B ⲙⲉⲧⲃ.), Pro 26 9 SA δουλεία; ShC 73 24 ⲧⲙ. ⲙⲡⲛⲟⲃⲉ, BAp 150 ⲙⲛ ⲗⲁⲁⲩ ⲙⲙ. ⲛⲁϣⲱⲡⲉ ⲛⲁⲛ (citing Col 2 16 ⲣ ϩⲁⲗ, l? ϩⲁⲡ), J 81 22 shall serve ϩⲛⲧⲙ. ⲛⲡⲉϥⲥⲱⲙⲁ; ⲣ ϩ. ⲥ ⲛ- dat: Deu 28 64 (B ϣⲉⲙϣⲓ), Ps 71 11 (B ⲉⲣ ⲃ.), Jo 8 33 SA²(B do), 1 Thes 1 9 SF(B do) δουλεύειν dat; ShA 2 252 ⲣ. ⲙⲡⲥⲁⲧⲁⲛⲁⲥ, CO 303 ⲡⲓⲱϣⲉ ... ⲧⲏⲣ. ⲛⲁⲕ ϩⲁⲣⲟϥ; qual: Pro 12 9 SA(B ⲟⲓ ⲛⲃ.), Ro 12 11 SF(B do), Cl 26 1 A δου. dat; Job 2 9 (B ⲉⲣ ⲃⲱⲕⲓ)λάτρις; CA 100 clergy ⲟ ⲛϩ. ⲛⲁϥ (sc altar), J 84 23 ⲟ ⲛϩ. ⲉϩⲟⲩⲛ ⲉⲡⲧⲟⲡⲟⲥ (cf 79 17 sim ϭⲁⲟⲡ); tr: Sa 19 13 ⲁⲁⲩ ⲛⲁⲩ ⲛϩ., Ac 7 6 sim(B ⲓⲣⲓ ⲙⲃ.) δου.; Miss 4 781 my sons ⲁϥⲁⲁⲩ ⲛϩ. ⲛⲁϥ, J 81 21 ⲁⲁⲩ ⲛϩ. ⲉϩⲟⲩⲛ ⲉⲡⲉⲕⲧⲟⲡⲟⲥ; ϫⲓ ⲛϩ.: Ge 43 17 (B ⲓⲣⲓ ⲙⲃⲱⲕ) εἰς παῖδα λαμβάνειν.

Cf ϣⲓⲣⲉ (ϩⲉⲣϣ.), ϩⲗⲗⲟ.

ϩⲁⲗ S nn, meaning unknown: BM 1067 lease of land ⲓⲱϩⲉ ⲛϩ. ⲉⲡⲁⲧⲗⲓⲕ (or l? ϩⲁⲗⲉ).

ϩⲉⲗ S nn m, meaning unknown: Ryl 301]ⲣ ϩⲱⲃ [...]ⲙⲡⲁϩ. ⲅⲁⲣ ⲁⲛ[.

ϩⲓⲗ F v ϩⲓⲣ.

ϩⲱⲗ SAA²BF, ϩⲏⲗ† SABF vb intr, *fly, go* (latter mostly BF): Hab 1 8 S(ϩⲁⲗⲁⲓ) πετάννύναι, Job 20 8 B(S ⲡⲱⲧ), Pro 7 10 B(S ϫⲓ ϭⲟⲥⲥ, A ϥⲓ ϭ.) ἐκπέτεσθαι; Job 30 15 S(B ϣⲉ) οἴχεσθαι; Mk 5 20 B(S ⲃⲱⲕ) ἀπέρχεσθαι; MG 25 210 B(S do) ὑπάγειν; ib 8 B ἀναχωρεῖν; Miss 4 113 B ⲛϯⲡⲁϩ. ⲁⲛ until I have entered it (sc temple, Mor 18 20 S diff), BSM 20 B ⲛ ⲧⲉⲛϩ. in shameful raiment = BMis 357 S ⲃ., C 86 19 B ϫⲛⲡⲁϩ. alive ... ⲛⲧⲉⲕⲓ dead, Ep 226 S]ⲛⲧⲁϩ. ⲡⲁϣⲛ ⲁϩⲣⲁⲓ[, KroppD 25 S of birds opp ⲟⲩⲱϩ; qual: Job 9 26 SB, Ps 90 5 S(B ϩⲁ.), Pro 9 12 SAB, Is 31 5 SB(F ϩ. ⲉⲃⲁⲗ), Zech 5 1 SA(B do) π., Ge 7 14 SB, Si 43 14 S πετεινός, Ps 77 27 S(B ⲟⲓ ⲛⲧⲉⲛϩ) πτερωτός, Aeg 276 S creatures ⲉⲧϩ. ἵπτασθαι, Is 16 2 B(S ϩ. ⲉⲃ.) ἀνίπ.; Mk 6 33 B(S ⲃⲏⲕ) ὑπάγειν; Sa 5 11 S διοδεύειν; PS 137 S ⲟⲩⲥⲟⲧⲉ ⲉϩϥ., Bor 251 293 S ϫⲗⲁⲙⲩⲥ ⲉⲧϩ. ϩⲓϑⲏ ⲙⲙⲟϥ (vision of emblems of Passion), DeV 2 236 B ark ceased ⲉϭϩ. ⲉⲥⲡⲏⲟⲩ (Ge 7 18).

With following preposition. ⲉ-: Ap 12 14 B(S ϩ. ⲉⲃⲟⲗ ⲉ-) πέτεσθ. εἰς, BHom 25 S ϩ.† ⲉⲧⲡⲉ ἀναπτερούσθαι; Jo 11 31 B(SA prob A² ⲃ. ⲉⲃ. ⲉ-), MG 25 208 B ϩ. ⲉⲕⲉⲙⲁ = Z 344 S ⲃ. ὑπαγ. εἰς; AM 277 B ϩ.† ⲉⲑⲱⲡ ποῦ πορεύεσθαι; EW 153 B ϩ.† ⲉⲛϭⲓⲥⲓ = ClPr 54 36 S ⲃⲏⲕ ⲉⲡϫ. εἰς ὕψος ἀνατείνειν; Job 10 19 B(S diff) ἀπέρχ.; PS 229 S soul ⲡⲁϩ. ⲉⲡⲭⲓⲥⲉ, MIE 2 338 B ⲙⲱⲓⲧ ⲛⲓⲃⲉⲛ ⲉⲣⲉⲡⲓⲣⲓ ϩ. ⲉⲣⲟϥ, BSM 36 B ⲛϩ.† ⲉⲑⲱⲡ = BMis 380 S ⲡⲁ, AM 22 B ⲛⲧⲛϩ. ⲉⲙⲁⲩ, Mani 1 A² eagle ϩ. ⲁⲙⲛⲏⲅⲉ, BM 590 (2) B, ib 1237 B ⲁⲓϩ. ⲉϫⲛⲧ, C 41 60 B ϩ. (ⲉ)ⲉⲣ ⲡⲟⲗⲉⲙⲓⲛ (cf ib ϣⲉ ⲉⲉⲣ ⲡ.); ⲉϩⲣⲏⲓ ⲉ- B: AM 178 ϩ. ⲉϩ. ⲉⲡⲓϯⲙⲓ, BSM 85 ϩ. ⲉϩ. ⲉⲡⲙⲱⲟⲩ for baptism = BMis 175 S ⲃⲟϣⲟⲩ ⲉⲡⲉⲥⲛⲧ; ⲉϩⲣⲏⲓ ⲉ- B: C 43 1 ⲁϥϩ. ⲉ. ⲉϯⲡⲟⲗⲓⲥ, ib 209 ⲉⲡⲓⲫⲛⲟⲩⲓ; ⲥ ⲉⲣⲁⲧ= B: C 43 244 ϩ. ⲉⲣⲁⲧϥ ⲙⲫϯ; ⲥ ⲉⲧⲉⲛ- B: BM 1227 ϥⲧⲱⲟⲩⲛ ⲉⲡⲕⲁⲥ ⲡⲧⲁϩ. ⲉⲧⲟⲧ; ⲥ ⲉϫⲛ-, *upon, over*: Ps 17 10 S(B ϩⲁ.), C 89 198 B ⲉⲟϩ. ⲉϫⲱⲓ like clouds πεταν. ἐπί; Z 345 S demons ϩ.† ⲉϫⲙⲡⲕⲟⲩⲓ (ⲛⲥⲟⲡ) = MG 25 210 B ⲡⲛⲟⲩ ⲉϩ. ἔρχεσθαι ἐπί; AM 197 B ⲉⲩⲙⲟϣⲓ ⲉⲩϩ.† ⲉ. ⲫⲓⲁⲣⲟ; ⲉϩⲣⲁⲓ, -ⲏⲓ ⲉϩ.: Ge 1 20 S(B ϩ. ϩⲓϫⲉⲛ-) π. ἐπί; Miss 4 191 B saints ⲉⲩϩ.† ⲉϩ. ⲉ. ⲡⲓⲃⲏⲙⲁ; ⲥ ⲛⲧⲉⲛ- B: DeV 1 108 fearing kingdom would not ϩ. ⲛⲧⲟⲧⲟⲩ ⲛⲡⲉϥϣⲏⲣⲓ; ⲥ ϣⲁ- B: Va 61 100 perfume ϩ. ϣⲁⲟⲩϣⲓϣϯ ⲛⲟⲅⲉⲓ, BSM 82 ϩ. ϣⲁⲧⲃⲁⲕⲓ ϯⲉⲡⲧⲓⲁⲥ = BMis 173 S ⲃⲱⲕ ⲉ-, PO 11

381 ⲉϥⲙⲟϣⲓ ⲉϩ.† ϣⲁⲡⲟⲩⲣⲟ; ⲋⲁ- B: ROC 27
162 ship ϩ. ⲋⲁⲣⲟⲛ ⲋⲉⲛⲫⲓⲟⲙ went (from) under us
(cf 2 Cor 11 25 S); ⲥ ⲋⲁⲧⲉⲛ- B: AM 181 ⲁϥϩ.
ⲋ. ⲡⲓⲁⲓⲕⲉⲟⲥ & became his disciple; ⲥ ϩⲁⲡⲉⲥⲛⲧ
ⲛ-S: LCyp 8 ⲉϥϩ.† ϩ. ⲙⲡⲉⲥⲧⲉⲣⲉⲱⲙⲁ ὑψιπετής; ⲥ
ϩⲛ-, ⲋⲉⲛ-: Is 11 14 S(var ⲛ-)B ⲡέⲧⲉⲥ. ἐν, Job 5 7†
S(B ⲉ-) ⲡέⲧⲉⲥ. acc; ShBerlSitz '29 430 S ⲉⲥϩ.† ϩⲙⲡⲁⲏⲣ, Mani 1 A² ⲕⲁ ⲡⲣⲁⲗⲁⲧⲉ ⲁϩ. ϩⲙⲡⲁⲏⲣ, BSM
68 B sun sets ⲛⲧⲉϥϩ. ⲋⲉⲛⲡⲓⲕⲁϩⲓ, C 86 344 lest ship
perish ⲛⲥⲉϩ. ⲋⲉⲛⲫⲓⲟⲙ (cf ⲥ ⲋⲁ-); ⲥ ϩⲓⲭⲉⲛ- B:
Ge 1 20 v above; AM 164 ϩ. ϩ. ⲡⲓⲏⲛⲙⲁ up on to.

With following adverb. ⲥ ⲉⲃⲟⲗ, fly, go forth or
as ϩ. alone: Ps 54 6 S(B ϩⲁⲗⲁⲓ) ⲡⲉⲧⲁⲛ., Is 30 6† SF(B
om ⲉⲃ.), Z 316 S took wings ⲁⲩϩ. ⲉⲃ. ⲡέⲧⲉⲥ., Hoʼs 9
11 A(B ϩⲁ.) ἐκπ., Is 16 2 S(B om ⲉⲃ.) ἀνίπτ., Sa 5 11
S ⲁⲓⲡⲧ; Is 41 2 S(B ϩⲓⲟⲩⲓ ⲉⲃ.) ἐξωθεῖσθαι; Lev 13
40 S(B diff) μαδᾶν; MIF 9 93 S ⲛⲡⲉⲡⲉⲕⲃⲱ ϩ. ⲉⲃ.,
Z 579 S ⲉⲣⲉⲧⲉⲩⲯⲩⲭⲏ ϩ.† ⲉⲃ. are distraught, Ep 170
S ⲉⲣⲉⲡⲁϩⲏⲧ ϩ.† ⲉⲃ. because of misfortunes, CO 339 S
sim, BKU 1 26 (81 16a)F bird's ⲕⲁⲕⲓϥ burnt ϣⲁⲩⲥⲁⲣ
ⲡⲉⲧϩⲉⲗ ⲉⲃ., BSM 41 B ⲓⲥϫⲉⲡⲉⲧⲁⲓϩ. ⲉⲃ. = BMis 386
S ⲃⲱⲕ ⲉⲃ., JKP 2 204 S of spear ⲁϥϩ. ⲉⲃ. ⲁϥⲃⲱⲕ ⲉ-
ⲡϫⲓⲥⲉ, AM 191 B open door ⲛⲧⲁϩ. ⲉⲃ.; ⲉⲃ. ⲉ-: Pro
23 5 S(A om), Ap 12 14 S(B om ⲉⲃ.) ⲡέⲧⲉⲥ. ⲉⲓⲥ; Sa
7 3 S(HT sic, Lag ϩⲱⲛ, var ⲉⲓ ⲉⲃ.) ⲥⲡⲁⲛ; C 86 124 B
ϩ. ⲉⲃ. ⲉⲡⲡⲟⲗⲉⲙⲟⲥ; ⲉⲃ. ⲉⲭⲛ- S: Bor 256 145 ⲉⲥϩ.†
ⲉⲃ. ⲉⲭⲙⲡⲉⲥⲗⲟϭ floating forth above, PBu 126 my opponent's words ϩ.† ⲉⲃ. ⲉⲭⲱϥ ⲉϥⲧⲁϩⲟ ⲙⲙⲟⲟⲩ; ⲉⲃ.
ⲡⲧⲉⲛ- B, from: Va 57 133 ⲁⲩϩ. ⲉⲃ. ⲛⲧⲟⲧϥ διαφεύγειν
acc; ⲉⲃ. ϣⲁ- B: C 41 36 ϩ. ⲉⲃ. ϣⲁⲡⲉⲡⲓⲥⲕⲟⲡⲟⲥ =
Bor 134 6 S(Vita Sin) ⲧⲁϩⲟ; ⲉⲃ. ϩⲁ- B, from: Jer
6 8 ἀφιστάναι ἀπό; ⲉⲃ ϩⲛ-, ⲋⲉⲛ-, from: Dan 2 5 B
ἀφιστ. ἀπό; DeV 2 194 B ϩ. ⲉⲃ. ⲋⲉⲛⲡⲉϥⲛⲓ; in: Bor
253 152 S eagle ϩ.† ⲉⲃ. ϩⲙⲡⲁⲏⲣ ⲡⲧέⲣⲩⲅⲁⲥ ἀνυψοῦν
ⲉⲓⲥ; R 1 4 21 S sim, Mani 1 A² birds ϩ. ⲁⲃ. ϩⲙⲡⲁⲏⲣ,
DeV 2 169 B ϩ. ⲉⲃ. ⲋⲉⲛⲡⲓⲡⲗⲁⲧⲓⲁ (sic l), ROC 25 246
B ⲡⲧⲁϣⲧⲉⲙϩ. ⲉⲃ. ⲋⲉⲛⲟⲩⲙⲏϣ ⲡⲥⲁϫⲓ, DeV 1 87 B
sim; ⲉⲃ. ϩⲓⲧⲉⲛ- B: TstAb 163 ere thou ϩ. ⲉⲃ. ϩⲓⲧⲟⲧ,
BSM 98 ⲉⲣⲉⲡϩⲁⲓ ⲡⲟⲩⲥϩⲓⲙⲓ ϩⲁⲣ. ⲉⲃ. ϩⲓⲧⲟⲥ; ⲉⲃ.
ϩⲓⲭⲛ-S, over: BMis 29 ⲡⲗⲓⲙⲏⲛ...ϩ.† ⲉⲃ. ϩ.ⲧⲉⲭⲱⲣⲁ
ⲧⲏⲣⲥ (cf above Bor 256), P 131¹ 8 Christ ϩ.† ⲉⲃ. ϩ.
ⲡⲉⲕⲗⲟⲟⲗⲉ; ⲥ ⲉⲡⲉⲥⲛⲧ B: BSM 76 ϩ. ⲉ. ⲉⲡⲓⲕⲁ-
ⲧⲁⲕⲓⲟⲡ (-ⲅⲉⲓⲟⲛ) = BMis 167 S ⲁⲙⲏⲓⲧⲛ ⲉ., C 86 152
an ell of spear ϩ. ⲉ. ⲋⲉⲛⲡⲓⲕⲁϩⲓ, ib 221 ⲟⲩϣⲓⲕ ⲉⲩϩ.†
ⲉ. ⲡⲗ ⲙⲙⲁϩⲓ; ⲥ ⲉⲡϣⲱⲓ B: AM 281 ⲁⲓϣⲁⲡ. ⲉ. ⲉ-
ⲫⲙⲁ ⲙⲡⲓⲑⲣⲟⲡⲟⲥ ἀνέρχ. ἔγγιστα; C 86 207 ϩ. ⲉ. ⲉⲡⲓ-
ⲫⲏⲟⲩⲓ, AM 323 ⲉⲣⲉⲡⲓⲣⲱⲙⲓ ϩ.† ⲉ. to be judged;
ⲥ ⲉϩⲟⲩⲛ (once), ⲉⲃ. ⲉ-: MG 25 234 ⲁⲩϩ. ⲉ. ⲉⲧⲉϥⲣⲓ
εἰσέρχ. εἰς, WHatch 351 ϩ. ⲉ. ⲉⲉϥⲉⲥⲟⲥ = Gu 69 S
ⲃⲱⲕ ⲉ. ⲉⲉϥ. εἰσέρχ. ἐν; BSM 44 ⲁϥϩ. ⲉ....ⲉⲡⲓⲙⲁ =
BMis 391 S ⲃ. ⲉ-, KroppM 14 S(obscure), C 86 320
ⲁⲩϩ. ⲉ. (var ⲉϩⲣⲏⲓ) ⲉⲡⲟⲩⲧⲁⲙⲓⲟⲛ, BSM 22 ⲉⲕϩ.† ⲉ.
ⲉⲡⲉϥⲁⲩⲗⲏⲟⲩ (varVa 63 1 ϩ. ⲉ-) = BMis 361 S ⲕⲡⲁⲃ.

ⲉ. ⲉ.; ⲉⲃ. ϣⲁ-: C 43 126 ⲁϥϩ. ⲉ. ϣⲁⲣⲟϥ; ⲥ ⲉ-
ϩⲣⲁⲓ S: AZ 23 1 13 ⲥⲁⲣⲧⲉ ϩⲁⲣⲟⲟⲩ (sc mixture ϩⲁⲗⲏⲧ?
طليق in covered bowl) ϣⲁⲡⲧⲟⲩϩⲟⲗ ⲉ. swell up (?);
ⲥ ⲧⲁⲓ B, hence: Lu 13 31 (varr ⲡⲧ., ⲉⲃⲟⲗ ⲧ., S ⲗⲟ
ⲙⲡⲉⲓⲙⲁ) ⲡⲟⲣⲉύ. ἐντεῦθεν.

ⲙⲁ ⲡϩ. S, exit: KroppD 26.

ⲙⲱⲓⲧ ⲛϩ. B, approach: BSM 82 = BMis 172 S
ϩ. vb.

ⲣⲉϥϩ. S, flyer: Deu 4 17 (B ⲉⲧⲣⲏⲧ ⲡⲧⲉⲡϩ) ⲡⲧⲉ-
ⲣⲱⲧός; Mun 180 ⲡⲉϫⲉⲓⲱⲧ ⲡⲣ.

ϭⲓⲛ-, ϫⲓⲛϩ., flight: Z 579 S ⲧϭ. ⲛⲓϭⲓϭⲗⲱ, BMis
57 S ϩⲛⲧϭⲟⲙ ⲡⲧⲉϥϭ. (cf Bel 36), P.Mich 601 S ⲧ-
ⲕⲓⲛϩ. ⲛⲟⲩⲱⲃⲧ, BSM 11 B ⲡⲓϫ. ⲉⲃⲟⲩⲡ ⲉⲡⲁⲓϫⲓⲡ-
ⲡⲟⲡ; ϭⲓⲛϩⲏⲗ ⲉⲃⲟⲗ S: Mich 550 24 of birds.

V ϩⲗⲟ.

ϩⲁⲗⲁⲓ B vb intr, fly of birds, insects: Ps 54 7 (S
ϩⲱⲗ ⲉⲃⲟⲗ) ⲡⲉⲧⲁⲛ., ib 90 5 (S ϩ.†), Dan 9 21 (S ϩ.†)
ⲡέⲧⲉⲥ., Nah 3 16 (A ϩⲱⲗ ⲁⲃ.) ἐκⲡⲉⲧⲁⲛ., Ez 39 4 ⲡⲧⲉ-
ⲧⲉⲓⲛός; MG 25 210 ϩⲁⲡⲁϥ ⲉⲩϩ. μυῖα, ib 8 ⲁⲡⲓϩⲁⲗⲏⲧ
ϩ., Mus 45 46 except they spread wings ⲙⲡⲁⲩϣ
ϩ.; ⲥ ⲉ-: MG 25 345 ⲉⲩϩ. ⲉⲡϭⲓⲥⲓ; ⲥ ⲉⲭⲛ-:
Ps 17 11 (S ϩ. ⲉⲭⲛ-) ⲡⲉⲧⲁⲛ. ἐⲡί; ⲥ ϩⲓⲭⲛ-: Va 57
175 ϩ. ϩ. ⲛⲓϩⲣⲱⲙⲓ; ⲥ ⲉⲃⲟⲗ: ib 258 ⲥⲉϭⲟϫⲓ ⲥⲉϩ.
ⲉⲃ. ἀφίⲡⲧⲉⲥθαι; BSM 129 ⲁⲥϩ. ⲉⲃ. ⲋⲉⲛⲡⲓⲛⲓ; ⲥ
ⲉⲡϣⲱⲓ V₃ 61 104 birds ⲙⲡⲁⲩϣ ϩ. ⲉ., FR 98 ϩ.
ⲥⲁⲡϣⲱⲓ ⲙⲙⲟϥ; as nn v next.

ϩⲁⲗⲟⲩⲅⲗⲓ B nn m, flight of bird: K 170 ⲡⲓϩ. (var
Montp 128 ⲡⲓϩⲁⲗⲁⲓ) طيران.

ϩⲱⲗ SB, ϩⲱ(ⲱ)ⲗⲉ S, ⲋⲱⲗ B vb intr, be hoarse:
Ps 68 3 SB ⲋ., cit BHom 71 S ϩⲱⲱⲗⲉ βραγχιᾶν; K
355 B ⲁⲥⲋ. حسر (sic l Pey); C 89 182 B ⲧⲁϣⲃⲱⲃⲓ ϩ.,
KroppE 29 S prayer for ⲟⲩϩⲣⲟⲟⲩ ⲡⲁⲧϩⲱⲗⲉ, BM 590
B ⲥⲡⲁϩ ⲡⲕⲟⲣⲟⲩ ⲡⲁⲧϩⲱⲗ (here?). V AZ 62 46. Cf
ϩⲉⲗϭⲓⲗⲉ & ϩⲱⲗ 4°.

ϩⲱⲗ, ϩ(ⲉ)ⲗ-, ϩⲟⲗ- S, ϩⲁⲗ- Sᶠ, ϩⲟⲗ⸗ S, ϩⲁⲗ⸗ Sᵃ A²F
vb tr, throw, bring: ShMIF 23 28 snake ⲡⲁϣ ϩⲉⲗ
ⲙⲟⲟⲩ (sc poison) ϣⲁⲧⲱⲡ?, ShP 130² 6 builders ϩⲗ
ⲟⲙⲉ, ⲡⲡⲧ ⲧⲱⲃⲉ, Miss 4 750 sand & water ⲉⲧⲣⲉϥϩ.
ⲙⲡϫⲟⲓ ⲡⲣⲏⲧⲟⲩ, RE 9 166 Sᵃ ⲁϥϣⲁⲡⲟⲩ ⲉⲣⲟⲓ ϫⲉ ⲁⲣ-
ϩⲁⲗⲟⲩ (sic l), Rec 6 65 ϣⲁⲕⲟⲩⲱϣ ⲑⲓⲛ ⲣⲱⲙⲉ, ϣⲁⲕⲟⲩⲱϣ ϩ. ⲡⲡⲉⲕⲥⲱⲙⲁ, v also ϩⲗ ⲟⲩⲱ ⲣ 475 a; ⲥ
ⲉ-: Miss 4 695 fruit of palm ⲛⲥϩⲟⲗϥ ⲉⲡⲕⲁϩ, BKU
1 26 (81 17) F ⲡⲱⲡⲓ (sic l)...ϩⲁⲗϥ ⲉⲡⲏⲣⲡ, Miss 4 751
ⲙⲙⲟⲟⲩ ⲁⲩϩⲟⲗⲁ ⲉⲡⲭⲟⲓ (cf ib 750 above); Mor 30 22
F Julian took blood ⲁϥϩⲁⲗϥ ⲉϩⲣⲏⲓ ⲉⲧⲡⲉ ῥίⲡⲧⲉⲓⲛ ⲉⲓⲥ
= BMis 247 S ⲡⲟϫϥ ⲉϩⲣⲁⲓ; ⲥ ⲉⲃⲟⲗ: Bodl(P)b 4
ⲁϥϩⲟⲗ ⲡⲉⲭⲏϥ ⲉⲃ. (no context), Mor 51 42 reapers
say ⲡⲧⲉⲡϩ. ⲡⲧⲕⲁⲗⲩⲃⲏ ⲉⲃ. & will return, ib 31 50 Sᶠ
she-camel sprang up ⲉⲥϩⲁⲗ ⲡⲟⲥϭⲉ ⲉⲃ. till reached
(other) camels, AM 327 B Susanna ⲉⲩϩ. ⲙⲙⲟⲥ ⲉⲃ.
ⲉⲧⲁⲕⲟⲥ, Wess 20 141 = PGM 2 181 F ⲉⲕⲉϩⲁⲗϥ ⲉⲃ.
(ⲡ)ⲑⲏ ⲡⲡⲓϩⲁⲗⲉⲧⲓ; ⲥ ⲁⲡⲁϩⲟⲩ: Mani 1 A² ⲁⲓϩⲁⲗⲧ ⲁ.

ϩⲱⲗ *S* nn, meaning uncertain : AJSL 46 247 ⲧⲡⲓϣⲉ ⲡⲕⲱϩⲧ, ⲧⲡ. ⲛϩ. *V* ⲡⲁⲓϣⲉ. *Cf* ? ϩⲱⲗ 2°.

ϩⲱⲗ, ϩⲟⲗ⸗ *B* sometimes for ⲱⲗ, ⲟⲗ⸗.

ϩⲁⲗⲁ *Sᶠ* vb tr, meaning unknown : BKU 1 21 heat water, put dye-stuff therein ⲛϩ. ⲛⲡⲓⲧⲟⲥ (ⲉⲓ̂ⲇ.) ⲉⲡⲉⲥⲏⲧ (*cf ib* ⲛ̄ⲛⲉϩ…ⲉⲡⲉⲥⲏⲧ). For χαλᾶν?

ϩⲁⲗⲉ *S*, ϩⲁⲁⲗⲓ *F* *v* ϩⲟⲟⲗⲉ.

ϩⲁⲗⲉ *SB* nn m, in place-names : ⲛϩ. (EW 85), ⲧⲉⲣⲱⲧ ϩ. (Ryl 196 n).

ϩⲁⲗⲏ *B* nn m, *miserly person* (?) : Bodl 325 154 (= Tatt 881) among *varia* ⲛϩ. ϫⲉ. Or ? ⲗʲϫⲉ.

ϩⲁⲗⲱ *S* vb intr c ⲉϩⲣⲁⲓ, meaning unknown : ST 359 ⲙⲁⲣⲉⲡⲕⲁⲙⲟⲩⲗ ⲧⲁϩⲟⲓ ⲛⲣⲁⲥⲧⲉ ⲙⲙⲟⲛ ⲁⲛⲣⲱⲙⲉ ϩ. ⲉϩⲣⲁⲓ.

ϩⲉⲗⲉ⸗, ϩⲓⲗⲉ⸗ *F* *v* ⲣⲟ(ϩⲓⲣⲡ-) & ϩⲁ 1° *s f*.

ϩⲉⲗⲓ, ϩⲉⲗ(?)*B* nn f, *fear* (cf ᒡⲛ AZ 50 89) : Job 13 11(*S* diff)δειλία; ϯ ϩ., *give fear, frighten* : Lev 26 36 (*S* ϩⲟⲧⲉ) δ. ἐπάγειν; Pro 13 3 (*SA* ϣⲧⲟⲣⲧⲣ), Jer 25 37 πτοεῖν; 2 Cor 10 9 (*S* ⲑⲣϣⲟ) ἐκφοβεῖν; ϩⲓ ϩ., *emit fear, terrify* : MG 25 4 ⲉⲣⲉⲣⲱϣ ϩ. ⲉⲃⲟⲗ φόβον ἀποβάλλειν, Va 63 17 ⲙⲡⲉⲣ ϩ. ⲉⲣⲟⲛ = BMis 395 *S* ϩⲓ ⲗⲁ = BSM 46 *B* ⲥⲱⲃⲓ; ϭⲓ ϩ. (?) : EW 172 ⲁϥ]ϭⲓ ϩⲉⲗ ⲉⲣⲱⲟⲩ saying Ye are spies (Ge 42 9).

ϩⲉⲗⲱ *v* ϩⲗⲗⲟ (ϩⲗⲗⲱ).

ϩⲏⲗⲉ *S* nn, a measure or container of bread : PLond 4 516 ⲟⲩϩ. ⲛⲡⲟⲉⲓ[ⲕ.

ϩⲟⲉⲓⲗⲉ *v* ϩⲟⲉⲓⲣⲉ.

ϩⲟⲟⲗⲉ, ϩⲟ. *S*(once), ϩⲁⲗⲉ *S*(once)*A*, ϩⲟⲗⲓ *B*, ϩⲁⲁⲗⲓ *F*, -ⲉ *Sᶠ* nn f m(once), *moth* : Job 32 22 *B*(*S* ϫⲟⲟⲗⲉⲥ), Pro 25 20 *SA*, cit ShMIF 23 88 ϩⲟⲗⲉ, Is 33 1 *SBF*, Mic 7 4 *SAB*, Mt 6 19 *SBF*(Rec 11 116), Lu 12 33 *S*(var ϫ.)*B*, Va 66 297 *B* ϣⲱⲡⲓ ⲛϩⲣⲉ ⲛ̄ϯϩ. σής; EpJer 11 *BF* βρῶμα tinea; Is 14 11 *B*(*S* ϫ.) σήψις; Pro 12 4 *S*(var*Sᶠ*)*A*(*B* Gk om), ⲣ, ⲉⲣ ϩ., *be moth-eaten, perished* : Job 19 20 *B*(*S* ⲗⲟϭⲗⲉϭ), EpJer 72 *F*(*B* ⲗ.) σήπειν, Job 13 28 *S*(*B* diff) σητόβρωτος; MG 25 246 *B* head ⲟⲓ ⲛϩ. through disease βιβρώσκειν; Sh(Besa)Bor 204 245 *S* sheep ⲉⲧⲟ ⲛϩ., Va 61 110 *B* ⲛⲉϥⲕⲁⲥ ⲉⲣ ϩ., C 86 245 *B* ⲡⲓ(ϣ)ϣⲏⲛ ⲉⲧⲁⲅⲉⲣ ϩ. = *ib* 302 ⲗ., C 43 68 *B* ϩⲃⲱⲥ ⲛⲁⲉⲣ ϩ., Mor 40 35 *S* books ⲁⲩⲣ ϩ. ⲉⲧⲃⲉⲡⲉⲭⲣⲟⲛⲟⲥ, Pcod 41 *S* led astray in their reason ⲉⲣⲉⲧⲉⲩϩⲉⲗⲡⲓⲥ ⲟ ⲛϩⲁ. = *F* ⲡⲓⲥⲧⲓⲥ ⲁⲓ ⲛϩ., BMis 50 *S* God's words ⲙⲉⲩⲣ ϩ. ⲉⲛⲉϩ; ⲁⲧⲣ, ⲉⲣ ϩ.: *incorruptible, indestructible* : Deu 10 3 *B*(*S* ⲙⲉⲩⲣ ϫ.), Is 40 20 *B*(*S* do) ἄσηπτος; Miss 8 234 *S* ⲥⲧⲉϥⲁⲛⲟⲥ ⲛⲁ.

ϩⲱⲗⲉ *S* nn f, meaning unknown : Kr 228 20 of ἀποθήκη to be disposed of ⲟⲩϩ. ⲉⲥⲡⲁϣⲧⲡⲓ ⲧⲁⲓ ⲉⲕⲥⲱⲕ ϩⲁⲣⲱⲥ (ⲱ for ⲟ often in this text), ST 55]ⲛⲧⲁϯ ⲟⲩϩ. ⲛⲁⲕ[same ?

ϩⲱⲱⲗⲉ, ϩⲱ., ϩⲁⲗ-, ϩⲟ(ⲟ)ⲗ⸗ *S*, ϩⲁⲗ⸗ *Sᶠ* vb tr, *pluck* : ShC 73 54 ⲉⲅⲱⲣⲥ ⲛⲣⲉⲛⲕⲁⲙ, ⲉⲩϩ. ⲛⲣⲉⲛⲃⲏⲧ, *ib* 109 sim, BP 9448 ⲁⲓϩⲱ. ⲡⲗⲓϫⲉ ⲛⲗⲁⲯⲁⲛⲉ, BMOr 6201 A 72 when flax hath grown we will come ⲧⲛϩⲟⲟⲗⲟⲩ ⲛⲁⲕ, Ryl 160 of flax (?) ⲧⲁϩⲟⲟⲗⲉϥ ⲧⲁⲥⲟⲙⲉϥ ⲧⲁⲕⲟⲕⲕϥ, Cai invent 218 account ⲛⲉⲡⲧⲁⲑⲱⲙ[ⲁⲥ] ϩⲟⲗⲉϥ, Ann 21 74 ⲡⲕⲟⲩⲓ ⲙⲙⲁϭⲉ ⲛ̄ⲧⲣⲉⲩϩⲁⲗⲉϥ, Cai CoptMus 1784 *Sᶠ* ⲁⲩⲧⲁⲙⲟⲓ ϫ(ⲉ)ⲁⲧϩⲁⲗ(*l* prob ⲁⲩϩ.) ϣⲟⲩⲕⲣⲉ ϥⲟ̄, R 1 5 35 to blasphemer ⲡⲱϫⲉ ⲛⲥⲉⲣ. ⲙⲡⲉⲕⲗⲁⲥ; ϩⲱⲗ ⲉⲃⲟⲗ (*l* ? ϩⲱⲗⲉ): ROC 7 143 ⲉⲩϩ. ⲉⲃ. ⲡⲥⲁⲛⲉⲃⲱ ⲛⲧⲉϥⲙⲟⲣⲧ, Mor 32 40 sim.

ϩⲱⲱⲗⲉ, ϩⲟⲗⲉ† *S*, ϩⲁ.† *Sʳ* vb intr, meaning unknown (prob not all same): BHom 12 man's nature to ϩ. ⲛⲟⲩϩⲱⲃ, but it is of Satan to ⲙⲟⲩⲛ ⲉⲃⲟⲗ ϩⲙⲡϩⲱⲱⲗⲉ (*ib* 309 3 ـوا كـلمـا / آيـه, Gkom, paral πίπτειν), CO 129 ⲛⲕⲟⲩⲥⲟⲡ ⲉⲧϩ.†…ⲡⲉⲧⲛⲁϩ. ϯⲛⲁϫⲟⲟⲩ ⲛⲁⲕ, *ib* 94 *Sᵃ* if God grant ⲛⲧⲁⲕⲃⲁϩ *that I recover* I will come, ⲉϣⲱⲡⲉ ⲧⲉϩ.† ϯⲛⲁ ⲡⲁⲕⲁ[ⲧⲁ]ϫⲓⲕⲏ (sic).

ϩⲗⲓ, ⲉϩ. *B*, ϩⲗⲉⲓ *A*, ϩⲓⲗ *F*(once)nn, used as pron, mostly = *S.A.A²F* ⲗⲁⲁⲩ *q v*, also *F* ⲗⲁⲡⲥ, ⲗⲁⲡϯ. **I** positive, *anyone, -thing, something*, without art : Ep Jer 33 (*F* ⲟⲩⲉⲉⲓ), Ac 21 37 (*S* ⲟⲩϣⲁϫⲉ) τις, Va 57 13 ϩ. ⲙⲡⲁⲓⲣⲏϯ ἄλλο τι; EpJer 45 (*F* diff) ἄλλος; AM 125 ⲁϩ. ⲟϩⲓ ⲥⲁⲃⲟⲗ, BSM 45 ⲛⲧⲉⲛϭⲓ ϩ. ⲛ̄ⲧⲟⲧⲕ = BMis 394 *S* ⲗⲁⲁⲩ (var Bor 155 ⲟⲩⲗ.); with indef art : Ge 19 12 (*S* diff), Lev 4 2 (*S* ϩⲱⲃ), Va 57 99 ⲓⲛⲓ ⲉϩⲟⲩⲛ ⲛⲟⲩϩ. τις, τι; C 89 123 ⲟⲩⲟⲛ ⲟⲩϩ. ⲛⲏⲟⲩ ⲉϫⲱϥ, *ib* 41 21 ⲁⲓⲡⲁϫⲓⲙⲁ ⲛⲉϣⲡ ⲛⲟⲩϩ. ?, Rec 6 180 ⲙ̄ⲫⲣⲏϯ ⲛⲟⲩⲉϩ.; as adj + ⲛ-: Ac 25 11 τι, Job 4 12 (*S* ϣⲁϫⲉ) τι ῥῆμα, 3 Kg 17 12, Ez 15 5 no Gk; Cat 217 ϩ. ⲛⲭⲣⲓⲥⲧⲓⲁⲛⲟⲥ, C 89 122 ⲕⲉϩ. ⲛⲉϩⲏⲟⲩⲓ; ϩ. ⲛⲓⲃⲉⲛ: TThe 193 of anchorite ⲁⲕⲣⲓ ⲛⲣⲟ ⲛϩ. ⲛⲓⲃⲉⲛ, Cat 13 ϩ. ⲛⲓⲃⲉⲛ ⲙⲡⲁⲑⲟⲥ; partitive : Ac 4 32 ϩ. ⲛⲧⲉ ⲡⲉϥ ϩⲩⲡⲁⲣⲭⲟⲛⲧⲁ (*S* diff) τι τῶν, ROC 17 405 ϩ. ⲛ̄ ⲛⲁⲓ τι τοιοῦτον; Va 57 182 ⲟⲩϩ. ⲛⲧⲉ ⲟⲩⲉⲧⲛⲓⲙⲁ (αἴτ.); K 172 ϩ. ⲉⲃⲟⲗ ϩⲉⲛⲡⲏ ـٔ.

II negative, *nothing* : Nu 20 19 (*S* ⲗ.), Job 26 7, 1 Cor 7 19 (*SF* do), MG 25 216 ⲁⲛⲟⲕ ϩ., Va 57 259 ϩ. ⲡⲉ ⲫⲃⲓⲟⲥ οὐδέν; AM 87 worldly obedience ϩ. ⲡⲉ; with art : Ps 38 6, Is 40 23, Hos 7 16 (*F* ⲛ̄ⲡⲓⲉ), Ac 5 36 (all *S* ⲗ.) οὐδέν; C 86 163 world is ⲙ̄ⲫⲣⲏϯ ⲛⲟⲩϩ., *ib* 43 231 ⲡⲉⲕⲃⲁⲥⲁⲛⲟⲥ ϩⲁⲛϩ. ⲡⲉ; partitive : Va 61 27 ⲉϥϫⲱ ⲛϩ. ⲛⲃⲏⲧⲟⲩ ⲉⲣⲱⲧ *suffering none* of herbs *to grow*.

III with Copt neg (oftenest), *no one, nothing*, without art : Ex 2 12 *AB*, Jos 23 9 (*S* ⲗ.), Mt 11 27 (*S* do), Jo 13 28 *BF* ⲙⲡⲉϩⲗⲓ ⲉⲓⲙⲓ (PMich 3521, *SA²*

do), Cl 27 5 *A* οὐδείς, Jer 47 15, Gal 6 3 (*S* do) μηδείς, Mt 9 33 (*S* ογⲟⲛ); Ez 34 28 (*S* ⲗ.)ⲟⲩⲕ...ⲟ̔; 1 Kg
2 2 ⲙⲙⲟⲛ ϧ. ⲉϧⲟⲓ (*S* ⲙⲛ ⲕⲉ-) ⲟⲩⲕ εἶναι; AM 273
ⲡⲧⲉϣⲧⲉⲙ ϧ. ⲉⲙⲓ μή τις; ib 87 ⲙⲡⲉⲣⲧⲁⲙⲉ ϧ., C 43
186 ⲡⲉⲙⲙⲟⲛ ϧ. ⲡⲉⲙⲁⲥ, MIE 2 419 ⲙⲡⲓⲥⲁϫⲓ ⲡⲉⲙ-
ϧ.; with art: Va 57 259 ⲙⲡⲉϥⲟⲡⲥ ⲉⲟⲩϧ. οὐδείς;
AM 226 ⲉⲡⲛⲁϣⲱ ⲁⲡ ⲡⲟⲩϧ.; ⲕⲉϧ.: Va 57 243
ⲡⲕ. ⲁⲡⲡⲉ ⲉⲃⲏⲗ ⲉ- ⲟⲩ̔δ.; C 43 111 ⲙⲡⲉϥϫⲁ ⲕ. ⲡⲣⲱⲃ
ⲡⲁϥ; as adj + ⲛ-: Ex 10 15, Job 16 18, 1 Cor 8 4
(*SF* ⲗ.) ⲟⲩ̔δ., Pro 2 12 (*SA* do), He 10 2 (*SF* do) μηδ.;
Cl 52 1 *A* needeth not ϧ. ⲛⲡⲗⲁϩⲉ οὐδὲν οὐδενός; MG
25 58 ⲡⲉϧ. ⲁⲡⲡⲉ, Dan 6 23 πᾶς; ib 3 92 no Gk; C 43
93 ⲙⲙⲟⲛ ϧ. ⲡⲓⲕⲁϩ in his body, ib 86 94 ⲕⲁⲧⲁ ⲉϧ.
ⲡⲥⲙⲟⲧ, Mus 34 199 ⲙⲡⲉϫⲉ ⲉϧ. ⲡⲥⲁϫⲓ, AM 19 ⲉϣⲧⲉⲙⲉⲣ ϧ. ⲙⲡⲉⲧϩⲱⲟⲩ, DeV 2 55 χωρὶς ϧ. ⲙⲙⲉⲧ-
ⲣⲉϥϭⲛⲁⲩ; partitive: Jer 49 17 ⲙⲡⲉϧ. ⲛϩⲏⲧⲟⲩ
ⲟⲩϫⲁⲓ αὐτῶν, Ro 14 7 ⲙⲙⲟⲛ ϧ. ⲙⲙⲟⲛ ⲡⲁⲱⲡⲃ
ⲟⲩ̔δ. ἡμῶν; BSM 43 ⲙⲙⲟⲛ ϧ. ϩⲉⲛⲡⲏ = BMis 390 *S*
ⲗ.; ⲁⲧϧ., *without any*: CDan 92 ⲉⲕⲟⲓ ⲡⲁ., HL
112 ⲁ. ⲡⲗⲟⲕⲗⲉⲕ.

IV advb, *at all*: 1 Cor 10 25 ⲡϧ. (*S* ⲗ.) μηδέν, Va
57 134 riches ⲉⲣ ⲱⲫⲉⲗⲓⲛ ⲙⲙⲟϥ ⲡϧ. οὐδέν, Bel 6
οὐδέποτε; Jer 7 4 ⲡϧ. τὸ παράπαν; Va 61 107 fire did
not ⲥⲓⲧⲟⲩ ⲛϧⲟⲓⲥ ⲡϧ., AM 122 words ⲡⲁϯ ϩⲛⲟⲩ
ⲡⲱⲧⲉⲛ ⲁⲡ ⲡϧ. ⲉⲡⲧⲏⲣϥ.
Concord. m: Jer 39 17 ϧ. ϥⲡⲁϩⲱⲛ, ib 28 43 ⲡⲡⲉϥ-
ϣⲱⲡⲓ ⲛϫⲉ ϧ., Ez 4 14 ϧ. ⲉϥϭⲁϫⲉⲙ; pl: DeV 2 149
ϧ. ⲛⲫⲁⲛⲟⲥ ⲉⲅⲙⲟϭ, C 89 147 ϧ. ⲙⲙⲉⲅⲓ...ⲉⲑⲣⲟⲅⲁ-
ⲗⲏⲓ ⲉϧⲣⲏⲓ.

ϧⲁⲗⲃ- *A²* vb p c in ϧⲁⲗⲃϧⲟ, *deceiver* or sim:
Mani 1 ⲟⲩϧ.ⲡⲉ ⲡⲕⲟⲥⲙⲟⲥ, ib be not beguiled ϩⲛⲡⲉϥⲙⲁ ⲡⲓⲱⲣϩ ⲏ ϩⲛⲡⲉϥⲙⲁ ⲡⲥⲱⲧⲙⲉ (ⲏ) ϩⲛⲧⲉϥⲙⲡⲧ.

ϧⲁⲗⲓⲃ, -ⲓϥ *S* nn, *casting-net*: CaiCoptMus 88
glossary ref to fishing ⲡⲟⲩϧⲟⲣⲉ, ⲡⲉϣⲡⲏⲅ, ⲧⲁⲃⲟ, ϧ.
ⲑⲁⲣⲧ, ⲡϣⲱⲡⲉ, CO 353 ⲧⲕⲟⲩⲓ (sic) ⲡϧⲁⲗⲓϥ.

ϧⲁⲗⲃϣⲉ *A²*, ϩⲉⲗ(ⲗ)ⲓⲃϣ, -ⲉⲃϣ *B* nn f, *breastplate*: Job 41 4, Is 59 17, 1 Thes 5 8 (var -ⲉⲃϣ, all
S ϧⲱⲕ)θώραξ; TEuch 1 174 ϩⲣϭ; ManiH 12 *A²* ⲉ-
ⲣⲉⲑ. ⲙⲡⲟⲗⲉⲙⲟⲥ ϧⲓⲱⲟⲩⲉ, ib 77 ⲁⲩϯ ⲑ. ⲁⲭⲡϧⲁⲓⲙⲉ, ib
8 ⲡⲟⲩⲣⲱⲙⲉ ⲡⲁϫⲓ ϧ. VSpg *Petubastis* Gloss no 235.

ϧⲁⲗⲁⲕ *SB*, -ⲉⲕ *S/F*, -ⲏⲕ *S*, ⲁⲗⲁⲕ *S*(? once)*B* nn
f, *ring* (cf ﺣﻠﻖ, ﺣﻠﻘﺔ): Ex 30 4 *B* ⲁ. ψαλίς (as if ψέλλιον); 4 Kg 19 28 *B* ϧ. (DeV 1 180) ἄγκιστρον;
Job 40 21 *SB* ϧ. ψέλλιον; ib *B* ϧ. (*S* ϣⲧⲟϥ) κρίκος;
Ez 16 12 *S*(*B* ⲗⲉⲟⲥ)τροχίσκος; C 41 19 *B* ⲕⲱⲗϩ ⲉϯⲁ.
=Miss 4 338 ﺣﻠﻘﺔ *door-knocker* (cf ⲙⲟⲩϭ BAp), K
127 *B* ⲡⲓⲁ. ﺃﻁﺮﺍﻕ metal *discs of nurâg* (AZ 12 124),
AM 260 *B* ⲡⲧⲁⲥⲱϫⲡ ⲙⲡⲉⲕϣⲁⲓϩⲉⲛⲟϧⲁ. (cf Is 37 29),
ShA 2 157 *S* luxurious monks ⲉⲩⲙⲏⲣ ⲡⲣⲉⲡⲙⲏⲛϣⲉ
ⲡϧ. ⲉⲡⲉⲩⲥⲟⲩⲛⲁⲣⲓⲟⲛ (*l* ϩⲱⲡ.), AM 147 *B* ϧⲁⲛϩ. ⲡⲉⲙ-
ϧⲁⲛⲛⲟϩ through martyrs' heels, PMich 3552 *S/*

ⲥⲡⲧ(ⲉ) ⲡϧ., ST 118 *S* ϧ. ⲡⲙⲁⲁϫⲉ, Ryl 243 *S* ⲟⲩϧⲁ-
ⲗⲏⲕ ⲡⲟⲩⲣⲓⲧⲉ, BM 708 *F* ϧ. ⲡⲁⲗ ϩⲉϧⲓ (?),Va 61 25 *B*
ⲁ. ⲡⲥⲱⲟⲩⲧⲉⲛ ⲛ ⲁⲗⲟϭ (but ⲁ. here prob = ⲁⲗⲟⲕ),Mor
46 21 *S* martyr in ship ⲁⲩⲡⲟϫϥ ⲉⲡⲁ. ⲉϧⲣⲁⲓ ⲉϫⲙⲡⲉϥ-
ⲡⲁⲧ (or ? = ⲁⲗⲟⲕ) ... ⲁⲩⲡⲟϫⲧ ⲙⲙⲟϥ ⲉⲡⲟⲅⲉⲛⲧ.
In names (?): Πανϧάλεκ, Τανϧάλεκ (Preisigke).

ϧⲱⲗⲕ *SBF*, -ⲗϭ, ϧⲟⲗⲕϭ *S*, ϧⲟⲗⲕ †*B* vb tr, *twist,
roll, braid*: ShIF 66 *S* ⲉⲁ[ⲧⲉ]ⲧⲡϧⲟⲗⲕϭ ⲡⲑⲉ ⲡⲟⲩϣⲧⲏⲡ
[ⲙ]ⲡⲟⲩⲡⲣⲏϣ, Bor 258 103 *S* Judith ⲁⲥϧ. ⲙⲡⲉⲥⲃⲱ
(in Jth 10 3 prob ϣⲱⲙ), Mor 41 99 *S* Herodias &
daughter ⲉⲩϧ. ⲙⲡⲁ̔ⲱ ⲡⲧⲉϧⲁⲡⲉ, DeV 1 155 *B* ⲟⲩϭⲓⲣⲁ
ⲉⲩϧ. ⲙⲙⲟⲥ; qual: MG 25 135 *B* deformed animals ⲉⲩϧ.† ⲉⲣⲉⲧⲟⲩⲙⲟⲣⲧ ϧⲓϫⲉⲡⲡⲟⲩⲥⲟⲓ; c ⲉ- *B*:
C 43 136 deformed woman's hand ϧ. ⲉⲣⲟⲥ (but prob
= Mor 48 72 *S* ⲱⲗⲕ ⲉ-); c ⲉϫⲉⲛ- *B*: Ex 28 14
πλέκειν ἐπί; c ⲡⲥⲁ- *B* emphatic: DeV 1 28 ⲉⲥϧ.
ⲡⲥⲁⲡϧⲱⲓ of daughter's head (cf Mor 41 above).

—— nn m, *twist, plait, hook*: Cant 7 5 *F*(*S* ϥⲱ)
πλόκιον, P 43 38 *S* ⲡⲣⲟⲕⲓⲟⲥ · ϧⲡϧ. ﺩﻻﻟﺔ, but = 44
68 ⲩⲡⲟⲕⲟⲙⲓⲟⲛ (*l* ⲩⲡⲟ.) · ϧⲡϧ. ⲡϥⲱ ﺩﻻﺋﻞ, Ex 39 18
B, Is 3 18 *SB* ἐμπλόκιον, 1 Pet 3 3 *B* ⲓⲉⲃ ⲡϧ. ⲡⲧⲉ ⲡⲓ-
ϥⲱⲓ (*S* ϧ. only, var BMis 114 -ϭ) ἐμπλοκὴ τριχῶν,
1 Tim 2 9 *SB* πλέγμα; K 354 *B* ϧⲟⲗⲕ ﻇﻔﺎﺋﺮ; R 1 2 38
S ⲛϣⲕⲓⲗ ⲙⲡⲡϧ. point to fornication, Mor 43 251 *S*
ⲕⲟⲥⲙⲏⲥⲓⲥ, ϧ., ϧⲟⲩⲣ.

ⲙⲉⲧϧⲟⲗⲕ *B*, *twisting* of cord &c: K 138 ⲙ.
among currier's or bookbinder's processes.

ϧ(ⲉ)ⲗⲕⲟⲩ *S*, ϧⲁⲗ. *SB*, ⲉⲗ. *F* nn f m, *sickle*: 1 Kg
13 20 *S* ⲧⲉϥϧ., Ap 14 18 *S* ⲑ.(var ⲟϧⲥ, *B* ⲥⲛϥⲓ) δρέπανον; K 127 *B* ⲡⲓϧ. ﻣﻘﻠﻢ (1 var ﻣﻘﻠﺪ), P 44 98 *S* ϧⲁⲗ.,
Montp 163 *B* ϧ. ﻣﻨﺠﻞ (*v* ϧⲣⲟⲃⲓ); ShA 1 384 *S* Kronos emasculated father ϧⲛⲟⲩϧ., BMOr 6230 (45) *S*
in list (cf PLond 4 no 1631) ⲥⲩⲡⲧⲉ ⲡϧⲉⲣⲕⲟⲩ ⲡⲟϧⲥ,
PMich 4545 *S* in list ϧⲁⲗ. ⲅ, CMSS 76 *F* ⲉⲗ. ⲡⲱϧⲥ.

ϧⲟⲗⲕⲓ *B* nn m, *catapult* (?), since between ⲥϥⲉⲛ-
ⲧⲟⲡⲓ & ⲙⲁⲛⲕⲁⲡⲓⲕⲟⲛ: K 117 ⲡⲓϧ. ﺣﺮﺝ (so most
MSS. Cf Almk 1 293 for different meaning).

ϧⲓⲗⲁⲕⲙⲓ, ϧⲩⲗ., ϧⲁⲗ. *B* nn m, *blear-eyed person*:
AZ 14 61 ϧⲓ., K 160 ϧⲩ., P 54 172 ⲡⲓϧⲁⲗ. ﺩﻣﻊ.

ϧⲟⲗⲟⲕⲱⲧⲥⲓ &c *v* ⲗⲟⲕϧⲟⲭⲓ.

ϧⲗⲟⲗ, ⲉϧ. *B*, ϧⲗⲁⲗ *F* nn m, *darkness*: Lev 13 21
(*S* ⲕⲣⲙⲣⲱⲙ, gloss ⲧⲁϧⲧϧ) ἀμαυρός; Ac 13 11 (*S*
ϧⲃⲥ) ἀχλύς paral ϧⲁⲕⲓ; Ps 147 5 (*S* ⲡⲓϥ), Is 29 18
(*S* ϧⲗⲟⲥⲧⲡ) ὁμίχλη; K 255 ⲡⲓϧ. ﺿﺒﺎﺏ; ROC 25 242
ⲟⲩϧ. ⲉⲡⲓⲃⲁⲗ, DeV 2 186 sim, C 86 126 ⲡⲓⲉϧ. ⲛϫⲁⲕⲓ
covered eyes; ⲉⲣ, ⲓⲗ, ⲟⲓ ⲡϧ., *become, be darkened*:
Deu 34 7 (*S* ⲣ ϧⲗⲟⲥ.), Lam 4 1 *BF* ἀμαυροῦσθαι; Lev
13 56 (*S* ⲕⲣ.) -ρός; Mic 4 8 (*S* ShP 130⁵ 43 ϣⲟⲃⲉ, *A*
ϣⲁ.)αὐχμώδης;Va 57 165 ⲡⲟⲩϧⲁⲗ ⲟⲓⲡϧ. ἀμβλυωπής;
DeV 2 181 eyes ⲉⲣ ϧ. ⲁⲥⲉⲣ ⲃⲉⲗⲗⲉ, Va 57 200 ⲟⲓ ⲡϧ.

ⲟⲩⲟϩ ⲡⲗⲓϫ ⲉⲡⲓⲟⲩⲱⲓⲛⲓ;   c e-: Ge 27 1 ⲉⲣ ϩ. ⲉϥ̄ⲡⲁⲩ ἀμβλύνειν gen; Is 44 18 sim (S ⲣ ⲃ̄ⲗⲗⲉ) ἀπαμαυρ. gen.

ⲑⲗⲟⲅⲗ B nn m, meaning uncertain: K 255 حقاف barber (? Egyptian), var (4 MSS) حقاف shoemaker, var (2 MSS) حقاف ridge of sand (or l 'ـﺐ). Kabis AZ 14 61 reads ﺟﻔﺎف dryness.

ϩⲁⲗⲓⲗ (hardly legible now) A nn, beetle (?): Hab 2 11 (S P 44 116 (ⲟⲩ)ⲁⲙⲟⲣⲏⲣⲉ q v, B = Gk) κάνθαρος, but var σκώληξ (cf? Berl Wörterb 3 150 hrrw, hrrt).

ⲑⲗⲏⲗⲓ F v ϧⲣⲏⲣⲉ.

ⲑⲗⲟⲉⲓⲗⲉ, -ⲉⲓⲗ, ϧⲣⲟⲉⲓⲣⲉ, ϧⲗⲉⲉⲓⲗⲉ, ϧⲉⲗⲉⲓⲗⲉ S, ϧⲗⲁⲓⲗⲉ Sᶠ, ϧⲗⲱⲓⲗⲓ (once), ⲗⲱⲓⲗⲓ B vb intr, be borne, float: Ac 27 17B(var ϧ., Sdiff)φέρεσθαι, Ge 7 18S(MS ϧⲗⲟⲟⲗⲉ, var ϣⲉⲉⲓ, B om)ἐπιφ.; Z 349 S when cast into water ⲁⲛⲟⲅⲁ ⲙⲡⲱⲛⲉ ϧ., BMEA 10587 S(Greg Naz) ⲡⲡⲉⲡⲓⲡⲉ ϧⲣ. (cf 4 Kg 6), BAp 87 S fish in water ⲉϧ. = MIE 2 359 B ⲛⲟⲙⲡⲓ, Cai 42573 2 Sᶠ recipe ϣⲁⲡⲧⲉⲡⲡⲉϧ ϧ. ⲧⲏⲣϥ; tr, bear S: MG 25 419 crocodile carrying man ⲁϥϧⲗⲁⲉ. (sic MS) ⲙⲙⲟϥ ϧⲙⲡⲓⲉⲣⲟ, BAp 134 Flood ϧ. ⲙⲡⲥⲱⲙⲁ ⲡⲁϫⲁⲙ, Mor 43 116 sim; c ⲉϫⲛ-: Mor 31 101 S ⲡⲉⲥⲕⲉⲩⲉ ⲉⲩϧⲗⲟⲉⲓⲗ ⲉϫⲙⲡⲡⲉϥ, DeV 2 229 B ark λ. ⲉ. ⲛⲓⲙⲟⲟⲩ; c ϧⲛ- HM 1 7 S stone ϧⲗⲟⲉⲓⲗ ϧⲙⲡⲙⲟⲟⲩ like ship; c ϧⲓⲣⲛ-: 4 Kg 6 6 S ἐπιπολάζειν; c ϧⲓⲡⲣⲁ-: P 129¹⁶68 S stone ϧ. ϧⲓϧⲣⲁϥ ⲙⲡⲙⲟⲟⲩ; c ϧⲓϫⲛ- S: SHel 29 boat -ⲗ ϧ. ⲑⲁⲗⲁⲥⲥⲁ, Bodl(P)a 2 19 recipe ⲡⲉⲧⲉϣⲁϥϧⲉⲗ ϧⲓϫⲱⲡⲙⲟⲟⲩ, ib 16 sim ϧⲉⲗϧⲓⲗⲉ; ⲣⲉϥϧⲗ. B, swimmer: K 113 عوام.

ⲗⲱⲓⲗⲓ B nn f (p 142 a), tail, buttocks: K 78 ✝ⲗ. الية does not belong here.

ⲑⲗⲟⲟⲗⲉ, ϧⲗⲱⲗⲉ (once) S, ϧⲗⲟⲗⲓ B (rare) vb tr, nurse, carry child: Ru 4 16 εἰς τιθηνὸν γίνεσθαι; BM 920 266 B ⲡⲉⲧⲟⲩϧ. ⲙⲙⲟϥ ﺣﻤﻞ; Bor 258 7 on Mary's knees, ⲉⲥϧ. ⲙⲙⲟϥ, ib 259 86 carrying child ϧⲓϫⲛⲡⲉⲥϭⲓϫ ⲛⲥϧ. ⲙⲙⲟϥ, BMis 9 ϧⲗⲙⲟⲟⲡⲉ ... ⲉⲧⲣⲉⲩϧ. ⲙⲙⲟⲟⲩ, P 131⁵ 105 ⲡⲉⲣⲉⲟⲩϧⲓϧⲁⲗ ⲛⲥϧⲓⲙⲉ ϧ. ⲙⲙⲟⲥ, BM 228 30 ⲛⲑⲉ ⲡⲟⲩⲉⲓⲱⲧ ⲉϥϧ. ⲙⲡⲉϥϣⲏⲣⲉ (on Lu 16 22), Aeg 12 ⲡⲉϭⲗⲟⲟⲧⲉ ⲡⲧⲁ ϧ. ⲙⲙⲟⲓ till I grew up, J 79 29 mother says ⲁⲓ ϧⲗⲱⲗⲉ ⲙⲡⲉⲓϣⲏⲣⲉ ϣⲏⲙ ⲁⲓⲛⲧϥ ⲉϧⲣⲁⲓ; with preposition: ShA 2 177 ϧ. ⲙⲙⲟϥ ϧⲓⲧⲛⲁϧⲃ (var P 131⁴ 142 ϧⲛ-) ⲛ ⲡⲉⲥⲡⲓⲣ ⲡⲟⲩϭⲣⲓⲙⲉ; KKS 583 ⲁⲓϧ. ⲙⲙⲱⲧⲛ ϧⲓⲛⲁϭⲓϫ; Lam 4 5 ϧ. ⲙⲙⲟⲟⲩ ϧⲓϫⲛⲡⲓⲕⲟⲕⲕⲟⲥ (B ϣⲁⲡϣ) τιθηνεῖν; BMis 122 Virgin ϧ. ⲙⲙⲟϥ ϧⲓϫⲛⲡⲉⲥϭⲓϫ; intr: R 1 2 27 of Virgin ⲁⲥ✝ ⲛⲁⲗⲕⲉ, ⲁⲥⲥⲁⲁⲡϣ, ⲁⲥϧ.; ϧ. ⲉϧⲟⲩⲛ ⲉ-: BMar 220 v ⲡⲟⲕⲡⲉⲕ; as nn m: P 44 87 ⲡⲉϧ. حضن (var 43 69 ـﻀ̆ـ, cf ϧⲁⲗⲟⲗⲓ); ⲣⲉϥϧ. S, nurse: Is 49 23 (B ⲣⲉϥϣⲁⲛϣ) τιθηνός. Cf LMis 282, 305, 357.

ⲑⲗⲗⲟ SA², ϧ. A, ϧⲉⲗⲗⲟ A², ⲥ̄. B, ϧⲉⲗ(ⲗ)ⲁ, ϧⲗ(ⲗ)ⲁ F, f ϧⲗⲗⲱ S, -ⲟⲩ SSᵃ, ϧⲗⲗⲟⲅ A, ⲥ̄ⲉⲗⲗⲱ B, pl ϧⲗⲗⲟⲓ S, ϧⲗⲗⲁ(ⲉ)ⲓ A, ⲥ̄ⲉⲗⲗⲟⲓ B, ϧⲉⲗⲗⲟⲅⲓ F & sg as pl, nn, old person (opp ϧⲣϣⲓⲣⲉ, ⲥ̄ⲉⲗϣ., v ϧⲁⲗ): Is 3 5 SB, Lu 1 18 B(S ⲣ ϧ.) πρεσβύτης, Deu 28 50 SB, Is 47 6 SB -βύτερος; MG 25 215 γέρων; Va 61 17 B ἀρχιμανδρίτης; ShC 73 122 S ⲡϧ. (sc abbot) ⲙⲛ ⲡⲉⲥⲛⲏⲩ, ShC 42 157 S ⲉⲅⲉⲧⲁⲙⲟⲓ ⲛ ⲛⲥⲉϫⲟⲟⲥ ⲉⲡϧ., MIE 2 383 B ⲛⲓⲥ̄. = BAp 107 S ⲡⲟϭ ⲡⲣⲱⲙⲉ, Pcod 18 S ⲁⲡϧ. ⲡⲁⲣⲱⲙ ⲣ ϧⲁϧ ⲛⲥⲟⲙ, AP 26 A² ⲟⲩϧ., Mor 40 39 S young saints called ϧ. because of piety = MG 25 266 B ⲛⲓⲥ̄ⲉⲗⲗⲟⲓ, BIF 22 107 F spare not ⲁⲗⲟⲩ ⲟⲩⲇⲉ ϧⲗⲗⲁ, CMSS 39 F ⲡⲉⲓϧⲗⲁ ⲥⲁϥϧⲁⲅⲡⲓ, ib 78 F ⲓⲱϧⲁⲛⲛⲏⲥ ⲫⲉⲗⲁ, Mor 27 11 F ⲡϧⲗⲁ; sg as pl: Job 29 8 S(B pl), Ps 148 12 S(B do), Pro 20 29 S(A pl), Ac 2 17 S(B do), MG 25 218 B ⲛⲓⲥ̄. ⲛⲧⲉ ⲡⲓⲧⲟⲟⲩ, BM 511 F ⲡⲉⲣⲉⲗⲗⲁ; f: AM 277 B, MG 25 215 B γραῦς; ShC 73 62 S ⲑ. (abbess) ⲙⲛ ⲕⲉⲥⲟ ⲛⲛⲟϭ ⲛⲥϧⲓⲙⲉ, ShMich 550 19 S ⲑ. ⲙⲛⲧⲉⲧⲛⲧⲏϣ ⲡⲙⲙⲁⲥ, Sh(?)Mor 54 90 S ⲟⲩϧ. (var ClPr 39 41 ⲛⲟϭ ⲛⲥϧⲓⲙⲉ, v CA 142), Win 13 Sᵃ ⲁⲛϧⲗⲗⲟⲅ ⲃⲱⲕ, Ora 4 25 S ⲃⲱ ⲡϧⲉⲗⲱ in recipe; pl: Jer 38 13 B(S sg) πρεσβύτης, Joel 1 14 A(S do, B = Gk) -βύτερος; Job 32 9 BF(P Mich 29) γέ.; Ex 24 9 S(B ⲛⲡⲣⲉⲥⲃ̄.), Jth 4 8 S(var sg) γερουσία; ShP 130¹ 141 S ϧⲉⲛⲕⲉⲛⲟϭ ⲛⲥϧⲓⲙⲉ ⲁⲩⲱ ⲡⲕⲉϧ., ShA 2 269 S ⲡⲕⲉϧ. ⲧⲏⲣⲟⲩ ⲉⲧϧⲁⲧⲏⲓ, ManiH 10 A² ⲡϧ., C 43 222 B ⲥ̄., ⲁⲗⲱⲟⲅⲓ, Hall 71 S ⲡⲉⲡⲓⲥⲕⲟⲡⲟⲥ ⲙⲛ ⲡϧ.; as adj, before nn: Ge 44 20 B πρεσβύτερος; Z 314 S ϧ. ⲡⲣⲱⲙⲉ γέ., BMis 540 S sim γηραλέος; BIF 13 105 S ϧ. ⲙⲙⲁⲛⲉⲥⲟⲟⲩ = MG 25 288 B, C 89 40 B ⲥ̄. ⲛⲥϧⲓⲙⲓ, BMis 446 S ϧⲗⲗⲟⲅ ⲛⲥ., Saq 317 S ϧ. ⲙⲙⲁⲩ, Leyd 215 S ϧ. ⲡⲉⲓⲱⲧ; after nn: Jud 19 16 S πρεσβύτης; 1 Tim 4 7 SB γραώδης; ShCambrUnivLibrAdd 1876 2 S Antonius ⲡⲉⲡⲉⲓⲱⲧ ⲡϧ., TT 118 S ⲣⲉϥⲕⲣⲙⲣⲙ ⲡϧ., ST 437 Sᵃ ⲧⲉϧⲉ ϧ., TstAb 161 B ⲓⲱⲧ ⲛⲥ̄.

ⲙⲛⲧϧ., ⲙⲉⲧⲥ̄., old age: Ge 15 15 SB, Ps 70 9 SB, Pro 16 31 SA γῆρας; Pcod 40 SF promising thee ⲟⲩϧ.; f -ϧⲗⲗⲱ: Pro 24 52 SA, Lu 1 36 SB, ROC 17 406 B ⲧⲁⲙ. γῆ.; ShC 73 26 S ⲙ. of Sarah, Mor 41 66 S of Elizabeth; pl(?): BM 185 1 S ⲧⲙⲛⲧϧⲃ̄ⲣⲣⲉ, ⲧⲙⲛⲧϧⲉⲗⲗⲟⲓ, ib 891 B ✝ⲙⲉⲧⲥ̄ⲉⲗⲗⲟⲓ of Jacob.

ⲣ ϧ., ⲉⲣ ⲥ̄., become, be old: Job 14 8 S(B ⲁⲓⲁⲓ), Jo 21 18 SB, He 8 13 SBF γηράσκειν, Is 46 4 SB καταγ., Jo 3 4 SA²B γέρων εἶναι; Jos 23 1 SB πρεσβύτερος; BG 28 S ⲡⲁⲓⲱⲛ ⲉⲧⲉⲙⲉϥⲣ ϧ., ViK 9557 S ⲡⲉⲡⲥⲕⲁⲫⲟⲥ ⲡⲧⲁϥ ϧ. ⲉϧⲟⲩⲛ ⲉⲡⲗⲓⲙⲛⲉ (l ⲗⲓⲙⲛⲏ), Mani H 86 A² ⲙⲁϥ ϧ., DeV 2 94 B ⲁⲡⲁⲓⲱⲧ ⲉⲣ ⲥ̄., C 41 31 B ⲉⲣ ⲥ̄. ⲡⲣⲱⲙⲓ; f: Ge 18 13 SB, Pro 23 22 SA γηρ.; ROC 17 400 B ⲑⲏ ⲉⲧⲁⲥⲉⲣ ⲥ̄. παρῆλιξ, J 68 39 Sᵃ ⲧⲁⲙⲁⲩ ⲁⲥⲣ ϧ.

As name: ϧⲗⲗⲟ, -ⲱ, ⲉⲗⲗⲱ (J pass), Ἑλλῶς, Φελῶς, Φελό (Preisigke), ϫⲉⲗⲱ (Cai 8196), ϧⲟⲩⲗⲟ,

ⲭⲱⲗⲟ, ⲭⲟⲅⲗⲟ, ⲧⲣⲟⲅⲗⲟ (Ep 401 n). In place-name : ⲡⲟⲩⲱϣ ϩⲗⲗⲟ (Saq 1912 p 49).

ϩⲁⲗⲱⲗⲓ (most MSS) -ⲟⲗⲓ, ϩⲉⲗⲟⲗⲓ, ϩⲁⲗⲱⲟⲩⲗⲓ (P 54 160, Montp 200, cf ϩⲱⲗ 1° s f) B adj, *light, frivolous*: K 231 eϩⲣ. طائش.

ϩⲁⲗⲗⲟⲩⲥ v ϩⲁⲗⲟⲩⲥ.

ϩⲁⲗⲱⲙ SA²B(once)F, -ⲟⲙ S, ⲁⲗⲱⲙ B nn m, *cheese*, now حلوم جبنة : Job 10 10 SB τυρός, C 99 141 S = C 89 47 B τυρίον χλωρόν = Va ar 172 29 'چ; K 200 B ⲡⲓ ⲁ. حالوم, جبن, P 54 163 B ⲡⲓ ⲁ. مصنوعات; BAp 107 S shepherd brings ϩⲉⲛϩ. = MIE 2 383 B ϩⲁⲡⲕⲟⲩϫⲓ ⲛⲁ. = PO 22 389 'چ, ShC 73 172 S ϫⲓⲣ, ⲧⲃⲧ, ϩ. allowed to sick, Va 63 14 B ϩ. = BSM 41 B ⲁ., Mani 2 A² unclean foods ϩ., ⲥⲁⲩϩⲉ, ⲧⲃⲧ, C 86 172 B ⲁ. eϥϩⲉϫϩⲱϥ, PCaiCoptMus 4 (4) S ϩ. ⲛⲃ̄ⲛ̄ⲡⲉ (not prob), ST 189 S gift to bishop (?) ⲡⲉⲓⲉⲗⲁⲭ(ⲓⲥⲧⲟⲥ) ⲛϩ., BM 1073 S as rent (as in Wess 20 116), Ryl 158 38 S sim; containers, measures : Mor 51 41 S no ϩ. ϩⲁⲡⲡⲉⲙⲉⲃⲁⲥⲱⲛ(quid? ἡμι-?), RE 9 176 S, WS 152 S ⲟⲣⲕⲟⲛ (ὄργ.), ib ⲁⲥⲕⲁⲗⲱⲡⲉ, ib 153 ⲕⲟⲗⲁⲑⲉ, ib 180 ⲥⲕⲉⲅ, ib 136 ϩⲟⲧⲥ, Bodl(P)d 47 S ⲗⲁⲕⲟⲛ ⲛ̄ϩⲁⲗⲟⲙ, BM 653 F ⲕⲉⲣⲁⲙⲙⲓ; ⲥⲁ ⲛϩ.(?) F : Aberdeen UnivLibr pap ⲛⲥ]ⲁ ⲛϩ.

Cf ⲧⲣⲟⲅⲁⲛ.

ϩⲱⲗⲙ, ϩⲉⲗⲉⲙ-, ϩⲟⲗⲙ⸗ B vb intr, *seize*: Lev 19 13 (S ⲧⲱⲣⲡ), Ps 49 22 (S do), ἁρπάζειν, Ez 22 29 διαρ.; Va 57 175 ϣⲁⲥⲭⲱⲣⲝ ⲉϩ.; tr : Job 20 19 (S do), Mt 13 19 (S do, F ϥⲓ), Jo 6 15 (SA² do), ἁρ., MG 25 196 ϩ. ⲡⲟⲩⲕⲟⲩϫⲓ ⲛⲥⲣⲟⲙ ἀφαρ., Is 5 17 (SF ⲧ.), Zeph 2 9 (A ⲧ.) διαρ., Ac 6 12 (S ϭⲱⲡⲉ) ⲥⲩⲛⲁⲣ.; Is 42 24 (S ϣⲱⲗ) προνομεύειν; Job 12 5 (S do) ἐκπορθεῖν; CDan 91 thy head ⲛⲧⲟⲩϩⲟⲗⲙⲉⲥ ἀπολλύναι; Va 66 312 ⲁⲩϩ. ⲓⲉ ⲁⲩⲕⲱⲗⲡ ⲛⲛⲉⲛⲭⲁⲓ of poor, C 86 344 ⲁⲡⲓⲑⲛⲟⲩ ϩ. ⲙ̄ⲡⲓⲭⲟⲓ.

With following preposition or adverb. ⲥ ⲉ- : Am 1 11 (A = Gk), 2 Cor 12 4 (S ⲧ. ⲉ-) ἁρ. εἰς; MIE 2 419 ⲁⲩϩ. ⲙ̄ⲡⲉϥϩⲟⲩⲥ ⲉⲡϫⲓⲥⲓ, MG 25 306 sim ⲉϩⲣⲏ ⲉ- = BIF 13 115 S ⲧ., DeV 2 141 ϩ. ⲛ̄ⲧⲁⲓϩⲓⲕⲱⲡ ⲉϩⲣⲏ ⲉⲭⲛⲙⲓ; ⲥ ⲛ̄-dat : Cai Euch 483 ⲁⲓϩ. ⲛⲏⲓ ⲛ̄ϯⲁ ⲡⲟ ⲫⲁⲥⲓⲥ ἁρ., Ps 43 11 (S ⲧ. ⲛ̄-) διαρ. dat, EW 153 ⲁϥ]ϩⲱⲗⲉⲙ (sic l) ⲡⲁϥ ⲙ̄ⲡ[ⲓϩⲙⲟⲧ = ClPr 54 36 S ⲧ. ⲡⲁϥ ⲡⲧⲉⲭⲁⲣⲓⲥ ὑφαρ.; ⲥ ⲉⲃⲟⲗ ⲛ̄- : Mic 3 2 (S ⲧ. ϩⲓ-, A ⲧ. ϩⲓⲭⲛ-) ἁρ. ἀπό; ⲥ ⲛⲥⲁ- : C 86 270 ϩ. ⲛⲥⲁⲡⲓⲣⲉϥϭⲓ ϣⲉⲡⲡⲟⲩϫⲓ ⲇⲁⲣⲁⲧⲟⲩ ⲡⲛⲓϣⲛⲟⲩⲓ ⲥⲩⲛⲁⲣ.; ⲥ ⲡⲧⲉⲛ- : Va 66 304 ϩ. ⲡⲟⲩⲙⲉⲣⲟⲥ ⲡⲧⲟⲧⲩ ⲙ̄ⲡⲓⲧⲣⲁⲡⲡⲟⲥ ἁρ. gen; C 43 91 ϩⲟⲗⲙⲉϥ ⲡⲧⲉⲛⲡⲉϥⲓⲱⲧ; ⲥ ϣⲁ- : 2 Cor 12 2 ϩⲉⲗⲉⲙ- (S ⲧ. ϣⲁ-) ἁρ. ἕως; ⲥ ϩⲉⲛ- : Pro 6 25 (SA ⲧ. ϩⲓ-) ⲥⲩⲛⲁⲣ. ἀπό; C 43 40 ϩ. ⲙⲙⲟϥ ϩⲉⲛⲡⲉϥϩⲁⲗⲁⲩⲝ *by his feet*; ⲉⲃⲟⲗ ϩⲉⲛ- : Ac 23 10 (S ⲧ. ⲉⲃ. ϩⲛ-) ἁρ. ἐκ, Jer 21 12 (S do) διαρ. ἐκ; DeV 2 100 ϩ. ⲡ̄ⲡⲓⲯⲩⲭⲏ ⲉⲃ. ϩⲉⲛ-

ⲣⲱϥ; ⲥ ⲉⲃⲟⲗ ϩⲓⲧⲉⲛ- : Jude 23 (S ⲧⲱⲕⲙ ϩⲛ-) ἁρ. ἐκ; ⲥ ⲉⲡϣⲱⲓ : AM 191 ϩⲟⲗⲙⲉϥ ⲉ. ⲉⲃ. ⲇⲉⲛⲡⲓ-ⲡⲁⲗⲗⲁⲧⲓⲟⲛ.

—— nn m, *rapine, spoil*: Lev 5 21 (S = Gk), Is 3 14 (S ⲧ.), He 10 34 (S do) ἁρπαγή, Nu 14 3 (S ϭⲱⲣⲙ), Zeph 1 13 (A ⲧ. vb) διαρ., Ps 61 11 (S ⲧ. vb) ἅρπαγμα, Phil 2 6 (S ⲧ.) -μός; Is 6 13 (S ϣⲱⲗ), ib 10 6 (S ⲟⲗⲥ) προνομή; Ez 38 13 σκῦλον; TstAb 259 ⲡⲓϭⲓ ⲛ̄ϭⲟⲛⲥ ...ⲡⲉⲙⲡⲓϩ.

ⲣⲉϥϩ., *seizer, ravener* : 1 Cor 6 10 (S ⲣⲉϥⲧ.) ἅρπαξ; C 86 109 death ⲛⲓⲣ. ⲛ̄ⲛⲓⲯⲩⲭⲏ; as adj : Ge 49 27 (S do), Mt 7 15 (S do) ἁρ.; C 43 42 ϩⲁⲗⲏⲧ ⲛⲣ. = Mor 39 17 S do, Va 63 104 opp ⲣⲉϥϯ; ⲙⲉⲧⲣⲉϥϩ. : Cat 18 those that live in ⲟⲩϩ. called dogs (on Mt 7 6), DeV 2 54 among sins ⲟⲩϩ.

ϫⲓⲛϩ. : Va 57 13 ⲡⲓϫ. ἁρπάζειν.

(ϩⲱⲗⲉⲙ), ϩⲉⲗⲉⲙ- S vb tr, *meaning unknown* : Mor 51 33 (parable) ⲁⲛⲕⲁ ⲡ̄ⲡⲟⲩϩ ⲡⲁⲧⲏⲣ ⲉϩⲣⲁⲓ ⲁⲛϩ. ⲡ̄ⲡⲟⲩϩ ⲡⲡⲟⲃ̄ⲗⲥ, (interpret) we abandoned strict rules, we entreated them to work.

ϩⲗⲱⲙ, ⲗ̄ϩⲱⲙ², ϩⲗⲟⲙ³ S, ⲗⲉϩⲗⲏⲙ⁴, ⲗⲉⲗ.⁵, ⲗⲉϩⲗⲉⲙ⁶ B nn m, *louse, flea*: Ex 8 12 B⁵(var⁶), ib 13⁴(var⁵) قمل, Ps 104 31 S¹(var²)B⁴(varr⁵ ⁶) σκνίψ; P 44 57 S ⲡⲉϩ.³ صرصار = BM 491; ShA 2 246 S ⲡⲉϩ.¹ as lowest of creation, Cat 147 B ⲕⲟⲩϫⲓ ⲛ̄ϩⲱⲟⲩⲧⲥ ⲡⲗ.⁵ on which ravens feed (Lu 12 24). Cf ⲉⲧⲛⲏϣⲓ 1°.

ϩⲁⲗⲙⲉ A² (Mani) nn f, *spring, fountain*: H 29 ⲧⲉ. ⲙⲙⲁⲩ ⲁⲩϣⲉⲕⲧⲥ, K 90 ϯⲡⲁ[ⲧⲉⲧ]ϩ. ⲉⲧⲁⲡ ⲃⲉⲃⲉ ⲡ̄ⲡⲉⲧⲁⲃⲉ, ib 64 sim. In name : Παθάλμε (var -ει Preisigke). Cf ϩⲟⲛⲃⲉ.

ϩⲁⲗⲙⲏ B nn as pl, *meaning unknown* : PO 14 325 withdrew from enticements of flesh eϥⲕⲱⲣϥ ⲛ̄ⲡⲉϥϩ. ⲙ̄ⲙⲁⲓϥⲛⲟⲃⲓ. Same ? as next.

ϩⲁⲗⲙⲓ B nn m, *dung, slime*: Ez 4 12 (S ⲙⲏ ⲟⲉⲓⲕ) βόλβιτον κόπρου; P 54 173 ⲡⲓϩ. وحل, قذر, MG 25 301 ⲟⲩⲙⲁ eϥⲟⲓ ⲛ̄ϩ. where camel fell = BIF 13 111 S ⲟ ⲛ̄-ⲥⲕⲟⲣⲁⲕⲓⲣ ϥⲩ = Psyr 235 47 ܠ̈ܘܩ ܐ ܚ ܠ ܘ ܐ(Polotsky). Job 39 6 ⲙⲁ ⲛ̄ϩⲁⲗⲙⲓ (sic l) ἁλμυρίς prob = Gk & in following ἅλμη : Va 68 187 ⲙⲱⲟⲩ ⲛ̄ϩ. ⲡⲧⲉ ⲡⲁⲓⲟⲙ, MG 25 160 ⲓⲟⲙ ⲛ̄ϩ. (sic l) & murky. Cf Rec 39 167.

ϩⲉⲗⲙⲏ,¹ ϩⲉⲣ.² (once), ϩⲉⲣⲙⲉⲥ³ S nn m, used in Copto-Arabic dying recipe : Bodl(P)a 1 e ϩ.¹ ⲡⲥⲟ-ⲫⲟⲥ (var³ ib 3 43, cf ⲕⲁϩ ⲡⲥ., ⲟⲙⲉ ⲡⲥ., ϩⲙⲭ ⲡⲥ.), ib f sim (var² ib 3 17), ib e ⲕⲟϭ ⲛ̄ϩ.¹ eϭⲟ ⲡϣⲓⲃⲉ (v ϣⲛⲃⲉ or ϣⲉⲡϭⲉ, var³ ib 3 44), ib c grind together gold & silver filings (ⲁⲗⲡⲟⲩⲗⲁⲧⲉ تراب), ϩ.¹ & copper, ib e (ⲟⲩ)ⲱϣⲙ ϩ.¹ ⲡ̄ⲣⲏⲧϥ (sc hot acid, var³ 3 48) ϣⲁⲡⲧⲉⲕⲗⲱ ⲉⲕⲡⲁϥ ⲉⲣⲟϥ eϥⲱ ⲡⲥⲱⲙⲁ. Prob not = ϩⲁⲗⲙⲓ since ⲥⲟⲧ used here (ib a 1 a, b, f, a 2 51, 65), nor = ἅλμη (v last word). Perhaps = ἑρμῆς *mercury* (though ⲥⲁⲡⲁⲕ زيبق ib a 1 g & in sim PChass; cf Berthelot *Chim du*

Moyen Âge 2 6, 4-12, JA '93 2 295 ⲙⲱⲟⲓⲟⲓ; but *ἑρ. arsenic* PHolkham 63).

ϩⲟⲙⲛⲙ *S*, ϩⲗⲁ. *A²* vb intr, *be entangled*: Mani K 125 *A²* ⲡⲗⲓϭⲙⲉ (*quid?*) ⲙⲁϩ. ⲁⲣⲟⲩⲛ ⲙⲛⲡⲧⲣⲟⲭⲟⲥ ⲉϥⲕⲱⲧⲉ; as nn m, *complication, entanglement*: Mus 40 256 world, its snares & ⲡⲉϩ. συμπλοκή; Mich 166 9 lest Lord destroy thee & lest ⲡⲉϩ. ⲉⲧϣⲟⲟⲡ ⲁⲙⲁⲣⲧⲉ ⲙⲙⲟⲕ. *Cf?* ϩⲁⲗⲙⲓ *slime*.

ϩⲉⲗⲙⲓⲥ *v* ⲙⲓⲥ, adding P 44 93 ⲛϩ. دعاميس (*l ﻣﻴﺼ-*). ϩ. *S* nn f, *different, v* ⲙⲁⲛⲕⲉ, ⲟⲩⲁϩⲣⲉ.

ϩⲁⲗⲙⲏϩⲉ¹, -ⲙⲏϩ², -ⲙⲉϩⲉ³, -ⲙⲉϩⲛ⁴, ϩⲉⲗⲙⲉϩⲉ⁵ *S*, ϭⲉⲗⲙⲉϩⲓ *B* nn f, *boat*: Ac 27 16 *B*(var ϭ. ⲛⲧⲉ ⲡⲓϫⲟⲓ, *S* = Gk) σκάφη; Saq 369¹, *ib* 373³(ⲗⲓϩⲉⲣⲡⲟⲥ, ϫⲟⲓ, ϣⲁⲧⲟⲟⲡⲧϥ also in these ostr), PFrankfurt 43 (copy Spg) ⲁⲕⲕⲱ ⲧϩ.¹ ⲉⲡⲁ[ϩⲟⲩ, CO 198 ⲑ.³, Ep 338⁴, PCaiCoptMus 4 (6) among *varia* ϩⲁⲥⲕⲁⲗⲉ ⲡⲕⲏⲡⲁⲣⲓⲥⲟⲥ ⲉϩ.² ϫⲟ[ⲓ, ViK 4707 ⲡϫⲟⲓ ... ⲙⲛⲑ.⁵ ⲁⲩⲱ ⲉⲧϩⲉⲡⲗⲉϩⲉⲣⲡⲟⲥ[(*sic?*). *Cf* θαλαμηγός.

ϩⲓⲗⲉⲛ- *F* v ⲣⲟ(ϩⲓⲣⲛ-).

ϩⲗⲟⲡ *S*, ϩⲗⲁⲡ *A*, pl ϩⲗⲟⲟⲡ *A* nn m, *vessel for pouring*: Zech 4 2 *A* ⲥⲁϩϥ ⲛϩ. (*S* ϫⲟⲗϩⲥ, *B* ⲗⲁϩⲉⲙ), *ib* 12 ⲛϩⲗⲟⲟⲡ (*SB* do) ἐπαρυστρίς; CO 472 *S* ⲟⲩϩ. ⲡⲟⲩⲧⲁϩ.

ϩ(ⲉ)ⲗⲡⲉ *S*, ϩⲏⲗⲡⲓ *Sⸯ*, ϩⲗⲡⲉ *A²*, ϭⲉⲗⲡⲓ, -ⲃⲓ *B*, ϩⲉⲗⲡⲓ, -ⲉ *O* nn f, *navel*: Job 40 11 *SB*, cit Br 267, ShA 1 396 *S*, MG 25 114 *B*, Cant 7 3 *S* ὀμφαλός; Lev 3 9 *B* ⲡⲉⲧⲥⲁⲡⲉⲥⲏⲧ ⲛⲑⲗϩ. (*S* ⳨ⲡⲉ) ὀσφύς; AZ 21 100 *O* ⲑⲉⲗⲡⲓ (gloss -ⲉ) ⲛⲟⲏ, BM 178 *S* ⲑ. of Virgin is baptismal font, R 2 1 71 *S* ⲟⲩϩ. ⲉⲡⲉⲥⲱⲥ ⲉⲥϣⲧϣⲱⲧ, Mor 51 11 *Sⸯ* ⲧⲉⲩϩ., *ib* *S*, MG 25 89 *B* as high as ⲧⲉⲩϭ.= Gött ar 114 22 ﻗﺎﺑﺖ, MIE 2 348 *B* ⲁⲧⲉⲥϭⲉⲗⲃⲓ ⲫⲱϭ, ManiK 90 *A²* ⲧⲉⲩϩ., BKU 1 1 *vo* *S* ⲡϣⲙⲧϣⲉ ⲙⲗⲟⲩⲧ ⲉⲧⲕⲟⲧⲉ ⲉⲧϩ. In name: Παθέλπε (Preisigke).

ϩⲗⲟⲡⲗ(ⲉ)ⲡ *S*, ⲗⲁⲡⲗⲉⲡ (once), ⲁⲗ., ⲁⲗⲁϩⲗⲉϩ *B*, ϩⲗⲡⲗⲱⲡ✓, ϩⲗⲉⲡⲗⲱⲡⸯ *S*, -ⲗⲁⲡⲧⸯ *Sᵃ* vb intr, *be weary, despondent*: Jer 15 9 *B* ⲗ. (*S* ⲉⲡⲕⲁϩⲉⲓ ἐκκακ.) ἀποκακεῖν; Z 290 *S* sitting in cell ⳨ϩ.ⸯ, BM 247 *ult* *S* ⲡⲓⲉⲧⲛⲯⲩⲭⲏ ϩ. saying When shall God hear?, ViK 9516 *S* while they talked ϩⲓϩ. ἀκηδιᾶν; ViK 4727 *S* neglect not τόπος for ⲧⲓϩ.ⸯ παραροκ, EW 194 (6) *B* to uphold commandments ⲡⲧⲉϥϣⲧⲉⲙϩⲁⲗ., Ep 271 *S* ϩⲓϩ. ⲡϩⲏⲧ; tr *S*, *weary, plague*: Jud 16 16 (P 44 108, var ϩⲟⲭϩ) στενοχωρεῖν (var παρενοχλεῖν); MMA 23 3 706 pray for me ⲙⲙⲟⲛ ⲡϩⲁⲗⲙⲱⲛ ϩ. ⲙⲙⲟⲓ; c ⲉ-: Mor 51 41 *S* ⲙⲡⲉⲣⲧⲣⲉⲡⲉⲕϩⲏⲧ ϩ. ⲉⲣⲟⲕ, OLZ '03 68 *Sᵃ* ⲡⲁϩⲏⲧ ϩ.ⸯ ⲉⲣⲟⲓ; c ⲉⲧϩⲉ-: Ep 514 *S* ⲧⲉⲧⲛϩ.ⸯ ⲉⲧⲃⲏⲛⲧⲛ; c ⲉϫⲛ-: ShA 1 260 *S* children destroy playthings ⲛⲥⲉϩⲗⲡⲗⲱⲡⲟⲩ ⲉϫⲛⲛⲉⲩⲉⲣⲏⲩ; c ϩⲛ- *S*: Wess 18 75 ⲙⲡⲉⲣϩ. ϩⲛⲗⲁⲩ ⲛ-

ϩⲓⲥⲉ ⲁⲕ. ⲉⲛ; BMOr 8810 480 ⲡⲉϩ. ⲉⲩⲧⲣⲟ ⲙⲡⲉⲡϩⲏⲧ ⲉϩ. ⲡϩⲏⲧⲟⲩ *labefacere*; Mor 51 34 ⲉϥϩ.ⸯ ϩⲛⲡⲉϥⲙⲉⲉⲩⲉ.

—— nn m *SB*, *weariness, distress*: Nah 2 10 *B* ϩ. ⲡϩⲏⲧ (*A* ⲡⲱϣ ⲡϩⲏⲧ?) ἐκβρασμός (var -γμός); BMOr 8810 *lc* ⲡⲉⲩϩ. *animi defectio*; PMusGuimet (*v* PSBA 26 178) *S* ϩ. ⲛⲡⲁⲁⲕⲉ, Mun 83 *S* demon of ⲡⲉϩ. where is idleness, Va 61 24 *B* ⲡⲁ. ⲙⲡⲓⲃⲓ, Mor 25 45 *S* ⲙⲛⲧⲕⲟⲩⲓ ⲡϩⲏⲧ paral ϩ., P 130⁴ 89 *S* ⲙⲛⲧⲣⲉϥϫⲛⲁⲁⲩ paral ϩ., MG 25 31 *B* angel strengthens him ⲟⲩϩⲉⲡⲓⲁⲗⲁϩ. (cf *ib supra* ⲧⲱⲗⲧ ἀκηδία), P 131⁴ 108 *S* hunger & thirst cannot ⲧⲣⲉϥϣⲱⲡⲉ ϩⲛⲟⲩϩ., DeV 1 124 *B* Herod dying ⲁϥϣⲱⲡⲓ ϭⲉⲡⲟⲩⲁⲗ. & slew self. *V* also ϩⲣⲟⲡⲣⲡ, ⲁⲡⲁⲗⲁϥ.

ϩⲁⲗⲟⲩⲥ¹ *SA²*, ϩⲁⲗⲗ.² *SB* (once) nn m, *spider's web* (cf نسوس Spg): Job 27 18², Ps 38 11¹ (var Rahlfs ϩⲁⲗⲟⲩⲥ), Is 59 5¹ *S*(var²)*B*(Va 98 202, elsewhere *B* ⲥⲧⲁⲭⲟⲩⲗ), AP 7 *A²* ἀράχνη; Sa 5 15¹ πάχνη (*l ?ἀρ.*); ShA 1 430 ⲉϥϩⲏⲗ ⲉⲃⲟⲗ ⲛⲑⲉ ⲙⲡⲉⲓϩ.¹, ShZ 595 ϩⲉⲛϩ.¹ ⲙⲡⲣⲉⲛϣⲟⲉⲓϣ, P 131⁴ 138 like ⲟⲩϩ.¹ ⲡⲁϩⲣⲡⲟⲩⲧⲏⲩ, BMar 75 gold & silver ϩⲉⲛϩ.¹ ⲡⲉ; ⲣ ϩ.: Job 8 14² (*B c.*) ἀρ. ἀποβαίνεσθαι.

As name: Θαλλοῦς (Preisigke).

ϩⲗⲟⲥⲧ(ⲉ)ⲛ *S*, ϩⲗⲁⲥⲧⲛ *SⸯA²* nn m, *mist*: Is 29 18 (*B* ϩⲗⲟⲗ) ὁμίχλη; PS 113 ⲟⲩϩ. ⲡⲕⲁⲕⲉ, ShA 1 53 ⲕⲉϩ. ⲏ ⲕⲉϩⲃⲥ covered her eyes, BMar 78 sim, Mor 29 22 ⲁⲡⲉϩ. ϣⲟϫⲟ ⲉⲡⲉⲥⲛⲧ ϩⲙⲡⲉⲥⲁⲛⲕⲉⲫⲁⲗⲟⲥ (ἐγκ.) like tears & she was blinded (var *ib* 30 27 ⲡⲙⲟⲩ ϩⲣⲟⲩⲛ), PMéd 166 ⲡⲙⲟⲩ ϩⲣⲟⲩ(ⲛ) ⲙⲛⲡⲉϩ., LDi 277 ⲡⲉϩ. ⲡⲧⲁϥⲣ ⲕⲁⲕⲉ ⲉϫⲙⲡⲣⲏ, Z 635 *Sⸯ* ⲡⲕⲁⲕⲉ ⲙⲡⲡⲉϩ., ManiK 72 *A²* ⲡϩ. ⲙⲡⲓϥ, Mor 41 9 *Sⸯ* ⲟⲩⲕⲟⲩⲓ ⲛϩ. ⲛⲣⲟⲩ bit me & ⲟⲩⲁⲅⲛⲁⲙⲓⲥ ⲡⲕⲁⲕⲉ overshadowed me (DeV 2 256 *B* om); ⲣ ϩ., *become misty, darkened*: Ge 27 1 (*B* ⲉⲣ ϩⲗⲟⲗ) ἀμβλύνειν; Deu 34 7 (*B* do) ἀμαυροῦν; BM 311 104 *Sⸯ* ⲙⲡⲉⲡⲉϥⲃⲁⲗ ⲣ ϩ., KroppM 59 sim ϩⲣⲟⲥⲧⲛ, PMéd 296 eye ⲟ ⲙⲙⲟⲟⲩ ⲉⲓ(ⲉ) ⲉϥⲟ ⲛϩ.; ⳨ ϩ., *darken*: Si 43 4 ἀμαυ.

ϩⲁⲗⲏⲧ *SAA²BF*, ⲁⲗ. *A*, pl ϩⲁⲗⲁ(ⲁ)ⲧⲉ *S*, -ⲉⲧⲉ *AA²*, -ⲉⲉⲧⲉ *A*, -ⲉ⳨ *AF*, -ⲁ⳨ *B* & sg as pl (rare), nn m, *flying creature* (cf ϩⲱⲗ 1°), *bird*: Ge 7 14 *SB*, Pro 6 5 *SA* ⲁ.*B*, EpJer 70 *BF* ὄρνεον, Mt 23 37 *SB* ὄρνις; MG 25 8 *B* ⲁⲡⲓϩ. ϩⲁⲗⲁⲓ πετεινός; Is 16 2 *B* ⲙⲁⲥ ⲛϩ. *S* sim νοσσός; PS 341 *S* ⲧⲃⲛⲏ, ϫⲁⲧϥⲉ, ⲑⲏⲣⲓⲟⲛ, ϩ., ShC 73 188 *S* bee ⲡⲉⲓⲕⲟⲩⲓ ⲛϩ., ShA 1 254 *S* grasshopper ⲟⲩϩ. ⲉϥϩⲱϭⲉ, Mor 41 163 *S* ⲟⲩϩ. ⲉϥⲛⲁⲧⲱⲣⲛ ⲡⲟⲩϩⲣⲟⲟⲙⲡⲉ, C 43 42 *B* ⲁϥϣⲱⲗ ⲙⲫⲣⲏ⳨ ⲡⲟⲩϩ., ManiH 92 *A²* ϩ. ⲡⲡⲟⲩϩ; pl: Ge 1 26 *SA*-ⲉ⳨ *B*, Ps 77 27 *S*-ⲁⲧⲉ (var -ⲁⲁⲧⲉ), Hos 2 12 *A* ⲁⲗⲉⲧⲉ *B*, Mt 13 32 *SBF* πετ.; Pro 9 12 *SA* -ⲉⲧⲉ *B*, Is 34 11 *SBF* ὄρνεον; Pro 1 17 *SA* -ⲉⲧⲉ *B* πτερωτός; PS 336 *S* ⲛϩⲁⲗⲁⲧⲉ, Mor 32 42 *S*-ⲁⲁⲧⲉ, El 64 *A* -ⲉⲉⲧⲉ, ManiK 32 *A²*, AM 215

B, Wess 20 141 *F*; sg as pl: Si 22 21 *S* ⲡⲉⲧ.; Is 31
5 *SF*(*B* pl) ⲟ̄ⲣ.; Aeg 282 *S*(var pl), LAl 11 *S* ⲛⲕⲟⲩⲓ
ⲡⲣ. As title (?) Baouit 2 31 *S* ⲛⲅⲩⲣⲓⲁⲕⲟⲥ ⲫ. In
name (?): Φαλῆτις, Παλίτ (Preisigke). In place-
name: ⲡⲉⲓⲱⲣⲉ ⲛⲡⲉϩⲁⲗⲁⲧⲉ (BM 1110, 1112).

ϩⲗⲁϯ *F* v ϭⲣⲟϯ.

ϩⲁⲗⲁⲧⲏⲩ *A²* nn, *tempest*(?): ManiK 116 clouds,
winds, ⲙⲡⲏ̄ⲉ ⲙⲛⲏϩ. Cf ⲥⲁⲣⲁⲑⲏⲩ.

ϩⲗⲁⲩ *F* v ϩⲣⲟⲟⲩ.

ϩⲗⲉⲩ *F* v ϩⲓ- s f.

ϩⲗⲟⲅⲓⲉ *Sᶠ* v ϩⲁⲗ *servant*.

ϩⲗⲟⲅⲱ v ⲟⲅⲱ 2° s f.

ϩⲗⲟⲅⲗⲱⲟⲩ *SBF*, ⲗⲟⲅⲗⲱⲟⲩ *S*(once)*B* vb qual
(Sethe *Verbum* 2 8?), *be high, exalted*: Is 30 25 *SB*
(var ϭⲟⲥⲓ)*F*, *ib* 17 6 (*S* var ⲗ., *B* ϭ.)μετέωρος, BHom
92 *S* ⲑⲁⲗⲁⲥⲥⲁ ⲉⲥϭ. ⲏ ⲉⲥϩⲟⲥⲉ μετεωρίζειν; Is 61 *S*(*B*
ϣⲏⲟⲩ ⲉⲡϣⲱⲓ) ἐπαίρεσθαι, cit OrChr 3 7 116, R 2 4
93 &c; P 44 122 *S* ⲡⲉⲧϩ. الطب.; BMOr 8775 119
ⲃⲉⲑⲗ. يلخ., P 54 119 *B* do; Z 616 *S* ϭⲓ ⲙⲡϩⲁⲗⲏⲧ
ⲉⲡⲉⲧϩ., Mor 41 114 *S* earth to bring forth ⲟⲩⲭⲟⲣ-
ⲧⲟⲥ ⲉⲩϩ.; ⲙⲡⲧ.: Tri 526 *S* طاول.

ϩⲁⲗⲱⲟⲩⲗⲓ *B* v ϩⲱⲗ 1° s f & ϩⲁⲗⲱⲗⲓ.

ϩⲁⲗϣⲏⲩ *S* nn as pl, meaning unknown (cf?
ϣⲏⲩ *long*): ST 171 ⲛⲕⲉⲧⲉ, ⲛⲕⲉϭⲱⲣⲉ, ⲛⲉϩ. Possibly a letter after ⲗ.

ϩⲁⲗⲓϥ v ϩⲁⲗⲓⲃ.

ϩⲱⲗϥ *B* as advb, *hastily*: MG 25 215 ⲁϥⲙⲟ
ⲛϩ. = Z 338 *S* ϩⲛ ⲟⲩϣ ⲛϣⲱⲡ ἄφνω. Cf? ⲭⲱⲗⲉⲙ.

ϩⲁⲗϩⲟ, ϩⲁⲗⲁϩⲟ v ϩⲟ Compounds.

ϩⲉⲗϩⲉⲗ *B* vb intr, *swim, float* (?): Job 11 12 (*S*
ⲡⲛⲏⲃⲉ) νήχεσθαι. Cf ϩⲗⲟⲉⲓⲗⲉ.

ϩⲟⲗϩⲗ, ϩⲉⲗϩⲱⲗ-, ϩⲉⲗϩⲱⲗⲥ, ϩⲉⲗϩⲱⲗ† *S* vb tr, *a
sprinkle, scatter* (?): Cai 42573 1 recipe ⲧⲉⲕ ϩⲉⲗϩⲱⲗ
ⲡⲣⲱⲙⲉ with water (cf ⲁⲛϣⲉⲩⲗⲉ), *ib* 2 ϭⲁⲛ ⲡⲉϩ-
ⲙⲟⲟⲩ ϩⲉⲗϩⲱⲗϥ ⲉⲡⲉⲥϩⲟ, PMéd 206 ϩⲉⲗϩⲱⲗⲟⲩ (sc
mixture) ⲉϫⲛ ⲡⲙⲟⲟⲩ ⲉⲧⲕⲏⲩ, cf ϩⲱⲗ 3°. **ⲃ** doubtful: Z 553 beheld fruitless tree ⲛⲑⲉ ⲉⲧⲉϥϩ.† ⲉⲃⲟⲗ
ⲙⲙⲟⲥ, PJkôw ⲁⲡⲙⲟⲥ ... ⲡⲣⲟⲗⲟⲕⲟⲧⲥⲉ [ ] ⲉϣⲁⲩ-
ϩⲉⲗϩⲟⲗⲟⲩ ⲛⲧⲟⲟⲧⲛ ⲁⲩⲧⲃⲁ ⲡⲗⲟⲉⲓⲥⲉ.

ϩⲟⲗϩⲗ *S* (once), ϩⲁⲗ. *A²*, ϭⲟⲗϭⲉⲗ, ϭⲉⲗϭⲱⲗ-
B, ϩⲉⲗϩⲱⲗⲥ *S*(once), ϭⲉⲗϭⲱⲗⲥ, -ϭⲟⲗ. *B*, ϩⲓⲉⲗⲁⲗⲧ†
A², ϭⲉⲗϭⲱⲗ† *B* vb intr, *slay*: Ez 40 41 (*S* ϣⲱⲱⲧ)
σφάζειν, *ib* 21 15 εἰς σφαγὴν γίνεσθαι; Zeph 1 10
(*A* ⲣⲱϧⲧ) ἀποκεντεῖν; Jer 27 11 (*S* ⲕⲱⲡⲥ) κερατίζειν; qual: Deu 28 31 (*S* ϣ.), Ap 5 6 (*S* ⲕ.), C 89
62 = C 99 147 *S* do σ.; Jer 28 4 κατακεντ.; ManiH
80 *A²* ⲥⲉϩ.; tr: Ex 22 1 (*S* ⲕ.), Lev 17 3 (*S* ϣ.),

Pro 9 2 (*SA* ⲕ.), Ap 6 4 (*S* ϩⲱⲧⲃ) ⲥ., Lu 19 27 (*S* ⲕ.)
ⲕⲁⲧⲁⲥ., ROC 17 405 ⲉϭⲉⲗϭⲱⲗϥ πρὸς τὴν σφάγην;
Nu 25 8 (*S* do), Hos 9 13 (*A* do) ἀποκεντ.; Ex 21 28
(*S* do) ⲕⲉⲣ.; Ez 27 21 ἐμπορεύεσθαι (mistaking *S* ⲣ
ⲉⲓⲉⲡϣⲱⲧ for ϣ.); Va 57 144 ⲡⲧⲉⲕϭⲉⲗϭⲱⲗ ⲡⲉⲕϣⲏⲣⲓ; DeV 1 124 took sword ⲁϥϭⲉⲗϭⲱⲗϥ ⲙⲙⲁϩ-
ⲁⲧϥ, BSM 55 ϭ. ⲛⲡⲉϥϫⲁϫⲓ = Va 63 22 *B* ϣⲁⲣⲓ =
BMis 409 *S* ⲡⲁⲧⲁⲥⲥⲉ, C 86 283 nails ϭ. ⲛⲡⲉⲥⲱⲙⲁ ⲙ-
ⲡⲓⲁⲧⲥⲓⲟⲥ (var ϭⲟⲙϭⲉⲙ), ManiH 29 *A²* sword ⲉⲧⲁϭ.
ⲡⲧ[ⲉⲡⲓ]ⲑⲩⲙⲓⲁ, My 70 *S* began to ⲑⲉⲗϩⲱⲗϥ ⲛϭⲓ ⲡⲉϥⲉⲓⲱⲧ, PMich 601 *S* like bitch ⲉⲥⲙⲟⲥⲉ ⲉⲩϩ. ⲙⲙⲟⲥ
ⲉⲥϯ ⲛⲧⲉⲥⲙⲏ; c ⲛⲥⲁ-: DeV 1 115 ϭ. ⲡⲉⲱⲟⲩ
without mercy; c ⲛⲧⲉⲡ-: Lam 4 9 (*S* ϫⲱⲧϩ, *F*
ⲡⲱⲗ) ἐκκεντ. ἀπό; c ϭⲉⲡ-, *with*: Ez 40 42 (*S*
ϣ.) ⲥ. ⲉⲛ; Is 14 19 (*S* ⲕ.) ἐκκεντ. dat; Ez 34 21 (*S*
do) ⲕⲉⲣ. dat; C 43 162 ϭⲉⲗϭⲱⲗϥ ϭⲉⲛⲧⲉϥⲗⲟⲩⲭⲏ.

—— nn m *B*, *slaughter*: Job 10 16 (*S* ⲡⲁϩⲥ), Is
34 6 (*SF* ⲕ.), Ob 10 (*SA* ϩⲱ.), Ja 5 5 (*SA* ⲕ.) σφαγή,
Am 5 25 σφάγιον.

ⲣⲉϥϭ. *B*, *slayer, gorer*: Ex 21 29 (*S* ⲣⲉϥⲕ.) κερατιστής; ROC 17 403 ⲥⲁϫⲓ ⲛⲣ.

ϫⲓⲛϭ. *B*, *slaying*: Ez 40 39 m (*S* ϣ.) σφάζειν;
DeV 1 115 f.

ϩⲉⲗϩⲉⲗⲉⲓ, -ϩⲉⲗⲗⲉⲓ nn f, as place-name: PLond
4 224 ⲧϩ., 223 ⲑ. Meaning unknown. ϩⲉⲗⲏ-
ϩⲉⲗⲏ WS 171 hardly same.

ϩⲉⲗϩⲓⲗⲉ *S*, ϭⲉⲗϭⲉⲗⲧ *B* nn f, *death rattle*: PSBA
33 116 *S* dying man ⲧϩ. ϣⲱⲡⲉ ϩⲛⲧⲉϥϣⲟⲩⲱⲃⲉ, Aeg
27 *S* sim ⲁⲧϩ. ⲙⲡⲉϩⲉⲗⲏⲥ ⲧⲱⲟⲩⲛ ⲉϩⲱϥ, Miss 4
170 *B* sim ϯⲛⲓϣϯ ⲛϭ. ⲉⲧⲱϣ ⲉⲃⲟⲗ ϭⲉⲛⲧϣⲃ̄ⲃⲓ like
saw. V LMis 374. Cf ϩⲱⲗ 2°.

ϩⲉⲗϩⲓⲗⲉ *S* v ϩⲗⲟⲉⲓⲗⲉ c ϩⲓϫⲛ-.

ϩⲁⲗⲁϩⲱⲗ[(or -ϩⲱⲧⲉ[ ) *S* nn: Bal, in list of
utensils ⲟⲩϩ.

ϩⲁⲗⲁϩⲱⲙ *S* nn m, *a vessel* (?): ST 298 ϣⲓ
ⲙⲛⲧⲉ ⲛⲣⲧⲟⲃ ⲛⲟⲣⲁϩ ϩⲙⲡϩ. ⲉⲧⲛⲧⲡⲉ ⲙⲡⲕⲁⲧⲁϩ ⲛ-
ⲡϣⲁϣⲟⲧ.

ϩⲱⲗϫ *B* v ϩⲱⲗϭ.

ϩⲗⲁϫ *F* v ϩⲱⲣϭ s f.

ϩⲗⲟϫ, ϩⲉⲗϫⲉ, ϩⲗⲏϫⲓ *B* v ϩⲗⲟϭ.

ϩⲗⲓϫⲓ *B* nn m, *diarrhoea*: K 160 ⲡⲓϩ. اسهال.

ϩⲗⲟϫⲗⲉϥ *S* nn, meaning unknown: Bodl copt
d 227 letter]ⲧⲁϩⲟ ϩⲉⲛϩⲗⲟϫⲗⲉϥ[.

ϩⲱⲗϭ *SF*, -ϫ *B*(rare), ϩⲉⲗⲏϭ (? same)*A²*, ϩⲱⲗϭⲥ
(once), ϩⲟⲗϭ† *S*, -ϫⲓ† *B* vb intr, *embrace*: Pro 7 18 (*B*
ⲥⲕⲉⲣⲕⲉⲣ) ἐγκυλίειν; Eccl 3 5 περιλαμβάνειν; c
ⲉ- as obj: BMar 123 ⲁϥϩ. ⲉⲣⲟⲟⲩ & kissed them ἐπιλ.,

Ge 29 13 (B ⲁⲙⲁⲗⲏⲝ), Cant 8 3 περιλ., Ac 20 10 (B ⲙⲟⲅⲗⲝ) συμπεριλ.; R 1 1 50 περιπτύσσειν; PS 122 ⲁϥϩ. ⲉⲣⲟⲕ, R 1 2 33 ϩ. ⲉⲡⲉϥⲉⲣⲏⲅ, C 43 107 B ⲡⲧⲁⲁⲙⲟⲡⲓ ⲙⲙⲟⲕ ⲛⲧⲁϩ. ⲉⲣⲟⲕ, ManiH 43 A² ⲡⲉⲧⲁⲩϩ. ⲁⲣⲁϥ ϩⲓⲧⲡ?, Mani 1 A² my father ⲉϣⲁϥϩ. ⲁⲣⲁⲓ ⲛ- ⲥⲏⲩ ⲛⲓⲙ; qual: Si 30 20 περιλ.; BMar 121 children ⲉⲧϩ. ⲉⲡⲉϥⲉⲣⲏⲅ καταφιλεῖν; MG 25 135 B ⲛⲁⲥⲣⲁϣⲓ ⲡⲉⲙϣⲟⲅⲡⲉ ⲉⲥϩ. ⲉⲣⲱⲟⲩ;   ⲉϩⲟⲩⲛ ⲉ- as c ⲉ-: Ro 12 10 F(S ⲡⲟⲕⲡⲉⲕ ⲉϩ. ⲉ-, B ⲭⲏ ϫⲉⲡⲟⲩⲙⲉⲓ ⲉϩ̄. ⲉ-) φιλόστοργος εἰς; ShViK 9101 ⲟⲩϩⲟⲟⲩⲧ ⲙⲛⲟⲩϩⲟⲟⲩⲧ ⲉⲩϩⲁϩ. ⲉϩ. ⲉⲡⲉϥⲉⲣⲏⲅ ϩⲛⲟⲩⲉⲡⲓⲑⲩⲙⲓⲁ ⲛⲥⲱⲟⲩϥ, Mor 48 85 ⲁϥϩ. ⲉϩ. ⲉⲣⲟϥ & kissed his mouth = C 43 142 B ⲉⲣ ⲁⲙ. ⲉ-, R 1 1 69 ⲉⲕϩ.† ⲉϩ. ⲉⲣⲟⲓ ϩⲙⲡⲉⲕⲟⲩⲱϣ ⲡ̄ϩⲏⲧ, C 43 193 B ⲉϥϩ.† ⲉϩ̄. ⲉⲡⲓⲣⲱⲙⲓ; as nn: JTS 9 383 greet brother ϩⲛⲟⲩϩⲱⲗϭ (l?ϩⲱⲗϭ) ⲉϩ. ⲉⲣⲟϥ;   c ϩⲛ-: PS 242 ⲡⲕⲉⲙⲩⲥⲧⲏⲣⲓⲟⲛ ⲉⲧϩ.† ϩⲛⲙⲙⲉⲗⲟⲥ.

—— nn m S: Eccl 3 5 περίληψις.

ϩⲱⲗϭ   v ϩⲱⲗⲕ & ϩⲱⲣϭ.

ϩⲗⲟϭ S, ϩⲗⲁϭ AA²F, ϩⲗⲁⲕ Sᵃ(nn), ϩⲗⲟϫ B, ϩⲟⲗϭ† S, ϩⲁⲗⲗⲉϫ† Sᶠ, ϩⲁⲗϭ† AA²F, ϩⲁⲗⲉϫ† A²F, ϩⲟⲗϫ† B, ϩⲁ.† F, p c ϩⲁⲗϭ- SA², ϩⲗϭ- A² vb intr, be sweet, take delight: Ex 15 25 SB, Si 49 2 S γλυκαίνεσθαι; Ps 140 6 B ἡδύνειν (S l δύνασθαι); BMis 195 S bitter waters ⲁⲩϩ., Cat 84 B dew on plants ⲑⲣⲟⲩϩ.;   qual: Eccl 11 7 SF-ⲝ, Is 5 20 SBF γλυκύς, Pro 9 17 SAB γλυκερός, Ez 3 3 B γλυκάζειν, Z 336 S ⲡⲙⲟⲟⲩ ϩ. γλυκαίν.; Ps 33 8 S(B ϩⲉⲗϫⲉ), Jer 24 3 B(S ⲛⲁⲛⲟⲩ-), Mt 11 30 S(var ϩⲗⲟϭϥ), Lu 5 39 B(S ⲡⲟⲩϭⲣ), χρηστός, Ro 16 18 SB χρηστο-; Ps 132 1 B(S ⲡⲟⲧⲙ) τερπνός; ib 134 3 B(S do) καλός; PS 214 S ⲡⲉⲕⲃⲟ ⲉⲧϩ., ShR 2 3 14 S ⲡⲡⲟⲃⲉ ϩ., BHom 115S ⲡⲉⲧⲥⲁϣⲉ, ⲡⲉⲧϩ., AM 121 B sim, Lant 11 D Sᶠ ⲧⲓⲣⲁⲗⲗ. ⲧⲓϣⲛϣⲏ, BIF 13 116 S ⲥⲙⲏ ⲉⲥϩ., C 89 93 B ϫⲓⲡⲉⲣ ⲯⲁⲗⲓⲛ ⲉⲥϩ. = C 99 154 S ⲡⲟⲧⲙ, AZ 23 103 S milk ⲉϥϩ., ManiBerlSitz '33 Taf 1 A² ⲧⲡⲉ ⲉⲧϩ., Ora 4 202 F ⲡⲓⲗⲉⲛ ⲉⲧϩ., BM 593 F ⲙⲉⲧⲥⲁⲛ ⲉⲧϩⲁⲗⲉϫ, ib 601 F sim -ϭ.

With following preposition. c ⲉ-, beyond, above: Ps 18 11 SB γλυκύτερος ὑπέρ; C 43 125 B ⲁⲙⲟⲛ ⲡⲉⲧϩ. ⲉⲡⲁⲓⲣⲁⲛ;   c ⲛ- dat: Job 21 33 B γλυκαίν. dat, Pro 27 7 SA γλυκὺς φαίνεσθαι; Ps 103 34 SB ἡδύν.; ib 51 11 B(S = Gk) χρ. ἐναντίον; BMis 139 S ⲁⲡⲉⲥⲧⲟⲓ... ϩ. ⲡⲁϥ;   c ⲛⲧⲛ-: Ps 54 15 B(S diff) γλυκαίν., Eccl 5 11 S(F ⲛⲁⲛⲟⲩ-) γλυκύς; Jer 38 26 B ἡδὺς γίν. dat; Mich 166 S thy cell ϩ.† ⲡⲧⲟⲟⲧⲕ, C 43 158 B ⲉϥϩ.† ⲛⲧⲟⲧϥ dear to him for his prowess;   c ⲡⲁϩⲣⲛ- S: BHom 44 sleep ϩ.† ⲡⲁϩⲣⲁⲕ, ST 270 ⲉϥϩⲁϩ. ⲡⲡⲁϩⲣⲁⲕ;   c ϩⲛ-: Ps 118 103 S(B ϩⲉⲗϫⲉ) γλυκύς dat, Ap 10 9 SBF(Lacau) γ. ἐν, Si 40 33 S γλυκαίν. ἐν, Z 325 S soul ϩ.† ϩⲛⲙⲡⲁⲑⲟⲥ ἐγγλ. dat; ShBM 193 3 S ⲉⲧϩ.† ⲡϩⲏⲧⲟⲩ (sc God's wishes) ⲛϩⲟⲩⲟ ⲉⲁⲩⲑⲟⲛ ⲛⲓⲙ, RAL '93 523 S ⲡⲉϥϩ.† ⲁⲛ ϩⲓⲧⲉϥϭⲓⲛⲧⲱⲙⲡⲧ ⲉ-

ⲣⲟϥ; Si 38 5 S ϩ.† ⲉⲃⲟⲗ ϩⲛ- γλυκαίν. ἀπό;   c ϩⲓ- ⲝⲉⲛ- B: BSM 31 remembrance ⲉⲧϩ.† ϩ. ⲡⲉϩⲛⲧ.

p c: Mus 40 45 S ⲟⲩϩ. ϣⲁⲝⲉ dulcia loqui; PS 8 S Jesus ⲡⲡⲁⲛⲧ ⲛϩⲁⲗϭ̄ϩⲏⲧ, ManiP A² ⲡⲓⲱⲧ ⲛϩⲗϩⲏⲧ; ManiK 79 A² ⲧⲉⲕⲟ ⲛⲧⲉⲧⲡⲙⲛⲧϩⲁⲗϭ̄ϩⲏⲧ, ManiP 45 A² ⲙ̄ⲧϩⲗϭ̄ϩⲏⲧ.

—— nn m SSᵃAA²BF, sweetness: Sa 16 21 S, BHom 3 S ⲡⲉϩ. ⲙⲡⲉⲃⲓⲟ γλυκύτης, Am 9 13 SA(B ϩⲗⲏⲝ) γλυκασμός; ShP 130⁴ 102 S v ⲡⲟⲕⲡⲉⲕ, BMis 178 S ⲡⲉϩ. ⲛⲓϫⲟⲉⲓⲧ, P 131³ 29 S after darkness ⲡⲉϩ. ⲙⲡⲟⲩⲟⲉⲓⲛ, TillOster 14 A ⲡϩ. ⲡⲡⲉⲧⲟⲩⲁⲁⲃⲉ, Mani 1 A² ⲡϩ. ⲡⲧⲉ ⲧⲥⲁⲣⲝ, AM 252 B ⲡϩ. ⲡⲡⲉϥⲗⲉϫⲓⲥ, Mor 24 20 F ⲡⲉϩ. ⲡⲧⲉⲕⲥⲙⲏ, CO 195 S I greet ⲡⲉϩ. ⲛⲧⲉⲕⲙⲛⲧⲉⲓⲱⲧ ⲉⲧⲟⲩⲁⲁⲃ, MMA 23 3 712 Sᵃ sim;   ϩⲛⲟⲩϩ. as advb S: BHom 8 ⲥⲱⲧⲙ ⲉϩⲉⲛⲕⲁⲧⲁⲗⲁⲗⲓⲁ ϩ., Ep 214 will give it you ϩ. with pleasure.

ⲙⲛⲧϩ. S sweetness: Tri 450 ⲧⲱⲛ ⲡⲧⲙ. ⸗̈, ⸉ .

† ϩ. SAA²B, make sweet, pleasant: Pro 5 3 SA(B † ⲕⲉⲛⲓ) λιπαίνειν; Sa 2 12 SB neg δύσχρηστος εἶναι, ShRE 11 16 S food ⲛⲁ†. ⲡⲧⲉⲕϣⲟⲩⲟⲃⲉ, ShHT F S demons †. ⲡⲁϥ ⲉϩⲟⲩⲛ ⲉⲡⲛⲟⲃⲉ, R 1 3 58 S of Salome ⲡⲥⲁⲧⲁⲛⲁⲥ †. ⲡⲧⲉⲥⲟ̈ⲡⲟⲣ̈ϫⲉⲓ, KroppE 32 S give me tongue ⲉϥ† ⲙⲡⲗⲁⲟⲥ, Miss 8 152 S ⲛ̄ⲇⲓⲁⲃⲟⲗⲟⲥ †. ⲡⲁⲕ ⲛϩⲟⲩⲟ, LCyp 3 S ϣⲉ ⲉⲧ†. sweet wood for magic, Mani 1 A² ⲉⲧ†. ⲡⲡⲕⲁⲣⲡⲟⲥ.

ϫⲓ ϩ., get sweetness: Z 617 S how doth honeydew ϫ. whilst yet in air?, TillOster 15 A ⲡⲕⲟⲥⲙⲟⲥ ⲧⲏⲣϥ ϫ. ⲁϩⲟⲩⲛ ⲁⲛⲡⲉ̄.

ϩ(ⲉ)ⲗϭⲉ S, ϩⲉⲗϫⲉ B, pl -ϫⲏⲩ B nn m f, sweetness: Ps 33 8 B(S ϩⲟⲗϭ), ib 118 68 B(S = Gk), Pro 2 21 B pl (S ⲛⲁⲛⲟⲩ-) χρηστός; Cant 5 16 S(F ⲛⲏⲛⲓ) γλυκασμός; Bodl Or 32 176 B chalice ⲟⲩϩ. to all that drink ⸗̈, ⸉; Mus 42 235 S of virginity ⲧϩ. ⲡⲁⲧⲣ ϩ̄ⲧⲥ, EW 37 B of God ⲡⲓϩ. ⲙⲙⲁⲅⲁⲧϥ, Va 57 235 B ⲡⲓϩ. ⲙⲛⲓⲡⲟⲛⲏⲣⲟⲥ, AM 136 B ϫⲉⲗϣⲓⲣⲓ ⲛϩ.;   ⲉⲣ ϩ. B: 1 Cor 13 4 (S as Gk) χρηστεύεσθαι; FR 96 01 ⲛ ... ϩ. ⲉϫⲟⲩⲛ ⲉⲣⲟⲥ;   ϫⲓⲡⲉⲣ ϩ.: Cat 13 ⲟⲩϫ. ⲉ- ϫⲟⲩⲛ ⲉⲡⲉⲡⲉⲣⲛⲟⲩ;   ⲙⲉⲧϩ.: Ps 118 66 (S as Gk) χρηστότης; MG 25 408.

ϩⲗⲛϭⲉ S, -ϫⲓ B nn f, as last: Job 6 6 B(S †ⲡⲉ) γεῦμα; Am 9 13 B-ϫ(SA ϩⲗⲟϭ) γλυκασμός; P 44 62 S ⲁⲛⲁⲗⲟⲩⲧⲓⲛ (? -λότης) ⲧⲉϩ. ⸗̈, ⸉; Cat 158 B ⲧϩⲩ- ϫⲟⲏ... ϣⲱⲡⲓ ⲛϩ. ⲛ†ⲯⲩⲭⲏ but afterward is as ⲟⲩ- ϣⲁϣϣⲉϥ, Dif 2 16 B ⲟⲩϩ. ⲛⲛⲏⲛⲓ, BMis 193 S ⲙⲟⲟⲩ ⲛϩ., Tatt 690 B ⲡⲓⲣⲁⲛ ⲉⲧⲟⲓ ⲛϩ.

ϩⲗⲱϭϥ S, be easy, pleasant: Mt 11 30 ⲉⲥϩ. (var & B ϩⲟⲗϭ) χρηστός, cit P 130⁴ 86 ⲉⲧⲛⲁϩ. ⲁⲅⲱ ⲉⲧⲁⲥⲱⲟⲩ, Bor 226 168 ⲛⲁⲗⲟⲥϥ.

ϩⲁⲗϭⲓⲥ S nn, among implements or vessels: Bodl(P)d 47]ⲟⲩⲉ ⲡⲗⲁⲕ,]ⲟⲩϩⲁⲙⲉ,]ⲟⲩϩ.   Coptic?

ϩⲗϭⲏⲧ A² v ϩⲗⲟϭ p c.

ϩⲁⲙ S, ϩⲁⲙ- SAA²BF, ϩⲙ- S, ⲁⲙ- B, pl ϩⲙⲏⲩ,

-ⲉⲩ S & sg as pl, nn m, *craftsman SF*: BKU 1 308
ⲏⲗⲓⲁⲥ ϥⲁⲙ, Hall 106 ϣⲉⲡⲟⲩⲧⲉ ⲛϥ., Saq 6 ⲡⲁⲓⲁⲕⲱⲛ
ⲓⲉⲣⲏⲙⲓⲁⲥ ϥ., CMSS 78 F ⲑⲉⲩⲧⲱⲥⲓ ϥ., WZKM 26
338 ⲁⲡⲁ ⲕⲩⲣⲟⲥ ϩ. (or ? name), Ep 76 ⲛϩⲉⲕⲉ ⲙⲛϩ.,
Hall 108 wage to ϥ. who mended cart, also to ϩⲉⲥⲡ-
ⲛⲓⲧ, Ryl 365 ⲛϥⲗϭⲓⲝ (*quid* ?) let him write to ⲛϩ.
ϥⲥⲙⲓⲧⲟⲩ, Ep 547 tools ⲉⲓⲛⲉ ⲛϩ., ⲙⲁⲭⲉ ⲛϩ.;   pl:
AZ 60 107 ⲧⲕⲟⲓⲛⲟⲧⲏⲥ ⲛⲛⲣⲙⲉⲩ ⲡⲁⲣⲁ (*ib* ⲛϩⲁⲙ ⲛⲁⲣⲁ), Ep 437 ⲛⲉϥⲙⲏⲩ will not work unpaid, ST 46
ⲛⲣⲙⲏⲩ doing woodwork in τόπος;   ϩⲁⲙⲕⲗⲗⲉ,
-ⲕⲉⲗⲓ *v* ⲕⲗⲗⲉ *sf*, ϩⲁⲙⲡⲟⲩϩ *v* ⲡⲟⲩϩ *sf*, ϩⲁⲙϣⲉ,
ⲁⲙϣⲉ *v* ϣⲉ *wood sf*, adding ManiK 132 *A²* ϩ., Saq 6,
78 *S* ϥⲙϣⲉ, ϩⲁⲙ ⲡⲁⲣⲁ, *chainsmith* (?), *v* AZ above,
ϩ. ⲛⲃⲟⲗⲃⲗ *v* ⲃⲟⲗⲃⲗ **I**, ϩ. ⲛⲕⲁⲗⲕⲉⲗ *v* ⲕⲟⲗⲕⲗ, ϩ. ⲥⲟⲩⲣⲉ (?) ST 352, ϩ. ⲁⲕⲏ WS 140 (*cf* 141 n & Φαμακεῖ
Preisigke), Φαμϧόι (Preis.), ϩⲁⲙⲡⲟⲓ *v* ⲡⲟⲓ. As
name (?): Φάμ (Preis.).

ϩⲁⲙ *A²* nn m, meaning unknown: AP 44 he said
ⲛϩ. ⲧⲣⲉⲡⲁⲩⲗⲟⲥ ϫⲱⲕ ⲁⲃⲁⲗ [ⲛ]ⲟⲓⲕⲟⲛⲟⲙⲓⲁ ⲛⲓⲙ.

ϩⲁⲙ in ϩⲁⲙⲡⲧⲱⲡ.

ϩⲁⲙⲓ† *v* ϩⲱⲱⲙⲉ.

ϩⲏⲙ *S* nn m, in list of utensils (σκεύη): Ep 543
ϣⲟⲙ(ⲧ) ⲛϩ.

ϩⲏⲙ, ϩⲙ *Sᵃ* *v* ϣⲏⲙ.

ϩⲟⲙ *B* nn m, *shoemaker*: K 132 ⲛⲓϩ. اسكاف,
WHatch 762 Mark ⲉⲧⲁϥⲡⲁⲩ ⲉⲟⲩϩ. (Anianus) he
gave him shoe to mend = PO 1 142 ـي.

ϩⲟⲙ *B* nn, *implement*: C 86 235 bade bring
ⲟⲩϩ. ⲡⲉⲙⲟⲩⲥⲙⲓⲗⲗⲁ (σμίλη) to scrape skin of head
= Budge *George of Lydda* 147 *b* ⲥⲡⲧⲛϩ. مَرْد.

ϩⲟⲉⲓⲙ *S*, ϩⲁ. *SSᶠ*, ϩⲁ(ⲉ)ⲓⲙⲉ *AA²*, ϩⲱⲓⲙⲓ *B*,
ϩⲁ(ⲉ)ⲓⲙ *F*, pl ϩⲛⲏⲙⲉ, ϩⲓⲙⲏ *S*, -ⲙⲉⲅⲉ *AA²*, -ⲙⲉⲉⲩ
A² & sg as pl, nn m, *wave*: Job 38 11 *S*(*B* ϫⲟⲗ), Ps
106 25 *S*(*B* do), cit(?)PMich 1192 *F*, Is 48 18 *SB*
(Lacr, var ϫ.), Jon 2 4 *SA* ϩⲁⲓⲉ (*sic* ?, *B* do), Mt
14 24 *F*(*S* pl, *B* do) κῦμα ; Pro 23 34 *SA*, Lu 8 24
SB κλύδων ; BM 216 80 *S* sailors ⲁⲓϣⲉ ⲙⲡⲛϩ. ⲛ-
ⲧⲁϥⲉⲓ ⲉϩⲣⲁⲓ ⲉϫⲱⲟⲩ ζάλη ; Ac 27 27 *B* (var ⲋⲗⲁ, *S*
Gk diff), Pcod 38 *SF* ⲁϥϧⲣⲟⲕ ⲛϭⲓ ⲡⲉⲓⲕⲉϩ. (*sc* of evil
thoughts), BHom 128 *S* sea raised ⲡⲉⲥϩⲁ., Ryl 289
S thy fatherhood knoweth ⲛϩ. ⲛⲧⲙⲛⲧϣⲏⲣⲉ [ϣⲏⲙ,
C 43 235 *B* ⲛⲓϩ. ⲛⲧⲉ ⲡⲁⲓϫⲁⲗⲕⲓⲟⲛ ⲁⲩϭⲓⲥⲓ *spray* (*cf*
BSG 185 *S* ⲡⲧⲉⲗⲧⲓⲗⲉ ⲉⲧⲩϭⲱϣⲉ ⲉϩⲣⲁⲓ), El 46 *A* fiery
sea ⲉⲛⲉⲥϩ. ϩⲉⲣⲟ, Mani 1 *A²* ⲛϩ. ⲧⲱⲣⲡ ⲙⲙⲁⲥ, *ib A²*
ⲛϩ. ⲙⲡⲃⲓⲟⲥ, DeV 1 161 *B* world ⲛⲉϥⲣⲱⲟⲩϣ ⲡⲉⲙ-
ⲡⲉϥϩ.;   pl: Job 38 11 *A*(Cl, *S* sg, *B* ϫ.), Mt 8 24
S ϩⲓ. (*B* sg), BHom 133 *S* ⲛϩⲓ. ϩⲱⲗ ⲉⲃⲟⲗ κῦ.; Tri
404 *S* ⲛϩⲓ. امواج; BAp 141 *S* ⲛϩ. (var JTS 8 141 ϩⲟⲉⲓⲙ); ManiK 40 *A²* ⲛϩⲓⲙⲉⲅⲉ ⲧⲏⲣⲟⲩ, Mani 1 *A²*
ⲛϩⲓⲙⲉⲉⲩ ⲙⲡⲓⲁⲙ; Mor 17 44 *S* as sg ⲡⲉⲓⲛⲟϭ ⲛϩⲓ.

ⲕⲗ.;   ⲣϩ., ⲟ ⲛϩ., *be covered with waves, be agi-
tated*: Is 5 30 *B*(var Lacr ϩⲓ ϩ., *S* ϩⲁϩ.) κυμαίνειν;
Jon 1 11 *SA*(*B* Gk diff), BM 256 221 *S* avoid much
talk lest enemy ⲁⲁⲕ ⲛϩ. (= C 73 41 Sh ?);   †ϩ.,
sim: Is 17 12 *SB*(prob) κυμαίν.; LCyp 5 *S* sea ⲉⲥ†
ϩ., SHel 48 *S* ⲟⲩⲡⲛⲥⲏ ⲉⲥ†ϩ., TstAb 259 *B* fiery
river †ϩ. ⲛⲡⲓⲣⲉϥⲉⲣ ⲛⲟⲃⲓ, Bor 264 41 *S* ⲛϣⲁϩ †ϩ.
ϩ.;   ϧⲓ, ⲃⲓ ϩ., *throw up waves*: ManiK 153 *A²* sea
ⲃ. ϫⲛⲛⲕⲣⲟ ⲁⲕⲣⲟ; ϧⲓϩ. ϩ. *S*, do so *repeatedly, be agi-
tated*: BMis 538 river ⲉϧϧ. κοχλάζειν; C 42 242 =
Miss 4 836 ϩⲏⲗⲟⲥ (ἐλ.) ⲙⲙⲟⲟⲩ sim, P 131⁵ 105 *Sᶠ*
ⲡⲛⲥⲏ sim, R 1 3 75 at this iniquity ⲁⲡⲉϩⲏⲧ ⲡⲟⲩⲟⲡ
ⲛⲓⲁ ϥ., BMar 241 eyes like fiery wheels ⲉⲩϥ.   ϩⲓ
ϩ. *B* as p ϩ.: Is 5 30 *v* above, TstAb 237 river ⲉⲩϩⲓ
(ϩ)ⲱⲓⲙⲓ;   ⲁⲧϩ. *B*: AM 228 ⲗⲩⲙⲏⲛ ... ⲡⲁ.

ϩⲟⲩⲙ *S* nn, meaning unknown: Bodl(P) d 47
in list of vegetables ⲥⲁϭⲥⲁϭ, ϭⲟⲩϫ, ϩ.   *Cf* ? ϩⲟⲩϭ.

ϩⲱⲙ *SAA²F*, -ⲙⲓ *B*, ϩⲙ- *S*, ϩⲉⲙ- *SB*, ϩⲟⲙ-
A², ϩⲁⲙ- *F*, ϩⲟⲙⲉ⸗ *SB*, ϩⲁⲙ⸗ *A*, ϩⲏⲙⲧ† *S*, ϩⲟⲙⲓ† *B*
vb intr, *tread, trample, beat*: Joel 3 13 *SAB*, BM
1130 *S* ⲛⲉϩⲱⲙ πατεῖν, Is 63 3 *S†B* καταπ., Nah 3 14
S(ShC 42 16)*AB* συμπ.;   Mor 51 35 *S* ⲥⲛⲏ ⲛϩ. opp
ⲥⲛⲏ ⲙⲡⲱⲛϣ (ref to vintage), C 86 152 *B* spear ϩ.†
ϫⲉⲡⲧⲉϥⲁϥⲉ;   tr: Is 32 20 *B*(*SF* c ⲉϫⲛ-), Lam 1
15 *BF* ϩⲁⲙ-, Zech 10 5 *AB*, Ap 14 20 *SB* π., 1 Kg
23 1 *S*, Ps 138 11 *S*(*B* c ⲉϫⲛ-), Lu 8 5 *S*(*B* ϩⲟⲙ ϩⲉⲙ)
καταπ., Va 68 165 *B* ϩ. ⲙⲡⲓⲥⲙⲁϩ ληνοπ., Ez 34 19 *B*
πάτημα ; Mic 6 15 *B*(*A* Gk om); Tri 336 *S* ⲉⲩϩⲙ
ⲡⲉϩⲉⲣⲏⲧ ساد;   ShA 1 462 *S* beasts ϩ. ⲛⲛⲙⲁ ⲙ-
ⲙⲟⲟⲛⲉ, ShC 42 167 *S* ⲛⲉⲧⲛⲁϩⲟⲙ with revilings &
cursings, HTO 191 *S* potter ϣⲁϥ. ⲙⲡⲉϥⲟⲙⲉ, Mani
K 137 *A²* ⲁϥϩ. ⲣⲉⲧϥ...ⲁϫⲱⲥ, Mani P 66 *A²* ⲙⲡⲓϩⲟⲙ
ⲣⲉⲧ ϩⲛⲡⲙⲁⲓⲧ.

With following preposition.   c ⲉ-: Is 16 10 *S*
ϩⲙ- (*B* ϫⲉⲡ-) π. εἰς, Ez 26 11 *B* καταπ. acc ; Mic 4
3 *B*(*SA* ⲟⲩⲱⲧϩ) κατακόπτειν εἰς, Joel 3 10 *B*(*SA* do)
συγκ. εἰς ; ⲉϩⲣⲁⲓ ⲉ- *S*: Ps 7 5 (*B* c ⲉϫ.) καταπ. εἰς ;
ShMun 162 beasts in fields ⲛⲥⲉϩⲟⲙⲟⲩ ⲉϩ. ⲉⲡⲟⲗⲉ ⲛ
ⲉϩ. ⲉⲡⲕⲁϩ;   c ⲉϫⲛ-: Is 42 5 *S*(*B* ϩⲓϫⲉⲛ-), Z 278
S ϩ. ⲉϫⲛⲡⲁⲙⲁϩⲧⲉ ⲙⲡⲙⲟⲩ (varWess 15 137 ϩⲓϫⲛ-)
π. acc, Lu 10 19 *SA*(TillOster 23)*B* π. ἐπάνω, Ps 90
13 *S*(*B* ϩⲟⲙⲉ.), Hos 5 11 *AB*, He 10 29 *B*(*S* ⲥⲱⲟⲩϥ)
καταπ., Mic 7 10 *SAB* εἰς καταπάτημα εἶναι, Dan 7
7 *B*(*S* acc) συμπ. acc ; Deu 33 29 *S*(*B* ⲁⲗⲏⲓ ⲉϫ.) ἐπιβαίνειν ἐπί ; Ps 107 9 *S*(*B* diff) ἐπιβάλλειν ἐπί ; Col
2 18 *B*(*S* ⲙⲟⲟϣⲉ) ἐμβατεύειν ; BG 106 *S* ⲉⲧⲉⲧⲛⲉϩ.
ⲉϫⲛⲧⲉϥⲡⲣⲟⲛⲟⲓⲁ, HM 1 6 *S* ⲁⲩϩ. ⲉϫⲛⲡⲉⲥⲛⲟϥ, Mani
1 *A²* ϩ. ⲁϫⲛⲧⲙⲛⲧϫⲁⲥⲓϩⲏⲧ, C 41 34 *B* ϫⲁ ⲡⲉϥϭⲁⲗⲁⲩϫ ⲉϩ. ⲁⲛ ⲉ. ⲡⲓⲕⲁϩⲓ = Bor 134 4 *S*(Vita Sin)
ⲙⲟⲟϣⲉ ϩⲓϫⲛ-;   ⲉϩⲣⲁⲓ ⲉϫⲛ-: 1 Kg 17 53 *B*(*S* diff),
Ez 32 13 *SB* καταπ. acc ; PS 141 *S* ϩ. ⲉϩ. ⲉϫⲛⲧⲉ-
ⲡⲣⲟⲃⲟⲗⲏ...ⲛⲥϩ. ⲉϫⲛ-, ShC 73 24 *S* ϩ. ⲉϩ. ⲉϫⲙⲡⲥⲁ-

ⲧⲁⲡⲁⲥ, Mani 1 A² ⲁⲅϩ. ⲁϩ. ⲁϫⲱⲥ, MG 25 36 B ⲉϣⲧⲉⲙϩ. ⲉϩ. ⲉ. ϩⲗⲓ ⲛϣⲉ ⲛⲧⲁⲧⲥⲓ ⲛⲥϩⲓⲙⲓ; ⲥ ⲛ-, *with*: Mt 7 6 SB ⲕⲁⲧⲁⲡ. ἐν, MG 25 234 B I swore not to ϩ. ⲡⲣⲁⲧ ⲙⲙⲁⲩ ⲡ. τὰ ἐκεῖ = EW 239 لا اتى برجلى, cf Mani 1 A² tr above, R 1 4 17 S ϩ. ⲉϫⲱⲟⲩ ⲛⲛⲉϥⲟⲩⲉⲣⲏⲧⲉ *pede calcare*; ⲥ ⲛⲥⲁ-: Tri 349 S ϩ. ⲛⲥⲁⲡⲉⲕⲥⲁⲧⲟⲟⲉ (*l?* ⲡⲉⲕⲟⲟⲉ) داس انارك; ⲥ ϩⲓ-: Is 42 16 S(B ϭⲉⲛ-) ⲡ. acc; Jer 29 13 B neg (S ⲙⲟⲟϣⲉ ϩⲓ-) ἄβατος; ⲥ ϩⲛ-, ϭⲉⲛ-, *with*: Ez 26 11 B ⲕⲁⲧⲁⲡ. ἐν; *in*: Is 16 10 B(S ⲉ-) ⲡ. εἰς, Is 1 12 B(P 104 8, S =Gk), Ap 11 2 B(S acc) ⲡ. acc, ShC 73 137 S ϩⲉⲙ ⲡⲣⲁⲕϩⲉ ⲛⲡⲧⲉⲣⲓⲣ; ⲥ ϩⲓϫⲛ-: Is 42 5 B(S ⲉϫⲛ-) ⲡ. acc, 4 Kg 13 7 S ⲕⲁⲧⲁⲡⲁⲧⲏⲥⲓⲥ; PO 14 332 B ϩ. ϩ. ⲛⲡⲁⲑⲟⲥ.

—— *SB* nn m, *treading, trampling*: Is 22 5 S(B ϩⲟⲙϩⲉⲙ) ⲕⲁⲧⲁⲡⲁⲧⲏⲙⲁ; P 44 87 S ⲛϩ. وزد; C 86 107 B ⲟⲩⲓⲟⲙ ⲉⲑⲃⲉⲡϩ. ⲙⲡⲓϩⲣⲁⲗⲟⲗⲓ.

ⲁⲧϩ. B, *untrodden*: Lev 16 22 (S ⲙⲉⲩⲙⲟⲟϣⲉ ⲡⲣⲏⲧϥ) ἄβατος.

ⲙⲁ ⲛϩ. B, *place of treading*: Is 7 25 (S ϣⲁⲓⲣⲉ) ⲕⲁⲧⲁⲡⲁⲧⲏⲙⲁ.

ⲣⲉϥϩ. B, *treader* of wine-press: Is 63 2 (S ⲙⲣⲓⲥ) ⲡⲁⲧⲏⲧⲟⲥ (*var* ⲡⲁⲧⲱⲛ *calcans*).

(ϩⲁⲙⲏⲧ), pl ϩⲁⲙⲉⲧⲉ A², as last: Mani 1 church is wine, wisdom wine-press, ⲛⲥⲱⲧⲡ ⲙⲡ̅ⲡ̅ⲉⲛⲉ ⲛϩ. (*Cf* ϩⲱⲗ, ϩⲁⲗⲏⲧ).

Cf ϩⲟⲙϩⲉⲙ.

ϩⲁⲉⲓⲙⲉ AA², ϩⲱⲓⲙⲓ B v ϩⲟⲉⲓⲙ.

ϩⲁⲙⲉ S nn f, *an implement*, *peg* (?) for marking height of inundation: Osir no 44 Thou (God) hast brought us the water ⲉⲣⲟⲩⲛ ⲁⲑⲁⲙⲉ, ib 38, 47 (*cf* P Oxy 1830 ἔνθεμα); in lists (same?): Bodl(P) d 47 ⲗⲁⲕ, ϩ., ϩⲁⲗϭⲓⲥ, ib f 44 ϩⲛϫⲉ, ϩ., ϣⲁⲗⲟⲟⲩ, PLond 4 516 ⲟⲩϩⲁⲙⲏ ⲙ[ⲛⲟⲩⲁ]ⲕⲉⲓⲥ (ἀκίς), Ryl 239 ⲟⲩϩ. *Cf?* ϩⲟⲙⲉ, if bowl or receiver could be thus used. ϩⲁⲙ(ⲉ) ⲡⲧⲱⲛ p 422 b is m.

ϩⲁⲙⲛⲓ S nn f, among σκεύη: Ep 546 ⲗⲁⲕⲏⲧ, ⲭⲏⲣⲉ, ⲥⲛⲧⲉ ⲛϩ., CO 459 varia ⲟⲩϩ. *Cf?* last.

ϩⲁⲙⲛⲓ B v ϩⲙⲟⲩ s f.

ϩⲁⲙⲟⲓ S, ⲁⲙ. S(once)B, ϩⲁⲙⲁⲓ S'A²F, ⲁⲙⲁⲓ F interj, *would, O that*, followed by various vbal prefixes. ⲉⲛⲉ-: Ex 16 3 B(S ⲛⲁⲛⲟⲩⲥ), Nu 14 2 B(S ⲟⲩⲛⲟϭⲣⲉ) ὄφελον; BHom 28 S ϩ. ⲉⲡⲉⲛⲧⲁⲩⲭⲡⲓⲉ ⲡⲉⲓⲣⲙⲙⲁⲟ εἴθε; ShViK 928 341 S of Judas ϩ. ⲉⲡⲉⲙⲡⲏⲅⲣ ⲁⲡⲟⲥⲧⲟⲗⲟⲥ ⲉⲛⲉϥ, ShRE 11 18 S ϩ. ⲉⲡⲉⲣⲉⲟⲩϭⲩⲛϩⲟϩⲟⲥ…ⲡⲁⲧⲁϩⲉ ⲡⲁⲓ, Wess 18 76 S ϩ. ⲉⲡⲉⲩⲛ ⲙⲉⲧⲁⲛⲟⲓⲁ ϣⲟⲟⲡ, ShC 73 180 S ϩ. ϭⲉ ⲉⲡⲉⲙⲛ ⲣⲱⲙⲉ ⲛⲕⲟⲧⲕ, Miss 4 775 S'ϩ. ⲉⲡⲉⲥⲡⲁϣⲱⲡⲉ ⲡⲁⲓ, Mor 41 105 S ⲁ. ⲉⲡⲉⲁⲑⲟⲟⲗⲉ ⲟⲩⲱⲙ ⲛⲡⲉⲕⲥⲁⲣⲝ, ib 27 5 F ϩ. ⲉⲡⲁⲓⲥⲁⲟⲩⲛ = BMis 324 S ϩ. ⲉⲛⲉ(ⲉ)ⲙⲟⲉⲓ, Mor 30 36 F ⲁ. ⲉⲡ(ⲉ)ⲙⲡⲓⲧⲁⲅⲁ = BMis 261 S ϩ. ⲙⲡⲉⲓϫⲱ, Va

57 87 B ⲁ. ⲉⲡⲉⲙⲡⲉϥϣⲱⲡⲓⲉ; ⲉⲣⲉ- B: C 43 117 ⲁ. ⲣⲱ ⲉⲣⲉⲧⲉⲡⲟⲩⲟϫ; ⲁ. ⲉⲥⲟⲩⲟⲧⲉⲃ ⲉⲃⲟⲗ; ⲡⲧⲉ-: Ps 118 5 B(S ⲛⲁⲛⲟⲩⲥ ⲉⲣⲉ-), Gal 5 12 B(S ⲉⲡⲉ-) ⲟϥ.; C 89 215 B ⲁ. ⲛⲧⲉⲡⲟⲩⲁⲓ ⲡⲟⲩⲁⲓ ϭⲟϫⲓ (S C 100 302 ϩ. ⲉⲣⲉ- ⲡⲁ-) εἴ.; ShA 1 231 S ϩ. ⲛⲧⲉⲧⲙⲡⲉⲓϣⲁϫⲉ ⲧⲱⲙⲛⲧ, MG 25 100 B ⲁ. ⲡⲧⲉϥⲙⲟⲩ, PcodMor 50 F ϩ. ⲧⲉⲡⲁϩⲓⲟⲩⲉ ⲥⲁⲧⲛ; ⲡⲁⲣⲉ- B: 2 Cor 11 1 (S ⲛⲁⲛⲟⲩⲥ ⲉⲡⲉ-) ⲟϥ.; AM 15 ⲁ. ⲡⲁⲓⲟⲓ ⲛⲥⲧⲣⲁⲧⲩⲗⲁⲧⲏⲥⲡⲉ; ⲁ- B: AM 270 ⲁ. ⲁⲓϭⲓ ⲙⲡⲉϥⲕⲉⲥⲙⲟⲧⲡⲉ εἴ., MIE 2 382 ⲁ. ⲁⲓⲙⲟⲩ ⲙⲫⲟⲟ ⲟⲩⲡⲉ; ⲡⲧⲁ-: KKS 587 S ϩ. ⲛⲧⲁⲕⲗⲟⲩϫⲓϭⲉ ⲙⲙⲟⲓ, JKP 2 150 S ϩ. ⲛⲧⲁⲕϭⲓ ⲃⲁⲡⲧⲓⲥⲙⲁ, FR 96 B ⲁ.….ⲛⲧⲁⲟⲩϫⲁⲓ; ⲉϣⲁⲣⲉ- S: JKP 2 242 ϩ. ⲉϣⲁⲕⲉⲓ; ⲉⲣⲉ- ⲡⲁ-: BMis 382 S ϩ. ⲉⲓⲛⲁϩⲉ ⲉⲣⲟϥ = Va 63 12 B ⲁ. ⲛⲁⲓⲛⲁϩⲉⲙϩ, DeV 1 74 B ⲁ. ⲉⲣⲉⲟⲩⲭⲱ ⲉⲃⲟⲗ ⲡⲁⲓϣⲱⲡⲓ; ⲡⲁⲣⲉ- ⲡⲁ- A²B: ManiP 58 ϩ. ⲡⲉⲧⲉⲧⲁϣ ⲡⲉϥ, AM 229 ⲁ. ⲡⲁⲓⲛⲁϣ ϫⲉⲙ ϫⲟⲙ; ⲛⲉⲁ- B: 1 Cor 4 8 (S ⲛⲁⲡ. ⲉϣϫⲉ-) ⲟϥ.; Cat 95 ⲁ. ⲡⲉⲁⲓⲡⲁⲩ, C 43 30 ⲁ. ⲡⲉⲁϥⲉⲣ ⲟⲩⲥⲓⲁⲡⲉ; ⲛⲛⲉ-: R 1 4 53 S ϩ. ⲡⲛⲉⲓⲛⲁϣ ϭⲙ ϭⲟⲙ ⲛⲕⲧⲟⲕ; ⲙⲡⲉ- S: BMis 261 ϩ. ⲙⲡⲉⲓϫⲱ.

With ⲉϣⲱⲡⲉ S: BMis 269 ϩ. ⲉϣ. ⲉⲡⲣⲏⲧ ⲙ-…ⲧⲏⲧ ⲛⲙⲙⲁⲛ, P 129¹⁸ 106 ϩ. ⲉϣ. ⲡⲟⲩϩⲙϩⲁⲗ (ⲛ)ⲡⲁϣⲧⲣⲁϥ ⲁⲡⲡⲉ = EW 44 B ⲁⲣⲏⲟⲩ.

Without vb: ShC 73 92 S ϩ. (ⲉ)ⲡⲉⲁⲛⲟⲡ ⲟⲩⲁ ⲙⲙⲟⲟⲩ, ShBor 246 85 S ϩ. ⲟⲛ ⲉⲡⲉⲉⲧⲃⲉⲟⲩⲙⲛⲧⲁⲧⲥⲟⲟⲩⲡ, EW 45 B ⲁ. ⲡⲓⲧⲉⲃⲛⲱⲟⲩⲓ ⲙⲙⲁⲅⲁⲧⲟⲩⲡⲉ, HB I cxlvii ⲁ. ⲡⲉ ⲡⲁⲙⲟⲕⲙⲉⲛ ⲟⲩⲡⲉ ⲧⲉⲥⲁⲡⲟⲗⲟⲅⲓⲁ?, Va 57 191 B ⲁ. ϣⲁϥⲁⲓ ⲙⲙⲁⲅⲁⲧⲩⲡⲉ εἴ.

ϩⲉⲙⲓ F v ϩⲙⲟⲙ (ϩⲙⲉ).

ϩⲉⲙⲓ B v ϩⲏⲙⲉ, ϩⲏⲙⲓ, ϩⲙⲙⲉ.

ϩⲏⲙⲉ SA, ϩⲉⲙⲉ², ϩⲙⲙⲉ³, ϩⲓⲙⲉ⁴ S, ϩⲏⲙⲓ⁵ BF, ϩⲏⲙⲙⲓ⁶ F, ϩⲉⲙⲓ⁷ B, ϩⲓⲙⲏ⁸ BF, ϩⲏⲙⲏ⁹ S'BF nn f, *fare, freight* on ship, camel: BMar 112 S sailor demands ⲧⲉϥϩ. ⲡⲧⲟⲟⲧϥ ⲛⲁⲩⲗⲟⲛ; ib 188 S to sailor ⲡⲉⲗⲕ ⲧϩ.² ⲛⲙⲙⲁⲛ μισθοῦν, ib ϩ.² ⲟⲩⲡⲟⲥⲧⲉ μισθὸς τοῦ πλοίου; K 233 B ⲧϩ.⁵ (varr⁸⁹) جملى, ⲕⲣⲁⲥ; ShC 42 71 S provisions & ϩ. for fugitives, Mor 53 6 S ⲙⲛ ϩ.³ ⲛⲧⲟⲟⲧⲟⲩ ⲉⲧⲣⲉⲩϫⲓⲟⲟⲣ, Bodl(P) d 32 S ⲑ. ⲙⲡⲉⲭⲓⲟⲟⲣ ⲛⲡⲧⲟϣ ⲁⲡⲧⲙⲟⲟⲩ, C 86 347 B †ϩ.⁵ (var⁷) ⲡⲉⲙⲡⲓⲭⲟ ⲉⲃⲟⲗ ⲛⲧⲉ ⲡⲓⲙⲱⲓⲧ, LAp 570 F would carry thee free ⲙⲡⲁⲣⲁ ϭⲓⲥⲧⲃⲉ ⲛϩ.⁶, J 5 R 14 S ϩ. ⲛⲭⲟⲓ, ST 133 S sim paid in wine, ib ϩ. ⲕⲁⲙⲟⲩⲗ, ib 38 S ⲧϩ. ⲛⲕⲁⲙⲟⲩⲗ shared, Kr 25 F ⲑ.⁹ (ⲉ)ⲡⲏⲣⲉⲡ for transport to town, Ep 299 S ⲙⲁⲁϫⲉ (of corn) ⲛϩ. paid by camel-herd, Tor 2 S will deliver barley ⲉⲡⲉⲕⲏ ϩⲛⲧⲁϩ., ib 7 S ϩⲛⲡⲁϩ., Kr 104 S' ⲧⲁⲣⲓϫⲓ ⲧⲁϩ.⁹ ⲡⲣⲟⲥ ⲫⲟⲣ[ⲁ; †ϩ., *pay fare*: Jon 1 3 SAB *v.* διδόναι, R 1 4 39 S ⲉϥⲛⲁ† ⲟⲩ ϩⲁⲟ.² ⲙⲡⲭⲟⲓ *naulum*; ShClPr 22 357 S ⲉⲧⲣⲉⲩ† ⲧⲉϥϩ. at ferry, Mor 50 34 S ⲧⲉⲧⲛⲛⲁϣ † ⲟⲩⲏⲣ ⲛϩ.³ ⲡⲁⲓ ϩⲁⲡⲁⲭⲟⲓ?, ib.³ ⲙⲡⲁϭⲓⲡ ⲙⲡⲁⲭⲟⲓ, Miss 4 237 S ⲁϥ† ϩ.³ ϩⲁⲣⲟⲟⲩ & put them aboard, BP 10589 S † ϩ. ϩⲓⲱⲟⲟⲩ, CO 160 S ⲛⲧⲁ† ⲧⲟⲩϩ. & deliver them

(wine), Ep 352 *S* will bring camels ⲛϭⲧ ⲧϭⲉⲙⲏ, Kr 132 *S* ⲧⲁⲧⲓ ⲧⲉϥϩ. ⲛⲁⲕ as husbandmen use, AZ 23 27 *Sf* ⲡⲉⲧⲁⲕⲧⲁⲁⲃ ⲉϩ. ϩⲁⲛⲣⲱⲥⲉⲙ; ⲁⲧϩ., *free of freight*: Kr 22 *F* will deliver wine ⲛⲁⲧϩ.⁹, BMOr 6201 A 34 *S* property ⲧⲉⲛⲟⲩ ⲍⲉ ⲉϥⲟ ⲙⲙⲁ ⲛⲧⲱⲕ ⲡⲁⲧⲏ ⲑ.⁴ ⲛ[(same ?).

— as measure (same ?): Hall 117 *S* ⲙⲡⲧⲉ ⲡϩ. ⲡⲣⲙⲟⲩ, BM 641 *F* ⲍ̄ ⲡϩⲛⲙⲙ ⲛⲏⲣⲉⲡ.

ϩⲏⲙⲉ *v* ϩⲟⲉⲓⲙ.

ϩⲏⲙⲙ, ϩⲉ. *B* nn m, *dower of divorced wife*: K 103 ⲡⲓϩ. ⲛ⳨ⲥⲟⲓⲙⲉ فرض المراة (var مهر). *V* AZ 14 62, Lane *Mod Eg* (1837) 1 140.

ϩⲓⲙⲙⲉ *v* ϩⲟⲓⲙⲉ & ϩⲏⲙⲉ.

ϩⲓⲙⲙⲏ *v* ϩⲟⲉⲓⲙ.

ϩⲓⲱⲙⲙⲉ. ϩⲓⲟ. *S*, ϩⲓⲟⲡⲉ (*sic*) *A*, ϩⲱⲙⲉ *SA²* nn f, *palm, hollow* of hand: 1 Kg 5 4 ἴχνος (opp ⲥⲃⲟⲓ καρπός); Pro 29 37 *SA*(*B* ⲁⲙⲁϩⲓ πῆχυς; Glos 278 ⲑⲱⲙⲉ ⲛϭⲓϫ · δράξ, θέναρ; ShZ 594 ϩ. ⲛϭⲓϫ (Dan 5 5 ἀστράγαλος, *B* ⲧⲱⲣⲓ); ShBM 212 how can he smite that hath not ⲧⲏⲛⲃⲉ ⲟⲩⲇⲉ ϩ. ⲛϭ.?, Tri 437 grasped thee ϩⲛⲧⲣⲓⲟ. ⲛⲧⲉϥϭ. اراج (var كف), Mani 1 *A²* ⲑⲱⲙⲉ ⲛⲧⲟⲟⲧ[ⲥ; MIF 9 57 ϩ. ⲛϭ. resting on Virgin's head, Mor 28 79 ϩ. ⲛϭ. ⲁⲥⲣⲱⲃⲉ ⲉⲃⲟⲗ ⲉϫⲙⲡⲥⲱⲙⲁ of martyr, BMar 235 ⲡⲉⲧⲛⲣⲟⲩⲡ ϩⲁⲧⲉⲣ. ⲛⲧⲉϥϭ.

ϩⲟⲙⲙ *S* nn f, *cup*: ShP 130ᵏ 65 vessels for eating & drinking ϣⲁϩⲣⲁⲓ ⲉⲛϫⲟⲡ ⲙⲛϩ., Cai 42573 2 ⲧϩ. ⲉⲧⲉⲣⲉⲡⲣⲱⲙⲉ ⲥⲱ ϩⲓⲟⲥ.

ϩⲱⲓⲙⲙ *B v* ϩⲟⲉⲓⲙ, adding MG 25 161 ⲱⲗⲕ ⲛⲥⲁϯϩ.

ϩⲱⲙⲙ *B v* ϩⲱⲙ.

ϩⲱⲱⲙⲉ, ϩⲱⲙ(ⲉ), ϩⲁ(ⲁ)ⲙⲧ *S* vb intr, *be thin, lean*, qual: Lev 13 30 (*B* om, but Va دقيق), Ge 41 6 ⲟ ⲛⲕⲏⲧⲩ ⲛϩ. حس (P 44 104 *sic*, *l* ? حـ, varr 43 87 ϩⲙ حش, Wess ⲟ ⲛϩⲟⲟⲙⲉ, *B* ϣⲟⲙ ⲥ) λεπτός; ⲥ ⲉⲃⲟⲗ, *be blighted, pine away*: Z 329 lifelong sickness ϣⲁⲛⲧⲉϥϩ. ⲉⲃ. ⲁⲩⲱ ⲁϥⲙⲟⲩ, Mor 29 45 declined daily ϣⲁⲛⲧⲉϥϩ. ⲉⲃ. & came nigh to death (BMis 275 om), *ib* 22 140 woman with ἀπόστημα ⲛⲧⲁⲥϩ. ⲉⲃ. ⲉⲡⲧⲏⲣϥ = BSM 131 *B* ϣⲙⲁ ⲉⲃ., Mus 48 290 sim dropsy ⲁⲥϩ. ⲉⲃ. ⲁⲥϣⲁⲃⲉ ⲧⲏⲣⲥ, J 104 14 ⲁⲓⲣ ϫⲏⲧⲩ ⲁⲓϩⲱ ⲙ(ⲉ)ⲉⲃ.; as nn : Deu 28 22 (*B* ⲭⲓⲗϥⲉϩ) ἀνεμοφθορία; R 2 4 58 ⲡⲟⲩⲟⲧⲟⲩⲉⲧ ⲛⲡⲉⲧⲉⲉⲧ, ⲛϩ. ⲉⲃ. ⲛⲡⲉⲧⲛⲁϫⲓ ⲟⲩⲱ; ϩⲟⲟⲙⲉ nn or adj *v* Ge 41 above. *Cf* ϩⲙⲡⲓϭⲉ p 239 *b* (though ϩⲙ-? = ϣⲏⲙ).

ϩⲙⲁ *A* prob for ϩⲙⲁⲙ, *v* ϩⲙⲟⲙ.

ϩⲙⲉ *SAA²B*, -ⲏ *Sf*, ϩⲙ *B* numeral m f, *forty* (*BF* mostly ⲙ̄): m Ge 18 29, Jud 12 14, Cl 53 2 *A*, Miss 4 767 *Sf* ϩ. ⲛⲣⲟⲟⲩ, Mus 34 195 *B* ϩⲙ ⲛⲉϩⲟⲟⲩ; f Ps 94 10, Am 2 10 *A*, Ac 7 23 (*BF* ⲙ̄), RA 188 *B* ϩⲙ

ⲡⲣⲟⲙⲡⲓ; Nu 1 37 ϩ. ⲧⲏ, Ap 11 2 ϩ. ⲥⲛⲟⲟⲩⲥ, Jo 2 20 *A²* ϩ. ⲧⲉⲥⲉ, Mani 1 *A²* ϩ. ⲧⲉⳓⲧⲉ, PS 21 ϩ. ⲯⲓⲧ, Lev 25 8 ϩ. ⲯⲓⲧⲉ, *cf* PO 11 703 ⲙ̄ⲏ̄ هماايسيت; *forty days* fast, *Lent*: Aeg 229 ⲡⲉϩ. ⲛⲣⲟⲟⲩ ⲉⲧⲟⲩⲁⲁⲃ ⲧⲉⲥⲥⲁⲣⲁⲕⲟⲥⲧⲏ; BAp 105 ⲡⲡⲁⲥⲭⲁ ⲙⲡⲉϩ. ⲛⲣⲟⲟⲩ, ShC 73 154 ⲧⲏⲛⲥϯ ⲛ ⲡⲉϩ. ⲛⲣⲟⲟⲩ, BM 954 lessons for ⲡⲉϩ. ⲛⲣⲟⲟⲩ, Mus 45 25 *B* ⲡⲓⲉϩⲙⲉ ⲛⲉϩⲟⲟⲩ, BM 157 1st Sunday of ⲡⲉϩⲙⲉ, HL 73 *B* 5th Sabbath ⲛⲧⲉ ⲡⲓϩ., Ep 136 ⲡⲛⲱⲗ ⲉⲃⲟⲗ ⲙⲡⲉϩ., Miss 4 760 *Sf* fasting ϩⲙⲡⲉϩ.; not Lent: MIE 2 339 *B* ⲡⲓϩ. ⲛⲧⲉ ⲡⲓϣⲱⲙ in Paône (*cf* Ep 1 171), Mor 53 34 fasted ϣⲟⲙⲛⲧ ⲛϩ. yearly = TstAb 231 *B* ⲍ̄ ⲛϩⲙ, Miss 4 212 *B* ϩⲙ ⲛⲉϩⲟⲟⲩ of penitence; *fortieth*: Nu 33 38 ⲙⲉϩϩ. ⲡⲣⲟⲙⲡⲉ (*B* ⲙⲁϩⲙ̄), Jos 14 10 ⲧⲙⲉϩϩ. ⲧⲏ.

ϩⲙⲏ, ϩⲏⲙⲙ, ϩⲩ. *B* nn m f, *pelican*: Lev 11 18 ⳨ϩ. (in P 44 105 حربا, *cf* Zeph 2 14), Deu 14 17 شاهين (confusion), Ps 101 6 (all *S* ϩⲣⲓⲙ) πελεκάν; K 168 ⲡⲓϩ. غيهب.

ϩⲙⲙ, or rather ⲁϩⲙⲓ vb, prob for احمى *make hot*: PChass 1 19 ⲧⲱⲣϭ ⲛ̄ⲣⲁⲧ ⲁ. ⲙⲙⲟⲩ ϥⲛⲁⲟⲩⲃⲁϣ, *ib* 2 22 ⲁ. ⲙⲙⲟⲩ ϩⲛⲡⲕⲱϩⲧ, Bodl(P) a 1 e ⲁ. ⲙⲙⲟⲩ ⲕⲁⲗⲱⲥ & put in vinegar, *ib* g ⲁϥⲁ. ⲙⲙⲟⲩ ⲛⲍ̄ ⲛⲥⲟⲡ.

ϩⲙⲟⲩ *SAB*, ϩⲉⲙⲟⲩ *F* nn m, *salt*: Lev 2 13 *SB*, Ez 16 4 *SB*, Mk 9 50 *SB*, Cl 111 2 *A* ⲥⲧⲏⲗⲏ ⲛϩ. ἅλς, ἅλας, Ps 106 34 *B* (*S* diff) ἅλμη; ShViK 9596 186 *S* ⲡⲉϩ. …ⲉⲩⲟⲩⲱⲙ ⲡⲛⲏⲧϥ ⲙⲡⲉⲩⲟⲉⲓⲕ ϣⲏⲙ, ShC 73 55 *S* ϯ ⲡⲉϩ ⲉⲡⲉϩ. ⲛ ⲉⲡⲗⲁⲯⲁⲡⲉ, BM 1001 *S* ⲟⲩⲟⲉⲓⲕ ⲉϥⲙⲉϩ ⲛϩ., CA 97 *S* ⲟⲉⲓⲕ ϩⲓϩ. during Pascha, Tri 496 *S* ϩ., ϩⲙϫ, ⲟⲉⲓⲕ food of monks, MG 25 263 *B* ⲡⲓⲧⲱⲟⲩ ⲛⲧⲉ ⲡⲓϩ. = *ib* ⲡⲓⲧ. ⲛⲧⲉ ⲡⲓⲣⲟⲥⲉⲙ, AM 235 *B* ϩⲉⲙϫ, ⲕⲟⲡⲓⲁ, ϩ. rubbed into wounds, ST 117 *S* ⲕⲟⲩϥ(ⲟⲛ) ⲛϩ., CO 212 *S* ⲑⲁⲗⲓⲥ ⲛϩ., RE 9 158 *S* ⲁⲣⲧⲟⲃ ⲛϩ., BM 657 *F* ⲉⲣⲧⲟⲩ ⲛϩⲉⲙⲟⲩ, BP 402 *S* ⲙⲁⲭⲉ ⲛϩ., KroppM 87 *S* ⲛⲕⲗⲁⲗ ⲛϩ., ShC 73 136 *S* ⲙⲟⲩ ⲛϩ. made fresh daily, Ryl 108 *S* sim as eye-disease; Ge 14 3 *S* ⲑⲁⲗⲁⲥⲥⲁ ⲛⲡⲉϩ., *B* ⲓⲟⲙ ⲛⲧⲉ ⲡⲓϩ. ἅλς, Nu 34 3 *S* sim (var ⲙⲁⲗϩ, *B* ⲉⲧⲙⲟⲗϩ) ἁλυκός, *v* also as place-name; *various sorts S*: AJSL 46 249 ϩ. ⲙⲡⲉⲧⲣⲁ, PMéd 273 ⲛ̄ⲧⲟⲟⲩ, *ib* 204 ⲛⲟⲩⲱⲙ, KroppJ 65 ϩ. ⲛⲡⲣⲣⲟ, AZ 23 116, PMéd 159 sim, Bodl(P) 2 9 ϩ. ⲡⲁⲗⲕⲉⲗⲓ (*cf* PMéd 312), Hall 65 recipes ϩ. ⲙⲡⲁⲣⲁ (*cf* p 267 *a*), KroppK 41 ⲛⲕⲱⲥ, ShC 73 144 ⲛⲧⲉ ⲧⲡⲩⲗⲏ opp ϩ. ⲉϥⲟⲩⲟϫ *unmixed*; ⲣ ϩ. *S, become salt*: Bor 226 175 if earth turn again ⲛϥⲣ ϩ.; ⳨ ϩ. *S, put, add salt*: Lev 2 13 (*B* ⲓⲛⲓ ⲉϩⲟⲩⲛ ⲛⲟⲩϩ.) ⲁ̆. προσφέρειν; ShViK 913 ⲛⲥⲉⲧⲛⲧ ϩ. ⲉⲣⲟϥ ϣⲁϥⲗⲱⲙⲥ, Wess 15 152 ⲁⲥⲧ ϩ. ⲉⲡⲉϥⲕⲟⲩⲓ ⲛⲥⲱⲙⲁ (*sc* babe's) ⲁⲥϩⲟⲕⲙⲉϥ; ϫⲓ ϩ. *S, be salted*: Kr 243 ⲧⲛ̄ⲧ ⲉⲩϫⲓ ϩ., Mor 51 34 (parable) ⲛϫⲓ ⲛϩ. *salt-cellar*, (interpr) ⲡⲛⲟϭ ⲛⲣⲉⲙⲛⲏ; ⲁⲧϩ., *unsalted*: Mk 9 50 *B* (*S* ϩⲁⲁⲃⲉ) ἄναλος, Job 6 6 *B* (*S* ⲁϫⲛϩ.) ἄνευ ἁλός; P

Méd 297 *S* swine's fat ⲛⲁ., BKU 1 1 *vo S* ⲟⲩⲁⲙϥ
ⲡⲁ.;   ⲙⲁ ⲡⲉϩ. *S*, *place where salt extracted*(?): Miss
4 778 he made ⲟⲩⲕⲟⲩⲓ ⲛⲙ. where brethren might
work; Turin papA 2 ⲡⲙⲁ ⲙⲡⲉϩ.;   ⲥⲁ ⲡϩ. *S*, *salt-
dealer*: WS 134 (*cf* ἁλοπώλης), PMich 3553 ⲯⲁⲛⲉϩ.
As name: Περμου (PBad 93), Saq 89, 158 ⲡⲓϩⲙⲟⲩ
(title?).

  ϩⲁⲙⲓ *B*, ⲙⲁ ⲛ-, *salt land*: Job 39 6 ἁλμυρίς.
Cf ? ⲗⲉϩⲙⲟⲩ.

In place-names: 2 Kg 8 13 ⲡⲓⲁ ⲡⲡⲉϩⲙⲟⲩ Γεμέ-
λεχ, PLond 4 597 Πουαμϩμου.

  ϩⲟⲙⲃⲉ *B v* ϩⲟⲩⲃⲉ.

  ϩⲉⲙⲕⲓ *B v* ϩⲛⲕⲉ.

  ϩⲙⲕⲟ *v* ⲟⲙⲕⲟ.

  ϩⲁⲙⲏⲗ *F v* ϩⲁⲙⲏⲣ.

  ϩⲁⲙⲟⲩⲗⲁϩⲭ *v* ⲙⲟⲩⲗⲁϩ.

  ϩⲙⲟⲙ, ϣⲙⲟⲙ (twice) *S*, ϩⲙⲁⲙ *A*, ϩⲙ. *S*/*A²F*,
ϩⲙⲟⲙ *B*, ϩⲛⲙ† *SA²F*, ϩⲛⲙ† *B* vb intr, *be hot*: Ps
38 3 *SB*, Is 44 15 *SB*, Hos 7 7 *AB*, Ja 2 16 *SAB* θερμαίνεσθαι, Ex 16 21 *SB* διαθ.; Ez 24 5 *B*(*S* ϩⲣⲃⲣ) ζεῖν;
Is 1 6 *B*(*S* † ⲧⲕⲁⲥ) φλεγμαίνειν; BMis 547 *S* ⲥⲉ-
ⲡⲁϣⲙ. ⲁⲛ (*cf* James *Apocr Anecd* 34 *calefiunt*); R 1
3 6 *S* antelopes (ϣⲟⲩ) surrounded him ϩⲱⲥⲧⲉ ⲛϥϩ.,
BKU 1 21 *Sʲ* ⲥⲁϩⲧⲉ ϩⲁⲣⲁϥ ϣⲁⲡⲧⲉϥϩ., ROC 25 250
B ⲁϥϩ. ⲛϫⲉ ⲡⲉϥⲡⲛⲁ;   qual: 1 Kg 21 6 *S* ⲉϥϩ.
ⲏ ⲉϥϩⲣⲟⲟⲩⲧ, Job 37 17 *SB* θερμός; Mt 8 14 *SBF*
(RChamp 543) πυρέσσειν; Ro 12 11 *B*(*SF* ϩ.) ζ., Ap
3 15 *SB* ζεστός; ROC 18 171 *S* ⲙⲡⲓⲟⲩⲉⲙ ⲡⲉⲧϩ.
ἕψημα; ShMiss 4 283 *S* water ⲉⲥⲕⲏⲃ opp ⲉⲥϩ., BMar
5 *S* ϭⲓⲟⲩⲱⲙ ⲉϥϩ., Mor 41 156 *S* ⲗⲁⲭⲁⲛⲟⲛ ⲉϥϩ.,
Ryl 106 21 *S* ⲉⲣⲱⲧⲉ ⲉⲥϩ., ManiK 54 *A²* sim, CA 101
S loaves ⲉⲩϩ. (opp ⲥⲕⲁⲡ), Rec 6 184 *B* sim, AZ 23
114 *S* ⲡⲕⲣⲟⲙ ⲉϥϩ. (*cf* 111 ⲡⲕⲟϩⲧ ⲉⲧϩⲏⲕ), Mor 41
199 *S* sick man ⲉϥⲥⲛϭ...ⲉϥϩ., AM 313 *B* ⲉϩⲟⲓ ⲛϩⲣⲟϣ
ⲓⲧⲉ ⲉⲩϩ.; Jer 38 2 *B* ⲙⲟⲩϩ. θερμός.

With following prepositions: C 43 76 *B* hast not
suffered (scalding water) ⲉϩ. ⲉⲣⲟⲕ;   1 Kg 4 19 *S*
ⲁⲡⲡⲁⲁⲕⲉ ϩ. ⲉϫⲱⲥ (Gk diff);   Job 31 20 *S* ϩ. ϩⲁ-
(*B* ⲉⲃⲟⲗ ϧⲉⲛ-) θ. ἀπό;   Bor 260 penult *S* ⲧⲉϥ-
ⲛⲁϩⲃⲉ ϩ. ϩⲙⲡⲥⲟⲣⲧ, BG 120 *S* ϩ. ⲉⲃⲟⲗ ϩⲙⲡⲛⲓϥⲉ.

—— nn m, *heat, fever*: Ps 18 7 *B*(*S* ϩⲙⲙⲉ), Ac
28 3 *B*(*S* do), Va 57 199 *B* ⲡⲟⲩϩ. ⲉϩⲟⲩⲛ ⲉϥ† θέρμη;
Deu 28 22 *SB*, Jo 4 52 *SA²BF*, BHom 40 *S* ⲟⲩϩ. ⲛ-
ϣⲱⲡⲉ πυρετός, Am 4 9 *SB* πύρωσις; Si 18 15 *S* καύσων; Ge 49 7 *B* μῆνις; P 44 79 *S* ⲡⲉⲛⲧⲩⲣⲟⲥ (ἴκτερος)·
ⲡⲉϩ. ﻟﺤﺲ; PS 348 *S* ⲕⲁⲅⲙⲁ, ϩ., ShA 1 105 *S* ⲡⲉϩ. ⲙ-
ⲡⲉϩⲣⲉⲩⲙⲁ, ShZ 593 *S* ⲟⲩϩ., ⲟⲩϩⲁⲣⲟϣ, C 438 5 *B* sim,
ManiK 119 *A²* sim, BM 1223 *A* sim ϩⲙⲁ, Kropp C
25 *F* sim ϩⲛⲙⲁⲙ (*sic* !), Ryl 105 *S* ⲁⲥⲓⲕ, ⲁⲣⲟϣ, ϩ.,
AM 125 *B* sun ⲉⲧϩⲓⲟⲩⲓ ⲉⲃⲟⲗ ⲛⲟⲩϩ. (*cf* R 1 466 *S* ϩⲙ-

ⲙⲉ), BMar 85 *S* at death ⲟⲩⲛⲟϭ ⲛϣⲙ. ⲕⲱⲧⲉ ⲉⲣⲟⲕ,
BMEA 10576 *F* ⲟⲩϩ., PO 11 312 *B* ⲡⲓⲡⲓϣϯ ⲛϩ. ⲉ-
ϩⲟⲩⲛ ⲉⲡⲓⲁⲅⲁⲑⲟⲛ.

  † ϩ. *B*, *give heat, burn*: Nah 3 19 (*A* † ⲧⲕⲉⲥ)
φλεγμ.; Va 57 32 ⲑⲉⲣⲙⲟⲥ ⲡⲣⲉϥϯ ϩ.

  ϭⲓ ϩ. *B*, *get heat, be warmed*: DeV 1 156 ⲙⲁ ⲛϭⲓ
ⲭⲃⲟⲃ in summer, ⲙⲁ ⲛϭⲓ ϩ. in winter.

  ϩⲙⲙⲉ *SA²*, ϩⲉⲙⲓ *B*(rare), ϩⲉⲙⲓ, ϩⲉⲓⲙⲓ *F* nn f m
(*B*), *heat, fever*: Job 6 17 (*B* ϩⲙⲟⲙ), Eccl 4 11, Ac 28
3 (*B* do) θέρμη, Sa 2 4 θερμότης; Tri 348 ⲧϩ. ⲛⲧⲧⲉ-
ⲣⲡⲡⲁ ﺣﺮ; ShR 2 3 6 ⲑ. ⲙⲡⲉϩⲙⲟⲙ burning thee,
ShRE 10 161 ⲡⲕⲃⲱ ⲙⲡⲛϩ., ShC 73 199 ⲗⲱϭ ⲛϩ.,
ShA 1 244 ⲧⲉⲕϩ. (*sc* of evil passions), BMar 150 ⲧⲉⲓϩ-
ⲥⲱ...ⲉⲓϣⲡⲉ ⲡⲧⲁϩ. ⲛ̄ⲣⲏⲧⲥ, MG 25 345 *B* ⲧϩ. ⲙⲡⲓϫ-
ⲣⲱⲙ, Ora 4 24 ⲃⲱⲕ ⲉϩⲣⲁⲓ ⲉⲧϩ. *hot bath* (? *cf* below),
BKU 1 26 (8117) *F* ⲡⲉⲧⲉⲑ. ϩⲓⲗⲉϥ, Stegemann 50
F ⲃⲓ ⲑⲉⲓⲙⲓ (*sic* collated) ⲁⲃⲁⲗ;   m *B*: Job 29 ϩⲛ.
(*S* Gk om) ﺣﺮ, K 58 ⲡⲓϩ. ﺣﺮﺍﻝ, O'Leary Th 46 wind,
earth, water & ⲡⲓϩ.;   ⲙⲟⲩϩ., *hot water*: Ap 3 16
B(var & *S* -ϩⲛⲙ) ζεστός; Ora 1c ⲧⲕⲟⲗⲟⲙ(ⲃ)ⲛⲑⲣⲁ
ⲙⲙ., ManiP 46 *A²* ⲙ. opp ⲙⲟⲩⲛⲕⲃⲃⲉ;   ⲣϩ.: BMis
539 ⲙⲡⲟⲩⲣ ϩ. (Ap 3 16);   † ϩ.: ShR 2 3 42 rich
man's abodes ⲉⲩϯ ⲕⲃⲟ in summer, ⲉⲩϯ ϩ. in winter,
ShBM 202 183 fire neglected ⲙⲉϥϯ ϩ., C 89 100 *B*
pit of hell ⲉϥϯ ϩ. like fire, Leyd 314 sun ϯ ⲛⲧⲉϩ.
ⲉϩⲣⲁⲓ ⲉϫⲱϥ;   ϫⲓ ϩ.: Mor 28 27 nails shield fingers
& toes ϫⲉⲡⲡⲉⲩϫⲓ ϩ. ⲏ ⲡⲥⲉϫⲓ ⲟϭⲃ.

Cf ⲑⲙⲟ.

  ϩⲙⲙⲉ *SAA²*, ϩⲉⲙⲓ *B*, ϩⲙⲙⲓ *F* always with ⲣ,
ⲉⲣ, forming vb intr, *steer, guide S*: Ac 27 11 (*B* ⲣⲉϥⲉⲣ
ϩ.) κυβερνήτης; Ja 3 4 (*B* do) εὐθύνειν; ShA 2 48
ⲛⲉⲧⲣ. ϩⲏⲡⲧⲟⲡⲟⲥ ⲙⲡⲛⲃ̄;   c ⲉ- *S*: Tri 264 ⲉⲧⲣ.
ⲉⲡⲁϫⲟⲓ ﻣﺮﺷﺪ; ShP 130⁵ 15 when winnowing ⲥⲉⲣ ϩ.
ⲉⲧⲙⲧⲣⲉⲩⲙⲃⲗⲃⲓⲗⲉ be mixed with chaff;   c ⲉϫⲉⲛ-
B: Salib 121 ⲁϥⲉⲣ. ⲉϫⲱⲟⲩ (His sheep) ⲉⲃⲟⲗ ϩⲓⲧⲟⲧϥ
ⲙⲡⲓⲃⲁϣⲟⲣ ﺣﺮﺱ.

  tr: Pro 12 5 *SAB*, Su 5 *SB*, Miss 8 127 *S* true faith
ⲉⲥⲣ. human race κυβερνᾶν, Sa 14 3 *S* διακυ.; Job 37
10 *SB* οἰακίζειν; Sa 12 18 *S* διοικεῖν; ib 9 3 *S* δι-
έπειν; ib 10 5 *S* φυλάσσειν; PS 357 *S* ⲉⲕⲣ. ⲡⲙⲟⲛⲁⲭⲟⲥ, BMis 347 *S* ⲁϥⲣ. ⲙⲙⲟⲛ = BSM 13 *B* ⲉⲣ
ⲟⲓⲕⲟⲛⲟⲙⲓⲛ, Mor 31 236 *S* thou (headstone of corner)
hast held firm 2 walls & ⲁⲕⲣ. ⲙⲙⲟⲟⲩ (RylBull 11
409 *a* ﺿﺒﻄﻢ), Pcod 27 *S* pots smeared with pitch
ϣⲁⲡⲧⲟⲩⲣ. ⲙⲡⲏⲣⲡ ⲉⲧⲟⲩⲛⲁⲡⲟⲭϥ ⲉⲣⲟⲩ *preserve*(?),
Mani 1 *A²* ⲁⲣⲓ ϩ. ⲙⲙ[ⲁⲓ] ⲡⲁⲣⲉϥⲥⲱⲧⲉ, AM 207 *B*
ⲁϥⲉⲣ. ⲙⲙⲱⲩⲥⲏⲥ before Pharaoh, Wor 323 *F* God
ⲉⲧⲉⲣ. ⲙⲙⲁⲟⲩ (*sc* waters).

—— nn m *SA*, *guidance*: Pro 1 5 *SA*(*B* ⲣⲉϥⲉⲣ.),
1 Cor 12 28 (*B* ⲙⲉⲧⲣⲉϥⲉⲣ.) κυβέρνησις; ShA 2 144
ⲕⲁ ⲡⲉⲕⲣ. ⲛϩⲏⲧⲟⲩ (*sc* congregation), ShWess 9 122
ⲛⲧⲉⲡⲉϥⲟⲩⲱϣ ⲙⲡⲉϩⲣ. ϣⲱⲡⲉ ⲉϫⲱⲛ.

ⲁⲧⲣϩ. *S, unguided*: Bor 240 54 lest we restrict our-selves (ἐγκρατεύεσθαι) over much ϩⲡⲟⲩⲙⲛⲧⲁ.

ⲙⲁ ⲛⲉⲣϩ. *B, guidance (?)*: TEuch 2 22 ⲟⲩⲙ. ⲛⲧⲉ ⲗⲟⲅⲓⲥⲙⲟⲥ ⲛⲓⲃⲉⲛ دلم.

ⲣⲉϥⲣϩ. *SA²B, pilot, guide*: Ez 27 8 SB, Ac 27 11 B(S ⲡⲉⲧⲣ.) κυβερνήτης; BHom 117 S ship ⲉⲙ ⲣ. ⲛⲉⲣⲏⲧϥ, Mani 1 A² ⲡⲣ. ⲁⲡⲉⲭⲏⲅ, BSM xi B ⲡⲓⲣ. ⲛⲡⲉⲯⲩⲭⲏ; ⲙⲉⲧⲣⲉϥⲉⲣϩ. *B*: Pro 11 14 (SA ⲣ. ⲛⲛ), 1 Cor *lc* -ⲛⲏⲥⲓⲥ, Mani K 114 A² ϯⲙ. ⲛⲁⲅⲅⲉⲗⲟⲥ.

ϭⲓⲛⲉⲣϩ. *S*, Bor 240 55 avoiding excess ⲧϭ. ⲉⲧⲛⲁ-ⲡⲟⲩⲥⲧⲉ ⲧⲁⲓ.

ϩⲙⲙⲉ   *v* ϩⲏⲙⲉ & ϩⲙⲟⲙ.

ϩⲙⲛ *S* nn, meaning unknown, part (?) of a gar-ment: Ry 262 in list of σκεύη ⲟⲩϩⲙⲛ ⲉϣⲧⲏⲛ (*l*? ⲛϣ.) ⲉⲥϩⲟ. [.

ϩⲁⲙⲁⲛⲉⲓ *S* nn, form doubtful, meaning un-known: PLond 4 515 list of *varia* ⲟⲩϩⲁⲙⲁⲛⲉⲓ ⲁϩⲉⲓ[(might be otherwise divided).

ϩⲙⲉⲛⲉ, ϩⲁⲙⲛⲉ   *v* ϣⲙⲟⲩⲛ.

ϩⲟⲙⲛⲧ *S*, ϩⲁ. *SᵃSᶠA²F*, ϩⲟⲙ(ⲉ)ⲧ *S* (esp ostr), ϩⲁⲙⲧ *SᵃAF*, ϩⲟ. *BO*, ϩⲁⲙⲉⲧ *F* nn m, *copper, bronze*: Ge 4 22 SB, Deut 8 9 SB, Ez 1 7 SB, Bor 253 151 *S* rust ϩⲙⲛⲉ. χαλκός; BG 74 *S* ⲛⲙⲉⲧⲁⲗⲗⲟⲛ ⲙϥ. ⲛⲛ-ⲡⲡⲉⲛⲓⲡⲉ, PS 212 *S* ⲑⲩⲗⲏ ⲙⲛϩ., LAp 570 *F* gold, silver, ϩⲁⲙⲉⲧ, Mor 24 21 *F* -ⲉⲧ ϩⲓⲧⲉⲣⲧ = *ib* 23 30 *S* ⲃⲁⲥⲓϭ;   as adj: Nu 21 9 SB, Is 48 4 SB, Zech 6 1 *AB* χαλκοῦς, Job 41 6 SB χάλκειος; ⲉⲓⲡⲉ ⲛϩ. *S, chain of copper*: Ps 104 18 (*B* = Gk) πέδη, *ib* 67 6 (*B* ϩⲣⲱⲟⲩ ⲙⲡⲉϩⲉⲥ) πεδᾶ-σθαι; Mk 5 3 (*B* = Gk) ἅλυσις; C 43 5 *B* ⲉⲣⲉ ⲛϩ., LMär 34 *S* ⲧⲟⲩⲱⲧ ⲛϩ., AM 103 *B* ⲥⲱϫⲓⲟⲛ (ζώδιον) ⲛϩ., El 44 *A* ⲡⲩⲗⲏ ⲛϩ., BIF 15 234 *Sᶠ* ⲧⲣⲓⲣ ⲛϩ., BKU 1 1 20 *Sᵃ* ϩⲣⲱ ⲛϩ., CO 459 *S* ⲕⲁⲗⲁϩⲧ ⲛϩ., Pap *penes* BHStricker *Sᶠ* ⲥⲕⲉⲟⲩⲉ ⲛϩⲁⲙⲛ (*sic bis*), J 66 40 *S* ⲗⲁⲕⲁⲡⲛ ⲃⲁⲣⲱⲧ, ⲭⲟⲩ ⲛϩ., KroppM 37 *S* ϣⲟⲩⲣⲏ ⲛϩ., Ryl 242 *S* ϩⲏⲃⲥ ⲛϩ., Bodl(P)b 6 *S* ⲕⲉⲣⲉⲥⲁⲡⲧⲛ (ⲛ)ϩ. (*v* Ep 544 n), AZ 21 100 *O* ϭⲁⲗⲁⲟⲩϭ ⲛϩ., *v* also ⲕⲁⲗ-ⲕⲓⲗ, ⲕⲟⲅⲛϫⲟⲩ;   ϩ. ⲛⲃⲁⲣⲱⲧ *v* ⲣ 44 *a*;   as cop-per coin, *money* (*cf* ϩⲁⲧ): EpJer 34 *B*(*F* diff?), Mk 12 41 SB χ.; Ex 21 11 *S*(*B* ϩⲁⲧ), Is 55 1 *S*(*B* do) ἀργύ-ριον; EpJer 24 *S*(ViK 2714, *BF* = Gk) τιμή; Ex 21 19 *B*(*S* ⲙⲛⲧⲥⲁⲉⲓⲛ) ἰατρεῖον; Deu 24 10 *S*(*B* diff) ὀφεί-λημα; ShC 73 122 *S* novice renounces ⲡⲟⲩϩ, ϩⲁⲧ, ϩ., *ib* 43 *S* ⲛⲡⲟⲩϩ ⲏ ϩ. paid for corn, BSM 47 *B* inherit-ing ⲟⲩⲭⲣⲏⲙⲁ ⲛⲉⲙⲟⲩϩ, P 129¹⁴ 127 *S* ϩⲙⲃⲁⲗ ϩⲁϩ., BKU 1 127 *Sᵃ* God shall cause you seek ⲛⲥⲁϥ. ⲉⲑⲟⲟⲩ (*cf* ϩⲉⲛⲓⲡⲉ ⲉϥϩⲟⲟⲩ ⲣ 41 *a inf*), CMSS 52 *B* ⲧⲁⲙⲟⲓ ϫⲉⲃⲛⲣⲃⲉ ⲡⲉⲥϩ., ViK 4727 *S* ⲛϩ. ⲙⲡⲉⲥⲕⲉⲟⲩⲉ ⲛⲏⲣⲡ, PMich 577 *F* account ϩⲁⲛⲉⲃϩⲁⲙⲉⲧ, ShC 42 69 *S* ⲧⲁⲓⲟⲩ ⲛⲧⲃⲁ ⲛϩ., Mor 17 13 *Sᶠ* ϣⲉ ϩⲙⲉ ⲛϩ., BKU 1 866 *S* ϫⲟⲟⲩ ⲧⲡⲁϣⲉ ⲛϩ., Kr 75 *S* ⲟⲩⲕⲁⲥ ϩⲣ.,

KroppK 35 *Sᵃ* ⲥⲁⲧⲏⲣⲉ (στατήρ) ⲛϩ., Ep 278 *S* ⲕⲉ-ⲣⲁⲧⲥⲉ (-άτιον) ⲛϩ., BKU 1 300 *S* ⲟⲩϩⲟⲗⲟⲕ/ ⲛⲛⲟⲩⲃ ⲛⲙⲛⲧⲥⲛⲟⲟⲩⲥ ⲛⲕⲉⲣⲁϯ ⲛϩ., BM 1211 *Sᵃ* ϫⲟⲩⲧ ⲛⲗⲓⲧⲣⲉ ⲛϩ., CO 174 *S* ⲟⲩⲕⲁⲥ ⲛⲗⲓⲕⲡⲁ ⲛϩ. (*v* Ep 313 n);   as pl: Mk 14 11 *S*(*B* ⲟⲩϩⲁⲧ) ἀρ.; Jo 2 15 *SA²*(*B* = Gk) κέρμα; Ac 16 16 *S*(*B* = Gk) ἐργασία; R 1 4 30 *S* ϩⲉⲛⲕⲉⲕⲟⲩⲓ ⲛϩ. *nummus*; ShA 2 337 *S* ⲛϩ. of Judas, AP 24 A² ϩⲛϩ., BM 544 *S* ⲛⲉϩⲟⲙⲉⲧ, CO 456 *S* ⲡⲗⲟⲟⲥ ⲛⲛϩ.

ϯ ϩ., *give, pay money*: Ex 22 25 *S*(*B* ϩⲁⲧ) ἀρ. ἐκ-δανίζειν, Lu 22 5 *S*(*B* do), ZNTW 24 90 *F* ἀρ. διδόναι; ShWess 9 138 *S* ϯ ⲛⲁϥ ⲛϩⲉⲛⲡ. ⲏ ⲟⲩⲛⲟⲩϩ, Ep 289 *S* ϯ ⲛϩ. ⲧⲏⲣⲟⲩ ⲡⲓⲱⲣⲁⲙⲛⲉ, EW 166 *B* ⲛⲓⲁⲣⲭⲱⲛ … ⲉⲩϯ ϩ. ⲉⲣⲱⲟⲩ ϩⲓⲧⲉⲛϯⲙⲉⲧⲙⲁⲓϩⲁⲧ (but Raabe *Petrus d. Iberer* 70 ܚܕܡ);   ϯ ϩ. ϩⲁ-: Deu 14 25 *S*(*B* ϩⲁⲧ) ἀποδ. ἀργυρίου; ShA 2 241 *S* ϯ ϩ. ϩⲁⲧⲉⲥⲃⲱ, DeV 1 69 *B* ϯ ϩ. ϫⲁⲡⲁⲓⲏⲣⲡ;   as nn: Deu 21 14 *S*(*B* diff) πρᾶσις ἀργυρίου.

ϣⲱⲡ ϩⲁϩ. *S, buy for money*: 2 Kg 24 24 κτᾶσθαι; BHom 18 ϣⲟⲡϥ ϩⲁϩ. ὠνεῖσθαι; nn: Jth 4 10 ἀργυρ-ώνητος; J 82 16 ϭⲁⲩⲟⲛ ⲛϣ. ϩⲁϩ. (*cf* above P 129¹¹).

ϫⲓ ϩ. *S, take bribe*: Miss 8 53 ⲛⲡⲟⲩϫ., CA 94 ⲛ-ⲛⲉⲩϫ. ⲛⲧⲛⲗⲗⲁⲁⲩ to ordain him, JKP 2 162 ϫⲓ ⲛⲛϩ. ⲡⲧⲉⲧⲛϯ ϩⲏⲩ (on Mt 28 12).

ⲙⲁⲓϩ., *money-loving*: Lu 16 14 *S*(*B* ⲙⲁⲓϩⲁⲧ) φιλ-άργυρος, Mani 1 A² Judas ⲡⲙ.; ⲙⲛⲧⲙ.: 1 Tim 6 10 *S*(*B* ⲙⲉⲧⲙⲁⲓϩⲁⲧ) φιλαργυρία.

ⲙⲁⲥ(ⲧ)ϩ., ⲙⲛⲧ- *S, hatred of money*: BMar 158 ἀκτημοσύνη.

ⲣ ϩ., ⲟ ⲛϩ., *become, be copper*: Lev 26 19 *S*(*B* ⲭⲱ ⲙⲫⲣⲏϯ ⲛⲟⲩϩ.) ὡσεὶ χαλκοῦν τιθέναι, Deu 28 23 *B*(*S* ϣⲱⲡⲉ ⲛϩ.) χαλκοῦς εἶναι, cit KroppE 23 *S*; PS 292 *S* ϯ ⲥⲁⲧⲉⲉⲣⲉ…ⲉⲥⲟ ⲛϩⲁⲧ ϩⲓϩ. (on Mt 22 19);   ⲣⲉϥⲣ ϩ., *copper-smith*: P 44 67 زبﺮ.

ⲥⲁ ⲛϩ. *S, copper-smith or -seller*: Sa 15 9 χαλκο-πλάστης; ShA 2 348, BMEA 54719 stele.

ⲓⲟⲡⲓ ⲛϩ. *B v* ⲉⲓⲟⲡⲉ.

As name: Φόμντ, Φομῆτ (Preisigke).

ϩⲁⲙⲛⲧⲱⲡ   *v* ⲧⲱⲙ 1° & ⲧⲱⲣⲡ 2°.

ϩⲙⲛⲧⲱⲣⲉ¹, ϩⲉⲙⲉⲧⲟⲣⲉ², ϩⲉⲃⲉⲧⲱⲣⲉ³, ϩⲉⲙⲛⲧⲱⲣ⁴, ϩⲁⲙⲡⲧⲱⲣ⁵, ϩⲉⲙⲉⲧⲱⲣ⁶, ϩⲙⲧⲱⲣ⁷, ϩⲟⲙⲱⲧⲱⲣ⁸ *S* nn m, *token, password (?)*: BerlOr 1611 6 messenger says This is the sign ⲙⲁⲉⲓⲛ; she replies ⲛϩ.³ ⲥⲙⲟⲛⲧ = BMOr 4723 10 ةمس الماⲗⲓ = Deubner *Kosm. u. Dam.* 94 σημεῖον ἐπιγινώσκω (*cf ib* ⲥⲏⲙ. ⲟⲡⲉⲣ ⲉ̂ⲓⲡⲉⲛ), R 2 1 7 (on Lu 1 40) ⲁⲥϫⲓ ⲛϩ.² ⲉϥⲥⲙⲟⲛⲧ & found Elisabeth pregnant, *ib* 2 1 33 (same MS, on Lu 2 16) ⲛⲥⲉⲡⲁϩ ⲉⲡⲙⲁⲉⲓⲛ ⲡⲥⲉϭⲛ ⲛϩ.¹ ⲉϥⲥⲙⲟⲛⲧ (*cf*? Is 7 14), WS 86 ⲫ.³ ⲡⲉ ⲡⲁⲓ ⲕⲁⲧⲁ ⲑⲉ ⲛⲧⲁⲕϫⲟⲟⲥ ϫⲉ-, BKU 1 311 ⲛϩ.⁴ ⲡⲉ ⲡⲁⲓ ϫⲉ-, ST 311 ⲛ]ϩ.⁴ ⲡⲉ ⲡ[ⲁⲓ, MMA 24 6 5 send money by bearer ⲫ.⁶ ⲁϥⲧⲁⲙⲓⲟ ⲟⲩϩⲟⲩⲣ ⲡⲁ-ⲙⲁⲑⲓⲁⲥ ⲁⲓⲭⲁⲣⲓⲍⲉ ⲡⲁϥ ⲡⲧⲉϥⲱⲡⲉ, ST 331 ⲁϥ(ϯ *v*

Ep 532 n) ⲛⲁⲓ ⲡ⳽.⁴ ⲝⲉⲧⲡⲡⲟⲟⲩϥ ⲡⲁⲕ, Turin ostr 5879 ⲙⲁⲣⲉϥϫⲓ (l ⲉⲓ) ⲉⲡⲟⲣⲁⲡⲟⲛ ⲡⲉⲓⲣ.⁵ ⲁⲕϣⲱⲕ (l ϭ.) ⲡ- ϩⲟⲙⲧ ⲉⲡⲍ ⲏⲥⲧⲓⲥ, ST 294 ⲡⲉⲓⲣ.⁷   *Cf* ? ⲧⲱⲣⲉ *hand*.

ϩⲁⲙⲡϣⲉ *S*, ⲁⲙⲡⲓϥⲓ *B* *v* ⲡⲓϣⲉ.

ϩⲁⲙⲏⲣ *S*, ⲁⲙⲏⲣ *B*, ϩⲁⲙⲏⲗ (?) *F* *nn m*, *arms, embrace*: Lu 2 28 *S*(*B* ϭⲡⲁϩⳝ) ἀγκάλη, BHom 95 *S* received His body ⲉⲡⲁϥ. ἀγκαλίζεσθαι; ShA 2 177 *S* ϫⲓⲧϥ (*sc* babe) ⲉⲝⲙⲡⲉϥϩ. ⲏ ⲡⲉϥϭⲃⲟⲓ, FR 12 *S* ⲁϭⲭⲓ ⲛⲧϣⲉⲉⲣⲉ ϣⲏⲙ ⲉⲡⲉⲥϩ., DeV 2 14 *B* ⲉϥϥⲁⲓ ⲙⲙⲟϥ ϩⲉⲡⲡⲉⲥⲁ., BMis 222 *S* ⲁⲥⲕⲁ ⲡⲉⲥϩ. ϩⲁⲣⲟϥ (*sc* cross, var Mor 16 79 ϫⲓⲧϥ ⲉⲡⲉⲥϩ.) & enfolded it, Miss 4 181 *B* ⲟⲩⲭⲱⲙ ϩⲉⲡⲡⲉϥⲁ.;   ⲣϩ. *SF*, *embrace*: Cant 2 6 *F* ⲉⲗ ϩⲁⲙⲏⲗ ⲙⲙⲁⲓ, Mor 19 53 ⲉⲅⲟⲗⲉⲙ ⲉⲣⲟϩⲡ …ⲉⲅⲣ. ⲙⲙⲟⲥ, Bor 253 162 ⲣ ϩ. ⲉⲡⲉϥⲥⲟⲛ περιλαμβάνειν, BIF 14 172 ⲁⲩⲉⲣ. ⲉⲣⲟϥ ⲁⳝⲁⲥⲡⲁⳃⲉ ⲙⲙⲟϥ, P 131⳽ 45 mothers ⲉⲣ. ⲉⲡⲉⲩϣⲏⲣⲉ;   † ϩ. *S*: P 129¹⁶ 7 ⲁⲥ† ⲙⲡⲉⲥϩ. ⲉⲡⲙⲁⲕ ⲙⲙⲁⲣⲧⲏⲣⲓⲁ & kissed her, Gu 95 kinsmen † ϩ. ⲉⲣⲟϥ (var KKS 263 ⲉⲣ ϩ.).

As name ϩⲁⲙⲏⲣ (CO 396, ϩⲁⲙⲉⲣ J 25 15 is ‿ⲉ).

ϩⲁⲙⲟⲣⲧ *v* ⲙⲟⲣⲧ.

ϩ(ⲉ)ⲙⲥ *SF*, ϩⲙϥ *S*(once), ϩⲛⲙⲥ *SF*, ϩⲉⲙⲥ *B* *nn m*, *ear of corn*: Ge 41 7 *S*(var ϩⲛ.)*B*, Job 24 24 *SB*, Mt 12 1 *SBF*, Mk 4 28 *S*(var ϩⲙϥ)*F* ϩⲛ. *B* στάχυς; K 194 *B* ⲡⲓϩ. سُنبُل; ShHT H 29 *S* ϩⲉⲛⲣⲟⲟⲩⲉ ⲉⲙⲛ ϩ. ϩⲓⲭⲱⲟⳟ, Miss 4 699 *S* ϩⲉⲛϩ. …ⲉⲩⲙⲉϩ ⲡⲉϩⲣⲁ, BAp 142 *S* ⲧⲃⲁ ⲛⲃⲛⲃⲓⲗⲉ ⲕⲁⲧⲁ ϩ., CA 103 *S* ⲥⲉⲣϩ ϩ., Miss 8 219 *S* ⲥⲉⲣⲥⲱϩ ϩ., Cat 210 *B* seed ϣⲁⲥⲣⲱⲧ ⲙⲛⲓϩ., *ib* 34 *B* ⲓⲁϩϩ. *cornfield*, Ryl 291 *S* ⲙⲁⲓⲣⲉ ⲛϩ.

ϩⲟ(ⲟ)ⲙⲉⲥ *S* *nn*, *water-jar* (?): ShC 73 138 he that serveth water shall wash ⲛϩⲟⲟ. ⲕⲁⲗⲱⲥ, BKU 1 105 have sent boys with ⲛⲓⲕⲟⳟ ⲛϩ. ϩⲟⲟⲙⲛⲉ *f* Kr 242 among *varia* (*cf* ⲁⲛⲟⲧ there).

ϩⲙⲁⲓⲥ *v* ϩⲙⲟⲟⲥ *s f*.

ϩⲙⲟⲟⲥ *SF*, ϩⲙⲉⲥⲧ², ϩⲙⲁⲥⲧ³, ϩⲙⲉⲥ⁴ *AA²*, ϩⲙⲟⲥⲧ *A*, ϩⲙ(ⲁ)ⲁⲥ⁶ *A²F*, ϩⲉⲙⲁⲥ⁷ *F*, ϩⲉⲙⲥⲓ *B*(in form all qual but this) *vb intr*, *sit, remain, dwell*: Ex 18 14 *SB*, Pro 3 24 *SA⁴B*, *ib* 6 10 *SA³B*, Hos 3 4 *A⁴B*, Jo 9 8 *SA²³B* καθῆσθαι, Is 30 22 *B*(*S* ⲛⲏϩ ⲉⲃⲟⲗ, *F* ϫⲉ- ϩⲉⲙ) ἀποκ., Nu 11 4 *SB*, Is 30 8 *SBF*, 1 Cor 10 7 *SB* καθίζειν, Lu 7 15 *SB*, Ac 9 40 *SB* ἀνακ., AM 274 *B* ⲉϥϩ. talking καθέζεσθαι; Ez 38 14 *B* κατοικίζειν; MG 25 231 *B* ⲁⲛⲓϩⲉⲗⲗⲟ ϩ. watching the road μένειν; AM 277 *B* ϩ. ⲙⲟⲩⲛ ⲉⲣⲟⲓ προσκαρτερεῖν; Ru 1 13 *S* κατέχειν; PS 5 *S* ⲉϥϩ. far from disciples, *ib* 32 *S* ⲉⲣⲉ- ⲫⲓⲗⲓⲡⲡⲟⲥ ϩ. ⲉϥϩⲣⲁⲓ (*cf* ⲥ ⲉϩⲣⲁⲓ), Mich 550 46 *S* sent them ⲧⲁⲣⲟⲩϩ. till summoned, MG 25 209 *B* went to see ϫⲉⲛⲁⲩϩ. ⲛⲁϣ ⲛⲣⲏ† *how they lived* = Z 344 *S* ⲕⲏ ⲉϩⲣⲁⲓ, ManiH 12 *A²* ⲡⲉⲧϩ.²…ⲉⲩⲥⲣⲁϥⲧ ⲁⲧⲥⲟⲫⲓⲁ, BM 580 4 *F* ⲉⲓϩⲙⲁ(ⲥ) ⲛⲁⲧϩⲟⲃ, Bodl(P) g 28 *S* wine

account ⲗⲁⲕⲟⲛ ⲉϥϩⲙⲟⲟⲥ, ⲗⲁⲕⲟⲡ ⲙⲡⲓⲥ(ⲉ), Leyd 240 *S* liturg rubric ϩ. (? κάθισμα), opp ϣⲧⲟ, *cf ib* 160. With following preposition.

—— ⲉ- *SAA²*, *on, at*: Jo 19 13 (*B* ϩⲓ-) καθ. ἐπί, BMis 238 Decius ϩ. ⲉⲡⲃⲏⲙⲁ προκ. ἐπί; Z 343 after rising, water ϩ. ⲟⲛ ⲉⲡⲉϥⲙⲁ ἀποκαθιστάναι εἰς; Mani K 52 *A²* ϩ.⁴ ⲁⲡⲓⲧⲛ, *ib* 103 *A²* ⲛⲓⲁⲧⲉ … ⲡⲁⲣ.² ⲁⲡⲟⲩ- ⲑⲣⲟⲡⲟⲥ, El 80 *A* ϩ. ⲁⲧⲱⲃⲉ *v* ⲧⲱⲃⲉ 1ⱽ, BMar 34 dux ϩ. ⲉⲡⲃⲏⲙⲁ;   *dat commodi*: R 1 5 50 ⲁϥϩ. (*sic l* = Mor 32 24) ⲉⲣⲟϥ ⲡⲣⲟ ⲃⲏⲙⲁⲧⲟⲥ ⲁⲅⲉⲛⲧϥ ϫⲉ ⲉⲡϩⲛ- ⲥⲉⲙⲙⲱⲡ ⲉⲭⲙⲡⲃⲏⲙⲁ, Miss 8 185 sim (*cf* BMar 20 ⲁⲡ- ⲕⲟⲙⲉⲥ ϩ. ⲡⲣⲟ ⲃ.), BAp 172 ϩ. ⲉⲣⲟⲕ ⲛⲑⲉ ⲛⲟⲩϩⲛⲧⲉ- ⲙⲱⲛ ⲛⲧⲕⲣⲓⲙⲉ.

—— ⲉⲭⲛ- *SAA²B*, *upon* = Lev 8 35 *SB*, Is 19 1 *B*(*S* ϩⲓϫⲛ-), Jo 12 15 *SA²³* (*B diff*) καθ. ἐπί, Mt 23 22 *S*(*B* ϩⲓϫ.) καθῆ. ἐπάνω, Ac 2 3 *B*(var ϩⲓϫ., *S* ⲉ- ϩⲣⲁⲓ ⲉⲭⲛ-) καθ. ἐπί; Z 280 *S* ϩ. ⲉ. ⲡⲕⲁⲑⲉⲭⲣⲁ, AM 21 *B* sim, ImpRussArS 18 028 *A* ϩ.⁵ ⲁⲭⲙⲡϩⲁⲣⲙⲁ, Mani 1 *A²* ϩ.⁴ ⲁⲭⲱϥ (*sc* ⲃⲏⲙⲁ), Mani 1 *A²* ⲉⲓϩ.⁶ sim. *V* also ⲥ ⲉϩⲣⲁⲓ.

—— ⲙⲛ-, ⲛⲉⲙ- *SA²BF*, *with*: 1 Kg 28 *B*(*S* ⲟⲛ- ⲥⲟ), Ps 25 5 *SB* καθ. μετά; PS 4 *S* disciples ϩ. ⲙⲛ- ⲡⲉⲧⲉⲣⲏⲩ, Rec 6 186 *B* ⲁⲛϩ. ⲡⲉⲙⲁϥ a year;   of married state: Est F 3 *S*, Mt 5 32 *S*(*B* ϭⲓ) γαμεῖν, 1 Cor 7 39 *SF*(*B* ⲇⲟ), AP 15 *A²* ² γαμεῖσθαι dat, Mt 24 38 *S*(*B* ⲇⲟ) ἐκγαμίζειν, AP C *A²* ⲛϥϩ.² ⲛⲙⲙⲉⲥ πρὸς γάμον λαμβάνειν; Mk 12 23 *S*(var & *B* ϫⲓ) γυναῖκα ἔχειν, Jud 14 20 *S*, Si 42 13 *S* συνοικεῖν, Deu 22 22 *B*(*S* ⲟⲩⲱϩ ⲙⲛ-) σ. dat; Ro 7 2 *S*(*B diff*) ὕπανδρος, BM 247 7 *S* wife ⲉⲥϩ. ⲙⲛⲡⲉⲥϩⲁⲓ μετὰ ἀνδρὸς εἶναι, Aeg 24 6 *S* ϩ. ⲙⲛⲟⲩⲥϩⲓⲙⲉ ⲛⲟⲩⲱⲧ μονόγαμος; ShC 73 45 *S* ⲉⲓⲛⲁⲃⲱⲕ ⲉϩ. ⲙⲛⲟⲩⲥϩⲓⲙⲉ, Aeg 10 *B* ⲉϥϩ. ϩⲉⲛⲡⲓⲧⲁⲙⲟⲥ ⲡⲉⲛⲧⲉϥϩⲥⲓⲙⲓ, C 86 111 *B* ⲓϩ. ⲛⲉⲙⲁⲕ as wife, BSM 103 *B* women ϩ. ⲡⲉⲙⲡⲟⲩϩⲁⲓ.

—— ⲛ- *SABF*, *in*: Lam 1 3 *F*(*SB* ϩⲛ-) καθ. ἐν; Mk 2 6 *S* ⲙⲡⲙⲁ ⲉⲧⲙⲙⲁⲩ (var ϩⲛ-, *B* ϩ. ⲙⲙⲁⲩ) ἐκεῖ καθη., *ib* 14 32 *S* ⲙⲡⲉⲓⲙⲁ (*B* ϩⲁⲙⲛⲁⲓ) καθη. ὧδε; EW 34 *B* ϥϩ. ⲙⲡⲁⲓⲙⲁ ἐνθάδε εἶναι, BMar 111 *S* sim. ἐνταῦθα περιμέν.; Ez 33 31 *SB* ϩ. ⲙⲡⲉⲛⲧⲟ καθη. ἐναντίον; PS 42 *S* ⲡⲉⲥϩ. ⲡⲉ ⲙⲡⲙⲁ ⲉⲧⲙⲙⲁⲩ, ShC 42 122 *S* ⲉⲩϩⲁⲣ. ⲙⲡⲉⲓⲙⲁ;   ethic dat: BMar 31 *S* ϩ. ⲡⲁⲕ ⲛⲧⲁⲥⲉⲓ ⲙⲡⲉⲕⲣⲟ, CO 385 *S* ϩ. ⲡⲁⲕ ϩⲙⲡ- ⲙⲓⲗⲓⲥ (*v* Ep 161), Va 61 17 *B* ⲭⲁⲧ ⲛⲧⲁϩ. ⲡⲏⲓ, BSM 40 *B* ϩ. ⲛⲱⲧⲉⲡ = BMis 385 *S* ϭⲱ ⲡⲁⲕ;   ϩⲣⲟⲩⲛ ⲛ- *S*: Tor 11 ϩ. ⲛ. ⲙⲡⲏⲓ, BMar 196 ϩ. ⲛ. ⲙⲛⲡⲩⲗⲱⲛ.

—— ⲥⲁ-, ⲛⲥⲁ- *S*(rare)*BF*, *on side*: Lev 13 46 *B* ⲥⲁⲡⲥⲁ (var ϣⲱⲡ, *S diff*) κεχωρισμένος καθη., C 41 47 *B* ⲡⲥⲁⲟⲩⲥⲁ (*cf ib* ϩⲉⲛⲟⲩⲉⲗⲕⲥ), AM 11 *B* ⲥⲁⲃⲟⲗ ⲛ†ⲡⲟⲗⲓⲥ; Ez 26 16 *B* ⲥⲁⲡⲉⲥⲏⲧ ἐπὶ γῆν καθη.; Cai Euch 464 *B* ⲥⲁⲡϣⲱⲓ ὑπερκαθῆ.; C 86 282 *B* ⲉⲩϩ. ⲥⲁϩⲟⲩⲛ ⲉⲩ† ϩⲁⲡ; Ps 109 1 *B* ⲥⲁⲟⲩⲓⲛⲁⲙ, *F* ⲛⲥⲁ- (*S* ϩⲓ-), sim Mk 14 62 *S* ⲛⲥⲁ-, *B* ⲥⲁ- καθη. ἐκ, Col 3 1 *B*(*S* ⲇⲟ) καθη. ἐν;   as nn: Mk 10 40 *SB* καθί.

—— ϩⲁ-, ϫⲁ- *SABF*, *under, at*: Hos 14 8 *SAB* καθί. ὑπό, Jon 4 5 *SA*(*B* ⲥⲁⲡⲉⲥⲏⲧ) καθη. ὑποκάτω; Jo 20 12 *SB* καθέ. πρός; Cant 2 3 *F* καθί. ἐν (σκιᾷ); WTh 186 *S* ϩ. ϩⲁⲣⲟⲟⲩ (*sc* prisoners); ϩⲁⲣⲁⲧ⸗, ϫ.: Hos 3 3 *AB* καθῆ. ἐπί; AP 11 *A*² ⲁⲥϩ.² ϩⲁⲣⲉⲧϥ καθί. παρά; ST 339 *S* ⲉⲧⲣⲉⲡⲃⲱⲕ ... ⲉⲧⲣⲉⲡϩ. ϩⲁⲣ[; ⲉⲡⲉⲥⲏⲧ ϫⲁ-: Nu 22 27 *B*(*S* ⲛⲕⲟⲧⲕ ϩⲁ-) ⲥⲩⲅⲕ. ὑποκάτω.

—— ϩⲓ- *SAA²BF*, *upon*: Job 28 *S*(*B* ϩⲓϫⲉⲛ-), Si 1 8 *S*(var & *B* do) καθῆ. ἐπί, Pro 20 8 *SA*ᶜ, Mt 23 2 *SB* καθί. ἐπί; Mt 11 16 *B*(*S* ϩⲛ-) καθῆ. ἐν, EpJer 42 *BF* ἐγκ. ἐν, AM 281 *B* ϩⲓⲡⲓϩⲩⲡⲟⲡⲟⲇⲓⲟⲛ καθέ. ἐν; Mt 20 21 *S*(*B* ⲥⲁ-) καθῆ. ἐκ; ShA 1 301 *S* ϩⲉⲛⲕⲁⲑⲉⲇⲣⲁ ... ϩ. ϩⲓⲱⲟⲩ, C 43 129 *B* ϩⲛⲧⲉⲩⲙⲱⲡ ϩ. ϩⲓⲡⲓⲃⲏⲙⲁ, *ib* 1 *B* ϩⲓⲡⲓⲑⲉⲁⲇⲣⲟⲛ, J 99 14 *S* ϩⲓⲡⲙⲟⲡⲁⲥⲧⲏⲣⲓⲟⲛ opp ϩⲓⲃⲟⲗ, PS 6 *S* ⲡⲉϥϩ. ϩⲓⲡⲉϥⲉⲣⲏⲩ, BIF 22 108 *F* captain ϩ. ϩⲓⲧⲟⲩⲱϣ ⲙⲡⲣⲣⲁ, ManiK 36 *A*² ϩ.² ϩⲓⲧⲉϥϩⲉⲣⲓ, AM 7 *B* ϩ. ϩⲓⲧⲛ ⲙⲡⲣⲟ ⲡ-.

—— ϩⲛ- ϫⲉⲛ- *SAA²BF*, *in*: Jer 21 9 *SB* καθῆ. ἐν, Deu 1 46 *SB* ἐγκαθῆ. ἐν, 1 Kg 24 1 *SB*, Mic 7 8 *SAB*, He 8 1 *F*(*S* ϩⲓ-, *B* ⲥⲁ-), citBM 511(4) καθί. ἐν, Jo 11 20 *SA²B* καθῆ. ἐν, Ex 16 29 *SB*, MG 25 220 *B* ϩ. ϫⲉⲛⲧⲉⲕⲣⲓ καθῆ. εἰς, 2 Kg 6 11 *B*(*S* ϣⲱ) καθῆ. εἰς, Jer 31 43 *S*(Cai 8316)*B* καθῆ. ἐπί, AP 11 *A*²³ καθῆ. οὗ; PS 90 *S* ϩ. ϩⲓⲡⲉⲑⲏⲥⲁⲩⲣⲟⲥ ⲙⲡⲟⲅⲟⲉⲓⲛ, ShBMOr 8810 366 *S* ⲡⲧⲏⲡⲁϩ. ⲁⲛ ϩⲛⲧⲉⲓϩⲉⲡⲉⲉⲧⲓ, ManiK 34 *A*² ⲉϥϩ.² ϩⲛⲧⲙⲏⲧⲉ of disciples, Miss 4 108 *B* ⲉⲑⲟⲩⲱϣ ⲉ-ϩ. ϫⲉⲛⲡⲉϥⲛⲟⲃⲓ, DeV 2 88 *B* ⲉϥϩ. ϫⲉⲛⲡⲉϥⲡⲁⲗⲁⲧⲓⲟⲛ.

—— ϩⲓⲣⲛ- *SAB*, *at, on*: Ge 18 1 *SB* καθῆ. ἐπί, Pro 9 14 *S.A*ᶜ*B* καθί. ἐπί, Jos 10 5 *S* ⲡⲉⲣⲓκαθί. acc, AM 273 *B* ϩ. ϩⲓⲣⲉⲡⲡⲓⲣⲱⲟⲩ παρακαθ. dat.

ϩⲁ(ϩ)ⲧⲛ-, *SA²*, *before, by, beside*: Mt 13 1 *S*(*B* ⲉ-ⲥⲕⲉⲡ-) καθῆ. παρά, LAp 570 *F* ⲁⲩϩ.⁷ ϩⲁⲧⲓⲡⲉϣⲧⲛ καθέ. παρά; Job 2 13 *S*(*B* ϫⲁⲧⲉⲛ-) παρακαθί. dat.; Z 334 *S* ϩ. ϩⲁϩⲧⲏϥ ⲡⲟⲩϭⲟⲟⲩ μέν. πρός; ManiH 59 *A*² ⲁⲩϩ. ϩⲁⲧⲛϥ & wept, AM 65 *B* ϩ. ϫ. ϯⲡⲩⲗⲏ, J 106 237 *S* ⲡⲉⲧϩ. ϩ. ⲁⲡⲓⲁ at time of her death.

—— ϩⲓϫⲛ- *SABF*, *upon*: Ge 8 4 *B*(*S* ⲉϩⲣⲁⲓ ⲉϫⲛ-), Is 6 1 *B*(*S* ϩⲓ-), Ap 6 16 *BF*(Lacau, *S* ϩⲓ-) καθῆ. ἐπί, Zech 6 13 *AB*, Mt 19 28 *F*ᶜ(PMich 538, *S* ⲉϩⲣⲁⲓ ⲉϫⲛ-, *B* ϩⲓ-) καθί. ἐπί, Lam 2 10 *B*(*F* ϩⲗⲏⲓ ⲉϫ.) καθί. εἰς; Ap 17 15 *SB* καθῆ. οὗ; PS 78 *S* ϩ. ϩ. ⲟⲩϭⲟⲙ, Pcod 15 *S* sat ϩⲁⲣⲁⲧϥ ... ϩ. ⲡϭⲩⲡⲟⲡⲟⲇⲓⲟⲛ, MG 25 159 *B* if Lord ϩ. ϩⲓϫⲱⲛ ϩⲓⲧⲉⲛϩⲁⲛϣⲱⲡⲓ, C 43 65 *B* ϩ. ϩ. ⲫⲓⲁⲣⲟ. *V* also ϭ ⲉϩⲣⲁⲓ.

With following adverb.

—— ⲉⲃⲟⲗ *S*, *outside* (?), *upright*: TT 39 at ship-wreck ⲉⲩϩ. ⲉⲃ. ϩⲓⲡⲭⲟⲓ, others ⲁϥⲉ ⲣⲁⲧⲟⲩ ϩⲓⲡⲭⲟⲓ, P 129¹³ 26 sick man can no longer ϩ. ⲉⲃ.; also ? CO 351, PLond 4 506.

—— ⲉϥⲁϩⲟⲩ *B*, *stay behind*: Miss 4 184 they departed, but we ⲁⲛϩ. ⲉ.

—— ⲉϩⲣⲁⲓ, ⲉϫ., *down*: Ru 3 18 *S* καθῆ., Nu 11 4 *S*(var & *B* om ⲉ.), Mk 9 35 *S*(*BF* do) καθί.; 1 Kg 24 16 *S* ⲡϥϩ. ⲉ. ⲡⲙⲗⲁⲕ ⲇⲓⲕⲁⲥⲁⲓ (ⲙⲟⲓ) ⲉⲕ χειρός σου; *ib* 1 7 *S* ϩ. ⲉ. ⲉⲟⲩⲱⲙ Gk om vb; PS 92 *S* ⲁⲓϩ. ⲉ. ϩⲙⲡⲕⲁⲕⲉ, ShC 42 203 *S* ϩ. ⲉ. opp ⲧⲱⲟⲩⲛ, Miss 8 60 *S* ⲉⲩϩ. ⲉ. ϩⲛⲧⲉⲕⲕⲗⲏⲥⲓⲁ (var om ⲉ.), WTh 186 *S* ⲁⲓϩ. ⲉ. ⲁⲕⲣⲓⲃⲱⲥ ⲁⲓⲥⲃⲁⲓ, C 89 27 *B* ⲡⲥⲉϩ. ⲉ. till visit ended, DeV 2 255 *B* dead arose ⲁϥϩ. ⲉ.; ⲉϩ. ⲉϫⲛ-: Ex 17 12 *S*, Ps 98 1 *S* καθῆ. ἐπί, Ex 2 15 *S*(all *B* ϩⲓϫⲉⲛ-), Ac 2 3 *S*(*B* ⲉϫ. only) καθῆ. ἐπί, Ge 31 34 *S*(*B* ϩⲓ.) ἐπικ. dat, Jo 4 6 *SA²*(*BF* do) καθέ. ἐπί; TT 124 *S* ⲁϥϩ. ⲉ. ⲉϫⲡⲡⲉϥⲡⲁⲧ, DeV 2 56 *B* ϩ. ⲉϫ. (*sic l*) ⲉ. ⲟⲩϭⲉⲣⲙⲓ; ⲉϩ. ϩⲓϫⲛ-: Pcod 1 *S* ϩ. ⲉ. ϩⲓϫⲱⲟⲩ (*sc* chariots).

—— ⲙⲙⲁⲩ, *there*: Ps 121 5 *SB*, Jer 29 18 *B*(*S* ϩⲙⲡⲙⲁ ⲉⲧⲙ.) καθῆ. ἐκεῖ; Mor 33 39 *S* ⲁⲥϩ. ⲙ. (var BMis 92 ϭⲱ), Aeg 6 *B* ⲁⲛϩ. ⲙ. (*sc* in Egypt) ⲡⲟⲩⲣⲟⲙⲡⲓ. *Cf* AM 289 *B* ⲡⲓⲙⲁ ⲉⲧⲉⲣⲉⲡⲓϩⲛⲧⲉⲙⲱⲡ ϩ. ⲙⲙⲟϥ (*v* ⲙⲁⲩ ⲑ).

—— ⲛϩⲟⲩⲛ, *within*: BMar 196 *S* suffered him to ϩ. ⲛ. ⲙⲡⲛⲅⲱⲛ, after being ϩⲓⲣⲙⲡⲣⲟ ⲙⲡ., C 43 92 *B* ⲁϥϩ. ϩⲓⲡⲓⲃⲏⲙⲁ ⲛϫ. ϫⲉⲛⲡⲓⲕⲁⲥⲧⲣⲟⲛ (*cf* Pey *Gr* 165 *S* ϩ. ϩⲓⲛⲃ. ⲛ. ⲉϣⲙⲟⲩⲡ), J 74 56 *S* wife ⲉⲥϩ. ⲛ. ϩⲁⲣⲟⲓ.

—— ⲛⲛ *B*, *excrement*: Is 36 12 (*SF* ⲙⲏ ⲟⲉⲓⲕ) κόπρος. Or *l*? ϩⲁⲗⲙⲓ.

ⲓϣ ⲛϩ. *B*, *urine* or ? *excrement*: 1 Kg 24 4 ⲉⲣ ⲓ. (*S* ⲥⲉⲡ ⲣⲁⲧ⸗) παρασκευάζεσθαι.

ⲙⲁ ⲛϩ. *SA²BF*, *seat, privy, anus*: Deu 28 27 *B*(*S* om), 1 Kg 5 3 *S* ἕδρα, Si 12 12 *S* καθέδρα, Mt 15 17 *SB*(*F* = Gk) ἀφεδρών, Mk 12 39 *SBF*(Mor 46 63) -καθεδρία, Jer 29 8 *B*(*S* om) κάθισις; Ez 43 8 *S*(ShA 1 235)*B* πρόθυρον; AM 281 *B* went in to ⲡⲓⲙ. σέκρετον; P 44 71 *S* ⲕⲗⲟⲩⲧⲣⲟⲥ (γλουτός)·ⲙ. ‏الدبر‎, K 78 *B* ⲡⲓⲙ. ‏‘ⲗ‎ (*cf Vita Pach* §92(143) καθισματήριον); ShC 73 196 *S* ⲙ. ϩⲓⲱⲱⲥ (*sc* table), Saq 14 *S* ⲡⲁⲓⲡⲉ ⲡⲙ. ⲛⲁⲡⲁ ⲓⲉⲣⲏⲙⲓⲁⲥ (*sc* abbot's seat), Ann 17 153 *S* martyrs seated on ϩⲉⲛⲙ. ⲙⲡⲉⲛⲓⲡⲉ (*cf* C 43 175 ⲥⲉⲙⲯⲉⲗⲓⲟⲛ ⲡⲑⲉⲛⲓⲡⲓ), Mani 1 *A*² ⲡⲙ.² ⲡⲓⲡⲁⲧⲉ, Miss 4 123 *B* ⲙ. bishop's throne (Mor 18 30 = 19 39 om), PO 11 329 *B* ⲁⲣⲓ ⲕⲁⲑⲁⲣⲓⲍⲓⲛ ⲡⲓⲙⲙ. *privies*, MG 25 156 *B* potter makes ⲡⲓⲙ. ⲡⲧⲉ ⲡⲓⲭⲫⲟ ⲡⲃⲉⲣⲓ, LMär 7 *S* snake came forth from ⲡⲉϥⲙ., MR 4 72 *S* ⲟⲩⲅⲩⲣⲓϩ ⲉⲓ ⲉⲃⲟⲗ ϩⲙⲡⲉⲥⲙ. = Miss 4 137 *B*, AM 294 *B* lamps ⲉϧⲟⲩⲛ ϫⲁⲡⲉϥⲙ., HL 112 *B* pain in his ⲙⲁ ⲛⲫⲉⲡ ⲙⲱⲟⲩ ⲉⲃⲟⲗ ⲛϩ., PBad 5 410 *Sᶠ* prayer ⲃⲓ ⲧⲉⲭⲁⲣⲓⲥ [ⲉ]ⲡⲉⲃϩⲁ ⲧⲉⲕϯ ⲡⲁⲃ ⲉⲧⲉⲭ. ⲉⲡⲉⲃⲙ.

ⲡⲕⲁ ⲛϩ. *S*, *thing whereon to sit*: C 99 121 set ⲟⲩⲛ. in midst of cell.

ϣⲫⲏⲣ ⲛϩ. *B* with ⲉⲣ, *be assessor*: Ex 23 1 (*S* diff) συγκαθί.; C 43 81 ⲑⲣⲉⲕⲉⲣ ϣ. ⲛⲉⲙⲁϥ.

ϭⲓⲛ-, ϫⲓⲛϩ. *SBF*, *manner of sitting, dwelling*: 3 Kg 10 5 *S*, Ps 138 2 *SB* f, Lam 3 63 *B* f(*F* ϩ. vb), CaiEuch 338 *B* m καθέδρα; ShP 130⁴ 135 *S* rich may not be favoured in ϭⲓⲛⲟⲩⲱⲙ, ϭⲓⲛϩ. or ϭⲓⲛⲛⲕⲟⲧⲕ, Sh(?) ViK 934⁴ 59 *S* wise know ⲧϭ. ϩⲁⲣⲧⲛⲙⲙⲛⲧⲉⲓⲱⲧ, BIF

13 1 10 *S* went to learn ⲧⲉⲩϭ.＝MG 25 297 *B* m, AM 264 *B* ⲧⲉⲩϫ. ⲥⲁⲟⲩⲓⲡⲁⲙ, JKP 2 188 *F* ⲧⲟⲩϭ.

ϩⲙⲁⲓⲥ *S* nn m, *buttocks*: P 43 41 ⲙⲟⲣⲓⲟⲛ · ⲡⲉϩ. ⲓ̈ⲁⲉⲓ̈ⲁ̈.

V ⲑⲙⲥⲟ.

ϩⲟⲙⲧ *SB*, ϩⲁ. *F* *v* ϩⲟⲙⲛⲧ.

ϩⲱⲙⲧ *F* nn, *shame, disgrace*: Is 30 3, 5 (*S* ⲛⲟϭⲛⲉϭ, *B* ϣⲱϣ) ὄνειδος.

ϩⲙⲟⲧ *SB*, -ⲁⲧ *AA²F*, ⲉϩⲙⲟⲧ *B*, pl ϩⲙⲟⲟⲧ *A²* (Ma), ϩⲙⲱⲧ (?)*B* nn. m, *grace, gift*: Ge 6 8 *SB*, Ps 83 12 *B*(*S*＝Gk), Pro 24 30 *SA*, 1 Cor 15 10 *SBF*, 3 Jo 4 *B*(*S* ⲣⲁϣⲉ) χάρις, Ro 12 6 *SBF*, MG 25 241 *B*.ⲟⲩϩ. ⲛⲧⲉ ⲟⲩⲡⲣⲟⲫⲏⲧⲓⲁ χάρισμα, Pro 11 16 *SA* ⲉⲟⲩⲛⲧⲉ ϩ. (*B* ⲣⲉϥϫⲉⲙ ϩ.) εὐχάριστος, Nah 3 4 *AB* sim ἐπίχαρις, Philem 19 *S* ⲕⲓⲧⲟⲟⲧ ϩⲱⲱⲕ ⲛϩ. (*B* diff) σεαυτόν προσοφείλειν; ShC 73 99 *S* let us pay tax ⲙⲡⲉⲛⲅⲁ ⲗⲁⲁⲩ ⲛϩ. ϩⲓⲱⲱⲛ *that no favour unto us be omitted* by such men(sc tax-gatherers),ShP 130² 74 *S* ⲟⲩⲛⲉ ⲡⲉϩ. ⲛⲟⲩⲣⲱⲙⲉ *what thanks, credit* if he leave bad & take good?, BMis 387 *S* ⲛⲉϩ. ⲛⲧⲁϥϣⲱⲡⲉ ⲙⲙⲟⲟⲩ＝BSM 41 *B*, R 1 4 32 *S* begged ⲟⲩϩ. ⲛⲧⲟⲟⲧϥ ⲙⲡⲉⲡⲁⲣⲭⲟⲥ, Mani K 43 *A²* ⲛϩ. ⲧⲏⲣⲟⲩ ⲉⲧⲁⲛⲓⲧ, AZ 21 151 *S* we tend thee not ϩⲛⲟⲩϩ. or from benevolence, PO 11 356 *B* ϩⲁⲛϩ. ⲛⲧⲁⲗϭⲟ, AM 214 *B*, ⲡⲁⲓⲉϩ. ⲫⲁⲓ, ib 224 *B* ⲛⲓⲉϩ. ⲛⲧⲉ ⲫϯ, LAp 562 *F* ⲙⲁ]ⲗⲉⲡⲉⲕϩⲉⲙⲁⲧ[ϣⲱ]ⲡⲓ; in neg phrases: ShA 2 102 *S* ⲙⲡⲱⲧⲛ ⲁⲛⲛⲉ ⲛϩ. *no thanks to you* that God forsake not His sanctuary, ib 321 *S* ⲛⲟⲩϩ. ⲁⲛⲛⲉ ⲉⲥⲁⲃⲉ ⲛⲓⲙ to bear troubles, ShC 73 110 *S* all bound to obey Christ ⲉⲙⲡⲟⲩϩ. (var ϩⲛⲩ) ⲙⲙⲁⲩ, R 1 5 38 *S* if thou release me ⲙⲛⲧⲁⲕ ϩ. ⲙⲙⲁⲩ, Mun 69 *S* will compel thee to pay ⲙⲛⲕⲟ. ⲁⲛⲛⲉ ＝ DeV 2 275 *B*, Ep 457 *S* ⲙⲡⲉⲛϩ. ⲁⲛⲛⲉ ϫⲱⲕ ⲧⲉⲕⲕⲉⲗⲉⲅⲓⲥ [ⲉⲃⲟⲗ], ib 327 *S* sim ⲛⲟⲩϩ. ⲉⲣⲟⲓ ⲁⲛⲛⲉ, ShIF 235 *S* ⲟⲩϩ. ⲉⲣⲟⲛ ⲁⲛⲛⲉ ϫⲉⲁⲛⲕⲉⲧ ϩⲉⲛⲧⲟⲡⲟⲥ, C 89 199 *B* ⲙⲏ ⲟⲩϩ. ⲉⲣⲟⲛⲛⲉ ⲫⲁⲓ ⲉⲧⲁⲛⲁⲓϥ?; pl: Mani BerlSitz '32 85 *A²* ⲛⲁⲣⲙⲟⲟⲧ ⲙⲡⲛⲁϩⲱⲣⲟⲛ, Mani 1 *A²* ⲛϩ. ⲛⲡⲉⲕⲁⲅⲅⲉⲗⲟⲥ, Pro 5 19 *B* ⲡⲉⲕϩⲙⲱⲧ (*sic* prob, but var ϩⲙⲟⲧ); as adj: Pro 7 5 *SA*(*B* ϯ ϩ.) πρὸς χάριν, cit MG 25 7 *B* χαριέστερος, Pro 17 8 *SA* χάρις, Si 18 16 *S* κεχαριτωμένος.

ⲁⲧϩ. *S*(mostly)*B*, *graceless, thankless*: Sa 16 29, Lu 6 35 *B*(*S* ϣⲡ ϩ. neg) ἀχάριστος; BMis 14 your enemies ϩⲉⲛⲣⲱⲙⲉ ⲛⲁ. ⲛⲉ, C 86 110 *B* Egyptians ϩⲁⲡⲁⲧⲉϩ. ⲡⲉ, BMis 41 I gave thee diadem ⲉⲡⲝⲓⲛϫⲏ ⲁⲓϯ ϭⲣⲱⲡⲉ ⲛⲣⲣⲟ ⲡⲁⲕ ⲛⲁ. & *had no thanks*; ⲙⲛⲧⲁⲧϩ.: Sa 14 26 Gk diff.

ⲣ, ⲉⲣ ϩ. *SA²B*(mostly)*F*, *give grace, favour*: Lu 7 21 (*S*＝Gk), CaiEuch 475 ⲁϥⲉⲣ. ⲛⲁⲛ ⲙⲡⲉⲓⲙⲓ, Va 66 288 ⲁϥⲉⲣ. ⲛⲛⲓⲥⲣⲁⲏⲗⲓⲧⲏⲥ ⲙⲛⲓⲱⲓⲕ, ZNTW 24 84 *F* ⲁⲕⲉⲣ. ⲛⲉⲡϩⲁⲕϯ ⲛⲉⲛ χαρίζεσθαι, Ac 25 9 (*S* ϯ ⲛⲟⲩϩ.) χάριν κατατίθεσθαι; ShC 73 167 *S* if he see to their needs ⲛⲉϥⲡⲁⲣ ⲟⲩϩ. ⲁⲛⲛⲉ *did it not of grace* ⲛⲉϥϩⲱⲃ

ϭⲁⲣⲡⲉ, R 1 3 31 *S* ⲡⲉϩ. ⲙⲡⲛϩⲟⲙ ⲉⲧϥⲉⲓⲣⲉ (*sc* God) ⲙⲙⲟⲟⲩ, Mor 41 127 *S* ⲁϥⲣ. ⲛⲁⲩ & *departed* (varr ib 40 12 ⲭⲁ[ⲣⲓ̇ⲍⲉ, Wess 15 121 ϯ ⲧⲉⲭⲁⲣⲓⲥ, Mor 39 17 ⲁⲥⲡⲁⲍⲉ) ＝ C 43 42 *B* ϯ ⲉⲝⲟⲩⲥⲓⲁ, BSM 13 ⲁϥⲉⲣ. ⲛⲏⲓ ⲛⲟⲩⲛⲟϩ ⲛϩⲁⲣⲓ ＝ BMis 346 *S* ⲭⲁⲣⲓⲍⲉ, C 43 243 ϯⲡⲁⲑⲣⲉⲕⲓⲣⲓ ⲛϩⲁⲛⲛⲓϣϯ ⲛϩ. ϩⲓϫⲉⲛⲡⲕⲁϩⲓ, Mani I *A²* ⲡⲉⲧⲁⲡⲕⲓⲱⲧ ⲣ. ⲙⲙⲁⲩ ⲛⲉⲕ; c ⲉϫⲉⲛ-: BSM 55 ⲁϥⲉⲣ ϩⲟⲩⲟ ϩ. ⲉϫⲱⲟⲩ by Incarnation, C 86 165 ⲛⲏ ⲉⲧⲁⲕⲉⲣ. ⲉϫⲱⲟⲩ; c ⲛⲛ-, ⲛⲉⲙ-: ROC 23 271 ⲛϩ. ⲉⲧⲁϥⲁⲓⲧⲟⲩ ⲛⲉⲙⲁⲛ, C 43 137 ⲁⲣⲓⲟⲩⲓ ⲛⲉⲙⲏⲓ ⲛⲟⲩϩ., BHom 69 *S* ⲡⲉϩ. ⲛⲧⲁⲥⲁⲁⲩ ⲛⲙⲙⲁⲛ, Hall 86 *S* ⲁⲛⲡⲉ ⲣ ⲟⲩⲛⲟϭ ⲛϩ. ⲛⲙⲙⲁⲕ; ⲛϩ., *as a favour, gift*: Miss 8 21 *S* ⲉⲕⲉⲓⲣⲉ ⲛⲛⲁⲓ ⲛϩ. ⲛⲡⲉⲥⲧⲱⲣⲓⲟⲥ.

ϯ ϩ. *SAA²BF*, *give grace, benefit, be kind*: Pro 7 5 *B*(*SA* diff) λόγοις πρὸς χ. ἐμβάλλεσθαι, Eph 4 7 *SB* χ. διδόναι, Ro 1 11 *SB* χάρισμα μεταδ., Eph 1 6 *S*(*BF* ϯ ⲛϩ.) χαριτοῦν, Pro 28 23 *SA* ϯ. ⲛϩⲙⲁⲥ γλωσσοχ.; HL 82 *B* ϯ. ⲛⲛⲓϫⲉⲗⲗⲟⲓ εὐεργετεῖν, Mani II 41 *A²* ϥⲁϯ. ⲛⲡⲉϥϩⲁⲙⲗⲁϭ, AM 94 *B* ⲉϣⲱⲡ ⲡⲧⲟⲩϯ. ⲛⲁϥ *if they give him gift* he admitteth them; ⲣⲉϥϯ ϩ.: ManiP 53 *A²* ⲡⲧⲁⲓⲃⲉⲕⲉ ⲛⲣ.; ⲙⲛⲧⲣⲉϥϯ ϩ.: Miss 8 33 *S* κεχαρισμένα; ϯ ⲛϩ., *as a favour, gift*: Ac 25 11 *B*(*S* ⲭⲁⲣⲓⲍⲉ acc), ib 27 24 *B*(*S* do), 1 Cor 2 12 *BF*(*S* do) χαρίζ.; AM 229 *B* gods ϯ ⲙⲙⲟϥ (sc life) ⲛϩ. ⲛⲛⲓⲣⲱⲙⲓ, RAl 108 *B* ⲁⲕϣⲁⲛϯ ⲙⲡⲓⲕⲟⲥⲙⲟⲥ ⲛⲏⲓ ⲛϩ. yet would I not worship ＝ BMar 10 *S* ⲭⲁⲣⲓⲍⲉ; cf AM 67 *B* ⲉⲣ ⲭⲁⲣⲓⲍⲉⲥⲑⲉ ⲛϩ.

ϣ(ⲉ)ⲡ ϩ. *SAA²BF*, *give thanks* (lit *take grace*): Mk 8 6 *B*(*S* ＋ ⲉϩⲣⲁⲓ ⲉϫⲛ-), Jo 6 11 *SA²B*, 1 Cor 11 24 *B*(*S* ⲥⲙⲟⲩ), ZNTW 24 84 *F* permit prophets ⲛⲥⲉϣ. εὐχαριστεῖν, Lu 6 35 *S* neg (*B* ⲁⲧϩ.) ἀχάριστος; ManiK 16 *A²* ⲧⲓϣⲟⲡ ⲙⲡⲉⲕϩ. ϫⲉⲁⲕⲥⲟⲉⲓ, TurM 13 *S* ϯϣ. ⲁⲡⲁϩⲏⲧ ⲙⲧⲟⲛ; c ⲛⲧⲛ-, *to* (lit *at hand of*): Jth 8 25 *S*, Lu 18 11 *SB*, Ro 14 6 *SB*, BM 320 149 *S* ⲉⲧⲁⲙϣ. ⲛⲧⲟⲟⲧϥ ⲁⲗⲗⲁ ⲛⲧⲁⲛⲡⲉ ⲉⲩⲭ. dat, MG 25 244 *B* ϯϣ. ⲛⲧⲟⲧⲕ χάριν ἔχειν dat; Z 314 *S* ⲁⲩϣ. ⲛⲧⲁⲛⲡⲉ ϩⲓⲭⲙⲡⲉⲛⲧⲁϥϣⲱⲡⲉ, AM 95 *B* ϣ. ⲛⲧⲉⲛⲫϯ, ShC 72 42 *S* ϩⲉⲛⲁⲧϣ. ⲛⲧⲡⲣⲱⲙⲉ, Ep 188 *S* ⲉϥϣⲱⲡ ϩ. ⲛⲧⲟⲟⲧⲉ ⲙⲡⲉⲛⲁⲅⲅⲉⲗⲟⲥ; c ⲉϫⲛ-, *for*: Aeg 267 *S* ϣ. ⲉ. ⲛⲟⲩϫⲁⲓ ⲙⲡⲉⲛⲧⲁⲩⲡⲓⲥⲧⲉⲩⲉ εὐχ. ἐπί; R 1 5 28 *S* ⲉϥϣ. ⲉ. ⲡⲉⲛⲧⲁϥⲧⲁϩⲟϥ; C 43 105 *B* ⲛⲥⲉϣ. ⲁⲛ ⲉ. ⲛⲟⲩⲍⲱⲣⲉⲁ; ⲉϩⲣⲁⲓ ⲉϫⲛ-: Phil 1 3 *SBF* ⲉⲩⲭ. ἐπί, Mt 15 36 *S*(*B* ⲥⲙⲟⲩ) ⲉⲩⲭ. only; c ϩⲁ-, as last: 1 Cor 1 4 *SB*, 1 Thes 1 2 *SF*(*B* ⲉϩⲣⲏⲓ ⲉⲝ.) ⲉⲩⲭ. περί; c ϩⲓϫⲉⲛ-, as last: FR 92 *B* ⲉⲩϣ. ϩ. ⲛⲏ ⲉⲧⲁϥϫⲟⲧⲟⲩ; as nn m: 1 Cor 14 16 *SB* εὐχαριστία, Mor 17 11 *S* ⲁⲛϯ ⲛϣ. ⲁⲛⲡⲉ -ⲧⲉⲓⲛ; DeV 1 182 *B*(var RAl 83 ⲉⲝⲟⲙⲟⲗⲟⲅⲏⲥⲓⲥ), ROC 23 285 *B* ϯⲉⲩⲭⲏ ⲛⲧⲉ ⲡⲓϣ. (cf BM 853 الشكر), BMis 443 *S* we ate & ⲁⲛϯ ⲙⲡϣ., Aeg 260 *S* eat ϩⲛⲟⲩϣ., AM 314 *B* made the offering ϫⲉⲛⲟⲩϣ.; qual: Ro 6 17 *SB* ⲡⲉϩ. ⲙⲡⲛ̄ⲉ ϣ. χάρις τῷ θεῷ; Miss 8 225 *S*, TstAb 229 *B* sim, Aeg 22 *SB* ⲡⲉⲕϩ. ϣ., ManiH 2 *A²* ⲡⲉⲕϩ. ϣ. ⲛⲁϥⲣⲉⲕ, ROC 27

160 B ⲡⲉϩϩ. ϣ. ϫⲉⲁϥϫϩⲁⲧ, C 89 208 B ⲛⲓϩ. ⲛⲧⲉ ⲫϯ ϣ. ⲉϩⲣⲏⲓ ⲉϫⲱⲓ ⲛⲥⲏⲟⲩ ⲛⲓⲃⲉⲛ ϫⲉ-; ⲁⲧϣⲓⲡ ϩ., *thankless*: ShC 42 109 S ⲡⲉⲓⲁ. ⲁⲩⲱ ⲡⲉⲓⲁⲧⲙⲛϣⲁ, AM 121 B *punish you* ϩⲱⲥ ⲛⲁ., ShIF 264 S ⲛⲁ. ⲛⲥⲟⲛ, ShA 1 461 S ⲡⲣⲱⲙⲉ ⲛⲁ. ⲛⲧⲟⲟⲧⲩ, AM 229 B ⲡⲓⲁⲥⲉⲃⲏⲥ ⲛⲁ. ⲡⲧⲟⲧⲩ; ⲙⲛⲧ-, ⲙⲉⲧⲁⲧϣⲓⲡ ϩ.: ShA 1 462 S ⲡⲉⲕⲙ., C 43 105 B ⲧⲉⲕⲙ. ⲉϧⲟⲩⲛ ⲉⲛⲛⲟⲩϯ; ⲣ ⲁⲧϣⲓⲡ.: ShA 1 376 S; ⲣⲉϥϣⲓⲡ ϩ., *grateful person*: Pro 11 16 B (SA diff), Col 3 15 SB εὐχάριστος; ⲙⲛⲧ-, ⲙⲉⲧⲣⲉϥϣⲓⲡ.: BMar 123 S ⲥⲏⲛ ⲙⲙ. -τήριος; P 129²⁰ 122 S ⲟⲩⲁϩⲝⲓⲟⲡⲡⲉ ... ⲉⲙⲟⲩⲛⲉ ⲉⲃⲟⲗ ϩⲛⲡⲉⲕⲙ., DeV 2 10 B *worshipping* ϧⲉⲛϩⲁⲡⲙ., ib 153 B ⲡⲁⲓⲣⲩⲙⲟⲥ ⲙⲙ. ⲙⲫϯ; ϫⲓⲛϣⲡ ϩ., *thanksgiving*: TEuch 2 86 B ϯⲉⲩⲭⲁⲣⲓⲥⲧⲓⲁ ⲉⲧⲉⲡⲁⲓⲛⲉ ⲛⲓⲝ.

ϫⲓ, ϭⲓ ϩ. *SAA²BF, obtain grace, favour*: Ro 1 5 B(S = Gk) χ. λαμβάνειν; AM 270 B ⲁⲙⲟⲓ ⲁⲓϫⲓ ⲙⲡⲉϥⲕⲉϩ. τρόπος, Bor 240*⁷ S ⲉⲅⲛⲁϫ. ⲉⲃⲟⲗ ⲙⲙⲱⲧⲛ, ib 251 219 S Jacob ⲉϥϫ. ⲉⲃⲟⲗ ϩⲓⲧⲟⲟⲧⲩ ⲛⲓⲱⲥⲏⲫ, Pey Gr 166 S ⲙⲡⲉⲕϫⲓ ⲡⲉϩ. *(sc advocate's) to plead for thee ?*, AP 20 A² ⲁⲩϫⲓ ⲙⲡⲉϩ. ⲛⲧⲉⲥϥⲣⲁⲛⲓⲥ; ⲥ ⲉⲧⲃⲉ-, *for*: TU 43 22 A *not able* ⲛⲝ. ⲉⲧⲃⲏⲧⲟⲩ; ⲥ ⲉϫⲛ-, *as last*: BMis 565 S *righteous shall* ϫ. ⲉϫⲱⲟⲩ πρεσβεύειν ὑπέρ; ShA 2 158 S *begging men to* ϫ. ⲉϫⲱⲟⲩ, AZ 21 157 S ϫⲓ ⲡⲉϩ. ⲙⲡⲡ̅ⲉ̅ ⲉϫⲱⲛ, ROC 20 51 S sim ⲛⲡⲁⲣⲭⲙ̅ⲭ̅ⲥ̅, BMis 364 S *Michael* ⲛϥϫⲓⲧⲟⲩ ⲛⲉϩ. ⲙⲡⲁⲣⲣⲏⲙⲡ̅ⲉ̅, Lant 1 S *that Michael may* ϫ. ⲉϫⲱⲟⲩ ϩⲙⲡⲛⲏⲙⲁ, ib 31 F sim ϫⲓ ⲡⲉϩ. ⲉⲛⲛⲟⲩϯ (ⲉ)ϫⲟⲃ, El 96 A ⲥⲉⲛⲁϫ. ⲁⲭⲏⲣⲉⲡⲕⲉⲕⲉⲛⲉ, Ora 3 239 B ϭ. ⲉ. ϩⲁⲡⲕⲉⲟⲩⲟⲛ ⲛⲧⲟⲧⲩ ⲙⲡⲭ̅ⲥ̅, C 86 168 B ⲛⲧⲉϥϭ. ⲉ. ⲡⲓⲱⲙⲓ ϧⲁⲧⲉⲛⲡⲟⲩⲣⲟ; ⲉϩⲣⲁⲓ ⲉϫⲛ-: BMis 145 S ϫⲓ ⲡⲉϩ. ⲙⲡⲡ̅ⲉ̅ ⲉ. ⲉϫⲱⲛ, BSG 187 S ⲁⲡⲣⲁⲧⲓⲟⲥ ϫ. ⲉ. ⲉϫⲱⲟⲩ ⲛⲡⲁⲣⲣⲙⲡ̅ⲉ̅, C 43 186 B, Lant 81 S sim; ⲥ ⲛⲧⲛ-: BMis 400 S ⲉⲓⲭⲓⲧⲛⲅⲧⲛ (sic l) ⲛⲉϩ. ⲛⲧⲟⲟⲧⲩ ⲙⲡ̅ⲡ̅ⲉ̅ (var ib ϫⲓ ⲙⲙⲱⲧⲛ) = Va 63 19 B ϫⲓ ⲙⲡⲉⲧⲛⲉϩ. ⲛⲧⲟⲟⲧⲩ = BSM 50 B ϣⲉⲡ; ⲥ ⲟⲩⲉ-, *against, over*: AM 227 B *martyr* ϭⲓ ⲛⲟⲩϩ. ⲟⲩⲃⲉⲛⲛ̅ⲛ̅ⲁ̅; ⲥ ϩⲓϫⲛ-, *as* ⲉϫⲛ-: Mor 23 38 S *souls* ⲉϣⲁⲣⲉⲙⲓⲭⲁⲏⲗ ϫ. ϩⲓ ϫⲱⲟⲩ = ib 24 27 F, Z 627 S *angel* ⲉⲧϫ. ϩ. ϣⲱⲡⲉ ⲛⲙⲁ., AM 316 B ⲁⲩϭ. ϩ. ϩⲁⲛⲙⲏϣ ⲛⲣⲉϥⲉⲣ ⲛⲟⲃⲓ.

ϭⲛ, ϫⲉⲙ ϩ. *SAB, find grace*: Ge 18 3 B(S ϭⲉ), Pro 3 4 B(SA ϫⲡⲟ), Ac 7 46 B(S ϭⲉ χ.) χ. εὑρίσκειν, Lu 1 28 S(B diff) χαριτοῦσθαι, Z 585 S *virginity caused Elisha's body to* ϭ. (4 Kg 4 35), BSM 115 B *dead husband* ϫ. ⲙⲡⲉⲙⲧⲟ ⲙⲫϯ.

As name: ⲡⲉϩⲙⲟⲧ (Ryl 194).

ϩⲁⲙⲉⲧⲉ A² v ϩⲱⲙ s f.

ϩⲓⲙⲉⲉⲩ A², -ⲙⲉⲩⲉ A A² v ϩⲟⲉⲓⲙ.

ϩⲁⲙⲟⲅⲉ v ϩⲁⲟⲅⲉ.

ϩⲁⲙϣⲉ S, -ϣⲉ A v ϣⲉ *wood s f*.

ϩⲙϩⲁⲗ S, ϩⲙϩⲉⲗ A, ϩⲉⲙϩⲉⲗ F v ϩⲁⲗ *servant*.

ϩⲁⲙϩⲉⲙ F v ϧⲟⲙϧⲉⲙ.

ϩⲙϩⲙ SS^f A², -ϩⲙⲉ A, ϩⲏⲙϩⲉⲙ S^f F, ϩⲉⲙϩⲉⲙ B vb intr, *roar, neigh* (cf ‏همهم‎ Acta Or 15 3), *of lion*: Jud 14 5 S, Ps 21 14 B(S ⲗϩⲙⲙ), Zeph 3 3 AB ὠρύεσθαι; Ap 10 3 B(S do) μυκᾶσθαι; Nu 23 24 B(S ϣⲟⲩϣⲟⲩ) γαυριοῦσθαι; Mich 550 25 S *whelps* etc. ϩⲓⲛⲁϩⲟⲩ ⲛⲛⲟⲙⲟⲩⲓ; *of horse*: Si 36 6 S χρεμετίζειν; ShIF 281 S ⲉⲧⲉⲧⲛϩ. *like horses*, OratCyp 117 S^f ⲉϭ. ⲉⲡⲑⲉ ⲛⲟⲩϩⲧⲁⲁⲣⲓ; *of demon*: R 1 4 25 S ⲁϥϩ. ⲉⲃⲟⲗ ⲛϩⲏⲧⲩ *rugire*; *of man*: EpJer 31 B(F ϩⲓ ⲕⲁⲥ) ὤρ., DeV 1 40 B *Herodias* ϩ. ⲙⲫⲣⲏϯ ⲛⲟⲩⲗⲁⲃⲟⲓ.

With following preposition. Mor 39 36 S^f ⲁϥϩⲛ. ⲉϩⲟⲩⲛ ⲉⲣⲟⲟⲩ = C 43 55 B; Jer 5 8 S ⲉϫⲛ- B χ. ἐπί, BIF 14 162 S^f *beasts* ϩⲛ. ⲉϫⲙⲡⲣⲁⲧⲓⲟⲥ, ManiP 18 A² ⲁⲩϩ. ⲁϫⲱⲓ *like lions*, Jer 2 15 B ⲉϩⲣⲏⲓ ⲉϫⲉⲛ- ⲱⲣ. ἐπί, ShBM 194 2 S ϥϩ. ...ⲉϩⲣⲁⲓ ⲉϫⲱⲟⲩ.

—— nn m, *roaring, neighing*: Ez 19 7 B(S ⲗ.) ὠρύωμα; Jer 13 27 SB, Am 6 7 AB χρεμετισμός; Job 39 25 B(no S) κραυγή; ShBMOr 8810 380 S *thy mocking & thy* ϩ. ⲉϫⲛⲛⲉⲧⲛⲉⲓⲟⲧⲉ, ShC 42 147 S sim, Mor 51 40 S ⲡϩ. ⲛⲛⲟⲩⲃ *sound (talk?) of gold*, BHom 72 S ⲡϩ. ⲛⲛⲉⲩⲥⲛⲟⲧⲟⲩ *of demons*, BMar 241 S sim, BIF 14 162 S^f ⲡϩⲛ. ⲛⲛⲉⲙⲟⲩⲓ.

ⲣ ϩ., *roar*: Mor 32 42 S ⲁϥⲣ. ⲛⲑⲉ ⲛⲛⲉⲙⲟⲩⲓ.

ϩⲟⲙϩⲉⲙ, ϧⲟⲙϧⲉⲙ, ϩⲉⲙϩⲉⲙ-, ϩⲉⲙϩⲱⲙ⸗ B vb tr, *tread, trample*: Ps 90 13 ϧ. (S ϩⲱⲙ ⲉϫⲛ-), Is 41 25 (P 104 168, S ϩⲱⲙ), ib ϩⲉⲙϩⲉⲙⲟⲛⲛⲟⲩ, Lu 8 5 (S do) καταπατεῖν; ⲥ ϧⲉⲛ-, *into*: C 86 152 *took spear &* ⲁϥϩ. ϧⲉⲛⲧⲁϥⲉ ⲙⲡⲓⲁⲣⲁⲕⲱⲛ; ⲥ ϩⲓϫⲉⲛ-, *upon*: Is 16 4 (S ϩⲱⲙ ⲉϩⲣⲁⲓ ⲉϫⲛ-) ⲕ. ἐπί; *as* nn m: Is 22 5 (S ϩⲱⲙ), ib 5 5 ϧ. (no var, S do), Lam 2 8 ϧ. καταπάτημα. Cf ϩⲱⲙ.

ϩⲙⲟϫ S, ϩⲟⲙϫ† SB, -ⲛϫ† S, ϩⲁⲙϫ† A², -ⲙⲛϫ† S^f vb intr, *become, be sour*: ShC 73 136 *not over much date-water to be made lest* ⲛⲉϩⲗⲟϭ ⲙⲡⲃⲛⲛⲉ ϣⲓⲃⲉ ⲉⲙⲡⲧⲣⲉϥϩ.; qual: P 54 172 B ⲉϥϩ. ‏حامض‎, Bor 295 99 S(v Z 635 n) ⲛⲛⲟⲩϫⲧ ⲛⲧⲕⲁⲕⲓⲁ ⲉⲧϩ. (cf Ex 12 8), ManiK 33 A² ϯⲡⲉ ⲉⲧϩ., opp ϯ. ⲉⲧϩⲁⲗϭ, PMéd 230 S ⲙⲟⲟⲩ ... ⲉϥϩⲟⲙϫ, Bodl(P)a 2 69 S^f ⲟⲩⲥⲱⲗ ⲣⲱⲙⲁⲛ (‏أصول الرمان‎) ϩ. ⲙⲡⲟⲩⲥⲱⲗ ⲣ. ϩⲱⲗⲱ (sic, l ϩⲱⲗⲉϭ, cf ῥόα ὀξεῖα & γλυκεῖα Meyerhof).

ϩⲙϫ SAA²F, ϩⲉ. SBF, ϩⲏ. SF nn m, *vinegar*: Nu 6 3 SB, Pro 25 20 SA, Jo 19 29 SA²B ὄξος; K 200 B ⲡⲓϩ. ‏خل‎; ShC 73 88 S *good & poor* ϩ. *to be mixed & eaten*, ShMich 550 19 S ϩ. ⲉⲙⲛ ⲙⲟⲟⲩ ⲛϩⲏⲧⲩ, Z 628 S ⲟⲩϩ. ⲛⲁⲥⲧⲩ ⲕⲁⲗⲱⲥ, AZ 23 109 S *pot filled with* ⲙⲙⲟⲟⲩ (v p 158 a) ⲕⲁⲡ ϩ., Tri 496 S *food of monks salt*, ϩ., *dry bread*, C 43 140 B ϩ. & ⲕⲟⲛⲓⲁ *on martyr's wounds*, El 94 A sim, Mani 1 A² ⲁⲩⲧⲥⲁⲩ ⲟⲩϩ., BSM 41 B *in storeroom* ⲧⲁⲣⲓⲕⲓ, ⲁⲗⲱⲙ, ⲉϩⲓⲱ, ϩ., CO 343 S ⲛⲉϩ....ϫⲟⲟⲩⲥⲟⲩ, Miss 4 644 S ⲏⲣⲡ ⲛⲉϩ. ϩⲓⲟⲩⲗⲱⲙⲓ *sold to poor*, Kr 29 S, ST 89 S, Tor 7 S *vintner's*

contracts sim (cf Wess 20 no 143), Mor 51 22 S vines diseased ⲉⲩⲟ ⲛⲧⲱ (l ⲥ̄ⲱⲛ = ⲥⲟⲛ) ϩⲓϩⲏ.;   various sorts: PMéd 277 S ϩⲛ. ⲛⲁⲡⲁⲥ, C 86 205 B sim, KroppK 31 S ⲁⲥ, Z 629 S ⲛⲁⲥ, BM 527 F prob do, BM 697 F ⲛⲃⲉⲣⲓ, AM 154 B ⲡⲁⲕⲣⲁⲧⲟⲛ, Mani 1 A² ⲛⲙⲉⲗ, Bodl(P)a 1 e ϩⲛ. ⲛⲥⲟⲫⲟⲥ, BMis 193 S, PMéd 190 S, C 43 167 B ⲉ̄ϫⲛⲏ̄ϫ, PMéd 177 S ⲉϫⲛⲟⲥⲉ, Z 629 S ⲉϫⲣⲁⲕϭ; ⲉⲗⲉⲗⲙⲭ υ ⲉⲗⲟⲩⲗⲉ·I;   vessels, measures: Ryl 317 S ⲗⲁⲕⲟⲛ, CO 217 S ⲕⲁⲕ, Bodl (P)a 1 f S ⲕⲟⲗⲗⲁⲟ(ⲉ), WS 147 S ϩⲟⲧⲥ, BP 4949 S ϩⲟⲧⲥ ⲟⲩ, WS 88 S ⲫⲟⲣⲛⲥ, BM 691 F δίπ(λοῦν), CO 212 S ϣⲛⲧⲁⲉⲥⲛ, ST 440 F, CO 498 F ϩⲛⲉⲩ, CO 505 F ⲥⲕⲛⲟⲩⲉⲓ.

ⲣ ϩ. S, *become, be sour*: CA 107 of wine ⲛ̄ϥⲧⲙⲣ. ⲛ̄ϥⲧⲙⲗⲱⲙⲥ, Kr 228 ⲁⲃⲏⲣ ϩⲛⲙⲛϫ, BMar 90 ο ⲛϩ., BMis 194 water ⲁⲩⲣ ϩ.

ⲧ ⲉⲛϩ. S, *be somewhat sour*: Wess 15 22 ⲟⲩⲏⲣⲡ ⲉⲩⲧ. οἰνάριον ὄξινον.

ϫⲓ ϩ. S, *use vin.* as cure: ShIF 155.

ϩⲁⲛ- A.A² nn m, *necessity* (?): Jo 3 7 A² ⲫⲁⲓ ⲧⲣⲟⲩϫⲡⲁⲧⲏⲛⲉ (S ϩⲁⲛⲥ, BF ϩⲱⲧ) δεῖ; El 56 A ⲫ. ⲧⲟⲩϩⲉⲓ ⲛⲛⲁⲧⲁⲑⲟⲟⲛ ⲙⲡⲛⲡⲉⲑⲁⲩ, TU 43 15 A ⲫ. ⲧⲟⲩϩⲱⲡⲉ. Cf ? ⲱⲡ bid (Rösch 184).

ϩⲁⲛ S nn m, meaning unknown: Hall 117 among *varia* ⲥⲛⲁⲩ ⲛϩ. ⲉϣⲱⲃ 2 ? *for shaving*.

ϩⲁⲛ- A prep υ ϩⲛ- (ⲉϩⲟⲩⲛ ϩⲛ-).

ϩⲁⲛ- (? ϩⲁ- ⲛ-) S in ⲫⲁⲛⲧⲟⲟⲩ υ p 441 b supra, adding ? BM 1024 ⲛⲙⲁ ⲛϩⲁⲛⲱⲛⲉ.

ϩⲁⲉⲓⲛ (?) S nn m, *sodden, soaked food* (??): Ryl 113 glossary ϫⲟⲙⲛ (ζωμίον, ψω. or ζωμός, ζουμί, cf P 44 85 vo) · ⲛⲥⲱⲛⲉⲛⲉ ⲫⲁⲉⲓⲛ.

ϩⲁⲛⲁ- B υ ⲣⲟⲩϩⲉ, ϩⲧⲟⲟⲩⲉ & AZ 51 124.

ϩⲛ- SA²FO, ϩⲛ- A, ϩⲉⲛ- B, ϩⲓⲛ-, ϩⲉ-, ϩⲛ- F, ϩⲉⲛ-FO, ϩ̄ⲛ-O, ⲛϩⲏⲧ⳽ (υ ϩⲛ belly) SA²F, ⲛϩ. A, ⲛϩ̄. B prep (constr of ϩⲟⲩⲛ) a of place *in, at, on*: Ge 3 10 SB, Job 19 24 S(B ϩⲓ-), ib 29 3 S(B ⲉ̄ϩⲣⲏⲓ ϩ̄.), Pro 22 13(2°) S(A ϩⲓ-), Eccl 7 11 SFϩⲓⲛ-, Is 1 21 B(S ϩⲣⲁⲓ ϩⲛ-), Lam 2 6 B(F ⲛ-), ib 3 1 BFϩⲓⲛ-, ib 4 2 B(F ϩⲗⲏⲓ ⲛ-), EpJer 3 BF, Mt 13 57 S(B ⲛ̄ϩ̄ⲣ. ϩ̄., F ϩⲗ. ϩ.), Mk 9 33 S(var & B ϩⲓ-), Jo 14 10 SA²B, Cl 32 2 A, ib 54 1 A ϩⲛⲧⲏⲛⲉ ἐν; Job 21 26 S(B ϩⲓ-ϫⲉⲛ-), Ps 83 10 SB, Lam 2 19 B(S ϩⲓϫⲛ-, F ⲛ-), Lu 21 8 SB(var ⲉ-), Ap 1 20 S(B ϩⲓ-) ἐπί; Pš 22 2 SB, Pro 24 39 SA, Mt 18 20 S(var ⲉ-)B εἰς; Ps 150 2 S (B = Gk), Mt 1 20 SB, Lu 1 18 S(B ⲛ̄ϩ̄ⲣ. ϩ̄.) κατά; EpJer 2 SBF, Sa 9 16 S, Mt 13 20 SBF μετά; Job 10 12 SB, Is 38 12 B(S diff) παρά; Ps 140 3 S(B ⲛ-) περί; Sa 11 5 S, Ac 13 49 SB διά; Ps 13 5 SB, Is 10 9 SB ⲟⲩ̄, Ap 2 13 S(B ⲛⲙⲟ̄ϥ), Mt 6 19 S(B om) ὅπου, Job 6 17 S(B diff) ὅπερ; Ps 16 10 SF(B ⲛ-), Pro 2 21 S(var & AB ϩⲓϫⲛ-), Sa 17 2 S, Mk 2 2 S(B

ⲛ-), BM 172 40 S ⲙⲟⲟϣⲉ ϩⲛⲟⲩϩⲓⲏ, BHom 38 S ⲱϣ ϩⲛⲡⲉⲩⲁⲅⲅⲉⲗⲓⲟⲛ acc; Lev 21 19 S(B diff), Mt 14 14 SBF, ROC 17 407 B ϣⲱⲡⲓ ϩ̄ⲉⲛⲫⲟⲩⲁϩⲥⲁϩⲛⲓ gen; Ge 13 2 S(B ⲛ̄ϩ̄ⲣ. ϩ̄.).), Job 33 26 SB, Ps 85 11 S(B ϩⲓ-), Mt 5 3 S(B ⲛ-), Jo 12 33 S(A²B do), Cl 23 1 A dat; often added after vb to complete sense: Is 6 11 SB ⲟⲩⲱϩ ⲛϩⲏⲧⲟⲩ κατοικεῖσθαι, ib 27 11 B ⲟⲩⲟⲛ ⲕⲁⲧ ⲛϩⲏⲧϥ σύνεσιν ἔχειν, Mt 5 19 S ϯ ⲥⲃⲱ ⲛϩⲏⲧϥ διδάσκειν, ib 18 20 S ⲥⲟⲟϩϩ ⲡϩⲏⲧϥ (B ⲙⲙⲟϥ) συνάγεσθαι; PS 11 S ⲧϫⲟⲙ ⲉⲧϣⲟⲟⲡ ϩⲓⲧⲏϩⲛ (cf ib ⲡ̄ϩⲏⲧⲧⲏⲛ̄), ib 141 S ⲁⲩϩⲉ ϩⲙⲡⲉⲭⲁⲟⲥ, ShC 73 21 S ⲉϥϣⲟⲟⲛ ϩⲙⲡⲥⲱⲧⲙ, ib 57 S ϩⲙⲡⲁϣⲁⲓ ⲙ̄ⲡⲣⲱⲕϩ (var ⲉⲧⲃⲉ-), ib 145 S loaves ϩⲓⲧⲉⲧⲣⲁⲡⲉⲍⲁ, Mor 30 23 Sꟷ ⲁϥϫⲁⲓ ⲉⲃⲟⲗ ϩⲛⲭⲱⲣⲁ ⲛⲓⲙ, C 86 209 B sim, R 1 3 5 S ⲡⲉϥⲣⲁⲛ ϩⲛⲡⲣⲱⲙⲉ *among*, Bor 241 148 S ⲙⲛⲟ̄ⲃⲥⲱ ⲛϩⲏⲧϥ save girdle, Ep 162 S ⲡⲓⲥⲭⲏⲙⲁ (monk's habit) ⲉⲧ̄ϩ̄ⲛϩⲏⲧϥ, BMis 115 S rings ϩⲛⲛⲉⲩⲧⲏⲛⲃⲉ, FR 32 S grieve not ϩⲙ̄ⲡⲉⲧⲛⲁϫⲟⲟϥ, ib 12 S not strangers ϩⲛ̄ⲡⲉⲩⲉⲣⲏⲩ, El 42 A ⲉⲩⲕⲱⲧⲉ ϩⲛⲛⲁⲏⲣ, ManiH 6 A² ϣⲱⲡⲉ ϩⲛⲟⲩⲥⲉⲣ̄ⲁϩⲣⲧ, PGM 1 60 O ϩⲛⲟⲩⲙⲉ, AP 1 A² place where corpse ⲕⲏ ⲁϩⲣⲏⲓ ⲛϩⲏⲧϥ, C 43 205 B ⲡⲓⲟⲩⲓⲧ ⲉⲧⲉⲛϩⲏⲧⲟⲩ, C 89 74 B ⲁ̄ⲭⲉⲙⲥ ϩ̄ⲉⲛⲟⲩⲕⲁⲧⲟⲩⲥ (κάδος), Kr 10 F ϩⲉⲛⲧⲁϣ, ib 13 F ϩⲉⲛⲡⲗⲉⲛ, ib 227 F ϩⲛⲣⲁⲛ, BM 597 F ϩⲉⲟⲩⲛⲁϫ ⲉⲣⲓⲥⲓ, JKP 2 50 F ϩⲛⲧⲁϭⲓϫ, KroppC 15 F child ϩⲉⲛⲧⲉⲥⲕⲁⲗⲁϩⲛ, AZ 21 94 O ⲡⲉⲧⲣⲉⲡⲛⲁⲏⲣ, ib 100 O ⲥⲱⲡ [ⲙ]ⲙⲟⲩ ⲉⲡⲛⲉⲥⲛⲟϥ, Hor 80 O ϩ̄ⲛⲟⲩⲉⲓⲉⲛⲡϣⲱⲧ;   varies with ⲛ-: Ge 31 37 S, Jos 5 10 S, Ps 20 8 S(B ⲛ-), Pro 7 16 B(S A ⲛ-), Lam 2 19 SB(F ⲛ-), PS 158 S ⲉⲧ̄ϩⲛⲛ̄ϭⲟⲛ, 157 ⲉⲧⲛ., ShC 73 138 S ϩⲙⲛⲣⲁⲛ ⲛⲧⲉ̄, var ⲙⲛ., MIF 9 51 S ⲱϣ ⲉⲃⲟⲗ ϩⲛⲧⲁⲥⲛⲉ, varBAp 12 ⲛⲧ.; cf b, c; with ϩⲓ-: 2 Kg 13 32 S, Job 19 24 S(B ϩⲓ-), Ps 85 11 S(B do), Pro 3 16 SA(B do), Jon 1 5 A(S ϩⲓ-), Ac 9 17 S, J 26 13 S ϩⲓⲧⲣⲁⲓⲉⲓⲧ, 17 ϩⲓⲧ.; υ also ϩⲓ- a s f.

b of time: Nu 1 18 S(var ⲛ-)B, Ps 1 3 SB, Pro 25 13 SA, Lam 2 19 SB(F ⲛ-), Mt 12 2 SBF ἐν; 2 Kg 7 19 S(var ⲉ-) εἰς; Deu 2 1 S(var & B ⲛ-), Ps 70 8 S(B ⲛ-) acc; Jos 14 7 S, Ps 21 2 SB, Is 36 1 SBF, Mk 5 42 SB gen; Jos 5 10 S(var ⲛ-), 1 Cor 15 4 SB (F ⲛ-), Ap 18 17 S(B ⲛ̄ϩ̄ⲣ. ϩ̄.) dat; PS 4 S ϩⲙⲡⲙⲛ̄ⲧⲏ ⲙⲡⲟⲟⲩ, AP 27 A² ϩⲓⲧⲟⲩϣⲏ ⲧⲏⲣⲥ, BMar 30 S ⲉⲓⲣⲙⲙⲛⲧϥ̄ⲓⲥ ⲛⲣⲟⲙⲡⲉ, Kr 10 F ϩⲉⲛⲕⲁⲣⲡ[ⲟⲥ] *harvest-time*.

c *by, with* as agent: 2 Kg 1 12 S, Ps 31 9 SB, Si 51 26 S, Lam 2 21 SB(F ϩⲗ. ϩⲓⲛ-), ib 4 14 B(S ⲛ-), Mk 1 8 SB ἐν; Pro 28 8 SA, Ac 13 17 SB μετά; Pro 24 56 SA(B ⲉⲃⲟⲗ ϩⲓⲧⲉⲛ-), Sa 11 5 S, Ac 8 20 S(var ϩⲓⲧⲉⲛ-, B do) διά; Pro 16 26 SA, Sa 12 27 S ἐπί; Ps 44 8 SB, Ap 3 18 S(B ⲛ̄ϩ̄ⲣ. ϩ̄.) ἐκ; Pro 24 22 a SA, Sa 16 5 S ἀπό; ib 11 7 S gen; Nu 14 43 S(B ⲛ-), Job 31 7 SB, Pro 14 1 S(varBHom 113 ⲛ-).AB, Is 6 2 SB, EpJer 10 B(F ⲛ-), Jo 11 2 S(A²B ⲛ-) dat; PS 157 S ⲁϥⲡⲁⲧⲁⲥⲥⲉ ⲙ̄ⲫⲟϥ ... ϩⲛⲛⲁϭⲓϫ (Od Solom 22 5 ⲁ),

ib 21 *S* bonds ⲉⲧⲟⲩⲙⲏⲣ ⲛϩⲏⲧⲟⲩ, R 1 3 81 *S* ⲁⲥϫⲁⲕ ϩⲙⲡⲉⲥⲟⲓⲝ, BMis 236 *S* ⲛⲛⲁⲩ ϩⲛⲡⲃⲁⲗ, J 71 39 *S* house I built ϩⲙⲡⲁⲣⲓⲥⲉ, Ep 198 *S* ⲉⲛⲧⲟⲩⲭⲏⲩ ϩⲙⲡⲉⲧⲛϣⲗⲏⲗ, Mani 1 *A²* ϫⲁⲣⲙⲉϥ ϩⲛⲟⲩϫⲉⲟⲩⲁ, BSM 119 *B* cried ϫⲉⲛⲧⲉⲥⲁⲥⲡⲓ (*cf* BAp 12 *S* sim ⲛ-), DeV 2 8 *B* ⲉⲣ ⲛⲟⲙ ⲉⲣⲱⲟⲩ ϫⲉⲛⲟⲩϫⲏⲛⲕⲁϯ, BIF 22 106 *F* shall die ϩⲛ- ⲧϭⲓϫ ⲛⲡⲉⲧⲛⲁϫⲱⲗⲟⲛ.

ⲉⲃⲟⲗ ϩⲛ- *SAA²BF*, *from in, from*: Ge 7 15 *SB*, Ps 16 14 *S*(*B* ⲉ̄ⲃ̄. ϩⲁ-, *F* diff), *ib* 17 47 *SB*(*F* ⲛⲧⲉⲛ-), Lam 3 19 *SB*(*F* ⲛ-), EpJer 20 *BF*, Ro 8 2 *S*(*B* ⲉ̄ⲃ̄. ϩⲁ-), MG 25 219 *B* ⲁⲛⲟⲛ ⲛⲁⲟⲩⲉ̄ⲃ̄. (*sic*) ϫⲉⲛⲟⲩⲁⲃⲏⲧ ἀπό; Ge 16 2 *S*(*B* ⲉ̄ⲃ̄. ⲛ-), Ps 21 9 *SB*, Lam 1 13 *B*(*F* ⲉ̄ⲃ̄. ⲛ-), Mt 7 9 *S*(*B* ϫ̄.), Z 344 *S* fetch wood ⲉ̄ⲃ̄. ϩⲙ-ⲡⲣⲉⲗⲟⲥ = MG 25 208 *B* ἐκ; Deu 27 5 *SB*, Ps 20 4 *SB* ἐκ made *from*; 2 Cor 5 8 *SB* ἐκ(δημεῖν) ἐκ, Ap 4 5 *S*(*B* ⲉ̄ⲃ̄. ϩⲁ-) ἐκ(πορεύεσθαι) ἐκ, Va 57 6 *B* ϧⲉⲓ ⲉ̄ⲃ̄. ϫⲉⲛⲡⲙⲉⲧⲃⲱⲕ ἐκ(πίπτειν) gen; Is 63 14 *S*(*B* ⲉ̄ⲃ̄. ϩⲓⲧⲉⲛ-), Ac 1 16 *B*(*S* ⲉ̄ⲃ̄. ϩⲓⲧⲛ-)διά; Ps 59 10 *S*(*B* diff), Mt 1 20 *S*(*B* diff) ἐν; Sa 14 22 *S* περί; *ib* 16 27 *S*, Is 30 2 *S*(*B* ⲉ̄ⲃ̄. ϩⲓⲧⲉⲛ-, *F* ⲛⲧⲉⲛ-) ὑπό; Sa 8 9 *S*, Is 34 16 *B*(*SF* ⲙⲙⲁⲩ), Lam 3 15 *B*(*S* ϩⲛ-) gen; ClPr 29 244 *S* ⲛⲟⲩϩⲟⲟⲩ ⲉ̄ⲃ̄. ϩⲛⲟⲩϩⲟⲟⲩ (*cf* 2 Cor 4 16 *S* ⲉⲧⲉ. *B* ϫⲁⲧⲉⲛ ⲛⲉϩ.) dat; MG 25 243 *B* cast him ⲉ̄ⲃ̄. ϫⲉⲛⲡⲁⲓⲙⲁ ἐντεῦθεν; PS 118 *S* ⲉⲥⲛⲏⲩ ⲉ̄ⲃ̄. ϩⲛⲡⲁⲓⲱⲛ, ShC 73 104 *S* ⲉⲩⲛⲏⲧ ⲉ̄ⲃ̄. ϩⲛⲙⲉⲓⲥⲩⲛⲁⲅⲱⲅⲏ, Mor 18 48 *S* ⲟⲩⲣⲱⲙⲉ ⲉ̄ⲃ̄. ⲛϩⲏⲧⲟⲩ (var *ib* 19 55 om ⲉ̄ⲃ̄.), Bor 226 175 *S* ⲣ ⲃⲗⲗⲉ ⲉ̄ⲃ̄. ϩⲙⲡⲟⲩⲟⲉⲓⲛ, El 94 *A* draw skins ⲁ̄ⲃ̄. ϩⲛⲟⲩⲅⲁⲡⲏⲅⲉ = *ib* 128 *S* ⲉ̄ⲃ̄. ⲛ-, ManiH 11 *A²* ⲛⲟⲩϫⲉ ⲙⲙⲁⲥ ⲁ̄ⲃ̄. ϩⲙ- ⲡⲕⲟⲥⲙⲟⲥ, DeV 2 25 *B* freed ⲉ̄ⲃ̄. ϫⲉⲛⲡϩⲓⲁⲣⲃⲉϥ, C 41 72 *B* saw them ϫⲉⲛⲛⲁⲃⲁⲗ ⲁⲓⲥⲟⲑⲙⲟⲩ ⲉ̄ⲃ̄. ϫⲉⲛⲡⲁⲙⲁϣϫ.

ϩⲛ- as if ⲉⲃⲟⲗ ϩⲛ-: Ex 2 10 *AB*, 2 Kg 12 3 *S*(var ⲉ̄ⲃ̄. ϩⲛ-), Ps 33 17 *S*(*B* ⲉ̄ⲃ̄. ϫ̄.), Is 36 16 *SF*(*B* do), Mic 1 3 *S*(var & *AB* do), Mt 28 2 *S*(*BF* do), Jo 13 4 *SA²*(*B* do), Cl 11 1 *A*, Z 295 *S* ⲁⲙⲟⲩ ⲉϩⲣⲁⲓ ϩⲙⲡ-ⲓⲉⲣⲟ, R 1 1 40 *S* (ⲉ)ⲡⲉⲥⲛⲧ ϩⲙⲡⲡⲏⲅⲉ ἐκ; 2 Kg 3 26 *S*(var ⲉ̄ⲃ̄. ϩⲛ-), Pro 10 5 *SA*(*B* do), Is 34 7 *SF*(*B* do), Mk 15 21 *SF*(*B* do), Cl 33 1 *A*, R 1 1 36 *S* followed Him ϩⲛⲧⲅⲁⲗⲓⲗⲁⲓⲁ ἀπό; Job 2 9 *S*(*B* do), Jer 26 12 *S*(*B* do), 1 Pet 4 1 *S*(*B* do, var ⲉ̄ⲃ̄. ϩⲁ-) gen; PS 144 *S* ⲁⲥⲉⲓ ϩⲙⲡϫⲓⲥⲉ, BG 26 *S* ⲙⲡⲉⲗⲁⲁⲩ ⲛϩⲏⲧⲛ ⲥⲟⲩⲛ, ShC 42 132 *S* ϥⲓⲧⲟⲩ ⲙⲙⲁⲩ ϩⲙⲡⲉϥϫⲱⲱⲙⲉ (*cf* Ex 32 33 ⲉ̄ⲃ̄. ϩⲛ-), El 128 *S* ⲕⲧⲟϥ ϩⲛⲙⲡⲟⲗⲓⲥ = *ib* 78 *A* ⲁ̄ⲃ̄. ϩⲛ-, Ann 19 232 *S* ⲁⲧⲁⲣⲉⲗⲡⲓⲥ ⲟⲩⲉⲓⲛⲉ ϩⲙⲡⲉⲓⲏⲓ = C 86 112 *B* ⲉ̄ⲃ̄. ϫ̄., BIF 13 107 *S* Jonah ⲛⲟⲩϩⲙ ϩⲛⲧⲕⲁ-ⲗⲁϩⲏ of whale = MG 25 292 *B* ⲉ̄ⲃ̄. ϫ̄., MIE 2 391 *B* (ⲧ)ⲥⲟϥ ϫⲉⲛⲡⲁⲓⲙⲱⲟⲩ = BAp 114 *S* ⲉ̄ⲃ̄. ϩⲛ-, J 75 49 *S* lest we ϣⲓⲃⲉ ϩⲙⲡⲉⲓⲱⲛϩ, *ib* 61 sim ⲉ̄ⲃ̄. ϩⲛ-, J 16 52 *S* whoso shall venture ϩⲓⲥⲟⲛ ϩⲛⲥⲱⲛⲉ (*cf* *ib* 18 45), TU 43 9 *A* ⲧⲟⲩⲛⲁⲥⲧ ϩⲙⲡⲉⲧⲙⲁⲩⲧ, BMis 33 *S* Theodore came ϩⲙⲛⲡⲟⲗⲁⲓⲙⲟⲥ, ROC 25 249 *B* ⲁϥⲓ ϫⲉⲛ-ⲑⲛⲉϫⲓ of Mary, Miss 8 47 *S* letter sent ϩⲛⲉϥⲉⲥⲟⲥ, Bor 226 158 *S* ⲟⲩⲁ ϩⲙⲡⲛⲉⲓⲟⲧⲉ.

ⲉϩⲟⲩⲛ ϩⲛ- *SB*, ϧⲁⲛ- *A*, *into, toward, at, within*: Job 6 28 *S*(*B* ⲉ-), Ez 37 9 *S*(ShA 1 370)*B*, Mk 8 23 *S*(*B* ϫ̄.) εἰς; Ac 26 14 *SB*, R 1 1 14 *S* crying ⲉϩ. ϩⲙ-ⲡⲕⲟⲩⲣⲥⲱⲣ πρός; Lev 4 6 *S*(*B* ⲙⲡⲉⲙⲑⲟ ⲛ-), R 1 1 27 *S* gnashing teeth ⲉϩ. ϩⲛ- κατά; Nu 21 9 *S*(var ⲉϩⲛ-, *B* ⲉ-), Ez 41 6 *SB*, Hos 11 4 *A*(*B* ϫⲉⲛ-) ἐπί; Ez 6 9 *SB*, R 1 1 36 *S* acc; Mt 7 25 *S*(*B* diff) dat; 1 Kg 9 16 *S* ⲉϩ. ϩⲙⲡⲛⲁⲩ ὡς ὁ καιρός, Nu 9 3 *S* sim (*B* ⲛ-) πρός; PS 322 *S* ϩⲓⲟⲩⲉ ⲉϩ. ϩⲛⲧⲉⲥⲙⲓⲥⲧϩⲏⲧ, BG 136 *S* ϯ ⲉϩ. ϩⲙⲡⲉϥϩⲏⲧ, *ib* 51 *S* ⲛϣⲉ ⲉϩ. ϩⲙ-ⲡⲉϥϩⲟ, MIE 2 413 *B* ⲙⲟϣⲓ ⲉϫ̄. ϫⲉⲛⲡⲓⲧⲱⲟⲩ, C 86 293 *B* pillar ⲉϫ̄. ϫⲉⲛⲡⲉⲥⲛⲓ; esp of *speaking to*: Lev 8 31 *S*(*B* ⲛ-), 2 Kg 2 14 *S*, Zech 3 2 *SA*(*B* ϫⲟ) πρός; 1 Kg 21 2 *S*, Ez 27 3 *SB* dat; R 1 1 60 *S* ⲡⲉϫⲁⲩ ⲉϩ. ϩⲙⲡⲉϥⲉⲣⲏⲩ εἰπεῖν only; BSG 198 *S* ⲡⲉϫⲁϥ ⲉϩ. ϩⲙ-ⲡⲕⲉϣⲟϫⲡ ⲛⲛⲉⲓϫⲱⲗⲟⲛ = *ib* 32 *B* ⲛ-, BMis 104 *S* none shall ⲧⲁϫⲉ ⲗⲁⲁⲩ ⲛϣⲁϫⲉ...ⲉϩ. ϩⲙⲡϩⲟ ⲙⲡⲣⲣⲟ.

ⲛϩⲟⲩⲛ ϩⲛ-, *within*: Ge 18 9 *B*(*S* ϩⲛ-), MG 25 6 *B* ⲟⲩⲱⲙ ⲛϫ̄. ϫⲉⲛⲡⲓⲃⲏⲃ ἐν; ShC 42 142 *S* ⲉⲛⲣⲙⲟⲟⲥ ⲛϩ. ϩⲙⲛⲏⲓ, ShA 1 257 *S* ⲟⲩⲱⲙ ⲉⲛⲡⲉⲧϩⲟⲩⲛ ⲛϩⲏⲧⲟⲩ (*sc* of fruits), C 43 92 *B* sat at βῆμα ⲛϫ̄. ϫⲉⲛⲡⲓ-ⲕⲁⲥⲧⲣⲟⲛ (*cf* PeyGr 165 *S* ⲛϩ. ⲉϣⲙⲟⲩⲛ).

ⲉⲥⲣⲏⲓ ϫⲉⲛ- *B*, *down in, into*: Jer 51 11 (*S* ϩⲛ-), Lam 3 3 (*S* ϩⲣⲁⲓ ϩⲛ-, *F* ⲉϫⲉⲛ-), Ez 22 9 (*S* ϫⲟ), Su 20 (*S* ϩⲛ-) ἐν; Jer 13 16 (*S* ⲉ-), Ez 13 11 (*S* ⲉϩⲣⲁⲓ ⲉ-) εἰς; Bel 17 παρά. Rarely, if ever, outside these books (1 Kg 17 22, Ro 1 24 prob not thus); ⲉϩ. ϫⲉⲛ- for ? ⲉϫ̄.: Dan 10 16 ἐν, Sa 5 3 (*S* ϩⲣⲁⲓ ϩⲛ-) dat.

ϩⲣⲁⲓ ϩⲛ-, ⲛϩ. ϩⲛ- (rare)*S*, ⲛϩⲣⲏⲓ ϩⲛ- *A*, ⲛϩⲣⲏⲓ ϩⲛ- *A²*, ⲛϫ̄., ⲛϩ. ϫⲉⲛ- *B*, ϧⲗⲏⲓ ϧ(ⲉ)ⲛ- *F*, *in*: Ge 2 3 *AB*, Ex 4 17 *A*(*S* ⲉϩ. ⲉ-, *B* ⲛϫ̄. ϫⲉⲛ-), 1 Kg 2 10 *B*(*S* ϩⲛ-), Ps 9 2 *S*(*B* ϫⲉⲛ-), *ib* 43 5 *SB*, *ib* 112 6 *B* ⲛϩ. (*S* ϩⲛ-), Eccl 7 10 *F*(*S* do), Mt 19 21 *SB*(var ⲛϩ.), Mk 8 3 *S* (varr ϩⲛ-, ϩⲓ-, *B* ϩⲓ-), Jo 10 38 *SA²*(*B* ϫ̄.), *ib* 14 13 *F* (MS Louvain, *SA²B* ϫⲉⲛ-) ἐν; Ps 105 29 *S*(*B* ⲉϩⲣⲏⲓ ⲉϫⲉⲛ-), Sa 12 17 *S*, Kandil 46 *B* ⲛϫ̄. ϫⲉⲛⲛⲁⲓ ⲉϥⲉϭⲓ ⲱⲟⲩ ἐπί; 1 Kg 17 49 *B*(*S* ⲉϩⲣ. ⲉ-), Is 49 4 *B*(*S* ⲉ-) εἰς; Sa 11 17 *S* διά; Ex 32 12 *B*(*S* ϩⲛ-) μετά; Ps 6 2 *B*(var ⲛϩ., *S* do), Sa 14 19 *S*, Ac 5 31 *B*(*S* diff), Cl 20 8 *A* Stras ⲛϩⲣ. ϩⲛ- (Berl ϩⲛ-), *ib* 20 5 *A* Berl ϩⲣ. ϩⲛ- (Stras ⲛϩⲣ.), BHom 17 *S* wash away sins ϩⲣ. ϩⲙⲛⲉⲕⲣⲙⲉⲓⲟⲟⲩⲉ dat; PS 64 *S* ⲁⲧⲁϫⲟⲙ ⲱϭⲣ ϩⲣ. ⲛ-ϩⲏⲧ, *ib* 346 *S* ⲃⲟⲗⲟⲩ ⲉⲃⲟⲗ ϩⲣ. ϩⲛⲙⲙⲣⲣⲉ, Br 232 *S* ⲉⲥⲣⲏⲓ ϩⲣ. ⲛϩⲏⲧϥ, ShC 73 103 *S* ⲣⲱⲙⲉ ϩⲣ. ⲛϩⲏⲧϥ (var om ϩⲣ.), ShA 2 175 *S* light ⲡⲉⲧϩⲣ. ϩⲙⲙⲡⲏⲅⲉ, ShC 73 204 *S* ⲉⲧⲥⲛϩ ϩⲣ. ϩⲙⲡϫⲱⲱⲙⲉ (*cf* 205 ⲥⲁϧⲟⲩ ⲉϩⲣ. ⲉⲛϫ.), El 52 *A* ϧⲟⲟⲛ ϩⲣ. ⲛϩⲏⲧⲟⲩ, TillOster 30 *A* ⲛϩⲣ. ϩⲛ-, Aeg 14 *B* ⲓⲣⲓ ⲙⲡⲉϥⲟⲩⲱϣ ⲛϫ̄. ⲛϩⲏⲧ, AM 294 *B* ⲛϩⲣ. ϫⲉⲛⲡⲓⲙⲁⲅ̄ ⲛⲉϩⲟⲟⲩ; ⲛϩⲣ. ϩⲛ- *S*: Nu 3 25 (*B* ϫ̄.) ἐν; ShA 1 447 place where fire ϫⲉⲣⲟ ⲛϩ. ⲛϩⲏⲧϥ, *ib* 75 ⲥⲉⲛϩ. ϩⲛⲧⲟⲩⲙⲏⲧⲉ, BMOr 8811 79 ⲥⲉⲛϩ. ϩⲛⲁⲙⲏⲧⲉ.

In adverbial expressions. Ps 37 19 *SB* ϩнογϫι н-ϭонс ἀδίκως, Mt 2 8 *S* ϩнογωρϫ (*B*=Gk) ἀκριβῶς, Sa 6 5 *S* ϩнογсοογтн ὀρθῶς, Mk 1 10 *S* ϩнтεγнογ (var н-, *B* diff) εὐθέως, Ac 24 4 *SB* ϩнογϣωωт εβολ συντόμως, Sa 14 15 *S* ϩнογϭεпн ταχέως, Ps 30 13 *S* ϩмпкωтε (*B* н-) κυκλόθεν, Sa 18 9 *S* ϩмфωп κρυφῇ, *ib* 2 9 *S* ϩмма нιм πανταχῇ, *ib* 19 21 *S* sim, Cl 23 1 *A* ϩнϩωβ нιм κατὰ πάντα; Deu 28 64 *S* ϩмпма εтммαγ (var н-, *B* diff), Mk 11 5 *S* sim ἐκεῖ; Job 1 20 *S* ϩмпαι (*B*= Gk) οὕτως, EpJer 63 *B* sim (*F* εт-βεпει) ὅθεν, ROC 17 408 *B* ϧεнпαι ἐπὶ τούτοις; Mor 40 39 *S* ϩмпαι αϥϣλнλ = MG 25 267 *B*, Cat 119 *B* ϧεнпαι ϫε ογн *whereupon* angel departed.

With art & causal pref (Stern 469 ff) ϩмптρε- *SA²F*, ϩмптε- *A*, ϧεнпϫιнθρε- or om θρε- *B*, *in the..., when*: Ps 29 9 *SB*, Is 37 1 *SF* (*B* diff), Hos 10 10 *SAB*, Mt 13 25 *S* (*BF* diff) ἐν τῷ inf; Jos 3 15 *B* (*S* нтερε-) ὡς δέ; AP 21 *A²* ϩмптρεϥнεγ, ShC 42 185 *S* ϩмптρεϥει ϣαρωтн, *ib* 73 206 *S* ϩмп-тρεϥειнε нтεϥϭιϫ εϩραι, C 89 110 *B* ϧεнпϫιн-θρογϩεϫϩωϫт.

εϩ(ε)н-*SO*, εϫεн- *O* as ϩн-: Sa 16 20 (var ϩн-) πρός; Ac 13 22 (var do, *B*=Gk) κατά, Ps 54 13 εт-ннγ εϩмпαϩнт (var ϩн-, *B* εтϣнн ϣ нεм-), Phil 2 20 sim (*B* do) ἰσόψυχος; PS 138 ει εϩεнпεγερнγ, *ib* 349 нсεсγмфωнι εϩмпсοογн, BG 18 εкр γγмнαζε εϩнтεсϩιмε like adversary, ShWess 18 143 εнтαγ-тαмιε нρωмε εϩεпθεικωн мпε̄, ShBMOr 8810 428 нεтннγ εϩмпεγϩнт εтεмε ммοογ (*cf* 430 нεтннγ εϩтнпεγϩнт = P 130⁵ 87, *v* αϩтн- πρός), BMis 288 αϥϯ нεϥογοι εϩмпмннϣε ннβαρβαρος (*cf* 289 sim εϫн- мм. *sic l* & εϩογн нβ.), AZ 21 98 *O* ппε̄ ο εтεϩнпε, 99 εϩεнпεροογ, 100 εϫεнтιογ-нογ; εβολ εϩн- *S*: KroppM 72 (*sic l*) нεϫ ϫαι-мωнιοн εβ. εϩнϫ̄ϫ̄, *cf* ? En Peterson (*Mart Claud*) εкпροсϫοкι εнογϩм нϩнпαϭιϫ; εϩογн εϩн- *S* (*cf* εϩογн ϩн-): Lev 18 1 (var ϩн-, *B* нεм-), Nu 14 11 (*B* do) πρός; R 2 2 27 ϭωϣт εϩ. εϩмпογϩαι ἐπί; Jo 20 22 (frag *penes* Crum, var & *B* ϩн-) ἐν-; PS 310 пεϫαϥ εϩ. εϩмпεтρος, R 1 2 19 αιϫοογ εϩ. εϩм-пρρο, CO 60 bishop bids р пϣα εϩ. εϩнтοογε ϩм-пϣα ω *celebrate in morning* (?).

αϩн-, αϩαн- *A²*(Ma)*S*(ST 240) has apparently no connexion with εϩн-.

ϩεн-, ϩαн- pl of indef art *v* ογα (ογ-) p 470 *a* & ϩοειнε.

ϩεн- *B* vb *v* (ϩιнε).

ϩιн *SB*, ειн *S* nn m, a *vessel*, *cup*, so *liquid measure* (הִין): Lev 23 13 *SB*, Nu 15 4 *B* (*S* ϣι), Ez 4 11 *S* ειн (*B* om, *ib* 46 5 *S* ϣι) εἶν; EW 160 drank ογϩ. м-мωογ, *ib* пεϥϩ. ммωογ. *Cf* JEA 10 284.

ρεϥм пϩ. εϩογн *S*, *diviner* by aid of cup: Deu 18 11 (*B* as Gk) ἐγγαστρίμυθος.

ϣεнϩ. *B*, *divination*, lit *inquiring of cup* (*cf* DM 1 9): Nu 23 23 (*S* ϩнααγ нϣιнε), Deu 18 10 (*S* ϣιнε nn) μαντεία, ROC 25 248 (Z 128) μάντις *v* αϣ-εβεн; мεтϣ.: Mic 3 6 (*SA* do) μαντεία; ρεϥϣ., *diviner*: Lev 19 31 (*S* ρεϥмογтε) ἐπαοιδός; Mic 3 7 (*SA* ρεϥϣ.) μάντις; K 114 ظانّ (var مُعزّم); мεтρ.: Is 44 25 (*S* тοптн) μαντεία; ερ ϣ., *be diviner*: Mic 3 11 (*SA* ϣιнε) μαντεύεσθαι; пϫιнερ ϣ.: Ez 21 29 (var ϣιнε nn) -εσθαι.

ϩογн *SA²F*, ϩ. *A*, ϧ. *B*, ϫ. *O* (constr ϩн- *q v*) nn m, *inward part* (rarely except as advb or + prep) *S*: Ex 26 33 (*B* сαϧ.), Is 22 11 (*B* do) ἐσώτερον; ViK 9518 пϩ. ммοс р κακε; *v* also мпϩ.; with poss: 2 Cor 4 16 (var пεтϩιϩ., *B* пεтсαϧ.) ὁ ἔσω, Mt 7 15 (*B* сαϧ.) ἔσωθεν, Si 19 22 τὰ ἐντός, *ib* 10 9 пεтпεϥϩ. τὰ ἐνδόσθια; PS 198 ογωтβ εпεϥϩ., ShViK 9298 пεтϩιθн ммοс н пεсϩ.; with poss art: Job 1 10 (*B* εтсαϧ.) τὰ ἔσω, Lev 4 8 (*B* do) τὰ ἐνδ.; Br 238 пαпϩ., *ib* 91 пεфγλαξ тαϩ. мпτ αβολ, ShC 42 215 пнι... пαпϩ., CO 185 пϩολοк/ εтϩ. (*l* ? εтнϩ., *cf* ST 298); мпϩ., *inside*, *within*: Nu 18 7 (var нϩ., *B* сαϧ.) τὸ ἔνδοθεν, Deu 5 14 (var пϩ., *B* do) ἐντός; PS 1 εтм. мпϣορп нтωϣ, ShA 2 270 м. мпκαтαпε-тαсмα, BMar 34 пωρϣ мпβнмα м. нтпγλн, BMis 570 walls ογα м. пογα, Miss 4 773 finished it м. προмпε сnтε, BM 1113 нсει п. пϣομнт пϩοογ, Bor 256 150 εпϩ. нϯογ пϩοογ; with poss: Ex 12 9 (*B* εтсαϧ.) ἐνδόσθια, Lev 1 9 (*B* нϧнт≈) ἐγκοίλια, Deu 22 2 (*B* нεм-) μετά; BMar 129 ογн сοн мпεкϩ. *further in* (desert) *than thou*?, Z 261 пεϥмαϩт мп-пεтмпεϥϩ.; without м-: Ac 20 6 (*B* diff) ἄχρις; PS 197 пϩ. мптοποс, Pcod 11 пϩ. мпκαтαпεтαс-мα, BMis 442 пϩ. нϩεнκογι пϩοογ; ϫιн(н)ϩ., *from within*: PS 17 пραε мγстнριοн ϫ., *ib* 328 ϫ. εβολ αγω ϫιнβολ εϩογн; as adj: PMéd 91 among eye-diseases пмογ пϩ., *ib* 283 ερεпεϥβαλ ογ пм. пϩ., *ib* 166 моγ ϩογн (*sic* prob), Mor 30 27 *S^f* αпм. пϩ. ϣογα εпεснт = ? BMis 258 λεγκοм(α) ммοογ.

р пϩ., *go within*: Deu 23 10 (*B* ι εϧ.) εἰσέρχεσθαι; PS 248 нсερ пεγϩ. *enter them*, ShRE 10 164 of roads εϥϣαпρ пεγϩ.; с ε-: 1 Kg 21 15 εἰσέ. εἰς; R 1 3 46 р пϩ. εнтαфοс; с н- gen: 1 Kg 9 13 εἰσέ. εἰς; BMis 557 р пϩ. нтпε *ingredi*; PS 252 р пϩ. нтοποс, ShIF 300 suffer you to р пϩ. ппεγρο.

εϩογн *SFO*, αϩ. *A*, αϩ. *A²*, εϧ. *B*, εϩοн *F*, *to inside*, *inward*, opp εβολ, appended to many vbs of motion, as βωκ, ει, εινε, κωтε, мοοнε 1°, моγр, мοοϣε, пα 2°, пογϫε, пωт, сωк, сιтε, сοογтн, сοογϩ, ϯ, тнпοογ, тωϩ, тαϩο, ογωтβ, ωλ, ωρεβ 1°, ϣε 1°, ϥι, ϥωϭε, ϩε, ϩωλ, ϩωп 1°, ϫι, ϭωтϩ; also to others as

ⲕⲣⲙⲣⲙ, ⲗⲓⲃⲉ, ⲙⲟⲕⲙⲉⲕ, ⲙⲟⲩⲧⲉ, ⲙⲉⲉⲩⲉ, ⲛⲓϥⲉ, ⲣⲓⲙⲉ, ⲥⲙⲙⲉ, ⲥⲟⲙⲥ, ⲥϩⲁⲓ, ⲧⲱϩⲙ 1°, ϣⲱⲡⲉ, ϣⲁϫⲉ, ⲣ ϩⲁⲗ, ϭⲱϣⲧ.

Often reinforcing following prep, ⲉ-: Ge 46 27 *S* ⲃⲱⲕ ⲉ. ⲉⲕⲏⲙⲉ εἰσ-, Mus 40 255 *S* name alone cannot ⲧⲟⲩϫⲟ ⲉ. ⲉⲧⲙⲛⲧⲉⲣⲟ εἰς, 1 Kg 17 49 *S* ⲣⲁϩⲧϥ ⲉ. ⲉⲧⲉϥⲧⲉϩⲛⲉ ἐπί, Zeph 3 2 *A* ϩⲱⲛⲧ ⲁ. ⲁⲡⲛ̅ⲉ̅ πρός, Ex 1 10 *A* ⲙⲉⲉⲩⲉ ⲁⲩϩⲱⲃ ⲁ. ⲁⲣⲁⲩ κατα-, PS 230 *S* ϩⲟⲧⲡ ⲉ. ⲉⲡⲉϥⲙⲉⲗⲟⲥ, ShC 42 39 *S* ϭⲙ ϭⲟⲙ ⲉ. ⲉⲣⲟϥ, BHom 30 *S* ⲙⲟⲟϣⲉ ⲉ. ⲉⲣⲟⲓ, AM 305 *B* ϣⲉ ⲉ. ⲉⲛⲓϣⲧⲉⲕⲟ, C 43 179 *B* ϩⲓⲧϥ ⲉ. ⲉⲡⲓⲭⲣⲱⲙ, BMis 481 *S* ⲣⲓⲙⲉ ⲉ. ⲉⲣⲟϥ, Va 57 15 *B* ⲛⲓⲥⲁϫⲓ ϭⲓ ⲉ. ⲉⲣⲱⲟⲩ; ⲉϩⲣⲛ-: Mt 5 39 *B* ϯ ⲉ. ⲉϩⲣⲉⲛⲡⲓⲡⲉⲧϩⲱⲟⲩ ἀντι-, Jud 9 29 *S* ϫⲟⲟⲥ ⲉ. ⲉϩⲣⲁϥ πρός, Mk 7 33 *S* ⲡⲉϫ ⲧⲁϥ ⲉ. ⲉϩⲣⲁϥ no Gk, ShBM 205 *S* ⲙⲟⲩⲧⲉ ⲉ. ⲉϩⲣⲁⲓ, Gu 59 *S* ϯ ⲧⲱⲛ ⲉ. ⲉϩⲣⲁⲕ, AM 153 *B* ϫⲟⲩϣⲧ ⲉ. ⲉϩⲣⲉⲛϩⲟ; ⲉϫⲛ-: Lev 21 11 *S* ⲃⲱⲕ ⲉ. ⲉϫⲛⲯⲩⲭⲏ ⲛⲓⲙ εἰσ-, C 86 303 *B* ⲡⲉⲧϥ ⲣⲱϥ ⲉ. ⲉϫⲱⲥ; ⲛ- dat *S*: Lu 23 14 ⲉⲓⲛⲉ ⲉ. ⲛⲁⲓ προσ-, Aeg 245 ϫⲓⲧⲟⲩ ⲉ. ⲙⲡⲭ̅ⲥ̅, Br 104 ⲟⲩⲱⲧⲃ ⲉ. ⲙⲫⲟⲩⲛ, *ib* 125 ϯ ⲉⲟⲟⲩ ⲉ. ⲙⲡⲛ̅ⲉ̅, J 107 19 ⲭⲱⲣⲓⲍⲉ ⲉ. ⲛⲏⲧⲛ; ⲛⲁϩⲣⲛ- *S*: Ps 42 4 ⲃⲱⲕ ⲉ. ⲛⲛ. πρός, Nu 14 4 ⲡⲉϫⲁⲩ ⲉ. ⲉⲛ. (var ⲉ. ⲛ-) dat; ϣⲁ- *S*: Mk 15 43 ⲃⲱⲕ ⲉ. ϣⲁⲡⲓⲗⲁⲧⲟⲥ πρός, ShA 2 256 ⲛⲏⲩ ⲉ. ϣⲁⲣⲟⲛ, Ge 8 7 ⲕⲧⲟϥ ⲉ. ϣⲁⲛⲱϩⲉ no Gk; ϩⲁ-, ϧⲁ-: Mt 8 8 *S* ⲉⲓ ⲉ. ϩⲁⲧⲁⲟⲩⲉϩⲥⲟⲓ εἰσ-, Si 51 30 (26) *S* ⲕⲁ ⲙⲁⲕϩ ⲉ. ϩⲁ- ὑπό; Ge 6 4 *B* ϣⲉ ⲉ. ϧⲁ-, Jer 45 14 *B* ⲙⲟⲩϯ ⲉ. ϩⲁⲣⲟϥ πρός, ShP 130[1] 141 *S* blows ⲉ. ϩⲁⲛⲉⲩⲟⲩⲉⲣⲏⲧⲉ.

Sim following nn: 4 Kg 5 7 *S* ⲟⲩⲗⲟⲓϭⲉ ⲉ. ⲉⲣⲟⲓ πρός, Mk 14 55 *S* ⲙⲛⲧⲙⲛⲧⲣⲉ ⲉ. ⲉⲓ̅ⲥ̅ κατά, Ro 3 22 *S* ⲧⲇⲓⲕⲁⲓⲟⲥⲩⲛⲏ ... ⲉ. ⲉⲟⲩⲟⲛ ⲛⲓⲙ εἰς, ShWess 9 93 *S* ⲡⲉϥⲟⲩⲱϣ ⲉ. ⲉϩⲉⲛⲥⲛⲏⲩ, Miss 8 33 *S* ⲧⲙⲛⲧⲉⲩⲥⲉⲃⲏⲥ ⲉ. ⲉⲡⲛ̅ⲉ̅, AM 238 *B* ϯϩⲉⲗⲡⲓⲥ ⲉ. ⲉⲡⲉⲕⲣⲁⲛ, Aeg 283 *S* ⲣⲉϥϯ ⲥⲃⲱ ⲉ. ⲉⲡⲉⲭ̅ⲥ̅, ROC 17 403 *B* ⲙⲉⲓ ⲉ. ⲉⲡⲟⲩϣⲏⲣⲓ.

Appended to nn: 4 Kg 14 25 *S* ϩⲓⲏ ⲉ., Ge 30 27 *B* ⲙⲱⲓⲧ ⲉ. εἴσοδος, Ez 40 15 *B* ⲡⲩⲗⲏ ⲉ. ἔσωθεν; J 50 43 *S* ⲣⲟ ⲉ., *ib* 6 41 ϩⲓⲣ ⲉ.; or nominal inf: Leyd 136 *S* ⲙⲟⲩⲣ ⲉ., BHom 38 *S* ⲉⲓ ⲉ., *ib* 54 *S* ⲧⲱⲕ ⲉ.

As prep (ellipse) *F*, *in payment for*, in accounts: CMSS 78 ⲉ. ⲧⲏⲃⲉⲧ, ⲉ. ⲡⲓⲛⲓⲛ, *ib* ⲉϩⲟⲛ ⲥⲁⲣⲉⲧ, ⲉϩⲟⲛ ⲁⲣϣⲓⲛ (*cf ib* ϫ = ὑπέρ), BP 5716 ⲉ. ⲡⲗⲉⲙⲧⲟⲩⲱ, ⲉ. ⲡⲛⲉϩ, Göteborg Stadsbibl P 82 ⲉ. ⲛⲉϩ, ⲉ. ⲡⲉⲛⲣⲉⲡ, BM 691 ⲭⲁⲛⲗ ⲉ. ⲧⲉⲃϣⲏⲗⲏⲧ, *ib* 709 ϑ ⲁ ⲡⲕⲁⲗⲁ ⲉ. ⲡ̅ⲕ̅ ⲛϩ(ⲛ)ⲉⲉⲩ.

ⲛϩ. *SAA²BF*, *within*: Ge 39 11 *S*(*B* ⲉϧ.), Jo 20 26 *SA²*(*B* do), AP 8 *A²* ἔσω, Ez 40 10 *B*(*S* diff) ἔσωθεν, Lev 18 9 *SB* ἐνδο-; Mor 48 54 *S* have left all for Thee ⲁⲓⲕⲁ ⲡⲉⲧⲛϩ. ⲛϩ. ⲁⲓⲕⲁ ⲡⲉⲧⲛⲃⲟⲗ ⲛⲃⲟⲗ, J 89 13 *S* we went to monastery ⲁⲛϭⲱ ⲛϩ., TU 43 2 *A* ⲁϥϭⲛⲧⲛⲉ ⲛϩ., Mun 66 *S* ⲕⲁⲁⲩ (*sc* crutches) ⲛϩ. ⲙⲙⲁⲩ as testimony, ShIF 99 *S* ⲡⲉⲧⲛⲡⲉⲧⲛϩ.; as nn m *S*, *inward parts*: BMis 285 ⲛⲧⲁⲉⲓⲛⲉ ⲉⲃⲟⲗ ⲛⲡϥⲛϩⲱⲛ (*sic*). With prep. c ⲉ-: 2 Kg 1 10 *S* ἐπί; FR 148 *S* born ⲛϩ. ⲉⲡⲙⲁ ⲛϭⲟⲓⲗⲉ, *ib* 86 *S* appeared to us ⲛϩ. ⲉⲛⲏⲓ (varr ⲛϩ. ⲙⲛ., ϩⲙⲛ.), KroppA 5 *S* Isis answered ⲛϩ. ⲉⲡⲣⲡⲉ, C 41 33 *B* came to me ⲛϧ. ⲉⲡⲓⲙⲁ, HSt 265 *S* spittle ⲛϩ. ⲉⲧⲉⲕⲧⲁⲡⲣⲟ (var ϩⲛ-), AZ 23 39 *F* ⲛⲟⲩϩⲓ ⲥⲛⲏⲧⲓ ⲛⲧⲁⲃⲕⲁⲣⲟⲩ ⲛϩ. (ⲉ)ⲗⲁⲃ; c ⲛ-: Ez 9 6 *B*, R 1 1 23 *S* set Jesus ⲛϩ. ⲙⲡⲉⲡⲣⲁⲓⲧⲱⲣⲓⲟⲛ, AP 13 *A²* ἔσω; Ge 7 23 *S*(varr ⲛϩ. ⲉ-, ϩⲛ-, *B* ϧⲉⲛ-) ἐν; PS 317 *S* ⲡⲉϥⲥⲁⲧ ⲛϩ. ⲛⲣⲱϥ, ShC 73 98 *S* ⲉⲩⲥϭⲣⲁϩⲧ ⲛϩ. ⲛⲛⲉⲩⲏⲓ, El 44 *A* ⲁⲩϩⲱϫⲧ ⲁⲣⲱⲓ ⲛϩ. ⲙⲙⲟ, TU 43 22 *A* ⲉⲧⲛϩ. ⲛⲛⲏⲓ, BMis 392 *S* ⲉⲣⲉⲟⲩ ⲛϩ. ⲙⲙⲟⲥ (var & Va 63 10 *B* ⲛϩⲏⲧⲥ) = BSM 44 *B* ⲥⲁϧ. ⲙⲙⲟⲥ = Mor 27 36 *F* ⲥⲁⲛϩ. ⲙ., PBu 44 *S* ⲥⲕⲉⲩⲏ ⲛⲧⲁⲩⲅⲓⲧⲟⲩ ⲛϩ. ⲙⲡⲁⲛⲓ, J 52 9 *S* sim, *ib* 39 33 *S* his share ⲛϩ. ⲙⲡⲏⲓ, *ib* 65 89 *S* ⲁⲡⲁⲣⲁⲅⲉ ⲛϩ. ⲙⲡⲧⲟⲡⲟⲥ (*cf* 86 sim ϩⲙ-); without ⲛ-: J 19 30 *S* ⲛⲏⲓ ... ⲛϩ. ⲫⲁⲅⲓⲟⲥ ⲫⲟⲓⲃⲁⲙⲱⲛ; c ϩⲁ-: Jo 1 48 *S*(*B* ϧⲁⲧⲉⲛ-) ὑπό; *ib* 5 3 *A²*(*S* om ⲛϩ., *B* ϧⲉⲛ-) ἐν; BMis 347 *S* ate with Him ⲛϩ. ϩⲁⲡϣⲏⲛ = BSM 14 *B* ϧⲁⲧⲉⲛ-, J 74 56 *S* wife ϩⲙⲟⲟⲥ ⲛϩ. ϩⲁⲣⲟⲓ; c ϩⲓ- *S*: Miss 4 661 ⲉⲓⲛϩ. ϩⲓⲛϫⲁⲓⲉ; c ϩⲛ- *S*: Lev 10 18 (*B* ϧⲉⲛ-) ἔσω, Bor 170 91 ⲛϩ. ϩⲙⲡⲧⲟⲟⲩ εἰς τὸ ἔσω ὄρος; Jo 19 42 (*B* ϧⲉⲛ-) ἐκεῖ; BM 174 ⲡⲉⲧⲛϩ. ϩⲙⲡⲉⲕⲏⲓ τὰ ἔνδον; PS 329 ⲉⲩⲛϩ. ϩⲛⲧⲙⲏⲧⲉ ⲛⲛⲕⲟⲗⲁⲥⲓⲥ, R 1 3 52 ϭⲱ ⲛϩ. ϩⲛⲑⲓⲗⲏⲙ; c ϩⲁϩⲧⲛ- *S*: BM 320 150 ϭⲱ ⲛϩ. ϩⲁϩⲧⲏϥ ἔνδον; J 65 94 ⲉⲓⲛϩ. ϩⲁϩⲧⲏϥ.

ⲥⲁϩ. *S*, ⲥⲁϧ. *B*(mostly), ⲥⲁⲭ. *O*, as ⲛϩ.: Ro 7 22 (*S* ϩⲓϩ.) ἔσω, Ez 40 23 (*S* do), Rec 6 168 ϣⲁϥⲉ ⲉⲧⲥ. = BMar 205 *S* do ἐσώτερος, MG 25 239 sim ἐνδότερος, 2 Chr 3 4, AM 272 ⲁϥⲕⲱⲗϩ ⲉⲃⲟⲗ ⲥⲁϧ. ἔσωθεν; Lev 8 7 ϩⲃⲟⲥ ⲛⲧⲉ ⲥ. (*S* = Gk) ὑποδύτης, DeV 1 100 ⲁϥⲱϣ ⲉⲃⲟⲗ ⲥ. *from within* (cell), MG 25 6 sim, Va 58 130 ⲡⲁⲣⲱⲙⲓ ⲉⲧⲥ. With prep. c ⲉ-: My 114 *S* all these ⲉⲩⲥ. ⲉⲡⲙⲉϩϥⲧⲟⲟⲩ ⲛⲥϩⲁⲓ, C 86 298 ϭⲓⲧⲕ ⲥ. ⲉⲡⲓⲡⲁⲗⲗⲁⲧⲓⲟⲛ ⲉⲧⲥ.; c ⲛ-: Bel 7, Mt 7 15 (*S* ϩ. nn) ἔσωθεν, MG 25 3 ⲕⲉⲟⲩⲁⲓ ⲥ. ⲙⲙⲟⲕ, RAl 91 ⲥ. ⲙⲙⲟϥ ⲛⲓⲃ ⲙⲩⲗⲓⲟⲛ, C 89 69 ⲉⲥⲥ. ⲙⲙⲱⲟⲩ ⲧⲏⲣⲟⲩ *innermost of all* = C 99 234 *S* ϩⲓϩⲟⲩⲛ ⲙ. ἐσώτ.; Ez 36 26 (var & *S* ⲉϧ. ⲉ-) ἐν, Ps 102 1 (*S* ϩⲙⲡⲥⲁ ⲛϩ.), Mt 23 26 (*S* do) ἐντός; Ac 1 18 (*S* ⲉⲧⲙⲡⲉϥϩ.) σπλάγχνα; ShA 1 381 *S* who worship wood, stone & clay ⲥ. ⲙⲙⲟⲟⲩ *in their houses* (?), ViK 9459 *S* seest those figures ⲉⲧⲥ. ⲙⲙⲟⲕ on thrones?, BIF 13 101 *S* city's port lay ⲥ. ⲙⲡⲉⲥⲥⲟⲃⲧ, C 86 205 ⲛⲏ ⲉⲧⲥ. ⲙⲙⲟϥ *intestines*, PGM 1 114 *O* ⲉⲑⲥⲁⲭⲟⲩⲛ (ⲡ)ⲛⲓⲥⲁⲥⲫⲓ; as nn: MG 25 18 forgetful of ⲡⲓⲥ., BSM 32 devoured ⲡⲁⲥ. = BMis 374 *S* ⲥⲁ ⲛϩ. ⲣ, ⲉⲣ ⲥ., *be within*: Gu 10 *S* ⲛⲧⲉⲣⲉⲛⲁⲡⲟⲥⲧⲟⲗⲟⲥ ⲣ ⲥ. ⲙⲡϩⲟⲩⲛ ⲙⲡⲣⲟ (*cf ib* ⲣ ⲛϩ. ⲙⲡⲣⲟ), DeV 1 81 ⲉⲧⲁⲓⲉⲣ ⲥ. ⲙⲡⲓⲣⲟ.

ⲥⲁ ⲛϩ. *SAA²F* nn m, *inner part*: Nu 3 10 (*B* ⲥⲁϧ.) ἔσω, He 6 19 *SF*(*B* do) ἐσώτ., Lu 11 7 (*B* ⲫⲏ ⲉⲧⲥⲁϧ.) ἔσωθεν, Ps 38 3 (*B* ⲥⲁϧ.), Lu 17 21 (*B* do) ἐντός, Job 21 24 (*B* ⲙⲁϧⲧ), Ps 50 10 *SA*(Cl, *B* ⲛⲏ ⲉⲧⲥⲁϧ.) ἐγ-

κατα, Z 328 ⲛⲁⲡⲥ. τὰ ἐν τῷ οἴκῳ; Si 36 5 σπλάγχνα, Ryl 94 109 ⲁⲡⲉⲥⲥ. ϣⲧⲟⲣⲧⲣ (3 K 3 26 μήτρα); PS 6 ⲛⲉⲩϭⲙⲛⲉⲅⲉ ⲉⲛⲥ. ⲛⲧⲉ ⲛⲓⲥ., Br 125 ⲟⲩⲱⲧⲃ ⲉϩⲟⲩⲛ ⲉⲛⲥ.,ViK 9461 he answered me ϩⲓⲛⲥ. (varBMar 129 ϩⲓⲛⲥ.) *from within* cave (cf above ⲥⲁϩ.), ManiK 53 A² ⲛⲥⲁ ⲛⲃⲁⲗ ⲙⲓⲛⲥ.; c ⲛ-: P 131³ 37 c. ⲙⲙⲉⲓⲙⲁ.

ϣⲁⲣ. SAA², ϣⲁⲉⲣ. SF, ϣⲁⲉⲥ. B, *towards inner part, inward*: PS 84 S all things on high ϫⲓⲛⲃⲟⲗ ϣ.; c ⲉ-: *until*: Ge 48 15 S(var ϣⲁϩⲣⲁⲓ)B, Ez 20 27 B(S ϣⲁϩⲣ.), Mt 26 58 S(B ϣⲁ-), 1 Cor 8 7 S (var ϣⲁⲉⲣ.)BF ἕως; Ac 2 29 B(S ϣⲁϩⲣ.) ἄχρι; Bor 253 160 S grieved ϣ. ⲉⲧⲉⲛⲟⲩ μέχρι; Jos 14 10 S I am 85 ϣ. (var ⲉϣ.) ⲉⲡⲟⲟⲩ σήμερον; PS 371 S ϩⲉⲱⲥ ϣ. ⲉⲡⲟⲟⲩ ⲛϩⲟⲟⲩ, ShC 73 41 S ϣ. ⲉⲧⲉⲛⲟⲩ (cf 42 ϣⲁϩⲣ.), ib 162 S covered ϣ. ⲉⲛⲉⲩⲕⲉⲗⲉⲛⲕⲉϩ (var ϣⲁ-), El 50 A upon earth ϣ. ⲁⲡⲟⲟⲩⲉ, ManiK 104 A² ϣ. ⲁⲛⲥⲏⲩ ⲉⲧⲉ-, BSM 84 B all worked ϣ. ⲉⲡⲟⲩⲣⲟ = BMis 175 S ϣⲁϩⲣ., EW 48 B to assemble ϣ. ⲉⲥⲟⲩⲛ (var ϣⲁ-) *by 20th day* of month, Va 57 42 B no one ϣ. ⲉⲟⲩⲁⲓ; c ⲉⲣⲁⲧ⸗: Ez 4 14 S ϣ. ⲉⲣⲁⲧϥ ⲙⲡⲟⲟⲩ (B ϣ. ⲉ-) ἕως τοῦ νῦν.

ϩⲓⲥ. SA², *within*: Ez 7 15 (B ⲥⲁϣ.), Mk 7 21 (B do) ἔσωθεν; Sa 17 12 ἔνδοθεν; ShA 1 334 ⲛⲉⲓⲥⲁ ϩⲓⲃⲟⲗ...ⲛⲉⲩⲭⲱⲣⲙ ϩ., ShBor 237 33 ⲧⲗⲙⲡⲧⲣⲙⲛϩⲏⲧ ϩ. before God, CA 89 ⲕⲁⲁϥ ϩ. after expulsion, R 2 1 71 bronze loseth not rust except ⲛⲥⲉⲣⲓⲧϥ ϩ. *into* furnace, Ep 163 ⲍⲟ ⲡⲉⲧⲩⲛⲟⲩⲣⲁ(ϥⲉ) ϩ. *on inner side* of sheet, ManiK 151 A² ⲛⲥⲱⲙⲁ ⲉⲧⲟⲩⲏⲥ ϩ., PMéd 169 use for eyes ϩ. ⲁⲩⲱ ϩⲓⲃⲟⲗ; with rel: Ro 7 22 (B ⲥⲁϣ.) ἔσω, Est 4 11, Ac 16 24 (B do) Mor 37 93 ⲧⲉⲣⲏ ⲙⲟⲥ ⲉⲧϩ. ἐσώτ.; 4 Kg 9 2 ἐν; BM 247 6 ⲟⲩⲗⲏ...ⲉⲥϩ. ἔνδοθεν; ShC 73 151 ⲡⲉⲡⲣⲱⲙⲉ ⲉⲧϩ., BMis 446 ⲡⲧⲟⲟⲩ ⲉⲧϩ. (cf 441 ⲛⲧ. ⲉⲧϩⲓⲃⲟⲗ), BAp 109 ⲧⲉⲣⲏ ⲉⲧϩ. = PO 22 392 ⲟⲩⲗⲉⲥ, BKU 1 92 sim, ManiK 139 A² ⲧⲁⲙⲓⲟⲛ ⲉⲧϩ.; as adj: ManiK 71 A² ⲛⲉⲥⲧⲁⲙⲓⲟⲛ ⲛϩ.; c ⲛ-: Ge 6 14 (B ⲥⲁϣ.) ἔσωθεν; BHom 138 ⲗⲏϭ ϩ. ⲙⲙⲟⲥ ἔνδον; Ez 40 10 (B ⲛⲥ.) κατέναντι; PS 107 ⲁⲧⲁϭⲟⲙ ⲥⲁⲗⲉⲅⲉ ϩ. ⲙⲙⲟⲓ, ShA 1 39 ⲛⲥⲁⲛⲥⲁ ⲛⲧⲭⲟ ϩ. ⲙⲙⲟⲥ, ShC 73 155 of what sort is man ϩ. ⲙⲙⲟϥ, ShIF 295 barbarians ⲉⲓ ϩ. ⲙⲡⲧⲟⲟⲩ *from within*, R 1 3 57 Satan answered ϩ. ⲛⲧⲙⲁⲁⲩ sim, Bor 306 145 ϣⲟⲟⲛ ϩ. ⲙⲡⲕⲁⲗⲅⲙⲁ (cf ib ⲙⲛϩ. ⲙ-), ManiK 36 A² ⲣ ⲁⲡⲉ ϩ. ⲛⲧⲁⲓⲕⲁⲓⲟⲥⲩⲛⲏ, J 35 49 ⲡⲧⲱⲣⲧ ϩ. ⲙⲡⲣⲟ, CO 294 ⲉϩ. (cf p 394 b sup) ⲛⲧⲉⲣⲉⲡⲉⲛⲏⲧ; ϩⲓⲛϩ.: Mor 28 212 stripped ⲟⲩⲕⲁⲙⲓⲥⲓⲟⲛ ϩ. ⲙⲙⲟϥ *undershirt*.

ⲣⲙⲛϩ. S, an ecclesiastical (?)official: CO 343 ⲡⲣ. (ⲛ)ⲡⲉⲡⲓⲥⲕⲟⲡⲟⲥ distributes vinegar, ib 255 ⲡⲣ. ⲅⲉⲱⲣⲅⲓⲟⲥ applied to regarding poor man.

ϩⲱⲛ SA²F, ϩⲛⲁⲛ Sᵃ(v ϩ. ⲉϩⲟⲩⲛ), ϩⲛⲁⲛ A, ϩⲱⲛⲉ A², ϩⲛ-,ϩⲟⲛⲥ S, ϩⲏⲛ† SA²F, ϩⲏⲛⲧ† A(B mostly ϧⲱⲛⲧ) vb intr, *approach, be nigh, comply with*: RNC 85 be patient ⲁⲕϩ. ⲁⲕϩⲱⲕ ⲉⲃⲟⲗ ⲛⲧⲉⲕⲙⲁⲣⲧⲩⲣⲓⲁ, ManiK 101 A² ⲛⲭⲱⲣⲁ ⲉⲧⲟⲩⲏⲟⲩ ⲙⲡⲛⲉⲧϩ.†

With following preposition.

—— ⲉ- intr: Am 9 10 SA, Lu 12 33 ἐγγίζειν, Ps 31 9 ⲉϩ. πρός, Eccl 4 17 F(S ϩⲱⲛⲧ ⲉϩⲟⲩⲛ ⲉ-) ἐγγύς gen; Ps 90 10 προσέρχεσθαι πρός; Is 34 1 (B ϩⲉⲛ ϩⲁ-, F ϩⲱⲛⲧ ⲉϩ. ⲉ-) προσάγειν; C 99 140 ⲁϥϩ. ⲉⲣⲟϥ = C 89 45 B πλησιάζειν; PS 229 ⲙⲡⲉⲩⲉϣ ϩ. ⲉⲣⲟϥ, ShBor 300 69 ⲙⲛ ⲗⲁⲁⲩ ⲙⲡⲉⲑⲟⲟⲩ ⲛⲁϩ. ⲉⲣⲟⲕ, R 1 2 32 ⲛⲧⲉⲣⲉϥϩ. ⲉⲧⲙⲟⲛⲏ, Ep 337 ⲁⲛϣⲁ ϩ. ⲉⲣⲟⲛ, ShC 73 105 ⲛⲥⲉⲟⲩⲱϣ ⲁⲛ ⲉϩ. ⲉⲛⲉⲛⲕⲁⲡⲛⲟⲛ, ShC 42 33 ⲉⲧⲣⲉϩⲁϩ...ϩ. ⲉⲛⲉϥⲇⲓⲕⲁⲓⲟⲛ, CO 297 am ready to ϩ. ⲉⲡϩⲁⲡ that God may ordain, J 37 76 ⲛϥϩ. ⲛϥⲥⲱⲡⲧ ⲉⲧϭⲟⲙ ⲙⲡⲉⲓⲉⲩⲅⲣⲁⲫⲟⲛ (cf below), CO 168 ⲛϥϩ. ⲉⲧⲉⲃⲗϭⲉ; *qual, nigh, related*: Deu 13 7, Ru 2 20, Pro 3 15 SA ⲉϩ. dat, Ps 21 11, Jo 11 54 (var & A² ϩ. ⲉϩⲟⲩⲛ), ViSitz 172 32 churches ⲉⲧϩ. ⲉⲣⲟⲟⲩ ἐγγύς, Si 26 12 σύνεγ.; Jth 4 6 πλησίον; Ps 79 6 (B ⲑⲉ ⲉϣⲉ) γείτων; Z 326 ⲣⲱⲙⲉ ⲉⲧϩ. ⲉⲣⲟϥ ἴδιος; Jos 9 13 κατοικεῖν; Mic 1 11 SA ἐχόμενος; Sh(?)P 78 41 clergy ⲉⲧϩ. ⲉⲡⲕⲁⲡⲛⲟⲛ, ShC 73 123 ⲡⲉⲧϩ. ⲉⲣⲟϥ *neighbour*, Aeg 253 concubine ⲉϩ. ⲉⲣⲟϥ ⲙⲁⲩⲁⲁϥ *cleaving to him alone*; vbal: Ac 21 27 (var & B om) μέλλειν; Mk 4 37 (B = Gk), ib 6 35 (B do) ἤδη; ShC 73 53 ⲡⲟⲩⲟⲉⲓⲛ ϩ. ⲉⲉⲓ ⲉϩⲣⲁⲓ, Mor 52 32 ⲁϥϩ. ⲉⲉⲓ (l ϥⲓ) ⲛⲧⲁⲛⲧⲛⲣⲱⲙⲉ *hath wellnigh captured mankind* by his teaching, Bor 256 153 ships ϩ. ⲉⲱⲙⲥ, CO 346 ⲁⲛϭⲁⲙⲟⲩⲗ ϩ. ⲉⲡⲱⲗϩ; tr: Si 36 12, Is 5 8 ⲉⲅ. πρός; ShA 1 53 ⲁϥϩⲟⲛⲥ ⲉⲣⲟϥ, ShP 130⁵ 65 ⲉⲧⲣⲉⲡⲉⲧⲙⲟⲕⲟ ⲛϣⲱⲡⲉ ϩⲟⲛϥ(sc pillow) ⲉⲣⲟϥ & lie thereon, COAd 14 ⲉϥϩⲟⲛⲓ ⲉϥⲑⲟⲙⲟⲗⲟⲅⲓⲁ (cf above), Win 73 ϫⲓ ⲧⲉ[.. ⲛ]ⲏⲣⲡ...ⲛⲉϩⲟⲛⲥ ⲉⲛⲏⲣⲡ ⲛⲡⲗⲁ ϣ(ⲁⲡⲉ).

—— ⲉϫⲛ-: Lu 10 9 (B ϧ. ⲉ-), ⲉⲅ. ἐπί; J 80 48 ⲛϥϩ. ⲉ. ⲧϭⲟⲙ ⲙⲡⲉⲓϫⲱⲣⲉⲁⲥⲧⲓⲕⲓ(ⲛ), cf above c ⲉ-.

—— ⲛⲥⲁ-, *toward*: Sh Berl Or 1611 5 40 ⲉⲁϥϩⲛ ⲧⲟⲟⲧϥ ⲛⲥⲁⲙⲁ where bread kept = P 131⁶ 87.

—— ϣⲁ-: Mic 1 9 SA(B diff) ἅπτεσθαι ἕως.

With following adverb. c ⲉϩⲟⲩⲛ intr: Ge 18 23, Is 33 13† (F ϩⲛⲏⲧ), Mt 26 45 ⲉⲅ., Ge 33 6 προσεγ., Si 32 16 συνεγ., Pro 27 10† SA, Jer 32 26† (ViK 9782) opp ⲟⲩϩⲏⲩ ⲉⲃⲟⲗ, Mt 24 32 (F do), Jo 2 13 SA² ἐγγύς, Ac 27 33 (var ϩ. ⲉϣⲱⲡⲉ, B ϣⲱⲡⲓ) μέλλειν; Miss 8 30 πλησιάζειν; PS 169 of time ⲁϥϩ. ⲉ., Sh 73 124 sitting ⲉⲩϩ. ⲉ. ⲉⲡⲉⲧⲣⲓⲧⲟⲩⲱϣ, MMA 24 6 4 Sᵃ ⲁⲧⲁ ϩⲁⲛ ϩⲛⲁⲛ ⲉ. (var ⲍⲟ ϩⲛⲁⲩ sic); tr (refl): Si 20 26 προάγειν ἑαυτόν; ⲉϩ. ⲉ-: Ps 106 18 (B ϣⲁ ⲉϩⲣⲏ ⲉ-) ⲉⲅ. ἕως, Job 33 22 (B ⲉ-), Mk 11 1 ⲉⲅ. εἰς, Pro 5 8 SA ⲉⲅ. πρός, Lev 10 3†, Ps 87 3 ⲉⲅ. dat, Jer 12 2†, Jo 6 19 SA², He 6 8 SF(all B do) ἐγγύς gen; Nu 5 8† (B diff) ἀγχιστεύειν dat; Su 4† (B ϫⲏ ϧⲁⲑⲟⲩⲉⲛ-) γειτνιᾶν dat; Deu 11 30† (B ⲧⲟⲙⲓ ⲉ-), Ps 67 26† (B ⲉ-) ἐχόμενος; Is 57 3 (B ϩⲉⲛ-) προσάγειν ὧδε, Ac 27 27 (B ϧ. ⲉϧ. ⲉ-) π. acc; BHom 15 ⲉⲧϩ.† ⲉ. ⲉⲛⲡⲣⲟ παριστάναι dat; Jos 17 10 συνάπτειν ἐπί; PS 152

ⲙⲡⲟⲩⲉϣ ϩ. ⲉ. ⲉⲣⲟⲓ, ShA 2 271 ⲛ†ϩ.† ⲉ. ⲉⲣⲱⲧⲛ ⲁⲡ ϩⲙⲡⲁϩⲏⲧ, BMar 103 captain ⲉϥ†ϩ.† ⲉ. ⲉⲡⲣⲣⲟ, El 46 *A* began ⲁϩ. ⲁ. ⲁⲣⲁⲓ, AP 26 *A²* ⲁⲩϩ. ⲁ. ⲁ-, FR 148 ⲁⲥϩ. ⲉ. ⲉⲙⲓⲥⲉ, Pcod 7 whoso shall cross fiery river ϥⲛⲁϩ. ⲉ. ⲉⲟⲩⲱϣⲧ; ⲉϩ. ⲛ-: Jth 16 24† ἔγγιστος gen (*cf ib* ⲉ-); Ro 5 2 as nn ⲡϩ. ⲉ. ⲛ- (var ⲉ-) προσαγωγή; ⲉϩ. ϣⲁ-: Si 51 7 ἐγ. ἕως.

ⲁⲧϩ., *unapproachable*: P 129²⁰ 133 He came ⲉⲃⲟⲗ ϩⲛⲕⲟⲩⲛϥ ⲙⲡⲉⲓⲁ. ⲉⲣⲟϥ.

ϩⲱⲛ *S A A² B* (*v c ⲡ-* & nn)*F*, ϩⲟⲡⲝ *S*, ϩⲁⲡⲝ *Sʃ A* vb intr, *bid, command* (*B* mostly ϩⲟⲛϩⲉⲛ): Ps 32 9 ἐντέλλεσθαι; Leyd 468 ⲁⲛⲟⲕ ⲉⲧϩⲱⲛ; tr: Ps 7 6, Lam 2 17 (*F* † ⲡⲥⲓⲙⲙⲓ) ἐντ.; AP 19 *A²* τάσσειν, Nu 30 2 (*B* ⲟⲩⲁϩⲥⲁϩⲛⲓ) συντ.; ShMIF 23 88 ⲛⲭ̄ⲥ̄ ⲉⲧϩ. ⲙⲙⲟⲥ, Mor 31 69 ⲡⲛ̄ⲛ̄ⲉ ⲡⲁϩ. ⲡⲧⲉϥϭⲟⲙ ⲉϩⲣⲁⲓ ⲡⲣⲏⲧⲕ.

With following preposition. ⲉ-: Ps 104 8 (*B* ϣⲁ-) ἐντ. εἰς, *ib* 118 4 ἐντ. inf, Job 37 6 ϩ. ⲉⲧⲣⲉ- συντάσ.; J 82 24 laws ⲉⲧϩ. ⲁⲩⲱ ⲉⲧⲉⲡⲓⲧⲣⲉⲡⲉ ⲉⲧⲣⲉ-; c ⲉⲧⲃⲉ-: Nah 1 14 *A*, He 11 22 ἐντ. περί; Ep 431 ⲁⲓϩ. ⲉⲧⲟⲟⲧⲕ ⲉⲧⲃⲉⲡⲣⲱⲙⲉ; c ⲉⲧⲛ- intr: Ge 2 16, Ps 90 11, Is 34 16 *SF*, Mk 13 34 *SF*, Jo 14 31 (*A²* † ⲁⲧⲛ-) ἐντ. dat, Mt 1 24 (*B do*) προστάσ. dat, *ib* 21 6 (*B do*), Lev 24 23 (*B* ⲟⲩⲁϩ.) συντ. dat; Ps 105 33 (*B* diff), Mk 5 43 διαστέλλειν dat; *ib* 6 8 παραγγέλλειν dat; *ib* 1 43 ἐμβριμᾶσθαι dat; PS 139 ⲁⲓϩ. ⲉⲧⲟⲟⲧϥ ⲛⲅⲁⲃⲣⲓⲏⲗ, BAp 155 †ϩ. ⲉⲧⲟⲟⲧⲕ ⲉⲙⲁⲧⲉ ⲉⲧⲣⲉⲕ-, Mor 24 7 *F* ⲉ ⲁⲛϩ. ⲉⲧⲁⲁⲧⲕ̄ ϫⲉ-; tr: Deu 6 1 ἐντ., Pro 5 2 *SA*, Mk 10 3 (*F* † ⲁⲛⲥⲉⲙⲙⲓ) ἐντ. dat; Ex 16 16 (*B* ⲟⲩⲁϩ.) συντάσ. dat; Mal 3 14 *A* ⲡⲉⲧⲁϥϩⲁⲛⲟⲩ ⲁⲧ. φύλαγμα; Br 125 commands ⲉⲛⲧⲁⲓϩⲟⲛⲟⲩ ⲉⲧⲟⲧⲧⲏⲩⲧⲛ, ShA 2 268 ⲁϥϩ. ⲉⲧⲟⲧⲧⲏⲩⲧⲛ ⲡⲟⲩⲇⲓⲁⲑⲏⲕⲏ, R 1 4 62 ⲁⲩϩⲟⲟⲡⲥ ⲉⲧⲟⲟⲧⲛ, Mor 32 51 *Sʃ* ⲁⲕϩⲁⲡⲟⲩ ⲉⲧⲟⲟⲧ, Mani 2 *A²* ϩ. ⲙⲙⲁⲥ ⲁⲧⲟⲟⲧⲟⲩ; c ⲛ- dat: Is 13 4 (*B* ⲟⲩⲁϩ.), Jer 23 32 *B* ἐντ. dat; Job 25 5 (var ϩⲱⲱⲛ, *B* ⲟⲩⲁϩ.) συντάσ. dat; Pcod 2 ⲁϥϩ. ⲡⲁϥ (*sic l*) ⲟⲩⲁⲁϥ ⲡⲧⲉϥⲁⲡⲟⲫⲁⲥⲓⲥ, Mor 31 210 manna ⲛⲧⲁⲡⲛ̄ⲛ̄ⲉ ϩⲟⲛ ⲙⲙⲟϥ ⲡⲛⲉⲛⲉⲓⲟⲧⲉ; c ⲡⲧⲛ-: Mt 28 20 ἐντ. dat; Jer 33 8 συντάσ. dat, Nu 15 23 (*B do*) σ. πρός; PS 339 ϣⲁϥϩ. ⲛⲧⲉ(ⲙ)ⲡⲁⲡⲧⲓⲙⲙⲟⲛ, BM 1180 ϩⲏⲛⲉ ⲛⲧⲟⲟⲧⲛ ⲑⲉ ⲡⲉⲕⲕⲉⲗⲉⲅⲉ; c ϣⲁ-: He 9 20 *SF* ἐντ. πρός.

—— nn m *S*(rare)*B*, *command*: Is 29 13 *S*, Col 2 22 *S*(both *B* ϩⲟⲛϩⲉⲛ) ἔνταλμα; He 11 23 (*S = Gk*) διάταγμα, Ge 47 26 (*S do*), Ps 98 7 (*S do*), Jer 51 10 (*S* ⲟⲩⲉϩⲥⲁϩⲛⲉ) πρόστ.; Dan 6 9 (*S = Gk*), Ac 17 7 (*S do*) δόγμα; Nu 19 2 (*S do*) διαστολή; ShA 2 106 *S* ⲡϩ. ⲉⲃⲟⲗ ϩⲓⲧⲙⲡⲛ̄ⲛ̄ⲉ, Ryl 94 100 *S* ⲛⲉϩ. of saints, Va 68 185 ⲛⲓϩ. of God…ⲛⲓϩⲟⲛϩⲉⲛ of Satan.

ⲣⲉϥϩⲱⲡⲧ (*l* ϩⲱⲛ)*S*, *commander, master*: Mor 36 53 Christ to sea (θάλ.) ⲁⲛⲟⲕⲡⲉ ⲡⲟⲩϩ.

ϭⲓⲛϩ. *S, command*: ShA 2 228 ⲧϭ. … ⲧⲉ ⲧⲁⲓ My son, keep my words.

ϩⲱⲛ *S B*(nn)vb intr, *go aground* in shallows: ShZ

637-8 ships ⲉⲩϣⲁⲛϩ. ⲛ ⲡⲥⲉⲱⲗⲥ are dragged off with ropes; nn *B* sim: AM 328 ⲁⲩⲙⲟⲛⲓ ⲉϩⲟⲩⲛ ⲉⲟⲩϩ. by western bank; ⲙⲁ ⲛϩ., *shallows* (*v* HOLange *Amenemope* 47): Miss 8 13 ship could not enter port for ⲟⲩⲡ ϩⲱⲙ. ⲡⲣⲏⲧϥ; ⲟ ⲛϩ., *be shallow*: Ac 27 17 ⲙⲁ ⲉϥⲟ ⲛϩ. (*B = Gk*) σύρτις (Va 75 ﺷﻮﻁ), *ib* 41 (var ϩⲱⲱⲛ, *B* as Gk) διθάλασσος; ShIF 221 ⲙⲁ ⲉϥⲟ ⲛϩ. ⲛ ⲉⲣⲉⲡⲙⲟⲟⲩ ⲥⲟⲃⲕ ϩⲁⲣⲟϥ, opp ⲙⲁ ⲉϥϣⲟⲕ.

ϩⲱⲛ *S* vb intr, *destroy* (?) c ϩⲛ-: Ex 15 9 (Ep 3, *B* ϩⲱⲧⲉⲃ) ἀναιρεῖν dat.

ϩⲱⲛ *SF*, ϩⲱⲱⲛ *S* nn m, *gift at betrothal* (?), with † *betroth*: LeipBer '02 144 ϩⲁⲙⲟⲓ ⲉⲛⲉⲡⲧⲁⲩ† ϩ. ⲙⲙⲟⲟⲩ ὑποπροίκειος γίνεσθαι; with ϫⲓ sim, c acc: Deu 20 7 (*B* ⲱⲡ ⲛⲥⲁ-) μνηστεύεσθαι; c ⲛ- dat: Mor 37 137 virgins ⲉⲁⲩϫ. ⲛⲁⲩ μνηστήρ; c acc & dat: Hos 2 20 *A*(*B do*) μ. dat; ShBMOr 8800 196 Christ died not for demons (so Origen) nor ⲙⲙⲛ ⲇⲁⲓⲙⲱⲛ ⲛⲁϫ. ⲛⲁⲩ ⲛⲟⲩⲟⲩϫⲁⲓ *promise selves salvation*, WTh 139 ⲁϥϫ. ⲛⲁϥ ⲛⲧϣⲉⲉⲣⲉ ⲡⲛⲟⲩⲙⲉⲣⲓⲁⲛⲟⲥ, BMis 274 ⲉⲓⲟⲩⲱϣ ϫ. ⲛⲧⲉⲕϣⲉⲉⲣⲉ ⲙⲡⲁϣⲏⲣⲉ = Mor 30 50 *F*, BMar 17 mother *loq* ⲉⲙⲁϫ. ⲛⲁⲕ ⲛⲧⲉⲕϣⲉⲗⲉⲉⲧ, Mun 126 husband ⲉⲧⲟⲩϫ. ⲙⲙⲟϥ ⲛⲧⲉⲓϣⲉⲉⲣⲉ ϣⲏⲙ; as nn m: R 1 1 20 ⲡϫⲓ ϩⲱⲱⲛ of Joseph & Mary, R 2 1 11, 12 as when mother seeks bride & girl's parents ⲛⲓⲟⲑⲉ ϫⲉ [ⲉ]ϫⲓ ⲙⲡϩ., so went Mary to Elizabeth ⲉⲧⲣⲉⲥϫ. ⲡⲓⲱϩⲁⲛⲛⲏⲥ.

ϩⲁⲁⲙⲛ *F* nn f, *some-, anything* (?): BM 586 9 ⲉⲓⲕⲥⲁⲟⲩ(ⲛ) ϫⲉⲙⲉ(ⲛ)ϩ. ⲛⲧⲁⲁⲧ ⲧⲁⲉⲓ ϣⲁⲗⲁⲕ, *ib* 582(1) 16 ϩ. ⲛⲓⲙ ϣⲁⲕϭⲁⲡⲁⲥ (*sic l*). Cf? ϩⲓⲛⲉ (*v* ⲛⲓⲙ), adding Jo 6 46 (PMich 3521) ⲉϩⲁϩⲓ(ⲛⲉ) ⲡⲉⲩ ⲉⲡⲓⲱⲧ (*SB* ⲟⲩⲁ, *A²* ⲗⲁⲩⲉ).

ϩⲁⲉⲓⲛⲉ *AA²*, ϩⲁⲓⲛⲓ *F* *v* ϩⲟⲉⲓⲛⲉ.

ϩⲏⲛⲉ *SAA²*, -ⲛⲓ *F* nn m, mostly as pl, *spice, incense*: Cant 1 2 (*F* ⲥⲁⲭⲓⲛ), Lu 24 1 (*B* ⲥⲑⲟⲓ), Jo 19 40 *SA²*(*B do*) ἄρωμα; Ez 27 17 (*B* ⲥ. ⲛⲟⲩⲩⲓ) μύρον; ShA 1 253 smoke of ⲡϣⲟⲟⲩⲉ ⲙⲛⲛⲕⲉϩ. … ⲉⲧⲟ ⲛⲥ† ⲛⲟⲩϩⲉ, ShC 42 105 ⲡⲉⲥⲧⲟⲓ…ⲉⲧϣⲟⲱϣ ⲉϩⲟⲩⲉ ϩ. ⲛⲓⲙ, Mor 29 15 perfume like ϩⲉⲛϩ. (varBMis 243 ϣⲟⲩϩ.), P 129²⁰ 133 ⲛϩ. ⲛⲧⲁϥ† ⲙⲁⲧⲉ, BAp 11 † ⲛϩⲉⲛϩ. ⲉⲣⲟϥ (*sc corpse*), Ryl 239 ⲟⲩⲙⲁϣϫⲉ ⲛϣⲓ ϩ. (or ? = one of following words); c†ϩ.: Cant 8 2 ⲏⲣⲡ ⲉⲧⲟ ⲛⲥ. (var ⲥ. ⲛϩ.) μυρεψικός; ShR 2 3 47 c]†ⲛϩ.; †ϩ., *offer incense*: 4 Kg 15 4 θυμιᾶν; c ⲉϩⲣⲁⲓ: *ib* 12 3 θ., Hos 4 14 *SA*(*B* ⲥⲑⲓ ⲛⲟⲩⲩⲓ) θύειν; KroppM 31 ⲁⲓ† ϩⲓⲛⲉ ⲛⲁⲕ ⲉϩ.

ϣⲟⲩϩ. *SAF*, ϣⲟϩⲉⲛ *B* (once) nn m, *incense* (*v* ϣⲟⲟⲩ): Nu 4 16 (*B* ⲥ. ⲛ.), Pro 27 9 *SA*, Is 1 13 *SF*(*B do*), Ap 8 3 (*B do*) θυμίαμα; Cant 5 1 (*F* ⲥⲁ.), Cl 25 2 *A*(var ϩⲁⲩ) ἄρ.; BHom 48 ⲥⲧⲟⲓ ⲛⲡⲥⲟⲃⲛ ⲙⲛⲛϣ. μύρισμα (for both), R 2 2 23 ⲛϣ. ⲙⲡⲥⲟⲃⲛ ⲙ. (do), Jos 22 23 μαναά? (var om); Ryl 19 ⲟⲩϣⲗⲏⲗ ⲛϣ.; BM

920 265 *B* ⲟⲩϣⲟϩⲉⲛ بخور; ⲧⲁⲗⲉ ϣ. ⲉϩⲣⲁⲓ: 4 Kg 14 4, Lu 1 9 (*B* ⲉⲛ ⲥ. ⲛ. ⲉϩ.) θυμιᾶν; Tri 448 بخر; Br 109 ⲧⲁⲗⲟ ⲉ. ⲛⲟⲩϣ.; ϯ ϣ. ⲉϩ.: Hos 11 2 *A*(*B* ϯ ⲥ. ⲛ. ⲉϩ.) θύειν.

In place-name (here or next?) PLond 4 224 τόπου νσανϩηνε.

ϩⲏⲛⲉ *S*(?)*A* nn f, *lime, dust*: Am 2 1 *A*(*B*=Gk) κονία; Mor 51 33 *S* ϣⲉϣ ⲉⲓⲧⲉⲛ ⲙⲡⲡⲧⲏⲩ ϩ. ⲙⲡⲡⲧⲟⲩⲣⲏⲥ; BKU 1 282 *S* ϫⲓ ⲧϩⲏⲛ[ⲉ ⲛ]ⲱⲛⲉ ⲛⲕⲱⲧ... ⲡⲱⲣⲕ ⲛⲱⲛⲉ ⲕⲁⲛ ⲉⲩϯ ϩ. ⲛⲁⲕ ⲕⲁⲛ ⲙⲡⲟⲩϯ (same?)

ϩⲏⲛⲉ, -ⲛⲏ, ϩⲉⲛⲏ *S* nn f, meaning unknown, relates to clothing: CO 465 ϯⲉ ⲛⲗⲓⲧⲣⲁ ⲛϩⲉ. ⲉⲩϩⲟⲥⲉ *5 litres of spun...*, Ep 284 ⲧϩⲏ. ⲛⲛϩⲃⲟⲟⲥ ⲛⲧⲏⲓ, BM 1096 in list ⲙⲓϣⲧⲱⲧⲉ, ⲕⲁⲗⲓⲅⲉⲛ(-γιον), ⲕⲁⲛϩⲏⲛⲏ, ⲟⲩϭⲟⲥ ⲛϩ., Ep 548 list of *varia* ϩⲉⲛϩⲉ. ⲛⲃⲉⲕⲉ (here?).

ϩⲏⲛⲉ *S* nn f, *body of cart*: Gloss 117 ⲧϩ.· πείρινθος; J 113 5 *S*[a] ⲕⲁⲧ ϩⲏⲙ, ⲃⲁⲓⲙⲁⲩ, ⲧϩⲏⲛ[ⲓ?] ⲙⲡⲓⲛⲓⲡⲉ (same?)

ϩⲏⲏⲛⲉ c ⲉⲓⲥ *v* p 85 *b*.

ϩⲓⲛⲉ *SA*[2], -ⲛⲓ *BF* vb intr, *move* by rowing: Is 33 21 *SF*(*B* ⲉⲣ ϩⲱⲧ), ἐλαύνειν; Ez 27 9 *SB*(*sic*) ⲉⲧϩ. κωπηλάτης (in 8 = ⲣⲉϥⲥⲱⲕ ⲛⲛⲟⲩⲟⲉⲣ), Cai 8024 *S* fish ϩⲓⲛⲁ (*sic*) ϩⲛⲛⲉⲩⲕⲁⲥ ⲉⲧϩⲛⲛⲉⲩϫⲓⲥⲉ ⲛϭⲉ ⲛϩⲉⲛⲟⲩⲟ[ⲉⲣ; tr: C 89 58 *B* ϩ. ⲙⲡⲓⲟⲩⲟⲥⲉⲣ=Va 172 36 تعب في جرّ المقذاف, MG 17 576 قذف (as if ϩⲓⲥⲉ) ἐλ.; Gu 101 *S* sim, BHom 88 *S* ship's oars ⲉⲩϩ. ⲙⲙⲟϥ, Mor 43 121 *S* ⲉⲩϩ. ⲙⲡϫⲟⲓ ⲥⲛⲁⲩ, *ib* 103 ⲡⲙⲁ ⲛϩ. ⲙⲡⲟⲩ.; ϩ. ⲉⲃⲟⲗ, *row forth*: Jo 6 19 *SA*[2]*F*(PMich 3521, *B* diff) ἐλ.; Lu 5 3 *S* ⲉⲃ. ⲛ- (*B* diff) ἐπανάγειν ἀπό.

ϩⲓⲛⲉ, ϩⲉⲛⲉⲓⲉ (pl? Griffith) nn m *S*, *steering-oar, rudder* (whence ϩⲓⲉ Dévaud): Ja 3 4 (P 44 54, var P 75 71 & *B* ϩⲓⲉ), Ac 27 40 ϩⲉ. (P 44 19, var & *B* do) πηδάλιον; P 44 121 ⲛϩ. ⲙⲡⲁⲗⲁⲥ سكّان; P 131[1] 22 steersman ⲉϥⲁⲙⲁϩⲧⲉ ⲙⲡⲉϥϩ., AZ 14 62 ϫⲟⲓ ⲉⲛⲁⲧϩ. (*cf* ⲁⲧϩⲓⲉ). *V* Rec 26 40.

(**ϩⲓⲛⲉ** *S*, -ⲓ), ϩⲉⲛ- as absol, ϩⲉⲛ⸗ *B*, ϩⲛⲧ⸗ *S*(very rare) vb refl, *move self* (*v* AZ 62 49), **a** *forward, toward* c ⲉ-: Ge 27 21 ἐγγίζειν dat; Is 57 3 (*S* ϩⲱⲛ ⲉϩⲟⲩⲛ ⲉ-) προσάγειν ὧδε; Mt 26 39 (*S* ⲙⲟⲟϣⲉ ⲉ-, *cf* Mk 14 35 *B* ⲥⲓⲛⲓ) προέρχεσθαι; c ϩⲁ-: Ge 45 4 ἐγ. πρός; Is 34 1 (*S* ϩⲱⲛ ⲉ-, *F* ϩⲱⲛⲧ ⲉϩⲟⲩⲛ ⲉ-) προσάγ. **b** *backward, away* c ⲉ: LIb 7 when threatened with drowning ⲙⲏ ⲙⲡⲓϩⲉⲛⲑⲏⲛⲟⲩ ⲉⲡⲓⲡⲉⲗⲁⲅⲟⲥ *remove from* (or ? *l* ⲛ-); c ⲛ- ethic dat: Ez 1 25 ἀνιέναι; Hab 2 4 (*A* diff), Gal 2 12 (*S* ⲥⲓϩⲉ) ὑποστέλλειν; MG 25 125 if mind neglectful ϣⲁⲣⲉϯϫⲟⲙ ϩⲉⲛⲥ ⲛⲁⲥ; **c** ⲉⲃⲟⲗ: Is 55 12 ϩ. ⲉⲃ. (*S* ⲉⲓ ⲉⲃ.) ἐξέρ., *ib* 52 11 (*S* ⲥⲟⲟϩⲉ ⲉⲃ.), Lam 4 15 (*S* do, *F* ϣⲱⲡ ϩⲁⲃⲁⲗ) ἀφιστάναι; C 89 11 ⲁϥϩⲉⲛϥ ⲉⲃ. ⲉϣⲧⲉⲙⲟⲩⲱⲙ=MG 17 351 امتنع ان لا; Va 58 131 ⲥⲉϩⲉⲛ ⲙⲙⲱⲟⲩ ⲉⲃ. ⲁⲛ ⲉⲩϯ ⲡⲉⲙⲏⲓ; ⲉⲃ. ⲛ-: Ex 23 7, Job 7 16 (both *S* do) ἀφ. ἀπό; 1 Tim 4 7 (*S*=Gk) παραιτεῖσθαι; Ps 36 8 (*S* ⲥ. ⲉⲃ.) παύεσθαι ἀπό; BG 38 *S* ⲁϥϩⲛⲧϥ ⲉⲃ. ⲙⲙⲟⲥ, C 86 25 ⲁⲕϩⲉⲛⲕ ⲉⲃ. ⲛⲧⲁⲅⲁⲡⲏ; ϫⲓⲛϩ. ⲉⲃ.: Va 58 178 ⲡⲓϫⲓⲛϩⲉⲛⲕ ⲉⲃ. ⲛⲛⲓϫⲓⲛⲟⲩⲱⲙ ὑπαλλαγή; ⲉⲃ. ϧⲉⲛ-: Nu 8 25 (*S* do) ἀφ. ἀπό; Va 61 219 ⲁϥϩⲉⲛϥ ⲉⲃ. ϧⲉⲛⲛⲓϩⲃⲏⲟⲩⲓ of world; ⲉⲃ. ϩⲁ-: Bar 3 8 (*S* do), Ac 5 38 (var ⲥⲁⲃ. ϩⲁ-, *S* do) ἀφ. ἀπό; Pro 9 18 (*SA* do), 1 Thes 5 22 (*S* do) ἀπέχειν ἀπό; C 86 240 ϩⲉⲛⲕ ⲉⲃ. ϩⲁⲣⲟⲓ, Cat 77 God's help ϩⲉⲛⲥ ⲛⲁⲥ ⲉⲃ. ϩⲁⲣⲟϥ; ⲥⲁⲃⲟⲗ ⲛ-: Ps 17 23, Dan 3 29, Ac 22 29 ἀφ. ἀπό, Nu 14 9 ἀποστάτης γίνεσθαι; Job 1 1, Ac 15 20 (all *S* do) ἀπέχ. ἀπό; *ib* 3 26 (*S* ⲕⲧⲟ ⲉⲃ. ϩⲛ-) ἀποστρέφειν ἀπό; Lu 5 3 (*S* ϩⲓⲛⲉ ⲉⲃ. ⲛ-) ἐπανάγ. ἀπό; C 43 175 ⲛⲧⲉϥϩⲉⲛϥ ⲥ. ⲙⲡⲁⲓⲣⲁⲛ ϫⲉⲥ̄, C 89 130 can demon ϩⲉⲛϥ ⲛⲁϥ ⲥ. ⲙⲙⲟⲓ?=C 99 258 *S* ⲥⲁϩⲱⲱϥ ⲉⲃ. ⲙⲙⲟⲓ; BG 61 *S* ⲁⲩϩⲛⲧⲟⲩ ⲙⲡⲥⲁ ⲛⲃⲟⲗ ⲙⲙⲟϥ; ⲛⲥⲁⲟⲩⲥⲁ *S*: PS 354 *S* ⲙⲁⲣⲟⲩϩⲛⲧⲟⲩ ⲛ.

ϩⲓⲛⲉ *F* *v* ⲛⲓⲛⲉ.

ϩⲟ(ⲉ)ⲓⲛⲉ, ϩⲟⲓⲛ (BG)*S*, ϩⲁⲉⲓⲛⲉ *AA*[2], ϩⲁⲓⲛⲉ *A*[2] (Ma), -ⲛⲓ *F*, constr ϩⲉⲛ- *SAA*[2]*F*, ϩⲓⲛ- *S*, ϩⲁⲛ- *B* used as pl of art ⲟⲩ- (*v* ⲟⲩⲁ), nn as pl, *some, certain*: Ex 16 20, Job 22 8, Ac 19 9 (all *B* ϩⲁⲛⲟⲩⲟⲛ), Cl 59 1 *A*, AP 5 *A*[2] τινες; Aeg 248 ἔνιοι; Mt 16 14 (*B* do), *ib* 22 5 (*B* ⲟⲩⲁⲓ), Ac 14 4 (*B* ϩ.) ὁ, οἱ, τὰ μέν, Sa 15 7 τά τε; Mk 4 20 *F*(Mus 49 188, *SB* ⲟⲩⲁ) ἕν; Mor 37 76 ⲛⲉⲛⲧⲁⲩⲛⲁⲩ ⲉⲣⲟⲟⲩ ϩⲓⲧⲛϩ., ZNTW 24 90 *F* ϫⲁⲁⲥ ⲉⲧⲃⲉϩ. ἄλλοι; BHom 21 ϣⲁⲛⲣⲁϣⲉ ⲉϫⲛϩ. ἕτεροι; Mk 6 5 (*B* ⲟⲩⲙⲏϣ) ὀλίγοι; Gk diff Ex 32 17 (*B*=Gk), Pro 13 23 (*B* as Gk); Gk & *B* om Mk 8 28 *SF*, Ap 2 14; PS 348 ⲉⲣϣⲁⲛϩ. ϭⲉ ⲉⲓ, *ib* 7 ⲉⲣⲉϩ. ⲟⲩⲟⲧⲃ ⲉⲛⲉⲩⲉⲣⲏⲩ, BG 99 ϣⲁⲣⲉϩⲟⲓⲛ ⲙⲟⲩⲧⲉ ⲉⲣⲟⲥ, Br 239 ϩ. ⲙⲉⲛ ⲁⲩⲣⲁϣⲉ...ϩⲉⲛⲕⲟⲟⲩⲉ ⲁⲩⲣⲓⲙⲉ, ManiK 51 *A*[2] ϩ. ⲙⲉⲛ...ϩ. ⲙⲉⲛ, ShC 73 160 ⲟⲩϫⲣⲟⲡ ⲧⲁϩⲉ ϩ., *ib* 42 184 ϩ. ⲉⲛⲁϣⲱⲟⲩ ϩⲁⲧⲛⲧⲏⲩⲧⲛ, *ib* 192 ⲙⲛⲣⲧⲱϩ ⲙⲛⲟⲩⲁ ⲏ ⲙⲛϩ. ⲉⲩⲙⲟⲩⲧⲉ ⲉⲣⲟϥ ϫⲉ-, ShA 1 62 ⲟⲩⲁ ⲏ ϩ. ϩⲣⲁⲓ ⲛϩⲏⲧⲉ, CA 96 ⲉⲧⲃⲉϩ. ⲉⲩⲛⲁϣⲁϫⲉ, Wess 11 168 ⲁϥϭⲱ ⲙⲛϩ. paral ⲙⲛⲕⲟⲟⲩⲉ, Miss 8 15 suffer not slanderers ⲉⲧⲣⲉⲩϩⲥⲁⲓ ϩ. ⲉⲛⲙⲁ ⲛϩ., ManiH 27 *A*[2] ϩ. ⲛϩⲁⲩⲧ ϩ. ⲛϩⲓⲙⲉ, AP 40 *A*[2] ϣⲁⲣϣⲣ ⲛⲧⲡⲓⲥⲧⲓⲥ ⲛϩ.; *such, of this sort* (*v* KKS 12): Ro 11 24 *SF* (*B* ⲛⲁⲓ) οὗτοι; AP 5 *A*[2] prob τίνες; Ap 3 9 (*B* ϩⲁⲛⲟⲩⲟⲛ) Gk om, ViSitz 172 4 19 ⲉⲛⲉϩ. ⲧⲁⲣⲛⲉ *if they were such* Gk om; ShA 1 254 beasts so named, but ⲛϩ. ⲁⲛⲛⲉ ⲉⲛⲉϩ, *ib* 2 16 ϩ. ⲧⲏⲣⲟⲩⲛⲉ, BM 288 78 ⲁⲛⲟⲛ ϩ. ⲁⲛ as thou dost think, KKS 13 ⲁⲛⲟⲛ ϩ. ⲁⲛ ϩⲛⲟⲩϣⲱⲡ ⲙⲛⲟⲩϯ ⲉⲃⲟⲗ (*cf* *HorSemit* 3 59 لسنا كما تبيع وتشتري); with art ϩⲉⲛ-: EpJer 31 *F*(*S* P 44 114 ϩ. only, *B* ϩⲁⲛⲟⲩⲟⲛ), Mk 14 4 *F*(*S* ϩ. only, *B* do) τινες, Cl 44 6 *A* ἔνιοι; *ib* 55 2 *A* ἕτ.; Pro 13 23 *A*(*S* do, *B* as Gk) Gk diff; Mor 18 109 ϩⲉⲛϩ. ⲛϩⲏⲧⲟⲩ (var LCyp

3 om ϩⲉⲛ-); as sg: Bor 263 24 ⲙⲡⲣⲧⲣⲉϥ. ⲉⲓ ⲉϩⲟⲩⲛ ⲉϥⲟ ⲛ̄ϭⲁⲃϩⲏⲧ, ib 31 sim ⲉⲣⲉ ⲟⲩⲙⲁⲧⲟⲩ ϩⲓⲡⲣⲟ̅. c ⲛ̄- gen: Mt 9 3 (B ϩ.); 1 Cor 10 7 (B do) ⲧⲓⲛⲉⲥ gen; Sa 16 1 ϩ. ⲛ̄ⲧⲉ ⲓⲙ̄ⲛⲉ ὅμοιοι; Mk 10 14 (B ⲛ̄ⲁⲓ ⲟ ⲅⲟⲛ, cf Mt 19 14 S ⲛⲁⲓ ⲛ̄ⲧ.) τοιοῦτοι; ib 2 16 (B do, var & Gk diff); c ϩⲛ-: Lu 6 2 (B ϩ.) τ. gen; Jo 6 64 SA²(B do), Ac 6 9 (B do) τ. ἐκ; Nu 22 6 (B ⲟⲩⲙⲏ̄ϣ) ἐξ αὐτῶν, Ap 2 10 (B ϩ.) ἐξ ὑμῶν.

ϩⲱⲡⲉ S, -ⲏⲓ F nn f, *canal*: Mor 41 234 horses washed ϩⲓⲑ.; in place-names: ⲑⲱⲡⲉ (Ryl 119, MR 2 66, ? Θῦνις), ⲗⲉϩ. (BM 542), ⲗⲓϩ. (Kr 228) البوصة, ⲗⲉϩⲱⲡⲓ (BM 592).
Cf DM 21 35 n.

ϩⲱⲡⲉ A² v ϩⲱⲡ *approach*.

ϩⲛⲉ- S (c ϩⲛ-), ⲉϩⲛⲉ- SB, ϩⲛⲁ⸗ S, ⲟⲡⲉ⸗ AA²F, ϩⲓⲏⲓ F, ⲉϩⲛⲁ⸗ SB, ⲉϩⲛⲉ⸗ AA²F nn, *will, desire* forming vbal phrases (properly vb ϩ + dat AZ 47 136), *be willing* (all ⲉϩ.): Ps 53 6 S(B ⲥⲉⲛⲁⲟⲩⲱ ϣ) ἑκουσίως, Philem 14 (B ⲥⲉⲛⲟⲩⲣⲱ ⲟⲩⲧϥ ⲛϩⲏⲧ) κατὰ ἑκούσιον; Si 32 15 S ἐν εὐδοκίᾳ, Phil 1 15 S(B ⲉⲑⲃⲉ ⲟⲩϯ ⲙⲁⲧ) δι᾽ εὐδ., Est 1 19 S δοκεῖν; Job 13 3 S(B ⲟ ⲩⲱϣ) βούλεσθαι; 1 Cor 9 17 SB ἑκών; Cl 31 3 A, AP 12 A² ἡδέως; Hos 14 5 SA(B om) ὁμολόγως; Jth 8 17 S ἀρεστός; 2 Cor 8 17 S αὐθαίρετος; ShC 73 74 S ⲉϥⲉⲙⲙⲉ ⲉⲣⲟⲛ ⲉϩⲛⲁⲩ, JA '05 117 S ⲁⲓⲙⲟⲩ ⲉϩⲛⲁⲓ, Ep 467 S ϩⲛⲟⲩ ⲅ̄ⲧⲟⲣ ⲁⲛ ⲁⲗⲗⲁ ⲉϩⲛⲏ ⲧⲓ, ib 131 S ⲉϩ ⲛⲁⲓ ⲉⲛⲉ ⲉϣⲁⲓϭⲛ ⲉⲅⲕⲁⲓⲣⲓⲁ I would have written, ViK 4701 S (ⲉ)ϩⲛⲏⲧⲛ ⲛ̄ⲧⲁⲧⲛⲉⲉⲓ, P 131⁶ 33 S that He enable us ⲉⲛⲉⲭⲱ ⲛⲏⲧⲛ ⲉϩⲛⲁⲩ *if it please Him* ⲛϥⲉⲛ ⲕⲟⲩⲓ, RE 9 136 S ⲉϩⲛⲁⲩ ⲙ̄ⲡⲉⲛⲉ, Aeg 36 B ⲉϩⲛⲱ ϩ ⲛⲉ ⲉⲁⲅⲕⲏⲡ ⲉⲙⲟⲩ, BM 228 29 S ⲉϩⲛⲉ ⲡⲉ ⲛⲉⲓⲱⲧ ⲁⲃⲣⲁ ϩⲁⲙ ⲛ̄ⲧⲁ ⲅ ⲥⲩⲛⲭⲱⲣⲉⲓ ⲛⲁϥ *would have been glad had he been suffered* to receive Nineve (Dives); neg: Lev 4 2 S ⲉϩ. ⲁⲛ (var ⲉⲛϩ. ⲁⲛ, B diff), ib 22 ⲛ̄ϩ. ⲁⲛ (B ⲉϩ. ⲁⲛ) ἀκουσίως, 1 Cor 9 17 S ⲉⲛϩ. ⲁⲛ B ⲉϩ. ⲁⲛ, Cl 2 3 A(Stras) ⲉϩ. ⲉⲛ ἄκων; Mor 37 113 S ⲉϩ. ⲁⲛ οὐχ ἑκών; Job 31 26 B ⲉϩ. ⲁⲛ (S ⲉⲭⲱⲟⲩ?) ἐπ᾽ αὐτοῖς; ShC 42 131 S ⲉϩ ⲛⲁⲓ ⲁⲛ ⲏ ⲙ̄ⲡⲁⲟ ⲩⲱ ϣ ⲁⲛⲡⲉ, BMis 263 S ⲛ̄ⲧⲁϥⲓⲧⲟⲩ ⲉϩⲛⲁⲩ ⲁⲛ, Z 283 S sim ϩ ⲛⲁ ϥ ⲁⲛ, C 86 351 B bade strip him ⲉϩⲛⲁ ϥ ⲁⲛ, Miss 4 817 S ⲛ̄ϩ ⲛⲁⲕ ⲁⲛ ⲁⲕ ϫ ⲟ ⲟ ⲥ; c rel ⲉⲧ- (all ⲉϩ.): Jth 8 15 S, Mt 17 12 B(S ⲟⲩⲱ ϣ), Jo 3 8 BF(SA² do) θέλειν, Ps 106 32 SB, Ac 13 22 B(S ⲟⲩ.) θέλημα; 1 Cor 12 11 B(S do), R 1 1 15 βού.; PS 204 S ⲛ̄ⲑⲉ ⲉⲧⲉϩⲛⲉ ⲡⲉ ⲩⲭ̄ⲥ̄, El 62 A ⲧ ϩⲉ ⲉⲧⲉϩ ⲛⲉ ⲩ, J 10 50 S ⲥ ⲙⲟⲧ ⲛⲓ ⲙ ⲉⲧ ⲉ ϩⲛⲏ ⲧ ⲓ, DeV 1 35 B ϩⲱⲃ ⲛⲓ ⲃ ⲉⲛ ⲉⲧ ⲉϩ ⲛⲏ ⲓ; c ⲡⲉⲧ-, ⲫⲓ ⲉⲧ- (all ⲉϩ.): Ps 39 9 B(S ⲟⲩ.), Mt 7 21 B -ⲉϩⲛⲉ ⲛ ⲁ ⲓ ⲱ ⲧ, F -ⲉϩ ⲛ ⲉϥ ⲙⲛ. (PMich 612, S do), Eph 1 5 BF -ⲉϩⲛⲏⲓ ϥ (S do) θέλημα; Dan 4 14 B, He 12 10 SB ⲇⲟⲕ., Ps 68 13 S(B ϯ ⲙⲁⲧ) εὐδοκία; Jer 31 30 S (Cai 8316, B diff), Mk 15 15 BF(S diff) ἱκανός; Deu 12 15 S-ⲉϩⲛⲉ ⲧⲉⲕ ⲯ ⲩⲭⲏ (B = Gk) ἐπιθυμία; Mt 10

29 B -ⲉϩ ⲛⲉ ⲡⲉⲧⲉⲛⲓⲱⲧ (SGk om); PS 360 S ϣ ⲓ ⲛⲉ ⲛⲥⲁ ⲡⲉⲧⲉϩ ⲛⲉ (f), ShBMOr 8810 391 S ⲡⲉⲧⲉϩ ⲛⲉ ⲡⲉ ϥ ϩⲏ ⲧ, Z 629 S recipe ⲥ ⲟ ⲟ ϣ ⲡⲉⲧⲉϩ ⲛⲁⲕ *what thou wilt*, C 43 52 B ⲫ ⲓ ⲉⲧⲉϩ ⲛ ⲱ ⲧⲉ ⲛ ⲁⲣ ⲓ ⲧ ϥ, ib 231 B ⲡⲉⲧⲉϩ ⲛⲁⲕ ⲁⲣ ⲓ ⲧ ϥ, BIF 22 106 F ⲕ ⲁ ⲧ ⲁ ⲡⲉⲧⲉϩ ⲛⲓ ⲛ ⲕ.

With following preposition. c ⲉ- (mostly S): ShBor 247 125 ⲧ ⲉⲓ ⲡ ⲗ ⲁ ⲕ ⲉ ⲉⲓ ϩ ⲛ ⲁⲛ ⲁⲛ ⲉ ⲣ ⲟ ⲥ; vbal: Deu 29 20 (B ⲟⲩⲱ ϣ), ROC 18 171 ⲉϩ ⲛ ⲁⲓ ⲉ ϫ ⲓ ⲟⲩ ⲉ ϩ ⲗ ⲟ θέλειν; 2 Cor 5 8, 1 Thes 2 8 SF(both B ϯ ⲙ.) εὐδοκεῖν; Ac 18 27 (B ⲟⲩ.) βού.; MG 259 B ⲥⲉ ϩ ⲛ ⲁⲕ ⲁⲛ ⲉ ⲕ ⲱ ϯ ⲛⲥ ⲁ- οὐ χρεία ἐστίν; ShC 73 23 ⲉϩ ⲛ ⲁⲛ ⲉ ⲕ ⲃ ⲉ ⲡⲉⲡ ⲗⲁⲥ, Pcod 19 ⲉϩ ⲛⲉ ⲛ̄ⲭ̄ⲥ̄ ⲉ ϯ, BIIom 72 *fierce against us* ⲉϩ ⲛⲁⲩ ⲉ ⲣ ⲟ ⲛ, JA '05 439 ⲧⲉ ϩ ⲛ ⲁ (f) ⲉ ⲧ ⲁ- ⲙ ⲟ ⲓ *be pleased to tell me*, ManiK 32 A² ⲛⲥ ⲁⲛ ⲉ ⲧ ⲉϩ ⲛ ⲉ ϥ ⲁ ⲙ ⲁ ϩ ⲉ, BM 1104 ⲙ ⲛ̄ ⲧ ⲁⲛ ⲕ ⲉ ⲣ ⲟ ⲟ ⲩ ϣ ⲉ ⲙ ⲁ ⲩ ⲛ̄ϩ ⲛ ⲁⲛ ⲉⲛ ⲁ ⲩ ⲉ ⲣ ⲱ ⲧ ⲛ̄ *we have no care save the wish to see you* (cf ib no thought to pray for but thy health); neg: Sa 17 9 ἀρνεῖσθαι; ShC 73 50 ⲉⲛϩ ⲛ ⲁ ⲩ ⲁⲛ ⲉⲥ ⲱ ⲧ ⲙ̄, ShR 2 3 6 ⲉϩ ⲛ ⲁⲕ ⲁⲛ ⲉ ⲕ ⲱ ⲛⲥ ⲱ ⲕ, Wess 18 111 ⲛ̄ ϩ ⲛ ⲁⲓ ⲁⲛ ⲉ ⲕ ⲁ ⲣ ⲱ ⲓ; c ⲉ ⲧ ⲣ ⲉ-: ShA 1 105 ⲉϩ ⲛ ⲁⲓ ⲁⲛ ⲉ ⲧ ⲣ ⲉ ⲅ ϣ ⲱ ⲡ ⲉ, ShC 42 119 ⲉϩ ⲛ ⲁⲛ ⲁⲛ ⲉ ⲧ ⲣ ⲉ ⲅ ⲡ ⲁ ⲣ ⲁ ⲅ ⲉ; c ⲛ̄- dat: Miss 8 89 S ⲡⲉⲧⲉϩ ⲛ ⲁ ϥ ⲙ̄ⲡ ⲕ ⲁ ⲛ ⲱ ⲛ τοῖς καν., ROC 17 406 B ⲡⲉⲧⲉϩ ⲛⲁⲕ ⲛ̄ ⲫ ⲁⲓ τὸ δοκοῦν ἐπί; Mor 17 118 S ⲕ ⲁ ⲧ ⲁ ⲡⲉⲧ ⲉϩ ⲛⲉ ⲛ̄ⲧ ⲟ ⲩ ⲯ ⲩ ⲭ ⲏ (sc woman's); c ϩⲛ- S: Ps 146 11 ⲉϩ ⲛ ⲉ ⲛ̄ⲭ̄ⲥ̄ ϩ ⲛ- (B ϯ ⲙ. ⲥ ⲉ ⲛ-), He 10 38 (B do) εὐδ. ἐν.

ⲣ ϩ ⲛ ⲁ⸗ &c SAA²F, *be willing, desire*: Ge 48 19 (B ⲟⲩ.) θ.; Jud 11 17, Gal 1 15 (B ϯ ⲙ.) εὐδ.; Ex 22 17 (B ⲟⲩ.) ἀνανεύειν; ShA 1 72 ⲙ̄ⲡⲉⲣ ϩ ⲛ ⲉ, Pcod 39 ⲛ̄ⲧ ⲉ ⲛ̄ⲭ̄ⲥ̄ ⲣ ϩ ⲛ ⲁ ϥ = F ⲉ ⲗ ϩ ⲛ ⲏ ϥ, Mani 1 A² ⲡ ⲉ ⲧ ⲁ ⲥ ⲣ ϩ ⲛ ⲉ ϥ ϫ ⲉ-; vbal: Ja 4 15 ⲣ ϩ. ⲛ̄ⲧ ⲛ ⲱ ⲛ ϩ (B ⲟⲩ.) θ.; ShC 73 111 ⲣ ϩ. ⲛ̄ⲧⲉ ⲧ ⲉ ⲓ ⲇ ⲓ ⲕ ⲁ ⲓ ⲟ ⲥ ⲩ ⲛ ⲏ ⲙ ⲟ ⲩ ⲛ̄ ⲉ ⲃ ⲟ ⲗ; c ⲉ-: Deu 1 26 ⲣ ϩ. ⲉ ⲃ ⲱ ⲕ, Hos 11 5 A ⲣ ⲉ ϩ. ⲁ ⲕ ⲧ ⲁ ϥ, 1 Thes 2 18 SF(all B ⲟⲩ.), Z 310 ⲙ̄ⲡⲉ ϥ ⲣ ϩ. ⲉ ⲟ ⲩ ⲱ ⲙ θ.; Jud 20 13, 1 Cor 1 21 (B ϯ ⲙ.) εὐδ.; 1 Kg 15 9 ⲣ ⲉ ϩ. ⲉ-, Ru 3 13 ⲧ ⲁ ⲣ ϩ. ⲉ- βού.; BG 36 ⲁ ⲥ ⲣ ϩ ⲛ ⲁ ⲥ ⲉ-, ShA 2 278 ⲛ̄ⲧⲉ ⲧ ⲛ ⲁ ⲣ ϩ ⲛ ⲏ ⲧ ⲛ ⲁ ⲛ ⲉ ⲛ ⲁ ⲩ, ShA 1 83 imperat ⲣ ϩ ⲛ ⲁ ⲕ ⲏ ⲟ ⲩ ⲱ ϣ… ⲉ ⲕ ⲱ, Miss 8 53 ⲁ ⲅ ⲣ ϩ ⲛ ⲁ ⲩ ⲙ ⲁ ⲅ ⲁ ⲁ ⲩ ⲉ ⲥ ⲙ ⲙ ⲉ, Mor 18 27 ⲁ ⲅ ⲣ ϩ ⲛ ⲁ ϥ ⲉ ⲥ ⲉ ϣ ⲛ̄ ⲣ ⲣ ⲟ = Miss 4 121 B ⲣ ⲁ ⲛ ⲁ ϥ, Mor 30 33 F ⲁ ⲥ ⲉ ⲗ ϩ ⲛ ⲏ ϥ ⲉ ⲝ ⲓ ⲧ ϥ; c ⲉ ⲧ ⲣ ⲉ-: Lu 1 3 (B ⲣ ⲁ ⲛ ⲏ ⲓ) δοκεῖν dat, Aeg 268 ϣ ⲁ ϥ ⲣ ϩ ⲛ ⲁ ϥ ⲉ. εὐδ.; ShC 73 29 ⲁ ⲅ ⲣ ϩ ⲛ ⲁ ⲩ ⲉ.; c ⲛ̄-: Ac 10 10 (var ⲉ-, B ⲟⲩ.) θ.; Deu 25 7 (B do) βού.; Miss 8 30 ⲁ ⲥ ⲣ ϩ ⲛ ⲁ ⲥ ⲛ̄- ⲇ ⲟ ⲕ. dat; Jth 11 1 αἱρετίζειν; ShC 42 200 ⲣ ϩ. ⲛ ⲉ ⲓ, Ming 292 ⲛ̄ⲧⲉ ⲧ ⲛ̄ ⲣ ϩ ⲛ ⲏ ⲧ ⲛ̄ ⲛ̄ ⲑ ⲉ ⲱ ⲣ ⲉ ⲓ ⲙ ⲙ ⲟ ⲩ; c ϩⲛ-: Jth 15 10, He 10 8 SFsim(B ϯ ⲙ.) εὐδ.

ϩⲛⲉ S nn, *meaning unknown*: PLond 4 196 &c Μωυσης ϩ ⲛ ⲉ. Cf ?? Ps 70 7 ϩ ϩ. (var PS ⲥ ⲟ ϭ, B ϣ ⲫ ⲏ ⲣ ⲓ) τέρας.

ϩⲛⲉ A v ϩ ⲛ ⲁ ⲁ ⲩ.

ϩⲛⲟ, -ⲱ SA v ϩ ⲛ ⲁ ⲁ ⲩ.

ϩⲓⲛⲏⲃ (ϩⲓ- ⲩ ϩⲓⲟϭⲉ) SS¹AA²F, -ⲛⲏϥ SF, -ⲛⲓⲙ, ϩⲓⲛⲓⲙ B vb intr, *sleep, doze*: Ps 75 7 B(S ϫⲓ ⲣⲉⲕⲣⲓⲕⲉ), Pro 6 10 B(SA do), Si 22 7 S νυστάζειν; Jer 14 9 B (S ⲱⲃϣ) ὑπνοῦν; Eccl 2 23 S(ShBor 247 104, var ⲛⲕⲟⲧⲕ) κοιμᾶσθαι; ShBIF 23 163 S ⲡⲉⲧⲛⲏⲝ...ⲁⲩⲱ ⲉⲧϥ., BerlOr 1607 3 95 S sailors ⲉⲛⲕⲟⲧⲕ ⲁⲩϩ., El 96 A sim, KroppA S ⲙⲡⲉⲟⲩϭⲓ ϩ. ... ϫⲓ ⲣ., Mani 1 A² ⲙⲡⲱⲣ ϩ., BM 527 F ϣⲁⲕⲣⲓⲛⲏϥ, OratCyp 9 S¹ ⲉⲙⲡⲓϩ., FR 94 B ⲁⲓϩ. ⲡⲟⲩⲕⲟⲩϫⲓ.

—— nn m SABF, *sleep*: Ge 31 40 SB, Nu 24 16 S(var ⲱⲃϣ, B ⲣⲁⲥⲟⲩⲓ), Pro 4 16 SAB, Eccl 5 11 S(F ⲛⲕⲁⲧ), ib 8 16 SF(PMich 3520), Mt 1 24 S(B ⲛⲕ.), Jo 11 13 AB(SA² ⲱⲃϣ) ὕπνος; Jer 23 31 B ⲛⲩⲥⲧⲁⲅⲙός; Ge 2 21 S(B ⲥⲣⲟⲙ ⲛϩ.) ἔκστασις; ShRE 10 160 S wake from ⲛϩ. ⲁⲩⲱ ⲡⲉⲛⲕⲟⲧⲕ, BIF 14 123 S ⲁⲛϩ. ϩⲣⲟϣ ⲉϩⲣⲁⲓ ⲉϫⲱⲛ, Mor 22 123 S ⲟⲩϩ. ⲉϥⲟϣ = BSM 112B,ClPr 46S before midnight named ⲛϣⲟⲣⲡ ⲛϩ., Mor 29 6 S ⲟⲃϣ ϩⲁⲛϩ., Mani 1 A² ϫⲓ ⳾ⲡⲉ ⲙⲡϩ., C 43 92 B ϩⲱⲣⲡ ⲛϩ., PO 11 341 B ϭⲓ ⲟⲩϭⲣⲟⲙ ⲛϩ.; ϩⲓⲛⲓⲙ B MG 25 23, 43, 163 &c (all Va 64).

ⲁⲧϩ. B, *without sleep*: TstAb 240 pass night ⲛⲁ.; ⲙⲉⲧⲁⲧϩ.: Va 61 9 ϣⲣⲱⲓⲥ, ⲛ.

ϭⲓⲛϩ. S, *manner of sleeping*: Mor 56 18 slept ⲛⲟⲉ ⲛⲧⲉϭ. ⲙⲙⲓⲛⲛⲏⲉ.

ϩⲟⲛⲃⲉ S, ϩⲟⲙ. B (once) nn f S m B, *spring, well*: Nu 33 9 f ϩ. ⲙⲙⲟⲟⲩ (var = Gk), Ps 41 1 sim, Ja 3 11 (cit BMOr 8810 473 ϩⲟⲃⲛⲉ, all B ⲙⲟⲩⲙⲓ) πηγή, P 44 53 ⲧⲏⲅⲏⲛ, ⲧⲙⲟⲩⲙⲉ, ⲧϩ., ﻋﻴﻦ, BMOr 920 265 = Ryl 453 336 B ⲛⲓϩ. ʻⲋ; Tri 664 ϩⲉⲛϩ. ⲙⲙ. ﻋﻴﻮن; ShC 42 70 when blessed ⲧⲕⲉϩ. ϣⲏⲙ sufficed for their drinking.

Cf ϩⲁⲗⲙⲉ.

ϩⲱⲛⲕ, -ⲧ, ϩⲉⲛⲕ- S, ϩⲁⲛⲕⲋ A² vb tr, *consecrate, appoint*: Deu 18 10 (B ⲥⲓⲛⲓ ⳾ⲉⲛⲟⲩⲭⲣⲱⲙ) περικαθαίρειν, διάγειν; Jud 17 5 ϩⲉⲛⲡ ⲧϭⲓⲝ πληροῦν, ἐμπιπλᾶν, τελειοῦν (cf ib 12 ⲧⲃⲃⲉ ⲧϭⲓⲝ same Gk); Mani 1 A² ⲁⲣⲓ ⲟⲩⲣⲉϥⲙⲟⲩⲧⲉ ⲛⲟⲩⲁⲓⲡⲉ ⲕⲣⲁⲛⲕⲟⲩ ϣⲁⲛϯϫⲱⲃⲉ ⲙⲙⲁⲩ. *Cf* OLZ '11 551. Same? as (ϩⲱⲕⲡ).

ϩⲓⲕⲉ S, ϩⲉⲗⲕⲓ B (once) nn m, *beer*: Is 19 10 SB ζῦθος; ShMich 550 18 ⲟⲩϩ. ⲏ ⲟⲩϥⲁⲕⲟⲛ allowed to sick, Ora 4 24 put mixture into ⲟⲩⲁⲡⲟⲧ ⲛϩ., PMéd 319 ⲧⲥⲟϥ ϩⲓϩ., Mor 51 35 ⲁⲛⲙⲁⲩ ⲙⲡⲅⲛⲕⲉ ⲟⲩⲉⲓⲛⲉ.

ϩⲁⲛⲕⲗϥ (? ϩⲁ for ϩⲟⲛⲕ.) ⲩ ϩⲁⲕⲗϥ.

ϩⲓⲛⲓⲙ B ⲩ ϩⲓⲛⲏⲃ.

ϩⲁⲛⲁⲙⲉⲣⲓ B ⲩ ⲙⲉⲉⲣⲉ.

ϩⲛⲁⲛ Sᵃ ⲩ ϩⲱⲛ *approach*.

ϩⲁⲛⲣⲟ, ⲁⲛⲣⲟ ⲩ ⲣⲟ p 289 b.

ϩⲁⲛⲁⲣⲟⲩϩⲓ B ⲩ ⲣⲟⲩϩⲉ.

ϩⲟⲛⲧ SB (once), ϩⲱ. (pl ?) S nn m, pagan *priest* (cf ⲟⲩⲏⲧⲉ): Ge 41 45 B(S ⲟⲩⲏⲏⲃ) ἱερεύς, Mor 18 108 ⲟⲩⲏⲏⲃ, ϩ., προφητης (varLCyp 1 om ϩ.) ἱεροφάντης only; Wess 15 10 ϩⲟⲙⲉⲣⲟⲥ ⲛϩ. = Miss 4 118 B ⲟⲩ., RNC 82 ⲛϩ. ⲙⲡⲁⲡⲟⲗⲗⲱⲛ, Miss 4 687 ⲟⲩ. & ϩ. of Apollo, P 129¹⁴ 128 ⲛⲛⲟϫ ⲛϩⲱ. of idol temple; Jos 9 6 (P 44 108) ⲛϩ. ⲙⲡⲕⲁϩ (= 43 97 ⲛϩⲱ.) اهل prob αὐτόχθων, so *l*? ⲛⲣⲱⲙⲉ as Nu 9 14.

ϩⲟⲛⲧ S vb qual, meaning unknown: BG 82 ⲧⲉϩⲟⲛⲧ ⲟⲩϭⲓⲉ ⲉⲙⲁⲥⲁⲓⲥⲑⲁⲛⲉⲧⲉ, *is one that understandeth not*, 81 διοίκησις of first created things is holy spirit or πρόνοια or ⲧⲉⲑ.

ϩⲱⲛⲧ S (rare, mostly ϩⲱⲛ or ϩ. ⲉϩⲟⲩⲛ) A²BF, ϩ. A, ⳾. B, ϩ(ⲉ)ⲛⲧ- S, ⳾. B, ϩⲟⲛⲧⲋ S, ⳾. B, ϩⲏⲛⲧ† SF, ϩⲁⲛⲧ†S¹A², ⳾ⲉⲛⲧ†B vb intr, *approach*: Ps 37 12, Is 5 19 BF, Ac 7 17 BF ἐγγίζειν, Mt 26 18 ἐγγύς εἶναι; 2Tim 4 6BF(Mus 49 202) ἐφιστάναι; MIE 2 419 ⲁϥ⳾. ⲛϫⲉ ⲡⲁⲥⲛⲟⲩ = BAp 124 S ⲁⲓϩⲱⲛ ⲉⲡⲱⲗⲕ; qual: 3 Kg 8 46, Dan 9 7, Zeph 1 7 (A = S), Mt 24 32 (F ϩⲱ.) ἐγγύς; MG 25 352 ⲉⲑⲟⲩⲏⲟⲩ, ⲉⲧ⳾.

With following preposition or adverb.

—— ⲉ- intr: Ex 32 19, Is 30 20 BF ἐγγίζ. dat, Lam 3 57, Mt 21 1 ἐγ. εἰς, Ps 31 6 ἐγ. πρός, Nu 8 19† προσεγ. πρός, MG 25 210 dared not ⲉ⳾. ⲉ- = Z 345 S ϩⲱⲛ ⲉϩ. ⲉ- ⲡⲣ. dat, Job 13 18†, He 8 13†(F = S) ἐγγύς gen, Ac 9 38† BF -ύς dat, Lev 21 2† (S ⲧⲏ⳾) ἔγγιστος dat; Ps 121 8†(S ϩⲓⲧⲟⲩⲱⲋ), Va 61 16 ⲟⲩⲗⲁⲕⲕⲟⲥ ⳾.† ⲉⲡⲓⲙⲟⲛⲁⲥⲧⲏⲣⲓⲟⲛ πλησίον gen, Phil 2 27 παραπ. dat; Ps 67 26†, He 6 9† ἐχόμενος gen, Ex 28 7† συνέχ. dat; ib 22 25†(S ϩⲁⲣⲧⲛ-) παρά only; C 89 67 ⲟⲩⲥⲟⲛ...ⲉϥ⳾.† ⲉⲡⲓⲙⲁ = C 99 233 S ⲉϥϩⲛⲙⲁ, C 89 204 ⲁⲛⲁⲥⲛⲟⲩ ⳾ⲱⲛ (sic MS) ⲉⲣⲟⲓ, TEuch 2 120 ⲛⲏ ⲉⲧ⳾.† ⲉⲣⲟⲓ ⲥⲁ ⲣⲓⲕⲟⲡ, MIE 2 381 ⲟⲩⲙⲁⲡⲉⲥⲱⲟⲩ ⳾. ⲉⲣⲟⲛ = BAp 106 S ⲛⲡ ⲉⲧⲓⲥⲅⲩⲅⲟⲣⲓⲁ, Miss 4 766 S¹ heard my voice ϩⲱⲥ ⲉϣϫⲉ ⲉϥϩ.† ⲉⲣⲟⲓ, Mani P 26 A² ⲡⲉⲧϩ. [ⲁⲣⲁϥ]; vbal: Ge 12 11, Is 26 17 ἐγγίζ. inf; Hos 5 11 A(B ⲉⲣ ϩⲏⲧⲥ) ἄρχεσθαι inf; EpJer 28 F ⲉⲥⲟ.† ⲉⲙⲓⲥⲓ (B ⲙⲏⲥⲓ) λεχώς; C 41 73 ⲁϥ⳾. ⲉⲉⲣ ⲣⲙⲛ ⲡⲣⲟⲙⲡⲓ = Miss 4 240 S ϩⲱⲛ ⲉϩ. ⲉ-, Mani P 39 A² ⲡⲉⲧϩⲁⲩϩ.† ⲁϣⲱⲡⲉ; tr: Is 5 8 ⳾ⲉⲛⲧ- ἐγγίζ. πρός; BSM 49 ⲁⲓⲕⲏⲛ ⲛ⳾. ⲙⲙⲱⲧⲉⲛ ⲉⲡⲁϫⲋ (BMis 400 S diff), Miss 4 615 S hath freedom ⲉϩⲓⲧ ⲛⲡⲉ ⲉⲛⲣⲱⲙⲉ, Mor 31 76 S she seized ⲛⲉϥϩⲟⲓⲧⲉ ⲛⲉϩⲟⲛⲧϥ ⲉⲣⲟⲥ; refl: Ps 54 19 ἐγγίζ. dat; Lev 18 20 S(B Gk diff); MG 25 294 ⲛⲁⲛ⳾. ⲙⲙⲟⲛ ⲉⲣⲟϥ ⲡⲉ = BIF 13 108 S ⲙⲟⲟϣⲉ ⲉ-; ⲉⲃⲟⲗ ⲉ-: Dif 2 97 ϯⲙⲓ ⲉⲧ⳾.† ⲉⲃ. ⲉⲛⲉϥⲑⲟⲱϣ; ⲉϩⲣⲏ ⲉ-: Ps 106 18 ἐγγίζ. ἕως.

—— ⳾ⲁ-: Is 50 8 (S ⲉ-) ἐγγίζ. dat.

—— ϩⲁ-: Ex 24 2 (S ⲉ-) ἐγ. πρός; ⲉⲃⲟⲗ ϩⲁ-: Job 17 12 ἐγγὺς ἀπό.

—— ⲉϩⲟⲩⲛ, ⲉϩ., ⲁϩ.: 3 Kg 2 1, Is 33 13† BF ἐγγίζ.; Lev 1 10 (S ⲉⲓⲛⲉ) προσάγειν; TstAb 159 ⲁⲩ⳾.

ⲉ. ⲡϫⲉ ⲡⲓⲉⲣⲟⲟⲩ, CMSS 41 *S/* ⲁⲡⲣⲱⲙⲉ ϩ. ⲉ., MIE 2 394 ⲁϥϭⲟⲡⲧⲩ ⲉ.;   ⲉϩⲟⲩⲛ ⲉ-: Ez 22 5, Zeph 3 2 *AB* ἐγγίζ. πρός, Ja 4 8 (var om ⲉⲥ.) ἐγ. dat, Ac 1 12† (var do) -ύς gen ; Is 34 1 *F(S* ϩⲱⲛ ⲉ-, *B* ϩⲉⲛⲍ ϩⲁ-) προσάγ.; Ez 11 22 ἐχ. gen; Va 57 123 ⲍ. ⲉ. ⲉⲡϫⲱⲕ ⲉⲃⲟⲗ φθάνειν πρός ; Mor 31 70 *S* ⲛⲧⲉⲣⲉϥϩ. ⲉ. ⲉⲣⲟϥ, Gu 80 *S* ϩϥ.† ⲉ. ⲉⲣⲟⲛ, AM 11 ⲁⲅⲥ. ⲉ. ⲉⲧⲡⲟⲗⲓⲥ, Aeg 6 ⲁⲥⲍ. ⲉ. ⲉⲙⲓⲥⲓ, C 89 205 ⲁϥⲍ. ⲉ.ϯ ⲙⲡⲉϥⲡⲛⲁ̅; tr (mostly *S* & refl): Hos 12 6 (BHom 60, *B* ⲍ. ϩⲁ-, *A* diff) ἐγγίζ. πρός, 2 Kg 20 16 ἐγ. ἕως, Ac 22 6 (*B* ⲍ. ⲉ-) ἐγ. dat, Lev 2 8 (*B* ⲑⲣⲟ ⲍ.) προσεγ. πρός ; Nu 16 10 (*B* ϣⲱⲡ ⲉ-) προσάγειν, Pro 24 15 ϩⲉⲛⲧ- (var ⲟⲡ-, *A* ⲧϩⲛⲟ)π. dat ; Ge 48 10 (*B* ⲑⲣⲟ ⲍ.) περιλαμβάνειν ; PS 357 ⲁⲥϩⲛⲧⲥ ⲉ. ⲉⲣⲟϥ,TstAb 251 *B* he said ϭⲟⲡⲧⲟⲩ ⲉ. ⲉⲣⲟⲓ;   ⲉⲥ. ⲡ-: Ez 1 15† ἐχ. gen.

—— nn m *B, nearness*: Ps 139 6 ⲡⲥ. ⲡⲱⲁⲡⲙⲱⲓⲧ (*S* ϩⲏⲡ) ἐχόμενα ; He 9 22 ⲕⲁⲧⲁ ⲟⲩϩ. (*SF*=Gk) σχεδόν.

ⲁⲧⲍ. *unapproachable*: FR 124 *B* ⲡⲓⲁ. ⲉⲣⲟϥ;   ⲁⲧⲙϩ ϩ., ⲍ.: P 44 48 *S* ⲟⲩⲁ. ⲉⲣⲟϥ · ⲁⲑⲟⲕⲧⲟⲥ (ἄθικ.); TEuch 2 272 *B* ἀπρόσιτος.

ⲣⲉϥϩⲛⲧ† *S*: Sa 15 8 ⲣ. ⲉⲡⲡⲉⲑⲟⲟⲩ (var ⲣⲉϥϩⲁⲥⲧⲩ better) κακόμοχθος.

ϫⲓⲛⲍ. *B, act of approaching*: BSM 49 ⲡⲁϫ. ⲉⲣⲱⲧⲉⲛ.

ϩⲉⲛⲉⲉⲧⲉ, -ⲧⲏ², ϩⲉⲛⲉⲧⲉ³, -ⲛⲧⲉ⁴, -ⲉⲧⲏ⁵, -ⲏⲧⲓ⁶, ϩⲏⲛⲉⲧⲉ⁷, -ⲛⲧⲉ⁸, -ⲛⲏⲧⲉ⁹ *S* nn f ⲏⲥⲗⲓⲁ (cf ⲡⲟⲛⲧⲉ) *monastery* of monks or nuns : Z 295, 320 μοναστήριον, R 1 4 14² *monasterium*, C 99 134=C 89 24 ⲙⲟⲛⲁⲥ., ib 99 218 =ib 89 33 *B* & Gk μονή, ib 100 304² μ., ib 99 112²= 89 22 *B* ⲙⲟⲛⲏ, ib 99 230 ⲧⲕⲉϣⲙ[ⲟⲩⲛⲉ ⲛ]ϩ. ⲛⲧⲥⲟⲟⲩ- ϩⲥ=ib 89 57 ⲙ., JA '75 5 244 ϩ. (var R 1 5 15 ⲙ.); Z 347 = MG 25 219 *B* ⲁϩⲏⲧ κοινόβιον ; PO 4 579 ⲡⲣⲟ ⲙⲡⲙⲟⲛⲁⲥ. = ib ⲡⲣⲟ ⲛϩ., Mor 37 28 ϩ. of Romanus called also ⲕⲟⲓⲛⲟⲃⲓⲟⲛ, ⲗⲁⲅⲣⲁ, ⲙⲟⲛⲁⲥ., J 106 135 ϩ. = ib 133 ⲙⲟⲛⲁⲥ., Pcod 37 ⲛϩ. (var ⲛⲥⲟⲟⲩϩⲥ), Mor 51 33 ⲛⲉϥⲥⲟⲟⲩϩⲥ...ⲉⲧⲉⲡⲁⲓⲡⲉ...ⲛⲉϥϩ.; ShWess 9 121 bequests to ⲑ.², 123 (same MS) ⲑ.⁴, Miss 8 5 ⲧⲏⲟϭ ⲛϩ. of Pbau, Mun 62 ϩ.⁵ of Pachom, Miss 4 648 ⲑ. of Shenoute, Lant 68 17 ⲑ.⁴ of Siut, ShA 2 44 ϩⲉⲛ- ⲕⲉⲉⲓⲟⲧⲉ ⲛϩ., Miss 4 738 ⲡⲉⲓⲱⲧ ⲛϩ., HT Z 394 οἰκο- νόμος of ⲛϩ.², JSch 43 προεστώς of ⲑ., Ryl 253 priest ϩⲓⲑ.⁹, BM 1031 ἱερεύς of ⲑ.⁷,Tur ostr 5980 δίκαιον of ⲑ.³, ST 436 ⲑ.³, CO 294 ϩ.⁶;   of nuns : Z 346 ϩ. ⲙⲡⲁⲣⲑⲉⲛⲟⲥ μονασ. ; Sh(Besa)BMOr 8810 493 ϩ.², Miss 4 748 man to ⲡⲙⲟⲛⲁⲥ., woman to ⲑ. ⲡⲙⲟ- ⲛⲁⲭⲏ, ib 720 sim, BIF 5 10 ⲧⲙⲁⲁⲩ ⲛⲑ., Osir p 41 sim, JKP 2 38 ⲑ.⁸. On ⲏⲥⲗⲓⲁ v TT 182.

ϩⲟⲛⲧⲉ *S* nn f, meaning unknown : PMich 3599 ⲁⲛⲟⲕ ⲉⲓϣⲱⲡ [   ]ⲉ ⲙⲛⲑⲟⲛⲧⲉ ⲙⲛϩⲣⲱⲃ ⲛⲓⲙ[.

ϩⲁⲛⲧⲟⲩⲥ DM   v ⲁⲛⲑⲟⲩⲥ.

ϩ(ⲉ)ⲛⲧⲟⲩ *SA²*, ϩⲏⲡ *S* nn m, *Hindu, Indian*: ⲧⲡⲟⲗⲓⲥ ⲛⲡϩ., ⲧⲙⲛⲧⲉⲣⲟ ⲛⲡⲉϩⲏⲡ. (KKS 5), ⲡⲣⲣⲟ

ⲡⲉⲡϩ. (S Hel 66), ⲧⲭⲱⲣⲁ ⲛⲡϩ. (Mani K 15), ⲡⲕⲁϩ ⲛⲡϩ. (ib 184).

ϩⲁⲛⲁⲧⲟⲟⲩⲓ, *B*   v ϩⲧⲟⲟⲩⲉ.

ϩⲛⲁ(ⲁ)ⲩ, ϩⲛⲁⲟⲩ, ϩⲛⲟ(ⲟ)ⲩ *S*, ϩⲛⲁ(ⲟ)ⲩⲉ *A*(or ? pl), ϩⲛⲟ (cf Till § 14), -ⲱ *SA*, ϩⲛⲉ *A*(once), ϩⲛⲉ(ⲉ)ⲩ, ϩⲉⲛⲉⲟⲩ, ϩⲛⲓⲟⲩ, ϩⲉⲉ(ⲟ)ⲩ *F* nn m **I** *vessel, pot, recep- tacle*: Ge 43 11, Is 30 14 (*F*=Gk), Lam 4 2 S*F*, Mt 13 48 (*F* do, all *B* ⲙⲟⲕⲓ) ἀγγεῖον, Ez 4 9 (*B* ⲥⲕⲉⲩⲟⲥ), Am 8 1 *SA*(*B* ⲙ.) ἄγγος ; Ex 24 6 (*B*=Gk), Pro 9 2 (*AB* do) κρατήρ ; Nu 7 13 (*B* do) τρυβλίον ; Z 317 ληκύθιον = MG 25 231 *B* ⲕⲛⲉⲓ ; Ps 2 9 (*B*=Gk), Jo 19 29 (*A²* ⲡⲕⲉⲉⲡ, *B* ⲙ.) σκεῦος ; 1 Kg 26 11 φακός ; Nu 4 7 ϩ. ⲛⲟⲩⲱⲧⲛ σπονδεῖον ; Mk 14 3 ϩ. ⲛⲁⲗⲁⲃⲁⲥ- ⲧⲣⲟⲛ (*B* do) ἀλάβ. ; Tri 303 ⲟⲩϩ. ⲛⲃⲗϫⲉ .ⳡⳑ; PS 370 ⲡⲉϩ. ⲛⲏⲣⲡ (cf 369 ⲁⲩⲧⲓⲟⲛ), ShRyl 68 270 ⲛⲉϩ. made by potter, ShC 42 83 ⲟⲩϩⲛⲟ ⲛⲥⲟϩⲟ, ShA 1 218 ϩⲛⲟ ⲛⲉⲓⲁ ϭⲓⲝ, BM 341 120 ⲡⲉϩ. ⲙⲙⲟⲟⲩ, ib 606 *F* ⲟⲩϩⲛ- ⲉⲉⲩ ⲛϩⲏⲙϫ, Kr 225 *F* ⳉ ⲡⲣⲉⲡⲉⲟⲩ ⲛⲏⲣⲡ, BM 706 *F* sim ϩⲛⲓⲟⲩ, Kr 22 *F* & BM 709 *F* sim ϩⲉⲉ(ⲟ)ⲩ, Ryl 238 ⲟⲩϩⲛⲟϭ ⲛϩ. ⲛⲃⲁⲣⲱⲧ, ib 186 ϩⲛⲟⲩ ⲛⲣⲟⲙⲉⲧ, BM 1064 ϩⲛⲟⲩ ⲛⲡⲉⲛⲓⲡⲉ ;   as pl : ShA 2 297 ϩⲉⲛϩ. ⲛⲕⲉ- ⲣⲁⲙⲉⲩⲥ, ib 119 wherein clothes kept, P 131⁵ 32 ϣⲟ- ϣⲟⲩ filled with wine ⲛⲥⲉⲥⲱ ϩⲛⲏⲉⲣ., Mor 27 34 ϩ. of wine = BMis 387 ϣⲁ- ϣⲟⲩ, Blake 306 ⲛⲉϩ.ⲉϣⲁ- ⲅⲉⲱ ⲛϩⲏⲧⲟⲩ.

II in general, *thing*, any material object : Nu 35 16, Ps 30 12, Hos 8 8 *A* ϩⲛⲱ, Lu 8 16 (all *B*=Gk) σκ.; Deu 23 19 (*B* ϩⲱⲃ) πρᾶγμα ; Aeg 243 ⲗⲁⲁⲩ ⲛϩ. μηδέν ; Ez 23 14 ϩ. ⲛⲥϩⲁⲓ (*B* ⲥⲕ. ⲛⲥ.) γραφίς (which Ex 32 4 *S* ⲥⲟⲧⲃⲉϥ); Cl 53 2 *A* ϩⲛⲉ (sic MS) ⲛⲟⲩⲱⲧϩ χώνευμα; Is 49 2 ϩ. ⲛⲕⲁ ⲥⲟⲧⲉ (*B* ⲙⲟⲕⲓ)φαρέτρα; ShC 42 38 ⲛⲉϩ. ⲉⲧⲕⲧⲏⲩ ⲉⲡⲉϥⲙⲁⲕϩ (var ϩⲛⲟ), ShViK 9596 187 ⲟⲩϩ. ⲉϩⲡⲟⲥⲉ, ShViK 9815 27 ϩ. ⲛⲟⲩⲱⲡ *key* ; ϩⲛⲟ, -ⲱ: Pro 19 14 *A*(*S* ⲛⲕⲁ) ὕπαρξις, RNC 30 ϩ. ⲛⲓⲙ ⲉⲡⲁϥⲁⲅⲥⲧⲓⲛⲓⲁⲡⲟⲥⲡⲉ ὑπάρχοντα ; ShIF 245 ⲟⲩϩ....ⲉⲅⲉⲟⲅⲟⲙϥ, ShBMOr 8810 410 ⲟⲩⲉⲗⲁ- ⲭⲓⲥⲧⲟⲛ ⲛϩ. ⲛⲟⲩⲱⲙ, ShA 2 2 ⲥⲧⲩⲗⲟⲥ ⲏ ⲛⲧⲟϥ ⲕⲉϩ., ib 346 ϩ. ⲛⲓⲙ ⲉⲧϩⲁⲣⲟⲥ ⲛⲧⲡⲉ, ShC 73 6 ⲟⲩϩ. (var ϩⲛⲁⲁⲅ)...ϣⲁⲣⲉⲡϭⲏⲣⲏⲥ ϭⲱⲣϭ ⲛϩⲏⲧⲩ, ShCai 8007 ϩ. ϩⲟⲗⲱⲥ...ⲏ ϩⲉⲗⲁⲁⲩ ⲛϩⲛⲁⲁⲩ, ShViK 934 222 ⲛⲉϩ. ⲛⲡⲓϣⲉ *blow-pipe*, ShMIF 23 25 ⲛϩ. ⲉⲧⲗⲟϭⲉ *what mad- ness!*, Mun 147 ⲉⲧⲙⲧⲣⲉϥϫⲓ ϩ. ⲛⲡⲡⲉϩⲛⲁⲁⲩ, Kr 162 ϩⲛⲱ ⲛⲣⲟⲙⲛⲧ, ST 117 ϩⲛⲱ ⲛⲃⲏⲛⲧ, J 66 38 ϩⲛⲱ ⲛⲓⲙ ⲉⲛϭⲣⲓⲙⲉ = 76 40 ⲉⲓⲁⲟⲥ;   as pl : Ge 31 37, Nu 18 3, Is 65 4, Nah 2 9 *A* ϩⲛⲁⲟⲩⲅⲉ, Mk 3 27 (all *B*=Gk) σκ., Deu 1 41 *S* ϩ. ⲙⲙⲓϣⲉ (*B*=Gk) σκ. πολεμικόν, Jth 15 11 σκευάσματα ; Pro 1 13 *A* ϩⲛⲁⲅⲉ (*S* ⲛⲕⲁ, *B* do) κτῆσις ; ib 20 25 *A* do (*S* do) τὰ ἴδια ; Ac 27 44 ϩⲉⲛϩ. ⲛⲧⲉ ⲡϫⲟⲓ (*B* ⲉⲛⲭⲁⲓ) τὰ ἀπό τ. πλοίου, Aeg 221 ⲛⲉϩ. of church τὰ τῆς ἐκκλ. ; Zeph 3 7 *A* ϩⲛⲱ ⲛⲓⲙ (*B* ϩⲱⲃ) πάντα ; Nu 22 7 ϩ. ⲛϣⲓⲛⲉ (*B* diff) μαντεία ; Jth 12 1 ϩⲛⲟⲩ ⲛϩⲣⲁⲧ ἀργυρώματα ; 2 Kg 17 28 ϩⲉⲛϩ. ⲛⲉⲗ-

ⲉⲗϣⲟⲅⲱⲟⲩ ἄλφιτον; Sh(Besa) Z 505 ϩⲛⲟ ⲛⲓⲙ ⲉⲩⲡⲁⲧⲁⲙⲓⲟⲟⲩ, ShC 42 50 ϩⲉⲛⲕⲉϩ. like dust (cf Ex 9 9),
ShR 2 3 58 gold, silver & ϩⲉⲛⲕⲉϩ. ⲙⲙⲛⲧⲣⲉϥϭⲁⲡⲁⲧⲁ,
ShMIF 23 15 swords, spears & ϩⲉⲛⲕⲉϩ., ShA 1 259
ⲡⲉⲅϩ. ⲛⲕⲱⲛⲥ, ShP 131⁴ 111 ⲛϩ. ⲛⲕⲱⲗϩ qv, Mor 18
13 ϩⲉⲛϩ. ⲛⲧⲟⲟⲧⲟⲩ like πυξίον (var 19 22 ϩⲉⲛⲥⲕⲉⲟⲥ)
= Miss 4 107 B ⲡⲁⲣⲑⲓ, R 2 4 71 monks ⲁⲛⲟⲅⲁⲥⲥⲉ ⲛ-
ⲡⲉⲅϩ., Pey Gram 165 ⲛⲉϩ. used for torture, CO 467
ⲡⲓϩⲛⲟⲟⲩ ⲉⲧⲥⲏϩ ⲉϯⲃⲗϫⲉ, ib 315 ϩⲛⲛⲁⲟⲩ ⲁϥⲓⲧⲟⲩ,
BM 1064 ⲡⲉϩⲛⲟⲩ ⲛⲛⲉⲛⲓⲡⲉ tools.

    ⲁⲧϩ., ⲙⲛⲧ-, state of being without property: Wess
11 167 ἀκτημοσύνη; ViK 9816 177 ⲧⲙ. as virtue,
opp ⲙⲛⲧⲉϣⲱⲧ.

    ϯ ϩ., pay fee: ShR 2 3 9 ⲛⲧϯ ϩ. ⲛⲡⲉϩⲣⲏⲧⲱⲣ (cf ib
23 ⲧϭⲛⲉ ϩⲣⲏⲧⲱⲣ).

    ϫⲓ ϩⲛⲁⲩ, bring offering, tribute (?): ShC 42 80 =
MIF 23 41 ⲙⲙⲛⲏϣⲉ ⲛⲧⲁⲕ(pagan)ϫⲟⲟⲥ ϫⲉⲥⲉ ϫ. ⲛⲁϥ
(sc? Christ) ⲉⲩϣⲁⲛⲛⲱⲛⲧ ⲡⲁⲓ ⲉϫⲛ ϯⲥⲟ, ib supra sim.
Same?

ϩⲛⲁⲩ B nn m, flowering branch of palm (Schweinf
ArPfl 229): Montp 173 ⲛⲓϩ. · ⲛⲓⲁⲗⲱⲟⲅⲓ اشرب, K
177 ⲛⲓϩ. ·ه·. Cf ⲁⲗⲱⲟⲅⲉ.

ϩⲓⲏⲛϥ F v ϩⲓⲏⲛⲃ.

ϩⲉⲛⲟⲩϥⲉ v ϩⲏ season.

ϩⲛⲱⲱⲣⲉ¹, ϩⲛⲱⲣⲉ², ϩⲛⲟⲣⲉ³ A nn f, fear (SB
mostly ϩⲟⲧⲉ): Jos 2 9¹(Cl), Pro 1 7², Mal 1 6¹ φόβος,
Hab 1 7¹ φοβερός, Pro 1 33 ⲁⲕⲛϩ.² ἀφόβως; Jon 2 4¹
(B ⲣⲟⲟⲩϣ b) μετεωρισμός; ⲁⲧϩ.: Cl 14 2 ϩⲛⲟⲩ-
ⲙⲛⲧⲁⲧϩ.¹ (var⁻) Gk diff; ⲡ ϩ.: Ex 1 17², Pro 14 2¹,
Jo 12 15¹ φοβεῖσθαι; Si 22 23² εὐλαβεῖσθαι; Si 22 18² δειλιᾶν; Pro 3 25² (B ⲛⲟⲩϣⲛ) πτόησις; El 46 ⲁⲓⲣ ϩ.¹ ⲛⲡϣⲁ, ib 76 ⲥⲉⲛⲁⲣ ϩ.², TU 43 3
ⲙⲛⲣ ϩ.³, ib 23 ⲉⲧⲉⲧⲓⲣ ϩ.³ ⲉⲛ ϩⲛⲧϥ; ⲣⲉϥⲣ ϩ.²:
Mic 7 2 εὐσεβής; ϯ ϩ.¹: Nah 2 11 ἐκφοβεῖν. Cf
AZ 68 57.

ϩⲟⲛϩⲉⲛ, ϩⲉⲛϩⲉⲛ-, ϩⲉⲛϩⲱⲛ⸗ B(for ϩⲉⲛϩⲱⲛⲧ Lu
6 38 l ⲛⲉϩⲛⲱⲛⲧ Cat 132) vb intr, bid(S mostly ϩⲱⲛ):
Ps 32 9, Lam 3 37 ἐντέλλεσθαι; Va 57 10 ⲡⲁⲓⲣⲏϯⲛⲉ
ⲉⲧⲁϥϩ. ἐπιτάσσειν; tr: Ge 45 19, Ps 7 7, Lam 2
17(F ϯ ⲁⲛⲥⲓⲙⲓ) ἐντ.; 1 Cor 11 17 (S=Gk) παραγγέλλειν; DeV 2 90 ⲡⲏ ⲉⲧⲁϥϯ ϩ. ⲙⲙⲱⲟⲩ.
    With following preposition. c ⲉ- remoter obj:
Ge 6 22 (S ϩ. ⲉⲧⲛ-), 3 Kg 2 3, Jo 15 14 (S.A² do) ⲉⲛⲧ.
dat; 2 Thes 3 4 (S ⲟⲩⲉϩⲥⲁϩⲛⲉ ⲛ-) παραγ.; MG 25 209
ϩⲱⲃ ⲛⲓⲙⲉⲛ ⲉⲧⲁⲓϩ. ⲙⲙⲟⲟⲩ ⲉⲣⲱⲟⲩ (S Z 344 as Gk)
εἰπεῖν dat; C 86 310 ⲑⲏ ⲉⲧⲁⲅϩⲉⲛϩⲉⲛⲛⲏⲡⲟⲩ ⲉⲣⲟⲥ,
MIE 2 417 ⲡⲁⲓ ⲉⲧⲁⲓϩⲉⲛϩⲱⲛⲕ ⲉⲣⲱⲟⲩ = BAp 123 S
ϩⲟⲛⲟⲩ ⲉⲧⲟⲟⲧⲕ; vbal: Ps 118 4 ⲉⲛⲧ., Deu 15 11
(var dat) ⲉⲛⲧ. inf; AM 253 ⲁϥϩ....ⲉϣⲧⲉⲙⲭⲟⲥ; c
ⲉⲑⲃⲉ-: Is 23 11, He 11 22 ⲉⲛⲧ. περί; AM 204 ⲡⲁⲓ
ⲉⲧⲁⲡⲓⲟⲅⲣⲱⲟⲩ ϩ. ⲉⲑⲃⲏⲧⲟⲩ; c ⲉⲧⲛ-: 3 Kg 17 4,

Jer 43 5, Ac 1 2 ⲉⲛⲧ. dat; Jos 4 8 συντάσ. dat; AM
267 ϩ. ⲉⲧⲟⲧϥ ⲛⲁϫⲓⲗⲗⲁⲥ παρατιθέναι dat; PO 11 326
ⲁϥϩ. ⲉⲧⲟⲧⲟⲩ ⲛⲛⲓⲥⲛⲏⲟⲩ (cf c ⲛ-), AM 261 ⲁϥϩ. ⲉⲧⲟⲧ-
ⲉⲛ ⲉⲑⲑⲉⲁⲣⲓⲟⲥ; tr: TstAb 228 ϩ. ⲙⲙⲱⲟⲩ...ⲉⲧⲟⲧⲕ,
BSM 108 sim ⲉⲧⲟⲧⲟⲩ ⲛⲛⲉϥⲁⲡⲟⲥⲧⲟⲗⲟⲥ; vbal:
Ac 5 28 (S=Gk) παραγ. dat inf; c ⲉϫⲉⲛ- Is 13
11 ⲉⲛⲧ. dat; ⲉϩⲣⲏⲓ ⲉϫ.: Jer 28 27 παραγ. ἐπί; c
ⲛ- dat: Ge 32 4, Dan 3 30, Jo 14 31 (A² ϯ ⲁⲧⲛ-) ⲉⲛⲧ.
dat; Jer 26 14 (S ϫⲓ ⲡⲟⲩⲱ ⲉϩⲣⲁⲓ ⲉ-) παραγ. εἰς, 1 Cor
7 10 (S=Gk) π. dat; Ez 24 18 ἐπιτάσ. dat; Mt 9 30
ἐμβριμᾶσθαι dat; BSM 50 ⲙⲫⲣⲏϯ ⲉⲧⲁϥϩ. ⲡⲱⲟⲩ, PO
11 326 ⲁϥϩ. ⲛⲛⲓⲥⲛⲏⲟⲩ (cf c ⲉⲧⲛ-); tr: Lev 27 34
ⲉⲛⲧ. acc dat; C 43 154 ⲡⲓⲟⲩⲁϩⲥⲁϩⲛⲓ ⲉⲧⲁϥϩ. ⲙⲙⲟϥ
ⲛⲱⲧⲉⲛ; + ⲉ-: 3 Kg 8 58 ⲁϥϩ. ⲛⲛⲉⲛⲓⲟϯ ⲉⲣⲱⲟⲩ ⲉⲛⲧ.
acc dat; Ac 16 18 ϯϩ. ⲛⲁⲕ...ⲉⲓ ⲉⲃⲟⲗ (S=Gk) παραγ.
dat inf; C 43 124 ϯϩ. ⲛⲁⲕ ⲉⲑⲣⲉⲕ-; c ⲛⲧⲉⲛ-: Nu
34 2, Mt 4 6 ⲉⲛⲧ. dat; 2 Thes 3 6 (S=Gk) παραγ. dat;
Jos 4 3 συντάσ. dat; Va 61 108 ϯⲛⲁⲓϣ ϩ. ⲛⲧⲟⲧϥ ⲛϩⲗⲓ.

   —— nn m, command: Is 29 13 (S ϩⲱⲛ), Col 2 22
ἔνταλμα; Ac 16 24 (S=Gk) παραγγελία; Deu 15 2
(S ⲇⲟ) πρόσταγμα; Va 57 9 παραίνεσις; ib 58 181
νομοθεσία; C 86 354 ⲡⲣⲟⲥⲧⲁⲅⲙⲁ, ϩ.

ϩⲱⲛϫ S(rare)F, ⳙ, B, ϩⲱⲛϫⲉ, ϩⲁⲛϫ, ϩⲟ., ϩⲱϫ,
ϩⲱⲛϭ F vb intr, entreat, exhort: Va 57 72 ⲉⲛ ϯⲣⲟ (ⲉ)ⲛϫ.
ⲉⲛⲧⲱⲃϩ, ib 61 94 = Mor 25 12 S ⲕⲱⲣϣ, Cai 8038-39-
42 F ϯⲱⲛϫⲉ ϯⲡⲁⲣⲁⲕⲁⲗⲓ, CMSS 45 F ϯⲣⲟⲗⲟⲕⲱⲧⲥⲓ
... ϩⲁⲛϫ (ⲛ)ⲛϫⲓⲧⲉ ⲛⲧⲁⲁⲧϥ (sic l, imperat?); c
ⲉ- obj: Ac 2 40 (S ⲥⲟⲛⲥ), ib 16 39 (S=Gk) παρακαλεῖν; ib 27 22 (S ϫⲟ) παραινεῖν; BIF 14 170 S ⲁⲓϩ.
ⲉⲡⲁⲉⲓⲱⲧ saying Guarantee me, Rec 6 173 ⲁⲓⳙ. ⲉⲣⲟϥ
ⲉⲑⲣⲉϥⲧⲁⲙⲟⲓ = BMar 209 S ⲥⲱⲣϣ, Mor 41 224 S
ⲁⲧϩ. ⲉⲣⲟⲟⲩ ⲉⲧⲣⲉⲩⲟⲩⲱⲙ, FR 100 ϯϯϩⲟ ⲟⲩⲟϩ ϯⳙ.
ⲉⲧⲉⲕⲙⲉⲧⲁⲅⲁⲑⲟⲥ help me, AM 288 ⲉⲩϯⳙ. ⲉⲛⲛⲟⲩϫⲓ
ⲛϩⲏⲧ, BM 583 12 F ϩⲟ. ⲉⲡⲁⲉⲓⲱⲧ ⲛⲃⲧⲁⲛⲉ, ib 22 ϩⲟ.,
BM 595 13 F ϯϩ.ⲉ ⲗⲁⲕ ⲛⲡⲉⲗⲉⲗ ⲛⲁⲱⲃⲉϩ, CMSS 39
F ⲁⲓϩⲱϫ ⲗⲁⲕ; c ϩⲓϫⲛ-: Mor 24 14 F Michael
hath naught to do ⲛⲥⲁϩ. ϩⲓϫⲛⲛⲉϥⲯⲩⲭⲁⲅⲓ = ib 23 21
S ⲥⲟⲛⲥ.

   —— nn B, entreaty: C 86 121 ϩⲓⲧⲉⲛⲟⲩⲙⲛϣ ⲛ⳧.
he (agreed to) appoint him.

ϩⲁⲡ SBO, ϩⲟⲡ S(ostr), ϩⲉⲡ A A²F, ⲉⲡ A² nn m,
judgment, inquest: Deu 4 1 SB, Pro 1 3 S.AB, Jo 9 39
S A²B, Ro 11 33 SBF, 1 Cor 11 29 B(S=Gk), C 89
80 B ⲓⲛⲓ ⲛⲏⲓ ⲙⲡⲁⲓϩ. ⲉⲑⲣⲓϥⲟⲗϫⲧ κρίμα, Ro 8 1 B(S
ⲧϭⲁⲉⲓⲟ) κατάκρ., Dan 4 21 B σύγκρ., Ge 18 19 SB,
Is 32 1 SBF, He 10 27 B(SF=Gk) κρίσις, Ro 2 5 ϩ.
ⲙⲙⲉ SB δικαιοκρισία; Lev 26 25 SB, Ac 28 4 B(S
ⲙⲡϣⲁ) δίκη, Ro 12 19 S(B ϭⲓ ⲙⲡϣⲓϣ) ἐκδίκησις;
Ac 23 29 S(B diff) ἔγκλημα; ib 25 20 S(B=Gk) ζήτησις; Mus 40 42 S(RegPach) ⲉⲓⲣⲉ ⲛⲁϥ ⲕⲁⲧⲁ ⲡⲉⲓϩ.
increpari; PS 50 S ⲉϥⲧⲁϩⲟⲟⲩ ⲛϭⲓ ⲡⲉⲕϩ., ib 365 ϫⲓ
ⲍⲱⲣⲟⲡ ⲉϫⲙ⳧. ⲙⲙⲉ, ShA 2 269 S ϯⲟⲩⲁⲁⲃ ⲉⲃⲟⲗ

ϩⲙⲡⲉⲧⲛϩ., BMis 451 *S* ⲛⲧⲅⲙⲟⲟⲥ ⲛⲥⲉⲧⲙ ⲡⲉⲡϩ.,
BM 475 *S* ⲡⲁⲣ. ⲕⲏ ⲙⲡⲭ̅ⲥ̅, CO 297 *S* ϩⲱⲛ ⲉⲡϩ. ⲉⲧ-
ⲉⲣⲉⲡⲛ̅ⲉ̅ ⲛⲁⲡⲧⲅ ⲉⲃⲟⲗ, ST 192 26 *S* ⲡⲁⲣ. ϭⲉⲉⲧ ⲉⲣⲟⲓ
ⲡⲙⲁⲅ, PBu 29 *S* ⲃⲱⲕ ⲉⲡϩ. ⲛⲙⲙⲁϥ, BKU 1 125 *S*
ⲃⲱⲕ ⲛⲓⲣⲱⲙⲉ ⲁⲡⲣⲟⲡ ⲡⲉⲙⲁⲓ, AZ 13 111 *S* ⲧⲁⲕⲉ ⲡϩ.
ⲡⲟⲩⲭⲏⲣⲁ, DeV 2 90 *B* ⲁϥϭⲁϫⲓ ⲡⲉⲙⲁϥ ⲡⲟⲩϩ. pronounced judgment on him (*cf* Jer 52 9 ϫⲉⲡ-), Hor
82 *O* ⲛⲧϥⲛⲁⲟⲩ ⲁϩ.

ⲁⲧϩ. *S, without* (going to) *law,* in undertakings to
deliver, pay &c : Ryl 159 20 will pay 6 *solidi* ⲛⲁ. ⲛⲁⲧ-
ⲡⲟⲙⲟⲥ ⲛⲁⲧⲗⲁⲁⲅ ⲡⲣⲱⲅ ⲛⲁⲙⲫⲓⲃⲟⲗⲉⲓⲁ, BM 1028 n,
PLond 4 500, BM 1061 sim. *Cf* δίχα πάσης ἀμφι-
βολίας κ. κρίσεως κ. δίκης (Preisigke *Wbuch* 72), ἄνευ
δίκης κ. κρίσεως (*ib* 840).

ⲉⲓⲣⲉ ⲙⲡϩ., -ⲡⲁⲣ. &c, ⲣ ϩ. *S A A²BF, give judgment,
avenge, go to law* : 1 Kg 2 10 *S*, Jer 23 5 *SB* κρίμα
ποιεῖν, Ps 9 4 *SB*, Jo 5 27 *A²B*(*S* = Gk) κρίσιν ποι.,
EpJer 63 *F*(*B* ϯ ϩ.) κρίσ. κρίνειν; Ps 42 1 *S*(*B* ϭⲓ ⲙⲡ-
ϣⲓⲙ) δίκην δικάζειν; PS 93 *S* ⲁⲣⲓ ⲡⲁϩ. ⲙⲡⲁⲕⲉⲇⲁ,
ShBor 300 77 *S* ⲣ ϩⲉⲡϩ. ⲙⲙⲉ, Mor 40 27 *S* ⲣ ⲡⲁϩ.
(var *ib* 39 37 ⲉⲣ ⲡⲁϩⲓ ⲕⲉⲇⲁ) = C 43 56 *B* ϭⲓ ⲙⲡⲁⲙ-
ⲡϣ.; ⲥ ⲙⲡ-, ⲡⲉⲙ-: Z 341 *S* ϯⲡⲁⲣ ⲡⲁϩ. ⲛⲙⲙⲁϥ
ἐκδίκησιν ποι. ἀπό; AZ 21 154 *S* ⲡⲛⲉ̅ ⲣ ⲡⲉϥϩ. ⲙⲡ-
ⲛⲉⲛⲧⲁⲅⲣⲱⲧⲉ̅ ⲙⲙⲟϥ, PGol 47 *A²* ⲉⲕⲁⲣ ⲡⲁⲉⲡ ⲙⲡ-,
BM 1223 *A* sim ϩⲉϥ, C 43 190 *B* ⲁⲣⲓ ⲡϩ. ⲙⲡⲁⲥⲡⲟϥ
ⲡⲉⲙⲫⲏ ⲉⲧⲁϥⲫⲟⲛϩ, ST 369 *S* ⲉϣⲱⲡⲉ ⲥⲟⲩϣ ⲉⲣ ⲫ.
ⲛⲙⲙⲁⲓ ⲙⲁⲣⲉⲥⲉⲓ; ⲥ ⲛ-gen or dat: Ps 145 7 *SB*
κρίμα ποι. dat, 2 Kg 8 15 *S*(var ϩⲛ-) do ἐπί, Ps 139
13 *B*(*S* ⲣ ⲕⲉⲇⲁ) κρίσ. ποι. gen; Jud 6 31 *S* δικάζ. ὑπέρ
(var περί), Cai 8010 1 He delayed not to ⲣ ⲡϩ. ⲛⲧⲉϥ-
ϣⲉⲗⲉⲉⲧ, Bor 267 103 *S* ⲉⲓⲣⲉ ⲙⲡϩ. ⲛⲛⲉⲡⲧⲁⲅⲡⲉⲣⲧ
ⲡⲉⲩⲥⲛⲟϥ; ⲥ ⲟⲩⲧⲉ-: Jer 7 5 *B* κρίσ. ποι. ἀνὰ μέσον; ⲥ ϫⲁ-: Jude 15 *B*(*S* ⲉϫⲛ-) κρίσ. ποι. κατά; ⲥ
ϩⲛ-, ϫⲉⲛ-: Ps 149 9 *SB*, Ez 28 26 *B*(*S*=Gk) κρίσ. ποι.
ἐν; ⲉⲃⲟⲗ ϩⲛ-: Lu 18 3 *S*(*B* ϭⲓ ⲙⲡ. ⲡⲉⲙ-) ἐκδ. ἀπό.

ϯ ϩ. *S A A²BF, give judgment* : Ps 57 2 *B*(*S*=Gk),
Mt 7 2 *SB*, Ro 2 1 *B*(*S* = Gk) κρίνειν, Ez 23 25 *SB*
κρί. διδόναι, Is 35 4 *B*(*SF* ⲧⲱⲃⲉ ⲡⲟⲩϩ.) κρίσ. ἀντα-
ποδ.; TU 20 5 6 *S* ⲡⲉⲧϯ ϩ. ⲉϥϫⲟⲟⲙⲉ, DeV 2 20 *B*
ⲁⲕϯ ϩ. ϫⲉⲟⲅⲣⲱⲃ ⲉϥⲙⲡϣⲁ ⲁⲓⲡⲉ *didst ordain, esteem,*
ManiK 80 *A²* ⲡⲉⲧϯ ϩ. ⲡⲟⲩϩ. ⲙⲙⲛⲉ, BM 1072 *S* ⲡ-
ⲧⲁⲓⲧⲓ ⲡⲓϩ. ⲛⲙⲙⲁϥ (*sc* colleague); ⲥ ⲉ-: Ps 50 4
S(*B* ϭⲓ ϩ.), Ac 23 3 *B*(*S* = Gk), Ro 14 13 *BF*(Mus
49 198, *S* do) κρίν. acc, Jo 16 11 *B*(*S* ⲧϭ., *A²* ⲧⲁⲭⲟ)
κρίν. gen, Eccl 3 17 *F*(*S*=Gk) κρίν. σύν, ZNTW 24
90 *F* ⲡⲉⲅϯ ϩ. ⲉⲗⲁϥ κρίνεσθαι, 1 Cor 4 4 *B*(*S* do) ἀνα-
κρίν. acc, Ps 81 1 *S*(PS)*B* διακ. acc, Dan 7 22 *B* κρί.
διδ. dat ; 1 Kg 8 5 *S* δικάζ. acc, Jud 6 31 *S* δ. dat ;
Jth 8 16 *S* διαιτεῖν; Ac 12 21 *S*(*B* ⲥⲁϫⲓ ⲡⲉⲙ-) δημη-
γορεῖν πρός; ShA 2 282 *S* ϯⲡⲁϯ ϩ. ⲉⲣⲱⲧⲛ, ManiK
51 *A²* ⲁⲧϯ ϩ. ⲁⲣⲁⲅ, DeV 1 120 *B* ⲉϥⲛⲁϯ ϩ. ⲉϯⲟⲓⲕⲟⲅ-
ⲙⲉⲡⲏ, Kr 164 *F* have chosen them ⲡⲥⲉϯ ϩ. ⲉⲗⲁⲡ,
C 43 45 *B* ϯ ϩ. ⲉⲣⲱⲟⲩ ⲉϥⲙⲓⲟⲩ; *vbal:* Is 41 6 *B*(*S*

diff), Ac 25 25 *B*(*S*=Gk) κρίν. inf; ⲥ ⲉϫⲛ-: BMis
126 *S* ϯ ϩ. ⲉⲭⲙⲡⲉϥⲭⲡⲓⲟ; ⲥ ⲛ-dat: Ps 34 24 *BF*
(Mus 49 180, *S*=Gk) κρίν. acc, *ib* 71 1 *SB*, Ap 20 4
SB κρί. διδ. dat, Jud 6 32 *S* δικάζ. ἐν; ⲥ ⲛⲉⲙⲏϯ
ⲛ-: Ez 34 22 *B*(*S*=Gk) κρίν. ἀνὰ μέσον; ⲥ ⲟⲩⲃⲉ-
Jer 27 34 *B* κρίν. πρός; ⲥ ⲟⲩⲧⲉ-: 1 Kg 24 13 *SB*
δικάζ. ἀνὰ μ.; ⲁⲧϯ ϩ. *B, not judging*: Cat 131
Christ ⲟⲓ ⲛⲁ. ⲉϩⲗⲓ & forgiving every one; Ja 3 17
(*S* ⲉⲙⲉⲥϫⲓⲁⲕⲣⲓⲛⲉ) ἀδιάκριτος *non judicans*; ⲙⲁ
ⲛϯ ϩ., *place of judgment*: Ex 21 6 *B*(*S* = Gk), 1 Cor
6 2 *SB* κριτήριον; Jer 15 17 *B*(*S* = Gk), Mk 15 1 *B*
(*SF* do) συνέδριον; BHom 27 *S* δικαστήριον; Ac 18
12 *B*(*S*=Gk) βῆμα; Mor 30 3 *F* ⲙⲁϯ ϩ. (*sic*); ⲣⲉϥ-
ϯ ϩ., *judge*: Deu 1 16 *SB*, Is 33 22 *SBF*, Hos 7 7
AB κριτής; Jos 23 2 *SB*, Ac 7 27 *SB* δικαστής; PS
175 *S*, C 86 291 *B*, ManiH 79 *A²*; ⲉⲣ ⲡ.: Mt 12 27
B(*S* ϣⲱⲡⲉ ⲡⲣ.) κριτ. εἶναι; ⲙⲉⲧⲣⲉϥϯ ϩ.: DeV 2 54
B among vices; ϭⲓⲡ-, ϫⲓⲛϯ ϩ.: BM 214 *S* ϯ ϩ.
ⲉⲣⲟ[ⲡ] ⲕⲁⲧⲁ ⲧϭ. ⲁⲅⲱ ⲕⲁⲧⲁ ⲧϫⲓⲛ[ⲉⲓ ?] ⲉⲧϥⲡⲏⲅ ⲙ-
ⲙⲟ[ⲥ], Va 58 137 *B* ϯϫ. ⲙⲙⲏⲓ.

ϩⲓⲟⲩⲓ ⲉⲡϩ. *BF, cast to law, condemn*: Su 48, Ro 2
1 (var ⲙ-, *S* ⲧϭⲁⲓⲟ), MG 25 217 ⲙⲡⲉⲣϩⲓ ϩⲗⲓ ⲉⲡϩ. κα-
τακρίν.; Ps 93 21 (*S* do) καταδικάζ.; AM 125 ⲡⲓⲣⲱⲃ
ⲉⲧⲉⲕϩⲓⲟⲩⲓ ⲙⲡⲉⲛϫⲉⲙϣⲓ ⲉⲡϩ. ⲡ̅ϩⲏⲧϥ; qual: 1 Cor
4 9 (K 243) ἐπιθανάτιος; MartIgn 876 (*S* R 1 4 69
ⲧϭⲁⲉⲓⲏⲅ) ὑπόδικος; TEuch 2 352 ⲁⲡⲟⲛ...ⲉⲧϩⲱⲟⲩⲓ
ⲉⲡϩ. κατάκριτος; as nn: DeV 2 50 ⲧⲁϩⲣⲟ ⲙⲡⲓϩ.
ⲉⲡϩ. *uphold condemnation*; ϩⲓⲟⲩⲓ ⲙⲡϩ. sim: Ro
8 34 (*S* do) κατακ.; Lam 3 36, Mt 12 7 *F*(*S* do, *B* ϯ
ϩ. ⲉ-) καταδ.; qual: Va 68 168 ϯϩⲱⲟⲩⲓ ⲙⲡϩ. κατακ.; Cat 29; as nn: Ro 5 18 (*S* do) κατάκριμα;
DeV 2 21 free me from ⲫⲓⲁϩⲃⲉϥ ⲙⲡⲓϩ. ⲙⲡϩ.; ⲁⲧϩ.
ⲉⲡϩ.: CaiEuch 453 may I stand ϫⲉⲛⲟⲩⲙⲉⲧⲁⲧϩⲣⲓⲧⲧ
ⲉⲡϩ. ἀκατακρίτως.

ϫⲓ, ϭⲓ ϩ. *S A A²BF, receive judgment, go to law* (*cf*
κρίμα αἴρειν ROC 14 366): Job 35 14 *SB*, Ps 50 6 *B*
(*S* ϯ ϩ. ⲉ-), Is 43 26 *SB* κρίνεσθαι, Deu 25 1 *S*(*B* ⲓ
ⲉⲡϩ.) εἰς κρίσιν προσέρχεσθαι; Va 58 155 ⲉⲅϭⲓ ϩ. ....
ⲉϣⲧⲉⲙϯ ⲙϥⲏ ⲉⲧⲁϥϭⲓⲧϥ; ϫⲓ, ϭⲓ ⲡⲟⲩϩ.: Ro 13
2 *SB*, Mk 12 40 *BF*(Mor 46 63, *S* = Gk) κρί. λαμ-
βάνεσθαι; 2 Thes 1 9 *SB* δίκην τίνειν; ϭⲓ ϩ. ⲉϫⲉⲛ-:
ROC 17 402 *B* ϭⲓ ϩ. ⲉ. ϯϥⲅⲥⲓⲥ; ⲥ ⲙⲡ-, ⲡⲉⲙ-:
Job 9 3 *S*(*B* ⲟⲩⲃⲉ-), Mt 5 40 *SB* κρίνεσθαι dat, Hos
2 2 *S*(ShA 2 293)*AB* κ. πρός; Jude 9 *S*(*B* diff) διακ.
dat, Ez 20 36 *SB* δ. πρός; Deu 33 7 *S*(*B* ⲉⲣ ϫⲓⲁⲕⲣⲓ-
ⲡⲓⲛ) δ. dat, Si 8 17 *S* δικάζ. μετά; Ac 23 30 *S*(*B* as
Gk) λέγειν πρός; Mt 5 25 *S* ⲡⲉⲧϫ. ⲙⲡ-(*B*=Gk) ἀντίδικος; CO 185 *S* ⲁⲓϫⲓ ϩⲟⲡ ⲡⲙ(ⲙ)ⲁⲕ ϩⲁⲣⲟⲟⲩ, Aeg
18 *B* ⲉⲡⲧ ⲉϩⲟⲩⲛ ⲉϭⲓ ϩ. ⲡⲉⲙⲏⲓ, ManiH 30 *A²* ⲁⲓϭⲓ ϩ.
ⲙⲛⲛⲓⲙ, Ryl 415 *F* ⲧⲉⲕⲯⲩⲭⲏ ϫⲓ ϩ. ⲙⲉⲧⲱⲓ; ⲥ
ⲟⲩⲃⲉ-: Ez 22 2 *SB* κρίν. acc, Job 31 13 *SB* κ. πρός,
Eccl 6 10 *F*(*S* ⲙⲡ-) κ. μετά, Job 11 3 *SB* ἀντικ. dat,
Lu 12 58 *S*(*B*=Gk) ἀντίδικος; ShBMOr 8810 497

S ϫⲓ ϩ. ⲟⲩⲃⲏ ⲛ ⲡⲁⲙⲉ;   ⲥ ϩⲁ-: Mor 50 51 *S* ϫⲓ
ϩ. ϩⲁⲣⲟⲥ ϩⲁⲧⲙⲡⲭ̅ⲥ̅;   ⲥ ϩⲓ-: 1 Cor 6 1 *SB* κρίν.
ἐπί; Z 311 *S* went to ϫⲓ ϩ. ϩⲓⲟⲩⲡⲟⲥ ⲡⲉⲗⲗⲟ δικάζεσ-
θαι πρός;   as nn: Si 29 22 (19) *S* κρίσις; Pro 23
29 *SA* ἀηδία;   ⲣⲉϥϫⲓ ϩ.: ShZ 600 *S* ⲛⲣ. called
δικανικός *advocates.*

ϩⲁⲁⲡ *F* v ϩⲟⲡ.

ϩⲓⲡ *B* v ϩⲓⲃⲱⲓ.

ϩⲟⲡ[1] *SB*, ϩⲟⲟⲡ[2] *S*, ϩⲁⲡ *A*[2], ϩⲁⲁⲡ *F*, ϩⲁⲡ- *SA*[2] nn
m, *feast, marriage feast, bride-chamber:* Jud 14 10 *S*[2],
2 Kg 13 27 *S*[2], 3 Kg 3 15 *S*[1], Jth 6 21 *S*[2] πότος; EpJer
31 *S*(P 44 114) ϩⲁⲡⲕⲱⲱⲥ (*B* ϫⲉⲓⲡⲡⲟⲡ, *F* diff) περί-
δειπνον ابه (glossed P 43 114 نزول من هدرل
ايسر (l ? ﺛﻴﺎ Sobhy)); Ge 29 22 *B*(*S* ϣⲉⲗⲉⲉⲧ), Mt 22
2 *B*(*S* do) Lu 12 36 *B*(*S* ⲙⲁ ⲛϣ.), ib 14 8 *F*(*S* om,
B ϩⲁⲛϩ., var ϫⲉⲓⲡ.), Ap 19 7 *B*(*S* = Gk) γάμος; R
1 5 32 *S* ϩⲉⲓⲡⲛⲟϭ ⲛⲣ.[1] ⲛⲣⲣⲟ for king's guests, BKU
1 31 8 sim ϩ.[2], R 1 3 46 *S* ⲛⲣ.[2] ⲙⲡⲓⲅⲩⲙⲫⲓⲟⲥ, BSM
22 *B* ⲁⲟⲅⲱⲡ ⲙⲡⲣⲟ ⲙⲡⲓϩ. = BMis 361 *S* ⲛⲅⲩⲙⲫⲱⲛ,
Mani 1 *A*[2] ⲉⲣⲉⲡϩ. ⲡⲁⲣϣ, ib ⲡⲣ.ⲡⲟⲩϭⲉ ⲉϥⲕⲱⲧⲉ ⲁⲡⲓⲱⲧ;   R 1 5 52 *S* ⲉⲓⲣⲉ ⲡⲟⲩϩ.[1] ⲉⲛϭⲱⲃ, PO 14 326 *B*
ⲁⲅⲓⲣⲓ ⲙⲡⲓϩ. ⲉⲣⲟϥ ⲛⲉⲙⲁⲥ, C 86 195 *B* desired to ⲓⲣⲓ
ⲛⲡⲉϥϩ. (*sc* saint's) ⲛⲉⲙⲧⲉϥϣⲉⲣⲓ.

ϩⲱⲡ *SAA*[2]*BF*, ϩⲉⲡ- *SB*, ϩⲁⲡ- *A*[2]*F*, ϩⲟⲡ- *SAA*[2],
ⲅⲱⲡ- DM, ϩⲟⲡ⸗ *SB*, ϩⲁⲡ⸗ *AA*[2]*F*, ϩⲏⲡ† *SAA*[2]*BF* vb
I intr, *be hidden, hide* (*B* often ⲭⲱⲡ): Sa 1 8 *SB*, Mk
7 24 *S*(*B* ⲱⲃϣ) λανθάνειν; Mt 5 14 *S*(*B* ⲭ.), 1 Tim
5 25 *SB* κρύπτειν, Ps 55 6 *S*(*B* do) κατακ.; Job 13 8
S(*B* do) ὑποστέλλειν; ShViK 9750 242 *S* ⲡⲉⲩϣⲛⲟϣ
ⲉⲧⲉⲙⲉϥϩ., Miss 8 159 *S* David's sin ⲛⲁϩ., ManiH 47
A[2] ϩ. opp ⲟⲩⲱⲛϩ;   qual: Bel 13 *B*, Jo 19 38 *S*(*B*
ⲭ.), Ap 2 17 *SB* κρ., 1 Cor 2 7 *SB* ἀποκρ., AM 267 *B*
ⲭⲣⲟϥ ⲉϥϩ. ἐγκ., Deu 15 9 *S*(var ϩⲱⲡ)*B*, Lu 8 17 *SB*
κρυπτός, Pro 9 17 *SAB* κρύφιος, Lam 3 10 *SB* κρυ-
φαῖος, Ps 16 12 *SB* ⲙⲁ ⲉⲧϩ. (*F* ⲡⲡⲉⲧϩ.) ἀπόκρυφος;
2 Cor 4 3 *B*(*S* ϩⲱⲃⲥ) καλύπτειν; Pro 1 6 *SA*(*B* ⲭⲁⲕⲓ)
σκοτεινός; Is 31 6 *SF*(*B* ϣⲏⲕ) βαθύς; 2 Cor 12 4 *S*
(*B* as Gk) ἄρρητος; BMis 354 *S* ⲉⲛϩ. ⲉⲧⲃⲉⲑⲟⲧⲉ,
Mani 1 *A*[2] ⲡⲙⲁⲣⲁⲓⲡⲉ ⲉⲧϩ., MG 25 70 *B* ⲁϩⲟ ⲉⲧϩ.
(var ⲭⲏⲡ), C 86 175 *B* ⲡⲉϥⲃⲁⲗ ϩ. *closed* (?), GriffStu
47 *F* ⲗⲉⲛ ⲉⲧϩ.;   ⲡⲉⲧ-, ⲡⲉⲧϩ.†, *what is hidden*: Mt
13 35 *SBF* κρ., Ps 18 12 *SB* κρύφιος, ib 138 15 *B*(*S*
ϩⲱⲡ nn) κρυφῇ, Si 14 21 *S* ⲡⲉⲥⲡⲉϩ., Mk 4 22 *SBF*
(Mus 49 188) ἀπόκρυφος, Is 29 10 *B*(*S* ⲙⲟⲩⲛⲅ ⲛϭⲓϫ
as if γλυπτά), Ro 2 16 *SB* κρυπτός; Job 19 29 *S*(*B*
= Gk) ἐπικάλυμμα; Ap 2 24 *S*(*B* ϣⲱⲕ) βάθος; Ro
1 20 *S*(*B* as Gk) ἀόρατος; Ps 50 6 *SB* ἄδηλος; PS
299 *S* ⲃⲱⲕ ⲉϩⲟⲩⲛ...ϩⲟⲩⲡⲉϩ., ShC 42 165 *S* ⲕⲣⲓⲛⲉ
ⲛⲁⲡⲉϩ., ib 73 2 *S* evil done ϩⲁⲛⲛⲉϩ., AZ 21 155 *S*
ⲥⲟⲟⲩⲛ ⲛⲡⲉϩ., DeV 2 8 *B* ⲥⲱⲣⲡ ⲛⲡⲏ ⲉⲧϩ., ManiK 16
A[2] ⲛⲛⲡⲉⲧϩ.

II tr: Job 14 13 *S*(*B* ⲭ.), Ps 9 15 *S*(*B* ϩⲱⲃⲥ), Jer
27 2 *F*(Mus 49 174, *B* ⲭ.), Jo 8 59 *SA*[2](*B* do) κρ.,
Is 26 20 *S*(*B* do) ἀποκρ., Lu 1 24 *SB* περικρ.; Pro 10
18 *SA*ϩⲱⲡ- (*B* ϩⲱⲃⲥ) καλ.; BHom 29 *S* ⲉⲛ(ⲛ)ⲁϩⲟⲡⲛ
ⲧⲱⲛ ? καταδύειν; PLond 4 457 *S* will arrest [& de-
liver] refugee ⲁⲭⲣⲟⲡϥ, ManiK 56 *A*[2] ⲁϥϩⲱⲡ ⲧⲉϥ-
ϩⲓⲕⲱⲛ, Ryl 106 57 *S* ϩⲱⲡ ⲡⲉϥⲣⲱ (*sc* vessel's), RE 9
167 *S* ⲁⲅϩⲉⲡ ⲡϭⲱⲃ until to-day, AM 203 *B* ⲁⲩϩⲟⲡⲟⲩ
for fear, Pcod 38 *F* ⲁⲅϩⲁⲡⲟⲩ = *S* ϩⲟⲃⲥⲟⲩ, DM 21 8
ⲅⲱⲡ *p-kke.*

With following preposition.

—— ⲉ-, *from:* Ge 18 17 *S*(*B* ⲉⲃⲟⲗ ϩⲁ-), Job 5 21
S(*B* ⲭ. ⲉⲃ. ϩⲁ-) κρ. ἀπό, Pro 1 11 *SA*(*B* ⲭ. ϫⲉⲛ-)
κρ. εἰς, Job 38 2 *SB* κρ. acc, Ps 30 4 *S*(*B* ⲭ.) κρ. dat,
Mt 11 25 *SB* ἀποκρ. ἀπό; Nu 5 27 *S*(*B* diff), C 99 140
S nothing ⲛⲁϩ. ⲉⲣⲟⲕ = C 89 45 *B* λαν. acc; Lu 24 31
S(*B* as Gk) ἄφαντος γίνεσθαι ἀπό; PS 16 *S* ϯⲛⲁϩⲉⲡ
ⲗⲁⲁⲩ ⲉⲣⲱⲧⲛ ⲁⲛ, ib 111 *S* ϯϩⲟⲙ...ⲛⲡⲉⲥϩ. ⲉⲣⲟⲕ, Sh
MIF 23 33 *S* ⲛϥϩ.† ⲁⲛ ⲉⲛⲥⲁⲃⲉⲟⲩ, Ryl 94 n *S* ⲉⲕⲛⲁ-
ϩⲟⲡⲕ ⲉⲧⲱⲛ ⲉⲟⲩⲙⲙⲉ ⲙⲡⲣⲛ?, Va 61 203 *B* ⲛⲓⲙⲱⲓⲧ ⲫⲏ
ⲉⲧϩ.† ⲉⲣⲟⲓ, Mani 2 *A*[2] ϣⲁⲣⲉⲡⲁⲡⲟⲥⲧⲟⲗⲟⲥ ϩⲱⲡ ⲡⲉϥ-
ⲙⲩⲥⲧⲏⲣⲓⲟⲛ ⲁⲡⲉⲧⲁⲛⲓⲧ, ib P 46 ⲧⲏⲣⲁⲛ ⲡⲛϣⲱⲛⲉ ⲁⲣⲁϥ,
Ryl 153 *S* ⲛⲛⲉⲩϩⲱⲡ ⲗⲁⲁⲩ ⲉⲣⲟϥ, Mor 24 30 *F* ⲙⲡⲉ
ϩⲁⲡ ⲗⲁⲟⲩ ⲉⲗⲁⲛ.

—— ⲉϫⲛ- *S*, *upon* as acc: Deu 13 8 (*B* = Gk) σκεπάζειν acc; ShC 73 58 ⲛⲡⲉϩ. ⲉϫⲛⲗⲁⲁⲩ ⲛϩⲱⲃ, ViK
9648 (colophon) if he sell book or ϩ. ⲉϫⲱϥ.

—— ⲛ- *S, for:* Ps 30 19 (*B* diff) κρ. dat; *in:* FR
180 Jews wished ⲉϩ. ⲙⲡⲉϥϯⲛ̇ⲟⲥ ⲛⲧⲙⲛⲧⲉ; *with* (or?
acc): Lam 3 44 *F*(*B* ϩⲱⲃⲥ) σκεπάζειν acc; ⲁⲃⲁⲗ
ⲛ- *A*[2]: ManiK 111 ⲡⲣⲏ̇ⲅⲉ ... ϩ.† ⲁ. ⲛⲛⲁⲓⲱⲛ, ib 78
ⲛϥϩ. ⲁ. (ⲛ)ⲛⲉϥⲥⲁⲙ;   ⲥⲁⲃⲟⲗ ⲛ- *B*: Ps 37 10 (*S* ⲉ-)
κρ. ἀπό;   ϩⲁⲃⲟⲗ ⲛ- *F*: Ap 6 16 (Lacau, *S* ⲉⲃ. ϩⲛ-,
B ⲭ. ⲉⲃ. ϫⲁ-) κρ. ἀπό;   ⲥⲁϧⲟⲩⲛ ⲛ- *B*: Cat 108
ⲭⲟⲡϥ ⲛⲧⲉϥⲭⲗⲁⲙⲓⲥ...ⲉϥϩ.† ⲥ. ⲙⲙⲟϥ;   ϩⲓⲣⲟⲩⲡ ⲛ-
A[2]: ManiK 71 ⲡⲉⲧϩ.† ϩ. ⲙⲡⲕⲁⲧⲁⲡⲉⲧⲁⲥⲙⲁ;   ϫⲁⲧ-
ⲟⲛ ⲛ- *B*: Ps 18 7 (*S* ⲉ-) ἀποκρ. acc.

—— ϩⲁ-, ϫⲁ-: Ps 53 tit *B*(ϩⲁⲧⲛ-) κρ. παρά, Ge
35 4 *S*(*B* ⲭ. ϫⲁ-) κατακρ. ὑπό; Am 9 3 *A*(*S* ⲙⲡⲙⲧⲟ
ⲉⲃ. ⲛ-, *B* ⲱⲙⲥ ⲉⲃ. ϩⲁ-) καταδύειν ἐκ;   ⲉⲃⲟⲗ ϩⲁ-
B: Ge 18 17 (*S* ⲉ-) κρ. ἀπό, Jer 16 17 (*S* ⲙⲡⲙ. ⲉⲃ.
ⲛ-) κρ. ἀπέναντι, Is 40 27 (*S* ⲉ-) ἀποκρ. ἀπό; AM 83
ⲁϥϩⲟⲡϥ ⲉⲃ. ϩⲁⲣⲟϥ.

—— ϩⲓ-: Am 9 3 *A*(*SB* ϩⲛ-) ἐγκατακρ. εἰς; ShC
73 49 *S* evil words ⲛⲁϩ. ⲁⲛ ϩⲓⲡⲃⲏⲙⲁ.

—— ϩⲛ-, ϫⲉⲛ-: Job 23 12 *S*(*B* ⲭ.), Mt 13 44 *SF*
(*B* do) κρ. ἐν, Ap 6 15 *SF*(Lacau, *B* do) κρ. εἰς; PS
19 *S* ⲡⲉⲟⲟⲩ ϩ.† ⲡϩⲏⲧϥ, BG 73 *S* ϩⲟⲡⲙ ϩⲛⲟⲩⲥⲓⲃⲱⲧⲥ,
C 89 152 *B* demon ϩ.⸗ ϫⲉⲛⲁϣ ⲙⲙⲉⲗⲟⲥ (*cf ib* demon
ⲭⲟⲡⲙ ⲛϧⲏⲧϥ), ManiK 31 *A*[2] ⲛϥϩ. ϩⲓⲛⲉϥⲙⲁⲧⲓⲁ;
ϩⲣⲁⲓ ϩⲛ-, ⲛϧ. ϫⲉⲛ-: Br 231 *S* ⲟⲩⲙⲟⲛⲟⲅⲉⲛⲏⲥ ϩ.† ϩ. ⲛ-
ⲣⲏⲧϥ, CaiThe 139 *B* ⲟⲩϣⲓ ⲙⲙⲁⲛⲡⲁ ϩ.† ⲛϧ. ⲛϧⲏⲧϥ.

—— ϩⲁⲧⲛ-, ϩⲁϩⲧⲛ-, ⳃⲁⲧⲉⲛ-: Ps 53 tit S(B ϩⲁ-), Pro 7 1 SA(B ⳝ. ⳃⲉⲛ-) κρ. παρά; C 99 199 S ⲉϥϩ.† ϩⲁⲧⲡⲧⲏⲩⲧⲛ = C 89 166 B (cf 167 sim ⳝ.†).

—— nn m: Is 4 6 S ϣⲱⲡⲉ...ⲛϩ. (B ⲙⲁ ⲉϥϩ.†) ἐν ἀποκρύφῳ; K 11 B ⲛⲓϩ. ةخ (sic l); ϩⲛⲟⲩϩ. SB (once), in hiding, secretly: Jud 9 31, Is 45 19 (B ⳃⲉⲛⲡⲉⲧϩ.†) ἐν κρυφῇ, Jer 13 17 (B do) κεκρυμμένως; R 1 1 24 λαθραίως; 1 Cor 9 26 SB ἀδήλως; ShC 73 40 ⲣⲕⲣⲟϥϩⲛⲟⲩϩ., BAp 94 ⲧⲓⲡⲟⲟⲩⲥⲟⲩϩⲛⲟⲩϩ.; ϩⲓⲛϩ. SA²: Job 13 10 (B do) κρυφῇ, Jo 7 4 SA²(B do) ἐν κρυπτῷ; Ps 10 2 (B do) ἐν σκοτομήνῃ.

ⲛϩ. SA, as last: Deu 28 57 (B ⲛⳝ.) κρυφῇ, Jud 4 21 ἐν κ.; 1 Kg 18 22, Hab 3 14 A(B do) λάθρα; ShA 1 464 ⲉⲓⲣⲉ ⲡϩⲉⲛⲕⲣⲟϥ ⲛ. ⲉⲛⲉⲥⲡⲏⲩⲧ, ShIF 73 ⲉϥⲣ ϩⲟⲃⲉ ⲛ., R 1 3 75 ⲛⲉϥ ϩⲙⲟⲟⲥ ⲛ ⲙⲙⲁⲥ ⲛ.

ⲁⲧϩ., unhidden: Mor 41 159 S † ⲡⲁⲓ ⲡⲟⲩⳝⲁⲣⲓⲥ ⲡⲁ.

ⲙⲁ ⲛϩ., place of hiding: 1 Kg 19 2 S κρυφῇ, Lu 11 33 B(S diff) κρύπτη; Mor 25 209 S ⲙ. ⲡⲕⲁⲕⲉ, Mani H 20 A² ⲡⲙ. ϩⲏⲓⲧⲟⲅⲓⲉⲅⲉ.

ϩⲏⲡⲓ B nn f, crypt, underground chamber: Ge 6 16 (S ⲟⲩⲏⲧ) κατάγαιος; K 153 †ϩ. ةربخم. Cf ⲥⲛⲏⲡⲉ.

In place-name (?): ⲡⲃⲗⲗⲉ ⲛϩⲱⲡ (CO 215).

ϩⲱⲡ, ϩⲱⲃ B nn, horn: Is 5 1 (Lacr, Va 34 40, 90 26, var ⲧⲁⲡ, S = Gk), ϩⲱⲃ (Va 98 47), ϩⲁⲡ (corr ⲧⲁⲡ BM 1247 36) κέρας ⲗⲓⲣ. Cf ⲧⲃ. (All Dévaud).

ϩⲁⲡⲉ S, -ⲓ B nn, god Apis: Jer 26 15 SB Ἆπις; BKU 1 31 5 S oath by ⲡⲭⲥ ϩ., ib ⲉⲣⲉϩ. ϩⲓ ⲙⲛ ϣⲉ, ib 8ϩ. ⲡⲉⲩⲡⲉ. Cf Leip Ber'02 142 ϩⲁⲡⲓⲥ. V KKS 110.

ϩⲏⲏⲡⲉ, ϩⲏⲓⲧⲉ, ϩⲏⲏⲡⲉ v p 85 b, adding F ϩⲉⲉⲓⲛⲉ Am 2 13 ἰδού (JEA 11 246), ϩⲉⲓⲡⲉ ⲁⲡⲟ[ⲕ (PMich 1291).

ϩⲏⲡⲓ B v ϩⲱⲡ s f.

ϩⲁⲡⲟⲣⲕ, -ⲡⲟⲣⲧ S, -ⲡⲁⲣⲕ S⸍ nn f, saddle, saddle-cloth: Ge 31 34 (var P 44 103 -ⲣⲧ, B ϣⲉⲛ†) σάγμα pl طبغ, Lev 15 9 ϩⲁⲡⲱⲣⲕ (P 44 105, B do) ἐπίσ. (ناك) فاك); Bodl(P) f 33 ϩ. ⲡ ⳝⲙⲟⲩⲗ, Cai 67324 vo S⸍ ϩ. ⲡⳝⲏⲡⲉ. Cf ? ⲡⲟⲣⲕ 1° or 2°.

ϩⲁⲡⲥ SAF, ϩⲟ. S impers vb, it is needful (B mostly ϩⲱ†), with ⲉⲧⲣⲉ-: Pro 22 29 A(S c ⲉ-), Is 30 29 S ϩⲟ. F, Lu 24 26 neg ⲛϩ. ⲁⲛ, Jo 3 7 (A² ϥϩⲁⲡ, BF ϩⲱ†) δεῖν; Pcod 44 ϩ. ⲉⲧⲣⲉⲡⲡⲓⲡⲉ ⲧϭⲁⲉⲓⲟⲩ, ShC 73 11 ϩ. ⲁⲛⲡⲓⲡⲉ ⲉⲧⲣⲉⲡⲡⲓ ϣⲱⲡⲉ ⲙⲙⲁⲉ; + -ⲡⲉ: 1 Cor 15 25 SF, BM 247 ϩⲟⲡⲥ ⲧⲁⲣⲡⲉ ⲉⲧⲣⲉ-δ., 1 Pet 1 6 (B ⲥϣⲉ) δέον εἶναι; He 7 12 SF(B as Gk) ἐξ ἀνάγκης; Br 126 ϩ. ⲧⲁⲣⲡⲉ ⲉⲧⲣⲉ-, Z 613 ϩⲟⲡⲥⲡⲉ ⲡⲧⲉ-; + vbal pref: BHom 10 ⲉϩ. ⲡⲉ ⲉⲧⲣⲉⲛⲉⲓ ἀνάγκη; Berl Sitz '29 430 if man's soul dark ⲉϩ. ⲟⲛ ⲉⲧⲣⲉϥⲣ ⲕⲁⲕⲉ; Ac 1 16 ⲛⲉϩ. ⲉⲧⲣⲉ- (var ϩ. ⲡⲉ) δεῖν; c ⲉ-: Pro 22 29 (A Gk om ⲉ-), BMis 234 ϩ. ⲉⲣⲟⲕ ⲉⲧⲣⲉⲕⲁⲅⲱⲛⲓⲍⲉ

δ.; Br 104 ϩ. ⲧⲁⲣⲡⲉ ⲉⲣⲱⲙⲉ ⲡⲓⲙ ⲉⲧⲣⲉϥ-, ShA 2 283 ϩ. ⲉⲣⲱⲧⲡⲉ ⲉⲧⲣⲉ-.

ϩⲱⲡⲥ B v ϩⲱⲃⲥ.

ϩⲟⲡⲧ B v ϩⲱⲧⲡ.

ϩⲡⲟⲧ, -ⲱⲧ S, ϩϥⲟⲧ, -ⲱⲧ B, ϩⲡⲁⲧ F nn, fathom: Ac 27 28 SB (both var -ⲱⲧ) ὄργυια; Leip 25 12 B when had dug down ⲡⲟⲩϩ., Mor 24 31 F sunk them in river ⲡⲕⲁ ⲛϩ.

ϩⲱⲡϣ S nn m, palm-branch with pendant dates: BMis 562 ⲟⲩⲧⳃⲁ ⲛϩ. ϩⲓⲭⲡⲟⲩⲧⳃⲁ ⲡⲗⲱⲟⲩ, ⲟⲩⲧⳃⲁ ⲡ ⲗⲱⲟⲩ ϩⲓⲡϩ. ⲛϩ. μύριοι ἀκρεμόνες κ. μύριοι βότρυες ἐφ' ἑκάστου κλήματος; Gu 47 ⲛϩ. ⲉⲧⲁϣⲉ ⲉⲧⲡⲏⲡⲉ, 48 handfuls of dates ϩⲓⲡⲟⲩⲁ ⲡⲟⲩⲁ ⲡⲡϩ. V LMis 86 & cf ⲗⲟⲟⲩ.

ϩⲟⲡϩⲛ S nn m, disturbance, excitement or sim: P 130³ 66 ⲛϩⲁⲧⲏⲩ ⲙⲛⲡϩ. ⲡⲧⲡⲟⲛⲏⲣⲓⲁ ⲙⲡⲭⲁⲕⲉ, ib ⲛ ϩⲁⲧⲏⲩ ⲉⲧⲟⲗⲓⲃⲉ ⲙⲙⲟⲛ ⲉⲧⲉⲡϩ. ⲡⲉ due to fleshly lusts. CO 383 ⲁⲛ[ⲡⲣ]ⲟⲩϩⲟⲡϩⲛ ⲉⲣⲟⲓ (collated), ST 338 (prob) this word?

ϩⲡⲟϭⲡϭ v ϩⳝⲟⲡⳝⲡ.

ϩⲁⲣ S nn m, meaning unknown: Cai 42573 1 recipe for sickness in village (ⲡⲉϥ†ⲙⲉ), take ⲛϩ. ⲡϣⲏϭⲉ ⲡ ϣⲁⲅⲉⲓ ϩⲓⲧⲉⲩⲭⲱⲣⲁ & smear face with sweet oil. ? l ϩ(ⲛⲡ)ⲁⲣ.

ϩⲁⲣ v ϣⲁⲁⲣ 1°.

ϩⲁⲣ- v ⲉⲓⲟⲡⲉ s f.

ϩⲣ-, ϩⲣⲉ- S, ⳃⲁⲣⲁ- B nn (?) as distributive prep: Ap 22 2 S tree bearing fruit ϩⲣⲉⲃⲟⲧ (var ϩⲣⲉⲉ.)B ⳃ. ⲁⲃⲟⲧ (var ⲕⲁⲧⲁ) κατά. V Spg Kopt Etym 14, PLille 1 66.

ϩⲉⲣ S nn as pl: Ep 231 ⲁⲙⲟⲩ ⲉϩⲟⲩⲡ ⲉⲡϩ. ⲡⲧⲛ ⲥⲩⲡⲁⲅⲉ. For ? ϩⲓⲣ.

ϩ(ⲉ)ⲣ- SA², ϩⲣ-A, ⳃⲉⲗ-, B, ϩⲉⲗ-, ϩⲉⲣ-F v ϣⲓⲣⲉ & ϩⲁⲗ servant.

ϩⲉⲣ-S, ϩⲁⲣⳅ F v ⳃⲱⲣ.

ϩⲏⲣ S nn m, meaning unknown: BM 1187]ⲡⲡⲟϭ ⲡⲣⲱⲙⲉ ⲥⲙⲉⲛ ⲡⲁϩ. ⲉⲡⲟⲟⲩ, ib ⲛϩ[ⲏ]ⲣ ⲡⲡⲉⲓⲏⲃⲧ. For ? ϩⲓⲣ.

ϩⲏⲣ† S vb qual, meaning doubtful, opp black: Ora 4 22 ⲉⲥⲟⲩ ϩ., ⲉⲥⲟⲩ ⲕⲁⲙⲉ; P 44 83 ⲉⲣⲉⲃⲓⲡⲱⲟ ⳃⲁⲃϣⲁⲃ ⲉⲧⲉⲣ صمح ﻰﻠﻘﻣ = 43 58 ⲉⲧϩⲏⲣ رﻮﺠﻣ ﺪ, cf 44 ib ⲉⲣ. ⲙⲁϩⲣⲟⲛ ⳝ. ⲉⲧⲕⲓⲙ رﻮﺳﺃ ﺪ. V Löw F 2 430. In ? ⲕⲓⲡⲉⲏⲣ, ⲥⲁⲙⲁϩⲏⲣ, ⲉⳃⲏⲣ = (χαμαιλέων) λευκός (Diosc.).

ϩⲓⲣ SSfA², ϩⲉⲓⲣ S, ϩⲓⲣ A, ⳃ. ⳃ. B, ϩⲓⲗ, ϩⲗ F nn m, road, street, quarter: BHom 141 S in bath or in ⲛϩ. ὁδός, Mk 11 4 SB, Z 296 S ϩ. ⲡⲓⲙ ⲡⲧⲉ ⲡ†ⲙⲉ, MG

25 203 *B* sim, AP 14 *A²* ἄμφοδος, Pro 7 8 *SA*(*B* ⲙⲱⲓⲧ) δίοδ., *ib* 1 20 *SA*(*B* do) ἔξοδ.; Ps 17 42 *S*(*B* ϣⲟⲉⲣ), Pro 7 6 *S*(*B* = Gk), Lam 2 1 1 *F*(*SB* = Gk), Ez 28 23 *B*(*S* = Gk) πλατεῖα; Si 9 7 *S*, Is 15 3 *B*(*S* πλ.), Ac 9 11 *SB*, CDan 87 *B* ⲛⲓϩ. of village ῥύμη; BMis 539 *S* ϩⲉⲛϩ. ⲉⲩⲃⲏⲕ ⲉⲡⲉⲥⲛⲧ (Lat Syr diff); Tri 696 *S* ⲡⲉⲥⲡⲗ. ⲙⲙⲡⲉⲥϩ. اﺯﺟ شوارﻳ; ShC 42 38 *S* ⲛϩ. ⲡⲡⲉⲓⲧⲟⲡⲟⲥ, Miss 4 242 *S* ⲟⲩϩ. ⲛⲧⲡⲟⲗⲓⲥ = C 41 39 *B*, ShA 2 63 *S* ⲡⲕⲗϫⲉ (*l* ⲡⲕ.) ⲙⲙⲡϩⲉⲓⲣ, R 1 3 38 *S* ⲡⲁⲅⲟⲣⲁ ⲙⲙϩ. ⲛⲁⲡⲟⲗⲓⲥ, ROC 20 49 *S* ⲛϩ. ⲙⲡⲉⲧⲉⲛ-ϯⲙⲉ, Mor 30 35 *Sᶠ* ⲛϣⲁⲣⲡ ⲛϩ., J 6 41 *S* ⲛϩ. ⲉϩⲟⲩⲛ, *ib* 47 34 *S* ⲉϩⲣⲁⲓ, *ib* 6 19 *S* ϩⲏⲙⲟⲥⲓⲟⲛ (*cf* ῥύμη δημ.), *ib* 1 62 ⲃⲗⲗⲉ (*cf* τυφλὴ ῥ.), Hall 95 *S* ⲛϩ. ϣⲏⲙ, Mor 51 37 *S* ⲛⲡⲥⲁϣⲧ, J 66 33 *S* ⲛⲡϩⲁⲕ, MélOr 6 510 *B* ⲛⲡⲛⲟⲩϫⲁⲓ, J 3 46 ⲛⲧⲡⲁⲓⲗⲁⲕⲁⲓⲡⲉ & vars, BM 323 *S* ⲫⲉⲣⲙⲏⲥ in Alexandria, Ricci (*Mirac Marci*) *S* ⲙⲡⲉⲡⲓⲥⲕⲟⲡⲟⲥ ⲁⲡⲓⲁⲡⲟⲥ, J 71 24 *S* ⲙⲫⲁⲅⲓⲟⲥ ⲃⲓⲕⲧⲱⲣ, others *v* J Index 468, BMis 164 *S* ϩⲣⲏⲙⲉ (ῥ.), ϩ., ⲣⲁⲅⲉ, C 86 172 *B* ⲛⲡⲡⲗⲁⲧⲓⲁ, ⲡⲓϥⲣⲁⲅⲙⲟⲥ, ⲡⲓⲭⲓⲣ, ROC 20 56 *S* ⲛϩ. ⲁⲩⲱ ⲡⲉϩⲓⲏ ⲙⲙⲟⲟϣⲉ, Dan*Vis* xiv 49 *B* sim, CA 90 *S* cleric & sick ϩⲙⲡⲉϥϩ. = *ib* rⲓ الشوار ع, Z 233 *S* after Christ's descent ϩⲉⲛϩ. ϩⲓⲁⲙⲓⲧⲉ ⲉⲩⲟ ⲡⲉⲣⲏⲙⲟⲥ, AM 313 *B* sim, PBad 5 402 *Sᶠ* bury charm ϩⲓⲟⲩϩ. ⲉⲥϯⲟⲥ (*l* ⲓⲥ.) *cross roads*, ManiK 134 *A²* left her chamber ⲛⲥⲓ ⲁⲛϩ., Ryl 252 *S* ⲣⲟ ⲛⲫ.;   f(error?)*S*: J 8 8 ⲧϩ. ⲃⲗⲗⲉ, *ib* 27 28 ⲛϩⲟⲩⲛ ⲛⲧϩ.;   ⲉⲛϩ., ⲉⲫⲓⲗ, *to the street*, so? *outside*: 2 Kg 13 17 *S* put her forth ⲉⲛϩ. ἔξω; PCol 2 *F* ⲁⲅⲉⲡⲧ ⲉⲫⲓⲗ ϩⲉ(ⲛ)ⲡⲉϣⲧⲉⲕⲁ, BM 593 *F* ⲉⲓⲟⲩⲉϣ ⲉⲓ ⲫⲓⲗ ϩⲓⲧⲡⲟⲗ(ⲓⲥ), *ib* 625 *F*]ⲕⲧⲉ ⲡⲁϣⲁⲙ ⲉⲫⲓⲗ ⲡⲉⲓ, *ib* 665 *F* ϣⲁⲓⲕⲟⲩ ⲫⲓⲗ ⲧⲁⲉⲓⲡⲧⲟⲩ ϩⲟⲩⲡ, MR 5 54 *F* ⲕⲟⲩⲉϣ ⲧⲁⲉⲓ ⲉⲫⲓⲗ ⲧⲁⲉⲓ ⲡⲉⲕ, Brussels Mus Cinq 6346 *F* ⲡϭⲁⲁⲩ ⲛⲧⲁⲉⲓ ⲫⲓⲗ ⲉϩⲟⲩⲛ ⲡⲁⲛⲓ, CMSS 28 *Sᶠ* ϣⲁⲓⲉⲓ ⲉⲫ., BM 708 *Sᶠ* ⲡⲉⲥⲕⲉⲅⲓ ⲛⲧⲁⲩⲡⲱⲧ ⲉⲫ., Ryl 348 *S* ⲡⲉⲥⲕⲉⲅⲉ ⲉⲧⲕⲏ ⲫ., PBad 5 361 *S* ⲧⲓⲛⲟⲟⲩⲥⲟⲩ ⲉⲛϩ.; BP 3248 *F* (ⲡ)ⲡⲓⲱ ⲧⲁ(ⲁ)ⲥ ⲉⲕⲣⲉⲫⲗ, BM 673 *F* ⲧⲗⲓ (ⲉ)ⲧⲥⲁⲫⲓⲗ.

ϩⲓⲣϩⲓⲣⲉ, ϩⲉⲣ-, ϩⲏⲣ *S* nn f, differs? from ϩⲓⲣ: J 1 64 ⲧϩ. ⲉⲣⲏⲥ, *ib* 13 25 ⲧϩ. ϩⲣⲟⲩⲡ, *cf* 9 42, *ib* 12 27 ⲛϩ. (*l* ⲧϩ.) ⲁⲃⲟⲗ, *ib* 13 24 houses ϩⲓⲟⲛϩⲣ., CO 145 house ϩⲓⲡϩⲓⲣ ⲛⲧⲡⲁⲓⲗⲁⲕⲓⲛⲉ ⲉⲧϩⲓϩⲟⲩⲛ ⲛⲧϩⲉⲣ., *ib* 147, Ep 503 no context.   J 41 56 ϯⲥ ⲛϣⲟⲡ ⲛϩⲓⲣϩⲓⲣ prob for ⲛϩⲓⲣ, *cf* TurM 16, CO 144.

ⲋⲓⲣ *B*, *stripe, line*, iterated: MG 25 57 many-coloured garment ⲟⲩⲟϩ ⲉⲥⲟⲓ ⲛⲋ. ⲋ. = MS Mingana 21...(confusion? στῦλος & στολή) اﺳطوانية ﻣﺴﺘﺮﻳﺗﺤﻄوط, *ib* 268 *v* ⲥⲓⲣ 2°.

ϩⲓⲣ† *B* vb qual (?), meaning doubtful: GPar 2 12 shaved ⲡⲓϥⲟⲓ ⲉⲧϩ. ⲡⲧⲉ ⲡⲉϥⲥⲫⲟⲧⲟⲩ = *ib* 8 *S* ϩⲧⲏⲩ ⲡⲡⲉϥⲥⲡⲟⲧⲟⲩ (*ib* 14 Gk om).

ϩⲟⲣ *S* nn, meaning unknown: ShA 2 118 ⲡⲁⲓ ⲉⲧⲟⲩϯ ϩ. ⲉⲣⲟϥ ⲉⲣ ⲡⲉⲓϩⲃⲏⲅⲉ ⲡⲥⲓϣⲉ.

ϩⲱⲣ, ϩⲣ-, ϩⲟⲣϩ, ϩⲏⲣⲧ† *S*, ⲟⲣϩ *B*, vb tr refl, mostly c ⲉ-, *guard against, take heed*: 2 Kg 20 10, Ez 33 4 *SB* (ⲟⲣϥϥ *l* ⲟⲣϥ) ϩ 5 *SB* (do) φυλάσσεσθαι, 2 Kg 22 24 ⲡⲣⲟϥ. ἀπό (which Ps 17 23 ϩⲁⲣⲉϩ ⲉ-); PS 280 ϩⲣ-ⲧⲏⲅⲧⲡ ⲉⲣⲱⲧⲡ ⲉⲡⲉⲥⲃⲱ (*cf* Mt 24 4), *ib* 309 ϩⲣⲧⲏⲡⲟⲩ ⲉⲣⲱⲧⲡ ⲙⲡⲣⲣ ⲛⲟⲃⲉ, ShIF 208 things ⲉⲧⲛⲛⲁϣ ϩⲟⲣⲡ ⲉⲣⲟⲛ ⲛϩⲏⲧⲟⲩ ⲁⲛ, ShViK 915 ϥϩ.† ⲉⲣⲉ ⲁⲩⲱ ⲉϣⲟⲣϣⲣ ⲉⲝⲡⲡⲉϥⲉⲣⲏⲩ, ShIF 263 ϩⲣⲱⲧⲛ ⲧⲉⲧⲛϩ.† ⲉⲛ ⲡⲟⲥⲉ ⲉϩⲟⲩⲛ ⲉⲣⲱⲧⲡ ⲉⲡϫⲓⲛϫⲏ?, *ib* 152 ϣϣⲉ ⲉⲡⲣⲱⲙⲉ ⲉϩⲟⲣϥ ⲡⲟⲩϩⲣ.

ϩⲱⲣ *SB*, ϩ(ⲉ)ⲣ- *S*, ϩⲱⲣ- *A*, ϩⲟⲣϩ *S* vb tr, *squeeze out* milk, *milk*: Job 10 10 *SB* ﺣﻠﺐ Lag, ﺟﺒﻞ Baudissin (*l*? ﺣﻠﺐ), Pro 24 68 *SAB* ἀμέλγειν; *ib* *S*(ShClPr 23 2, var & *A* ⲱϥⲉ) *B* ἐκπιέζειν; Is 7 22 *S* ϩⲣ ⲉⲣⲱⲧⲉ (*B* ⲉ. only) γάλα ποιεῖν;   as nn: Job 20 17 *SB* ἄμελξις.

ϩⲱⲣ, god *Horus* in Hor 79, 85 *O* ϩⲣ-, ϩⲁⲣⲡϣⲱⲧ planet *Jupiter* & in many names, as ϩⲱⲣ, ϩⲱⲗ (Baouit 2 35), ϩⲱⲣⲥⲓⲛⲥⲓⲟⲥ, ϩⲁⲣⲥⲓⲛⲥⲉ, ϩⲉⲣⲟⲩⲟⲝ, ⲡⲓϩⲱⲣ, ⲧⲁ-ϩⲱⲣ, *cf* Preisigke 44-59; & place-names, as ⲧⲁϩⲁⲛ-ϩⲱⲣ, ⲧⲉⲩϩϩⲱⲣ.   *V* ⲥⲓⲟⲩ.

ϩⲱⲣⲁ *S* nn f, meaning doubtful: 2 Kg 13 20 ⲉⲥⲟ ⲛ̄ⲭⲏⲣⲁ ⲉⲥⲟ ⲛϩ. ϩⲙⲡⲏⲓ (var om) gloss or ? = ἐκψύχουσα (elsewhere = ⲕⲁ ⲡⲧⲏⲩ, ϩⲱⲥⲃ, ⲙⲟⲩ).

ϩⲉⲣⲉ *v* ϩⲣⲉ.

ϩⲉⲣⲉ *S* nn, meaning unknown: CO 466 in list of *varia* ϩ. ⲁ̄ (var Univ College Lond ⲟⲩϩ.).

ϩⲉⲉⲣⲉ *S* nn m, meaning unknown, title or occupation: Kr 50 25 ⲁⲃⲣⲁϩⲁⲙ ⲫⲉⲉⲣⲉ.

ϩⲉⲣⲓ *B* *v* ϩⲣⲣⲉ.

ϩⲏⲣⲉ *S* nn, meaning unknown: Ep 546 ⲟⲩⲗⲱϯϩ̄ ⲗⲁⲩ ⲡϩ.

ϩⲟ(ⲉ)ⲓⲣⲉ, -ⲗⲉ *S*, ϩⲁⲓⲣⲉ *Sᶠ*, (ϩ)ⲁⲓⲣⲉ *A*, ϩⲱⲓⲣⲓ *B* nn f, *dung* human or animal: Lev 4 1 1 *B* pl (*S* ⲥⲟⲧ), *ib* 16 27 *B*(*S* = Gk), Nu 19 5 *B* pl (*S* ⲥ.), Is 30 22 *B*(*S* ⲙⲏ ⲟⲉⲓⲕ, *F* ⲙⲉ ⲙⲏ), ROC 25 273 *B* ⲟⲩⲱⲙ ⲛⲡⲉϥϩ. ⲥⲱ ⲡⲧⲉϥⲙⲏ, Z 336 *S* sim (*cf ib* ⲟⲩⲉⲙ ⲥⲟⲧ), R 2 40 *S* ϩⲉⲛϩⲟⲉⲓⲗⲉ κόπρος; Ez 4 15 *SB*, Zeph 1 17 *SAB* βόλβιτον, Si 22 2 *S* ϩ. ⲛⲥⲟⲧ β. κοπρίων; Mor 25 19 *S* ϩ. ⲉⲧⲗⲟⲙⲥ wherein animal (prob scarab) burrows (?) = Va 61 101 *B*(*v* ⲥⲣⲟϥⲣⲉϥ), Miss 4 699 *S* their purity is as ⲧϩⲟⲉⲓⲗⲉ ⲙⲛⲧⲃⲗⲝⲉ, Z 628 *Sᶠ* in recipe ⲧϩⲁⲓⲣⲉ of dog (*album graecum* Dulaurier), Ora 4 193 *S* sim ϩ. ⲛⲡⲟⲉⲓⲧ ⲉϥϣⲟⲙⲉ *dung ground fine*.

In place-name: ⲡⲗⲁⲗ ⲛϩⲟⲓⲣⲉ (WS 120).

ϩⲣⲁ *SA²*, ϣⲣⲁ *S* vb tr, *drive, compel*: 1 Kg 30 20 ἀπάγειν; Lam 1 6 (*B* ϭⲟϫⲓ) διώκειν; Mor 17 8 shepherd ⲉϥϩ. ⲡⲛⲉϥⲉⲥⲟⲟⲩ ἐλαύνειν; BMis 27 angels ϩ. ⲙⲡⲉⲩϩⲣⲟⲟⲩ *sent forth*.

With following preposition or adverb.   c ⲉ-, *to*: ShMing 322 ridden by devil ⲉⲧⲣⲉϥϩ. ⲙ̄ⲙⲟⲟⲩ ⲉϩⲉⲛⲙⲁ ⲙ̄ⲙⲟⲟϣⲉ ⲉϩⲟⲩⲛ, ShClPr 22 362 ⲉϥϩ. ⲙ̄ⲙⲟⲟⲩ ... ⲉⲧⲃⲁⲃⲩⲗⲱⲛ, *Bucheum* 2 78 ⲉⲕⲛⲁϣ. ⲉⲛ[, Ep 255 ⲡⲟⲥⲉ ⲛⲛ̄ⲧⲃⲛⲟⲟⲩⲉ ⲉⲡⲧⲁⲓⲙⲟⲟⲩⲧⲟⲩ ⲉⲧⲣ. ⲉⲣⲟϥ (meaning?), ShHTG ⲛ̄ⲥⲉⲣ. ⲙ̄ⲙⲟⲛ ... ⲉϩⲣⲁⲓ ⲉⲁⲙⲛ̄ⲧⲉ;   c ⲛⲥⲁ-, emphatic: ShC 42 220 ϩ. ⲛ̄ⲥⲱⲟⲩ ⲉϩⲉⲛⲙⲁ ⲛ̄ϫⲁⲓⲉ, ShR 2 3 16 death ϩ. ⲛ̄ⲥⲱⲟⲩ ⲉϩⲟⲩⲛ ⲉⲡⲕⲱⲧ, WTh 152 ⲉϥϩ. ⲛ̄ⲥⲁⲛ̄ⲃⲁⲣⲃⲁⲣⲟⲥ & overcame them, ManiK 114 *A*² ⲁϥϩ. ⲛ̄ⲥⲱϥ ϩⲓⲧⲛ̄ⲧⲉⲡⲣⲟⲓⲁ, *ib* 30 *A*² ⲉϥϩ. ⲛ̄ⲥⲱⲟⲩ ⲁⲧⲕⲟⲗⲁⲥⲓⲥ;   c ϩⲛ-, *with*: ShIF 202 ⲉⲩϩ. ⲙ̄ⲙⲱⲧⲛ ϩⲙ̄ⲡⲟⲩϩⲉⲣⲥⲁϩⲛⲉ like mules with scourge;   c ϩⲓ-: J 73 14 ⲗⲁⲁⲩ ⲛⲓⲙ ⲉϥϩ. ϩⲓⲡⲕⲁϩ (same word?);   c ⲉⲃⲟⲗ, *forth*: ShA 1 463 ⲙ̄ⲡⲣ̄ϣⲓⲡⲉ ϩ. ⲙ̄ⲙⲟⲟⲩ ⲉⲃ., *ib* ϩ. ⲙ̄ⲙⲟⲟⲩ ⲉⲃⲟⲗ ⲛ̄ϩⲏⲧⲉ; BMis 324 wind ϩ. ⲙ̄ⲙⲟⲟⲩ ⲉⲃ. ⲉⲡⲡⲉⲗⲁⲅⲟⲥ; J 50 70 ⲛ̄ⲥⲉϩ. ⲙ̄ⲙⲟⲛ ⲙ̄ⲡϣⲁⲃⲟⲗ to observe terms of deed, *ib* 75 57 sim ϣ.

ϩⲣⲁ⸗, ϩⲣⲱ⸗ *B* vb(?), *it is fitting*: 1 Tim 2 10 ⲡⲉⲧϩⲣⲁⲩ (varr ⲡⲉⲧϩⲣⲱⲟⲩ, ⲡⲉⲧⲉ-) ⲛ̄ⲛⲓϩⲓⲟⲙⲓ (*S* ⲡⲉⲧⲉϣϣⲉ) πρέπειν.

ϩⲣⲁⲓ, *S*, ϩⲣⲏⲉⲓ *AA*²*O*, ϩⲣⲏⲓ *A*²*BO*, ϩⲗⲏ(ⲉ)ⲓ *F*, ϩⲣⲉ *SAB*(ⲥⲁϩⲣⲉ), ϩⲣⲏ *S*ᵃ nn m, *upper part* (cf ϩⲟ, ϩⲓ-, AZ 44 93), rarely except as advb or + prep: ShP 130¹ 115 *S* other worlds ⲙ̄ⲡⲣⲉ ⲙ̄ⲡⲁⲓ, opp *ib* ϩⲁⲣⲟϥ ⲙ-, TU 43 9 *A* shall be taken ⲁⲡ̄ⲣⲉ ⲛ̄ⲛⲡⲏⲩⲉ; & v as nn below;   with rel, *above*: Pro 8 29 *S* ⲕⲗⲟⲟⲗⲉ ⲉⲧϩⲣⲁⲓ (*A* ⲛ̄ϩ., *B* om), Is 36 2 *SF*(*B* ⲥⲁⲡϣⲱⲓ) ἄνω; BKU 1 41 *S* ⲡⲏⲓ ⲉⲧϩ. (cf ⲉⲧⲛϩ.);   with ⲧⲁ- v p 390 *a*;   ⲣ ⲛϩⲣⲉ *A*, *be above*: Mic 4 1 (*S* ⲡⲉⲧⲡⲉ, *B* ⲥⲁⲡϣⲱⲓ) ὑπεράνω.

Mostly reinforcing following preposition.   c ⲛ̄- (or ? for ϩⲛ-): Ex 20 11 *S*(*B* ⲛϩ. ϧⲉⲛ-) ἐν; Is 15 5 *S* (*B* ϩ. ϩⲓ-) ἐπί; AZ 21 100 *O* ⲁⲓⲧⲟⲩ ⲣⲏⲓ ⲛ̄ϥⲏⲧ ⲛ-;   c ⲟⲩⲧⲉ- *q* v;   c ϩⲓ-: J 13 24 *S* houses ϩ. ϩⲓⲟⲩϩⲣ̄ⲓⲣⲉ;   c ϩⲛ-: Nu 14 16 *S*(*B* ⲛϩ. ϩⲓ-), Eccl 7 10 *F*(*S* ϩⲛ-), ἐν, v also ϩⲛ-;   c ϩⲓϫⲛ- *S*: Ex 16 14 (*B* ⲛϩ. ϩ.), Nu 7 9 (*B* ϩⲓ-), Ps 136 1 (*B* ϩⲓϫ.) ἐπί, Mt 23 22 (var ⲉϩ. ⲉϫⲛ-, *B* do) ἐπάνω; Br 106 laid branches ϩ. ϩⲓϫⲙ̄ⲡⲧⲟⲡⲟⲥ, RNC 82 stones ⲉⲩϩ. ϩⲓϫⲱⲟⲩ.

ⲉϩⲣⲁⲓ *SSfF*, ⲁϩ. *S*ᵃ, ⲁϩⲣⲏ(ⲉ)ⲓ *S*ᵃ*AA*²*O*, ⲁϩⲣⲏ *S*ᵃ *A*, ⲁϩⲣⲉ *S*ᵃ, ⲉϩⲣⲏⲓ *BF*, ⲉϩⲗ., ϩⲗ. *F*, *to above, upward*, opp ⲉϩⲣⲁⲓ, ⲉϩ. *downward* (from which *S* cannot always be distinguished & with which *B* sometimes confused), appended to vbs of motion, as ⲁⲗⲉ, ⲃⲱⲕ, ⲃⲣ̄ⲃⲣ̄, ⲉⲓ, ⲉⲓⲡⲉ 1°, ⲕⲱⲧⲉ, ⲙⲟⲟϣⲉ, ⲙⲟⲩϩ 1°, ⲡⲁ 2°, ⲡⲱⲧ, ⲣⲱⲧ, ⲥⲱⲕ, ⲥⲓⲧⲉ, †, ⲧⲁⲗⲟ, ⲧⲓⲡⲟⲟⲩ, ⲧⲱⲟⲩⲛ, ⲟⲩⲱⲧⲃ̄, ⲱⲗ, ⲱϣ, ϣⲉ, ϭⲓ, ϭⲱϣⲉ, ϩⲱⲗ, ϫⲓⲥⲉ, ϫⲟⲟⲩ; also to others, as ⲙⲟⲩⲧⲉ, ⲛⲉⲣⲥⲉ, ⲣⲁϣⲉ, ⲥⲙ̄ⲙⲉ, ⲥⲟⲗⲥ, ⲧⲟⲉⲓⲧ, ϣⲗⲏⲗ, ϭⲱϣⲧ.

Represents prep where prefixed to vb: Ge 3 18 *S* (*B* diff), 2 Kg 6 17 *SB*, Ps 46 5 *S*(*B* ⲉⲡϣⲱⲓ), Is 34 3

SF(*B* do), Hos 1 11 *A*(*B* do), Mt 13 48 *SF*(*B* diff) ἀνα-, *ib* 21 18 *S*(*B* do) ἐπανα-; Nu 16 47 *SB*, Ps 36 35 *S*(*B* ⲉⲡϣ.) ἐπι-; Ac 1 13 *S*(var & *B* ⲉϩⲟⲩⲛ) ⲉⲓⲥ-; Ps 56 8 *S*(*B* om), Pro 20 5 *SA*, Sa 19 10 ἐκ-(?); Jos 13 1 *S* προ-; Lev 21 17 *SB*, Mt 8 4 *S*(*B* ⲉϩⲟⲩⲛ) προσ-; not in Gk: Sa 18 9 *S* ⲧⲁⲗⲉ ⲑⲩⲥⲓⲁ ⲉϩ. θυσιάζειν, Ps 87 1 *S* ⲱϣ ⲉϩ. (*B* ⲉⲃⲟⲗ) κράζειν, Lam 5 12 *SB* ⲉⲓϣⲉ ⲉϩ. κρεμαννύναι, Ps 62 4 *S* ϥⲓ ⲉϩ. (*B* ⲉⲡϣ.) αἴρειν, Ja 3 11 *SA* ⲧⲁϩⲟ ⲉϩ. (*B* ⲃⲉⲃⲓ) βρύειν, R 1 1 21 *S* ⲥⲟⲟϩⲉ ⲉϩ. χωρίζεσθαι; PS 134 *S* ⲛ̄ⲧⲥ ⲉϩ. from Chaos, *ib* 71 *S* ⲁϥϩⲟⲥϥ ⲉϩ., Aeg 254 *S* ⲧⲟⲩⲛⲟⲥⲟⲩ ⲉϩ., R 1 3 27 *S* ϫⲁⲥⲧⲟⲩ ⲉϩ., Ep 374 *S*¹ ⲛ̄]ⲧⲉⲉⲓ ⲁϩ., Hall 69 *S*ᵘ ⲥⲟⲩϥⲧⲟⲟⲩ ⲡⲓⲉⲧⲉⲓ ⲁϩⲣⲉ, *ib* 62 *S*ᵃ ⲁⲥⲓⲛⲁ ⲉⲓ ⲁϩⲣⲏ, PMéd 131 *S* abscess ⲉⲓ ⲉϩ. *burst*, Kr 1 4 *S* inundation ⲙⲟⲩϩ ⲉϩ., AM 288 *B* ⲧⲱⲡⲕ ⲉϩ., *ib* 227 *B* fruit † ⲟⲩⲱ ⲉϩ., C 43 167 *B* ⲧⲁⲗⲉ ⲗⲓⲃⲁⲛⲟⲥ ⲉϩ., ManiH 3 *A*² †ⲛⲁⲣⲧ ⲁϩ., *ib* 27 *A*² ⲡⲏⲩ ⲁⲡⲓⲧⲛ ... ⲉⲓ ⲁϩ., Hor 82 *O* ⲛⲉⲟⲩ ⲁϩ.;   doubtful *up* or *down*: ShC 42 210 *S* ⲡⲉⲥⲕⲱⲧⲉ ⲉϩ., ST 227 *S*ᵃ ⲕⲱⲧⲉ ⲁϩ., COAd 40 *S* ⲧⲁϩⲟⲓ ⲉϩ., Kr 233 *F* ⲧⲁϣϥ (ⲉ)ⲗⲁⲛ ϩ.

Appended to nn *SO* (presumably *up*): J 47 34 ⲡϩⲓⲣ ⲉϩ., *ib* 42 23 ⲡⲧⲱⲣⲧ ⲉϩ., *ib* 67 75 ⲧⲕⲉϫⲟⲉ ⲉϩ.; JA '75 5 216 ϫⲓⲡϩⲟⲟⲩ ⲉϩ., CO 128 ϫⲓⲡⲧⲛⲥⲧⲓⲁ ⲉϩ., *ib* 148 ϫⲓⲡⲧⲁⲕ ⲛ̄ϫⲟⲓ...ⲉϩ., Hor 83 *O* ⲛ̄ⲭⲓⲣⲁⲙⲡⲉ ‾ⲙ̄ⲃ̄‾ ⲁϩ. (but *cf* ? ϩⲣⲁⲓ *down*, ⲥⲁϩⲣⲏⲓ); *cf* BMis 126 ϫⲓⲡⲙ̄ⲙⲟⲥ ⲉϩ. ⲙ̄ⲡⲉⲓⲟⲩⲁⲥ ⲥⲟϭⲉⲡ ⲑⲁⲙⲁⲣ (on Ge 38 26).

As nn, also ϩⲣ. *B*, *person above, superior, magnate*: Jer 25 38 ⲟⲩⲉϩ., Pro 8 16 ⲛⲓⲉϩ. (*SA* ⲛⲟϭ), Jer 24 8 ⲛⲉϥⲉϩ. (*S* = Gk), *ib* 41 10 ⲛⲓϩⲣ., Is 34 12 ⲛⲉⲥϩ. (*S* ⲁⲣⲭⲱⲛ, *F* ⲛⲁϭ), Nah 3 10 ⲛⲉⲥϩⲣ. ⲛ̄ϭⲛⲧⲟⲩ (wrongly added, *SA*=Gk) μεγιστάν.

Reinforcing following preposition, often with *upward* sense.   ⲉ- (mostly *S*): Deu 17 8 (*B* ⲉ-), Ac 24 11 *S*(var ⲉ-)*B*, AP 4 *A*² ἀνα- ⲉⲓⲥ, Lu 1 9 (var & *B* ⲉϩⲟⲩⲛ) ⲉⲓⲥ- ⲉⲓⲥ, Deu 11 5 (*B* ⲉ-), Mt 8 14 (*B* ⲉϩⲟⲩⲛ ⲉ-) ⲉⲓⲥ, Is 36 10 *SBF* ⲉϩⲣⲏⲓ ἀνα- ἐπί, Ex 34 1 (*B* ϩⲓ-), Is 19 2 *F*(BM 1221, *SB* ⲉϫⲛ-), Mt 14 34 (*B* ⲉϩⲟⲩⲛ ⲉ-, *F* ⲉ-) ἐπί, Ps 19 9 (*B* ⲟⲩϩⲉ-), Hos 2 13 *A*(*B* diff) ἐπι-, 2 Kg 7 27 προσ- πρός, Ps 119 1 (*B* ⲟⲩ.), Eccl 1 6 *F*(*S* diff), Is 32 6 *SF*ⲉϩⲣⲁⲓ (*B* ⲟⲩ.) πρός, Jud 3 10, Lam 1 4 *BF*, Mt 26 6 (*F* ⲉ-, *B* diff) ἐν, Ge 7 24 (*B* ϩⲓϫ.) ὑψοῦσθαι ἐπί; PS 58 ϩⲩⲙⲛⲉⲩⲉ ⲉϩ. ⲉⲡⲟⲩⲟⲉⲓⲛ, ShMIF 23 70 ϥⲓ ⲟⲩϭⲉⲣⲱⲃ ⲉϩ. ⲉⲣⲟⲓ, BHom 14 ⲡⲱⲡⲉ ⲉⲃⲟⲗ ϩⲙ̄ⲡⲕⲁϩ ⲉϩ. ⲉⲧⲡⲉ, BMis 387 jars full ⲉϩ. ⲉⲣⲱⲟⲩ (var BM 305 ϣⲁⲉϩ. ⲉ-), ManiH 44 *A*² ⲁϥⲧⲉⲗⲟ ⲁϩ. ⲁⲕⲧⲏⲥⲓⲫⲱⲛ, C 43 209 *B* ϩⲱⲗ ⲉϩ. ⲉⲡⲓⲫⲛⲟⲩⲓ;   *toward*: BG 74 ⲉⲓ ⲉϩ. ⲉⲧⲩϫⲟⲕⲡⲉ, PS 191 ϣⲁϫⲉ ⲛⲓⲙ ⲉϩ. ⲉⲧⲥⲩⲡⲧⲉⲗⲉⲓⲁ, *ib* 239 ϫⲟⲟϥ ⲉϩ. ⲉⲡⲉϥⲙⲁⲁⲭⲉ, BMis 247 ⲧⲟⲩϫⲟ ⲛ̄ⲡⲉϩⲣⲱⲙⲁⲓⲟⲥ ⲉϩ. ⲉⲡⲅⲙⲁ, J 18 9 I betake me ⲉϩ. ⲉⲧⲉⲡⲣⲁⲥⲓⲥ, Ryl 216 money received ⲉϩ. ⲉⲧⲧⲓⲙⲏ, AP 41 *A*² brought letter ⲉϩ. ⲁⲛⲉϥⲫⲓⲗⲓⲡⲡⲟⲥ;   *up ... down SA*: ShA 1 404 sun's ⲙⲁ ⲡⲉⲓ ⲉϩ. & his ⲙⲁ ⲛ̄ⲃⲱⲕ ⲉϩ., *ib* sun ⲡⲏⲩ ⲉϩ. ⲁⲩⲱ ⲟⲛ ⲉϥⲛⲁ

ⲉϩ., R 2 1 59 ⲥⲱⲕ ⲙⲙⲟⲟⲩ ⲉϩ. ⲉⲡⲉⲡⲓⲑⲩⲙⲓⲁ ⲉⲧⲥⲟⲟϥ … ϫⲓ ⲙⲟⲉⲓⲧ ϩⲏⲧⲟⲩ ⲉϩ. ⲉⲧⲡⲉ, El 106 *A* ⲡⲁ ⲁϩ. ⲡⲏⲩ ⲁϩ.; ⲉⲝⲛ- (often neither *up* nor *down*): Ge 32 31 *S*(*B* ⲉ-) ἀνα- dat, Ps 77 31 *SB*, Cant 7 8 *F*(*S* ⲉϩ. ⲉ-), Lam 2 10 *F* ϩ. (*B* ϩⲓϫ.) ἀνα-ἐπί,' Jth 16 17 *S* ἐπανα-dat, Ps 3 1 *SB* ἐπανα-ἐπί, Ge 1 20 *S*(*B* ϩⲓϫ.), Ps 9 15 *B*(*S* ⲉⲝⲛ-), Eccl 10 7 *F* ϩ. (*S* ϩⲓϫⲛ-), Is 30 1 *F* ⲉϩⲗ. (*SB* ⲉⲝⲛ-), Mic 4 8 *AB*, Mt 14 14 *S*(*BF* ϩⲁ-) ἐπί, 3 Kg 8 46 *B*, Sa 16 4 *S*, Mt 17 5 *S*(*B* ⲉⲝ.), BHom 49 *S* ⲡⲱⲧ ⲉϩ. ⲉϫⲱⲥ ἐπί, Ps 90 13 *S*(*B* do), Is 31 3 *SBF* ⲉϩⲣⲏⲓ, Jo 13 18 *SA²B* ἐπι-ἐπί, Deu 10 1 *S*(*B* ⲉⲡϣ. ϩⲁ-), Ps 23 3 *B*(*S* ⲉϩ. ⲉ-) ἀνα-εἰς, 3 Kg 8 52 *B*(*S* ⲉ-) εἰσ-εἰς, Ps 120 1 *S*(*B* ⲉⲝ.), Lam 2 2 *F*(*B* ⲉ-), Mt 4 8 *S*(*B* ⲉⲝ.) εἰς, Ps 17 41 *SB*, ib 90 10 *B*(*S* ⲉ-), Is 3 5 *A* (Cl, *SB* ⲟⲩⲃⲉ-) πρός, Mt 5 23 *SB* προσ-ἐπί, Mic 3 4 *SAB* ἐν, 2 Kg 1 19 *B*(*S* ⲉⲝⲛ-), MG 25 2 *B* martyred ⲉϩ. ⲉⲝⲉⲛⲡϥⲣⲁⲛ ὑπέρ, Dan 11 23 *B* ὑπερ-, Ps 34 15 *B* (*S* om), Ac 19 16 *S*(var & *B* ⲉ-) κατά, 1 Chr 16 21 *B* (Ps 104 14 ὑπ.), Bar 1 13 *B* περί, Nu 25 3 *S*(*B* ⲉⲝ.), ROC 17 400 *B* ⲣⲁϣⲓ ⲉϩ. ⲉⲝ. ⲧⲱϩⲣⲁ dat, Ge 1 26 *S* (*B* ⲉ-), Ps 104 21 *B*(*S* ⲉⲝⲛ-) gen; Br 241 *S* ⲧⲁⲗⲟ ⲙⲟⲟⲩ ⲉϩ. ⲉⲝⲛ-, ShC 73 175 *S* ⲃⲱⲕ ⲉϩ. ⲉⲝⲛⲟⲩⲧⲟⲟⲩ لمّ ال, MIF 9 53 *S* sun ϣⲁ ⲉϩ. ⲉϫⲙⲡⲕⲁϩ (var BAp 13 ⲉⲝⲛ-), Imp Russ Ar S 18 029 *Sᵃ* ⲉⲓⲙⲉ ⲁϩⲣⲏ ⲁϫⲱⲟⲩ, BM 1224 *Sᵃ* sim, C 43 98 *B* if war ⲧⲱⲛϥ ⲉϩ. ⲉϫⲱⲓ, AM 117 *B* ⲧⲱϩ ⲉϩ. ⲉϫⲱⲓ; without direction: PS 113 *S* ⲡⲛⲉⲅⲁⲙⲁⲣⲧⲉ ⲉϩ. ⲉϫⲱⲓ, Br 119 *S* ⲟ ⲡⲣⲣⲟ ⲉϩ. ⲉⲝⲛ-, ib 94 *S* ⲧⲱⲧ ⲛϩⲏⲧ ⲉϩ. ⲉϫⲱⲓ, ShC 73 90 *S* ⲙⲟⲕϩ ⲛϩⲏⲧ ⲉϩ. ⲉⲝⲛ-(var ⲉϫⲛ-), BHom 13 *S* burning with lust ⲉϩ. ⲉϫⲡⲧⲉⲥϩⲓⲙⲉ, Mor 41 44 *S* ϫⲓ ⲛⲧⲁⲡⲣⲟⲥ-ⲉⲩⲭⲏ ⲉϩ. ⲉϫⲱⲟⲩ *on their behalf*, Aeg 260 *S* ⲧⲉⲛⲥⲙⲟⲩ ⲉⲣⲟⲕ ⲉϩ. ⲉϫⲙⲡⲁⲓ, Mani P *A²* ⲛⲧⲟⲩ ⲁϩ. ⲁϫⲱⲟⲩ, AM 20 *B* ⲱⲟⲩ ⲛϩⲏⲧ ⲉϩ. ⲉϫⲱϥ, ib 85 *B* ⲁϥϭⲓⲛⲓ ⲉϩ. ⲉϫⲱϥ, ib 325 *B* gnashed teeth ⲉϩ. ⲉϫⲱϥ, ib 153 *B* marvelled ⲉϩ. ⲉϫⲉⲛⲧⲟⲩⲙⲉⲧⲥⲁⲓⲉ, C 43 222 *B* ⲁϥⲧⲁⲕⲟ ⲛⲧⲡⲟⲗⲓⲥ ⲉϩ. ⲉϫⲱⲛ; ⲉϩⲣⲏ-: Mk 3 5 *S* ϭⲱϣⲧ ⲉϩ. ⲉϩⲣⲁⲩ (var ⲉϩⲟⲩⲛ, *B* ⲉ-) περι-acc; ⲟⲩⲃⲉ-: Is 57 13 *S*(*B* ⲉⲃⲟⲗ) ἀνα-, Job 27 10 *S*(*B* ⲟⲩ.), Ps 101 2 *S*(*B* ⲉⲡϣ.) ἐπί-, Si 8 2 *S* ἀντι-; AP 37 *A²* ⲁϣ ⲉϩⲙ ⲁϩ. ⲟⲩϭⲉⲡⲝⲥ, BKU 1 23 *F* ⲧⲓⲱ ⲙ ⲉⲗⲏ ⲟⲩⲏⲕ; ϣⲁ- *S*: Ps 73 23 (*B* ⲉⲡϣ.) ἀνα-πρός; PS 16 ⲁⲙⲟⲩ ⲉϩ. ϣⲁⲣⲟⲛ; ϩⲁ- *B*, *up to*: ROC 18 36 ⲓⲟⲣⲉⲙ ⲉϩ. ϩⲁⲣⲟϥ ἀνα-πρός, Ps 30 23 (*S* ⲟⲩ.), Lam 2 18 (*S* ⲉϩ. ⲉ-) πρός; AM 151 ϣⲗⲏⲗ ⲉϩ. ϩⲁⲡⲛⲧ; ϩⲁ- *SA²*, *up beneath*: BHom 7 ϭⲓ ⲉϩ. ϩⲁⲡⲉⲗⲏⲧⲏ, ManiK 35 *A²* ⲡⲉⲧⲃⲓ ⲁϩ. ϩⲁⲡⲉ ϩⲏⲅⲉ, J 83 13 ⲥⲱⲕ ⲉϩ. ϩⲁⲡⲉⲕⲣⲓⲙⲁ; ϩⲓ-: Mk 6 54 *SB*(var ⲉⲃⲟⲗ ϩⲓ-) ἐκ-ἐκ (cf + ϩⲛ-), Dan 5 5 *B* ἐπί; Cl 12 4 *A* ⲃⲱⲕ ⲁϩ. ϩⲓⲡⲓϩⲟ dat; C 43 61 *B* ϫⲟⲩϣⲧ ⲉϩ. ϩⲓⲱⲧϥ, Br 118 *S* paths ⲉⲧⲉⲧⲛⲡⲏⲩ ⲉϩ. ϩⲓⲱⲟⲩ; ϩⲛ-, ϩⲉⲛ-, *up from*: Jos 4 19 *S*, Dan 7 3 *SB* ἀνα-ἐκ, Mt 3 16 *S*(*B* ⲉⲡϣ.) ἀνα-ἀπό, Jud 16 14 *S*, Ez 21 3 *S*(*B* ϩⲉⲛ-) ἐκ-ἐκ, Ge 30 16 *SB* εἰσ-ἐκ, Deu 26 2 *S*(*B* diff) ἀπό, Ac 7 14 *B*(varr ⲛϩ.,

ⲛϩ., *S* diff) ἐν; PS 78 *S* ⲛⲧⲉ ⲉϩ. ϩⲙⲡⲭⲁⲟⲥ, Br 118 *S* ⲃⲱⲕ ⲉϩ. ϩⲙⲙⲁ, BAp 1 *S* ⲉⲓ ⲉϩ. ϩⲙⲡⲙ̄ⲧⲉ, Mani K 11 *A²* ϫⲉⲥⲧϥ ⲁϩ. ϩⲙⲡⲕⲟⲥⲙⲟⲥ, AM 254 *B* ⲑⲁⲣⲙⲉϥ ⲉϩ. ϩⲉⲛⲛⲓⲃⲁⲑⲙⲟⲥ; ϩⲓϫⲉⲛ- *B*: 2 Kg 1 24 (*S* ⲉⲝⲛ-) ἀνα-ἐπί, Dan 9 19 (*S* ⲉϩ. ⲉⲝⲛ-) ἐπι-ἐπί, Bel 36 ἐπάνω; AM 33 ϣⲉⲛ ϭⲓⲥⲓ ⲉϩ. ϩ. ⲡⲉⲕⲣⲁⲛ.

ⲛϩ. *SAA²B*(mostly) *upward, above*: Jud 11 31 (*S* ⲉϩ.) ἀνα-, Pro 8 29 *A*(*S* ⲉⲧϩ., *B* om) ἄνω; ShA 1 245 *S* some roots ⲉⲧⲙⲡⲉⲥⲏⲧ, others ⲛⲉⲧⲛϩ., TRit 546 ⲉⲛϥ ⲛϩ. ⲡⲟⲩϭⲗⲓⲗ; ⲛϩ. ⲉϫⲉⲛ-: Ex 34 27 (*S* ⲉϩ. ⲉⲝⲛ-) ἐπί; ⲛϩ. ϩⲓ-, *on, in*: Ex 15 22 (*S* ϩⲓ-), Jer 9 26 (*S* ϩⲛ-), ib 39 12 (*S* ⲉ-) ἐν; Ez 18 6 ἐπί; Mani 1 *A²* testify to me ⲛϩ. ϩⲓⲡϫⲓⲥⲉ; ⲛϩ. ϩⲉⲛ-: Ex 8 19 ἐν; AP 19 *A²* light shone ⲛϩ. ⲛⲣⲏⲧϥ ὅπου; MG 25 105 (cf Z 48) ⲛⲁϥⲛϩ. ϩⲉⲛⲓⲍ̄ ⲛⲣⲟⲙⲡⲉ; *v also* ϩⲛ- *b*; ⲛϩ. ϩⲓϫⲉⲛ-: Jer 2 34 (*S* ϩ. ϩⲓϫⲛ-) ἐπί, ib 38 6 ἐν.

ⲥⲁϩ. *SFO, on upper side, above*: P 130⁵ 35 ⲁⲕⲉⲓ ⲉⲃⲟⲗ ⲥ. ⲁⲕⲟⲩⲟⲛϩⲕ ⲛⲥⲁⲡⲉⲥⲏⲧ, AZ 23 114 lay drugs ⲥ. ⲁⲩⲱ ⲥⲁⲡⲉⲥⲏⲧ, Bodl(P)g 6 stood ⲥ. ⲛ[ⲡⲙⲁ ⲛϣⲱ]-ⲡⲉ, PSBA 34 174 have named ⲛⲉϥⲣⲁⲛ ⲥ., Rec 37 46 monastery ⲉⲧⲥ. (cf 48 do ⲉⲗⲙⲉ ϩⲁⲗⲗⲁⲭⲁ äẛ ⲙ), PGM 1 114 *O* Son of Father ⲉⲑⲥⲁⲣⲏ (ⲛ)ⲡⲓⲥⲁⲥϥⲉ; ⲛⲥ.: Lu 14 10 *F*(*S* ⲉϩ. ⲉⲡϫⲓⲥⲉ, *B* ⲉⲡϣ.) προσανα-ἀνώτερον; ⲥⲁϩⲣⲉ ⲛⲛ ⲙ *SAB*: Zech 4 3 *A* ⲛⲛⲥ. (*S* ⲛⲧⲡⲉ ⲛ-, *B* ⲥⲁⲡϣ. ⲛ-) ἐπάνω, Mic 3 2 *A* ⲙⲛⲥ. ⲛ-(*S* ϩⲓⲧⲡⲉ ⲛ-, *B* diff) ἀπό desuper; Cl 12 3 *A* ⲙⲁ ⲛⲛⲥ. ὑπερῷον (cf Jos 2 6 *S* ⲭⲉⲛⲉⲡⲱⲣ), MIE 2 335 *B* stood to pray in ⲟⲩⲙⲁ ⲛⲥ. = PO 22 352 مكان (var P ar 4878 71 مكان); PS 202 *S* ⲉⲛⲥ. opp ⲉⲛϩⲃⲃⲉ, ib 297 *S* ϩⲓⲛⲥ. ⲛⲡⲉⲭⲁⲟⲥ, ib 205 *S* ⲉⲧⲛⲉⲩⲥ. opp ⲉⲧⲛⲉϥⲉⲥⲏⲧ.

ϣⲁϩ. *SAA²*, ϣⲁⲉϩ. *BF*, *upward*: Br 263 *S* ϫⲓⲛⲙⲡⲉⲥⲏⲧ ϣ.; ϣ. ⲉ-, *up to*: Ge 13 3 *S*(*B* ϣⲁ-), ib 48 15 *S*(var & *B* ϣⲁϩⲟⲩⲛ), Ps 13 1 *S*(*B* do), Is 30 28 *B*(*SF* diff), Jo 5 17 *SA²*(*B* do) ἕως; PS 5 5 *S* ϫⲓⲛⲡⲉⲥⲏⲧ ϣ. ⲉⲙⲡⲏⲩⲉ, ShC 73 142 *S* ϫⲓⲛⲙ̄ⲡⲛⲟϭ ϣ. ⲉⲡⲕⲟⲩⲓ, CA 90 *S* ϣ. ⲉⲡⲟⲟⲩ ⲛϩⲟⲟⲩ, Miss 4 244 *S* fame reached ϣ. ⲉϩⲣⲱⲙⲏ, El 92 *A* ⲡⲱⲧ ϣ. ⲁⲑⲟⲩⲣⲁⲓⲁ= ib 122 *S* ⲉϩ. ⲉ-, ManiK 12 *A²* ϣ. ⲁⲧϭⲓⲛⲉⲓ, AM 287 *B* went south ϣ. ⲉⲡⲓⲉⲑⲁ ϣ, Mor 30 24 *F* ϣ. ⲉⲡⲁⲧⲛⲟⲩ† Julian; *even to, except*(?)*SB* (once, cf ϣⲁ-ⲉ): ShA 1 419 have we heard of wrong done to his neigh-bour ⲟⲩⲁⲉ ϣ. ⲉⲡⲉϥϣⲁϫⲉ?, ShC 42 81 fasts kept by all ϣ. ⲉⲡⲕⲉⲣⲣⲱⲟⲩ, ib 43 none dieth without Creator ϣ. ⲉⲡⲉⲛⲧⲁⲟⲩⲑⲏⲣⲓⲟⲛ ⲟⲩⲟⲙϥ, Sh(?)ClPr 39 41 = Mor 54 90 let no priest sport with woman ϣ. ⲉⲩϣⲉⲉⲣⲉ ϣⲏⲙ ⲙ̄ⲡⲟⲩⲛⲟϭ ⲛⲥϩⲓⲙⲉ, ShC 73 145 none may talk ϣ. ⲉⲟⲩⲁ ⲉϥϣⲱⲡⲉ, ib 10 I marvel ϣ. ⲉⲑⲉ ⲉⲛⲧⲁⲩϫⲓ ⲟⲩⲁ, JTS 8 243 they shall not know Hell ϣ. ⲉⲡⲉⲓⲉⲣⲟ ⲛⲕⲱϩⲧ that all must cross (cf BMar 135 *sup*), TstAb 171 *B* all sins soul had committed ϣ. ⲉⲡⲓⲡⲉⲧϩⲱⲟⲩ (corrupt?).

ϩⲓϩ. *S*, *upward*: P 129¹⁶ 69 ϩⲓⲡⲉⲥⲏⲧ trees joined,

ⲁⲩⲡⲱⲣⲝ ⲙⲉ ⲣ., BMOr 6203 shalt possess ⲙⲁ ⲛϣⲱⲡⲉ ⲣ. ⲣⲓⲡⲉⲥⲏⲧ, BM 1015 terms of lease]ⲉϩⲁⲓⲥⲟⲩ ⲣ. *above*, *ib* 217 27 ⲥⲧⲉⲣⲉⲱⲙⲁ ⲉⲧⲣ.; ϩⲓϩⲣⲉ S: ShA 1 150 fire ⲛⲉϧⲥⲉ ⲣ. after smouldering in depths.

ϩⲣⲁⲓ S, ϩⲣⲏⲓ A, ϩⲣⲏⲓ Jo Ma), ϩⲣⲛⲉⲓ (AP) A², ϩ̄ⲣⲏⲓ B, ϧⲗⲏⲓ F nn m, *lower part*, opp to ϩⲣⲁⲓ *upper part q v.* As nn m once: J 25 21 S ⲛⲁⲁⲛⲣ ⲉⲧⲁⲛⲣ. ⲙⲙⲟϥ, *cf ib* 11 ⲉⲧⲛⲡⲉⲓⲧⲏ ⲙⲡⲛⲓ. Otherwise only in compounds.

ⲉϩⲣⲁⲓ, -ⲣⲏ (once) S, ⲁϩⲣⲏⲓ, -ⲣⲏ A, ⲁϩⲣⲏ(ⲉ)ⲓ, -ⲣⲏ, ⲉϩⲣⲏ A², ⲉϩ̄ⲣⲏⲓ B (but often ⲣ.) O, ⲉϩⲗⲏⲓ F, *to below, downward*, appended to vbs of motion, as ⲃⲱⲕ, ⲉⲓ, ⲉⲓⲛⲉ, ⲕⲱ, ⲕⲧⲟ, ⲙⲟⲟϣⲉ, ⲛⲁ, ⲡⲏⲅ, ⲡⲟⲩϫⲉ, ⲣⲱϩⲧ, ϯ, ϯⲕⲉ, ⲧⲁϩⲟ, ⲑⲙⲥⲟ, ⲟⲩⲱϩ, ⲱⲙⲥ, ϣⲟⲅⲟ, ϩⲉ, ϩⲙⲟⲟⲥ, ϩⲓⲟⲩⲉ, ϫⲓ, ϫⲟ & to others, as ⲧⲱⲱⲃⲉ, ⲑⲃ̄ⲃⲓⲟ, ϩⲱⲙ, ϣⲁϫⲉ, ϭⲱϣⲧ.

Represents preposition prefixed to vb. Nu 11 4 S (var & B om), Jos 3 16 B (S om), Job 11 10 S (B ⲉϩ.), Ps 55 7 S (B ⲉⲡⲉⲥⲏⲧ), Hag 2 22 A (S ⲉⲡⲉⲥⲏⲧ, B diff), Jo 4 47 A²BF (S do) κατα-, MG 25 233 B ϫⲟⲩϣⲧ ⲉⲅ̄. κάτω; Lev 23 22 S (B om), Jo 4 28 F (SA²B do), Col 3 8 B (S ⲛⲥⲁ-), Cl 13 1 A ἀπο-; Mt 13 24 SF (B diff) παρα-; Mic 2 13 A (B ⲉⲃⲟⲗ) ἐκ-; not in Gk: Jos 6 5 ϩⲉ ⲉϩ., Zech 11 2 A do (SB om) πίπτειν, Deu 26 4 S ⲕⲱ (B om), Jo 13 4 SA²B τιθέναι, Is 33 23 BF sim (S diff) χαλᾶν, *ib* 45 8 S (B diff) ῥαντίζειν, Deu 11 10 S ϫⲟ ⲉϩ. (B do) σπείρειν; PS 233 S how doth ⲕⲟⲥⲙⲟⲥ ⲕⲏ ⲉϩ., El 92 A ⲕⲟⲩ ⲁϩ. ⲡⲧⲥⲁⲣⲝ̄ = *ib* 128 S, ShC 73 59 S ⲉⲅϩⲙⲟⲟⲥ ⲉϩ., AP 21 A² ⲛⲉⲁϥⲟⲁⲉⲓⲉⲡⲉ ⲁϩ., BSM 93 B ϭⲁ ⲥⲱⲙⲁ ⲉⲅ̄., BP 5561 F ⲧⲁⲟⲩⲉϩ ⲡⲉⲓⲧⲓⲕⲉⲱⲛ (δίκαιον) ⲉϩ.

Reinforcing following preposition, mostly with downward sense. ⲉ-: Jud 14 1 S, Ps 21 15 SB, Is 30 2 BF (S ⲉⲡⲉⲥ. ⲉ-), Am 9 3 SA (B ϫⲉⲛ-), Ac 8 5 SB κατα- εἰς, Va 57 14 B ϩⲉⲓ ⲉⲅ̄. ⲉⲧⲕⲁⲕⲓⲁ κατα- πρός; Ge 18 22 SB, Ps 142 3 S (B ϣⲁ ⲉⲅ̄.), Lam 1 8 BF, Jo 5 7 A²B (S ⲉⲡⲉⲥ.) εἰς, Ge 46 26 SB εἰσ- εἰς, Joel 2 20 AB ἐκ- εἰς, Ge 50 14 SB, Ac 7 9 SB (var ⲉϩ.) ἀπο- εἰς, Nu 5 17 SBF (BM 1221), Aeg 222 S ⲉⲓ ⲉϩ. ⲉⲣⲉⲛⲛⲟϭ ⲛⲣⲓⲥⲉ ἐν- εἰς, Ac 21 11 SB, 2 Cor 4 11 B (S ⲉ-) παρα- εἰς, Pro 9 18 AB (S ⲉⲡⲉⲥ.) ἐπί, Lev 11 35 S (B ⲉ-) ἐπι- ἐπί, Am 1 7 A (B ⲉⲅ̄.) ἐκ- ἐπί, Ez 20 23 S (B ⲉⲅ̄. ϫⲉⲛ-) δια- ἐν, Jo 3 35 SBF ἐν; PS 350 S Christ ⲉⲓ ⲉϩ. ⲉⲡⲕⲟⲥⲙⲟⲥ, RChamp 539 A ⲛⲧϣ (*l* ⲛⲧⲥ) ⲁϩⲣⲏ ⲁⲩϭⲁⲉ, Mun 110 S ϫⲟⲥ ⲉϩ. ⲉⲡⲕⲁϩ, *ib* 162 S beasts in fields ⲛⲥⲉϩⲟⲙⲟⲩ ⲉϩ. ⲉⲛⲟⲙⲉ, PLond 4 448 S ⲧⲁⲁϥ (*sc* money) ⲛⲁⲓ ⲉϩ. ⲉⲛⲁϭⲓϫ, ST 393 Sᵃ ϩⲛⲓⲉ ⲁϩ. ⲁⲧⲙⲏ[, C 86 275 B ϩⲓⲧϥ ⲉⲅ̄. ⲉⲟⲩⲭⲁⲗⲕⲓⲟⲛ, Miss 4 184 B went from Ephesus ⲉⲅ̄. ⲉϫⲛⲙⲓ, C 86 210 B ⲥⲁϩⲉ ⲉⲅ̄. ⲉⲛⲓⲙⲁϣϫ ⲛ-; ⲉϫⲛ-: Jos 15 10 S, Sa 7 3 S, Mt 19 28 S (BF ϩⲓ-), Jo 4 6 SA² (BF ϩⲓϫ.) κατα- ἐπί, Ex 4 3 A (B ϩⲓϫ.), Ps 118 41 SB (var ⲉϩ.), Sa 18 23 S, Mt 3 16 S (B ϩⲁ-), Cl 21 6 A ⲧⲁϩⲣⲁϥ ⲁϩ.

ⲁⲝⲙⲡⲁϭⲁⲑⲟⲛ ἐπί, Ps 15 6 S (B ⲉ-) ἐπι- dat, Ge 35 14 S (B ϩⲓϫ.) ἐπι- ἐπί, CaiEuch 652 B send Paraclete ⲉⲅ̄. ⲉϫⲱⲡ ἐξαπο- ἐπί, Jo 12 24 S (B ⲉⲝ., ϩⲓϫ.) εἰς; PS 287 S ϩⲉ ⲉϩ. ⲉϫⲙⲡⲉϩⲟ (*cf ib* 289 ϩⲉ ⲉϫⲙ-), *ib* 65 S looked from on high ⲉϩ. ⲉϫⲛⲟⲩⲗⲏ, AP 22 A² sim, ShC 73 24 S ϩⲱⲙ ⲉϩ. ⲉϫⲙⲡⲥⲁⲧⲁⲡⲁⲥ, Mun 116 S ⲉⲓ ⲉⲡⲉⲥⲏⲧ …ⲉϩ. ⲉϫⲙⲡⲕⲁϩ, BIF 13 108 S ⲡⲧⲟⲩ ⲉϩ. ⲉϫⲛⲧⲡⲉⲧⲣⲁ = MG 25 293 B, Aeg 255 S ⲉⲩⲭⲁⲣⲓⲥⲧⲉⲓ ⲉϩ. ⲉϫⲙⲡⲛⲉϩ, El 66 A sun ⲡⲣⲣⲓⲉ ⲁϩ. ⲁϫⲙⲡⲕⲁϩ, *ib* 38 A ⲧⲉⲗⲏⲗ ⲁϩ. ⲁϫⲱⲟⲩ, PGol 47 A² may curse ⲉⲓ ⲉϩⲣⲏ ⲉϫⲟⲩ-, BM 1224 A² ⲉⲓⲛⲉ ⲁϩⲣⲏ ⲁϫⲱⲟⲩ, KroppC F 1 ⲉϩ. ⲉϫⲉⲛⲡⲉⲕϫⲟⲧⲓⲟⲛ (ζῷδ.), Miss 4 180 B ⲉⲣ ⲙⲉⲧⲁⲛⲟⲓⲛ ⲉⲅ̄. ⲉϫⲉⲛⲡⲟⲩⲛⲟⲃⲓ; ⲉϩ. ⲉⲝ. B often where sense seems *down upon*: Ps 88 46 ϫⲱϣ ⲉϩ. ⲉⲝ. κατα-, AM 59 ϥⲱⲛ ⲉϩ. ⲉⲝ. (but C 43 120 ϥⲟⲛⲟⲩ ⲉⲅ̄. ⲉ-), *ib* 60 ⲉⲣ ⲉⲡⲓⲕⲁⲗⲓⲥⲑⲉ ⲛϭⲁⲛⲣⲁⲛ ⲉϩ. ⲉϫⲱϥ, *ib* 146 ⲟⲩⲱⲣⲡ ⲙⲡⲉⲕϩⲙⲟⲧ ⲉϩ. ⲉϫⲱⲡ, C 43 87 ⲙⲟⲩϯ ⲉϩ. ⲉⲝ. = AM 330 ⲙ. ⲉⲅ̄. ϩⲓϫ.; or varies with ⲉⲅ̄.: Ps 139 11, Lu 1 12, Ac 19 17 πίπτ. ἐπί; AM 268 ⲡⲓⲣⲁⲥⲙⲟⲥ ⲓ ⲉϩ. ⲉⲝ. συμβαίνειν dat, *ib* 249 give life ⲉϩ. ⲉϫⲱⲟⲩ; ⲁϩ. ⲁⲝ. A where ⲉϩ. ⲉϫⲉⲛ- B: Hos 4 9, 5 10, Mic 4 7, Zeph 3 17, 18 ἐπί (*cf* Joel 3 9, Hab 3 16 ⲁϩ. ἀνα-); ϩⲁ-: Jer 43 14 B κατα- πρός, Jo 13 37 SA² (B ⲉϩ. ⲉⲝ.) ὑπέρ, Eccl 2 14 F (S ϩⲛ-) ἐν; ϩⲛ-, ϫⲉⲛ-: Ge 22 18 S (B ⲛⲅ̄. ϫⲉⲛ-), Ro 1 24 B (S ϩⲛ-) ἐν, Eccl 5 1 F (S ϩⲓϫⲛ-) ἐπί … κάτω, Lam 1 2 F ϩⲗⲏⲓ ⲛ- (*l* ϩⲛ-, B ⲉⲝ.) ἐπί, Ez 21 4 S (B ⲉⲅ̄. *sic?*) ἐκ- ἐκ; El 58 A ⲁⲙⲥ ⲁϩ. ⲡϩⲏⲧⲥ, AM 189 B ⲭⲁϥ ⲉϩ. ϫⲉⲛⲡⲓⲛⲁⲗⲗⲁⲧⲓⲟⲛ; ϩⲓϫⲉⲛ- B: C 43 215 ⲧⲣⲉⲙⲥⲟϥ ⲉϩ. ϩ. ⲟⲩϭⲗⲟϫ.

ⲛϩⲣⲁⲓ, ⲛϩ., ⲛⲅ̄., *below*: Mk 14 66 B ⲛⲉϥⲛⲅ̄. (S ⲛⲉϥϩⲣ.), Jo 8 23 B ⲛⲏ ⲉⲧⲉⲛⲉⲅ̄. (var ⲉⲛⲉⲅ̄., SA² diff) κάτω; ShA 1 245 S ⲡⲉⲧⲛϩ. … ⲡⲉⲧⲛⲧⲡⲉ; ϩ ϩⲓ-B, *in, on*: Ge 12 9 (S ϩⲛ-), Jer 3 21 ἐν; ϩ ϩⲛ-, ϫⲉⲛ- AB sim: Nu 14 11 (S do), Hos 5 4 A (B ϫⲉⲛ-), Jo 11 38 AB (S ϩⲛ-, A² ϩⲣ. ϩⲛ-), C 86 275 nails ⲛⲅ̄. ⲡϩⲏⲧⲟⲩ *wherewith* to tear flesh ἐν; Jer 3 10 ἐπί; ϩ ϩⲓϫⲛ-: Deu 31 13 B, Joel 2 30 A ἐπί.

ⲥⲁϩ. S (rare), ⲥⲉϩ., ⲥⲁϩⲣⲉ A, ⲥⲁⲅ̄. B, ⲥⲉⲅ̄. O, *downward, below*: Ex 26 24, Va 63 84 ⲓⲥϫⲉⲛⲥ. ⲉⲧϥⲉ κάτωθεν; El 80 A ⲭⲛ-…ⲥ. (= Mt 2 16 SB ⲉⲥⲏⲧ, *cf* ϩⲣⲁⲓ *upper part p* 699 *b*), Va 61 204 left servants ⲥ. ⲁϥϩⲱⲗ ⲉⲛϣⲱⲓ (*cf* Ge 22 5), C 89 195 ⲉϥϭⲟⲥⲓ ⲉⲩⲥ., Miss 4 157 wherefore didst not read ⲛⲓⲭⲱⲙ ⲥ.? = Mor 19 97 S ⲉⲡⲉⲥⲏⲧ = Gött ar 114 75 اخر الى, MG 25 248 ⲙⲉⲗⲟⲥ ⲉⲧⲥ. *lower limbs*, Hor 84 O ⲉⲧⲥ., ShA 1 256 S some ϯ ⲕⲁⲣⲡⲟⲥ ⲛⲥ. others ⲛⲥⲁⲧⲛⲉ; ⲥ ⲛ- S (once) B: Ge 1 7 ὑποκάτω; Va 66 304 body cannot ϣⲱⲡⲓ ⲥ. (*sic, l?* ⲥⲁϩ.) ⲡⲧⲁⲫⲉ ὑπέρ; PMéd 318 S ϣⲟⲩ ⲥⲛⲟϥ ⲉϩⲣⲁⲓ ⲥ. ⲙⲙⲟϥ, MIE 2 398 lay ⲥ. ⲡⲟⲩϣⲏⲛ = BAp 97 S ϩⲁ-, BSM 40 ⲟⲩⲡⲉ ⲉⲧⲉⲡⲡⲁⲫⲟⲣϣϥ ⲥ. ⲙⲡⲓⲁⲣⲭⲱⲡ? = BMis 386 S ϩⲁ-; as nn: TU 43 13 A ⲉⲓ ⲁⲃⲁⲗ … ⲛⲡⲥⲁ. ⲥⲉⲃⲱⲕ ⲁϩⲣⲏ ⲁ- = PO 9 209

ⲗⲅ̄ϯⲁ̄ⲃ̄ϯ; ⲉⲣ c. *B, be below*: Lam 1 9 καταφέρεσθαι (var καταβαίνειν); C 86 320 when digging
ⲉⲧⲁϥⲉⲣ ⲥ. ⲡⲟⲩⲕⲟⲩϫⲓ.

ϣⲁⲣ. *S*(rare), ϣⲁⲉⲋ̄. *B, down to*: Is 29 4 (*S* ⲉ-),
Ez 12 3 (*S* ⲉϩ. ⲉ-) εἰς; *ib* 29 10 *SB* ἕως; He 12 4 (*S*
diff) μέχρι, Ap 2 10 *SB* ἄχρι; EW 149 ϣ. ⲉϯⲡⲟⲩ.

ϩⲣⲉ *SA²*, ϩⲉⲣⲉ *S*, ϩⲣⲓⲉⲓ, ϩⲣⲅⲉⲓ *Sᵃ*, ϩⲣⲉ *A*, ϣ̄ⲣⲉ
B, ϩⲣⲏ *F*, pl ϩⲣⲏⲩⲉ *SA²*, ϩⲣⲉⲟⲩⲉ, ϩⲣⲉⲟⲟⲩ *S*, ϩⲣⲏⲟⲩⲉ, -ⲏⲩ *A*, ϣ̄ⲣⲏⲟⲩⲉ *B*, ϩⲣⲏⲟⲩⲓ *F* & sg as pl, nn f m
(*SF* rare), *food of men*: Ps 68 22 *SB*, Ro 14 15 *SB*
βρῶμα, Nu 14 9 *SB* κατάβ., Ge 9 3 *B*(*S* ⲟⲩⲱⲙ), Deu
23 19 *B*(*S* ⲉⲃⲣⲁ), Jo 4 32 *SA²BF*, He 12 16 *B*(*S* ϭⲓⲛⲟⲩⲱⲙ) βρῶσις, Ge 31 15 *B*(*S* ⲟⲩ.) κατάβρωσις; Ps
64 9 *SB*, Pro 6 8 *SAB*, He 5 14 *SBF* τροφή; Job 3 24
SB pl, Pro 4 17 *SAB* pl σῖτος, Lev 26 26 *S*(*B* ⲥⲟⲩⲟ)
σιτοδεία, Lu 12 42 *SB* -μέτριον, Jud 7 8 *S* ἐπισιτισ-
μός; Lam 4 9 *S*(*BF* ⲟⲩⲧⲁϩ) γέννημα; Ge 27 7 *B* ἔδεσμα; Lu 10 7 *B*(*S* ⲃⲉⲕⲉ) μισθός; Dan 1 5 *B* ⲧϩ̄. ⲛ̄ⲧⲉ
ⲡⲓⲉϩⲟⲟⲩ τὸ τῆς ἡμέρας; ShC 73 195 *S* ϩ. ⲣⲓⲥⲱ, ShA
1 4 19 *S* ⲧⲉⲣ. ⲛ̄ⲙⲙⲟⲛⲁⲭⲟⲥ, Bor 265 93 *S* ⲟⲩϩ. ⲛⲱⲡⲉ,
BSM 27 *B* ⲉⲧϣⲁⲧ ⲛ̄ϩ̄.; *of beasts, fodder*: Ge 1
30 *B*, Jer 41 20 *SB* βρῶσις, Job 6 5 *SB* βρῶμα, Ez 34
8 *SB* κατάβ.; Job 38 39 *SB* βορά; *ib* 15 23 *SB* pl σῖ.;
Ge 24 25 *S*(ShA 2 167, *B* ⲥⲱⲟⲩ ϩⲉⲛ) χόρτασμα; BMis
232 *S* ϩ. ⲡⲡⲉⲑⲏⲣⲓⲟⲛ, C 43 91 *B* ⲛ̄ⲛⲓⲟⲩϩⲱⲣ, CMSS
78 *F* ⲛⲉⲃⲁⲗⲡⲓ, BM 602 *F* ⲛϩ. ⲡⲡⲉⲧⲉⲃⲛⲁⲅⲉⲓ, Ryl 34
6 *S* sow ⲥⲟⲩⲟ, ⲉⲓⲱⲧ, ϩ., PMich 4571 *S* about sowing
ⲧⲉϥ]ⲡⲁϣⲉ ⲛϩ. ⲧⲉϥⲡⲁϣⲉ ⲛⲟⲩϩⲣⲱ, CMSS 20 *Sf* ⲛⲱⲥⲉ
ⲓⲉ ⲛⲉϩ ⲉⲧⲣⲉⲡⲁⲁⲩ, ViK 1112 *S* ⲟⲧⲡ ϩ. ⲉⲣⲟⲩⲏⲡ, Ostr
penes Crum *S* ⲡϣⲗⲟⲡ (*wisp*?) ⲛϩ. [ⲉ]ⲧⲉⲓϭⲱⲗ ⲙⲙⲟⲩ,
BM 1140 *S* ⲛⲉϩⲣⲏ ⲉϥⲫⲏⲩ, *ib* 1141 *S* ⲧⲛⲟⲟⲩ ⲛⲉϩ.,
BMOr 6201 B 19 *S* ⲥⲉⲧⲓⲁϩ ϩ., PLichatschev (Jernstedt)*S* ⲥⲓⲧⲓⲱϩⲉ ϩⲉⲣⲉ = *ib* χορτ(ου) αρου(ρας), PStras
124 *S* ⲙⲟⲉⲓⲁϩ ⲛϩⲉⲣⲉ, ST 421 *Sᵃ* ϩⲣⲅⲉⲓ; pl forms:
ϩⲣⲏⲩⲉ *SA²* Jth 11 12, Job 30 4, ShRE 11 15, PMich
1298 ⲛⲉϩ. ... ϯⲡⲁⲕⲱⲧⲉ ⲉⲣⲟⲟⲩ ⲧⲁⲧⲥⲟⲟⲩ (so growing
crop), Mani 1 *A²*, ϩⲣⲉⲟⲩⲉ *S* Ge 6 21 (*P* 44 102), ϩⲣⲉⲟⲟⲩ *S* Ryl 356; ϩⲣⲏⲟⲩⲉ *A* Pro 24 60, ϩⲣⲏⲩ (?)
Joel 1 16; ϩⲣⲏⲟⲩⲓ *F* Jo 4 8; ϣ̄ⲣⲏⲟⲩⲓ *B* Ge 6 21,
ROC 25 255 (var *ib* 273 ϣ̄ⲣⲏⲃⲓ.)

ⲁⲧϩ̄., ⲙⲉⲧ- *B, lack of food*: Va 58 73 ⲛⲓⲙ. more
painful than blows.

ⲣ ϩ., ⲟ ⲛϩ̄., *become, be food*: Hab 3 17 *B*(*A* + ⲃ̄ⲣⲉ)
βρῶσιν ποιεῖν, Deu 32 24 *SB* βρῶσις; Mani 1 *A²*
ϣⲁⲥⲣ ϩ. ⲛⲓⲡ̄ⲡ̄.

ϯ ϩ., (ⲛ)ⲟⲩϩ., *give food*: Ps 135 25 *SB* ⲧⲣⲟ. διδόναι; Ge 43 24 *SB* χορτ. δ.; Pro 29 33 *SAB* βρώματα
δ.; C 99 190 *S* steward ϯ ϩ. ⲛⲡⲉϥϩⲙϩⲁⲗ, AZ 23 39
F ⲙⲡⲉⲃⲕⲉⲧ ⲧⲁⲧⲓ ϩ. ⲛⲉⲥ (*sc* cow).

ⲟⲩⲉⲙϩⲣⲉ *B v* p 479 a.

ϫⲓ ϩ., *get fodder*: Ep 373 *Sᵃ* send asses ⲛⲧⲁϫⲓ
ϩⲣⲓⲉⲓ ⲛⲉⲙⲁⲟⲩ; as nn: CO 222 *S* ⲛϫ., ⲛϫⲓ ⲧⲱϩ,
ⲛϫⲓ ⲉⲓⲱⲧ.

ϭⲓ ϩ̄. *B, take food*: MG 25 371 forgot to ϭ. ⲡⲉⲙ-
ϩⲓⲛⲁⲙ. ⲣⲉϥϭⲓ ϩ̄., *taking, needing food*: Va 57 10
ⲥⲁⲣϫ ⲛⲣ.

ϩⲣⲉ *v* ϩⲣⲁⲓ *upper part*.

ϩⲣⲓ *S* nn, *endive*(?): PMéd 316 ϩ. ⲛ̄ⲧⲟⲟⲩ *wild e.*,
P 44 83 ϩ. ⲛ̄ⲧⲟⲩ· ⲥⲓⲗⲗⲓⲟⲃⲟⲧⲁⲛⲏ (*cf* ? ⲥⲓⲗⲓⲥ = σέρις
Keimer) ﺑﻠﻴﺲ (*cf* ⲁⲡⲛⲟϣⲉⲣ). Or ? for ϩⲣⲉ.

ϩⲣⲟⲉⲓ *S* nn, *meaning unknown*: El 114 be of
one mind always ⲉⲣ ⲣⲓ.ⲁⲕⲉ ϩ.ⲛ̄ⲡⲉϩ. (Miss 1 273 reads
ⲉⲣⲣⲓⲥⲁⲉ· ϩ.ⲛ̄ⲡⲉⲣⲣⲟⲉⲓ) ϫⲉⲉⲧⲉⲧⲛⲁⲡⲟⲉⲓ ⲛⲡⲱⲃ ⲛⲓⲙ =
ib 74 *A* om.

ϩⲣⲱ *SB*, ϩⲣⲟⲩ *A*, ⲉϩⲣⲱ *B* (once) nn f, *oven, furnace*: Nu 25 8 *S*(var = Gk)*B*, Pro 16 30 *SA*, Dan 3
22 *SB*, Mt 13 50 *SB*(*F* = Gk) κάμινος, Ex 9 8 *B* κα-
μιναῖος; Lev 11 35 *SB* κυθρόπους; Sa 3 6 *S* χωνευτήριον; BHom 36 *S* ϩ. ⲡⲥⲁⲧⲉ κλίβανος; Hos 13 3 *B*
ϩ. ⲛϭⲱⲣ (*A* ϩ.) καπνοδόχη; Tri 462 *S* اﻟﺘﻨﻮﺭ; ShR 2
3 19 *S* ϩ. ⲡⲕⲱϩⲧ, DeV 2 185 *B* ϩ. ⲛⲭⲣⲱⲙ, AM 206
B sim ⲉϩ., Mich 550 25 *S* ϩ. ⲙⲡⲉⲛⲓⲡⲉ, BKU 1 1 *ro*
S ϩ. ⲛⲣⲁⲙⲉⲧ, PMéd 208 *S* ϩ. ⲛⲁϣ, Pcod 27 *S* ϩ. of
potter, BM 1179 *S* ϩ. ⲛⲧⲱⲕ ⲕⲟⲩⲫⲟⲛ; ⲙⲁ ⲛⲧⲉϩ.
S: ShC 73 73 both for baking & heating.

ϩⲣⲃ̄ *SA²*(Jo), ϩⲣⲃⲉ, ⲣⲃⲉ *A*, ϩⲣⲃⲉ *A²*(Ma), ϣ̄ⲉⲣⲉⲃ,
ⲭ. *B* nn m, *form, likeness*: Est 2 2 *S*, Is 53 3 *A*(Cl,
S ⲉⲓⲛⲉ, *B* ⲥⲙⲟⲧ), Jo 5 37 *SA²*(*B* do) εἶδος; Deu 4 12
S(*B* do) ὁμοίωμα (var μορφή), Ro 2 20 *S*(*B* ⲙⲟⲣⲫⲓ)
μόρφωσις, Mt 17 2 *B* ϣⲱⲃⲧ ⲛϩ. (var ⲭ. *S* ϣⲓⲃⲉ only)
μεταμορφοῦσθαι; HL 109 *B* sim ⲭ. μετασχηματίζεσθαι; Joel 2 4 *A*(*B*=Gk), Nah 2 5 *A* ⲣ. (*B* do) ὅρασις;
1 Cor 13 12 *S*(*B* ⲑⲟⲛⲧⲉⲛ) αἴνιγμα, cit Va 66 304 *B*
ϣ̄.; 1 Pet 2 16 *S*(*B* ⲕⲁⲗⲩⲙⲙⲁ) ἐπικάλ.; Sa 13 10 *S*
ἀπείκασμα; *ib* 17 14 *S* τέρας; Lev 13 2 *S*(*B* diff)
ἀφή; 2 Kg 14 27 *S* ⲛⲉⲥⲉ ϩ. καλός; ShR 2 3 69 *S*
ⲟⲩϩ. ⲛⲣⲟⲧⲉ, ShClPr 24 360 *S* ⲉⲣⲉⲛϩ. ⲙⲡⲥⲁⲧⲁⲡⲁⲥ
ϭⲟⲟⲗⲉ ⲙⲙⲟⲩ, BMOr 8811 80 *S* ⲛϩ. ⲛⲧⲙⲛⲧⲉⲩⲥⲉⲃⲏⲥ, C 100 278 *S* in vision saw ⲛϩ. ⲙⲡⲉⲛⲉⲓⲱⲧ, Till
Oster 21 *A* ⲥⲙⲁⲧ, ϩ., Mani 1 *A²* ⲛϩ. ⲉⲧⲁϥⲟⲩⲱⲡ[ϩ]
ⲛϩⲏ[ⲧϥ.

ϫⲓ ϩ., *take form, likeness*: Hos 12 10 *S*(BMOr 8800
201)*A*(*B* ϭⲓ ⲥ.) ὁμοιοῦσθαι; 2 Cor 11 13 *S*(*B* ϣⲓⲃ̄ϯ
ⲙⲡⲥ.) μετασχ.; Z 586 *S* devil ⲉⲧⲭ., Mor 18 113 *S*
spirits ⲛⲱⲱⲡⲉ ⲙⲡⲉⲩⲥⲙⲟⲧ ⲛⲥⲉϫⲓ ⲛϩⲣⲃ., CaiThe 442
B ⲁϥϭⲓ ⲭ. ⲙⲡⲟⲩⲙⲟϩⲟ (*cf* Mt 17 2 ϣⲟⲃⲧⲉϥ ⲛϩ̄.); c
ⲛ-: Ro 12 2 *S*(*BF* ⲥ.) μεταμ. dat, Phil 3 10 *S*(*B* ϣ.
ⲛⲥ.) συμμ. dat; C 99 217 *S* ⲁϥϫⲓ ⲛϩ. ⲛⲟⲩⲥϩⲓⲙⲉ =
89 14 *B* ⲉⲣ ⲛⲥ. σχημ. εἰς, 1 Pet 1 14 *S*(*B* diff) ⲟⲛⲟⲥⲭ.
dat; EW 148 *B* ϭⲓ ⲙⲡϩ̄. ⲛⲟⲩⲟⲅⲏⲃ̄ ἱεροπρεπής; Sh
MIF 23 22 *S* to devil ⲉⲕⲣ ⲡⲕⲉϫⲓ ⲙⲡϩ. ⲛⲣⲉⲡⲙⲛⲓⲛϣⲉ
ⲛⲣⲱⲙⲉ, ManiH 11 *A²* ϫⲓ ⲟⲩϩ. ⲛⲥⲱⲙⲁ; c ϩⲛ-
S: Wess 18 40 ⲛⲉⲥⲧⲁⲓⲟ ... ϫ. ϩⲛⲧⲉⲕⲕⲗⲏⲥⲓⲁ *taketh*

shape in; iterated: ManiP *A*² ⲁⲕϫⲓ ⲉ. ⲉ. ϣⲁⲧⲉⲕ-
ⲙⲟⲩϣⲧ ⲁⲡⲣⲉⲓⲧⲉ ⲡⲓⲙ; ϭⲓⲛϫⲓ ⲉ. *S*: Bor 248 58
ⲧϭ. ⲙⲡⲉϥⲙⲟⲩ (*cf* Ro 6 5 ⲡⲉⲓⲡⲉ ὁμοίωμα).

ⲉⲣⲃ̄ *S* nn, *leg*: Lev 11 21 ⲉ. ⲛⲧⲡⲉ ⲡⲣⲁⲧⲟⲩ (*B* ⲥⲛⲏⲓ)
σκέλος; ⲉⲃ̄ⲣ *S*, ⲉⲣⲏϥ *F*, *wand*, same?: BMis 338
S ⲉ. ⲡⲕⲁⲕⲉ opp ⲉⲣⲁⲃ̄ⲥⲟⲥ ⲡⲟⲩⲟⲉⲓⲛ = Mor 27 14 *F* ⲉ.

ⲉⲣⲉⲃ̄ *S*, ⲉⲣⲏϥ *Sⳑ*, ⲉⲣⲉϥ *B* nn m, *chisel*: BMOr
8775 139 *B* = P 54 155 ⲡⲓⲙⲁⲃⲟⲅⲗ, ⲡⲓⲉ. both مِنقار;
CO 468 *S* ⲡⲥⲁⲣϥ, ⲡⲉ. ⲡⲣⲁⲧⲏⲣ, Ep 547 *S* ⲉ., ⲥⲁⲣϥ ⲱ,
Pap *penes* BHStricker *Sⳑ*.

ⲉⲣⲟⲩⲃ̄ *B* *v* ⲉϥⲟⲩⲣ.

ⲉⲱⲣⲃ̄ *SB*(once), -ϥ, ⲉⲟⲣⲃ̄⳿ *S*, ⲉⲁⲣⲃ̄⳿ *A*, ⲉⲟⲣ(ⲉ)ϥ⳿
S vb intr, *be broken*: Sa 4 5 περικλᾶσθαι; 1 Kg 2 4
(*B* ϣⲱⲛⲓ) ἀσθενεῖν; Mor 46 36 fallen idol's head &
hands ⲉ. ⲉⲓⲭⲁⲡⲕⲁⲣ, Mor 31 254 ⲁⲡⲉϥϫⲁⲡ ⲡⲟⲩⲡⲁⲙ ⲉ. = BMEA 10578 *F* ⲥⲱⲗⲡ ⲉⲃⲁⲗ = RylBull 11
416 *b* انكسر; qual: MIF 9 46 ⲡⲉϥⲣⲟ ⲟⲩⲟⲛⲃ̄…
ⲙⲟⲭⲗⲟⲥ ⲉ. (var BAp 9 ⲣⲟ ⲉ. ⲙ. ⲟⲩ.), Mor 51 40
ⲟⲩⲕⲁⲥ ⲉ. ⲉⲛⲧⲉϥϭⲓⲥⲉ, Bodl (P) f 78]ⲟ ⲥⲡⲧⲉ ⲉⲣⲉⲟⲩⲉⲓ
ⲉⲟⲣⲉϥ; tr, *break*: Lev 1 17 (*B* ⲕⲱⲣϫ) ἐκκλᾶν, Ez
19 12 (*B* ϫⲱϫⲓ) κατακ., Ps 45 9 (*B* ⲕⲱϣ), Lam 2 3
(ShC 73 77, *B* do) συγκ.; Zech 11 16 (*B* diff) ἐκτρίβειν, Deu 33 20 (*B* ⲃⲟⲩⲃⲉⲙ), Mk 5 4 (*B* do) συντ.;
ShA 2 172 sickness ⲉϥⲉ. ⲡⲛⲉϥⲕⲉⲉⲥ, P 129²⁰ 133 ⲁϥⲉ.
ⲁⲡⲉⲓⲉⲓⲃ̄ ⲙⲡⲙⲟⲩ = Mus 45 44 *B*; as nn: ShBM
212 ⲟⲩⲉ. ⲉⲛⲛⲉⲕⲕⲉⲉⲥ after fall.

ⲉⲣⲏⲃⲉ, ⲉⲣⲉ. *S* nn f, *meaning unknown*: Hall 68
ϣⲁⲓⲉⲓ ⲉⲃⲟⲗ ⲉⲧⲉⲣⲏ. ⲛ[, ST 224 ⲧⲉⲣⲣⲉ. ⲡⲣⲛⲥ. As
place-name (?) ⲧⲉⲣⲣⲏϥⲉ (Ep 1 122, AZ 66 123).

ⲉⲁⲣⲁⲃⲉⲓ *F* *v* ⲉⲣⲟⲟⲩ (ⲉⲣⲟⲩⲃ̄ⲃⲁⲓ).

ⲉ(ⲉ)ⲣⲃ̄ⲱⲧ, ⲉⲉⲣⲃⲟⲟⲃⲉ (*sic* MS)*S*, ⲁⲣⲃ̄ⲟⲧ, -ⲱⲧ *B*
nn f *S* m *B*, *staff*, *wand*: Z 339 *S* moved it ⲛⲧⲉϥ-
ⲉ. βαινὴ ῥάβδος (*cf* ϣⲃ̄ⲱⲧ); *ib* 340 *S* monk walking
ⲉⲣⲉⲧⲉϥⲉ. ⲛⲧⲟⲟⲧϥ, Miss 4 712 *S* ⲕⲟⲩⲓ ⲛⲉ. in his
hand, R 1 2 32 *S* ⲉϥⲧⲁⲭⲣⲏⲩ ⲉⲭⲧⲉϥⲉ., Mor 51 37 *S*
ⲉⲛⲕⲉⲗⲉⲉⲗⲉ & ⲉⲉⲛⲉ. ⲙⲡⲁⲕⲡⲁⲣⲟⲩ *broad-backed
staves* for fighting, RA1 92 *B* ⲁⲩϭⲓ ⲙⲡⲉϥⲁⲣⲃ̄ⲱⲧ ⲁⲩ-
ⲙⲟϣⲓ ⲉⲃⲟⲗ, Montp 173 *B* ⲡⲓⲃ̄ⲛⲧ, ⲡⲓⲃⲁⲓ, ⲡⲓⲁⲣⲃ̄ⲱⲧ
جريد, AZ 25 106 *S* ⲟⲩⲉⲣⲃ̄ⲟⲟⲃⲉ ⲉⲧⲗⲏⲕ for stirring; K
126 *B* among weaver's tools ⲡⲓⲁⲣⲃ̄ⲱⲧ كسور *cylinders*
for winding (Lab); *ib* 133 *B* parts of ship ⲡⲓⲁⲣⲃ̄ⲟⲧ
جاغوص (*sic* MSS) *beam* staying sides of ship apart
(BIF 20 60), *prop* supporting mast (Lab).

ⲉⲱⲣⲕ *S*, ⲉⲁⲣⲕ *Sⳑ*, ⲉⲟⲣⲕ⳿ *S* vb intr, **a** *sit down, be
quiet* (?): Mor 31 228 in cool shade ⲧⲁⲉ. ⲧⲁⲙⲓⲕⲉ ⲙ̄-
ⲙⲟⲓ = RylBull 11 406 *a* أجلس, *ib* ⲁϥⲛⲕⲟⲧⲕ ⲉϥⲉ. = *ib*
ني only. **b** *sit in ambush*: Nu 14 45⳿ (*B* ϣⲟⲡ), *ib*
22 5⳿(var & *B* ⲟⲩⲟⲉ) ἐγκαθῆσθαι; Jos 8 4⳿ ἐνεδρεύειν;
Jer 5 6 (*B* ⲣⲱⲓⲥ) γρηγορεῖν; **c** ⲉ-: 1 Kg 19 2 ⲉⲟⲣⲕ

ⲉⲣⲟⲕ (var ⲉⲁ. om ⲉ-) φυλάσσειν; Si 14 22 ⲉ. ⲉⲣⲟⲥ
ⲉⲛⲉⲃ. *V* next word.

ⲉⲣⲟⲕ *S*, ⲉⲣⲁⲕ *SAA*²*F*, ⲉⲟⲣⲕ⳿ *S*, ⲉⲁ.⳿ *AA*², p c
ⲉⲣⲕ- *A*² vb **I** intr, *be still, cease*: Nu 11 2 (varrP 44
107 ⲉⲣⲏϭ, Mor ϭⲱ, *B* ⲉⲣⲟⲩⲣ), Hos 8 10 *A*(*B* ⲉⲉⲣⲓ),
Mk 4 39 (*B* ⲕⲏⲡ) κοπάζειν; C 99 231 ⲁϥⲉ. ⲛϭⲓ ⲡϫⲁⲓⲙⲱⲛ = C 89 65 *B* ⲉⲉⲣⲓ παύεσθαι; Job 11 19(*B*=Gk)
ἡσυχάζειν; ShA 1 56 ⲉⲧⲣⲉⲟⲩⲕⲱⲧ ⲉϥⲭⲣⲟ ⲉ., ShC 42
18 ⲉ. ⲛⲧϭⲱ, Mor 40 10 war ⲉ. for 3 years (var 39 15
ⲕⲁⲧⲁⲥⲧⲉⲗⲓ) = C 43 41 *B* ⲥⲃⲟⲕ (from *S* ⲉⲣⲟⲕ?), BMis
70 may fiery river ⲉⲣⲁⲕ (var FR 38 ⲉⲥⲩⲭⲁⲍⲉ ⲙ̄ⲙⲟϥ),
ManiH 59 *A*² his mouth ϭⲱ ⲁϥⲉ., Bor 310 5 ⲧⲣⲉⲡ-
ϫⲓⲙⲱⲛ ⲉ., P 131⁵ 144 wine left in house ϣⲁⲛⲧⲉϥ-
ⲉⲣⲁⲕ, CMSS 7 to woman ⲉⲣϣⲁⲛⲉ. ⲛϭⲛⲁⲡⲓⲥⲧⲉⲩⲉ ⲡⲉ
ⲁⲛ; qual: Pro 7 9 *SA*(*B*=Gk) ἡσυχία, Is 66 2 *A*
(Cl, *SB* ⲣⲙⲣⲁϣ), 1 Tim 2 2 (*B* ⲣⲉⲙⲣⲁⲩϣ), -χιος;
Aeg 245 εὐσταθής; Hos 13 8 *S*(ShViK 9868 157)*A*
(*B* ⲟⲛϣ?) ἀπορεῖσθαι; Br 237 ⲉⲣⲉⲡⲧⲏⲣϥ ⲉ., ShClPr
22 356 ⲉⲩⲥⲃ̄ⲣⲁⲅⲧ ⲁⲩⲱ ⲉⲩⲉ., P 130³ 70 ϭⲓ ⲡϣⲁϫⲉ ⲉⲧⲉ.,
BMis 563 ⲡⲉⲧⲉ. ⲙ̄ⲡⲓⲡⲁⲣⲑⲉⲛⲟⲥ (*l*? ⲉⲟⲕⲣ *esurientes*),
Mani 1 *A*² ⲡⲓⲁⲙ ⲉ. **II** tr, *quiet*: R 2 1 63 sea ⲉ.
ⲡⲛⲉⲥⲟⲉⲓⲙ; refl: Jer 26 27 *F*(Mus 49 174, *B* ⲉⲉⲣⲓ)
ἡσυχάζειν; BAp 57 ϭⲱⲡⲧ ⲟϣⲙ, ⲙⲁⲡⲓⲁ ⲉ. ⲙⲙⲟⲥ
ἠρεμεῖσθαι; ShBMOr 8810 366 ⲉ. ⲙⲙⲱⲧⲛ, Mor 24
15 *F* ⲉ. ⲙⲙⲁⲩ, *ib* 22 79 storm ⲉ. ⲙⲙⲟϥ (var *ib* 26 13
ⲉ. only), LMär 28 may (spirits) on left ⲉ. ⲙⲙⲟⲟⲩ &
those on right lead on.

With following preposition. ⲉ ⲉ-: ManiK 41
*A*² ⲡⲉⲛⲧ…ⲉ. ⲁⲣ[ⲁϥ]; vbal: 2 Kg 13 39 κοπ. gen;
ShViK 926 127 ⲛⲧⲉⲡⲉⲡⲛⲁ ⲉ. ⲉⲧⲙⲧⲣⲉϥⲥⲓⲙⲉ ⲉⲉⲣⲁⲓ
ⲉⲣⲟⲕ; ⲉ ⲁⲃⲁⲗ ⲛ- *A*², *from*: Mani 2 ⲛϥⲉ. ⲁⲃ.
ⲙⲡⲉϥⲁⲅⲁⲑⲟⲛ, Mani K 11 *A*² ⲡⲟⲩ]ⲁⲓⲉ ⲉ. ⲙⲙⲁⲩ…
ⲁⲃⲁⲗ ⲙⲡⲣⲓⲥⲉ; ⲉ ⲉⲛ- sim: Nu 25 8 (var ⲗⲟ, *B*
ⲗⲱϫⲓ) παύ. ἀπό; Cl 63 1 *A* ⲁⲛⲉ. ⲙⲙⲁⲛ ⲉⲛⲧⲥⲧⲁⲥⲓⲥ
ἠσ. gen; ShC 42 32 ⲁⲩⲉ. ⲉⲛⲧⲉⲩⲙⲛⲧⲁⲉ ⲛϣⲁϫⲉ,
Mor 31 25 ⲁϥⲉ. ⲉⲛⲡⲉϥϣⲱⲡⲧ, Pcod 38 *SF* ⲁϥⲉ. ⲡⲉⲛⲧ
ⲛϭⲓ ⲡⲙⲉⲉⲩⲉ; ⲉⲃⲟⲗ ⲉⲛ-: Jos 7 26 παύ. gen; Est
2 1 κοπ. gen; PSBA 10 197 ⲉ. ⲉⲃ. ⲉⲛⲡⲛϣⲱⲡⲉ.

—— nn m *SA*², *quietness*: Br 105 ⲥⲓⲧⲛ ⲉⲓⲉ., ShC
73 144 ⲭⲡⲟⲩϥ ⲉⲛⲟⲩ. ⲭⲱⲣⲓⲥ ⲟϣ ⲉⲃⲟⲗ, ManiK 41
*A*² ⲧⲉⲣⲕⲟ ⲡⲣⲱⲙⲉ ⲉⲛⲡⲁⲥⲡⲁⲥⲙⲟⲥ ⲙⲡⲛⲉⲥ., *ib* K 103
*A*¹ ⲟⲩⲉ. ⲙⲡⲟⲩⲕⲁⲣⲁⲓⲧϥ, *ib* 70 sim.

ⲟ ⲛⲉ. *S*, *be quiet*: Tri 618 ⲉⲓⲟⲩⲧⲥⲁⲡⲟ ⲕⲟ ⲛⲉⲟⲣⲕ
(*l* ⲉⲣ.) هاد (var ساكن).

✝ ⲉ. *S*, *give quiet, calm*: BHom 33 wine ✝. ⲛⲧⲗⲩⲡⲏ
παύειν, Nu 25 11 (*B* ✝ ⲉⲙⲧⲟⲛ) καταπ.; R 1 4 52 ✝.
ⲙⲡⲉⲩⲡⲛⲁ = MartIgn 866 *B* ⲉⲉⲣⲓ πραΰνειν; Ep 592
2 ✝. ⲙⲡⲟⲩⲅⲟⲉⲓ ἡμεροῦν; Ming 313 ✝. ⲙⲡⲉⲓⲙⲟⲟⲩ
ⲡⲓⲕⲧⲣⲉϥⲉⲓ ⲉⲡⲉⲥⲉⲣⲁⲅⲧ ἀποκαθιστάναι εἰς κατάστασιν.
(Si 39 36 *l* ⲧⲉⲣⲕⲟ).

p c *A*²: ManiK 183 ⲉⲛⲁⲅⲁⲑⲟⲥⲡⲉ ⲡⲉⲣⲕⲏⲧ; *ib* H 81
ⲙ̄ⲡⲧⲣ̄ⲣⲕⲏⲧ.

ϩⲣⲱⲕⲉ nn S sim (?): Mor 31 255 ϯ ⲉⲟⲟⲩ ⲡⲁⲩ ϯ ϩⲣⲱⲕⲉ ⲡⲁⲩ.

ϩⲣⲏϭ, -ⲝ S vb intr, as ϩⲣⲟⲕ: Nu 16 50 (var ϩⲣⲣⲉ, B ⲧⲁϩⲛⲟ), ib 11 2 v I above ⲕⲟⲡ.; Tri 515 fiery river ϩ. خدد; Wess 151 39＝BAp 3 Gehenna ⲱϣⲙ ⲁⲥϩ., Mor 32 11 smite him anew ⲧⲁⲣⲉⲡⲉⲓⲁⲡϭⲟⲥⲓⲟⲥ ϩⲣⲏⲝ ϩⲡⲉϥⲙⲛⲧⲣⲉϥϣⲁϫⲉ (var R 1 5 50 ϩⲣⲟⲕ ⲙⲙⲟϥ).

ϩⲟⲣⲕϥ S nn (adj), silent, quiet: Si 26 14 σιγηρός; PS 260 ϣⲱⲡⲉ ⲛϩ.
V last word & ⲑⲣⲕⲟ.

ϩⲉⲣⲕⲟⲩ　　v ϩⲗⲕⲟⲩ.

ϩⲣⲉⲕⲣⲓⲕⲉ　　v ⲣⲕⲣⲓⲕⲉ.

ϩⲟⲣⲕϥ　　v ϩⲣⲟⲕ s f.

ϩⲣⲓⲙ SB, nn m, pelican: Lev 11 18 S(B ϩⲙⲏ) no Ar (P 44 105 ＝ .حرل), Deu 14 17 S(B do), Ar confused, Ps 101 7 S(B do) غيهم πελεκάν; K 168 B ⲡⲓϩ. ′ⲅ̄; BKU 1 ro S ϩ. ⲡⲧⲟⲟⲩ; ϩⲣⲓⲙ B K 167 مخلب bird's claw, same ?

ϩⲣⲓⲙ B nn m, plant artemisia: K 192 ⲡⲓϩ. (1 var ϩⲣⲉⲙ) شيح.

ϩ(ⲉ)ⲣⲙⲁⲛ SB(Jer), -ⲙⲏⲛ S f, -ⲙⲉⲛ F, ⲗⲉⲣⲙⲉⲛ A, ⲉⲣⲙⲁⲛ B nn m, pomegranate tree or fruit: Nu 13 24 SB, Jer 52 22 B ϩ. ῥόα, 2 Chr 3 16 B ῥοΐσκος; K 177 B رمان; Aeg 261, Ryl 108 S ⲡϩ., BMar 219 S ϩⲉⲡϩ. (var Mor 48 33 S f)＝Rec 6 185 B, BM 309 S f, BMis 10 S ϩ(ⲉ)ⲛϩ. ⲡⲛⲟⲩⲃ ϩⲓⲣⲁⲧ; ⲕⲟⲩⲕⲉ ⲛϩ. SF, rind of p.: Cant 6 6 SFϩⲉⲣⲙⲉ[ⲛ λέπυρον ῥόας, P 44 81 ⲝⲉⲣⲙⲱⲣⲉⲁⲥ· ⲕ. ⲛϩ. قشر الر; in recipes Z 628 ϩ(ⲉ)ⲛⲕ. ⲛϩ., PMéd 321 do; Ryl 106 38 ⲟⲩⲁⲣⲣⲁ[ⲙ]ⲏⲛ (sic l? ＝الرمان) ⲉϥⲕⲏⲕ; ⲟⲩⲥⲱⲗ ⲣⲱⲙⲁⲛ S, p. roots transcribes أصول الر Bodl(P)a 2 69; ⲃⲱ ⲛϩ., p. tree: Deu 8 8 S(B ⲉ. only), 1 Kg 14 2 S, Cant 8 2 SFϩⲉⲣⲙⲉⲛ, Hag 2 19 SAB ῥόα; P 44 81 S ⲃⲁⲗⲁⲩⲥⲧⲓⲟⲛ· ⲧⲃ̄. شجرة الر; ⲙⲁ ⲛϩ.: Zech 12 11 SA(B ⲓⲁϩ ⲡⲉ.) κοπετὸς ῥοῶνος. As name: f ⲁⲣⲙⲁⲛ (? RylSuppl 39), ⲗⲁϩⲙⲁⲛ (BKU 1 262), m ? (Hall 18).　V R Champ 723.

ϩⲉⲣⲙⲉⲥ　　v ϩⲉⲗⲙⲏⲛ.

ϩⲁⲣⲛ-, ϩⲁⲣⲉⲛ-　　v p 289 b.

ϩⲓⲣⲛ-　　v p 290 a.

ϩⲱⲣⲡ SAA²B(mostly), ϩⲟ.† SB vb intr, sleep, doze: Job 3 13 (S ⲱⲃϣ), Ps 3 6 A(TU 43 8)B(S do), Pro 4 16 A(S do, B ⲛⲕⲟⲧ), Mus 34 186 ⲁϥϩ. ⲛⲉⲛⲕⲟⲧ ὑπνοῦν; ShBMOr 8810 412 S ϩ. ⲙⲙⲉⲣⲉ, ⲛⲕⲟⲧⲕ ⲡⲧⲉⲩϣⲏ, BAp 93 S ⲁⲓϩ. ⲡⲟⲩⲕⲟⲩⲓ, MG 25 235 sim, C 43 92 ⲁϥϩ. ⲡⲣⲓⲙⲁ ⲡⲟⲩⲕⲟⲩϫⲓ, DeV 2 35 ϩ. ⲡⲕⲁⲕⲱⲥ ϩⲉⲛⲟⲩϩⲓⲛⲓⲙ ⲉϥϩⲱⲟⲩ, ManiP A² ⲧⲏϩ. ⲛⲧⲛⲡⲛ-

ⲕⲁⲧⲉ, PO 11 325 ϩ. ⲡⲟⲩⲙⲛⲧϣ ⲛⲡⲁⲩ̈; qual: MG 25 211 made as though ⲡⲉⲓϩ. διυπνίζειν (as if ὑπ., Z 345 S ⲡⲉⲣⲥⲉ); ShMIF 23 30 S ⲉⲩϩ. ⲛ ⲉⲩϣⲁⲡⲧⲱⲟⲩⲛ, ViK 9780 133 S ⲉϥϩ. ⲉϥⲣⲏⲥ, AM 80 seemed as if ⲡϯϩ. ⲁⲛ; ϫⲓⲛϩ. B: Mus 34 198 ⲧⲝ. in tomb.

ϩⲱⲣⲡ SBF, ϩ(ⲉ)ⲣⲡ- S, ϩⲟⲣⲡϭ, ϩⲟⲣⲡ† SB vb I intr, be wet, drenched: AZ 25 114 S ϯ ⲁⲗⲕⲓⲛ (القين) ⲉⲣⲟϥ (sc molten metal) ϣⲁⲡⲧϥϩ. (this word ?); c ⲛ-, with, in: Is 34 3 S(B ⲉⲃⲟⲗ ϩⲉⲛ-, F ϩⲛ-) βρέχεσθαι ἀπό; WTh 150 S ⲡⲕⲁϩ ϩ. ⲛⲥⲛⲟϥ, Mor 31 245 S feet ϩ. ⲙⲙⲟⲟⲩ, MIE 2 415 B sim; c ϩⲛ- sim; Jos 3 15 S ϩ. ϫⲱⲗⲕ (B ϫ. ⲱⲙⲥ) βάπτεσθαι εἰς; ShA 2 106 S hands ϩ. ⲛⲣⲏⲧⲟⲩ (sc blood), PSBA 10 197 S earth ϩ. ⲛⲡⲉⲥⲣⲙⲉⲓⲟⲟⲩⲉ, Va 59 5 B sim; ⲉⲃⲟⲗ ϩⲉⲛ-: DeV 2 45 B earth ϩ. ⲉⲃ̄. ϩⲉⲛⲛⲉⲣⲙⲱⲟⲩⲓ; qual: C 41 13 B ϣⲃⲓⲛ ⲉⲧϩ.; Is 14 20 B(S ⲧⲟⲗⲙ) φύρεσθαι ἐν; BIF 37 57 S ⲛⲃⲏⲛⲧ ⲉⲩϩ., Va 61 18 B lentils ⲉϥϩ. ⲙⲙⲟⲟⲩ βρεκτός; ib 57 41 S ⲉϥϩ. ⲙⲙⲟⲟⲩ ὑγρὸς καὶ διαλελυμένος; ShViK 910 S ⲉⲩϩ. ⲛⲥⲛⲟϥ, ShIF 152 S sim ϩⲛ-, Job 24 8 B ⲉⲃⲟⲗ ϩⲉⲛ- ὑγραίνεσθαι ἀπό.

II tr, wet, drench: Wess 11 169 S ϩ. ⲡϩ(ⲉ)ⲛⲕⲟⲩⲓ ⲛⲃⲏⲛⲧ βρέχειν; Deu 33 24 S(B ⲥⲱⲡ) βάπτειν, Lu 11 38 S(B ϭⲓ ⲱⲙⲥ) -τίζειν; Tob 2 6 S λούεσθαι; ShRyl 70 246 S ϩⲟⲣⲡϥ (sc sponge) ϣⲁⲡⲧϥⲙⲟⲩϩ, Mor 40 29 S ϩⲉⲣⲡⲧⲏⲩⲧⲛ in river (var ib 39 38 & C 43 57 B ⲱⲙⲥ), ib 16 14 S ⲉϥϩ. ⲙⲙⲟⲟⲩ (sc vessels, var BMis 188 ϭϣϩⲱⲟⲩϥ ϩⲛⲟⲩⲙⲟⲟⲩ), HL 104 B ⲁϥϩ. ⲙⲡⲉϥⲱⲓⲕ for journey, C 41 20 B sim＝Miss 4 636 S ⲧⲱϩⲃ, C 89 10 B ϩ. ⲛ[ϩⲁⲛ]ⲕⲁⲗ, PO 14 340 B sweat ϩ. ⲙⲡⲉϥⲥⲱⲙⲁ ⲧⲏⲣϥ; c ⲛ-, with: Lu 7 38 SB βρ. dat, MG 25 243 B ϩ. ⲡⲡⲉϥⲃⲏⲛⲧ ⲙⲙⲟⲟⲩ βρ.; C 86 274 B ϩ. ⲙⲡⲉϥⲥⲱⲙⲁ ⲛⲣⲙⲟⲩ καταπάσσειν; BMis 491 S ϣⲁϩ. ⲡⲧⲉⲩⲗⲩⲃⲏⲧⲱⲡ (λεβί.) ⲙⲙⲟⲟⲩ; c ϩⲛ- sim: Ps 6 7 SB βρ. ἐν; Lev 11 32 S(B ⲱⲙⲥ) βα. εἰς; Bor 151 128 S sweet odours ⲛⲥⲉϩⲣⲡ ⲡⲉⲕⲥⲱⲙⲁ ⲛⲣⲏⲧⲟⲩ; c ⲉ-, for, because of: Si 31 27 S βαπτίζ. ἀπό.

ϩⲣⲁⲛ A² nn, meaning unknown: ManiP ⲁϥⲃⲱⲕ ⲁϥ[ⲙⲟⲩⲧⲉ ?] ⲁⲣⲁⲩ ϩⲛⲟⲩϩ. Cf ? next word (HT).

ϩⲣⲟⲡⲣⲉⲡ S, ϩⲗⲟⲡⲗⲉⲡ S f, ϩⲣⲁⲡⲣⲉⲡ A² vb intr, blink, open (?) eyes, spread wings (cf ? رفرف Dévaud): ViK 9403 14 let mouth be closed till eyes see, lips silent till ⲛⲕⲟⲩϩⲉ ϩ. ⲉϫⲛⲡⲕⲉⲕⲉ (on Lu 1 20); tr: Mor 53 55 S f ⲛⲃⲁⲗ ⲉⲧⲉⲥϩ. ⲙⲙⲟⲟⲩ ϩⲛⲟⲩⲣⲅⲱⲡⲏ from them she shed tears (on Lu 7 38), Z 616 birds ϩ. ⲡⲡⲉⲩⲧⲏⲣ; as nn: ManiK 71 A² ⲟⲩϩ. ⲛⲃⲉⲗ twinkling of an eye.

ϩⲁⲣⲡⲥ F nn f, outspread hand: Eccl 4 6 ⲟⲩϩ. ⲉⲥⲙⲉϩ ⲛ[(PMich 3520, S ⲙⲙⲟⲩϩ ⲛⲟⲩϭⲓϫ) πλήρωμα δρακός.

ϩⲁⲣⲡϣⲱⲧ O　v ϩⲱⲣ god Horus.

ϩⲣⲏⲣ *S* nn m, title or occupation: Ryl 165 ⲃⲓⲕⲧⲱⲣ ⲡⲉϩ., *ib* ⲃⲓⲕ/ ϥⲣⲏⲣ (in both ⲏ doubtful).

ϩⲣⲣⲉ *S*(once), ϩⲉⲣⲓ, ϩⲟⲩⲣⲱⲟⲩ† *B* vb intr, *cease, be still*: Nu 16 50 *S*(var ϩⲣⲏⲥ, *B* ⲧⲁϩⲡⲟ, cf 48 *S* ϩⲣⲟⲕ), Ps 105 30 (*S* ⲥⲱ), Hos 8 10 (*A* ϩⲣⲁⲕ), Mt 14 32 (*S* do, *F* ⲗⲁ) κοπάζειν; Lu 8 24 (*S* ⲗⲟ), C 89 65 ⲁϥϩ. ⲛϫⲉ ⲡⲧⲏⲙⲟⲛ = C 99 231 *S* ϩⲣⲟⲕ παύεσθαι, Job 26 12 ⲑⲣⲉ- ϩ. (*S* ⲥⲙⲓⲛⲉ) καταπ.; Ac 19 35 sim (*S* = Gk) καταστέλλειν; Job 37 17 (*S* ⲥⲱⲧ), Jer 26 27 (*F* Mus 49 174 ϩⲣⲁⲕ) ἡσυχάζειν; Si 22 18 (*S* ⲥⲱ, *A* ⲱϩⲉ) ὑπομένειν; TRit 522 ⲁϥϩ. ⲛϫⲉ ⲡⲓϩⲏⲧ (of dead) ١ﺩﺍ; Aeg 54 may unresting worm ϩ., AM 58 ⲑⲣⲉ- ⲡⲓⲙⲁⲧⲟⲓ ϩ. ⲉⲩⲣⲓⲟⲩⲓ ⲉⲣⲟⲟⲩ; qual: Ex 24 14, Ez 38 11 ἡσ.; 1 Tim 2 2 (*S* ⲥϩⲣⲁϩⲧ) ἤρεμος; 1 Pet 3 4 (*S* ⲣⲙⲣⲁϣ) πραΰς; K 56 ⲉⲧϩ. ﺩﺍﺩ; MG 25 49 ϫⲓⲡ-ⲱⲡⲥ ⲉϥϩ.; tr: MartIgn 866 ⲙⲡⲉⲣⲗⲓ ϩ. ⲙⲡⲟⲩ-ϫⲱⲡⲧ = R 1 4 52 *S* † ϩⲣⲟⲕ πραΰνειν; C 86 272 sim καταστ.; refl: Ge 4 7 (*S* C 100 335 ⲕⲁ ⲣⲟ, *A* Cl ⲁⲣⲏϩ), Ps 75 9 (*S* ⲥⲱ), C 89 45 ⲁⲣⲏⲟⲩ ⲩⲡⲁⲣ. ⲙⲙⲟϥ = C 99 140 *S* ⲥϩⲣ. ⲏⲥ.; Am 7 5 ⲕⲟ.; Ps 82 2 (*S* ⲥⲱ) καταπρ.; c ϩⲉⲛ-, ⲉⲃⲟⲗ ϩⲉⲛ-: Va 61 116 ⲁϥϩ. ϩⲉⲛⲡⲉϥϫⲱⲡⲧ, C 89 *lc* sim ⲉⲃ. ϩⲉⲛ- = *lc S* ϩⲣⲟⲕ ⲏⲥ. ἀπό; ⲉⲃ. ϩⲁ-: Ez 43 10 (BM 1247 127, var diff) ⲕⲟ.; as nn: Abst 412 ⲙⲟⲓ ⲡⲁⲡ ⲡⲟⲩϩ.; ⲙⲉⲧ-ϩⲟⲩⲣⲱⲟⲩ: PasH 16 ⲟⲩⲱⲡⲃ ⲙⲙ. *Cf* ϩⲣⲟⲩⲣ.

ϩⲣⲏⲣⲉ *SAA²*, -ⲣⲓ, ϩϩⲏⲣⲓ *B*, ϩⲗⲏⲗⲓ, ϩⲣⲏ. *F* nn m *S*(once *B*), f *A²BF*(twice *S*), *flower*: Job 15 30 *S* m *B* f, Cant 2 12 *F*, cit TillOster 24 *A*, Is 5 24 *S* m *BF* f, *ib* 61 11 *S*(*B* ⲣⲱⲧ), Zeph 2 2 *S* m *B* f (*A* † ⲟⲩⲟⲩ), Ja 1 11 *S* m *B* f ἄνθος, Ex 28 34 *B* ἄνθινος; *ib* 25 31 *B*, Nu 8 4 *S* f (var ⲉⲓⲉⲡ., *B* ϫⲁⲗ), Cant 2 1 *F* f (*S* = Gk), *ib* 16 *F* ϩⲣ., Mt 6 28 *B*(*S* = Gk) κρίνον, JA '05 1 450 *S* ⲟⲩϩ. ⲛⲕⲣⲓⲛⲟⲛ ⲉϥⲧⲣⲉϣⲣⲱϣ; Job 14 7 *B* f (*S* † ⲟⲩⲱ) ῥάδαμνος; Va 57 15 *B* πόα; Mor 41 83 *S* ⲡⲉϩ. ⲡⲡⲉⲃⲱϫⲁⲛⲏ (βοτ.), LCyp 12 *S* ⲡⲁⲅⲁⲡ ⲙⲡⲉϩ., KroppR 16 *S* ⲧⲉϩ. ⲡⲧⲁⲥ† ⲟⲩⲱ, Va 57 2 *B* ⲫⲟⲅⲟⲧⲟⲅⲉⲧ ⲡⲧⲟⲩϩ., ManiP *A²* ⲛ̅ϩ̅ⲥ̅ ⲧϩ. ⲙⲡⲓⲱⲧ; Si 50 8 *S* ϩ. ⲡⲟⲩⲣⲧ ἄ. ῥόδων; Job 15 33 *SB* ϩ. ⲡϫⲟⲉⲓⲧ ἄ. ἐλαίας; JTS 4 394 *S* ϩ. ⲡⲥ†ⲡⲟⲩϫⲉ, Lacr 92 *B* sim; MG 25 319 *B* ϩ. ⲡⲧⲉ ϩⲁⲡⲁⲣⲱⲙⲁⲧⲁ, PMéd 172 *S* ϩ. (ⲛ)ϣⲟⲡⲧⲉ, *ib* 321 *S* ϩ. ⲛϭⲟⲩϩ, ϩ. ⲡⲧⲉ ⲡⲓⲕⲉⲡⲓ *v* ⲕⲡⲏ nn, Ryl 94 (33 2)*S* ⲡⲉϩ. ⲡⲧⲉⲧⲡⲛⲏⲗⲓⲕⲓⲁ, ROC 17 401 *B* m sim, ManiP *A²* John ⲧϩ. ⲡⲧⲡⲁⲣⲑⲉⲛⲓⲁ.
ⲉⲓⲉⲡϩ. *v* Nu 8 above.
ⲣ ϩ. *S*, *come to flower, blossom*: Job 14 2 (*B* ⲫⲓⲣⲓ ⲉⲃⲟⲗ) ἀνθεῖν; ⲧⲉⲕ ϩ. ⲉⲃⲟⲗ *S*, *put forth blossom*: Nu 17 8 (*B* ⲫⲉⲣ ϩ. ⲉⲃⲟⲗ) ἐξαν.; ⲟⲩⲁⲙϩ. *S flower-eater*, a beetle: Hab 2 11 (P 44 116, *A* ϩⲁⲗⲓⲗ, *B* = Gk) κάνθαρος, P 44 56 do ﺍﺳﻮﺩ ﺯﻧﺒﻮﺭ; ϩⲓ ϩ. ⲉⲃⲟⲗ *B*: MG 25 175 staff ⲉⲧⲁϥϩⲓ (sic) ϩ. ⲉⲃ., cf *ib* † ⲟⲩⲱ ⲛϩ. ⲉⲃ., Mus 34 191 ϩⲓ ⲉϩ. ⲉⲃ.

As name: Θρῆρις, Τελῆλις (Preisigke).
On ϩ. = ? λείριον-λείλιον *v* Lagarde *Mitteil.* 2 21, *Mém Soc Ling Paris* 15 163, *JAOS* 56 197.

ϩⲣⲟⲉⲓⲣⲉ *v* ϩⲗⲟⲉⲓⲗⲉ.

ϩⲣⲉⲥⲓⲛ *S* nn m (?), *saddle*: P 44 84 ⲥⲉⲗⲗⲁⲡ · ⲡϩ. ﺳﺮج (43 61 ϩⲣⲉⲥⲉⲡ, 248 ϩⲣⲏⲥⲓⲛ); *ib* ⲥⲉⲗⲗⲟⲩⲣⲧⲟⲥ · ⲣⲉϥⲧⲁⲙⲓⲉ ϩ. ﺳﺮج. For ? (ὑ)πηρέσιον (R McKenzie).

ϩⲁⲣⲁⲧ⸗, ϩⲓⲣⲁⲧ⸗ *v* ⲣⲁⲧ⸗.

(ϩⲱⲣⲧ), ϩⲟⲣⲧ⸗ *B* vb tr, *seize, wrest*: C 86 101 πρόσταγμα brought by soldier ⲁϥϩⲟⲣⲧϥ ϩⲉⲛⲡⲉϥϫⲓⲝ & rent it in pieces.

ϩⲣⲁⲉⲓⲧ *SA²* *v* ϩⲟ p 648 *a*.

ϩⲣⲱⲧ *SS f ABF*, ⲉϩ. *B* nn f, *wine-press, vat*: Ex 22 29 *SB*, Pro 3 10 *B*(*SA* ⲉⲓⲟⲙ), Lam 1 15 *BF*, Hos 9 2 *S f*(JEA 11 245)*ABF*, Joel 3 13 *AB*, *ib* 2 24 *B*(*SA* ⲉⲓ.), Ap 19 15 *SB* ληνός, Is 16 10 (*S* ⲉⲓ.), Zech 14 10 *SAB* ὑπολήνιον, Is 5 2 *B*(*S* do) προλ.; *ib* 63 2 *S* ⲙⲣⲓⲥ ⲡϩ. (*B* Gk diff); Dif 1 67 *B* martyrs crushed in †ϩ. ﻧﻮﺭج (but Synax 1 117 ﻣﻌﺼﺎ); P 44 63 *S* ⲉⲡⲑⲣⲟⲡⲓⲟⲡ · ⲧⲉϩ. ﺟﺮ̈ⲝ, K 446 *B* sim; Ann 19 232 *S* set up ⲧⲉϩ. ⲡⲥⲉϥⲣⲏ ⲙⲡⲉⲓⲟⲙ ϩⲡⲧⲉⲥⲙⲛⲧⲉ = C 86 107 *B* ⲉϩ., P 131³ 85 *S* ϣⲓⲕⲉ ⲡ[ϩⲉⲛ]ϩ. = Va 61 96 *B* ⲕⲱⲧ ⲡϩⲁⲛϩ., CA 107 *S* ϩⲱⲱⲗⲉ ⲙⲡⲉϥϭⲱⲙ ⲉⲧⲉϩ., BMis 207 *S* ⲛⲓⲟⲙ ⲡⲏⲣⲡ...ⲡϩ. ⲙⲁ ⲡⲉⲣϩⲱⲧ *B* (*l* ⲉϩⲣ.) in which saint confined C 86 105. As place-name(?): ﺩﻫﺮﻭﻁ opposite Maghâgha.

ϩⲣⲧⲉ *S a*(once, *v* HT *St John* p xx)*A²* nn f, *fear*: Jo 20 19 (*SB* ϩⲟⲧⲉ) φόβος; He 5 7 *S a*(*SBF* do) εὐλάβεια; Mani 1 ⲁⲭⲡϩ., *ib* ⲡϩⲟⲟⲩⲉ ⲡϩ., ManiK 41 [ⲧ]ϩ. ⲡⲡϫⲁⲓⲱⲡ, ManiH 59 ⲑ. ⲙⲡⲣⲣⲟ; ⲟ ⲡϩ.: ManiH 20 ⲟⲩⲃⲗⲕⲉ ⲉⲥⲟ ⲡϩ.; † ϩ.: ManiK 32 ϥ† ϩ. ⲡⲡⲉϥϭⲁⲙ ϩⲡⲧⲉϥⲥⲙⲏ. *V AZ* 63 154.

ϩⲟⲣⲧϥ *B* nn m, *phantasm, ghost*: Nu 16 30 (*S* = Gk), Is 28 7 (*S* ⲣⲁⲥⲟⲩ) φάσμα, Mt 14 26 (*SF* = Gk) φάντασμα, Hab 3 10 ⲡⲉϥϩ. (*S* ⲟⲩⲱⲛϩ ⲉⲃⲟⲗ, *A* = Gk) -ασία; Job 4 16 (*S* diff) αὔρα; Jer 27 39 ἴνδαλμα; Rec 6 169 he thought ϫⲉⲁⲡⲟⲕ ⲟⲩϩ. = BMar 206 *S* ⲡⲡⲁ, PO 14 351 terrifying him ϩⲉⲛϩⲁⲡⲥⲙⲟⲧ ⲡϩ.; ⲙⲉⲧϩ., *appearance*: K 70 †ⲙ. ﻧﺨ̍ﻞ (cf *AZ* 14 63).

ϩⲁⲣⲏⲩ *v* ⲁⲣⲏⲩ.

ϩⲣⲉⲩ *A* *v* ϩⲟⲟⲩ *day*.

ϩⲣⲟⲟⲩ *S*, ϩⲣⲁⲩ *A*, ϩⲣⲁⲩ *A²*, ϩⲣⲱⲟⲩ *B*, ϩⲗⲁⲩ, ϩⲣⲁⲁⲩ *F*, ϩⲣⲟⲩ- *SA²*, ϩⲣ- *S*(Jo 12 29), ϩⲁⲣⲁ-, ϫ.- *B*, ϩ.-*F*, ϩⲣⲁ⸗ *S*, ϩⲣⲉ⸗ *A²*, ϫⲁ⸗ *O* nn m, *voice, sound* of God or man: Ge 3 17 *S*(*B* ⲥⲙⲏ), Eccl 10 20 *S*(*F*

c.), Sa 1 7 *SB*, Is 30 19 *SF*, (*B* c.), Mk 15 34 *S*(*B* do)
ⲫⲱⲛⲏ, Jth 14 16 *S* ϩ. ⲫ.... ⲥⲙⲏ βοή; 2 Kg 6 15 *B*
(*S* ⲗⲟⲅⲗⲁⲓ), Ps 101 2 *B*(*S* ⲁϣⲕⲁⲕ), Jer 14 2 *SB*,
Zeph 1 10 *B*(*A* ⲁϣϭⲁⲡ), He 5 7 *B*(*S* ⲁϣ., *F* ⲱϣ ⲉⲃⲁⲗ)
κραυγή; Ps 41 4 *S*(*B* c.), Joel 3 14 *SB*, 1 Kg 14 19 *S*
ⲡⲟϭ ⲛϩ. ἦχος, Job 4 13 *S*(*B* do) ἠχώ; 1 Kg 2 24 *S*
(Wess 9 87), Jer 29 15 *S*(*B* do), Jo 12 38 *SA²*(*B* do),
Ro 10 16 *S*(*BF*Mor 43 300 do) ἀκοή; Is 15 8 *B*(*S*
ⲁϣ.) βοή; Ps 18 4 *SB* φθόγγος, Deu 32 2 *S*(*B* do)
ἀπόφθεγμα; Sa 1 10 *S* θροῦς; PS 63 *S* ⲛϩ. ⲛϩⲟⲧⲉ,
ShBor 233 245 *S* ⲧⲁϣⲉ ⲡⲉϩ. ϩⲛⲟⲩⲛϣⲟⲧ, Gu 95 *S*
ⲡⲉⲓϩ. ⲛⲧⲁⲓⲥⲱⲧⲙ ⲉⲣⲟϥ ... ⲧⲉⲓⲥⲙⲏ ⲛⲧⲁⲓⲥ. ⲉⲣⲟⲥ, Mor
28 184 *S* ⲡⲉⲓϩ. ⲡⲧⲉⲓⲙⲓⲛⲉ (*sc* what hast just said), El
98 *A* ⲛϩ. ⲛⲁⲕⲓⲙ ⲁⲧⲡⲉ, ManiK 143 *A²* ⲛϩ. ⲛⲥⲉϫⲉ,
DeV 2 49 *B* ⲛϩ. ⲙⲡⲁⲓⲟⲭⲗⲟⲥ, PO 11 322 *B* ⲁⲩϣⲱⲡⲓ
ⲉⲛⲟⲩϩ. ⲛⲣⲁϣⲓ, TEuch 1 364 *B* ⲡⲓⲱⲃϩ ⲡⲉⲕϥⲱ-
ⲛⲏⲥⲓⲥ ϫⲟⲥ ⲉⲛⲟⲩϩ. بلعل, Hor 82 *O* ⲡⲧⲟⲩⲉⲓⲣⲉ ⲁ-
ϩⲣⲁϥ. **b** of beasts, things: Lev 26 36 *SB*, Ps 92 3
S(*B* c.), Eccl 7 7 *S*(*F* c.), Joel 2 5 *A*(*B* do), Mt 24 31
S(*BF* do) ⲫ.; Ps 64 7 *S*(*B* do), Is 13 21 *S*(*B* ⲥⲉⲛⲥⲉⲡ)
ἦ., BHom 35 *S* ϩ. of trumpet ἤχησις, c. of judge;
1 Cor 14 7 *S*(*B* do) φθ.; Jer 4 19 *B* ⲕⲣ.; Sa 17 17 *S*
ῥυθμός; *ib* 11 19 *S* βρόμος; Z 292 *S* of falling walls
ψόφος; Mor 37 96 *S* ϩ. ⲛⲣⲟⲡⲗⲟⲛ κτύπος; Si 45 15 *S*
ⲥⲱⲧⲙ ⲉⲡⲉϩ. ἀκουστὸς ποιεῖσθαι; ShA 1 397 *S* ⲕⲓ-
θαρα...ⲡⲉϩ. ⲛⲡⲉⲥⲟⲩⲉⲗⲗⲉ, BHom 111 *S* ⲛⲣⲁⲧⲏⲣ,
Ora 4 208 *S* maladies ⲣⲁϩⲧⲉ ⲛⲓⲙ ϩⲓⲧⲏⲩ ⲛⲓⲙ ϩⲓϩ.
ⲛⲓⲙ (? *tinnitus*), MG 25 255 *B* ⲛϩ. of breaking cup,
DeV 2 45 *B* ϩ. of cattle.

ⲁⲧϩ., ϩ., *voiceless*: 1 Cor 12 2 *B*(*S* ⲙⲉⲩϣⲁϫⲉ)
ἄφωνος; My 164 *S* ⲥϩⲁⲓ ⲛⲁ. consonant (*cf* ϯ ϩ.).

ⲃⲱⲕ ϩ. *v* ⲥⲉⲕ ϩ.

ⲛⲟⲩϫⲉ, ⲛⲉϫ ϩ. *SA²*, *throw voice, let a cry*: Ez 27
36 (*B* ϥⲓ ϩ. ⲉϩⲣⲏⲓ) συρίζειν; BAp 110 wolf ⲛⲉϫ ⲟⲩⲛⲟϭ ⲛϩ., ManiH 74 *A²* ⲛⲟⲩϫⲉ ⲛⲟⲩϩ.; c ⲉⲃⲟⲗ:
Mk 15 37 (*B* ⲙⲟⲩϯ ⲉⲃⲟⲗ ⲟⲩⲥⲙⲏ) φωνὴν ἀφιέναι; BIF
13 98 ⲛⲉϫ ϩ. ⲉⲃ. = MG 25 277 *B* ϯ ϩ. ⲉⲃ.

ⲣ ϩ., *make noise*: Ez 6 11 *S*(*B* diff) ψοφεῖν.

ⲥⲉⲕ ϩ., ϩ., *draw sound, snort*: ShC 73 200 *S* ϣⲁϥ-
ⲥⲉ(ⲕ) ϩ. ϩⲛϣⲁⲛⲧϥ, LMär 18 *S* ⲁϥⲥⲉⲕ ϩ. ϩⲛϣⲁⲛⲧϥ,
Mor 24 10 *F* ⲥⲁⲕ ⲟⲩϩ. ⲉⲃ. ϩⲛϣⲉⲉⲛⲧⲃ, BSM 111 *B*
ⲥⲉⲕ ϩ. ⲉⲃⲟⲗ ⲉⲛⲡⲉⲭⲉⲃϣⲁⲓ; sim BP 12491 *S* com-
plaints of ill-treatment ⲁⲩⲃⲱⲕ ϩ. ⲛϣⲁ ⲉϩⲣⲁⲓ ϩⲓⲱⲓ.
Cf DM 1 17, 6 19 *sq* n ϩⲣⲱ.

ϯ ϩ., ϩ., *give, utter voice*: Pro 2 3 *B*(*SA* ⲙⲟⲩⲧⲉ
ϩⲛⲟⲩⲥ.), Joel 3 16 *SA*(*B* ⲱϣ), 1 Cor 14 8 *S*(*B* ϯ c.)
ⲫ. διδόναι, Si 45 15 (9) *S* ⲫ. ἠχεῖσθαι; Jth 10 13 *S* διαφωνεῖν (misunderst); Lam 3 8 *B*(*S* ϫⲓ ϣⲕⲁⲕ, *F* ⲱϣ
ⲉⲃⲁⲗ) κράζειν; Jos 10 21 *S* γρύζειν; 1 Cor 13 1 *S*(*B*
ⲥⲉⲛⲥⲉⲡ) ἠχεῖν; TEuch 1 246 *B* deacon shall ϯ ϩ.
saying صر, AZ 33 54 *F* bird ϯ ⲛⲟⲩϩ., KroppE 31 *S*
tongue ϯ ϩ. ⲙⲙⲟⲩⲥⲓⲕⲟⲛ, My 164 *S* ⲥϩⲁⲓ ⲉϥϯ ϩ.
vowel (*cf* ⲁⲧϩ.), Mor 37 106 *S* caused him to ϯ ϩ. ⲛⲁϥ

ⲉⲧⲙⲭⲟⲟⲥ *give promise* ἀπαιτεῖν μηδενὶ λέγειν;   c
ⲉⲃⲟⲗ: Mk 5 38 *S*(var ⲟⲩⲉⲛ ⲣⲟ, *B* ⲉϣ ⲗⲏⲗⲟⲅⲓ) ἀλαλάζειν; Jos 6 8 *S* σημαίνειν; Br 51 *S* ϯ ⲛⲟⲩϩ. ⲉⲃ.,
OrChr '32 116 *S* fiery river ϯ ϩ. ⲉⲃ. ⲉⲙⲁⲧⲉ, C 43 208
B ϯ ⲛⲟⲩⲛⲓϣϯ ⲛϩ. ⲉⲃ.;   ⲣⲉϥϯ ϩ.: My 35 *S*
birds ⲛⲣ.

ⲱϣ, ⲉⲱ ϩ., ϩ., *utter voice*, mostly c ⲉⲃⲟⲗ: BIF 13
112 *S* camel ⲁϥⲉϣ ϩ. ⲉⲃ. = MG 25 302 *B*, Va 58 72
B ⲥⲛⲁⲱϣ ⲟⲩϩ. ⲉⲃ. & will be helped, C 43 239 *B* ⲟⲱϣ
ⲟⲩⲛⲓϣϯ ⲛϩ. ⲉⲃ., C 86 167 *B* ⲁϥⲉϣ ⲟⲩϩ. ϣⲁⲡⲟⲩⲣⲟ
saying; *ib* 173 ⲣⲉϥⲉϣ ϩ. *herald*.

ϥⲓ ϩ., ϩⲣⲁ⸗ *S*, ϩⲣⲉ⸗ *A²*, *raise voice*: Lu 11 27 *S*(var
ϫⲓ ϣⲕ. ⲉⲃⲟⲗ, *B* ϥⲓ ⲥⲙⲏ) ⲫ. ἐπαίρειν; AP 44 *A²* ⲁⲩϥⲓ
ϩⲣⲉⲩ; c ⲉⲃⲟⲗ: 1 Kg 24 17 (*B* ϥ. ⲥ. ⲉⲛϣⲱⲓ) ⲫ.
αἴρειν, Jud 2 4, Ac 14 11 (*B* ϭⲓⲥⲓ ⲥ. ⲉϩⲣⲏⲓ) ⲫ. ἐπαί.,
Lu 1 42 (*B* ⲱϣ ⲉⲛϣ.) ἀναφωνεῖν; Z 322 ⲁⲩϥⲓ ϩⲣⲁⲩ
ⲉⲃ. ϩⲛⲟⲩⲛⲟϭ ⲛⲥⲙⲏ μιᾷ φωνῇ ἀναβοᾶν; Aeg 23 ⲁⲩϥⲓ
ϩⲣⲁⲩ ⲉⲃ. ⲁⲩⲅⲣⲓⲙⲉ = *ib B* ϭⲓⲥⲓ ⲥⲙⲏ ⲉϩⲣⲏⲓ, AP 56 *A²*
ⲁϥϥⲓ ϩⲣⲉϥ ⲁⲃ.;   c ⲉϩⲣⲁⲓ: PS 79 *S* ⲁⲥϥⲓ ϩⲣⲁⲥ ⲉ.
ⲉⲡⲭⲓⲥⲉ saying, Ez 27 36 *B v* ⲛⲉϫ ϩ.

ϫⲓ ⲛⲡⲉϩ., ⲛϩⲣⲁ⸗ *S*, *take voice, cry*: Mor 17 42
began to shout ⲉⲩϫⲓ ⲛϩⲣⲁⲩ ἀνακράζειν; *hear* (*cf* ϫⲓ
ⲥⲙⲏ): ShC 73 96 ϣⲁⲣⲉⲛϩⲁⲗⲏⲧ ϫⲓ ⲛⲡⲉϩ. ⲛⲛⲉⲧⲕⲣ-
ⲙⲣⲙ. *Cf* p 648 *a*.

ⲛⲁϣⲧϩ. *S*, *hard-voiced*: ⲙⲏⲧⲛ. ϩ. Mor 25 45.

ⲡⲟϭϫ ⲛϩ. *S*, epithet of Isaiah (*cf* Ro 9 27): Leyd
125 ⲡⲁⲡⲉⲛ. ⲉⲛϩ. (prob *l* ⲡⲟϭ ⲛϩ. as in Ryl 42, *cf* Pas
H 213 *B* ⲫⲁⲡⲓⲛⲓϣϯ ⲛϩ., Brooks *Select Let Severus*
1 447 ⲕⲕⲇ ⲟⲃ, Va ar 172 163 العظيم الصوت صاحب).

ϩⲣⲟⲩⲙⲡⲉ *SA²* nn m, *voice of sky, thunder*: Jo 12
29 *S*(var ϩⲣⲁⲙⲡⲉ)*A²* ϩ. ⲛⲧⲡⲉ (*B* ϩⲁⲣⲁⲃⲁⲓ), Ap 6 1 (*B*
do) βροντή; Gu 70 ἦχος; ManiK 32 *A²* ϩⲣⲟⲩⲙⲡⲉ.

ϩⲣⲟⲩ(ⲃ)ⲃⲁⲓ *S*, ϩⲁⲣⲁⲃⲁⲓ, ⲭ. *B*, ϩⲁⲣⲁⲃⲉⲓ, -ⲁⲓ *F* nn
f m(once) sim: Job 26 14 *S* m *B*, Ps 76 18 *SB*, Si 35
10 *S*, Ap 10 4 *S* f *BF*, Jo 12 29 *B* f β.; Miss 4 690 *S*
ϩⲉⲛⲉⲃⲣⲏϭⲉ ⲙⲛⲣⲉⲛϩ., AM 155 *B* ϩⲁⲛⲃ. ⲁⲩϣⲱⲡⲓ,
FR 102 *B* sim ⲭ., LAp 528 *F*, GriffStu 162 *F* ϩⲁⲣⲁⲃⲁⲓ ⲛⲣⲉⲛ ⲉⲙⲛⲧ ⲙⲙⲉⲧⲃⲏ;   ϯ ϩ. *S*, ⲉⲣ ϩ. *B*: 1 Kg
2 10 *SB*, Ps 28 3 *B*(*S* ⲱϣ ⲉⲃⲟⲗ) βροντᾶν.

ϩⲣⲟⲩⲟ, -ⲱ *S*, ϩⲣⲟⲩⲟ, ϩⲣⲃⲟ *A*, ϩⲉⲣⲟⲩⲱ, ⲭ. *B* nn,
great voice, boastful talk: Zech 9 2 *B* ⲙⲉⲅⲓ ⲉϩⲁⲛⲃ. (*A*
diff) σοφίζειν;   mostly ⲙⲛⲧϩ., -ϩ., ⲙⲉⲧϩ., *boastfulness*: 1 Kg 2 3 *SB* μεγαλορρημοσύνη, Ps 11 4 *B*(*S*
ⲡⲟϭ ⲛϣⲁϫⲉ), Ob 12 *AB* -ρήμονεῖν, Si 48 22 *S*, Zeph
3 11 *AB* μεγαλαυχεῖν, *ib* 28 *SA*(*B* Gk diff), 2 Pet 2 18
S -ⲱ *B*(*sic l*?), Jude 16 *S* -ⲱ (*B* ϩⲉⲛⲟⲩϩⲣⲟⲩⲟ) ὑπέρογκος; ShWess 9 90 *S* ϣⲁϫⲉ ⲙⲙ. spoken against God,
ShR 2 3 80 *S* among sins ⲙⲛⲧϩⲣⲟⲩⲟ, AM 204 *B* ⲭⲉ
ⲙⲉⲧⲭ.= BM 321 5 *S* ⲡⲟϭ ⲛϣⲁϫⲉ;   ⲣ ⲙⲛⲧϩ. *S*:
Ryl 62 2 ⲙⲛⲣⲣ ⲙ. *Cf* ⲙⲛⲧ ϩⲣⲟⲩⲟ. *V* Dévaud
Études 35.   Distinct from ϩⲗ, ϩⲣ ⲟⲩⲱ p 475 *a*.

ϩⲣⲟⲩⲣ *B* vb intr, *cease, be quiet*: Ge 8 1 (*S* ϭⲃⲟⲕ),

Nu 11 2 (*S* ϩⲣⲟⲕ *q v*), AM 275 let tempest ϱ. κοπάζειν; Ps 88 10 (*S* ϭⲱ) καταπραΰνειν; ib 106 29 (*S*
ϱⲏ ⲡⲧⲏⲩ ϣⲱⲡⲉ) εἰς αὔραν ἵστασθαι; AM 218 ⲑⲣⲉⲡ-
ⲃⲉⲣⲃⲉⲣ⳽ ϱ.; c ϫⲉⲛ-: Va 58 72 ⲁϥϱ. ϫⲉⲛⲧⲉϭ-
ⲭⲱⲡⲧ; c ⲉⲃⲟⲗ ϱⲁ-: Jon 1 11 (*S* ⲗⲟ, *A* ⲗⲁϭⲉ) ⲕⲟ.
ἀπό; c ⲉⲃ. ϩⲓϫⲉⲛ-: Ge 8 11 (*S* c.) ⲕⲟ. ἀπό; tr
(refl): Jer 14 21 ⲕⲟ. *Cf* ϩⲣⲣⲉ. *V* Griffith
Stories 96.

ϩⲣⲟⲩⲱⲣ⳽   *v* ϩⲃⲟⲣⲃⲉⲣ.

ϩⲣⲟⲩⳅ(ⲉ)ⳃ *S* nn as pl, *pebbles*: 1 Kg 14 14, κόχ-
λαξ, cit P 44 109 الرَّزُّ (misunderst).

ϩⲣⲟⲩⲟⲩⳅϥ *S* nn with ⲡ, *perish*(?) or *disinte-
grate* (*cf* last), *putrefy*: PS 271 ⲯⲩⲭⲏ ⲛⲁⲣ ϱ. ⲁⲩⲱ
ⲛⲥⲁⲛϩⲁⲗⲓⲥⲕⲉ ⲉⲡⲁϥ ⲙⲡⲕⲱϱⲧ, ib 321 sim ϱⲙⲡϩⲁϥ
ⲙⲡⲉⲭⲁⲗⲁⳅⲁ, ib 380 sim ⲛⲥⲃⲱⲗ ⲉⲃⲟⲗ, ib 304 trans-
gresssor ⲛⲁⲣ ϱ. ϩⲙⲡⲕⲟⲗⲁⲥⲓⲥ. *Cf* AZ 14 63.

ϩⲱⲣⳡ *S*, ϩⲁⲣⳡ† *Sᵃ* vb intr, *break*(?): BP 5657 *S*
ⲧⲁⲥϣⲛⲉ...]ϱ. ⲡⲉⲥⲭⲡⲁϱ, COAd 34 ⲡⲁⲛⲥⲏⲛ (ἀγγεῖον)
ⲛϱ., TurM 24 ⲟⲩⲛⳡⲓⲥ (*cf* ST 439, WS 123) ⲉⲣⲉ-
ⲧⲉⲥⲟⲩⲣⲏⲧⲉ ϱ.†

(ϩⲱⲣϣ), ϩⲉⲣϣ- *B* vb tr, *run* ship *aground*: Ac
27 41 (*S* ⲙⲟⲟⲛⲉ) ἐπικέλλειν.

ϩⲣⲟⲩϣ *SBF*(once), ϩⲣⲁⳡ *SᵃAA²F*, ⲉϩⲣⲟⲩϣ *B*,
ϩ(ⲉ)ⲣⳡ- *S*, ϩⲟⲣⳡ† *SB*, ϩⲁ.† *SᵃS/AA²*, ⲟⲣⳡ- *O*, ⲡ c
ϩⲁⲣⳡ- *SAA²F*, ⲁⲣⳡ- *A* vb **I** intr, *be heavy, slow,
difficult*: Is 33 15 *SBF*, Lam 3 7 *BF*(*S* ⲧⲁϣⲟ), Hab 2
6 *AB* βαρύνειν, Ge 48 17 *B*(*S* ⲛⲁϣⲧ) Ex 17 12 *SB*,
βαρύς; ShIF 227 *S* ⲡⲉⲧⲭⲱ ⲡⲛⲁⲓ ⲛⲁϱ. ⲣⲱ ⲛϩⲉⲛⲕⲉ-
ⲣⲟⲙⲡⲉ, BMis 259 *S* body ϱ. like lead, ST 335 *Sᵃ*
ⲧⲉⲥⲁⲅⲛⲉ (= ⳿ⲥⲟⲟⲩⲛ) ⳅⲉⲁⲕϱ., TstAb 246 *B* ⲁⲛⲉϥ-
ⲃⲁⲗ ⲉϱ., MG 25 105 *B* ⲁϥϱ. ϩⲓⲧⲉⲛⲡⲓϣⲱⲡⲓ, Mor 30
20 *F* ⲛⲧⲉⲗⲉⲡⲡⲟⲗⲩⲙⲟⲥ ϱ. = ib 29 17 *S* ⲡϣⲟⲧ; qual:
Ps 34 18 *B*(*S* ⲟϣ), ib 47 14 *B*(*S* ⲧⲁⲉⲓⲏⲩ), Mt 23 4
SB βαρύς, Lam 2 7 *B*(*F* ⳅⲁⲣ) as if -ύς, Mt 26 43 *SB*
βαρεῖν, Joel 2 8 (*A* diff) καταβαρύν., Ps 121 7 *B*(*S*
diff) -βαρις; Ex 18 22 *B*(*S* ⳅⲟⲥⲉ), Dan 11 36 *B*(*S*
ⲛⲟϭ) ὑπέρογκος; Is 3 16 *B*(*S* ⲇⲟ) ὑψηλός; Ez 3 5 *B*
βαθυ-; ib 6 *B* profundus; Ja 1 19 *B*(*SA* ⲱⲥⲕ) βραδύς;
R 2 2 28 *S* ⲛⲛⲟⲃⲉ ϱ. ⲁⲛ χαλεπός; Lu 11 46 *S*(*B*
ⲙⲟⲕϩ) δυσ-; PS 153 *S* ϩⲩⲗⲏ ⲉⲥϱ., ShP 130² 3 *S*
wolves ⲉⲩϱ. will seize lambs, BIF 13 114 *S* ϩⲙⲟⲙ
ⲉϥϱ. = MG 25 305 *B* ⲟϣ, Vi ostr 429 + 396 *S* ⳁϱ.
ⲉⲙⲁⲧⲉ ⳿ϣⲱⲡⲉ, J 79 23 *Sᵃ* ϣⲱⲡⲉ ⲉⲩϱ., TillBau 128 *S*
ⲟⲩϩⲟⲟⲩ ⲉⲩϱ.ⲡⲉ (unlucky day), Z 286 *S* ⲡⲁⲓⲁⲥⲧⲙⲁ
ϱ. ⲛⲡⲁϩⲣⲁⲕ, P 131³ 36 *S/* ⲁⲛⲁϣ ⲛⲛⲟⲩϩ ⲉⲧϱ., MIE
2 362 *B* ⲉⲧϥⲱ ⲉⲧϱ., Va 58 70 *B* ⲉⲙⲃⲟⲛ ⲉϥϱ.

II tr, *make heavy*: Ge 31 35 *S*(*B* ⲛϣⲟⲧ) βαρέως
φέρειν, Is 33 15 *SF*(*B* ⲑⲣⲟ...ϱ.) βαρύνειν; Am 8 5 *S*
ϱⲉ. (*B* ⲉⲣ ⲡϣⳁ) μεγαλύνειν; Ez 39 26 *B* ϱ.† (*l*? ϱⲣ.)
ἐκφοβεῖν; Tri 696 *S* ⲛⲃⲁⲣⲟⲥ ⲉⲧϱ.† (? ϱⲣ.) ⲙⲙⲟⲛ.
With following preposition.

— ⲉ- *SA²BF*, *for, beyond*: Va 63 102 *B* ⲙⲙⲟⲛ
ϩⲗⲓ ⲡⲉⲧϥⲱ ϱ.† ⲉⲣⲟⲥ βαρύς, Job 15 10 *B* βαρύτερος
gen, 2 Cor 11 9 *S* neg(*B* ⲟⲩⲁϩ ⲃⲁⲣⲟⲥ ⲉⲭⲉⲛ-) ἀβαρής,
1 Thes 2 7 *SF*(*B* ϣⲱⲡⲓ ϩⲁⲟⲩⲃⲁⲣⲟⲥ) ἐν βάρει εἶναι,
Is 6 10 *B*(*S* ⲱⲥⲕ) βαρέως, 2 Thes 3 8 *S*(*B* ⲟⲩⲁϩ ⲃ.
ⲉⲭ.) ἐπιβαρεῖσθαι acc; Ps 21 25 *B*(*S* ⲙⲉⲥⲧⲉ) προσοχθίζειν dat, *v* also ⲟⳃ; ShA 1 72 *S* ⲁⲛϱ. ⲉⲡⲛ̄ⲉ̄ so
that He forgive us not, BIF 13 114 *S* ⲉϥϱ. ⲉⲡϣⲱⲡⲉ
= MG 25 305 *B* ϱ. ϫⲉⲛ-, Ora 4 7 *S* ⲉⲕⲉⲧⲣⲉⲃϩⲉⲣⲟϣ
ⲉⲣⲟⲥ like millstone, ManiK 110 *A²* ⲉⲥϱ.† ⲁⲛⲓⲣⲙ-
ⲙⲁⲟ; *dat commodi*: Ge 48 10 *S*(var ϩⲧⲟⲙⲧⲙ, *B*
om ⲉ-), Ps 4 2† *S*(*B* ⲇⲟ) βαρυ-; ShWess 9 107 *S* ⲡⲉⲩϱ-
ⲣⲏⲧ ϱ.† ⲉⲣⲟⲟⲩ, Mor 31 256 *S* ⲧⲁⲁⲡⲉ ϱ.† ⲉⲣⲟⲓ after
sleep, PSBA 10 196 *S* ⲕⲉϩⲛⲃⲉ ⲉϥϱ.† ⲛϩⲟⲩⲟ ⲉⲡϣⲟ-
ⲣⲡ; *vbal*: Sa 2 14 *S*(*B* diff) βαρύς, Ac 28 27 *SB*
βαρέως; ShZ 594 *S* ϥⲛⲁϱ. ⲉⲧⲙϥⲟⲧⲟⲩ ⲉⲃⲟⲗ *hardly
shall He not destroy them*, PMéd 229 *S* ⲡⲙⲁⳅⲉ ⲉⲧϱ.†
ⲉⲥⲱⲧⲙ; ϱⲣⲟⲩⲡ ⲉ-: BM 358 = Mor 47 183 *S*
sins ⲉⲩϱ.† ⲉϱ. ⲉⲡⲱϱ.

— ⲉⲭⲛ-, *upon*: Jud 1 35 *S*, Mal 3 13 *A*(*B* ⲉϩⲣⲏⲓ
ⲉⲭ.) βαρύν. ἐπί, 2 Cor 5 4 *B*(*S* = Gk) βαρεῖν ἐπί; ib
12 13 *B*(*SF* ⲟⲩⲉϩ ϩⲓⲥⲉ ⲉ-) καταναρκᾶν gen; Lev 18
25 *B*(*S* ϩⲱⲧⲉ) προσοχ. dat; Deu 30 11 *S*(*B* om ⲉⲭ.)
ὑπέρογ. εἶναι; Jud 6 2 *S* ⲓⲥⲭⲩⲉⲓⲛ ἐπί; ShC 73 146 *S*
bread ϱ. ⲉⲭⲙⲡϩⲏⲧ, CO 324 *S* sickness ϱ. ⲉⲭⲙⲡⲉⲛ-
ⲉⲓⲱⲧ, BSM 31 *B* ⲙⲏ ⲁ(ⳡ)ϱ. ⲉⲭⲱ ⲛϫⲉ ⲡⲉⲣ ⲫⲙⲉⲅⲓ?
(varVa 63 6 ⲉϱ. ⲉⲣⲟ) = BMis 373 *S* ⲗⲟ ϩⲙⲡⲟⲩϩⲏⲧ,
ManiP *A²* ⲙⲡⲉϥ. ⲁⲭⲱⲓ, Mor 30 39 *F* camel threw
him ⲁϥϱ. ⲉⲭⲱϥ = BMis 264 *S* ⲛⲕⲟⲧⲕ ⲉⲭⲱϥ; ⲉ-
ϩⲣⲁⲓ, -ⲛⲓ ⲉⲭⲛ-: Ps 31 3 *SB* βαρύν. ἐπί; Jth 13 2 *S*,
Ac 20 9 *S*(*B* Gk diff); ShBM 230 158 ⲉⲕϱ.† ⲉϱ. ⲉⲭⲱⲟⲩ ϱⲛⲧⲉⲕⲟⲙⲙⲉ, ShC 42 165 *S* Christ ϱ. ⲉϱ. ⲉⲭⲛⲡⲟ-
ⲟⲩ ⲟⲛ ⲡⲁⲓ (as if ϱ. ⲛϩⲏⲧ), BMar 6 *S* let Thy mercy ϱ.
ⲉϱ. ⲉⲭⲱⲓ, C 43 163 *B* ⲛⲛⲓⲡⲟⲗⲉⲙⲟⲥ ⲉⲉϱⲟⲩϣ ⲉϱ. ⲉⲭⲱⲕ.

— ⲛ- dat: Ex 18 18† *SB*, Nu 11 14† *SB* βαρύς
dat; *with, in*: Nu 16 15 *B*(*S* ϱ. ⲛϩⲏⲧ) βαρυθυμεῖν,
Lu 9 32 *B*(*S*† ϱⲁ-) βαρεῖν dat; 1 Kg 4 19 *S* ϱ.† ⲡⲱ
συλλαμβάνειν; Ming 336 *S* if one cleave to God
ϣⲁϥⲗⲟ ⲉϥϱ.† ⲛⲛⲟⲃⲉ, Mor 34 32 *S* ⲡⲣⲱⲃ ϱ.† ⲡⲉⲓⲙⲉ
ⲉⲣⲟϥ (varBMis 108 ⲙⲟⲕϱ), Va 61 20 *B* ⲛⲏ ⲉⲧϱ.† ⲛⲥⲱⲧⲉⲙ ⲛⲥⲁⲡⲓⲉⲛⲧⲟⲗⲏ; *as to*: AZ 21 100 *O* ⲉϥⲟⲣϣ
ⲛⲛⲉⲃⲗⲁ[ⲥ].

— ϱⲁ- *S* *v* Lu 9 32 above.

— ϱⲛ-, *in*: Ex 4 10 *A*(*SB* diff) βραδύ-; ShC 42
185 *S* ⲁⲓϱ. ϩⲙⲡⲁϣⲱⲛⲧ, Va 57 34 *B* ship ϱ.† ϫⲉⲛⲡⲁⲟ-
ⲟⲩⲛⲓ, MG 25 315 *B* sick ⲉⲧϱ.† ϫⲉⲛⲡⲟⲩⲥⲱⲙⲁ.

— ϩⲓϫⲛ- *S*, *upon*: BHom 50 ⲟⲩϱⲟⲃ ⲉϥϱ.† ϱ.
ⲥⲟⲩⲥⲁⲡⲛⲁ.

— nn m *SAA²BF*, *weight, burden*: Z 307 *S* ⲡⲉϱ.
ⲧⲏⲣϥ ⲡⲡⲉⲥⲛⲏⲩ βαρύς; ShC 73 190 *S* ⲟⲩϱ. ⲛⲥⲱⲙⲁ
paral ⲙⲡⲧⲁⲥⲑⲉⲛⲏⲥ; PS 282 *S* ⲡⲉϱ. ⲛ̄ⲧⳃϣⲉ, BMis
89 *S* ⲡⲉϱ. of child in womb, TillOster 15 *A* ϭⲓ ⲡⲓϱ.
ⲁ̄ⳃ[ⲁⲗ ϱ.]ⲛⲡⲉⲧⲛ̄ϩⲏⲧ, ManiP *A²* ⲡϱ. ⲙⲡⲥⲱⲙⲁ, Va 57

4 *B* his goods doubled ⲥⲉⲛⲟⲩϩ., *ib* 61 10 *B* ⲡⲓϩ. opp ⲡⲓⲁⲥⲓⲁⲓ, C 41 53 *B* ⲛⲁϥⲙⲟϣⲡⲉ ⲥⲉⲛⲟⲩϩ. = Miss 4 413 متواني كسلان, Mor 30 15 *F* ⲛⲉϩ. ⲙⲡⲱⲡⲓ; as adj: ShA 1 42 *S* ⲟⲩⲟⲩⲟⲉⲓϣ ⲛϩ.

ⲁⲧϩ. *S*, *without weight*: Mor 25 77 ⲥⲱⲙⲁ ⲛⲁ.

† ϩ. *S*, *give, add weight*: Bor 260 119 ⲉϥ† ϩ. ⲙⲡⲉϥⲛⲁⲣⲃ.

ϩ. ⲛϩⲏⲧ *SAA²F*, *be slow of heart, long-suffering*: Job 7 16 (*B* ⲱⲟⲩ ⲛϩⲏⲧ), Pro 19 8 *A*(*S* ⲣ ϩⲁⲣϣϩⲏⲧ), Ja 5 7 (*B* do), AP 14 *A²* ⲙⲁⲕⲣⲟⲑⲩⲙⲉⲓⲛ; ShIF 297 is not forgiveness ϩ. ⲛϩ. ⲁⲩⲱ ⲁⲡⲉⲭⲉ?, BMis 37 ϩ. ⲛϩ. ⲡⲟⲩⲕⲟⲩⲓ ϣⲁⲛⲧⲉ-, Mor 27 34 *F* ϩ. ⲛϩ. ⲧⲁⲥⲱⲡⲉ = BMis 387 *S*; *be heavy with wrath*: Nu 16 15 *S*(var ⲙⲟⲩϩ ⲛϭⲱⲛⲧ, *B* ϩⲣⲟϣ ⲡⲉⲙⲃⲟⲛ) βαρυθυμεῖν; c ⲉ- vbal: ShA 1 99 ⲁϥϩ. ⲛϩ. ⲉⲧⲙⲉⲓⲣⲉ; c ⲉϫⲛ-: Lu 10 12 (*B* ⲉⲙⲧⲟⲛ ϣⲱⲡⲓ ⲛ-) ἀνεκτὸς εἶναι dat; ⲉϩⲣⲁⲓ ⲉϫⲛ-: Si 32 18, Mt 18 26 (*B* ⲱⲟⲩ ⲛϩ. ⲡⲉⲙ-) μακ. ἐπί; BHom 41 ϩ. ⲛϩ. ⲉϩ. ⲉⲭⲱⲓ ἐάν acc; ShA 2 315 ⲁϥϩ. ⲛϩ. ⲉϩ. ⲉⲭⲱⲓ; qual: 2 Pet 3 9 (*B* ⲱⲟⲩ ⲛϩ.) μακ.; Sa 12 11 ἄδειαν διδόναι; Cl 19 3 *A* ϥϩ. ⲛϩ. ⲙⲡ ⲡⲉϥⲥⲱⲡⲧ ἀόργητος ὑπάρχειν; Job 19 3 *B* ⲁⲣϣⲏⲧ ⲉⲭⲉⲡ- (*S* ⲉⲧⲉⲧⲛϩⲓⲭⲱⲓ) ἐπικεῖσθαι dat.

ⲣ ⲥ ϩ. ⲗⲉⲥ *A*, *heavy-tongued*: Ex 4 10 (Cl, var ϩ.† ϩⲁⲡⲗⲉⲥ, *SB* diff) βραδύγλωσσος; ϩ.ϩⲏⲧ, *long-suffering*: Ex 34 6 (*B* ⲙⲉⲧϣⲉⲛϩⲏⲧ), Ps 85 15 (*B* ⲣⲉ ϥⲱⲟⲩ ⲛϩ.), Pro 15 18 *SA*, Eccl 7 9 (*F* ⲛⲁϫ ⲛϩ.) μακρόθυμος; BAp 25 Job ⲛϩ.(varMIF 9 60 ⲣⲉϥϫⲣⲡⲟⲙⲓⲛⲏ), BM 511(3)*F* ⲟⲩϩ., Z 284 ⲟⲩϩ. ⲉⲭⲛⲡⲣⲱⲙⲉ, ManiP 33 *A²*; pl *ib* 145 ⲡⲓϩ. ϩⲉⲧⲉ; ⲙⲛⲧϩ. ϩⲏⲧ, *patience*: Is 57 15 (*B* ⲙⲉⲧⲣⲉϥϣⲟⲩ ⲛϩ.), Ro 2 4 (*B* do) μακροθυμία; Sa 2 19 (*B* ϭⲩⲡⲟⲙⲟⲛⲏ) ἀνεξικακία; *ib* 12 21 ἀκρίβεια; CA 88 ⲙⲛⲧϩⲣⲟϣ (*sic*) ϩ. opp ϣⲧⲟⲣⲧⲣ, TU 43 22 *A* ⲙⲛⲧⲁ.ϩ., PBu 23 hear us ϩⲣⲟⲩⲙ., ManiK 91 *A²* ⲧⲙ.; ⲣ, ⲟ ⲛϩ.ϩⲏⲧ, *be patient*: Pro 19 8 (*A* ϩⲣ. ⲛϩ.), Z 300 ⲁⲣⲓ ϩ. ϣⲁⲛⲧϥϫⲱⲱⲧ ⲙⲡⲧⲃⲧ μακροθυμεῖν; PS 175 ⲉϥⲟ ⲛϩ., Br 125 ⲁⲣⲓ ϩ. (*cf ib* ϩⲣ. ⲛϩ. imperat) C 99 141 ⲣ ϩ. ⲉⲭⲱⲓ = C 89 46 ⲱⲟⲩ ⲛϩ. ⲉⲭⲱⲓ.

ϩⲣⲏϣⲉ *SA²*, ϩⲉⲣϣⲉ *S*, ϩⲣⲏϣⲓ, ⲉϩ. *B*, ϩⲣⲉ. *S*(?)*B*, nn f, *weight*: Si 13 2 *S*, Ap 2 24 *S*(*B* = Gk) βάρος; Nu 7 25 *S*(var&*B* ϣⲓ) ὁλκή; Gk om Lev 24 5 *S*(*B* do), 2 Kg 12 30 *S*, Ez 4 10 *S* -ϣⲓ *B*; ShR 2 3 28 *S* ⲟⲩⲱϩ ⲡⲕⲉϩ. ⲉϩⲣⲁⲓ ⲉϫⲱⲛ, Mor 39 17 *S* ⲁⲩϣⲓ ⲛⲟⲩⲃ...ϣⲁⲧⲉϥϩ. (varWess 15 122 ⲁϫⲓ ⲛⲧⲉϥϩ.) = C 43 43 *B* ϣⲁⲧⲟⲩ†ⲛⲧⲉϥϩ., P 129¹⁶ 38 *S* ⲁⲡⲉⲓⲱⲧ † ⲛⲧⲁϩ. ⲛⲛⲟⲩⲃ (*cf* AM 194 *sup*, but diff), C 86 142 *B* sim ϩ., Z 553 *S* ⲧⲁⲓⲟⲩ ⲡⲕⲉⲡⲁⲅⲛⲁⲣⲓⲟⲛ ⲛϩⲉⲣ., ManiK 85 *A²* ϩⲓ ⲁϩⲣⲏⲓ ϩⲁⲡϩ. ⲧⲏⲣⲟⲩ, BSM 2 *B* ship ⲥⲁⲧϩⲣⲉϣⲓ ⲛⲡⲓⲟⲑⲱⲟⲩ = BMis 323 *S* ⲡⲏϣⲟⲧ, *ib* 43 *B* ⲧⲁⲗⲉ ϩ. ⲉⲭⲉⲡⲛⲉⲡ ⲯⲩⲭⲏ (varVa 63 15 ⲟⲩⲁϩ ⲃⲁⲣⲟⲥ) = *ib* 390 *S* ⲟⲩⲉϩ ϩⲓⲥⲉ.

V ⲧⲉⲣϣⲟ.

ϩⲣⲟϣ *B*, ϩⲟⲣϣ† *SB*, *be cold*   *v* ⲱⲣϣ & ⲁⲣⲟϣ.

ϩⲣϣⲓⲣⲉ, ϩⲣ., ⲥⲉⲗϣⲓⲣⲓ, ϩⲉⲣϣⲏⲗⲓ   *v* ϣⲓⲣⲉ.

ϩⲁⲣϣⲏⲧ   *v* ϩⲁϣⲏⲧ.

ϩⲣⲉϥ, -ⲛϥ   *v* ϩⲣⲉⲃ.

ϩⲣⲏϥ *F*   *v* ϩⲣⲃ *leg*.

ϩⲣⲟϥ *S* nn f, *an iron utensil*: Ryl 243 36 ⲥⲛⲧⲉ ⲛϩ. ⲙⲡⲉⲡⲓⲡⲉ.

ϩⲁⲣⲉϩ *S*, ⲁⲣ. *SB*, ϩⲁⲣⲏϩⲉ (rare), ⲉⲣⲉϩ, -ⲏϥ *S* (rare)*A*, ⲁⲣⲏϩ *A*(rare)*A²*, ⲉⲣⲏϩⲧⲉ, ⲁⲣ. *A*(*v s f*), ⲁⲗⲉϩ *F* vb intr, *keep, guard*: Job 36 21 *S*(*B* ⲥ ⲉ-), Ps 126 1 *B*(*S* ⲥ ⲉ-), EpJer 69 *F*(*B* do) φυλάσσειν; 2 Cor 11 9 *SB*, Ap 3 3 *SB* τηρεῖν, Dan 3 30 *B*(*S* do) συντ.; Zeph 2 3 *S*(*AB* Gk diff); ShA 1 57 *S* ϩ. ⲙⲡⲣⲧⲣⲉⲩⲧⲁϩⲱⲧⲛ, GFr 313 *S* to see if His steward ϩ. ⲕⲁⲧⲁ ⲧⲉⲡⲧⲟⲗⲏ, PLond 4 436 *S* we swear ⲉⲧⲣⲛϩ. ⲧⲓⲣⲟⲉⲓⲥ according as above written, J 50 71 *S* ⲧⲁⲣⲉⲛϩ. ⲡⲣⲟⲥ ⲧⲉϭϭⲟⲙ, DeV 2 111 *B* ⲭⲁ ⲡⲓⲙⲁⲧⲟⲓ ⲉⲩⲁ.; tr *B*: Ge 3 24 (*S* ⲥ ⲉ-), 2 Chr 6 14 ϥ.; refl *A* ⲁ.: Ge 4 7 (Cl, *S* ⲕⲁ ⲣⲟ, *B* ϩⲉⲣⲓ) ἡσυχάζειν.

With following preposition.

—— ⲉ- obj: Ge 3 24 *S*(var ⲁ., *B* tr), Nu 3 10 *S* (var ⲣⲟⲉⲓⲥ)*B*, Job 14 13 *SB*, Ps 16 4 *SBF*, Pro 2 11 *SAB*, Cant 1 6 *F*(*S* ⲡ.), Sa 6 5 *S*(var ⲁ.), Si 21 12 *S* (var do), Hos 12 6 *S*(ShA 1 412)*A* ⲁ. *B*, Ro 2 26 *SB* ϥ., Job 2 6 *SB*, Zech 3 7 *AB* διαφ.; Ge 3 15 *SB*, Jo 17 11 *SA²B*, Ap 3 10 *S*(var ⲁ.)*B*, AP 15 *A²* ⲧ., Dan 7 28 *B* διατ., Ac 9 24 *SB* παρατ., Si 41 14 *S* ⲁ. συντ.; 2 Cor 11 32 *SB* φρουρεῖν; Deu 23 14 *S*(*B* ⲡⲟϭⲉⲙ) ἐξαιρεῖν; Jud 21 11 *S* περιποιεῖσθαι; Va 57 13 *B* ⲁ. ⲉⲛⲓⲥⲁⲉⲩ ⲛⲉⲡⲓⲧⲁⲥⲙⲁ ἐπιλαμβάνεσθαι gen; Br 92 *S* ϩ. ⲉⲣⲱⲧⲛ ⲙⲡⲣⲭⲟⲟⲩ, BG 103 *S* sent to world ⲉⲁ. ⲉⲣⲟϥ, *ib* 139 *S* ⲧⲟⲓⲕⲟⲛⲟⲙⲓⲁ...ⲁⲓⲉⲣⲉϩ ⲉⲣⲟⲥ, ShBM 253 58 *S* ϩ. ⲉ-ⲡⲉⲛⲥⲱⲙⲁ ⲉϥⲟⲩⲁⲁⲃ, Aeg 262 *S* ϩ. ⲉⲣⲟⲕ ⲉⲙⲁⲧⲉ & spill not therefrom (*sc* chalice), AM 182 *B* ⲁ. ⲉⲣⲟϥ ⲉϥⲧⲟⲩⲃⲏⲟⲩⲧ, Ryl 337 *S* in letter ⲉⲣⲉⲡⲟⲥ ϩ. ⲉⲡⲟⲩⲱⲡⲉϩ, Lant 14 58 *S* in colophon, JKP 2 72 *S* ϩⲁⲣⲏϩⲉ ⲉⲧⲁⲓⲕⲉⲟⲥⲓⲛⲉ, DeV 2 99 *B* ⲁ. ⲉⲛⲓⲉⲡⲧⲟⲗⲓ, Worr 325 *F* ⲁ. ⲉⲛⲓⲯⲏⲭⲛⲟⲩ, Kropp Cl1 *F* ⲁ ⲕⲗⲁⲉⲓⲥ ⲕⲁ. (ⲉ)ⲡⲉϥⲋ̄ ⲛⲥⲉ; + 2d obj: Jer 3 5 *B*, Bor 170 85 *S* ⲁϥϩ. ⲉⲣⲟϥ ⲉⲧⲛⲟϥⲣⲉ (ⲛ)ⲛⲕⲟⲟⲩⲉ φυλ. εἰς; Jo 12 7 *SA²B*, Ac 25 21 *SB* ⲧ. εἰς; vbal: Jos 23 11 *SB* ϥ. gen; Pcod 18 *S* ϩ. ⲉⲧⲙⲕⲁⲡⲏⲗⲉⲅⲉ, C 43 50 *B* ⲁ. ⲉϣⲧⲉⲙⲭⲁ ϩⲗⲓ ⲉϣⲉ; vbal + obj: Ps 38 1 *SB*, Ez 20 21 *SB* ϥ. acc gen; ShC 73 56 *S* ⲉⲩϩ. ⲉⲣⲟⲟⲩ ⲉⲧⲙⲧⲣⲉⲩ-, BHom 61 *S* ϩ. ⲉⲣⲟⲕ ⲉⲧⲙⲁⲁⲥ; + ⲛ- dat: 3 Kg 8 24 *B*, Ps 88 28 *SB* ϥ. acc dat; Lev 19 20 *SB* διαφ. dat, Pro 25 10 *SA* ⲧ. acc dat, Ex 12 6 *SB* διατ.; Ps 30 20 *B*(*S* ϩⲱⲡ) κρύπτειν dat; ShC 73 150 *S* ⲉⲧⲣⲉϥϩ. ⲛⲁⲛ ⲉⲡⲉϥⲛⲁ, BMEA 10579 *S* ⲡⲛ̄ⲉ ⲉⲃⲁϩ. ⲉⲣⲱⲧⲛ ⲛⲁⲛ, J 92 40 *S* ⲉ-ⲧⲣⲉⲛϩ. ⲛⲱⲧⲛ ⲉⲧⲥⲟⲙ of this deed (*cf* ST 104 sim ⲛⲧⲥⲟⲙ), ST 244 *S* †ⲛⲁϩ. ⲛⲁϥ ⲉⲡⲗⲟⲅⲟⲥ, AM 192 *B* ⲁ. ⲉⲡⲁⲓⲁⲗⲟⲩ ⲛⲏⲓ; *from*: ClPr 53 20 *S* monk must

ϩ. ⲉⲡⲥⲉⲓ ⲙⲡⲛ†ⲅⲉ; sim (2d obj): Si 35 21 S(var ⲁ.), Mic 7 5 SA ⲁ. B, 2 Thes 3 3 S(B ⲉⲃⲟⲗ ϩⲁ-) ϕ. ἀπό; Si 11 35 S, Lu 12 1 S(B † ϩⲏⲧ) προσέχειν ἀπό; Ac 15 29 S(B ⲥⲁⲃⲟⲗ ⲛ-) διατ. ἐκ; ShA 2 58 S ⲙⲁⲣⲉϥϩ. ⲉⲣⲟϥ ⲉⲡⲓⲑⲃⲏⲅⲉ ⲙⲡⲟⲛⲏⲣⲟⲛ, PSBA 25 269 S ϩ. ⲉⲣⲟⲕ ⲉⲣⲟϥ = Miss 4 98 B ⲥⲁⲃⲟⲗ ⲙⲙⲟϥ, CA 112 S ϩ. ⲉⲣⲟⲕ ⲉⲣⲉϭⲧ ⲗⲁⲁⲩ, TstAb 232 B ⲁ. ⲉⲣⲟⲕ ⲉⲡⲓⲱⲟⲩ ⲉⲧ-ϣⲟⲩⲓⲧ; sim ⲉⲃⲟⲗ ⲛ-S: Bor 239 53 ⲛϥϩ. ⲁⲛ ⲉⲣⲟϥ ⲉⲃ. ⲛⲡⲁⲓ παραϕ. gen; sim ⲉⲃ. ϩⲁ-B: Ps 139 5 (S ⲉ-) ϕ. ἐκ, AM 269 ⲁ. ⲉⲣⲱⲧⲉⲛ ⲉⲃ. ϩⲁⲣⲟϥ ϕ. ἀπό; C 89 68 ⲁ. ⲉⲣⲱⲧⲉⲛ ⲉⲃ. ϩⲁⲛⲟⲩⲙⲉⲅⲓ = C 99 234 S ⲉ-, MG 25 356 ⲛⲧⲉϥⲁ. ⲉⲣⲟϥ ⲉⲃ. ϩⲁⲡⲉϥⲥⲟⲛ = ROC 18 58 مـصد حذر; sim ⲉⲃ. ϩⲛ-, ϩⲉⲛ-: Ps 17 23 S(B ⲥⲁⲃ. ⲛ-) ϕ. ἀπό; Jo 17 15 SAʸ(B ⲉⲃ. ϩⲁ-), Ap 3 10 S(B do) τ. ἐκ; Mor 42 55 S ϩ. ⲉⲡⲉⲛⲉϩⲏⲧ ⲉⲃ. ϩⲛⲙⲉⲉⲅⲉ ⲛⲓⲙ (var ib 43 55 ⲉ-), C 86 163 B ϣⲁⲝ. ⲉⲣⲟⲩ ⲉⲃ. ϩⲉⲛϭⲓⲛϫⲟⲛⲥ; sim ⲥⲁⲃ. ⲛ-: Ps 17 B ut sup; Ac 15 29 B(S ⲉ-) ἀπέχ. gen; MR 5 47 Sʲ may Lord ϩ. ⲉⲣⲟⲕ ⲥ. ⲙⲡⲉⲑⲁⲩ ⲛⲓⲙ, PO 11 384 B ⲁ. ⲉⲣⲟⲕ ⲥ. ⲛ†ⲉⲕⲕⲗⲏⲥⲓⲁ.

—— nn m SABF, watch, guard: Ps 38 1 SB, ib 129 6 B(S ⲟⲩⲣⲓϣⲉ), Pro 20 28 SA, Hab 2 1 A(SB ⲙⲁ ⲛϩ.) ϕυλακή, Ac 12 6 B(S ⲁⲛⲟⲩⲣⲏϣⲉ) ϕύλαξ; Si 35 22 S(var ⲁ.), 1 Cor 7 19 SBF τήρησις; Pro 28 25 SA ἐπιμέλεια; Va 58 191 B crieth out ⲁⲧϭⲛⲉⲁ. ⲁⲧⲁⲙίευτος; ShZ 598 S who take mysteries once a year ⲉⲅⲉⲓⲣⲉ ⲙⲡⲁⲓ ϩⲓⲟⲩϩ. in self-restraint, R 1 2 51 S ϣϣⲉ ⲉⲁⲁϥ ϩⲓⲟⲩⲛⲟⲥ ⲛϩ. with great care, WS 48 S doors signed ⲉⲅⲁ. ⲛⲡⲗⲁⲟⲥ (cf Ex 12 22), Pcod 20 S ⲛⲁⲡⲟⲩ ⲛϩ. in things of flesh, Mus 40 277 S ϩⲁⲣⲏϩⲉ, Va 58 68 B monk ⲙⲙⲁⲓⲧⲟⲩⲃⲟ ⲉⲣⲉⲡⲓⲁ. ⲛⲧⲟⲧⲩ, Cat 99 B ⲉⲣ ⲡⲛⲏⲫⲓⲛ ϩⲉⲛⲟⲩⲁ., TstAb 235 B we need ⲟⲩⲛⲓϣ† ⲛⲁ. to escape wrath.

ⲙⲛⲧⲁⲧϩ. S, heedlessness: Bor 252 176 eyesight ϣⲱⲡⲉ ϩⲓⲟⲩⲙ. ⲉⲥⲃⲗⲁⲡⲧⲉⲓ ἀπὸ καχεξίας βλάπτεται.

ⲙⲁ ⲛϩ. SABF, watching-place: Ps 76 5 B(S ⲟⲩⲣ-ϣⲉ), Lam 2 19 BF(S do) ϕυλακή, Va 58 145 B arrested by ⲡⲓϩⲟⲩⲅⲓⲧ ⲙⲙ. προϕ. (v Euseb iii 23 15), Is 1 8 SBF, Mic 1 6 SAB-ϕυλάκιον (cf ⲃⲟⲛⲧⲉ); Nu 23 14 B(S ⲙⲁ ⲛϣⲱϣⲧ ⲉⲃⲟⲗ), Is 41 9 B(S diff) σκοπιά; ib 22 9 S(B = Gk) ἄκρα.

ⲣⲉϥϩ. SB, watcher, guard: 1 Kg 17 20 B(S ⲣⲉϥ ⲣⲟⲉⲓⲥ), Is 62 6 SB, Ac 5 23 B(S ⲁⲛⲟⲩ.) ϕύλαξ; MG 25 215 B natron guards τηρητής; Mor 41 44 S ⲡⲉⲕ-ⲁⲅⲅⲉⲗⲟⲥ ⲛⲣ., C 43 135 B ⲡⲓⲣ. ⲡⲧⲉ ⲡⲓϣⲧⲉⲕⲟ, N & E 39 337 B ⲡⲓϫⲉⲗⲗⲟ ⲛⲣ. ⲉⲡⲥⲱⲙⲁ; ⲣⲉϥϩ ⲁ. B: 1 Kg 17 22 (S ⲡⲉⲧϩ.) ϕ.; ⲙⲉⲧⲣⲉϥⲁ. B, watchfulness: Cat 170 give heed ϫⲉⲛⲟⲩⲛⲓϣ† ⲁⲙ.

ϭⲓⲛ-, ϫⲓⲛϩ. SB(mostly)F, act of watching, guard-ing: Nu 3 25 S ϭⲓⲛⲉⲣϩ. (var&B ⲟⲩ.), Pro 4 23 (S ϩ. A ⲉ.), Mt 14 25 F(SB ⲟⲩ.), Va 57 9 ⲡϫ. ⲉⲣⲱⲟⲩ ϕυλα-κή, Lev 8 35 (S = Gk), Mal 3 14 (A diff) ϕύλαγμα, Ps 18 12 (S ϩ. vb) ϕυλάσσειν; C 89 134 vintner is care-

ful ϫⲉⲛⲧⲁⲭⲣⲟ ⲛⲉⲙⲝ. ⲛⲓⲃⲉⲛ, TEuch 1 302 μύρον shall be for ⲟⲩⲝ. ⲉⲡⲓⲉⲥⲱⲟⲩ of church.

ⲉⲣⲓϩ̄ⲧⲉ A: Pro 3 21, 7 5, Mal 3 14, El 38, TU 43 18; ⲁⲣⲓϩ̄ⲧⲉ A: Hos 4 10.

ϩⲣⲟϩ, -ⲟⲟϩ (pl ?) S nn, meaning unknown: ShA 1 216 ϩⲉⲛⲣ.....ⲙⲙⲁⲓϩⲛⲑⲟⲡⲏ opp righteous & God-fearing, ib 220 we have reproved ⲛϩⲣⲟⲟϩ as to this abuse (πλάνη, sc divination by relics).

ϩⲁⲣⲟⲩϩⲣ, ϩⲓⲣ. v ⲣⲟⲩϩⲣ.

ϩⲣ̄ϩⲣ̄ S, ϩⲣ̄ϩⲣⲉ A, ϫⲉⲣϫⲉⲣ B vb intr, snore (cf خرّ IgR): Jon 1 5 SAB, BHom 6 S ⲙⲁⲣⲉⲗⲁⲁⲩ ⲉϥ-ⲟⲃϣ ⲉϥϩ. winneth prize ῥέγκειν; P 43 234 S ⲛⲉⲥ-ⲡⲓⲛⲓⲧⲉⲥ (δυσπνοικός)· ⲡⲉⲧϩ̄. بجّ الذي; K 234 B ⲉϥϩ̄. (var ϫⲉⲗϫⲉⲗ) نخّ; Mor 256 S ⲉⲛⲣ. ⲉⲓⲡⲱⲱⲣⲉ ⲣⲁⲥⲟⲩ = Va 61 89 B; as nn B: K 160 ⲡⲓϩ̄. النخير.

ϩⲣⲟϩ(ⲉ)ⲣ S vb tr, urge forward or sim: Mor 37 256 pushing me & ⲉϥϩ. ⲙⲙⲟⲓ ⲉⲧⲙⲛⲧⲉ ⲙⲡⲥⲩⲛϩⲉ-ⲣⲓⲟⲛ; nn: Bodl ostr 433]ⲟⲩⲗⲁⲁⲩ ⲉϥ. ⲛⲧⲁⲁϥ ⲛⲕⲁⲧⲁ ϩ. ⲁⲡⲛⲉ (obscure).

ϩⲓⲣϩⲓⲣⲉ v ϩⲓⲣ.

ϩⲁⲣⲓϩⲁⲣⲟ⳯ S, ϩ. A, ϫ. B v p 634 a.

ϩⲁⲣⲁϫ, ϩⲁϫⲁⲣ B nn as pl, branches: BMOr 8775 117 ϩ., P 54 116 ϩⲁϫ. اغصان (which P 55 2 = ⲕⲗⲏⲙⲁ, 44 80 ⲕⲗⲁⲇⲟⲥ).

ϩⲱⲣϫ, ϩⲣⲟϫ v ϩⲱⲣϭ.

ϩⲱⲣϫ A v ⲱⲣϫ.

ϩⲣⲱⲝⲉ S nn as pl, boundary or sim: J 18 26 ⲛϩ. ⲛⲉ ⲡⲁⲓ ⲉⲅⲕⲱⲧⲉ (cf ⲧⲟϣ, ϭⲉⲓⲧⲛⲓⲁ J pass).

ϩⲣⲟϫⲣ(ⲉ)ϫ S, ϩⲣⲟϫⲣⲉϫ Sʲ, ϫⲣⲁϫⲣⲉϫ, ⲣ.(once) B vb tr, grind (teeth), rub (cf חרק Dévaud): Ps 111 10 SB, Lam 2 16 SB βρύχειν; Mk 9 18 SB τρίζειν; R 1 4 24 S ⲛϥϩ. ⲛⲛⲉϥⲟⲃϩⲉ fremere; MG 25 371 B ⲛⲧⲉϥϫ̄. ⲛⲛⲉϥⲛⲁϫϩⲓ; intr, be set on edge: MIF 67 168 Sʲ ⲛ]ⲛⲁϫⲉ ⲙⲡⲣⲱⲙⲉ ϩ. ϩⲓⲧⲉⲙⲡⲉ[ϩⲉⲙ]ϫ(?), v ⲣⲁϫⲣⲉϫ.

With following preposition. ⲥ ⲉϩⲟⲩⲛ, ⲉϩ. ⲉ-, against: Ac 7 54 S(B ⲉϩⲣⲏⲓ ⲉϫ.) β. ἐπί; PS 93 S ⲁⲩϩ. ⲛⲛⲉϥⲟ. ⲉϩ. ⲉⲣⲟⲓ, C 43 217 B ⲁϥϩ̄. ⲛⲛⲉϥϩⲓ. ⲉⲃ. ⲉⲡⲓⲁⲅⲓⲟⲥ (cf ib 93 sim ⲉϩⲣⲏⲓ ⲉϫ.); ⲥ ⲉϩ. ϩⲛ-: R 1 1 27 S ⲁⲩϩ. ⲛⲛⲉϥⲟ. ⲉϩ. ϩⲛⲡⲉⲓⲕⲟⲇⲙⲓⲟⲥ ⲧ. κατά; ⲥ ⲉϩⲣⲁⲓ ⲉϫⲛ-: Job 16 9 SB, Ps 36 12 SB (var ⲣ.) β. ἐπί; Ac 5 33 B(S diff) διαπρίεσθαι; Mor 31 23 Sʲ ⲁϥϩ̄. ⲛⲛⲉϩⲟ. ⲉϩ. ⲉϫⲱϥ.

—— nn m S, gnashing: BHom 72 ⲛⲉϩ. of teeth; meaning uncertain: P 129¹² 16 beware of boys' bright

eyes, clean faces & ⲡⲉϩ. ⲡⲡⲉⲩⲟⲩⲅⲉⲣⲏⲧⲉ ; ϩ.ⲉⲃⲟⲗ :
Sh(?)ViK 9006 224 ϩⲉⲡϩ. ⲉⲃ. ⲡⲡⲉⲩϩⲟ ⲙ̄ⲡⲉⲩⲥⲁⲣⲝ
(for these ⲩ ⲣⲟⲭⲣⲉⲭ, prob same).

ⲥ́ⲣⲓⲭ, ⲥ̅ⲗ. B nn m, (tooth-)ache: Am 46 ⲥ̅. ⲡⲡⲁⲭⲣⲓ
(S ⲡⲟⲩϣⲥ) γομφιασμός ὀδ.; K 159 ⲡⲓⲥ̅ⲗ. ⲡⲡ. ضربان
الاسنان.

ϩⲱⲣϭ[1] SA[2], -ⲗϭ[2], -ⲣⲭ[3], ϩ(ⲉ)ⲣϭ- S, ϩⲟⲣⲭ SB
(rare), ϩⲁⲣϭⲍ A[2], ϩⲟⲣϭ†, -ⲣⲭ† S, ϩⲁⲣϭ† A[2] vb intr,
be heaped up, set in order: Ru 3 7† στοιβή ; Lev 3 5†
(var -ⲣⲭ,† B Gk om) ; ClPr 28 word in moderation is
good ⲉϣϫⲉ ϩϭ.† ϫⲉ ϩⲟⲗⲱⲥ ⲡⲏⲧⲡ, ManiK 41 A[2] ⲥⲉϩ.
ⲡⲥⲉⲕⲱⲧ ϩⲣⲧⲁⲗⲛⲉ, ib 62 A[2] ⲁϩϭ. ⲁϥⲥⲁⲡⲛⲉ, ib 106 A[2]
ⲡⲁⲣⲭ̄ⲱⲛ ⲡⲉⲓ ⲉⲧϩ.† ϩⲛⲁ[ⲡⲏⲩ]ⲉ ;   tr: BHom 126
ⲁϥϩ.[1] ⲡⲁⲡⲏⲩⲉ in His wisdom (cf Jer 10 12), ManiK
53 A[2]]ϩ. ⲡⲡⲁⲣⲭ̄ⲱⲡ ⲉⲩⲥⲏⲣ ⲁⲃⲁⲗ, ib 72 A[2] ⲁϥϩⲁⲣϭⲟⲩ
ⲁϥⲥⲁⲣⲟⲩ ⲁⲃⲁⲗ, ib 102 A[2] ⲁⲡⲓⲱⲧ…ϩ. ⲡⲓⲣⲃⲏⲩⲉ ⲙ̄ⲡ-
ⲡⲕⲟⲥⲙⲟⲥ.

With following preposition or adverb.   ⲥ ⲉϫⲡ- :
Lev 1 7 ϩⲉⲣϭ-(B ⲥⲓ†) ἐπιστοιβάζειν ἐπί ; 2 Kg 18 17
ϩ.[1] στηλοῦν ἐπί ; Si 30 18† παράκεισθαι ἐπί ; BHom
54 ϩ.[1] ⲡⲡϣⲉ ⲉⲭⲱϥ (sc altar, varR 2 2 36 ϩ.[2]) ἐπιτιθέναι ; HM 1 15 ϩ.[2] ⲉⲭⲱϥ (sc grave) ⲡⲟⲩⲛⲟϭ ⲛⲥⲟⲟⲩϩⲥ
ⲡⲱⲡⲉ (var BMar 218 ϭⲱⲗ ⲉϩⲣⲁⲓ ⲉϫⲡ-) = Rec 6 183
B ϩⲓⲟⲩⲓ ϩⲓ-, Mor 31 249 ϩ.[3] ⲡⲡϣⲉ ⲉϫⲡⲡⲉⲩⲉⲣⲏⲩ,
RNC 82 stones ϩ.† ⲉϫⲡⲡⲉⲩⲉⲣⲏⲩ, MIE 2 403 B corpses ϩⲟⲣⲭⲟⲩ ⲉ.ⲡⲟⲩⲉⲣⲏⲟⲩ = PO 22 421 رمي ;   Mor
52 46 logs ⲁϥϩⲟⲣϭⲟⲩ ⲉϩⲣⲁⲓ ⲉϫⲛ- (cf 3 Kg 18 33
στοιβ. ἐπί) ;   ⲥ ⲡ-, *with, by* (cf ⲥ ⲉϩⲣⲁⲓ): PMich 4945
mount ⲉⲩϩ.† ⲡϩⲉⲡⲡⲁϩⲉ ⲡⲁⲣ[ⲉ = PO 8 105 حندحد ;
احسل ;   ⲥ ϩⲓ-, *upon*: Jos 2 6† ⲥⲧⲟⲓ. ἐπί ;   ⲥ ϩⲓϫⲡ-
sim : Lev 6 12 ϩ.[1] (B Va ⲥⲁⲧⲟ l ? ⲥⲓ†) ⲥⲧⲟⲓ. ἐπί جعل
علي ; Jos 7 26 ϩ.[1] ἐφιστάναι dat ;   ⲥ ⲉϩⲣⲁⲓ, *fill full*:
ShP 130⁵ 65 ϩⲣϭ ϩⲉⲡϣⲟⲧ ⲉ., BMis 123 ϩ.[2] ⲉ. ⲉⲙ-
ⲙⲁⲁⲭⲉ ⲙ̄ⲡⲉⲧϩⲏⲧ ⲡⲡϣⲁϫⲉ ⲉⲧⲙⲉϩ ⲡⲣⲏⲩ, P 131¹ 30
ⲧⲏⲣ.[1] ⲉ. ⲉⲡⲉⲧⲡⲙⲁⲁⲭⲉ ⲡⲓⲕⲁⲣⲡⲟⲥ ⲡⲧⲡⲧⲁⲡⲣⲟ.

—— nn m SA[2], *order, harmony*: PS 243 ⲡϩ.[3]
ⲡⲡⲉⲩⲙⲉⲗⲟⲥ, BG 50 ⲡϩ.[1] ⲡⲁⲙⲙⲉⲗⲟⲥ ⲡϩⲁⲣⲙⲟⲥ, ShP
130⁴ 141 beauty & hue of body & ⲡϩ.[1] ⲡⲁⲙⲙⲉⲗⲟⲥ,
ManiK 57 A[2] ⲡⲕⲟⲥⲙⲟⲥ ⲛ]ϩⲣⲏⲧϥ ⲙ̄ⲡⲡⲉϩ. ;   as
title Saq 227 ϣⲉⲡⲟⲩⲧⲉ ⲡϩ.[3]

ϩⲣⲟⲭ S, ϩⲗⲁⲭ F vb, *pile up, support*: Cant 2 5 F
ϩ. (for ? ϩⲁⲗⲭⲧ) ϩⲗⲏⲓ ⲡⲣⲉⲡϫⲓⲙⲡⲉϩ (S ViK 9763 3
ⲕⲧⲟ ⲉ-) στοιβ. ἐν ; BMEA 10587 S(Jesus *loq*) waters
(of Jordan) ϩ. ⲉⲓϣⲁⲡⲃⲁⲡⲧⲓⲍⲉ.

Cf Kémi 2 13.

ϩⲣⲏϭ · v ϩⲣⲟⲕ.

ϩⲁⲥ S, ϩⲟⲥ B, ϩⲉⲥ F nn m, *dung* (of animals,
birds), in recipes: PMéd 281 S ϩ. ⲡⲁⲗⲟⲩⲕ, ϩⲟⲓⲧⲉ,
ⲟⲩⲱⲡϣ, ib 305 ⲡϩ. ⲡⲡⲉⲥⲧⲣⲟⲩⲑⲟⲥ, ib 319 as emetic
ϫⲁϫ ⲡⲃⲡⲛⲉ ; Cai 42573 1 S ϭⲉⲣⲱⲙⲡⲉ, ⲁⲗⲕⲏⲣⲧ
(قرل), ⲡⲁⲡⲁⲓ, ⲕⲏⲧⲉⲥ(? κῆτος), Ora 4 203 F ϩ. ⲡⲁⲃⲱⲕ,

ⲃⲁϣⲁⲣ, ⲙⲉⲥⲉϩ (ⲙⲥⲁϩ), BM 527 21 F ⲡϩ. ⲉⲡⲁⲗ-
ϩⲉⲣⲧ(?) ;   ⲉⲣ ϩ. B, *let dung* as nn : K 161 ⲡⲓⲉⲣ ϩ.
تغريط.

ϩⲁⲉⲓⲥ (or ? ϩ., all uncertain now) A nn f, *widow-
hood*: Mic 1 16 (SB ⲙ̄ⲡⲧⲭⲏⲣⲁ) χηρεία. If ϩ. *cf*
ḥꜣy lament, if ϩ. ḥrt widow (Kuentz). *Cf* Rösch 85.

ϩⲉⲥ, ϩⲏⲥ interj v p 86 a.

ϩⲱⲥ SA[2]B vb intr, *sing, make music* (*cf* Sethe
Verbum 1 264): Ps 20 14 B(S ϫⲱ), Eph 5 19 B(S ⲇⲟ)
ᾄδειν ; Dan 3 91 B(FMus 49 187 ⲥⲙⲟⲩ) ὑμνεῖν ; ib 4
34 B αἰνεῖν ; BMis 507 S ⲉⲓϩ. ⲉⲓⲥⲙⲟⲩ ⲉⲓϯ ⲉⲟⲟⲩ,
MG 25 341 B ⲉⲩϩ. ⲉⲩⲉⲣ ϩⲩⲙⲛⲟⲥ, ManiH 24 A[2]
ⲉⲩϩ. ⲕⲁⲧⲁ ⲡⲟⲗⲓⲥ ⲡⲟⲗⲓⲥ, Aeg 238 B ⲫⲁⲡⲓⲱⲧ ⲁϥϩⲟⲥ
= ابو طبل ;   tr B: Nu 21 17 (S ϫⲱ), Ps 7 1 (S ⲇⲟ)
ᾄδ. ; FR 126 ϩ. ⲡⲟⲩⲱϣ.

With following preposition or adverb.   ⲥ ⲉ-,
to: Ps 136 3 B(S ⲇⲟ) ᾄδ. ; Is 38 18 SB, Bar 3 6 B(S
ⲥ.), Lu 2 13 B(S ⲇⲟ) αἰ. ; Dan 3 24 SB ὑμ. ;   Z 324 S
angels ⲉⲩϩ. ⲉⲣⲟⲟⲩ εὐφημεῖν ; My 20 S ⲉⲩϩ. ⲉⲣⲟϥ
ⲛϭⲓ ϩⲡⲗⲁⲟⲥ, ManiP 30 A[2] ⲁⲩϩ. ⲁⲧⲕⲓⲗⲡⲁϭ, DeV
2 19 B ⲉⲓϩ. ⲉⲡⲉⲕⲡⲁⲓ ;   ⲁϩⲟⲩⲡ ⲁ- A[2] : ManiP A[2]
ϩ. ⲁϩ. ⲁⲡⲓⲱⲧ, ⲉϩⲟⲩⲡ ⲉϩⲣⲉⲡ- B: 1 Kg 186 ⲉⲩϩ. ⲉⲥ̄.
ⲉ. ⲍⲁⲅⲓⲁ (S ⲉⲃⲟⲗ ϩⲏⲧϥ ⲡ-) χορεύειν εἰς συνάντησιν ;   ⲥ ⲡ-dat B: GPar 1 5 ⲧⲉⲡϩ. ⲡⲁⲕϫⲉⲁⲙⲏⲡ ;   ⲥ
ϩⲛ-, ⲥⲉⲛ-, *in* B: Ap 14 3 (S ϫⲱ) ᾄδ. acc ; 1 Chr 15
22 Gk diff ; Aeg 53 ϩ. ⲉⲣⲟⲥ ⲥⲉⲡⲓϩⲱⲥ ; *with* S : BM
Or 7561 136 ⲉⲩϩ. ϩⲡⲡⲉⲩⲕⲓⲑⲁⲣⲁ ;   ⲉⲃⲟⲗ ⲥⲉⲡ-
B: Va 57 191 ϩⲁⲛⲥⲩⲣⲓⲧⲟⲥ (σύριγξ) ⲉⲩϩ. ⲉⲃ. ⲥⲉⲡ-
ⲡⲁⲓ ;   ⲥ ϩⲁⲧⲏ S, ⲥⲁⲭⲉⲡ- B, *before*: WTh 182 S
seraphs ϩ. ϩⲁⲧⲉⲕⲣⲏ, AM 170 B ⲉⲩϩ. ⲥⲁϫⲱⲟⲩ ;   ⲥ
ⲉⲡϣⲱⲓ B, *upward*: Miss 4 224 ϩ. ⲉ. ⲙ̄ⲡⲓⲧⲣⲓⲥⲁⲅⲓⲟⲛ.

—— nn m SA[2]B(mostly), *song, hymn* هوس (v Z f
Semitistik 9 258): Ps 39 4 (S ϫⲱ), Va 57 191 ᾆσμα ;
Is 42 10 (S ⲥⲙⲟⲩ) ὕμνος ; Ge 31 27 (S = Gk) μουσικός ; Mic 2 4 (SA ⲧⲱϣ) μέλος ; Ex 15 20 χορός ; Am
5 23 S(ShIF 248, B ϩⲣⲱⲟⲩ) ἦχος ; P 44 2ᵇ S ⲡϣⲟⲣⲡ
ϩ. ⲙⲙⲱⲅⲥⲉ (Ex 15 ᾠδή) ; 2 Kg 6 13 S ⲟⲩϣⲡⲏⲣⲉ
ϣⲟⲟⲡ ϩⲙⲡⲉϩ. (var χορος) Gk om ; Miss 4 160
ⲉⲩϩⲡⲟⲥ, ⲯⲁⲗⲙⲟⲥ, ϩ., ϩⲱϫⲏ, ManiP A[2] ϣⲗⲏⲗ, ϩ.,
ⲯⲁⲗⲙⲟⲥ, FR 120 ϩⲁⲡϩ. ⲡⲉⲙϩⲁⲛⲥⲙⲟⲩ, TEuch 2 243
ⲡⲓϩ. consists of sequence of Ps verses.

ⲣⲉϥϩ. SB, *singer*: Eccl 2 8 B(Va 57 259, SF diff)
ᾄδων ; 4 Kg 11 14 S ᾠδός ; P 44 64 S ϩⲩⲙⲛⲱϩⲟⲥ·
ⲣ.ⲉⲡⲡⲱϩⲏ, BMar 138 S ⲣ. ⲉⲡ̄ⲡⲉ̄ ;   ⲙⲉⲧⲣ. B, *singing*: CaiEuch 476 ϯⲙ. of seraphs ὑμνῳδία.

ϭⲓⲡ-, ϫⲓⲡϩ. SSᶠB, *singing, song*: RylSuppl 11 S
ⲥⲙⲟⲩ, ϭ., AZ 21 155 S ⲟⲩϭ. ⲡⲑⲉ ⲙⲡⲉⲧⲣⲓⲥⲁⲅⲓⲟⲥ, C
43 70 S ϯϫ. of cherubs, OratCyp 155 Sᶠ ϭ. ϩⲓⲥⲙⲟⲩ
of heavenly powers, TRit 549 B ⲡⲓϫ. ⲉⲧⲟⲩⲱϣ ⲙ-
ⲙⲱⲟⲩ throughout year (Ps verses) هوسات.

ϩⲱⲥ *B* nn m, *big drum* (*v* AZ 14 63, *cf?* *sh* Dévaud, Berl Wörterb 4 205 ; if so, not same as ϩⲱⲥ *sing*): K 14 ⲡⲓϩ. طبل, *ib* 259 خز, 'ذ .

Cf ϩⲁⲥⲓⲉ

ϩⲱⲥ *SA*, ϩⲉⲥ-, ϩⲱⲥ⸗, ϩⲟⲥ⸗ *S*, ϩⲁⲥ⸗ *A* vb intr, *be blocked, filled, covered up*: Zech 14 5 *A*(*B* ϣⲟⲣ) ἐμφράσσειν ; ShRE 10 160 wells ⲉⲩϣⲁⲛϩ. wherewith shall they be opened?;   tr: Ge 26 15 (MS Louvain, *B* ϣ.) ἐμφ.; Jos 11 13 χωματίζεσθαι, Tob 8 16 ϩⲉⲥ-χωννύναι ; ShP 130⁵ 65 ⲡⲉⲧϩⲱⲥ ⲛⲟⲩⲡⲁϣ ⲡⲉⲧ.ⲡⲟⲩϩⲟⲉⲓⲧ (*l* ϩⲓ.), BMis 219 ⲡⲉⲓⲟⲧⲉ ⲉⲧϩⲟⲥⲟⲩ (*sc* earth on Jesus' tomb), R 1 3 43 father commanded ⲉϩ. ⲙⲡⲧⲁⲫⲟⲥ ⲛⲡ̄ⲥ̄, MIF 9 46 ϩ. ⲛⲡⲉⲧⲣⲓⲣ (var BAp 9 ⲧⲁⲕⲟ prob).

With following preposition.   ⲉ ⲉϫⲛ-: Mor 17 18 when digging foundations they cast in maiden ⲁⲩϩ. ⲉϫⲱⲥ ϩⲛⲉ(ⲉ)ⲡⲱⲡⲉ κατακλείειν dat ; BMis 209 ⲁⲩϩ. ⲉϫⲛⲡϣⲉ ⲙⲡⲉⲥ†ⲟⲥ so as to hide it, *ib* 218 ϩⲉⲥ ⲉⲓⲧⲛ ⲉϫⲛⲡⲧⲁⲫⲟⲥ ; ⲉⲃⲟⲗ ⲉϫⲛ-: BMar 146 eagle came ⲛϩ. ⲉⲃ. ⲉϫⲛⲡⲙⲁ ⲛⲛⲓⲕⲟⲧⲛ (confusion? with ϩⲱⲃⲥ, as Eccl 6 4 in BMar 84 8); ⲉ ⲛ-, *with*: Mor 31 44 found church ⲉⲁⲥϩ. ⲛϣⲱ, BMis 206 ⲙⲁⲣⲟⲩ ϩⲟⲥⲥ (*sc* tomb) ⲛⲛⲉ ⲓⲧⲛ ;   ⲉ ϩⲛ- *A* sim: Zech 9 15 (*B* ⲑⲱⲙⲥ ϩⲉⲛ-) καταχωννύναι . ἐν ;   ⲉ ϩⲓϫⲛ-, *upon*: Mor 32 49 martyr in pit ⲁⲩϩ. ϩⲓϫⲱϥ.

ϩⲱⲥ *SBF*, ϩⲱⲱⲥ, ϩⲟⲩⲥ *S*, ϩⲟⲥ *B* nn m, *thread, cord*: Ge 14 23 *SB*, Jos 2 18 *S*, Cant 4 3 *S* ϩⲱⲱⲥ (var ϩⲟⲩⲥ)*F*, Ez 40 3 *B*(HConst 288, var & *S* diff) σπαρτίον ; Nu 15 38 *B*(*S* ⲧⲱⲧⲉ), Jud 16 9 *S*, Si 6 31 *S* κλῶσμα ; Ez 47 3 *SB* μέτρον ; P 44 95 *S* ⲡϩⲟⲩⲥ كز ; ShC 73 123 *S* ϩ̄ⲉⲥⲱ, ϩⲟⲩⲥ, ⲙⲟⲩⲥ, Mus 40 277 *S* ⲁⲩⲕⲧⲟ ⲉⲣⲟϥ ⲡⲟⲩϩ. ⲛ̄ⲥⲟⲟⲩⲛⲉ (var better BAp 169 ϩⲟⲃⲥⲟⲩ ⲛⲟⲩϩⲱⲃⲥ ⲛϩ.); ϩ. ⲛ̄ⲕⲟⲕⲕⲟⲥ: Lev 14 6 *S*(*B* ϩ. ⲉⲧⲥⲁ†) κλωστός ; Ez 16 11 *SB* κάθεμα ; Griff Stu 163 *F* ⲉϥⲙⲏⲣ ⲙⲡⲓϩ. ⲡⲕⲟ. ⲉϫⲉⲛⲧⲉⲃⲙⲉⲥⲧⲛϩⲧ ; ⲕⲁⲡ ⲛϩ. ⲛ ⲕⲁⲡ 1°.   *Cf?* ϩⲓⲥⲉ spin.

ϩⲱⲥ *A²* nn, *weakling, coward* or sim: ManiH 75 feeble & strong ⲛϩ. ⲙⲛⲛⲓϫⲁⲗⲁϣⲓⲣⲉ, ManiP ⲁϥⲥⲁⲡⲉ ⲛϩ. ⲛⲣⲏⲕⲉ, *ib* ⲉⲣⲉⲛⲓϩ. ⲙⲉⲉⲩ ϩⲙⲡⲟⲩϩⲏⲧ ϫⲉ-, *ib* ⲛⲓϫⲱⲃ ⲛϩ. ⲉⲧⲛⲧ ⲛⲥⲱⲓ.

ϩⲁⲥⲓⲉ *SA²*, -ⲉⲓⲉ, -ⲓⲏ *S*, ⲉⲥⲓⲉ *B* nn m, *drowned* (lit *praised person, cf* ϩⲱⲥ 1°, AZ 46 132); with preceding vb: *be drowned, shipwrecked*: Mor 17 8 *S* ⲛⲧⲁⲡⲣ ⲃⲟⲗ ⲛϩ. ναυαγίῳ περιπίπτειν ; EW 29 *B* ⲁⲛϩⲱⲗ ⲛⲉ. ϩⲉⲛ ⲫⲓⲟⲙ (*S* Wess 15 130 = Gk diff), ManiK 28 *A²* souls [ⲉⲧ]ϫⲏⲩ ⲛϩ.;   ⲃ̄ⲱⲕ ⲛϩ. *S* sim: Mor 18 148 many ⲃ. ναυαγεῖν ; R 1 4 46 those ⲃ. *submersus esse* ; Tri 673 خسر ; ShA 1 59 ⲃ. ϩⲙⲡⲓⲉⲣⲟ, Bor 251 296 ⲃ. ϩⲙ ⲡⲛⲟⲃⲉ, Mor 41 25 ship ⲃ. = DeV 2 281 *B* ϩⲱⲗⲕ, Gu 62 leave us lest city ⲃ̄ⲱⲕ ⲛϩⲁⲥⲓⲛ, BHom 48 ϣⲁⲥⲃⲱⲕ ϩⲙⲛϩ. (var R 2 2 32 ⲛϩ.);   ϣⲉ ⲛϩ., ⲛⲉ. *SA²B* sim: 1 Tim 1 19 *S*(*B* ⲃⲓϫⲓ), Va 66 308 *B* ⲫⲏ ⲉⲧⲁϣϣ. ⲣⲁⲩⲁⲅ.;

ShMIF 23 97 *S* ⲁϩⲁϩ ϣ. ⲡϩⲏⲧⲟⲩ (*sc* worldly affairs), ManiP *A²* ⲡⲉⲓⲧⲁ ⲡϩ ⲁϣ., EW 191 *B* ships ⲱⲙⲥ ⲡⲥⲉϣ.; ⲙⲛⲧⲁⲧ ϣ. *S*, *undrownableness*: BHom 100 ⲧⲙ. ⲡⲟⲩ ⲡⲟⲙⲟⲡⲛ ;   ⲉⲣ ⲉ. *B* sim: Va 58 171 sin ⲉⲣ ⲡⲁⲓⲣⲱⲙⲓ ⲛⲉ. ναυάγιον, *ib* 57 33 ⲱⲙⲥ ⲉϩⲣⲏⲓ … ⲉⲣ ⲉ. ναυάγια ὑπομένειν ; *ib* 172 ⲛⲏ ⲉⲧⲁⲩⲉⲣ ⲉ. ὑποβρύχιος γίνεσθαι ; *ib* 69 ⲁⲛⲉⲣ ⲉ. ϩⲉⲛⲡⲓⲭⲣⲱⲙ ; ⲟ ⲛϩ. *A²*: ManiK 147 ⲥⲉⲟ ⲛϩ. ⲥⲉⲱϫⲛⲉ ;   ⲙⲉⲧⲉ. *B*, *drowning*: Va 57 2 ⲱⲙⲥ ⲉⲡⲉⲥⲏⲧ ϩⲉⲛⲟⲩⲙ.;   P 131⁴ 126 *S* have told you all ye should do & ⲁⲓⲧⲥⲁⲃⲉⲧⲏⲩⲧⲛ (ⲉ)ⲛⲣⲁⲥⲉⲓⲛ ⲡϩⲏⲧⲟⲩ *warned you of* (risk of) *shipwreck therein*.

In names: Ἀσιῆς, Ἐσ., Πιεσιῆς, Φεσιῆς, Θασιῆς, Ταφεσιῆς (Preisigke).

ϩⲏⲥⲉ *F* nn, meaning unknown: Kropp C 119 virtues of angels ⲥⲁⲣⲁⲫⲁⲏⲗ ⲧⲓ ϩ. ϩⲓⲙⲉⲧⲥⲁⲓⲛ (*sic* MS) ϩⲓⲧⲟⲗϭⲁ.

ϩⲓⲥⲉ *SA²*, ϩ. *A*, ϩⲓⲥⲓ *B*, ϩ. *F*, ϩⲁⲥⲧ- (2d pl) *S*, ϩⲁⲥⲧ⸗ *SF*, ϩⲟ.⸗, ϩⲓ.⸗ *S*, ϩⲉ.⸗ *A²*, ϩⲁⲥ⸗ *B*, ϩⲟⲥⲉ† *S*, ϩⲁ.† *Sᵃ A²*, ϩⲁ.† *A*, ϩⲟⲥⲓ *B*, ϩⲁ.† *F*, p c ϩⲁⲥⲧ- *S* vb **I** intr **a** *toil, be troubled, difficult*: Ps 126 1 *S*(*B* ϭⲓ ϩ.), Is 49 4 *B*(*S* ϣⲛ ϩ.), Mt 6 28 *S*(*B†*) κοπιᾶν, Si 22 13 *B*(*S* do) κόπον ἔχειν ; Z 288 *S* ⲁⲥϩ. ⲉⲥϣⲱϣⲧ ⲙⲙⲟϥ (var Miss 4 618 ⲙⲟϩⲛ ⲉⲃⲟⲗ) σπουδάζειν ; Bor 226 162 *S* if thy word be disdained ⲛⲧϥ. πονεῖν ; ShC 73 60 *S* ⲁϥϩ. ϩⲛⲟⲩⲡⲟⲗⲓⲧⲉⲓⲁ, C 99 177 *S* ⲁⲓϩ. ⲉⲓⲉⲡⲓⲑⲩⲙⲉⲓ (var *ib* 266 ⲟⲛⲧⲱⲥ ⲁⲓⲉⲡ. ⲧⲱⲛⲟⲩ), BMar 63 *S* ⲙⲏ ⲛⲧⲁⲡⲙⲁⲣⲧⲩⲣⲓⲟⲛ ⲉⲧⲛϩ ⲣⲱⲙⲛ ϩ. *is shrine at Rome difficult* (of access)?, Ora 4 20 *S* child's teeth grow ⲉⲡⲛⲉϥϩ., C 86 154 ⲁⲥϩ. ⲙⲡⲉⲥϣ ⲃⲟⲗⲟⲩ ⲉⲃⲟⲗ.   **b**, *be wearied, suffering*: 1 Kg 14 31 *S*, Pro 4 12 *SAB*, Is 31 3 *SBF*, Lam 5 5 *BF*, Z 338 *S* heavy laden ⲁϥϩ. ⲁϥϩⲙⲟⲟⲥ = MG 25 200 *B* ⲕⲟ., Jth 13 1 *S* κοπιᾶσθαι ; Nah 2 6 *A*(*B* ϣⲱⲡⲓ) ἀσθενεῖν ; R 1 4 60 *S* ⲁⲓϩ. ⲁⲓⲕⲁ ⲧⲟⲟⲧ ⲉⲃⲟⲗ ⲛⲡⲁ ϩⲣⲁⲕ ἀποκάμνειν εἰς ; C 43 105 *B* sim, C 99 180 *S* (ⲉ)ⲛϩ. ϫⲉⲉⲡⲏⲡ ⲉⲣⲟⲕ *are weary* (of saying) *we are thine*, Miss 8 174 *S* ⲙⲏ ⲛⲧⲁⲡⲡⲉ̄…ϩ. ⲛ ⲡⲧⲁ ϥⲥⲕ?, *ib* 147 *S* heal me ϫⲉⲁⲓϩ. ⲉⲙⲁⲧⲉ, MR 5 49 *F* ⲁⲧⲁⲡⲥⲩⲭⲏ ϩ. ⲕⲁⲕⲟⲥ (-ῶς), MIE 2 400 *B* fetch water ϫⲉⲁⲕϩ. = BAp 98 *S* ⲑⲗⲓⲃⲉ, CaiThe 375 *B* ⲁⲓϣⲁⲛⲥⲁϫⲓ…ⲡⲁⲗⲁⲥ ⲡⲁϩ. ⲁⲛ ;   + 2d vb: Ps 68 3 *SB* ⲕⲟ. κράζων, Jo 4 6 *SA²*(*BF* diff) ⲕⲟ.; R 2 1 72 *S* ⲉⲛ ϣⲁⲛϩ. ⲉⲡⲧⲱⲣ ⲉⲣⲟⲩ ⲛ, BM 1102 *S* ⲁⲓϩ. ⲉⲓⲥϩⲁⲓ ⲡⲁⲕ, ManiH 14 *A²* ⲁⲡⲁⲡⲟⲥⲧⲟⲗⲟⲥ ϩ. ⲉ ⲩⲣⲓⲙⲉ, Miss 4 181 *B* ⲁⲓϩ. ⲉⲓⲟⲣⲓ ⲉⲣⲁⲧ *whilst they talked* (var C 41 79 ϫⲁ ⲧⲟⲧ ⲉⲃⲟⲗ), C 43 67 *B* ⲁⲛϩ. ⲉⲡⲕⲱ† ⲛⲥⲱϥ, Gu 22 *S* ⲁ ⲧⲉⲧⲛϩ. ⲉⲧⲉⲧⲛⲥⲱⲣⲙ *have laboured to mislead* ; qual: Is 33 24 *SBF*, 1 Cor 4 12 *SB*, Z 297 *S* †ϩ. ϫⲉ†ⲡⲁ ⲡⲱⲣϫ ⲉⲃⲟⲗ ⲙⲡⲁⲥⲟⲛ ⲕⲟ., Eccl 1 8 *F*(*S* ϣⲁⲁⲧ) ἔγκοπος, Job 3 17 *S*(*B* ϩⲉⲛϩⲱⲙ) κατάκ.; ROC 27 142 *B* wherefore ⲉⲕϩ. ⲙⲡⲁⲓⲣⲏ†? κάμνειν ; Mk 6 48 *S*(*B* ⲧⲣⲉⲙⲕⲛⲟⲏⲧ) βασανίζεσθαι ; BMar 158 *S* ϩⲓⲟⲟⲩⲉ… ⲉⲩ ϩ. τραχύς ; ShC 73 153 *S* ⲉϥϩ. opp ⲉϥⲙⲟⲧⲉⲛ, ShP

129¹² 8 *S* Paône Epêp Mesorê ⲛⲉⲓⲉⲃⲟⲧ ⲉⲧϩ., BM
1223 *A²* ⲟⲩⲱⲛⲉ ⲉϥϩ., ViK 9759 73 *S* Adam expelled
ⲉϥⲉϣⲱⲡⲉ ⲉϥϩ. for ever, COAd 63 *Sᶜ* ⲛⲕⲉⲣⲟⲥ (ⲕⲁⲓ.)
ϩ. ⲧⲱⲡⲉ, MMA 23 3 701 *Sᵃ* ⲧⲉⲓⲣⲁⲙⲡⲉ ϩ., LMär 34
S ⲉϣⲱⲡⲉ ⲡⲉⲕϩⲏⲧ ϩ. I will pay thee more, ManiK
106 *A²* ⲟⲩⲙⲣⲣⲉ ⲉⲥϩ. ⲉⲥⲡⲁϣⲧ, BSM 58 *B* ⲡⲓⲛⲟⲩⲛ ϩ.
= BMis 416 *S* ⲡⲡⲉⲗⲁⲧⲟⲥ ⲡⲁϣⲧ, C 43 190 *B* ⲁⲥⲕⲩⲥⲓⲥ
ⲉⲧϩ.

II tr, *trouble, weary* (mostly refl): Is 43 22 *S*(*B*
ⲑⲣⲟ ϩ.) κοπιᾶν ποιεῖν, Mor 37 97 *S* was careful ⲉ-
ⲧⲣⲉϥϩⲁⲥⲧϥ ⲁⲩⲧ ⲱ ⲕ., Job 16 7 *S*(*B* ϯ ϩ. ⲛ-) κατάκοπον
ποι.; Eccl 5 17 *SF* μοχθεῖν, Sa 15 7 *S* ἐπίμοχθος; Ac
15 19*S*(var ϯ ϩ., *B* ⲟⲩϩ ϩ.) παρενοχλεῖν; C 99 239
S in weaving ⲉⲧⲁϩ. ⲛⲛⲕⲁⲡ ⲛⲕⲁⲙ = C 89 74 *B* λῶμα
στρέφειν = Va 172 45 نہ, but MG 17 441 لم, so
confusion; ShIF 184 *S* ⲉⲣϣⲁⲛⲡⲣⲱⲙⲉ ϩⲁⲥⲧϥ ⲛϥ-
ϣⲓⲡⲉ, ShP 130² 116 *S* ⲙⲡⲣϩⲁⲥⲧⲧⲏⲩⲧⲛ, ManiK 165
A² ϩⲉⲥⲧⲧⲏⲛⲉ, LMis 92 *S* ⲉⲓⲛⲁϩⲟⲥⲧ ⲉⲡⲭ ⲓⲛϫ ⲏ, Ep 196
S ⲁϥϩⲓⲥⲧⲛ, ST 225 *S* ⲙⲡⲣϩⲓⲥ(ⲉ) ⲛⲁϩⲏⲧ, PBu 96 *S*
ⲉⲛϩ. ⲡⲧⲉⲧⲛⲙⲛⲧⲭ̄ⲥ̄ by writing, DeV 1 158 *B* ⲙⲁⲣⲉⲛ-
ϩⲁⲥⲧⲉⲛ opp ⲙⲧⲟⲛ ⲙⲙⲟⲛ;   ⲙⲁⲓϩⲁⲥϥ *B*, *labour-
loving*: MG 25 212 ⲡⲓⲙ. καματηρός; K 232 مٔس
الٔٮ;   ⲙⲉⲧⲙⲁⲓϩ.: MG 25 372 πολιτεγεσθε ϩⲉⲛⲟⲩⲙ.;   ⲣⲉϥϩⲁⲥⲧϥ *S*: Sa 15 8 κακόμοχθος.

With following preposition.

—— ⲉ-, *as obj* (mostly)*S*: BMar 29 ⲙⲡⲉϩ. ⲉⲣⲟⲕ
ϫⲉⲙⲙⲟⲩ, Mor 51 27 ⲡⲉϥϩⲏⲧ ϩ. ⲉⲣⲟϥ against wife,
BMOr 6201 B 47 ⲁⲓϩ. ⲉⲓⲱⲥⲏⲡ but he would not, CO
241 ⲁⲩϩ. ⲉⲣⲟⲓ ⲛⲥⲡⲁⲩ ⲛⲛⲉⲓⲟ *importuned me*, J 42 21
ⲛⲧϩ. ⲉⲡⲓⲧⲛ ϩⲓⲃⲁⲗ ⲛⲡⲣⲟ (meaning?);   qual: 1 Cor
9 13 (CA 93, var ⲥⲣⲟϩⲧ, *B* ⲙ ⲏ ⲡ) παρεδρεύειν dat; Sh
ClPr 22 359 ⲛⲉⲧϩ. ⲉⲣⲟⲟⲩ…ϩⲙⲡⲉϣⲱⲡⲉ, ShBMOr
8800 202 Origen spends days ⲉϥϩ. ⲉⲡⲧⲏⲩ (cf Eccl 5
15), BMOr 8811 244 ⲧⲉⲓⲟⲉⲓⲙⲉ…ϩ. ⲉⲛⲉⲕⲟⲉⲓⲙⲉ ⲧⲏⲣⲟⲩ *beyond*;   tr (refl), *for SA²*: Col 1 29 (*B* ⲥ ⲓ
ϩ.) ⲕⲟ. εἰς; Eccl 5 15 μοχ. εἰς; ShBor 246 49 ⲁϥ-
ϩⲁⲥⲧϥ ⲉⲡⲧⲏⲩ (cf last), ManiK 10 *A²* ϣⲁϥϩⲉⲥⲧϥ ⲁ-
ⲡⲉϥⲕⲁⲣⲡⲟⲥ ⲛϥⲥⲁⲛⲟⲩϣⲟⲩ;   ⲉϩⲟⲩⲛ ⲉ- *B*, *against*:
BSM 75 ⲉⲣⲉⲡⲉϥϩⲏⲧ ϩ.⁺ ⲉϩ. ⲉⲛⲁⲓⲣⲱⲙⲉ = BMis 166
S ⲟ ⲛⲁⲧϩⲣⲓⲟⲥ ⲉϩ. ⲉ-;   ⲉ-vbal: Jer 17 16 *B*, Jo 4 6
F(*SA²*ϩ. ⲉϥ-, *B* ϩ. ⲉⲃⲟⲗ ϩⲉⲛ-) ⲕⲟ.; ShC 73 51 *S* ϩⲱⲃ
ⲛⲓⲙ ⲉⲧϩ.⁺ ⲉⲣ ϩⲱⲃ ⲉⲣⲟⲟⲩ, Ming 328 *S* ⲙⲡⲉⲣϩ. ⲉⲧⲱⲃϩ,
Dif 2 107 *B* ⲧⲉⲛⲛⲁϩ. ⲁⲛ ⲉⲧⲁⲓⲟ, GMir 17 *S* ⲛⲧϩ.⁺ ⲁⲛ
ⲉⲧⲣⲉⲕϩⲉ ⲉⲣⲟⲥ.

—— ⲉⲧⲃⲉ, *because of*: BIF 13 107 *S* ⲁⲩϩ. ⲉ. ⲡⲉⲟⲙ-
ⲕⲟ = MG 25 291 *B*, TstAb 230 *B* ⲛⲁϩⲏⲧ ϩ.⁺ ⲉⲑⲃⲏⲧⲕ, Mor 31 48 *S* ⲉⲓϩ.⁺ ⲉ. ⲧⲁϣⲛ ⲛⲡⲉⲥⲛϣⲉ.

—— ⲙⲛ-, ⲛⲉⲙ-, *with*: Eccl 2 21 *F*(*S*⁺ ⲛ-) μόχθος
ἐν; Is 30 5 *F*(*S* ⲉⲣⲁⲧϩ, *B* ϩⲁ-) ⲕⲟ. πρός; C 86 306 *B*
ⲁⲓϩ. ⲛⲉⲙⲡⲁⲓⲅⲉⲛⲟⲥ ἐκκακεῖν πρός; BG 71 *S* ⲛⲉⲡ̄ⲛ̄ⲁ̄
ⲛⲧⲁϩ. ⲛⲙⲙⲁⲛ, ShMiss 4 281 *S* ϩⲁⲥⲧⲕ ⲙⲛⲡⲉⲛⲧⲁϥϩ.
ⲉⲧⲃⲏⲏⲧⲕ.

—— ⲛ- dat: Eccl 2 21⁺ *S*(*F* ϩ. ⲙⲉⲛ-) μόχθος ἐν;

R 1 5 50 *S* ϯⲛⲁϯ ϩⲱⲃ ⲉϥϩ.⁺ ⲛⲁⲕ, ShIF 250 *S* ⲉⲛϩ.⁺
ⲛⲛⲓⲙ?, DeV 1 104 *B* hour of death ⲉⲥϩ.⁺ ⲛⲣⲱⲙⲓ ⲛⲓⲃⲉⲛ;   vbal: ROC 25 248 *B* ⲥⲉϩ.⁺ ⲛϥⲣⲟ ⲉⲣⲱⲟⲩ
δυσαγώνιστος; C 43 242 *B* woman ⲉⲑⲛⲁϩ. ⲙⲙⲓⲥⲓ,
BM 581(2) *F* ⲁⲛϩ. ⲛⲧⲓ ⲡⲉⲧⲉⲙⲟⲥⲓ (δημ.), KKS 552
S ⲁⲓϩ. ⲛϥⲟⲣϭ ⲉⲣⲟⲕ, C 89 99 *B* ⲕⲟⲗⲁⲥⲓⲥ ⲉⲧϩ.⁺ ⲛϥⲁⲓ
ϩⲁⲣⲱⲟⲩ.

—— ⲛⲧⲛ- *S, concerning*: Ep 339 ⲡⲉ]ⲕϩⲏⲧ ϩ. ⲛⲧⲟⲟⲧ,
BP 5667 sim.

—— ϩⲁ-, ϩⲁ-, *from, by reason of*: PS 219 *S* ⲉⲧϩ.⁺
ϩⲁⲧⲉⲅⲉⲧⲡⲱ, JTS 8 243 *S* ⲛϯϩ.⁺ ϩⲁⲣⲟⲕ ⲁⲛ for canst
avail naught against me, Ep 459 *Sᵃ* ⲡⲁϩⲏⲧ ϩ.⁺ ϩⲁⲣⲟⲕ,
MIE 2 377 *B* ⲛⲁϥϩ.⁺ ⲡⲉ ϩⲁⲡⲉⲓⲕⲁϩ ⲛϩⲏⲧ.

—— ϩⲁ- *B, for*: Is 30 5 (*S* ⲉⲣⲁⲧϩ, *F* ⲙⲛ-) ⲕⲟ. πρός.

—— ϩⲛ-, ϩⲉⲛ-, *in, with*: Ps 6 6 *SB*, Is 47 13 *SB*
ⲕⲟ. ἐν; R 1 59 *S* ϩ. ϩⲛⲟⲩϣⲱⲡⲉ βαρεῖσθαι ἐπί; Eccl
1 3⁺ *S*(*F* Mich 3520 ϣⲉⲛ ϩ.) μοχ. dat; ShC 73 57 *S*
ⲉⲧϩ.⁺ ϩⲛⲣⲉⲛⲓⲟϭ ⲙⲡⲟⲗⲓⲧⲉⲓⲁ, Bor 264 11 *S* ⲁⲛⲉⲥⲛⲏⲩ
…ϩ. ϩⲛⲡⲁⲓⲁⲥⲧⲏⲙⲁ (sc their long journey), Ming 296
S ϩⲁⲥⲧⲕ ϩⲙⲡⲉⲕⲥⲱⲙⲁ, Mani 2 *A²* ⲡⲉϥⲙⲕⲁϩ ⲉⲧ[ϥ]ϩ.⁺
ⲛϩⲏⲧϥ, AM 158 *B* ⲁⲓϩ. ϩⲉⲛⲧⲁⲓⲃⲁⲥⲁⲛⲟⲥ;   ⲉⲃⲟⲗ
ϩⲉⲛ- *B*: Jo 4 6 (*SA²F* diff) ⲕⲟ. ἐκ.

ϩ., ϩ. ⲛϩⲏⲧ, *be troubled in mind, disheartened*: Mor
18 131 *S* exhorted them ⲉⲧⲙϩ. ἀθυμεῖν; Va 58 178
B ⲉϥϩ.⁺ ⲓⲉ ⲉϥⲟⲓ ⲡⲉⲙⲕⲁϩ.

ⲣ ⲕ *S*, *troubled, anxious* (?), *v last*: ST 264 all
brethren are ϩ(ⲉ)ⲛⲣⲁⲥϩⲛⲧ ⲛⲣⲱⲙⲉ.

—— nn m *SAA²BF*, *labour, product of labour,
weariness, suffering*: Ge 31 42 *S*(*B* ⲙⲕⲁϩ), Jo 4 38
SA²B, 1 Cor 3 8 *SBF*(Mor 38 103) κόπος, Sa 16 20
S ⲁϫⲛϩ. ἀκοπιάτως; Pro 3 9 *SAB*, Ap 21 4 *SB*, Aeg
243 *S* ⲛ ϩ. ⲛⲛⲉⲕϭⲓϫ πόνος; Nu 20 14 *SB*, Eccl 10 15
SF, Lam 3 65 *SF* μόχθος; BHom 44 *S* opp ⲁⲛⲁⲡⲁⲩ-
ⲥⲓⲥ, Z 316 *S* flew ϩⲛⲟⲩϩ., MG 25 19 *B* κάματος; Cl
6 1 *A* αἰκία;   Deu 31 17 *S*(*B* ⲡⲉⲧϩⲱⲟⲩ) κακός; Si 29
15 *S* κάκωσις; He 2 9 *SF*(*B* ⲙⲕ.) πάθημα; Job 4 8 *S*
(*B* do) ὀδύνη; Si 5 10 *S* ἐπαγωγή; Phil 3 1 *S*(*B* diff)
ὀκνηρός; AM 271 *B* πειρασμός; BM 189 170 *S* ⲧⲟⲓⲛ-
ⲡⲉⲓⲣⲁ ⲛⲛⲉϩ. συμφορά; Aeg 270 *S* δυσχερής; BHom
7 *S* ἱδρώς;   Mus 40 46 *S*(Reg Pach) ⲙⲉϥ̄ⲁⲟⲑⲉⲧⲉⲓ ⲉⲧ-
ⲃⲉⲛϩ. lassitudo; PS 81 *S* ⲁⲛⲁⲩ ⲉϥ. ⲙⲡⲁⲣⲱⲭ, Sh
Wess 9 156 *S* fasts, vigils, ϩ. ⲧⲏⲣⲟⲩ, ShC 42 97 *S*
women ⲉⲧϫⲓ ⲛⲛϩ. ⲛⲡⲉⲩϩⲁⲓ, C 99 103 *S* ⲁⲩϯ ⲙⲛⲉϥϩ.
ⲙⲙⲛⲧⲛⲁ, Ryl 94 100 *S* gather wealth ⲉⲃⲟⲗ ϩⲛϩⲉⲛϩ.
ⲙⲙⲉ, J 85 19 *S* ϫⲓ ⲛϥϩ. & spend it, HL 98 *B* have
not eaten ⲉⲃⲏⲗ ⲉⲡⲓϩ. ⲛⲧⲉ ⲛⲁϫⲓϫ, Miss 4 162 *B* ⲁϥⲑⲁⲙⲓⲟϥ (sc book) ⲉⲃⲟⲗ ϩⲉⲛⲡⲉϥϩ. ⲙⲙⲓⲛ ⲙⲙⲟϥ,
Hyvernat Alb 28 *B* ⲁϥϣⲱⲡⲓ ⲉⲃⲟⲗ ϩⲉⲛⲡⲉϥϩ. ⲛϫⲁⲓⲟⲛ,
Ep 532 *S* payments ϩⲁⲣϩ., Gu 93 *S* ⲙⲏ ⲟⲩϩ. ⲡⲉ ϭⲓ
ⲡⲱⲛⲉ ⲙⲙⲁⲩ?, FR 26 *S* ⲛⲟⲩϩ. ⲁⲛⲛⲉ ⲉⲓϣⲁϫⲉ ⲉⲣⲟⲥ (var
BMis 64 ⲙⲡⲉⲧϣ. ⲉ.), MG 25 394 *B* ⲙⲟⲧⲓⲥ ϩⲉⲛⲟⲩϩ.
ⲉⲩⲥⲱⲧⲙ ⲉⲧⲉϥⲥⲙⲏ *hardly*, ManiH 13 20 *A²* sim?,
ClPr 40 1 *S* shall eat soft meat ⲁϫⲛϩ., C 41 69 *B* sim,

BMis 437 *S* I rested ⲉⲓⲙⲧⲟⲛ. ⲡⲡⲉϩⲓⲟⲟⲩⲉ, EpApp 1 115 *S* ϣⲁϥⲁⲓⲥⲟⲁⲛⲉ ⲉⲡϩ. ⲡⲧⲉⲣⲓⲛ; ϩⲁⲥⲉ ⲛⲛ R 1 3 11 *l* ϩ[.]ⲥⲉ (collated), so prob ϩⲓⲥⲉ.

ⲁⲧϩ., ⲥ., *unwearied*: Va 57 197 *B* ⲡⲓⲁ. ⲥⲉⲛϩⲓⲁⲧⲱⲛ ἀκαμπής; ViK 9777 *S* Christ brought up from hell ⲧⲉⲭⲙⲁⲗⲱⲥⲓⲁ ⲛⲁ. *without difficulty. Cf* ⲁⲧϩⲓⲥⲉ.

ⲙⲛⲧⲙⲁⲓϩ., ⲥ., *love of toil*: ROC 20 51 *S* keeping vigil ϩⲛⲟⲩⲙ., P 44 32 *S* ⲥⲕⲟⲗⲁⲍⲉ (σχ.) ϩⲛⲟⲩⲙ., N & E 39 333 *B* ascetic life ⲁⲥⲕⲱⲕ ⲉⲃⲟⲗ ⲥⲉⲛϩⲟⲩⲙ.

ⲣ ϩ. *SA*, *take trouble*: Mic 6 3 *A* v below; Bor 226 166 ⲁϥⲣ ϩ. ⲡⲧⲉⲣⲓⲛ πορείας δρόμον ποιεῖν; RE 10 34 ⲣ ϩⲉⲛⲛⲟϭ ⲛϩ. till he established his faith; *make trouble*: PS 42 ⲛϩ. ⲉⲛⲧⲁϥⲁⲁⲩ ⲛⲁⲥ.

† ϩ., ⲥ., *give trouble*: Col 1 29 *S*(*B* ϭⲓ ⲥ.) ⲕⲟ., Si 29 4 *S*, Mt 26 10 *S*(*Bo* ⲩⲁϩ ⲥ.), Lu 11 7 *B*(*S* ⲟⲩⲉϩ ϩ.) κόπον παρέχειν, RNC 38 *S* † . ⲡⲡⲉⲛⲕⲉⲉⲓⲟⲧⲉ εἰς κ. ἐμβάλλειν, Ac 24 4 *S*(*B* ⲧⲁϩⲣⲟ) ἐγκόπτειν, Job 19 2 *SB* ἔγκοπον ποιεῖν; C 99 215 *S* = C 89 10 *B* καταπονεῖν; MG 25 251 *B* vain thoughts † . ⲡ- ὀχλεῖν, Dan 6 18 *B* παρενοχ., Z 362 *S* ⲡⲡⲉϥ†. ⲡⲗⲁⲁⲩ ὀχληρὸς γίνεσθαι; Lam 3 5 *B*(*S* ⲑⲙⲕⲟ) μοχθεῖν; MG 25 205 *B* that none † . ⲡⲏⲓ θλίβειν; Mk 5 35 *S*(var † ϩⲟⲓ) *B* σκύλλειν; 1 Thes 2 2 *F* passive (*S* ⲭⲛⲁϩ ϩ., *B* ϭⲓ ⲥ.) -πάσχειν; Nu 22 29 *S*(*B* ⲥⲱⲃⲓ) ἐμπαίζειν (which 1 Kg 6 5 *S* ⲑⲙⲕⲟ, *cf* above); 1 Kg 16 15 *S*(var ⲱϫⲧ) πνίγειν; ROC 25 246 *B* ⲙⲁ ⲥ. ⲛⲁⲕ ⲁⲙⲟⲩ ὡς θέλεις ἐλθέ; Jer apocr(Balestri lxiv)*S* ⲡⲥⲉ†. ⲙⲡⲣⲉϥⲧⲁⲗϭⲟ = *ib B* ⲉⲣ ⲃⲗⲁⲃⲧⲓⲛ (βλάπ.), ShA 2 57 *S* Philistines † . ⲡⲓⲥⲁⲁⲕ, BM 337 98 *S* ⲛⲉⲭⲣⲟⲡ ⲉⲧ†. ⲡⲡⲉⲅⲉⲛⲏⲙⲁ (*cf* Mt 13 7 ⲱϫⲧ), DeV 1 123 *B* ⲡⲓϭⲛⲉⲡ †. ⲙⲡⲉⲩⲙⲁⲥⲧ, PBu 187 *S* to judges †. ⲡⲧⲉⲧⲛⲙⲉϣⲧ ⲡⲉⲡⲣⲱⲃ, *ib* 262 sim †. ⲛⲏⲧⲛ, CO 325 *S* † . ⲡⲁⲕ ⲡⲧⲉⲓ.

ⲟⲩⲉϩ ϩ., ⲟⲩⲁϩ ⲥ., *as last*, *c* ⲉ-: Lu 11 7 *S*(*B* † ⲥ.) ⲕⲟ. παρέχειν; 2 Cor 12 13 *SF*(*B* ϩⲣⲟϣ ⲉϫⲉⲛ-) καταναρκᾶν; Mic 6 3 *S*(ViK 9560, *A* ⲣ ϩ., *B* ϩⲟϫϩⲉϫ)παρενοχλεῖν; 1 Thes 2 9 *SF*(*B* ⲟⲩⲉϩ ⲃⲁⲣⲟⲥ ⲉϫ.) ἐπιβαρεῖν; PS 33 *S* †ⲟⲩ. ⲉⲣⲟⲕ many times, ShMun 93 *S* sim, BMis 390 *S* ⲙⲡⲉⲟⲩⲉϩ ⲗⲁⲁⲩ ⲛϩ. (var ⲃⲁⲣⲟⲥ) ⲉⲣⲟⲛ = BSM 43 *B* ⲧⲁⲗⲉ ϩⲣⲉϣⲓ ⲉϫ., C 86 109 *B* ⲡⲡⲉⲕⲟⲩ. ⲉⲡⲁⲥⲟⲛ on the road, C 41 47 *B* ⲟⲩ. ⲉⲣⲟⲕ ⲡⲧⲉⲕⲡⲉⲣⲥⲓ ⲙⲡⲓⲥⲟⲛ = Miss 4 404 اِ ﻦﻣ ﻞﻌﺟ (ⲁⲣⲓ ⲧⲁⲅⲁⲡⲏ); *c* ⲉϫⲛ-*S*: PS 50 ⲟⲩ. ⲉϫⲙⲡⲁⲑⲃⲃⲓⲟ; *c* ⲛ- dat *B*: Dan 6 2 (*S* = Gk) ἔνοχ.

ϣ(ⲉ)ⲡ ϩ., ⲥ., *take trouble, labour, suffer*: Si 30 27 *S*, 1 Cor 15 10 *SF*(*B* ϭⲓ ⲥ.) ⲕⲟ., Sa 18 11 *S* ϣⲟⲡ ⲡⲛϩ., Mk 8 31 *S*(*BF* do), Lu 13 2 *S*(*B* ϭⲓ ⲙⲕⲁϩ) πάσχ., Va 66 289 *B* ⲁⲅ ϣ. ϩⲓⲧⲉⲛ†ϩⲉⲗⲡⲓⲥ κακοπαθ.; Job 17 2 *S*(*B* ⲥ.†), Va 66 309 *B* sick ⲙⲁⲣⲟⲩϣ. κάμν.; Si 3 26 *S* κακοῦσθαι; PS 98 *S* ⲁⲥϣⲉⲛ ⲡⲉⲓⲛⲟϭ ⲛϩ., ShA 2 270 *S* brethren ⲉⲓⲟⲩⲁⲃ ⲁⲅⲱ ⲉⲧϣ., Pcod 25 *S* of Son ⲁϥϣ. (var ⲣ ⲡⲁⲑⲏⲧⲟⲥ), AM 121 *B* recant ⲛⲛⲁⲧⲉⲛϣ., Leyd 418 *S* ⲁϥϣ. died & rose, Cai ostr 47401 *S* ⲉϣⲱⲡⲉ ⲙⲡⲣⲧⲁⲁⲩ

(2d f) ϣ. ⲛⲧⲉⲧⲁⲁⲩ, C 43 173 *B* after tortures was as if ⲙⲡⲉϥϣⲉⲡ ϩⲗⲓ ⲛⲥ., JKP 2 144 *F* ⲁⲓϣ. ⲡⲧⲉⲓⲟⲩϣⲓ (Mt 27 19); *c* ⲉ-, *for*: Job 2 9 b *S*(*B* ϭⲓ ⲥ.), Jo 4 38 *SA*²(*B* ⲥ. ⲉ-) ⲕⲟ.; Z 311 *S* ⲟⲩⲃⲉⲕⲉ ⲙⲡⲓϣ. ⲉⲣⲟϥ *laborare*; ShBor 246 61 *S* plant ⲛⲧⲁϥϣⲡ ⲡⲉϥϩ. ⲉⲣⲟϥ, DeV 2 49 *B* sim ⲙⲡⲉⲕϣ. ⲉⲣⲟϥ, Mor 25 14 *S* ⲡⲏⲓ ⲛⲧⲁⲅϣⲟⲡ ⲡⲉϥϩ. ⲉⲣⲟϥ = Va 61 96 *B* ⲉⲧⲁⲅϣ. ⲉⲣⲱⲟⲩ; *c* ⲉⲧⲃⲉ-, *because of*: Wess 15 138 *S* ⲁⲅϣ. ⲉ. ⲧⲡⲓⲥⲧⲓⲥ πάσχ.; ShBor 246 37 *S* ⲉⲛϣ.... ⲉ. ⲓⲏⲥⲟⲩⲥ, BM 82 *B* ⲁϥϣ. ⲉ. ⲡⲉⲡⲟⲥ ⲛⲛⲓⲣⲱⲙⲓ; *c* ⲉϫⲡ-, *for, about*: Jos 24 13 *S* ⲕⲟ. ἐπί; Phil 1 29 *SF*(*B* ϣⲉⲡ ⲙⲕⲁϩ)πάσχ. ὑπέρ; WTh 134 *S* ϣ. ⲉϫⲙⲡⲣⲁⲛ ⲙⲡⲉⲛⲧⲁϥϣ. ϩⲁⲣⲟⲛ, PO 11 316 *B* ⲉⲅϣ. ⲉ. ⲡⲟⲅⲉⲣⲛⲟϭ; ⲉ-ϩⲣⲏⲓ ⲉϫ. *B*: Miss 4 149 ϣ. ⲉⲣ. ⲉ. ⲡⲓⲡⲁⲣϯ; *c* ⲙⲛ-, ⲛⲉⲙ-, *with*: Si 37 5 *S* συμπον. dat; Va 66 301 *B* ϣ. ⲡⲉⲙⲡⲏ ⲉⲧⲙⲟⲕϩ συναλγεῖν dat; BMar 114 *S* ⲉⲅϣ. ⲛⲙⲙⲁϥ, EW 28 *B* sim συμπάσχ.; BG 53 *S* Eve ⲉⲧⲣ ϩⲱⲃ ⲉⲡⲥⲱⲧ ... ⲉⲥϣ. ⲛⲙⲙⲁϥ, BMis 516 *S* Michael ⲡⲉⲡⲧⲁϣ. ⲛⲙⲙⲁϥ (*sc* Christ) from tomb to hell, Ep 348 *S* ⲡⲉⲕϩ. ⲉⲧⲉⲕϣⲟⲡ ⲙⲙⲟϥ ⲛⲙⲙⲁⲓ; *c* ⲡⲧⲉⲛ-*B*, *from*: AM 152 ye must ϣⲟⲡ ⲟⲩⲙⲏϣ ⲛⲥ. ⲡⲧⲟⲧϥ; *c* ϩⲁ-, ⲥⲁ-, *for*: BHom 125 *S* ⲁϥϣ. ϩⲁⲣⲟⲛ, AM 118 *B* ⲉⲑⲛⲁϣ. ⲥⲁⲣⲟϥ; *c* ϩⲛ-, ⲥⲉⲛ-, *in*: 2 Kg 23 7 *S* ⲕⲟ. ἐν; Pro 16 26 *SA* ⲡⲟⲛ. ἐν; Eccl 1 3 *F*(Mich 3520, *S* ϩ.†) μοχ. dat; Job 10 1 *S*(*B* ⲥ.†) κάμ. dat; ShWess 9 172 *S* ϣ. ϩⲣⲉⲡⲛⲏⲥⲧⲓⲁ, RE 9 160 *S* I hear that ⲧⲉⲧⲛϣ. ϩⲛⲧⲉⲧⲛⲕⲟⲅⲓ ⲙⲏ, C 86 172 *B* ϣ. ⲥⲉⲛⲡⲓⲭ̄ⲙⲡⲓⲟⲩϣⲓ; *c* ϩⲓϫⲉⲛ-*B*, *for*: AM 205 ⲛⲓⲥ. ⲉⲧⲉⲕⲡⲁϣⲟⲡⲟⲩ ϩ. ⲡⲁⲣⲁⲛ; as nn m, *labour, product of labour*: Ann 10 60 *S* built it ϩⲛⲡⲉϥϣ. ⲙⲙⲓⲛ ⲙⲙⲁϥ, Lant 81 25 *S* sim, DeV 1 60 *B* finished ⲡⲉϥϣ. ϩⲓϫⲉⲛ ⲡⲓⲥⲧⲟⲥ, BSM 45 *B* ⲟⲩϣ. ⲥⲉⲛⲟⲩⲙⲉⲧⲣⲟⲅⲟ = BMis 393 *S* ⲟⲩⲙⲏⲛϣⲉ ⲡⲁⲡϩⲟⲗⲟⲙⲁ, AM 85 *B* devil jealous of saint's ϣ.; ⲁⲧϣ. ϩ., *without suffering, sympathy*: AM 267 *B* am not pitiless & ⲁ. ἀσυμπαθής; Pcod 25 *S* Word ⲟⲩⲁ. (var ⲁⲡⲁⲑⲏⲥ); ⲣⲉϥϣ. ϩ., *who labours, suffers*: BM 216 109 *S* of hermit πονικός; BM 261 65 *S* ⲥⲁⲣϩ ⲛⲣ., Aeg 34 *B* sim, BAp 103 *S* wast ⲣ. ϩⲛⲧⲁⲓⲁⲕⲟⲛⲓⲁ ⲛⲛⲓⲛⲕⲉ; ⲙⲛⲧ-, ⲙⲉⲧⲣ-, *suffering*: Bor 226 158 *S* κακοπάθεια; Z 301 *S* ⲧⲙ. of body κόπος; BAp 168 *S* opp ⲙⲛⲧⲣⲉϥϫⲛⲁⲁⲩ, AM 85 *B* rejoiced ⲥⲉⲛⲡⲉϥⲙ.; ϭⲓⲛⲣ. *S*, *as last*: P 129¹⁴ 53 ϭⲓⲛϩⲕⲟ, ϭⲓⲛⲉⲓⲃⲉ, ϭⲓⲛⲱⲃϣ, ⲥ. of Jesus.

ϥⲓ ϩⲁϩ., *bear trouble*: Deu 1 12 *S*(*B* ϥⲁⲓ tr) κόπον φέρειν; BMis 173 *S* ⲃⲓ ϩⲁⲟⲩⲕⲟⲅⲓ ⲛϩ. ⲛⲧⲃⲱⲕ (*cf* † ϩ.), C 86 275 *B* ϥⲁⲓ ϩⲁⲛⲁⲓⲥ.; ⲙⲛⲧⲣⲉϥϥⲓ ϩⲁϩ., *patience in suffering*: Aeg 270 *S* ἀνεξικακία.

ϭⲓ ⲥ. *BF*, *labour, suffer*: Ps 126 1 (*S* ϩ.) ⲕⲟ.; *ib* 37 9 (*S* ⲙⲕⲁϩ) κακοῦσθαι; Ja 5 13 (*S* ϣⲡ ϩ.) κακοπαθ., Mk 8 31 *BF*(*S* do) πάσχ.; He 12 3 (*S* do) κάμ.; *c* ⲉ-: Job 2 9 (*S* do) ⲕⲟ. acc; Is 62 8 (*S* do) μοχ. ἐπί; *c* ⲡⲉⲙ-: Phil 4 3 (*S* ϣⲙϣⲉ) συναθλεῖν dat; *c* ⲥⲁ-: Ro 16 6 (*S* ϣⲡ ϩ.) ⲕⲟ. εἰς; *c* ⲥⲉⲛ-: Col 1 29 (*S* †

ϩ.) ⲕⲟ. εἰς; ⲥ ϩιⲭⲉⲛ-: C 43 126 ϭι ⲡⲟⲩⲙⲏϣ ⲛϩ̄.
ϩ. ⲡⲁⲣⲁⲡ.

ϣⲫⲏⲣ ⲛϩ̄. B, *fellow-labourer*: Phil 1 27 (S diff) συναθ.

ϫⲓⲛϩ̄. B, *labour*: BSM xi made it (book) ⲉⲃⲟⲗ ϩⲉⲛⲡⲉϥ. ⲙⲙⲏⲓ.

ϩιⲥε S, -ⲥⲓ B (once), ϩⲉⲥⲧ- F, ϩιⲥⲧ⸌, ϩⲁ.⸌, ϩⲟⲥⲉ† S vb tr, *spin*: Ex 35 26 B νήθειν جَ; ViK 9811 153 ϩ. ⲛⲣⲉⲛϭⲱ ⲛⲃⲁⲗⲗⲡⲉ, BMOr 9533 ⲁⲛⲧⲁⲁϥ (*sc* flax) ⲉⲧⲣⲉϥⲣϩιⲥⲧⲟⲩ ⲁⲗⲗⲁ ⲙⲡⲟⲩϩ. ϣⲁⲧⲟⲩⲡⲛϣⲉ, TurM 13 ⲛⲧⲁϫⲟⲟⲩ ⲛⲗⲁⲥ ⲉⲣⲏ[ⲥ] ⲛⲧϩιⲥⲧⲟⲩ, Aegyptus 3 282 ⲛⲛⲁⲁⲩ ⲛⲉⲛⲧⲁϩⲁⲅⲉⲓⲁ ϩιⲥⲧⲟⲩ ⲛⲁⲓ, Hall 120 flax (?) ⲛⲧⲁϩιⲥⲧⲟⲩ ⲛⲏⲧⲛ...ⲉⲛϣⲁⲛⲁⲙⲫⲓⲃⲁⲗⲉ ⲉⲣⲁⲥⲧⲟⲩ, BM 585 16 F ⲁⲩϩⲣⲉⲥⲧ ⲛⲉⲥⲁⲣⲉⲧ; Lu 12 27 ϩ. νή., but var κοπιᾶν & B ϩ̄., so prob *toil*; qual: Ex 26 31 ⲉϥⲥⲏⲧ ⲉϥϩ. (B cⲁϥ only) κεκλωσμένος (var νενησμένος), ib 25 4 (P 44 104 ابريسم, B do), Si 45 17 κεκ.; Mor 37 257 κοκκος ⲉϥⲥⲏⲧ ⲙⲡϣⲛⲥ ⲉϥϩ., Ep 547 λίτρα ⲛⲃ̄ⲛⲕ ⲉϥϩ., CO 465 sim. *V* OLZ '24 568. *Cf*? ϩⲱⲥ *thread*.

ϩιⲥⲧ⸌ S KroppK 52 ⲟⲩⲧⲁⲡ ⲡⲉⲉⲓⲟⲩⲗ ϩιⲥⲧϥ ⲛⲁⲡⲟⲩⲕⲁⲗⲁⲙⲱⲡ (ὁποκάλαμος) &c can scarcely belong here.

ϩⲱⲥⲉ S nn, an implement relating to clothing: Vi ostr 237 in list ⲟⲩϩ. ⲛⲟⲩⲱϫⲉ ⲛⲧⲱⲛⲉ (σινδόνιον, *cf* Ep 558 n), ⲟⲩϩ. ⲛⲟⲩⲱϫⲉ ⲛⲏⲃⲓⲕⲟⲥ (λιβυ.?, *cf* ST 121 ⲗⲉⲃⲉϭⲟⲥ).

ϩⲟⲥⲃ̄, -ⲃⲉ S nn f, *market*: Mor 48 53 ⲑⲟⲥⲃⲉ ⲛⲧⲡⲟⲗⲓⲥ ⲡⲉⲙϫⲉⲡⲉ = C 43 126 B ϣⲡⲁⲩ, Mor 44 35 ⲁⲩϫⲓ ⲛⲛⲟⲉⲓⲕ ϩⲛⲧϩ., ib 36 ⲑⲟⲥϥ; ⲣⲙⲛϩ. (var -ⲃⲉ): Ac 17 5 (B = Gk) ἀγοραῖος. *V* Sethe *DemUrk* 265.

ϩⲟⲥⲙ², -ⲛⲙ⸌, -ⲙⲉ³ S, -ⲉⲙ B, ϩⲁⲥⲙ⸌ SF, ϩⲱⲥⲉⲙ⸌ SS⸍ nn m, *natron* (carbonate of soda): Jer 2 22 S (B ϩⲁⲓ) νίτρον; ib B (S ⲥⲙⲣⲱϩⲉ) ποία; BHom 49 S ⲟⲩϩ. ⲙⲡⲟⲩⲁⲛϫⲓⲣ (var R 2 2 33 ϩ.⸌ σμῆγμα only); P 44 88 S, K 204 B ⲡⲓϩ. طرون; MG 25 296 B watchman ⲉϥⲣⲱⲓⲥ ⲉⲡⲓϩ., ib 303 B ⲙⲁ ⲛⲉⲣ ϩⲱⲃ ϩⲉⲛⲡⲓϩ. = BIF 13 112 S, ib 56 B ⲉⲛ ϩ. ⲉⲃⲟⲗ, WS 146 S ⲣⲧⲟϥ ⲛϩ., AZ 25 116 S ϩ.³ ⲟⲩϣⲓ, ib 112³, PMéd 216 S², Z 627 S ⲟⲩϩ.⁴ ⲛⲧⲛⲟⲡⲟϥ, AZ 25 27 Sⁱ ϩⲏⲙⲉ ϩⲁⲡ.⁵, BKU 121 vo F pound ⲟⲩⲕⲗⲉⲗ ⲛϩ.⁴, Bodl(P)a 2 32 S ϩ.⁵, CO 250 S ⲛⲡⲁ[ⲣⲁϫⲉⲓ]ⲥⲟⲥ ⲙⲛϩ. *sc* book of Apophthegmata; various sorts S: ϩ. ⲡⲁⲣⲁⲃⲓⲕⲟⲛ Z 627⁴, PMéd 176; ⲛⲁⲣⲥⲉⲡⲓⲕⲟⲛ Ora 4 25; ⲃⲉⲣⲛⲓⲕⲁⲣⲓⲟⲛ· ϩ. ⲉϥⲧⲣϣⲣⲱϣ احمر 'ⲟ̀ P 44 65, ϩ.⁴ ⲉϥⲧⲟⲣϣ PChass 2 14, ⲛⲕⲟⲕⲟⲥ Bodl(P)a 1 a; ⲉϥⲣⲱϫ PMéd 162; ϩ.⁴ ⲛⲧⲉ ⲣⲁⲕⲟⲧⲉ Z 628.
In place-name: ⲡⲧⲟⲟⲩ ⲙⲡϩ. ὄρος τῆς Νιτρίας (Z 346), ἐρῆμος τῆς N. (HM 1 141), ἡ N. (Mor 37 105), ⲡⲧ. ⲙⲡϩ. (Wess 15 127) = ⲡⲧ. ⲛⲧⲡⲓⲧⲣⲓⲁ (ib 125), ⲧ. ⲛⲧⲉ ⲡⲓϩ. = ib ⲛⲧⲉ ⲡⲓⲣⲙⲟⲩ (MG 25 263). *V* EW *Hist* 18 & CO *l c* n.

ϩⲁⲧ SB, ϩⲁⲧⲉ, ϩⲁⲁⲧ[ⲉ] S, ϩⲏⲧ SᵃF, ϩⲉⲧ Sᵃ AA²F nn m (f B in ḇ), **a** *silver*: Ps 114 1 SB, Pro 3 14 SAB, Eccl 7 13 SF ἀργύριον, Ac 17 29 SB -ρος, Ps 67 13 S (B ⲓⲉⲃ ⲛϩ.), Is 30 22 SF (B do) -ἀργυροῦσθαι; ShIF 271 S ⲡϣⲏⲃⲉ ⲙⲛϩ., SHel 35 S ⲕⲁϩ ⲟⲩⲟⲃϣ ⲛⲑⲉ ⲛⲟⲩϩ., DeV 2 86 B sim of water, BerlSitz '33 Taf 1 .1² ⲟⲩϩ. ⲡⲉ ⲡⲟⲩⲥⲱⲙⲁ. **b** *silver coin, money*: Ex 21 21 B (S ⲁⲥⲟⲩ), Lev 25 37 SB, Jud 16 5 S, Mt 27 6 S (var ϩⲟⲙⲛⲧ, *cf* 28 15) B, ib 26 15 S (var ϩⲁⲧⲉ) B, Ac 7 16 BF (S ϩⲟ.) -ριον, Zech 11 13 B f ϯⲗ̄ ⲛϩ. -ροῦς, Ex 12 44 B ϣⲱⲡ ϩⲁⲣ. ἀργυρώνητος; Mor 56 16 S ⲟⲩϩ. ⲛϥⲥⲟⲣϥ ⲡⲓⲛⲏⲕⲉ, J 24 130 Sᵃ have settled with thee all ⲡⲟⲩⲃ, ϩⲛⲧ, ϩⲟⲓⲧⲉ, Ep 525 Sᵃ ⲧⲁⲓⲟⲩ(ⲟⲩ)ⲉ ⲛϩⲉⲧ; as adj: Nu 10 2 SB, Is 31 7 S (BF nn), Ac 19 24 SB ἀργυροῦς, EpJer 38 B ⲓⲉⲡ ⲛϩ. F ⲓ. ϩ. περίαργυρος; Bor 134 3 S (Vita Sin) τράπεζα ⲛϩ. = C 41 27 B, Mor 56 42 S ⲥϥⲣⲁⲅⲓⲥ ⲛϩ., Ep 546 S ⲕⲗⲏⲗ ⲛϩ., ib 545 S ϣⲱⲡ ⲛϩ., ST 122 S ϣⲏϭⲉ ⲛϩ., Ryl 238 S ⲡⲟⲧⲏⲣⲓⲛ ⲛϩ., AM 15 B ⲉⲓⲉⲗ ⲛϩ., AZ 21 144 S ⲥⲁⲧⲉⲉⲣⲉ ⲛϩ., ManiP A² ⲥⲧⲁⲧⲉⲉⲣ ϩ., PMéd 230 S ⲙⲟⲟⲩ ⲛϩ. (ὑδράργυρος); **c** *white* SA²: Lev 23 40 ϩⲏⲧ ϩ. κάλλυνθρον; KroppD 54 ⲃⲉⲑⲁⲧ, ROC 18 ('13) 174 ḇ. ϩⲁⲧⲉ λευκάς (v LMis 88), BIF 14 166 ḇ. ϩⲁⲁⲧ[ⲉ (v ⲙⲉⲗϩⲉ); Kr 4 F]ⲗⲁⲟⲩ ⲛⲃ̄ϩⲏⲧ (?), Ora 4 20 ϩⲧⲟ ϩ. ϩⲧⲟ ⲕⲁⲙⲉ, KroppJ ⲁⲙϩ. (v ⲟⲙⲉ), ManiP A² ϭⲣⲁⲙⲡ-ϩ., v ? also ϩⲁⲧⲁⲓⲗⲉ (HT).

ⲁⲧϩ., ⲁⲧϭⲛ ϩ. B *without money, payment*: Ex 21 11 (S ⲡⲟⲩⲉϣ ⲛⲣⲟ.) ἄνευ ἀργυρίου; ⲁⲧϭ. ϩ.: TRit 223 ⲛⲧⲁⲗϭⲟ ⲛⲁ. (*cf* ⲛⲭⲓⲛϫⲏ).

ⲙⲁⲓϩ. SB, *money-loving*: Lu 16 14 B (S ⲙⲁⲓϩⲟ.), Br 102 S φιλάργυρος; He 13 5 neg B (S do) ἀφ.; ⲙⲉⲧⲙ. B, *love of money*: Va 57 6 φιλαργυρία.

ⲙⲉⲛⲧ- S, ⲙⲁⲛⲕϩ. B, *silver-smith*: Ac 19 24 B (S ⲣⲉϥⲣ ϩ.) ἀργυροκόπος, K 111 B صائغ; ⲣⲉϥⲙ. sim: Jer 6 29 B ἀργυροκ.; ShViK 934 222 S.

ⲥⲁ ⲛϩ., *silver-dealer*: BMOr 6201 B 37 S ⲛⲙⲁ ⲛⲯ.

ⲣ, ⲟ ⲛϩ. S, *be, work silver*: PS 292 ⲥⲁⲧⲉⲉⲣⲉ...ⲉⲥⲟ ⲛϩ. ϩⲓⲣⲟⲙⲡⲧ; ⲣⲉϥⲣ ϩ., *silver-smith*: Jud 17 4, Ac 19 24 (B ⲙⲁⲛⲕϩ.) ἀργυροκόπος; Sa 15 9 -χόος.

ϯ ϩ., *give, pay silver (money)*: Deu 15 6 S (B as Gk) δανείζειν; Ac 5 8 B ϯ ϩⲁϩ. (S ϩⲟ.) ἀποδιδόναι gen; Ostr Chicago 2499 S ⲁⲓϯ ⲡⲁⲓ (ⲗ ⲡⲉ) ⲡⲟⲩϩ. ⲛⲧⲟ ⲉⲧⲟ ⲙⲡⲉϥϩⲥ̄.

ϩⲁⲧ S nn m, meaning doubtful: Jud 15 19 λάκκος (varr τραῦμα, ὅλμος). *Cf*? R 2 4 37 ⲛ]ϩⲏⲧ ⲛⲧⲙⲉⲣⲟⲩⲟⲟⲥⲉ (v LMis 57).

ϩⲁⲉⲓⲧ¹, ϩⲁⲓⲉⲓⲧ², -ⲉⲓⲏⲧ³, ϩⲁⲓⲧ⁴, ϩⲉⲉⲓⲧ⁵, ϩⲏⲉⲓⲧ⁶, ϩⲏⲓⲉⲓⲧ⁷, ϩⲟⲉⲓⲧ⁸ S nn f, *gateway, porch, forecourt*: Ge 43 18¹ (B ϣⲑⲟⲙ), 2 Kg 11 9¹ (var⁸), Ac 12 13¹ (B = Gk), Z 335 sat in ϩ.¹ ⲡⲟⲩⲣⲙⲙⲁⲟ πυλών; P 131² 83 Lazarus lay ϩⲓⲡⲉϥϩ.⁸ (var Mor 25 10 & Va 61 93 B πυλών); P 44 58 ⲑ.¹· ⲧⲁⲅⲗⲏ جل, Mk 14 68¹ (B ⲙⲁ

ⲉⲧⲥⲁⲃⲟⲗ) προαύλιον; ViK 9169 ⲑ.¹ ⲡⲉⲑⲣⲓⲟⲛ (αἴθριον) ⲡⲉⲧⲣⲓⲕⲗⲓⲛⲟⲛ, Mor 43 264 ⲧⲉⲕⲣ.ˣ ⲉⲧⲉⲡⲉⲕⲗⲗⲁ
ⲡⲉⲓ ⲉⲃⲟⲗ ⲙⲡⲉⲕⲗⲗⲁ ⲡⲃⲱⲕ ⲉⲣⲟ ⲟⲩⲛ, BM 1015 ⲣ.¹, cf
ib 1023 ⲟⲣⲉ, J 39 27 ⲧⲣⲓ ⲧⲏⲣⲥ ⲉⲧⲉⲣⲡⲟ.⁶, ib 26 8 ⲡⲥⲓⲙ
ⲡⲟⲥⲓⲟⲛ ⲉⲧⲣⲧⲣ.², ib 43 34 ⲧⲁⲡⲟⲑⲏⲕⲏ ⲉⲧⲣⲧⲣ.⁷ (36ⲣ.⁶,
28 ⲣ.²), ib 48 5 ⲣⲏⲧⲣ.⁴ ⲗⲡⲏⲓ, ib 20 53 ⲡⲣⲁⲧⲟⲟⲩ ⲡⲑ.⁵,
RNC 49 ⲡⲣⲟ ⲡⲑ.¹, J 39 87 ⲉⲣⲉⲧⲣ.² ϣⲧⲁⲙ, J 42 22 ⲑ.⁵
(sic), ϩⲁⲓⲙⲟⲟⲩ, ⲣⲟ ⲡⲃⲁⲗ, ⲧⲱⲣⲧ ⲉⲣϩⲁⲓ shall be in
common, TurM 16 ϩⲁⲓⲙⲁⲩ ⲣⲏⲟ.⁶, ib ⲧⲱⲣⲧ ⲡⲧⲉ ⲑ.⁶ Cf
PLond 5 175, PMon 131 πρόθυρον & πυλών. Not to
be confused with ⲣⲓⲉⲓⲧ.

ϩⲉⲧ, ϩⲧ F interj v p 86 a.

ϩⲉⲧ F   v ϩⲁⲧ 1°.

ϩⲏⲧ SAA²BFO, ϩⲉⲧ DM, ϩⲧⲏⳍ SAA²FO, ϩⲧⲉⳍ O,
ϩⲟⲏⳍ B, ⲏⲧⳍ A(ⲣⲗⲛⲣ.), ⲉⲣⲧⲏⳍ B, pl ϩⲉⲧⲉ AA², ϩⲉ†F,
-ⲏⲧ in compounds SABF (v list at end) nn m, heart,
mind: Ge 20 5 SB, Pro 3 1 SAB, Mt 13 15 SBF, Jo
12 40 SA²B καρδία; Is 40 13 SB, 1 Cor 14 14 SB
νοῦς; Deu 28 47 SB, Pro 2 10 SAB διάνοια; Ps 106
18 S(B=Gk), Is 58 10 S(B do) ψυχή; PS 28 S ⲉⲣⲉ
ⲡⲉ ⲣ. ϫⲟⲕⲣ, ShC 73 210 S drink ϣⲁⲛⲧⲉ ⲡⲉⲧⲣ. ⲕⲃⲟ,
ShA 2 283 S ⲥⲁ ⲙⲡⲉⲧⲣ. ⲉⲡⲁⲩ ⲉⲣⲟⲛ, BIF 14 115 S
ⲗⲁⲁⲩ ⲡⲣⲱⲙⲉ ⲉⲣⲉⲣ. ⲙⲙⲟⲟⲩ, Aeg 266 S ⲡⲧⲱⲧⲛ ⲡⲉⲧ
ⲉⲟⲩⲉⲛⲣ. ⲙⲙⲟⲟⲩ, BMar 84 S weepest as if ⲉⲗⲡ
ⲗⲁⲁⲩ ⲡⲣ. ⲙⲙⲟⲕ, Miss 4 713 S ⲡⲉϫⲣ. ⲗⲟ ⲙⲙⲁⲩ (var
ⲡⲱϣⲥ ⲉⲣⲟⲟⲩ), Mor 44 15 S let us go ⲡⲧⲓϣⲁϫⲉ ⲉ
ⲡⲉⲧⲣ. ViK 9182 (?) S ⲡⲥⲉ ⲡⲱϣ ⲙⲡⲉⲛⲣ. with groans,
AM 52 B ⲙⲡⲉ ⲡⲁⲣ. ⲗⲧⲟⲡ ⲉⲣⲟⲓ, MR 4 69 S what
lacketh it ⲕⲁⲧⲁ ⲡⲉⲕⲣ.?=Miss 4 135 B ⲕⲁⲧⲁ ⲣⲟⲕ, DeV
1 105 B ⲉⲓⲟⲩⲱϣ ⲉⲕⲟⲥϥ ⲕⲁⲧⲁ ⲡⲁⲣ., ib 2 238 B ⲡⲓⲣ.
ⲧⲁⲕⲟ from hunger, AM 290 B ϫⲟⲙϥ (sc molten lead)
ⲉϩⲣⲏⲓ ⲉⲣⲟ ⲛⲣ, MG 25 382 B entering ⲡⲣ. ⲡⲧⲯⲩⲭⲏ
of each (cf ROC 18 295 سلطمو ... الحشا
الصفر(حشا)), MR 5 32 S ⲧⲓⲡⲣⲟⲥⲕⲩⲛⲉⲓ...ⲣⲁⲙⲡⲁⲣ. ⲙⲡⲧⲁ
ⲯⲩⲭⲏ, AZ 21 100 O ⲉⲣⲉⲧⲛⲥ ⲭⲁⲉⲣⲟⲙ, ib 104 O ⲫⲏⲧ,
PGM 1 52 O sim, Hor 82 O ⲣⲧⲉϥ, DMV 32 12 pe·f
ϩⲉⲧ;   ⲣ. ⲉⲓ ⲉ-, come to senses: Ac 12 11 B(S ⲣ. ϣⲱⲡⲉ
ⲗⲗⲟⳍ) ἐν ἑαυτῷ γίνεσθαι; Lu 15 17 B(S ⲙⲟⲕⲙⲉⲕ)
εἰς ἑαυτὸν ἔρχεσθαι; Z 329 S εἰς ἔννοιαν ἔρ.; DeV 2
126 B after trance ⲁ ⲡⲁⲣ. ⲓ ⲉⲣⲟⲓ, Mor 41 24 S ⲡⲧⲉⲣⲉ
ⲡⲉ ⲣ. ⲉⲓ ⲉⲣⲟϥ=DeV 2 279 B ϫⲉⲙ ⲡⲉϥ ϩⲟⲩⲥ; ϣⲱ
ⲡⲉ ⲙⲙⲟⳍ: Mor 22 29 S ⲡⲧⲉⲣⲉⲡⲉϥⲣ. ϣ. ⲙⲙⲟϥ=
BSM 80 B ⲥⲉⲗⲡⲓ ⲉⲣⲟϥ;   pl: Cl 2 1 A written
ϩⲛ[ⲡ]ⲉⲧⲏⲣ. σπλάγχνον; v also ⲣⲁⲙⲣ., F v ⲁⲧϩⲏⲧ &
v ϩⲣⲟϣ p c A².

ⲣ. ϩⲱⲱⲛ, evil-hearted: ManiP A², MG 25 122 B.
ⲣ. ⲡⲟⲩⲱⲧ SBF, single heart, one mind: Ps 54 15
B(S ⲣⲓⲟⲩⲥⲟⲛ) ὁμόνοια; Ap 17 13 S(B=Gk) μία
γνώμη;   ⲗⲡⲧ-, ⲙⲉⲧⲣ. ⲡⲟⲩ., unanimity: ClPr 54
40 S ⲧⲙ. ⲉⲣϩⲩⲛ ⲉⲡⲉ ⲩⲉⲣⲏⲧ, CaiEuch 502 B ⲧⲙ. ⲛⲧⲉ
†ⲁⲅⲁⲡⲏ ὁμόνοια; ShA 2 314 S ⲟⲩⲙ. ⲙⲡⲉⲧ ⲩⲟⲩⲏⲣ

ⲛⲁⲙⲁⲩ, FR 90 B He gave disciples †ⲙ.;   ⲣ ⲣ.
ⲡⲟⲩ.: BM 247 7 S ϣⲁ ⲉⲣ ⲟⲩⲣ. ⲡⲟⲩ. ⲙⲓⲁ ⲕ. γίνε-
θαι; Aeg 245 S ⲣ ⲟⲩⲣ. ⲡⲟⲩ. ⲙⲡⲟⲩⲥⲡⲱⲙ ⲡⲟⲩ. ἴση
βουλή; ShViK 924 S Rahab ⲁⲥⲣ ⲟⲩⲣ. ⲡⲟⲩ. ⲙⲛⲡⲕⲁ
ⲧⲁⲥⲕⲟⲡⲟⲥ;   Mor 30 16 F martyr ⲁⲓ ⲛⲑⲉ ⲡⲟⲩⲣ.
ⲡⲟⲩ., (var ib 29 14 & BMis 241 S ⲛⲑⲉ ⲡⲟⲩⲡⲉ ⲡⲁⲗⲁ
ⲙⲁⲥ) ὁ ὄντως ἀδάμας (cf ⲟⲩⲱⲧ Sa 17 13).

ⲣ. ⲥⲛⲁⲩ SAA²F, ⲣ. ē B, two hearts, double-minded:
Ja 4 8 SAB δίψυχος; C 99 219 S obedience χωρὶς
ⲣ. = C 89 33 B ἀδιάκριτος; Mani 1 A² ⲁⲓⲭⲓ ⲁⲕ ⲡ.ⲣ.,
J 106 26 S ϩⲡ(ⲟⲩ)ⲟⲩⲱϣ ⲡⲁⲧⲣ ⲣⲧⲏϥ...ⲁⲕ ⲡ.ⲣ., BSM
104 B I will take husband ⲁ ⲧⲛⲉ ⲣ. = Mor 22 116 S
ⲁⲕⲛⲉⲧⲕⲁⲕⲉⲓ;   ⲗⲡⲧ-, ⲙⲉⲧⲣ. ⲥ.: Gu 105 S ⲧⲉⲕ ⲙ.
O Didymus, Z 626 S is evident ⲁⲕ ⲡ ⲙ., C 86 187 B
faith ⲁⲥϥⲉⲣⲗⲓ ⲙ ⲙ.;   ⲗⲡⲧ-, ⲙⲉⲧⲁ ⲧⲣ. ⲥ.: My 18 S
believed ⲣ ⲛⲟⲩ ⲙ., ROC 25 250 B fell on knees ϩⲉⲛ
ⲟⲩ ⲙ.;   ⲣ, ⲉⲣ ⲣ. ⲥ., be of 2 minds, doubtful: Mt
14 31 BF(S = Gk) διστάζειν; ib 21 21 SB, ZNTW
24 86 F(ⲙ)ⲡⲉⲣ(ⲉⲣ)ⲣ. ⲉⲧⲃⲏⲧϥ διακρίνεσθαι; Aeg 243
S, Cl 23 2 A διψυχεῖν; Va 57 128 B δυσχεραίνειν;
Leip 24 6 B ⲡⲓⲣ ⲃⲏⲟⲅⲓ ⲉⲧⲉⲕⲟⲓ ⲡⲣ. ⲉⲣⲱⲟⲩ ἀμφισβη-
τεῖν; PS 13 S ⲁⲧⲉⲡⲓⲣ ⲣ., Mor 56 21 S ⲡⲉⲧⲛⲁⲣ ⲣ.
ⲉⲧⲉϥ ⲁⲛⲁⲥⲧⲁⲥⲓⲥ, AP 55 A² ⲉⲙⲡⲉⲧⲛⲁⲣ ⲣ., DeV 2 253 B
ⲁⲕⲉ ⲣ. ⲉϥⲛ ⲉⲧⲁ ⲭⲟϥ = Mor 41 6 S ⲣ ⲁⲡⲓⲥⲧⲟⲥ, Mor
31 32 S ⲙⲡⲉ ⲩⲉⲣ ⲣ. but went ⲣ ⲛⲟⲩ ⲣ. ⲡⲟⲩⲱⲧ.

ⲣ. ⲡⲱⲛⲓ, ⲙⲉⲧ- B, stony-heartedness: Cat 176.

ⲣ. ϣⲏⲙ SA, small, faint heart, impatient: Pro 14
29 SA ⲡⲣ., 1 Thes 5 14 (B ⲕⲟⲩϫⲓ ⲛⲣ.) ὀλιγόψυχος;
ShA 1 74 ⲣⲉϥϣⲱⲡⲧ ϩⲓⲣ. (cf Si 23), BMOr 7561 49 not
vengeful, quick to wrath ⲛⲟⲩⲣ. ⲁ ⲡⲛⲉ;   as adj: Pro
18 14 SA ὀλ.; Si 23 20 (Lag & Ryl Suppl 7) θερμός
(cf ? šⲙ Dévaud);   ⲗⲡⲧⲣ. ϣ. S, timidity, impatience: Ps 54 8 (B ⲙⲉⲧⲕ. ⲛⲣ.) ὀλιγοψυχία; BHom 20
ὀλιγωρία paral ⲗⲡⲧⲁ ⲙⲉⲗⲏⲥ, Bor 253 114 do paral
ⲗⲡⲧⲥⲁ ⲃ ⲏⲧ; Z 249 μικροψυχία; C 99 108 ⲁⲓ ϣⲱⲡⲉ
ϩⲛ ⲟⲩ ⲙ. ⲉⲣ ϩⲛ ⲉⲣⲟⲕ = MG 17 361 عليك, ib 89
cursed not ϩⲛ ⲟⲩ ⲙ. & wrath = Va ar 172 94 نفجر,
ShBMOr 8810 472 ⲗⲡⲧⲣⲉϥ† ϭⲱⲛⲧ, ⲙ., ⲗⲡⲧⲣⲉϥ
ⲥⲱϣ, P 131⁶ 65 ⲡϣⲁϩ ⲡⲧⲙ.;   ⲣ ⲣ. ϣ.: Nu 21 4
(B ⲉⲣ ⲕ. ⲛⲣ.), Cl 59 4 A ὀλιγοψυχεῖν; Pro 3 11 A(SB
ⲣ ⲕⲟⲩⲓ ⲛⲣ.) ὀλιγωρεῖν; BMar 110 μικροψ.; ShViK
9593 they that summon to prayer shall neither ⲣ ⲣ.
ⲉⲩ ϣⲗⲏⲗ nor delay, ShC 73 37 ⲧⲉ ⲡⲟ ⲡⲣ. ⲉⲧⲁ ϥϫⲓ ⲉⲣⲟⲛ
to hear God's word.

ⲁⲧϩⲣ. SAA²BF, without mind, senseless: Pro 1 22
SAB, Eccl 7 6 SF, Ro 2 20 SB, Cl 3 3 A ἄφρων;
Deu 32 31 S(B=Gk) ἀνόητος, Hos 7 11 A(B ⲁⲧⲕⲁ†)
ἄνους; Job 13 2 S(B do) ἀσύνετος; Jer 27 2 F(Mus
49 174, B as Gk) ἀπτόητος (reading ? ἀνόητος); B
Hom 55 S μωρός; Mani 1 A² ⲡⲓⲁ. ⲡⲣⲣⲟ, C 43 98 B
ⲱ ⲡⲓⲁ.;   pl: Eccl 4 17, 7 10 F;   as adj: Ps 73
18 SB, Cl 21 5 A ἀφ.; Sa 19 3 S ἄνοια (nn); Deu 32
21 S(B ⲙⲙⲟⲛ ⲕⲁ† ⲙⲙⲟϥ) ἀσύν.; J 67 121 S ⲣⲉⲛ-

ⲣⲱⲙⲉ ⲛⲡⲁ., BSM 120 *B* ⲁⲗⲱⲟⲩⲓ ⲛⲁ.;   ⲙⲛⲧ-, ⲙⲉⲧⲁϩ.: Deu 22 21 *SB*, Ps 37 5 *S*(*B* ⲙⲉⲧⲁⲧⲉⲙⲓ), Eccl 2 13 *SF*, Mk 7 22 *S*(*B* ⲙⲉⲧⲁⲧⲕⲁϯ) ἀφροσύνη; Pro 14 8 *SA*(*B* do) ἄνοια; BG 62 *S* ⲁϥⲙⲟⲩϩ ⲙⲙ., J 80 24 *S* ⲁⲓⲁⲁⲥ ϩⲛⲧⲁⲙ., ManiP *A*² ⲧϧⲙ., DeV 1 122 *B* thought ⲋⲉⲡⲧⲉϥⲙ.;   ⲣ ⲁⲧϩ.: Jer 10 21 *B* ἀφρονεύειν, 2 Cor 12 11 *B*(*SF* ϣⲱⲡⲉ ⲛⲁ.) ἀφ. γίνεσθαι; Mk 7 18 *S*(*B* ⲁⲧⲕ.) ἀσύν. εἶναι.

ⲃⲁⲗϩ. *SAB*(once)*F*, *open, simple-minded*: Job 8 20 (*B* ⲁⲧⲕⲁⲕⲓⲁ), Pro 1 4 *SA*(*B* ⲁⲧⲡⲉⲧϩⲱⲟⲩ), He 7 26 *SF*(*B* do), Cl 14 4 *A* ἄκακος; Nu 14 23 (*B* ⲁⲧⲉⲙⲓ) ἄπειρος; C 99 148 ⲟⲩϧ. = C 89 74 *B* ἁπλοῦς; Mor 23 76 opp ⲡⲁϣⲧϩ., DeV 2 102 *B* ⲋⲉⲗⲗⲟ ⲙϧ.;   ⲙⲛⲧ-ϧ.: Job 27 5 (*B* ⲙⲉⲧⲁⲧⲕⲁⲕⲓⲁ), Ps 77 72 (*B* do) ἀκακία; Cl 21 7 *A* ἀκέραιος; PS 210 ⲧⲙ. ⲙⲛⲡⲉϧⲃⲓⲟ, JTS 9 383 opp ⲙⲛⲧⲙⲁⲣϩ.

ⲙⲁⲣϩ. *S*, *with bound, closed heart, guileful*, ⲙⲛⲧⲙ. v JTS above.

ⲣⲙⲛϩ. *SAA²B*(rare)*F*, *man of heart, wise man*: Aeg 244 σώφρων; Hos 14 10 *A*(*B* ⲕⲁⲧϩⲏⲧ) συνετός, Ro 3 11 (*B* ⲡⲉⲧⲕⲁϯ) συνίων; Pro 1 5 *SA*(*B* ⲛⲉϥϩⲏⲧ) νοήμων; Ja 3 13 (*B* ⲕⲁⲧϩ.) ἐπιστήμων; Job 5 12 (*B* = Gk) πανοῦργος; AP 23 *A²* ⲡⲁϩⲏⲧ ⲙⲛⲡⲣ., AM 54 *B* wise steward, ⲕⲩⲣⲓϩ (κῆρυξ) ⲛⲣ.; as adj: Ac 13 7 (*B* ⲕⲁⲧϩ.) συνετός; Ro 12 1 *S*(*BF* Ryl Suppl 1 = Gk, var MR 2 69 = *S*) λογικός; Si 10 26 ἐπισ.; ShC 73 32 ⲡϣⲏⲣⲉ ⲛⲣ., Miss 4 640 ⲥϩⲓⲙⲉ ⲛⲣ.;   pl: TU 43 21 *A* ⲡⲣⲙⲛϩⲉⲧⲉ;   ⲙⲛⲧⲣ., *wisdom, understanding*: Deu 4 6 (*B* ⲕⲁϯ), Ps 31 tit (*B* do) σύνεσις, ib 46 7 *SA* ⲙⲉⲧⲣⲉⲙⲉⲛϩⲏⲧϧ (bis MIF 67 76, *B* do) συνετῶς; Pro 1 2 *SA*(*B* ⲙⲉⲧⲥⲁⲃⲉ), Sa 4 9 φρόνησις, Lu 16 8 (*B* do) φρονίμως; Is 33 6 *SF*(*B* = Gk) ἐπιστήμη; Aeg 239 νουνεχία; ShC 73 41 opp ⲙⲛⲧⲁⲑⲏⲧ, ShA 2 309 ⲧⲙ. ϩⲓⲃⲟⲗ ⲛⲡⲁϩⲣⲛⲣⲱⲙⲉ;   ⲣ ⲣⲙⲛϩ.: Is 44 18 (*B* ⲕⲁϯ) φρονεῖν, Ro 12 3 *SF*(*B* ϭⲓ ⲥⲃⲱ) σωφ.; 1 Kg 18 14 συνιέναι; Pro 10 19 *SA*(*B* ⲉⲣ ⲛⲉⲃϩ.) νοήμων εἶναι.

ϣⲥ, ϣ(ⲉ) ⲛϩ. *SB*(once)*F*, ϣⲓ ⲛϩ. *F*, *grief*: Job 7 19 (*B* ⲉⲙⲕⲁϩ ⲛϩ.), Is 30 26 *F*(*S* ⲧⲕⲁⲥ, *B* do), Ro 9 2 *B*(*S* ⲙⲕⲁϩ ⲛϩ.) ὀδύνη; Lam 1 22 *F* ϣⲓ ⲛϩ. (*S* = Gk, *B* ϩ. ⲙⲟⲕϩ) καρδία λυπεῖσθαι; Ps 54 3 (*B* diff) ἀδολεσχία (var μέριμνα); ShC 73 138 ⲡϣ. & gnashing of teeth, R 1 3 77 comforted ⲉⲧⲟ ⲡϣ.

Forming noun. ⲕⲱⲗϫ ⲛϩ., *compunction*: BHom 75 *S* may ⲕ. be to such as squander life; ⲕⲣⲟϥ ⲛϩ., *guile*: Ro 1 29 *S*(*B* ⲭⲣ. only) δόλος; ⲙⲟⲕⲙⲉⲕ ⲛϩ., *thought*: ShC 42 134 *S* ⲙ. ⲉⲑⲟⲟⲩ; ⲡⲁϭ ⲛϩ., *long-suffering*: Eccl 7 9 *F* ⲡⲁϭ ⲛϩ. (*S* ϩⲁⲣϣϩ.) μακρόθυμος; 1 Cor 9 12 *F*(BM 507) ⲁⲓ ⲛⲡ. (*B* ⲱⲟⲩ ⲛϩ., *S* diff) στέγειν; El 36 *A* [ϣⲁ]ⲧⲉⲟ ϩⲱⲡⲉ ⲉⲕⲉⲉ [ⲡ]ⲡ.; ⲡⲱⲣⲕ ⲛϩ., *breaking of heart*: R 1 3 74 *S*; ⲡⲱϣ ⲛϩ., *rending of heart*: Nah 2 10 *A*(*B* ⲁⲗⲁⲡⲗⲉⲡ ⲛϩ.) ἐκβρασμός(-γμός); ManiK 150 *A²* ⲡ. ⲁⲣⲁⲩ; ⲣⲁϣⲓ ⲛϩ.,

joy of heart: CaiThe 126 *B* grief turned to ⲟⲩⲣ.; ⲟⲩⲛⲟϥ ⲛϩ. sim (v p 486 a); ⲥⲟⲟⲩⲛ ⲛϩ., *knowledge*: Ps 138 6 *S*(*B* ⲉⲙⲓ) γνῶσις; ⲑⲃⲃⲓⲟ ⲛϩ., *humility*: Z 307 *S* ταπεινοφροσύνη, AM 252 *B*;   also ⲙⲉⲥⲟϩⲏⲧ q v.

ⲕⲱ ⲛϩ., ⲕⲁ ϩ. *SAA²BF*, *set heart, trust*: Job 11 18 *SB* πείθειν; Ps 30 14 *S*(*B* = Gk) ἐλπίζειν; PS 315 *S* ⲕⲁ ϩⲧⲏⲧⲛ that ye will attain, Va 61 88 *B* ⲉϥⲭⲱ ⲛϩⲑⲏϥ that there is no repentance;   c ⲉ-, *upon*: Pro 3 29 *SAB*†, Is 30 32 *SB*†*F* π. ἐπί, Jer 12 5 *SB*, Phil 3 4 *S*(*B* ϩⲱⲧ ⲛϩ. ⲋⲉⲡ-) π. ἐν, Job 31 24 *SB* π. dat; Is 30 12 *SF*(*B* as Gk) ἐλ. ἐπί, Jth 9 7 *S* ἐλ. ἐν, Si 5 1 *SB* ἐπέχειν ἐπί, Job 27 6 *S*(*B* ϯ ϩ. ⲉ-) προσέχ. dat, Is 48 2 *S*(*B* om) ἀντέχ. dat; BAp 162 *S* ⲁϥⲕⲁϩⲧⲏϥ ⲉⲣⲟϥ, ArchivOr '37 124 ⲛⲉⲃⲁⲗ ⲡⲟⲩⲱⲡ ⲛⲓⲙ ⲕⲟ ⲡⲉϩⲧⲏⲩ ⲉⲣⲟⲕ, Ryl 439 30 *B* ϩⲟⲛⲟⲩ ⲭⲛ ⲉⲣⲟⲩ; vbal: Sh A 2 146 *S* ⲕⲱ ϩⲧⲏⲕ ⲉⲧⲣⲉⲩϯ, Mor 18 38 *S* ⲉⲅⲕⲱ ⲡϩⲧⲏⲩ ⲉⲥⲅⲛⲁⲧⲉ; ShC 73 116 *S* ⲧⲉⲅⲙⲡⲧⲣⲉϥⲕⲁ ϩⲧⲏⲩ ⲉⲣⲟⲟⲩ ⲙⲁⲩⲁⲁⲩ *selfconfidence*;   c ⲉⲝⲛ- sim: Ps 145 3 *B*(*S* ⲡⲁⲣⲧⲉ ⲉ-), Is 30 3 *S*(*B*†*F* ⲉ-) πεί. ἐπί;   c ⲛ- sim: Is 28 17 *B*(*S* do) πεί. dat;   c ϩⲓ- sim: 1 Kg 9 20 *S* καρ. τιθέναι dat; as nn m, *confidence*: Mani K 126 *A²* ⲧϩⲉⲗⲡⲓⲥ ⲙⲛⲡⲕⲁ ϩⲧⲏⲩ;   c ⲉⲃⲟⲗ, *loosen heart, relax, be careless*: C 86 292 *B* ⲁⲡⲉⲕϩ. ⲭⲱ ⲉⲃⲟⲗ ληρεῖν; ShC 73 25 *S* if rich man ⲛϥⲕⲁ ⲡⲉϩϩ. ⲉⲃ. thieves will come, BMar 161 *S* weepest to-day, to-morrow ⲛⲧⲕⲁ ϩ. ⲉⲃ. ⲛⲉⲙⲟⲟϣⲉ ϩⲛⲟⲩϩⲏⲣ, MG 25 97 *B* ⲙⲡⲉϥⲭⲁ ⲡⲉϥϩ. ⲉⲃ. till death, BM 217 1 *S* ⲛⲛⲉⲕⲕⲁ ⲡⲉⲕϩ. ⲉⲃ. ⲙⲛⲧⲉⲅⲙⲛⲧⲉⲛⲣⲓⲟⲛ, C 86 345 *B* ⲁⲩⲭⲁ ⲡⲟⲩϩ. ⲉⲃ. ⲡⲉⲙⲗⲁϥ;   ⲙⲉⲧⲕⲁ ϩ., *reason, sense* (?): Mart Ign 867 *B* ⲉⲥⲟⲛⲥⲓⲥ (αἴσ.) ⲙⲙ. = R 1 4 54 *S* ⲙⲛⲧⲣⲙⲛϩ.;   ϭⲓⲛⲕⲁ ϩ., *reliance*: Leyd 352 *S* σ. ⲉⲡⲭ̄ⲥ̄.   ⲕⲁⲣⲧⲁⲓⲧ† *A²*: ManiP 7 ⲉⲛⲕ. ⲁⲡⲉⲕⲡⲁⲉ (cf ⲕⲁⲣⲁⲉⲓⲧ p 288 b), ib 93 sim.

ⲣ ϩ., ⲉⲓⲣⲉ ⲛϩ. *SAA²B*(once)*F*, *reflect, criticize* (?): ShBM 209 35 let not sick ⲣ ϩ. ⲉⲩϩⲟⲟⲩ lest God be wroth, COAd 14 we make this agreement ⲛⲧⲉⲧⲛⲣ (l ⲛⲧⲛⲣ) ϩ. ⲁⲩⲱ ⲛⲣⲏϣⲉ (sic, l ? ⲣⲁϣⲉ) ⲉⲛⲡⲱ (l ⲉⲛⲟ) ⲛⲟⲩϩⲏⲧ ⲛⲟⲩⲱⲧ, Win 14 will obey my elders (cf CO 29)...ⲛⲛⲡⲣ ϩ. ⲉⲣⲟⲟⲩ;   *repent, regret*: 1 Kg 15 35, Ps 109 4 (*B* ⲟⲩⲱⲙ ⲛϩ.), He 7 21 *SF*(*B* do) μεταμέλεσθαι; Nu 5 6 (*B* diff) πλημμελεῖν; Si 17 19, Zech 8 15 *AB*(Lakân 152, var ⲟⲩ. ϩ.) μετανοεῖν; Si 20 1 ἀνθομολογεῖσθαι; R 2 1 52 ⲉϥⲉⲓⲣⲉ ⲛϩⲧⲏϥ weeping for what had done;   c ⲉ-: Mt 21 32 (*B* ⲟⲩ. ϩ. ⲉ-) μεταμ. gen, Sh(Besa)Bor 205 368 ⲉⲙⲡⲟⲩⲣ ϩⲧⲏⲩ ⲉⲧⲣⲉⲛⲕⲧⲟⲟⲩ;   c ⲉϫⲛ-: Pro 14 15 *SA*(*B* do) εἰς μετάνοιαν ἔρχεσθαι; Sh(Besa)Z 513 ⲉⲕⲉⲓⲣⲉ ⲛϩⲧⲏⲕ ⲉϫⲛⲛⲕⲁⲕⲓⲁ, BMar 56 ⲣ ϩⲧⲏⲕ ⲉϫⲛⲡⲉⲛⲧⲁⲕⲉⲣⲓⲧ ⲙⲙⲟϥ;   c ⲛ- dat: Nu 5 8 (*B* ⲉⲣ ⲛⲟⲃⲓ ⲛ-) πλημ. dat;   c ⲛⲥⲁ-: Pro 11 3 *SA*(*B* ⲭⲱ ⲛⲥⲱϥ ⲛ(ⲟⲩ)ⲟⲩ. ⲛϩ.) μετάμελον λείπειν; ShIF 242 ⲛⲉⲡⲧⲁⲩⲣ ϩⲧⲏⲩ ⲛⲥⲱⲟⲩ at death;   as nn m: Nu 5 7 (*B* ⲙⲉⲧⲁⲙⲉⲗⲉⲥ) πλημμελία; ManiP *A²* ⲡⲣ ϩⲧⲏϥ;   ⲁⲧⲣ ϩⲧⲏⲥ, *un-*

repentant: Ro 11 29 *SF*(*B* ⲁⲑⲟⲩ. ⲡϩ.) ἀμεταμέλητος;
Mus 42 235 virginity ⲧⲣⲗⲥⲉ ⲡⲁⲧⲣ ϩⲧⲏⲥ, J 104 3 ⲣⲡ-
ⲙⲏ ⲡⲁⲧⲣ ϩⲧⲏⲥ; ⲙⲏⲧⲣ ϩⲧⲏⲍ: Si 17 22 ἀνθομο-
λόγησις; ⲙⲏⲧⲣⲉϥⲣ ϩⲧⲏϥ: HSt 459 ⲧⲙ. of those
chosen priests(var Aeg 244 ⲣⲩⲡⲟⲙⲟⲡⲏ?) τὸ προσεχές
= PO 8 584 لَاِـﻲٰ; BM 228 60 ⲟⲩⲙ. ⲡⲁⲟⲩⲏⲣ & what
grief if we die in sins ?, Miss 8 177 shalt repent at
last & thy ⲙ. shall profit nothing.

ⲥⲱⲕ ϩ. *S, draw heart, persuade*: 2 Cor 10 5 (*B*=
Gk) αἰχμαλωτίζειν; RNC 49 ⲁϥⲥⲉⲕ ⲡϩ. ⲙⲡⲉϥⲉⲓⲱⲧ,
BMis 17 ⲥⲉⲕ ⲡϩ. ⲙⲡⲣⲣⲟ…ⲉϩⲟⲩⲏ ⲉ-.

ϩ. ⲥⲙⲓⲛⲉ, ⲥⲉⲙⲛⲓ *SB, heart be established, mind
steadied*: Mk 5 15 *S*(*B* ϩ. ⲙⲙⲟϥ), 2 Cor 5 13 *S*(*B*
ⲕⲁⲧ) σωφρονεῖν; LMär 25 *S* threw water in his face
ϣⲁⲡⲧⲉⲡⲉϥϩ. ⲥⲙⲛⲧϥ ⲉⲣⲟϥ, AM 322 *B* ⲁⲡⲉϥϩ. ⲥ. ⲉⲣⲟϥ
ⲉⲃⲟⲗ ϩⲉⲛⲡⲓϩⲓⲥⲓ. *V* also ⲥⲙⲓⲛⲉ ⲉ-.

ⲧ ϩ., ⲡϩ. *SAA²BF, pay heed, observe*: EstE 8 *S*,
Pro 1 24 *SAB* προσέχειν; Is 5 12 *F*(*S* ⲙⲟⲩϣⲧ, *B*
ⲡⲁⲩ), ib 59 16 *S*(*B* ⲧ ⲡⲓⲁⲧⲍ), Ac 11 6 *B*(*S* ⲙⲟⲩϩ), ib
27 39 *B*(*S* ⲉⲓⲱⲣϩ) κατανοεῖν; Ps 2 10 *S*(*B* ⲕⲁⲧ) συνιέναι; 1 Kg 25 17 *S* γινώσκειν; Deu 1 8 *S*(*B* ⲡ.),
Lu 12 15 *S*(*B* ⲇⲟ) ὁρᾶν; Su 12 *B* παρατηρεῖν; Jer 13
15 *S*(*B* ϭⲓ ⲥⲙⲏ) ἐνωτίζεσθαι; Mk 4 24 *S*(*B* ⲡ.) βλέπειν, Nah 2 8 *A*(*B* ⲭⲟⲩϣⲧ) ἐπιβ.; Si 11 32 *S* κατάσκοπος, Eccl 2 3 *S*(*F* ⲭⲱϣⲧ) κατασκέπτειν; PS 356 *S*
ⲁϥⲧ ϩⲧⲏϥ ϩⲉⲥⲉⲣ ⲭⲣⲓⲁ, Bor 248 10 *S* ⲁ ⲩⲧ ϩⲧⲏⲩ as
I came forth; c ⲉ-, *give mind, devote self to*: Si
30 21 *S* ψυ. διδόναι εἰς, Bor 226 160 *S* ⲧ ⲡⲉϩϩ. ⲉϣⲓⲡⲉ
ⲕⲁⲣ.ⲇ. ζητεῖν; ShC 73 119 *S* cursed whoso ⲧⲙⲡⲉϩϩ.
ⲉⲣϩⲟⲉⲓⲧⲉ to adorn it, BSM 69 *B* ⲁⲡⲓⲣⲱⲙⲓ ⲧ ⲙⲡⲉϥϩ.
ⲉⲫⲧ; *give heed to, be careful of*: Ex 23 21 *SB*, Ps 34
23 *SBF* (Mus 49 180), He 2 1 *SBF*, 1 Tim 1 4 *B*(*S*
ⲭⲓ ⲣⲣⲁⲍ) προσέχ. dat; Ps 36 32 (*B* ⲭ. ⲛⲥⲁ-), Lu 12 27
S(*B* ⲧ ⲡⲓⲁⲧⲍ) κατανο.; Mic 4 9 *A*(*B* ⲥⲱⲟⲩⲛ) γινώσ.;
Pro 2 11 *SA*(*B* ⲁⲣⲉϩ) τηρεῖν, Ps 129 3 *SB*, Z 316 *S*
sat ⲉϥⲧ ⲡϩⲧⲏϥ ⲉⲧⲉϩⲓⲏ = MG 25 231 *B*(var ⲡ-), AP
8 *A²* παρατ.; Ro 16 17 *B*(*S* ϭⲱϣⲧ) σκοπεῖν, Nu 33 52
S ⲡⲉⲧⲟⲩⲧ ⲡϩⲧⲏⲩ ⲉⲣⲟⲟⲩ (var & *B* diff) σκοπιά, 1 Kg
20 18 *S* ἐπισκέπτεσθαι; Deu 32 7 *S*(*B* ⲕⲁⲧ) συνιέναι;
Mk 13 9 *S*(*B* ⲡⲁⲩ) βλ.; Job 35 5 *S*(*B* ⲧ ⲡⲓⲁⲧⲍ) καταμανθάνειν; Lev 13 3 *S*(*B* ⲡ.) ὁρᾶν; Aeg 282 *S* ⲉⲧⲧ
ⲡⲟⲧⲏϥ ⲉⲡϣⲁϫⲉ (var ⲧ ϩ.) φυλάσσειν; PS 80 *S* ⲧ
ϩⲧⲏⲕ ⲉⲣⲟⲓ & save me, ShC 73 2 *S* ⲧ ϩⲧⲏⲕ ⲉⲡⲉⲧⲣⲅⲣⲁⲫⲏ,
ManiP *A²* ⲉⲅⲁ ⲧ ϩⲧⲏⲩ ⲁⲡⲉϥⲥⲁⲓⲉ, C 43 115 *B* magistrate ⲧ ⲡⲣⲟϩⲏϥ ⲉⲡⲓⲣϩⲏⲟⲩⲓ ⲛⲧⲉ ⲡⲟⲩⲣⲟ; vbal: Ps 39
13 *SB* ⲡⲣ. ⲉⲓⲥ: BHom 2 *S* ⲧ ϩⲧⲏ ⲉⲧⲙ̄ϫⲓⲥⲉ βλ.; Deu
6 25 *S*(*B* ⲁⲣⲉϩ) φυλ.; PS 79 *S* ⲧ ϩⲧⲏⲕ ⲉⲧⲣⲉⲕⲛⲟⲩϩⲙ̄
ⲙ̄ⲙⲟⲓ; ⲉϩⲣⲁⲓ ⲉ-: Jos 2 16 *S*(Gk diff); + 2d ⲉ-:
Mt 7 15 *S*(*B* ⲁⲣⲉϩ ⲉ- ⲉⲃⲟⲗ ϩⲁ-) ⲡⲣ. ἀπό, Mk 12 38 *S*
(*B* ⲡⲁⲩ, *F* Mor 46 63 ⲥⲁⲙⲉⲥ ⲉ- ϩⲁⲃⲁⲗ ⲡ-) βλ. ἀπό; Sh
A 1 335 *S* ⲧ ϩⲧⲏⲧⲛ ⲉⲣⲱⲧⲛ ⲉⲣⲟⲟⲩ, DeV 2 49 *B* ⲧ ϩⲟⲏⲓ
…ⲉⲡϩⲣⲱⲟⲩ; vbal: Ex 19 12 *SB* ⲡⲣ. dat gen; + ⲉ-
ⲃⲟⲗ ϩⲁ- *B*, ϩⲛ-, ϩⲓⲧⲛ- *S*: Mt 10 17 *SB*, Lev 22 2 *SB*

ⲡⲣ. ἀπό; Bor 243 148 *S* ⲧ ϩⲧⲏⲧⲛ ⲉⲣⲱⲧⲛ ⲉⲃ. ϩⲓⲧⲛⲡ-
ⲣⲱⲙⲉ; c ⲉⲭⲛ-: Miss 4 744 *S* ⲁϥⲧ ⲡⲉϥϩ. ⲉⲭⲛⲡ-
ⲙⲡⲣⲉϥϫⲓ ⲟⲩⲁ ⲡⲁⲣⲓⲟⲥ; Ge 4 5 *B*(*A* Cl ⲁ-) ⲡⲣ. ἐπί;
MIE 2 404 *B* ⲁⲓ ⲧ ϩⲑⲓ ⲉ. ⲟⲩⲁⲓ ⲡⲡⲓⲥⲧⲩⲗⲟⲥ, TT 57 *S*
ⲧ] ϩⲧⲏⲕ ⲉⲭⲛ[ⲟⲩⲟⲡ] ⲛⲓⲙ in trouble; c ⲛ- dat:
Dan 7 8 *B*(*S* ⲉ-) προσνοεῖν dat; Lu 17 3 *F*(Mor 30 1,
SB ⲇⲟ) προσέχ. dat; Ez 46 18 *B* ⲙⲁⲣⲟⲏϥ ⲡⲕⲗⲏⲣⲟ-
ⲡⲟⲙⲓⲁ κατακληρονομεῖν dat; PS 30 *S* ⲡⲉⲧⲛⲁ ⲧ ϩⲧⲏϥ
ⲡⲁⲩ ϥⲡⲁⲉⲓⲙⲉ; c ϩⲓ- *S*: Mk 6 52 (*B* ⲕⲁⲧ ⲉⲭ.)
συνι. ἐπί; c ⲉϩⲛ- *S*: Jer 12 11 (*B* ⲭⲱ ϩⲉⲡ-) τιθέναι
ἐν; c ⲉϩⲟⲩⲛ *S*: Mor 37 35 ⲁϥ ⲧ ⲙⲡⲉϥϩ. ⲉ. ⲁϥ
ϣⲟⲭⲡⲉ διάνοιαν συνάγειν; as nn m: Sa 6 19 *S*
προσοχή; Lu 17 20 *S*(*B* ⲙⲉⲧⲣⲉϥⲧ ϩⲟⲏϥ) παρατή-
ρησις; BAp 77 *S* ⲥⲱⲧⲙ ϩⲛⲟⲩⲧ ϩⲧⲏϥ, TstAb 159 *B*
sim, Ostr BP 12489 *S* ϩⲁⲣ]ⲉϩ ⲉⲡⲕⲁⲓⲟⲡ … ϩⲛⲟⲩ ⲧ
ϩ.; ⲙⲛⲧ-, ⲙⲉⲧⲁⲧ ⲧ ϩⲧⲏϥ, *heedlessness*: BHom 5
S ⲁⲕⲁⲁⲩ ϩⲛⲟⲩⲙ. ἀπροσεξία; K 100 *B* غَفْلَة; ClPr
25 1 *S* as if ignorant ϩⲛⲟⲩⲙ.; ⲣⲉϥ ⲧ ϩⲧⲏⲍ, *giving mind, attentive*: Pro 22 29 *SA* ὁρατικός; ⲙⲛⲧ-,
ⲙⲉⲧⲣⲉϥ ϩ.: HL 83 *B* ⲧⲙ. ⲉⲣⲟⲡ ἰδιοπραγμοσύνη
(but 84 = ⲙⲉⲧⲁⲧⲉⲙⲓ); Mus 42 217 *S* said through
ⲟⲩⲙ.; ϫⲓⲛⲧ ϩ. *B, observation*: Su 15 (var ⲡϫⲓⲛ
ⲧⲟⲩ ⲧ ⲡϩ.) παρατηρεῖν.

ϣⲡ ϩ. *SA², ϣⲉⲡ ϩ. A²BF, ϣⲁⲛ ϩ. B*(once), ϣⲡ
ϩ. *F*, ϣⲡ ϩⲧⲏⲍ *SAA², ϣⲉⲡ(ⲉ)ϩⲧⲏⲍ S, ϣⲁⲡϩⲧⲏⲍ SA
A²BF, ϣⲁⲡⲉϩⲧⲏⲍ S*(rare)*BF, ϣⲁⲡⲉϩⲧⲏⲍ S, pitiful
of heart* (v ϣⲟⲟⲡⲉ or ? ϣⲱⲡⲉ, cf ManiH 15) ⲁ as vb,
have pity: Ps 36 21 *SB*, Pro 13 9 *SAB* οἰκτείρειν, Ps
111 5 *B*(*S* ⲛⲛ) -μων; Mt 18 27 *S* ϣⲡ- (var ϣⲉⲡⲉ-)
B σπλαγχνίζεσθαι; BMar 157 *S* who seeing them
ⲡⲩⲧⲁⲙϣⲡϩⲧⲏⲩ ? κατανύσσεσθαι; Ac 7 24 *BF*(*S* Gk
diff); Bor 260 *penult S* ⲙⲡⲉⲕϣⲉⲡϩⲧⲏⲕ, DeV 1 37
B ⲉⲟⲣⲉϥϣⲉⲡ ϩⲏⲧ; c ⲉⲭⲛ-: Ps 4 1 *S*(*B* ϩⲁ-), Is
30 18 *SF*(*B* ⲇⲟ), Mic 7 19 *SAB* οἰ.; Mk 6 34 *S*(*B*
ⲇⲟ) σπ. ἐπί; ShC 73 ix *S* ϣⲉⲡ ϩⲧⲏⲕ ⲉ. ⲡⲉⲧⲡⲏⲧ, Bor
284 191 *S* ϣⲁⲡϩⲧⲏϥ ⲉⲭⲱⲡ, ManiP 17 *A²* ϣⲡ ϩⲧⲏⲕ
ⲁⲭⲱⲓ; ⲉϩⲣⲁⲓ, -ⲣⲏⲓ ⲉⲭ-: Mt 14 14 *S*(*BF* ϩⲁ-) σπ.
ἐπί; BG 52 *S* ϣⲡ ϩⲧⲏϥ ⲉⲣ. ⲉ. ⲧⲥⲟⲙ, ShA 1 81 *S*
ⲉⲙⲡⲟⲩϣⲡ ϩⲧⲏⲩ ⲉⲣ. ⲉⲭⲱⲓ ⲏ ϩⲁⲣⲟⲓ, Mani 1 *A²* ϣⲡ
ϩⲧⲏⲕ ⲁϩ. ⲁⲭⲱⲓ, C 43 190 *B* ϣⲁⲡⲁϩⲟⲏⲕ ⲉⲣ. ⲉⲭⲱⲓ; c
ϩⲁ-, ϩⲁ-, ϩⲁ-: Ex 33 19 *SB*, 4 Kg 13 23 *S* ϣⲉⲡⲉ-,
Is 30 18 *B*(*SF* ⲉⲭⲛ-) οἰ., Jer 13 14 *S*(*B* ⲉⲃⲟⲗ ϩⲁ-) οἰ.
ἀπό, MG 25 247 *B* ϣⲉⲡ ϩ. ϩⲁⲡⲁⲓⲣⲱⲙⲓ ⲕⲁⲧⲟⲓ.; ROC
17 406 *B* ⲡⲁⲕⲡⲁϣⲉⲡ ϩ. ϩⲁⲣⲟⲡⲉ ἐλέειν; Bor 170 90
S ⲁϥϣⲉⲡⲉⲣⲧⲏϥ ϩⲁ- φείδεσθαι gen; PS 107 *S* ϣⲡ
ϩⲧⲏⲕ ϩⲁⲣⲟⲓ, ShC 42 191 *S* ϣⲡ ϩⲧⲓ ϩⲁⲣⲟ, ib 198 *S*
ⲛ ⲧ ⲡⲁϣⲁⲡⲁⲣⲧⲛⲓ ⲁⲡ ϩⲁⲡⲉⲩⲧⲁⲕⲟ, BHom 74 *S* ⲉϥϣⲁⲡ-
ⲁⲣⲧⲏϥ ϩⲁ-, Z 330 *S* ϣⲉⲡⲉⲣⲧⲏ ϩⲁⲣⲟⲓ, El 66 *A* ⲁϥϣⲡ
ϩⲧⲏϥ ϩⲁⲣⲱⲧⲡⲉ, MIE 393 *B* ϣⲡ ϩ. ϩⲁⲣⲟⲓ, Mor 24
12 *F* ⲡⲉⲧⲛⲁϣⲁⲡⲁⲣⲧⲏⲕ ϩⲁⲗⲁⲕ; as nn m: Jud 5 30
S ϣⲁⲡ ϩⲧⲏϥ (var ϣⲁⲡⲉ-), Ps 77 38 *S*(*B* ⲣⲉϥϣ.), Jon
4 2 *SA* ⲛⲧⲕ ⲟⲩϣⲁⲡϩⲧⲏϥ (*B* ⲇⲟ), Lu 6 36 *S*(*B* ⲡⲁⲛⲧ)
οἰκτίρμων, Phil 2 1 *B*(*SF* ⲙⲛⲧϣ.) -μός; Cl 54 1 *A*

εὔσπλαγχνος, Ja 5 11 S(B ϣⲁⲛⲑⲙⲁϩⲧ) πολύσπ.; PS
269 S ϧⲉⲛϣⲁⲛϧⲧⲏϥ, ShC 73 49 S ⲛⲡⲉ ⲛϣⲁⲛϧⲧⲏϥ, ib
104 ⲣⲱⲙⲉ ⲛϣⲁⲛϧⲧⲏϥ (var ϣⲉⲛ-), C 99 236 S ⲛϣⲉⲛ-
ϧⲧⲏϥ = C 89 71 B ⲣⲉϥϣ., P 130¹ 89 S ⲉⲓⲱⲧ ⲛϣⲉⲛⲉ-
ϧⲧⲏϥ, AP 35 A² ϧⲉⲛϣⲉⲛϧ., ManiP A² ⲛϣⲁⲛϧⲧⲏϥ, ib
K 147 A² ϫⲓ ϣⲛϧ. ⲉⲧⲃⲉⲡⲉⲥϣⲏⲣⲉ, C 43 190 B ⲛⲑⲟⲕ
ⲟⲩϣⲁⲛϧⲑⲏϥ, DeV 1 95 B ϥϯ...ⲛϣⲁⲛⲁϧⲑⲏϥ, MR
5 33 F ⲛϣⲁⲛϧⲧⲏϥ; ⲁⲧϣⲉⲛϧⲏⲧ B, pitiless: 2 Tim 3 3
(S ⲟⲩⲁϧⲓⲏⲧ) ἄστοργος; ⲙⲛⲧ-, ⲙⲉⲧϣ., pity, mercy:
Ps 24 6 SB, Ro 12 1 SBF, He 10 28 SB(F ⲙⲉⲧⲛⲁⲏⲧ)
οἰκτιρμός; Pro 12 10 SA(B ⲙⲁϩⲧ), Lu 1 78 SB
σπλάγχνον; PS 358 S ⲙ., ShC 73 1 S ⲙ., ib 42 28
S -ϣⲁⲛⲉϧⲧⲏϥ, ShA 1 236 S -ϣⲛϧⲧⲏϥ, BHom 102
S -ϣⲁⲛⲉϧⲧⲏϥ, RNC 48 S -ϣⲛϧⲧⲏϥ, ManiP 28 A²
thou art ⲟⲩⲙ. ⲧⲏⲣⲕ, DeV 2 34 B ⲙ., BSM 63 B
-ϣⲁⲛϧⲑⲏϥ, ib 42 B-ϣⲁⲛⲁϧⲑⲏϥ, Mor 24 15 F-ϣⲁⲛⲁ-
ϧⲧⲏⲃ; ⲣ, ⲟ ⲛϣ. S: PS 201 ⲟ ⲛϣⲁⲛϧⲧⲏϥ ϧⲁⲣⲟⲛ,
ShMIF 23 98 ⲉⲧⲟ ⲛϣⲁⲛϧⲧⲏϥ, Bor 265 88 ⲉⲣ ϣⲛ-
ϧⲧⲏϥϧⲉⲣⲟⲩⲛ ⲉⲣⲟⲟⲩ; ⲣⲉϥϣⲉⲛ ϧ. B, compassionate
person: Ps 108 12 (S ϣⲁⲛϧⲧⲏϥ), Lam 4 10 (S -ϧⲧⲏϥ,
F ⲛⲁⲏⲧ) οἰκτίρμων, Eph 4 32 (S -ϧⲧⲏϥ) εὐσπ.; DeV
2 39 ϧ. ⲉϩⲟⲩⲛ ⲉⲡⲉϥⲡⲗⲁⲥⲙⲁ; ⲙⲉⲧⲗⲉϧϣⲉⲛ ϧ. F:
Ro 12 1 (RylSuppl 1, varr BM 506 ⲙⲉⲧϣ., MR 2 70
ⲙⲉⲧϣⲁⲛϧⲧⲏϥ) οἰκτιρμός.

ϥⲓ ϧ. SA², take, captivate heart, delight: Cant
4 9 (F ⲧⲗⲉ- ⲟⲩⲡⲁϥ) καρδιοῦν; ib 6 4 ἀναπτεροῦν;
Jo 10 24 SA²(B ⲱⲗⲓ ψ.) ψυχὴν αἴρειν; ⲙⲛⲧⲃⲁⲓϧ.:
Mor 28 27 lamb upon throne (Ap 5 6) ⲉⲧⲉⲧⲁⲓⲧⲉ
ⲧⲙ.

V also ⲕⲟⲩⲓ II (adding ManiK 98 A² ⲙⲛⲧⲕ. ⲛϧ.),
ⲕⲁϯ s f (adding Eccl 9 11 F ⲕⲁϩⲏⲧ συνετός), ⲙⲉ love,
ⲙⲕⲁϩ, ⲙⲉⲥⲱⲏⲧ, ⲙⲧⲟⲛ I s f, ⲙⲉⲉⲩⲉ nn, ⲙⲟⲩϣⲧ ⲣⲥ,
ⲡⲁ 1° (ⲡⲁⲏⲧ), ⲡⲛⲃ lord, ⲛϣⲟⲧ (ⲛⲁϣⲧ), ⲡⲁⲕⲉ, ⲡⲱϧⲥ,
ⲡⲱϧ break II, ⲥⲱⲣⲙ I (adding C 41 34 B ⲁϥϣⲱⲡⲓ
ⲉϧⲥ.ⲛϧ.), ⲥⲱⲧⲙ (ⲥⲧⲙⲏⲧ, add A² ManiK 191), ⲥⲱⲱϥ,
ⲧⲱⲕ 1°, ⲧⲁⲕⲟ I, ⲧⲱⲕⲙ s f, ⲧⲱⲙ shut, ⲧⲉⲣ-, ⲧⲱⲧ, ⲧⲁϫⲣⲟ,
ⲟⲩⲱⲗⲥ, ⲟⲩⲱⲙ, ⲟⲩⲣⲟⲧ nn, ⲟⲩⲱϣ desire nn, ⲟⲩⲱϣϥ
s f, ⲟⲩⲓϧⲉ ⲣ ⲥ (-ⲏⲧ), ⲱⲕ be content, ⲱⲟⲩ, ϣⲓ s f, ϣⲗⲁϧ,
ϧⲗⲟϭ (-ⲏⲧ), ϧⲣⲟⲕ ⲣ ⲥ (-ⲏⲧ) ϧⲣⲟϣ, ϫⲓⲥⲉ, ϫⲣⲟ ⲣ ⲥ, ϫⲓⲥⲉ
ⲣ ⲥ, ϭⲃⲃⲉ ⲣ ⲥ, ϭⲓⲛⲉ, ϭⲱⲧⲡ nn.

ϧⲁϧⲧⲛ- SA², ϧⲁ(ϧ)ⲧⲉ- S, ϧⲁϧⲧⲉ- A, ϧⲁⲑⲏ-F, ϧⲁ-
(ϧ)ⲧⲏ﹕ SA²F, ϧ. A, ϧⲁⲑⲏ﹕ F prep, below heart of, so
with, beside (cf ϧⲁⲧⲛ- p 428 b, with which confused,
except in pronom forms): Ge 29 27 (B ⲡⲉⲙ-), Ex 2
3 A(B ϧⲁⲧⲉⲛ-), ib 33 21 (B ϧⲁ-), Nu 11 15 (var ⲛⲁ-
ϧⲣⲛ-, B ⲙⲡⲉⲙⲑⲟ), Deu 32 34 (B ⲛⲧⲉⲛ-), Ps 38 7 (B
ⲉⲃⲟⲗ ϧⲓⲧⲉⲛ-), Pro 2 1 SA(B ϧⲉⲛ-), Jo 4 40 SA²(B
ϧⲁⲧ-), Cl 21 8 A, Z 273 ⲡⲉⲧϧⲁⲧⲏϥ παρά, BHom 41
ⲛⲡⲛⲃ ϧⲁⲧⲏϥ παρεῖναι, Sa 9 10 συμπ. dat, Job 2 13 (B
ϧⲁⲧ-), Ps 5 4 (B ϧⲉⲛ-) παρα- dat; Deu 32 50 (B ϧⲁⲧ-),
Mt 13 56 (B ϧⲁ-, ϧⲁ-, F ϧⲁⲧⲉⲛ-) πρός, Ps 93 20 (B
ⲡⲉⲙ-) συμπρος- dat; Ge 29 14 (B do), Jud 13 9 μετά;
Deu 1 1 (B ⲛϧⲣⲏⲓ ϧⲓ-) ἐν; Mk 3 34 (B ⲙⲡⲉϥⲕⲱϯ)

περί; Lu 1 56 (B ⲡⲉⲙ-) σύν; Lev 6 3 (B ϧⲁⲧ.) ἐχόμενος; Aeg 274 ϧ. ⲡⲉⲑⲩⲥⲓⲁⲥⲧⲏⲣⲓⲟⲛ πλησίον; Z 336
ϧ. ⲑⲁⲗⲁⲥⲥⲁ εἰς ὄχθην; Tri 338 ⲙⲛ ... ⲡⲓⲥⲧⲓⲥ ϧⲁⲧⲏϥ
ⲓⲁ﹕; PS 361 ⲛⲥⲉϧⲁϧⲧⲏϥ ⲁⲡ, ib 37 ⲕⲁⲧⲉⲭⲉ ⲙⲙⲟϥ
ϧⲁⲧⲏϥ, BG 26 ⲟⲩⲛ ⲕⲉⲟⲩⲁ ϧⲁⲧⲏϥ, ShC 73 62 ϧⲁϧⲧⲏⲛ, ib ϧⲁⲧⲏⲛ, ib 42 157 ϧⲁϧⲧⲛⲧⲏⲩⲧⲛ...ϧⲁϧⲧⲉⲧⲏⲩⲧⲛ-
ⲧⲛ...ϧⲁⲧⲉⲧⲏⲩⲧⲛ, CO 137 ϧⲁⲑⲉⲧⲏⲩⲧⲛ, Bodl(P)d 203
ϧⲁϧⲧⲏⲧⲛ, TU 43 6 A ϧⲁϧⲧⲉⲧⲏⲛⲉ, BM 628 F ϧⲁⲑⲏ-
ⲧⲏⲛⲟⲩ, BMis 333 ϭⲛ ⲡⲁⲣⲣⲏⲥⲓⲁ ϧⲁⲧⲏϥ (var ⲛⲡⲁ-
ϧⲣⲁϥ), ib 381 ⲃⲱⲕ ϧ. ⲛϣⲱⲥ = Va 63 11 B ϧⲁⲧⲉⲛ- =
BSM 37 B ϣⲁ-, BHom 50 ⲙⲛ ϧⲙϧⲁⲗ ϧⲁⲧⲏⲥ (var R
2 2 33 ϧⲁϩ.), BAp 120 ⲟⲩⲛ ⲟⲩⲭⲣⲉⲟⲥ ⲉⲣⲟⲓ ϧ. ⲟⲩⲣⲱⲙⲉ, J 56 8 ⲁⲛⲃⲱⲕ ϧ. ϫⲁⲏⲗ, ManiH 59 A² ϧⲙⲉⲥⲧ
ϧⲁⲧⲏϥ, ib K 89 A² ϣⲟⲟⲡ ϧⲁⲧⲏϥ, BM 589 F ⲉⲗ ϧⲱⲃ
ϧⲁⲧⲏⲕ, CMSS 49 F ⲉⲓⲥⲧⲉ (ⲉ)ⲅϧⲁϧⲧⲏⲃ, ib 41 F ⲡⲱⲧ
ϧⲁⲑⲏⲙⲟⲩⲥⲛ, Kr 3 F ⲉⲅϧⲁⲑⲏⲛⲟⲩ; from beside:
1 Kg 6 20 ⲗⲟ ϧⲁϧⲧⲏⲛ ἀπό; BMOr 8811 238 ⲙⲡⲛⲛ-
ⲥⲁⲧⲣⲉⲡⲁⲓ ⲧⲱϧⲛ ϧⲁϧⲧⲏϥ (cf ib ⲧⲱϧⲛ ϧⲁⲧⲏⲥ), BP
8098 we heard ϧⲓⲧⲛ[ⲛⲡⲣⲁⲛ]ⲙⲁⲧⲉⲩⲧⲏⲥ ... ⲉⲅⲏⲏⲩ
ϧⲁⲧⲏⲧⲛ, OLZ '03 67 ⲁϥⲧⲥⲁⲃⲟ (sc pupil) ⲉⲱϣ ⲙⲡⲁⲧ-
ϥⲃⲓⲧϥ ϧⲁⲧⲏϥ (var 68 ϧⲁϧⲧⲏϥ) ere he (his father) took
·him from him (? teacher); cf ? Sa 11 12 ⲉⲅϧⲁⲧⲏϥ ἀπεῖναι opp ⲙⲡⲉϥⲁⲧⲟ ⲉⲃⲟⲗ.

ϧⲏⲧ SSᵃS'F, ϩⲏⲧ, ⲭ. B nn m, north (lit down-
stream on Nile, not bibl, cf ⲙϧⲓⲧ): ST 308 S ⲁⲅⲗⲟ
ⲉⲩϯ ⲥⲟⲩⲟ ⲉⲃⲟⲗ ⲙⲡϧ., J 47 27 S ⲡⲙⲉⲣⲟⲥ ⲉⲧⲙⲡϧ., ib
25 24 S ⲡⲏⲓ ⲙⲡϧ., Kr 36 F ⲟⲩⲉϩⲉ ϩⲣⲁ ϧⲉⲡⲡⲉϧ., J 12
26 S as boundary ⲡϧ. ⲡⲣⲟ ⲡⲁⲩⲑⲉⲛⲧⲏⲥ, KroppF 45
S ϧ. ⲣⲏⲥ ⲡⲉⲓⲛϧⲧ ⲙⲡⲡⲉⲙⲛⲧ.

With preceding preposition. ⲥ ⲉ-, ⲁ-, northward: PS 353 S ⲉⲩⲕⲛⲧ ⲉ., BAp 110 S ⲃⲱⲕ ⲉ. (var
BMOr 7561 ⲉⲡϧ.), BM 346 1 S ⲡϧⲱⲧ ⲉⲣⲏⲥ...ⲥⲑⲏⲣⲉ.,
C 43 225 B ϣϧⲓⲣ ⲉⲣⲏⲥ ... ⲧⲁⲥⲉⲟ ⲉϧ., HM 1 81 S ⲣ
ϧⲱⲧ ⲉ., P 129¹⁴ 122 S ⲉⲓⲛⲏⲩ ⲉ. = DeV 1 76 B from S
to Achmim, AM 63 B ⲁϥⲓ ⲉ. to Alexandria, C 43 133
B ϣϧⲓⲣ ⲉ. sim, ib 227 B ⲥⲱⲕ ⲉ. sim (cf ib 240 ⲥⲱⲕ
ⲉⲣⲏⲥ), PLond 4 518 S ⲉⲩⲥⲏⲕ ⲉ., AZ 16 15 S ⲁⲕⲛⲧⲥ
ⲉ. ⲁⲓⲧⲥⲟⲥ ⲉⲣⲏⲥ, BM 1153 S ⲉⲓ ⲉ. ϧⲙⲙⲁⲣⲏⲥ, Hall 63
S ⲃⲱⲕ ⲉ., J & C 97 Sᵃ ⲡⲛⲟⲩ ⲉ., Ryl 321 S ⲥϧⲁⲓ ⲡⲁⲓ
ⲉ., ib ⲧⲛⲟⲟⲩϥ ⲉ. ST Sᵃ 257 ϫⲟⲟⲩ ... ⲁ., ib 336 sim,
CMSS 41 S' ⲡⲱⲧ ⲉ., BM 1237 B ϧⲱⲗ ⲉϫϧⲛⲧ, Kr 125
S ⲡⲣⲟ ⲛϥⲓⲣ ⲟⲩⲛ ⲉ., Ryl 165 S ⲧϫⲟ ⲛⲡⲁⲛⲉ ⲉ.; without ⲉ-: BM 544 S ⲉⲓ ϧ., ib 1127 S ⲛⲧϥ ⲛⲁⲓ ϧ., Cai
8074 S ⲕⲱ ϧ., PBu 211 S ⲃⲱⲕ ϧ.

ⲛϧ. with preceding ⲉ- S, meaning as last: BP 9419
ⲉⲓ ⲉⲛϧ. ϧⲓⲛϫⲟⲓ, Ep 337 ⲧⲁⲗⲉ ⲛⲡⲉϧ ⲉⲛϧ., ib 401 ϥⲓⲧϥ
ⲉⲛϧ., ib 253 ϫⲟⲟⲩ...ⲉⲛϧ., J 45 32 ⲡⲣⲟⲟⲩⲛ ⲉⲛϧ.; ⲛ̄-
for ⲉⲛ-: ST 48 ⲉⲓ ⲛϧ., ib 215 ϣⲛ ⲛϧ., Ostr olim ER
Ayrton ⲃⲱⲕⲥ ⲛϧ., Ostr olim ER sim: HCons 390 ϣⲁⲡⲧⲉϥ-
ⲕⲱϯ ⲛϧ. ϩⲉⲡⲧⲉⲥϫⲟⲓ...ⲕⲱϯ ⲉⲣⲏⲥ; or ⲁ- S: Sh
Wess 9 121 ϫⲟⲟⲩ ⲙⲫⲟⲡⲉⲩⲥ ⲁⲡϧ., CO 177 ⲉⲓ ⲁⲡϧ.,
Hall 100 ⲃⲱⲕ ⲁⲡϧ. ⲃⲱⲕ ⲉⲣⲏⲥ, J 35 28 ⲡⲉϫⲣⲟ ⲟⲩⲛ
ⲁⲡϧ.; ⲧⲁⲛϧ. S, on north side: J 24 124 (ⲧ)ⲧⲟⲓⲉ ⲧ.

ⲛⲧⲉϩⲉⲗⲣⲁ, *ib* 93 16 ⲛⲧⲟϣ ⲧ.; ⲧⲁϩ. sim: Lant 111 ⲧⲡⲉⲗⲓⲁⲥ ⲧ. ⲛⲧⲡⲟⲗⲓⲥ, Bodl ostr 151 ϫⲟⲟⲩ ⲧ.; ϣⲁⲡϩ. *S*, *as far as north*: ShC 73 120 ϣ. ⲉⲡⲉⲓⲁ, J 46 7 ϫⲓⲛ- ... ϣ. ⲉϫⲱⲥ ⲙⲡⲏⲓ (*cf ib* 45 33); ϩⲁⲡϩ. *S*, *on north*: ShC 73 102 ⲧⲥⲩⲛⲁⲅⲱⲅⲏ ⲉⲧϩ. (var ϩⲁϩ.), ST 131 ⲑⲉⲟⲇⲱⲣⲟⲥ ϩ. (*cf ib* 199 ⲡⲏⲩ ϩⲁⲣⲏⲥ).

ⲥⲁϩ. *S*, *northern side*: P 129[16] 19 ⲟⲩⲕⲟⲧⲥ ⲛⲧⲉ ⲡⲓⲉⲣⲟ ⲥ., Miss 4 719 ⲣⲱⲙⲉ ⲛⲧⲉ ⲥ., Mor 31 5 ⲭⲱⲣⲁ ⲉⲧⲥ. (var Miss 4 771 ⲙⲡⲙϩⲓⲧ); ⲥⲁ ⲡϧ. *B*: HCons 389 ⲉⲣ ⲁⲅⲓⲁⲍⲓⲛ ⲉⲡⲓⲥ.; ⲡⲥⲁϩ. ⲛ- *S*: Kr 104 ϣⲉⲧ[ⲡⲟⲩ]ⲃⲉ ⲡⲥ. ⲛⲃⲁⲃⲩⲗⲱⲛ, WS 93 ⲡ]ⲥ. ⲙⲡⲙⲁ ⲡⲥⲏⲡⲁⲕⲉ (*συνάγειν*); ⲥⲁϧ. ⲛ- *B*: MG 25 230 ⲥ. ⲙⲙⲟϥ = Z 316 *S* ⲙⲡⲉⲥⲏⲧ ⲙ. *παρακάτω*; AM 329 ⲉⲡϥ ⲥ. ⲛϯⲃⲁⲕⲓ, *ib* 200 ⲥ. ⲡⲉⲙⲉⲛⲧ *north-west*; ⲣⲉⲙⲥⲁϧ. *B*: C 43 237 ⲟⲩⲣ. ϧⲉⲛⲡⲑⲟϣ ⲛⲓⲙⲉⲛϣⲟϯ.

In place-names(?): ⲣⲱⲙⲉ ⲁϩ.(ST 222), ϫⲏⲣⲉ (*l* ⲧϫ.) ϩⲉⲛⲁϩⲓⲧ, ⲡⲣⲱⲙⲉ ⲁϩ. (BM 1103), ⲣⲙⲁⲛϩ. (Aegyptus 3 280), ⲣⲱⲙⲏ ⲁⲛϩ. (Hall 97), ⲣⲙⲫ. (PLond 4 511, *cf ib* 185 &c *τόπος Φῆτ*), ⲡⲁⲓⲁⲕ(ⲱⲛ) ⲙⲡⲁϩⲧ (ST 376, *cf Παχητος* Ep 1 115); also ⲡⲁⲡⲟⲩϥ ϧ. (Amélineau *Géog* 250), شبرا خيت in WDelta.

ϩⲏⲧ *SB*, ϩⲧⲏ⸗[1] *SA*[2]*F*(?), ϩⲧⲉ⸗ *S*(once), ϩⲑⲏ⸗[2] *B*, ϩⲏⲧ⸗[3] *SB*, ϩⲉⲧ⸗ *S*(once), pl ϩⲧⲉⲉⲩ *S* nn m, *tip*, *edge*: Ge 47 31 *B*[2], Lev 8 23 *S*[1]*B*[3], Is 28 4 *S*[1](*B* ⲗⲁⲕϩ), He 11 21 *S*[1]*F*(? Mich 550 9)*B*[2] *ἄκρον*, LCyp 1 *S* ⲡϩ. ⲛⲛϣⲏⲛ (var Mor 18 107 ϩ[1]) *ἀκρόδρυα*; P 44 70 *S* ⲁⲕⲣⲟⲇⲁⲕⲧⲩⲗⲟⲓ · ϩⲧⲏⲩ ⲛⲛⲧⲏⲏⲃⲉ اطراف; Ex 28 32 *B*[2], Job 30 18 *B*[2] *περιστόμιον*; Lev 14 14 *S*[1] (var om, *B*=Gk) *λοβός*; 3 Kg 7 15 *S*[1](P 44 111) *ἐξεχόμενος*; 2 Kg 4 12 *S* ϣⲉⲉⲧ ϩⲧⲏⲩ ⲛⲛⲉⲩϭⲓϫ *κολοβοῦν χεῖρας*; P 44 68 *S* ⲉⲗⲓⲝ · ϩⲧⲏⲩ ⲛⲙⲙⲁⲁϫⲉ اط'; BMis 562 *S* from roots ϣⲁϩⲣⲁⲓ ⲉⲡⲉϥϩ. *ad summos ordines*; ShP 130[2] 88 *S* robe covered ϩⲧⲏⲩ ⲛⲣⲁⲧⲥ, R 1 3 71 *S* ϣⲱⲛⲧ ⲉϩⲧⲏⲥ of a robe, LAl 7 *S* ϩⲧⲏⲥ ⲛⲧⲉϥⲡⲟⲣⲫⲩⲣⲁ, BAp 68 *S* ϩⲧⲏϥ ⲛⲛⲉϥⲧⲏⲏⲃⲉ ⲉⲧⲉⲛⲉϥⲉⲓⲉⲓⲃⲉ, AJSL 46 248 *S* ϩⲧⲉϥ ⲙⲡⲉϣⲧⲉ of ship, GPar 2 8 *S* shave ϩⲧⲏⲩ ⲛⲛⲉⲩⲥⲡⲟⲧⲟⲩ, ManiK 188 ϩⲧⲏϥ ⲛⲛⲁⲟⲩⲣⲏⲧⲉ, Mor 15 62 *S* giraffe reaches ⲉⲡϩ. ⲛⲛϣⲏⲛ, C 86 12 *B* demon seized ϩⲑⲏϥ ⲙⲡⲉϥ[ⲗⲁⲥ] & dragged it from mouth, Bodl Copt g 1 *B*(Theot) ϯⲛⲁϣⲉ ⲛⲏⲓ ϩⲓϫⲉⲛⲡϩ. ⲙⲡⲓⲃⲉⲛⲓ (*cf* Cant 7 8), Ryl 62 1 *S* ⲟⲩⲥⲧⲣⲁⲅⲅⲓⲗⲟⲩⲛ ⲉⲧⲉⲡⲁⲓⲛⲉ ϩⲏⲧϥ ⲛⲟⲩⲁⲡⲟⲧ, Ora 4 22 *S* ϩⲏⲧϥ ⲙⲡⲉⲩⲧⲟⲟⲩⲉ, BMar 42 *S* ϩⲉⲧⲟⲩ (of palms) ⲧⲱⲣⲕ ⲉⲛⲉⲩⲉⲣⲏⲩ (*cf* ⲙⲁⲛⲓⲛ); pl: BP 11349 ⲡⲓⲱϩⲉ ... ⲡⲟⲉⲓⲕ ⲉⲧϩⲓϫⲛⲡⲉϥϩ. *reeds along its edges*.

ϩⲓⲉⲓⲧ *SA*, ϩⲉⲓⲉⲓⲧ *S*, ϩⲓⲧ *SA*[2]*B*(once), ϩⲓⲓⲧ *A*[2] nn m, *pit* (*B* mostly ϣⲓⲕ): Ps 7 15, Pro 22 14 *SA*, Eccl 10 8 (*F* ϣⲉ[ⲓ]) *βόθρος*, Is 24 17 *SB*, Mt 12 11 *βόθυνος*; P 44 53 ⲃⲗⲉⲑⲣⲟⲥ (? *βόθρ.*), ⲗⲁⲕⲕⲟⲥ · ⲡⲉϩ. جب ,حفرة; PS 257 ⲡϩ. ⲛⲕⲱϩⲧ, ShZ 595 ⲡϩ. ⲁⲩⲱ ⲡϣⲏⲉⲓ, Mor 53 42 ϩⲉⲛϩ. full of worms = TstAb 42 *B* ϣⲱϯ, BMis 152 ⲡϩⲓⲧ whither devil goeth, TillOster 21 *A* fall into ⲡϩ., ManiK 109 *A*[2] cast into ⲡϩ., *ib* 111 ϣⲁⲙⲧ ⲡϩⲓⲓⲧ. Not to be confused with ϩⲁⲉⲓⲧ.

ϩⲟⲧ (oftenest), ϩⲱⲧ[2], ϩⲟⲧⲉ[3], ϩⲱ.[4] *S*, ϩⲁⲁⲧⲉ *S*[f], ϩⲁⲧⲉ *F* nn m, *presence*(?) + art or poss & ⲉⲃⲟⲗ, *opposite* (*B* ⲙⲑⲟ ⲉⲃ.): Nu 3 4[4] (var ⲙⲡⲉⲙⲧⲟ ⲉⲃ.), *ib* 8 13 ⲙⲡⲉⲙ. ⲉⲃ. ⲛ- ... ⲁⲩⲱ ⲙⲡϩ. ⲉⲃ. ⲛ- *ἔναντι*, Jth 5 21 *ἐναντίον*, Ps 22 5 *SF* (on dalmatic *penes* Th Whittemore) *ἐξ ἐναντίας*, Ez 40 2 ⲙⲡⲉϥϩ. *ἀπέναντι*, Am 4 3[3] *κατέν.*; Lev 16 15, Mor 17 34 ⲙⲡϩ.[3] ⲙⲡⲉⲡϩⲟ *κατὰ πρόσωπον*; 1 Kg 12 16 *S*[f], 4 Kg 14 3[2] *ἐν ὀφθαλμοῖς*; Ez 40 13 *ἐπί*; Miss 8 36 put fear ⲙⲡϩ.[3] ⲛⲛⲉⲡⲓⲥⲕⲟⲡⲟⲥ dat; PS 41 ⲡⲉⲩϥⲧⲟⲟⲩ ⲛⲕⲟⲟϩ ⲙⲡⲡⲉⲩϣⲟⲙⲛⲧ ⲛⲕ. ⲙⲡⲉⲧⲙⲡⲉⲩϩ., RE 9 146 monastery ⲙⲡϩ. ⲙⲡϣⲡϩⲱⲣ, BAp 112 ⲡⲁⲣⲁⲅⲉ ... ⲙⲡϩ.[2] ⲙⲡϩⲟⲓ = PO 22 396 عرب (var على), ViK 9248 154 sitting ⲙⲡϩ.[4] ⲛⲧⲉϥⲙⲁⲁⲩ = Aeg 53 *B* ϧⲁⲧⲉⲛ-.

ϩⲱⲧ *S*, ϩⲟⲧ *SB*(once) nn m, *sack*, *bag*: Jos 9 10, Mk 2 22 (*B* = Gk) *ἀσκός*; Job 32 19 (*B* ϩⲟⲓ ⲛⲛⲓϥⲓ) *φυσητήρ*; Nu 6 15 (var P 44 106 ϩⲟⲧ قفة, *B* = Gk) *κανοῦν*, K 231 *B* ⲡⲓϩ. زق; Pey *Gr* 165 ϩ. ⲉϥⲙⲉϩ ⲡϣⲱ, Z 614 ϩ. ⲛⲛⲟⲩⲃ, BMar 195 ⲟⲩϩ. ⲛⲧⲁϥⲣ ϩⲣⲏⲥⲥⲉ (*ῥήσσειν*).

ϩⲱⲧ *SS*[f]*AA*[2]*B*, ϩⲱⲱⲧ *S* nn with ⲣ, ⲉⲣ, *make sail*, *float*: Lu 8 23 *SB*, BMar 111 *S* *πλεῖν*; Is 33 21 *B*(*SF* ϩⲓⲛⲉ) *ἐλαύνειν*; Pro 24 54 *SA* *ποντοπορεύειν*; Lu 8 22 *S*(*B* ⲥⲱⲕ) *ἀνάγεσθαι*; Ac 27 15 *S*(*B* do) *φέρεσθαι*; ShC 73 174 *S* ⲕⲁ ϫⲟⲓ ⲉⲃⲟⲗ ⲉⲣ ϩ. سفر; C 99 186 *S* ⲁⲩⲣ ϩ. ⲉⲩⲡⲏⲩ ⲉⲣⲏⲥ, Mor 51 34 *S* ⲁⲙⲡⲟⲗⲩⲕⲟⲡⲟⲛ (-*κωπος*) ⲙⲟⲟⲛⲉ ⲁⲛⲁⲕⲏ ⲛⲕⲉⲗⲉⲉⲗⲉ ⲉⲣ ϩ., PSBA 30 131 *S* stone ⲣ ϩ. like ship, Mani 1 *A*[2]]ⲣ ϩ. ⲥⲉϣϭⲏⲣ; tr: Ja 3 4 *S*(var Woide ϩⲱⲱⲧ, *B* ⲥ.) *ἐλ.*

With following preposition. ⲥ ⲉ-, *to*: Jon 1 3 *B*(*SA* ⲥϭⲏⲣ), Ac 27 2 *SB* *πλεῖν εἰς*, Lu 8 26 *B*(*S* ⲥϭ. ⲉϩⲣⲁⲓ) *καταπ. εἰς*; BerlOr 1607 3 95 *S* ship ⲉⲣ ϩ. ⲉⲧⲉⲭⲱⲣⲁ, ManiP *A*[2] ⲛⲧⲛⲣ. ⲁⲡⲕⲁϩ, C 86 344 *B* ship ⲉⲣ. ⲉⲧⲁⲛⲧⲓⲟⲭⲓⲁ, BMar 26 *S* set sail & ⲁⲩⲣ. ⲉⲣⲏⲥ, Z 282 *S* ⲣ. ⲉⲣⲏⲥ ⲉⲑⲉⲃⲁⲉⲓⲥ, C 86 122 *B* sim ⲉⲣⲏⲥ ϧⲉⲛⲫⲓⲁⲣⲟ, ViK 9531 *S* ⲣ ϩⲱⲱⲧ ⲉⲡⲙⲁⲣⲏⲥ (*ib* ⲣ ϩⲱⲧ), Mor 30 7 *S*[f] ⲡⲉϫⲏⲩ ⲉⲣ. ⲉⲣⲏⲥ on sea = BMis 235 *S* ⲥϭⲏⲣ, HM 1 81 *S* on river ⲣ. ⲉϩⲏⲧ (*cf ib* ⲥϭ. ⲉϩⲏⲧ); ⲉⲃⲟⲗ ⲉ-: Ac 27 6 *S*(var & *B* om ⲉⲃ.) *πλ. εἰς*; ⲥ ⲙⲛ-, ⲛⲉⲙ-: Mani 1 *A*[2] ⲣ ϩ. ⲙⲛⲧⲓⲱⲧⲉ ⲛⲧⲏⲩ, AM 328 *B* ⲉⲣ ϩ. ⲛⲉⲙⲁϥ ⲉⲭⲏⲙⲓ; ⲥ ⲛ-: Ac 27 40 *SB* ⲣ ϩ. ⲙⲡⲧⲏⲩ *τῇ πνεούσῃ κατέχειν*; ⲥ ϣⲁ-: Miss 8 195 *S* ⲣ ϩ. ⲉⲣⲏⲥ ϣⲁⲡⲙⲁ, C 43 154 *B* ⲉⲣ ϩ. ϣⲁϯⲁⲡⲉⲙⲣⲱ; ⲥ ϩⲛ-, ϧⲉⲛ-: ClPr 54 45 *S* lake ⲉⲧⲟⲩⲣ ϩ. ⲛϩⲏⲧⲥ *πλώιμος*; Mor 22 57 *S* ⲉⲧⲡⲗⲉⲁ ϩⲛⲑⲁⲗⲁⲥⲥⲁ ... ⲣ ϩ. ϩⲛⲛⲉⲓⲉⲣⲱⲟⲩ, ManiK 125 *A*[2] waters ⲉⲣⲉⲡⲉϫⲏⲩ ⲣ ϩ. ⲛϩⲏⲧⲟⲩ, AM 202 *B* ⲉⲣ ϩ. ϧⲉⲛⲫⲓⲁⲣⲟ; ⲥ ϩⲓⲧⲟⲩⲛ: Miss 8 13 *S* ⲁⲛⲣ ϩ. ϩ. ⲟⲩⲛⲏⲥⲟⲥ.

ⲙⲁ ⲛⲣ ϩ. *S*, *sailing course*: Mus 42 228 (on 1 Tim 1 20) rest sailed with Paul ⲙⲡⲙⲁ. ⲛⲧⲉ ⲧⲙⲉ. ShA 2 49 *S* obstacles ⲉⲧϩⲙⲙⲁⲙⲟⲉⲓⲧ ⲛⲣ ϩ. sim.

ⲝⲓⲡⲉⲣ ϩ. *B* nn m, *sailing, voyage*: Ac 27 10 (*S* om) πλοῦς; MG 25 282.

ϩⲱⲧ, ϩⲟⲧ† *S* vb intr, meaning unknown: CO 133 I departed as bidden ⲁⲥϣⲱⲡⲉ ⲁⲓϫⲱϩⲉ ⲉⲡⲧⲓⲙⲉ ϫⲉⲉⲓϩ.ⲉⲣⲟⲓ, PMich 4939 ⲡⲉⲓⲛⲟϭ ⲛϣⲉ ⲛϣⲟⲡⲧⲉ ⲉϥϩ.†ⲕⲁⲗⲱⲥ (cf? ϩⲱⲧⲉ 1°, ϣⲉ ⲛϩⲱⲧ). Prob not same.

ϩⲱⲧ in ϣⲉ ⲛϩ. *v* ϩⲱⲧⲉ.

ϩⲁⲧⲉ, ϩⲁⲁ. *S*, ϩⲉⲧ† *S*/*A²F*, ϩⲉⲧⲉ, -ⲧⲉ *A²*, ϭⲁⲧ *B*, ϩⲁⲁⲧ⸗ *S*, vb intr, *flow*: Ps 147 7 *B*(*S* ϣⲟϯⲟ), Is 48 21 *B*(*S* ϣ. ⲉⲃⲟⲗ) ῥεῖν, Job 22 16 *B* ἐπιρρ., He 2 1 *S*(*B* ⲣⲓⲕⲓ ⲉⲃⲟⲗ, *F* ⲥⲗⲉϭⲗⲉϭ) παραρρ., cit ShP 131⁴ 92 ϩⲁⲁ. (*v* ⲟⲩⲱⲧϩ ⲉⲃⲟⲗ) & BMar 89 ϩⲁⲁ.; Jos 4 18 *S*, Ez 32 14 *SB* πορεύεσθαι, Is 32 2 *B*(*SF* ⲥⲱⲕ) φέρεσθαι, Ez 47 2 *B* καταφ.; Si 50 8 *S* ἔξοδος; ClPr 54 43 *S* ⲙⲟⲟⲩ ⲉϥϩ. ἐπίκλυσις; K 201 *B* metals ⲉⲧϩⲛⲉ & ⲉⲧϭ. ⸢آبذ⸣, ⸢ٲذابة⸣; ShZ 593 *S* ⲡⲉⲓⲉⲣⲱⲟⲩ...ⲥⲱⲕ, ⲡⲙⲟⲩⲉⲓⲟⲟⲩⲉ ϩ., R 2 64 *S* fountains ϣⲟϯⲟ ⲉϩⲣⲁⲓ like ⲟⲩⲙⲟⲟⲩ ⲉϥϩ., Miss 4 209 *B* ⲓⲁⲣⲱⲟⲩ ⲉⲧϭ., Mor 30 13 *S*/ ⲥⲛⲟϥ ⲉⲧϩ., ViK 9320 182 *S* flax pressed ϣⲁⲛⲧⲉⲡⲉϥⲛⲉϩ ϩⲁⲁⲧ(ⲉ); BAp 87 *S* ⲡⲙⲟⲩ ⲛϩⲁⲁⲧⲉ ⲛ̄ⲙⲙⲟⲩ ⲛⲉⲓⲟⲟⲩⲉ *stream of* (river's) *waters*; tr, *let flow, pour*: Deu 26 9 *B*(*S* ϣ.), Ez 20 6 *B*(*S* do), Joel 3 18 *B*(*SA* ⲧⲁϩⲟ ⲉⲃⲟⲗ) ῥ.; ShA 1 459 *S* ⲟⲩⲙⲁ ⲉϥϩ. ⲙⲡⲙⲟⲟⲩ, MG 25 151 *B* eyes ϭ. ⲛⲣⲁⲡⲉⲣⲙⲱⲟⲩⲓ; refl: Tri 324 *S* waters ⲛⲧⲁⲩϩⲣⲃⲣⲃ ⲁⲩⲱ ⲁⲩϩⲁⲁⲧⲟⲩ ⸢الحارية⸣.

With following preposition. ⲉ ⲁϫⲛ-: ManiH 8 *A²* blood ϩⲉⲧⲉ ⲁϫⲱϥ; ⲉ ⲛ-, *with*: Job 29 6 *S*(*B* ϥⲟⲡⲡⲉⲛ) χεῖν dat; *from*: Cai The 317 *B* fountain ϭ. ⲙⲡⲓⲗⲓⲃⲁⲛⲟⲥ (var TThe 162 ⲉ-, cf Cant 4 15 *S* ϣ. ⲉⲃⲟⲗ ϩⲛ-); ethic dat: Cant 2 11 *F* ⲁϥϭ. ⲡⲉϥ ⲛⲁⲟⲩⲉϥ; ⲉ ϩⲛ-*S*, *in*: BHom 125 water ϩ. ϩⲛⲡⲉⲓⲉⲣⲱⲟⲩ, Bor 256 150 ship ϩ. ϩⲛⲙⲟⲩⲙⲉ of waters; *upon*: Miss 4 753 water ϩⲁⲁ. ϩⲛⲡⲉⲛⲗⲁⲝ; *with*: P 129¹⁴ 127 their backs ϩ. ϩⲛⲡⲉⲥⲛⲟϥ, Mor 31 242 garments ϩ. ϩⲛⲡⲛⲏⲣⲡ; *from B*(? ⲉⲃⲟⲗ ϭ.): C 41 13 tears ϭ. ϩⲉⲛⲡⲉϥϩⲁⲗ: ⲉ ϩⲓϫⲛ-: SHel 85 *S* blood ϩ. ϩ. ⲛⲕⲁϩ.

With following adverb. ⲉ ⲉⲃⲟⲗ: Ps 104 41 *B*(*S* ϣ. ⲉⲃ.) ῥ., P 131² 117 *S* wine drunk ⲛⲁϩ. ⲉⲃ. = Va 58 192 *B* διαρρ., Va 66 301 *B* things temporary & ⲥⲉϭ. ⲉⲃ. ῥευστός; ManiH 56 *A²* tears ϩⲉⲧⲉ ⲁⲃ., Cat 61 *B* food ϭ. ⲉⲃ. ⲟⲩⲟϩ ⲉⲧⲥⲱⲕ ⲉⲡⲓⲙⲁ ⲛϩⲉⲗⲥⲓ; tr: Ez 20 15 *B*(*S* ϣ. ⲉⲃ.) ῥ.; Gu 94 *S* eyes ϩ. ⲉⲃ. ⲙⲙⲟⲟⲩ (var KKS 262 ϩⲟⲧⲉ), C 86 99 *B* streets ϭ. ⲉⲃ. ⲛⲥⲛⲟϥ; ⲉⲃ. ⲉ-: Jos 3 16 *S* καταβαίνειν εἰς; ⲁⲃ. ⲛ-: ManiP *A²* ⲡⲡⲁⲉ ⲉⲧϩ. ⲁⲃ. ⲙⲡⲓⲱⲧ; ⲉⲃ. ϩⲁ-, ϭⲁ-: Ez 47 1 *B* ⲉⲕⲡⲟⲣ. ὑποκάτωθεν; Ora 4 184 *S* oil ϩ. ⲉⲃ. ϩⲁⲡⲉϥⲣⲟⲥ; ⲉⲃ. ϩⲛ-, ϭⲉⲛ-: Jo 7 38 *SA²B* ῥ. ἐκ, ROC 17 400 *B* milk ϭ. ⲉⲃ. ϭⲉⲛⲟⲏ ἐπιρ.; BG 26 *S* fountain ϩ. ⲉⲃ. ϩⲛⲡⲙⲟⲟⲩ ⲉⲧⲟⲛϩ; ⲉⲃ. ϩⲓϫⲛ-: Aeg 255 *S* water ⲥⲱⲕ ⲉϩⲟⲩⲛ or ϩⲁⲁⲧⲉ ⲉⲃ. ϩ. the font, KroppR 15 *S* fountain ϩ. ⲉⲃ. ϩ. ⲧⲁⲡⲉ ⲙⲡⲓⲱⲧ, C 43 80 *B* blood ϭ. ⲉⲃ. ϩ. ⲡⲓ-

ⲕⲁϩⲓ, ib 41 20 *B* blessing ϭ. ⲉϩ. ϩⲓϫⲱⲛ; ⲉ ⲉⲡⲉⲥⲏⲧ: Ez 47 1 *B* καταβαίνειν; BMar 40 *S* honey ⲉϥϩ. ⲉϩ. ϩⲛⲧⲁϣⲟⲩⲱⲃⲉ, BMis 192 *S* rivers ϩ. ⲉ. ⲉⲣⲟⲥ (*sc* sea), Mor 23 39 *S* ⲉⲧϩ. ⲉ. ⲛϩⲉⲛⲁⲅⲁⲑⲟⲛ = ib 24 28 *F*.

—— nn m *SA²B*, *flow, rush of water*: Ez 47 5 *B* (BM 1247, var diff) ῥοῖζος; Sa 7 25 *B*(*S* om) ἀπόρροια *emanatio*; K 103 *B* ⲡⲓϭ. of semen ⸢انزال⸣ (var ⸢قيض⸣); Blake 240 *S* ⲛϩ. ⲙⲡⲓⲉⲣⲟ casts it (*sc* emerald) on shore, ManiK 109 *A²* ⲛⲟⲉϯⲉ ⲉⲧⲛⲁϭⲱ ⲉⲩⲥⲱⲕ ⲁⲡⲓⲧⲛⲉ; ⲉⲗ ϭ. *B*: Va 63 81 ⲟⲩⲓⲁⲣⲟ ⲉⲩⲉⲗ ϭ. ῥεῖν; Is 30 25 (*SF* ⲥⲱⲕ) διαπορ.; ⲉⲣϩ. *B*: Cat 198 ⲡⲛⲧⲛ ⲉⲥⲉⲣϭ.; ⲥⲉⲕ ϭ. *B*: Aeg 26 river c. like sea's waves, C 43 6 water ⲉⲩϭ. at his touch.

ⲙⲁ ⲛϩ. *S*, *water-course, channel*: 4 Kg 2 21 (PMich 607), Ps 1 3 (*B* ϥⲟⲓ) διέξοδος; P 44 53 ⲭⲓⲗⲟⲥ (χεῖ.)· ⲙ. ⸢مجرى⸣; BHom 97 ⲙⲙ. ⲛⲧⲥⲟⲫⲓⲁ (ALR '96 191 ⸢اذهاب⸣), ShC 42 49 ⲡⲉⲕⲣⲱⲟⲩ ⲛⲙⲙⲁ ⲛϩⲁⲁ., P 131¹ 74 Jordan ⲉϥ(ⲥ)ⲕⲣⲕⲣ ϩⲛⲡⲉϥϩ. (PO 22 290 ´ⲁ), ib ⲙⲙ. ⲉⲧⲟ ⲛϭⲟⲉⲓⲙ, R 1 2 28 whom Father revealed ϩⲛⲙⲙ. of Jordan, Mor 31 123 when he drank water ⲛϥⲧⲁϩⲉ ⲙⲙ. ⲉⲃⲟⲗ & *it reached outflow* pain was great.

V Dévaud *Études* 37.

ϩⲁⲧⲉ *A*, El 74 prob = ϩⲟⲧⲉ *hour*.

ϩⲁⲧⲉ *A* *v* ϩⲟⲧⲉ 2°.

ϩⲁ(ⲁ)ⲧⲉ *v* ϩⲁⲧ 1° & ϩⲟⲧ.

ϩⲁϯ *F* *v* ϩⲟⲧⲉ 1°.

ϩⲏ(ⲏ)ⲧⲉ *SA*, ϩⲉⲓⲧⲉ, ϩⲉⲧ, ϩⲉⲓⲧⲥ *F* *v* ⲉⲓⲥ (adding AZ 21 100 *O* ⲛⲧⲉ).

ϩⲓⲧⲉ *SA²F*, ϩ. *A*, ϭⲓϯ, ϩⲓϯ (rare) *B*, ϩⲉⲧ- *S*, ϭⲁⲧ- *B*, ϩⲁⲧ⸗ *S*, ϩⲉⲧ⸗ *A*, ϩⲉⲧ⸗ *A²*, ϭⲁⲧ⸗ *B*, ϩⲓⲧ⸗ *B* (prob confusion with forms of ϩⲓ 1°) vb, a mostly tr, *move to & fro, rub, whet*: JTS 9 379 *S* ϩ. ⲙⲡⲉϥⲥⲱⲙⲁ ϩⲛⲣⲉⲛⲡⲟϭⲉ ⲛϭⲟⲟⲩⲛⲉ, C 86 205 *B* sim, ib 83 *B* ϭ. ⲙⲙⲟⲟⲩ (borers) ⲛϭⲏⲧⲟⲩ (ears, cf ϩⲱⲧⲉ 1°), C 43 218 sim ϩⲓϯ ⲙⲙⲟⲟⲩ, AM 59 *B* ϭ. ⲙⲙⲟⲟⲩ (swine's fat) ⲉⲡⲉϥⲥⲱⲙⲁ, BMar 41 *S* bade ϩ. ⲙⲡⲉϥⲥⲱⲙⲁ, Mor 41 342 *S* iron tool in martyr's eye ⲁϥⲧⲣⲉⲩϩ. ⲛⲥⲱϥ (cf ϩⲱⲧⲉ P 129¹⁶), Miss 4 751 blessed sand & water ⲉϥϩ. ⲛⲙⲙⲁϥ *rubbed (self) therewith* till healed, Va 61 200 *B* ϯ ⲥⲏϥⲓ ⲁϥϭⲁⲧⲉ, ib 211 *B* ⲁⲓϭⲁⲧⲉ ⲉⲣⲟϥ (*sc* ram, Ge 22 13).

b intr, *be worn with age, old*: Deu 29 5 *S*(*B* ⲉⲣ ⲁⲡⲁⲥ), Job 13 28 *S*(*B* do) παλαιοῦν; Mor 37 143 *S* teeth ϩ. through age τρίβειν, Pro 5 11 *SAB* κατατρ.; Jos 9 10 *S* καταρρηγνύναι; C 99 92 *S* ⲡⲛⲏϣ ⲉⲁϩ. = Va ar 172 95 ⸢خلق⸣, MIE 2 337 *B* when aged ⲛⲉⲡⲕⲁⲥ ϭ. = PO 22 354 ⸢فصل⸣; ShP 130³ 3 *S* shall wear raiment ϣⲁⲛⲧⲟⲩϩ., Mor 33 11 *S* Virgin's robe did not ϩ. (var BMis 77 ⲡⲱϣ), EW 160 *B* garments ϭ. ⲁⲩⲉⲣ ⲫⲉⲗϫⲓ; tr, *wear out*: Job 9 5 *S*(*B* ⲉⲣ ⲁⲡⲁⲥ) παλ.; Si 6 37 *S* ϩⲉⲧ-

ἐκτρ.;   with prep or advb : P 129¹³ 37 *S* ⲡⲉⲡⲣⲏϣ
ⲡⲧⲁϥⲣ. ⲡⲧⲟⲟⲧϥ; Deu 8 4 *SB* ϩⲓ- ⲡⲁⲗ. ἀπό; JA '05
1 431 *S* ⲡⲉⲥⲥⲁⲣϩ ϩ. ϩⲙ̅ⲡⲟϩⲉ, P 131⁴ 130 *S* sim ϩⲓⲧⲡ-;
Job 30 13 *B* ⲉⲃⲟⲗ ἐκτρ., Va 58 156 *B* feet of money-
lovers ⲥ̄. ⲡⲡⲓϫⲓⲕⲁⲥⲧⲏⲣⲓⲟⲛ ⲉⲃ. ⲕⲁⲧⲁⲧⲣ.; Is 41 15 *S*
ⲉⲃ. (*B* ⲧⲱⲙⲟ) λεπτύνειν, ManiH 39 *A²* ⲡⲥⲁⲣϫ ⲡⲁⲣ.
ⲁⲃ.;   *spend time, loiter S* : ShA 2 232 ⲉⲧⲣⲉϩ. at
church time, ShMiss 4 280 who are careless in refectory ⲉⲩϩ.,ShViK 976ʹ96 ⲉⲩϩ. ϣⲁⲡⲧⲟⲩⲣ ⲡⲉⲟⲟⲩ
ⲧⲏⲣϥ ⲉⲭⲡⲉⲛⲉⲗⲁⲭⲓⲥⲧⲟⲛ ⲛⲣⲱϩ, ShC 73 92 one toil-
eth all day ⲛⲉⲟⲩⲁ ϫⲉ ⲉⲩϩ.,*ib*158 let none ϩ.ϩⲙⲡⲣⲟⲟⲩ-
ⲧⲛ; tr : ShA 2 29 ⲥⲉϩ. ⲙⲡⲉⲟⲩⲟⲉⲓϣ,ManiP 82*A²*sim.

c intr, *be convulsed, tormented* : Mt 15 22 *S*(*B* as
Gk) δαιμον-ίζεσθαι, P 43 50 *S* ⲟ ⲛⲇⲁⲓⲙⲟⲛⲓⲟⲛ ⸱ (ⲇⲁⲓ-
ⲙⲟⲛⲓ)ϫⲱⲙⲉⲡⲟⲥ ⸱ ⲡⲉϩ. مصروع; Mt 4 24 *S*(*B* ⲟⲓ
ⲙⲡⲉⲣⲙⲟ) σεληνιάζεσθαι; Mk 9 20 *S*(*B* ⲥⲱⲟⲩⲧⲉⲣ)
κυλίεσθαι; Va 57 165 *B* ⲡ ⲟⲩϫⲓϫ ⲥ̄. χειραλγία; R 1
4 39 *S* ⲁⲡϣⲏⲣⲉ ... ϩ. ϩⲓⲧⲛ ⲟⲩⲇⲁⲓⲙⲟⲛⲓⲟⲛ *arreptus* ;
Bor 288 40 *S* may bones ⲡⲧⲁ ϩ. ⲙⲟⲩⲣ ϩⲣⲟⲩⲛ ⲉⲡⲉⲩⲉⲣⲏⲩ, C 43 85 *B* among maladies ⲟⲩⲁⲓ ⲉϥϩ̄., Miss
4 102 *B* eye ⲉⲧϩ. = Mor 18 7 *S* ⲧⲓ ⲧⲕⲁⲥ;   tr : Lu
9 39 *S*(*B* ⲣⲱϣⲧ ⲉϩⲣⲏⲓ) σπαράσσειν; He 11 35 *S*(*B*
ⲟⲩⲟϣⲟⲩⲉϣ) τυμπανίζειν; MG 25 362 *B* demon ⲥ̄.
ⲙⲙⲟⲥ (ROC 18 124 ܠܡܐ ܘܠܡ), C 99 132 *S*
sim = C 89 15 *B* = Va ar 172 10 روح مصر, ShMIF 23 68
S God ϩ. ⲡⲓⲣⲱⲙⲉ that sin thus, ShRE 10 161 *S*
among tortures ⲁⲩⲅⲁⲧⲟⲩ, ShZ 596 sim, Mor 40 49
S threw him to ground ⲁϥϩ. ⲙⲙⲟϥ = MG 25 275 *B*,
Mor 30 59 *F* ⲟⲩϫⲉⲙⲱⲛ ϩ. ⲙⲙⲁⲥ;   **c** ϩⲓϫⲛ- : BMis
280 *S* ϩ. ⲙⲙⲟϥ ϩ. ⲡⲕⲁϩ;   **c** ϩⲓⲡⲉⲥⲛⲧ : Mk 9 26 *S*
(var ⲣⲱϩⲧ ⲉⲡⲕⲁϩ, *B* ϣⲟⲟⲣⲧⲉⲣ)σπαρ.;   as nn m,
spasm, pain : HL 89 *B* ϩⲁⲡϣⲱⲛⲓ...ϩⲁⲡⲥ̄. ὀδυνᾶν; C
86 336 *B* ⲡⲁⲓⲥ̄. (sc gout), BHom 138 *S* hair ⲡⲣⲉⲥ-
ⲣⲁⲥⲧ ϩⲁⲡⲣ., Va 58 192 *B* after drinking ⲟⲩⲥ̄. ⲥ̄ⲉⲡ-
ⲧⲉⲕⲁⲃⲉ, Miss 4 101 *B* ⲟⲩⲛⲓϣϯ ⲡϩ. ⲟⲩⲱⲙ ⲡⲱϣ (sc
eye) = Mor 18 6 *S* ϯ ⲧⲕⲁⲥ (cf PEbers *ḥꜣtï*, Dévaud).

d tr, *flay* : Lev 1 6 *B*(*S* om), Mic 2 8 *SAB*(Lacr,
var ⲣⲱϣⲧ) ἐκδέρειν; ShA 1 240 *S* ⲡⲉⲩϣⲁⲁⲣ ⲁⲩⲅⲁⲧⲟⲩ, P 129¹¹ 96 *S* Mani's death ⲁⲩϩⲉⲧ ⲡⲉⲩϣⲁⲁⲣ (*v*
PSBA 24 77), HM 1 161 *S* ϯⲡⲁϩ ⲡⲡⲉⲧⲛϣⲁⲁⲣ ⲧⲁⲉⲛ-
ⲧⲟⲩ ⲉⲃⲟⲗ ϩⲡⲡⲉⲧⲛⲥⲱⲙⲁ, *ib* ⲧⲁⲧⲁⲗⲟⲟⲩ ⲉϫⲡⲡⲉⲧⲛⲥ.,
ManiK 51 *A*]ϩⲁⲧⲃⲟⲩ ⲁϩⲉⲧⲟⲩ ⲙⲡⲟⲩϣⲁⲣⲉ, C 43 138
B ϩⲁⲧ ⲡⲉϣⲁⲣ, BM 912 *B* ϩⲓϯ ⲙⲡⲟⲩϣ., DeV 2 221
B ⲁⲩϣⲁⲡⲥⲁⲧ ⲡⲉϣϣⲉ *if its* (tree's) *wood peeled* ;   **c**
ϩⲓ- *S* : P 129¹⁸ 90 ⲁⲩϩ. ⲙⲡⲉϥϣⲁⲁⲣ ϩⲓⲱⲱϥ. Gu 7 sim.

ⲁⲧϩ., -ⲥ̄.,*unworn,untormented* : R 1 5 49 *S* despite
tortures ⲟⲩⲥⲁⲣϫ ⲛⲁ. ⲧⲉⲧⲧⲟ ϩⲓⲱⲱϥ (var Mor 32 22
ⲁⲧϩⲓⲥⲉ), P 131⁶ 7 *S* ϩⲃⲥⲱ ⲛⲁ., Cat 104 *B* ⲥⲱⲙⲁ ⲡⲁ-
ⲑⲟⲙⲟⲩ ⲛⲁ. ⲡⲁⲧⲃⲱⲗ ⲉⲃⲟⲗ.

ⲙⲛⲧⲣⲉϥϩ. *S, convulsion* : Leyd 448 ⲙⲛⲧⲣⲉϥϣⲗϥ
ⲙ., ⲙⲛⲧⲉⲙⲛⲟ & other maladies, ShA 2 29 ⲟⲩⲙⲛⲧⲁ-
ⲙⲉⲗⲏⲥ ⲟⲩⲙ. ⲙⲡⲟⲩⲟⲉⲓϣ *wasting of time.*

Cf ϩⲓ 1°, ϩⲱⲧⲉ & ? (ϭⲱⲧ).

ϩⲟ(ⲉ)ⲓⲧⲉ *S*, ϩⲁ(ⲉ)ⲓⲧⲉ *A*, ϩⲁⲉⲓⲧⲉ *A²*, ϩⲁⲓⲧⲓ *S^f F*,
ϩⲓⲧ- *S* (once) nn m f, *garment*   m : Ps 108 19 (var
ϩⲃⲥⲱ, *B* ϩⲃⲟⲥ), Job 13 28 (*B* do), Mt 14 36 *F*(*S* pl,
B do), Ap 19 16 (*B* do) ἱμάτιον, Ru 3 3 -τισμός; Lu
6 29 (*B* do) χιτών; Lev 19 28 ϩ. ⲉϥⲡⲏϩ (*B* diff) ἐντομίς; BMis 316 ⲡϩ. ⲉⲧⲣⲟⲃⲥ ⲉϫⲱϥ, CA 89 ⲟⲩϩ.
ⲉⲡⲁϣⲉ ⲥⲟⲩⲛⲧϥ, Vict & AlbMusT 162-1928 *F* ⲧⲉⲕ-
ϩⲉⲙϩⲁⲗ ... ⲉⲧⲁⲥϫⲉⲧ ⲡⲓϩ.; Bodl(P)a 1 *b* ⲡϩ.;   f:
Pro 27 13 *A*(*S* ϣⲧⲏⲛ), Hag 2 13 *A*(*S* do, *B* ϩ.), Jo
19 23 *A²*(*SB* ϣ.), BHom 4 ἱμάτιον; Zech 8 23 *A* ⲧⲁⲡ
ⲡⲧϩ. (*B* ϣⲧⲁϯ ⲛⲣϩ.) κράσπεδον; Cant 5 3 (ShIF 143,
var ϣ.) χ.; EstD 4 ἔνδυσις; ShC 73 157 ⲑ. ⲡϣⲟⲩ-
ⲡⲁⲣϭ, CO 465 ⲧϩ. of wife ⲙⲡⲉⲥϩⲱⲡⲛ, R 1 3 32
ⲟⲩϩ. ⲉⲥⲥⲁϣⲧ, Ryl 217 ⲟⲩϩ. ⲁⲥⲉⲓ ⲉⲧⲟⲟⲧ, ⲟⲩⲡⲁⲗⲗⲓⲛ,
ⲟⲩⲡⲉⲛⲧⲉⲡⲧⲏⲥ (? ἐπενδύ.), AZ 16 15, Ep 533; ShA 2
349 ⲣⲉⲩⲣ ϩⲱⲃ ϩ., Sh(Besa)Z 504 ϩ., ⲡⲣⲏϣ, ⲕⲗⲁϥⲧ,
BM 239 5 ⲟⲩϣ. ⲙⲡⲟⲩϩ. (cf Jo 19 23);   as pl : Ex
19 10 (*B* ϩⲃ.), Ps 44 8 (*B* do), Am 2 8 *A*(*B* do), Z 334
ἱμάτιον, Mk 5 15 (*B* do) -τίζεσθαι; Lev 8 13 (*B* ϣ.),
Is 36 22 *SF*(*B* ϩⲃ.) χ.; Pro 29 40 *SA* ἔνδ., 2 Kg 13-
18 ⲛⲣ. ⲉⲧϩⲓⲃⲟⲗ ἐπενδύτης; Deu 22 12 (*B* ⲉⲣϣⲱⲛ)
περιβόλαιον; 2 Kg 10 4 μανδύας; Br 259 ⲡⲉⲓϩ., ϣⲧⲏⲛ,
ⲣϣⲱⲛ, ShA 1 108 ϩⲉⲛϩ. ⲛ ϩⲉⲛϩⲃⲟⲟⲥ, *ib* 156 ⲡⲁⲡⲉ
ⲡⲓϩ.,OratCyp 101 *S^f* ⲉⲣⲉⲡⲉⲥϩ. ⲉⲣ ⲕⲱϩⲧ,Mor 28 199
ϩⲉⲛϩ. ⲉⲩⲣⲁϩⲉ;   various sorts : Jer 4 30 ϩ. ⲡⲕⲟⲕ-
ⲕⲟⲥ (*B* ⲟⲩⲕⲟⲕ.) κόκκινος, MR 4 141 *F* ⲡⲕⲱϩⲛⲥ; *ib*
F ⲡⲕⲁⲗⲗⲁⲡⲓ (-αίνος); Ez 16 10 ⲛⲁϭⲉⲓⲛⲁⲅⲁⲡ (*B* ϩⲃ.)
ποικίλος; Nu 4 7 ⲡⲭⲏϭⲉ ⲧⲏⲣϥ (*B* do) ὁλοπόρφυρος;
Mor 31 98 ⲛⲣⲟⲗⲟⲥⲩⲣⲓⲕⲟⲛ; C 99 235 ⲛϥⲱ = C 89 70
B do τρίχινος; ShMIF 23 34 ϩ. ⲡⲕⲣⲙⲧⲥ, CO 100 *S^a*
ⲕⲁⲙⲛ, Ostr *penes* Crum ⲥⲡⲧⲉ ⲡϩ. ⲛⲣⲃⲟⲥ, Bodl(P)a
1 *b* ⲡⲁⲗⲁϥ, ViK 76 *F* ⲡⲁⲣⲉⲩ, BP 4977 ⲉϥϫⲓ ϫⲉⲣⲓⲥ
(χει.), *ib* ⲛⲥⲁϫⲱ, R 1 3 37 ⲉⲅⲧⲟⲥⲥ ⲡⲡⲟⲩϩ ϩⲓⲏⲛⲥ, C
O 459 ⲙⲙⲟⲡⲁⲭⲟⲥ, *ib* ⲡϣⲏⲣⲉ ϣⲏⲙ;   † ϩ. ⲉϫⲡ-,
clothe : J 90 9 (cf 87 25 ⲡⲉϫ ϩⲃⲥⲱ);   ϩⲓⲧϣⲱⲙⲉ
S : Ez 16 13 (*B* ϩⲃ. ⲡϣⲱⲙ) τρίχαπτος (*ib* 10 = ϩ.
ⲡϣⲱⲙⲉ).   On gender cf AZ 56 99, 59 162.

ϩⲟ(ⲉ)ⲓⲧⲉ *S*, ϩⲁⲓ. *S^a*, ϩⲱⲓϯ *B*, ϩⲉⲓϯ *F* nn f, *hyena* :
Si 13 20 *S*, Jer 12 9 *SB*, MG 25 6 *B* ⲟⲩⲛⲓϣϯ ⲡϩ.
ⲉⲥⲥⲟⲭⲓ ὕαινα; K 164 *B* ϯϩ. ضبع; BG 42 *S* ϥⲟ ⲡϩ.,
R 1 2 57 *S* ⲑ. is bisexual, CO 469 *S^a* ⲧϩ. ⲟⲩϣⲁⲃⲉ
ⲫⲉⲥⲛⲥ (φύσις), BM 528 *F* beside picture of animal
ⲟⲩϩ., PMéd 281 *S* ϩⲁⲥ ⲡϩ.

ϩⲟⲧⲉ *S*, ϩⲁ. *S^f A*(onlyTillOster)*A²*, ϩⲁϯⲉ *A²*(AP),
ϩⲟϯ *B*, ϩⲁϯ *F* nn f, *fear* : Ge 15 12 *SB*, Is 33 3 *SBF*,
Mt 14 26 *SBF*, Jo 19 38 *SA²B* φόβος, Ps 46 2 *S*(*B*
ⲟⲓ ⲡϩ.), He 10 31 *S*(*B* ⲉⲣ ϩ.) φοβερός, Ac 22 9 *S* ϣⲱⲡⲉ
ϩⲛⲟⲩϩ. (*B* om) ἔμφοβος γίνεσθαι, Is 19 17 *SB* φόβηθρον, Sa 17 4 *S* ⲁⲭⲓⲛ., 1 Cor 16 10 *SB* do ἀφόβως;
Ps 54 4 *SB*, 2 Tim 1 7 *B*(*S* ⲙⲛⲧϭⲱⲃ) δειλία; Ez 7 18
SB θάμβος; He 5 7 *SBF*(*S^a* ϩⲣⲧⲉ) εὐλάβεια; Nu 13
33 *S*(*B* diff) ἔκστασις; PS 5 *S* ϣⲱⲡⲉ ϩⲛⲟⲩⲛⲟϭ ⲡϩ.,

ib 80 *S* ⲁⲩⲥⲃⲟⲕ ϩⲓⲧⲛ ϩ., ShC 73 14 *S* ⲟⲩϩ.ⲡⲉ ⲡⲁⲩ ⲉⲣⲟⲥ, Bor 260 120 *S*ᶠ Zebulon means ϩⲡ. ⲏ ⲡϣⲟⲣϣⲣ ⲡⲧⲉⲩϣⲏ, TillOster 12 *A* ϩⲡⲟ. ⲛⲡⲭ̅ⲥ̅, *ib* 13 *A* ⲟⲩϩ. ⲧⲏⲡⲛ̄, DeV 2 86 *B* ⲟⲩϩ. ⲭⲏ ϩⲓⲭⲉⲛⲡⲓⲁⲉⲙⲱⲛ, BSM 50 *B* awaited him ϩⲉⲡⲟⲩϩ.;   as pl: 2 Cor 7 5 *SB* φόβος, Ps 65 3 *SB*, Z 321 *S* God's works ϩⲡ. ⲡⲉ -ⲉⲣⲟ́ⲥ, Ps 87 16 *SB* -ⲉⲣⲓⲥⲙⲟⲥ; Sa 17 8 *S* δεῖμα; PS 70 *S* ϩⲡ. ⲉⲡⲧⲁⲕⲧⲟⲙϣⲟⲩ ⲉⲣⲟⲓ;   as adj: Is 11 3 *SB* φό.; C 99 148 *S* ϣⲁϫⲉ ϩⲡ. = C 89 74 *B*, *ib* 41 79 *B* ⲥⲙⲟⲧ ϩⲡ., Mor 24 24 *F* ⲙⲟⲩ ϩⲡ.

ⲁⲧϩ., *without fear*: RNC 72 *S* Jesus ⲡⲓⲁ., Sh(?) Mor 54 21 *S* ⲣⲱⲙⲉ ⲡⲓⲙ ⲡⲁ.;   ⲙⲛⲧ-, ⲙⲉⲧⲁⲧϩ., *fearlessness, impudence*: Z 361 *S* ⲧⲙ. ἄφοβος, Pro 15 16 *S*(*A* -ϩⲛⲱϩⲉ), Bor 235 117 *S* open not mouth when laughing ⲟⲩⲙ. ⲧⲁⲣⲧⲉ ἀφοβία; ShC 73 130 *S* to lift head when prostrating ⲟⲩⲛⲟⲥⲧⲉ ⲙⲙ., Mus 30 14 *S* ⲧⲙ. of youth, AM 120 *B* boldness & ⲙ.;   ⲣ ⲁⲧϩ.: BM 247 7 *S* in husband's absence ϣⲁⲥⲉⲣ ⲁ. ἄφοβος γίνεσθαι.

ϩⲁϩ. *S*, *under, in fear, fearful* (cf p 632 b): Bor 226 167 ⲉϥⲛⲁϣⲱ ⲉϩ. ὑπὸ φόβου, BHom 27 ⲉⲛϣⲱⲡⲉ ⲉⲛϩ. ἐναγώνιος; Bor 260 121 sword & spear ⲉⲧϩ. (var *ib* 261 188 ⲙⲉϩ ϩⲡ.), BM 260 ⲡⲣⲁⲡ ⲉⲧϩ., J 65 14 ⲛⲓⲁⲡⲁⲩϣ ⲉⲧϩ.

ⲣ, ⲉⲣ ϩ. *SA²BF, be afraid*: Ge 3 10 *SB*, Jer 26 27 *BF*(Mus 49 173), Jo 6 19 *SA²B*, Ro 11 20 *SBF* φοβεῖν; Job 13 25 *SB* εὐλαβεῖσθαι; *ib* 41 1 *SB* δείδειν; Mt 8 26 *S*(*B* ϣⲟⲗϩ ⲡϩⲏⲧ) δειλὸς εἶναι; PS 8 *S* ⲁⲩⲣ. ⲉⲙⲁⲧⲉ, AP 37 *A²* ⲁⲩⲣ. ⲁⲩⲡⲱⲧ, Mun 149 *S* ⲉⲓⲣ. ϫⲉⲙⲉⲓⲉⲓⲉϩⲣⲁⲓ, BSM 41 *B* ⲁⲩϩⲉⲣ. = BMis 386 *S* ϣⲧⲟⲣⲧⲣ, BKU 1 26 (81 16 *b*) *F* ⲙⲉϩⲉⲣ.;   qual: Deu 8 15 *SB*, Ps 88 8 *B*(*S* ϩ. nn), He 10 27 *BF*(Mus 49 203, *S* do) φοβερός, *ib* 12 21 *SB* ἔκφοβος; Va 57 8 φρικτός; PS 239 *S* ⲟ ⲡϩ. ϩⲏⲧϥ ⲙ-, ShViK 9040 182 *S* ⲉⲧⲟ ⲡϩ. ϫⲉⲙⲛⲡⲟⲧⲉ;   ⲥ ⲉ-: Mt 1 20 *SB*, Z 294 *S* ⲡⲉϥⲣ. ⲉϩⲱⲕ φ. inf, Ps 90 5 *S*(*B* ⲉⲃⲟⲗ ϩⲁ-) φ. ἀπό; PS 87 *S* ⲁⲩⲣ. ⲉⲃⲟϩⲉⲓ ⲉⲣⲟⲓ, C 99 150 *S* ⲁⲛⲣ. ⲉⲧⲁⲗⲟϥ = C 89 87 *B* ⲛⲧⲁⲗⲟϥ;   ⲥ ⲉϫⲛ-: PS 130 *S* when they beheld ⲁⲩⲣ. ⲉ. ⲡⲉϥⲉⲣⲏⲩ;   ⲥ ⲉⲧⲃⲉ-: Is 19 17 *SB* φ. διά; Va 57 15 *B* ⲡⲉⲧⲟⲩⲉⲣ. ⲉⲟⲃⲏⲧϥ δεί. ἀπό; PS 7 *S* ⲣ. ⲉ.ⲛⲛⲟϭ ⲛⲕⲓⲙⲧⲟ;   ⲥ ⲡ-: Ann 22 271 *S* ⲛⲥⲉⲟ ⲡϩ. ⲁⲡ ⲡⲧⲛⲟϭ ⲙⲙⲛⲧϫⲓ ⲟⲩⲁ; vbal: Nu 12 8 *S*(*B* ⲉ-) φ. inf; C 89 183 *B* ⲉⲣ. ⲛϣⲱⲓⲧ ⲉϩⲟⲩⲛ; ⲥ ⲡⲁϩⲣⲉⲛ-*B*: C 43 49 ⲁⲓⲉⲣ. ⲛⲁϩⲣⲁϥ, DeV 2 38 ⲧⲉⲩⲕⲱⲏ (εἰκ.) ⲟⲓ ⲛϩ. ⲛⲁϩⲣⲁϥ;   ⲥ ϩⲁϩⲉⲛ-*B*: Va 57 132 ⲥⲉⲙⲡϣⲁ ⲁⲛ ⲉⲉⲣ. ϩⲁⲭⲱⲟⲩ φ. acc; AM 28 ⲉⲣ. ϩⲁϫⲱⲓ;   ⲥ ⲉⲃⲟⲗ ϩⲁ-*B*: Ps 90 supra, Jer 1 8 φ. ἀπό;   ⲥ ϩⲁⲑⲏ, ϩⲁⲧϩⲏ ⲛ-: Is 51 7 *B*(*S* ϩⲏⲧ⸗ ⲛ-), EpJer 68 *BF* φ. acc; 1 Kg 18 12 *S* φ. ἀπό; Jer 15 17 *SB* εὐλ. ἀπό, Job 6 16 *B*(*S* ϩⲏⲧ⸗ ⲛ-) διευλ. acc; PO 11 321 *B* ⲉⲣ. ϩⲁⲧϩⲏ ⲙⲫϯ;   ⲥ ⲉⲃⲟⲗ ϩⲛ-, ϩⲉⲛ-: Job 19 29 *S*(*B* ϩⲁⲧϩⲏ ⲛ-) εὐλ. ἀπό; Ez 36 31 *B* προσοχθίζειν ἐν; ⲥ ϩⲏⲧ⸗ ⲛ-(*B* ϩⲁⲧϩⲏ ⲛ-): Ge 32 11, Ps 26 1, Pro 3 7 (*A*

ⲣ ϩⲛⲱϩⲉ), Eccl 5 6 (*F* ⲁⲟⲏ), Jo 9 22 *SA²*, AP 7 *A²* φ. acc, Ps 3 6 φ. ἀπό; Job 3 19 δεί. acc; Is 57 11 (var ⲧⲣⲣⲉ, *B* ϭⲱⲧⲡ) εὐλ.; Ps 32 8 *B*(*S* ⲥⲧⲱⲧ ϩⲏⲧ⸗) σαλεύεσθαι ἀπό; PS 64 ⲣ. ϩⲏⲧϥ ⲙⲡⲉⲕⲟⲩⲟⲉⲓⲛ, TillOster 12 *A* ⲣ. ϩⲏⲧⲟⲩ, ManiH 82 *A²* ⲣ. ϩⲏⲧϥ ⲙⲡⲉⲧ[, Mor 27 19 *F* ⲡⲏ ⲉⲧⲉⲣ. ⲛϩⲏⲧϥ, Mor 31 171 ⲣ. ϩⲏⲧϥ ⲙⲡⲉϣⲧⲉⲕⲟ;   ⲉⲣ ϩ. as nn *B*: He 10 31 (*S* ϩ.) φοβερός; ⲁⲧⲉⲣ ϩ. *B*: Phil 1 14 (*SF* ⲁⲧⲛϩ.) ἀφόβως; AM 213 ⲡⲁⲣⲣⲏⲥⲓⲁ ⲡⲁ.;   ⲙⲛⲧⲁⲧⲣ ϩ. *S*: Z 328 ἄδεια;   ⲣⲉϥⲣ ϩ. *S*(mostly)*B*: Ac 8 2 *SB* εὐλαβής, Miss 8 35 ⲡⲣ. ⲡⲉⲡⲓⲥⲕⲟⲡⲟⲥ -έστατος, *ib* 31 θεοσεβέστατος; J 75 27 ⲣ. ⲙⲙⲟⲛⲁⲭⲟⲥ, CO 61 ⲡⲁϣⲏⲣⲉ ⲡⲣ. ⲡⲗⲁϣⲓ(ⲁⲛⲉ), *ib* 75 ⲣⲱⲙⲉ ⲡⲣ. ⲁⲩⲱ ⲡⲣⲉϥϣⲙϣⲉ ⲡⲉ̅, HCons 355 *B* ⲡⲣ. in orthodox lands اتقى;   ⲙⲛⲧ-, ⲙⲉⲧⲣ.: Miss 8 76 εὐσέβεια, *ib* 40, C 89 27 *B* εὐλάβεια; ShC 42 225 Cyril to Shenoute ⲧⲉⲕⲙ., R 1 3 80 Herod showed ⲟⲩⲙ. ϩⲡⲣⲉⲛⲁⲛⲁϣ *respect* (on Mk 6 26).

ϯ ϩ. *SB, give fear, terrify*: Ps 65 5 *S*(*B* ⲙⲉϩ ϩⲡ.), Si 1 8 *SB* φοβερός, Bor 253 119 *S* ⲉⲃⲏⲧⲉ ⲉⲧϯ φόβητρον, BMar 175 *S* ⲥⲁⲗⲡⲓⲛⲝ ⲉⲥϯ. μετὰ φόβου; Cant 6 3 *S*(*F* ϩ. nn) θάμβος εἶναι; BMis 285 *S* tortures ⲉⲧϯ.;   ⲥ ⲉ-: Bor 253 118 *S* ϯ. ⲉⲙⲁ ⲡⲓⲙ τὰ σύμπαντα ἐκφ.; C 86 67 *B* ⲉⲕϯ. ⲛⲏⲓ ⲉⲟⲩⲭⲣⲱⲙ ἀπειλεῖν acc;   ⲥ ⲛ- dat: Ez 34 28 *SB* ἐκφ. acc, Dan 4 2 *B*, C 89 109 *B* ϯ. ⲡⲱⲟⲩ ⲉϣⲧⲉⲙ- φοβερίζειν acc; ShA 2 330 *S* ϯ. ⲛⲡϩⲁⲓⲙⲱⲛ, JTS 10 391 *S* ⲉϥϯ. ⲡⲁⲩ ϫⲉⲕⲁⲥ;   ⲥ ⲉϫⲛ-: Bar 3 6 *B*(*S* ⲉϩⲣⲁⲓ ⲉϫⲛ-), Ez 32 26 *SB* φόβον διδόναι ἐπί; DeV 2 52 *B* ⲙⲁ ϩ. ⲉ. ⲡⲏ ⲉⲟⲣⲁⲕⲓ;   ⲣⲉϥϯ ϩ. *S*: Deu 10 17 (*B* ⲉⲧⲟⲓ ⲡϩ.) φοβερός; My 167 ⲡⲣⲱⲃ ⲡⲣ. ⲡⲧⲉ ⲡⲕⲁⲧⲁⲕⲗⲩⲥⲙⲟⲥ.

ϩⲓ ϩ. *B, cast, put fear*: Va 58 191 drunkard ⲉϩϥ.; AM 230 ⲡⲏ (*sc* tortures) ⲉⲧⲉⲕ. ⲙⲙⲱⲟⲩ;   ⲥ ⲉ-: AM 270 ⲉⲧϩ. ⲉⲣⲟⲓ ⲡⲟⲩⲙⲟⲩ ἀπειλ. dat acc; MG 25 81 ⲙⲁⲣⲉⲛϩ. ⲉⲣⲟϥ, AM 230 ⲕⲣ. ⲉϩⲉⲛⲃⲁⲥⲁⲛⲟⲥ *wouldest terrify with tortures*;   ⲥ ⲉⲃⲟⲗ: C 43 49 ⲡⲉϥϩ. ⲉⲃ. = Mor 39 27 *S*ᶠ ⲙⲏϩ ϩⲣⲟ.;   ⲣⲉϥϩⲓ ϩ.: Va 61 28 serpent obedient & showed no ⲥⲙⲟⲧ ⲡⲣ.

ϫⲓ ϩ. *S, bring fear, frighten*: Mor 17 17 *S* smote him ⲉⲥϫ. ⲙⲙⲟϥ ἐκφοβ.

Cf ϩⲣⲧⲉ.

ϩⲟⲧⲉ *S*, ϩⲁ. *AA²*, ϩⲟⲧ *B*, ⲟⲧⲓ, ⲁⲧⲉ *O* nn f, *hour, moment*: Job 24 6 *B*(*S* ⲧⲏ) ὥρα, Pro 10 6 *B* neg(*SA* diff) ἄωρος; Is 50 4 *B* ⲁⲣⲉϣⲁⲛⲧϩ. ... ϣⲱⲡⲓ (*S* ⲟⲩⲟⲉⲓϣ) ἡνίκα δεί; ShP 78 45 *S* ϩⲣⲟⲕ ⲡⲟⲩⲕⲟⲩⲓ, ⲕⲃⲟ ⲡⲟⲩϩ., TU 43 5 *A* ⲟⲩϩ. ϩⲙⲛ, El 74 *A* ⲁⲧⲉⲧⲛⲡⲁⲣ ⲛⲟⲉⲓⲉ (νοεῖν) ⲡϩ. ⲡⲓⲙ (but = *ib* 114 *S* ϩⲱⲃ), Mani 2 *A²* preaching ⲡϩ. ⲛⲓⲙ, Mani P *A²* ⲉⲡⲧⲱⲣⲡ ϩ. ϩ. ⲉⲛⲛⲟⲩϫⲉ ϩⲟⲟⲅⲉ ϩⲟⲟⲅⲉ, AZ 23 115 *S* recipe ϫⲉϥϫⲟⲃⲟⲩ ⲛϣⲟⲙ(ⲧⲉ) ⲡϩ. (*cf* 111 ⲡⲉ̅ ⲡⲟⲩⲡⲟⲩ).

ⲛⲟⲩϩ. ϩⲉⲛⲟⲩϩ. *B, on a sudden*: Ac 2 2 (*S* ϩⲛⲟⲩϣⲥⲡⲉ) ἄφνω; Job 1 19 (*S* do), Mk 13 36 (*S* do, *F* = Gk) ἐξαίφνης; AM 280 ἀφνιδίως; C 86 281 thunderstorm ⲡ.;   ⲛⲧϩ. ϩⲉⲛⲟⲩϩ.: Lu 1 64 (var ⲛⲧϩ. ⲛⲧϩ.,

S do) παραχρῆμα; ⲛ̀ϯϩ. ϣⲉⲛϯϩ.: Jer 13 14 (*S* ϩⲓⲟⲩⲥⲟⲡ) ἐν τῷ αὐτῷ;   AZ 21 100 *O* ⲉⲭⲉⲛⲧⲓⲟⲧⲓ ⲧⲓⲁⲧⲉ
paral ⲧⲓⲟⲩⲛⲟⲩ.

ⲣ ϩ. *S, spend time*: R 2 4 69 ⲁϥⲣ ⲟⲩⲛⲟϭ ⲛϩ. ⲉϥϣⲁϫⲉ, Miss 4 832 sim, *ib* 700 ⲣ ⲧⲉⲧⲛϩ. ⲡⲟϣϣ ⲙ̅ⲡⲛⲁⲩ
ⲛ̅ϣⲱⲣⲡ.

ϩⲟⲧⲉ *B* with preceding ⲉ-, prep, *beyond, more
than*: 2 Kg 1 23 (*S* ⲉϩⲟⲩⲉ ⲉ-), Ps 96 9 (*S* do), *ib* 18 11
(*S* ⲉ-), Lam 4 6 (*F* ⲉϩⲟⲩⲁⲥⲧⲉ), Eph 3 20 (*S* ⲡⲣⲟϩⲉ)
ὑπέρ, Dan 7 23 ὑπερ-; 1 Kg 17 43 (*S* ⲙⲡⲁⲣⲁ), EpJer
58 (*F* do), Mt 10 15 (*S* ⲉϩ.) ἤ; Ps 134 5 (*S* = Gk), Ez
29 15 (*S* do) παρά; Pro 29 28 (*SA* ⲉ-), 1 Cor 1 25 (*S*
ⲛϩ. ⲉ-) gen; C 89 53 ⲧⲉⲧⲉⲛⲗⲟϥ ⲉϩ. ⲟⲩⲙⲛ̅ϣ, AM 177
Simeon was young ⲉϩ. ⲓⲱⲁⲛⲛⲏⲥ, RAl 86 sins ⲁϣⲁⲓ
ⲉϩ. ⲥⲟⲇⲟⲙⲁ (var Leip 24 42 ⲡϩⲟⲅⲟ ⲉ-), PO 11 369
chose Judas's part ⲉϩ. ⲡⲭ̅ⲥ̅; AM 273 better to sur-
render ⲉϩ. ⲡⲧⲁⲕⲟ ⲙ̅ⲡⲓⲗⲁⲟⲥ;   c following ⲉ-:
Ex 1 9, Ps 37 20 (*S* ⲉϩⲟⲩⲉⲣⲟⲥ), Dan 6 3 (*S* ⲉ-) ὑπέρ,
Ps 64 4 (*S* do) ὑπερ-; Dan 11 2 παρά; EpJer 67 (*F*
ⲉϩⲟⲩⲁ.), Mt 3 11 (*S* do) gen; AM 111 ⲛⲁⲛⲉⲕ ⲉϩ.
ⲉⲣⲟⲓ, C 43 115 ⲧⲁⲓϩⲟⲩⲧ ⲉϩⲟⲧⲉⲣⲟⲕ; vbal: Ge 29 19
(*S* ⲡϩⲟⲩⲉ), Ps 117 8 (*S* ⲉϩ.), 1 Cor 7 9 (*S* do, *F* do) ἤ;
HL 85 better wine ... ⲉϩ. ⲉⲥⲉ ⲙ̅ⲙⲟⲟⲩ gen; C 86 338
better to die ⲉϩ. ⲉⲱⲛⲃ̅, *ib* 89 149 chose to be devil's
ⲉϩ. ⲉⲑⲣⲉϥϣⲱⲡⲓ ⲡⲥⲕⲉⲩⲟⲥ ⲡⲥⲱⲧⲡ;   *when*: Is 30
19 ⲉϩ. ⲉⲧⲁϥⲡⲁⲩ (*SF* ⲡⲧⲉⲣⲉϥⲡⲁⲩ) ἡνίκα; Dan 5 20
ⲉϩ. ⲉⲧⲁϥϭⲓⲥⲓ ὅτε; DeV 2 27 ⲉⲛⲉⲣ ⲙⲉⲗⲉⲧⲁⲛ ... ⲉϩ.
ⲉⲛⲛⲁϭⲓ ⲙ̅ⲡⲓⲥⲱⲙⲁ ⲡⲣⲉϥⲧⲁⲛϩⲟ. These prob for ὅτε.

   Cf ϩⲟⲩⲟ.

ϩⲱⲧⲉ *S*, -ϯ *B* (nn) vb intr, *rub, bruise*: C 73 54
ⲉⲩϩ. ⲛ ⲉⲩⲧⲱϣ at time of bread-making;   tr: Jer
7 18 (P 44 113, *B* ⲟⲩⲱϣⲉⲙ) τρίβειν;   *pierce* or ?
rub to & fro (diff word ? *cf* ϩⲓⲧⲉ a): TT 77 ϩ. ⲙ̅ⲡⲉϥ-
ϯⲃⲥ ⲛ̅ⲟⲩⲥⲁϩ ⲉϥⲗⲟⲃ̅ϣ, BMar 28 sim ϩ. ⲙ̅ⲙⲟⲟⲩ ⲡⲣⲏⲧⲟⲩ (sc ears), P 129[16] 62 borers into ears ⲡⲥⲉϩ. ⲛ̅ⲥⲱⲟⲩ
(*cf* ϩⲓⲧⲉ Mar 41);   as nn f, that wherewith ring or
hole is *pierced*, so rod, pole: Nu 13 24 *SB* (var ϣⲉ ⲛϩ.)
ἀναφορεύς هود (v KKS 436); K 157 *B* parts of house
ⲛⲓϩ. اساطير، دهوفات;   ϣⲉ ⲛϩⲱⲧ *S*, ⲛϩⲱϯ *B, wooden
pole*: Ex 30 4 *B* σκυτάλη حامل; *ib* 37 4 *B* διωστήρ
عارضة; Nu 4 6 *B* (*S* ⲟⲩⲁϩ) ἀναφ. عمد; 2 Kg 23 21 *S*
ϣ. ⲡⲇⲓⲁⲃⲁⲑⲣⲁ ξύλον διαβ. (P 44 110 مجاز) not
understood); Mor 51 34 *S* ⲁⲡⲥϩⲟⲟⲩ ⲉⲃⲟⲗ ϩⲙ̅ⲡϣⲏⲛϩ.,
PMich 4545 *S* list ϣⲉ ⲛϩ. β, ϭⲟⲗⲃⲉ η.

   Diff words *S*: ? Glos 224 γαστροφόρος· ⲛ̅ϩⲗϭ. ⲛ̅
ⲃⲗϫⲉ *earthenware...-holder* (*cf* γάστρα belly-shaped
pot); Ep 543 list of σκεύη ⲟⲩϩⲱⲧⲁⲇⲉ, Baouit 1 52 on
a vase ϩⲱⲧⲉ.   *Cf* ϩⲁⲧⲉ.

   As place-name (?): ⲡϩⲱⲧⲉ (BM 1130).

ϩⲱⲧⲉ *S* (?), -ϯ *BF* nn m, *tribute*: Lam 1 1 *BF* φόρος, Deu 28 33 *B* (var ⲟⲩⲟϯ, *S* diff) ἐκφόριον; C 43
35 *B* Persians demand ⲛⲟⲩϩ. = Mor 39 6 *S* φορος,

ib 75 *B* imprisoned ⲉⲟⲃⲉϩⲁⲛϩ. ⲡⲧⲉ ⲡⲟⲩⲣⲟ ⲉⲅⲥⲁⲃⲟⲗ
ⲙ̅ⲙⲟⲓ (*cf*? AM 315 ⲉⲅⲁⲙⲟⲛⲓ ⲙ̅ⲙⲟⲛ ⲉⲣⲱⲟⲩ), ST 85
S ⲧⲏⲭⲣⲉⲱⲥⲧⲉⲓ ⲉⲧⲁⲁⲩ (*sc* corn) ⲛⲁⲕ ϩⲙ̅ⲡⲉϩ., CO
140 *S* field & ⲡⲉϩϩ.;   ϯϩ., *pay tribute*: Lu 23 2 *B*
(*S* ϯ ϣⲱⲙ)ϩ. διδόναι, Ro 13 7 *B* ⲡⲓϩ. (*S* do) φ. ἀποδ.;
Mk 12 14 *BF* (Mich 545, *S* = Gk) κῆνσον δ.; C 43
66 *B* ⲁⲛⲟⲕ ⲟⲩⲉⲗⲉⲩⲑⲉⲣⲟⲥ ⲉⲓϯ. ⲙ̅ⲡⲟⲩⲣⲟ, CO 206 *S*
sowing contract ⲛⲥϯ ⲡⲉϩ. ⲡⲁⲓ;   ⲣⲉϥϯϩ. *B*: Deu
20 11 (*S* ϯ ϣ.) φορολόγητος;   ⲁⲧϩ. *B, tax-free*:
AM 285 ⲭⲁ ⲡⲟⲩⲕⲁϩⲓ ⲡⲱⲟⲩ ⲉⲃⲟⲗ ⲛⲁ. prob = C 43
122 ⲁⲧⲧⲉⲗⲟⲥ.

ϩⲱϯ *S*[f] (once) *BF* nn, *necessity*, as impers vb *it is
needful* (*S* mostly ϩⲁⲡⲥ): Jo 3 7 (*A*[2] ⲫⲁⲡ, *F* ϩ. ⲡⲉ),
Ac 1 21 (*S* ϣϣⲉ), 1 Cor 11 19 δεῖν; Or Chr NS 3 48
ϩ. ⲡⲧⲉϥⲭⲉⲙ ϯⲡⲓ ⲙ̅ⲫⲙⲟⲩ;   ϩ.-ⲡⲉ: Is 30 29 (*F* =
S), Mt 24 6, Jo 3 14 (*F* om -ⲡⲉ) δ.; MG 25 231 ϩ. ⲡⲉ
ⲡⲧⲉⲟⲩⲁⲓ ⲣⲁⲡⲁϥ (*SZ* 317 & Gk om), Va 57 233 ⲡⲉϩ. ⲡⲉ
ⲡⲧⲉϥϯ ⲭⲱ ⲛⲁⲛ ⲉϩ̅ⲣⲏⲓ, Mor 24 29 *F* ϩ. ⲡⲉ ⲡⲧⲁⲭⲓ,
Cat 20 ϩ. ⲡⲉ ⲉⲑⲣⲉϥⲗⲁⲟⲥ ⲛⲁϯ;   c ⲉ-, *for*: Lu 2
49, Jo 4 4 *BF*, 1 Cor 15 25, He 9 26 (*SF* ϣϣⲉ) δ.
acc inf; Aeg 19 ϩ. ⲉⲣⲟ ⲡⲧⲉⲙⲟⲩ = *ib S* ⲧⲁⲡⲁⲅⲅⲏⲧⲉ;
vbal: Ac 14 22 (*S* diff) δ. acc inf; MG 25 206 ϩ.
ⲉⲣⲟϥⲡⲉ ⲉⲉⲣ ⲕⲟⲗⲁⲍⲓⲛ ⲙ̅ⲙⲟϥ μέλλειν inf; Mor 30 7
S[f] ϩ. ⲡⲉ ⲉⲛⲧⲣⲉⲕⲁⲅⲱⲛⲓⲍⲉ (sic) = *ib* 29 6 *S* ϩⲁⲡⲥ ⲉ-
ⲧⲣⲉⲕ-;   c ⲛ-, *dat*: AM 145 ϩ. ⲡⲱⲧⲉⲛ ⲡⲧⲉⲧⲛ-.
V Sethe *DemUrk* 32.

ϩⲧⲁⲓ *S* (once), ϩⲧⲉⲓ *F* nn, with vb ϩⲓⲟⲩⲉ, *deceive,
mislead, disregard* or sim: Cant 1 6 ⲡⲧⲁϥϩⲓ ϩⲧ[(*S* ⲕⲱ
ⲡⲥⲁ-) παραβλέπειν; Lam 1 19 ⲁⲩϩⲓ ϩ. ⲙⲙ[ⲁⲓ (*B* ϩⲓ
ⲡϩⲟ) παραλογίζεσθαι; *ib* 2 7 ⲁϥϩⲓ ϩ. ⲡⲧⲉϥϣⲛⲟⲩϯ (*B*
ⲭⲱ ⲡⲥⲁ-) ἀπωθεῖν; He 10 28 ⲁⲗⲉϣⲁ(ⲡ)ⲟⲩⲉⲓ ϩⲓ ϩ.
ⲙ̅ⲡⲛⲟⲙⲟⲥ (Mus 49 204, *S* = Gk, *B* ϣⲟϣ) ἀθετεῖν;
Mor 31 215 *S* ⲙⲉⲓⲣⲓ ϩ. ⲛ̅ⲛⲁⲡⲣⲟⲫⲏⲧⲏⲥ;   ⲙ̅ⲡⲧⲣⲓ
ϩ. *F*: Cant 8 7 (*S* ϣⲟⲥ̅ϥ) ἐξουδενώσις.

ϩⲧⲁ(ⲉ)ⲓ, ⲉϩⲟ. *S*, ϭⲟⲁⲓ *B*, ϩⲧⲉⲓ *F*, ϭⲟⲧ†, ϭⲁⲟ† *B*
vb intr, *become, be fat*: Deu 32 15 *S* (var ⲉϩⲟ. P 44
20) *B* (sic Va), Eccl 12 5 *S*, Mt 13 15 *F* (*S* ⲛϣⲟⲧ, *B*
ⲟⲩⲙⲟⲧ), *Vizant Vrem* 14 190 *B* ⲡⲓⲗⲟⲧⲟⲥ ⲁϥϭ. = Cai
The 202 ظلف παχύνεσθαι, Va 58 186 *B* ⲡⲓϭⲉⲡⲧ ... ⲁⲕ-
ⲑⲣⲉϥϭ. παχὺν κατασκευάζειν, Ps 143 14 *S* (var ⲧⲏⲕ
P 44 20, *B*†) παχύς; P 44 72 *S* ⲗⲓⲡⲁⲣⲁ· ⲉⲥϭ. سمين;
qual *B*: Nu 24 8 (*S* nn) πάχος, Ps 143 14 *v* above, Va
58 188 ϫⲓⲛⲟⲩⲱⲙ ⲉⲧϭ., C 89 21 ropes ⲉⲩϭ. παχύς;
K 73 ⲫⲏ ⲉⲧϭⲁⲟ سمن;   as nn m: Nu 24 8 *S v* above;
Mor 17 12 *S* ⲡⲉϩ. ⲙ̅ⲡⲉⲥⲥⲱⲙⲁ εὐσαρκία; MIE 2 403
B ⲛⲁϣⲉ ⲡⲉϥϭ., BM 332 *S* fingers ⲉⲣ [ⲑⲉ ⲛ]ⲡⲉϩ.
ⲡⲣⲉⲛϣⲱⲡⲉ, Mor 28 262 *S* serpent ⲙ̅ⲡⲉϩⲧⲟⲓ ⲡⲟⲩⲣⲱⲙⲉ ϩⲙ̅ⲡⲉϥⲥⲱⲙⲁ, DeV 2 139 *B* ⲡⲓϭ. ⲡⲧⲉ ⲧⲟⲩ-
ϣⲃⲱⲃⲓ of serpents, MG 25 372 *B* ⲡϭ. ⲡⲧⲉⲡⲓⲑⲩⲙⲓⲁ,
Va 57 87 *B* ⲡⲓϭ. ⲉⲑⲟⲩⲟⲙⲧ of flesh;   adj: Ez 16
26 *B* (*S* ⲛⲟϭ ⲛ̅ⲥⲁⲣⲝ) μεγαλόσαρκος.

ϭⲟⲏ *B* nn f, *thickness*: Job 15 26, Jer 52 21 πάχος.

ϩⲧⲏ S nn f, *shaft of spear* : 1 Kg 17 7 κοντός, cit
P 44 109 طرب (as if ϩⲏⲧ *tip*);   BMis 564 golden
ship ⲉϥϫⲓ ⲡⲟⲩϩ. ⲡϩⲁⲧ (*cf* AJSL 46 248 ϣⲧⲉ *mast*,
var ϩⲧⲉ).

ϩⲧⲟ, -ⲱ SA, ⲉϩⲧⲟ S(rare), ϩⲟⲟ B, (ⲉ)ϩⲧⲁ F, ϩⲧⲉ-
A, f ϩⲧⲱⲣⲉ, ϩⲧⲟⲟⲣⲉ S, ϩⲧⲱⲣⲏ, ϩⲧⲟ. A², (ⲉ)ϩⲟⲟⲣⲓ B,
(ⲉ)ϩⲧⲁ(ⲁ)ⲣⲓ F,   pl (ⲉ)ϩⲧⲱⲱⲣ SF, -ⲉ S, ϩⲧⲱⲣ SAF,
(ⲉ)ϩⲟⲱⲣ, ϩⲟⲟⲣ B, ϩⲧⲟⲩⲣⲉⲩⲉ A & sg as pl, nn m,
horse: Ps 32 17 SB, Pro 21 31 SA, Is 31 3 S(B pl)F
ⲉϩ., Nah 3 2 A-ⲱ B, Zech 14 20 S(BM 185)A-ⲱ B,
Ap 18 13 SB ἵππος, P 44 54 S ἵππαγρος · ϩ. ϩⲟⲟⲩⲧ;
Glos 75 S ⲙⲟⲥⲙⲉⲛⲓⲛ (? μουσμόνιον)· ⲕⲟⲩⲓ ⲛϩ.; K 166
B ⲟⲩϩ. خيل, ⲡⲓϩ. فرس P 44 83 S ϩⲓⲏϩ. جـ; Tri 270 S
ⲡⲉϩ. حصان; BM 346 1 S *tail of* ⲟⲩϩ., BMar 14 S sim
-ⲱ, C 43 197 Bⲧⲁⲗⲛⲟⲩⲧ ⲉⲡⲉϩϩ., Mor 30 39 F sim ⲉϩ.,
ib 16 64 S ⲉϩ., BM 1068 S *its price* [ⲥ]ⲡⲁⲩ ⲙ[ⲙⲁ]ⲏⲧ
ⲡⲣⲟⲗⲟⲕ, Bodl(P)a 2 65 S ⲥⲟⲧ ⲛϩ. *as wrapping for
phial*;   f, *mare*: Cant 1 9 S(P 131⁶ 1)F ἵπ.; ROC
25 242 B φοράς, ib ϩ. ⲛⲥϩⲓⲙⲓ φ., Mich 601 S ⲟⲩϩ.
[ⲉⲥ]ⲗⲟⲃⲉ ⲛⲧⲟⲟⲧϥ ⲡⲟⲩ(ϩ)ⲧⲱ, LAl 13 S ϥⲧⲟ ⲛϩ., Bodl
(P)d 37 S ⲧⲉϩⲧⲟⲟⲣⲉ, BMOr 6201 B 136 S do, ManiP
111 A² ⲡⲁϩⲧⲱ., ManiH 77 A² ⲁⲩⲟⲩⲱⲣϩ ⲛϩⲧⲟ., Orat
Cyp 117 F *neighing like* ⲟⲩⲉϩⲧⲁⲁⲣⲓ, Ep 271 S ⲧⲉϩ.
to be sold;   pl: Deu 11 4 S(var ϩⲧⲱⲣ)B, Jth 1 13 S,
Eccl 10 7 SF ϩⲧⲱⲣ, Sa 19 9 S ϩⲧⲱⲣ, Is 5 28 S ⲉϩ. B,
ib 30 16 S ⲉϩⲧⲱⲱⲣⲉ BF ⲉϩ., Hos 14 4 AB. Ap 9 7 S
(var ϩⲧⲱⲣ)B ἵπ., Hab 3 8 A ϩⲧⲟⲩⲣⲉⲩ(ⲉ?, S= Gk, B
diff) ἱππασία; ShC 42 70 S(var ϩⲧⲱⲣ), P 132¹ 10 S
ϩⲉⲡⲉϩ., R 1 3 49 S ⲛⲉϩⲧⲱⲣ, Mor 31 254 S ⲉϩ. =
BMEA 10578 F ϩ., C 43 36 B ⲡⲓⲥⲧⲁⲅⲗⲟⲡ ⲛⲧⲉ ⲡⲓϩ.,
C 86 234 B ⲡⲁⲉϩ., ib 174 B ϩⲟⲟⲣ; Bodl(P)d 32 S
ⲯⲁⲉⲓⲡ ⲛⲉϩⲧⲱⲣ;   various sorts: Ap 6 2 SB ⲟⲩⲱⲃϣ λευκός, ib 5 SB ⲕⲁⲙⲉ μέλας, ib 8 SB ⲟⲩⲉⲧⲟⲩⲱⲧ
χλωρός, Zech 1 8 A ⲙⲣϣ B ⲡⲁⲟⲩⲁⲛ ⲛⲭⲣⲱⲙ πυρρός,
Zech 1c A ⲡⲉⲟⲩⲉⲛ ⲉⲟⲩⲉⲛ, B ⲁⲟⲩⲓ ⲁⲟⲩⲁⲡ ποικίλος,
Ora 4 20 S ϩⲁⲧ, Mor 51 41 S *nickname* ⲡⲉϩ. ⲡϣⲉ.
   As title (?): BMOr 6201 B 210 S ⲙⲟⲩⲓ ⲡⲉϩ.
   ⲙⲁⲥ ⲛϩ. S, *foal*: ShBor 247 110.
   ⲙⲁⲛⲉϩ. S, *horse-keeper, groom*: BMis 37 ⲥⲧⲁϥ-
ⲗⲓⲧⲏⲥ (σταβ.) ⲙⲙ.
   ⲣⲱⲙϩ. S, ⲣⲉⲙⲛϩ.B, *horseman* : Is 22 7 B(S diff)
ἱππεύς;   same? Kr 48 S ⲛϩ., Ryl 208 S, BMOr 6201
A 24 S ⲁⲡⲟⲕ...ⲛϩ. ApaVictor, ib 74 S ⲛϩ. ApaTheo-
dore ⲡⲉⲭⲣⲩⲥⲱⲏⲥ.   Cf AZ 43 89.
   ⲋ̄ⲁⲥⲓϩ., ⲛϩ. B, *raised on horse, rider*: Ex 14 9, Jer
4 29 (S = Gk), Hos 1 7 (A ⲡⲉⲧϩⲙⲁⲥⲧ ϩⲓⲭⲱⲟⲩ) ἱππεύς; Ex 14 23 (var ⲛϩ.), Is 36 8 (SF ⲣⲉϥⲁⲗⲉ) ἀναβάτης; K 136 ⲡⲓⲋ̄ⲁⲥⲟⲩ ⲡⲧⲉ ⲡⲓϩ. سياس.
   In place-name: ⲧⲱϩⲉ ⲧⲁⲡⲉϩⲧⲱⲱⲣ = طرخ الخيل (R 1
5 49, Amélineau *Géog* 524).
   V ϩⲱⲧⲣ.

ϩⲧⲟⲓ S nn as pl, *meaning unknown, a crop*?: P

Mich 4543 *promise to pay* ϩⲁⲡϩⲱⲃ (ⲡ)ⲡⲭⲉⲙⲟⲥⲓⲟⲡ...
ϩⲁⲡϩ. ⲡⲧⲁⲓⲭⲓⲧⲩ... ⲧⲁⲁⲡⲟⲗⲟ(ⲧⲓϩⲉ) ⲙⲟⲟⲩ ⲡⲁⲕ... ⲙ-
ⲡⲉ(ⲓ)ⲧⲁⲁⲩ ⲡⲁⲕ ⲉⲓⲁ† ⲧⲁⲡⲁⲣⲭ(ⲏ) ⲛϩ. ⲡⲁⲕ ϩⲁⲣⲟⲟⲩ
(on ἀπαρχή Ep 1 193, adding Z 317 = γεῦμα), Bodl(P)
d 31 *account* ⲁⲡⲟⲗⲗⲱ ϩⲉⲛⲉϩ. ⲩ̂ γ (*l* ϩⲉⲛ- ⲉϩ. ?).

ϩⲱⲧⲃ SA², -ⲉⲃ SF, ϩⲱⲧⲃⲉ A, ϩ. A², ⲑ̄ⲱⲧⲉⲃ B,
ϩⲉⲧⲃ̄-S, ϩⲁⲧⲃ̄- A², ⲑ̄ⲉⲧⲉⲃ-, ⲑ̄ⲁ.(ⲣⲉϥ-)B, ϩⲁⲧⲉⲃ̄-(do)
F, ϩⲟⲧⲃ̄- S, ϩⲁ. A, ϩ. A²F, ⲑ̄ⲟⲉⲃⲋ̄ B, ϩⲟⲧⲃ† S(once),
ϩⲁⲧⲃⲉ† A², p c ϩⲁⲧⲃ̄- S, ϩⲁⲧⲃⲉ- A, ϩⲁ. A². ⲑ̄ⲁⲧⲉⲃ̄- B
vb I intr, *kill*: Pro 22 13 SA, Mt 19 18 SB φονεύειν;
2 Cor 3 6 B(S ⲙⲟⲩⲟⲩⲧ) ἀποκτείνειν; Jer 8 17 B θανατοῦν; Ez 9 8 B κόπτειν; Is
28 6 B(S ⲧⲁⲕⲟ) ἀναιρεῖν; Deu 21 2 S(B ⲙⲁϣⲓ) τραυ-
ματίας;   qual: Is 26 21 S(B tr) ἀναιρεῖσθαι; Mani
K 176 A² ⲧⲯⲩⲭⲏ...ⲉⲥϩ.

II tr: Ge 4 14 SB, Ps 104 29 B(S ⲙ.), Mt 14 5
BF(S do) ἀποκ.; Pro 1 32 SAB, Mt 23 31 SB φ.;
Jer 4 31 SB, Ac 7 28 SBF, He 10 9 B(SF ϥⲓ) ἀναι.;
Job 5 2 B(S ⲙ.), Mk 14 55 BF(S do) θα.; Jer 47 15
B πατάσσειν; ib 52 10 B, 1 Jo 3 12 B(SF ⲕⲱ.), Ap 6
4 S(B ⲑ̄ⲟⲗⲑ̄ⲉⲗ) σφάζειν; Dan 2 24 B ἀπολλύναι; Job
3 8 B(S ⲧⲁ.) χειροῦσθαι; Col 3 5 B(S ⲙ.) νεκροῦν;
MG 25 204 B ϣⲁⲑⲛⲁⲩ ⲧⲉⲧⲉⲡⲑ̄. ⲙⲡⲓⲑ̄ⲉⲗⲗⲟ? τύπτειν; PS 345 S *incited beast* ϣⲁⲛⲧϥϩ. ⲙⲙⲟϥ, Pcod
28 S ϩⲉⲧⲃ̄ ⲟⲩⲣⲱⲙⲉ, El 134 S ⲙⲏ ⲁⲣⲉⲡⲭ̄ⲣⲥ̄ ϩ. ⲇⲓⲕⲁⲓⲟⲥ?=ib 98 A ϩ. ⲇ., AP 21 A² ⲁⲩϣⲓⲡⲉ ⲛⲥⲁϩⲧ-
ⲃⲉϥ, ManiH 12 A² ⲁⲥϩ. ⲡⲛⲓϩⲣⲁⲙⲡⲉ, ib 77 A² ϩⲁⲧⲃⲟⲩ,
BIF 22 107 F ϩⲁⲧⲃⲟⲩ, AM 164 B ⲑ̄ⲟⲉⲃⲉⲛ.
   With following preposition.   c ⲉ-: Ez 9 6 B
ⲁⲡⲟⲕ. εἰς, Ap 13 3 S(B diff)σφ. εἰς;   c ⲉϫⲛ-: AM
196 B ⲑ̄ⲟⲉⲃⲟⲩ ⲉ. ⲫⲣⲁⲛ ⲙⲡⲭ̄ⲥ̄; ⲉϩⲗⲏⲓ ⲉϫ.: Lam 2
11 F(B Gk diff) c ϩⲓϫⲉⲛ-: C 86 98 B ⲑ̄. ⲙⲙⲟⲟⲩ
ϩ. ⲫⲣⲁⲛ;   c ⲡ-, *with* (cf ϩⲡ-): AM 265 B ⲑ̄ⲟⲉⲃⲟⲩ
ⲛⲧⲥⲏϥⲓ κατακόπ.;   c ⲡⲥⲁ- *emphatic*: Ps 77 34 B
(S diff) ἀποκ. acc; Lam 3 53 F(B acc) θαν. acc; Mor
31 38 S *began to* ϩ. ⲛⲥⲁⲡⲇⲓⲕⲁⲓⲟⲥ (var Miss 4 776 ⲛ-),
ib 16 8 S ⲉϥϩ. ⲛⲥⲱⲟⲩ (var BMis 186 ⲙⲙⲟⲟⲩ), AM
104 B ⲁⲩⲑ̄. ⲛⲥⲁⲡⲙⲏⲛϣ, BIF 22 107 F ϩ. ⲛⲥⲁⲡⲉⲣⲙ-
ⲑⲉⲗ;   c ⲡⲧⲉⲡ-: Ex 17 3 B(S ⲙ. ϩⲁ-)ⲁⲡⲟⲕ. dat;   c
ϩⲡ-, ⲑ̄ⲉⲡ-, *with*: Job 1 17 S(B ⲡ-) ⲁⲡⲟⲕ. ἐν; ib 14 30
B(S ⲱⲭⲡ) ἀναιρ. ἐν, Ez 26 11 B ἀν. dat; DeV 2 69
B ⲑ̄ⲟⲉⲃⲟⲩ ⲑ̄ⲉⲡⲧⲥⲏϥⲓ, AM 244 B sim ⲑ̄ⲉⲡϩⲓⲡⲙⲟⲩ
ⲛⲓⲃⲉⲛ.
   p c : 1 Tim 1 9 B ⲑ̄. ⲣⲱⲙⲓ (S ⲣⲉϥϩⲉⲧⲃ̄ ⲣ.) ἀνδρο-
φόνος; 1 Jo 3 15 B(S do) ἀνθρωποκτόνος; JA '75 5
263 S ⲟⲩϩ. ϣⲏⲣⲉ (var Lammayer 48 ϩⲉⲧⲃ̄-), My 106
S *Jews* ⲛϩ.ⲡ̄ⲉ, ManiP 39 A² ⲟⲩϩ. ⲣⲱⲙⲉ, DeV 1 23 B
ⲑ̄.ⲥⲟⲡ; Cl 4 7 A ⲙⲡⲧϩ̄.ⲥⲁⲡ ·ἀδελφοκτονία.
   —— nn m SABF, *slaughter, murder*: Nu 21 24
SB, Mt 15 19 SBF φόνος; Ac 8 1 SB ἀναίρεσις; Pro
1 11 SA(B diff) αἷμα; PS 362 S ⲡⲧⲉⲣⲉϩ. ϣⲱⲡⲉ, BAp
136 S ⲛϩ. ⲛ̄ⲡϣⲏⲣⲉ ⲕⲟⲩⲓ, C 43 40 B ⲁⲩⲛⲓϣ† ⲛⲑ̄. ⲧⲁϩⲉ

ⲡⲓⲡⲉⲣⲥⲏⲥ = Mor 39 14 *S* ϩⲁϭⲧⲥ, DeV 1 122 *B* wiped out ⲉⲃⲟⲩⲥ. ⲡⲉϩⲟⲩⲙⲟⲩ;   *thing slain, corpse*: Nu 31 8 *B*(*S* ϩⲁⲧⲃⲉⲥ), 1 Kg 17 52 *B*(*S* do), Is 34 3 *BF*(*S* do), Lam 4 9 *B*(*F* ϩ. vb, *S* ϣⲱⲱϭⲉ), Zeph 2 12 *B*(*A* ϣ.) τραυματίας; Ps 109 6 *S*(*B* ϩⲧⲟⲡ) πτῶμα; Ez 32 18 *B*(*S* ⲙⲟⲟⲩⲧ) νεκρός.

ⲉⲣ ϩ. *B*, *slay*: Ro 13 9 (*S* ϩ.) φονεύειν; C 43 189 ⲟⲩϩ. ⲉⲧⲁϭⲁⲓϭ.

ⲣⲉϥϩ., -ϩ., *slayer, murderer*: Mt 22 7 *SB*, Ap 22 15 *SB* φονεύς, Nu 35 16 *SB* φονευτής; R 1 3 62 *S* ⲡⲣ. = DeV 1 45 *B* ⲥⲕⲉⲡⲱⲗⲁⲧⲱⲣ (ⲥⲡⲉⲕⲟⲩ., K 403 ساقان), AP 22 *A²* ⲁⲡⲁⲕⲟⲩⲣ. ⲉⲡ, ManiK 19 *A²* ϩⲱⲧⲃⲉ, MG 25 238 *B* serpent ⲟⲩⲣ. ⲡⲉ, C 86 274 *B* Jezebel †ⲣ., DeV 2 233 *B* ⲣ. ⲡⲥⲁⲡⲟⲩϣⲏⲣⲓ; ⲣⲉϥⲣⲉⲧⲃ- *S*, -ϩⲁⲧⲃ- *A²*, -ϩⲁⲧⲉⲃ- *B*, -ϩⲁⲧⲉⲃ- *F*: Jo 8 44 *SA²B*-κτόνος; Aeg 227 *S* ⲣ. ⲥⲟⲛ φονεύειν; ROC 23 283 *B* ⲣ. ⲡϫⲥ̄, JKP 2 134 *F* ⲗⲉϩⲣ. ⲥⲁⲛ;   as adj: CaiEuch 466 *B* thoughts ⲡⲣ. θανατηφόρος; ShMich 550 20 *S* ϣⲟⲭⲡⲉ ⲡⲣ., Cat 159 *B* ⲡⲁⲑⲟⲥ ⲡⲣⲉϥϩ. ψυχη; ⲙⲛⲧ-, ⲙⲉⲧⲣ., *slaughter, murder*: ShC 73 6 *S*, Bor 243 146 *S*, Cat 144 *B*; ShBor 204 249 *S* ⲙ. ϩⲉⲧⲃ ψυχη, EW 46 *B* ⲙ. ϩⲁⲧⲉⲃ ⲁⲗⲟⲩ; ⲣ ⲣ. *S*: Aeg 215 ⲁϥⲣ ⲣ. ⲉⲣⲟϥ ⲙⲙⲓⲛ ⲙⲙⲟϥ αὐτοφονευτής εἶναι.

ϫⲓⲛϩ. *B*, *act of slaying*: 3 Kg 17 20, Su 28 θανατοῦν; Aeg 6 sought me ⲉⲡϫⲓⲛϩⲟⲟⲑⲃⲉⲧ.

ϩⲁⲧⲃⲉⲥ, ϩⲟ. *S*, ϩⲁ. *A* nn f, *slaughter*: ShA 2 104 ϩⲟ. ⲡⲣⲱⲙⲉ, ib 1 457 wept for ⲧϩ., R 2 1 43 ⲧⲉⲓⲛⲟϭ ⲛϩ. (on Nu 25 9), Mor 40 10 sim (var ib 39 14 ϩⲟϩⲧⲥ);   *thing slain* (*cf* above nn): Jud 15 17 gloss on ⲁⲛϩⲁⲓⲣⲉⲥⲓⲥ; Nah 3 3 *A*(*B* ϩⲉⲓ) πτῶσις; BHom 120 devour ⲛϩ. ⲛⲛⲉⲧⲙⲟⲟⲩⲧ.

ϩⲉⲧⲃⲉ *A²*, nn f, as last: ManiH 83 †ϩ. ⲡⲧⲉ †ⲥⲧⲁⲩⲣⲱⲥⲓⲥ, Mani P ⲁⲩⲣⲉϣⲉ ⲁⲭⲡⲧⲉⲕϩ.;   *burial*(?) *A*: Is 53 9 (Cl, *SB* ⲕⲁⲓⲥⲉ) ταφή.

ϩⲁⲧⲏⲗ *F*   *v* ϩⲁⲧⲏⲣ.

ϩⲁϯⲗ *A²* nn as adj, meaning uncertain, *humble*, *lowly*(?): ManiP 52 ⲉϥⲁϩⲱⲗ ⲁϩⲟⲩⲛ ⲁⲩⲙⲛⲧⲣⲁ ⲡⲟⲩⲥⲓⲙⲉ ⲛϩ., opp ⲡⲉⲧⲁⲓ, ib 16 ⲛⲧⲕ ⲟⲩϣⲙⲙⲟ ⲛϩ. a poor man lacking all.

ϩⲁⲧⲁⲓⲗⲉ¹, -ⲁⲗⲏ², -ⲁⲗ(ⲉ)³, -ⲁⲗⲉⲉⲗⲉ⁴ *S* nn, an eye disease: Lev 21 20 (Miss 6 75¹, MS Louvain = Rec 8 27¹, P 44 106², 43 92³ مزروق, Mor 1⁴, *B* ⲁⲟⲩⲁⲡ ⲛϫⲗⲟ, no corresponding Ar) prob ἔφηλος.   *V* KKS 49. Cf ⲗⲉⲯ, ⲕⲗⲟ (λεύκωμα is rather var of πτίλος).

ϩⲁⲧⲗⲟⲟⲩⲧⲥ *S* nn, meaning unknown: Mor 51 36 bring forth to harvest ⲛⲉⲓϩ. ⲡⲣⲉⲙⲛⲏ ⲡⲉⲓⲟⲩⲉⲙ ⲕⲁⲗⲓⲣⲓⲟⲛ (κολλούρ.) ⲡⲣⲱⲙⲉ ⲉⲧϣⲱⲡⲉ. Cf? ϩⲁⲧ ⲥ.

ϩⲁⲧⲙⲉ (*sic* l) *S* nn, a vessel or measure: CO 239 ⲟⲩϩ. ⲡⲧⲉϣ.

ϩⲧⲟⲙⲧⲙ *S*, (ϩ)ⲧⲁⲙⲧⲙⲉ *A*(nn), ⲑⲟⲙⲧⲉⲙ, ⲧ. *B* (nn), ϩⲧⲁⲧⲁⲙ- *S*, ϩⲧⲁⲧⲱⲙ⳽ *A²*, ϩⲧⲁⲧⲱⲙⲧ†, ϩⲧⲁⲧⲟⲙⲧ† *S*, ⲧⲉⲙⲑⲱⲙⲧ† *B* vb **I** intr, *be darkened* (prob confused with ⲧⲱⲧⲙ): Z 571 by much vigil ⲛϩⲏⲧ ϩ. σκοτοῦσθαι; R 1 4 8 eyes ϩ. caligare; Ge 48 10 (var & *B* ϩⲣⲟϣ) βαρυωπεῖν; Gu 70 sea's water ϩ. ἰλιγγιᾶν(?); PS 5 ⲁⲡⲉⲛⲃⲁⲗ ϩ. through bright light, ShA 1 53 blinded woman ⲁⲡⲉⲥⲟⲩⲟⲉⲓⲛ ϩ. ⲏ ⲁϥⲧⲱⲣ, ShC 42 94 sim, Mich 550 45 ⲡⲉⲡⲗⲟⲛⲓⲥⲙⲟⲥ ϣⲧⲟⲙⲧⲁⲙ (*sic*) ⲉⲡϣⲁⲡⲙⲉⲉⲩⲉ ⲉⲡϫⲓⲥⲉ;   qual: Is 42 3 (*B* ⲟⲓ ⲛ̄ⲭⲣⲉⲙⲧⲥ) καπνίζειν; Mt 12 20 (*B* do) τύφειν; Jude 13 (*B* ⲡⲧⲉ ⲧⲭⲉⲙⲥ) σκότος; C 89 130 *B* hell ⲉϥⲧ. = Va ar 172 75 مظلم, Tri 365 sim; Aeg 26 ϩⲣⲟⲟⲩⲉ ⲉⲧϩ. = ib *B* ϩⲉⲭϩⲱϫ, ShA 1 110 midday light ϩ., ib 2 116 ⲡⲉⲩϩⲏⲃⲥ ϩ. ⲏ ⲁϥⲭⲉⲛⲁ, ShP 130⁴ 117 ⲡⲥⲟⲟⲩⲛ ⲉⲧϩⲧⲟⲙⲧ of heretics, P 131⁴ 99 ⲕⲁⲡⲡⲟⲥ…ⲉϥϩ.

II tr, *darken*: R 2 2 25 cloud ϩ. ⲛⲡⲁⲕⲧⲓⲛ ⲙⲡⲣⲏ ἀμαυροῦν; R 1 1 78 ϩ. ⲛⲡⲃⲁⲗ ⲛⲡⲉⲓⲁⲧⲡⲉ̄, ManiP *A²* powers & dominions ⲁϥϩⲧⲓⲧⲱⲙⲟⲩ, BHom 111 lest noise of craftsmen ϩ. ⲛⲓⲙⲁⲁϫⲉ of Solomon.

—— nn m *SAB*, *darkness, mist*: Zeph 1 15 *SA*(*B* ⲡⲓϭ) ὁμίχλη; Jude 6 *S*(*B* ⲭⲁⲕⲓ) ζόφος; Va 58 181 *B* ⲡⲁⲓⲙⲏϣ ⲡⲧ. ⲡⲧⲉ ⲫⲃⲓⲟⲥ ἐπιθολοῦν; ShA 2 94 *S* ⲟⲩϩ. like that of Sodom, ShMIF 23 34 *S* ϩⲟⲓⲧⲉ ⲛⲕⲣⲙⲧⲥ ϩⲧϩ., C 89 100 *B* †ϩⲉⲙⲓ ⲡⲉⲙⲡⲓⲑ. in hell;   ⲣ ϩ. *S*: Ming 283 ⲡⲁⲏⲣ ⲟ ⲛϩ.

ϩⲁⲧⲡ-   *v* ⲧⲱⲣⲉ p 428 *b*.

ϩⲧⲡ-, ⲉ- *S*(Sh) = ⲉϩⲡ-, *v* p 685 *a*.

ϩⲓⲧⲡ-   *v* ⲧⲱⲣⲉ *lc*.

ϩⲟⲧⲡ (*l*? ϩⲱⲧⲡ) *Sᵃ* vb c ⲉ-, meaning unknown: Ep 531 in mercantile record ⲁⲓϫⲓ ⲕⲟⲩⲭⲟ (*l* ϩⲟ) ⲡⲥⲟⲩⲟ ⲁϫⲱⲓ ⲛⲁⲥ ⲁⲥϩ. ⲉⲣⲟϥ.

ϩⲱⲧⲡ *SAA²BF*, ϩⲱⲡⲧ *SF*, ϩⲉⲧⲡ-, ϩⲟⲧⲡ⳽ (often ϩⲟⲡⲧ⳽) *SB*, ϩⲟⲧⲡ† *SB*, ϩⲁ.† *A²* vb **I** intr, *join, attune, be reconciled, sink* (sun, stars): 2 Kg 6 5 *B*(*S* ⲧⲱϣ) ἁρμόζειν; Ge 15 12 *SB*, Eccl 1 5 *SF*, Mk 1 32 *SB* δύειν; Job 31 26 *S*(*B* ⲕⲏⲡ), Lu 23 45 *S*(*B* ⲙⲟⲩⲛⲕ) ἐκλείπειν; ShMIF 23 197 *S* ⲡⲉⲧϫⲓ ϩⲁⲡ…ϣⲁⲡⲧⲟⲩϩ., RE 9 153 *S*]ⲁⲡⲁⲧϩⲁϫⲉ ⲙⲙⲟⲥ ⲉⲧⲣⲉⲥϩ., ManiH 50 *A²* ⲁϥϩ. ⲁϥⲙⲧⲁⲡ ⲙⲙⲁϥ, BHom 128 *S* ⲁⲡⲣⲓ ϩ., AM 11 *B* sim, ManiK 165 *A²* ⲉϥϣⲁⲡⲛⲟⲩⲉ (*sc* sun) ⲉϩ., ManiP *A²* ⲥⲉϩ.† ⲧⲏⲣⲟⲩ.

II tr: Ps 151 2 *B*(*S* ⲧ.), Nah 3 8 *B*(*A* ⲧ.) ἁρ.; Ex 40 18 *B* διεμβάλλειν رزقي; Is 49 8 *B*(*S* ⲥⲙⲓⲛⲉ) καθιστάναι; Joel 3 15 *B*(*SA* † neg) δύ.; RE 9 172 *S* ⲙⲡⲣϩⲟⲧⲣ ⲡⲉⲥϩⲁⲓ ⲉⲧⲣⲉϥϩⲟⲧⲡⲥ, C 89 38 *B* canon bids ⲉ-ⲑⲣⲉⲛϩ. ⲙⲛⲓⲃ (*sc* fast days) = Va ar 172 24 نجب, Cai The 273 *B* ⲁϥϩⲟⲧⲡⲟⲩ ⲉⲩⲥⲟⲡ like lyre القيثارة.

With following preposition.

—— ⲉ- *SABF* intr: 1 Kg 29 4 *S*, Mt 5 24 *S*(var ⲙⲛ-)*B* διαλλάσσειν dat, 1 Cor 7 11 *SBF* καταλ. dat,

C148 1 *A* ἐπικαταλ. dat; Eph 4 16 *B*(*S* ϣⲱⲡ̅) συναρμολογεῖσθαι; Va 57 249 *B* ⲉⲧϩ.† ⲉⲣⲟⲕ συμπλέκεσθαι dat, ib 250 *B* ⲁϥϩ. ⲉⲣⲟⲥ ⲛⲁϥ συνάπτειν dat; Jer
15 9 *S*(Wess 18 100, *B* ⲩ ϩⲁⲓ) ἐπιδύειν dat; ShBor
246 67 *S* not able ⲉϩⲟⲧⲡ ⲉⲛ̅ⲡ̅ⲉ̅, Mor 53 41 *S* ϩ. ⲉ-
ⲡⲉⲅⲉⲣⲏⲅ = TstAb 236 *B* ⲉⲣϩⲓⲣⲏⲛⲓ ⲡⲉⲙ-, MIF 9 60
S ⲁⲓϩⲱⲧⲡ ⲉⲧⲁϩⲓⲕⲱⲛ (εἰκ., var *B*Ap 22 ⲙⲛ-), Bor 226
181 *S* ⲁⲛϣⲱⲙⲛⲧ ⲛϩⲁⲧⲓⲟⲥ ϩ. ⲉⲛⲕⲱⲣⲧ regardless of
their bodies, COAd 29 *S* wife ⲛⲁϩ. ⲉⲣⲟⲩ ⲁⲛ, DeV 2
51 *B* ϯ-ⲭⲟⲡⲧ ⲉⲣⲱⲟⲩ...ϯϩ.† ⲉⲣⲱⲟⲩ, Amer School Or
Res 6 109 *B* ⲁϥⲙⲉⲧⲡⲟⲩϯ ϩ. ⲉϥⲙⲉⲧⲣⲱⲙⲓ; tr:
2 Cor 5 19 *B*(*S* ⲛ-) καταλ. acc dat, Eph 2 16 *S*(*B* ⲛ-)
ἀποκ. acc dat, Ac 7 26 *SBF* ⲥⲩⲛⲁⲗ. acc εἰς; Ez 1 11
B συζευγνύναι πρός; Miss 4 220 *B* ϩⲟⲡⲧⲉⲛⲛⲟⲩ ⲉⲧϯ-
ⲙⲁⲩ συνάπτειν dat, GFr 425 *S* ϩⲉⲧⲛ ⲡ̅ⲡ̅ⲉ̅ ⲉⲣⲟⲕ ἐξι-
λεοῦν; Aeg 243 *S* ϩⲉⲧⲛ ⲛⲉⲧⲙⲓϣⲉ ⲉⲅⲉⲓⲣⲏⲛⲓ εἰρηνεύειν; ShBor 246 73 *S* ⲁⲥϩⲉⲧⲛ ⲧⲉϥⲉⲕⲕⲗⲏⲥⲓⲁ ⲉⲣⲟϥ
ⲉⲅⲉⲓⲣⲏⲛⲓ, ShLeyd 372 *S* ⲉⲣⲉⲛⲡ̅ⲡ̅ⲉ̅ ϩ. ⲙⲙⲟⲛ ⲉⲩⲙⲛⲧ-
ϣⲏⲣⲉ ⲛⲁϥ, Sh(?)Mor 54 15 *S* ⲡⲧⲉϥϩⲟⲡⲟⲩ ⲉⲛⲉϥ-
ⲉⲓⲱⲧ, MG 25 54 *B* ϩⲟⲧⲡⲉϥ ⲛⲉⲙ-ϯⲥϩⲓⲙⲓ ⲉⲟⲩⲅⲁⲙⲟⲥ,
TEuch 1 2 *B* ⲁⲭⲱ ⲧⲉⲩⲭⲏ ... ϩ. ⲉⲣⲟⲥ ⲛⲧⲁⲓⲕⲉⲉⲩⲭⲏ
لهذا; ⲉϩⲟⲩⲛ ⲉ- *B*: DeV 2 105 ϯ-ⲥⲁⲣⲝ ... ⲁϥ-
ϩⲟⲧⲡⲥ ⲉϩ. ⲉⲣⲟϥ.

—— ⲉϫⲛ- *SB*: Eph 4 26 *B*(*S* ⲉ-) ἐπιδύ. ἐπί; Sh
MIF 23 152 *S* ⲡⲣⲏ ϩ. ⲉϫⲛⲁϣ ⲛⲭⲱⲣⲁ.

—— ⲙⲛ-, ⲛⲉⲙ- *SA²B*: Mt 5 24 *S*(var & *B* ⲉ-, cf
ManiP 39) διαλ. dat; BMar 99 *S* ⲉⲣⲉⲛⲡ̅ⲡ̅ⲉ̅ ϩⲁⲣ. ⲛⲓⲙⲁⲛ-
ⲙⲁⲛ, C 43 37 *B* ⲉⲑⲣⲟⲩ-ϩ. ⲛⲉⲙⲡⲟⲩⲉⲣⲛⲟⲩ = Mor 39
10 *S* ϣⲱⲡϥ, ManiK 148 *A²* ϩ. ⲙⲛⲧⲟⲩⲛⲉⲙ ⲓⲧⲉ ϯⲣ-
ⲏⲛⲓ, Mun 151 *S* ⲁⲛⲡ̅ⲡ̅ⲉ̅ ⲗⲟ ⲉϥϩ.† ⲛⲓⲙⲙⲁⲛ, C 86 27 *B*
wife ⲉⲧϩ.† ⲛⲉⲙⲛⲏⲓ since youth; tr: ROC 17 402
B ϩⲟⲧⲡⲉϥ ⲛⲉⲙⲟⲩⲅⲁⲙⲟⲥ συναρμ.; Va 57 189 *B* ⲁⲩ-
ϩⲟⲧⲡⲥ ⲛⲉⲙⲟⲩⲣⲱⲙⲓ συζ. dat; MartIgn 870 *B* ϩⲉⲧⲛ
ϯⲙⲉⲑⲛⲟⲩϫ ⲛⲉⲙϯⲙⲉⲑⲙⲏⲓ = R 1 4 58 *S* ⲧⲉϩ- συγκρίνειν dat; BSG 188 *S* ⲛϥϩ. ⲛⲓⲙⲙⲁⲛ ⲙⲡⲉϥϩⲁ, R 2
4 94 *S* ϩⲟⲧⲡⲛ...ⲙⲛⲡ̅ⲡ̅ⲉ̅, Va 63 3 *B* ⲁⲩϩⲟⲧⲡⲟⲩ ⲛⲉⲙⲡⲟⲩⲉⲣⲛⲟⲩ = BSM 26 *B* ⲑⲱⲟⲩϯ = BMis 365 *S* ϩⲟⲧⲣⲟⲩ; ⲉϩⲟⲩⲛ ⲛⲉⲙ- *B*: Va 66 293 ϩⲟⲧⲡⲥ ⲉϩ. ⲛⲉⲙ-
ⲧⲉⲛⲫⲩⲥⲓⲥ συζ.

—— ⲛ- dat *SB*: Eph 2 16 *B*(*S* ⲉ-) *v* c ⲉ-; Mor 53
63 *S* ϩ. ⲛⲁϥ ⲙⲡⲕⲟⲥⲙⲟⲥ; ⲁⲃⲁⲗ ⲛ- *A²*: from: Mani
K 164 ⲡⲣⲏ ϩⲁⲣ. ⲁⲃ. ⲙⲡⲕⲟⲥⲙⲟⲥ.

—— ϩⲓ- *B*: Ex 26 9 συνάπτ. ἐπί.

—— ϩⲛ-, ϩⲉⲛ- *SAB*: Col 1 22 *SB* ἀποκαταλ. ἐν;
Miss 4 223 *B* ⲁϥϩ. ⲡⲛⲉϥⲉⲕⲕⲗⲏⲥⲓⲁ ϩⲉⲛⲡⲓⲛⲁϩϯ; for
ⲉⲃⲟⲗ ϩⲛ-: Pro 6 35 *SA*(sic l, *B* ϯ ⲟⲩⲱ) ἀνταπαλ. acc,
Si 27 21 *S* διαλλαγή gen; TEuch 2 270 *B* ⲁⲕϩ. ⲛϯ-
ⲕⲧⲓⲥⲓⲥ ⲉ̅ⲃ̅. ϩⲉⲛⲡⲓ̅ ⲛⲥⲧⲟⲓⲭⲓⲟⲛ συναρ.

—— ϩⲓⲧⲛ- *SA*: Z 270 *S* ϩⲉⲧⲛ ⲟⲩⲟⲛ ⲛⲓⲙ...ϩ.ⲡⲉϥ-
ⲥⲡⲟϥ; ⲉⲃⲟⲗ ϩ.: Pro 15 28 *SA* φίλος γίνεσθαι διά.

—— nn m *SB*, *joint, joining, reconciliation*: He 4
12 *B*(*S* = Gk) ἁρμός; Is 9 5 *B*(*S* ϣⲃⲉⲓⲛ), Ro 5 11
SB καταλλαγή; K 54 *B* ⲡⲓϩ. اتّصال · Va 61 30 *B* ⲡⲣϩ.

ⲛϯⲯⲩⲭⲏ ⲛⲉⲙⲡⲓⲥⲱⲙⲁ, ROC 17 404 *B* ⲡϩ. ⲙⲡⲧⲁ-
ⲙⲟⲥ; *sinking of sun*: Ge 15 17 *S*(*B* vb) δυσμή,
Lev 22 7 *S*(*B* do) δύειν.

ⲁⲧϩ. *A²B*, *unsinking*: ManiP *A²* ⲡⲓⲣⲏ ⲛⲁ.,TstAb
249 *B* ⲟⲩϣⲓⲛⲓ ⲛⲁ.

ⲙⲁ ⲛϩ. *SAB*, *place of sinking* of sun, west: Nu 22
1 *SB*, Ps 74 6 *B*(*S* ⲉⲙⲛⲧ), Zech 8 7 *AB*, Lu 13 29
SB δυσμή, Miss 8 37 *S* bishops ⲉⲧϩⲛⲙⲁ. δύσις;
Mor 31 236 *S* ⲧⲕⲣⲏⲧⲏ ⲉⲧⲉⲛⲙⲁ. ⲙⲡⲉⲣⲡⲉ where were
priests' vestments.

ⲙⲉⲧϩ. *B*, *union*: K 57 اتّحاد.

ⲥⲁ ⲛϩ. *AA²*, *sunset side, west*: TU 43 16 *A* ⲛⲥ.,
ManiK 7 *A²* ⲡⲕⲁϩ ⲛⲥ., ManiBerlSitz '33 86 *A²* ⲛⲥ.
ⲙⲡⲉ opp ⲛⲥⲁ ⲙⲡⲣⲓⲉ ⲙⲡⲉ.

ⲣ ϩ., *reconcile*: Ro 11 15 *SB* καταλλαγή.

ⲣⲉϥϩ. *B*, *reconciler*: Va 58 188 fasting ⲟⲓ ⲡⲣ. ⲉⲣⲟⲛ
ⲙⲫϯ.

ϭⲓⲛ-, ϫⲓⲛϩ. *SA²B*, *union, reconciliation, sinking* of
sun: Va 68 167 *B* ⲧⲁⲓϫ. ⲛϣⲉⲙⲙⲟ of prodigal's welcome, ib 57 123 *B* ⲟⲩϫ. ⲉϥϯ καταλλαγή, P 44 50 *S*
ϭ. · ⲕⲁⲧⲁⲗ(ⲗ)ⲁⲧⲏ (ﺿ,); Va 57 124 *B* ⲟⲩϫ. ⲛⲡⲏ
ⲉⲧϣⲟⲡ συνάπτεσθαι; TRit 241 *B* ⲡⲟⲩϫ. (sc of bridal
pair) اتّصال; ib 6 *B* ⲡⲓϫ. ⲉϩⲟⲩⲛ ... ϫⲉⲡⲧⲕⲟⲓⲛⲱⲛⲓⲁ,
ManiK 164 *A²* ϭ. of sun.

ϩⲟⲧⲡ (Va), ϩⲟⲡⲧ (Lag) *B* nn, *thing joined*(?), *chain,
rim*: Ex 25 11, 25 κυμάτιον (var κλεῖσμα) طوق.
In place-name: ⲡⲛϩⲱⲧⲡ بندهدج (Ep 269, *ib* 1 120).
In month-name: ⲡⲁⲣⲙϩⲟⲧⲡ, -ϩⲁⲧⲡ *q v.*

ϩⲱⲧⲡ *B* v ⲱⲧⲡ 1°.

ϩⲧⲟⲡ *SB*, ϩⲧⲁⲡ *A²* nn m, *fall, destruction*: Job 16
15 *SB*, ib 33 17 *S*(*B* ϩⲉⲓ), ib 37 16 *S*(*B* ⲟⲩⲱϫⲡ), Ps
109 6 *B*(*S* ϩⲱⲧ̅) πτῶμα, Si 35 20 *S* ⲁⲛⲧⲓⲡ., Ps 90 6
SB συμπ., Si 20 17 *S*, Jer 6 15 *B* πτῶσις; PS 345 *S*
ⲉϥⲛⲁϩⲉ...ϩⲛⲟⲩϩ., BMis 110 *S* arise from ⲛⲉϩ. ⲙⲡⲇⲓⲁⲃⲟⲗⲟⲥ, BP 10587 *S* ϩⲉⲧⲁϥⲉ ⲙⲙⲟϥ ϩⲛⲟⲩϩⲧⲟⲡ (sic)
ⲛ̅ⲇⲁⲓⲙⲟⲛⲓⲟⲛ, ManiK 15 *A²* ⲛϩ. ⲙ̅ⲙⲓϣⲉ ⲙⲛⲛⲡⲟⲗ[ⲉ-
ⲙⲟⲥ; as if ? from ϩⲱⲧⲡ: MG 25 67 *B* ⲁⲩϩⲉⲓ ϫⲉⲛ-
ⲡⲓⲣⲧⲟ̅ⲃ̅ & lost virginity, BMis 69 *S* ⲁⲓⲭⲡⲟϥ (sc Jesus)
ⲁϫⲛϫⲱϩⲙ ⲁϫⲛϩ. (var FR 38 ⲥⲩⲛⲟⲩⲥⲓⲁ), Mor 33 124
S ⲟⲩⲙⲛⲧⲟⲩⲁ ⲡⲧⲉ ⲧⲥⲁⲣⲝ ⲁϫⲛⲡⲗⲁⲁⲩ ⲛϩ. (var BMis
62 ϫⲣⲟⲡ).

ϩⲧⲟⲡ *SB*, -ⲁⲛ *S*ᵃ nn m, a measure (cf Berl *Wörterb*
3 196): K 127 *B* husbandman's tools ⲛⲓϩ. (var ϩⲟⲧⲡ)
مفال tin vessels; CO 350 *S* ⲉϣⲱⲡⲉ ⲟⲩⲟⲛ ϫⲁⲕ ⲙⲙⲁⲩ
ⲭⲟⲟⲩ ⲟⲩⲕⲟⲩⲓ ... ϣⲁⲡϣⲁⲩ ⲛⲭⲟⲩⲱⲧ ⲛϩ., Vi ostr 164
*S*ᵃ ⲥⲛⲁⲩ ⲛϩ. ⲛⲡⲓⲕⲧⲉ (for ? ⲡⲉⲓⲕⲧⲉ).

ϩⲁⲧⲏⲣ, -ⲣⲉ *S*, ϩⲁⲑⲏⲣ, ⲁⲑ., ⲁⲡⲑ., ⲁⲡⲑⲉⲣⲁ *B*,
ϩⲁⲧⲏⲗ *F* nn m f, *hammer* (cf ܗܐܛܘܪ *Kémi* 2 14): Jud
4 21 *S*, Jer 10 4 *SB*ϩ., Is 41 7 *SB*, BHom 111 *S*
ϩⲣⲟⲟⲩ ⲛϩ. (on 3 Kg 6 7) σφῦρα, P 44 67 *S* ⲛϭⲫⲏⲣⲁ ·
ϩ., 43 62 *S* ﻣ·, ⲙⲣⲍⲓⲛⲉ, K 124 *B* ϯϩⲁⲑⲏⲣ ﻣﺮ-
ⲁⲧⲣⲉⲥⲉ, ⲇⲟⲧⲁⲕ مطرقة

الجارّ, *ib* 123 *B* ϯⲁⲡⲑⲉⲣⲁ ʼⲗ.; *ib* 151 *B* ⲟⲩϩ. ʼⲋ; Mor
17 112 *S* ϩ. ⲙⲡⲉⲡⲓⲡⲉ, Pap *penes* BH Stricker *S* ⲟⲩ-
ⲣⲁⲧⲏⲣⲉ ⲙⲡⲉⲛ[ⲓⲡ]ⲉ, Pcod 39 *S* ϩⲓⲟⲩⲉ ⲉϫⲱϥ ⲙⲡ. (*sic*
prob)*F*, Mor 18 63 *S* ϩⲓⲟⲩⲉ ⲉϫⲱϥ ⲡⲛⲉϣⲥⲉ ⲡϩ. =
Miss 4 138 *B* ⲡⲓⲁⲛⲑ., *C* 86 45 *B* ⲡⲁⲙⲛϣ ... ϩⲓⲟⲩⲓ
ⲉⲣⲟϥ ⲭⲉⲡⲟⲩⲏⲣ ⲡⲁⲑ., BMis 47 *S* ⲡⲉⲧⲛⲓⲃⲧ ⲙⲡⲉⲧⲛϩ.,
CO 468 *S* ⲡⲥⲁϥϥ, ⲡϩⲣⲉⲃ, ⲡϩ.;   ⲣⲉϥϩⲓⲟⲩⲉ ⲙⲡϩ.:
Ge 4 22 *SB* σφυροκόπος;   ϯ ϩ.: AZ 23 113 *S* ϯ
ϩ. ⲡⲁⲩ (*sc* compound of metals).

ϩⲱⲧ(ⲉ)ⲣ *S*, -ⲧⲣⲉ *A²*, ϩⲉⲧ(ⲉ)ⲣ-, ϩⲟⲧ(ⲉ)ⲣ- *S*, ϩⲁⲧⲉⲣ-
F, ϩⲟⲧⲣⲝ, ϩⲟⲧⲣ†, -ⲣⲉ† *S*, ϩⲟⲧⲉⲣ *B* vb intr, *be joined,
doubled*: ShBMOr 8810 453 of them that fast over-
much ⲥⲉϩ. ⲧⲏⲣⲟⲩ fasting 4 days or week on end, ShC
73 103 none may abstain from eating ⲉⲩϩ. ⲥⲛⲁⲩ ⲥⲛⲁⲩ
(var ⲉⲩⲉⲓⲣⲉ ⲡⲥ. ⲥ.);   qual: Deu 15 18 hireling ⲉϥϩ.
ⲧⲣⲣⲟⲙⲡⲉ (*B* ⲣⲉⲙⲃⲉⲭⲉ ⲡⲣⲟⲙⲡⲓ) ἐφέτιος; Va 66 305
B course of sun & moon ⲉⲧϩ. *attuned* like lyre εὐαρ-
μοστία; ClPr 30 10 ⲉⲥϩⲟⲧⲣⲉ ⲛϭⲓ ⲧⲉⲭⲁⲣⲓⲥ διπλάσιος;
P 54 123 *B* ح.ـ ، موصول; Z 579 ⲡⲣⲱⲙⲉ ϩ. ⲉϥⲟ ⲛ-
ⲥⲛⲁⲩ body & soul, Pcod 46 ⲡⲉⲧϩ. in fellowship of
marriage, Wor 227 ⲉⲩϩ. ⲉⲩϩⲣ ϩⲱⲃ ϩⲁⲡⲉϥⲃⲉⲕⲉ *hireling*,
TurM 18 ϣⲟⲙⲛⲧ ⲡⲕⲉⲣⲟⲓ (κηρίον? Ep 545)...ⲡⲡⲁ-
ⲕⲟⲧ (?) ⲡϩⲏⲧⲟⲩ ϫϩ. ⲡⲥⲛⲁⲩ ⲡϩⲣⲉⲃ;   tr: BMOr
6807(5) ⲉⲩϩ. ⲙⲙⲟⲟⲩ (*sc* ὑποστάσεις) ϩⲱⲥ ⲕⲁⲧⲁ ⲟⲩⲁⲍⲓⲁ συνιέναι; P 44 90 ὁμοφωνεῖν; ShZ 603 ⲁϥϩ. ⲙⲡϣⲁϫⲉ ⲙⲡⲉⲓϣⲱⲛϥ (of birth & death), BMis 19 ⲡⲥⲉ-
ϩⲟⲧⲣⲧ ϩⲛⲟⲩⲅⲁⲙⲟⲥ, BM 173 216 announcing Easter
ⲧⲡⲛⲁϩ. ⲡⲧⲕⲉⲥⲁϣϥⲉ ⲡϩⲣⲃⲗⲟⲙⲁⲥ (cf Gött N '01 329
ⲧⲡⲛⲁϩ. ϣⲁ ⲟⲡ ϩⲓⲧⲕⲉ-), BM 1152 ⲧⲁϩⲟⲧⲉⲣ ⲡⲓⲱ *yoke*
(or ? *hire*) asses, RE 9 172 ⲙⲡⲣϩⲟⲧⲣ ⲡⲉⲥϩⲁⲓ ⲉⲧⲣⲉϥϩⲟⲧⲡⲥ *constrain not*.

With following preposition. ⲥ ⲉ-, *join, be hired,
hire to*: PS 42 ⲡⲉⲥⲁϩⲟⲣⲁⲧⲟⲥ ⲉⲧϩ.† ⲉⲣⲟⲥ, ShMun 157
ⲉⲧⲣ ϩⲟⲩⲟ ϩ. ⲙⲙⲟⲕ ⲉⲧⲙⲡⲧϣⲃⲏⲣ of Christ, Bor 260
121 ϩⲉⲧⲣ ⲡⲉⲥϩⲁⲓ ⲙⲡⲡⲟⲙⲟⲥ ⲉⲡⲉⲩⲁⲅⲅⲉⲗⲓⲟⲛ, Mor 46
47 rich man ⲉⲣⲉⲟϥ(ⲟⲩ)ⲟⲉⲓⲉ ϩ.† ⲉⲣⲟϥ working & getting wage, AZ 67 102 contract ⲁⲓϩⲟⲧⲣⲉⲕ ⲉⲣⲟⲓ to do
year's work, Ryl 185 ⲉⲓϩ.† ⲉⲣⲟⲕ ϩⲁⲡⲕⲁⲣⲡⲟⲥ;   ⲉ-
ϩⲟⲩⲛ ⲉ-: PS 230 ⲉⲥϩ.† ⲉϩ. ⲉⲡⲉϥⲙⲉⲗⲟⲥ, ShIF 155
strips fit to ϩⲟⲧⲣⲟⲩ ⲉϩ. ⲉⲩϩⲟⲓⲧⲉ ⲛϣⲁⲓ, BMis 131 ϩⲟⲧⲣⲟⲩ ⲉϩ. ⲉⲡⲉⲅⲉⲣⲏⲩ, BAp 111 ϩⲟⲧⲣϥ ⲉϩ. ⲉⲡⲛⲁⲙⲟⲥ =
MIE 2 386 *B* ϯ ⲡⲁϥ ⲡⲧⲉϥϭⲓⲁⲓ;   ⲥ ⲙⲛ-, *agree with*:
Ryl 64 Christ's flesh ϩ.† ⲡⲙⲙⲁϥ ⲕⲁⲧⲁ ⲟⲩⲁⲍⲓⲁ συνάπτεσθαι dat (cf above BMOr 6807), ShR 2 3 54 ⲡⲁⲡⲟⲩ ⲧⲁⲙⲡⲧⲛⲟϭ ⲉⲣϣⲁⲛⲡⲉϩⲏⲅⲉ ϩ. ⲡⲙⲙⲁⲥ, ShClPr
22 356 ⲡⲗⲟⲓⲟⲛ...ⲙⲡⲧⲉⲡⲣⲁⲍⲓⲥ ⲉⲧϩ.† ⲡⲙⲙⲁϥ, ROC
19 75 ⲧⲁⲙⲡⲧⲛ̄ ϩ. ⲁⲛ ⲙⲛⲧⲥⲁⲣⲝ ϩⲓⲟⲩϣⲱⲛϥ, Mor 40
7 ϩ. ⲙⲡⲛⲉⲅⲉⲣⲏⲩ ⲉⲩⲅⲁⲙⲟⲥ (var *ib* 39 10 ϣⲱⲛϥ ⲙⲡⲛ.
ϩⲛ-), Ryl 72 352 ϫⲉⲕ ⲥⲛⲁⲩ of pearl ⲉⲩϩ.† ⲙⲡⲛⲉⲅⲉⲣⲏⲩ;   tr, *join with*: ClPr 30 11 ⲁϥϩⲉⲧⲉⲣ ⲡⲧⲱⲙⲉ
ⲡⲣⲉⲛⲥⲛⲏⲩ ⲙⲡⲛⲉⲅⲉⲣⲏⲩ διπλῆ καλεῖσθαι (Jo 1 41);
ShLeyd 157 ⲁⲡⲡⲛ̄ ϩ. ⲡⲧⲙⲡⲧⲉⲣⲟ ⲙⲡⲧⲙⲡⲧⲟⲩⲏⲏⲃ,

Mus 42 229 ϩⲉⲧⲣⲧⲏⲩⲧⲛ ⲙⲡⲡⲉⲭ̄ⲥ̄, Mor 22 122 ⲁⲥ-
ϩⲉⲧⲣ ⲁⲭⲁⲃ ⲡⲙⲙⲁⲥ ⲉⲧⲉⲥⲡⲁⲣⲁⲛⲟⲙⲓⲁ = BSM 112 *B*
ϭⲱⲧⲃ (*l* ϩⲱⲧⲡ) ⲡⲉⲙ., BMis 365 ⲁⲩϩⲟⲧⲣⲟⲩ ⲙⲡⲡⲉⲅⲉⲣⲏⲩ = Va 63 3 *B* ϩⲟⲧⲡⲟⲩ = BSM 26 *B* ⲑⲱⲟⲩϯ
ⲡⲉⲙ-, ManiK 48 *A²* ϩ. ⲙⲙⲁⲩ ⲙⲡⲡⲟⲩⲉⲣⲏⲩ;   ⲉ-
ϩⲟⲩⲛ ⲙⲡ-: Leyd 270 ⲡⲧⲁⲛⲥⲁⲓⲁ ϩⲟⲧⲣⲟⲩ ⲉϩ. ⲙⲡⲡ-
ϩⲟⲡⲟⲕⲉⲛⲧⲁⲩⲣⲟⲥ (Is 34 14).

—— nn m *SA²*, *joint yoke, union*: BHom 47 ⲡϩ.
ⲙⲡⲡⲅⲁⲙⲟⲥ (var R 2 2 31 ⲡϣⲱⲛⲃ) συζυγία; Ryl 113
ϩⲉⲅⲅⲟⲥ · ⲡⲥⲟⲉⲓϣ ⲡϩ. ⲡϣⲱⲛⲃ, Mani P *A²* ⲡϩ. ⲙⲡ-
ϫⲱⲣⲙⲉ.

ⲣⲁⲙⲡϩ. *S*, *hireling*: R 1 3 57 Herod (Mt 14 6) ⲡⲣⲣⲟ
ⲡⲁϥⲏⲥ ⲡⲁⲣⲁ ⲟⲩⲣ. (as term of contempt), Mor 46
51 victuals (χρεία) for ⲡⲣ.

ϭⲓⲛϩ. *SA²*, *union, agreed hire*: Deu 15 18 (*B* ⲃⲉⲭⲉ)
μισθός; Pap *olim penes* GHorner ⲟⲩϭ. (*sc* of Trinity),
Mani P 86 *A²* ⲧϭ. ⲡⲧⲥⲁⲣⲝ.

In place-name: ⲡⲣⲱ]ⲙⲉ ϩⲱⲧⲣ (Ryl 185).

ϩⲱⲧⲏⲣ *B* nn, among maladies &c, in ⲡϩⲉⲓ ϩ. الخلاء اخ
secretions K 159 (gloss BM 924 سعيدى *Sa'idic*).   Cf
ϣⲃⲉⲗⲧ.

ϩⲁⲧⲣⲉ *SA²*, ⲁⲧⲣⲉ *B*, ⲉ̀. *O*, pl ϩⲁⲧⲣⲉⲉⲩ¹, -ⲉⲉⲅⲉ²,
-ⲉⲩⲉ³ *S*, ⲁⲑⲣⲉⲩ, ⲁⲧ. *B*, ϩⲁⲧⲣⲏⲟⲩ *F* nn m, *a doubled
thing, twin*: Mani P *A²* ⲡϩ. ⲙⲡⲓⲡⲉⲧⲭⲏ[ⲕ, BMis 272
S ϣⲏⲣⲉ ⲥⲛⲁⲩ ⲡϩ. (var Mor 29 41 ϩ.³) = Mor 30 48 *F*
ϩⲁⲧⲣⲏⲟⲩ, AZ 21 100 *O* ⲓⲃⲧ ⲡϩⲉⲛⲓⲡⲉ ⲡⲁ̄., *C* 86 271 *B*
ϣⲉ ⲉϩⲟⲓ ⲡⲁ. *double-pronged*;   pl: Ge 25 24 *B*(*S*
MS Louvain ⲉⲩⲟ ⲛ]ⲥⲛⲁⲩ), Cant 4 5 *S²*(var sg) δίδυμος, *ib* 2 *S³*(var do, *F* ⲥⲡⲉⲩ ⲥⲡⲉⲩ) διδυμεύεσθαι; Br
99 *S* ⲡϩ.¹, PasH 56 *B* all things (creatures) ⲟⲓ ⲡⲁⲧ.;
as if sg: PS 194 *S* ⲡⲥⲱⲧⲏⲣ ⲡϩ.¹ *ib* 197 ϕ.¹ ⲡⲥⲱⲧⲏⲣ,
ib 223 ⲡϩ.¹ ⲙⲙⲩⲥⲧⲏⲣⲓⲟⲛ;   *testicles B*: Lev 21 20
(*S* = Gk) μόνορχις; Deu 25 11 (*S* diff) δίδ.

As name: ϩⲁⲧⲣⲉ (Z 299, BM 1224), -ⲏ (J 107),
ⲁⲧⲣⲉ (CO 29), ⲁⲑⲣⲉ (*AmerJPhilol* 56 110), Ἀθρέ (PG
65 372), Ἀθρῆς, Ἀτ. (Preisigke) هدرا، هدرى (Synax 1
151, 327), ⲑⲁⲧⲣⲉ (Rec 11 147), -ⲏ (Cai ostr 44674
39), Θατρῆς, Παθατρῆς (Preisigke).

ϩⲉⲧⲣⲉ *S* nn f, *part of body*, ? *Sⁱ* for ϩⲁⲧⲣⲉ: PMéd
319 boy ⲉⲣⲉⲧⲉϩ. ⲡⲏⲩ ⲉⲃⲟⲗ.

ϩⲁⲧⲣⲉⲥ *S* nn f, *yoke, pair* (of mules): P 130ᵇ 66
Plato's chariot ⲧϩ. ⲙⲡⲥⲛⲁϥ ⲥⲛⲁⲩ ⲉⲧⲡⲁϩⲃ ⲉⲣⲟϥ.

V also ϩⲧⲟ.

ϩⲧⲟⲣ *S*, -ⲁⲡ *AA²* nn m, *necessity, constraint*:
Philem 14 (*B* = Gk) opp ϩⲡⲛⲁ̄, Bor 253 167 ⲙⲡ ϩ.
ϩⲓϫⲱⲛ ἀνάγκη; BMOr 6203 A deed drawn up ⲁⲭⲛ-
ⲗⲁⲁⲩ ⲡϩ.;   ⲥ ⲉ-: 1 Cor 9 16 (*B* do) ἀν. dat; ShC
73 84 Lent & Pascha ϩⲉⲛϩ.ⲡⲉ ⲉⲟⲩⲟⲛ ⲡⲓⲙ to fast,
BM 1149 ⲟⲩϩ. ⲉⲣⲟⲓⲡⲉ ⲉⲥϩⲁⲓ, Bor 282 164 ⲟⲩϩ. ⲉⲣⲟⲛ-
ⲡⲉ ⲉⲧⲣⲉⲛ-;   ϩⲛⲟⲩϩ. advb: Wess 15 135 ⲁⲛϯ ⲡⲉⲛ-
ⲟⲩⲟⲓ ϩ. ἀναγκαίως, 1 Pet 5 2 (*B* ⲭⲉⲛⲟⲩϭⲓ ⲡϩⲟⲡⲥ)
ἀναγκαστῶς, 2 Cor 9 7 (*B* as Gk) ἐξ ἀνάγκης, Ac 15

28 (*B* do) ἐπάναγκες; ShC 73 56 those disobedient
ϥⲓⲧⲟⲩ ⲙⲙⲁⲩ ϩ., ShC 42 149 ⲉϩⲣⲁϥ ⲁⲛ ⲁⲗⲗⲁ ϩ., ShC
73 74 epistles read 4 times yearly ϩ., Mus 40 44 (Reg
Pach)sim, Mor 28 76 thy bidding ⲧⲏⲡⲁⲁ(ⲁ)ⲥ ϩ., ST
250 15 ϩⲛⲟⲩϣⲧⲟⲣ; c ϩⲁ- & poss, *on own authority, of own accord*: 2 Cor 3 5 ϩⲁⲡⲉⲛϩ. (*B* ϩⲱⲥ ⲝⲉⲉⲃⲟⲗ
ⲙⲙⲟⲛ) ἐξ ἑαυτῶν, ib 8 3 ϩⲁⲡⲉⲛϩ. οὐ ϩⲁⲧⲟⲩ (*B* ϫⲉⲛ-
ⲡⲟⲩⲣⲱⲟⲩⲧϥ ⲙⲙⲁⲩⲁⲧⲟⲩ) αὐθαίρετος; Wess 11 167
ϩⲁⲡⲉⲩϩ. ⲉϣⲁⲅⲁⲙⲁⲣⲧⲉ ⲡⲣⲟϩⲟ ἑκούσιος; Z 333 chose
to die ϩⲁⲡⲉϥϩ. ⲙⲙⲛ ⲙⲙⲟϥ, Sh(Besa)Z 506 none
shall give aught away ϩⲁⲡⲉⲩϩ. ⲙⲁⲩⲁⲁϥ, ShIF 203
ⲧⲉⲧⲛϣⲟⲟⲡ ϩⲁⲡⲉⲧⲛϩ. ⲙⲁⲩⲁⲁⲧⲧⲏⲩⲧⲛ, BMis 452 ⲙ-
ⲡⲉϥϭⲣⲟϣ ⲉⲣ ⲡⲣⲱϩ ϩⲁⲡⲉϥϩ. οὐⲁϥ for he fled vain
glory; c ϩⲛ- sim: ShViK 908 253 ϩⲙⲡⲁϩ. ⲙⲙⲛ
ⲙⲙⲟⲓ as man in authority, BHom 125 Christ came
ϩⲁⲡⲉϥϩ. ⲙⲛⲧⲉϥⲁⲅⲁⲡⲏ, ManiH 3 *A*² ⲁⲓⲡϣⲉ ϩⲙⲡⲁϩ.
οⲩⲁϩⲉⲧ; c ϩⲓⲧⲛ- sim: R 2 4 96 we serve evil ϩ.
ⲡⲉⲡϩ. ⲙⲁⲩⲁⲁⲛ.

ⲣ ϩ. *S, constrain* c ⲉ-: Nu 23 12 (*B* ⲁⲣⲉϩ) φυλάσσειν; Si prol προάγειν; Mich 550 24 ⲁⲥⲣ. ⲉⲣⲟⲟⲩ
ⲉⲧⲣⲉⲩϣⲡ ⲧⲟⲟⲧⲥ ... ⲙⲡⲉⲗⲗⲟ, R 2 1 30 ⲁⲩⲣ. ⲉⲛⲡⲣⲟ
ⲉϣⲓⲛⲉ, Z 283 ⲡⲥⲉⲣ. ⲉⲡⲓⲥⲓⲟⲩⲣ to admonish *dux*, Cl
Pr 30 14 ⲁⲥⲉⲣ. ⲉⲣⲟⲛ ⲉϩⲉⲣⲙⲏⲛⲉⲩⲉ what we have set
down; c poss, *take authority*: Si 20 6 ⲉⲧⲉⲓⲣⲉ ⲙⲡⲉϥ-
ϩ. ἐνεξουσιάζεσθαι; 1 Cor 9 18 (*B* = Gk) καταχρᾶσθαι
τῇ ἐξουσίᾳ; Miss 4 229 suffered none ⲉⲣ ⲡⲉⲩϩ. ϩⲓⲗ-
ⲗⲁ(ⲁ)ⲩ ⲡⲣⲱϩ.

ϯ ϩ. *SA, put constraint, compel, give authority* c
ⲉ-: 2 Mac 6 1 *A* ἀναγκάζειν; R 1 1 64 ϯ. ⲉⲣⲟⲛ ⲉⲧⲃⲏⲛⲧⲟⲩ ἐντέλλειν; Mor 37 62 ⲡⲉⲧϯ. ⲉⲣⲟⲛ κατεπείγειν; ShBor 246 *ult* ⲡⲧⲁϥ. ϯ. ⲉⲛⲓⲙ ϫⲉⲡⲛⲉⲅⲭⲟⲟⲥ (*cf*
Mt 17 9 ϩⲱⲡ), ShViK 9750 242 ⲟⲩⲧⲱϣ ⲉⲩϯ. ⲉⲣⲟⲛ
ⲡⲣⲏⲧⲩ, MR 4 68 ⲁϥϯ. ⲉⲣⲟⲓ ⲛϭⲓ ⲡⲣ ⲡⲙⲉⲉⲩⲉ = Miss
4 134 *B* ϩⲓ ⲁⲡⲁⲅⲕⲏ, Mor 50 58 ⲁⲡⲣⲱϩ ϯ. ⲉⲣⲟⲓ ⲉⲧⲣⲁ-,
Blake 300 ϯ. ... ⲉⲧⲙⲧⲣⲉ-; c ⲛ- *dat*: Si 30 29
ἐξουσίαν διδόναι dat.

ϩⲧⲱⲣⲉ *S*, ϩⲧⲟⲩⲣⲉ *A*   *v* ϩⲧⲟ.

ϩⲧⲉⲣⲧⲁⲣⲧ *S*ᵃ   *v* ϣⲧⲟⲣⲧⲣ.

ϩⲉⲓⲧⲉⲥ *F*   *v* ⲉⲓⲥ *s f.*

ϩⲟⲧⲥ, ϩⲁ. *S* nn f, *vessel or measure* (*cf* hꜣṯ
Dévaud): Glos 232 κεράμιον · ϩⲁ., ib 223 ⲡⲉⲧϩⲓ ϩⲟ.
ⲛϣⲉ · ἀσιλλοφόρος *wooden yoke-bearer* (ἀσ. ? misunderst); Turin ostr 768 ⲛⲟϭ ⲡϩⲁ., ϩⲁ. ϣⲏⲙ; contains wine Ryl 347, WS 88, 133; vinegar *ib* 147, BP
4949; herbs λαψάνη Turin ostr 426; salted fish ϫⲓⲣ
WS 147; olives PMich 4927; cheese WS 153; mustard ϣⲗϭⲟⲙ CO 348; ⲥⲁϩⲡⲉ BP 402, Vi ostr 740;
ⲉⲧϩ(?)WS 144.

ϩⲧⲁⲓⲧ *A*²   *v* ϩⲏⲧ (ⲕⲱ ⲛϩ.).

ϩϯⲧ, ϩⲧⲓⲧ *SB* nn m, *beet B*: Is 51 20 (*S* ϫⲡⲏ)

σευτλίον; K 195 ⲡϩ. سلق (*cf* P 44 82 ⲥⲉⲩⲡⲗⲟⲡ, *l* ⲥⲉⲩⲧ.
'‑); *onion S*: P 44 82 ⲡⲉϩ. · ⲡⲉⲙϫⲟⲗ بصل, Tri 422 '.ϩ
(*cf* Nu 11 5 *SB* ⲙϫⲱⲗ); PMéd 247 (*v n*), *ib* 304 ϭⲱⲃⲉ
ⲡϩ., *ib* 235 ⲙⲟⲟⲩ ⲡϩ.

ϩⲁⲧⲏⲩ   *v* ⲧⲏⲩ.

ϩⲧⲟⲟⲩⲉ, ⲧⲟⲟⲩⲉ *S*, ⲧⲁⲩⲉ *S*ᵃ(*v* ⲥⲓⲟⲩ), ϩⲧⲁⲩⲉ *S*ᶠ*A*²
(Ma), ϩⲓⲧⲁⲩⲉ *AA*²(JoAP), ϩⲓⲧⲁⲩ *A*²(AP), ⲧⲟⲟⲩⲓ *B* ⲛⲛ
m, ϩⲁⲛⲁⲧ. *B* f *dawn, morning*: Ge 1 19 *AB*, Ps 29 5 *S*
(*B* ϣⲱⲣⲡ), Jer 21 12 *S*(*B* ⲏⲧ.), Hos 7 6 *A*(*B* ϣ.), Jo 18
28 *SA*²(*B* do) πρωί, Mt 21 18 *SB*, Cl 43 5 *A* πρωία,
Job 38 12 *SB* ϩⲁ. πρωινός; Ex 14 24 *B* ϩⲁ. ἑωθινός;
Job 7 4 *S*(*B* ϣ.), Ac 16 35 *S*(*B* ⲉϩⲟⲟⲩ) ἡμέρα; Ex 16
23 *B*(*S* ⲣⲁⲥⲧⲉ) αὔριον; ShC 73 65 *S* ϩ. ⲡϣⲱⲣⲡ ⲛⲧⲕⲩⲣⲓⲁⲕⲏ, C 89 206 *B* ϩⲁ. ⲉⲙⲁϣⲱ ⲛϯⲅⲣ., Mor 19
58 *S* ϩ. ⲙⲡⲉϥⲣⲁⲥⲧⲉ, *ib* 22 76 *S* ϩ. (var *ib* 26 9 & *B*
Mis 158 ϣⲱⲣⲡ), AP 23 *A*² ϩⲓⲧⲁⲩ *in morning*, Mani
P 146 *A*² ⲡϩ. ⲁϥϣⲱⲡⲉ ⲉ[ⲧⲁ]ⲡⲣⲏ ϣⲁⲓⲉ, Va 63 6 *B*
ⲁϣ ⲡⲉϩⲟⲟⲩⲡⲉ ⲧ. = BMis 373 *S* ⲣⲁⲥⲧⲉ, C 41 11 *B*
arose ϩⲁ., CaiThe 272 = TThe 144 *B* ϫⲉⲛⲧⲁⲓϩⲁ.
سر; with poss: Lev 22 30 *B*(*S* ⲛⲁⲩ ⲛϩ.), Jud 6
28 *S*, 1 Kg 15 12 *S* τὸ πρωί; MG 25 11 *B* ⲁϥⲓ ⲉⲡⲉϥⲧ.
ἑξῆς.

ⲡⲛⲁⲩ ⲛϩ. *SAB, time of dawn, morning hour*: Ex 16
7 *SB* ϩⲁ., Eccl 10 16 *S*(*F* ⲛϣ.), Mk 13 35 *SB* ϩⲁ. (*F*
Mor 21 3 do) πρωί, Ps 89 14 *B* ϩⲁ.(*S* ⲛⲟⲩ ⲛϣ.), Zeph
3 3 *A*(*B* ⲛϣ.) τὸ π., Ps 72 14 *SB* ⲛⲧⲉ ⲧ., Lam 3 22 *B*
pl ϩⲁ. πρωία, Ge 49 27 *S*(*B* ⲧ.), Ap 22 16 *S*(*B* ⲛⲧ.)
-νός; Ps 21 tit *S*(*B* ⲛϣ), Jon 4 7 *SA*(*B* do) ἑω.; Ps
62 7 *B* pl (*S* ⲛϣ.) ὄρθρος; AM 50 *B* ⲙϥⲛⲁⲩ ⲛϩⲁ.;
ϣⲁⲡⲛ. ⲛϩ., ⲛϩⲁ.: Lev 6 9 *SB*, Nu 9 15 *S*(*B* ϣⲁϩⲁ.)
ἕως(τὸ) πρωί.

ⲥⲟⲩ ⲛϩ., ⲛⲧⲉ ϩⲁ. *v* ⲥⲓⲟⲩ.

ⲉϩ. *S*, ⲁϩ. *A*, ⲉⲧ., ⲉϩⲁ. *B, at dawn, in morning*: Ge
21 14 *S*(*B* ⲛϣ.), Nu 22 13 *S*(*B* ⲏⲧ.), Ps 89 6 *S*(*S*ᶠ
tablet Cai Copt Mus ϩ., *B* ϩⲁ.) τὸ πρωί, Ex 34 25 *B*
ⲉϩⲁ. (*S* ϣⲁϩ.) εἰς τὸ π., Zeph 3 5 *A*(*B* ϣ.), Mk 11 20
S(*B* ⲛϩⲁ.) πρωί, Ps 64 8 *S*(*B* ⲛⲧⲉ ϩⲁ.) πρωία; Ex 32
6 *S*(*B* ⲉⲡⲉϥⲣⲁⲥⲧϯ) τῇ ἐπαύριον; Lu 24 22 *S*(*B* ⲛϣ.)
ὀρθρινός; Mt 28 1 *SB* ⲉⲧ. ἐπιφώσκειν; ShMIF 23 145
S ϩⲓⲣⲟⲩϩⲉ...ⲉϩ., R 1 2 42 *S*(var Lammeyer 45 ⲙⲡⲛⲁⲩ ⲛϣ.).

ⲛϩ. *SB, as last*: Ge 28 18 *S*(var ⲉϩ.)*B*, Deu 28 67
S(*B* ϩⲁ.), Ps 58 17 *SB* τὸ π., Is 50 4 *B* ⲛϩⲁ. (*S* ⲉϩ.),
Mk 16 2 *B* do (*S* BMis 501 ϩ.) πρωί, Ap 2 28 *B*(*S* as
adj) πρωινός; Ps 56 9 *B* ⲛϩⲁ. (*S* ⲙⲡⲛ. ⲛϣ.) ὄρθρου,
2 Kg 15 2 *S* ϣⲟⲣⲡϥ ⲛϩ. (var ⲉϩ.) ὀρθρίζειν; AZ 21
154 *S* ⲧⲱⲟⲩⲛ ⲛϩ., C 43 122 *B* ⲁϥⲧⲱⲟⲩⲛ ⲛϩⲁ., DeV 2
132 *B* ⲁϥϣⲟⲣⲡϥ ⲛⲧ., BSM 67 *B* ⲁⲡⲓⲧ ⲡⲉⲙⲟⲧⲉⲛ ⲛⲧ.

ϣⲁϩ. *SAB, till morning*: Ex 12 10 *S*(*B* ⲉϣ.), *ib* 23
18 *SB* ϣⲁϩⲁ., Job 7 4 *S*(*B* ϣⲁϣ.) ἕως πρωί; Pro 7
18 *SAB* ϣⲁⲧ. ἕως ὄρθρου; BAp 216 *S* = Rec 6 181
B ϣⲁⲧⲉϣ. ϣⲱⲡⲓ, C 89 14 *B* ϣⲟⲡⲧ ⲉⲣⲟⲕ ϣⲁϩⲁ.

ϩⲓⲧⲟⲟⲩⲉ S(Sh), *at dawn*: Bor 246 89 ϣⲓⲡⲉ ⲛⲥⲱϥ ϩ., C 73 81 first prayer ϩ., A 2 233 early at church ϩ. ⲁⲩⲱ ϩⲓⲣⲟⲩϩⲉ.

ⲉϩⲓⲧⲟⲟⲩⲉ S, as last: CO 60 ⲣ ⲡϣⲁ ⲉϩⲟⲩⲛ ⲉ. ϩⲁⲙⲡϣⲁ ⲱ (ⲟ ⲡ 685 a).

ⲭⲓⲛϩ. S, *from morning*: Ac 28 23 (B ⲓⲥⲭⲉⲛϣ.) ἀπὸ πρωί, Job 4 20 (B ϣ.) ἀπὸ πρωίθεν.

V Rec 24 206, AZ 51 124, GöttN '20 133.

ϩⲓⲧⲟⲩⲛ, ϩⲓⲧⲟⲩⲱⲝ ⲩ ⲧⲟⲩⲱⲝ.

ϩⲱⲧϥ B vb tr, *nail* (*l* -ϭⲧ = ⲱϭⲧ): C 86 205 ⲁϥⲑⲣⲟⲩϩ. ⲛⲛ̄ ⲡⲓϭⲧ ⲉⲡⲉϥⲥⲱⲙⲁ ⲉϩⲟⲩⲛ ⲉⲡⲓⲥⲗⲟⲝ, *ib* 216 sim.

ϩⲁⲑⲱⲣ (BMis 156, J 16 2, Kr 5, Ryl 265), ϩⲉⲱⲣ (CO 478, Tor 12) S, ⲁⲑⲱⲣ (ShMiss 4 590, BMis 133, Lant 51) S, (AM 247, LIb 3, BSM 34) B, ϩⲁⲑⲱⲗ (Mor 24 3), ϩⲉ. (MR 2 48), ϩⲁⲑⲟⲗ (Kr 25), -ⲧⲟⲗ (BM 1226) F, name of 3d month, Gk Ἀθύρ, Ἀθῆρ, Ar هاتور. In place ⲛϩⲁⲧⲱⲣ (J & C 92, *cf* 49) goddess's, not month's name. *Cf* GöttN '25 52.

ϩⲟⲧϩⲧ S, ϩⲁⲧϩⲧ S/A², ϩⲁⲧϩⲧ A, ϩⲟⲧϩⲉⲧ B, ϩⲁⲧϩⲉⲧ F, ϩⲉⲧϩ(ⲉ)ⲧ- S, ϩⲉⲧϩⲉⲧ- B, ϩⲉⲧϩⲟⲩⲧϩ SF, ϩⲧϩⲱⲧϩ A, ϩⲉⲧϩⲱⲧϩ B, ϩⲧϩⲟⲧϩ O, ϩⲉⲧϩⲱⲧϩ⁺ SSᵃ, ϩⲉⲧϩⲱⲧ⁺ B vb **I** intr, *inquire, examine*: Ge 31 33 B(S ⲙⲟⲩϣⲧ), Jo 7 52 SA²B ἐρευνᾶν, Sa 13 6 S διερ., Ps 63 7 SB ἐξερ.; Deu 17 4 S(B ⲕⲱⲧ) ἐκζητεῖν; Job 8 8 SB ἐξιχνιάζειν, ClPr 54 38 S συνεξετάζειν; Su 48 B ἀνακρίνειν; AM 265 B ⲁϥϩ. ⲟⲩⲟϩ ⲁϥⲉⲙⲓ περιεργάζεσθαι; ShC 42 195 S physician's remedy ⲉⲧϩ. ⲛ ⲉⲧⲟⲩⲟⲙ, opp ⲉⲧⲕⲏⲃ, Pcod 46 S ϣϣⲉ ... ⲉϩ. ϩⲉⲛⲡⲉϥϩⲉ ⲉϩⲣⲁⲓ, *ib* 28 F ⲉⲧϩ. ⲉⲛⲉⲟⲩⲁ = S ⲇⲓⲁⲕⲣⲓⲧⲓⲕⲟⲥ, ManiK 123 A² ⲁⲧⲉⲧⲛϩ....ⲁⲧⲉⲧⲛϣⲓⲛⲉ; qual: Ps 110 2 B(S ⲙⲟϣⲧ) ἐκζ.; He 5 14 B(SF = Gk) γυμνάζεσθαι; DeV 2 35 B scriptures ⲥⲉϩ. ϩⲉⲛⲟⲩⲥⲓⲛⲕⲁⲧ, CO 385 Sᵃ ⲧⲉⲣⲏⲧ[ϩⲱ]ⲧ ⲁⲩⲱ ⲧⲕⲡ ⲁⲓⲕ ⲁⲡ.

II tr: Jer 27 26 B, Pro 20 27 A(Cl, var & S ⲙ.), Jo 5 39 SA²(B ϩ. ϩⲉⲛ-), Ro 8 27 B(S ⲙ.) ἐρ., Ps 108 11 B ϩⲉⲧϩⲉⲧ- (S do), Ob 6 SAB ἐξερ.; Sa 6 9 S ἔρευνα ἐφιστάναι; Job 5 27 SB, Si 1 3 SB ἐξιχ.; Ac 17 11 SB, 1 Cor 2 15 B ϩⲉⲧϩⲉⲧ-(S do) ἀνακρ., Jer 15 10 B(S = Gk) διακρ., 1 Cor 2 13 F(S diff, B = Gk) συγκρ.; Aeg 280 S ϩⲉⲧϩⲉⲧ ⲡⲉⲩϩⲃⲏⲩⲉ ἀκριβοῦν, Si 51 21 S διακριβ., Nu 23 10 B(S diff) ἐξα.; Ps 7 10 B(S = Gk) ἐτάζειν, Jth 8 13 S ἐξετ.; Deu 23 21 S(B ⲕⲱⲧ ⲛⲥⲁ-) ἐκζη.; Jer 17 10 B δοκιμάζειν; Va 63 95 B ϣϭⲉ ⲡⲉⲛϩⲉⲧϩⲱⲧϥ ⲉⲡⲓϩⲟⲅⲟ = Mich 550 31 S ⲙ. σαφέστερον ῥηθῆναι; R 1 4 42 S ϩ. ⲛⲁⲙⲁ ⲡⲭⲁⲓⲉ *penetrare*; Sh Wess 9 147 S ⲉⲓϩⲁϩⲉⲧϩⲉⲧ ⲡⲉⲭⲡⲟ ⲙ ⲡⲛϣⲏⲣⲉ, ShIF 155 S vinegar ⲡⲧⲁϩ. ⲡⲉⲧⲛϣⲟ, Mor 32 29 S/ ⲛⲉⲧϩ. ⲡⲡⲉⲣⲏⲧ, C 89 139 B ϩⲉⲧϩⲱⲧⲟⲩ ϣⲁⲡⲧⲟⲩⲉⲣ ⲟⲙⲟⲗⲟⲅⲓⲛ = Va ar 172 80 بحث, Hor 83 O ϩⲧϩⲟⲧϥ.

With following preposition.   c ⲉ- obj: Dan 5

16 B συγκρ. acc; Va 58 169 B ⲉⲧϩ. ⲟⲩⲟϩ ⲉⲧⲥⲟⲙⲥ ⲉⲑⲙⲉⲧⲥⲁⲓⲉ ⲛⲧⲉ ϩⲁⲛⲣⲓⲟⲙⲓ; vbal: ShA 2 170 S ⲛⲉϩⲧ. ⲉⲧⲣⲉⲩⲛⲁⲩ, Mun 154 S ⲙⲡⲛⲥⲁⲧⲣⲉϥϩ. ⲉϫⲟⲟⲥ ϫⲉ;   c ⲉⲧⲃⲉ-: 1 Cor 10 25 B(S = Gk) ἀνακρ. διά, Ac 24 8 B(S do) ἀ. περί; 1 Pet 1 10 SB ⲉϩⲉⲣ. περί; BMOr 6807 5 S ϩ. ⲙⲙⲁⲧⲉ (*l* ⲉⲙ.) ⲉ. ⲡⲙⲩⲥⲧⲏⲣⲓⲟⲛ πολυπραγμονεῖν; ClPr 53 19 S ϩ. ⲉ. ⲧⲟⲩⲥⲓⲁ ⲛⲧⲉⲧⲣⲓⲁⲥ, C 86 130 B ⲁⲡⲟⲩⲅⲣⲟ ϩ. ⲉⲑⲃⲏⲧⲕ ϫⲉⲛⲟⲩⲥⲡⲟⲩⲁⲕ;   c ⲛⲥⲁ-: Miss 8 79 S ϩ. ⲛⲥⲁⲡⲉϩⲃⲏⲩⲉ regarding faith ⲉⲣ., 1 Pet 1 11 B(S ϣⲓⲛⲉ) ⲉⲣ. εἰς, Va 58 180 B ϩ. ⲛⲥⲁⲧⲉϥⲙⲉⲧⲁⲣⲭⲉⲟⲥ ⲁⲛⲉⲣ., Sa 64 S ⲇⲓⲉⲣ., Ps 63 7 B(S ⲡ-), *ib* 118 69 B(S ϣ.), Pro 2 4 SAB, Am 9 3 B(S ⲧ ⲟⲩⲟⲓ, A ⲕⲱⲧⲉ) ⲉⲝⲉⲣ.; Job 10 6 S(B ⲕⲱⲧ) ⲉⲝⲓⲭ.; Si 3 21 S ⲉϫⲉⲧ.; Mt 2 7 B(S ϣ.) ἀκρ.; RChamp 372 S let your piety ϩ. ⲛⲥⲱϥ (*sc* heretic), BMis 83 S ϩ. ⲛⲥⲁⲡⲉⲓⲁⲡⲧⲗⲟⲅⲓⲁ, Z 619 S ϩⲱⲃ...ⲡϣⲟⲩϩ. ⲛⲥⲱϥ, C 43 157 B ⲉⲩϩ. ⲛⲥⲁⲡⲓⲭⲣⲓⲥⲧⲓⲁⲛⲟⲥ, Mor 39 21 F sim;   c ϩⲛ-: Mt 2 16 B(S ⲉⲃⲟⲗ ϩⲓⲧⲛ-) ἀκρ. παρά; ShA 2 311 S man's thoughts ⲥⲉϩ.⁺ ⲛⲧⲟⲟⲧϥ ⲙⲡ̄ⲡ̄ⲉ̄;   c ϩⲛ-, ϩⲉⲛ-, *in*: Jo 5 39 B(SA² ⲛ-) ⲉⲣ. acc; He 5 13⁺ B neg (S ⲁⲧⲥⲟⲟⲩⲛ) ἄπειρος gen; Va 66 293 B ⲙⲁⲣⲉϥϩ. ϩⲉⲛⲡⲁⲓⲥⲁϫⲓ φιλοσοφεῖν; 1 Chr 28 21 B πρόθυμος; ShC 73 152 S ϣⲱⲡⲉ ⲉⲛϩ. ϩⲛⲣⲉⲛⲕⲟⲩⲓ *be diligent* (but *cf* Mt 25 21 ϩⲣⲟⲧ), ROC 23 156 B παιδ. ϩⲉⲛⲡⲓϩⲱⲙ, ManiP 39 A² ⲉⲛϩ. ϩⲛⲡⲥⲉϫⲉ;   *with*: Zeph 1 12 B(A ⲙⲟⲩϣⲧ) ⲉⲝⲉⲣ. μετά.

—— nn m SB(rare), *inquiry, question*: Miss 8 58 ⲛϩ. ⲡⲧⲉ ⲡⲛⲟⲩⲙⲁ ἔρευνα; Wess 15 135 ⲛϩ. ⲡⲁⲙⲡⲧⲁⲥⲉⲃⲏⲥ ⲉⲛⲧⲁϥϫⲟⲟⲩ ⲉⲝⲉⲧⲁⲥⲓⲥ; Ro 14 1 (B ϩⲓⲟⲓ) διάκρισις; BM 274 8 some will answer ϩⲉⲛⲟⲩϩ. ϫⲉ-, R 1 2 27 ⲡⲓⲥⲧⲉⲩⲉ ⲡⲟⲩⲉϣ ⲛϩ., BSM 109 B ⲟⲩⲟⲙⲟⲩ ⲁⲧϩⲛⲉϩ.;   *inquirer* B: He 4 12(S ⲣⲉϥϭⲣⲓⲡⲉ) κριτικός.

ⲁⲧϩ., -ϩ. SB, *unfathomable, -searchable*: Job 9 10 B(S ⲁⲧⲁⲣⲏⲭⲝ) ἀνεξιχνίαστος; Ro 11 33 B(SF ⲙⲟⲩϣⲧ neg) ἀνεξερεύνητος; P 44 48 S ⲁⲡⲉⲣⲁⲧⲁⲥⲧⲟⲥ (? ⲁⲛⲉⲣⲱⲧ.)·ⲡⲓⲁⲧϩⲉⲧϩⲟⲧϥ لا ي; R 1 2 23 S Trinity unknowable ⲛⲁⲧϩⲉⲧϩⲱⲧⲥ, DeV 1 70 B ⲥⲟⲫⲓⲁ ⲛⲁⲧϩⲉⲧϩⲱⲧⲥ; ⲁⲧϣ ϩ. B: CaiEuch 473 ⲡⲓⲁⲧϣ ϩⲉⲧϩⲱⲧϥ ἀπερινόητος; DeV 2 15 ϫⲟⲙ ⲡⲁⲧϣ ϩⲉⲧϩⲱⲧⲥ; ⲙⲛⲧ-, ⲙⲉⲧⲁⲧϩ., *unquestioningness*: BHom 100 S ⲧⲙ. ⲛⲥⲁⲧⲡⲓⲥⲧⲓⲥ (ALR '96 194 المساءلة ل), Mor 28 161 S giving charity ϩⲛⲟⲩⲙ., DeV 2 42 B accept service ϩⲉⲛⲟⲩ(ⲉⲩ)ⲧⲛⲙⲟⲥⲩⲛⲏ ⲛⲉⲙⲟⲩⲙ.

ⲣⲉϥϩ., -ϩ. SB *inquirer*: Bar 3 23 S(prob)B ἐκζητητής, 1 Cor 1 20 B(S = Gk) συνζ.; Mus 34 206 B Thomas ⲛⲓⲣ., l'O 2 169 S sim ⲧⲉⲕⲥⲓⲝ ⲡⲣ.; ⲙⲛⲧ-ⲣ.: Bor 248 47 S running after ⲟⲩⲙⲛⲧⲡⲉⲣⲓⲉⲣⲅⲟⲥ ⲙⲡⲟⲩⲙ., Cat 133 B ⲙ. ⲡⲣⲟϩⲟ of heretics, Va 57 91 B ⲓⲣⲓ ⲡⲟⲩⲙ. ⲛⲥⲁⲡⲓⲡⲟⲛⲏⲣⲁ.

ϭⲓⲛϩ. S, *inquiry*: BHom 100 marvel beyond ϭ. ⲛⲓⲙ (ALR *l* c الحدس), P 130⁵ 35 sages seek ⲧϭ. ⲛⲥⲱⲕ.

ϩⲁⲩ Sᵃ nn m, *something due*, named with forced

labour: ST 101 hath settled with wife…ϩⲁϥ. ⲉⲓⲍⲉ ϩⲁⲕⲃⲁ, ib ⲙⲡⲉϥ ϩ. ϥ̄ⲭⲣ(ⲉ)ⲟⲥⲧⲉ ⲛⲧⲁ(ⲁ)ϥ. For ϩⲁ(ⲁ)ⲩ *day* unlikely.

ϩⲁⲩ- *SA²* v ϩⲓⲟⲅⲉ p c.

ϩⲁⲩ- v ⲡⲟⲩϩ *sf*, but ? p c of ϩⲓⲟⲅⲉ.

ϩⲏⲩ *SAA²F*, ϩⲏⲟⲩ *SABF*, -ⲟⲩⲓ *F* nn m, *profit, usefulness*: 2 Kg 18 22 *S*, Job 22 3 *B*, Ro 3 1 *SB*, Z 324 *S* ϣⲁⲭⲉ ⲉⲧⲃ̄ⲛⲉⲡϩ. ὠφέλεια, Jer 16 19 *B* -λημα, 2 Tim 3 16*S*(*B* ⲟⲓ ⲛϩ.) -λιμος, EpJer 67 *B*(*F* ϭⲉⲙ ϩ.) -λεῖν, 1 Cor 15 32 *SBF* ὄφελος; Phil 1 21 *SBF*, Aeg 267 *S* ⲡⲟⲩϩ. ⲛⲁⲛ ⲁⲛ κέρδος, R 1 5 11 *S* ⲟⲩϩ. ⲉϥϩⲟⲟⲩ αἰσχροκερδής; Sa 13 19 *S* πορισμός; 2 Tim 2 14 *SB* χρήσιμος; Eccl 10 12*F*(*S*=Gk) χάρις; MG 25 166 *B* δαψίλεια opp ⲟⲥⲓ; Si 29 4 *S* εὕρεμα; Sa 3 11 *S* neg ἀνόητος; Bor 253 171 *S* ⲉⲅⲭⲓ ⲉⲣⲟⲩⲛ ⲉⲛϩ. λυσιτελής; Mus 40 46 *S* (Reg Pach) false witness ⲉⲧⲃⲉⲟⲩϩ. *lucrum*; Jer 21 9 *S*(*B* ϣⲱⲗ) σκῦλον; Jud 18 24 *S* ⲟⲩⲡⲉ ⲡⲁⲣ. τί ἐμοι?, Ez 15 2 *B* ⲟⲩⲡⲉ ⲛϩ. τί ἂν γένοιτο?; PS 365 *S* ⲡⲣⲟⲟⲩϣ ⲉⲧⲉⲙⲛ ϩ. ⲛⲣⲏⲧϥ, ManiP 105 *A²* ⲧⲥⲃ̄ⲱ ⲉⲧⲉⲙⲛ ϩ. ⲛⲥⲱⲥ, ShC 42 110 *S* ⲛϩ. ⲉⲧϣⲟⲟⲡ ⲉⲃⲟⲗ ϩⲛⲡⲉϩⲃⲏⲩⲅⲉ, Lant 70 *S* book dedicated ⲉⲩϩ. ⲙ̄ⲡⲟⲩϭⲟⲗϭⲗ̄ ⲛⲛⲉⲧⲛⲁϣⲱ, COAd 14 *S* ⲛϩ. ⲡⲟⲥⲉ *come profit come loss*, Ryl 349 9 *S*(ⲉ)ϣⲱⲡⲉ ⲁⲡⲡⲉ ϫⲓ ⲙⲟⲉⲓⲧ ⲉⲡⲛϩ., TillOster 28 *A* ⲉⲙⲁⲧⲉ ⲁⲅⲛⲁϭ ⲛϩ., ManiP *A²* ⲙⲛ ϩ. ⲁⲧⲉϥϩⲁⲏ, C 89 176 *B* ⲟⲩⲛⲓϣϯ ⲛϩ. in this Epistle = C 100 283 *S* ⲡⲟⲃⲣⲉ, ib 43 119 *B* ⲟⲩϩ. ⲡⲟⲩ will money bring you?, MR 5 33 *F* write us of thy health ⲉⲧⲙⲉϩ ⲛϩ. ⲙ̄ⲯⲩⲭ(ⲏ) ϩⲓⲥⲱⲙⲁ, Mor 24 3 *F* words ⲉⲧⲙⲏϩ ⲛ̄ϩⲛⲟⲩⲅⲓ; as adj: BMar 180 *S* ϣⲁⲭⲉ ⲛⲓⲙ ⲛϩ., MG 25 250 *B* sim.

ⲙⲁⲓϩ. *SB*, *profit-loving*: 1 Tim 3 8 *S* ⲙ. ⲛϣⲱⲗⲟϥ *B* ⲙ. ⲡϣⲏⲛϣ αἰσχροκερδής; ⲙⲛⲧⲙ.: ClPr 54 4 *S* ⲧⲙ. ⲉⲧⲁⲣⲃ̄ⲣ ⲡⲛϩⲏⲧⲟⲩ, Cat 93 *B* ⲡⲣⲟⲅⲟ ⲡⲧⲟⲩⲙ.

ⲣ, ⲉⲣ ϩ., *profit*: Tit 3 8 *B*(*S* ϯ ϩ.) ὠφέλιμος; AM 270 *B* ⲉⲧⲟⲓ ⲛϩ. ⲛⲡⲉⲧⲓⲯⲩⲭⲏ χρήσιμος; ROC 17 405 *B* ⲙ̄ⲡⲉⲡⲓϩⲱⲃ ⲉⲣ ϩ. ⲛⲁϫⲁⲗ συμφέρειν; Aeg 213 *S* ⲉⲉⲣ ⲟⲩϩ. ⲛⲡⲉⲧϩⲙⲡⲙⲁ κερ. συμβάλλεσθαι.

ϯ ϩ. *SAA²BF*, *give profit, benefit* intr: Pro 10 32 *SAB*, Sa 6 27 *S*, Z 299 *S* speak to the ⲛⲁⲡⲁⲥ ⲧⲁⲣⲉϥϯ. ὠφελεῖν; Aeg 231 *S* ⲡⲉⲡⲧⲁⲩϯ. κερδαίνειν; 1 Kg 13 13 *S* neg ματαιοῦσθαι; ShC 73 131 *S* laughter & play ⲛⲥⲉϯ. ⲁⲛ, BHom 28 *S* let speech be of judgment ⲉⲧⲣⲉⲕϯ., JKP 2 162 *S* to soldiers ϫⲓ ⲛⲡⲓϩⲣⲟⲙⲛⲧ ⲛⲧⲛϯ. (Mt 28 12), Rec 6 65 *S* ϣⲁⲕϯ. ⲡⲱⲕⲛⲉ ϣⲁⲕϯ ⲟⲥⲉ ⲡⲱⲕⲛⲉ, Va 57 64 *B* spirit is willing but flesh ϯ ϩⲗⲓ ⲛϩ. ⲁⲛ (Mt 26 41 ⲁⲥⲑⲉⲛⲏⲥ); as nn (adj): Sa 15 12 *S* ἐπικερδής; tr *S*(mostly), *gain*: Is 30 5 *SBF*, Jer 23 32 *B*, Mk 7 11 (*B* ϫⲉⲙ ϩ.), Jo 6 63 *SA²B*, Z 338 ⲡⲗⲟⲅⲅⲓⲛⲟⲥ ⲡⲁϣ ϯ. ⲙⲙⲟ ⲁⲛ ὠφ.; Mt 18 15 (*B* ϫⲫⲟ), 1 Cor 9 20 (*B* ⲇⲟ), BHom 41 believing thief ⲁϥϯ. ⲙ-

ⲡⲡⲁⲣⲁⲍⲓⲥⲟⲥ, Z 309 ⲉϥⲟⲩⲱϣ ⲉϯ. ⲙⲙⲟϥ ⲕⲉⲣⲇ.; PS 79 ⲧⲁϭⲟⲙ ⲛⲥⲉⲛⲁϯ. ⲙⲙⲟⲥ ⲁⲛ *shall have no profit of it*, ShBor 246 59 worldlings wish ⲉϯ. ⲙⲙⲟⲟⲩ ⲙⲁⲅⲁⲁⲩ, ShMIF 23 71 ⲟⲩ ⲡⲉⲧⲛⲁϯ. ⲙⲙⲟϥ ⲉⲓϣⲁⲛⲣ ⲛⲟⲃⲉ?, ShBor 233* 1 ⲛⲧⲛⲁϯ. ⲡⲗⲁⲁⲩ ⲁⲛ, CA 102 ⲕⲛⲁϯ. ⲛⲡⲉⲩⲯⲩⲭⲏ, DeV 2 209 *B* ⲁⲓϯ. ⲛⲧⲁⲙⲉⲧϣⲟⲩⲧ; c ⲉ- *S*(mostly), *profit by*: ShMun 162 beasts lay waste fields ⲉⲧⲁⲧⲣⲉⲩϯ. ⲉⲣⲟⲟⲩ ⲛ̄ϭⲓ ⲡⲉⲛⲧⲁⲩϫⲟⲟⲩ, ShA 2 57 they have prophesied (Mt 7 22) but ⲛⲥⲉⲛⲁϯ. ⲉⲗⲁⲁⲩ (cf tr), BAp 151 ⲙⲁⲣⲉⲣⲱⲙⲉ ⲛⲓⲙ ϯ. ⲉⲣⲟⲕ ϫⲉⲕⲉϯ. ⲡⲣⲱⲙⲉ ⲛⲓⲙ, C 86 244 *B* ⲁⲓϯ. ⲉⲣⲟⲕ ⲙⲙⲁϣⲱ; c ⲛ- dat: Is 30 6 *B*(*SF* acc), Jer 7 4 *B*, Gal 5 2 *B*(*S* ⲇⲟ) ὠφ. acc; HL 73 *B* houses ⲉⲧⲉⲙⲡⲟⲩϯ. ⲡⲱⲟⲩ ὠφ. gen; Cl 19 1 *A* ⲥⲉϯ. ⲡⲉⲛ βελτίονα ποιεῖν; AM 235 *B* ⲡⲉⲕⲙⲁⲧⲓⲁ ⲛⲁϯ. ⲛⲁⲕ ⲁⲛ ⲛϩⲗⲓ; c ⲙⲛ-: C 99 69 *S* consort not with one ⲉⲛϥ̄ⲛⲁϯ. ⲁⲛ ⲛⲙⲙⲁϥ = MG 17 430 ﻻ; c ϩⲛ-, ϧⲉⲛ-: Ps 88 22 *S*(*B* ϫⲉⲙ ϩ. ϧⲉⲛ-) ὠφ. ἐν; Va 61 215 *B* ⲙ̄ⲡⲁϯ. ⲉ̄ⲃⲟⲗ ⲙⲙⲟⲥ ϧⲉⲛⲟⲗⲓ οὐδὲν κερδ.; ⲁⲧϯ ϩ. *B*: Tit 3 9 (*S* vb) ἀνωφελής; ⲙⲉⲧⲁⲧ.: He 7 18 (*SF* ⲙⲛⲧⲁⲧⲡⲟⲩⲣⲉ) ⲁⲛⲱ.; ⲣⲉϥϯ. ϩ. *S*: Blake 298 ⲟⲩⲁ ⲙ(ⲉ)ⲛ ⲁϥϯ ⲟⲥⲉ ϩ(ⲉ)ⲛⲕⲟⲟⲩⲉ ⲁⲩⲁⲩ ⲛⲣ.; ⲙⲛⲧⲣ.: Wess 11 170 spake of ⲧⲙ. ⲛⲧⲉⲯⲩⲭⲏ ⲥⲱⲧⲏⲣⲓⲁ *utilitas*.

ϫⲫⲉ ϩ. *B*, *acquire gain*: PasH 194 ⲁϥϫⲓ ⲡⲣⲟ ⲙⲡⲓϩⲙⲟⲧ ⲁϥϫ. ⲙⲫⲛⲟⲃⲓ ﺍﻛﺴﺐ; ⲙⲉⲧⲣⲉϥϫ. ϩ.: Ac 19 25 (*S* diff) εὐπορία.

ϭⲛ ϩ. *S*(rare).*AA²F*, ϫⲉⲙ ϩ. *B*, *find profit, gain*: Is 47 12, Mk 8 36 *BF*, Jo 12 19 *A²B* ὠφ.; Ac 27 21, 1 Pet 3 1 κερδ. (all *S* ϯ ϩ.); 2 Cor 1 8 neg (*S* diff) ἐξαπορεῖσθαι; Pro 22 18 *A*(*S* ϯ ϩ.) καλὸς εἶναι; C 43 139 if I confess Him ϯⲛⲁϫ. ⲉⲙⲁϣⲱ, MartIgn 872 ϥⲛⲁϫ. ⲛϩⲗⲓ; R 1 4 61 *S* ϯ ϩ. ⲗⲁⲁⲩ = AM 123 ϫⲉⲙ ϩⲟⲙ ⲛϩⲗⲓ, C 89 99 glad as one ⲉⲁϥϫⲓⲙⲓ ⲡⲟⲩⲛⲓϣϯ ⲛϩ. = Va ar 172 58 ﻭﺟﺪﻭﺍ, AM 297 be obedient & ϫ. ⲡⲣⲁⲡⲗⲏⲛϣ ⲛⲃⲁⲥⲁⲛⲟⲥ *gain* (remission of), Mani 1 *A²* ⲛϩ. ⲉⲧⲉⲣⲉⲡⲣⲱⲙⲉ ⲛⲁϭⲡⲧϥ (cf Mt 16 26 *S* ϯ ϩ., *B* ϫ.); c ⲉ-: ShC 73 115 *S* ⲉⲧⲣⲉⲛϭ. ⲉⲡⲉⲡⲉⲣⲏⲩ, Miss 4 209 *B* ⲛⲧⲁϫ. ⲉⲡⲭ̄ⲥ̄ (cf 201 sim ⲙⲡⲭ̄ⲥ̄); c ϩⲛ-, ϧⲉⲛ-: Jer 2 11 *B* ⲱϥ. ἐκ, Ps 88 23 *B*(*S* ϯ ϩ.) ὠφ. ἐν; Tri 501 *S* ϭ. ϩⲛⲧⲉⲡⲣⲁⲅⲙⲁⲧⲓⲁ, CA 97 *S*, BSM 50 *B* ⲁⲧⲉⲧⲉⲛϫ. ϧⲉⲛⲛⲓ ⲉⲧⲁⲣⲉⲧⲉⲛⲥⲱⲧⲉⲙ ⲉⲣⲱⲟⲩ? = BMis 402 *S* ⲡⲗⲏⲣⲟⲫⲟⲣⲉⲓ; ⲣⲉϥϭ., ϫ. *A²B*, *one who finds gain*: ManiP *A²* ⲟⲩⲉϣⲟⲧ ⲛⲣ.; ⲙⲉⲧⲣ. *B*: Cat 104 ϯⲙ. ⲉϩⲣⲏⲓ ⲉϫⲉⲛⲡⲓⲥⲁϫⲓ ⲛⲧⲉ ⲫϯ.

In many names: ϩⲏⲩ (J 45 35), ⲛϩⲏⲩ (Lant 112), ⲡⲉϩ. (Kr 145), ⲡⲓⲛⲩ (Baouit 2 9), Φήου (Preisigke), ⲧⲉϩⲏⲩ (Bodl(P)d 27), ⲁⲙⲁϩⲏⲩ (or ⲁⲙⲁ ϩ. MG 30 pl 1), ⲁⲡⲁⲥⲧⲁϩⲏⲩ (MR 5 26), ⲕⲩⲣⲁϩⲏⲩ (or ⲕⲩⲣⲁ ϩ. ib 120, cf ﻗﻴﺮ Grohmann *ArPapyri* 1 186), ⲕⲟϩⲏⲩ (J 24 62) = ⲕⲟⲛϩⲩ (ib 6), ⲗⲁⲗϩⲏⲩ (JSch 10) = ⲗⲁⲗⲏⲩ (ST 415), ⲗⲁϩⲛⲟⲩ (BM 1252), Λαήου (Preisigke), ⲙⲓⲕⲁϩⲏⲩ (Ora 4 2081 16), ⲧⲁⲡⲣⲏⲩ (RChamp 541), ⲡⲓⲗⲓϩⲏⲩ (JA '88 372, cf Grohmann *lc* ﻟﻴﺐ). In place-name

ϯⲙⲟⲩⲓ ⲛⲡⲁⲡⲉϩⲛⲟⲩ جزيرة السواقي (Miss 4 395) ϩ. prob pl of ϩⲟⲓ q v.

Cf ϩⲟⲧ̅ϩⲉ & *v* RylDem 3 370.

ϩⲟⲟⲩ *SA²F*, ϩⲟⲟⲩⲉ *Sᵃ AA²*, ϩⲱ. *A*, ⲉϩⲟⲟⲩ *B*, ϩⲁ-(ⲟ)ⲩ *F*, ϩⲁⲁ(ⲟ)ⲩ *S/F*, ϩⲟⲩ(ⲙⲓⲥⲉ) *SAF*, pl ϩⲣⲉⲩ *AA²* (Ma) & sg as pl, nn m, *day*: Ge 2 3 *A* ϩⲱ. *B*, Eccl 2 3 *SF*, Mk 9 2 *SBF*, Jo 6 39 *S.A²B* ἡμέρα; PS 4 *S* ⲡⲉϩ. ⲉϣⲁⲣⲉⲛⲟⲟϩ ϫⲱⲕ ⲛⲣⲏⲧϥ, *ib* 344 ⲡⲉϩ. ⲛⲧⲁⲩⲙⲟⲩⲣ, Sh A 2 268 *S* ⲁϥⲉⲓ ϣⲁⲣⲱⲧⲛ ⲛⲁϣ ⲡ., *ib* 1 249 *S* ϩⲣⲉⲡϩ. ϣⲁⲛⲧⲃ̅ⲃⲟⲟⲩ ϩⲣⲉⲡϩ. ϣⲁⲭⲁⲣⲙⲟⲩ, ShC 42 41 *S* ⲡⲉϩ. ⲙⲡⲟⲩⲁ ⲡⲟⲩⲁ (fated) *days* (of life), ViK 9749 *S* ⲛϩⲣⲁⲟⲩⲉ ⲛϩ. (on Mt 18 28), El 126 *Sᵘ* ⲥⲁⲯ ⲛϩ., TU 43 15 *A* ⲟ⳿ⲅⲏ ⲟⲩϩ. ⲛⲏⲅ, ManiK 27 *A²* ⲫⲟⲟⲩ ⲙⲡⲧⲟⲩϣⲏ, BKU 1 26 (8116 *b*) *F* ϣⲁⲙ̄ϯ (sic) ⲛϩⲁⲁⲩ, AZ 23 54 *S/* ϣⲁⲙⲧ ⲉϩ., AM 313 *B* ⲡⲓⲉϩ. ⲧⲟⲩ ⲧⲣ̅ *tertian fever* (cf p 567 a), C 43 240 *B* ⲟⲩⲉϩ. ⲛⲕⲩⲣⲓⲁⲕⲏ (but Bodl(P)d 203 *S* ⲣ ⲟⲩⲕⲩⲣⲓⲁⲕⲏ ⲛϩ.), Lant 7 *F* ⲡⲉϩⲁⲩ (ⲡ)ⲡⲁϭⲓ ⲛϣⲓⲛⲓ; pl form: Ge 4 3 *A*(ClBerl, Stras ϩⲟⲟⲩⲉ), Ps 33 12 *A*(Cl) ἡμ.; Cl 25 2 *A* ⲛϩ. of its dissolution; ManiK 22 *A²* ⲛⲉϩ. ⲛϣⲱⲡⲉ; ϩ. ⲛⲟⲩⲱⲧ: 2 Pet 3 8 *SB* (cf Ps 89 4 *S/* ϩⲁⲟⲩⲱⲧ tablet Cai Copt Mus) μία ἡμ., Sa 5 15 *S* ϩ. ⲟⲩ. μονήμερος; ⲕⲟⲩⲓ ⲛϩ.: Jo 2 12 *SA²*(*B* as Gk) οὐ πολλαὶ ἡμ.; ShC 42 42 *S* ⲙⲡⲡⲥⲁⲣⲉⲡⲕ. J 61 16 *S* left him there ⲛⲣⲉⲡⲕ.; ϩ. ⲉⲧⲙⲙⲁⲩ: Is 30 23 *SBF*, Hos 2 16 *AB*, Mk 13 32 ἡμ. ἐκείνη, El 134 *Cᵃ* ⲡⲉϩⲟⲟⲩⲉ ⲉ.; ⲣⲁⲥⲧⲉ ⲛϩ.: Ge 30 33 *S*(*B* ⲉϩ. ⲡⲧⲉ ⲣ.) ἡμ. ἡ αὔριον; ⲥⲁϥ ⲛϩ.: Miss 8 79 *S* χθές; ⲣⲟⲙⲡⲉ ⲛϩ.: BIF 13 103 *S*, Kr 140 *F*; ⲉⲃⲟⲧ ⲛϩ.: J 96 50 *S*, ManiK 157 *A²*. *V* also ⲙⲟⲟϣⲉ (p 206 a), ⲡⲟⲩϭⲉ (p 240 a).

Prepositional & adverbial expressions. ⲙⲡⲉϩ., ⲙⲡⲓⲉϩ., *on, in day, by day*: Lev 8 34 *S*(*B* ⲛϩⲣⲏⲓ ϩⲉⲛ-), Ps 58 17 *S*(*B* ϩⲉⲛ-) ἐν ἡμ.; Jer 14 17 *SB*, Ap 7 15 *SB* ἡμέρας, Mt 20 2 *S*(var ⲉ-)*B* τὴν ἡμ., Job 2 1 *SB* ὡς ἡ ἡμ.; PS 125 *S* ⲙ. ⲉⲕⲡⲁϫⲓ ⲃⲁⲡⲧⲓⲥⲙⲁ, ShC 42 208 *S* ⲙ. ⲛⲧⲟⲣⲅⲏ (var ϩⲙ-), J 65 27 *S* ⲛⲡⲉϩ. ⲙⲡⲧⲉⲩϣⲏ, *ib* 67 89 *S* mayest not cast her forth ⲉⲥⲟⲛϩ ⲛⲛⲉⲥϩ., BM 529 *S* ⲛⲧⲁⲛϣⲟⲡϥ ⲙⲡⲓϩ. *to-day*; ⲉⲡⲉϩ. *S, some day*: ShP 130⁴ 96 this house ⲉⲩⲉϣⲣϣⲱⲣϥ ⲉ., *cf ib* foundations shall be removed ⲉϩⲣⲉⲛϩ.; ⲛⲟⲩϩ. *S, on, for a day, one day*: BMar 9 ⲁⲡⲉⲕⲥⲱⲙⲁ ⲧⲁⲣⲁⲥⲥⲉ ⲉⲣⲟⲕ ⲛ., JKP 2 12 ⲙⲡⲉⲧⲉⲥ[ϩⲓⲙⲉ ϭ]ⲱϣⲧ ⲉⲣⲟⲩ ⲛ. *ever*, Hall 118 tell him to come ⲛ. (sic l) ⲛϥϣⲗⲏⲗ ϩⲙⲡⲧⲟⲡⲟⲥ, AZ 23 108 *S* recipe ⲧⲥⲟⲟⲩ ⲉϩⲙⲁⲕ ⲛ.; BG 19 ⲛⲟⲩⲁ ⲛⲡⲉⲓϩ.; ⲛⲟⲩϩ. ⲉⲃⲟⲗ ϩⲛⲟⲩϩ.: Is 58 2 *S*(*B* ⲛ. ϩⲁⲧⲉⲛ ⲛⲟⲩⲉϩ.) ἡμέραν ἐξ ἡμ.; ϩⲛⲟⲩϩ. ⲉⲃ. ϩⲛⲟⲩϩ.: Ps 60 6 *S*(*B* ϩⲁⲛⲉϩ. ⲉⲝⲉⲛϩⲁⲛⲉϩ.) ἡμέρας ἐφ' ἡμ., *ib* 8 sim ἡμ. ἐξ ἡμ.; R 1 4 61 *S* = AM 123 *B* do *from day to day*; ⲛⲟⲩϩ. ⲉⲩϩ.: 2 Cor 4 16 *S*(*B* do) ἡμέρα κ. ἡμέρα; ϣⲁⲡⲉϩ., *till the day*: Ps 60 6 *S*(*B* ϣⲁⲣⲁⲡⲉϩ.) ἕως ἡμ.; BMis 160 *S* ϣ. ⲙⲡⲉⲡⲙⲟⲩ = BSM 70 *B*; ϣⲁⲣⲉϩ.: Lam 5 20 *SB* εἰς μακρότητα ἡμ.;

ϣⲁⲉⲃⲟⲗ ⲉⲡⲁⲓⲉϩ.: Ez 20 31 *B* ἕως τ. σήμερον ἡμ.; ϩⲁⲑⲏ ⲛⲡⲉⲓϩ., *before now*: CO 376 *S*; ϫⲁϩⲉⲡⲡⲓⲉϩ. *B* sim: C 86 191, Ac 5 36 ϫⲁϩⲱⲟⲩ ⲛⲡⲁⲓⲉϩ. (*S* ϩⲁⲑⲏ ⲛ.) πρὸ τούτων τ. ἡμ., Miss 4 220 ϫⲁϩⲱϥ ⲛⲡⲁⲓⲉϩ. πώποτε; ϩⲙⲡⲉϩ., ϩⲉⲛⲡⲓⲉϩ., *in day*: Ps 19 1 *SB*, Mt 10 15 *SB*, Ro 2 5 *SB* ἐν ἡμ.; ϩⲣⲁⲓ ϩⲛ-, ⲛϩ. ϩⲉⲛ-: Ac 1 15 *SB*, Ap 10 7 *S*(*B* ϩⲉⲛ-) ἐν ἡμ.; ϩⲙⲡⲓⲉϩ.: Jos 4 14 *S* ἐν ἐκείνῃ τῇ ἡμ.; ⲛϫⲓⲛⲡⲉϩ. ⲉⲧⲙⲙⲁⲩ: Miss 8 173 *S*; ϫⲓⲛϩ. ⲉϩ., *from day to day*: Lev 23 37 *S*(*B* ⲙⲙⲏⲛⲓ ⲙⲙⲏⲛⲓ) καθ' ἡμέραν εἰς ἡμ.; Ez 28 14 *SB* ἀφ' ἧς ἡμ.; ⲟⲩϩ. ⲉⲃⲟⲗ ϩⲛⲟⲩϩ., *on a certain day* (cf above ⲛⲟⲩϩ.): BMar 185 *S* ἐν μιᾷ τῶν ἡμ.; DeV 2 272 *B*; ShC 42 89 *S* ϩⲣⲉⲡϩ. ⲡⲉ ⲉⲃ. ϩⲛ-ϩⲣⲉⲡϩ. *days* (there shall) *be when*; ⲙⲡⲓⲉϩ. ϩⲉⲛⲡⲓⲉϩ., *on this same day*: Pro 12 16 *B*(*SA* ⲙⲙⲏⲛⲉ) αὐθημερόν.

Iterated: R 1 2 50 *S* wasteth life ϩ. ϩ. *from day to day*; Tob 10 1 *S*, Va 57 262 *B* ⲡⲉϩ. ⲡⲉϩ. ἑκάστη ἡμ., ShA 2 278 *S* see each other ⲛⲉϩ. ⲛⲉϩ. ⲁⲩⲱ ⲙⲙⲏⲛⲉ ⲙⲙ., Mt 6 34 *SB* ⲉⲡⲉϩ. ⲡⲉϩ. τῇ ἡμ., Ja 2 15 *S* ⲙⲡⲉϩ. ⲡⲉϩ. (*B* ⲛⲧⲉ ⲡⲓⲉϩ.) ἐφήμερος; Sh(?)ViK 9332 *S* ⲉϥϩⲱϥⲧ ⲙⲡⲉϩ. ⲡⲉϩ.; Z 353 *S* sim.

In dates: Est 7 2 *S* ⲛⲙⲁϩ. ⲥⲛⲁⲩ δευτέρα ἡμ.; R 1 3 58 *S* sim, Ge 1 31 *A* ⲛⲙⲁϩⲥ]ⲟⲩ ⲛϩⲱ. *B* ⲉϩ. ⲙⲙⲁϩⲋ̄ ἡμ. ἕκτη, Ez 1 1 *B* ⲛ ⲡⲓⲙⲁϩⲥⲟⲟⲩⲉ ⲛⲉϩ. (*S* ⲥⲟⲩϥⲟⲩ) πέμπτη, 1 Cor 15 4 *F* ⲛⲡⲉϩⲣ̄ ⲡⲣⲟ. ἡμ. τρίτῃ; Ep 284 *S* ⲛⲙⲁϩⲥⲛⲁⲩ ⲛϩ., AP 27 *A²* ⲡⲉϥⲙⲁϩϣⲁⲙⲛⲧ ⲛϩ., Hor 83 *O* ϩⲟⲩⲗⲁ̄ (doubtful). For days of month *v* ⲥⲏⲩ(ⲥⲟⲩ-).

Commemorative days & sim: BAp 120 *S* ⲡⲉϩ. ⲙⲡⲁⲣⲭⲓⲉⲡⲓⲥⲕⲟⲡⲟⲥ Severus, Saq 226 *S* list of saints' days, often ⲛⲉϩⲟⲩ ⲛ-, C 86 336 *B* ⲡⲉϥⲛⲓϣϯ ⲡⲉϩ. (sc of St George), Rec 5 62 *S* epitaph ⲡⲉϩ. ⲙⲡⲣ ⲡⲙⲉⲉⲩⲉ ⲙⲡⲙⲁⲕⲁⲣⲓⲟⲥ..., Ostr *penes* G. Jéquier ⲛϩ. ⲛⲧⲁⲙⲁⲁⲩ, CO 103 *S* ⲛϩ. ⲛⲓⲣⲱⲙⲉ ⲛⲧⲁⲩⲙⲟⲩⲧⲟⲩ, AP 6 *A²* ⲡⲉϩ. ⲙⲡⲉϥϣⲓⲣⲉ, ViK 4912 ii *S* whoso shall contest (this will) ... ⲙⲡⲛⲥⲁⲡⲁⲛⲟϭ ⲛϩ. (meaning?), ManiP 26 *A²* ⲛϩ. ⲛⲣⲏ ⲛⲣⲁⲙⲡⲉ; *v* also ϩ. ⲛⲣⲁⲛ (p 298 b), ϩ. ⲛⲟⲩⲁⲥⲃⲉ (p 493 a), ϩ. ⲛⲟⲩⲱⲛϩ ⲉⲃⲟⲗ (pp 486 b, -7 b), ϩ. ⲛⲟⲩⲱϣ (p 501 b inf), ϩ. ⲛϣⲁ (p 543 b), ϩⲟⲩⲙⲓⲥⲉ (p 185 a inf), ⲥⲟⲟⲩ, ϩⲙⲉ.

Omitted: Jo 11 39 *SA²B* ⲡⲉϥϥⲧⲟⲟⲩ, Ac 28 13 *SB* ⲡⲉⲛⲥⲛⲁⲩ, ShMiss 4 281 *S* ⲡⲉϥⲥⲛⲁⲩ ⲏ ⲡⲉϥϣⲟⲙⲛⲧ, BMar 43 *S* ⲡⲁⲙⲛⲧⲟⲩⲉ, ⲡⲁϩⲟⲩⲧⲁϥⲧⲉ, ROC 25 243 *B* ⲡⲉⲥϣⲟⲙⲧ, BM 346 1 *S* ⲡⲉϥⲙⲏⲧⲛⲉ ⲡⲟⲟⲩ, KroppK 34 *S* ⲡⲉϣⲙⲟⲩⲛ ⲙⲡⲱϩ (*l* ⲟⲟϩ), MIE 2 352 *B* ⲡⲓⲋ̄ ⲙⲡϣⲁⲓ.

ⲣ ϩ., ⲡⲉϩ., ⲡⲓⲉϩ., *spend day*: Ac 20 16 *SB* τὴν ἡμ. γίνεσθαι *diem facere*; Ps 37 7 *B*(*S* Gk no vb), BM 1001 *S* ⲁϥⲉⲣ ⲡⲉϩⲙⲉ ⲛϩ. eating naught, BMis 436 *S* ⲣ ϩⲣⲉϩ. ϩⲁⲣⲧⲏϥ; ⲣ ϩⲁϩ ⲛϩ. *S*: Deu 30 18 (*B* ⲁϣⲁⲓ) πολυήμερος γίνεσθαι; J 91 20 ⲁⲛⲣ. tending him.

† ϩ. *S*: BAp 155 ⲉⲕϯ ϩ. ⲛⲥⲁϩ. (cf ⲛⲟⲩϫⲉ ⲛⲥⲁ-).

ϫⲓ ϧ. *S*: ShC 42 118 ⲉⲛϫⲓ ϧ. ⲉⲡⲉⲩϣⲁⲡ (*sic l ?*).

ⲡⲟⲟⲩ (for ⲡⲣⲟⲟⲩ) *SA²*(AP)*O*, ⲡⲟⲟⲅⲉ *A²*(Ma), ⲫⲟⲟⲩ *B*, ⲡⲁ(ⲁ)ⲟⲩ *F*, *the day, to-day*: Ex 16 25 *SB*, He 3 13 *SB* ⲥⲏⲙⲉⲣⲟⲛ; BM 244 1 *S* ⲉⲧⲃⲉⲛ. *because to-day* (is Easter), ST 265 *S* ⲉⲓⲥ ⲡⲕⲉⲡ. (ⲡ)ⲛⲉⲓⲡⲁⲩ ⲟⲩⲣⲱⲙⲉ, Mor 24 3 *F*, Kr 236 *F* ⲡⲉⲕⲥϧⲉⲓ ⲡⲥⲉⲃ ⲙⲡⲉⲕⲥϧⲉⲓ ⲙⲡ., Lant 62 *S* ⲡ. ⲡⲁⲓ ⲥⲟⲩⲁ, Ryl 339 *S* ⲙⲡⲁⲧⲉⲡ. ϣⲱⲡⲉ; ⲙⲡ., ⲙⲫ., *to-day* (lit *on to-day*): Ps 2 7 *SB*, Mt 6 11 *SBF* ⲥⲏⲙ.; PS 128 *S* ⲉⲧϣⲟⲟⲡ ⲛⲁⲕ ⲡⲥⲱⲙⲁ ⲙ., ShC 42 95 *S* ⲡⲉⲡⲧⲁⲩ ϫⲡⲟϥ ⲙ., BHom 134 *S* ⲥⲁϥ ⲁⲡⲁⲅⲗⲟⲥ... ⲙⲡ. ⲙⲁⲑⲁⲓⲟⲥ (*cf ib* ⲥⲁϥ... ⲡⲟⲟⲩ *bis*), ManiBerlSitz '33 Taf 1 *A²* ⲉⲧⲟ ⲛⲣⲣⲟ ⲙⲡ., AP 22 *A²*, C 43 2 *B*, Kr 236 *F*, BM 592 6 *F* ⲉⲡ., AZ 21 99 *O*, PGM 1 50 420 *O*(*sic* MS), Kr 75 *S* ⲛⲡ. ⲡⲁⲓ, KroppD 1 *S* ⲡ. for ⲙⲡ.; ⲙⲛⲛⲥⲁⲡ. *S*: J 99 31 ⲙ. ⲙⲛⲛⲥⲁⲣⲉⲡⲕⲉⲟⲅⲟⲉⲓϣ *from to-day henceforth*, CO 172 ⲙ.ⲡ. ⲉⲃⲟⲗ *sim*; ⲡⲣⲟⲥ ⲡ. *S*: ST 318 *as from to-day*; ϣⲁⲡ. *SF*: 2 Cor 3 15 (*B* ϣⲁⲉϧⲟⲩⲛ ⲉⲫ.) ⲉⲱⲥ ⲥⲏⲙ.; PS 200 I have spoken with you ϣ., ST 202 ⲁⲅⲁⲡⲉⲗⲉⲓ (ἀπει.) ⲉϫⲱϥ ϣ.; Kr 234 *F* rent received ϣⲉⲛ. *so far*; ϣⲁϩⲣⲁⲓ ⲉⲡ. *S*: ShC 42 166, Pcod 15; ϣⲁⲉϧⲟⲩⲛ ⲉⲫ. *B*: Jer 3 25 ⲉⲱⲥ ⲧⲏⲥ ⲏⲙ. ⲧⲁⲩⲧⲏⲥ, Ac 2 29 (*S* ϣⲁϩⲣⲁⲓ ⲉⲡ. ⲛϧ.) ⲁⲭⲣⲓ ⲧ.ⲏⲙ.ⲧ.; ϧⲁⲑⲏ ⲙⲡ. *SA²*: R 1 3 16 ϯⲥⲟⲟⲩⲛ ⲙⲙⲟϥ ϧ. ⲙⲡ., TT 66 Egypt ⲉⲧⲗⲟ-ⲃⲉ ϧ. ⲙⲡ. *in idolatry*, J 67 77, ManiK 16 *A²*; ϧⲁϫⲉⲛⲡ.ϥ. *B*: AM 269 ⲡⲣⲟ ⲧⲟⲩⲧⲱⲛ ⲧ.ⲏⲙ., *ib* 47; ϫⲓⲙⲡ., -ⲉⲡ. *SF*, ⲓⲥϫⲉⲛⲡⲫ. *B*: Is 38 19 *SB* ⲁⲡⲟ ⲧ. ⲥⲏⲙ.; Kr 136 *F* ⲉϫⲓ(ⲛ)ⲡⲁⲩ; PS 8 *S* ϫ. ⲉⲃⲟⲗ, ShR 2 3 86 *S sim*, FR 36 *S sim* (var BMis 69 ϫⲓⲛⲧⲉⲛⲟⲩ), MG 25 280 *B* ⲓⲥ. ⲫ. ⲉϥ.; JA '75 5 216 *S* ϫ. ⲉϩⲣⲁⲓ, BMOr 6203 ϫ. ⲡⲁⲓ... ⲉⲑⲏ, Ryl 144 *S* ϩⲁϫⲓⲙⲉⲡ. ⲉⲑⲏ, J 76 48 *S* ϫ. ⲉⲡⲁϩⲟⲩ = *ib* 66 46 ϣⲁⲉⲡⲉϩ; ⲣ ⲡⲟⲟⲩ: BMis 381 *S* ⲕⲛⲁⲣ. ⲉⲣⲟⲓ = Mor 27 31 *F wilt devote to-day to me* = BSM 37 *B* ⲭⲛⲁϣⲟⲡⲧ ⲉⲣⲟⲕ ⲙⲫ. = *ib* 145 تضيفني; ϣⲙ(ⲡ)ⲧ ⲉⲡ. v p 566 *b inf*.

ⲡⲟⲟⲩ ⲛⲣⲟⲟⲩ, ⲫ. ⲡⲉϧ. *SBF*, *this day*: Ge 31 2 *SB* ϣⲙⲧ ⲉⲡ. ⲡϧ. ⲧⲣⲓⲧⲏ ⲏⲙ.; ⲙⲡ. ⲡϧ.: Lu 19 42 *S*(*B* ϧⲉⲡⲡⲁⲓⲉϩ.) ⲉⲛ ⲧⲏ ⲏⲙ. ⲧⲁⲩⲧⲏ; Lant 5 16 *S book completed* ⲙ.; ϣⲁⲡ. ⲡϧ.: Mt 11 23 *S*(*B* ϣⲁⲉϧⲟⲩⲛ ⲉⲫ.) ⲙⲉⲭⲣⲓ ⲧ.ⲥⲏⲙ.; Br 104 *S* ϣⲁⲡ. ⲡϧ.; ϣⲁϩⲟⲩⲛ ⲉⲡ. ⲡϧ.: Ez 20 29 *B* ϣⲁⲉϧ. ⲉⲫ. ⲡⲉϧ. (*S* ϣⲁϩⲣⲁⲓ ⲉⲡ.) ⲉⲱⲥ ⲧⲏⲥ ⲥⲏⲙ.ⲏⲙ.; PS 4 *S*, Pcod 40 *F* ϣⲁⲉϧ. ⲉⲡⲁⲁⲟⲩ ⲡϧ. = *S do*; ϣⲁϩⲣⲁⲓ ⲉⲡ. ⲡϧ. *S*: Mt 27 8 (*B* ϣⲁⲉϧⲟⲩⲛ ⲉⲫ.) ⲉⲱⲥ ⲧⲏⲥ ⲥⲏⲙ.; CA 90; ϧⲡⲡ. ⲡϧ., ϧⲉⲡϥ. ⲡⲉϧ. *B*: Jos 3 7 *SB* ⲉⲛ ⲧⲏ ⲏⲙ. ⲧⲁⲩ., Ac 20 26 *B* ϧⲉⲡⲡⲁⲓⲉϩ. ⲡⲧⲉ ⲫ. (*S* ⲙⲡ. ⲡϧ.) ⲉⲛ ⲧⲏ ⲥⲏⲙ. ⲏⲙ.; J 16 2 *S*, *ib* 78 7 *S* ϧⲣⲁⲓ ϧ.; ϫⲓⲙⲡⲡ. ⲡϧ. *S*, ⲓⲥϫⲉⲛⲡⲫ. ⲡⲉϧ. *B*: Ez 24 2 *SB* ⲁⲡⲟ ⲧ. ⲏⲙ. ⲧ. ⲥⲏⲙ.; J 2 18 *S*.

In name: ⲧⲁⲡⲣⲟⲟⲩ (Aegyptus 11 444).

V Rec 24 201.

ϩⲟⲟⲩ *S*, ϩⲁⲩ *AA²F*, ϩⲱⲟⲩ *B*, ϩⲁⲟⲩ *FO* vb intr (qual), *be putrid, so bad, wicked*: Lu 6 43 *SB* ⲥⲁⲡⲣⲟⲥ,

Job 25 6 *S*(*B* diff) ⲥⲁⲡⲣⲓⲁ; Sa 6 25 *S* ⲧⲏⲕⲉⲓⲛ; Ge 28 8 *SB*, Is 56 11 *B*(*S* = Gk), Jo 3 19 *SA²BF* ⲡⲟⲛⲏⲣⲟⲥ ⲉⲓⲛⲁⲓ, Nu 20 5 *SB*, Eccl 10 13 *F*(*S* = Gk), Eph 5 16 *SB* ⲡⲟ.; Pro 1 18 (19) *SAB*, 1 Cor 15 33 *SBF*, AP 15 *A²* ⲕⲁⲕⲟⲥ, Ps 34 17 *S* ϣⲟϫⲡⲉ ⲉⲑ. (*B* ⲙⲉⲧⲥⲁⲙⲡⲉⲧϩ.) ⲕⲁⲕⲟⲩⲣⲅⲓⲁ, Ro 1 29 *B* ⲙⲉϧⲓ ⲉϧⲣ. (*S* diff) ⲕⲁⲕⲟⲏⲑⲉⲓⲁ, Mk 7 10 *SB* ϣⲁϫⲉ ⲉϧⲣ. -ⲗⲟⲅⲉⲓⲛ; Sa 3 19 *S*, Is 18 2 *B*(*S* ⲛⲁϣⲧ) ⲭⲁⲗⲉⲡⲟⲥ; Job 6 3 *B*(*S* ⲥⲟϣϥ), Ro 9 11 *B*(*S* ⲡⲉϩ.) ⲫⲁⲩⲗⲟⲥ; ManiH 3 *A²* ϯⲁⲡⲓⲧ ϯϧ., PS 25 *S* ⲡⲉⲩⲡⲣⲁⲝⲓⲥ ⲉⲑ., R 1 5 47 *S* ⲟⲩϧⲧⲟ ⲉϧⲣ., PMd 242 *S* (ⲟⲩⲁ)ⲙⲟⲙⲉ ⲉⲑ., ManiK 99 *A²* ⲡ̄ⲛ̄ⲁ̄ ⲉⲧϩ., C 43 244 *B* ϫⲉⲙⲱⲡ ⲉϧⲣ.

With following preposition. c ⲉ-, *bad beyond, worse than*: Si 34 14 *S*, Mt 12 45 *SB* ⲡⲟⲛⲏⲣⲟⲧⲉⲣⲟⲥ gen; Sa 15 18 *S*, Jo 5 14 *SA²*(*B* ⲡϧⲟⲩⲟ), Va 57 9 *B* ⲉⲧϩ. ⲉⲕⲟⲗⲁⲥⲓⲥ ⲡⲓⲃⲉⲛ ⲭⲉⲓⲣⲱⲛ gen; ShRE 11 18 *S* ⲛⲁⲓ ϧ. ⲉⲡⲣⲟϥ, R 1 5 28 *S* ϭⲉⲃⲁⲥⲁⲛⲟⲥ ⲉϧⲣ. ⲉⲡⲁⲓ; *for, to*: ManiK 53 *A²* fruit ⲉϧⲣ. ⲁⲡⲟⲅⲱⲙ; ⲡϧⲟⲩⲟ ⲉ-: Va 57 8 *B* ⲥⲉϩ. ⲛϧ. ⲉⲙⲉⲧⲃⲱⲕ ⲡⲓⲃⲉⲛ ⲭ. gen; BHom 50 *S* ⲉⲧϩ. ⲛϧ. ⲉⲡⲓⲙⲟⲅⲓ; c ⲉϩⲟⲧⲉ- *B*: 1 Kg 17 43 (*S* ⲡⲁⲣⲁ) ⲭ.; DeV 2 237 ⲥⲉϩ. ⲉϧ. ⲣⲱⲟⲩϣ ⲡⲓⲃⲉⲛ; c ⲉⲃⲟⲗ ⲟⲩⲧⲉ- *B*: Dan 3 32 (*S* = Gk) ⲡⲟⲛⲏⲣⲟⲧⲁⲧⲟⲥ ⲡⲁⲣⲁ; c ⲡⲁⲣⲁ: PS 260 *S* ⲧⲉⲧⲓⲕⲟⲗⲁⲥⲓⲥ ϧ. ⲡ.ⲣⲱⲙⲉ ⲡⲓⲙ, AM 56 *B* these days ϧ. ⲛⲏⲓ ⲡ. ⲡⲁⲥⲛⲟⲩ ⲧⲏⲣϥ; c ⲛⲉⲙ-: C 89 116 *B* none might work with him ϫⲉϧ. ⲡⲉⲙⲱⲟⲩ (*cf* ⲏⲛ ⲥⲕⲗⲏⲣⲟⲥ), Mani 1 *A²* ⲡⲉⲧⲁⲧⲥⲉⲧⲉ ⲃⲓ ⲙⲡⲛⲉϫⲁⲕⲉ ⲉⲥϧ. ⲡⲉⲙⲉϥ.

ⲡⲉⲑⲟⲟⲩ, ⲡⲉⲧϩ. as nn *SAA²BFO*, *who, what is evil, wickedness*: Ge 3 22 *SB*, Sa 3 14 *S*, Mt 5 11 *B*(*S* ϩⲱⲃ ⲉⲑ.)ⲡⲟ., Eccl 11 10 *F*(*S* = Gk) ⲡⲟⲛⲏⲣⲓⲁ; Job 13 4 *SB*, Ps 87 4 *SB*, Ap 2 2 *SB* ⲕⲁ., Mt 15 4 *S* ϫⲉ ⲡⲉⲑ. (*BF* ϧ. vb) ⲕⲁⲕⲟⲗⲟⲅⲉⲓⲛ; 2 Cor 5 10 *SB* ⲫⲁⲩ.; Mt 13 48 *SBF* ⲥⲁⲡ.; Sa 13 13 *S* ⲁⲡⲟⲃⲗⲏⲙⲁ; Ac 13 10 *SB* ⲣⲁⲇⲓⲟⲩⲣⲅⲓⲁ; ShC 42 189 *S* ⲡⲕⲉⲡ. ⲉⲡⲧⲁⲛⲁⲁⲩ, TillOster 11 *A* ⲣⲁⲉⲓⲥ ⲁⲣⲱⲡⲉ ⲁⲡ., C 100 333 *S* men ⲡⲉⲧϩ. opp ⲡⲉⲧⲛⲁⲡⲟⲩⲟϥ, CO 110 *S* ⲉⲡⲉⲗⲁⲁⲩ ⲛⲡ. ⲡⲁⲣⲁⲧⲉ ⲙⲙⲟⲕ, BSM 67 *B* save us ϧⲁⲡ. ⲛⲓⲃⲉⲛ, Hor 83 *O* ⲡⲉⲧϩⲁⲟⲩ; with art or pron: Ps 33 13 *SB* ⲛⲡ., *ib* 27 3 *S* ⲛⲡ. (*B* ϯⲙⲉⲧⲡ.), *ib* 34 26 *SB* ⲛⲁⲡ., *ib* 39 14 *SB* ϧⲉⲛⲡ., Is 7 16 *S* ⲛⲡ. *B* ⲟⲩⲛ., *ib* 31 2 *SBF* ϩⲉⲛⲡ., Dan 9 13 *SB* ⲛⲉⲓⲡ. ⲕⲁ.; Ac 28 21 *S* ⲟⲩⲛ. (*B* diff) ⲡⲟ.; PS 101 *S* ϧⲉⲛⲡ., ShC 42 165 *S* ⲡⲉⲩⲡ., AP 3 *A²* ⲟⲩⲛ. ⲁⲡⲙ[ⲁ ⲛ]ⲟⲩⲛ., ManiP 1 34 *A²* ⲡⲉⲧⲛⲛ., C 43 166 *B* ⲛⲁⲓⲛ.; ⲙⲉⲧⲡ. *B*: Ps 27 3 above; ⲁⲧⲡ. *B*, *guileless, unharmed*: Jer 11 19 (*S* ⲃⲁⲗϩⲏⲧ) ⲁⲕⲁⲕⲟⲥ; HCons 361 preserve him ⲛⲟⲩϫ ⲛⲁ.; ⲙⲉⲧⲁⲧⲡ. Va 61 4 *innocence*.

ⲉⲓⲣⲉ ⲙⲡ., ⲣ ⲡ., *do evil*: Ps 33 16 *SB*, 2 Cor 13 7 *SBF* ⲕⲁ. ⲡⲟⲓⲉⲓⲛ, Is 11 9 *B*(*S* om) ⲕⲁⲕⲟⲡⲟⲓ., BM 172 40 *S* ⲣ ⲡ. ⲙⲡⲉⲧϩⲓⲧⲟⲩⲱⲡ ⲕⲁ. ⲉⲣⲅⲁⲍⲉⲥⲑⲁⲓ; Ps 50 4 *SB* ⲡⲟ. ⲡⲟⲓ., *ib* 91 11 *SB* ⲡⲟⲛⲏⲣⲉⲩⲉⲥⲑⲁⲓ; Jo 3 20 *SA²B*(*F* ϩⲱⲃ ⲉϧⲣ.) ⲫⲁⲩⲗⲁ ⲡⲣⲁⲥⲥⲉⲓⲛ; Ez 17 15 *B* ⲉⲛⲁⲛⲧⲓⲁ ⲡⲟⲓ.; PS 50 *S* ⲡⲧⲁϩⲣ ⲛⲉⲓⲡ., CO 268 *S* ⲡⲉⲡⲃⲓⲟⲥ ⲙⲉϧⲣ ⲡ.

ⲛⲗⲁⲁⲩ, AM 102 B ⲉⲣ ⲡ. ⲡⲧⲉϥϩⲱⲕⲓ ;   ⲣⲉϥⲣ ⲡ.:
Pro 2 14 A(S ⲉⲧⲣ ⲡ., B ⲡⲉϩ.), Mor 37 61 S(sic l) ⲕⲁ.;
ShC 42 152 S ⲛⲣ....ⲡⲣⲉϥⲣ ⲡⲟⲃⲉ, Pcod 38 F ϩⲛϩⲟⲡⲛ
ⲛⲗⲉϥⲉⲗ ⲡ.= S ⲉⲥⲃⲗⲁⲡⲧⲉⲓ;   ⲙⲛⲧ-, ⲙⲉⲧⲣ.: Z 270
S, CaiEuch 124 B;   ⲥⲁ ⲙⲡ., doer of evil: Si 11
35 S κακοῦργος ; Ps 9 36 B(S=Gk), Mt 12 34 S(B
ϩ.) ⲡⲟ.; My 83 S ⲡⲉ. ⲡⲇⲓⲁⲃⲟⲗⲟⲥ, AM 216 B slain
as c.;   ⲙⲛⲧ-, ⲙⲉⲧⲥ.: Ps 34 17 B(S ϣⲟⲭⲡⲉ ⲉⲑ.) κακουργία ; Mt 22 18 B(S=Gk) πονηρία ; Bor 254 173
S;   ⲉⲣ ⲥ.: Deu 19 19 B(S om) πονηρεύ.;   ⲙⲉⲧⲣⲉϥ-
ⲉⲣⲥ.: Cat 95 B.

ϩⲱⲟⲩ SAA²BF, ϩⲟⲩ- S vb intr, rain: Ap 11 6 S
(B ⲙⲟⲩ ⲡϩ. ⲓ ⲉϩⲣⲏⲓ) βρέχειν ; Ps 67 8 S(B ⲑⲗⲏ ⲉⲃⲟⲗ)
στάζειν ; Ge 8 2 S(B Gk not vb), C 41 46 B ⲁⲧϥⲉ ϩ.,
MG 25 339 B sim;   tr S : Ps 143 6 (B as Gk) ἀστράπτειν ; Deu 33 28 (B Gk diff); BHom 103 heaven
ⲁⲥϩ. ⲙⲡⲟⲉⲓⲕ (ALR '96 196 ‌).
   With following preposition.   ⲉ ⲉϫⲛ-: Ge 19 24
SB, AM 4 7 SB β. ἐπί, Ps 10 6 SB ⲉϫⲓⲃ. ἐπί ; HM 1
115 S ϩ. ⲉϫⲱⲕ ... ⲡⲟⲩⲙⲟⲟⲩ, ViK 9798 111 S ⲉⲙⲡ
ⲓⲱⲧⲉ ϩ. ⲉϫⲱϥ, ManiP 10 A² ⲁϥⲧⲣⲉⲥϩ. ⲁⲭⲱⲟⲩ like
clouds, AM 155 B ⲟⲩϭⲏⲡⲓ...ϩ. ⲉϫⲱⲟⲩ;   ⲉϩⲣⲁⲓ, -ⲛⲓ
ⲉⲭ.: Ja 5 17 S(B ϩⲓⲭⲉⲛ-) β. ἐπί, Ex 9 18 B ⲩⲉⲓⲛ
only;   ⲉ ϩⲓⲭⲉⲛ- B: Ge 2 5 β. ἐπί ; Va 61 92 ⲉⲑⲣⲉⲧ-
ϥⲉ ϩ. ⲛⲛⲟⲩⲃ ϩ. ⲛⲕⲁϩⲓ;   ⲉ ⲛ- dat : Ps 77 24 SB,
Joel 2 23 SAB β. dat ;   ⲉ ⲉⲃⲟⲗ ϩⲛ-, ϫⲉⲛ-: Lu 17
29 SB β. ἀπό ; Ap 16 21 S(B as Gk) καταβαίνειν ἐκ ;
ShRyl 71 93 S fire ϩ. ⲉⲃ. ϩⲓⲧⲡⲉ.
    —— nn m S AF(B mostly ⲙⲟⲩ ⲛϩ.), rain, moist-
ure : Job 29 23, Pro 25 14 SA, Is 30 23 SF, He 6 7,
Mor 37 75 ⲡⲁ̣ϩ ⲡϩ. in Ethiopia ὑετός ; Ez 21 7 B(Lacr,
PasLect 130, var & S ⲑⲱⲗⲉⲃ) ὑγρασία ; Ps 104 32, ib
67 9 (B ⲙⲟⲩ ⲡⲱϣⲓ), Mt 7 25 βροχή ; Lu 12 54 ὄμβρος ; Pro 27 15 SA σταγών ; Z 311 diseased body
ⲧⲁ̣ϥⲉ ϩ. ⲉⲃⲟⲗ ⲉϥⲟ ⲛⲥⲧⲟⲓ πύον.
   ⲙⲟⲩ ⲛϩ. SA²BF, as last : Ge 7 4 S(B ⲙ. ⲛⲕⲁⲧⲁ-
ⲕⲗⲩⲥⲙⲟⲥ), 2 Kg 1 21 SB, Eccl 12 2 F(S ϩⲟⲩⲙⲡⲉ), Ep
Jer 52 BF, Ez 22 24 S(ShC 42 159)B ⲩⲉ.; PS 213
S ⲛⲙ., ManiK 114 A² cloud ϣⲟⲅⲟ ⲛⲟⲩϩ., ib 175
exuded by wounds, C 86 213 B sim ⲙⲟⲩϩ., AM 144
B ϭⲏⲡⲓ ⲙⲙ.;   ⲙⲉⲧⲁⲧⲙ. ⲛϩ. B Va 57 76.
   ϩⲟⲩⲙⲡⲉ S, ϩⲱⲟⲩ ⲙⲡⲉ A, as last (lit rain of sky):
Deu 32 2, Job 38 28, Hos 6 3 SA(all B ⲙⲟⲩ ⲛϩ.), Lev
26 4 (B ⲙ. ⲡⲱϣⲓ), Deu 11 11 (B do) ⲩⲉ.; BHom 125
ⲛϩ. ⲙⲛⲧⲱⲧⲉ ; Jer 14 1 neg (B ϣⲁⲣⲕⲉ) ἀβροχία.
   ϭⲓⲛ-, ϫⲓⲛϩ., act of raining : Si 43 19 S ⲩⲉ.; Va 57
206 B ⲡⲓϫ. ⲉϫⲱⲟⲩ (sc Sodom) ⲛⲧⲉ ⲡⲓϫⲣⲱⲙ.

ϩⲁⲟⲩⲉ S nn m, tailor : P 44 67 ⲣⲁϥⲉⲩⲥ · ⲡϩ. خِيَاط
(but 43 37 ϩⲁⲙⲟⲩⲉ, cf ? ϩⲁⲙ ⲡⲧⲱⲡ) ; Ryl 239 ⲥⲡⲁⲗⲓⲥ
(ψαλίς) ⲛϩ., Baouit 1 108 ⲟⲩⲉⲡⲟⲃⲣⲉ ϥⲁⲩⲉ.

ϩⲓⲉⲉⲩ(ⲉ)   v ϩⲟⲓ 1°.

ϩⲓⲟⲩⲉ SAA¹, ϩⲓⲟⲩⲓ BF, ϩⲓ- SBF, ϩⲟⲩ- S(tr ⲉ ⲉ-)
AA², ϩⲓⲧϥ SB, ϩⲱⲟⲩⲓ†, ϩⲟ.† B, p c ϩⲁⲩ- SA² vb intr,
be struck, whetted : Ps 56 4 B(S ⲧⲏⲙ), Ap 2 12 B(S
do) ὀξύς, Ez 21 9 B(var ϣⲉⲃϣⲱⲃ, S ⲧⲱⲙ) ὀξύνειν ;
ib 11 B sim ἐξακονᾶν ;   qual B : ϩⲱ. ⲙⲡⲉϫⲏⲥ (πέ-
δαις) Ps 78 11 (S ⲧⲟ ⲙⲡⲉⲓⲡⲉ) πεδᾶσθαι ; Is 42 7 (S
ⲙⲏⲣ) δεῖσθαι ; O'Leary H 24]ⲉⲧϩ. ⲡⲧⲉⲃⲥ ;   tr,
strike, cast, lay : Lu 22 63 S(B ⲉ-) δέρειν ; Bar 2 21
B καταβάλλειν ; Ac 21 3 B(S ϣⲟϭⲟ) ἀποφορτίζεσθαι ;
Tob 11 8 S Gk diff, Am 6 5 B ϩⲓ ⲧⲉⲣⲧⲱⲣⲓ (v p 425 a) ;
ShIF 307 S entreating him ⲉⲩϩⲓ ⲣⲱϥ, Z 613 S ⲡⲧⲏϥ
ϩ. ⲙⲙⲟϥ, J 7 31 S price ⲁⲓⲣⲓⲧⲟⲩ ⲁⲓⲭⲓⲧⲟⲩ ⲛⲥϫⲭ ⲉⲥϫⲭ
(or ? for ϣⲓⲧⲟⲩ), BM 1089 S ⲡⲧⲁⲧⲡⲉ ϩⲓ ⲙⲟⲟⲩ, Mani
P 8 A² ⲡⲕⲉⲕⲁ̣ϩ ⲁⲡ ϩⲟⲩ ⲣⲉϣⲣⲉϣ (sic l, v ⲣⲁϣⲣⲉϣ),
ManiK 123 A² ⲛϩⲟⲩⲅⲉ ⲉⲧⲁⲩϩⲟⲩ ϩⲏⲧⲟⲩ, AM 172 B
ⲁϩⲉ. ⲛⲛⲓⲧⲉⲃⲛⲱⲟⲩⲓ, C 43 79 B ϩ. ⲛϣϫⲱⲧ ... ⲉⲙⲏⲣ
ⲛϩⲏⲧⲟⲩ (sc martyr's heels), BSM 3 B I fear lest
ⲛⲧⲁϩ. ⲛⲧⲁⲯⲩⲭⲏ cast away my life.
   With following preposition.
     —— ⲉ obj, intr : Ex 2 13 SB(A ⁑), Deu 25 11 S(B
ⲙⲓϣⲓ), Lu 12 45 S(B ⲡ-), Aeg 216 S ⲡⲉⲩϩ. ⲉⲣⲟϥ, MG
25 203 B sim τύπτειν ; Jo 18 23 SA²B, Ac 5 40 SB
δέρ.; Jer 44 15 B πατάσσειν, Jon 4 8 SA(B ⲉϫⲛ-) π.
ἐπί ; Mt 26 67 B(S ⁑ ⲁⲁⲥ) ῥαπίζειν ; Si 30 1 S μαστι-
γοῦν ; Job 5 4 S(B ⲧⲣⲉⲙⲕⲟ) κολαβρίζειν ; 1 Pet 2 20
S(B ⁑ ⲕⲉϥ) κολαφίζειν ; ShMiss 4 280 S ⲉⲩ† ⲕⲗⲯ
ⲉⲩϩ. ⲉϩⲉⲛϣⲏⲣⲉ ϣⲏⲙ, Mor 31 34 S ϩ. ⲉⲣⲟϥ (var Miss
4 774 ⲉⲩⲃⲣⲓϫⲉ (ὑβ.). ⲙⲙⲟϥ), ManiK 51 A² ϩ. ⲁⲣⲁⲩ, AM
58 B ϩ. ⲉⲣⲟϥ, Mor 30 31 F ϩⲓⲟⲩⲉ ⲓⲉ ⲉⲛⲗⲱⲙⲓ ;   into : Mt 6 26 B(S ⲥⲱⲟⲩϩ ⲉϩⲟⲩⲛ ⲉ-) συνάγειν εἰς ;
qual, cast, lying B : Lu 16 20 (S ⲛⲏⲭ ϩⲛ-) βάλλειν
πρός ; MG 25 201 ⲡⲉ.ⲣϩⲁⲡ ϩⲟ. ⲉⲡⲓⲧⲁⲣⲧⲁⲣⲟⲥ ;   tr,
cast to, into (mostly B) : Is 19 8 (S ⲡⲟⲩϫⲉ), Mt 13 42
BF(S do), Jo 18 11 (S A² do) βαλ. εἰς, Jer 11 19 (S
do) ⲉⲙⲃ. εἰς, Mt 12 20 (S ⲉⲓⲡⲉ ⲉⲃⲟⲗ) ⲉⲕⲃ. εἰς, Is 11 8
(S ⲭⲓ ⲉϫⲛ-) ⲉⲡⲓⲃ. ἐπί, Lam 4 5 (F ϣⲧⲁ, S diff) περιβ. ;
Ez 5 4 (S ⲡ.) ῥίπτειν εἰς, Ps 54 33 (S do) ἐπιρρί. ἐπί ;
Sa 5 11 S μαστίζειν ; Jer 13 1 διέρχεσθαι ἐν, Ez 22 20
εἰσδέχεσθαι εἰς ; Pro 6 10 ϩⲓ ⲡⲉⲕⲭⲓϫ ⲉⲕⲙⲟⲩⲗϫ ⲙ-
ⲙⲟⲟⲩ ⲉ- (SA diff) ἐναγκαλίζειν ; C 89 11 ϩⲓ ⲕⲉⲣⲙⲓ
ⲉⲡⲓϩⲙⲟⲩ μίσγειν dat ; Mart Ign 869 ϩ. ⲛⲟⲩϩⲙⲟⲩ
ⲉⲛⲉϥϣⲁϣ = R 1 4 57 S ϩⲓ ἀνατρίβειν (cf p 643 b) ; Ac
8 3 (S ⲡ.) παραδιδόναι εἰς ; Ez 36 19 (S ⲥⲱⲣ ⲉⲃⲟⲗ)
λικμᾶν εἰς ; Ps 25 2 ϩⲓ ⲭⲣⲱⲙ ⲉ- (S ⲡⲓⲥⲉ) πυροῦν, Jer
28 25 ϩⲓ ⲥⲁⲧ ⲉ- ἐμπ.; Miss 4 134 ⲡⲓⲣⲱⲃ ϩⲓ ⲁⲛⲁⲅⲕⲏ
ⲉⲣⲟⲓ = MR 4 68 S ϩ. ϩⲧⲟⲣ, AM 184 new ship ⲁϥϩⲓⲧϥ
ⲉϥⲗⲱⲟⲩ, C 43 117 ⲁⲓⲣⲓⲑⲛⲟⲩ ⲉⲡⲓϣⲧⲉⲕⲟ, ib 133 ϩ.
ⲡⲟⲩⲃⲉⲛⲓⲡⲓ ⲉⲡⲉϥϭⲁⲗⲁϫ, MG 25 135 ϩⲓ ⲡⲓⲙⲏⲛⲓ
ⲛⲧⲉ ⲡⲓⲥⲧⲁⲩⲣⲟⲥ ⲉⲣⲱⲟⲩ, BHom 62 S ⲡⲉⲛⲧⲁϥϩⲟⲩ ⲗⲁ
ⲉⲣⲟϥ (v Lu 19 8), Mani 1 A² ⲁⲩϩⲟⲩ ⲱⲡⲉ ⲁⲣⲁϥ, AP 3
A² sim.
     —— ⲉϫⲛ-, upon : Am 9 1 SB(A ⲣⲱϩⲧ) ⲡⲁⲧ. ἐπί ;
Z 330 S teeth ϩ. ⲉⲭⲡⲛⲉⲅⲉⲣⲏⲧ συγκρούειν ; Mor 31

47 S ϩ. ⲉ. ⲧⲉϥⲁⲡⲉ, C 43 13 B sim ;   qual B : 3 Kg 8 54 ⲉϥϩ. ⲉ. ⲡⲉϥⲕⲉⲗⲓ ⲟⲕⲗⲁⲕⲱⲥ ἐπί ; C 89 66 ⲉϥϩⲟ. ⲉ. ⲡⲉϥϩⲟ = C 99 232 S ⲡⲁⲣⲧ πίπτειν ἐπί ;   tr : Mt 26 12 B(S ⲛ.) βαλ. ἐπί, Ge 2 21 B(S do) ἐπιβ. ἐπί ; Ez 16 5 B(S do) ἀπορρί. ἐπί ; Tri 586 S ϩ. ⲉ.ⲡⲉϩⲟ ⲛⲣⲉⲡⲗⲁⲁⲥ, Aeg 30 B ϩ. ⲡⲟⲩⲗⲙⲟⲩ ⲉ.ⲛⲥⲱⲙⲁ ;   refl B : Ge 17 17, 1 Cor 14 25 (S ⲡⲱⲣⲧ ⲉϫⲛ-) πί. ἐπί ; Mk 15 19 (S as Gk, F ϩ. ⲉϩⲟⲩⲛ ⲉϩⲗⲉⲛ-) γόνατα τιθέναι ; AM 141 ϩⲓⲧⲟⲩ ⲉ. ϩⲏⲧⲟⲩ, MIE 2 416 ⲁⲓⲣⲓⲧ ⲉ.ⲡⲁϩⲟ ; ⲉ-ϩⲣⲏⲓ ⲉϫ. B : Hos 7 12 (A ⲡⲱⲣϣ ⲁϩ. ⲁϫⲛ-) ἐπιβάλ. ἐπί ; Ez 19 8 (S ⲡⲱ. ⲉϩ. ⲉϫⲛ-) ἐκπεταννύναι ἐπί.

——— ⲙⲛ-, strike (fight) with : BMOr 6201 A 28 S ⲁⲡⲛⲁϭⲟⲩ(ⲟ)ⲡ ϩⲓⲉϥⲉ (sic) ⲙⲛⲛⲉⲧⲉ(ⲛ)ⲣⲱⲙⲉ, BKU 1 26 (8117) F drunkards ϣⲁⲩϩⲓⲟⲩⲉⲓ ⲙⲉⲡⲉⲩⲉⲣⲏⲩ.

——— ⲛ- dat : Ge 48 12 S(B as Gk) ἐξάγειν ἀπό (misunderst) ; with instrum : Nu 22 23 SB ⲡⲁⲧ. dat, Lu 22 49 SB ⲡ. ἐν ; Is 41 7 SB ⲧⲩ. dat ; Ac 16 22 SB, 2 Cor 11 25 S(B ⲟⲩⲟϣⲟⲩⲉⲙ) ῥαβδίζειν ; Si 12 18 B (S ϣϭⲁ) ἐπικροτεῖν dat ; Gu 41 S ϩ. ⲉⲣⲟϥ ⲛⲣⲛϭⲉ-ⲣⲟⲟϩ, Wess 18 60 S ϩ. ⲉϫⲱϥ ⲛⲣⲉⲡⲛϭⲉ, AM 207 B ϩ. ⲉⲣⲟϥ ⲛⲣⲁⲡⲕⲟⲩⲗⲫⲟⲥ (κόμβος).

——— ⲛⲥⲁ-, after, upon or emphatic : 2 Kg 1 1 S ⲧⲩ. ; Mt 26 51 B(S ⲣⲱϩⲧ) ⲡⲁⲧ. ; Jos 10 10 S κατακόπ. ; ib 7 5 S συντρίβ. ; Jo 18 10 B(S do, A² ϣⲱϣⲉ) παίειν ; Ex 21 30 B(S ⲛ. ⲉϫⲛ-) ἐπιβάλ. dat ; Ps 21 11 B(S ⲛ. ⲉ-) ἐπιρρί. ἐπί ; 2 Pet 2 17 S(B ϭⲱⲣⲉⲙ ⲛⲥⲁ-) ἐλαύνειν ; Lev 26 16 S(B diff) σφακελίζειν ; Deu 22 14 B(S ⲧⲱⲱϣⲉ ⲉϩⲟⲩⲛ ⲉ-) ἐπιτιθ. dat ; OrChr NS 3 40 B ϩⲓⲧϥ ⲛⲥⲁⲫⲟⲩⲱϣ ⲙⲫϯ ἀναφέρειν ἐπί ; Gal 4 14 B ϩ. ⲑⲁϥ ⲛⲥⲁ- (S diff) ἐκπτύειν ; Ja 3 6 B ϩⲓ ⲁϭⲛⲓ ⲛⲥⲁ- (S ϫⲱϩⲙ) σπιλοῦν ; P 131² 117 S wine drunk ϥϩ. ⲛⲥⲁⲧⲉⲕ-ⲁⲡⲉ throb in = Va 58 192 B, C 43 60 B ϫⲛⲁϩⲓ ⲙⲉⲣⲉϩ ⲛⲥⲱⲓ ; cast behind, repel : Ps 43 24 B(S ⲕⲱ ⲛⲥⲁ-) ἀπωθεῖν.

——— ϩⲁ- B, ϧⲁ- F, beneath : Jer 34 8 ἐμβάλ. ὑπό ; MG 25 12 refl προσπί. dat ; TstAb 251 ⲁⲓⲱⲥⲏⲫ ϩ. ⲙ-ⲙⲁⲡⲁⲥⲥⲛ ϧⲁⲧⲉϥϫⲓϫ ⲡⲟⲩⲓⲛⲁⲙ (Ge 48 13), AM 243 ϩⲓⲧϥ ϧⲁⲛⲉⲛϭⲁⲗⲁⲩϫ, BP 3285 F ⲁⲓϩⲓ ⲡⲗⲓⲙⲁ (λεῖμμα) ϩⲁⲗⲁⲓ.

——— ϩⲛ- (rare), ϧⲉⲛ-, in, on : Mt 27 30 (S ⲣⲱ. ⲉ-ϩⲣⲁⲓ ⲉϫⲛ-) ⲧⲩ. εἰς, Ac 23 2 (var ⲉϫⲟⲩⲛ ϧ., S ⲣⲱ. ⲛ-) ⲧⲩ. acc ; 2 Cor 11 20 (S ⲉϩⲟⲩⲛ ⲉ-) δέρ. εἰς ; Pro 1 14 (S ⲡⲟⲩϫⲉ, A ⲧⲱⲕⲉ) βάλ. ἐν, 1 Cor 7 35 (S ϯ ⲉϩⲏⲧⲋ) ἐπιβ. dat ; DeV 2 181 ⲛⲁϥϩ. ϧⲉⲛⲡⲉϩⲟ ; with instr (cf ⲛ-) : Ez 26 9 καταβάλ. ἐν ; ib 25 6 ἐπιψοφεῖν dat ; C 86 275 ϩ. ⲉⲭⲉⲡⲧⲉϥⲁϥⲉ ϧⲉⲛϩⲁⲡⲓϥⲧ, ib 274 ϧⲉⲛϩⲁⲡⲗ-ⲙⲟⲩⲧ, ShA 2 304 S ⲉⲓϩ. ⲉⲣⲟϥ ϩⲛⲡⲁϭⲓϫ.

——— ϩⲁⲧⲉⲛ- B, beneath : Jo 19 29 (SA² ⲥⲟⲟⲩⲧⲛ ⲉ-) προσφέρειν dat.

——— ϩⲓϫⲉⲛ- B, upon : Ez 19 12 (S ⲛ. ⲉϫⲛ-) ⲣⲓ. ἐπί ; 1 Kg 24 9 (S ⲡⲱⲣⲧ ⲉϫⲛ-) κύπτειν ἐπί ; C 86 296 ϩ. ⲡⲟⲩⲃⲁⲥⲓⲥ (? ⲕⲁⲥⲥ.) ϩ.ⲧⲉϥⲁϥⲉ ⲧⲓⲑ. ἐπί ; C 43 220 ϩ. ⲙⲡⲓⲁⲧⲓⲟⲥ ϩ. ⲡⲉϥⲥⲟⲓ.

With following adverb.

——— ⲉⲃⲟⲗ (mostly B), cast out, put forth : Job 5 3, Mt 5 13 βάλ., Is 1 30 (all S ⲛ. ⲉϩ.), MG 25 4 ⲣⲱϧ ϩⲓ ϧⲉⲗⲓ ⲉϩ. ἀπόβ., Ps 16 11 (S do, F ⲥⲓⲧⲓ), Lam 3 16 (S ⲑⲓⲟ), Jo 9 34 BF (Mich 3521, SA² do) ἐκβ. ; Mt 19 3 (S do) ἀπολύειν ; Is 30 22 (SF ⲥⲱϩⲣ) ὤθ., Ps 77 67 (S ⲕⲱ ⲛⲥⲁ-), Lam 3 45 (F ϩⲱⲣⲓ ϩⲁⲃⲁⲗ), Ez 5 6 (S ⲧⲥⲧⲟ) ἀπωθ., Jer 23 2 (S ⲡⲟⲩϫⲡ) ἐξωθ. ; ROC 25 271 ϩⲓⲧⲥ (sc wife) ⲉϩ. ⲣⲓ., Hos 10 7 (S ⲡⲟⲩϫⲉ, A ϯⲕⲉ ?) ἀπορρί. ; Deu 22 19 (S do), Is 50 1 (S do) ἐξαποστέλλειν ; Ac 7 19 BF (S do) ἐκτιθ. ; Ps 65 20 (S ⲥⲟⲟϩⲉ ⲉϩ.) ἀφι-στάναι : BMis 571 ⲥⲟⲩⲥⲧⲟⲗⲏ…ⲉⲥϩⲓ ⲣⲁϣⲉ ⲉϩ.,TT 19 S sim, RE 9 144 S bade ϩⲓ (sic ?) ⲙⲙⲱⲧⲛ ⲉϩ., ROC 25 246 heretic ⲛⲁϥϩ. ⲙⲡⲓⲧⲁⲙⲟⲥ ⲉϩ., C 43 222 ϩ. ⲛⲛⲓϩⲉ-ⲙⲱⲡ, C 86 286 wood ϩⲓ ϫⲱϩⲓ ⲉϩ., C 89 95 ϩⲓ ⲉ-ϩⲣⲏⲭ ⲉϩ. ;   qual B : Jer 22 30 (S ⲧⲥⲧⲟ ⲉϩ.) ἐκκήρυκ-τος, 1 Tim 4 4 (S ⲧⲥⲧⲏⲩ) ἀπόβλητος, Lev 21 7 (S ⲛ. ⲉϩ.) ἐκβάλ. ; Mt 5 32 (S do) ἀπολύ. ; Is 41 2 (S ⲣⲏⲗ ⲉϩ.) ἐξωθ. ; 2 Cor 4 8 (S = Gk) ἐξαπορεῖσθαι ; Ex 25 27 εἰς θήκας εἶναι جل ;   as nn B : Ro 11 15 (S ⲧⲥ. ⲉϩ.) ἀποβολή, Ex 11 1 ἐκβ., Jer 12 12 (S ⲛ. ⲉϩ.) διεκβ. ; ib 39 36 ἀποστολή ; Lev 16 10 (S ⲙⲁ ⲡⲟⲩ-ⲱⲱⲧⲉ ⲉϩ.) ἀποπομπή ; MIE 2 396 ⲡϩ. ⲉϩ. ⲡⲟⲩⲥⲟⲟ-ⲛⲉϥ = BAp 122 S ⲛⲛ. ⲛⲟⲩⲥ. ;   ⲉϩ. ⲉ- : Ez 47 8 (S om) ἔρχεσθαι ἕως ἐπί ;   ⲉϩ. ⲉϫⲉⲛ- : Va 61 216 ⲁⲩϩⲓ ⲧⲟⲩϥⲁⲧ ⲉϩ. ⲉϫⲱϥ ὑποσκελίζειν ; C 43 169 ⲁϥϩ. ⲡⲧⲉϥ-ϫⲓϫ ⲉϩ. ⲉϫ. ⲡⲉϥⲥⲱⲙⲁ & healed it (cf AM 326 be-low) ;   ⲉϩ. ϩⲉⲛ- : C 89 79 ϩⲓⲧϥ ⲉϩ. ϩⲉⲛⲡⲓⲥⲛⲟⲩ βάλ. ἔξω (var ἐξελαύνειν gen), Jer 12 14 ἐκβ. ἐκ, Ez 30 22 καταβ. ἐκ ; Nu 5 2 (S ⲛ. ⲉϩ.), Jer 24 5 (S ϫⲟⲟⲩ ⲉϩ.) ἐξαπος. ἐκ ; ib 16 13 (BM 1247, var ϩⲟⲣϩⲉⲣ ⲉϩ., S P 129⁵ 173 ⲛ. ⲉϩ.), Ez 11 16 ἀπορρί. ἀπό, MG 25 242 ϩⲓⲧⲧ ⲉϩ. ϩⲉⲛⲧⲉⲕⲙⲟⲡⲏ ἐκρί. gen ; C 43 58 ϩⲓⲧϥ ⲉϩ. ϩⲉⲛⲧⲫⲉ, AM 326 ⲁϥϩ. ⲡⲧⲉϥϫⲓϫ ⲉϩ. ϩⲉⲛⲡⲥⲱⲙⲁ (cf C 43 169 above & ib 230 below) ;   ⲉϩ. ϩⲁ- : MG 25 6 ϩⲓ ϯϩⲟϯ ⲉϩ. ϩⲁⲣⲟϥ ἀποβάλ. ἀπό, Ge 4 14 ἐκβ. ἀπό ; Lam 3 17 ἀπωθ. ἐκ ; Ge 45 1 ἐξαπος. ἀπό ; Va 61 205 ⲛⲧⲁϩⲓ ⲡⲁⲓⲣⲱⲟⲩϣ ⲉϩ. ϩⲁⲣⲟⲓ ;   ⲉϩ. ϩⲁⲧⲉⲛ-ⲛ- : Ps 77 55 (S ⲛ. ⲉϩ. ϩⲁ-) ἐκβ. ἀπὸ προσώπου ;   ⲉϩ. ϩⲓϫⲉⲛ- : Ps 2 3 (S ⲛ. ⲉϩ. ϩ.) ἀπορρί. ἀπό ; ROC 17 405 ⲁϥϩⲓⲧⲟⲩ ⲉϩ. ϩⲓϫⲱϥ ἀποδύεσθαι ; Ez 32 3 περιβ. ἐπί ; C 43 230 ⲁϥϩⲓ ⲧⲉϥϫⲓϫ ⲉϩ. ϩ.ⲡⲉϥⲥⲱⲙⲁ (cf AM 326 above).

——— ⲥⲁⲃⲟⲗ ⲛ- B : Ac 5 34 (S ⲣ ⲛⲃⲟⲗ) ἔξω ποιεῖν ; ib 13 46 (S ⲛ. ⲉϩ.) ἀπωθ. ; ib 50 (S do) ἐκβάλ. ἀπό ; Va 58 147 ⲁϥϩ. ⲥ. ⲙⲙⲟϥ ⲡⲧⲥⲩⲛⲏⲑⲓⲁ ἀποβ. ; Ps 118 29 (S ⲥⲟⲟϩⲉ ⲉϩ.) ἀφιστάναι ἀπό ; AM 36 ⲁⲩϩⲓⲧ ⲥ. ⲛϯ-ⲃⲁⲕⲓ.

——— ⲉⲡⲉⲥⲏⲧ B (mostly refl) : Mt 4 6 (S ⲛ. ⲉⲡ.) βάλ. κάτω ; BSM 45 ⲁⲩϩⲓⲧⲟⲩ ⲉ. = BMis 393 S ⲁⲩ-ⲡⲁⲣⲧⲟⲩ ;   ⲉⲡ. ⲉ- : C 43 57 ⲁⲩϩⲓⲧⲟⲩ ⲉ. ⲉ.ⲫⲓⲁⲣⲟ, ib 151 bade ϩ. ⲉ. ⲉⲣⲟϥ (ⲡ)ⲟⲩⲟⲏⲛⲓ ;   ⲉⲡ. ϧⲁⲣⲁⲧ⸗ : Va 66 308 beggar ϩ.† ⲉ. ϧⲁⲣⲁⲧⲕ.

—— ⲥⲁⲡⲉⲥⲏⲧ ⲛ- *B*: Ps 44 6 (*S* ϧⲉ ϧⲁⲣⲁⲧ⸗) πί. ὑποκάτω; Jer 45 12 τιθ. ὑποκ.

—— ⲥⲁⲧϧⲏ ⲛ- *B*: C 89 198 ϧⲓ ϧⲁⲡⲉⲡⲏⲟⲩ ⲥ. ⲙⲙⲟϥ *obviam ei*.

—— ⲉⲡϣⲱⲓ *B*: C 89 2 wine drunk ⲁϥϧⲓⲧϥ ⲉ. ἐξαίρειν; Miss 4 95 when come to land ϧⲓⲧⲟⲩ ⲉ. *set ashore* = Mor 19 6 *S* ⲕⲁⲁⲩ ⲉⲃⲟⲗ, AM 307 ϧ. ⲙⲡⲓⲗⲓⲃⲁⲛⲟⲥ ⲉ. ⲉϥϣⲏⲟⲩⲓ, MG 25 76 ϧⲓ ϧⲟⲥⲉⲙ ⲉⲡ. *throw (dig) up*.

—— ⲉϥⲁϧⲟⲩ *B*: Ps 88 39 (*S* ⲧⲁⲩⲟ ⲉϧⲣⲁⲓ), Ac 24 22 (*S* ⲡ. ⲉⲡⲁϧⲟⲩ) ἀναβάλ.; Ez 23 35 (*S* ⲡ. ϧⲓⲏ.) ἀπορρί. ὀπίσω; ⲣⲓϥⲁϧⲟⲩ: AM 307 ⲁϥϧ. ⲡⲡⲉϥⲭⲓϫ ϧ. ⲙⲙⲟϥ.

—— ⲉϧⲟⲩⲛ, ⲉϧ. (mostly): Jer 34 12 εἰσάγειν; Ge 39 22† (*S* ⲟⲧⲡ ⲉϧ.) ἀπάγεσθαι (var ἐγκλείσθαι); 1 Cor 16 2 *BF*(Mus 49 200, *S* ⲥⲱⲟⲩϧ ⲉϧ.) θησαυρίζειν; EW 33 ϧⲓ ϧⲗⲓ ⲡⲣⲱⲙⲓ ⲉ. = Gu 66 *S* ⲟⲧⲡ ⲉ. ϥⲩⲗⲁⲕίζειν; C 43 116 ⲁⲡⲓϧⲛⲧⲉⲙⲙⲟⲛ ϧⲓⲧⲉⲛ ⲉ. *imprisoned us* = AM 306 ⲉⲡϧ.† ⲉ.;   ⲉϧ., ⲉϧ. ⲉ-: Jo 3 24 *F*(*B* ⲉ-, *S* ⲡ. ⲉ-) βάλ. εἰς, Is 37 7 (*S* ⲇⲟ) ἐμβ. εἰς; Jer 39 3 ⲕⲁⲧⲁⲕⲗ. ἐν; Lu 18 13 *S*(varr ϧⲛ-, ⲉⲭⲛ-, *B* ⲕⲱⲗϧ ϧⲉⲡ-) τύ. εἰς; Lam 3 13 (*S* ⲭⲱⲧⲉ ⲉ.) εἰσάγειν dat; Ac 4 3 (*S* ⲡ. ⲉ-) τιθ. εἰς; 2 Cor 11 20 *S*(*B* ϧⲉⲡ-) δέρ. εἰς; Mor 31 37 *S* ϧ. ⲉ. ⲉⲣⲱϥ (var Miss 4 776 ⲉ. ϧⲛ-), C 89 4 ϧⲓⲧⲟⲩ ⲉ. ⲉⲡⲓϣⲧⲉⲕⲟ = C 99 213 *S* ⲟⲧⲡⲟⲩ ⲉ. ⲉ-, DeV 2 26 ⲁⲡϧⲓⲧϥ ⲉ. ⲉⲣⲱⲡ, C 43 209 ⲁϥϧ. ⲡⲡⲉϥⲙⲁϣⲧ ⲉ. ⲉⲧⲉϥⲡⲉⲭⲓ ⲡⲕⲉⲥⲟⲡ, AZ 23 37 *F* ⲁⲕϧⲓ ⲡⲉⲕⲗⲉⲡ ⲉ. ⲉⲧⲁϣⲁ (? ἐγγύα);   ⲉϧ. ⲉϧⲣⲡ-: Ac 27 14 *S*(*B* ⲡⲓϧⲓ ⲉ. ⲉ.) βάλ. κατά; Ez 3 13 *B*(*S* Ep 31 ⲉ. ϧⲏ-) of wings πτερύσσεσθαι πρός; ShA 1 459 *S* water ϧ. ⲉϧ. ⲉϧⲣⲁⲥ ⲛⲧϣⲱⲙⲉ;   ⲉϧ. ϧⲁ- *B*: Ex 4 6 (*A* ⲧⲱⲕⲉ ⲁϧ. ϧⲁ-) εἰσφέρειν εἰς; Jer 34 11 εἰσάγ. ὑπό; C 41 34 ⲁϥϧⲓ ⲧⲉϥϫⲓⲭ ⲉ. ϧⲁⲧⲉϥⲥⲧⲟⲗⲏ = Bor 134 4 *S*(Vita Sin) ⲥⲟⲟⲩⲧⲡ ⲉϧ. ϧⲁ-;   ⲉϧ. ϧⲛ-, ⲉϧ. ϧⲉⲡ-: R 1 1 36 *S* ϧ. ⲉ. ϧⲓⲡⲉⲛϧⲏⲧ τύ., C 89 11 *B* sim ⲡⲉϧⲟⲩ τύ. εἰς; Lu 6 48 *S*(*B* ⲕⲱ. ⲉ. ⲡⲥⲁ-) προσρηγνύναι dat; Ex 26 29 *B*(*S* ⲡ. ⲉ. ⲉ-) εἰσάγ. εἰς; PS 322 *S* ⲁⲥϧ. ϧⲛⲧⲉⲥⲙⲓⲥⲧⲏⲣⲓⲧ, Mor 41 25 *S* wind ϧ. ⲉ. ϧⲙⲡⲭⲟⲓ = DeV 2 281 *B* ⲡⲓϧⲓ ⲉ. ϧⲉⲡ-, R 1 1 68 *S* ϧ. ⲡⲣⲉⲡⲁⲥ ⲉ. ϧⲛ-, C 43 175 *B* ϧⲓⲧⲟⲩ (sc nails) ⲉ. ϧⲉⲡⲧⲉϥⲡⲁϧⲃⲓ, BMis 149 *S* ⲟⲩϧ. ⲙⲡⲁⲧ ⲉ. ϧⲛⲡⲉⲩⲉⲣⲏⲩ; ⲙⲁ ⲡϧ. ⲉϧ. *B*: Jer 36 26 ἀπόκλεισμα.

—— ⲉϧⲣⲁⲓ, ⲉϧⲣⲏⲓ (mostly), *cast down*: Dan 3 5, Mt 2 11 (*S* ⲡⲱⲣⲧ) πί., Ps 71 9 (*S* ⲇⲟ) προπί.; Is 46 6 (*S* ⲇⲟ) κύπτειν; AM 35 ⲁϥϧⲓⲧϥ ⲉ. ⲁϥⲟⲅⲱϣⲧ; ⲉϧ., ⲉϧ. ⲉ-: Bel 31 βάλ. εἰς, Mk 1 16 *S*(*B* ϧ. ⲉ-) ἀμφιβ. ἐν; Ez 24 4 (*S* ⲡ. ⲉϧ. ⲉ-) ἐμβ. εἰς; Ge 37 20 ῥί. εἰς; Lam 1 13 (*F* ⲟⲩⲃⲓⲁ) κατάγ. ἐν; 2 Pet 2 4 *F*(Mich 3520, *S* ⲡ. ⲉⲡⲉⲥⲏⲧ ⲉ-, *B* as Gk) ταρταροῦν; AM 207 ϧⲓⲧϥ ⲉ. ⲉⲟⲩⲭⲁⲗⲕⲓⲟⲡ; ⲉϧ. ⲉⲭⲉⲡ-: Ez 28 17 (*S* ⲡ. ⲉⲭⲡ-) ῥί. ἐπί; MG 25 218 ⲁⲩϧⲓⲧⲟⲩ ⲉ. ⲉ.ⲡⲟⲩϧⲣⲟ πί. ἐπί; ⲉϧ. ϧⲓⲭⲉⲡ-: AM 119 ϧⲓⲧⲟⲩ ⲉ. ϧ.ⲧⲉϥⲡⲁϧⲃⲓ; ⲉϧ. ϧⲁ-: Mk 7 25 (*S* ⲡ. ϧⲁⲣⲁⲧ⸗) προσπί. πρός; C 43 135 ϧⲓⲧϥ

ⲉ. ϧⲁⲡⲉⲛϭⲁⲗⲁⲩⲝ; ⲉϧ. ϧⲁⲣⲁⲧ⸗ Ac 16 29 (*S* ⲡⲱⲣⲧ ϧⲁⲣⲁⲧ⸗) προσπί. dat.

p c: ManiP *A²* ⲟⲩϧⲁⲩϣⲛⲉⲧⲉ ⲙⲁⲣⲓϧⲁⲙ, P 44 96 *S* ⲡⲓϧⲁⲩⲧⲟⲟⲧϥ مذرىىن (sic l?) *winnowing-shovels* (cf HAWinkler *Bauern* 101); also ? ϧⲁⲩⲡⲟⲩϩ.

—— nn *S*: 4 Kg 14 10 τύπτων. ⲱⲡⲉ ⲡϧ., ϣⲡⲉ ⲡϧ. q v.

ⲙⲉⲧⲁⲧϧⲓⲧϥ *B*, *undauntedness*: TThe 183 ⲁϥⲭⲱⲕ ⲙⲡⲉϥⲁⲅⲱⲡ ϧⲉⲛⲟⲩϧ. ⲁⲩⲱ ⲡⲁⲧⲕⲓⲙ غىر سق. ⲉ.

ⲣⲉϥϧ., *smiter, thrower*: Ge 4 22 *SB* σφυροκόπος; ⲣⲉϥϧⲓ- *BF*: Ac 23 23 -ⲗⲟⲛⲭⲏ (*S* diff) δεξιολάβος; Am 2 15 *B* -ⲥⲟⲑⲛⲉϥ, *F* -ⲥⲁⲧⲉ τοξότης; Is 19 8 -ϫⲉⲗⲓ (*S* ⲡⲉⲭ ϣⲡⲉ) ἀμφιβολεύς; Va 61 104 -ϣⲡⲉ, ib 16 -ⲙⲁⲑⲟⲩⲓ; K 110 -ⲡⲗⲁϫ طىل; ib 112 -ⲁⲟ ϧⲁⲣ حبال.

ϭⲓⲛ-, ⲭⲓⲛϧ., *act of smiting, casting*: LDi 274 *S* ⲧϭⲓⲛϧ. ⲙⲡⲕⲁϣ ⲉⲭⲛⲧⲉϥⲁⲡⲉ, MG 25 162 *B* ⲡⲭⲓⲡϧⲓⲧⲥ ⲉⲡⲓⲕⲟⲗⲁⲥⲓⲥ, Va 58 69 *B* ⲡⲉⲧⲉⲡⲭⲓⲡϧⲓⲧ ⲉⲃⲟⲗ.

ϧⲓ ⲡⲏⲃ, -ⲡⲓⲙ *v* ϧⲓⲡⲏⲃ.

ϧⲓ ⲧⲟⲟⲧ⸗ *SBF*, ϧⲟⲩ ⲧ. *AA²*, *lay hand, undertake, begin, attempt*: Jer 28 12 *B* ἐγχειρίζειν, Ac 19 13 *SB* ἐπιχειρεῖν; Mk 14 72 *SB* ἐπιβάλ.; Jer 30 3 *B* ἐπιλημπτεύεσθαι; PS 116 *S* ⲁϧⲓ ⲧⲟⲟⲧⲥ ⲁⲥϧⲩⲙⲡⲉⲩⲉ, Mor 28 190 *S* †ⲡⲁⲣⲓ ⲧⲟⲟⲧ ⲧⲁⲭⲱ, AM 94 *B* ⲁϧⲓ ⲧⲟⲧϥ ⲁϥⲙⲟϣⲓ;   ⲉ ⲉ-, *upon*: Deu 12 18 *SB*, Pro 23 2 *SA*, Is 25 11 *S*(*B* ⲉⲡ ⲭⲓⲭ ⲉϧⲣⲏⲓ ⲉⲭⲉⲡ-) χεῖρα ἐπιβ., Jer 18 22 *SB* ἐγχ. εἰς, Est 9 25 *S* ἐπιχ.; Mic 1 12 *SA*(*B* ⲉⲣ ϧⲏⲧⲥ) ἄρχεσθαι εἰς, 2 Cor 8 10 *B*(*S* ⲁⲣⲭⲉⲓ) -ⲉⲛⲁⲣⲭ.; Ex 21 14 *S*(*B* ⲟⲩⲱϧ ⲉⲭⲉⲡ-) ἐπιτιθ. dat; Jth 10 8 *S* ἐπιτήδευμα; ROC 17 409 *B* ⲁⲡⲓⲱⲧ ϧⲓ ⲧⲟⲧϥ ⲉⲡⲉϥϣⲏⲣⲓ ἄπτεσθαι gen; PS 170 *S* ⲡⲁⲓ ⲭⲉ ⲉϥⲛⲁϧⲓ ⲧⲟⲟⲧϥ ⲉⲣⲟⲟⲩ *attempt*, ShC 73 142 *S* things ⲉⲧⲛⲡⲁⲣⲓ ⲧⲟⲟⲧⲛ ⲉⲣⲟⲟⲩ ⲉⲁⲁⲩ, BSM 28 *B* ⲁⲩϧⲓ ⲧⲟⲧⲟⲩ ⲉ†ⲙⲁϧ-ⲧϥ = BMis 368 *S* ⲁⲣⲭⲉⲓ, ib 31 *B* ⲁϥϧⲓ ⲧⲟⲧϥ...ⲉⲧⲉϥⲉⲩⲥⲉⲃⲏⲥ ⲡⲥϧⲏⲓ = ib 373 *S* † ⲡⲉϧⲟⲩⲟⲓ, RNC 65 *S* ⲁⲕϧⲓ ⲧⲟⲟⲧⲕ ⲉⲡⲡⲟⲗⲟⲥ *attacked*, ManiH 34 *A²* ⲁϥϧⲟⲩ ⲧⲟⲧϥ ⲁⲡⲉⲩⲡⲓⲥⲧⲟⲥ;   vbal: Ac 12 1 *S*(*B* ⲓⲛⲓ ⲡⲧⲭⲓⲭ ⲉϧⲣⲏⲓ) ⲭ. ἐπιβάλ.; Ge 11 6 *B* ἐπιτιθ.; Mk 8 31 *F*(*S* = Gk, *B* do) ἄρχ. Deu 2 31 *S*(*B* ⲉⲣ ϧⲏⲧⲥ) ἐνάρχ.; EstE 12 *S* ἐπιτηδεύειν; Is 37 26 *S*(*B* Gk diff) *adducere*; Nu 16 40 *S*(*B* ⲓ) προσέρχεσθαι; Lu 24 28 *S*(*B* ⲉⲣ ⲙⲫⲣⲏϯ) προσποιεῖσθαι; BMar 112 *S* ⲁϥϧⲓ ⲧⲟⲟⲧϥ ⲉⲛⲟⲭϥ πειρᾶσθαι; ROC 17 399 *B* †ⲡⲁⲣⲓ ⲧⲟⲧ ⲉⲭⲉ- διηγήσομαι *only*; PS 25 *S* ⲁⲩϧⲓ ⲧⲟⲟⲧⲟⲩ ⲉⲡⲟⲗⲉⲙⲓ, RE 9 146 *S* ⲙⲡⲓϧⲓ ⲧⲟⲟⲧ ⲉⲡⲕⲟⲧⲕ ⲡⲙⲙⲁⲥ, J 79 64 *S* ⲁϥϧⲓ ⲧⲟⲧϥ ⲉⲧⲁⲕⲱ (cf ib 104 35 ἐπιχειρεσθε), El 88 *A* ϥⲛⲁϧⲟⲩ ⲧⲟⲟⲧϥ...ⲁⲱϧⲉ, DeV 2 281 *B* ⲁϥϧⲓ ⲧⲟⲧϥ...ⲉϧⲟⲭϥ ⲉϥⲓⲟⲙ;   ⲉ ⲉⲭⲡ-: Ex 4 13 *B*(*SA* diff) προχειρίζειν; Is 11 14 *S*(*B* ⲓⲛⲓ ⲭⲓⲭ ⲉⲭ.) ⲭ. ἐπιβάλ. ἐπί;   ⲉ ⲡ-: Jer 18 22 *B*(*S* ⲉ-) ἐγχ. acc; Mk 15 18 *F*(*S* = Gk, *B* ⲉⲣ ϧⲏ.) ἄρχ.; PS 51 *S* ⲁⲩϧⲓ ⲧⲟⲟⲧⲟⲩ ⲡⲟⲩⲱϧⲙ, AM 75 *B* ⲁϥϧⲓ ⲧⲟⲧϥ...ⲡⲥⲟⲧϧⲉⲧ;   ⲉ ⲡⲥⲁ-: Mk 10 16 *B*(*S* ϣⲟⲡϣⲡ) ἐναγκαλίζεσθαι; Ac 27 19 *B*(*S* om) αὐτόχειρ

ρί.; ⲥ ⲉϩⲟⲩⲛ ϩⲛ-: BMis 474 *S* ⲁⲓⲣⲓ ⲧⲟⲟⲧ ⲉ. ϩⲙⲡⲧⲟⲟⲩ *set out.*

ϩⲓ ⲁⲣⲭⲏ *B, make beginning:* MG 25 208 ⲁϥϩ. ⲙⲙⲟⲣⲧ (*qv*) ἀρχὴν βάλ.; DeV 2 77 *when man* ϩ. ⲡⲥⲱ, TstAb 171 ⲁϥϩ. ⲛⲝⲱ, MIE 2 343 ⲁϥϩ. ⲙⲡⲓⲃ̄ ⲙⲡⲣⲟⲫⲏⲧⲏⲥ, GöttN '99 38 ⲁϥϩⲓ ⲧⲁⲣ. ⲡⲟⲩⲕⲟⲩϫⲓ ⲛⲣⲓ ⲝⲉⲡⲧⲉϫ̔ⲕⲟⲧⲉ.

ϩⲓ ⲕⲗⲏⲣⲟⲥ *BF, cast lots:* C 43 160 *B* ⲁϥϩ. ⲡⲉⲙⲛⲟⲩⲅⲉⲣⲛⲟⲩ, LAp 520 *F* sim = *ib S* ⲛⲉⲝ-. *Cf* ϩⲓ ⲱⲡ (p 527 *b*).

ϩⲓ ⲥⲧⲁⲩⲣⲟⲥ *B, cast (sign of) cross:* PO 11 373 *eat without* ⲛⲧⲉϥϩ., *ib* 376 ⲁϥϩⲓ ⲡⲓⲥ. ⲉⲛⲓⲃⲉⲛⲓ.

V also ⲁϭⲛⲓ, ⲃⲁⲗ, ⲉⲃⲣⲏϭⲉ, ⲓⲉⲗⲗⲉ, ⲕⲣⲱⲙ, ⲕⲁⲥ 1°, ⲕⲱⲧⲉ (p 127 *a inf*), ⲗⲁ 1° (adding BHom 62 *S* ϩⲟⲩ-), ⲗⲁⲧⲃⲥ, ⲙⲁⲧⲟⲩ, ⲟⲉⲓϣ, ⲥⲱⲛⲧ 1° (ⲥⲓⲧⲉ), ⲥⲟⲧⲃⲉϥ, ⲥϧⲃⲏⲧⲉ, ⲥⲁⲣⲧⲉ, ⲧⲱⲱⲃⲉ 2° (ⲧⲟⲟⲃⲉⲥ), ⲧⲉⲃⲣ, ⲧⲏⲩ, ⲧⲁϥ, ⲭⲟⲥ, ⲱⲡⲉ, ⲱⲡ, ⲱⲣⲥ(ⲟⲣⲥ), ϣⲕⲁⲕ, ϣⲓⲛⲉ (ϣⲙⲛⲟⲩϭⲉ), ϣⲡⲉ, ϣⲱⲧ(ϣⲁⲧⲥ), ϣⲁⲣ, ϩⲛ 2°, ϩⲟ (p 647 *b*), ϩⲉⲗⲓ, ϩⲟⲉⲓⲙ, ϩⲁⲡ, ϩⲣⲏⲣⲉ, ϩⲟⲧⲉ 1°, ϩⲧⲁⲓ, ϩⲱⲧⲣ *sf*, ⳓⲁⲗ, ϫⲟⲗ, ϫⲉⲗⲓ, ϭⲱⲱⲃⲉ, ϭⲗⲁ, ϭⲣⲟϭ.

Cf Sethe *Verbum* 2 650, 683 6.

ϩⲟⲩⲟ *SAA²B,* ⲟⲩϩⲟ *B,* ϩⲟⲩⲁ, ⲟⲩϩⲁ *F,* ϩⲟⲩⲉ- (here abbrev -ⲉ) *SA²F nn m, greater part, greatness* (from ϩⲟⲩ + ⲟ, so Sethe *Verbum* 1 161 *a*, Indices 91): Ex 16 17 *SB,* Is 55 7 *B*(*S* ⲉⲙⲁⲧⲉ) πολύς, Ps 89 10 *SB,* Mal 3 14 *AB,* 1 Cor 15 6 *SBF* πλείων, Mt 21 8 *B* (*S* ⲉⲧⲛⲁϣⲱϥ), Mor 37 55 *S* ⲛⲉϩ. ⲡⲛⲉⲥⲛⲏϥ πλεῖστος. Lev 25 37 *S*(*B* ⲙⲉⲧϩ.), Ez 22 12 *SB* πλεονασμός; Nu 4 26 *S*(*B* ⲉⲣ ϩ.), Jo 10 10 *SA²B* περισσός, Eccl 2 11 *F* ⲟⲩϩⲁ (*S* ϩⲱⲃ ⲛϩ.), Ro 5 17 *SB,* Z 312 *S* ϯ ⲙⲡⲉϥϩ. ⲡⲛⲉⲧϣⲁⲁⲧ -σεία, Mt 12 34 *SB* ·ⲥⲉⲩⲙⲁ, Mk 12 44 *S* (*B* ⲉⲣ ϩ.) -σεύειν; 2 Cor 4 17 *S*(*B* ⲙⲉⲧϩ.) ὑπερβολήν, Eph 1 19 *SB*(*F* ⲙⲉⲧϩ.) -βάλλειν; Jude 16 *B*(*S* diff) ὑπέρογκος; Br 246 *S* *could not bear it* ⲉⲧⲃⲉⲡⲉϩ. ⲙⲡⲉⲥⲟⲩⲟⲉⲓⲛ, ShBM 195 1 *S* ⲟⲩⲛⲉ ⲛⲉϩ. ⲛⲧⲁϥϣⲱⲡⲉ ⲛⲏⲧⲛ *to have wrought gold & silver?,* ShBor 247 107 *S is vanity &* ⲙⲛ ⲗⲁⲁⲩ ⲛϩ. *therein,* Pcod 10 *S* ⲟⲩⲛⲉ ⲛⲉϩ. ⲙⲡⲁⲣⲭⲓⲇⲓⲁⲕⲟⲛⲟⲥ ⲡⲁⲣⲁ ⲛⲕⲉⲥⲉⲉⲡⲉ ? (these three as if ϩⲟⲩ), Mus 42 217 *S* ⲟⲩϩ. ⲡⲉ ⲉⲝⲟⲟϥ *superfluous (cf* c ⲉ-), ROC 19 76 *S* sim, Bor 282 174 *S up to heavens* ϣⲁⲡⲉϩ. ⲙⲡⲁⲏⲣ, ClPr 53 20 *S sell corn* ⲉⲝⲛⲟⲩϩ. *at a profit,* CO 243 *S* ⲛⲉϩ. ⲛⲛⲁⲓ ϯⲁⲥⲡⲁϫⲉ ⲡⲡⲉⲥⲛⲏⲩ, Va 57 236 *B* ⲛⲟⲩϩⲟ ⲛⲣⲱⲙⲓ ⲛⲓⲃⲉⲛ, C 86 287 *B* *fled* ϩⲓⲧⲉⲛⲡⲓϩ. ⲛⲧⲉ ⲡⲓϣⲁⲣ, AM 261 *B* ⲡⲉⲧⲉⲛϩ. ⲥⲱⲟⲩⲛ *most of you,* BIF 22 107 *F* ⲛⲉϩ. ⲛⲧⲡⲱⲗⲓⲥ = Mor 41 193 *S* ⲧⲡⲟⲗⲓⲥ ⲧⲏⲣⲥ, Va 61 88 *B once, twice* ⲡⲉⲙⲡⲓϩ.; *as adj before nn,* **a** *great, much:* Ac 26 24 *S*(var -ⲉ, *B* ⲗⲛⲓϣⲧ)πολ.; ShViK 9812 83 *S* ⲟⲩϩ. ϩⲟⲧⲉ *before God,* BMar 207 *S* ϭⲓⲛⲉ ⲛⲟⲩϩ. ϩⲉⲉⲕⲉ, R 1 5 39 *S* ⲡⲥⲥⲟⲟⲩⲛ ⲁⲛ ⲙⲡⲉϩ. ⲟⲩⲉⲉⲓⲛⲓⲛ, Aeg 258 *S* ⲙⲛ ϩ. ⲡⲣⲉⲥⲃⲩⲧⲉⲣⲟⲥ ⲙⲙⲁⲩ = PO 8 607 لم يكن قسا, Mani 2 *A²* ⲙⲛ ϩ. ⲙⲛⲧⲡⲁⲉ ⲡⲏⲩ ⲁⲧⲟⲟⲧϥ, C 89

120 *B* ⲛⲓϩ. ⲣⲓⲙⲓ, Cat 142 *B* ⲉϭϥ ⲣⲱⲟⲩϣ ⲉⲡⲓϩ. ⲭⲣⲓⲁ (Lu 10 40), BSM 6 *B* ⲟⲩϩ. ⲥⲁϫⲓ ⲛⲧⲏⲓ ⲉⲑⲣⲓ- = BMis 323 *S* ⲟⲩϩ. ⲉⲣⲟⲓⲡⲉ ⲉⲧⲣⲁ-; ϩⲟⲩⲉ- sim *S:* ShP 130⁴ 119 ⲡⲉⲓϩ. ϫⲁϫⲉ ⲡⲣⲱⲙⲉ, ShA 1 400 ⲛϩ. ⲡⲣⲟⲫⲏⲧⲏⲥ *John,* Blake 238 *sold* ϩⲁⲟⲩϩⲟ. ϯⲙⲏ. **b** *greater, more:* Jo 15 2 *B*(*SA²* -ⲉ), He 11 4 *B*(*S* -ⲉ)πλεί.; 1 Cor 7 38 *SB*(*F* -ⲉ) κρείσσων; ShC 73 101 *S* ϩⲉⲛϩ. ⲃⲗⲗⲉ *leading blind,* ShA 1 86 *S* ⲙⲁⲣⲉⲡⲓⲣⲉϥⲣ ⲛⲟⲃⲉ ϣⲱⲡⲉ ⲛϩ. ⲣⲉϥⲣ ⲛⲟⲃⲉ, ShC 42 183 *S* ⲉⲓⲙϫⲉ ⲟⲩⲙⲟⲓϩⲉⲧⲉ … ⲟⲩϩ. ϣⲡⲏⲣⲉ ϫⲉ, ShA 2 155 *S* ⲟⲩϩ. ⲛⲟϭ ⲛⲥⲁϩⲟⲩ, BMis 216 *S* ⲉⲓⲥ ϩ. ⲥⲟ ⲡⲛⲉⲡⲁⲓⲁ (-εά), DeV 1 82 *B* ϩ. ϩⲟⲩⲉ- sim *S:* Lu 11 31 (var & *B* ϩⲟⲩⲟ ⲉ-) πλεί.; Mt 11 9 (var & *B* do), 1 Cor 12 23 (var do, *B* ⲛϩ.) περισσότερος; Eccl 7 24 ϣⲱⲡⲉ ⲛϩ. ⲥⲟⲫⲟⲥ σοφίζεσθαι; 1 Kg 10 23 ὑπέρ-; ShC 73 111 ⲟⲩϩⲟⲧⲉⲡⲉ ϫⲟⲟⲥ ⲟⲩϩ.ⲁⲡⲟⲙⲓⲁⲧⲉ ⲡⲡⲉⲧⲛⲁⲁⲥ; *after* nn: Dan 6 3 *SB* ⲟⲩⲓⲛⲁ̄ ⲛϩ., Miss 8 130 *S* ⲟⲩϩⲱⲃ ⲛϩ. περισσός, Lu 20 47 *SB* -σότερος, Eccl 2 11 *S* sim -σεία; Ro 15 23 *B* ⲙⲉⲓ ⲛϩ. ἐπιποθία; PMéd 157 *S* ⲁⲁϥ ⲛϩ. *proudflesh;* ⲧⲟ ⲛϩ. *v* p 396 *b*.

c ⲉ-, *beyond, more than:* Jon 4 11 *SA*(*B* om ⲉ-), Mt 12 41 *SB,* BHom 46 *S* ϯ ϩⲟⲩⲉ ⲉⲡⲉⲧⲁⲣⲟⲛ (var R 2 2 30 -ⲟ)πλεί. gen; 2 Cor 9 1 *S*(*B* ⲛ-) περισσός dat, Mt 11 9 *B*(*S* om ⲉ-)-σότερος gen; *ib* 12 6 *B*(*S* ⲣ ⲛⲟϭ ⲉ-)μείζων gen; 1 Cor 15 6 *F*(*S* ⲛϩ. ⲛ-, *B* ⲥⲁⲡϣⲱⲓ ⲛ-) ἐπάνω dat, Mk 14 5 *S*(*B* do)ἐπ. gen; Leip 24 29 *B* ϫⲉ ϩ. ⲉⲓⲏ προσθήκην διδόναι παρά; Si 40 26 *S* -ⲉ ὑπέρ; ShC 73 99 *S* ϯ ⲡⲁϥ ϩ. ⲉⲡⲉⲩⲫⲟⲣⲟⲥ, BMar 27 *S* ⲙⲛⲧⲟⲩ ϩ. ⲉⲡⲁⲓ, Mor 36 69 *S* *physician rejoiceth at cures* ⲟⲩϩⲟⲩⲉ ⲉⲃⲉⲕⲉ, ManiK 147 *A²* ⲛϭⲱϣⲃⲉ ⲁⲡⲉⲓ… ⲛϩ. ⲁⲡⲉⲓ, C 41 55 *B accompanying him* ϣⲁϩ. ⲉⲟⲩ ⲙⲩⲅⲗⲗⲓⲟⲛ, Ryl 94 104 *S* ⲟⲩϩ. ⲉⲣⲟⲓⲡⲉ ϣⲁⲭⲉ ⲉⲣⲟⲥ.

ⲉϩⲟⲩⲟ ⲉ- *SF, more, rather than:* Si 22 16 (var -ⲉ, *B* ⲉϩⲟⲧⲉ), Mk 9 43 (*B* do) ἤ; Nu 12 3 (var do, *B* ⲉⲃⲟⲗ ⲟⲩⲧⲉ-)παρά; Phil 1 12 *F*(*S* ⲛϩ., *B* = Gk)μᾶλλον; Si 3 2 (var ⲉⲝⲛ-)ἐπί; *ib* 25 16 (var παρα) Gk om; ShC 73 3 *better* ⲉⲧⲁϫⲟⲟⲩ ⲉϩ. ⲉⲧⲁⲩⲟⲟⲩ; ⲉϩⲟⲩⲉ ⲉ- sim: Ps 17 17 (*B* ⲉϩⲟⲧⲉ), Eccl 4 6 (*F* ⲉϩⲟⲩⲁⲓⲥⲧⲉ) ὑπέρ; Job 19 13, Mt 11 22 ἤ; Nu 13 32 ⲉ. ⲉⲣⲟⲛ (var ⲉⲣⲟⲛ ⲛϩ., all *B* do), Sa 8 6 μᾶλ., Job 20 2 (*B* do) μ. ἤ; Z 303 ϯⲁⲥⲕⲉⲓ ⲉ. ⲉⲣⲟϥ ἀσκητικώτερος εἶναι; ShC 73 121 ⲡⲥⲱⲧⲙ ⲥⲟⲧⲛ ⲉ. ⲉⲧⲣⲉ-, C 99 175 *were burnt* ⲉ. ⲉⲣⲟⲥ ⲉⲧⲣⲉⲩϩⲁⲣⲡⲁ, RNC 50 ⲡⲛⲡⲁⲣ ⲥⲁϩ ⲁⲛ ⲉ.ⲉⲡⲥⲁⲉⲓⲛ; ⲉ-ϩⲟⲩⲉ- sim: Deu 30 5, Ps 118 72 *v.,* Jo 12 43 (*A²* ⲛϩ. ⲁ-) μ. *v.*; Ps 117 9 (all *B* do), Mt 19 24 (*B* ⲓⲉ, *F* ⲉϩ. ⲓⲥⲧⲉ) ἤ, Ge 29 30 (*B* ⲉϩⲟⲧⲉ) μ. ἤ; Jth 12 18 παρά; Mt 5 20 (*B* ⲉⲣ ϩ. ⲉ-)πλεί. gen; *ib* 9 13 (var ⲛϩ., *B* as Gk) καὶ οὐκ; Sa 7 24 (κινητικ)ώτερος gen, 1 Cor 1 25 (var ⲛϩ., *B* ⲉϩⲟⲧⲉ) (σοφ)ώτερος gen; PS 305 ⲧⲉⲩⲕⲣⲓⲥⲓⲥ ϩⲟⲟⲩ ⲉ. ⲕⲣⲓⲥⲓⲥ ⲛⲓⲙ, ShP 130⁵ 100 ⲉⲧⲧⲱⲕⲥ ⲉ. ⲧⲟⲩⲟϩⲉ, ShMun 96 *nearer to death* ⲉ. ⲡⲱⲛϩ, C 99 171 *ill-conducted* ⲉ. ⲡⲉⲥⲛⲏⲩ ⲉⲧⲁⲡⲁⲭⲱⲣⲉⲓ = C 89 136 *B* ⲛϩ., Mich 550 29 *outspoken* ⲉ. ⲉⲟⲩⲟⲛ ϩⲓⲛⲁⲡⲟⲥⲧⲟⲗⲟⲥ.

ⲉϩⲟⲩⲟ ⲉⲓⲥⲧⲉ S(once), ⲉϩⲟⲩⲁ (ⲓ)ⲥⲧⲉ F: Eccl 4 6 (P Mich 3520), ib 7 6 (Schmidt) ⲉϩⲟⲩⲁⲥ., ib 6 3 ⲉϩⲟⲩⲁⲥⲧ ⲉⲗⲁϥ (S ⲉ-), Cant 1 2 do, Mk 12 43 (Mor 46 63), Jo 3 19, 1 Cor 7 9, Pcod 40; S: P 131⁴ ⲓⲟⲟⲧ ϭⲓⲛⲁⲩ ⲉϩⲟⲩⲟⲛ ⲉⲃⲟⲗ ⲉϩⲟⲩⲟ ⲉⲓⲥⲧⲉ ⲉⲧϭⲓⲛⲥⲱⲧⲙ. Cf ⲛϩ.ⲉⲓⲥⲧⲉ below.

ⲉⲛⲉϩ. (mostly S) advb, greatly, very: Eccl 7 17, Mk 3 12 (B ⲛⲟⲩⲙⲏⲏϣ), Ac 18 27 (B ⲉⲙⲁϣⲱ) πολύ, πολλά, Jud 20 40, Ps 61 2 (B ⲛϩ.) ἐπὶ πλεῖον; Mk 10 26 (B do) περισσῶς; ib 16 4 (B ⲉⲙ.) σφόδρα, Ac 27 18 (B do) σφοδρῶς; Ge 30 30 (B ⲉⲣ ⲙⲏϣ) εἰς πλῆθος; 1 Cor 12 31 (B ⲛϩ.) καθ' ὑπερβολήν; Miss 8 76 ⲥⲭⲣⲓⲥⲓⲙⲉⲅⲉ ⲉ. χρειωδέστατος; Va 66 288 B ⲛⲁⲡⲉϥ ⲉ. κάλλιστος; Blake 256 ⲉⲧϣⲓⲟⲕⲉ ⲉ. profundissimus; PS 101 ⲁⲥϣⲱⲡⲧ ⲉ., ShC 73 146 ϣⲁϥϩⲣⲟϣ ⲉ. (var ⲛϩ.), BAp 79 ⲛⲥⲟϥⲟⲥ ⲉ., CA 91 ⲟⲩⲅⲗⲗⲟ ⲉ., ROC 23 279 B ⲟⲩⲍⲱⲅⲣⲁⲫⲟⲥ...ⲛⲧⲉⲭⲛⲓⲧⲏⲥ ⲉ., Mor 29 6 ⲁϥ ⲣⲁϣⲉ ⲉ. (var BMis 234 ⲉⲙⲁⲧⲉ, Mor 30 6 F ⲉⲙⲁϣⲁ), Va 63 85 B ⲛⲛⲉⲛⲥⲱⲕ ⲛⲛⲓⲥⲁϫⲓ ⲉ.

ⲛϩ. advb, greatly, very, more: Nu 13 32 S(B ⲙⲁⲗ ⲗⲟⲛ ⲉϩⲟⲧⲉ), Mt 10 28 S(B ⲛϩⲟⲟⲩ), 1 Cor 7 21 SF(B = Gk) μᾶλ.; EpJer 12 B(F ⲁⲧⲉ-), Lu 7 42 SB πλείων, ViSitz 172 4 15 S ⲛϩ. ϣϣⲉ ⲉⲣⲟⲓ ⲉⲣ ϩⲟⲧⲉ πλέον, Ps 50 4 B(S ⲉⲙⲁⲧⲉ) ἐπὶ πλεῖον, Dan 7 7 B(S do), Mk 15 14 SB περισσῶς, He 2 1 SBF, AP 16 A² -σοτέρως; Ac 20 38 S(B = Gk) μάλιστα; He 10 29 B ϩⲱⲟⲩ ⲛϩ. (S om) χείρων; Mt 20 31 SB μείζων, Sa 13 3 S βελτίων; Cai Euch 598 B ⲛϩ. ϫⲉ ⲑⲏ ⲉⲑⲟⲩⲁⲃ...ⲙⲁⲣⲓⲁ ἐξαιρέτως; Dan 3 22 B ὑπερ(ισχύειν); Ro 7 13 B(S ⲣ ϩ.) καθ' ὑπερβ.; Jer 38 37 B ⲉⲛⲓϣⲱⲓ ⲛϩ. εἰς τὸ μετέωρον; Pro 15 5 SA (πανουργ)ότερος; Sa 19 13 S (χαλεπ)ώτερος; Va 57 15 B ϥⲧⲁⲓⲏⲟⲩⲧ ⲛϩ. τιμιώτερος; P 44 99 S ⲟⲥⲓⲟⲧⲁⲧⲟⲥ · ⲡⲉⲧⲧⲃⲃⲏⲩ ⲛϩ., PS 50 S ⲁⲩ ϫⲓⲱⲕⲉ ⲙⲙⲟⲓ ⲛϩ., ShC 73 3 S what they deem corn ⲉⲩⲧⲱϣ ϩⲱⲱϥ ⲛϩ.ⲡⲉ, Wess 15 127 S ⲧⲉⲛⲟⲩ ⲛϩ.†ⲉⲣⲭⲣⲓⲁ ⲙⲙⲟϥ, BMis 228 S ⲛϩ. ⲁϥϯ ⲉⲟⲟⲩ ⲛⲁⲛ He rather did us honour by incarnation, ib 326 S ⲕⲁⲗⲱⲥ ⲛϩ. ϫⲉⲛⲁⲡⲕⲁϩ ⲣⲁϣⲉ, BSM 17 B ϯ ⲣⲁϣⲓ ⲛ. = BMis 352 S ⲧⲱⲛ ⲟⲩ, TU 43 23 A fear no one ⲛϩ. ϫⲉ ⲡⲣⲱⲙⲁⲉⲓ, C 41 14 B sins ⲥⲉⲟϣ ⲛ. = ViK 9471 S ⲉⲙⲁⲧⲉ, DeV 2 53 B knowledge ⲉⲧϣⲟⲙ ⲛϩ., C 43 2 B I would release thee ⲛϩ. ϫⲉ ϫⲉⲛⲑⲟⲕ ⲟⲩⲙⲁⲧⲟⲓ, CMSS 41 S⸍ ⲧⲓϣⲓⲛⲉ ... ⲛϩ. ⲧⲉ ⲡⲁ⳥, Dif 1 32 B brought him ⲉϥⲥⲟⲛϩ ⲛϩ.; ⲛϩ. ⲉⲙⲁⲧⲉ S: Ro 5 15 (B ⲛ. ⲙⲁⲗⲗⲟⲛ) πολλῷ μᾶλ.; ⲛϩ. ⲛⲧⲟϥ S: 1 Pet 3 9 (B ⲡⲉⲧⲟⲩⲃⲏϥ) τοὐναντίον; B1F 37 54 ⲁⲗⲗⲁ ⲛ. ⲛⲧ. ἀλ. μᾶλ.; CA 97 ⲁⲗⲗⲁ ⲉϥϩⲟⲟⲩⲧ ⲛⲧ. ⲛ.; ⲉⲙⲁϣⲱ ⲛϩ. B: BSM 77 ⲡⲓⲣⲁⲥⲙⲟⲥ ⲉϥⲛⲁϣⲧ ⲉ. ⲛ.; ⲛϩ. ⲙⲁⲗⲗⲟⲛ: 1 Cor 9 12 BF(ⲙ. ⲛ., var ⲉϩ. ϫⲉ, S ⲛϩ. ⲥⲉ) οὐ μᾶλ., Phil 1 14 (SF om ⲙ.) περισσοτέρως; ⲙⲁⲗⲓⲥⲧⲁ ⲛϩ.S: BMis 377 woman to be veiled ⲙ. ⲛϩ. ϩⲓⲧⲉⲕⲕⲗⲏⲥⲓⲁ; ⲛϩ. ⲉ-, more than: Lu 21 3 S(B ⲉϩⲟⲧⲉ), MG 25 216 B whither flee ⲛϩ. ⲉⲛⲁⲓϣⲁϫⲉ? πλεῖ gen; Va 57 8 B bad ⲛϩ. ⲉⲙⲉⲧϩⲱⲕ ⲛⲓⲃⲉⲛ χεί.

gen; Job 13 2 S(B ⲉϩⲟⲧⲉ ἀσυνετ)ώτερος gen, Pro 6 6 A(S ⲉϩⲟⲩⲉ, B do) (σοφ)ώτερος; Pro 3 14 A(SB do), Lu 10 12 S(var ⲉϩⲟⲩⲟ, B do)ἤ, Nu 14 12 S(var ⲉϩⲟⲩ ⲉ-, B do), Jo 3 19 A²(S ⲉϩⲟⲩⲉ-, B ⲙⲁⲗ. ⲉ.) ⲙⲁⲗ ἤ; Ge 48 22 S(B ⲉϩⲟⲧⲉ), Ps 68 31 A prob (Cl, SB do), Si 8 16 S(var παρά) ὑπ.; Nah 2 9 A(B do) ἐπί; Mt 12 7 S(var do, BF as Gk) καὶ οὐκ; PS 321 S ϥϫⲏϥ...ⲛ. ⲉⲛⲕⲱⲧ, ShBMOr 8810 492 S ⲙⲉⲣⲉ ⲡⲥⲁϩⲟⲩ ⲛ. ⲉⲛ ⲥⲙⲟⲩ, ⲡⲕⲁⲕⲉ ⲉϩⲟⲩⲟ ⲉⲛⲟⲩⲟⲉⲓⲛ, ShC 42 167 S ⲉⲑⲟⲟⲩ ⲛ. ⲉ ϣⲱⲡⲉ (var ⲉϩⲟⲩⲟ ⲉ-), Aeg 282 S ⲥⲉⲧⲡ ⲡϣⲁϫⲉ... ⲛ. ⲉϩⲱⲃ ⲛⲓⲙ (var ⲉϩⲟⲩⲉ-), Wess 18 63 S ⲥⲉⲥⲟⲧⲡ ⲛ. ⲉⲣⲟⲕ (var Mor 19 54 παραροκ), BSM 55 B caused sun to stand ⲛ. ⲉⲟⲩⲉⲣⲟⲟⲩ (Jos 10 13), Aeg 40 B exalted ⲛ. ⲉⲧⲫⲉ; vbal: He 11 25 S(var ⲉϩⲟⲩⲉ, B ⲉ ϩⲟⲧⲉ)ἤ; ShC 73 46 S better to go ⲛ. ⲉⲧⲣⲉ-, C 41 38 B ⲁⲛⲛⲁⲩ ϣⲱⲡⲓ ⲛ. ⲉⲑⲣⲉⲛⲓⲥⲛⲏⲟⲩ...ⲟⲩⲱⲙ it was high time, BMis 371 S better we die ⲛ. ⲉⲣⲟⲥ ⲛⲧⲓⲣ ⲡⲱϩⲥ, Va 63 5 B sim; without ⲉ-: Ge 34 19 S ⲛ. ⲡⲉⲧ ϣⲟⲟⲡ ϩⲙⲡⲏⲓ (B ⲉϩⲟⲧⲉ ⲉⲛⲇⲟⲝ)ότατος gen; 1 Kg 9 2 S ⲛ. ⲟⲩϣⲓ ⲛⲓⲁⲣⲃⲉ (var ⲉϩⲟⲩⲉ ⲉⲟϩⲛ.) ὑπερ- κ. ἐπάνω; Bor 264 6 S great number ⲛ. ⲛⲣⲉⲑⲛⲟⲥ ⲧⲏⲣⲟⲩ, BKU 1 92 S thy sons ⲉⲧⲙⲟⲟⲛ ⲛⲁⲛ ⲛ. ⲥⲟⲛ, C 86 221 B flames rose ⲛ. ⲓ̄ ⲙⲙⲁϩⲓ; ⲛϩⲟⲩⲉ- sim S: Ge 49 26 (B ⲉϫⲉⲛ-) ὑπερ- ἐπί; ib 29 19 (B ⲉϩⲟⲧⲉ ⲉ-) βέλτιον ἤ; ShA 1 453 ⲛⲁⲛⲟⲩⲥ ⲉⲧⲣⲁϫⲓ ⲛ. ⲁⲡⲟⲧⲁⲥⲥⲉ, BMis 170 ϫⲟⲥⲉ ... ⲛ. ⲧⲁϫⲓⲥ ⲛⲓⲙ, ib 211 ⲛⲉⲩⲟⲩ ⲛϩ. ⲛⲏ; ⲛϩⲟⲩⲉ ⲉ- S: Nu 22 6 (B ⲉϩⲟⲧ(ⲉ) ⲉ-), BHom 52 ⲛ. ⲉⲣ ⲛⲟⲃⲉ (var R 2 2 35 ⲛϩⲟⲩⲟ ⲉ-)ἤ; Ps 50 7 (var ⲉϩⲟⲩⲉ ⲉ-), Cant 1 3 (ShC 42 53, var ⲛ. only) ὑπ.; BHom 27 ⲧⲁⲓⲏⲩ ⲛ. ⲉⲛⲕⲁ ⲛⲓⲙ τιμιώτερος; ⲛ. ⲉϩⲟⲧⲉ B sim: PO 11 338 better that I suffer ⲛ. ⲉ. ⲛⲥⲉⲛϩⲟⲩ.

ⲉϩⲟⲩⲟ, rather as ⲛϩ.: ShR 2 3 11 S we hold it loss but ⲉⲟⲩⲣϩⲏⲩ ⲛⲁⲛ ⲉ. ⲡⲉ, 1 Cor 9 12 F ⲉ. ϫⲉ (var ⲙⲁⲗ. ⲛϩ., S ⲛ. ⲥⲉ, B ⲛϩ. ⲙⲁⲗ.) οὐ μᾶλ.

ⲛϩ. ⲛϩ. iterated for emphasis SA²B: PS 272 S ϯⲛⲁϭⲟⲗⲡⲟⲩ ⲛⲁⲕ ⲉⲃⲟⲗ ⲛ. ϩⲛⲟⲩⲡⲁⲣⲣⲏⲥⲓⲁ, BAp 151 S ⲛ. ⲥⲱⲧⲙ ⲛⲥⲁⲡⲡⲉ, ManiK 180 A² ⲛ. ϣⲁϥⲫⲱⲛⲉ[, MG 25 33 B ⲛⲧⲉⲕϣⲧⲉⲙϫⲓ ⲣⲱⲟⲩϣ ⲛ. ⲉⲡⲉⲕⲭⲓⲱⲡⲥ, Va 16 99 B blessings invoked ⲛ. ⲛⲓⲥⲙⲟⲩ of Trinity; ⲛϩ. ϫⲉ ⲛϩ., most of all: Z 333 S his enemies ⲛ. ϣⲁϥ ⲥⲟⲧⲡⲟⲩ ⲉⲗⲁⲩ ⲛⲁϥ ⲡⲣⲏⲛⲓ πολλῷ μᾶλ., CA 113 S ⲙⲁⲗⲓⲥ]ⲧⲁ ϩⲙⲡⲉϯⲟⲟⲩ ⲙ[ⲡⲛⲥⲟⲟ]ⲩ ⲛ. ⲙⲡⲥⲁⲃⲃⲁⲧⲟⲛ, Cat 140 B upbraided Chorazin ⲛ. ⲕⲁⲫⲁⲣⲛⲁⲟⲩⲙ; ⲛϩ. ⲣⲱ ⲛϩ., all the more: Mor 17 61 S ⲛ. ϫⲉⲕⲉϣⲟⲟⲡ ϩⲛⲧⲉⲓⲁⲣⲭⲏ ⲙⲁⲗ....περισσοτέρως (var καὶ μάλιστα).

ⲛϩ. ⲉⲓⲥⲧⲉ, more than: Sh(?)Mor 54 8 S⸍ wretched ⲛ. ⲉⲣⲱⲙⲉ ⲛⲓⲙ.

ⲙⲉⲧϩ. BF, abundance, superfluity: Va 57 202 ⲙ ⲙⲟⲛ ϩⲗⲓ ⲙⲙ. ⲛⲁϣⲱⲡⲓ πλέον, Lev 25 37 πλεονασμός; 2 Cor 10 15 περισσεία; ib 4 17 ὑπερβολή (all S, ⲟⲩϩ.), Eph 1 19 F(SB ⲛⲉϩ.) ὑπερβάλ.; Va 61 8 †ⲙ. ⲛⲛⲓⲍ̄ⲣⲏ ⲟⲩⲓ; ⲍⲉⲛⲟⲩⲙ. advb: Dan 7 28 ἐπὶ πολύ; Ps 30 24 (S ⲉⲙⲁⲧⲉ), Ac 26 11 (S ⲉⲛⲉϩ.) περισσῶς, Dan 3 22

(Sⲉⲙ.) ἐκ περισσοῦ; Gal 1 13 (S επεϩ.) καθ' ὑπερβ.;
Va 58 156 ϣⲁϥⲣⲱϣⲓ ⳦. καθαρώτερος γίνεσθαι; C 86
101 ⲛⲁⲥⲱϣ ⲉⲃⲟⲗ ⳦., AM 217 ⲥⲁϩϯ ⳦ⲁⲣⲟϥ ⳦.;   c
ⲉ-, beyond: Eph 3 20 (var ⲛ-, S ⲉϩⲟⲩⲉ-) ὑπερεκπερισσοῦ gen, cit AM 249 ⲛ ⲉϩⲟⲧⲉ.

ⲡ, ⲉⲡ ϩ., be, have more, exceed: 1 Kg 2 33 S, Phil
1 26 SBF περισσεύειν, Jud 21 7† S περισσός; Si 23 3
SAB, Ez 23 32† SB πλεονάζειν; Pro 11 24 B (SA ⲡ
ϩ. ⲛ-) πλείονα ποιεῖν; Eph 2 7 B (S ϩ. ⲛⲛ) ὑπερβάλ.;
4 Kg 12 10 S πολύς; ShC 73 153 S one hath naught
ⲕⲉⲟⲩⲁ ⲉϥⲉⲣ., ShZ 602 S ⲉⲥⲟ ⲛϩ. opp ⲉⲥⲥⲟⲝⲉ̀, ShP
130⁴ 150 S ⲉⲡⲥⲱϣⲧ ⲙⲡⲣⲱⲃ ϣⲁⲛⲧⲉⲡⲛⲁⲩ ⲣϩ., CA 108
S ⲁⲡⲉⲥⲙⲟⲧ ⲡⲧⲉϥⲙⲉⲧⲁⲛⲟⲓⲁ ⲣ.= ⲡ ϩ. زاد, RE 9 161
S have pity for ⲧⲉϥⲙⲛⲧϩⲏⲕⲉ ⲟ ⲛϩ., Mani K 100 A²
ⲕⲉϩⲱⲃ ⲉϥⲟⲩⲁⲧⲃⲉ ⲉϥⲣ.; ⲣ ⲡⲉϩ.: Ez 45 9 B ἱκανοῦσθαι; Mun 40 S ⲛⲉϣⲁⲥⲣ ⲡ. ⲙⲡⲉϩⲟⲟⲩ spent most
of day; ⲣ ⲟⲩϩ.: Miss 4 236 S ⲙⲡⲟⲩⲕⲱⲗϫ ⲛⲗⲁⲁⲩ
ⲉⲣ.; ⲣ ϩ. ⲉ-, be, have more than: Mt 5 20 SB
περισσεύ. πλεῖον gen, Ac 23 13 SB πλείων εἶναι; Ez
16 47 SB ὑπερκεῖσθαι acc; 4 Kg 2 10 S (PMich 607)
ⲁⲕⲣ. ⲉⲡϫⲓ σκληρύνειν; Va 66 288 B ⲁϥⲉⲣ. ⲉⲟⲩⲁⲓ
ϣⲉⲡⲛⲉϣⲓ προέχειν gen; BG 68 S ⲁⲥⲣ. ⲙⲁⲗⲗⲟⲛ
ⲉⲡⲁⲛⲧⲓⲙⲓⲙⲟⲛ, ShBor 233 248 S ⲛⲛⲉϥⲣ. ⲉⲛⲉϥϣⲓ,
CA 112 S gifts ⲉⲧⲣ. ⲉⲡⲣⲱⲃ ⲛⲧⲉⲕⲕⲗⲏⲥⲓⲁ = ib ⲡ ϥⲛ
فضلوا عن, Bodl (P) d 30 S what thou wilt ϣⲁ(ⲓ)ⲁⲟⲩ
ⲧⲁⲉⲣ. ⲉⲣⲟⲟⲩ I will do & will do yet more, Ryl 106 71
S drink it (drug) & ⲛⲡⲉⲕⲣ. ⲉⲣⲟϥ, C 89 9 B ⲡⲥⲉⲡⲓ ⲉ-
ⲛⲁⲉⲣ. ⲉⲧⲉⲡⲭⲣⲓⲁ; ⲉ-, for: Tob 4 16 S, Mt 13 12
BF (S ⲡ. only), Lu 15 17 B (S ⲥⲛⲏⲩ), Jo 6 13 SB (A²
ⲥⲉⲉⲡⲉ, F ⲥⲱⲭⲡ), Ro 5 15 B (S ⲁϣⲁⲓ ⲉϩⲟⲩⲛ) περισσ.,
Z 310 S ⲡⲁⲓ...ⲉⲅⲣ. ⲉⲣⲟⲓ περισσὰ ἔχειν, MG 25 18 B
ⲫⲏ ⲉⲧⲟⲓ ⲛϩ. ⲉⲣⲟϥ περισσεία; Ex 16 23 S (B ⲉⲡ. only)
πλεονάζειν; ShR 2 3 30 S ⲭⲣⲏⲙⲁ ⲉⲧⲣ. ⲉⲣⲟⲕ;
vbal (ⲉ- superfluous?): Ryl 94 108 S ⲛⲉⲥⲣ. ⲉⲥⲟⲗⲥⲗ
was the more comforted, ClPr 42 10 S ⲣ. ⲉⲣⲁϣⲉ ⲛⲙⲙⲁⲛ; ⲉⲣ ϩ. ⲉϫⲉⲛ- B: C 86 163 years ⲉϩ. ⲉϫⲱϥ; ⲣ
ϩ. ⲙⲛ- S: Si 30 27 περισσ. ⲉⲛ; ⲣ ϩ. ⲛ-: Pro 11 24
SA (B Gk om ⲛ-) πλεί. ποιεῖν; J 106 55 S ⲙⲡⲉⲥϭⲉ
ⲉⲛⲉⲧⲣ. ⲛⲁⲥ (Mk 12 42), Z 247 S ⲉⲅⲟ ⲛϩ. ⲡⲟⲩⲁ one
too many; ⲉⲣ ϩ. ⲛⲧⲉⲛ- B: Nu 3 46 (S ⲡⲁⲣⲁ) παρά;
ⲣ ϩ. ϩⲛ-: Eccl 3 19 S (F ϩ. ⲛⲛ), Ac 16 5 S (B diff),
1 Cor 15 58 SBF (Mus 49 200), Aeg 280 S ⲣ. ϩⲛⲛⲉ-
ⲡⲣⲟⲥⲫⲟⲣⲁ περισσ., 2 Cor 7 4 B (S + ⲉⲙⲁⲧⲉ) ὑπερπ.;
Ex 26 12 B πλεονάζ.; 2 Cor 9 14 B (S ⲛⲁϣⲉ) ὑπερβάλ.; Dan 7 24 B ὑπερφέρειν; TEuch 1 341 B ⲣ. ⲥⲉⲛ-
ϩⲱⲃ ⲛⲓⲃⲉⲛ ⲛⲁⲅⲁⲑⲟⲛ تفاصل; ShC 73 19 S limbs ⲉⲧⲉ-
ⲣⲉⲡⲉⲓϣⲱⲡⲉ ⲣ. ⲛⲣⲏⲧⲟⲩ, ShIF 149 S blood-suckers
ⲣ. ϩⲙⲡⲥⲛⲧⲗⲁⲧⲟⲩ, ShMich 550 19 S ⲁⲛⲣ. ⲉⲙⲁⲧⲉ
ϩⲁⲡⲥⲓ, ShP 131⁵ 19 S ⲉⲧⲉⲧⲛⲟ ⲛϩ. ϩⲁⲡⲧⲱⲃϩ, BMis
135 S ⲛⲛⲉⲡⲣ. ϩⲁⲙⲡϣⲁϫⲉ, ManiK 110 A² fire ⲛⲁⲣ.
ϩⲁⲙⲡϣⲏⲛ; ⲣ ϩ. + obj (nn or vb) immediately following, be the more, do greatly: Ps 137 3 B (S ⲧⲁϣⲟ)
πολυ-; ib 36 35 B (S diff), Dan 3 52 B (S om), Joel

2 24 SA (B om), Ro 5 20 SB (cit Mor 18 82 S ⲉⲡ. ⲉ-,
Miss 4 151 B ⲟⲩϩⲟ, cf F ⲟⲩϩⲁ) ὑπερ-; Pro 9 9 A (S
ϩⲟⲅⲉ-, B ⲛϩ. ⲥⲟⲫ)ώτερος εἶναι; ShR 2 3 41 S ⲣ. ϫⲓ
ⲙⲡⲱⲡ ϣⲁⲉⲛⲉϩ, ShP 131⁴ 141 S ⲁⲥⲣ. ⲥⲛⲧϥ (sc grace)
ⲉⲧⲃⲉⲡⲉⲥⲃⲃⲟ, Miss 8 247 S ⲥⲉⲛⲁⲣ. ⲟⲩϫⲁⲓ ⲉⲃⲟⲗ ϩⲙ-
ⲡⲉⲕⲙⲁⲣⲧⲩⲣⲓⲟⲛ, WZKM 26 339 S ⲧⲓⲣ. ϣⲓⲛⲉ ⲛⲥⲁ-
ⲡⲉⲧⲟⲩϫⲁⲓ, J 2 9 S ⲉⲓⲣ. ϫⲉ ⲧⲁⲭⲣⲟ ⲙⲙⲟϥ (sc deed)
ϩⲓⲧⲛⲣⲉⲛⲙⲛⲧⲣⲉ, BSM 55 B ⲁϥⲉⲣ. ϩⲙⲟⲧ ⲉϫⲱⲟⲩ =
BMis 410 S ⲕⲁⲧⲁⲝⲓⲟⲩ ⲙⲙⲟϥ (as in ib 139, BAp 84),
C 89 89 B ⲉⲣ. ⲥⲙⲟⲩ ⲉⲡ⳨ⲥ = ib 99 153 S ϩⲟⲅⲉ-, Va 58
189 B ⲁⲣⲓ ϩ. ⲕⲁⲑⲁⲣⲓϫⲓⲛ ⲛⲧⲉⲕⲯⲩⲭⲏ;   ⲣ ϩⲟⲅⲉ-
(mostly S) sim: Jo 7 31 A² (SB ⲣ ϩⲟⲅⲟ ⲉ-) πλ. ποιεῖν,
Bor 253 162 ϯϩⲁⲣ. ⲙⲟⲩ μᾶλ.;   Dan 3 88 F (Mus 49
187, B ϩⲟⲅⲟ) ὑπερ-, Mk 7 37 (B ⲛϩ.) ὑπερπερισσῶς;
Pro 1 5 (A ϩⲟⲅⲟ, B ⲛϩ. ⲥⲟⲫ)ώτερος εἶναι; Mk 4 24
(B ⲧⲟⲩϩⲟ) προσ-; PS 21 they beheld & ⲁⲩⲣ. ϣⲧⲟⲣⲧⲣ,
ShRyl 68 262 ⲁⲩⲣ. ⲫⲩⲥⲓⲥ ⲛⲧⲉⲡⲏ, ShC 42 217 ϥⲛⲁⲣ.
ϣⲱⲡⲉ ⲉϥⲟⲩⲁⲁⲃ (varr ⲣ ϩⲟⲅⲟ, ϣⲱⲡⲉ ⲛϩⲟⲅⲟ), ShA
1 266 men ⲉⲧⲣ. ⲥϩⲟⲩⲟⲣⲧ, ib 418 not only...ⲁⲗⲗⲁ ⲧⲓⲣ.
ⲡⲕⲉⲣ. ϯϩⲱⲡⲧ, Bor 253 152 eagle seeing snares ϣⲁϥⲣ.
ϩⲱⲗ ⲉⲡϫⲓⲥⲉ; ⲣ ⲟⲩϩ.: ShC 73 81 ⲁϥⲣ ⲟⲩϩ. ⲛⲉⲑⲟⲟⲩ;
ⲙⲛⲧⲣ ϩⲟⲅⲟ S: Deu 1 12 (B = Gk) ἀντιλογία; ShRyl
68 265 ⲉⲩϫⲉ ⲙ. ⲉⲛⲡⲉ̄, ShP 130⁴ 119 ⲛⲉⲛⲛⲟϭ ⲙⲙ. of
heretics (but? all l ⲙⲛⲧⲣⲟⲅⲟ, v ϩⲣⲟⲟⲅ sf);   ⲙⲉⲧⲣⲉϥⲉⲣ ϩ. ⲥⲁϫⲓ B: HL 82 φλυαρία.

ϩⲟⲟⲅⲉ SᵃAA², ϩⲱⲟⲅⲉ A   v ϩⲟⲟⲅ day.

ϩⲟⲩⲙⲁⲣⲉ   v ϣⲟⲩⲙⲁⲣⲉ.

ϩⲟⲟⲅⲛⲧ O   v ϩⲟⲟⲅⲧ.

ϩⲟⲩⲱⲣ   v ϩⲃⲟⲣⲃⲉⲣ (place-name).

(ϩⲟⲟⲅⲣⲉ cf Sethe Verbum 2 632), ϩⲟⲩⲣⲉ- SA²,
ϩⲟⲩⲣ-, ϩⲟⲩⲣⲱ-, ϩⲟⲩⲣⲱ(ⲱ)⳦, ϩⲟⲩⲣⲟ⳦ S, ϩⲟⲩⲣⲱ⳦ B
(once) vb tr, deprive c double acc: Ge 48 11 ϩⲟⲩⲣⲟⲧ
ἐστερήθην (B ϣⲱⲡϩ), Ps 20 2 (B do), Si 28 16, BMar
113 ⲁⲩϩⲟⲩⲣⲱ ⲡⲉⲧⲙⲙⲁⲩ ⲡⲛⲉϥⲛⲕⲁ στερεῖν, Ex 21
10 (B ϫⲱϫⲉ), Si 4 1 ϩⲟⲩⲣ- (P 44 118), ib 31 24 ϩⲟⲩⲣⲉ-
(var ϥⲱϫⲉ), Ja 5 4 (AB ϫⲱϫⲉ) ἀπος.;   Ge 31 7 ϩⲟⲩ-
ⲣⲱⲱⲧⲉ ⲙⲉ (B diff), ib 41 (B ϣⲱϥⲧ) παραλογίζεσθαι;
RNC 35 ϩⲟⲩⲣⲱⲥ ⲛⲧⲉⲥⲥⲱϣⲉ ἀποσπᾶν; Tri 518 ϩⲟⲩ-
ⲣⲟϥ ⲛⲧⲉϥⲯⲩⲭⲏ اغرها; ShC 73 38 ⲁⲩϩⲟⲩⲣⲱϥ ⲙⲁⲅⲁⲁϥ ⲛⲡⲁⲅⲁⲑⲟⲛ, Mor 43 94 ⲙⲡⲣϩⲟⲩⲣⲱⲛ ⲛⲡⲙⲟⲟⲩ
ⲛⲱⲛϩ (var R 2 4 33 -ⲣⲱⲛ), Bor 304 82 ⲁⲩϩⲟⲩⲣⲱⲧ
ⲛϣⲟⲙⲛⲧ (ⲛϣⲏⲣⲉ), BMis 377 ⲉⲕⲛⲁϩⲟⲩⲣⲱⲧ ⲙⲡⲁⲙⲉ
ⲉϩⲟⲩⲛ ⲉⲡⲁⲣⲭⲁⲅⲅⲉⲗⲟⲥ = Va 638 B ⲱⲗⲓ ⲛⲧⲟⲧ, P 129²⁰
125 ⲙⲡⲣϩⲟⲩⲣⲱϥ ⲙⲡⲉⲕⲗⲁⲟⲥ ⲡⲧⲉⲭⲁⲣⲓⲥ, Mani 1 A²
ϯⲛⲁϩⲟⲩⲣⲉⲧⲏⲛⲉ ⲉⲛ ⲙⲡⲉⲧⲁⲓϣⲡ ⲱⲡ ⲙⲙⲁϥ, Mus 45
25 B ⲁⲩϩⲟⲩⲣⲱⲟⲩ ⲛⲛⲓⲕⲟⲟⲩⲓ;   c ⲉ- sim: BMis 22
ⲁⲩϩⲟⲩⲣⲱⲧ ⲉⲛⲉⲕⲣⲟ (cf KKS 507 ϩⲟⲩⲣⲱⲡ ⲙⲡⲉϥϩⲟ), ib 46 ϩⲟⲩⲣⲱⲧ ... ⲉⲛⲉⲕⲁⲅⲁⲑⲟⲛ;   passive:
2 Cor 2 11 (B ϭⲓ ⲛϫⲟⲛⲥ) πλεονεκτεῖσθαι.

ϩⲟⲩⲣⲱ⳦   v preceding word.

ϩⲟⲩⲣⲓⲧ *SA²*, ϩⲱ. *S*, ⲟⲩ. *B*, pl ϩⲟⲩⲣⲁⲧⲉ, ϩⲱ. *S*, ϩⲟⲩⲣⲉⲧⲉ *A²*, ⲟⲩⲣⲁϯ *B* & sg as pl, nn m, *watcher, guardian*: Ge 4 9 *S*(cit BodlP d 54)*B* φύλαξ, قيس; K 113 *B* ⲡⲓⲟⲩ. حارس; P 54 177 *B* ⲡⲟⲩⲟⲩⲣⲓⲧ (*l* ⲡⲟⲩⲣ.) اهتدى (confusion ? with ϩⲉⲣⲓ *q v*); Mus 40 277 *S* ⲡϩ. ⲁⲩⲱ ⲡⲉϥⲏⲗⲁⲅ ⲛⲉⲛⲕⲁⲣⲡⲟⲥ, MG 25 296 *B* ⲟⲩϭⲉⲗⲗⲟ ⲛⲟⲩ. ⲉϥⲣⲱⲓⲥ ⲉⲛϩⲣⲟⲥⲉⲛ = BIF 13 109 *S*, BMOr 6201 *B* 80 *S send* ⲟⲩϩ. ⲛⲛⲕⲟⲩⲓ ⲣⲉϩⲣⲟⲉⲓⲥ, J 117 5 *S* ⲟⲩⲧⲉⲣϩⲟⲁⲛ ⲛⲡϩ., BP 11349 28 *S* ϩⲉⲕⲉ ⲡϩ. (*cf* ϩ. ⲣⲟⲉⲓⲥ), ST 170 *S* ⲛⲡⲟⲩϩ̄ ⲛϩ., CO 482 *S* [wages of] ⲛ̄ϫⲁⲉⲓⲁⲥⲕ ⲛⲛⲡϩ., ViK 4749 *S* ⲁⲛϩⲣⲱ. ⲧⲓ ⲡⲉⲥϩⲁⲓ ⲡⲧⲉⲡⲉ[, Kropp M 1 *S invoking* ⲡⲉⲧ̄ ⲡϩ. ⲛ̄ϫⲱⲣⲉ ⲉⲧⲣⲟⲉⲓⲥ, ManiK 11 *A²* ϣⲱⲡⲉ ⲛⲉⲩ ⲛⲉⲃⲟⲏⲑⲟⲥ ϩⲓϩ., *ib* 91 *A²* ϯⲟⲩ ⲡϩ. ⲛⲛⲡⲁⲧⲛ̄ⲕⲁⲧⲉ; ⲁⲡⲉ ⲡϩ. *S, head watchman* (*cf* πρωτοφύλαξ, ἀρχιφ. Wess 19 47): J 115 18 ⲁⲡⲟⲕ…ⲡⲁ. ⲛ̄ϫⲏⲙⲉ, *ib* 42 7 ⲉⲣⲉⲥⲁⲙⲟⲩⲏⲗ ⲟ ⲛⲡⲁ.; pl: Z 344 *S* Nitrian ascetes' work (baskets) given to ⲡϩ. to sell = MG 25 209 *B* φ. (*cf* above *ib* 296), *ib* 76 *B sim* = Gött ar 114 16 الحالين الذين يحملون النطرون, Kr 239 *S* ⲡϩ.…. ⲁϣⲟⲙⲛⲧ ϩⲓⲱⲟⲩ ⲕⲱⲧ ⲉⲅⲕⲟⲧⲉ ⲡⲣⲟⲉⲓⲥ *made a round of inspection*, BM 1031 *S* ⲧⲡⲁϣⲛⲉ ⲧⲏⲣⲥ ⲛⲛⲉϩ. *of village*, ViK 4720 *S* ⲡⲁⲡⲏⲅⲉ ⲡⲛⲉⲧⲙⲉ … ⲛⲛⲡⲉⲩϩ., *ib* 4708 *S* ⲛ[ⲉⲓ]ϩⲱ. ⲧⲏⲣⲟⲩ, ManiK 141 *A²* ⲡϩ. ⲉⲧⲣⲁⲓⲥ, *ib* ⲛϩ.…ⲉⲅϭⲙⲉⲥⲧ ϩⲓⲣⲙⲡⲣⲟ *holding keys*.

ϩⲟⲩⲱⲣⲧ *S* nn m, a part or disfigurement of body: P 129²⁰ 178 *recipe begins* ⲉⲧⲃⲉⲡⲉϩ.[(*rest illegible*).

ϩⲟⲩⲁⲥⲧⲉ *F* v ϩⲟⲩⲟ p 736 *a sup*.

ϩⲓⲱⲟⲩⲧ *B* v ϩⲉ *fall*.

ϩⲟⲟⲩⲧ *A²* nn m, *meaning unknown*: ManiK 44 *five sayings spoken* ⲛⲙⲛⲧⲡⲁⲣⲁ ⲡⲉϩ.

ϩⲟⲩⲏⲧ *S.A²*, pl ϩⲟⲩⲁⲧⲉ *S* & sg as pl, nn, *passenger on board ship*(?): Ez 27 29 ⲡⲉϩ. (*B om*) ἐπιβάτης (var ναύτης) *nauta*; P 131² 156 ⲡⲛⲉⲉϥ…ⲛⲛⲡⲉϩ. ⲉⲧⲧⲁⲗⲏⲅ ⲛⲙⲙⲁⲩ ναύ.…ἐπ., BHom 88 *ship of faith* ⲉⲣⲉⲡⲛⲉⲉϥ ϩⲓⲱⲱϥ *that is clergy*, ⲉⲣⲉⲛⲉϩⲟⲩⲁⲧⲉ ⲧⲁⲗⲏⲅ ⲉⲣⲟϥ *that is Christian folk*, Mani P 123 *A²* ⲁⲡⲥⲧⲁⲩⲣⲟⲥ ⲣ ϫⲁⲓ ⲁⲙⲯⲩⲭⲁⲩⲉ ⲣ ⲉϩ.; P 44 54 ⲡⲉϩ. قراىل *yards of mast* (*v* BIF 20 64 n, Almk 2 101, HA Winkler *Volksk*. 60, *here misunderst* ?).   V Griffith *Stories* 100, HO Lange *Amenemope* 133.

ϩⲟⲩⲉⲓⲧ *SF*, ϩⲟⲩⲓⲧ *A²BFO*, f ϩⲟⲩⲉⲓⲧⲉ *S*, -ⲓⲧⲉ *SAA²*, -ⲓϯ *BF*, pl (*v* AZ 47 29) ϩⲟⲩⲁⲧⲉ *S*, -ⲁϯ *B*, -ⲉϯ *F* nn, *first*: Is 44 6 *B*(var & *S* ϣⲟⲣⲡ), Jer 27 17 *BF*(Mus 49 176, *S do*), Lu 19 16 *BF*(Mor 30 2, *S do*), Ac 28 7 *B*(*S* ⲁⲣⲭⲱⲛ) πρῶτος; Deu 21 17 *S*(*B* = Gk), Ap 21 6 *S*(*B do*) ἀρχή, Jer 3 4 *B* ἀρχηγός; PS 356 *S* ⲡⲉϩ. ϫⲉⲕⲣⲟⲡⲟⲥ, BSM 72 *B* ⲡⲓϩ. *eldest* = BMis 162 *S* ⲛⲟϭ, ManiH 53 *A²* ⲡϩ. ⲛⲧⲁⲓⲕⲁ[ⲟⲥⲏⲡ, DeV 2 164 *B* ⲡⲓϩ. … ⲡⲓⲙⲁϩⲃ̄, *ib* 55 *B* ⲁⲡⲟⲕⲡⲉ ⲡⲓϩ.

ⲛⲛⲱⲟⲩ, C 43 200 *B* ⲡⲓϩ. ⲉⲧⲉⲡϩⲏⲧⲟⲩ, PGM 1 50 *O* ⲁⲡⲧ ⲕⲱⲟⲩ ϩⲱⲟⲩ ⲡϣⲱⲥⲙ [ⲡⲉ]ϩ.; *as adj, after nn*: Ge 8 13 *B*(*S* ϣ.), 1 Cor 15 45 *BF*(*S do*) π.; Ez 21 21 *B* ἀρχαῖος; Br 115 *S* ⲡϣⲟⲣⲡ ⲡⲣⲁⲙⲏⲛ ⲡϩ., AM 43 *B* ⲡⲓⲥⲟⲡ ⲛϩ.; *before nn*: Ex 12 2 *B*(*S* ϣ.), Ac 1 1 *B*(*S do*) π.; Job 40 14 *SB* ἀρχή, 1 Pet 5 4 *F*(Mus 49 196, *S* ⲛⲟϭ, *B diff*) ἀρχι-; BG 33 *S* ⲡⲉϩ. ⲡⲁⲓⲱⲛ, ManiBerlSitz '33 86 *A²* ⲡϩ. ⲡⲥⲩⲙⲃⲟⲩⲗⲟⲥ, AM 304 *B* ⲡⲓϩ. ⲡⲣⲱⲙⲓ, ViK 7033 *F* ⲛⲉϩ. ⲉϣⲉϫⲓ.

nn f, *beginning, first*: Ps 118 160 *S*(*B* = Gk), Eccl 7 9 *F*(*S* = Gk), Zech 12 7 *A*(*B* ϣ.), R 1 2 35 *S* ἀρχή, Is 23 16 *S*(*B* ⲣⲏϯ ⲡⲧⲉ ϣ.) ἀρχαῖος; Jud 20 32 *S*, Mt 12 45 *S*(*B* pl), He 8 7 *B*(*SF* ϣ.) π., Deu 9 18 *S*(*B* ϣ.) πρότερος; Joel 2 3 *A*(*S* ⲡⲉⲧϩⲓⲣⲏ, *B sim*) πρὸ προσώπου, Jos 8 6 *S* ἔμπροσθεν; PS 7 *S* ⲧⲁⲙⲉϩⲥⲡⲧⲉ…ⲧⲉϩ., ShC 73 61 *S* ⲛⲑⲉ ⲡⲧⲉϩ. *as formerly*, ShA 1 376 *S* ⲡϩ. ⲛⲛⲕⲁⲣⲡⲟⲥ, ManiH 7 *A²* *taught us* ⲛⲧϩ., ManiK 32 *A²* ⲧⲟⲩϩ. ⲛⲙⲧⲟⲩⲣⲁⲛ, C 43 30 *B* ϯϩ. ⲧⲉ ϯⲗⲁϩⲟⲓ *let loose against him*; ϩⲛⲧⲉϩ. *SA²*, *in the beginning*: Sa 14 6, Jo 1 1 (*B* = Gk) ἀρ.; BHom 81 ϩ. ⲛ̄ϫ̄ⲡⲉ… ⲛ̄ⲡⲉ, BM 248 115 ⲛⲛⲉϥϣⲟⲟⲡ (*sc* Adam) ⲁⲛⲡⲉ ϩ., AP 42 *A²*; ϫⲓⲡⲧⲉϩ. *SA²*, *from beginning*: Jos 24 2, Sa 6 24, Mk 10 6(*B* ⲓⲥ̄ϫ. ⲧⲁⲣⲭⲏ, *F* ⲛ̄ϫ. ⲛϣ.) ἀπ'ἀρ., EstC 8 ἐξ ἀρ., Ps 101 25 (*B* ⲓⲥ̄ϫ. ϩⲏ) κατ' ἀρ.; BHom 116 ϫ. ϣⲁⲁϩⲣⲁⲓ ⲉⲧⲉⲛⲟⲩ, ManiH 75 *A²* ϫ. ϣⲁⲑⲁⲏ, J 105 16 *ye have cared for* τόπος ϫ.; ϯϩ. *A²*, *make beginning*: ManiK 158 ⲁⲩϯ. ⲛⲧⲉⲟⲩⲟ ⲁⲡⲉϥⲙⲁⲑⲏⲧⲏⲥ, *ib* 94 *they give place to enmity* ⲁⲧⲟⲩϯ. ⲛϣⲱϯ; *f adj, after nn*: Dan 9 1 *B*(*S* ϣ.), Eph 6 2 *B*(*S do*) π.; Br 136 *S* ⲧⲁⲩⲡⲁⲙⲓⲥ ⲛ̄ϩ.; *before nn*: Ez 10 11 *B* μία; PS 355 *S* ⲧⲉϩ. ⲡⲧⲁϫⲓⲥ, AM 284 *B* ϯϩ. ⲛⲡⲟⲗⲓⲥ.

pl: Job 8 7 *B*(*S* ϣ.), Eccl 1 11 *F*(*S do*), Ac 13 50 *B*(*S* ⲛⲟϭ) π.; Is 41 26 *S*(*B* ϣ.) ἔμπρ.; Pro 3 9 *S* ϯ ⲛⲉϩ. (*AB* = Gk) ἀπάρχεσθαι; Eccl 1 10 *F*(PMich 3520, var Schmidt ϩⲁⲧⲉⲛϩⲏ, *S as* Gk) γενόμενος αἰών; AM 176 *B* ⲡⲓϩ. ⲛⲧⲉ ⲡⲉϥϯⲙⲓ.

ⲉⲣ, ⲟⲓ ⲛϩ. *B*, *be first*: Ac 24 5 ⲟⲓ ⲛϩ. (*S* ⲥⲁϩ) πρωτοστάτης; 3 Jo 9 ⲡⲓⲙⲁⲓⲉⲣ ϩ. (*S* ⲙⲁⲓⲣ ϣ.) φιλοπρωτεύειν; Cat 98 ⲡⲓⲡⲁⲑⲟⲥ ⲛⲧⲉ ϯⲙⲁⲓⲉⲣ ϩ.; Va 57 59 ⲙⲉⲧⲙ.

ϩⲟⲟⲩⲧ, ⲉϩ., (ⲉ)ⲓϩ., ϩⲉⲟⲩⲧ *S*, ϩⲉⲩⲧ *SA*, ϩⲁⲩⲧ *AA²*, ϩⲏⲩⲧ *A²*, ϩⲱⲟⲩⲧ *S*(once)*B*, ϩⲁ(ⲟ)ⲩⲧ, ⲉϩ. *F*, ϩⲟⲟⲩⲓⲧ *O*, ϩⲟⲩⲧ- *S* nn m, **a male** of men, gods, *husband*: Ge 1 27 *SA*(Cl)*B*, Is 66 7 *SB*, Mk 10 6 *SBF*(Mor 21 141) ἄρσην, Nu 5 3 *SB* ἀρσενικός; Deu 22 5 *SB*, Jer 51 19 *S*(*B* ϩⲁⲓ), 1 Cor 7 11 *SF*(*B do*) ἀνήρ; BMis 542 *S* women ⲉⲟⲩⲛⲧⲁⲩ ⲙⲙⲁⲩ ⲛⲛⲉϩ. *vir*; ShA 2 279 *S* *to nuns* ⲛⲉⲧⲡⲥⲏⲩ, ⲛⲉⲧⲡϣⲏⲣⲉ, ⲛⲉⲧⲡϩ. (*cf* 277 ⲛⲉⲧⲡϣ., ⲛⲉⲧⲡⲥ., ⲛⲉⲧⲡⲣⲱⲙⲉ), Sh(?)Mor 54 117 *S bride* & ⲡⲉⲥϩ., Lammeyer 40 ⲡⲟⲩϩ. (var JA '75 5 259 *S* ϩⲁⲓ), PBad 5 376 *S* ⲧⲣ(ⲁϥⲉ) ⲛ̄ⲡⲁⲡϩ. (*male member* ?) ⲉⲧⲁⲗϭⲉⲉⲙⲓⲁ (? Arab), J 76 52 *S* ⲡⲛⲉⲥϩⲓⲙⲉ ϫⲓ (*inherit*) ϩⲁⲉϩ., *ib* 66 47 *S* ⲟⲩⲉϩ., ManiK 26 *A²* ⲡϩ. ⲛⲛⲡⲉϩⲣⲓ

ⲁⲙⲉ, C 43 223 B ⲛϩ., BG 96 S ⲡⲡⲁ ⲛϣⲙⲧϩ.; ⲣⲉϥ-
ⲛⲕⲟⲧⲕ ⲙⲛϩ. v ⲛⲕⲟⲧⲕ s f;   as adj (often without
ⲛ-): Nu 3 43 S(B as nn), Ez 16 17 SB ἀρσενικός,
Aeg 241 S ⲁⲁⲓⲙⲟⲛⲓⲟⲛ ⲛϩ. ἀρρενικός; ib 214 S ⲥⲙⲟⲧ
ⲛϩ. τὰ ἀνδρῶν; Nu 27 8 B ϣⲏⲣⲓ ⲛϩ. (S om ϩ.) υἱός;
Eccl 2 7 SF, Joel 2 29 SA ϩⲙϩⲁⲗ ⲛϩ. (B ⲃⲱⲕ) δοῦλος;
ib 3 3 B ⲁⲗⲟⲩⲅⲓ ⲛϩ. (A ϣⲏⲣⲉ ϣⲏⲙ) παιδάριον; PS
377 S ⲥⲡⲏⲩ ⲛϩ., J 76 50 S sim ⲛⲓϩ.; ϣⲣ ϩ., male child
v p 585 b, ShMich 550 15 S ⲙⲉⲗⲟⲥ ⲛϩ., KroppM 114
S ⲙⲁ ⲛϩ., Rec 6 174 B sim = BAp 210 S ⲥⲙⲟⲧ ⲛϩ.,
DeV 1 123 B sim, PBad 5 394 S ⲥⲱⲙⲁ ⲛϩ., PMéd
146 S & CR '87 376 S sim, PBad 5 406 S ⲉⲡⲓⲑⲉⲙⲓⲁ
(-θυμία) ⲛϩ., AZ 21 100 O ⲛⲟⲩ ⲛ́ⲟⲟⲅⲛⲧ, KroppC 43
F ⲧⲉⲙⲁⲛ (δαίμων) ϩⲁⲟⲧ, ib R 19 S ⲉⲛⲧⲏⲣ ⲛϩ., AZ 21
88 O ⲛⲧⲉⲣ ϩ., ib 33 132 S ⲙⲁⲅⲓⲁ ⲛϩ., Mor 33 138 S
ⲡⲁⲣⲑⲉⲛⲟⲥ ⲛϩ., ib 123 S bare Him without ⲙⲁ ⲡⲉⲛⲕⲟⲧⲕ ⲛϩ., PO 11 323 B ⲥⲓⲛⲟⲩⲥⲓⲁ ⲛϩ., ManiK 27 A²
ⲥⲁⲣⲝ ⲛϩ. ϩⲓⲥϩⲓⲙⲉ.

male animal: Ge 7 16 SB ἄρσην, Lev 4 23 S ⲃⲁⲁⲙ-
ⲛϩ. (B ⲃⲁⲣⲏⲓⲧ) χίμαρος ἄρ.; Ez 43 22 B sim ἔριφος;
PS 354 S ⲇⲣⲁⲕⲱⲛ ⲛϩ., BMis 264 S ⲥⲁⲙⲟⲩⲗ ϩ. =
Mor 30 39 F ⲥ̄. ⲉϩ., Hall 121 S ⲙⲁⲥ ϩ., ϩⲉⲓⲉⲃ ϩ., Mani
1 A² ⲟⲩⲱⲛϣ ⲛϩ. (wild?), BKU 1 26 (8 117) F ⲁⲗⲉⲕⲧⲱⲣ
ⲉⲛϩ. (wild?).

inanimates: PMéd 308 S ⲙⲉⲭⲡⲱⲡⲉ ⲛϩ. v ⲙⲉⲭⲡ.,
Ryl 102 S ⲡⲉⲡⲓⲡⲉ ⲛϩⲟⲟⲩⲧ (cf use of ♂), J 76 44 S
ϩⲓⲧⲱ ⲛⲓⲙ ⲛⲓϩ., PMich 3554 S ⲥⲙⲏⲣⲡⲉⲅⲏ (? σμυρ-
ναῖος cf Ryl 244) ⲛⲉϩ., Ostr *penes* Crum S ϩⲟⲓⲧⲉ ⲛⲉϩ.,
OstrBristolMusH 1847 S sim ⲛⲉⲓϩ., ST 118 S ⲑⲣⲁⲕⲉ
(θωράκιον?) ⲛϩ., ViK 76 F ⲗⲟⲧⲓⲥ (λῶδιξ) ⲛⲁⲣⲉⲩ ⲛϩ.

b *wild*, savage man, beast: Job 39 5 S ⲉⲓⲁ. ⲛϩ. (B
ⲛⲧⲱⲟⲩ), Ps 79 13 S ⲉⲓⲁ ϩ. (B do) ὄνος ἄγριος, ShA 2
7 S ⲉⲓⲱ ⲛϩ., Ps 79 13 ⲡⲓⲣ ϩ. (B do) σῦς ἐκ δρυμοῦ, MS
Louvain 5 90 S ϩ. ⲛϩ. ⲛⲧⲟⲟⲩ, El 42 A ϣⲁϩⲉⲩⲧ (cf
DM 21 34); ManiP 61 A² ⲟⲩⲱⲛϣ ϩⲛ., P 44 55 S
ⲁⲅⲣⲓⲟⲧⲣⲁⲅⲟⲥ· ⲥⲓⲉ ϩ. جدي بري; R 1 3 74 S ⲁϥ ⲛϩ. *bee*
(v ⲁϥ 2° & ⲃⲟⲗⲃⲗ I); Mt 3 4 S ⲉⲃⲓⲉ ϩ. (B ⲛⲧⲉ ⲧⲕⲟⲓ)
ἄγ.; ShP 129¹⁴ 130 S wild man ⲕⲁⲧⲁ ⲡⲣⲁⲛ ⲉⲧⲟⲩⲙⲟⲩⲧⲉ ⲉⲣⲱⲧⲛ ϫⲉϩⲉⲟⲩⲧ, P 131² 136 S sim;   JKP
2 92 S lion wolf & bear ⲧⲉⲩⲙⲁⲡⲓⲁ ϩ. ⲉⲡϣⲟⲙⲛⲧ.

wild plant SF: Ro 11 24 SF ϫⲓⲧϩ. (B ϫⲱⲓⲧ ⲛϣⲁϣⲓ) ἀγριέλαιος opp -ⲛⲟⲩⲧⲙ; Z 628 ⲕⲡⲧⲉ ⲛϩ., BKU
1 40]ⲃⲓⲛ ϩ. (? cf DM 24 2 a), KroppK 57 ⲗⲱⲣⲥⲏⲡⲉ
ϩ., PMéd 321 ϣⲁⲙⲁⲣ ϩ., P 43 59 ⲁⲅⲣⲓⲟⲛ ⲕⲩⲙⲓⲟⲛ·
ⲧⲁⲡⲉⲛ ϩ. بري, فقوس بري ib 235 ϣⲟⲡ ϩⲉⲩⲧ, ib
ⲉⲛⲭⲟⲗ ϩⲉⲩⲧ بصل, عنصل, ib 59 v ⲉⲗⲟⲟⲗⲉ I, KroppM 35
ⲑⲁⲣⲙⲟⲥ (sic l) ϩⲉⲟⲩⲧ, ib E 60 ⲗⲓⲃⲁⲛⲟⲥ ϩ., ⲙⲁⲥⲧⲓⲭ(ⲏ)
ϩ., PBad 5 394 ϣⲁⲗ ⲛϩ.
Obscure is BM 1020 S lease of ⲟⲩⲛⲁⲧ ⲛⲥⲱϩⲉ ⲛϩ.
ⲧⲏⲣϥ.

ϩⲟⲩⲧ- S in ϩ. ⲥϩⲓⲙⲉ: BG 28 ϥⲟⲩⲧⲥϩⲓⲙⲉ ⲛⲧⲁϥⲉⲓ
ⲉⲃⲟⲗ ϩⲓⲧⲉϥⲡⲣⲟⲛⲟⲓⲁ, ib 29 ⲧⲙⲉϩϯ ⲛϩ., ib 97 ⲡⲉϥ-
ⲡⲣⲟⲧⲟⲅⲉⲛⲏⲧⲱⲣ ⲛϣⲏⲣⲉ ⲛϩ.

ⲙⲛⲧ-, ⲙⲉⲧϩ.: BG 103 S ⲧⲉϥⲙ., opp ⲧⲉϥⲙⲛⲧⲥϩⲓ-
ⲙⲉ *male element*, MG 25 240 B ⲉⲧⲉⲣ ⲁⲥⲕⲓⲛ ϩⲉⲛⲟ-
ⲩⲃⲓⲟⲥ ⲙ.

o ⲛϩ. A² ManiP ⲡⲟⲛⲏⲣⲟⲛ ⲉⲧⲟ ⲛϩⲏⲧ.

ϩⲟⲟⲩⲧⲏ S, ϩⲟⲩⲧⲉⲛ F nn m, *road, highway*: Z
295 corpse lying ϩⲓⲙⲛϩ. ὁδός; BMis 125 Tamar sat
ϩⲁⲣⲧⲛϩ. ⲙⲙⲟⲟϣⲉ (cf Ge 38 14 πρὸς ταῖς πύλαις...
ἐν παρόδῳ), Mor 31 35 ⲁϥⲕⲧⲟϥ ⲉⲕⲉϩ. (var Miss 4 775
ϩⲓⲏ), BAp 111 ⲡϣⲟⲣⲡ ⲛϩ. ⲙⲡⲉⲕϯⲙⲉ = PO 22 395
طرق, ShC 73 1 58 none shall ϩⲓⲧⲉ ϩⲁⲙⲛϩ. *loiter on road*,
LMär 27 field ϩⲓⲧⲟⲩⲱϥ ⲙⲛϩ., KroppD 30 ϥ. ⲉⲉⲓ
ⲉϩⲣⲁ(ⲓ), Ryl 381 amîr coming south ϩⲓⲛϩ., ib 323 ϩⲛ-
ⲡⲧⲣϥⲉⲣ ⲡⲁϣⲉ ⲛⲛϩ. ⲉϥⲛⲏⲩ ⲉⲣⲏⲥ, ib 158 ⲡⲧⲉⲧⲁⲣⲧⲟⲛ
ⲙⲉⲣⲟⲥ ϩⲓⲛϩ., Kr 63 F ⲛⲉϩⲧⲟⲩ ⲛϩ. *cross-roads*(?); as
boundary ib 130, 190;   as measure of distance S: Ac
1 12 ⲟⲩϩⲓⲏ ⲛⲥⲁϣϥ ⲛϩ. (B as Gk) σαββάτου ὁδός, so
ϩ. = ca 150–200 yards or 1 furlong (Enc. Bibl. 5294).

ϩⲟⲩⲧⲉⲛ A² nn as epithet of beauty: ManiP ⲙⲛⲧ-
ⲥⲁⲓⲉ ⲛϩ.;   ⲙⲛⲧϩ.: ManiK 132]ⲟⲩⲉ ⲙⲙⲁⲩ ⲁⲩ-
ⲥⲁⲓⲉ ⲙⲡⲟⲩⲙ., ib 162 rising sun ϣⲱⲗ ⲟⲩⲥⲁⲓⲉ ⲙⲡⲟⲩⲙ.
upon all creation.

ϩⲟⲩⲛⲟⲩ B vb qual: Va 57 71 ⲡⲓⲣⲁⲛ ϥϩ. ⲟⲩⲟϩ
ϥⲟⲣϣ ⲉϫⲉⲛⲡⲓⲣⲉϥⲉⲣⲛⲟⲃⲓ. Prob ⲟⲩⲛⲟⲩ (cf Is 59 9).

ϩⲁⲩϣ S nn m, a title, occupation or epithet: Saq
66 ⲫⲓⲗⲟⲑⲉⲟⲥ ϥ., cf ? ib 207 ⲡⲁⲥⲟⲛ ϥ. ϣ ⲁⲡⲁⲧⲏⲣ.
ϩⲟⲓϣ prob different.

ϩⲟⲟⲩϣ S, ϩⲁⲟⲩϣ A²F, ϩⲁϣ A², ϩⲱⲟⲩϣ B vb
intr, *abuse, curse*: Nu 20 13 B(S ⲥⲁϩⲟⲩ) λοιδορεῖν;
Va 57 42 B καταρᾶσθαι;   c ⲉ- obj: Ge 49 23 B λ.
εἰς, Ex 17 2 B(S do) λ. πρός, Jo 9 28 A²B(S do) λ. acc,
Jer 36 27 B συλλ. acc; Nu 23 8 b S(B ⲥⲁϩⲟⲩⲓ), Eccl
7 22 F(S do) καταρ. acc, Nu 5 19 S(B ⲥϩⲟⲩⲟⲣⲧ) ἐπι-
κατ.; MG 25 126 B ϩ. ⲉⲡⲓⲣⲉϥⲙⲟⲟⲩⲧ, Va 57 200 B
thine enemy ⲁϩϩ. ⲉⲣⲟⲕ ὑβρίζειν; ib 252 B ἐπηρεάζειν
opp ⲥⲙⲟⲩ; ShRyl 68 265 S ⲥⲱϣ ⲙⲡⲛ̄, ϩ. ⲉⲡⲉϥⲡⲉⲧ-
ⲟⲩⲁⲁⲃ, ShViK 9814 21 S ⲁϩϩ. ⲉⲣⲟⲓ ϩⲛϣⲁϫⲉ ⲛⲓⲙ
to humiliate me, ManiP 40 A² ⲡⲉⲓ ⲉⲧⲁϩϣ ⲁⲣⲁⲕ (cf
Lu 6 28 καταρ.), DeV 2 65 B ⲁϥϩ. ⲉⲡⲉϥϩⲣⲟⲟⲩ ⲙⲙⲓⲥⲓ;   ⲥⲉϫⲉⲛ- B: C 86 177 ⲁⲡⲓⲙⲁⲧⲟⲓ ϩ. ⲉⲭⲱⲟⲩ;   c
ⲡⲉⲙ- B: Ex 21 18 (S c.) λ.;   tr: Deu 33 8 B(S
do) λ.; Nu 23 8 b S(B c.) καταρ.;   as nn m: Si
29 8 S, 1 Pet 3 9 B(S do) λοιδορία, Ex 17 7 B(S do)
-ρησις; Va 57 262 B ὕβρις;   ⲉⲣ ϩ. B: MG 25
204 ⲉⲣ ⲟⲩⲙⲏϣ ⲛϩ. ⲉⲣⲟϥ ὑβρίζειν; ib 126 sim ἀτιμάζειν;   ϯ ϩ. B: Cat 131 ϯ ⲡⲟⲩϩ. ⲥⲁⲟⲩϩ., C 86
175 ϯ. ⲉⲣⲟϥ... ⲥⲁϩⲟⲩⲓ ⲉⲣⲟϥ;   ⲣⲉϥϩ. B: 1 Cor 5
11 (S ⲣⲉϥⲥ.) λοίδορος; Va 57 186 ⲣⲱⲙⲓ ⲛⲣⲉϥϩ. ὑβριστής.
V PLille 1 68.

ϩⲟⲩϫⲉ SA², ⲟⲩϫⲉ B, ϩⲟⲩϫⲏ F nn m, *untimely
birth*: Nu 12 12 SB, Eccl 6 3 SF ⲛⲓϩ., 1 Cor 15 8

SBF ἔκτρωμα, P 44 73 *S* ⲉⲕⲧ. · ⲍⲉϥⲣⲟⲥ (*cf?* δίφρος as bearing-stool) · ϩ. قفص, K 71 *B'*⸺, Glos 340 *S* ἀκύλινον, ἄμβλωσις · ϩ.; BG 46 *S* ⲛ̄ⲧⲉⲣⲉⲥⲉⲓⲙⲉ ⲉϥ. ... ⲍⲉⲛϥⲡⲟⲩϫⲱⲕ ⲁⲛ, ShZ 603 *S* ⲡⲉⲭⲡⲟ ⲙ̄ⲡⲉϥⲧⲉ ⲁⲩⲱ ⲡⲉⲧⲉⲛⲟⲩϩ. ⲁⲛ, *ib* ⲉϣⲁⲛϫⲡⲟⲛ ⲙⲙⲓⲛ (*sic*) ⲙⲙⲟⲛ ⲛϩ. ⲙ̄ⲡⲁⲧⲉⲡϫⲱⲕ ⲉⲃⲟⲗ, ManiK 93 *A*² ⲁⲛϩ. ⲉⲓ ⲁⲡⲓⲧⲛ, *ib* 123 ⲛϩ. ⲉⲧⲁⲩϭⲟⲩ ϩⲏⲧⲟⲩ.   *V* AZ 58 56.

ϩⲁⲩϭⲁⲗ *S*, ⲁⲩϫ. *B*, ϩⲁⲩϭⲏⲗ *F* nn m, *anchor, hook*: Ac 27 29 *SB*, He 6 19 *SBF* ἄγκυρα; K 133 *B* ⲡⲓⲁ. مرسى; R 2 1 56 *S* ϩ. ⲙ̄ⲡⲉⲛⲓⲡⲉ, AZ 21 148 *S* ⲧⲁⲭⲣⲉ ⲛ̄ⲡϫⲟⲓ ϩⲓⲧⲛ̄ϩ., BerlOr 1607 4 104 *S* ⲛϩ. ⲉⲧⲁⲙⲁⲣⲧⲉ ⲙ̄ⲡϫⲟⲓ, Va 61 104 *B* ⲥⲓϯ ⲛϩⲁⲛⲁ. *fore & aft.* موجل is wooden or iron rake, *cf* ⲙⲁⲛϭⲁⲗⲉ & *v* HA Winkler *Bauern* 99, *Volksk.* 152, BIF 20 72 n (where equated with ϣⲱϣ, *v* here p 606 *a*), *ib* 206.   From ἄγκυρα? (Stern 22, Sethe GöttN '25 53).

ϩⲓⲁⲓϣ *F*   *v* ⲟⲉⲓϣ.

ϩⲟⲓϣ *S* nn m, *title or occupation*: Saq 13]ⲛⲇⲓⲁⲕⲟ(ⲛⲟⲥ) ⲫ. ⲡⲉⲧⲣⲁⲫⲉⲩⲥ.   *Cf?* ϩⲟⲓϣⲉ.

ϩⲱϣ *SA*²*BF*, ϩⲉⲱ-, ϩⲟⲩϣ-, ϩⲱⲟⲩϣⲉ(ⲗϩⲟⲩϣⲉ)*S*, ϩⲁⲩϣⲉ *A*²(?), ϩⲏϣ† *SA*²*B* vb intr, *be in distress*: Ps 106 6 *S*(*B* ϩⲟⲭϩⲉⲭ) θλίβεσθαι; Eccl 10 9 *F*(*S*=Gk) κινδυνεύειν, 2 Cor 11 26 *B*(*S* om) κίνδυνος; PS 99 *S* ϩⲙ̄ⲡⲧⲣⲉⲓϩ. ⲁⲕϭⲱⲧⲙ̄ ⲉⲣⲟⲓ, BMis 481 *S* will require thy capital ϥⲛⲁⲧⲣⲉⲕϩ., TSBA 9 368 *B* ⲛⲏ ⲉⲑⲛⲁϩ. ϫⲉⲛϥⲓⲟⲙ (var Ryl 438 ϩ.†);   qual: 1 Kg 28 15 *S*, Z 342 *S* ⲉⲧⲃⲉⲟⲩ ⲕⲣ. ? θ.; Su 22 *S*(*B* ϩⲉⲭϩⲱϫ) στενός; 1 Kg 14 6 *S* συνέχεσθαι, BMar 103 *S* helpeth ⲡⲉⲧϩ. καταπονεῖσθαι; Ez 34 21 *S*(*B* do) ἐκλείπειν; PS 49 *S* turn not away ϫⲉϥ. ⲉⲙⲁⲧⲉ, ShC 42 210 *S* beast attacked by others ⲉϥϩ. ⲡⲧⲉⲩⲙⲛⲧⲉ, WTh 177 *S* ⲉⲧϩ. ϩⲛⲣⲉⲛϣⲱ-ⲛⲉ, C 43 98 *B* ⲛ̄ⲡⲗⲩⲙⲏⲛ(ⲗⲓ.) ⲛⲟⲩⲟⲛ ⲛⲓⲙ ⲉⲧϩ., ManiH 9 *A*² ⲉⲩϩ. ⲉⲙⲡⲟⲩϫⲡ ⲙⲁ ⲛ[;   tr *S*: Lev 25 14 ϩⲉϣ-(*B* ϩⲟⲭ.) θ.; ShP 130⁵ 56 ⲡⲉⲧⲛⲁϩ. ⲛⲟⲩⲣⲱⲙⲉ, R 1 3 82 worldly cares ϩ. ⲙ̄ⲙⲟⲓ, ST 226 ⲛ̄ⲧⲁⲓϩⲟⲩϣ ⲉⲓϫⲧ ⲟⲩ ϩⲛ̄ⲡⲕⲉϩⲟⲓ [(same ?).

With following preposition.   c ⲉ-: ManiP 122 *A*² ϩⲁⲩϣ ⲁⲩⲁⲧⲉ, N&E 39 341 *B* ⲉⲡⲕⲟⲧ ⲡⲁⲕ ϩⲟⲗⲱⲥ ⲣⲱ ϯϩ.† ⲉⲣⲟⲕ ⲁⲛ (*cf* ÉtLeem 91 *S* sim ϩⲁⲣⲟⲕ);   c ⲉⲧⲃⲉ- *S*: RE 9 164 ⲧⲏϩ.† ⲉⲙⲁⲧⲉ ⲉ.ⲡⲉⲛϩⲱⲃ ⲛ̄ϭⲓⲭ, Ryl 273 ϥϩ.† ⲉ.ⲟⲩⲡⲣⲁⲅⲙⲁ;   c ⲙⲛ-, ⲛⲉⲙ-: ShR 2 3 67 *S* ⲁⲓϩ. ⲙ̄ⲡⲉⲓⲅⲉⲛⲟⲥ of Christians, AM 106 *B* sim;   c ⲛ-*S*: Hall 102 send the things ϫⲉϯϩ.† ⲙ̄ⲙⲟⲟⲩ, LouvreR 1780 ⲧⲉϩⲉϣ ⲡⲉⲧⲁⲅⲉ (*v* ⲉⲧⲱ) ⲉⲙⲁⲧⲉ;   c ⲛⲧⲛ-: Ac 5 16† *B*(*S* ⲙⲟⲕⲏ) ὀχλεῖσθαι ὑπό; ShViK 933 *S* father ⲉϥϩⲁⲛⲡ. ⲡⲧⲟⲟⲧϥ̄ ⲙ̄ⲡⲉϥϣⲏⲣⲉ, C 43 27 *B* ⲁⲓϩ. ⲛ̄ⲧⲟⲧϥ̄ ⲙ̄ⲡⲁⲓⲁⲛⲟⲥⲓⲟⲥ;   c ϩⲁ-, ϣⲁ-: Mor 37 51 *S* ⲛϩ.† ⲁⲛ ϩⲁⲭⲣⲏⲙⲁ φροντίζειν gen; R 1 5 40 *S* ϯϩ.† ⲁⲛ ϩⲁⲡⲉⲕⲃⲁⲥⲁⲛⲟⲥ, C 43 9 *B* sim, Ep 219 *S* ϯϩ.† ϩⲁⲡⲉⲣⲕ[ⲟ, RAl 101 *B* ϯϩ.† ⲁⲛ ϩⲁⲡⲁⲓⲃⲁⲗ for I have spiritual eyes;   c ϩⲓⲧⲉⲛ- AM 38 *B* ⲁⲓϩ. ϩ.ⲡⲁⲓⲧⲉ-ⲡⲟⲥ (*cf* c ⲙⲛ-).

With following adverb.   c ⲉⲃⲟⲗ: P 44 120 *S* ⲁϥϩⲱϣϥ̄ ⲉⲃ. ⲙ̄ⲙⲓⲛ ⲙ̄ⲙⲟϥ الرب نفس of Ninevites ⲥⲉⲛⲁϩ. ⲉⲃ. ϩⲓϫⲉⲛ (?ⲗ ϩⲓⲧⲉⲛ) ⲛ̄ⲛⲓⲙⲟⲟⲩ ⲉⲧⲟϣ (*cf* Synax 1 135);   c ⲉϩⲟⲩⲛ: 4 Kg 9 8† *S* συνέχεσθαι; TurO 13 *S* ⲁⲓϩ. ⲉ. ⲙ̄ⲡⲓⲛϭⲓ ⲑⲉ ⲛⲉⲓ, ManiH 53 *A*² ⲡⲉⲧϩ.† ⲁ., *ib* K 148 *A*² ⲉⲧⲃⲉⲧⲁⲡⲁⲥⲕⲏ ⲁⲩϩⲁϣⲟⲩ ⲁ. ⲁⲣⲁϥ (but this prob = ⲱϣ 2°).

—— nn m, *distress, straits*: 1 Kg 22 2 *S* ἀνάγκη; Jer 19 9 *B* περιοχή, *ib* 52 5 *B* συνο.; Va 66 309 *B* ⲛⲏ ⲉⲧϩⲉⲛϩⲁⲛϩ. δυστυχεῖν; PS 49 *S* ⲡⲁϩⲱⲭ ⲙ̄ⲡϩⲁϣ., ShA 1 427 *S* help every one ⲉⲧϩⲛⲣⲉⲛϩ., ShMich 550 15 *S* ϣⲁⲛⲧⲩϯ ⲟⲩⲱ ⲙ̄ⲙⲟⲩ ϩⲙ̄ⲡⲉϥϩ., C 43 190 *B* ⲉ-ⲑⲣⲉϥⲙⲧⲟⲛ ⲉⲃⲟⲗ ϫⲉⲛⲡⲉϥϩ., C 99 107 *S* ⲕⲁⲁⲧ ⲉⲃⲟⲗ ϩⲙ̄ⲡⲉⲓϩ. (*cf ib* 213 & C 89 5 *B* θλῖψις), Ep 277 *S* I beg ⲛ̄ⲧⲃⲁⲗⲧ ϩⲙ̄ⲡⲉⲓⲕⲉϩ., Balestri xlii *S* either in ϩⲉⲛϩ. or in ⲡⲉϣⲧⲉⲕⲱⲟⲩ.

ⲙⲁ ⲛϩ. *S*, *place of constraint, distress (?)*: Pcod 7 ⲙ̄ⲙ. ⲉⲧϩⲙ̄ⲡⲉⲓⲕⲟⲥⲙⲟⲥ where those awaiting Judgment.

ϩⲁϣⲉ nn f, *constraint*: Is 30 6 *F*(*S* ⲗⲱⲭϩ, *B* ⲧⲁⲕⲟ) στενοχωρία; ManiH 96 *A*² ϩⲛ̄ⲧⲁⲕⲉϩ.   *Cf* ϩⲁϣϣ.

(ϩⲱⲟⲩϣ) ϩⲟⲩϣ⸗   *v* ⲱϣ 2°.

ϩⲟⲓϣⲉ *S* nn m, *meaning unknown*: MR 4 131 in word-list ⲫⲟⲓϣⲉ.   *Cf?* ϩⲟⲓϣ.

ϩⲁϣⲥ   *v* ϩⲱϣ *s f*.

ϩⲁϣⲏⲧ¹ *SA*², -ⲓⲧ², ϩⲁⲣϣⲏⲧ³ *S* nn m, *falcon*: Deu 14 15³ (Ciasca, Mor diff, *B* = Gk) καταρράκτης (*cf* ϣⲗⲱⲙⲃⲏϫ); P 44 55 ϩⲉⲣⲁⲕⲓⲟⲩ (ἱέραξ) · ⲉⲓⲕⲧⲓⲥ (ἰκτῖνος) · ⲛϩ.² صنف سقر · س̆. ⲛϩ.² , ⲛϩ.² =43 22 ⲧ. سقر. · ⲉⲕ. شاهين, *ib* 22 ⲛϩ. صقر̇ ش̇ ايضب = P 45 73 ايضب ش̇ , Tri 627 ϩ.² سقر̇.; ManiH 9 *A*² [birds] ⲛ̄ⲓⲧ ϩⲓⲧⲟⲩ ⲙ̄ⲡϩ.¹ P 129¹⁴ 105 ⲑⲗⲟ ⲉⲃⲟⲗ ⲛ̄ⲡⲉϩⲣⲁⲧⲟⲩ ⲙ̄ⲡⲡⲉϩ.¹ ⲉⲃⲟⲗ ϩⲓⲡⲉⲧⲙⲁ ⲛ̄ϣⲱⲡⲉ ⲛ̄ⲛⲁⲕⲉ *hurricanes & cataracts (?) sc* enemies of church.

ϩⲱϣϥ *S* vb tr, *break*: BG 121 ⲁⲓⲃⲱⲗ ⲉⲃⲟⲗ ⲛ̄ⲡⲛ̄-ⲥⲛⲟⲟⲩⲥ...ⲁⲓϩ. ⲛ̄ⲡⲓⲡⲩⲗⲏ, *ib* 126 ⲡⲧⲉϩ. ⲙ̄ⲡⲉⲩⲡⲁϩ-ⲃⲉϥ.   Same as ϩⲱϣϥ *q v*.

ϩⲁϣⲱϣ, ϩⲉϣϩⲱϣ⸗, ϣϩⲁϣⲧ† *A*² (Mani) vb tr, *press, oppress (cf ϩⲱϣ) or consume*: K 54 ⲁϥⲙⲁⲣⲟⲩ ⲁϥϩⲉϣϩⲱϣⲟⲩ as fire burneth trees, P ⲙ̄ⲡⲉϥϭⲛ̄ ⲕⲉⲥ ϩⲓⲙⲟⲩⲧ ⲡⲧⲉϩ. ⲙ̄ⲙⲁⲩ, K 176 soul ⲉⲥϩ.† ⲉⲥⲙⲁⲣⲧ.

ϩⲟϥ *SB*, ϩⲟⲃ, -ⲡ, ϩⲱⲃ *S*, ϩⲁϥ *AA*²*F*, f ϩϥⲱ *SB*, ϩⲃⲱ *SA*²*F*, ϩⲃⲟⲩ *A*, pl ϩⲃⲟⲩⲓ *SB*(once) & sg as pl, nn m f, *serpent*: Ge 3 13 *SB*, Ex 4 17 *S* ϩⲟⲃ, Eccl 10 11 *SF*, Mic 7 17 *SAB*, Jo 3 14 *SA*²*BF*, Ap 9 19 *S*(*B* ϩϥⲱ) ὄφις; Ps 57 4 *S*(*B* do), Is 30 6 *SB* ϣⲏⲣⲉ ⲛϩ. *F* ⲙⲉⲥ ⲛϩ., R 1 4 57 *S* ϩ. ⲡⲣⲉϥⲛⲉϫ ⲙⲁⲧⲟⲩ = MartIgn 869 *B* ἀσπίς; Sa 16 10 *S*, Jer 27 8 *B*(*S*=Gk) δράκων;

Pro 23 32 *A* ϧ. ⲛⲧⲉⲡ (*S* = Gk) κεράστης; K 172 *B* ⲡⲓϧ. ‮نعبان‬; BG 37 *S* ⲟ ⲡϧⲁ ⲛϧ., ShC 42 208 *S* ⲟⲩϧⲟϥ ⲏ ⲟⲩϧⲁⲣⲁⲕⲱⲡ, Mor 51 6 *S* ⲡⲉϧⲣⲁⲕⲱⲡ ⲛϧ. of Euchaita, BIF 13 114 *S* ϧ. ⲛⲁⲣ., C 43 232 *B* ⲡⲓϧ....ⲙⲫⲣⲏϯ ⲡⲣⲁⲡⲕⲁⲡⲱⲛ ⲡϣⲉ, 233 called ⲛⲓⲁⲣ., Miss 4 99 *B* ⲛϧ. ⲉⲩⲡⲏⲟⲩ ⲉⲃⲟⲗ ϧⲉⲛⲣⲱϧ ⲙⲡⲓⲁⲣ., PS 156 *S* ϧ. ⲛⲥⲓⲧ, *ib* 138 ⲥⲓⲧ ⲛϧ., C 86 155 *B* ⲁⲣ. ⲛⲉⲙϧ. ⲛⲥⲓⲧ, El 48 *A* ⲛⲓϧ., ManiP 60 *A²* ϥ. ⲛⲣⲉϥϩⲱⲧⲃⲉ, AP 43 *A²* ⲧⲡⲓⲥⲧⲓⲥ ⲙⲫ., BMar 37 *S* ⲟⲩϧⲗⲟ ⲙⲡⲟⲩⲙⲁⲧⲟⲩ ⲛϧ.; ϭⲁⲗ ϧⲟϥ (collated) *S*, *serpent-charmer* (?): R 1 5 30 ⲙⲁⲧⲟⲥ ⲛϭ.; ϭⲁⲡ ϧ. *BF*, *serpent-catcher*: C 43 232 ⲡⲓⲣ̄ ⲛϭ. bringing serpents to slay martyr, BM 1230 *F* among workmen ⲛϭ. (same?); ⲣⲉϥϭⲉⲡ ϧ. *S*: Mor 50 42 no ϧ. could remove snake from her neck.

f: Lu 3 7 *S*, Ac 28 3 *S* (both *B* ⲁ̄ⲭⲱ) ἔχιδνα, P 44 56 *S* ⲁⲓⲭ̄ⲣⲁⲡⲁⲡ · ⲧⲉⲣϩⲟ ‮لىا‬; Is 13 22 *SB*, *ib* 34 15 *SF* (*B* do), Zeph 2 14 *S* (P 44 116) *A* (*B* do) ἐχῖνος (as if ἔχιδ.); Is 14 29 *B* (*S* ϧⲟϥ) ἀσ., Mor 37 48 *S* ϧⲟϥ ⲟϥ̄., ϧϩⲱ ἀσ.; K 172 *B* ϯ̄ϧ. ‮حيّة‬; BM 363 115 *S* wild beasts & ⲛⲉϧ. in desert, BMis 514 *S* ⲛⲉϧ. ⲛⲣⲟⲩϧ, *ib* 191 *S* ⲛⲣⲱϧ ⲛⲥⲓⲧ ⲉⲧⲉⲧⲁⲓⲧⲉ ⲧϧ., Mor 52 24 *S* Thomas preached in land of ⲛⲉϧⲃⲱⲱ (*l* ?? ϧⲛⲧⲟⲩ), Mani 1 *A²* ⲡⲓⲁϭ ⲛⲁⲣⲁⲕⲱⲛ ⲧϧ.; pl: Mt 3 7 (*B* ⲁ.) ἔχιδνα; Tri 424 ⲛⲉϧ. ‮لىا‬; BMis 514 ϧⲉⲛϧ. ⲙⲛⲣⲉⲛⲥⲓⲧ; as sg: *ib* 557 ϧⲟ ⲛϧ., TstAb 178 *B* ϧⲟ ⲛⲉⲃⲟⲩϧⲓ (*l* ⲛⲉϧⲃ., *cf Texts & Stud* 2 (2) 138, Vassiliev *Anecd Gr Byz* 306 8), Bor 282 173 ⲙⲁⲧⲟⲩ ⲛⲟⲩϧ. (*Cf* pl of ϧⲓⲃⲱⲓ).

In name: ⲡϣⲉⲛⲧϧⲃⲱ (C 89 55) = ϣⲉⲛⲧⲉϧ. (TT 182 n) = ‮شندفو‬ (Va ar 172 35), Ψεντφοῦς (Preisigke).

ϩⲟⲩϥ *SB* nn m, *vetch, pulse*: P 46 159 *S* ⲡⲓϧ. ‮جلبان‬, K 193 *B* do, Bodl(P)b 7 *S* among herbs ϭⲟⲩϭ, ϧ., ϩⲉⲣⲥⲓⲙ, PMich 3561 *S* ϧ. ⲁⲣ̄ β ν̄ ⲁϫ; K 259 *B* ‮ج.المطروح‬, Montp 151 *B* ⲡⲓϧ. · ⲡⲓⲁⲣⲁⲕⲓ (ἄρακος Langkavel 4, *cf* P 44 83, WS 154) ‮ج.‬; K 197 *B* ⲡⲉⲗⲡⲉⲡⲉⲡ (μηλοπέπων) ⲛϧ. ‮بطيخ اصفر‬; ⲥⲁ ⲡⲣⲟ ⲩϧ *S*, *pulse-seller*: Saq 4 pl 47. ⌐*Cf* ? ϩⲟⲩⲙ.

ϩⲁϧⲉ *A²* *v* ϧⲁⲁⲃ.

ϩϧⲱ *v* ϧⲟϥ.

ϩⲁϧⲗⲉ(ⲉ)ⲗⲉ¹ *S*, ϧⲁⲃ.², ϩⲁϧⲗⲉⲗⲓ³ *S*, ⲁϧⲗⲉⲗⲓ *B*, ϩⲁϧⲗⲉⲗⲁ⁴, ϩⲉϧⲗⲉⲗⲉ⁵ DM nn f, *lizard*: Lev 11 30 *S¹* (var²) *B* σαύρα; ‮سام ابرص‬; P 46 169 *S* ⲧϧ.³ ‮حلمة‬; Ora 4 26 *S* ⲟⲩϧ.² ⲉⲥⲟⲩⲉⲧⲟⲩⲱⲧ, DM 13 23 ϧ.⁴, *ib* 24 26 ϧ.⁵ ⲛⲥⲉⲧ ⲛ *two-tailed lizard*.

ϩϥⲟⲩⲣ, ϩⲣⲟⲩⲃ *B* nn m, *young fish*: K 170 ⲡⲓϧ. ‮زرزق‬ (*cf* Dozy 1 596), BMor 8775 136 ⲛϧⲣ. ‮قازريق‬.

ϩⲱϧⲉⲥ *F* *v* ϧⲱⲃⲥ.

ϩⲱϭⲧ, -ϧⲧ, ϧⲟϥⲧ, ϧⲉϥⲧ-, ϧⲟϥⲧ⸗, -ϧⲧ⸗ *S* vb intr, *steal* (*cf* ϧⲏⲡⲡ Dévaud): Jo 10 10 (*AA²B* ⲭⲓⲟⲩⲉ) κλέπτειν; BMis 311 ⲁϥϧⲟ. ⲛⲭⲓⲟⲩⲉ; tr: Ge 31 19 (*B*

ⲕⲱⲗⲡ), Ex 21 17 (*B* ⲱⲗⲓ), BM 216 110 ϧ. ⲡⲛⲉⲥⲕⲉⲩⲏ ⲕⲗ.; Jo 12 6 (*A* ϥⲓ ⲛⲭ., *A²* ⲭ., *B* ⲧⲱⲟϧⲡ) βαστάζειν; Aeg 230 ϧ. ⲡⲟⲩⲅⲕⲩⲙⲏⲗⲓⲟⲛ from church ἀφαιρεῖν; *ib* ⲁϥϧⲟⲃⲧϥ λαμβάνειν; ShClPr 22 366 ϧ. ⲡⲛⲉⲣⲛⲁⲁϥ, BHom 87 Achar ⲉϥϧⲱⲃⲧ ⲛϧⲉⲛⲁⲛⲁⲑⲉⲙⲁ (Jos 7 1), CA 112 ϩⲁⲣⲉϩ ⲉⲣⲟⲕ ⲉϧⲉϥⲧ ⲗⲁⲁϥ, BP 9104 ⲁⲩϧⲟϥⲧⲟⲩ (*sc* crops) ⲙⲡⲟⲩⲕⲁⲁϥ ⲉϯ ⲁ̄ⲏⲙⲟⲥⲓⲟⲛ.

With following preposition or adverb. ϧ ⲡⲥⲁ-: *ib* ⲛⲓⲧⲁⲩϧⲟϥⲧⲟⲩ ⲛⲥⲱⲓ; ϧ ⲛⲧⲛ-: Sh(?)ViK 9332 ⲉϧ.....ⲛⲧⲟⲟⲧⲛ; ϧ ϧⲓ-: Pcod 8 entrusted with ⲉⲩⲟⲓ ⲕⲟⲡⲟⲙⲓⲁ...ⲛϧ. ϧⲓⲱⲥ; ϧ ϧⲛ- *from*: CA 99 ⲁϧ. ϧⲛⲧⲧⲓⲙⲏ ⲙⲡⲉϥϭⲱⲙ (Ac 5 2), Pcod 8 ⲡⲉⲛⲧⲁϧ. ϧⲁ-ⲡⲉⲅⲗⲱⲥⲥⲟⲕⲟⲙⲟⲛ; ⲉⲃⲟⲗ ⲛ-, ϧⲛ-: BHom 49 none can ϧ. (*sic*!) ⲉ̄ϧ. ⲙⲡⲛⲁ ⲉⲧⲙⲙⲁⲩ ⲙⲡⲥⲁ ⲛⲧⲡⲏⲩⲏ, Pcod 3 ⲉϧϧ. ⲉ̄ϧ. ⲛϧⲏⲧϥ (*sc* purse).

—— ⲛⲛ m, *theft*: Ex 22 3 (*B* ϭⲟⲩⲱ) κλέμμα, Tob 2 12 κλεψιμαῖος, Si 41 19 κλοπή.

ⲣ ϧ : Lu 18 20 (*B* ϭⲓⲟⲩⲓ) κλέπτειν.

ⲣⲉϥϧ., *thief*: Si 20 24, 1 Cor 6 10 (*B* ⲣⲉϥϭ.) κλέπτης; ShViK 941 47 among sinners, Wess 18 48 ⲛⲥⲉ-ⲟⲡ̄ ϧⲱⲥ ϧ. if we hide marvels that befell, ViK 9328 107 unstamped coin ϥⲙⲟⲧⲛ ⲛⲡⲣ. ⲉϧⲟⲩϥⲧϥ; ⲙⲛⲧ-ⲣⲉϥϧ. (*sic l* ?): PS 209 ⲧⲙⲛⲧⲣⲉϥϧⲱⲧϥ.

(ϩⲱϥⲧ), ϧⲉϥⲧ-, ϧⲟϥⲧ⸗ *S* vb tr, *send forth, eject*: ShMIF 23 29 ⲡⲣⲟϥ ⲉϣⲁϥϧⲉϥⲧ ⲙⲙⲟⲟⲩ ⲉⲡⲃⲁⲗ (*cf* 28 ϧⲟϥ ⲡⲁϣ ϧⲉⲗ ⲙⲟⲟⲩ), ShViK 918 ϯⲛⲁⲡⲟϩⲉ ⲛ ϧⲟϥ-ⲧⲉ; ϧ ⲉⲃⲟⲗ: ShMun 177 (ⲡ)ⲛⲉϥϧⲟⲩⲧⲛ ⲉⲃ. ⲙⲙⲟϥ paral ϧⲟⲟⲡⲉⲛ ⲉⲃⲟⲗ ⲛ-, Miss 4 696 evil thoughts ϧⲟϥⲧⲟⲩ ⲉⲃⲟⲗ.

ϩⲟϥⲧ⸗ *B* *v* ⲱϥⲧ.

ϩϥⲟⲧ, -ⲱⲧ *B* *v* ϧⲣⲟⲧ.

ϩⲓϥⲟⲩⲓ *B* *v* ϧⲓⲃⲱⲓ.

ϧⲁϧ *SA A²* nn as pl, *many, much* (*B* mostly ⲙⲏϣ): Job 11 19, Pro 8 18 *SA*, Mt 7 22 (*F* PMich 612 ⲁⲧⲁ), Jo 4 39 *A²* (*SB* ⲙⲏⲛϣⲉ) πολλοί, Job 16 2, Hag 1 6 *A* -ⲗⲁ̄, Mt 26 9 -ⲗⲟⲩ, BHom 30 ⲉϥϣⲁⲡⲟⲩⲉⲙ ϧ. πολύ, Ps 143 13 (*B* ⲛⲁϣⲉ), Si 25 8 πολυ-; BHom 8 ⲙⲛⲧ-ⲟⲩⲉⲙ ϧ. γαστριμαργία; ShIF 221 ⲡⲣⲙⲉⲓⲟⲟⲩⲉ ⲛϧ., ShViK 928 342 ⲛⲛⲓⲭⲉ ϧ., ShMich 550 13 ⲁϧ. ⲭⲟ ⲛ-ϧⲉⲛⲕⲁⲥ...ⲁⲩⲃⲱⲕ ⲁⲩⲕⲁⲁⲩ, C 100 356 ϧ. ⲛϧⲏⲧⲧⲏⲩⲧⲛ ⲉⲣⲉⲡⲙⲉⲉⲩⲉ ϯ ϧⲓⲥⲉ ⲛⲁϥ, El 76 *A* ⲟⲩⲏ ϧ. ⲛⲁⲣ ⲉⲡⲓⲟⲩ-ⲙⲉⲓ = *ib* 116 *S* ⲟⲩⲙⲏⲛϣⲉ, AP 40 *A²* ϧ. ⲡⲉⲛⲧⲁⲩⲧⲁⲩ ⲁⲃⲁⲗ; as adj: Ge 17 4 (BMis 460) πλῆθος; Mk 4 5, Aeg 246 ϧ. ⲡⲓⲣⲡ πολύς, Mt 13 17 (*F* ⲁ.) πολλοί, Ps 118 162, Pro 4 10 *SA* -ⲗⲁⲓ, Sa 8 8 πολυ-; Mt 18 24 μύριοι; *ib* 13 5 (*B* ϣⲱⲕ) βάθος; ShC 73 100 ⲡⲱⲣⲧ ϧ. ⲛⲥⲡⲟϥ ⲉⲃⲟⲗ, *ib* 55 ϧ. ⲛⲓⲉϧ not to be used, TU 24 1 5 ϧ. ⲡⲣⲓⲙⲉ, BKU 1 296 as greeting ϧ. ⲡⲣⲟⲙⲡⲉ ⲡⲁⲙⲉⲣⲓⲧ ⲛⲉⲓⲱⲧ (*cf* πολλὰ τὰ ἔτη), *ib* 297 ϧ. ⲡⲟⲩⲟⲉⲓϣ, Mani K 68 *A²* ϧ. ⲛⲥⲱⲡⲧ.

p ϩ., *be, do many*: Mt 13 58 (*F* ⲁ.) πο. ποιεῖν, Deu 30 18 (*B* ⲁϣⲁⲓ) πολυ-γίνεσθαι; *ib* 11 21 (*B* do) μακρο-; Ac 9 13 (*B* diff) ὅσος; J 91 20 ⲁⲡⲣ. ⲡϩⲟⲟⲩ ⲉⲡϩⲩⲡⲟⲣϭⲓ ⲉⲣⲟϥ, ManiK 145 *A²* ⲉⲅⲣ. ⲡⲁϩⲉ, OrChr 3 7 112 ⲉⲧⲟ ⲡϩ. ⲡⲃⲁⲗ.

ⲙⲛⲧϩ., *multitude*: Mt 6 7 ⲙ. ⲡϣⲁϫⲉ πολυλογία; BMis 227 ⲧⲙ. ⲛⲡⲉ̄ of gentiles (*cf* EpApp 1 23 ϩ. ⲙⲙⲛⲧⲡⲉ̄).

ϩ. ⲛⲥⲟⲛ *v* p 350 *b*, adding Jo 18 2 *A²* & Br 249 *S* ⲡϩ. ⲡϩ. ⲡⲥ. (or *l*? ⲡϩ. once).

ϩ. ⲛⲡϣⲁϫⲉ *v* p 614 *a*.

In place-name: ϩⲁϩ ⳟⲏⲛⲓ ابيار (Amélineau *Géogr* 556).

ϩⲁϩ *B* nn (adj?), meaning unknown, in ⲫⲓⲟⲙ ⲡϩ.: Ex 23 31, Deu 1 1 (both *S* = Gk) ἐρυθρὰ θάλασσα. Ar as in ϣⲁⲣⲓ *q v*.

ϩⲱϩ *SA* (nn), ϩⲱϩ *B*, ϩⲟϩ⳽ *S*, ϩⲁϩ⳽, ϩⲏϩ† *B* vb intr, *be scraped, itch*: Tob 11 7 *S* δάκνειν; 2 Tim 4 3 *S* (*B* tr) κνήθειν; EpJer 7 *B* (*S* ϩⲱⲕ) καταξύειν; TRit 522 *B* ⲁⲩϩ. ⲛϫⲉ ⲡⲓⲙⲁⲩϩ of corpse انصم (var ⲙ̄ⲥⲙ̄, *cf* ⲥϩⲙⲉ); P 44 90 *S* ⲁⲥϩ. تكد; P 54 119 = BMOr 8775 119 *B* ϩ. تنزع (*l*? غزغ Sobhy); ShIF 101 *S* malady ⲉϥϩ. ⲡⲣⲟϥⲟ ⲉϥϩⲱⲣⲁ ⲡⲓⲙ, ShA 1 46 *S* ⲧⲟⲟⲧϥ ⲙⲛⲣⲁⲧϥ ϩ., GMir 19 *S* eyes watered & ⲁⲩϩ., PMéd 299 *S* ⲡⲉϥⲃⲁⲗ ϩ., *ib* 257 ⲯⲱⲣⲁ ⲉⲥϩ.; ϭ ⲉ-: Job 7 5 *B* (*S* ϩⲱⲱⲕⲉ) ξύ. جراحي ادلك (Baudissin).

tr, *scrape, scratch*: Job 2 8 *B* (*S* do) ξύ., Lev 14 41 *B* (*S* ShIF 131 ϩⲱⲕ ⲉⲃⲟⲗ), *ib* 42 *B* ϩⲁϩⲟⲩ (var ⲑⲟⲧⲟⲩ, *S* do) ἀποξύ.; 2 Tim *B* ut sup; ShIF 108 *S* ϯ ⲛⲧⲉⲩϫⲓⲥⲉ ⲡⲛⲉⲧϩ. ⲙⲙⲟⲥ ⲛ ⲛⲉⲡⲧⲁⲩϩⲟⲣⲥ ⲡⲁⲩ, ShA 2 101 *S* ⲉⲧⲙⲧⲣⲉⲣⲱⲙⲉ ⲉⲡⲓϣⲱⲛⲉ ϩⲓⲱⲱϥ ϩ. ⲙⲙⲟϥ, ShR 2 3 47 *S* luxurious rich ⲉⲧⲟⲩϩ. ⲡⲛⲉⲟⲩⲉⲣⲏⲧⲉ ⲁⲩϣⲉ[ⲡ ϩⲓ]ⲥⲉ ⲙⲙⲟⲟⲩ ϣ[ⲁⲡ]ⲧϥⲱⲃϣ; ϭ ⲉⲃⲟⲗ: Rec 6 172 *B* ϩⲁϩⲟⲩ (*sc* ulcers) ⲉⲃⲟⲗ = BMar 209 *S* ϩⲟⲕⲟⲩ.

—— nn m *SA*, ϩⲁϩⲟⲩ *B* (once) *scratching, itching*: Deu 28 27 *SB* κνήφη زحير (?); ShA 2 96 ⲡⲓϣⲱϣⲉ ⲙⲡⲉⲩⲟⲩⲱϣ ⲁⲡⲡⲉ ⲁⲙⲁϩⲧⲉ ⲙⲙⲟⲟⲩ ⲉⲡⲉϥϩ., *ib* 105 ϣⲟⲟϭⲉϥ ϩⲓⲡⲉϥⲉⲓⲃ ϩⲓⲡϩ. ⲉⲧⲣⲟⲗϭ, ShIF 107 ⲑⲏⲗⲟⲓⲏ ⲉⲧϣⲟⲟⲡ ⲡⲁⲩ ⲉⲃⲟⲗ ϩⲓⲡϩ. ⲙⲡϣⲱⲛⲉ, ShViK 907 ⲛ[ⲉⲡ]ⲧⲁⲩⲧⲁⲕⲟⲟⲩ ϩⲓⲙⲡϩ., BM 1223 *A* bring upon her ⲟⲩ(ⲉ)ⲣⲁϣ ⲙⲡⲟⲩⲡⲟⲩϭⲥ ⲡⲟⲛⲧ ⲙⲡⲟⲩϩ., P 129¹² 16 ⲧⲉⲓⲯⲱⲣⲁ ⲙⲡⲡⲉⲥⲕⲉϩ., PMéd 320 ϩ. ⲡⲥⲁϣ, *ib* 314 ⲡϭ. ⲉϫⲛⲡⲉⲛⲕⲉⲣⲧⲉ, *cf* Z 629 ⲡⲉⲧϩ. ϩⲓϫⲛⲧⲉⲩⲕ., BMOr 9533 send ⲟⲩⲕⲟⲩⲓ ⲛⲥⲓⲡⲡⲱⲛ...ⲡⲥⲉⲣⲓⲧⲟⲩ ⲙⲡⲁⲧⲉϥϩⲱ ⲡⲱⲗϭ ⲉⲃⲟⲗ (*cf*? ϩⲱⲱⲕⲉ of flax-combing).

ϩⲱϩⲃ *v* ϩⲱϩϥ.

ϩⲟϩⲡ *v* ϩⲟⲡϩⲡ.

ϩⲓϩⲣⲁ⳽ *v* ϩⲟ p 650 *a*, adding ManiK 165 *A²* ⲉⲩⲥⲁϣⲧ ϩⲓϩⲣⲙⲡⲣⲟ.

ϩⲁϩⲧⲏ- *SA²* *v* ϩⲏⲧ 1° *s f*.

ϩⲓϩⲱⲧⲏⲣ *B* *v* ϩⲱⲧⲣ *s f*.

ϩⲟϩϥ *S* nn, *article of camel's furniture*: ST 120 ⲟⲩϩ. ⲡⲕⲁⲙⲟⲩⲗ.

ϩⲱϩϥ, -ⲃ *S* nn f, *hand* as measure: Is 40 12 (*B* ϯϫ) χείρ, paral ⲣⲧⲱ, ϫⲁⲙⲏ. *Cf* ḥf' (Dévaud).

ϩⲁϫ *v* ϩⲱϫ *s f*.

ϩⲱϫ *SF*, -ϫⲉ (once), ϩⲟϫ, ϩⲉϫ-, ϩⲏϫ† *S* vb intr, *be in straits*: JTS 10 400 when dying ⲉϥϣⲁⲛϩ. ϩⲓϫⲙⲡⲉⲩϭⲗⲟϭ, *ib* ⲉⲥϣⲁⲛϩ. *when in straits* of death; qual: EstD 5 ἀποστενοῦσθαι; PS 261 ⲡⲉⲧϣⲱⲡⲉ ⲙⲡⲛⲉⲧϩ., *ib* 49 ϯϩ. ϩⲣⲁⲓ ϩⲙⲡⲕⲁⲕⲉ, Cai 67324 in list ϭⲉⲗϭⲓϫ ⲉⲩϩ. *tight-fitting* (?); ϭ ⲉ-: Mor 30 13 *F* shut him in dark place ⲡⲥⲉϩ. ⲉⲣⲟϥ = BMis 239 *S* ⲱⲣϫ ⲉⲣⲟϥ κατακλείειν; BM 1014 lease ⲙⲡⲉⲧⲉⲣϩ. ⲉⲧⲁⲟⲓⲥ (meaning ?); ⲉϩⲟⲩⲛ ⲉ-: ShA 2 48 waters ⲉⲧϩⲱϭⲉ ⲉⲡϫⲟⲓ...ⲏ ⲉⲧϩⲱϫⲉ ⲉϩ. ⲉⲣⲟϥ; ⲉϩⲟⲩⲛ ⲉϩⲣⲡ-: Miss 4 697 ⲡⲣⲟⲉⲓⲙ ⲉⲧϩ. ⲉϩ. ⲉϩⲣⲁϥ (*sc* ship); tr: PS 47 ⲡⲉⲩϩ. ⲙⲙⲟⲓ ϩⲡⲟⲩϩⲓ ⲛϭⲟⲡⲥ, *ib* 46 ⲁⲩϩⲕⲱⲧⲉ ⲉⲧⲥⲟⲫⲓⲁ ⲁⲩϩ. ⲙⲙⲟⲥ, ShA 2 3 is folly if craftsmen should say ϫⲉⲉⲩⲛⲁϩⲉϫ ϩⲉϩⲟⲡⲁϭ ⲏ ⲡⲥⲉⲥⲗⲉϭⲗⲱϭⲟⲩ ere they are finished, Mor 31 62 spake in wrath ⲉϥϩ. ⲡⲛⲉϥⲃⲁⲗ *frowned* (? lit *narrowed eyes*) ⲉϥⲕⲓⲙ ⲛⲧⲉϥⲁⲡⲉ (Ethiop Pereira *Abba Samuel* 101 495 om).

—— nn m, *straits*: Deu 28 53 (*B* ϩⲟϫϩⲉϫ), Sa 5 3 (varr ϩⲟϫϩⲉϫ, ⲗⲱϩϫ, *B* ⲙⲉⲧⲯⲗⲁϭ ⲛϩⲏⲧ) στενοχωρία; PS 81 ⲡⲁⲑⲗⲓⲯⲓⲥ ⲙⲡⲡⲁϩ., *ib* 49 ⲡⲁϩ. ⲙⲡⲡⲁϩⲱϣ, Sh C 42 91 ⲧⲉⲩⲙⲛⲧⲏⲕⲉ ⲙⲡⲡⲣⲟϫ ⲉⲧⲟⲩⲛϩⲏⲧϥ, PMich 3546 ⲡϩ. ⲉⲧϩⲓⲱⲱϥ.

ϩⲁϫ *S* nn m, *a disease*: Aeg 27 of dying man ⲉⲣⲉⲡϩ. ϯ ⲛⲥⲱϥ like strong wind & devouring fire, Ryl 104(3) recipe for ⲡϩ. (potion of cumin, rue & wine). *V* also ϩⲟϫϩⲉϫ.

ϩⲱϫ *B* adj, *cold*: Mt 10 42 (*S* ⲱⲣϣ), Ap 3 16 (*S* do) ψυχρός.

ϩⲁϫⲓ *B* *v* ϩⲁϭⲉ.

ϩⲟϫⲉ *S* nn f, *a malady, paral chill*: Ostr *penes* Crum ⲁⲓⲥⲕⲩⲣⲕⲣ ϩⲁⲡⲁⲣⲟϣ ⲁⲑ. ⲙⲟⲟⲩⲧ, Ep 237 ⲧϩ. same ? *Cf*? ϩⲱϫ *cold*.

ϩⲱϫⲉ (reading doubtful) *S* nn as adj, meaning unknown: Ryl 115 ⲧⲥⲱϣⲉ ⲡϩ.

ϩⲱϫⲉ *v* ϩⲱϫ.

ϩϫⲁ, ϣϫⲁ *SSᵃ* nn f (?), *vessel or measure*: BM ostr 44748 ϫⲟⲟⲩ ⲟⲩϩ. ⲙⲙⲟⲩⲗϭ, Ep 368 ϩ. ⲡⲃⲁⲗⲁⲧ, CO 466 ϩ. ⲡϣ[ⲉ], duplic Univ Coll Lond ϫⲁ ⲡϣⲉ,

ST 297 ϣ. ⲡⲡⲁⲣⲥⲉⲡⲓⲕⲱⲡ (orpiment), BKU 1 137 ⲧϣ. (no context).

ϩϫⲉ or ? ϩϫⲉ[.]S, nn, *eel*: Glos 417 [μ]ῦρος · ϩ.

ϩⲁϫ(ⲉ)ⲛ-, ϩⲁϫⲏ-, ϫⲁϫⲉⲡ- *v* ϫⲱ head.

ϩⲓϫ(ⲉ)ⲛ- *v* ϫⲱ head.

ϩⲱϫⲡ SAA², ϩⲉϫⲡ- S, ϩⲟϫⲡϩ SB, ϩⲟϫⲡ†(?)S vb tr, *shut*: Cl 43 3 A κλείειν, Ps 34 3 (B ϣⲑⲁⲙ) συγκ.; ViSitz 172 4 18 ϩ. ⲡⲡⲉⲧⲙⲁⲁϫⲉ κωφοῦσθαι, Mic 7 16(A ϩⲱϫⲧ, B diff) ἀποκ.; Z 306 ⲁϥϩ. ⲡⲛⲉϥⲃⲁⲗ καμμύειν; Sh ib 515 ⲁϥϩ. ⲡⲛⲉⲩⲙⲁⲁϫⲉ, Mor 22 51 ⲡϥϩ. ⲡⲡⲉϥϭⲃⲱϣ, ViK 9518 ⲁϥϩⲟϫⲡⲥ ⲛⲥⲁⲥⲁ ⲛⲓⲙ, ManiH 96 A² ϩ. ⲡⲡⲣⲱⲟⲩ; c ⲉ-: Deu 15 7 (B ϣ. ⲉⲃⲟⲗ ϩⲁ-) συσφίγγειν ἀπό; ⲉϩⲟⲩⲛ ⲉ- B: C 43 92 ⲁϥϩⲟϫⲡϥ ⲉϩ. ⲉⲟⲩⲙⲁ ⲙⲙⲁⲅⲁⲧϥ; c ⲉϫⲡ-: P 131⁵ 21 ⲛⲧⲣⲟϫⲡ… ⲉϫⲡⲡⲉⲕⲃⲁⲗ; c ϩⲛ-: BHom 85 ⲛⲉϣⲁϥϩⲉϫⲡ ⲧⲉϥϭⲓϫ ϩⲛⲧⲕⲏ (*l ?* ϩⲉⲣⲡ, *cf* Mt 26 23 ϭⲱⲛ or Si 34 15 ϩⲟϫϩϫ); as nn: Si 27 14 ἐμφραγμός.

ϩⲱϫⲧ S(once)AA², -ϫϭ A vb, as last, intr: ShP 130² 75 S ⲉⲣⲉⲣⲱⲛ ⲛⲁϥ. ⲛϥⲟⲩⲱⲛ; tr: Pro 21 13 (S ϣⲧⲁⲙ) φράσσειν; Zech 7 11 (B ϩⲣⲉ-ϩⲣⲟϣ) βαρύνειν; c ⲁ-: Pro 4 12 (SB ϣ.) συγκλείειν; Mic 7 16 (S ϩⲱϫⲡ) ἀποκωφ.; El 44 ⲁϥϩ. ⲁⲣⲱⲓ ⲛϩⲟⲩⲛ ⲙⲙⲟ, ib 104 ⲥⲉϩⲱϫϭ ⲙⲙⲁⲥ ⲁⲣⲟⲟⲩ, ManiK 93 A² ⲁⲙⲙⲁⲓⲧ ϩ. ⲁⲛⲟⲩ[; c ⲁⲣⲏ-: TU 43 22 ⲛⲁⲩϩⲱϫϭ ⲁⲣⲏⲡⲉⲧ- [ⲁⲩϩⲱϫϭ ⲁⲣⲁϥ].

ϫϩⲟⲡϫⲡ, ϩⲛⲟϭⲡϭ, ϩⲡⲟϫ., ϫⲟⲛϫⲡ (oftenest)S, ϫⲁⲛϫⲡ, ϫⲉⲡϫⲱⲡϩ A², vb intr, *grope, feel* as blind man: Is 59 10 (varr ϩⲛⲟϭ., ϩⲡⲟϫ., ϫ. ShBMOr 8810' 395, B ϫⲟⲙϫⲉⲙ) ψηλαφᾶν; Sh(Besa)Bor 204 246 ⲉⲧϫ. ⲙⲙⲉⲉⲣⲉ as if midnight, ShCaiCoptMus *Catal* 1 01 ⲉⲩϫ. ϩⲙⲛⲥⲟⲟⲩⲛ…like blind ⲉⲧϫ. ϩⲓⲧⲉϩⲓⲏ; c ⲉ-: ShC 73 169 cursed whoso approacheth fellow's bed ⲛϫ. ⲉⲣⲟϥ ⲏ ⲛϥϭⲙϭⲱⲙϥ; c ⲛ-, *with*: ShA 1 53 ⲉϫ. ⲡⲡⲉⲥⲟⲩⲉⲣⲏⲧⲉ ϩⲓⲧⲉϩⲓⲏ; c ⲉϩⲟⲩⲛ ϩⲛ-: ib 54 ⲉϥϫ. ⲉ. ϩⲣⲉⲡⲙⲁ ⲡⲕⲁⲕⲉ.

tread A² intr: ManiH 5 A² sharp [claws?] ⲁⲩϫ. ⲁⲩϩⲱⲙ; tr A²: ManiP 70 sea's waves ⲁⲕϫⲉⲡ- ϫⲱⲡⲟⲩ ϩⲡⲧⲉⲕϭⲓⲛϭⲏⲣ, ManiH 76 ⲛⲧⲃⲛⲁⲅⲉ…ⲁ]ⲩϫⲉⲡϫⲱⲡϥ; as nn A², *thing trodden upon*: ManiK 105 ⲟⲩⲡⲟⲡⲟϫⲓⲟⲛ ϩⲓϫ.

ϩⲁϫⲁⲣ B *v* ϩⲁⲣⲁϫ.

ϩⲱϫⲧ *v* ϩⲱϫⲡ *s f.*

ϩⲱϫϥ S vb, meaning unknown: Sph 10 158 incantation addressed to (?)corpse ϩ. ⲡⲓⲕⲱⲥ; ϩⲟϫϥ† (same ?): PMéd 105 ⲡⲃⲁⲗ ϩ. (for ? ⲉⲧϩ.).

ϩⲁϫϩ *v* ϩⲟϫϩϫ.

ϩⲟϫϩϫ S, -ϩⲉϫ SB, ϩⲁϫϩϫ SS'A, ϩⲟϫϫ S, ϩⲁϫ- ϩ(ϫ)S", ϩⲁϫϫ A, ϩ(ⲉ)ϫϩ-, -ϩⲉϫϫ- S, ϩϫϩϫ-A², ϩⲉϫ- ϩⲉϫ- B, ϩⲉϫϩⲱϫϩ SB, ϩⲉϫϩⲁϫϩ A², ϩⲉϫϩⲱϫϩ(?)F, ϩⲉϫϩⲱϫϩ†SBF, -ϩⲟϫϩ†B vb intr, *be distressed, restricted, narrow*: 1 Kg 30 6 S, Ps 106 6 S(B ϩⲱϣϩ)θλίβειν; Pro 29 2 SA ϩⲁϫϩ στένειν; Ac 16 18 S(var ϩⲟϫϩ, B ⲙⲕⲁϩ ⲛϩⲏⲧ) διαπονεῖν; Nu 22 3 S(B ⲉⲣ ϣⲗⲁϩ ⲛϩⲏⲧ) προσοχθίζειν; ShBM 204 64 S ⲁⲓϩ. ⲁⲩⲱ ⲁⲓⲙⲉⲥⲧⲉ ϫⲱ ⲡϣⲁϫⲉ, Bor 139 179 S ⲁϥϩ. until Lord's wrath past, BMis 219 S ⲁϥϩ. … ⲁϥⲟⲩⲟⲗⲥ ⲛϩⲏⲧ = Mor 16 74 S ϩ ϩⲃⲁ, Mor 28 225 S after month's waiting ⲁⲕϩ. as if after year's imprisonment, DeV 2 65 B ⲁⲩϩ. ⲛϫⲉ ⲡⲉϥⲡⲣⲟⲫⲏⲧⲏⲥ; qual: Ps 30 10 B(S = Gk), Is 28 14 B (S ⲗⲟϫϩ), Lam 1 20 B(F ⲙⲁϫϩ, S ViK 9685 = Gk) θλ.; Job 24 11 S(B ϫⲛⲟⲩ), Is 30 20 SF(B do), C 89 169 B ⲟⲩⲡⲉⲧⲣⲁ ⲉⲥϩⲟⲥⲓ … ⲉⲥϩ. στενός, 2 Cor 4 8 SB στενοχωρεῖν; ShViK 9298 Sⲧⲉϩⲓⲏ ⲉⲧϩ. ⲟⲣⲣⲉⲧⲟⲩⲟϫⲥ, ShZ 593 S ϩⲓⲏ ⲉⲧϩⲏϫ ⲉⲧϩ., C 89 62 B ⲛⲉⲧϩ. = C 99 147 S λυπεῖ, Va 63 11 B ⲥⲛⲟⲩ ⲉⲧϩ. = BMis 381 S ⲕⲁⲓⲣⲟⲥ ⲛϩⲓⲥⲉ, DeV 2 171 B ϩⲓⲣ ⲉϥϩ., ST 189 S ⲟⲩⲣⲧⲟ]ϩ ⲛⲣⲱⲙⲉ ⲉϥϩ. opp ⲧⲏⲙ (meaning?); tr, *straighten, compel*: Deu 23 16 B(S ⲙⲟⲩⲕϩ), Ps 105 42 B(S = Gk), Lam 1 5 B(F ⲗⲱϫ), 1 Thes 3 4 B(SF = Gk) θλ., Nu 22 25 B(S ⲗⲟϫⲗϫ) ἀποθλ., Lev 22 24 B(S ϭⲟⲟⲃ) ‎؎, Ps 17 39 B(S ⲗⲱϫϩ), Mic 7 2 SB(A ⲗⲁϫⲗⲉϫ), Zeph 1 17 SB(A ϩϫϩϫ-) ἐκθλ., Lu 8 42 SB συνθλ. prob; Jud 16 16 S στενοχ., Va 57 103 B στενοχωρίαν ποιεῖν; C 89 14 B ⲥⲉϩ. ⲙⲙⲟⲓ for debt (S ib 99 132 = Gk) ἐνοχλεῖν, Dan 3 50 B παρενοχ.; Nu 29 7 B(S ⲑⲙⲕⲟ) κακοῦν; Lu 19 43 B(S ⲱⲧⲡ ⲉⲣⲟⲅⲡ) συνέχειν; Ez 22 29 B ἐκπιέζειν; PS 360 S ⲛⲥⲉϩⲉϫϩⲱϫⲟⲩ ⲛⲥⲉⲑⲗⲓⲃⲉ ⲙⲙⲟⲟⲩ, ShR 2 3 34 S ϩⲁ. ⲙⲡⲉⲩϣⲡϩ, Pcod 28 S ⲁⲩϩⲉϫϩⲱϫⲧ F ϩⲉϫ[ⲱ]ϫⲉⲛ by questioning, Mus 40 272 S ⲉⲧϩ. ⲙⲡⲉⲡ̄ⲛ̄ⲁ̄ ⲉⲧⲟⲩⲁⲁⲃ (cf Eph 4 30 λυπεῖ), BAp 77 S ⲙⲡⲣϩϫϩⲱϫ (sc debtor), C 43 227 B possessed woman fell upon them ⲁⲥϩ. ⲙⲙⲟⲟⲩ, C 99 149 S ⲉⲧϩ. ⲙⲙⲟϥ ⲟⲩⲧⲱϣ ⲙⲛϩⲟ ⲥⲛⲧⲉ = C 89 75 B.

With following preposition. c ⲉ-: Is 49 20† B(sic l, S ϭⲏⲅ) στενός dat; MIF 9 85 S'ⲁⲡⲉⲙⲛⲏϣⲉ ϩ. ⲙⲙⲟϥ ⲉⲛⲁⲩ ⲉⲣⲟϥ, Win 55 Sᵃ ⲙⲡⲣϩⲁϫϩ(ϫ) ⲉⲣⲟⲓ for thou givest to all; ⲉϩⲟⲩⲛ, ⲉϩ. ⲉ-: Nu 22 25 B (S ⲗⲱϫϩ) προσθλ. πρός; c ⲉϩⲟⲩⲛ ⲉϫⲡ- S: Mor 18 35 ⲉⲧϩ.† ⲉϩ. ⲉϫⲛⲁⲙⲙⲁⲧⲟⲓ eager to be martyred; c ⲉϩⲣⲏⲓ ⲉϫⲉⲛ- B: 2 Cor 1 6 (S = Gk) θλ. ὑπέρ; c ⲛⲧⲉⲛ- B: CDan 85 ⲁϥϩ. ⲛⲧⲟⲧⲟⲩ & thought to flee, De V 2 46 ⲁⲩϩ. ⲡⲧⲟⲧⲥ ⲛϥⲙⲉⲧⲁⲑⲟⲟⲩⲙ; c ϩⲁ-, ϩⲁ-: ClPr 54 35 S ⲉⲧⲉⲧⲡ.† ϩⲁⲟⲃⲁⲃⲉⲥ ⲛⲧⲡⲉ = EW 153 B στενοχ. dat; c ⲉⲃⲟⲗ ϩⲁ- B: Deu 15 7 (var ϣⲑⲁⲙ ⲉⲃ. ϩⲁ-, S ϩⲱϫⲡ ⲉ-) συσφίγγειν ἀπό; c ϩⲛ-, ϩⲉⲛ-: 2 Cor 4 8 B(S = Gk) θλ. ἐν, Si 34 15 S ϩ. ⲧⲉⲕϭⲓϫ (var ϩⲉϫϫ ⲉ-) συνθλ. ἐν; 2 Cor 6 12 S(B ⲛϩⲣⲏⲓ ϩ.) στενοχ. ἐν; PS 178 S ⲡⲉⲥϩⲱϫ ⲡⲧⲁⲩϩⲉϫϩⲱϫⲥ ⲛϩⲏⲧⲟⲩ, ShViK 9593 S ⲛⲡⲉⲡⲟⲩⲁ ⲡⲟⲩⲁ ϩⲟϫϩ(ϫ ϩ)ⲙⲡⲉⲧϥⲙⲉ-

ⲉⲅⲉ ⲉⲣⲟϥ, R 1 2 11 S ⲁⲡⲉⲥⲡⲏⲅ ϩ. ϩⲛⲧⲁϭⲃⲉⲥ, Miss 4
232 S ⲥⲉϩ.† ϩⲛⲧⲉⲭⲣⲓⲁ ⲡⲧⲉⲅϩⲃϭⲱ, ManiK 52 A² ⲉⲅ-
ϩⲉⲭϩⲁⲭⲧϩⲛⲟⲩⲙⲣⲣⲉ, BSM 90 B ⲡⲓϩⲛⲕⲓ ϩ.† ϩⲉⲛⲡⲓϣ-
ⲧⲉⲕⲟ = BMis 181 S ⲣ ϭⲣⲱϭ; ϩⲣⲁⲓ ϩⲛ-, ⲛϭ. ϭ.:
2 Cor 6 12 B ut sup; R 1 5 51 S spirit ϩ. ϩ. ⲡⲣⲏⲧⲩ (var
Mor 32 26 Sᶠ ⲁϥϩ. ϩⲓⲡⲉϥⲡ̄ⲛ̄ⲁ̄); c ϩⲓⲧⲛ-: Miss 4
640 S ⲁϥϩ. ϩ. ⲛⲃⲁⲥⲁⲛⲟⲥ, DeV 2 191 B ⲁϩϩ. ϩ. ⲫⲗⲓⲏⲓⲡ
ⲙⲡⲓⲥⲧⲁⲅⲣⲟⲥ; ⲉⲃⲟⲗ ϩ.: ShC 73 125 S ⲉⲣⲉⲡⲛ̄ⲛ̄ ⲡⲁϩ.
ⲉϩ̄. ϩⲓⲧⲟⲟⲧⲟⲩ.

—— nn m, *distress, need*: Ps 31 7 B(S = Gk), Is
28 10 B(S do), Ro 2 9 B(SF do) θλῖψις, Ex 3 9 SB,
Deu 26 7 B(S = Gk) θλιμμός; Si 10 27 S, 2 Cor 12
10 B(S ⲗⲱⲭϩ, F ⲗⲱⲭ) στενοχωρία, C 89 169 B ⲡⲓϩ.
of road στένος, RNC 23 S ⲟⲩⲛⲟ[ϭ … ⲡ]ϩ. ϩⲙⲛ[ⲛⲓ
στένωσις; PS 180 S ⲡϩ. ⲛⲧⲉ ⲡⲉⲭⲁⲟⲥ, ShP 131⁷ 34
S ⲡϩ. ⲛⲧⲉϩⲓⲛ ⲉⲧϭⲏⲅ, ShMIF 23 10 S ⲡϩ. ⲙⲡϭⲓⲥⲉ
that body suffered, ShBor 233 245 S ⲟⲩϩ. ⲉⲧⲃⲉⲧⲉϥ-
ⲭⲣⲓⲁ, Gu 90 Sᶠ save from ⲡϩ. (of hunger), Pcod 8
S after Adam's fall ⲡⲉⲥⲧⲟⲓⲭⲉⲓⲟⲛ…ϣⲱⲡⲉ ⲡⲁϥ ϩ.,
BMis 546 S scarce could one man descend into pit
ϩⲛⲟⲩϩ., Rec 6 174 B ⲡϩ.…ⲉⲑⲃⲉⲡⲓⲉⲣⲕⲟ = BMar 210
S ⲡϭⲓⲥⲉ, DeV 1 36 B ⲡϩ. ⲙⲡⲓϣⲧⲉⲕⲟ, C 43 55 B ⲡϩ.
ⲙⲡⲓϣⲉⲙⲙⲉⲣϭ; C 100 295 S ⲑⲗⲓⲯⲓⲥ, ϩ. ⲡϩⲏⲧ = C
89 179 B ⲙⲕⲁϩ ⲛϩ., J 68 26 Sᵃ ⲡⲉⲓⲣⲟⲙⲡⲉ ⲡϩⲁⲭⲣ(ⲝ).
  Cf ϩⲟⲝⲝ.

ϩⲟⲝⲝ, ϩⲉⲝⲝ S, ϩⲁⲝⲝ, ϩⲝⲝ A v ϩⲟⲝϩ.

ϩⲱⲝϭ A v ϩⲱⲝⲡ s f.

ϩⲁϭⲉ, ϩⲁⲁϭⲉ S, ϩⲁϫⲓ B nn m, *snare*: Pro 6 5 S
(cit BAp 148 ϩⲁⲁ., A ⲁⲗⲟⲅ)B, 1 Cor 7 35 B(S ⲉⲗⲱ)
βρόχος; Eccl 7 27 S(var cit Mor 43 254 ϭⲟⲣϭⲥ) δεσμός; TEuch 2 475 B ⲡⲓϩ. of devil خانق; P 44 88 S
ϩⲉⲛϩⲟⲥⲉ اشراك; PS 100 S ⲛϭⲟⲣϭⲥ, ⲛϩ., Mor 43 222
S ⲡϩ. ⲙⲡⲙⲙⲣⲣⲉ ⲙⲡⲙⲟⲩ, ib 28 44 S ⲁⲓⲥⲉⲛ ⲟⲩⲟⲡ
ⲡⲓⲙ ϩⲁⲡⲁϩ., MG 25 146 B eagle soaring escapes
ⲫⲁϣ, if descends is taken in ⲡⲓϩ., O'Leary Th 25 B
ⲁϥϩⲉⲓ ϩⲉⲛⲡⲓϩ.; ⲙⲉⲧϩ. B: TRit 426 ϯⲙ. ⲛⲧⲉ
ϯⲉⲡⲓⲑⲩⲙⲓⲁ اختناق.
  In place-names (this word ?): ϩⲁϭⲉ, ⲧⲙⲟⲩ ⲛϩ.,
ⲧⲟⲟⲩ ⲛϩ., ⲧⲱⲣⲱ ⲛϩ. (LMis 47, WS 180 n), ϩⲁⲁϭⲉ
(P 129¹⁵ 24).

ϩⲏϭⲉ S vb intr, *be disturbed, concerned*: Ez 2 6
ϣⲧⲟⲣⲧⲣ ⲟⲩⲧⲉ ϩ. (B ⲧⲱⲙⲧ) ἐξιστάναι; Mk 12 14 (var
ⲣⲟⲟⲩϣ ϩⲁ-, B = Gk) μέλειν; Mor 40 19 when he saw

me ⲉⲓϩ. ⲡⲁϩⲣⲁϥ (var *ib* 39 26 Sᶠ ⲁⲓⲉⲣ ϩⲁⲧⲉ) = C 43
49 B ⲉⲓⲥⲑⲉⲣⲧⲉⲣ.

ϩⲱϭⲃ, -ϭϥ, -ⲕⲙ S, -ϭⲙⲉ A², ϩⲟϭⲉϥ F, ϩⲉϭⲃ-,
ϩⲉϭⲙ-, ϩⲟϭⲃ S, -ϭⲡϩ B, ϩⲟϭⲃ†, -ϥ† S, p c ϩⲁϭⲃ-
SA, ϩⲁϭⲉⲃ- F vb I intr, *wither, fade, expire*: Job 24
24 (B ⲗⲱⲙ), Ja 1 11 (B do) μαραίνειν, 1 Pet 1 4 neg
(B ⲁⲧⲗ.) ἀμάραντος; Mt 24 12 v ⲱϭⲃ ψύχειν, Ez 21 7
(B ⲗ.) ἐκψ.; Mk 4 6 (B = Gk) καυματίζειν; Bor 253
270 ⲧⲗⲩⲡⲏ ⲡⲧⲁϭ. ⲡϩⲏⲧ σβεννύναι; Ps 68 3 F(Pcod
Mor, SB ϩⲱⲗ) βραγχιάζειν; PS 107 ⲁⲧⲁϭⲟⲙ ⲧⲁⲕⲟ…
ⲁⲧⲁⲣⲅⲗⲏ ϩⲱⲕⲙ, BG 120 ⲁϭ. ⲁⲥⲡⲕⲟⲧⲕ ⲉⲃⲟⲗ ϩⲛⲧⲁϩ-
ϣⲉ, ShBM 194 3 ⲉⲛϩ. as grass without water, ShBM
Or 8800 1 ⲁϭ. ⲛϭⲓ ⲧⲉⲕⲥⲙⲏ ⲁⲥⲱϩⲙ, Mor 43 147 lips
ϩ. ϩⲓⲧⲙⲡⲕⲁⲩⲥⲱⲙ ⲁⲩⲱ ⲁⲩϣⲱⲕϩ, R 2 1 23 Arius ⲁϥϩ.
ϩⲁⲑⲏ ⲡⲧⲉϥⲟⲩⲛⲟⲩ (cf in ϣⲟⲩⲉ qual), ManiP 133 A²
ⲛⲕⲗⲟⲙ…ⲙⲁⲩϩ.; qual: ShA 1 466 ⲙⲟⲗⲟⲭⲏ ⲉⲧϩ.
ϩⲙⲡⲕⲁⲩⲙⲁ (cf Job above), ROC 7 143 breasts ϩ. ⲉⲧ-
ϩⲉⲧⲁⲥⲕⲛⲥⲓⲥ, HM 1 96 martyr to judge ⲡⲉⲕⲣⲁⲡ ϩⲟϭϥ.

II tr, *wither, destroy*: Job 15 30 (B ⲗ.) μαρ., Mor
18 147 ⲉⲓⲙⲁϩⲉϩⲃ ⲧⲁⲯⲩⲭⲏ ϩⲣⲁⲓ ϩⲓⲧⲁⲗⲩⲡⲏ ⲕⲁⲧⲁⲙ.;
Si 43 23 ϩⲉϭⲙ- ἀποσβ.; Ez 26 12 B καθαιρεῖν; ClPr
47 80 had Sarah grieved at Isaac's sacrifice ⲛⲥϭ. ⲡⲧⲉ-
ⲟⲩⲥⲓⲁ, BMOr 6201 B 296 not weakened by age ⲙⲉ-
ⲣⲉⲡⲉϩⲟⲟⲉⲓϣ (sic) ϩⲟϭⲃⲟⲩ.

p c ϩ.ⲥⲙⲏ: Ex 4 10 SA(var Cl ϩⲛⲙ, B ϣⲟⲙ) ἰσχνόφωνος; Is 33 19 SF(B as Gk) βαθύφωνος.
  —— nn m, *feebleness*: Eccl 12 4 ἀσθένεια; P 131¹
32 ⲡϩ. ⲡⲧⲉⲡⲣⲱ κρυερός.
  ⲁⲧϩ., *unfading*: Br 240 ⲡⲟⲩⲟⲉⲓⲛ ⲛⲁⲧⲧⲁⲕⲟ ⲡⲁ.,
Mich 550 24 ⲧⲣⲓⲁⲥ … ⲉⲡⲁ., Ep 79 ⲁⲩⲣⲁϣⲉ ⲡⲁ. ⲧⲁ-
ϭⲟⲡ, ManiP 1 A² ⲡⲥⲁⲓⲉ ⲡⲁ.
  Cf ⲱϭⲃ (confusion ?).

ϩⲓϭⲗⲱ v ϭⲗⲱ.

ϩⲱϭⲙ, -ⲕⲙ v ϩⲱϭⲃ.

ϩⲁϭⲓⲛⲓ S, ⲁϭⲓⲛ B nn m, *scented herb, mint*: P 46
152 S ⲡϩ. نعنع, HCons 2 B ⲍ̄ ⲙⲙⲓⲛⲓ ⲡⲁ. = اوراق خفر;
TEuch 1 463 B ⲡⲭⲁⲓ ⲡⲟⲩⲟϥ ⲡⲉⲙⲡⲓⲁ. ; ϩ. ⲡ-
ⲥⲧⲟⲓ, ⲁ. ⲛⲥⲑ.: Mt 23 23 SB, Lu 11 42 SB ἡδύοσμον;
P 43 58 S ⲡⲁϭⲓⲛ ⲥⲧⲟⲓ, K 179 B ⲁϣⲓⲛⲥⲑ. ريحان; AJSL
46 247 S ⲟⲩϩⲁⲕⲓⲛ ⲡⲥ. ⲡ̄ⲁⲁϥ ⲡⲟⲩⲕⲗⲟⲙ, KroppJ 50
S recipe ϩⲁϭⲓⲝ(ⲗ-ⲓⲛ) ⲡⲝⲏϭⲉ ϩⲁϭⲓⲛ ⲡⲉϭⲟⲟϭⲉ. With
ϩ. ⲡⲥ. cf ? Diosc ἡδύοσμον · μακιθῶ (var -ηθό).

(ϩⲱϭⲡ), ϩⲟϭⲡϩ B v ϩⲱϭⲃ.

ϫ

ϫ, 30th (or 31st, v Hall pll 28, 29, MR 4 130, RE 14 147 n) letter of alphabet, called ϫⲁⲛϫⲓⲁ (K 1, Stern p 7), ϫⲉⲛϫⲉ (ib p 418), جَنجا (Lab ⲡⲓϧⲟϫⲓⲧ ⲛⲧⲱⲣⲧⲉⲣ 4, Rec 12 38), اَجَنجا (Stern lc). Derived from hierogl ṯ(S, B ϭ), as ϫⲓ, ϫⲏⲙⲉ, ϣϫⲏⲛ; or ḏ(SB), as ϫⲟⲓ, ⲟⲩϫⲁⲓ, ϧⲙⲝ; or g(B, S ϭ), as ϫⲱⲃⲓ, ⲥⲟϫⲉⲛ, ϭⲗⲟϫ; or k(B, S ϭ), as ⲃⲏϫ, ϭⲱϫⲓ, ⲥⲱⲗϫ; or ḳ(B, S ϭ), as ⲕϫⲓ, ϫⲓϫⲓ. In O AZ 21 93 ff dem ⳨ (or ⲓ⳨) = ϫ thrice, ϫ = ϫ once (98 16), ϭ = ϫ & ϣ often; in P Mimaut (PGM 1 48, 60) ⲓ⳨ mostly, ϫ once (670), ϭ = ϣ; in Hor, PMich 6131 & DM glosses ⳨. Replaced by ϭ, as ⲗⲟϭⲗⲉϭ, ⲛⲟϭⳠ (Bodl P c 11), ⲱⲣϭ (JKP 2 160), ϭⲡⲟⳠ (Bodl P f 24), ϭⲓϭ (J & C 98), ϧⲡⲟϭ-ⲡⲉϭ; B(rare) ⲁⲓϭⲉⲣⲟⲕ (C 43 233); converse, as ⲙⲁⲛϫⲁⲗⲉ, ⲡⲁϫ (MR 5 55), ϫⲣⲟⲟⲙⲡⲉ (Gu 19), ϫⲁⲣ-ϫⲉⲣ (Mt 24 51), ϧⲱⲣϫ (Mor 31 249). Replaces ⲧϣ, as ⲁϫⲉⲩ (AZ 71 87 A), ⲡⲉϫⲏⲕ (PS 53), ϫⲉ (Kr 81), ϫⲟⲩϫⲙⲏⲛ (ib 154), ϫⲏⲛ (Jo 20 15 A²), ⲡⲁϫⲉⲗⲉⲉⲧ (Mani P 150 A²), ϫⲃⲓⲱ (ib 174), ϫⲱϣⲓ (Eccl 5 8 F), ϫⲡⲓⲟ, ϫⲡⲟ, ϫⲏⲗⲓ (Lam 2 10 F), ϫⲟⲅⲓⲁ (JEA 11 246 F), ϫⲉⲡϧⲱⲣ (Bristol Mus H 4124), ϫⲡⲃⲓⲕⲧⲱⲣ (P 130¹ 139); converse, as ⲡⲉⲧϣⲁϥ (AZ 23 100 O), ⲧϣⲏⲙⲉ (CO 165), ⲧϣⲛⲱⲟⲩ (ἅλων P 44 62); ⲧϣ for ⲧϫ, as ⲉⲧϣⲱⲗⲉ (ib 80), ⲧϣⲛⲡⲉⲡⲱⲣ (Kr 125); converse, as ⲧϫⲏⲅⲉ (Mor 31 204). Replaces ⲧϫ, as ⲁϫⲓ (B Hom 97), ϫⲉⲡⲉⲡⲱⲣ (Mt 24 17), ϫⲕⲱⲟⲩ (PLond 4 pass), ⲉϫⲁⲥⲓ (Is 34 13 F), ⲙⲛϫⲁϫⲉ (Mic 7 10 A); converse, as ⲡⲉⲧϫⲉ (Pcod Mor 17), ⲉⲧϫⲏⲅ (Mani P 42 A²). Replaces ϣ after ⲧ, as ϫⲟⲩⲧϫⲁⲗⲧⲉ (Mor 32 23), ⲙⲛⲧϫⲉⲙⲟ (Kr 102), ⲧϫⲁⲧⲥ (Ryl 343), ⲁⲧϫⲏⲗⲓ (Lam 1 20 F), ⲧϫⲓⲡⲉⲗⲁ (Σινελαεύς Kr 113); converse, as ⲙⲉⲧϣϥⲓⲛⲧ (1 Tim 2 9 B), ⲉⲧϣⲱⲗⲉ (P 44 80), cf My 39 ⲉⲧϭⲓⲛ = ⲉϫⲓⲛ. Replaced by ϣ, as ϣⲱϫⲡ (ϣⲱⲡϣ Nu 6 19), ⲙⲁⲁϣⲉ (Ac 7 57), ϣⲟϣⲡⲉ (ib 27 12), ϣⲉϭⲉ (P 44 67), ϣⲡⲁ (Cant 6 5 F); converse, as ⲡⲟⲩϫⲉ (Ge 32 25), ϫⲙⲟⲅⲉ (P 43 65). Varies with ⲧ, as ⲁⲣⲏⲧⲉ (Deu 30 13 Budge), ⲡⲟⲧⲉ (ib 22 19), ϯϭⲉ-ϫⲓϫⲓ, ⲙⲓⲧⲱⲗ-ⲙⲉϫⲧⲱⲗ (v p 214 b), ⲕⲁⲧⲟⲧⲉ-ⲕⲁϫⲱϫ (Καθύτος, Κατύτις BM 1075, AZ 28 1), ϣⲗⲓⲧ-ϣⲗⲓϫ (p 563 a), ϧⲟⲗⲟⲕⲟⲧⲧⲓⲛⲟⲥ-ⲉⲗⲉⲕⲟϫⲓⲛⲟⲥ (Amer J Philol 56 110), ϧⲟⲧⲥⲓ, ϧⲟϫⲥⲓ (p 627 b); or ⲑ, as ⲑⲟⲕⲧⲉⲕ-ϫⲟⲕϫⲕ (Lev 19 28), ⲟⲣⲛⲓϫⲓ (ὀρνίθιον? Pro 24 66). Replaces ⲧ, as ⲁⲡⲁⲗⲗⲁϫⲓⲛ (-αγῆναι Va 57 64), ⲁⲡⲧⲓⲗⲉϫⲉ (CO 171), ⲉϫⲉⲡⲡⲉⲧⲟ (ἐγένετο Pap penes Maggs Bros 1937), ⲑⲁⲣⲁⲡϫⲓⲃⲓⲛ (Montp 146, cf K 190), ϫⲓⲙⲁ (γίμελ Lam 1 3 B, ib 2 3 ⲅⲓⲙⲁ); or ⲕ, as ⲧⲱϫ (Saq 1909 p 101), ⲑⲟⲩⲣⲁϫⲓ-ⲑⲟⲣⲁϭⲓ (θωράκιον K 120, TEuch 1 175), Σαρραϫηνος (Rev Épigr 1913 151); converse: BMis 485 ⲕⲛⲁⲁⲩ; or

ⲕⲥ(ⳅ), as ⲃⲓⲛⲁϫ (p 41 b), ⲧⲁϫⲓⲧⲛ (PLond 4 435 n); or ⳅ in ⲁⲥⲡⲁϫⲉ (Hall 83); Varies with ⳍ AA²F, rarely S (archaic), too often to justify explanation proposed p 516 a, q v, adding ⲉϫⲙⲁⲗⲱⲥⲓⲁ (Lam 2 14 F), ⲧⲉϫⲛⲓⲧⲏⲥ (Cant 7 2 F) & ⲥⲁϫⲛⲓ, ϫⲓ, ⲉϫⲱ (O Beatty's Isaiah xi), ⲣⲉϫⲡⲁⲩ (JEA 11 245 F), Πεσχαλ, -ϫⲁⲗ (BM 1075), Ταρούχις cf ⲧⲁⲣⲣⲟⲩϫ (WS 175); also ? names as Πχώωρ, Πχόχ (POxy 2058), Χεκούλ (ib 2037) & f Χενοννῶφρις (var Σεν- for Τσεν-), Χενψόις (var do), cf sim ϫ(ⲉ)ⲛ- above. Transcribed in Gk by τζ, as Πτζωτζ (var -ωτς), Τζιτζοι (Preisigke, var Τζιτσοι, cf MG 25 399 ϫⲓϭⲱⲓ), Τσεκλουτζ (ib, var -κλουτς, -κρουχ), Πετζρωτζ (Ryl 149), ουτζαι, τζεν- (CMSS 59), κουτζι, τζομ (MR 5 41, 2 57), σατζι, τζωπ (EW 86); or τσ, as κοντσου-ⲕⲟⲩⲛϫⲟⲩ q v, τσαερⲃⲏⲛⲓⲥ cf ϫⲁⲣϫⲉⲣⲃⲏⲛⲉ (Hall 113, 38); or σ, as σισόη (ϫⲓϫⲱⲓ Lev 19 27); or γχ in Ἀρουώγχιος-ϧⲉⲣⲟⲩϫ (BM 1028); or transcribes τι ⲕⲉⲣⲱⲛϫⲓ (BM 1252, cf ⲕⲉⲣⲟⲡⲧⲥⲓ Kr 72, Κεροντζι Wess 10 157), ⲁⲡⲟⲕⲣⲁϫⲱⲡ-Ἀρποκρατίων (PSBA 29 295). Transcribes Ar ج, as ϥⲁⲣⲁϫ جَرّ (BM 618), ⲥⲉⲛϫⲁⲣ جَنجار (L Al xvii, cf ⲥⲓⲛϭⲁⲣ AZ 23 118), ⲉⲥⲡⲛⲓⲧⲉϫ اِسفيداج (ib), ϭⲁⲗⲓϫ خَليج (BSM xi), ⲉⲙϫⲉⲁ مَجد (BM 726), ϫⲉⲡⲉⲗ جَبل (EW 234 ff); transcribed by ج, as ⲁⲡϫⲓϫ الجيج, ⲡⲉⲣⲛⲟⲩϫ برنوج, ⲡϫⲉⲗⲃⲁϧ جلفة, ⲙⲁⲣ-ϫⲱϫⲉ برجوج (p 184 a); or ش (cf B ϭ), as ⲡⲉⲗϫⲱⲃ بلشوم, ⲧⲙϫⲓⲣ دمشير (? Τεμσιρ Wess 3 133) ϫⲉⲗϥⲁⲩ, ϫⲱⲱⲣⲉ شورى (Synax 1 323 ult), ϫⲕⲱⲟⲩ (for ⲧϫ.) شنشيف; or ϫⲉⲃⲣⲟ شبرا, ϫⲏⲙⲉ شامة, ϫⲡϫⲏⲃ اشقوا, (ⲧ)ϫⲁⲁⲡⲉ صان, ϫⲓⲣ صير; or ⲥ (rare): ϫⲉⲙⲡⲟⲩϯ سمنود, or ص, as ϯⲗⲟϫ دلاص, ϫⲓⲣ صير.

On pronunciation of ϫ v Worrell Coptic Sounds, esp 21, 24, 107-9, 131-8.

ϫⲁ F   v ϫⲟ 1° & 2°.

ϫⲁⲓ B vb intr, meaning doubtful: ROC 25 241 ⲧⲉⲕϭⲁⲏ ϫⲁϫ. ⲙⲫⲣⲏϯ ⲛⲧⲓⲉϫⲓ ἥκειν; as nn m (same?): HL 87 on Mt 9 11 ⲛⲁⲩϫⲉⲙ ⲁⲣⲓⲕⲓ ⲁⲛ ⲉⲡⲓϫ. (sic), ⲉⲃⲏⲗ ϫⲉϫⲉⲡⲟⲩⲙⲉⲑⲙⲏⲓ ⲁϥⲟⲩⲱⲙ ⲟⲩⲟϩ ⲁϥⲥⲱ ⲟⲩⲕ ἂν ἐπὶ ἄρτου καὶ ὕδατος ἐπιλαμβάνοντο, ἀλλά (var εἰ μή).

ϫⲁⲓ AA²F   v ϫⲟⲓ ship,   AF   v ϫⲟⲉ wall.

ϫⲁ(ⲉ)ⲓⲉ SAA², ϫⲁⲉ S, ϫⲁ(ⲓ)ⲏ S^fF nn m, desert (B ϣⲁϥⲉ): Ex 19 1 (var ⲧⲟⲟⲩ), Job 1 19, Hos 2 3 A, Mt 14 15 (F = Gk), Jo 11 54 A²(S = Gk) ἔρημος, Ps 101 6 -μικός, Mor 17 108 ⲡϫ. ⲙⲡⲣⲡⲉ -ⲙⲱⲥⲓ (cf 110 ⲡϣⲟⲣϣⲣ ⲉⲣ.); ShViK 9814 22 ϧⲓⲛ ⲙⲡϫ. opp ϧⲓⲛ

ⲙⲡⲣⲣⲟ, Faras 3 pl 69 ⲡⲉⲯⲁⲗⲙⲟⲥ ⲙⲡⲭⲁⲉ (sc Ps 90), Bodl Hunt 3 160 ⲧⲕⲩⲣⲓⲁⲕⲏ ⲙⲡⲭ. = الأحد الأول الصوم, BIF 13 108 ⲟⲩⲭ. ⲉϥⲣⲟⲥⲉ = MG 25 295 B ⲱ., CO 227 ⲡⲧⲟⲡⲟⲥ ⲟⲩⲭ. ⲡⲉ, Ep 84 ⲡⲧⲟⲡⲟⲥ ⲛⲁⲡⲁ ⲓⲱⲁⲛⲛⲏⲥ ⲙⲡⲭ., P 68 1 ⲡⲭ. ⲛⲁⲡⲁ ϣⲉⲛⲟⲩⲧⲉ, Lant 77 sim, BMar 129 ⲙⲟⲟϣⲉ ⲉϩⲟⲩⲛ ⲉⲙⲡⲭ., ib 128 sim ϩⲙⲡⲭⲧⲧⲟⲟⲩ, Miss 4 732 ⲃⲱⲕ ⲉϩⲣⲁⲓ ⲉⲡⲭ.; JKP 2 134 Sf ⲃⲱⲕ ⲉϩⲟⲩⲛ (ⲉ)ⲡⲉⲓⲭⲁⲛ, Z 551 ⲉⲓ ⲉⲃⲟⲗ ϩⲓⲡⲭ. come forth from, BMar 205 ⲡⲭ. ⲉⲧⲣⲓⲣⲟⲩⲛ = Rec 6 168 B ϣ. ⲉⲧⲥⲁⲃ. (cf ib 213 ⲉⲣⲏⲙⲟⲥ ⲉⲧⲣ.);   f: Hos 13 15 A(sic MS) ⲉⲣ.; as adj: Ps 62 1 ⲉⲣ.; Hall 87 ⲧⲟⲡⲟⲥ ⲛⲭ.; ⲙⲁ ⲛⲭ.: Si 9 7, Mal 1 4 A(B ⲱ.) ⲉⲣ., Mt 14 13 (B ⲙⲁ ⲛϣ., F ⲙⲉ ⲡⲉⲣⲏⲙⲟⲥ) ⲉⲣ. τόπος; BMar 213 ⲙ. ⲛⲡⲧⲉⲣⲏⲙⲟⲥ ⲉⲧⲣⲓⲣⲟⲩⲛ = Rec 6 178 B ⲙⲁ ⲡϣⲱⲡⲓ ⲉⲧⲃⲉⲡⲛⲓϣ., Ep 162 9 withdraw to ⲟⲩⲙ. ⲏ ⲛⲣⲟⲩⲙⲟⲛⲁⲥⲧⲏⲣⲓⲟⲛ, J 79 35 monastery is ⲟⲩⲙ. & hath need of such vows (sc oblates), Mor 24 16 F ⲭⲓⲧⲕ ⲉⲟⲩⲙⲁ ⲛϣⲁⲓⲛ; ϩⲓⲡⲭ.: Ps 54 7 (B ϩⲓⲡϣ.), Jo 3 14 A²(S ⲉⲣ.) ἐν τῇ ἐρ.; Mani P A² ⲕⲁⲁⲧ ⲡⲥⲱⲕ ϩ.; ϩⲓⲡⲙⲭ.: Ps 62 tit(B ϩⲓ-), Lu 3 4 (var ⲉⲣ., B do) ἐν τῇ ἐρ.; Pcod 37 Christian ⲉϥⲟϩⲏϩ ϩⲓⲡⲭ. (var ϩⲓⲡⲧⲟⲩⲉⲓⲏ); ϩⲣⲁⲓ ϩⲙ-: Mt 3 1 (B do) ἐν.

ⲙⲁⲓⲭ., *loving desert, solitude*: Miss 4 815 Chrysostom's ἀσκητικόν to Demetrius ⲉⲛⲭ. (cf PG 47 393 μονάζοντα ἀσκητήν).

ⲙⲛⲧⲭ., *desolation*: Mor 17 79 ἐρήμωσις.

ⲕⲱ ⲛⲭ., *make desert*: Ps 106 33 τιθέναι εἰς ἐρ., Is 13 9 ἐρ. τιθ.

ϯ ⲛⲭ., sim: Jer 41 22 (B diff) ἐρ. διδόναι.

ϣⲱⲡⲉ ⲛⲭ., *become desert*: Is 5 9 (BF ⲉⲛϣⲱϥ) εἰς ἐρ. εἶναι; LAl 12 ⲁⲡⲁⲙⲁ ⲡⲥⲱ ϣ. ⲛⲭⲁⲉ.

ⲣ ⲭ., *be desert, abandoned*: Lev 26 22 (B ϣⲱⲡⲓ ⲉⲩϣⲏⲛ), Is 33 8 SF(B ϣⲱϥ), Lu 11 17 (B do) ἐρημοῦν, Ex 23 29 ἔρημος γίνεσθαι, Ps 72 19 (B ϣⲱⲡⲓ ϩⲓⲛϣⲁϥⲉ) εἰς ἐρήμωσιν γίν.; Jer 39 43 (B as Gk) ἄβατος εἶναι *desertus esse*; ShA 2 137 ⲡⲉⲧⲓⲣⲡⲛⲓϩⲉ ⲡⲧⲁ ⲣ., El 86 A ⲡⲡⲉⲕⲁϩ ⲣ., WTh 184 corpse ⲡⲁⲣ. ⲙⲁⲅⲁⲁϥ ϩⲙⲡⲙⲁ ⲉⲧⲙⲙⲁⲩ till kinsmen fetch it;   c ⲉ-, to: ShA 2 331 ⲛⲁⲣ. ⲉⲡⲉⲡⲛ̅ⲁ̅ ⲉⲧⲟⲩⲁⲁⲃ; *dat commodi*: Deu 7 22 (B Gk om ⲉ-) ⲉⲣ. γίν.; c ⲉⲃⲟⲗ ϩⲛ-: BM 187 147 ⲙⲁⲣⲉⲡⲉⲧⲟⲣⲡ ϩⲛⲧⲁⲡⲏ ⲙⲡⲃⲓⲟⲥ ⲣ. ⲉⲃ. ϩⲛ-ⲡⲉⲧⲣⲟⲟϣ, Tri 296 let him not ⲣ. ⲉⲃ. ϩⲛⲡⲉⲕⲭⲁⲣⲓⲥⲙⲁ;   tr: Ps 78 7 (B ϣⲱϥ tr), Sa 5 24 ἐρημοῦν, Zeph 3 6 A(B do) ἐξερ., Ap 17 16 (B do) ἠρημωμένον ποιεῖν; Jos 8 28 χῶμα (var βουνὸν) τιθέναι; C 99 236 devil ⲁϥⲣ ⲧⲟⲓⲕⲟⲩⲙⲉⲛⲏ ⲛⲭ.;   qual: Is 61 4 (B ϣⲁ.) ἔρημος; Miss 8 206 ⲕⲁⲥⲧⲣⲟⲛ ⲉϥⲟ ⲛⲭ.

As vb (?)S: Si 39 17 ⲟⲩⲙⲟⲟⲩ ⲉϥⲭ. ῥεῦμα ἀγροῦ (var ὑγροῦ); Ryl 340 reeds ⲛⲁⲧⲉⲧⲱ ⲛⲧⲭ. (ⲗ ⲧⲧⲟ ⲉⲧⲭ.). Cf ⲧⲟⲟⲩ, ϣⲱϥ(ϣⲁϥⲉ).

ⲭⲁⲉⲓⲟ A², ⲭⲁⲓⲉ-, ⲭⲁⲓⲟ∕ B   v ⲧⲥⲁⲉⲓⲟ.

ⲭⲁⲓⲟ S, ⲭⲁⲓⲁ F   v ⲧⲭⲁⲉⲓⲟ.

ⲭⲉ B nn m, *spathe* of date-palm: K 177 ⲡⲓⲭⲉ قلب (P 44 66 = ἐλάτη, v Schweinf *Ar Pfl* 229).

ⲭⲉ- SAA²BFO, ⲭ(ⲉ)- SAF, ⲛⲭⲉ- (rare) SBF (v sf), conjunction (from ⲭⲱ *say*), **a** apposition, *namely*: Jo 11 49 SA² ⲟⲩⲁ...ⲭⲉⲕⲁⲓⲫⲁⲥ (B ⲉⲡⲉϥⲣⲁⲛ-ⲡⲉ), Ac 16 12 S ⲟⲩⲡⲟⲗⲓⲥ ⲭⲉⲕⲟⲗⲟⲛⲓⲁ (B ⲛⲕ.), Ora 4 190 S ⲟⲩⲛⲧⲓϣ ⲭⲉⲡⲥⲓⲙ, Baouit 1 116 F ⲁⲡⲁⲕ ⲡⲓⲉⲗⲁ-ⲭⲓⲥⲧⲱⲥ ⲭⲉⲫⲓⲃⲁⲙⲱⲛ, C 43 166 B ⲫⲁⲓ ⲭⲉⲑⲉⲟⲇⲱⲣⲟⲥ, ShA 1 155 S ⲧⲉⲭⲛⲓⲧⲏⲥ ⲡⲉⲓⲟⲡⲉ ⲭⲉⲥⲱⲣⲉ, ShBM 253 58 S ⲡⲉⲡⲧⲁⲩϯ ⲡⲉⲓⲥⲭⲛⲓⲁ ⲉⲭⲟⲩⲩ ⲭⲉⲙⲟⲡⲁⲭⲟⲥ, Va 58 71 B leaving none alive ⲭⲉⲙⲟⲡⲁⲭⲟⲥ, BMis 166 S ⲡⲉⲓⲣⲱⲃ ⲭⲉⲓⲟⲩⲉ.   **b** after vbs call, name: Lu 1 13 SB ⲙⲟⲩⲧⲉ ⲉⲡⲉϥⲣⲁⲛ ⲭⲉⲓⲱϩⲁⲛⲛⲏⲥ, Cl 10 1 A ⲡⲉⲧⲟⲩⲙⲟⲩⲧⲉ ⲁⲣⲁϥ ⲭⲉ-, Ac 1 23 SB ϯ ⲣⲓⲛϥ ⲭⲉⲓⲟⲩ-ⲥⲧⲟⲥ.   **c** before direct statement or question: Ge 31 12 SB ⲡⲉⲭⲁϥ ⲛⲁⲓ ⲭⲉϥⲓ ⲓⲁⲧⲕ ⲉϩⲣⲁⲓ, Sa 2 13 S ϥϫⲱ ⲙⲙⲟⲥ ⲭⲉϯⲥⲟⲟⲩⲛ, Ap 5 12 SB ⲉϥϫⲱ ⲙⲙⲟⲥ...ⲭⲉ-ⲙⲡϣⲁ, ManiK 34 A² ϯϫⲱ ⲙⲙⲁⲥ...ⲭⲉⲟⲗ ⲡⲉⲧ[ⲛϩ]ⲏⲧ, PS 40 S ⲁⲩⲱϣ ⲉⲃⲟⲗ ... ⲭⲉⲡⲱⲥ ⲁⲡⲭ̅ⲥ̅ ⲟⲩⲧⲁϩⲛ ⲉⲃⲟⲗ, CO 61 S ϯⲣ ϣⲡⲏⲣⲉ ⲙⲙⲱⲧⲛ ⲭⲉⲙⲁⲧⲛⲉϣⲓⲡⲉ ϩⲏⲧϥ, Kr 48 S I swear ⲭⲛⲛⲉⲓϣ ⲡⲁⲣⲁⲃⲁ, AZ 21 100 O ⲁϩ-ϣⲉⲡⲥ ⲭⲉⲁⲣϩⲟ, (om after ⲡⲁⲭⲉ∕ in ManiK: 17, 64, 76, 184, not so ManiH, P); or indirect: Ac 10 28 S ⲉⲧⲙ-ⲉⲡ ⲗⲁⲁⲩ ⲛⲣⲱⲙⲉ ⲭⲉϥϫⲁϩⲙ (B ϫⲟⲥ ⲛϩⲗⲓ ⲭⲉ-), Cl 3 1 A ⲡⲉⲧⲥⲛϩ ⲭⲉⲁϥⲟⲅⲱⲙ, ib 24 4 A ⲙⲁⲣⲡϯ ϩⲧⲏⲛ ⲭⲉⲁⲣⲉⲡⲃⲣⲉ ϩⲱⲡⲉ ⲡⲉϩ ⲡϭⲉ (var ⲉⲧⲉϩⲁⲣⲉ-), Jer 22 30 SB ⲥϩⲁⲓ ⲙⲡⲉⲓⲣⲱⲙⲉ ⲭⲉⲟⲩⲣⲱⲙⲉⲡⲉ ⲉⲁⲩⲧⲥⲧⲟϥ ⲉ-ⲃⲟⲗ, PS 28 S ⲉⲓⲙⲉ ⲭⲉⲟⲩⲡⲉⲧⲉⲣⲉⲡ̅ⲭ̅ⲥ̅ ⲛⲁⲁⲁϥ, CO 82 S ϯⲟ ⲙⲙⲛⲧⲣⲉ ⲭⲉⲁⲡⲉⲥⲡⲧⲉ ϩⲟⲟϥ, ManiK 55 A² ⲡⲉⲓ ⲭⲉ-ⲁⲧⲣⲁⲛ ⲉ[ϥⲁⲡ]ⲉⲣⲥⲉ;   ὅτι: Ge 28 6 SB ⲁϥⲛⲁⲩ ⲭⲉ-ⲁⲉⲓⲥⲁⲁⲕ ⲥⲙⲟⲩ, Sa 8 17 S ⲁⲓⲙⲉⲕⲙⲟⲩⲕⲧ ⲭⲉⲟⲩⲡ ⲟⲩ-ⲱⲛϩ ϣⲟⲟⲡ, Cl 27 3 A ⲧⲏⲣ ⲡⲟⲓⲉ ⲭⲉⲡⲧⲏⲣϥ ϩⲏⲡ ⲁⲣⲁϥ, Eccl 7 8 F ⲭⲉⲧⲙⲓⲛⲧⲡⲟⲩⲭ ϣⲁⲥⲕⲓⲙ, S sim;   καθότι: Is 54 9 B ⲁϥⲭⲟⲥ ... ⲭⲉⲁⲓⲱⲣⲕ;   διότι: ib 3 9 SB.   **d** explicative, *because*: Ps 29 1 SB ϯⲛⲁ-ⲭⲁⲥⲧⲕ ⲭⲉⲁⲓϣⲟⲡ, Hos 7 13 SAB ⲟⲩⲟⲓ ⲛⲁⲩ ⲭⲉⲁⲩ-ⲡⲱⲧ, Lu 14 17 S ⲁⲙⲏⲓⲧⲛ ⲭⲉⲁⲡⲕⲁ ⲛⲓⲙ ⲥⲟⲃⲧⲉ, Jo 16 6 SA²B ⲁⲗⲗⲁ ⲭⲉⲁⲓⲭⲉ ⲡⲁⲓ all ὅτι, Ro 8 7 SB ⲭⲉⲡⲙⲉⲉⲩⲉ ⲅⲁⲣ (var om) ⲛⲧⲥⲁⲣⲝ ⲟⲩⲙⲛⲧϫⲁϫⲉⲧⲉ διότι; Mt 13 6 B ⲭⲉ ⲙⲙⲟⲛⲧⲟⲩ ⲛⲟⲩⲛⲓ (S ⲉⲃⲟⲗ ⲭⲉ) διὰ τό; PS 61 S ⲡⲟⲩϫⲙ ⲙⲙⲟⲓ ⲭⲉⲁⲓϣⲱⲧ, ShA 1 241 S Moses in foreign land ⲭⲉⲁϥⲁⲣⲁⲱ ϣⲓⲡⲉ ⲡⲥⲱϥ, El 140 S ⲉⲛⲁ-ⲧⲁⲕⲟ... ⲭⲉⲁⲛⲣ ⲁⲧⲥⲱⲧⲙ, CO 111 S thou mayest return ⲭⲉⲉⲛⲉⲛⲥⲩⲅⲭⲱⲣⲉⲓ ⲉⲗⲁⲅⲉ...ⲉⲡⲁⲣⲉⲗⲑⲉ ⲙⲙⲟⲛ, ib 343 S send them ⲭⲉⲧⲉⲭⲣⲓⲁⲧⲉ, J 20 123 S ⲁⲓⲥⲣⲁⲓ ϩⲁⲣⲟϥ ⲭⲉⲙⲉϥⲛⲟⲓ, Kr 40 S sim ⲭⲛⲃⲛⲟⲓ ⲁⲛ, C 43 4 B delayed to torture him ⲭⲉⲛⲉⲥⲱϥ ⲅⲁⲣⲡⲉ, GöttN '99 38 B he set about small cell ⲭⲉⲡⲧⲉϥⲕⲟⲧⲥ, Va 57 184 B remember him ⲭⲉⲛⲉϩⲟⲩ ⲁⲧϥⲓ (ⲗ ⲉⲧ-) ϥⲣⲱⲟⲩϣ ⲛⲡⲓ-ⲅⲣⲁⲫⲏ, ManiH 33 A² ⲡⲉⲓⲉⲧⲛ ⲭⲉⲁⲡⲉⲕⲃⲉⲗ ⲛⲟ, AZ 21 99 O ⲁⲙⲟⲩ ... ⲭⲉⲁⲡⲟⲕⲛⲉ ⲃⲁⲣⲃⲁⲣⲓⲱ, PGM 1 60 O ⲭⲉⲁⲡⲕ ⲓⲉⲑⲟⲣ.   **e** final, ἵνα (B mostly = Gk): Ge 18 21 (var ⲭⲉⲕⲁⲥ), Pro 2 12 SA ⲭⲁϥⲛⲁ-, Ap 20 3, Va

57 7 B ϫⲉϩⲓⲡⲁ; ὅπως: Jos 4 24, Ez 19 9 SB; καί:
Deu 10 2 (B subj); ὅτι: Ps 20 6 SB; εἰς τό: Eph 1
12 B(S ⲉⲧⲣⲉ-); παρὰ τό: Jer 9 11 B(var ἵνα, S ⲉ-) ut
(cf Job 24 8 S, Bar 3 28 SB);   vb inf: Ge 22 10 S
ϫⲉϥⲡⲁ- (B ⲉ-), Is 5 2 S ϫⲉⲉϥⲉ- B ϫⲉϥⲡⲁ-; PS 36 S
ϣⲁⲅⲱⲓⲕ ⲡⲧⲉⲩⲅⲣⲩⲗⲏ ϫⲉⲡⲡⲉⲅⲣ ⲁⲧⲥⲟⲗ, Br 42 S ϯ-
ⲡⲁⲧⲁⲗⲱⲧⲡ ... ϫⲉⲉⲧⲉⲡⲁⲥⲟⲩⲱⲡϥ, El 46 A ⲉⲉⲓⲥⲁⲡⲥ
ⲙⲙⲁϥ ϫⲁϥⲡⲁⲧⲟⲩϫⲁⲓ, ShA 2 50 S ⲟⲩⲥⲉⲣⲱⲃ...ϫⲉⲡ-
ⲡⲁϫⲟⲟⲥ ϫⲉⲟⲩⲥⲏϥⲉ, Mani P 62 A² ⲡⲟⲩⲣⲉ ⲡⲧⲕⲗⲟⲟⲗⲉ
...ϫⲉⲉⲓⲡⲁϣ ϫⲱⲃⲉ, Mani K 13 A² sent them ϫⲉⲩⲡⲁ-
ⲧⲁϣⲉⲁⲓϣ, Ora 4 19 S recipe ⲉⲧⲃⲉⲡⲃⲟⲩϭⲉ ϫⲉⲡⲡⲉⲅ-
ⲣⲱⲧ, Ep 244 S ⲣϣⲁⲡⲡⲥⲁϩ ⲉⲓ ϫⲉⲉϥⲡⲏⲅ ⲉϩⲣⲧ, BSM
17 B ⲁⲙⲟⲩ ϫⲉⲡⲧⲉⲕⲧⲁⲗⲟⲡ, AZ 21 104 O ϫⲉⲉⲓⲉⲗⲗⲓ
ⲡⲉⲧⲉⲛⲡⲉⲥϩⲛⲧ, C 43 186 B went to bath ϫⲉϩⲓⲡⲁ ⲡⲧⲉⲥ-
ϫⲱⲕⲉⲙ.   f ellipse: Ac 17 32 SB ⲡⲧⲉⲣⲟⲩⲥⲱⲧⲙ
ϫⲉⲧⲁⲡⲁⲥⲧⲁⲥⲓⲥ, Lu 23 6 S sim, Cl 47 1-2 A ϫⲓ ⲧⲉⲡⲓⲥ-
ⲧⲟⲗⲏ ⲙⲡⲁⲩⲗⲟⲥ...ϫⲉⲡⲁϥϭⲣⲉⲓ ⲟ, ShA 2 46 S why ate
ye of tree? ⲉϥϫⲁ ⲙⲉⲛ ϫⲉⲡⲣⲟϥ ⲡⲉⲡⲧⲁϥ-, ShC 42 81 S
ⲁⲕⲧⲡⲡⲟⲟⲩ ϣⲁⲣⲟⲓ ϫⲉⲁⲙⲟⲩ, ShIF 248 S ⲡⲁⲓ... ⲡ ϯ-
ⲡⲁⲥⲱⲧⲙ ⲁⲡ ⲉⲣⲟⲟⲩ ⲁⲩⲱ ϫⲉⲙⲡⲣⲁⲁⲩ ⲣⲱ, C 99 180 S
ⲡϭⲓⲥⲉ ϫⲉⲉⲡⲏⲡ ⲉⲣⲟⲕ are weary (saying) we are thine,
BMis 52 S stretched forth hand to me ϫⲉⲱ ⲕⲩⲣⲓⲗⲗⲟⲥ,
Pcod 9 S bestow them on bishop ϫⲉⲧⲁⲁⲩ ⲙⲙⲛⲧⲡⲁ,
BMar 29 S ⲙⲡⲉⲓⲣⲓⲥⲉ ⲉⲣⲟⲕ ϫⲉⲁⲙⲟⲩ, C 41 41 B ϩⲣⲓⲟⲩⲓ
ⲉⲡⲓⲱ ϫⲉⲗⲟⲩϣⲓ, C 89 140 B ⲉⲑⲃⲉⲟⲩ ⲁⲕⲓⲛⲓ ⲙⲡⲁⲓⲡⲧⲏϫ
ϫⲉⲁⲣⲓⲧϥ ⲙⲙⲟⲡⲁϫⲟⲥ?, Mani K 10 A² ⲧϭⲉ ⲙⲡⲟⲩⲁⲓⲉ
ϫⲉⲡⲡⲉⲩⲉϥⲡⲁ[, ib 78 ⲟⲩⲡ ⲕⲉϣⲁⲙⲧ ⲁⲡ ⲡⲣⲏⲧϥ, [ⲡϣⲁ-
ⲣ]ⲡ ⲙⲉⲛ ϫⲉ[..., ⲡⲙⲁϣϣⲁⲙⲧ ϫⲉⲡⲉϥⲥⲱⲙⲁ ⲧⲏⲕ, Kr 72
F we write (saying) ϫⲉⲓⲧ (l ϫⲉϩⲉⲓⲧ), ib 3 F ⲧⲉⲓⲧⲟⲩ (sc
apprentices) (ⲡ)ⲡⲉⲥⲉϩ ϫⲉⲧⲥⲁⲙⲁⲩ (ⲡ)ⲡⲉⲧⲉⲭ ⲛⲓ, BM
706 F he sent man ϫⲓⲟⲩⲉϣ ⲁⲓⲕ, J 5 10 S ⲁⲡⲟⲛ ...
ϫⲁⲓⲣⲉⲓⲡ ϫⲉⲡⲣⲟⲙⲟⲗⲟⲅⲉⲓ, Mor 31 79 S ⲱ ϫⲉⲟⲩⲏⲣⲡⲉ
ⲡⲉϫⲁⲣⲓⲥⲙⲁ, Aeg 43 B ⲱ ϫⲉⲟⲩⲟⲓ ⲡⲱⲧⲉⲛ, KroppM
19 S ⲁⲓⲟ ⲁⲓⲟ ϫⲉϯⲱⲣⲕ, Hall 89 S letter begins ϫⲉ-
ⲉϣⲱⲡⲉ, Ep 280, 455, BKU 1 299 sim.   g εἰ, if,
whether: Ex 4 18 A ⲧⲁⲡⲟ ϫⲉⲉⲧⲓ ⲥⲉⲁⲛϩ (SB ϫⲉⲉⲡⲉ),
Job 35 14 S(B ⲓⲥϫⲉ), Mt 26 63 SB, Mk 3 2 S(B
ϫⲉⲁⲛ).   h after Gk particles: Va 57 135 B ⲡϭⲟⲓ
ⲡⲉⲡⲁⲛⲧⲓⲟⲡ ⲁⲡ...ⲁⲗⲗⲁ ϫⲉⲉⲣ ⲡⲕⲉⲥⲩⲙⲫⲱⲛⲓⲡ ἀλλὰ
καί, PO 14 368 B accept gift ⲕⲁⲛ ϫⲉϥϫⲟϫⲉⲃ, ShMIF
23 136 S none is greater ⲟⲩ ⲙⲟⲛⲟⲛ ϫⲉⲣⲱⲙⲉ ⲁⲗⲗⲁ,
BAp 75 S sim, J 67 81 S ⲙⲟⲛⲟⲛ ϫⲉϯϭⲟⲉ ⲧⲁⲓ ⲁⲗⲗⲁ
(cf ib 68 66), Ep 365 S ⲡⲗⲏⲛ ϫⲉ-, DeV 2 119 B ⲟⲩⲭ
ⲟⲧⲓ ϫⲉ- ... ⲁⲗⲗⲁ, Va 57 15 B ϩⲱⲥ ϫⲉⲙⲫⲣⲏϯ ⲉϥϫⲱ
ⲙⲙⲟⲥ ὡσανεί, C 99 239 S ⲉⲡⲓⲧⲓⲙⲁ ⲙⲡⲕⲟⲩⲓ ϩⲱⲥ
ϫⲉⲁϣϣⲁϫⲉ = C 89 74 B ϩⲱⲥ ⲁϥ-, Va 57 16 B ϩⲱⲥⲧⲉ
ϫⲉⲉϥⲟⲩⲱϣ, ib 127 B ⲧⲟⲩⲧⲉⲥⲧⲓⲡ ϫⲉⲡⲁϫⲓⲡⲉⲣ ⲟⲩⲱ (sc
Ps 103 34), BMEA 10583 S ⲉⲡⲉⲓϫⲏ ϫⲉⲙⲡⲉⲡⲁⲡⲟⲃⲉ
ⲕⲁⲁⲧ ⲧⲁⲉⲓ.

ⲡⲭⲉ: Lu 2 4 B(Va 57 102) ⲟⲩⲡⲟⲗⲓⲥ ⲡ.ⲡⲁⲍⲁⲣⲉⲑ,
PS 260 S ⲟⲩⲟⲓ ⲡⲏⲧⲡ...ⲡ.ⲉϣⲱⲡⲉ, GriffStu 163 F ⲁⲓⲁ
ⲡ.ϯⲧⲁⲗⲕⲁ ⲙⲁⲕ, ib ϯⲡⲁⲣⲁⲕⲁⲗⲓ ... ⲡ.ⲉⲕⲉⲓ, BM 1227
F ⲉⲡⲥ(ϩ)ⲁⲓ...ⲡ.ⲁⲡⲉⲣ ⲧⲉⲕⲓ (δέχεσθαι).

V also ⲉⲃⲏⲗ, ⲡⲥⲁⲃⲏⲗ ϫⲉ-p 35 b, ⲉⲃⲟⲗ ϫⲉ-p 34 b,
ⲉⲧⲃⲉⲭⲉ- p 61 b, ⲉϥⲙⲁ ϫⲉ-p 154 a, ϫⲉⲟⲩⲏⲓ p 471 b,
ϫⲉⲕⲁⲁⲥ.

ϫⲉ B again v ϭⲉ.

ϫⲉ SAF v ⲡϭⲓ & ϫⲡ-.

ϫⲏ SB nn f, dish, bowl for food, incense (cf ḏꜣ·t,
ل، Dévaud): Si 34 15 S, Mt 26 23 S(B ⲃⲓⲡⲁϫ),
ءاناً, Mk 14 20 SB ءاناً τρύβλιον; Ex 25 29 S(P 44
104)B 'ꜣ, Nu 7 14 B(S ϫⲏⲛⲥ) כַּף θυΐσκη; Ge 25 34
B ⲉϥⲉⲙⲁ; K 130 B ϯϫ. ءناً; ROC 23 275 B ⲡⲟⲧⲏ-
ⲣⲓⲟⲡ, ⲁⲓⲥⲕⲟⲥ, ϫⲏ for church.   Cf ϫⲏⲛⲥ.

ϫⲏ, ϫⲓ S(?), ϫⲓⲉ A², ϫⲏⲓ B nn m, chip, mote of
straw, dust: Mt 7 3 SB κάρφος قذً; ShBor 233 231
S ⲟⲩϣⲉ ⲏ ⲟⲩϭⲗⲙ ϣⲁϩⲣⲁⲓ ⲉⲟⲩϫⲏ, ShA 1 294 S ϧⲉⲛ-
ϫⲏ ⲙⲡⲣⲉⲡϣⲟⲉⲓϣ that wind scattereth, BIF 37 55 S
ⲁϥϥⲓ ⲡⲟⲩⲕⲟⲩⲓ ⲡϫⲏ from ground, ManiP 40 A² ⲡϫ.
ⲉⲧⲉⲛⲡⲉϥⲃⲉⲗ, Hall 148 S charm to recover sight ⲡϫⲓ
ϭⲡⲁⲗⲟ ⲡⲉϩⲗⲟⲥⲧⲛ ϭⲡⲁⲃⲱⲗ ⲉ[ⲃⲟⲗ.   Cf ϣϫⲉ 2°.

ϫⲏ S(mostly)A²BF, ϫⲓ A in nn m ϫⲓⲛϫⲏ, emptiness, vanity(?), cf preceding word (Spg): Job 20 18
ϩⲉⲡϫ. (B ⲡⲉⲧϣⲟⲩⲓⲧ) κενός; Ps 34 19 ⲉϫ. (PS 96,
var & B ⲡϫ.) δωρεάν; ⲉⲡϫ.(B once), for naught, in
vain: Lev 26 16 (B ⲉⲡⲉⲧϣ.), Job 9 17 (B ϫⲉⲛⲟⲩⲡⲉⲧ-
ϣ.), Pro 23 29 SA διὰ κενῆς, Is 49 4 (B do), Ja 4 5 (B
ⲉϥⲗⲏⲟⲩ) κενῶς, Job 21 34 (B ⲉⲡⲁⲛⲏⲣ) κενά, 1 Thes
3 5 SF(B ⲉϥϣⲟⲩⲓⲧ) εἰς κενόν; Ps 34 7 (B ϫⲉⲛⲟⲩⲙⲉⲧⲉϥ.), Is 30 5 (B ⲉϥ., F ⲡⲓϭⲉⲉⲓ), Mt 15 9 (B ⲉϥ.) μάτην,
Is 30 15 SF(B ⲡⲟⲩⲉϥ.) μάταιος, Ps 3 9 SA(TU 43 9,
B ϫⲉⲛⲟⲩⲙⲉⲧⲉϥ.) ματαίως, ib 62 9 (B do) εἰς.μάτην;
ib 68 4 (B ⲡϫ.), Jo 15 25 SA²(B do) δωρεάν; Bor 253
267 ϣⲱⲡⲉ ⲡⲕⲗⲉⲡⲧⲏⲥ ⲉ. ἄφνω; PS 25 ⲡⲟⲗⲉⲙⲓ ⲉ. ϩⲣⲁⲓ
ϩⲙⲡⲟⲅⲟⲉⲓⲛ, ShC 42 139 will beg forgiveness ϫⲉⲁⲓ-
ⲉⲙⲕⲟⲟⲩ ⲉ., ShC 73 92 ϩⲟⲓⲛⲉ ⲉⲩⲕⲱⲧⲉ ϩⲛⲧⲥⲟⲟⲩϩⲥ ⲉ.,
ShA 1 298 ϩⲉⲡⲁⲡⲁϣ ⲉ., BerlOr 1607 3 102 ⲡⲉⲓⲥⲁⲉⲓⲛ
ⲉϥⲧⲁⲗϭⲟ...ⲉ. gratis, MIE 2 341 B ⲁⲓϣⲉⲡ ⲡⲁⲓϭⲓⲥⲓ ⲉ.,
CO 209 ⲁϥϭⲟⲡⲛ ⲉ. arrested us without cause;   ⲡϫ.
sim: Ge 29 15 SB, Job 1 9 SB, Ps 108 3 B(S ⲉⲡϫ.),
Ap 21 6 SB δω., Ez 6 10 B εἰς δω.; R 1 5 14 S ⲟⲩⲱⲙ
ⲡⲟⲩⲟⲉⲓⲕ ⲡ. ἀργός; Ps 43 13 B(S ⲁϫⲡⲁⲥⲟⲩ) ἄνευ τιμῆς;
ShC 42 83 S ⲡ. opp ϩⲁⲣⲉⲡⲕⲟⲩⲓ ⲡⲧⲓⲙⲏ, Miss 8 169 S
penitent thief ⲁϥⲟⲩⲉⲙ ⲡⲁⲧⲡⲉ ⲡ., AM 93 B ϯ ⲡⲟⲩ-
ⲙⲱⲟⲩ ⲡ. ⲡⲡⲉⲧⲟⲃⲓ.

ϫⲏⲓ B v ϫⲏ 2°.

ϫⲓ SAA²F, ϫⲉⲓ (Ro 1 27 CBeatty), ϫⲓⲉⲓ S(same?),
ϫⲉ Sʲ(Mor 30 9), ϭⲓ B, ϫⲓ- SAA²FO, ϫⲉ- SF, ϫⲉⲓ-
S, ϭⲓ- BF(once), ϫⲓⲧ⸗ SAA²F, ϭⲓⲧ⸗ B, ϫⲏⲅ† SAA²,
ϫⲛⲟⲩ† A, ϭⲛⲟⲩ† B, ρ c ϫⲁⲓ- SAA²F, ϫⲁⲉⲓ- A²O,
ϭⲁⲓ- B, ϫⲁⲩ- SA², ϭⲁⲩ- B vb I intr, receive, take:

Mt 7 8 *SB*, Ap 3 3 *SB* λαμβάνειν, BMis 560 *S* each may ϫⲓ ⲕⲁⲧⲁ ⲡⲉϥϭⲃⲏⲅⲉ ἀπολ., Aeg 276 *S* let bishop ϫⲓ ⲡϣⲟⲣⲡⲙⲉⲧⲁⲗ.; Pro 9 9 *B*(*SA* diff), Z 292 *S* ⲙⲡⲟⲩϫⲓ took not (wine) δέχεσθαι; 1 Cor 9 10 *B*(*SF* = Gk) ⲙⲉⲧⲉⲭⲉⲓⲛ; 2 Cor 5 10 *SB* κομίζεσθαι; ShC 42 198 *S* ⲡⲉⲧϯ ⲁⲅⲱ ⲡⲉⲧϫⲓ ϩⲏⲟⲩⲕⲣⲟϥ, Aeg 256 *S* ⲡⲉⲧϫⲓ (sc baptism), P 129²⁰ 134 *S* ⲡⲉⲩⲭⲁⲣⲓⲥⲧⲓⲁ ⲙⲡⲛⲥⲁⲧⲣⲉⲩϫⲓ (communion), AM 258 *B* opened mouth ⲉϭⲓ, Hyvernat Alb 28 *B* whoso shall say Amen ⲉϥⲉϭⲓ ⲕⲁⲧⲁ ⲡⲓⲥⲙⲟⲩ;   take wife, *marry:* Mt 19 10 *B*(*S* ϫⲓ ⲥϩⲓⲙⲉ), 1 Cor 7 9 *SBF* γαμεῖν;   *touch, reach, hit:* Jer 9 8 *S*(*B* ⲑⲟⲩⲕⲥ) τιτρώσκειν, cit ShClPr 22 359 & BMOr 8811 220 all ϫⲓⲉⲓ, PS 5 *S* ⲡⲟⲩⲟⲉⲓⲛ…ϫⲓ ϫⲓⲛⲡⲉⲥⲏⲧ ϣⲁϩⲣⲁⲓ ⲉⲙⲡⲏⲅⲉ, ShC 73 162 *S* ⲛⲥϫⲓ ⲁⲛ it matters not (cf c e- intr), Bor 260 98 *S* ⲟⲩⲡⲛⲁ ⲡⲉⲧϫⲓ ⲟⲩϣⲏⲣⲉ ⲡⲡⲉ ⲡⲉⲧⲟⲩϫⲓ ⲙⲙⲟϥ (evil) *spirit aimeth, Son of God is struck* (on Mt 4 1 ff);   qual: ShA 1 458 *S* art as net ϩⲉⲛⲣⲁⲗⲁⲧⲉ ⲉⲧϫ. ⲡⲣⲏⲧⲕ; ϫ. ⲡⲕⲟⲧⲉ, *crooked, guileful:* Pro 2 15 *SA*(*B* ⲕⲟⲗϫ) καμπύλος; ib 8 8 *SA*(*B* ⲟⲩⲟⲡ ⲕ. ⲡⲣⲏⲧϥ) στραγγαλώδης; BM 190 158 *S* ϭⲓⲛϣⲁϫⲉ ⲉⲧϫ. [ⲡⲕⲟ]ⲧⲥ of heretics (= PO 8 253 ܠܘ̈ܐ ܐ̈ܟܢܐ). V also c e-, ⲛⲧⲛ-, ⲉϩⲟⲩⲛ & ϭⲟⲡⲥ, ϫⲓ ⲛ-.

II tr, *take, get, bring, accept:* Lev 18 17 *SB*, Is 21 3 *B*(*S* ⲧⲁϩⲟ), EpJer 9 *F*(*B* ⲱⲗⲓ), Hos 4 8 *SA*(*B* do), Mt 13 20 *SB*(*F* ϣⲱⲡ), He 9 15 *SBF* λαμβ., Job 17 9 *SB*, Ez 3 14 *B*(*S* Ep 31 91) ἀναλ., Lu 16 25 *SB* ἀπολ., Job 3 5 *SB* ἐκλ., Va 57 11 *B* ϭⲓ ⲙⲡⲓⲡⲁⲣⲁϫⲓⲥⲙⲁ ἐπιλ., Ac 24 25 *B*(var ϫⲓⲁⲓ, *S* ϭⲉ) μεταλ., Lam 3 2 *SBF*, Mt 1 20 *S*(*B* ϣⲱⲡ), Aeg 288 *S* ⲡϣⲙⲙⲉ ⲡⲧⲁϥϫⲓⲧϥ παραλ., Jer 39 24 *B* συλλ.; Ge 18 10 *B*(*S* ⲭⲡⲟ), Is 13 8 *B*(*S* ⲧⲁ.), Jo 4 18 *SBF* ἔχειν, Lam 5 7 *F* ϫⲣⲓ (*B* ϥⲁⲓ) ὑπέχ.; Ge 4 11 *S*(ShA 2 112)*B*, Mt 10 14 *S*(*B* ϣ.), Lu 16 6 *S*(*B* ⲙⲟ), Aeg 214 *S* ϫⲓⲧϥ ϩⲱⲥ ⲕⲗⲏⲣⲓⲕⲟⲥ δέχ., MartIgn 865 *B* ⲁϥϭⲓ ⲡϯⲙⲉⲧⲉⲡⲓⲥⲕⲟⲡⲟⲥ διαδ., Ez 22 20 *B* εἰσδ., BM 158 *S* ϫⲓ ⲡⲡⲉϣⲗⲏⲗ προσδ.; Ps 39 16 *SB*, Lu 7 37 *SB* κομίζειν; EpJer 1 *B*, Mk 13 11 *S*(*B* ⲓⲛⲓ) ἄγειν, Ps 136 3 *S*(*B* ⲱ.), Lu 13 15 *S*(var ϥⲓ) *B* ἀπάγ.; Eccl 10 20 *S*, Ap 21 10 *S*(*B* ⲱ.) ἀποφέρειν, Jude 12 *B*(*S* diff) παραφ., Pro 10 24 *B* ϭⲓ, ⲓⲛⲓ (*SA* diff) περιφ., Sa 16 21 *S* προσφ.; Lu 20 35 *S*(*B* om) τυγχάνειν, Job 3 22 *B*(*S* ϩⲉ) κατατ.; Is 10 15 *B*(*S* ϥⲓ) αἴρειν; Lev 25 30 *S*(*B* ϣ.) κτᾶσθαι; Mt 5 32 *B*(*S* ϩⲙⲟⲟⲥ ⲙⲡ-) γαμεῖν, AP 10 *A²* ϫⲓ ϩⲉⲉⲓ γάμος γίνεσθαι; Pro 8 9 *SA*(*B* ϫⲓⲙⲓ) εὑρίσκειν; Is 30 13 *SF*(*B* ϭⲣⲟ) ἁλίσκεσθαι; Va 58 154 *B* fish in water ⲉⲩϭⲓ ⲙⲙⲱⲟⲩ ϩⲁⲙⲡⲏ ⲡⲉⲙⲣⲁⲙⲡⲁⲓ ὧδε κἀκεῖσε περιφέρεσθαι; Mk 9 6 *S* ⲁⲑⲟⲧⲉ ϫⲓⲧⲟⲩ (*BF* diff) ἔκφοβος γίνεσθαι; PS 35 *S* ϫⲓⲧⲟⲩ…ⲁⲁⲩ ⲙⲯⲩⲭⲏ ⲡⲣⲱⲙⲉ, ShR 2 3 82 *S* ⲉⲙⲡ ⲥⲧⲱⲧ ⲡⲁϫⲓⲧⲡ, ib 77 *S* ⲙⲡⲕϫⲓ ⲗⲁⲁⲩ ⲛⲙⲙⲟⲕⲥ, ShC 73 47 *S* ϫⲓ ⲧⲱⲧ ⲡⲣⲏⲧ, Miss 4 237 *S* ⲡⲉⲡⲧⲁⲩϫⲓ ⲥⲟⲧⲉ *struck by arrows*, MIE 2 345 *B* women ⲉⲩϭⲓ ϭⲛⲓⲃⲓ, Pcod 20 *S* ⲡⲥⲉⲡⲁϫⲓ ⲡⲟⲃⲉ ⲁⲛ, BHom 117 *S* ϫⲓ ⲡⲟⲩⲡⲟⲗⲓⲥ in war, AP 3 *A²* ⲁϥϫⲓ ⲙⲙⲁϥ & brought

him, BAp 86 *S* ⲁϥϫⲓ ⲙⲡⲉϥⲕⲉⲗⲱⲗ to draw water = MIE 2 358 *B*, Mor 31 22 *S* ⲡⲧⲡⲭⲓ ⲁⲡ ⲡⲧⲥⲩⲡϩⲟⲟⲥ of Chalcedon, ib 55 102 *S* ⲡⲧϫⲓ ⲁⲡ ⲙⲡⲉⲓⲱⲧ when He saith, paral ib ⲡⲧⲡⲓⲥⲧⲉⲩⲉ ⲁⲡ ⲉ-, ViK 9661 28 *S* ⲁⲯⲩⲭⲟⲛ opp ⲉⲧϫⲓ ⲧⲉⲯⲩⲭⲏ, C 100 320 *S* ⲡⲉⲡⲧⲁⲁⲗⲁⲙ ϫⲓ ⲡⲉⲩⲧⲩⲡⲟⲥ whereof A. was type, AZ 14 82 *S* ⲡⲉⲡϫⲓ ⲙⲙⲟⲕ ϩⲱⲥ ⲣⲱⲙⲉ ⲡⲉⲗⲉⲅⲑⲉⲣⲟⲥ (var BMar 9 ult ⲡⲁⲣⲁⲧⲏⲣⲉⲓ) = RAl 108 *B* ⲥⲟⲙⲥ, HM 1 95 *S* ⲁⲕϫⲓ ⲡⲧⲁⲣϫⲏ ⲡⲛⲉⲃⲁⲥⲁⲛⲟⲥ hast felt first tortures, KroppB *S* ⲙⲡⲉⲥⲟⲩⲱϣ ⲉϫⲓ ⲡⲧⲁⲡⲓ, Ep 140 *S* ⲁⲓϫⲓ ⲡⲉⲥϩⲁⲓ ⲡⲧⲉⲕⲁϫⲓⲱⲥⲩⲛⲏ, Hall 127 *S* money ⲡⲧⲁⲕϫⲓ ⲧⲟⲧ ⲙⲙⲟⲟⲩ, CO 252 *S* ⲁⲓϫⲓ ⲧⲟⲟⲧⲩ ⲡⲟⲩⲣⲱⲙⲉ *got his promise* to deliver letter, Kr 5 *S* ⲁⲡϫⲓ ⲁⲡⲡⲗⲏⲣⲟⲩ ⲡⲙⲁϥⲧⲁⲥⲉ ⲡⲣⲟⲗⲟⲕ/, LMär 31 *S* ⲡⲁⲡⲡⲱⲡⲁ ⲉϥϫⲓ ⲙⲙⲟⲟⲩ ⲙⲙⲏⲡⲉ, PLond 4 492 *S* ⲁⲧⲧⲓⲉ ⲡⲕⲟⲓⲉ ϫⲓ ϣⲟⲙⲧ [ⲡⲣⲟⲗⲟⲕ/ *are assessed at*, BMOr 6230(45) ϩⲉⲥⲧⲁⲥ (sic) ⲡϫⲓ ⲙⲟⲟⲩ, El 78 *A* market-places ⲡⲁϫⲓ ϩⲁⲓϩ, ManiP 37 *A²* ϫⲓ ⲟⲩⲗⲗⲉ with angels, ib K 147 *A²* ϫⲓ ϣⲡϩⲧⲏϥ, DeV 2 18 *B* ϭⲓ ⲡⲟⲩⲣⲁϣⲓ, Mor 30 9 *Sᶠ* ⲕⲡⲉϫⲉ ⲡⲉⲡⲡⲟϭ ⲡ̄ⲱⲣⲉⲁ = BMis 23 6 *S* ϫⲓ, Va 61 112 *B* dead bones gathered ⲡⲥⲉϭⲓ ⲙⲡⲟⲩⲕⲱϥ as before, BM 915 18 *B* ⲧⲉⲧⲉⲛϭⲓ ⲡⲡⲁⲓⲥⲑⲟⲥⲓ ⲃⲱⲛ ? *perceive*, ManiP *A²* ⲡⲧⲉⲡⲁⲡⲡ̄ⲛ̄ ϫⲓ ⲥ̄ⲡⲟⲩϥⲉ, AZ 23 38 *F* ϭⲓ ϫⲉ ⲃⲓⲱ (*l* ⲧϣ.), Hor 83 *O* ⲥϭⲓⲙⲉ…ⲁϥⲁϫⲓ ⲟⲅⲓⲥ (?);   *have, be provided with S:* BAp 55 ϣⲧⲏⲡ…ⲉⲥϫⲓ ⲧⲟⲧⲉ ⲉⲡⲥⲁ ⲥⲛⲁⲩ δικρόσσιον; Mt 21 12 ϫⲓ ⲕⲟⲗⲅⲙ ⲃⲟⲡ (κόλλυβος); Mor 18 115 ⲃⲁⲗ ⲉⲩϫⲓ ⲥⲟⲧⲉ βέλη ἔχειν; ShIF 154 ⲥⲗⲡⲉ… ⲉⲧϫⲓ ⲧⲟⲉⲓⲥ, BMar 5 women ϫⲓ ⲙⲁⲡⲓⲁⲕⲏⲥ ⲡⲡⲟⲩⲃ, RE 9 164 ϣⲧⲏⲡ ⲉⲩϫⲓ ⲭⲉⲣⲓⲥ (sic MS), CMSS 70 *Sᶠ* sim ϫⲓ ⲥⲧⲁⲩⲣⲟⲥ, Ryl 244 sim ϫⲓ ⲕⲟⲩⲓ ϣⲱⲡⲧ, BSG 178 ⲧⲣⲟⲭⲟⲥ … ⲉϥϫⲓ ⲣⲁ ⲡⲥⲡϥⲉ, Mor 37 168 ϭⲉⲣⲱⲃ ⲡϣⲉ ⲉϥϫⲓ ⲡⲟⲩⲃ, BMis 564 ship ⲉϥϫⲓ ⲡⲟⲩϭⲧⲏ, Ep 574 ⲑⲓⲛ(ⲑⲏⲡ) ⲉⲁⲩϫⲓ ⲕⲱϩⲧ burnt, ViK 4716 ⲡⲡⲉⲣϫⲓ ⲡⲉⲡⲓⲡⲉ *be not put in irons*, PBu 200 ⲡⲣⲁⲥⲓⲥ … ⲉⲥϫⲓ ⲙⲁⲣⲧⲩⲣⲟⲥ;   *touch, reach, hit:* Cant 2 5 *S*(ShC 42 56) τιτρ.; BM 174 1 *S* ⲙⲡⲉⲡⲟⲃϩⲉ (of lions)…ϫⲓ ⲙⲡⲉϥⲥⲱⲙⲁ, Mor 40 9 *S* arrows ϫⲓ ⲙⲡⲣⲏⲧ ⲙⲡⲉⲣⲧⲟ (var ib 39 12 ϫⲁⲧ-) = C 43 39 *B* ⲧⲁϩⲉ-, Mor 52 38 *S* ⲁⲧⲥⲟⲩⲣⲉ ϫⲓ ⲙⲡⲉϥⲧⲏⲏⲃⲉ, P 129¹⁶ 4 *S* thinkest that tortures ϫⲓ ⲙⲙⲟⲛ ?, ⲡⲥⲉϫⲓ ⲉⲣⲟⲛ ⲁⲛ, C 41 51 *B* ⲁϥⲟⲣⲉⲡⲓⲙⲱⲟⲩ…ϭⲓⲡⲣⲟ ⲙⲡⲓⲕⲁⲣⲓ, Kr 116 *S* ⲁ ⲙⲙⲟⲟⲩ ⲉⲓⲁϥϫⲓ ⲙⲓⲭⲁⲏⲗ *reached St Michael's* (church);   *learn (by heart):* MG 25 253 *B* ⲁϥϭⲓ ⲡϯⲡⲁⲗⲉⲁ ⲡⲁⲡⲟⲥⲑⲏⲧⲓⲥ ἀποστηθίζειν; C 89 37 *B*, MIE 2 325 *B* sim, CO 30 *S* ordinand will ϫⲉⲓ ⲡⲉⲩⲁⲅⲅⲉⲗⲓⲟⲛ of John ⲛⲁⲡⲟⲥ. (cf ib 29 ϫⲱⲣ), BP 12486 *S* promises to ϫⲓ ⲟⲩⲙⲉⲣⲟⲥ ⲡ ⲭⲱⲙⲉ ϩⲓⲡⲉⲅⲅⲉⲗⲓⲟⲛ, ShC 73 133 *S* ⲛⲅⲡⲁϫⲓ ϩⲟⲩⲟ ⲁⲡ ⲉⲧⲙⲧⲣⲉϥϭⲱⲃ ⲉⲙⲡⲧ ⲙⲙⲉⲣⲟⲥ, Ep 72 *S* ⲡⲗⲉϫⲓⲥ …ⲡϫⲓⲧⲟⲩ ϩⲡⲟⲩⲥⲡⲟⲩⲁⲏ, HL 93 *B* ⲡⲱⲥ ⲙⲡⲉⲕⲓ ⲉϭⲓ ⲙⲡⲓⲯⲁⲗⲙⲟⲥ ?;   *buy S:* FR 36 go to them that sell ⲡⲧϫⲓ ⲡⲟⲩⲥⲧⲟⲓ (var BMis 69 ϯⲥⲁⲧⲉⲉⲣⲉ ⲡⲧϫⲓⲧⲉ ⲡⲥⲧⲟⲓ), BMis 376 ⲁϥⲧⲁⲁⲥ (sc cloak) ⲁϥϫⲓ ⲙⲡⲉⲥⲟⲩⲟ, R 1 5 11 ⲙⲡⲣϫⲓ ⲗⲁⲁⲩ ⲡⲁⲣⲁ ⲧⲧⲓⲙⲏ (var Bor 239 56

ϣⲉⲡ), TillBau 131 ⲙⲡⲣϫⲓ ⲕⲁϩ on that day; paral
with ϯ pp 392 a **A**, 395 b **D** s f.

With following preposition.

—— e- SAA²BF, lead, relate to, attain to intr: Nu
35 27 B(S as Gk) ἔνοχος εἶναι; Deu 22 26 B(S ⲉⲣⲟⲩⲛ
e-) εἰ. dat; Mt 12 5 B(S no vb) -αίτιος εἰ.; Gal 2 6
S(B diff) διαφέρειν dat; Ez 42 1 SB ducere ad; Pro
12 28 B(SA diff) εἰς; Jer 27 5 B(S as Gk) ἕως; Is 10
26 B(S as Gk), Ac 25 27 B(S om) κατά; Ez 41 11 SB,
Phil 2 30 B(S diff) πρός; Miss 8 92 S ⲛϭⲓ ⲁⲡ ⲉⲣⲟⲓ
ϩⲁⲡⲉⲓϣⲁϫⲉ οὐ πολὺς ὁ λόγος ἐμοί; ShA 1 52 S ⲉϭⲁⲓ
ⲉⲣⲟⲓ, BAp 5 S ⲛϭⲁⲓ ⲉⲣⲟⲕ ⲁⲡ (var Wess 15 142 ⲙⲉⲗⲓ),
PS 139 S ⲡⲉⲥⲟⲩⲉⲣⲏⲧⲉ ϫⲓ ⲉⲡⲕⲁⲕⲉ, ShC 73 209 S one
will ϫⲓ ⲉⲡⲉⲧⲣⲓⲧⲟⲩⲱϥ ⲉϥⲥⲟⲟⲩⲛ, another will not befoul body yet will sate it with (evil) desires, AncientEg
'27 97 S inquire ϫⲉⲉⲣⲉⲡⲓⲁⲥⲉⲑⲏⲥ ⲛⲁϫⲓ ⲉⲡⲓⲁ ⲛⲡⲣⲱⲙⲉ
ⲡⲧⲉ ⲡⲓⲧⲟⲡⲟⲥ, Viostr 293 Sᵃ will not suffer aught ⲁϫⲓ
ⲁⲣⲟⲕ (cf CO 108 ⲉⲧⲁⲣⲟⲕ) whether as to tax or debt,
Mor 23 32 S ⲙⲡⲉⲟⲩⲱⲡⲉ ϫⲓ ⲉⲣⲟϥ hit him, Va 57 45 B
ⲙⲟⲕⲙⲉⲕ ⲉϥϭⲓ ⲉϥⲙⲟⲩ; qual B: MG 25 223 ⲉⲣⲉ-
ⲡⲓⲥⲛⲁⲩϩ ⲡⲧⲉ ⲧⲁⲓⲉⲡⲧⲟⲗⲏ ϭ. (var ϭⲓ) ⲉⲣⲟⲕ ⲁⲡ, Va 57
75 ⲙⲙⲟⲡ ϩⲗⲓ ⲡⲉⲧⲓⲁ (αἰτ.) ϭ. ⲉⲣⲱⲟⲩ ⲁⲡ; tr, to,
for: Jer 28 8 S(BMOr 6954)B λαμβ. dat, Mt 20 9 SB
λ. ἀνά, Ac 7 53 SB λ. εἰς, Nu 23 27 S(B diff) παραλ. εἰς;
Job 38 20 S(B ⲱⲗⲓ ϣⲁ-) ἄγειν εἰς, BMar 121 S ϫⲓⲧ
ⲉⲧⲁⲡⲁⲧⲣⲓⲥ ἀνάγ. εἰς, Ps 30 17 S(B ⲉϩⲣⲏⲓ ⲉ-) κατάγ.
εἰς; ib 103 11 S(B ϣⲱⲡ) προσδέχ. εἰς; Ex 20 25 S(B
ϩⲓⲟⲩⲓ) ἐπιβάλλειν ἐπί; 1 Cor 15 19 BF(Mor 38 4) ⲧⲉⲡ-
ϭⲓ ⲟⲩⲡⲁⲓ ⲉⲣⲟⲡ (SAFZ diff) ἐλεεινὸς εἰ.; Jud 17 10 S
ⲡⲉⲧⲕⲡⲁϫⲓⲧⲟⲩ ⲉⲣⲟⲕ ⲉⲡⲉⲕⲱⲡϩ τὰ πρός; Ro 7 10 B sim
(S diff) ἡ εἰς; PS 56 S ⲡϭⲁⲓⲧ ⲉⲡϫⲓⲥⲉ, BG 69 S ⲡϥⲥⲱⲕ
ⲙⲙⲟⲥ... ⲡϥϫⲓⲧⲉ ⲉⲧⲃⲱϣⲉ, ShC 73 25 S ⲡⲉϥϩⲏⲧ ⲡⲁϫⲓ
ⲟⲩⲟⲉⲓⲛ ⲉⲣⲟϥ in Scriptures, ib 61 S ⲉⲩⲛⲁϫⲓⲧⲟⲩ (sc
grave-clothes) ⲉⲣⲣⲟⲩ ⲁⲡ not to be provided for them,
Miss 4 242 S ⲧⲉϫⲣⲓⲁ ⲧⲏⲣⲥ ⲉⲧⲉⲩϣⲁⲛϫⲓⲧⲉ ⲉⲣⲟⲟⲩ that
they used to receive, JSch 3 S ⲧⲉⲩⲉⲥⲩⲅⲁ ⲁⲡϫⲓⲧⲉ ⲉ-
ⲡⲉⲩⲡⲣⲟⲥⲱⲡⲟⲡ according to their persons, BMis 222
S grasped it (cross) ⲁⲩϫⲓⲧϥ ⲉⲡⲉⲩⲅⲁⲗⲙⲏⲣ (cf 223 sim
ϥⲓⲧϥ), ViK 9064 S ϫⲓⲧ ⲉⲧⲉϩⲓⲏ ⲡⲓⲙⲙⲁⲕ = DeV 2 137
B ϭⲓⲧϥ ⲡⲉⲙⲁⲕ, El 78 A ⲥⲉϫⲓⲧⲟⲩ ⲁⲧⲙⲏⲧⲣⲟⲡⲟⲗⲓⲥ,
ManiK 165 A² ⲉⲩⲁϫⲓ ⲁⲣⲁⲩ ⲡⲧⲟⲩⲛⲟⲩ take occasion,
MIE 2 348 B ⲉⲥϭⲓ ⲙⲡⲓϣⲱ...ⲉⲡⲉⲥⲡⲓ, BMar 24 S ⲉϥϫⲓ ⲡⲉⲡⲡⲉ ⲉⲡⲉϥϭⲓϫ handcuffed, ROC 23 278 B ⲡⲓⲙⲁ
ⲉⲧⲉⲡϭⲓ ⲙⲡⲓⲡⲁⲓ ⲉⲣⲟⲡ ⲡϩⲏⲧϥ, BKU 1 1² S cried saying
ⲉⲓϫⲓ ⲡⲛⲥⲉ ⲧⲁ[ⲙⲁⲁ]ⲩ ⲉⲣⲟⲓ appeal to (?), Mor 24 12 F
ϫⲓ ⲙⲙⲁⲩ ⲉⲡⲉⲕⲟⲗⲁⲥⲓⲥ; vbal: Nu 23 20 S ⲁⲩϫⲓ
ⲙⲙⲟⲓ ⲉⲥⲙⲟⲩ (B diff) παραλ. inf; ShC 73 103 S
ⲡⲛϫⲓ ⲁⲡ (var ⲡⲧⲉϫⲣⲓⲁ ⲁⲡⲧⲉ) ⲉⲱⲣϫ ⲙⲡⲣⲟ, HL 85 B
ⲡⲓⲣⲱⲃ ϭⲓ ⲉⲑⲣⲉⲡϭⲥⲓ of man be in moderation; e-
ⲣⲁⲧ: Mk 14 53 S(B ϩⲁ-) ἀπάγ. πρός; Ac 23 24 S(B
as Gk) διασώζειν πρός; PS 240 S ϫⲓⲧϥ ⲉⲣⲁⲧⲥ ⲡ-, PO
11 305 B ϭⲓⲧϥ...ⲉⲣⲁⲧϥ ⲙⲡⲓⲉⲡⲓⲥⲕⲟⲡⲟⲥ.

—— ⲉϫⲡ- SABF, **a** take upon tr: Lev 18 18 SB,
Is 2 4 B(S ⲁⲙⲁⲣⲧⲉ), Mic 2 4 SAB λαμβ. ἐπί, Cai
Euch 491 B ϭⲓ ⲡⲟⲩⲱⲓⲕ ⲉ. ⲡⲉⲕϫⲓϫ λ. ἐν, Jer 15 15 B
(S ⲉⲧⲃⲉ-) λ. περί; Ps 89 13 B ϭⲓ ϯⲣⲟ ⲉ. (S ⲥⲟⲡⲛ ⲉ.)
παρακαλεῖν ἐπί; Deu 1 40 S(var e-, B Gk no vb) ἐπί;
AZ 21 157 S we pray thee ϫⲓ ⲡⲉϩⲙⲟⲧ ⲙⲡⲛⲧ ⲉϫⲱⲡ,
El 34 A ⲁϥϫⲓⲧ ⲁϫⲡⲧⲁⲡⲟⲗⲓⲥ, BSM 25 B ϭⲓ ⲙⲡⲥⲟⲃⲛⲓ
ⲉϫⲱⲟⲩ = BMis 364 S ϫⲓ ⲕⲉⲗⲉⲩⲥⲓⲥ ϩⲁ-. **b** take
upon, for, borrow (mostly S) intr: Deu 15 6 (B ⲉⲣ
ϫⲁⲡⲓⲥⲧⲏⲥ ⲉ-), Ps 36 21 (B ϭⲓ ⲉⲑⲗⲏⲥⲓ), Is 24 2 SB
(opp ϯ ⲉⲙⲏⲥⲉ, ϯ ⲉⲡⲟⲩϣⲁⲡ), δανείζεσθαι; Mun 43
ϫⲓ ⲉϫⲱⲟⲩ ⲡⲧⲡⲣⲛⲕⲟⲟⲩⲉ, ShLMis 414 ⲁⲩϫⲓ ⲉϫⲱⲟⲩ
ⲡⲧⲟⲟⲧⲟⲩ, Kr 41 F ⲁⲓϫⲓ ⲉϫⲱⲓ ⲡⲧⲁⲁⲧⲕ, Aegyptus 3
280 ⲁⲓϫⲓ ⲉϫⲱⲓ ⲡⲧⲟⲟⲧϥ...ⲡⲥⲡⲁⲩ ⲡⲧⲉⲣⲙⲉⲥⲓⲟⲡ, Mor
41 19 went to ϫⲓ ⲉϫⲱϥ ϩⲁⲧⲏϥ (sc rich man) = DeV
2 270 B ϭⲓ ⲡⲧⲟⲧϥ ⲙⲡⲟⲩϣⲁⲡ; tr: ShA 1 454 ⲁϥϫⲓ
ⲉϫⲱϥ ⲡⲟⲩϭⲣⲟⲥ, ib 242 ⲧⲥⲁⲃⲟ ⲉϫⲉⲓ ϫⲱⲣⲟⲡ ⲉ. ⲡⲉⲧⲟⲩⲁⲁⲃ, PMich '24 ϧⲉⲛⲡⲟⲩⲃ ⲡⲧⲁⲓϫⲓⲧⲟⲩ ⲉϫⲱⲓ, ST
201 ⲑⲉ ⲉⲧⲉⲣⲡⲁϫⲓⲧϥ ⲉϫⲱ ⲡⲧⲉⲡⲡⲟⲟⲩ ⲟⲩϩⲟⲗⲟⲕ/ ⲡⲁⲓ
whatever canst borrow, Pcod 35 S pledged church
vessels ⲁϥϫⲓ ϧⲉⲛⲡⲥⲕⲉⲩⲏ ⲡⲥⲱⲙⲁⲧⲓⲕⲟⲡ ⲉϫⲱⲟⲩ, Ryl
353 ⲓⲁϫⲓ ⲡⲉⲧⲣⲓⲙⲏⲥⲓⲡ ⲉϫⲱⲥⲟⲩⲟ in return for corn,
Kr 32 F ⲁⲓϫⲓ ⲁⲣⲑ ⲁ ⲡⲧⲁⲧ ⲉϫⲱⲏⲗⲡ, ib 29 ⲡϣⲁⲣⲉ
ⲉϣⲁⲣⲉ) ⲡⲉϣⲟⲧⲉ ϫⲓ ⲙⲙⲟϥ ⲉϫⲙⲡϫⲓϫⲱϥ (quid?), Mor
25 3 ⲉⲓⲡⲁϫⲓ ⲡⲧⲁⲣⲭⲏ ⲙⲡⲉⲡⲣⲟϭⲟⲓⲗⲓⲟⲡ ⲉϫⲱⲓ ⲡⲧⲉ(ⲡ)-
ⲡⲓⲙ ? = Va 61 87 B.

—— ⲙⲛ-, ⲛⲉⲙ- SAB (mostly), be concerned with,
touch intr: Ge 20 6 (S ⲕⲱϩ ⲉ-), Job 20 6 (S ⲡⲱϧ ϣⲁ-),
Pro 6 29 (SA ϫ. ⲉ-), Is 6 7 (S ⲧⲱϭⲉ ⲉ-), Lam 4 14
(S ϫ. ⲉ-), Mt 14 36 (SF do) ἅπτεσθαι, Am 6 3 ἐφάπ.;
Ex 19 12 (S do) θιγγάνειν; Va 68 171 cannot ϭⲓ ⲡⲉⲙ-
ⲧⲁⲓϣⲫⲏⲣⲓ with impure lips προσψαύειν; MG 25 356
ⲉϣⲱⲡ ⲡⲧⲉϥϭⲓ ⲡⲉⲙⲡⲓⲁⲣⲛⲟⲩ (Göttar 114 126 جدر)),
TstAb 232 ⲙⲡⲉⲣϭⲓ ⲡⲉⲙⲣⲱⲙⲓ = Mor 53 35 S ϫⲱⲣⲙ
ⲙⲛ- (l ϫⲱⲗⲙ), MIE 2 382 ⲙⲡⲉϥϫⲁϥ ⲉϭⲓ ⲡⲉⲙⲡⲉϥ-
ϫⲓϫ, Mor 29 28 Sᶠ ⲁϥϫⲓ ⲡⲉⲙⲡⲥⲱⲙⲁ; qual: MG
25 87 in cell am sheltered ⲛⲁϩⲏⲧ ⲙⲙⲁⲅⲁⲧϥ ⲡⲉϯϭ.
ⲡⲉⲙⲁϥ in contact, communion with; tr, take with:
Hos 14 3 AB, MG 25 215 ⲁϥϭⲓ ⲡⲡⲓⲥⲡⲏⲟⲩ ⲡⲉⲙⲁϥ λ.
μετά, Mt 12 45 SB παραλ. μ., Job 1 4 SB συμπαραλ.

—— ⲛ- SBF, dat: Ps 71 3 SB ἀναλ. dat; ib 44 14 S
(B ⲓⲡⲓ ⲉϩⲟⲩⲛ ⲉ-) ἀποφέρειν dat; 1 Kg 9 8 S διδόναι
dat; R̄ 2 1 10 S ⲉⲥⲡⲁϫⲓ ⲡⲟⲩϣⲉⲗⲉⲉⲧ ⲙⲡⲉⲥϣⲏⲣⲉ,
BAp 82 S ϫⲓⲧϥ ⲙⲡⲡⲁⲧⲣⲓⲁⲣⲭⲏⲥ, Ep 85 S ⲁⲕϫⲓ ⲥⲓⲁⲩ
ⲛⲟⲗⲟⲕ/ ⲡⲁⲡ ⲉⲧⲛⲭⲣⲓⲁ, PMich 777 F ⲁⲕϫⲓ ⲟⲩⲡⲉϣⲓ
ⲡⲣⲱⲗⲱⲕ/ ⲡⲉⲓ ⲉⲡⲟⲩϣⲉⲡ, Ryl 196 S undertake to ϫⲓ
ⲉⲡⲧⲁⲧⲓ(ⲟ)ⲛ ⲡⲏⲧⲛ ⲉⲣⲟⲟⲩ (sc money); Ryl 215 S ⲁⲓϫⲓ
...ⲡⲧⲡⲁϣⲉ ⲡⲧⲃⲟⲡⲧⲉ for, Kr 234 S ⲁⲡϫⲓⲧⲟⲩ ⲡϣϭⲟⲗ
as rent, BM 1061 S ϫⲓⲧⲟⲩ (sc fields) ⲡⲉⲙⲫⲩⲧⲉⲩⲙⲁ,
BM 580 F ϫⲓ ⲡⲉⲃϩⲁⲙⲧ ⲉⲥⲟⲩⲁ; towards: Ez 47 8 S
(B ⲉ-) πρός; ethic dat: Ge 11 29 S(B om ⲛ-), Jer
50 9 SB λ. dat, Eph 6 13 SB ἀναλ.; Z 326 S went to
ϫⲓ ⲟⲉⲓⲕ ⲛⲁϥ ἀποφ. dat; Sa 8 2 S ἄγειν dat; PS 131
S ⲁⲩϫⲓ ⲡⲁⲩ ⲡⲟⲩϭⲟⲙ, CA 99 S ⲁϥϫⲉ ⲡⲕⲁ ⲡⲁϥ (or

from ϫο *spend*?), Bess 7 7 *B* ϭι πακ мϕн ετεκογαϣϥ *take what* (price) *thou wilt*, BSM 104 *B* πταϭι пηι πεγϕнлια to *wife*; in recipes: PMéd 208 *S* ϫι πακ πογκογϫι πκρлєс, Bodl(P)a 1 a *S* ϫι мπεϭлоог πακ; *from* (*cf* c πτη-): BMar 44 *S* ϫι πτειсηϥε πτϭιϫ мπειαπолос & *dispatch me*.

—— πτη- *SAA²BF*, *from* intr: Lev 25 14 *S*(*B* ϣωπ) κτᾶσθαι παρά; Cant 5 8† *S*(BM 192, *F* λα[ϩτ] τιτρώσκειν gen; 2 Cor 11 20 *B*(*S* Gk vb only); BG 25 *S* πϥϫι απ πτηκεογα; tr: Job 31 37 *S* ϫε- *B*, Is 37 14 *SB* λ. παρά, Mt 17 25 *SB* λ. ἀπό; CaiEuch 476 *B* ϭι πτотєπ πτεπсλη δέχ; 1 Cor 6 19 *B*(*SF* єϩол ϩιπ-) ἔχ. ἀπό; Aeg 279 *S* ϫι ψηϕος πτооτογ ψ. κομίζειν gen; Mus 40 44 *S*(RegPach) *do naught* εϫιϫι τεϭπωлη πτηποικономос *nisi quod pater jusserit*; PS 79 *S* αγϫι τεсметαποια πτооте (*cf* c ετη-), Ryl 189 *S* αιϫι αιπληρογ πτооτκ...πταικαια τιмн, CO 168 *S* sim, Kr 22 *F* αιϫι ν̅ β пταλι (= πτα- ατι), Mani 2 *A²* ϫι πτооτϥ πογмπτрαммао, C 43 15 *B* ϫι мπατωϩϩ птот, MR 2 47 *F* сπαγ πλογκωтсι αιϫιτογ πτατк (*cf* c εϫπ- **b**); ετη- *SF* for πτη-: PS 118 ϫι ετоотє πτεсметαποια, Ryl 188 акϫι ταπαρакλнсιс ετоот, Kr 112 καιπαϣє...αιϫιτє ετοотηγτη, AZ 23 35 *F* αιϫι τεϩτιмηп εταα(τ)κ.

—— ϣα- *SB*, *to*: Z 340 *S* ϫιτϥ ϣαπϩλло προσφ. dat; BM 849 31 *B* road ετϭι ϣαϕιωτ, BIF 13 106 *S* ϫιτεπ ϣαроϥ = MG 25 289 *B* ολтєπ; ϣαεϩрнι є- *B*: Jer 4 10 (*S* do) ἀπτ. ἕως; ϣαεϩрнι є- *B*: Ge 28 12 (*S* πωϩ) ἀφικνεῖσθαι εἰς; C 43 47 sim.

—— ϩα- *SF*, *instead*, *on account of*: ShC 73 43 ϫι πογϩ... ϩαсого, J 26 15 αιϫι... πτооτє ϩαπсιπпосιοπ, Kr 152 ταϫι ϩαπαθєκє πлμπτсоогϲ πρτοϥ, J 76 51 πпεϩоогт ϫι ϩαсϩιмє, MR 5 33 *F* єϥєϫι πεκϣлнλ ϩαλαπ.

—— ϩι- *SB*, *on*, *in*: Jer 7 29 *B* ἀναλ. ἐπί; ShC 73 152 *S* ϫι ϩεπκογι πιπηϭ ϩιπραϣλнϥ, RE 14 28 *S* book ερεπαϣηρє παϫι ϩιωϥ *learn by heart therein* (*cf* ϫι tr *learn*).

—— ϩп-, ϧεп- *SB*, *in*, *from* intr: ShMun 176 *S* πεγϣηρє ϫωλϫ ϩπογли πсεϫι ϩонтϲ, Mich 550 29 *S* chrysolite пκωϧт ϣωπε εϥϫι ϩонтϥ *inherent in*, Aeg 18 *S* αϥογω εϥϫι ϩιπϩαϭє; tr: Ez 29 14 *SB* ὅθεν λ., ib 39 10 *B* λ. ἐκ, Deu 14 24 *S*(var єιпє, *B* π- ϩрнι ϧєπ-) λ. ἐν; JTS 38 118 *S* ϫι πογβετсπιρ ϩπ- πκεєс (Ge 2 21), PBad 5 377 *S* ϫι πιταρκο ϩппєκ- мλαϫє, BSM 131 *B* ϭι...пєϩ ϧεппιϕαпос; ϩραι ϩп-, єϧ. ϧєп-: Ez 22 12 *SB* λ. ἐν; пϧрнι ϧєп- *B*: Jer 43 14 λ. εἰς.

—— ϧατєп- *B*, *by*, *beside*: BSM 35 ϭι пθαι ϧα- тотк = BMis 379 *S* καас πτооτκ.

—— ϩιτη- *SA²*, *by*, *through*: Ps 49 16 (*B* diff) ἀναλ. διά; ShC 73 198 ϫι огоєιπ ϩ. пєϩнрϭє, Mani K 162 *A²* ϫι асπасмос ϩιτоотϥ (*sc rising sun*), J 15

57 αιϫι... ϩιтоотк πττελεια тιмн, Win 53 ϫι ϥтоог мληρ πпωϩ ϩιтоотϥ.

—— ϩαϫη- *S*, *in advance*, *from before*: 2 Kg 8 4 ϫι ϩαϫωϥ (var ϩαϩωϥ) π- προκαтал. gen.

—— ϩιϫη- *SB*, *upon*: DeV 2 5 *B* αϥϭιτϥ ϩ. πєϥ- ϫιϫ (*cf* Lu 2 28), Z 627 *S* ϫι πтϧλλε πтсоогϩє ϩ. ϩ(є)пϫϧϧєс.

With following adverb.

—— єϧол *SAA²BF*, *out*: Lu 23 26 *S*(*B* ιпι єϧ.), BHom 55 *S* пεϥϫι псогсαппα єϧ. ἀπάγειν; EpJer 9 *B*(*F* om єϧ.) λαμβ.; єϧ. є-: Mt 27 31 *S*(*B* ωλι) ἀπάγ. εἰς; Bor 253 130 *S* ϫιтog єϧ. επмϩααγ сυσ- τέλλειν ἐν; Miss 4 195 *B* sim, ManiP 212 *A²* ϫι ммαγ αϧ. ατκολασιс; єϧ. εϫп-: Jos 27 *S* ἐπί no vb; єϧ. ммαγ: Jer 45 11 *B* ἐκεῖθεν; єϧ. π-: Is 64 1 *SB* λ. ἀπό, Cai Euch 654 *B* ετπαϭι єϧ. ммωог метαλ. ἐκ; єϧ. ϩп-, ϧєп- intr: Ge 8 20 *SB* λ. ἀπό, Ez 5 4 *SB* λ. ἐκ, CaiEuch 341 *B* εθπαϭι єϧ. пϧнтϥ ме- тαλ. ἐκ, Aeg 212 *S* ϫι єϧ. ϩптεπροσφορα μ. dat; 1 Cor 9 12 *B*(*SF* = Gk) μετέχ. gen, ib 10 17 *SB* μ. ἐκ; PS 84 *S* ατετпϫι єϧ. ϩлпαп̅п̅α, FR 162 *S* ϫι єϧ. ϩп- тεрωтє, JA '05 2 117 *S* πειεκιϧє... ϫι єϧ. ϩнптog, TT 97 *S* ϫι єϧ. ϩппκε[ϫω]ωмє *get by heart*, TU 43 8 *A* ϫι αϧ. ϩптмпт[, DeV 2 66 *B* ϭι єϧ. ϧεппсϧоι пписоϫεп, Mor 24 26 *F* αϫι єϧ. ϩεмпєксωмα; tr: Jud 11 5 *S* λ. ἀπό, Jer 13 7 *B*(*S* ϥι) Ap 10 10 *SB* λ. ἐκ, Jos 4 8 *S* ἀναλ. ἐκ, Job 22 22 *S* ἐκλ. ἐκ; ib 2 10 *S* (*B* єϧ. ϩιτπ-) δέχ. ἐκ; ib 21 17 *SB* ἔχ. ἀπό; PS 14 *S* ϫι мπετпмεрος єϧ. ϩптсолм, BM 219 *S* сарϩ пταϥϫιτϥ єϧ. ϩптπαρθεпος; єϧ. ϩιτп- Jo 10 18 *SA²*(*B* πтεп-) λ. παρά, 1 Cor 11 23 *SB* παραλ. ἀπό; Is 40 2 *S*(*B* єϧ. ϧєп-) δέχ. ἐκ χειρός; Va 57 13 *B* ατε(τε)пϭιτє єϧ. ϩιτoтєп παρέχ.; C 43 107 *B* ϭι єϧ. ϩιτoтκ мπιϫλом.

—— επεснт *SB*, *down*: 1 Kg 2 6 *S*(*B* ω. є-), Pro 5 5 *S*(*A* αϧрнι, *B* єϧ.) κατάγ. Ez 31 16 *B* καταβιβάζειν; ShR 2 3 16 *S* ϫιтog є. ελмπτε παραλ. (BM 285 1 a), MIE 2 367 *B* sim, Mor 23 31 *S* *turning wheel* єсϫι є. εсειпє єϩрαι.

—— επϣωι *B*, *up*: Ez 40 2 (*S* єιпє єϩрαι) τιθέναι ἐπί.

—— єϩогп, єϧ. *SAA²BF*, *in*: Ez 44 7 *B*, Jo 18 16 *SA²*(*B* ιпι) εἰσάγ., Mt 22 10 *S*(*B* θωoϥ†) συνάγ.; Lev 10 1 *S*(*B* ιпι) προσφέρ.; Aeg 218 *S* ϫι єϩ. ϩωс κληρικος προσδέχ.; Job 5 26 *S*(*B* ω.) συγκομ.; PS 60 *S* ετπαϫιτϥ єϩ., JTS 10 398 *S* compelling hus- bands to ϫι ϫρнма παγ єϩ., Mani 1 *A²* ϫιτ αϩ. пϫωрοп; мα πϫι єϩ.: Is 36 2 *F* мα πϫι мαγ єϩ. (*S* ϥω, *B* = Gk) ὑδραγωγός; єϩ. є- intr: Nu 35 27 *S*(*B* пηϥ ϧα-) ἀγχιστεύειν; 2 Kg 19 42 *S* ἐγγί- ζειν πρός; Jos 23 14 *S*(*B* diff), Cl 62 1 *A* ἀνήκειν dat; ib 9 1 *A* ἀγ. εἰς, Ge 6 19 *S*(*B* ω.) εἰσάγ. εἰς; Ez 40 32 *B*(*S* є-) βλέπειν κατά; Col 1 22 *S* neg (*B* αταρικι)

ἀνέγκλητος; Deu 22 26 S(B e-) sim εἶναι dat; Va
66 306 B ϯⲕⲁⲧⲏⲅⲟⲣⲓⲁ ⲉⲧϭⲓ ⲉⲃ. ⲉⲡⲏ ⲡⲣⲟⲥⲧⲓⲑ.; GFr
435 S ⲉϥϫⲓ ⲉⲣ. ⲉⲧⲉⲯⲩⲭⲏ ψυχῆς εἶναι, Va 57 10 B
ⲃⲗⲁⲃⲏ ⲉⲥϭⲓ ⲉⲃ. ⲉⲣⲱⲧⲉⲡ ὑμῖν ἡ β., 2 Pet 1 3 S(B ϣⲱⲡⲓ
ⲉⲃ. e-) τὰ πρός; ViSitz 172 4 24 S ⲧⲛϣⲱⲗⲏ ⲉⲧϭⲓ ⲉⲣ.
ⲉⲡⲡⲉ ἡ εἰς θεόν γν., Ps 118 38 S(B Gk om vb), Su 63
BF(Mus 49 181) Gk do, Mic 6 2 A(B Gk do), 2 Cor
8 4 S(B ϣⲱⲡⲓ ⲛ-) Gk do; ShC 73 126 S sin ⲉϥϫⲓ
ⲉⲣ. ⲉⲡⲙⲟⲩ, ManiP A² road ⲉⲧϭⲓ ⲁϭ. ⲁⲡⲱⲛⲅ, Cat 142
B ⲡⲓⲭⲣⲓⲁ ⲉⲧϭⲓ ⲉⲃ. ⲉⲡⲓⲥⲱⲙⲁ, CO 140 S will fulfil
ⲡⲉⲧϫⲓ ⲉⲣ. ⲉⲣⲟⲛ ⲧⲏⲣϥ, PLond 4 483 S any man ⲉϥϫⲓ
ⲉⲣ. ⲉⲣⲟⲛ ⲉⲓϫⲉ ⲉⲅⲥⲁⲃⲟⲗ ⲙⲙⲟⲛ, J 37 31 S go to law
ϩⲁⲗⲁⲁⲩ ⲡⲣⲱⲃ ⲉϥϫⲓ ⲉⲣ. ⲉⲧⲉⲓⲕⲗⲏⲣⲟⲡⲟⲙⲓⲁ (cf ib 44 69
ⲇⲓⲁⲫⲉⲣⲓⲥⲑⲁⲓ e-);   tr: Ge 12 15 S(B ⲱ.), Ps 77 54
S(B ⲓⲛⲓ) εἰσάγ. εἰς, Sa 6 21 S ἀνάγ. ἐπί, Aeg 210 S
ϫⲓ ⲗⲁⲁⲩ ⲉⲣ. ⲉⲡⲉⲑⲩⲥⲓⲁⲥⲧⲏⲣⲓⲟⲛ προσάγ. εἰς; ib 230
S ϫⲓ ⲡⲉϩ ⲉⲣ. ⲉⲡⲉⲣⲡⲉ ἀναφέρ. εἰς, Mt 6 13 S(BF do)
εἰσφ. εἰς, 1 Kg 17 18 SB εἰσφ. dat, Ge 43 26 S(B do)
προσφ. dat; Lu 16 4 S(B ϣⲱⲡ) δέχ. εἰς, Ez 22 19 S
(ShViK 907)B εἰσδ. εἰς, Aeg 281 S ϫⲓⲧϥ ⲉⲣ. ⲉⲕⲟⲓⲛⲱ-
ⲛⲉⲓ προσδ. εἰς; PS 247 S mysteries ⲉⲧⲛⲁϫⲓ ⲙⲡⲉⲛⲉ-
ⲛⲟⲥ ... ⲉⲣ. ⲉⲡⲧⲟⲡⲟⲥ, ShC 73 139 S ϫⲓ ⲡⲉⲩϭⲡⲏⲩ ⲉⲣ.
ⲉⲡⲙⲁ ⲡϣⲉⲗⲉⲉⲧ, AM 16 B ⲁϥϭⲓⲧⲟⲩ ⲉⲃ. ⲉⲡⲉϥⲡⲁⲗⲁ ϯ-
ⲟⲛ;   ⲉⲣ. ⲡ- S: Ac 23 18 (B ⲓⲛⲓ) ἄγ. πρός; Aeg 245
ϫⲓⲧⲟⲩ ⲉⲣ. ⲙⲡⲭ̅ⲥ̅ προσφ. dat;   ⲉⲣ. ⲡⲓⲁϩⲣⲡ- S: Lu
12 11 (B do) εἰσφ. ἐπί;   ⲉⲃ. ⲡⲉⲙ- B: Eph 1 15 (S
e-) εἰς;   ⲉⲣ. ϣⲁ-: Ge 8 9 S(B ⲓⲛⲓ ⲉⲃ. ϩⲁ-) εἰσάγ.
πρός; Va 57 194 B ⲡⲓⲧⲁⲓⲟ...ϭⲓ ⲉⲃ. ϣⲁⲡⲓⲟⲩⲣⲟ ἀναβαίνειν εἰς; ⲥⲁⲃ. e- B: C 86 298 ⲛⲧⲁϭⲓⲧⲕ ⲥ. ⲉⲡⲓⲡⲁⲗⲗⲁⲧⲓⲟⲛ.

—— ⲉϩⲣⲁⲓ, -ⲏⲓ, ⲁϭ. SAA²B, up: Jos 18 12 S προσ-
αναβαίν.; Ex 33 12 S(B ⲱ. ⲙⲡϣⲱⲓ) ἀνάγ.; Bor 248
58 S ⲟⲩⲥⲙⲟⲧ ⲡⲥⲟⲣⲁϩⲧ...ϫⲓ ⲙⲡⲟⲩⲥ ⲉⲣ., TU 43 4 A
give me power ⲁⲧⲁϫⲓⲧⲏⲡⲉ ⲁⲣ.;   ⲉⲣ. e- intr: Deu 11
24 S(B Gk om vb), 1 Kg 26 3 S Gk do; BM 315 55
S ⲡⲱⲛⲅ ⲉⲧϫⲓ ⲉⲣ. ⲉⲧⲡⲉ, ManiK 122 A² ⲡⲗⲓⲣⲙⲉ (v ib
120 n) ⲉⲧϫⲓ ⲁⲣ. ⲁⲡⲥⲧⲉⲣⲉⲱⲙⲁ, C 43 50 B ⲡⲓⲙⲱⲓⲧ
ⲉⲧϭⲓ ⲉⲣ. ⲉⲧⲫⲉ = Mor 39 28 Sᶠ ϫⲓ ⲙⲁⲉⲓⲧ ⲉⲣ.;   tr:
Ez 20 10 SB ἄγ. εἰς, Mt 4 1 S(B ⲱ. e-), Lu 2 22 S(B
ⲓⲛⲓ) ἀνάγ. εἰς; 1 Kg 17 54 S(var ϫⲓ, ⲛⲧⲥ ⲉⲣ.) λαμβ.
εἰς; Mk 16 19 S(B ⲱ. ⲉⲡϣⲱⲓ e-) ἀναλ. εἰς; BMis 3
S ϫⲓⲧⲟⲩ ⲉⲣ. ⲉⲅⲡⲟⲗⲓⲥ, AP 41 A² ϫⲓ ⲡⲧⲉⲡⲓⲥⲧⲟⲗⲏ ⲁⲣ.
ⲁⲡⲉⲫⲓⲗⲓⲡⲡⲟⲥ, AM 299 B ϭⲓⲧⲟⲩ ⲉⲣ. ⲉⲡⲁⲏⲓ;   ⲉⲣ.
ⲉⲧⲛ-: BMis 123 S ϫⲓ ⲉⲣ. ⲉⲧⲟⲟⲧⲕ ⲙⲡϫⲱⲙⲉ;   ⲉⲣ.
ⲉϫⲉⲛ-: Is 14 4 B(S ⲉϫⲛ-) λ. ἐπί; 1 Cor 4 6 S ϫⲓ ⲡⲥⲙⲟⲧ ⲉⲣ. ⲉϫⲛ- (B ϣⲱⲡ ⲡⲥⲭⲏ. e-) μετασχηματίζειν
εἰς; RNC 59 S ϫⲓⲧϥ ⲉⲣ. ⲉϫⲙⲡⲉⲑⲉⲁⲧⲣⲟⲛ;   ⲉⲣ. ϣⲁ-:
BHom 129 S ϫⲓ ⲡⲛⲉⲯⲩⲭ ⲟⲟⲩⲉ ⲉⲣ. ϣⲁⲁⲡⲉϫⲉⲓⲱⲧ.

—— ⲉϩⲣⲁⲓ, ⲁⲣ., ⲉⲃ. SAB, down, ⲉⲣ. e-: Ps 21 15
S(B ⲓⲛⲓ ⲉⲃ. e-), Pro 5 5 AB(S ⲉⲡⲉⲥⲛⲧ e-) κατάγ.
εἰς; ⲁⲣ. ⲁⲭⲛ-: Zeph 3 18 AB λ. ἐπί; ⲉⲃ. ϣⲁ-:
Va 58 179 B profit of fasting ϭⲓ ⲉⲃ. ϣⲁϯⲯⲩⲭⲏ ἀναβιβ. πρός.

ⲣ c: ϫⲁⲓⲃⲉⲕⲉ v ⲃⲉⲕⲉ, adding Mor 30 35 F = BMis
261 S; ϫ. ⲙⲗⲁϩ v ⲙⲗⲁϩ, adding ManiH 41 A² ϯ
ϩⲙⲁⲧ ⲛⲡⲉϥ. ⲙ.; ϫ. ⲟⲣϭ v ⲱⲣϭ; ϫ. ⲟⲩⲣⲁⲧ ManiP
200 A²; ϫ. ϭⲣⲏⲡⲉ ManiP 43 A² ⲣⲣⲟ ⲛϫ.; ϫⲁⲅ- v
ⲙⲟⲉⲓⲧ, adding Mani 1 A² ⲁⲣⲓ ϫⲁⲩⲙⲁⲓⲧ ⲡⲧⲉⲓⲣⲏⲛⲏ,
ib K 168 A² ⲥⲓⲟⲩ ⲡⲣⲉϥ. (on ϫⲁⲅ- v Sethe Verbum 2
649, but cf A ϫⲁⲓ- ⲡ 188 b); ϭⲁⲩϭⲣⲟϥ v ⲕⲣⲟϥ s f.

—— ⲛⲛ m SB, taking, bringing: Z 262 S ⲡϫⲓ ⲡⲉⲡ-
ⲕⲉⲉⲥ of Baptist (to Egypt), Gu 100 S ⲡϫⲓ ⲡⲟⲩⲱϣⲉ (cf
Mt 4 19), CO 222 S ⲡϫⲓ ϭⲣⲉ, -ⲧⲱϭ, -ⲉⲓⲱⲧ provision
of fodder, straw, barley, Va 57 144 B Samaritan woman is judged (δικάζειν) ⲉⲑⲃⲉⲑⲁⲡⲥ ⲛⲥⲱ ⲡⲧⲉ ϩⲁⲡⲙⲟⲩ (or ? ⲓ ϫⲓⲛⲥⲱ).   V also ⲡ 395 b E.

ⲁⲧϫⲓ, -ϭⲓ v ⲥⲁⲃⲉ(ⲥⲃⲱ), ⲧⲁⲥⲥⲉ, ⲱⲡ(ⲏⲡⲉ) &c.
ⲉⲣ ϭⲓ B, v ⲙⲟⲟⲩ (ⲡ 198 b), ⲥⲁⲡⲓⲥ.
ⲣⲉϥϫⲓ S, taker: ShC 42 221 ⲕⲣⲓⲧⲏⲥ ⲡⲣ. t. (of
bribes), R 1 2 71 ⲟⲩⲣ. ϩⲙⲡⲥⲱⲙⲁ of Christ, ib 1 1 80
ladder ⲡⲣ. ⲣⲱⲙⲉ ⲉϩⲣⲁⲓ ⲉⲙⲡⲏⲩⲉ.

ϭⲓⲛϫⲓ, ϫⲓⲛϭⲓ SB, partaking: CaiEuch 395 B ⲡⲉⲡϫ.
ⲉⲃⲟⲗ ϩⲉⲛⲡⲉⲕⲙⲩⲥⲧⲏⲣⲓⲟⲛ μετάληψις, Mor 17 14 S ϭ.
ϩⲙⲡⲥⲱⲙⲁ σωματική μετάλ.; Va 57 154 B ⲡⲓϫ. ⲙ-
ⲕⲁϩ & in many compounds.

Combined with following nouns & many others:
ⲁⲉⲓⲕ, ⲃⲉⲕⲉ, ⲃⲟⲧⲉ, ⲉⲕⲓⲃⲉ, ⲉⲟⲟⲩ, ⲉⲅⲱ, ⲕⲗⲟⲙ, ⲕⲱⲧⲉ
(ⲕⲟⲧⲥ), ⲙⲕⲁϩ, ⲙⲏⲥⲉ, ⲙⲟⲉⲓⲧ, ⲙⲟⲟⲩ, ⲙϣⲓϣ, ⲡⲁϩⲣⲉ,
ⲣⲟ, ⲣⲁⲛ, ⲣⲟⲩϩⲉ, ⲥⲙⲟⲩ, ⲥⲱϣ, ⲥⲣⲁⲓ, ⲧⲁⲉⲓⲟ, ⲑⲁⲃ, ⲟⲩⲟⲓ
(ⲟⲩⲁⲉⲓⲉ), ⲟⲩⲱ 1° s f, 2°, 3°, ⲟⲩⲟⲉⲓⲛ, ⲱⲙⲥ, ⲱⲡ(ⲏⲡⲉ),
ϣⲕⲁⲕ, ϣⲏⲙ 2°, ϣⲓⲡⲉ, ϣⲁϫⲉ (adding HCon 463 S if
bishop ⲟⲩⲱϣ ⲉϫⲓ ⲟⲩϣ. hear a word, PBu 265 S ⲙⲉⲣⲉⲗⲁⲁⲩ ϫⲓ ϣ. ⲡⲧⲟⲟⲧϥ ⲡⲣⲱⲙⲉ χωρὶς ἀπόδειξις),
ϣⲟⲭⲡⲉ, ϥⲱϭⲉ(ϥⲟϭⲥ), ϩⲁⲉ, ϩⲱⲃⲥ(ϩⲃⲟⲟⲥ s f), ϩⲁⲡ,
ϩⲣⲟⲟⲩ(ϩⲣⲁ), ϫⲡⲓⲧ, ϫⲡⲁϩ, ϫⲣⲟⲡ, ϭⲟⲡⲥ; with Gk
nouns as ϫⲓ ⲁⲅⲁⲡⲏ take alms P 131³ 85 S = Va 61 97
B, ⲗⲉϥϫⲓ ⲁ. beggar CMSS 78 F; ϫⲓ ⲃⲁⲡⲧⲓⲥⲙⲁ βαπτίζεσθαι Mk 1 5 S; ϫⲓ ⲅⲁⲙⲟⲥ γαμεῖν Aeg 28 S; ϫⲓ
ⲇⲱⲣⲟⲛ δ. λαμβ. Ps 14 5 S; ϫⲓ ⲗⲟⲅⲟⲥ get promise DeV
2 91 B, ST 352 S; ϫⲓ ⲙⲟⲣⲫⲏ μορφοῦσθαι Gal 4 19
SB; ϫⲓ ⲙⲩⲥⲧⲏⲣⲓⲟⲛ PS 232 S (cf ⲉⲣ- ⲡ 57 b); ϫⲓ
ⲡⲟⲗⲟⲥ litigate(?) PBu 146 S; ⲣⲉϥϫⲓ ϩⲟⲡⲗⲟⲛ ὁπλίτης
Nu 32 21 S; ϫⲓ ϩⲟⲣⲟⲥ(ὅρ.) J 44 9 S; ϫⲓ ⲡⲓⲣⲁ πειράζειν
Sa 12 26 S, DeV 2 40 B; ϫⲓ ⲡⲟⲗⲉⲙⲟⲥ make war SHel
17 S, ⲣⲉϥϭⲓ ⲡ. C 86 91 B; ϫⲓ ⲥⲁⲣⲝ (cf σαρκοῦσθαι)
BHom 91 S.

ϫⲓ in ϫⲓⲟⲟⲣ, ϫⲓ ⲡⲓⲟⲣ v ⲡ 82 a, adding A²(Mani)
ϫⲓⲟ(ⲟ)ⲣⲉ: P 42 ⲁⲩϫ. ⲙⲙⲁⲕ, K 15 ⲁⲓϫ. ⲁⲧⲭⲱⲣⲁ ⲡⲡ-
ⲏⲡⲧⲟⲩ;   ⲙⲁ ⲡϫ.: ib 91 ⲙⲙ. ⲛⲧⲛⲁϭ ⲡⲥⲉⲧⲉ, ib 111
ⲁⲡⲓⲱⲧ ϣⲟⲩⲟ ⲡϣⲁⲙⲧ ⲙⲙ. ⲁⲃⲁⲗ ⲙⲡⲥⲁ ⲡⲧⲡⲉ, ib ⲙⲙ.
ⲙ. ⲡⲧⲁϥϣⲟⲩⲟⲩϩ ⲁϫⲙⲡⲓⲕⲁϩ.   Distinct from last
(v Sethe Verbum 2 648).

ϫⲓ S(once), ϭⲓ B nn m, breast, pap: C 86 145 her
clothes rent ⲉⲣⲉⲡⲉⲥϭⲓ ⲡⲛⲟⲩ ⲉⲃⲟⲗ ⲡϩⲏⲧⲟⲩ, C 43 229
ⲡⲉϥϭⲓ ⲃ̅ of man; Mich 601 S like bitch on its chain,

like sheep e(ⲩ)ⲧⲁⲁⲥ ⲁⲡ[ⲉ]ⲥϫⲓ(same ?);   ϯϭⲓ, ϫⲓ,
suckle: Ge 21 7 (Sⲧⲥⲛⲕⲟ), Ex 2 7 (A ⲧⲉ ⲕⲉⲓⲃⲉ), Mt 24
19 (S do) θηλάζειν; Ge 33 13 (S Gk diff); Ora 4 185 S
ⲟⲩⲗⲁⲃⲟⲓ [ⲉⲥⲟⲩ]ⲱϣ ⲉϯ ϫⲓ (ⲛ)ⲛⲉⲥϣⲏⲣⲉ;   ⲟⲩⲉⲙ
ϭⲓ, *take suck*: Job 3 12 (S ϫⲓ ⲉⲕⲓⲃⲉ), Lam 2 11 (F
ⲡⲉⲧ[ⲁⲩ]ⲧⲥⲉⲛⲕⲁ ⲙⲙⲁⲩ) θη., ib 2 20 (S do, F ⲟⲩⲱⲙ
ⲁⲣⲱϯ), Joel 2 16 (A ϫⲓ ⲉ.) θ. μαστούς; K 71 ⲉⲑⲟⲩⲉⲙ
ϭⲓ (var ϣⲓ) مرض; CDan 98 ⲛⲓⲕⲟⲩϫⲓ ⲡⲟⲩⲁⲙⲉⲣⲱϯ
ⲉⲧⲉⲡⲛⲏⲡⲉ ⲉⲑⲟⲩ., ROC 25 258 ⲁⲗⲱⲟⲩⲓ ⲡⲟⲩⲁⲙϭⲓ, C
43 100 ⲉⲓⲟⲩ. ⲡⲧⲁⲙⲁⲩ, DeV 1 116 ⲉⲩⲟⲩ. ϭⲛⲡⲉⲛⲡⲙ-
ⲡⲟϯ;   as vb tr, *suckle*: C 41 69 ⲓⲥϫⲉ ⲧⲉⲣⲁϭⲓ (or ? *l*
ϯϭⲓ) ⲡⲉϣⲏⲣⲓ ⲁⲛ, wherefore didst bear him ? (Miss
4 394 ازفر, GöttN '89 54 ܚܠܡ܁ܣ).

ϫⲓ S nn m, a metal vessel or utensil: ST 439 ⲥⲡⲁⲩ
ⲡϫⲓ ⲡⲣⲟⲙⲡⲧ, *ib* ⲟⲩϫⲓ ⲡⲕ. ϣⲏⲙ, BP 69109 sim, Mor
51 34 ⲁⲡϫⲓ ⲡⲉⲙⲟⲩ ⲃⲱⲕ ⲁⲧⲕⲟⲡⲓⲥ ⲃⲱⲕ ⲡⲉⲙⲙⲁϥ, WS
146 ⲟⲩϫⲓ (?) ⲡⲏⲣ.

ϫⲓ A   *v* ϫⲏ 3°.

ϫⲓ A[2]   *v* ⲡϭⲓ.

ϫⲓⲉ A[2]   *v* ϫⲏ 2°.

ϫⲟ SAA[2], ϫⲱ S, ϭⲟ, ⲧϭⲟ (*v* p 466 a)B, ϫⲁ F, ϫⲉ-
SA, ϫⲟ- S, ϭⲉ- B, ϫⲁ-, ϭⲁ- F, ϫⲟⲋ SF, ϫⲁⲋ S[a] A[2]F,
ϭⲟⲋ B, ϫⲏⲅ† S, ϭⲛⲟⲩⲧ† B vb intr, *sow*, *plant* (caus of
? ⲧⲱⲱϭⲉ): Lev 25 11 S(B ⲥⲓϯ), Mt 13 18 S(BF do),
Jo 4 36 SA[2](B do) σπείρειν; Is 65 22 B(S ⲧⲱϭⲉ), Lu
13 6† SB φυτεύειν, Jer 1 10 B(S ⲧ.) καταφ.; P 44 53 S
ⲕⲁϥ ⲉⲩϫ.† ⲁⲣⲟⲩⲣⲁ; ShC 42 86 S fields ⲉⲧϫ.† opp ⲉⲧⲕⲏ ⲉⲃⲟⲗ, ShP 130[2] 80 S ⲙⲁ ⲡⲉⲗⲟⲟⲗⲉ ⲉⲩϫ.†, ShMun
162 S ⲥⲱϣⲉ ⲉⲥϫ.†;   tr: Ex 23 10 S(B ⲥ.), Job 31
8 SB, Hag 1 6 A ϫⲉ-(B do), Mt 13 37 S(BF do), Bor
226 167 S ⲡⲟⲩⲟⲉⲓⲉ...ϫⲉ ⲡⲉϥϭⲣⲟϭ ⲥⲡ.; Ge 2 8 B(S
ShC 73 37 ⲧ.), Ps 79 16 B(S do), 1 Cor 9 7 B(S do) φ.;
BHom 7 S ϫⲟ ⲡⲡⲉϥⲣⲱⲟϣ προκαταβάλλειν;   corn,
flax: ShA 1 454 S ⲟⲩϭⲣⲟϭ ⲡϫⲟ, ManiP 153 A[2] ⲡⲣⲉ-
ⲥⲱϣⲉ...ⲧⲡϫⲁⲥ, CO 138 S ϫⲱ ⲡⲉⲓⲱⲣⲟⲩⲙⲁⲩ, BM
1146 S ⲡⲉⲓⲱⲣⲉ ⲡⲧⲁϥϫⲟⲟⲩ, Ryl 346 S ϫⲟ ⲟⲩⲛⲣⲏⲥⲟⲩⲟ,
Ostr *penes* Crum ϫⲱ ⲉⲓⲱⲣⲉ, J 32 8 S[a] hast right ⲉϫⲁϥ
(*sc* land bought), BM 849 41 B ϭⲟ ⲡⲟⲩⲓⲟⲩⲣⲓ ⲓⲉ ⲁⲗⲟⲗⲓ,
Kr 137 F ⲧⲉⲡϫⲁ ⲟⲩⲡⲱⲥⲱⲛ (ⲡⲟⲥⲟⲛ) ⲓⲱⲩⲣⲓ, *ib* 129 F ⲡⲁ-
ⲓⲱⲣⲓ... ⲉⲕϫⲁⲃ, BMEA 10585 F ϭⲁ ⲡⲓⲱⲩⲣⲓ;   trees:
ShBM 198 29 S ϫⲟ ⲡⲣⲉⲡⲕⲏⲡⲟⲥ, ShMun 110 S palm
ⲙⲡⲁⲧⲕϫⲟⲥ, Rec 6 185 B ⲁϥϭⲟⲟⲩ ⲡⲡⲁⲓⲙⲁ = BMar
219 S ⲧ., DeV 2 48 B gourd ⲙⲡⲉⲕϭⲟⲩϭ;   2d acc:
C 99 211 S field ϫⲟϥ ⲡⲟⲩϭⲣⲟϭ = C 89 4 B, Ep 85 S
ⲡⲧⲡϫⲟ ⲡ...ⲕⲁϩ ⲡⲁⲕ ⲙⲙⲁⲣⲉ, ST 37 S ⲙⲉⲣ(ⲟⲥ) ⲡⲟⲙⲉ ... ⲡⲧϫⲟⲟⲩ ⲡⲉⲓⲱⲣⲉ ⲡⲡⲁϣⲉ, BM 1073 S ⲧⲁϫⲟⲥ
ⲡⲕⲁⲣⲡⲟⲥ ⲡⲓⲙ ⲉⲓⲟⲩⲁϣϥ.

With following preposition or adverb.   c ⲉ-:
ShMIF 23 99 S field ϫⲟ ⲉⲣⲟⲥ ⲙⲡⲓϭⲣⲟϭ, Pcod 29 S
ϫⲟϥ ⲉⲡⲕⲁϩ, Va 61 91 B ϫⲣⲟϫ ⲉⲑⲣⲉϥϭⲟⲩ ⲉⲧⲉϥⲕⲟⲓ;

ⲉⲣⲟⲩⲡ, ⲉⲋ. ⲉ-: Mus 45 47 B ⲉⲡϭ.† ⲉⲋ. ⲉϯⲃⲱ ⲡⲁⲗⲟⲗⲓ,
J 107 16 S ⲕⲁϭ ... ⲉⲧⲉⲧⲡϫⲱ ⲙⲙⲟϥ ⲉ. ⲉⲡⲙⲟⲡⲁⲥⲧⲏ-
ⲣⲓⲟⲛ (this word or next ?);   ⲉϩⲣⲁⲓ ⲉ-: Mk 4 31 (B
ⲥ. ⲉϫⲉⲛ-) ⲥⲡ. ἐπί; ShMun 110 ϫⲟⲥ ⲉ. ⲉⲡⲕⲁⲅ;   c
ⲉϫⲛ-: Hos 2 23 A(B ϥⲓϫⲉⲛ-) ⲥⲡ. ἐπί, Bor 239 80 S
ϫⲉ ⲡⲉϥⲥⲟⲩⲟ ⲉ. ⲟⲩⲡⲉⲧⲣⲁ;   c ϥⲓϫⲛ-: Mk 4 16 S
(var ⲉϫⲛ-, B ⲥ. ⲅ.) ⲥⲡ. ἐπί;   c ⲡ- dat S: J 59 4
ⲉⲧⲣⲁϫⲟ ⲟⲩⲥⲧⲱⲩ ... ⲡⲁⲕ, COAd 20 field ⲡⲧⲁⲩϫⲟⲟⲥ
ⲡⲁⲕ, ST 437 ⲡⲙⲁⲣⲉ ⲡⲧⲁⲓϫⲟⲩ ⲡⲁϣⲉⲡⲟⲩⲧⲉ;   c ϩⲛ-,
ϩⲉⲛ-: Mt 13 27 SF ϫⲁⲋ (BM 499, var & B ⲥ.) ⲥⲡ.
ἐν, Lev 19 19 S(var ⲛ-, B ⲥ. ϩⲉⲛ-) κατασπ.; PS 49 S
ⲡⲉⲡⲧⲁⲩϫⲟⲓ ϩⲛⲡⲉⲓⲡⲉⲑⲟⲟⲩ, ManiK 101 A[2] ⲁⲓϫⲟ ⲡⲧ-
ⲙⲛⲉ ϩⲛⲡⲭⲱⲣⲁ ⲧⲏⲣⲟⲩ, Miss 4 117 B ⲡⲛⲟⲩϭⲉ ϫⲣⲟϫ
ⲡϩⲏⲧϥ; ϩⲣⲁⲓ ϩⲛ-, ⲡϩⲣ. ϩⲉⲛ-: Mt 13 31 S(var ⲉ-)
F ϫⲟϭ (B ⲥ.) ⲥⲡ. ἐν; CaiEuch 393 B ⲡⲉϥϫⲓⲛⲕⲓⲙ ⲉⲧϭ.†
ⲡϭ. ⲡϩⲏⲧⲉⲡ ἔμφυτος dat; C 86 39 B believer ⲉⲧϭ.†
ⲡϭ. ϭⲉⲛϯⲃⲱ ⲡⲁⲗⲟⲗⲓ ⲙⲙⲏⲓ, ManiP 75 A[2] ⲡⲙⲁ...ϫⲟ
ⲡϩⲣⲏⲓ ⲡϩⲏⲧϥ ⲙⲡϣⲏⲡ;   c ⲉϩⲣⲁⲓ S: Deu 11 10
(B ⲥ.) ⲥⲡ.; ShC 42 144 ⲡϭⲟⲟⲙ ⲡⲧⲁⲧⲉⲧⲡϫⲟⲟⲩ ⲡⲁⲓ
ⲉϩ.;   as nn: (*cf* κατασπορά): ST 37 ⲡⲧϫⲟⲟⲩ ϩⲛⲡϫⲟ
ⲉϩ. ⲡϯⲣⲟⲙⲡⲉ, Ep 85, BKU 1 79 sim.

—— nn m SAA[2]BF, *sowing*, *planting* : Ge 8 22
S(B ϫⲣⲟϫ) σπέρμα; Is 32 10 SBF, Am 9 13 SA(B
ⲥⲓϯ) σπόρος; Is 60 21 B(S ⲧⲱϭⲉ) φύτευμα, Va 57 276
B ⲟⲩϭⲟ ⲡⲧⲉ ⲟⲩϣϣⲏⲡ φυτόν, Ps 127 3 B ϭⲟ ⲙⲃⲉⲣⲓ (S
ⲧ. ⲙⲃ.) νεόφυτος; ShA 1 454 S ⲧⲁⲣⲭⲏ ⲙⲡϫⲟ, ⲑⲁⲏ
ⲙⲡϫⲟ, BMar 47 S ϩⲉⲛϭⲣⲟϭ ⲡϫⲱ, BAp 134 S divers
trees ϣⲁϩⲣⲁⲓ ⲉⲡϫⲟ ⲡⲧⲥⲱϣⲉ, AP 44 A[2] ⲟⲩϫⲟ ⲙⲡϣⲉ[ϫⲉ], AM 88 B ⲡⲥⲏⲟⲩ ⲙⲡⲓϭⲟ, Wess 188 S rubric
ⲉϩⲙⲡϫⲟ at sowing, Kr 137 F ⲡⲕⲉⲣⲟⲥ (και.) (ⲡ)ⲡϫⲁ.

ⲙⲁ ⲡϫⲟ, *place of sowing*, *planting* : Mic 1 6 AB
(S ⲧ.) φυτεία; P 44 53 S ⲁⲡⲣⲓϫⲓ(ⲟ)ⲡ ⲕⲁⲧⲁⲥⲫⲟⲣⲁ·
ⲙ. ازرع;   ⲙⲁ ⲉⲧϫ.†: Lu 6 1 S(B ⲣⲟϯ) σπόριμος.

ⲣⲉϥϫⲟ, *sower* : Z 583 S opp ⲣⲉϥⲱⲗ; ⲣⲉϥϫⲉ ⲡⲧⲏϭ
ib 271 S.

Cf ϫⲟⲉⲓⲧ vb.

ϫⲟ SF(once), ϫⲱ S, ϭⲟ B, ϫⲁ F, ϫⲉ- SAF, ϫⲓ-
S, ϭⲉ- BF, ϫⲟⲋ S, ϫⲁⲋ AA[2]F, ϭⲟⲋ B, ϭⲁⲋ F vb tr, *put*,
send forth, *spend* (*cf* ϫⲟⲩ): PMich 562 F account
ⲡⲉⲧⲁϥϭⲁϥ (*bis*), C 86 346 B ⲉϥϭⲟ ⲡϭⲱⲃ ⲡⲓⲃⲉⲛ ⲉⲧϣⲟⲡ
ⲡⲁϥ (but var c ⲉⲃⲟⲗ).

With following preposition.   c ⲉ-: Jo 20 27 A[2]
(S ⲡⲟⲩϫⲉ, B ϩⲓⲟⲩⲓ) βάλλειν εἰς; Job 31 8 S neg (B
diff) ἄρριζος γίνεσθαι; ROC 17 406 B ϭⲟ ⲛϯϭⲛϩⲓ ⲉⲃⲏⲧ
χρᾶσθαι κατά; Bel 3 B δαπανᾶν εἰς; Ryl 72 351 S ϫⲉ
ⲕⲉⲗⲉⲃⲓⲛ ⲉⲡⲉϣϣⲏⲛ;   c ⲉϫⲛ-: Jos 9 4 S, Is 11 8 S
(B ϩⲓ.) ἐπιβ. ἐπί;   c ⲛ-: BMis 262 S to quarrelsome ox ⲡⲡⲕⲁⲙ ϭⲟⲙ ⲉϫⲱ ⲙⲙⲟⲥ (*sc* ⲧⲕⲁⲡⲉ) ⲡⲕⲉⲥⲟⲡ
ⲡⲗⲁⲁⲩ ⲡⲣⲱⲙⲉ (var Mor 29 31 ⲣⲱⲣⲧ) = Mor 30 37 F
ϫⲁⲡⲥ (*cf* c ⲉϩⲣⲏⲓ ϩⲁ-), BM 582(2) F ϭⲉ ⲟⲩⲕⲁⲡⲉⲣⲧⲁⲃ
ⲡⲉⲃ;   c ϩⲛ-, ϩⲉⲛ-: Mor 30 41 F ⲁϥϫⲉ ⲧⲉϥϭⲓϫ ϩⲙⲡⲁⲥⲱⲙⲁ = BMis 265 S ϫⲱⲣ ⲉ-, AM 102 B ϭⲱⲟⲩ (*sc*
nails) ⲡϩⲣⲏⲓ ϭⲉⲛⲡⲓⲕⲁⲙ.

With following adverb.

—— ⲉⲃⲟⲗ: Jth 12 4 *S*, Mk 5 26 *SB*, 2 Cor 12 15
SBF ϫⲁϩ ⲇⲁⲡ., Va 58 153 *B* withering grass, dying
herb ⲧϥⲅⲥⲓⲥ ⲉⲧⲙⲟⲧⲉⲛ ⲛ̄ϭⲟ ⲉⲃ. εὐδαπάνητος; Ps 68
31 *A*(Cl, *S* ⲡ., *B* ⲧⲁⲟⲅⲟ) ἐκφέρειν; Deu 32 22 *S*(*l*?
ϫⲉⲣⲟ, *B* as Gk) φλέγειν; Nu 17 12 *S*(var ϩⲱⲧⲉ ⲉⲃ.,
B ⲙⲟⲅⲛⲕ) παραναλίσκεσθαι; ib 32 13 *S*(var ⲥⲟⲣⲙ,
B ⲕⲱϯ ⲡⲉⲙ-) καταπλανᾶν; Col 1 23 *S* ϫⲉ ⲥⲓⲧⲉ ⲉⲃ.(*B*
ⲧⲁⲭⲣⲏⲟⲩⲧ) θεμελιοῦν; Va 58 156 *B* ⲁⲅϭⲟ ⲉⲃ. ⲛ̄ⲡⲓⲁ-
ⲡⲁϣ πιπράσκειν (sic prob); ShR 2 3 71 *S* wealth ⲁⲕ-
ϫⲟⲥ ⲉⲃ. ϩ̄ⲛⲟⲅⲙ̄ⲛⲧϣⲛⲁ, CA 99 *S* alms ϫⲟⲟⲩ ⲉⲃ. ⲕⲁⲗⲱⲥ, C 43 163 *B* ϭⲟ ⲛⲟⲩⲙⲏϣ ⲛ̄ⲉⲗⲉⲏⲙⲟⲥⲓⲟⲛ ⲉⲃ., AZ
16 15 *S* ⲁⲓϫⲟ ⲛ̄ⲣⲃⲟⲟⲥ ⲉⲃ. ⲁⲓϫⲓ ⲡⲥⲛⲁⲩ ⲛ̄ϩⲟⲗⲟⲕ/ *sold*
linen & got 2 solidi, Cai Copt Mus ostr 4998 (*v* Catal
1 57) list of *varia* ⲡⲁⲓ ⲧⲏⲣⲟⲩ ⲛ̄ⲧⲁ ϫⲟ ⲉⲃ. ϩ̄ⲛⲑⲏⲡⲓⲧⲉ
expended, sold (?), BM 605 *F* ⲡⲉⲧⲉϫⲁ ⲃⲁⲗ ⲉⲟⲩⲕⲗⲁⲥ-
ⲙⲁ; of time: BHom 9 *S* ϫⲉ ⲡⲉⲡⲁϩⲉ ⲉⲃ. ⲁⲡϫⲓⲛ-
ϫⲏ, Va 57 238 *B* ϭⲉ ⲡⲟⲩⲥⲛⲟⲩ ... ⲉⲃ. ϩ̄ⲛⲡⲓϣⲧⲉⲕⲟ
ἀναλίσκ.; Z 288 *S* ⲕⲁⲧⲁⲛ.; Va 58 190 *B* ϭⲉ ⲛⲓⲉⲣⲟⲟⲩ
ⲉⲃ. ⲇⲁⲡ.; Job 14 14 *B*(*S* ϫⲱⲕ ⲉⲃ.) συντελεῖν; BMar
83 *S* ⲉϥϫⲱ ⲙⲡⲉϥⲁϩⲉ ⲉⲃ., Pcod 48 *S* sim ϫⲱ, HL 113
B ϭⲟ ⲙⲡⲉϥ ... ⲥⲛⲟⲩ ⲉⲃ.; as nn, *expenses*: BM
358 *S* service of poor & ⲛ̄ϫⲟ ⲉⲃ. ⲙ̄ⲡⲧⲟⲡⲟⲥ, Bodl(P)
c 12 *S* ⲛ̄ϫⲟ ⲉⲃ. ⲛ̄ⲡⲏⲣⲡ ⲛⲧⲁⲓⲁⲕⲟⲛⲓⲁ, J 99 17 *S* ⲡⲉⲩ-
ϫⲏⲙⲟⲥⲓⲟⲛ ... ⲉⲡϫⲟ ⲉⲃ. ⲡⲧⲉⲡⲣⲟⲥⲫⲟⲣⲁ, CMSS 64
S' ⲛ̄ϫⲟ ⲉⲃ. ⲉⲛϣⲉⲉⲓ, JSch 1 30 *S* money ⲉⲛⲁϫⲱ ⲉⲃ.,
KroppM 57 *S* ⲛϫⲱ ⲉⲃ. *application* of charm, BM 691
F ⲛ̄ϫⲁⲃⲟⲗ, PAberdeenUniv *F* ⲛ̄ⲗⲟⲩ(ⲟⲥ) ⲉⲡϫⲁⲃⲁⲗ,
CO 509 *F* ⲧϫⲁⲃⲟⲗ (*sic*); ϫⲓⲛϭⲟ ⲉⲃ. *B*: Va 57
48 ⲛ̄ϫ. ⲛ̄ⲡⲓϩⲏⲕⲓ ἀναλίσκ.; ⲉⲃ. ⲉ-: Ac 21 24 *SB*
ⲇⲁⲡ. ἐπί, Lu 10 35 *SB* προσδ., EpJer 9 *BF* ⲕⲁⲧⲁⲛⲁⲗ.
εἰς; 1 Cor 9 18 *S* ⲛⲟⲩⲉϣ ⲛ̄ϫⲟ ⲉⲃ. ⲉ- (*B* as Gk) ἀδά-
πανος; Z 346 *S* ϫⲟϥ ⲉⲃ. ⲉⲣⲟⲛ εἰς τ. χρείαν ἡμῶν; ShC
42 93 *S* gifts offered ⲉⲛⲉ ⲉϩⲉⲥⲧⲓ ⲉ ... ϫⲟⲟⲩ ⲉⲃ. ⲉⲣⲟⲟⲩ
ⲛⲁⲅⲁⲁⲩ, BMar 92 *S* ϫⲱ ⲉⲃ. ⲉⲛⲉⲧϣⲱⲡⲉ ⲛ̄ⲣⲏⲧⲟⲩ (sc
wine), HM 1 42 *S* ϫⲟ ⲉⲃ. ⲉⲣⲟⲟⲩ (sc temples) ϩ̄ⲙⲡ-
ⲧⲁⲙⲓⲟⲛ ⲙⲡⲣⲣⲟ, AM 285 *B* sim, C 99 146 *S* ship's
cargo ϫⲟϥ ⲉⲃ. ⲉⲡⲉⲥⲡⲏⲩ, Ep 348 *S* ⲥⲡⲁⲩ ⲛⲥⲟⲉⲓϣ ...
ϫⲟⲟⲩ ⲉⲃ. ⲉⲣⲟⲕ ϩⲁⲡⲉⲕⲣⲓⲥⲉ, J 85 19 *S* fruits of toil ϫⲟϥ
ⲉⲃ. ⲉⲛⲗⲟⲅⲟⲥ ⲙ̄ⲡⲗⲉⲭⲛⲟⲥ (λύχ.), MélOr 6 517 *B* his
goods ϭⲱⲟⲩ ⲉⲃ. ⲉϯⲇⲓⲁⲕⲟⲛⲓⲁ; ⲉⲃ. ⲉϫⲛ- *S*: BMar
136 ⲁⲡⲥⲱⲧⲏⲣ ϫⲉ ⲧⲟⲟⲧϥ ⲉⲃ. ⲉϫⲙ̄ⲡⲣⲟ, Mor 38 27 ⲁϥϫⲉ ⲧⲟⲟⲧϥ ⲉⲃ. ⲉϫⲙ̄ⲡⲉϩⲣⲟ, ib 31 26 sim ⲧⲉϥϭⲓϫ; ⲉⲃ.
ⲡ-: Va 57 244 *B* ϭⲱⲟⲩ ⲉⲃ. ⲛ̄ⲣⲁⲡⲕⲉⲭⲱⲟⲩⲛⲓ εἰς ἑτέ-
ρους κενοῦν; BMar 56 *S* ϫⲉ ϩⲉⲛⲛⲟϭ ⲛ̄ⲁⲡⲣⲁⲗⲱⲙⲁ ⲉⲃ.
ⲛ̄ⲡⲥⲁⲉⲓⲛ; ⲉⲃ. ϩⲁ-: 2 Cor 12 15 *SF*(*B* ⲉϩⲣⲏⲓ ⲉϫ.)
ἐκδαπ. ὑπέρ; ⲉⲃ. ϩⲓ- *SA²*: R 1 5 36 ⲁ̄ⲡ̄ⲛ̄ⲉ̄ⲙ̄-
ⲱⲡ ϫⲉ ⲧⲟⲟⲧϥ ⲉⲃ. ϩⲓⲡⲉϥϩⲣⲟ (sic, *l*? ⲛⲉⲥ-), ManiP 226
sim; ⲉⲃ. ϩⲛ-, ϩⲉⲛ-: Ja 4 3 *SB*(*A* ⲱϫⲛⲉ) ⲇⲁⲡ. ἐν;
Cant 5 4 *S*(var ⲉϩⲟⲩⲛ, *B* ParisInstCath 151 ϫⲉⲩ ⲉⲃ.
ⲟⲩⲛ) ἀποστέλ. ἀπό; ShC 42 97 *S* ϫⲟ ⲛⲧⲉϥⲥⲛϥⲉ ⲉⲃ.
ϩ̄ⲛⲣⲏⲧϥ ⲛⲡⲉⲩⲉⲣⲏⲩ, Aeg 22 *S* ϫⲉ ⲧⲉⲕϭⲓϫ ⲉⲃ. ϩ̄ⲙⲡⲉϥ-
ⲥⲱⲙⲁ = *B* ⲭⲱ ϫⲓϫ ⲉϫⲉⲛ-; ϫⲉ ⲛⲟⲩⲛⲉ ⲉⲃ., *put*

forth, take root: Jer 12 2 *S*(*B* ϭⲉⲡ-), Eph 3 17 *SB*
ⲣⲓⲍⲟⲩⲥⲑⲁⲓ, Hos 14 6 *A*(*S* ⲡ. ⲉⲃ., *B* ϩⲓ.) ῥίζας βάλ.; Sa
12 10 *S* ἔμφυτος; ShMIF 23 146 *S* ϫⲟϥ ⲉϩⲣⲁⲓ ⲉⲡⲕⲁϩ
... ⲁϥϫⲉ ⲛⲟⲩⲛⲉ ⲉⲃ., BMis 554 *S* plants ⲙⲡⲟⲩϫⲉ ⲛ.
ⲉⲃ., C 41 19 *B* ϭⲉ ⲛ. ⲉⲃ.; Si 24 13 *S* ϫⲉ ⲛ. ⲉⲃ.
ϩⲛ- ⲣⲓϫ. ἐν, Is 40 24 *S* sim (var ⲉϩⲣⲁⲓ ⲉ-, *B* diff) ⲣⲓϫ.
εἰς; ShA 1 465 *S*, C 43 123 *B* sim.

—— ⲉϩⲟⲩⲛ ⲉ- *S*: Lam 3 13 (but var ⲛⲟⲩϫⲉ, *B*
diff) εἰσάγειν ἐν; PS 369 ϫⲟ ⲛ̄ⲡⲗⲟⲩ ⲭⲏ ⲉϩ. ⲉⲡⲁⲥⲡⲓⲣ,
ShA 2 130 ϫⲟ ⲛ̄ⲡⲉⲩⲧⲃ̄ⲛⲟⲟⲩⲉ ⲉϩ. ⲉⲙⲙⲁ ⲛⲟⲉⲓⲕ, J 107
16 land ϫⲱ ⲙⲙⲟⲟϥ ⲉϩ. ⲉⲡⲙⲟⲛⲁⲥⲧⲏⲣⲓⲟⲛ; ⲉϩ. ϩⲁ- *S*:
P 129[16] 3 bull ϫⲟ ⲙ̄ⲡⲉϥⲧⲁⲡ ⲥⲡⲁⲩ ⲉϩ. ϩⲁⲣⲟϥ; ⲉϩ.
ϫⲉⲛ- *B*: C 43 60 ϭⲱⲟⲩ (sc nails) ⲉϩ. ϫⲉⲛ̄ⲡⲓϣ̄ⲃⲉ.

ϫⲟ *A* nn, *wind, tempest* (*d'* Dévaud, *v* Spg 305):
Hos 8 7 (*B* ϫⲓⲙⲫⲉ) ἀνεμόφθορα.

ϫⲟ *SB*, ⲁ̄ϫⲱ *B* nn m, *crook-back*, ⲟ, ⲟⲓ ⲛ-: Lev
21 20 *B*(*S* = Gk), 3 Kg 21 11 *S* κυρτός; K 74 *B* ⲡⲓⲁ.
احدب, opp ⲉⲧⲥⲟⲩⲧⲱⲛ. (Dévaud *Ét.* 41 doubts
identity of ϫⲟ, ⲁ̄ϫⲱ).

ϫⲟ *S*, ⲁϭⲟ *B*, pl ϫⲱⲟⲩ *S* nn m, *arm-pit*: Tri 485
S ⲛⲉϥϫⲟ باط, K 260 *B* ⲡⲓⲁ. '؛ ShC 73 171 *S* cursed
whoso shall pluck out hair ⲉⲧⲣⲱⲧ ⲛⲣⲟⲩⲛ ϩ̄ⲛⲡⲉϥϫⲟ,
ib 162 arms bared ϣⲁϩⲟⲩⲛ ⲉⲡⲉⲛϫⲱⲟⲩ (var ϣⲱⲡϣ).
V Rec 39 161.

ϫⲟⲉ, ϫⲟⲓⲉ[2], ϫⲟⲉⲓ[3], ϫⲟⲓ[4] *S*, ϫⲟ[5] (oftenest) *SS'F*,
ϫⲱ[6] *SB*, ϫⲁⲓ[7], -ⲓⲉ[8] *A*, ϫⲟⲓ, ϫⲱⲓ *B*, ϫⲁ(ⲁ)ⲓ *F*, ϫⲉ- *S*,
ϫⲓ- *SB*, pl ⲉϫⲏ *S* & sg as pl, nn f, *wall* (*cf* ⲥⲟⲃⲧ): Lev
5 9 *S'B*, Jud 16 13 *S'*, Ps 61 3 *S'B*, Cant 2 9 *F* ϫⲁⲓ, Si
22 18 *S'A'*, Tob 2 9 *S*, Hab 2 11 *A'B'*, Ac 23 3 *S'B*,
MG 25 359 *B* in weaving he reached ϯϫ. (but Gött
ar 114 128 حائل as if *border*) τοῖχος; Mic 7 11 *S'A'*
maceria; Ps 88 40 *S'*(*B* ⲥⲟⲃⲧ), Eccl 10 8 *S*(*F* ϫⲁⲗϫⲉⲗ),
Mk 12 1 *S'B* φραγμός; Ez 41 21 *S'B* paries; ShP 130[2]
25 *S* ϩⲉⲛϫⲟ ⲁⲩⲱ ϩⲉⲛⲥⲟⲃⲧ, ShRE 10 163 *S* ϩⲉⲛϫⲟ...
ⲕⲏⲧ ⲉϫⲙ̄ⲡϣⲱ, BAp 69 *S* ϭⲱϣⲧ ⲉⲧϫ., ib sim ϫⲟ, Wess
159 *S* ⲛϫ. ⲙ̄ⲡⲣⲡⲉ, HM 1 78 *S* ⲧϫ. ⲡⲧⲉⲧⲣⲓⲣ, DeV 2 86
B ⲛⲓⲭ. ⲛ̄ⲧⲉ ϯⲅⲣⲱ, MG 25 23 *B* ⲡⲉⲛⲭ. ⲛ̄ϯⲣⲓ, C 43 28 *B*
ϯϫⲱⲓ, BMis 570 *S* size of Paradise ϥⲧⲟⲟⲩ ⲛ̄ϣⲉ ⲛ̄ⲕⲁϣ
ⲉⲧϫⲟ each *side* of area, *cf* BM 528 *F* in title of § I ⲃⲧⲁ
ⲛϫ. ⲙ̄ⲡⲓⲱⲣⲓ, Mor 29 22 *S'* ⲛⲉϫⲟ of room, ib 41 98
S', ib 30 25 *F* ϫⲁⲁⲓ sim, J 67 74 *S* ⲟⲩⲉⲓ ⲛϫ., ib 11 60
S ⲧϫ.[2] ... ⲣ ⲕⲟⲓⲛⲟⲛ, ib 51 4 *S* ⲧϫ.[2] ⲧⲁⲃⲁⲗ ⲛ̄ⲫⲓⲣ, TurM
16 *S* ⲧϫ.[3] (sic) ⲧⲁⲣⲏⲥ, ib ϫ., ST 109 *S* ⲛ̄ⲧⲉⲩϫ.[4] ⲉⲃⲟⲗ,
CO 148 *S* ⲛ̄ⲧⲁⲕ ⲛϫ.[4], Mor 16 109 *S* ϫⲟⲟⲓ; pl *S*:
2 Kg 5 11, Ez 41 13 ⲛⲉϫⲉ.ⲧ.; Cant 8 9 (var ⲉϫⲉ, *F* sg)
ἔπαλξις; Nu 22 24 (var P 44 107 & *B* ⲧⲗⲟⲙ) αὐλαξ;
R 1 3 32 e. of κοιτῶν; ⲙⲁ ⲛ̄ϫⲟ *S*, *piece of wall*:
ShC 42 202 ⲁ̄ϩⲉⲛ. ϣⲉ ⲉϫⲱⲟⲩ, BMis 174 site pleased
him save for ϩ̄ⲛⲕⲟⲩⲓ ⲙⲙ. ⲉⲩⲣ̄ⲡⲧⲙⲛⲧⲉ (var Mor 26
34 ⲕⲟⲩⲓ ⲛ̄ϫⲟ); ϫⲉⲡⲧ-, ϫⲉⲡⲉⲧⲙⲏⲛⲧⲉ *S*, ϫⲓⲡⲉⲙⲏϯ
B nn f, *middle wall*: Eph 2 14 *SB*, cit Miss 4 615 *S*

μεσότοιχον; Ge 38 29 B ϥⲣ.; P 131³ 61 S ⲧϫⲉⲛⲉⲧⲙ.,
Mor 16 20 S ⲛϫⲓⲛⲉⲧⲙ., COAd 4 S ⲧϫⲟⲉ ⲛⲧⲙ.
Once m : Tri 528.

ϫⲟⲓ SB, ϫⲟⲉⲓ² S, ϫⲁⲓ³ AA²(M2)F, ϫⲁⲉⲓ⁴ S²AA²
(Jo), pl ⲉϫⲏⲩ SA²F, -ⲛⲟⲩ B & sg as pl, nn m, *ship,
boat*: Is 33 21 SBF, Jon 1 4 S²A², Mt 14 13 SBF, Jo
6 17 SA²B πλοῖον, Job 40 26 S(B pl) πλωτός; ib 9
26 S(B pl), Pro 31 14 SA⁴B ναῦς; P 44 54 S, K 133
B سفينة, opp ⲕⲁⲧⲟ كرم; Tri 482 S, P 55 13 B 'ⲗ; P
43 246 S πλωρα (πρ.)· ⲉⲑⲏ(ⲙ)ⲛϫ., ⲡⲣⲩⲙⲛⲁ·ⲉⲡⲁⲣ-
ⲟⲩ ⲙⲛϫ.; PS 354 S ⲟⲩϫ. v ⲣⲓⲉ 1°, ShA 2 48 S water
ϫⲱⲥⲉ ⲉⲛϫ.², ShA 2 151 S(var² BM 206 83), ShBM
198 30 Sᵃ cattle, vineyards ⲉⲓϫ.⁴, C 86 129 B ⲣⲁⲡ-
ⲗⲏϣ ⲛϫ. ⲡⲉⲙⲣⲁⲡⲕⲟⲙⲁⲣⲓⲟⲛ (πωμ.), Br 236 S ⲟⲩϫ.
ⲉϥⲟⲧⲡ, J 5 R 14 S ⲣⲏⲙⲉ ⲛϫ., TillBau 130 S ⲥⲁⲧ ⲟⲩϫ.
ⲉⲡⲙⲟⲟⲩ, AM 184 B ⲟⲩϫ…. ⲣⲓⲧϥ ⲉϥⲛϫ., BM 1117
S², El 56 A ⲁⲩⲧⲁⲗⲁⲉⲓ ⲁⲡⲛϫ.⁴, AM *lc* B ⲧⲁⲗⲉ ⲟⲩⲁⲟⲩⲡ
ⲉⲛϫ., Mani K 25 A² ⲛϫ.⁵ ⲡⲟⲩⲁⲓⲛⲉ, Mor 30 51 F
ⲣⲛϫ. = ib 29 44 S ⲥⲓⲛⲟⲩⲏⲗ, ViK 4707 S opp ⲣⲁⲗ-
ⲗⲏⲛⲣⲉ, DeV 2 77 B ⲟⲩϫ. ⲉϥⲉⲣ ⲣⲱⲧ ϩⲉⲛⲫⲓⲟⲙ, AM
88 B ϫ. ⲉϥⲣⲏⲗ ⲉⲣⲁⲕⲟϯ, ib 185 B ⲁⲩϣⲟⲓⲣ ⲉⲛϫ., ib
67 B ⲁⲡⲛϫ. ⲗⲟⲡⲓ ⲉⲡⲓⲣⲟⲣⲙⲉⲥ, C 43 227 B ϫⲱⲟⲩⲡ ⲙ-
ⲡⲛϫ. ⲉⲃⲟⲗ, ib 212 B ⲑⲟⲕ ⲛⲧⲉ ⲡⲓϫ., ib 213 B ⲥⲕⲁⲗⲁ
do, AM 296 B ⲟⲩⲉⲛⲧ do ; Ryl 238 S ϫ. ⲛⲃⲁⲣⲱⲧ ⲛ-
ⲉϩⲁⲗⲩⲭⲡⲟ(ⲡ, *cf* πλοιάρια χαλκᾶ Preisigke) ; pl :
Ge 49 13 SB, Ps 47 7 SB, Ap 8 9 SB πλοῖ., Jo 6 23
SA²BF(PMich 3521) -άριον; Dan 11 40 SB ν.; Sa 14
5 S σχεδία ; BMis 179 S, ManiK 110 A², AM 149 B.

ⲣ ϫ. A², *act as ship, transport* (?) : ManiP 84 ⲧⲁ-
ⲗⲉⲉⲩ…ⲧⲉⲧⲁⲣ ϫ. ϩⲁⲣⲁⲓ till she convoy me to city.

In names(?) : Ψανετσῆβ (PLond 4 428), ⲡⲁⲡⲉϫⲏⲩ
(BM 1085, Baouit 2 13). In place-name : Φαμϫόι
(PLond 4 204), -ϫάι (PCai 3 121).

ϫⲟⲩ A   v ϫⲱ *say & cup.*

ϫⲟⲩ O   v ϭⲱ.

ϫⲱ SA²BFO, ϫⲟⲩ AA², ϫⲟⲟⲩⲉ A² (c e-), ϫⲉ-
SAA²BF, ϫⲓ- SAF, ϫⲁ- F, ϫⲟⲟ⳿ SA², ϫⲓⲧ⳿ S(3d pl
once), ϫⲓ⳿ S(imperat)AA²O, ϫⲉⲓ⳿ A, ϫⲟ⳿ A²B, ϫⲟⲧ⳿
B (3d pl), ϫⲁ(ⲁ)⳿ F, imperat ⲁϫⲓ- S, ⲁϫⲓ⳿ SAA²F,
ⲉϫⲓ⳿ AA²ODM, ⲉϫⲉⲓ⳿ A, ⲁϫⲉ- SBF, ⲁϫⲟ⳿, ⲁϫⲟⲧ⳿
B(BSM 97), ⲣ ⲥ ϫⲁⲧ- SA² **A** vb **I** intr (rare), *say,
speak, tell* : 1 Kg 16 2 B(Str) ἐρεῖν; Ac 4 14 S(B diff)
ἀντειπεῖν; ShA 2 281 S ⲛⲡⲉⲧⲛϭⲛ ϣⲁϫⲉ ⲉϫⲱ, ROC
19 72 S ⲕⲁⲧⲁ ⲡϣⲁϫⲉ ⲛϫⲱ *as the saying is*, AM 179
B ⲛⲧⲉⲟⲩⲁⲓ ϭⲓ ϭⲣⲟⲡ ⲟⲩⲗⲉϫⲓⲥ ⲉϥϫⲱ *whilst reciting*,
Hor 82 O ⲛⲧϥϫⲱ ⲛⲧⲟⲩⲉⲓⲣⲉ.

II tr : Ps 34 25 SBF(Mus 49 180), Eccl 2 15 SF,
Jo 12 49 SA²B, Cl 13 2 A εἰπεῖν; Ge 32 4 SB, Pro 1
11 SAB, Lu 9 31 S(B ϫⲁϫⲓ), AP 7 A² ⲡⲉⲧϫⲟⲩ ⲙⲙⲁⲩ
λέγειν; Job 19 4 SB, 1 Cor 14 9 SB λαλεῖν; Ps 9 1
S(B c.), Is 43 21 S(B ϥⲓⲣⲓ) διηγεῖσθαι, Si 34 12 S
ἐκδ.; Job 32 6 S(B ⲧⲁⲗⲟ), Ps 50 15 SA(Cl)B, Is 12

4 S(B ⲣⲓ ⲱⲓϣ) ἀναγγέλλειν, Ps 54 17 SB, Pro 12 17 SA
(B c.) ἀπαγγ., Sa 2 13 S ἐπαγγ.; Ps 77 2 S(B c.) φθέγγεσθαι; Ps 118 171 S(B ϩⲉⲃⲓ) ἐξερεύγεσθαι; MG 25
211 B ϫⲱ ⲙⲡⲓⲃ̄ ⲙ̄ⲯⲁⲗⲙⲟⲥ βάλλειν; PS 115 S ⲡ-
ϣⲁϫⲉ ⲉⲛⲧⲁⲥϫⲟⲟⲩ, ib 7 S ⲡⲁⲓ ⲥⲉ ⲉⲩϫⲱ ⲙⲙⲟⲟⲩ, ShA
1 241 S ϣⲁⲩⲑⲙⲕⲟϥ ϫⲉⲛⲡⲁϩⲟⲟⲥ ϫⲉⲙⲟⲟⲩⲧϥ *not to
say slay him*, Z 268 S didst never see Jesus ⲧⲁϫⲟⲟⲥ
ϫⲉⲛⲧⲕⲟⲩⲙⲉⲥⲧⲉ ⲡⲙⲙⲁϥ, BM 267 191 S ϫⲱ ϭ̄ⲉ ⲡⲁⲡ
ⲙⲡⲃⲱⲗ (imperat), AP 11 A² what ill have I wrought ?
ϫⲟⲟⲥ (sim), BMis 322 S ⲡⲉⲡⲧⲁⲕⲟⲩⲱ ⲉϫⲓⲧⲟⲩ = BSM
5 B ⲡⲧⲉⲕϫⲱ, ROC 17 407 B ⲡⲓⲥⲁϫⲓ ⲉⲧⲉⲥⲁⲣⲣⲁ ⲡⲁϫⲟⲧⲟⲩ ;   *as for saying* : Mk 9 23 S ⲉϫⲟⲟⲥ (*sic* Mor 4)
ϫⲉ- (*cf* B Gk), ShC 73 64 S ⲉϫⲟⲟⲥ ϫⲉ ϫⲉ-, ShWess 9
148 S sim, Sh(?)Leyd 332 S ⲛⲑⲉ ⲉϫⲟⲟⲥ ϫⲉ-, BM 267
S ⲉϣⲱⲡⲉ ⲧⲉⲧⲛⲣⲡⲧⲃⲁ̄ⲅⲗⲱⲡ ⲛⲑⲉ ⲉϫ. *as it were*, BMis
387 S ⲉϫϫⲉⲟⲡ ⲉϫⲟⲟⲥ (var ib c. ⲛⲥⲉϫⲟⲟⲥ), DeV 2 186
B eyes smarted ⲣⲱⲥ ⲉϫⲱⲥ (var ϫⲟⲥ) ϫⲉⲡⲉϥϩⲁⲗⲗⲟⲩ
ⲡⲁϫⲱϫⲓ ⲉⲃⲟⲗ; ϫⲉ-, ϫⲓ-, ϫⲁ- : Job 11 2 A ϫⲉ ⲣⲁⲣ
(Cl, S ⲟ ⲛⲣ., B ϫⲱ), Pro 23 9 SA ϫⲉ ⲗⲁⲅⲉ, Jo 11 13 S
ϫⲉ ⲡⲉⲡⲕⲟⲧ (A² ϫⲉⲣⲁ-, B ϫⲟ⳿), ib 6 6 SA² ϫⲉ ⲡⲁⲓ (B
ϫⲟ⳿) λέγ., Pro 15 23 S ϫⲉ ⲗⲁⲅⲉ A ϫⲓ, Jo 3 12 BF(S ϫⲱ
e-) ⲉⲓⲡ.; Job 42 7 S ϫⲓ ⲗⲁⲁⲩ, B ϫⲉ, Mk 4 34 F ϫⲉ ⲗⲁⲡⲥ
(SB ϣⲁϫⲉ) λάλ.; Si 18 2 S ϫⲉ ⲡⲉϥϧⲣⲏⲅⲉ ἐξαγγ.; Ob
12 A ϫⲓ ⲡⲟϭ ⲡϣⲁϫⲉ, B ϫⲉ μεγαλορρημονεῖν; PS 71
S suffer me ⲛⲧⲁϫⲓ ⲡⲃⲱⲗ, Br 91 S ϫⲉ ⲡⲉⲓⲣⲁⲡ, ShC
42 109 S ϫⲉ ⲣⲉⲡϣⲏⲙ, BMis 299 S ϫⲓ ⲡⲁⲓ, Mor 30
24 F ϫⲁ ⲣⲏⲕⲟⲩⲓ, ib 47 ϫⲉ ϫⲱϩ ⲡⲓⲙ, AM 204 B ϫⲉ
ⲙⲉⲧϫⲉⲣⲟⲩⲱ; imperat forms : Is 43 26 S(BHom
136) ⲁϫⲓ ⲡⲉⲕⲛⲟⲃⲉ (var ϫⲱ)B ⲁϫⲉ λέγε; PS 33 S ⲁϫⲓ
ⲡϣⲁϫⲉ, Mun 38 S ⲁϫⲓ ⲡⲉⲧⲉⲕⲟⲩⲁϣϥ = C 86 285 B
ⲁϫⲉ, BMar 23 S ⲁϫⲉ ⲟⲩϣⲁϫⲉ, DeV 2 173 B ⲁϫⲉ ⲡⲉϥⲣⲁⲡ, Mor 24 34 F ⲁϫⲉ ⲡⲉⲣⲃⲏⲟⲩⲓ; Mt 4 3 S ⲁϫⲓⲥ B
ⲁϫⲟⲥ, Jo 10 24 A² ⲉϫⲓⲥ ⲉⲓⲡέ, Jer 27 2 F ⲁϫⲓⲥ B do ⲉⲓ-
πατε, Hag 2 2 A ⲁϫⲓⲥ B do, Cl 8 3 A ⲉϫⲉⲓⲥ ⲉⲓⲡⲟⲛ,
ManiK 42 A² ⲁϫⲓⲥ, DM 6 32 O ⲉϫⲓⲥ, Mt 10 27 S
ⲁϫⲓϥ B ⲁϫⲟϥ ⲉⲓⲡⲁⲧⲉ, 1 Kg 15 16 S ⲁϫⲓⲥⲟⲩ λάλησον;
HM 1 157 S ⲁϫⲓⲥⲟⲩ ⲉⲣⲟⲓ, BSM 97 B ⲣⲱⲃ ⲡⲓⲃⲉⲡ…
ⲁϫⲟⲧⲟⲩ.

With following preposition.
—— e-, *to* : Dan 2 7 B, Jo 4 29 SA²(BF ⲡ-) ⲉⲓⲡ.
dat; Job 9 7 S(B do), Ps 44 1 S(var & B ⲡ-) λέγ. dat,
Mor 17 12 S ϫⲱ ⲙⲙⲟⲥ ⲉⲧⲁⲓ λέγ. acc, Ps 17 tit S(B
ⲥⲁϫⲓ ⲡⲉⲙ-) λαλ. dat, Lu 12 3 S(B c. ϩⲉⲡ-) λαλ. πρός,
Aeg 275 S ϫⲱ ⲉⲡⲗⲁⲟⲥ προσλαλ. dat, Deu 17 11 S(var
& B ⲡ-) ἀνάγγ. dat, 1 Cor 2 1 S(B ⲧⲁⲙⲟ) καταγγ. dat;
Ex 18 8 S(B c. ϩⲁⲧⲉⲡ-) διηγ. dat, Ps 47 14 S(B ϥⲓⲣⲓ
e-) δ. εἰς; Si 46 27 (20) S ὑποδεικνύαι dat; PS 4 S
ϣⲁⲣⲉⲕ̄ ϫⲟⲟⲥ ⲉⲡⲉϥⲙⲁⲑⲏⲧⲏⲥ, BG 26 S ⲡⲧⲁϫⲉ ⲡⲁⲓ
ⲉⲣⲟⲛ, ShC 42 35 S ⲉϥϫⲱ ⲉⲣⲟⲟⲩ ⲙⲡⲉⲡⲧⲁϥϣⲱⲡⲉ,
Mor 18 15 S ϯⲛⲁϫⲱ ⲉⲣⲟⲕ (var ⲡⲁⲕ) ⲡⲟⲩϣⲡⲏⲣⲉ =
Mis 4 110 B, ManiK 166 A² ϯϫⲱ ⲙⲙⲁⲥ ⲁⲣⲱⲧⲛ,
ManiH 45 A² ⲁⲡⲙⲁⲧⲓⲥⲧⲱⲣ ϫⲟⲟⲩⲉ ⲁⲡⲣⲣⲟ, Mor 30
62 F ⲡⲁⲓⲟⲩϣϣ ⲉϫⲉ ϩⲉⲡⲕⲟⲩⲓ ⲉⲗⲁⲧⲡ, C 86 358 B ⲁⲩ-

ϫⲱ ⲉⲣⲟϥ ⲛⲛⲓϫⲟⲙ; *of, against*: Ps 70 10 S(B ⲛ-) ⲉⲓⲡ. dat, Mt 12 32 S(var ⲉⲣⲟϥⲛ ⲉ-, B ⲛⲥⲁ-) ⲉⲓⲡ. κατά; Tit 2 8 S(B ϩⲁ-) λέγ. περί; Ex 21 16 S ϫⲉ ⲡⲉⲑⲟⲟⲩ ⲉ- (B ⲇⲟ) κακολογεῖν acc; Ps 72 8 S(B ⲥ. ϣⲁⲉϩⲣⲏⲓ ⲉ-), Ac 6 11 B(S ⲉⲣⲟⲩⲛ ⲉ-) λαλ. εἰς; ShWess 9 142 S Martha & Mary ⲉⲧⲟⲩϫⲱ ⲙⲙⲟⲥ ⲉⲣⲟⲟⲩ ϫⲉⲡⲉⲭ̅ⲥ̅ ⲁⲉ ⲙⲙⲟⲟⲩ (Jo 11 5), Z 278 S ϣⲁϫⲟⲟⲥ ⲉⲡⲉⲭ̅ⲥ̅ that He died for us, Va 57 141 B ⲙⲁⲧⲑⲉⲟⲥ ... ϫⲱ ⲙⲙⲟⲥ ⲉⲡⲓⲥⲱⲧⲏⲣ ϫⲉ-; vbal: Ps 105 23 S(B ⲉⲡϫⲓⲛ-) ⲉⲓⲡ. gen, Dan 2 2 SB ⲉⲓⲡ. inf; PS 87 S ⲁⲅϫⲟⲟⲥ ⲉϥⲓ ⲡⲁⲟⲩⲟⲉⲓⲛ, DeV 2 33 B ⲁϥϫⲟⲥ ⲉⲁⲓϥ; ⲉⲣⲟⲩⲛ, ⲉϩ. ⲉ-: Ez 33 8 S(B ⲛ-) ⲉⲓⲡ. dat, Mt 5 11 S(B ⲛⲥⲁ-) ⲉⲓⲡ. κατά, Ez 37 5 B(S ⲉⲛ-) λέγ. dat, Ac 2 25 S(B ⲉ-) λ. εἰς; Ps 30 18 S(B ⲥ. ϩⲁ-) λαλ. κατά; Sh(Besa)Z 505 S ϫⲟⲟⲥ ⲉϩ. ⲉⲣⲟⲛ in wrath; ⲉⲣⲟⲩⲛ ⲉϩⲣⲏ-: Lu 22 65 S(var ⲉϩ. ⲉ-, B ⲉ-) λέγ. εἰς; v ϫⲉⲣⲟ- below & p 649 b.

—— ⲉⲧⲃⲉ-: Ps 121 8 SB λαλ. περί; Z 299 S ⲁⲩϫⲟⲟⲥ ⲉ. ⲁⲡⲁ ⲡⲟⲓⲙⲏⲛ λέγ. περί; MG 25 203 B ϫⲟⲥ ⲉⲑⲃⲏⲧⲩ διηγ. περί; He 7 9 B(ⲤF ϩⲓⲧⲛ-) ⲉⲓⲡ. διά; Ryl 72 351 S ϫⲉ ϩⲉⲛⲕⲟⲩⲓ ⲉ. ⲧⲥⲱϣⲉ, Mani K 42 A² ϫⲟⲥ ⲉⲧⲃⲏ[ⲧⲟⲩ], Aeg 56 B ϫⲟⲧⲟⲩ ⲉⲑⲃⲏϯ.

—— ⲉϫⲛ-: Ez 24 3 SB ⲉⲓⲡ. ἐπί; Jer 11 21 SB λέγ. ἐπί; ib 15 16 S(B ⲙⲟⲩϯ ⲉϩⲣⲏⲓ ⲉϫ.) ἐπικαλ. ἐπί; ib 32 29 SB ὀνομάζεσθαι ἐν; BMis 303 S ϫⲉ ⲡⲣⲁⲛ ⲙⲡⲭ̅ⲥ̅ ⲉ. ⲟⲩⲱϩ ⲉϥϣⲟⲩⲉⲓⲧ, C 86 99 B ⲡⲉⲛⲛⲓⲅⲙⲁ (αἴνιγ.) ... ⲉⲧⲁϥϫⲟϥ ⲉ. ⲓⲗⲏⲙ; ⲉϩⲣⲁⲓ, -ⲛⲓ ⲉϫⲛ-: Ez 26 2 B ⲉⲓⲡ. ἐπί; Ps 34 26 S ϫⲉ ⲛⲟϭ ⲡϣⲁϫⲉ ⲉⲣ. ⲉ. (B ϫⲉ ... ϩⲁ-) μεγαλορρημονεῖν ἐπί; ShMun 111 S ϫⲟⲟⲥ ⲉϩ. ⲉϫⲱ ⲏ ⲉϩⲟⲩⲛ ⲉⲣⲟ, Aeg 56 B ϫⲱ ⲛⲛⲁⲓ ... ⲉϩ. ⲉϫⲱⲥ.

—— ⲛ- dat: Job 11 10 SB, Jo 3 12 SA²BF ⲉⲓⲡ. dat; Ps 39 15 SB, λέγ. dat; Mk 12 1 S(B ⲥ. ⲡⲉⲙⲁ-) λαλ. dat; Ps 51 tit S(B ⲧⲁⲙⲟ) ἀνάγγ. dat, Mt 11 4 S(B ⲇⲟ) ἀπάγγ. dat, Ps 55 8 S(B diff) ἐξάγγ. dat; Pro 1 23 SA(B ϩⲁⲧⲉⲛ-) προιέναι dat; PS 11 S ⲁⲓϫⲟⲟⲥ ⲛⲏⲧⲛ, BMis 67 S sim (var FR 32 ⲉⲣⲱⲧⲛ), El 54 A ϫⲟⲩ ⲙⲙⲁⲥ ⲛⲉⲓ, HL 93 B ϫⲉ ϯϩⲟⲩⲓϯ ⲡⲗⲉⲍⲓⲥ ⲛⲁϥ, BM 1239 F ⲁⲓϫⲁⲥ ⲛⲉⲃ.

—— ⲛⲥⲁ-, *against*: Lev 20 9 SB ⲉⲓⲡ. acc, Mt 12 32 B(S ⲉ-) ⲉⲓⲡ. κατά, Pro 20 20 SA (κακο)λογ. acc; Ac 6 13 B(S ⲉⲣⲟⲩⲛ ⲉ-) λαλ. κατά; Deu 22 14 B(S ⲥⲱⲣ ⲛⲥⲁ-) καταφέρειν; ShIF 215 S ϫⲉ ϩⲟⲩⲟ ⲉⲡⲁⲓ ⲛⲥⲱϥ ⲏ ⲉϩⲟⲩⲛ ⲉⲣⲟϥ, DeV 2 85 B ϫⲉ ⲟⲩⲥⲁϫⲓ ⲛⲥⲁϥϯ.

—— ⲟⲩⲃⲉ- B: Jude 9 (S ϣⲁϫⲉ ⲙⲛ-) διακρίνεσθαι dat; FR 114 ⲁϥϫⲟⲧⲟⲩ ... ⲟⲩⲃⲉⲡⲓⲱⲧ *to the Father*.

—— ϩⲁ-, ϩⲁ-: Jer 18 20 S(B ⲥ. ϩⲁ-) συλλαλ. κατά; Ez 22 7 B(S ⲛⲥⲁ-, κακο)λογ. acc.

—— ⲉϩⲟⲩⲛ ϩⲉⲛ-, ⲉⲣ. ϩ.: C 86 97 B ϫⲉ ⲡⲁⲓ ⲉϩ. ϩⲉⲛⲡⲣⲟ ⲙⲡⲟⲩⲅⲣⲟ, Mor 24 10 F ⲁϥϫⲱ ⲙⲙⲁⲥ ⲉϩ. ϩⲉⲙⲡⲁⲓⲱⲧ.

p c: ManiP 14 A² ϫⲁⲧⲃⲱ(ⲱ)ⲛ *evil-speaker*; ib 173 ⲛϫⲁⲧⲃⲁⲓⲛⲉ *harpers* ⲉⲩⲣⲱⲥ ⲁⲟⲩⲛ ⲁⲡⲓⲱⲧ; ϫⲁⲧⲟⲩⲁ *blasphemer* v p 468 b.

ⲁⲧϫⲱ S, *ineffable*: BG 24 ⲡⲓⲁ. ⲙⲡⲉϥⲣⲁⲛ, My 115 ϯⲁ. ⲙⲡⲉⲥⲥⲙⲟⲧ; Br 260 ϩⲉⲛⲁⲧϫⲟⲟⲩ ϩⲛⲗⲁⲥ ⲛⲥⲁⲣϫ.

ⲣⲉϥϫⲉ- SB, ϫⲓ- S, *sayer, speaker*: Job 8 2 B ⲣ. ⲙⲛⲏϣ ⲛⲥⲁϫⲓ (S diff) πολυρρήμων, Ps 113 S ⲣ. ⲛⲟϭ ⲛϣⲁϫⲉ (B diff) μεγαλορρήμων, Tit 1 10 S ⲣ. (var ⲣⲉϥϫⲓ)ϣⲁϫⲉ ⲛⲉⲡⲣⲁ (B ⲣⲉϥⲥ.) ματαιολόγος, 1 Tim 1 10 B ⲣ. ⲙⲉⲑⲛⲟⲩϫ, S ⲣⲉϥϫⲓ ϭⲟⲗ ψεύστης; PS 158 S ⲣ. ⲛⲉⲑⲟⲟⲩ, Mor 44 17 S ⲣ. ⲁⲉ, DeV 2 37 B ⲣ. ⲥⲁϫⲓ ⲉϥϣⲟⲩⲓⲧ; ⲙⲛⲧⲣⲉϥϫⲉ-: 1 Tim 4 2 S ⲙ. ϣⲁϫⲉ ⲛϭⲟⲗ (B ⲣⲉϥϫⲉ-) ψευδολόγος.

ϭⲓⲛϫⲟⲟⲥ, ϫⲓⲛϫⲟⲥ, *saying, speech*: Va 57 247 B ⲡⲓϫ. ⲉⲓⲡⲉῖⲛ; Mor 31 15 S ⲟⲩϭ. ... ϫⲉⲕⲱ ⲡⲁⲓ ⲉⲃⲟⲗ, Cat 231 B ⲡⲉϥϫ. ϫⲉ- (Jo 21 16); Sh(?)ViK 9344 60 S ⲧϭⲓⲛϫⲉ ⲟⲩϣⲁϫⲉ.

V also ⲁⲉ (p 157 b), ⲙⲧⲁⲩ, ⲡⲟⲩϫ (p 247 a), ⲟⲩⲁ (p 468 b, adding as nn ManiP 86 A²), ϣⲕⲁⲕ (p 556 a), ϭⲟⲗ.

ϫⲉⲣⲟ- SA², ϫⲉⲣⲁ- A², ϫⲉⲣⲉ-, ϫⲉⲉⲣⲉ- B(once), *mean* (from ϫⲉ ⲉⲣⲟϥ, so Spg Rec 34 155): Jo 11 13 A² ⲉϥϫⲉⲣⲁ ⲡⲉⲉⲓⲕⲁⲧⲉ (S ϫⲉ-, B ϫⲟⲥ ⲉⲑⲃⲉ-) λέγ. περί; Br 34 S ⲉⲓϫⲉⲣⲟ ⲧⲥⲁⲣϫ[ⲁⲛ, Mani K 33 A² (cf Berl Sitz '33 I, Taf 1) powers of world ⲉⲓϫⲉⲣⲟ ⲡⲉⲓ ⲉⲧⲟ ⲛⲣⲣⲟ; ϫⲉⲣⲉ- B: Jo 13 22 ⲁϥϫⲉⲉⲣⲉ ⲛⲓⲙ (SA² as Gk, 1 Jo 5 16 sim (S ⲉⲓϫⲱ ⲙⲙⲟⲥ ϫⲉ-) λέγ. περί; 1 Cor 5 10 ⲡⲉⲓϫ. ⲛⲓⲡⲟⲣⲛⲟⲥ (S ⲇⲟ) Gk no vb اغبل, Cat 32 ⲉⲩϫ. ⲛⲓⲙ ϫⲉⲁⲛϫⲱ (Mt 11 17)?, C 43 128 ⲉⲕϫ. ⲛⲓⲙ ⲛⲡⲟⲩϯ? = Mor 48 56 S ϫⲉ-; c ⲉ- B: C 86 303 ⲉⲓϫⲉⲣⲉ ⲉⲣⲟⲕ ⲛⲑⲟⲕ (var ⲉⲓⲥⲉⲣⲟⲕ) = BSG 197 S ⲉⲓϫⲱ ⲉⲣⲟⲕ (cf BSM 45 ⲉⲓϫⲱ ⲉϫⲱⲣⲟⲑⲉⲟⲥ *I mean* D. & P 132¹ 3 S ⲉⲓϣⲁϫⲉ ⲉⲣⲟⲕ ⲛⲧⲟⲕ); ϫⲉⲣⲟϥ SA²B, ϭⲉⲣⲟϥ B, ϫⲉⲗⲁϥ F, *say to*: Dan 3 4 B ⲁⲩϫⲉⲣⲱⲧⲉⲛ (var ϫⲉ ⲉⲣⲟⲧⲉⲛ), cit BKU 1 183 S ⲉⲩϫⲉⲣⲱⲧⲛ, Lu 7 14 S ⲉⲓϫⲉⲣⲟⲕ (var & B ϫⲱ ⲙⲙⲟⲥ ⲡⲁⲕ), MG 25 4 B ⲁⲓϭⲉⲣⲟⲕ λέγ. dat, Jo 13 18 SA² ⲡⲉⲓϫⲉⲣⲱⲧⲛ (B ϫⲱ ⲉⲑⲃⲉⲑⲏⲛⲟⲩ) λέγ. περί; Mor 31 236 S ⲁⲓϫⲉⲣⲟⲕ ⲡⲱⲡⲉ ⲡⲕⲟⲟⲥ = Ryl Bull 11 436 b ايها الحبر, P 129¹⁴ 96 S ⲉⲓϫⲉⲣⲱⲧⲛ ⲡⲧⲱⲧⲛ = *Alexandr. Patriarchengesch.* (Hamburg) 36 انا اقول لكم, LMär 35 S ⲁⲓϫⲉⲣⲟⲕ ⲛ ⲧⲟⲕ ⲱ ⲡⲉⲧⲟⲩⲱⲧ, BAp 60 S ⲉⲓϫⲉⲣⲟⲕ ϫⲓ ⲙⲡⲁⲙⲉⲣⲓⲧ ⲉⲙⲡⲏⲩⲉ, Mich 601 S ⲉⲓϫⲓⲣⲟⲕ ⲡⲓⲣⲁⲛ, HM 1 158 S ⲉⲓϫⲉ ⲉⲣⲟⲕ, Ryl 430 136 B ⲁⲓϫⲉ ⲉⲣⲱⲧⲉⲛ, Mor 41 335 S ⲉⲓϫⲉⲣⲱⲧⲛ = BIF 22 106 F ⲁⲓϫⲉⲗⲁⲧⲉⲛ, C 41 67 B ⲁⲓϫⲉⲣⲟⲕ ⲱ ⲡⲓⲣⲉϥⲙⲱⲟⲩⲧ, ib 42 ⲉⲓϫⲉⲣⲟ ⲛⲑⲟ (var ⲉⲓϫⲱ ⲉⲣⲟ), TSBA 9 357 B ⲁⲕϭⲉⲣⲟ (sic MS, ⲗⲁⲓ-) ⲛⲑⲟ, C 43 233 B ⲁⲓϭⲉⲣⲟⲕ, Cat 31 B ⲉϥϭⲉⲣⲟϥ ⲛⲑⲟϥ *signifying himself*.

Cf ⲡⲉϫⲉ, ϫⲉ- conjunct.

B *sing* (same ?) S(mostly)AA²BF intr: Ps 56 7 (B ϩⲱⲥ), Is 23 16 (B ⲇⲟ) ᾄδειν, Hos 7 2 A(B ⲇⲟ) συνᾴ.; BMis 32 ⲉϥϫⲱ ⲉϥϭⲟⲥϭ, CA 89 ⲛⲡⲉⲩϫⲁⲕ ⲟⲩⲉ ⲛⲡⲉⲩϫⲱ *as heathen do*, Mani P 200 A² ⲡⲁⲩⲗⲟⲥ ⲉⲩϫⲟⲩ; tr: Ex 15 1 F(BB́CMSS 13 ϩ.), Ps 58 16 (B ϩ. ⲉ-) ᾄ.; Pro 29 49 SA ὑμνεῖν, Z 312 ϫⲱ ⲙⲡϣⲟⲙⲛⲧ

ⲡⲉⲁⲅⲓⲟⲥ τρισάγιον ψάλλειν; 1 Cor 14 7 *SB* αὐλεῖν;
Mic 2 4 *SA* ⲕⲱ ⲡⲟⲩⲧⲟⲉⲓⲧ θρηνεῖν; R 1 3 50 ⲕⲱ ⲙ-
ⲡⲉⲓⲣⲅⲙⲡⲟⲥ, JA '05 450 ⲕⲱ ⲡⲣⲏⲟⲩⲏⲗⲗⲉ, FR 114 *B*
ⲕⲱ ⲛⲧϥⲣⲱⲁⲛ.

With following preposition.   c ⲉ-: Ps 12 6 (*B*
ⲅ.), *ib* 149 1 *SB*, Is 5 1 *SB* ⲁ̈. dat; Ps 136 3 (*B* ⲅ.)
ὑμ. dat; Mt 11 17 *SB* αὐλ. dat; P 131³ 83 on Lu 16
19 ⲡ̄ⲭⲟⲣⲁⲅⲗⲏⲥ ⲉⲩⲕⲱ ⲉⲡⲓⲡⲉⲅⲏ = Va 61 93 *B*, Mor
41 106 ⲕⲱ ⲉⲣⲟⲟⲩ with sweet voice = DeV 1 38 *B*;
ⲉⲁϩⲟⲩⲛ ⲁ-: ManiP 133 *A²* harp in hand ⲉⲩⲕⲱ ⲥ.
ⲁⲡⲓⲱⲧ;   c ⲛ-: Ps 103 33 (*B* ⲅ.) ⲁ̈. dat; Aeg 281
ⲡⲉⲧⲕⲱ ⲡ̄ⲧⲗⲅⲣⲁ *sing to lyre* λυριστής; BMis 184 ⲕⲱ
ⲡⲟⲩⲧⲉⲗⲏⲗ ⲙⲡⲕⲁⲣ;   c ⲉⲛ-: 2 Kg 6 13 (var ⲙⲛ-,
B as Gk) reading ᾖσαν, Hos 7 2 *A*(*B* ⲅ.) ⲁ̈. dat; ShA
2 136 ⲡⲉⲧⲕⲱ ⲣ̄ⲡⲟⲩⲕⲓⲑⲁⲣⲁ *sing to*, Mor 18 19 sim, *ib*
22 102 ⲕⲱ ⲅⲏⲣⲉⲡⲟⲣⲅⲁⲡⲟⲛ ⲙⲙⲟⲩⲥⲓⲕⲟⲛ, Aeg 39 *B*
sim, Miss 4 113 *B* lyre cords ⲛ̄ⲧⲉⲡⲕⲱ ⲉⲡⲉⲛⲡⲟⲩϯ
ⲡ̄ⲃⲏⲧⲟⲩ.

—— nn m *SABF*, pl ⲕⲱⲟⲅⲓ *B* (*cf* ⲣⲉϥⲕⲱ)& sg as
pl, *song*: Ps 39 3 *S*(*B* ⲅ.), Eccl 7 6 *SF*, Cant 1 1 *SA*
(TillOster 24) ᾆσμα; Ps 64 2 *B*(*S* ⲥⲙⲟⲩ) ὕμνος; Va
57 42 *B* μέλος; ShR 2 3 67 *S* ⲕⲱ ⲡⲁⲧϣⲁⲩ, R 2 1 58
S ⲕⲱ ⲙ̄ⲡⲟⲣⲡⲏ, ROC 20 51 *S* ⲡ̄ⲕⲱ ⲙ̄ⲡⲡⲭⲁⲕ ⲅ̄ⲡⲡⲉⲧ-
ⲧⲡ̄ⲥⲓⲝ, Z 581 *S* ⲟⲩⲏⲗⲗⲉ, ⲕⲱ, ⲱⲇⲏ, MG 25 358 *B*
ⲅⲁⲡⲕⲱ ⲉⲩⲃⲏⲗ ⲉⲃⲟⲗ ⲡⲧⲉ ⲡⲓⲕⲟⲥⲙⲟⲥ (Gött ar 114 127
غنى من ذي العالم), Aeg 39 *B* ⲛ̄ⲕⲩⲑⲁⲣⲓⲱⲧⲏⲥ (κιθαρῳδός
or -ιστής)...ⲧⲁⲟⲩⲟ ⲡ̄ⲣⲁⲛⲕⲱ;   pl: O'LearyTh 12*B*
ⲥⲉⲡⲥⲉⲛ ⲡ̄ⲕ. (*cf* O'Leary H 35 c. ⲡⲕⲱ);   ⲙⲁ ⲡⲕⲱ *S*,
singing place: BMis 13 ⲙ. ⲡⲟⲣⲅ̄ⲁⲡⲟⲛ.

ⲥⲛⲏⲃⲉ ⲡ̄ⲕⲱ *v* ⲥⲛⲏⲃⲉ;   ⲟⲩⲗⲗⲉ ⲡ̄ⲕⲱ *S*: R 2 2 32 ᾆσμα;
ShA 1 386 ⲅⲉⲡⲟⲩ. ⲡ̄ⲕⲱ without profit, Mor 41 121
ⲕⲓⲑⲁⲣⲓⲍⲉ ⲅ̄ⲛⲡⲟⲩ. ⲡ̄ⲕⲱ ⲛ̄ⲑⲉ̄ⲃⲉⲟⲥ (var *ib* 40 7 ⲟⲩ. ⲡⲟⲣ-
ⲅ̄ⲁⲡⲟⲛ ⲡⲟⲛⲏⲃⲁⲓⲟⲥ).

ⲣⲉϥⲕⲱ *SB*, pl · ⲕⲟⲟⲩⲉ *S*, -ⲕⲱⲟⲅⲓ *B*, *singer, min-
strel*· Ap 18 22*SB* αὐλητής; RNC 70*S* ⲟⲩⲣ. ⲡ̄ⲭⲟⲣⲁⲅ-
ⲗⲏⲥ ⲉϣⲁϥⲕⲱ, ClPr 56 11 *S* ⲅⲉⲡⲣ. χορεύε ⲙ̄ⲡⲣⲉⲡ-
ⲭⲱⲣⲁⲅⲗⲏⲥ, P 131³ 83 *S* ⲡⲣ. ⲙ̄ⲡⲡⲉⲭⲟⲣ. = Va 61 93
B ⲅ., ⲣⲉϥⲥⲁⲕ, Miss 4 168 *B* ⲣ. ⲛ̄ⲕⲩⲑⲁⲣⲓⲱⲧⲏⲥ (*v* nn
above), BM 255 9 *S* ⲡⲟⲣⲅ̄ⲁⲡⲟⲛ ⲙ̄ⲡⲉⲓⲣ.;   pl: Dan
3 10*B* ⲣⲉϥⲭ. μουσικός; Mt 9 23 *S* ⲣⲉϥⲭ. *B* do αὐλ.;
Dif 1 16 *B* ⲡⲓⲣ. ملاه (*cf* Synax 1 29, K 14 *b* ⲡⲓⲕⲱ-
ⲟⲩⲓ); PasH 15*B* مزمرون.

ⲕⲱⲥ *SAA²BFO* (from ⲕⲱⲥ *q v*, Sethe *Verbum* 1
60 *bis*) nn m, *head*: Lev 13 45 *S*(*B* ⲁⲫⲉ) κεφαλή; PS
344 *S* ⲉⲡⲁⲣⲟⲩ ⲡ̄ⲕⲱϥ, El 120 *S* = 90 *A* ⲅⲓⲭⲛ ⲡ̄ⲕⲱϥ,
ROC 19 69 *S* ladder ⲡⲏⲅ ϣⲁⲕⲱⲥ ⲉⲧⲡⲉ, ManiP 207
A² ϯⲡⲁⲭⲁⲣⲡ ⲡⲉⲩϫⲓⲥⲉ ⲅ̄ⲛ̄ⲕⲱⲓ, C 86 217 *B* ⲡⲓⲡⲩⲣⲅⲟⲥ
ⲡⲧⲉ ⲕⲱϥ, AZ 21 100 *O* ⲕⲱϥ, ⲣⲉⲧⲃ̄, ⲡⲉⲃⲗⲁ[ⲥ; in-
animate: Ge 28 12 *B*(*S* ⲁⲡⲉ) κε.; Nu 23 28 *S*(*B* ⲁ.),
Am 9 3 *S* ⲡ̄ⲕⲱϥ *A*(*B* do) κορυφή; ShC 42 22 *S* of
tower (Ge 11 4), ManiK 11 *A²* church ⲙ̄ⲛ̄ⲕⲱⲥ; co-

ⲟⲩⲅⲉ ⲡ̄ⲕⲱⲥ, *crown of head* *v* p 374 *a*;   ⲙⲏⲧⲉ ⲡ̄ⲕⲱⲥ
SF sim: Deu 33 16 (*B* ⲥⲱⲟⲩⲅⲓ ⲡⲧⲉ ⲧⲁ.), Ps 7 16 (*B*
do) κορ.; Mor 24 9 *F* ⲧⲙ. ⲡ̄ⲕⲱⲕ.

With preceding preposition.   c ⲉ-*S*: Est 4 1
Gk om, Br 252 ϯ ⲡⲁϥ ⲡⲟⲩⲕⲗⲟⲙ ⲉⲕⲱϥ, ShC 42 88
ⲉⲩⲡⲏⲧ ⲕⲁⲅ ⲉⲕⲱⲟⲩ, BAp 142 from roots ϣⲁⲅⲣⲁⲓ
ⲉⲕⲱⲟⲩ;   c ⲡⲥⲁ-, ⲥⲁ-, *behind head, backward, head
down*: Kropp B *S* ⲁⲓⲃⲱⲕ ⲉⲅⲟⲩⲛ ⲡⲥⲁⲕⲱⲓ paral ⲡⲥⲁ-
ⲣⲁⲧ, Mor 25 19 *S* its gait not straight but ⲉϥⲙⲟⲟϣⲉ
ⲡⲥⲁⲕⲱϥ = Va 61 101 *B* ⲉⲡⲁϩⲟⲩ, BMis 241 *S* ⲁϣⲧϥ
ⲡⲥⲁⲕⲱϥ, ManiK 51 *A²* ⲉϣⲧⲟⲩ ⲥⲁⲕⲱⲩ, C 43 212 *B*
ⲁϣⲓ ⲉⲅⲣⲏⲓ ⲥⲁⲕⲱϥ, Cat 232 *B* sim ⲡⲥⲁⲕⲱϥ;   c
ⲅⲁ-, ϣⲁ-: Jth 13 6 *S* πρὸς κε., Job 29 3 *S*(*B* ⲥⲁⲡϣⲱⲓ
ⲡⲧⲁⲫⲉ) ὑπὲρ κε., Ez 32 27 *SB* ὑπὸ τ. κε.;   ShC 73 82
S ⲡⲡⲉⲓⲕⲁ ⲟⲩ ⲅⲁⲕⲱⲓ, *ib* 161 ⲉ̄ⲓ ⲅⲁⲕⲱϥ ⲁⲩⲱ ⲅⲁⲣⲁⲧϥ;
as nn m *S*: Mor 51 36 ⲁⲣⲁⲕⲱⲥ ⲉⲣ ⲑⲉ ⲡ̄ⲃⲁⲣⲁⲧⲥ, Kr
245 ϥⲁⲕⲱϥ ⲡⲧⲁϣⲧⲏⲡ;   c ⲅⲓ-: Deu 28 23 *S*(*B*
ⲥⲁⲡϣ. ⲡⲧⲁ.) ὑπὲρ κε.; Br 234 *S* ⲟⲩⲥⲣⲏⲡⲉ ⲅⲓⲕⲱⲟⲩϥ;
MG 25 4 *B* ⲅⲁⲡⲧⲁⲡ ⲅⲓⲕⲱⲟⲩϥ;   ⲉⲃⲟⲗ ⲅⲓ-: Ez 26 16 *B*
ἀπὸ κε.;   c ⲕⲓⲡ-... ϣⲁ-*SB* (rare): Deu 13 7 (*B*
ⲁⲣⲏⲕⲥ) ἀπ' ἄκρου... ἕως ἄκ.; ShZ 593 ⲕⲓⲡⲕⲱⲥ ⲡⲟⲩ-
ⲭⲱⲣⲁ ϣⲁⲕⲱⲥ; C 89 89 *B* ⲁⲩⲣⲏⲕⲥ ⲡ̄ϯⲟⲓⲕⲟⲩⲙⲉⲡⲓ
ⲓⲥⲕⲉⲡⲕⲱⲥ ϣⲁⲕⲱⲥ = C 99 153 *S* ⲕⲓⲡⲕⲱⲥ ⲉⲕⲱⲥ.

With various verbs.   BM 851 1 *B* ⲕⲱϥ ⲃ̄ⲛϣ ⲉⲃⲟⲗ
(var TEuch 1 1 ⲁⲫⲉ); Si 12 10 *S* ⲕⲱϥ ⲃ̄ⲛⲣ ⲉⲡⲉⲥⲛⲧ
συγκύπτειν; ShZ 528 *S* ⲉⲓⲉⲃⲉⲅ ⲕⲱⲓ; My 23 *S* ⲕⲁ
ⲕⲱⲟⲩ *submit selves*, Mal 4 2 *A* ⲕⲁ ⲕⲱⲟⲩ ⲁⲃⲁⲗ (*B* diff)
ἀνειμένος, Ac 27 40 *SB* sim ζευκτηρίας ἀνιέναι; Wess
18 59 *S* ⲁⲓⲕⲁ ⲕⲱⲟⲩ ⲉⲃ̄. ⲉⲧⲣⲉⲩⲃⲱⲕ, J 80 40 *S* sim, Mor
23 23 *Sⁱ* ⲁⲧⲃ̄ⲱ ⲕⲉ ⲕⲱⲥ ⲉⲡⲉⲥⲛⲧ = *ib* 24 21 *F*, DeV 2
77 *B* ⲭⲁ ⲕⲱⲥ ⲉⲅⲣⲏⲓ; MG 25 246 *B* ⲕⲱϥ ⲕⲏⲕ ⲉⲃⲟⲗ
ⲕⲉⲫ.; ViK 9616 *S* ⲡⲁⲣⲧ ⲕⲱϥ; Ac 19 16 *B* ⲕⲱⲟⲩ
ϥⲏⲅ τραυματίζειν; Deu 2 24 *S* ⲥⲙⲛ ⲕⲱⲥ (*B* diff)
ἐνάρχεσθαι; JTS 10 402 *S* continent & patient ϣⲁⲡ-
ⲧⲟⲩⲥⲙⲉⲛ ⲕⲱⲟⲩ ⲡⲡⲉⲩϣⲏⲣⲉ *begat* (?); Si 21 24 *S*
ⲥⲟⲩⲧⲛ ⲕⲱⲥ παρακύπτειν; MIF 9 17 *S* ⲁⲩϯ ⲕⲱⲟⲩ
ⲉⲅⲟⲩⲛ ⲅⲁⲡⲉⲕⲣⲓⲙⲁ, Wess 18 56 *S* ϯ ⲕⲱϥ ⲉⲣ. ⲅⲁⲡ-
ⲡⲁⲣⲃ̄, C 86 334 *B* ⲁϥϯ ⲕⲱⲟⲩ ⲉⲃ̄. ⲉⲡⲓⲁⲅ ϣϣⲏⲡ, Bor
290 144 *S* ⲡϣⲱⲡⲉ ϯ ⲕⲱⲟⲩ ⲉⲅⲣⲁⲓ ⲡⲥⲉⲭⲁⲧⲉ; Mor 18
18 *S* ⲉⲑⲃⲓⲟ (*sic*) ⲕⲱⲟⲩ; ManiK 111 *A²* ⲟⲩⲱⲡⲅ ⲕⲱⲟⲩ;
Lu 9 58 *B* ⲟⲩⲁⲅ ⲕⲱϥ (*S* diff) κε. κλίνειν; AZ 21 153
S ⲙⲁⲣⲡⲟⲩⲉⲅ ⲕⲱⲡ; Ez 7 18 *B* ϣⲃ̄ ⲕⲱⲟⲩ (*S* ⲅⲉⲕⲉ-)
φαλάκρωμα, 1 Cor 11 6 *S* ϣⲃ̄ ⲕⲱⲥ (*B* ⲃⲱⲕⲣ) κείρειν;
Deu 33 11 *S* ϥⲓ ⲕ. ⲉⲅⲣⲁⲓ (*B* ⲧⲱⲟⲩⲛ) ἀνιστάναι, Is 8 8
S sim (*B* ⲧ. ⲡⲧⲁⲫⲉ), Zech 1 21 *A* sim (*B* ϥⲓ ⲁ. ⲉⲡϣⲱⲓ)
αἴρειν, Job 10 15 *S* sim *B* ϥⲓ ⲕ. ⲉⲡϣ. ἀνακύπ., HL 96
B ϥⲁⲓ ⲡ̄ⲕⲱϥ ⲉⲡϣⲱⲓ ἀνανεύειν; 1 Kg 13 3 *S* ⲁⲩϥⲓ ⲕⲱⲟⲩ
(gloss? on ⲁⲑⲉⲧⲉⲓ); P 129¹⁵ 24 *S* ⲉⲙⲛ ϭⲟⲙ ⲙⲙⲟⲥ ⲉϥⲓ
ⲕⲱⲥ ⲉⲅⲣⲁⲓ, ManiK 149 *A²* ⲃⲓ ⲕ. ⲁⲅ.; 1 Cor 11 6 *SB*
ⲅⲃⲥ ⲕⲱⲥ κατακαλύπτειν, Mor 27 28 *F* sim; Nu 6 9 *SB*
ⲅⲉⲉⲕⲉ ⲕⲱϥ ξυρᾶν (*cf* *ib* *S* ⲅⲱⲱⲕⲉ ⲡⲧⲁⲡⲉ); Va 63 98 *B*
ⲁⲩⲟⲩⲁⲙⲉⲧ ⲥⲓ ⲕⲱⲟⲩ ⲡⲓϣⲁϣ ἕλκη, σηπεδών;   as
nn m *S* (meaning?): Kr 29 wine sold ⲡⲛⲅⲁⲁⲣⲉ ⲉϣⲁ-

(ⲣⲉ)ⲡⲉϣⲟⲧⲉ ϫⲓ ⲙⲙⲟϥ ⲉⲛϫⲓ ⲝⲱϥ, *ib* ⲛϫⲓ ϫ. ⲡⲙⲉⲥⲟⲣⲏ; *V* also ⲕⲁⲗⲧ-, ϫⲱⲃⲥ, ϫⲧⲟ, ϭⲛⲟⲛ *bend.*

ⲉϫⲛ- *SF*, ⲁ. *SSᵃAA²*, ⲉⲓϫ(ⲉ)ⲛ- *S*, ⲉϫⲉⲛ- *BFO*, ⲉϫⲉ- *F*, ⲉϫⲱⲛ- *F*, ⲉϫⲱ- *SF*, ⲉϫⲱϩ *SA²BF*, ⲁϫⲱϩ *SᵃAA²O* prep, **a** *upon, over*: Ge 2 21 *SB*, Nu 21 8 *S* (var ϩⲓϫⲛ-, *B* ϩⲓ-), Pro 2 14 *SAB*, Eccl 2 3 *S*(*F* ⲛ-), *ib* 10 7 *F* ⲉϫⲱⲛ- (*S* ϩⲓϫⲛ-), Cant 7 8 *S*(*B*Hom 33, var ⲉϩⲣ. ⲉ-, *F* ⲉϩⲗ. ⲉϫⲱⲛ-), Is 30 3 *S*(*BF* ⲉ-), Mt 23 36 *S*(var ⲉϩⲣ. ⲉϫⲛ-)*B*, Mk 1 10 *S*(*B* ⲉϩⲣ. ⲉϫ.), *ib* 4 16 *F*(Mus 49 188, *SB* ϩⲓϫⲛ-), Jo 12 15 *S*(var ϩⲓϫⲛ-)*A²* (*B* ⲉ-), He 11 21 *B*(*S* ⲛ- *F* ⲉϩⲗ. ⲉϫ.), Ap 3 12 *S*(*B* ϩⲓ-), ἐπί, Job 13 11 *SB*, *ib* 21 17 *S*(*B* ⲉϩⲣ. ⲉϫ.), Mk 3 10 *SB*, Lu 23 26 *S*(*B* ⲉ-), MG 25 240 *B* ⲧⲱϩϩ ⲉ. ⲟⲩⲡⲉϩ, Aeg 242 *S* ⲙⲧⲟⲛ ⲉ. ⲡⲉⲩϣⲁϫⲉ ἐπί-, Job 3 5 *SB*, Jer 26 9 *SF*(*B* ⲉ-) ἐπί- ἐπί, Lu 19 17 *SB* ἐπάνω; Sa 5 19 *S*, Mk 15 36 *SB*(*F* ϩⲓϫ.) περί-; Jon 4 6 *SA*(*B* ⲉϫ. ⲧⲁϥⲉ ⲛ-) ὑπέρ; Ge 7 20 *S*(*B* ⲥⲁⲡϣⲱⲓ) ὑπεράνω; Ps 56 3 *SB*, Si 17 4 *S* ⲕⲁⲧⲁ-; Ps 7 16 *SB*, Lam 2 11 *F* ⲉϫⲱⲛ- (*B* ϩⲓϫ.), Lu 22 17 *S*(*B* ⲉⲣⲣⲉⲛ-), AP 19 *A²* ⲁⲥⲡⲁⲣⲧⲉ ⲁⲡⲉⲥⲛⲧ ⲁ. ⲡⲙⲁ εἰς; Mt 15 29 *S*(*B* ⲉⲥⲕⲉⲛ-), Ac 16 13 *S*(*B* ϩⲁⲧⲉⲛ-) παρά, Is 51 23 *S*(*B* diff), Ac 1 10 *S* (var ϩⲓϫⲛ-, *B* ⲡⲁⲣⲣⲉⲛ-) παρα-; Job 16 10.*S*(*B* ⲉϩⲣ. ⲉ.) ἔν-; Gu 71 *S* ⲉⲓ ⲉⲡⲉⲥⲛⲧ ⲉ. ⲧϫⲛⲉⲡⲱⲣ opp ⲁⲗⲉ ⲉ-ϩⲣⲁⲓ ⲉϫⲛ- ἀπό; Deu 13 8 *S*(*B*=Gk), Mt 26 67 *S*(*B* ⲛ-)acc; Ge 3 16 *S*(var & *B* ⲉ-), Jos 11 10 *S*, Lu 3 1 *S*(*B* do)gen; Ge 34 19 *SB*, Pro 1 27 *SAB*, Is 13 11 *SB* dat; Gk om: Lev 24 15 *S*(*B* as Gk), Deu 28 44 *S*(*B* do), Lu 23 34 *S*(var & *B* ⲉ-); PS 132 *S* ⲁⲥⲕⲟⲧⲉ ⲉ. ⲡⲉⲣⲡⲉ (OdSolom 6 8 ⲍ), Br 254 *S* ⲁⲙⲁϩⲧⲉ ⲉ. ϩⲉⲛⲡⲟϭ ⲛⲉⲟⲟⲩ, ShC 73 171 *S* ϫⲓ ϭⲟⲗ ⲉ. ⲟⲩⲣⲱⲃ, *ib* 213 *S* each one ⲙⲟⲩϩ ⲉϫⲱϥ *observing him*, Aeg 255 *S* ϣⲗⲏⲗ ⲉ. ⲡⲙⲟⲟⲩ, Wess 18 6 *S* rubric ⲛⲁⲡⲁⲅⲛⲱⲥⲓⲥ... ⲉ. ⲡⲙⲟⲟⲩ, P 129²⁰ 142 *S* sim ⲉ. ⲡⲕⲩⲣⲏⲅⲙⲁ (κήρυ.) followed by ὑπὲρ τ. ἀρχιερέως ... πεμψάντος ... κήρ., Leyd 158 *S* when archons come ⲉⲩⲛⲁⲧⲁⲅⲉ ⲛⲁⲓ ⲉ-ϫⲱⲟⲩ(*cf* Rec 7 144 ⲧⲁⲅⲟⲟⲩ ⲉⲣⲟϥ),*ib* 184 *S* ⲧⲕⲩⲣⲓⲁⲕⲏ ⲉ.ⲡⲁⲣⲭⲁⲅⲅⲉⲗⲟⲥ followed by ⲡϣⲁ ⲙⲡⲁⲣⲭ., *ib* 136 *S* ⲧⲩⲙⲟⲥ ⲉ.ⲡⲉⲩⲁⲅⲅⲉⲗⲓⲟⲛ, J 56 22 *Sᵃ* houses ⲉⲓ ⲁϫⲱⲛ from parents, *ib* 92 39 *Sᵃ* powers ⲉⲧⲁⲣⲭⲉⲓ ⲁϫⲱⲛ, El 34 *A* ⲁϥϫⲓⲧ ⲁ. ⲧⲡⲟⲗⲓⲥ, ManiK 41 *A²* ⲕⲱⲁϫⲱⲩ ⲛⲧⲟⲩ-ⲛⲉⲙ, *ib* P 223 *A²* they say ⲁ. ⲡϫⲁⲓϭⲣⲏⲡⲉ *concerning*, C 86 325 *B* ⲟⲩϫⲉⲙⲱⲛ ⲉϫⲱⲓ (var ⲡⲉⲙⲛⲓ), DeV 2 176 *B* stand ⲉ. ⲡⲉⲕϭⲁⲗⲁϫϫ (var ϩⲓϫ.),Griff Stu 163 *F* girt ⲉ. ⲧⲉⲃϯⲡⲓ, AZ 21 104 *O* ϯ ⲡⲙⲟϥ (*sc* crown) ⲉϫⲛⲡⲉⲣⲟ, Hor 82 *O* ϫⲓ ⲕⲗⲙ...ⲁϫⲱⲟⲩ.

b *for, on account of:* Lam 1 10 *BF* ⲉϫⲱⲛ-, Jon 4 2 *SAB*, Mk 6 34 *S*(*B* ϩⲁ-), *ib* 9 12 *S*(var ⲛ-)*B*(*F* ⲉⲧⲃⲉ-) ἐπί; Lev 9 7 *S*(*B* ⲉϩⲣ. ⲉϫ.), *ib* 23 28 *S*(*B* ⲉⲑⲃⲉ-), Ez 43 19 *B*(HCons 304,var ⲉⲑ.), Ro 14 12 *B*(*S* ϩⲁ-)περί-; Jud 9 17 *S*, 1 Cor 15 29 *B*(*SF* ϩⲁ-), AP 16 *A²* ϣⲗⲏⲗ ⲁ. ⲧⲁϣⲉⲉⲣⲉ ὑπέρ, Deu 33 29 *S*(*B* ⲉ-),Sa 10 20 *S* ὑπέρ-; Pro 8 31 *SAB*, Eccl 10 9 *S*(*F* ⲉϩⲗ. ⲉ.) ἔν; 1 Kg 28 20 *S*(var ϩⲁⲑⲏ ⲛ-) ἀπό; Ps 4 4 *S*(*B* ⲉϩⲣ. ⲉ.)acc; PS 324

S ⲉⲧⲉⲧⲛⲁⲉⲩⲭⲉ ⲉϫⲱⲥ, *ib* 130 *S* ⲁⲅⲣ ϩⲟⲧⲉ ⲉ. ⲡⲉⲩⲉ-ⲣⲏⲩ, ShC 42 283 *S* λυπει ⲉ. ⲕⲉⲟⲩⲁ (var ⲛ-), ShA 2 312 *S* punished ⲉⲧⲃⲉⲟⲩ ⲏ ⲉ. ⲟⲩ ⲡⲣⲱⲃ, ShC 73 30 *S* they expound prophet ⲉ. ⲡⲉⲩⲟⲩⲱϣ *as they will,* Sh (Besa)Z 503 *S* cried out ⲉ. ⲧⲉⲥⲡⲗⲁⲕⲉ, TU 43 21 *A* grieved ⲁ. ⲛⲉⲧⲁⲩⲛⲕⲁⲧⲉ, LAp 528 *S* ⲥⲟⲡⲥ ⲉϫⲱⲧⲛ = *ib* *F*, Ep 201 *Sᵃ* entreat Christ ⲁ....ⲡⲁϣⲏⲣⲉ, Ryl 94 105 *S* ⲣ ⲙⲁⲣⲧⲩⲣⲟⲥ ⲉ. ⲡⲉϥⲣⲁⲛ, CA 105 *S* ⲁϥⲡⲱϣ ⲉϫⲱϥ ⲡⲙⲁϥ, J 63 7 *Sᵃ* ϯ ⲟⲩⲡⲛϣⲉ ⲡⲣⲟⲗⲟⲕ/ⲡⲛⲓ ⲁ. ⲏⲡⲡⲉ *in return for,* *ib* 26 10 sim, Aeg 19 *B* my death ⲉ. ⲡⲱⲛϩ ⲙⲡⲓⲕⲟⲥⲙⲟⲥ = *ib* *S* ϩⲁ-, PO 11 321 *B* ⲥⲁϫⲓ ⲉϫⲱⲓ ⲡⲁϩⲣⲉⲡⲛⲁⲓⲟϯ.

c *against:* Deu 21 10 *B*(*S* ⲉⲣⲛ-), Job 19 5 *S*(*B* ⲉϩⲣ. ⲉϫ.), Is 5 25 *SBF* ἐπί, *ib* 14 22 *S*(*B* do) ἐπί-, Lev 17 10 *SB* ἐπί- ἐπί; Lu 9 50 *S*(*B* ϩⲓ-) ὑπέρ; Job 16 4 *S*(*B* ϩⲁ-) κατά; PS 24 *S* ⲁⲩⲕⲓⲙ ⲉ. ⲡⲉⲩⲉⲣⲏⲩ, JA '75 5 210 *S* heretics ⲥⲱⲟⲩϩ ⲉ. ⲧⲕⲁⲑⲟⲗ. ⲉⲕⲕⲗⲏⲥⲓⲁ, Wess 18 88 *S* ⲧⲱⲟⲩⲛ ⲉϫⲱⲛ opp ⲙⲓϣⲉ ⲉϫⲱⲛ, Dif 161 *B* ⲟⲩⲟⲛⲧⲏⲓ ⲉϫⲱϥ ⲛⲧ ⲡⲥⲁⲑⲉⲣⲓ (Synax 1 107 ⲡ ⲇⲗ, *cf* p 481 *b* **III**), C 41 50 *B* ⲉⲓⲟⲩⲉⲙ ⲁⲡⲁⲗⲱⲙⲁ ⲉϫⲱⲧⲉⲛ *at your expense,* Miss 4 126 *B* blood crieth out ⲉ. ⲓⲟⲩⲃⲉⲛ-ⲡⲁⲗⲓⲟⲥ.

d *to (cf* ⲉϩⲟⲩⲛ ⲉ.): Lu 10 33 *S*(*B* ⲉϩⲣ. ⲉϫ.) κατά; Is 2 1 *S*(*B* ϩⲁ-) πρός; Br 123 *S* ⲃⲱⲕ ⲉϩⲟⲩⲛ...ⲉ. ⲙⲡⲩ-ⲗⲏ, BMis 132 *S* ⲉⲧⲣⲁϯ ⲙⲡⲁⲟⲩⲟⲓ ⲉϫⲱⲥ, J 93 18 *S* ⲉϥϣⲁⲛⲕⲧⲟϥ ⲉϫⲱⲛ, P 131³ 62 *S* ⲉⲕⲛⲏⲧ ⲉϩⲟⲩⲛ ⲉⲕⲛⲏⲩ ⲉⲃⲟⲗ ⲉϫⲱϥ *to & fro past him,* BSM 35 *B* ⲁϥⲓ ⲉϫⲱⲛ = BMis 378 *S* ϣⲁⲣⲟⲛ, BMar 149 *S* ⲉⲓ ⲉⲃⲟⲗ ⲉ. ⲡⲣⲟ, J 106 174 *S* ϯⲱⲣⲕ ⲉϫⲱⲧⲛ ϫⲉ-.

e *in addition to, after:* Lev 26 23 *S*(*B* ⲉϩⲣ. ⲉϫ.) ἐπί; Ge 28 9 *S*(*B* ϩⲁ-) πρός, Ru 1 17 *S*, Tob 2 11 *S* προσ-; Lev 26 18 *S* ⲉ. ⲡⲁⲓ (*B* ϣⲁ-) ἔως; PS 172 *S* ⲟⲩⲉϩ ϭⲱⲛⲧ ⲉ. ϭⲱⲛⲧ, LMär 34 *S* will give thee others ...ⲉ. ϯⲕⲉⲙⲁⲁⲃⲉ ⲉⲓϯ ⲙⲙⲟⲟⲩ ⲛⲁⲕ, Miss 8 72 *S* ⲙⲡⲁ-ⲧⲉϩⲁϩ ⲛⲣⲟⲟⲩ ϫⲱⲕ ⲉⲃⲟⲗ ⲉ. ⲧⲉϥⲭⲓⲣⲟⲇⲟⲡⲓⲁ, J 75 127 *S* ⲧⲉⲓⲇⲓⲁⲑⲏⲕⲏ...ⲛⲥⲉⲟϣⲥ ⲉⲁⲣⲭⲏ ⲛⲓⲙ...ⲉ. ⲧⲩⲡⲟ-ⲅⲣⲁⲫⲏ of witnesses, Va 66 294 *B* ⲟⲩϣⲱⲡⲓ ⲉ. ⲧⲟⲩⲕⲉ-ⲙⲉⲧⲣⲏⲕⲓ, Ryl 110 *S* recipe ⲛⲡⲉⲣⲥⲉ ⲙⲟⲟⲩ ⲁⲛ ⲉϫⲱⲥ, AJSL 46 244 *S* recipe ⲟⲩⲁⲙⲥ (*sc* egg) ⲉ. ⲡⲉⲃⲓⲱ, AZ 23 111 *S* ϯ ⲟⲩϣⲓ ⲛⲛⲟⲩⲃ ⲉϫⲱϥ;   ⲉϫⲛⲡⲁⲓ: BHom 143 *S* ⲉ. ϫⲉ ⲧⲏⲣⲟⲩ ὑπέρ; Miss 8 73 *S* sim πρός; J 10 58 *S* sim, BKU 1 21 vo *F* ⲉ. ⲡⲕⲓϣⲱⲙ ⲉⲣⲁϥ.

Mor 31 72 *S* idiot ⲙⲉϩ ⲣⲱϥ ⲉ. ⲡⲉϥϩⲟⲓⲧⲉ *chewed (saint's) raiment (cf* p 209 *a).*

Abnormal forms. BMis 53 *S* ⲡⲱϣ ... ⲉⲓϫⲉⲛⲡⲉ-ϣⲏⲣⲉ, 67 (same MS) ⲉⲓϫⲛⲛⲟⲩⲃⲁⲗ (var FR 32 ϩⲓ-ϫⲛ-), Ryl 61 *S* liturg rubric ψαλλει ⲉϫⲱⲧⲛⲓ, JKP 2 104 *S* sim ⲉϫⲱⲡⲗⲁⲟⲥ, BMOr 6201 *A* 168 *S* ⲟⲩⲁϩ ⲛⲓⲥⲟⲓ ⲙⲛⲛⲓⲃⲁ ⲉϫⲱⲡϣⲧⲁ, BMEA 10579 *S* ⲧⲛⲣⲱⲕ ⲉϩⲟⲩⲛ ⲉϫⲛⲡⲥⲉⲉⲡⲉ ⲛⲧⲁⲧⲡⲉⲧⲁⲥⲥⲉ ⲛⲁⲛ ⲙⲙⲟⲟⲩ, Ryl 346 *S* ⲉⲣⲟϣ ⲉϫⲛⲡⲣⲱⲙⲉ, *ib* 353 *S* ϫⲓ ⲡⲉⲧⲣⲓⲙⲛⲥⲓⲛ ⲉϫⲱⲥⲟⲩ, AZ 23 112 *S* ϯ...ⲉϫⲟⲣ ⲛⲧⲉⲣϫⲙ (*cf* 115 ϯ ...ⲉϫⲛⲓ), PGol 47 *A²* ⲉϫⲟⲩⲙⲁⲕⲁⲣⲉ, Kr 32 *F* ⲁⲓϫⲓ

...ⲉϫⲱⲏⲗⲡ, BKU 1 26 (8116a) *F* ⲙⲁⲣⲟⲩ ⲉϫⲱⲟⲩⲣⲱⲙⲓ, Cant 7 8 *F,* Lam 1 10 *F* ⲉϫⲱⲡ- (*v* above), Kr 16 *F* ⲉϫⲉⲥⲟⲩⲁ, *ib* 11 *F* ⲉϫⲩϩⲣⲉⲉⲓ, BKU 1 23 *F* ⲉⲓϫⲏⲧⲏⲗⲟ ⲫⲏⲗⲓ, *ib* ⲉϫⲉⲗⲟⲙⲓ ⲛⲓⲃⲓ, Ora 4 202 *F* ⲉϫⲉⲧⲁⲡⲏ, Sph 10 4 *F* ⲉϫⲉⲡⲧⲓⲙⲉ.

ⲉⲃⲟⲗ ⲉϫⲛ-, *out upon:* Deu 33 12 *S*(*B* om ⲉⲃ.) ἐπί; Jos 3 15 *S*(*B* ϣⲁ-) κατά; Bess 7 10 *B* ⲥⲉⲡⲁϣϩⲁⲙ ⲡⲡⲓⲣⲱⲟⲩ ⲉⲃ. ⲉϫⲱ.

ⲉϩⲟⲩⲛ ⲉϫⲛ- *v* p 686 *a,* add *S* BAp 80 ⲃⲱⲕ ⲉϩⲟⲩⲛ ⲉϫⲱϥ *go into his presence,* COAd 10 sim, J 67 57 at marriage ⲙⲡⲉⲥⲉⲛ ⲗⲁⲁⲩ ⲉϩ. ⲉϫⲱⲓ, Rec 11 134 additional books ⲛⲧⲁⲅⲉⲓ ⲉϩ. ⲉϫⲱⲟⲩ.

ⲉϩⲣⲁⲓ ⲉϫⲛ- *v* pp 699 *a,* 700 *a.*

ⲣ ⲉϫⲛ- *S be over, superesse* (?): BMOr 9533 they have spun but half ⲧⲕⲉⲡⲏϣⲉ ⲥⲉⲣ ⲉϫⲱⲟⲩ ⲟⲛ or ? *are yet at work thereon.*

(ϩⲁϫⲛ-*S,* ϩ. *A*), ϩⲁϫⲱⲡ-*S*(once), ϩⲁϫⲉⲛ-*B,* (ϩⲁϫⲉⲛ-*F*), ϩⲁϫⲱⲥ *SF,* ϩ. *A,* ϩ. *B* prep, *before* (mostly *B*) **a** of place: 2 Kg 6 4 (*S* ϩⲓⲣⲏ), Ps 104 17 (*S* ϩⲁⲑⲏ) ἔμπροσθεν; Mal 3 14 (*A* ⲙⲡⲁⲧⲟ ⲁⲃⲁⲗ), Ac 14 13 (*S* ⲙⲡⲃⲟⲗ) πρό, Mt 2 9 (*S* ϩⲏⲧⲥ), cit BMis 99 *S* ϩⲁϫⲱⲟⲩ, 2 Kg 8 4 *S* ⲡⲣⲟ-; Is 28 10 (*S* ϩⲏⲧⲥ) προσ-, Ro 16 2 (*S* diff) προστάτις; Lu 2 25 *F*(*S* ⲛⲏ-, *B* ϩⲓϫ.), Ez 32 4 ἐπί; Mt 25 1 *Sᶠ*(PcodMor, *S* ⲉⲧⲱⲙⲛⲧ, *B* ⲉϩⲣⲉⲛ-) εἰς ὑπάντησιν, MG 25 232 ⲁⲅⲓ ⲉⲃⲟⲗ ϩⲁϫⲱϥ = Z 317 *S* ϩⲏⲧϥ εἰς ἀπάντ., Deu 10 11 *SB* ἐναντίον; ⲙⲟⲟϣⲉ ϩ. Mic 2 13 *SA*(*B* diff) ἡγεῖσθαι; ϭⲓ ⲙⲱⲓⲧ ϩ. Ps 79 2 (*S* ϩⲏⲧⲥ) ὁδηγεῖν, Jer 2 6 καθοδ.; Mor 27 35 *S* ⲉⲓ ⲉⲃⲟⲗ ϩⲁϫⲱϥ (var BMis 389 ϩⲏⲧϥ), AM 31 *B* sim, Gu 58 *S* sim (var *ib* ϩⲁⲧⲉϥϩⲏ), BMis 37 *S* ⲁϥⲧⲱⲟⲩⲛ ϩⲁϫⲱϥ & greeted him, Graz Univ Libr *F* ⲁⲓⲙⲁϣⲓ ϩⲁϫⲱⲟⲩ, PLond 4 516 *S* ϩⲁϫⲱⲡⲡⲣⲏⲥ ⲛⲡϭⲟⲙ, Miss 4 717 *S* ⲥⲱⲕ ϩⲁϫⲱⲟⲩ *precede,* AM 330 ϩⲱⲥ ϩⲁϫⲱⲥ, El 86 *A* living shall go ϩⲁϫⲟⲟⲩ ⲛⲡⲉⲧⲙⲁⲩⲧ *to meet,* Va 61 94 ⲡⲧⲉϥϫⲟⲡϥ ϩⲁϫⲱϥ ⲙⲡⲓⲣⲁⲙⲁⲟ = P 131³ 83 *S* ϩⲁⲡϩⲟ ⲛ-, AM 33 ϯϣⲓⲡⲓ ϩⲁϫⲱⲥ, PO 11 321 ⲡⲁϥϫⲏ ϩⲁϫⲱⲟⲩ ⲡⲛⲉϥⲥⲩⲅⲅⲉⲛⲏⲥ ϩⲱⲥ ⲓⲱⲧ, BM 661 *F* may God ⲕⲉⲉⲕ ϩⲁϫⲱⲓ ⲡⲟⲩⲙⲏⲛϣⲉ ⲡⲗⲁⲙⲡⲓ, *ib* 1114 *S* ⲕⲓⲧⲃⲁ ⲡⲣⲟⲙⲡⲉ ⲟⲛ ⲉⲕⲟⲡⲁϩ ⲉⲕϩⲁϫⲱⲓ. **b** of time: Is 43 10 (*S* ϩⲁⲑⲏ), Jo 3 28 *BF*(*S* do) ἔμπ.; Ps 54 20 (*S* do), Pro 8 23 (*SA* do), Eph 1 4 (*SF* do), Am 4 7 (*S* do, cf OLZ '30 878), AM 276 archbishops ⲉⲧⲁⲩϣⲱⲡⲓ ϩⲁϫⲱϥ πρό, Mk 15 42 (*F* ⲑⲉⲕⲧⲓ ἕκτη) προ-; Lam 2 16 *BF* προσ-; MG 25 20 died ϩ. (*sic!*) ē ⲛⲉϩⲟⲟⲩ ἐντός (cf Am 4 above); Is 51 5 (*S* diff) ὑπο-; Ac 17 16 ⲥⲟⲗⲥ ⲉⲃⲟⲗ ϩ. (*S* ϩⲏⲧⲥ) ἐκδέχεσθαι; Va 58 123 spoken ϩ. ϯⲡⲏⲥⲧⲓⲁ νηστειῶν ἀρχή, Ez 37 11 ϫⲟⲩϣⲧ ⲉⲃⲟⲗ ϩ. (*S* do) ἐλπίς; *ib* 21 22 Gk om; BAp 20 *S* Christ ⲉⲧϣⲟⲟⲡ ϩⲁϫⲱϥ ⲙⲡⲧⲏⲣϥ, BSM 101 ϩ. ⲟⲩⲕⲟⲩϫⲓ, C 43 107 unto Whom glory ϩ. ⲡⲓⲉⲛⲉϩ (cf πρὸ αἰώνων), Mus 34 206 thou (Joseph) didst touch Him ϩ. ⲑⲱⲙⲁⲥ, Miss 4 123 swear by God ϩⲁϫⲱϥ ⲙⲡⲁⲡⲧⲉⲕⲥϧⲁⲓ *ere thou subscribe* = Mor 18 31 *S* ϩⲁⲑⲏ ⲛ- = Gött ar 114 31

من قبل ان, Mor 31 2 *S* fathers ⲉⲧϩⲁϫⲱⲟⲩ, *ib* 95 sim, Va 57 79 to benefit thee ϩⲁϫⲱⲥ ⲉⲑⲣⲉⲥϣⲱⲡ ⲉⲃⲟⲗ ⲛϫⲉ ϯⲁⲡⲟⲗⲓⲁ.

ⲓⲥϫⲉⲛϩ., *since before:* Miss 4 218 ι. ϩ. ⲟⲩⲙⲏϣ ⲡⲥⲛⲟⲩ ἀπὸ πλείστων χρόνων, Va 57 208 ι. ϩⲁϫⲱϥ ⲡⲛⲉϣⲟⲣⲡ ⲡⲓⲟⲧ ἐκ προγόνων.

ⲣ ϩⲁϫⲱⲥ *S, go toward:* Miss 4 766 ⲁϥⲉⲣ ϩⲁϫⲱϥ ⲉⲡⲁⲉⲓⲱⲧ & fell at his feet, JA '05 450 sim, Mor 46 52 ⲁⲣⲓ ϩⲁϫⲱⲓ ⲉⲧⲡⲟⲗⲓⲥ.

ϩⲓϫⲛ-*SAA²,* ϩⲓϫⲉⲛ-*BF,* ϩⲓϫⲱ-*SF,* ϩⲓϫⲟ-*S,* ϩ(ⲉ)ⲓϫⲉ-, ϩⲓϫⲓ-*F,* ϩⲓϫⲱⲥ *SAA²BF* prep, lit *on head of,* so *upon, over:* Ge 6 5 *SB,* Ex 16 14 *B*(*S* ϩⲓⲣⲛ-), Deu 31 13 *S*(*B* ⲛϩⲣⲏⲓ ϩ.), Si 1 8 *S*(var ϩⲓ-) *B,* Is 49 22 *S*(*B* ⲉ-), Jer 23 5 *SBF,* Lam 4 21 *B*(*F* ϩⲗⲏⲓ ⲉϫⲱⲡ-), *ib* 2 19 *S*(*B* ϩⲉⲡ-, *F* ⲡ-), Mt 14 8 *S*(*BF* ϩⲓ-), *ib* 27 25 *S*(*B* ⲉϩⲣ. ⲉϫ.), Lu 8 16 *S*(var ⲉϫⲛ-)*B,* Jo 3 36 *BF*(*S* ⲉϩⲣ. ⲉϫⲛ-), *ib* 6 19 *SA²B,* Ac 9 33 *SB*(*F* ⲉϫ.), Cl 17 5 *A,* Aeg 274 *S* gospels laid ϩ. ⲧⲁⲡⲉ of ordinand, CaiEuch 497 *B* ι ⲉⲡⲉⲥⲏⲧ ϩ. ⲡⲕⲁϩⲓ ἐπί, Lev 2 15 *S*(*B* ⲉϩⲣ. ⲉϫ.), Jer 4 23 *B*(*S* ⲉϫⲛ-), 1 Cor 9 16 *B*(*S* diff) ἐπι-, Ge 18 2 *S,* Is 14 13 *S,* Jo 3 31 *SF*(*B* all ⲥⲁⲡϣⲱⲓ) ἐπάνω; Is 61 7 *SB,* Phil 2 9 *S*(*B* ϩⲟⲥⲓ ⲉ-) ὑπέρ, Dan 3 60 *S*(*B* ⲥⲁⲡ. ⲉ-) ὑπεράνω; Br 263 *S* ⲛϭⲟⲙ ⲉⲧϩ. ⲡⲙⲟⲟⲩ, PS 142 *S* ⲁⲓⲁϩⲉ ⲣⲁⲧ ϩⲓϫⲱⲥ & robbed her of power, *ib* 335 ⲉϥϣⲟⲟⲡ ϩ. ⲧⲉϥⲉϫⲟⲩⲥⲓⲁ ⲙⲙⲓⲛ ⲙⲙⲟϥ *being of independent authority* (?), ShMIF 23 69 *S* ⲙⲛ ⲕⲣⲓⲙⲁ ϩⲓϫⲱⲟⲩ, ShC 42 190 *S* ⲥⲟϭⲛ ϩ. ⲧⲁⲡⲉ ... ⲥⲟϭⲛ ⲉⲧϩⲓⲧⲁⲡⲉ, ShBor 247 121 *S* ⲙⲟⲟϣⲉ ϩ. ⲟⲩⲉⲣⲏⲧⲉ ⲥⲛⲧⲉ, BMis 38 *S* ⲡⲉⲓⲡⲟⲗⲉⲙⲟⲥ ⲉⲧϩⲓϫⲱⲛ, JKP 2 52 *Sᶠ* ⲧⲙⲉⲧϩⲏⲕⲏ ⲉⲧϩⲓϫⲟϥ, Kr 228 12 *S* ⲡⲉⲥϫⲓⲕⲉⲱⲛ (-καιον) ϩⲓϫⲱⲕ *her rights are thy care,* BSM 46 *B* ⲡⲁⲓ ... ⲉⲧⲉⲛⲧⲱⲧⲉⲛ ϩⲓϫⲱⲓ *what ye (may claim) of me* = Va 63 16 *B* ...ⲧⲁϩⲟ ⲙⲙⲟⲩ ⲉⲣⲟⲓ = BMis 395 *S* ...ⲧⲁϩⲟ ⲙⲙⲟⲩ ⲉϫⲓⲧⲟⲩ ⲡⲧⲟⲟⲧ, Z 267 *S* ⲡⲉⲥϭⲉⲣⲱϥ ϩ. ⲡⲁⲑⲓⲙⲉ ⲙⲡⲣⲡⲟ her (Pulcheria's) authority above queen's, ManiH 62 *A²* ⲉϥⲕⲏ ϩ. ⲡϭⲗⲁϭ, J 69 16 *S* ϩⲙⲟⲟⲥ ϩ. (cf *ib* 106 100 ⲉϫⲛ-), DeV 2 166 *B* ⲟⲩⲙⲏϣ ⲡⲣⲱⲟⲩϣ ⲭⲏ ϩⲓϫⲱⲓ, *ib* 23 *B* ⲡⲧⲉϥϫⲓⲧϥ ϩ. ⲡⲉϥϫⲓϫ, BSM 35 *B* ⲁϥⲓ ϩ. ⲟⲩⲙⲁⲡⲉⲥⲱⲟⲩ = BMis 378 *S* ⲉϫⲛ-;   *upon, in:* Ge 22 14 *SB,* Jud 6 26 *S*(var ⲉϫⲛ-), Pro 2 21 *SA*(*B* ϩⲓ-), Jer 15 10 *B*(*S* ϩⲛ-), Jo 4 20 *SA²B* ἐν; Jos 9 26 *S, ib* 10 12 *S* κατά, Ge 12 6 *SB,* Ps 36 29 *S*(*B* ϩⲓ-), Jer 10 18 *SB* κατα-; PS 230 *S* ⲟⲩⲣⲱⲙⲉ ⲉϥϩ. ⲡⲕⲟⲥⲙⲟⲥ; *upon,* motion *to:* Ez 9 3, *ib* 11 16 *B* εἰς; DeV 2 89 *B* ⲙⲁⲣⲉⲡⲧⲁⲥϭⲟⲡ ϩ. ϯϩⲓⲥⲧⲟⲣⲓⲁ; *on, at, beside:* Ps 1 3 *S*(*B* ϩⲁⲧⲉⲛ-), Ac 10 6 *S*(*B* do) παρά, Ez 25 9 *B,* Ac 1 10 *S*(var ⲉϫⲛ-, *B* ⲛⲁϩⲣⲉⲛ-) παρα-; BMis 560 *S* set me ϩ. ⲟⲩⲛⲅⲗⲱⲛ πρό ad, C 86 270 *B* ϩⲉⲙⲥⲓ ϩ. ⲡⲓⲃⲏⲙⲁ προ(καθίζειν); Sa 12 16 *S,* Ps 131 7 *S*(*B* ϩⲉⲡ-), Ez 37 24 *SB* gen; Ge 15 11 *SB,* Job 21 9 *SB,* Mk 7 32 *S* (var & *B* ⲉϫⲛ-), Ac 12 7 *S*(*B* om) dat; Br 232 *S* ⲁϩⲉ ⲣⲁⲧϥ ϩ. ⲧⲉⲧⲣⲁⲡⲉⲍⲁ, PO 11 365 *B* sim (cf 364 ⲉϫ.), Mor 18 16 *S* ⲉⲣⲉⲡⲥⲱⲧⲏⲣ ϩ. ⲡⲁⲙⲁ ⲡⲛⲕⲟⲧⲕ = Miss 4

110 B ϧⲉⲙⲥⲓ ϧ., ShA 2 51 S ⲕⲣ. ⲡⲉⲑⲩⲥⲓⲁⲥⲧⲏⲣⲓⲟⲛ ⲡⲓⲙⲁⲓ, ManiH 11 A² ϥⲁϣⲱ ϩⲓϫⲱⲥ, Gu 88 S ⲟⲩⲏ ⲟⲩⲏⲣ ⲡⲣⲱⲙⲉ ϩⲓϫⲱⲓ come to baptism, BSM 37 B ⲁϥ- ⲥⲓⲛⲓ ϩⲓϫⲱⲕ = BMis 381 S ⲡⲁⲣⲁⲅⲉ ⲙⲙⲟⲕ, BM 1073 S ⲉⲣⲉⲡⲉⲕⲣⲱⲙⲉ ϣⲓ ⲙⲙⲟⲟⲩ (sc corn) ϩⲓϫⲱⲓ in my presence, DeV 2 93 B ϧ. ⲡⲁⲓ ⲧⲏⲣⲟⲩ after all this, CO 187 S sim (cf ⲉϫⲛ- ⲉ);   upon, for: Lev 5 8 B(S ϧⲁ-), Si 45 37 (23) S περί, Ex 29 9 S(B ⲉϫ.), Mk 15 17 SB(F ⲉϫ. ⲧⲉϥⲁⲡⲏ) περι- ; Mor 31 36 S shed blood ϧ. ⲡⲣⲁⲛ ⲙⲡⲁⲭ̄ⲥ̄ (var Miss 4 775 ⲉϫⲛ-), DeV 2 267 B ϯ ⲱⲟⲩ ϧ. ⲡⲓⲣⲙⲟⲧ (cf ib sim ⲉϫ.), FR 98 B give me courage ϧ. ϯⲁⲡⲟⲫⲁⲥⲓⲥ;   through: Deu 15 1 S (var ϩⲓⲧⲛ-, B ⲕⲁⲧⲁ), Sa 10 4 S, Is 19 7 S(B ⲙⲡⲕⲱϯ ⲛ-) διά;   from upon SAA²(B rare, cf ⲉⲃⲟⲗ ϧ.): Ge 48 17 (B ⲉⲃⲟⲗ ⲉϫ.), Nu 17 10 (B 16 25 diff), Job 2 9 (B ⲉⲃ. ϧ.), Pro 2 22 SA(B ϧⲓ-), Ps 103 34 (B ⲉⲃ. ϧⲁ-), Is 53 8 A(Cl, var & SB ⲉⲃ. ϧ.) ἀπό, Est 4 4 ⲁⲡⲟ- ἀπό; Jos 15 18, Jer 10 11 (Miss 8 229, var ⲉⲃ. ϧ., B ⲉⲃ. ϧⲁ-) ἐκ; Lu 4 9 ϧ. ⲡⲉⲓⲙⲁ (var ⲉϫⲛ-, B ⲉⲃ. ⲧⲁⲓ) ἐντεῦθεν; ShMIF 23 18 ϥⲓ ⲛⲧⲉϥⲁⲡⲉ ϩⲓϫⲱϥ, TT 40 ϥⲓ ⲧⲉϥⲟⲩⲉⲣ- ⲏⲧⲉ ⲙⲙⲁⲩ ϧ. ⲡⲕⲁϩ, Faras (3) lxix 17 ⲙⲡⲉϥⲕⲓⲙ ⲉⲧⲉϥⲟⲩⲉⲣⲏⲧⲉ ϩⲓϫⲱⲥ (sc snake), Ryl 72 353 ⲕⲁⲁⲧ ⲉ- ⲡⲉⲥⲏⲧ ϧ. ⲡⲉⲓⲱ, BMis 33 ⲁϥⲧⲟⲩⲛⲟⲥⲟϥ ⲉϩⲣⲁⲓ ϧ. ⲡⲉ- ⲑⲣⲟⲛⲟⲥ, Miss 4 167 B thy memory ⲡⲁⲕⲛⲏ ϧ. ⲡⲕⲁϩⲓ, ManiP 4 A² ⲡⲁⲣⲕϥ (sc tree) ϧ. ⲡⲉⲩⲕⲁϩ.   not literal: Est 8 15 S ⲟⲩⲕⲗⲟⲙ ϩⲓϫⲱϥ στέφανον ἔχων, Mk 14 13 S ⲟⲩϣⲟϣⲟⲩ ϩⲓϫⲱϥ βαστάζων, Dan 4 14 B ⲉⲧϭⲟⲥⲓ ϧ. ὕψιστος, Jo 10 29 SA² ϧ. ⲟⲩⲟⲛ ⲛⲓⲙ πάντων μεῖζον, Ac 1 18 B ϧⲉⲓ ϧ. ⲡⲉϥϩⲟ πρηνὴς γενόμενος.

ⲡⲉⲧ-, ⲡⲉⲧϧ., who is over, in command: Ge 39 21 S (B diff) ἀρχι(δεσμοφύλαξ), AP 11 A² ⲡ. ⲡⲉⲧⲙⲏⲣ δεσ- μοφ., Pro 23 5 SA προεστηκώς, Ru 2 5 S ἐφεστὼς ἐπί, Dan 3 2 B ὁ ἐπί, Jth 12 10 S ὁ πρός, Job 5 8 S(B ⲡⲛⲃ̄) δεσπότης, Lu 22 26 S(B = Gk) ἡγούμενος; PS 318 S ⲡⲉⲧϩⲓϫⲱⲟⲩ, ShA 2 243 S sim, ShC 73 x S ⲡⲉⲧϧ. ⲡⲉ- ⲕⲟⲗⲁⲥⲓⲥ, DeV 1 37 B ⲫⲏ ⲉⲧϧ. ⲡⲓϣⲧⲉⲕⲟ.

Abnormal forms. Bodl(P) a 2 47 S ϩⲓϫⲱⲡⲕⲱⲣⲧ, Kr 233 F ϩⲓϫⲱⲡⲥⲟⲩⲁ, ib 8 F ϩⲓϫⲱⲟⲩⲣⲱ, BM 661 F ϩⲓϫⲱⲡⲉⲓ, AZ 23 110 S ϩⲓϫⲟⲣ̄ ⲡϣⲓ, CMSS 35 F ⲟⲩⲁ- ⲁⲧⲟⲩ ⲡⲁⲡ ϩⲓϫⲟⲕⲉⲥⲁⲛ, BM 594 F ϩⲓϫⲟⲡⲡⲉⲙⲡⲧ (cf ⲉϫⲱⲛ- F), Kr 10 F ϩⲉⲓϫⲉⲃⲣⲉⲉⲓ, ib 33 F ϩⲓϫⲉⲛⲣⲉⲡ, Mor 24 5 F ϩⲓϫⲉⲡⲧⲁⲩ, BM 580 13 F ϩⲓϫⲓⲛ(ⲡ)ⲗⲁⲧ- ⲥⲏⲛⲓ (? πλαστήριον).

ⲉⲃⲟⲗ ϧ. SABF, from upon: Ge 8 3 S(B as Gk), Deu 22 8 B(S ⲉⲃ. ϧⲛ-), Is 30 11 SF(B ⲉⲃ. ϧⲁ-), Nah 1 13 A(B do), Ac 13 29 B(var ⲉⲃ. ϧⲓ-, S ϧⲓ-) ἀπό; Pro 1 12 SAB, Ez 11 23 B(S ⲉⲃ. ϧⲛ-) ἐκ; Ac 9 32 B(varr ⲉⲃ. ⲉϫ. & S ⲉⲃ. ϩⲓⲧⲛ-) διά; ShA 1 452 S ⲧⲱϭⲛ ⲉϩⲣⲁⲓ ⲉⲃ. ϧ ⲡⲕⲁϩ, ib 2 336 S ⲧⲁⲕⲟ ⲛⲧⲁⲡⲧⲁⲥⲉⲃⲏⲥ ⲉⲃ. ϧ. ⲡⲕⲁϩ, BSG 188 S ϥⲓ ⲙⲙⲁⲩ ⲛⲡⲣⲓⲥⲉ ... ⲉⲃ. ϩⲓϫⲱⲡ, BIF 13 108 S come down ⲉⲃ. ϧ. ⲧⲡⲉⲧⲣⲁ, CDan 95 B ϭⲟϫⲓ ⲡⲥⲱⲟⲩ ⲉⲃ. ϧ. ⲡⲟⲩⲑⲣⲟⲡⲟⲥ, DeV 2 235 B deluge ⲡⲁⲕⲏⲛ ⲉⲃ. ϩⲓϫⲱⲧⲉⲛ.

ϩⲣⲁⲓ ϧ., ⲡϧⲣⲏⲓ ϧ. SB, upon: Ex 16 14 S(B ϩⲓϫ.), Nu 6 7 S(B do), Jer 2 34 SB, Mt 9 6 S(B do) ἐπί; Ex 24 18 S(B ⲛϧⲣ. ϧⲓ-), Jer 38 6 B ⲉⲛ; PS 117 S ϯ ⲟⲩⲱ ϧ. ϩⲓϫⲱⲓ (Od Solom 1 4 ـܥ ـ), ShBor 281 99 S ⲡⲥⲁϩⲟⲩ...ϧ. ϩⲓϫⲱ as it was ⲉⲭⲡⲥⲩⲡⲁⲧⲱⲧⲏ of old; ⲉϩⲣ. ϧ. v p 699 b; ⲛϧⲣ. ϧ., ⲛⲉ̄ⲥ̄. v p 700 b.

ⲡ ϧ. S, be over: Deu 28 43 (B ϭⲓⲥⲓ ⲉⲡϣⲱⲓ) ἀναβαί- νειν ἐπί; Is 43 24 (B diff) προιστάναι; PS 44 ⲁⲥⲟⲩⲉϣ ⲃⲱⲕ ⲉⲡϫⲓⲥⲉ ⲛ̄ⲥⲉⲣ ϩⲓϫⲱⲟⲩ.

ϩⲓϫⲱⲟⲩ nn m S, meaning obscure: PStras 409 letter of bishop's envoy ⲁⲓⲧⲁⲁⲗⲉ ⲡⲉⲙⲟⲟⲩ ⲉⲡⲉϥϩⲓ- ϫⲱⲟⲩ (cf ? ⲡⲓϩⲣⲓⲫⲁϩⲟⲩ p 285 a 25).

ϫⲱ SA², **ϫⲟⲩ** Sᵃ A nn m, cup (B always ⲁⲫⲟⲧ): Ps 22 5, Pro 23 31 S(var ⲁⲡⲟⲧ) A, Jer 32 1 (var Cai 8316 do), Lu 22 20, Jo 18 11 SA² ποτήριον, P 44 60 ⲡⲟⲧⲏⲣⲓⲟⲛ, ⲁⲡⲟⲧ, ϫⲱ س̄ك; ShP 130¹ 141 ⲡⲓⲡⲁϩ, ϫⲟⲡ, ϫⲱ, ST 411 sim, Blake 318 ϩⲛⲭⲱ ⲛ ϩⲛⲁⲡⲟⲧ of onyx, PMich 597 ⲡⲡⲟⲩϩ, J 66 40 Sᵃ ⲡⲣⲟⲙⲡⲧ, Mor 44 30 ϫⲱ ⲙⲙⲁⲧⲟⲩ, ManiH 7 A² ⲡⲥⲡⲁϥ;   ⲉⲡϫⲱ (l ?? ⲉⲓⲉⲡ-): Vi Sitz 172 4 16 ⲡⲉⲧⲛⲁⲥⲱ (sic) ⲉⲡⲟⲩⲉⲡϫⲱ ϩⲓⲏⲣⲡ ϩⲓⲉⲃⲓⲱ θανάσιμον φάρμακον μετὰ οἰνομέλιτος. V also ? ⲗⲁⲗ.

ϫⲱⲓ B nn m, earthen basin: K 150 ⲡⲓϫ. (3 varr ϫⲱⲣ, l ϫⲱ), ib 260 do مَاجُور (= also λακάνη P 55 11, ⲕⲁⲡⲓⲕⲟⲛ K 150). Cf ? ـ & ϫⲱⲣ.   Prob not same as last.

ϫⲉⲃ- in ϫⲉⲃϣⲁⲓ v ϣⲁ nose.

ϫⲏⲃ v ϫⲟⲩϥ.

ϫⲟⲃ F, **ϫⲟⲃ⸗** S v ϫⲱϥ be costly.

ϫⲱⲃ B v ϭⲃ̄ⲃⲉ.

ϫⲱⲃⲓ B v ϭⲱⲱⲃⲉ.

ϫⲱⲱⲃⲉ, -ϭⲉ, ϫⲱ(ⲱ)ϭⲉ S, ϫⲟⲩⲟⲩⲃⲉ A, ϫⲱⲃⲉ A², ϫⲉⲉⲃ-, ϫⲟⲟⲃ⸗ S, ϫⲁⲃ⸗ A A² vb intr, pass by, over: Mani H 85 A² ⲥ]ⲉϫ. ⲥⲉⲡⲁⲣⲁⲅⲉ, ib P 39 A² ⲧⲡⲡⲁϫ. ⲡⲧⲡⲭⲓⲟⲣⲉ;   tr, pass by, surpass, reach: LeipBer '02 146 ⲁϥϫⲉⲉⲃⲉ ⲧⲣⲟⲉⲓⲁ παραπλεῖν; Mor 37 110 ⲥⲓ- ⲡⲉ ⲙⲙⲟⲟⲩ ⲁⲩⲱ ϫ. ⲙⲙⲟⲟⲩ διαβαίνειν; 1 Tim 6 16 ⲙⲉⲣⲉⲗⲁⲁⲩ ϫⲟⲟⲃⲉϥ (B ϣ ϭⲱⲡⲧ ⲉⲣⲟϥ) ἀπρόσιτος; ShA 2 240 ϩⲉⲙⲡⲟⲉⲓⲧ ⲛϫ. ⲡⲧⲉⲩⲯⲩⲭⲏ ⲉϩⲣⲁⲓ ϩⲓⲡⲁ- ⲏⲣ, BAp 138 ⲁϥϫ. ⲛⲧⲙⲉϩϣⲟⲙⲧⲉ ⲁⲡⲉ, Miss 8 253 perfume ϫ. ⲙⲡⲁⲏⲣ ⲧⲏⲣϥ till reached us, Mor 37 160 ⲙⲁⲣⲉⲡϫⲉⲉⲃⲉ ⲡⲟⲩⲁ ⲡⲟⲩⲁ & ascend to heaven, BM Ad 31290 304 escaped & ⲁϥϫ. ⲙⲡⲭⲁⲓⲉ (on Ex 2 15), BMar 92 ϫ. ...ⲙⲡⲉⲗⲁⲅⲟⲥ, Z 271 took Syria captive ⲁϥϫⲱϫⲉ ⲡⲡⲙⲉⲣⲟⲥ ⲛⲧⲁϥⲧⲁϩⲟⲟⲩ, Till Oster 24 A ϫ. ⲙⲡϫⲉⲓⲙⲱⲛ (cf Cant 2 11), Ming 288 ⲁϥϫⲟ- ⲟⲃⲟⲩ (sc heavens) ϩⲓⲡⲉϥⲙⲟⲛⲙⲉⲛ, TU 43 4 A ⲁⲓϫⲁ- ⲃⲟⲩ, ManiP 40 A² ⲁⲩϫ. ⲙⲙⲁϥ ⲧⲏⲣⲟⲩ (cf Lu 10 31).

With following preposition or adverb.　ⲥ ⲉ-:
Mor 18 162 ⲁ̄ⲝ. ⲉⲡⲕⲟⲥⲙⲟⲥ without distraction, CO
133 ⲁⲓ̄ⲝ. ⲉⲡⲧⲓⲙⲉ ⲉⲓⲣⲱⲧ ⲉⲣⲟⲓ, ManiP 62 *A*² ⲉⲓⲡⲁⲩ̣ ⲝ.
… ⲁⲛⲉⲕⲙⲁ, Till Bau 119 ⲉⲣⲩ̄]ⲁⲛⲥⲟⲩⲥⲟⲟⲩ ⲉⲧⲱⲃⲉ
ⲝⲱⲱϭⲉ [ⲉⲧⲕⲩⲣⲓ]ⲁⲕⲏ *fall upon*, 121 sim -ϥⲉ;　ⲥ
ⲙⲛ-: ST 101 ⲉϥϣⲁⲛⲝⲱϭⲉ ⲟⲛ ⲙⲛⲧⲉϥⲥ(ⲣ̄)ⲓⲙⲉ none
shall molest them(same?);　ⲥ ⲣⲛ-: ManiK 356 *A*²
ϯ̄ⲕⲉⲥⲙ…ⲝ. ⲣⲙⲡⲕⲁⲣ;　ⲥ ⲥⲓⲣⲛ-: ManiP 224 *A*²
ⲝ. ⲣ. ⲡⲣⲟ;　ⲥ ⲣⲁⲧⲛ-: Nu 20 19 (var ⲙⲟⲟⲩϣⲉ ⲣⲁ-
ⲣⲁⲧⲝ, *B* ⲥⲓⲛⲓ ⲉⲃⲟⲗ ⲉⲥⲕⲉⲛ-) παρέρχεσθαι παρά;　ⲥ
ⲉⲃⲟⲗ: ShA 2 321 ϯⲛⲁⲝⲱϭⲉ ⲉⲃ ϩⲓⲧⲡⲧⲗⲅⲡⲏ … ⲛⲟⲉ
ⲙⲡⲉϣⲁϥⲝⲱⲃⲉ ⲉⲃ. ⲣ. ⲣⲉⲛⲥⲣⲁⲣⲟⲟⲩⲉ, ManiP 227 *A*²
ⲛ]ⲥⲉⲛⲉⲁ ⲝ. ⲁⲃ. ϩⲓⲧⲟⲟⲧⲕ;　ⲥ ⲉⲣⲟⲩⲛ: Mor 37 1̄13
hindereth them ⲉⲧⲙⲧⲣⲉⲩⲝ. ⲉⲣ. διέρχ.; AZ 16 15
ⲁⲓ̄ⲝ. ⲉⲣ. & visited the brethren.

ⲁⲧⲝⲟⲟⲃⲉ̄, *impassable*: P 131³ 1 fire ⲛⲡⲟⲉⲧⲟⲛ ⲁⲩⲱ
ⲛⲁⲧⲝⲟⲟⲃⲉϥ.

ⲝⲃ̄ⲃ(ⲉ)ⲥ, ⲝⲉⲃ̄ⲃⲉⲥ², ⲝⲉⲃ̄ⲃ̄ⲥ³, ⲝ(ⲉ)ⲃ̄ⲥ⁴, ⲝⲏⲏⲃⲥ⁵, ⲝⲏ-
ⲃ̄ⲥ⁶, ⲝⲏⲓⲃⲉⲥ⁷, ⲝⲁ(ⲉ)ⲓⲃⲉⲥ⁸ *S*, ⲝⲃ̄ⲃⲉⲥ *Ā*, ⲝⲉⲃ̄ⲥ *B*, ⲝⲏⲃ̄-
ⲃⲉⲥ *F* nn, *coal* f: 2 Kg 14 7 *S*⁵, Is 6 6 *SB* ἄνθραξ, *cit*
ViK 9221 *S*, *ib* 9538 *S*⁵; P 46 155 *S* ۮۥۦ, P 55 7 *B*
ٔۦ;　m *B*: Is 44 19 (*S* pl) ἄν.; DeV 2 17 on Is 6 6,
Absal 578 ⲁⲥϫⲁⲓ ϩⲁⲡⲓⲝ ⲡⲧⲉ ϯⲙⲛⲧⲛⲟⲩϯ; Ez 24 6
(*S* ϣⲏⲏⲃⲉ) ἰός;　no gender: Lev 16 12 *SB*, Pro 6
28 *SAB*, Is 5 24 *SBF*, *ib* 54 11 *B* (*S* = Gk), BHom 44
S ⲡⲉⲣϣ ⲣⲉⲛⲝ. ϩⲁⲣⲟⲟⲩ (sc martyrs, cf BMar 28) ἄν.,
RNC 45 *S* ἀνθρακιά; C 89 13 *B* ϩⲁⲛⲝ. ⲛ̄ⲭⲣⲱⲙ ⲡⲩⲣ-
ⲕⲁⲓⲁ; Lam 4 8 *S*⁵ (*B* ⲁϣⲙ̄ⲓ), Z 331 *S* faces like ⲣⲉⲛⲝ.⁸
ἀσβόλη; ShC 73 49 *S* ⲕⲣⲟⲙⲣⲙ ⲛⲟⲉ ⲡⲟⲩⲝ., BMar
144 *S* ⲝ. ⲡⲥⲁⲧⲉ, *ib* ⲝ. ⲛ̄ⲕⲱⲣⲧ, CO 335 *S* ⲃⲓⲣⲉ ⲛ̄ⲝ.²,
Mor 42 11 *S* ⲟⲩⲝ.⁷ ref to Is 6;　various kinds *S*:
Ora 4 25 ⲝ.⁴ ⲛ̄ⲡϣⲉ ⲛ̄ⲡⲟⲩⲝⲉ, Cai 42573 2 ⲝ.³ ⲛ̄ϣⲉ ⲛ̄-
ⲧⲱⲣⲉ, KroppF 55 ⲝ.⁶ ⲛ̄ⲡⲗⲉⲛⲕ(ⲟⲛ, cf *ib* R Introd 9 ⲕⲁⲣ-
ⲃⲱⲛⲉ ϩⲏ[ⲗⲟⲡ] ⲡⲗⲉⲛⲕⲟⲛ), Saq 103 ⲝ]ⲉⲃ̄ⲥ ⲛ̄ϫⲟⲓⲧ; as
adj: Ge 2 12 *B* ⲱⲛⲓ ⲛⲁⲟⲩⲁⲛ ⲛ̄ⲝ. *hue of (red) coal* ἄν.
(cf Blake 250); ROC 23 280 *B* sim.

ⲡ̄ ⲝ., *become charcoal*: BMis 445 *S* lay on wood &
light fire beneath ϣⲁⲛⲧⲟⲩⲣ̄ ⲝ.
V AZ 47 28, Rec 17 157.

ⲝ(ⲉ)ⲃⲏⲗ, ⲝⲓⲃ., ⲝⲉⲃⲉⲗ *S* nn, *spear* (= ? ζιβύνη):
Jth 1 15, Is 2 4 (*B* ⲡⲁⲣⲃⲓ), Jer 6 23 (P 44 113 خٔۦ,
B ⲡⲁⲅⲓ) ζ. (which Mic 4 3 *S* = ⲙⲉⲣⲉϩ); P 44 57 ⲟⲝⲩ̄-
ⲫⲁⲣⲓⲛ ϩⲉⲛⲝ.ʹ, Tri 525ʹ, TMina *Epima* 27 ⲉϥⲥⲟⲛⲣ̄
ⲉⲡⲁϩⲟⲩ ⲙⲙⲟϥ ⲛⲟⲩⲝⲓⲃ. *bound to spear*;　*shoot,
sucker*(?): BMOr 8811 242 ⲡⲝⲉⲃⲉⲗ ⲛ̄ⲧⲃⲛⲛⲉ if planted
groweth apace, 243 ⲛⲝ. ⲛ̄ⲧϣⲟⲡⲧⲉ grow likewise.

ⲝⲃⲓⲛ *S* nn m, *blemish*: Lev 21 17 (*B* ⲁϭⲛⲓ), Cant
4 7 (*F* ⲧⲱⲗⲟⲙ *sic*), Dan 1 4 (*B* ⲃ̄ⲇⲟ, *F* Mus 49 183 ϣⲉⲛ
? same word) μῶμος; Sa 13 14 κηλίς; R 1 4 29 ⲣ̄ⲡⲁϩⲣⲉ
ⲉⲡⲉϥⲝ. ⲉⲧⲣⲓⲱⲱϣ (sc ⲛ̄ⲥⲟⲛ ⲛ̄ϫⲓϥ) *vitium*; Wess 18 92
ⲝ. ⲛⲓⲙ wrought on land by man, BMis 519 wrought

on field by beasts, BP 4906 let camelherds examine
this camel ⲉⲧⲃⲉ ⲝ. & fix its price;　*without blemish*
ⲉⲙⲛ̄ ⲝ. ϩⲛ-, ϩⲓ-: Lev 23 12 (*B* ⲁⲧⲁ.) ἄμωμος;　Br
46; ⲁⲧⲝ.: Bor ?53 114 ἄχραντος; P 129²⁰ 126 bring
fruits to fullness ⲉⲅⲟ ⲛⲁ. ἀβλαβής.

ⲝⲉⲃⲣⲟ, ⲝⲉⲡ. *B*　*v* ϭⲱⲡⲣⲟ.

ⲝⲁ(ⲉ)ⲓⲃⲉⲥ, ⲝⲏⲓⲃⲉⲥ *S*, **ⲝⲉⲃ̄ⲥ** *B*　*v* ⲝⲃ̄ⲃⲉⲥ.

ⲝⲱⲃ̄ⲥ, ⲝⲉⲃ̄-, ⲝⲟⲃ̄ⲥ́, ⲝⲟⲃ̄ⲥ† *B* vb tr, *bend, bow*:
TEuch 1 316 ⲙⲁⲣⲉⲡⲓⲁⲣⲭⲓⲉⲡⲓⲥⲕⲟⲡⲟⲥ ⲝⲉⲃ̄ⲥ ⲝⲱϥ
خٔۦ, *ib* 369 ⲉⲩⲭⲏ ⲛ̄ⲝ. ⲝⲱϥ خٔۦ; Leip 26 22 ⲁⲛⲓⲥⲩ-
ⲣ̄ⲡⲟⲛ (σίγ.) ⲝⲉⲃ̄ⲥⲉ ⲝⲱⲟⲩ (or ? ⲉⲝ.), BSM 45 ⲁⲩⲝⲱ-
ⲃ̄ⲥⲟⲩ ⲙⲡⲉⲙⲑⲟ ⲙⲡⲓⲁⲣⲭⲱⲛ = BMis 393 *S* ⲡⲁϩⲧⲟⲩ
ⲛ-.　With following preposition or adverb. c ⲛ-:
Va 61 209 ⲙⲡⲉⲕⲝⲱⲡⲥ ⲛ̄ⲡⲓⲗⲁⲟⲥ, *ib* 28 ⲡⲁϥⲝ. ⲛ̄ⲝⲱϥ
ⲛⲁϥ, TEuch 2 351 ⲉⲩⲝ.† ⲛⲁⲕ ⲛ̄ϫⲉ ⲡⲉⲡⲡⲁⲣⲃⲓ;　c
ⲉⲡⲉⲥⲏⲧ: C 86 295 ⲝⲱϭ ⲝ.† ⲉⲡ. κεφαλὴν κλίνειν; Mus
34 202 ⲡⲉϥⲃⲁⲗ ⲝ.† ⲉⲡ.;　c ⲉⲝⲣⲏⲓ: Mk 1 7 (*S* ⲡⲱⲣⲧ)
κύπτειν; EW 148 ⲁϥⲝⲟⲃ̄ⲥϥ ⲉⲝ. συγκλ.

ⲝⲁⲃⲁⲁⲧ *A*² vb qual, *be hard* or sim: ManiK 31
ϥ̄ⲝ. ⲛ̄ⲡⲣⲟⲅⲟ ⲁ[ⲃⲁ]ⲡⲓⲡⲉ, *ib* [body] ⲝ. ϥ̄ⲧⲏⲕ, *ib* 101 ϯ̄ⲧⲉ-
ⲛⲉⲁ ⲉⲧⲝ.

ⲝⲉⲃⲓⲱⲟⲩ *B*　*v* ϭⲃⲃⲉ.

ⲝⲁⲃ̄ⲝⲓⲃ *B* nn, *small* in stature: MG 25 4 ⲟⲩⲣⲱⲙⲓ … ⲉϥⲟⲓ ⲛ̄ⲝ. μικροφανής *haud grandis homunculus*.

ⲝⲟⲃ̄ⲝⲃ *S*, **ⲝ̄ⲃ̄ⲝⲱϥ́** *F*　*v* ϫⲟϥϫϥ.

ⲝⲁⲕ *S*, **ϭⲁⲕ** *B*, **ⲝⲉⲕ** *F* vb intr, *clap* hands, *flap*
wings: Mor 37 83 *S* ⲉ̄ⲩ̄ⲝ. κροτεῖν; CA 89 *S* at sub-
deacon's marriage ⲛ̄ⲛⲉⲩⲝ. ⲟⲩⲇⲉ ⲛ̄ⲛⲉⲩⲝⲱ. With
following preposition or adverb.　c ⲉ- DeV 2 94
B brought idols ⲁⲩϭ. ⲉⲣⲟⲟⲩ (cf Dan 5 4 αἰνεῖν); ⲉ-
ⲣⲟⲩⲛ ⲉ-: JKP 2 122 *S* winds ⲝ. ⲉⲣ. ⲉⲡⲁⲕⲏⲡⲟⲥ (cf Cant
4 16 ⲡⲓϭⲉ ⲉⲣ. διαπνεῖν);　c ⲉⲝⲛ-: Lam 2 15 *S* (P
131⁵ 14, *B* ⲕⲱⲗϩ ⲉϩⲣⲏⲓ ⲉⲝ., *F* acc) κρ. ἐπί, Pro 17 18
S (*A* ⲝⲁⲁⲝⲉ) ἐπικρ. dat, Ez 29 7 *S* (*B* ⲕ. ⲉⲝ.) ἐπικρ.
ἐπί; LMär 17 *S* ⲁϥ̄ⲝ. ⲛ̄ⲛⲉϥϭⲓⲝ ⲉ. ⲛⲉⲅⲉⲣⲏⲩ;　ⲉ-
ⲝⲣⲏⲓ ⲉⲝ. *B*: Job 27 23 κρ. ἐπί; DeV 2 37 ⲛⲁⲩϭ. ⲉⲣ.
ⲉⲝⲱⲥⲡⲉ;　c ⲛ-, *with* (or ? acc): Ps 46 1 *S*, Lam ut
sup *F*, Ez 21 14 *S* κρ. acc, Ps 97 8 *S* (all *B* ⲕ.), Ez 6 11
S ⲝ. ⲛ̄ⲧⲉⲕϭⲓⲝ ⲣ̄ ϩⲣⲟⲟⲩ ⲛ̄ⲧⲕⲟⲩⲉⲣⲏⲧⲉ κρ. dat, *ib* 21
12 *S* κρ. ἐπί (both *B* ⲕ.), Is 55 12 *B* (*S* ⲧⲁⲁⲧⲉ) ἐπικρ.
dat; Dif 1 56 *B* ϭ. ⲛ̄ⲡⲟⲩⲧⲉⲛ صفق; Mor 28 71 *S*
ⲉⲥⲧⲉⲗⲏⲗ ⲉⲥ̄ⲝ. ⲛ̄ⲡⲉⲥϭⲓⲝ; *v* also nn;　c ⲉⲣⲟⲩⲛ ϩⲁ-
F: PMich 4946 ⲁⲩⲝⲏⲕ ⲛ̄ⲛⲉⲩϭⲓⲝ ⲉⲣ. ϩⲁⲡⲁⲣⲁ;　c
ϩⲛ- *S*: Jer 31 26 (Cai 8316, *B* ⲕ.) ἐπικρούειν ἐν; R 1
3 81 ⲁⲥⲝ. ϩⲛ̄ⲛⲉⲥϭⲓⲝ.

——— nn m *SB* (once), *palm of hand, clapping, flap-
ping*: Mor 18 173 shall not hear ⲉⲩⲝ. κρότος; P 44
70 ⲑⲉⲛⲁⲣ · ⲡⲁⲗⲁⲙⲏ · ⲛ̄ⲝ. ⲛ̄ⲧϭⲓⲝ كٔۦ; Mor 31 203

ⲧⲁⲁⲩ ⲉϩⲣⲁⲓ ⲉⲡⲉⲝ. ⲡⲡⲉⲕϭⲓⲝ = Ryl Bull 11 399 *a* في خلب, ROC 20 51 ⲛⲝⲱ ⲙⲡⲛⲝ. ϩⲡⲡⲉⲧⲛϭⲓⲝ, BM 840 47 *B* cherubim ϩⲓ ϭ. ⲛⲛⲟⲩⲧⲉⲛϩ.

ⲣⲉϥϫ., -ϭ. *clapper* of hands: ROC 20 46 *S* ⲣⲉϥ ϫⲏⲣ, ⲣⲉϥⲥⲱⲃⲉ, ⲣ. ⲛⲛⲉⲩϭⲓⲝ, Va 61 93 *B* ⲣⲉϥϫⲱ, ⲣ. = P 131³ 83 *S* ⲭⲟⲣⲁⲅⲗⲏⲥ.

ⲝⲁⲕ, ⲝⲁⲕⲍ *S* vb, cut (?): ShA 2 20 ⲟⲩⲧⲟⲉⲓⲥ ⲙⲡⲗϭⲉ ... ⲣϣⲁⲩ ⲡⲝⲁⲕⲉ ⲉⲩϩⲟⲓⲧⲉ ⲛϣⲁⲓ (*cf*? Lu 5 36), BMOr 7561 108 let none ⲝ. ϩⲛⲛⲉⲩⲥⲁ[ⲣⲍ] ⲉⲝⲡⲣⲉϥⲙⲟⲟⲩⲧ (*cf* Deu 14 1 κατατέμνειν) nor uncover head. *Cf* ⲝⲟⲕⲝⲕ.

ⲝⲁⲕ *hair* v ⲝⲟⲕ.

ⲝⲉⲕ *S* nn m, *valve* of shell: Ryl 72 352 pearl-shell ⲥⲁⲁⲡϣ ϩⲛⲝ. ⲥⲡⲁⲩ ⲉϩⲣⲟⲧⲣ ⲙⲡⲛⲉⲅⲉⲣⲏⲩ, *ib* ⲛⲝ. ⲉⲣⲉ ⲡⲙⲁⲣⲅⲁⲣⲓⲧⲏⲥ ⲛϩⲏⲧⲟⲩ, PBad 5 393 marginal rubric ⲥϩⲁⲓ ⲡⲉⲡⲣⲁⲛ ⲉⲩⲝ. ⲡⲟⲩⲛⲉ (*l* ⲱⲛⲉ) ⲛⲁⲙⲉ *sherd* (lit *shell*) of clay; different word?: Vi ostr 293 *S*ᵃ ⲛⲧⲁϭⲙ ⲡⲁⲝ. (context useless).

ⲝⲉⲕ *F* v ⲝⲁⲕ 1°.

ⲝⲓⲕ *F* nn, meaning unknown (? not complete): BM 627 ⲥⲛⲉⲩ (ⲙ)ⲙⲉⲧⲣⲟⲩ (μέτρον) ⲛⲝⲓⲕ[.

ⲝⲟⲕ¹ *SA*, **ⲝⲁⲕ**² *S* nn m, *hair* of man or beast (*cf* ⲣⲱ̄, (?) ابرة, σάκκος): Pro 23 7 *A*(*S* ⲃⲱ), Glos 6 ⲛⲝ.² θρίξ; ShC 73 113 ϣⲱϣ ⲙⲡⲝ.¹ ⲛⲧⲉϥⲁⲡⲉ, *ib* 171 accused whoso ⲡⲁϣⲃ ⲝ.¹ ϩⲓⲗⲁⲁⲩ ⲙⲙⲁ ⲡⲧⲁϥ, ShA 1 467 ⲟⲩⲱⲙ ⲛⲛⲝ.¹ ⲡⲧⲉⲕⲙⲟⲣⲧ, ShBerlOr 1611 5 35 ⲉⲓⲁⲁⲩ, ⲝ.¹, ⲡⲟⲩϭ, ⲕⲟⲧ, ⲝⲱⲱⲙⲉ (*cf* C 73 43 ⲕⲟⲧ, ϭⲟⲟⲩⲡⲉ, ⲝⲱⲱⲙⲉ, C 89 9 ⲡⲟϩ, ϥⲱⲓ), P 131¹ 59 ϩⲉⲛⲝ.² ⲡⲃⲁⲁⲙⲡⲉ ⲉⲧⲁⲙⲓⲟ ⲛⲧⲁⲉⲣⲓⲥ ⲛϣⲁⲁⲣ (*cf* Ex 26 7 δέρρεις τρίχιναι var αἴγειαι, Ep 1 157 n), Ep 438 ⲡⲕⲟⲩⲓ ⲛⲝ.² ... ⲝⲟⲟⲩ ⲟⲩⲑⲁⲗⲓⲥ, ST 294 ⲡⲣⲏϣ ⲛⲝ.², *ib* 298 ⲥⲁⲕⲓⲁ ⲛⲝ.², COAd 53 ϣⲟⲙⲛⲧ ⲛⲱⲡⲉ (a measure) ⲛⲝ.², Hall 60 sim ⲝ.¹, ST 445 ⲛⲝ.² ... ⲙⲛⲧⲟⲅⲉ ⲛⲱⲡⲉ ⲡⲁⲣⲁ ⲥⲡⲧⲉ ⲟⲩϭⲟⲥ ⲡⲗⲓⲧⲣⲁ, ST 129 ⲙⲁϥ ⲡⲗⲓⲧⲣⲁ ⲡⲭⲁϥ (?) ⲛⲝ.²; same? ShP 131⁶ 76 Christ seeketh not ϩⲉⲛⲛⲟϭ ⲛⲝ.¹ ⲉϩⲟ ⲛ[ⲥⲧ]ⲓ ⲛⲥⲓϥⲉ from His servants. In names: Παπⲝάκ, Κακτⲝάκ *hairless* (Preisigke).

ⲝⲱⲕ *SAA²BF*, **ⲝⲉⲕ-** *SB*, **ⲝⲁⲕ-** *SA²F*, **ⲝⲟⲕⲍ** *SB*, **ⲝⲁⲕⲍ** *AA²F*, **ⲝⲁⲁⲕⲍ** *AF*, **ⲝⲏⲕ**† *SAA²BF* vb **A I** intr, *be completed, full, end* life: Lu 13 32 *S*(*B* ⲝ. ⲉⲃⲟⲗ) τελεῖσθαι, Nu 7 1 *B*(*S* ⲝ. ⲉⲃ.), Dan 11 36 *B*(*S* do), Mal 3 9 *A*(*B* ⲝ. ⲉⲃ.) συντ.; 4 Kg 13 20 *S* ἔρχεσθαι; Cant 4 6 *S*(*F* ⲓ) διαπνεῖν; PS 6 *S* ⲛⲉϩⲟⲟⲩ ⲉϣⲁϥⲝ. ⲡⲣⲏⲧϥ (*sc* moon), BG 121 *S* ϣⲁⲛⲧϥⲝ. ⲛ̄ϭⲓ ⲡⲁⲣⲓⲱⲙⲟⲥ, P 131¹ 78 *S* subscription to Cant ⲛⲝⲱ ⲛⲧⲉ ⲡⲓⲝⲱ ⲁϥⲝ., AZ 23 115 *S* end of recipe ⲁϥⲝ. (oftener ⲁϥⲝ. ⲉⲃ.), Kr 1 38 *S* ⲁⲓⲍ ⲉⲙⲁϩⲉ ⲝ. in river's rise, ManiP 11 *A*² ⲡⲧⲟⲩⲛⲟⲩ ⲉⲧⲝⲁⲕ. ⲛⲝⲓ ⲡⲉⲕⲱⲧ, Tst Ab 255 *B* ⲁⲩⲝ. ⲛϫⲉ ⲡⲓⲉϩⲟⲟⲩ, C 86 312 *B* town ⲉⲧⲁϥⲝ. ⲛ̄ϩⲏⲧϥ

(var ⲝ. ⲉⲃ.) *where died*; qual: Ps 138 22 *B*(*S* ⲛⲟϭ) τέλειος; Ap 3 2 *S*(*B* ⲝ. ⲉⲃ.) πληροῦσθαι; Lev 23 15 *S*(*B* do) ὁλόκληρος; PS 117 *S* fruits ⲥⲉⲙⲉϩ ⲥⲉⲝ. (Od Solom 1 5 ܡܛܠܢ), ShC 42 43 *S* living 100 years ⲉⲩⲝ. ⲛ ⲉⲩϣⲁⲁⲧ ⲛⲣⲉⲡⲕⲉⲣⲟⲙⲡⲉ, Ep 84 *S* ϣⲁⲛⲧⲕⲣ ⲧⲉⲕⲣⲟⲙⲡⲉ ⲉⲥⲝ., BKU 1 66 *S* ⲁⲓⲝⲓ ⲧⲉⲩⲧⲓⲙⲏ ⲉⲥⲝ., ManiP 151 *A*² ⲟⲩϩⲟⲟⲩ ⲉϥⲝ., *ib* 167 ⲛⲡⲉⲧⲝ.

II tr, *complete, finish*: He 10 1 *B*(*SF* ⲝ. ⲉⲃ.) τελεῖν, *ib* 8 5 *B*(*SF* do) ἐπιτ., Is 44 24 *B*(*S* do), EpJer 61 *B*(*F* ⲝ. ⲉⲃ.) συντ.; Mt 5 17 *B*(*S* do), AM 282 *B* what people asked ⲁϥⲝⲟⲕϥ ⲡⲗⲏ., 1 Thes 2 16 *B*(*S* do), 1 Cor 16 17 *B* v p 289 *a* (*S* do) ἀναπ.; Is 65 20 *S*(*B* ⲙⲟⲣ ⲉⲃ.) ἐμπιπλάναι; Br 231 *S* ⲛⲥⲉⲭⲟⲕⲟⲩ ⲛⲥⲉ ⲝⲓⲧⲟⲩ, Mk 2 3 *S* ⲉⲩⲝⲕ ϥⲧⲟⲟⲩ (*B* diff) ὑπὸ τεσσάρων, *ib* 5 9 *S* ⲝⲉⲕ ϩⲁⲣ (*B* ⲉⲣ ⲟⲩⲙⲏϣ) πολλοὶ εἶναι; R 1 4 38 *S* ⲁⲩⲝⲉⲕ ⲟⲩⲣⲟⲙⲡⲉ *exigere*; BMar 21 *S* ⲛⲉⲩⲝⲉⲕ ⲙⲛⲧⲥⲛⲟⲟⲩⲥ *amounting to 12* (*cf* p 208 *b*), COAd 44 *S* will not depart ϣⲁⲛⲧⲁⲝ. ⲡⲭⲟⲩⲧⲁϥⲧⲉ ⲛϩⲟⲟⲥ, Mani P 51 *A*² virginity ⲁⲓⲝⲁⲕⲥ ϩⲛⲛⲉⲕⲣⲉⲛ, Ryl 444 *B* ⲉϥ ⲝⲏⲕ ⲡⲉϥϩⲁⲣⲟⲙⲟⲥ *bravely*.

With following preposition.　　ⲥ ⲉ-: Nu 3 3 *B*(*S* ⲝ. ⲉⲃ.) τελ. inf, Si 24 28 *S* συντ. inf; Jer 32 34 *B*(*S* ⲝ. ⲉⲃ.) πλ. εἰς; Br 232 *S* ⲉϣⲁⲥⲝ. ⲉⲩⲝⲉⲕⲁⲥ ⲉⲃⲟⲗ ϩⲛⲧⲙⲟⲛⲁⲥ;　　ⲥ ⲉⲝⲉⲛ- *B*: ROC 25 253 ⲛⲧⲉⲡⲥⲁⲭⲓ ⲝ. ⲉⲝⲱϥ ἁρμόζειν ἐπί; PO 11 355 ⲝ. ⲉⲝⲱϥ (*sc* new pontiff) ⲙⲡⲛϣⲉⲙϣⲓ;　　ⲉϩⲣⲏⲓ ⲉⲝ.: Ez 5 13 (*S* ⲝ. ⲉⲃ.) συντ. ἐπί;　　ⲥ ϩⲛ- *A*²: ManiP 18 mysteries ⲁⲩⲝ. ⲡϩⲏⲧⲕ, ManiK 179 ⲉⲩⲝ.† ϩⲙⲡⲡⲁⲣⲧⲉ.

—— nn m *SBF*, *completion, end, total*: Is 19 15 *B*, Mt 26 58 *B*, 1 Cor 15 24 *BF*(Mor 38 4, var Z & all *S* ϩⲁⲕ), Ap 21 6 *S*(*B* ⲝ. ⲉⲃ.) τέλος, Ex 29 22 *B*, He 7 11 *F*(*SB* do) τελείωσις; Ez 19 7 *SB*, Jo 1 16 *S*(*B* ⲙⲟϩ) πλήρωμα, Ez 5 2 *SB* -ωσις, CDan 85 *B* this day ⲛⲝ. ⲛ̄ϯ̄ ⲡⲣⲟⲙⲡⲉ πληροῦσθαι; Ps 38 5 *B*(*S* ϩ.), He 6 16 *B*(*SF* do) πέρας; Deu 33 14 *S*(*B* ⲑⲱⲟⲩⲧⲥ) σύνοδος; Mor 17 126 *S* ⲛⲝ. ⲛⲣⲟⲟⲩ ⲥⲡⲁⲩ μετὰ δύο ἡμ.; PS 4 *S* ⲡⲉⲡⲗⲏⲣⲱⲙⲁ ⲙⲡⲛⲝ. ⲧⲏⲣϥ, ShA 2 3 *S* handiwork ⲉⲙⲡⲁⲧⲟⲩⲥⲙⲓⲛⲉ ⲉⲙⲡⲁⲧⲟⲩⲉⲓ ⲉⲡⲉⲩⲝ., ShBor 246 61 *S* ⲛⲝ. ⲙⲡⲉⲓϣⲁϫⲉ ⲛⲕⲉⲙⲁ, BAp 81 *S* ⲧⲁϯ ⲡⲝ. ⲉⲣⲟⲓ = MIE 2 357 *B* ⲡⲓⲙⲩⲥⲧⲏⲣⲓⲟⲛ, *ib* 125 *S* ⲛⲕⲥⲟⲟⲩⲛ ⲙⲡⲁⲝ. ⲧⲏⲣϥ = *ib* 418 *B* ⲡⲁⲃⲓⲟⲥ, Z 622 *S* ⲟⲩⲉϩ ⲟⲩⲝ. ⲉⲝⲡⲡⲉⲓϣⲁϫⲉ, Pcod 26 *S* ⲛⲝ. ⲡⲉ ⲡⲁⲓ *in short*, BM 1139 *S* ⲛⲝ. ⲧⲏⲣϥ ⲁⲓⲧⲡⲛⲟⲟⲩⲥϥ ⲛⲁⲕ, Hall 22 *S* ⲥϩⲁⲓ ⲛⲝ. ⲡⲁⲓ, AM 128 n *B* ⲙⲙⲟⲛⲧⲉϥ ⲁⲣⲭⲏ ⲟⲩⲇⲉ ⲝ., FR 108 *B* ⲓⲥⲝⲉⲛⲡⲉⲥ. *death*, Miss 8 211 *S* thou seest ⲛⲝ. ⲧⲏⲣϥ ⲙⲡⲁⲥⲱⲙⲁ *exhaustion* & poverty, BIF 13 114 *S* after sunset ⲛⲝ. ⲙⲡⲉϩⲟⲟⲩⲡⲉ, MG 25 240 *B* ⲛⲝ. ⲛⲧ̄ⲉ ⲡⲉϩⲟⲟⲩ ⲁⲥⲙⲟⲩ, AM 284 *B* Apollo & ⲛⲝ. ⲙⲡⲓⲟ̄ ⲛ̄ⲛⲟⲩ ϯ = C 43 120 *B* ⲛⲥⲱϣⲡ, JSch 10 22 *S* ⲧⲁⲡⲗⲏⲣⲟⲩ ⲙⲙⲟⲕ ⲙⲡⲝ. ⲡⲧⲉⲕⲁⲥⲫⲁⲗⲓⲁ, Mor 30 9 *F* ⲉⲓⲙⲉ ⲉⲡⲝ. ⲛ̄ ⲡⲉⲛⲧⲁⲓⲝⲁⲁⲩ ⲛⲏⲕ;　　with vbs. ⲓⲣⲓ *B*: Jer 5 10, Zeph 1 18 (*S* = Gk, *A* ϩⲁⲉⲓ) συντέλειαν ποιεῖν; ϯ: BMis 73 *S* ⲙⲁⲣⲉⲛϯ ⲛⲟⲩϯ. ⲉⲡϣⲁϫⲉ, C 43 92 *B* pray

Him to ϯ ⲡⲟⲩϫ. ⲛ̄ⲡⲓⲡⲓⲣⲁⲥⲙⲟⲥ, BM 1072 *S* ϯ ⲛ̄ϫ. ⲉⲡⲉⲧⲣⲓⲙⲏⲥⲓⲛ ⲉⲙⲁⲣⲕⲟⲥ *remainder*; ϫⲓ, ϭⲓ: Va 57 212 *B* ⲁⲩⲕⲏⲛ ⲉⲩϭⲓ ⲡⲟⲩϫ. τέλ. λαμβάνειν; RNC 48 *S* ϫⲓ ⲙⲡ̄ϫ. ⲛ̄ⲧⲡⲓⲥⲧⲓⲥ *have faith confirmed*, DeV 2 16 *B* ⲁⲩϭⲓ ⲡⲟⲩϫ. ϩⲁⲧⲟⲛ ⲡⲟⲩⲕⲟⲩϫⲓ *things lately fulfilled*.

With preceding preposition. c ⲉ-: Jos 10 13 *S* εἰς τέλ., 1 Chr 29 19 *B* ἐπὶ τ.; Dan 9 2 *B*(*S* ϫ. ⲉⲃ.) εἰς συμπλήρωσιν; J 8 6 *S* have paid other 5 ⲉⲡϫ. ⲛ̄-ⲥⲛⲁⲩ ⲡⲣⲟⲗⲟⲕ/, ST 194 *S* cannot deliver corn ⲉⲡϫ. *in full*, BMis 77 *S* ⲡⲉⲥⲉⲓ ⲉⲡϫ. ⲛ̄ϣⲟⲙⲧⲉ ⲡⲣⲟⲙⲡⲉ, RAl 88 *B* ⲓ ⲉϩⲣⲏⲓ ⲉⲡϫ. ⲛ̄ⲣⲙ̄ ⲡⲣⲟⲙⲡⲓ; c ⲉϫⲛ-: 2 Kg 24 8 *S* ἀπὸ τέλους; c ⲛ-: C 86 190 *B* ⲁⲩⲓ ϣⲁ-ⲣⲟϥ ⲛ̄ⲡϫ. ⲡⲉ̄ ⲡⲣⲟⲙⲡⲓ; c ϣⲁ-, ϣⲁ-: Deu 31 30 *S*(*B* ϣⲁⲃⲟⲗ) εἰς τέλ.; Dan 11 35 *B* ἕως πέρας; PS 56 *S* ⲙ̄ⲡⲣⲕⲁⲁⲧ ... ϣⲁⲡϫ. ⲙ̄ⲡⲁⲟⲩⲟⲉⲓϣ, *ib* 10 *S* ϫⲓⲛⲧⲁⲣ-ⲭⲏ ... ⲉⲱⲥ ϣⲁⲡⲉⲥϫ., J 89 16 *S* ϣⲁⲡϫ. ⲡⲟⲩⲣⲉϩⲃⲟ-ⲙⲁⲥ *after a week* He heard us, CO 29 *S* will learn gospel ϣⲁⲡϫ. ⲙ̄ⲡⲧⲁⲓⲟⲩ *by end of Pentecost*, Va 61 13 *B* none knew ϣⲁⲡϫ. ⲡⲟⲩⲣⲟⲙⲡⲓ, BM 1001 *S* ϩⲁⲡϫ. ⲛ̄ⲧⲣⲉϩⲱⲙⲁⲥ *till week's end*, Ep 97 *S* paid ϩⲁⲡϫ. ⲙ̄-ⲙ̄ⲡⲧⲉ *to complete 15*; c ϩⲛ-, ϩⲉⲛ-: Br 43 *S* ϩⲙⲡϫ. ⲙ̄ⲡⲉⲡⲗⲏⲣⲱⲙⲁ, Ep 398 *S* I greet ϩⲙ̄ⲡϫ. ⲛ̄ⲧⲁⲯⲩⲭⲏ, DeV 2 135 *B* ϫⲉⲛⲡϫ. ⲡⲣⲁⲛⲕⲟⲩϫⲓ ⲡⲉϩⲟⲟⲩ; ϩⲛ-, ϫⲉⲛⲟⲩϫ.: CaiEuch 466 *B* ὁλοτελῶς, R 1 2 66 *S* came to save man ϩ. τελεῖν; CaiThe 165 *B* ϫⲱⲧⲉⲃ ϫ. ⲛ̄ϯ-ⲙⲉⲧϫⲁϫⲓ كلّها; BG 46 *S* ⲛ̄ϥϩ. ⲁⲛ *not complete*, Gött N '98 171 *S* scriptures suffice to ϯⲥⲃⲱ ⲛⲁⲛ ϩ., Cat 11 *B* ⲥϣⲉ ⲉϩⲓⲧⲟⲩ ⲉⲃⲟⲗ ϫ., Miss 4 214 *B* ϫⲟⲩϣⲧ ϫ. ⲉ-ϩⲣⲏⲓ (*l* ⲉϫ.) ⲉϫⲉⲛⲡⲁⲑⲉⲃⲓⲟ, C 43 112 *B* ye are ϩⲁⲡⲁⲑⲟ-ⲛⲟⲩϯ ϫ., DeV 2 33 *B* have turned from evil ways ϫ., Ep 190 *S* ⲡⲁⲛⲟⲩⲟⲩ ⲉⲙⲁⲧⲉ ϩ.

ⲁⲧϫ., *without end*: P 44 48 *S* ⲁⲡⲓⲣⲟⲥ · ⲡⲓⲁ. الذي ل مثله, TRit 424 *B* life to come ⲛⲁ.

ⲣⲉϥϫ. *B, perfecter*: He 12 2 (*S* ⲣⲉϥϫ. ⲉⲃ.) τε-λειωτής.

B ϫ. ⲉⲃⲟⲗ (oftener)*SAA²BF*, meanings as ϫ., **I** intr: Is 55 11 *SB* τελεῖν, Z 273 *S* ⲉⲕⲉϫ. ⲉ. ⲉⲕⲟⲩ-ⲟϫ διατ., Dan 3 40 *B* ἐκτ., Job 1 5 *SB*, Mk 13 4 *SB* συντ., Z 343 *S* found him ⲉⲁϥϫ. ⲉ. *dead*, MG 25 2 *B* opp ⲉⲣ ϩⲏⲧⲥ τελειοῦν, RNC 35 *S* ⲁϥϫ. ⲉ. in exile τε-λευτᾶν, Lu 8 14 *S*(*B* diff) τελεσφορεῖν; Nu 6 5 *SB*, Mt 2 15 *SB* πληροῦν, Ge 15 16 *SB*, Is 60 20 *SB* ἀναπ.; PS 17 *S* ϣⲁⲡⲧⲉⲡⲉϥⲟⲩⲟⲉⲓϣ ϫ.ⲉ., Mani 2 *A²* ⲁⲩⲥⲁϣⲧϥ ...ϣⲁⲡⲉϥϫ. ⲁ., C 41 53 *B* stayed by him ϣⲁⲧⲉϥϫ. ⲉ. *died*, DeV 2 163 *B* ⲁⲡⲉϥⲥⲛⲟϥ ϫ. ⲉ., BSM 38 *B* ⲁϩⲱⲃ ⲛⲓⲃⲉⲛ ⲕⲏⲛ ⲛ̄ϫ. ⲉ. = BMis 383 *S* ⲣ ϣⲁⲩ; qual: Ge 6 9 *SB*, Ro 12 2 *SBF* τέλειος, Is 28 22 *SB* συν-τελεῖσθαι; Ps 72 10 *SB* πλήρης; CaiEuch 452 *B* ⲙⲁ-ⲧⲟⲩⲃⲟⲓ ⲉⲓϫ. ⲉ. ὅλος, Sa 15 3 *S* ὁλόκληρος; BG 24 *S* ⲡⲟⲩⲟⲓⲛ ... ⲉⲧϫ. ⲉ., Br 229 *S* ⲙⲉⲗⲟⲥ ⲛⲓⲙ ϫ. ⲉ., BMar 196 *S* ⲟⲩⲣⲟⲙⲡⲉ ⲉϫ. ⲉ., ManiK 92 *A²* ⲡⲣⲱⲙⲉ ⲉⲧϫ. ⲉ., C 86 222 *B* arose from dead ⲉϥϫ. ⲉ., PBu 112 *S* preserve you ⲉⲧⲉⲧⲛϫ. ⲉ. body, soul & spirit.

II tr: Ru 3 18 *S*, Mt 19 1 *S*(var ⲟⲩⲱ)*B*, Gal 5 16 *SB*, Z 342 *S* ⲛ̄ϯⲛⲁϫⲉⲕ ⲡⲉⲓⲁⲡⲟⲧ ⲉ. ⲁⲛ τελεῖν, Zech 4 9 *SAB*, Phil 1 6 *SBF* ἐπιτ., Ge 2 2 *AB*, Deu 31 24 *B* ϫⲉⲕ ⲧⲟⲧⲥ ⲉⲃ. (*S* ⲟⲩⲱ), Lam 2 17 *SBF* συντ., Nu 3 3 *S*(*B* om ⲉ.), Jo 17 4 *SA²BF* τελειοῦν; Ps 15 11 *S*(*B* ⲙⲟⲩϩ), *ib* 126 5 *SBF* ϫⲁⲕ- (Mor 30 19), Ro 13 8 *SB* πλη., Ex 23 26 *S*(*B* ⲙ.), 1 Cor 14 16 *SB* ἀναπ.; Job 33 25 *S*(*B* diff), Mk 9 12 *S*(*BF* ⲧϥⲟ) ἀπο-καθιστάναι; Hab 2 5 *AB* περαίνειν; BMar 118 *S* ϫⲕ ⲙ̄ⲛ̄ⲧⲏ ⲡⲣⲟⲟⲩ ⲉ. διανύειν; PS 60 *S* ϯⲛⲁϫⲉⲕⲧⲏⲩⲧⲛ ⲉ. ⲙ̄ⲡⲗⲏⲣⲱⲙⲁ ⲛⲓⲙ, *ib* 35 *S* ⲡⲉⲩϫ. ⲉ. ⲙ̄ⲙⲟⲟⲩⲡⲉ, ShA ϩ 282 *S* ⲧⲉⲧⲛⲥⲛⲟϭ opp ⲧⲉⲧⲉⲟⲩⲛ ϭⲟⲙ ⲙⲙⲟⲥ ⲉϫⲉⲕ ⲟⲩ-ϩⲱⲃ ⲉ., PLond 4 510 *S* ⲧⲛⲥⲙⲓⲛⲉ ⲙ̄ⲙⲟⲥ (*sc* deed) ⲧⲛ̄-ϫⲟⲕ ⲙ̄ⲙⲟⲥ ⲉ. ⲇⲏⲙⲟⲥⲓⲁ, ManiP 183 *A²* ⲡϫ]ⲱⲕ ⲧⲉ-ϫⲁⲕϥ ⲁ., AP 44 *A²* ϫ. ⲁ. ⲡⲟⲓⲕⲟⲡⲟⲙⲓⲁ ⲛⲓⲙ, BSM 27 *B* ϣⲁⲧⲟⲩϫ. ⲉ. ⲙ̄ⲡⲟⲩⲱⲙ = BMis 366 *S* ⲟⲩⲱ, Mor 27 42 *F* ϫⲁⲕ ⲧⲡⲓⲥⲧⲓⲥ ⲉ., *ib* 45 *F* ϫⲁⲁⲕϥ ⲉ., Lant 4 *F* ⲡϭⲭⲁⲕ ⲧⲉϥⲅⲁⲛ ⲉ., Miss 4 762 *S^f* may Lord ϫⲁⲕⲧ ⲉ. ⲕⲁⲗⲱⲥ.

With following preposition. c ⲉ-: Ez 27 11 *B* (*S* tr) τελειοῦν acc ; c ⲉϫⲛ-: *ib* 13 15 *SB* συντε-λεῖν ἐπί; C 89 19 *B* vision ⲛⲁϫ. ⲉ. ⲉϫⲱⲕ, Miss 8 246 *S* ⲁϫϫ. ⲉ. ⲉϫⲱⲕ ⲛ̄ϭⲓ ⲡϣⲁϫⲉ; *ib* 243 sim ϩⲓϫⲱⲕ; c ⲙⲛ-, ⲡⲉⲙ-: 3 Kg 11 4† *S*(Miss 8 159) τέλειος μετά, JEA 20 51 *S* bring me her ⲛ̄ⲧⲁϫ. ⲉ. ⲙ̄ⲡⲁⲟⲩⲱϣⲉ ⲛ̄-ⲙⲁⲥ, BSM 113 *B* sim ; c ⲛ-: dat: Lu 1 57 *S*(*B* ⲙ. ⲉⲃ.) ⲡⲓⲙⲡⲗⲁⲛⲁⲓ dat; Job 19 27 *S*(*B* om ⲛ-) συντελ. dat; Mt 13 14 *SF*(*B* ⲉϫⲛ-) ἀναπλη. dat; ShC 73 43 *S* ⲉⲡⲉⲥϫⲛ̄ ϫ. ⲉ. ⲙ̄ⲡⲡⲉ ⲛ ⲉϩⲟⲩⲛ ⲉ-, DeV 2 163 *B* ⲉ-ⲟⲣⲉϥϫ. ⲡⲁϥ ⲉ. ⲛ̄ⲧⲉⲡⲓⲟⲩⲙⲓⲁ, PBad 5 401 *S^f* ϫⲁⲕⲟⲩ ⲛⲁⲓ ⲉ. ϩⲛ̄ⲟⲩϭⲉⲡⲏ; *with, of*: Ac 9 36† *SB* ⲙ. ⲛ-) πλήρης gen, Ro 1 29† *S*(*B* do) πληροῦν dat; BG 94 *S* ⲉϥϫ.† ⲉ. ⲙ̄ⲡⲟⲩⲟⲉⲓⲛ, ShMIF 23 141 *S* ⲉ ⲣⲉⲧⲉⲕⲕⲗⲏⲥⲓⲁ ϫ.† ⲉ. ⲙ̄ⲙⲟⲟⲩ; *in space of*: BMis 175 *S* ⲁⲩϫⲉⲕ ⲧⲉⲕ-ⲕⲗⲏⲥⲓⲁ ⲉⲃ. ⲛ̄ⲭⲟⲩⲧⲁⲥⲉ ⲛ̄ϩⲟⲟⲩ = BSM 84 *B*; c ϩⲁ-, ϫⲁ-: CaiEuch 486 *B* ϫⲉⲕ ⲡⲉⲕⲡⲟⲗⲟⲥ ⲉ. ϫⲁⲣⲟⲓ ⲡⲗⲏ. ὑπέρ; El 50 *A* face ⲙ̄ⲡⲉⲧϫ.† ⲁⲃ. ϩⲁⲡⲉϥⲉⲁⲩ (*l*? ϩⲙ-, *cf ib sup*); c ϩⲛ-, ϫⲉⲛ-: Ge 6 9† *SB* τέλειος εἶναι ἐν, Jo 17 23† *B*(*S* ⲉ-, var ⲛ-) τελειοῦσθαι εἰς, ZNTW 24 84 *F* ϫⲁⲕⲥ ⲉ. ϩⲉⲡⲧⲉⲕⲁⲅⲁⲡⲏ τελ. ἐν, 2 Cor 7 1 *SB* ἐπιτελ. ἐν, Ez 7 8 *B*(*S* ⲉϩⲣ. ϩⲛ-) συντελ. ἐν; Gal 5 14 *SB*† πληρ. ἐν; Ro 13 9 *SB*† ἀνακεφαλαιοῦν ἐν; PS 262 *S* ⲉϥϫ.† ⲉ. ϩⲛ̄ⲧⲙ̄ⲛ̄ⲧⲇⲓⲕⲁⲓⲟⲥ, ShBM 198 20 *S* ϫⲟⲕⲟⲩ ⲉ. ϩⲛ̄ⲙ̄ⲡⲁⲣⲁⲫⲩⲥⲓⲥ, BM 194 *S* may God ϫⲟⲕⲧ ⲉ. ϩⲛ̄ⲟⲩⲡⲟⲙⲟⲡⲏ, TillOster 12 *A* ϫⲁⲁⲕⲟⲩ ⲁ. ϩⲛ[, BSM 27 *B* plied them ϣⲁⲧⲟⲩϫ. ⲉ. ϫⲉⲡⲡⲓⲥⲱ = Va 63 3 *B* ϣⲁⲧⲟⲩϭⲓ (BMis 366 *S* diff); ϩⲣⲁⲓ ϩⲛ-, ⲛ̄ϩⲣ. ϫ.: Jo 17 13 *SA²BF*, Ro 8 4 *B*(*S* om ϩⲣ.) πληρ. ἐν.

—— nn m *SA²B*: Ps 23 1 *SB*, *ib* 95 11 *S*(*B* ⲙⲟϩ), Eph 1 10 *SB* πλήρωμα; Ps 4 tit *SB*, 1 Pet 1 9 *S*(*B* om ⲉ.), Miss 8 109 *S* ϣⲁⲡⲁϫ. ⲉ. *death* τέλος, Jer 2 2 *S*(ShHTϯ1)*B*, Lu 1 45 *SB* τελείωσις; Ez 7 3 *B* πέρας;

Mani P 23 *A²* ⲟⲩⲁ. ⲁ. ⲛⲧⲛⲥⲃ̄ⲱ, DeV 1 116 *B* ⲛⲁ. ⲉ. of Innocents, Mor 41 41 *S* ϣⲁⲡⲁ. ⲉ. ⲛⲁⲟⲩⲧⲟⲩⲉ ⲛ̄ⲣⲟⲟⲩ, Z 377 *S* to know ⲣⲛⲟⲩⲁ. ⲉ.

ⲣⲉϥⲁ. ⲉⲃⲟⲗ *S* *v* **A** *s f.*

ϭⲓⲛ-, ⲁⲓⲛⲁ. ⲉⲃ., *completion, death* : ROC 23 154 *B* ⲛⲁ. ⲙⲡⲓⲡⲁⲗⲁⲧⲓⲟⲛ, Mor 18 88 *S* ⲧϭ. ⲡⲁⲡⲁ ⲙⲁⲕⲁⲣⲓⲟⲥ = Miss 4 154 *B* ⲁⲓⲛⲓ ⲉⲃ. ϩⲉⲛⲥⲱⲙⲁ, MIE 2 421 *B* sim.

ⲀⲎⲕⲉ, Ⲁⲉⲕⲉ *v* Ⲁⲱⲱϭⲉ (Ⲁⲏϭⲉ).

Ⲁⲱ(ⲱ)ⲕⲉ, ⲁⲟⲩⲟⲩⲕⲉ, Ⲁⲉⲉⲕⲉ-, ⲁⲉⲕ- *S*, **ⲁⲁⲕⲁ-** *F*, **ⲁⲟⲟⲕⲥ̄** *S* vb intr, *prick, sting, goad* : R 1 371 coarse raiment ⲧⲱⲕⲥ ⲁⲩⲱ ⲥⲁⲱⲕⲉ (collated);   tr : Am 7 14 (P 43 119) Ⲁⲱⲕⲉ ⲛⲣⲏⲕⲙⲡⲉ (*l* ⲕⲡⲧⲉ, *v* ⲟⲩⲟⲩⲕⲉ which prob *l* ⲁⲟⲩⲕⲉ) κνίζειν; Ap 9 5 (var ⲁⲉⲕ-, *B* Ⲁⲱⲕⲣ) παίειν; Mor 17 113 ⲁⲩⲀⲉⲉⲕⲉ ⲡⲉⲥⲣⲏⲧ, *ib* 122 ⲉⲩⲁ. ⲙⲡⲁⲡⲟⲩⲥ κεντεῖν; Eccl 10 11 *F*(*S* ⲗⲱⲕⲥ) δάκνειν; Tri 666 whip Ⲁ. ⲛⲡⲉⲥⲟⲟⲩ سٰ, *ib* words Ⲁ. ⲛ̄ⲡⲣⲏⲧ جرّ; PS 383 ⲉϥⲀ. ⲙⲡⲉⲥⲣⲏⲧ, ShIF 101 sickness ⲉϥⲧⲱⲕⲥ ⲛ ⲉϥⲀ. ⲛⲡⲣⲏⲧ like scorpion, Mor 55 39 ⲟⲩⲣⲟⲃ Ⲁⲉⲉⲕⲉ ⲟⲩⲣⲱⲙⲉ; c ⲣⲛ-, *with* : Stegemann 81 ⲛ̄ⲡⲉⲗⲁⲟⲩ ⲛ̄ⲭⲁⲧⲃⲉ...ⲁⲟⲩ. ⲣ̄ⲡⲉϥⲥⲟⲩⲣⲉ; c ⲣⲓⲧⲛ-, *by* : ShP 130² 69 ⲁⲩⲀⲟⲟⲕⲟⲩ (*sc* fruit) ⲣ.ⲛⲃⲏⲧ;   as nn (same ?) : P 43 74 ⲡⲀⲱⲕⲉ جحر *hole* (*cf* Ⲁⲟⲕⲁⲕ جحر).

Ⲁⲟⲟⲕⲉϥ, Ⲁⲟ. (once)*S*, **Ⲁⲁⲕϥ** *AA²* nn m, *goad* : Pro 26 3 *SA*, Hos 5 12 *A*(*B* Ⲁⲟⲕⲣϥ) κέντρον, Eccl 12 11 Ⲁ. ⲡⲉϥⲉ βούκ.; ShZ 601 ⲡⲉⲓⲀ. ⲉⲅⲕⲱⲡⲥ ⲛⲧⲉⲯⲩⲭⲏ, Sh *ib* 637 ⲧⲱⲃⲥ ... ⲛ̄ⲧⲃⲛⲏ ⲣⲙ̄ⲡⲉϥⲀⲟ., ShA 2 130 ⲣⲱⲃⲕ ⲉⲣⲟⲟⲩ ⲛ̄ⲣⲉⲛⲀ., Mani P 226 *A²*.

Cf ⲁⲟⲩⲕⲣ, Ⲁⲟⲕⲁⲕ.

Ⲁⲕⲟ, Ⲁⲕⲟⲥ̄ *SB*(mostly)vb tr, *sell, trade, spend* : Llb 6 wealth Ⲁ. ⲙⲙⲟⲥ ⲉⲡⲓϣⲉⲙⲙⲱⲟⲩ, MG 25 358 took baskets ⲀⲉⲛⲧⲉϥⲀⲕⲱⲟⲩ (Gött ar 114 127 باع), *ib* 372 sim Ⲁⲕⲱⲟⲩ ϩⲁⲣⲁⲡⲕⲟⲩⲀⲓ ⲛⲟⲓⲕ (*ib* 133 do); c ⲉⲃⲟⲗ : Ryl 349 *S* *v̄* μὴ ⲁⲓⲀⲕⲟⲥ ⲉ., C 41 21 where may I find ⲛ̄ⲧⲁⲀ. ⲉ. ⲉⲡⲓⲧⲟⲡⲟⲥ to build it ? = Miss 4 637 *S* Ⲁⲟ ⲉⲃⲟⲗ = *ib* 353 نفق, C *lc* Ⲁⲁⲝ. ⲉ. ⲉⲡⲓⲧⲟⲡⲟⲥ = EW 163 *B* ⲧⲀⲟ (sic MS) ⲉ., C 86 321 Ⲁ. ⲉ. ⲛϩⲏⲧⲟⲩ ⲉⲡⲕⲱⲧ, BM 689 (2) *S* ⲡⲗⲟⲅⲟⲥ ⲛⲧⲁⲓⲀⲕⲟϥ (collated) ⲉ. ⲉ[,Va 63 10 ⲁⲧⲉⲧⲉⲛⲀ. ⲟⲩⲙⲏ̄ϣ ⲉ. ⲉⲟⲃⲏⲧ = BMis 393 & Mor 27 18 *S* Ⲁⲟ ⲉⲃ.;   as nn m, *cost* : MG 25 69 ⲧ̄ ⲙⲡⲓⲀ. ⲉ. ⲛⲧⲉ ⲧⲉⲥⲙⲏⲥⲓ & child's keep, C 86 347 ⲧ̄ ⲣⲙⲙⲓ ⲡⲉⲙⲡⲓⲀ. ⲉ. of journey, Ryl *lc* *v̄* ⲁ...ⲉⲩⲀⲕⲱ ⲉ.

Ⲁⲁⲕⲟⲩⲗ *S* nn m, *sparrow* : P 44 56 ⲥⲉⲧⲣⲟⲩⲟⲥ· ⲛⲁⲀⲁⲝ· ⲛⲀ.,عصفر. As name : Ⲁ. (CO 481, PLond 4 180), Ⲁⲁⲕⲟⲩⲣ (AZ 33 58 corrected from ϣⲁⲕ.), Χεκοῦλ (POxy 2037).

Ⲁⲱⲕⲙ *SA²*, **-ⲙⲉ** *AA²*, **Ⲁⲱⲕⲉⲙ** *BF*, **Ⲁⲉⲕⲙ-** *S*, **Ⲁⲉⲕⲉⲙ-** *B*, **Ⲁⲁⲕⲉⲙ-** *F*, **Ⲁⲟⲕⲙⲥ̄** *SB*, **Ⲁⲁⲕⲙⲥ̄** *SS^f A²F*, **Ⲁⲟⲕⲙ†** *S*, **Ⲁⲁ.†** *S^a f*, **Ⲁⲁⲕⲙⲉ†** *A²*, **Ⲁⲟⲕⲉⲙ†** *B* vb intr,

wash : 2 Kg 11 2 *S*, Is 1 16 *A*(Cl, *SBF* tr), Jo 13 10 *SA²B* λούεσθαι; TU 24 1 4 *S* saw maiden ⲉⲥⲀ., Aeg 264 *S* ⲛⲉⲛⲧⲁⲩⲀ. (var + ⲣⲓⲧⲙⲡⲃⲁⲡⲧⲓⲥⲙⲁ), Mani P 76 *A²* ⲁⲓⲀ. ⲛⲣⲏⲧ[ϥ ⲣⲓ]ⲧⲛⲡⲥ̄ⲓⲝ ⲛ̄ⲛⲡⲉⲧⲟⲩⲁⲃⲉ, C 44 144 *B* went to bath Ⲁⲉϥⲓⲁ., Mani P 99 *A²* ⲉⲓⲀ.† ⲉⲓⲧⲟⲩⲃⲁⲓⲧ;   tr, *wash, wet* : Ps 66 *SB*, Is 1 16 *F* v above, Ac 9 37 *SBF* Ⲁⲁⲕⲙⲉⲥ λ., 1 Cor 6 11 *SB* ἀπόλ.; BHom 5 *S* ⲁϥⲀⲉⲕⲙ ⲡⲉϥϭⲗⲟϭ καταβρέχειν; ShC 73 82 *S* ⲛⲥⲉⲭⲟⲕⲙⲉϥ ⲛ̄ⲥⲉⲉⲓⲁⲁϥ (*sc* corpse), Mani P 59 *A²* ⲡⲉⲕⲙⲉⲗⲟⲥ Ⲁ. ⲙⲙⲁⲓ, *ib* 100 ϥⲁϩⲀⲕⲙⲉ (f), C 43 3 *B* blood Ⲁ. ⲙⲡⲉϥⲥⲱⲙⲁ, PO 11 351 *B* lamp broke ⲁϥⲀⲟⲕⲙⲉϥ ⲧⲏⲣϥ.

With following preposition.   c ⲉ-, *in* : Br 263 *S* Ⲁ. ⲉⲛⲣⲁⲛ ⲙⲡⲁⲛⲧⲟⲩⲟⲉⲛⲓⲥ;   c ⲛ-, dat : Ez 23 40 *SB* λ. *quibus*; ethic dat : BIF 13 100 *S* Ⲁ. ⲛⲏⲧⲛ;   *with* : Cant 5 12 *F*(*S* ⲣⲛ-) λ. ἐν, Deu 23 11 *S*(*B* ϩⲉⲛ-) λ. dat;   Mus 34 206 *B* hands ⲉⲧⲀ.† ⲛⲥⲛⲟϥ αἱμορροεῖν; ShIF 177 *S* ϥⲀ.† ⲛⲣⲉⲛⲥⲛⲱϣ, Mor 48 58 *S* sim = C 43 130 *B* ϩⲟⲣⲡ ⲉⲃⲟⲗ ϩⲉⲛ-, Mor 29 21 *S^f* lance Ⲁ.† ⲛ̄ⲥⲛⲟϥ, Mani P 103 *A²* ⲉⲓⲀ.† ...ⲁⲃⲁⲗ ⲛⲕⲱⲗⲡ;   c ⲣⲓ-: Z 628 *S* Ⲁⲁⲕⲙⲉϥ ⲣⲓⲟⲣⲙⲱⲛ (θερμόν); c ϩⲛ-, ϩⲉⲛ-, *with, in* : Ez 16 4 *SB* λ. ἐν, Lev 8 6 *SB*, He 10 22† *SBF* λ. dat, Job 9 30 *SB* ἀπόλ. dat, Jth 10 3 *S* περικλύζειν dat; ShC 73 118 *S* cursed whoso ⲛⲁⲀ. ⲛ̄Ⲁⲓⲟⲩⲉ ⲣⲛⲟⲩⲙⲟⲟⲩ, JTS 4 391 *S* ⲙⲡⲉϥⲀ. ⲉⲛⲉⲣ ⲣⲛⲟⲩⲙⲟⲟⲩ since became bishop, ViK 9574 *S^f* ⲁⲩⲀⲁⲕⲙⲉⲧ ⲛ̄ⲣⲏⲧⲥ (*sc* lake), Mani P 103 *A²* Ⲁⲁⲕⲙⲉⲧ ϩⲛⲙⲙⲟⲩ ⲡⲓⲱⲧⲉ, *ib* 41 *A²* Ⲁⲁⲕⲙ(ⲛ) ⲣⲛⲏⲧⲗ̄ⲧⲗⲉ, C 43 49 *B* Ⲁⲟⲕⲙⲟⲩ ϩⲉⲛ-ⲧⲗⲩⲙⲏⲛⲓ;   ⲉⲃⲟⲗ ϩⲛ-, ϩⲉⲛ- : Ac 16 33 *SB* λ. ἀπό, Ap 1 5 *B* λ. ἐκ; Ps 50 7 *S*(*A* Cl ⲉⲓⲱ, *B* ⲣⲱϣⲓ) πλύνειν ἐκ; Mor 55 42 *S* Ⲁⲁⲕⲙⲉⲧ ⲉⲃ. ⲛⲣⲏⲧⲥ, DeV 2 86 *B* ⲁⲩϣⲁⲛⲀ. ⲉⲃ. ϩⲉⲛⲧϩⲣⲱ *cleansed by furnace.*

—— nn m *SA²B*, *washing, cleansing* : Eph 5 26 *S* (*B* ⲱⲙⲥ),Tit 3 5 *SB*, λουτρόν; Aeg 283 *S* ⲛⲡϣⲁ ⲙⲡⲀ. τῶν ἐπιφανίων ἑορτή; Mani P 76 *A²* ⲡⲀ. ⲛ̄ⲧⲙⲛⲧⲁⲧⲙⲟⲩ, KroppR 16 *S* ⲡⲀ. ⲛⲧⲁⲡⲓⲱⲧ ⲁⲓⲧϥ ⲉϥⲛⲁⲡⲗⲁⲥⲥⲉ ⲡⲁⲁⲙ, Mallon *Chrest* 39 *B* ⲛⲀ. in Egypt where Jesus raised spring.

ⲧ̄ Ⲁ., *give washing, baptize* : Jo 3 22 *F*(*S* = Gk, *B* ⲧ̄ ⲱⲙⲥ) βαπτίζειν; Mor 40 26 *S* ⲁϥⲧ̄. ⲛⲏⲧⲛ (var *ib* 39 35 ⲃⲁⲡⲧⲓⲍⲉ);   ⲗⲉϥⲧ̄ Ⲁ. *F*: Mt 14 2 (*S* = Gk, *B* ⲣⲉϥⲧ̄ ⲱⲙⲥ) βαπτιστής.

Ⲁⲓ Ⲁ., *take washing, be baptized* : Jo 3 23 *F*(*S* = Gk, *B* ϭⲓ ⲱ.) βαπτίζεσθαι; Mor 36 8 *S* Ⲁ. ϩⲉⲛⲡⲉϥϭⲓⲝ, Leyd 434 *S* do, Mor 22 37 *S^f* Ⲁ. ϩⲙⲡⲉⲕⲣⲁⲛ (var BMis 176 *S* ⲃⲁⲡ. ⲉ-) = BSM 85 *B* ϭⲓ ⲱ., Mani P 99 *A²*.

ⲁⲧⲀ. *S*, *without washing* : Munich Landesbibl 21 (phot NReich) asceticism of Severus ⲉϥⲟ ⲛⲁ. (PO 2 243 ܠܐ ܠܡܘܣ); ⲙ̄ⲛⲧⲁⲧⲀ. of ascetes : Mor 37 256.

ⲙⲁ ⲛⲀ. *A²B*, *washing place* : AP 47 *A²* ⲙⲁ ⲛⲀⲱ]ⲕⲙ (prob) βαλανεῖον; Va 57 247 *B* ⲡⲭⲟⲕⲙⲉϥ ϩⲉⲛⲡⲛⲓ., C 43 144 *B* as part of ⲥⲓⲱⲟⲩⲛⲓ = Mor 48 90 *S* ⲑⲟⲗⲟⲥ, Mani P 8 *A²* ⲟⲩⲙ. ⲙⲡⲉⲱⲣ.

ϫⲓⲛϫ. *B* nn f, *washing*: BM 768 43 ϯⲉⲕⲕⲗⲏⲥⲓⲁ ⲛⲧⲉ
ϯϫ. كَنِيسَة الْمَعْمُودِيّة. Synax 2 156, Amélineau *Géog* 236.

ϫⲱⲕⲣ *S*, -ⲣⲉ *A²*, ϫⲟⲩⲕⲉⲣ *B*, ϫⲉⲕⲣ-, ϫⲟⲕⲣ⸗, ϫⲁ.,
ϫⲟⲕⲣ⁺ *S*, -ⲉⲣ⁺ *B* vb tr, *salt, season, cure*: Wess 15 22
S if victuals lack salt ϣⲁⲓϫⲁⲕⲣⲟⲩ (sic prob) ἀρτύειν;
BHom 87 *S* cannot ϫ. ⲙⲡⲗⲱⲙⲥ ⲡⲓⲟⲩϫⲁⲥ, ib 88 *S*
ϫⲉⲕⲣ ⲣⲉⲛⲯⲩⲭⲏ, Mor 40 37 *S* ϫ. ⲡⲛⲉⲯ. ⲛⲧⲁⲩⲃⲁⲁⲃⲉ,
Dif 1 19 *B* sim مَلَّحَ, MG 25 263 *B* salt ⲉⲧⲁⲩϫ. ⲡⲛⲓⲯ.
ⲉⲧⲁⲩⲗⲱϭ, P 131⁴ 94 *S* ϯⲛⲁϫ. ⲙⲡⲉⲕⲥⲱⲙⲁ ϫⲉⲛⲡⲉϥ-
ⲕⲡⲟⲥ (var R 1 1 70 ϫⲱⲕⲙ);   qual: Mich 550 29
S his words ϫ. ⲛⲑⲉ ⲛⲟⲩϩⲙⲟⲩ, Mor 52 13 *S* ⲟⲩϭⲡⲉ
ⲉϥϫ. (ⲩ ⲁⲃⲉⲣϫ), MG 25 140 *B* ϯⲛⲁⲫⲣⲓ ⲛϣⲉⲗⲧⲁⲙ
ⲉϣⲟⲙ ⲥϫ. (cf Mk 4 31), C 41 13 *B* epistles ⲉⲩϫ.

    With following preposition.   ⲥ ⲉϩⲟⲩⲛ ⲉ-: PS
28 *S* ⲡⲉϥϩⲏⲧ ϫ.⁺ ⲉ. ⲉⲧⲙⲡⲧⲉⲣⲟ;   ⲥ ⲛ-, *with*: Lev
2 13 *S*(*B* ⲙⲟⲩⲗϩ) ἁλίζεσθαι dat; Col 4 6⁺ *S*(*B* ⲥⲉϩ-
ⲡⲛⲟⲩⲧ), cit C 89 27 *B* ἀρτ. dat;   ⲥ ϩⲛ-, *with*: Mk
9 49 *S*(*B* ⲙ.) ἁλ. dat; ib 50 *S*(*B* ⲇⲟ) ἀρτ. dat; FR 150
S ⲯⲩⲭⲏ ⲛⲓⲙ ⲛⲁϫ. ⲛⲣⲏⲧⲟⲩ = Aeg 9 *B* ⲉⲣ ⲕⲁⲑⲁⲣⲓⲍⲓⲛ, Mani P 101 *A²* ⲁⲓϫ. ⲛⲧⲁⲯⲩⲭⲏ ϩⲛ ϯⲥⲃⲱ.

    ⲣⲉϥϫ. *S*, *cleanser*: Sh(?)Mor 54 99 ϩⲙⲟⲩ ⲡⲣ.

—— nn m *B*, *seasoning*: Cat 7 He calleth teachers
' salt ' ⲉⲧⲃⲉⲡ ϫ. ⲛⲡⲓⲥⲁϫⲓ ⲉⲑⲟⲩⲁⲃ, Va 58 185 fasting
ⲧϣⲉⲣⲓⲧⲉ ⲙⲡⲓϫ. νήψεως σύνοικος.

ϫⲟⲩⲕⲣⲉ *S* nn, meaning unknown: Ep 519 account ϣⲟⲙⲧ [ⲛ ?] ⲡϫ. ⲙϣⲁⲛ ϩⲁⲥⲟⲩⲟ ⲕⲉϣⲟⲙⲧ
ⲛ[? ⲛ]ⲕⲁⲕⲉ ϩⲁⲥⲟⲩⲟ. Something edible, ? salted
(v last word or cf ϣⲟⲩⲕⲣⲉ). As name: ϫⲟⲕⲣⲉ
(*JAmOrSoc* 48 152).

ϫⲓⲕⲣⲓⲥ¹, -ⲉⲥ², ϭⲁϭⲣⲏⲥ³ *S*, ϫⲓⲕⲣⲏⲥ⁴, -ⲟⲥ⁵, ϫⲉⲕ-
ⲣⲏⲥ⁶ *B* nn m, *tiger, panther* (= τίγρις): K 164 *B*
ⲡⲓϫ.⁴, P 46 158 *S* ⲡϭ.³ نمر; P 44 121 *S¹*, K ib *B* ⲡⲓϫ.⁶
نمر; SHel 26 *S* ⲟⲩϫ.² ⲙⲡⲟⲩⲗⲁⲃⲟⲓ, Mor 48 96 *S* ϫ.²,
ⲗⲁⲃⲟⲓ, ⲗⲉⲟⲡⲁⲣⲁⲗⲓⲥ = C 43 146 *B* ⲡⲁⲣⲁⲗⲓⲥ, C 43
30 *B* ϫ.⁵, ⲙⲟⲅⲓ, ⲡⲁⲣⲁⲗⲓⲥ, AM 327 *B* ⲡⲓϫ.⁶ ⲟⲩⲧ ⲉⲛⲟⲥ
ⲉϥϩⲱⲟⲩ.

ϫⲉⲕⲁⲁⲥ *SAA²*, -ⲕⲁⲥ *SA²*(Mani K 29), -ⲕⲁⲁⲥⲉ *SA*
(AP), -ⲕⲁⲥⲉ *A²*(Jo, Ma), -ϫⲁⲥ *B*, (ⲡ)ϫⲉⲕⲉ(ⲉ)ⲥ *F*,
ⲕⲁⲁⲥ *A*, ϫⲁⲥ *B*, ⲕⲉ(ⲉ)ⲥ *F* conjunct (cf ⲕⲱ g), *that, in
order that* (*B* mostly = Gk), followed by 2d pres: Deu
10 13 ϫ. ⲉⲣⲉⲡⲉⲧⲁⲡⲟⲩϥ ϣⲱⲡⲉ ⲙⲙⲟⲕ, Mt 18 16 ϫ.
ⲉⲣⲉϣⲁϫⲉ ⲛⲓⲙ ⲁϩⲉⲣⲁⲧϥ, Ac 5 15 ϫ. ⲉⲣⲉⲧⲉϥϩⲁⲓⲃⲉⲥ ⲧⲁ-
ϩⲉ- (*B* ⲕⲁⲡ) ἵνα; Ps 59 5 ϫ. ⲉⲣⲉⲡⲉⲕⲙⲉⲣⲓⲧ ⲡⲟⲩϩⲙ (*B*
ϩⲓⲛⲁ), ib 77 6 ϫ. ⲉⲣⲉⲕⲉⲛⲉⲡⲁ ⲉⲓⲙⲉ ὅπως ἄν; Mt 23 5
ϫ. ⲉⲣⲉⲡⲣⲱⲙⲉ ⲛⲁⲩ (*B* ⲉⲑⲣⲉ-) πρὸς τό; PS 111 ϫ. ⲉⲣ-
ⲉⲡⲉⲕⲧⲱϣ ϫⲱⲕ ⲉⲃⲟⲗ, BG 105 ϫ. ⲉⲣⲉⲡⲉϩⲟⲟⲩ ⲟⲩⲱⲛϩ ⲉⲃⲟⲗ, J 104 44 ϫ. ⲉⲣⲉⲡ⳨ⲥ ⲥⲙⲟⲩ ⲉⲣⲟϥ, Lant 24
F sim; by 2d fut: Pro 3 6 *A* ϫ. ⲁⲥⲡⲁⲥⲁⲩⲧⲛⲉ (*S* 3d
fut), Mt 7 12 ϫ. ⲉⲣⲉⲡⲣⲱⲙⲉ ⲛⲁⲁⲩ, Jo 3 17 *SA²* ϫ.

ⲉⲣⲉⲡⲕⲟⲥⲙⲟⲥ ⲡⲁⲟⲩϫⲉⲉⲓ, Cl 55 1 *A* ϫ. ⲁⲉⲓⲁⲉⲓⲡⲉ ἵνα;
AP 16 *A²* ϫ. ⲉⲥⲡⲁϣⲗⲏⲗ, ib 10 ϫ. ⲉⲉⲓⲡⲁϩⲙⲟⲩ, Cl
44 2 *A* ϫ. ⲁϩⲉⲛⲕⲉⲅⲉ ⲡⲁⲭⲡⲉ ⲡⲉⲩ ὅπ.; PS 31 ϫ. ⲉⲩⲡⲁⲣ ϩⲃⲁ, ShC 42 89 ϫ. ⲉⲓⲡⲁⲉⲓⲙⲉ, El 62 *A* ϫ. ⲁⲕⲡⲁⲣ
ⲟⲩⲡⲁⲉ, Mani 2 *A²* ϫ. ⲉⲩⲡⲁⲱⲛ ϩ, Wess 18 35 ⲧⲉⲡⲟⲩⲱϣ
ϫ. ⲉⲕⲡⲁⲣ ⲙⲟⲛⲁⲭⲟⲥ, CO 152 ϫ. ⲉⲓⲡⲁⲉⲩⲭⲁⲣⲓⲥⲧⲁ,
BSM 122 *B* ϫ. ⲉⲣⲉⲧⲟⲩⲧⲉⲭⲏⲛ ⲡⲁϭⲓ ⲱⲟⲩ;   by 3d
fut: Deu 2 30 ϫ. ⲉϥⲉⲧⲁⲁϥ ⲉϩⲣⲁⲓ, Is 36 12 *SF*(*B* ϩⲟ-
ⲡⲱⲥ), Mt 14 15 ϫ. ⲉⲩⲉⲃⲱⲕ (var ϫⲉ-, *F*=*B*), 2 Cor 2 4
ϫ. ⲁⲛ ⲉⲧⲉⲧⲛⲉⲗⲩⲡⲉⲓ ⲁⲗⲗⲁ ϫⲉⲉⲧⲉⲧⲛⲉ- *B* ϫⲉ- ... ϫⲉϩⲁⲥ
ἵνα; Ge 50 20 ϫ. ⲉⲥⲉϣⲱⲡⲉ (*B* ϣⲁⲧⲉⲧⲛϣ.), Ps 9 14
ϫ. ⲉⲓⲉϫⲱ, ib 50 4 *SA*(Cl) ϫ. ⲉⲕⲉⲧⲙⲁⲓⲟ ὅπ. ἄν, Sa 16
28 ϫ. ⲉⲩⲉⲉⲓⲙⲉ, Jon 1 6 *A* ⲕⲁⲁⲥ ⲁϥⲁⲧⲟⲩϫⲁⲡ ὅπ. (*SB*
εἴπως); ZNTW 24 19 *F* ⲁⲣⲓ ⲡⲁⲙⲟⲩⲓ ... ⲕⲉⲥ ⲉⲕⲉ-
ⲡⲉⲣⲙⲉⲥ τοῦ ῥύσασθαι; Ro 15 8 *B* ϫ. ⲉϥⲉⲧⲁϩⲣⲉ- (*S*
ⲉⲡⲧ.) εἰς τό; PS 11 ϫ. ⲉⲧⲉⲧⲛⲉϣ ϭⲙ ϭⲟⲙ, BG 64
ϫ. .... ⲉϥⲁⲧⲁϩⲟⲟⲩ, ShR 2 3 48 ϫ. ⲉϥⲉⲕⲱ ⲡⲁϥ, FR 86
bade ϫⲉϩⲁⲁⲥ ⲉⲅⲉⲭⲓⲧϥ (var om), Kropp F 18 I adjure
thee ϫ. ⲉⲕⲉⲧⲱϣ, BKU 1 9 sim ⲉⲕⲁⲧⲣⲉϥ-, Gu 97 ⲟⲩ-
ⲣⲁϣⲉ ⲡⲁⲡⲉ ϫ. ⲉⲩⲉⲁⲁⲕ ⲛⲉⲣⲣⲟ, J 84 23 ϫ. ⲉϥⲉϣⲱⲡⲉ
ⲉϥⲟ ⲛⲟϩⲣⲁⲗ, AP 40 *A²* ϫ. ⲁⲛ ⲉⲡⲁⲥⲱⲧⲙ, Mani 1 *A²*
ϫⲉⲕⲁⲥⲉ ... ⲉⲣⲁⲟⲩⲱⲛϩ, C 43 7 *B* ϫ. ⲉϥⲉⲥⲱϯ, BSM
100 *B* ϫ. ⲉⲕⲉⲣⲱⲓⲥ, Mor 24 29 *F* ϫ. ⲉⲩⲉⲕⲟⲗⲁⲍⲉ, Stegemann 67 *F* ⲛϫ. ⲉⲕⲉⲛ ⲉ(ϩ)ⲣⲓⲛ, Griff Stu 162 *F* ⲛϫ.
[ⲉⲕ]ⲉϫⲁⲟⲩ;   by neg 3d fut: Deu 17 20 ϫ. ⲉⲛ-
ⲛⲉϥⲣ ⲛⲃⲟⲗ (*B* ⲛⲧⲉϥϣⲧⲉⲙ-), Jos 22 24 ϫ. ⲉⲛⲛⲉⲡⲉ-
ⲧⲛϣⲏⲣⲉ ϫⲟⲟⲥ, Ps 16 5 ϫ. ⲛⲛⲉⲩⲕⲓⲙ (*F*=*B*), Mt 24 20
ϫ. ⲛⲛⲉⲡⲉⲧⲛⲡⲱⲧ ϣⲱⲡⲉ, Jo 3 20 *S* ϫ. ⲛⲛⲉⲩϫⲡⲓⲉ- (*A²*
ϫⲉ-), *F* ⲕⲉⲥ ϫⲉ-, AP 8 *A²* ϫ. ⲉⲛⲟⲩϫⲓ ἵνα μή; Jos 23 7
ϫ. ⲉⲛⲛⲉⲧⲛⲃⲱⲕ, Hos 14 3 *A* ϫ. ⲛⲉⲧⲛϫⲟⲟⲩ, Zech 12 7
A ϫ. ⲡⲉϥ- ὅπ. μή, Ex 20 26 ϫ. ⲛⲛⲉⲕϭⲱⲗⲡ (cit CA 91
ϫⲉ-), Ps 124 3 ϫ. ⲉⲛⲉⲡⲁⲓⲕⲁⲓⲟⲥ ⲥⲟⲩⲧⲛ- (*B* ϩⲓⲛⲁ) ὅπ.
ἄν μή, Hos 4 4 *A* ϫ. ⲡⲉⲗⲁⲟⲅⲉ ϫⲓ ὅπ. μηδείς; PS 27
ϫ. ⲉⲡⲡⲉⲩⲉϣ ϭⲙ ϭⲟⲙ, ib 168 sim ⲡⲡⲉⲩ-, J 9 59 ϫ.
ⲉⲡⲉⲗⲁⲁⲩⲉ ⲡⲣⲱⲙⲉ ⲉϣ, ib 94 27 ϫ. ⲡⲡⲉⲧⲣⲉ ⲉⲣⲟϥ (var
ib 87 21 ϫⲉ-), El 72 *A* ϫ. ⲡⲉϥϣⲱⲃϩ, AP 41 *A²* ϫ. ⲉⲡⲉⲥ-
ⲥⲕⲁⲛⲇⲁⲗⲓⲍⲉ, Mani P 33 *A²* ϫⲉⲕⲁⲥⲉ ⲡⲛⲭⲓ ϭⲁⲗ, BSM
97 *B* ϫ. ⲡⲡⲛϩ ⲁ ⲧⲟϯ ⲉⲃⲟⲗ;   by subjunct, *S* rare
except in dependent clause: Sa 16 3 ϫ. ⲉⲩⲉⲛⲓⲟⲩⲙⲓ ...
ⲡⲥⲉⲧⲙϭ ϭⲟⲙ, Mor 55 75 ϫ. ⲉⲣϣⲁⲡⲟⲩϭⲣⲟⲟⲙ(ⲡⲉ)
ⲉⲣ ⲥⲁⲃⲟⲗ ⲡⲥⲉⲟⲩⲟⲙϥ, Lant 31 (2) *S^f* ϫ. (ⲡ)ⲧⲉⲡⲁⲣⲭ-
ⲁⲅⲅⲉⲗⲟⲥ ϫⲓ ⲡⲉϥⲙⲁⲧ;   *ABF*: Ac 3 26 *B* ϫ. ⲡⲧⲉ-
ⲡⲓⲟⲩⲁⲓ ... ϩⲉⲛϥ ⲥⲁⲃⲟⲗ (*S* ϩⲙⲡⲧⲣⲉ-) ἐν τῷ; Jo 3 16 *F*
ⲕⲉⲉ[ⲥ ⲟ]ⲩⲟⲛ ⲛⲓⲃ[ⲓ ⲉⲧ]ⲡⲉ- ... ⲡϥ-, ib 4 8 *F* ⲡⲉⲁⲩϣⲏ
ⲕⲉⲥ ⲡⲥⲉϣⲱⲡ (*S* ⲉϣⲱⲡ), 2 Cor 2 4 *B* ϫ. ⲡⲧⲉⲧⲉⲡⲉⲙ
(*S* ϫⲉ-) ἵνα; EpJer 17 *F* ϫⲉⲕⲉⲥ ⲡⲥⲉϣⲧⲉⲙⲃⲓⲧⲟⲩ, Cl
10 2 *A* ϫ. .... ϭⲣ ⲕⲗⲏⲣⲟⲛⲟⲙⲓ ὅπ.; Ro 12 2 *F* ⲕⲉⲥ ⲡⲧⲉ-
ⲧⲉⲛⲓⲙⲓ (*SB* ⲉⲧⲣⲉ-) εἰς τό, Ac 15 33 *B* ϫ. ⲡⲥⲉϣⲉ (var
ⲉⲑⲣⲟⲩ-, *S* Gk diff); AM 199 *B* ϫ. ⲡⲧⲉⲕⲟⲩⲟⲣⲡⲟⲩ,
C 43 178 *B* ϫ. ⲡⲧⲁⲉⲣ ⲡⲉⲙⲡϣⲁ;   by ⲉ-: Ac 15 38
B ϫ. (var ϫⲁⲥ only) ... ⲉϣⲧⲉⲙⲟⲗϥ (*S* om) μή; JEA
20 52 *S* ϫ. ⲉⲧⲁⲁϥ ⲡⲛⲓⲙ;   ⲙⲡⲉⲣϫⲁⲥ as neg subjunct *B* (Till *Dialektgram* 61, Gött Anz '34 59): Ps

2 12 ⲙ. ⲡⲧⲉⲡⲟⲥ ⲭⲱⲡⲧ (*S* = Gk) μήποτε; ROC 25 239 ⲙ. ⲡⲧⲉϩⲁⲡⲟⲅⲟⲛ ⲙⲉⲅⲓ. *Cf* ⲭⲉ-.

ⲭⲟⲕⲥ *B* nn m, *crepitus ventris*: K 160 ⲡⲓⲭ. ضراط. *Cf* ⲥⲁⲣϭⲁⲧⲥⲉ.

ⲭⲟⲟⲕⲉϥ *S*, ⲭⲁⲕϥ *A* *v* ⲭⲱⲟⲕⲉ *s f.*

ⲭⲟⲩⲕϩ, ⲭⲱ., ⲭⲟ.(once), ⲭⲉⲕⲣ-, ⲭⲟⲕⲣ⸱ *B* vb intr, *prick, bite*: Job 16 11 ὀξύς ݣ (Baudissin), Va 57 226 thorns ⲉⲩⲑⲟⲩⲅ̄ ⲉⲩⲭⲱ. κεντεῖν τιτρώσκειν, *ib* ⲉⲥⲭⲱ. ⲉⲥⲗⲟⲩⲅ̄; tr: Job 2 7 ⲭⲟ. (*S* ϣⲁⲁⲣ), Ap 9 5 (*S* ⲭⲱⲕⲉ) παίειν; Am 9 3 (*S* ⲗⲱⲕⲥ, *A* ⲡⲱϩⲥ) δάκνειν; C 89 106 be patient ϣⲁⲡⲧⲉⲡⲟⲥ ⲭⲟⲕⲣϥ κατανύσσειν (Va ar 172 62 لظ); Ac 28 3 (*S* ⲙⲉⲣ ⲣⲱϥ) καθάπτειν; Cat 78 ⲛⲓⲙⲁⲥⲧⲓⲅⲝ ... ⲁϥⲭⲉⲕϩ ⲁⲇⲁⲙ ⲛⲃⲏⲧⲟⲩ, Tst Ab 161 remembrance of death ⲭ. ⲙⲡϩⲏⲧ, C 86 141 ⲁⲟⲩⲕⲩⲣⲁⲥⲧⲏⲥ (ⲕⲉⲣ.) ⲭⲟⲕⲣϥ; as nn m: Jer 8 16 ὀξύτης.

ⲭⲟⲕⲣϥ nn, *goad*: Hos 5 12 (*A* ⲭⲁⲕϥ), ROC 17 403 κέντρον; Va 57 266 ⲡⲓⲭ. ⲡⲧⲉ ⲫⲗⲙϣ ⲛⲡⲓⲕⲁⲧⲏⲅⲟⲣⲓⲁ νιφάς (confused ? with σκνίψ). *Cf* ⲭⲱⲟⲕⲉ, ⲭⲟⲕⲭⲕ.

ⲭⲉⲕⲭⲓⲕ *SB*, ⲭⲓⲕ. *S* nn, *ant* or other insect (*cf* زقز̈ AZ 21 22 n): P 44 57 *S* ⲙⲉⲣⲙⲉⲡⲓⲅ (μύρμηξ)· ⲡⲓⲭⲓ. نمل (*sic*), Or 8771 *B* ⲡⲓⲭ. الذّ; Sa 19 10 *S* σκνίψ; Wess 9 51 *S* ϩⲛⲭⲓ. to devour you (Ryl Bull 11 401 *b* (دباب وقمل, Pcod 29 *S* ⲭⲓⲡⲡⲣⲱⲙⲉ ϣϩⲟⲣⲁⲓ ⲉⲛⲭ. (var Mich 550 27 ⲭⲓ.). *Cf* ϭⲁⲭⲓϥ (ⲭⲁϥⲭⲓϥ).

ⲭⲟⲕⲭⲕ *S*, ⲭⲁⲕⲭⲉⲕ *S f*, ⲭⲟⲕ. *B*, ⲭⲉⲕⲭⲱⲕ⸱ *S*, ⲭⲉⲕⲭⲱⲕ⸥ *SB*, -ⲭⲟⲕⲧ⸥ *S* vb intr, *prick, brand, braid*: Lev 19 28⸥ *B* (var ⲑⲉⲕⲑⲱⲕ, *S* tr) στίζειν صنع وشم; R 2 2 23 *S* ⲑⲏⲇⲟⲡⲏ ⲭ. ϩⲓⲣⲟⲩⲡ ⲙⲙⲟϥ γαργαλίζειν; MG 25 403 *B* ϩⲃⲟⲥ ⲛⲁⲡⲁⲥ ⲉϥⲭ.⸥ (Gött ar 114 147 قديمة خلقان, ROC 19 44 ⲇⲕⲗⲁ only); ShP 130² 104 *S* things craftsman maketh ⲉϥⲕⲟⲥⲙⲉⲓ ⲙⲙⲟⲟⲩ ⲉϥⲭ. ⲉϥϯ ⲉⲓⲉⲛⲥⲁ ⲉⲣⲟⲟⲩ, PLond 4 462 *S* request on behalf of man ⲉϥϩⲉⲕϩⲟⲕⲧ ϩⲛⲡⲙⲁ ⲛⲡⲁⲣϩⲓ[ⲥⲧⲁ (*cf* στίζειν); tr: BHom 28 *S* conscience ⲭ. ⲙⲙⲟⲛ ⲉⲭⲛ ⲡⲉⲛⲧⲁⲡⲗⲁⲁⲩ κεντεῖν; P 44 120 *S* ⲉϥⲭ. ⲙⲙⲟⲛ يلغزنا (*l* ? يلدغنا, *cf* ⲭⲱⲟⲕⲉ nn), ShP 130² 88 *S* maiden ⲉⲧⲭ. ⲙⲙⲟⲥ ⲉⲥϯ ⲥⲁ ⲉⲣⲟⲥ, Sh(?)Mor 54 138 *S f* ⲭ. ⲡⲡⲉⲧⲛⲟⲩⲟϭⲉ & make smooth hair, *ib* 41 106 *S* ⲭ. ⲡⲡⲟⲩ(ⲟⲩ)ⲟϭⲉ (DeV 1 38 *B* om), *ib* 37 168 *S* ⲭⲉⲕⲭⲱⲕⲟⲩ (*sc* words) ⲛⲑⲉ ⲡⲟⲩϣⲧⲏⲛ ϩⲣⲟⲩⲭⲛⲥⲉ, *ib* 51 35 *S v* ⲡϣⲓⲧ (where ⲟⲩⲱϭ = ? ⲟⲩⲟϭⲉ), PLond 4 463 *S* ⲡⲣⲱⲙⲧⲉⲡⲕⲟⲓⲉ ⲁⲩⲭⲉⲕⲭⲟⲕⲟⲩ (*cf ib* 462 above).
With following preposition. c ⲉ-: Sh(?)Mor 54 60 *S* sinners shave beards ⲉⲩⲭ. ⲉⲣⲟⲟⲩ (*sc* bodies) ⲛϩⲣⲉⲡⲣⲁⲡ ⲙⲡⲣⲉⲡⲕⲉⲓⲧⲟⲥ (ⲉⲓⲇ.), MélOr 6 504 *B* took needle ⲛⲧⲉⲥⲭ. ⲉⲣⲟϥ (*sc* blessed bread); c ⲉϫⲛ-: KroppE 40 *S* letters ⲉⲧⲭ.⸥ ⲉϫⲛⲧⲙⲉⲥⲧ ⲛϩⲏⲧ, Ryl 103 *S* sim; c ⲛ-, *with*: WTh 197 *S* ⲭ. ⲙⲙⲟⲟⲩ (finger

nails) ⲛⲣⲉⲡⲛⲕⲁ ⲛⲧⲱⲣⲡ; c ϩⲛ-: ShA 1 299 *S* ⲉⲣⲁⲓⲥⲟⲩ ⲉⲣⲟϥ (*sc* house) ⲭⲉⲕϩⲱⲕⲟⲩ ⲛϩⲏⲧϥ, Sh(?) Mor 54 59 *S f* ⲭ. ⲛⲡⲉⲧⲛⲥⲱⲙⲁ ϩⲣⲉⲛⲥϩⲁⲓ.

—— nn *B* f, *stamp, brand*: P 54 163 *varia* +ⲭ.; الرسم ,الختم; *S*(same?), *provocation*: Si 34 33 (29) ἐρεθισμός, 2 Cor 12 20 (*B* ϣⲉⲣϣⲓ, *F* ⲭⲏⲗϫⲉⲗ) ἐριθεία; cit ? ShWess 9 155 ⲡⲭ. ⲛⲕⲁⲧⲁⲗⲁⲗⲓⲁ.

ⲣⲉϥⲭ. *S*, *slanderous*(?): Si 28 15 ⲗⲁⲥ ⲛⲣ. τρητός (gloss τετρυπημένος).

Cf ⲭⲱⲟⲕⲉ, ⲭⲟⲩⲕϩ.

ⲭⲁⲗ *B* nn m, *branch*: Lev 23 40, Dan 4 11, Mt 13 32 (*F* ⲧⲉⲗ), Ro 11 19 (*F* = *S*, all *S* = Gk) κλάδος; Ez 19 11 (*S* ϣⲗϭ) κλῆμα; Job 15 32 (*S* ⲧⲁⲣ) ῥάδαμνος; Ps 79 11 (*S* ϯ ⲟⲅⲱ) ἀναδενδράς; Nu 8 4 (*S* ϩⲣⲏⲡⲉ) κρίνον عرج; Jer 17 8 στέλεχος; Aeg 39 ⲃⲁⲓ ⲛⲃⲛⲧ, ⲭ. ⲛⲭⲱⲓⲧ, BSM 57 ⲭ. ⲛⲥⲉⲟⲓ ⲛⲟⲩϥⲓ = BMis 412 *S* ⲕⲗⲁ., MG 25 141 birds in tree ⲟⲩⲟϩ ⲉ̄ⲭⲉⲛⲡⲉⲥⲭ.; ⲓⲣⲓ ⲛϩⲁⲡⲭ.: Ez 17 23 βλαστὸν ἐκφέρειν; ϩⲓ ⲭ. ⲉⲃⲟⲗ: C 86 293 κλάδους ἀπολύειν. ⲗⲁⲭⲁⲗ *v* p 135 *a.*
hayfork: P 54 135 ⲡⲓⲭ. مذرى (*cf* ⲧⲁⲣ).

ⲭⲏⲗ *S* nn m, *a fish*: P 46 237 ⲡⲭ. شيلان (prob = Coptic, not شال).

ⲭⲓⲁⲁⲗ *F* *v* p 82 *a infra.*

ⲭⲓⲗ *F* *v* ⲭⲓⲣ.

ⲭⲟⲗ, *BF* ϭⲁⲗ *BF* nn m, *wave*: Ex 15 8 *B f* (CMSS 13), Job 6 15 (*S* ϩⲟⲉⲓⲙ), Jon 2 4 (*SA* do), Mt 14 24 (*SF* do) κῦμα; Ja 1 6 (*S* do) κλύδων; Aeg 26 ⲡⲓⲭ. ⲛⲧⲉ ⲫⲓⲟⲙ, MG 25 160 ⲛⲓϩⲱⲓⲙⲓ... ⲡⲉⲙⲡⲓⲭ.; ϩⲓ ⲭ., *throw up waves*: Jer 6 23 κυμαίνειν; FR 94 river ⲉϥϩ. ...ⲥⲉϭⲟⲥⲓ ⲛϫⲉ ⲛⲉϥϩⲱⲓⲙⲓ.

ⲭⲟⲗ *S* Tri 259 بصل = ⲙⲭⲟⲗ. *Cf* ⲭⲱⲗ 2°.

ⲭⲟⲗ *B* *v* ϭⲱⲟⲗⲉ vb & nn.

ⲭⲟⲩⲗ *B* nn m, *fragment* or sim (*cf* ◣ IgR): MG 25 194 ⲭ. in serpent's eye, ⲁϥϩⲉⲓ ⲛϫⲉ ⲡⲓⲭ. ϧⲉⲛⲡⲉϥ ⲃⲁⲗ at saint's touch.

ⲭⲱⲗ *B* nn m, *honeycomb*: P 54 119, BMOr 8775 119 ⲡⲓⲭ. شهد.

ⲭⲱⲗ *S* nn as adj, ? for ⲙⲭⲱⲗ, *onion* (-coloured): Ryl 244 ϣⲧ(ⲏ)ⲛ ⲛⲭ., ⲡⲁⲗⲗⲓⲛ ⲛⲭ., *ib* 262 sim. *Cf* ⲭⲟⲗ 2°.

ⲭⲱⲗ *B* *v* ϭⲱⲗ *return* & ϭⲱⲟⲗⲉ 1°.

ⲭⲁⲗⲉ- *F* *v* ⲭⲱⲟⲗⲉ 1°.

ⲭⲁⲗⲉ- *B* *v* ϭⲟⲉⲓⲗⲉ **B.**

ⲭⲉⲗⲁ *F* *v* ⲭⲉⲣⲟ *kindle.*

ϫⲉ ⲁ⸗ *F* *v* ϫⲱ vb (ϫⲉⲣⲟ-).

ϫⲉⲗⲉ *S* nn, meaning unknown: ST 171 ⲉϣⲱⲡⲉ ϫ. ϧⲁⲧⲏⲧⲛ tell me, for I have none. *Cf ?* ϫⲗⲗⲉ.

ϫⲉⲗⲓ *B* nn, *net*: Is 19 8 ⲣⲉϥϫⲓ ϫ. (*S* ⲡⲉϫ ϣⲛⲏ) ἀμφιβολεύς.

ϫⲉⲗⲱ *A²* vb tr, meaning uncertain: ManiP 165 ϥϫ. ⲧⲉⲧⲡⲱ ⲉⲧⲁϫⲱⲓ.

ϫⲉⲓⲗⲓ *F* = ⲧϣⲉⲓⲗⲓ (*v* ϣⲁⲓⲣⲉ): CMSS 78 ⲡⲉϩⲁⲙ-ⲡⲓ ϩⲉⲧϫ., BP 9544 ⲡⲉⲗⲉⲙϫ. *Cf ?* place-name ⲧϫⲉⲗⲓ (Amélineau *Géog* 488).

ϫⲓⲉⲓⲗⲉ *S* nn, meaning unknown: BM 1088 among vegetables ⲙⲛⲧⲏ ⲛⲧⲙⲏ ⲛϫ. *Cf ?* ϫⲓⲉⲓⲣⲉ.

ϫⲟⲗⲓ *B* *v* ϫⲟⲟⲗⲉⲥ.

ϫⲟⲩⲓⲗⲓ *B* *v* ϭⲟⲉⲓⲗⲉ.

ϫⲱ(ⲱ)ⲗⲉ *SF*, ϣⲱⲗⲉ *S*, ϫⲟⲩ(ⲟⲩ)ⲗⲉ *A*, ϭⲱⲗ, ϣⲱⲗ *B*, ϫⲟ(ⲟ)ⲗⲉ *F* (Hos 6 10), ϫⲉ(ⲉ)ⲗⲉ- *S*, ϫⲱⲗⲉ- *SA²*, ϭⲉⲗ-, ϭⲟⲗ-*B*, ϫⲁⲗⲉ-*F*, ϫⲟ(ⲟ)ⲗ⸗*S*, ϫⲁⲗ⸗*A²*, ϭⲟⲗ⸗*B*, ϭⲟⲗ†*B* vb intr, *gather harvest* (fruit, corn, flowers): Jer 6 9 *B* τρυγᾶν, Si 30 26 *S*, P 44 80 *S* ⲡⲉⲧϣ., Glos 222 *S* τρυγητής; P 54 118 *B* ⲉϭ⸗.† ٯطف; tr: Lev 25 11 *SB*, Job 15 33 *SB*, Cant 5 1 *SF* ϫⲱ., Ryl 62 3 *S* ϫⲉⲉⲗⲉ ⲟⲩⲙⲁ ⲡⲉⲗⲟⲟⲗⲉ, Va 63 90 *B* ϭⲉⲗ ⲡⲉⲥⲟⲩⲧⲁϩ τρ., Am 6 1 *B* ἀποτρ., Lev 25 5 *SB* ἐκτρ.; Deu 24 20 *B*(*S* ϭⲣⲓⲧ) καλαμᾶσθαι; Is 18 5 *S*(*B* ⲱⲗⲓ) ἀφαιρεῖν; ShP 129¹⁴ 130 *S* ⲡⲉⲧⲛϭⲱⲙ ... ϫⲟⲟⲗⲟⲩ, Bor 292 204 *S* ϫ. ⲡϣⲗϩ ⲡⲓⲙ, CA 106 *S* ϫ. ⲡⲡⲉϥϫⲗⲉ, ManiP 99 *A²* rose ϫⲁⲗⲉⲥ, *ib* K 11 *A²* fruits ϫⲁⲗⲟⲩ, C 86 47 *B* cypress ⲁⲩϣⲁⲛϭⲟⲗϥ (but = GMir 261 *S* ϫⲟⲗϥ⸗, *cf* Assemani *AcMartOr* 255 ܡܣܘ), CMSS 37 *F* ϫⲁⲗⲉ ⲡⲉⲕⲁⲡⲁⲗⲁⲗⲓ, BKU 1 181 *F*; *collect* taxes (*cf* Sethe *DemUrk* 111): ST 227 *S* ⲁⲓϫ. ⲟⲩⲧⲣ(ⲙⲏ)ⲥⲓⲟⲛ ... ⲉϣⲱ-ⲡⲉ ⲧⲁϭⲟⲙ ⲧⲁϫ. ⲡⲉϥⲧⲉⲙⲟⲥⲓⲟⲛ.

With following preposition. ⲉ ⲉ-: Hos 10 12 *B*(*A* ⲱⲉϩ) τρ. εἰς; Deu 23 25 *S*(*B* diff) ἐμβάλλειν εἰς; Mor 53 71 *S* ϣⲁⲣⲉⲡ[ⲣⲉϥ]ϫ. ϫ. ⲉⲡⲉϥⲕⲟⲧ *gather into basket*; ⲉ ⲛ- dat: Hos 6 10 *AB*(sic l)*F*(JEA 11 245) τρ. dat; C 41 65 *B* ϭⲟⲗ ⲃⲟⲩ† (l ⲟⲩⲟⲩ†) ⲛⲡⲓ-ⲥⲡⲏⲟⲩ; ⲉ ⲛⲥⲁ-: Miss 4 752 *S* ϫ. ⲛⲥⲁⲛⲥⲱⲧⲡ ⲛϭⲓⲥ-ⲧⲣⲉ; ⲉ ϩⲓ-: ManiK 11 *A²* ϫ. ϩⲓⲱⲱϥ (sc tree) ⲛⲡⲛ ⲉⲧⲁⲡⲱϩ; ⲉⲃⲟⲗ ϩⲓ-: Lu 6 44 *B*(*S* ⲉⲃ. ϩⲛ-) τρ. ἐκ; ⲉ ϩⲛ-, ϭⲉⲛ-: Ps 79 12 *S*(*B* tr) τρ. acc; Va 66 288 *B* each flower ⲉⲑⲣⲉϥϭ. ⲡⲃⲏⲧϥ δρέπειν; ⲉⲃ. ϩⲛ-*S* *v* Lu above.

—— nn m *SABF*, *harvest*: P 44 80 *S* ⲡϣⲱⲗⲉ · τρύγη · ٯطاف, Lev 26 5 *SB*, 1 Kg 13 21 *S* ⲡϫ. ⲛ ⲡⲱϩⲥ, Is 16 9 *SB* ϣⲱⲗ, *ib* 32 10 *SBF*, Am 9 13 *SAB* τρυγη-τος, Va 57 160 *B* lest unbelievers say ⲉϥϫⲏ ⲉⲃⲣⲏⲓ ⲛϫⲉ ⲟⲩϭ. ⲥⲁϭⲟⲩⲛ τρύξ (on Jo 2 7); Is 18 5 *B* ⲥⲛϥⲓ

ⲛϣ. (*S* ⲟϩⲥ) δρέπανον; ShP 131⁴ 149 = *ib* 131² 69 *S* time for ϫⲟ, ϫ., ⲱⲗ, Kr 152 *S* ⲏⲣⲡ ⲛϫ. (τρύγησις ?) included in wage, *ib* 153 sim, *cf* BP 4929 *S* ⲏⲣⲡ ⲉⲡϫ.; Cant 2 12 *SA*(*F* ϣⲁⲧϫⲏ *v* p 592 *a*) τομή; K 258 *B* ⲡⲓϭⲟⲗ قطاف; ShA 2 130 *S* ⲛϫ. of vineyards, P 131² 69 *S* ⲡϫⲟ, ⲡⲱϩⲥ, ⲡϫ., DeV 2 237 *B* ⲙⲙⲟⲛ ϭⲣⲏ, ⲥϫⲁⲓ, ϭ., Mor 31 255 *S* fruits ⲉⲣⲉⲡⲉϫϫⲟⲟⲗⲉ (ⲉ)ϥⲧⲁ-ⲅⲉ ⲁⲣⲱⲧⲉ ⲉⲃⲟⲗ ⲁⲩⲱ ⲡⲉϫϣⲗϩ ⲉⲩⲣⲟⲟⲩⲧ ϩⲓⲱⲟⲩ = Ryl Bull 11 435 *b* عليها (sic) ورق الاخضر الذى كانت, CO 160 *S* wine due ϩⲙⲡϫⲱⲗ(ⲉ) ⲉⲧⲏⲩ ⲉϩⲟⲩⲛ, Hall 52 *S* wine ϩⲙⲡϫ. ⲛⲧⲣⲓⲧⲏ, ST 88 *S* sim ⲡϫⲱϫⲉⲕⲁⲧⲉ, *ib* 89 sim ⲉⲡⲓ ⲧⲏⲥ ⲧⲉⲧⲁⲣⲧⲏⲥ, COAd 17 sim ⲡⲧⲁⲣϫⲏ ⲡⲉⲛⲧⲏ, Kr 22 *F* ⲡϫ. ⲙⲡⲕⲁⲣⲡ(ⲟⲥ) ⲉⲧⲥⲉⲡ ⲍ̄, Ryl 255 *S* ⲛⲡⲧⲁⲡ-ϫⲟϥ ⲉⲃⲟⲗ ⲉⲡϫ., BM 706 *F* ⲡϩⲣⲟⲟⲩ ⲛϫⲱⲱⲗⲓ. Once f: ST 247 *S*.

ⲙⲁ ⲛϫ. *S*: WS 132 wine as wage ⲕⲁⲧⲁ ⲙ., ? = ϫ.
ⲣⲉϥϫ., -ϭ. *SAB*, *harvester*: Jer 29 9 *SB*(sic l), Ob 5 *S*(MR 1934 10)*AB* τρυγητής; ShA 2 63 *S*.

ϫⲗⲗⲉ *SA* nn f, *grapes of gleaning, left over*: Jud 8 2 ϫⲗ. opp ϫⲱⲱⲗⲉ, Mic 7 1 *SA*(*B* ϫⲱⲃⲓ), Ob 5 *S* *ut sup A*(*B* do) ἐπιφυλλίς (which Zeph 3 7 *A* ϭⲉⲉⲡⲉ); Glos 203 καρπον (*l* ? καρπίον); ShP 131⁴ 161 ϫⲱ-ⲱⲗⲉ ⲥⲙⲁϩ ... ⲕⲱⲧϩ ϫ., ShP 130² 72 ϫ. ⲡ(ⲉ)ⲗⲉϩⲙⲉϫ ⲉⲧⲡⲁϣⲧ ⲉⲃⲟⲗ ⲟⲩⲧⲉ ⲡⲉⲥⲙⲁϩ, *ib* 4 foxes eat ⲥⲙⲁϩ, ϫ., ⲃⲗⲃⲓⲗⲉ (on Cant 2 15). In place-name (?) ⲧϫⲉⲗ-ⲗⲉ (BM 346).

Cf ϭⲱⲗ *collect*, ϫⲱⲗϩ 1°.

ϫⲱⲱⲗⲉ *SA²*, ϫⲱⲗⲉ *A²*, ϫⲟⲟⲗⲉ† *S* vb intr, *be hin-dered* (?): ShP 130² 26 = ViK 9345 canals ⲥⲱⲕ ϩⲡⲡⲉⲩⲙⲁ ⲡⲉⲓ ⲉⲃⲟⲗ ⲙⲡⲟⲩϫ. ⲏ ⲙⲡⲟⲩϭⲱ, ManiH 28 *A²* ⲧⲉⲕⲕⲗⲏⲥⲓⲁ ⲡⲁϫⲱ. ⲉⲛ ϫⲡⲙⲡⲓⲛⲟ, *ib* K 94 ⲁⲙⲙⲁⲓⲧ ϫ. ⲁⲛϩⲁⲗⲙⲉ ⲥⲱϣⲧ ⲙⲡⲧⲏⲩ, ShC 73 158 ⲉⲧϫ.† ⲉⲡⲁ-ϩⲟⲩ opp ⲉⲧⲙⲟⲟϣⲉ ⲉⲑⲏ; tr *A²*, *stop, make cease*: ManiH 12 ⲁⲥϫⲱ. ⲣⲱⲟⲩ ⲛⲡⲓⲣⲉϥⲥⲉ[ϫⲉ, *ib* ⲁⲥϫ. ⲧⲟⲩⲗ-ⲗⲉ ⲡⲓⲯⲁⲗⲙⲟⲥ, ManiP 53 ϫⲱⲗ ⲧⲉⲣⲙⲓⲛ.

ϫⲗⲉ *A·* nn, *hindrance* (?): ManiP 58 ⲕ]ⲁⲁⲡ ⲉⲡ-ⲟⲩⲁϫ ⲁϫⲗⲉ.

Cf ? ϭⲱⲗ *return*.

ϫⲗⲁ *S* nn m, meaning unknown: PMich 3584 ϩⲓ ⲣⲟⲟⲩϣ ϩⲁⲡⲉϫ. ⲡⲁⲛⲧⲏ[. *Cf* ? Πετλα-ρης (var -κλα, Sethe *DemUrk* 111).

ϫⲗⲱⲃ *v* ϫⲗⲱⲙ.

ϫⲟⲗⲃⲓ *B* nn f, baker's *wooden shovel*: K 132 ϯϫ. مجرفة.

ϫⲁⲗⲃⲉⲗ *A²* nn, meaning unknown: ManiH 31 ⲟⲩⲉⲡⲓⲑⲩⲙⲓⲁ ... ⲥⲁⲣ ϫ. ⲉⲡ.

ϫⲉⲗⲃⲉⲥⲓ *F* *v* ϭⲉⲗⲃⲉⲥⲓ.

ϫⲱⲗⲕ *SAF*, ϭ. *B*, ϫⲉⲗⲕ-*S*, ϭ., ϭⲟⲗⲕ-*B*, ϫⲁⲗⲉⲕ-*F*(?), ϫⲟⲗⲕ⸗*S*, ϫⲁⲗⲕ⸗*S/A²*, ϭⲟⲗⲕ⸗*B*, ϫⲟⲗⲕ†*S*, ϫⲁ.†,

-ϭ† A², ϭⲟⲗⲕ† B vb intr **A**, *stretch, extend*: MG 25 16
B of bow τείνειν, Ps 44 5 B(S ⲥⲱⲙⲛⲧ) ἐντ.; 4 Kg 13
18 S Gk om; P 54 171 Bⲡⲓϭⲓϭⲓ ⲉⲧϭ. شدّد; P 129¹⁶ 69
S ⲁⲩϯ ⲙⲁⲗⲓⲗ ⲛⲁⲩ (sc 2 palms) ϣⲁⲡⲧⲟⲩϫ. ⲕⲁⲗⲱⲥ (cf
ϫⲗⲁⲕ), Mor 18 110 S ⲡⲙⲟⲩⲧ ⲉⲧⲉϣϫⲁϫ. (var LCyp
4 ⲱⲗⲕ);   qual: Is 21 15 SB διατ., Jer 4 29 SB
ἐντ., Va 57 181 B prayers ⲉⲧϭ. ἐκτενής; MG 25 258
B rained 2 days & nights ⲉⲩϭ., C 89 145 B ϧⲁⲡⲁⲥ-
ⲕⲏⲥⲓⲥ ⲉⲩϭ. ⲉⲡⲓⲣⲟⲅⲟ, ib 204 B ⲁⲣⲉⲧⲏ ⲉⲩϭ., Va 61 207
B who hath tied my hands ϧⲉⲛϩⲁⲛⲥⲁϫⲓ ⲉⲩϭ. ? (on
Ge 22 11, 12);   tr: Jer 27 14 SB τεί., Is 44 24 B
(S ⲡⲱⲣϣ) ἐκτ., Ps 10 2 B(S ⲥⲱ.), Jer 26 9 SBF(Mus
49 173), Lam 2 4 S(ShC 73 77 ϫⲱⲣⲕ sic)B(F diff), ib
3 12 SBFϫⲁⲗⲉ[ⲕ ἐντ., 3 Kg 22 34 S ἐπιτ.; Job 9 8
B(S diff) τανύειν; P 44 96 S ⲧⲕⲁⲧⲁⲇⲓⲕⲏ ⲉⲧϫ. ⲙⲡⲟ-
ⲍⲏⲧⲟⲥ (ζυ.) نصب; Mor 41 12 S ⲡⲉⲧⲟⲩⲡⲁⲕⲓⲙ ⲉⲡⲉ-
ⲛⲟⲩϩ (to raise pillar) ⲡⲥⲉϭⲟⲗⲕϥ = DeV 2 261 B ϭ.
ⲛⲡⲓⲙⲁⲛϭⲁⲛⲟⲡ, DeV 2 40 B ⲡⲥⲟⲟⲡⲉϥ...ϭⲟⲗⲕϥ.

With following preposition.   ⲥ ⲉ-: Hab 3 9 A
(S ⲉϫⲛ-, B ϧⲓⲣⲁ.) ἐντεί. ἐπί; Ex 19 13 B κατατοξεύειν,
Leip 24 12 B legs in stocks ⲙⲡⲉϥϭⲟⲗⲕⲟⲩ ⲉϩⲁⲡⲙⲏϣ
ⲡⲭⲟⲗ κεντήμασιν ἐμβάλλειν; ShA 2 303 S ϧⲉⲛⲛⲟϭ
ⲛϣⲉ ⲉⲡϫ. ⲉⲣⲟⲟⲩ ⲛⲛⲓⲛⲟⲩϩ, BIF 13 101 S chains ⲉⲧϫ.†
ⲉⲡⲙⲁ ⲡⲉⲓ ⲉϩⲟⲩⲛ (of port) = MG 25 282 B, Miss 4
212 B ϣⲓⲛⲟⲩ...ϭⲟⲗⲕⲟⲩ ⲉⲣⲟⲓ, AM 309 B ϭⲟⲗⲕ ⲥⲟⲟ-
ⲡⲉϥ ⲉⲣⲟϥ, Mor 30 13 Sᶠ ϫⲁⲗⲉⲕϥ ⲉⲡⲭⲓⲥⲉ, RNC 87 S
woman ⲛ[ⲉⲁⲥ]ϫ. ⲉⲙⲓⲥⲉ;   ⲉϧⲟⲩⲛ ⲉ-: ShA 2 12 S
shooters ⲉⲧϫ. ⲉϩ. ⲉⲧⲉ̄ψⲩⲭⲏ (cf Jer 27 29);   ⲥ
ⲉϫⲛ-: KroppR 10 S ϫ. ⲡⲧⲉⲕⲡⲓⲧⲉ ⲉ. ⲡⲁⲣⲭⲏⲡⲗⲁⲥ-
ⲙⲁ;   ⲥ ⲛ- dat: Zech 9 13 SAB ἐντ. dat, Ps 139 6
B(S ⲥⲱ.) διατ. dat; *with*: Pro 7 16 A(S do, B ϧⲉⲛ-)
τ. dat; C 86 281 B ⲁⲧϥⲉ ϭⲗⲱⲕ (sic) ⲛϭⲏⲡⲓ (cf 215
ϧⲱⲃⲥ ⲛϭ.), ST 223 S sick man ⲉⲓⲭ.† ⲡⲧⲏⲩ *short* (?) of
breath;   ⲥ ϣⲁ-: B: AM 263 Libya ⲉⲧϭ.† ϣⲁⲗⲉⲃ-
ⲧⲓⲛ (Λεπ.);   ⲥ ϩⲁ-: Va 61 202 ϭ. ⲛⲣⲁⲛϩⲣⲱⲟⲩ
ϩⲁϥϯ;   ⲥ ϩⲛ-, ϧⲉⲛ-: Pro l c B τ. dat, Hos 11 4
B(A ⲥⲱⲕ) ἐκτ. ἐν, ROC 25 250 B ⲉϥϭ.† ϧⲉⲛⲡⲓⲧⲱϧⲥ
παρατ., Ac 22 25 B(S ⲥⲱ.) προτ. dat; Nu 24 8 S(var
ⲥⲱ., B ϧⲓ ⲥⲟⲟⲛⲉϥ) κατατοξ. dat; Job 6 2 S(B ⲱⲗⲓ)
αἴρειν ἐν; MG 25 245 B ⲡⲁϩⲏⲧ ϭ.† ϧⲉⲛϥϯ ἀπερί-
σπαστον ποιεῖν ἀπό; BMar 21 S ϫⲟⲗⲕϥ ϩⲣϩⲉⲛⲗⲱ-
ⲣⲟⲥ;   ⲉϧⲟⲗ ϧⲉⲛ-: Ex 39 21 B συσφίγγειν ἀπό;   ⲥ
ϫⲓⲛ- A²: ManiK 125 ⲛⲗⲓϭⲙⲉ ⲉⲧϫ.† ϫⲛⲛⲙⲏⲛⲅⲉ ⲁⲡⲕⲁϩ, ib P 221 ⲡⲁⲥⲁⲧⲉ...ϫⲁⲗⲕⲟⲩ ϫⲛⲛⲕⲣⲟ ⲁⲕⲣⲟ.
With following adverb.

—— ⲉϧⲟⲗ: ROC 18 170 S ϫⲉⲗⲕ ⲧⲉⲧⲛⲁⲥⲕⲏⲥⲓⲥ ⲉϧ.,
Ming 290 S ⲛⲟⲩϩ ⲉⲧϫ.† ⲉϧ. of rope-dancer τεί.,
ROC 17 399 B ϭ. ⲉϧ. ⲛⲧⲣⲉⲗⲡⲓⲥ παρατ.; Va 57 70 B
ⲙⲁⲣⲉⲛϭ. ⲉϧ. ⲛⲧⲉⲛϫⲓⲛⲙⲟϣⲓ ὀξυποδεῖν; Bor 248 11
ϫⲟⲗⲕϥ (sc time) ⲉϧ. (= Brooks *SelLetSeverus* 1 201
ولبس) opp ϭⲱⲟⲩ ⲉϩⲟⲩⲛ, HM 1 100 S ⲉϥϫ.† ⲉϧ. ⲉⲧ-
ϧⲉⲛⲛⲟϭ ⲛϯ ⲧⲕⲁⲥ, JTS 8 244 S he split in twain ⲛⲟⲉ
ⲉⲧⲉϥϫ. ⲉϧ. ⲙⲙⲟⲥ so (*tightly*) *was he stretched*, P 130⁵

—— 36 S sun rising causeth ⲛⲓϩⲛⲃⲉ ⲉⲧϫ.† ⲉϧ. to cease,
BMis 293 S bade ⲛⲥⲉϫⲟⲗⲕϥ ⲉϧ. & scourge him, AM
292 B sim, Mor 31 117 S ⲁⲥⲕⲏⲥⲓⲥ ⲉⲧϫ.† ⲉϧ.;   +ⲛ-,
with, on: RNC 68 S bade ϫ. ⲉϧ. ⲡⲁⲥⲕⲗⲁ ⲛϥⲧⲟⲟⲩ
ⲙⲙⲟⲥ, C 86 208 B sim ⲛϫ̄ ⲡϣⲙⲟⲩ; *as to*: Va
59 5 B bade ϭⲟⲗⲕϥ ⲉϧ. ⲛⲛⲉϥϫⲓϫ & feet;   +ϩⲛ-,
ϧⲉⲛ-: Z 330 S ⲉⲓϭ.† ⲉϧ. ϩⲛⲟⲩϩⲣⲁⲡ ⲛⲧⲉⲓϭⲟⲧ, C 43 172
B ϭⲟⲗⲕϥ ⲉϧ. ϧⲉⲛϩⲁⲛⲗⲱⲣⲟⲥ;   +ϩⲓⲧⲛ-: Job 26 7
B ἐκτ. ἐπί; P 131² 157 S ⲛϫ. ⲙⲙⲟⲛ ⲁⲛ ⲉϧ. ϩ. ϧⲉⲛ-
ⲛⲟⲩϩ, Mor 30 12 Sᶠ ϫⲁⲗⲕⲟⲩ ⲉϧ. ϩⲓ[ⲧⲛ ? ⲙ]ⲙⲁⲧⲟⲓ; *as*
nn m, *stretching, extent, endurance*: P 131² 157 S we
need ⲟⲩϫ. ⲉϧ. lest worldliness intrude τάσεως δεῖν;
P 44 59 S تشيع; BMar 197 S ⲡⲛⲟϭ ⲛϫ. ⲉϧ. ⲛⲛⲉϥⲁ-
ⲥⲕⲏⲥⲓⲥ, MIE 2 337 B bore ⲡⲁⲓⲛⲓϣϯ ⲛϭ. ⲉϧ. ⲛⲧⲉ ⲡⲁⲓ-
ⲕⲟⲅⲙⲁ.   ϩⲛⲟⲩϫ. ⲉϧ. S, *continuously, strenuously*:
Miss 4 676 praying ϩ., Wess 18 53 sim ⲛⲟϭ ⲛϫ.,
BMis 277 hastened on road ϩⲛⲟⲩⲛⲟϭ ⲛϫ.;   ϫⲓⲛϫ.
ⲉϧ. S, *persistence*: Mor 31 16 ⲧⲉϫ. ⲉⲡⲉϣⲗⲏⲗ.

—— ⲉⲡϣⲱⲓ B: Va 68 168 ϭ. ⲛⲡⲁⲃⲟⲗ ⲉ. ⲉⲧϥⲉ
ἀνατ. εἰς, MG 25 210 sim = Z 345 S ⲡⲱⲣϣ ⲉϧⲟⲗ,
AM 278 sim ἐκτ. εἰς; ib 129 thoughts ϭ.† ⲉ. ϩⲁϥϯ.

—— ⲉϩⲣⲁⲓ, -ⲛⲓ: Lev 8 7 B ⲉϩ. ⲉϫⲛ- (S ⲥⲱ.
ⲉϩⲟⲩⲛ ⲉ-) συσφίγ. ἐν (var ἐπί); BIF 13 116 S hands
ϫ. ⲉϩ. ⲉⲧⲡⲉ = MG 25 308 B, Bor 254 172 S ⲡⲉⲩ-
ⲡⲟⲩⲥ...ϫⲟⲗⲕϥ ⲉϩ. ϣⲁⲡⲡⲉ.

—— **nn m**, *strain, tension* B: AM 280 ⲁϥϣⲱⲡⲓ
ⲛϫⲉ ⲟⲩⲛⲓϣϯ ⲛϭ. στάσις; MG 25 349 ⲛϭ. ⲙⲡⲉϥ-
ⲙⲉⲩⲓ ϩⲁⲡⲟⲧⲉ (Gött ar 114 123 الامر, ROC 17 375
الاسو), HL 90 ⲥⲉⲛⲁϣ ⲃⲱⲗ ⲙⲡⲉⲕϭ. (sic) ⲉϧⲟⲗ ⲁⲛ
strictness, Cat 26 ⲛϭ. ⲛϯⲁⲥⲕⲏⲥⲓⲥ, ROC 25 253 lest
he fall away ϩⲁⲡⲉϥϭ. ⲉⲧⲧⲟⲙ ⲉϥϯ;   ϩⲛⲟⲩϫ., -ϭ.,
strenuously: Hab 3 9 SAB ἐντείνων, HCons 463 B
ϯϩⲟ ϭ. ἐκτενῶς; HL 107 B sim ἱκετεύων; BSM 17
B ⲛⲁϩⲃⲱⲧⲥ ⲟⲩⲃⲏⲓ ϭ.

ⲟ ⲛϫ. S, *be in anxiety* (?): Ryl Suppl 27 mother
greeteth thee & co ⲛϫ. ϫⲉⲛⲡⲉⲕϫⲓ ⲡⲗⲁⲁⲩ [.

ϫⲗⲁⲕ S, ϭ. B **nn m**, *stretching, strain, punishment*:
KroppK 34 S a malady ?; K 354 B ⲡⲓϭ. تعذيب;   ϯ
ϫ., ϭ.: P 78 52 S ϯ ϫ. ⲛⲁⲩ (sc 2 palms, cf ϫⲱⲗⲕ
intr) till they met; Mk 5 7 B(S = Gk) βασανίζειν.
Cf ⲙⲁⲛϫⲏ.

ϫⲟⲗⲕⲥ S, ϭ. B **nn f**, *strain* on cord, *stringency* of
exercises: MG 25 242 B ϫⲛⲁϫⲁⲓ ϫⲁⲧⲟⲩϭ. ⲁⲛ πόνος;
Mor 55 66 S fish on hook ⲉϥϯ ϫ. ⲉϥϯ (ⲉⲡⲉⲓ)ⲥⲁ ⲙⲛⲡⲁⲓ yet is the more entangled.

B *sew*, by drawing, stretching thread SA²(cf ϣⲱⲗⲕ): Ge 3 7 (cit ShA 2 47) ⲁⲩϫ. ⲛⲣⲉⲛϭⲱⲃⲉ (var & B
ⲧⲱⲣⲡ) ῥάπτειν, Jo 19 23 A² ϫⲁⲗⲉϭ (SB do) ἄρραφος;
ShC 42 109 ⲛⲥⲉϫⲟⲗⲕⲥ ⲉⲩϭⲟⲓⲧⲉ ⲙⲡⲗϭⲉ = Lu 5 36
ⲧⲱⲣⲡ ἐπιβάλλειν; ShA 2 349 among crafts ⲡⲉϥⲡ ϩⲱⲃ
ⲉϭⲟⲓⲧⲉ ϣⲁⲣⲁⲓ ⲉⲡⲉⲧϫⲱⲗ[ⲕ, Sh(Besa)Z 506 among
crafts ⲡⲉⲧϫⲉⲗⲕ ϩⲟⲉⲓⲧⲉ, ShP 130⁴ 157 ⲥⲟⲩⲣⲉ ⲛϫⲉⲗϭ
ⲧⲟⲟⲩⲉ, Mor 51 38 tailors ϫ. ⲛⲛⲉⲧⲁⲙⲡⲁϩⲉ, ShP 131⁴ 111

among weaving tools ⲕⲗⲁⲗ ⲛ̄ϫⲟⲗⲕⲟⲩ; as nn: ShP 130⁵ 19 garment wrought by needle ⲉⲣⲉⲡⲉϥϫ. ⲟⲩⲟⲛϩ ⲉⲃⲟⲗ ϩⲓⲱⲱϥ ⲛ̄ϩⲣⲏⲧϥ ⲙⲁ ⲙⲁ; ⲅ ⲉϩⲟⲩⲛ ⲉ-: ShP 130⁵ 49 ill-woven garments ⲡⲉⲧⲛⲁⲣ ϩⲛⲁϥ ⲛ̄ϫⲟⲗⲕⲟⲩ ⲉϥ. ⲉⲡⲉⲅⲉⲣⲏ ⲙ̄ⲡϥ̄ϭⲙ̄ ϭⲟⲙ, ib 95 ϩⲉⲡⲧⲟⲉⲓⲥ ⲛ̄ϣⲣⲱ [ⲉⲧ]ϫ.† ⲉϥ. ⲉⲣⲟⲟⲩ.

ϫⲱⲗⲕ S(rare)B, ϭ., ϫⲟⲗⲕⲥ, ϫⲟⲗⲕ† B, ⲣ ⲥ ϫⲁⲗⲕ- A², be submerged, overwhelmed: Jos 3 15 S ϩⲱⲣⲡ ϫ. (B tr ϫ. ⲱⲙⲥ) βάπτεσθαι; Jer 28 39 καροῦσθαι; DeV 2 281 great storm ϩⲱⲥⲧⲉ ⲛ̄ⲧⲉϥϫ.; tr: Is 66 12 (S ⲥⲱⲕ) ἐπικλύζειν, Ps 77 20 ϭ. (S do), Dan 11 26 κατακλ.; EW 126 ὑποβρύχιος γίνεσθαι; Ps 21 17 (S ⲱϭⲧ) ὀρύσσειν. With following prep or advb. ⲅ ϩⲛ-, ϩⲉⲛ-: Ps 67 24 S(B ϭⲱϫ) βάπ. ἐν; Mt 18 6 (cit Va 57 262, var ⲱⲙⲥ) καταποντίζεσθαι ἐν; Sa 5 7 (var ϭ., S Gk diff); BMis 149 S ϫ. ϩⲙ̄ⲡⲓⲉⲣⲟ, AM 211 ⲛ̄ⲧⲁϫⲟⲗⲕ(ⲕ) ϩⲉⲛⲡⲓⲡⲉⲗⲁⲧⲟⲥ, C 89 137 ship ϭ. ϩⲉⲛ-ϥⲓⲟⲙ; ⲅ ⲉⲡⲉⲥⲏⲧ: MG 25 345 ⲉϥϫ.† ⲉ. ⲉϥⲛⲟⲩϥ ⲉⲡϣⲱⲓ=Z 316 S ⲱⲙⲥ ⲕⲁⲧⲁⲡ.; CaiEuch 466 ϩⲙⲉⲧⲁⲥⲑⲉⲛⲏⲥ ⲟⲩⲟϩ ⲉⲧϫ.† ⲉ. ⲛ̄ⲧⲉ ⲡⲉⲛⲡⲗⲁⲥⲙⲁ κάτω βρῖθος; ⲅ ⲉϩⲣⲏⲓ: 2 Pet 3 6 (S ⲱⲙⲥ) κατακλ.; Lu 4 29 (S ⲛⲟⲩϫⲉ ⲉⲃⲟⲗ ⲛ̄ϩⲟϭⲧⲡ) κατακρημνίζειν; MG 25 18 ϫⲟⲗⲕϥ ⲉϭ. (sic l) ϣⲁⲧⲉϥⲡⲁⲣⲃⲓ ⲕⲁⲧⲁⲡ.

ⲣ ⲅ: ManiH 12 ⲛ̄ϫⲁⲗⲕⲙⲥⲉ divers that bring up pearls, Mani 1 we thy pearls, thou ⲛ̄ⲡϫ. [ⲙⲥⲉ ⲉⲧ]ⲁⲧ-ϭⲛ ⲁϩⲣⲏⲓ from sea.

ϫⲗⲁⲕ v ϫⲱⲗⲕ 1° A s f.

ϫⲉⲗⲕⲉⲥ, -ⲛⲥ B nn as pl, bugs: K 173 ⲛⲓϫ. بقّ.

ϫⲟⲗⲕⲥ v ϫⲱⲗⲕ 1° A s f.

ϫⲁⲗⲓⲗ B v ϭⲁⲗⲓⲗ.

ϫⲗⲗⲉ S nn f, meaning unknown: CO 459 among metal objects ⲥⲛⲧⲉ ⲛ̄ϫ., OstrUnivCollLondon ⲙⲁⲣ-ⲕⲗⲗⲉ (v ? p 182 a supra) ⲛ̄ϫ. (var CO 466 om).

ϫⲗⲗⲉ SA v ϫⲱⲗⲉ 1° s f.

ϫⲓⲗⲗⲉⲓ F nn, shield: Cant 4 4 ϣⲁ ⲛ̄ϫ. ⲉϣⲓ (S= Gk) θυρεός. Cf ϭⲗ.

ϫⲁⲗⲟ (?) S vb tr (caus), meaning unknown, ⲅ ? ⲉⲃⲟⲗ: Ep 458]ⲉⲛⲁϩⲱⲃ ϣⲁⲅ̄ϫⲁⲗⲁⲗⲱⲓ ⲉⲃⲟⲗ ϫⲉ(ⲡ)-ⲡⲉⲩϯ ⲗⲁⲁⲩ ⲛ̄ⲡⲕ[ⲁ.

ϫⲉⲗⲗⲏⲥ vb v ϫⲱⲗϩⲥ.

ϫⲓⲗⲗⲉⲥ¹, -ⲛⲥ², ϫⲉⲗⲗⲏⲥ³, ⲕⲉⲗ.⁴, ⲭⲉⲗⲗⲉⲥ⁵ (ⲗ ϫ.) S nn m, box, wallet (cf ϫⲱⲱⲗⲉ gather Dévaud): 1 Kg 17 40¹(varr²³, B ⲕⲁⲧⲟⲥ) κάδιον (var πήρα); cit P 44 120⁴=43 127⁵ زبيل, cit PO 4 582².

ϫⲁⲗⲓⲙ B nn as pl, chickens: K 169 ⲛⲓϫ.(sic), Bodl 325 155 -ⲙ فراريج; Lab 2 143 ⲥⲙⲁϩ ⲛ̄ϫ. (whence ?).

ϫⲱⲗⲙⲉ, -ⲣⲙ S, ϫⲱⲗⲙⲉ A², ϭⲱⲗⲉⲙ B (nn), ϫⲟⲗⲙ†, -ⲣⲙ† S, ϫⲁ.† Sf, ϫⲁⲗⲙⲉ† A² vb intr, a make merry, or sim: Tri 368 ⲛ̄ⲧⲏϫ. ⲛ̄ⲧⲛⲉⲩϥⲣⲁⲡⲉ نتنعّم, P 44 122 ϩⲟⲥⲉ ⲉϩⲟⲅⲉ ϫ. استنشاق (as if ϣⲱⲗⲙ), وتفرح, R 1 3 36 =RylSuppl 20 Eudoxia would have audience ⲙ̄ⲡⲁⲧⲉⲡⲡⲁⲗⲁⲧⲓⲟⲛ ϫ.; ϫ. ⲉϩⲟⲩⲛ: BKU 1 275 ⲥⲟⲩⲣⲟⲩⲥ ⲙⲡⲓⲥⲁⲕ ⲉⲩⲛⲁ ⲉ. (sic) ⲛ̄ⲥⲉϫⲓ ⲥϭⲓⲙⲉ make (marriage) festival (?).

b be implicated, involved (same ?, cf ϭⲗⲟⲙⲗⲙ): Mani K 10 A² husbandman ϣⲁϥϫ. ϫⲛ̄ⲡⲧⲁⲣⲭ ⲛ̄ⲡ-[ⲭⲟ] ⲛ̄ⲟⲩϩⲣⲉ; ⲅ ⲉ-: Mor 28 83 Sf heard not ⲉⲃⲟⲗ ϫⲉⲡⲉϥϫ.† ⲡⲉ ⲉⲡⲉⲡⲗⲁⲕⲙⲁ (? πλέγμα) ⲙⲡⲙⲁ ⲛ̄ⲥⲱ (cf ϫⲟⲗⲙⲉⲥ), PapAntinoe penes HT ⲧⲓϫ.† ⲉⲡⲛⲟⲩϥ ⲉϫⲓ-ⲧⲟⲩ, Mani 2 A² ⲉⲩϫ.† ⲁ̄ⲡⲣⲟⲥⲫⲟⲣⲁ ϩⲣⲟⲩⲧⲟⲩⲃⲟ; ⲅ ⲙⲛ-: HM 1 130 ⲁⲓϫ. ⲙⲡⲟⲩⲥⲟⲡ ⲁⲩⲱ ⲁⲓⲕⲁⲁⲥ ϩⲙ̄ⲡⲁϩⲏⲧ ⲉⲧⲙⲧⲣⲁⲃⲱⲗ ⲛⲙⲙⲁϥ (cf ⲙⲟⲩⲣ ⲙⲛ-), Mor 53 35 ϩⲁⲣⲉϩ ⲉⲣⲟⲕ ⲉϫⲱⲣⲙ (l-ⲗⲙ) ⲛ̄ⲡⲣⲱⲙⲉ=TstAbr 232 B ϭⲓ ⲛⲉⲙ-, ST 282 let him fill basin with water ϫⲉⲉⲓϫ.† ⲙⲛ..ϩⲙⲟⲟⲥ; ⲅ ϩⲛ-: BM 217 238 ⲛ̄ⲧ-ⲟⲩⲱϣ ⲁⲡ ⲉⲁⲙⲉⲗⲉⲓ ⲏ ⲉⲧⲣⲉⲕ. ϩⲛⲣⲁϩ ⲙⲙⲉⲉⲅⲉ, Mor 47 209 he observed that ⲥⲉϫ.† ⲧⲏⲣⲟⲩ ϩⲙ̄ⲡⲕⲱϩⲧ all intent upon the fire, Ann 8 95 ⲉⲓϫⲟⲣⲙ ϩⲛ̄ⲛⲣⲟⲟⲩϣ ⲙⲡⲉⲓⲃⲓⲟⲥ; tr: Ep 297 tell not brethren that I am sick ⲛ̄ⲧϫ. ⲡⲉⲩϩⲏⲧ (or ? ϫⲱⲗ).

—— nn m SB(rare), a festivity, dissipation: Sh P 130³ 2 did I not fear our appetites ⲡⲉⲛⲛⲁϥⲓ ⲡⲉⲓϣⲓ ⲙⲙⲁⲅⲡⲉ ⲡⲧⲉⲛⲉⲓⲛⲉϫ. ⲧⲏⲣⲟⲩ ϥⲓ ⲙⲙⲁⲩ ϫⲉϣⲓ, CA 113 ϣⲁⲡ]ⲧⲉⲡϫ. ⲟⲩ[ⲱ=ib ⲟⲓ ⲡⲓϭ. حتّى ينقضى, ib ⲉⲣⲥⲁ ⲁⲩⲟ (var om) ϭ., P 129¹⁴ 116 ⲛ̄ϫ. opp ⲡⲉⲥϭⲣⲁϩⲧ, Mor 28 189 never desired ⲛ̄ϫ. ⲙ̄ⲡⲉⲓⲕⲟⲥⲙⲟⲥ; **b** distraction, care: BMOr 7561 71 ⲛ̄ϫ. ⲧⲏ[ⲣϥ ⲙ̄ⲡ]ⲥⲁⲧⲁⲛⲁⲥ, Va 61 96 B planteth vines &c ϩⲱⲥⲧⲉ ⲉϥⲓⲣⲓ ⲛ̄ⲣⲁⲛⲓϣϯ ⲛ̄ϭ.=Mor 25 14 ⲛⲟϭ ⲛ̄ⲭⲟⲣ-ⲙⲉⲥ = P 131³ 85 S ⲛⲟϭ ⲛ̄ϩⲏⲅⲉ, Ming 295 ⲣ ⲭⲣⲓⲁ ⲙⲡⲥⲉⲉⲡⲉ ⲛ̄ϫ. ⲉⲡⲥⲟⲃⲧⲉ ⲛ̄ⲧⲧⲉⲭⲛⲏ τὸ ἔργον προσθεῖναι δεῖ.

ϫⲟⲗⲙ(ⲉ)ⲥ, ϫⲟⲣ. S nn, cares, distractions: TT 27 ⲡⲥⲟⲗⲥⲗ ⲛ̄ⲛⲁⲅⲟⲣⲁ ⲙⲛ̄ϫ. ⲛⲙⲙⲁ ⲛⲥⲱ, BMar 80 what profit ⲡⲉⲓϫ. ⲙ̄ⲡⲛⲉⲓϩⲓⲥⲉ ⲧⲏⲣⲟⲩ ?, P 130⁵ 121 ϣⲧⲟⲣⲧⲣ ϩⲓϫ. ⲛ̄ⲧⲉ ⲡⲓⲃⲓⲟⲥ, BodlCopt g 1 ⲙⲛ̄ϩⲉⲡ ⲑⲉ ⲛ̄ⲡⲙⲉⲉⲩⲉ ⲙⲡⲡⲉ ⲛ̄ϩⲏⲧⲟⲩ (sc riches) ⲉⲧⲃⲉⲛⲉⲩϫ.; ϫⲟⲣ. v Mor 25 above.

ϫⲱⲗⲙ Sf v ϫⲱⲣⲙ.

ϫⲗⲱⲙ¹, ϫⲗⲱⲃ², -ϥ³ S nn m, brazier: Lev 6 39¹ (B=Gk) ἐσχάρα; ShC 73 137 ⲡⲁⲥⲧϥ...ϩⲓⲛⲉϫ.³ ⲉⲓⲧⲉ ϩⲓⲧⲉⲧⲣⲓⲣ (cf ⲁϣ 2°), R 1 5 36 as tortures ⲛⲉϫ.² ⲙ̄ⲛⲛ-ⲗⲁⲕⲏⲧ. Cf ϭⲣⲱⲡ & ? χλουβοκεραμεύς (POxy 1913).

ϫⲓⲗⲙⲁ F nn, meaning unknown, epithet of a garment: AZ 23 41 ⲁⲗϫⲁⲥ ⲛ̄ⲡⲉⲡⲛⲏⲧⲓ (v ⲛ̄ϭⲉ), ⲁⲗⲭⲁⲥ ⲛ̄ϫ. Or ? cf جلّة shorn wool (Grohmann).

ϫⲓⲗⲙⲓⲛ or -ⲙⲓ *v* ϭⲉⲗⲙⲁⲓ.

ϫⲟⲗⲙⲉⲥ *v* ϫⲱⲗⲙ *sf*.

ϫⲗⲁⲡ *F* *v* ϫⲣⲟⲡ.

ϫⲉⲗⲉⲡⲟⲗ *F* *v* ϫⲉⲛⲉⲡⲱⲣ.

ϫⲟⲗ(ⲉ)ⲥ *v* ϫⲱⲗϩ 2° (ϫⲟⲗϩⲉⲥ).

ϫⲟⲟⲗⲉⲥ *S*, ϫⲁ(ⲁ)ⲗⲉⲥ *A*, ϫⲟⲗⲓ *B*(rare), [ϫⲁⲁ]ⲗⲓ *F* nn f, *moth*: Job 32 22 (*B* ϩⲟⲗⲓ), Pro 14 30 *SA*, Mt 6 19 *SF*(*B*=βρῶσις), Lu 12 33 (var & *B* ϩ.) σής, P 44 57 ⲥⲏⲥ· ⲧϩⲟⲟⲗⲉ· ⲧϣⲟⲗⲉⲥ سوس; Is 14 11 (*B* do) σῆψις, cit ShA 1 373 ⲡϫ. (*sic*); Hab 3 16 *A*(*B* diff) *putredo*; K 350 *B* ϯϫ. الآكلة (which Tri 397 *S*=ϩⲟⲟⲗⲉ); ShWess 9 172 ⲑⲟⲟⲗⲉ ⲙⲛⲧϣⲟⲟⲗⲉⲥ, Sh(?)Mor 54 104 ⲧϫ. ⲙⲛⲡⲁⲡⲟⲩⲓ (*v* ϩⲁⲃⲟⲩⲉⲓ) ⲧⲁⲕⲟⲟⲩ, MIF 9 44 of Judas ⲁⲩϩⲟⲃⲥϥ ⲛⲟⲩϫ.; ⲣ ϫ., *be moth-eaten*, *rotten*: Jos 9 11 βιβρώσκειν; Job 27 18 (*B* ϣⲱⲡⲓ ⲙⲫⲣⲏϯ ⲛϩⲁⲛϩ.) ἀποβαίνειν; neg: Ex 26 26 (*B* ⲁⲧⲉⲣ ϩ.), Is 40 20 (*B* do) ἄσηπτος; BHom 123 corpses ⲉⲛⲧⲁⲩⲣ., R 1 4 39 *v* ⲕⲛⲭ, TillOster 13 *A* ⲣ. ϩⲛⲛⲕⲉⲉⲥ (*cf* Pro 14 above).

ϫⲁⲗⲁⲩ *S*: BKU 1 22 ⲧⲁⲧⲥ ⲉⲥⲕⲱⲧⲉ ⲁⲡⲣⲏ ⲉϫ. ⲕⲱⲧⲉ ⲁⲡⲟϩ, for ? ⲧϣⲁⲗⲁⲩ (ϣⲁⲗⲟⲟⲩ).

ϫⲁⲗⲁⲩϫ *SF* *v* ϭⲁⲗⲟϫ.

ϫⲗⲱϥ *v* ϫⲗⲱⲙ.

ϫⲉⲗϥⲁⲩ *B* *v* ϭⲗⲃⲟⲟⲩ.

ϫⲱⲗϩ *SA*², -ⲉϩ *S*(once)*F*, ϫⲗϩ-, ϫⲟⲗϩ⸗ *S*, ϫⲁ. *A* *A*², ϫⲁⲗ(ⲉ)ϩ† *F* vb tr, *cut*, *prune*: Lev 25 3 ϫⲗϩ (var ϫⲱⲱⲗⲉ, *B* ϣⲱⲧ) τέμνειν, Gloss 382 ⲡⲉⲧϫⲱⲗⲉϩ ϭⲱⲩ[ⲉ] κλαδοτομεῖν; Cl 23 4 *A* ϫⲁⲗϩⲥ (*sc* vine) φυλλορροεῖν; GMir 261 cypress ⲙⲛⲡⲁⲩ ⲡⲧⲁⲩϫⲟⲗϩϥ (*v* ϫⲱⲱⲗⲉ tr), BMar 82 ⲛⲥⲉϫⲟⲗϩⲕ like sour grapes, ClPr 47 5 vine ⲉⲧⲟⲩϫ. ⲙⲡⲉϥⲥⲱⲙⲁ, ManiK 158 *A*² ⲉⲩⲛⲁϫ. ⲛϩⲏⲧϥ ⲙⲡⲟⲩⲁⲓⲛⲉ ⲛⲥⲉⲥⲁϣⲧϥ; intr *F*: Eccl 6 2† (or *v* ϭⲣⲱϩ, *S* ϣⲱⲱⲧ), *ib* 10 3 (*sic l* ?, *S* do) ὑστερεῖν, *ib* 1 15† (*S* do) -ημα; *ib* 10 18 (*S* diff) στάζειν; c ⲛ-, *with*: *ib* 9 8 *F*]ⲧⲉⲕⲁⲡⲏ ϫ. ⲛⲛ[ⲏϩ ὑσ.; as nn m: Job 15 32 (*B* ϣⲁⲧϣⲉ) τομή, Jer 11 16 (ShMIF 23 152, *B* ⲕⲱⲣϫ) περιτομή, ShC 42 161 ⲡⲥⲏⲩ ⲙⲡϫ. of vineyard.

ϫⲱⲗϩ *SAB*, -ⲗⲁϩ, -ⲣⲁϩ *S*, ϭⲱⲗϩ *B*, ϫⲁⲗⲉϩ *F*, ϫⲉⲗⲉϩ- *S*, ϫⲟⲗϩ⸗ *SB*, ϫⲁⲗϩ⸗ *A*² vb intr, *draw*, *scoop* water, wine (*cf* دلو IgR, or ? دلى): BMar 91 *S* ⲉϥϫ. ⲉϥⲡⲱⲛϭ ⲛⲥⲁⲧⲡⲩⲅⲏ, DeV 2 69 *B* ⲉϥⲙⲁϩ ⲙⲱⲟⲩ ϧⲉⲛ ⲟⲩⲡⲩⲅⲏ ... ⲁϥϣⲁⲛϫ.; tr: ShA 2 48 *S* sailors ⲡⲣⲟⲥⲉϫⲉ ⲉϫ. ⲏ ⲉⲡⲱⲛϭ ⲉⲃⲟⲗ ⲙⲙⲟⲟⲩ, C 89 195 *B* (grapes) to be trodden ⲛⲧⲉⲛϭ. ⲙⲡⲟⲩⲏⲣⲡ, Va 61 213 *B* ⲟⲩⲡⲩⲅⲏ ... ϫⲟⲗϩⲥ; c ϩⲛ-: Hag 2 17 *SA*(*B* ⲫⲱⲛⲕ) ἐξαντλεῖν; c ϩⲓϫⲛ-: Mor 32 22 *S* in cauldron ⲁϥϫⲉⲗⲉϩ ⲙⲟⲟⲩ ϩⲓϫⲱϥ; c ⲉⲃⲟⲗ: BMis 64 *S* ϫ. ⲛⲟⲩⲙⲟⲟⲩ ⲉⲃ. ϩⲛⲟⲩⲡⲩⲅⲏ (var Mor 33 129 = FR 26 ⲡⲱⲛϭ), *ib* ϩⲓ ⲧⲟⲟⲧϥ ⲉϫ. ⲉⲃ. (var *llc* ϣⲓⲕⲉ), BM 1130 *S* ϫ. ⲡⲏⲣⲡ ⲉⲃ., *ib* 1174 *S* about wine-jars (?)]ⲕⲱⲧⲟⲩ ⲱϥⲧⲟⲩ ϫⲟⲗϩⲟⲩ (ⲉ)ⲃ. ... ⲧⲟⲟⲃⲟⲩ, *ib* 1036 wine from ⲡⲕⲁϫⲟⲩⲥ ⲉⲕⲁϫⲱⲣⲁϩ ⲉⲃ. ⲉⲙⲟⲃ ϩⲓϫⲡⲡⲉⲕⲓⲟⲙ, Ryl 409 *S* ϫⲱⲗⲁϩ ⲡⲙⲟⲟⲩ ⲉⲃ., TillOster 10 *A* ϫ. ⲁⲃ. ⲥⲉⲛⲉⲧⲡⲕⲁⲣⲡⲟⲥ *draw from store of wine*, ManiK 111 *A*² ⲁϥⲡⲁⲛⲕⲟⲩ ⲁϥϫⲁⲗϩⲟⲩ ⲁⲃ. ⲙⲡⲓⲕⲁϩ, BM 636 *F* ϫ. ⲡⲏⲣⲉⲡ ⲉⲃ.; c ⲉⲡϣⲱⲓ: Va 68 169 *B* ϫ. ⲉ. ⲛⲛⲓⲙⲱⲟⲩ ἐπαντ.

ϫⲟⲗϩ(ⲉ)ⲥ, ϫⲟⲗ(ⲉ)ⲥ *S* nn f, *vessel*, *tube for pouring*: Nu 4 9 (*B* Va om), Zech 4 2 (var -ⲗⲥ, *A* ϩⲗⲁⲡ, *B* ⲗⲁϧⲉⲙ) ἐπαρυστρίς; Ex 25 31 -ⲗⲉⲥ (P 44 104, *B*=Gk) καυλός فتيلة.

ϫⲱⲗϩ, ϫⲟⲗϩ⸗, ϫⲟⲗϩ† *B* vb tr, *swathe*, *clothe*, *cover* (*SA* mostly ϭⲱⲱⲗⲉ), qual: Ps 44 10 περιβάλλεσθαι; Ez 41 26 κρυπτός. With following preposition. c ⲉ-: Deu 22 12 (*S* ϯ ϩⲓ-) περιβ. ἐν, Si 23 12† ἀντιπ. dat; Is 11 5† (*S* diff) εἰλεῖν acc; c ⲛ-, *with*, *in*: Ge 38 14, Ez 16 10 περιβ. dat, *ib* 27 7, Jon 3 6, Jo 19 2 (*SA*² ϯ ϩⲓ-), Ap 12 1†, Va 57 49 ⲉϥϫ.† ⲛϩⲁⲛⲫⲉⲗϫⲓ περιβ. acc, Ps 103 2 ἀναβ. acc; *ib* 108 18 (*S* ϯ ϩⲓ-) ἐνδύειν acc, C 86 312 ϯⲥⲩⲛϫⲟⲛⲓⲟⲛ ... ⲉⲥϫ.† ⲙⲙⲟϥ, DeV 1 47 ⲉϥϫ.† ⲛϯⲥⲧⲟⲗⲏ, Va 57 168 ⲁϥϫⲟⲗϩϥ ⲙⲡⲓϣⲁⲣ; c ϧⲉⲛ-: Ps 44 14 περιβ. ἐν; Ez 16 4 (*S* ⲥⲟⲩⲗⲱⲗ⸗) σπαργανοῦν ἐν; FR 124 ϥϫ.† ϧⲉⲛⲡⲱⲟⲩ; as nn (adj): Ps 103 6 ϩⲃⲱⲥ ⲛϫ., Is 59 17 do (*S* ⲣϣⲱⲛ) περιβόλαιον.

ϫⲓⲛϫ., *clothing*, *vestments*: HL 91 ⲡϫ. ⲛⲧⲉ ⲛⲟⲩϩⲃⲱⲥ στολισμός; MIE 2 418 ⲡⲁϫ. ⲛⲧⲉ ⲡⲁϣⲉⲙϣⲓ = BAp 125 *S* ϭⲟⲟⲗⲉⲥ = PO 22 476 مزرة (مئزر).

ϫⲟⲗϩϥ nn m, *grating*, *lattice*: Ex 37 (Lag p 225 8) ⲡⲓϫ. ⲛϩⲟⲙⲧ παράθεμα غطاء, *ib* 38 (*ib* p 226 11) do.

(ϫⲗⲁϩ), ϫⲟⲗϩ† *S* vb qual, *be smallest*, *least*: Mt 2 6 (*B* ⲕⲟⲩϫⲓ) ἐλάχιστος εἶναι, Tri 483 on Mic 5 2 ⲛⲧⲉϫ. ⲟⲩϫⲉ ⲥⲟⲃⲕ ⲁⲛ حقيرة, صغيرة.

ϫⲗⲁϩⲙⲉⲥ *S* nn, meaning unknown: CO 466 among *varia* = dupl Univ Coll London.

ϫⲟⲗϩⲉⲥ *v* ϫⲱⲗϩ 2°.

ϫⲱⲗϩⲥ *S* vb intr, *be exhausted* (?): 2 Kg 4 4 ⲉⲁϥ(*sc.* the child)ϫ. ⲁϥϩⲉ ἀναχωρεῖν. But -ⲥ ? suff, *sc* ⲧⲙⲟⲟⲛⲉ.

ϫ(ⲉ)ⲗϩⲏⲥ, ϫⲗϩⲥ, ϫⲉⲗⲗⲏⲥ *S* vb, *be exhausted*, *pant*: Si 34 20 (var -ϩⲥ) ἀσθμαίνειν (P 44 119 لهث); Sa 11 19 ⲗϩⲏⲥ (var ⲗϩⲏⲙ) φυσᾶν; C 99 159 ⲑⲉ ⲉⲧⲟⲩϫ. ⲙⲙⲟⲥ from much torturing = C 89 98 *B* ϧⲟⲥⲓ = Va 172 57 ϯ, P 44 88 ⲉϥϫ. ϯ, انبهر, Mor 25 12 Dives in hell ϫⲉⲗⲗⲏⲥ ϩⲁⲡⲉⲓⲃⲉ (var P 131³ 84 ⲁϣ ⲁϩⲟⲙ) = Va 61 94 *B* ⲙⲟⲕϩ; as nn m, *exhaustion*, *panting*: BM 332 Nestorius dying ϩⲛⲟⲩⲛⲟϭ ⲛⲧⲁⲗⲁⲓⲡⲱⲣⲓⲁ ⲙⲛⲟⲩϫ., Aeg 27 sim ⲧϩⲉⲗϩⲓⲗⲉ ⲙⲛⲡϫ. ⲧⲱⲟⲩⲛ ⲉϫⲱϥ, Miss 4

757 of pursuing dogs ⲁⲓⲥⲱⲧⲙ ⲉⲡⲉⲩⲭ. as they gnashed teeth, BAp 109 sim ⲛⲁϣⲁⲓ ⲙⲡⲉⲩⲭ.

ⲉⲗⲟⲏⲥ B nn (same ?, cf Sa 11 above): Va 58 182 overfull belly ⲉϭⲣⲓ ⲉ. διαρρήγνυσθαι, στένειν.

ⲭⲗⲁϭⲧⲥ S nn f, meaning uncertain: Z 298 ⲉⲓⲣⲏⲟⲩⲭ. ⲉⲥϣⲟⲕⲣ ϣⲁⲡⲁⲙⲟⲧⲉ deep pit, vessel or sim.

ⲭⲟⲗⲣϥ v ⲭⲱⲗⲣ 3°.

ⲭⲱⲗⲭ SA²B v ϭⲱⲗⲭ.

ⲭⲉⲗⲭⲟⲩ B v ϭⲓⲛϭⲗⲱ.

ⲭⲁⲗϫⲉⲗ F v ⲭⲟⲣⲭⲣ.

ⲭⲉⲗϫⲉⲗ S nn, wantonness (?): Lammayer 39 woman going to church ⲕⲟⲥⲙⲉⲓ ⲙⲙⲟⲥ ⲣⲛⲟⲩⲭ. (varr om). Cf ? ϫⲏⲣ.

ⲭⲉⲗϫⲉⲗ B v ϭⲟⲗϭⲉⲗ.

ⲭⲉⲗϫⲓⲗ S nn, meaning unknown: Bodl (P) e 51 ⲙⲁⲣ[ⲉ]ϥϭⲱⲕⲉⲧϥ (? -ⲟϭⲧⲉϥ) ⲉⲧⲡⲟϭⲉ ⲭ. ϭⲩϣⲡⲥⲉϭⲱⲥ (? ϣⲓⲡⲉ ⲡⲥⲱϭ). Cf ? ϭⲉⲗϭⲓⲗ (v ⲕⲁⲗⲕⲓⲗ).

ⲭⲏⲗϫⲉⲗ F v ϫⲏⲣ (ⲭⲣϫⲣⲉ).

ⲭⲟⲗϫⲗ S, ⲭⲁⲗϫⲗⲉ A, -ϫⲗ A², ⲭⲁⲗϫⲉⲗ S/F (nn), ⲭ(ⲉ)ⲗϫⲗ- S, ⲭⲱⲗϫⲗ- A, ϫⲗϫⲱⲗⲝ, ⲭⲗϫⲱⲗ† S vb tr, surround with hedge: BMOr 8811 242 trees enclosed in walls ⲁⲩⲱ ϣⲁϥϫⲗϫⲱⲗⲟⲩ, RNC 76 shoot arrows into body & ⲭⲗϫⲱⲗϥ from head to foot; ⲥ ⲛ-, with: Si 28 26 περιφράσσειν; ShBM 194 1 ⲉⲩⲕⲱⲛⲥ ⲙⲡⲣⲱⲙⲉ… ⲉⲩⲭ. ⲙⲙⲟϥ ⲡⲥⲟⲧⲉ, HM 1 118 martyrs ⲭⲉⲗⲭⲉⲗ ⲡⲉⲩⲥⲱⲙⲁ ⲧⲏⲣϥ ⲡⲥⲟⲧⲉ, BMar 21 irons put on hands & feet ⲁϥⲭⲣⲭⲱⲗϥ ⲧⲏⲣϥ ⲙⲡⲉⲓⲡⲉ; ⲥ ⲣⲛ-: Hos 2 6 S (ShA 2 336) A ⲭⲱⲗϫⲗ- (B ϭⲗⲟ) ϥⲣ.; Mor 37 165 ⲉⲣⲉⲣⲉⲛⲃⲟⲩⲣⲉ ⲭ.† ⲣⲓⲡⲉⲣⲛⲃϭ (v ⲧⲁⲥⲣ).

—— nn m SAA²F, hedge: Nu 22 24 (B ⲥⲟⲃⲧ), Job 38 31 (var ⲕⲧⲟ, B = Gk), Pro 24 46 SA, Eccl 10 8 F ⲭⲁⲗϫ(ⲉⲗ, S ϫⲟⲉ), Is 5 2 (B ϭⲗⲟ), Eph 2 14 (B ⲑⲱⲙ) φραγμός; Is 31 9 F (S ϣⲗⲣ, B ϭ.) χάραξ; P 46 169 ⲡⲭ. سيل; ShViK 9099 ⲁⲡⲧⲓ ⲧⲣⲉⲩⲙⲉϣⲧ ⲡⲭ. ⲙⲙⲏⲛⲉ, Mor 32 7 S/ sitting in garden ⲉϥϩⲉⲱⲣⲉⲓ ⲙⲡⲉⲩⲭ., ⲙⲁⲛⲓK 110 A² ⲡⲁϭ ⲡⲭ. ⲙⲡⲣⲏⲥⲃⲧⲉⲣⲉ, BMar 236 ⲡⲭ. of Paradise, PBad 5 406 S/ Eve ⲥⲉⲛⲉⲣⲟⲩⲛ ⲉⲡⲭ.

ⲭⲟⲗϫ(ⲉ)ⲗ S, ϫⲁ. S/, ϫⲗϫⲗ-, ϫⲗϫⲱⲗⲝ S, ⲭⲉⲗ B (once) vb, intr, let drip, drip: BKU 1 21 vo S/ recipe ⲛⲕⲉϣⲧ(ϥ) ⲉϩⲣⲁⲓ ϣⲁⲛⲧⲉϥⲭ.; tr, ShViK 9764 95 spread herbs ⲉⲧⲣⲉⲩϫⲗϫⲗ ⲡⲉⲩⲙⲟⲟⲩ; ⲥ ⲉϫⲛ-: Lev 1 15 (B ⲧⲉⲗⲧⲉⲗ ⲥⲁⲧⲉⲛ-) στραγγίζειν πρός, ib 5 9 SB (ⲉϩⲣⲏⲓ sic ⲉⲭ.) καταϭ. ἐπί; 3 Kg 22 35 ἀποχύνειν εἰς; Mor 46 13 ⲉⲣⲉⲡⲉϥⲥⲛⲟϥ ⲭ. ⲉ. ⲡⲕⲁϩ; ⲥ ⲉⲃⲟⲗ ⲣⲛ-: BMar 41 hanged head downward till blood ⲭ. ⲉⲃ. ⲣⲛⲣⲱϥ. Cf ϭⲟⲗϭⲗ.

ⲭⲙ- A v ⲭⲉⲡⲉⲡⲱⲣ.

ⲭⲟⲙ B nn f, cauldron, basin: Ps 59 10 (S = Gk) λέβης, though Ar ابّ (no var) as if ⲭ. strength.

ⲭⲟⲙ B, ⲭⲁⲙ F v ϭⲟⲙ.

ⲭⲱⲙ SAA²F, ⲭⲱⲱⲙⲉ S (once), ⲭⲱⲙⲉ, ⲭⲙ- A² nn m, generation (B mostly ⲭⲱⲟⲩ): Nu 9 10 (B = Gk), Ps 48 19, Is 34 10 SF, Joel 3 20 SA, Ac 14 16 (var ⲭⲱⲙⲉ, B do) γενεά; ⲭⲓⲛ(ⲟⲩ)ⲭ. ϣⲁ(ⲟⲩ)ⲭ.: Ps 9 26 ἀπὸ γ. εἰς γ., Pro 27 24 SA ἐκ γ. εἰς γ., Lu 1 50 εἰς γ. καὶ γ.; ⲉⲩⲭ. ⲡⲛⲭ.: Ps 105 31 εἰς γ. καὶ γ.; ⲡⲣⲉⲡⲭ. ⲡⲭ.: Joel 2 2 SA εἰϭ. γ. γενεῶν; ⲙⲡⲭ. ⲡⲭ. A², from g. to g.: ⲙⲁⲛⲓH 14 ⲧⲉⲟⲩⲟ…ⲙⲡⲭ. ⲡⲭ. ⲭⲡⲡⲁϫⲁⲙ; ϣⲁϫⲉ ⲡⲭ. (B ⲭⲱⲟⲩ ⲡⲥⲁⲭⲓ): 1 Tim 1 4, Tit 3 9 ϣⲭⲭ. (var ϣⲭ.) γενεαλογία; ⲁⲧⲥⲁϫⲓ ⲉⲭ. BF: He 7 3 (S as Gk) ἀγενεαλόγητος; ⲭⲙ- A²: ⲙⲁⲛⲓH 28 ⲡⲓⲭⲙⲡⲣⲱⲙⲉ, ib K 55 ⲣ ⲣⲏⲭⲙⲡⲣⲱⲙⲉ.

ⲭⲱⲙ A² vb, meaning uncertain: ⲙⲁⲛⲓP 4 ⲁⲩⲭ. ⲁⲡⲣⲱⲃ.

ⲭⲱⲙ SB nn m, meaning uncertain, in place-name ⲡⲭ. ⲡⲧⲕⲉⲙⲏⲛ (TMina Epima 30 S = C 43 150 B), var ⲧϭⲱⲙ S ⲡϭⲱⲙ B. Cf ? ḏm troop, garrison (Mina lc xxx), or for ϭⲱⲙ q v.

ⲭⲱⲙ B v ⲭⲱⲱⲙⲉ.

ⲭⲁⲙⲁⲓ F v ϭⲱⲱⲙⲉ.

ⲭⲁⲙⲏ SA²B nn f, calm: Mt 8 26 SB γαλήνη, Va 58 193 B ⲱⲣϥ ⲡⲭ. γ. βαθεῖα, Si 3 15 S, Mt 16 2 B (no S) εὐδία; Ez 32 14 B (S ϭⲣⲁⲣⲧ) ἡσυχάζειν; ShRE 10 161 S ⲡⲧⲏⲩ ⲙⲡⲛⲭ.; BHom 103 S ⲧⲭ. ⲡⲡⲣⲟⲉⲓⲙ (ALR '96 197 لمـو), BAp 167 S ϯ ⲡⲟⲩⲭ. ⲙⲡⲟⲩϩⲣⲟⲕ ⲙⲡⲥⲱⲙⲁ, Mor 28 191 S ⲙⲡⲉⲣϣⲱⲡⲉ ⲣⲛ ⲟⲩⲁⲙⲉⲗⲓⲁ ⲁⲗⲗⲁ ϯ ⲡⲟⲩⲭ. ⲙⲡϣⲁϫⲉ hearken calmly, ⲙⲁⲛⲓP 157 A² hour when ⲧⲭ. ⲡⲁϣⲱⲡⲉ, BSM 84 B went ϩⲉⲡⲟⲩⲡⲓϣϯ ⲡⲭ. = BMis 174 S ⲛϯⲙⲏ (prob l ⲭ.), TEuch 1 339 B ⲟⲩⲗⲩⲙⲏⲛ ⲡⲭ.

ⲭⲁⲙⲏ fist v ϭⲁⲭⲙⲏ.

ⲭⲓⲙⲓ B v ϭⲓⲛⲉ.

ⲭⲱⲱⲙⲉ SF, ⲭⲱⲙⲉ² SA²F, ⲭⲟⲩⲟⲩⲙⲉ³, ⲭⲟⲩⲙⲉ⁴ A, ⲭⲱⲙ B, ⲭⲱⲱⲙ⁵, ⲭⲱⲙⲓ⁶, ⲭⲟⲟⲙⲉ⁷, ⲭⲟⲙⲉ⁸ F, pl ⲭⲙⲉ AA² & sg as pl, nn m, a sheet, roll of papyrus, written document, book, (rarely parchment, v below): Is 8 1 B (S = Gk), 2 Jo 12 B (S do), Va 58 148 B ϩⲁⲡⲭ. χάρτης, Jer 43 6 SB χαρτίον, ib 4 B (S ⲭ. ⲡⲭ.) χ. βιβλίου; MIE 2 417 B ⲡⲁⲭ. = BAp 123 S χαρ., DeV 2 153 B ⲡⲓⲭ. whereon all recorded = MG 25 425 S ⲭ., ShBMOr 8800 54 S ⲡⲉⲭ. ⲉⲧⲕⲏ ⲉϩⲣⲁⲓ ⲛ ⲡⲭ. ⲉⲧⲉⲧⲛⲱϣ ⲙⲙⲟⲟⲩ, ShMun 115 S ⲡⲱⲱⲛⲉ ⲡⲡⲉⲧⲥⲏϩ ⲣⲛⲡⲉⲭ.…ⲉϩⲣⲁⲓ ⲉⲡⲉⲓⲭ. (of parchment), Mor 41 260

S confession written on ϫ., then ⲁⲩϫⲓ ⲙⲡϫ. & read it, CO 457 *S* ϫ.[2] ⲛϫ., AJSL 46 247 *S* write charm on ⲟⲩϫ. ⲛⲕⲁⲑⲁⲣⲟⲛ, 249 sim ϫ. ⲛⲕⲁⲑⲁⲣⲟⲛ, CMSS 23 *F* apologizes ⲙⲡⲓϭ ϫ. ⲛⲕⲁⲑⲁⲣⲱⲛ (cf CO 97 &c ⲙⲡⲉⲓϣⲛ ϫⲁⲣ. & Arabic A Grohmann *Aperçu* 1932 38); Ex 32 32 *SA*[1](Cl)*B*, Dan 7 10 *SB*, Phil 4 3 *SB*, Z 278 *S* βίβλος, Deu 17 18 *SB*, Is 30 8 *SBF*, Mal 3 16 *A* ϫ.[3] *B*, He 9 19 *SBF*[5], Gu 74 *S* ϫ. whereon letter written βιβλίον (var χάρτης), Mor 17 124 *S* ⲁϥⲥⲙⲓⲛⲉ ⲛⲟⲩϫ. ϣⲁⲓⲱⲅⲣⲁⲡⲏⲥ β. ποιεῖν; Va 57 271 *B* ϫ. ⲛϣⲁⲣ δέρμα; PS 246 *S* ⲛⲛⲟϭ ⲥⲡⲁⲩ ⲛϫ., ShC 73 163 *S* ⲡⲉⲅⲣⲁⲫⲏ ⲁⲩⲱ ⲛϫ. ⲉⲧⲥⲏϩ ⲛⲁⲛ, ib 72 *S* ϥⲉⲛϫ. if needed for writing, ib 43 *S* ⲕⲟⲧ, ϭⲟⲟⲩⲛⲉ, ϫ., Mor 16 79 *S* ⲁⲥϫⲓ ⲛⲟⲩϫ. & wrote to son, ib 28 239 *S* ⲙⲟⲩϣⲧ ϩⲛ ⲛϫ. & bring forth contract (γραμμάτιον) of So-&-so, El 58 *A* ⲛϫ.[4] ⲛⲡⲉⲧⲁⲛϩ, Mani H 24 *A*[2] ⲛⲓϫ. ⲉⲧⲥⲏϩ, MG 25 322 *B* ⲛⲁⲓϫ. named 'Paradise', MG 25 118 (Z 120 n)*B* ⲙⲏ̄ⲣ̄ⲉ̄ ⲟ ⲛϫ. *page*?, C 43 142 *B* take ⲕⲁϣ, ⲙⲉⲗⲁ, ϫ., ib 50 *B* ⲟⲩϫ. ⲉϥⲧⲟⲃ ⲡⲧⲉⲃⲥ, ShP 130[1] 157 *S* ⲟⲩⲛⲕⲟⲉⲓϩ ⲛϫ., BMis 451 *S* he closed & ⲁϥⲙⲟⲩⲣ ⲙⲡϫ., ib 309 *S* ⲕⲁⲡⲥⲁ wherein ⲛⲉⲕⲣⲁⲙⲙⲁⲧⲓⲟⲛ ⲙⲛ ⲛϫ., Mor 40 35 *S* ⲑⲏⲕⲏ ⲛϫ., P 43 29 *S* ⲟ ⲩⲛ ϫ. ⲇⲣⲁⲓⲏ, Mor 51 35 *S* ⲛϣⲟⲩϣⲧ ⲉⲩⲙⲉϩ ⲛϫ., J 65 54 *S* contents of monastery ⲉⲓⲧⲉ ⲅⲣⲁⲙⲙⲁⲧⲓⲟⲛ ⲉⲓⲧⲉ ϫ.[2], Rec 11 134 *S* works of Shenoute ϩⲓⲟⲩϫ.[2] ⲛⲡⲁⲗⲁⲓⲟⲛ (palimpsest?), but ib ϫ., BM 1227 *B* ⲁⲛⲓⲥⲛⲧ ⲛⲁⲓϫ. (sc ἀσφάλεια) ⲛⲁⲕ, Kr 14 *F* ⲁ]ⲓⲥⲛ ⲡⲉⲓϫ.[2] ⲥⲟⲩⲕ̄ⲃ̄ ⲧⲱⲃⲓ, AZ 23 35 *F* ⲡⲓⲗⲟⲙⲓ ⲉⲧⲉ ⲡⲙⲉⲧⲣⲓ ϩⲗⲏⲓ ⲡⲉⲓϫⲱⲙⲉ, BM 1226 *F* witness ⲉⲛⲉⲣϫ.[7], CMSS 61 *F* ⲛⲉϫ.[5] ⲛⲧⲁⲡⲥ ⲧϥⲥⲓ (στίζειν as PG 65 132γ) ⲙⲙⲁⲩ, COAd 50 *S* ⲛϫ. ... ϭⲟⲧϥϭ ⲛⲧϣⲁⲗ[ⲕ]ϥ, RE 14 28 *S* bring needle & stitch ⲡⲉⲓⲙⲟⲩϩ ⲛⲧⲁⲅⲱⲗⲡ ϩⲓⲛⲉϫ., Imp Russ Ar *S* 18 026 *S* ⲛϣⲁⲣ ⲙⲡϫ. ⲙⲛⲧⲉϥⲧⲓⲙⲓ ⲧⲏⲣϥ, Ep 392 *S* ⲛⲉⲓϫ. ... ⲛⲧⲉⲧⲛⲟⲩⲱϩ ⲟⲙⲉ ⲉⲣⲟϥ (v n), ST 384 *S* ⲛϭⲉⲓ ...ⲛⲛⲧⲥⲁⲛⲟ ⲛϫ.[2] *put papers in order*, C 86 269 *B* ⲁϥ ϥⲓ ϥⲣⲱⲟⲩϣ ⲛⲛⲁⲓϫ. ⲁϥ ⲑⲁⲙⲓⲟϥ, RNC 4 *S* 14 works ⲥⲛⲏ ⲉⲡⲉⲓϫ., RE 9 158 *S* Apostle (Paul) & John ϩⲓⲟⲩϫ. ⲛⲟⲩ ⲱⲧ; as adj: Is 18 2 *SB* βύβλινος; Va 57 101 *B* ϫⲁⲣ. ⲛϫ. κῶδιξ; Miss 4 99 *B* ⲧⲟⲙⲟⲥ ⲛϫ. = Mor 18 4 ⲛϫ., (cf ⲧ. ⲛϣⲁⲣ, C 43 184 *B* ⲧⲱⲙⲁⲣⲓⲟⲛ ⲛϫ. (cf RChamp 495 *S* ⲧ. ⲛϫ.); ⲕⲉⲫⲁⲗⲓⲥ ⲛϫ.: Ps 39 7 *S* (*B* ⲕⲁ ϩ ⲛϫ.), Ez 2 9 *B*, cit BMis 353 *S* = BSM 17 *B* ⲡⲓϫ. ⲕ. βιβλίου; Lant 5 *S* ⲕⲉⲫⲁⲗⲁⲓⲟⲛ ⲛϫ., ib 22 *F*[6] ϫ., ib 74 ro *S* ⲡⲉⲓϣⲟⲙⲛⲧ ⲛⲕ. ⲛϫ. (sc Pro, Eccl, Job) in 1 volume; ϫ. ⲙⲙⲉ(ⲙ)ⲃⲣⲁⲛⲟⲛ: Mor 44 7 *S*, MIE 2 404 *B* ⲧⲟⲙⲁⲣⲓⲟⲛ ⲛϫ. ⲙⲙⲉⲙ(ⲃ)ⲣⲁⲛⲟⲛ = PO 22 422 طومار ورق, Mor 40 35 *S* ⲣⲉⲛⲧⲉⲧⲣⲁⲥ (quaternion?) ⲛϫ. ⲙⲙⲉⲙⲃ., CMSS 61 *F* ϫ.[5] ⲙⲙⲉϥⲣⲱⲛ, cf ϫ. ⲛϣⲁⲣ above; ϫ. ⲛⲟϣ, *reading book*: CMSS lc *F* opp ϫ.[5] ⲛⲅⲣⲁⲫⲏ *scriptures*, Leip 24 31 *B* sermons, Miss 4 162 *B* encomium, ib 179 acts, AM 93 *B* ϫ. ⲛⲟϣ or προσφορά dedicated, PSBA 29 195 *S* sim, AM 285 *B* bade burn ⲛϫ. ⲛⲟϣ = Mor 48 43 *S* ϫ. only,

BM 594 *F* ⲟⲩϫ.[8] ⲉⲡⲟϣ;   pl form (v OLZ '27 655): Cl 25 5 *A* ⲛϫ. ἀναγραφή; Mani H 23 *A*[2] ⲛϫ. ⲛⲧⲥⲟⲫⲓⲁ, ManiP 29 *A*[2] ϫ. ⲛⲛⲓⲡⲟⲙⲟⲥ.

b *bundle, parcel* made of papyrus(?)*S*: Miss 4 722 ϫ. ⲛⲥⲧⲟⲓ offered to monastery, BM 1103 ⲡⲓⲃⲁⲥ ⲉⲥⲧⲏⲙ (l ⲡⲥ.) ⲉⲣⲉϥⲁⲩϥ ⲉϫ.[2] ϩⲓⲱϥ, OstrCai 47401 ⲉϣⲱⲡⲉ ⲁⲣ[ϭⲛ ϫ. ⲧⲓⲡⲟⲟⲩⲥⲟⲩ ... ⲕⲁⲛ ⲉⲡⲉⲓⲱ (v p 88 a) ⲕⲁⲛ ⲡⲗⲟⲩⲙⲁⲧⲉ (-μάκιον).

Cf also ? ⲕⲉⲭⲉⲙ (ⲕⲉ- **II a**).

ϫⲓⲉ *S* nn m, *sowing* of seed: Lev 26 5 (P 44 106 زراعة = 43 93 قطاف, var ϫⲟ, *B* ⲥⲓϯ) σπόρος. l? ϫⲗⲗⲉ (v ϫⲱⲱⲗⲉ 1°).

ϫⲓⲉ *AA*[2] v ϫⲱⲱⲙⲉ.

ϫⲓⲏ *S* or ⲛ̄ϫⲓⲏ (? ⲉⲛϫ.) nn in prescription for worms (ἕλμις): PMéd 318 ⲛϫ. & dried grapes boiled & drunk.

ϫⲓⲟ *S* vb caus or nn: Bodl(P) e 33 among varia ϩⲟⲩⲣ ⲛϫ.   Cf ? ⲧⲙ̄ⲙⲟ or ϫⲉⲙⲙⲟ.

ϫⲁⲙⲟⲩⲗ *B* v ϭⲁⲙⲟⲩⲗ.

ϫⲉⲙⲙⲟ *B* vb caus, *be at ease* or sim, c ⲛⲉⲙ-: Pro 11 29 (*SA* ϣⲉⲉⲓ ⲙⲛ-) συμπεριφέρεσθαι dat (in 5 19 *S* ⲙⲟⲟϣⲉ ⲙⲛ-) تصرّف في.   Cf ? ϫⲁⲙⲏ (AZ 20 200).

ϫⲓⲙⲡⲏⲓ *AA*[2] v ϫⲉⲡⲉⲡⲱⲣ.

ϫⲓⲙⲡⲓⲗ *S* nn, meaning unknown, in charm to impoverish an ἄρχων: KroppK 42 ⲥⲁϣϥ ⲛϫ. ⲉⲩⲣⲁⲕϩ.

ϫ(ⲉ)ⲙⲡⲉϩ, ϫ(ⲉ)ⲙⲡⲏϩ[2], ϫⲉⲡⲏϩ[3], ϫⲏⲡⲉϩ[4], ϫⲓ.[5], ϫⲱ.[6] *S*, **ϫⲁⲙⲡⲏϩ[7], ϫⲛ.[8]** *A*, **ϫⲉⲙⲫⲉϩ** *B*, **ϫⲓⲙⲡⲉϩ[9], ϫⲉⲡⲉϩ[10]** *F*, **ϫⲛⲟϩ** DM nn m, *apple* (תפוח, تفاح IgR): Pro 25 11 *SA*[7], Cant 7 8 *SF*[9], Joel 1 12 *A*[8]*B* μῆλον, Ge 30 15 *B* ϫ. ⲛⲛⲟⲩⲧⲉⲙ (*S* ϫ. ⲙⲙⲁⲛⲇⲣⲁⲅⲱⲣⲟⲥ) μ. μανδ. يبروح, P 43 233 *S* ϫ.[2] ⲅⲉⲡⲡⲉⲧⲱ (? κυδόνη) · ⲥⲁⲙⲁⲣⲓ(ⲧⲓ)ⲕⲏ شامين [5], P 44 81 *S* ϫ.[4] [5], K 177 *B* [5]; ShP 130[2] 3 *S* ϩⲱ ⲛϫ., BAp 66 *S* ⲟⲩϫ ⲙⲟⲧ ⲛϫ. was fruit of Tree of Knowledge, BM 1140 *S* ⲟ ⲩϫ.[5] ⲛⲟⲩⲱⲧ, PCol 7 (inv 50) *S* ⲥⲡⲁⲩ ⲉϫ.[6] ⲉⲛⲁϣϣⲉⲙ (cf P 43 above), BM 528 *F* ϫ.[10], DM 24 15 ϫ.; *apple-hued*: Ryl 244 *S* ⲁⲩⲁⲛ ⲛϫ.[6], ST 191 *S* ⲗⲟⲧⲓϩ (λῶδ.) ⲛϫ.   As name m: ϫ.[3] (PapAntinoe *penes* HT).

V MR 4 142, AZ 63 142 n & v ⲫⲉϫ.

ϫⲉⲙⲧⲁⲩ *B* v ⲙⲧⲁⲩ.

ϫⲙⲁⲁⲩ *S* nn as pl, *testicles, castrated parts*: P 43 41 among genital organs ⲛϫ. مخاصى, انثيين

ϫⲉⲙⲫⲉϩ *B* v ϫⲉⲙⲡⲉϩ.

ϫⲓⲙⲫⲉϩ, ϫⲓⲛ.[2], ϫⲓⲙⲫⲉ[3], -ⲫⲟϩ[4] *B* nn, *blight*: Deu 28 22 (*S* ϩⲱⲱⲙⲉ ⲉⲃⲟⲗ) شور, 2 Chr 6 28 ϫ. ⲡⲉⲙ ⲓⲕⲧⲉⲣⲟⲥ (var[4]), Hag 2 18 (*SA* ϣⲱⲡⲉ ⲛⲓⲕⲧ.) ἀνεμο-

φθορία, Hos 8 7³ (A ⲝⲟ) -φθορος;   ⲉⲣ ⲝ.: Ge 41 6
(S ⲝⲓⲧⲏⲩ sic, not as on p 440 b) ضربتهن السموم, Pro 10
5 (varr²⁴, SA ϣⲱⲥⲙ), Is 19 7³ (S ⲝⲡⲧ.) -φθορος.   Cf
Spg 271, 305.

ⲝⲉⲙϣⲁⲓ B   v ϣⲁ nose p 544 a.

ⲝⲙⲝⲙ   v ⲕⲙⲕⲙ & ϭⲛϭⲛ.

ⲝⲟⲙⲝⲉⲙ B   v ϭⲟⲙϭⲙ.

ⲝⲛ- SA², ⲝⲉⲛ-², ⲝⲓⲛ-³ S, ⲝⲉ-⁴ SB(once)F conj,
or (B ϣⲁⲛ-): Eccl 2 19 (ShBor 246 46, var ⲏ ⲝ.², F
ⲓ...ⲓ), Mt 11 3 (var⁴R 1 3 78, var³ BAp 132), ib 27 17,
Lu 5 23 (B ⲓⲉ), ib 12 41 (var⁴), Jo 9 2 SA², Ac 8 34
(var²), Ro 4 10 (varr²⁴ & = Gk), Z 334 ⲡⲣⲁⲡ ⲡⲉⲧⲛⲟⲩ-
ⲝⲙ ⲝⲉⲡⲣⲱⲃⲉ, C 86 289 B ⲡⲉⲕⲛⲟⲩϯ...ⲝⲉⲡⲉⲛⲛⲟⲩϯ
ⲏ̄; PS 332 ϣⲁⲉⲓ...ⲝⲉⲙⲉϭⲉⲓ, ShA 2 235 ⲡⲛ̄ⲉ...ⲝⲛ-
ⲡⲣⲱⲙⲉ, ShBor 300 71 ⲉⲧⲃⲏⲛⲧϥ ⲝⲡⲉⲧⲃⲏⲛⲧⲓ, ShC
42 16 which is greater ⲛ̄ⲝ̄ⲥ̄ ⲙⲡⲁⲡⲁϣⲡⲉ ⲝⲛⲡⲁⲡⲁϣ-
ⲡⲉ?, ShMiss 4 283 ⲟⲉⲛⲛⲟϭ ⲛ̄ϭⲓⲙⲉⲛⲉ ⲝⲡⲣⲉⲡϣⲉⲉⲣⲉ
ϣⲏⲙⲉ, Pcod 9 which is chief virtue ⲡⲉⲓⲱⲣⲡⲉ ⲝⲡⲟ-
ⲟⲩⲛⲉ?, Mor 51 101 ⲉϥϣⲁϫⲉ ⲉⲧⲃⲉⲧⲥⲁⲣⲝ ⲝⲉⲉϥϣⲁϫⲉ
ⲉⲧⲃⲉⲧⲙⲛⲧⲡⲛ̄ⲁ̄?, ib 41 138 ⲕⲏⲛⲩ ⲡⲙⲙⲁⲛ ⲝⲉⲕⲛⲁⲃⲱⲕ?,
ÉtLeem 91 ⲉⲧⲉⲧⲛϣⲱⲡ ⲝⲉⲉⲧⲉⲧⲓ̈ϯ ⲉⲃⲟⲗ?, BMar 41
to know ⲝⲉⲡⲉϥⲟⲛⲟ ⲝⲛⲁϥⲙⲟⲩ, Ep 332 ⲙⲟϣⲧϥ (sc
sesame) ⲝⲉϥⲟⲩ ⲛⲃⲁⲣ ⲝⲡⲉϥϣⲁⲣ, Mor 41 91 ⲙⲡⲛⲁⲩ
ⲛϣⲟⲣⲡ ⲝⲉⲙⲡⲛⲁⲩ ⲙⲙⲉⲉⲣⲉ ⲝⲉⲙⲡⲛⲁⲩ ⲡⲣⲟⲩⲅⲉ, ib
24 5 F because of man ⲝⲉⲉⲧⲃⲉⲙⲁⲥⲧⲓⲙⲁ = ib 23 8 S
ⲝⲡⲙⲙⲟⲛ ⲉⲧⲃⲉ-, ib 30 12 Sf did parents name thee
ⲝⲉⲡⲉⲙⲁⲧⲟⲓ = BMis 238 ⲝⲓⲡⲙⲙⲟⲛ ⲙⲙⲁⲧⲟⲓ.

ⲝⲛ-, ⲝⲓⲛ-, ⲝⲉⲙⲙⲟⲛ, or not (B ϣⲁⲛⲙⲙⲟⲛ, cf p
168 b): Ex 17 7 (var³), Deu 8 2 (var³) ἤ ὄυ; PS 262
ⲥⲉⲃⲁⲥⲁⲡⲓⲍⲉ ⲙⲙⲟϥ...ⲝⲡⲙ.,ib 303 ⲥⲉⲛⲁⲕⲱ ⲛⲁϥ ⲉⲃⲟⲗ
ⲝⲡⲙ.,ShC 73 20 doth lamp outshine sun ⲝⲡⲙ.(var
ⲝⲡ-)?, Mor 24 30 F is soul brought first to heaven
ⲝⲉⲙ.?   not neg: 1 Cor 9 10 F(S ⲝⲡ- only), ClPr
54 44 to save one child ⲝⲡⲙ. ⲉⲭⲁⲣⲓⲍⲉ ⲙⲡⲟⲩⲝⲁⲓ
ⲛϣⲣϣⲓⲣⲉ ⲥⲛⲁⲩ ⲏ̄; ShBM 215 ⲟⲉⲛⲯⲩⲭⲏ ⲛⲁⲧⲛⲟⲃⲉ
ⲝⲡⲙ. ⲟⲉⲛⲯ. ⲛⲣⲉϥⲣ ⲛⲟⲃⲉ, ShA 1 227 ⲡⲁⲡⲟⲩⲛⲏⲃ
ⲝⲡⲙ. ⲡⲁⲡⲗⲁⲟⲥⲡⲉ, ShZ 368 haul ships ⲟⲓⲟⲉⲛⲛⲟⲩⲟ
ⲝⲡⲙ. ⲟⲛⲡⲉⲣⲛⲁⲁⲩ ... ⲡⲉⲓⲉⲡⲥⲁ, BM 331 45 those I
slew ⲝⲓⲙⲙ. ⲛⲉⲝⲓⲱⲧⲙⲟⲥ...ⲝⲉⲡⲁⲣⲑⲉⲛⲟⲥ (var Mor
18 143 both ⲝⲓⲙⲙ.),ManiK 111 A² ⲙⲏ ⲡⲧⲁϣϣⲟⲩⲱ
ⲁⲡⲟⲩⲣⲓⲧ...ⲝⲡⲙ. ⲡⲧⲁϣϣⲟⲩⲱ ⲁⲡⲓⲕⲁⲟ?, Mor 24 31
F are they brought back to earth ⲝⲉⲙ. ⲛϣⲁⲝⲓⲧⲟⲩ
ⲉⲡⲉ(ⲉ)ⲱⲡ?;   ⲝⲛ-, ⲝⲓⲡⲙⲡⲉ, or not (cf p 178 a b):
CA 99 ⲉⲡⲉⲁϥⲝⲟⲟⲩ ⲉⲃⲟⲗ ⲕⲁⲗⲱⲥ ⲝⲡⲙ., BAp 68 when
God made Adam ⲁϥⲧⲁⲙⲉ ⲧⲕⲉⲉⲩⲣⲁ ⲡⲙⲙⲁϥ ⲝⲡ-
ⲙ.?;   ⲝⲡⲡⲱⲣ, or rather: 3 Kg 22 15 ⲝ. ⲧⲁϭⲱ ⲏ̄.

ⲝⲁⲛ B nn in ⲗⲁⲝⲁⲛ q v.

ⲝⲏⲛ   v ϣⲏⲡ.

ⲝⲏⲛ B   v ϭⲛⲟⲡ 1°.

ⲝⲓⲛ- SSfF, ⲝⲛ- SAA²O, ⲝⲉⲛ- SF, ϭ(ⲉ)ⲡ-, ⲕⲡ-,
ϣⲉⲡ- S, ϭⲓⲡ- SSfF, ⲓⲥⲝⲉⲛ- B, ϭⲏⲡ-, ⲝⲓ-, ⲝⲉ- F preposition, from (starting from), since, a before nn:
1 Kg 3 20 S, Ps 18 6 SB, ib 60 2 S(B ⲉⲃⲟⲗ ⲝⲉⲡ-), Mt
17 18 S(var ⲝⲓⲡⲉ-)B, Jo 19 27 SA²B, C 99 235 S ⲝⲓⲡ-
ⲣⲟⲩⲅⲉ = ib 89 69 B ⲡ- ἀπό; Job 31 12 S(B diff), Ps
87 15 SB, Pro 29 33 B(SA ⲡ-), Mt 12 42 S(B ⲉⲃ.
ⲝⲉⲡ-), Mor 37 36 S ⲡⲉϥⲕⲧⲏⲥⲓⲥ...ⲝⲓⲡⲡⲉϥⲉⲓⲟⲧⲉ ἐκ;
Cl 23 3 A ⲝⲓⲡⲡⲉⲓⲁⲧⲉ ἐπί; Ps 101 25 SB κατά; Va
57 131 B ⲓ. ⲡⲁⲓⲙⲁ ἐντεῦθεν; PS 247 S ⲝⲓⲡⲡⲥⲁ ⲡⲃⲟⲗ,
BG 16 S ⲉⲣⲉⲡⲏⲩ ⲝⲓⲧⲱⲛ?, ShBor 246 61 S plant
dieth ⲝⲓⲡⲡⲉϥⲛⲟⲩⲛⲉ, CA 111 S ⲝⲓⲡⲝⲟⲩⲱⲧⲉ ⲡⲣⲟⲙⲡⲉ, CO 383 S ⲝⲓⲡⲧⲉⲩϣⲏ ⲉⲓ[ⲟ]ⲅⲱ ⲉⲓⲛⲁⲩ ⲉⲣ[ⲟⲕ], Aeg
45 B following her ⲓ. ⲓⲉⲣⲟⲩⲥⲁⲗⲏⲙ,Va 61 119 B ⲟⲱⲗ
ⲉⲧⲉⲕⲕⲗⲏⲥⲓⲁ ⲓ. ⲟⲁⲡⲁⲣⲟⲅⲣⲓ; Mor 19 53 S ⲝⲓⲡⲟⲉ ⲡ-
ⲧⲁⲓⲉⲓ (var Wess 18 62 ⲝⲓⲡⲧⲁⲓⲉⲓ), BM 1113 S ⲝⲡⲟⲉ
ⲉϣⲁⲕⲉⲓ ⲡⲁⲓ,ib 1107 ⲝⲓⲡⲉⲟⲏ ⲡⲧⲁⲓⲉⲓ(v p 640 a. Jernstedt compares ἀφ'ὡς BGU 1141 18, POxy 528);
as nn m: J 57 12 S ⲡⲧⲁⲩⲉⲧⲏⲡⲉⲩⲅⲉ (κινδυ.) ⲁⲣⲟⲥ ⲛⲁⲕ
ⲉⲙⲛⲧⲉ (ⲉἰⲙ.) ⲉⲡⲝⲓⲡⲧⲉ;   b before vb: 2d pres,
while yet Ps 70 6 SB ἀπό; Ac 3 2 S(var ⲝⲓⲡ-)B ἐκ;
Lu 24 6 S(B = Gk) ἔτι; PS 92 S ⲝⲓⲡⲉⲓϣⲟⲟⲡ ⲟⲙ-
ⲡⲁⲁⲓⲱⲛ, BSG 180 S ⲝⲓⲡⲉϥⲟⲛⲟ, Bor 260 121 S ⲝⲓⲡⲉ-
ⲣⲉⲡⲧⲉⲭⲡⲓⲧⲉ ⲣ ⲟⲱⲃ, Mor 55 54 S taken to heaven
ⲝⲓⲡⲉϥⲟⲙⲡⲥⲱⲙⲁ (on 2 Cor 12 2), DeV 2 10 B ⲓ. ⲉϥ-
ⲟⲓϥⲟⲅⲉⲓ, Mor 30 18 F ⲝⲉⲟ ⲡⲣⲉⲗⲗⲏⲛ = BMis 284 S
ⲝⲉⲡ-;   2d perf (ⲝⲓⲡⲧⲁ- = ⲝⲓⲡⲓⲧⲁ-): Job 20 4 SB,
2 Pet 3 4 S(var ⲝⲉⲛ)B, Ap 16 18 SB ἀφ'οὗ; Mk 9 21
SB ὡς (var ἔως); Ge 16 3 S ⲙⲡⲡⲥⲁⲙⲛⲧⲉ ⲡⲣⲟⲙⲡⲉ
ⲝⲓⲡⲧⲁⲥⲟⲩⲱⲟ ⲙⲡ- (B as Gk) μετὰ ῑ ἔτη τοῦ οἰκῆσαι;
Mk 15 44 S ⲉⲡⲉⲁϥⲱⲥⲕ ⲝⲓⲡⲧⲁϥⲙⲟⲩ (B ⲁϥⲟⲅⲱ ⲁϥⲙⲟⲩ) πάλαι ἀπέθανε; ShA 2 268 S ⲙⲡϥⲱⲥⲕ ⲝⲓⲡ-
ⲡⲧⲁϥⲛⲕⲟⲧⲕ, ShBM 215 90 S ⲝⲓⲡⲧⲁⲡⲡⲉ̄ ⲧⲁⲙⲓⲉ ⲡⲣⲱⲙⲉ, Ep 519 S ⲕⲉⲛⲧⲁ(ⲓⲉ)ⲓ, ib 216 S ⲕⲓⲧⲁ-, ST 227 S
ϭⲉⲡⲧⲁϭⲉⲓ, RE 9 160 S ϭⲡⲧⲁⲓⲥⲟⲁⲓ;   other tenses:
Pcod 5 S ⲝⲓⲡⲧⲉⲣⲉⲧⲁⲡⲟⲫⲁⲥⲓⲥ ⲧⲁⲅⲟⲩ; Mani 1 A² ⲝⲓⲡ-
ⲡⲧⲉⲉⲓ ⲁⲧⲥⲁⲣⲝ; ib P 43 A² ⲝⲙⲡⲛⲕϯ ϣⲡⲉ ⲡⲧⲉⲩⲡⲗⲁⲛⲏ,
ib 165 ⲝⲓⲡⲧⲟⲩⲣⲱⲛⲉ ⲁⲙⲁⲡⲉ, Lu 2 21 B ⲓ. ⲙⲡⲁⲧⲟⲩⲉⲣ
ⲃⲟⲕⲓ (S ⲉⲙⲡⲁⲧⲥ-).

c prefixed to other prep.   ⲝⲓⲡⲉ- S: Lev 23 32
(var ⲝⲓⲡ-), Jer 38 8 ἀπό; Ge 9 11 (var do) ἔτι, Z 362
ⲙⲡⲣ-...ⲝ. ⲡⲉⲓⲙⲁⲩ μηκέτι; BMis 46 ⲝ. ⲧⲁⲙⲉ(ⲛ)ⲧ-
ⲕⲟⲩⲓ, BM 1065 ⲝ. ⲡⲟⲟⲩ, ib 1088 list of things put
on boat ⲝ. ⲡⲟⲟⲩ this day, ST 181 ϣⲉⲡⲉϯⲛⲟⲩ, v also
ⲡⲝⲓⲡ- below;   ⲝⲓⲡⲡ- S, ⲝⲛⲡ- SAA²: Ac 23 23
(var ⲝⲓⲡ-) ἀπό; Deu 15 20 (var do, B ⲥⲁⲙⲉⲡⲏ ⲡ-),
Pro 29 21 A(S ⲝⲓⲡ-) ἐκ; BG 17 ⲝ. ⲡⲓⲡⲁⲩ, PS 70 ⲝ.
ⲡⲉⲟⲅⲟⲉⲓϣ, ib 10 ⲝ. ⲟⲟⲩⲡ (but 17 ⲝⲓⲡⲟ.), ShLeyd
332 ⲝ. ⲡⲉⲓⲙⲁ, El 50 A ⲝ. ⲧⲣⲁⲉⲓ, PLond 4 486]ⲝⲓⲡ-
ⲡⲡⲣⲟⲟⲩ ⲙⲙⲟⲥ ⲡⲧⲁⲡⲡⲉ̄[(cf ⲝⲓⲡ- ... ⲉⲟⲣⲁⲓ), ManiK
10 A² ⲝ. ⲧⲁⲣⲭⲏ, ib P 112 A² ⲝ. ⲡⲥⲏⲩ, ST 314 ⲝⲓⲡ-
ⲙⲡⲙⲟⲩⲣ ⲁⲟⲟⲩⲡ, J 86 44 ⲝ. ⲧⲉ(ⲡⲟⲩ);   ⲓ. ⲝⲁ-

ⲧⲣⲏ B: BSM 29 ı. ⲛⲥⲁⳓ = BMis 369 S ⲉⲓⲥ ⲕⲉⳟⲟⲟⲩ
ⲥⲛⲁⲩ; ı. ⲍⲁⲭⲉⲛ-ⅴ ⲡ758a; ı. ⳟⲛ ⳟ ⲩ ⲣ642b; ⲍⲓⲛ-
ⳟⲛ-, ı. ⲍⲉⲛ-: Ps 57 3 S(B ı. ⲉⲩⲍⲉⲛ-) ἀπό; Is 44 2 B(S
ⲉⲃⲟⲗ ⳟⲛ-) ἐκ;   or advb: Ez 41 7 B ı. ⲉⲡⲉⲥⲏⲧ ἐκ.

d with ⲛⲛ intervening, *from...to.* ⲉ-: Sa 8 1 S,
Mt 23 34 SB ἀπό ... εἰς; ShZ 598 S ⲍⲓⲛⲟⲩⲕⲁⲓⲣⲟⲥ
ⲉⲟⲩⲕⲁⲓⲣⲟⲥ, Mani K 41 A² ⲍⲛ̄ⲡ̄ⲕⲉⲕⲉ ⲁⲡⲟ ⳓⲁⲓⲛⲉ,
BSM 133 B ı. ⲡⲟⲗⲓⲥ ⲉⲡⲟⲗⲓⲥ;   ⲁⲭⲛ- A²: Mani 1
ⲍⲛ̄ⲡ̄ⲡⲏⲩⲉ ⲁⲭ̄ⲡ̄ⲕⲁⳉ; ⳝⲁ-: Jon 3 5 SAB, Ac 28
23 SB ἀπό...ἕως, Ro 5 14 SB ἀπό...μέχρι; Ez 41 20
SB ἐκ ... ἕως, Pro 27 24 SA ἐκ ... εἰς; PS 10 S ⲍⲓⲛ-
ⲧⲁⲣⲭⲏ ⳟⲉⲱⲥ ⳝⲁⲡⲉⲥⲱⲕ, Br 249 S ⲍⲓⲛⲡⲉⳝⲉⲓ ⲉⲃⲟⲗ
ⳝⲁⲡⲉⳝⲉⲓ ⲉⳉⲟⲩⲛ, ShA 2 269 S ⲍⲓⲛⲡⲡⲉⲕⲟⲩⲓ ⳝⲁⲡⲉⲛ-
ⲛⲟ ⳓ, El 136 S sim ⲍⲛ-, BMEA 10585 F sim ⳓⲓⲛ-, CO
186 S sim ⲍⲛ-, El 86 A ⲍⲛ̄ⲡⲥⲁ... ⳝⲁⲛⲥⲁ, Mani P 112
A² ⲍⲛ̄ⲡⲧⳟⲟⲩⲓⲧⲉ ⳝⲁⲑⲁⲏ, Ora Chr Period 3 535 B ı.
ⲑⲱⲡ ⳝⲁⲑⲱⲛ اﻟﻰ (أتّﻲ); ⳝⲁ(ⲉ)ⳉⲣⲁⲓ ⲉ-: Ge 15 18 S(B
ı....ⳝⲁ-), Lu 23 5 S(B do) ἀπό...ἕως; PS 6 S ⲍⲓⲛ-
ⲍⲛ-...ⳝ. ⲉⲍⲛ-, Mani P 61 A² ⲍⲛ̄ⲡ̄ⲡ̄ⲕⲁⳉ ⳝ. ⲁⲙⲡⲏ-
ⲩⲉ;   ⳝⲁⲉⳉⲟⲩⲛ ⲉ- B: Ac 1 22 (S ⳝⲁ ⳉ ⲣⲁⲓ ⲉ-) ἀπὸ
...ἕως; ı. ⲍⲁⲭⲉⲛ-ⅴ ⲡ 758a;   or advb. ⲉⲃⲟⲗ,
from...onward: Hag 2 18 SA(B om ⲉⲃ.) ἀπό; ShR
2 3 86 S ⲍⲓⲛⲙⲡⲟⲟⲩ ⲉⲃ., BIF 13 100 Sᶠ ⲍⲓⲛⲉⲡⲟⲟⲩ
ⲉⲃⲟⲗ = MG 25 280 B, CA 98 S ⲍⲓⲛⲡ̄ⳝⲱⲙ ⲉⲃ., Ep
192 S have relied on thee ⲍⲓⲛⲡⲡⲉ̄ ⲉⲃ. *from (after) God,*
ib 373 am friendless ⲍⲉ[ⲛ]ⲡⲡⲉ̄ ⲉⲃ., DeV 1 92 B art our
father ı. ⲫ̄ⳁ ⲉⲃ., C 43 221 B arms cut off ı. ⲛⲉⳑⲁⲗⲱⳝ
ⲉⲃ., Mani H 27 A² ⲍⲛ̄ⲡ̄ⲡⲛⲁ ⳓ ⲙ̄ⲡⲟⲗⲉⲙⲟⲥ ⲁⲃ.;   ⲉ-
ⳉ ⲣⲁⲓ S, as last: BMis 35 ⲍⲓⲛⲉⲡⲟⲟⲩ ⲉⳉ., BM 1079 none
omitted ⲍⲓⲛⲉⲙⲛ̄ⲧⲁⲃⲧⲉ ⲡⲣⲟⲙⲡⲉ ⲉⳉ., BMis 126 on
Ge 38 26 ⲍⲓⲛⲙⲟⲥ ⲉⳉ. ⲙ̄ⲡⲉⲓⲟⲩⲁⲁⲥ ⲥⲟⳟⲉⲡ ⲑⲁⲙⲁⲣ
(cf PLond 4 above);   ⲉⲡⲉⲥⲏⲧ S, ⲉ ⳉ ⲣⲏⲓ B, *downward*: Mk 15 38 SB ἀπό...ἕως, Mt 2 16 S(B as Gk)
ἀπό...καὶ κατωτέρω.

e preceded by other prep. ⲉ- SF: Is 32 12 F
ⲉⲍⲛ-(S ⲍⲓⲛ-, B ⲉⲃⲟⲗ ⳉⲁ-) ἀπό; Jo 4 52 F ⲉⲍⲓⲛ-(S
ⲛ-, B ⲍⲉⲛ-, A² Gk om), P 131⁵ 103 archbishops ⲉⲍⲓⲛ-
ⲉⲙⲁⲣⲕⲟⲥ, FR 8 ⲉ ⳓ ⲉⲛⲥⲟⲩⲁ ... ⳝⲁⲥⲟⲩⲁ (cf ib ⲍⲓⲛ-
ⲥⲟⲩⲁ), BM 1140 ⲉⲧ ⳓ ⲙⲟⲩ ⲍⲓⲛⲉⳉ ⲉⲛⲟⲩⲱⲧ, Kr 1 9
ⲁ ⲍⲓⲛⲡⲉⲛⲏ, Orat Cyp 94 F ⲉ ⳓ ⲛⲡⲉⲓⲛⲃ̄ ... ⳝⲁⲛⲃⲱ, L
Ap 548 F ⲉⲍⲓⲛⲡⲉⲩ[ⲕⲟⲩⲓ] ⳝⲁ-, BM 612 F ⲉⲍⲉⲛⲟⲩ-
ⲕⲟⲩⲓ, ib 666 F sim ⲉ ⳓ ⲓⲛ-, Kr 3 F give George a mount
ⲉⲍⲓⲛⲡⲉⲧⲛⲉⲧⲓⲙⲓ ⳝⲁⲕⲉⲧⲓⲙⲓ, ib 136 F ⲉⲍⲓⲛⲡⲁⲩ *from
to-day*;   ⲛ- SSᶠFO: Ge 7 23 (var ⲍⲓⲛ-), Eccl 1 10
F(PMich 3520, var Schmidt & S ⳉⲁⲧⲛ̄), Jer 27 3 F
(Mus 49 175) ἀπό; Pro 8 21 (A ⲍⲛ-) ἐκ; Is 30 20 F
(S ⲍⲓⲛ-, B ⲍⲉ-) -ἔτι; Eccl 11 9 F(S ⳟⲛ-, B ⳉⲛ-) ἐν; Mor 48 7
ⲉⲓ ⲛ ⲍⲓⲛⲡⲟⲩⲉ (var BMar 206 ⲙⲛⲟⲩⲉ), LMär 31 three
days ⲛ ⲍⲓⲛⲧⲁⲩ ⲍⲡⲟ ⳑ, Mor 31 176 ⲛ ⲍⲓⲛⲡⲉⳝⲟⲣⲡ, ib 93
Sᶠ ⲉⲍⲓⲛⲟⲟⲩ ⲉ ⲑⲏ, FR 2 blasphemed her ⲛ ⲍⲓⲛⲉⲥⲟⲛ-
ⲟⳟ *whilst she lived*, Mor 30 47 Sᶠ ⲛ ⳓ ⲓⲛⲉⳑ ⲙⲛ̄ⲕⲟⲥⲙ-
ⲙⲟⲥ = BMis 271 S ⲍⲉⲛ ⳑ-, BIF 22 107 F ⲛ ⲍⲓⲛⲡⲉⲟⲩ-
ⲕⲟⲩⲓ ⳝⲁ-, Hor 83 O ⲛ ⲍⲛⲡⲣⲁⲙⲡⲉ ⲙ̄ⲃ̄;   ⳉⲁ- S:

Ryl 144 ⳉⲁ ⲍⲓⲛⲉⲡⲟⲟⲩ, ib 324 ⳉ. ⲉⲡⲉⲓⲙⲁ ⲉⲡⲁ ⳉ ⲟⲩ, BM
1054 ⳉ. ⲉⲡⲁⳝⲟⲡⲥ;   ⳉⲓ- S: Ac 20 9 ⳉⲓⲭ ⲓⲛ ⲙ ⲉ ⳑ-
ⳝⲟⲙⲧⲉ ⲛ ⳉ ⲉ (var ⲍⲓⲛ-) ἀπό; ST 266 ⳉⲓⲭⲉ ⲛ ⲡⲟⲟⲩ.

V also ⲉⲛⲉ ⳉ (p 57 b), ⲛⲁⲩ (p 235 a h), ⲧⲉⲛⲟⲩ (p
485 a), ⳝⲱⲣⲡ (p 587 b), ⲍⲱⲙ.

ⲍⲓⲛ- B *v* ⳓⲓⲛ-.

ⲍⲓⲛ A A² nn m, *power, capacity*: TU 43 4 A ⲁⲓⳁ
ⳉⲓⲱⲧ ⲛ ⲧⲁⳟⲛⲁⲙⲓⳓ ⲙ̄ⲡ ⳑ ⳝ. (PO 9 196 ⳁⲣⲅ), ib 7 sim,
Mani K 9 A² ⲕⲁⲧⲁ ⲡⲉ ⲧ ⲓ ⳝ. ⲙ̄ⲛ̄ⲧ ⲣⲉ ⲉ ⲧ ⲉ ⲧⲛⲁ ⳓ [ⲛ]ⳓⲁⲙ,
ib P 166 A² ⲡ ⳝ. ⲙ̄ⲡⲓⲗⲉⲙⲛⲥⲉ (= -ⲙⲛⳝⲉ), ib 190 ⳁ
ⳓⲁⲙ ⲉ ⲧ ⳁ ⳝ. ⲛ̄ⲥ ⲧⲟⲓⲭ ⲉⲓⲱⲛ. Nah 2 3 B ⲍⲓⲛ f δυναστεία (A ⳓⲁⲙ) can hardly be this word.

ⲍⲓⲱⲛ A² AP 28, prob for ⳝⲓⲱⲛ as in Ex 4 6 A,
Cl 8 4 A.

ⲍⲟⲛ B *v* ⳓⲟⲛ.

ⲍⲁⲛⲉ¹ S A², ⲍⲁⲁ.², ⲍⲟⲟ.³, ⲍⲁⲡⲏ⁴ S, nn, *ark, box*:
4 Kg 12 9³ (varr P 44 111¹, 43 108⁴) κιβωτός, صندوق,
T ri 510 κιβωτος ⲉⲧⲟⲩⲙⲟⲩⲧⲉ ⲉⲣⲟⲥ ⲍⲉⳝ.⁴ ⳅ; Mani P
167 A²] ⲍ. ⲙ̄ⲡⲁ ⲅⲁ ⲑⲟⲛ ⲧ ⲕ ⲓⲃ̄. ⲙ̄ⲡⲥⲱⲧⲉ, LAl 5 (ⲕ)ⲛⲁ-
ⳓ ⲉⲛ ⳉ ⲁ ⳉ ⲛ ⲍ.¹, ST 117 ⲟⲩ ⲍ.² ⲛ̄ⲃⲏⲧ ⲕⲟⲩⲓ, Bodl(P)f 24
in list ⲥ ⲫ ⲁⲗⲓⲥ[, ⲍ.³ ⲛⲛ[, ⳝ ⲧ ⲛⲛ.

ⲍⲁⲛⲉ, -ⲏ B, **ⲍⲁⲡⲓ** F *v* ⳓⲟⲛ.

ⲍⲁⲛⲉ B *v* ⳓⲛⲟⲛ, *be soft.*

ⲍⲁⲛⲏ B nn f, *hoe*: K 127 among husbandman's
tools ⳁ ⲍ. ﻣﺰق (var + ﻣﻠﻮﻩ, cf Dozy 2 558), Montp
170 ﻣﻐﺮﻓﺔ (unlikely).

ⲍⲁⲛⲟ B nn m, *basket* (?) full of earth (cf בצו IgR,
נוצ Dévaud): C 41 53 ⲙⲟ ⳝ ⲓ ⳓ ⲉⲛⲟ ⲩ ⳉ ⲣⲟ ⳝ ⲛ ⲉⲙⲡⲓ ⲍ.
ⲛ̄ⲕⲁ ⳉ ⲓ, ib ⲛⲓ ⲍ. ⲛ̄ⲕⲁ ⳉ ⲓ ⲧⲁ ⲗ ⲛⲟⲩⲧ ⲉⲣⲟⳑ (Ar Miss 4 413
om).

ⲍⲓⲛⲓ F *v* ⳓⲓⲛⲉ.

ⲍⲱⲱⲛⲉ A² vb, meaning unknown: Mani K 184
]ⲁⲩ ⲍⲱⲱⲛⲉ[, no context.   Cf? Leyd 445 S ⲛⲁⲧ-
ⲍⲟⲟⲛ ⳑ (or this = ⳝⲟⲟⲛ ⳑ).

ⲍⲛⲁⳁ, **ⲍⲛⲟⳁ** (once) S, **ⲍⲁⲡⳁ** F vb tr, *strike, deal
blows*: Lu 12 48 (B ⳁ ⳝ ⲁ ⳝ) δέρειν; ib 10 30 ⲍⲛⲟⳁ
(B ⳁ ⲉⲣ ⳓ ⲱⲧ), Ac 16 23 (var ⲍⲛ ⲁ ⲁ ⳁ, B ⳁ ⳝ.) πληγὰς
ἐπιτιθέναι, RNC 41 ⲁⲩ ⲍⲛⲁⲓ ⳉⲉ ⲛ ⲥ ⳝ ⲏ ⳝ ⲉ πλ. προσφέρειν
dat, Mor 37 46 ⲍⲛⲁⳑ ⲛ ⳉ ⲉⲛ ⲛ ⲟ ⳓ ⲛ̄ⲥⲏ ⳝ ⲉ πλ. κόπτειν;
1 Thes 2 2 ⲁⲩ ⲍⲛⲁⲡ ⳉ ⲓ ⲥⲉ (B ⳓ ⲓ ⳓ ⲓ ⲥ ⲓ, F ⳁ ⲛ ⳉ ⲛ ⳉ.) προ-
πάσχειν; ShP 130¹ 132 ⲡⲉⲧⲛⲁ ⲍⲛⲁⳑ ⲟⲩ ⳝ ⲥ ⲛ̄ⳓ ⲉⲣⲱⲃ
... ⲛⲟⲩ ⲁ; Miss 8 20 ⲁⲩ ⲍⲛⲁⲡⲁⲩ ⳉ ⲓ ⲥ ⲛ ⳝ ⲉ, HM 2 108
ⲍⲛⲁⳑ ⲛ ⳝ ⲉ ⲛ̄ⲃⲟⲩ ⲛ ⲉⲩⲣⲟⲛ ⲉⲛ ⲉ ⳑ ⲥ ⲟ ⲓ, Mor 30 37 F thou
(ox) shalt not be able ⲉⲍⲛ ⳑ (sc thy head) ⲗⲁⲁⲩ ⲛ̄-
ⲗⲱⲁⲓ = ib 29 31 Sᶠ ⲣⲱⳉⲧ = BMis 262 S ⲍⲱ ⲙⲙⲟⲥ
(sic, l ?? ⲍⲟⲛ ⳑ) ⲛⲗⲁⲁⲩ.

ϫⲛⲁϫ S, ϫⲉⲡⲉϫ A, ϭⲁⲡⲡⲁ-, ϭⲉⲡⲁϫ, ϭⲁⲡⲡⲁϫ F vb tr, *send*: Ge 21 14 (B ⲟⲩⲱⲣⲡ ⲉⲃⲟⲗ), Ex 4 13 SA(B ⲟⲩ.) ἀποστέλλειν, Lu 20 10 (var ϫⲟⲟⲩ, B ϯ ⲧⲟⲧϫ ⲉⲃⲟⲗ) ἐξαπ.; PMich 524 F ϭⲁⲡⲡⲁ ⲡ[ⲉ]ⲕϣⲉϫⲓ ⲙⲏⲡⲛⲏ, *ib* ϭⲁⲡⲡⲁⲥ ⲙⲏⲡⲛⲏ, CMSS 28 F ϭⲁⲡⲡⲁ ⲡⲉⲧⲣⲉⲙⲁⲥ (? τριμήσιον), BM 582 (1)F ϱⲁⲡⲓ ⲡⲓⲙ ⲡϣⲁⲕϭⲁⲡⲁⲥ(*sic l*); c ⲉ-: PS 91 ϫⲛⲁⲩ ⲉⲡⲕⲁⲕⲉ; ⲉϱⲣⲁⲓ ⲉ-: *ib* 112 ϫⲛⲁⲥ ⲉϱ. ⲉⲡⲉⲭⲁⲟⲥ; c ⲛ-F: Kr 3 ϭⲁⲡⲡⲁⲥ ⲡⲏ[ⲡ, *ib* ϭⲁⲡⲡⲁ ⲧⲉⲅⲕⲁⲧⲁⲅⲣⲁⲫⲓ ⲡⲏⲡ, BM 628 ϭⲁⲡⲡⲁ ⲛ̄ ⲙⲡⲁⲣⲉⲥ ⲡⲁⲛ. Also ? Kr 226 F ϭⲁⲁⲡⲁⲕ, CMSS 56 F]ϭⲁⲡ ⲡⲉⲃϣⲉⲣⲉ ϧⲁⲗ[.

ϫⲛⲁϫ O vb tr = ? one of preceding words: Hor 84 ϫⲡⲁϥ ⲡϣⲉⲣⲉ ⲡϫⲡⲣⲁⲙⲡⲉ ⲙ̄ⲃ̄.

ϫ(ⲉ)ⲛⲁ S, ϫⲉⲡⲉ A², ϫⲡⲉ S, ϭⲉⲛⲟ B, ϫⲡⲉ-, ϫⲉⲡⲁϫ S, ϭⲉⲛⲟϫ, ϭⲉⲡⲛⲟⲩⲧ† B vb intr, *be quenched*: Job 4 10 B(S ⲱϣⲙ), Pro 10 7 SB(A ϧⲱⲕ), Si 28 13 S ϫⲡⲉ, Is 34 9 B(SF ⲱ.), BHom 35 S ϫⲡⲁ σβεννύναι; Mk 9 43 S neg (B ⲁⲧϭ.), Va 57 67 B ἄσβεστος; BIF 13 115 S lamp ⲛⲧⲁϥϫ. = MG 25 306 B, R 1 2 42 S sim ϫⲡⲁ, ManiP 191 A² sim ϫ., ShA 1 457 S fire ⲉⲙⲉϥⲱϣⲙ ⲟⲩⲇⲉ ⲉⲙⲉϥϫ., My 140 S stars ϫ., BMar 85 S in age voice ϫ., Va 61 94 B fire ⲙⲡⲁϥϭ. = P 131³ 84 S ⲱϫⲡ; qual B: Va 57 186 lamp ⲉϥϫ. σβ.

tr, *quench, make cease*: 2 Kg 14 7 S, Jer 21 12 B(S ⲱϣⲙ), 1 Thes 5 19 S(B ⲱϣⲉⲙ)σβ., Va 58 125 B lamp ⲁⲓϭⲉⲡⲟⲥ ἀποσβ., KKS 584 S sim ϫⲉⲡⲁϥ, Miss 4 202 B ⲡⲓⲙⲟⲩⲉ...ⲁⲡϭⲉⲛⲟϥ, Mor 53 63 S I am light come ⲉⲭⲡⲉ ⲡⲕⲁⲕⲉ ⲡⲓⲡⲁⲑⲟⲥ, ManiP 204 A² ϫϥ. ⲙⲡⲉⲩⲕⲱϥⲧ.

With following preposition or adverb.   c ⲉ-, *dat com*: Job 18 6 S(B ⲛⲁϱⲣⲉⲛ-)σβ. dat; c ⲛⲧⲛ-: BMis 374 S ⲡⲡⲉⲧⲛⲑⲩⲥⲓⲁ ϫ. ⲡⲧⲟⲟⲧⲛ = Va 63 7 B ⲕⲱⲣϥ = BSM 32 B ⲧⲁⲕⲟ, C 43 219 B ⲁⲡⲟⲩⲃⲁⲗ ϭ. ⲡⲧⲟⲧⲟⲩ; c ϱⲓϫⲛ-: Job 30 8 B ⲡⲓϣⲟⲩϣⲟⲩ ⲉⲧⲁϥϭ. ϱ. ⲡⲓⲕⲁϱⲓ (S ⲱ.) σβ. ἀπό.

ⲁⲧϫ., ⲁⲧϭ., *unquenchable*: Lu 3 17 B(S ⲱ. neg) ἄσβεστος; R 1 2 54 S fire ⲛⲁ., C 89 146 B sim = *ib* 99 174 S ϫ. neg.

o ⲡϫⲛⲉ: ShR 2 3 43 S rich man abandoned in hell ⲉϥⲟ ⲡϫ. ⲁⲩⲱ ⲉϥϣⲓⲡⲉ ⲛⲃⲟⲏⲑⲓⲁ ⲛⲓⲙ.   This word ?

ϫⲛⲉ- S *bend* v ϭⲛⲟⲛ 2°.

ϫⲛⲉ, -ⲏ, ϫⲛⲏⲛ S nn m, *beet* or *green herbs* generally: Is 51 20 -ⲏ (B ϱⲣ̄ⲧ) σευτλίον, cit ShA 1 466 -ⲉ; P 44 83 ⲁⲡⲑⲉⲁⲥ ϩⲟⲧⲁⲡⲏ· ϫ. ϱⲟⲟⲩⲧ ﺑﺮﻟﻖ =43 59 ϫ. ⲡϫ. ﺍﺷﻨﺎﻥ ﺟﺒﻠﻲ (Löw 42); ViK 9549 28 sick man's vomit ⲟⲩⲉⲧⲟⲩⲱⲧ ⲛⲑⲉ ⲛⲟⲩϫ., PMéd 308 ⲛⲟⲩⲡⲉ ⲛϫ. (v Chassinat *in loc*), Ryl 106 64 ⲙⲡⲉⲣⲟⲩⲉⲙ ... ϫⲏ. ⲟⲩⲇⲉ ⲉⲣⲱⲧⲉ.   V ϫⲁⲡⲟⲣ ﺑﺸﻨﻲ.

ϫⲉⲛⲉϫ A v ϫⲛⲁϫ *send*.

ϫⲛⲟ SA v ϫⲛⲁⲩ.

ϫⲛⲟⲩ SAA²FO, ϫⲓⲛⲟⲩ, ϫⲛⲟ S(both rare), ϭⲛⲟⲩ B, ϫⲉⲛⲁ(?)F, ϫⲡⲉ- SA², ϫⲛⲟⲩ- SF, ϫⲛ- S, ϫⲛⲟⲩϫ SAA²F, ϫⲛⲁⲩϫ Sª, ϭⲛⲟⲩϫ B, ϫⲓⲛⲟⲩϫ S, ϫⲉⲛⲟⲩϫ S/F, ϫⲉⲛⲟⲩⲟⲩϫ S, ϫⲛ. F vb tr, **I** *ask, question, require* (B mostly ϣⲓⲛⲓ): Ge 40 7, Jo 9 19 SA², Z 310 ⲁⲩϫⲟⲡ ϫⲡⲉ ⲟⲩϩⲗⲗⲟ ϫⲉ-, *ib* 347 ⲁⲓϫⲛⲟⲩⲟⲩ ϫⲉ-=MG 25 219 B ϣ. ἐρωτᾶν, Deu 32 7, Ez 20 1 (B ⲉⲣ ⲉⲧⲏ), Mk 15 2 ἐπερ.; Ps 10 4 ϫⲡⲟ (cit ShBM 195 ⲉⲓⲟⲣⲙ ⲉϫⲛ-), Si 23 10 (var ϫⲛⲟ), BM 216 110 speak not ⲙⲡⲁⲧϥϫⲛⲟⲩⲕ ἐξετάζειν; Lu 15 26, Ac 10 18 (var ϣⲓⲛⲉ) πυνθάνεσθαι; Is 65 1 ζητεῖν; Ps 81 1 (B ϯ ϱⲁⲡ) διακρίνειν; P 54 122 B (ⲁⲩ)ϭⲛⲟⲩⲡ ﺍﺳﺘﺨﺒﺮﻭﺍ(?); BG 69 ⲡⲧⲁⲣⲓϫⲛⲟⲩⲡ, ShC 4 119 ⲉⲣϣⲁⲡⲟⲩⲁ ϣⲓⲛⲉ ⲉϥϫ. ⲙⲙⲁⲓ, *ib* 73 125 ⲉⲩⲉϫⲛⲉ ⲡϱⲗⲗⲟ for leave (*cf* 124 ϣ. ⲡⲧⲟⲟⲧϥ ⲙⲡϱⲗⲗⲟ), C 99 140 ⲁϥϫⲛⲟⲩϥ ϫⲉⲟⲩ ⲡⲉⲧϣⲟⲟⲡ =*ib* 89 45 B ϣ., BAp 142 ⲡⲙⲁ ⲡⲉⲗⲟⲟⲗⲉ ⲛⲧⲁⲧⲉⲛϫⲛⲟⲩⲓ (concerning it), Mor 40 42 ⲁⲡⲛϫⲛⲟⲩϥ ϫⲉⲁϫⲓ ⲟⲩϣⲁϫⲉ=MG 25 268 B ϣ., Mor 41 92 ⲉⲩϣⲁⲛϫⲉⲛⲟⲩⲓ, El 52 A ⲁⲓϫⲛⲟⲩϥ ϫⲉⲡⲓⲙⲡⲉ, J 2 49 ⲡⲥⲉϫⲛⲟⲩⲡ ⲛⲧⲉⲛϱⲟⲙⲟⲗⲟⲅⲉⲓ, ST 378 Sª ⲁⲣⲓ ⲧⲁϭⲁⲡⲛ ⲛⲥϫⲛⲁⲩϥ, Miss 4 104 B ⲁⲩϭⲛⲟⲩⲩ ϫⲉⲁⲡ ⲑⲁⲓⲧⲉ ϯϣⲟⲛⲏ, DeV 1 39 B ⲁϥϣⲁⲛϭⲛⲟⲩ (f) ϫⲉ-, BSM 75 B ⲉϥϫ. ⲙⲙⲱⲟⲩ, Mor 30 22 F ⲡⲉ(ⲧ)ϫ. ⲙⲙⲁⲓ; imperat ⲙⲁϫ.: Job 12 7, Jo 18 21 (A² ϫⲛⲟⲩ), R 1 4 65 ⲙⲁϫⲛⲉ ⲡⲣⲉϥⲛⲟⲥ ⲉⲣ., Jo 9 23 SA² ἐπερ.; BMis 23 ⲙⲁϫⲛⲟⲩϥ ⲧⲁⲣⲉϥⲥⲉⲓ.

With following preposition.   c ⲉ- further obj: Mt 21 24, Mk 4 10 (B ϯ ϱⲟ), Z 304 ϯⲛⲁϫⲛⲟⲩⲕ ⲉⲩϣⲁϫⲉ ⲉⲣ., Nu 27 21, Hag 2 11 SA ἐπερ., Ge 43 7 ἐπερώτησις; Jo 4 52 SA²(BF ϣ.), BMar 118 ϫⲛⲟⲩϥ ⲉⲧⲁⲓⲧⲁ πυνθ.; PS 277 ⲡⲁⲓⲡⲉ ⲉⲧⲉⲧⲛϫ. ⲙⲙⲟⲓ ⲉⲣⲟϥ, ShC 42 92 ⲁⲣⲉⲡⲉⲡⲓⲥⲕⲟⲡⲟⲥ ϫⲛⲟⲩⲓ ⲉⲣⲟϥ (*cf* 93 ⲁⲣⲉⲡⲣⲉⲥⲃⲩⲧⲉⲣⲟⲥ ϣⲓⲡⲉ ⲉⲧⲃⲏⲛⲧⲩ), BMar 8 ⲙⲡⲉⲓϫⲛⲟⲩⲕ ⲉϣⲉⲗⲉⲉⲧ *asked for*, Pcod 20 ⲥⲉⲛⲁϫⲛⲉ ⲡϫⲱⲥ ⲉⲡⲉⲥⲟⲟⲩ, J 67 42 ϫ. ⲧⲉϥⲥϱⲓⲙⲉ ⲉⲡⲁⲡⲁϣ, Tor 12 ⲁⲛϫⲛⲟⲩⲕ ⲉⲡⲁⲓⲙⲟⲥⲓⲟⲡ, BKU 1 37 ⲡⲛⲉⲓϫⲛⲟⲩⲕ ⲉⲗⲁⲁⲩ (= ⲡⲁⲣⲉⲗⲑⲉ CO 111, v PRussGeorg 4 41), MG 25 307 B ⲉϥϫ. ⲙⲙⲟⲩ ⲉϥϱⲣⲁⲡ, DeV 1 92 B ⲉⲓⲟⲩⲱϣ ⲉϫⲛⲟⲩⲕ ⲉⲟⲩⲥⲁϫⲓ, *ib* 93 sim ϭⲛⲟⲩⲕ, Miss 4 157 B ⲟⲩⲅⲩⲡⲟⲅⲣⲁⲫⲓ ... ⲉⲕϫⲡⲟⲩ ⲙⲙⲟⲓ ⲉⲣⲟⲥ, Mani 2 A² ⲡⲥⲉϫ[ⲉ ⲡ]ⲉⲧⲁⲕϫⲛⲟⲩⲓ ⲁⲣⲁϥ, AZ 21 94 O ⲫⲱⲃ ⲉⲧⲓϫⲛⲟⲩ ⲙⲙⲟⲟⲩ ⲉⲣⲟϥ (for ⲉⲣⲟϥ); vbal: Ez 20 3 B(S ϫ. only), Mt 16 1 ἐπερωτᾶν; Ep 157 ⲙⲡⲟⲩϫⲛⲟⲩⲓ ⲉϱⲁⲣⲓⲁⲍⲉ ⲙⲙⲟⲥ, Mani K 68 A² ⲁϥϫⲛⲟⲩϥ ⲁⲣ ⲟⲩⲡⲟⲗⲉⲙⲟⲥ (refl?); c ⲉⲧⲃⲉ-: Is 45 11 (B diff), Jo 18 19 SA² ⲉⲣ. περί, Mk 7 17 (var ⲉ-) ἐπερ. περί; PS 251 ⲥⲉⲛⲁϫⲛⲉ- ... ⲉ. ⲡⲉⲩⲧⲃⲃⲟ, ShC 73 44 God shall ϫⲛⲉ ⲡⲣⲱⲙⲉ ⲉ. ϱⲱⲃ ⲛⲓⲙ, C 99 251 ϫ. ⲙⲙⲟⲟⲩ ⲉ. ⲡⲉⲅⲓⲱⲧ = *ib* 89 103 B ϣ., Miss 4 188 B ϭⲛⲟⲩⲓ ⲉ. ⲡⲁⲓϱⲱⲃ, BM 585 F ⲁⲓϫ. ⲡ(ϩ)ⲓⲁⲕⲟⲩⲉ. ϑ a (or ? *tell*); c ⲛⲙ-, *consult, debate with*: BMis 51 ⲁⲙⲏⲓⲧⲛ ... ⲧⲁϫⲛⲟⲩⲓ

ⲡⲓⲁϩⲏⲧⲛ (var Mor 33 99 ϣⲁϫⲉ), ManiK 32 A² ⲕⲣⲁϥ
ⲡⲓⲁ ⲉⲧⲟⲩⲛⲁϫⲛⲟⲩⲟⲩ ⲁⲛⲛⲟⲩⲉⲣⲏⲩ;   ⲥ ϩⲁ-: Pcod
8 ⲥⲉⲛⲁϫⲛⲉ ⲡⲉⲡⲓⲥⲕⲟⲡⲟⲥ ϩⲁⲡⲉϥⲗⲁⲟⲥ, Mun 33 ϫⲛⲟⲩⲓ
ⲁⲛ ϩⲁⲡⲉⲓϩⲱⲃ.

—— nn m, *questioning, inquiry* : Pro 1 32 ϫⲛⲟ (*A*
Cl prob *sic l*) ἐξετασμός; H S I 645 on Mk 8 27 ⲡⲉϫ-
ⲛⲟ ⲛⲧⲕⲁⲓⲥⲁⲣⲓⲁ, *ib* on 12 28 (?) ⲡⲉϫⲛⲟⲩ ⲉⲡⲭ̅ⲥ̅.

II *tell, say* : ShLeyd 374 ϩⲁⲓⲡⲧⲣⲉⲩϫⲛⲟⲩϥ ϫⲉⲉⲓⲥ
ⲧⲉⲕⲙⲁⲁⲩ (Lu 8 20 ϫⲓ ⲡⲟⲩⲱ), BAp 131 on Mk 6 35
ⲁⲙⲁⲑⲏⲧⲏⲥ ϫⲛⲟⲩϥ ϫⲉⲕⲁ ⲁⲙⲙⲏϣⲉ ⲉⲃⲟⲗ (var JTS
8 241 ⲡⲉϫⲁⲩ), Aeg 17 ⲁⲓϫⲛⲟⲩⲕ ... ϫⲉⲛⲥⲩⲭⲁⲍⲉ = *B*
ⲥⲁϫⲓ ⲛⲉⲙ-, Mor 23 5 ⲁⲩϫⲛⲟⲩϥ = *ib* 24 3 *F* ⲧⲁⲙⲁ,
Bodl (P) a 3 *S'* ⲁϥ (*sc* teacher) ϫⲉⲛⲟⲩⲓ ϫⲉⲡⲡⲉⲣⲟⲉⲛⲱ
= *ib* 1 *f* ⲧⲁⲙⲟⲓ, Mor 30 52 *F* ⲁⲙⲡⲉϫ. ⲗⲁⲁⲩ (var BMis
275 ⲧⲁⲙⲉ-), HM 2 29 ⲁϥϫⲛⲉ ⲕⲉⲙⲁⲧⲟⲓ ϫⲉⲁⲡⲧⲟⲩ-
ⲭⲣⲏⲥⲧⲓⲁⲛⲟⲥ, Mor 28 205 healed cripple ⲡⲉϫ. ⲁⲙ-
ⲡⲟⲩⲁ ⲡⲟⲩⲁ ⲡⲡⲉⲛⲧⲁⲩϣⲱⲡⲉ, Miss 4 664 ⲁⲩϫⲛⲟⲩⲥ ...
ϫⲉⲙⲉⲩⲛⲁ ⲗⲁⲁⲩ ⲉⲃⲱⲕ ⲛⲁϥ ⲉϩⲟⲩⲛ, Mor 31 36 ⲁⲡ-
ⲕⲁⲩⲭⲓⲟⲥ ϫⲛⲉ ⲛⲛⲙⲙⲁⲧⲟⲓ ϫⲉⲁⲛ(ⲉⲓⲙ)ⲉ ⲛⲁⲓ, BMis
278 ⲁϥϫⲛⲟⲩϥ ϫⲉϯ ⲧⲉⲕϣⲉⲉⲣⲉ, BM 613 ⲁⲕϫⲓⲛⲟⲩϥ
ϫⲉⲧⲁⲓⲉⲓ, ST 199 ⲁⲡⲁϫⲁⲙ ... ϫ. ⲙⲛⲛⲁ ϫⲉⲉⲓⲏⲩ, Ep
191 ⲁⲩϫⲛⲟⲩⲓ ϫⲉⲁⲙⲛⲛⲁ ϩⲧⲩⲃⲣⲓⲍⲉ, CMSS 39 *F* ⲁⲡⲉⲓ-
ϩⲗ(ⲗ)ⲁ ϫⲛⲟⲩⲓ ϫⲉⲁⲕⲡⲟⲧ, ViK 1101 *F* ⲁⲓϫⲛⲟⲩⲟⲩⲕ
ϫⲉⲡⲱⲧ;   intr : Mor 30 11 *F* ⲡⲉ]ⲧⲉⲣⲉⲡⲁⲅⲅⲉⲗⲟⲥ ϫⲉⲛⲁ (prob) ⲛⲁϥ (var BMis 238 ϫⲟⲟⲩ ⲉⲣⲟϥ);   ⲥ ⲉ- :
Mor 44 23 Judas went ⲁϥϫⲛⲉ ⲧⲉϥϭⲣⲓⲙⲉ ⲉⲡⲡⲧⲁⲩ-
ϣⲱⲡⲉ, Miss 4 618 ⲡⲉⲕϣⲁϫⲉ ⲉⲧⲉⲕϫ. ⲁⲙⲟⲓ ⲉⲣⲟⲟⲩ
ϫⲉ- (var Z 288 ϫⲱ λέγειν), Mor 30 43 *F* ⲁϥϫⲛⲟⲩϥ
ⲉϩⲱⲃ ⲛⲓⲃⲓ (var BMis 267 *S* ⲡⲁⲣⲁⲅ(ⲅ)ⲓⲗⲉ).

ϫⲛⲛⲉ *S* nn m, meaning unknown : CO 261 ϯ ⲡϫ.
ⲁⲙⲡⲛⲕⲁⲕⲉ ⲛⲁⲓ.

ϫⲉⲛⲉⲡⲱⲣ *S*, -ⲫⲱⲣ *B*, ϫⲓⲡⲛⲏ *AA²*, ϫⲉⲗⲉⲡⲟⲗ *F*
nn f *SF*, m *B*, *roof* : Deu 22 8 *SB*, 2 Kg 11 2 *S*, Pro
25 24 *SA*, Zeph 1 5 *AB*, Mt 10 27 *SB*, C 99 149 *S*
ⲧϫ. ⲁⲙⲡⲥⲱⲟϩ = *ib* 89 75 *B* ⲡⲓⲭ. ⲛⲧⲉ ⲡⲓⲙⲁ ⲛⲉⲱⲟⲩ ϯ
δῶμα; Tri 657 *S* ϣⲱⲭⲧ ϩⲓⲛⲧϫ. طم; Miss 4 716 *S*
went up ⲉϫⲛⲧϫ. of church, BMis 94 *S* stood ⲉϫⲛ-
ⲧⲉⲥϫ., Kr 125 *S* ⲧϭⲏⲛⲉⲡⲱⲣ, ManiH 10 *A²* cast down
from ⲛⲧϫ., Miss 4 114 *B* ⲡⲓⲭ. of temple, C 86 230 *B*
tree grew up through ⲡⲓⲭ., Kr 36 *F* ⲡⲉⲥϩ[ⲟⲩ]ⲛ ⲁⲙⲡ-
(ⲧ)ϫ.   *Cf* ⲗⲱⲃϣ 2°, ⲡⲉⲣ-.

ϫⲓⲛⲓⲟⲣ *B*   *v* pp 82 *a*, 751 *b*.

ϫⲓⲛⲓⲣⲓ, ϫⲓⲛⲓⲓⲣⲓ *B*   *v* ϫⲏⲣⲓ & ϫⲓⲉⲓⲣⲉ.

ϫⲟⲓⲥ *B*, ϫⲁ(ⲓⲓ)ⲥ *F*   *v* ϭⲟⲓⲥ.

ϫⲓⲛⲧ *S* nn m, reading doubtful, meaning unknown : Br 267 he created small intestine ⲁⲙⲡⲛⲉ
ⲡⲣⲉⲛⲓⲁⲥ ⲉⲡϫ. ⲁⲙⲡⲛϩⲉⲑⲉⲅⲥ (illegible C Baynes III).

ϫⲱⲛⲧ *SAA²BF*, ϭ. *B*, ϫ(ⲉ)ⲛⲧ-, ϫⲟⲛⲧ-, ϫⲟⲛⲧⲥ *S*,
ϫⲁⲛⲧ⸗ *AF*, ϭⲟⲛⲧ⸗ *B*, ϫⲟⲛⲧ† *SB*, ϭ.† *B* vb intr, **I** *try*,

test : Mt 4 3 *B*(*S* = Gk), 1 Thes 3 5 *B*(*SF* do) πειράζειν; C 89 117 *B* crop ⲉⲧⲓ ⲉⲥⲟⲓ ⲛⲥⲓⲁ ⲁⲙⲡⲁⲧⲉⲥϫ. χωρὶς
σπέρματος (Va ar 172 68 قبل ان يبس, MG 17 581 قبل
ولى (ان يلوى); ShA 2 75 *S* ⲉⲩϫ. now finding, now finding
not;   qual : Va 57 13 *B* ⲉⲛⲁ(ⲩ)ϭ....ⲛⲁⲩⲟⲓ ⲛⲉⲡⲓ-
ⲧⲓⲁⲓⲟⲛ ἐπιτήδειος εἶναι; 1 Kg 17 39 *S* ⲛⲉϥϫ. ⲁⲛ
ⲁⲙⲙⲟⲟⲩ ἄπειρος εἶναι; Ge 41 7 *B*(var ϫ., *S* ϫⲏⲧ)
πλήρης لوس; Z 265 *S* fled ϫⲉⲛⲥⲉϫ. ⲁⲛ ⲛⲁⲡⲁⲥⲕⲏⲥⲓⲥ,
Mor 18 151 *S* pregnant women ⲉⲣⲉⲛⲉⲩϣⲏⲣⲉ ϫ. ⲛ-
ϩⲏⲧⲟⲩ, BM 979 *S* ⲉϥϣⲱⲡⲉ ⲉϥϫ. ⲛⲧⲟⲟⲧⲕ, PMéd 190
S sim, Ryl 106 31 sim ?;   tr : Ex 20 20 *S*(*B* = Gk),
Dan 1 14 *SB*, 2 Cor 13 5 *SF* (prob, *B* = Gk), C 89 61
B ϣⲁⲛⲧⲉⲛϭⲟⲛⲧϥ ⲛⲕⲉⲥⲟⲡ ⲡⲉⲓ., Si 31 9 *S* ⲡⲉⲛⲧⲁⲩϫⲛⲧ
ⲅⲁⲣ πολύπειρος, He 11 29 *S* (var ShZ 638 ϫⲟⲟⲛⲧⲥ, *B*
as Gk) πεῖραν λαμβάνειν; Lu 14 19 *S*(*B* do) δοκιμάζειν; ShBor 247 107 *S* ⲛϥⲧⲁⲛϫⲛⲧ ⲡⲓⲟⲩ, ShA 1 156
S ⲡⲉⲛⲧⲁⲩⲥⲁⲓⲛⲧⲟⲩ (*sc* clothes) ⲛⲧⲁϫⲟⲛⲧⲟⲩ, BMis
293 *S* ⲁⲕⲭⲛⲧ ⲧⲁⲣⲭⲏ ⲛⲛⲃⲁⲥⲁⲛⲟⲥ ϫⲉⲥⲉϩⲟⲟⲩ, Mor
41 140 *S* arise ⲛⲧⲁϫⲟⲛⲧⲕ (var *ib* 40 25 ϫⲛⲟⲩⲕ = C
43 54 *B* ϣⲉⲡⲕ), Miss 8 196 *S* ⲁⲩϫⲟⲡⲧ ⲟⲩⲙⲏⲛϣⲉ
ⲁⲙⲡⲟⲗⲉⲙⲟⲥ, Tri 690 *S* ϫⲟⲛⲧ ⲛⲉⲣⲓⲟⲟⲩⲉ, ManiH 14
A² ϫ. ⲡⲉⲧⲟⲛⲕ, Va 61 199 *B* God ϭ. ⲡⲁⲃⲣⲁⲁⲙ.

With following preposition.   ⲥ ⲉ- as obj : ShC
73 89 *S* foods good for sick ⲉⲧⲣⲉϥϫ. ⲉⲣⲟⲟⲩ, ShClPr
23 *S* ⲉⲧⲛⲱ...ⲡⲉⲧⲛⲁϫ. ⲉⲣⲟⲥ;   vbal : Deu 4 34 *B*(*S* ϫⲓ
ϫⲛⲧ), Pro 26 18 *SA*, Ac 16 7 *BF*(*S* = Gk), *ib* 26 21
B(*S* ϩⲓ ⲧⲟⲟⲧⲥ), C 86 69 *B* ⲁϥϭ. ⲉⲃⲟⲗ ⲉⲃⲟⲗ ⲁⲙⲡⲉϥ-
ⲑⲱⲟⲩⲓ ⲡⲉⲓ., Deu 28 56 *S*(*B* diff) πεῖραν λαμβ.; Va
57 72 *B* ⲛϭ. ⲉⲫⲱⲧ δοκιμάζειν; Mor 53 74 *S* ⲛ†ϫ.†
ⲁⲛ ⲉⲡⲱⲧ, BMar 181 *S* ⲉⲩϣⲁⲛϫⲟ(ⲛ)ⲧⲕ ⲉⲥⲁⲣⲧⲉ ⲡⲁⲕ
if art tempted to, Va 66 311 *B* ⲛⲡⲁϭ. ⲉϯ ⲡⲱⲧⲉⲛ ⲛϯ-
ϩⲣⲩⲡⲟⲇⲉⲓϫⲓⲥ;   ⲥ ⲉϫⲛ- : Zech 11 13 *SA*(*B* = Gk)
δοκ. ὑπέρ;   ⲥ ⲁⲛ- : ShA 1 69 *S* ϫ. ⲛⲕⲉⲥⲟⲡ ⲁⲙⲡ-
ⲧⲟⲩϣⲉⲉⲣⲉ;   ⲥ ϩⲛ-, ϫⲉⲛ- : Eccl 2 1 *SF* ϫⲁⲛⲧⲥ ⲡⲉⲓ.
ἐν, He 4 15† *S*(*B* = Gk) ⲡⲉⲓ. κατά; Phil 4 12† *S*(*B*
ⲧⲥⲁⲃⲏⲟⲩⲧ) μυεῖσθαι ἐν; Hab 1 8 *SA* ϫⲟⲡⲧⲟⲩ ⲉⲣⲡⲉⲩ-
ϩⲧⲱⲣ (*B* diff) ἐξιππάζεσθαι; ShC 42 103 *S* ⲁⲙⲡⲁⲧ-
ⲟⲩϫⲟⲛⲧⲕ ϩⲓⲣⲉⲛⲃⲁⲥⲁⲛⲟⲥ, BM 915 17 *B* ⲉⲩϭ. ⲁⲙⲟⲓ
ϫⲉⲛϯⲡⲟⲣⲛⲓⲁ, DeV 2 44 *B* ⲛⲁϥϭ.† ⲡⲉ ϫⲉⲛⲟⲩϫⲟⲙ ⲉϥ-
ⲫⲱⲣⲕ ⲛⲉⲛⲟⲩⲡⲓ.

II *begin SA*, ⲥ ⲉ- : Jud 1 35, Tob 2 12, Mic 6 13
A(*B* ⲉⲣ ϩⲏⲧⲥ) ἄρχεσθαι, Deu 2 25 (*B* do) ἐνάρ.; Mk
13 28 (var ϣⲱⲡⲉ, *B* = Gk, *F* om) ἤδη; ShZ 603 ⲁϥϫ.
ⲉⲣ ⲁⲧⲥⲟⲙ.

—— nn *SB*, *trial* : 1 Pet 4 12 *S*(*B* = Gk) πειρασμός, Job 7 1 *B*(*S* ⲁⲁ ⲡⲭ.) πειρατήριον; He 3 9 *B*(*S*
= Gk) δοκιμασία.

ⲁⲧϭ. *B*, *untried, untempted* : TEuch 2 371 may we
pass night ⲛⲁⲧϭⲟⲡⲧⲉⲛ ἀπείραστος; Va 61 199 ⲡⲓⲟⲩⲁⲓ
ⲛⲁⲧϭⲟⲛⲧϥ (*sc* God).

ⲁⲁ ⲡϫ., ϭ. *SB*, *place of trial* : Ge 49 19 *B*, Ps 17
30 *B*(*S* ⲁⲁ ⲛⲥⲟⲟⲛⲉ) πειρατήριον; Va 58 154 *B* mortals are ⲁⲁⲁ. ⲡⲡⲓⲥⲁⲁⲫⲱⲣⲁ γυμνάσιον; ShA 1 201 *S*

martyrs' shrines ye have made ⲙ̅. ⲛⲛⲉⲧⲛ̅ⲙⲁⲥⲉ ⲙⲁ
ⲙ̅ⲡⲱⲧ ⲙ̅ⲡⲉⲧⲛⲉⲓⲱ.

ϫⲟⲛⲧⲥ, ϭ. nn, *trial*: Mor 37 82 *S* this I say ϩⲛ̅ⲟⲩϭ.
ⲙ̅ⲡⲟⲩⲙⲉ ἀπὸ πείρας; P 44 121 *S* ⲉⲓⲧⲉ (43 129 ✝) ϫ.
ⲉⲧⲉⲕⲕⲗⲏⲥⲓⲁ امت¹; Cat 173 *B* devils ask souls ⲉⲟⲩϭ.
ⲡⲉⲙⲟⲩⲉⲧⲁⲥⲙⲟⲥ.

ϫⲡⲓⲧ *SA* nn with vb ϫⲓ, *try*, tr: Deu 13 3 (*B*= Gk)
πειράζειν, *ib* 8 16 (*B* do) ἐκπ.; Mor 17 16 ⲉⲥϫ. ⲙⲙⲟϥ
λόγος δοκιμαστικός; 2 Kg 10 3 κατασκέπτεσθαι; ShA
1 458 ⲁϥϫ. ⲙⲙⲟϥ saying;   ⲥ ⲉ-: Deu 4 34 ϫ. ⲉⲧⲣⲉϥ
(*B* ϭⲱⲡⲧ ⲉ-) ⲡⲉⲓ.;   ⲥ ⲛⲥⲁ-: ST 339 ⲙⲏⲡⲟⲧⲉ ⲡⲧⲉ
ⲣⲱⲙⲉ ϫ. ⲛⲥⲱⲡ; as nn m: Deu *lc* (*B*= Gk) πειρασμός; Si 6 22 δοκιμασία; P 44 59 ⲛ̅ϫ.· ⲡ̅ϫⲟⲕⲓⲙⲁⲍⲉ,
ⲡⲓⲣⲁⲍⲉ; ⲣⲉϥϫⲓ.: Hos 6 9 *SA* (Till *in loc* p xxix,
B ⲣⲉϥⲉⲣ ⲡⲓⲣⲁⲍⲓⲛ) πειρατής; ShIF 98.

ϫⲱⲛⲧ *B*, ϫⲡⲉⲧ *F*   *v* ϭⲱⲛⲧ.

ϫⲓⲛⲧ✝ *F*   *v* ϭⲱⲡⲧ.

ϫⲛⲧⲏⲩ (*sic*, not as p 440 *b*) *v* ⲧⲏⲩ.

ϫⲛⲁ(ⲁ)ⲩ *S*, ϫⲛⲟ *S* (once) *A*, ϭⲛⲁⲩ, ϭⲛⲁⲩϩ *B* vb
intr, *delay*: Pro 6 11 neg *SA* (*B* ⲁⲧϭ.) ἄοκνος; Va 57
219 *B* ⲧⲉⲛϭ. ⲉⲡⲟⲓ ⲡⲣⲉϥϥ ⲥⲃⲱ ῥυθμίζειν (*l* ? ῥαθυμεῖν); TU 43 1 *A* ⲙ̅ⲡⲉⲛϫ. ⲉⲁⲡⲉϩⲣⲁⲓ ⲡⲏⲧⲓⲉϭ, Miss 4
205 *B* ⲡⲧⲉⲧⲛ̅ϣⲧⲉⲙϭ. ⲉⲣⲉⲧⲉⲛ✝ ϩⲟ;   ⲥ ⲉ-: Nu 22
16 *SB*, Ac 9 38 *SB*, Mor 18 170 *S* (var LCyp 22 ϫⲛⲟ),
ROC 25 239 *B* ✝ϭ. ⲉⲥϫⲛⲧⲟⲩ ὀκνεῖν, GöttN '98 174
S not fitting ⲉⲧⲣⲉⲛϫ. ⲉⲧⲁⲩⲟⲟⲩ, Mor 37 70 *S* ✝ⲛⲁϫ.
ⲉⲧⲣⲁⲭⲱ ὀκνητέος, BMar 169 *S* ⲉϥϫ. ⲉⲯⲁⲗⲗⲉⲓ τῷ
ὄκνῳ συνέχεσθαι εἰς; BHom 4 *S* ϫ. ⲉⲣϩⲙⲟⲟⲥ ⲉϩⲣⲁⲓ
ξενίζειν; ShC 73 51 *S* woman ⲉⲥϫ. ⲏ ⲉⲥϭⲟⲧⲡ ⲉⲥⲱϩⲉ,
ROC 20 420 *S* none will ϫ. ⲉⲙⲟⲩⲧⲉ ⲉⲣⲟⲥ ϫⲉⲙⲁⲣ-
ⲧⲩⲣⲟⲥ, BSM 362 *S* ⲙ̅ⲡⲣ̅ϫ. ⲉ✝ = BSM 23 *B* ⲉⲣ ⲁⲣⲕⲟⲥ
(-γός);   ⲥ ϩⲛ-: Ro 12 11 *S* (*B* ⲟⲓ ⲛ̅ϭ., var ⲣⲉϥϭ.,
F ⲁⲓ ⲡⲱϫⲉⲡ) ὀκνηρός dat.

ϭⲛⲁⲩϩ *B*: BSM 59 ⲙ̅ⲡⲉⲣϭ. ⲙⲙⲟⲕ ⲁⲡ ⲉⲥⲱⲧⲉⲙ =
Va 63 26 ϭⲛⲁⲩ, *ib* 50 ⲙ̅ⲡⲉⲣϭ. ⲙ̅ⲙⲱⲧⲉⲛ ⲁⲛⲡⲉ ϭⲉⲡ-
ⲡⲓⲭⲓⲛⲓⲛⲓ ⲉϩⲟⲩⲛ = Va 63 19 do = BMis 402 *S* ϫ.,
AM 247 ⲛ̅✝ⲛⲁϭ. ⲁⲛ ⲉⲥⲁϫⲓ.

—— nn m, *sloth*: Phil 3 1 *B* (*S* ϩⲓⲥⲉ) ὀκνηρός; Sh
MIF 23 100 *S* ⲡⲉϫ. of my body ✝ ⲟⲩⲃⲏⲓ, Mich 550
24 *S* worketh ⲁϫⲛⲗⲁⲁⲩ ⲛ̅ϫ.;   BMis 485 *S* is not
dead but ⲉϥⲟ ⲛ̅ϫⲛⲁⲁⲩ (*sic* MS).

ⲁⲧϫ., -ϭ., *without delay*: Pro 6 11 *B* (*SA* vb) ἄοκνος;   ⲙ̅ⲛ̅ⲧ-, ⲙⲉⲧⲁ.: Va 57 276 *B* ✝ⲙ. of Paul
ἀνεπαχθής; Bor 287 2 *S* among virtues.

ⲣⲉϥϫ., -ϭ., *sluggard*: Pro 6 6 *SA* (*B* ϭⲉⲡⲡⲉ), Si 22 1
S, Mt 25 26 *S* (*B* do) ὀκνηρός; ShMiss 4 282 *S* let
porters not be ϩⲉⲛⲣ. neglecting duties, BMar 170 *S*
ⲣ. opp ⲥⲡⲟⲩⲇⲁⲓⲟⲥ, AM 225 *B* ⲡⲟⲩⲥ ⲡⲣ.;   ⲙ̅ⲛ̅ⲧ-,
ⲙⲉⲧⲣⲉϥϫ., *delay, sloth*: Eccl 10 18 *S* (*F* ⲙ̅ⲛ̅ⲧⲱϫ),
Bor 226 158 *S* ⲡⲉⲣⲃⲏⲅⲉ ⲛ̅ⲧⲙ. ὀκνηρία; BHom 134
S ⲧⲙ. ⲟⲩⲉⲗⲥ ⲧⲉⲯⲩⲭⲏ ῥαθυμία; ShC 42 226 *S* ⲟⲩⲙ.

ⲁⲡ ⲧⲉⲡⲧⲁⲥⲕⲁⲧⲉϫⲉ ... ⲁⲗⲗⲁ ⲟⲩϣⲱⲡⲉ, Miss 4 742 *S*
ⲙ̅ⲡⲧⲁⲙⲉⲗⲏⲥ ⲁⲅⲱ ⲙ., Va 63 86 *B* ⲙⲉⲧⲁⲣⲅⲟⲥ, ⲙ.

ϭⲉⲡⲡⲉ *B*, pl ϭⲉⲡⲡⲉⲩ nn, *sluggard, delayer*: Pro 6 6
(*SA* ⲣⲉϥϫⲛⲁⲁⲩ), Va 57 220 ϣⲱⲡⲉ ⲛⲁⲣⲅⲟⲥ ⲟⲩⲟϩ ⲛϭ.
ὀκνηρός;   pl: Pro 11 16 (*SA* do) ὀκ.;   ⲉⲣ ϭ.:
Deu 32 36 (*S* ⲛⲁ ⲧⲟⲟⲧϥ ⲉⲃⲟⲗ) παρειμένος; EW 29 ⲉⲉⲣ
ϩⲱⲃ ϣⲁⲕⲉⲣ ϭ. = Wess 15 129 *S* ϣⲁⲕⲙⲟⲕⲣ̅ⲕ ⲥⲓⲁίνειν;
Va 61 90 ⲉⲣ ϭ. ⲉ̇ϣⲧⲉⲙϫⲱⲕ ⲉⲃⲟⲗ ⲙ̅ⲡⲓϣⲉⲙϣⲓ; ⲁⲧ ϭ.:
C 86 164 ⲁϥⲧⲱⲛϥ ⲛⲁⲧ ϭ.;   ⲙⲉⲧ ϭ.: HL 81 ⲟⲩⲙⲉⲧ-
ⲁⲙⲉⲗⲉⲥ ⲡⲉⲙⲟⲩⲙ. ὄκνος.

ϫⲛⲟⲟⲩ, ϫⲛⲁⲁⲩ, ϭⲛⲟⲟⲩ (once) *S*, ϭⲛⲱⲟⲩ *B*, *S/F*
v ⲣ̅ϫⲛⲟⲟⲩ below, pl ϫⲛⲟⲟⲩⲉ *S* & sg as pl, nn m,
threshing-floor, grain *heaped* there: 2 Kg 6 6 *SB*, Job
5 26 *S* (var -ⲟⲩⲉ) *B*, Joel 2 24 *SB* (*A* ϩⲓⲧ), Lu 3 17 *SB*
ἅλων, Jud 15 5 *S* ϫ̆. (var στοιβή), Lev 26 5 *B* (*S* diff)
ἀλοητός; Ex 8 10 *B*, Jos 5 3 *S* ϫⲛⲁ. (Wess), Si 20 28
S (ShR 2 3 62 ϫⲛⲁ., Br 241) θιμωνιά; K 128 *B* ⲡⲓϭ.
اندر ,بيدر ,جرن (cf HAWinkler *Bauern* 99), ViK 9471
S ⲡⲉϫ. ⲙ̅ⲡⲁⲧⲙⲉ = C 41 14 *B* = Miss 4 323 مجرنة;
ShP 130⁵ 23 *S* vines, meadows & ⲡⲉϫ. (ⲛ)ⲡⲉⲡⲟⲓⲕⲓⲟⲛ,
BMOr 6201 A 24 *S* ⲡⲕⲁⲓⲣⲟⲥ ⲙ̅ⲡⲉϫ., CO 187 *S* ⲥⲓⲙⲥⲓⲙ ⲉϩⲟⲩⲛ ⲉⲡⲁϫ., Mun 37 *S* scattered like ⲟⲩϣⲟⲉⲓϣ
ⲛ̅ϫ. ϩⲛ̅ⲛ̅ϣⲱⲙ, DeV 2 172 *B* trodden like ⲟⲩⲥⲟⲩⲟ
ϩⲓⲭⲉⲛⲟⲩϭ., Va 57 4 *B* ⲭⲱ ⲙ̅ⲡⲓⲥⲟⲩⲟ ϭⲉⲛ✝ϩⲣⲟⲓ ⲛ̅ⲧⲉ
ⲡⲉϥϭ., BKU 1 65 *S* ⲡⲁⲕⲧⲟⲡ...ϩⲓⲛ̅ϫ.;   pl form:
P 43 16 ⲛ̅ϫ.', 'ϩ, *ib* 46 159 ⲡⲉϫ. جرن, ⲛⲉϫⲛⲟⲟⲩⲉ جرن.

ⲣ̅ϫⲛⲟⲟⲩ¹, ⲣⲉϫ.², ⲗⲉϫ.³, ⲣⲓϫ.⁴, ⲣ̅ϫⲛⲟⲟⲩⲉ⁵ *S*, ⲣ̅-
ϫⲛⲁⲩ *S/*, ⲣⲉϫⲛⲁⲩ, ⲗⲁϭⲛⲁⲩⲩ *F* nn f, meaning as ϫ.:
Ge 50 10¹ (*B* ϭⲛⲱⲟⲩ), Jud 6 37² (var³), 1 Kg 19 22¹
(varᵇ), Hos 9 2 *F* p. (JEA 11 245, *A* ϩⲓⲧ, *B* do) ϭ̆., Mor
25 158², Miss 8 227 *S/* ⲛⲧϩⲓ ϩⲛ̅ⲧⲉⲕⲣ., Kr 11 *F* ⲛ̅ⲕⲉ-
ⲣⲱⲥ (καιρός) ⲧⲗ.

ϫⲉⲛⲉⲫⲱⲣ *B*   *v* ϫⲉⲡⲉⲡⲱⲣ.

ϫⲓⲛϥⲉϩ *B*   *v* ϫⲓⲙⲫⲉϩ.

ϫⲱⲛϥ *SA*², ϣ. *S*, ϫⲟⲟⲡⲉϥ† *S*, ϫⲁ(ⲁ)ⲛϥ† *A*² vb
intr, *happen, befall*: BM 358 28 ⲁϥϫ. ⲡⲟⲩⲥⲟⲡ...ⲁϥⲉⲓ
(var Mor 47 184 ⲁⲥϫ.), JTS 9 379 ⲁϥϫ. .... ⲉⲧⲣⲉϥⲉⲓ,
J 75 55 ⲡⲉⲧⲛⲁϫ. ⲡⲥⲉⲱϣ ⲡⲡⲉⲧⲥⲛ̅ϩ, PCol 1 witness
says ⲉⲓϫ.† *chanced* (to be present), Mani K 173 *A*²
ⲥⲉϫ.† ⲁⲧⲣⲉⲛϭⲙ̅ ⲧⲁⲡⲉ, *ib* 174 ⲥⲉϫⲁⲁⲡϥ ⲥⲉϣⲛⲏϣ; impers: BAp 106 ⲁⲥϫ. ϩⲙ̅ⲡⲉϩⲟⲟⲩ ⲉⲧⲙⲙⲁⲩ = MIE 2
381 *B* ⲁⲥϣⲱⲡⲓ, *ib* 80 ⲡⲉⲁⲥϫ. ⲉⲣⲉⲡⲡⲉⲧⲟⲩⲁⲁⲃ ϩⲁϩⲧⲏϥ,
Miss 8 210 ⲉⲥϣⲁⲛϫ. ⲡⲟⲩⲥⲟⲡ ⲡⲧⲉⲡⲉⲧⲣⲟⲉⲓⲥ ✝ ⲡⲁⲓ,
BM 1131 ⲁⲥϫ. ⲉⲓⲡϩⲟⲩⲛ ⲉⲡⲏⲓ;   tr, *meet with, fall
upon*: Z 325 ⲙ̅ⲡⲉϥϫ. ⲗⲁⲁⲩ ⲡⲧⲉⲓⲣⲉ οὐδενὸς τυγχάνειν;
Wess 18 8 ⲉⲡ(or ⲉϥ)ϣⲁⲛϫ. ⲧⲕⲩⲣⲓⲁⲕⲏ, BM 298 ⲉⲧⲕⲩⲣⲓⲁⲕⲏ...ϫ. ⲁⲗⲕⲏ ⲙ̅ⲡⲁⲣ̅ⲙⲟⲩⲧⲉ, MⲁniK 52 *A*² ⲁⲩ
ⲣ ⲣⲱϥ...ⲁⲩϫ. ⲡⲛⲉϥϩⲃⲏⲩⲉ ⲁⲡⲟϭⲣⲏⲧⲉ;   ⲥ ⲉ-: BM
216 80 those sailing ⲉⲙⲁϣⲱ. [ⲉⲟⲩ]ⲧⲏⲩ ⲡⲟⲩϫⲁⲙ
τυγχ.; Aeg 264 ⲛ̅ϫ. ⲉⲡⲕⲁⲓⲣⲟⲥ ⲉⲧⲙⲙⲁⲩ, BMis 156
ⲁⲡϣⲁ ... ϫ. ⲉⲣⲟⲥ (*sc* Sunday) that year = BSM 63 *B*

ⲉⲣ ⲁⲡⲁⲛⲧⲁⲛ ⲉ-, J 94 31 ⲡⲉⲧⲛⲁϫ. ⲉⲡⲉⲓⲭⲁⲣⲧⲏⲥ, Win 31 witnesses say ⲁⲛϫ. ⲉⲡⲧⲟⲡⲟⲥ (cf PCol above); ⲉ- ⲣⲟⲩⲛ ⲉ-: RylSuppl 50 naught can ϫⲱⲛϥⲉ ⲉⲣ. ⲉⲡⲧⲟ- ⲡⲟⲥ ⲉⲧⲙⲙⲁⲩ (var Leyd 469 ϫⲱⲣ ⲉⲣ.), BM 313 ⲁⲩϫ. ⲛⲣⲉⲡⲛⲟϭ ⲛⲕⲁⲧⲏⲅⲟⲣⲉⲓⲁ ⲉⲣ. ⲉⲣⲟϥ.

—— nn m, *chance*: Aeg 218 ⲕⲁⲧⲁ ⲟⲩϫ. ⲛⲧⲉⲡⲉ- ⲡⲓⲥⲕⲟⲡⲟⲥ ⲙⲟⲩ κ. συγκυρίαν, Mor 17 118 sim κ. συν- τυχίαν; JTS 4 39 ⲁⲛϫ. ϣⲱⲡⲉ ⲉϥⲛⲁⲡⲣⲟⲛⲗⲑⲉ, Mor 26 8 God τρⲉⲩϫ. ϣⲱⲡⲉ so that pagan be converted, *ib* 39 30 ⲉϥⲡⲏⲛ ⲉⲃⲟⲗ...ⲣⲡⲟⲩϫ.

ϫⲡⲟϥ, ϫⲉⲡⲟϥ², -ⲃ³ S ϫⲡⲁϥ S*f*, ϭⲡⲟϥ⁴, ϣⲡ.⁵, ϣⲡⲟⲩϥ⁶ B nn m, *basket, crate* (? خَشَبَة): Z 344 S full of bread = MG 25 208 B ⲥⲱⲕ ἀναβολίδι(ο)ν; K 151⁶ مقطف كراي, Montp 168 B ⲡϣ.⁶, Bodl 325 154 B⁵ زرد; for bread: Miss 4 749 S*f*, Kr 242 S² ⲛϭⲁⲁϭ[ⲉ; beans: WS 124 S(paral ⲃⲓⲣ, ⲃⲁⲗⲟⲧ, ⲥⲟⲟⲕ); chaff: C 86 180 B⁴; wood: Kr 154 S³; wine: ST 132 S ϣⲏ ϥⲧⲟⲟⲩ ⲛϫ., CO 160 S ⲧⲉⲓⲟⲩ ⲛϫ., also Ep 90, Tor 7; of bronze: Pap *penes* BHStricker S ⲟⲩϫ. ⲉⲣⲁⲙⲏ(ⲧ).

ϫⲡⲟⲩϥ *v* ϫⲟⲩϥ.

ϫⲡⲁⲣ SAA²F(once), ϫⲡⲣ S*f*, ϫⲡⲁ A, ϭⲡⲁⲣ B, ϫⲡⲉⲣ, ϫⲉⲡⲣ F, pl ϫⲡⲁⲅⲣ S, ϭ. B(also sg) & sg as pl, nn m, *a forearm*: P 44 70 S ⲕⲁⲥ ⲙⲡⲉϫ.· ⲕⲉⲣⲕⲓⲥ عظم الدراع; Job 1 17 B(S Gk Ar diff); LMär 2 S cut off ⲡⲉϥϫ. ⲛⲟⲩⲛⲁⲙ = C 43 40 B, BMis 46 S raised ⲡⲉϥϫ. ⲥⲡⲁⲅ, Mor 32 20 S bade bind his ⲕⲉⲗⲉⲛⲕⲉⲣ ⲣⲓϫⲛ- ⲡⲉϥϫ. ⲛⲟⲩⲛⲁⲙ, *ib* 31 202 S*f* pass ropes ⲣⲁⲛⲉⲕϫ. (cf Jer 45 12 ἀγκών), Miss 4 749 S ⲛⲟⲩⲗ ⲛϫ. of cross, ManiK 174 A² ⲙⲟⲩⲧ, ⲡⲁⲣⲃ, ϫ. ⲥⲡⲉⲩ, C 43 221 B cut off ⲡⲉϥϭ. ⲃ̄ ⲓⲥϫⲉⲛⲛⲉϥⲁⲗⲱϫ ⲉⲃⲟⲗ, Mor 40 10 S ϫ. ⲛⲟⲩⲛⲁⲙ (var *ib* 41 124 ϭⲃⲟⲓ)= *ib* 39 14 F ϫⲡⲉⲣ = C 43 40 B ⲡⲉϥϭⲡⲁⲅ, Mor 30 6 F ⲛⲉⲃϫ. ⲣⲓⲥⲉ ⲉϥⲙϣⲓϣⲉ = BMis 233 S ϭⲃⲟⲓ, MG 25 150 B ⲁϥϫⲁⲗⲁ ⲡⲉϥϭ. ⲉϩⲣⲏⲓ into boiling cauldron, BKU 1 26 (8116a)F ⲙⲁⲣⲁϥ (sc amulet) ⲣⲓϫⲟⲡⲉⲕϫⲉⲣ, BM 527 F(same MS)ϫⲡⲁⲣ, ST 398 S eagle's *wing*; pl forms: Lu 2 28 B(S ⲣⲁⲙⲏⲣ), ROC 17 405 B ⲉⲥⲧⲁⲕⲧⲟ ⲉⲣⲟϥ ⲛ- ⲡⲉⲥϭ. ἀγκάλη; Jer 38 21 B ὦμος; Ps 118 48 B(S ϭⲓⲭ), Pro 10 4 B(SA do)χείρ; Aeg 6 B ⲣⲉⲙⲥⲓ ⲉϫⲉⲛ- ⲡⲉⲥϭ.حضفه; ShC73 162S uncover ⲛⲉⲧⲓϫ. (var ϭⲃⲟⲓ) ϣⲁⲣⲟⲩⲛ ⲉⲡⲉⲧⲛϣⲱⲡϣ, J 13 25 S *boundaries*]ⲣⲁⲓ ϫ. (obscure).

b, *strength, violence* SAA²: Mor 17 11 ⲛⲉϫ. of waves βία, Wess 11 167 ϣⲁⲩⲧⲣⲉⲅⲕⲱⲧⲉ ⲣⲡⲟⲩϫ. βι- αίως; JSch l 37 they tend me ⲣⲓⲛⲉⲩⲣⲓⲥⲉ ⲛϫ.; ⲛϫ. adverbial: Jer 18 14 (B ⲛϫⲟⲛⲥ) βιαίως, Ac 5 26 (B do)μετὰ βίας, Bodl(P)c 23 ⲥⲱⲕ ⲙⲙⲟϥ ⲛ. βιάζεσθαι; Pro 25 26 S(var ⲛϫⲓⲛϭⲟⲛⲥ)A ἔξοδος (of rushing water); ShViK 915 ⲉⲩⲁⲙⲁⲣⲧⲉ ⲛ. ⲣⲓⲛⲉⲩϭⲓⲭ, ShCl Pr 36 200 ⲟⲩϣⲱⲧⲉ ⲉⲥⲃⲉⲉⲃⲉ ⲛ., ShC 42 200 ⲉⲙⲟⲧⲥ ...ⲛϥⲛⲁⲩ ⲉⲣⲟⲩ ⲛ. *with effort*, ShA 2 299 ⲉⲙⲟⲧⲥ

ⲁϥⲧⲱⲟⲩⲛ ⲉϩⲣⲁⲓ ⲛ. sim; ☨ ϫ.: Ryl 94 100 ⲙⲛⲧ- ⲣⲉϥϫⲓ ⲛϭⲟⲛⲥ ... ⲙⲛⲧⲣⲉϥ☨ ϫ. ⲛⲡϩⲏⲕⲉ; ϫⲓ ϫ., ⲛϫ., *use violence, compulsion*: Ge 33 11 (B ϭⲓ ⲛϫⲟⲛⲥ), BM 320 150 though bidden depart ⲁϥϫⲓⲧϥ ⲛϫ. ⲁϥϣⲱ βιάζ., Pro 16 26 SA ϫⲡⲁ ἐκβ., Ge 19 3 SB παραβ., Aeg 229 ϫⲓ ⲛⲟⲩⲡⲁⲣⲑⲉⲛⲟⲥ ⲛϫ. βιασάμενος ἔχειν; Pro 19 10 SA ϫⲓ ⲛⲟⲩϫ. δυναστεύειν, Hos 12 7 A(B ⲉⲣ ⲙⲉⲧϫⲱⲣⲓ) κατⲁδ.; Sa 10 14 (var ϫⲓ ⲛϭⲟⲛⲥ) τυραν- νεῖν; ShC 73 99 ϫⲓⲧⲟⲩ ⲛϫ. ⲉⲧⲣⲉⲅⲃⲱⲕ, C 99 274 ⲙⲟⲧⲥ ⲁⲩϫⲓⲧⲁ ⲛϫ. ϣⲁⲡⲧⲉϥⲁⲥⲡⲁⲍⲉ ⲙⲙⲟⲟⲩ; as nn m: P 129¹¹ 61 who have sacrificed ⲣⲡⲟⲩϫ. μετὰ βίας; Sa 10 11 πλεονεξία; ⲙⲛⲧϫⲓ ⲛϫ. A²:ManiH 78; ⲣⲉϥϫⲓ ϫ.: Job 6 23 (B ϫⲱⲣⲓ) δυνάστης; Sa 16 4 τύραννος; ShA 2 237 p ⲣⲱⲃ ⲛⲣ., ClPr 45 cruci- fied ⲣⲓⲧⲛⲣⲉⲛⲣ.; ⲙⲛⲧⲣⲉϥϫⲓ ϫ.: Am 3 9 (B ⲙⲉⲧ- ⲣⲉϥϭⲉⲛ ϫⲱⲣⲓ) καταδυναστεία; ShR 2 3 34 ⲧⲙ. ⲛⲡ- ⲣⲏⲕⲉ.

ⲙⲟⲩϫⲡⲁⲣ S, ⲙⲁⲣϣ.¹, ⲙⲟⲣϣⲡⲁⲣ, -ϭⲡⲁⲅⲣ³ B nn f, *what is bound on shoulders, scapular* of monks: MG 25 210 B ⲡⲟⲩⲃⲱⲕ ⲡⲉⲙⲡⲟⲩⲙ.¹ = Z 345 S ⲙⲟⲧϫⲣ ἀνάλαβος; Mor 40 41 S = MG 25 268 B¹(BMAdd 17262 23 *b* صمّاء), BIF 13 110 S sim = MG 25 298 B om, MG 25 40 B ⲕⲟⲗⲟⲃ, ⲙ.¹, ⲭⲗⲁϥⲧ, TEuch 1 85 B ☨ⲙ.³ ⲉⲧⲉ(*sic l*)ⲡⲓⲥϫⲛⲓⲙⲁ ⲡϣⲁⲣⲡⲉ اسكيم الجلد, BodlMarsh 32 92 B ☨ ⲣⲓⲱⲧϥ ⲛ☨ⲙ.³ دِرْع, P 54 170 B². *Cf* ? ϭⲗⲣ.

ϫⲉⲡⲣ B nn m, *a garment*: BMOr 8775 119 ⲛϫ. ثوب.

ϫⲡⲉⲣ F nn m, *a container or measure*?: AZ 23 39 ⲋ̄ ⲛϫ. ⲛⲃⲁⲣⲛⲉⲣ. *Cf* ?? ϫⲁⲡⲉ.

ϫⲁⲏⲏⲣⲓ B nn f, *meaning doubtful*: K 137 among parts of waterwheel ☨ϫ. زٖلط (rope to which pots at- tached AZ 14 84).

ϫⲱⲛϫ B nn m, *colocynth*: BMOr 8771 104 ⲛϫ. حنظل (cf ⲗⲁⲕⲁⲙⲟⲩ).

ϫⲁⲛⲓϫⲓ B nn m, *palm-fibre* for rope-making: K 138 ⲛϫ., P 55 2 ⲛⲓϫⲁⲛϫⲓ ليف (cf ϣⲛⲃⲏⲛⲉ).

ϫⲓⲛϫⲏ *v* ϫⲏ 3°.

ϫⲓⲛϫⲛ S, ϫⲉⲛϫⲉⲛ B *v* ϭⲛϭⲛ.

ϫⲓⲛϫⲓⲛ *v* ϭⲛϭⲛ & ϭⲓⲛϭⲓⲛ.

(ϫⲟⲛϫⲛ) S vb tr, *inquire*: Si 21 19 words ⲉⲙⲡⲟⲩ- ϫⲛϫⲱⲛⲟⲩ ἀδιεξέταστος. *Cf* ϫⲛⲟⲩ.

ϫⲓⲛϭⲱⲣ B *v* ϭⲓⲛϭⲱⲣ.

ϫⲡ- SA²F, ϫⲉⲡ- SF, ⲁϫⲡ- S(once)B, pl(?)ⲁϫⲡⲓ B nn f m, *hour*, mostly with following numeral: Ac 2 15 S(var ϣⲡ-)B ὥρα; K 62 B ☨ⲁ. ساعة; BIF 14 182 S ⲛⲧⲉⲣⲉϫⲡ☨ ⲙⲡⲉⲣⲟⲟⲩ ϣⲱⲡⲉ; m: BM 1249 B

ⲡⲓⲁϫⲡⲛ̄, but *ib* ⳁ ⲁϫⲡⲛ̄, EW 214 n *B* title of Horologium ⲡⲓⲁϫⲡⲓⲁ اجبة‎; pl(?): PO 14 337 *B* ⲛⲓⲥⲩⲡⲁϫⲓⲥ ⲡⲧⲉ ⲡⲓⲁ. ⲉⲑⲣⲉϥϣⲗⲏⲗ each hour.

With preceding preposition.   ⲥ ⲛ-, *at*: BMis 163 *S* ⲁϥⲉⲓ ⲛ̄ϫⲡⲁⲙⲛ̄ⲧⲟⲩⲉ, Mor 23 27 *S* sim = *ib* 24 12 *F* ⲧⲥⲉⲡⲓⲁ̄, AM 302 *B* ⲡⲁ. ⲥ̄ⳁ ⲙ̄ⲡⲓⲉϩⲟⲟⲩ, ManiP *A²* ⲡ̄ⲧⲁⲡⲥⲟⲉ, BIF 22 107 *F* ⲡ̄ⲭⲡⲛ̄ ϣⲁϫⲡⲛ̄; ⲥ ϣⲁ-, *till*: KKS 25 *S* continued talking ϣⲁⲡⲥⲁϣϥⲉ, MG 25 233 *B* ϣⲁⲁ. ⲥ̄ⳁ, AM 104 *B* ⲓⲥϫⲉⲛⲫⲛⲁⲩ̄ ϣⲁⲁ. ⲥ̄ⳁ; ⲥ ϩⲉⲛ- *B*, *in, at*: C 86 283 ϩⲉⲛⲁ. ⲥ̄, AM 288 ⲛ̄ϧⲣⲏⲓ ϩⲉⲛⲁ. ⲓⲁ̄; ⲥ ϫⲓⲛ-, ⲓⲥϫⲉⲛ-, *from*: PS 6 *S* ϫⲓⲛⲡϣⲟⲙⲧⲉ, KroppA *S* ϫⲓⲛⲉϫⲡϣⲟⲙⲧⲉ, C 43 212 *B* ⲓ. ⲁ. ⲥ̄; Jo 4 52 *F* ⲉϫⲓⲛⲧϫⲡⲛ̄ (*SA²* ⲙ̄ⲡⲛⲁⲩ ⲛ̄ϫⲡ-, *B* ϩⲉⲛⲁ.).

ⲙ̄ⲡⲛⲁⲩ ⲛ- *SB*, *at time of, about the … hour*: Mt 20 5 *SF* ⲧϫⲡ- (PMich 539, *B* ⲡⲁϫⲡ-) περὶ ὥ., *ib* 27 45 *S* (var ⲙ̄ⲡⲛ̄ⲭ-) *B* ἀπὸ ὥ., Lu 23 44 *SB* ὡσεὶ ὥ., Mk 15 34 *SBF* ⲭⲥ̄ (MR 1934 29) τῇ ὥ.; BG 136 *S* ⲡⲡ. ⲛ̄ϫⲡ-(ⲡ)ⲥⲓⲧⲉ, BMis 374 *S* ⲡⲡ. ⲛ̄ϫⲡⲟⲩⲉⲓⲉ = Va 63 7 *B* = Mor 27 27 *F* ⲥⲡ, AP 2 *A²* ⲡⲡ. ⲛ̄ϫⲡⲯⲓⲧⲉ.

ϫⲉⲡ-, ϫⲟⲡ *B* v ϣⲱⲡⲉ.

ϫⲟⲡ *S*, **ϫⲁⲡ** *SªA²* nn m, *dish, bowl*: ShC 73 136 ϫ. ⲛⲟⲩⲱⲙ ϫⲓⲣ, *ib* 137 ϫ. ⲛ̄ⲃⲗϫⲉ, ShP 130¹ 141 ⲡⲓⲡⲁϫ, ϫ., ϫⲱ, ShC 42 40 their hands ϩⲁⲡⲉⲓϫ. ⲛⲟⲩⲱⲧ on table, ShPCol 6 (inv 25) ⳝⲓⲛⲟⲩⲱⲙ … ⲉϣⲁⲟⲅⲟⲙⲥⲯ ϩⲣ̄ⲡⲭ., ST 411 ⲟⲩϫ. ⲙ̄ⲡⲟⲩϫⲱ ⲛ̄ⲣⲱⲙ, Win 44 ⲟⲩⲡ ⲯⲓⲥ ⲛϫ.[?]ϫⲟⲡ ⲟⲩϣⲗⲟⲡ ⲛⲟⲩⲱⲧ, Vi ostr 164 *Sª* ϫ. ⲛ̄ⲃⲁⲣⲟⲧ (prob), Ep 543 *Sª*, Mani K 132 *A²* among wooden σκεύη; ⲙⲁ ⲛϫ., meaning uncertain: C 73 211 let none touch aught in refectory till seated, ⲉⲥⲉϩ ⲟⲩⲙⲁ ⲛ̄ϫⲟⲡ (or ? ϫⲡⲟ) ⲏ ⲟⲩⲙⲁ ⲛⲟⲩⲟⲟⲧⲉ.

ϫⲟⲡ *B* vb qual, *be hard, cruel*: BMOr 8775 119 in varia ⲉϫ. قاسية‎; Va 57 226 ⲕⲁϩⲓ ⲉⲧϫ. ⲉⲧⲟⲓ ⲛⲥⲙⲟⲧ ⲡⲱⲡⲓ λιθώδης; MG 25 228 demon ⲡⲥⲙⲟⲧ ⲉϥϫⲟⲡⲧ ⲟⲩⲟϩ ⲉϥϫ.

ϫⲁⲡⲓ *B* nn, with vb ⳝⲓ, *stray, swerve*(?): MG 25 123 rudderless ship ⲉϥϫⲓ ϫ. ⲙ̄ⲡⲏ ⲡⲉⲙⲙⲛⲁⲓ.

ϫⲉⲡⲓ *B* nn f, *chip, slice, morsel*: K 232 ⲡⲓϫ. قطع‎, جزلات, هبر‎; P 54 175 ⲡⲓϫ. حشائش‎; EW 175 ⲧⲁⲓⲕⲟⲩϫⲓ ⲡϫ. ⲛ̄ϣⲉ.

ϫⲏⲡⲓ *F* v ⳝⲏⲡⲉ.

ϫⲓⲡⲉ *S* vb tr, meaning unknown: ShViK 9814 22 ⲙⲡⲥⲁⲧⲣⲉϥϫ. ⲛⲟⲩⲙⲡⲧⲅⲉⲙⲱⲛ. *L* ϫⲓ ⳁⲡⲉ.

ϫⲱⲡⲓ *F* v ϣⲱⲡⲉ.

ϫⲡⲓ-¹ *S*, **ϫⲡⲉ-²** *SA* vb followed by other vb, *must*, with 1st fut pref: Pro 23 2 *S¹*(var²)*A*, Mk 8 31¹(var² *BF* ϩⲱⳁ) δεῖν; Lu 14 18¹ (*B* as Gk) ἀνάγκην ἔχειν; 1 Kg 8 19¹(var²) εἶναι fut, Tob 14 8¹(var²) πάντως do, 2 Kg 4 11² ἐκζητεῖν fut; PS 346 ⲥⲉⲡⲁϫ.¹ ⲃⲱⲕ, ShC

42 145 ⲡⲉϣⲁϫⲉ ⲡⲁϫ.¹ ϣⲱⲡⲉ, ShP 131⁴ 157 ⲓ̄ⲥ̄ ⲡⲁϫ.¹ ⳁ ⲥⲟ ⲉⲣⲟⲟⲩ, BMar 206 ϥⲡⲁϫ.² ⲉⲓ (var Mor 486 ϣⲁϥⲉⲓ), Aeg 20 ⳁⲡⲁϫ.¹ ⲙⲟⲩ = *ib* *B* ⳁⲡⲁⲙⲟⲩ, BMar 234 ⲕⲡⲁϫ.² ⲃⲱⲕ; with other tenses: *ib* 135 ϣⲁⲣⲉⲟⲩⲟⲡ ⲡⲓⲁ ϫ.² ⲡⲉⲣⲁ (περᾶν), COAd 47 ϣⲁⲓⲭ.² ⲉⲓ, Mor 37 10 ⲡⲉϣⲁϥϫ.² ⲡⲱⲧ, BM 187 129 girdle ⲉⲣⲉⲡⲉⲧⲟⲩⲱⲙ ϫ.¹ ⲙⲟⲣⲟⲩ ⲙⲙⲟϥ, PStras 114 ⲁϣⲡⲉ ⲡⲉⲥⲓⲅⲅⲟⲩⲗⲁⲣⲓⲥ ⲡⲧⲁϫⲡ(ⲉ) ⲟⲩⲱⲛ ⲉⲣⲟⲥ, J 73 6 ⲃⲁⲓⲭ.¹ (for ⲟⲩⲁⲓ-) ⲃⲱⲕ; as absolute: Tri 438 ϫ.¹ ⲡⲉ ⲉⲧⲣⲉⲡⲭ̄ⲥ̄ … ⲟⲩⲟϩ ان ل Y, *ib* 464 ϫⲡⲉⲓ ⲉⲧⲣⲉⲡⲡⲛ̄ⲁ̄ ⲟⲩⲱⲛϩ ⲉⲃⲟⲗ do.

ϫⲡⲓⲟ (for ⲧϣⲡⲓⲟ) *SAA²*, **-ⲓⲁ** *F*, **ϫⲫⲓⲟ** *B* (rare), **ϫⲡⲓⲉ-** *S*, **ϫⲡⲓⲁ-** *A²*, **ϫⲡⲓⲟⳝ** *S*, **ϫⲡⲓⲁⳝ** *AA²*, **ϫⲡⲓⲏⲧ**† *S*, **ϫⲫⲓⲏⲧ**† *B* vb intr, *blame, upbraid* (caus of ϣⲓⲡⲉ, *B* mostly ϭⲟϩⲓ): Ge 31 37, Job 13 3 ἐλέγχειν; Ps 34 26 *F* (Mus 49 180, *S* ⲟⲩⲱⲗⲥ, *B* ϭⲓ ϣⲱϣ) ἐντρέπειν; tr: Job 5 17, Pro 9 8 *SA*, Hos 4 4 *SA*, Jo 3 20 *SA²* ϫⲡⲓⲁ- (*BF* c.), Aeg 243 ϫⲡⲓⲉ ⲡⲉⲛⲧⲁϥⲣ̄ ⲡⲟⲃⲉ ἐλ., Mic 4 3 *SA* ἐξελ., Ac 18 28 διακατελ.; 1 Cor 4 14 *B*(*S* ⳁ ϣⲓⲡⲉ) ἐντ.; Is 43 12 (*B* ⳁ ϣⲱϣ) ὀνειδίζειν; Aeg 267 ⲧϭⲟⲙ … ⲛⲁϫⲡⲓⲟⲟⲩ δυσωπεῖν; ShZ 637 ϫⲡⲓⲉ ⲡⲣⲙⲙⲁⲟ, R 2 15 ⲉϥⲉⲗⲉⲛϭⲉ ⲁⲩⲱ ⲉϥϫ. ⲛⲁⲣⲓⲟⲥ, Mor 31 4 ⲉⲓϫⲡⲓⲟⲓ ⲙ̄ⲙⲁⲅⲁⲁⲧ, Mani H 80 *A²* ⲥⲉϫ. ⲙⲙⲁⲓ, C 43 91 *B* ϫ. ⲛ̄ⲛⲓⲁⲡⲟⲙⲟⲥ; qual, *ashamed, modest*: Pro 10 5 (*AB* om) αἰσχύνη (Hexap); ClPr 29 245 ⲟⲩⲁⲧ ϣⲓⲡⲉ ⲡⲉϣⲁϥϣⲱⲡⲉ ⲛ̄ϫ., BHom 68 ⲟ ⲛ̄ϫ. ϩⲁⲧⲛⲟⲩⲟⲡ ⲛⲓⲙ.

With following preposition.   ⲥ ⲉⲧⲃⲉ-: Jo 16 8 *SA²* ϫⲡⲓⲁ- ἐλ. περί, Ps 104 14 ἐλ. ὑπέρ; MIE 2 378 *B* ϫ. ⲙⲙⲱⲟⲩ ⲉ. ⲛⲟⲩⲛⲟⲃⲓ = BAp 94 *S* ⲥⲟϩⲉ; ⲥ ⲉϫⲛ-: Ps 49 8 ἐλ. ἐπί; Tri 488 ϫⲡⲓⲉ ⲡⲓⲟⲩⲅⲁⲓ ⲉ. ⲡⲉⲛⲧⲁⲅⲕⲟⲧⲟⲩ على‎; ShC 42 33 ϫⲡⲓⲟϥ ⲉ. ⲡⲉϥⲙ̄ⲛⲧϣⲁϥⲧⲉ; ⲥ ⲙⲛ-: Ep 1 134 n come ⲛ̄ϫⲡⲓⲟⲓ ⲙ̄ⲡⲁⲡⲁⲥ ϫⲉⲁϥⲃⲱⲗ ⲛⲁ ⲙⲟⲛⲁⲥⲧⲏⲣⲓⲟⲛ ⲉⲃⲟⲗ (meaning?); ⲥ ϩⲁ-: TT 35 ⲉⲩϫ. ⲙⲙⲟⲡ ϩⲁⲡⲉⲛⲧⲁⲡⲁⲁⲩ; ⲥ ϩⲛ-: 2 Kg 7 14 (var ⲛ-) ἐλ. ἐν, Job 33 19 ἐλ. ἐπί; Mani H 11 *A²* ⲁϥϫⲡⲓⲁⲥ ϩⲛ[; ⲥ ϩⲓⲧⲛ- (passive): 1 Cor 14 24 ἐλέγχεσθαι ὑπό, BHom 98 ⲁⲩϫ. ⲛ̄ⲃⲁⲗⲁϩⲁⲙ ϩ. ⲟⲩⲉⲱ; ⲉⲃⲟⲗ ϩ. sim: Ja 2 9 ἐλ. ὑπό; Aeg 268.

—— nn m, *blame*: Job 6 26, Pro 1 23 *SA*, Sa 2 14 (*B* ⲣⲉϥϫ.) ἔλεγχος, Nu 5 18, Is 37 3 *SF* ἐλεγμός, Job 21 4 ἔλεγξις; Eccl 7 6 ἐπίτιμησις; 1 Cor 15 34 *B*(*SF* ⳁ ϣⲓⲡⲉ) ἐντροπή; ShA 2 271 ⲥⲓϣⲉ, ϫ., ⲥⲟⲡⲥ, BMis 359 ⲡⲉϫ. ⲛ̄ⲧⲁⲓϥⲓ ϩⲁⲣⲟⲟⲩ = BSM 21 *B* ϣⲱϣ, AM 131 *B* ⲡⲓϫ. ⲉⲧⲟⲩⳁ ⲙ̄ⲙⲱⲟⲩ.

ⲙⲛⲧϫ.†, ⲙⲉⲧϫ.†, *shamefacedness, modesty*: 1 Tim 2 9 *B*(*S* ⲙⲛ̄ⲧⲣⲉϥϣⲓⲡⲉ) αἰδώς; Mus 40 275 ⲟⲩⲙ. ⲙ̄ⲡⲟⲩⲙⲛ̄ⲧⲁⲕⲁⲓⲣⲓⲟⲥ (ἀκέραιος) = BAp 167.

ϫⲓⲛϫ.† *B*, *modesty* or sim: TRit 434 ⲟⲩϫ. ⲡⲧⲉ ⲟⲩⲱⲟⲩ اقتناء المجد‎ (confused with ϫⲫⲟ) opp ⲟⲩⲙⲉⲧ ϣⲗⲁϩ ⲛ̄ϩⲏⲧ.

ϫⲡⲟ (for ⲧϣⲡⲟ) *SA²*, ⲧϩⲡⲟ *A*, ϫⲫⲟ *B*, ϫⲡⲁ *F*, ϫⲡⲉ- *SAF*, ⲧϩⲡⲉ-, ⲧϩⲡⲟ- *A*, ϫⲡⲟ- *SA²*, ϫⲡⲁ- *A²F*,

ϣⲡⲁ-*F*(BKU 1 23), ϫϥⲉ-, ⲧϫϥⲉ-*B*(ⲣⲉϥⲧ.), ϫⲡⲟ⸗*S*, ⲧϫⲡⲁ⸗*A*, ϫⲡⲁ⸗*A²F*, ϫϥⲟ⸗*B*, ϫⲡⲁⲉⲓⲧ†*S*(?), ϫϥⲏ-ⲟⲩⲧ†*B* vb tr **I**, *beget*, *bring forth* of male or female (caus of ϣⲱⲡⲉ): Ge 5 6 m *SB*, Eccl 6 3 pl *SF*, Ez 16 20 f *SB*, Zech 13 3 pl *SAB*, Mt 2 4 *S* pl (*B* ⲙⲓⲥⲓ), Lu 1 57 *S* f (*B* do), Jo 9 19 *SA²* pl (*B* do), Aeg 241 *S* ϣⲁϫⲡⲉ ⲟⲩϥⲟ̄ⲡⲟⲥ γεννᾶν, Ps 109 3 m *SB* ἐκγ., Eccl 7 2 *F* pl (*S* ⲙⲓⲥⲉ nn) γέννησις, Sa 7 12 f *S* γένεσις; Eccl 1 11 *F* pl (*S* ϣⲱⲡⲉ), Ap 16 18 *S* pl (*B* ϣⲱⲡⲓ) γίνεσθαι; Ge 3 16 *S* f (*B* ⲙ.), ib 31 43 *S* pl (*B* do), Pro 17 25 f *SA*, Lu 1 31 *S* f (*B* do) τέκειν, Ge 11 30 f *SB*, Jer 38 8 m *S*(ShA 2 340)*B* τεκνοποιεῖν, ROC 17 400 *B* ϥⲏ ⲉⲧⲁⲩϫϥⲟⲩ τόκος; Ja 1 15 *B*(*SA* ⲙ.) ἀποκυεῖν; Ge 18 10 *S*(*B* ϭⲓ), Gal 4 22 *SB* ἔχειν; Col 2 19 *B*(*S* ⲕⲱⲧ) συμβιβάζειν; Aeg 215 *S* ⲁϥϫⲡⲟϥ ⲡⲧⲉⲓⲣⲉ φύειν; Br 237 *S* ⲁϥϫⲡⲟϥ ⲙⲙⲓⲛ ⲙⲙⲟϥ, BG 88 *S* ϫ. ⲡϩⲏⲕⲁⲣⲡⲟⲥ, BMis 55 *S* ⲡⲧⲉⲣⲉϥϫⲱⲕ ⲉⲃⲟⲗ ⲛϭⲓ ⲡⲉⲣⲟⲟⲩ ⲙⲡⲉⲥⲙⲓⲥⲉ ⲁⲥϫ. ⲡⲟⲩϣⲉⲉⲣⲉ, Aeg 10 *S* ⲁⲧⲁⲙⲁⲁⲩ ϫⲡⲟⲓ = ib *B* ⲙ., BMar 104 *S* ⲁϫⲥ ⲡϣⲏⲣⲉ ⲥⲛⲁⲩ, R 1 2 40 *S* ⲁⲥϫⲡⲟϥ (var Bor 239 76 ⲙⲁⲥⲧϥ), Ep 100 *S* ⲉϥϫⲡⲟ ⲟⲩϣⲉⲉⲣⲉ, Mani H 61 *A²* ⲁϥϫⲡⲁⲩ, Mani P 71 *A²* ϫ. ⲙⲙⲁⲓ, ib 234 *A²* ϣⲁⲕϫⲡⲟ ϣⲏⲣⲉ, Aeg 41 *B* ⲁϯⲡⲁⲣⲑⲉⲛⲟⲥ ... ϫ. ⲙⲡⲭⲣⲓⲥⲧⲟⲥ, Kropp C 17 *F* children ϣⲁⲥϫⲡⲁⲁⲩ (sic), BKU 1 23 *F* ⲁⲥϫⲡⲁ (sic *l*) ⲡⲓⲗⲱⲙⲁⲓ; intr: AM 186 *B* ⲉⲑⲛⲁϫ. χωρὶς ⲉϭⲓⲙⲓ; qual: O'Leary Th 14 branches of candle-stick ⲉⲅϫ. ⲉⲃⲟⲗ ⲙⲙⲟⲥ (cf Ex 25 31), ib 15 chains ⲉⲅϫ. ϩⲉⲛϯⲡⲁⲣⲟⲯⲓⲥ.

II *acquire*: Ex 21 2 *B*(*S* ϣⲱⲡ), Lu 18 12 *SB*, Ep 592 *A* ϫⲡⲉ ⲙⲡⲧⲣⲙⲛⲣⲏⲧ κτᾶσθαι, Lev 25 13 *B*(*S* = Gk) κτῆσις; Pro 10 16 *SA*(*B* ⲓⲣⲓ) ποιεῖν, Ge 31 18 *S* (*B* ⲑⲁⲙⲓⲟ), Ps 78 11 *B*(*S* ⲧⲟⲩϫⲟ), Is 43 21 *SB* περιπ.; Pro 31 16 *B*(*SA* ⲧⲱϭⲉ) as if *καταφύεσθαι; CDan 84 *B* ⲡⲁϫ. ⲡⲣ̄ ⲡⲁⲣϭⲓⲱⲛ (ἀργύριον) καταλύειν; Lu 19 16 *S*(*BF* Mor 30 2 ⲓⲣⲓ) προσεργάζεσθαι; Cl 25 3 *A* ϭⲧⲟⲛⲉ ⲧⲏⲅ πτεροφύειν; Si 27 1 *S* ϫⲡⲉ ϩⲁⲣ πληθύνειν; BMar 207 *S* wage ϯϫ. ⲙⲙⲟϥ = Rec 6 171 *B* ϭⲓⲧϥ, Ryl 252 *S* ⲡⲉⲥⲡⲏⲗⲁⲓⲟⲛ ⲡⲧⲁⲓϫⲡⲟϥ, J 75 53 *S* testament shall ϫ. ϭⲟⲙ ⲛⲓⲙ, ManiK 155 *A²* ⲁϥ]ϫ. ⲣⲉⲧϥ ϫⲓⲛⲛ̄ϯⲛ ⲁⲧⲡⲉ *planted foot*(?); qual *S*(once) *B*: Eph 2 21 (*S* ϣⲱⲡⲃ) συναρμολογεῖσθαι; Bodl(P)e 13 *S* c]ⲛⲧⲉ ⲛⲟⲓⲛⲉ ⲉⲅϫ., ib ϣⲙⲟⲩⲛ ⲉⲅϫ. (meaning?); as nn K 141 ⲡⲓϫ. حبر المركّب (*compounded ink*).

With following preposition.   c ⲉ-, *for*, *to*: Si 41 9 *S*, Jo 18 37 *SA²*(*B* ⲙ.) ⲅⲉ. εἰς, Job 5 7 *S*(*B* do) ⲅⲉ. dat, Pro 17 17 *SA* ⲅⲉ. χάριν; MG 25 359 *B* ϣⲁⲧⲉϥϫ. ⲉϩ̄ϫⲟⲓ προσεγγίζειν dat (Gött ar 114 128 وصل الي); BG 80 *S* ⲁⲅϫⲡⲟⲟⲩ ⲉⲡⲕⲁϩ AZ 21 142 *S* ⲟⲩ ⲡⲉⲛⲧⲁⲓⲭⲡⲟϥ ⲉⲡⲉⲓⲕⲟⲥⲙⲟⲥ ? cf *to* every man ⲡⲧⲁⲩϫⲡⲟϥ ⲉⲡⲉⲓⲕ., ManiH 21 *A²* ⲁⲩϫⲡⲁⲡ ⲁⲡⲕ., Va 61 109 *B* sim, R 1 3 49 *S* ⲁⲣⲱⲟⲩ ϫ. ⲉⲡⲕⲁϩ (*l* ? ϫⲧⲟ, cf c ϩⲁ-), N & E 39 345 *B* ⲡⲁϫ.† ⲉⲣⲱⲟⲩⲡⲉ ϩⲉⲛⲟⲩⲙⲉⲧϫⲱⲣⲓ *took upon selves*; ⲉϩⲣⲟⲩⲛ ⲉ-: ShBor 247 127 *S* ⲟⲩⲟⲅⲟⲉⲓϣⲛⲉ

ⲡⲟⲩⲱⲧ ⲡⲉⲧⲉϣϣⲁϥϫ. ⲉϩ. ⲉⲡⲱⲡⲣ, J 37 36 *S* may not take occasion against you ⲟⲩϫⲉ ⲉϫ. ⲉϩ. ⲉⲣ. ⲉⲣⲱⲧⲛ; c ⲉϫⲛ-: Ge 50 23 *S*(*B* ⲙ.) τίκ. ἐπί; Ez 36 12 *B* ⲅⲉ. ἐπί; c ⲙⲛ-, ⲡⲉⲙ-: ViK 9670 81 *S* ⲙ̄ⲡⲓϫ. ⲙⲛⲡⲉⲕϣⲏⲣ, BSM 117 *B* ⲉⲣⲉϫ. ⲡⲟⲩϣⲏⲣⲓ ⲡⲉⲙⲁϥ, J 88 5 *S* ⲁⲓϫⲡⲟϥ ⲉⲃⲟⲗ ϩⲛ̄ⲡⲁⲙⲉⲗⲟⲥ ⲙⲡⲧⲉϥⲙⲁⲁⲩ, ib 68 39 *S* ⲁⲓϫⲡⲟϥ ⲙⲛ ... ⲡⲁϣⲟⲣⲡ ⲛ̄ⲣⲁⲓ; c ⲛ-mostly ethic dat, *beget*: Deu 23 8 *S*(*B* ⲙ.), Lu 1 13 *S*(*B* do) ⲅⲉ. dat; Nu 26 59 *S*(*B* diff) τ. dat, Mor 17 67 *S* ⲧⲁⲥϫⲙⲓⲉ ... ϫ. ⲛⲁⲓ ⲡⲟⲩϣⲏⲣⲉ τεκνοῦν; TU 24 14 *S* ⲁ̄ϫⲡⲟⲥ (sc daughter) ⲛⲁⲓ, Wess 15 152 *S* ⲁϫⲡⲉ ϣⲏⲣⲉ ⲙⲡⲉⲓⲥⲓⲟⲩⲣ, AP 30 *A²* ⲁϫⲡⲁϥ ⲡⲉϥ; *acquire*: Ps 77 54 *S*(*B* om ⲛ-), Pro 16 22 *SA*, Mt 10 9 *S*(*B* ⲭⲱ) ⲕⲧ., BHom 18 *S* virtue ⲉⲡⲧⲁⲕϫⲡⲟϥ ⲛⲁⲕ πρὸς κτ.; Ez 18 31 *S*(*B* ϭⲓ) ποιεῖν, Pro 7 4 *SA* περιπ.; Cl 44 2 *A* διαδέχεσθαι; 2 Tim 4 3 *S*(*B* ⲥⲱⲕ) ἐπισωρεύειν; 1 Cor 9 11 *F*(*S* ϫⲟ, *B* ⲥⲓϯ) σπείρειν dat, Sa 8 18 *S* λαμβάνειν, Pro 1 13 *SA*(*B* ⲧⲁϩⲟ) καταλ.; Mt 19 21 *B*(*S* ⲕⲱ) ἔχειν; Pro 3 4 *SA*(*B* as Gk) εὑρίσκειν; Z 309 *S* ⲁϥϫ. ⲛⲁϥ ⲡⲧⲕⲟⲗⲗⲩϭⲉ (κολλήγιον) κερδαίνειν; LMär 3 *S* ⲙⲡⲧϫⲁⲥⲓⲣⲏⲧ ⲡⲧⲁϥϫⲡⲟⲥ ⲛⲁϥ, TT 95 *S* ⲁϫ. ⲛⲁϥ ⲡⲟⲩⲡⲣⲟϩⲁⲓⲣⲉⲥⲓⲥ, J 185 *S* of property sold ⲉϫⲡⲟϥ ⲛⲁⲕ ⲉⲟⲩⲉϩⲙ ϫⲡⲟϥ ⲛⲁⲕ ⲉϫⲓⲟⲓⲕⲉⲓ ⲙⲙⲟϥ (cf κτᾶσθαι PMon 142, PLond 5 176), Mani 1 *A²* ϫ. ⲡⲉ ⲡⲟⲩⲡⲁⲣⲣⲏⲥⲓⲁ, C 41 70 *B* ⲁϥϫ. ⲛⲁϥ ⲡⲟⲩⲙⲏ̄ϣ ⲡⲥⲟⲩⲟ; ⲉⲃⲟⲗ ⲛ-: Mt 19 12 *S*(*B* ⲙ.) ⲅⲉ. ἐκ, Ge 16 2 *B*(*S* ⲉⲃ. ϩⲛ-) τεκνοποιεῖν ἐκ; Mani K 27 *A²* ⲡⲉⲛⲧⲁⲩϫⲡⲁⲩ ⲁⲃ. ⲡⲡϭⲁⲙ; c ⲡⲧⲉⲛ-*B*: Ge 25 10 (JTS 2 263, var & *S* ϣⲱⲡ) ⲕⲧ. παρά; c ϩⲁ-*S*: ShC 73 161 bearers of corpse to burial ⲉⲩϣⲁⲡⲟⲩ ⲉϫ. ϩⲁⲡⲉϥⲉⲣⲏⲩ *replace* (lit *make to be for*); ⲉϩⲣⲟⲩⲡ ϩⲁ-: BMar 23 bade ϫ. ⲥⲟⲉ ⲡⲗⲁⲙⲡⲁⲥ ⲉ. ϩⲁⲡⲉϥⲥⲡⲓⲣⲟⲟⲩⲉ (or *l* both ? ϫⲧⲟ, cf c ⲉ-); c ϩⲛ-, ϩⲉⲛ-: Ja 1 18 *SAB* ἀποκυεῖν dat; Ac 8 20 *S*(var & *B* ϩⲓⲧⲛ-)ⲕⲧ. διά; BAp 125 *S* ⲁⲓϫⲡⲟϥ ϩⲛ̄ⲡⲁⲣⲱⲃ ⲛϭⲓϫ, J 96 81 *S* ⲡⲉⲧϥⲛⲁϫⲡⲟϥ ϩⲙ̄ⲡⲉϥⲉⲣⲧⲱϣϭⲉⲓⲣⲱⲡ; ⲉⲃⲟⲗ ϩⲛ-: Sa 4 6 *S*, Jo 1 13 *SF*(BP 5569, *B* ⲙ.) ⲅⲉ. ἐκ; Sa 15 8 *S*(var ⲧⲁⲙⲓⲟ) πλάσσειν ἐκ; BG 75 *S* ⲁϫ. ⲡⲣⲓϣⲏⲣⲉ ⲉⲃ. ϩⲁⲡⲕⲁⲕⲉ, Mor 41 59 *S* ϫⲡⲟⲕ ⲙⲙⲓⲛ ⲙⲙⲟⲕ ⲉⲃ. ϩⲛ̄ⲧⲉⲥⲕⲁⲗⲁϩⲏ, AP 42 *A²* ⲁⲅϫⲡⲁϥ ⲁⲃ. ϩⲛ̄ⲙⲁⲣⲓⲁ, AM 227 *B* ⲁⲅϫϥⲟϥ ⲉⲃ. ϩⲉⲛⲣⲁⲛⲓⲟϯ; c ⲉⲃⲟⲗ ϩⲓⲧⲛ-: Aeg 283 *S* ⲧⲣⲉⲩϫ. ⲛⲁⲡ ⲙⲡⲛ̄ⲅⲉ ⲉⲃ. ϩ. ⲧⲉⲑⲉⲟⲧⲟⲕⲟⲥ ⲅⲉ. ἐκ; Ge 4 1 *B* ⲕⲧ. διά; Ac 20 28 *SB* περιπ. διά.

——nn m *SAA²BF*, ⲙⲭⲟ *S*(error), *birth*, *begetting*: Ge 6 9 *S*(*B* ϫⲓⲛϫ.), ib 11 10 *S*(*B* ϫⲓⲛⲙ.), Ez 16 4 *S*(*B* ϫⲓⲛϫ.) γένεσις, Mt 19 28 *S* ϫ. ⲡⲕⲉⲥⲟⲡ (*B* ⲟⲩϫⲉⲙⲥⲱⲡⲧ, *F* ⲟⲩϭⲉⲙ.) παλιγγενεσία, Jud 1 10 *S* γέννημα, R 1 1 19 *S* ⲡⲉⲕϫ. ϩⲓⲃⲉⲑⲗⲉⲉⲙ γέννησις, Job 11 12 *SB* γεννητός, Jo 3 6 *F*(*SA²* vb, *B* ⲙ.) γεγεννημένος, Deu 7 13 *S*(*B* do), Pro 23 18 *SA* ἔκγονος, Am 7 1 *B* ἐπιγονή; 1 Tim 2 15 *S* ϫⲡⲉ ϣⲏⲣⲉ (*B* ⲙⲉⲧⲣⲉϥϫ. ϣ.) τεκνογονία; Job 21 8 *S*(*B* ⲟⲩⲧⲁϩ) σπόρος; Lev 11 29 *S* ϫ. ⲙⲡⲕⲁϩ (var ⲙⲭⲟ P 44 105, *B* diff) χερσαῖος; Br

227 S ⲡⲉϫ. ⲛ̄ⲕⲉⲥⲟⲡ, ShRE 10 161 S each ⲕⲁⲧⲁ ⲡⲉϥ-
ⲉⲓⲡⲉ ⲙ̄ⲡⲉϥϫ., Bor 239 50 S Christ ⲟⲩϫ. ⲡⲟⲩⲥⲱⲡⲧ
ⲁⲛ, R 2 1 21 S Melchisedek ⲟⲩϫ. ⲛ̄ⲑⲉ ⲡⲣⲱⲙⲉ ⲛⲓⲙ,
BMar 48 S pure ϫⲓⲛⲡⲉϥϫ. ϣⲁⲡⲉϥϫⲱⲕ ⲉⲃⲟⲗ, P 131¹
24 S rubric ⲧⲕ̄ⲩⲣⲓⲁⲕⲏ ⲡⲛⲉϫ. in month Choiahk,
ManiP 41 A² ϫ. ⲡⲁⲧⲙⲟⲩ, DeV 2 6 B ϫ. ⲕⲁⲧⲁ ⲥⲁⲣⲝ,
MG 25 156 B ⲛⲓϫ. ⲛ̄ⲃⲉⲣⲓ new-born babes, EpApp 1
58 S was virgin ⲙ̄ⲡⲛ̄ⲥⲁⲡⲉϫ., Bor 241 56 S ⲧⲕⲟⲓⲛⲱ-
ⲛⲓⲁ ⲙ̄ⲡⲉϫⲡⲉ ϣⲏⲣⲉ; possession, gain: Ge 23 4 B,
Pro 10 15 SAB ⲕⲧῆⲥⲓⲥ, Job 20 29 SB ⲕⲧῆⲙⲁ; Va 57
44 B ⲕⲉⲣⲇⲟⲥ; DeV 2 273 B ⲛⲓϫ. opp ⲡⲓⲕⲉⲫⲁⲗⲉⲟⲛ =
Mun 68 S ⲗⲓⲙⲙⲁ (ⲗῆ.), Leyd 352 S ⲟⲩⲛⲟϭ ⲛ̄ϫ. ⲙⲙⲉ
ϣⲟⲟⲡ ⲛⲁⲩ, BSM 51 B ⲉⲑⲛⲁϯ ⲙ̄ⲡⲉϫ. = BMis 403
S ⲙⲛ̄ⲥⲉ, ib 47 B ϭⲓ ϫ. = ib 395 S ϫⲓ ⲙⲛ̄ⲥⲉ.

ⲁⲧϫⲡⲟϥ, unbegotten: BG 88 S ⲡⲓⲁ. ⲡⲡⲉ, BiblMar-
ciana Or 193 12 S ⲁϫ. ⲙ̄ⲡⲉⲓⲁ., ManiP 96 A² ⲡⲓⲁ.

ⲣⲉϥϫ. SB, begetter, maker: Bor 227 159 S ⲣ. ⲛⲓⲙ-
ⲡⲉⲑⲟⲟⲩ ⲅⲉⲛⲛⲏⲧⲓⲕⲟⲥ; BM 980 306 S faith & unfaith
ϩⲉⲛⲣ. ⲡⲧⲥⲛ̄ⲧⲉ; ⲣⲉϥϫⲡⲉ-: R 1 2 66 S ⲣ. ⲡⲉ ⲑⲉⲟ-
ⲧⲟⲕⲟⲥ, BSM 60 B sim, Bar 3 23 B ⲣⲉϥⲧϥ̄ⲫⲉ (no var)
ϣϣⲱ ⲙⲩⲑⲟⲗⲟⲅⲟⲥ; BG 87 S ⲟⲩϭⲟⲙ ⲡⲣ. ⲟⲩⲥⲓⲁ, Br 253
S ⲁⲣⲥ(ⲉⲡ)ⲟⲩⲥⲉⲛⲓⲁ ⲉⲧⲉⲧⲣ. ϩⲟⲟⲩⲧⲧⲉ, SHel 83 S ⲡⲓⲉⲃⲟⲧ
(sc Parmhotp) ⲡⲣ. ϣⲱⲡⲉ; ⲙ̄ⲛⲧ-, ⲙⲉⲧⲣⲉϥϫⲡⲉ-:
1 Tim 2 15 B ⲛⲛ; ROC 17 399 B ⲙ. ϣⲏⲣⲓ ⲡⲁⲓⲇⲟ-
ⲡⲟⲓⲓⲁ; Ac 19 25 B ⲙ. ϩⲛⲟⲩ (S diff) ⲉⲩⲡⲟⲣⲓⲁ; ShIF
293 S ⲣ̄ⲱⲃ ⲙⲙ. ⲡⲟⲃⲉ.

ϭⲓⲛ-, ϫⲓⲛϫ., begetting, generation: Ge 6 9 B(S ϫ.)
ⲅⲉⲛⲉⲥⲓⲥ; ShBor 247 127 S ⲧϭ. ⲉⲧⲛⲁⲡⲟⲩϭ, BMis 142
S she redeemed world ϩⲓ̄ⲧ̄ⲛⲧⲉⲥϭ., ManiK 147 A²
ⲧ̄ⲙ̄ⲥⲉ ⲛ̄ⲧϭ. ⲛ̄ⲡⲣⲱⲙⲉ, DeV 2 6 B angels ⲉⲣ ϩⲩ̄ⲙ̄ⲡⲟⲥ
ⲉⲡⲉϫ., MartIgn 875 B ϩⲁⲡϫ. (var AM 128 ϫⲫⲟ)
ⲡⲉⲙϩⲁⲡⲅⲉⲛⲉⲁⲗⲟⲅⲓⲁ.

ϫⲁⲡⲗⲉ S nn f, part ? of water-wheel: BKU 1 94
ⲧϫ. ⲁⲓⲕⲁⲁⲥ ϩⲁⲡϩⲟⲓ (named with ⲟⲩⲁϩⲣⲉ, ⲙⲁⲡⲕⲉ,
ϩⲉⲗⲙⲓⲥ, ⲕⲗⲟⲟⲗⲉ).

ϫⲁⲡⲟⲣ, -ⲱⲣ S nn, kind of mallow: P 43 56 ϫ.
بامية (hibiscus, althaea), but ib 44 82 ⲉⲧⲓⲛⲏⲓ (quid?)·
ϫ. بشني (ⲡⲉϫⲛⲉ p 774 a).

ϫⲉⲡⲣⲟ B v ϭⲱⲡⲣⲟ.

ϫⲡⲓⲏⲧ v ϣⲓⲡⲉ (ϣⲡⲓⲏⲧ).

ϫⲡⲟϩ DM, ϫⲉⲡⲉϩ F, ϫⲱⲡⲉϩ S v ϫ(ⲉ)ⲙⲡⲉϩ.

ϫⲁⲡϫⲓ B. v ϭⲁⲡϫⲉ.

ϫⲁⲡϫⲉⲡ B v ϭⲁⲡϭⲉⲡ.

ϫⲁⲡϫⲓⲡ B v ϭⲁϫⲓϥ.

ϫⲟⲡϫⲡ S, ϫⲁⲡ. A² v ϭⲭⲟⲡϫ̄ⲡ.

ϫⲁⲁⲣ, ϫⲁⲣ- F v ϫⲣⲟ (ϫⲱⲱⲣⲉ).

ϫⲏⲣ SAA² vb intr, be wanton, merry: Nah 2 4 A
(B ⲥⲱⲃⲓ), Pro 27 7 ϫ. + ⲧⲥⲧⲟ ⲉⲃⲟⲗ (A om) ⲉⲙⲡⲁⲓⲍⲉⲓⲛ;

BMar 160 ⲧⲛ̄ⲥⲱⲃⲉ ⲧⲛⲭ., BHom 128 ⲉⲩϫⲗⲉⲅⲁⲍⲉ ⲙ-
ⲙⲟϥ ⲉⲩϫⲱⲃⲉ ⲉⲩϫ., CA 89 at sub-deacon's marriage
ⲡⲛⲉⲩϫ. ⲛ̄ⲧⲉϥⲡⲟⲙⲡⲏ, Mor 2588 theatres & circuses
& ⲙⲙⲁ ⲉⲧⲟⲩϫ. ⲛ̄ⲣⲏⲧⲟⲩ, ManiH 14 A² ⲉⲙⲡⲟⲩϫⲁ-
ⲡⲟⲗⲁⲅⲉ ... ⲙ̄ⲡⲟⲩϫ. ϩⲛ̄ⲡⲉϥϫⲏⲟⲡⲁϫⲉ; c ⲉϫⲛ-:
1 Tim 5 11 (B ϫⲉⲣϫⲉⲣ) ⲕⲁⲧⲁⲥⲧⲣⲏⲛⲓⲁⲍⲉⲓⲛ gen; c
ⲙⲛ̄- Ap 18 9 (B do) ⲥⲧⲣⲏⲛⲓⲁⲍⲉⲓⲛ, JTS 10 398 rich men
ⲉⲩϫ. ϩⲛ̄ⲡⲕⲏⲡⲟⲥ ⲙ̄ⲙⲛ̄ⲡⲁⲗⲗⲁⲕⲏ.

—— nn m, wantonness, sport, revelling: Ro 13 13
(B ϫⲉⲣ.), Gal 5 21 (B ϣⲉⲣϣⲓ) ⲕⲱⲙⲟⲥ; Ap 18 3 (B
ϫⲉⲣ.) ⲥⲧⲣⲏⲛⲟⲥ; Jer 29 17 (B ⲥⲱⲃⲓ) ⲡⲁⲓⲅⲛⲓⲁ, Is 66 4 (B
do), Mor 17 18 tricks of sorcerer ⲉⲙⲡⲁⲓⲅⲙⲁ; BMar
161 ⲟⲩϫ. ⲙ̄ⲡⲟⲩⲥⲱⲃⲉ ⲅⲉⲗⲱⲥ ⲕ. ⲁⲇⲓⲁⲫⲟⲣⲓⲁ; Wess 18
14 ⲡ̄ⲛⲉⲡϫ. ϯ ϫⲣⲟⲡ ⲛⲁⲩ ⲉⲧⲙ̄ⲧⲥⲁⲃⲟ ⲥⲫⲁⲓⲣⲁ ⲕ. ⲟⲥⲁ
ⲧⲟⲓⲁⲩⲧⲁ, BHom 47 eyes ϣⲱⲡⲉ ϩⲛⲟⲩϫ. ⲁⲧⲁⲕⲧⲟⲥ; Si
30 8 ⲉⲁⲅⲕⲁ ϫ. ⲉⲃⲟⲗ ⲛ̄ⲥⲱϥ ⲁⲛⲉⲓⲙⲉⲛⲟⲥ (but cf Mal 4 2
A ⲕⲁ ϫⲱϥ ⲉⲃ. ⲁⲛ.), Aeg 223 ϩⲉⲛϫ. ⲙ̄ⲛⲣⲉⲛϯⲅⲉ ⲙⲉⲑⲏ;
Tri 525 ⲟⲩϫ. ْجَدْ; ShBMOr 8810 431 ϯϩⲉ, ϫ., ⲥⲱ,
ShMich 550 15 ⲙ̄ⲛⲧⲣⲉϩ ⲛ̄ϣⲁϫⲉ ϩⲛⲟⲩϫ., C 99 170
after feast ye brake my chattels ϩ̄ⲙ̄ⲡϫ. ⲛ̄ⲧⲉⲧⲛ̄ⲯⲩⲭⲏ
= C 89 136 B ϫⲉⲣ., C 99 6 some mounted ass ϩⲛⲟⲩϫ.,
ManiK 135 A²] ⲕⲁⲧⲁ ⲟⲩϫ. ϩⲛ̄ⲟⲩⲗⲁⲗⲉϩ; c ⲉⲓⲣⲉ:
Mor 17 26 ⲉⲓ. ⲛ̄ⲣⲉⲛⲛⲟϭ ⲛ̄ϫ. .... at festival ⲫⲁⲛⲧⲁⲍⲉ-
ⲥⲑⲁⲓ; BMis 547 ⲥⲉⲉⲓ. ⲛⲡⲉⲩϫ. ϩⲓϫ̄ⲙ̄ⲡⲕⲁϩ ⲙⲁⲧⲁⲓⲟⲧⲏⲥ;
P 131⁴ 115 where devil ⲉⲓⲣⲉ ⲛ̄ⲡⲉϥϫ. opp where is
Christ's body.

ⲣⲉϥϫ., wanton: Jude 18 (A ⲣⲉϥϫⲣϫⲣⲉ, B ⲣⲉϥ-
ⲥⲱⲃⲓ) ⲉⲙⲡⲁⲓⲕⲧⲏⲥ; Mor 37 34 ⲣ. ϩⲱⲥ ϣⲏⲣⲉ ϣⲏⲙ ⲣⲁ-
ⲑⲩⲙⲉⲓⲛ; ROC 20 46 ⲣ., ⲣⲉϥⲥⲱⲃⲉ, R 1 2 55 ⲣ., ⲣⲉϥⲕⲁ
ⲟⲩⲛⲟⲩ, ⲣⲉϥⲙⲟⲩⲧⲉ.

ϭⲓⲛϫ. nn m, wantonness: Tri 383 ⲡⲉⲧⲛⲁⲧⲟϭϥ
ⲉⲡϭ. جَدّ.

ϫⲣϫⲣⲉ A, -ϫⲓⲣ A², ϫⲉⲣϫⲣ S (once), -ϫⲉⲣ B, ϫⲉⲣ-
ϫⲓⲣ B (nn), ϫⲏⲗϫⲉⲗ F (nn) vb intr, as ϫⲏⲣ: 1 Tim 5 6
B (S = Gk) ⲥⲡⲁⲧⲁⲗⲁⲛ; Dif 1 62 B in youth ⲛⲁⲕϫ. ⲁⲛ
لعب; Va 58 189 B ⲁⲩϫ. in gluttony & drink (cf ?
Ez 16 49), ib 68 177 ⲉⲧϫ. to-day, to-morrow they repent; c ⲛⲥⲁ-: 1 Tim 5 11 B (S ϫⲏⲣ ⲉϫⲛ-) ⲕⲁⲧⲁ-
ⲥⲧⲣⲏⲛ. gen; TSBA 9 374 B sim; as nn m: 2 Mac
6 4 A, Ro 13 13 B (S ϫⲏⲣ) ⲕⲱⲙⲟⲥ; Ap 18 3 B (S do)
ⲥⲧⲣⲏⲛⲟⲥ; 2 Cor 12 20 F (S ϫⲟⲕϫⲕ, B ϣⲉⲣϣⲓ), Gal
5 20 B (S ⲙ̄ⲛ̄ⲣⲉϥϯ ⲧⲱⲛ) ⲉⲣⲓⲑⲉⲓⲁ; Bodl 325 153 B
ⲛ̄ϫⲉⲣϫⲓⲣ بطر; Mor 43 251 S guard sons from ⲛ̄ϫⲉⲣ-
ϫⲣ ⲛ̄ϣⲉⲉⲣⲉ ⲛ̄ⲥϩⲓⲙⲉ ⲛⲓⲟⲩϫⲁ, ManiP 7 A² ⲡⲟⲩⲛⲁϥⲉ
ⲛⲭ., Va 58 193 B ⲛⲓϫ. ⲛⲉⲙⲡⲓϩⲓϫⲓ; ⲣⲉϥϫ. A v
ⲣⲉϥϫⲏⲣ.

ϫⲏⲣ spy v ϫⲱⲣ 2°.

ϫⲏⲣ be black v ϫⲱⲣ 3°.

ϫⲓⲣ SB, ϫⲓⲗ F nn m, brine, small salted fish: P 44
54 S ⲙⲉⲡⲁⲥ (ⲙⲁⲓⲛⲓⲥ?, -ⲛⲏ)· ⲟⲩϫ. صير = 43 242; ib 91
S ⲧⲁⲣⲓⲭⲓⲟⲛ· ⲛⲭ. ص; R 1 5 14 S ⲟⲩϫ. ⲏ ⲟⲩⲧⲃ̄ⲧ
ⲅⲁⲣⲟⲥ; K 269 B أزربة, ص; P 46 168 S among fish

ⲙⲥⲁϩ, ⲣⲏⲓ, ⲛ̄ⲍ., ib 237 S ⲛ̄ⲍ., ⲕⲁϣⲱ, ⲍⲏⲗ, ShC 73 119 S ⲍ. ⲛ̄ⲧⲃ̄ⲧ, ⲧⲃ̄ⲧ ⲉϥⲡⲟⲥⲉ, ⲧⲁⲣⲓⲭⲓⲟⲛ, ib 55 S ⲍ., ϩⲙⲟⲩ, ⲗⲁⲯⲁⲛⲉ, ib 172 S ⲍ. ⲛ̄ⲧⲃ̄ⲧ, ϩⲁⲗⲱⲙ may be given to sick, ShPCol 6 (inv 25) S ⲡⲙⲟⲩ ⲡϩⲙⲟⲩ ⲛ̄ ⲡ[ⲍ]ⲓⲣ ⲡⲗⲉⲯⲁⲛⲉ, BP 402 S ϣ̄ⲧⲁⲉⲥⲉ ⲛ̄ⲍⲓⲣⲗⲁⲯ, RE 10 38 S ⲍ. & ⲧⲁⲣⲓⲭⲓⲟⲛ in same list, TMena Epima 20 S testicles torn out ⲁⲩϯ ⲉⲣⲟⲟⲩ ⲛⲟⲩⲍ. = C 43 140 B ⲡⲉϥ ⲉϥⲃⲉⲣⲃⲉⲣ, C 86 83 B ϥⲱⲛ ⲛⲟⲩⲍ. upon wounds (var ϩⲉⲙⲍ), Saq 319 S ⲧⲣⲓ (ⲛ)ⲛⲉⲍⲓⲣ pickle store-room;   vessels, measures: ShC 73 136 S ⲍⲟⲡ ⲛⲟⲩ ⲱⲙ ⲍ., PMich 1539 S ⲕⲟⲗⲗ(ⲁ)ⲑ(ⲉ) ⲛ̄ⲧⲁⲣⲓⲭ(ⲉ), ⲕⲟⲗⲗ(ⲁ)ⲑ(ⲉ) ⲛ̄ⲍ., PLond 4 524 S sim, BM 606 F ⲕⲟⲩⲣⲓ, Hall 117 S ⲕⲟⲩⲧⲱⲛ (v Ep 543 n), WS 149 S ⲕⲁⲥ, ib 85 ⲗⲁϧⲏ, ib 89 ⳅⲉⲥⲧⲏⲥ (cf same text ϥⲟⲣⲏⲥ ⲛ̄ⲧⲁⲣⲓ ⲭⲉ), ib 134 ⲥⲓⲡⲗⲟⲩⲛ (v ib 112), ib 147 ϩⲟⲧⲥ, ib 149 ϭⲁⲗⲁϧⲧ ⲛ̄ⲍ. ⲗⲁⲟⲥ (l ? ⲗⲁⲡⲥ).   V JEA 14 33 & on جص v Dozy 1 856, AZ 14 85, MIF 30 341, ib 33 96 n, CHBecker Beiträge 146; on زلية Saq 1912 27.

ⲁⲛⲍⲓⲣ S nn m, lotion, paste of salt, as soap: Su 17 (P 44 115, B = Gk) σμῆγμα زلود, cit BHom 49 ⲟⲩ ϩⲣⲟⲥⲙ ⲙⲡⲟⲩϥ. (var R 2 2 33 ϩ. only) σμ., Tri 525 ⲛⲥⲓ ⲟⲟⲩⲡⲉ ⲙ̄ⲡⲛⲁ.ˈⲋ; BM 1111 ⲡⲛⲉⲛϩ (l ⲙⲡⲉϩ), ⲡⲁ., Ryl 307 ⲡⲁ. ⲁⲓⲥⲁⲛⲧϥ, ib 159 expenses of husbandry ⲉⲓⲧⲉ ⲁ. ⲉⲓⲧⲉ ⲁⲛϩⲁⲗⲱⲙⲁ ⲛⲓⲙ (cf σμῆγμα PLond 1 209), BMOr 6201 B 115 ⲍⲓ ⲛⲁ. ⲙⲁⲣⲟⲩⲧⲁⲁⲩ ⲛ̄(ⲡ?)ϭⲟⲟⲙ[.

ⲍⲓⲣ B in ⲁϥⲍⲓⲣ q v.

ⲍⲓⲟⲟⲣ   v pp 82 a, 751 b.

ⲍⲱⲣ SAB, ⲍⲱⲱⲣ (once), ⲍⲉⲣ- S, ⲍⲟⲣ⸗ SB, ⲍⲟ ⲟⲣ⸗ S, ⲍⲏⲣ† SBF vb tr, sharpen, whet (cf جرب Dévaud): Pro 27 17 A(S ⲧⲱⲙ), Sa 5 21 S ὀξύνειν, Deu 32 41 S(B diff) παροξ.; Ez 21 11 S(ShC 73 12, B ϣⲟ ⲃ̄ ϣⲉ ⲃ̄) ἐξακονᾶν; Ps 7 12 S(B as Gk) στίλβειν; ShC 73 16 S sword ϣⲁⲩⲍⲟⲣⲥ, JTS 38 120 S ⲉϥϣ. ⲡⲟⲩ ⲗⲟⲩⲭⲏ, Mun 20 S sim ⲍⲱⲱⲣ, TT 18 S reaper ⲍ. ⲙⲡⲉϥϩⲟⲣⲥ, Va 61 207 B sword ⲉⲧⲁϥ ⲍⲟⲣⲥ (on Ge 22 6);   intr: Ez 21 9 S(ShC 73 12, var ⲧ., B ut sup); qual: Job 41 21 S(ShA 1 396, var ⲧⲏⲙ, B ϣⲉⲡϣⲱⲡ) ὀξύς; C 86 278 B sword's edges ⲉⲩⲍ. ἀκονᾶν; ib 275 B ⲓ̈ⲁⲧ ⲉⲩⲍ. جلب; P 44 69 S ⲛⲁⲍⲣⲉ ⲉⲧⲍ. ˈⲋ; Tri 525 S ⲍⲉⲃⲏⲗ ⲛ̄ⲍ. (as if adj) مسنون; KroppD 58 S ⲛⲉⲩⲥⲏⲃⲉ ⲍⲣ ⲉⲩⲧⲙ, Mor 30 13 F ϭⲁⲗ†ⲉⲩⲍ., ShC 42 117 S ⲥⲟⲧⲉ ⲉⲩⲍ., R 2 1 63 S worm ⲉⲧⲍ. like nail, C 43 94 B martyr dragged over ⲙⲁ ⲛ̄ⲱⲛⲓ ⲉⲩⲍ., BMis 476 S cut self with ⲛ̄ⲱⲛⲉ ⲉⲧⲍ., P 131¹ 52 S ⲙⲉⲍⲛ̄ⲱⲛⲉ ⲉⲥⲍ. & incurable.

With following preposition.   ⲉ ⲉ-, to, against: Va 57 173 B ⲛ̄ⲑⲱⲟⲩ...ⲉⲧⲍ. ⲉⲣⲱⲟⲩ ⲛ̄ϯⲥⲏϥⲓ ἀκ. κατά; ShRE 10 162 S ⲉⲩⲍ. ⲡⲧⲉⲩⲥⲏϥⲉ ⲉⲣⲟϥ, ROC 20 50 S ⲉϥ ⲍⲉⲣ ϭⲟⲣⲧⲉ ⲉⲣⲟϥ ⲙⲁⲩⲁⲁϥ;   as to: BSG 178 S knives ⲉⲩⲍ.† ⲉⲡⲣⲟ ⲥⲛⲁⲩ;   ⲉ ⲟⲩⲃⲉ-, against: BM 257 328 S ⲍⲉⲣ ⲡⲉⲩⲥⲏϥⲉ ⲟⲩⲃⲏⲥ (sc church), Z 268 S

of Julian ⲁⲕⲍ. ⲙⲡⲉⲕⲗⲁⲥ ⲟⲩⲃⲉⲡⲡⲉ̄;   ⲥ ⲉⲃⲟⲗ ϩⲛ-, by (instr): ShC 73 16 S ϣⲁⲩⲍⲉⲣ ⲥⲛϥⲉ ⲛⲓⲙ ⲉⲃ. ⲛ̄ϩⲏⲧⲥ (sc sword in Ez 21).

—— ⲉⲃⲟⲗ B: DeV 2 40 ⲁϥϣⲁⲛⲍ. ⲙⲡⲱⲥ̄ⳅ ⲙ̄ⲡⲉϥ ⲍⲱⲡⲧ ⲉⲃ.

—— ⲛⲛ m S, sharpness: ShC 73 16 ⲡⲉⲥⲍ. (sc sword's) ⲟⲩⲉⲃⲟⲗ ⲛ̄ϩⲏⲧⲥⲡⲉ, ShRE 10 159 surgeon's ⲥⲟⲧⲃⲉϥ ⲙ̄ⲡⲉⲩⲍ.

ⲍⲱⲣ S, ⲍⲉⲣ- B, ⲍⲟⲟⲣ⸗ S, ⲍⲟⲣ⸗ B, ⲍⲏⲣ† (?) SB vb tr, examine, study: Nu 13 2 B ⲍⲉⲣ ⲡ̄ⲕⲁϩⲓ, ib 32 B ⲍⲟⲣϥ, Gal 2 4 ⲍⲉⲣ- (all S ⲛⲁⲩ) κατασκέπτεσθαι; CO 29 S ordinands promise to ⲍ. ⲡⲉⲩⲁⲅⲅⲉⲗⲓⲟⲛ ⲛ̄ⲧ̄ⲛ ⲁⲡⲟⲥⲧⲟⲗⲓⲍⲉ ⲙⲙⲟϥ, BP 12489 S ⲛ̄ⲥⲉⲍ. ⲡⲉⲩⲁⲅ. ⲛ̄ ⲥⲉⲣ ⲡⲉⲩϣⲗⲏⲗ, Ep 381 S here is book ⲉⲕⲍ. ⲙ̄ⲡⲣⲟⲥ ⲉⲩⲭⲏ, Hall 108 S wage to smith ⲛ̄ⲧⲁϥⲍⲟⲟⲣⲉ (sc shaft of cart);   as nn, examiner, spy: He 11 31 S (Beatty, var ⲍⲱⲱⲣⲉ, B ⲍⲏⲣ) κατάσκοπος;   ⲍⲏⲣ sim: Ge 42 34 SB, Ja 2 25 B(SA diff) κ.;   ⲣⲉϥ ⲍⲏⲣ: P 44 63 S ⲛ̄(ⲕⲁ)ⲧⲁⲥⲕⲟⲡⲟⲥ ˙ ⲣ. روقبا, جواسيس.

ⲍⲱⲣ SSⁱ, ⲍⲏⲣ† S vb, be, make black as with soot: JTS 38 126 faces ⲛ̄ⲛ ⲛ̄ⲑⲉ ⲡⲟⲩϭⲁⲗⲁϩⲧ ⲉⲥⲍ.† (cf Nah 2 10 A), PBad 5 401 Sⁱ ⲡϭⲁⲗⲁϩⲧ (ⲛ̄)ⲁⲥⲁⲣ† ϩⲁⲣⲁⲥ ϣⲁⲛⲧⲉⲥⲍ. (ⲉ)ⲛ̄ⲕⲉⲍ. ⲉⲡⲣⲁ (ⲛ̄)ⲍ̄ⲗ, R 1 3 76 Baptist's face ⲍ.† tanned (?) from desert air.   Cf ? Ps 73 20 S ⲉⲧⲍⲟⲟⲣ(ⲉ) σκοτοῦσθαι.

ⲍⲱⲣ B   v ⲍⲱⲱⲣⲉ scatter & ⲍⲱⲓ.

ⲍⲉⲣⲟ SAA², -ⲣⲱ S, ⲍⲉⲗⲁ Sⁱ F, ϭⲉⲣⲟ B, ⲍⲉⲣⲉ- SA², ⲍⲉⲉⲣⲉ- S, ⲍⲉⲣⲟ- A², ϭⲉⲣⲉ-, ϭⲉⲣⲟ- B, ⲍⲉ(ⲉ)ⲗⲉ-, ⲍⲉⲗⲁ- F, ⲍⲉⲣⲟ⸗ SA², ⲍⲉⲣⲱ⸗ SA², ϭⲉⲣⲟ⸗, ϭⲉⲣⲱ⸗ B, ⲍⲉⲣⲁⲓⲧ† A², ϭⲉⲣ ⲛⲟⲩ† B, -ⲗⲏⲟⲩⲧ† F vb I intr, blaze, burn: Lev 6 6 S(var -ⲣⲱ, B ⲙⲟϩ), Is 4 5 S(var & B ⲙⲟⲩϩ), Mal 4 1 A(SB do) καίειν; Lu 12 49 S(var & B do), Va 58 141 B ϥⲙⲉⲅⲓ ⲛ̄ⲡⲓⲥⲱⲙⲁ ϭ. ἀνάπτειν, ib 57 215 B ϣⲁϥϭ. ϩⲣⲟⲅ ἐξάπ.; 2 Cor 11 29 S(B ⲣⲱⲕϩ) πυροῦσθαι; Pro 29 1 SA φλέγειν; ib 26 20 A (S ⲙ.) θάλλειν; C 89 33 B ϭ. ⲙ̄ϥⲣⲏ† ⲛ̄ⲟⲩⲭⲣⲱⲙ ὡς πῦρ γίνεσθαι; Ac 20 8 S(var -ⲱ, B Gk om); ShC 73 25 S ϩⲛⲃⲥ ⲉⲩϭ., R 1 5 31 S ⲁⲩⲥⲁⲣⲧⲉ [ϩⲁ]ⲣⲟϥ ⲁⲩⲍ. ⲧⲏⲣϥ, Bor 100 42 S devil's arrows ⲉⲧⲍ., El 46 A waves ⲍ. like pitch, ManiK 5 A² ⲧⲥⲉⲧⲉ ⲍ.;   qual: Ez 20 47 B(S ⲍⲉⲣⲟ) ἐξάπ.; Is 5 24 F(S ⲥⲱⲕ, B ⲛ̄ ⲭⲣⲱⲙ) ἀνειμένος; ManiP 204 A² ⲧⲥⲉⲧⲉ ⲍ., Va 61 94 B ⲙ̄ⲡⲁϥϭⲉⲡⲟ ⲁⲗⲗⲁ ⲛⲁϥϭ. = P 131³ 84 S ⲣⲱⲕϩ.

II tr, kindle: Lev 24 3 S(B ⲧⲉⲙⲙⲟ) καί., Ez 24 10 SB ἀνάκ., ib 20 48 S ⲍⲉⲣⲱϥ B ἐκκ.; Mk 4 21 S ⲍⲉⲉⲣⲉ-, BF(Mus 49 188) ⲍⲉⲗⲉ-, R 1 4 59 S dip papyrus in oil ⲛ̄ⲧⲉⲧⲛ̄ⲍⲉⲣⲱϥ ἅπτειν, Jer 21 14 SB, Lam 2 3 F ⲍⲉⲉⲗⲉ- (B ⲙ. ⳅⲉⲡ-) ἀνάπ., Nu 8 3 SB ἐξάπ.; Jo 18 18 SA²B ⲍⲉⲣⲉ ⲟⲩϣⲁϩ ἀνθρακιὰν ποιεῖν; Mus 40 40 S ⲍⲉⲣⲉ ⲁϣ focum facere; Miss 8 13 S ⲧⲉⲩⲛⲁϩⲓⲥ...

ⲙⲡⲛⲁⲩ ⲛϫⲉⲣⲉ ⲡⲣⲏⲃ̄ⲥ (cf τὸ λυχνικόν), ManiP 173 A²
ⲣⲏⲃ̄ⲥ ⲉⲧⲁⲕϫⲉⲣⲟϥ, ib H 69 A² ϫⲉⲣⲟ ⲧⲥⲉⲧⲉ, MIE 2 360
B ϭⲉⲣⲟ ⲭⲣⲱⲙ, MG 25 306 B ϭⲉⲣⲟ ⲡⲓϫⲏⲃ̄ⲥ, AM 307
B ϭ. ⲡⲧϣⲏⲟⲩⲓ.

With following preposition.   c ⲉ-, for: EpJer
18 BF ϫⲉⲗⲁ- ⲕ. dat; Mor 41 8ὸ S fire ⲁⲕϫⲉⲣⲟϥ ⲉ-
ⲣⲟⲕ; ⲁϫⲟⲩⲡ ⲉ-A: Ob 18 (S ⲙ. ⲉϩ. ⲉ-, B ⲣ.ⲉϩ̄. ⲉ-)
ἐκκ. εἰς;   c ⲡ-: ShR 23 22 S ⲡϣⲁⲣ...ϫⲉⲣⲱϥ ⲡⲁⲕ,
C 43 101 B ⲣⲓⲣ...ϭⲉⲣⲱⲥ ⲛⲭⲣⲱⲙ;   c ϩⲛ-, ϫⲉⲛ-:
Ap 19 20 S(B ⲙ. ϫⲉⲛ-) ⲕ. ἐν; Joel 1 19 A(B tr) ἀνάπ.
acc; Va 57 44 B soul ⲉⲧϭ.† ϫⲉⲛⲡⲓⲭⲣⲱⲙ πυροῦσθαι;
BHom 42 S spark ϫ. ϩⲛⲟⲩϭⲣⲏⲃ̄ⲗⲏ ἐπιλαμβάνεσθαι gen;
ⲉⲃⲟⲗ ϩⲛ-: Deu 32 22 S(B ⲙ. ϫⲉⲛ-) ἐκκ. ἐκ;   c
ϩⲓⲧⲛ-: Is 5 24 F(S ⲙ., B ⲣ.) ⲕ. ὑπό; Sh(?)Mor 54
146 Sᶠ ϣⲁϥⲧⲣⲉⲡⲉϥⲛⲓ ϫ. ⲣ. ⲡⲓⲛⲓϣⲉ.

—— ⲉⲃⲟⲗ: Nah 2 10 A ⲁϫ. ⲁⲃ̄. ⲡⲧⲣⲉ ⲡⲟⲩϭⲁⲗⲁϫⲧ
ὡς πρόσκαυμα χύτρας nigrido ollae (cf ϫⲱⲣ 3°).

ⲁⲧϭ. B, unlit: Va 58 128 lamp ⲟⲓ ⲛⲁⲧϭⲉⲣⲱ (sic) μὴ
ἅψας; BM 857 2 ⲡⲓϩ̄ ⲛⲥⲟⲗ ⲛⲁⲧϭ.† بغير وقيد.

ϫⲉⲣⲟ-   v ϫⲱ say p 755 b.

ϫⲏⲣⲉ SF, **ϫⲉⲉⲣⲉ** S, **ϫⲏⲣⲓ** B, **ϫⲉⲣⲉ** F nn f, threshing-floor: Jud 6 37 S(P 44 108, var ⲣⲉϫⲛⲟⲟⲩ) ἅλων
صبر (sic); C 41 53 B ϯ ⲕⲁⲣⲓⲉϯϫ. ⲙϥⲟⲣϣ ⲱⲓⲕ (Miss 4
413 يلقوا الطين only), J 10 36 S ϫ. ⲙⲡⲧⲟⲡⲟⲥ, ib 20 55
S ϫⲭⲉⲉⲣⲉ ⲛⲧⲡⲉ ⲙⲡⲥⲁⲡⲡⲱⲥⲓⲟⲛ (συμπό.), ib 35 30 S
ⲡⲧⲡⲉ ⲛⲧϫⲁⲣⲁⲟⲩ (ἐξέδρα), ib 49 S ⲡⲣⲟ ⲡⲧⲉϫ., Ep 563
S ⲡⲕⲏⲅⲏⲗ(ⲉⲩⲧⲏⲣⲓⲟⲛ) ⲡⲧϫ., BM 673 F sale of rooms
(ⲗⲓ) & ⲡⲉⲛϫⲉⲣⲉ;   corn threshed or season of threshing (cf ϫⲛⲟⲟⲩ): PLond 4 500 S ϫⲟⲩⲧⲁϥⲧⲉ ⲡⲉⲣⲧⲟⲃ
ⲧⲁⲧⲁⲁⲩ ϩⲓⲧⲭ. ⲉⲧⲏⲛⲩ, Bodl(P) e 48 S corn ⲉⲩϭⲱϣⲧ
ϩⲁⲣⲟϥ ϩⲛⲧ., BP 11349 S shall pay share ⲡⲣⲟⲥ ⲡϣⲁⲁⲣ ⲛⲧ.;   CMSS 78 F ϫⲧϫⲏⲣⲉ = ? ⲧϫⲉⲉⲣⲉ. Τχῆρε
PMon 131 (var Τχρῆρε ib 121, PLond 5 170) may be
this word; cf ? also PFior 1 no 65 μηχανῆς καλου-
μένης Τζήρας.

ϫⲏⲣⲓ B nn, meaning uncertain: Ex 23 24 ⲡⲉⲩ-
ⲥⲧⲏⲗⲏ ⲡⲉⲙⲡⲟⲩϫ. ⲛⲥϫⲁⲓ written ... (S Gk om) قمـر.
Cf ? next word.

ϫⲏⲣⲓ, **ϫⲓⲡⲓⲣⲓ** B nn m, filth: Is 4 4 (varr BM 1247
ϫⲓⲡ., P 104 64 ⲑⲱⲗⲉⲃ, S ⲧⲱⲗⲙ) ῥύπος; Va 68 169
ⲡⲓϫ. ⲉⲧϣⲏϣ ⲡⲧⲉ ⲛⲓϫⲱ αἰσχρὰ ᾄσματα.

ϫⲓⲉⲓⲣⲉ S, **ϫⲏⲣⲓ**, **ϫⲓⲡⲓⲣⲓ** B nn m, pod of carob &
of other plants: K 176 B ⲛⲓϫ. خرنوب; Lu 15 16 B
ϫⲓⲡ. (S ϭⲁⲣⲁⲧⲉ) κεράτιον عـ, cit Cat 158 B ϫⲓⲡⲛ.;
PMéd 156 S ϫ. ⲛϣⲟⲡⲧⲉ, Ann 18 285 S in recipe
ⲙⲟⲟⲩ ⲙⲛϫ., ShC 73 111 S ⲉⲩϭⲱⲣⲙ ⲙⲡϫ. ϣⲏⲙ,
Bal S ⲡϣⲏⲙ ⲛϫ. ⲉⲧⲉⲭⲣⲓⲁ ⲡⲉⲧⲛⲏⲓ. Cf ? ϫⲓⲉⲓⲗⲉ.
V Rec 15 125, OLZ '27 565.

ϫⲱⲱⲣⲉ S, **ϫⲱⲣⲉ** S, **ϫⲱⲣ** S (rare) B, **ϫⲟⲩ(ⲟⲩ)ⲣⲉ** Sᵃ
A, **ϫⲣⲁⲣⲉ** A²(Ma), **ϫⲉ(ⲉ)ⲣⲉ-**, ϭⲉⲣ- S, ϫⲉⲣ- B, ϫⲟⲟⲣ⸗

S, ϫⲟⲣ⸗ SB, ϫⲁⲁⲣ⸗ AF, ϫⲁⲣ⸗ AA²F, ϫⲣⲁⲣⲱ⸗ A²
(Ma), ϫⲟⲟⲣⲉ† S, ϫⲁⲁⲣⲉ† A, ϫⲣⲁⲣⲁⲧ† A²(Ma), ϫⲏⲣ†
B vb tr, scatter, disperse (cf הזר Dévaud): Lu 11 22
B(S ϭⲱⲣ) διαδιδόναι; Si 43 14 S καταπαύειν;   qual:
Miss 4 223 B ⲡⲉϥϩⲟⲣⲓ ⲉⲧϫ.

With following preposition.   c ⲉ-: Bar 3 7 B(S
ϫ. ⲉⲃⲟⲗ) διασπείρειν ἐκεῖ; Mt 25 24 S(B ϫ. ⲉⲃ̄.) διασκορπίζειν; PLond 5 132 S ϭⲉⲣ ⲉⲡⲉⲅⲉⲣⲏⲧ;   c
ⲡⲉⲙ-: Ez 12 14 B(S do ⲉ-) διασπ. εἰς;   c ⲛⲥⲁ-:
Tri 339 S ϫⲉⲉⲣⲉ ⲡⲥⲱⲟⲩ ⲛ(ⲡ)ⲕⲟⲧⲥ فرق;   c ⲥⲁⲃⲟⲗ
ⲛ-: PS 155 S ϫ. ⲥ. ⲙⲙⲟⲓ;   ⲥⲥⲁⲡⲉⲥⲏⲧ ⲛ-: Deu 9
14 B(var & S ϣⲱⲧⲉ ⲉⲃ̄.) ἐξαλείφειν ὑποκάτωθεν.   As
nn: Jer 15 7 B(S ϫ. ⲉⲃ̄.) διασπορά.

—— **ⲉⲃⲟⲗ**, as ϫ. & bring to naught, hinder intr: Ps
111 9 S(B ϭⲱⲣ ⲉⲃ̄.), Lu 11 23 S(B tr), Va 58 149 B
ⲁϫ. ⲉⲃ̄. ⲧⲏⲣⲟⲩ σκορπίζειν, Nu 10 35 SB, Ez 5 2 S
(B ⲡⲟⲩϫ ⲉⲃ̄.), Ac 5 37 S(B ⲃⲱⲗ ⲉⲃ̄.) διασκ..; Nah 1
14 A(B nn) σπείρειν, Is 35 8 BF(S†), Ac 8 4 S(B c.
ⲉⲃ̄.) διασπ.; Ex 32 25 S(B ϣⲱⲡ ⲉⲃ̄.) διασκεδαννύναι;
Ps 72 2 S(B ϣⲱⲡ ⲉⲃ̄.) ἐκχέειν, Ge 11 9 S(B ϣⲱⲣϫ)
συγχ.; Ps 34 15 S(B do) διασχίζειν; Va 57 70 B ⲁⲣⲉ-
ϣⲁⲛϯⲁⲡⲧⲉⲗⲉⲥ ϫ. ⲉⲃ̄. λύεσθαι; Gu 70 S ⲁⲛⲁⲗⲟ-
ⲡⲓⲟⲛ ϫ. ⲉⲃ̄. ἀπολλύναι; Mor 17 83 S ⲧⲣⲉϥϫ. ⲉⲃ̄.
ⲕⲁⲕⲱⲥ ὀλλύναι; Si 43 15 S διαθρύπτειν; Aeg 232 S
παρεμποδίζειν; C 99 210 S pursuing dogs ⲁⲩϫ. ⲉⲃ̄.
= C 89 2 B, ManiH 75 A² bones ϫⲣ. ⲁⲃ̄. κατὰ χώρα,
PMéd 297 S sore ⲉⲧⲣⲉϥϫ. ⲉⲃ̄. ⲉⲓ(ⲉ) ⲧⲉϥⲟⲩⲱⲛ, Miss
4 96 B heretics ϫ. ⲉⲃ̄. like smoke;   qual: Jo 11 52
SB διασκ.; Zeph 3 10 A(B ϫⲱⲣ ⲉⲃ̄.) διασπ.; 4 Kg
14 26 S σπανίζειν; Sa 2 3 S χαῦνος; K 228 B ⲛⲓⲥⲁϫⲓ
ⲉⲧϫ. ⲉⲃ̄. قطـ;   Br 79 S limbs ⲉⲧϫ. ⲉⲃ̄., BHom 123
S gather ⲡⲉⲧϫⲟⲟⲣ(ⲉ) ⲉⲃ̄., ManiP 213 A² sim ϫⲣⲁⲣⲁⲧ,
P ar 203 151 B sim, Ep 455 S ϩⲁⲡⲥ ⲧⲁϫ. ⲉⲃ̄.;   tr:
Ps 17 14 SB, Jo 10 12 SAA²B ⲥⲕⲟ., Jer 23 2 SB, Zech
1 19 SA ϫⲟⲩⲣⲉ B ϫⲉⲣ- διασκο.; Lev 26 15 SB, Job
16 12 SB διασκεδ.; Is 32 6 SF(B ϫⲓⲡϫ. ⲉⲃ̄.), ib 41 16
B(S ⲑⲗⲟ) διασπ.; ib 30 22 SF(B ϣⲟϣϣ) λικμᾶν; Jer
27 17 SB(F Mus 49 176 ⲥⲓϯ ⲉⲃ̄.) ἐξωθεῖν; Mic 5 8
AB διαστέλλειν; Nah 2 3 A ϫⲁⲁⲣ⸗ (B diff) ἐκτινάσσειν; Is 23 9 B(S ⲃⲱⲗ ⲉⲃ̄.) παραλύειν; ib 17 13 SB
ἀποσκορακίζειν; Z 274 S ϥϫ. ⲉⲃ̄. ⲡⲡⲉϥϩⲡⲏ of our
fathers ἀφαιρεῖν; Si 35 3 S ἐμποδίζειν; ShA 2 339 S
ϫⲉⲉⲣⲉ ⲟⲩⲙⲏⲛϣⲉ ⲉⲃ̄., BMOr 8811 235 S that destroy
hope & ⲉⲧϫ. ⲉⲃ̄. ⲡⲛⲉⲩⲅⲣⲓⲥⲉ, BMis 38 S urge on troops
ϣⲁⲡⲧⲉⲕϫⲉⲣⲉ ⲡⲡⲟⲗⲁⲓⲙⲟⲥ ⲉⲃ̄. prepare (cf ⲥⲱⲣ ⲉⲃ̄.),
BMar 144 S ⲡⲡⲉⲛϫ. ⲉⲃ̄. ⲙⲡⲱϫⲁϫⲉ divert discourse, let
us return & finish story, Miss 8 26 S ⲁϥⲟⲩⲱϣ ⲉϫⲉ-
ⲣⲉ ⲡϣⲁϫⲉ ⲉⲃ̄. sim (?), ManiH 74 A² ϫⲣ. ⲁⲃ̄. ⲡⲡⲉϥ-
ⲥⲁϫⲣⲥ, TurM 9 S ⲉⲕⲟⲩⲱϣ ⲉϫⲟⲣⲟⲥ (sc ⲧⲁⲗⲡⲉⲥⲟⲩⲣ
روسب) ⲉⲃ̄. ⲧⲁⲣⲥ ⲛⲁⲧⲣⲁⲧⲱⲣ (ἄκρατος), Mor 24 23 F let
not enemy ϫⲁⲁⲣⲉⲛ ⲉⲃ̄., BM 633 F σκεύη of wine ⲁⲃ̄-
ϫⲁⲣⲟⲩ ϩⲁ(ⲗ) ⲕⲁⲕⲱⲥ.

ϫ. ⲉⲃ̄. ⲉ-: Lev 26 33 S(B ϫⲉⲛ-) διασπ. εἰς; Jer 24

9 *SB* οὗ ἐξωθ.; Jo 16 32 *SB* σκο. εἰς; ShC 42 99 *S*
ϫⲟⲟⲣⲟⲩ ⲉⲃ. ⲉⲡⲉϧⲱⲣⲁ, Mich ostr 25120 *S* ⲉⲅⲭ.† ⲉⲃ.
ⲉⲣⲁϩ ⲡϭⲓϫ, BMis 215 *S* riches ϫⲱⲱⲣⲟⲩ ⲉⲃ. ⲉⲡⲕⲱⲧ
of church; ⲉϩⲣⲁⲓ ⲉ-: Jth 7 32 *S* σκο. εἰς; Gu 65 *S*
cloud ϫ. ⲉⲃ. ⲉϫ. ⲉⲑⲁⲗⲁⲥⲥⲁ; ⲉϩⲣⲁⲓ ⲉϫⲛ-: Ex 32
20 *S*(*B* ⲥⲓ†ⲉϫ̅. ⲉ-) ⲥⲡ. ἐπί; ⲛ-: Dan 11 24 *B* διασκ.
dat; Jer 52 8 *B* διασπ. ἀπό; ManiK 99 *A*² ⲡⲛⲟⲩⲥ ...
ϫⲣ. ⲁⲃ. ⲙⲙⲁϥ ⲡϭⲃⲱⲕ; ⲡⲉⲙ-: Ez 5 10 *B*(*S* ⲉ-)
διασκ. εἰς; ⲟⲩⲧⲉ-: ManiK 76 *A*² wealth ϫⲣ. ⲁⲃ.
ⲟⲩⲧ[ⲱ] ⲡⲡⲉϥϫⲁⲝⲉ; ϧⲁ-: ShWess 9 120 *S* ϩⲉⲛⲣ-
ⲣⲱⲙⲉ ⲡϫⲉⲉⲣⲉ ⲡⲉⲩⲟⲉⲓⲕ ⲉⲃ. ϩⲁⲣⲱⲟⲩ, DeV 2 34 *B*
ⲁϫϫ. ⲙⲡⲉϥⲙⲃⲟⲛ ⲉⲃ. ϩⲁⲣⲟⲛ, Kropp R 8 *S* ϫⲱⲟⲣ(ⲉ)
ⲉⲃ. ϩⲁⲑⲏ ⲙⲙⲟⲓ ⲙⲡⲡⲁ̅ ⲛⲓⲙ; ϩⲛ-, ϩⲉⲛ-: Ez 29 12
SB, Joel 3 2 *SAB* διασπ. ἐν, Lev 13 22 *B*(*S* ⲡⲱⲣϫ)
διαχέ. ἐν; Ps 105 27 *SB* διασκ. ἐν; Job 19 10 *B*(*S*
ⲧⲁⲕⲟ) διασπᾶν dat; ShZ 597 *S* ϫⲉⲣⲉ ⲡⲉⲩⲕⲁⲕⲉ ⲉⲃ.
ⲡϩⲣⲧⲟⲩ, ManiK 144 *A*² ϫⲣⲁⲣⲱⲟⲩ ⲁⲃ. ϩⲛⲙⲙⲁ, AM
245 *B* flock ϫ.† ⲉⲃ. ϩⲉⲛⲙⲁⲓ ⲡⲓⲃⲉⲛ; ⲡϩⲣⲏ ϩⲉⲛ-:
Mic 6 14 *B*(*S* diff) ἐξωθ. ἐν; ϩⲓϫⲛ-: Ge 9 19 *S*(*B*
ⲉϫⲉⲛ-) διασπ. ἐπί; Ez 11 16 *B* διασκ. εἰς; C 99 230
S endured ϣⲁⲡⲧⲉⲡ̅ⲭ̅ⲥ̅ ϫⲟⲟⲣⲟⲩ ⲉⲃ. ϩⲓϫⲱϥ = C 89 56
B, BHom 120 *S* men when dead ϫ.† ⲉⲃ. ϩ. ⲡⲣⲟ ⲙⲡⲕⲁϩ, BKU 1 259 *S* may He ϫⲱⲣⲉ ⲡⲉⲓϭⲓⲥⲉ ⲉⲃ. ϩ. ⲡ-
ⲣⲏⲕⲉ *from off*;   as nn m, *scattering, dissolution*:
Deu 30 4 *SB*, Ja 1 1 *B*(*S* = Gk) διασπορά; R 1 4 58 *S*
ⲡϫ. ⲉⲃ. ⲡⲛⲕⲉⲉⲥ σκορπισμός, Dan 12 7 *B* διασκ.; Ge
11 9 *S*(*B* ⲫⲱⲣϫ ⲉⲃ.) σύγχυσις; Mor 17 100 *S* ⲉϥϣⲟⲟⲡ
ⲡϫ. ⲉⲃ. to your souls ἀπόλλων; *ib* 95 *S* ⲡϫ. ⲉⲃ. that
befell temple (var Gu 259 ϣⲱϥ) ἐρήμωσις; Ps 89 17
S(*B* Gk om, Rahlfs *Sept Stu* 2 159); ShP 130² 78 *S*
gatherest us ϩⲙⲡⲉϫ. ⲉⲃ., Worr 315 *S* man's ϫ. ⲉⲃ.
ϩⲙⲡⲧⲁⲫⲟⲥ, Leip 24 31 *B* sim, ManiP 228 *A*² ⲡϫⲣ.
ⲁⲃ., Mus 45 35 *B* shall be to him ⲟⲩⲕⲣⲓⲙⲁ ⲡⲉⲙⲟⲩϫ.
ⲁⲃ. as to Judas, RE 9 136 *S* lest poor suffer ⲟⲩϫ. ⲉⲃ.,
PBad 5 410 *S* among evils invoked ϫⲟⲣⲓ ⲉⲃ. ⲡⲓⲙ, Ora
4 3 *S*ᵃ sim ⲡϫⲟⲩⲣⲉ ⲁⲃ.; ⲯ ϫⲓⲛϫ. ⲉⲃ. nn m *B*: Is
32 6 (*SF* ϫ. vb) διασπ.; Zech 11 14 (*A* ϫ. vb), Lev
26 44 (*S* do) ⲡϫⲓⲡϫⲉⲣ ⲧⲁⲓⲁⲑⲏⲕⲏ ⲉⲃ. διασκ.

ϫⲱⲱⲣⲉ *strong* v ϫⲣⲟ.

ϫⲣⲓ *S* v ϭⲣⲉ *B* nn.

ϫⲣⲟ *SAA*², ϭ. *S*(Sh)*AA*²*B*, ϫⲣⲁ *F*, ϫⲣⲁⲉⲓⲧ† *SA*²,
ϭ.†(Sh), ϫⲣⲟ.†, ϭ.†*S*(Sh), ϭⲣⲁⲓⲧ†*A*², ϫⲣⲏⲩⲧ†*S*(once),
ϭⲣⲏⲟⲩⲧ† *B*, ϫⲁⲣⲏⲟⲩⲧ† *F* vb intr, *be, become strong,
firm, victorious*: Ps 26 14 *S*(*B* ϫⲉⲙ ⲡⲟⲙ†), *ib* 30 24
S(*B* do) ἀνδρίζεσθαι; Is 28 22 *S*(*B* ϫⲉⲙ ϫⲟⲙ) ἰσχύειν;
Job 41 15 *S*(*B* ϭⲏⲥ) πηγνύναι; Deu 32 15 *A* ϫ. (Cl, *SB*
ϩⲧⲁⲉⲓ) παχύνειν (this word? *Cf* Ps 21 29 *S* ϫⲱⲱⲣⲉ);
Ps 50 4 *SA* ϫ. (Cl)*B*, Ap 2 7 *SB* νικᾶν, Aeg 270 *S* ⲉ-
ⲧⲣⲉϥϫ. πρὸς τὴν νίκην; BMis 37 *S* when had become
king ⲡϫϫ. ⲡⲟⲩⲕⲟⲩⲓ *somewhat established*, PMéd 230
S pound it ϣⲁⲡⲧⲉϥϫ. ⲧⲉϥϣⲟⲟⲩⲉ, PBad 5 349 *S* in

every war ϣⲁϥϫ., Miss 8 46 *S* Christ ⲡⲉⲡⲧⲁⲕϫ., ⲡ-
ϫⲣⲁ.†;   as acclamation (*cf* ἀνδρίζου): ShA 1 379
S ϧⲁⲓⲣⲉ ⲡⲣⲏ ϫ. ⲡⲟⲟⲣ, El 54 *A* ϫ. ϭⲡ ϭⲁⲙ, BMar
38 *S* ϫ. ⲡⲉⲛⲧⲁϫϫ. ϭⲁⲙ ϭⲟⲙ ⲡⲉⲛⲧⲁϥϭ. ϭ., ManiP 210
*A*² ϫ. ⲙⲡⲓⲁⲕ (*cf* ⲙⲓⲟⲍ), AM 67 *B* ϭ. ⲟⲩⲟϩ ⲡⲧⲉⲕϫⲉⲙ
ϫⲟⲙ;   qual: Ap 6 2 *S*(var *BP* 11965 35 ϫⲣⲟ.)*B*,
BHom 133 *S* contending with her ⲉϭ. ⲛⲓ.; Ro 4 16
F(JEA 13 26, *SB* ⲧⲁϫⲣⲏⲩ) βέβαιος εἶναι; Ex 32 18
S ϫⲣⲟ. (*B* ϭⲟⲣ) κατ' ἰσχύν; Jo 20 26 *A*²(*SB* ϣⲟⲧⲙ)
κλείσθαι; Mor 28 62 *S* ⲉϥⲙⲓϣⲉ ⲉϥϫ., MG 25 83 *B*
came forth from trials ⲉϥϭ., ManiP 195 *A*² ⲥⲡⲁϥ ⲉⲧϭ.

tr: Wess 15 138 *S* ⲛⲧⲁϫϫ. ⲁⲡ ⲙⲡϧⲁⲡ κυροῦν *ratify*;
ROC 17 408 *B* ⲁⲧⲥⲙⲏ ϭ. ⲡⲉⲡⲥⲡⲗⲁϫ ⲡⲟⲡ δριμύσσειν;
LAp 572 *F* ϫ. ⲙ[ⲡⲉⲧ]ⲉⲡⲣⲓⲧ with food ἰσχύειν (not
exact transl); Tri 347 *S* ϫ. ⲡϩⲟⲩϩⲟⲣⲙ ⲡⲓⲣⲉⲑⲛⲟⲥ
لغ.;   refl(mostly acclamation): Deu 31 6 *B*(*S* ϭⲙ
ϭⲟⲙ), HL 76 *B* ϫⲉⲙ ⲡⲟⲙ† ⲟⲩⲟϩ ϭ. ⲙⲙⲟⲕ ἀνδ.;
ROC 27 157 *B* ϭ. ⲙⲙⲟ σώζειν; RNC 79 *S* ϫ. ⲙⲙⲟⲕ
ⲱ ⲁⲣⲓⲁⲡⲟⲥ, Ann 17 152 *S* ϫ. ⲙⲙⲱⲧⲡ, El 56 *A* ϫ. ⲙ-
ⲙⲁⲕ, Mor 39 39 *F* ϫ. ⲙⲙⲁⲧⲛ = *ib* 40 29 *S* ⲧⲱⲕ.

With following preposition.

—— ⲉ-, *upon, over*: Pro 6 25 *SA*ϭ.*B*, Lu 11 22 *SB*,
Jo 16 33 *SA*²*B*, R 1 4 56 *S* ⲁⲩϫ. ⲉⲣⲟϥ ϩⲓⲧⲟⲩϭⲣⲙⲉ
ⲛⲓ.; He 11 33 *SB* καταγωνίζεσθαι gen; Col 2 18 *B*
(*S* ⲃⲱⲱⲣⲉ) καταβραβεύεσθαι; Is 30 31 *B*(*SF* ϭⲱⲧⲡ),
2 Pet 2 19 *S* ϫⲣⲏⲅⲧ (*P* 44 18, var ϭⲱ.)*B*† ἡττᾶσθαι,
Wess 15 135 *S* ⲙⲉⲩϣ ϫ. ⲉⲣⲟⲥ ἀήττητος; BMis 234
S ⲁϫϫ. ⲉⲡⲡⲟⲗⲩⲙⲟⲥ κρατεῖν; Is 30 13 *B*(*SF* ϫⲓ) ἁλίσκεσθαι; PS 115 *S* ⲁⲩϫ. ⲉⲣⲟⲟⲩ, ShC 73 39 *S* ⲡϩⲟⲟⲩⲧ ⲉⲧⲟⲩϫ. ⲉⲣⲟⲟⲩ, TillOster 21 *A* ⲁ[ⲩ]ϭ. ⲁⲣⲁⲩ, El
54 *A* ϭ. ⲁⲡⲕⲁⲧⲏⲅⲟⲣⲟⲥ, ManiK 49 *A*² ⲁϥϭ. ⲁⲣⲁϥ, C 43
204 *B* ϭ. ⲉⲡⲓⲃⲁⲥⲁⲡⲟⲥ, DeV 2 69 *B* ⲁⲩϭ. ⲉⲡⲓⲡⲟⲗⲉⲙⲟⲥ
victorius in war;   qual: 1 Jo 5 5 *SB*, Va 63 98 *B* ⲡⲓⲡⲁⲑⲟⲥ ... ϭ. ⲉϥ†ⲧⲉϧⲡⲏ ⲛⲓ., Z 329 *S* ⲡⲉⲥϭⲁ ϫ. ⲉϣⲁϫⲉ
ⲡⲓⲙ ἐκνι.; Va 57 232 *B* ⲉⲩϭ. ⲉⲡⲓⲉⲑⲛⲟⲥ ⲕⲣ.;   Mor 18
146 *S* iniquity ϫ. ⲉⲣⲟⲓ περιγίνεσθαι; ShR 2 3 48 *S*
ⲉⲩϫ. ⲉⲣⲟϥ, ShC 42 77 *S* ⲡⲉⲧⲕϭ. ⲉⲣⲟⲟⲩ, *ib* 73 25 ⲉϥ-
ϭⲣⲟ. ⲉⲣⲟϥ, Pcod 45 *S* water ϫ. ⲉⲡⲕⲱⲧ, BSM 111 *B*
ⲉⲣⲉϭ. ⲉⲣⲟⲓ = Mor 22 122 *S* ⲁⲣϫⲣⲟ.

—— ⲉϫⲛ-: BSM 15 *B* ϣⲁⲧⲉⲡϭ. ⲉ. ⲡⲉⲡϫⲁϫⲓ; BG
46 *S* ⲡⲉϥϧⲣⲟ (*sic*) ⲡϩⲏⲧ ⲉϩⲣⲁⲓ ⲉϫⲱⲟⲩ.

—— ϩⲛ-, ϩⲉⲛ- instr: Hab 3 19 *SB*(*A* ϭ. ⲡϩⲣⲏⲓ
ϩⲛ-), Z 297 *S* one thing ⲉⲧⲉⲕϫ.† ⲉⲣⲟⲓ ⲡϩⲏⲧϥ = MG
25 207 *B* ⲛⲓ., BMar 6 *S* ⲡⲉϥϫ.† ⲡⲉ ϩⲙⲡⲉϣⲗⲏⲗ, Till
Oster 21 *A* ⲁ[ⲩ]ϭ. ⲁⲣⲁⲩ ϩⲙⲡⲕⲉⲕⲉ ⲡⲧⲙⲡⲧⲁⲑⲏⲧ.

—— nn m *SAA*²*BF*, *victory, strength*: Pro 22 9
S(*A* ⲧⲁϫⲣⲟ), BMar 123 *S* ⲡⲉϫ. ⲡⲡⲃⲁⲣⲃⲁⲣⲟⲥ *over
barb*. νίκη, 1 Cor 15 55 *SA* ϭ. (TillOster 22)*B* νῖκος,
Am 1 11 *B*(*A* † ⲧⲱⲡ), *ib* 8 7 *SB* ⲉⲅⲭ. εἰς ν.; CaiEuch
478 *B* hymn of ⲡⲓϭ. ἐπινίκιον; Va 58 146 *B* ⲡⲓϭ. ϩⲉⲛ-
†ⲁⲡⲁⲥⲧⲁⲥⲓⲥ τρόπαιον; Cant 5 8 *F*(*S* ⲡⲟⲙⲧⲉ) ἰσχύς;
Sa 7 10 *S* ὑγίεια; Phil 2 1 *B* ϭ. ⲡϩⲏⲧ (*SF* ⲥⲟⲡⲥ) παράκλησις; HM 2 134 *S* ⲡⲉϫ. ⲡⲡⲉⲩϩⲏⲧ toward Christ,

ShC 42 77 *S* ⲛⲟⲩϭ. ⲛⲁⲕ ⲁⲛⲛⲉ = MIF 23 36, ManiP 41 *A²* ⲟⲩϭ. ⲙⲡⲉⲕⲃⲏⲙⲁ, AM 8 *B* ⲁⲣⲉϣⲁⲛⲛⲓϭ. ϣⲱⲡⲓ ⲛⲱⲧⲉⲛ; ϯ ϫ., ϭ.: 1 Chr 28 20 *B* ϯ ϭ. ⲙⲙⲟⲕ ἴσχυε κ. ἀνδρίζου; BG 67 *S* ⲡⲉⲡ̅ⲛ̅ⲁ̅ ⲛϫⲱⲣⲉ...ϣⲁϥϯ ϫ. ⲛⲧϭⲟⲙ, ShR 2 3 48 *S* ⲉⲩⲉϣ [ⲗⲟⲩ]ⲗ[ⲁⲓ] ⲉⲃⲟⲗ ⲉⲩ[ϯ] ⲛⲁϥ ⲙⲡⲉϭ. ϩⲙⲡϣⲁϫⲉ ⲙⲡⲉⲩⲧ[ⲁⲡⲣⲟ] *acclaiming him*, P 130³ 71 *S* we must ϯ ϫ. ⲛⲛⲉⲥⲛⲏⲩ...ⲉⲛⲥⲟⲗⲥⲗ ⲙⲙⲟⲟⲩ, ManiH 5 *A²* ϯ ⲡϭ. ⲛⲏⲓ; ϫⲓ, ϭⲓ ϭ. *A²B*: ManiP 56 *A²* ⲁⲓϫⲓ ⲡϭ., C 43 162 ⲁϥϭⲓ ⲙⲡⲓϭ. ϧⲉⲛⲡⲓⲡⲟⲗⲉⲙⲟⲥ, AM 9 rejoicing at ⲡⲓϭ. ⲉⲧⲁⲩϭⲓⲧϥ; ⲥⲙⲛ ϫ. *S*, *establish victory*: Mus 40 257 Jesus ⲡⲣⲉϥⲥ. νικοποιός; ⲣ ϫ., ϭ., *be victorious*: Va 63 82 *B* ⲁⲥⲉⲣ ⲡⲕⲉϭ. ⲉⲛⲏ ⲉⲧϯ ⲟⲩⲃⲏⲥ περιγίνεσθαι; Mani K 55 *A²* ⲁϥⲣ ϩⲛϫ., *ib* ⲣ ⲟⲩⲛⲁϭ ⲛϫ., PMich 1291 *F* ϩⲉⲣϣⲓⲣⲉ ...ⲉⲣ ϫ. ⲉⲣⲁⲓ.

ⲁⲧϫ., -ϭ., *unconquerable*: Mor 17 120 *S* ϭⲟⲙ ⲛⲁ(ⲧ)ϫ. ⲉⲣⲟⲥ ἀνίκητος; Mus 34 187 *B* ⲁⲙⲏϣ ⲛⲁ. ἀήττητος; J 75 45 *S* ⲇⲓⲁⲑⲏⲕⲏ ⲛⲁ. ⲉⲣⲟⲥ.

ⲙⲁⲓϫ., -ϭ., *victory-loving*: Mart Ign 877 *B* man is ⲍⲱⲟⲛ ⲙⲙ. = R 1 4 71 *S* ⲣⲉϥϫ. φιλόνικος; R 1 3 81 *S* ⲧⲕⲁⲕⲓⲁ...ⲟⲩⲙ. ⲧⲉ.

ⲣⲉϥϫ., -ϭ., *victor*, epithet of emperors, martyrs: Miss 8 29 *S* νικητής; PSBA 10 198 *S* ⲡⲣ. ⲍⲏⲛⲱⲛ, ManiP 53 *A²* ⲡⲣⲉϥϭ. ⲁⲛⲕⲉⲕⲉ, AM 222 *B* ⲟⲩⲣⲱⲟⲩ ⲛⲣ., C 86 90 *B* ⲡⲓϫⲱⲣⲓ ⲛⲣ., J 98 4 *S* ⲣ. *sc* St Phoebammon (prob not to be joined with ⲕⲗⲁⲙ, *cf* p 105 *a*).

ϭⲓⲛϫ., *victory*: ShP 130³ 2 *S* ⲧϭ. ⲉⲛⲉⲩϫⲁϫⲉ.

V ⲧⲁϫⲣⲟ, ϫⲟⲣϫⲣ.

(ϫⲱⲱⲣⲉ *SA*, ϫⲱⲣⲉ *AA²*, ϫⲱⲣⲓ *BF* all as nn only), ϫⲉⲣ- (once), ϫⲟⲟⲣ† *S*, -ⲣⲉ†, ϫⲱ(ⲱ)ⲣⲉ† *A*, ϫⲟⲣ†, ϫⲟⲣⲓ† (once)*B*, ϫⲁ(ⲁ)ⲣ† *F*, p c ϫⲁⲣ- *SBF* vb intr (qual), *be strong, hard, bold*: Ge 14 5 *B*, Is 43 16 *B*(var & *S* ⲟϣ), Joel 1 6 *SA* ϫⲟ. *B*, Lu 11 21 *S*(*B* nn), 2 Cor 10 10 *B* (*S* ϭⲙϭⲟⲙ), He 6 18 *B*(*SF* ⲧⲁϫⲣⲏⲩ) ἰσχυρός, Mt 9 12 *B*(*S* ⲧⲏⲕ) ἰσχύειν, Ez 19 14 *SB* ἰσχύς; Nu 8 4 *S*(*B* ⲧⲁϫ.), Is 5 28 *B*(*S* ⲛⲁϣⲧ), He 5 14 *SBF* στερεός; Ex 6 1 *A* ϫⲱⲣⲉ (var Cl 60 3 ϫⲟ., *B* ⲁⲙⲁϩⲓ), Job 30 21 *SB*, Pro 23 11 *S*(var ϫⲱⲱⲣ)*A*, Am 2 14 *A* ϫⲱⲱⲣⲉ *B* (*S* nn), 1 Pet 5 6 *SF*(Mus 49 197, *B* ⲁⲙ.) κραταιός; Job 16 14 *S*(*B* nn), Ac 7 22 *BF*(*S*=Gk) δυνατός, Ge 49 24 *B*(Va, *S* nn) δυνάστης; Deu 28 52 *B*(*S* ⲟⲣϫ), Is 26 5 *B*(*S* ϫⲟⲥⲉ) ὀχυρός, Lam 2 2 *F* ϫⲁⲣ (*B* ⲧⲁϫⲣⲟ nn), Mic 5 11 *B*(*A* ⲁⲣϫ) ὀχύρωμα; Deu 33 28 *B*(*S* ⲧⲁϫ.), Is 32 18 *B*(*SF* ⲧⲁϫ. nn) πείθειν; Col 1 23 *B*(*S* ⲧⲁϫ.) ἑδραῖος; MG 25 213 *B* ϩⲏⲧ ⲉϥϫ. θαρσαλέος; ShA 2 163 *S* ⲕⲁϩ ⲉⲧϫ. ⲉⲙⲛ ϣⲟⲉⲓϣ ⲛϩⲏⲧϥ, ShC 73 153 *S* ⲧⲙⲛⲧϫⲱⲱⲣⲉ ⲛⲛⲉⲧϫ., Mor 31 124 *S* ⲛⲉⲣⲉⲛⲉϥϣⲁϫⲉ ϫ. when praying, Z 630 *S* dissolve them ϩⲓⲏⲣⲡ ⲉϥϫ., Ryl 62 1 *S* ⲕⲁⲡⲛⲟⲥ ⲉⲧϫ., MG 25 383 *B* ⲡⲉϥϩⲏⲧ ϫ. as lion's, C 43 18 *B* ⲥⲁϫⲓ ⲉⲧϫ., Pcod 40 *F* sinners ⲥⲉϫ. (*S* ⲣ ϩⲟⲩⲟ).

tr *S*: Mor 28 29 ⲁⲕϫⲉⲣ ⲡⲉⲕⲃⲁⲗ ϩⲛⲧⲕⲁⲕⲓⲁ (*cf* p c).

With following preposition. c ⲉ-, *over, than*: Deu 7 1 *S*(*B* ⲉϩⲟⲧⲉ-), Pro 24 65 *SAB*(*sic l*), Mk 1 7 *S*(*B* ⲉϩ.) ἰσχυρότερος gen; Ps 34 10 *SB*, Jer 38 11 *S* (ShA 2 340)*B* στερεώτερος gen; Sa 10 12 *S* δυνατώτερος gen; BM 174 *S* body ϫ. ⲉⲧϭⲟⲙ ⲛⲙⲙⲟⲩⲓ ἀδάμαστος dat; PS 142 *S* ⲛⲉⲥϫ. ⲉⲣⲟⲟⲩ, Pcod 45 *S* nature of iron ϫ. ⲉⲡⲱⲛⲉ (*cf ib* ⲡⲱⲛⲉ ϫⲣⲟ ⲉⲡⲉⲛⲓⲡⲉ), BSM 112 *B* ⲉⲛϫ. (? error) ⲉⲛⲏ whom we can capture = Mor 22 123 *S* ⲉⲛϭⲱⲣϭ, Bor 254 171 *S* Three Children ⲉⲩϫ. ⲉϩⲟⲩⲉⲛⲕⲱϩⲧ; c ⲉϫⲉⲛ-: Va 58 185 *B* ⲉϥϫ. ⲉ. ⲫⲙⲟⲩ ἰσχ. κατά; c ⲛ-: Dan 3 20 *B* ⲉⲩϫ. ⲛⲛⲟⲙϯ ἰσχ. ἰσχύι; c ϩⲛ-, ϧⲉⲛ-: Leyd 303 *S* ⲯⲩⲭⲏ ⲉⲧϫ. ϩⲛⲧⲁⲣⲉⲧⲏ, Bor 240 53 *S* ⲉⲩϫ. ϩⲙⲡⲉⲩⲥⲱⲙⲁ, AM 136 *B* ⲉϥϫ. ϧⲉⲛⲧⲉϥϩⲉⲍⲓⲥ.

p c: ϫⲁⲣⲃⲁⲗ Pro 27 20 *S*(*A* ϫⲁⲣ-) στηρίζων ὀφθαλμόν (*cf* ⲧⲁϫⲣⲉ ⲃ. Pro 16 30, Am 9 4, Jer 24 6); ⲙⲛⲧϫ. *S*: Eccl 11 9 (*F* ⲓⲱⲣϩ ⲛⲃ.) ὅρασις ὀφ. (error?), cit (?) JA '75 5 229 ἀκαιροπερίσπαστος; BMis 521 ⲡⲟⲣⲛⲓⲁ, ⲙⲛⲧⲁⲧϣⲓⲡⲉ, ⲙⲛⲧϫ.; ϫⲁⲣϩⲏⲧ AM 2 16 *S*(*B* diff) κραταιός; BM 185 *S* opp ϭⲁⲃ[ϩⲏⲧ], C 43 36 *B* ϫ. ϧⲉⲛⲡⲓⲡⲟⲗⲉⲙⲟⲥ, BAp 154 *S* ϣⲱⲡⲉ ⲛϫ., Bor 234 10 *S* ⲁⲣⲓ ϫ.; ⲙⲛⲧ-, ⲙⲉⲧϫ.: BMis 237 *S* θαρσαλέος; Bor 260 99 *S* ⲙ. ϩⲓⲛⲟⲙⲧⲉ, Miss 4 200 *B* ϣⲱⲡⲓ ϧⲉⲛⲟⲩⲙ., Mor 30 10 *F*; ϯ ⲙ.: BMis 197 *S* ⲁⲡⲇⲓⲁⲕⲟⲛⲟⲥ ϯ ⲙ. ⲛⲁϥ (var Mor 16 33 ϯ ⲧⲱⲕ ⲛϩⲏⲧ), Cat 75 *B* ⲉϥϯ ⲙ. ⲛⲱⲟⲩ, BIF 22 107 *F* sim; ϫⲓ, ϭⲓ ⲙ.: Ac 28 15 *B*(*S* ⲧⲱⲕ ⲛϩ.) θάρσος λαμβάνειν; BMis 194 *S* ⲁϥϫⲓ ⲛⲁϥ ⲛⲟⲩⲙ. & cast out fear.

ϫⲱⲱⲣⲉ *SAF*(once), ϫⲱⲱⲣ, ϫⲱⲣ *S*(rare), ϫⲱⲣⲉ *S* (rare)*AA²*, ϫⲟⲟⲣⲉ *S*(once)*A*, ϫⲱⲣⲓ *BF*, ϫⲱⲱⲣⲓ *F*, *strong*, **a** as nn: Ps 77 65 *S*(*B* ⲉⲟⲩⲟⲛ ϣϫⲟⲙ ⲙⲙⲟϥ), *ib* 88 8 *S*(*B* ϫⲟⲣ), *ib* 119 4 *S* ϫⲱⲱⲣ, ϫⲱⲣ *B* δυνατός, Ge 49 24 *S*(*B* Va ⲡⲉⲧϫⲟⲣⲓ), Ps 102 20 *S* ϫ. ϩⲛⲧⲉⲩϭⲟⲙ δ. ἰσχύι (*v* AZ 71 81), Job 6 23 *B*(*S* ⲣⲉϥϫⲓ ϫⲛⲁϩ), Pro 8 3 *SAB*, *ib* 23 1 *SA* ϫⲱⲣⲉ, *ib* 25 6 *SA* ϫⲟ. δυνάστης; Jer 9 23 *A*(Cl) ϫⲱⲣⲉ *B*, Lam 1 15 *BF* ϫⲱⲣⲁ, Ap 6 15 *SBF* ϫⲱⲱⲣⲓ, 1 Cor 4 10 *B*(*S* ϫⲟⲟⲣ) ἰσχυρός, Is 5 22 *SBF*-ⲣⲉ ἰσχύειν; Ps 53 3 *SB*, Am 2 14 *S*(*AB* vb†) κραταιός; Pro 10 4 *SA* ϫⲱⲣⲉ (*B* ⲁϣⲓⲣⲓ), Mor 17 12 *S* ⲟⲩϫ. ϩⲙⲡⲉⲥⲥⲱⲙⲁ ἀνδρεῖος; Job 29 9 *SB* ἁδρός; Pro 21 16 *SA* γίγας; Zech 11 2 *A*(*B* diff) μεγιστάν; Ps 21 29 *S*(*B* ⲕⲉⲛⲓⲱⲟⲩⲧ) πίων; BMar 119 *S* youths ϩⲉⲛϫ. ϩⲛⲧⲉⲩϭⲟⲙ εὐμεγέθης; C 99 212 *S* ⲛϫ. = C 89 4 *B* τίρων; PS 175 *S* ⲟⲩϫ., BG 68 *S* ⲧϭⲟⲙ...ⲟⲩϫⲱⲣⲉⲧⲉ, BM 256 222 *S* ⲟⲩϭⲱⲃ, ⲟⲩϫ., ManiK 102 *A²* ϩⲛϫ., BSM 48 *B* ⲙⲓⲭⲁⲏⲗ ⲡⲓϫ. = BMis 397 *S* ⲇⲩⲛⲁⲧⲟⲥ, KroppM 17 *S* ⲡⲛⲟϭ ⲛϫⲱⲣⲉ.

b as adj, after nn: Ex 17 9 *S*(*B* om), Ps 17 17 *S*(*B* ϫⲟⲣ) δυνατός; Pro 12 4 *SA* ϫⲟ. *B* ἀνδ.; Ps 7 11 *S*(*B* ϫⲟⲣ) ἰσχυρός; BG 67 *S* ⲡⲉⲡ̅ⲛ̅ⲁ̅ ⲛϫⲱⲣⲉ, PS 101 *S* ϯ ϭⲟⲙ ⲛϫⲱⲱⲣ, LMär 14 *S* ⲇⲩⲛⲁⲧⲟⲥ ⲛϫ., AZ 71 81 n *S* sim ϫⲟⲟⲣⲉ, ManiP 153 *A²* ⲧⲉⲕⲛⲁϣⲧⲉ ⲛϫ., Mani 1 *A²* ⲡⲡ̅ⲉ̅ ⲛϫ., MG 25 198 *B* ⲉⲣ ϩⲏⲧ ⲛϫ.; before nn: BHom 127 *S* ⲛϫ. ⲛⲧⲩⲣⲁⲛⲛⲟⲥ, Mor 31 62 *S* ⲟⲩϫ. ⲛ-

ⲣⲱⲙⲉ, C 86 270 B ⲡⲓϫ. ⲙⲙⲁⲣⲧⲩⲣⲟⲥ; c following ⲉ-, ⲉϧⲟⲧⲉ ⲉ-, *stronger than*: Eccl 6 10 *SF* ϫⲱⲣⲓ
ἰσχυρότερος ὑπέρ, 1 Cor 10 22 *B*(*S* ϫⲟⲟⲣ ⲉ-) ἰσ. gen;
ViK 9763 4 *S* ⲡⲓⲙ ⲛϭⲱⲃ...ⲡϫ. ⲉⲣⲟϥ.

ⲣ, ⲉⲣ ϫ., *be strong*: 1 Kg 4 9 *S* εἰς ἄνδρας γίνεσθαι;
Jer 13 18 *B*(*S* ϭⲙ ϭⲟⲙ) δυναστεύειν, Ja 2 6 *B*(*S.A* ϫⲓ
ⲛϭⲟⲛⲥ) καταδ. gen; R 2 1 50 *S* ⲛⲥⲱⲙⲁ ⲣ. ⲛϥϭⲙ ϭⲟⲙ,
ManiK 144 *A²* sin ⲣ. ⲁⲭⲓⲧⲛⲏⲉ, TstAb 175 *B* ⲧⲁⲥⲁⲣⲝ̄
ⲉⲣ.; ϫⲓⲡⲉⲣ ϫ. *B*: Cat 13 +ϫ. ⲟⲩⲃⲉϥⲛⲟⲃⲓ.

ϫⲙ ϫ. *B*, *use strength, force*: Va 58 71 ⲁϥϫ. ⲉϫⲱⲥ
ⲁϥϧⲉⲃⲓⲟⲥ.

ϭⲉⲡ ϫ. *S*(once)*B*, ϣⲉⲡ ϫ. *B*, as last : Va 58 155
ⲥϭ. ⲛϫⲉ +ⲙⲉⲧⲙⲁⲓⲧⲟⲓ ⲡⲣⲟϥⲟ, paral ⲥⲁⲙⲁϧⲓ καταδυναστεύειν; AM 123 even if one ϭ. he shall not profit
= R 1 4 61 *S*ⲉⲡⲓⲭⲉⲓⲣⲉⲓ; c ⲉ-: Lakân 45 mankind
ⲉⲁⲩϣⲉⲡ ϫ. ⲉⲣⲟϥ ϧⲓⲧⲉⲛⲡⲓⲇⲓⲁⲃⲟⲗⲟⲥ; c ⲉϫⲉⲛ-: Ex
21 16(*S* ϫⲓ ⲛϫⲛⲁϧ), Deu 24 7(*S* ϭⲙ ϭⲟⲙ ⲉ-)καταδ.;
Jer 15 18 (*S* do) κατισχύειν; TEuch 2 273 ⲁⲩϣⲉⲡ
ϫ. ⲉϫⲱϥ τυραννεῖν; MG 25 197 ⲉⲣⲉⲡⲓϫⲁϫⲓ ϭ. ⲉϫⲱⲥ;
ⲉϧⲣⲏⲓ ⲉϫ.: Jer 27 33 καταδ.; Cat 49; c ϧⲛ- *S*:
P 130⁵ 35 wise cannot fathom Thee ⲁⲩϫⲣⲟ ⲅⲁⲣ ⲛϭⲓ
ⲡⲓⲟⲩⲱⲣⲉ (*sc* disciples) ⲁⲩϭ. ⲛϭⲓ ⲡⲉⲧⲣⲁⲙⲙⲁⲧⲕⲟⲥ
ϧⲙⲡⲉⲛⲧⲁϣⲉⲟⲓϣ *were overpowered*(?); ⲙⲉⲧϭ. ϫ.:
TEuch 2 225 saved us ⲉⲃⲟⲗ ϧⲁϫⲙ. of devil; ⲙⲉⲧⲣⲉϥϫ. ϫ.: Am 3 9 καταδυναστεία; Miss 4 149 ⲧⲟⲩϫ.
ⲉϫⲱⲛ (Gött ar 114 67 قَهَرَ).

ⲙⲛⲧ-, ⲙⲉⲧϫ., *strength, prowess, feat*: Ex 6 6 *B*(*A*
ϫⲓ ⲛϫⲟⲙⲥ), Ps 19 7 *B*(*S* ϭⲟⲙ) δυναστεία, 1 Cor 15 43
F(*SB* do) δύναμις; Pro 21 30 *S.A* -ϫⲱⲣⲉ ἀνδρεία; Sa
10 12 *S*(var -ϫⲱⲱⲣ) ἰσχυρός, Ps 32 16 *B*(*S* ⲡⲟⲙⲧⲉ),
Aeg 268 *S* ⲧⲙ. ⲛⲡⲣⲱⲙⲉ ἰσχύς; C1 5 6 *A* -ϫⲱⲣⲉ γενναῖος; Jer 31 30 *B* ἱκανός; BHom 50 *S* ἄθλησις; MG
25 27 *B* +ϫ. of man is to accept blame before God
ἐργασία; ShC 73 164 *S* opp ⲙⲛⲧϭⲱⲃ, ib 134 *S* food
& raiment acquired by ⲧⲉϥϫ., Lammeyer 51 *S* ⲧⲙ. of
Christ's body & blood (var R 1 2 48 ⲙⲡⲧⲁⲩⲑⲉⲡⲧⲏⲥ),
BAp 150 *S* ⲡⲟⲩϫ. ϫⲓⲡⲉ + ⲟⲉⲓⲕ in time of plenty,
ManiP 90 *A²* ⲧⲙ. ⲙⲡⲉⲕϧⲣⲁϥ, AM 78 *B* ⲧⲉϥϫ. ⲛⲉⲙ-
ⲧⲉϥⲙⲉⲧϧⲁⲣϧⲏⲧ, Mor 30 36 *F* ⲙⲛⲧϫⲱⲣⲓ; ϧⲛ-,
ϧⲉⲛⲟⲩϫ. advb : Va 58 145 *B* horseman ⲁϥϭⲱⲣⲉⲙ
ϭ. ἀκρατῶς; BHom 68 *S* ⲉⲧⲁⲥⲕⲉⲓ ϧ., Mun 37 *S* bore
tortures ϧ. = C 86 283 *B*; ⲣ ⲙⲛⲧϫ.: Pro 29 47
SA δύναμιν ποιεῖν; ShViK 9593 *S* who pray too often
ϧⲱⲥ ⲉϣϫⲉ ⲛⲧⲁⲩⲉⲓⲣⲉ ⲛⲟⲩϫ., HT *X* 1 *S* ⲉⲓⲣⲉ ⲛⲟⲉⲡ
ⲛⲟϭ ⲙⲙ. ϧⲙⲡⲡⲟⲗⲉⲙⲟⲥ.

ⲣⲉϥϫⲟⲟⲣ *S*, *strong man*: Tri 383 قُوَّة.
As name : ϫⲱⲣⲉ (R 1 5 25 = شُور Synax 1 323),
ⲡⲭ.(RNC 3, 4), ⲡϫⲟⲣ(Ora 4 3), ? Σωρέ(PLond 4 36).
V AZ 67 77.

(ϫⲱⲣⲉⲃ), ⲣ c ϫⲁⲣⲉⲃ-, ϫⲁⲣⲡ-, ϫⲉⲣⲉⲃ- *B* vb tr,
cut open (?): He 4 13 ϫ. ⲛⲁⲣⲃⲓ (*S* ϣⲁⲁⲧ) مَكُشُوف, Va
57 67 sad & humbled ⲉⲛⲟⲓ ⲛϫⲁⲣⲡⲛⲁⲣⲃⲓ τραχηλίζειν;
BM 841 82 ϫⲉⲣⲉⲃⲛⲁϧⲃⲓ.

ϫⲟⲣⲃⲉⲥ *B* nn f, a small (?) vessel : K 150 = P 55
11 +ϫ. صَاقُل (1 var جُرّ).

(ϫⲱⲣⲕ), ϫⲁⲣⲕ⳿ *O* vb tr, meaning unknown : Hor
83 ⲡⲧⲟⲩϫⲁⲣⲕϥ ⲛⲡⲛⲣⲁⲙⲡⲉ ⲙ̄ⲃ̄ ⲁϧⲣⲏⲉⲓ.

ϫⲱⲣⲙ *SA²*(once), -ⲙⲉ *AA²*, ϭⲱⲣⲉⲙ *B*, ϫⲱⲗⲙ
S¹, ϫⲁⲣⲙⲉ- *A²*, ϫⲟⲣⲙ† *S* vb intr, **A** *make sign, beckon*:
Va 57 68 *B* eyes of them ⲉⲧϭ. ⲕⲁⲕⲱⲥ διανεύειν; Mani
P 225 *A²* sim ; tr: Pro 4 25 *B*(var & *S* ⲉⲓⲱⲣⲙ, *A*
ⲙⲟⲩϭ) νεύειν; Ac 19 33 *SB*(or ? prep ⲛ-) κατασείειν,
TMina*Epima* 21 *S* dumb man ϫ. ⲙⲙⲟϥ(*sc* bystander)
ⲉⲡⲙⲁⲕⲁⲣⲓⲟⲥ...ϫⲉⲕⲁⲥ ⲉϥⲛⲁⲕⲱⲣϣ ⲉⲣⲟϥ = C 43 142
B + ϧⲟ ⲉⲣⲟϥ ϧⲓⲛⲁ, Bess 7 5 *B* eyelids ⲉⲓϭ. ⲙⲙⲱⲟⲩ
ϣⲁⲛⲧⲁⲣⲱϧⲧ ⲛⲛⲓⲁⲗⲱⲟⲩⲓ ⲉⲡⲁⲧⲥⲉⲃⲟ; c ⲉ-, *to*: Jo
13 24 *B*(*S* ⲟⲩⲃⲉ-), Z 344 *S* ⲁϥϫ. ⲉⲡⲕⲟⲩⲓ ⲉⲧⲣⲉϥⲃⲱⲕ
= MG 25 209 *B*, Aeg 275 *S* ⲡⲛⲉⲟⲩⲁ ϫ. ⲉⲟⲩⲁ in
church νεύ., Lu 1 22 *B*(*S* ⲟⲩ.) διαν., ib 62 *B*(*S* do)
ἐνν., Pro 26 24 *SA* ἐπίν., Lu 5 7 *S*(var ⲟⲩ.)*B* κατάν.;
Ac 12 17 *B*(*S* ⲕⲓⲙ) κατασ.; Tri 732 *S* ϫ. ⲉⲧⲉⲥϧⲓⲙⲉ
ⲉⲃⲱⲕ رَمْز; PS 107 *S* ⲉϥϫ. ⲉⲣⲟⲓ (*cf* Ps 108 25 ⲕⲓⲙ
ⲡⲛⲉⲩϧⲁⲡⲉ), P 131⁶ 4 *S* Jesus ⲁϥϫ. ⲉⲡⲁⲅⲅⲉⲗⲟⲥ & he
took away stone, Mor 23 46 *S* ⲁϥϫ. ⲉⲡⲣⲱⲙⲉ ϫⲉⲧⲱ-
ⲟⲩⲛ, El 42 *A* ⲁϥϫⲱⲣⲙ (sic) ⲁⲣⲁⲩ & they turned
away, ManiP 98 *A²* ϫⲱⲣⲙ ϧⲱⲕ ⲁⲣⲁⲓ, ib 76 *A²* ⲁϥ-
ϫⲁⲣⲙ ⲓⲉⲧϥ ⲁⲙⲡⲉⲧⲟⲩⲁⲃⲉ, BM 917 *B* ⲁϥϫ. ⲉϥⲣⲏ
(Pereira *Abba Samuel* 99 ⲓⲋⲍ as if ⲓⲱⲣⲙ, Mor 31 57
diff), Miss 4 117 *B* ⲁⲡⲁⲓⲱⲧ ϭ. ⲉⲛⲓⲥⲛⲏⲟⲩ ϫⲉⲙⲟⲛⲓ
ⲙⲙⲟϥ = Mor 19 32 *S* ⲕⲓⲙ; c ⲛ- instr : Ps 34 19
S(*B* ϧⲉⲡ-) διαν., Pro 10 10 *AB*(*S* ϧⲛ-) ἐνν.; Dif 2 16
B ⲁϥϫ. ⲉⲣⲟⲕ ⲙⲡⲉϥⲧⲏⲃ; dat: ManiK 178 *A²* ⲉϥϫ.
ⲛⲉⲩ ⲁⲧⲟⲩⲙⲁⲣⲉ, Ryl 430 88 *B* ⲁϥϫ. ⲡⲉ ϫⲉⲛⲡⲓⲧⲟⲩⲃⲟ
'ⲻ; c ⲟⲩⲃⲉ-: Mor 37 46 *S* ⲁϥϫ. ⲟⲩⲃⲏϥ that he
should draw nigh νευ., ib 17 78 *S* ϧⲙⲧⲣⲉϥϫ. ⲟⲩⲃⲉ-
ⲕⲁⲣⲟⲥ διαν.; BMis 550 *S* ⲁⲡⲁⲅⲅⲉⲗⲟⲥ ϫ. ⲟⲩⲃⲏⲓ ϫⲉ-
innuere; BMis 554 *S* ⲡⲉϥϫ. ⲟⲩⲃⲏⲓ *intueri*; Mor 43
39 *S* ⲁϥϫ. ⲟⲩⲃⲉⲓⲱϧⲁⲛⲛⲏⲥ (Jo 19 27), C 100 278 *S*
ⲁϥϫ. ⲟⲩⲃⲏϥ ... ⲉⲧⲣⲉϥϣⲱⲡ ⲉϧⲟⲩⲛ; c ϧⲛ-, ϧⲉⲛ-
instr : Si 27 22 *S* διαν. dat, Pro 6 13 *SA*(*B* ⲛ-) ἐνν.; Sh
A 2 258 *S* ϫ. ϧⲛⲡⲉϥⲃⲁⲗ ⲉⲉⲓⲣⲉ ⲛⲟⲩⲕⲣⲟϥ; as nn m:
Is 3 16 *B*(*S* ⲕⲓⲙ) νεῦμα, Pro 6 13 *SAB* ἔννευ.; C 99
88 ϧⲙⲡϫ. ⲙⲡⲉϥⲧⲏⲛⲃⲉ ⲡⲉϫⲁϥ, ManiK 163 *A²* ⲁⲡⲥⲱⲧⲏⲣ ⲛⲟⲩϫⲉ ⲡⲟⲩϫ. ⲛⲛⲉϥⲙⲁⲑⲏⲧⲏⲥ ϫⲉ-, ib H 44 *A²*
ⲁϥⲟⲩϫⲉ ⲛϧⲓϫ. ϧⲁⲧⲉϥⲥⲧⲁⲩⲣⲱⲥⲓⲥ, ib P 104 *A²* ϣⲁⲓ+
ϫ. ϧⲁⲡⲣⲉϥⲣ ⲛⲁⲃⲉ brought to my tribunal; ϭⲓⲛϫ.
A², *beckoning*: ManiK 32 ⲧϭ. ⲉⲧⲟⲩⲛⲁⲧⲉⲉⲥ ⲙⲡⲛⲟⲩ-
ⲉⲣⲏⲩ.

B *urge, drive, ride, hasten* (same ?) intr : Va 58 145
B horseman ϭ. ϧⲉⲛⲟⲩⲙⲉⲧϫⲱⲣⲓ ἐλαύνειν, Ps 97 6 *B*
(but *S* ϫⲁϧϫ) ἐλατός, Zech 9 8 *AB*(*S* ⲣⲉϥϫ.) ἐξελαύ.;
Va 57 123 *B* ⲉⲧϫ. ϧⲉⲛⲡⲓⲁⲣⲟⲙⲟⲥ δρομεύς; 2 Kg 13
29 *S*(var & Gk om), JA '05 434 *S* horseman ⲁϥϫ. &
reached city, BM 995 102 *S* invaders ϫ. ϧⲙⲡⲧⲟⲟⲩ,
ViK 4701 *S* they told us ϫⲉⲁⲧⲛⲉϫ. ⲁⲧⲛⲉⲕⲱ ⲡϣⲟⲧⲉ

(place), CO 436 *S* charioteer ⲉϥϫ. ϧⲙⲡⲁϭⲱⲛ (ⲁⲅ.), BMis 278 *S* ⲁⲡϣⲏⲣⲉ ϫⲏⲗ ϫ. (on horse?) ⲉⲛⲟⲩⲛⲟϭ ⲛϭⲟⲙ = Mor 30 56 *S^f* = ib 29 49 *S* ⲧⲱϫⲙ, WTh 156 *B* messengers ϭ. ϫⲉⲛⲛⲓⲙⲁ ⲛⲛⲱϣ like birds, TSBA 9 367 *B* ⲙⲱⲟⲩ ⲛϧⲱⲟⲩ ⲉϥϭ.; tr: 1 Kg 6 8 *S* ⲁⲡⲉⲗ.; 2 Kg 6 3 *S*(*B* ⲏⲓⲓ) ⲁⲅⲉⲓⲛ; R 1 5 31 *S*(collated) soldiers bidden ϫⲉⲉⲅⲉϫ. ⲛⲡⲉϥ[.. ϧⲏⲡ]ⲉⲅϭⲓϫ, C 41 15 *B* mounted on beast ⲉϥϭ. ⲙⲙⲟϥ. ⲥ ⲉ-: 3 Kg 22 34 *S* ⲡⲏⲛⲓⲟⲭⲟⲥ ⲉⲧϫ. ⲉⲡⲉϥϩⲁⲣⲙⲁ (Gk om), BMis 32 *S* horseman ϫ. ⲉⲡⲉⲓⲥⲁ ⲙⲛⲛⲁⲓ, FR 20 *S* to muleteer ϫ. ⲉⲑⲏ ⲛⲕⲉⲟⲩⲓ, C 86 324 *B* ⲁⲅϭ. ⲉⲣⲟϥ but could not catch him; ⲉⲣⲟⲩⲛ, ⲉⲃ. ⲉ-: LA 113 *S* ⲁⲅϫ. ⲉ. ⲉⲡⲕⲁⲕⲉ, C 86 150 *B* ⲁϥϭ. ⲙⲡⲉϥⲉⲣϩⲟ ⲉ. ⲉⲛⲓⲑⲣⲁⲕⲱⲛ; ⲥ ⲉϫⲛ-: BMis 220 *S* ϫ. ⲉϩⲟⲟⲩ ⲉⲣⲟⲩⲛ ⲉⲧⲉⲣⲅⲁⲥⲓⲁ (var Mor 16 76 ϫ. ⲛⲥⲱⲟⲩ); ⲥ ⲙⲛ-, ⲛⲉⲙ-: DeV 2 184 *B* startled horse ϭ. ⲛⲉⲙⲁϥ (*sc* rider) & dragged him, MG 25 103 *B* many ⲉⲧϭ. ⲛⲉⲙⲱⲧⲉⲛ (Gött ar 114 44 الذي معكم); ⲥ ⲛⲥⲁ-: Lu 8 29 *B*(*S* ϫⲓ passive), 2 Pet 2 17 *B*(*S* ϩⲓⲟⲩⲉ) ⲉⲗ.; Lam 1 4 *B*(*S* pap *olim* BP Grenfell, *F* ϭⲓ) ⲁⲅ.; Ge 33 13 *S*(*B* ϭⲟϫⲓ) ⲕⲁⲧⲁⲇⲓⲱⲕⲉⲓⲛ; C 89 100 *B* ⲉⲅϭ. ⲛⲥⲱⲟⲩ ϫⲉⲛⲟⲩϣⲱⲟⲣⲧⲉⲣ (Va ar 172 58 سر as if? ⲓⲱⲣⲉⲙ); ShA 2 157 *S* ⲡⲉⲧϫ. ⲛⲥⲱⲕ ⲉⲣⲟⲩⲛ ⲉⲛⲱⲛⲣ, Miss 4 718 *S* ϫ. ⲛⲥⲁⲡⲉⲧⲉⲃⲛⲟⲟⲩⲉ, Mani K 116 *A²* ϫ. ⲛⲥⲱⲥ ⲁⲙⲙⲁ, Cat 102 *B* be thou His colt ⲉⲑⲣⲉϥϭ. ⲛⲥⲱⲕ, ROC 27 155 *B* devil ϭ. ⲛⲥⲱϥ (*sc* ship) ϫⲉⲛⲫⲓⲟⲙ. ⲥ ϩⲁ-: Worr 220 *S* ⲉϥϫ. ϩⲁⲣⲟϥ (*sc* his rider) ϣⲁⲛⲧϥⲛⲧϥ ⲉⲣⲟⲩⲛ; ⲥ ϩⲓ-*S*: BMis 277 ⲁϥϫ. ϩⲓⲧϩⲏ (ϣⲁⲛⲧϥ)ⲉⲓ ⲉⲧⲡⲟⲗⲓⲥ, ViK 4719 ⲉⲓⲥ ϩⲏⲏ(ⲧⲉ?) ⲛϫ. ϩⲓⲡⲟϣ; ⲥ ⲉⲃⲟⲗ *B*: C 86 324 saying ϭ. ⲙⲁϣⲉ ⲛⲁⲕ ⲉⲃⲟⲗ ... ⲁⲅϭ. ⲉⲃ. ⲁϥϣⲉ ⲛⲁϥ, ib 96 ϣⲁⲅϭ. ⲉⲃ. ϫⲉⲛⲧⲟⲩⲙⲏϯ (*sc* of battle).

ⲙⲁ ⲛϫ., -ϭ., *training stable*: MIF 13 103 *S* ⲡⲉⲥⲧⲁⲃⲗⲟⲛ ... ⲉⲧⲉⲙⲙ. ⲛⲧⲉ ⲛⲉϩⲧⲱⲣⲛⲉ = MG 25 283 *B*.

ⲣⲉϥϫ., -ϭ., *driver, rider*: Zech 9 8 *S*(*AB* ⲡⲉⲧϫ.) ⲉⲝⲉⲗⲁⲩⲛⲉⲓⲛ; Ex 1 11 *B* ⲉⲡⲓⲥⲧⲁⲧⲏⲥ ... ⲛⲣ. (*A* ⲥⲁϩ) ⲉⲡⲓⲥⲧⲁⲧⲏⲥ; K 246 *B* ϩⲩⲡⲉⲩⲥ (ⲓⲡⲡ.) · ⲡⲓⲣ. فارس.

V AZ 54 134.

ϫⲱⲣⲙ *v* ϫⲱⲗⲙ.

ϫⲣⲁⲙⲡⲓ *F* *v* ϭⲣⲟⲟⲙⲡⲉ.

ϫⲁⲣⲁⲙⲡⲟ *B* nn, plant with edible leaves: MG 25 243 in Lent he ate only ϫⲱⲃⲓ ⲛϫ. ⲕⲣⲁⲙⲃⲏ (Gött ar 114 100 ورق الشجر). *Cf*? the Gk word.

ϫⲟⲣⲙⲉⲥ *v* ϫⲱⲗⲙ *s f*.

ϫⲱⲣⲡ *S* *A²*, ϫⲁⲣⲡ- *A²* vb intr, *stumble, trip*: Ro 11 11 (*B* ⲥⲗⲁϯ) ⲡⲧⲁⲓⲉⲓⲛ; Jud 5 22 ⲉⲙⲡⲟⲇⲓⲍⲉⲓⲛ; Si 34 18 ⲡⲣⲟⲥⲕⲟⲡⲧⲉⲓⲛ; Is 3 5 (*B* ϧⲉⲓ) ⲥⲩⲙⲡⲓⲡⲧⲉⲓⲛ; Deu 19 5 (*B* diff) ⲉⲕⲕⲣⲟⲩⲉⲓⲛ; ShViK 9101 ⲉⲧⲣⲉⲅⲭⲱϫ ⲛ ⲉⲧⲣⲉⲅϫ. ⲏ ⲉⲧⲣⲉⲅⲁⲙⲁϩⲧⲉ ⲛⲙⲙⲉⲗⲟⲥ ⲛⲡⲉⲅⲉⲣⲏⲩ in impurity, BM 363 116 whilst walking ⲁϥϫ., Mani 2 *A²* ⲁϥⲧⲣⲟ ⲙⲙⲁⲥ ⲁⲧⲣⲉⲥϫ.; tr: *v* ⲥ ⲉ-, ϧⲛ-.

With following preposition. ⲥ ⲉ-, *stumble against, touch*: Ro 9 32 (var ⲛ-, *B* ϭⲓ ϭⲣⲟⲡ) ⲡⲣⲟⲥⲕⲟⲡ. dat; Si 13 3 ⲡⲣⲟⲥⲕⲣ., R 1 4 36 came not again ϫ. ⲉⲡⲟⲩⲟⲟⲧⲉ *contingere*; ShIF 93 his garments ⲛϥⲟⲩⲱϣ ⲁⲛ ⲉⲧⲣⲉⲅϫ. ⲏ ⲉⲧⲣⲉⲅⲧⲱϭⲉ ⲉⲣⲟϥ, P 131³ 83 shoving away poor ϫⲉⲛⲛⲉϫ. ⲉⲛⲉⲅϩⲟⲓⲧⲉ ⲛϣⲟⲩϣⲱ (var Mor 25 11 ϫⲱⲣ) = Va 61 94 *B* ⲑⲱⲗⲉⲃ, Mun 137 ⲉϥϫ. ⲉⲡⲥⲱⲙⲁ of prophet (4 Kg 13 21), HM 2 114 ⲁϥϫ. ⲉⲧⲉϥⲟⲩⲉⲣⲏⲧⲉ & fell, BHom 85 disciples careful ⲉⲧⲁⲕⲁ ⲧⲉⲅϭⲓϫ ϫ. ⲉⲧⲁⲡⲥⲱⲧⲏⲣ (Mt 26 23), Mani H 85 *A²* ⲡⲉⲧⲁϫ. ⲁⲣⲁⲥ; tr: Ps 90 12 (*B* ϭⲓ ϭ.) ⲡⲣⲟⲥⲕⲟⲡ. ⲡⲣⲟⲥ; ⲥ ⲙⲛ-: CO 129 reconciled them so that ⲛⲡⲉⲅϩⲟⲡ ⲛ ⲣⲏⲧⲟⲩ ϫ. ⲙⲛⲡⲉϥⲉⲣⲏⲩ; ⲥ ϧⲛ-: ShMIF 23 9 ⲉⲧⲁϫ. ϧⲙⲡⲉⲕϩⲏⲧ ... ⲉⲟⲩⲡⲟⲣⲛⲉⲓⲁ, ManiP 207 *A²* ϯⲛⲁϫⲁⲣⲡ ⲛⲉⲅϫⲓⲥⲉ ϧⲓϫⲱⲓ; ⲥ ⲉⲃⲟⲗ(?): COAd 22 lay wine ϩⲓⲡⲧⲟⲟⲩ ... ⲙⲡⲣⲕⲁⲁⲩ ϫ. ⲉⲃ[ⲟⲗ].

ϫⲣⲟⲡ *S*, -ⲁⲡ *A A²F*, ϭⲣⲟⲡ *B*, ϫⲗⲁⲡ *F* nn m, *obstacle, impediment*: Ex 23 33 *SB*, Ro 14 13 *SBF* ϫⲣ. (Mus 49 199), 1 Cor 8 9 *SBF* ϫⲗ. ⲡⲣⲟⲥⲕⲟⲙⲙⲁ; Cl 20 3 *A* ⲡⲁⲣⲉⲕⲃⲁⲥⲓⲥ; Lev 19 14 *B*(*S* = Gk), 1 Jo 2 10 *S* (*B* = Gk) ⲥⲕⲁⲛⲇⲁⲗⲟⲛ; Deu 7 16 *SB* ⲥⲕⲱⲗⲟⲛ; Ez 44 12 *B* ⲕⲟⲗⲁⲥⲓⲥ, Job 13 27 *S*(*B* ϣⲓⲕ) ⲕⲱⲗⲩⲙⲁ; Ps 124 5 *B*(*S* ⲙⲛⲧⲥⲁⲛⲕⲟⲧⲥ) ⲥⲧⲣⲁⲅⲅⲁⲗⲓⲁ; Jud 11 35 *B*(*S* diff) ⲉⲙⲡⲟⲇⲟⲥⲧⲁⲧⲉⲓⲛ; Mor 29 37 *S* lest they steal again ⲛⲡⲉⲟⲩϫ. ⲧⲁⲣⲟⲟⲩ = ib 30 43 *S^f* ⲟⲩⲛⲉⲑⲟⲟⲩ ϣⲱⲡⲓ ⲙⲙⲁⲩ, BMis 278 *S* ⲛⲛⲉⲕⲉϫ. ⲧⲁⲣⲟⲥ *mishap*, BM 337 98 *S* ⲕⲁⲑⲁⲣⲓⲍⲉ ⲛⲡⲉϫ. ⲉⲧϯ ϭⲓⲥⲉ ⲛⲡⲓⲡⲉⲛⲛⲁⲓ, Ep 455 *S* come ⲉⲕⲥⲙⲓⲛⲉ ⲛⲛⲉϫ., Ostr *penes* GJéquier *S* ⲛ ⲣⲱⲙⲉⲛⲉ ⲉⲙⲡⲧⲟⲩ ϫ. ϩⲁⲡⲉⲓⲙⲉⲣⲟⲥ (obscure), PMich 3549 *S* messenger ⲁⲟⲅϫ. ⲧⲁⲣⲟ ⲧⲉϥⲡⲁⲧ, PSBA 10 198 *S* God keep kingdom ⲉϫⲛⲡⲗⲁⲁⲩ ⲛϫ., Mani P 17 *A²* sim, BMis 62 *S* sim (var Mor 33 124 ϩⲧⲟⲡ), AM 289 *B* road ⲉⲧⲉⲙⲙⲟⲛ ϭ. ⲛϧⲏⲧϥ; as adj, ϣⲛⲉ ⲛϫ.: Is 8 14 *S*(*B* reversed), Ro 9 32 *SB* ⲗⲓⲑⲟⲥ ⲡⲣⲟⲥⲕⲟⲙⲙⲁⲧⲟⲥ, ManiH 85 *A²*.

ⲁⲧϫ., ϭ., *unimpeded*: Ac 24 16 *B*(*S* ⲁϫⲛϫ.), Phil 1 10 *BF* ϫⲗ. (*S* diff) ⲁⲡⲣⲟⲥⲕⲟⲡⲟⲥ, P 130³ 60 *S* ⲟ ⲛⲁ. ⲛⲡⲉⲛⲉⲣⲏⲩ.

ⲣ, ⲟ ⲛϫ., -ϭ., *be stumbling-block, difficult*: Ps 48 13 *S* (*B* = Gk) ⲥⲕⲁⲛⲇⲁⲗⲟⲛ, Jo 6 61 *F*(PMich 3521, *SB* = Gk) ⲥⲕⲁⲛⲇⲁⲗⲓⲍⲉⲓⲛ; Si 39 31 (24) *S* ⲡⲣⲟⲥⲕⲟⲙⲙⲁ; ShC 73 138 *S* beware ⲉⲧⲙⲣ ϫ. ϩⲟⲗⲱⲥ, BMis 459 *S* ⲟⲩⲛ ⲟⲩ ϣⲁϫⲉ ⲟ ⲛϫ. ⲉⲣⲟⲓ, DeV 2 168 *B* those dead & those ⲉⲧⲁⲅⲁⲓⲧⲟⲩ ⲛϭ. (= ib ϭⲓ ⲉⲣϭⲟⲧ).

ϯ ϫ., -ϭ., *give scandal, trip up*, ⲥ ⲛ- dat: BM 216 79 *S* go not back ⲉⲣⲉⲛϫⲁⲕⲉ ϯ. ⲛⲁⲕ ⲉⲕⲕⲟⲡ., 1 Thes 2 18 *S*(*B* ⲧⲁϩⲣⲟ, *F* ⲕⲱⲗϭ) ⲉⲅⲕⲟⲡ.; ROC 17 407 *B* ⲉⲙⲡⲟⲇⲓⲟⲥ ⲅⲓⲛⲉⲥⲑⲁⲓ; Aeg 247 *S* ϯ. ϩⲙⲡⲉϥϩⲁⲣⲟⲙⲟⲥ ⲡⲁⲣⲁⲧⲉⲙⲛⲉⲓⲛ; BM 255 10 *S* flutes (Is 5 12) ϯ. ⲁⲛ ⲛⲡⲉⲧⲥⲱⲧⲙ ⲉ[ⲣⲟⲟⲩ], BMar 49 *S* threats cannot ϯ. ⲛⲁⲕ ⲉⲣⲟⲩⲛ ⲉⲡⲉⲕⲉⲓⲱⲧ, BSM 89 *B* ⲙⲡⲉⲛⲁⲓ ϣ ϯ. ⲛⲁϥ ⲉϩⲟⲩⲛ ⲉⲡⲓϫⲟⲥⲉⲙ = BMis 180 *S*; ⲥ ⲉ- *S*: Si 18 21 ⲉⲙⲡⲟⲇⲓⲍ. gen; Mor 31 129 ⲙⲡⲣϯ. ⲉⲟⲩⲁ ⲛϧⲏⲧⲟⲩ; ϯ

ⲡⲟⲩϫ. *SF*, ϧⲗⲓ ⲡϭ. *B*: 1 Cor 9 12 *SBF* ἐγκοπὴν διδόναι, 2 Cor 6 3 *SB* προσκοπὴν δ.

ϫⲓⲝ., ϭⲓϭ., *stumble, be impeded*: Pro 4 19 *SAB*, Jer
13 16 *SB*, Jo 11 9 *SA²B* προσκόπ.; Pro 3 6 *SAB* neg
ὀρθοτομεῖν; ShC 42 203 *S* ϑⲉ ⲡⲧⲁⲡⲁⲓ ϫ. ⲙⲙⲟⲥ, AM
179 *B* if reciter should ϭ. ⲡⲟⲩⲗⲉϫⲓⲥ;　c ⲉ-: Ps 90
12 *B*(*S* ϫⲱⲣⲡ), Is 3 5 *B*(*S* do) προσκόπ. πρός, 1 Pet
2 8 *SB*, Cl 21 5 *A* π. dat, Ro 15 22 *S*(*B* ⲧⲁϧⲛⲟ) ἐγκόπ.
gen; AM 245 *B* ⲙⲡⲉⲡⲑⲣⲟⲩϭ. ⲉⲣⲟⲓ *impede*;　c ϧⲛ-,
ϫⲉⲡ-: Si 30 13 *S*, Ro 14 21 *SB* προσκόπ. ⲉⲛ; ManiH
73 *A²* ϫ. ϧⲣⲏⲡ[, MG 25 187 *B* ⲁⲓϭ. ϫⲉⲡϥⲏ ⲉⲧⲁⲕⲕⲏⲛ
ⲉⲉⲙⲓ ⲉⲣⲟϥ.
V PSBA 38 184.

ϫⲣⲁⲣⲉ *A²* v ϫⲱⲱⲣⲉ 1°.

ϫⲉⲣⲏⲧ *S* nn m, *meaning unknown*: PLond 4 515
among metal (?) objects ⲡⲉⲥϫ. ⲙⲡⲡⲉⲥⲧⲃⲏⲗ ⲙⲡⲡⲉⲥⲕⲏⲗ
ⲛⲃⲉⲛⲓⲡⲉ.

ϫⲟⲣϯ *B* v ϭⲟⲣⲧⲉ.

ϫⲁⲣϧ *F*, ϫⲟⲣϧ *B* v ϭⲣⲱϧ.

ϫⲱⲣⲁϧ *S* vb intr, *limp, be lame*: 1 Kg 17 39 ⲁϥϫ.
ⲡϭⲓ ϫⲁⲅⲉⲓⲁ ⲡⲧⲉⲣⲉϥϫⲱⲡⲧ ⲉⲙⲟⲟϣⲉ ⲡϧⲏⲧⲟⲩ (var
Wess ϫⲟⲩϧⲉ, *B* om) χωλαίνειν.

ϫⲱⲣϧ *BO* v ϫⲱⲣϧ.

ϫⲉⲣϧⲟϥ *S* nn, *a malady*: PMéd 240 ⲟⲩϫ. as title
of recipe to be applied with ibis feather.

ϫⲣϫ *S* nn m, *meaning unknown, related ? to*
vineyards: Ryl 385 *vo* sued.me for a *tremis* ϧⲁⲛϭⲟⲟⲙ
ⲉⲡⲁϫ.

ϫⲉⲣⲏϫ *B* v ϭⲱⲣϭ 1° (ϭⲉⲣⲏϭ).

ϫⲣⲟϫ *B* v ϭⲣⲟ(ⲟ)ϭ.

ϫⲱⲣϫ *BF* v ϭⲱⲣϭ 1° & 2°.

ϫⲱⲣϫ *B* v ϭⲱⲣϭ 3°.

ϫⲉⲣϫⲓ *B* v ϭⲟⲣϫ.

ϫⲣϫ(ⲉ)ⲣ *S* nn m, *meaning unknown*: TurO 9
(reading uncertain) ⲉ ... ⲁⲩϫ. ⲉⲓ ⲉϧⲟⲩⲛ ⲡⲁⲕ ⲉⲕⲡⲁϥ
ϯⲉ ⲙⲙⲁϫⲉ ⲡⲥⲟⲩⲟ, Win 54 ϯⲟⲩ ⲡⲗⲓ[, ϯⲟⲩ ⲡϫⲣϫⲣ[.

ϫⲣϫⲣⲉ *A*, ϫⲣϫⲓⲣ *A²*, ϫⲉⲣϫⲉⲣ *SB*, -ⲓⲣ *B*, ϫⲏⲗϫⲉⲗ *F* v ϫⲏⲣ.

ϫⲟⲣϫⲣ *S*, ϫⲁⲣϫⲉⲣ *S*ᶠ, ϫⲁⲗϫⲉⲗ *F*(all nn), ϭⲉⲣ-
ϭⲱⲣϧ, ϫⲉⲣϫⲱⲣⲧ† *S* vb tr, *overcome* or sim: Ryl 94
(33 1) ϯ ⲟⲩⲟⲓ ⲉϧⲟⲩⲛ (ⲉ)ⲛⲃⲁⲣⲃⲁⲣⲟⲥ ⲡⲧⲉⲡϭⲉⲣϭⲱⲣ-
ⲟⲩ;　qual, *be hard*: Leyd 304 ⲥⲱⲙⲁ ⲉϥϫ. ⲁⲩⲱ
ⲉϥϫⲁϫⲱ is enfeebled by soft raiment τραχὺς καὶ
σκληρός; R 1 4 39 desert ⲉⲧϫ. ⲁⲩⲱ ⲉⲧϧⲣⲟⲥⲉ *vastus* (cf

ib 35 sim ⲉⲧϫⲁϫⲱ *vastus*),MIF 67 171 ⲉϥⲉⲧⲁϫⲣ[ⲟ ?]
ϧⲛⲛⲓⲕ[ⲁⲓ]ⲣⲟⲥ ⲉⲧϫ.;　　as nn m: HM 2 28 behold
ⲡϫ. ⲙⲡⲉϥⲥⲱⲙⲁ & humility (var Mor 32 3 *S*ᶠ), MR
5 49 *F* I could not come ⲉⲧⲃⲏⲡϫ. ⲡⲧⲁⲉⲓⲛ ⲧⲁⲯⲩⲭⲏ
(ⲉ)ⲗⲁϩ.　　V ϫⲣⲟ &c.

ϫⲟⲣϫⲥ *B* v ϭⲱⲣϭ 1° (ϭⲟⲣϭⲥ).

ϫⲁⲥ (ⲭⲁⲥ)*A* v ϭⲣⲟⲥ.

ϫⲏⲥ *B* vb qual: 1 Kg 16 6 ⲁⲗⲗⲁ ⲉϥϫ. ⲙⲡⲉⲙⲑⲟ
ⲙⲡϫⲟ̄ⲥ (*S* ⲉⲓⲥ) ἀλλὰ καί (var πλὴν ἄρα). *L* ? ⲉϥⲭⲏ.

ϫⲏⲥ *S*, nn m, *meaning unknown*: Win 12 (mostly
illegible) ϩⲓⲧ ⲉⲣⲏⲥ ⲉⲡⲁ[ⲧⲟⲩ]ⲃⲁⲥ[ⲧⲏ] ⲉⲣⲉⲡⲉϥϫ. (or
ϫⲉⲓⲥ) ϧⲁⲣⲟⲛ.

ϫⲏⲏⲥ *S* nn f, *bowl, censer*: Nu 7 14 (*B* ϫⲏ) θυΐσκη; P 43 64 ⲟⲣⲑⲟⲙⲉⲗⲓⲁⲛ (-μίλιον) · ϣⲏⲥ, ⲧϣⲉⲉⲥ
سُكلر.　　*Cf* ϫⲏ.

ϫⲟ(ⲉ)ⲓⲥ *SS*ᶠ, ϫ̄ⲥ *SAF*, ϫⲁⲉⲓⲥ *AA²F*, ϫⲁⲓⲥ *A²F*,
ϭⲟ̄ⲥ *S*ᶠ(BM 544) ⲟ̄ⲧ, ⲟ̄ⲥ (vary in MSS, here only ⲟ̄ⲧ
used; rhymes ⲡⲁⲟⲥ, ⲡⲉⲧⲟⲡⲟⲥ K 424-5 merely graphic)*S*(late & *S*ᶠ)*BF*, ⲧϲⲥ *B*(EW 86), شيس (BIF 5 93),
pl ϫⲓⲥⲟⲟⲩ(ⲉ)*S*, -ⲉⲩⲉ *AA²*, ϭⲓⲥⲉⲩ *B*, ϫⲓⲥⲛⲟⲩⲓ *F*, -ⲏⲏ-
ⲩⲉ *S*ᶠ & sg as pl (rare *S*)nn m f, *lord*: title of God *pass*
κύριος; MR 5 42 *B* ⲡⲉⲕϫⲓⲟⲩⲥ (same?);　　of man,
master, owner: Job 3 19, Mt 18 25, ib 20 8 all *SB*, MG
25 215 *B* ⲡϫⲟ̄ⲥ ⲛϯⲡⲁⲣⲁⲑⲏⲕⲏ = Z 338 *S* ⲡⲉⲡⲧⲁϥϭⲁ-
ⲗⲱⲟⲩ ⲕⲩ́.;　Mt 13 27 *SB* οἰκοδεσπότης; Is 50 1 *B*(*S*
Gk diff);　Mor 56 27 *S* ⲡϫ. ⲙⲡⲧⲟⲟⲩ, Mun 69 *S* ⲡϫ.
ⲙⲡⲡⲟⲩϩ = DeV 2 276 *B* (cf ib 272 *B* ϫⲡⲛϩⲃ), Ep 271
S ⲡϫ. ⲛⲧⲉ ⲡⲉⲭⲩⲣⲟⲛ, ShC 42 16 *S* ⲡϫ. ⲙⲡⲁⲡⲁϣ,
CO 140 *S* ⲧⲁⲗⲟⲟϥ ⲙⲡⲉϥϫ.;　vocative ending letter
ⲡⲉⲡϫ. Kr 232 (cf δέσποτα);　　of saint: Sph 10 2 *S*ᶠ
ⲡⲉⲡϫ. ⲡⲃⲁⲡⲧⲓⲥⲧⲏⲥ, Ryl 196 *S* ⲡⲁⲓⲕⲁⲓⲟⲛ ⲉⲧⲟⲩⲁⲁϩ
ⲛⲡⲁϫ.[;　ϫ. & ⲟ̄ⲧ in same *S* text: Is 51 20 &c (Mor),
BM 153 581, Ryl 24, 104(4), CMSS 23, 28;　ⲡⲟ̄ⲧ
for ⲟ̄ⲧ: BM 599 *F*, Lant 17 *S*ᶠ, BP 5567 *F*;　ⲡⲁⲡⲟ̄ⲧ
ⲉⲡⲓⲱⲧ: BM *lc*;　ϫ̄ⲥ: *S* BG 131 (ib ϫⲟⲉⲓⲥ), 138,
BAp 79, BMar 132, BMis 240, 359 (Edfu MSS);　*A*
Ex 4 10; *F* Jo 9 36 (PMich 3521);　f: Ge 16 4 *B*,
Pro 24 58 *SA*, AP 8 *A²*, EW 30 *B* κυρία;　Cai Euch
539 *B* δέσποινα; ShWess 9 123 *S* ⲧϫ. ⲙⲡⲡⲣⲁⲅⲙⲁ,
BMis 62 *S* ⲧⲉⲡϫ. ⲧⲏⲣⲥ Mary, Aeg 38 *B* sim;　pl
forms: Ge 18 3 *S*(*B* Gk sg), Ps 122 2 *SB*, Ac 16 19
SB, Col 3 22 *SB*(var ϭⲓⲥⲛⲟⲩ) ⲕ.; Pro 17 2 *SA* δεσπότης; BHom 20 *S*, J 15 25 *S* ⲡⲉⲡϫ. ⲉⲧⲁⲣⲭⲉⲓ ⲉϫⲱⲛ,
ib 104 5 *S* ϫⲓⲥⲟⲟⲩ, ManiH 47 *A²*, Mor 39 42 *S*ᶠ, BM
588 *F*, AM 122 *B*;　　sg as pl: C 41 42 *B* ⲡⲓϫⲟ̄ⲧ ⲛⲧⲉ
ⲡⲓϭⲟⲙ, CO 397 *S* ⲡⲉϥϫ., CMSS 41 *S*ᶠ ⲡⲁϫⲟ̄ⲧ, ib 26
B sim, MR 5 49 *F* ⲡϫⲁⲉⲓⲥ;　　attributive: BMar
121 *S* ϫ. ⲛⲥⲟⲡ, Sph 10 3 *S* ϫ. ⲡⲓⲱⲧ ⲁⲩⲱ ⲡϣⲏⲣⲉ,
BSM 8 *B* ⲟ̄ⲧ ⲡⲓⲱⲧ, Abst 334 *B* ⲧⲉⲡⲟ̄ⲧ ⲡⲛⲏϩ, C 43
109 *B* ⲡⲁⲟ̄ⲧ ⲛⲓⲟϯ.

ⲣ, ⲟ ⲛϫ., ⲉⲣ, ⲟⲓ ⲛⲟⲥ̄ *SAA²BF, be lord, rule*: Jos
12 2 *S*, Lu 22 25 *S*(*B* ⲥ ⲉ-) κυριεύειν, Ps 71 7 *SB* ⲕⲁⲧⲁⲕ.; Va 57 8 *B* δεσπ. εἶναι; Va 66 307 *B* ⲟⲓ ⲛⲟⲥ̄ ⲙ-
ⲙⲓⲛ ⲙⲙⲟϥ αὐτεξούσιος; ShC 42 145 *S* ⲁⲩⲣ ⲡⲉϫ.
ⲁⲅⲡⲱⲧ, *ib* 136 *S* ⲥⲉⲟ ⲙⲡⲉϫ. & none constraineth
them, BMis 56 *S* ⲛ̄ⲧⲉⲣⲉⲥⲣ ⲡⲉⲥϫ. ⲛⲟⲩⲕⲟⲩⲓ she withdrew to place alone (*cf* FR 14 ⲣ ⲡⲟϫ), J 79 49 *S* that
monastery may ⲣ ⲡⲉϫ. (*sc* oblate) ϣⲁⲉⲡⲉϩ, *ib* 35 78
S ⲧⲓⲧⲓⲁⲗⲏⲥⲓⲥ (διάλυσις) ⲥⲟⲣϫ ⲥⲟ ⲛϫ., Ryl 293 *S* ⲕⲟ
ⲙⲡⲉⲕϫ. to undo agreement, CO 294 *S* ⲧⲉⲧⲛⲡⲱ ⲙⲡϫ.
ⲡⲧⲉⲧⲛⲡⲟϫⲧ [ⲉⲃⲟⲗ], ST 265 *S* ⲉⲓⲟ ⲙⲡⲁϫ. ⲁⲛ, DeV
1 109 *B* if I slay Him not ⲧⲁϫⲓϫ ⲛⲁⲉⲣ ⲟⲥ̄ ⲁⲛ;   ⲥ
ⲉ-, *over*: Nu 24 7 *SB*, Lam 5 8 *S*(Mus 50 229)*BF*,
Ro 6 14 *SB* ⲕⲩⲣ. gen, Ge 9 1 *B*(*S* ⲥ ⲉⲭⲛ-), Mt 20 25
SB, Ac 19 16 *S*(var ⲉϩⲣⲁⲓ ⲉϫⲛ-)*B* ⲕⲁⲧⲁⲕ. gen, Ge
23 20 *B* κυροῦν dat, Bel 5 *B* κυρίαν ἔχειν gen; Eccl 7
20 *F*(*S* as Gk), Lu 22 25 *S*(*B* ⲉⲣ ϣⲓϣⲓ) ἐξουσιάζειν,
Aeg 221 *S* ἐξουσίαν ἔχ.; Job 27 17 *S*(*B* ⲁⲙⲟⲛⲓ) ⲕⲁ-
ⲧⲉⲭ.; Sa 9 2 *S* δεσπόζειν gen, 1 Tim 5 14 *S*(*B* ⲉⲣ ⲡⲛⲏⲃ)
οἰκοδεσποτεῖν; Pro 28 15 *SA* τυραννεῖν; Aeg 217 *S*
ⲉⲣ ϫ. ⲉⲡⲉⲓⲁϩⲓⲱⲙⲁ ἐγκρατὴς γίνεσθαι gen; Jud 3 28
S προκαταλαμβάνειν; BG 72 *S* ⲉⲥⲟ ⲛϫ. ⲉⲟⲩⲟⲛ ⲛⲓⲙ,
BMis 394 *S* ⲛ̄ⲧⲟ ⲁⲛ ⲛϫ. ⲉⲡⲉⲡⲥⲱⲙⲁ = BSM 45 *B*
ⲑⲏⲩ ⲉϫⲉⲡ-, JSch 10 21 *S* ⲉⲕⲱ ⲙⲡϫ. ⲉⲣⲟϥ, Mani 2
A² ⲣ ϫ. ⲁⲧⲉϥⲙⲛⲧⲓⲉⲡϣⲱⲧ, C 86 275 *B* ⲉⲣ ⲟⲥ̄ ⲉⲡⲓϭ
ⲛⲟⲩⲣⲟ;   vbal: Ex 21 8 *SB* κύριος εἶναι; ShC 42
136 *S* ⲡⲧⲡⲟ ⲁⲛ ⲙⲡⲉⲛϫ. ⲉⲃⲱⲕ, Hall 109 *S* ⲕⲱ ⲙ-
ⲡⲉϫ. ⲉϥⲁⲁϥ (= ⲉⲧ.) ⲉⲃⲟⲗ;   ⲥ ⲉϫⲛ-, as last: Ge 3
16 *S*(*B* ⲉ-), Dan 5 21 *B* ⲕⲩⲣ. gen, Ps 118 133 *S*(*B* ⲉ-)
ⲕⲁⲧⲁⲕ gen; Lev 27 21 *S*(*B* diff) κατάσχεσις; Pro 28
22 *SA* κρατεῖν gen; Ps 88 9 *S*(*B* ⲟⲓ ⲡⲡⲛⲏⲃ) δεσπόζειν
gen, Deu 15 6 *S*(*B* ⲉ-) ἄρχειν gen; J 16 26 *S* (ⲛ)ⲧⲁⲥⲁ-
(ⲁ)ⲧ ⲛϫ. ⲉϫⲛⲡⲉⲧϣⲟⲡ ⲛⲁⲥ;   ⲉϩⲣⲁⲓ ⲉϫⲛ-: Ps 104 21
B(*S* = Gk) κύριον καθιστάναι gen; Ge 1 26 *SB* ⲁ̄ⲣ.
gen; PS 61 *S* ⲁ̄ⲡⲣϫ. ⲉϩ. ⲉϫⲱⲥ, AP 21 *A²* ⲣ ϫ. ⲁϩ. ⲁϫⲛ
ⲧⲉϥⲟⲩⲥⲓⲁ;   ⲥ ⲛ-: 1 Cor 7 4 *S* ⲟ ⲙⲡϫ. ⲛ- (*F* ⲉ-, *B*
ⲉⲣϣ. ⲛ-) ἐξουσιάζειν gen; BSM 118 *B* ⲉⲣ ⲟⲥ̄ ⲛⲛⲓ-
ⲭⲣⲏⲙⲁ, J 4 50 *S* ⲡⲥⲕⲉⲗⲉⲅⲉⲥⲑⲁⲓ(ⲗ ⲅⲣⲓⲉⲅ.) ⲁⲅⲱ ⲛⲧⲣ
ⲛϫ. ⲛⲡⲭⲱⲣⲏⲙⲁ, *ib* 48 15 *S*, CO 144 *S* sim (*cf* ⲣ ϫ.
ⲉ-);   ⲥ ϩⲓϫⲛ-: Ge 47 *B*(*ACI* ⲁϫⲛ-) ⲁ̄ⲣ. gen; ⲣⲉϥⲣ
ϫ., *ruler*: P 131¹ 1 *S* sun, moon as ⲣ. ⲛⲧⲟⲓⲕⲟⲩⲙⲉⲛⲏ
(*v* TU 20 4 46).

ⲙⲛⲧϫ. ⲙⲉⲧⲟⲥ̄, *lordship*: Is 40 10 *SB*, Dan 4 19 *B*
κυρεία, Eph 1 21 *SBF* κυριότης; Ps 144 13 *S*(*B* ⲙⲉⲧ-
ⲡⲛⲏⲃ) δεσποτεία; ManiP 193 *A²* ⲛϫⲁⲙ ⲙⲛⲛⲁⲙ., C 43
166 *B* ⲁⲧⲉⲕⲙ. ⲉⲣ ⲕⲉⲗⲉⲅⲓⲛ, J 9 51 *S* ⲛ̄ⲧⲁⲙⲁⲣⲧⲉ ϩⲡⲙ.
ⲛⲓⲙ, BM 1013 *S* ⲧⲙⲛⲧϫ. ⲉⲧⲓⲥⲧⲱⲧⲉ ⲡⲉⲓⲱⲣⲉ, AZ 23
28 *F* ⲙⲉϫⲁⲓⲥ ⲛⲥⲁⲡ.

ⲝⲟⲥ *B* *v* ϭⲟⲥ.

ⲝⲱⲥ *S*. ϭ., ϭⲁⲥ- *B*, ⲝⲟⲥ⳽, ϫⲏⲥ† *S*, ϭ.† *B* vb a, *become, be hard, solid intr*: Ex 15 8 *B*, Job 6 16 *B*(*S*
ⲱϭⲣ), *ib* 15 7 *B*(*S* ⲧⲱⲕ), Is 42 5 *B*(*S* ⲧⲁⲭⲣⲟ) ⲡⲏⲅ-

ⲛⲩⲛⲁⲓ; Ps 67 17† *B*(*S* ⲧⲏⲕ, var ϫⲟⲥⲉ ⲛϧⲏⲧ), Lam 4 7
B(*S* ⲧⲱⲕ) τυροῦν; Job 41 14† *S*(*B* ⲧⲟⲙⲓ) κολλᾶν; *ib*
3 12 *S*(*B* ⲧⲁϫ.) συναντᾶν; Lam 3 8 *S* l? ϫⲱⲥ (*B* ϣ-
ⲑⲁⲙ ⲡⲣⲱ) ἀποφράσσειν; C 86 275 *B* martyr's body
ϭ. ⲛⲥⲛⲟϥ like lead μολύνεσθαι (as if μολυβδοῦσθαι);
Ez 20 40† *B*(*S* as Gk) ὑψηλός (cf Ps 67 above), *ib* 26
5† *B*(Gk diff); K 201 *B* ⲛⲓⲡⲏⲅⲏ (? πηγός) ⲉⲧϭ.† opp
ⲉⲧϭⲁϥ اادن ﻣﻌﺎﺩﻥ; BMar 152 *S* ⲁⲧⲕⲟⲗϫⲙⲉⲛⲑⲟⲣⲁ
ϫ. ⲁⲥⲣ ⲱⲡⲉ, opp ⲣ ⲙⲟⲟⲩ ⲡⲧⲉⲥϩⲉ, KKS 502 *S* water
ϫ. like lead, OrChrNS 3 50 *B* blood ⲉϥϭ.† like stone,
HM 1 6 *S* blood ϫ. ϩⲓⲭⲙⲡⲕⲁϩ, Mor 34 32 *S* ⲉⲕⲓⲃⲉ
ⲁⲩϫ. ⲛⲉⲣⲱⲧⲉ (var *ib* 33 70 & BMis 108 ⲙⲟⲩϩ).

b, *pack, load, harden* tr: MG 25 156 *B* after forming
pots ϣⲁϥϭⲁⲥ ⲫⲕⲁⲙⲓⲛⲓ (-ⲛⲟⲥ) & fireth them (cf *ib* 195
ⲑⲱⲕ), *ib* 143 *B* having made divers links ϣⲁϥϭⲁⲥ
ⲫⲁⲗⲩⲥⲓⲥ ⲡⲧⲉϥⲧⲁⲣⲟⲥ ⲉⲣⲁⲧ⸗ = EW 238 ﻳﻘﻴﻢ...ﻳﻜﻤﻠﻬﺎ;
WZKM '02 268 *S* ϫ. ⲡϫⲁⲙⲟⲩⲗ ⲛⲥⲟⲧ, ST 236 *S* send
cart ⲛⲧϫ. ⲛϣⲉ ⲙⲡⲁϣ ⲉϩⲟⲩⲛ (ⲡ)ⲁⲡ;   qual: Win 48
S send camel ⲉϥϫ. ⲡϫⲁϣⲟⲩ...ⲡⲧϫⲟⲥϥ ⲕⲁⲗⲱⲥ for I
will pay freight, Bodl copt inscr 469 *S* camel ⲉϥϫ.
ⲙⲙⲟⲟⲩ.

ϫⲏⲥⲉ *v* ϫⲓⲥⲉ 2°.

ϫⲓⲥⲉ *SAA²*, ϭⲓⲥⲓ *B*, ϫ. *F*, ϫⲉⲥⲧ- *SA²*, ϫⲁⲥⲧ- (Si
84, Ja 4 10)*S*, ϭⲉⲥ-, ϭⲁⲥ- *B*, ϫⲁⲥⲧ⳽, ϫⲓⲥⲧ⳽ (ⲩ ⲥ ϧⲛ-)*S*,
ϫⲉⲥⲧ⳽ *AA²F*, ϭⲁⲥ⳽ *B*, ϫⲟⲥⲉ† *S*, ϫⲁⲥⲉ† *AA²*, -ⲓ† *A²*(AP)
F, ϭⲟⲥⲓ† *B*, ⲣ ⲥ ϫⲁⲥⲓ- *SAA²F*, ϭⲁⲥⲓ- *B* vb **I** intr, *become, be high*: Ge 48 19 *SB*, Ps 17 46 *SB*, 2 Cor 11 7
SB ὑψοῦσθαι, Pro 17 16 *SA* ὑψηλός; 1 Kg 3 19 *S*,
Lam 1 9 *F*(*B* ⲉⲣ ⲡϣⲱⲧ) μεγαλύνεσθαι; Is 5 24 *S*(*B* ⲓ
ⲉⲡϣⲱⲓ) ἀναβαίνειν; Ps 46 9 *SB* ἐπαίρεσθαι; Ob 4 *AB*
μετεωρίζειν; Ez 47 5 *SB* ἐξυβρίζειν; 1 Cor 8 1 *SB*
φυσιοῦν; Jo 3 30 *SF*(*B* ⲁⲓⲁⲓ) αὐξάνειν; BM 187 130
S ⲡⲥⲟⲟⲩⲛ ⲡⲧⲉ ⲭⲁⲣⲓⲥ ϫ., RE 9 166 *S* letter ends ⲟⲩϫⲁⲓ ϫ. ϭⲙϭⲟⲙ ⲟⲩϫⲁⲃ (cf ⲥ ϧⲛ-), PO 11 343 *B* ⲁⲕ-
ϣⲁⲛϭ. remember brethren;   qual: Job 31 28 *SB*,
Mk 11 10 *SB*, AP 16 *A²* ὕψιστος, Ge 7 19 *SB*, Eccl
7 9 *S*(*F* ϫⲁⲥⲓϩⲏⲧ), Mk 9 2 *SBF* ὑψηλός, Job 14 19 *B*
ὕπτιος; Is 30 25 *SB* (var ϩⲗⲟⲅⲗⲱⲟⲩ) *F* μετέωρος,
BHom 92 *S* sea ⲉϭ. -ⲱⲣⲓζⲉⲓⲛ; Nu 13 29 *S*(*B* ϫⲟⲣ)
ὀχυρός, Lam 2 2 *S*(ShC 73 77, *B* ⲧⲁⲭⲣⲟ) ὀχύρωμα;
Bar 3 22 *SB* ἐπιμήκης; Nu 13 32 *B*(*S* ϣⲟⲓ) ὑπερμ.;
Ro 13 1 *SB* ὑπερέχειν; Ps 103 3 *SB*, Ac 1 13 *B*(*S*
ⲛⲧⲡⲉ) ὑπερῷος; Ex 18 22 *S*(*B* ϩⲟⲣϣ) ὑπέρογκος; Ps
103 8 *S*(*B* ⲛⲁ ⲉⲡϣⲱⲓ) ἀναβαίνειν; Ez 39 18 *B* ⲥⲧⲉⲁ-
τοῦσθαι (cf ? ϫⲱⲥ Ps 67 17); PS 181 *S* ϥϫ. ⲛϭⲓ ⲡⲁ-
ⲡⲟⲛⲏⲙⲁ, ShC 73 4 *S* ⲙⲡ ⲣⲱⲙⲉ ϫ. ⲉⲧⲑⲉⲣⲁⲡ ϩⲓⲥϫⲏ-
ⲙⲁ, *ib* 49 *S* ⲛⲡⲉⲧϫ., R 2 1 71 *S* nose ϫ. ⲛϩ̄ⲧⲙⲛⲧⲉ
ⲛⲡⲃⲁⲗ, Mor 44 27 *S* ⲉϥϫ. opp ⲕⲟⲗⲟⲃⲟⲥ, PSBA 10
196 *S* ϣⲁϫⲉ ⲉϥϫ., Mor 33 12 *S* never ate ⲧⲣⲟⲫⲏ
ⲉϥϫ. (var BMis 77 ⲛⲟϥ ⲛϭⲓⲡⲟⲅⲱⲙ), C 43 36 *B* recruits ⲉⲩϭ. (*S* Mor 40 5 ⲗⲁϣⲓⲛ), *ib* 86 112 *B* ⲉⲩϭ.
ϭⲉⲡⲧⲉϥϭⲙⲁⲓⲏ = Ann 19 233 *S* ⲉϥⲧⲏϣ, Mani K 157
A² ⲧⲣⲓⲕⲱⲛ ⲙⲡⲡⲉⲧϫ., C 86 263 *B* ϩⲁⲡⲙⲩⲥⲧⲏⲣⲓⲟⲛ

ⲉⲩ ⲋ., PO 11 328 *B* ϭⲉⲡⲟⲥ ⲉⲩϭ., AZ 33 55 *F* ϩⲣⲁⲁⲩ
ⲉⲧⲝ.;   ⲙⲁ ⲉⲧⲝ., -ⲋ.: Cant 7 8 *S*(*F* ⲡⲉⲧⲝ.) ὕψος,
Is 36 7 *BF*, Bor 170 84 *S* ὑψηλός ; Ps 88 40 *S*(*B* ⲧⲁ-
ⲣⲏⲟⲩⲧ) ὀχύρωμα ; Jer 22 13 *B* ὑπερῷος.

II tr, *exalt*: Jos 3 7 *SB*, Pro 4 8 *SAB*, Is 1 2 *SBF*,
Jo 12 34 *SA²B*, Ja 4 10 *S* ⲝⲁⲥⲧ(ⲧ)ⲏⲩⲧⲛ *B* ὑψοῦν, Dan
3 60 *S*(*B* ⲉⲣ ⲟⲅⲟ ϭ.) ὑπερυψ. ; Nu 15 3 *S*(*B* ⲉⲣ ⲡⲓϣ-
ϯ), Ac 10 46 *B*(*S* ⲉ ⲉⲟⲟⲩ) μεγαλύνειν ; Ps 82 2 *SB*
αἴρειν, ib 27 9 *SB*, Ob 3 *AB* ἐπαί. ; Dan 3 97 *B* αὐξάνειν ; Jon 1 11 *A*(*SB* ⲡⲉⲣϭⲉ) ἐξεγείρειν ; Ps 9 22 *SB*
ὑπερηφανεύεσθαι ; ib 130 1 *SB* μετεωρ. ; Si 8 4 *S* ⲣⲱⲙⲉ ⲛ̄ⲝⲁⲥⲧ ⲥⲙⲏ γλωσσώδης (cf ib 9 23 ⲣⲉⲩⲱⲱ ⲉ̄ⲃⲟⲗ);
PS 101 *S* ⲁⲥⲝ. ⲙⲙⲟⲥ, RNC 84 *S* martyrs ⲉⲛⲧⲁⲕ-
ⲝⲁⲥⲧⲟⲩ *raise* (on rack ?), cf Miss 8 253 *S*, ManiP 148
A² ⲥⲉⲛⲁⲝⲉⲥⲧⲉ, DeV2 96 *B* ϣⲁⲩϭⲁⲥⲟⲩ, TstAb 226 *B*
ⲁⲩϭ. ⲛ̄ⲧⲉⲩⲥⲙⲏ.

With following preposition.

—— ⲉ- *SAA²BF*, *over*, *above* : Ge 7 17 *S*(*B* ⲉ̄ⲃⲟⲗ
ϩⲁ-) ὑψοῦν ἀπό, Job 35 5† *SB* ὑψηλός ἀπό, Va 57 13 *B*
ⲉⲧϭ.† ⲉⲛⲁⲓ -ⲟⲧⲉⲣⲟⲥ gen ; Ps 8 2 *S*(*B* ⲥⲁⲡϣⲱⲓ ⲛ-) ἐπαί.
ὑπεράνω, Si 48 15 *S* ὑπεραί. ; Pro 5 19 *SA*(*B* ϣⲱⲡⲓ
ⲉⲥⲧⲁⲓⲏⲟⲩⲧ) ἡγεῖσθαι gen, Ro 12 10 *SF*(*B* ⲭⲱ ⲛ̄ⲧⲉⲛ-)
προηγ., Dan 6 3† *S*(*B* ⲧⲁⲓⲏ. ⲉ̄ⲣⲟⲧⲉ-), Lu 6 40 *S*(*B*
ⲟⲩⲟⲧ ⲉ-) εἶναι ὑπέρ ; Mk 4 32 *S*(*B* ⲟⲓ ⲛⲓϣ̄ϯ ⲉ-) μείζων γίνεσθαι gen ; PS 154 *S* ⲁⲓⲝ. ⲉⲣⲟⲟⲩ, ShR 2 348 *S*
ⲛⲉ ⲟⲩⲥⲓⲁ ⲉⲧϭ.† ⲉⲣⲟϥ, Miss 8 230 *S* ⲉⲣⲉⲟⲅⲁ ⲝ.† ⲉⲟⲅⲁ,
BMis 207 *S* ⲉⲩ̄ϫⲟⲟⲥⲉ ⲉⲧⲡⲟⲗⲓⲥ ⲧⲏⲣⲥ (cf 219 ⲝ.† ⲉⲝⲛ-
ⲧⲛ. ⲧ.), ManiP 9 *A²* ⲡⲉⲧⲝ.† ⲁⲣⲁⲩ, C 43 255 *B* waves
ϭ. ⲉⲧⲁⲁⲫⲉ, ManiK 14 *A²* ⲧⲉⲕⲕⲗⲏⲥⲓⲁ ⲝⲉⲥⲧⲉ ⲁⲡⲝⲓⲥⲉ
up to ; vbal : Ps 36 34 *S* ⲉ̄ⲧⲣⲉ- *B* ⲉⲡ̄ⲝⲓⲛ-, Is 30 18
SF ⲉ- *B* do ὑψοῦν gen ; ⲉⲣⲟⲅⲟ, ⲡ̄ϩ. ⲉ-, ⲉⲣⲟⲧⲉ : Ps
96 9 *SB* ὑπερυψ. ὑπέρ, Dan 7 23 *B* ὑπερέχειν ; BG 54
S ⲁⲩϭ. ⲛ̄ϩ. ⲉⲣⲟⲟⲩ, BMis 121 *S* ⲝ.† ⲉⲣⲟⲅⲉ (sic) ⲉⲣⲟⲟⲩ,
ShBM 198 29 *S* ⲣ ⲟⲅⲟⲉ ⲉⲣⲟⲛ ; ⲉϩⲣⲁⲓ ⲉ- : Dan
12 7 *B* ὑψοῦν εἰς, Job 11 13 *S*(*B* ϥⲁⲓ ⲉⲡϣⲱⲓ ϩⲁ-) ὑπτιάζειν πρός ; ϣⲁϩⲣⲁⲓ ⲉ- : Mt 11 23 *SB* ὑψ. ἕως ;
Ps 56 10 *S*(*B* ⲉⲣ ⲡ.) μεγ. ἕως.

—— ⲉⲝⲛ- *SAA²B*, *over*, *upon* : Ps 26 6 *SB*, Ez
29 15 *SB* ὑψοῦν ἐπί, Ge 7 20 *S*(*B* ⲥⲁⲡϣ.) ὑ. ἐπάνω, Ps
98 2 *SB* ὑψηλός ἐπί ; Jer 31 26 *S*(Cai 8316)*B*, Zeph 2
8 *SAB* μεγ. ἐπί, Pro 3 5 *SA*(*B* ⲉ̄ϩⲣⲏⲓ ⲉⲝ.) ἐπαί. ἐπί ;
Aeg 247 *S* ⲝ. ⲙⲙⲟⲟⲩ ⲉ. ⲡⲣⲏⲕⲉ ὑπεροπτεύειν ; Job
3 14 *S*(*B* ϣⲟⲩϣⲟⲩ) γαυριᾶν ἐπί ; PS 173 *S* ⲝ. ⲡ̄ⲧⲉⲕ-
ϭⲟⲙ ⲉ. ⲛⲁⲭⲁⲭⲉ, ManiP 50 *A²* sim, ib 44 *A²* thy head
ⲝ. ⲁ̄ⲝⲡⲉⲅⲡⲅⲗⲏ, BSM 69 *B* waves ϭ. ⲉ. ⲛⲓⲝⲟⲓ =
BMis 160 *S* ⲡ̄ϣⲟⲧ ⲉ̄ϩⲣⲁⲓ ⲉⲝⲛ- ; ⲉ̄ϩⲣⲁⲓ ⲉⲝⲛ- : Jth 9
7 *S*, Ps 107 6 *SB* ὑ. ἐπί, Is 37 23 *S*(*B* ⲟⲩⲃⲉ-) ὑψ. πρός ;
1 Cor 4 6 *B*(*S* ϣⲟⲩϣⲟⲩ ⲉⲝⲛ-) φυσιοῦν ὑπέρ ; Dan 3
47 *S*(*B* ⲉⲣ ⲥⲁⲡϣ.) διαχεῖν ἐπάνω ; ManiK 105 *A²* ⲁⲩ-
ⲝⲉⲥⲧⲩ ⲁ̄ϩ. ⲁⲝⲡⲧⲙⲡⲛⲁ̄ϭ.

—— ⲛ- *SAB* dat : 3 Kg 8 8† *B* ὑπερέχειν acc ; Ac
5 31 *SB* ὑψοῦν acc ; *as far as* : Jth 1 4 *S* ὕψος ποιεῖν
gen ; *in* : Zeph 1 11 *A*(*B* ϧⲉⲛ-) ἐφαίρ. dat.

—— ⲛⲧⲛ- *S*, *with*, *for* : Miss 8 153 ⲛ̄ⲧⲉⲣⲉⲡⲉϥϩⲏⲧ
ⲝ. ⲡ̄ⲧⲟⲟⲧϥ & had forgotten God, Ming 332 ⲙ̄ⲡⲉⲣⲕⲁ
ⲡⲉⲕϩⲏⲧ ⲉⲝ. ⲛⲧⲟⲟⲧⲕ.

—— ⲛⲁ̄ϩⲣⲉⲛ- *B*, *beside*, *before* : Ps 88 28 (*S* ⲡⲁⲣⲁ)
ὑψηλὸς παρά.

—— ⲟⲩⲃⲉ- *B*, *toward* : Job 15 25 (*S* ⲙⲡⲙ̄ⲧⲟ ⲉⲃⲟⲗ
ⲛ-) αἴρ. ἐναντίον ; Is 37 23 v above.

—— ϣⲁ- *SB*, *up to* : Lu 10 15 *S*(var & *B* ϣⲁϩⲣⲁⲓ
ⲉ-) ὑ. ἕως ; HL 117 *B* ⲁϥϭⲁⲥⲧ(ⲧ) ϣⲁⲡⲓϭⲏⲡⲓ.

—— ⲉⲃⲟⲗ ϩⲁ- *B*, *from off* : Deu 17 20 (*S* ⲉⲝⲛ-) ὑ.
ἀπό, Ps 112 7 v below.

—— ϩⲛ-, ϩⲉⲛ- *SAA²BF*, *in*, *among* intr : Ps 45 10
SB ὑ. ἐν, Deu 8 14 *SB*, Ez 19 11 *SB* ὑ. dat ; PS 61 *S*
ⲁⲩⲝ. ⲡ̄ϩⲏⲧ ⲡ̄ϭⲓ ⲡⲉⲡⲡⲁ, WTh 197 *S* ⲡⲁⲓ ⲉⲧⲝ.† ⲡ̄ϩⲏ-
ⲧⲟⲩ *loftiest of them*, TillBau 128 *S* child's days ⲛⲁⲝ.
ϩⲙⲡⲉⲕⲏⲓ, RE 9 153 *S* letter ends ⲝ. ϩⲙ̄ⲡ̄ϫⲟⲉⲓⲥ, Till
Oster 24 *A* ;   tr : 2 Chr 5 13 *B*, Ps 60 2 *S*(*B* ϩⲣⲓⲝⲉⲛ-)
ὑ. ἐν, ib 65 17 *S*(*B* diff) ὑ. ὑπό ; Lam 4 2 *SB*(*F* om)
ἐπαίρ. ἐν ; ManiH 50 *A²* ⲝⲉⲥⲧⲩ ϩⲛ[ⲧ, AM 141 *B*
ⲡ̄ⲧⲉϥϭⲁⲥⲏⲟⲩ ϩⲉⲛⲡⲓⲡⲁⲗⲗⲁⲧⲓⲟⲛ, BMis 236 *S* ⲝⲓⲥ-
ⲧⲩ (sic) ϩⲙ̄ⲡⲁϩⲓⲱⲙⲁ = Mor 30 9 *F* ⲝⲉⲥⲧⲩ ;   ϩⲣⲁⲓ
ϩⲛ- : Ps 65 7 *SB* ὑ. ἐν ;   ⲉⲃⲟⲗϩⲛ- : Ps 112 7 *S*(*B* ⲉ̄ⲃ.
ϩⲁ-) ἀνυ. ἀπό ; ManiH 60 *A²* ⲝⲉⲥⲧⲩ ⲁ̄ⲃ. ϩ[ⲙⲡⲥⲱ]ⲙⲁ.

—— ϩⲓⲝⲛ- *SB*, *upon* : Dan 4 14† *B* ὕψιστος gen ;
ⲉⲃⲟⲗ ϩ. : Jo 12 32 *S*(*A²* ⲁⲩ̄ϩⲣⲏⲓ[, *B* ⲉ̄ⲃ. ϩⲁ-) ὑ. ἐκ (var
ἀπό) ; Ez 10 19 *B* μετεωρ. ἀπό ; AM 305 *B* ⲛⲁⲩϭ.†
ⲉ̄ⲃ. ϩⲓⲝⲱⲟⲩ ⲧⲏⲣⲟⲩ.

With following adverb.

—— ⲉⲡϣⲱⲓ *B*, *upward* : Jer 38 37 ὑ. εἰς τὸ μετέωρον ; Ez 24 3 (*S* ⲉϩⲣⲁⲓ) ἐφιστάναι ; Va 63 89 ϭ.
ⲙ̄ⲡⲟⲩⲙⲟⲩⲧ ⲉ. ἐπαί. ; C 41 72 ⲁⲩϭ. ⲉ. like palm, C
43 215 flame ϭ. ⲉ. ;   ⲥⲁⲡϣⲱⲓ *B* : Ge 7 20 ὑ. ὑπεράνω ;   ⲉ ⲡ-, *higher than* : He 7 26 (*SF* ⲉ-) ὑψηλότερος γίνεσθαι gen.

—— ⲉϩⲣⲁⲓ, -ⲏⲓ, ⲁϩ. *SA²BF*, *up* : Ac 2 33 *S*(*B* ϭ.
only) ὑ. ; Ap 8 4 *S*(*B* ϣⲉ ⲉⲡϣⲱⲓ) ἀναβαίνειν ; Ac 4
24 *B*(*S* ϥⲓ ⲉϩ.) αἴρ. ; He 5 7 *SF*(*B* ⲓⲛⲓ ⲉϩ.) προσφέρειν ;
R 1 3 27 *S* ⲡⲥⲟⲃⲧ ... ⲝⲁⲥⲧⲟⲩ ⲉ., ManiH 55 *A²* ⲉϥⲁ-
ⲝⲉⲥⲧⲩ ⲁ., Aeg 23 *B* ϭ. ⲡⲧⲟⲩⲥⲙⲛ ⲉ.

ⲣ ⲉ, *who raises*, *mounts*.   ⲝⲁⲥⲓⲃⲁⲗ : Pro 24 36 *SA*
ὑψηλοὺς ὀφθ. ἔχειν, Aeg 241 *S* ὑψηλόφθαλμος, Ps 100
5 *S*(*B* ⲣⲉϥϫⲓ ⲡⲣⲟ ϭⲉⲛⲡⲉⲩⲃⲁⲗ) ὑπερήφανος ὀφθ. ;
ⲙ̄ⲡⲧⲝ. : Si 26 9 *S* μετεωρισμὸς ὀφθ. (cf ⲧⲁϭⲃ.) ; ϭⲁⲥⲓ (var ϭⲁⲥ) ⲡⲁ̄ϩⲃⲓ *B* : 2 Tim 3 4 (*S* ⲝⲁⲥⲓϩⲏⲧ) τυφοῦσθαι ; ϭⲁⲥⲓϩⲟ v p 723 a ;   ⲝⲁⲥⲓ, ϭ. ϩⲏⲧ (cf
below ⲝⲓⲥⲉ ⲡϩⲏⲧ) : Ps 17 27 *S*(*B* ⲣⲉϥϫⲓ ⲡⲣⲟ), Pro 3
34 *SAB* ὑπερήφ. ; Is 2 12 *SB* μετέωρος ; AP 23 *A²* ⲡⲝ.
ⲁϥϣⲱⲡⲓ ϩⲡⲟⲩⲟⲑⲉⲓⲟ, BSM 100 *B* cast down ⲡⲓϭ. ;
as adj : Nu 15 30 *S*(*B* ⲙⲉⲧϭ.), Ps 35 11 *S*(*B* do) ὑπερηφανία ; Eccl 7 9 *F*(*S* ⲝ.†) ὑψηλός ; Mor 24 18 *F* ⲡⲝ.
ⲡ̄ⲇⲓⲁⲃⲟⲗⲟⲥ ; ⲣ ⲝ., ⲉⲣ ϭ. : Ro 1 30 *SB* ὑπερήφανος ;
HSt 469 (var ⲝⲓⲥⲉ ⲡϩ.) κατεπαίρεσθαι ; Pro 21 4 *S*(*A*
ⲝ. adj) μεγαλόφρων ;   ⲙⲛ̄ⲧⲝ., ⲙⲉⲧϭ. : Ex 18 21 *S*(*B*

ⲙⲉⲧⲣⲉϥϩⲓ ⲡⲣⲟ), Ps 16 10 *SF*(Mor 33 1, *B* ⲇⲟ), Pro 8
13 *SAB* ὑπερηφανία; Ro 12 16 *SBF* ὑψηλός, Eccl 10
6 *F*(*S* ϫⲓⲥⲉ nn) ὕψος; CaiEuch 503 *B* ⲡⲓⲙ. ⲡⲧⲉ ⲡⲓ-
ϧⲉⲣⲉⲥⲓⲥ φρύαγμα; He 12 1 *SB* ὄγκος; BMar 157 *S*
ἀλαζονεία; BMis 565 *S superbia*; Hab 3 14 *SA*(*B*
Gk diff); ManiP 45 *A²* ⲁⲧⲙ. ⲣ ϧⲉⲗ ⲙⲙⲁϥ, DeV 2 25
B ⲡϣⲱⲡⲓ ⲛϯⲙ.

—— nn m *SAA²BF*, pl form *v* below, *height, top*:
Ge 6 15 *SB*, Eccl 10 6 *S*(*F* ⲙⲉⲧϫⲁⲥⲓϩⲏⲧ), Is 35 2 *SBF*,
Am 2 9 *AB* ὕψος, Job 24 24 *SB*, Ro 8 39 *SB* ὕψωμα;
1 Cor 2 1 *SB* ὑπεροχή; Ez 24 25 *B* ἔπαρσις; *ib* 25 9
B ἀκρωτήριον; *ib* 43 12 *B*(var ⲁϥⲉ) κορυφή; Pro 21
22 *SA* ὀχύρωμα; Ps 92 4 *S*(*B* diff) μετεωρισμός;
Jth 9 10 *S* ἀνάστημα; Si 47 5 *S* γαυρίαμα; GFr
359 *S* ⲡ̄ϫ̄. ⲡⲡⲉϧⲟⲟⲩ μακροημέρευσις; Nu 24 6 *B*(*S*
ⲕⲣⲟ), Jer 14 6 *B*(*S* diff) νάπη; PS 26 *S* mysteries ⲡⲧⲉ
ⲡⲁⲡ̄ϫ̄., BG 71 *S* ⲡ̄ϫ̄. ⲡⲧⲉϥⲙⲛⲧⲥⲁⲃⲉ, ShViK 98 15 27
S ⲡ̄ϫ̄. ⲉⲧⲟⲩϫⲱ ⲙⲙⲟⲟⲩ *proud words*, ShC 42 112 *S*
ⲥⲉ ⲙⲙⲁϧⲉ ⲡ̄ϫ̄., R 1 1 78 *S* raised ⲉⲡ̄ϫ̄. ⲙⲡⲉϥϯⲟⲥ,
ManiP 207 *A²* ϯⲛⲁϫⲁⲣⲙ ⲡⲉϥϫ̄. ϧⲓϫⲱⲓ, EW 64 *B* we
(Pharisees) are ⲡ̄ϫ̄. ⲙⲡⲓⲗⲁⲟⲥ; pl forms (*cf* Spg
278 *supra*): Ps 17 33 *S* ϫⲓⲥⲓⲉⲉⲩ (varr ϫⲓⲥⲓⲉⲟⲩ, -ⲥⲉⲉⲩⲉ,
B ⲡⲏ ⲉⲧϭ.†) ὑψηλά; K 136 *B* ⲛⲓϭⲁⲥⲟⲩ ⲛⲧⲉ ⲡⲓⲣⲟ
سياس; ⲉⲡ̄ϫ̄., ⲉⲩϫ., ϭ.: Ps 74 6 *B*(*S* ⲉⲧⲡⲉ), Eph
4 8 *SB* εἰς ὕψος; BM 174 1 *S* ⲉⲧⲃⲏⲕ ⲉⲡ̄ϫ̄. ἄνω, BHom
30 *S* ϧⲱⲗ ⲉⲡ̄ϫ̄. εἰς τὴν ἄνοδον; PS 78 *S* ⲁⲥⲕⲟⲧⲥ ⲉⲡ̄ϫ̄.,
R 1 3 67 *S* ⲏ ⲉⲡ̄ϫ̄. ⲏ ⲉⲡⲉⲥⲏⲧ *more or less*, DeV 2 99 *B*
ⲛⲧⲟⲩⲥⲟⲕⲧⲉⲛ ⲉⲡϫ., J 20 91 *S* ⲕⲱⲧ ⲙⲙⲟϥ ⲉⲡ̄ϫ̄.; ⲉ-
ϫⲏ-: Is 10 12 *SB* ἐπὶ τὸ ὕψος, Hab 3 19 *B*(*SA* ⲙⲁⲉⲧ̄ϫ̄.†)
ἐπὶ τὰ ὑψηλά; Lu 4 29 *B*(*S* ⲕⲟⲟϩ) ὀφρύος; ⲡ- *S*,
in: PS 42 ⲡⲟⲩⲟⲉⲓⲛ ⲉⲧⲙⲡ̄ϫ̄., Miss 4 238 set him ⲙⲡ̄ϫ̄.
ⲙⲡⲃⲏⲙⲁ (var Z 378 n ⲙⲡⲉⲧⲡⲉ); ⲥⲁ- *F*: Eph 1 21
(Mich 550 9, *S* ϫ̄.† ⲉ-, *B* ⲥⲁⲡϣⲱⲓ ⲛ-) ὑπεράνω; ϧⲓ-
S: Deu 11 11 (*B* ⲛⲧⲱⲟⲩ) ὀρεινός; ϧⲛ-, ϫⲉⲛ-: Jos
15 19 *S* ἄνω opp ϧⲁⲡⲉⲥⲏⲧⲉ, Va 57 9 *B* ἀνωτάτω, Ac
19 1 *S*(*B* ⲥⲁⲡϣⲱⲓ) ἀνωτερικός; ⲉⲃⲟⲗ ϧⲓ-, ϫⲉⲛ-: Ps
17 16 *SB*, Lam 1 13 *B*(*F* ⲉⲃ. ⲛ-) ἐξ ὕψους, Is 32 15
SBF ἀφ' ὑψηλοῦ, Sa 9 17 *S* ἀπὸ ὑψίστων; ⲙⲁⲓϭ.
B, *loving high rank*: Cat 101 ⲧⲛⲱⲙⲛ ⲡⲕⲉⲛⲟⲇⲟϫⲟⲛ
ⲟⲩⲟϩ ⲙⲙ.

ϫⲓⲥⲉ, ϭ. ⲛϩⲏⲧ *SA²BF*, *be high-hearted, vain*: Ro 11
20 *SBF* ὑψηλὰ φρονεῖν, BHom 18 *S* μέγα φρ.; 1 Cor
4 18 *SB* φυσιοῦσθαι; 1 Tim 6 4 *SB* τυφοῦσθαι; Ps 30
23 *S*(*B* ϧⲓ ⲡⲣⲟ) ὑπερηφανίαν ποιεῖν; Jer 13 15 *B*(*S* ϫ̄.
tr) ἐπαίρεσθαι; Pcod 9 *S* exhort them ⲉⲧⲙ̄ϫ̄. ⲛϧ.; ⲥ
ⲉϫⲛ- *S*: BHom 2 ϫ̄. ⲛϧ. ⲉ. ⲡⲟⲩϭⲁ ἐπαί., Aeg 268 ϫ̄.
ⲛϧ. .... ⲉ. ⲡⲉⲧ- ἐπαί. κατά; nn m: 2 Cor 12 20
SBF φυσίωσις; ManiP 105 *A²* ⲡ̄ϫ̄. ⲛϧ. ⲙⲡ[, Cat 98
B ⲁⲓⲧⲟⲩ ϫⲉⲡⲟⲩϭ ⲛϧ. *V* also p c.

ϫⲟϭⲉ nn *S* m f, *exalted person, place*: Jos 3 16 ⲡϩⲏ
ⲙⲡ̄ϫ̄. (*B* ϣⲟϭ ⲉϩⲣⲏⲓ) ἄνωθεν; P 131³ 17 Joseph
tempted ⲡⲉⲣⲉⲧⲉϥϫ̄. ⲁⲡⲓⲗⲏ ⲡⲁϥ ⲙⲡⲙⲟⲩ ⲉⲥⲥⲟⲡⲉ
ⲙⲙⲟϥ.

ϫⲓⲥⲉ *SS𝒻*, ϫⲉ., ϫⲏ. *S* ϫⲓϭⲓ *S𝒻F*, nn f, *land measure*, prob $\frac{1}{100}$ arura (HT): Ryl 323 *S* sow ⲟⲩϫ. ⲡⲉⲓⲱϧⲣⲉ, RE 14 23 *S* ϧⲙⲉϫⲉ (*l* ⲧⲉ) ⲡϫⲉ. ⲡⲉⲓⲱϧⲣⲉ, Kr 92 *S*
ⲥⲉⲧⲓⲁϧ ⲙⲁϧⲉ ... ⲡⲥⲉ ⲡϫⲓⲥ[ⲉ, BM 1013 *S* ⲥⲉ ⲙⲃ̄ⲧⲟ
ⲡϫ., Pcod Mor 25 *S* result of arithm problem ϣⲁⲩⲉⲣ
ϫ., *cf* BM 528 1 *S𝒻* sim, *ib* 16 ϫⲓϭⲓ, Win 35 *S* ϯⲟⲩ
ⲡⲛⲱϧ ⲙⲡϣⲟⲙⲛⲧ(ⲉ) ⲡ̄ϫ̄ⲏ., Ostr *penes* GJéquier *S*
ⲙⲛⲧⲁⲥⲉ ⲡ̄ϫ̄ⲏ. ⲛϧⲣⲉ ⲉⲡⲕⲁϧ, Ostr *penes* CSchmidt *F*
ⲓ̄ⲃ̄ ⲡ̄ϫ̄. ϧⲓⲡ̄ⲓ̄ⲱ̄ϧ̄ⲣ̄, BMOr 6201 *B* 28 *S* about land-tax
ⲁⲕⲧⲓ ⲟⲩϧⲟⲗⲟⲕ/ ⲉϫ.

ϫⲓⲥⲉ *S*, -ⲓ *F*, ϭⲓϭⲓ *B* nn f, *back*: Ge 9 23 *S*(*B* ⲥⲟⲓ),
Ps 80 6 *SB*, Ro 11 10 *SB*, R 1 4 70 *S* ϧⲱⲱⲕⲉ ⲡⲧⲉϥϫ.
= MartIgn 876 *B* νῶτος; ShC 73 67 *S* ⲕⲱⲗϫ ⲡⲧⲉϥϫ.
ⲉⲡⲉⲥⲏⲧ, ShMun 166 *S* ⲕⲧⲟ ⲡⲧⲟⲩϫ. ⲉⲣⲟϥ, J 106 64 *S*
found naught ⲉⲧⲉⲓⲡⲁⲣⲉⲕⲧ ⲧⲁϫ. ⲉϫⲱϥ, BM 1001 *S*
ϯ ⲡⲧⲉϥϫ. ⲉϧⲟⲩⲛ ⲉϧⲓⲥⲉ ⲛⲓⲙ, AM 207 *B* beaten with
ⲕⲟⲩⲙⲫⲟⲥ (κόμβ.) ϧⲓϫⲉⲛⲧⲉϥϭ.; *spine, vertebra*:
ⲕⲁⲥ ⲡⲧϫ.: 1 Kg 5 4 *S*, Job 40 13 *S*(*B* ϭ.) ῥάχις; K
76 *B* ϯϭ. ظهر (*l* قفا), AZ 14 118), Mor
51 40 *S* ⲟⲩⲕⲁⲥ ϧⲟⲣϧ ϧⲛⲧⲉϥϫ., BMEA 10578 *F* ⲁⲡⲕⲉⲥ
ⲡⲧⲉϥϫ. ⲟⲩⲱⲡϫ (*sic*) = Mor 31 254 *S*.

ϫⲟⲥⲉⲙ *B*, ϫⲁ. *F* *v* ϭⲟⲥⲙ.

ϫⲓⲥⲙⲓⲥ *B* *v* ⲧⲏϭⲙⲉⲥ.

ϫⲁⲥϥⲉ *S* nn f with vb ϫⲓ, *set in order, repair*:
2 Chr 24 4 (P 44 112, var 43 110 ϫⲓ ⲙⲡⲥⲁϣϫϥ) ἐπι-
σκευάζειν ترميم; Si 50 1 ὑπορράπτειν; ShP 130⁵
16 aiding devil ⲉⲛⲕⲱⲧ ⲡⲓⲙⲁϥ ⲁⲩⲱ ⲉⲕϫⲓ ϫ. ⲡⲡⲉⲧⲉ-
ⲣⲉⲡⲭ̄ⲥ̄ ϣⲟⲣϣⲣ ⲙⲙⲟⲟⲩ.

ϫⲓϧⲟⲙⲉ *S* nn, meaning unknown: ST 120 list
of *varia* ⲟⲩϫ.

ϫⲁⲧ *F* nn m, meaning unknown: PMich 1193 13
ⲗⲓⲡⲱⲛ ⲡⲁⲥⲡⲉ[ⲟ]ⲩ ⲙⲓϫ. ϣⲟⲡ ⲡⲉϣⲱⲣⲓ, 15 ⲉⲓⲙⲓ ϫ.
ϣⲟⲡ ⲡⲉϣⲱⲣⲓ, *vo* 24 ⲧⲁⲙⲁⲓ ϫⲉϫⲏⲛⲧⲁⲡϫ. ⲧⲁⲗⲁ ⲧⲓ-
ⲗⲁⲙⲧⲓ.

ϫⲏⲧ *S* vb qual, *be narrow*: P 43 234 ϫⲉⲥⲡⲉⲅⲉⲑⲏⲥ
(δυσπνιγετός?) · ⲡⲉⲧⲉⲣⲉⲡⲟⲩⲛⲓϥⲉ ϫ. ضيق النفس (*cf*
p 239 b ϧⲉⲙⲡⲓϥⲉ). *L* ? ϫⲏϥ for ϭⲏϥ.

ϫⲏⲧ *v* ϫⲧⲁⲓ.

ϫⲉⲓⲁⲓⲧ *A* *v* ϫⲟⲉⲓⲧ vb.

ϫⲓⲧ *A* *v* ϣⲓⲧⲉ.

ϫⲟⲉⲓⲧ *S*, ϫⲁ. *SS𝑎A*, ϫⲁⲓⲧ *A²F*, ϫⲱⲓⲧ *B*, ⲑⲱⲏⲧ *O*
(? PGM 2 46) ϫⲓⲧ- *SAF* nn m, *olive tree, its fruit*:
Job 15 33 *SB*, Ps 127 3 *SB* ἐλαία, Is 17 6 *SB* ῥῶξ
ἐλαίας, Ac 1 12 *S* ⲡϫ., *B* ϥⲁⲡⲓϫ., ἐλαιών, Deu 24 20
B ⲥⲉⲕ ϫ. (*S* ⲙⲁ ⲡϫ.) ἐλαιολογεῖν; K 178 *B* ⲟⲩϫ.
زيتون, P 43 233 *S* ⲙⲟⲟⲩ ⲡϫ. · ⲅⲗⲉⲅⲉⲟⲥ (γλυκέος?)
ما الزيت *juice of (cultivated) olive* (? Meyerhof); Miss 4

231 *S* planted ϩⲉⲛ ⲃⲛⲛⲉ ⲙⲡϥⲉⲛ ϫ., G Par 2 2 *S* ⲕⲁⲣⲡⲟⲥ ⲛ ϫ. ⲉⲧⲉⲡⲉⲓⲥⲟϭⲛ, *ib* sim ⲉⲧⲉⲡⲉⲓⲛⲉϩⲡⲉ, Sph 10 4 *S* ϫⲁ. ⲙⲙⲟ(ⲟ)ⲩ (*cf* اللّٰه; Dozy), Saq 103 *S* ϫ]ⲉⲃⲥ ⲛ ϫ., PMich 4927 *S* ϩⲟⲧⲥ ⲛ ϫ., Bodl(P) b 9 *S* ⲟⲣϭⲟⲡ (*v* WS 153) ⲛ ϫ., MR 5 32 *S* ⲗⲁϥⲛ ϫ., CO 216 *S* ⲙⲟⲥⲡ ⲛ ϫ., J & C 98 *S*ᵃ ⲉⲣⲧⲁⲃ ⲛ ϫ., AZ 23 39 *F* ⲉⲗⲧⲁⲃ ⲛ ϫ. (*sic*) PBad 5 402 *F* ⲕⲁⲥ ⲛ ϫ., CO 338 *S* ϭⲉⲣⲱⲃ ⲛ ϫ.; as adj: Lev 24 2 *S*(*B* diff) ἐλάϊνος; ϩⲱ ⲛ ϫ., *olive tree* : Ps 51 10 *SB*, Hos 14 7 *SAB*, Ro 11 17 *SBF* ἐλαία; ⲓⲟϩⲓ ⲛ ϫ. (once), ⲓⲁϩϫ. *B*, *olive garden* : Deu 6 11 (*S* ⲙⲁ ⲛ ϫ.), Jer 5 17 ἐλαιών; C 86 234 10.; ⲙⲁ ⲛ ϫ. *S* : Deu *lc* (var ϣⲏⲛ ⲛ ϫ.); ϣⲏⲛ ⲛ ϫ. *S* : Deu 28 40 (*B* ϫ. only) ἐλαία, Jos 24 13 -ών; ϣⲉ ⲛ ϫ. *SB* : DeV 2 191 *B* cross of ϣ., AM 309 *B* saw of ϣ. (death of Isaiah), Mor 43 113 *S* ϣⲗⲉϭ ⲛϣ. = C 43 154 *B* ; ϭⲃϫ. *S*, ϫⲱⲃⲓ ⲛ ϫ. *B* : Ge 8 11 φύλλον ἐλαίας; ϫⲁⲗ ⲛ ϫ. *B* : BSM 131 picture put forth ϩⲁⲛ ϫ. = Mor 22 140 *S* ⲕⲗⲁϫⲟⲥ, DeV 1 121 ϩⲁⲛ ϫ. in hands; ⲧⲁⲣ ⲛ ϫ. *B* : *ib* 2 234; ⲧⲟⲟⲩ ⲛⲛ ϫ. *SA*², ⲛⲧⲉ ⲛ ϫ. *B* : Mt 21 1 *SB* ὄρος τ. ἐλαιών; BG 79 *S* ⲡⲧ. ⲡⲁⲛ ⲓ ϫ. (*sic* prob), ManiP 123 *A*²; ϫⲓⲧ- : Zech 4 14 *SA* ϩⲱ ⲛ ϫ. ⲡⲟⲩⲧⲙ (*B* as Gk) ἔλαιον (Hex); Ro 11 24 *SF* sim (*B* ϫⲱⲓⲧ ⲛⲛ.) καλλιέλαιος, *ib* 17 *SF* ϫ. ϩⲟⲟⲩⲧ (*B* ϫⲱ. ⲛϣⲁϣⲓ) ἀγριέλ.   Olive oil *v* ⲛⲉϩ.

In place-names : ⲫⲁⲛ ϫⲱⲓⲧ (C 86 161) = ⲡⲓⲉⲍⲍⲉⲓⲑⲟⲩⲛ (*ib* 173 = الزيتون, *v* Amélineau *Géog* 327), ⲙⲁⲕⲁⲣⲉ ⲡⲁⲛ ϫⲟⲉⲓⲧ (BMOr 6201 A 4).

—— *SA*²*F* nn m f, *testicle* : Lev 21 20 (*B* ⲁⲗ) -ορχίς, MR 4 128 ⲟⲣⲭⲓϫⲓⲁ· ⲛ ϫ.; P 43 234 ϫⲁ. (*l* ? ⲧ ϫ.) ⲙⲡⲣⲱⲙⲉ خصوتيه; Tri 364 ⲛⲉ ϫ. called ⲛⲁⲛⲁⲅⲕⲁⲓⲟⲛ انثيان (*cf* ⲥⲁⲙⲃⲉϩⲓ); PMéd 285 ⲛⲉ ϫ. ϣⲱⲡⲉ, CR '87 376 ⲛ ϫ. ....ⲉⲧⲙⲟ ϫⲣ, Cai 42573 2 anoint ϫ. with sweat of black ass, ManiK 173 *A*² ⲛⲉ ϫ. ⲥⲛⲉⲩ, BKU 1 26 (8117) *F* ⲛⲉ ϫ. (*sic l*) ἐπαλέκτωρ in recipe.   *Cf* ὀρχάς, ὄρχις kind of olive.

ϫⲟⲉⲓⲧ ϫⲱ., ϫⲟⲉⲓⲧ ϫ *S*, ϫⲁⲓⲧ ϫ *S*ᵃ, ϫⲉⲓⲁⲓⲧ† *A*, ϫⲁⲓⲧ† *A*², p c ϫⲁⲉⲓⲧ- *S*, vb tr, *plant* (?): Hall 79 ⲁⲕϭⲟⲡⲧ ϫⲉⲉⲓⲁ ϫⲱ. ϩⲉⲛ ⲉⲓⲁϩⲟⲩ, CO 304 ⲛⲧⲁ ϫⲟⲉⲓⲧⲥ (*sc* ⲧⲏ ⲛϣⲉ of land) ⲛⲁⲕ, Win 69 ⲁⲥ ϫⲟⲉⲓⲧ[, RE 14 23 (68) *S*ᵃ fields ⲛ ϭ ϫⲁⲓⲧⲟⲩ (ⲙ)ⲙⲁϩⲉ, TurM 16 ⲡⲉⲧⲛⲁⲧⲁϩⲟ ⲡⲓⲉⲣⲟⲥ (*cf* Ep 102 & refs) ϩⲓⲑⲛ ⲉ ϫⲛⲁϫ. ⲧⲏ ⲛⲉⲓⲧ; qual : Hos 9 13 *A* ⲉⲡⲉⲥϣⲏⲣⲉ ϫ. ⲡ ϩⲏⲧⲥ πεφυτευμένοι (Hexap), ManiK 173 *A*² wheel ⲡⲉⲧⲟⲩⲧⲣⲁⲓⲧ ⲉⲩⲁϥⲧ ⲉⲩ ϫ. ⲛ ϩⲏⲧⲩ (same ?); p c : CO *lc* ⲛ ϭⲉ ⲛⲛ ϫⲁⲉⲓⲧⲟⲩⲟⲧ[ⲉ ⲧⲏ]ⲣⲟⲩ (*sic*, correct p 444 *b* 1).   *Cf* ϫⲟ 1°.

ϫⲱⲧ *S*(Theban) vb tr, *long for, have affection for* or sim : COAd 67 come south that we meet thee ϫⲉ ⲁⲛ ϫ. ⲙⲙⲟⲕ, Ep 356 that I come & meet you for ⲁⲓ ϫ. ⲙⲙⲱⲧⲛ ⲉⲙⲁⲧⲉ, BKU 1 290 ⲁⲓ ϫ. ⲙⲙⲟⲕ ⲉⲙⲁⲧⲉ & have thirsted for thee.

ϫⲱⲧ *B* nn f, *pillar* (so Ar): C 86 329 ⲓϣⲓ ⲙⲙⲟϥ ⲉⲟⲩⲛⲓϣ† ⲛ ϫ. ⲉⲥ ϫⲱ عمود عال (but Budge *St George of Lydda* 58 *b* ⲛ ϭⲟⲗ).   ϫⲱⲧ = ϭⲱⲧ unlikely.

ϫⲱⲧ *B* *v* ϫⲟ ϫⲱⲧ & ϭⲱⲧ.

ϫⲁⲧⲉ, ϫⲁⲁ., ϫⲟⲧⲉ† *S* vb intr, *advance in age, become, be ripe* : Jud 13 25 (var ϫⲁⲁ.), 2 Kg 12 3 ἀδρύνεσθαι; 1 Kg 1 22 ἀναβαίνειν; Ge 41 22† (*B* ϫⲟⲡⲧ) πλήρης; Tri 502 ⲁϥ ϫ. ϩⲛ ⲧⲉⲥⲕⲉⲡⲏ ⲙⲁⲉⲗ (same ?); TT 154 after birth ⲡⲕⲟⲩⲓ ϫ. ϣⲏⲙ ϣⲏⲙ ϣⲁⲛⲧϥ ⲧⲉⲗⲉⲓⲟⲥ, KKS 299 sim, ShZ 602 ϩⲉⲛ ϩⲙⲗⲥ ⲙⲡⲁⲧⲟⲩ ϫⲁⲁ. ϩⲙ ⲡⲉⲩⲥⲏⲩ, *ib* ⲛ ⲡϣⲱⲡⲉ † ϫⲱⲟⲩ ⲉϩⲣⲁⲓ ⲛⲥⲉ ϫ., *ib* 603 (same MS) ⲁϥ ϫⲁⲁ. opp ⲣ ⲃⲃⲣⲉ, Mich 550 24 ⲛⲉ ϭⲣⲱⲟϭ ⲛⲧⲁ ϫ.

ϫⲓ† *v* p 395 *b*.

ϫⲱⲧⲉ *SAA*², ϫⲱⲧ *SA*², -† *F*, ϫⲉⲧ- *S*, ϫⲁⲧ- *SS*ᶠ*A*², ϫⲟⲧ ϫ *S*, ϫⲁⲧ ϫ *S*ᶠ*A*² vb intr, *pierce, penetrate* (*cf* ḏdt *Kémi* 2 17): Sa 7 24 (*B* ⲫⲟϩ) διήκειν; Mich 550 31 sim ϫ. ⲛⲥⲉⲛⲁⲩ = Va 63 94 *B* ϭⲓ ⲟⲩⲱⲓⲛⲓ βλέπειν, 1 Kg 14 27 eyes ⲛⲁⲩ ⲁⲩ ϫ. ἀναβ.; *ib* 29 ⲛⲁⲃⲁⲗ ϫ. ὁρᾶν; PMéd 156 recipe for eyes ⲧⲣⲉⲡⲟⲩⲟⲉⲓⲛ ϫ., Mor 24 28 *F* ⲁⲡⲉⲃⲏⲗ ϫ. ⲁⲡⲡⲉⲩ = *ib* 23 39 *S* ⲉⲓⲱⲣϩ;   tr, *pierce* (of weapon), *traverse* : Job 20 24 (*B* ϫⲱⲧϩ) τιτρώσκειν, BIF 37 54 ⲛⲥⲉⲧ ⲙⲉϣ ϫ ⲟⲧⲛ ἄτρωτος εἶναι; Si 32 16, He 4 14 (*B* ⲥⲓⲛⲓ) διέρχεσθαι; 1 Kg 17 49 διαδύειν διά; BHom 14 ⲙⲡⲟⲩ ϫ ⲟⲧⲟⲩ πλήσσειν; Tri 502 ϫ. ⲙⲡⲡⲉⲗⲁⲧⲟⲥ ⲣⲃⲍ; PS 186 light ϫ. ⲛⲟⲩⲙⲏⲏϣⲉ ⲛⲕⲁⲧⲁⲡⲉⲧⲁⲥⲙⲁ, ShRE 10 162 ϫⲟⲧ ϥ ...ⲛ ϫ ⲟⲩⲟ ⲉⲣⲉⲡⲗⲟⲩⲭⲏ, R 2 1 49 ⲡⲉⲓϣⲁ ϫⲉ ϫ. ⲙⲙⲟⲓ, Mor 39 12 *S*ᶠ arrow ϫⲁⲧ ⲛ ϩⲏⲧ (var *ib* 40 9 *S* ϫⲓ) = C 43 39 *B* ⲧⲁ ϭⲉ-, PBad 5 398 *S*ᶠ nails ϫⲁⲧ ϥ ⲛ ϭⲉ ⲛⲟⲩ ⲕⲱϩⲧ, Mich 554 ⲁⲓ ϫⲉⲧ ⲡⲓⲉⲣⲟ, Mor 50 69 sailing to Constantinople ⲁⲛ ϫ ⲉⲧ ⲡⲁⲗⲁⲥⲧⲏⲙⲁ ⲡ ⲕⲛⲙⲉ, *ib* 37 106 ϫⲉⲧ ⲡⲉⲥ ϩⲏⲣ ⲙⲡⲉⲓⲃⲓⲟⲥ & come to port, Mani K 127 *A*² fire could not ϫ. ⲙⲙⲁϥ, *ib* H 61 *A*² ⲁϥ ϫⲁⲧ ⲡⲕⲟⲥⲙⲟⲥ ⲁϥⲃⲱⲕ, BP 9418 † ⲡⲁⲉⲓ ⲉϩⲟⲩⲛ ⲛⲧⲁ ϣⲱⲧⲉ ⲙⲡⲣⲟ & require my money (same ? or *l* ϣⲱⲧⲉⲙ).

With following preposition.   c ⲉ- : Ez 41 3 (*B* ϣⲉ ⲉϩⲟⲩⲛ ϣⲁ-) εἰσέρχ. εἰς; R 1 1 61 ⲁⲩ ϫⲟⲧϥ ...ⲉⲡⲉϥ ⲥⲡⲓⲣ ἐκκεντεῖν; Mor 40 25 ϫⲟⲧϥ ⲉⲡⲉϥ ⲁⲡⲕⲉⲫⲁⲗⲟⲥ (ἐγκ., var *ib* 39 34 ⲣⲁϩⲧϥ) = C 43 54 *B* ⲑⲟⲩ ϩ, Bor 267 103 ⲁϥ ϫ. ⲉⲡⲉⲥⲏⲧ ⲉⲁⲙⲡⲧⲉ, ManiP 204 *A*² ⲁϥ ϫ. ⲁⲡⲓⲧⲛ ⲁⲡⲛⲟⲩⲛ; vbal : BMar 181 ⲉⲩ ϣⲁⲛ ϫⲟⲧⲕ ⲉⲥⲁϩ ⲧⲉ ⲛⲁⲕ *if art impelled to kindle*; ⲉϩⲣⲁⲓ ⲉ- : Jos 18 15 διέρχ. εἰς; ShA 1 455 thieves ϫ. ⲉ. ⲉⲩ ϭⲱϣⲉ, J 106 43 prayers ϫ. ⲉ. ⲉⲙⲡⲏⲩⲉ;   c ⲉ ϫⲛ- : Jos 16 3 διέρχ. ἐπί; 2 Kg 2 23 τύπτειν ἐπί;   c ⲛ- instr : Mor 22 101 ϫⲉⲧ ⲛ ⲡⲉ ⲛⲟⲩ ⲗⲟⲅⲭ ⲏ = BSM 95 *B* ϫⲟⲧϥ, Ryl 94 110 ϫⲟⲧϥ ⲛ ⲧⲉⲡⲗⲏⲧⲏ ⲙⲡⲟⲩ ϫⲱ (Job 1 20), ManiP 196 *A*² ϫⲁⲧϥ ⲙⲡⲃⲉⲣ ϩⲉ;   c ⲟⲩⲧⲉ- : Ex 26 28 (*B* ⲥⲟⲩⲧⲱⲛ ⲉⲃⲟⲗ ϫⲉⲛⲧ ⲙⲛⲧⲉ) ἀνὰ μέσον δικνεῖσθαι;   c ϣⲁ- : He 4 12 (*B* ⲛⲁ ⲉϫⲟⲩⲛ ϣⲁ-) διικ. ἄχρι; Jon 2 6 *A*(*S* ⲉⲓ ⲉϩⲟⲩⲛ ϣⲁ-) *B* Gk diff; Br 227 light ϫ. ϣⲁ ⲡⲧⲟⲡⲟⲥ;   c ϩⲛ-, *into* : Br 226 voice ϫ. ϩⲓ ⲙⲁ ⲛⲓⲙ, Leyd 401 ϣⲁⲥ ϫ. ϩⲛ ⲡⲁⲗⲧⲕⲁⲥ, ManiH 77 *A*² ϫⲱⲧ

ⲡⲥⲁⲧⲉ ⲣ̄ⲙⲡⲟⲩϩ[ⲟ; instr: ShA 1 394 ϫⲟⲧϥϩⲛⲟⲩⲙⲉ-
ⲣⲉϩ, Mor 55 39 *S*ᶠ snake ϫⲁⲧⲟⲩ ϩⲛⲧⲉϥⲙⲁⲧⲟⲩ; c
ϩⲓⲧⲛ-: Sa 7 23 χωρεῖν; BHom 44 ϫⲟⲧⲕ ϩ. ⲡⲥⲟⲧⲉ;
c ϫⲓⲛ-: Sa 8 1 διατείνειν ἀπό.

With following adverb. c ⲉⲃⲟⲗ: ShC 42 185
was wroth ϩⲱⲥⲧⲉ ⲉⲧⲣⲁϫ. ⲉⲃ. ⲛⲧⲁⲃⲱⲕ, Mor 19 63 ⲁⲡ-
ⲃⲁⲣⲃⲁⲣⲟⲥ ϫⲉⲧ ⲡⲙⲏⲛϣⲉ ⲉⲃ. (var *ib* 18 55 om ⲉⲃ.) =
Miss 4 131 *B* 1 ⲉⲃ. ϩⲉⲛ-, Hall 106 ⲛⲧⲉϫⲱⲧ ⲉⲃ. ⲉⲣⲟϥ
go (f) *out to him*; ⲉⲃ. ϩⲛ-; 2 Kg 2 23 διέρχ. ἐκ; c
ⲉϩⲟⲩⲛ: 4 Kg 9 2 εἰσέρχ.; P 131³ 52 ϫ. ⲉ. ϩⲓⲧⲡⲟⲩⲣⲟ
ⲉϥϣⲟⲧⲙ (Jo 20 19); ⲉϩ. ⲉ-: 3 Kg 22 30 εἰσέρχ. εἰς;
Jos 3 15 εἰσπορεύεσθαι ἐπί; Lam 3 13 (*B* diff) εἰσάγειν ἐν; Ez 41 6 (*B* ϣⲉ ⲉⲃ. ⲉ-) διάστημα ἐν; BMar
119 ϫ. ⲉ. ⲉⲧϫⲱⲣⲁ ⲉⲧϩⲓⲣⲟⲩⲡⲓ ἀναβαίνειν εἰς; BMis
127 ⲙⲁⲣⲓϫ. ⲉ. ⲉⲑⲓⲥⲧⲟⲣⲓⲁ ⲡⲕⲉⲕⲟⲩⲓ, ManiP 163 *A*²
ϫⲁⲧⲥ ⲁ. ⲁⲡⲟⲏⲧ; ⲉϩ. ϣⲁ-: HM 2 20 ϩⲙⲡⲧⲣⲉⲛϫ. ⲉ.
ϣⲁⲣⲟϥ; ⲉϩ. ϩⲛ-: ShC 42 38 ⲁϥϫ. ⲉ. ϩⲓⲣⲱⲟⲩ, Mor
25 65 ϫ. ⲉ. ϩⲙⲛϣⲁϫⲉ, Mor 30 6 *S*ᶠ ⲁϥϫ. ⲉ. ϩⲛⲧⲉⲅ-
ⲙⲏⲧ = BMis 233 ⲃⲱⲕ ⲉ. ϩⲛ-.

—— nn m, *penetration, separation*: P 44 95 his
preaching ⲣ ⲟⲩⲟⲉⲓⲛ ⲉⲡϫ. ⲛⲧⲕⲁⲧⲁⲡⲟⲏⲥⲓⲥ بلوغ الى حدّ
الفهم; P 131⁴ 113 at creation of waters ⲁⲩϫⲁ ⲟⲩϫ. ⲟⲩⲧⲱⲟⲩ (Ge 1 7); f: PMich 3560 ⲡⲉⲕⲙⲉⲣⲟⲥ ϩⲡⲧϫ.
ⲙⲡⲣⲓⲣ, J 51 4 (ⲥ)ⲁⲃⲁⲗ ⲛⲫⲓⲣ ⲙⲁ ⲡⲧϫ. (same ? or *l*
ϣⲱⲧⲉ).

Cf ϭⲱⲧϩ.

ϫⲧⲁⲓ, ϫⲏⲧ⁺ *S* vb intr, *ripen* (cf ϫⲁⲧⲉ): Ge 41 7⁺
(*B* ϭⲟⲏⲧ, ϫⲟⲏⲧ) πλήρης; ShA 2 29 grain ⲙⲡⲟⲩϫ.
for was scorched by wind.

ϫⲧⲟ (for ⲧϫⲧⲟ) *SAA*², ϣⲧⲟ *SB*, ϫⲧⲉ- *S*, (ⲉ)ϣⲧⲉ-
B, ϣⲧⲁ- *F*, ϫⲧⲟ⸗ *S*, ϣⲧⲟ⸗ *SB*, ϣⲧⲁ⸗ *SF*, ϣⲧⲏⲟ *B* (c
ⲉϩⲣⲏⲓ), ϫⲧⲏⲟⲩ⁺, ϣ.⁺ *S*, ϣⲧⲏⲟⲩⲧ⁺ *BF* vb tr, *lay down*:
Job 24 10 *S*(*B* ⲑⲣⲉ-...ⲛⲕⲟⲧ), Nah 3 18 *AB* κοιμίζειν;
Jer 40 12 *S*(*B* diff) κοιτάζειν; Job 26 12 *B*(*S* ⲡⲱⲣϣ)
στρωννύναι; C 41 53 *B* ⲉϣⲧⲉ ⲕⲁϩⲓ = Miss 4 413 الق;
LMis 196 *S* ⲁϥϣ. ⲛⲛϭⲁⲙⲟⲩⲗ = EW 44 *B* = Hor Sem
3 60 عرس; Mor 31 75 *S* ϣ. ⲙⲙⲟⲥ ⲙⲡⲁⲧⲟ ⲉⲃⲟⲗ
ⲙⲡⲣⲏ; qual, *lying down*: AM 256 *B* being sick
ⲉⲓϣ., MG 25 88 *B* sim, BMOr 6948 (2)*F* ⲉⲥϣ. ⲉⲥⲉⲛ-
ⲕⲁⲧ.

With following preposition. c ⲉ- *S* ϫ. ⲉⲡϣⲱⲡⲉ,
succumb to sickness: 2 Kg 13 2 (var ϣ.) ἀρρωστεῖν;
Aeg 10 = *ib B* ⲉⲛⲕⲟⲧ ϩⲉⲛⲡⲓϣ., BMis 466 ⲁϥϣ. ⲉⲡϣ.,
ib 470 (same MS) ϫ.; *in, on*: Ge 43 21 *B*(*S* ⲟⲩⲉϩ)
καταλύεσθαι; Lam 2 12 *S*(Pap *olim* BPGrenfell, *BF*
diff) ἐκχέειν εἰς; TEuch 1 151 *B* ϣⲧⲟϥ (sc novice) ⲉⲡⲕⲁϩⲓ على مُذ; BIF 13 116 *S* ϣⲧⲟϥ (sc corpse) ⲉⲡⲕⲁϩ
= MG 25 308 *B* ϣ. ⲉϫⲉⲛ-; ⲉϩⲟⲩⲛ, ⲉⲃ. ⲉ-: Mor 40
20 *S* ⲡⲉϫϫ(ⲧ)ⲏⲩ ⲉ. ⲉⲧϣⲟⲣⲡⲉ ⲙⲡⲏⲛ = C 43 49 *B* ϣ.⁺
ⲉⲃ. ⲉ-; c ⲉϫⲛ-, ⲁϫⲛ-, *upon*: Ac 9 33⁺ *F*(*B* ϩⲓϫⲉⲛ-,
S ⲛⲏϫ ϩ.) κατακεῖσθαι ἐπί; MG 25 291 *B* ⲡⲁⲡϣ.⁺
ⲡⲉ ⲉ. ϯⲡⲉⲧⲣⲁ = BIF 13 107 *S* ϣ.⁺ ϩⲓϫⲛ-, ManiK 161

*A*² ⲧϩⲣⲏϣⲉ...ϫ. ⲁϫⲱⲩ; tr: Mor 38 51 *S* ϫⲧⲟϥ ⲉ.
ⲧⲉϥϫⲓⲥⲉ, BIF 15 233 *S* ϣⲧⲁϥ ⲉ. ⲟⲩⲙⲁ ⲛⲛⲕⲟⲧⲕ, C 43
80 *B* ϣⲧⲟϥ ⲉ. ϩⲏⲧϥ; ⲉϩⲣⲏ ⲉϫ. *B*: 3 Kg 17 19 κοι.
ἐπί; c ϩⲛ-, ϩⲉⲛ-: Lu 2 7 *S*(*B* ⲭⲱ) ἀνακλίνειν ἐν;
Lam 4 5 *F* ϣⲧⲁⲩ ϩⲓⲡⲓⲧⲓⲛ (*S* ϭⲟⲟⲗⲉ, *B* ϩⲓⲟⲅⲓ) περιβάλλεσθαι gen; C 86 295 *B* ⲁⲥϣⲧⲟϥ ϩⲉⲛⲕⲉⲛϥ (cf 231
ⲭⲁϥ) κοιμίζ. εἰς; ShA 2 62 *S* ⲡⲧⲉⲛϫⲁⲧⲉ ϩⲉⲛϣⲏⲣⲉ
ⲁⲛ ϩⲙⲡⲟⲩⲧⲟⲡ, Miss 4 783 *S* ⲁⲩϣⲧⲁϥ ϩⲛⲧⲕⲁⲗⲓⲃⲉ
(-ύβη); CaiEuch 584 *B* ⲉⲩϣ.⁺ ϩⲉⲛⲡⲛⲓⲁⲃⲓ προκατακεῖ.
ἀρρωστήμασι; Z 617 *S* ϫ. ϩⲙⲡⲟⲅⲟⲙϥ, MG 25 163
B ⲉϥϣ.⁺ ϩⲉⲛⲡⲉϥϣⲱⲡⲓ; c ϩⲓϫⲛ-: 4 Kg 4 21 *B*
κοιμίζ. ἐπί; Mk 4 38 *S* ϫⲧⲉ ϫⲱⲥ (*B* ⲛⲕⲟⲧ ϩⲓⲫⲁϩⲟⲩ)
καθεύδειν; C 43 229 *B* ϣⲧⲟϥ ϩ. ⲡⲉϥⲥⲟⲓ; qual: Mt
9 2 *B*(*S* ⲛⲏϫ ϩ.) βάλλ. ἐπί; cf c ⲉϫⲛ-.

With following adverb. c ⲉⲡⲉⲥⲏⲧ: Job 12 23 *B*
καταστρωννύναι; Bor 138 ult *S* ⲁⲩϫⲧⲉ ⲡⲉϥⲥⲱⲙⲁ ⲉ.;
c ⲉϩⲣⲏ *B*: C 89 42 of unloading cargo ⲁϥϣⲧⲏϥ ⲉ.
ⲡⲉⲙⲡⲓⲥⲛⲏⲟⲩ = C 99 138 *S* ⲡⲟⲡⲕϥ ⲉ. μεταφορὰ γίνεσθαι = Va ar 172 26 الاخوة الى به وانو حماره, MG 17
554 الاخوة انفذ لیحملوا (this word ?).

ϣⲧⲟ nn *S*, as liturgical rubric, alternating with
λέξις, τάγμα, ϩⲙⲟⲟⲥ, before successive ἑρμηνεῖαι:
Leyd 240, 242, P 68 65, *prostration*(?); KroppM 85
ⲟⲩϣⲧⲟ as title of charm to produce a *lying-ill* (cf
PGM 1 150 2496 ἐπὶ κατακλίσεως).

ⲣⲉϥϫ. *A*², *who knocks down*: ManiP 221 ⲧⲣⲉϥⲣⲱ-
ϩⲧ, ⲧⲣ.

ϫⲁⲧⲙⲉ *S*, ϫⲉⲧ. *A* nn, *heap* of grain: Job 5 26 (*B*
ϩⲟⲓ), Cant 7 3 (var ϫⲟⲧ.), Zeph 2 9 *A*(*B* prob ϩⲟⲓ)
θημωνιά.

ϫⲱⲧⲡ *B* *v* ϭⲱⲧⲡ.

ϫⲁⲧϥⲉ, -ⲃⲉ *S*, ϫⲉⲧⲃⲓ *S*ᶠ, ϫⲉⲧϥⲉ *AA*², ϭⲁⲧϥⲓ *B*,
ϫⲉ. *F* nn m, *reptile*: Ge 1 25 *SAB*, Lev 11 29 *S*(var
-ⲃⲉ)*B*, EpJer 19 *BF*, Ac 10 12 *SB* ἑρπετόν; PS 35 *S*
ⲧⲃⲛⲏ, ϫⲁⲧⲃⲉ, ⲑⲏⲣⲓⲟⲛ, *ib* -ϥⲉ, BMar 24 *S* ϫ., ϭⲏⲧ,
Sh(?)Mor 54 122 *S*ᶠ, Mani K 160 *A*², *ib* P 167 *A*²
ϫⲉϥⲧⲉ, MIE 2 409 *B* place full of ϭ., Ryl 104 § 4 *S*
spell against bite of ϫⲁⲧⲃⲉ; ϫ. ⲛⲃⲁⲕⲙⲁⲧⲟⲩ *S*:
Z 552 ἰοβόλος; ϫ. ⲉⲧⲛⲉϫ ⲙⲁⲧⲟⲩ *S* R 1 1 44. As
name (?): BM 1252 *F* ⲛϫⲁⲧϥ.

ϫⲱⲧϩ, ϫⲟ.⁺ *S* vb intr, *fail, cease*: Deu 28 65⁺ (*B*
ⲥⲁⲃⲉⲗ), Jer 14 6 (*B* ⲙⲟⲩⲛⲕ) ἐκλείπειν; ShC 73 24
ⲡⲉϥⲃⲁⲗ ϫ. ⲉⲧⲃⲉⲡⲉⲓⲃⲉ, BMis 479 about to bear ⲁⲡⲉⲥϣⲏⲣⲉ ϫⲟϩⲧ (*l* ϫⲱⲧϩ) ⲡϩⲏⲧⲥ & died.

ϫⲱⲧϩ *SB* *v* ϭⲱⲧϩ.

ϫⲧⲁϩ *O* vb (?), *meaning unknown*: Hor 78 ⲁϥ-
ⲁϣⲛ ⲁϫ. *Cf* ? ϫⲱⲧϩ 1°.

ϫⲟⲧϫⲉⲧ *v* ϣⲟⲧϣⲧ.

ϫⲁⲓⲱⲟⲩ *B* *v* ⲧϭⲁ(ⲉ)ⲓⲟ.

ϫⲉⲩ *S*ᶠ nn m, unknown animal : Orat Cyp 115 let her be as ⲟⲩⲓⲱ ⲉⲥϩⲁⲡⲓⲱ, ⲟⲩⲙⲟⲩⲧ ⲉⲥϩⲁⲡϫ., ⲟⲩ-ⲟⲩϩⲁⲁⲣⲓ ϩⲁⲡⲟⲩϩⲁⲣ.

ϫⲏⲟⲩ *B* *v* ϭⲱⲟⲩ.

ϫⲓⲟⲩ *S* nn m, meaning unknown : Baouit 140 ⲡⲁⲡϫ. epithet after name.

ϫⲟⲟⲩ, ϫⲟⲩ (rare)*S*, ϫⲁⲁⲩ *S*ᵃ, ϫⲁⲩ *SS*ᵃ*AA*²*F*, ϫⲁⲟⲩ *S*ᵃ, ϫⲉⲩ *B* (ⲥ ⲉϩⲟⲩⲡ), ϫⲉⲩ-, ϫⲟⲟⲩ- *S*, ϫⲁⲩ-*SA*²*F*, ϫⲁⲟⲩ- *F*, ϫⲟⲟⲩ϶, ϫⲁⲩⲟⲩ϶, ϫⲟⲩ϶ *S*, ϫⲁⲁⲩ϶ *S*ᵃ, ϫⲁⲩ϶ *S*ᵃ*AA*², ϫⲁ(ⲟ)ⲩⲧ϶ *F*, vb intr (rare), *send* (cf ϫⲟ 2°, *B* mostly ⲟⲩⲱⲣⲡ): Ge 31 4, Job 1 5 ἀποστέλλειν; Mt 14 10 *SF* πέμπειν; Ep 253 ⲁⲓϫ. ⲁⲓⲡ ⲅⲓⲕⲧⲱⲣ, MMA 24 64 *S*ᵃ ⲁⲕϫⲁⲁⲩ ⲁⲕⲕⲁⲁⲧ ϩⲓⲃⲟⲗ;   tr: Nu 22 15, Ps 106 20 (*B* ⲧⲁⲟⲩⲟ), Pro 25 13 *SA*, Mt 13 41 (*BF* ⲧ.), Mk 4 29 (*F* ⲧⲛⲁⲩ Mus 49 189), Jo 7 32 *SA*², Ac 9 38 (*F* ⲧϣⲉ-) ἀπ., Ex 24 5, Jud 6 8 (var ⲧⲛⲛⲟⲟⲩ), Lu 20 10 (var ϫⲡⲁ϶, *B* ϯ ⲧⲟⲧ϶ ⲉⲃⲟⲗ) ἐξαπ.; Lu 7 10 πέ., AP 14 *A*² ϫ. ⲡⲟⲡⲛⲉⲓⲫⲟⲣⲟⲥ ἀποπέ., Pro 16 28 *SA* διαπέ., ib 22 21 *A* ϫⲁⲩ϶ (*S* ϫⲡⲁ϶) προβάλλεσθαι (var ἀποστ.); PS 139 ⲁⲓϫ. ⲛⲅⲁⲃⲣⲓⲏⲗ, C 99 233 ⲁϥ-ϫⲉⲩ ⲑⲉⲟⲇⲱⲣⲟⲥ = C 89 67 *B* ⲟⲩ., Mor 29 32 ϫ. ⲡⲟⲩ-ⲉⲣⲅⲁⲧⲏⲥ (var BMis 263 ⲧⲛ.), WS 89 ϫⲉⲩ ⲃⲧⲟ ⲛⲟⲓⲡⲉ, Ep 431 ϫⲟⲟⲩ ⲡⲁⲣⲱⲙⲉ, Hall 22 ⲛⲧⲁϫⲁⲩ ⲡⲁϣⲓⲛⲉ, ST 347 *S*ᵃ ⲧⲁϫⲁⲁⲩϥ, ib 290 ⲙⲡⲉⲕϫⲟⲟⲩⲥⲉ, ib 298 ϫⲟⲟⲩ-ⲥⲟⲩ, JKP 2 134 *F* ⲁⲡⲡⲱⲣⲡⲓ (*l* ⲁⲧⲡ.) ϫⲁⲟⲩ ⲧⲉⲥϣⲏⲗⲓ, BM 588 *F* ϫⲁⲩⲧⲟⲩ (sc books, ib sim ⲟⲩⲁⲁⲧⲉ).

With following preposition.   ⲉ ⲉ- Is 36 2 *SF*, Mk 8 26 *SF* ϫⲁⲟⲩⲧ϶, Jo 17 18 *SA*² ⲧⲁ-ⲅⲟⲓ...ϫⲟⲟⲩⲥⲟⲩ ἀπ. εἰς both; Ac 10 32 πέ. εἰς, Cl 1 22 *A* ἐκπέ. εἰς; PS 63 ϫⲟⲟⲩⲥⲟⲩ ⲉⲡⲉϫⲁⲟⲥ, ViK 9180 ⲁⲩϫⲟⲟⲩⲕ ⲉϩⲣⲱ-ⲙⲏ, KKS 583 ⲁⲡⲡⲣⲟ ϫⲟⲟⲩⲧ ⲉⲡⲉⲓⲙⲁ (var ⲧⲛ.), ST 237 ⲁⲕϫⲟⲛⲧ ⲉϫⲉⲙⲉ, Mich 597 ⲧⲁϫⲁⲟⲩⲕ ⲉⲡⲱⲛⲉ, ManiP 112 *A*² ⲁⲕϫⲁⲩⲧ ⲁⲡⲓⲧⲡ, ib K 39 *A*² ϫⲁⲩϥ ⲁⲡ-ⲡⲗⲁϩ (sic);   vbal : Ps 58 tit ἀπ. καί, Mt 22 3 (var ϫ. ⲉⲃⲟⲗ), Jo 4 38 *SA*²*F* ϫⲁⲩⲧ[ⲏⲛⲟⲩ ἀπ. inf, Zech 1 10 *A* ϫⲁⲩⲥⲟⲩ ἐξαπ. inf; 1 Thes 3 5 *F* ϫⲁⲩ (sic MS, *S* ⲧⲛ.) πέ. εἰς; BHom 83 ϫⲟⲟⲩⲥⲟⲩ ⲉⲣ ϩⲱⲃ, Mor 24 17 *F* ϫⲁⲟⲩⲧⲃ ⲉϯ ⲟⲩⲱ;   ⲉ ⲉⲣⲡ-: 4 Kg 15 37 ἐξαπ. ἐν;   ⲉ ⲉⲣⲁⲧ϶: 2 Kg 11 6 ⲁϥϫ. ⲉⲣⲁⲧϥ saying ⲧⲛ. ⲡⲁⲓ ἀπ. πρός both, Tob 10 9 ἐξαπ. πρός; BHom 74 ϫⲟⲟⲩⲥ ⲉⲣⲁⲧϥ ⲙⲡⲉⲓⲉ;   ⲉ ⲉϫⲛ-: Ps 77 45 ἐξαπ. εἰς;   ⲉ ⲛ- dat : Lu 11 49 ἀπ. εἰς, Pro 21 8 *SA* ἀπ. πρός, Ge 32 18 ἀπ. dat; Ap 11 10 πέ. dat, Pro 6 19 *SA* ἐπιπέ. ἀναμέσον; PS 115 ⲁⲓϫⲟⲟⲩⲥ ⲛⲁⲥ, Aeg 264 ϫⲉⲩ ⲡⲉϣⲏⲣⲉ ⲛⲁⲩ, Ep 377 ⲧⲛⲡⲟⲟⲩϥ ⲛⲁⲓ ⲛⲧⲁϫⲟⲟⲩϥ ⲛⲁϥ, CO 241 *S*ᵃ ⲁⲓϫⲁⲩϥ ⲛⲉⲕ, Jern 1 ⲁⲧⲡⲉϫⲁⲩ (ⲟⲩ)-ϣⲓⲛⲉ ⲛⲁⲓ, BM 1103 ϣⲁⲓϫⲟⲩ ⲧⲁⲓⲟⲩ...ⲛⲁⲕ, Bodl(P) b 5 ⲁⲓϫⲟⲩⲥⲟⲩ ⲛⲁⲕ;   *for*: C 99 193 ϫⲟⲟⲩϥ ⲡⲟⲩϩⲱⲃ, BKU 1 22 ⲉⲓϫⲟⲟⲩⲕ ⲙⲡⲁⲣⲱⲃ;   ⲉ ⲡⲥⲁ-: Jth 1 7 ἀπ. ἐπί, RNC 27 ⲁϥϫ. ⲛⲥⲁⲉⲡⲓⲫⲁⲛⲓⲟⲥ ἀπ. πρός; Ac 20 1 μεταπέ. acc; Aeg 213 ϫ. ⲛⲥⲱϥ προσκαλεῖσθαι;

ShC 42 42 ϫ. ⲡⲥⲱⲟⲩ, BKU *lc* ϫⲟⲟⲩⲕ ⲡⲥⲁⲛⲁⲓ paral ϧⲁⲃⲕ ⲡⲥⲁ-, BP 10589 ϫ. ⲛϣⲁⲙⲟⲩⲗ ⲡⲥⲱⲟⲩ, AP 3 *A*² ⲁⲩϫ. ⲡⲥⲁⲁⲧⲭⲁⲣⲏⲥ, ManiP 131 *A*² ⲁⲡⲁⲓⲱⲧ ϫⲁⲩⲧ ⲡⲥⲱⲕ;   ⲥ ⲥⲡⲧⲛ-: Ep 291 ϫ. ⲧⲁⲡⲟⲕⲣⲓⲥⲓⲥ ⲛⲧⲟⲧϥ ⲛ-, ib 364 sim;   ⲥ ϣⲁ-: Ex 3 10, Jo 5 33 *SA*² ἀπ. πρός; Lu 4 26 πέ. πρός; Mor 33 134 ϯⲛⲁϫⲉⲩ ⲡⲉⲡⲡ̄ⲁ̄...ϣⲁ-ⲣⲱⲧⲛ (var BMis 66 ⲧⲛ. ⲡⲓⲧⲛ), Mani K 182 *A*² ⲁϥ-ϫⲁⲩⲥ ϣⲁⲡⲉϥⲥⲁⲡ.

With following adverb.   ⲥ ⲉⲃⲟⲗ : Ge 8 6 (var om ⲉⲃ.), Mt 24 31 (*BF* ⲧⲁⲟⲩⲟ) ἀποσ., Deu 21 14 (*B* ⲭⲱ ⲉⲃ.), Zech 9 11 *SA* ἐξαπ.; BHom 54 ϫ. ⲉⲃ. ⲛⲡⲣⲙ-ϩⲁⲗ ἀπολύειν;   ⲉⲃ. ⲉ-: Lev 16 10 ἀποσ. εἰς, Mk 3 14 ἀπ. inf;   ⲉⲃ. ⲉϫⲛ-: Ap 5 6 ἀποσ. εἰς;   ⲉⲃ. ⲛ-: Deu 15 12 ἐξαπ. ἀπό; ST 360 ϫ. ⲉⲃ. ⲛⲁⲓ, PSBA 30 204 sim;   ⲉⲃ. ϣⲁ-: Ob 7 *SA* (prob ϫⲁⲩⲕ) ἐξαπ. ἕως;   ⲉⲃ. ϧⲏ-: Jer 24 5 (*B* ϩⲓⲟⲩⲓ ⲉⲃ. ϧⲉⲛ-) ἐξαπ. ἐκ, Aeg 234 ἐξαπ. gen;   ⲉⲃ. ϩⲓⲧⲛ-: Ge 25 6 ἐξαπ. ἀπό; Mt 11 2 πέ. διά; PS 359 ϫ. ⲉⲃ. ϩⲓⲧⲙⲡⲉⲩⲕⲣⲱⲙ;   ϫ. ⲉⲃ. confused with ϫⲟ ⲉⲃ. *spend*: ALR '93 527 ϫⲏⲩ (*l* ϫⲉⲩ) ⲧⲉⲩϣⲏ ⲉⲃ. ϩⲛϩⲉⲛⲅⲩⲙⲛⲟⲥ, J 5 R ⲡⲉⲛⲧⲁⲓϫⲟⲟⲩϥ ⲉⲃ.;   ⲥ ⲉϩⲟⲩⲡ ⲉ-: Nu 13 28 ἀπ. εἰς; Mk 5 12 πέ. εἰς; BKU 1 22 ⲉⲓⲁϫⲟⲟⲩⲕ ⲉϩ. ⲉⲡⲓⲙ?;   ⲉϩ. ⲛ-: Mk 3 31 ἀπ. πρός, ViK 9471 ⲁϥϫ. ⲡⲁϥ ⲉϩ. ϫⲉⲉⲓⲟⲩⲱϣ ⲉϫⲓ ⲥⲙⲟⲩ = Miss 4 14 *B* ⲟⲩ. ⲉϩ., ST 260 *S*ᵃ ϫⲁⲩ ⲁϩ. ⲡ[;   ⲉϩ. ϣⲁ-: ST 235 ⲁⲕϫ. ⲉϩ. ϣⲁⲧⲉⲡⲙⲡⲧⲉⲗⲁⲭ(ⲓ-ⲥⲧⲟⲥ);   ⲉϩ. ϧⲉⲛ-: Cant 5 4 *B* (Biblica 16 48) ϫⲉⲩ ⲛⲧⲟⲧⲩ ⲉϩ. ϧⲉⲛ- (var & *S* ϫⲉ-, cf ϫⲟ) ἀπ. ἀπό;   ⲥ ⲉϩⲣⲁⲓ : EpApp 1 143 ϫ. ⲉϩⲣ. ⲛϧⲉⲛϣⲗⲏⲗ, Ryl 284 ⲁⲓϫ. ⲉϩⲣ. ⲁⲓ̈ϫⲁϫⲉ ⲡⲉⲙⲁⲟⲩ, ManiP 226 *A*² ϫⲁⲩⲥⲟⲩ ⲁϩⲣ.;   ⲉϩⲣ. ⲉ-: Mt 14 35 (*BF* ⲟⲩ. ⲉⲃⲟⲗ ϧⲉⲛ-), Mk 8 26 (*F* ϫⲁⲟⲩⲧⲩ ⲉ-) ἀπ. εἰς; Ac 10 5 πέ. εἰς, BM 174 1 ϫ. ⲙⲡⲉⲩϣⲗⲏⲗ ⲉϩⲣ. ⲉⲧⲡⲉ ἀναπέ. εἰς; TMina Epima 29 ϫⲟⲟⲩϥ ⲉϩⲣ. ⲉⲕⲙⲉ;   ⲉϩⲣ. ⲉϫⲛ-: Ps 77 49 (*B* ⲧⲁ. ⲉϩⲟⲩⲡ ⲉ-) ἐξαπ. εἰς; Mich 597 ⲉⲓϫⲁⲩ ⲙ-ⲙⲟⲕ ⲉϩⲣ. ⲉ. ⲛⲓⲁⲡⲟⲧ;   ⲉϩⲣ. ⲛ-: BMar 124 ϫ. ⲉϩⲣ. ⲙⲡⲁⲣⲣⲟ ἀναπέ. dat; BM 159 ⲧⲱ ⲕ̄ⲱ̄ ⲅ̄ⲙⲡⲟⲡ ⲁⲡⲁ-ⲡⲉⲙⲛⲱⲛ[ⲉⲛ]· ⲧⲓϫ. ⲡⲁⲕ ⲉϩⲣ. ⲛϧⲉ[ⲡϩⲩⲙⲟⲥ]; Sa 18 9 προαναμέλπειν;   ⲥ ϩⲁⲑⲏ : Ps 104 17 ἀπ. ἔμ-προσθεν, Lu 9 52 ἀπ. πρὸ προσώπου, Ex 23 28 ἀπ. πρό-τερον;   ⲥ ϩⲓⲣⲏ : BHom 22 ϫ. ⲟⲩⲉⲓⲱⲧⲉ ϩ. ⲙⲙⲟⲕ.

V AJSL 48 53, AZ 47 145.

ϫⲱⲟⲩ *B* nn m, *generation* (*SAA*²*F* mostly ϫⲱⲙ): Ge 9 12, Ps 77 6 (*S*=Gk), Mt 16 4 (*S* do), Joel 2 2 ϩⲁⲡϫ. ⲛϫ. γενεά; C 41 11 enduring ϣⲁϩⲁⲡϫ.;   ⲓⲥ-ϫⲉⲛϫ. ϣⲁϫ.: Is 58 12 γενεῶν γενεαῖς, Lam 5 19 εἰς γ. καὶ γ.;   ϫ. ⲡⲥⲁϫⲓ (*S* ϣⲁϫⲉ ⲛϫⲱⲙ) 1 Tim 1 4 γενεαλογία, Tit 3 9 sim (*S* ϣϫϫⲱⲙ);   ⲥⲁϫⲓ ⲉϫ. He 7 6 (*S* ⲧⲁϫⲉ ⲅⲉⲛ. ⲉⲃⲟⲗ) γενεαλογεῖν.

ϫⲓⲟⲩⲉ *SAA*², ϭⲓⲟⲩⲓ *B*, ϫ. *F* vb intr, *steal*: Lev 19 11 *SB*, Pro 6 30 *SAB*, Jo 10 10 *AA*²*B* (*S* ϩⲱϥⲧ) κλέ-πτειν; Br 102 *S* ⲡϥⲧⲙϫ.;   tr: Jo 12 6 *A*² (*A* ϥⲓ ⲛϫ., *S* ϩ., *B* as Gk) βαστάζειν; Miss 4 112 *B* ϥⲣⲏϯ ⲉⲧⲟⲩϭ.

ⲡⲡⲓⲕⲟⲩϫⲓ ⲛ̄ⲁⲗⲱⲟⲅⲓ = Mor 18 18 *S* ϭⲱⲡⲉ ;   c e-
S: Wess 18 74 ⲡⲡⲉⲧⲕⲉⲛⲟⲍⲟϫⲓⲁ ϫ. ⲉⲣⲟⲕ ⲕⲗ.; Mor
47 211 ⲁϫ. ⲉⲣⲟⲓ ⲁϥϫⲓ ⲙ̄ⲡⲁⲡⲣⲓⲱϥ, Ep 222 cannot
quit house ϫⲉⲉⲛⲉϥϫ. ⲉⲣⲟⲓ, Bor 253 266 ϫ. ⲉⲡⲉⲥ-
ⲕⲉⲩⲟⲥ;   c ⲡⲥⲁ- *S*: JTS 10 403 gates & bolts ϫⲉⲡ-
ⲡⲉⲩϫ. ⲛ̄ⲥⲁⲡⲉⲅⲉⲣⲏ, JA '88 376 ⲁϥϫ. ⲛ̄ⲥⲱⲕ; c ϧⲛ-
S: CA 112 ⲁϥϫ. ϧⲛⲛ̄ⲁⲱⲣⲟⲛ; ShViK 9101 8 ⲡⲉⲧⲛⲁϫ. ⲉⲃⲟⲗ ϧⲛ̄ⲧⲧⲟ ⲙ̄ⲡⲉϥⲥⲟⲛ.

—— nn m *SAA²BF*, ϭⲟⲩⲱ *B* f(once), *theft, fraud*:
Sa 14 25 *S*, Jer 31 27 *S*(Cai 8316)*B*, Mt 15 19 *SBF*
ⲕⲗⲟⲡⲏ́; Ge 31 39 *SB*, Ex 22 3 *B* f(BMOr 8787 92
ⲡⲉⲧⲁϥϭⲓⲟⲩⲓ اخرى خِـفْـيَـة, *S* ϧ.) ⲕⲗⲉ́ⲙⲙⲁ; BM 260 *S*
ϧⲉⲛϫ. ⲙⲡⲣⲉⲡⲧⲱⲣⲡ, Mun 33 *S* ⲡⲉⲓⲥⲕⲉⲩⲏ ϧⲉⲛϫ. ⲡⲉ,
PLond 4 502 *S*(ⲡ)ⲡⲉⲓⲕⲁ ⲗⲁⲁⲩ ⲛ̄ϫ. ⲉϣⲱⲡⲉ ⲡⲣⲏⲧⲥ,Ep
459 *S* ⲉⲓⲣⲉⲓ (ⲙ̄)ⲙⲟⲟⲩ ϧⲛⲟⲩϫ., C 43 217 *B* among
sins ⲟⲩϭ.;   adj, *stolen, secret*: Pro 9 17 *SAB* ⲕⲗⲟⲡⲏ́;
BMOr 8802 2 *S* ⲙ̄ⲡⲁⲑⲟⲥ ⲛ̄ϫ.;   ⲛ̄ϫ. advb, *stealthi-
ly*: Deu 13 6 *S*, Mt 1 19 *S*, Jo 11 28 *SA²*(*B* all ⲛ̄ϭⲱⲡ)
ⲗⲁ́ⲑⲣⲁ; Ge 31 26 *S*(*B* do) ⲕⲣⲩⲃⲏ̄, Is 29 15 *S*(*B* ϩⲉⲛⲡⲉ-
ⲧⲣⲉⲡ) ⲉⲛ ⲕⲣⲩ́ⲫⲏ; Jer 2 34 *B* ϣⲁⲧⲥ ⲛ̄ϭ. (*S* ⲙⲁ ⲉϥϧⲏⲡ) ⲇⲓⲟ́ⲣⲩⲅⲙⲁ; Sa 19 3 *S* ⲉⲧⲛⲏⲧ ⲛ̄ϫ. ⲱ̀ⲥ ⲫⲩ́ⲅⲁⲥ; FR
180 *S* disciples went ⲉⲛⲧⲁϥⲟⲥ ⲛ̄ϫ., C 41 26 *B* belongings ⲉⲧⲁⲣⲉⲧⲉⲛⲟⲗⲟⲩ ⲛ̄ϭ.;   ⲛ̄ϫ. ⲉ-, *unbeknown to*:
ShC 73 153 *S* eating ⲛ̄ϫ. ⲉⲡⲉⲧⲟⲩⲏϧ ⲡ̄ⲙ̄ⲙⲁⲩ, HM 1
191 *S* fleeing ⲛ̄ϫ. ⲉⲡⲉⲩⲥⲏϧ (for ⲥⲁϧ), RE 9 151 *S* babe
she conceived ⲛ̄ϫ. ⲉⲣⲟⲓ, C 89 101 *B* polluting bodies
ⲛ̄ϭ. ⲉⲛⲟⲩⲅⲓⲟⲩ = Va ar 172 59 عـ خِـفْـيَـة;   ϥⲓ ⲛ̄ϫ., *steal*:
Ge 30 33 *S*(*B* ⲕⲱⲗⲡ), Mt 27 64 *S*(*B* ⲱⲗⲓ) ⲕⲗ., EpJer
17 *F*(*B* ⲕⲱ.) ⲥⲩⲗⲁ̄ⲛ; Jo 12 6 *A²* v ϫ. tr; ShC 42 187
S ϥⲓ ϧⲉⲛⲣ̄ⲗⲁⲁⲩ ⲛ̄ϫ., ManiP 187 *A²* ⲃⲓ ⲛⲉⲡⲉ̄ ⲛ̄ϫ.;
J 76 76 *S* ⲁⲡⲁⲥⲛⲏⲩ ϥⲓⲧϥ ⲉϫ. ⲉⲣⲟⲓ.

ⲙⲁ ⲛ̄ϫ. *S*, *secret place*: ShA 2 62 ϧⲟⲡⲟⲩ ϧⲛ̄ⲟⲩⲣⲙ.

ⲣⲉϥϫ., -ϭ. *SAA²B*, *thief*: Job 30 5 *SB*, Zech 5 4
SAB, Mt 24 43 *S*(*B* ⲥⲟⲛⲓ) ⲕⲗⲉ́ⲡⲧⲏⲥ; PS 377 *S* ⲡⲥⲟⲟ-
ⲡⲉ ⲡⲣ., ShBM 214 = R 2 44 5 *S* ⲁⲩϭⲟⲡⲧ ⲛⲟⲉ ⲛ̄ⲟⲩⲣ.,
Miss 8 250 *S* ⲣⲉϥϧⲱⲃⲧ, p., ManiP 19 *A²*;   ⲙ̄ⲛ̄ⲧⲣⲉϥϫ.
S: Aeg 242 ⲕⲗⲟⲡⲏ́.

ⲥⲁ ⲛ̄ϫ. *A²* = *SB* ⲣⲉϥϫ.: Jo 10 10 ⲕⲗⲉ́ⲡⲧⲏⲥ.

ϫⲓⲟⲩⲉ *S*, 1 Kg 22 2 ⲟⲩⲟⲛ ⲛⲓⲙ ⲉⲧϫ. (var Mor ⲉⲧ-
ϫⲱⲟⲩⲉ) ⲩ̀ⲡⲟ́ⲭⲣⲉⲱⲥ, prob *l* ⲉⲧϫⲓ ⲉ(ⲟ)ⲩⲱ.

ϫⲟⲟⲩⲉ *S*, ϫⲱⲟⲩⲓ *B*, ⲣⲉϥ- v ϫⲱ 1° **B**.

ϫⲟⲟⲩⲉ *A²* v ϫⲱ 1° **A**.

ϫⲁⲩⲗⲉ *A²* vb intr, *support, bear* or sim, c ϧⲁ-:
ManiK 25 ⲉⲧϫ. ϧⲁⲡϧⲣⲓϣⲉ ⲧⲏⲣⲟⲩ ⲙ̄ⲡⲕⲟⲥⲙⲟⲥ, *ib* P 2
ⲉϥϫ. ϧⲁⲛⲕⲁϧ ϧⲛ̄ⲡⲉϥϭⲓϫ, *ib* K 63]ⲧⲟⲩⲥⲓⲁ ⲙ̄ⲡⲟⲩⲁⲓⲛⲉ
ⲉⲧϫ. ϧⲁⲛⲡⲉ̄ ⲧⲏⲣⲟⲩ.

ϫⲱⲟⲩⲛ *B* v ϭⲱⲟⲩ.

ϫⲁⲩⲛⲓ *F*, ϫⲱⲟⲩⲛⲓ *B* v ϭⲟⲟⲩⲛⲉ.

ϫⲁⲩⲉⲓⲧ *S* nn: Mor 37 174 ⲙ̄ⲙⲉⲗⲟⲥ ⲉⲧⲙ̄ⲙⲁⲩ

(*sc* genital organs) ⲁⲛ ⲡⲉⲧⲟ ⲛ̄ϫ. ⲙ̄ⲡϣⲓⲡⲉ, but knowledge of their potency.   Prob *l* ϫⲁⲩⲙⲟⲉⲓⲧ.

ϫⲟⲟⲩⲧ *S*, ϫⲁⲟⲩⲧ *F* nn, *base, rejected person* or
thing: 2 Cor 13 5 *SF*(*B* = Gk), 2 Tim 3 8 (*B* do), Tit
1 16 (*B* ⲁⲧϣⲁⲩ), ViSitz 172 4 21 ⲛ̄ⲡⲉϧⲣⲉ ⲉⲣⲟⲓ ⲛ̄ϫ.
ⲁⲇⲟ́ⲕⲓⲙⲟⲥ; Sa 2 16 (*B* ϩⲁⲉ) ⲕⲓ́ⲃⲇⲏⲗⲟⲥ; ShA 2 308 ⲡⲁⲓ
ⲡⲁϣⲱⲡⲉ ⲛ̄ϫ. ⲉⲡⲉϧⲟⲩⲟ;   as adj: Ro 1 28 (*B* = Gk)
ⲁⲇ.; Sh(?)Ep 66 ⲟⲩⲥⲟ[ⲟ]ⲩⲛ ⲛ̄ϫ.;   ⲙⲛ̄ⲧϫ.: ShA
2 260 careless in liturgical reading ϧⲛⲟⲩⲙ.;
ⲙⲛ̄ⲧⲣⲉϥϫ.: Z 281 prophet hath rebuked their ⲙ.
(Hab 1 4);   p ϫ.: Z 270 on George of Cappadocia
ⲁϥⲣ. ϧⲓⲧⲡⲓⲥⲧⲓⲥ, ShHT *L* 1 ⲡⲉⲧⲡϧⲣⲏⲧ ⲧⲁⲕⲏⲩⲧ ⲁⲩⲱ
ⲉⲧⲉⲧⲛⲟ ⲛ̄ϫ. ϧⲛ̄ϧⲱⲃ ⲛⲓⲙ.

ϫⲟⲩⲱⲧ *SAF*, ϫⲱⲧ *B*(very rare), ϫⲟⲩⲧ- *SSᵃAA²F*,
ϫⲟⲩⲱⲧ-, ϫⲁⲩ. *S*, ϫⲱⲧ- *S*, ϫⲟⲧ- *SF*, f ϫⲟⲩⲱⲧⲉ *SA²F*,
ϫⲟⲩⲟⲩⲱⲧⲉ *SA²*,(*B* ⲛ̄, literary *S* rare: BIF 14 183) nn,
twenty: Ge 18 31, Hag 2 16 *SA* ⲉⲓ́ⲕⲟⲥⲓ; BM 1113
ⲡⲉⲕϫ. ⲡⲟⲟⲩ, K 67 *B* ϫⲱⲧ · ⲕ̄ (so MSS), CCVa 1 103
ϫⲟⲩⲧ, *ib* 676 عشـر;   adj: Ge 32 14, 2 Kg 9 10, Ac
27 28 ⲉⲓ̈.; BAp 11 ϫ. ⲡϣⲟ, PLond 4 497 ϫ. ⲛ̄ϧⲟⲗⲟⲕ/,
BM 1211 A 7 ϫⲟⲩ(ⲱ)ⲧ ⲛ̄ⲗⲓⲕⲡⲉ, PStras 124 ϫⲉϫⲱⲧ
(*sic*) ⲛ̄ⲙⲟⲩⲉⲓⲁϧ, Kr 11 *F* ϫ. ⲡⲉⲗⲧⲁⲃ̄;   f: ShC 42 158
ⲙⲛⲧⲉ ⲡⲥϧⲓⲙⲉ ⲛ̄ϫ., BHom 106 ϫ. ⲛ̄ⲣⲟⲙⲡⲉ, WS 97 ϫ.
ⲛ̄ⲗⲓⲧⲣⲁ, BM 596 *F* sim, *ib* 1126 ϫⲟⲩⲟⲩ. ⲛ̄ϭⲁⲗⲁϧⲧ,
ManiP 224 *A²* ϫⲟⲩⲟⲩ. ⲛ̄ⲥⲧⲁⲧⲉⲉⲣ, *ib* ϫ.;   constr:
Ep 298 ϫⲟⲩⲱⲧⲟⲩϭⲁ, ST 325 ϫⲟⲩⲧⲟⲩϭⲉ, Jud 10 3 ϫⲟⲩⲧ-
ⲥⲛⲟⲟⲩⲥ, *ib* 2 ϫ. ϣⲟⲙⲧⲉ, Ryl 104 ⲛ̄ϫⲟⲧⲏ̄. a recur-
rent fever(?), PS 102 ϯϫⲟⲩⲧⲁϥⲧⲉ ⲙ̄ⲡⲣⲟⲃⲟⲗⲏ, Ap 11
16 ⲛ̄ϫ.ⲁϥⲧⲉ ⲙ̄ⲡⲣⲉⲥⲃ̄ⲩⲧⲉⲣⲟⲥ, Ep 535 ϫⲟⲩⲱⲧⲁϥⲧⲉ,
Nu 8 24 ϫⲟⲩⲧⲏ ⲛ̄ⲣⲟⲙⲡⲉ, BM 1103 ϫⲱⲧⲏ, KroppK
24 ⲛ̄ϫⲟⲩⲧⲉ ⲙ̄ⲡⲱϧ (ⲗⲟⲟϧ), Jo 6 19 *A²*, BM 1252 *F* ϫⲟⲩⲧⲏ, ManiP 43 *A²* ϫⲟⲩⲧⲉⲥⲉ, Cai 8608 ϫⲟⲧⲁⲥⲉ, Lepsius
Denk 6 103 39 ϫⲁⲩⲱⲧⲥⲁϣϥⲉ, Ep 537 *Sᵃ* ϫⲟⲩⲧⲥⲁϣⲃⲉ,
PLond 4 484 ϫⲟⲩϧⲙⲏⲛ, JSch 2 1 ϫⲱⲧϣⲙⲏⲛ, WS
150 ϫⲧϧⲙⲏⲛⲉ, PLond 4 442 ϫⲟⲩⲧⲯⲓⲥ, 4 Kg 14 2
ϫⲟⲩⲧⲯⲓⲧⲉ ⲛ̄ⲣⲟⲙⲡⲉ;   multiples of *twenty*: JTS
5 556 ϣⲟⲙⲉⲧⲉ ⲛ̄ϫⲟⲧ, El 132 ϣⲉⲙ̄ⲧϫⲟⲩ(ⲱⲧ) = *ib* 96 *A*
ϧⲛ̄ⲧϫ. *sixty*, PSBA 29 194 ϥⲧⲟⲟⲩ ⲛ̄ϫⲟⲩⲱⲧ, BM 1088
ⲃ̄ⲧⲟⲟⲩ ⲛ̄ϫⲟⲩⲱⲧⲉ ⲛⲁⲥⲕⲁⲗⲱⲡⲉ, PMich 6865 ϥⲧⲉⲩ-
ϫⲟⲩⲱⲧ *eighty* (v AZ 33 130), Hall 120 ϯⲟⲩ ⲛ̄ϫⲟⲩⲱ[ⲧ
hundred;   remarkable are BMis 570 ⲧⲁⲓⲟⲩ ϫⲟⲩⲧ-
ⲥⲛⲟⲟⲩⲥ *seventy-two*, BSG 191 ⲧⲁⲓⲟⲩ ϫ. ⲯⲓⲥ *seventy-
nine* (cf ⲧⲁⲓⲟⲩ ⲙⲁϧ);   *twentieth &c day*: BM 1107
ⲥⲟⲩϫⲟⲩⲱⲧ, Z *Deut Paläst Ver* 7 Taf ii ⲥⲟⲩϫⲟⲩⲕ (*sic*)
ⲛ̄ⲡⲁϣⲓⲣ, Hag 2 1 *A* ⲥⲟⲩϫⲟⲩⲧⲉϥⲧⲉ, Ostr Louvre SN
114 ⲥⲟⲩϫⲟⲩ]ⲱⲧⲥⲁϣⲃⲉ ⲛ̄ⲡⲁⲱⲡⲉ, BP 8700 ⲥⲟⲩϫⲟⲩ-
ⲱ(ⲧ)ⲯⲓⲥ;   ordinals: BAp 8 ⲡ̄ⲙⲉϧϫⲟⲩⲱⲧ, R 1 5
45 ⲧ̄ⲙⲉϧϫⲟⲩⲱⲧⲉ, *ib* 14 49 ⲧ̄ⲙⲉϧϥⲧⲟⲩϫⲟⲩⲱⲧⲉ, PS 81
ⲙⲉϧϫⲟⲩⲧⲁϥⲧⲉ, 4 Kg 15 1 ⲧ̄ⲙⲉϧϫⲟⲩⲧⲥⲁϣϥⲉ.

In place-names: ⲛ̄ϫⲟⲧⲏ *F* = ⲭⲱⲣⲓ́ⲟⲛ Ⲉⲓ̈ⲕⲟⲥⲓⲡⲉⲛⲧⲁ-
ⲣⲟⲩ́ⲣⲱⲛ (Kr 47); ⲡⲁⲛϫⲟⲩⲧⲏ (BMOr 6201 A), ⲛⲁⲡ-
ϫⲟⲩⲧⲏ (PMich 6858), طـحـا نشـودي (? *Ṭaha nšodî*, PRosi

Geor 5 224) = χ. Εἴκοσιπ.; ⲡⲉϥⲧⲟⲟⲩ ⲛ̄ϫⲟⲩⲱⲧ (Ryl 158 25).

ϫⲟⲟⲩϥ *S*, ϭⲟⲙϥ, -ⲛϥ *B* nn m, *papyrus*: Job 8 11 *SB*(cit P 44 117 بوص), *ib* 40 16 *SB*, Is 19 6 *SB*-ⲙ̄ϭ πάπυρος; Mor 41 181 *S* magician casts on fire ⲟⲩⲙ ϣⲛⲧⲉ ⲙ̄ⲛⲟⲩϫ & other plants.   *Cf* ⲧⲣⲃⲏⲓⲛ.

ϫⲟⲟⲩϭ *S* vb tr c ⲉⲃⲟⲗ, meaning unknown, relates to preparation of flax: Ann 21 74 ⲙ̄ⲡⲣⲧⲣⲉⲩϭⲁⲗⲉϥ ...delay not, lest it spoil ⲁⲩⲱ ⲛⲧⲭ̄ϫⲟⲟⲩϭϥ ⲕⲁⲗⲱⲥ.

ϫⲉⲩϫ &c *F*   *v* ϭⲓϫ.

ϫⲱⲟⲩϫ *B*   *v* ϭⲱⲟⲩϭ.

ϫⲟⲩϫⲟⲩ *SA²*, ϭⲟⲩϭⲟⲩ *S* vb, *fly* (?) of birds: PMich 601 ⲧⲕⲛ̄ϫⲟⲩϫⲟ[ⲩ] ⲡ(ⲟⲩ)ⲃⲏⲛⲉ, ⲧⲉⲥⲡⲟⲩϫⲉ (-δή) ⲡⲟⲩⲃⲏⲕ, ⲧϭⲓ(ⲡ)ⲙⲟⲟϣⲉ ⲡⲟⲩⲁⲣⲱⲙ, ⲧⲕⲛ̄ⲡⲱⲗ ⲡⲟⲩⲱⲃⲧ̄, P 44 121 ⲛⲣⲁⲗⲁⲁⲧⲉ ⲉⲧⲛⲏⲗ ϩⲓϫⲱⲟⲩ ⲉⲧϭ. في الجدارات السود, ManiP 182 let doves dwell with you ⲛⲥⲉϫ. ⲙ̄ⲡⲉⲧⲛ̄ⲣⲟ, *ib* 158 sim.

ϫϥⲓ *B* vb intr, meaning doubtful: P 54 120 ⲁⲓ-ϫϥⲓ ⲡⲱⲧⲉⲛ بحيّكم, so an adjuration. *Cf* K 493 ϫϥⲓⲉϯ حيا (so ? from ϫϥⲓⲟ).   Hardly related to ϫⲡⲓ-.

ϫϥⲓⲟ *B*   *v* ϫⲡⲓⲟ.

ϫϥⲟ *B*   *v* ϫⲡⲟ.

ϫϥⲟⲓ *B*   *v* ϭⲃⲟⲓ.

ϫⲁϥⲁⲧ *B*   *v* ϭⲁⲡⲉⲧ.

ϫϥⲟⲧ (?), ϫϥⲱⲧ, -ϯ *B* nn m (?), a part of body whereof there are two, *thighs, buttocks, testicles* (?): C 86 219 nails driven ϩⲉⲛⲡⲉϥϫϥⲟⲓ (*l* ϫϥⲟⲧ Hyvernat) ⲃ̄, *ib* nails drawn ⲉⲃⲟⲗ ϩⲉⲛⲡⲉϥϫϥⲱϯ, C 43 131 nails ⲇⲟⲕⲥⲟⲩ (*sic l*) ⲉⲡⲉⲥⲛ̄ⲧ ϩⲉⲛⲡⲉϥϫϥⲱⲧ so that they pierced seat beneath him (TMina *Epima* 10 *S* om. Parallels C 43 11 ⲁⲡⲁⲥⲕⲉⲟⲛ, *ib* 175 ⲥⲟⲓ).

ϫϥⲓⲉϯ *B*   *v* ϫϥⲓ.

ϫϥⲓⲏϯ *B*   *v* ⲡ 577 *b* ϣⲡⲓⲛⲧ.

ϫⲱϥⲉϩ *B*   *v* ϫⲉⲙⲡⲉϩ.

ϫⲁϥⲟⲭⲓ, ϫⲁⲡ. *B* nn m, *spine, vertebrae* (cf ? *bkśw* Dévaud): K 77 ⲡⲓϫ. فقار وهي سلسلة الظهر.

ϫⲉⲭⲁⲥ *B*   *v* ϫⲉⲕⲁⲁⲥ.

ϫⲓϣ *S* nn m, meaning unknown: ShP 130² 75 at Judgment ⲉⲣⲉⲡⲓⲥⲗⲟⲧ ⲉⲧⲥⲁϣⲉ ⲕⲱⲧⲉ ⲉⲣⲟⲕ ⲛ̄ ⲡϲⲟ ⲛ̄ ⲡⲓϫ. ⲱ ⲡⲣⲱⲙⲉ.

ϫⲟϣ *B*   *v* ϭⲱϣ.

ϫⲉϣⲥ *B*   *v* ϫⲉⲥⲥ.

ϫⲟⲩϣⲧ *B*, ϫⲱ. *F*   *v* ϭⲱϣⲧ.

ϫⲟϣϫⲉϣ *B*   *v* ϭⲟϣϭⲉϣ.

ϫⲁϥ *SB*, ϫⲁⲃ *S*, ϫⲉϥ *AA²*, ϫⲉⲃ *F* nn m, *frost*: Ex 16 14 *S*(*B* ⲓⲱϯ ⲉⲁϥϭⲱⲥ), Zech 14 6 *SAB* πάγος, Ge 31 40 *SB*, Bar 2 27 *B* παγετός, Job 38 24 *S*(*B*= Gk), Ps 77 47 *S*(*B* do) πάχνη; Job 37 9 *SB*, Jo 18 18 *SA²*(*B* ϥⲣⲱ), Ac 28 2 *S*(*B* ⲱⲝⲃ) ψῦχος; Va 57 49 *B* ⲉϥⲟϫⲉⲃ ϩⲉⲛⲡⲓϫ. κρυμός; Cant 5 2 *S*(*F* ⲓⲱϯ) ψεκάδες νυκτός; P 44 53 *S* ⲁⲣⲁⲭⲛⲏ (=P 45 116, *l* prob πάχ.)· ⲡⲭ. جَلِيد; BMis 547 *S* ⲡⲭ. *nives*; PS 259 *S* ⲡⲭ. ⲙ̄ⲡⲉⲭⲁⲗⲁⲍⲁ, *ib* 317 *S* from dragon's mouth come ϫ. ⲡⲓⲙ ⲙⲛ̄ϣⲟⲉⲓϣ ⲛⲓⲙ, ShR 2 3 18 *S* naked ϩⲛ̄ⲧⲙⲛ̄ⲧⲉ ⲙ̄ⲡⲭ., R 1 1 71 *S* sim, ShBM 263 *S* ⲕⲃⲟ, ϫ., Sh(?)ViK 9317 *S* ⲁϭⲃⲉⲥ, ⲟⲩⲁⲥϭⲉ, ϫ., Ryl 94 102 *S* ϫ., ⲭⲓⲱⲡ, ⲭⲣⲩⲥⲧⲁⲗⲗⲟⲥ, MG 25 180 *B* ϫ., ϣⲁⲣⲃⲁ, MIE 2 414 *B* ⲕⲁⲙⲁ opp ϫ., Mor 24 25 *F* ϫ. ⲛⲕⲗⲁ= *ib* 23 35 *S* ⲱⲃ̄ ⲛ̄ⲑⲉ ⲙ̄ⲡⲉⲕⲗⲟ *q v*;   ⲙⲁ ⲛ̄ϫ.: BMis 543 *S locum glacie*(*i*);   ⲙⲉⲧϫ. *B*: K 58 برد.

ϫⲁϥ *B* nn, a disease (?): Leip 27 1 father shall ⲉⲣ ϫⲁϥ ϫⲁϥ ⲙⲛ̄ ⲡⲓⲙⲟⲩ & shall die=BMar 17 *S* ⲣ ϣⲟⲩⲙⲛ (*v* ⲙⲛ *s f*, var *Mart Viktor ed* Lemm 25 ⲣ ⲡϣⲟⲩⲁⲙⲁⲙⲉ).

ϫⲉϥ- *S* vb tr, *strike* (?) blow, *v* ⲁϫⲉ.   For ϫⲉ ⲟⲩⲁⲁϫⲉ improbable.

ϫⲏϥ†, p c ϫⲁϥⲓ- *B* vb, *be of kin*: Lev 25 25 ⲉⲧϫ. (*S* ϩⲛ), *ib* ⲉⲧϫ. ϩⲁ⸱ (*S* ϩⲏⲡ) ἀγχιστεύειν ولي, Deu 19 6 ⲉⲧϫ. ϩⲁⲡⲓⲥⲛⲟϥ (*S* ϫⲓ ⲉϩⲟⲩⲛ) ἀγ. τοῦ αἵματος الدم; p c: ϫⲁϥⲓϩⲛⲧ (var ϫⲉϥⲓ-) Nu 5 8 ⲣⲱⲙⲓ ⲛ̄ϫ. (*S* ϩⲏⲡ ⲉϩⲟⲩⲛ) ἀγ. قرابة.

ϫⲏϥ *S* vb qual, meaning unknown: ShA 1 459 (*cf* Z 473) ⲧⲁⲕⲁⲑⲁⲣⲥⲓⲁ [ⲡⲟⲩϩ]ⲁⲗⲏⲧ ⲉⲧⲡⲏⲩ [ⲉⲃⲟ]ⲗ ⲡ̄ϩⲏⲧϥ ⲉ[ϫⲡⲓⲙ]ⲙⲁ ⲉⲧϫ.   *L* ? ϣⲏϥ (Zoega).

ϫⲓϥ *S* nn, *niggard*: Si 14 3 μικρολόγος; R 1 4 29 ⲉⲩϫ. ⲡⲉ, *ib* ⲛ̄ⲥⲟⲡ ⲛ̄ϫ. *parcus*.   *Cf* ? ϫⲁⲃϫⲓⲃ.

ϫⲟⲩϥ *SAA²B*(once), -ⲃ, ϫⲛⲟⲩϥ *S*, ϫⲟϣ *S*(once) *B*, ϫⲉϥ- *SB*, ϫⲟⲩϥ- *A*, ϫⲟϥ- *B*, ϫⲏϥ† *SSᶠA²B*, -ⲃ† *SSᶠ*, p c ϫⲁϥ- *B* vb intr (rare) **I** *burn, scorch*: Is 43 2 *S*(*B* ⲣⲱⲕϩ tr) κατακαίεσθαι; ShC 42 50 *S* ⲟⲩⲡⲗⲏⲛ ⲛ̄ϫⲏ.; qual, *burnt, burning*: Ex 9 9 *B* ἀναζεῖν; PS 321 *S* ⲡⲕⲱⲧ ⲉⲧⲣⲁⲙⲡⲧⲉ ϫ., BMis 198 *S* words ϫ. ⲛ̄ⲑⲉ ⲡⲟⲩⲕⲱⲧ, BKU 1 21 *vo Sᶠ* ϥⲁⲥⲙ ⲉϫⲏ. (*cf* ⲉϥⲣⲱⲭ PMéd 162), OratCyp 93 *Sᶠ* ⲟⲩⲱϣ ⲉⲧϫ., Cat 89 *B* mustard ϭⲝ. ϩⲉⲛⲧⲉⲥⲕⲁⲩⲥⲓⲥ; tr: Va 57 76 *B* surgeon's patients ⲉϥϫ. ⲙ̄ⲙⲟⲩ καίειν, Va 63 102 *B* sim ϫⲟϥ ⲙ̄ϥⲑⲉⲡⲓⲡⲓ, *ib* 103 ⲛ̄ⲧⲁϫⲉϥⲑⲏⲛⲟⲩ ⲁⲛ ⲕ., Pro 6 28 *SA* ϫⲟⲩϥ-, *B*(var ϫⲟϥϫⲉϥ) κατακ.; P 54 116 *B* ϫⲟϥϥ كيّ (*sic* prob); ShC 73 73 *S* ⲡ̄ⲛⲉⲗⲁⲁⲩ ϫⲉϥ ⲕⲱⲣⲧ ⲉⲗⲁⲁⲩ ⲙⲙⲁ (*cf ib* ϫⲉⲣⲉ ⲕ.), ShWess 9 158 *S* ⲉϥϫ. ⲙ̄ⲙⲟⲛ ⲡⲟⲩⲕⲱⲣⲧ, BMis 277 *S* ⲡⲁⲥⲡⲗⲁ ⲛ̄ϫ-

ⲛⲟⲡ ⲉϥϫⲏϥ (sic) ⲙⲙⲟⲕ = Mor 30 56 S⸍ (var ib 29 48
S ⲣⲱⲕϩ ⲙⲙⲟⲓ ⲉⲧⲃⲛⲏⲧⲕ), Cat 40 B mustard ⲉⲧϫ.
ⲟⲩⲟϩ ⲉⲧⲉⲣ ⲥⲧⲩⲫⲓⲛ wounded ; ⲥ ⲉⲃⲟⲗ, flare up :
ST 278 S ⲡⲣⲱⲃ ϫⲉϥ ⲉⲃ. ⲛⲑⲉ ⲙⲡⲕⲱⲣⲧ.

—— nn m SAA²B, burning, ardour : Pro 25 13 SA
ⲕⲁῦⲙⲁ, Ex 21 25 SB ⲕⲁⲧⲁ́ⲕ. ; BMis 148 S fiery river
ⲡⲉϫ. ⲏ ⲡⲉϥⲣⲱⲕϩ, P 129¹⁶ 3 S martyr in red-hot
brazen bull ⲙⲡⲉⲗⲁⲁⲩ ⲛϫ. ϣⲱⲡⲉ ⲙⲙⲟϥ, PMéd 265
S, CR ’87 376 S among maladies, MG 25 394 B & Va
58 77 B ϫⲟⲩϥ ⲩ ⲕⲉⲗⲕⲁ, ManiP 40 A² ⲛϫ. ⲛⲡⲡⲁϩⲣⲉ,
Mor 43 102 S ⲡⲉϫ. ⲉϩⲟⲩⲛ ⲉⲣⲟϥ.

ϫⲓⲛϫ. B, burning : Va 57 76 ⲡⲓⲕⲁⲩⲧⲏⲣⲟⲥ ⲉⲧⲉⲡⲓϫ.
ⲕⲁⲩⲧⲏ́ⲣ.

ϫ. ⲛϩⲏⲧ, be warm at heart, feel warmly : 1 Kg 22 8
S ϫⲏⲃ ⲛϩ. ⲉϩⲣⲁⲓ ⲉϫⲱⲓ ⲡⲟⲛⲉⲓ͂ⲛ ⲡⲉⲣⲓ́ ; as nn m :
Bor 226 159 S pray ϩⲛⲟⲩϫ. ⲡⲟ́ⲛⲟⲥ ⲕⲁⲣⲇⲓ́ⲁⲥ ; Pro 13 4 B
(SA ⲱⲣϫ) ⲉⲡⲓⲙⲉ́ⲗⲉⲓⲁ, cf ib 24 B ; Va 57 71 B repentance ϫⲉⲛⲟⲩϫ. ⲉ̓ⲙⲙⲉ́ⲣⲓⲙⲛⲟⲥ ; Bor 263 24 S passover
eaten ϩⲛⲟⲩϫ., IIL 78 B ⲁⲓϫⲓ ⲣⲟⲟⲩϣ ϫⲉⲛⲟⲩϫ., BMis
5 S wept ϩⲛⲟⲩϫ., Cat 89 B we believe ϫⲉⲛⲟⲩϫ., Mor
44 34 S ϩⲓⲛϫ. ⲙⲡⲉϥϩⲏⲧ ⲉϩⲟⲩⲛ ⲉⲡⲉⲭ̅ⲥ̅, BMis 275
S sim ϫⲟⲩ, Ryl 94 106 S sim ϫⲏ.   p c B, zealous
or sim : Va 68 166 ϫⲁⲩϩ. ⲡⲁⲣⲁⲗ ⲣⲉϥϥⲓ ⲣⲟⲟⲩϣ ⲕⲏⲇⲉⲙⲱ́ⲛ
(prob) ; Cat 150 ⲕⲱϯ ⲛⲥⲱⲟⲩ ϫⲉⲛⲟⲩⲙⲉⲧϫⲁⲩϩ.

II be sharp, bitter : P 44 53 S ⲟⲩϫⲅⲥ· ⲉϥϫⲏⲃ ;
ShMiss 4 284 S food ⲉϥ]ⲙⲟⲗϩ, ⲉϥϩⲁⲃⲟⲧ, ⲉϥϫ.†,
ShIF 151 S ⲡⲁϩⲣⲉ ⲉⲧϫ. ⲏ ⲉⲧⲟⲩⲱⲙ (cf C 42 195 ⲡⲁϩⲣⲉ
ⲡⲓⲃⲉⲟ...ⲡⲉⲧ[ⲛϥ ?]), Mor 16 27 S water ⲉϥϫ.† (var B
Mis 194 ⲁϥⲣ ϩⲙϫ ⲉϥⲥⲁϣⲉ), ib 52 18 S agate ϫ.† ϩⲓ-
ⲧⲉϥϯⲡⲉ like ⲡⲣⲓ͂ⲛⲟⲥ, BMis 193 S ϩⲙϫ ⲉϥϫ.† ⲉϥⲥⲁϣⲉ,
PMéd 291 sim (v note ib 180, but cf Z 627 ϩ. ⲛⲟⲣ-
ⲙⲱⲡ), DeV 245 B ⲉⲣⲙⲱⲟϥⲓ ⲉⲩϫ.†, ManiK 33 A²ϯⲡⲉ
ⲉⲧϫ.†, opp ib ϯⲡⲉ ⲉⲧϩⲁⲗϭ, Aeg 27 S ⲧⲉⲩⲡⲟⲩ ⲉⲧϫ.†
of death.

Cf ϫⲟϥϥ.

ϫⲟⲩϥ S, ϫⲱϥ SB, ϫⲟⲃ F, ϫⲟⲃ⸱ S, ϫⲏϥ† SBF,
ϫⲏⲃ†, ϫⲁϥ† S, ϫⲟϥ B vb intr, be costly, rare : P 131⁴
151 S ⲉⲣⲉⲡⲁⲃⲟⲧ ⲡⲁⲟⲩⲱ ⲧⲡⲁⲩ ⲧⲁⲣⲉⲡⲉⲥⲟⲩⲟ ϫⲱϥ ? (cf
Am 8 5), BM 1103 17 S ⲁⲡⲧⲉⲛⲙⲁ (-ⲏⲙⲁ) ϫⲟⲩϥ ⲉϩⲣⲏ
ϩⲁⲣⲧⲏⲛ ⲡⲧⲃⲱⲕ ⲉⲕϣϣⲡ ⲧⲉⲛⲉⲙⲁ ⲉϥϫ.†, ib 580 20 F
ⲁⲡⲥⲓⲡⲡⲓ (ⲥⲓ́ⲡⲡⲓⲟⲛ) ϫ. ⲕⲁⲗⲱⲥ, ... ϣⲁⲃϫ., TillBau 123
S ⲛⲧⲉⲛⲛⲙⲁ ϫⲉⲁϣⲡⲉ ϣⲁϫ. [ⲛⲁϣ]ⲡⲉ ϣⲁϥⲟⲩⲱⲗⲉ ;
qual : BMis 375 S price not sufficient ϫⲉⲡⲉⲥⲟⲩⲟ
ϫⲁϥ ⲧⲱⲛⲟⲩ = Va 63 7 B ϫⲟϥ = Mor 27 28 F ϫⲏϥ =
BSM 33 B ⲛϫⲱϥ ⲙⲡⲓⲥⲟⲩⲟ = ib 142 ناخ, Mor 43 268
S sold them ⲉⲩϫⲏⲃ ϩⲁⲡⲟϭ ⲛϯⲙⲏ, P 131⁴ l c S grain-
hoarders ⲉⲩⲉϯ ⲉⲃⲟⲗ ⲉϥϫ., Va 58 142 B ϩⲁⲡⲓⲁⲟⲥ
(ⲉⲓ̓ⲇ.) ⲉⲩϯ ⲙⲡⲟⲩⲥⲱⲓⲧ...ⲉⲩϫⲏϥ, Ryl 348 S loaves ϩⲁ
ⲩ̄ ⲁⲇ′ ⲁⲡϣⲏⲧⲟⲩ (l ϭⲡ.) ⲉⲩϫ. ;   tr, value : P 44 49
S ⲡⲁⲧϫⲟⲃⲉϥ ⲁⲗⲟⲩ الذي, Ryl l c ⲉϣⲱⲡⲉ ⲁⲕϫⲟⲃⲉϥ
ϩⲓⲭⲱ[;   as nn m v BSM above.   Cf ? ϫⲓϥ.

ϫⲁϥⲓ- B   v ϫⲏϥ 1°.

ϫⲱ(ⲱ)ϥⲉ   v ϫⲱⲱⲃⲉ.

ϫⲱϥⲓ B nn m, fenugreek : P 54 144, BMOr 8775
133 ⲛⲓϫ. ابله.   Cf ⲧⲓⲗⲓ.

ϫⲟϥⲧⲛ S, ϫⲁ. S⸍, ϭⲟϥⲧⲉⲛ B nn c adverbial ⲛ-,
headlong, over the edge : Lu 4 29 S ⲛⲟϫϥ ⲉⲃⲟⲗ ⲛϫ. (B
ϫⲟⲗⲕϥ ⲉϩⲣⲏⲓ) ⲕⲁⲧⲁⲕⲣⲏⲙⲛⲓ́ⲍⲉⲓⲛ, Mor 17 31 S ⲉⲓⲟⲩⲱϣ
ⲉⲛⲟϫⲧ ⲉⲃ. ⲛϫ. ⲕⲁⲧⲁ̀ ⲕⲣⲏⲙⲛⲟⲩ̂ ⲣⲓ̂ⲯⲁⲓ ; Jo 10 1 B (var
ⲉϭ., SAA² ϩⲓⲕⲉⲥⲁ) ⲁ̓ⲗⲗⲁⲭⲟ́ⲑⲉⲛ ; ShP 131⁷ 33 S slay
thy son or ⲛⲟϫϥ ⲉⲃ. ⲛϫ., Mor 28 218 S⸍ ⲁⲡⲣⲱⲙⲉ ϩⲉ
ⲉⲃⲟⲗ ⲛϫ. = BMOr 4723 53 اسفل الى ;   ϩⲓ ϭ. ⲉϩⲣⲏⲓ
B, leap over : Va 61 22 made as if to ϩⲓ ϭ. ⲉ. ⲡⲥⲁϯ-
ⲭⲟⲓ ⲉ̓ⲡⲓ̀ ⲧ. ⲧⲟⲓ̂ⲭⲟⲛ ⲥⲕⲁⲗⲁⲃⲁⲧⲁ̂ⲛ (sic ?).   Cf ? ṯ f jdnw
(Erman in Lange Amenemope 66).

ϫⲁϥϫⲓϥ B   v ϭⲁϫⲓϥ.

ϫⲟϥϥ, ϫⲟⲃϫⲃ S, ϫⲟϥϫⲉϥ, ϫⲉϥϫⲱϥ⸱ SB, ϫⲃ-
ϫⲱⲃ⸱ F, ϫⲉϥϫⲱϥ† SB vb intr, burn, cook : Va 57 206 B
ⲣⲟⲕϥ ϫⲉⲛⲟⲩⲭⲣⲱⲙ ⲡⲧⲉϥ. & become ashes ⲕⲁⲧⲁ-
ⲕⲁⲓ́ⲉⲓⲛ, Ps 50 18 B ϫⲗⲓⲗ ⲛϫ. (S ϭⲗⲓⲗ only) ⲟ̔ⲗⲟⲕⲁⲩ́-
ⲧⲱⲙⲁ, Z 331 S ϣⲁϫ. ⲛⲥⲉⲣⲱⲕϩ ⲡⲉⲣⲓⲫⲗⲉ́ⲅⲉⲓⲛ ; P 131¹
16 S ⲁϥⲧⲣⲉ(ⲡⲉ)ⲡⲓⲃⲟⲩⲗⲟⲥ ϫⲟⲃ. ϩⲓⲧⲙⲡⲉϥⲑⲟⲛⲟⲥ, C
43 59 B ⲉⲣⲉⲧⲉⲛϫ. in hell ;   qual (mostly B) : Deu
29 23 (S ⲣⲟⲕϩ) ⲕⲁⲧⲁⲕ. ; Nu 6 19 (S = Gk) ⲉ̔ⲯⲉⲓⲛ ; Ex
12 9 (S ϭⲏⲥ) ⲟ̓ⲡⲧⲁ̂ⲛ, Lu 24 42 (S do) ⲟ̓ⲡⲧⲟ́ⲥ ; MG 25
394 ⲟⲩϣⲉ ⲉϫϫ. = Gött ar 114 143 جمر ; P 131³ 84
S lips ϫ. ϩⲓⲧⲙⲡϣⲁϩ = Va 61 94 B, C 86 172 ⲁⲗⲱⲙ
ⲉϫϫ. ;   tr : Deu 16 7 B (var BM 787 ϫⲉϥϫⲱϥ(ϥ),
S ϭⲱϭ), Is 44 16 B (S do) ⲟ̓ⲡⲧⲁ̂ⲛ ; Lev 6 10 B (S ⲧⲱϭ)
ⲡⲉ́ⲥⲥⲉⲓⲛ ; Bor 295 99 S ⲡⲧⲁⲩⲡⲉⲥ ⲡⲉⲥⲟⲟⲩ ⲁⲛ ⲁⲗⲗⲁ
ⲡⲧⲁⲩϫⲉⲃϫⲟϥϥ (cf Ex 12 9 S ϭ.), Mor 51 21 S ⲁϥ
ⲛⲣⲓⲣ ϫⲉϥϫⲱϥ(ϥ), AZ 23 115 S ⲛⲡⲡⲁϩⲣⲉ...ϫⲉϥϫⲟⲃ-
ⲟⲩ, BKU 1 26 (8117) F [ⲛ]ⲉⲭⲁⲓⲧ (sic l) ⲉⲡⲁⲗⲉⲕⲧⲱⲣ
ϫⲃϫⲱⲃⲟⲩ ;   as nn m S : Z 302 demon could not
suffer ⲛϫ. ⲙⲡⲉⲑⲃⲃⲓⲟ ⲡⲩ́ⲣⲱⲥⲓⲥ.

Cf ϫⲟⲩϥ 1°.

(ϫⲱϩ) A   v ϫⲱϩ smear.

ϫϩⲟⲩ A vb intr, meaning uncertain : Cl 25 4
phœnix having kindled altar ⲁϥϣⲁϫ. ϫⲉ ⲁⲟⲩ ϥⲣ
ⲉⲧⲛⲓϩ.

ϫⲱϩⲙⲉ A   v ϫⲱϩⲙ.

ϫⲁϩϫϩ A   v ϭⲟϣϭϣ.

ϫⲁϩ A nn, dissoluteness : 2 Mac 6 4 ⲙⲛⲧϫ. ⲁ̓ⲥⲱⲧⲓ́ⲁ
(elsewhere S ⲙⲛⲧϣⲛⲁ).

ϫⲓϩ S nn m, spittle : 1 Kg 21 13 ⲡⲉϥϫ., Is 40 15
(B ⲑⲁϥ) ⲥⲓ́ⲉⲗⲟⲥ ; ShZ 595 ϣⲟⲉⲓϣ, ϫ., ϩⲃⲏⲧⲉ, ShIF
200 ⲡⲉϥϫ. ⲉⲧⲟϣ ⲡⲧⲁϣϣⲟⲩⲟ ⲉⲃⲟⲗ ϩⲓⲣⲱϥ, BHom
122 babe’s mouth ⲡⲛⲓϣ ⲛϫ. ϩⲓⲉⲓⲧⲛ, cf BMar 84 (same
text), Ora 4 22 ⲉⲣⲁϥ (= ⲣⲟⲟⲩ) ϩⲁϫ., ib ⲁϥⲣⲟⲕ ϩⲁϫ.?
In name (?) : Παπϫⲓϩ (PCai 2 74).

ϫⲱϧ *SAA²FO,* -ϧⲉ *S*(once), ϭⲟϧ *B,* ϧⲟϧ *SF*(once each), ϫⲉϧ- *SF*(do), ϫⲏϧ† *S* vb intr, *touch* (*B* mostly ϭⲓⲛⲉⲙ-), c ⲉ- as obj: Ge 3 3 *SB,* Job 5 19 *SB,* EpJer 28 *BF* ϫⲟϧ, Hag 2 13 *SA,* Mt 14 36 *SBF,* Jo 20 17 *SA²,* AP 14 *A²* ἅπτεσθαι, Va 58 124 *B* ⲁϥ̄ϫ. ⲉⲛⲉⲡϭⲁⲗⲁϫ ⲉϥⲁⲡ.; Lu 11 46 προσψαύειν; Ez 9 6 *B* ἐγγίζειν, Nu 27 11 (*B* ϩⲉⲛⲧ) ἔγγιστα; BMar 114 could not ϫ. ⲉⲣⲟⲥ πλησιάζειν; Ac 10 28 (*B* ⲧⲱⲙ) κολλᾶσθαι; Jo 4 9 *S*(var & *F* ⲧⲱϧ, *B* ⲙⲟⲩϫⲧ)*A²* συγχρᾶσθαι; Aeg 285 συμμολύνεσθαι; MartIgn 879 *B* ⲙⲡⲟⲩϭ. ⲉⲡⲉϥⲥⲁⲣⲝ θιγγάνειν; PS 240 fire ⲛⲁϫ.ⲉⲣⲟϥ ⲁⲛ, TMina*Epima* 8 to martyr ⲕⲟⲩⲱϣ ⲛⲧⲛϫ. ⲉⲡⲉⲕⲥⲁⲣⲝ ? = C 43 129 *B* ⲧⲁⲕⲟ, BMis 265 ⲁϥⲭⲱⲣⲉ ⲉⲡⲁⲥⲱⲙⲁ (var Mor 29 35 ϫⲉϧ ⲧⲉϥϭⲓⲝ ϧⲓⲡⲁⲥ.) = Mor 30 41 *F* ϫⲉ(ϧ) ⲧⲉϥϭⲓⲝ ϧⲙ-, Wess 18 62 ⲙⲡⲉⲕⲉϧⲟⲟⲩⲧ ϫ. ⲉⲣⲟⲓ (var Mor 19 54 ⲥⲟⲩⲱⲡⲧ), RE 9 146 ⲙⲡⲓϫ. ⲉⲣⲟⲥ ϧⲓⲟⲩⲡⲁⲑⲟⲥ, MG 25 356 *B* one of 3 temptations ⲡⲓⲁⲣⲏⲟⲩ ⲉϧ. ⲉⲣⲟϥ (but Gött ar 114 126 المأخذة الصاحب, ROC 18 58 واطّل جلّ), BM 351 34 by marrying niece ⲁⲕϫ. ⲉⲛⲉϭⲃⲟⲓ ⲛⲧⲉⲕⲥⲱⲛⲉ = Miss 4 320 نست اعنال; ShC 73 169 ⲡⲉⲧⲛⲁϫ. ⲉⲡⲉⲧⲣⲓⲧⲟⲩⲱϥ ... ϧⲓⲟⲩ(ⲟⲩ)ⲱϣ ⲉϥϩⲟⲟⲩ, C 41 39 *B* ⲁⲩϭ. ⲉⲟⲩⲣⲟ = Miss 4 242 *S* ⲧⲱϩⲛ, R 1 3 37 ⲁϥϫ. ⲉⲡⲁϩⲏⲧ, Hor 84 *O* ϫ. ⲁⲣⲁϥ, J 66 56 ⲉⲧⲡⲁⲡⲁⲣⲁⲃⲁ ⲛⲧⲁⲇⲓⲁⲑⲏⲕⲏ ⲏ ⲛϥϫ. ⲉⲣⲟⲥ ϧⲟⲗⲟⲥ; ⲉ-ϧⲟⲩⲛ ⲉ-: Leyd 469 cannot approach ⲟⲩⲇⲉ ϫ. ⲉ. ⲉⲡⲧⲟⲡⲟⲥ (or ? *l* ϫⲱⲧϧ), J 52 20 any man ⲉϥϫ.† ⲉ. ⲉⲡⲁⲧⲉⲛⲟⲥ; c ⲛ- dat: Kr 50 what shall result ⲉϥϫⲟϧ ⲛⲡⲉⲩⲟⲓⲉ; c ⲛⲉⲙ-: BodlMarsh 24 *B* art charged ⲉϧ. ⲛⲉⲙⲡⲏ ⲉⲑⲟⲩⲁⲃ ⲛⲥⲕⲉⲟⲥ; c ⲛⲥⲁ-: BMis 261 ⲁⲡⲟⲩ̄ϫ (sc ox) ϫ. ⲛⲥⲁⲡⲟⲩ̄ϫ; c ϧⲛ-, ⲉⲃⲟⲗ ϧⲉⲛ-: ShC 73 119 beguile us ⲉⲧⲣⲉⲛϫ. ⲏ ⲉⲧⲣⲉⲛⲧⲱⲡⲉ ϧⲓⲛⲁⲓ, CDan 92 *B* ⲉⲩϫⲟϧ ⲉⲃ. ⲛϧⲏⲧⲥ (*l* ? ϭⲟ, Pereira *Abba Daniel* 449 ϫⲩ-ⲛ).

tr: Job 6 9 *B*(*S* diff) τιτρώσκειν; BMis 246 *S* ⲙⲡⲉⲡⲕⲱⲧ ϫ. ⲙⲙⲟⲟⲩ (var Z 263 ⲉⲣⲟⲟⲩ); c ⲉ-: Blake 236 *S* ϫ. ⲙⲙⲟϥ ⲉϧⲉⲛⲙⲁ ⲉϥⲧⲓ ⲧⲕⲁⲥ.

—— nn m, *touching, contagion*: Lev 13 31 *B*(*S* ϧⲣⲃ), Deu 17 8 *B*(*S* ⲙⲛⲧⲗⲁ) ἁφή; J 5 45 *S* ⲟⲩ̄ϫⲉ ϫ. ⲟⲩ̄ϫⲉ ϫ. ⲛϫ. kinsman, near or distant, ib 37 61 ϣⲏⲣⲉ, ⲕⲗⲏⲣⲟⲛⲟⲙⲟⲥ, ϫ., ϫ. ⲛϫ., ViK 4912 *S* ϧⲡⲛⲁϧ (sic) ⲏ [ϩ]ⲛⲛⲉⲧⲏⲡ ⲉⲣⲟⲓ ⲕⲁⲧⲁ ⲃⲁⲑⲙⲟⲥ ⲛⲓⲙ ⲛⲥⲩⲅⲅⲉⲛⲓⲁ.

ⲁⲧϫ., *untouchable*: P 44 49 *S* ⲁⲡⲁⲫ (? ἄναπτος)· ⲡⲓⲁⲧϫ. ⲉⲣⲟϥ.

ϫⲱϧ, ϫⲉϧ- *S,* ϫⲁϧ- *Sᶠ,* ϫⲁϧ⸗ *S,* ϫⲁϧ⸗ *A,* ϫⲏϧ† *SA²*(?), -ϧ† *A,* ϭⲉϧ† *B* vb intr, *smear, anoint* (*cf* טוח Dévaud): Ez 13 12 (*B* ⲱⲙϫ) ἀλείφειν; qual: Job 33 24 (*B* do) ἀλοιφή; Pro 21 9 *SA,* Mt 23 27 (*B* ⲟⲩϫ ⲡⲕⲟⲛⲓⲁ) κονιᾶν; Si 22 18 *SAB* ξυστός; P 54 174 *B* ⲉⲥϭ. ذاشه; Mani P 220 *A²* tombs ⲉⲧϫ[; tr: Ez 13 10 (*B* ⲑⲱϧⲥ) ἀλ., Jo 9 11 (*A²* ⲥⲱⲗϭ, *B* ⲗⲁⲗⲉ) χρίειν; LAp 368 blood ϫⲉϧ ⲛϥⲧⲏⲛ πυτίζειν εἰς; BMis 199 ϫ. ⲡⲛⲉⲟⲅⲉϧⲣⲟ (var Mor 16 38 ⲥⲱⲗϭ ⲉ-), Mor 40 25 ϫⲉϧ ⲡⲉϥⲣⲟ = C 43 55 *B* ϣⲟϭⲟ ⲉϫⲉⲛ-.

With following preposition or adverb.   c ⲉ-, *upon*: Jo 9 6 (*A²* c., *B* λ.) ἐπιχ. ἐπί; Miss 8 216 ⲡⲉϥⲥⲛⲟϥ ϫ. ⲉⲛⲉⲡⲗⲁⲧⲓⲁ, BMis 200 ⲛⲧⲁⲩϫⲉϧ ⲡⲉϥⲥⲛⲟϥ ⲉⲟⲩ?, ib 3 ⲡⲥⲛⲟϥ ϫ.† ⲉⲣⲟϥ, HM 16 ⲡⲥⲛⲟϥ ϫ. ⲉⲣⲟⲟⲩ (sc paving-stones), Mor 55 104 ϫⲁϧ (sc clay) ⲉⲛⲃⲁⲗ;   c ⲛ-, *with*: Ex 2 3 *A* ϫⲁϧⲥ (sic Sdff) ⲛⲁⲙⲡⲣⲏⲉ (*B* ⲱ. ⲛ-), Sa 13 14 κατάχ. dat; Ge 6 14 (*B* ϯ ⲛ-) ἀσφαλτοῦν; Deu 27 2 (*B* ⲱ.) κονιάζειν dat; BAp 69 ϫⲉϧ ⲡⲭⲟ ⲛⲕⲟⲛⲓⲁ, AZ 23 109 bottle ϫⲁϧⲥ ⲉⲡⲟⲙⲉ (*cf* 108 ⲥⲟⲗϭⲥ), PBad 5 410 *Sᶠ* images ϫⲁϧ ⲡⲉⲩⲣⲁ (ⲛ)ⲱⲣⲟ;   c ϧⲛ-: Sa 15 4 ϫ.† ϩⲣⲉⲛⲁⲅⲁⲛ σπιλοῦσθαι dat; BMis 4 ϫ.† ϧⲛⲡⲉϥⲥⲛⲟϥ;   c ϧⲓⲃⲟⲗ: Miss 4 699 tombs ⲉⲧϫ.† ϧ., Z 613 ϫⲁϧⲥ ⲛⲧⲁⲣⲧ ϧ.

—— nn: Ez 13 12 (*B* ⲱ.) ἀλοιφή; ShP 130² 96 ϧⲉⲛⲕⲱⲧ ϧⲉⲛϣⲟⲣϣⲣ ⲙⲛϫⲉⲛϫ.

ϫⲟⲩϧⲉ *S,* ϭⲟⲩⲓ *B*(once) vb intr, *limp, halt*: He 12 13 (*B* ⲙⲉⲧϭⲁⲗⲉ) χωλός, 1 Kg 17 39 v ϫⲱϧⲁϧ; P 43 50 ⲕⲟⲧⲥⲟⲓ (ⲕⲟⲧϫⲟⲥ)· ⲡⲉⲧϫ. (var 44 79 ϣⲟⲩϫⲉ) زمن. c ⲉ-: 3 Kg 18 21 (P 131¹ 80) ϫ. ⲉⲧⲉⲧⲛⲟⲩⲉⲣⲏⲧⲉ χωλαίνειν ἐπί;   c ⲉϫⲛ-: ib (Miss 8 169);   c ϧⲓ-: ib (ShWess 9 139);   c ϧⲓϫⲛ-: ib (Bor 226 174); c ⲛ-: BMis 452 ⲉϥϫ. ⲛⲧⲉϥⲟⲩⲣⲏⲛⲧⲉ; c ϧⲛ-, ϫⲉⲛ-: BM 185 ⲛⲛϫ. ϧⲛⲛⲉⲕⲗⲟⲧⲓⲥⲙⲟⲥ, Va 61 19 *B* ⲉⲧϭ. sim.

ϫⲁϧⲗ *F* v ϫⲱⲗϧ *draw.*

ϫⲁϧⲗⲉ *S* nn f, meaning unknown: Ryl 243 37 among metal utensils ⲥⲛⲓⲧⲉ ⲛϫ. For ? ϫⲁⲗϧⲉ.

ϫϧⲙ *S* nn with ⲣ-, *be left, neglected*: Pro 24 46 (*A* om) ἐκλελειμμένος γίνεσθαι.

ϫⲱϧⲙ *SA²*(AP), -ϧⲙⲉ *A,* -ϧⲙⲉ *A²*(Ma), ϭⲱϫⲉⲙ *B,* ϫⲉϧⲙ- *S,* ϭⲁϫⲉⲙ- *B*(once), ϫⲁϧⲙ⸗ *SA²,* -ϧⲙ⸗ *A,* ϭⲁϫⲙ⸗ *B,* ϫⲁϧⲙ† *SA²,* -ϧⲙⲉ† *A,* -ϧⲙⲉ† *S*(once) *A²*(Ma), ϭⲁϫⲉⲙ† *B,* ϫⲉϧ(ⲉ)ⲙ† *F* vb I intr, *be defiled*: Deu 24 4 *S*(*B* ⲥⲱϥ), Ez 7 24 *SB,* Hos 6 10 *AB,* He 12 15 *B*(*S* ⲥⲱⲱϥ) μιαίνεσθαι; Pro 19 19 *SA* λοιμεύεσθαι; 1 Cor 8 7 *B*(*S* ⲧⲱⲗⲙ) μολύνεσθαι; Jer 3 2 *B* ἐκφύρεσθαι; Jud 2 19 *S* διαφθείρειν; Ap 22 11 *S*(*B* ⲑⲱⲗⲉⲃ) ῥυποῦσθαι; BHom 29 *S* ⲡⲥⲱⲙⲁ ϫ. σπιλοῦσθαι; Deu 32 5 *S*(*B* ⲙⲉϧ ⲡⲁϧⲛⲓ) μωμητός; ShA 1 286 *S* ⲛϣⲏⲣⲉ ⲉⲛⲧⲁⲩϫ., ShC 73 48 *S* ⲡϧⲏⲧ ⲙⲡⲣⲱⲙⲉ ϫ., CA 113 *S* enter brothel ⲉϫ., ManiH 23 *A²* ⲉϥⲟⲩⲁⲃⲉ ϥⲧⲙ̄ϫ., Miss 4 105 *B* ⲡⲛⲉⲡⲟⲩⲙⲁϣϫ ϭ.; qual: Lev 10 10 *SB,* Lam 4 15 *BF*(*S* = Gk), Am 7 17 *SA* -ϧⲙⲉ *B,* 1 Cor 7 14 *B*(*SF* = Gk) ἀκάθαρτος; Mk 7 5 *S*(*B* ⲑⲱⲗⲉⲃ), He 10 29 *SBF*(Mus 49 203) κοινός, ib 9 13 *SBF* κοινοῦσθαι; Lev 21 14 *S*(*B* ⲥⲱϥ), Ps 9 26 *B*(*S* ⲥⲱϧϥ) βεβηλοῦν; Sa 12 4 *S,* BMar 127 *S* Hadrian ⲡⲉⲧϫ., AP 15 *A²* ⲧⲉⲉⲓⲕⲣⲓⲥⲓⲥ ϫ. ἀνόσιος; 2 Pet 2 13 *S*(*B* ⲑⲱⲗⲉⲃ) μῶμος; Cl 1 1 *A* -ϧⲙⲉ μιαρός, Va 66 308 *B* ⲛⲭⲁⲓ ⲉⲧϭ. μίασμα; Is 30 22 *F*(*SB* diff) ἀποκαθῆσθαι, Deu 7 26 *S*(*B* = Gk) ἀνάθεμα εἶναι

ⲕⲣⲟⲙ; 2 Kg 3 29 S γονορρυής; 1 Cor 8 12 F(var ϣⲱⲡⲓ as SB Gk), BG 82 S ⲧⲧⲣⲓⲃⲏ ⲉⲧϫⲁϧⲙⲉ (106 sim -ϧⲙ), ShP 131⁵ 71 S ⲕⲁϧ ⲉϥⲥⲟⲧⲡ ... ⲕⲁϧ ⲉϥϫ., Aeg 264 S ⲡⲧⲉⲧϧϫ. ⲁⲡ, Mani 2 A² ⲧⲣⲟⲫⲁⲅⲉ ⲉⲅϫ., DeV 2 93 B ⲉⲡⲓⲑⲩⲙⲓⲁ ⲉⲧϭ., C 86 204 B ⲉⲧϭ. ⲟⲩⲟϧ ⲉⲧⲥⲟϥ, Mor 30 32 F ⲧⲁⲡⲣⲁ ⲉⲧϫ.

II tr, *defile, pollute*: Ge 34 5 S(B c.), Lev 13 3 SB, Aeg 232 S ⲡⲁϣ ϫⲁϧⲙⲉϥ ⲁⲡ μιαί.; Ps 88 32 B(S ⲥⲱϧϥ), Ac 24 6 S(B c.) βεβ.; Mk 7 15 S(B do) κοινοῦν; Ez 23 11 SB διαφθ.; Va 58 125 B ϭ. ⲙⲡⲉⲕⲉⲣⲫⲉⲓ ⲥⲡⲓⲗ.; Zech 14 2 SAB μολ.; BG 62 S ⲁϥϫⲁϧⲙⲉⲥ & begat son, ShC 73 40 S ϫⲉϧⲙ ⲡⲁⲥⲱⲙⲁ, Mor 19 53 S ϫ. ⲡⲧⲁⲥⲱⲫⲣⲟⲥⲩⲛⲏ (var Wess 18 62 ⲥⲟⲟϥ), Mani P 69 A² ⲡⲉⲓ ⲉⲧϫ. ⲙⲙⲁⲓ, C 43 201 B ⲡⲥⲟϩⲓ...ϭ. ⲙⲡⲓⲁⲏⲣ, BSM 89 B ⲙⲡⲉⲧⲁⲙⲟⲥ ... ϭⲁϧⲉⲙ ⲣⲱⲙⲓ = BMis 180 S.

With following preposition. c ⲉ-obj: Ez 16 25 SB λυμαίνεσθαι; MR 4 73 S ⲙⲡⲣϫⲱⲣ(ⲙ) ⲉⲡⲙⲁ = Miss 4 137 B ϧⲓ ⲁϧⲛⲓ = Gött ar 114 56 ⲛⲥⲓⲛ, BP 12489 S ordinands ⲉⲧϫⲱⲣ(ⲙ?) ⲉⲡⲉⲅⲙⲁ ⲡⲓⲕⲟⲧⲕ during Lent (cf CO 30 ⲣⲟⲉⲓⲥ); c ⲉϫⲡ-: Nu 5 2† S(B = Gk) ἀκάθ. ἐπί; ⲉϧⲣⲏⲓ ⲉϫ.; ib 6 9 B(S om) μι. ἐπί; c ⲙⲡ-, ⲡⲉⲙ-: Aeg 282 S ϫ. ⲙⲙⲟⲥ ⲙⲡⲣⲉⲡⲕⲟⲟⲅⲉ ⲁⲥⲉⲗ-γαίνειν πρός; ShR 2 3 10 S ⲁϥϫⲁϧⲙⲉϥ ⲙⲡⲟⲩⲧⲃⲏⲓ, C 43 187 B ⲙⲡⲓϭ. ⲙⲡⲁⲥⲱⲙⲁ ⲡⲉⲙⲟⲩⲣⲱⲙⲓ; c ⲡ-, *with*: Ez 7 17 B(S ⲧⲱⲗⲙ) μολ. gen; c ⲡⲧⲉⲡ-: Ro 14 14† BF(Mus 49 199, S ⲥⲟⲟϥ) κοινός dat; c ϧⲡ-, ϭⲉⲡ-: Nu 6 7 B(S ⲥⲱⲱϥ ⲉϧⲣⲁⲓ ⲉϫⲡ-) μι. ἐπί; Ez 20 30 B(S ϧⲣⲁⲓ ϧⲡ-) μι. ἐν; Ps 13 1 B(S ⲥⲱⲱϥ) βδελύσσεσθαι ἐν; Mich 550 31 S ϫ. ϧⲡⲟⲩⲙⲏⲧⲡⲟⲉⲓⲕ ῥυποῦν ὑπό; Mani P 86 A² ϫⲁϧⲙⲉϥ (sc tongue) ϧⲡ-ⲡⲭⲉⲟⲩⲁ, AM 70 B ϭ. ⲙⲡⲓⲕⲁⲣⲓ ... ϧⲉⲡⲡⲓⲟⲩⲥⲓⲁ; ⲡϧⲣⲏⲓ ϧⲉⲡ-: Ez 23 17 B(S ϧⲡ-) μι. ἐν; ⲉϧⲣⲏⲓ ϧⲉⲡ-: ib 30 B(S ϧⲣⲁⲓ ϧ.) do; ⲉⲃⲟⲗ ϧⲡ- S: Eccl 7 19 (F ⲱⲣⲉⲃ ⲡⲥⲁ-) μι. ἀπό; PS 299 ϫ. ⲉⲃ. ϧⲛⲟⲩⲗⲏ; c ϧⲓⲧⲡ-: Ez 36 17 S(B ϧⲓ-) μι. ἐν; Mich 550 31 S ⲁⲡⲉϥ-ϧⲏⲧ ϫ. ϧ. ⲡⲁⲓ = Va 63 95 B ϭⲉⲡ-; ⲉⲃⲟⲗ ϧ.: Ro 14 14† B(S ⲥⲟⲟϥ ϧⲁ-) κοι. διά.

—— nn m SAA²B, *uncleanness, pollution*: Lev 18 19 B(S = Gk), Mic 2 10 SAB, 2 Cor 12 21 B(SF = Gk), AP 10 A² ἀκαθαρσία; Ac 15 20 S(B diff) ἀλί-σγημα; Ro 13 13 S(B ⲥⲱϥ) ἀσέλγεια; Lev 7 8 S(B ⲱⲣⲉⲃ), Jth 13 16 S μίασμα; Job 11 15 B(S ⲧⲱⲗⲙ) ῥύπος; Eph 5 27 S(B ⲁϭⲡⲓ) σπίλος; Lev 12 2 B(S ϣⲣⲱ) ἄφεδρος; BG 135 S ⲟⲩϭⲱⲱϥ ⲙⲡⲟⲩϫ., Mun 152 S given over to ⲡϫ. ϫⲓⲛⲉⲩⲣⲡⲗⲏⲧⲉ ⲡⲣⲟⲗⲡⲉ, BMis 542 S defiled ⲙⲡⲁⲧⲟⲩⲣ ⲧⲏ ⲙⲡϫ., Mani P 206 A² ⲡⲁϫ ⲡⲟⲩϫ. ⲁⲃⲁⲗ, C 43 21 B ϭ. ⲡⲡⲱⲓⲕ; as adj: Mani K 175 A² ⲙⲟⲩ ⲡϫ. from wounds.

ⲁⲧϫ., -ϭ. SA²B, *undefiled*: 1 Pet 1 4 B(S ⲁⲧⲧⲁⲕⲟ) ἀμίαντος; Ep 592 A S ⲃⲓⲟⲥ ⲡⲁ. ἄχραντος; Br 262 S ⲡⲁⲧⲟⲩⲗⲏ, ⲡⲁ., ⲡⲁⲧϣⲁⲭⲉ, Mani P 61 A² ⲡⲣⲓⲉ ⲡⲁ. ⲣⲉϥϫ., *defiled person*: TstAb 259 B.

ϫⲁϧⲛⲓ B nn f, *baking-oven*: K 132 ϯϫ. طابونة. Cf HA Winkler *Volkskunde* 127.

ϫⲁϧⲧ B, BMOr 8775 118 = ⲙϫⲁϧⲧ.

ϫⲁϧⲁⲟⲩϫⲉⲓ S nn, meaning unknown: BP 9109 among metal utensils ⲕⲉⲣⲁⲡⲧⲏⲥ, ⲙⲟⲅⲓ, ϫ., ⲉⲣ-ⲙⲟⲩⲧⲉ.

ϫϧⲁϧ S nn m, meaning unknown: ST 383 ⲁ-ⲡⲉϥϫϧⲁϧ · [(context lost).

ϫⲁϧϫ¹ S, -ϫⲉϧ B(once), ϫⲁϧ² SB, ϫⲁϧϭ³ S, ϫⲁϫ⁴ SB, ϫⲁⲗϫⲉϧ⁵(?) B, ϭⲁϧϫ⁶, ϭⲁϧϭ(ⲉ)ϧ⁷, ϭⲟϧ.⁸, ϭⲁϧ⁹, ϭⲟϧϭ¹⁰, ϫⲉϫⲱϧϫ S vb tr, *strike, gnash*: BIF 37 57 S ⲕϫ.⁴ ⲡⲡⲥⲱ κόπτειν; P 131⁵ 80 S ⲁϫ.¹ ⲡⲡⲉⲅ-ϭⲓϫ, Mor 38 61 S ⲉϥϫ.³ ⲡⲡⲉϥⲟⲃϧⲉ, BHom 10 S ⲉⲡ-ϣⲁⲡϭ.⁸ ⲡⲡⲉⲡⲟⲃϧⲉ; With following preposition or adverb. c ⲉ-: BKU 1 2 S ⲁϧϫ.² ⲡⲡⲉϥϭⲉⲣⲟϥ ⲉⲡ-ⲕⲁϧ; c ⲉϫⲡ-: Ez 22 13 S¹(B ⲕⲱⲗϧ) πατάσσειν πρός; P 129¹⁶ 17 S ⲁϫ.¹ ⲡⲡⲉϥϭⲓϫ ⲉ. ⲡⲉϫⲉⲣⲏⲩ, Mor 31 24 S sim ϧⲟϫϧⲉⲭ (sic); c ϧⲓϫⲡ-: Mor 28 132 S ⲁϫ.² ⲡⲡⲉϥϭⲓϫ ϧ. ⲡⲉϫⲉⲣⲏⲩ (var P 129¹⁶ ut sup); c ϧⲡ-: Ez 21 14 S¹(var ϫⲁⲕ ⲡ-, B ⲕ.) κροτεῖν χεῖρα ἐπί χ. ROC 20 50 S singers ⲉⲧϫ.² ϧⲣⲡⲉⲡⲃⲁⲕⲗⲉ (-λον), Mor 52 15 S ϣⲁϥϫⲉⲣϫⲱϧϥ (sc anthrax) ϧⲙⲡϧⲁⲧⲏⲣ; c ⲉⲃⲟⲗ: Bodl(P) a 2 2 recipe ⲉⲡⲧⲩ ⲉⲃⲟⲗ ϫⲉϫⲱϧϧ ⲉⲃ.

—— nn m, *beating, gnashing*: Hab 2 19 B² ἔλασμα; Lu 13 28 S⁸(varr² ³ ⁷ ¹⁰), Mt 8 12 S⁷(varr² ⁹), ib 13 42 S⁶(var⁷), ib 22 13 S⁷(var⁴), ib 24 51 S⁷(var¹, all B ϭⲟⲉⲣ-ⲧⲉⲣ) βρυγμός; PS 259 S ⲡϭ.⁷, BHom 5 S⁷(cf ib above⁸), MIF 9 46 S², ShMus 45 31 B ⲡϫ.⁵ ⲡⲟⲃⲓ {var ϫⲁϫϫⲉϧ); as adj, *beaten*: Nu 10 2 S¹(var²)B²(var⁴), Ps 97 6 S¹(but B ϭⲱⲣⲉⲙ), Si 50 17 S¹ ἐλατός; ib 9 S² ὁλοσφύρητος; Job 42 11 S¹(var², B diff) ἄσημος; ShViK 934 222 S ϧⲡⲟ ⲡϫ.¹ ⲙⲡⲥⲁ ⲡⲣⲟⲙⲧ, R 1 3 39 S trumpets ⲡⲡⲟⲩⲃ ⲡϫ.², ib 50¹(same MS); hence *re-fined, pure*: P 44 21 S¹ ابريز خالص (cf TThe 59 B ⲉⲧ-ⲧⲟⲩⲃⲏⲟⲩⲧ), P 43 31 S ⲡⲟⲩⲃ ⲡϫ.⁴ مصفّى; Dif 1 16 B⁴ ⲋ.

ϫⲁϫ S, ϫⲉϫ AF, ϭⲁϫ B nn m, *sparrow*: Lev 11 15 S(B = Gk), Pro 26 2 SA στρουθός, Job 40 24 SB, Lam 4 3 SBF, Mt 10 29 SB στρουθίον; MG 25 13 B πετεινόν; Glos 161 S ⲡϫ. καιφος- κεφ. &c (= ? κέπ-φος v Liddell & Scott⁹ 860); Tri 328 S عصفور; ShZ 592 S lowly creatures such as ⲡϫ. ⲁⲩⲱ ⲡϭⲁϫⲓϥ, Mor 51 35 S ⲡϫ. ⲙⲡⲡϧⲓⲙⲃⲗⲱ devoured fat of land.

ϫ. ⲙⲃⲏⲡⲉ, ϭ. ⲙⲃⲓⲣⲓ v p 40 a.

ϫ., ϭ. ⲡⲗⲓⲗ SB, *a bird*: P 54 139 B ابو الفصاد, P 46 146 S ⲡⲓϫ. ابو صفادة (prob l as last), BM 920 266 B ⲡⲓϭ. ابو فصاد, Bodl 325 155 B ⲡⲓϭ. دروري (l ? دوري) or cf P 43 24 زرزور دروري).

As name: ⲡⲭⲁϫ (BM 1075, cf Στρουθός, Spg *Dem Stud* 1 no 320). In place-name (?) ⲡⲓⲁϧϫ. (PLond 4 200).

ϫⲁϫ *Sf* nn m, meaning unknown: PBad 5 409 incantation ⲛϫ. ⲡⲁⲗϭⲏⲡⲓ, I adjure thee.

ϫⲁϫ- *v* ϫⲱϫ 1°, ϫⲁⲁϫⲉ 1°, ϭⲱⲱϫⲉ **A**.

ϫⲉϫ *Sf* vb intr (?), meaning unknown: BKU l 21 *ro* in dyeing recipes ⲱⲡⲉ ⲛϫ., paral ⲱ. ⲛⲥⲉⲕⲧ.

ϫⲓϫ *B* *v* ϭⲓϫ.

ϫⲟⲩϫ *B* *v* ϭⲟⲩϭ.

ϫⲱϫ, ⲁⲛϫ. *SA²BF*, ϫⲁϫ- *B*, *head, capital* (cf ϫⲱⲥ): Ps 117 22 *B*(*S* ⲁⲡⲉ)κεφαλή, Nu 4 2 *S*(*B*=Gk) κεφάλαιον; Dan l 3 *B*(*F* prob ⲁⲛϫ.), ι Pet 5 4 *B*(*S* ⲛⲟϭ), Va 58 147 *B* ϫ. ⲛⲥⲟⲡⲓ (cf *ib* ⲁϥⲉ ⲡⲥ.) ἀρχι-, ROC 25 248 *B* ϫ. ⲛⲧⲉ ⲡⲓⲡⲗⲁⲛⲟⲥ αἱρεσιάρχης; Is 28 16 *B* (*S* ⲁ.) ἀκρο-; MG 25 243 *B* ϫ. ⲡⲁⲃⲏⲧ ἡγούμενος; Mor 30 53 *F* brought ⲟⲩⲥⲧⲣⲟⲩⲃⲓⲗⲗⲁ (στρόβιλος) ⲁϥⲥⲙⲓⲛⲧⲟⲩ ⲛϫ. of martyr's couch = BMis 275 *S*]ϫ. (var Mor 29 46 *S* ⲁⲡⲉ), CO 267 *S* beg him ⲛϥϫⲓ ⲛϫ. ⲡⲧⲟⲟⲧ; ϫⲁϫⲃⲱⲛ *B*: Ps 21 17 (*S* ⲡⲟⲛⲏⲣⲟⲥ) πονη- ρεύεσθαι (cf κακὴ κεφαλή), cit Dif 1 146 ⲧⲁⲧⲃ. (*v* p 39 *b*), cf Win 2 3 ⲡⲕⲁⲕ (for ? ϭⲁϭ) ⲃⲱⲛ, epithet of addressee; ϣⲛϫ. *S*, *headache*: AJSL 46 246; ⲁⲛ- ϫⲱϫ: Dan *ut sup F*; Jth 14 12 *S* ἥγ.; BHom 134 *S* ⲛⲁ. ⲙⲡⲕⲁϩ ἀκροθίνιον; LMär 2 *S* ⲛⲁ. ⲛⲛⲡⲉⲣⲥⲟⲥ = C 43 41 *B* ⲁⲣⲭⲱⲛ, R 2 1 20 *S* patriarchs, prophets ⲛⲁ. ⲛⲧⲉⲅⲣⲁⲫⲏ, AM 248 *B* Peter ⲡⲓⲁ. ⲛⲛⲓⲁⲡⲟⲥⲧⲟⲗⲟⲥ, Baouit pl 84 *S* sim ⲛⲁⲛϭⲱϭ (sic), Saq 139 *S* ⲛⲁⲛⲧⲱϫ, PBu 40 *S* ⲉⲓⲛⲁϫⲉ ⲡⲣⲱ ⲉϥⲉⲛⲁ. *magnates*, ManiK 32 *A²* ⲛⲁ. ⲛⲛⲁⲓⲱⲛ.

ⲣ, ⲉⲣ ϫ., *make, be head*: Deu 28 13 *S*(*B* ⲁϥⲉ) εἰς κεφ. καθιστάναι, Lam l 5 *F* ⲉⲅⲉⲓ ⲛϫ. (*B* do) εἰς κ. γίνεσθαι, Is 19 15 *S*(*B* do) κ. ποιεῖν; *ib* 40 23 *B*(*S*= Gk) ἄρχειν; ι Tim 2 12 *B*(*S* ⲣ ϫⲟⲉⲓⲥ) αὐθεντεῖν; Mani K 173 *A²* ⲁⲩⲉⲉⲩ ⲛϫ., C 43 51 *B* ⲟⲓ ⲛϫ. ⲙⲡⲓⲥⲧⲣⲁ- ⲧⲉⲩⲙⲁ = Mor 39 30 *S* ⲁⲛϫ.; ⲟ ⲛⲁⲛϫ.: Wess 15 18 *S* ⲟ ⲛⲁ. ⲉⲧⲉⲅⲁⲡⲟⲥⲧⲁⲥⲓⲁ, ManiK 175 *A²* sim; ⲙⲉⲧ- ⲣⲉϥⲉⲣ ϫ.: Va 57 59 *B* ⲡⲓⲙ. ⲉⲧⲉⲧϭⲁⲓⲏ ⲛⲧⲁϩⲓⲥⲧⲉ τὰ πρωτεῖα.

As name (?) ⲡϫⲱϫ (Kr p 204), Τζῶτζ (Preisigke); place-name (?) ⲡϫⲱϫ (C 89 55) = Va ar 172 35 بشت (? ابو تشت).

V also ⲗⲁⲕϩ.

ϫⲱϫ *S* nn, *needle*: Mor 31 209 sew torn garments with ϩ(ⲉ)ⲛϫ. ⲡⲕⲛⲛ (var P 132¹ 16 ⲗⲁⲥ ⲡⲕⲁⲙ).

ϫⲟϫ *S* nn m, *same*?: Cai 67324 ϫ. ⲥⲛⲉⲩ ⲙⲡⲟⲩⲅⲛⲃ.

ϫⲱϫ *B* *v* ϭⲱϭ.

ϫⲁ(ⲁ)ϫⲉ, ϫⲁϫⲱ†, ϫⲁϫⲱⲟⲩ† (once) *S* vb intr, *be hard, rough*: Ryl 127 arable land ⲁϥϫ. (ⲛ)ⲡⲉⲕϣ ϫⲟ ϩⲓⲱⲱϥ, ShViK 9757 193 iniquities ⲁϥϫⲓⲙⲉ ⲉⲣⲟⲟⲩ ⲛ- ϭⲓ ⲡⲉⲧϫ. ⲉⲧⲉⲛⲛⲏⲧⲟⲩ, Ryl 320 (ⲙ)ⲡⲣϫ. ⲙⲛ(ⲛ)ⲣⲱⲙⲉ, *ib* ϫ. ⲙⲛⲡⲥⲁϩ (or ? ⲣ ϫⲁϫⲉ *enemy*), Pcod 48 dying

man's ϣⲟⲩⲟⲃⲉ[ⲟⲛ or ? ⲟ ⲛ]ϫ. ϩⲁⲡⲉⲓⲃⲉ (cf Dévaud *Ét.* 41); qual: Z 319 nature of stone (*l* ⲱⲛⲉ) ϫ. opp ϭⲏⲛ σκληρός, BIF 37 55 ϭⲓⲛⲱⲡⲁϭ ⲉⲥϫ. σκληραγωγία, R 1 4 59 ⲡⲉⲡⲓⲡⲉ ⲉϥϫ. = MartIgn 870 *B* ⲛⲁϣϯ ἀπε- σκληκώς; Z 329 ⲧⲉϥⲥⲙⲓⲏ ϫ. τραχύς, Bor 253 169 ϭⲓⲛ- ⲱⲛϩ ⲉⲧϫ. τραχύτης; BHom 15 road ⲙⲟⲕϩ ⲁⲩⲱ ⲉⲥϫ. σκόπελος; Aeg 242 αὐθάδης; Jud 1 35 ⲡⲉⲧϫ. gloss on ⲟ ⲛⲃⲗϫⲉ ὀστρακώδης; BMar 105 ⲧⲟⲟⲩ ⲉⲧϫ. δα- σύτερος; Nu 13 21 opp ⲕⲓⲱⲟⲩ (*B* Gk diff), ι Kg 25 3 (var om, Gk diff); R 1 4 35 ⲉⲣⲏⲙⲟⲥ ⲉⲧϫ. *vastus* (cf ϫⲟⲣϫⲣ); ShC 42 141 ⲕⲁϩ ⲉⲧⲙⲟⲗϩ ⲉⲧϫ., P 129¹³ 49 ⲧⲟⲟⲩ ... ⲉϥϫ. opp ⲧⲏⲕ, PSBA 32 29 stone either ϫ. or ⲗⲉⲕⲗⲱⲕ, Blake 290 aspect of amethyst ⲉϥⲧⲉⲣⲧⲱⲣ ⲁⲩⲱ ⲉϥϫ. (cf *ib* 152), ShBM 202 184 trees ⲉⲩϫ. full of thorns, P 129¹⁴ 101 rind of pomegranate ϫ., ShA 1 248 wine ⲉϥϫ., ShP 130⁴ 148 garments ⲉⲩⲛⲁϣⲧ ⲛ ⲉⲩϫ., BMis 439 ⲁⲥⲕⲏⲥⲓⲥ ⲉⲥϫ., BMar 48 ϭⲓⲛⲛⲥⲧⲉⲩⲉ ⲉⲥϫ., *ib* 173 ⲉⲕϫ. ϩⲛⲡⲉⲕϫⲓ ⲙⲛⲡⲉⲕϯ, ClPr 43 groans soften thee not ⲛϫ. ⲕⲛⲁϣⲧ;   Cl Pr 25 2 warrior terrible & ⲉϥϫⲁϫⲱⲟⲩ ⲉⲧⲃⲉⲡⲉⲧϯ ⲛⲙⲙⲁϥ;   as nn m: P 44 91 ⲛϫ. غلظ العنز, *ib* ⲛⲁϣⲧ ⲙⲁⲕϩ do; P 130¹ 94 ϣⲱⲡⲉ ⲛϫ. ⲛⲛⲁϩⲣⲉⲛⲛⲁⲡⲁⲑⲟⲥ;   adj: ShP 131⁶ 37 ⲡⲣⲏϣ ⲛϭⲗⲱ ⲛϫ. no longer used by monks.

ⲁⲧϫ., *not rough (hoarse)* of voice: KroppE 30.

ϫⲁϫⲣⲓⲙ *B* nn m, *cliff*: Mt 8 32 (*S* ϣⲱⲱⲙⲉ) κρημ- νός, Va 57 173 ⲙⲱⲓⲧ ⲛϫ. σκοπελὸς καὶ κρ., *ib* 226 ⲙⲁ ⲛϫ. ἀποκρ.; *ib* 164 ὄχθη; K 215 ⲛϫ. لوف; MG 25 291 ⲕⲟϭ ⲙⲡⲉⲧⲣⲁ ⲉϥⲟⲓ ⲛϫ. = BIF 13 107 *S* ⲟ ⲛϫⲁϫⲱ ⲉⲙⲁⲧⲉ.

ϫⲁϫ-, ϭⲁϫⲙⲟⲉⲓⲧ *v* p 188 *b*.

ϫⲁⲁϫⲉ *SA* vb intr, *clap* hands: Pro 17 18 *A*(*S* ϫⲁⲕ) ἐπικροτεῖν;   c ⲛ-: ShlF 268 ϫ. ⲛⲧⲟⲟⲩⲛ ⲡⲡⲉⲧⲛϭⲓϫ;   c ϩⲛ-: ShC 73 81 ⲛⲧⲛϫ. ϩⲛⲛⲉⲛϭⲓϫ.

ϫⲁϫⲉ *SAA²O*, -ϫⲓ *B*, ϫⲉϫⲓ *F*, pl ϫⲓϫⲉⲉⲩ¹, -ⲅⲉ², ϫⲓϫⲉⲟⲩ³ (old MSS), ϫⲓⲛϫⲉⲉⲩ⁴, -ⲅⲉ⁵, -ϫⲉⲅⲉ⁶ *S*, ϫⲓ- ϫⲉⲅⲉ⁷ *AA²*, -ϫⲉⲟⲩⲅⲉ⁸ *SA* & sg as pl, nn m f, *enemy*: Ex 23 4 *SB*, Job 19 11 *SB*, Mt 13 25 *SBF* ἐχθρός; Pro 14 7 *B*(*SA* ϯ ⲟⲩⲃⲉ) ἐναντίος; Ge 22 17 *S*(*B* ⲉⲧϯ ⲟⲩ.), Sa 11 9 *S* ὑπεν.; Br 101 *S* ⲛϫ. ⲛⲧⲙⲛⲧⲉⲣⲟ, ShA 1 130 ⲡⲉϥϫ. ⲧⲏⲣⲟⲩ, BM 217 1 *S* ⲛϫ. ⲉⲑⲏⲡ, Bor 286 34 *S* ⲟ ⲩϫ. ⲉⲡⲛⲃ, Mani P 55 *A²* ⲡⲥⲱⲙⲁ ⲉⲧⲣⲁⲩ ⲙⲛϫ., C 86 131 *B* ⲙⲓϣⲓ ⲡⲉⲙⲟⲩϫ.;   f: ShP 130² 72 *S* ⲛⲧⲟ ϫ. ⲙⲡⲉⲟⲟⲩ;   as adj: Jer 37 14 *S*(*BP* 8712) *B*, Mt 13 28 *SBF* ἐχ.; ShC 42 70 *S* ⲣⲱⲙⲉ ⲛϫ., ShBM 194 1 *S* ϫ. ⲡⲣⲱⲙⲉ, Hor 76 *O* ⲥⲟⲩ ⲛϫ., *ib* 77 ⲥⲟⲩϫ.;   pl forms: Nu 24 8¹ (var⁴), Jud 2 14¹ (var²), Ps 58 10¹ (var²), *ib* 109 1¹ (varr³⁵), Sa 15 14¹, Mk 12 36¹ (varr²⁶⁸), PS 294¹, Ac 2 35² (var sg), Deu 12 10³ (var⁵), Mor 34 47⁴, Mic 7 6⁵ (*A*⁸), Lev 26 17⁵ (var sg), ManiP 112⁷ *A²*, Am 9 4⁸ *A*.

ⲙⲁⲓϫ., *loving enmity, quarrelsome*: Pro 3 30 *SA*(*B* ⲙⲉⲓ ⲡⲉⲣ ϫ.), cit Ep 258, Aeg 247 *S* φιλεχθρεῖν.

ⲙⲛⲧ-, ⲙⲉⲧϫ., *enmity*: Ge 3 15 *SB*, Pro 10 18 *SAB*,
Ro 8 7 *SB* ἔχθρα; Is 27 4 *S*(BM 256 191, var ⲣⲉϥⲙⲓϣⲉ, *B* ⲃⲏⲧⲥⲏ)πολεμία; ShC 42 118 *S* ⲙ.ϩⲓⲙⲟⲥⲧⲉ,
ib 148 ϣⲁϫⲉ ⲙⲙ., ManiK 119 *A²* ⲛϭⲁⲙ ⲛⲧⲙ., DeV
2 26 *B* ⲛⲓⲫⲑⲟⲛⲟⲥ, ⲡⲓⲙⲟⲥϯ, ⲛⲓⲙ., Mor 27 8 *F*;   ⲙ.
ⲉⲣⲟⲩⲛ ⲉ- *S*: R 1 59 ⲕⲁ ⲙ. ... ⲉϩ. ⲉⲗⲁⲩ κατὰ ψυχὴν
ἔχειν; Miss 8 33 ⲟⲩⲙ. ⲉϩ. ⲉⲡⲉⲥⲧⲱⲣⲓⲟⲥ δυσμένεια
κατά; PS 284 ⲙ. ⲉϩ. ⲉⲧⲉⲯⲩⲭⲏ.

ⲣ ϫ., ⲟ ⲛϫ., *be at enmity*: Ro 5 10 *SB* ἐχθρὸς εἶναι,
Si 28 6 *S* ἐχθραίνειν; ⲥ ⲉ-: Deu 2 9 *SB*, Ps 34 19
SB ἐχθραί., Ex 23 22 *S*(B ⲛ-) -θρεύειν, Aeg 285 *S*
-θρὸς εἶ., Gal 4 16 *SB* -θρὸς γίνεσθαι; PS 283 *S* ⲉϥⲟ
ⲛϫ. ⲉⲣⲟⲥ, ShBor 246 41 *S* ⲉⲛⲡⲟⲩⲁⲁⲩ ⲛϫ. ⲉⲣⲟϥ,
ManiK 96 *A²* ⲣ ϫ. ⲁⲡⲉⲥⲓⲱⲧ, C 89 2 *B* ⲡⲟⲩⲛⲟⲩϯ ⲟⲓ
ⲛϫ. ⲉⲣⲟϥ, Hor 79 *O* ⲣ ϫ. ⲁⲣⲁⲥ; ⲥ ⲉⲧⲃⲉ-: Ro 11
28 *SBF* ἐχθρὸς διά; ⲥ ⲙⲛ-, ⲛⲉⲙ-: Nu 25 17 *B*(S
ⲉ- prob) ἐχθραίνειν dat; BM 245 1 *S* ⲉϥⲱ (ⲗ ⲟ) ⲛϫ.
ⲙⲛⲛⲉⲩⲉⲣⲏⲩ, DeV 1 164 *B* sim (cf PS 283 *S* ϣⲱⲡⲉ
ⲛϫ. ⲙⲛ-); ⲥ ⲛ-: Ex 23 22 *B*(*S* ⲉ-)-θρεύειν dat; as
vb (?): El 122 *S* ⲡⲉⲧⲁϫⲉ. ⲉⲉⲡⲉⲧⲟⲩⲁⲁⲃ = ib 92 *A* ⲣ
ϫ., Mor 28 56 *S* ⲡⲉⲧϫ. ⲙⲛⲡⲉ.

ϫⲁϫⲉ *F*   *v* ϫⲁϭⲏ.

ϫⲁϫⲱ   *v* ϫⲁⲁϫⲉ *be hard.*

ϫⲁϫⲱ *B* nn, *sort of fuel*: Ps 101 4 (S ⲱⲡⲉ) φρύγιον.   Cf? *Religionsgesch. Vers. u. Vorarb.* 3 362
λίθος γαγάτης *lapis qui celerrime accenditur.* ϫⲁϭⲟ
JTS 8 242 (var BAp 138 ⲕⲓⲕⲁⲥ) not this.   Cf? ϭⲱϭ
& ϭⲉϭⲟⲩ.

ϫⲉϫⲟⲩ *B*   *v* ϭⲓⲛϭⲗⲱ.

ϫⲓϫⲓ *B*   *v* ϯϭⲉ.

ϫⲓϫⲓ *B* vb with ⲣⲉϥ-, *brigand*: K 88 (var -ϫⲁϫⲓ)
لِصّ.   Cf? ϭⲱⲱϫⲉ **A**.

ϫⲓϫⲱⲓ, ϭⲓ. *S*, ϫⲓϭⲱⲓ *B*, *single lock* or *plait of hair*
left on head (cf ظِفر): Lev 19 27 *S*(var ϭⲓ.)*B* σισόη
ضَفِير; BM 920 266, Ryl 453 337 *B* ⲛⲓϫ. مَخَارِف (but
PG 28 720 ἀπόκαρσις).   *V* Spg *Dem Stud* 1 45*.
As name ϫⲓϫⲱⲓ(Z 299)=Σισώης (PG 65 372), ϫⲓϭⲱⲓ (BM 915, MG 25 323 = Gött ar 114 112 شيشاي)
ϭⲓϭⲱⲓ (Bristol Mus H 2684), Τιθώης (PG *l c* 428)=
Σισώης, Σισῶις, -όις (ib ⲛ), ϯⲧⲟⲅⲉ (C 99 73), Τζιζόι,
Τζατζῶι (Preisigke), Διδῶει (AZ 23 38).

ϫⲱϫⲓ   *v* ϭⲱⲱϫⲉ.

ϫⲱϫⲉⲃ *B*   *v* ϭⲱϫⲃ.

ϫⲁϫⲃⲱⲛ *B*   *v* ϫⲱϫ.

ϫⲁϫⲓⲑⲱⲗ *B*   *v* ϭⲁϭⲓⲧⲱⲛ.

ϫⲉϫⲣⲉ *B* nn m, *sorrel*: K 178 ⲟⲩϫ., Montp 174
ⲛⲓϫ. حَمَّاض.   Cf? σέσελι (D'Arcy Thompson).

ϫⲉϫⲣⲓⲙ *B*   *v* ϫⲁⲁϫⲉ 1°.

ϫⲉϫⲣⲏⲥ *B*   *v* ϫⲓⲕⲣⲓⲥ.

ϫⲉϫⲥ, -ϣⲥ, ϫⲟϫⲥ *B* nn f, *ingot* of metal among
silversmith's properties: Montp 138 ϯϫⲟ, P 54 160
ϯϫⲉϣⲥ, P 55 9 ⲟⲩϫⲉϫⲥ سَبِك, K 129 ⲛⲓϫⲉ. سَبَائِك.

ϫⲁϫϩ *SB*   *v* ϫⲁⲣϫϩ.

ϫⲓϫϩ, ϫⲉⲟⲩϫϩ *F*   *v* ϭⲓϫ.

ϫⲁϭⲉ, pl ϫⲁϭⲉⲩ, ϭⲁϭⲉⲩ *B* nn, *bent, maimed person*: Va 57 194 ⲛⲓϫ. ἀνάπηρος; MG 25 280 hands
ϣⲱⲡⲓ ⲛϫⲁϭⲟ (*l*? -ϭⲉ) = BIF 13 100 *S* ϭⲁⲛⲁϩ; ⲟⲓ
ⲛϫ.: Mt 18 8 (*S* ϭⲁ.) χωλός; C 89 49 ⲛⲉϥϫⲓϫ ⲟⲓ ⲛϫ.
= C 99 226 *S* ϣⲟⲟϭⲉ = Va ar 172 30 أَجْذَم; Va 61 20
ⲉⲧⲟⲓ ⲛϫ. ϫⲉⲛⲛⲟⲩϫⲓϫ;   pl: Mt 15 30 (*S* ϭⲁ.) χω.;
MG 25 279 ϭⲁⲛϭ. ⲛⲕⲉⲗⲁⲫⲟⲥ = BIF 13 99 *S* do, Ora
3 237 ⲛⲓϫ. ⲁⲩⲑⲣⲟⲩ ⲥⲱⲟⲩⲧⲉⲛ.

ϫⲁϭⲏ *B*, ϫⲁϫⲉ¹, ϭ.² *F*, pl ϫⲁϭⲁⲩ *B* nn f, *left hand*
(*S* ϩⲃⲟⲩⲣ): Job 23 9 (BM 1247), Mt 6 3 *BF²*, ZNTW
24 90 *F²*, Va 68 171 ⲛⲓϣⲱⲃϣ ⲛϫⲁϭⲁⲩ ἀριστερός;
Cant 2 6 *F¹*, Ap 10 2 *BF¹*(Lacau) εὐώνυμος; Ps 90 7
κλίτος; C 43 47 ⲧⲉϥϫ.;   as adj: Ez 4 4 ἀρ.; ROC
18 36 λαιός; KroppC 7 *F* ⲧⲉⲕϫⲓϫ ϭ.²;   ⲥ ⲉ-: Ge
13 9 εἰς ἀρ.;   ⲥ ⲥⲁ-: Ge 14 15 ἐν ἀρ., Ez 1 10 (var
ⲛⲥⲁ-) ἐξ ἀρ., Mt 25 33 (*S* ϩⲃ.) ἐξ εὐ., AM 267 ⲥⲁ-
ⲧⲉϥϫ. τῇ εὐ.

ϫⲓϫⲱⲓ *B*   *v* ϫⲓϫⲱⲓ.

ϫⲱ(ⲱ)ϭⲉ, ϫⲱϫⲉ (once)*S*, ϭⲱϫ *B*, ϫⲉϭ-, ϫⲟϫ⸗,
ϫⲟϫ⸗, ϫⲁⲕ⸗ *S*, ϫⲁϭ⸗ *S¹*, ϭⲟϫ⸗ *B*, ϫⲏϭ† *S*, ϭⲏϫ† *B*
vb intr, *be dyed, stained*: ShA 2 304 *S* beaten ϣⲁⲛ-
ⲧⲉⲡⲉⲩⲥⲱⲙⲁ ϫ. *black & blue*, Miss 4 699 *S* hands of
those plucking blighted ears ϫ. ⲛⲑⲉ ⲙⲛⲥⲉϭⲟⲩ, Cat
147 *B* colour of raven ϭ. ⲡⲧⲉϥⲉⲣ ⲭⲁⲙⲉ;   qual:
Ez 23 15 *S*(var & *B* nn) παραβαπτός; Blake 254 *S* ⲡⲉⲓ-
ⲱⲛⲉ ⲉϥϫ. in hue βαθύς; Mor 25 63 *S* ⲡⲉϫⲱϣ ⲉⲧϫ.,
Va 66 297 *B* ϩⲁⲛⲁⲟⲩⲁⲛ ⲉⲩϭ. in divers colours;   tr:
P 129¹¹ 97 *S* ⲛⲡⲙⲁ ⲛⲛⲉⲧϫ. ⲛⲡⲁϭⲁⲛ ἀλουργοῦ βαφή;
Bodl(P) a 1 b *S* ϫ. ⲛⲣⲟⲓⲧⲉ ⲛⲁⲗⲁⲩ ⲛⲕⲟⲕⲕⲟⲥ, JA '75 5
262 *S* ⲧⲉⲧϫ. ⲛⲧⲉⲥⲃⲥⲱ (var R 1 2 43 ϫⲟⲟϭⲉ), Mor 25
218 *S* ϩⲉⲛⲥⲟⲣⲧ ⲉⲧⲣⲉⲛϫⲟϭⲟⲩ, BKU 1 21 ro *S¹* ⲛⲓⲧⲟⲥ
(ⲉⲓⲇ.) ⲛϣⲁⲕϫⲁϭϥ, Bodl(P) a 1 e *S* ⲛⲣⲟⲓⲧⲉ...ⲉⲕⲟⲩⲱϣ
ⲉϫⲟϫϥ, Hall 115 *S* ϩⲉⲛⲉⲓⲱ...ⲁⲕϫⲁⲕⲟⲩ (*sic l*);   ⲥ
ϩⲛ-, ϧⲉⲛ-: Ps 67 24 *B*(*S* ϫⲱⲗⲕ), Job 9 31 *SB* ϭⲟϫ⸗
βάπτειν ἐν, Ap 19 13 *S*(B ⲛⲟϫϭ) β. dat; ShIF 148
S ϩⲟⲓⲧⲉ ⲉⲩϫ.† ϩⲙⲡⲉⲥⲛⲟϥ, Pap from Magâga *per*
HRanke 1929 sim ϫⲱϫⲉ, Mor 43 76 *S* wool ϫⲟϫϥ
ϩⲛⲙⲙⲓⲧϫⲁⲛⲁⲅⲁⲡ;   ⲉⲃⲟⲗ ϩⲛ-, ϧⲉⲛ-: Dan 4 30 *B*
β. ἀπό; Mor 48 21 *S* ⲥⲁⲣ̅ϫ̅ ϫ. ⲉⲃ. ϩⲛϯⲱⲧⲉ (var BMar

213 ϭⲱϭ) = Rec 6 179 *B* ;   as nn m : Jud 5 30 *S* βάμμα; K 125 *B* ⲛⲓϭ. (*sic*) اصباغ; ShIF 150 *S* ⲛϫ. ⲙⲡⲉⲥⲛⲟϥ, BKU 1 21 *ro S* thing to be dyed ⲉⲁⲃϭⲉⲛ ϫ., K 487 *B* ⲛⲓϭⲟⲝ صبغ;   ⲣⲉϥϫ., *dyer* : R 1 3 19 *S* ⲣⲉϥϫⲉϭ ⲥⲟⲣⲧ.

ϫⲏϭⲉ *SAA*[2], -ⲕⲉ, ϫⲉⲕⲉ *S*, ϭⲏϫⲓ *B*, ϫⲏϭⲓ *F* nn m, *purple dye* : Ex 26 31 *SB* ارجوان, Pro 29 40 *SA*, Cant 3 10 *S*(*F* ϫⲉⲗⲃⲉⲥⲓ), EpJer 71 *F*(*B* = Gk), Lu 16 19 *B* ϭⲏ-ϫⲏ (Cat 87, var = Gk) πορφύρα; Mor 18 123 *S* βάμμα; P 43 35 *S* ⲟⲩϫ. سنجوني, برفيري, 44 67 *S* ϣⲉϭⲉ ʾ; Aeg 252 *S* ⲉϥϯ ϩⲓⲱⲟϥ ⲛⲟⲩϫ. = PO 8 597 يلبس احمر; Mor 37 168 *S* embroider them like ⲟⲩϣⲧⲏⲛ ⲛϩⲟⲩϫ., BMis 79 *S* ⲡ ϩⲱⲃ ⲉⲛϫ. ⲙⲡⲕⲁⲧⲁⲡⲉⲧⲁⲥⲙⲁ, P 131[1] 61 *S* ⲟⲩϫ. ⲙⲡⲟⲩⲕⲟⲕⲕⲟⲥ, ST 120 *S* ⲥⲛⲧⲉ ⲛⲗⲓⲧⲣⲁ ⲛϫ., BKU 1 21 *ro S*ᶠ ⲟⲩϫ. ⲉϥⲧⲁⲣϣ, ⲟⲩϫ. ⲉϥⲕⲏⲙ (*cf* BM 849 below), JA ʼ05 3 413 *S* ϫ. ⲙⲙⲉ (*v* p 157 a);   as adj :

Est 8 15 *S*, EpJer 11 *BF*, Jo 19 2 *SB* πορφύρεος, Mk 15 17 *SB*(*F* = Gk) -ρα, Nu 4 7 *SB* ὁλοπόρφυρος, Is 3 21 *B* ⲓⲉⲃ ⲛϭ. (*S* diff) περιπόρ., R 2 2 21 *S* ⲁⲅⲁⲡ ⲛϫ. πορφυρίζων; TEuch 2 47 *B* ⲙⲁⲛⲡⲁ ⲛϭ. ملو (var BM 849 (خرق السود); R 1 1 68 *S* ϫⲗⲁⲙⲩⲥ ⲛϫ. (var Mor 43 286 ⲛⲕⲟⲕⲕⲟⲥ), J 76 39 *S* ϩⲟⲓⲧⲉ ⲡϫⲏⲕⲉ ⲛϭⲣⲓⲙⲉ (*ib* 66 38 om ⲛϫ.), ManiP 196 *A*[2] sim, BP 4977 *S* ⲗⲁⲁⲩ ⲛϫⲉⲕⲉ, DeV 2 96 *B* ϧⲃⲟⲥ ⲛϭ., KroppJ 50 *v* ϩⲁϭⲓⲛ; as title *S* : BIF 3 204 ⲫⲟⲓⲃⲁⲙⲙⲱⲛ ⲛϫ., or name : Ryl 115, PMich 3541 ⲁⲡⲁ ⲛϫ.;   ⲉⲓⲉⲛϫ.*S*, ⲓⲉⲃ ⲛϭ. *B*, *purple embroidery* : Jud 8 26 *S* πορφύρεος; Is 3 21 *B* ut sup;   ⲟ ⲛϫ.*S* : Is *l c*;   ⲥⲁ ⲛϫ., ⲛϭ., *purple-seller* : Ac 16 14 *SB*(*F* ϭⲉⲗⲃⲉⲥⲓ) πορφυρόπωλις صباغة; K 337 *B* ⲃⲏⲁⲉⲁ الارجوان; C 86 122 *B* ϫⲟⲓ ⲛⲥⲁ ⲛϭ.   *Cf* PLond 4 162 Σαντσιτζε (or ? = ⲥⲁ ⲛϫⲓϫⲉ, *v* ϯϫⲉ).

ϭ

ϭ, 31st (or 30th, *v* p 745 *a*, adding LMis 127 ϭ ϫ (*sic*), Win 39) letter of alphabet, called ϭⲓⲙⲁ (K 1, Stern pp 7, 418), شيما (K Stern *ll cc*, *cf* جشيما Lab ⲡⲓ-ϩⲟⲩⲓⲧ ⲛⲧⲱⲧⲉⲣ 4). Early *F* MSS & *A* once (ImpRuss Ar S 18, tab i) use form ⲁ.   Derived from hierogl *g*(*S*, *B* ϫ), as ϭⲃⲟⲓ, ⲥⲟϭⲛ, ⲧⲱϭⲉ; or *B* ϭ, as ϭⲱⲗⲡ, ϭⲁϩⲥⲉ;   or *k*(*S*, *B* ϫ), as ϭⲱϭ, ϥⲱϭⲉ, ⲃⲏϭ; or *B* ⲧ, *v* below;   or *k*(*S* rare, *B* ϫ), as ϩⲁϭⲉ;   or *t*(*B*, *S* ϫ), as ϭⲓ, ϣϭⲏⲛⲓ;   or *d*(*B*, *S* ϫ), as ϭⲛⲱⲟⲩ nn. Not found in *O* (though in DM cipher) or oldest *F*(Schmidt's Eccl Cant Lam, Ch. Beatty's Isaiah glosses, where 16 8 ⲧⲁⲕⲥ would be *S* ⲧⲟϭⲥ). Replaced by ϫ, as ϫⲱ (Ep 244), ϫⲱϣⲧ (BodlP d 17), ϫⲟ-ⲟⲗⲉ (KroppR 15), ϫⲁϩϫⲉϩ (Mt 24 51);   converse, as (ⲉ)ϭⲱⲟⲩ (Kr 116), ϫⲓϭ (Ora 4 7), ϭⲓϭ (J & C 98), ⲙⲉϭⲉϥ (ST 227), ϭⲱⲕ (Ora 4 10), ⲟⲣϭ (ST 181), ⲛⲟⲩϭ? (AZ 23 109).   Replaced by ⲕ, as ⲕⲓⲛ- (P Mich 601), ⲕⲱ (Hall 88, CO 83), ⲕⲗⲟⲙⲗⲙ (J 51 10), ⲕⲗⲟⲧⲉ (ϭⲗⲟⲟϭⲉ Ep 222), ⲕⲁⲙ *F*(& ϭⲁⲙ PGM 2 181), Πεκῦσις (ⲡⲉϭⲱϣ), Πελκεῆσις (Preisigke *W. buch* 3 320); *cf* also ⲕϭⲟⲗ (ST 280);   converse, as ϭⲉ-(pass), ⲛⲉϭ- (ST 246), ϭⲛⲁ- (BM 1211 C), ϫⲉϭⲁⲥ (Br 41), ϭⲓⲙ (*ib* 247), ϭⲟⲓ (ⲕⲟⲅⲓ Ep 554), ϩϭⲟ (CO 209), ⲥϭⲓⲙ (El 120, *cf* BerlSitz ʼ12 1039), ϭⲓⲃⲱⲧⲟⲥ (Ex 26 33), ϭⲑⲁⲣⲁ (Ps 150 2), ⲉⲧⲕⲁϭⲉⲓ (PS 359), ⲉⲛⲏϭⲓ(ἐποίκιον Kr 137), ⲡⲣⲟⲥϭⲟϭⲓⲁ(J 74 21).   Replaces ⲧ, as ⲛϭ- (pass), ⲁⲗⲟϭⲟⲛ (*Rev ÉgAnc* 1 154), ⲁϭⲱⲡ (CO 436), ⲗⲟⲩϭⲓⲛⲉ (BP 8709), ϭⲉⲱⲣϭⲓⲟⲥ (ST 378), ⲙⲉⲛⲧⲉϭⲉ (μέντοιγε J 76 37), ⲡⲁⲣⲁϫⲓϭⲓ *A*?(AP 23);   converse, as -ⲧⲏ (-ϭⲉ J 69 29), ⲧⲁⲥ (Ep 532), ⲛⲧⲓ (& ⲛϭⲓ BKU 1 8), ϣⲧⲱⲣ (*ib* 267).   Varies with

ⲧ, as ⲁⲧⲃⲉⲥ (p 26 *a*), ⲛⲟⲧ (BP 8095), ⲛⲁⲧ *F*(MR 5 54), ⲙⲟⲩϫⲧ (p 214 *a*), ⲧⲣⲁ (p 429 *b*), ⲃⲟⲧⲉ (Mor 31 50), ⲧⲟⲟⲧⲉ (p 407 *a*), ⲟⲩⲟⲧⲉ? (PMich 6861), ⲕⲱⲛϭ (ϭⲱⲡⲧ El 136), ⲡⲁⲧⲥⲉ (p 286 *b*), ⲧⲟⲩϣⲧ (PBad 5 332), ⲡⲓ-ϣⲧⲉⲣⲱⲟⲩ (Saq 10 *n*), ⲧⲙⲟⲩⲡⲉⲧⲣⲏⲧⲉ (or ? *l* -ϭⲣⲏⲥⲉ Baouit 2 44), ⲧⲁⲧⲥⲓ *B* (p 466 *b*), ϣⲗⲓⲧ *B*(p 563 *a*); *cf* also ⲧⲥⲓϫ, ⲧϭⲁⲙ (BM 524), ⲧϭⲗⲟⲧⲉ (Ps 25 2 Rahlfs), ⲛⲁⲧϭ (Stegemann 67).   Replaced by ϩ, ϫ, as ϩⲗⲁⲙ-ⲗⲙ (ManiK 125, *cf ib* ϭⲗ.), ϫⲗⲟⲙⲗⲉⲙ *B*(PO 11 330); *cf* ? ϩⲃⲟⲩⲣ.   Varies with ϣ, rarely *S*, as ϭⲓⲛⲉ (PS 251), ϣⲱⲡⲉ (Ac 1 16), ϣⲱϣⲧ (Ap 11 12), ϭⲱⲕⲉ (RNC 83), ⲥⲛϣ (*ib* 54), ⲛⲟϣ (Mor 38 57), ϭⲗⲓϭ (*ib* 32 31), ϣⲁⲛ (PChass 2); *cf* also ϭⲙⲟⲟϣⲉ (Lant 73), ϣϭⲟⲥ for, ϭⲣⲟⲥ;   often in late *B*, as ⲁϣⲓⲛ (p 744 *b*), ϣⲓⲛ (Ez 43 12), ⲉⲙⲟⲩ (p 65 *a*), ϣⲓ breast, ϭⲓ (2 Cor 10 13), ϣⲟⲧϣⲉⲧ, ϣⲱⲛ (Ac 3 7), ⲧⲁⲛϭⲟ (Ps 17 15), ϭⲱⲟⲩϯ(p 601 *b*), ϣⲉⲛ- (Deu 24 7), ϭⲟⲩⲣⲏ(Nu 16 18), ⲙⲟⲣϣⲛⲁϭ (p 777 *b*).   Transcribes Ar ج, as ϭⲟⲩⲡⲡⲉ جبّة (MR 5 55), ϭⲉⲗⲗⲟⲩϫ جلوز (P 44 81), ⲥⲓⲛϭⲓⲛⲓⲗ زنجبيل (PMéd 89); ϩⲁϭⲉϭ حجاج (Ryl 235), ϯⲡⲁϭ دياج (*ib* 343), ⲃⲁⲣⲁϭ برج (Kr 236, *cf* ϥⲁⲣⲁϫ BM 618); transcribed by ج, as ⲃⲉⲣϭⲟⲩⲧ فرجوط (also فرشوط Amélineau *Géog* 178), ⲛⲁϩϭⲁⲩⲣⲉ الجور (AZ 55 70), ⲙⲟⲩⲛϭⲟⲩϭ منجوج (TT 73 *n*);   or ش, as ϭⲙⲟⲩⲛⲓ اشمون (AM 74), ϭⲓⲛⲟⲩⲣⲟⲟⲧⲉ شنواد (TMina *Epima* xxxi), ϭⲉⲛⲉⲙⲟⲩ-ⲗⲟⲥ شرملس (Amélineau *lc* 183, *cf* ? شبرا ملس Ibn Giʼân 83), ϭⲣⲟ اشرو, ϭⲗⲓⲗ اشليل (BIF 5 93, 94).   In EW 234 ff not used.

On pronunciation of ϭ *v* Worrell *Coptic Sounds*, esp 21, 24 ff, BerlSitz ʼ12 1036 ff, Gött Nachr ʼ16 123.

ϭⲁ *S* nn m, *ugliness, deformity* (?): Si 11 2 ὅρασις (var θράσος), opp ⲥⲁ. *Cf* ⲧϭⲁⲉⲓⲟ. *V* KKS 190; different etymol AZ 46 125.

ϭⲁ *S ƒ*, ⲕⲁⲓ *S* nn **m**, a vessel (ḳʃj Lange *Amenemope* 117): BKU 1 21 boil water ⲛⲕⲧⲁⲁϥ ⲉⲡϭ., *ib* ⲡⲁϥⲧϥ ⲉⲡϭ., *ib* ⲧⲁⲁⲃ ⲉⲡⲙⲁⲩ ϩⲓⲟⲩϭ., PMich 3552 ⲟⲩⲕ. ⲛⲁⲣϣⲓⲛ.

ϭⲁⲓⲟ *S*, ϭⲁⲓⲁ *F*   *v* ⲧϭⲁⲉⲓⲟ & ⲧϭⲁⲉⲓⲟ.

-ϭⲉ *S A A² F*(rare), -ⲭⲉ *S*(rare)*B*, -ϭⲏ *F*, ⲛϭⲉ *S*, ⲛⲕⲉ *O* enclitic particle **I**, *then, therefore, but*: Ge 12 13 *S*(*B*=Gk), Job 1 5 *S*(*B* ⲟⲛ), Mt 3 10 *S*(var ⲟⲛ, *B*=Gk) *ib* 13 40 *S*(*BF*=Gk), *ib* 22 9 *S*(*B* ⲍⲉ), Mk 9 11 *S*(var & *F* om)*B*, BHom 50 *S* ⲛⲧⲉⲣⲉⲡⲁⲓϭⲉ ⲉⲃⲧⲱⲧⲟⲩ(var R 2 234 ⲍⲉ), Va 57 174 *B* ⲉⲑⲃⲉⲟⲩⲭⲉ ⲛϣⲱⲃ?, BMar 116 *S* ⳁϭⲉ ⲡⲁⲓ ⲡⲟⲩϩⲣⲉ, Cl 14 1 *A* ⲟⲩⲁⲓⲕⲁⲓⲟⲛϭⲉⲡⲉ, AP 8 *A²* ⳁⲉⲣⲛⲧϭⲉ ⲛⲏⲧⲓ ⲟⲩⲛ, BHom 55 *S* ⲁⲓϭⲉ ⲛⲥⲟⲩⲁⲛⲡⲁ ⲉⲃⲟⲗ γοῦν; Job 22 25 *S*(*B* om), Pro 24 38 *SA*, Jon 4 11 *SA*(*B*=Gk), Ac 19 2 *S*(var & *B* do), Miss 8 42 *S* ⲉⲡⲉⲓⲁⲛϭⲉ ⲁⲡⲥⲱⲧⲙ, Aeg 240 *S* ⲡⲧⲟⲕϭⲉ ⲡⲉⲧⲣⲟⲥ δέ; Cl 62 1 *A*, Aeg 267 *S* ⲡⲉⲭⲁⲣⲓⲥⲙⲁϭⲉ ⲉⲧⲉⲡⲁⲓⲛⲉ μέν; Jos 24 18 *S*, BMar 167 *S* ⲙⲏⲡⲱⲥϭⲉ ἀλλά; Sa 1 11 *S*, BHom 24 *S* ⲉⲣⲉⲡⲁⲓϭⲉ ϣⲟⲟⲡ ⲛⲧⲉⲓⲣⲉ, Miss 8 140 *S* ⲟⲩϭⲉⲡⲉ ⲡⲉϥϣⲡⲏ? τοίνυν; Mk 4 41 *S*(*B*=Gk), Ac 21 38 *S*(*B* om) ἄρα; Mt 26 45 *SB*, BHom 12 *S* ⲙⲁⲣⲡⲧⲱⲟⲩⲛϭⲉ, CDan 86 *B* ⲙⲁⲣⲉⲡϣⲉ ⲡⲁⲡ ⲉϣⲓⲛⲧⲭⲉ λοιπόν; C 43 131 *B* ⲗ. ⲭⲉ ⲭⲱ ⲛⲥⲱⲕ, BMis 201 *S* ⲁϣϭⲉⲡⲉ ⲡⲉⲕϣⲁ (var Bor 267 41 ⲁϣ λοιποππε); 3 Kg 19 4 *S*(ViK 9687), Ps 49 22 *S*(*B* om), Mic 3 1 *SA*(*B* do), R 1 5 13 *S* ⲙⲡⲣⲣ ϩⲟⲧⲟϭⲉ δή; Nu 4 34 *S* (var ⲁⲩⲱ, *B* do), Deu 22 17 *S*(*B* ⲟⲩⲟϩ), 1 Kg 25 11 *S*(var om), Eccl 1 4 *F*(PMich 3520, *S* ⲍⲉ), Ez 3 3 *S* (*B* ⲍⲉ), Va 66 309 *B* ⲟⲩⲟⲛ ⲕⲉⲙⲩⲥⲧⲏⲣⲓⲟⲛⲭⲉ ϩⲏⲡ, Z 301 *S* ⲁⲡⲟⲛϭⲉ ⲣⲱⲱⲛ καί, Eccl 5 15 *S*, Lam 3 8 *S*(*B* om) καίγε, Jth 11 17 *S* καὶ νῦν; Cl 12 6 *A* ⲟⲩⲁⲛϭⲉ ⲡⲓⲙ ⲉⲧⲟⲩⲛⲁⲃⲓⲧⲟⲩ, Va 57 268 *B* ⲟⲩⲭⲉ, Gu 33 *S* ⲡⲉϥϣⲡⲉϭⲉⲡⲉ γάρ; Ro 13 11 *S*(*B*=Gk) ἤδη;   Gk om: Ex 6 6 *A*(*B* om), Jos 4 18 *S*, 4 Kg 4 13 *B*, Ps 88 47 *B* (*S* om), Is 30 16 *F*(*SB* om), Ez 16 42 (*SB* ⲟⲩⲟϩ), Cl 436 6 *A*, Ja 3 10 *B*(*S* om), Ap 6 10 *B*(*S* diff); PS 152 *S* ⲡⲁⲓϭⲉ ⲱ ⲡⲭ̅ⲥ̅ⲡⲉ ⲡⲃⲱⲗ, BG 122 *S* ⲉⲧⲃⲉⲡⲁⲓϭⲉ ⲁⲓⲉⲓ, Br 124 *S* ⲡⲁⲓϭⲉⲡⲉ ⲡⲉⲩⲣⲁⲛ, ShBM 204 64 *S* ϩⲁⲥ ⲙⲉⲡϭⲉⲛⲉ ⲡⲟⲩⲁ, ShC 73 76 *S* ⲟⲩϭⲉⲡⲉ ⲡϣⲁⲩ, *ib* 25 *S* ⲉϣⲱⲡⲉϭⲉ ⲉⲩϣⲁⲡⲉⲓ *but*, ShC 42 169 *S* ⲉϣⲭⲉⲁⲡⲉⲛⲥⲱⲧⲏⲣϭⲉ ... ⲭⲟⲟⲥ sim, ShA 1 252 *S* ⲡⲁⲓ ⲁⲡϭⲉ ⲡⲉⲧϣⲟⲟⲛ ⲁⲗⲗⲁ, *ib* 2 174 *S* others have known ⲁⲡⲟⲛϭⲉ (var ⲍⲉ) ⲙⲡⲉⲛⲥⲟⲩⲱⲛϥ, ShlF 197 *S* ⲉⲛⲉⲟⲩⲱϣ ⲁⲡⲡⲉ ⲉⲧⲣⲉⲩⲉⲓⲣⲉ ⲁⲅⲉⲓⲣⲉϭⲉ *yet they did it*, BMis 293 *S* if Christ but help me ⳁⲅⲛⲏϣϭⲉ ⲁⲡ, BHom 112 *S* if ye do right ..., ⲉⲧⲉⲧⲛϣⲁⲛⲡⲁⲣⲁⲃⲁϭⲉ, El 74 *A* ⲫⲱⲡⲉϭⲉ ⲉⲧⲉⲧⲛⲉⲓⲉ ⲡⲟⲩϩⲣⲏⲧ ⲡⲟⲩⲱⲧ = *ib* 114 *S*, *ib* 52 *A* ⲁⲓⲭⲡⲟⲩϥ-

ϭⲉ ⲭⲉⲡⲓⲙⲡⲉ, ManiP 64 *A²* ⲙⲁⲣⲉ ⲡⲉⲕϭⲉ, ManiK 122 *A²* ⲉⲓⲧⲉϭⲉ ⲟⲩⲙⲛⲧⲣⲙⲙⲁⲟ...ⲏ ⲙⲙⲁⲛ ⲟⲩⲙⲛⲧⲣⲏⲕⲉ, C 43 81 *B* ⲕⲏⲡ ⲉⲣⲟⲕⲭⲉ ϩⲉⲛⲧⲁⲙⲁⲡⲓⲁ, C 86 120 *B* ⲕⲟⲧⲕⲭⲉ, Pcod 39 *F* ⲙⲁⲗⲉⲡⲡⲉⲥⲓⲛⲟⲩϭⲏ...ⲉⲗ ⲡⲟⲓⲡ; -ϭⲉ ⲟⲩⲛ: Va 57 7 *B* ⲁⲡⲁⲭⲉ ⲟⲩⲛ γοῦν; *ib* 32 *B* ⲟⲩⲭⲉ ⲟⲩⲛⲡⲉ ⲡⲓϩⲛⲟⲩ τοίνυν; ShC 73 xii *S* ⲙⲁⲣⲉⲛⲉⲩⲭⲁⲣⲓⲥⲧⲉⲓϭⲉ ⲟⲩⲛ, Pcod 5 *S* ⲉⲧⲃⲉⲟⲩϭⲉ ⲟⲩⲛ, AM 62 *B* ⲥⲱⲧⲉⲙⲭⲉ ⲟⲩⲛ (*cf* Bor 289 51 *S* ⲥⲱⲧⲙϭⲉ ⲟⲛ); ⲟⲩⲛϭⲉ: Pcod 8 *S* ⲕⲟⲅⲟϣ [ⲟⲩ]ⲛϭⲉ ⲉⲧⲣⲉⲩ-, DeV 1 131 *B* ⲙⲁⲣⲉⲡϭⲓ ⲉ̇ⲃⲱ ⲟⲩⲛϭⲉ; ⲡⲗⲏⲛϭⲉ: PS 60 *S* ⲡ. ⲥⲱⲧⲙ, DeV 1 158 *B* sim; ⲧⲉⲛⲟⲩ-, ⳁⲛⲟⲩϭⲉ: Ge 12 19 *S*(*B* om), Ex 4 12 *A*(*B* ⲟⲩⲟϩ ⳁⲛⲟⲩ), Hos 2 10 *Sƒ*(JEA 11 244, *B* do) καὶ νῦν, Is 5 13 *SF*(*B* ⳁ. ⲍⲉ) τοίνυν, Ge 30 30 *SB*, Ac 23 15 *S*(*B* ⳁ. ⲟⲩⲛ) ν. οὖν, Jos 9 18 *S* ν. δέ, Ac 17 30 *S*(var & *B* ⲍⲉ) τὰ ν.; Su 20 *B* (*S* ⲉⲧⲃⲉⲡⲁⲓϭⲉ) διό; Cl 64 1 *A* λοιπόν; PS 117 *S* ⲧ. ⳁⲕⲉⲗⲉⲅⲉ, ST 224 *S* ⳁ. ⲉⲡⲓⲁⲏ ⲁⲡⲉⲓ, PMich 1526 *S* ⳁ. ⲭⲉ, El 104 *A* ⳁ. ⲁ̇ⲕⲡⲁⲧⲉⲕⲟ, AM 230 *B* ⳁ. ⳁⲏⲥ, C 86 349 *B* ⳁ. ⲓⲥ ⲡⲉϩⲟⲟⲩ (var om ⲭⲉ), Mor 24 14 *F* ⳁ. ...ⲧⲉⲡⲗⲉϣⲓ;   -ϭⲉ ⲧⲉⲛⲟⲩ: Miss 8 57 *S* ⲁⲡⳁ ⲉⲡⲧⲟⲗⲏϭⲉ ⲧ., Va 57 14 *B* ⲙⲁⲣⲉⲡⲉⲣ ⲡⲟⲓⲡⲭⲉ ⳁ. τοίνυν, C 99 234 *S* = *ib* 89 68 *B* τοιγαροῦν; Jud 16 13 *S* δή; PS 198 *S* ⲗⲟⲓⲡⲟⲛϭⲉ ⲧ., ShC 73 xi *S* ⲁⲡⲟⲛϭⲉ ⲧ. ⲙⲁⲣⲡⲡⲱⲧ; ⲁⲣⲁϭⲉ: ROC 17 405 *B* ϩⲁⲣⲁⲭⲉ ⲁⲁⲃⲣⲁϩⲁⲙ ⲭⲉ- ἄρα; ShC 73 179 *S* ⲁ. ⲡⲕⲁⲓⲣⲟⲥⲡⲉ, *ib* 193 ⲁ. ⲉⲕⲧⲙⲗⲁⲉⲓⲏⲩ, *ib* 129 *S* ⲙⲏ ⲁ. ⲉϥⲥⲟⲧⲡ?

II *again, once more*, **a** in neg phrase: Ge 8 21 *SB*, Job 7 9 *B*(*S* ⲕⲧⲟ ⲉ-), Is 54 9 *B*(*S* ⲭⲓⲛⲧⲉⲡⲟⲩ), He 10 17 *SBF* ἔτι, Jos 22 33 *S*, Mk 2 2 *B*(*S* diff), Ro 6 6 *B*(*S* ϭⲉ ⲭⲓⲛⲧ.), Z 322 *S* ⲉⲧⲙⲉⲣ ϩⲱⲃϭⲉ, MG 25 248 *B* ⳁⲡⲁϣⲉ ⲛⲛⲓ ⲁⲡϣⲉ μηκέτι, Ge 9 11 *B*(*S* om), Nu 32 19 *S*(*B* om), Is 32 3 *SBF*, Mic 4 3 *SAB*, Jo 15 15 *SA²B*, WHatch 352 *B* ⲛⲉⲙⲙⲟⲛ ⲉⲣⲫⲉⲓ ⲙⲙⲁⲩ ⲁⲛⲭⲉⲡⲉ, MG 25 206 *B* ⲡⲁⲭⲉⳁ ⲛⲁϥ ⲁⲡⲡⲉ οὐκέτι; Gk om: Deu 12 31 *S*(*B* om), Ps 27 5 *B*(*S* om), Jo 4 5 *BF*(*SA²* om), Z 344 *S* ⲙⲡⲟⲩⲉⲓⲥϭⲉ ⲡⲕⲉⲥⲟⲡ; BG 106 *S* ⲡⲥⲧⲙⲟⲩⲱⲛϩϭⲉ, ShBMOr 8810 479 *S* ⲉⲧⲙⲣ ϩⲟⲧⲉϭⲉ ϩⲏⲧϥ, P 131² 139 *S* ⲙⲏ ⲑⲉϭⲉ ⲙⲙⲉⲧⲁⲡⲟⲉⲓ ⲡⲕⲉⲥⲟⲡ, C 86 305 *B* ⲙⲡⲉϥⲭⲉⲙ ⲥⲁⲭⲓⲭⲉ ⲉⲭⲱ, Tst Ab 173 *B* ⲙⲙⲟⲛ ⲛⲧⲏⲓ ⲡⲟⲩⲥⲁ ⲭⲓ ⲉⲭⲟⲩⲭⲉ, Va 57 157 *B* ⲙⲡⲁⲣⲉⲃⲓⲭⲉ λοιποπ, MG 25 357 *B* ⲙⲡⲁⲩⲭⲉⲟⲩⲁϩ ⲧⲟⲧ ⲭⲉ (*sic*) ⲉⲣⲉⲓ, *ib* 346 *B* ⲙⲡⲉϥⲭⲉⲉⲣ ⲉⲧⲓⲛ (αἰτεῖν) ⲙⲫ ⳁⲭⲉ, Miss 4 182 *B* ⲙⲡⲓⲭⲉⲡⲁⲩ ⲉⲣⲟⲥ, DeV 2 139 *B* ⲙⲡⲓⲡⲁⲩ ⲉⲣⲱⲟⲩⲭⲉ, BM 917 *B* ⲙⲡⲉϥⲭⲉⲉⲣ ⲁⲡⲁⲧⲕⲁⲍⲓⲛ ⲙⲙⲟϥ, DeV 2 9 *B* ⲡⲁⳁⲭⲉⲥⲟⲟⲩⲛ ⲙⲙⲟϥ ⲁⲡ, AZ 23 27 *S* ⲙⲁⲓⲟⲩⲱⲣⲉⲡ ⲗⲁⲁⲩ ⲡⲁⲕϭⲉ; ⲁⲩⲱϭⲉ *S*: Nu 11 25 (*B* ⲟⲩⲟϩ...ⲭⲉ), Is 65 19 (*B* ⲛⲡⲉ-...ⲭⲉ) οὐκέτι, Ps 73 9 (*B* ⲭⲉ) ἔτι; Pcod 32 made poor that he might seek God ⲁ. ⲙⲡⲉϥϣⲓⲛⲉ; ⲛϭⲉ *S*: Zech 13 2 (*AB* om) οὐκέτι; PMéd 299 ⲉⲧⲁⲧⲣⲉⲩϩⲣⲱⲧ ⲛϭⲉ, BP 11349 (ⲛ)ⲥⲉⲧⲙⲁⲙⲫⲓⲃⲁⲗⲉ ⲛϭⲉ, PBu 15 ⲙⲁⲓϭⲉ ⲉⲣⲟϥ ⲛϭⲉ. (Not to be confused with *B* ⲛⲭⲉ p 747 *a infra*).

b not negative: Is 1 5 *SF*(*B* ⲟⲛ), Jer 13 27 *SB*,

Mk 14 63 S(B ⲟⲛ) ἔτι; PS 211 S ⲉⲧⲓϭⲉ ⲡⲁⲙⲁⲑⲏⲧⲏⲥ
ⲥⲱⲧⲙ, ShViK 9313 69 S flesh ⲥⲛⲁⲧⲱⲟⲩⲛϭⲉ.

V Rec 30 142, 34 154.

ϭⲉ, ϭⲓ *A*   *v* ⲛϭⲓ.

ϭⲉ, ϭⲏ   *v* ⲕⲉ.

ϭⲏ *B* nn m, *quince*: K 178 (1 var ϣⲉ) سفرجل, صَفٌ,
Montp 174 ⲡⲓϭⲏ.

ϭⲓ *B*   *v* ϫⲓ vb & *breast*.

ϭⲓ-, ϫⲓ-   *v* p 660 a.

ϭⲓⲉ *SAA²*, ϭⲓⲉⲓⲉ, ϭⲓⲏ *S*, ϭⲓⲓⲉ *B*(once), ⲕⲓⲏ *BF*,
pl ⲕⲓⲕⲟⲩ *F* nn m, *he-goat* (*B* ⲃⲁⲣⲏⲓⲧ): Ge 31 10 (var
Z 583 ϭⲓⲉⲓⲉ), Pro 24 66 *SA*, Is 34 6 *SF* pl, He 9 13
SF, R 1 4 57 among Egypt's gods ⲟⲩϭ. = Mart Ign
869 *B* ⲃ. τράγος; Miss 4 766 demon stank like ⲡⲉⲓϭⲓⲏ
ⲛⲃⲁⲗⲗⲉ, Mani 2 *A²* ⲃⲁⲗⲗⲡⲉ, ⲁⲓⲗⲉ, ϭ. among unclean foods, BSM 110 *B* ⲟⲩϭ., MG 25 134 *B* ⲟⲩ-
ⲃⲟⲓϣⲓ...ⲉⲥⲣⲓⲙⲓ ⲓⲥϫⲉⲕ ⲉⲥⲟⲓ ⲓⲕ. (? this word).

ϭⲓⲏ, ϣ. *B* nn m, *border, limit* (*S* ⲧⲟϣ): Ex 34 24
ϭⲓⲏ ⲟⲩⲟⲥⲟⲉⲛ (Va), Nu 35 27 (cf 26 ⲑⲟϣ), Is 15 8, Ez
43 12 ⲡⲉϭ. (var HCon 301 ⲡⲉϥϣⲓⲏ), ib 48 22 ⲡⲓϭ.,
Mt 19 1 ὅριον; Ez 38 6 ἔσχατος; ib 43 13 γεῖσος; ib
20 βάσις; ib 44 14 φύλαξ; Dif 1 38 Alexandria & the
Lake (*sc* Mariût) ⲡⲉⲙⲡⲟⲩϣⲓⲛ نُحُو, CDan 93 robber
ϩⲉⲛⲡⲓϭ. ⲉⲧⲉⲙⲙⲁⲩ, C 86 171 to king ⲁⲡⲉⲕⲣⲙⲟⲧ ⲧⲁϩⲉ ⲡⲉϭ. ⲧⲏⲣⲟⲩ;   3 Kg 8 16 ϯϭⲓⲏ (var HCon 226
ⲡⲓϭⲣⲏⲡⲓ) σκῆπτρον (error ?).

ϭⲟ *B*   *v* ϫⲟ 1°, 2°.

ϭⲱ *SA²F*, ⲕⲱ *S*, ϭⲟⲩ *AA²*(Jo), ϫⲟⲩ *O*, ϭⲱⲱⲧ *F*,
ϭⲉⲉⲧ† *SAA²*, ϭⲏⲛⲧ† *SF* vb intr, a *continue, persist*
(mostly followed by 2d pres): Job 15 29 (*B* ⲟϩⲓ),
1 Cor 3 14 *SF* ϭⲱⲱⲧ (*B* ⲟϩⲓ ⲉⲣⲁⲧ⸗), He 13 1 (*B* ϣⲱⲡⲓ
ⲉⲥⲥⲙⲟⲛⲧ), Aeg 220 ϥϭⲱ ϥⲟ ⲛⲉⲡⲓⲥⲕⲟⲡⲟⲥ, Wess 15
137 ⲉϥϣⲁⲛϭⲱ ⲉϥⲙⲏⲛ ⲉⲃⲟⲗ μένειν, Job 2 9 (*B* ⲟⲩⲱⲙ
ⲉ-) ἀναμ., BMar 109 ⲁϥϭⲱ ⲙⲁϥϣⲁϥ ἀπομ., Lu 1 22
(*B* ⲟ.), He 1 11 *F* -ⲱⲧ (*SB* ϣⲱⲡⲉ) διαμ., Miss 8 43
ⲁⲩϭⲱ ⲉⲅⲁϩⲉⲣⲁⲧⲟⲩ ἐπιμ., Aeg 211 παραμ., Job 14 14
(*B* ⲁⲙⲟⲛⲓ ⲛⲧⲟⲧ⸗), 1 Pet 2 20 (var†, *B* ⲱⲟⲩ ⲛϩⲏⲧ) ὑπομ.;
AP 8 *A²* ϭⲱ ⲉⲣⲉⲡⲟⲩⲁⲁⲃ τηρεῖν; Ge 8 10 (*B* do) ἐπέχειν; Job 8 15 (*B* ⲥⲉⲙⲛⲓ) ἱστάναι; Mk 15 36 *SF*(*B*
ⲭⲱ) ἀφιέναι; Ge 2 18 ϭⲱ ⲙⲁⲅⲁⲁ⸗ (*B* ϣⲱⲡⲓ ⲙ.), cit
Mor 24 7 *F* ϭⲱⲧ μόνος εἶναι, Mk 12 25 (var ϣⲱⲡⲉ, *B*
ⲉⲣ ⲙⲫⲣⲏϯ) εἶναι; Si 48 18 καταλείπεσθαι; Gk om:
1 Kg 19 24, Lu 7 38 (var ϣⲱ., *B* as Gk), ROC 18 169
each one ϭⲱ ⲉϥⲥⲱⲕ ⲙⲡⲉⲧⲣⲓⲧⲟⲩⲱϥ, C 99 141 ⲁϥϭⲱ
ⲉϥⲣⲟⲧⲣⲧ = C 89 47 *B* ⲟ.; PS 24 ⲁϥϭⲱ ⲉϥⲡⲏⲧ, BG 64
ⲁϥϭⲱ ⲡⲣⲟⲥ ⲟⲩⲟⲓϣ, ShC 73 98 ⲉⲅⲛⲁϭⲱ ⲉⲩϭⲣⲁϩⲧ
(var ϣⲱ.), C 99 150 ⲁⲩϭⲱ ⲉⲩⲙⲏⲛ ⲉⲃⲟⲗ ⲉⲩϣⲗⲏⲗ =
C 89 86 *B* ⲟ.ⲉⲩⲙ.ⲉⲃ., BMis 362 ϥⲛⲁϭⲱ...ⲉϥⲥⲟⲡⲉ =

BSM 23 *B* ϥⲙⲏⲛ, ib 494 Nile ϭⲱ ⲉϥⲙⲟⲩϩ ⲉⲡⲟⲩ-
ⲙⲟⲩⲡ ⲉⲃⲟⲗ, BMar 246 ϭⲱ ⲧⲁϣⲁϫⲉ ⲙⲡⲁⲉⲓⲱⲧ, B
Hom 48 = R 2 2 32 soul ϭⲱ ϩⲁⲣⲓϩⲁⲣⲟⲥ ⲉⲥⲟϫⲟⲝ, Miss
4 570 went to desert ⲛⲧⲁϭⲱ ϩⲁⲣⲓϩⲁⲣⲟⲓ, Till Oster 16
A ϭⲟⲩ ⲉⲧⲉⲧⲛⲉ ⲛⲡⲁϩⲧ ϩⲏⲧ, ManiK 191 *A²* ⲉⲩϣⲁⲛϭⲱ
ⲉⲩⲙⲏⲛ ⲁⲃⲁⲗ ⲛϩⲏⲧⲟⲩ, Pcod 39 ⲉⲕϣⲁⲛϭⲱ ⲉⲕ⸗ = ibF
ϭⲱⲱⲧ, BIF 22 108 *F* ⲛⲧⲉⲗⲟⲩϭⲱⲱⲧ ⲉⲩⲱϣ ⲉⲃⲁⲗ, Kr
36 *F* ⲛⲉⲓϩⲱⲙⲉ ϭⲱ ⲉⲃⲥⲙⲁⲛⲧ, AZ 23 111 ⲡϣⲓ ⲛⲃⲁⲣⲟⲧ
ⲡⲟⲧ ⲛⲧⲉⲡⲟⲟϫ ϭⲟ;   qual: Lev 13 5 (*B* ⲟ. ⲉⲣⲁⲧ⸗)
μ., Sa 7 27 ϭ. ϩⲁⲣⲓϩⲁⲣⲟⲥ μ. ἐν αὐτῇ; Jo 16 32 ϭ.
ⲙⲁⲅⲁⲁ⸗ (*A²* ϣⲟⲟⲡ, *B* ⲭⲏ) μόνος εἶναι; Aeg 216 ⲛ-
ⲧⲟⲩ ϫⲉ ⲛⲉϭ. ⲡⲉ οὐκ ἀντιτύπτειν; ib 255 ⲟⲩⲁⲡⲁⲥ-
ⲕⲏⲧⲉ ⲉⲥϭ. ⲁⲩⲱ ⲉⲥϭⲉⲡⲓ.

b *desist, stop*: Ge 8 2 (*B* ⲧⲁⲣⲡⲟ) συνέχ., Cl 21 7 *A*
παρέχ.; Lu 8 44 (*B* ⲟ.) ἱστάναι, Ac 27 28 (*B* ⲉⲣ ⲟⲩⲱϣ)
διισ.; Ps 75 8 (*B* ϩⲉⲣⲓ), Lu 23 56 (*B* = Gk) ἡσυχάζειν;
Ps 82 1 (*B* ϩ.) καταπραΰνειν; Job 6 7 (*B*? ⲕⲏⲡ) παύεσθαι; 1 Kg 15 16 ἀνιέναι; Nu 11 2 (var ϩⲣⲟⲕ, *B* ϩⲣⲟⲩⲣ),
Mt 14 32 (*B* ϩ., *F* ⲗⲁ) κοπάζειν; Hab 1 13 *A*(*SB* ⲕⲁ
ⲣⲟ) παρασιωπᾶν; Lu 22 51 (var ϩⲱ, *B* ⲕⲏⲡ) ἐᾶν;
Ac 18 20 (*B* diff) ἐπινεύειν; Mk 5 29 (*B* ϣⲱⲟⲩⲓ) ξηραίνειν; R 1 29 ⲁⲥϭⲱ ⲛϭⲓ ⲧⲡⲛⲧⲥⲏ στέλλειν; PS 42 ⲛⲧⲉ-
ⲣⲉⲥϭⲱ ⲉⲥϭⲩⲙⲛⲉⲅⲉ, Br 260 ⲁⲡⲁⲓⲱⲛ ϣⲧⲟⲣⲧⲣ ⲁⲩⲱ
ⲁϥϭⲱ, ShP 131⁴ 89 of preacher ⲉϥⲛⲁϭⲱ ⲡⲁϣ ⲛⲛⲁⲩ?,
ShC 73 13 saith to sword ϫⲉⲕⲱⲛⲥ...ⲟⲩϫⲉ ϫⲉϭⲱ
ⲉⲣⲉⲕⲱⲛⲥ, Z 342 ⲁϥϭⲱ ⲙⲡⲉϥⲃⲱⲕ, Leyd 126 ⲧⲁⲡⲣⲟ
ⲡⲁⲧⲕⲁ ⲣⲱⲥ, ⲗⲁⲥ ⲉⲧⲉⲙⲉϥϭⲱ, ManiH 59 *A²* ⲁⲧϥⲧⲁ-
ⲡⲣⲟ ϭⲱ, Mor 19 100 ⲁϥϭⲱ ⲉϥⲟ ⲛⲉⲙⲡⲟ (var ib 18 99
ⲗⲟ), COAd 13 ϣⲁⲓⲕⲱⲧ ⲛⲏⲧⲛ ϩⲓⲃⲟⲗ ϣⲁⲡⲧⲉϭⲱ ⲉⲥ-
ϣⲧⲟⲣⲧ, ib 240 ⲧⲁⲁⲥ ⲡⲁϥ ⲙⲡⲣϭⲱ, BKU 1 26 (8117)
F if prescription followed ϣⲁϥϭⲱ (cf ⲗⲟ **b**), BIF 22
107 *F* ⲛⲧⲉⲗⲟⲩϭⲱ ⲉⲩϩⲱⲧⲉⲃ.

With following preposition.

—— ⲉ-, *wait for*: Job 36 2 (*B* ⲟ. ⲛ-), Ac 20 5 (*B*
do), BHom 21 ϭⲱ ⲉⲧⲁⲡⲟⲫⲁⲥⲓⲥ, R 2 2 25 ϩⲉⲛⲡϣⲧⲉⲕⲟ
ϭ.† ⲉⲣⲟⲕ μ., Job 7 2 (*B* ϫⲟⲩϣⲧ ⲉⲃⲟⲗ ϩⲁ-) ἀναμ., Is
30 18† *SF*(*B* ⲙⲟⲩⲛ) ἐμμ. ἐπί, Ac 1 4 (*B* ⲟ.) περιμ., Mk
8 2 (var ⲡⲣⲟⲥⲕⲁⲣⲧⲉⲣⲉⲓ, *B* do) προσμ. dat, Ps 141 7 (*B*
do) ὑπομ.; Phil 2 16 (*B* ⲁⲙⲟⲛⲓ) ἐπέχ.; PS 45 ⲉⲧⲁϩⲉ ⲛ
ⲉⲧϭ.† ⲉⲡⲙⲩⲥⲧⲏⲣⲓⲟⲛ, TT 52 ⲣⲡⲓⲥⲉ ⲉⲧϭ.† ⲉⲣⲟⲛ, BMis
168 ϭⲱ ⲉⲣⲟⲓ ⲡⲟⲩⲕⲟⲩⲓ;   vbal: Jos 19 47 ὑπομ. τοῦ;
Ac 14 18 (var om, *B* ϩⲉⲣⲓ) καταπαύ. τοῦ; P 129¹⁴ 54
we must not ϭⲱ ⲉⲉⲣ ⲡⲉϥⲙⲉⲉⲩⲉ.

—— ⲉϫⲛ-: Jud 5 9 εἰς no vb; ⲉϩⲣⲁⲓ ⲉ.: Jth 8 7,
Jo 3 36 (*B* ϣⲱⲡⲓ ϩⲓϫⲉⲛ-) μ. ἐπί.

—— ⲙⲛ-: Lu 24 29 μ. μετά, Si 46 14 διαμ. dat,
BHom 10 ϣⲁϥϭⲱ ⲛⲙⲙⲁⲕ παραμ.; Z 317 will come
& ϭⲱ ⲛⲙⲙⲁⲓ καταλύειν παρά; Aeg 244 ⲙⲁⲣⲉϥϭⲱ
ⲛⲙⲙⲁⲥ (*sc* wife), El 36 *A* ⲉⲕϭ.† ⲙⲡⲉⲧⲟⲩⲁⲁⲃⲉ, Mor
27 33 *F* -ⲱⲧ ⲛⲁⲕ...ⲙⲡⲧⲕⲥϭⲓⲙⲉ.

—— ⲛ- dat: Mk 14 34 (*B* ⲟ. ⲛ-) μ., Si 41 12 διαμ.
dat; Ex 24 14 (*B* do) ἡσυχ.; Eccl 2 10 *F* ϫⲱ ⲛ[ⲏⲓ ? (*S*
ⲁϩⲉ ⲣⲁⲧ⸗ ⲛ-) ἱστάναι dat; BSG 190 ϭⲱ ⲛⲏⲧⲛ ⲡⲟⲩ-

ⲕⲟⲩⲓ = *ib* 25 *B* ⲟ. ⲡⲏⲓ, BM 604 *F* ϭⲱ ⲡⲉⲕ;   *for, during* &c: ZNTW 24 86 *F* ϭⲱ ⲡⲟⲩⲃⲁⲟⲩ μ. acc; PS 332 ⲡⲕⲁⲕⲉ ϭⲱ ⲡⲗⲓⲕⲧⲩ ⲙⲡⲣⲏ;   *in*: Mt 26 38 (*B* ⲟ.) μ. ⲱⲇⲉ; Mk 9 5 SF(*B* ⳛⲱ.) εἶναι ⲱ̅.; Aeg 275 let no unbeliever ϭⲱ ⲙⲡⲉⲓⲙⲁ μή τις no vb; ManiH 40 *A²* ⲉⲅⲁϭⲱ ⲙⲡⲓⲙⲁ, PS 140 ⲁⲧⲡⲓⲥⲧⲓⲥ ϭⲱ ⲡⲧⲙⲏⲧⲉ, P Mich 6865 ⲙⲡⲣϭⲱ ⲙⲡⲉⲛⲃⲟⲗ.

—— ⲛⲧⲛ-: Lev 19 13 (*B* ⲡⲕⲟⲧ) κοιμᾶσθαι παρά; CA 112 ⲛⲧⲉⲟⲩⲥϥⲣⲁⲅⲓⲥ ϭⲱ ⲛⲧⲟⲟⲧϥ, PBu 67 ⲧⲁⲣⲟⲩϭⲱ ⲛⲧⲟⲟⲧⲛ ⲉⲓⲟ ⲡ⳨ⲥ̅ ⲉⲣⲟⲟⲩ.

—— ϣⲁ-: Is 5 11† *F*(*S* diff, *B* ⲟ.) μ. acc, Mt 11 23 (*B* ⳛⲱ.) μ. μέχρι; Sa 11 26 διατηρ.; BHom 25 ϭⲱ ϣⲁⲁⲧⲉⲡⲣⲟⲑⲉⲥⲙⲓⲁ στέγειν; CO 354 ϭⲱ ϣⲁⲧⲓⲕⲩⲣⲓⲁⲕⲏ.

—— ϩⲁ-: CA 95 ϭⲱ ϩⲁⲧⲉϥⲉ[ⲍ̣ⲟⲩⲥⲓⲁ (*cf ib* ⲣⲣ ⲥⳠⲖ.), Pap *penes* Maggs Bros 1937 ϭⲱ ϩⲁⲧⲟⲩⲉⲣϭⲟⲓ, AZ 21 100 *O* ⲉⲧϩⲟⲩ ⲁϣⲟⲓϣ.

—— ϩⲓ-: Jo 19 31 (*B* ⲟ. ϩⲓϫⲉⲛ-) μ. ἐπί; PS 194 ⲥⲉⲛⲁϭⲱ ϩⲓϩⲃⲟⲩⲣ, P 129¹⁶ 2 ⲙⲡⲉⲟⲩϭⲱ ⲡⲟⲩⲱⲧ ϭⲱ ϩⲓⲱⲱⲥ (*sc* head).

—— ϩⲛ-: Lu 10 7 (*B* ⳛⲱ.), Jo 8 31 SA²(*B* ⲟ.) μ. ἐν, Si 6 21 ἐμμ. ἐν, Is 8 10 (*B* ⳛⲱ.) ἐμμ. dat, 1 Cor 16 8 (*B* do) ἐπιμ. ἐν, Ac 11 23 (*B* ⲟ.) προσμ. dat; Pro 7 11 SA(*B* = Gk) ἡσυχ. ἐν; Ru 1 16 αὐλίζεσθαι; Ez 21 30 (ShC 73 12, *B* ⳛⲱ.) καταλύ. ἐν; Deu 9 9 (*B* ⳨ⲏ) καταγίνεσθαι ἐν; Z 353 ⲡⲉϥϭ.† ⲙⲁⲅⲁⲁⲩ ⲉⲙⲡⲧⲟⲟⲩ καθῆσθαι; PS 121 ⲉⲓϭ.† ⲟⲩⲃⲏϥ ϩⲙⲡⲉⲓⲧⲟⲡⲟⲥ, Pcod 19 ⲉϥϣⲁⲛϭⲱ ϩⲓⲡⲉϥⲧⲟϣ *keep within bounds*, JTS 10 398 ϥϭ.† ϩⲛⲧⲉϥⲉⲥⲓⲥ (φύ.) ⲡⲧⲉϥϭⲣⲓⲙⲉ ⲙⲙⲁⲧⲉ, BMar 202 ⲁⲡⲉⲧⲕⲁⲥ ϭⲱ ϩⲛⲡⲉⲥⲟⲩⲣⲏⲧⲉ, ManiH 8 *A²* world shall ϭⲱ ϩⲛⲟⲩⲥⲁⲧⲉ, Mor 30 31 *F* ϭⲱ ϩⲛⲧⲡⲟⲗⲓⲥ, *ib* 24 31 *F* ⲡⲉⲧⲙⲡϣⲏⲛ ⲛϭⲱⲱⲧ ϩⲛⲧⲉⲓⲁϭ ⲡϣⲱϣⲓ;   ϩⲣⲁⲓ ϩⲛ-: Jo 6 56 SA²(*B* ⳛⲱ.) μ. ἐν; Aeg 236 ϭ.ϩ. ⲡϩⲏⲧⲟⲩ; as ⲛⲣ ⲙ: Phil 1 24 SF(*B* ⳛⲱ.) ἐπιμ. dat.

—— ϩⲓⲣⲡ-: Deu 20 12 (*B* ϭⲗⲟ ⲉϩⲣⲏⲓ Va) περικαθίζειν; Ob 14 SA(*B* ⲟ. ⲉⲣⲁⲧϥ ϩⲓϫⲉⲛ-) ἐφιστάναι ἐπί; 2 Kg 17 12 παρεμβάλλειν ἐπί; Hab 1 10 SA(*B* ⲁⲙⲟⲛⲓ) κρατεῖν gen; Mor 47 88 ⲁⲩϭⲱ ϩⲓⲣⲱϥ *encamp against*.

—— ϩⲁ(ϩ)ⲧⲛ-: Jo 14 17 SA²(*B* ⳛⲱ. ⲛⲉⲙ-) μ. παρά; R 1 140 ⲉⲧϭ.† ϩ. ⲡⲧⲁⲫⲟⲥ παραμ. dat; Ge 29 14 (*B* ⳨ⲏ ⲛⲉⲙ-) εἶναι μετά; Ps 54 (*B* ⳛⲱ. ϫⲉⲛ-) παροικεῖν dat; Miss 4 638 ⲉⲓⲟⲩⲱϣ ⲉⲥϭⲱ ϩⲁⲣⲧⲏⲕ = C 41 34 *B* ⲟ. ϫⲁⲧⲟⲧⲕ, ManiH 22 *A²* ϭⲱ ϩ. ⲡⲉϥϣⲃⲏⲣ.

—— ϩⲓϫⲛ-: 1 Tim 4 16 (*B* ⲙⲏⲛ ⲛϭⲣⲏⲓ ϫⲉⲛ-) ἐπιμ. dat; Job 37 17 (*B* ϩⲉⲣⲓ) ἡσυχ. ἐπί; Deu 32 11 (*B* diff, Ps 41 1 (*B* ϣⲱ. ϩ.) ἐπιποθεῖν ἐπί; Nu 9 19 (*B* ⲱⲥⲕ) ἐφέλκεσθαι ἐπί; Zech 3 7 (*B* as Gk) διακρίνειν; C 99 144 ⲁϥϭⲱ ϩⲓϫⲱⲟⲩ (*sc* new monasteries) = C 89 52 *B* ⲑⲱⲙ ⲉϫⲱⲟⲩ = Miss 4 568 يبقى يتردّد اليهم = Va ar 172 32 مذاكرة; ShC 73 93 ϭⲱ ϩⲓϫⲱⲟⲩ (*sc* brethren?) ϩⲛⲧⲉⲥⲃⲱ, Ep 244 send ⲧⲉⲕⲥⲃⲱ ⲛⲥϭⲱ (*sic*) ϩⲓϫⲱⲓ ⲙⲙⲡⲁⲛⲓ, BMis 224 ⲡⲉⲡⲓⲧⲣⲟⲡⲟⲥ ϭⲱϩ. ⲡϩⲏⲅⲉ of workshops, WS 142 ϭⲱ ϩⲓϫⲱⲟⲩ (*sc* sacks) ⲛⲥⲟⲩ-

ⲥⲙⲧⲟⲩ, ManiH 11 *A²* ϥⲁϭⲱ ϩⲓϫⲱⲥ *till world's end*; ϩⲣⲁⲓ ϩ.: Jth 7 13 παρεμβάλ. ἐπί.

With following adverb.   ⲥ ⲙⲙⲁⲩ: Ac 17 14 (*B* ⲥⲱϫⲡ) ὑπομ. ἐκεῖ;   ⲥ ⲡϩⲟⲩⲛ: J 89 13 we went to monastery ⲁⲛϭⲱ ⲛ. beseeching;   ⲥ ϣⲁⲃⲟⲗ: Sa 1 14 ⲉⲧⲣⲉⲩϭⲱ ϣ. εἰς τὸ εἶναι; ManiP 86 *A²* ⲁⲓϭⲱ ϣ. ⲉⲓⲙⲉⲗⲉⲧⲁ.

With following negative: Ru 3 18 ⲡⲣⲱⲙⲉ ⲛⲁϭⲱ ⲁⲛ ⲉⲙⲡⲉϥϫⲱⲕ ἡσυχ.;   Mor 53 10 ⲡⲧⲁⲙⲓⲙ ϭⲱ ⲡⲁⲧⲙⲟⲩ?, Bor 254 172 ⲉⲅϭ.† ⲡⲁⲧⲟⲩⲱⲙ, CO 83 ⲙⲡⲣⲕⲱ ⲡⲁⲧⲭⲓⲧϥ, BM 581 *F* ⲙⲡⲉⲣϭⲟ ⲡⲁⲧⲧⲁⲟⲩⲁ;   Jos 10 19 ⲙⲡⲣϭⲱ ⲁⲭⲙⲡⲱⲧ ἱστάναι; Pro 1 33 ϭⲱ ⲁⲭⲓϩⲣⲟⲧⲉ (*AB* ⲙⲧⲟⲛ ⲙⲙⲟϥ) ἡσυχ.;   Ac 14 17 ⲙⲡϥϭⲱ ⲡⲟⲩⲉϣ ⲛⲣⲙⲛⲧⲣⲉ- ἀφιέναι; ShBMOr 8810 371 ⲙⲡⲣϭⲱ ⲡⲟⲩⲉϣ ⲡⲧⲁⲙⲟⲟⲩ, HM 1 75 ⲧⲡⲛⲁϭⲱ ⲡⲟⲩⲉϣ ⲛⲧⲡⲡⲟⲟⲩ ⲡⲥⲱⲥ = EW 115 *B* ϩⲉⲙⲥⲓ;   CO 322 ⲙⲡⲣⲕⲱ ⲡϣⲟⲩⲉⲓ (*v* p 601 a).

ⲁⲧϭⲱ: ShIF 239 a visible malady ⲟⲩⲁ. ⲡⲉ ⲉⲧⲣⲉϥϩⲱⲛ.   Prob *l* ⲁⲧϭⲟⲙ.

ϭⲓⲛϭⲱ, *keeping silence*: Sh(?)ViK 9344 60 ⲧϭ. ⲁⲩⲱ ⲧϭⲓⲛϫⲉ ⲟⲩϣⲁϫⲉ, ShViK 9764 101]ⲧⲉϥϭ. (no context).

ϭⲱ *S* nn, meaning unknown, epithet of rope: Copt Mus ostr ⲣⳠⳠⲗ (*Guide* 1 57) ⲡⲱϩ ⲛϭⲱ *paral* ⲡⲱϩ ⲛϭⲗⲟϭ, Turin ostr *v* p 425 *a*.

ϭⲱ *B* *v* ⲉϣⲟ.

ϭⲃ- *A²* in ϭⲃⲥⲉⲓⲣⲉ (ManiK 54, P 23) *v* ⲥⲓⲣ 1°.

ϭⲱⲃ *v* ϭⲃⲃⲉ.

ϭⲱⲃ *B* *v* ϣⲱⲃ *s f.*

ϭⲁⲃⲓ- *A*, ϫⲁⲃⲓ- *B* *v* ϭⲃⲃⲉ.

ϭⲓⲃⲉ *v* ⲕⲏⲡⲉ *s f.*

ϭⲱⲱⲃⲉ¹ *S*, ϭⲱⲃⲉ² SAA², ϫⲱⲃⲓ *B*, ϭ. *S/F*, ϭⲃ- *S* nn f (once), *leaf*: Ge 3 7 S²(Mus 50 8)*B*, Pro 11 14 S²AB, Mt 24 32 S²BF, Ap 22 2 S¹B φύλλον; Ob 5 *B* (SA ϫⲗⲗⲉ) ἐπιφυλλίς; Ap 6 13 S¹(*B* ⲃⲛϣ) ὄλυνθος; Ja 1 11 S²m(Ryl 94 101, var & *B* ϩⲣⲏⲣⲉ *qv*) ἄνθος; Ez 47 12 *B* folium, BMis 565 S¹ fol.; ϭ. ⲛⲣⲡⲱ S¹F(*B* ϫ. only) φύλ.; BMOr 8771 68 *B* scribe's tools ⲡⲓϫⲱⲃ چوب (*cf* K 141 ϫⲁⲣⲧⲏⲥ ⳧,); PMéd 195 *S* ϭ. ⲛⲕⲟⲥ (*quid*?) ⲉⲧϣⲟⲟⲩⲉ, BG 56 *S* ⲡⲉϥϭ.², BMar 210 *S* ϩⲉⲛϭ.¹ *covered him* = Rec 6 174 *B*, Pcod 22 ϭ.¹ (var²), R 2 1 76 *S* ϣⲗⲉ ... ⲉϥⲟϣ ⲛϭ.², PBad 5 398 S/, ManiP 8 *A²*, AZ 33 56 *F* ϭⲟⲃⲓ, Va 63 117 *B* in rubric ϯⲉ ⲛⲭ. *leaves of book*; ϭⲃ- *S*: Ge 8 11 ϭⲃⲭⲟⲉⲓⲧ φ. ἐλαίας; KroppJ 49 ϭⲃⲧⲁⲫⲏ(ⲛ); ϭⲃϣⲁ *v* p 544 *a*;   ⲁⲧϭ. *S*, *without leaves*: Kr 6 ⲥⲟⲣⲡ (*sic* MS, *l*? ⲥⲟⲣⲙ) ⲡⲁ.; ⲗⲁϭ.,-ϫ. *v* p 135 *a*, adding Ez 20 28 *B*(var ⲟⲓ ⲛϭⲛⲓⲃⲓ, *S* sim) κατάσκιος & as name in pap *penes* HT;   ⲕⲁⲧϥ ϭ. *S*:

Glos 226 φυλλολόγος· [ⲡⲉⲧ- or ? ⲣⲉϥ]ⲕ. ϭ.; ⲧⲉϭⲟ
ϭ. A: Cl 23 4 φυλλοροεῖν; ϩⲓ ϫ. ⲉⲃⲟⲗ B: Mk 13
28 (SF ϭ. ϯⲟⲩⲱ) φ. ἐκφύειν; ϫⲓ ϭ., ϭⲓ ϫ.: Lam 2
20 B(S diff) ἐπιφυλλίζειν, Mic 7 1 B(SA ⲕⲉⲧϥ ϫⲗⲉ)
ἐπιφυλλίς; Blake 300 S ⲁⲥⲁⲣⲭⲉⲓ ⲛϫⲓ ϭ.
Cf ϭⲱⲃϭⲱⲃⲉ.

ϭⲱⲃⲉ S nn f, meaning unknown: CO 454 ⲕⲁⲗⲕⲓⲗ,
ⲙⲣⲱϩⲉ, ϭ. ⲡⲁⲗⲁ[ⲩ, AZ 16 17 among σκεύη ϣⲟⲙⲧⲉ
ⲛϭ., BP 419 *varia* ϣⲧⲏⲛ ⲛⲉⲣⲓⲙ[ⲉ ?]ⲛϭ. ⲙⲛⲟⲩⲣ-
[ϣⲱⲛ ?]ⲛⲕⲟⲕⲕⲟⲥ, ST 334 same ?

ϭⲃⲓⲉ A² vb intr, meaning unknown: ManiP 164
fight with dragon ⲁⲡⲉϫⲣⲁⲕⲱⲛ ϭ. *Cf* ϭⲃⲃⲉ.

ϭⲃⲟⲓ, ϭⲃⲟⲉ S, ϭϥⲟⲉⲓ Sᵃ, ϭⲃⲁ(ⲉ)ⲓ AA², ϫϥⲟⲓ B,
ϭⲃⲁⲓ F nn m, *arm* of man, *leg* of beast: Ge 49 24 S(B
ϣⲱⲃϣ), Nu 18 18 S(var & B ϣⲱⲡϣ), Deu 18 3 S
ϭⲃⲟⲉ (var -ⲟⲓ, B do), Si 38 38 S -ⲟⲉ (collated, *cf* AZ
47 43), Is 30 30 SBF, Zech 11 17 A(B ϣ.), Jo 12 38
SA²(B do) βραχίων; 1 Kg 5 4 S καρπός opp ϩⲓⲟⲙⲉ;
Pro 5 20 SA(B ⲁⲗⲱϫ), Va 58 127 B ⲫⲉⲣϣ ⲛⲉⲕϫ. ⲉⲃⲟⲗ
ἀγκάλη; Deu 33 12 B(S diff), Job 31 20 B(S ⲛⲁϩⲃ),
Ez 24 4 B(S ϣ.) ὦμος; ShC 73 162 S uncover ⲛⲉⲧⲛ-
ϭ. (var ϫⲛⲁϩⲣ), BodlMarsh 32 35 B lay ⲟⲩⲣⲁⲛⲓⲟⲛ
(ὡράριον) on deacon's ϫ. ⲛϫⲁϭⲏ (var TEuch 1 13
ⲙⲟϯ); BMis 77 S mother set her down ϩⲓϫⲛⲛⲉⲥϭ.,
P 68 31 S ⲛϭ. ⲛⲧⲉⲥⲧⲟⲗⲏ, BM 351 34 *v* ϫⲱϩ 1° ⲉ-,
Imp Russ Ar S 18 029 Sᵃ, ManiH 54 A² ⲡⲱⲣϣ ⲁⲃⲁⲗ
...ⲛⲛⲉϥϭ., GMir 263 S ⲥⲱⲗⲡ ⲛⲛⲁϭ. = Va 59 19 B.

ϭⲃⲃⲉ, ϭⲟⲟⲃ†, -ϥ† S, ϭⲁⲃ†(?)A², ϫⲉⲃⲓⲱⲟⲩ†, ϫⲱⲃⲓ†,
ϫⲱⲃ† B(all rare), p c ϭⲁⲃ- SF, ϭⲁⲃⲓ- A, ϫ. B vb intr,
become, be feeble, timid: Ps 17 36 (B ϣⲱⲛⲓ), Ro 4 19
(B do, F ⲡⲟϣⲥ ⲛϩⲏⲧ) ἀσθενεῖν, ViSitz 172 4 27 ἔξασ.;
Ps 118 161 (B ⲉⲣ ϩⲟⲧ) δειλιᾶν; Sa 17 12 ἥττων; BM
216 110 ⲧⲉⲯⲩⲭⲏ ϭ. λεπτύνειν opp ϯⲟⲩⲱ, Mor 18 115
ⲛϣⲁϫⲉⲓ ⲛϭ. λεπτότερος γίνεσθαι; Mor 37 53 body
ⲕⲏⲙⲉ opp ϭ. ἰσχνοῦν; P 131² 147 ⲧⲉⲯⲩⲭⲏ ϭ. ⲛϭⲣ
ϭⲱⲃ; ShR 2 3 71 martyrs ⲙⲛⲟⲩϭ. ϩⲟⲗⲱⲥ, C 99 127
ⲥⲱⲙⲁ ϭ. through sickness; qual: Is 28 20 (B
ϩⲉϫϩⲱϫ), Ez 17 6 B ϫⲱⲃ, Ro 8 3 (B ϣ.) ἀσ., Ge 29
17 (var ϭⲟⲟϥ, B ϫⲁⲓⲏ), Ez 34 20 (ShR 2 3 35, B ϫⲟ-
ϫⲉⲃ), 1 Cor 4 10 S(B ϫⲱⲃ nn), Aeg 248 opp ϫⲟⲟⲣ
ἀσθενής; Sa 9 14 δειλός; Ge 41 19 (B ϣⲟⲙ) λεπτός;
Lev 22 24 (B ϩⲟϫϩⲉϫ) ἐκθλίβεσθαι; K 73 B ⲉⲧϫⲱⲃⲓ
ⲋⲋⲋ; ShMich 550 19 victuals ⲉⲧϭ. ⲉⲧⲣ ⲁⲡⲁⲛ ⲁⲛ, Sh
Bor 300 71 wroth with sheep ⲛⲥⲉϭⲟⲟⲃⲉ ⲁⲛ, but because disobedient, Z 271 ⲛⲉⲧϭⲟⲟϥ...ϩⲙⲡⲉⲩⲙⲉⲉⲩⲉ,
ManiP 70 A² ⲟⲩⲏⲓ [ⲉϥ]ϭⲁⲃ ⲛⲉⲧⲕⲛⲉⲣϩⲧϥ(this word?),
C 41 68 B young camel ϫⲉⲃ. for lack of milk = Miss
4 394 ⋯; p c ϭ., ϫ. ϩⲏⲧ: Ap 21 8 S(B ϣⲗⲁϩ
ⲛϩⲏⲧ) δειλός; Pro 12 8 SA(B do) νωθροκάρδιος; *ib*
18 8 SA ἀνδρόγυνος; BM 185 S ⲛϭⲁⲃ[ϩⲏⲧ] opp ϫⲁⲣϩⲏⲧ, BKU 1 31 5 S ⲛϭ. ⲏ ⲡⲣⲉϥⲣ ϩⲟⲧⲉ; ⲙⲛⲧϭ.,

ⲙⲉⲧϫ.ϩ.: Wess 11 168 S δειλία; ShZ 602 S opp
ⲙⲛⲧⲛⲁϣⲧϩⲏⲧ, BMis 285 S ⲁⲅⲛⲟϭ ⲙⲙ. ⲧⲁϩⲣⲟⲩ, C
89 162 B, Mor 24 28 F; p ϭ., ⲉⲣ ϫ.ϩ.: Ps 26 1
B(S p ϭⲱⲃ) δειλιᾶν, Mk 4 40 S(B ϣⲱⲛⲓ) -λός; Ann
17 151 S ⲙⲡⲉⲣⲣ ϩⲟⲧⲉ ⲟⲩⲇⲉ ⲙⲡⲉⲣⲉⲣ ϭ., DeV 2 15 B
ⲙⲡⲉⲣⲉⲣ ϫ., Mun 143 S ⲁⲛϣⲱⲡⲉ ⲉⲡⲟ ⲛϭ.

―――― nn m S, *weakness*: Sa 17 14 προδοσία; Tri
237 ϩⲉⲛⲉⲃⲓⲏⲛ ⲁⲩⲱ ϩⲉⲛϭ. ⋯.
Cf ⲕⲟⲟⲃⲉϥ ⋯ p 99 a, which may belong here.

ϭⲱⲃ SAA²F, ϭⲁϥ Sᶠ, ϫⲱⲃ, -ⲃⲓ (once) B, ϭⲟϥ, ϫ.
F, f ϫⲟⲃⲉ S(once), -ⲃⲓ B nn, *weak person*: Job 4 3 S
(B ⲁⲧϫⲟⲙ) Is 32 4 SF(B ⲉⲧϣⲱⲛⲓ) ἀσθενεῖν, Pro 6 8
SAB, 1 Cor 8 10 SF(B ⲟⲓ ⲛϣ.), MG 25 220 B ⲁⲛⲟⲕ
ⲟⲩϫ., Cl 6 2 A ⲛϭ. ϩⲓⲧⲟⲩⲥⲁⲣϫ -νής; Job 5 15 S(B
ⲁⲧϫ.) ἀδύνατος; Am 8 4 B(S ϩⲏⲕⲉ) πτωχός; *ib* 4 1 B
(S ⲉⲧⲙⲟⲕϩ) πένης; Si 37 12 S δειλός; Ap 3 17 B(S
ⲉⲃⲓⲏⲛ) ἐλεεινός; EpJer 35 B(F ⲑⲉⲃⲓⲏⲟⲩⲧ) ἠτ.; K
73 B ⲛⲓϫⲱⲃⲓ ⋯ BMOr 8775 87 B ⲛⲡⲣⲁⲕⲧⲟⲓ· ⲛⲓϫ.
⋯; TU 24 1 3 S didst succour ⲛϭ. & give them
strength, BHom 117 S ⲛⲕⲱ ⲱⲣⲉ...ⲛϭ., ManiP 211
A² ⲛⲓϭ. ⲛⲣⲱⲥ, MIE 2 383 B ⲙⲛⲓⲧⲟⲩ ⲛⲁⲅⲁⲡⲏ ⲛⲛⲓϫ.
= BAp 107 S ⲛϩⲏⲕⲉ; as name (epithet): PLond 5
132 S ⲫⲟⲓⲃⲁⲙⲙⲱⲛ ⲛϭ.; f B: ROC 27 144 ⲁⲛⲟⲕ
ϭⲁϥϫ., C 86 77 sim; as adj: Ac 4 9 SB, Cl 10 2
A ἀσθενής; Ac 14 8 S(B ⲁⲧϫⲟⲙ) ἀδύν.; BMar 198
S ⲥⲛⲏⲩ ⲛⲕⲱⲃ πένης; Si 22 19 S δει.; Pro 22 29 SA
νωθρός; 2 Kg 6 22 S(var nn) ἀχρεῖος (varr εὐτελής,
ταπεινός); BHom 50 S ϭⲟⲓⲙⲉ ⲛϭ., Mani K 13 A²
ϩⲏⲧ ⲛϭ., C 43 48 B ⲉϫⲙⲁⲗⲱⲧⲟⲥ ⲛϫ., *ib* 41 32 B ϫ.
ⲙⲙⲟⲛⲁⲭⲟⲥ, BM 545 (2) F ⲛⲓϫⲟϥ ⲛⲣⲟⲅⲙⲉ; f:
Saq 317 S ⲧⲁϫⲟⲃⲉ ⲛⲯⲩⲭⲏ, ROC 25 257 B ⲭⲏⲣⲁ
...ⲛϫ., *ib* 27 144 B ⲭⲟⲩⲃⲓ; ⲙⲛⲧϭ., ⲙⲉⲧϫ., *weakness, folly*: Ro 8 26 SB, 2 Cor 12 10 F(S ⲙⲛⲧⲁⲧϭⲟⲙ,
B ϣⲱ.) ἀσθένεια, 1 Cor 1 27 B(S ϭⲟϭ) -νής; Pro 19
12 SA, C 86 63 B δειλία; *ib* 288 B ταπείνωσις; PS
40 S strength diminished ⲁⲩϣⲱⲛⲉ ϩⲛⲟⲩⲙ., ShA 2
341 S swore not again to do ⲧⲉⲓⲙ. (sc filing teeth),
ShC 73 95 S ⲙ. ... ⲉⲩⲙⲉϩ ⲙⲛⲧϭⲟϥ, Miss 4 591 S
demon came forth ϩⲛⲟⲩⲙ., MIE 2 390 B help ⲧⲉⲛⲙ.,
Archiv Or '37 126 Sᶠ spirit of ⲙⲉⲧϭⲁϥ = CaiEuch 59
B ⲛⲧⲉ ⲛⲓϣⲱⲛⲓ; p ϭ., ⲉⲣ ϫ. (rare), intr: 1 Kg 2 5
(B ϣⲱ.), Lam 5 13 (BF do), Hos 4 5 SA(B do) ἀσθενεῖν, Mor 37 107 ⲟ ⲛϭ. ϩⲓⲡⲉⲥⲥⲱⲙⲁ ἀσθενής; Ps 26 1
(B ⲉⲣ ϫⲁⲃⲓϩⲏⲧ), Jo 14 27 (B ⲉⲣ ϣⲗⲁϩ ⲛϩⲏⲧ) δειλιᾶν;
Is 8 15 (B ⲉⲣ ⲁⲧϫⲟⲙ) ἀδυνατεῖν; *ib* 19 1 (var ϭⲱⲧⲡ)
ἡττᾶσθαι; Jos 5 1 καταπλήσσεσθαι; PS 36 ⲛⲥⲉⲣ.
ϩⲛⲧⲉⲩϭⲟⲙ, ShP 130² 96 overburdened workmen ⲣ.
ⲛⲛⲉⲩϩⲁⲣⲃ, ShIF 84 let none ⲣ. ϩⲓⲧⲉⲩϭⲩⲡⲟⲙⲟⲛⲏ,
ShMIF 23 87 ⲟⲩϭⲁⲛⲁϩ ⲉⲣⲉⲧⲉϥϭⲓϫ...ⲣ., Mor 22 52
ⲙⲏ ⲛⲧⲁⲡⲡⲉ̄ ⲣ. ⲛⲡⲁϩⲟⲙⲉⲛ?, Bor 238 1 ⲛⲉⲧⲟ ⲛϭ. ⲉⲛⲉⲩ-
ⲟⲩⲣⲏⲧⲉ, ManiH 27 A² ⲉⲕ]ⲕⲗⲏⲥⲓⲁ ⲡⲁⲣ. ⲉⲛ, PO 11 343
B ⲁϥⲉⲣ. ⲛⲟⲩⲱⲓⲛⲓ *had weak sight*, Mor 30 5 F ⲉⲣ ϭⲟϥ
ⲛϩⲏⲧ = BMis 233 S ϣⲗⲁϩ, CMSS 78 F ⲛⲙⲉⲥⲓ ⲛⲧⲁⲃ-

ⲉⲗ ϭⲟϥ;   tr: 1 Kg 2 10 ἀσθ. ποιεῖν; Ps 16 9 B(S ⲙⲟⲩⲕⲣ) ταλαιπωρεῖν; Nah 2 12 A(B ⲱⲭⲣ) ἀποπνίγειν; 1 Kg 17 50 (B om) πατάσσειν; ShC 73 16 enemy ⲁⲁⲩ ⲛϭ. ϩⲓⲧⲛⲡⲉϥⲥⲟⲧⲉ, ShMIF 23 18 smote him & ⲁϥⲁⲁϥ ⲛϭ., RNC 56 ⲛϩⲁⲥⲁⲡⲓⲥⲧⲏⲣⲓⲟⲛ ⲁⲕⲁⲁⲩ ⲛϭ., Ep 176 ⲁⲩⲣ ⲡⲁϭⲓⲝ ⲛϭ., BSM 124 B ⲁⲓϥ ⲛⲟⲩϭ. ⲉⲙⲁϣⲱ = Mor 22 133 S.

ϭⲃⲓⲣ A, ϭⲃⲟⲩⲣ A² v ϩⲃⲟⲩⲣ.

ϭⲃⲥⲉⲓⲣⲉ A² v ϭⲓⲣ 1°.

ϭⲁⲃⲱⲧ B nn, material or instrument used in cleansing sheep: MG 25 155 when sheep ⲉⲣ ϫⲉⲣϫⲓ ϣⲁϥⲧ ϭ. ⲡⲁϥ ϣⲁⲧⲉϥⲕⲱⲕ ⲛⲛⲓϫⲉⲣϫⲓ.

ϭⲃϣⲁ v ϣⲁ nose.

ϭⲁⲃϭⲁⲃ¹, ϭⲁϥϭⲁϥ², ⲕⲁϥⲕⲁϥ³, ⲅⲁϭⲕ.⁴, ϭⲁⲃϩⲏⲃ⁵ S nn, chick-pea: P 44 83 ⲉⲣⲉⲃⲓⲛⲑⲱ (-θος)· ϭ.¹ ⲉⲧϭⲣ = 43 58 ϭ.⁵ (v ϩⲏⲣ†), حمص مقلي ‎, ib ⲧⲣⲱⲧⲁⲗⲓⲥⲟⲛ (l ? -λιος)· ϭ.¹ do, ib ⲉⲣⲉⲃⲓⲛⲑⲟⲥ ⲙⲁⲩⲣⲟⲛ . ϭ.¹ (sic l) ⲉⲧⲕⲏⲙ حاسود ‎ '; Miss 4 723 bread, dates & ϩⲉⲡⲕⲟⲩⲓ ⲛϭ.¹ (Synax 1 322 15 om word), Bodl(P) d 47 among herbs ϥⲁⲥⲓⲗⲉ, ϭ.², ϭⲟⲩϫ, RE 9 150]ⲛⲧⲉ ⲛⲕ.³ named with ⲟⲩⲟⲧⲉ ⲡⲛⲓⲥⲉ, Cai Copt Mus ostr ⲅϥⲅⲗ (Guide 1 57) ⲧⲟ ⲣⲧⲟⲃ ⲛⲧ.⁴   ϫⲟϥϫⲟϥ· ⲙⲟⲗⲟϫ[ⲏ medical MS penes W. Erichsen 112 prob not this.

V BIF 28 82.

ϭⲉⲃϭⲓⲃ, ϭⲓⲃ. S nn as pl, fragments, shreds (?): ShA 2 19 ϩⲉⲛϭ. (var ϭⲓⲃ.) ⲛϣⲉ as firewood.

(ϭⲟⲃϭⲃ), ϭⲃϭⲱⲃ⧸ S vb tr, tread to pieces or sim: ShIF 89 ⲁⲩϫⲟⲙⲟⲩ (sc bandages) ϩⲓⲛⲡⲉϥⲧⲟⲟⲩⲉ ⲁϥϭⲃϭⲱⲃⲟⲩ ⲉⲁϥϩⲣⲓⲧⲟⲩ.   Cf preceding word & ϭⲃⲃⲉ.

ϭⲱⲃϭⲱⲃⲉ S nn, leaf of melon (so Ar): P 44 82 ⲕⲉⲩⲭⲣⲓⲥⲁⲑⲱϫⲱⲡ· ⲟⲙⲟⲫⲟⲟⲩ· ϭ. ورق فقوس = 43 57 ⲱⲙⲟⲫⲟⲟⲩ فقوس only.   Cf ϣⲱⲡⲉ 'ⲃ, so ? ϭⲱⲃⲉ + ϣⲱⲡⲉ.

ϭⲁⲕ B v ϫⲁⲕ 1°.

ϭⲓⲕⲥ B nn m, spindle (?): K 126 ⲡⲓϭ. جزل (no var, l ? مغزل Sobhy, but v AZ 14 115).

ϭⲗ, ϭⲁⲗ S nn m, weapon: Si 29 16 ἀσπίς, Jth 9 7 γαῖσος or ? ἀσ.; Is 13 4 ⲣⲉϥⲙⲓϣⲉ ⲙⲡϭⲗ ὁπλομάχος, cit P 44 112 رمح ‎; BKU 1 31 (5) ⲟⲩϭⲁⲗ ⲙⲛⲟⲩⲡⲛⲓⲧⲉ. Cf ? ϫⲓⲗⲗⲉⲓ.

ϭⲁⲗ F v ϧⲟⲗ wave.

ϭⲏⲗ A² nn m, cry: ManiP 206 ⲡϭ. ⲉⲧⲁⲡⲁⲥⲡⲏⲩ ⲡⲁϫϥ, ib 205 ⲉⲩⲕⲁ ϭ. ⲁⲃⲁⲗ ⲁⲭⲱⲓ;   with vb ⲱϣ (ⲁϣ-): AP 36 ⲁ]ϥⲁϣ ϭ. ⲉϥϫⲟⲩ ⲙⲙⲁⲥ;   ⲥ ⲁⲃⲁⲗ (mostly), cry out: Jo 11 43 (S ⲁϣⲕⲁⲕ, A ⲁϣϭⲁⲡ prob, B ⲱϣ ⲉⲃⲟⲗ) κραυγάζειν; AP 15 κράζειν; ib 14

ἀνακ.; ib 13 βοᾶν; ManiP 123 ⲁⲕⲁϣ ϭ. ⲁⲃ. ϫⲉ-, ib H 93 ⲉϥϣⲗⲏⲗ ϩⲱⲥⲧⲉ ⲁⲧⲩⲁϣ ϭ. ⲁⲃ.;   as nn m: Mani H 21 ⲡϩⲣⲁ[ⲩ ⲙⲡⲁϣ]ϭ. ⲙⲛⲡⲣⲓⲙⲉ.   Cf ⲁϣ ⲁⲗ (ⲁⲗ 3°), ϣⲕⲁⲕ, ϣϭⲁⲡ.

ϭⲟⲗ S, ϭⲁⲗ Sᶠ AA²F nn m f(rare), lie, liar (B mostly ⲛⲟⲩϫ, ⲙⲉⲑⲛ.): Ps 5 6, Pro 6 19 SA, Is 30 12 SF, Jo 8 44 (A² ⲣⲉϥϫⲉ ϭ.) ψεῦδος, Ro 3 4 ψεύστης; Ac 21 24 (B ϩⲗⲓ) οὐδέν; ShC 73 11 ϣⲁϫⲉ ⲙⲡϭ., ib 42 135 ⲣ ⲧⲏⲩⲧⲛ ⲙⲙⲉ ⲉⲛⲧⲉⲧⲛϩⲉⲛϭ., BM 255 ⲧⲱϩ ⲛⲧⲁⲙⲉ ⲙⲛⲡϭ., Ep 503 ⲛϫⲁⲧⲁϭⲟ ϭ., ManiK 79 A² ⲡⲱⲡⲉ ⲡⲉⲧⲉⲛⲙⲓⲛⲉ ⲁⲩϭ., PMich 4547 F ⲙⲉ(ⲛ) ⲗⲁⲁⲩ ⲛϫ. (sic);   f: Is 44 20 ⲟⲩϭ. (var Sᶠ) ⲧⲉⲧⲛⲧⲁⲟⲩⲓⲛⲁⲙ ψεύ., Ro 3 7 ⲧⲁϭ. ψεῦσμα;   as adj: Ex 20 16, Pro 8 7 SA ψευδής, 2 Thes 2 9 -δος; ShIF 300 ϣⲏⲣⲉ ⲛϭ., ϣⲉⲉⲣⲉ ⲡⲛⲟⲩϫ, LMär 27 ϣⲁϫⲉ ⲛϭ., El 52 A, ManiH 30 A², ViK 7033 F all sim, BMis 134 ⲫⲁⲡⲧⲁⲥⲓⲁ ⲛϭ., Ep App 1 85 ⲙⲛⲧⲟⲩⲁ ⲛϭ.

ⲣ ϭⲟⲗ, be lie, false: Jos 23 14 διαφωνεῖν; Mani 2 A² ⲡⲥⲉϫⲉ…ⲛⲁⲣ ϭ.;   make liar, stultify: ShC 42 135 ⲁⲧⲉⲧⲛⲉⲓⲣⲉ ⲛⲧⲥⲩⲛⲁⲅⲱⲅⲏ ⲛϭ., BMis 245 ⲡⲧⲁⲣ ⲡⲉϥϣⲁϫⲉ ⲛϭ., Mor 55 18 ⲕⲛⲁⲣ ⲗⲁⲅⲉⲓⲁ ⲛϭ. when he saith &c.

ϫⲓ, ϫⲉ ϭⲟⲗ, speak lie: Lev 19 11, Job 31 28, Ro 9 1 (var ϫⲉ), He 6 18 SF ϫⲉ, Cl 27 2 A ϫⲉ ψεύδεσθαι; BG 15 ⲡⲱⲥ ⲧⲉϫⲓ ϭ.?, Sh(?)ViK 9345 15 ϫⲉ ⲙⲉ, ϫⲓ ϭ., ST 280 ⲉⲓϫⲉ ⲛϭⲟⲗ ⲁⲛ, ManiP 139 A² ⲙⲁϥϫⲉ ϭ.;   as nn m: Ps 58 12 ψεῦδος;   ⲥ ⲉ-: Jos 24 27 ψεύ. dat, Hos 9 2 Sᶠ ϫⲉ (JEA 11 245) A ψ. acc, Mt 5 11 ψ. ἕνεκεν, Col 3 9 ψ. εἰς; PS 92 ⲁⲛϫⲓ ϭ. ⲉⲣⲟⲓ, ShC 73 91 ϫⲓ ϭ. ⲉⲧⲁⲙⲉ, CO 94 ⲉϥϫⲓ ϭ. ⲉⲣⲟⲓ;   ⲥ ⲉϫⲛ-: ShC 73 171 ⲡⲉⲧⲛⲁϫⲓ ϭ. ⲉ. ⲟⲩⲱⲃ, ShR 2 3 7 ⲛϭϫⲓ ϭ. ⲉϫⲱⲕ saying thou wast not there;   ⲥ ⲛ-: Jth 11 5 ψεῦδος ἀναγγέλλειν dat,   ⲁⲧϫⲓ ϭ., unlying: BM 245 ⲧⲉϥϣⲡⲏ ⲛⲁ. of Saviour; ⲙⲛⲧⲁ.: My 68;   ⲣⲉϥϫⲓ, ϫⲉ ϭⲟⲗ, liar: Si 15 8, Jo 8 55 (A² ⲥⲁ ⲡϫⲉ ϭ.) ψεύστης, ib 44 A²(S ϭ. nn) -δος, Is 30 9 F ⲗⲉϥϫ. (S do) -δής; LCyp 15 ⲣⲉϥϫⲉ ϭ.; ⲙⲛⲧⲣ.: R 1 2 47; ⲣ ⲣ.: Pro 24 32 SA -δής γίνεσθαι; CO 224. ⲥⲁ ⲡϫⲉ ϭⲟⲗ: Jo 8 55 as above.

ϭⲟⲗ B v ϭⲗⲟ 2°.

ϭⲱⲗ, ϭ(ⲉ)ⲗ-, ϭⲱⲗ- S, ϭⲁⲗ- F, ϭⲟ(ⲟ)ⲗ⧸, ⲕⲟⲗ⧸, ⲕⲉⲗ†, ⲡ ϭ ϭⲁⲗ- S vb tr, collect, gather: Z 337 ⲉϥϭⲉⲗ ϣⲉ συλλέγειν; Ac 28 3 (B diff) συστρέφειν; ShA 2 19 ϭⲉⲗ ϩⲉⲛⲗⲁⲕⲙ ⲛϣⲉ, ib 1 455 ⲛ. ⲛⲉⲛⲧⲁⲩϭⲟⲟⲣⲟⲩ ⲉⲃⲟⲗ, ShC 73 98 paral ⲕⲱⲧϥ, BMar 218 ϭ. ⲡⲟⲩⲁϣⲏ ⲡⲱⲡⲉ ⲉϩⲣⲁⲓ ⲉϫⲱϥ = Rec 6 183 B ϩⲓⲟⲩⲓ ϩⲓⲣⲉⲛ-: Wess 18 87 ϭ. ⲛⲡⲉⲧⲛⲕⲗⲟⲙ = Miss 4 99 B ⲱⲗⲓ, Ryl 94 (33 3) ϭⲗ ⲃⲃⲓⲗⲉ ϩⲓⲡⲁϩⲟⲩ ⲙⲙⲟⲟⲩ, J 87 30 ⲁⲓⲕⲟⲗϥ ϩⲓⲡⲧⲓⲙⲉ to adopt him as son, BM 1113 wine-jars ⲛⲏⲝ ⲉⲃⲟⲗ…ⲛⲡⲉⲕϭⲟⲗⲟⲩ, ST 273 ϣⲁⲡⲧ(ⲕ)ⲕⲱⲗ ⲧⲁⲗⲱⲡⲓⲁ ⲙⲡⲕⲁⲙⲟⲩⲗ, Ryl 356 ⲁⲥϭⲱⲗ ϩⲣⲉⲟⲟⲩ, BM 678 F ⲙⲁ

ⲡϭⲁⲗ ϩⲣⲏ; ⲥ ⲉϩⲟⲩⲡ: Mor 18 65 ⲉⲕϭⲗ ϣⲁϫⲉ ⲉϩ.
ⲉⲃⲟⲗ hindering others from speaking (ib 19 74, Miss
4 139 B om), BKU 1 313 ⲉⲟⲩⲡ ⲕⲉⲙⲛⲏϣⲉ ⲕⲉⲗ (l? ϭⲏⲗ)
ⲉϩ. saying shameful things; p c: Glos 225 ⲕⲟⲕ-
ⲕⲟⲗⲉⲕⲧⲏⲥ · ⲡϭⲁⲗⲃⲗⲃⲓⲗⲉ, R 1 5 30 ⲙⲁⲅⲟⲥ ⲡϭⲁⲗⲣⲟϥ
(collated) this word?; ⲣⲉϥϭⲗ ϣⲉ: Deu 29 11 (B
ⲣⲉϥϥⲉϩ ⲣⲟⲕϩ) ξυλοκόπος.
Cf ϫⲱⲱⲗⲉ.

ϭⲱⲗ *SA²*(Ma)*F*, ⲕⲱⲗ *SA²*(Ma)*B*, ϭⲱⲗⲉ *A²*(Jo),
ϫⲱⲗ *B*, ϭⲗ- *S*, ϭⲱⲗ- *A²*(Ma), ⲕⲉⲗ-, ϫⲉⲗ- *B*, ϭⲟ(ⲟ)ⲗϩ
S, ⲕⲟⲗϩ, ϫⲟⲗϩ *B*, ϭⲁⲗϩ *F*, ϭⲏⲗ† *S*, ϫⲏⲗ† *B* vb **I** intr,
return, roll back, curl up (cf krj Dévaud): Is 34 4 *SBF*
ἐλίσσειν; Ap 6 14 *S*(*B* tr) ἀποχωρίζειν; Mor 19 78 *S*
ⲁⲡⲥⲱⲃⲁϩ ϭ. ⲛⲑⲉ ⲡⲟⲩϩⲏⲃⲥ (*v p* 659 *b supra*), TMina
Epima 20 *S* martyr roasted till ⲡⲉⲕⲟⲩⲕⲉ ⲙⲡⲉϥⲥⲱⲙⲁ
ϭ. = C 43 140 *B* ϫ., Gu 61 *S* ⲁⲡϣⲁⲁⲣ ⲡⲧⲉⲩⲁⲡⲉ ϭ.,
MIF 9 93 *S* ⲡⲡⲉⲡⲉⲕⲉⲓⲃ ϭ. nor hair fall, P 131¹ 54 *S*
ⲙⲡⲁⲧⲉⲛⲁ(ⲉ)ⲓⲡⲟⲛ ϭ. ⲡⲥⲉⲧⲁϩⲉ ⲉⲣⲟⲛ ⲡϭⲏⲧϥ (*cf* Lu
12 36), Mani K 175 *A²* ⲡⲡⲗⲏⲛ ⲕ. ⲡⲥⲉϣⲟⲩⲟ ⲡⲟⲩⲙⲟⲩ ⲡⲣⲱⲟⲩ, *ib* P 190 *A²* ⲡⲧⲏⲣϥ ⲛⲁϭ. ⲕⲁϭ. ⲡⲧⲁⲕ ⲉⲡ,
ib 223 ⲥⲉⲛⲁϭ. ⲡⲥⲉⲟⲩⲛⲉ *paral* ⲟⲩⲱⲥϭ., Mor 24 24 *F*
heat caused skin of feet to ϭ. ⲛϥϭⲛⲏⲓ = *ib* 23 34 *S* ϭ.
ⲉⲃⲟⲗ; qual: Ap 6 14 *S* ⲟⲩϭⲱⲙⲉ ⲉϥϭ. (*B* om)
ⲉⲗ.; ⲥ ϩⲛ-: BAp 81 *S* as one ⲉⲁϥϭ. ϩⲛⲟⲩⲙⲁ ⲛⲥⲱ =
MIE 2 356 *B* ⲧⲱⲛ ⲉⲃⲟⲗ ϩⲉⲛ-.

II tr: He 1 12 *B*(*S* ⲥⲁϩⲥϩ, *F* ⲕⲱϥ), Ap *ut sup* ⲉⲗ.;
Lu 4 20 *B* ⲕⲉⲗ- (*S* ⲕⲱⲃ) πτύσσειν; PS 6 *S* ⲙⲉϣⲁⲕ
ⲉⲅⲡⲁϭⲗ ⲡⲕⲟⲥⲙⲟⲥ, Br 137 *S* ⲉⲓϣⲁⲡⲉⲓ ⲡϭ. ⲡⲛⲁⲓⲱⲛ,
ManiP 70 *A²* ⲛϭⲉⲣⲉϭⲉ...[ⲁⲕ]ϭ. ⲡⲉϥϣⲡⲏⲩ, MélOr
6 506 *B* ⲕ. ⲛⲛⲓⲙⲉⲗⲟⲥ ⲡⲧⲉ ⲡⲭⲥ (*sc* eulogies), BKU 1
21 *vo F* hang it up till ⲛⲕϭⲁⲗϥ ⲁⲅⲱ ϣⲁⲕϩⲁⲃ-
ⲉⲥϥ; ⲁⲧϭ.: Miss 8 249 *S* ⲙⲡⲧⲣⲣⲟ ⲡⲁ. *paral* ⲙⲉϥ-
ⲟⲩⲉⲓⲛⲉ; ⲣⲁ ϭ. *A²* *rolling up, end*: ManiK 105
third plague is ⲡⲣ. [ⲡⲧ]ϩⲁⲏ, *ib* 165 ⲡⲣ. ⲡϭⲱⲃ ⲛⲓⲙ.
As nn *prob* ⲕⲱⲗ p 102 *a*.

ϭ. ⲉⲃⲟⲗ *S*, ⲕ., ϫ. ⲉⲃ. *B*, a *return*: Jud 11 35 *B* ϫ.
(*S* ⲕⲧⲟ ⲉⲡⲁϩⲟⲩ) ἐπιστρέφεσθαι; Lu 12 36 *S*(*var* &
R 1 5 29 om ⲉⲃ., *B* ϯ ⲟⲩⲱ) ἀναλύειν; Mor 25 218 *S*
ϣⲁⲡⲧⲟⲩϭ. ⲉⲃ. (*sc* guests) & went home, P 132² 106
S barbarians] would ϭ. ⲉⲃ. ϩⲛⲡⲧⲟϣ ⲉⲧⲙⲙⲁⲩ *scour
those parts* & make captives, Mor 28 245 *S* found that
war ⲉⲁϥϭ. ⲉⲃ. ϩⲓϫⲛⲟⲩⲙⲉⲣⲓⲁⲛⲟⲥ *had receded from*,
ib 23 34 *v* **I** above] ; *tr, turn back*: Jer 31 2 *B* ϫ.
κόπτειν *disperdere*; ShC 73 141 *S* overseer's duty ⲉⲕ[ⲱ
ⲡⲡ]ⲥⲛⲏⲩ ⲉⲃ.... & ⲉϩⲟⲗⲟⲅ ⲉⲃ., *ib* 152 ⲡⲓⲁⲩ ⲉⲧⲉϣϣⲉ
ⲉⲙⲟⲟϣⲉ ⲉⲃ. ⲙⲡ...ⲉϩⲟⲟⲗⲟⲅ ⲉⲃ.; Mor 25 68 *S* ⲥⲉⲛⲁ-
ϭⲟⲗⲥ ⲉⲃ. like book (*cf* Is 34 above), BSM 20 *B* ⲕⲱⲗ-
ⲧⲉⲛ ⲉⲃ. in shame = BMis 357 *S* ⲃⲱⲱⲣⲉ (*cf* Mt 22 13),
ib 14 *B* ⲁⲡⲁⲥⲟⲛ ⲕⲟⲗⲧ ⲉⲃ. = *ib* 349 *S* ⲁⲓⲱⲕⲉⲓ ⲡⲥⲱⲓ,
AM 94 *B* he sought to ⲕⲟⲗⲟⲩ ⲉⲃ., C 41 17 *B* millstone ground so much that ⲙⲡⲟⲩϣ ϫⲉⲙ ϫⲟⲙ ⲡⲕⲟⲗϥ
ⲉⲃ. = Miss 4 326 ﺣﻞ, AZ 23 108 *S* ϭⲟⲡ ⲛⲡⲁⲧⲧⲟⲗⲕ

(الطلق) ϭⲁⲗϥ (*sic* MS) ⲉⲃ. ⲁⲁϥⲡⲥⲓϣϥ; refl *BS*(once),
turn: Va 63 100 rich man ⲁϥϭⲟⲗϥ ⲡϥⲙⲉⲧⲣⲏⲕⲓ ⲡⲧⲱ-
χὸς γίνεσθαι; *ib* 66 301 ⲡⲁⲓ ⲡⲧⲉϥϫⲟⲗϥ ⲙⲙⲟⲩ, opp
ⲉⲣ ⲕⲁⲧⲁⲫⲣⲟⲛⲓⲛ ἔπεσθαι; TDi 254 ⲙⲁⲣⲟⲩϫⲟⲗⲟⲩ
ⲡϫⲉ ⲡⲓϭⲟⲣⲙⲏ ﻛَﺐ; Bor 297 4 *S* on 1 Cor 7 29 ⲁϣⲧⲉ
ⲧϭⲛⲡⲟⲗⲓ ⲉⲡⲛⲁϭⲟⲗⲡ ⲙⲙⲟⲥ? (but ? *l* ⲡⲁⲟⲗⲡ). *Cf*
ⲕⲱⲗⲉ ⲉⲃⲟⲗ.

b *deny A²B* ϫ.: C 86 168 ⲁⲓϫⲉⲗ ⲙⲡⲁϭⲥ ⲓⲏⲥ, Abst
566 sim; ϫ. ⲉⲃⲟⲗ, *deny*: Ge 18 15, Jo 18 27 *A²B*,
Ac 4 16 (all *S* = Gk), C 86 66 besought him ⲉⲟⲣⲉϥϫ.
ⲉⲃ. ἀρνεῖσθαι; qual (here?): Cat 34 on Mt 12 1
disciples ϫ. ⲉⲃ. taking no thought for food; tr,
deny, reject: Mt 10 33, Ap 2 13 ἄρ., Mt 16 24 ἀπαρ.
(all *S* = Gk); Ps 14 4 (*S* ϭⲱϣⲉ) ἀθετεῖν; Jer 4 30, Ac
7 27 (*SF* ⲧⲱϣⲡ) ἀπωθεῖν; MG 25 219 refl (*S* Z 347
= Gk) ἀποτάσσειν; Va 57 13 ⲁⲩϫⲟⲗⲟⲩ ⲉⲃ. ⲙⲡⲓⲉⲡ-
ⲧⲏⲣϥ ἀποδύεσθαι; C 43 113 ⲡⲧⲁϫⲉⲗ ⲫϯ ⲉⲃ. ⲡⲉ, Mus
45 52 ⲉⲧϫ. ⲙⲡⲓⲡⲟⲙⲟⲥ ⲉⲃ.; as nn m: Cai Euch
399 ἀπάρνησις; Va 57 6 ϯⲁⲕⲧⲏⲙⲟⲥⲩⲛⲏ ⲉⲧⲉⲡⲓϫ. ⲉⲃ.
ⲡⲉ, MG 25 333 ascetic virtues ⲡⲓϫ. ⲉⲃ. = Gött ar 114
117 ﺟﺤﺪ الهوى; ⲁⲧϫ. ⲉⲃ.: Va 58 153 ⲡⲓϫⲣⲉⲟⲥ ⲡⲁⲧ-
ϫⲟⲗϥ ⲉⲃ. of death ἀνυπέρθετος; ⲙⲉⲧⲣⲉϥϫ. ⲉⲃ.:
Miss 4 202 plunged in ⲫⲓⲟⲅⲡ ⲛϯⲙ.; ϫⲓⲛϫ. ⲉⲃ.,
apostasy: C 86 27 grieved at ⲡⲁϫ.
Cf? ϫⲱⲱⲗⲉ 2°.

ϭⲱⲗ *B* v ϫⲱⲱⲗⲉ 1°.

ϭⲁⲗⲉ *SB*, -ⲏ *S* (rare)*F*, ϣⲁⲗⲉ *B*, pl ϭⲁⲗⲉⲉⲩ¹ *SA²*,
-ⲉⲩⲉ² *SA*, ϭⲁⲗⲉⲅⲉ³ *SA²*, ϭⲁⲗⲉⲩ *B* & sg as pl, nn,
lame, crippled person: Deu 15 21 *SB*, Job 29 15 *S*(*var
cit* Mor 25 10 -ⲏ, *B* pl), Is 33 23 *SBF* χωλός; Aeg
282 *S* λώβη ποδῶν; BG 128 *S* ⲧⲣⲉⲛϭ. ⲙⲟⲟϣⲉ, MG
25 405 *B* ⲟⲩϭ. ⲙⲙⲓⲥⲓ, Mor 24 34 *F* ⲟⲩϭ., C 43 79 *B*
ⲟⲩϣ. ϣⲁϥⲙⲟϣⲓ, BM 1077 *S* after names ϭ.;
c following prep *S, as to*: 2 Kg 9 13 ⲉ- (*var* ⲛ-) ϫ.
dat; ShMIF 23 87 ⲟⲩϭ. ⲉⲧⲉⲟⲩⲉⲣⲏⲧⲉ ⲥⲛⲧⲉ, ShA 2
245 sim ϩⲛ-; as adj.: Lev 21 18 *SB* χ.; PS 378 *S*
ⲥⲱⲙⲁ ⲛϭ. ⲁⲩⲱ ⲛϭⲁⲛⲁⲡ, AZ 21 152 ϣ ϣⲱⲡⲉ ⲛϭ.; pl
forms: Mt 11 5 *B*(*S* sg), Jo 5 3 *A²* ϭ.¹ *B*(*S* do), R 1 1
12 *S²* χ.; PS 279 *S¹*, ClPr 45 201 *S¹*, El 118 *S³* = *ib* 88
A, Leyd 463 *S²*, ManiH 10 *A²* ϭ.³, AM 224 *B*; ⲙⲛⲧ-,
ⲙⲉⲧϭ.: He 12 13 *B*(*S* ϫⲟⲩϭⲉ) χ., Mor 37 123 *S* ⲧⲙ.
ⲛⲡⲉϥⲥⲧⲟⲥ ("Ηφαισ.) χωλότης; ⲣ ϭ., ⲟ, ⲟⲓ ⲛϭ.:
2 Kg 4 4 *S*, Ps 17 45 *SB* χωλαίνειν, Mk 9 45 *SB* χωλός; BM 529 *vo S* send a beast ϫⲉⲁⲡⲱϩ ⲉⲣ ϭⲁⲗⲏ.

ϭⲁⲗⲉ-, ϭⲁⲗⲟ- v ϭⲟⲉⲓⲗⲉ.

ϭⲉⲗⲓ *B* nn m, *butter*: Ge 18 8, Deu 32 14, Job 29
6 (all *S* ⲥⲁⲉⲓⲣⲉ) βούτυρον; 1 Kg 17 18 *v* cip 1°; K
200 ⲛⲓϭ. ﺑﻴﺮﺍﻁ (*var* ﺑﺮﺍﻥ, ﺳﻤﻦ, cf? ﺩ، ﺑﻴﺮﺍﻁ Dozy).

ϭⲟ(ⲉ)ⲓⲗⲉ, ⲕⲟⲓⲗⲉ *S*, ϭⲁⲉⲓⲗⲉ *A*, ϭⲁⲓⲗⲉ *AA²*, ϫⲱⲓⲗⲓ
B, ϭⲁⲓⲗⲓ, ϫⲁⲁⲗⲓ, ϭⲁⲗⲓ (nn), ⲕⲁⲗⲓ *F*, ϭⲁⲗⲉ- *S*, ϭⲁⲗⲟ-

A, ϭⲁⲗⲱⲱ⸗, ϭⲁⲗⲱⲟⲩ[1†], ⲕ.[†] (ⲥ ϧⲓϫⲡ-), ϭⲁⲗⲏⲅ[2†], ϭⲁⲗⲏⲅⲧ[3†], -ⲗⲟⲟⲩⲧ[4†] (once each) *S*, -ⲗⲓⲧ[†] *A*, ϭⲉⲗⲓⲧ[†] *A²*, ϫⲁⲗⲏⲟⲩⲧ[†], ϭ.[†] *B* vb intr, **A** *dwell*: Ps 55 6 *SB*, Lam 4 15 *F* ϭ. (*S* ϣⲱⲡⲉ ϩⲓⲡⲙⲁ ⲛϭ., *B* ϣⲱⲡⲓ only) παροικεῖν; Mor 31 64 *S* ⲉϥⲛⲁϭ. ϣⲁⲣⲧⲟⲟⲩⲉ; qual: Mor 17 66 *S* ⲉⲣⲉⲡⲁⲡⲟⲥⲧⲟⲗⲟⲥ ⲙⲡⲉⲓⲙⲁ ⲉϥϭ.[4]? ξενίζειν; Ps 38 12 *S¹*(*B* ⲣⲉⲙⲛϫ.) παρεπίδημος; Mor 17 78 *S* ⲁⲡⲣ ⲡⲣⲟϭⲉ ⲉⲡϭ.[1], CaiCoptMus pap 4-2 *S* ϥϭ.[4]

With following preposition.

—— ⲉ-, *dwell at, visit* intr: Deu 18 6 *S*(*B* ϣⲱⲡⲓ ϩⲓ-) ⲟⲩ παροικ., Ps 60 4 *S*(*B* ϣ. ϫⲉⲛ-) π. ἐν, Lev 18 3 *S*(*B* ⲉⲣ ⲣⲉⲙⲛϫ.) κατοικ. ἐπί; Ac 21 16 *SB* ξ. παρά, Pro 21 7 *SA* ἐπίξ. dat, Ro 16 23 *S* ⲡⲉϯϣⲁⲓϭ. ⲉ- (*B* ⲡⲁϣⲉⲙⲙⲟ) ξένος; Jos 2 1 *S* καταλύειν ἐκεῖ, Ez 23 17 *S*(*B* ⲟϩⲓⲉ-) κ. εἰς, Lu 19 7 *S*(*B* ⲙⲧⲟⲛ) κ. παρά; Ez 47 23 *B* προσήλυτος εἶναι; Tob 5 6 *S* αὐλίζεσθαι παρά; Bor 235 118 *S* ⲕⲟⲩⲱϣ ⲉⲧⲣⲁϭ. ⲉⲡⲙⲁ? παραβάλλειν; PS 122 *S* ⲧϭⲟⲙ ⲉⲛⲧⲁⲥϭ. ⲉⲣⲟⲓ, ShMIF 23 76 *S* Babylon ⲁⲛϫⲁⲓⲙⲱⲛ ⲧⲏⲣⲟⲩ ϭ. ⲉⲣⲟⲥ, Pcod 38 *S* ⲁϥϭ. ⲉⲣⲟⲓ ⲛϭⲓ ⲟⲩⲣⲱⲙⲉ = *ib F*, C 99 136 *S* had need ⲉⲧⲣⲉϥϭ. ⲉⲟⲉⲛⲉⲉⲧⲉ = C 89 30 *B*, C 99 210 *S* ⲡⲉⲛⲧⲁϥϭ. ⲉⲣⲟϥ *his host*, BAp 106 *S* when clergy ϭ. ⲉⲡⲉⲛⲡⲉⲧⲟⲩⲁⲁⲃ ⲡⲉⲓⲱⲧ = MIE 2 381 *B* ⲉⲣ ⲁⲡⲁⲡⲧⲁⲛ ⲉ-, J 67 18 *S* ⲁϥϭ. ⲉⲡⲕⲟⲥⲙⲟⲥ, PGol 47 *A* ⲟⲩϫⲉⲙⲟⲡⲓⲟⲛ ϭ. ⲉ[, ManiP 151 *A²* ϣⲁϥϭ. ⲁⲛⲡⲁⲣⲑⲉⲛⲟⲥ ⲛϭⲟⲩⲱϩ ϩⲛ-, *ib* H 11 *A²* ⲁⲥϭ. ⲁⲛⲙⲁ, AM 88 *B* ⲁϥϭ. ⲉⲟⲩⲛⲁⲡⲧⲟⲭⲓⲟⲛ, Mor 24 21 *F* ⲛⲧⲉⲡⲣⲣⲁ ϭ. ⲉⲗⲁ, KroppC 29 *F* (ⲛ)ⲡⲉⲗⲕⲉⲟⲩ ⲉⲕⲁⲗⲓ ⲉⲗⲁⲥ; qual: Jud 19 16 *S¹* παροικ. ἐν, Pro 3 29 *S¹AB* π. ἐπί, Lev 25 6 *S¹*(var², *B* ⲣⲉⲙⲛϫ.) πάροικος πρός; Ac 10 6 *B*(var ϭ., *S* ⲟⲩⲛϩ ϩⲁⲧⲛ-) ξ. παρά, Mor 17 56 *S* ⲡⲙⲁ ⲉⲧⲉϥϭ.[1] ⲉⲣⲟϥ ξ. ἐν, ViSitz 172 4 58 *S* ⲡⲉⲧϭ.[1] ⲉⲣⲟⲓ ξένος; PS 342 *S* ⲡⲙⲉⲣⲟⲥ ⲉⲧϭ.[3] ⲉⲛⲕⲟⲥⲙⲟⲥ, ShC 73 54 *S* strangers ⲉⲧϭ.[1] ⲉⲡⲣⲟ, Mor 52 40 *S* ⲡⲉϥϭ.[2] ⲉⲡⲛⲓ, JTS 9 379 *S* demon ϭ.[2] ⲉⲡⲉⲓⲁⲱⲗⲟⲛ, BMis 177 *S¹* sim = BSM 87 *B* ϭ., C 86 303 *B* sim ϫ. (var ϭ.), RE 9 135 *S* cattle ⲥⲉϭ.[1] ⲉⲡⲁⲧⲭⲉ (place), AZ 30 40 *S* stolen goods ⲉⲧϭ.[3] ⲉⲣⲟⲩ, ManiK 94 *A²* body ⲡⲣⲙⲛⲉⲥ ⲉⲧϭ. ⲁⲣⲁϥ, *ib* P 139 *A²* wisdom ⲉⲧϭ. ⲁⲡⲉϥⲅⲣⲁⲫⲁⲅⲉ, TSBA 9 358 *B* widow (of Sarepta) ⲉⲧϭ. ⲉⲣⲟⲥ; tr, *give lodging*: Si 11 36 *S* ἐνοικίζειν; P 131³ 78 *S* ϭⲁⲗⲉ ⲡⲉⲧⲟ ⲛϣⲙⲙⲟ ⲉⲣⲟϥ, Mor 47 187 *S* let us make ⲙⲁ ⲛϭ. & whoso passeth by ϣⲁⲡϭⲁⲗⲱⲟϥ ⲉⲣⲟⲛ; ⲉϩⲟⲩⲛ ⲉ- *B*: C 89 31 ⲁⲓϫ. ⲉϭ. ⲉⲧⲁⲃⲉⲡⲛ̅ⲛⲓ, MG 25 182 ⲙⲡⲉⲣϫ. ⲉϭ. ⲉⲣⲟϥ.

—— ⲛ- *B, as last*: PO 11 312 ⲁϥϫ. ⲙ̄ⲫⲙⲟⲡⲁⲥⲧⲏⲣⲓⲟⲛ.

—— ϩⲁⲧⲉⲛ- *B*: Ge 20 1 παροικ. ἐν.

—— ϩⲁ- *S*: JA '05 438 ϣⲁϥϭ. ϩⲁⲣⲟⲥ.

—— ϩⲛ- *S*: Ex 12 13 (*B* ⲭⲏ) κατοικ. ἐν; BMis 106 ⲉⲓϭ.[1†] ϩⲓⲟⲩⲙⲁ ⲛϭⲟⲉⲓⲗⲉ.

—— ϩⲓϫⲛ- *S*: J 65 18 ⲉⲓⲕⲁⲗⲱⲟⲩ ϩ. ⲡⲕⲁϩ, *cf* Ps 38 12 ⲣⲙⲛϭ. ϩⲙⲡⲕ.

—— ⲛⲛ m *S, sojourn*: Zech 9 12 (*A* ⲙⲁ ⲛϭ., *B*

ϫⲓⲛϫ.) παροικεσία; Miss 8 104 ϣⲁⲡⲣⲁⲉ ⲛϭ. ⲙⲡⲁⲃⲓⲟⲥ (Gk diff); BM 673 *F* ⲧⲗⲓ (ⲉ)ⲧⲥⲁⲫⲓⲗ ⲛϭⲁⲗⲓ or ? *place-name*;   *furniture, plenishings*: J 70 40 ⲛϭ. ⲙⲡⲁⲛⲏⲓ ⲧⲏⲣϥ ⲉⲧⲉⲟⲩϭⲉⲣⲱⲡⲉ &c ⲁⲡⲗⲱⲥ ⲡⲉⲧⲟⲩⲙⲁⲛⲏ ⲧⲏⲣϥ, *ib* 76 46 sim ⲕⲟⲓⲗⲉ, CO 296 ⲡⲁϭ. ⲧⲏⲣϥ sim.

ⲙⲁ ⲛϭ., ϫ. *SAA²BF, dwelling-place, station*: Ps 33 4 *S*(*B* ⲙⲁ ⲛϣⲱⲡⲓ), *ib* 64 tit *S*(*B* ⲟⲩⲧⲉ⸗ ⲉⲃⲟⲗ), Lam 2 22 *SBF*, Hab 3 16 *S*(ShMIF 23 13)*AB*, Ac 13 17 *S*(*B* = Gk) παροικία; Jer 14 8 *SB*, Lu 2 7 *S*(*B* ⲙⲁ ⲛⲟⲩϭ⸗) κατάλυμα, Ge 24 23 *S*(ShA 2 167, *B* as Gk) τόπος τοῦ καταλῦσαι; Nu 33 1 *S*(*B* = Gk) σταθμός; ShA 2 277 *S* ⲡⲓⲙ. opp eternity, Mor 28 210 *S* ϩⲙⲙ. for passing strangers, Mani 1 *A²* ⲡⲓⲙ[ⲁ] ⲛϭ., C 86 196 *B* bring my bones ⲉⲡⲁⲙⲁ ⲛϫⲱⲗⲓ (sic), Mor 30 29 *F*; ⲣ ⲙⲁ ⲛϭ. *A²*: Mani 1 we are thy temple ⲉⲛⲁⲣ. ⲡⲉⲕ. As place-name ⲡⲓⲙⲁ ⲛϫ. (Amélineau *Géog.* 572).

ⲣⲙⲛϭ., ϫ. *SAA²BF, sojourner*: Ex 2 22 *SB*, Zeph 2 5 *SAB*, Eph 2 19 *SB* πάροικος; He 11 13 *SB* παρεπίδημος; Sa 5 15 *S* καταλύτης; CaiEuch 594 *B* προσήλυτος; 2 Kg 12 4 *S* πάροδος; ManiP 181 *A²* ⲣ. ⲁⲡⲧⲟ; ⲣ, ⲟ ⲡⲣⲙⲛϭ.: Ge 15 13 *SB*, Ps 118 19 *SBF* ⲣⲟⲙⲉϭ. (Pcod Mor 3) πάροικος εἶναι, *ib* 104 23 *B*(*S* ϭ. vb), Hos 10 5 *SAB*, He 11 9 *B*(*S* ⲟⲩⲱϩ) παροικεῖν; ShA 1 241 *S* ⲣ ⲣ. ϩⲛⲟⲩϩⲁϭ, AM 92 *B* ⲡⲙⲁ ⲉⲧⲁⲓⲉⲣ ⲣ. ⲛϧⲏⲧϥ;   ⲙⲉⲧⲣⲉⲙⲛϫ. *B*: Ps 119 5 (*S* ⲙⲁ ⲛϣⲱⲡⲉ) παροικία; CaiEuch 589 παρεπιδημία.

ϭⲓⲛϭ., ϫⲓⲛϫ.: Ex 12 40 *B* ⲡⲓϫ. κατοίκησις, Zech 9 12 *B* v ϭ. nn, JA '88 370 *S* ⲧⲁϭ. ⲉϩⲁⲗⲟⲅⲁⲛ.

B ϭⲟ(ⲉ)ⲓⲗⲉ *S*, ϭⲁⲓⲗⲉ *A²*(nn), ϫⲱⲓⲗⲓ *B*, ϭⲁⲗⲉ- *SB*, ⲕ., ⲕⲁⲗⲱ- *S*, ϭⲉⲗⲱ- *Sᵃ*, ϫⲁⲗⲉ- *B*, ϭⲁⲗ(ⲱ)ⲱ⸗ *S*, ϭⲉⲗⲱ⸗, ⲕⲁⲗⲟ⸗ *Sᵃ*, ϫⲁⲗⲱ⸗, ϭ. *B*, ϭⲗⲱ⸗, ⲕ. *F*, ϭⲁⲗⲱⲟⲩ[1†], -ⲏⲩ[2†], -ⲏⲩⲧ[3†], ⲕⲉⲗⲟⲓⲧ[4†] *S*, ϭⲉⲗⲓⲧ[†] *A²*, ϫⲁⲗⲏⲟⲩⲧ[†], ϫ. *B* tr, *deposit, assign, entrust*; ⲉ ⲉ-, *to*: Lev 6 4 *S* ϭⲁⲗⲱⲱ⸗ *B* ϫⲁⲗⲱ⸗, Lu 12 48 *SB* ϫⲁⲗⲉ-, 1 Tim 1 18 *B*(*S* ⲕⲱ) παρατιθέναι dat, Ps 30 5 *S*(*B* ⲭⲱ) π. εἰς (cf Lu 23 46 †), Jer 48 10 *B* ϫⲁⲗⲱ⸗ παρακαταιθ., Ex 22 8 *B* ϫⲁⲗⲱ⸗ (*S* ϭ. nn) παρακαταθήκη Deu 23 15 *S* ϭⲁⲗⲱⲱ⸗ (*B* diff) προστιθ. dat; ShA 2 280 *S* ⲡⲣⲱⲃ ⲛⲧⲁⲡ̄ⲓⲃ̄ ϭⲁⲗⲱⲱϥ ⲉⲣⲟⲓ, *ib* 326 *S* ⲁⲓⲧ̄ ϭⲁⲗⲉ ϩⲉⲛⲣⲱⲙⲉ ⲉⲣⲟⲟⲩ, Bor 294 117 *S* ⲟⲩⲡⲁⲣⲁⲑⲏⲕⲏ ⲁⲩϭⲁⲗⲱⲟⲥ ⲉⲣⲟⲓ, R 1 2 40 *S* ⲁⲩϭ. ⲉⲣⲟⲥ ⲙⲡⲉϥϣⲏⲣⲉ, Ep 531 *Sᵃ* ⲁⲕⲟⲩⲥ(ϩ)ⲓⲙⲉ ⲕⲁⲗⲱ ϩⲉⲡⲕⲁⲕⲉ ⲉⲣⲟⲓ, *ib* ⲕⲉⲗⲱ-, Ostr *penes* Crum *Sᵃ* ⲁⲡϫⲉⲗⲱ ϩⲉⲡⲥⲕⲛⲏⲅⲉ ⲉⲙⲁⲣⲓⲁ, Ep 338 *Sᵃ* wine ⲉⲓϭⲉⲗⲱⲟⲩϥ ⲉⲣⲱⲉⲓ(?), ST 284 *Sᵃ* corn ⲛⲧⲁⲓⲕⲁⲗⲟⲩ ⲁⲣⲟⲕ, AM 112 *B* ⲡⲁⲣⲁⲑⲏⲕⲏ ⲉⲧⲁⲓϫⲁⲗⲱⲥ ⲉⲣⲟⲕ, *ib* 113 same MS ϭⲁⲗⲱⲥ, Aeg 49 *B* ⲁⲕϭⲁⲗⲟⲛ ⲉⲧⲉⲕⲙⲁⲩ *entrusted to us Thy mother*, MG 25 253 *B* ⲁϥϭⲁⲗⲉ ⲡϣⲏⲣⲓ ⲙⲡⲓⲁⲟⲩϫ ⲉⲣⲟϥ, P 129¹⁸ 100 *S* Christ & Thomas's flayed skin ⲁϥϭⲁⲗⲱⲟϥ ⲉⲡⲉϥⲥⲱⲙⲁ, J 66 24 *S* ⲡⲉϥⲛ̄ⲛ̄ⲃ̄ ⲛⲧⲁϥϭⲁⲗⲱⲟϥ ⲉⲣⲟⲓ = *ib* 76 19 ⲧⲁⲁϥ, Kr 47 *F* ⲧⲁϭⲗⲱⲟⲩ ⲉⲗⲁⲕ, *ib* 129 *F* ⲓⲱⲣⲓ ⲉⲧⲁⲁⲕⲗⲱⲉⲃ ⲉⲣⲟⲩⲛ (ⲉ)ⲑⲁⲓⲱϭ(? ⲧⲁⲡⲱⲧⲏ);   intr *S*: Mus 40 39 (Reg Pach) none may

receive aught ⲛⲧⲛⲣⲱⲙⲉ ⲉϭ. ⲉⲣⲟϥ *commendatum accipere*, Kr 228 ⲉⲥϭ. ⲉⲡⲛⲉ ⲉⲣⲙⲁⲕ (ⲛⲙⲙⲁⲕ);   qual: Z 338 *S* ϩⲛⲡⲕⲁ ϭ.[1] ⲉⲣⲟϥ παραθήκην ἔχειν τινός; ShA 2 282 *S* every one ⲉⲧⲉⲟϭⲟⲡ ⲣⲱⲙⲉ ϭ.[1] ⲉⲣⲟⲟⲩ *to whom man hath been entrusted*, ib 81 *S* ⲛⲉⲩϭ.[2] ⲁⲛ ⲉⲣⲟϥ, ShR 2 3 5 *S* ⲡⲉⲕⲣⲡⲁⲁⲩ ⲉⲧϭ.[1] ⲉⲡⲣⲱⲙⲉ *deposited with*, ShA 1 34 *S* oath ⲕϭ.[1] ⲉⲣⲟⲟⲩ *lieth upon them*, C 99 234 *S* ⲡⲉϯϭ.[1] ⲉⲣⲟϥ *entrusted to me* = ib 89 68 *B* ϭ., BMar 212 *S* angel ⲉⲧϭ.[2] ⲉⲣⲟⲕ since childhood (Mor 48 19, Rec 6 177 *B* om), Mus 45 24 *B* ⲡⲓⲣⲱⲙⲓ ⲉⲧⲉϥϫ. ⲉⲣⲟϥ *man with whom* (angel) *is entrusted*, BMis 79 *S* ⲉⲥϭ.[1] ⲉⲣⲟⲕ (var[2] Mor 34 8), AZ 30 40 *S* ⲡⲉⲧϭ.[3] ⲉⲣⲟϥ, CO 378 *S* ⲧⲁⲕⲉⲣⲁⲥ (?) ⲉⲧⲕ.[4] (*sic* prob) ⲉⲣⲟϥ, ManiP 218 *A²* ⲡⲭⲣⲏⲙⲁ ⲉⲧϭ. ⲁⲣⲁⲩ, C 86 134 *B* king's son ϭ. ⲉⲡⲁⲣⲭⲏⲉⲡⲓⲥⲕⲟⲡⲟⲥ;   c ⲉⲃⲟⲗ: Ryl 240 *S* chattels ⲛ]ⲧⲁⲓϭⲁⲗⲱⲟⲩ ⲉⲃ.

—— nn m *SA²B*, *deposit*: 2 Tim 1 14 *SB*, Z 339 *S* ϫⲓ ⲛⲟⲩϭ. ⲛⲧⲉ ⲟⲩⲁ παραθήκη; Ex 22 11 *SB* παρακαταθ.; ManiK 140 *A²* whenever they require of her ⲡⲟⲩϭ. (*cf* παραθηκη just before).

ϭⲱⲱⲗⲉ *S*, ϭⲱⲗⲉ *SA²*, ϫⲱⲗ, ⲁϫϫⲱⲗ *B*, ϭⲉ(ⲉ)ⲗⲉ-*S*, ϭⲁ(ⲁ)ⲗⲉ-*S^f*, ϭⲗ-*S*, ϫⲉⲗ-*B*, ϭⲟⲟⲗⲉ⸗*S*, ϭⲁⲗⲉ⸗*SAA²*, ϭⲁⲁⲗ⸗*AF*, ϫⲟⲗ⸗*B*, ϭⲟⲟⲗⲉ[†], ϫⲟⲟⲗⲉ[†](once)*S*, ϭⲁⲁⲗⲉ[†] *AF*, ϭⲁⲗⲉ[†] *A²F*, ϫⲏⲗ[†] *B*, ϭⲁⲗⲓ[†] *F* vb tr, *swathe, clothe, cover*: Si 43 22 *S* ἐνδύειν; ib 38 17 *S* περιστέλλειν, Ac 5 6 *B*(*S* ⲕⲱⲱⲥ) συστ.; SHel 46 *S^f* cloud ⲁⲥϭⲁⲁⲗⲉ ⲡⲥⲱⲙⲁ, ManiK 180 *A²* ⲡⲉⲧⲛⲁϭⲁⲗⲧ;   refl: Ge 24 65 *S*(Mich 550 1, *B* ϫⲱⲗϩ) περιβάλλειν;   qual: Ez 41 26 *S*(*B* do) κρυπτός; C 100 269 *S* bed ⲉϥϭ. adorned (?), opp ⲉϥⲧⲏⲕ (*cf* R 1 3 32 below).

With following preposition.

—— ⲉ-: P 129[18] 111 *S* took his (Thomas's) skin ⲁϥϭ. ⲙⲙⲟϥ ⲉⲡⲉϥⲥⲱⲙⲁ (*cf* ϭⲟⲉⲓⲗⲉ **B** c ⲉ- sim), MIF 9 95 *S* ⲉⲓⲛⲁϭⲟⲟⲗⲉ (*l* ϭⲱ.) ⲉⲡⲉⲧⲣⲟⲥ ⲡⲟⲩⲥⲧⲟⲗⲏ (*cf* c ⲛ-), ManiP 206 *A²* ⲧⲁⲣⲃⲥⲱ ... ϭ. ⲁⲡⲉⲧⲁⲣⲫⲟⲣⲉ ⲙⲙⲁⲥ;   qual: RNC 26 *S* ⲡⲉⲥⲕⲉⲟⲥ ⲉⲧϭ. ⲉⲛⲉⲑⲣⲟⲛⲟⲥ σκέπασμα; BAp 2 *S* napkin ϭ. ⲉⲡⲉϥϩⲟ, B Hom 120 *S* flesh ϭ. ⲉⲡⲕⲁⲥ, ManiK 108 *A²* ⲡⲣϣⲱⲡ ⲉⲧϭ. ⲁⲣⲁⲥ.

—— ⲁϫⲛ- *A²*: ManiK 177 ⲡϩⲃⲥⲱ ... ϭⲁⲗⲟⲩ ⲁ. ⲡⲉϥⲥⲱⲙⲁ, ib 164 ⲡⲉϥ†ⲟⲩ ⲡϣⲏⲣⲉ ⲉⲧϭ. ⲁ. ⲡⲉϥⲥⲱⲙⲁ (*cf* ib 20).

—— ⲛ-, *with, in* (mostly *S*): Jth 4 12 περιβ. dat, Bar 5 2 *B*, Zech 3 5 *SA*(*B* ϯ ϩⲓ-) π. acc; Job 38 9 (*B* ⲕⲟⲩⲗⲱⲗ) σπαργανοῦν dat; Ex 26 29 ϭ. ⲛ̄ⲡⲟⲩϭ̄ (*B* ⲗⲁⲗⲟ) καταχρυσοῦν; ShC 42 94 ⲛⲧⲟⲉⲓⲥ ⲡⲉⲛⲧⲁⲩϭⲉⲗⲉ ⲡϣⲏⲣⲉ ⲙⲙⲟⲟⲩ, ClPr 47 5 ⲛⲧⲟⲉⲓⲥ ⲛⲧⲁⲡⲉⲡⲭ̄ⲥ̄ ϭⲟⲟⲗⲟⲩ ⲙⲙⲟϥ, ShA 2 177 ϭⲟⲟⲗⲉϥ ϩⲣⲉⲡⲧⲟⲉⲓⲥ, Gu 34 ⲉⲓⲛⲁϭⲉⲉⲗⲉ ⲡⲉⲧⲣⲟⲥ ⲡⲟⲩⲥⲧⲟⲗⲏ, ViK 9754 116 ϭⲟⲗⲥ ⲙⲡⲃⲱ ⲛⲃⲁⲗⲡⲉ, Mor 41 29 ⲁⲓϭⲟⲟⲗⲉϥ (*sc* pillar) ⲛ̄ϩⲁⲧ, ManiP 50 *A²* ⲁϥϭ. ⲙⲙⲁⲓ ⲛⲧⲥⲧⲟⲗⲏ, ib 67]ϭⲁⲗⲉⲧ ⲙ̄ⲙⲁⲥ;   refl: Est 6 8 ⲧⲥⲟⲗⲏ ... ⲡⲣⲣⲟ ϭⲟⲟⲗⲉϥ ⲙⲙⲟⲥ,

Ps 70 13 (*B* ϯ ϩⲓ-), *ib* 108 29 *B*(var ϫⲟⲗϩ, *S* ϯ ϩⲓ-), Is 37 1 *SF*(*B* ϯ ϩⲓ-), Mic 7 10 *SA*(*B* ϫⲟⲗϩ) περιβ. acc, Ps 103 2 (*B* ϯ ϩⲓ-) ἀναβ. acc; Is 49 18 *SB* περιτιθ. acc; Job 29 14 *B*(*S* ϯ ϩⲓ-) ἀμφιάζειν; Jth 10 3 στολίζειν ἐν; PS 106 ⲙⲁⲣⲉϥϭⲟⲟⲗⲉϥ ⲙⲡⲉⲭⲁⲟⲥ like garment, ShIF 149 ϭⲉⲗⲉⲧⲏⲩⲧⲛ ⲙⲙⲟⲟⲩ (*sc* garments), BMar 217 half of garment ⲁⲓϭⲟⲗⲧ ⲙⲙⲟⲥ = Rec 6 183 *B* ϫⲟⲗϩⲧ, El 92 *A* ⲥϭⲁⲁⲗⲉⲥ ⲙⲡⲉⲥϩⲃⲁⲥ = ib 122 *S*, ManiP 95 *A²* ⲁⲓϭⲁⲗⲉⲧ ⲙⲡⲓϫⲓϩⲃⲁⲥ;   qual: Ps 44 13 (*B* ϫⲟⲗϩ ϭⲉⲡ-), Ap 4 4 (*B* ⲕⲧⲏⲟⲩⲧ ⲛ-) περιβ. ἐν, EpJer 11 *BF*, Mk 14 51 *SBF*(var ϭⲁⲗⲉ) π. acc, 1 Kg 28 14 ἀναβ. acc; Ap 1 13 (*B* ⲧⲟⲓ ϩⲓ-) ἐνδύ. acc; He 9 4 *SF*(var Pcod Mor ϭⲁⲗⲓ) περικαλύπτειν dat; Is 30 22 *SF*(*B* ⲟⲓ ⲡⲓⲉⲙ̄ ⲛϩⲁⲧ) περιαργυροῦν; PS 229 ⲡⲟⲩⲟⲉⲓⲛ ... ⲉⲧϭ. ⲛⲧⲉϥⲯⲩⲭⲏ, ib 353 ⲉⲩϭ. ⲛⲣⲉⲛϩⲃⲟⲥ, ShC 73 11 sword's ⲕⲟⲉⲓϩ ⲛ ⲡⲉⲧϭ. ⲙⲙⲟⲥ, ShBM 198 19 ⲉⲕϭ. ⲙⲡⲉⲥⲭⲛⲙⲁ, C 100 279 ⲧⲉⲥⲧⲟⲗⲏ ⲉⲧϭ. ⲙⲡⲉⲡⲉⲓⲱⲧ, R 1 3 32 bed ⲉⲧϭ. ⲛⲡⲟⲩϩ̄, BMOr 6230 (44) ⲟⲩⲟⲓⲡⲉ ⲡϣⲉ ⲉⲥϭ. ⲡⲛⲉⲡⲓⲛ[ⲉ, El 60 *A* ⲉⲩϭ. ⲛⲣⲉⲡⲧⲙⲉⲓ, ManiP 193 *A²* ⲉϥϭ. ⲛⲧⲥⲧⲟⲗⲏ, DeV 2 129 *B* ⲉⲩϫ. ⲛ̄ϩⲁⲛϩⲃⲱⲥ, Mor 24 22 *F* ϭ. ⲛⲟⲩⲥⲧⲟⲗⲏ;   qual c ⲙⲙⲟ⸗: Jer 15 12 (*B* diff) περιβόλαιον; ViSitz 172 4 21 ⲡⲉⲕⲗⲏⲣⲟⲥ ⲉⲧⲉϥϭ. ⲙⲙⲟⲓ ⲟⲩ περίκειμαι ἐπιτυχεῖν; BAp 67 righteousness ⲉⲧϭ. ⲙⲙⲟϥ (*cf* ib sim ⲧⲟ ϩⲓⲱⲱϥ), Mor 16 47 ϩⲃⲟⲩⲥ ⲉⲧϭ. ⲙⲙⲟϥ(var BMis 205 ϭⲗⲙ̄ⲗⲟⲙ ⲉⲣⲟϥ), BMar 206 ⲡⲉϥϩⲃⲱ ... ϭ. ⲙⲙⲟϥ = Rec 6 169 *B* ϫⲟⲗϩ, KroppR 15 ⲥⲧⲟⲗⲏ ... ⲉⲣⲉⲡⲓⲱⲧ ϫ. ⲙⲙⲟⲥ, Mani P 185 *A²* virtues ⲉⲣⲉⲧⲁⲅⲁⲡⲏ ϭ. ⲙⲙⲁⲩ.

—— ϩⲛ-, ϩⲉⲛ-: Nu 4 10 *S*(*B* ϩⲓⲟⲩⲓ ⲉϩⲣⲏⲓ ⲉ-) ἐμβάλ. εἰς, Ps 146 8 *S*(*B* ϩⲱⲃⲥ), Bor 253 152 *S^f* ϭⲁⲗⲉ ⲧⲉⲯⲩⲭⲏ ϩⲛⲧⲁⲣⲉⲧⲏ περιβ. ἐν; AM 279 *B* ϫ. ⲙⲡⲉⲥⲱⲙⲁ ... ϩⲉⲛⲡⲓϣⲁⲣ περιείλειν dat; ShA 1 376 *S* ϭⲟⲟⲗⲟⲩ ϩⲓⲛⲡϣⲓⲡⲉ, P 131[4] 114 *S* ⲁϥϭⲉⲗⲉ ⲧⲡⲉ ϩⲓⲛⲡⲉⲕⲗⲟⲟⲗⲉ, Ryl 89 *S* ⲉⲩϭ.[†] ϩⲛⲟⲩⲗⲓⲡⲟⲛⲏϩⲟⲛ.

—— ⲁϫϫⲱⲗ *B*: MG 25 404 ⲁϫⲁ. ⲙⲡⲉϥⲥⲱⲙⲁ = Gött ar 114 147 كسا, ib 355 thieves ⲁ. ⲛⲛⲓⲥⲕⲉⲩⲟⲥ = 126 اخذوا, ib 86 ⲁⲛⲁ. (*sic* var) ⲙⲡⲉϥⲥⲱⲙⲁ, Aeg 49 ϯⲛⲁⲁ. ⲙⲡⲉⲥⲱⲙⲁ ϩⲉⲛⲡⲓⲉⲡⲧⲏⲙⲁ (-δυμα).

—— nn, *covering, cloak*: CO 49 *S* ⲧⲏⲡⲟⲟⲩ ⲧⲁⲡⲟⲕⲣⲓⲥⲓⲥ ⲛ[ⲡ]ϭⲱⲗⲉ ⲡⲁⲓ (this word?);   adj: Is 50 3 *B* ϩⲃⲱⲥ ⲛϫ. (*S* ϩ. only) περιβόλαιον; Tor 43 *S* ⲗⲟⲧⲓϩ ⲛϭⲱⲗⲉ (or ? ϭⲟⲓⲗⲉ).

ϭ(ⲉ)ⲗⲓϫ *S* nn as pl, *gloves* (?): Cai 67324 *v* ϩⲱϫ, Ryl 365 ⲛϭ. .... ϩϫⲁⲓ ⲙⲡⲣⲁⲙ ϥⲥⲛⲧⲟⲩ.

ϭⲟ(ⲟ)ⲗⲉⲥ *S* nn f, *covering, garment*: Is 47 2 (*B* ϩⲱⲃⲥ) κατακάλυμμα; Si 19 26 στολισμός; ShIF 66 garment ⲥⲙⲛⲧϥ ⲛⲁⲓ ⲡⲧⲩⲡⲟⲥ ⲛϭ., BAp 125 = MIE 2 418 *B* ϫⲓⲛϫⲱⲗϩ ⲛⲧⲉ ⲡⲁϣⲉ ⲉϣϣⲓ = PO 22 476 مزمل, which P 44 91 = ϭⲁⲗⲟⲧ (ⲃⲁⲗ.), RE 9 164 ⲥⲛⲧⲉ ⲛ̄ϣⲧⲏⲛ, ⲥⲛⲧⲉ ⲛϭⲟⲗⲥ, ib 157 ⲟⲩⲕⲟⲩⲓ ⲛϭ.

ϭⲱⲱⲗⲉ *S* vb intr, *burst, split* (?): WTh 176 fire beneath martyr's body ϣⲁⲛⲧⲉⲡⲉϥⲥⲡⲓⲣⲟⲟⲩⲉ ϭ., ShR

2 3 50 (collated) feedest thy dogs ϣⲁⲛⲧⲟⲩϭⲉⲓ ⲛⲥⲉϭⲱⲗⲉ ⲉⲃⲟⲗ.   *Cf* ? ⲕⲱⲗⲉ ⲉⲃⲟⲗ.

ϭⲱⲱⲗⲉ, ⲕⲱⲗⲉ S, ϫⲟⲗ, ϫⲱⲗ B(once)nn m, *flat cake, loaf*: Nu 6 15 (B=Gk) قرص, 2 Kg 6 19 B(var ϫⲱⲗ HCons 166'ⲋ, S ⲟⲣⲃⲉ) λάγανον; P 43 36 ϭⲟⲩⲗⲏ (*cf ib* ⲕⲁⲑⲁⲣⲟⲛ 'ⲍ, رغيف &طلمة); ShC 73 146 ⲡⲉⲧⲛⲱϫϭ ⲡϣⲱⲧⲉ ⲉⲃⲟⲗ ⲉⲁⲁⲩ ⲛϭ., Kr 242 among gifts ϫⲟⲩⲧⲁⲥⲉ ⲛϭ., RE 9 174 ϯ ⲟⲩⲕ. ⲡ[ⲛⲉⲧⲡⲁ]ⲣⲁⲅⲉ, BP 9445]ⲧⲱϭ ⲡⲓⲕ.

ϭⲗⲁ SA²B, ⲕ., ϭⲗⲟ S, ϭⲗⲉ S*ᶠ*, ϭⲗⲁϩ B nn m, *wave*(?): Ac 27 27 B ϫⲏ ⲥⲁⲡϭ. (var ϧⲱⲓⲁⲓ, S ⲣϧⲱⲧ) διαφέρεσθαι; ManiP 208 A² ⲁⲩϭ. ⲛⲃⲁⲗ ⲧⲉⲣⲟ ⲡⲉϥϫⲁⲓ;   ϯ ϭ., *sway, stagger*: 2 Kg 6 6 B(S ⲡⲱϣⲥ ⲉⲃⲟⲗ) περισπᾶν; Is 29 9 S(var ϭⲗⲟ, B ⲑⲓϭⲓ), *ib* 24 20 S(B diff) κραιπαλᾶν, cit P 44 112 S متمايل; ϩⲓ ϭ. sim: 1 Kg 21 13 S(var Bodl(P) c 16 ϯ ϭ.) παραφέρεσθαι (?); ShClPr 22 363 S ⲁⲧⲉⲧⲛⲧⲣⲉϩⲁϩ ⲥⲣⲟⲙⲣⲓ ⲁⲩⲱ ⲁⲩϩ., BMis 521 S drunkard ϩⲓ ⲕ. ⲉⲡⲉⲓⲥⲁ ⲙⲡⲁⲓ, Sh(?)Mor 54 148 S*ᶠ* sim; MG 25 105 B ⲛⲁϥϩ. going from side to side, AZ 28 62 S ϩⲓ ⲕ.;   tr, *push* B: Va 68 173 ⲉϥϩ. ⲙⲙⲟϥ ⲉⲡⲕⲁϩⲓ πρόσωπον εἰς τ. γῆν ὠθεῖν; C 41 63 ⲁⲩϩ. ⲙⲙⲟϥ (*sc* door) but could not open it = Miss 4 647 S ⲣ ⲧⲉⲩϭⲟⲙ = *ib* 449 لكزوا, Miss 4 159 ⲛⲁϩ. ⲙⲙⲟϥⲡⲉ (*sc* cripple) ⲉⲡⲁⲓⲥⲁ ⲡⲉⲙⲫⲁⲓ, C 43 211 ⲉⲩϩ. ⲙⲙⲟϥ for he could not walk, DeV 1 78 ⲛⲁϩ. ⲉⲡⲁⲓⲥⲁ ⲡⲉⲙⲫⲁⲓ ⲙⲡⲓⲕⲗⲏⲣⲟⲥ = P 129¹⁴ 123 S ⲛⲟⲩϫⲉ;   as nn m B: K 99 ⲡⲓϭ., اجتهاد, تمايل, سكران, سكر Va 58 192 ⲟⲩⲟⲓϭⲓ ⲡⲉⲙⲟⲩϩⲓ ϭⲗⲁϩ; ⲙⲛⲧⲣ.S: Tri 526'ⲋ;   ϭⲓ ϭ.B, *throng, press upon*: Miss 4 184 ⲉⲩⲧϭⲟ ⲙⲙⲟⲛ ⲉⲃⲟⲗ ⲉⲩϭ. ⲙⲙⲟⲛ.

ϭⲗⲁ A   *v* ϭⲗⲟ 1°.

ϭⲗⲏ B nn f, *scorpion*: Ez 2 6, Lu 10 19 (S both ⲟⲩⲟⲟϩⲉ) σκορπίος; BSM 77 ⲟⲩϭ. ⲙⲁϩ ⲣⲱⲥ ⲉⲣⲟϥ = BMis 168 S ⲕⲉⲣⲁⲥⲧⲏⲥ, C 89 123 ⲟⲩϭ....ⲛⲧⲉⲥⲗⲟⲕⲥϥ.

ϭⲗⲏ S vb tr, meaning uncertain, *strengthen, support*(?): Mor 43 232 ⲡⲉⲧϭⲃⲃⲉ ⲙⲡⲉⲧϭ. ⲙⲙⲟϥ (*cf ib* scattered...gathered, fallen...raised).

ϭⲗⲟ S, ϭⲗⲁ A nn m, *vanity, futility*: Is 49 4 (same MS as ϭⲗⲟ *s v* ϭⲗⲁ, B ⲙⲉⲧⲉⲫⲗⲏⲟⲩ) ⲉⲡⲉϭ. εἰς μάταιον; ⲁⲡϭ. A: Cl 7 2 ⲣⲁϧϣ...ⲛⲁ. μάταιος; ⲙⲛⲧⲁ. A: Am 2 8 (B om) συκοφαντία (*v* AZ 62 129 & *cf* meanings of ⲗⲁ).

ϭⲗⲟ B vb tr, *surround, besiege*: Hos 2 6 (SA ϫⲗϫⲗ) φράσσειν; ⲥ ⲉϩⲣⲏⲓ: Deu 20 12 (*sic* Va, Lag ϭⲟⲗ, S ϭⲱ ϩⲓⲣⲏ-) περικαθίζειν;   as nn m, ϭⲣⲱ f, *hedge, fence* (*drw* Dévaud): Is 5 2 (S ϫⲟⲗϫⲗ) φραγμός; *ib* 31 9 (S ϣⲗϩ, F ϫⲁⲗϫⲉⲗ), *ib* 37 33 (S ϣⲱⲗϩ) χάραξ; K 397 ⲟⲩϭ. (var BMOr 8775 117 ϭⲣⲟ) سياج;

Montp 201 ϯϭ. حائط.; Cat 117 ⲡⲓϭ., MG 25 210 ⲧⲁⲕⲧⲟ (*sic*) ϭ. ⲉⲣⲟϥ περιχαρακοῦν.

ϭⲗⲟ   *v* ϭⲗⲟϭ 2°.

ϭⲗⲟⲓ B nn f, *ball*: K 243 περικαθερμα (-αρμα)· ⲡⲓϭ. ⲡⲉⲥⲱⲃⲓ اكرة اللعب, Montp 169 ϯϭ. 'ⲓⲥ(*cf* Fleischer *De Glossis* 40. In 1 Cor 4 13 B περικ.= نفاية); MG 25 81 demons cast ϩⲁⲛϭ. ⲛⲭⲣⲱⲙ into saint's cell.

ϭⲗⲱ, ⲕ., ϭⲗⲟⲩ (once) S nn f, *twig, firewood*: Dan 3 46 (B ϣⲉ ⲛⲁⲗⲟⲗⲓ) κληματίς, cit P 44 115 زرجون (*cf* ⲥⲁⲣϭⲉ) & Cai 8027 ϭⲗⲟⲩ; Job 24 19 (B Gk diff, *cf* Hexap καῦμα); ShP 131⁶ 37 ⲡⲣⲏϣ ⲛϭ. ⲉⲧⲁϫⲱ, CO 335 send ⲟⲩϭ. ⲡⲉⲛⲡⲉ ⲯ (? ⲉⲡⲉⲡⲥ) ⲡⲉⲥⲧⲉⲡⲟⲩϭⲉ ⲉϩⲣⲁⲓ, Ep 533 paid so much ϩⲁⲕ., *ib* 542 ⲥⲡⲁⲩ ⲛⲓⲟ ⲛⲕ., ST 232 ⲛⲟⲩϭ ⲛϭ.;   Turin ostr 5926 ⲡⲣⲉϥⲛ ⲕ.

ϭⲗⲏⲃ F nn, *muzzle*, with ϯ: 1 Cor 9 9 (S ϣⲱⲧⲃ, B ⲥⲁϫⲟⲗ) κημοῦν.   V KKS 185.

ϭⲗⲃⲉ A   *v* ϭⲉⲗⲙ.

ϭⲟⲗⲃⲉ S, -ⲓ, ϣⲟⲗⲃⲓ B nn f, *garment of wool* (so Ar): K 257 B ϯϭ., AZ 14 22 B ϣ. ⲓ̈, فرو, P 54 168 B 'ⲋ, خص, سطبر (as if καλύβη); BIF 13 115 S ⲙⲧⲟⲛ ⲙⲙⲟⲕ ϩⲓϫⲛⲧⲉⲓϭ.= MG 25 307 B, *ib* 308 ϣⲧⲟϥ ⲉϫⲉⲛ ϯϭ.= 116 S, Bodl(P) f 55 S ϭ. ⲛⲃⲁ, PMich 4545 S list ϣⲉⲛϩⲱⲧ ⲃ, ϭ. ⲏ (*cf* p 722 a).   *Cf* κολόβιον (Stern 144, ThReil *Beiträge* 118) & ? جلابية (Dozy 1 204).

ϭⲗⲱⲃⲓ B nn m, *scissors* (*cf* ܡܚܕܒܐ كلابة Dévaud): K 128 among silver-smith's tools ⲡⲓϭ. كازم وهو كالمقص (*v* Almk 2 82).

ϭⲉⲗⲃⲉⲥⲓ, ϫ. F nn, *purple*: Cant 3 10 ϫ. (S ϫⲏϭⲉ), *ib* 7 6 (S do) πορφύρα;   ⲥⲁ ⲛϭ.: Ac 16 14 (Mus 42 195, S ⲥⲁ ⲛϫⲏϭⲉ, B ⲥⲁ ⲛϭⲏϫⲓ) πορφυρόπωλις.   *Cf* καρπάσιον (St Paul Girard).

ϭⲗⲃⲟⲟⲩ, ϭⲉⲗⲃⲁⲩ S, ϫⲉⲗϥⲁⲩ B nn, fish, *silurus mystus*: Glos 412 S among fish [....]ⲧⲓⲥ· ϭ., K 171 B ⲛⲓϫ. شلبا; *v* JEA 14 29;   ϭⲓϣⲉ ⲛϭⲉⲗ.: PBad 5 406 in recipe.

ϭⲉⲗⲃⲟⲟⲩ S nn m, meaning unknown, plant, cereal?: Mor 51 33 Pachom's community of old was as harvest ϩⲙⲡⲉϥⲟⲉⲓϣ ⲙⲡϭ. ⲙⲡⲡⲥⲓⲙⲟⲩϭ.   *Cf* ? جلبان, جلبة or ? ϭⲱⲗ 1° & *v* ⲃⲟⲟⲩ 2° p 46 *b*.

ϭⲱⲗⲕ B   *v* ϫⲱⲗⲕ 1° & 2°.

ϭⲗⲁⲕ, ϭⲟⲗⲕⲥ B   *v* ϫⲱⲗⲕ 1° (ϫⲗⲁⲕ).

ϭⲁⲗⲟⲩⲕⲥ, ϣ. B nn f, *scarabaeus beetle*: K 172 ϯϭ. خنفسا., Montp 132 ϣ.

ϭⲁⲗⲓⲗ S *v* ⲕⲁⲗⲕⲓⲗ p 103 a, adding ϫⲁⲗⲓⲗ B nn m: C 43 13 cast martyr into ⲟⲩϫ. ⲛϣⲉ...ⲛⲧⲉⲧⲉⲛ

ⲟⲩⲁⲥϥ ϫⲉⲡⲧⲉϥⲙⲏϯ, TillBau 126 S good day [for building] house or ⲟⲩϭ. *water-wheel* (?).

ϭιλϫ̄ S nn (abbreviated), meaning unknown: Ryl 348 ⲡⲉⲥⲓⲡⲡⲉ (σίππιον) ⲡϭ., ib ⲡⲁϭ.

ϭⲗⲓⲗ SABF nn m, *burnt-offering* : Ex 18 12 SB, Lev 9 2 S(B ϭ. ⲡⲭⲟϥϫⲉϥ), Ps 50 16 S(A Cl ⲥ̄ⲃⲛⲥⲉⲧⲉ, B do), Is 1 11 B(SF ϣⲟⲩⲥⲟⲟⲩϣⲉ), Hos 6 6 SAB, He 10 6 SBF ὁλοκαύτωμα, 1 Kg 7 9 S, Dan 3 40 B -καύτωσις; Lev 6 8 S(B ⲥⲱⲟⲓ), ib 22 27 S(B ⲟⲩⲧⲁϩ) κάρπωμα, Is 43 23 B(S ϣ.) ὁλοκάρπωσις, Lev 6 3 SB ⲕⲁⲧⲁⲕ. V Sethe *Dem Urk*. 199.

ϭⲗⲓⲗ S nn as pl, *axe* : Tri 534 ⲕⲟⲣⲉ ⲛ̄ⲧⲡⲟⲩⲡⲉ... ϩⲛϩⲉⲡϭ. زواليج. *Cf?* ⲕⲁⲗⲉⲗⲉ (Miss 4 308).

ϭ(ⲉ)ⲗⲙ, ϭⲁⲗⲙ, ⲕⲉⲗⲙ S, ϭⲗⲃⲉ A(prob) nn, *dry sticks, twigs* : Is 41 2 (var ϭⲁⲗⲙ), Hos 10 7 SA, Ac 28 3 (var ϭⲗϭⲙ, all B ⲗⲉⲃⲙ), LeipBer '02 156 carried down by torrent like ϩⲛϭ. φρύγανον; ShA 2 252 snake cannot carry ⲟⲩϣⲉ ⲏ ϩⲉⲛϭ., GMir 180 ϭ. ⲏ ϣⲉ as fuel, Bor 240 54 broken wood ⲉⲧⲟ ⲛ̄ϭⲗⲗⲙ, Sh(Besa) Z 504 ϩⲉⲛϭⲗⲗⲙ ⲙ̄ⲡⲣⲉⲡⲣⲟⲟⲩⲉ carried by wind, Sh MIF 23 34 ⲟⲩⲅⲩⲗⲏ ⲛ̄ϭⲗⲗⲙ, ShA 2 163 ⲙⲁ ⲛⲓⲙ ⲉⲧⲟ ⲟⲩϣ ⲛ̄ϭ. ϩⲓϣⲟⲉⲓϣ, J 43 31 ⲥⲉϯ ⲱϣ ⲕ. (same ?).

ϭⲱⲗⲉⲙ B v ϫⲱⲗⲙ.

ϭⲗⲁⲙ, ϣ. B vb†, *kindle* : K 231 = P 50 116 ⲉⲩϭ. (var Montp 201 = P 54 162 ⲉⲩϣ.). *Cf* ϫⲗⲟⲙ.

ϭⲗⲁⲙ AA² v ⲕⲱⲗⲉⲙ, adding ManiK 51 A² ⲟⲩϣⲡ ⲡ̄ϣⲱⲡⲉ ⲙ̄ⲡⲟⲩϭ., ib P 188 ⲕⲱⲧ ⲛ̄ϭ. ⲡⲉⲕⲁⲧⲉ, Jo 13 27 A² ϩⲛⲟⲩϭ. (S ϭⲉⲡⲏ, B ⲛ̄ⲭ., F ⲧⲕⲟⲩⲣ) τάχιον, ManiH 53 A² ⲧⲱ]ⲃⲣ ϩⲛⲟⲩϭ.; Pro 22 29 A ⲣⲉϥϭ. (S ⲣⲉϥϭⲉ.) ὀξύς.

ϭⲗⲟⲙ S vb = ⲧⲗⲟⲙ (v Addenda to p 411).

ϭ(ⲉ)ⲗⲙⲁⲓ¹, ϭⲉⲗⲙⲁ², ⲕ.³, ϭⲁⲗ.⁴, ϭⲉⲗⲙⲏⲡ⁵, ⲕ̄ⲅⲗⲙⲁⲡ⁶ S, ϭⲉⲗⲙⲁⲉⲓⲡ S/F, ϫⲓⲗⲙⲓⲛ F nn m, *jar, vase* (cf Aram קלב κάλπη Dévaud): Ex 16 33¹, He 9 4¹ SF ϭ. (both B = Gk) στάμνος, P 44 60 among church furniture ⲥⲧⲁⲙⲛⲟⲥ · ⲛϭ.¹ (sic) قسط القليلة = 43 28² درن; BHom 11¹, BMis 85⁴, ib 87 ⲛϭ.⁵ ⲡⲡⲟⲩⲃ, BMOr 7029 78 ⲡⲕ.⁶ ⲡⲡ[ⲟⲩⲃ], Mor 33 26 S/ ⲛϭ. ⲡⲡⲟⲩⲃ, ib 30 S/ ϭ. ⲡⲉⲧⲉⲙⲙⲁⲩ, Hall 48 ⲕ.³ ⲛⲏⲣⲡ (cf? ST 116 ⲕⲗⲉⲙ), BP 8095 F ⲟⲩⲭ. ⲛⲃⲁⲣⲱⲧ (l ⲉⲃ. = ⲛⲃ.).

ϭⲗⲏⲓⲙⲓ B v ϣⲗⲁⲉⲓⲛ.

ϭⲗⲟⲙⲗⲙ, ⲕ. (nn)S, ϭⲗⲁⲙⲗⲙ AA², ϭⲗⲟⲙⲗⲉⲙ, ⲕ. (once), ⲭ. (do)B, ϭⲗ(ⲉ)ⲙⲗⲱⲙ- S, ϭⲗⲓⲗⲱⲙⲉ S A², ⲗⲓⲗⲱⲙⲉ SS/, ϭⲗⲉⲙⲗⲱⲙⲉ SB, ϭⲗⲓⲗⲱⲙⲧ SA², -ⲗⲟⲙ†, -ⲗⲟⲙⲧ†, ⲗⲓⲗⲱⲙⲧ†, ⲗⲁⲗⲏⲙⲧ S, ϭⲗⲉⲙⲗⲱⲙⲧ†, ⲗⲉⲙⲗⲏⲙⲧ B vb intr, *be twisted, implicated* (cf קלב AZ 49 94): Pro 28 18 SA ἐμπλέκεσθαι, Nah 1 10 SA(B ⲙⲟⲗϫ) περιπ.; Ps 19 9 S(B ⲥⲱⲡϩ) συμποδίζεσθαι; ShViK 9346 when tempest strikes them ϣⲁⲛϣⲟⲧ ⲡⲥⲉϭ. ⲡⲥⲉⲱⲗⲕ ⲡⲥⲉⲱϭⲣ, DeV 1 103 B ⲁⲡⲁⲗⲁⲥ ϭ. cannot speak clearly; qual: Job 40 12 SB συμπλέκ.; Cl Pr 54 39 S ⲙⲡⲧⲣⲉⲟⲩⲱ ⲉⲧⲗⲙⲗⲱⲙ ⲉⲩⲙⲟⲕϩ ⲡⲃⲟⲗⲟⲩ δυσδιεξόδευτος πλοκή; Va 57 200 B ⲡⲟϭ ⲉⲧϭ. σχοινίον; Jo 20 7 S(B ⲕⲟⲩⲗⲱⲗ) ἐντυλίσσεσθαι; R 2 1 71 S bodily beauties ϩⲉⲛⲙⲁⲣⲧ ⲉⲩϭ. ⲉⲩⲕⲱⲧⲉ, MIF 9 17 S corpse ⲉϥϭ. ⲡⲥⲁⲟⲩⲥⲁ in cistern; tr, *embrace* : Ps 49 19 SB περιπ. acc; BMar 165 S ⲡⲥⲉⲙⲟⲣⲡ ⲡⲥⲉϭⲗⲓⲗⲱⲙ, Mor 41 192 S seized him by neck ⲡⲥⲉϭⲗⲓⲗⲱⲙϥ, ManiK 29 A² ⲁϥϭⲗⲓⲗⲱⲙⲥ (sc soul).

With following preposition.   c ⲉ- : Ps 118 61 S (B ⲙⲟⲩⲗϫ ⲉ-) περιπλέκειν dat, Hos 4 14 S(ShP 131⁶ 80)A(B ⲡⲉⲙ-)συμπ.μετά; Mor 37 99 S camel's rope ϭ. ⲉⲩⲱⲡⲉ περιειλεῖν εἰς; ib 17 118 S ⲡⲥⲉϭⲗⲉⲙⲗⲱⲙ ⲥⲱⲥⲓⲡⲁⲧⲣⲟⲥ ⲉⲣⲟⲟⲩ (sc snakes) ἐλίσσειν; Va 57 95 B snake ϭ.† ⲉⲣⲟⲥ καμπύλος; ShA 1 407 S passions ϭ. ⲉⲣⲟⲛ, BMis 205 S ⲡϩⲟⲟⲥ ⲉⲩϭⲗⲓⲗⲟⲙ ⲉⲣⲟϥ (var Mor 16 47 ϭⲟⲟⲗⲉ ⲙⲙⲟϥ), Bor 248 47 S ⲙⲉⲩϭ. ⲉⲡⲉⲡⲟⲩⲉⲣⲏⲧⲉ, PBad 5 410 S/ ⲗⲉⲙⲗⲟⲙⲟⲩ ⲉⲩⲧⲁⲓⲥ, BM 6201 B 120 S ⲉⲩⲗⲓⲗⲏⲙⲧ† ⲉⲣⲟⲟⲩ, CDan 98 B tongue ϭ. ⲉⲣⲟⲓ, PO 11 330 B viper ⲁⲥⲭ. ⲉⲧⲉϥϫⲓϫ; ⲉϩⲟⲩⲛ ⲉ- : Zech 14 13 A(B ⲙ. ⲉϭ. ⲉ-) συμπλέκ. πρός; BMis 544 S snakes ϭ.† ⲉϩ. ⲉⲡⲉⲩⲙⲁⲕϩ circumvolvi; PS 50 S may they be for them snare & ⲙⲁⲣⲟⲩϭ. ⲉϩ. ⲉⲣⲟⲟⲩ, ShA 2 75 S ⲟⲩⲉⲓⲁⲟⲥ (net ?, rake ?) cast into water ⲛⲉϥϭ. ⲉϩ. ⲉⲡⲛⲟⲩⲃ ⲁⲩⲱ ⲉⲡⲣⲁⲧ, Mor 56 72 S shroud ⲃⲟⲣ̄ϫⲣ ⲉⲃⲟⲗ ⲙⲙⲟϥ, opp ϭ. ⲉϩ. ⲉⲣⲟϥ ⲡⲕⲉⲥⲟⲡ, C 89 123 B snakes ⲕ. ⲉϭ. ⲉⲡⲉϥϭⲁⲗⲁϫⲭ (124 ϭ.†); c ⲉϫⲛ- : ShMIF 23 22 S devil is ϩⲣⲛⲟ ⲉⲧϭⲗⲓⲗⲟⲙⲧ ⲧⲏⲣϥ ⲉ. ⲡⲉϥⲉⲣⲏⲅ ⲏ ⲉⲃⲟⲗ ϩⲛⲡⲉϥⲉⲣⲏⲅ self-involved, participant in naught besides; c ⲡⲉⲙ- B : Hos 4 14 v above; ⲁϩⲟⲩⲛ ⲙⲛ- A² : ManiK 92 ⲁϥϭ. ⲁϩ. ⲙⲛⲡⲟⲩⲁⲓⲛⲉ; c ⲛ- : Gu 94 S ⲉϥϭ.† ⲡⲣⲉⲡⲕⲉⲣⲉⲁ (κειρία), Mor 54 70 S ϭⲗⲉⲙⲗⲱⲙϥ ⲡⲡⲉⲧⲟⲉⲓⲥ; c ϩⲛ-, ϩⲉⲛ- : 2 Tim 2 4 B(S ⲧⲱϩ ⲙⲛ-), 2 Pet 2 20 S(B refl) ἐμπλέκ. dat, Nah 2 4 B(A ⲁ-) συμπ. ἐν; 1 Kg 21 9† S (var ⲛ-) ἐνειλεῖν ἐν, Mk 15 46 S(B ⲕⲟⲩⲗⲱⲗ) ἐν. dat; Lu 23 53 S(var ⲕⲱⲥ, B do) ἐντυλίσσειν dat; Job 18 8 B(S ⲥⲁϩⲥϩ) ἐλίσσειν ἐν; Va 57 260 B worms ⲉⲩⲗ.† ϫⲉⲡ̄ⲡⲓⲕⲁⲣⲓ ἐγκαλινδεῖσθαι περί; ShBMOr 8810 443 S ⲡⲧⲉⲓⲡϭ. ϩⲛⲡⲉϥϣⲏⲛⲉ, ShMIF 23 81 S ⲧⲏϭⲗⲗⲟⲙⲧ ⲡϩⲏⲧⲥ, Mor 25 18 S perfume ⲡⲥⲉϭⲗⲓⲗⲱ[ⲙϥ ϩ]ⲡⲡⲉⲩϩⲟⲉⲓⲧⲉ = Va 61 100 B ⲡⲥⲉⲭⲟⲡϥ ϩⲉⲛ-, Aeg 12 SB tongue & lips ⲁⲩϭ. ϩⲁⲡϫⲓ ⲛ̄ϭ̄ⲟⲛⲥ, PMich 4558 S ⲁⲓⲗⲓⲗⲱⲙϥ ϩⲡⲧⲁⲥⲧⲟⲩⲗ[ⲏ, ManiK 30 A² ⲉϥϭ. (ⲙ)-ⲙⲁⲩ ϩⲁⲡϯ ⲥⲃⲱ.

ϭ., ⲕ. S nn, *complication* (?) in legal texts : J 51 10 ⲡⲁⲧⲗⲁⲁⲩ ⲡⲕ., ST 41 ⲉϫⲡⲗⲁⲁⲩ ⲡϭ. ⲟⲩϫⲉ ⲗ. ⲡⲁⲙⲫⲓⲃⲟⲗⲓⲁ, ib 429 ϫⲱⲣⲓⲥ ⲁⲙⲫ. ϩⲓϭ. ϭ. ⲉϩⲟⲩⲡ B sim : Va 57 62 ⲡϭ. ⲉ. ⲡⲡⲓⲣⲃⲛⲟⲩⲓ ⲛ̄ⲃⲓⲱⲧⲓⲕⲟⲡ.

Cf ? ϫωλμ b.

ϭελμη, ϭελμαειπ   *v* ϭελμαι.

ϭολμες B   *v* ϣολμες.

ϭλαμϭλ[μ] A^2 vb intr, meaning unknown:
Mani K 180]ε παρϭοπ ϩ[πογ]παρϭε πϭ.   *Cf*
ϭλομλμ.

ϭλαπϭωϣ   *v* ϭαραϭωϭϣ, adding ϭλ. F
BKU 1 26 (8116 b) ϣεερ πογϭ.

ϭλαπ F   *v* καλωπογ.

ϭλπ B   *v* ϭλαπ.

ϭωλπ SAA^2F, κ. *SF*, ϭωρπ B, ϭ(ε)λπ-, ϭολπ⸗,
κ.*S*, ϭλαπ⸗ A^2, ϭορπ⸗B, ϭολπ†, κ.† *SF*, ϭα.† S^aAA^2F,
ϭορπ† B, p c ϭλαπ- S vb tr, *uncover, open, reveal*: Ez
23 18 B(S c εϧολ) ἀποκαλύπτειν; C 86 320 B αϥϭ.
πϯκολλαϑι, TRit 247 B αϥϭ. μπικαρι with flowers
ظهر; Bess 7 66 Sπετπαϭ. ποϒκηρπ in thy name, Mor
46 49 S οϒλακοτε πηρπ...αϥϭολπς, ManiP 158 A^2
πηρπ πϧρρε αϒϭαλπϥ, *cf* c πϭα-, Ep 531 S ϩεπκακε
...ασκωλπογ & took half thereof.
With following preposition.
—— ε-: Si 1 6 *SB*, Jo 12 38 *SB*(A^2 c εϧολ) ἀποκ.
dat; Z 321 S πεπταϥϭ. εροϥ ὁρᾶσθαι dat; ShR 2 3
90 S ϑε ετππαϭ. επ̄ϩ̄ μμος, Ep *lc* S others too she
took ππεϥκ αροι; qual SA^2: ShWess 9 141 ετϭ.
εροϥ απτι πετϩηπ, ShA 2 295 ϥϭ. επϩητ πηετο πϭα-
ϧε, ST 268 have sold all shrouds save one πςκ. εροι
απ *which I did not find*, *ib* 448 εϣωπε πϩωϧ ϭ. ετεκ-
μπτειωτ ετϧεπϩολοκοτϭε ... let me know, Ep 299
S^a μπ οϒοπ ϭ. εροπ, J 44 145 μπ λαϒε ϭ. εροι εαϥ-
ϭϩαιϥ ετϩιαϑηκη, ManiK 32 A^2 πει τηροϒ ϭ. α-
ραϥ;   tr: Jer 11 20 S(B c εϧ. ϩα-) ἀποκ. πρός, EW
148 B ἐκκ.; PS 60 S αιϭ. ερωτπ ππειμϒςτηριοπ,
ShA 1 281 S devil ϭ. μμοοϒ εροοϒ, Pcod 13 S
αϒϭλπ πϩωϧ εροϥ, ManiP 8 A^2 ϭ. αραϥ ππιπετ-
ϩηπ, DeV 2 8 B sim.
—— εϫπ-: Corpus Cambridge 541 F μμπ[πετ]-
πεκολπ εϫοκ;   εϩρηι εϫ.: Jer 13 26 B(S c εϧολ)
ἀποκ. ἐπί.
—— π- dat: Dan 2 19 B ἀποκ. dat, MG 25 243 B
πτεϥϭ. μπρωϧ μπιϫελλο παϥ ἀποκ. dat; Bor 253
149 S εϥπαϭ. παϒ in bride-chamber.
—— πϭα-: Mor 51 24 S αϒϭ. πϭαπελακοπ πηρπ
(*cf* 23 οϒλακοπ πτερεϥϭολπϥ).
—— ϩα-: ManiP 105 A^2 ϭεϭ.† ϩαπ[.
With following adverb.
—— εϧολ: 2 Kg 6 20 S, Nah 2 7 AB, 1 Cor 3 13
SBF(Mor 38 103) ἀποκ., 2 Cor 3 18 $S^†$B ἀπακ.; Hab
3 2 *SAB* ἀναδεικνύειν; Mk 4 22 F(Mus 49 188, S tr,
B οϒωπϩ εϧ.) φανεροῦσθαι; BHom 50 S plans παϭ.

εϧ. (var R 2 2 34 οϒωπϩ εϧ.), JTS 5 559 S απμα ϭ.
εϧ., ManiK 13 A^2 αϒϫικαιος ϭ. αϧ.;   qual: Nu
5 18 F(BM 1221, S tr, B ϫω εϧ.), Pro 27 5 S(var
οϒοπϩ εϧ.)A ἀποκ., EpJer 30 B(F κη εϧ.) ἀκάλυπτος
εἶναι; 1 Cor 11 5 S(B ϩωϧϲ απ) ἀκατακάλ., R 1 5 16
S πεϒϩο ϭ. εϧ. απ φαίνεσθαι; BMis 358 S limbs ϭ.
εϧ., ManiK 151 A^2 eyes ϭ. αϧ.;   tr: Ge 8 13 B(S
οϒωπ), Lev 18 6 S(B ϧωϣ), Mic 1 6 *SAB*, Gal 1 16
SB ἀποκ., Job 12 22 *SB*, Jer 29 10 *SB* ἀπακ., Pro 26
26 *SA* ἐκκ.; Jth 9 1 S γυμνοῦν; Deu 22 17 S(B φορ-
περ) ἀναπτύσσειν; Mk 2 4 *SB* ἀποστεγάζειν; ClPr
54 44 S αϥϭ. εϧ. πτπαποϒργια φωρᾶν; BG 59 S ϭ.
εϧ. μφϧϲ, BMis 37 S bade send & ϭ. εϧ. μπεσταϒρος
discover, P 131⁵ 100 S ακϭ. εϧ. μπλεπτιοπ = Mus 35
203 B ωλι, BIF 14 125 S her son ϭολπϥ. μπεπ-
πρηϣ *divested self of*, ManiH 40 A^2 ϭ. πεϒϩο αϧ.; C
89 13 B αϥϭ. πϯϣιω εϧ., DeV 2 234 B αποε ϭ. εϧ.
πϯϧαϫμι (*v* p 510 b);   εϧ. ε- S: Lu 10 21 (B π-)
ἀποκ. dat; Miss 4 777 ατεϩιη...ϭ. εϧ. ερωμε πιμ;
εϧ. εϫεπ-: Lam 2 14 B ἀποκ. ἐπί;   εϧ. π- dat: Ps
36 5 B(S οϒωπϩ ε-) ἀποκ. πρός, Jo 12 38 A^2(SB e-)
ἀ. dat; Ac 16 9 S(B οϒωπϩ ε-) ὁρᾶν dat; PS 81 S
ακϭ. παπ εϧ. ππειϣαϫε, *ib* 4 S ϭλπ παι παπ εϧ.,
ShA 1 391 S πειραπ...πταϥϭ. παι εϧ., AP 40 A^2 αϒϭ.
αϧ. πϑεοπϭπ, ManiK 155 A^2 ϭαλποϒ πεπ αϧ.; DeV
2 165 B is right εϑριϭορπϥ πακ εϧ.;   εϧ. πτεπ-:
Ps 17 16 B(S π-) ἀνακ. ἀπό;   εϧ. ϩα-: Ru 3 4 S,
Jer 20 12 B ἀποκ. πρός; ManiP 57 A^2 αϒϭ. αϧ. ϩαπ-
κεκε;   as nn m: 1 Kg 20 30 S, Eph 1 17 *SB* ἀπο-
κάλυψις, 1 Pet 1 5 S(B vb) ἀποκαλύπτεσθαι; Dan 10
7 S(B παϒ), Lu 1 22 S(B οϒωπϩ), Z 307 S παϒ επϭ.
εϧ. πϩπαϒϒελος, AM 276 B πιϭ. εϧ. of Virgin ὀπτασία; EW 147 B truth revealed ϩιτεποϒϭ. εϧ. ἐμφά-
νεια; ShP 130² 91 S ϩεποϒωπϩ εϧ. μπϩεπϭ. εϧ., Sh
P 131¹ 37 S cursed whoso ϭωϣτ ... ϩποϒεπιϑϒμια
εϩραι εϫπϭ. εϧ. ππετϩιτοϒϩοϒ *nakedness*, *ib* or
εϫμπεϒϭ. εϧ. μμιπ μμοοϒ, BMis 1194 S worthy
to see ϩαϩ πϭ. εϧ. (meaning ?).   ϫιπϭ.
εϧ. B: Dan 11 35 ἀποκ. vb.

p c S, *who or which uncovers, is bare*: MélChMoeller
1 228 οϒϭαλπϫωϥ (*cf* ἀναφάλαντος *recalvaster*), Mor
18 1000 οϒϭαλπϩραϥ (var *ib* 19 101 φϒλακρος *l* φαλ.)
= Miss 4 159 B κακϩραϥ.

ατϭ. S, *not uncovered*: BM 1127 πεκϩμϫ ... πα.
αϒω πατπαρτοϒ εϧολ.

ρεϥϭ. αϧ. A^2, *revealer*: ManiK 16 πρ. πππετϩηπ.

ϭωλπ, ϭολπ⸗ B vb tr, *create*: Ge 2 8, *ib* 19 (S =
Gk) πλάσσειν; جبل   ;   ρεϥϭ., *creator*: K 44 مكون.

ϭωλπ B nn m, *faggot*, used as *raft*: K 134 ship's
appurtenances πιϭ. (1 var ϭλωπ) طن الرومس, شرش،
اذش.   *Cf* μρωμ.   V BIF 20 76 n.

ϭⲱⲗⲡ *B* nn, *projecting roof, veranda*: K 154 سقيفة (which 153 = ⲥⲟⲉⲕⲉⲑⲉ).   *V* Almk 2 7.

ϭⲗⲁⲡ, ϭⲁⲗⲡ *B* nn m, *mass, lump*: Job 38 28 (*S* diff) βῶλος ; C 89 6 dew fell ⲁϥⲉⲣ ⲟⲩϭ. ⲛⲉϩⲓⲱ ⲥⲧⲉⲣⲉⲟⲛ = MG 17 345 ارض = Va ar 172 6 قوام ; P 54 175 (var K 232 ϭⲁ.) حفنة, كبثة, قبضة ; EW 64 ⲡⲓϭ. ⲛⲥⲟⲣⲧ (on Jud 6 38).   ϭ. عنقود P 43 (so Pey) not found ('ⲥ = ⲥⲙⲁϭ P 43 54) ; the MS is *S* only.

ϭⲁⲗⲟⲡⲟⲩ   *v* ⲕⲁⲗⲱⲡⲟⲩ.

ϭⲁⲗⲉⲥ *S* nn f, meaning unknown, part of a mill (? μηχανή, *cf* ⲙⲁⲭⲁⲡⲏ Deu 24 6 *B*): PLond 4 517 among varia ϣⲙⲟⲩⲛⲉ ⲛϭ. ⲛⲙⲁⲭⲁⲡⲉ.

ϭⲟⲟⲗⲉⲥ *S* nn f, *thigh*: GMir 257 ⲧϭ. ⲛⲧⲟⲩⲉⲣⲏⲧⲉ ⲡⲟⲩⲛⲁⲙ ⲡⲧⲥⲛϥⲉ, ib 260 sim = C 86 46, 47 *B* ⲕⲉⲗⲓ ⲛⲧⲉ ⲧϥⲁⲧ = SE Assemani *AcMartOr* 1, 254, 255 ܠܗܐ.

ϭⲟⲟⲗⲉⲥ   *v* ϭⲱⲱⲗⲉ 1° s f.

ϭⲁⲗⲓⲧ *A*, ϭⲉⲗ. *A²*   *v* ϭⲟⲉⲓⲗⲉ.

ϭⲗⲟⲧ *B*   *v* ϭⲗⲟϭ 2°.

ϭⲗⲱⲧ[1] *SA²B*, ϣ. *B*, ϭⲗⲱⲧⲉ *A²*, dual ϭⲗⲟⲟⲧⲉ[2], ϭⲗⲟⲧⲉ[3], ϭⲗⲟⲟϭⲉ[4] *S*, ϭⲗⲁⲧⲉ *A²* nn m f, *kidney* (*cf* כליות IgnR), also other internal organs: Lev 3 4 *S* ⲥⲟⲉⲓϣ ⲛϭ.[1] *B* ⲡⲓϭ. ⲃ̄, ib 8 16 *S* ⲛⲉϭ.[1] ⲥⲛⲁⲩ *B* do, Job 16 14 *S* ⲛⲁϭ.[2] *B*, Ps 7 11 *B*(var ϣ.), ib 25 2 *S³*(so Budge Ps always, varr², ⲧϭ.[3])*B*, Sa 1 6 *S³*, Jer 12 2 *B*(*S* ϩⲏⲧ), Ap 2 23 *S²*(varr³⁴)*B* νεφρός ; 2 Kg 3 27 *S²* ψόα ; Ge 49 6 *B*(*S* diff) ἧπαρ ; BMis 247 *S* spear smote him ⲉϫⲛⲡⲉϥϭ.[2] (var⁴ Z 264) = PO 1 420 كلية, Aeg 12 ⲛⲉϭ.[2] ⲛⲧⲁⲅⲣⲗⲟⲟⲗⲉ ⲙⲙⲟⲓ when babe = *B* ⲛⲓⲭⲓⲝ, ManiK 91 *A²* ϩⲛⲡⲁⲣ, ⲟⲩⲁϭ, ⲡⲁⲓϣ, ϭⲗⲁⲧⲉ, MG 25 152 *B* ruminated food enters ⲛⲓϭ. ⲛⲧⲉ ⲡⲉϥϩⲏⲧ ;   f: Ex 29 13, 22 *B* ⲧϭ. ⲥⲡⲟⲩϯ *v*. ; ManiK 173 *A²* ⲧⲉϥϭ. ⲥⲛⲧⲉ, ib 174 ⲧϭⲗⲱⲧⲉ ⲛϭⲃⲟⲩⲣ.

ϭⲗⲧⲉ *S* nn, meaning unknown: Hall 115 among things pledged ϩⲉⲛⲉⲓⲕⲧⲉ, ϩⲉⲛⲍⲟⲟⲩⲣ, ⲟⲩϭ.

ϭⲁⲗⲓⲧⲉ *S* nn f, *vessel or measure*: WS 88 ⲙⲟⲩϩ ⲧⲉⲩϭ. ⲡⲛⲉϩ, paral ϩⲟⲧⲥ, PHeidelb 497 (copy Crum) ϫⲟⲩⲱⲧ ⲡⲉⲣⲧⲟϥ ⲛⲧⲁϣⲣ ϩⲁϭ., Mor 51 34 ⲡⲥⲁ ⲛϭⲁⲗⲓⲧⲁ, paral ⲡⲉϣⲟⲧⲉ.   *Cf* ?? κόλλαθον (ⲕⲟⲗⲁⲑⲓ, ⲕⲁⲣⲁⲑⲉ BM 1119), often f (Ryl 350 n).

ϭⲁⲗⲟⲩⲃⲓϩ *S*, ⲃⲁⲗⲙⲃⲉϭ, -ⲃⲁϭ (Dévaud *Ét.* 30 n), ⲁⲗⲟⲩⲃⲉϭ *B* nn m, *bald-headed person*: Lev 13 41 *SB* ἀναφάλαντος ; El 120 *S* ⲉⲟⲩⲡ ⲟⲩⲧⲟⲉ ⲡⲥⲟⲓⲙ ϩⲓⲑⲏ ⲡⲭⲱϥ ⲛϭ. = ib 90 *A* ⲡϣⲁⲧⲙⲉⲣⲏⲗ (*cf* AZ 24 125 n), BMar 135 *S* Peter came to me ⲉⲩϭⲁⲗⲟⲩⲃⲟⲥⲡⲉ (*cf* *Synax Cpolit* 778 ἀναφάλας, Peter bald *v* FXKraus *Realencycl* 2 612, but here ? confused with κολοβός); ⲙⲛⲧϭ., ⲙⲉⲧⲁⲗ.: Lev 13 42 ἀναφαλάντα ⲙⲁ ذبل (P44

105 مقشورة).   With ⲟⲩⲃⲓϩ *cf* ? ⲟⲩⲃⲁϣ *s f* & ⲁⲗ 2°. *Cf* also ⲕⲁⲗⲧ-.

ϭⲗⲱⲟⲩϣ, ϣ., ϭⲁⲗⲱⲟⲩϣ *B* nn m, *maimed, paralysed person*: Va 57 193 ϩⲁⲛϭⲁⲗ. ⲉⲣⲉⲡⲟⲩⲙⲉⲗⲟⲥ ϥⲉⲧϥⲱⲧ διεστραμμένος τὰ μέλη ; MG 25 405 ⲟⲩϭ. in hands & feet = Gött ar 114 148 مفلوج, K 101 ⲡⲓϭ. (var ϣ.) شلش, شلوش, تشعيت (*cf* Dozy = ? this word), var فجيت (diff word ?) ; Miss 4 159 ⲁⲩϭⲓϯ ⲙⲡⲓϭ. (*sc* crawling cripple) ϩⲓϫⲉⲛⲡⲉⲛⲕⲁⲥ ⲙⲡⲓⲙⲁⲣⲧⲩⲣⲟⲥ & was healed = Mor 19 101 *S* ⲕⲉⲣϭⲟⲥ (κυρτ.).

ϭⲁⲗⲁⲟⲩϭ *O*   *v* ϭⲁⲗⲟϫ.

ϭⲁⲗⲁϣⲓⲣⲉ *A²* nn m, *strong man, giant* (?): Mani K 119 ⲧⲁϫⲣ ?]ⲁⲓⲧ ϩⲛⲟⲩⲙⲛⲧⲁϣⲓⲣⲉ ⲉⲧⲃⲉⲡⲛⲁϭ ⲛϭⲁⲙ ...ⲙⲛⲛϭ. [ⲉⲧⲟ] ⲛϩⲏⲧⲥ, ib H 61 ⲁⲩϫⲁⲧ ⲡⲕⲟⲥⲙⲟⲥ... ⲛⲑⲉ ⲡⲟⲩϭ., ib 75 ⲛϩⲱⲥ ⲙⲛⲛϭ. (*v* ϩⲱⲥ 4°), ib P 138 ⲡⲓϩⲁⲣϣϩⲏⲧ ⲛϭ., ib 46 ⲡⲭⲱⲙⲉ ⲛⲛϭ. (*v* n there & Berl Sitz '33 39 γραφὴ τῶν γιγάντων).   As name *S*: ϭ. (BM 1130), ⲕⲁⲗ. (Cai 8724), Καλασῖρις (Preisigke). For etymol *v* Spg *Dem Stud* 1 17*, AZ 43 88, but ? wrongly held related to ⲁϣⲓⲣⲉ (*v* p 84 a, adding ManiK 100 *A²* ⲧⲁⲙⲛⲧⲭⲱⲣⲉ ⲙⲛⲧⲁⲙⲛⲧⲁ., ib 72 ⲡⲟⲩⲧⲉ ⲛϫⲱⲣⲉ ⲡⲁ.).

ϭⲗⲟϥ *B*   *v* ϣⲗⲟϥ.

ϭ(ⲉ)ⲗϩ, ϭⲗⲁϩ (once) *S* nn m, *shoulder*: R 1 4 17 ⲁϥⲕⲧⲉ ⲛⲉϥϭⲓϫ ⲙⲡⲉⲧⲡⲉ ⲡⲛⲉϥϭ. *humerus* ; ShP 131⁶ 37 ϩⲉⲛϣⲧⲏⲛ...ⲉϫⲛⲡⲉⲩϭⲓϫ ⲙⲡⲛⲉⲩϭ., Ming 341 ⲁⲓⲁⲙⲁϩⲧⲉ ⲙⲡⲉϥϭ. (varr Mor 48 6 ϭ. ⲥⲛⲁⲩ, BMar 205 ϭⲃⲟⲓ) = Rec 6 168 *B* ϭⲛⲁϩ, R 1 5 49 ⲡⲉϥϭⲉ. ⲥⲛⲁⲩ (var Mor 32 23 ϭⲗⲁϩ), HM 1 95 sim, P 129¹⁶ 12 ⲛⲕⲉⲉⲥ ⲛⲡⲉϥϭⲉ. *Cf* ϫⲛⲁϩ.

ϭⲗⲁϩ *B*   *v* ϭⲗⲁ.

ϭⲗⲉϩ *B*   *v* ϣⲗϩ.

ϭⲱⲗϩ *B*   *v* ϫⲱⲗϩ 2°.

ϭⲁⲗϩⲏ *F*   *v* ϭⲱⲗ 1°.

ϭⲟⲗⲉⲥ *B*   *v* ϣⲟⲗⲉⲥ.

ϭⲁⲗⲁϩⲧ *SA*, -ⲧⲉ *S*(once), -ⲉϩⲧ *Sᶠ F*, ⲕⲁⲗⲁϩⲧ *S* nn f, *pot*: Nu 11 8 (*B* ϣⲓⲱ), 1 Kg 2 14, Si 13 3 opp Ⲭⲁⲗⲕⲓⲟⲛ, Mic 3 3 *SA*(*B* do), Wess 15 22 ϯ̄ⲟ ⲡⲉⲡⲓⲥⲕⲟⲡⲟⲥ ⲉⲡⲉϣ. χύτρα, Cl 17 6 *A* ⲗϣⲱⲃ ⲁⲃⲁⲗ ϩⲛⲟⲩϭ. κύθρα ; ShA 1 240 ϩⲉⲛⲁϥ ⲉⲩϭ., ShC 73 137 ⲛϭ.... ⲡⲣⲟⲕϩⲉ ⲉⲧϩⲣⲟⲟⲩ, C 99 210 ⲧϭⲁⲗⲁϩⲧⲉ ⲛⲁϥ = ib 89 3 *B* ϣ., ib 158 his hope is ϩⲛⲟⲩϭ. = ib 89 97 *B* do, C 99 104 ⲟⲩⲕⲟⲩⲓ ⲛϭ. wherein bread kept, BMar 81 man's life as ⲡⲗϩⲟ(ⲃ) ⲡⲟⲩⲕ. (*cf* Cl above), JTS 38 126 faces black ⲛⲑⲉ ⲡⲟⲩϭ. ⲉⲥⲕⲏⲣ, PBad 5 401 *Sᶠ* ⲡϭⲁⲗⲉϩⲧ (*sic* ?) (ⲧ)ⲁⲥⲁϩϯ ϩⲁⲣⲁⲥ ϣⲁⲛⲧⲉⲥϫⲱⲣ, Mor 38 62 *Sᶠ* sim, PMéd 238 ⲡⲁⲥⲧⲟⲩ ϩⲛⲟⲩϭ. ⲛⲃⲣⲣⲉ, BKU 1 26

(8116b)*F* ϭ. for cooking, WS 149 ϭ. ⲛ̀ϫⲓⲣ, BM 1126 ϭ. of honey, CO 368 ⲕⲁ(ⲗⲁ)ⲅⲧ ⲛ̀ϣⲱⲡⲉ, *ib* 459 ⲕ. ⲛ̀ⲣⲟⲙⲡⲧ, KroppF 49 ϭ. ⲛⲁⲃⲁⲥⲉⲓⲛ, *ib* J 63 ⲧϭ̄. ⲛⲁⲧⲙⲁⲁϫⲉ.

ϭⲁⲗⲟϫ *B*, -ⲁϫ *F*, pl ϫⲁⲗⲁⲩ(ϫ)*S*(once), ϭⲁⲗⲁϫ *BF*, ϫ., ϫⲁⲗⲁϫⲣ *F*, ϭⲁⲗⲁⲟⲩϭ *O* nn f, *foot, knee*: Ps 65 6 (*S* ⲣⲁⲧ⸗), *ib* 120 3 (*S* ⲟⲩⲉⲣⲏⲧⲉ), EpJer 25 *F*(*S* do, *B* om), Mt 4 6 (var pl, *S* do), Ap 10 2 *BF*(Lacau, *S* do)ποῦς; C 41 43 ϯⲓⲡⲓ ⲛⲧⲉ ⲧⲉϭ., *ib* 43 229 ⲧⲉϭ. ⲃ̄; pl forms: Ge 18 4 (*S* ⲟⲩ.), Ps 98 5 (*S* do), Is 1 6 (*SF* do), Lam 2 1 *BF* ϫ. (*S* do), *ib* l 13 *BF* ϫⲁⲗⲁⲩϫⲣ, EpJer 16 *BF*(*S* Mus 50 230 do), 1 Cor 15 25 (*SF* do), MG 25 216 fell ϩⲁⲛⲉϭ. ⲡ.; Bar 5 6 ⲙⲟϣⲓ ⲛ̀ⲡⲟⲩϭ. πεζός; Ez 1 7 (*S* do), Am 3 12 (*S* do)σκέλος; Cant 7 1 *F* ϫ. (*S* ⲧⲁϭϭⲉ)διάβημα; BKU 1 22 *S* ⲧⲁⲧⲥ ⲉⲥⲕⲱⲧⲉ ⲁⲡⲣⲏ ⲉϫⲁⲗⲁⲩ(ϫ) ⲕⲱⲧⲉ ⲁⲡⲟϭ, C 43 219 ⲑⲟ ⲟⲩ̈ ⲉⲧⲧⲟⲓ ⲉⲡⲉϭ., AM 43 ⲁϥⲟϩⲓ ⲉⲣⲁⲧϥ ϩⲓϫⲉⲡⲡⲉϭ., Aeg 12 ⲡⲓϭ. ⲉⲧⲁⲓⲣⲉⲙⲓⲥⲓ ϩⲓϫⲱⲟⲩ = *ib* S ⲡⲁⲧ, C 43 162 fell beneath ⲡⲉⲛϭ. of horse, CMSS 45*F* dust of ⲛⲉϭ., AZ 21 100 *O* ⲡⲁⲡⲓϭ. (prob) ⲛ̀ⲣⲟⲙⲡⲧ; ⲙⲁ ⲛ̀ϫⲁ ⲛⲓϭ.: Va 57 185 ἴχνος; AM 280 ἀναβάθρα.

ϭⲱⲗϫ *S*, ϫ. *SA²B*, -ϭ *S*(once), ϭⲱⲗϭ *Sʲ*, ⲕⲱⲗϫ *B*, ϭ(ⲉ)ⲗϫ-, ϫⲉⲗⲉϫ-, ϭⲟⲗϫ⸗, ϭⲟⲗϭ⸗ *S*, ϫⲟⲗϫ⸗ *SB*, ϭⲁⲗϫ⸗ *AA²*(AP), ϫⲁⲗϫ⸗ *A²*(Ma), ϭⲟⲗϫᵗ *S*, ϭⲁⲗϭᵗ*Sʲ*, ϫⲟⲗϫᵗ *SB*, ϭⲁⲗϫᵗ *A*, ϫⲁⲗϫᵗ *A²*(Ma) vb intr, *be entwined, implicated* (cf ⲗⲱⲕϭ metath. & ⸗ⲅ̣⸗ Dévaud): Lam 1 14 *B*(*F* ϭⲗⲁⲙⲗ?]ⲉⲙ ϩⲗⲏⲓ ϩⲓⲡ-)συμπλέκειν; ShBM 204 77 *S* nets for prey ϣⲁⲡⲧⲟⲩϫ., Mor 55 66 *S*(on Ps 103 26) serpent turning about ⲉϥⲛⲁⲉⲓ ⲛϭ. ⲉⲡⲉϩⲟⲩⲟ, MG 25 161 *B* sim, AM 298 *B* ⲁⲩϫ. ⲛ̀ϫⲉ ⲡⲉⲛⲥⲫⲟⲧⲟⲩ ⲙ̀ⲡⲓϩⲩⲅⲅⲉⲙⲱⲡ *clave together*; qual *A²*: ManiK 133 bonds ⲉⲧϭϫ. ⲉⲥⲙⲏⲣ ⲛ̀ϩⲏⲧⲟⲩ, *ib* 85 soul ⲉⲧϫ. ⲟⲩⲧⲱⲟⲩ, *ib* P 201 ⲡⲉϥⲫⲟⲥⲥⲁⲧⲟⲛ ϫ. ϧⲉⲙⲁϩⲧⲉ ⲛ̀ⲡⲓⲗⲁϣⲁⲡⲉ (meaning?); tr, *entangle, ensnare*: Job 40 19 *B* ἐνσκολιεύεσθαι; C 42 101*S* ⲡⲉϥⲟⲓⲙⲉ ⲡⲁϫⲟⲗϫⲕ ⲁⲡ; BHom 135 *S* ⲧⲟⲉⲓⲙ...ϭⲉⲗϫ ⲡⲉϫⲙⲁⲗⲱⲧⲟⲥ (αἰχ.), Bor 258 104 *S* Judith & Holofernes ⲁⲥϫⲟⲗϥⲟⲩ (sc baited hook)ⲁⲥⲡⲁϩϥ ϩⲓⲣⲟⲩⲛ, BMis 557 *S* ϩⲉⲛϣⲗⲓϭ...ⲉⲩϭ. ⲡⲡⲉⲯⲩⲭⲟⲟⲩⲉ, LA1 9 *S* ⲉϥϭⲟⲗϭⲉϥ *withhold, conceal self* (cf c e- refl), ManiK 177 *A²* ϯϭⲁⲙ ⲉⲧⲟⲩϫ. ⲙⲙⲁⲥ.

With following preposition.

—— e-: Ps 21 16 *SB*, *ib* 136 6 *B*(*S* ⲧⲱϭⲉ) κολλᾶσθαι dat, Lam 2 2 *B*(*S* ShC 73 77 ϣⲱϣ ⲙⲡ-, *F* ⲧⲱϫⲉ ⲉϩⲗⲏⲓ) κ. εἰς; *ib* 4 8 *B*(*SF* ⲧ.) πηγνύναι ἐπί, Va 57 260 *B* ϣⲁⲑⲛⲁⲩ ⲛϫ.ᵗ ⲉⲡⲁⲡϫⲁⲣⲓ? ⲛⲣⲟⲙⲡ. dat; Pro 6 21 *B*(*SA* ⲙⲟⲩⲣ) ἀφάπτειν ἐπί; Is 26 3ᵗ *S*(var ϩⲓⲡ-, *B* diff)ἀντιλαμβάνειν; Va57 146 *B* ⲁⲡⲓⲧⲉⲃⲧ ϫ. ⲉϯⲱⲓⲙⲓ; Wess 9 51 *S* ⲟⲩϣⲟⲉⲓϣ...[ⲡϥ]ϭ. ⲉⲡⲉⲧⲛⲥⲱⲙⲁ= RylBull 11 401 *b* صق ; ShA 2 157 *S* ⲙ̀ⲡⲣϭⲟⲗϫⲉϥ ⲉⲛⲗⲟⲓϩⲉ ⲛⲙⲙⲁⲕ, TMina *Epima* 21 *S* martyr's skin & hair ϭ. ⲉⲛⲱⲡⲉ = C 43 141 *B*, *ib* *B* lips ϫ. ⲉⲛⲉⲩⲉⲣⲏⲟⲩ

= *ib* S ⲗⲱⲭⲣ, Mor 55 66 *S* hook & fish ϣⲁⲥϭ. ⲉⲡⲉϥⲙⲁⲣⲧ, Gu 99 *Sʲ* ⲉⲩϫ.ᵗ ⲉⲡⲉⲩⲥⲡⲟⲧⲟⲩ, Va 61 19 *B* ⲡⲓⲗⲟⲅⲓⲥⲙⲟⲥ ⲉⲧϫ.ᵗ ⲉⲛⲕⲁϩⲓ; refl *S*, ViK 9572 17 ⲁⲓϭⲟⲗϭⲧ ⲉⲩⲛⲁϭⲉ ⲛϣⲉ; *withdraw, abstain from*: C 73 212 ⲧⲁⲟⲩⲉⲙ ⲡⲉⲓϩⲣⲟ ϫⲓⲛⲙⲙⲟⲛ ⲧⲁϭⲟⲗϫⲧ ⲉⲣⲟϥ, ShA 1 418 any food ⲉⲣⲉⲡⲣⲱⲙⲉ ⲛⲁϭⲟⲗϫϥ ⲉⲣⲟⲟⲩ.

—— ⲉϫⲛ-: Ge 25 26 *S*(Mus 50 19, *B* ⲁⲙⲟⲛⲓ) ἐπιλαμβ. gen.

—— ⲛ- instr *SA²*: *cleave, adhere to* refl: Is 56 4 (*B* do), RNC 38 able to [ϭⲟ]ⲗϫϥ ⲛ̀ⲧⲙⲛⲧⲟⲩⲏⲏⲃ ἀντέχεσθαι gen; Is 3 6 (*B* ⲁⲙⲁϩⲓ) ἐπιλαμβ. gen; Ps 2 12 (*B* ⲁⲙⲟⲛⲓ) δράσσεσθαι gen; 1 Pet 5 5 ϫⲉⲗⲉϫ- (*B* ϫⲱⲗ) ἐγκομβοῦσθαι dat; AP 14 *A²* ⲁϥϭⲁⲗϫϥ ⲛⲙⲁⲥ περιπλέκειν dat; ShMIF 23 153 ⲉϭⲟⲗϫⲡ ⲡⲡⲉⲧⲱⲫⲉⲗⲉⲓ, P 131⁵ 17 ⲡⲧⲓϭⲟⲗϫⲡ ⲙ̀ⲡⲉⲓⲣⲁⲩϭⲁⲗ ⲉⲧⲟⲣϫ, Z 578 ⲛ ϭⲟⲗϫⲕ ⲙ̀ⲡⲟⲉⲓⲕ...ⲧⲥⲓⲟⲕ ϫⲉ ϩⲱⲱϥ ⲙⲙⲛⲧⲡⲟⲉⲓⲕ *abstain from*; qual *SA*: Pro 1 22 *SA*(*B* ⲁⲙⲟⲛⲓ) ἔχεσθαι gen, Zeph 1 6 *A*(*B* ϣⲱⲡ) ἀντέχ. gen, 1 Tim 6 2 (*B* ⲁⲙⲟⲛⲓ) ἀντιλαμβ. gen; Tri 617 ⲉⲁⲩϭ. ⲛ̀ⲣⲉⲡⲥⲧⲟⲗⲏ (var تخف) *swathed in*; Pro 4 22 *SA* ⲡⲉⲧϭ. ⲙⲙⲟⲟⲩ (*B* Gk diff); ShC 42 151 *S* ⲉⲩϭ. ⲙ̀ⲡⲓϣⲁϫⲉ ⲉⲧⲟⲩϫ, ShMiss 4 285 ⲟⲩⲱⲙ (ⲙ)ⲡⲉ ⲡⲟⲉⲓⲕ opp ϭⲟⲗϫ ⲙⲙⲟϥ, BHom 57 ⲉⲥϭ. ⲛ̀ⲧⲃⲟⲛⲑⲓⲁ ⲙ̀ⲡⲛⲉ̄.

—— ⲛⲥⲁ-: R 1 2 12 *S* ⲉⲛϭⲟⲗϫ[ⲡ?]ⲛⲥⲁⲡⲛⲉ̄, MG 25 161 *B* ϫ. ⲙ̀ⲡⲓϫⲓⲁⲃⲟⲗⲟⲥ ⲛⲥⲁⲡⲉϥϫⲉ̄ϣⲁⲓ.

—— ϩⲓ-: Z 340 *S* beheld one ⲉⲩϭ.ᵗ ϩⲓⲱⲱϥ ϩⲓⲧⲛϩⲟⲓⲛⲉ κρατεῖσθαι *closely guarded*, ShC 73 6 *S* ⲉⲛⲁϣⲱⲧ ⲁⲛ ⲛ̀ϫ. ϩⲓⲧⲉⲩⲧⲣⲁⲡⲉⲍⲁ; JTS 38 122 *S* nail ⲁϥϭ. ϩⲓⲡⲁϩⲟⲩ ⲙ̀ⲡϣⲉ, *ib* another ⲁⲩϭⲟⲗϫϥ ϩⲓⲡⲙ̀ⲡϣⲉ.

—— ϩⲛ-, ϩⲉⲛ-: ROC 11 305 *S* ⲡⲥⲉϫ. ϩⲛ̀ⲡϣⲱⲡⲉ ἐμπλέκ. εἰς; Is 24 18 *S*(*B* ⲣⲁⲟⲩϭ) ἁλίσκεσθαι ὑπό; Deu 30 20 *S*(*B* ⲧⲱⲙⲓ) ἔχεσθαι gen, Eccl 7 19 *S*(*F* diff) ἀντέχ. ἐν; Tri 528 *S* Balaam's ass ⲁⲥϭⲟⲗϫ (*l* ϭⲱ.) ϩⲁⲛⲡⲭⲟ (sic) التصق ; ShMIF 23 77 *S* bait ⲥⲉⲛⲁϫⲱⲗϭ ⲛ̀ϩⲏⲧϥ, ShMiss 4 285 *S* sim, Gu 99 *Sʲ* many ⲛⲁϭⲱⲗϭ ϩⲛ̀ⲧⲟⲓⲙⲉ, P copte 155 (= PSBA 26 176) *S* sword ⲉⲧϭ.ᵗ ϩⲛ̀ⲧϫⲱⲡⲛ, BMOr 8811 211 *S* ⲟⲩⲟⲛ ⲛⲓⲙ ⲉⲧϫ.ᵗ ϩⲛ̀ⲡⲁⲡⲟⲗⲓⲁ, ManiP 81 *A²* ⲉⲩϫ.ᵗ ϩⲛ̀ⲡⲟⲅⲱⲙ ⲙ̀ⲡⲛⲥⲱ, *ib* K 173 *A²* Zodiac signs ⲉⲩϫ.ᵗ ⲉⲩⲙⲏⲣ ϩⲙ̀ⲡⲓⲧⲣⲟⲭⲟⲥ, Aeg 32 *B* ϫⲟⲗϫⲥ (sc shroud) ϫⲉⲛⲣⲉⲡⲫⲉⲣⲟⲡⲓ (περόνιον); ⲁⲃⲁⲗ ϩⲛ-: Zech 8 23 *A*(*B* ⲁⲙⲟⲛⲓ) ἐπιλαμβ. ἐκ.

—— ϩⲓⲧ(ⲉ)ⲛ-: Va 63 95 *B* ⲁⲡⲉϥⲥⲛ̄ⲁ̄ ⲕ. ϩ. ϯⲁⲕⲁⲑⲁⲣⲥⲓⲁ ῥυπᾶσθαι ὑπό (this word?); ⲉⲃⲟⲗ ϩ.: Sh ClPr 24 359 *S* ⲧⲉⲧⲛϫ. ⲉⲃ̄. ϩ. ⲡⲉⲧⲡⲉⲣⲏⲧ like snares.

With following adverb. ⲉ ⲉⲡⲉⲥⲏⲧ: Ps 43 26 *B* (*S* ⲧⲱϭⲉ) ⲕⲟⲗ. εἰς; ShC 73 201 *S* ⲉϥϭ.ᵗ ⲉ. like dog, BMis 514 *S* scarce could man ϭ. ⲉ. ⲛ̀ϩⲏⲧϥ (sc whirlpool, or ? = ⲕⲱⲗϫ) ⲉ ⲉϧⲟⲩⲛ, ⲉϭ̄.: BM 1141 *S* obscure; ⲉϩ. ⲉ-: 2 Kg 189 *S*(var ϫ.) περιπλ. ἐν; Aeg 32 *B* ⲁϯⲕⲁⲓⲥⲓ ϫ. ⲉϭ̄. ⲉⲡⲉϥⲥⲱⲙⲁ, Mor 41 246 *S* horse's feet ϭ. ⲉϩ. ⲉⲣⲟϥ so could not move; ⲉϩ. ϩⲁ-: ShC

73 136 Ϩⲛⲉⲡⲡⲁⲧ ⲉⲧϭ.† ⲉϩ. ϩⲁⲣⲟⲛ; ⲡϩⲟⲩⲡ ⲉ-: Mor 41 259 S lips & tongue ϭ. ⲛϧ. ⲉⲣⲱϥ.

—— nn m S, *entanglement*: ShC 73 7 ⲡⲁϣ, ϭⲟⲣϭⲥ, ⲭ.; *abstinence*: Z 578 n ⲛϭ. ⲛⲡϭⲛⲟⲩⲱⲙ, ShP 131⁷ 46 mourn ϩⲛⲟⲩⲗⲩⲡⲏ ⲙⲛⲟⲩϭ., MMA 23 3 710 ostr ⲟⲩⲡⲁϣⲉ ⲛⲧⲛⲃⲉ ⲛϭ. *quid* ? (no context).

ϭⲱⲗϫ *SAA²*   *v* ⲕⲱⲗϫ *bend*.

ϭⲗⲟϫ *BF*   *v* ϭⲗⲟϭ 1° & 2°.

ϭⲗϫⲉ *S* nn BMis 93 = ⲕⲗϫⲉ.

ϭⲱⲗϭ   *v* ϭⲱⲗϫ.

ϭⲗⲓϭ *S* = ϣⲗⲓϭ *q v*, adding Mor 32 31 ϭ. ⲥⲛⲁⲩ red-hot ⲧⲣⲧⲱⲣⲟⲩ ϩⲛⲡⲉϥⲉⲕⲓⲃⲉ, (BSG 178 ⲟⲩϭ. ⲡⲣⲁⲙϣⲉ, prob *l* ϭⲗⲓⲗ).

ϭⲗⲟϭ, ⲧⲗ. *S*, ϭⲗⲟϫ *BF*, ⲭⲗ. *B*(AZ 61 109n), ϭⲗⲁϭ *AA²F*, ϭⲁⲗⲉϫ *F* nn m, *bed, bier*: Ge 48 2 *S*(var ⲙⲁ ⲡⲛⲕⲟⲧⲕ)*B*, Job 7 13 *SB*, Pro 7 16 *SAB*, Mk 4 21 *SB* (*F* Mus 49 188 ⲙⲁ ⲡⲉⲛⲕ.) κλίνη, Ac 5 15 *SB* κλινά-ριον (paral ⲙⲁ ⲛⲛⲕ. κράβαττος); Ex 21 18 *S*, Ps 35 4 *S*(both *B* ⲙⲁ ⲡⲉⲛⲕ.), Pro 7 17 *SA*(*B* ϣⲁⲓⲣⲓ) κοίτη; Mk 2 4 *SB*, Jo 5 8 *SA²B* κράβ., R 1 4 69 *S* will burn thee ϩⲓϫⲙⲡⲉϭ. ⲙⲡⲉⲛⲓⲡⲉ = MartIgn 876 *B* κραβατ-τοπυρίαις ἀναιρεῖν; Ps 62 6 *S*(*B* ϥⲣⲏϣ) στρωμνή; Va 58 123 *B* night thoughts ϩⲓϫⲉⲛⲡⲓϭ. ⲡⲉⲙⲡⲓⲙⲁ ⲡⲉⲛⲕ. κλίνη, στρ.; Lu 7 14 *S*(*B* ⲥⲗⲏ) σορός; Mor 37 139 *S* σκιμπόδιον; PS 121 *S* ⲡⲉⲧⲙⲏⲣ ⲉⲡⲉϭ., ShC 73 161 *S* ⲡⲉⲧϭⲉⲓ ϩⲁⲡⲉϭ. *bier*, BMis 71 *S* ⲕⲱ ⲙⲡⲉϭ. ⲉⲡⲉⲥⲏⲧ (*cf* 70 sim ⲙⲁ ⲛⲛⲕ.), Z 328 *S* corpse upon ϭ., AM 54 *B* sim, Mor 30 50 *F* sim = BMis 274 *S* ⲙⲁ ⲡⲛⲕ., TstAb 231 *B* lay not ⲉϫⲉⲛⲟⲩⲙⲁ ⲡⲉⲛⲕ. ⲟⲩⲇⲉ ϩⲓϫⲉⲛⲟⲩϭ., AP 37 *A²* ϥⲓ ϩⲁⲡⲉϭ., ManiH 57 *A²* ϩⲙⲉⲥⲧ ⲁⲭⲛⲡϭ., *ib* 62 corpse ϩⲓϫⲙⲡϭ., *ib* 73 ⲡⲱⲣϣ ⲛⲡⲟⲩϭ., C 43 147 *B* ϭ. ⲛⲃⲉⲛⲓⲡⲓ = TMina *Epima* 28 *S* ⲙⲁ ⲡⲛⲕ. ⲛⲃⲉⲛⲓⲡⲉ, C 86 271 *B* ϭ. ⲛⲣⲟⲙⲧ, ST 116 *S* ϥⲧⲟⲟⲩ ⲛϭ., PMich 3559 *S* ⲡⲟϭ ⲛⲧⲗⲟϭ, *ib* 4567 *S* do, BM 708 *F* among iron articles ϭⲁ. Ⲁ̄.

ϭⲗⲟϭ, ⲉϭ. *S*, ⲉϭⲗⲁϭ *A*, ϭⲗⲟϫ, -ⲧ (Jon), ⲉϭⲗⲟϫ, ⲉϫ., ϣⲗⲱϫ *B* nn m, *gourd* (*cf* ? *dn(l)g* Berl *Wörterb* 5 470): K 259 *B* ϣ. قثّاء (but *ib* 199 كرنب, *l* كزنيب); DeV 2 48 *B* Jonah's ⲃⲱ ⲡⲉϭ., 49 ⲡⲉϫ., AM 47 *B* as if one should scrape ⲟⲩϭ. ⲙⲃⲟⲛϯ (that feels not), *cf* p 41 *b*, Z 630 *S* ⲡⲉⲧⲥⲁⲛϩⲟⲩⲛ ⲉⲡⲉϭ. in recipe, RAl 87 *B* Jonah comforted ϩⲓⲧⲉⲛⲡⲓⲕⲁⲥ ⲡⲉϭ. (var DeV 1 195 ⲕⲟⲩϫⲓ ⲙϥⲉⲛⲧ ⲛϭ.); Ryl 72 351 *S* field ⲙⲡⲟⲩⲭⲟ ϭ. ⲉⲣⲟⲥ (for ? ϭⲣⲟϭ); CO 347 *S* ⲛⲟϭ (*l* ? ⲡⲉϩ) ⲛϭ., Cai Copt Mus *Catal* 1 ov *S* among *varia* ⲡⲱϩ (not for ⲡⲉϩ which is ⲛⲏϩ *ib*) ⲛϭ.; ⲃⲛⲧ ⲛ(ⲉ)ϭ.*S*, ϥ. ⲡⲉ. *A*, ϥⲉⲛⲧ ⲛ(ⲉ)ϭ., ⲡⲉϫ. *B* nn m, *colocynth*: Jon 4 9 *SAB* κολόκυνθα اصل القرع, Tri 304 *S* do; DeV 2 48 *B* ϥ. ⲡⲉϭ., *ib* ⲡⲉϫ.

ϭⲗⲟ *S* nn f, sim : P 44 82 ⲕⲟⲗⲟⲕⲩⲛⲑⲟⲥ · ⲧⲉϭ. قرع, (var EW 222 glossary 'ϭ, on which *v* Almk 1 370). *Cf* ? ⲕⲗⲟ in DM 24 27 (*v* p 102 *b*).

ϭⲗⲟϭ *S* nn, meaning unknown, context broken: Hall 150 (collated) record of work (or task) ⲡⲁⲓⲡⲉ ⲡⲁⲣⲱⲃ ⲛϭⲓϫ...ⲗⲓⲧ(ⲣⲁ) ⲡⲉⲓⲟⲉ (? ⲉⲓⲱ *linen*)...ⲛⲛⲟⲩϭ. ⲙⲙⲁϫⲉ.

ϭⲗⲟⲟϭⲉ¹, ϭⲗⲟϭⲉ² *SA²*, ⲕⲗⲟϭⲉ³, ⲧⲗⲟⲟϭⲉ⁴, ⲧⲗⲱϭⲉ⁵ *S*, ⲧⲗⲁϭⲉ *F* nn f, *ladder* (*cf* ? درجة Dévaud): Ge 28 12⁴ *sic*(*B* ⲙⲟⲩⲕⲓ), cit ShA 2 77¹ κλίμαξ; P 44 21 ⲧⲉϭ.² = CaiThe 177 *B* ⲙ. سلّم; ShViK 915 ϩⲉⲡⲧⲱⲣⲧⲣ, ϩⲉⲛϭ.¹, ShA 1 306 cannot mount without ⲧⲱⲣⲧⲣ ⲏ ϩⲡⲟⲩⲧ.⁵, TT 40 ⲡϣⲟⲣⲡ ⲙⲡⲟⲉⲓϣ ⲡⲧⲉϭ.¹, WTh 136 serpent ϩⲁⲣⲁⲧⲥ ⲡⲧⲉϭ.¹ = *ib* 4 *B* ⲥⲁⲡⲉⲥⲏⲧ ⲛϯⲙ., Ep 222 send man ⲛϥϥⲓ ⲧⲕ.³, ManiP 167 *A²* ⲡⲛⲧⲱⲣⲧ, ⲧⲛϭ.¹, *ib* 177 *A²* ⲁ]ⲥⲣ ϭ.¹ for those mounting, *ib* 8 *A²* ⲟⲩϭ.² ⲁⲡ-ϫⲓⲥⲉ, PcodMor 20 *F* ⲧⲉⲧ. of Jacob.

ϭⲗⲟⲟϭⲉ   *v* ϭⲗⲱⲧ.

ϭⲉⲗϭⲓⲗ, ϭⲉⲓⲗϭⲉⲓⲗ   *v* (ⲕⲟⲗⲕⲗ) ⲕⲁⲗⲕⲓⲗ & *cf* ? ϫⲉⲗϫⲓⲗ.

ϭⲟⲗϭ(ⲉ)ⲗ *S*, ϭⲁⲗϭⲗ *A²*, ϫⲉⲗϫⲉⲗ *B*(nn), ϭ(ⲉ)ⲗϭⲱⲗ⸗, ⲕⲗⲕⲱⲗ⸗ *S*, ϫⲉⲗϫⲱⲗ⸗ *B*, ϭ(ⲉ)ⲗϭⲱⲗ⸗⁺ *S* vb tr, *spread to dry*: Nu 11 32 *SB*, Jer 8 2 *B* ψύχειν; Ostr *penes* EES *S* ref to palm cultivation ⲉⲕⲧⲁⲕⲗⲕⲱⲗϥ; ⲥ ⲉⲃⲟⲗ: 2 Kg 21 6 *S* ⲉⲩϭ.† ⲉⲃ. ϩⲁⲡⲣⲏ, *ib* 9 ϭⲉⲗϭⲱⲗⲟⲩ ⲉⲃ. ϩ. ἐξηλιάζειν; Jer 4 29 *S* ⲡⲕⲁϩ ⲧⲏⲣϥ ⲁϥϭ. ⲉⲃ. (*B* Gk &com, ? gloss on ἀναχωρεῖν), cit P 44 113 = 43 113 اختلج, تزلزل; ShC 73 162 *S* not seemly to ϭ. ⲛⲡⲉⲧⲛ-ⲭⲛⲁϩ ⲉⲃ. (var ϭⲃⲟⲓ) ⲉⲃ. (var ϭⲱⲗⲡ ⲉⲃ.), ManiK 113 *A²* ⲁϥϭ. ⲁⲃ.(ⲡ)ⲙⲙⲁⲩ ⲙⲡⲛⲉⲕⲉ, *ib* 159 ϣⲁϥϭ. ⲁⲃ. ⲡⲧ-ϩⲣⲧⲉ, WS 89 *S* ⲡϭⲣⲕⲗⲕⲗ ⲉⲃ. (this word ?); as nn: Nu *lc SB* ϫⲉⲗϫⲉⲗ (Va) ψυγμός; ⲙⲁ ⲛϫ.: Ez 47 10 *B* ψυγ. (in 26 14 ⲙⲁ ⲙ̄ϥⲱⲣϣ). *Cf* ϫⲟⲗϫⲉⲗ 2° (same word ?).

ϭⲗϭⲓϫ   *v* ϭⲱⲱⲗⲉ 1° *s f*.

ϭⲁⲙ *S* nn, *bull* (?): Is 11 6 (Rec 23 112, 124, var ⲕⲧⲏⲣ, *B* = Gk) ταῦρος. *Cf* ? ḳmꜣ (Berl *Wörterb* 5 38 Dévaud).

ϭⲉⲙ *Sᵃ*   *v* ⲕⲁⲙ.

ϭⲟⲙ *S*, ϭⲁⲙ *AA²F*, ϫⲟⲙ *B*, ϫⲁⲙ (rare)*F* nn f, *power, strength* (for ϭ., ϫ. with ϣ- *v* below): Nu 2 3 *SB*, Is 36 22 *SBF*, Mk 13 25 *SBF*, Cl 11 2 *A* δύ-ναμις, Ps 64 6 *S*(*B* ⲙⲉⲧϫⲱⲣⲓ), *ib* 79 2 *SB* δυναστεία; Job 6 11 *SB*, Ps 21 15 *S*(*B* ⲛⲟⲙϯ), Pro 14 4 *SAB*, Eph 1 19 *SBF*, BHom 40 *S* ⲧϭ. ⲙⲡⲥⲱⲙⲁ ἰσχύς; Job 4 10 *SB* σθένος; Pro 6 8 *SAB* ῥώμη; Sa 87 *S* ἀνδρεία; *ib* 17 5 *S* βία; Ps 45 3 *S*(*B* ⲁⲙⲁϩⲓ) κραταιότης; 2 Cor 8 20 *B*(*S* ⲧⲁϫⲣⲟ) ἀδρότης; Cant 6 3 *S* τάγμα (Hexap);

PS 118 *S* ⲧⲏⲡⲟⲟⲩ ⲡⲁⲓ ⲛⲟⲩⲛⲟϭ ⲛϭ., *ib* 91 ⲟⲩϭ. ⲛⲣⲟ
ⲙⲙⲟⲅⲓ, Br 231 *S* ⲡⲉⲧⲟⲩⲱⲛⲣ ⲉⲃⲟⲗ ⲛⲧⲙⲧϭ. (*cf ib* τρι-
δύναμις), ShA 2 317 *S* smiting ⲣⲓⲧⲉϥϭ. *with (all) his
might*, ShC 73 84 *S* ⲉⲧⲉⲩϭ. ⲧⲉ ⲉϭⲱ, ShIF 264 *S* ⲧⲉⲩϭ.
ⲁⲛⲧⲉ *it is not in their power*, BMis 212 *S* ⲛⲧⲛϭ. ⲁⲛⲧⲉ,
SHel 36 *S* ⲛⲧⲉⲕϭ. ⲁⲛⲧⲉ ⲉϯ ⲧⲱⲛ, AZ 21 158 *S* ⲛϭ.
ⲙⲛⲡⲉϣⲏⲣⲉ, COAd 42 *S* oath ϣⲉ ⲡⲓⲧⲟⲡⲟⲥ ϣⲉ ⲧⲉϥ-
ϭ., PBu 112 *S* when they heard ⲧϭ. ⲛⲛⲁⲓ *authority
of these* (documents), ST 104 *S* ⲛⲧⲛϩⲁⲣⲉϩ ⲛⲁⲕ ⲛⲧϭ.
ⲙⲡⲉⲓⲗⲟⲧⲟⲥ, J 75 119 *S* shall demand them ⲣⲓⲟⲩϭ.,
AP 22 *A²* will turn ⲧⲉⲧⲛϭ. ⲁⲩⲗⲁⲭⲗⲉϩ, ManiK 60 *A²*
ⲛϭ. ⲙⲡⲕⲉⲕⲉ, DeV 2 56 *B* ⲧϫ. ⲛϯⲙⲉⲧⲁⲛⲟⲓⲁ, PO 11
306 *B* at school learned ⲧϫ. ⲡⲛⲓⲥϫⲁⲓ;   as adj : Ps
109 2 *SB*, 1 Cor 12 10 *SB* δύναμις; 3 Kg 19 11 *S* ⲟⲩϭ.
ⲙⲡⲛⲁ μέγας; DeV 2 37 *B* ⲟⲩⲣⲁⲛ ⲛϫ.

ⲁⲧϭ., *powerless, unable, as nn impotence* : Job 5 16
SB, EpJer 27 *BF*, Mt 19 26 *S*(*B* ⲙⲉⲧⲁⲧϫ.), MG 25 6
B ⲟⲩϭⲱⲃ ⲛⲁ. ἀδύνατος; Sa 13 17 *S* ἀσθενής; Leyd
305 *S* luxury ⲧⲣⲉⲡⲉⲣⲓⲟⲙⲉ ϣⲱⲡⲉ ⲛⲁ., R 1 3 15 *S* ⲟⲩⲁ.
ⲡⲁⲓ, Pcod 26 *S* ⲟⲩⲁ. ⲡⲉ ⲉⲧⲣⲉⲧⲉⲓⲥⲁⲣϫ ⲧⲱϭⲛ, J 66 21
S ⲗⲁⲁⲩ ⲛⲁ. ⲣⲙⲡⲁⲥⲱⲙⲁ, AP 20 *A²* ⲁⲛ ⲗⲁⲁⲅⲉ ⲛⲁ.
with God, MG 25 344 *B* wings ⲛⲁ., ROC 25 256 *B*
ⲛⲁ. ⲛⲭⲏⲣⲁ, Pap Liverpool Mus *F* ⲛⲁⲧⲧϭ. (*sic*);
ⲙⲛⲧ-, ⲙⲉⲧⲁ. : Ro 8 3 *SB*, He 6 4 *B*(*S* ⲁⲧϭ.) ἀδύν.;
Lam 1 7 *B*(*F* ⲙⲁⲛ ϣϫⲁⲙ) οὐκ ἰσχύς; He 7 18 *SF*(*B*
=Gk) ἀσθ.; ShC 73 84 *S* hindered ⲣⲓⲧⲛⲧⲙ., *ib* 51
ϣⲱⲡⲉ ⲛ ⲟⲩⲙ., ManiP 92 *A²* ⲧⲁⲙ., DeV 2 10 *B* ⲑⲙ.
of old age;   ⲣ ⲁ. : Ge 18 14 *SB*, Is 8 15 *B*(*S* ⲣ ϭⲱⲃ),
Lu 1 37 *SB* ἀδυνατεῖν; Is 40 30 *B*(*S* ⲕⲁ ϭ. ⲉⲃⲟⲗ)
ἄνισχυς εἶναι; 2 Cor 12 10 *SF*(*B* ϣⲱⲡⲓ) ἀσθενεῖν; Miss
4 529 *S* fasted ϣⲁⲓⲧϥⲣ. ἀτονεῖν; PS 36 *S* ⲛⲡⲉⲅⲣ.
ⲡⲥⲉⲁⲧⲟⲡⲓ, LMär 13 *S* ⲡⲁⲥⲱⲙⲁ ⲣ. ⲉⲣⲟⲓ, BSM 53 *B*
ⲟⲩⲁⲓ ⲉϥⲟⲓ ⲛⲁ. = BMis 406 *S* ⲟⲩϭⲱⲃ, C 43 189 *B*
ⲉϥⲉⲣ. ⲉϣⲧⲉⲙⲧⲱⲛϥ.

ⲣⲙⲛϭ., ⲣⲉⲙⲛϫ., *mighty man* : 1 Kg 17 51 *v* ⲗⲉⲙⲏ-
ⲛϣⲉ, Bar 1 4 *B* δυνατός, Ac 8 27 *B*(*S*=Gk) δυνάστης;
C 89 52 *B* ⲟⲩⲣ. = C 99 145 *S* ⲁⲩⲡⲁⲧⲟⲥ; KroppD 25
S ⲡⲓⲣⲙⲉϭ. (*l* ⲛϭ.).

ⲕⲁ ϭ. ⲉⲃⲟⲗ *S*, *abandon strength* : Is 40 30 *ut sup*;
He 11 12 (*B* diff) νεκροῦσθαι; BM 311 104 sim, JTS
38 124 ⲛϭⲕ. ⲣⲓⲧⲉϥⲙⲛⲧⲣⲗⲗⲟ.

ⲉⲓⲣⲉ, ⲓⲣⲓ, ⲣ, ⲉⲣ ϭ., ϫ., *do mighty deeds, wonders* : Ps
117 16 *SB*, Mt 7 22 *SB* δύναμιν ποιεῖν; Lu 1 51 *S*(*B*
ⲁⲙⲁϩⲓ) κράτος π.; R 1 3 32 *S* ⲛϭ. ⲉⲧϥⲉⲓⲣⲉ ⲙⲙⲟⲟⲩ,
Pcod 18 *S* ⲁⲛⲣⲗⲗⲟ ⲣ ⲣⲁϩ ⲛϭ.;   ⲥ poss, *do utmost* :
Si prol *S* ἰσοδυναμεῖν; ShC 42 165 *S* ⲙⲛⲡⲓⲥⲁⲧⲣⲉⲩⲣ
ⲧⲉⲩϭ. ⲙⲡⲉⲣⲉⲡⲕⲟⲟⲅⲉ, Mor 22 30 *S* ϯⲡⲁⲣ ⲧⲁϭ. ⲛⲧⲁⲃⲓ
ⲡⲛⲁⲙⲁⲓ, ST 194 *S* ⲁⲛⲣ ⲧⲉⲛϭ. ⲡⲛⲙⲏⲧⲛⲓ, C 86 115 *B*
ϯⲛⲁⲓⲣⲓ ⲛⲧⲁϫ. ⲡⲉⲙⲁⲕ ⲉⲡⲓⲛⲉⲧⲣⲱⲟⲩ.

ϯ ϭ., ϫ., *give power* : Ps 67 29 *SB*, Eccl 10 10 *S*(*F*
ϫⲛ ϫⲁⲙ) δυναμοῦν, Lu 9 1 *SB* δύναμιν διδόναι; Ps
147 1 *B*(*S* ⲧⲁϫⲣⲟ), Ez 34 4 *S*(*B* ϯ ⲡⲟⲙϯ) ἐνισχύειν,
Ps 88 21 *SB* κατισ., *ib* 28 10 *SB* ἰσχὺν διδ.; *ib* 104 24

S(*B* ⲑⲣⲉⲁⲙⲁϩⲓ) κραταιοῦν; Pro 21 6 *SA* ἐνεργεῖν;
PS 132 *S* ⲁⲩϯ. ⲡⲧⲉⲩⲡⲁⲣⲣⲏⲥⲓⲁ (Od Solom 6 17 ⲁⲥⲟⲃ
ⳑⲗⲱ), ShC 42 181 *S* ⲉⲩϯ. .... ⲙⲡϣⲁⲣ, ManiK 72 *A²*
ϯ. ⲡⲛⲉϥϣⲏⲣⲉ, BSM 88 *B* ⲉϥϯ. ⲛⲱⲟⲩ & *healeth
them*; ⲙⲛⲧⲣⲉϥϯ ϭ. : Mor 22 45 = R 2 441 *S* ⲟⲩⲙ.
ⲙⲡⲛⲟⲃⲉ, MélOr 6 508 *B* sim.

ⲟⲩⲛ ϭ. *SAA²*, *there is power, have power* : Mk 2 19
(*B* ⲟⲩⲟⲛ ϣϫⲟⲙ) δύνασθαι, *ib* 14 35 (*B* do) δυνατός;
ShViK 940 219 ⲉⲡⲉⲟⲩⲛ ϭ. ⲡⲉ;   ⲥ ⲛ-, ⲙⲙⲟ⸗ :
Job 42 2 (*B* do), Mt 12 29 (*BF* do) δύνασ., Ps 23 8 (*B*
do), Pro 3 28 *SA*(*B* do), Lu 1 49 (*B* ⲉⲧϭⲟⲣ) δυνατός;
ShMun 164 ⲟⲩⲛ ϭ. ⲙⲙⲟⲟⲩ ⲉⲣⲟⲟⲩ, CA 103 ⲉϣⲱⲡⲉ
ⲟⲩⲛ ϭ. ⲙⲙⲟϥ, AP 23 *A²* ⲟⲩⲛ ϭ. ⲙⲙⲁϥ...ⲁⲧⲣⲉϥ-.

ⲟⲩⲛ ϣϭ. *SA²F*, ⲟⲩⲟⲛ ϣϫ., *B as last* : Ge 13 16
SB, Mk 14 5 *SB* δύνασ., Va 57 8 *B* δυνατός; J&C 92
S ⲉϣϫⲉ ⲟⲩⲛ ϣϭ., AP 40 *A²* ⲟⲩⲛ ϣϭ. ⲛⲡⲉⲓ;   ⲥ ⲛ-,
ⲙⲙⲟ⸗ : Is 36 8 *SBF*, Mt 8 2 *S*(var ⲟⲩⲛ ϭ.)*B*, MG
25 214 *B* ⲟⲩ. ϣϫ. ⲙⲙⲟⲕ ⲉⲛⲟⲣⲉⲙ δύνασ., Ro 4 21 *B*
(*S* ⲟⲩⲛ ϭ.) δυνατός εἶναι; Jer 31 14 *B* ἰσχύειν; Ac 14
12 *S*(var do, *B*=Gk) ἡγούμενος εἰ.; PS 184 *S* ⲟⲩⲛ
ϣϭ. ⲙⲙⲟϥ ⲉⲭⲱ, C 43 231 *B* ⲟⲩ. ϣϫ. ⲙⲙⲟϥ ⲉϯⲯⲩ-
ⲭⲏ, MIE 2 392 *B* ⲟⲩ. ϣϫ. ⲛⲣⲱⲃ ⲛⲓⲃⲉⲛ = BAp 115
S ⲟⲩⲛ ϭ., Mani 2 *A²* ⲟⲩⲛ ϣϭ. ⲙⲙⲁϥ ⲁⲧⲣⲉϥ-.

ⲙⲛ ϭ. *SAA²*, *there is not power, have not power* :
Ps 68 2 (*B* ⲙⲙⲟⲛ ϣϫ.) οὐκ ὑπόστασις εἰ.; Lu 14 26
(var ϣϫⲟⲙ, *B* do) οὐ δύνασ.; PS 234 ⲙⲛ ϭ. ⲛⲥⲟⲩⲛ
ⲡϣⲁⲭⲉ, ShIF 81 ⲉⲙⲛ ϭ. ⲉⲧⲣⲉⲩ-;   ⲥ ⲛ-, ⲙⲙⲟ⸗ :
Ge 31 35 (*B* do), Pro 24 56 *A*(*S* ⲉ-), Jo 3 2 *SA²*(*B* do),
Ac 27 15 (var ϣϫ., *B* do) οὐ, μή δύνασ.; Lu 16 3 (*B*
ϣϫⲉⲙ ϫⲟⲙ ⲁⲛ) οὐκ ἰσ.; BG 50 ⲉⲙⲛ ϭ. ⲛⲧⲥⲁϣϥⲉ...
ⲉⲧⲟⲩⲛⲟⲥϥ, ShC 42 36 ⲙⲛ ϭ. ⲙⲡⲛⲧⲉ ⲉⲣⲱⲃ ⲛⲓⲙ.

ⲙ(ⲙ)ⲛ ϣϭ. *SA²F*, ⲙⲙⲟⲛ ϣϫ., *B as last* : Si 17 25
S, Jo 3 5 *BF*(*S* ϭ.) οὐ δύνασ., 1 Cor 12 3 *SB*, Ap 7 9,
SBF(Lacau) οὐδεὶς δ., Ac 2 24 *SB* οὐ δυνατός εἰ.; Br
137 *S* ⲙⲛ ϣϭ. ⲉⲧⲣⲉ-, DeV 2 109 *B* ⲙ. ϣϫ. ⲡⲧⲉⲫⲙⲟⲩ
ϫⲱⲛⲧ, ManiP 52 *A²* ⲙⲛ ϣϭ. ⲁⲧⲣⲉ-;   ⲥ ⲛ-, ⲙⲙⲟ⸗ :
Is 36 14 *F*(*S* ϭ., *B* ⲭⲉⲙ ϫ.), EpJer 7 *BF*, Mt 5 14 *SB*,
Ro 8 7 *SB* οὐ δύνασ.; Gal 5 6 *B*(*S* ϭⲙ ϭ.) οὐκ ἰσ.,
Dan 8 7 *B* οὐκ ἰσχὺς εἰ.; AZ 21 158 *S* ⲙⲛ ϣϭ. ⲛⲗⲁⲁⲩ,
Br 235 *S* ⲙⲛ ϣϭ. ⲙⲙⲟⲟⲩ ⲉⲛⲟⲓ, ManiH 96 *A²* ⲉⲙⲛ
ϣϭ. ⲙⲙⲁ[ⲓ, PS 24 *S* ⲡⲉⲙⲛ ϣϭ. ⲙⲡⲕⲟⲥⲙⲟⲥ ⲉⲧⲟⲩⲛ,
Aeg 258 *S* ⲙⲙⲛ ϣϭ. ⲙⲙⲟϥ ⲉⲧⲣⲉϥ-, DeV 2 106 *B*
ⲙⲙⲟⲛ ϣϫ. ⲙⲙⲟⲕ...ⲉϥⲱⲣϫ, MG 25 206 *B* ⲙⲙⲟⲛ
ϣϫ. ⲙⲙⲟⲓ ⲟⲩⲃⲏⲕ.

ϩⲉ ϭ. *S*, *find power* : ViK 4802 ⲛⲛⲓϩⲉ ϭ. ⲉⲣⲟⲟⲩ.

ϭⲓ ϫ. *B*, *get strength* : Job 17 9 (*S* ϫⲓ ⲧⲱⲕ) θάρσος
ἀναλαμβάνειν.

ϭⲙ, ϭⲛ ϭ., ϫⲉⲙ ϫ., *find power, be strong, able* : 2 Kg
10 12 *S*, Ps 30 24 *S*(*B* ⲧⲁϫⲣⲟ), *ib* 104 4 *S*(*B* ⲁⲙⲁϩⲓ)
κραταιοῦσθαι; Pro 7 1 *SAB*, Is 5 22 *F*(*S* ϫⲱⲱⲣⲉ, *B*
ϫⲟⲣ), Aeg 243 *S* ⲙⲉⲣⲉⲧⲙⲛⲧⲣⲙⲙⲁⲟ ϭ., MG 25 3 *B*
ⲉⲧⲁⲡⲓⲣⲏ ϫ. ἰσχύειν, Ge 48 2 *S*(*B* ϫⲉⲙ ⲡⲟⲙϯ), Ac 9
19 *SB* ⲉⲛⲓⲥ., Lu 23 5 *B*(*S* ⲧⲱⲕ ⲉⲣⲟⲩⲛ) ἐπισ., Ex 17 11

S(*B* ϫ. ⲛ.), Lu 23 23 *SB* ⲕⲁⲧⲓⲥ., Dan 3 22 *SB* ὑπερισ., Ap 5 2 *S*(*B* ϫⲟⲣ) ἰσχυρός ; Jer 5 4 *SB*, Lam 4 14 *SF* ϫⲓⲛ ϫ. (*B* ϣϫ. ϫ.), Mk 6 19 *S*(var & *B* do), 2 Cor 1 4 *B*(*S* ϣϭ.) δύνασ., Ac 9 22 *SB* ἐνδυναμοῦσθαι ; Job 27 14 *S*(*B* ϫ. ⲛ.) ἀνδροῦν, Dan 10 19 *B* ἀνδρίζεσθαι ; Mt 14 27 *F*(*S* ⲧⲱⲕ ⲡϩⲏⲧ, *B* ϫ. ⲛ.) θαρσεῖν ; Ps 17 17 *S*(*B* ⲧⲁϫ.) στερεοῦσθαι ; PS 152 *S* ⲁⲓϣⲱⲡⲉ ⲁⲓϭ., Aeg 264 *S* ⲟⲩϣⲗⲏⲗ ⲉϥϭ., J 89 29 *S* ⲡⲉⲛⲧⲁⲡϭ. ⲉⲡⲁⲁϥⲡⲉ ⲡⲁⲓ, El 54 *A* ⲁⲕϭ. ⲁⲕϭⲣⲟ, ManiH 31 *A*² wickedness ⲥⲁϭⲛ ϭ. ⲉⲡ, TstAb 256 *B* grief ⲉϥϭ. ⲙⲙⲁϣⲱ ; as surname : R 1 35 *S* ⲁϥϭⲟⲩ ⲉⲩⲙⲟⲩⲧⲉ ⲉⲣⲟϥ ϫⲉⲡⲉⲧϭ. ; c ⲉ- : Nu 13 31 *S*(*B* ⲟⲩ ⲃⲉ-) δύνασ. πρός, Jer 20 10 *B* δ. dat, Deu 24 7 *S*(*B* ϭⲉⲛ ϫⲱⲣⲓ) καταδυναστεύειν acc ; Ps 12 5 *S*(*B* ⲟⲩ ⲃⲉ-) ἰσ. πρός, BHom 51 *S* naught could ϭ. ⲉⲧⲉⲓⲥⲣⲙⲉ (var R 2 2 34 ϫⲣⲟ) ἰσ. gen, Sa 7 30 *S*(*B* ϣϫ.) ἀντισ. gen, CaiEuch 582 *B* death cannot ϫ. ⲉⲣⲟⲛ ⲕⲁⲧⲓⲥ. κατά ; Pcod 29 *S* another arose ⲁϥϭ. ⲉⲣⲟϥ, ROC 23 286 *B* ⲉⲣⲉⲡⲁⲓⲡⲁⲣⲁⲡⲟⲙⲟⲥ ϫ. ⲉⲣⲟⲕ ; vbal : Jos 9 25 *S*, Ps 17 38 *S*(var & *B* ⲛ-), Pro 24 73 *A*(*S* ϣϭ.), BHom 4 *S* ⲛϭ. ⲉϫⲟⲟⲥ δύνασ. ; Deu 28 32 *SB*, Lu 14 29 *S*(*B* ϣϫ.) ἰσ., MG 25 239 *B* ϣⲧⲉⲙϫ. ⲉⲥⲱⲟⲩⲧⲉⲛ οὐκ εἶναι inf ; PS 43 *S* ⲙⲛⲥϭ. ⲉⲃⲱⲕ, BG 26 *S* ⲡⲉⲧⲛⲁϭ. ⲉⲛⲟⲓ ⲙⲙⲟϥ, ShC 42 138 *S* ⲉⲩϣⲁⲛϭ. ⲉⲟⲩⲱϣⲃ, BSM 58 *B* ⲛϯ ϫ. ⲁⲛ ⲉⲉⲣ ϫⲓⲛⲓⲟⲣ ; ⲉⲣⲟⲩⲛ ⲉ- : ShC 42 39 *S* ⲁⲓϭ. ⲉϥ. ⲉⲣⲟϥ ⲏ ⲉϩⲣⲁⲓ ⲉϫⲱϥ, Sh Bor 246 84 *S* no arrow ϭ. ⲉϥ. ⲉⲣⲟϥ ; c ⲉϫⲛ- : Jud 16 5 *S* δύνασ. dat ; Dan 11 5 *B* ⲉⲛⲓⲥ. ἐπί, Jer 15 18 *S* (*B* ϭⲉⲛ ϫⲱⲣⲓ) ⲕⲁⲧⲓⲥ. gen ; Vi Sitz 172 4 62 *S* ⲉⲩϭ. ⲉ ⲡⲙⲟⲩ ; ⲉϩⲣⲁⲓ ⲉϫⲛ- : Ps 51 7 *S*(*B* ⲉϫ. only) δύνασ. ἐπί ; Ac 19 16 *S*(var ϭ. ⲉ-)*B* ⲓⲥ. κατά, Ge 12 10 *S*(*B* ϩⲓϫ.) ⲉⲛⲓⲥ. ἐπί ; BHom 41 *S* ⲡⲣⲏⲟⲟⲡⲏ ϭ. ⲉϥ. ⲉϫⲱⲟⲩ ⲕⲣⲁⲧ. ; c ⲙⲛ- : Ge 32 28 *SB* ⲉⲛⲓⲥ. μετά ; c ⲛ-, ⲙⲙⲟ⳯ : Hos 10 11 *B*(*A* diff) ⲉⲛⲓⲥ. dat ; Deu 28 27 *B*(*S* ϣϭ.), Bar 4 17 *B* ⲟⲩ ⲡⲉⲧϫ. ⲙⲙⲟϥ ? δύνασ. ; Mus 42 229 *S* ⲉⲓϭ. (*sic* prob) ⲙⲙⲟⲓ ⲉⲧⲣⲁⲥϭⲁⲓ, El 48 *A* ⲙⲡⲓϭⲛ ϭ. ⲡⲣⲱⲣⲉ (*sic*) ⲁⲣⲉⲉⲧ, MG 25 5 *B* ⲁϥϫ. ⲡ ⲕⲁϯ ; c ⲟⲩ ⲃⲉ- *B* : Nu 13 31 *ut sup* ; Ps 12 5 (*S* ⲉ-) *ut sup* ; c ⲉⲛ-, ϩⲉⲛ- : Si 30 14 *S* ⲓⲥ. dat, Jer 45 22 *B* ⲕⲁⲧⲓⲥ. ⲉⲛ ; He 11 34 *SB* δύνασ. ἀπό, Ps 111 2 *S*(*B* ϩⲓϫ.) δυνατός εἶ. ἐν, Ro 4 20 *SB* ἐνδυναμοῦσθαι dat ; Lu 1 80 *S*(*B* ⲁⲙⲁϩⲓ) κρ. dat ; Br 231 *S* ⲡⲁⲓ ⲉⲧϭ. ϩⲓϭⲟⲙ ⲛⲓⲙ, ShA 1 83 *S* my body ⲛⲛⲉⲡϣⲱⲡⲉ ϭ. ⲡϩⲏⲧϥ ⲏ ⲉⲣⲟϥ, J 106 34 *S* ⲉⲓϭ. ϩⲙⲡⲁⲥⲱⲙⲁ *bodily potent* (cf ib 66 21 ⲉⲓⲧⲏⲕ) ; c ϩⲓϫⲛ- : Jer 9 3 *S*(BM 173 219, *B* ⲧⲁϩⲣⲟ) ⲉⲛⲓⲥ. ἐπί.

ϣϭⲙ ϭ. *SA²F*, ϩϭ. *A*, ϣϫⲉⲙ ϫ. *B*, meaning as ϭⲙ ϭ. : Mk 2 7 *S*(var ⲟⲩⲛ ϭ., *B* ⲟⲩⲟⲛ ϣϫ.), ib 6 19 *S*(var ϭⲙ ϭ.)*B* δύνασ. ; Ap 12 8 *SB* ⲓⲥ. ; PS 172 *S* ⲉⲙⲡⲥ ϣϭⲙ ϭ., ib 168 *S* ⲛⲡⲉϣ ⲟ ϭ ⲟⲡ ⲙⲙⲟⲟⲩ ϭⲙ ϭ., TillOster 9 *A* ⲧⲉⲧⲛ ϩϭⲛ ϭ., DeV 2 114 *B* ⲛⲁⲥϣϫⲉⲙ ϫ. ⲁⲛⲡⲉ ; c ⲉ- Ps 128 2 *SB* δύνασ. dat ; Mt 16 18 *SB* ⲕⲁⲧⲓⲥ. gen ; PS 50 *S* ⲛⲛⲉϥⲡⲁϣϭⲙ ϭ. ⲉⲣⲟⲓ ⲁⲛ, DeV 2 87 *B* ⲛⲡⲉⲥϣϫⲉⲙ ϫ. ⲉⲣⲟϥ ; Ge 13 6 *SB*,

---

Is 36 9 *SBF*, Mt 17 16 *SB*, Jo 9 4 *SA²B* δύνασ. ; Lu 21 36 *S*(*B* ⲛ-) ⲕⲁⲧⲓⲥ. ; PS 26 *S* ⲛⲛⲉⲩⲉϣϭⲙ ϭ. ⲉϫⲱⲕ ⲉⲃⲟⲗ, ib 146 *S* ⲛⲧⲉⲣⲟⲩⲧⲙⲉϣϭⲙ ϭ. ⲉⲧⲱⲟⲩⲛ, BMis 203 *S* ⲙⲡⲉϥϣϭⲙ ϭ. ⲉⲁⲗⲉ ⲉϫⲛ- ; c ⲛ- vbal : Nu 22 11 *B*(*S* ⲉ-), Jer 13 23 *B*(*S* ϣ-), MG 25 205 *B* ⲙⲡⲉⲥ ϣϫⲉⲙ ϫ. ⲙⲙⲓⲥⲓ δύνασ. ; Eph 3 18 *B*(*S* ⲉ-) ἐξισ. ; PS 12 *S* ⲉϥⲉϣϭⲙ ϭ. ⲛⲧⲁϣⲉⲟⲉⲓϣ, ShC 42 158 *S* ⲙ ϣϭⲙ ϭ. ⲛϫⲱ (cf ib ⲉϫⲱ), DeV 1 124 *B* ⲙⲡⲉϥϣϫⲉⲙ ϫ. ⲛⲁⲙⲟⲛⲓ ⲛⲧⲟⲧϥ ; c ⲟⲩ ⲃⲉ *B* : Ps 138 6 (*S* ⲉ-), Jer 15 20 δύνασ. πρός.

Cf AZ 54 122 & Spg 270.

ϭⲟⲙ *S* nn f, *court, hall* (?) : Ez 40 47 (*B* ⲉⲣⲃⲓ) αὐλή. *Cf* ib 23, 27 same Gk.

ϭⲱⲙ *SAA²BF*, ϭⲟⲙ. ⲕ. *S*, ϫⲱⲙ *B*(place-name), ϭⲱⲙⲉ *S*(once), pl ϭⲟⲟⲙ *SAA²*, -ⲙⲉ *A²*, ⲕⲁⲁⲙ *S* & sg as pl, nn m, *garden, vineyard, property* : Deu 11 10 *B*(*S* ϣⲏⲛ), EpJer 70 *B*(*F* ϣⲏ *l* ϣⲏⲛ), Jo 18 1 *B* (*SF* P 129¹⁸ 124? do, *A²*=Gk) κῆπος ; Pro 24 45 *SA* ἀμπελών ; ib 23 10 *SA*, Ac 5 1 *S*(*B* ⲓⲟϩⲓ) κτῆμα ; Mt 26 36 *SF*(*B* do), Jo 4 5 *SF*(ViK 10112, var & *B* do) χωρίον ; Bodl 325 55 *B* ⲛⲓϭ. ; بستان المقلة ; Tri 443 *S* appeared to Cleopas & Luke ⲉⲩϩⲙⲡϭ. حقل. (cf Lu 24 18 & Tischendorf on ib 13), C 41 42 *B* ϩⲁⲛϭ. = Miss 4 394 كرم = ib 643 *S* ϭⲟⲙ (*l* ϭⲟⲟⲙ) ; ShBM 198 30 *S* flocks ϩⲓϭ. ϩⲓⲕⲏⲡⲟⲥ, ShA 1 260 *S* ϭⲉ(?ϫⲉ)ϭ., Mor 28 192 *S* ϩⲛⲁϣ(ⲉ) ⲛϭ. ϩⲓⲕⲟⲙⲁⲣⲓⲟⲛ (πομ.), P Lond 4 516 *S* sim, Br 45 *S* ⲛϭ., ⲛⲉⲓⲱⲣⲉ, ST 396 *S* ⲡⲉϥⲉⲓⲁⲣⲟⲩ ⲙⲡⲉϥⲕⲟⲙ, TU 24 1 6 *S* ⲟⲩⲥⲱⲧ ⲛϭ., BMar 5 *S* ⲥϯ ⲱⲣⲉ ⲛϭ., Ryl 158 *S* ⲥⲉⲧⲓⲁ ϩϭ., Pcod 3 *S* ⲛ]ϭ. ⲙ ⲡⲉⲥⲡⲟϥ (cf Mt 27 8 *S* ⲥⲱϣⲉ), CA 107 *S* ϫⲱⲱⲗⲉ ⲙ ⲛⲉϥϭ., BMOr 8811 242 *S* wine of ⲛϭ., ManiP 178 *A²* ⲛϭ. ⲡⲉⲗⲁⲗⲉ, C 86 201 *B* ϭ., ⲕⲟⲓ, ⲙⲁ ⲡⲁⲗⲟⲗⲓ, CO 347 *S* ⲡⲉϩ ⲛϭ. ; BP 11938 *S* ⲟⲩ ⲥⲁⲓⲉ ⲛϭⲙⲉⲉⲡⲉ ϣⲁϥⲥⲙⲛ ⲧϥⲧⲟ ⲛϭⲱⲙⲉ. *V* ⲥⲁⲣϥⲉ.

Plur forms : Joel 1 11 *A*(*B* om), Ac 2 45 (var ϭⲱⲙ, *B* ⲓⲟϩⲓ) κτ. ; ib 28 7 (*B* do) χ. ; Nu 22 24 (*B* ⲓⲁϩⲁⲗⲟⲗⲓ) ἀμ. ; Mt 22 5 (*B* ⲓⲟ.) ἀγρός ; ShC 42 114 ⲡⲥⲱϣⲉ, ⲛϭ., ib 144 ⲛϭ. that ye have planted, ShA 1 402 ⲛϭ. (var ϭⲱⲙ) ⲁⲩⲱ ⲡⲕⲁⲓⲉ, R 2 1 24 *S* ⲟⲩⲥⲓⲁ, ϭ., ⲕⲏⲡⲟⲥ, Leyd 445 ⲧⲥⲱϣⲉ, ⲛⲣⲟⲓ, ⲛϭ., Mor 51 23 God caused ⲛⲉϭ. ⲉⲣ ⲟⲩⲙⲏⲛϣⲉ ⲛⲏⲣⲡ, Br 40 ⲛⲓⲕⲁⲁⲙ (var ib 45 ϭⲱⲙ) ⲙⲛⲡⲉⲡⲉⲓⲟⲣⲉ, ManiH 12 *A²* ⲛϭⲟⲟⲙⲉ ⲉⲧⲥⲙⲁⲙⲁⲧ, ib P 195 *A²* ⲡⲓⲁ ϩ ⲟⲩ ⲙⲙⲡ ϭⲟⲟⲙ. *Cf* KKS 210, Rec 28 213.

ϭⲙⲉ *SB*, -ⲏ *SS′B*, ϭⲓⲙⲏ *F*, pl ϭⲙⲏⲩ *SAA²*, ϭⲙⲓⲛ ⲟⲩ, -ⲉⲉⲩ *S*, ϭⲙⲁ ϭⲉⲓ *S′* & sg as pl, nn m, *gardener, vinedresser* : Lu 13 7 *S*(*B* ⲟⲩ ⲱⲓ ⲛⲁⲗⲟⲗⲓ) ἀμπελουργός ; Jo 20 15 *B* ϭⲙⲏ ⲙⲡⲓϭⲱⲙ (var ⲛϭ., *SA²* ⲡⲁⲧⲉϣⲛⲏ) κηπουρός ; K 301 *B* حارس ; ShA 2 18 *S* ⲡⲟⲩⲟⲉⲓⲉ... ⲛⲉϭⲙⲏ, Mor 31 16 *S* vine ⲡⲉϥϭⲙⲏ ⲕⲁⲑⲁⲣⲓⲍⲉ ⲙⲙⲟϥ, C 89 134 *B* vineyard tilled by ⲟⲩϭ. = Va ar 172 77 كرم, Mich 550 24 *S* vine pruned by ⲡⲉϭⲙⲏ, BM

1013, 1036, 1040 *S* ϭ. supplies wine, CMSS 63 *Sf*
ⲛⲉϭ., *ib* 73 *F* ϭⲓⲙⲏ, Ryl 159 *S* ⲁⲡⲟⲕ...ⲡⲟⲩⲟⲉⲓⲉ ⲁⲩⲱ
ⲛⲉϭ.;   adj: DeV 2 182 *B* ⲣⲱⲙⲓ ⲛϭ., BM 289 *S*
ⲧⲉⲭⲛⲓⲧⲏⲥ ⲡϭⲙⲏ;   pl forms: *S* R 2 4 67 ⲛⲉⲩϭ.,
Ryl 207 ⲛⲉϭ., *ib* 193 ϭⲙⲏⲟⲩ, Kr 133 ϭⲙⲉⲉⲩ; *A* Joel
1 11; *A²* ManiH 12; *Sf* CMSS 63; ⲁⲧϭ. *S*, *un-
tilled*: Ryl 385 ⲣⲟ ⲙⲁⲓⲟⲩⲙⲁ ⲏⲣⲁ.; ⲙⲛⲧϭ., *vine-
dressing*: Ryl 159 *S* wage for ⲙ. ϩⲓⲙⲛⲧⲟⲩⲟⲉⲓⲉ.
In place name: ⲡϭⲱⲙ ⲛⲧⲕⲉⲙⲏⲡ *B*(C 43 150, but =
S ⲧϭ. TMina *Epima* 31, *cf ib* p xxx), var *ib B* ⲛϫⲱⲙ.

ϭⲁⲓⲙⲉ *S* nn, *hen, domestic fowl*: P 44 56 ⲟⲣⲛⲓⲥ,
ⲟⲣⲛⲓⲑⲟⲛ · ϭ. دجاجة; *ib* ⲛϭ. ⲡⲕⲟⲩⲓ · ⲧⲗⲁⲣⲟⲥ ⲕⲁⲓⲡⲟⲥ
شامرك (*cf* P 45 139 ϭⲗ. ʾ.ـ, ⲕⲁⲓⲡⲟⲥ ʾ.ـ, K 169 ⲕⲗ. ﺟﺎﻣﺮﻙ
for ⲕⲁⲓ. *l* ? ⲕⲁⲓⲙⲉ);   ϭ. ⲛⲉⲑⲱϣ, *Ethiopian hen*:
P 43 24 ﺍﻟﺤﺒﺶ ʾ. Cf ⲕⲁⲓⲙⲓⲟⲛ *GöttGAnz.* ’22 104 & ?
name Πκαῖμις (Preisigke).

ϭⲓⲙⲉ, -ⲏ *B* vb intr, *take pleasure*: Hel 1 25 -ⲏ(*S* as
Gk) ἀπόλαυσιν ἔχειν, 1 Tim 6 17(*S* = Gk) ἀπόλαυσις;
Dif 1 63 ϭ. ϩⲉⲛⲡⲓⲣⲱⲟⲩϣ ⲙⲃⲓⲱⲧⲓⲕⲟⲛ ... , *ib* 94 sim
... ;   as nn m, *satiety, debauch*: Lu 21 34 (*S* ⲥⲉⲓ)
κραιπάλη; HL 112 life full of ease ⲡⲉⲙⲟⲩϭ. βίος
τρυφηλός; K 13 ⲛⲓϭ., AZ 14 117 ϭⲙⲏ...; Cat 16
ϭ., ⲟⲩⲱⲙ, ⲥⲱ, τρίφη (τρυ.).

ϭⲓⲙⲓ *F* v ϭⲓⲡⲉ.

ϭⲱⲱⲙⲉ *S*, ϭⲟⲩⲟⲩⲙⲉ *A*(nn), ϭⲉ(ⲉ)ⲙⲉ-, ϭⲟⲟ-
ⲙⲉ† *S*, ϭⲁⲁⲙⲉ† *SA*, ϭⲁⲙⲉ† *A*, ϫⲁⲙⲁⲓ† *F* vb intr, *be
twisted, crooked*: Ps 17 26 (*B* ϥⲱⲛϫ), Pro 6 14 (*B*
ϥⲱⲛϫ) διαστρέφειν; Mich 550 31 ⲁⲡⲉϥⲏⲡⲉ ϭ. ϩⲛⲟⲩ-
ⲁⲕⲁⲑⲁⲣⲥⲓⲁ = Va 63 95 *B* ⲕⲱⲗϫ διαφθείρεσθαι (?);
Pcod 35 (ⲛ)ⲧⲁⲡⲉϥϩⲏⲧ ϭ. ⲙⲡⲛⲡⲉ;   qual: Job 9 20,
Pro 2 15 (*A* ϭⲁⲩϭ), Lu 3 5 (all *B* ⲕⲟⲗϫ) σκολιός, Pro
10 8 (*A* do, *B* ⲥⲙⲟⲡⲧ ⲁⲛ) σκολιάζειν; Deu 32 5 (*B*
do), Eccl 1 15 *SF*, Is 59 8, Hab 1 4 *SA* διαστ., Deu
32 20 (all *B* ϥⲱⲛϫ) ἑκοτ.; Ps 77 57, Si 36 28 στρεβλός; Ps 100 3 σκαμβός; Hos 7 16 *SA* ϭⲁⲙⲉ (all *B*
ⲕ.) ἐντείνεσθαι; BG 72 ⲟⲩⲙⲉⲉⲩⲉ...ⲉϥϭ., ShA 1 66
ϩⲉⲛⲡⲣⲱⲙⲉ ⲉⲩϭⲁⲁⲙⲉ, *ib* 2 333 whence ⲛⲓϩⲃⲏⲩⲉ ⲉⲧϭ.
ⲁⲩⲱ ⲛⲥⲱϣ ?, Bor 240 62 ⲛⲥⲡⲟⲩⲇⲁⲓⲟⲥ opp ⲉⲧϭ.,
Pcod 44 ⲥⲉϭ. ϩⲙⲡⲉϥϩⲏⲧ;   tr, *twist, pervert*: Deu
27 19 (*B* ⲣⲓⲕⲓ) ἐκκλίνειν; Ac 13 10 (*B* ϥⲱⲛϫ) διαστ.;
2 Pet 3 16 (*B* = Gk) στρεβλοῦν; ShP 130² 77 ⲁⲩϭⲉⲙⲉ
ⲡϩⲁⲡ, Sh(Besa)Z 504 ⲉⲧϭ. ⲛⲡⲉⲧⲥⲟⲩⲧⲱⲛ, BMis 150
ⲟⲩⲕⲣⲓⲧⲏⲥ ⲉϥⲛⲁϭⲉⲉⲙⲉ ⲡϩⲁⲡ;   as nn m, *perversion*:
Job 4 18 (*B* diff), Pro 23 33 *SA* σκολιός, Ez 16 5 (*B*
ⲛⲓϥ.) -ότης; P 44 78 ⲁⲙⲡⲟⲧⲓϫⲉ (ἐμποδ.) · ⲡϭⲟⲟⲙⲉ
اعوجاج; ShA 2 309 woman ⲡⲁϣⲁⲓ ⲙⲡⲉϭ., Mor 18
62 ⲛϭ. ⲛⲧⲁⲡⲓⲥⲧⲓⲥ (var *ib* 19 71 & Miss 4 137 *B* ⲛⲟⲃⲉ),
Bor 234 8 ⲙⲡⲣⲙⲟⲟϣⲉ ϩⲛⲟⲩϭ.
ⲙⲛⲧϭⲟⲟⲙⲉ, *crookedness*: Tri 261 ⲡⲧⲉⲛⲟⲣⲑⲟⲩ
ⲛⲧⲙ. ʾⲁ.
ⲣⲉϥϭ., *perverter*: ROC 20 47 ⲣ. ⲙⲡϩⲁⲡ; ⲙⲛⲧ-
ⲣ.: ShA 1 3ⲋ8 among vices ⲙ. ⲙⲡϩⲁⲡ.

ϭⲙⲉ, -ⲏ *SB*, ϭⲓⲙⲏ *F* v ϭⲱⲙ.

(ϭⲱⲱⲕ), ϭⲱⲕ⳿ *S* vb tr, *make, form*: Sa 14 2 (sic,
var ⲙⲟⲩⲛⲕ which prob intended) κατασκευάζειν.

ϭⲁⲙⲟⲩⲗ *SABF*, ⲕ. *S*(esp Theban), ϫ. *B*, ϭⲉⲙ.
DM, f ϭⲁⲙⲁⲩⲗⲉ[1], ⲕⲁⲙⲟⲟⲩⲗⲉ[2], ⲕⲁⲙⲏⲗⲉ[3] *S*, ϭⲁⲙⲉ-
ⲩⲗⲉ *Sf*, ϫⲁⲙⲁⲩⲗⲓ[4], ϭ.[5], ϫⲁⲙⲉⲩⲗⲓ[6] *B*, pl ϭⲁⲙⲁⲩⲗⲉ[7],
ϭⲁⲙⲟⲩⲗⲉ[8], ⲕⲁⲙⲟⲟⲩⲗⲉ[9], ⲕⲁⲙⲁⲩⲗⲉ[10] *S*, ϫⲁⲙⲁⲩⲗⲓ[11],
ϭ.[12] *B*, ϭⲁⲙⲉⲩⲗⲓ *F* & sg as pl, nn m f, *camel*: Ge 31
17 *S*(*B* ⲛⲓϫ.[11]) ﺟﻤﻞ, *ib* 34 *S*(*B* ϯϫ.⁴) ﺑﻌﻴﺮ, Is 30 6 *SF*
(*B* pl), Ez 25 5 *B* ϫ., *ib* 27 21 *B* ϭ., Zech 14 15 *A*(*B*
pl), Mt 3 4 *SB*(var ϫ.) ﺍﺑﻞ κάμηλος; ShC 42 70 *S*
herds of ϭ., ⲉⲥⲟⲟⲩ, ⲙⲁⲥⲉ, C 43 64 *B* ⲛⲓϭ., BM 678
F ⲛⲉϭ., *ib* 591, 639 *F* ϭⲁⲙⲟⲗ, Hall 73 *S* ⲕⲁⲙⲟⲗ,
DM 24 29 blood of ϭ.;   camel-loads *SF*: OstrG
Jéquier ⲟⲩϭ. ⲛⲧⲱ, WS 89 ϣⲟⲙⲛⲧ ⲛϭ. ⲛⲏⲣⲡ, *ib* 155
ⲥⲛⲁⲩ ⲟⲩϭⲟⲥ ⲛϭ. ⲛⲥⲟⲩⲟ, CO 230 ⲟⲩⲕ. ϩⲣⲁ, Ep 548
ⲟⲩⲕ.³ ⲛⲃⲛⲛⲉ, BM 585 *F* ϭ. ⲛϣⲃⲏⲛⲓ, Ep 543 ⲕⲁⲙⲏⲗ
of ?;   contracts to tend camel: CO 218, 220, 221
S;   f: Ge 24 64 *B* ϯϫ.⁴ ﺟﻤﻞ, *ib* 32 15 *S*¹ ⲕ. ﻧﺎﻗﺔ; K
165 *B* ϯϫ.⁶ ʾⳝ; Miss 4 778 *S* ⲧⲕⲟⲩⲓ ⲛϭ.¹, Mor 31 48
S ⲧϭ.¹, *ib* ⲧϭ. *Sf*, Ep 341 *S* ⲧⲕ.², Tor 29 *S* ⲟⲩⲕ.³, C
41 68 *B* ⲟⲩϭ.⁵, C 43 64 *B* ϩⲁⲛϭⲁⲙⲟⲩⲗ ⲛⲉⲙϩⲁⲛϭ.⁵,
OratCyp 117 *Sf*;   pl: Ge 12 16 *B*¹¹(Lag -ⲙⲟⲩⲗⲓ,
S ϭ.) ﺍﺑﻞ, Job 1 17 *B*¹¹(*S* do) ﺟﻤﻞ ἡ κ., Ge 37 25 *B*¹¹
ʾⲓ ⲟ κ., Jer 30 29 (7) *B*¹²(*S* do) ⲕ.; BMEA 10578 *F* =
Mor 31 254 *S* ϩⲉⲛϭⲁⲙⲟⲩⲗ, P 129¹⁶ 11 *S* ⲛϭϥ.⁸, Ep
346 *S* ⲛⲕ.¹⁰, CO 226 *S* ⲛϭ.⁷, Hall 102 *S*⁹;   ⲙⲁⲛϭ.,
camelherd: MG 25 215 *B* ϫ. (var ϭ.) καμηλίτης; J
66 82 *S*, Ep 84 *S* ⲙⲁⲛⲕ., BP 5182 *S* ⲙⲁⲛⲕⲁⲙⲁⲩⲗⲉ,
BM 691 *F* ⲙⲁⲛϭ.   ⲙⲁⲥ ⲛϭⲁⲙⲁⲩⲗⲉ *S*: Mor 31
83.
ⲥⲉⲣϭ., ⲥⲟⲩⲣϭ. v ⲥⲟⲩⲣⲉ.
As name: ϭⲁⲙⲟⲩⲗ (martyr WTh 175, AM 99), ϭ.
(BM 588, Rec 6 64), ⲁⲡⲁ ϭ., ⲕ. (BM 529, CO 357),
Καμοῦλ, Κιαμοῦλ (Preisigke), ﺟﻤﻮﻝ (PO 17 715);
place-name v ϩⲟⲓ 1° s f.
V also ϣⲉⲣⲃⲉⲥ, ϩⲁⲡⲟⲣⲕ, ϩⲟⲟⲩⲧ p 739 *a*.

ϭⲓⲙⲟⲩⲧ *B* v ϭⲓⲙⲟⲩⲧ.

ϭⲟⲙϥ, ϭⲟⲛϥ *B* v ϫⲟⲟⲩϥ.

ϭⲱⲙϩ *S* vb tr, meaning unknown: Mun 20 at
crucifixion one sharpened spear, ϩⲉⲛⲕⲟⲟⲩ(ⲉ) ⲉⲩϭ.
ⲡⲣⲉⲛⲉⲓⲃⲧ.

ϭ(ⲓ)ⲙϩⲟⲩⲧ v ϭⲓⲙⲙⲟⲩⲧ.

ϭⲁⲙϭⲙ v ϭⲛϭⲛ.

ϭⲟⲙϭ(ⲉ)ⲙ *S*, [ϭⲁⲙ]ϭⲙⲉ *A*, ϭⲁⲙϭⲙ *A²F*, ϫⲟⲙ
ϫⲉⲙ *B*, ϭⲁⲙϭⲛⲙ *F*, ϭⲁⲙϭⲙ- *A²*, ϭⲛϭⲱⲙ⳿ *SAA²*,
ϫⲉⲛϫⲱⲙ *B*, vb intr, *touch, grope*: Deu 28 29 *SB*,
Job 5 14 *SB*, Ps 134 17 *SBF*-ⲛⲙ (Pcod Mor 55), ψηλαφᾶν; 2 Pet 1 9 *B*(*S* Gk diff) *manu temtare*; Gu

84 S ⲡⲉⲩϭⲓⲝ ⲙⲙⲟⲟⲩ ⲙⲉⲩϭ., C 43 214 B were blind ⲉⲡϭ. ϣⲁⲧⲉⲡⲓ ⲉⲡⲁⲓⲙⲁ;   tr: Zech 3 9 SAB, Ac 17 27 S(B ⲝ. ⲡⲥⲁ-) ψ.; Mor 31 2 S ⲁⲡⲉⲩϭⲓⲝ ϭⲗ-ϭⲱⲙⲥ, ManiP 223 A² ⲁⲓϭⲁⲙⲓϭⲙ ⲡⲕⲟⲥⲙⲟⲥ, ib K 151 A¹ limbs ⲙⲁⲩϭⲙϭⲱⲙⲟⲩ, DeV 2 11 B ⲡⲓⲁⲧϣ ⲧⲁϭ-ⲟϥ ⲁⲩϫⲉⲙϫⲱⲙⲕ.

With following preposition.   c ⲉ-: Ge 27 12 B, Is 59 10 S(B ϩⲓ-), Lu 24 39 SB ψ., Va 58 149 B ⲁⲩϫ. ⲉⲡⲉϥϭⲗⲟϫ ψ. ⲉⲛ; R I 4 13 S ⲁϥϭ. ⲉⲛⲉⲩⲙⲉⲗⲟⲥ *con-signare*; ShViK 9101 8 S cursed whoso shall ϫⲱϩ ⲏ ⲡϥϭ. ⲉⲩϣⲏⲣⲉ ϣⲏⲙ, ShC 73 124 S sim, RE 9 146 S ⲙⲡⲓϭ. ⲉⲣⲟⲥ ⲙⲡⲓϫⲱϩ ⲉⲣⲟϥ, TU 43 3 A a[ⲡϭⲁⲙ]ϭⲙⲉ ⲁⲣⲁϥ (PO 9 196 ﬡﬡ), ManiK 151 A² ⲉⲩϭ. ⲁⲣⲁⲩ, Aeg 21 B ⲉⲓϫ. ⲉⲡⲉϥⲥⲱⲙⲁ;   c ⲡⲥⲁ-: Sa 19 16 S (*sic l*) ζητεῖν; Ac 17 27 B *ut sup*;   c ϩⲓ-: Is 59 10 B *ut sup*;   c ϩⲛ-, ϩⲉⲛ-, *with*: Sa 15 15 S ψηλάφησις Mor 34 48 S ⲁⲓϭⲙϭⲱⲙⲟⲩ ϩⲛ ⲡⲁϭⲓⲝ = Aeg 44 B; *in, upon*: Job 12 25 S(B ⲉ-) ψ. acc; PS 366 S blind ⲉⲩϭ. ϩⲙ ⲡⲕⲁⲕⲉ, ShCai Copt Mus *Catal* 1 ⲟⲓ S ⲉⲩϭⲟⲡ ϩⲛ ⲣⲙⲡⲥⲟⲟⲩⲛ ⲏ ⲉⲩϭ. ϩⲛⲛⲉⲩ̄ⲅⲣⲁⲫⲏ, Mor 29 22 S ⲉⲥϭ. ϩⲛⲛⲉϩⲟ = ib 30 27 F.

—— nn m, *sense of touch*: BHom 48 S ⲡϭⲙϭⲟⲙ (var R 2 2 32 vb) ἁφή; Mani K 140 A² ⲡϭ. ⲡⲡⲓϭⲓⲝ; as adj: Ex 10 21 SB ψηλαφητός, He 12 18 B(S vb) -ϥⲁⲛ.

ⲁⲧϭ., *untouchable*: Leyd 442 S ⲡⲁⲧϭⲙϭⲱⲙⲉϥ = Kropp 2 169 ἀψηλάφητος; Br 273 S ⲡⲓⲁⲧϭⲙϭⲱⲙⲏ̄ϥ ⲙⲁⲅⲁⲁϥ, ib 234 S ϩⲟ ⲡⲁⲧϭⲙϭⲱⲙϥ, ManiP 121 A² ⲡⲓⲁ.

ϫⲓⲛϫ. B, *act of touching*: CaiEuch 393 ϫⲓⲛⲕⲓⲙ, ϫⲓⲛⲡⲁⲩ, ϫ. ἁφή.

ϭⲓⲛ- (for ϭⲓ ⲛ-)SA²(ϭⲓⲙ-)F, ⲕⲓⲛ- S(rare), ϭⲛ-SA, ϫⲓⲛ- S(once)BF, mostly f SA²F, m B vbal pref forming nn of action, *act of, manner of*: Ge 32 22 B ϫⲓⲛⲥⲓⲛⲓ(S ⲙⲁ ⲡϫⲓⲟⲟⲣ) διάβασις, Ex 23 16 B-ⲑⲱⲟⲩϯ (S ⲥⲱⲟⲩϩ ⲉϩⲟⲩⲛ) συναγωγή, Ps 54 14 S -ⲟⲩⲱⲙ (B ϩⲣⲉ) ἔδεσμα, Cant 4 3 SF ϫⲓⲛϣⲉϫⲓ, Jo 8 43 SA² do λαλιά, Dan 9 27 B-ϣⲱϥ (S ϣ. nn) ἐρήμωσις, Mt 14 25 F-ⲁⲗⲉϩ (SB ⲟⲩⲣⲱϣⲉ) φυλακή, 1 Pet 2 12 BF-ⲙⲟϣⲓ (S=Gk) ἀναστροφή, BHom 44 S -ϩⲉ ⲡⲧⲱⲙⲁ, Miss 8 33 S-ⲱϣ ἀνάγνωσις, ib 38 S-ⲧⲁⲗⲉ ϭⲓⲝ χειροτονία; Tri 637 S-ⲟⲩⲱϣ̄ⲃ̄ مباني, K 151 B-ⲕⲱⲧ مباني; ib 142 B-ϣⲓ احداث; PS 38 S-ϭⲱϣⲧ, ib 278 S-ⲁϩⲉⲣⲁⲧⲟⲩ, ShA 1 90 S-ⲕⲱ ⲉⲃⲟⲗ, Bor 248 61 S ϭⲓⲛⲙⲉϩ ⲡϣⲱⲧ (*cf* Col 1 24), BM 332 S ϭⲓⲙⲙⲟⲩ, ib 975 S-ⲣ ⲣⲱⲙⲉ, PMich 601 S ⲧⲕⲓⲛϭⲱⲗ, Mor 32 24 S ϭⲉⲛ̄ϩⲱⲕ, JSch 3 8 S ϭⲛⲱⲡϩ, ManiK 164 A² ϭⲓⲙⲡⲣⲓⲉ, ib 144 ϭⲓⲙⲙⲓⲥⲉ, Va 61 8 B-ⲙⲟⲩⲛ ⲉϯⲡⲣⲟⲥⲉⲩⲭⲏ, Cat 118 B-ⲁϣϥ, ib 61 B-ⲕⲟⲧⲟⲩ ⲉⲣⲟϥ, Va 58 31 B-ⲥⲟϭⲉⲡ ⲡⲱϣ, ib 57 187 B-ϫⲉ ⲡⲓⲥⲁϫⲓ, ib 33 -ϣⲧⲉⲙⲥⲟϯ, Pcod 40 F-ⲱⲡϩ;   with Gk vbs: BHom 103 S, -ⲙⲁⲥⲧⲓⲅⲟⲩ, Aeg 27 S-ⲡⲁⲣⲁⲅⲉ, ManiK 137 A² ϭⲓⲙⲡⲗⲁⲥⲥⲉ, Cat 131 B-ⲉⲣ ⲁⲅⲁⲡⲁⲛ, Rec 6 182 B-ⲉⲣ ⲁⲡⲁⲓⲧⲁⲛ;   m

S(rare): Lev 11 34 -ⲟⲩⲱⲙ (B ϩⲣⲉ) βρῶμα; ShC 73 54, BMar 5, Z 262 sim (*cf* above f), P 44 31 -ⲉⲓⲙⲉ, Tri 383 -ϫⲏⲣ, Gu 100 ϫⲓⲛⲟⲩⲱⲣⲉ;   f B: Ge 33 14 -ⲙⲟϣⲓ πόρευσις, 1 Chr 28 19 -ⲉⲣ ϩⲱⲃ κατεργασία, Ps 70 6 -ⲥⲙⲟⲩ ὕμνησις, ib 103 34 -ⲥⲁϫⲓ (*cf* Cat 81 m) διαλογή, Ro 16 18 do (var m) -λογία, Ps 138 2, Lam 3 63 -ϩⲉⲙⲥⲓ καθέδρα, CaiEuch 462 -ⲉⲣ ϩⲱⲃ ἐνέργεια; MG 25 331 -ϭⲟϫⲓ, ib 333 ϫⲓⲛⲙⲟϣⲓ, ROC 25 254 -ⲡⲁⲩ (ib m), Va 57 36 -ⲙⲓⲥⲓ (ib m), Cat 150 -ⲥⲱⲧⲉⲙ (ib 198 m), ib 119 -ⲉⲣ ⲣⲱⲙⲓ (ib 128 m);   with pre-ceding prep B, ⲉ-: Ge 3 22 ⲉⲡϫⲓⲛⲥⲟⲩⲉⲛ (S ⲉⲧⲣⲉ-) τοῦ γιγνώσκειν, Ps 26 13 ⲉⲡϫⲓⲛⲡⲁⲩ (S ⲉⲡ.) τοῦ ἰδεῖν, Ro 1 11 ⲉⲡϫⲓⲛⲧⲁϫⲣⲉⲑⲏⲛⲟⲩ (S ⲉⲡⲧ.) εἰς τὸ στηριχ-θῆναι, 1 Cor 8 10 ⲉⲡϫⲓⲛⲑⲣⲉϥⲟⲩⲱⲙ (S ⲉⲟⲩ.) εἰς τὸ ἐσθίειν;   ϩⲉⲛ-: Nu 4 15 ϩⲉⲡⲡϫⲓⲛⲧⲱⲟⲩⲛ (S ϩⲙ-ⲡⲧⲣⲉⲥ.) ἐν τῷ ἐξαίρειν, Ps 18 12 ϭⲉⲡⲡϫⲓⲛⲁⲣⲉϩ (S ϩⲙⲡⲧⲣⲉϥⲣ.) ἐν τῷ φυλάσσειν, Ac 8 6 ϭⲉⲡⲡϫⲓⲛⲑⲣⲟⲩ-ⲥⲱⲧⲉⲙ (S ϩⲙⲡⲧⲣⲉⲩⲥ.) ἐν τῷ ἀκούειν; Aeg 49 ϭⲉⲡ-ⲡϫⲓⲛⲑⲣⲉⲕⲧⲱⲛⲕ, BSM 39 ϭⲉⲡϫⲓⲛ̄ϯⲑⲉⲥⲟⲡⲓⲥⲧⲉ ⲡ-ⲥϭⲓⲁⲓ ϫⲱ ⲡⲛⲁⲓ = Va 63 13 ⲉⲥϫⲱ ⲡⲛⲁⲓ;   ϭⲓⲛ-, ϫⲓⲛ-+ suff: Ps 106 19 B ⲉⲡϫⲓⲛⲧⲟⲩϭⲟϫⲣⲉϫ (S ϩⲙⲡⲧⲣⲉⲩ-ⲣⲱϣ) ἐν τῷ θλίβεσθαι; Z 269 S ⲧϭⲓⲛⲧⲁⲩϭⲣⲓⲗⲁ, My 32 S ⲧϭⲓⲛⲧⲁϥϣⲃⲏⲧϥ, PCol 2 F ⲧϭⲓⲛⲧⲁⲕϭⲣⲉⲓ, Va 61 23 B ⲉⲡϫⲓⲛⲧⲉϥϣⲙⲏⲗ, FR 100 B ⲉⲡϫⲓⲛⲧⲁⲟⲩⲱⲛϩ; *v* also preceding groups.

With following nn S(incorrect ?): ShBor 246 37 ⲫⲁⲛⲧⲁⲥⲓⲁ ⲡϭⲓⲙⲙⲁⲧⲟⲥ, P 44 75 ⲧⲉⲃⲉⲗⲏ (τὰ β.) · ⲡ-ϭⲓⲛⲥⲟⲧⲉ سهام, Mor 44 9 -ⲟⲩⲱⲣⲉ (*cf* Gu 100 above). *V* Stern 180, 470, Chaîne 673 ff & Rec 27 153.

ϭⲓⲛ- S'F, ϭⲏⲡ- F   *v* ϫⲓⲛ-.

ϭⲟⲛ S, ϭⲁⲡ Sᵃ, ϫⲟⲡ B nn m, *low, hollow place*: Ge 37 14 B κοιλάς, ib 23 2 B -λωμα, Is 8 14 S(MS ϭⲟⲙ, B ϩⲉⲗⲗⲟⲧ) -λασμα; Ge 26 17 B φάραγξ; Deu 11 11 S(B ⲙⲉϣϣⲱⲧ) πεδεινός opp ⲡϫⲓⲥⲉ, Jud 1 9 S ⲕⲁϩ ⲉⲧⲣⲓⲡϭ. gloss on πεδ., ClPr 54 45 S ⲡϭ. ⲡⲧⲉⲭⲱⲣⲁ ὕπτιος; BMOr 8781 B ⲡⲓϫ. هيش جون; PS 157 S ⲙⲙⲁ ⲉⲧⲙⲡϭ. ⲙⲡⲉⲥⲏⲧ (OdSolom 22 1 اسفل) opp ⲉⲧϫⲟⲥⲉ, Miss 4 235 S ϩⲙⲡϫⲓⲥⲉ ϩⲛⲧⲁⲣⲉⲧⲏ...ϩⲓ-ⲡϭ. ϩⲛⲧⲉⲩϭ̄ⲃⲱ, Mich 550 45 S ⲡⲉⲧϩⲙⲡϭ. gazing up-ward, Ep 103 Sᵃ dwelling-place ϩⲙⲡϭ.

ϭⲟⲟⲡⲉ S(once), ϫⲁⲡⲉ, -ⲏ B, -ⲓ F, pl ϫⲁⲡⲉⲩ B nn m f, as last: Lev 13 31 (S ⲑⲃⲃⲓⲏⲩ) ἔγκοιλος, ib 34 ⲟⲓ ⲡϫ. (Sdo) κοῖλος, Cant 2 1 F(S ⲉⲓⲁ) -άς; MG 25 186 παρεπίστυλος ⲡⲛⲟⲩ ⲉⲡϫ. (*cf* below) = Gött ar 114 31 الي; C 41 18 ⲡⲓϫ. ⲙⲙⲟⲟⲩ = Miss 4 328 كلب = *RevSémit* 7 162 الحمى; BMOr 8775 137 ⲡⲓϫⲁⲡⲏ, ⲡⲓⲥⲧⲟⲙⲁⲭⲟⲥ اسم; f: BIF 14 122 S ⲧϭ. outside city, ib 178 S sim (var HM 1 203 ⲡⲟϭ ⲡⲉⲓⲁ), MG 25 185 ϯϫⲁⲡⲏ of Abba Moses =ʹẕ(*cf* ? EW *The Mon-asteries: Architecture* 228);   pl: Lev 14 37 (S ⲟⲩⲗ-ⲡⲉ ShIF 132) κοιλάς; Ps 112 6 (S ⲑ.) ταπεινός.

ϭⲟⲛ, ϭⲱⲡ *v* ϭⲛⲟⲡ 1°.

ϭⲉⲛⲁ⳿, ϭⲁⲡⲛⲁ⳿ *F* v ϫⲛⲁ⳿ 2°.

ϭⲉⲛⲟ *B* v ϫⲉⲛⲟ.

ϭⲓⲛⲉ *SAA²F*(rare), ϫⲓⲛⲓ *B*, ϭⲓⲙⲓ, ϭⲓⲛⲓ, ϫⲓ. *F*, ϭⲛ- *SAA²F*, ϭⲉⲛ- *SF*, ⲕⲛ-, ϭⲓⲛ- *S*, ϭⲙ- *S^f*, ϫⲉⲙ- *B*, ϫⲓⲛ- *F*, ϭⲛⲧ⳿ *SAA²*, ϭⲉⲛⲧ *SF*, ⲕⲛⲧ⳿, ϭⲛⲛⲧ⳿, ϭⲛ⳿ *S*, ϫⲉⲙ⳿ *B*, ϭⲏⲧ⳿, ϫⲓⲛⲧ⳿, ϭⲛ⳿, ϭⲏⲛ⳿ *F* vb intr (rare), *find*: Eccl 8 17 *S*, Jer 14 3 *SB*, Mk 14 55 *BF(S* ϧⲉ) εὑρίσκειν; BMEA Hartwell pap 1936 *S* ⲕⲛⲁϭ. ⲡⲛ̄-ⲧⲁⲁⲩ (*sc money*), Mor 18 45 *S* ⲉϣⲱⲡⲉ ⲁⲕϭⲛ ϩⲙⲟⲧ… ϯⲥⲟⲟⲩⲛ ϫⲉⲁϭ., MMA 23 3 704 *S* ⲙⲡⲛϭ. (*sc corn*) ⲡⲧⲣⲟⲙⲡⲉ, Kr 227 *F* ⲁⲡⲕϭⲱϯ… ⲙⲡⲉⲛϭⲓⲛⲓ, BMis 376 *S* ⲉⲛϣⲁⲛϭ. = BSM 33 *B*.

tr: Ge 5 24 *B(S* ϧⲉ), Ex 22 2 *B(S* ⲧⲁϩⲟ), Ps 88 20 *SB*, Pro 2 5 *AB*, Eccl 11 1 *F* ϫⲓⲛⲧϥ, ib 7 15 *F* ϫⲓⲛ-, Cant 8 10 *F* ϫⲓⲛⲓ (all *S* ϧⲉ), Si 34 8 *S*(var ϧⲉ), Is 35 9 *BF*, Jo 11 17 *AA²B*, 2 Cor 12 20 *BF*(all *S* ϧⲉ), Cl 9 4 *A* ⲁⲩϭⲛⲧϥ ⲙⲡⲓⲥⲧⲟⲥ εὑ., Bar 3 17 *B* ἐξεύρεσις; Jer 45 20 *B* ⲉⲓⲛⲁⲓ dat; Ex 20 12 *B(S* ϣⲱⲡⲉ ⲡ-) γίνεσθαι dat; 1 Pet 4 12 *B(S* ⲧⲁϩⲟ) συμβαίνειν; Pro 25 8 *A(S* ϧⲉ) προσπίπτειν; Am 2 15 *F* ϭⲓⲛⲉ (JEA 11 246, *SB* ⲛⲟⲩϫⲙ) σῴζειν; Job 17 1 *SB* τυγχάνειν; PS 31 *S* ⲥⲉⲛⲁϭⲛ ⲗⲁⲁⲩ ⲁⲛ, ShC 73 111 *S* ⲥⲟⲡ ⲛⲓⲙ ⲉⲧⲟⲩⲛⲁϭⲛ ⲡⲉϭⲉⲣⲏⲩ, *B* Mis 450 *S* ⲡⲉⲛⲣⲁⲛ ϩⲟⲥⲉ ϭⲛⲡⲟⲩ *for are names of gods* (*cf* Mk 14 68 below), Mor 48 17 *S* ⲉⲩ ⲛⲁϭⲛ ⲧⲣⲟⲫⲏ ⲡ̄ⲧⲱⲛ (var *BMar* 211 ϧⲉ), PMéd 130 *S* ⲁⲓϭⲛⲧⲥ ⲙⲙⲉ, Miss 8 244 *S* who can ϭⲛ ⲡϫⲱⲕ ⲛⲡⲉⲕⲁⲣⲉⲧⲏ ?, Ep 213 *S* come to us ⲛ̄ⲧⲛϭⲛⲧⲕ, CO 195 *S* ⲙⲡⲉⲓⲥⲉⲣϩⲉ ⲛ̄ⲧⲁⲉⲓ ⲧⲁⲕⲛ̄ⲧⲕ, ib 254 *S* ⲉⲓϣⲁⲛϭⲛ ⲟⲩⲁ, El 74 *A* ⲁⲩϣⲁⲛ-ϭⲛⲧϥ, ManiH 26 *A²* ⲕⲁϭⲛ ⲧⲟⲩⲥⲛ, ib 28 ⲛⲥⲉⲛⲧⲟⲩ, FR 98 *B* ⲁⲥϣⲁⲛϫⲉⲙⲧⲉⲛ, Va 57 130 *B* ⲉⲉϩⲣⲟⲩϫⲉⲙ-ⲧⲉⲛ, DeV 2 183 *B* ⲛ̄ⲧⲉⲟⲩⲡⲉⲧϩⲱⲟⲩ ϫⲉⲙⲕ, CMSS 23 *S^f* ⲗⲓⲡⲓϭⲙ ϫⲱⲙⲉ, BM 587 *F* ϣⲁⲧⲉⲕϭⲛⲧⲃ, ib 663 *F* ⲁⲓϭⲛⲧⲥ, ib 593 *F* (ⲙ)ⲡⲓϭⲏⲡⲕ, ViK 1120 *F* ⲧⲁⲉⲓ ⲧⲁϭⲛⲕ, ib 7033 *F* ⲉⲕϭⲓⲛⲓ ⲙⲁⲃ; with other vb following: Dan 5 27 *B*, Mt 1 18 *B(S* ϧⲉ), 1 Cor 15 15 *BF(S* do) εὑ.; BMis 168 *S* ⲁⲩϭⲛ ⲡⲣⲱⲙⲉ ⲉϥⲙⲏⲝ = BSM 78 *B*, C 99 243 *S* ϣⲁⲩϭⲛⲧⲟⲩ ⲉⲩϩⲟⲥⲉ = C 89 88 *B*, Mor 19 33 *S* ⲁⲩϭⲉⲛⲧⲟⲩ ⲉⲅⲉⲓⲣⲉ, DeV 2 169 *B* ϭⲛⲁ-ϫⲓⲙⲓ ⲡⲣⲱⲙⲓ ⲃ̄ ⲉϥⲣⲉⲙⲓⲥⲓ, AZ 23 38 *F* ϣⲁⲧⲡⲉϭⲛⲧϥ ⲉϥⲕⲏⲃ; He 12 11 *B(S* Gk diff), PS 43 *S* ⲁⲓϭⲛⲧⲥ ⲉⲥⲙⲡⲉⲥⲛ̄ⲧ, ShA 1 208 *S* ⲁⲛϭⲛⲧⲟⲩ ⲉⲣⲉⲛⲕⲉⲉⲥ ⲡⲟⲩ-ϩⲟⲟⲣⲡⲉ, CA 108 *S* ⲉⲩϣⲁⲛϭⲛ ⲟⲩⲁ ⲉϥⲕⲱⲧⲉ, DeV 2 163 *B* ⲁⲛϫⲉⲙϥ ⲉϥⲱⲗⲓ ⲙ̄ⲙⲟϥ; Bel 12 *B* ⲛ̄ⲧⲉⲕϣⲧⲉⲙ-ϫⲉⲙⲟⲩ ⲉⲁϥⲟⲩⲟⲙⲟⲩ, Z 298 *S* ⲕⲛⲁϭⲛⲧ ϩⲱⲥ ⲉⲁⲓⲣⲁϣⲉ, Cl 43 5 *A* ⲁⲩϭⲛ ⲡⲥⲉⲣⲱⲃ ⲉⲁϥϯ ⲟⲩⲟⲩ εὑ.; DeV 2 231 *B* ⲁⲩϫⲉⲙⲥ ⲉⲁⲩⲙⲁϣⲑⲁⲙ ⲡⲣⲱⲥ; Ro 4 19 *B* ⲁϥ-ϫⲉⲙϥ ⲁϥⲙⲟⲩ (*S* diff) κατανοεῖν; C 86 259 *B* ⲁⲩ-ϫⲉⲙⲟⲩ ⲁⲡⲟⲥ ϭⲟⲧⲟⲩ ⲉⲃⲟⲗ; Lu 19 48 *S* ⲙ̄ⲡⲟⲩϭⲛ ⲉⲩⲛⲁⲣ ⲟⲩ εὑ.; Is 13 *SF* ⲙⲡⲟⲩϭ(ⲉ)ⲛ ⲡⲁⲛⲧ ⲛⲓⲙ συνιέναι; Mk 14 68 *S* ⲛ̄ϯϭⲛ ⲁⲛ ⲉⲣⲉϫⲱ ἐπίστασθαι; ShMIF

23 73 *S* ⲙ̄ⲡⲟⲩϭⲛ ⲉϥⲛⲁⲁⲙⲁϩⲧⲉ ⲙⲙⲟϥ ϩⲛⲟⲩ, ManiP 151 *A²* ⲙⲁⲓϭⲛ ⲉⲓⲁⲧⲡⲧⲱⲛⲕ ⲁⲡⲓⲙ, PBu 141 *S* ⲁⲛⲙⲟⲩ ϭⲛ ⲁⲛϣⲁϫⲉ… ϭⲱ (for these *cf* AZ 58 157); + -ⲥ impers: Cl 25 5 *A* ⲥⲉϭⲛⲧⲥ ⲉⲁϥⲣ ϯⲟⲩ εὑ.; Miss 8 27 *S* ⲛ̄ϭⲛⲧⲥ ⲉⲩϩⲁⲣⲡⲁⲍⲉ ⲙ̄ⲡⲉⲧⲕⲣⲁⲧⲟⲥ, Pcod 23 *S* ⲥⲉ-ⲛⲁϭⲛⲧⲥ ϫⲉⲟⲩϭⲉⲧ (var ⲥⲉⲛⲁϩⲉ ⲉⲣⲟϥ ⲉⲟⲩϭⲉⲧ), PJkôw *S* ⲙⲁⲣⲉⲕϭⲛⲧⲥ ϫⲉⲡⲧⲟⲕ ⲉⲧⲟ ⲙⲡⲣⲟⲥⲟⲡⲟⲛ, BristolMusH 3041 *S* ⲁⲓϭⲛⲧⲥ ⲁⲩⲡⲁⲣⲁⲃⲁ, El 44 *A* ⲁⲓϭⲛⲧⲥ ϭⲉⲡⲡⲩⲗⲏ ⲡⲣⲁⲙⲡⲉ, ib 52 *A* ⲁⲓϭⲛⲧⲥ ⲡⲁⲡⲁⲃⲉ… ⲥⲛϩ ϭⲓⲧⲟⲟⲧϥ, Kr 3 *F* ⲡⲧⲟⲩϭⲛⲧⲥ ⲉⲁϩⲣⲁⲡ ⲟⲩϭⲟⲩ (ϩⲱⲃ), Ep 173 *S* ϭⲛⲧⲥ ⲁⲓⲉⲓ *suppose I were come*, sim OstrChicago 2482 *S* ϭⲛⲧⲥ ⲕⲛⲁⲥϫⲁⲓ ⲡⲁⲓ ⲡϩⲁϩ ⲛⲥⲟⲡ.

With following preposition. ⲉ ⲉ-: Pro 27 26 *A(S* ϧⲉ ⲉ-) ἔχειν εἰς; Ex 1 10 *B* ϫⲉⲙ ⲟⲩϭⲃⲱ ⲉ-κατασοφίζεσθαι acc; ShA 2 171 *S* ⲁⲣⲁ ⲉⲕⲛⲁϭⲛ ⲡϣⲏⲣⲉ ⲙⲡⲉⲓⲁⲓⲱⲛ ⲉⲣⲟⲕ in time of need ?, CO 129 *S* ⲁⲓϭⲛⲧⲥ ⲉⲡⲕⲟⲩϭⲟⲛ as they told me, DeV 1 56 *B* ϣⲁⲕϫⲉⲙⲥ ⲉⲣⲱⲟⲩ ⲉⲩ-ⲧⲱⲟⲩⲛ ϩⲁ- *shalt find it to their credit that they*, MIE 2 398 *B* ⲛⲁϫⲉⲙⲟⲩ ⲉⲣⲟⲛ *for us* (*our needs*); vbal: Ac 4 14 *S(B* diff) ϭⲛ ϣⲁϫⲉ ⲉϫⲱ ἔχειν, ShR 2 3 40 *S* sim ϭⲓⲛ-; Nu 11 13 *S* ϭⲛ… ⲉϯ (var ϧⲉ) *B* Gk no vb; BMis 345 *S* ϭⲛ ⲉⲣⲱⲧⲉ ⲉⲧⲥⲡⲕⲟ ⲙⲙⲟⲓ = BSM 12 *B* ⲉⲱ-ⲣⲉⲥ-, Kr 38 *F* ⲙⲡⲉⲃϭⲛⲧⲃ ⲉⲡ ⲉⲁⲡⲟⲗⲟⲅⲓⲍⲉ; ⲉϩⲟⲩⲛ, ⲉϫ. ⲉ-: Ac 7 19 *B* cf Ex 1 10 above; Tit 1 7 *S* ϭⲛ ϩⲱⲃ ⲉⲣ. ⲉ- (*B* diff) -ἔγκλητος εἶναι; ShClPr 39 41 *S* ϭⲉⲛ ⲗⲁⲁⲩ ⲡϣⲁϫⲉ ⲉⲣ. ⲉ-; ⲥ ⲙⲛ-, ⲡⲉⲙ-: BIF 37 51 *S* ⲉⲙⲡⲧⲣⲁⲧⲟ ϭⲛ ϩⲱⲃ ⲙ̄ⲡⲗⲁⲁⲩ μὴ ἔχειν τι μετά τινος; Miss 8 238 *S* conspiring with woman ϣⲁⲛ-ⲧⲉⲕϭⲛ ⲡⲉⲕⲡⲁⲑⲟⲥ ⲛⲙⲙⲁⲥ; ⲥ ⲡ- dat: Ge 2 20 *B(S* ϧⲉ) εὑ. dat; BM 596 *F* ϭⲉ(ⲡ) ϫⲟⲩⲱⲧⲉ ⲡⲗⲓⲧⲣⲉ ⲛⲁϥ; *dat commod*: Ps 83 3 *SB*, Is 34 14 *BF(S* ϧⲉ), Hos 12 8 *AB*, MG 25 204 *B* ⲁ̄ⲕϫⲉⲙ ⲟⲩϭⲣⲓⲙ ⲡⲁⲕ εὑ. dat; ⲥ ⲛⲥⲁ- *SF*, *against* (of misdeeds): ShC 73 58 ϩⲉⲛⲟⲉⲓⲕ ⲉⲁϭⲛⲧⲟⲩ ⲛ̄ⲥⲟⲅⲟ ⲛⲥⲁⲟⲉⲓⲡⲉ, Mus 48 80 (*RegPach*) ϣⲁϫⲉ ⲛⲥⲟⲗ ⲉⲩϣⲁⲛϭⲛⲧϥ ⲛⲥⲁⲟⲅⲁ *deprehendi*, CO 221 ⲡⲡⲉⲕⲕⲛ ⲕⲁⲧⲁⲫⲣⲟⲛⲏⲥⲓⲥ ⲡⲥⲱⲓ, PLond 4 509 ⲁⲩϭⲛ ⲗⲁⲁⲩ ⲡⲥⲱⲥ, BM 604 *F* ϣⲁⲓϭⲛ ⲗⲁⲟⲩ ⲥⲉⲕ; ⲥ ϩⲁ- *B* sim: Dan 6 4 (*S* ϧⲉ ⲉϩⲟⲩⲛ ⲉ-) εὑ. κατά; C 41 64 ϫⲉⲙ ⲛⲟⲃⲓ ϩⲁⲣⲟϥ.

ϭⲛ-, ϫⲉⲙ ϩⲏⲧ, *find heart, learn wisdom*: Ps 93 8 *SB* φρονεῖν, 1 Pet 4 7 *S(B* ϫⲉⲙ ⲕⲁϯ) σωφρ.; Ps 81 5 *S(B* ⲕⲁϯ) συνιέναι; ShBMOr 8810 457 *S* ⲉⲙⲡⲕϭⲛ ⲡⲉⲕⲣ. ⲉⲧⲣⲉⲕⲉⲓⲙⲉ, ViK 9530 *S* whilst yet child ⲙⲡⲁⲧⲉⲕϭⲛ ⲡⲉⲕⲣ., AM 216 *B* ⲁⲣⲉⲧⲉⲛϫⲉⲙ ϩ. to forsake your god ?, C 43 244 *B* ⲉⲧⲁϥϫⲉⲙ ϩⲣⲏϥ *come to self*, J 93 15 *S* sim.

—— nn m *SB*, *finding, thing found*: Si 13 30 *S* εὕρεσις, Jer 45 2 *B* εὕρημα.

ⲁⲧϫ. *B*, *not to be found*: Lev 25 47 ⲉⲣ ⲁ. (*S* diff) ἀπορεῖσθαι; ⲙⲉⲧⲁ.: Deu 28 22 (*S* ϩⲃⲁ) ἀπορία.

ⲙⲉⲧϫ. *B*, *existence*: K 58 ϯⲙ. وجود (*transl from Ar ?*).

ⲣⲉϥϭ., ϫ., *finder*: Mor 37 119 *S* ⲡⲣ. ⲛⲡⲉⲥϩⲁⲓ, Pro

16 20 *SA* ⲣⲉϥϭⲛ- εὑρετής, Ro 1 30 *B*(*S* ⲣⲉϥⲕⲱⲧⲉ) ἐφευρ.

ϫⲓⲛϫ. *B*, *act of finding*: Cat 111 ⲡⲓϫ. of Cross, Va 61 203 ⲉⲛⲕⲱ⳨ ⲉⲡϫⲓⲛϫⲉⲙ.

V also ⲁⲣⲓⲕⲉ, ⲕⲁ⳨, ⲗⲟⲓϭⲉ, ⲡⲟⲗⲧⲉ, ⲣⲁⲧ⳽, ⲣⲏ⳨, ⲧⲱⲡⲉ(⳨ⲡⲉ), ⲟⲩⲱ 2°, ⲟⲩⲟⲉⲓϣ, ϣⲁ 4°, ϣⲓⲡⲉ (adding ⲣⲉϥϭⲛ ⲡϣ. ManiP 141 *A²*), ϩⲉ 2°, ϩⲟ, ϩⲙⲟⲧ, ϭⲟⲙ.

ϭⲓⲛⲉ *S* nn, meaning unknown, in some way related to (epithet of) goat's gall: PMéd 296 ⲥⲓϣⲉ ⲛϭ. ⲙⲃⲁⲙⲡⲉ.   ϭ. = ⲕⲛⲛⲉ not probable.

ϭⲟⲟⲛⲉ *v* ϭⲟⲛ & ϭⲛⲟⲛ 1° s f.

ϭⲛⲟ *B*, ϭⲉⲛⲛⲏⲩⲧ† *S*, ϭⲛⲏⲟⲩⲧ† *B* (*cf* ϭⲛⲟⲛ 1°) vb intr, *be hard*: Job 41 15 *B*(var 1 MS ϭⲛⲥ, *S* ϫⲣⲟ) πηγνύναι ϫⲁⲙⲇ; Va 57 33 *B* ⲕⲁϩⲓ ⲙⲡⲉⲧⲣⲁ ⲉϥϭ.† χαλεπός (?); PMéd 281 *S* ⲛⲡⲣⲕⲁⲁⲩ (sc ingredients) ⲉⲩϭ.† ⲉⲛⲉϥⲟⲩⲟ, AZ 14 117 *B* I felt body, found it ⲉϥϭ.† *stiff* & knew he was dead, BM 1127 8 *S* ⲛⲕⲟⲗⲗⲁⲑ(ⲉ) ⲉⲩϭⲉⲛⲛⲏⲩⲧ (this word ?).

ϭⲛⲟⲩ *B* *v* ϫⲛⲟⲩ.

ϭⲱⲛⲙ *O* vb intr, *be blinded*: DM 13 12 'r f ϭ. n p byl ⲓⲓ.

ϭⲓⲛⲙⲟⲩⲧ¹, ϭⲓⲙ.², ϭⲓⲛⲙⲟⲧ³, ⲕⲛⲙⲟⲩⲧ⁴, ϭⲙⲙ.⁵, ϭⲓⲛϩⲟⲩⲧ⁶, ϭⲓⲙ.⁷, ϭⲙ.⁸, ϭⲉⲙ.⁹ *S*, ϭⲓⲙⲟⲩⲧ *B* nn f, *the Pleiades* (*cf ?* ⲕⲛⲙ·ⲧϫ Berl *Wörterb* 5 133 HT): Job 9 9 ⲧϭ.¹ *B* no art, ib 38 31 ⲧϭ.²(var¹)*B* do Πλειάς; P 44 52 ⲧϭ.¹ ⲉϩⲁⲥⲧⲣⲟⲛ ⲛⲣ̄ⲛ (*cf* K 51 ⲱⲣⲓⲁⲥ · ⲉϩ. '⳽), P 43 131 ⲧⲉⲡⲣⲁϩⲓⲥ (ⲡ)ⲧϭ.¹ اعمال الٮ (from كتاب ديوناسيوس, sc Dionysius Areop.); PS 349 ⲡⲁⲣⲭⲱⲛ ⲉⲧϩⲓϫⲛϭ.⁵, BKU 1 7 ⲧϭ.³ in midst of heaven, ib 22 sim ⲧⲕ.⁴, L Cyp 3 ⲧϭ.⁷ (var Mor 18 109⁹), Mor 41 152 ⲡϣⲱⲡϣ ⲙⲛⲧϭ.⁸, P 132² 47 morning star & ⲧϭ.⁶, Mor 46 32 wizard ⲁϥⲁⲗⲉ ⲉⲧϭ.¹, Orat Cyp 25 *Sᶠ* sim⁸.   No proof that ¹⁻⁵ are equivalent to ⁶⁻⁹.

ϭⲛⲏⲛ *B* *v* ϣϭⲛⲏⲛ.

ϭⲛⲟⲛ *SB*, ϭⲛⲁⲛ *Sᶠ F*, ϭⲏⲛ† *SAF*, ϭⲟⲛ† *S*, ϭⲁⲛ† *A²*, ϫⲏⲛ†, ϭⲛⲏⲟⲩⲧ† *B* (*cf* ϭⲛⲟ) vb intr, *be soft, smooth, weak*: Job 33 25 *S*(*B* ⳨ ⲗⲟⲕⲗⲉⲕ), Ps 54 22 *B*(*S* ⲕⲛⲛⲉ), ἀπαλύνειν, Mt 24 32 *BF*(*S* ⲗⲛⲕ) ἀπαλὸς γίνεσθαι, Va 58 185 *B* ⲑⲣⲉⲡⲓⲣⲏⲧ...ϭ. μαλάσσειν, ib 57 198 *B* sim ⲥⲩⲙⲙ., ib 199 *B* heart ⲕⲏⲛ ⲟⲩⲟϩ ⲁϥϭ. καταψύχειν; ShC 73 147 *S* ⲧⲣⲉⲡϣⲱⲧⲉ ϭ. by overwatering, ALR '93 519 *S* tree's sap ⲥⲧⲩϥⲉⲓ in some ϣⲁϥϭ. in others, BMar 95 *S* wine ⲁⲩⲧⲁⲕⲟ ⲁⲩϭ. ⲁⲩⲣ ϭⲏⲡⲧ, Miss 8 252 *Sᶠ* ϣⲁⲡⲗⲱⲃ̄ϣ...ϣⲁⲡϭ. ϩⲙⲡⲉⲡⲙⲉⲉⲩⲉ, BSM 70 *B* waves subsided ⲁⲩϭ., ib 134 *B* ⲑⲣⲟⲩ ϭ. (sc natures).   qual (a) ϭⲏⲛ, ϫⲏⲛ: Ge 18 7 *S*(var ⲗⲏⲕ)*B*, ib 33 13 *B*(*S* ϭⲟⲃ̄ⲕ, Is 47 1 *S*(*B* ⲗⲏⲕ?), Z 319 *S* ⲧⲉϥϭⲩⲥⲓⲥ ⲙⲡⲙⲟⲟⲩ ϭ. opp ϫⲁϫⲱ ἀπαλός; Pro 26 22 *SA*, Mt 11 8 *S*(*B* ϭⲁⲛⲉ, *cf* Lu 7 25 ϫⲏⲛ) μαλακός; Jer 27 2 *BF*

(Mus 49 174), Mic 1 16 *SB*(*A* ϣⲛⲣⲏⲧ for ? ⲥⲁⲡⲁϫⲧ), Z 344 *S* ϩⲛⲥⲱⲙⲁ ⲉⲩϭ. = MG 25 208 *B* τρυφερός; R 2 2 24 *S* ϣⲁϫⲉ ⲉⲧϭ. θωπεία; Ge 27 11 *B*, Ez 24 7 *B* (*S* ⲥⲗⲉϭⲗⲱϭ), Lu 3 5 *B*(*S* do) λεῖος; Is 40 4 *B* ⲙⲱⲓⲧ ⲉⲩϭ. (*S* do) πεδίον; Ps 16 10 *B*(*S* ⲱⲧ, *F* ⲕⲓⲛⲟⲩⲧ) στέαρ; Ez 26 5 *B* ⲙⲁ ⲉϥϭ. ⲉϥϩⲛⲥ (Gk diff); P 44 82 *S* ⲙⲉⲣⲓⲁϥⲓⲗⲟⲛ (μυριόφυ.) (ⲉ)ⲧϭ. رخص = 43 58 (*l* ?? قشاء), ib 53 *S* ⲅⲧⲣⲟⲧⲏⲥ, ⲅⲩⲣⲁⲥⲓⲁ · ⲉϥϭ. طب, Tri 426 *S* ⲡⲣⲏϣ ⲉⲧϭ. رطب (as if ϭⲟⲛ nn); ShC 42 149 *S* ϣⲁϫⲉ ⲉⲩⲛⲁϣⲧ opp ⲉⲩϭ., ShIF 180 *S* clothes sim, R 2 4 38 *S* ⲧⲉⲧϭ. ⲉⲧⲉⲧⲉⲥϭⲓⲙⲉⲧⲉ, AZ 23 111 *S* ⲛⲕⲟⲣⲧ ⲉⲧϭ. (v ⲁⲕⲧ), TillOster 13 *A* ϭⲓⲛϣⲉϫⲉ ⲉⲥϭ., MG 25 291 *B* ⲉⲩϭ. ϭⲉⲛⲛⲟⲩⲥⲱⲙⲁ = BIF 13 107 *S*, Rec 6 184 *B* loaves ⲉⲩϭ. = BMar 218 *S* ⲣⲟⲟⲩⲧ; (*b*) ϭⲟⲛ *S*, ϭⲁⲛ *A²*: PSBA 27 168 ⲕⲉⲥⲓⲗⲉⲓ (κίσηρις) ⲉⲧϭ. opp ϫⲁϫⲱ, ShMIF 23 30 ⲕⲁⲡ ⲛⲡⲟⲩϭ ⲉϥⲙϣⲟⲓ ⲉⲩϭ., Z 628 ⲗⲁⲙϩⲁⲡⲧ ⲉϥϭ. (ὑγρός, opp λ. ⲛϫⲛⲣⲟⲡ PMéd 340), ManiP 46 *A²* ⲥⲡⲟⲛⲧⲟⲥ ⲉⲧϭ.; (*c*) ϭⲛⲏⲟⲩⲧ *B*: Va 58 141 τροφὴ ⲉⲧϭ. πολύυγρος; BMOr 8775 102 ⲙⲁⲗⲟⲧⲟⲛ (-ακός) · ϥⲏ ⲉⲧϭ. لڦا, P 54 163 ⲉⲩϭ. رخو, طب; Miss 4 200 ϩⲁⲛⲡϥⲁϫⲣⲓ ⲉⲩϭ. = *Amer Journ Theol* '05 722 soothing emollients, Ora 3 235 ⲛⲓⲑⲛⲟⲩ ⲉⲧϭ. (cf BAp 70 *S* ⲧⲏⲩ ⲉⲧϭⲏⲛ).

  —— nn m *SB*, *softness*: Deu 28 56 *SB* ἀπαλότης (or τρυφερότης); Lu 8 6 *B*(sic *l*, *S* ⲁϭⲃⲉⲥ) ἱκμάς; AZ 13 57 *B* = Va 57 226 νοτίς *v* ⲕⲟⲗⲕⲉⲗ; K 92 *B* ⲡⲓϭ. (ib 91 for ϭ. *l*, as varr, ϣⲛⲏⲡ); ShIF 181 *S* ⲡⲁⲕⲉ, ϭ., ⲛϣⲟⲧ, P 131⁷ 31 *S* ⲟⲩϭ. ⲙⲡⲟⲩⲙⲛⲧⲏⲙⲉⲣⲟⲥ, Z 633 *S* our nature ϩⲱⲕ ⲉⲃⲟⲗ ⲙⲡⲉ. ⲛⲡⲉⲡⲣⲏ ⲏⲟⲡⲛ, ViK 9828 *S* surgeons strive to cut ϩⲛⲟⲩϭ., DeV 2 282 *B* after storm ⲟⲩⲛⲓϣ⳨ ⲛϭ.; ⳨ϭ.: Va 58 150 *B* not ⲉ⳨ ϭ.....ⲛⲡⲉⲧⲉⲛⲯⲩⲭⲏ χαυνοῦν, but to edify you; ClPr 43 13 *S* sighs will not ⳨ ϭ. ⲙⲡⲉⲕϩⲏⲧ, P 129¹⁷ 70 *S* ⳨ ϭ. ⲙⲡⲓⲡⲓⲥⲧⲟⲥ ⲉⲧⲣⲉϥⲥⲗⲁⲁⲧⲉ.

ϭⲟⲡ, ϭⲟⲟⲛⲉ, ϭⲱ(?)*S*, ϭⲱⲡ *SA*, ϫⲁⲡⲉ *B* adj, *soft*: Pro 25 15 ϭⲱⲡ *SA*, Mt 11 8 *B*(*S* ϭⲏⲛ) μαλακός; P 54 137 *B* رطب, ملس;   nn m, of wine *S* PMich 4237 d ϥⲓϫ ⲙⲡⲛϭⲟⲡ ⲙⲡⲡⲗⲱⲙⲛⲥ ⲡⲉϣⲁⲕ[ϭⲡⲧⲉ, ib 6863 ⲧⲁϭⲱⲡ ⲉⲣⲟⲟⲩ (sc wine) ⲡⲁⲕ ⲛⲣⲏ(ⲙ)ϫ ϭⲓϭⲱⲡ, Mor 51 22 vines healed ⲙⲡⲉⲣϫⲓⲭ ⲟⲩϫⲉ ϭⲱ ϣⲱⲡⲉ ⲛⲣⲏ ⲧⲟⲩ;   ⲣ ϭ.: BMar 95 wine ⲁⲓⲧⲣⲉϥⲣ ϭⲟⲛ ϩⲓⲗⲱⲙⲥ, ib 94 ⲧⲣⲉⲛⲏⲣⲡ...ⲡⲱϣⲛⲉ ⲁⲩⲣ ϭⲟⲟⲛⲉ ⲉϥⲗⲟⲙⲥ (? ⲉⲩ-) ϩⲓϩⲙϫ, Mor *lc* vines ⲟ ⲛⲧⲱ ϩⲓϩⲙⲁϫ. Meaning here doubtful; *cf ?* ἀποίητος Wess 20 144, *Tell Edfou* 1 178; & for ϭⲱ *cf ?* g*ꜣw* loss, default, Berl *Wörterb* 5 152 (HT).

ϭⲛⲟⲛ, ϭⲛⲟ(ⲛ)², ϭⲛⲉ-³ *B*, ϫⲛⲉ- *S* (once) vb tr, *bend, bow* with ϫⲱ⳽ *head*: Ro 8 20³(*S* ⲑⲃⲃⲓⲟ), 1 Cor 14 34⁵ (*S* = Gk) ὑποτάσσειν; ROC 17 400 ⲉϥϭ.¹ ⲡϫⲱϥ ὑπακούειν; C 89 147 ⲉⲕϭ.² ⲡϫⲱⲕ ⲉⲕⲥⲱⲧⲙ ⲛⲥⲁ-, Tri 332 *S* ϫ. ϫⲱⲕ ⲛⲧⲅⲩⲡⲟⲧⲁⲥⲥⲉ حتّى.   With following preposition.   c ⲉ-: Ro 10 3¹(var ⲛ-, *S* = Gk), ib 13 1⁵ (var *S* do) ὑποτ. dat;   c ⲛ-: Ps 36 7³(*S* do), Dan

11 39³(S ⲑ.), Lu 2 51²(S ⲥⲱⲧⲙ ⲛⲥⲁ-), 1 Cor 15 28³ (SF = Gk), Ja 4 7³(A ⲑ., S [　]) ὑποτ. dat, Ps 17 48³ (S = Gk) ὑ. ὑπό, CaiEuch 596 ⲙⲁⲣⲟⲩϭ.³ ϫⲱⲟⲩ ⲛⲁϥ ⲕⲁⲑⲩ. dat; C 86 280 all things ⲥⲉϭ.¹ ⲛϫⲱⲟⲩ ⲛⲁⲕ ὑπακ. dat; Va 57 9 ⲉⲧⲥ.¹ ⲛϫⲱⲟⲩ ⲛⲁϥ ὑποκλίνειν dat; Ja 3 7²(SA ϭⲱⲙ) δαμάζειν dat; Va 57 65 ⲥⲉϭ.¹ ⲛϫⲱⲟⲩ ⲡⲣⲁⲛⲡⲁⲑⲟⲥ, C 43 93 ⲙⲡⲉϥϭ.³ ϫⲱϥ ⲛⲛⲓϫⲱⲗⲟⲛ, AM 126 ⲉϥϭ.¹ ⲛϫⲱϥ ⲛⲛⲓⲡⲁⲑⲟⲥ = R 1 4 66 S ⲅⲩⲡⲟⲕⲓⲥⲑⲁⲓ ⲛ-; ⲥ ⲉⲡⲉⲥⲛⲧ: Va 61 118 ϣⲁϥϭ.³ ϫⲱⲟⲩ ⲉ.; ⲥⲁ-ⲡⲉⲥⲛⲧ: Eph 1 22³(S ⲑ.) ὑποτ. ὑπό.

—— nn m, *submission, obedience*: Gal 2 5³(S = Gk) ὑποταγή; MG 25 126 ⲡⲓϫⲓⲛϣⲱⲡⲓ ϩⲁⲡⲓϭ.³, PO 11 343 ϩⲁⲡϭ.³ ⲛⲧⲉ ⲡⲉϥⲓⲱⲧ.

ϭⲁⲛⲛⲁ- F *v* ϫⲡⲁⲓ 2°.

ϭⲏⲛⲉ *v* ⲕⲏⲛⲉ 1°.

ϭⲉⲛⲏⲉ B *v* ϫⲡⲁⲩ *s f*.

ϭⲁⲛⲛⲁⲥ (?) F, meaning unknown, as epithet (?) of 2 implements: CMSS 76 ⲧⲣⲁⲡ ϭⲁⲛⲛⲁⲥ ⲁ[.], ⲙⲉ-ⲥⲱⲃⲓ ϭⲁⲛⲛⲁⲥ.　Or ? *cf* ϫⲡⲁⲓ 2°.

ϭⲉⲛⲏⲏⲩⲧ S, ϭⲏⲛⲟⲩⲧ B *v* ϭⲛⲟ.

ϭⲟⲛⲥ SA (once), ϭⲁⲛⲥ AA²(Ma)F, ϭⲁⲁⲛⲥ A²(AP), ϫⲟⲛⲥ B, ϫⲁ(ⲛ)ⲥ F (once) nn, *might, violence* or sim, as adj: Ex 14 21 B, Ps 47 7 S(B ⲛⲁϣⲧ), Is 11 15 SB βίαιος, Si 20 2 S ἐν βίᾳ; adverbial: Sa 5 11 S, Is 30 30 SB(F ⲛⲡⲁⲙⲧ) βίᾳ, Hab 3 6 B(SA ϩⲛⲟⲩϭⲟⲙ) βίᾳ, Ac 5 26 B(S ⲛϫⲛⲁϩ) μετὰ β., Jer 18 14 B(S diff) βιαίως, Lu 24 29 B ⲁⲙⲟⲛⲓ ⲛϫ. (S om) παραβιά-ζεσθαι; C 86 63 B enticed beasts toward him ⲛϫ. προσβιάζεσθαι; RE 10 39 S ⲁϥⲧⲱⲣⲡ ⲡⲟⲩϣⲉⲉⲣⲉ ϣⲏⲙ ⲛϭ., MG 25 252 B ⲁⲛⲓⲧ ⲉⲃⲟⲗ ⲛϫ.; *hardly B*: 1 Pet 4 18(S = Gk) μόλις; MG 25 345 ⲙⲟⲛⲓⲥ ⲛϫ. ⲁϥⲓ ⲉⲙⲏⲣ = Z 316 S ϩⲛⲟⲩⲡⲟϭ ⲛⲑⲗⲓⲯⲓⲥ = Gött ar 114 121 جلب.

ϫⲓ ⲛϭ., ϭⲓ ⲛϫ., *use violence, do evil* intr: Job 8 3 SB, 1 Cor 6 8 SB ἀδικεῖν; Ps 37 12 S(B ⲉⲣ ϭⲓ ⲛϫ.) ἐκβιάζ.; CO 73 S ⲡⲉⲧϫ. ⲛϥϭⲩⲡⲁⲧⲉ ⲁⲛ; qual: Ps 145 7 SB, Is 1 17 SA(Cl)B ἀδ., 1 Pet 2 19 B(S ϣⲡ ϩⲓⲥⲉ ⲛⲟⲩϫ.) ἀδίκως πάσχειν; BMis 541 S ϯϫⲏⲩ ⲛϭ. *noceri*; BM 1223 A ⲛⲉ(ⲧ)ϫⲏⲩ ⲛϭⲟⲛⲥ, ManiP 45 A² sim; tr, *hurt, ill-treat, constrain*: Pro 1 32 SAB, EpJer 17 B(F ⲉⲗ ⲙⲉⲧϫⲓ ⲛϭ.), Ac 7 24 SBF, Ap 11 5 S(B ⲉⲣ ⲁϫⲓⲕⲓⲛ) ἀδ.; Est 7 8 S, Z 310 S ϫⲓ ⲙⲡⲉⲕ-ⲙⲉⲉⲩⲉ ⲛϭ., AP 14 A² ϫⲓ ⲛⲟⲩϣⲙⲙⲟ ⲛϭ., AM 282 B ⲡⲧⲉⲡⲓⲗⲁⲟⲥ ϭⲓⲧ ⲛϫ. βιάζ., Jon 1 13 B(SA ⲉⲓⲣⲉ ⲛⲁⲡⲁ-ⲧⲟⲟⲧϥ) παραβ.; 1 Chr 16 21 B δυναστεύειν, Sa 2 10 S ⲕⲁⲧⲁⲇ.; Eccl 4 1 F ϫⲓ ⲛϫⲁ(ⲛ)ⲥ (S ϩⲓ ⲗⲁ), Lu 3 14 B (S do) συκοφαντεῖν; 2 Cor 2 11 B(S ϩⲟⲅⲣⲱϥ) πλεο-νεκτεῖν; Sa 10 14 S τυραννεῖν; *ib* 11 S κατισχύειν; Wess 18 74 S ϫⲓⲧⲕ ⲛϭ. ⲉⲧⲣⲉⲕⲉⲣ ϩⲱⲃ ἀναγκάζειν; Br 258 S ϫⲓ ⲛⲡⲉϩⲉⲣⲏ ⲛϭ., ShC 42 144 S ⲉⲓⲉϫⲓⲧⲏⲩⲧⲛ

ⲛϭ., Ryl 310 S ⲁϥϫⲓⲧϥ ⲛϭ. ϣⲁⲡⲧϥϭⲣⲁⲓ; c 2d acc: Ac 25 10 SB ⲙⲡⲓϫⲓⲧⲟⲩ ⲛϭ. ⲛⲗⲁⲁⲩ οὐδὲν ἀδ., Philem 18 S ⲁϥϫⲓⲧⲕ ⲛϭ. ⲛⲟⲩϩⲱⲃ τι σε ἀδ.; With following preposition. c ⲉ-: Lu 16 16 SB β. εἰς; c ⲉϩⲣⲏⲓ ⲉϫⲉⲛ-: Bar 2 13 B ἀδ. ἐπί; c ⲉⲃⲟⲗ ⲛ-: Ge 16 5† SB ἀδ. ἐκ; c ⲡⲧⲛ-: BMis 444 S ⲥⲉϫ.† ⲛϭ.....ⲡⲧⲟⲟⲧⲟⲩ; c ϩⲛ-: Deu 24 14 S(B diff) ἀπαδ. acc; c ⲉⲃⲟⲗ ϩⲓⲧⲛ- (passive): BMis 1198 S ⲉⲧⲟⲩϫⲓ ⲙⲙⲟⲟⲩ ⲛϭ. ⲉⲃ. ϩ. ⲡⲇⲓⲁⲃⲟⲗⲟⲥ.

—— nn m SABF, *violence, iniquity*: Deu 32 4 S (B ⲙⲉⲧϭⲓ ⲛϫ.), Job 11 14 SB, Ps 54 11 S(B = Gk), 2 Cor 12 13 SBF ἀδικία, Lev 16 16 SB, Jer 16 17 B (S ⲛⲛⲧϫⲓ ⲛϭ.), Ap 18 5 SB ἀδίκημα, Job 6 29 SB ἄδικος; Ac 21 35 B(S ϭⲟⲣⲙⲏ) βία; Ps 118 36 S(B ⲙⲉⲧϭ.) πλεονεξία; Ez 37 23 SB ἀσέβεια; Ex 6 6 A (B ⲙⲉⲧϫⲱⲣⲓ) δυναστεία; Ps 44 7 S(B = Gk) ἀνομία; Ge 6 5 S(B do) κακία; *ib* 31 36 SB ἁμάρτημα; ShR 2 3 49 S ⲛϫⲓ ⲡⲟⲩⲙⲛⲛϣⲉ ⲛϭ. ϭⲛⲣⲱⲃ ⲛⲓⲙ, ShC 42 113 S ⲛϫ. ⲙⲛⲡⲧⲱⲣⲡ, BM 256 221 S ⲛϫ. ⲙⲛⲡⲁⲙⲟⲥ is honoured in heaven, ViK 950 S ϭⲱⲧⲙ (ⲉ)ⲡⲁϫ. ⲙⲛ-ⲡⲁⲩⲗⲟⲥ, AZ 34 86 S I adjure thee ⲣ ⲡⲁϭⲁⲡ ⲙⲛⲡⲁⲕⲃⲁ ⲙⲛⲡⲁϫ., J 106 24 S ϫ., ⲁⲡⲁⲧⲏ, ⲥⲩⲛⲁⲣⲡⲁⲅⲏ (var *ib* 30 ϩⲓⲁ), DeV 2 46 B ⲡⲓϭ. ⲉⲧϩⲛⲡⲟⲩϫⲓϫ, BM 581 (2) F ⲛϫ. ⲡⲧⲁϩⲉⲓ ⲉϫⲱⲓ, COAd 60 S ⲉⲡⲉⲧⲛⲉⲕⲟ (= ⲛⲛⲉⲧ-ⲛⲕⲱ) ⲗⲁⲅⲉ ⲛϫ. ϩⲓϫⲛⲡⲟⲩⲁ; as adj: Ps 17 48 S(B ⲟϫⲓ), Is 32 7 SBF, Aeg 241 S ϩⲛⲏⲅⲉ ⲛϫ., Cl 3 4 A ⲕⲱϭ ⲛϫ. ἄδικος; LMär 35 S ⲛⲛⲱⲡⲛⲁ ⲛϫ.; ϩⲓⲟⲩ-ϫ. advb: Job 24 10 SB, Pro 1 17 A(S ⲉⲛⲣⲁ, B ⲙⲉⲧ-ⲟϫⲓ) ἀδίκως; PS 47 S ⲉⲛⲉⲅⲣⲱϫ ⲙⲙⲟⲓ ϩ., BMis 452 S ⲛϫⲙⲟⲟϣⲉ ϩ. being lame, BSM 73 B seized their property ϭ.

ⲙⲛⲧϫⲓ ⲛϭ., ⲙⲉⲧϭⲓ ⲛϫ. (S rare): Ge 44 16, Is 33 15 (SF ϫ. nn), Ro 2 8 (SF do) ἀδικία, Jer 16 17 S(B ϭ. nn) ἀδίκημα; Is 28 8 (S ϩⲱϭⲉ), Eph 4 19 (S ⲙⲛⲧ-ⲙⲁⲓⲧⲟ ⲛϩⲟⲩⲟ) πλεονεξία; ManiH 32 A² ⲟⲩⲃⲓⲁ ⲙⲛ-ⲟⲩⲙ.; EpJer 17 F ⲉⲗ ⲙ. (B ϭ. vb) ἀδικεῖν.

ⲣ ϫ., ⲉⲣ ϭ.: Deu 28 29 B(S ⲑⲙⲕⲏⲩ), Aeg 281 S ἀδικεῖν, Deu 25 16 S(B = Gk) ἄδικον ποιεῖν, Job 36 23 S(B ⲉⲣ ⲙⲉⲧϭ.) ἀδ. πράσσειν; Nu 14 44 B(S ⲙⲟⲩ-ⲕϩ) διαβιάζ.; ShR 2 3 28 S bribing ⲉⲧⲃⲉⲣ ϫ., Lant 102 *vo* S ⲁⲩⲣ ϩⲛⲡⲟϭ ⲛϫ. ϩⲓϫⲙⲡⲕⲁϩ.

ⲣⲉϥϫ., ϭ.: Ex 23 1 SB, Job 24 20 SB, Is 54 14 B (S ϫ. nn), He 6 10 B(SF = Gk) ἄδικος; Mt 11 12 SB βιαστής; 1 Cor 5 10 B(S ⲙⲁⲓⲧⲟ ⲛϩⲟⲩⲟ) πλεονέκτης; ShBM 230 147 S; as adj: Job 13 4 SB, Sa 3 19 S, Dan 3 32 SB ἀδ.; ⲙⲛⲧ-, ⲙⲉⲧⲣⲉϥ-: Ps 71 14 B(S ϫ. nn) ἀδικία; BMOr 8802 3 S ⲙⲛⲧⲣⲉϥϣⲡ ϩⲓⲥⲉ & ⲙⲛⲧⲣⲉϥϫⲓⲧⲛ ⲛϭ. to save us from sloth; ⲟⲓ ⲣⲉϥϭ.: DeV 2 100 B Saracens ⲉⲧⲟⲓ ⲛⲣ.

ϭⲱⲛⲧ SAF, ⲕⲱⲛϭ S (nn), ϭⲱⲱⲛⲧ S (once) A², ϫⲱⲛⲧ B, ϭⲟⲛⲧ† S, ϭⲁ.† AA²F, ϭⲁⲁ.† A², ϫⲟⲛⲧ† B vb intr, *be wroth*: Ps 59 3 B(S ⲛⲟⲩϭⲥ), Mt 18 34 B(S do) ὀργίζειν, Ps 105 16 B ⲑⲣⲉⲭ. (S ϯ ⲛ.) παρορ.; Ez

21 9 *SB*, Mt 2 16 *S*(*B* ⲙⲃⲟⲛ) θυμοῦσθαι; 1 Cor 13 5
B(*S* ⲛ.) παροξύνειν; Bel 28 *B* ἀγανακτεῖν; Ac 5 33 *S*
(*B* Gk diff); PS 101 *S* ⲁⲥϭ. ⲉⲡⲉⲣⲟⲅⲟ, C 99 3 *S* ⲙⲡⲉϥ-
ⲟⲩⲱⲣ ⲉⲧⲟⲟⲧϥ ⲉϭ., BM 1158 *S* ⲁⲕϭⲱⲱⲛⲧ, BSM 46
B lest he hear ⲛⲧⲉϥϫ., BIF 22 107 *F* ⲁϥϭ. ⲉⲗⲁϣⲁ,
BM 493 *vo F* ⲙⲁⲩϣⲁϣⲕ ⲡⲉⲗϭⲱ(ⲛ)ⲧ;   qual: Va
58 191 *B* ϥⲏ ⲉⲧϫ. ⲟⲣ.; *ib* 153 ἀπειλεῖν; C 99 235 *S*
ⲡⲉϭ. ⲉⲙⲁⲧⲉ = C 89 69 *B* λυπεῖσθαι; Jud 18 25 *S*
πικρός (var κατώδυνος); PS 104 *S* ⲉϥϭ. ⲉⲗⲁϣⲟ,
ShA 1 69 *S* words he said ⲉϥϭ., BHom 130 *S* they
scorned Him ⲉⲛϥϭ. ⲁⲛ, AP 1 *A²* ⲡⲉⲥϭ. ⲡⲉ, AM 127 *B*
ⲉⲑⲃⲉⲟⲩ ⲕϫ. ?

With following preposition.   c ⲉ-, *at, against*:
Deu 29 27 *S*(*B* ϫ. ⲡⲉⲙⲃⲟⲛ ⲉϫⲉⲛ-), Lam 5 22 *S*(*BF*
Quatrem. ⲉϩⲣⲏⲓ ⲉϫ., var Schmidt ϩⲱⲣⲉⲕ), Ap 12 17
S(*B* ϩⲓϫⲉⲛ-) ⲟⲣ. ἐπί, Is 28 28 *B*(*S* ⲡⲟⲩϭⲥ) ⲟⲣ. dat;
Lev 10 16 *S*(*B* ⲉϫ.) θυ. ἐπί; Ge 30 2 *S*(*B* ⲙⲃ.) θυ. dat;
Zech 11 8 *A*(*B* ϩⲣⲟϣ ⲉ ϩ. ⲉϫ.) βαρύνειν ἐπί; Jo 7 23
B(*S* ⲛ.) χολᾶν dat; Mk 14 5 *S*(*B* ⲙⲃ.) ἐμβριμᾶσθαι
dat; R 1 1 37 *S* λυπ. κατά; PS 381 *S* ⲁ̄ⲥ̄ ϭ. ⲉⲡⲕⲟⲥⲙⲟⲥ, Sh(?)Mor 54 87 *S* ⲁⲕϭ. ⲉⲣⲟⲛ (var ClPr 39 39
ⲛ.), ST 209 *S* ⲙⲡⲣϭ. ⲉⲣⲟⲛ, C 43 118 *B* ⲁϥϫ. ⲉⲣⲱⲟⲩ;   qual: Ac 12 20 *S*(*B* ϣⲟⲡ ϩⲉⲛⲟⲩⲙⲃ.) θυμομαχεῖν dat; Va 58 159 *B* ⲕϫ. ⲉⲣⲱⲟⲩ ἀγαν.; Mk 6 19 *S*
(*B* ⲙⲃ.) ἐνέχειν dat; Ac 26 11 *S*(*B* ⲗⲓⲃⲓ nn) ἐμμαί-
νεσθαι dat; Zech 11 8 *A*(*B* ϩⲣ.) ἐπωρύεσθαι ἐπί; PS
138 *S* ⲉⲡⲉϥϭ. ⲉⲧⲡⲓⲥⲧⲓⲥ, R 1 5 50 *S* ⲉⲓϭ. ⲉⲣⲟⲕ (var Mor
32 25 ⲣ ⲭⲱⲗⲏ), *ib* 1 3 77 *S* Herodias ⲛⲉⲥϭ. ⲉⲧⲁⲡⲉ ⲡ-
ⲓⲱϩⲁⲛⲛⲏⲥ, longing to slay him, ManiK 220 *A²* ⲉⲩϭ.
ⲁⲧⲥⲁⲣⲝ, AP 20 *A²* ⲛⲉϥϭⲁⲁ. ⲡⲉ [ⲁ]ⲡⲁⲩⲗⲟⲥ, PO 11
360 *B* ⲡⲁⲓⲣⲱⲙⲓ ϫ. ⲉⲧⲉⲕⲙⲉⲧⲁⲧⲓⲟⲥ, Mor 24 15 *F* ⲧⲉⲧⲛϭ. ⲉⲡⲉⲗⲱⲙⲓ;   ⲉϩⲟⲩⲛ ⲉ- *B*: C 86 66 ⲁϥϫ. ⲉϩ.
ⲉϩⲣⲁϥ ἐμβρ. τῷ προσώπῳ;   c ⲉⲑⲃⲉ-: 2 Kg 3 8 *S* θυ.
περί; Jer 40 9 *SB* πικραίνειν περί;   c ⲉϫⲛ-: Ex 4 14
S(*A* ⲁ-, *B* ⲙⲃ. ⲉ-), Nu 24 10 *B*(*S* ⲛ.), Is 5 25 *SBF*
θυ. ἐπί; Ps 73 1 *B*(*S* ⲛ.) ⲟⲣ. ἐπί;   ⲉϩⲣⲏⲓ ⲉϫ. *B*: Ps
79 5 (*S* do) ⲟⲣ. ἐπί;   c ⲛ- dat *B*: Jer 11 17 παρορ.
acc;   c ϩⲛ-, ϩⲉⲛ-: Nu 11 1 *B*(*S* ⲙⲟⲩϩ) θυ. dat;
Sa 12 27 *S* ἀγαν. ἐπί; C 43 174 *B* ⲁϥϫ. ϩⲉⲛⲟⲩⲙⲓϣϯ
ⲛⲑⲩⲙⲟⲥ;   c ϩⲓⲧⲛ- *S*: ShMiss 4 275 ϯϭ.† ... ϩ.
ⲡⲉⲓⲙⲕⲁϩ ⲛϩⲏⲧ;   c ϩⲓϫⲉⲛ- *B*: Ap 12 17 (var ⲉϫ.,
S ⲉ-) ⲟⲣ. ἐπί.

—— nn m *SAA²BF*, *wrath*: Ge 49 6 *S*(*B* ⲙⲃ.),
Pro 6 34 *SA*(*B* do), Is 5 25 *SB*(*F* ϭⲡⲉⲧ), *ib* 30 27 *SF*
(*B* do), Lam 3 1 *SB*(*F* ϩⲱⲗⲕ), Mic 5 14 *AB*, 2 Cor 12
20 *SBF*, AP 9 *A²* θυμός; Ps 55 8 *B*(*S* = Gk); Ro 5 9
B(*S* do) ὀργή; Hab 3 12 *SAB*, Ac 4 29 *SB* ἀπειλή;
ib 15 39 *B*(*S* = Gk) παροξυσμός; He 3 8 *B*(*S* ϯ ϭⲡⲁⲧ)
παραπικρασμός; Is 50 2 *S*(*B* ⲙⲃ.) ἐλεγμός; BG 65
S ⲭⲱⲣⲓⲥ ϭ. ϩⲓⲕⲱϩ, ShIF 268 *S* ϭ. ⲛⲡⲁⲣⲁⲕⲟⲡ, ⲙⲁⲧⲟⲩ
ⲛ̄ϩⲟⲩ, El 136 *S* ⲡⲕⲱⲛϭ = *ib* 100 *A* ϩⲗⲕⲉ, BMis 102
S ⲛϭ. ⲛⲧⲛⲙⲁⲅⲟⲥ (var Mor 33 58 ⲛⲙⲁⲅ.) *against*
wizards that had fooled him, ManiK 92 *A²* ⲟⲩϭ., AM

240 *B* ⲁϥⲙⲟⲣ ⲛϫ., *ib* 217 *B* ⲁϥⲉⲙⲃⲟⲛ ϩⲉⲛⲟⲩⲙⲓϣϯ
ⲛϫ.;   as adj: Ez 16 38 *SB* θ.; TstAb 232 *B* ⲥⲁϫⲓ ⲛϫ.

ⲁⲧϭ., -ϫ. *SB*, *unangered, not to be angered*: Aeg
244 *S* bishop must be ⲟⲩⲁ., Mor 27 13 *S* God ⲛⲁ.,
Lakân 259 *B* sim;   ⲙⲛⲧⲁⲧϭ. *S*: Bor 226 176, *ib*
240 61.

ⲣⲉϥϭ., -ϫ. *SAB*, *wrathful person*: Pro 11 25 *SAB*
θυμώδης; Ps 17 49 *B*(*S* ⲣⲉϥⲓ.) ὀργίλος; TEuch 2 476
B ⲟⲩϩⲟⲣ ⲛⲣ. اسد; ShA 1 74 *S*, MG 25 30 *B*;   ⲙⲛⲧⲣ-
ⲣ. *S*: BHom 24 ὀργίζεσθαι;   ⲉⲣ ⲣ. *B*: C 89 97 =
C 99 158 *S* ⲛ. vb.

ϯ ϭ., ϫ. *SABF*, *cause anger, provoke*: Nu 14 11 *S*(*B*
ⲙⲃ.), Is 5 24 *BF*(*S* ϯ ⲛ.) παροξ.; Ps 77 40 *SB*, Lam
1 18 *B*(*F* ϫⲓⲛϯ), Ez 12 9 *SB* παραπικ.; Is 1 4 *B*
(*SF* ϯ ⲛ.), Mic 2 7 *B*(*SA* do) παρορ.; PS 81 *S* ⲛⲡⲁϯ.
ⲡⲁⲩ, Mor 33 53 *S* ϯ. ⲡⲁϥ (var BMis 99 ϯ ⲛ.), El 72
A, C 41 73 *B*;   ⲣⲉϥϯ ϭ., ϫ.: Ez 2 8 *B*(*S* ϯ ϭ. vb);
adj: Ps 77 8 *B*(*S* ϯ ⲛ.) παραπικ.; Mor 31 22 *S* ⲙⲟⲛⲁⲭⲟⲥ ⲛⲣ.;   ⲙⲛⲧⲣⲉϥϯ ϭ. *S*: ShBMOr 8810 472
ϥⲓ ⲧⲉⲓⲛ. ⲉⲃⲟⲗ ⲙⲙⲟ.

ϭⲛⲁⲧ *S*, -ⲉⲧ, ϫⲡⲉⲧ *F* vb intr, *be wroth*: Lam 2 6 *F*
ϫ. (*B* ϯ ϫⲱ.) παροξ.; Mk 10 14 (var ⲛ., *B* diff) ἀγαν.;
Z 617 if in temptation ⲙⲡⲣϭ.;   as nn m: Is 5 25 *F*
(*SB* ϭⲱ.) θυμός;   ⲣⲉϥϭ. Tit 1 7 (*B* ⲣⲉϥϫⲱ.) ὀργίλος;   ϯ ϭ.: He 3 16 (*B* ϯ ϫⲱ.) παραπικ.;   nn m:
Ps 94 8 (*B* ϫⲱ.) παραπικρασμός; P 44 91 ⲙⲛⲧⲁⲅ-
ⲑⲁⲧⲏⲥ (-δης)· ⲛⲧϯϭ.;   ⲣⲉϥϯ ϭ.: Miss 8 251.

ϫⲓⲛϯ, ϫⲉⲛϯ *F* nn f, *wrath*: Lam 1 12 (*B* ⲙⲃ.) θυ.
or ὀρ., *ib* 2 2 (*B* do), *ib* 2 6 ϫⲉ. (*B* ϫⲱ.) ὀρ.

ϭⲱⲛⲧ, ϭⲟⲛⲧⲉ *B*   *v* ϫⲱⲛⲧ.

ϭⲛⲟⲩⲧ *A²* nn, meaning unknown: ManiP 226
weave crown for my head ⲙⲁⲣⲟⲩⲥⲣⲁϥⲣⲉϥ ⲁⲕⲟⲩⲡⲧ
ⲛϫⲓ ⲡⲉⲕⲙⲁϩ ⲛϭ.

ϭⲉⲛⲧⲱⲗⲓ *B*   *v* ϣⲉⲛⲧⲱⲗⲓ.

ϭⲛⲁⲩ *B*   *v* ϫⲡⲁⲁⲩ.

ϭⲛⲟⲟⲩ *S*, ϭⲛⲱⲟⲩ *B*   *v* ϫⲛⲟⲟⲩ.

ϭⲓⲛⲟⲩⲏⲗ¹, ϭⲉⲛ.², ϭⲓⲛⲟⲩϩⲁⲗ³, -ⲟⲩⲃⲁⲗ⁴, ⲕⲓⲛⲃⲏⲗ⁵
S, ϭⲓⲛⲟⲩⲉⲗ *A²*, ϭⲉⲟⲩⲏⲗ *F* nn m, kind of *ship* (cf
kbnjt ship of Byblos): P 44 54 ϭ.² ϩⲣⲟⲙⲁⲛⲓⲙ (sic
δρομάδιον, cf K 133) حراقة دروق; BMis 268 ⲟⲩⲛⲟϭ
ⲛ.⁵ built of ϣⲟⲩⲉⲃⲉ wood = Mor 30 44 *F*, Mor 29 44
ϩⲉⲛϭ.¹ sailing on sea = *ib* 30 51 *F* ϫⲁⲓ, BMar 5 ⲙⲛⲧ
ⲛϣⲉ ⲛϭ.⁴ sim, BMis 281 (ϭⲓⲛ)ⲟⲩⲁⲗ³ sim, Mich 550
46 send him not by ϫⲟⲓ ⲟⲩ ϭ.¹, SHel 26 ⲕⲟⲧⲓ ⲛ-
ⲥⲕⲁⲫⲟⲥ ⲛϭ.¹, HM 2 89 ⲟⲩⲗⲓⲛⲛⲓϣⲉ ⲛϭ.³, ManiP 213
A² ⲛϭ. of traders ⲡⲉⲭⲏⲩ of merchants.   *V* BIF 30
453.   Hence ? شنابر (Kremer *Beitr* 265).

ϭⲛⲏⲟⲩⲧ *B*   *v* ϭⲛⲟ & ϭⲛⲟⲛ 1°.

ϭⲛⲁⲩϩ *B*   *v* ϫⲛⲁⲁⲩ.

ϭⲟⲛϥ, ϭⲟⲙϥ B v ϫⲟⲟⲩϥ.

ϭⲛⲟϥ B v ϫⲛⲟϥ.

ϭⲛⲟⲩϥ, ϭⲡⲱϥ B nn m, *heavy object*: K 261 ⲡⲓϭ. قبن *iron hammer* (K), possibly so in Upper Egypt (Sobhy), P 54 132 -ⲱϥ 'ز, رزين.

ϭⲁⲛⲁϩ S, -ⲉϩ S/F nn, *maimed, crooked person*: Mk 9 43 SF(Mor 21 142, B ϫⲁϭⲏ)Mor 18 128 κυλλός; Tri 408 عـ; ShMIF 23 87 ⲟⲩϭ. ⲉⲣⲉⲧⲉϥϭⲓϫ...ⲥⲟⲩⲧⲱⲛ ⲁⲡ ⲁⲥⲣ ϭⲱ̄ⲃ, ShC 73 59 abusive names ϭⲁⲗⲉ, ϭ., ϭⲁⲅⲗⲉ, PSBA 25 270 ⲁϥⲱⲗⲕ ⲛⲧⲉϥϭⲓϫ ⲉⲣⲟϥ ... ⲛⲑⲉ ⲛⲟⲩϭ., BIF 13 99 ϩⲉⲛϭ. ⲡⲕⲉⲗⲁⲫⲟⲥ = MG 25 279 B ϭⲁϭⲉⲩ (cf ib 280 ⲭⲁϭⲟ), Mor 38 53 S/, Jern 4 ⲡⲣⲁϣⲉ ⲛϭ., BM 1079 Ἀπα Τηρ ϭ.; adj: PS 378 ⲥⲱⲙⲁ ⲛϭⲁⲗⲉ ⲁⲩⲱ ⲛϭ., KroppE ϭⲓⲝ ⲡⲟⲩⲛⲁⲙ, ϭⲓⲝ ⲛϭ. (cf ϫⲁϭⲏ κυλ. above); p ϭ.: Lev 22 22 (var ϭⲁϫⲉⲗⲁⲥ, B Gk sim), R 1 52 ⲡⲉⲧⲟ ⲛϭ. ϩⲡⲡⲉⲩⲥⲱⲙⲁ. As name: Πκανᾶχ, Κάναχ (Preisigke).

ϭⲛⲁϩ, ϭⲡⲁϩⲣ B v ϫⲛⲁϩ.

ϭⲓⲛϩⲟⲩⲧ v ϭⲓⲛⲙⲟⲩⲧ.

ϭⲟⲛⲁϭ[1], ϭⲟⲩⲡⲁϭ[2], ϭⲱⲛϭ[3], ϭⲟⲩⲛⲁϭⲉ(?)[4], ϭⲟⲩⲡⲁϭⲉⲥ[5], ⲕⲁⲅⲡⲁⲕⲉⲥ[6], -ⲕⲟⲥ[7] S nn m = κανύάκης, γαυ., *cloak* (not of fur, Reil *Beitr.* 132): Ryl 246 ϭ.[1] ⲡⲁⲓⲅⲩⲡⲧⲓⲟⲛ ⲡⲁⲅⲁⲡ, BMEA 10579 ⲡⲙⲏⲧ ⲛϭ.[1], ϭ.[3], ViK 4787[2], ib 4745[1,2], Ep 339[4], P 131[5] 37 ϭ.[5] ⲡⲗⲁⲁⲩ, Ryl 245[6], MR 4 141 ⲕ.[7] ⲡⲁⲅⲁⲡ, ⲕ.[7] ⲡⲣⲁⲥ[ⲉ]ⲥ (? πράσιος). Cf Lagarde *GesAbh* 206.

ϭⲱⲛϭ[1], ϭⲱϭ[2], ϭⲱⲛϭⲛ[3], ϭ(ⲉ)ⲛϭ-[4], ϭⲡϭⲛ-[5] S vb tr, *wring, nip off*: Lev 5 8[1] (varr[2], P 44 105[3], B ϭⲱⲣⲡ), ib 1 15[5] (B ⲫⲱⲣϫ) ἀποκνίζειν; Deu 23 24[4] (B ⲑⲟⲩⲱϯ) συλλέγειν.

ϭⲓⲛϭⲉ, ϭⲓϭⲉ S nn, meaning uncertain, ? *scale*, *link* of armour: 1 Kg 17 5 ϩⲱⲕ ⲛⲣⲉ ⲛϭ. (var P 44 109 ϩ. ⲉⲣⲉ ⲛϭⲓϭⲉ, 43 100 ϩ. ⲙⲡⲛⲣⲛϭⲓϭⲉ درع وجوش) θώραξ ἁλυσιδωτός.

ϭⲓⲛϭⲗⲱ[1], -ϭⲗⲟ[2], -ϭⲉⲗⲱ[3], -ϭⲗⲟⲩ[4], -ⲧⲗⲱ[5], ϭⲡϭⲉⲗⲱ[6], ϭⲉⲡϭⲗⲱ[7], ϭⲡϭⲉⲗⲟ[8], ⲕⲁⲡⲕⲗⲱ[9], ϭⲓϭⲗⲱ[10], ϭⲱⲗϭⲉⲗⲱ[11] S, ϫⲉⲗϫⲟⲩ[12], ϫⲁⲗϫⲟⲩ[13], ϫⲉϫⲟⲩ[14] B, ϭⲓⲛϭⲓⲗⲱ[15], ϭⲉⲣϭⲱ[16] F, ϭⲉⲡϭⲗⲱ DM nn f, *bat* (cf with B *drgj·t* Dévaud *Ét.* 26): Deu 14 17 S[1](var[3])B[12] خفاش, Is 2 20 S[1]B[13], EpJer 21 S[7](Mus 50 231)B[12]F[16] νυκτερίς; P 44 56 S ⲛⲉⲟⲁⲥⲟⲥ(?νεοσσός) ϭ.[8] طبر, ib 105 S[2] ·خ; BMOr 8771 88 B ϫ.[14] ',; ShC 42 51 S ⲧϭ.[1] ⲙⲡⲡⲓⲕⲧⲓⲕⲟⲣⲁⲝ, ShP 130[2] 81 S idolaters worship ⲛϭ.[5] (var RE 10 163[1]), Mor 51 35 S ⲛϫⲁϫ ⲙⲛⲛϭ.[1] devour fat of land, Z 579 S ⲛϭ.[10] that see not, P 131[7] 77 S ⲛϭ.[1] ⲃⲱⲕ ⲉϩⲟⲩⲛ ⲉⲡⲉϣⲕⲁⲗ; in recipes (cf POslo 1 90): BKU 1 26 (8117)F ⲛϭ.[15] boiled, Cairo 42573 2 S contents of stomach of ϭ.[6], Ora 4 19 S

blood of ϭ.[10](or ?[1]), Mus 51 77 S sim[11], DM 24 32 sim, KroppK 30 S blood of ⲕ.[9] as ink, PMéd 296 S urine of ϭ.[4], AZ 23 108 S prob sim.

ϭⲓⲛϭⲏ[1] SA[2], ϭⲉⲛϭⲉⲛ[2], ϭⲛϭⲛ[3], ϫⲡϫⲛ[4], ϫⲓⲛϫⲓⲛ (nn)[5], ϫⲁϫⲁ̄[6] S, ϫⲉⲛϫⲉⲛ B vb intr, *make music* with instrument or voice (cf meanings of ϩⲣⲟⲥ, ϫⲱ): R 2 1 18 = Leyd 379 S David ⲙⲡⲉϥⲕⲓⲑⲁⲣⲁ ⲁϥϭ.[1] ⲉϥϫⲱ ⲙⲙⲟⲥ ϫⲉ-, ManiP 117 A[2] ⲧⲁϭ. ⲙⲡⲛⲉⲧϩⲣⲱⲥ ⲁⲣⲟⲕ; with following preposition: Mun 126 S David ⲁϥϭ.[2] ⲉⲧⲉϥⲕⲓⲑ. ⲉϥϫⲱ ⲙⲙⲟⲥ ϫⲉ-, ManiP 133 A[2] ⲡⲟⲩⲕⲓⲑ. ϩⲛⲡⲉϥϭⲓϫ ⲉⲩϭ. ⲁⲣⲁϥ, ManiK 187 A[2] ⲁⲓϭ. ⲁⲧⲃⲁⲓⲛⲉ, ib P 164 A[2] ϭ. ⲁⲧⲕⲓⲑ., BMis 351 S sim ϭ.[1] ⲛ- (var ϩⲛ-) = BSM 16 B ⲕⲓⲙ ⲛ-, Aeg 56 B sim ϫ. ⲛ-, Dif 3 31 B ϫ. ⲙⲡⲉⲕⲗⲁⲥ ⲙⲫⲣⲏϯ ⲛⲟⲩⲟⲣϭⲁⲛⲟⲛ حرج; *sing*: TT 18 S birds ⲉⲩϭ.[6] ϩⲛ[ⲧⲉϥⲁ]ⲥⲡⲉ (var Mich 550 24 ⲕⲁⲕⲓⲙ qv),Worr 256 S Virgin ⲉⲥϭ.[3] ⲉⲡⲉⲥϣⲏⲣⲉ; ⲣⲉϥϭ., drummer, singer: Ps 67 26 S -ϫ.[4](B ⲣⲉϥⲕⲉⲙⲕⲉⲙ)τυμπανίστρια; Worr *l c* ϭⲣⲟⲙⲡⲉ ⲡⲣϥϭ.[3]; nn: Ps 150 5 S ϫ.[5](B = Gk) κύμβαλον; P 46 232 S ⲛϫ.[5] صلصل (K 139 = ⲕⲩⲙⲃ.); Jth 15 12 S ϫ.[5] (var MS *penes* JG Smyly ϫⲓⲛϫⲓⲛ) Gk diff. V Dévaud *Ét.* 53 (ϭ. & ϫ. independent).

ϭⲓⲛϭⲓⲛ S, ϫⲓⲛϫⲓⲛ B nn m, *rocket* (plant): BMOr 8775 1 33 = P 54 144 B ⲛⲓϫ. ·ⲉϩ ⲱⲙⲟⲩ (εὔζωμον) جرجير; PMéd 285 S ⲉϩⲣⲁ ϭ.

ϭⲱⲛϭⲛ, ϭⲡϭⲛ- v ϭⲱⲛϭ.

ϭⲓⲛϭⲱⲣ SA[2]F, ϭⲛ. A, ϫⲓⲛ. B nn m, *talent*, weight or coin: Ex 25 39 B, 2 Kg 12 30 S, Zech 5 7 SAB, Mt 25 15 SBF(PMich 540)τάλαντον, Ap 16 21 S ⲓⲥϭ. B ϫⲓⲛ. ταλαντιαῖος; ShHT H 4 S ⲡⲥⲁⲧⲉⲉⲣⲉ ⲛ ⲛϭ., BM 219 S ⲡⲣⲁⲡ ⲙⲙⲁⲣⲓⲁ, ⲡⲉⲥⲧⲟⲩ ⲛϭ. (sc 5 letters), Ryl 310 S ⲙⲛⲧⲥⲁϣϥⲉ ⲛⲧⲃⲁ ⲛϭ., ManiP 224 A[2] ⲙⲏⲧ ⲛϭ., PO 14 367 B ⲡⲓⲉ̄ ⲛϫ.

ϭⲁⲛϭⲟⲩϣ F v ϭⲁⲣⲁϭⲱⲟⲩϣ.

ϭⲓⲛϭⲉϩ, ϭⲉⲛϭⲉⲛⲉⲣ S nn m, *elephantiasis*: P 44 79 ⲛⲟ ⲕⲓⲗⲫⲓⲁ (κελε-) ⲛϭ. ·جذم (cf K 158 B ⲕⲉⲫⲁⲗⲟⲥ 'أج), ⲣⲟ ⲉⲗⲅⲫⲁⲓ· ⲛϭ. ·مجذين, EW 222 scala ⲛϭⲉⲛϭ. ·ج.

ϭⲁⲡ v ⲕⲁⲡ 2° & ϭⲟⲡ.

ϭⲟⲡ SB, ⲕⲁⲡ S, ϭⲁⲡ S/AA[2], ϣⲟⲡ B nn f, *sole* of foot, *foot*: Glos 57 S/ ⲧϭ. ταρσός, P 44 71 S ⲧⲁⲣ. ϭⲱⲡ ⲡⲣⲁⲧ ضب; Deu 28 35 B(Va, var & S ⲥⲛⲃⲉ), Pro 5 5 SA(B ⲧⲁⲧⲥⲓ) ἴχνος; Ac 3 7 SB(prob, cf ϯϩⲃ), Mor 17 30 S cannot stand ϩⲓⲭⲛⲡⲉϥϭ. βάσις; Lev 11 26 B (S ⲣⲁⲧϥ) ὁπλή; Mor 37 97 S centaur's ϭ. like ass's πούς; Jos 9 11 S ⲛϭ. ⲡⲡⲉⲩⲧⲟⲟⲩⲉ κοῖλος; R 14 17 S ⲡⲉϫⲟⲩⲉⲣⲏⲧⲉ ⲙⲙⲛϭ. ⲡⲣⲁⲧⲩ planta; BMis 556 S sore became like ⲟⲩⲕ. ⲡⲉⲓⲱ pes asini; K 78 B ϯϣ. قدم; Tri 435 S stand upon ⲡⲉⲕϭ. لبي(cf P 44 71 ⲧⲁϭ ϭⲉ ',); Aeg 21 S ⲛϭ. ⲡⲡⲉϥⲟⲩⲉⲣⲓⲧⲉ = ib B ϭⲁⲗⲁϫ, BMis

140 S child learning to walk ⲉϥⲧⲟϭⲥ ⲛⲛⲉϥⲕⲟⲅⲓ ⲛϭ., Mun 125 S' sim ⲧⲁⲭⲣⲟⲥ ϭⲛⲡⲉⲥⲕ. ⲛϭⲁⲡ, Miss 8 235 S ⲁⲧϭ. ⲡⲟⲅⲡⲁⲙ ... ⲡⲱϣ & oil flowed forth, Mor 41 121 S live coals beneath ⲛϭ. ⲡⲣⲁⲧⲟⲩ, ib 187 S cut off ⲛϭ. ⲡⲛⲉϥⲟⲩⲉⲣⲏⲧⲉ, C 86 275 B nails into ⲡⲓϣ. ⲛⲧⲉ ⲣⲁⲧϥ, ManiK 174 A² ⲛϭ. ⲡⲡⲉϥⲟⲩⲣⲏⲧⲉ ⲟⲣⲣ ⲥⲛϥⲉ ⲡⲣⲉⲧϥ, KroppB S tears covered ⲛϭ. ⲡⲣⲁⲧⲕ, MG 25 134 B cast self down ⲉϫⲉⲛⲡⲓϭ. ⲛⲧⲉ ⲣⲁⲧⲧ.

ϭⲟⲡ SB, ⲕⲁⲡ Sᵃ, ϭ. A² nn f, cutting instrument: SHel 32 S martyr's thighs scored with ϩⲉⲛϭ. ⲙⲡⲉⲛⲡⲡⲉ, Pap penes BHStricker S ϭ. ⲉϣⲱⲗϭ, CO 468 Sᵃ ⲧⲕⲁⲡ ⲡϣ. ManiK 132 A² carpenter's ⲃⲁϣⲟⲩⲣ ... ⲗⲉⲡⲧⲏⲡ ... ϩⲛⲧϭ. ⲛϥⲥⲗⲟϭⲗⲱϭϥ, MG 25 222 B ϣⲉ ⲛϭ. stroke of tool in mat making.

ϭⲟⲡ v ϭⲟⲡⲉ.

ϭⲱⲡ A² nn, meaning unknown: ManiH 29 ⲛϭ. ⲡⲁϣ[?]ⲟⲩⲱϭⲡ.

ϭⲱⲡ v ϭⲱⲡⲉ.

ϭⲱⲡ B v ϣⲱⲃ.

ϭⲁⲡⲉⲓ v ⲕⲁⲡⲁⲓ & ϭⲟⲡⲉ.

ϭⲉⲡⲏ SA²F, ϭⲓⲡⲏ S, ϭⲏⲡⲉ F vb intr, hasten (SA²): Jos 4 10, Lu 2 16 (B ⲓⲏⲥ), Ac 20 16 (B do) σπεύδειν; Mor17 117 ϥⲡⲁϭ. ⲛⲧⲁⲕⲧⲟⲓ εὐθέως; BHom 22 ⲙⲁⲣⲉϥϭ. ⲡⲅⲧⲱⲟⲩⲛ διανιστάναι (ib 320 ⲥⲟⲓⲧⲱⲟⲩⲛ); PS 38 ⲁⲓⲧⲣⲉϭ., BIF 14 133 ⲁϥϭ. ⲁϥⲉⲓ (var LMär 29 ⲁϥⲧⲁⲭⲏ), HSt 463 let each ϭ. ⲡϥⲃⲱⲕ (var Aeg 263 ⲥⲡⲟⲩⲁⲍⲉ), Mor 39 11 ⲁϥϭ. ⲁϥⲟⲩⲱϣⲧ = C 43 38 B ⲁϥϭⲱⲗⲉⲙ, EnPeterson ϣⲁⲕϭ. ⲡⲡⲟϭⲧⲉⲃⲟⲗ; imperat: Ps 137 3 ϭ. ⲡⲥⲱⲧⲙ (B ϭⲱⲗⲉⲙ c.), ib 101 2 ϭ. ⲥⲱⲧⲙ (B ϭ. c.) ταχύ; Lu 19 5 ϭ. ⲁⲙⲟⲩ (B ϭ. ⲙⲙⲟⲕ) σπ.; 2 Tim 2 15 (B ⲓⲏⲥ ⲙ.) σπουδάζειν; PS 93 ϭ. ⲁⲣⲓ ⲡⲁⲣⲁⲡ, ib 61 ϭ. ⲡϭⲡⲁϩⲙⲉⲧ, BM ostr 82 12-12 6 ϭ. ⲟⲩⲁϩⲟⲩ, Ep 380 ϭ. ⲡⲡⲛⲧⲟⲩ; tr (refl): Ge 18 6 (B ⲓⲏⲥ) σπεύ.; Mun 27 ⲉⲡⲉϥϭ. ⲙⲙⲟⲟⲩⲡⲉ, BMar 86 ϭ. ⲙⲙⲟⲕ ⲡⲧⲥⲱⲧⲉ, ManiP 161 A² ϭ. ⲙⲙⲟ ... ⲡⲧⲉⲃⲱⲕ.

With following preposition: ⲉ e-: Job 31 5 (B do) σπου. εἰς; Mich 550 41 ϭ. ⲙⲙⲟⲕ ⲉⲧⲉⲅⲡⲁⲍⲓⲥ; ⲉϩⲟⲩⲛ ⲉ-: Si 21 23 ταχὺς εἰς; MIF 67 166 ⲟⲩⲅⲕⲱϭⲧ ⲉϥϭ. ⲉϩ. ⲉⲕⲉⲕⲱⲣⲧ; vbal: Jth 13 1 σπου., Pro 20 21 (A ϭⲗⲁⲙ) ἐπίσπου.; Ex 2 18 (B ϭ.), Ps 105 13 (B do), AP 13 A² ⲁⲕϭ. ⲁⲧⲉⲉϥ ταχύνειν, Is 59 7 (B ⲓⲏⲥ) ταχινός, Jo 20 4 (B diff) τάχιον; Ps 13 4 (B ⲓ.) ὀξύς; BAp 52 ⲉⲓϭ. ⲉϯ ⲡⲁⲟⲅⲟⲓ ἐπείγεσθαι; Br 45 ⲉⲧⲉⲧⲡϭ. ⲉϣⲱⲡ, ShC73 130 ϭ. ⲉⲧⲟⲟⲩⲡ, Bor 294 120 ⲙⲁⲣⲉⲡϭ. ⲙⲙⲟⲛ ⲉⲧⲁϩⲟⲛ ⲉⲣⲁⲧⲛ; ⲥ ⲉⲣⲁⲧϥ: Si 18 13 καταⲥⲡⲉⲩ. ἐπί; ⲥ ⲉⲝⲛ-: Mor 36 30 death ϭ. ⲉⲝⲛⲟⲩⲡ ⲡⲓⲙ, BMis 154 devil ϭ. ⲉⲝⲙⲡⲣⲱⲙⲉ; ⲥ ⲡ-: P129¹⁸ 162 ⲙⲡⲉϥϭ. ⲙⲡⲓⲥⲧⲉⲩⲉ, ViK 4720 ⲙⲡⲉⲕϭ. ⲙⲡⲣⲟ-

ⲃⲁⲗⲉ ⲡⲁⲓ; ⲥ ϩⲛ-: Is 16 5(var ⲛ-) σπεύ. acc, Si 43 5 καταϭ. acc.

As advb: Is 9 1 ⲁⲣⲓⲥ ϭ. (B ⲛⲭ.) ταχύ, Lu 16 6 (B do) ταχέως; ShA 1 34 cleansed from ⲧⲉⲅⲙⲛⲧⲣⲉϥⲣ ⲙⲡⲧⲣⲉ ϭ.(cf ib ⲧⲉⲅⲙⲛⲧⲣⲉϥϣⲱⲣⲕ ϩⲛⲟⲩϭ.), Blake 306 ⲥⲉϭⲓⲡⲉ ⲙⲙⲟϥ (sc beryl) ⲁⲛ ϭ. not readily found in woman's ornaments; ϩⲛⲟⲩϭ. SA²F, forthwith: Ps 78 8, Is 32 4 SF, Jo 11 29 (A² ϩⲛⲟⲩϭⲗⲁⲙ) ταχύ, ib 13 27 (A² do, F ϩⲓⲧⲕⲟⲩⲣ) τάχιον, Deu 9 12 τὸ τάχος, Ps 6 10 διὰ τάχους, Ac 25 4 ἐν τάχει (all B ⲛⲭ.), Sa 4 16 ταχέως; Ps 77 33 (B ϭⲉⲛⲟⲩⲭ.), Mk 6 25 (B = Gk) μετὰ σπουδῆς, Sa 2 6 σπουδαίως; 2 Pet 3 10 (B ϭⲉⲛⲟⲩⲟⲩⲟⲓ) ῥοιζηδόν; Ap 22 12 (B ⲛⲭ.) ἔτι; 3 Jo 14(B ⲥⲁⲧⲟⲧϥ) εὐθέως; PS 240 ⲥⲡⲟⲩⲁⲍⲉ ϩ., ib 33 ⲉⲅⲡⲁⲥⲟⲩⲧⲟⲩ ϩ. ⲡⲁϣ ⲡⲥⲙⲟⲧ?, R 1 2 9 prayed & raised dead ϩ., BIF 13 107 ⲁϥⲕⲧⲟϥ ϩ. = MG 25 292 B ⲛⲭ., BMis 246 var ϩⲛⲟⲩϭⲁⲥⲁⲓ, Ep 327 ϫⲟⲟⲩ ⲡⲛϭⲓⲧⲉ ϩ., ib 361 ϩⲛⲟⲩϭⲓⲡⲏ, AP 42 A², GriffStu 162 F ϩⲛⲡⲟⲩϭⲏⲡⲉ.

ⲣⲉϥϭ., one who is quick, hasty: Pro 22 29 (A ⲣⲉϥϭⲗⲁⲙ) ὀξύς, Ps 44 1 (B ϣⲉⲡϣⲱⲡ) ὀξυ-; P 131⁴ 100 ⲧϭⲓⲛⲥⲱⲧⲙ ⲟⲩⲣ. ⲧⲉ ⲉϩⲟⲩⲉ ⲉⲧϭⲓⲡϣⲱⲗⲙ, ib 101 ⲉⲧⲟ ⲡⲣ.; ⲙⲛⲧⲣ.: LeipBer '02 142 ⲟⲩⲙ. ϩⲙⲡⲗⲁⲥ ὀξύτης; P 131¹ 32 ⲧⲙ. ⲉϫⲱ of birds κλαγγὴ πολύφθογγος.

Cf ϭⲁⲡϭⲉⲡ.

ϭⲏⲡⲉ S(rare), ⲕ. A, ϭⲏⲡⲓ BF, ϫ. F nn f, cloud (S ⲕⲗⲟⲟⲗⲉ): Ge 9 13, Lam 3 44 BF ϫ., Mk 9 7 BF ϭ. νεφέλη, Job 7 8, Is 14 14 νέφος; PS 213 S ⲛϭ., ⲥⲓⲟⲩ, ⲁⲏⲣ, BG 73 S shaded by ⲟⲩϭ. ⲛⲟⲩⲟⲓⲛ, Mor 23 30 S = ib 24 21 F ϭ. sim, El 86 A ⲡⲕ. ⲡⲧⲡⲉ, C 89 169 reaching unto ⲡⲓϭⲓⲡⲏ (sic), AM 155 ⲟⲩϭ. ⲙⲙⲟⲩ ⲡⲣⲱⲟⲩ, BM 580 14 F ϣⲁⲡⲧⲉⲧⲉⲓϭ. ⲟⲩⲱⲧⲉⲃ.

ϭⲟⲡⲉ¹, ϭⲟⲡ², ϭⲁⲡⲉ³, -ⲕ⁴, -ⲉⲓ⁵ S nn, small vessel, so small quantity (cf ⲕⲟϫ ⲗⲟ Dévaud): Deu 26 5 ϭ.¹ (no var, B ⲛⲡⲓ) ἀριθμός; Ap 3 4 ϭ.² ⲡⲣⲱⲙⲉ (B Gk diff); C 99 3 ⲟⲩⲕⲟⲅⲓ ⲛϭ.¹ ⲡⲣⲱⲙⲉ (var ib 112 ⲕ. ⲡⲟϫⲉ), ShP 130⁴ 135 ϭ.¹ ⲕⲟⲅⲓ ⲡⲣⲛⲁⲁⲩ ⲡⲟⲩⲱⲙ, ShC 73 54 ⲟⲩⲙ ⲟⲩⲕⲟⲅⲓ, ⲥⲉ ⲟⲩϭ.¹ ⲙⲙⲟⲟⲩ, ShC 42 181 ⲙⲟⲟⲩ ⲉⲡⲁϣⲟⲩ ⲟⲡⲡ ⲟⲩϭ.¹ ⲕⲟⲅⲓ ⲙⲙⲟⲟⲩ, ShMiss 4 283 ϣⲟⲩⲉ ⲟⲩϭ.¹ ⲙⲙⲟⲟⲩ ⲉϫⲱϥ to wash, ShP 130⁴ 157 among small chattels ⲟⲩϭ.² (for ? ϭ.¹) ⲡⲥⲱ ⲙⲡⲣⲉⲡϩⲁⲁⲩ ⲡⲃ[ⲗ]ⲝⲉ, P 132⁴ 361 ⲥⲉ ⲟⲩϭ.¹ ⲙⲙⲟⲟⲩ, BMis 479 ϫⲓ ⲟⲩϭ.⁴ ⲙⲙⲟⲟⲩ ⲡⲧⲟⲟⲧϥ (cf ib ⲁⲡⲓⲡⲉ ⲡⲁⲓ ⲡⲟⲩⲕⲟⲅⲓ ⲙⲙⲟⲟⲩ), ib 487 ⲟⲩϭ.⁵ ⲙⲙⲟⲟⲩ sprinkled on nets, Ora 4 26 ϭ.¹ ⲡⲉⲣⲱⲧⲉ, Ryl 397 ⲟⲩϭ.³ (no context); ϭ.¹ ϭ.¹, little by little: ShC 73 199 he let fall water ϭ. ϭ., ib 210 (not Sh) ⲥⲱ ϭ. ϭ. ... ⲙⲡⲣⲥⲉ ⲗⲟⲕ ⲥⲡⲁⲩ ⲡⲥⲁ ⲡⲉⲅⲉⲣⲏⲩ.

ϭⲱⲡⲉ SAA²F(nn), ⲕⲱⲡⲉ, ϣⲱⲡⲉ (bis), ϭⲱⲡ, ⲕⲱⲡ S, ϭⲱⲡⲓ BF, ϫ. F, ϭⲉⲡ- SB, ϭⲡ-, ϣⲁⲡ- S, ϭⲱⲡ- SA, ϭⲟⲡ- S, ϭⲁⲡ- SS'A²(Ma)F, ⲕⲉⲡ- SO(?), ϫⲉⲡ- B,

ⲕⲁⲡ-*F*,ϭⲟⲡⲍ*SB*,ϭⲁⲡⲍ*SS^fAA²F*,ⲕⲁⲡⲍ,ⲕⲟⲡⲍ,ⲕⲱⲡⲍ,
ϭⲱⲡⲍ*S*, ⲭⲟⲡⲍ*B*, ⲭⲁⲡⲍ*F*, ϭⲏⲡ† *SS^fA*, ⲕⲏⲡ†, ϭⲉⲡ†,
ⲕⲉⲡ†*S*, ⲭⲏⲃ̅†*B*, p c ϭⲁⲡ-*BF* vb(*B* rare) **I** intr, *seize,
take*: Lu 5 4 (*B* ⲭⲟⲣⲭⲥ) ἄγρα;   qual: Nu 2 2 (var
ⲏⲡ, *B* ϭⲉⲡⲧ) ἔχεσθαι, 1 Kg 21 7, Lu 12 50 (*B*=Gk)
συνέχ.; Mk 15 6 (var ⲙⲏⲣ, *B* ⲥⲟⲛϭ) δέσμιος.

II tr: 1 Kg 19 20 (var ϭⲱⲛ), Is 31 4 *F* ϭⲁⲡⲥ (*S*
ⲧⲁϭⲟ, *B* ⲱⲗⲓ) λαμβάνειν, Deu 25 11 (*B* ⲁⲙⲟⲛⲓ), Lu
20 20 (*B* ⲧⲁϭⲟ) ἐπιλ., Jo 18 12 *SA²*(*B* ⲁⲙ.), Ac 1 16
(var ϣ., *B* ⲁⲙ., var ⲁⲙⲁϩⲓ), BMar 105 ⲁϥⲟⲩⲱϣ ⲉⲕⲟ-
ⲡϥ, Cl 12 2 *A* ϭⲁⲡⲟⲩ συλλ., C 99 212 bade ϭⲉⲡ ⲣⲉⲡ-
ⲡⲟϭ ⲛⲧⲓⲣⲱⲛ = C 89 4 *B* ⲧⲁϭⲟ συναναλ.; Cant 2 15 *S*
(ShA 1 293)*F* ϭ., Jo 7 30 *SA²*(*B* ⲧⲁ.), Ac 12 4 *SB* ϭⲟⲡⲍ
πιάζειν; Pro 6 30 *SA* ϭⲱⲡ-*B* ⲭⲉⲡ-, *ib* 31 *SAB* ⲭⲟⲡⲍ,
Is 22 3 (*B* ⲧⲁ.) ἁλίσκεσθαι; Am 3 4 (*B* ϭⲱⲗⲉⲙ) ἁρπάζειν, Ac 6 12 (*B* do) συναρ.; Lev 17 13 ϭⲱⲣϭ ⲉϭ. (*B*
ⲧⲁϩⲟ ⲭⲟⲣⲭⲥ) θήρευμα θηρεύειν; Lu 5 10 (*B* ⲧⲁ.) ζωγρεῖν; Mk 14 1 (*B* ⲁⲙⲟⲛⲓ, *F* ⲁⲙⲉⲣⲓ), ROC 18 171 ϭⲉⲡ
ⲧⲉϥⲟⲩⲉⲣⲏⲧⲉ κρατεῖν; Lu 21 12 (*B* as Gk) χεῖρας ἐπιβάλλειν; ShA 2 129 ⲛⲱⲧ...ⲉⲧⲃⲉϭⲛ ⲥⲁⲣⲁϭⲱⲟⲩϣ, *ib*
29 wind drieth grain ⲉⲙⲡⲁⲧⲟⲩϭⲉⲡ ⲉϩⲣⲁ ⲛ ⲁⲅⲁⲣⲭⲉⲓ
ⲛϭ., El 118 ϭ. ⲛⲥⲁⲃⲉⲟⲅⲉ = *ib* 78 *A*, Mor 19 12 ϭⲉⲡ
ⲡⲉⲧⲛⲕⲗⲟⲙ (var *ib* 18 4 ϭⲓ) = Miss 4 99 *B* ⲱⲗⲓ, BM
214 ⲁⲩϭⲟⲡⲧ like ʼhief, BIF 15 253 ϭ. ⲛⲡⲉϥϭⲓⲭ ⲙⲛ
ⲡⲉϥⲟⲩⲉⲣⲏⲧⲉ, ʙM 346 1 ϭ. ⲛϩⲉⲡⲉⲭⲏⲅ & set him on
board, BMis 258 ⲁⲥϭⲱⲡ ⲛⲁⲡⲛⲓϣⲉ & brake them,
HM 1 34 *S^f* ⲁⲩϭⲁⲡϥ, BKU 1 1 (ⲓⲓ) ⲁϥϭⲱⲡ ⲟⲩⲃⲏϭ,
ib 21 ro *S^f* ϭⲁⲡ ⲟⲩⲅⲟⲩⲓ ⲛⲁⲡⲉⲓ...ⲡⲧⲟⲩϭ̄ⲓⲧϥ ⲉⲁϥϭⲉⲡ
ⲭⲱϫⲉ (cf ϭⲉⲡ ⲉϩⲣⲁ above), Cai 8090 rubric ϭⲟⲡ ⲛⲁ-
ⲥⲟⲩⲅ̅ *begin at* (lessons) *for 7th day*, Cat 23 *B* on Mt
8 29 ⲁϣ ⲡⲥⲛⲟⲩ?, ⲉϥϭⲉⲡ ⲥⲛⲟⲩ ⲛϯⲕⲟⲗⲁⲥⲓⲥ, BM 1124
ⲉⲕϣⲁⲛϭⲱⲡ ⲟⲩϭⲟⲟⲩ ⲉⲕⲛⲏⲃⲉ, RE 9 152 ⲁⲓϭⲱⲡ ⲡⲣⲁⲅⲓⲟⲥ ⲛⲡⲁϣⲧⲉ, J 65 95 ⲁⲓⲡⲁⲣⲁⲕⲉ ⲉⲧⲣⲁϭⲱⲡ (ⲡ)ⲉⲡⲉⲓⲱⲧ
visit (?), Ryl 339 ⲉϥϭⲱⲡ ⲗⲟⲉⲓϭⲉ ⲭⲉ-, PLond 4 465
ⲁⲧⲉⲧⲛϭⲱⲡⲧ *arrested me*, BMOr 9536 *vo* ⲉⲣϣⲁⲛⲡⲕⲁ-
ⲡⲟⲛ... ⲕⲱⲡⲧ, Turin ostr 5929 ⲁⲓⲕⲟⲡϥ, ST 378 ⲉϥϭⲱⲡ ϭⲣⲟⲙⲡⲉ, Cai 42573 1 ϣⲏⲛ ⲉϭⲁⲡ ⲧⲃ̅ⲧ, TurO
11 ⲕⲉⲡ ⲧⲃ̅ⲧ, ST 290 ⲁⲓⲕⲱⲡⲉ ⲛⲡⲉⲓⲣⲱⲙⲉ, Ryl 370
ϭⲟⲡ ⲛⲉϭⲁϭⲉ, CO 133 ⲉⲕⲕⲁⲡⲥ, El 80 *A* ϭ. ⲛⲥϩⲓⲙⲉ
ⲡⲓⲙ, AP 15 *A²* ⲡⲉⲧϭ. ⲙⲙⲁⲩ, ManiP 206 *A²* ⲁⲩⲥⲧⲱⲧ
ϭⲁⲡ ⲡⲟⲩⲁⲣⲭⲱⲛ, PGM 1 60 665 *O* ϣⲁⲛⲧⲕⲕⲉⲡ ⲛⲥⲟ-
ⲡⲧⲉ, BM 615 *F* ϭⲁⲡ ⲛⲉⲃⲛⲏⲓ, *ib* 627 *F* ⲡⲓⲱⲣⲓ ⲛⲧⲁⲓϭⲁ-
ⲡϥ, PMich 4380 *F* unfortunates ⲉⲩϭ. ⲙⲙⲁⲩ;   in
recipes (cf PMéd ⲭⲓ ⲛⲁⲕ): AZ 23 115 ϭⲟⲡ ⲟⲩϣⲓ
ⲡⲧⲁⲣⲧ, Ryl 106 45 ϭⲟⲡ β̅ ⲛⲗⲓⲧⲣⲁ, Cai 42573 1 ϭⲁⲡ ⲍ̅
ⲛⲃⲏⲧ (but *ib* 2 ⲭⲓ ⲛⲁⲕ), PChass 2 ϣⲁⲡ ⲟⲩϣⲓ.
   With following preposition.

—— ⲉ- (not *B*): He 3 14 (var ⲛ-, *B* ⲉⲣ ϣⲫⲏⲣ ⲉ-)
μέτοχος γίνεσθαι gen; ShC 73 141 ϯ [ⲡⲟⲩ]ⲧⲓⲙⲏ ⲙ-
ⲡⲉⲓⲁ[ⲟⲥ] ⲕⲁⲧⲁ ⲡⲉⲧⲟⲩⲛⲁϭ. ⲉⲣⲱⲧⲛ, Leyd 151 rubric
ⲡⲓⲁ ⲛⲧⲁⲛϣⲟⲣⲡ (sc previous chanter) ⲕⲁⲁϥ ⲉⲃⲟⲗ
ϣⲁϥϭ. ⲉⲣⲟϥ ⲟⲛ *take up again*, BM 112 sim ⲟⲩⲟϩ
ⲉⲃⲟⲗ ⲙⲡⲉⲓⲙⲁ ϭ. ⲟⲛ ⲉⲧⲉⲭⲛⲥⲟ, Ryl 287 instructions

as to buying fodder ⲉϥϣⲁⲛϭ. ⲉⲣⲱⲧⲛ *hath account
against you* ⲧⲉⲧⲛⲉⲧⲓ ⲛⲁϥ, BM 1103 ⲁⲩϭ. ⲉⲣⲟϥ ⲡⲁⲓ,
PMich 6863 ⲧⲁϭⲱⲡ ⲉⲣⲟⲟⲩ (sc wine) ⲛⲁⲕ ⲡⲣⲏ(ⲙ)ⲭ
ϩⲓϣⲟⲡ, BM 5808 *F* (ⲁ)ⲧⲁⲥⲱⲡⲓ ϭⲁⲡⲟⲩ ⲉⲣⲓⲛⲉϭ (Hnês),
ManiP 188 *A²* may thy mercy be spark ⲛϭ. ⲁⲛϣⲏⲁ
ⲉⲧⲣⲏⲧ (cf ⲉϩⲟⲩⲛ ⲉ-);   qual, *liable, guilty*: Deu
19 10 (*B*=Gk), Jos 2 19 ἔνοχος εἶναι, Ja 2 10 *SA*(*B*
ⲣⲁⲟⲩϭ) ἔν. γίνεσθαι; Eph 5 7 (*B* ⲟⲓ ⲛϣⲫⲏⲣ) συμμέ-
τοχος γίν.; Pro 1 23 *SA*(*B* p.) ὑπεύθυνος; BHom 21
ⲉⲛϭ. ⲉⲟⲩⲕⲟⲗⲁⲥⲓⲥ ὑπέχειν; R 1 4 60 ⲉⲧϭ. ⲉⲡⲉⲓⲥⲱϣ =
MartIgn 871 *B* ⲟⲓ ⲡⲉⲡⲟⲭⲟⲥ ὑποκεῖσθαι; ShA 2 112
ⲉⲧⲉⲧⲛϭ. ⲉⲣⲉⲡⲉⲛⲡⲱϣ, Mich 550 36 ⲉϥϭ. ⲉϩⲁϩ ⲙⲛⲑⲟ-
ⲛⲟⲥ (φθ.), RE 9 141 ⲉⲩϭ. ⲉⲡⲉⲛⲕⲗⲏⲙⲁ (sic l), J 18 56
ⲉϥⲕ. ⲉⲡⲁⲛⲁϣ, Mor 30 9 *S^f* ⲉⲕϭ. ⲉⲩⲛⲟϭ ⲛⲁⲓⲙⲱ-
ⲣⲓⲁ;   tr: PO 4 580 ⲡⲉⲧⲟⲩⲱϣ ⲉϭⲉⲡ ⲱⲡⲉ ⲉⲣⲟⲓ (*ib*
621 ⲱ̄ⲗ̄ⲍ̄:ⲛ̄ⲗ̄ⲗ̄ⲛ̄ϯ), Kr 237 *get money from X, give it
to Y*, ⲉⲩϭ. (ⲙ)ⲙⲱϥ ⲉⲣⲱⲓ *can claim it of me*, Ep 537
ⲁⲛⲕⲱⲡⲧ ⲉⲡⲓⲡⲣⲟⲥ, BM 530 *vo* his account (λόγος)
ⲉⲙϣⲁϥϭⲟⲡϥ ⲉⲣⲟⲓ *I will pay him it*, BP 5561 *F* tax due
ⲛⲧⲁⲕⲁⲡ ⲩ̄ⲥ ⲉⲗⲁⲓ ϩⲉ(ⲡ)ⲡⲟⲉⲙⲁⲧⲓⲥⲙⲟⲥ *am responsible
for*;   ⲉϩⲟⲩⲛ ⲉ-: Nu 14 18 (var ⲟⲩⲡ ⲡⲟⲃⲉ ⲉ-, *B* ⲣⲉϥⲉⲣ ⲛ.) ἔνοχος; PS 271 ⲧⲉⲧⲛϭ.† ⲉⲣ. ⲉⲩⲛⲟϭ ⲛⲕⲣⲓⲙⲁ,
ShA 1 447 fire ϭ. ⲉⲣ. ⲉⲡⲟⲩⲁ ⲡⲟⲩⲁ ⲛⲡϣⲏⲡ;   ⲉϩⲗⲏⲓ
ⲉ- *F*: Cant 1 7 ⲁⲙⲉⲛⲧⲟⲩⲭⲁⲡⲧ ⲉⲣ. ⲉϩⲉⲡ- (*S* Gk diff).

—— ⲁⲙⲉⲛ-*F*: BM 706 account ⲉⲩϭⲱⲡⲓ ⲁⲙⲉⲡⲉϩⲁ-
ⲗⲏⲅ ⲧⲏⲣⲟⲩ.

—— ⲛ-*SBF* dat: 2 Kg 2 21 *S* κατέχειν σεαυτῷ;
C 43 232 *B* ϭ. ⲛⲏⲓ ⲛⲣⲁⲓⲣⲟⲩϭ, BP 5178 *S* ⲕⲱⲡ ⲡⲉⲥⲟⲟⲩ
ⲛⲁⲓ, BM 618 *F* ϭⲁⲡϥ ⲛⲉⲓ;   *in* (=ϩⲛ-): Balestri LX
S rubric ϭ. ⲁⲙⲛⲓⲙⲁ (cf ⲥ ⲉ-), ViK 9477 *S* sim.

—— ⲛⲥⲁ-*SA²F*: Lam 4 18 *F* ϭⲱⲡⲓ (*S* diff, *B* ⲭⲱ-
ⲣⲭ) θηρεύειν; Wess 18 61 *S* ϭ. ⲛⲥⲁⲡⲉϩⲓⲟⲗⲉ, ManiP
196 *A²* ⲁϥϭ. ⲥⲁⲡⲟⲩⲙⲏ[ⲧ;   ⲛⲥⲁⲡⲁⲣⲟⲩ: Ora 4 24
S ⲛⲥⲉϭⲡ ⲡⲉⲕⲟⲩⲉⲣⲏⲧⲉ ⲛ.

—— ⲛⲧⲛ-*SS^fF*: Wess 15 152 ⲁⲧⲙⲉⲥⲓⲟ ϭⲟⲡϥ (sc
babe) ⲛⲧⲟⲟⲧⲕ, Win 70 ⲟⲩⲡ ⲡⲟⲩⲃ ⲕⲏⲡ ⲛⲧⲟⲟⲧⲕ, Ep
327 ⲟⲩⲡ ⲟⲩⲡⲁϣⲉ ⲛϩⲟⲗⲟⲕ/ ϭⲉⲡ ⲛⲧⲟⲟⲧ, Tor 28 sim
ⲕⲉⲡ, BM 660 *S^f* ϭⲁⲡⲟⲩ ⲛⲧⲟⲟⲧϥ, Kr 225 *F* ϭⲁⲡ ϑ̄ ⲁ
ⲛⲧⲁⲁ(ⲧ)ⲃ̅.

—— ϩⲁ-*SB*: BM 327 ϥϭ.† ⲁⲡ ϩⲁⲗⲁⲁⲩ ⲡⲉⲧⲛⲕⲗⲏ-
ⲙⲁ, WZKM ʼ02 265 we will require naught ϩⲁ(ⲡ)-
ⲭⲏⲙⲟⲥⲓⲟⲡ ⲛⲧⲡⲕⲁⲡⲕ ϩⲁⲣⲟϥ, Ryl 423 105 b *B* ⲛⲧⲁ-
ϣⲱⲡⲓ ⲉⲓⲭⲏⲃ̄ ϩⲁⲡⲉⲧⲉⲛⲛⲟⲃⲓ.

—— ϩⲛ-*SA²*: Ps 58 12 (*B* ⲧⲁ.), Ez 12 13 ϣ. (*B*
ⲁⲙⲁϩⲓ) συλλ. ἐν; Mt 22 15 παγιδεύειν ἐν; Mk 12 13
ἀγρεύειν dat; Lu 11 54 (var ⲛ-, all *B* ⲭⲱ.) θηρ.; BHom
19 ϭ.† ϩⲛϩⲁϩ ⲛⲡⲟⲃⲉ ὑπεύθυνος εἶναι; 1 Cor 3 19 (*B* ⲁ-
ⲁⲙⲁϩⲓ, cf Job 5 13 ⲧⲁ.) δράσσεσθαι ἐν; ShA 1 59 ϭ.
ⲛⲡⲣⲁⲗⲏⲧ ϩⲙⲡⲡⲁϣ, ShBIF 23 72 ⲉϥϭ. ⲛⲡⲣⲱⲙⲉ ϩⲡⲛⲉ-
ⲡⲉⲩⲟⲩϣ, P 129¹⁴ 52 Council of Chalcedon ϭ.† ϩⲛ-
ⲡⲕⲁⲡⲱⲛ of Ephesus *answerable to, condemned by*, Cai
8313 rubric ⲕⲁⲑⲏⲛⲥⲓⲥ of Liberius (cf BIF 23 200)
ⲛϥϭ. ϩⲛⲧⲉⲥⲁⲣⲭⲏ *start at*, ViK 2617 sim ϭ. ⲁⲙⲡⲉⲓⲙⲁ

ϩⲡⲉⲓⲣⲏⲙⲓⲁⲥ (Jer 388), FR 8 ⲙⲡⲧⲁϥⲧⲉ ⲡϩⲟⲟⲩ ⲁⲥϭⲁⲡⲟⲩ ϩⲙⲡⲙⲁⲣⲯⲓⲥ ⲡⲉϩⲟⲧ, ManiP 15 *A²* ϭⲁⲡ ⲡⲁⲡⲉ ϩⲙⲡⲉⲧⲛϭⲓⲝ; ⲉϩⲟⲩⲛϩⲛ- *S*: BP 9446 of new door ⲡϩⲃⲥ ⲙⲡⲧⲏⲡⲏ ⲕⲁ(ⲁ)ⲩ ⲉⲧⲣ[ⲉⲩ]ϭ. ⲉⲙⲁⲧⲉ ⲉϩ.ϩⲛⲧⲭⲟ; ⲛⲉϩⲣⲏⲓϩⲛ- *A²*: ManiP 10 ⲉϥⲁϭⲁⲡϥ ⲛ. ⲛϩⲏⲧϥ (*sc* snare).

—— ϩⲓϫⲛ- *S*: PMich 6862 5 ⲯⲁⲩϭⲟⲡ ϩⲁϥ ⲉϩⲟⲩⲙⲉⲧ ϩⲓϫⲱⲛ.

—— ϫⲓⲛ- *S*, take up, start from: Jud 1 36 ⲛⲧⲟϣ ⲁⲩϭ. ϫⲓⲛⲧⲁⲡⲁⲃⲁⲥⲓⲥ ἀπό no vb, 4 Kg 15 16 sim do (*cf* c ϩⲛ- in rubrics).

ⲣ ⲉϭⲁⲡ-   *v* p 741 *a*.

—— nn *S*, taking, draught of fish: CaiCoptMus 88 (EW 222) ⲛϭ. مصيد; BMOr 6201 *B* 189 ⲁⲡⲁ (ⲁ)ⲙⲟⲩⲛ ⲡⲁⲡⲉ ⲛϭ. (or ⲡⲁⲡⲉⲛϭ., same?); BKU 1 15 *F* amulet ⲛϭⲱⲡⲉ ⲛⲡⲃⲉⲗ, *ib* 16 sim ⲛⲃⲉⲗ ϩⲟⲣ (meaning ?).

ⲁⲧϭ. *S*, not to be taken: Bor 253 152 (1°) ⲉϥⲟ ⲛⲁⲧϭⲟⲡϥ οὐδὲ λαθρίαν ἀδικίαν ὑφιστάναι.

ⲙⲁ ⲛϭ. *S*, place of taking up, beginning: Vict & Alb Mus 434⁸-1888 rubric ⲙⲙ. ⲛⲡⲥⲱⲕ ⲉⲃⲟⲗ (var Leyd 150 ⲙⲙ. ⲉϩⲟⲩⲛ ⲛⲡⲥⲱⲕ ⲉⲃ.).

ⲣⲉϥϭⲉⲡ- *S*, taker: Mk 1 17 (*B* ⲣⲉϥⲧⲁϩⲉ-) ἁλιεύς; Gu 99 ⲣⲉϥϭⲉⲡⲧⲉⲃⲧ, Mor 50 42 -ϩⲟⲩ.

ϭⲓⲛϭ. *S*, taking, grasping: Z 330 ⲁϥ ... ⲥⲟⲕⲧ ϩⲛⲧⲉϥϭ. ἕλκειν τῆς χειρός; P 131⁴ 106 ⲧϭ. ⲙⲡⲉϥϭⲓⲉⲓⲃ in trap.

ϭⲟⲡⲥ *S* nn, capture: R 1 1 66 will conquer enemies ϩⲛⲟⲩⲛⲟϭ ⲛϭ., AZ 14 117 (no context).

V also ⲗⲟⲓϭⲉ, ⲡⲟⲩⲛⲉ, ϫⲣⲟ (ϫⲱⲱⲣⲉ).

ϭⲁⲡⲗⲏϭⲉ *S* nn f, meaning doubtful: Glos 433 σαλαμηρα (? σαλμούρα Bell) · ⲧϭ.

ϭⲱⲡⲣⲟ *S* (once), ϫⲉⲡⲣⲟ *SB*, ϫⲉⲫ., ϫⲉⲃ. *B* nn f, farmstead, hamlet (?) = شبرا, شبرى, which *PSchott-Reinhardt* 1 106 = ἐποίκιον: EW 92 *B* he shall build ⲟⲩⲕⲟⲩϫⲓ ⲛϫ. ⲛⲧⲁⲓⲟ ⲛⲁⲕ ... ⲟⲩⲟϩ ⲡⲓϫⲁⲓ ⲛⲁⲉⲣ ⲟⲩⲛⲓϣϯ. In place-names: ⲧⲱⲣⲉ ⲙⲛⲧϭ. ⲛⲡⲉⲗⲟⲟⲗⲉ (Cai Copt Mus pap 4-5 *S*, *cf* شـ بلولة thrice, but in Delta), ϫⲉⲡ. ⲙⲉⲛⲉⲥⲙⲁ (BIF 13 111 *S*) = ϫⲉⲃ. (MG 25 301 *B*) = شـ منسينا (PO 5 82), ϫⲉⲡ. ⲙⲟⲩⲛⲟⲡⲥⲱⲛ (PO 14 324 *B*) = شـ منصور (*ib* 3 519), ϫⲉⲃ. ⲡⲁⲑⲏⲛⲓ (PO 11 335), ϯϫⲉⲫ. ⲡⲉϫϭⲏⲧ (C 86 269 *B*) *cf* شـ خنيت (Ibn Gi'ân 129); ⲥⲁⲡⲣⲟ ϩⲃⲱ (BIF 1 176) شـ رحمة, this word, not as p 656 *b*.

ϭⲓⲡⲥ *B* nn m, wrinkle on skin, bark: K 75 ϭ., ⲭⲣⲱϣ غضون (BM 924 ومهم تجاعيد الجبهة), *ib* 198 ⲛϭ. خبَّت (*v* AZ 14 117, Lane 1 692 *a*).

ϭⲟⲡⲥ   *v* ϭⲱⲡⲉ *s f*.

ϭⲟⲩⲯ *S* nn m, meaning unknown, among sailors' requirements: WS 97 ⲡⲕⲟⲩⲓ ⲙⲁϣⲣⲧ ⲙⲡϭ.

ϭⲁⲡⲁⲧ *S* nn f, collar-bone: P 44 70 ⲕⲗⲓⲥ (-εἰς) · ⲧϭ. كتف (43 41 كتب, by error); Ora 4 26 recipe ⲥⲁϣϥ ⲛϭ. ϩⲓⲟⲩ(ⲉ)ⲥⲟⲟⲩ (*sic* prob) ⲛⲕⲁⲙⲉ, this word ?

ϭⲁⲡⲉⲧ *A²*, ϫⲁϥⲁⲧ *B* nn as pl, fibre (?) of palm tree: ManiK 18 *A²* of palm ⲛⲉⲥϭ. ⲙⲡⲉⲥⲃⲗⲉ, MG 25 351 *B* garment of ⲛϫ. ⲛⲧⲉ ⲛⲓⲃⲉⲛⲓ = Gött ar 114 124 ليف من النخل = ROC 18 54 ܟܐܦܐ. *Cf* ? ⲕⲁϥⲁϫⲓ.

ϭⲱⲡⲧ *S/F*   *v* ϭⲱⲧⲡ.

ϭⲁⲡ(ⲉ)ⲓϫⲉ¹, ϭⲁⲡⲓϫⲏ², ⲕⲁⲡⲓϫⲉ, ϭⲁⲡⲓϫⲟⲩ³ *S*, ϫⲁⲡⲓϫⲓ, ϫⲁϥ⁴., ϫⲁⲡⲁ.⁵ *B* nn m f, a dry measure: Ap 6 6 *S*¹ (var³ BP 11965 2 cit) *B* (var⁴) χοῖνιξ; P 44 22 *S*² ⲛϫ., K 143 *B* ⲡⲓϫ. مِدّ الكيل, *ib* 130 *B*⁵ صاع, *ib* 145 *B* ϯϫ. مُدّ الـ; Hall 108 *S* ⲧⲕ., *ib* ⲧϭ.¹, *ib* 131 among iron σκεύη ⲕ. ⲓϫ, Bodl(P) f 55 *S* ϥⲓⲣ ⲥⲛⲁⲩ ⲛϭ.³ *Cf* ⲛⲓⲡⲉⲣ- قفيز -ⲕⲁⲡⲓⲑⲏ &c Lagarde *Ges. Abh.* 81, *Mitth.* 2 27 (Jernstedt), also Dévaud *Ét* 54.

ϭⲁⲡϭⲉⲡ, ϭⲉⲡϭⲡ *S*, ϫⲁⲡϫⲉⲡ *B* vb intr, be hurried, anxious: Si 2 2 *S* ϭⲉⲡ. *B* (varr ϫⲁⲃϫⲉⲃ, ϫⲁⲡϫⲁⲡ) σπεύδειν; Bor 260 106 *S* ⲛⲡⲉⲕϭ. ϩⲉⲛⲛⲉⲑⲗⲓⲯⲓⲥ; nn m: P 54 174 *B* ⲡⲓϫ. استرخا انحلال. *Cf* ϭⲉⲡⲏ.

ϭⲁⲣ- *S* in BM 1160 ⲡⲉⲓϭⲁⲣⲃⲁⲙⲡⲉ prob = ϣⲁⲡⲁⲥ in Nu 31 20.

ϭⲟⲣ   *v* ⲕⲟⲩⲣ 3°.

ϭⲱⲣ, ϭⲟⲩⲣ *B* nn m, smoke, cinder: BM 915 saw ⲛϭ. of his cooking, Va 57 194 ϩⲁⲡⲃⲏⲓⲃⲓ ⲡⲉⲙϩⲁⲛϭ., *ib* 41 ϭⲟⲩⲣ ⲛⲕⲁⲡⲛⲟⲥ, *ib* ⲣⲟⲕϩ ⲉⲧϯ ϭ. καπνός, Hos 13 3 ϩⲣⲱ ⲛϭ. (*A* ϩ. only) καπνοδόχη; Va 58 153 ⲡⲓϭ. ⲛⲣⲉϥϣⲁⲙⲓⲟ ϣⲟⲣⲧⲉⲣ τέφρα; Is 1 31 (var ϭⲟⲩⲣ P 104, *S* Gk diff); ϯϭ.: MG 25 146 of honey ⲁⲩϣⲧⲉⲙϯ ⲛⲁϥ it cannot be robbed of its sweetness; P 54 115 = BMOr 8775 117 ⲡⲓϭⲟⲩⲣ مشاق (confusion ?? with στιππύον preceding word in Is 1 31).

ϭⲱⲣ   *v* ⲕⲱⲣ.

ϭⲁⲓⲣⲓ *B*   *v* ϭⲣⲱ.

ϭⲉⲣⲟ *B*   *v* ϫⲉⲣⲟ.

ϭⲉⲣⲁ *B*   *v* p 755 *b*.

ϭⲓⲣⲁ ϭⲓⲣⲉ-, ϭⲓⲣⲟ- *A²*, ϭⲓⲣⲁ ϭⲓⲣⲓ- *S*, ⳟⲉⲣⲟ ⳟⲉⲣⲱ- *S*ᵃ vb, be like, resemble (?): ManiK 153 ⲡⲓⲉⲣⲟ ... ⲉϭⲓⲣⲁϥ ϭⲓⲣⲟ ⲧⲛⲁϭ ⲛⲑⲁⲗⲁⲥⲥⲁ, *ib* 151 ⲡⲓϫⲁⲓ ⲥⲛⲉϥ ... ϭⲓⲣⲁⲩ ϭⲓⲣⲟ ⲛⲃⲉⲗ ⲥⲛⲉⲩ, *ib* 172 ⲡⲉⲧⲛⲁⲣ ϫⲁⲓⲥ ... ϭⲓⲣⲁϥ ϭⲓⲣⲉ ⲡⲱⲙⲟⲫⲟⲣⲟⲥ, Pap *penes* Maggs Bros 1937 *S*]ⲡⲣⲁⲅⲙⲁⲧⲓⲁ ⲙⲡⲡⲉⲡⲉⲣⲛⲟⲩ[ ] ϭⲓⲣⲟⲛ ϭⲓⲣⲓ ⲛⲉⲡⲉⲣⲛⲟⲩ ϩⲓⲧⲉⲡⲣⲁⲅⲙⲁⲧⲓⲁ, Ep 280 *S*ᵃ ⳟⲉⲣⲟⲓ ⳟⲉⲣⲱ ⲡⲣⲱⲙⲉ ⲛⲧ[, (CO 314 12 *S*ᵃ prob not same). *V* AZ 72 141, Till *Schutzbriefe* 121.

ϭⲱⲣⲉ A² vb intr c ⲁⲃⲁⲗ, meaning unknown : ManiK 152 river's flood ⲁϥϩⲱϧⲧ ⲁϥϩⲣⲃ̄ⲣ ⲁϥϭ. ⲁⲃ. ϩⲁⲧⲛⲁϭ ⲡⲉⲙⲡⲣⲉ (prob not = ϫⲱⲣⲉ ⲉⲃ. S).

ϭⲣⲁ v ⲧⲣⲁ, adding ManiK 168 A² ⲧⲃ̄ⲛⲁⲩⲉ ⲛϥ̄-ⲧⲟⲩϭ. quadrupeds.

ϭⲣⲉ S nn, meaning uncertain, (1) *cattle, sheep* or *stags* (Ar *buffaloes*), or (2) *birds* (so Spg) : 3 Kg 4 23 (P 44 110 = 43 105) ϩⲛϭ. ⲉⲩⲥⲱⲧⲡ (l ⲥⲟ.) ⲛⲣⲉϥⲙⲓⲥⲉ جواميس. *Leg* ? ⲉϩⲉ.

ϭⲣⲉ, ϭⲣⲏ B nn f, *ladle* : K 129 cook's utensils ⲧϭ., P 55 12 among wooden tools, K 150 (var ϭⲣⲏ, ϭⲗⲉ) آلة. *Cf* 3 Kg 7 40 S(P 44 111 = 43 107) ⲑ(ⲉ)ⲣⲙⲁⲥⲧⲣⲓⲟⲛ ⲉⲧⲉⲡⲉⲭⲣⲓⲛⲛⲉ (l ? ⲭⲣⲓⲛⲉ).

ϭⲣⲏ SB, ϭⲣⲓ A vb intr, *dig* (*cf* כרה Dévaud) : Lu 16 3 SB, Glos 381 S ⲡⲉⲧϭ. σκάπτειν, Ps 79 16 S(B tr) ἀνασκ.; Hos 10 11 A Syro-Hexap *dig* (or ? l ϭⲣⲟ ἐνισχύειν as B); ShViK 9315 179 S ⲁϥϭ. ⲁϥϭⲱϧⲉ, ShA 2 240 Sϭ. ϩⲙⲡⲕⲁϩ, ib 101 S one with itch ⲧⲉϥ-ⲉⲛⲉⲣⲅⲓⲁ ⲉⲧϭ. ϩⲛⲟⲩϩⲱⲣ, ShIF 267 S ⲥⲟⲧⲃⲉϥ ⲛϣⲓⲕⲉ ⲁⲩⲱ ⲛϭ.; tr : Is 5 6 SB σκ., Ps 7 15 SB ἀνασκ., Jer 28 58 B κατασκ.; ShA 1 388 S ϩⲓⲉⲓⲧ...ϭ. ⲙⲙⲟϥ ⲛⲥⲉϣⲁⲕⲧϥ̄, Ann 19 232 Sϭ. ⲙⲡⲉⲓⲟⲙ in wine-press, Ryl 72 351 S ⲧⲥⲱϣⲉ...ϭ. ⲙⲙⲟⲥ, C 86 38 B ⲧϩⲱ ⲛⲁ-ⲗⲟⲗⲓ...ϭ. ⲙⲙⲟⲥ, ManiP 208 A² ϭ. ⲙⲡⲟⲩⲕⲁϩ ⲛⲧⲁ-ⲕⲉⲥ; nn m : Tri 521 S ⲣⲃ̈; ShC 42 107 S ⲉⲩ-ⲧⲱⲡⲡⲉ ⲛϩⲱⲥ ⲉⲩⲧⲱⲡ ⲛϭ.?, BM 1115 S ⲉⲣⲉⲛϭⲟⲟⲙ ⲁϣ ϩⲣⲁⲓ ⲉⲡⲉϭ., DeV 2 237 B ⲙⲙⲟⲛ ϭ. ⲙⲙⲟⲛ ⲥⲭⲁⲓ. *Cf* ϭⲣⲓ MIF 67 107 (Jernstedt).

ϭⲣⲟ SAA²B v ϫⲣⲟ.

ϭⲣⲟ B v ϭⲗⲟ 2°.

ϭⲣⲱ B nn f, *dew, fine rain* : AZ 14 118 Scala (not found) ⲧϭ. جل; ib ϭⲁⲓⲣⲓ do.

ϭⲉⲣⲱⲃ SAA²F(Is 36), -ϥ S, ϭⲁⲣⲱⲙ S/F, ϭⲁ-ⲣⲱⲛ B(once), ϫⲁⲣⲱⲃ F(once), pl ϭⲉⲣⲟⲟⲃ SA², -ⲱⲃ S & sg as pl, nn m, *staff, rod* (B ϣⲃⲱⲧ) : Ex 4 2 A, Job 9 34, Lam 3 1 F ϫ., Mic 5 1 SA, He 1 8 SF, Ap 11 1 F(Lacau) ῥάβδος; 1 Kg 17 40, Pro 13 24 SA βακ-τηρία; ib 25 18 SA ῥόπαλον; ShA 1 464 send them ⲛ-ⲥⲉⲟⲩⲱⲙ ϩⲁⲛϭ., Sh(?)Mor 54 98 S/ ⲕⲱⲕ ⲛⲛⲉϥ. ⲉⲃⲟⲗ (Ge 30 37), Z 267 Pulcheria ⲡⲉⲥϭⲉⲣⲱϥ ϩⲓϫⲛⲡⲁϣⲱⲙⲉ ⲙ̄ⲡⲣⲣⲟ her authority (?) above queen's, OraChrPeriod 3 82 ⲡⲉϥⲛⲟϭ ⲛϭⲉⲣⲱϥ, J 66 21 ⲉⲓⲙⲟⲟϣⲉ ϩⲓϫⲛⲡⲁϭⲉ-ⲣⲟⲃ (var ib 76 15 ⲡⲁϭⲉⲣⲟⲟⲃ), C 86 224 B ⲕⲟⲩϫⲓ ⲛϭⲁ-ⲣⲱⲛ = ib 288 ϣ., Mor 53 7 S/; pl : Nu 17 7 (var sg) ῥ., Ac 16 22 (do) ῥαβδίζειν; Mt 26 47 (var -ⲟⲟϥ), Mk 14 48 S(var -ⲱⲱⲃ)F(B ϣⲉ) ξύλον; Ex 12 11 βακ.; ShBM 210 to συναγωγή ⲉⲣⲉϣⲟⲩϣⲟⲩ ⲙⲙⲟ ϩⲛϩⲉⲛϭ. ⲙ̄ⲡⲛϣⲱ ⲡⲧⲟⲩⲁⲡⲉ *locks, curls* (?), TT 135 bade bring ϩⲉⲛϭ. & beat lad = MG 17 430 جرد, RNC 87 smite

them ⲛϩⲉⲛϭ., Mor 28 78 sim ϭⲉⲣⲱⲱⲃ, AP 22 A² ⲛⲉϥ-ϭ.; various kinds : Is 36 6 SF ⲛⲕⲁϣ καλάμινος; Ge 30 37 ϭ. ⲛϣⲉ ⲛⲥⲧⲩⲣⲁϩ στυράκινος; Jer 1 11 ⲛϣⲉ ⲛⲕⲁⲣⲉⲓⲁ (cf Tri 662) καρύινος; CO 338 ⲛϫⲟⲓⲧ; Est 4 11 ⲛⲛⲟⲩⲃ χρυσοῦς; Ps 2 9, Ap 12 5 ⲙⲡⲉⲛⲓⲡⲉ σιδη-ροῦς; LMär 34 idol with ϭⲉⲣⲱϥ ⲙⲛ. in hand; ✝ ϭ., *smite with rod* : ShBM 200 177 ⲛⲡⲉⲣⲱⲙⲉ ✝ ⲉⲣⲱⲙⲉ ...ϩⲛⲟⲩϭ., Mor 55 73 ✝ ⲛⲁϥ (sc snake) ⲡⲟⲩϭ. ⲡⲟⲩⲱⲧ ⲉⲧⲉϥϣⲁⲡⲉ; ϣⲥ ⲛϭ., *blow of rod* : ShA 1 44 ⲟⲩⲧⲣⲟⲡ ⲛ ⲟⲩϣ., ShP 130¹ 139 ⲙⲗⲁⲃ ⲛϣ. for thievish nun (cf Leipoldt *Schen.* 142).

ϭⲱⲣⲃ S v ⲕⲱⲣϥ.

ϭⲱⲣⲙ S/F v ϭⲉⲣⲱⲃ.

ϭⲱⲣⲙ S vb tr, *seize* or sim : ShMIF 23 195 ⲁⲩϭ. ⲙ̄ⲡⲉⲛⲧⲁⲥⲧⲁⲁϥ ... ⲏ ⲁⲩϭⲓⲧϥ ⲛⲧⲟⲟⲧⲉ · ⲛⲓⲧⲱⲣⲡ ϩⲟⲟⲩ ⲉⲧⲱⲣⲡ ⲛⲓⲙ, so ? = ⲧⲱⲣⲡ.

ϭⲱⲣⲉⲙ B v ϫⲱⲣⲙ.

ϭⲣⲓⲙ S nn, meaning doubtful, *bit, fragment* ? : ViK 9345 16 = P 130² 26 ⲡⲙⲟⲟⲩ ⲉϥ✝ ⲉϩⲟⲩⲛ ⲉϩⲣⲏⲓ ϣⲱⲙⲉ ⲉⲩⲟⲩⲱϣⲡ ⲉϩⲣⲁⲓ ϭ. ϭ. *bit by bit*.

ϭⲣⲟⲟⲙⲡⲉ, ϭⲉⲣⲟⲙ. S, ϭⲣⲁⲙ. AA²F(?), ϭⲣⲁⲁ. A, ϭⲣⲟⲙⲡⲓ B, ϭⲉⲣⲁⲙⲡⲉ, ϫⲣⲁⲙⲡⲓ F(constr v below) nn m f, *dove* (same ? as *columba*, Mus 44 120 n, *Bull SocLing* 39 181, but v Spg 292, Berl *Wörterb* 5 181) : Ge 8 8 SB, Ps 54 6 SBF(Pcod Mor 58) ϭⲉⲣ., Cant 2 10 S(ShC 42 52)A(TillOster 24) ϭⲣⲁⲁ. F ϫ., Zeph 3 1 AB, Jo 2 14 SA²B περιστερά; PS 129 S descended ⲛⲑⲉ ⲛⲟⲩϭ., Sh(Besa)Z 513 Sϭ. ⲉϥⲟⲩⲱⲧ ⲛ ⲉϥⲙⲟⲗϩ for sick, PMich 3552 S among victuals ⲟⲩⲁⲥⲕⲛ⸗ (ἀγ-γεῖον)ⲛϭⲉⲣⲟⲙⲡⲉ (cf Preisigke *W.buch* s v περιστερίον), KroppH 113 S ⲛϭⲟϥ ⲛϭ., PMéd 196 S ⲕⲟⲡⲣⲟⲥ ⲛϭⲉⲣ., Mor 51 35 S ⲡⲥⲁⲙⲛⲧ ⲛϩⲣⲟ ⲛϭ. (v p 339 b, cf ManiP 161), ManiH 12 A² slew ⲛⲛϭ., MG 25 12 B ϩⲁⲛϭ. ⲉⲩ-ϩⲏⲗ; ⲙⲁⲥ ⲛϭ. : Lev 5 7 SB, Lu 2 24 SBF ϭⲣⲁⲙ[(BM 502) νοσσὸς περ.; ⲙⲁⲛⲉϭ. S : Baouit 130. ⲥⲓⲙ ⲛϭ. v ⲥⲓⲙ c. ⲕⲁϩ ⲛⲧⲣⲁⲙⲡⲉ J 3 21 prob = κράμβη.

ϭⲣⲙⲡϣⲁⲛ S, ϭⲉⲣⲉⲡ. S/, ϭⲣⲟⲙⲡϣⲁⲗ. ϭⲣⲉⲙⲡ. B, ϭⲣⲉⲙⲡ. F(?) nn f, *turtledove* : Lev 1 c S(varr ϭⲉⲣⲙ-, ϭⲏⲣⲙ-)B, Cant 2 12 S ⲛⲉϭ. (cit Wess 18 44 S/ ⲧϭ.), Jer 8 7 S(P 44 113), ib 32 30 B ϭⲣⲉⲙⲡ-, Lu 1 c SBF ϭⲣⲉⲙ[, Va 57 12 B ⲧϭ. τρυγών; Tri 342 S ⲧⲉϭ. آلة. R 2 2 28 S ⲧⲉϭⲣⲏⲙⲡ-, Sh(?)Mor 54 107 S/ ⲟⲩϭ., ib 22 129 S ϭⲣⲙⲡϣⲏⲛ = BSM 119 B.

ϭⲣⲁⲙⲡⲉⲧ A², *white dove* (v ϩⲁⲧ c) : ManiP 167 ⲧϭ. ⲧⲁⲛⲓⲧⲛϩ ⲉⲧⲟⲩⲁⲃϣ, ib 156 sim.

ϭⲣⲟ(ⲟ)ⲙⲡⲉ, ⲧⲣⲟⲙⲡⲉ S, ⲕⲣⲁⲙⲡⲉ S^a nn m, *vessel in form of dove*(?) : Ryl 238 among church furniture ⲕⲟⲩⲓ ⲛϭ. ⲛϩⲁⲣⲱⲧ (v FXKraus *Realencycl.* 2 821, as lamp Strzygowski *Kopt. Kunst* 291, JEA 21 pl xxi),

Hall 86 ⲟⲩϣⲁⲁⲣ ⲛϭ. ⲡⲣⲟⲙⲧ (meaning?); measure: TurM 22 ⲛⲧ. ⲛ ... ⲥⲟ̄ⲟ̄, JSch 10 15 will pay ⲟⲩϭ. ⲡⲛⲟⲩϩ ⲉⲡⲣⲟⲗⲟⲕ/ as instalment of debt, CO 202 Sᵃ ϯ𝕩ⲣⲉⲓⲱ[ⲥⲧⲉ ⲡⲁⲕ ⲛ- ? ⲙ]ⲡⲟⲩⲕ. ⲡⲛ[?]ϣⲟⲙⲛⲧ ⲛⲣⲧⲟⲃ.

As name ϭⲣⲟⲙⲡⲉ (CO 337), ⲅⲣⲁⲙⲡⲉ (OstrUniv CollLond), ⲧⲉϭ. (Ryl 232), ⲧⲉϭⲣⲟⲟ. (BodlP b 3), ⲧⲉϭⲣⲁ. (BP 9543), ϭⲉⲣⲟⲡ ? (BM 1120), Τεκράμπε, Τεκρομπία (Preisigke, cf Περιστερά).

ϭⲁⲣⲱⲡ *B v* ϭⲉⲣⲱϩ.

ϭⲱⲣⲡ *B v* ϭⲱⲗⲡ 1° & ϭⲱⲣϥ.

ϭⲣⲟⲡ *B v* 𝕩ⲱⲣⲡ (𝕩ⲣⲟⲡ).

ϭⲣⲱⲡ *B nn m, oven*: K 153 ⲡⲓϭ. مدخن, Rec 6 184 bread hot from ⲡⲓϭ. = BMar 218 *S* ⲧⲣⲓⲣ, MG 25 222 ⲡⲓϭ. ⲛⲧⲉ ⲡⲓⲁⲙⲣⲉ, C 41 21 ⲕⲉⲣⲙⲓ...ⲉⲃⲟⲗ ϩⲉⲛⲡⲓ̄ ⲛϭ. = Miss 4 637 *S* ⲧ. = *ib* 352 تنور. *Cf* 𝕩ⲗⲱⲙ & ? χλουβοκεραμεύς (POxy 1913 21), κλουβός (*ib* 1923 14), also place-name ⲕⲁⲣⲡⲉ (Kr 13 *F*) prob = Καμίνων (*ib* 146).

ϭⲣⲏⲡⲉ *SAA², -*ⲡⲓ *SʲBF nn f, a diadem*: Est 8 15 *S*, Sa 18 24 *S*, Ap 12 3 *S*(*B* 𝕩ⲗⲟⲙ) διάδημα; 2 Kg 1 10 *S* βασίλειον; P 44 59 *S* ⲥⲧⲉⲫⲁⲛⲟⲥˑ ⲧⲉϭ. ⲅⲣⲁⲃⲓⲟⲛ (βρα.) ﺍ, Tri 583 *S* ⲕⲗⲟⲙ, ϭ. 'ﺝ, اكليل; Br 234 *S* ⲟⲩϭ. ϩⲓ𝕩ⲱⲟⲩ, P 132¹ *S* ⲧⲉϥϭ. ⲛⲣⲣⲟ adorned with jewels, *ib* 6 jewels ⲉⲡⲉϥⲕⲗⲟⲙ ⲙⲛⲧⲉϥϭ., BMar 234 *S* ⲕⲱ ϩⲓ𝕩ⲱϥ ⲡⲟⲩⲕⲗⲟⲙ ⲙⲡⲟⲩϭⲣⲏⲛⲡⲉ, OratCyp 21 *Sʲ* ⲕⲗⲟⲙ, ϭ., ManiP 213 *A²* ⲙⲁⲣ ⲟⲩϭ. ⲁ𝕩ⲏⲧⲟⲅⲁⲡⲉ, *ib* 136 *A²* ⲧϭ. ⲉⲧⲉⲙⲁⲥⲡⲟⲩϩⲉ, ROC 23 276 *B* ⲟⲩ𝕩ⲗⲟⲙ ⲙⲙⲁⲣⲅⲁⲣⲓⲧⲏⲥ ⲥⲁⲡϣⲱⲓ ⲛϯϭ., C 86 264 *B* ⲟⲩϭ. ⲛⲡⲟⲩⲃ ⲉⲣⲉϩ̄ ⲡ𝕩ⲗⲟⲙ ϩⲓ𝕩ⲱⲥ, Miss 4 168 *B* ⲛⲧⲉⲕⲉⲣ ⲫⲟⲣⲓⲛ ⲛⲟⲩϭ., BMEA 10578 *F* ⲧⲉϭ[ⲣⲏ]ⲡⲓ ⲉⲧⲟ𝕩ⲉ[ⲛ]ⲧⲉϥⲁⲡⲏ, Mor 24 13 *F* sim. *b sceptre*: Sa 7 8 *S*, *ib* 10 14 *S*, Cl 16 2 *A* σκῆπτρον; K 119 *B* ϯϭ. عصا, 'ﺝ الذهب; Ryl 94 (33 1) *S* ⲟⲩⲕⲗⲟⲙ ϩⲛⲧϭⲓ𝕩 ⲙⲡⲉϥⲭ̄ⲥ̄, ⲟⲩϭ. ⲛⲣⲣⲟ ϩⲛⲧϭⲓ𝕩 ⲙⲡⲉϥⲛⲉ̄, BMis 208 *S* ⲡⲉⲥϯⲟⲥ... ⲉⲩⲕⲱ ⲙⲙⲟϥ ⲛϭ. ⲛⲁⲩ (*sc* kings) ⲁⲩⲱ ... ϩⲓ𝕩ⲉⲡⲉⲩ ϩⲣⲁⲃⲧⲟⲥ ϩⲛⲡⲉⲩϭⲓ𝕩.

ⲣ ϭ. *A²*, *form, be crown*: ManiP 54 ⲁⲩⲣ ⲟⲩϭ. ⲁ𝕩ⲱ. 𝕩ⲓ ϭ. *A²*, *be crowned*: ManiH 42 new king ⲁϥ𝕩. ⲁⲡⲉϥⲙⲁ; 𝕩ⲁⲓϭ., *crown-bearing*: *ib* P 136 ⲛ𝕩. ⲉⲧⲉⲙⲁϩⲧⲉ.

ϭⲣⲉⲡⲣⲉⲡ *B nn as pl, meaning uncertain*: P 54 117 = BMOr 8775 118 ϩⲁⲛϭ. خروب (*l* ? خروب *carob*).

ϭⲉⲣⲏⲧ *S nn as pl, meaning unknown*: BAp 153 ⲧⲉⲃϣⲉ, ⲧⲙⲁⲁⲩ ⲛⲛϭ. ⲧⲏⲣⲟⲩ (or *l* ? ϭⲉ = ⲕⲉ-).

ϭⲁⲣⲁⲧⲉ *S nn, carob pod* = κεράτιον: Lu 15 16 (*B* 𝕩ⲓⲛⲓⲣⲓ) ⲕⲉⲣ., P 44 66 𝖟ⲩⲗⲟⲕⲉⲣⲁⲧⲁˑ ϭ. خرنوب. *Cf* 𝕩ⲓⲉⲓⲣⲉ.

ϭⲟⲣⲧⲉ, ⲕ. *S*, ϭⲁⲣⲧⲉ *SF*, ⲕⲁⲣⲧⲉ *Sᵃ*, ϭⲁⲣϯ *SʲF*, 𝕩ⲟⲣϯ *B*(once), ϭⲁⲗϯ *F nn f, knife, sword*: Ge 22 6 (*B* ⲥⲏϥⲓ), Jud 3 16, Z 299 for cutting fish, BM 174 ⲧϭ. ⲡⲁⲙⲁⲥⲉⲓⲣⲟⲥ μάχαιρα; Mor 18 53 draw ⲧϭ. from ⲕⲟⲉⲓϩ, BMis 239 score his body with ϩⲉⲛϭ. ⲉⲩ𝕩ⲏⲣ, Mor 30 13 *F* sim ϭⲁⲗ., Mor 32 50 *Sʲ* fell him ⲡⲟⲩϭⲥⲉ (*v* p 375 *a*) ⲛϭ., Ryl 94 107 ⲧϭⲁ. for Isaac, PasH 179 *B* sim ϯ𝕩., BM 525 *F* ⲥⲏⲃⲉ, ⲗⲱⲡ𝕩ⲏ (ⲗⲟⲩ.), ϭⲁⲣⲧⲉ, CMSS 76 *F* -ⲧⲓ ⲡⲉⲡⲓⲡ[ⲓ, RE 14 28 *Sᵃ*; ⲁⲧϭ. *S, without knife*: BKU 1 1 ⲩⲟ ϣⲁⲧϥ ⲡⲁⲧϭ., *ib* ⲡⲁⲧϭⲁ., PMich 602(3) 𝕩ⲓ ⲡⲁⲕ ⲡⲟⲩϭⲱⲃⲉ ⲙⲙⲟⲗⲟ𝕩ⲉ (-χη) ⲡⲁⲧⲕ. *not cut.* For ⲁ𝕩ⲟⲗϯ *B* C 89 181 *l* ? 𝕩ⲟⲣϯ.

ϭⲁⲣⲁⲧⲏⲓⲏ *v* ϭⲁⲣϭⲁⲧⲁⲡⲉ.

ϭⲱⲣϣ *v* ⲕⲱⲣϣ.

(ϭⲱⲣϥ) *S*, -ⲣⲡ *B*, ϭⲟⲣϥϩ, ⲕ. *S vb tr, nip off*: Lev 5 8 *B*(*S* ϭⲱⲡϭⲛ), Ez 17 4 *S*(P 44 115, var 43 115 ⲕ., wrongly *s v* ⲕⲱⲣϥ, *B* ⲱⲗⲓ) ἀποκνίζειν.

ϭⲱⲣϩ *SA²F*, ⲕ., ϭⲱⲣⲁϩ *S*, 𝕩ⲱⲣϩ *BO*, ⲉ𝕩. *B*, *nn m, night*: Ge 19 33 *B*(*S* ⲟⲩϣⲏ), Jer 29 9 *B*(*S* ⲇⲟ) νύξ; PS 145 *S* ⲡⲉ𝕩ⲁⲟⲥ ⲉⲧⲉⲡⲧⲟ𝕩ⲡⲉ (ⲡ)ϭ. (cf 146 sim ⲡⲧⲟ𝕩ⲡⲉ ⲧⲉⲩϣⲏ), Mich 550 33 *S* ⲉⲓⲧⲉ ϭ. ⲉⲓⲧⲉ ⲙⲉⲉⲣⲉ, Mor 30 27 *F* sim, PMéd 196 *S* ⲕⲁⲁⲩ ⲡ(ⲛⲙⲉ)ⲣⲁ ⲁ̄ ⲙⲡⲟⲩϭⲱⲣⲁϩ, Cat 197 *B* ⲡ𝕩...., ⲡⲓⲉ𝕩...., ⲟⲩⲉ𝕩.; as adj: Job 4 13 *S*(*B* ⲛⲧⲉ ⲡⲓⲉ𝕩.), Ps 90 5 *S*(*B* ⲇⲟ) νυκτερινός; PGM 1 60 670 *O* ⲁⲡⲕⲡⲉ ⲡⲡ[ⲛ]ϥ ⲡ𝕩.; ⲡϭ., ⲡ𝕩. adverbial: Deu 16 1 *B*(var ⲙⲡⲓⲉ𝕩., *S* diff), Is 34 9 *B*(*SF* ⲡⲧⲉⲩϣⲏ), 1 Thes 2 9 *S*(*B* ⲧⲉⲩ.) νυκτός, Lu 21 37 *S*(but var ϩⲛⲛϭ., *B* ⲡⲓⲉ𝕩.) νύκτας, Z 296 *S* ⲣ ϩⲱⲃ ⲛϭ. νύκτα, Pro 29 33 *S*(*A* diff) ἐκ νυκτῶν, Va 61 24 *B* διὰ τῆς ν.; AJSL 46 246 *S* ⲡⲉⲧⲉⲣ ϩⲟⲧⲉ ⲡⲕ., ManiP 223 *A²* ⲣ ⲯⲁⲗⲉ ⲛϭ., Miss 4 196 *B* ⲁϥϩⲟⲗⲧ ⲡ𝕩. ⲉⲣ ⲉ𝕩.: Va 66 290 *B* ⲟⲓ ⲡⲉ𝕩. ⲡϣⲣⲱⲓⲥ ἀγρυπνεῖν.

ϭⲣⲱϩ *SF*, ⲕ., ϭⲣⲱⲱϩ, ⲕⲣⲟϩ *S*(ⲛⲛ), ϭⲣⲟϩ, 𝕩ⲟⲣϩ† *B*, 𝕩ⲁⲣϩ† *F vb intr, be in want, needy, diminished* (*S* rare): 1 Cor 8 8 (*SF* ϣⲱⲱⲧ) ὑστερεῖν; Pro 13 11 (*S* ⲣ ϭ., *A* ⲣ ϣⲧⲁ) ἐλάσσων γίνεσθαι; Is 8 22 (*S* ⲕⲁ ⲧⲟⲟⲧϥ̇ ⲉⲃⲟⲗ) ἀπορεῖσθαι; Va 61 213 ⲡⲏⲓⲏ...ⲥⲡⲁϭ. ⲁⲡ ⲟⲩⲇⲉ ⲥⲡⲁⲟⲩⲛⲕ ⲁⲡ; *c e*-: Nu 9 7 (*S* ⲣ ϩⲁⲉ) ⲩⲟ. inf; 2 Cor 12 13 (*SF* ϣ.) ἡττᾶσθαι; *c ⲡ*-: *ib* 11 (*SF* ⲇⲟ) ⲩⲟ.; Tit 3 13 (var ϭⲉⲡ-, *S* ⲇⲟ) λείπειν; Mor 33 84 *S* poor ⲥⲉϭ. ⲡⲁⲅⲁⲑⲟⲛ ⲡⲓⲙ; *c ϭⲉⲡ*-: Ez 4 17 (*S* ⲣ ϭ.) ἐνδεὴς γίν.; *c ⲉⲃⲟⲗ ϩⲁ*-: Ps 77 30 (*S* ⲣ ϭ. ϩⲓ-) στερεῖσθαι ἀπό; qual: Dan 5 27, ZNTW 24 90 *F* ⲩⲟ.; Va 57 121 ⲟⲩⲧⲟⲓ ⲉⲥ𝕩. κολοβός; *c ⲡ*-: Ja 1 5 (*S* ϣ.) λ. gen; Va 57 163 ⲉⲩ𝕩. ⲡⲉⲗⲓ ⲡⲁⲓⲁⲫⲟⲣⲁ ⲁⲡ ⲟⲩⲇⲉⲛ διαφέρεσθαι; tr *S*(*l* ? ⲣ ϭ.): Si 31 21 (var ⲣ ϭ.) ἐπιδεῖσθαι gen; ViK 4727 ⲙⲡⲣϭ. ⲉⲙⲟⲕ ⲉⲗⲁⲁⲩ.

—— *nn m SBF, want, need*: Ps 33 9 *S*(*B* ⲉⲣ ϩⲁⲉ), 1 Cor 16 17 *B*(*SF* ϣ.), 2 Cor 9 12 *SB*(var ⲭⲣⲓⲁ) ὑστέρημα; Pro 6 11 (*A* ϣⲟⲩⲟ̣ⲩϭⲉ, *B* ⲙⲉⲧⲣⲉϥⲉⲣ ϭ.), Ez

4 16 *SB* ἔνδεια; Ro 11 12 *B*(*S* ϣ.) ἥττημα; MG 25
220 *B* ἐλάττωμα; Hag 2 17 *S*(*A* ϣⲟⲩⲧ, *B* ⲙⲉⲧⲁⲧⲟⲩ-
ⲧⲁϩ) ἀφορία; ShBor 246 53 *S* ⲡⲣⲏⲕⲉ...ⲡⲉϥϭ., BMis
371 *S* ⲱⲡⲣ ⲣⲟⲩϭⲣⲱⲱϭ, ViK 9527 *S* do, C 99 137 *S*
ⲡⲉϭ. = C 89 41 *B* ⲙⲉⲧⲣⲏⲕⲓ, *ib* 162 *B* ⲡⲭ. ⲛⲡⲉⲡⲯⲩ-
ⲭⲏ, COAd 54 *S* when I settle thy account ⲛⲧⲁⲃⲓ
ⲡⲕⲟⲩⲅⲣⲟϭ, ST 385 *S* ⲕⲣⲱϭ (context lost), AM 257
B ⲛϩⲟⲩⲟ ⲛⲡⲏ, ⲛϭ. ⲛⲡⲁⲓ;   c ⲛ- *S, want of*: Am 4
6 (*B* ⲙⲉⲧⲣⲉϥⲉⲣ ϭ.) ⲉⲛⲇ.; Deu 28 48 (*B* do) ἔκλειψις;
ShP 130⁵ 33 ⲡⲉϭ. ⲛⲣⲡⲗⲁⲁϥ ⲛⲓⲙ.

ⲁⲧϭ. *B, without needs*: TEuch 1 466 ⲙⲉⲑⲛⲟⲩϯ
ⲛⲁ., Bess 14 340 grant us ⲟⲩⲱⲛϩ ⲛⲁ. (*Cf* ἀνέκλει-
ⲡⲧⲟⲥ, ἀνυστέρητος).

ⲣ ϭ. *S, be in want*: Pro 27 7 (*A* ϣⲁⲁⲧ) ἐνδεῖν, Si 4 3
ⲡⲣⲟⲥⲇ., Deu 24 14 (*B* ⲉⲣ ϭ.) ἐνδεής; Si 13 5 ὑστερεῖν,
1 Jo 3 17 (var ϣ., *B* ⲉⲣ ⲭⲣⲓⲁ) χρείαν ἔχειν; ShBor
281 102 ⲉϥⲣ. ϩⲛⲟⲩⲙⲛⲧⲣⲏⲕⲉ;   c ⲛ-: Job 30 4 (*B*
ⲉⲣ ϭ.), Pro 9 13 (*AB* ϣ.) ἐνδεής; Si 11 13 ὑσ.; Pro 29
29 (*A* do) ἀπορεῖσθαι; 2 Kg 3 29 ἐλασσοῦσθαι; Si 31 21
(var ϭ.) ἐπιδ.; ShLMis 414 ⲣ ϭⲣⲱⲱϭ ⲙⲡⲟⲉⲓⲕ, ShA
2 30 ⲉⲧⲟ ⲛϭ. ⲛⲡⲉⲣϩⲏⲅⲉ ⲛⲧⲙⲛⲧⲉⲩⲥⲉⲃⲏⲥ;   c ⲟⲛ-:
Si 37 26 καθ ὑσ. gen; Ps 77 30 *v* intr;   as nn m:
Deu 15 8 (*B* ⲉⲣ ϭ.) ἐνδεῖσθαι.

ϭⲣⲏϭⲓ *B* nn m, *rawness, raw* (*fruit*): BMOr 8775
125, K 347, Montp 113 ⲡⲓϭ. اجلاف.

ϭⲣⲉϭⲧ, ϭⲣⲉϭⲧ   *v* ϭϭⲣⲁϭⲧ nn.

ϭⲟⲣϫ, -ϫⲉ (rare) *S* nn m, ϫⲣϫⲓ *B* f, *filth*: 1 Pet
3 21 *S*(*B* ⲑⲱⲗⲉⲃ) ῥύπος; P 44 68 *S* ⲕⲉⲯⲉⲗⲏ (ⲕⲩ.)·
ⲛϭ. ⲙⲡⲙⲁⲁϫⲉ; Va 68 169 *B* ⲡⲓϫ....ⲛⲧⲉ ⲡⲓⲭⲱ αἰσχύνη; BMis 360 *S* filthy raiment & ⲡⲉⲓϭⲱⲣϫⲉ ⲛⲧⲉⲡ-
ⲥⲱⲙⲁ (but var *ib* ⲕⲟⲩⲅⲃ̄=ϭⲱϫⲃ, BSM 22 diff) P
131¹ 51 *S* wash away ⲛϭ. ⲙⲡⲥⲱⲙⲁ, DeV 1 135 *B*
sim, BM 265 *S* ⲟⲩⲉⲓⲱ ⲉⲃⲟⲗ (ⲛ)ⲡϭⲟⲣϫⲉ ⲛⲧⲉ ⲧⲥⲁⲣⲝ,
MG 25 126 *B* stone rolled over corn ϣⲁϥⲕⲱⲕ ⲡⲧⲉϥϫ.
ⲧⲏⲣⲥ (husks &c) ⲉⲃⲟⲗ;   a disease *B*: Deu 28 27
(*S* = Gk) ψώρα ἀγρία اجلب (*cf* ⲉⲣ ϫ.);   ⲙⲉⲧϫ. *B*: Va
57 165 maladies of soul ⲡⲉⲥⲙ. ἀηδία;   ⲣ ϭ., ⲉⲣ
ϫ.: Lev 22 22 *B*(*S* do) ψωραγριᾶν منتشر الشعر; Mor
18 116 *S* ⲡⲉϥⲥⲱⲙⲁ ⲟ ⲛϭ. ῥυποῦν; MG 25 155 *B* sick
sheep ⲉϥⲉⲣ ϫ...., ⲕⲱⲕ ⲛⲓϫ.

ϭⲣⲏϫⲓ *B*   *v* ϭⲣⲏϭⲉ.

ϭⲉⲣⲏϭ *S*, ϫⲉⲣⲏϫ *B*, ϭⲣⲏϭ *F*   *v* ϭⲱⲣϭ 1° s f.

ϭⲱⲣϭ *SAA²*, ϫⲱⲣϫ *BF*(nn), ϫⲉⲣϫ- *B*, ϭⲁⲣϭ⸗
A², ϫⲟⲣϫ⸗ *BF*(ϫⲱⲣϫ⸗), ϭⲟⲣϭ†*S*, ϭⲁ.† *AA²*, ϫⲟⲣϫ†*B*,
ϭⲁⲣⲉϫ† *F* vb intr, *waylay, hunt*: Ps 9 30 *B*(*S*†), Lam
3 10 *SB* ἐνεδρεύειν; ShA 1 278 *S* ϩⲛⲁⲁⲩ ⲛϭ., Mun
74 *S* ⲛⲕⲁ ⲛϭ.;   qual: Job 38 40 *S*(*B* ⲭⲱ.) ἐν.;   tr:
Ge 27 3 *S*(Mus 50 20)*B* ϫⲉⲣϫ-, Lam 3 52 *BF* ϫⲱⲣⲓ
θηρεύειν.

With following preposition.

—— e- intr, obj: Pro 26 19 *S*(var ϭⲱⲱⲣϭ)*A*, Lam
4 19 *B*, Lu 11 54 *S*(*B* ϭⲓ ⲭⲣⲟϥ) ἐν.; Ps 58 3 *SB*, B
Hom 3 *S* ⲁⲧϭ. ⲉⲣⲟⲕ ϩⲓⲧⲛⲡⲉⲕⲃⲁⲗ θ.; Pro 5 22 *SAB*
ἀγρεύειν; Jth 12 16 *S* τηρεῖν; PS 91 *S* ⲁⲧϭ. ⲉⲣⲟⲓ
ⲡⲟⲩϭⲟⲗ ⲡⲣⲟ ⲙⲙⲟⲅⲓ, ShWess 9 86 *S* ⲙⲏ ⲡⲉⲑⲏⲣⲓⲟⲛ
ϭ. ⲁⲛ ⲉⲡⲉⲥⲟⲟⲩ ?, Mus 42 224 *S* ⲉϥⲟⲩⲱϣ ⲉϭ. ⲉⲡⲉⲡ-
ⲯⲩⲭⲏ, ManiK 129 *A²* ϭ. ⲁⲡⲉⲥⲧⲃ̄ⲧ, Pcod 18 *S* ϭ.
ⲉⲣⲟϥ ϩⲓⲣⲡⲧⲡⲩⲗⲏ, Va 61 13 *B* ⲉⲧⲁϥϭ. ⲉⲣⲟϥ ⲁϥⲭⲉⲙϥ
ⲉϥⲓⲣⲓ ⲙⲡⲁⲓ;   qual: Mic 7 2 *S*(Hex, *A* ϭⲱ., *B* diff),
Ac 23 21 *S*(*B* ⲭⲱ.) ἐν.; C 89 67 *B* ⲡⲓⲙⲥⲁϩ ⲉⲧϫ. ⲉⲣⲱⲟⲩ
= C 99 233 *S* ϭⲱ. ⲧⲏⲣ., 2 Kg 3 30 *S* διαπαρατ.; Job
10 16 *S*(*B* ⲭⲱ.) ἀγ.; Am 3 5 *S*(*B* do) ἰξευτής; ShA
1 455 *S* ⲡⲉⲧϭ. ⲉⲣⲟϥ, Sh(?)Mor 54 19 *S* ϭ. ⲉⲣⲡⲥⲡⲱ-
ⲱⲃ, ManiP 205 *A²* ⲡⲁϣⲅ ⲉⲧϭ., MG 25 38 *B* snares
ⲉⲧϫ. ⲉϥⲙⲉⲧⲣⲱⲙⲓ, JKP 2 206 *F* ⲉⲣⲉⲡⲉⲑⲏⲣⲓⲱⲛ ϭ.
ⲉⲣⲁ;   tr: Ps 139 12 *B*(*S* vbal) θ. εἰς, 2 Tim 2 26 *B*
(*S* ϭⲏⲡ) ζωγρεῖσθαι; ManiP 53 *A²* snare ⲁϥϭⲁⲣϭⲟⲩ
ⲁⲣⲁϥ;   vbal: Lev 17 13 *S*(*B* diff) θ.; Ps 9 29 *S*†*B*
ἐν.; ShViK 9343 78 *S* ϭϥ.† ϩⲣⲡⲣⲱⲃ ⲡⲓⲙ ⲉⲧⲁⲕⲉ ⲡⲉⲏⲧ
(or next word ?), MG 25 394 *B* ⲉϥϫ. .... ⲉⲱⲗⲓ ⲙⲡⲉϥ-
ⲱⲡϭ.

—— ⲉϫⲉⲛ- *B*: Ps 93 21 (*S* e-) θ. ἐπί.

—— ⲛ- dat: Job 38 39 *SB* θ. dat.; Mt 22 15 *B*(*S*
ϭⲱⲡⲉ) παγιδεύειν ἐν.

—— ⲛⲥⲁ- *B*: Jer 16 16 θ. acc.

—— ϩⲛ-, ϩⲉⲛ-: Job 24 11 *B*(*S* e-) ἐν. ἐν, Si 5 16
S ἐν. dat; Pro 6 25 *SAB* ἀγ. dat; ShP 130⁴ 117 *S*
ⲉϣⲁϥϭ. ϩⲛⲡⲓⲙ ⲏ ⲉϣⲁϥⲣ ⲡⲓⲙ ⲡϭⲟⲣϭⲉ?

—— ϩⲁⲧⲛ-, ϩⲁⲣⲧⲉ-: Pro 7 12† *SA*(*B* ⲉⲥⲕⲉⲛ-) ἐν.
ἐν; *ib* 8 3† *SA*(*B* ⲙⲏⲡ) παρεδ. παρά.

—— nn, snare: Job 25 3 *S*(*B* ⲭⲟⲣϫⲥ), BHom 6 *S*
ⲛϭ. ⲙⲡⲉⲕⲣⲟϥ ἐνεδρα; Lam 3 52 *BF* ϫⲱⲣ(ϫ) θ. vb.

ⲙⲁ ⲛϭ., ⲛϫ.: Ps 9 28 *S*(*B* ⲭⲟⲣϫⲥ) ἔνεδρα; Nah
2 13 *A*(*B* do) θήρα; Va 58 151 *B*.

ⲣⲉϥϭ., -ϫ., *hunter*: Ps 90 3 *B*(*S* ϭⲉⲣⲏϭ) θηρευτής;
Job 19 12 *B*(*S* ⲣⲉϥⲣ ⲕⲣⲟϥ) ἐγκάθετος; Si 14 22 *S* ἰχ-
ⲛⲉⲩⲧής; R 2 2 28 *S* ἰξευτής; K 135 *B* صياد; Va 57 142
B ⲟⲩϭⲟⲣⲓ ⲛⲣ. ⲉⲡⲓⲧⲃ̄ⲧ.

ϭⲓⲛϭ., ϫⲓⲛϫ.: ShMIF 23 25 *S* ϭ. of devil, Cat
206 *B* ⲟⲩϫⲓⲛϫⲟⲣϫⲩ ϩⲉⲛⲟⲩⲥⲁϫⲓ.

ϭⲟⲣϭⲥ *S*, ϭⲁ. *AA²F*, ϫⲟⲣϫⲥ *B* nn f, ϭⲁⲣϭϥ *A*,
ambush, snare: Jos 23 13 *S*(*B* ϥⲁϣ), Job 22 10 *SB*,
Ps 9 16 *B*(*S* ⲡⲁϣ), Pro 6 2 *SA* -ϥ (*B* ⲫ.), Hos 9 8 *B*
(*A* ⲡⲁⲥϭϥ) παγίς; Nu 23 24 *B*(*S* ⲡⲁⲣϭ), Ps 16 12 *BF*
(*S* do), Pro 12 27 *SAB*, Is 31 4 *B*(*SF* ⲓⲓ.), Nah 2 12
B(*A* ⲡⲁϩ̄ϭ) θήρα, Lev 17 13 *B*(*S* diff) θήρευμα; Sa 14
21 *S*, Ob 7 *B*(*SA* ⲕⲣⲟϥ) ἔνεδρον; Lu 5 4 *B*(*S* ϭⲱⲡⲉ)
ἄγρα; Si 13 21 *S* κυνήγιον; PS 100 *S* ⲛϭ. ⲥⲏⲣ ⲉⲃⲟⲗ
ⲙⲡⲓϩⲣⲁϭⲉ, ShC 73 6 *S* ϣⲱⲡⲉ ⲉⲩϭ. ⲙⲛⲟⲩⲡⲁϣ, Lant
111 *S* ⲧⲟⲩϫⲟϥ ⲉⲛϭ. ⲙⲡⲁⲓⲁⲃⲟⲗⲟⲥ, Ryl 277 *S* if art
neglectful ⲛⲕ(? ⲛⲧⲕ)ⲟⲩⲣⲱⲙⲉ ⲛⲣⲉϥⲕⲁⲧⲁⲫⲣⲟⲛⲉⲓ ⲉⲃ-
ϣⲟⲟⲡ ϩⲁⲟⲩϭⲟⲣϭⲥ, ManiP 166 *A²* ⲧϭ. ⲙⲡⲓϭⲉⲣⲏϭ,
Va 61 105 *B* lion ⲛⲁⲭⲓⲙⲓ ⲡⲟⲩϫ. *quarry*;   ⲉⲓⲣⲉ, ⲣ ϭ.

S: LCyp 1 ἐνεδρεύειν; ViK 9658 8 woman ⲣϭ., paral
ⲉⲣ ⲙⲟⲟⲗⲉ; ⲟ ⲛϭ.: Eccl 7 27 θήρευμα.

ϭⲉⲣⲏϭ SAA², ⳃⲉⲣⳃ B, ϭⲣⲏϭ F, pl ϭⲉⲣⲁϭⲉ S,
ϭⲉⲣⲉϭⲉ AA² & sg as pl, nn m, *hunter*: Ps 90 3 S(B
ⲣⲉϥϭ.) Jer 16 16 B θηρευτής; Ge 10 9 S(CorpusCam-
bridge 541)B κυνηγός; Am 8 1 SB ἰξευτής; Hos 9 8
A(B Gk diff); ShC 736 S ⲟⲩⲅⲛⲁⲁⲩ... ϣⲁⲣⲉⲛϭ. ϭⲱⲣϭ
ⲛⲣⲏⲧϥ, Mani 1 A² ⲛϭ. ⲉⲧⲕⲟⲗⲁⲕⲉⲅⲉ ⲁⲅⲑⲏⲣⲓⲟⲛ, Mor
25 18 S ⲡⲉϭ. ϭⲱⲣϭ ⲉⲣⲟϥ = Va 61 100 B, AZ 33 55 F
ⲡⲉϭ. ϭⲟⲡⲉ ⲙⲁϥ;   pl forms: Hos 5 2 A(B ⲛⲏ ⲉⲧⳃ.)
ἀγρεύειν; R 1 3 16 S bade ⲛϭ. ϭⲱⲣϭ ⲉⲣⲟϥ, ViK 9332 S
bird ⲛⲏⲅ ⲉⲛⲛⲥⲓⳃ [ⲛⲛ]ϭ., ManiP 70 A² ⲛϭ. ⲉⲧⲟⲩⲱϣ
ϭⲱⲣϭ ⲁⲣⲁⲕ;   ⲙⲉⲧϭ. B: Ge 25 27 κυνηγεῖν.

In place-name (?): ⲧⲙⲟⲩϭⲉⲣⲏϭⲉ (*Deir el-Gebrawi*
2, pl xxix, 3), ⲧⲙⲟⲩⲛϭⲣⲏϭⲉ (PLond 4 505), Μου-
νκρῆκις (*ib* 5 79).

ϭⲱⲣϭ SA², ⳃⲟⲣⳃ B, ⳃⲁⲣⳃ- F, ϭⲟⲣϭⳅ S, ϭⲁ. A²,
ⳃⲟⲣⳃⳅ B, ϭⲟⲣϭ†, ϭⲟⲗϭ† S, ϭⲁⲣϭ† A², ⳃⲟⲣⳃ† BF, vb
tr, *prepare, provide*: 1 Kg 3 3 S ἐπισκευάζεσθαι; Sh
Mich 550 18 S ⲉⲅⲩⲁⲛⲛⲟⲩ ⲉⲥⲟⲃⲧⲉ ⲛⲛⲣⲏⲃⲉ ⲛⲥⲉϭⲟⲣ
ϭⲟⲩ, ManiH 28 A² table & ⲛⲉⲧϭ. ⲙⲙⲁⲥ, ManiK 140
A² ϣⲁⲥϭⲁⲣϭ (*sc* ϯϯⲡⲉ) ⲡⲥⲧⲉⲉⲥ, Va 57 88 B physician ⲉⲣ ⳃⲣⲁⲥⲟⲉ ⲟⲩⲟⳉ ⲉϥ ⳃ. ⲡⲟⲩⲥⲕⲉⲅⲁⲥⲓⲁ, Leip 26
29 B ⲡⲓⲧⲣⲟ ⲭⲟⲥ ⲉⲧⲁⲩ ⳃⲟⲣ ⳃϥ;   qual: Nu 8 4 B(S
ⲧⲏⲕ) στερεός ⳬⳮ; Ez 23 41 S(B ⲥⲃⲧⲱⲧ) κοσμεῖσθαι;
AP 9 A² ⳃⲉⲡⲧⲣⲁⲡⲉⳎⲁ ⲉⲅⳃ. λαμπρός; Jer 5 27 B ἐφί-
στασθαι; Bor 248 53 S ⲡⲟⲩⲱϣⲙ...ⲉϥϭ. ⲁⲩⲱ ⲉϥⲕⲉ
ⲣⲁ (κεραννύναι) ⲉⲃⲟⲗ ⳉⲙⲡⲉⲟⲁⳃ, Mor 37 146 S ⲡⲏⲣⲡ
ⲉⲧϭ. ⲙⲙⲓⲛⲉ ⲛⲓⲙ, WS 123 S ⲟⲩⳉⲟⲓ ⲉϥϭⲟⲣⲉϥ, Mani
P 205 A² ⲡⲉⲩⲡⲁⲩⳋϥ ⲉⲧϭ., Va 58 66 B priest sent with
chalice ⲉϥϭ., C 86 212 B ⲙⲁⲛⲕⲁⲛⲟⲡ ⲉⲧⳃ. *fitted* (with
knives &c).

With following preposition: Mor 55 39 S ϣⲁⲣⲉⲛ-
ⲥⲁⳉ ϭ. ⲡⲟⲩⲁⲡⲟⲧ ⲛⲁϥ, ROC 23 282 B sim;   DeV
2 149 B ⳃ. ⲛⲛⲓ ⲫⲁⲛⲟⲥ ⲛⲛⲉⲣ, Ryl 240 S ⲛⲁⲛⲁⲗⲏⲛ
(-άριον) ⲛⲃⲁⲗⲱⲧ (ⳃⲁⲣ.) ⲉϥ ϭⲟⲗϭ ⲛⲃⲏ ⲃ[.], Lam 1 13 F
ⲁϥ ⳃⲁⲣⳃ ⲟⲩϣⲏⲛ ⳉⲗⲏⲓ ⲛⲛⲁⳉⲁⲗⲁ ⳃⳃ(B ⲫⲟⲣⳃⳃ)διαπε-
τάζειν dat;   ShC 73 195 S τράπεζα...ϭ.† ⳉⲛⲟⲩ?
ⳬⳮ, Mor 37 165 S feathers ⲉⲅϭ.† ⳉⲛⲧⲧⲁⲣ ⲛⲧⲥⲁⲣ ⳇ;
or advb: ClPr 43 13 ⲧⲉⲧⲣⲁⲡⲉⳎⲁ ⲉⲥϭ.† ⲉⲃⲟⲗ, Ryl 158
S part of rent ⲟⲩ ⳃⲓⲥⲕⲁⲣⲓⲛ ⲉϥϭ.† ⲉⲃ. (*cf* Wess 20 116
δισκάριον μεστόν), ManiP 100 A² ⲛϥⳃⲁⲣⳃⲉ (f) ⲁⲃ.
ⳉⲛⲡⲉⲧⲛⳉ;   as nn: PLond 4 515 S ending list of
implements ⲙⲛ[ⲛⲉⲥ]ϭⲟⲗⲉϭ ⲉⲃ.

—— nn m SF, *preparation, mixed contents*: Eccl
10 1 (ShC 42 47) σκευασία, Ex 31 11 (P 44 104, B
ⲥⲉⲙⲛⲓ), Lev 16 12 (B ⲥⲁⲧⲛⲟⲩⲧ *v* p 366 *b*), Nu 4 16
(B ⲙⲟⲩ ⳃ ⲧ) σύνθεσις; Cant 7 3 F(S diff) κρᾶμα; Mus
40 46 (Reg Pach) ⲛϭ. ⲛⲟⲩⲧⲣⲁⲡⲉⳎⲁ *dapes lautioris
mensae*; P 131⁴ 105 victuals ⲥⲙⲛⲧⲟⲩ ⳉⲓⲧⲛⲣⲉⲛϭ. ⲉⲅ-
ⲥⲟⲧⲛ, Bodl(P) b 6 ⲛⲛⲁⳉ ⲛϭ., WS 121 ⲕⲁⲛⲓⲥⲕⲉ ⲛϭ.,
KroppJ 49 ⲛϭ. ⲛⲧⳃⲁⲗⲁⳉⲧ, BKU 1 8 31 sim, KroppM

---

26 ⲧⲉⲓⲁⲡⲁⲣⲭⲏ ⲛⲛⲉ ⳉ...ⲉⲥⲉⲩⲱⲡⲉ ⲡⲁⲓ ⲛϭ. *in all my
undertakings*, BM 532 in bishop's pastoral ⲟⲩⲥⲙⲟⲩ
ⲙⲛⲟⲩϭ. ⲉϥⲙⲏⲛ [ⲉⲃⲟⲗ.

ⲣⲉϥϭ. S, *preparer*: BMis 151 among sinners ⲛⲣ.
ⳉⲙⲛⲁⲡⲟⲧ, Tri 614 phoenix ⲛⲛⲟϭ ⲛⲣⲁⲗⲏⲧ ⲛⲣ. ⳬⳮ.

ϭⲱⲣϭ SA, -ⳃ A, ⳃⲱⲣⳃ, ⳃⲟ. B, ϭⲟⲣϭⳅ, S, ⳃⲟⲣⳃⳅ
B, ϭⲟⲣϭ† S, ϭⲁ.† AA², ⳃⲟⲣⳃ† B vb intr, *be in habited*:
Si 10 3 S οἰκίζεσθαι, *ib* 16 5 S ϭⲱⲣϭ (*sic* MS) συνοικ.,
Ps 92 tit B(S ⲟⲩⲱⳉ), Ez 36 33 B ⳃⲟ., Joel 3 20 SAB
κατοικεῖν; P 131⁵ 77 S paradise deserted ⲁⲙⲛⲧⲉ ⳉⲱⲱϥ
ⲁⳃ., Mor 22 31 S after deluge earth ϭ. ⲛⲕⲉⲥⲟⲡ, MG
25 311 B ⲁⲛⲓⳋⲁϭⲉ ⳃ. ⲛⲕⲁⲗⲱⲥ;   qual: Pro 8 26
SA(B ⳋⲟⲡ ϭⲉⲛ-) οἰκεῖν, 1 Kg 27 8 S, Ez 38 12 B, Zech
1 11 A(B ⳃⲟ) κατοι.; BM 256 189 S ⲧⲡⲉⲣⲓⲭⲱⲣⲟⲥ ϭ.
ⲁⲩⲱ ⲉⲥⲧⲥⲛⲩ (*cf* Ge 13 10), ManiH 13 A² ⲛⲉⲥϯⲙⲉ
ⲉⲧϭ.;   tr, *inhabit, people*: El 82 A ⲥⲉ ϭⲱⲣⳃ ⲙⲙⲁⲥ
(*sc* Jerusalem) ⲥⲉⲟⲩⲱⳉ ⲙⲙⲟ. With preposition: Tri
297 S ϭ. ⲉⲧⲉϥⲣⲥⲱ ⳬⲉ, TT 11 S ⲛϥϭ. ⲉⲛⲕⲁⳉ;   ShRE
1117 S ⲛⲡⲟⲗⲓⲥ...ⲁⲩϭ. ⲛⲁⳉⳉⲉⲗⲟⲥ, Leyd 277 S ⲛⲧⲟⲩ-
ⲉⲓⲏ ⲁⲩϭ. ⲙⲙⲟⲛⲁⲭⲟⲥ, Mor 43 110 S ⲁⲩ ϭⲟⲣϭϥ (*sc*
Paradise) ⲙⲯⲩⲭⲏ;   P 131² 163 S ⲡϣⲁⲭⲉ ⲉⲧⲟⲩ-
ⲛⲁϭ. ⲛⲧⲟⲓⲕⲟⲩⲙⲉⲛⲏ ⲛⲣⲏⲧⲟⲩ, BMis 342 S ⲛⲉⲓⲕⲟⲥ-
ⲙⲟⲥ...ϭ. ⲉⲃⲟⲗ ⳉⲙⲡⲉⲓⲛⲉ ⲛⲁⲗⲁⲙ;   MG 25 88 B ⲛⲁⲓ-
ⲙⲁ...ⲁⲡⳍⲧ ⳃⲟⲣⳃϥ ⲉⲃⲟⲗ ⳉⲓⲧⲟⲧⲕ;   as nn: ShA 2 137
S ⲁⲥ ϣⲱⲡⲉ ⲉⲩⳋⲱϥ ⲛⲡⲉⲧⲛⲣⲏⲅⲉ ⲉⲅϭ. ⲛⲧⲉⲕⲕⲗⲏⲥⲓⲁ.

In place-names (this or ? preceding words): ⲡⲣⲙⲛ-
ⲛϭ. (Ann 8 90), ⲡⲧⲙⲉ ϭ. (BM 1134), Πτεμεγκύρκις
(PG 25 368), Τεμενκῶρκις (Preisigke *W.buch*), ⲧⲥⲓ ⲛϭ.
(BM 1040).

ϭⲣⲟ(ⲟ)ϭ SA, ϭⲗⲟϭ S, ϭⲣⲁϭ A²F, ⳃⲣⲟⳃ B, pl ϭⲣⲱ-
(ⲱ)ϭ, ⲕⲣⲱⲱϭ (once) S, ϭⲣⲟⲟϭ SF, ⳃⲣⲱⳃ B, ϭⲣⲱⲱⳃ
F & sg as pl, nn m, *seed*: Ge 8 22 B(S ⳃⲟ), Is 30 23
SBF, Mt 13 24 SBF σπέρμα, Lev 26 20 S(B ⲟⲩⲧⲁⳉ),
Mk 4 26 SBF(Mus 49 189) σπόρος; Ex 22 5 S(B ⳃⲟ)
γένημα; Br 275 S ⲡⲉϭ. ⲛⲡⲁⳃⲁⲑⲟⲛ ⲧⲏⲣⲟⲩ, ShViK
9315 S ⳃⲟ ⳉⲣⲁⲓ ⲛⲣⲏⲧϥ ⲛⲟⲩ ϭⲣⲟⲟϭ, Ryl 72 351 S field
ⲛⲡⲟⲩⳃⲟ ϭⲗⲟϭ ⲉⲣⲟⲥ, Wess 18 92 S ⲛϭ. ⲙⲡⲙⲁ ⲛⲉ-
ⲗⲟⲟⲗⲉ, ManiK 173 A² ⲛⲙⲉⲗⲟⲥ ⲉⲧⲉⲣⲉ ⲛ. ⲛⲏⲅ ⲁⲃⲁⲗ
ⲙⲙⲁϥ, BM 849 41 B ⳉⲓ ⳃ. ⳃⲉ ⲛⲟⲩ ⲕⲁⳉⲓ;   of man
B: Ps 104 6 (S = Gk), Is 57 3 (S do) σπέρμα; Lev 15
3 γόνος; BSM 12 human race ⲉⲃⲟⲗ ϭⲉⲛ ⲛⲁⳃ.;   pl
forms: Lev 26 16 S(var ϭⲣⲟϭ, B sg), Mt 13 32 S(varr
ϭⲣⲟⲟϭ, ϭⲣⲟϭ)BF, 1 Cor 15 38 S(var ϭⲣⲟⲟϭ)B σπέρμα; Deu 28 51 S(var ϭⲣⲱϭ, B ⲟⲩ.), Si 24 20 S(var
do) γέν.; JA '75 5 264 S ⲛⲉ ϭⲣⲱⲱϭ...ⲛⲉ ϭⲣⲟϭ, BAp
95 S ⲡⲉⲕ. ⲙⲛⲕⲁⳉ, Ryl 158 S ⲧⲁ ⳃⲟⲟⲩ (*sc* fields) ⳉⲛ-
ⲛⲁ ϭⲣⲱⲱϭ, Va 57 5 B ⲛⲓⳃ. ⲉⲧⲟⲩⲥⲓϯ ⲙⲙⲱⲟⲩ, BMOr
6201 A 89 F ⲛⲉϭ. ⲛⲉⲃⲣⲉⲓ, BMis 462 S corn, barley,
lentils, beans ⲙⲛⲛⲥⲉⲉⲡⲉ ⲛⲛⲉϭⲣⲟⲟϭ;   as adj: Nu
5 2 S ⲉⲣⲉⲙⲟⲟⲩ ⲛϭ. ϣⲟⳃⲟ ⲛⲥⲱϥ (B diff) γονορρυής;
Lev 15 16 B ⳋⲁⲓⲣⲓ ⲛ ⳃ. κοίτη σπέρματος; JTS 8 241
S ⲛⲉ ⳃⲟ ⲛϭ.

CR '87 377 *S* in recipe ϧⲙⲙⲁϧⲧ ⲛϭ. for anointing breasts.

ⲁⲧϭ., -ⲝ., *seedless*: Deu 7 14 *B*(*S* ⲁⲧϣⲏⲣⲉ) ἄγονος; Mor 55 81 *S* ⲕⲁϧ...ⲡⲁⲧϭ.

ⲉⲓⲣⲉ ⲡⲟⲩϭ.: Is 37 31 *SB* σπέρμα ποιεῖν, Ex 9 31 *B* σπερματίζειν.

† ⲝ.: Lev 18 23 *B*(*S* as Gk) σπερματισμός.

ⲝⲓ ϭ., ϭⲓ ⲝ.: Lev 12 2 *SB* σπερματίζεσθαι; *ib* 19 19 *B*(*S* diff) κατοχεύειν.

ϭⲉⲣϭⲱ *F*   *v* ϭⲓⲛϭⲗⲱ.

ϭⲣⲏϭⲉ *S*, -ⲝⲓ *B*, -ϭⲓ *F* nn f (once), *dowry*: Ge 34 12 *SB*, Ex 22 16 *SB* φερνή; Mor 18 182 *S* ⲧⲉϭ. ⲛⲧⲉⲥⲙⲛⲧⲡⲁⲣⲑⲉⲛⲟⲥ προίξ; K 103 = P 54 162 *B*(no var) ⲡⲓϭ. ; WTh 139 *S* † ⲙⲡϣⲧⲟⲟⲧϥ ⲙⲛⲧⲉϭ. ⲛⲧ- ϣⲉⲉⲣⲉ ϧⲁⲣⲟϥ, BMis 274 *S* youth's father says †ⲡⲁ- ⲧⲁϣⲟ ⲧⲉϭ. (*sic l*) ϧⲙⲡⲛⲟⲩⲃ ⲙⲡⲣⲁⲧ ⲁⲩⲱ ϧⲉⲛϧⲙⲅⲁⲗ &c = Mor 29 44 ϭⲣⲏϭⲉ, *ib* 30 50 *F*, Mor 38 71 *S* bridegroom brings silver & gold as ϭ., C 86 201 *B* gave bride's father ⲧⲉϭ. ⲛⲛⲟⲩⲃ besides many gifts.

(ϭⲟⲣϭⲣ), ϭⲉⲣϭⲱⲣ⸗   *v* ϫⲟⲣϫⲣ.

ϭⲟⲣϭⲥ *S*, ϭⲁ. *AA²F*, ϭⲁⲣϭϥ *A*   *v* ϭⲱⲣϭ 1°.

ϭⲁⲣϭⲁⲧⲁⲛⲉ, ϭⲁⲣⲁⲧⲏⲡⲓ *S* nn f, *bread-basket* or sim: Mor 51 41 ⲡⲛⲉϭⲁϭⲉ ϣⲱⲡⲉ ϧⲓⲧϭⲁⲣϭ., *ib* 42 ϧⲓⲧϭⲁⲣⲁ...., ⲧϭⲁⲣⲁ. ϫⲉⲡⲉ ϧⲏⲧϥ ⲙⲡⲣⲱⲙⲉ. Not Coptic? *Cf* γυργαθός, -αθίον.

ϭ̄ⲥ, ϭ̄ⲥ̄, ⲟ̄ⲥ̄ *BF*   *v* ϫⲟⲉⲓⲥ.

ϭⲁⲥ   *v* ϭⲟⲥ.

ϭⲉⲥ *S* nn (adj), meaning unknown, epithet of iron: PMich 1547 list of σκεύη some ⲛϧⲟⲙⲛⲧ, others ⲛⲡⲓⲡⲓⲡⲉ, one ⲛ]ϧⲟⲙⲛⲧ ⲛϭ.

ϭⲉⲥ *S* nn, meaning unknown, epithet appended to names in Greek corn-assessment BM 1075, as Ἀπολλως ϭ., Βικτωρ ϭ., Τατιανου ϭ. *Cf*? ϭⲁⲗⲉ sim in BM 1077.

ϭⲟⲥ *S*, ϭⲁⲥ *SᵃF*, ⲕ. *S*, ϫⲟⲥ *B*, ϭⲓⲥ- *SF*, ϭⲉⲥ- *S*, ⲕⲥ- *A²*, ϫⲉⲥ- *B* nn m, *half*: CA 98 *S* ⲟⲩϭ. ⲛⲥⲟⲩⲟ = *ib* ⲣ̄ⲉ نصف اردب; CO 174 *S* ⲟⲩⲕ. ⲡⲗⲓⲕⲛⲁ ⲛϧⲟⲙⲛⲧ; after nn or numeral, without *and*: Ez 40 42 *SB* ⲟⲩ- ⲙⲁϧⲉ ⲟⲩϭ., Ap 11 9 *S* ϣⲟⲙⲧ ⲛϧⲟⲟⲩ ⲟⲩϭ. (*B* ⲫⲁϣⲓ) ἥμισυ; Jud 8 10 *S* ⲧⲃⲁ ⲟⲩϭ. δέκα πέντε χιλιάδες; ST 445 *S* ⲥⲛⲧⲉ ⲟⲩϭ. ⲡⲗⲓⲧⲣⲁ, J 59 4 *Sᵃ* ⲟⲩϭⲟⲗⲟⲕ/ ⲟⲩϭⲁⲥ, *ib* 117 8 *S* ⲥⲟ ⲟⲩⲕ. ⲕⲉⲣⲁⲧⲥⲉ, ST 117 *Sᵃ* ⲟⲩϭⲁⲣⲧⲁⲃ ⲛ- ϧⲙⲟⲩ ⲟⲩϭ., Miss 494 *B* ⲟⲩϫ ⲓ ⲟⲩⲝ. λογκοχι, BM 556 *F* ⲓ̄ⲁ̄ ⲛⲕⲉⲥ ⲟⲩϭ.; ⲙⲁϫϭⲟⲥ *v* ⲣ 213 *a*; ϭⲓⲥ-, ϫⲉⲥ-: Ez 43 17 *B* ϫⲉⲥⲙⲁϧⲓ (HCons 303, var ⲫ. ⲁⲙⲙ.) ἥμ., Ap 8 2 *S* ϭⲓⲥⲟⲩⲛⲟⲩ (*B* diff) ἡμιώριον; *ib* 16 21 *S* ϭⲓⲥ- ϭⲓⲛϭⲱⲣ (*B* Gk diff); Ac 27 40 *S* ϭⲓⲥⲗⲁⲅⲟ (*B*=Gk) ἀρτέμων; PS 244 *S* ϭⲉⲥⲧⲃⲁ ⲛϧⲟⲙⲡⲉ, ShMiss 4 280

S ⲧⲕⲉϭⲓⲥⲟⲩⲛⲟⲩ, ShA 2 236 *S* ϭⲓⲥⲧⲏⲛⲃⲉ, Mor 40 31 *S* ⲟⲩϭⲓⲥⲙⲁϧⲉ (var *ib* 41 146 ⲡⲁϣ-), ManiP 217 *A²* ⲉϧⲟ ⲛϫⲉⲟⲩⲓⲡ, LAp 570 *F* ϭⲓⲥⲧⲃⲉ ⲛϧⲏⲙⲙⲓ, CMSS 76 *F* ϭⲓⲥⲗⲁⲕ; ϭⲓⲥⲕⲓⲧⲉ *v* ⲡ 124 *a*.

(ϭⲱⲥ), ⲕⲉⲥ† (*l* ϭⲏⲥ)*S* vb intr, *be hard, dry*: P 43 51 among diseases ⲯⲟⲣ(ⲁ) ⲉⲥⲕ. جرب اليابس, opp ⲯ. ⲉⲥⲗⲁⲕ (*l* ⲗⲏⲕ) جـ' اللين. Prob = ϫⲱⲥ *q v*.

ϭⲱⲥ *B*   *v* ϫⲱⲥ.

ϭⲱⲥ *B* nn m, *flatus ventris*: K 161 ⲡⲓϭ. نـ. *Cf* ϫⲟⲕⲥⲓ.

ϭⲏⲥⲉ *F* vb intr, meaning unknown: BM 581(1) ⲙⲡⲉⲛϣ ϭⲏⲥⲉ ϣⲁⲡⲁⲁⲩ.

ϭⲓⲥⲓ *B*   *v* ϫⲓⲥⲉ vb & nn.

ϭⲓⲥⲗⲁⲅⲟ   *v* ⲗⲁⲅⲟ.

ϭⲟⲥⲙ *S*, ϭⲁⲥⲙⲉ *AA²*, ϭⲁⲥⲙ *A²F*, ϫⲟⲥⲉⲙ *B*, ϫⲁ. *F* nn m, *darkness, tempest*: Ex 20 21 *S*, Deu 4 11 *S* with ⲕⲁⲕⲉ, Ps 17 9 *SF* ϭ. (Pcod Mor 55), Zeph 1 15 *S* Aγνόφος, Job 10 21 *S* -ⲉⲣⲟϭ (all *B*=Gk), Lam 2 1 *F* ⲝ. (*B* as Gk) γνοφοῦν; AM 273 *B* great wind & ⲟⲩϭ. χειμῶνος ὥρα; C 86 270 *B* ⲡⲓϣⲧ ⲛⲝ. ὄμβρος; HL 110 *B* ⲝ. ⲛϫⲙⲟⲙ ⲡⲁⲣⲟϣ περίστασις πυρετοῦ; Sh MIF 23 34 *S* ⲕⲣⲙⲧⲥ, ϧⲧⲟⲙⲧⲙ, ϭ., ShC 42 35 *S* light scattereth ⲛϭ., ShA 2 163 *S* ϧⲁⲧⲏⲩ ⲛϭ., ManiP 180 *A²* ⲡⲉϧⲟ, ⲧⲟⲩⲙϧⲣⲓⲧ, ϭ., *ib* 192 James died ϧⲁⲡϭⲁⲥⲙ ⲙⲡⲱⲛⲉ, *ib* 63 ⲙⲡⲉϭ. ⲛⲉϧⲥⲉ ⲁⲣⲁϥ (*sc* ship), C 43 149 *B* ⲡⲓⲝ. ⲛⲧⲉ ⲡⲓⲑⲏⲟⲩ; ⲁⲧϭ. *B*, *without storm, unperturbed*: MG 25 37 if I stay in closed cell †ⲟⲓ ⲛⲁ.

ϭⲁⲥⲧ, -ⲧⲉ *F* vb intr, *dance*: Mt 14 6 (*SB* ϭⲟⲥϭⲥ) ὀρχεῖσθαι; cit Mor 24 4 ⲁⲥϭⲁⲥⲧⲉ ϧⲉⲡⲧⲙⲏ†. For? ϭⲁⲥϭ, *cf* ϭⲟⲥϭ(ⲉ)ⲥ.

ϭⲟⲥⲧ, ϭⲁ., ⲕⲁ., ⲧⲁ. *S*(Theban) nn m, a measure of length, less than ⲡⲟⲩϧ: Win 35 †ⲟⲩ ⲛⲡⲱϧ ⲡⲁⲣⲁ ϥⲧⲟⲟⲩ ⲛϭ., ST 160 †ⲟⲩ ⲛϭ. ⲙⲛϧⲧⲟⲟⲩ ⲛϣⲱⲡⲉ (or? ϣⲟⲡ), Ep 562 ⲯⲁⲓⲧⲁⲥⲉ ⲛⲓⲕ., ST 401 ⲟⲩⲅ. in instructions for weaving, J 28 7 ⲙⲏⲧ ⲛϭⲁ. of land.

ϭⲁⲥⲟⲩ *B*   *v* ϫⲓⲥⲉ 1° nn (pl).

ϭⲟⲥϭ(ⲉ)ⲥ *S*, ϭⲟⲥϫⲉⲥ *B* vb intr, *dance*: 2 Kg 6 16 *B*(*S*=Gk), Is 13 21 *SB*, Mt 14 6 *SB*(*F* ϭⲁⲥⲧ) ὀρ- χεῖσθαι; ShC 73 48 *S* ⲛⲉⲡⲡⲛⲁ ⲛⲁϭ. ϧⲛⲧⲟⲩ (*cf* Is *lc*), Mor 31 224 *S* ϧⲉϫⲓⲟⲙⲉ ϭ. ϧⲓϫⲛ ⲛⲛⲉϥϫⲱⲗⲟⲡ; as nn: Va 57 276 *B* ϧⲁⲛϭ. ⲛⲧⲉ ⲡⲉⲧⲉⲛϣⲏⲣⲓ ὄρχησις; Sh R 2 3 67 *S* ϫⲱ ⲛⲁⲧϣⲁⲩ ⲙⲡϧⲣⲉⲡϭ., Va 57 42 *B* ⲡⲓϭ. ⲧⲉⲧⲉⲛⲓⲣⲓ ⲙⲙⲱⲟⲩ. *Cf* ϭⲁⲥⲧ.

ϭⲁⲧ- *F*   *v* ϭⲱⲥ 1°.

ϭⲁⲓⲧ *A²* vb prob qual of ⲧϭⲁⲉⲓⲟ: ManiK 96 ⲉⲧϭ. ϧⲛⲡⲟⲩⲉⲓⲛⲉ, *ib* 68 ⲙⲟⲣⲫⲁⲅⲉ ⲉⲧϭ., *ib* 218 ⲥⲉϫⲉ ⲉⲩϭ.

ϭⲟⲧ S, ϭⲁⲧ A²F nn f, *size, age, form*: Ez 19 11 (B
ⲙⲁⲓⲏ), Eph 1 19 (B ⲙⲉⲧⲡⲓϣϯ, F ⲙⲉⲧⲡⲁϭ), Mor 37
64 ϩⲉⲛϭ. ⲛⲥⲱⲙⲁ, *ib* 65 ⲉⲩⲡⲟϫⲧ ⲟⲛⲧⲉⲩϭ. μέγεθος,
1 Kg 9 2 ϫⲟⲥⲉ ⲟⲛⲧⲉⲩϭ., Bar 3 26 sim (B ⲡⲓϣϯ) εὐμεγέθης, 1 Kg 16 7 (B=Gk) ἕξις μεγέθους; Job 29 18
(B ⲙⲁ.), Si 26 17, Lu 19 3, He 11 11 ἡλικία, Gal 1 14
(all B do)συνηλικιώτης; R 22 21 ϣⲏⲣⲉ ϣⲏⲙ ⲟⲛⲧⲉⲩϭ.
B Mar 192 ⲟⲩⲕⲟⲩⲓ ⲟⲛⲧⲉⲕϭ. νέος; P 44 87 ⲙⲉⲧⲣⲟⲡ·
ⲧϭ. · ⲡϣⲓ مقدار‎, جد‎; Ann 19 233 ⲡⲉϥⲧⲛⲓϣ ⲟⲛⲧⲉⲩϭ. =
C 86 112 B ⲙⲁ., Bor 255 252 ⲙⲉϥϭⲃⲟⲕ ⲟⲛⲧⲉϥϭ., P
Méd 130 ⲁⲁϥ ⲡⲥⲟⲗ ⲛⲧϭ. ⲙⲡϣⲓ ⲛⲧⲛⲏⲣⲉ, TurM 13
ϫⲟⲟⲩ ⲧϭⲟⲟⲧ ⲛⲧⲁⲣⲟⲩ, ManiK 152 A² ϣⲁⲟⲩⲏⲣⲧⲉ
ⲧⲉⲥϭ.; Mor 41 73 ⲧϭ. ⲡⲧⲁⲣⲅⲗⲏⲕⲓⲁ for I am 14 years
old, Bodl(P) f 8 prayer ⲛⲧⲟⲩ (sc children) ⲉϩⲣⲁⲓ ⲉⲡϣⲓ
ⲛⲧⲉⲩϭ., PS 282 ⲧϭ. ⲉⲧⲁⲥⲉⲓ ⲉⲡⲕⲟⲥⲙⲟⲥ ⲛ̇ϩⲏⲧⲥ, B Hom
122 ⲡⲛⲟϭ ϭⲓ ⲛϭ. ⲛⲓⲙ, *young, old, small, great*, AP
21 A² ⲡⲁⲧⲉⲩϭ. *of his sort*, ManiH 32 A² ye see ⲧϭ.
ⲙⲡⲣⲉϣⲉ; Mor 40 46 ⲱ ⲧϭ. ⲡⲛⲓϩⲙⲟⲧ = MG 25 272
B ⲱ ⲡⲉⲙⲛⲁⲓϩ., AZ 38 59 ⲱ ⲧϭ. ⲉⲡϣⲓⲕ ⲡⲧⲥⲟⲫⲓⲁ, Gu
5 ⲱ ϫⲉⲟⲩⲏⲣⲧⲉ ⲧϭ. ⲡⲛϭⲟⲙ;   ⲡⲧⲉⲓϭ., *of this sort,
size, such*: Jos 10 14, Mk 13 19 (B ⲣⲏϯ) Z 325 ⲉⲟⲟⲩ
ⲡ. τοιοῦτος, Lu 7 9 (B ⲙⲁ.), Z 274 ⲟⲩⲛⲟϭ ⲡϩⲟⲧⲉ ⲡ.
τοσοῦτος, 2 Cor 1 10 (B ⲡⲓϣϯ), Ap 16 18 (B ⲣ.) τηλικοῦτος, Gal 6 11 (B ⲙⲁ.)πηλίκος; Br 246 ⲧ̇ⲛⲧ̇ϣⲏⲣⲉ
ⲡ., ShA 2 241 ⲙⲁ ⲛⲓⲧⲟⲡ ⲛⲧⲉⲓⲙⲓⲛⲉ, ⲧⲁⲉⲓⲟ ⲡⲧⲉⲓⲣⲉ,
ⲁⲅⲁⲑⲟⲛ ⲡ., LMär 14 ϩⲱ ⲉⲣⲟⲕ ⲟⲛⲧⲓⲙⲁⲓⲏ ⲡ., ManiK
52 A² ϯⲣⲣⲉ ⲡ.;   ⲁϣ ⲛϭ., *of what size, sort*: Col
2 1 (B ⲙⲁ.) ἡλίκος, He 7 4 SF(B do), B Hom 24 ⲟⲩ-
ⲥⲓϣⲉ ⲡⲁ. πηλ.; Mk 13 1 ϩⲉⲛⲁ. (var ϩⲉ, B ⲣⲏϯ) ποταπός; B Hom 21 ⲕⲟⲗⲁⲥⲓⲥ ⲡⲁ. ποῖος; Z 322 ⲟⲩⲁ.
ⲧⲉ ⲧ̇ⲛⲧ̇ⲁⲅⲁⲑⲟⲥ ὅσος; PS 185 ⲟ ⲡⲁϣ ⲙ̇ⲙⲓⲛⲉ, ⲡⲁϣ
ⲡⲧ̇ⲩⲡⲟⲥ, ⲡⲁ., ShC 42 37 ⲟⲩⲥⲁϩⲟⲩ ⲡⲁ. paral ⲥⲙⲟⲩ
ⲡⲁϣ ⲡⲁⲉⲓⲛⲥ, Wess 18 111 ⲟⲩⲁ. ⲡⲉ ⲉⲧⲟⲩ̇ⲡⲁⲁⲥ ⲙ̇ⲙ-
ⲡⲟⲩⲁ ⲡⲟⲩⲁ ⲙ̇ⲙⲟⲛ?;   ⲣ, ⲟ ⲡⲧϭ., *be like*: Ja 3 4 (B
ⲙⲁ.) τηλ. εἶναι; RNC 73 my sin ⲡⲁⲣ ⲧϭ. ⲁⲡ ⲙ̇ⲡⲁ-
ⲅ̇ⲁⲑⲟⲛ ⲡⲧⲁϥϣⲱⲡⲉ, B Mar 192 ⲉⲩⲟ ⲛ̇ⲧⲉⲕϭ., ManiH
17 A² ⲧⲁⲩ̇ⲣ ϯϭ. ϩⲛⲧⲝ[, Mor 24 27 F broad place ϣⲁϥⲉⲗ ⲧϭ. ⲙ̇ⲡⲕⲟⲥⲙⲟⲥ ⲧⲏⲣϥ̄.   V LAl 54.

ϭⲱⲧ SA(?), ⲝ. B(once) nn f, *drinking trough* (cf ?
ⲛⲁ Dévaud): Ge 24 20 (Mus 50 17, P 44 103, B ⲙⲁ
ⲡⲧⲥⲟ) ποτιστήριον; Ex 2 16 A ϭⲱ[ⲧ] (S uncertain, B
ⲙⲉⲣⲁⲡ) δεξαμενή (var ποτίστρα); Ge 30 38 (B ⲙⲁ
ⲡⲧⲥⲟ) ληνός; Tri 672 ⲧϭ. حوض‎; ShC 42 220 flocks
ⲥⲱ ϩⲡⲛⲓϭ. ⲡⲟⲩⲱⲧ, LIb 7 B ⲧⲁⲓⲝ. ⲡⲱⲛⲓ wherein James
Persian's body laid, ViK 4741 list ⲟⲩϣⲁⲗⲟⲟⲩ, ⲟⲩϭ.,
ⲟⲩϣⲟⲧⲉ.

ϭⲱⲱⲧ F *v* ϭⲱ.

ϭⲓϯ B *v* p 395 *b*.

ϭⲓⲱϯ B nn, *tip of scorpion's tail* (so Ar), a lunar
station: K 52 ϭ. شولة‎ (cf ib ⲁⲧⲧⲓⲁ '؎).

ϭⲱⲧⲡ SA²BF, -ⲧϥ, -ϥⲧ B, ϭⲱⲡⲧ S(nn)S'F, ϭⲉⲧⲡ-,
ϭⲱ., ϭⲟⲧⲡ⸗ S, ϭⲟⲧⲡ† SB, ϭⲁⲡⲧ† F, ⲣ c ϭⲁⲧⲡ- A²
vb intr, *be defeated, overcome*: Deu 20 3 B -ⲧϥ (var
-ϥⲧ, S?) θραύειν; Is 8 9 S(B ϭⲣⲟ ⲉ-), *ib* 31 4 F -ⲡⲧ
(SB om) ἡττᾶσθαι; 1 Kg 14 22 S φεύγειν; C 89 58
B ⲁⲟⲩⲁⲓ ϭ. by drowsiness ὀλιγωρεῖν = Va ar 172 36
أجل‎; ShMIF 23 16 S ⲁⲩϭ. ⲁⲩϭⲉ, ShP 131¹ 157 S
ⲡⲉⲧϫⲟⲟⲣ ϭ., Miss 4 705 S ⲛϯⲙⲉ ⲛⲧⲁϥϭ. opp ⲛϯ.
ⲛⲧⲁϥϣⲣⲟ, Bor 295 109 S not unbelieving because of
His flesh nor ⲛⲧϭ. ⲁⲛ ⲉⲧⲃⲉⲡⲉϥϫⲙⲟ *dismayed*, B Mar
124 S ⲙ̇ⲡⲟⲩϭ. by threats, ManiK 180 A² ⲛϥ̇ⲧⲙϭ.
ⲛϥ̇ⲧⲙⲧⲣⲓⲉ;   qual: Deu 28 33 B(Va, Lag ⲉⲣ ϭⲱϥⲧ,
S ⲟⲩⲱⲙ̇ϣ) θρ.; Is 31 8 SF(B ϭⲣⲟ ⲉ-) ἥττημα; Ex
32 18 S(B ⲕⲱⲧⲥ) τροπή; Jth 15 3 τρέπεσθαι; ShA
1 392 S ⲉϥⲛⲱⲧ ⲉⲃⲟⲗ ⲛϭ., EpApp 1 93 S enemies of
faith ⲉⲩϭ. ⲁⲩⲱ ⲉⲩϣⲟⲩⲉⲓⲧ.

tr, *defeat, overcome*: B Hom 51 S ⲉⲛⲉⲟⲩⲥⲟⲙⲉ ϭⲟⲧⲡⲟⲩ ⲛ̇ⲧ. ὑπό; Nu 14 45 S(B ϩⲓⲟⲩⲓ ⲛⲥⲁ-) τρ.; B Hom
133 S περιγίνεσθαι; ShA 1 394 S spreading out of
hands ⲡⲁϭⲟⲧⲡⲩ, C 86 119 B send Michael ⲛⲧⲉϥϭ.
ⲛⲛⲓⲡⲟⲗⲉⲙⲟⲥ & scatter them.

With following preposition.   c ⲉ- S: Ep 252 ye
have not inquired for me, ⲡⲗⲏⲛ ⲁ̇ⲡⲁϩⲏⲧ ϭ. ⲉⲣⲟⲓ, Sh
C 73 51 ⲟⲩⲥϭⲓⲙⲉ ⲉⲥ̇ϩⲡⲁⲁⲩ ⲏ ⲉⲥϭ.† ⲉⲥⲱϩⲉ *wearied of*,
ShMIF 23 101 ϯϭ.† ⲉⲣ ⲧⲕⲉⲡⲏⲥⲧⲓⲁ;   c ⲡ-: MG
25 147 B ⲟⲩⲟⲛ ⲟⲩⲙⲏϣ ⲛⲁϭ. ⲡ̇ⲣⲱⲗ ⲉϥⲉⲕⲕⲗⲏⲥⲓⲁ from
fear of the powers; ⲙⲡⲉⲙⲧⲟ ⲉⲃⲟⲗ ⲛ- S: 1 Kg 31 1
(var ϩⲓⲑⲏ ⲛ-) φεύ. ἐκ προσώπου, *ib* 7 10 sim ⲡ̇ⲧⲁⲓⲉⲓⲛ
ⲉⲛⲱⲡⲓⲟⲛ;   c ⲡⲁϩⲣⲛ-: BMis 61 S ⲁⲓϭ. ⲡ. ⲧⲉⲕⲛⲟϭ
ⲛⲥⲟⲫⲓⲁ (var Mor 33 120 S' ϭⲱⲡⲧ);   c ϩⲁ-: R 1 4
60 S but for magic ⲛⲉⲕⲛⲁϭ. ⲡⲉ ϩⲁⲛ̇ⲃⲁⲥⲁⲛⲟⲥ = Mart
Ign 871 B ϭ. ⲉⲁⲕϣⲉⲛ ⲡⲁⲓⲇⲓⲥⲓ εἴκειν; ManiP 58 A²
ⲡⲉⲧⲁϭ. ϩⲁⲧⲉϥϩⲉⲧⲡⲱ;   ϩⲁⲧⲛ, ⲝ̇ⲁ-: 2 Kg 10 13 S ἀπὸ
προσώπου φ.; 4 Kg 14 12 S ⲡⲧ. ἀπὸ πρ.; Jud 4 23 S
τροποῦν ἔμπροσθεν; Is 57 11 B(S as Gk) εὐλαβεῖσθαι;
EW 151 B ⲛⲏ ⲉⲧⲁⲩϭ. ϩⲁⲧⲟ̇ϩⲣⲏ νικᾶσθαι; Mor 16 64
S ⲁⲩϭ. ϩⲁⲧⲉϥϩⲏ (var BMis 214 ⲡⲱⲧ ϩ.), Mor 29 6 S
ⲁⲩϭ. ϩ. ⲛⲡⲉⲣⲣⲱⲙⲁⲓⲟⲥ (var BMis 233 ϩⲓϩⲏ ⲛ-), Z 286
S ⲛ̇ⲛϭ. ⲛⲛⲉⲕϫⲁϫⲉ ϩⲁⲧⲉⲕϩⲓⲏ (sic), AM 242 B ⲡ̇ⲧⲉⲩϭ.
ϭ. ⲡ̇ϫⲟⲙ ⲡⲧⲉ ⲫϯ;   c ϩⲓⲣⲏ, ϩⲓⲑⲏ S: 2 Kg 2 17
ⲡⲧ. ἐνώπιον, Jos 11 6 ⲧⲣ. ἐναντίον; Deu 28 7 (B ϩⲱⲧ)
φεύ. ἀπὸ πρ., Mor 16 58 ⲡⲟⲗⲉⲙⲟⲥ ⲛⲓⲙ...ϣⲁⲣⲉ ⲡⲡⲉ
ϭⲟⲧⲡⲟⲩ ϩ. ⲙ̇ⲙⲟϥ (var BMis 211 ⲟϥⲃⲃⲓⲟⲟⲩ ϩ.);   c ϭⲡ-,
ϭⲉⲡ-: Is 30 31 SF -ⲡⲧ (B ϭⲣⲟ ⲉ-) ⲛ̇ⲧ. dat; 2 Kg 14
S φεύ. ἐκ; ShR 2 3 12 S ⲙⲡϥϭ. ϩⲙⲡⲡⲟⲗⲉⲙⲟⲥ ⲥⲡⲁⲩ,
AM 225 B ⲁⲓϣⲁⲛϭ. ϭⲉ ⲡⲡⲓⲥⲁϫⲓ ⲡⲟⲩⲕⲟⲩϫⲓ *fail*; Is
19 1 S ϭ. ϩⲣⲁⲓ ϩⲡ- (var ⲣ ϭⲱⲃ, B ϣⲑⲟⲣⲧⲉⲣ) ⲛ̇ⲧ. ἐν;
c ϩⲏⲧⲥ SF: Z 306 ⲁ̇ϥϭ. ϩⲏⲧϥ ⲙⲡⲡⲣⲗⲟ ⲛ̇ⲧ. ὑπό, BIF 37
54 ⲡⲡⲁⲑⲟⲥ ⲉϣⲁⲣⲉ ⲧⲉⲯⲩⲭⲏ ϭ. ϩⲏⲧϥ ⲛ̇ⲧ. dat; B Hom
34 ϥⲛⲁϭ. ⲁⲛ ϩⲏⲧϥ (sc misfortune), Mor 19 8 sim =
Miss 4 96 B ⲉⲣ ϩⲟϯ, Mor 30 11 F ⲙ̇ⲡⲣϭ. ϩⲏⲧϥ ⲛⲡⲉⲁ-
ⲡⲏⲗⲛ (ἀπει.) = BMis 237 S ⲣ ϩⲟⲧⲉ.

With following adverb.   c ⲉⲃⲟⲗ S: 2 Kg 8 1 ⲧⲣⲟ.;

Hall 91 ογпε.πρωⲃ ⲛϭ. ⲡϭⲏⲧ ⲙⲡⲗⲁⲟⲥ ⲉⲃ. ⲉⲧⲣⲉⲩⲃⲱⲕ ⲛⲁⲩ?; ⲉⲃ. ⲛ-, *scare away from*: ShC 42 167 ⲉⲛϭ. ⲙⲙⲟⲟⲩ (sc teachers) ⲉⲃ. ⲙⲙⲟⲛ ϩⲣⲁⲓ ϩⲙⲡⲉⲙϣⲓϣⲉ ⲙⲡⲡⲉⲛⲥⲱϣ, *ib* 168 ⲁⲛϭⲟⲧⲡ ⲙⲁϭⲁⲁⲡ ⲉⲃ. ⲙⲡⲡⲉ, *ib* 73 69 ϭⲟⲧⲡϥ (sc evil thought) ⲉⲃ. ⲙⲙⲟⲛ; ⲉⲃ. ϩⲛ-: ShC 42 82 ⲡⲣⲱⲙⲉ...ϭⲟⲧⲡⲟⲩ ⲉⲃ. ϩⲛⲡⲉⲅⲏⲓ.

—— ⲡϩⲏⲧ *S*, *be afraid*: Wess 18 88 ⲙⲡⲣϭ. (var Mor 19 13 ⲣϩⲟⲧⲉ), CA 103 disciples ⲙⲡⲟⲩϭ. ϣⲁϩⲣⲁⲓ ⲉⲧⲣⲉⲩⲥⲉϩⲥ ϩⲙⲥ (Lu 6 1); as nn *S*: Mor 41 37 ⲁⲗⲟⲧⲛ ⲉⲧⲉⲧⲛϯ ϭ. ⲡⲁⲓ *when going to my Lord*.

ⲡ ⲥ *A²*: ManiH 76 ϩⲁⲗⲁⲧⲉ ⲛϭⲁⲧⲡϩⲏⲧ.

—— nn m *SA²*, *intimidation, discouragement*: B Hom 134 ⲧⲉⲩⲥⲩⲛⲉⲓⲇⲏⲥⲓⲥ ⲧⲉⲧϯ ϭ. ⲛⲁⲩ ⲉⲧⲙⲓϣⲉ ⲡⲙⲙⲁⲩ τὸ συνειδὸς πολέμιον ἔχειν, Wess 18 134 on Eph 6 16 ⲡⲧⲁⲣⲉ ⲣⲁⲧⲛ ⲁⲭⲛϭ., BMOr 6954 (45) ⲥⲧⲱⲧ, ⲡⲉϩϣⲉⲗϥ, ϭⲱⲡⲧ, ⲙⲟⲕⲣⲉⲥ, ManiP 181 *A²* ⲡϭ. (no context).

ⲁⲧϭ. *SB*, *without defeat, unconquered*: R 1 2 24 *S* ⲁⲑⲗⲟⲫⲟⲣⲟⲥ ⲛⲁ., Miss 8 248 *S* ⲁ. ϩⲛⲧⲉϥⲯⲩⲭⲏ, DeV 2 160 *B* ⲁⲧⲱⲡⲓⲥⲧⲏⲥ ⲛⲁ., MG 25 110 *B* ⲟⲓ ⲛⲁ. ϩⲓⲧⲉⲡⲡⲉϩⲙⲟⲧ; ⲙⲛⲧ-, ⲙⲉⲧⲁⲧϭ.; BMar 124 *S* ἀμετάθετος; C 86 187 *B* ⲑⲗ. ⲛⲧⲉ ⲡⲉϥϩⲏⲧ.

ⲉⲣ ϭⲟϣⲧ *B* v above qual.

ⲣⲉϥϭ., ϭⲉⲧⲡ-*S*: P 44 58 ⲣⲉϥⲭⲣⲟ·ⲣⲉϥϭ. ظافر; 1 Tim 1 10 ⲣⲉϥϭⲉⲧⲡ ⲣⲱⲙⲉ ⲉⲃⲟⲗ (*B* ⲣⲉϥϯ ⲣⲉⲙϩⲉ ⲉⲃ.) ἀνδραποδιστής; ⲙⲛⲧⲣⲉϥϭ. ⲣ. ⲉⲃ. ShRyl 65.

ϭⲟⲡ *B* nn, *defeat*: TEuch 2 476 turn enemy's powers ⲉⲩϭ. رجعوا مغلوبين.

ϭⲟⲧⲡⲥ *SB*, ϭ ⲁ. *S^f* nn f, *defeat*: 2 Kg 18 7 *S* θραῦσις; *ib* 17 8 *S* ϯ ϭ. καταλύειν; *ib* 3 34 *S^f* ⲛⲑⲉ ⲡⲟⲩϭ. ὡς Ναβάλ (נבל for נפל GRDriver); ClPr 54 41 *S* ⲡⲥⲣⲟⲙⲟⲗⲟⲅⲓ ⲛⲧⲉⲥϭ.=EW 154 *B* ἡττᾶσθαι; ShClPr 22 360 *S* such as flee are naught but ⲧⲁⲙⲛⲧϭⲱⲃ ⲙⲛⲧϭ., Z 617 *S^f* show forth ⲧϭ. ⲙⲡⲭⲁϫⲉ, Va 58 178 *B* ⲡⲓϭⲣⲟ ⲓⲉ ⲧϭ. ⲡⲛⲉϥϫⲁϫⲓ.

ϭⲓⲧⲣⲉ, ⲕ. *S* nn f (?), *cedrate, kind of lemon*: P 44 81 ⲕⲓⲧⲣⲟⲡ·ϭ. أترج, *ib* ⲕⲱⲧⲣⲓⲫⲩⲗⲟ (κιτρόφυλλον)· ϭⲱⲃⲉ ⲛⲓϭ., MR 5 53 ϣⲟⲙⲧⲉ ⲉϭ., ST 345, PMéd 230 (cf 232), BMar 219 ⲕ.=Rec 6 185 *B* ⲕⲓⲱⲣⲓ (K 178 ⲕⲉⲧⲣⲓ ϫ); *Cf* RE 9 156 ϣⲟⲙⲧ ⲡⲕⲓⲧⲣⲁ, TurM 5 ϥⲧⲟⲟⲩ ⲡⲕⲓⲧⲣⲁ. From κίτρον or converse, v Rec 15 102.

ϭⲓⲧⲥ *B* v ϣⲓⲧⲉ.

ϭⲱⲧⲥ *B*, ϭⲁⲧⲥ† *S* vb tr, *bend, lower*: Job 22 29 *B* ⲉⲧϭ. ⲡⲛⲉϥⲃⲁⲗ (*S* om) κύφειν طأطأ Baud, حارب Lag; ST 287 *S* perhaps she will take pity on me ⲙⲙⲟⲛ ϯϭ.† ⲉⲃⲟⲗ (same ?).

ϭⲁⲧϥⲓ *B* v ϫⲁⲧϥⲉ.

ϭⲱⲧϩ *SB*(rare). ϫ. *SB*, ⲕ., ϭⲱⲣⲧ *S*, ϫ. *B*, ϭⲟⲧϩ̇ *S*, ϫ. *B*, ϭⲟⲧϩ† *SB*, ϫ.† *SB*, ϭⲁⲧϩ†, ⲕ.† *A* vb intr,

wound, pierce (cf قدّ AZ 49 94): Pro 12 18 *B*(*SA* ⲕⲱⲡⲥ) τιτρώσκειν; Mor 42 7 *S* in spring ⲡⲉⲧⲣⲏⲧ...ⲡⲥⲉϫ., SHel 51 *S* tortured so that ⲡⲉϥⲁⲡⲉⲫⲁⲗⲟⲥ (ἐγκ.)ϭ., HM 1 36 *S* weights on his hands ϣⲁⲡⲧⲟⲩϭ. ⲛϭⲓ ⲡⲉⲣⲓⲱⲙⲉ ⲡⲡⲉϥϭⲓⲝ, Va 57 145 *B* ⲁⲥϫ. ⲧⲉⲛϩ & called Him Lord (Jo 4 11); qual: Job 36 25 *B*(*S* ⲧⲁⲕⲟ tr) ⲧⲓⲧ.; Pro 23 27 *SAB*(cit Va 58 192), τετραίνειν; Hag 1 6 *A* ⲕ. (*B* ⲟⲩⲟⲧⲉⲡ) τρυπᾶν; ShIF 268 *S* ⲧⲱⲱⲙⲉ ⲉⲥϭ., Bodl(P)a 1 *a S* ⲟⲩϭⲁⲣⲁⲉⲓⲉ (قُرْئَةٌ) ⲉⲩϭ. as strainer, TillOster 10 *A* ⲥⲕⲉⲟⲥ ⲉⲩϭ., C 89 53 *B* ⲉⲣⲉⲡⲟⲩⲥ(ⲁ)ϫⲓ ϭ.

tr: Job 20 24 *B*(*S* ϫⲱⲧⲉ), Pro 7 26 *B*(var ⲱϩⲣ, *SA* ⲕⲱⲡⲥ) ⲧⲓⲧ.; ShA 1 238 *S* ⲁⲡⲥⲁⲧⲁⲡⲁⲥ ϭ. ⲙⲡⲉⲕⲛⲏ... ⲁϥⲃⲟϣⲕ, Mor 48 83 *S* ⲁⲩϭ. ⲡⲡⲉϥϯⲃⲥ, J 45 36 *S* ϭ. ⲡⲣⲟ ⲉⲡⲣⲏⲥ, *ib* 47 73 sim ⲕ., C 43 130 *B* bade ϫ. ⲙⲡⲉϥϣⲁⲓ, DeV 2 66 *B* ϫⲱⲣⲧ ⲙⲡⲉϥⲙⲟⲕⲓ ⲡⲥⲟⲭⲉⲡ, COAd 50 *S* here is book ⲡ ⲡⲡⲁ ⲡϭⲟⲧⲣϥ ⲡⲧϣⲁⲗ[ⲕ]ϥ *pierce & stitch it*.

With following preposition or adverb. ϭ ⲉ-: Mt 6 19 *S*(var ϣⲟⲭⲧ, *B* ϩⲓ ϣⲁⲧⲉ) διορύσσειν, Ex 22 2 *S*(*B* ϣ.) διόρυγμα; Jer 52 7 *S*(*B* diff) διακόπτειν; 4 Kg 12 9 *S* τετρ. ἐπί; PS 308 *S* ϭ. ⲉⲡⲛⲓ...ϭ. ⲉⲡⲉϭⲛⲓ, Sh BM 206 84 *S* ⲡⲉⲧⲛⲁϭⲱⲣⲧ ⲉⲣⲟϥ ϥⲡⲁⲧⲁⲕⲟϥ, Mor 28 143 *S* ⲙⲡⲉⲡⲉⲥⲡⲟⲩⲥ ϭ. ⲉⲡⲉⲓϣⲁϫⲉ; ϭ ⲡⲥⲁ- *B*: AM 273 ϫ. ⲡⲥⲁϯϣⲟⲓ τέμνειν; ϭ ϩⲁ- *S*: Lam 4 9 ϫ.† ϩⲁⲡⲉⲣⲕⲟ (*B* ϭⲉⲗϭⲱⲗ, *F* ⲡⲁⲗϩ) ἐκκεντεῖν ἀπό; ϭ ϩⲡ-, ϭⲉⲡ-: C 89 34 *B* ⲁϥϭ. ϭⲉⲡⲟⲩⲡⲓϣϯ ⲡⲉⲥⲟⲛⲥⲓⲥ (ⲁⲓϭ.) κατανύσσειν dat =Va ar 172 22 استقفل; ShA 2 25 *S* dark places ⲉⲡⲧⲁϫ. ⲡϩⲏⲧⲟⲩ, ShMIF 23 27 *S* ⲡⲉⲡⲧⲁⲭ. ϩⲛⲧⲉⲕϣⲟⲩⲱⲃⲉ that thou couldst not swallow, Va 61 20 *B* ⲡⲁϥϫ. ⲙⲙⲱⲟⲩⲛⲉ ϭⲉⲡⲡⲥⲁϫⲓ; ϭ ϩⲓⲧⲡ- *S*: ShP 131ᵇ 15 ⲡⲉⲩⲃⲁⲗ ϭ. ϩⲓⲧⲙⲡⲓⲃⲉ; ϭ ⲉϩⲟⲩⲛ, ⲉϭ.: R 1 5 28 *S* scraped him till ⲡⲉϥⲥⲡⲓⲣⲟⲟⲩⲉ ϩⲱⲛ ⲉϭ. ⲉϩ. *be pierced* (?), C 43 171 *B* sim.

—— nn m *SAB*, *pierced place, hole*: P 44 73 *S* ⲧⲣⲩⲡⲓⲧⲓⲡ· نقب; ShP 131ᵇ 49 *S* ship will sink ⲉⲧⲃⲉⲡⲉⲓϭ. ⲡⲟⲩⲱⲧ, ShC 73 90 *S* ϩⲉⲡϭ. ϣⲏⲙ...ϩⲓⲣⲉⲡⲧⲛⲏⲉ, Mor 25 41 *S* tree ⲟⲩⲕⲟϭⲓ ⲛϭ. ϩⲓⲱⲱⲥ, CO 473 *S* dimensions of sack ⲥⲛⲁⲩ ⲟⲩϭⲁⲥ ⲡⲧⲛⲏⲃⲉ ⲉⲡϭ., Till Oster 10 *A* ⲛϭ. in honey-pot, C 86 212 *B* torture-wheel with ⲗⲁϭⲉⲙ ⲃ̄ ⲡⲭⲱⲓⲧ ϭⲉⲡⲟⲩϫ., C 89 203 *B* ⲡⲭⲱϭⲧ of words he had heard; ϫ. ⲡϩⲏⲧ *B*: Va 57 190 ⲟⲩⲡⲓϣϯ ⲡⲕⲁⲧⲁⲡⲓϫ ⲓⲥ (-νυξις) ⲡⲧⲉ ⲟⲩϫ. iterated *S*, ⲣ, ⲟ ⲛϭ. ϭ., *become, be all holes*: Z 316 ϩⲃⲟⲥ ⲉⲥⲟ ⲛϭ. ϭ.=MG 25 231 *B* ⲭⲟⲗ. ϫ. τρωγλωτός; Sh Mun 160 ⲟ ⲛϭ. ϭ. ⲛⲑⲉ ⲡⲧⲟⲉⲓⲥ ⲛϣⲣⲱ, ShZ 636 n corn ⲡϭⲏⲧ ⲁⲁϥ ⲛϭ., ϭ., Mor 38 23 martyr scraped till ϭⲱⲙⲁ ⲧⲏⲣϥ ⲉⲣ ϭ., Miss 8 255 diseased eyes ⲉⲣ ϭ. ϭ.

ⲁⲧϫ. *B*: Va 57 45 ⲟⲓ ⲛⲁ. ⲡⲟⲩⲟϫ ἀνάλωτος; *ib* 174 ⲑⲏⲥⲁⲩⲣⲟⲥ ⲛⲁ.

ϭⲁⲧϩⲉ *S* nn, *hole*: Miss 8 263 ϩⲛⲕⲟⲩⲓ ⲛϭ....ⲛⲑⲉ ⲛϩⲛⲥⲉ ⲙⲙⲉϩⲧⲱⲡ in diopsical body.

ϭⲟⲧϭⲉⲧ *B v* ϭⲟⲝϭ(ⲉ)ⲝ.

ϭⲁⲩ *A²* nn (?), meaning unknown: ManiH 67]ⲙⲟ ⲛϭⲁⲩ ⲛ̄[.

ϭⲏⲟⲩ *B* nn m, *coriander* plant: P 55 8 ⲛⲓϭ. كُزْبُرَة (*cf* K 185 ⲕⲟⲗⲓⲁⲡⲧⲣⲟⲡ *'S*); BMOr 8775 127 ⲛⲓϭ. فرس *traganum nudatum* (AIssa 181), *cf ib* 128 ⲛⲓϭⲟ *'ذ*.

ϭⲟⲩ *B* nn, ingredient in poison: AM 60 ⲟⲩⲉⲡϣⲁϣⲓ ⲡⲉⲙⲟⲩϭ. ⲡⲉⲙⲟⲩⲓⲁⲃⲓ. *v* KKS 45 n. *Cf?* ϣⲟⲩ 1°.

ϭⲱⲟⲩ *S*, ϭⲟⲩ *A²*(Ma), ϭⲟⲟⲩ⸗ *S*, ϭⲏⲩ† *SA*(once) *A²*, ϭⲏⲟⲩ† *S*(Br 257) *A A²*, ⲭⲏⲟⲩ† *B* vb intr, *be narrow*: Leyd 314 ⲁⲥϭ.[ⲁⲥϩ]ⲟⲭⲣⲝ ⲛϭⲓ [ⲧⲡⲩⲗ]ⲏ ⲙⲡⲱⲡϩ; tr, *make narrow*: Jos 17 15 ⲥⲧⲉⲛⲟⲭⲱⲣⲉⲓⲛ; qual: Nu 22 26 *S*(*B* ϩⲉϫϩⲱϫ), I Kg 24 23 *SB*, Pro 23 27 *SA*, Is 30 20 *B*(*SF* ϩ.), Zech 10 11 *AB*, Lu 13 24 *SB* ⲥⲧⲉⲛⲟⲥ; ShIF 180 *S* ϩⲉⲛⲡⲣϣⲱⲛ...ⲉⲩϭ., ShLeyd 354 *S* let none concern self with ⲡⲉϫⲏⲧⲛⲙⲁ ⲉⲧϭ., Mor 31 211 *S* bottom of pit ϭ.(*v* ⲡⲟⲡⲕϫ p 266*a*), PChass 1 *S* glass vessel ⲉⲣⲉⲣⲱϥ ϭ., TU 43 11 *A* ⲛ ϩⲟ...ⲉⲧϭⲏⲩ, ManiK 95 *A²* each one ϭ. ϥⲑⲗⲓⲃⲉ, FR 94 *B* roads ϭⲉⲭ. ⲉⲙⲁϣϣⲱ.

With following preposition or adverb. ϭ ⲉ-*SA²*: Jth 4 7† ⲥⲧⲉⲛⲟⲥ ⲉⲡⲓ, Is 49 20† (*B* ϩ.) ⲟⲧ. dat; ManiK 223 *A²* ⲉϥϭ. ⲁⲡⲡⲉⲑⲁⲩ, Louvre 10029 ⲉⲣⲉⲡⲕⲟⲥⲙⲟⲥ ϭ.† ⲉⲣⲱⲡⲛ; ϭ ⲛⲧⲛ-*S*: Jos 19 48 ⲑⲗⲓⲃⲉⲓⲛ ⲁⲡⲟ; ϭ ϩⲛ-*S*: BHom 120 ⲡⲕⲁϩ ϭ.† ϩⲛⲡⲧⲁⲫⲟⲥ *crowded with*; ϭⲃⲟⲗ ϩⲛ-: Is 49 19 (*B* ϩ. ⲛⲧⲉⲛ-) ⲥⲧⲉⲛⲟⲭ. ⲁⲡⲟ; ϭ ⲉϩⲟⲩⲛ, ⲉϭ.: TEuch 1 191 *B* ϯⲡⲩⲗⲏ ⲉⲧϫ.† ⲉϭ. ⲉⲡⲉⲕⲛⲓ ضيق, C 99 108 *S* ϩⲱ ⲉⲣⲟⲕ...ⲉⲕϭ. ⲁⲡⲥⲟⲃⲧ ⲉϩ. = Va ar 172 14 ضاق الى داخل; ShC 73 16 *S* sword (Ez 21) ⲉϭⲟⲩⲉϣ ϭ. ⲉϩ. opp ⲟⲩⲱϣⲥ ⲉⲃⲟⲗ, ShMIF 23 179 *S* ⲡⲕⲟⲥⲙⲟⲥ ϭ.ⲉϩ. ⲉⲡⲣⲉϥⲣ ⲛⲟⲃⲉ; ShA 1 156 *S* ⲟⲩⲟϣⲥⲟⲩ ⲉⲃⲟⲗ, ϭⲟⲟⲩⲥⲟⲩ ⲉϩ. (*v* AZ 73 137), Mor 43 64 *S* Christ ϭⲟⲟⲩϥ ⲉϩ. ⲙⲙⲓⲛ ⲙⲙⲟϥ & set self in her womb.

—— nn m, *narrowness*: ShIF 180 *S* ⲡⲉϭ., ⲡⲉⲩⲟⲩⲱϣⲥ, BMis 121 *S* ⲛϭ. ⲙⲡⲁϩⲏⲧ; P 50 97 *B* ⲡⲓϫ.† ⲛⲧⲉ ⲡⲓⲛⲓϣϯ *v* ϩⲁⲙⲛⲓϥⲓ (*sic l*) p 239 *b*.

ϭⲱⲟⲩ *SA²*, ⲭⲱⲟⲩⲛ *B*, ϭⲉⲩ-*S* vb tr, *push*: Ps 61 4 *B*(*S* ⲟⲩⲱⲗⲥ) ⲱⲑⲉⲓⲥⲑⲁⲓ; ϭ ⲉⲃⲟⲗ intr, *push out to sea, set sail*: Ac 21 1 *B*(*S* ⲕⲱ ⲉⲃⲟⲗ), *ib* 28 10 *S*(var ⲕⲱ ⲉϩ., *B* ⲓⲛⲓ ⲉϩ.) ⲁⲛⲁⲅⲉⲥⲑⲁⲓ; Wess 15 125 *S* went aboard ⲁⲩϭ.ⲉϩ., DeV 2 41 *B* ⲉⲧⲁⲩϫ. ⲉϩ. ⲡⲁⲩⲉⲣ ϩⲱⲧⲡⲉ, ManiP 193 *A²* ⲉⲡⲁϭ.ⲁϩ. ⲡⲉⲙⲉϥ; tr, *put* (ship) *to sea*: BMar 190 *S* ⲁⲩⲧⲁⲗⲟⲟⲩ...ⲁⲩϭⲉⲩ ⲛ̄ϫⲟⲓ ⲉϩ. ⲡⲗⲉⲓⲛ; SHel 54 *S* ϭ. ⲉϩ. ⲙⲛϫ.,Mor 28 139 *S* ⲁⲛⲁⲅⲅⲉⲗⲟⲥ ϭⲉⲩ ⲛϫ. ⲉϩ., Miss 4 185 *B* ⲁⲩϫ. ⲙⲡⲓϫⲟⲓ ⲉϩ. ⲁⲩⲉⲣ ϩⲱⲧ. With prepositions. ϭ ϩⲁ-*B*: AM 280 ⲁⲩϫ. ⲉϩ. ϩⲁⲡⲓⲭⲣⲟ ⲁⲡⲟⲃⲁⲓⲛⲉⲓⲛ gen; ϭ ϩⲛ-, ϧⲉⲛ-: Ac 27 21 *B*(*S* ⲕⲱ ⲉϩ. ϩⲛ-) ⲁⲛⲁⲅ. ⲁⲡⲟ; *ib* 13 *B*(*S* ⲧⲱⲟⲩⲛ ⲉϩ. ϩⲛ-) ⲁⲓⲣⲉⲓⲛ acc, Mor 17 44 *S* ϭ. ⲉϩ. ϩⲛⲡⲙⲁ

ⲉⲧⲙⲙⲁⲩ ⲉⲡⲁⲓ. ⲉⲕⲉⲓⲑⲉⲛ; Mor 19 10 *S* ⲙⲡⲁⲧⲉⲛϭ. ⲉϩ. ϩⲣⲁⲕⲟⲧⲉ = Miss 4 98 *B*, C 43 147 *B* ϫ. ⲙⲙⲟϥ ⲉϩ. ϧⲉⲛⲫⲓⲟⲙ; instr: Mor 51 34 *S* ⲁⲛϭ. ⲉϩ. ϩⲁⲙⲡϣⲏϩⲣⲱⲧ *pushed off with pole* (*v* p 722 *a*).

ϭⲓⲟⲩⲓ *B v* ϫⲓⲟⲩⲉ.

ϭⲟⲩⲓ *B v* ϫⲟⲩϩⲉ.

ϭⲟⲩⲱ *B v* ϫⲓⲟⲩⲉ nn.

ϭⲟⲩⲏⲗ *S* nn m, kind of *locust*: Lev 11 22 ⲛϭ. (var om, *B* = Gk) ⲁⲧⲧⲁⲕⲏⲥ جندب.

ϭⲉⲟⲩⲏⲗ *F v* ϭⲓⲡⲟⲩⲏⲗ.

ϭⲁⲩⲗⲉ *S* nn m, meaning unknown: ShC 73 59 among abusive names ⲛϭⲁⲗⲉ, ⲛϭⲁⲛⲁϩ, ⲛϭ., ⲛϭⲁⲩⲟⲛ, ⲡⲕⲁⲥⲉ, so either bodily defect or (despised) trade. *Cf* ϭⲟⲟⲩⲣⲉ, ϭⲁⲩⲣⲉ.

ϭⲟⲩⲗⲏ *S* nn, *thin loaf, cake*: P 43 36 ϭ. رغيف (which 44 85 = ⲕⲟⲗⲗⲟⲩⲣⲓ(ⲟ)ⲡ).

ϭⲁ(ⲟ)ⲩⲟⲛ, ϭⲁⲩⲟⲩⲟⲛ, ⲕⲁⲩⲟⲡ *S*, ϭⲁ(ⲟ)ⲩⲁⲡ *Sa Sf A²F*, ⲕ. *Sa*, ϭⲁⲩⲛ- *A²*, f ϭⲁⲩⲱⲡⲉ *S*(once) & m as f, pl ϭⲁ(ⲟ)ⲩⲟⲡⲉ *A²*, ⲕⲁⲩⲡⲉ *F* & sg as pl, nn, *slave, servant*: Lev 25 39 (*B* ⲃⲱⲕ) ⲟⲓⲕⲉⲧⲏⲥ; 2 Kg 11 9 (var ϩⲙϩⲁⲗ), 2 Cor 4 5 (var do, *B* do) ⲇⲟⲩⲗⲟⲥ; Tri 268 عبد; ShC 73 59 among abusive names ϭⲁⲩⲗⲉ, ϭ., ⲕⲁⲥⲉ &c, *ib* 46 sim ⲛϭ. ϩⲱⲱⲃⲉ ⲏ ⲛϭ. ϩⲱⲱⲡⲉ, BM 1113 ⲛϭ. ϩⲱⲱⲛ, ManiP 81 *A²* ϭⲁⲩⲛϩⲱⲱⲛ, TillBau 131 ϣⲟⲡ ϭⲁⲩⲟⲅⲟⲛ, J 82 16 ⲟⲩϭ. ⲡϣⲟⲡ ϩⲁⲣⲟⲙⲛⲧ, Miss 4 721 *Sf* ⲡⲉⲧϯ ⲉⲃⲟⲗ ⲛⲡⲉϭ., Mor 31 78 *Sf* ⲛⲁϭ. filled my house, J 86 19 oblate as ϭ. ⲉϩⲟⲩⲛ ⲉⲡⲙⲟⲛⲁⲥⲧⲏⲣⲓⲟⲛ, *ib* 90 7 to serve rest of his days as ϭ. ⲛⲁⲡⲁⲥ, BM 1134 letter from ⲡⲉⲕϭ. ⲡⲁⲛⲏⲩⲉ, Ryl 302 sim ⲡⲉⲕϭ. (on this formula MR 5 30 ff, *cf* Kr 238, Ryl 308 ⲡⲉⲧⲛⲉϩⲙϩⲁⲗ), Ep 333 *Sa* ⲁⲓⲧⲛⲁⲅⲥⲟⲩ ⲙⲡⲛⲕⲁⲟⲩⲟⲛ, ST 193 ⲡⲉⲧⲛⲕ. ⲛⲕⲗⲏⲣⲓⲕⲟⲥ, AZ 23 31 ϣⲃⲣϭ., MR 5 29 *F* ⲡⲉϭ.; f: PStras 169 ⲧⲉⲕϭ. ϣⲏⲡⲉ ⲛⲥⲟⲕ; m as f ℞P 8098 ⲧⲉⲕϭⲁⲩⲟⲛ ⲉⲧⲉⲧⲁⲥϩⲓⲙⲉⲧⲉ, ManiP 61 *A²* ⲧⲉⲕϭ.; pl: ManiH 16 *A²* ⲛϭ. ⲛⲧⲥⲉⲧⲉ, *ib* 111 ⲛϭ. ⲛⲧⲥⲁⲣⲝ, *ib* H 61 ⲡⲉϥ]ϭ., Baouit 138 *F* ⲡⲣ]ⲱⲙⲉ ⲡⲉⲕ.; adj: Eph 6 6 ⲙⲛⲧⲉⲓⲁ ⲛϭ. (*B* ⲙⲉⲧⲃⲁⲗ ⲙⲃⲱⲕ) ⲟⲫⲑⲁⲗⲙⲟⲇⲟⲩⲗⲉⲓⲁ; Tri 319 ⲡⲁⲓϫⲛⲕⲛⲕ ⲛϭ. ذل; ShMiss 4 287 ⲟⲩⲡⲣⲟϩⲁⲓⲣⲉⲥⲓⲥ (ⲛ)ϭ., ManiK 12 *A²* Jesus took ⲟⲩⲙⲟⲣⲫⲏ ⲛϭ. (Phil 2 7 ⲛϩⲙϩⲁⲗ).

ⲙⲛⲧϭ.: PS 211 ⲧⲙ. opp ⲙⲛⲧⲣⲙⲙⲁⲟ ⲙⲡⲕⲟⲥⲙⲟⲥ, J 95 6 ⲣ ϩⲙϩⲁⲗ ⲉⲣⲟϥ (*sc* monastery) ϩⲙⲙ. ⲛⲓⲙ, *ib* 69 25 *S* ⲉϥϥⲓⲗⲟⲕⲁⲣⲉ (-ⲕⲁⲗⲉⲓⲛ) ⲁⲣⲟⲓ ϩⲛⲙⲛⲧⲕ ⲛⲓⲙ, *ib* 81 36 ϩⲣⲓⲥⲉ ⲛⲡⲉϥϭⲓϫ ⲙⲛⲧⲙ. (ⲛ)ⲡⲉϥⲥⲱⲙⲁ, Mani H 9 *A²* ⲡⲛⲩ ⲁⲩⲙ.

ⲣ, ⲟ ⲛϭ.: J 79 28 ⲛϥⲣ ϭ. ⲙⲡⲡⲉ, *ib* 46 ⲉϥⲱ ⲛϭ. ⲉⲣⲟϥ, ManiP 103 *A²* ⲙⲡⲓⲣ ϭ. ⲛⲧⲕⲁⲕⲓⲁ, MR 5 29 *F* ⲁⲓⲉⲣ ϭⲁⲟ(ⲩ)ⲁⲡ (ⲛ)ⲕⲁⲗⲁⲙⲱⲡ.

ϭⲁ(ⲟ)ⲩⲟⲛ S nn m, a drink: ShMich 550 18 food
for sick ϭ., ⲉⲏⲕⲉ, ⲫⲁⲕⲟⲡ, Mor 51 33 ⲁⲛⲧⲱϣⲣ ⲉⲛⲧⲉ-
ⲣⲱⲧⲉ ⲁⲛⲉⲃⲗⲱⲉ ⲉⲙⲡϭ., BM 1165 in list of victuals ϭ.

ϭⲟⲟⲩⲛⲉ S, ϭⲁⲩ. SS ᶠA, ϭⲁⲟⲩⲡⲉ A, ϫⲱⲟⲩⲛⲓ B
(once), ϭⲁⲩⲛⲓ, ϫ. (?)F nn f, hair-cloth, sacking, sack:
Ge 42 35 (MR 1934), Job 16 15, Is 37 1 SF, Lam 2
10 F ϫ. (prob), Jon 3 5 SA (all B ⲥⲟⲕ) σάκκος; Zech
13 4 SA (B ⲥⲟⲕ ⲙϭⲱⲓ) δέρρις τριχίνη; Ap 6 12 (B
do) ϭ. τ.; Ge 43 12 μάρσιππος (B do); ShC 73 43
ⲕⲟⲧ, ϭ., ϫⲱⲱⲙⲉ bartered, Mor 28 199 saint's under-
garment ⲟⲩϭ., ib 31 238 ⲉⲣⲉⲧϭ. ϧⲓⲱⲱϥ = RylBull 11
409 b ليس مسح جلد (var BMOr 3599 118 شو 'ـ), Saq
324 among saints ⲁⲡⲓⲕⲟⲡⲉ ('Επίγονος?) ⲡⲁⲧϭ., Mor
24 11 F ⲕⲛⲙ ⲛⲧⲉⲏ ⲡⲟⲩϭ. (Ap 6 12), CMSS 70 S ᶠ in
list of clothing ϭ., PMich 524 F ⲡⲥⲛⲏⲡ ⲡⲉϭⲁⲩⲛⲓⲱ
(cf ? p 253 a), BM 637 F ⲡⲁϭ ⲛϭ.; adj: R 1 449 ϣⲧⲏⲡ
ⲛϭ. tunica saccea (v p 597 a), ST 189 ⲥⲧⲣⲱⲙⲁ (ⲛ)ϭ.
ⲡⲟϭ ⲉϥϣⲟⲡ, Miss 4 236 ⲡⲟϭⲉ ⲛϭ. for tabernacle
(? Ex 26 7), Mus 40 277 ϧⲱⲥ ⲛϭ. to hold καταπέτα-
σμα in place (cf Encycl Bibl 4867, but var BAp 169
ϧⲱⲃⲉ ⲛϭ.).
As measure, sackful: Montp 176 B ⲡⲓⲑⲁⲗⲓⲥ, ϯϫ.
غرا (K 143 ϯⲑ. only); of bread BM 1166, CO 197;
corn Bodl(P)g 17, BP 5567 F; dates ϥⲡⲉ AZ 67 102;
onions WS 86; salt Pap penes MaggsBros 1937; Sph
10 1 ⲧϭ. ⲉⲥⲥⲟⲗⲉϭ ⲉⲥⲧⲟⲟⲃⲉ; sand BIF 14 123.
ⲥⲁ ⲛϭ., sack-seller: BM 1094 ⲯⲁ ⲛϭ., ib 1095 ⲯⲁ
ⲡϭⲟⲩⲛⲓ, Osir pl 37 ⲡⲥⲁ ϭⲁⲩⲡⲉ.
ⲥⲁϭⲧ-, ⲥⲁϭϭ sack-weaver: Sh(Besa)Z 506 ⲡⲥ., MIF
59 268 ⲡⲥⲁϭϭ., ib 205, WS 142 sim, CMSS 39 F ⲥⲁϭϭ.
(Cf σακκοράφος Arch. f. Pap 8 100).
The place-name(?) ⲡⲁϭⲟⲟⲩⲡⲉ-Πακαΰνις PLond 4
pass (for ? ⲡⲁⲧϭ.) = قبنو (PSchott-Reinhardt 1 106).

ϭⲟⲟⲩⲣⲉ, ϭⲁⲩⲣⲉ S nn, slave or sim as term of
contempt: ShC 73 46 who calls neighbour ⲡϭⲁⲩⲟⲛ
ⲃⲱⲛⲉ ⲛϭ. ....ϫⲉϥⲥⲱϣ ⲙⲡⲉⲧϧⲓⲧⲟⲩⲱϥ, ib ⲟⲩϧⲙϧⲁⲗ
ⲛ ⲟⲩϭ., ib 47 ⲛⲣⲙϧⲁⲗ ⲛ ⲡϭⲁⲩⲣⲉ. Cf LBib 1 267
ⲯⲁϫⲱ (as name p 384 a) ⲡϭⲁⲩⲣⲉ. In place-
name (?) ⲡⲁϭϭⲁⲩⲣⲉ (AZ 55 70) جوبر (Ibn Giân 192).
Cf ϭⲁⲩⲗⲉ.

ϭⲱⲟⲩϭ SA, ϫⲱⲟⲩϫ B (nn), ϭⲟⲟⲩϭ† S, ϭⲁⲟⲩϭ†,
ϭⲟⲟⲩϫ† S ᶠ, ϭⲁⲩϭ† AA² vb intr, be twisted, crooked:
ShC 42 215 iⲛ-built rooms ⲁⲩϭ. ⲁⲩⲱ ⲁⲩϭⲱⲧⲣ, Mor
22 140 ⲟⲩⲃⲁⲗ ⲡⲧⲁϥϭ. = BSM 131 B ⲥⲱⲧⲏⲣ, Mor 19
99 ⲁⲡⲉϥϧⲟ ϭ. ⲡⲥⲁⲡⲁϧⲟⲩ = Miss 4 158 B ⲫⲱϧ ⲉϥⲁϧⲟⲩ, P 131⁵ 1 look not back lest ⲡⲉⲕⲧⲗⲟⲙ ϭ.; qual:
Deu 32 5 (B ⲕⲟⲗϫ), Pro 4 24 A(S ϭⲟⲟⲙⲉ, B do) σκολιός, ib 10 8 A(S do, B ⲥⲙⲟⲡⲧ ⲁⲡ) σκολιάζειν; Jud 5
6, Pro 6 14 A(S ϭⲟⲟⲙⲉ, B ⲫⲟⲡϫ) διαστρέφεσθαι; Ps
17 26 A(Cl, S do, B = Gk) στρεβλός; Mor 18 109 S ᶠ
-ϫ λοξός; Tri 259 جرب; ShViK 908 254 ϣⲏϣ ϧⲡⲧ-

ⲙⲉ opp ϭ. ϧⲙⲡϭⲟⲗ, ShC 73 3 ⲉⲧⲥⲟⲩⲧⲱⲡ opp ⲉⲧϭ.,
LCyp 3 ϧⲓⲁ (l ϧⲓⲛ) ⲙⲙⲟⲟϣⲉ ⲉⲩϭ., Mor 41 77 S ᶠ ϧⲏ-
ⲣⲱⲏⲥ ⲡⲉⲧϭ., ManiP 189 A² ⲡⲉⲕⲕⲱⲧ ⲡⲗⲁⲉⲓ ⲁϧⲣⲏⲓ
ⲉϧϭ.; 　　tr: Pro 14 2 SA σκολιάζ.; Ex 23 6 (B ⲫⲱⲛϧ) διαστ.; ShA 1 258 ϣⲁϭ. ⲡⲧⲉⲩϭⲓϫ ⲏ ϣⲁⲩⲡⲟⲟ-
ⲡⲉⲥ; 　　nn m: ShA 1 455 his hand on plough ϧⲛⲟⲩ-
ⲥⲟⲟⲩⲧⲛ ⲁⲡ ⲁⲗⲗⲁ ϧⲛⲟⲩϭ., Z 579 bat flies ϧⲛⲟⲩϭ., K
159 B among maladies ⲡⲓϫ. أول (Montp 178 أؤ, cf
Dozy 2 558) = BM 924 + مصع.

ϭⲟⲩϭⲟⲩ v ϫⲟⲩϫⲟⲩ.

ϭⲱϣ S (once), ϫ., ϫⲉϣ- B, ϭⲟϣϥ S (once), ϫⲟϣϥ,
ϫⲏϣⲧ† B vb intr, pour forth: 2 Chr 4 2 ϧⲟⲗⲧ ⲡϫ.
χυτός; CaiThe 163 at Incarnation ⲙⲡⲉϥϫ., ⲙⲡⲉϥ-
ⲑⲱϣ; 　　qual, molten, cast: Job 40 13 (S ⲟⲩⲱⲧϧ)
ϫ.; 　　tr: Lam 2 4 (S ShC 73 77 ⲡⲱϧⲧ, F ⲃⲱⲗ ⲉⲃⲁⲗ),
Dan 11 15 ἐκχέειν; Ps 147 5 (S = Gk) πάσσειν; AM
290 ⲁⲩϭⲟϣϥ (sc molten lead).
With following preposition. ϭ ⲉ-, into, onto: Jer 31
11 ἐγχ. εἰς; Ge 24 20 ἐκκενοῦν ἐπί (var εἰς); C 89 60
ϫⲉϣ ⲙⲙⲟⲟⲩ ⲉⲣⲟϥ (sc herbs), BSM 2 ϫ. ⲙⲡⲉϥⲥⲡⲟϥ
ⲉⲡⲡⲟⲧⲏⲣⲓⲟⲛ = BMis 322 S ⲥⲱⲧϥ; ⲉϭⲟⲩⲛ ⲉ-: ROC
25 247 ϫⲉϣ ⲉⲩϧⲟⲡⲏ ⲉϭ. ⲉⲡⲓⲥⲱⲙⲁ; ⲉϭⲣⲏⲓ ⲉ-: Nu
19 17 (S ⲡⲱ.) ἐκχ. εἰς, C 89 60 ϫ. ⲉϭ. ⲉⲣⲟϥ (sc food)
κατάχ. ἐν; C 43 72 bade ϫⲟϣⲟⲩ ⲉϭ. ⲉⲧⲉϥϣⲃⲱϧⲓ;
ϭ ⲉϫⲉⲛ-: Jer 7 20 χ. ἐπί, Ps 78 6 (S ⲡⲱ.) ἐκχ. ἐπί, Ex
29 7 (S ⲟⲩⲱⲧϧ) ἐπιχ. ἐπί, MartIgn 877 ϫ. ⲡⲟⲩϧⲙⲟⲩ
...ⲉ. ⲡⲉϫϣⲁϣ = R 1 470 S ⲡⲱ. καταχ., Lev 1 5 (S do)
προσχ. ἐπί; Mus 34 204 ϫ. ⲡⲟⲩⲥⲟϧⲉⲡ ⲉϫⲱϥ; intr:
ShC 42 87 S ⲡⲉϥϭ. ⲁⲡ ⲉϫⲙⲡⲕⲁϧ, TSBA 9 363 ⲁⲩϫ.
ⲉϫⲱⲟⲩ ϣⲁⲛ ⲡⲥⲟⲡ (cf 3 Kg 18 34); ⲉϭⲣⲏⲓ ⲉϫ.: Ez
21 31 (var PasLect 296 ⲫⲱⲡ), ib 36 18 (S ⲡⲱ.) ἐκχ.
ἐπί, Nu 5 15 (S do) ἐπιχ. ἐπί; AM 53 bade ϫⲉϣ ϧⲉⲙϫ
ⲉϭ. ⲉϫⲱⲟⲩ; ⲉϧ. (for ? ⲉϭ.) ⲉϫ.: Ps 106 40 (var ⲉϭ.,
S do), Hos 5 10 (A ⲡⲱ.) ἐκχ. ἐπί, Mt 26 7 (S do, F
ⲡⲡⲁϫ) καταχ. ἐπί; C 43 26 ϫⲉϣ ϧⲉⲙϫ ⲉϧ. ⲉϫ. (cf AM
53 above); intr: Jon 2 6 (SA diff) περιχ. dat; ϭ ⲡ-,
in, into: C 43 141 ϫⲟϣϥ (sc lead) ϧⲣⲟⲏϥ, AZ 23 116
S ϭⲟϣϥ ⲙⲡⲃⲁⲣⲟⲧ; with: Job 38 38 ϫ.† ⲡⲕⲟⲡⲓⲁ (S
ⲡⲱ. ⲉⲃⲟⲗ) χ.; C 86 320 bottle ⲉⲣⲉⲣⲱⲥ ϫ. (var ϫ.†)
ⲡⲕⲟⲡⲓⲛ (γύψος ?) = BM 335 96 S ϧⲱⲥ [ⲧⲟ]ⲟⲃⲉ; ϭ
ϧⲉⲡ-, with: Lev 2 4 (S ⲧⲱⲣⲥ ⲉ-) διαχρίειν (as if διαχ.)
ἐν; ϭ ϧⲁⲧⲉⲡ-: Ez 43 18 (HCons 303, var ⲫⲱⲡ)
προσχ. πρός; ϭ ϧⲓϫⲉⲡ-: Lam 2 11 (F ϧⲱⲧⲉϧ l
ⲡⲱϧⲧ ⲉⲣϧⲛⲓ ⲉϫ.) ἐκχ. εἰς, Am 9 6 (S ⲡⲱ., A ⲡⲱⲣϧ)
ἐκχ. ἐπί; Bodl Marsh 32 123 ϫ. ⲡⲧⲉⲕϫⲱⲣⲉⲁ...ϧ.
ⲧⲉⲕⲃⲱⲕⲓ.
With following adverb. ϭ ⲉⲃⲟⲗ: Ez 16 36 (S ⲡⲱ.
ⲉⲃ.) ἐκχ.; Mk 9 18 (S ⲧⲁϧⲟ) ἀφρίζειν; C 86 274 tortured till ⲡⲉϥⲙⲁⲥⲧ ϫ. ⲉⲃ. ῥίπτεσθαι; Cat 71 ϫ. ⲉⲃ.
ⲡⲡⲓⲥⲟϧⲉⲡ, Va 57 164 ⲡⲁⲓⲃⲓⲟⲥ ⲉⲧϫ.† ⲉⲃ. like water;
ⲉⲃ. ⲉϫⲉⲡ-: Ez 16 15 (S ⲡⲱ. ⲉⲃ. ⲉϫⲡ-); Ps 41 5 ⲉⲃ.
ⲉϧ. ⲉϫ. (S ⲡⲱ. ⲉϧ. ⲉ.) ἐκχ. ἐπί; ⲉⲃ. ϧⲉⲡ-: Ps 44 3 (S

ⲡⲱⲡ ⲉ̅. ϩⲓ-) ἐκχ. ἐν, Lev 14 39 (S ϫⲱϣⲣⲉ ⲉ̅.) διαχ.
ἐν; C 86 275 martyr's brain ϫ. ⲉ̅. ϩⲉⲡⲣⲱϭ, AM 221
ϩⲙⲟⲧ ⲉⲧϫ. ⲉ̅. ϩⲉⲡⲡⲉϭϩⲟ; as nn m: Lev 4 12 (S
ⲡⲱ. ⲉ̅.) ἔκχυσις; Deu 23 10 (S ϫⲱⲣⲙ) ῥύσις; ⲥ ⲉⲡⲉⲥⲏⲧ: Ap 16 1 (S ⲡⲱ.) ἐκχ.; C 43 114 tortured till
ⲡⲉϥⲙⲁⲥⲧ ϫ. ⲉ., DeV 2 169 ϫⲟϣϥ (sc potion) ⲉ.
ϩⲉⲡⲣⲱⲟⲩ.

—— nn, *pouring, confusion*: Miss 4 219 ⲟⲩϭⲫⲁⲛ-
ⲧⲁⲥⲓⲁ ⲓⲉ ⲟⲩϫ. in Christ's nature συγχέειν.

ⲁⲧϫ., *unmixed*: Cat 184 ⲅⲩⲡⲟⲥⲧⲁⲥⲓⲥ ⲡⲁ. ⲡⲁⲧϣⲓ̅ⲃ̅ϯ.

ϭⲁⲓϣⲉ A² nn as pl, meaning unknown, something
terrifying: ManiP 65 ⲁⲕⲣ ⲃⲁⲗ ⲁⲓϭ. ⲉⲧⲟ ⲛϩⲣⲧⲉ, *ib* K
154 ⲡⲓⲁⲣⲭⲱⲡ ⲟ ⲡⲧⲣⲉ ⲡⲛϭ.

ϭⲏϣⲉ, ϭⲉ. S nn m, *goose* or *large duck* (*cf* g̃š Berl
Wörterb 5 208): P 44 55 ⲭⲓⲛ (χήν), ⲭⲏⲡⲁⲣⲓⲛ·ⲛϭ.
ط, زر, P 43 233 ⲅⲁⲛⲱⲥ (?)· ⲥⲓⲙ ⲛϭ. زن, الدد دن; P
46 146 among birds ⲛϭⲉ. ﻙﻙ (misplaced or? *cf* ⲉⲧⲏϣⲓ
2°); Cai 42573 1 recipe ⲛϩⲁⲣ (*v* p 696 *b*) ⲛϭ. ⲛϣⲁⲅⲉⲓ
ϩⲓⲧⲉⲛⲭⲱⲣⲁ *when migrating*.

ϭⲟⲱϣⲉⲛ B nn, herb *dill*: K 255 شبت (beside ϣⲱϣⲉⲛ خزم, *cf* Stern 146).

ϭⲱϣⲧ SA², ϣ. S(once), ϫⲟⲩϣⲧ, ϣ. B(rare),
ϫⲱϣⲧ F, ϭⲟϣⲧ⁺ S(c ϩⲁ-), ϭⲁϣⲧ⁺ A², vb intr, *look,
see* (*cf* dem g̃p Griff *Stories* 148, but *v* Spg *Mythus
Gloss* 670 n): Ps 9 31 SB, Pro 12 13 B(SA ϯ ϩⲧⲏϥ),
Mt 24 4 S(B ⲡⲁⲩ), BHom 4 S ϭ. ⲙⲏⲡⲱ βλέπειν, Is
42 18 B(S ϭⲓ ⲃⲁⲗ ⲉϩⲣⲁⲓ) ἀναβ., *ib* 37 17 SB εἰσβ., Bel
40 B ἐμβ., Lam 1 11 B(F ⲥⲁⲙⲥ ⲉⲃⲁⲗ), Nah 2 8 B(A
ϯϭ.) ἐπιβ., Ps 36 13 S(B ⲉⲣ ϣⲟⲣⲡ ⲡⲛ.) προβ.; Ex 33 5
S(B ⲛ.), Mk 1 44 S(B do) ὁρᾶν, Ps 34 16 SB ἐφο.; Jud
1 24 S, Job 4 16 S(B do) ἰδεῖν; Mk 15 40 S(BF do)
θεωρεῖν; Lu 11 35 S(B do) σκοπεῖν, Hab 2 1 S(ClPr
27 76)B(A ϭⲱϣⲧ) ἀποσκοπεύειν, Ac 7 32 S(B ϯ ⲛⲓⲁⲧϥ)
κατανοεῖν; Lu 21 28 S(B ϫ. ⲉⲡϣⲱⲓ) ἀνακύπτειν, Lam 3 50 BF διακ.; He 10 13 B(S ϭ. ⲉⲃⲟⲗ, F ⲥⲁ. ⲉⲃ.) ἐκδέχεσθαι; BHom 32 S ⲛⲃⲁⲗ ⲉⲡⲧⲁϭ. ⲕⲁⲕⲱⲥ, BMis
95 S ⲁⲩϭ. ⲁⲩⲛⲁⲩ, MIE 2 336 B ⲉⲧⲁϥϫ. ⲁϥⲛⲁⲩ ⲉⲡⲓⲥⲟⲡ; qual: ManiP 199 A² ⲉⲣⲉⲧⲙⲉⲩ ϭ.

With following preposition.

—— ⲉ-, *at, to*: Cant 1 5 S(F ⲥⲁ. ⲉ-), Mt 6 4 S(BF
ⲛ.), 1 Cor 1 26 S(B do) βλ. acc, Pro 16 25 S(A ⲥⲱ.),
Mk 12 14 SB(F PMich 545 ϫⲓ ϩⲁ.) β. εἰς, Si 25 10 S
β. ἐπί, Ez 9 2 BB. πρός, Ps 9 28 S(B ϫ. ⲛⲥⲁ-) ἀποβ.
εἰς, Si 36 17 S, Is 5 30 B(S ϭ. ⲉϩⲣⲁⲓ ⲉ-, F ⲥⲁ. ⲉ-) ἐμβ.
εἰς, Lu 22 61 S(B ⲥⲟⲙⲥ ⲉ-) ἐμβ. dat, Nu 21 9 SB,
Ja 2 3 SB(F ⲓⲱⲣⲉⲙ) ἐπιβ. ἐπί, Mk 3 5 B(S ϭ. ⲉⲣⲟⲧⲛ ⲉ-) περιβ. acc; Jer 13 20 B(S ⲛ.) ἰδ., 1 Kg 16 7
SB ὁρ. εἰς, He 12 2 SB ἀφορ. εἰς, Job 21 16 S(B ⲛ.)
ἐφορ.; 2 Cor 4 18 SB σκ., Lam 4 17 B(S ϭ. ϩⲏⲧϥ)
ἀποσκοπεύ., R 2 2 34 S ⲉϥϭ. ⲉⲣⲟⲛ (var BHom 51 ⲛ.)
κατάσκοπος, Eccl 2 2 F(S ϯ ϩⲧⲏϥ) κατασκέπτεσθαι;

Ap 11 12 S(var ϣ., B ⲛ.) θε.; Lu 12 24 S(B ϯ ⲛⲓⲁⲧϥ)
κατανο.; *ib* 4 20 S(B ⲉϩⲣⲏⲓ ϩⲓ-) ἀτενίζειν dat; 2 Cor 3
18 B(S ⲉⲓⲱⲣϩ) κατοπτρίζεσθαι; Ja 1 25 S(B co.) πα-
ρακύπ. εἰς; Mt 6 28 S(B ϯ ⲛ.) καταμανθάνειν; Ro 12
16 S(B ⲙⲉⲅⲓ, F ⲥⲁ.) φρονεῖν; Z 334 S no man ϭ.
ⲉⲣⲟϥ ἐπιμελεῖσθαι gen; Ru 2 9 S, Ps 22 2 SB, Ez 40 4
SB all Gk om; PS 35 S ϭ. ⲉⲧⲡⲉ ⲛⲥⲉⲡⲁⲩ, *ib* 31 S ϭ.
ⲉⲣⲃⲟⲩⲣ, ShA 1 405 S sailors ϭ. ⲉⲣⲟⲩ (sc stars), Mor
31 67 S ϭ. ⲉⲡϫⲱⲕ ⲉⲃⲟⲗ *wait for*, P 131³ 56 S ⲉϥϭ.
ⲉⲣⲱⲧⲛ ⲉⲣⲟⲅⲉ ⲉⲣⲟⲓ *pay heed to*, BMis 540 S ϭ. ⲉⲡⲉⲓⲥⲁ
(541 ϩⲓⲛ.), Mor 28 221 S ϭ. ⲉⲣⲟⲕ ⲛⲥⲁⲑⲏ *take heed to
self*, AP 21 A² ⲉϥϭ. ⲁⲣⲁⲥ, ManiP 162 A² ⲥⲉϭ.⁺ ⲉϩⲟⲟⲩ
ⲉϩⲟⲩⲛⲅ, C 41 8 B ⲛⲧⲉϥϫ. ⲉⲛⲉⲥⲱⲟⲩ ⲡⲉⲙⲏⲓ = Miss
4 633 S ϫ]ⲓ ϩⲣⲁϥ ⲉ- (collated), BSM 50 B ϫ. ⲉⲣⲟϥ
whilst he went up = Va 63 19 B co. ⲛⲥⲱϥ = BMis 402
S ϭ. ⲛⲥⲱϥ, Aeg 21 B ϫ. ⲉⲣⲟⲓ = *ib* S ⲉⲓⲟⲣⲙ ⲛⲥⲱⲓ;
vbal: Eccl 2 12 S(F ⲥⲁ.) ἐπιβλ.; Lu 1 25 SB ἐπιδ.

—— ⲉϫⲛ-, ⲉϫⲉⲛ-: Ps 39 4 SB ἐμβλ. εἰς, 2 Kg 9 8
S, Is 66 2 SB ἐπιβ. ἐπί, Jud 6 14 S ἐπιβ. πρός, Lam
4 16 SB ἐπιβ. dat, Ge 18 16 S(var ϭⲓ ⲉⲓⲁⲧϥ ⲉϩⲣⲁⲓ ⲉ-)B
καταβ. ἐπί; Ps 89 16 B(S ⲉϩⲣ. ⲉ-) ἰδ. ἐπί, *ib* 30 7 SB,
Ob 12 SB(A ⲥⲱ.) ἐπιδ., Aeg 221 S ⲡⲉⲧϭ. ⲉϫⲱϥ ἐφορ.,
EstD 2 S ἐπόπτης; Pro 5 21 SB(A ⲥⲱ.) σκοπ. εἰς, Sa
7 23 S ϭ. ⲉ. ⲡⲧⲏⲣϥ παντεπίσκοπος; Deu 11 12 SB,
Ps 32 18 SB, Jer 16 17 B all Gk om; TU 24 1 7 S
ⲧⲙⲡⲧⲁⲅⲁⲑⲟⲥ...ⲡⲁϭ. ⲉϫⲱⲛ, ShA 2 258 S ⲡⲡⲉ̅ ϭ. ⲉ.
ϩⲱⲃ ⲛⲓⲙ, Mor 22 53 S ⲉⲡϭ. ⲉϫⲱⲛ ϫⲉⲡⲡⲉⲗⲁⲁⲩ ⲛⲁⲩ
ⲉⲣⲟⲛ, JTS 10 396 S ⲉϥϭ. ⲉϫⲡⲧⲉⲓⲙⲛⲧⲣⲙⲙⲁⲟ *expect*,
AP 44 A² ϭ. ⲁ. ⲡⲓⲙⲁⲉⲓⲛ, ManiP 29 A² ϭ. ⲁ. ⲡⲉⲕⲙⲉ-
ⲣⲉⲧⲉ, Mus 45 49 B ⲛⲧⲁⲓⲃⲉⲕⲉ ⲙⲙⲉ ϫ. ⲉϫⲱⲟⲩ (sc con-
tenders).

—— ⲛ-B, *toward*: Ez 40 46 (S ⲉ-)βλ. πρός; instr:
Ge 13 14 (S ϭⲓ ⲓⲁⲧϥ ⲉⲣ.) ἀναβ. dat; Is 60 4 (var HCons
270 ϥⲁⲓ, S do) αἴρειν ὀφθαλ.; AM 330 ⲁϥϭ. ⲛⲡⲉϥⲃⲁⲗ.

—— ⲛⲥⲁ- SB, *after, at*: Jud 13 20 (var θε.), Mt
5 28 SB, AP 16 A² βλ.; Jo 1 36 S(B ⲉ-) ἐμβ. dat, Pro
29 41 S(A ⲥⲱ. ⲥⲉ-) περίβλεπτος, 1 Kg 18 9 B(S diff)
ὑποβλέπεσθαι; Nu 21 8 S(var & B ⲉ-) ἰδ.; Ez 7 19
S(B co.) ὑπερορ.; Jth 10 10 S ἀποσκοπεύ.; He 10
24 S(B ϯ ϩⲑⲏϥ) κατανο.; Lam 3 26 B ὑπομένειν εἰς;
Ac 28 6 S(B diff) προσδοκᾶν; P 44 48 S ⲁⲡⲉⲛϫⲟⲧⲟⲥ·
ⲙⲉϭ. ⲛⲥⲱϥ; Ps 118 82 S(B Gk om); PS 6 S ⲡⲉ-
ⲣⲉⲙⲙⲁⲑⲏⲧⲏⲥ ϭ. ⲛⲥⲱϥ as He ascended, ShIF 102 S
ⲛⲧⲣ ϩⲛⲁⲕ ⲁⲛ ⲉϩⲱ ⲉⲣⲟⲕ ⲉⲕϭ. ⲛⲥⲱⲟⲩ, ShA 1 108 S
ϩⲁϩ ⲉⲡⲓⲟⲩⲙⲉⲓ ⲉⲣⲟϥ ⲛ ⲉϭ. ⲛⲥⲱϥ, P.132¹ 31 S ⲙⲡⲉϥϭ.
ⲛⲥⲱϥ ⲉⲡⲧⲏⲣϥ *took no heed of him*, BAp 3 S ⲁϥϭ. ⲛ.
ⲡⲙⲟⲩ (var Wess 15 139 ⲉ-), MR 5 50 S ⲑⲉ ⲉⲧⲕϭ. ⲛⲥⲱⲓ
ⲙⲙⲟⲥ, Pey *Gram* 166 S ⲙⲁⲣⲉⲟⲩⲟⲛ ⲛⲓⲙ ϭ. ⲛⲥⲱⲕ
ⲕⲁⲗⲱⲥ *look favourably on thee*, ManiP 104 A² ϭ. ⲛ.
ⲡⲁϩⲟ, C 89 20 B demons gambolling ϫⲉϥⲛⲁϫ. ⲛⲥⲱⲟⲩ
= Va ar 172 16 ﻨﻈﺮ.

—— ⲟⲩⲃⲉ- A²: ManiP 206 ⲉⲓϭ.⁺ ⲟⲩⲃⲉⲛⲁⲥⲛⲏⲩ.

—— ϩⲁ- S: Bodl(P)e 48 will pay thee corn ⲉⲩϭ.⁺

ϩⲁⲣⲟϥ ϩⲡ(ⲧ)ⲭⲏⲣⲉ, Miss 4788 let none ϭ. ϩⲁⲡϩⲟ ⲡⲟⲩⲁ
...but each ϭ. ⲉⲣⲟϥ ⲙⲁⲩⲁⲁϥ, ViK 9402 47 Zacharias
loq (*cf* Lu 1 18) ⲉⲓⲡⲁϣ ϭ. ⲡⲁϣ ⲡϭⲉ ϩⲁⲡϩⲟ ⲡ.... ⲉⲗⲓⲥⲁ
ⲃⲉⲧ? ; ϩⲁⲑⲏ, ϩ. ⲡ-: Si 2 7 *B*(*S* ⲉⲃⲟⲗ ϩⲏⲧϩ) ἀναμένειν; Phil 3 20 *B*(*S* do) ἀπεκδέχ.; He 11 40 *B*(*S* ⲉ-)
προβλ.; PO 2 177 *S* ϭ. ϩⲁⲑⲏ ⲙⲡⲝⲥ ⲉⲧⲣⲉϥⲉⲓ.

—— ϩⲛ- *S* instr: BHom 6 ⲁⲓϭ. ⲕⲁⲕⲱⲥ ⲡϩⲏⲧⲟⲩ
(*sc* eyes) ⲓⲇ.; J 65 39 ϭ. ϩⲛϩⲉⲛⲃⲁⲗ; *in*: Pro 15 3 *S*(*A*
ⲥⲱ.) σκοπ. ἐν.

—— ϩⲏⲧϩ *S*, *toward*: Ac 17 16 (*B* ⲥⲟ. ⲉⲃⲟⲗ ϩⲁ-
ⲭⲉⲡ-), Z 334 ϭ. ϩⲏⲧⲥ ⲡⲧⲉϥϭⲟⲩⲡⲟⲩ ἐκδέχ., Ru 1 13,
Lu 7 19 (*B* ⲭ. ⲉϩ. ϩⲁⲭ.) προσδ.; BHom 7 ϭ. ϩⲏⲧϥ
ⲙⲡⲉⲕⲗⲟⲙ ἀποβλ.; Miss 4 243 sent food ⲉⲛϥϭ. ϩⲏⲧϥ
ⲁⲛ, CO 199 delay not for ⲉⲛϥϭ. ϩⲏⲧϥ, Mor 31 105
ⲁϥϭ. ⲡϩⲏⲧϥ (*cf* ⲉⲃⲟⲗ ϩⲛ-) ⲙⲡⲉⲧⲛⲁϣⲱⲡⲉ.

—— ϩⲁⲧⲛ-, ϩⲁⲧⲉⲛ-: Ex 33 8 *SB* σκοπεύ. παρά,
Ge 49 18 *B* περιμένειν.

—— ϩⲁⲭⲛ-, ϩⲁⲭⲉⲛ-: Mt 24 50 *B*(*S* ϩⲏⲧϩ) προσδοκᾶν; Jer 13 16 *B*(*S* do) ἀναμέν. εἰς, Hab 2 3 *B*(*A*
ⲱϭⲉ ⲁ-) ὑπομέν.; Miss 4 826 *S* tarried for them ⲉⲓⲥϭ.
ϩⲁⲭⲟⲟⲩ (*l* -ⲭⲱⲟⲩ), C 89 34 *B* since dawn ⲧⲉⲡⲭ.
ϩⲁⲭⲱⲕ.

—— ϩⲓⲭⲉⲛ- *B*: Jer 4 23 (*S* ⲉⲭⲛ-) ἐπιβλ. ἐπί; AM
205 ⲁϥⲭ. ϩ.ⲡⲉϥⲥⲱⲙⲁ.
With following adverb.

—— ⲉⲃⲟⲗ: Ap 19 10 *S*(*B* diff) ὁρ.; Ez 32 10 *B*
προσδέχ.; Jth 7 30 *S* διακαρτερεῖν; Br 230 *S* ⲡⲕⲉⲟⲩⲁ
ϭ. ⲉϩ. ⲉⲣⲟⲩⲛ ⲉ-, BMis 94 *S* standing on roof ⲉⲥϭ.
ⲉϩ.; ⲉϩ. ⲉ-: ShC 73 25 *S* ⲉⲩϭ. ⲉϩ. ⲉⲧⲁⲡⲟϥⲁⲥⲓⲥ; ⲉϩ.
ⲉⲭⲛ-: Ge 4 4 *B*(*A* ⲥⲱ. ⲁⲭⲛ-) ἐπιδεῖν ἐπί; Br 236 *S*
ϭ. ⲉϩ. ⲉ. ⲡⲧⲣⲓⲁ̄ⲅⲛⲁⲙⲓⲥ, Lammeyer 44 *S* ⲁⲡⲛ̄ ϭ. ⲉϩ.
ⲉ. ⲡⲥⲱⲡⲧ (var R 1 2 42 ⲉϩ. ϩⲛ-), C 89 102 *B* strove
not to ⲭ. ⲉϩ. ⲉ. ⲡⲓⲗⲁⲟⲥ ⲡⲡⲉϥⲃⲁⲗ = C 99 162 *S* ⲉϩ.
ϩⲛ-; ⲉϩ. ⲙⲛ-: ShR 2 3 74 ϭ. ⲉϩ. ⲙⲡⲡⲉⲧϣⲁⲭⲉ ⲡⲙⲙⲉ; ⲉϩ. ⲛ-: Br 230 *S* ϭ. ⲉϩ. ⲡⲧⲡⲩⲗⲏ; ⲉϩ. ⲡⲥⲁ-:
Aeg 265 *S* ϭ. ⲉϩ. ⲡⲥⲁⲡⲉϩⲟⲟⲩ, BMar 78 ⲕⲉⲓⲟⲣⲙ ⲉⲃⲟⲗ
...ⲉⲕϭ. ⲉϩ. ⲡⲥⲁⲡⲉϩⲟⲩⲥⲓⲁ come to fetch thee; ⲉϩ.
ϩⲁ-: Mk 8 15 *B*(*S* ϭ. + ϯ ϩⲧⲏϩ ⲉϩ. ϩⲛ-) βλ. ἀπό; ⲉϩ.
ϩⲛ-, ϩⲉⲛ-: Ps 32 13 *SB* ἐπιβλ. ἐκ; Deu 26 15 *SB*
ⲕⲁⲧⲓⲇ. ἐκ; Ps 84 11 *SB* διακ. ἐκ, Jud 5 28 *S* παρακύ.
ἐκτός; PS 42 *S* ϭ. ⲉϩ. ϩⲙⲡⲟⲅⲟⲉⲓⲛ; ⲉϩ. ϩⲏⲧϩ *S*,
ϩⲁⲧϩⲛ *B*: 1 Cor 16 11 *S* ⲉϩ. ⲡϩ. (*cf* ϭ. ϩⲏⲧϩ, *B* ⲥⲟ. ⲉϩ.
ϩⲁⲭ.), He 11 10 *SB* ἐκδέχ., Ro 8 19 *S*(*B* ⲥⲟ. ⲉϩ. ϩⲁⲧϩⲛ) ἀπεκδ., Job 2 9 *SB*, Is 55 12 *S*(*B* ϩⲁⲭ.), Ac 23 21
B(*S* ϣⲁⲛⲧϩ) προσδ.; Deu 32 2 *SB* προσδοκ.; Is 59
11 *B*(*S* ϣⲱ ⲉ-), 1 Thes 1 10 *SB*(*F* ⲥⲁ. ⲉϩ. ϩⲁⲧϩⲛ) ἀναμέν., Sa 8 12 *S* περιμ., ib 3 9 *S* προσμ. dat, Ps 32 19 *B*
(*S* = Gk) ὑπομ. dat; ib 24 15 *B*(*S* ⲉⲓⲟⲣⲙ ⲉ-) Gk om;
BG 66 *S* ⲉⲩϭ. ⲉϩ. ϩⲏⲧⲟⲩ ⲭⲉⲉⲩⲛⲁⲡ̄ⲧⲟⲩ, ShBM 253
56 *S* ⲡⲉⲧϭ. ⲉϩ. ϩⲏⲧⲧⲏⲩⲧⲛ whither ye go, Mor 31 106
S ⲁⲩϭ. ⲉϩ. ⲡϩⲏⲧϥ (*cf* 1 Cor 16 above) ⲙⲡⲟⲩⲱ, ManiP
7 *A*[2] ⲉⲧⲉⲟⲩⲁⲡ ⲡⲙ ϭ.† ⲁϩ. ϩⲏⲧϥ, BodlMarsh 32 28 *B*
ⲉϥⲭ. ⲉϩ. ϩ. ⲡⲧⲉⲕϩⲱⲣⲉⲁ (*cf* 44 sim ϩⲁⲭⲱⲥ ⲡ-); ⲉϩ.

ϩⲓⲧⲛ-: Si 14 23 *S* παρακύ. διά; ⲉϩ. ϩⲁⲭⲡ- (once),
ϩⲁⲭⲉⲡ-: Lam 2 16 *BF*, Mt 11 3 (*S* do) προσδοκ., Ge
49 10 (*S* ⲉϩ. ϩⲏⲧϩ)-δοκία; Is 51 5 (*S* ϭⲉⲉⲧ), ib 60 9 (*S* =
Gk) ὑπομ.; Gal 5 5 (*S* ϭ. ⲉϩ. ϩⲏⲧϩ) ἀπεκδέχ., Job 29
23 (*S* do) προσδ.; ROC 17 399 ἐλπίζειν; Wess 15 140 *S*
ⲡⲁⲓⲕⲁⲓⲟⲥ...ϭ. ⲉϩ. ϩⲁⲭⲱϥ (var BAp 4 ϩⲏⲧϥ), Va 63 15
ⲁⲅⲭ. ⲉϩ. ϩⲁⲭⲱϥ ⲙⲡⲓⲁⲣⲭⲱⲛ = BMis 389 *S* προσ-
καρτηρει ϩⲁⲭ.; ⲉϩ. ϩⲓⲭⲛ- *S*: Ps 101 19 (var & *B*
ⲉⲭⲡ-) ἐκκύ. ἐκ; as nn m *S*: Is 66 9 (*B* = Gk) προσδοκία; Si 40 8 σκοπία; Phil 1 20 (*B* ⲭⲓⲛⲭ.) ἀποκαραδοκία.

—— ⲉⲡⲉⲥⲏⲧ: Is 8 22 *S*(*B* ⲥⲟ.) ἐμβλ. κάτω; Bar 2
20 *B* κύπτειν; AM 281 *B* κά. νεύειν; Z 317 *S* ϭ.ⲉ. opp
ϭ. ⲉⲧⲡⲉ = MG 25 233 *B* ⲭ. ⲉϩⲣⲏⲓ προσέχειν κά.; PS
171 *S* ⲁϥϭ. ⲉ. ⲉⲡⲧⲟⲡⲟⲥ, ib 13 *S* ϭ. ⲉ. ⲉⲭⲙⲡⲕⲟⲥⲙⲟⲥ,
C 43 37 *B* ⲁⲥⲭ. ⲉ. ⲉⲡⲓⲥⲧⲁⲩⲗⲟⲛ.

—— ⲉⲡϣⲱⲓ *B*: Su 9 (var ⲥⲟ.) βλ. εἰς, Ge 15 5 (*S*
ⲉϩⲣⲁⲓ), Mt 14 19 (*S* ϥⲓ ⲉⲓⲁⲧϩ ⲉⲣ., *F* ⲥⲁ. ⲉϩⲗ.) ἀναβ. εἰς.

—— ⲉⲡⲁϩⲟⲩ, ⲉϥ.: Lu 9 62 *SB* βλ. εἰς τὰ ὀπίσω,
Jud 20 40 *S* ἐπιβ. ὀπ., Jos 8 20 *S* περιβ. εἰς τὰ ὀπ.;
BMis 71 *S* ⲁⲡⲁⲡⲟⲥⲧⲟⲗⲟⲥ ϭ. ⲉ., AM 199 *B*; ⲥⲁϥ.:
1 Kg 24 9 *B*(*S* diff) ἐπιβ. εἰς τὰ ὀπ.

—— ⲉϩⲟⲩⲛ, ⲉϩ̄.: Lu 24 12 *S*(*B* ⲥⲟ. ⲉϩ̄.) παρακύ-
ψας βλ.; ⲉϩ. ⲉ-: BG 29 *S* ⲁⲥϭ. ⲉ. ⲉⲣⲟϥ, ShA 2 283
S ϭ. ⲉ. ⲉⲡⲣⲟ, Miss 4 180 *B* sim; ⲉϩ. ⲉϩⲣⲡ-: Job 2
10 *S*(*B* ⲉ-) ⲉⲙⲃ., Mk 10 21 *S*(*B* do) ἐμβ. dat, Mor 17
13 *S* ϭ. ⲉ. ⲉϩⲣⲁⲓ ⲉⲙⲃ. εἰς, Job 21 5 *S*(*B* do) εἰσβ. εἰς;
Cant 7 4 *S* σκοπεύ. πρόσωπον; Ex 25 20 *B* Gk om;
ShA 2 284 *S* ϭ. ⲉ. ⲉϩⲣⲡⲡⲉⲧϣⲏⲣⲉ, AM 153 *B* ⲭ. ⲉ.
ⲉϩⲣⲉⲛⲡⲣⲟ; ⲉϩ. ⲉⲭⲛ-: Ez 21 2 *S*(*B* ⲥⲟ. ⲉϩ̄. ⲉⲭ.) ⲉⲙⲃ.
ἐπί; CDan 90 *B* ⲭ. ⲉ. ⲉⲭⲱⲓ προσέχειν; ⲉϩ. ϩⲁ-:
PLond 4 522 *S* ⲙ]ⲉⲕϣ ϭ. ⲉ. ϩⲁⲡⲁϩⲟ ϣⲁⲉⲡⲉⲣ; ⲉϩ.
ϩⲛ-, ϩⲉⲛ-: Jo 13 22 *SA*[2] ϭⲱϣⲧ (*B* ⲥⲟ. ⲉ-) β. εἰς, Nu
12 10 *S*(var ⲉⲭⲛ-, *B* ⲉϩⲣⲏⲓ ⲉⲭ.) ἐπιβ. ἐπί; 2 Cor 3 7
B(*S* ⲉϩ. ⲉ-) ἀτενίζειν εἰς; Is 36 9 *SF*(*B* as Gk) ἀποστρέφειν εἰς; ShC 73 131 *S* ϭ. ⲉ. ϩⲁⲙⲡⲣⲟ ⲡⲡⲉϥⲉⲅⲣⲏⲅ,
C 89 147 *B* ⲭ. ⲉ. ϩⲉⲛⲡⲣⲟ.

—— ⲉϩⲣⲁⲓ, ⲉϩ̄., *down*: MG 25 233 *B* ⲙⲡⲉⲣⲭ. ⲉ.
κάτω προσέχ.; ⲉϩ. ⲉⲭⲛ-: Ps 73 20 *S*(*B* ⲉⲭ.) ἐπιβλ.
εἰς, ib 24 16 *SB* ἐπιβ. ἐπί; Ac 4 29 *S*(*B* ⲥⲟ. ⲉϩ̄. ⲉⲭ.)
ἐπιδ. ἐπί; PS 47 *S* ⲉⲩϭ. ⲉ. ⲉⲭⲱⲓ, C 43 194 *B* ⲁϥⲭ. ⲉ.
ⲉⲭⲱϥ, AP 22 *A*[2] ϭ. ⲁ. ⲁⲭⲛ(ⲡ)ⲟⲩϣⲁⲭⲡⲉ.

—— ⲉϩⲣⲁⲓ, ⲉϩ., *up*: BMis 94 *S* ⲁϥϭ. ⲉ. & saw
woman at window; ⲉϩ. ⲉ-: Su 35 *S*(Mus 50 235)*B*
(var ⲉⲡϣⲱⲓ) ἀναβλ. εἰς, Is 5 30 *S*(*B* ⲉ-) ἐμβ. εἰς; Eccl
12 5 *S* ὁρ. εἰς; ⲉϩ. ϩⲓ-: C 43 61 *B* ⲭ. ⲉ. ϩⲓⲱⲧϥ (*sc*
tree whereon he hung); ⲉϩ. ϩⲓⲭⲉⲛ-: Lam 3 63 *B*
ἐπιβ. ἐπί.

—— nn m, *look, glance*: C 99 134 *S* ϩⲁⲣⲉϩ ⲉⲡϭ.
ⲡⲡⲃⲁⲗ = C 89 24 *B*, PO 2 169 *S* ⲡⲉⲥⲃⲁⲗ ⲡⲉϥϩⲧⲟ
ⲙⲡⲉⲥϭ. ⲉⲡⲉⲥⲏⲧ, BAp 56 *S* ⲡϭ̄. ⲏ ⲡⲉⲓⲱⲣϩ ⲡⲡⲉⲣⲓⲟⲙⲉ.
ⲁⲧⲭ. *B*: Va 58 132 ⲧⲉⲕⲙⲉⲧⲁ. ⲥⲡⲁϣⲱⲡⲓ ⲛⲁⲛ ⲡⲟⲩ-
ϩⲉⲓ παρόρασις.

ⲙⲁ ⲛϭ., -ϫ., *look-out place*: Is 21 6 B(S=Gk) σκοπός; *ib* 8 B(S ⲛⲁⲩ) σκοπιά; ⲙⲁ ⲛϭ. ⲉⲃⲟⲗ: Nu 23 14 S(B ⲙⲁ ⲡⲁⲣⲉϧ), Hos 5 1 S(ShMun 176, B do, A ⲙⲁ ⲡϣⲱⲡⲧ) σκοπιά; 2 Chr 3 7 B ὀρόφωμα.

ⲣⲉϥϭ., *one who sees*: Job 35 13 S(B ⲛⲁⲩ vb) ὁρατής; ⲣⲉϥϭ. ⲛⲥⲁ-: 1 Pet 4 15 B(S diff) -ἐπίσκοπος; ⲣⲉϥϭ. ⲉⲃⲟⲗ: Si 37 20(14)S σκοπός; ⲙⲉⲧⲣⲉϥϭ.: Ja 2 1 B(SA ⲙⲛⲧⲣⲉϥϫⲓ ϩⲟ) προσωποληψία.

ϭⲓⲛϭ., ϫⲓⲛϫ.: MG 25 246 B ⲛⲓϫ. ⲡⲉⲙⲡⲓⲣⲱⲟⲩϣ of world θεωρία; Phil 1 20 B(S ϭ. ⲉⲃ.) ἀποκαραδοκία; PS 38 S ⲡⲧⲏⲣⲁⲡⲡⲟⲥ...ⲧⲉⲩϭ., TT 27 S ⲧϭ. ⲉⲧϣⲟⲩⲉⲓⲧ, ROC 20 49 S ⲧϭ. ⲡⲡⲉⲧⲛⲃⲁⲗ, DeV 1 138 B ⲛⲓϫ. ⲕⲁⲕⲱⲥ ⲡⲥⲁⲡⲓϧⲓⲟⲩⲙⲓ; ϫⲓⲛϫ. ⲉⲃⲟⲗ: He 10 27 B(S ϭ. ⲉⲃ., F ⲥⲁ. ⲉⲃ.) ἐκδοχή.

ϭⲓϣϣⲟⲩ B v ϣϣⲟⲩ.

ϭⲟϣϭ(ⲉ)ϣ S, ϫⲟϣϫⲉϣ (nn), ϫⲉϣϫⲟϣ (once) B, ϭⲁϣϭⲉϣ F, ϭⲉϣϭⲉϣ- S, ϭⲉϣϭⲱϣ- F, ϭⲉϣϭⲱϣ⳾ ϭϣ. (once)S, ϫϧⲱϫ⳾A, ϭⲉϣϭⲱϣ†S vb tr, *sprinkle*: Mk 7 4(B diff), Mor 18 141 ϣⲁϥϭⲉϣϭⲉϣ [ⲡⲉⲕⲗ]ⲟⲙ ῥαντίζειν, Lev 14 7 (B ⲡⲟⲩϫϭ ⲉϩⲣⲏ ⲉϫⲉⲛ-) περιρ.; Job 36 27 B ϫⲉϣ. ἐπιχέειν; LAp 541F ϣⲁϭ. ⲛⲏⲓ ⲙⲡⲉⲩⲥⲡⲁϥ=P 129¹⁸ 102 S ⲥⲱⲧϥ(EW 38 B diff); c 2d acc: He 9 13 SF ϭⲉϣϭⲱϣ- (B ⲛ. ⲉϫ.) ῥ., Nu 19 20 (var ⲉϩⲣⲁⲓ ⲉϫⲉⲛ-, B do)περιρ.; qual: Ryl 110 recipe ⲙⲭⲱⲗ ⲉϥϭ.(ⲉϥ)ϣⲏⲩ. With preposition. ⲥ ⲉϫⲛ- BMis 452 ϭ. ⲉ. ⲧⲉϧⲟⲩⲣⲏⲧⲉ; ⲥ ⲛ- instr: Ps 50 7 S(var ϧⲛ-)A(Cl) ῥ. dat; ⲥ ϧⲛ-: Nu 8 7 (B ⲛ. ⲉϫ.) περιρ.; BMis 188 ϭⲉϣϭⲱϣⲟⲩ (sc vessels) ϧⲛⲟⲩⲙⲟⲟⲩ (var Mor 16 14 ϧⲱⲣⲡ); ⲉⲃⲟⲗ ϧⲛ-: Nu 19 4 (B ⲛ.), He 10 22 SF(B ⲛ. ⲉⲃ. ϧⲁ-) ῥ. ἀπό; C 99 232 ϭ. ⲉⲃ. ϧⲛⲟⲩⲛⲟϭ ⲡⲣⲓⲙⲉ (l? ⲡⲟⲩ-)=C 89 67 B ⲣⲓⲙⲓ ⲇⲉⲛⲟⲩⲣⲓⲙⲓ ⲉϥⲟϣ; ⲉⲃⲟⲗ ϧⲓϫⲛ-: Ex 24 8 (B ⲛ. ⲉϫ.) κατασκεδαννύναι gen.

—— nn m, *sprinkling, outpouring*: Nu 19 9 S(B ⲛ.), 1 Pet 1 2 S(B do) ῥαντισμός; Job 36 17 B κατάχυσις; Deu 4 49 B ⲛϫ. (S om, cf ἀσηδώθ) مقفر; Tri 273 S ⲛϭ. ⲙⲡⲉⲥⲛⲟϥ نضح; MG 25 56 B ⲛϫ. ⲛⲧⲡⲉⲧⲣⲁ =Gött ar 114 7 اسفل الجبل; ib 292 B ϯⲡⲉⲧⲣⲁ ⲑⲏ ⲉⲧⲉⲛⲓϫ. ⲙⲙⲱⲟⲩ ⲥⲁⲣⲏⲥ ⲙⲙⲟⲥ=BIF 13 107 S ϧⲉⲗⲗⲟⲥ (ἕλος) ⲙⲙⲟⲟⲩ, Wess 18 84 S water used ϧⲛⲟⲩϭⲱ, ⲟⲩϭ., ⲟⲩϭⲓⲱ ⲉⲃⲟⲗ, O'LearyTh 25 B ⲁⲩϭⲉⲓ...ⲇⲉⲛⲛϫ. ⲙⲡⲓⲕⲁϩⲓ, PMéd 189 S ⲟⲩϭⲱϣϭⲉϣ ⲉⲛⲃⲁⲗ, BP 419 S list of *varia* ⲕⲁⲃⲟⲥ ⲁ̄, [ϭ]ⲟϣϭ ⲉ̄.

Cf? ⲧⲟⲥⲧⲉ.

ϭⲁϥ Sᶠ, ϭⲱϥ, ϭⲟϥ F v ϭⲃⲃⲉ(ϭⲱⲃ).

ϭⲟⲩϥ F nn, *meaning unknown, an article made or sold*: BMOr 11289 (14) after names ⲛⲉⲓⲥⲁ ⲛϭ. (ⲉ)ⲧⲁⲅⲓ ϧⲗⲏⲓ.

ϭⲱϥ Sᶠ nn m, *meaning unknown*: Mor 32 35 martyrs taking leave of friends ϥⲥⲏϥ ϫⲉⲡⲉⲧⲉⲟⲩⲛⲧϥ ⲟⲩϭ. let it suffice him (cf? Mk 6 8 ϭⲉⲣⲱⲃ).

ϭⲁϥⲏ B nn f, prob=ϣⲁϥⲏ *desert* (p 610 a): BM Or 1325 151 ϯϭ. مقفر, (l'ϳ) لكا, ib 8780 100 ϯϣ. do, K 311 'ϳ.

ϭⲱϥⲧ B v ϭⲱⲧⲡ.

ϭⲟⲩϥⲧⲉⲛ B v ϫⲟϥⲧⲡ.

ϭⲁϥϭⲁϥ v ϭⲁⲃϭⲁⲃ.

ϭϭⲉⲗⲧ B v ϣϫⲉⲗⲧ.

ϭⲱϭⲉⲙ B v ϫⲱϧⲙ.

ϭⲉϧ B vb qual (?), *be exalted*: CaiThe 494 Son of God ϧⲁⲡⲓⲣⲁⲛ ⲉⲥϭ. (l as TThe 245 ⲉⲧϭ.) رفع.

ϭⲉϧ, ϭⲟϧ B v ϫⲱⲣ 2°.

ϭⲓϧⲃⲟⲥ B v ϧⲱⲃⲥ (ϧⲃⲟⲟⲥ).

ϭⲣⲟⲥ¹, ϭⲟϧⲥ², ϫⲣⲟⲥ³, ϣϭⲟⲥ⁴, ϣϫⲣⲟⲥ⁵, ϣϫⲟⲥ⁶ S, ϫⲁⲥ A, ϭⲣⲁⲥ F, ϭⲣⲉⲥ DM; ϭⲟϧⲥⲉ⁷, ϭⲁ.⁸ S, ϭⲁⲣⲥⲓ B nn f, *gazelle*: Deu 12 15 S¹B, 2 Kg 2 18 S⁸, Prio 6 5 S³(var⁶, cit BHom 6⁴, ShA 1 59⁸, ShBMOr 8810 436¹, Sh(Besa)Bor 206 586⁷)AB, Cant 4 5 S ⲙⲁⲥ ⲛϭ.ᴷ (cit ShC 42 53⁸), Si 27 20 S¹(var⁵), Ac 9 36 BF(S=Gk) δορκάς, P 44 54 S ϫⲟⲣⲕⲁⲥ· ⲧⲉϭ.¹, ⲧϭ.⁸(l ظبى) غزل، ضبى, Is 13 14 S¹(varr⁶ ⁷)B δορκάδιον; JTS 10 400 S², DM 5 12, 13 7.

ϭⲁϧϭ, ϭⲟϧϭ, ϭⲁⲣϫⲉϧ, -ϭⲉϧ, ϭⲟϧϭⲉϧ v ϫⲁⲣϫϧ.

ϭⲁϫ-, ϫⲁϫ- v ⲙⲟⲉⲓⲧ p 188 b & p 799 b.

ϭⲁϫ B v ϫⲁϫ 1°.

ϭⲏϫ S v ϭⲱⲱϫⲉ *dig*.

ϭⲏϫ B v ϫⲱⲱϭⲉ.

ϭⲓϫ SAA²F, ϫ. B, ϫⲓϧ F, pl ϫⲉⲩϫ¹, ϫⲉⲟⲩϫ², -ϫ³, -ϧϫ⁴ F & sg as pl, nn f, *hand*: Ge 3 22 SB, Job 5 18 SA(Cl)B, Ps 16 14 SBF, ib 103 28 S(B ⲧⲟⲧϥ), Lam 1 10 BF -ϫϧ, Hag 1 3 AB, Jo 10 28 SAA²B χείρ; Eccl 4 6 S(F ϧⲁⲣⲡⲉ), Ez 10 2 B δράξ; PS 87 S ⲡⲁⲧⲱϣ ...ϣⲟⲟⲡ ϧⲛⲡⲉⲕϭ., ShC 73 73 S ⲡⲉⲧⲟⲙⲟ ⲡⲡⲉⲩϭ., ib 81 S let us not ϫⲁⲁϫⲉ ϧⲛⲡⲉⲛϭ., BM 1064 S wage ϧⲁⲡⲉⲕϭ. *for thy handiwork*, CO 29 S if we comply not ⲙⲛ ϭ. ϧⲓϫⲱⲛ, ib 40 sim, LouvainBiblUniv 6 S I swear by ⲧϭ. ⲉⲧϧⲓϫⲱⲓ, CO 107 S ⲁⲓⲥⲙⲛ ⲡⲓⲗⲟⲅⲟⲥ ⲛⲧⲁϭ., PLond 4 463 S ⲉⲩϧⲣⲁⲓ ⲡⲧⲉⲩϭ., El 54 A ⲉϥⲥⲏϧ ϧⲛⲧϭ., ManiH 33 A¹ ⲛⲉϥϭ., AP 37 A² ⲧϭ. of maiden, AM 318 B ⲧⲉϫϧ. ⲥⲡⲟⲩϯ, BSM 129 B ⲁⲧϭⲡⲉϫ. ⲛⲣⲱⲙⲓ, JKP 56 F ⲛⲭⲏϭ(sic MS)ⲛⲓⲥⲁⲕ; Ps 72 24 SB ϭ. ⲛⲟⲩⲛⲁⲙ χ. δεξία, P 129¹⁶ 9 S ⲧϭ. ⲛⲟⲩ. ...ⲧⲉϩⲃⲟⲩⲣ, Ez 39 3 B ϫ. ⲛϩⲁϭⲏ χ. ἀριστερά; C 86 151 B horse ϧⲣⲓ ⲉⲣⲁⲧϥ ⲉⲭⲉⲛⲡⲉϥϥⲁⲧ ⲉϥϧⲓⲟⲅⲓ ϫⲉⲛⲡⲉϥϫ. *forefoot*, BMis 32 S sheep ⲛⲉⲩϭ. ⲙⲡⲉⲩ ⲟⲩⲉⲣⲏⲧⲉ sim, HM 2 107 S ϭ. ⲙⲡⲉⲛⲓⲛⲉ called ⲁⲛⲁⲕⲗⲏ-

ⲥⲧⲟⲥ (? ὄγκιστρον) = C 86 271 *B*, *cf* ? CO 466 ϭ. among utensils, Ep 319 ⲟⲩϭ. ⲛ[ϣⲙ]ⲟⲩⲉⲓ; ϩⲁⲧϭ.: Sa 9 16 *S* ⲡⲉⲧϩⲁⲡⲉⲛϭ. τὰ ἐν χ.; Miss 8 43 *S* ⲡⲉⲡⲓⲥⲕⲟⲡⲟⲥ ⲉⲧϩⲁⲧⲉϥϭ. *under his control*, RChamp 372 *S* ⲉϥϩⲁⲧⲉϥϭ. sim, ManiK 128 A^2 ⲑⲃⲓⲟⲧⲏⲛⲉ ϩⲁⲧϭ. ⲙ-; ⲛϭ. ⲉϭ.: J 3 39 *S* ⲁⲛϫⲓⲧⲥ (*sc* price) ⲛϭ. ⲉϭ.; ⲛϭ. ⲙⲛϭ.: Ryl 346 *S* ⲁϥϣⲱⲡ ⲛϭ. ⲙⲛϭ.; ϭ. & ⲧⲟⲟⲧ⸗ (*v* ⲧⲱⲣⲉ 2°): Lev 8 22 *S* ⲕⲱ ϭ. ⲉϫⲛ-, *ib* 14 ⲕⲁ ⲧ. ⲉϫⲛ-, Ps 21 20 *S* ϭ. *B* ⲧ., Is 1 12 *S* ϩⲓⲧⲉⲛⲧⲏⲩⲧⲛ *B* ϧⲉⲛⲛⲉⲧⲉⲛϫ., Mk 8 23 *S* (var ⲧ.) all χ.; ShC 73 20 *S* ϭ. ⲛⲛⲁⲅⲅⲉⲗⲟⲥ (var ⲧ.), ShMIF 23 187 *S* ϩⲛⲃⲥ ⲛⲧⲟⲟⲧϥ ... ϩⲛⲃⲥ ϩⲛⲛⲉϥϭ., KroppR 9 *S* ⲥⲏⲃⲉ ⲃⲏϣ ⲛⲧⲟⲟⲧϥ ⲉⲥϩⲛⲧⲉϥϭ. ⲛⲟⲩⲛⲁⲙ; pl forms *F*: Eccl 2 11^2, *ib* 4 6^1, *ib* 10 18^4, Jer 22 25^1 (MR 1934 22), Lam 1 14^2, *ib*^{3} (all *S* ϭ.).

With various verbs. ⲉⲓⲱ, *wash hands*: Ps 57 10 *SB*, *ib* 72 13 *SB*; ⲉⲓⲛⲉ ⲉϫⲛ-, *lay h. on*: Is 11 15 *SB*, R 1 1 39 *S*; ⲉϩⲣⲁⲓ ⲉϫⲛ-: Jo 7 30 *SA^{2}B*, Is 31 3 *SBF*; ⲕⲱ sim: HL 104 *B* ⲭⲁ ϫ. ⲉϫⲱϥ προχειρίζειν, Ac 14 23 *B* (*S* ⲥⲙⲓⲛⲉ) χειροτονεῖν, RNC 58 *S* ⲕⲁ ϭ. ⲉϫⲱⲟⲩ; nn He 6 2 *B* (*SF* ⲧⲁⲗⲟ), Cat 198 *B* ⲡⲟⲩⲭⲁ ϫ., Bodl Marsh 32 115 *B* title of prayer ⲟⲩⲭⲁ ϫ.; ⲣ ⲛⲟϭ ⲛϭ. *S*, *be free-handed*, *generous*: R 1 4 30 ⲇⲁⲯⲓⲗⲓⲥ (-ής) ⲏ ⲉϥⲟ ⲛⲛ.; ϯ *S*, *promise*: BM 1137 ⲁⲕϯ ϭ. ⲛⲁⲓ ⲉⲣⲟⲟⲩ (*sc* money), BP 11349 ⲙⲛⲛⲥⲁⲧⲣⲉϥϯ ⲧⲉϥϭ. ⲉⲧⲟⲟⲧϥ ... ⲙⲡⲇⲏⲙⲟⲥⲓⲟⲛ, WS 95 ⲁⲛϯ ⲧⲉⲛϭ. (ⲉ)ⲛⲕⲟⲩⲓ ⲥⲟⲛ ϫⲉ-, Ryl 357 ϯ ϭ. ⲛⲁϥ ϩⲁⲣⲟⲓ; ⲧⲁⲗⲟ as ⲕⲱ *S*: Mor 52 14 ⲧ. ϭ. ⲉϫⲱⲟⲩ ⲉⲧⲉⲡⲁⲓⲛⲉ ⲥⲩⲛⲁⲅⲉ ⲙⲙⲟⲟⲩ, BMis 463 ⲧ. ϭ. ⲉϫⲙⲡⲉⲕⲥⲟⲛ ⲛⲛⲟϣⲛⲉϥ, Miss 8 38 ϭⲓⲛⲧ. ϭ. χειροτονία; ϣϭⲁ *v* ϣⲱⲱϭⲉ *sf*; ϥⲱⲧⲉ: ⲃⲁⲧϭ. *v* p 625 *a* (though Bodl e 33 may be ⲃⲁⲓ-); ϫⲓ, ϭⲓ: AM 265 *B* supplicants ⲁⲩϭⲓ ϫ. ⲛⲧⲟⲧϥ χ. *κατασπάζεσθαι deosculare got his blessing* (? *cf* PO 1 391); Vi K 9605 33 *S* ⲡⲉⲛⲧⲁⲩϫⲓ ⲛⲧⲉϥϭ. (*sc* Meletius's) ϩⲁⲑⲏ ⲛⲧⲕⲁⲑⲉⲣⲉⲥⲓⲥ, Mor 28 98 *S* ⲉϥϫⲓ ϭ. ⲙⲛ- ... ⲉⲩⲟⲗⲙ ⲉϩⲟⲩⲛ ⲉⲛⲉⲩⲉⲣⲏⲩ, RE 9 151 *S* ⲁϥϫⲓ ⲧⲁϭ. [ϫⲉ]ⲛϣⲁϫⲉ ⲙⲡⲛ̄ⲉ ⲡⲁⲓ; ϫⲁⲕ *v* p 760 *b*; ϭⲱⲗⲉ: ϭⲗϭ. *v* p 809 *b*.

As adj: ⲕⲉⲗⲉⲃⲓⲛ ⲛϭ. *v* p 102 *b*, ⲙⲟⲩⲛⲅ ⲛϭ. *v* p 175 *a*, ⲥⲃⲃⲉ ⲛϭ. Eph 2 11 *S* (*B* Gk diff), ⲥϧⲓ ⲛϫ. Col 2 14 *B v* p 383 *b*, ⲧⲱⲣⲓ ⲛϫ. Dan 5 24 *B* ἀστράγαλος χειρός, ϩⲱⲃ ⲛϭ. *v* p 654 *a*.

Hand of script *S*: HM 1 57 ⲧⲕⲟⲩⲓ ⲛϭ., ⲧⲛⲟϭ ⲛϭ. taught in school, J 74 91 confirmed by ⲧϭⲟⲙ ⲁⲩⲱ ⲧϭ. ⲛⲛⲁⲣⲭⲱⲛ (or ? hand given in promise); ϭ. ⲛⲥϩⲁⲓ: BMar 29 ⲛⲅⲥⲟⲟⲩⲛ ⲧϭ. ⲛⲥ. ⲙⲡⲉⲕⲉⲓⲱⲧ, Faras pl 71 26 place ⲉⲧⲟⲩⲛⲁⲧⲱϭⲉ ⲉⲃⲟⲗ ⲛϩⲏⲧϥ ⲛϯϭ. ⲛⲥ. = Leyd 468.

As measure *S*: Miss 4 723 ϣⲟⲙⲧⲉ ⲛϭ. ⲛⲕⲉⲣⲉⲁ (κειρία), ST 268 ⲡⲥⲁⲉⲓϣ ⲛⲕⲩⲣⲉⲁ ... ⲏⲙⲛⲧⲓ (εἰμ.) ⲛⲟⲩϭ. ⲛⲛⲟⲩⲱⲧⲉ, BKU 1 265 ⲉϣⲱⲡⲉ ⲟⲩⲛⲧⲁⲕ ⲕ[ⲉ]ⲣⲏ (? κειρ.) ⲛⲧⲛⲛⲟⲟⲩ ⲟⲩϭ. ⲛⲁⲓ, WS 94 ⲥⲱ (ⲛ)ϭ. ⲛⲥⲓⲛⲛⲟⲛ, Ep 305 ϥⲧⲟⲉ ⲛϭ. ⲉⲩⲟ ⲛϯⲉ ⲙⲙⲁϫⲉ of corn (?), *ib* 534 ⲕⲟⲩϭ. ... ⲁⲩⲣ ϯⲟⲩ ⲛⲥⲟⲉⲓϣ, BM 1066 ⲟⲩⲥⲟⲉⲓϣ ⲛϭ., WS 118 of wine ⲙⲛⲧⲉ ⲛϭ., Pap Dundee Mus (*olim* Rev C Campbell) ⲟⲩϭ. ⲛⲃⲛⲛⲉ, BP 11349 crop so poor that ⲙⲛⲓϭⲛ ⲟⲩϭ., Ryl 319 18 ⲟⲩϭ[ⲓϫ] ⲛⲥⲟⲩⲟ.

ϭⲟⲩϫ^1, ⲕ.^{2}, ϭⲱϫ^3, ϭⲟⲩϭ^4, ⲕⲟⲩⲕ^5 *S*, ϫⲟⲩϫ, ϣⲟⲩϫ *B* nn m, *safflower*, *cardamum*: P 44 82 *S* ⲕⲛⲏⲕⲟⲥ · ⲁⲧⲣⲁⲕⲧⲉⲗⲟⲥ (ἀτρακτυλίς) · ⲛϭ.^{4} قرطم, K 193 *B* ⲛϫ. 'ق, Bodl 325 151 *B* ⲛϣ. 'ق (but BMOr 8775 134 كراث *leek*); R 1 4 9 *S* ⲟⲩ]ϭ.^{3} ⲛϥⲥⲁϩⲛϥ (*l* ? ⲥⲁϩⲙϥ) *olus comminutum*, Z 351 ⲟⲩϣⲏⲙ ⲛϭ.^{1} ⲉϥϩⲛϭ ⲉϩⲣⲁⲓ, PMéd 318 ⲛⲟⲉⲓⲧ ⲛϭ.^{4} ⲛϩⲟⲕⲉ (*cf* BM 1165 ϭ.^{4} ⲉϩⲱⲕⲉ), *ib* 321 ϩⲣⲏⲣⲉ ⲛϭ.^{4}, Hall 115 ϩⲙⲉ ⲛⲕ.^{5}, Sph 10 4 ⲁⲓⲛⲉ ⲛϭ.^{1}, CO 476 ⲙⲁϫⲉ ϩⲁⲕ.^{2}, ST 117 ⲕⲟⲉⲓⲥ ⲛϭ.^{1}, Win 29 ⲑⲁⲗⲉ (-λίν) ⲛⲕ.^{5}, Bodl(P) d 47 among edibles ϭⲁϥϭⲁϥ, ϭ.^{1}, ϩⲟⲩⲙ, *ib* b 7 sim ⲥⲟⲩⲟ, ϭ.^{4}, ϩⲟⲩϥ.

ϭⲟⲩϫ *B* *v* ϭⲱϭ 2°.

(**ϭⲱϫ**), ϭⲉϫ, ⲕⲁϫ⸗ *v* ϭⲱϭ 1°.

ϭⲱϫ *v* ϭⲱⲱϫⲉ **A**.

ϭⲱϫ *B* *v* ϫⲱⲱϭⲉ.

ϭⲁϫⲉ *S*, ϭⲉϫⲉ *F* nn m, *earring* (*B* ⲗⲉⲟⲛ): Ge 24 22 (Mus 50 17), Jud 8 24 ⲟⲩⲗⲉⲟⲛ ⲏ ⲟⲩϭ., Pro 11 22 *ib* 25 12 m (*A* ⲕⲁϣⲁⲃⲉⲗ), Is 3 20 (var ϭⲁⲁϫⲉ), Hos 2 13 *F* (*A* do) ἐνώτιον; JTS 10 397 ϫⲓⲛⲟⲩϭ. ϣⲁⲟⲩϩⲟⲩⲣ; ⲁⲛϭⲉϫⲓ *Sf*: Sh(?)Mor 54 134 ⲟⲩⲁ. ⲉϥⲁϣⲉ ⲉⲡⲙⲁⲁϫⲉ ⲛⲟⲩⲉϣⲟⲩ (*cf* Pro 11. For ⲁⲛ- *cf* ? ʿ*n*- AZ 37 27 HT).

ϭⲁϫⲉ *F* *v* ϫⲁϭⲏ.

ϭⲏϫⲓ *B* *v* ϫⲱⲱϭⲉ (ϫⲏϭⲉ).

ϭⲓϫⲱⲓ *v* ϫⲓϫⲱⲓ.

ϭⲟϫⲓ *B* vb intr, *run* (*S* mostly ⲡⲱⲧ): Ge 24 28, Ps 58 5, Gal 5 7 τρέχειν, Ex 21 7 (*S* ⲃⲱⲕ ⲉⲃⲟⲗ) ἀποτ., Nah 2 4 (*A* ϥⲱϭⲉ) διατ., Va 57 203 ⲥⲉϭ. ⲛϫⲉ ⲛⲓⲁⲅⲅⲉⲗⲟⲥ περιτ., Ac 8 30 (*S* ϯ ⲟⲩⲟⲓ) προστ.; Lam 1 6 (*S* ϩⲣⲁ), Lu 17 23 διώκειν; Jer 4 28 (*S* ϯ ⲟⲩ.) ὁρμᾶν; *ib* 27 4 (*S* ⲃⲱⲕ) βαδίζειν; Ora 3 241 ⲉⲕϭ. ⲉⲕϭⲓⲟⲩⲓ, Miss 4 125 ⲁϥϭ. ⲁϥⲁⲗⲏⲓ ⲉϩⲣⲏⲓ = Mor 18 32 *S* ⲃⲟϭϥ.

With following preposition. c ⲉ-: Nu 17 12 τρ. εἰς, Is 59 7 τ. ἐπί; Hos 6 3 (*A* ⲡⲱⲧ) διώ. inf; Va 61 105 ϭ. ... ⲉⲡϣⲉⲙⲙⲟ, AM 126 ϭ. ⲉⲡⲉϥⲙⲱⲓⲧ = R 1 4 66 *S* ⲡ. ⲛⲧⲉϥϩⲓⲏ; vbal: Ac 14 5 (*S* ϯ ⲟⲩ. ⲉ-) ὁρμὴ γίνεσθαι inf; CaiEuch 484 ϭ. ⲉⲕⲱϯ ⲛⲥⲁ- τ. εἰς; AM 279 ⲉⲥϭ. ... ⲉⲡⲁⲩ; ⲉⲃⲟⲗ ⲉ-: C 43 118 ⲁⲥϭ. ⲉⲃ. ⲉⲡⲓⲡⲩⲗⲱⲛ; ⲉϧⲟⲩⲛ ⲉ-: Va 58 180 προστ. dat; Miss 4 130 ϭ. ⲉ. ⲉⲡⲟⲩⲣⲟ; ⲉϧⲣⲏⲓ ⲉ-: C 43 69; c ⲉⲃ. ⲉϩⲣⲉⲛ-: Ge 18 2 (*S* ⲡ. ⲉⲃ. ϩⲏⲧ⸗) προστ. εἰς; Jer 28 31 διώ. εἰς; c ⲉⲣⲁⲧ⸗: DeV 1 202 ϫⲟϫⲓ ⲉⲣⲁⲧϥ ⲙⲫϯ; c ⲉϫⲉⲛ-: MartIgn 879 lion ϭ. ⲉϫⲱϥ = R 1 4 73 *S* ⲡ. ⲉϫⲱϥ τ. ἐπί, Ac 21 32 κατατ. ἐπί; DeV 2 52 ϭ. ⲉ. ϯⲙⲉⲧⲁⲛⲓⲁ, *ib* 175 zealous masons ⲉⲩϭ. ⲉ.

ⲡⲓⲕⲱⲧ; ⲉϩⲟⲩⲛ ⲉⲭ.: AM 80 ⲁⲓϭ. ⲉϩ. ⲉϫⲱϥ; ⲉϧⲣⲏⲓ
ⲉⲭ.: Su 38 ⲧ. ἐπί, Ac 7 57 (S ϯ ⲟⲩ. ⲉϧ. ⲉⲭⲡ-) ὁρ. ἐπί;
C 43 114 ⲁⲩϭ. ⲉϧ. ⲉ. ⲡⲓⲃⲏⲙⲁ; ⲥ ⲛⲥⲁ-: Is 5 11
(SF ⲡ. ⲛⲥⲁ-), Lam 5 5 (F ⲡ. ⲛⲥⲉ-), Jo 5 16 (A² ⲡ. ⲥⲁ-,
S = Gk), Ro 12 14 (SF ⲡ. ⲛⲥⲁ-) ⲇⲓⲱ́., Lam 3 43 ἀποδ.,
Ps 100 5 (S ⲡⲟⲩϫⲉ ⲉⲃⲟⲗ), Joel 2 20 (S do, A ϯⲕⲉ ⲁⲃ.)
ⲉⲕⲇ., Ge 14 15, Ps 30 16 ⲕⲁⲧⲁⲇ.; CaiEuch 584 ϭ. ⲛⲥⲱϥ
(sc sickness) ἐξελαύνειν; DeV 1 43 ⲁⲥϭ. ⲛⲥⲁⲏⲗⲓⲁⲥ =
R 1 360 S ϫⲓⲱⲕⲉ ⲛⲥⲁ-, Va 63 23 ϭ. ⲛⲥⲁⲡⲓⲡⲁⲓ = BMis
411 S ⲡ. ⲛⲥⲁ-; ⲥ ϣⲁ: Ac 14 14 (var ϧⲁ-, S ⲡ. ⲉϧ.
ⲉ-) ἐκπηδᾶν εἰς; ⲥ ϩⲉⲡ-: Ps 118 32 ⲧ. acc, 1 Cor
9 24 ⲧ. ἐν; instr: C 43 40 ⲁϥϭ. ϩⲉⲡⲡⲉϥϭⲁⲗⲁϫ;
ⲥ ϧⲁ-: Su 19 (S ⲡ. ⲉϧⲣⲁⲓ ⲉⲭⲡ-) ἐπιτ. dat; ⲉⲃⲟⲗ ϧⲁ-:
Jer 5 1 ⲡⲉⲣⲓⲧ. ἐν; ⲥ ϧⲓ-: Ps 18 67 ⲧ. acc; ⲥ ⲉⲃⲟⲗ
ϧⲓⲣⲉⲛ-: CDan 93 ⲁⲩϭ. ⲉϧ. ϧ. ⲡⲓⲣⲟ.

With following adverb. ⲥ ⲉϩⲟⲩⲛ: Ac 12 14 ⲉⲓⲥⲧ.;
C 86 272 ⲁⲩϭ. ⲉ. ⲙ̄ⲡⲉⲙⲑⲟ ⲛ̄ⲛⲓⲟⲩⲣⲱⲟⲩ; ⲥ ⲙⲙⲁⲩ:
Mk 6 33 (S ⲡ. ⲉⲣⲁⲧⲋ) ⲥⲩⲛⲧ. ἐκεῖ; ⲥ ⲥⲁⲙⲉⲛϩⲏ: Hos
2 7 (A ⲡ. ⲛⲥⲉ-) ⲕⲁⲧⲁⲇ. acc; ⲥ ⲥⲁⲫⲁϩⲟⲩ: 1 Kg 17
53 (S diff) ἐκκλίνειν ὀπίσω; C 41 15 ⲁⲓϭ. ⲥ. ⲙⲙⲟϥ;
ϧⲓⲫ.: Ex 14 4 ⲕⲁⲧⲁⲇ. ὀπ.

——— nn m, course: MG 25 11 ⲡⲁⲓⲡⲓϣ̄ϯ ⲛϭ. δρόμος, Ac 21 30 (S ⲥⲱⲟⲩϩ vb) συνδρομή; PO 11 322
ⲟⲩϭ. ⲛ̄ⲧⲉ ⲡⲓⲧⲓⲙⲓ ⲧⲏⲣϥ.

ⲙⲁ ⲛϭ., place of running, path: Pro 4 26 (SA diff)
τροχιά.

ⲣⲉϥϭ., runner: Pro 6 11 (SA ⲣⲉϥⲡ.) δρομεύς; Va
58 136 δραπέτης; pursuer, dispeller: TEuch 2 274
blessed water ⲟⲩⲣ. ⲛ̄ⲣⲁⲛϣⲱⲡⲓ (Bute Morn Serv 146
ἀλεξητήριον جلاب).

ϫⲓⲛϭ., act of running: He 12 13 (S ϧⲓⲛ) τροχιά (cf
Pro 4 26); DeV 1 178 ⲉⲧⲁⲥⲓⲱⲟⲩ ϩⲉⲡⲧⲉⲥϫ.

ϭⲱⲱϫⲉ S, ϭⲱϫⲉ S A A², ϭⲱϫ S(?), ϫⲱϫⲓ B, ϫⲉϫ-
S B, ϫⲁϫ- B, ϭⲟϫⲋ S, ϫⲟϫⲋ B, ϭⲟⲟϫⲉ† S, ϭⲁⲁϫⲉ†
S/F, ϫⲏϫⲓ† B, p c ϭⲁ(ⲁ)ϫⲉ- S/F, ϫⲁϫ- B, vb A, cut
(cf ذرب AZ 49 94), intr: Mic 2 13 B (SA ϣⲱⲱⲧ) διακόπτειν; MG 25 208 B ϫ. ⲡⲱⲧⲉⲛ ⲙ̄ⲡⲁⲓⲙⲁ = Z 344 S
ⲥⲉⲗⲡ ⲱⲡⲉ λατομεῖν; Is 32 4† S (var S/, B ϫⲟϫⲉϧ), ib
29 24† SF (B do) ψελλίζειν; tr: Ge 38 29 B ϫⲉϫ-
δⲓⲁⲕ., Mt 5 30 B (S ⲥⲱⲗⲡ), ib 18 8 B (S ϣ.), 2 Cor 11
12 B (S ϭ. ⲉⲃⲟⲗ), Cl 63 2 A ἐκκ., Deu 9 21 S ϭⲟϫϧϥ
(var om, B ϭⲟⲧϭⲉⲧ), Jer 31 12 B συγκ.; Ez 19 12 B
(S ϧⲱⲣⲃ) κατακλᾶν; Tri 314 S ⲙⲛ ϭⲟⲙ ⲉϭ. ⲙ̄ⲡⲉϥ-
ⲡⲉⲗⲁⲅⲟⲥ جلاب; ManiP 178 A² ⲁⲭⲉ ⲡⲉⲧⲁⲩϭ. ⲛ[, ib 16
A² ⲕϣⲱⲧ ⲛ̄ⲕϭ. ⲛⲧⲣⲉⲓⲧⲉ ⲛ̄ⲛⲓϣⲁⲃϩⲣⲟ, BSM 30 B ⲛ-
ⲡⲉⲛϫ. ⲙ̄ⲡⲉⲕϫⲱⲣⲟⲛ = BMis 370 S ⲟⲩⲱⲥϥ, C 43 146
B ϫ. ⲛ̄ⲡⲉⲛⲙⲟϯ = TMina Epima 25 S ϩⲱⲗ; ⲥ ⲛⲥⲁ-
B: Jer 23 29 κ. acc; C 86 38 ϫ. ⲛ. ⲡⲓⲧⲏⲃ ⲛ̄ⲧⲉ ⲡⲉϥϫⲓϫ; ⲥ ⲉⲃⲟⲗ: Deu 25 12 B ϫⲉϫ-(S ϭ. ⲉϧ.), Gal
5 12 SB ἀποκ., 2 Cor 11 12 S ut sup; Lev 21 18† B
(S ⲥⲟⲗⲡ) -τμητος; Mt 26 51 B (S ϥⲓ ⲉϧ.), Ap 22 19
B ϫⲱϫ (S do) ἀφαιρεῖν; N&E 39 341 B ⲁⲩϫⲉϫ ⲧⲉϥ-

ⲁⲫⲉ ⲉϧ.; ϭⲱϫ ⲉϧ. S (this word?): Ep 298 they found
solidus deficient ⲁⲩϭ. ⲉϧ. ⲡⲣⲟⲥ ⲧⲁⲡⲁⲗⲟϭⲓⲁ, CO 257
sim (imperfect); ⲉϧ. ϧⲁ- B, from: Va 57 162 ϫ. ⲉϧ.
ϩⲁⲣⲱⲟⲩ ⲡ̄ⲧⲁⲓⲕⲉϩⲩⲡⲟⲯⲓⲁ ἐκκ.; CaiEuch 393 ϫ. ⲉϧ.
ϩⲁⲣⲟⲛ ⲡⲡⲓϩⲟⲣⲙⲏ ἀναχαιτίζειν ἀπό عن جلب, Cat 48 ϫ.
ⲉϧ. ϩⲁⲣⲱⲟⲩ ⲙ̄ⲡⲓⲡⲁⲑⲟⲥ, BSM 49 ⲙ̄ⲡⲁⲧⲉⲧⲣⲉⲗⲡⲓⲥ…
ϫ. ⲉϧ. ϩⲁⲣⲟⲛ, ib 153 قضيب = BMis 399 S ⲱϫⲛ; ⲉϧ.
ϧⲓ- B: Deu 8 9 (S ϣ.) μεταλλεύειν; ⲉϧ. ϧⲛ-, ϩⲉⲡ-:
Va 57 64 B ⲡⲓⲉⲥⲟⲛⲥⲓⲥ ⲉⲧⲁⲟⲩⲁⲓ … ϫ. ⲉϧ. ⲛ̄ϧⲏⲧⲟⲩ
τρανότερος, BP 11349 S ⲉⲁϩϭ ⲉⲣⲟϥ ⲛ̄ϭ. ⲉϧ. ⲛ̄ϧⲏ-
ⲧⲟⲩ (sc crop); ϫⲓⲛϫ. ⲉϧ. B: Va 57 76 ⲛⲓϫ. of sur-
gery. ⲣ ⲥ: ϫⲁϫⲗⲁⲕϩ v p 140 b (more prob cut than
hard), ϭ., ϫ. ⲗⲁⲥ v p 144 b, ϫ. ⲟⲙⲓ v p 255 a, ϫ. ϣⲁⲓ
v p 544 a.

——— nn m B: Ge 14 17 (S ϭⲟϫϭϫ) κοπή.

ⲣϭ. S: Tri 238 ⲡⲉⲓϣⲁϫⲉ ϭⲟ ⲛϭ. ⲛ̄ⲧⲁⲡⲟⲗⲟⲅⲓⲁ جلب.

ⲙⲁ ⲛϫ.: MG 25 208 B ⲡⲉⲧⲣⲁ ⲛ̄ⲧⲉ ⲡⲓⲙⲁ ⲛϫ. πέτρα
σκληρά; BIF 13 109 S ⲙⲁ ⲛ̄ϫⲉϫ ⲱⲡⲉ = MG 25 296
B ⲙⲁ ⲛ̄ϫⲁϫ ⲱ.

ϭⲱϫⲉ SA², ϭⲱⲱϫⲉ, ϫⲟϫⲉ (once) S, ϫⲱϫⲓ B (rare),
ϭⲉϫ-, ϭⲏϫⲧ† S B, dig intr: Lu 6 48 SB σκάπτειν; Tob
2 7 ὀρύσσειν; Deu 6 11† (B ϣⲏⲕ) λατομεῖν; BM 329
ⲡⲕⲁ ⲛϭ., Mor 16 75 ⲡⲉⲩⲥⲕⲉⲩⲉ ⲛϭ. (var BMis 219 c.
ⲡϣⲓⲕⲉ); tr: Mor 17 134 ⲉⲩϣⲓⲕⲉ ⲙ̄ⲡⲧⲟⲡⲟⲥ ⲉⲧⲟⲩϭ.
ⲙⲙⲟϥ (var BAp 55 ⲉⲩϭ. … ⲉⲧⲟⲩϣ.) σκάμμα (var
ὄρυγμα); Tob 8 9 ϭⲉϫ- ὀρ.; Ex 21 33 (B ϣⲱⲕⲓ) λατ.;
ShP 130⁵ 82 ⲁϥϭⲣⲏ ⲁϥϭ. ⲙ̄ⲡⲉⲧⲣ ϩⲟⲩⲟ ⲛ̄ϩⲏⲧϥ, BMis
533 ϭ. ⲙ̄ⲡⲙⲟⲟⲩ ⲉⲡⲉⲧⲗⲟⲙ = ViK 9543 ϫⲟϫⲉ, Miss
4 231 ⲁⲩϭ. ⲛⲟⲩϣⲏⲓ, ManiP 79 A² ϭ. ⲛ̄ⲧⲉϥⲛⲟⲩⲡⲉ.

With following prep or advb: BAp 67 ⲁϥϭ. ⲉⲡⲕⲁϩ, ib 55 ϣⲓⲕⲉ ⲉⲡⲉⲥⲛⲧ…ϭ. ⲉⲡⲉⲥⲛⲧ, DeV 2 255 B
sim; BMar 206 ⲁⲓϭ. ⲛ̄ⲡⲁϭⲓϫ = Rec 6 169 B ϣ. ⲛ-;
Miss 4 672 ⲥⲕⲉⲩⲉ … ϭ. ⲛ̄ϩⲏⲧⲟⲩ, R 1 3 44 ϭ. ϩⲣⲏ-
ⲙⲁ ⲉⲧⲙⲙⲁⲩ.

——— nn A², what is dug, spadeful: ManiP 217
ⲁⲓⲏⲥ ϣⲓⲕⲉ … ⲛϭ. ⲉⲧⲁϥⲡⲁⲛⲕⲟⲩ ⲁϩⲣⲏⲓ.

ⲣⲉϥϭⲱϫ S, digger (or cutter?): PMich 1549 ⲁⲛⲁ-
ⲧⲟⲗⲗⲉ ⲣⲉⲃϫ.

ϭⲱϫⲃ, -ϥ S, -ⲉϧ SF, ⲕⲟⲩϫⲃ S (nn), ϭⲱϫⲃⲉ AA²,
ϫⲱϫⲉϧ B, ϭⲉϫⲃ- S, ϭϫⲃⲉ- A, ϫⲉϫⲉϧ- B, ϭⲟϫⲃⲋ S,
ϭⲁϫⲃⲋ Sᵃ, ϭⲟϫⲃ†, ϭⲁ.†, ϭⲟϫϥ† S, ϭⲁ.† S/F, ϭⲁϫⲃⲉ† A
A², ϫⲟϫⲉϧ† B, ϭⲁϭϥ†, ϫⲁϫⲉϥ† F, p c ϫⲁϫⲉϧ- B vb
I intr, be small, less, humble (cf صغر Stricker ActaOr
15 5): Ex 30 15 B, Si 42 27 S ἐλαττονεῖν; EW 150 B
opp ϭⲓⲥⲓ ἐλάσσων γίνεσθαι; BHom 90 S loquacity
ⲙⲁⲣⲉⲥϭ. ἡττᾶσθαι; Ez 21 7 B (PasLec, var ⲗⲱⲙ, S
ϩⲱϩⲃ) ἐκψύχειν; R 1 4 66 S of moon μειοῦσθαι opp
ⲙⲟⲩϩ; Job 31 26 S sim (B ⲙⲟⲩⲛⲕ) φθίνειν; Is 60
20 S sim (B do) ἐκλείπειν; Cl 20 4 A Gk diff; PS 36 S
ⲛⲥⲉϭ. ⲛⲥⲉⲁⲧⲟⲡⲓ, ManiK 120 A² ϣⲁⲩⲣ ϩⲟⲩⲟ ⲛⲥⲉϭ.,
ib P 190 moon ⲙⲁϭ., BSM 59 B ϥϫ. ⲛ̄ϫⲉ ⲡⲁϫⲱⲣⲟⲡ
= BMis 418 S ⲥⲟⲃⲕ; qual: Jth 9 11 S, Jo 2 10

S(*B* cⲃⲟⲕ) ἐλάσ.; Cl 57 2 *A* μικρός; Ez 34 20 *B*(*S* ϭⲟⲟⲃ)ἀσθενής; Is 53 3 *A*(Cl, *S* ⲟⲕⲙ, *B* ⲗⲟⲡⲕ) ἐκλ.; Va 58 148 *B* scale of balance ϣⲉ ⲉⲡϭⲓⲥⲓ ⲉϭ. ἀνακουφίζειν; Z 278 *S* ⲉϥⲧⲏϭ ⲉⲡⲡⲉ ϩⲡⲟⲩϣⲱⲃ ⲉϥϭ. ψιλός; *ib* ⲗⲟϭⲙⲁ ⲉⲧϭ. ψυχρός, P 129¹⁷ 77 *S* ⲧⲁϭⲉ ϣⲁⲭⲉ ⲉⲩϭ. ψυχρολογεῖν; Is 32 4 *B*(*SF* ϭⲁⲁϫⲉ)ψελλίζειν, cf Mor 36 19 *S* on Lev 22 22 ⲡⲉϭⲗⲁⲥ ϭ.; BHom 46 *S* προσφορα ⲉⲧϭⲟⲭϥ βραχύς; R 2 2 21 *S* ϣⲏⲣⲉ ϣⲏⲙ ⲉⲧϭ. εὐτελής; PS 203 *S* ⲉⲣϫⲓ (*v* p 57 *b*)...ⲉⲧϭ. opp ⲉⲧⲭⲟⲥⲉ, ShA 2 166 *S* ⲡⲉⲧⲥⲟⲧⲡ...ⲛⲉⲧϭ., ShC 73 162 *S* ⲧⲟⲡ of garments...ⲉⲩϭ. ⲏ ⲉⲩⲙⲉϩ, BHom 119 *S* ⲥⲙⲏ ⲉⲥϭ. ⲉⲥⲟⲕⲙ, P 129¹⁴ 53 *S*/ ϣⲁⲭⲉ ⲉⲧϭⲁⲭϥ, Blake 304 *S* beryls ⲥⲉϭⲁⲭⲃ for those near by, ⲥⲉⲧⲁⲉⲓⲏⲩ for distant, P 129¹⁴ 127 *S* ϩⲉⲛⲣⲱⲙⲉ...ⲉⲩϭ. opp ⲛⲟϭ ⲛⲣⲱⲙⲁⲟ, DeV 2 161 *B* ⲧⲣⲟⲫⲏ ⲉⲥϭ., Mor 27 5 *F* ⲡⲁϫⲁⲓ ϭⲁϫϥ = BSM 3 *B* ϫⲱϫⲉⲃ, Mus 51 79 *F* ⲉⲣⲉ(ⲡⲁⲁϩ)ϫ., PStras 334 *F* sim ϭⲁϭϥ; as adj: Kr 153 *S* Phoebammon ⲡⲉⲧϭ. ⲡϫⲓⲁⲕ(ⲱⲛ), *ib* 92 sim (cf AZ 23 73 ⲧⲁⲗⲏⲧⲉⲗⲁⲭ(ⲓⲥⲧⲟⲥ) ⲉⲧϭ.).

II tr, *lessen*: He 2 7 *S* ϭⲟϫⲃ̄ *F*(*B* ⲑⲉⲃⲓⲟ) ἐλαττοῦν; Mk 13 20 *B*(*S* ⲧⲥⲃⲕⲟ, *F* ⲉⲗⲕⲟⲩϭ) κολοβοῦν; Ex 5 8 *B* ἀφαιρεῖν; Ps 76 8 *S*(*B* ϣⲱⲧ) ἀποκόπτειν; Cl 47 5 *A* ⲁϥϭⲭⲃⲉ ⲡⲣⲉⲡ μειοῦν; BM 216 80 *S* hymns ϭⲱⲭϫⲡ ⲡⲁⲡⲟⲗⲩⲙⲟⲥ *sublevare*; ShBM 198 30 *S* ϭⲉⲭⲃ ⲡⲁⲧⲉ ψⲩⲭⲏ...ⲉⲧⲃⲉⲡⲁⲡⲥⲱⲙⲁ, ShPStras 25 *S* ⲉⲧⲙⲧⲣⲉϭ. ⲡⲟⲅⲟⲩⲅⲟⲩ (varViK 9223 68 ⲉⲅⲟⲩⲅⲟⲩ), CA 111 *S* ⲡⲡⲉϭ. ⲡⲧⲕⲓⲧⲉ *not fall below penny* in his alms, CO 244 *S*ᵃ ⲙⲁⲓϭⲁⲭⲃⲏⲕ, ManiP 216 *A*² ⲡⲟⲩϭ. ⲡⲧⲉⲩϭⲁⲙ.

With following preposition.   c ⲉ-: ShC 73 109 *S* ⲡⲡⲉⲩϭ. ⲉⲡⲉⲩϣⲗⲏⲗ (cf 102 ϭ. ⲙⲡⲉⲡϣ.), *ib* 133 *S* when repeating scripture ⲉⲧⲙⲧⲣⲉϥϭ. ⲉⲙⲏⲧ ⲙⲙⲉⲣⲟⲥ; Va 57 13 *B* ⲉⲧϫ.† ⲉⲡⲓϩⲉⲗⲏⲡⲟⲥ ἐλάσσων gen, *ib* 58 193 *B* ⲡⲧⲉⲣⲁⲥϯ ϣⲱⲡⲓ ⲉϥϫ.† ⲁⲡ ⲉⲫⲟⲟⲩ ἀπολείπειν; Aeg 289 *S* ⲡⲉⲧϭ.† ὑποβαίνειν; DeV 2 24 *B* ⲧⲉⲡϫ.† ⲉⲣⲟϥ ⲁⲡ ⲡϩⲗⲓ, ShC 42 43 *S* ⲧⲁⲓⲟⲩ(ⲟⲩ)ⲉ ⲡⲣⲟⲙⲡⲉ ⲁⲅⲱ ⲡⲉⲧϭ.†ⲉⲡⲁⲓ; R 1 5 13 *S* ϭ. ⲙⲡⲉϥⲥⲱⲙⲁ ⲉⲣⲉⲛⲧⲣⲟⲫⲏ, Pcod 40 *SF* ϭ. ⲡⲧⲉⲕ ψⲩⲭⲏ ⲉⲡⲉⲥⲙⲟⲩ;   c ⲁⲃⲁⲗ ⲡ- *A*²: ManiK 122 ⲉϥⲁϭ. ⲁⲃ. ⲙⲡⲕⲁϩ;   c ϩⲡ-, ϩⲉⲡ-: C 99 158 *S* ⲡⲉϫϣⲱⲟⲧ ⲉⲧⲟⲩϭ.† ⲡⲣⲏⲧϥ = C 89 96 *B* ⲡⲉⲧⲟⲩϣⲁⲧ ⲙⲙⲟϥ, BMar 94 *S* ⲁϥϭ. ϩⲡⲧⲁⲅⲁⲡⲏ that his father used to do, BSM 59 *B* ϯϫ. ϩⲉⲡⲡⲁⲣⲑⲏⲟⲅⲓ = BMis 417 *S* ϭ.†;   ⲉⲃⲟⲗ ϩⲡ- *S*: Lev 27 18 (*B* diff) ἀνθυφαιρεῖν ἀπό; ShZ 602 ⲉⲥϭ.† ⲗⲁⲁⲩ ⲉⲃ. ϩⲁⲡϣⲓ opp ⲟ ⲡϩⲟⲅⲟ.

p c *B*: Va 61 5 ⲡⲓϫⲁⲭⲉⲃⲗⲁⲥ (cf Is 32 4 ⲗⲁⲥ ⲉⲧϫ.†).

—— nn m *SA*²*B*, *inferiority, diminution*: JA '73 1 242 *S* if sick & thou eat meat ⲟⲩϭ. ⲡⲁⲕⲡⲉ ἥττημα; BM 174 2 *S* ⲡⲉⲟⲃⲃⲓⲟ...ϣⲱⲡⲉ ⲡϭ. ⲙⲡⲁϩ ϫⲱⲙⲁ ἐλάττωσις; V 58 151 *B* ⲡϫ. ⲡϯⲙⲉⲧⲣⲱⲙⲓ εὐτέλεια; *ib* 132 ⲡϫ. ⲙⲡⲓⲭⲣⲟⲡⲟⲥ ἔκλειψις; Mor 18 63 *S* good is faith of Dioscorus ⲙⲡ ⲗⲁⲁⲩ ⲡϭ. ⲡⲣⲏⲧⲥ = Miss 4 138 *B* ⲁⲭⲡⲓ(ⲗⲁϭ.) = Göttar 114 57 عـ,Mus 42 232 *S* ⲡⲉⲓϭ.

---

frailties belong not to divinity, OrChrPeriod 4 49 *S* ⲟⲩϭ. ⲙⲡⲉⲥⲧⲟⲓⲭⲓⲟⲡ (*sc* moon), Turin *Atti* 30 806 *S* ⲟⲩⲅⲟϭ ⲡϭ. ⲙⲡⲉⲡⲃⲓⲟⲥⲛⲉ (*sic l*) that worldlings outstrip us, BMis 359 *S* be ye not found ϩⲙⲡⲉⲓⲕⲟⲩϫⲃ (var ϭⲱ.), ManiK 169 *A*² ϣⲁⲣⲉⲟⲩϭ. ϣⲱⲡⲉ ϩⲡⲡⲓⲗⲟⲅⲓⲉⲅⲉ, *ib* P 203 *A*² ⲙⲡ ϣⲧⲁ ⲙⲡ ϭ. ⲡⲣⲏⲧⲟⲩ, Cat 193 *B* ⲡⲓϫ. ⲙⲡⲟⲩⲅⲉⲡⲟⲥ opp ⲡⲓϣϯ ⲡϭ., AM 247 *B* ⲡϫ. ⲙⲡⲁⲗⲁⲥ, C 89 122 *B* ⲁⲑⲉⲟⲇⲱⲣⲟⲥ ϣⲱⲡⲓ ⲡⲟⲩϫ. =Va ar 172 70 نقص مـارّي opp ⲟⲩⲟⲥⲟⲉⲡ ⲉⲃⲟⲗ ϩⲉⲡϯⲡⲣⲟⲕⲟⲡⲏ, *ib* 39 *B* lest I be found ϩⲉⲡⲟⲩϫ. ⲡⲁⲣⲣⲉⲡⲡⲟⲥ;   ϯ ϭ., ϫ.: EW 150 *B* ϯ ⲡⲟⲩⲙⲉⲧⲡⲓϣϯ...ϯ ⲡⲟⲩϫ. ἐλαττοῦν; Mor 37 227 *S* Arius ⲁϥϯ ⲡⲟⲩϭ. ⲡⲧⲟⲩⲉⲓ ⲡⲛϩⲩⲡⲟⲥⲧⲁⲥⲓⲥ, MIE 2 367 *B* ϯ ⲡⲟⲩϫ. ⲙⲡⲓⲥⲱⲙⲁ that God made;   ϫⲓ ϭ. *S*: Blake 298 Reuben ϫⲓ ⲡⲟⲩϫ. ⲉⲧⲃⲉⲟⲩⲥϩⲓⲙⲉ.

ⲁⲧϭ., ϫ., *unfailing, undiminished*: ManiP 68 *A*² ⲭⲣⲏⲙⲁ ⲡⲁ., MG 25 397 *B* ⲧⲣⲓⲁⲥ...ⲡⲁⲧϫ.

ⲟⲓ ⲡϫ. *B*: Ez 34 4 (*S* ϭⲃⲃⲉ) ἀσθενεῖν.

ϭⲓⲛϭ. *S*, *waning* of moon: ShP 130¹ 105 ϭⲓⲛⲙⲟⲩϩ, ϭ.

ϭⲁϫⲙⲏ, -ⲉ, ϫⲁⲙⲏ *S* nn f, *fist, handful* (cf קֹמֶץ Dévaud): Is 40 12 (var ϫ., *B* ϩⲟⲣⲡⲥ) δράξ; P 44 22 قفـة; BMOr 6201 *B* 229 account]ⲧⲓ ϩⲁϭⲁⲭⲙⲉ.

ϭⲁϫⲙⲉⲥ *S* nn, same: J 65 24 hoping for ⲟⲩϭ. ⲡⲡⲁ & drop of dew at Judgment.

ϭⲁϫⲓϥ¹ *SA*, -ⲃ², ⲕⲁϫⲓϥ³ *S*, ϫⲁϥϫⲓϥ⁴, ϫⲁⲡϫⲓⲡ⁵, ϫⲉϥϫⲓϥ⁶, ϫⲉⲃⲭⲓⲡ⁷ *B* nn m f (once), *ant*: Pro 6 6 *S*¹ *AB*⁴, cit Bor 253 166 *S*², Mor 18 123 *S*², Va 57 259 *B* ⲡⲓϫ.⁶ ⲡⲉⲙⲡⲓϣⲟⲗⲙⲉⲥ, *ib* 12 *B* ⲡⲓϫ.⁴ μύρμηξ; K 173 *B* ϯϫ.⁵ (varr⁴⁶, BMOr 8771 88⁷) نمـل; ShZ 592 *S* ⲡϭ.¹, Gu 47 *S* ⲟⲩⲕ.³, KroppM 115 *S* may his penis be as ⲟⲩⲕ.³ ⲉⲥⲁⲕϥ ϩⲏⲧⲉⲡⲣⲱ (cf RChamp 541), MG 25 147 *B* ⲡⲓϫ.⁴ ⲉⲧⲟⲱⲟⲩϯ ⲉϩⲟⲩⲡ in summer;   ⲣ ϭ.*S*, *suffer from warts or itch*: Lev 22 22¹ (var ⲟ ⲡⲁⲣϣⲁⲡ, *B* ⲑⲟⲩⲑⲟⲩ) μυρμηκιᾶν, LCyp 4 ⲡⲉⲙⲟⲩⲧ ⲡϣⲁϫⲱⲗⲕ ⲡⲥⲉⲉⲣ ϭ.¹ (var Mor 18 110²)-κιασμός; P 44 122 ⲁϥⲥⲕⲟⲧⲉⲅⲉ ϣⲁⲡⲧⲉⲡⲉϥⲥⲱⲙⲁ ⲉⲣ ⲕ.³ نمـل.

As name: Καχιβ (PCai 1 205), Πχιπχιπ? (PLond 4 216), ϫⲁⲡϫⲓⲡⲉ (J 43 44).
Cf ϫⲉⲕϫⲓⲕ.

(ϭⲱϫϩ), ϭⲟϫϩ⸗ *v* ϭⲱⲱϫⲉ **A**.

ϭⲟϫϭ(ⲉ)ϫ *S*, ϭⲁϫϭⲉϫ *S*/, ϭⲁϫϭ *A* (nn), ϭⲟⲧϭⲉⲧ, ϣⲟⲧϭⲉⲧ *B*, ϭⲉⲧϭⲱⲧ- *B*(once), ϭⲉⲭϭⲱϫ⸗, ϭⲉⲧϭⲱϫ⸗, -ϭⲱϭ⸗ *S*, ϭⲉⲧϭⲱⲧ⸗ *B*, ϭⲉⲭϭⲟϫⲧ† *S* vb tr, *cut, smite, slaughter* (cf ϭⲱⲱϫⲉ): Jer 26 5 *B* κόπτειν, Is 18 5 *S* (*B* ⲱⲗⲓ) ἀποκ., Ge 32 8 *SB*, Job 42 18 *S*(var ϭⲟϭϭⲉϭ, *B* ϫⲱϫⲓ) ἐκκ., Zeph 1 11 *B*(var ϣⲟⲧ., *A* ⲧⲉⲕⲟ) κατακ., Deu 9 21 *B*(*S* ϭⲟϫϭ⸗) σύγκ.; Lam 2 21 *S*(*B*=Gk, *F* ϣⲱⲧ) μαγειρεύειν; Jud 1 10 *S* πατάσσειν; Ez 13 13 *B* ϭⲉⲧϭⲱⲧ-(*S* ϩⲣⲱϩⲧ) ῥηγνύναι; ShA 1 448 *S* ⲁϥϭ. ⲡⲣⲉⲛⲁϣⲏ ⲡⲧⲁⲣ, ShA 2 345 *S* ϣϣⲱⲧ ⲙⲙⲟⲟⲩ...ϭ.

ⲛϩⲉⲛⲕⲟⲟⲩⲉ, ShC 42 112 *S* ϭⲉⲧϭⲱϫⲥ ⲏ ϭⲉⲧϭⲱϭⲟⲩ, ShP 130² 86 *S* ⲉⲩⲕⲟⲛⲥ ⲉⲩϭ.†, BMis 504 *S* ⲁϥϭ. ⲛϩⲉⲛⲣⲣⲟ (Ps 134 10 ⲙⲟⲩⲟⲩⲧ), C 86 37 *B* ⲉⲩⲛⲁϭⲉⲧϭⲱⲧⲕ ⲕⲁⲧⲁ ⲡⲉⲕⲣⲁⲧⲱⲙⲓ.

With following preposition or adverb. c ⲛ- *B* instr: C 86 216 ϭⲉⲧϭⲱⲧⲟⲩ ⲛⲧⲥⲏϥⲓ; c ⲛⲥⲁ-: Nu 14 45 *B*(*S* tr) *κατακ.*; ShMIF 23 9 *S* sword ⲉⲧϭ. ⲛⲥⲱⲟⲩ, C 41 51 *B* ⲡⲓⲃⲁⲣⲃⲁⲣⲟⲥ ⲁϥϭ. ⲛⲥⲱⲟⲩ, Mor 39 44 *S^f* bade ϭ. ⲛⲥⲱⲟⲩ = *ib* 40 33 *S*; c ϩⲛ-, ϧⲉⲛ-: Dan 9 26 *B*(*S* ϣⲱⲱⲧ) *ἐκκ. ἐν*, Ez 5 2 *S*(*B* ⲥⲱⲗⲡ) *κατακ. ἐν*; *ib* 23 25 *B*(*S* p.) *καταβάλλειν ἐν*; ⲉⲃⲟⲗ ϩⲛ-: ShHT *J* 1 *S* ⲛϥϭ. ⲛⲧⲡⲟⲣⲛⲓⲁ...ⲉⲃ. ⲛϩⲏⲧϥ; c ⲉϧⲣⲏⲓ *B*: MG 25 27 dogs & birds ϭⲉⲧϭⲱⲧϥ ⲉϧ. ⲧⲏⲣϥ (*sic l*) *κατατέμνειν*; c ⲉⲡⲉⲥⲏⲧ *S*: WTh 196 fire beneath martyr ϣⲁⲛⲧⲉⲡⲉⲥⲥⲡⲓⲣⲟⲟⲩⲉ ϭ. ⲉⲡ. (this word ? *Cf* ⲡⲟⲧⲡⲧ).

—— nn m, *cutting, slaughter*: Ge 14 17 *S*(*B* ϫⲱϫⲓ), Deu 28 25 *B*(*S* diff) *κοπή*, Pro 6 15 *SA*(*B* ϣⲱⲧ ⲉⲃⲟⲗ) *διακ.*, 1 Chr 15 13 *B* ⲓⲣⲓ ⲡⲟⲩϣ. *διακόπτειν* قطع, R 1 4 59 *S* ϭ. ⲛⲙⲙⲉⲗⲟⲥ = MartIgn 870 *B* ϭⲟⲧϫⲉⲧ *συγκ.*; Lev 21 5 *B*(*S* ϣⲱⲗϩ vb) *ἐντομίς*; Va 57 167 *B* ϯⲥⲫⲁⲅⲏ ⲛⲉⲙⲡⲓϭ. of war; ϣⲱⲧ ⲛϭ. *B*: Lev 19 28 (*S* ⲥϩⲁⲓ ⲉϫⲉⲕϫⲱⲕⲟⲩ) *ἐντ.*

ⲣⲉϥϭ. *B*, *slayer*: OraChrPeriod 3 547 ⲫⲓⲣ. ⲛⲛⲓϫⲱⲣⲓ.

Cf ϣⲟⲧϣⲧ.

(ϭⲁϭ-) ⲕⲁⲕ- *v* ϫⲱϫ 1° (ϫⲁϫⲃⲱⲛ).

ϭⲟⲩϭ *v* ϭⲟⲩϫ & ϭⲱϭ 2°.

ϭⲱϭ *S*, ϫⲱϫ *B*, ϭⲁⲁϭⲓ *F*(?), ϭⲉϭ-, ϭⲉϫ- *S*, ϭⲁⲧ- *F*, ϭⲟϭ⸗, ϭⲁϭ⸗, ϭⲉϭ⸗, ⲕⲟϫ⸗ *S*, ⲕⲁϫ⸗, ⲕⲁⲧϣ⸗ *S^a*, ϫⲟϫ⸗ *SB*, ϭⲏϭ†, -ϫ† *S*, ϫⲏϫ† vb intr, *roast, bake* (= ? ⲧⲱϭ): Deu 16 7 *S*(*B* ϫⲟϥϫⲉϥ) *ὀπτᾶν*; Ps 101 4 *SB* *συμφρύγειν*; Job 30 17 *S*(*B* ⲣⲱⲕϩ) *συγχεῖσθαι*; SHel 32 *S* fire beneath cauldron so that ⲡⲉϥⲥⲱⲙⲁ ϭ. ⲉⲙⲁⲧⲉ; qual: Lev 2 4 *B*(*S* diff) *πέπτειν*; *ib* 23 14 *B* (*S* diff) *φρ.* (prob); Ex 12 8 *S*(*B* ⲫⲟⲥⲓ), Lu 24 42 *S*(*B* ϫⲉϥϫⲱϥ) *ὀπ.*, cit Tri 259 مشوى; ShViK 9596 187 *S* ⲉⲃⲣⲁ ⲉϥϭ. not eaten in Lent, PSBA 27 168 *S* ⲉⲩϭⲏϫ ⲙⲡⲉⲩⲉⲣⲏⲩ, Z 627 *S* ⲥⲟⲟⲩϩⲉ ⲉⲥϭ. ϩⲓϫⲛϩⲛϫⲃⲃⲉⲥ, PMéd 184 *S* ⲧⲉⲡⲛ ⲉϥϭⲏϫ, *ib* 304 ϭⲏϭ; tr: Ex 16 23 *B*(*S* ⲧⲱϭ) *πέπ.* (var *ζυμοῦν*) paral ⲫⲓⲥⲓ, Lev 26 26 *B*(*S* do, *F* ϭⲁⲧ- BM 1221) *π.*; Is 44 16 *S*(*B* ⲫⲓⲥⲓ) *ὀπ.*; ShP 130¹ 124 *S* ϭ. ⲛϩⲉⲛⲁϥ in fire, ShRyl 68 259 *S* ϩⲉⲛⲉⲓⲧⲟⲥ (-δος) ⲉⲩⲣ ϩⲟⲩⲟ ⲛϭⲉϭⲟⲩ ⲏ ⲉⲩⲙⲉϩ (*v* ⲙⲟⲩϩ 2°) ⲉⲙⲁⲧⲉ, Bor 307 4 *S* ⲁϥⲥⲁϩⲧⲉ...ϣⲁⲛⲧⲉϥϭⲉϭ ⲡⲉⲩⲥⲁⲣⲝ, Ep 575 *S* ⲃⲗⲃⲓⲗⲉ ⲙⲡⲓⲡⲉⲣ (*πέπερι*) ⲛⲕⲟϫⲟⲩ, BKU 1 27 *S^a* ingredients [ⲕ]ⲁⲕⲁϫⲟⲩ ⲕⲁⲗⲟⲥ (-ῶς), *ib* ⲛⲕⲁⲧϣϥ ⲛⲁϥϥ, AZ 23 108 *S* ⲥⲧⲱϥ (*sc* mixture) ⲉⲛⲕⲟϩⲧ ϭⲟϭϥ, Cai 42573 2 *S* ϭⲁϭⲟⲩ ϩⲓⲛⲉϩ, PSBA *lc S* ϭⲉϫ ⲟⲩⲕⲟⲩⲓ ⲙⲯⲉⲙⲓⲑⲉⲓ (*ψιμύθιον*), Ann 18 284 *S* ⲛⲁⲥⲥⲓⲣⲓϫ (الشيرج, *cf* BodlP 1 a *f* ⲁϣϣⲓⲣⲓϫ, Ryl 110 ⲁϣϣⲉⲣⲓϭ) ⲛⲛϫⲟϫϥ, PBad 5 398 *F* ⲛⲑⲉ ⲛⲟⲩⲕⲱϩⲧ ⲉⲕϭ. ⲙⲙⲁϥ.

ϭ. ⲉⲃⲟⲗ *S*: ShC 73 146 ⲡⲉⲧϭⲉϫ ϣⲱⲧⲉ ⲉⲃ. ⲉⲁⲁϥ ⲛϭⲱⲱⲗⲉ.

ϭ. ⲉϩⲣⲁⲓ *S*: Z 351 ⲟⲩϣⲏⲙ ⲛϭⲟⲩϫ ⲉϥϭ.† ⲉϩ.

—— nn m *B*, *baked* bread: K 132, 263 ⲡⲓϫ. قلى, خبز. *Cf* AZ 14 88.

ⲙⲁ ⲛϭⲟϭ *S* nn m, *baked, roasted food*: Tri 239 ⲁⲩⲟⲩⲱⲙ ⲙⲡⲙ. مُحَمَّر (word still thus used in Upper Egypt, Sobhy).

ϭⲁⲁϭⲉ¹, ϭⲁϭⲉ², ⲕⲁⲕⲉ (Theban), ϭⲉϭⲉ³ (this ?) ϭⲟⲟϭⲉ⁴ *S*, ϭⲁϭⲉ DM, ⲕⲁⲕ- *S* n m f, *baked loaf, cake* (*cf* كعكة Spg 295): ShC 73 144 ⲡⲣⲱⲙⲉ ⲙⲡϭ.¹ (var²) shall put plenty of bread (ⲟⲉⲓⲕ) into basket, *ib* 145 ⲛϭ.¹ ⲉⲧⲗⲏⲕ, *ib* ⲛϭ.¹ ⲉⲩⲡⲟⲥⲉ, *ib* 211 ⲧⲉϥϭ.¹ ⲉⲧϣⲏⲩ *long loaf*, ShIF 302 ⲟⲩⲗⲁⲕⲙ ⲛϭ.¹, Mor 51 41 if ye will not reap ⲛⲛⲉϭ.² ϣⲱⲡⲉ ϩⲛⲧϭⲁⲣϭⲁⲧⲁⲡⲉ, *ib* 42 ϭ.¹, Ep 541 ⲥⲟⲩⲟ ⲛⲕ., *ib* 309 ⲛⲥⲟⲩⲟ ⲁⲩⲧⲟⲕϥ ⲛⲕ., Ryl 280 ⲧⲱϭ ⲡϣⲏⲙ ⲛϭ.², *ib* 159 as wage ⲧⲁⲓⲟⲩ ⲛⲏⲓ ⲛϭ.¹ (*v* p 66 *b*), ViK 4794 ⲃⲧⲟ ⲛϭ.¹, J 5 R victuals ⲏⲣⲡ, ⲕ., ⲁϥ, Z 630 in recipe ⲟⲩϭ.¹ ⲉϥϣⲟⲩⲱⲟⲩ, BM 472 ⲛ]ⲧⲉⲛϭ.⁴ ϣⲱⲟⲩ (*l* ϣⲟⲩⲱⲟⲩ) ⲕⲁⲗⲱⲥ, *ib* 1150 ⲛϭ.¹ (ⲛ)ⲧⲁⲕⲥⲙⲏⲛⲧⲟⲩ, DM 24 16 *ntek 'rf n* ϭ., Ryl 158 38 ϭ.¹ ⲛⲡϫⲱⲱⲗⲉ, BM 1090 ϭ.¹ ⲛⲥⲓⲙⲁⲭⲉ (? *σύμμαχος*), CO 361 ⲕ. ϣⲏⲙ, Ep 280 ⲃⲓⲣ ⲛⲕ., *ib* 531 ⲥⲁⲗⲱ ⲛⲕ., Ostr 3050 Univ Coll Lond ⲡⲗⲓⲯⲉ ⲛϭ.³ BP 402 ⲑⲁⲗⲓⲥ ⲛⲕ., CO 366 ϣⲁⲧⲓⲗⲁ ⲛⲕ., WS 88 ϭⲟⲟⲩⲛⲉ ⲛϭ.²; ⲕⲁⲕϣⲱⲧ: Ep 540 so many ⲕ., paral ⲟⲉⲓⲕ ϣⲏⲙ, ⲟⲉⲓⲕ ⲟⲩ; ⲕⲁϫⲕⲁⲕⲉ, a crop or field ?: Ann 22 272 sowing contract ⲧⲁⲣⲉⲕϫⲟ ⲛⲕ. ϩⲙⲡϫⲟ ⲉϩⲣⲁⲓ ⲛⲧⲉⲣⲟⲙⲡⲉ. KroppJ 50 ϭⲟⲟϭⲉ same? *v* p 744 *b infra*. Ryl 280 ⲧⲁⲕⲉ = ? this word, *v* p 404 *b infra*.

In place-name (?) ⲧⲁⲧϭⲁⲁϭⲉ (BM 1030).

ϭⲱϭ *S* vb intr, *swell*: BMar 66 man with elephantiasis ⲁϥϭ. ⲧⲏⲣϥ.

ϭⲟⲩϭ *S*, ϭⲟⲩϫ *B* nn, *swelling, boil*: BMOr 8775 118, P 54 117 *B* نفخة, PMéd 262 *S* lay remedy on ⲛϭ. ⲙⲡⲛⲥⲓⲣⲉϥⲉ, *ib* 265 *S* ⲡⲉϣⲱ, ⲛϭ., ⲡϫⲟⲩϥ.

Place-names ⲡⲁⲡⲉϭⲟⲩϭ (Kr 255), ⲙⲟⲩⲛϭⲟⲩϭ (TT 74 مُحَمَّر) hardly belong here.

ϭⲁⲁϭⲉ *v* ϭⲱϭ 1°.

ϭⲁⲁϭⲓ *F* *v* ϭⲱϭ.

ϭⲉϭⲟⲩ *S* nn m, a dark substance, ? charcoal: Miss 4 699 hands ϫⲱⲱϭⲉ ⲛⲑⲉ ⲙⲡϭ. *Cf* ϭⲱϭ 1°, ϫⲁϫⲱ 2° & ? السود *s v* ϫⲟⲩϫⲟⲩ.

ϭⲓϭⲉ *v* ϭⲓⲛϭⲉ.

ϭⲓϭⲗⲱ *v* ϭⲓⲛϭⲗⲱ.

ϭⲁϭⲣⲏⲥ *v* ϫⲓⲕⲣⲓⲥ.

ϭⲁϭⲉⲧⲟⲗ *S* nn, a light ship: P 44 54 ⲕⲁⲣⲁⲣⲓⲛ (*l* -ⲃⲓⲛ *καράβιον*)· ϭ. سَلَّارِيّة (which K 133 = ⲥⲁⲗⲗⲁⲣⲓⲟⲥ *i q* Montp 172 ⲗⲁϩⲁⲣⲓⲁ, P 55 13 ⲗⲉϩⲱⲣⲓⲟⲛ).

ϭⲁϭⲓⲧⲱⲛ, -ⲡⲉ (twice) *S*, ϫⲁϫⲓⲑⲱⲗ *B* nn m f, *coarse linen, tow*: Dan 3 46 *B* (*S* ⲥⲁⲁϭⲉ) *στιππύον*; K 360 *B* سَرَاية : DeV 282 *B* ⲛⲓϫ. ⲡⲉ ⲡⲓⲧⲟϩ ⲉⲑⲛⲏⲟⲩ ⲉⲃⲟⲗ ϩⲉⲛⲡⲓⲙⲁϩⲓ, BIF 14 117 *S* brazen bull heated with ϩⲛⲗⲁϭⲓⲧⲱⲛ (*l* ⲕⲁϭ. or ϫⲁϭ.) ⲙⲡⲣⲏⲥⲁⲁϭⲉ, Va 61 107 *B* furnace heated with ⲑⲏⲡ, ⲗⲁⲙϫⲁⲧⲡ, ⲣⲟⲕϩ ⲛϫ. (*cf* Dan *l c*); garment thereof *S*: Si 40 5 (var P 44 119 ϭⲁϭⲓⲛⲧⲟ) *ὠμόλινον* (Hebr [ ], *v* NPeters *Ecclesiasticus Hebraice* 94); ShViK 9764 95 ⲡⲡⲉⲣⲱⲙⲉ ⲡⲉⲣϣ ⲧⲉϥϭⲁϭⲓⲧⲱⲡⲉ ⲉⲃⲟⲗ ⲛ ⲧⲉϥϩⲟⲓⲧⲉ, C 99 104 ϩⲃⲥⲱ ⲙⲙⲟ ⲛⲁϫⲟⲥ ⲉⲧⲉⲟⲩϭ. ⲧⲉ, *ib* 102 ⲧϭ. ⲟⲣⲣ ϣⲧⲏⲛ ⲡϭⲟⲟⲩⲡⲉ, Miss 4 232 ϩⲉⲛϭ. woven on loom, Mor 51 38 monks wear ϭ. ϩⲓⲧⲟⲗⲟⲙⲱⲛ (*cf* Mus 40 36) ϩⲓⲙⲟϫϥ, *ib* ⲛϭ. of Apa Pachôm, Z 351 ⲟⲩⲕⲗⲁϥⲧ ⲛϭ., *ib* ϭ. = ϣⲧⲏⲛ in Lu 3 11, ST 121 ϯⲟⲓⲉ (*l*? ϯⲉ) ⲡϭⲁϭⲉⲧⲱⲡⲉ.

  Cf? ϣⲉⲛⲧⲱⲗⲓ.

ϭⲁϭⲟⲩϩⲟⲣ, ⲕⲁⲕⲟⲩϩⲟⲟⲣ *S* nn, meaning unknown: Bal, in list of utensils]ϭ.[, Ostr *penes* Crum ϣⲟⲩⲟ ⲡⲓⲕ. Contains ? ϭⲁⲁϭⲉ & ⲟⲩϩⲟⲣ.

ENGLISH INDEX

This index is strictly alphabetical, *e g. break* and *broken, sick* and *sickness* are independent entries. The repeated occurrence of a word in the same column is not indicated.

Entries in roman type are those of words not amenable to more precise translation.

(*Add*) indicates Additions and Corrections.

contain *520 a, 575 a*
contemn *110 b*
contempt *110 b, 375 b*
contend *615 a, 618 b*
content *195 a, 309 b*
— nn *195 b*
—, be *194 a, 325 a, 519 b*
— heart *438 a*
contents *209 b*
contest *615 a*
continue *171 b, 530 b, 803 a*
continually *172 a*
continuance *171 b, 172 a*
continuously *171 b, 767 b*
contract nn *385 b*
contracted, be *525 a*
contradict *510 a*
contradictor *510 b*
contrary to, *34 a, 143 b*
contribution *513 b*
contrite *419 a*
contrition *419 a*
control nn *10 b*
—, under *840 a*
converse *648 a*
— with *421 a, 502 b*
conversion *107 b*
convocation *459 a*
convulse *720 a*
convulsion *720 a*
cook *273 a, 387 a, 796 b*
cooked (food) *387 a*
cooking grease *388 b*
cool, be, become *100 a*
—, make *100 a, 322 b*
coolness *100 a*
coping *138 a*
copper *678 a, b*
— -smith *678 b*
copulate *243 b*
copy (written) *383 b*
cord *100 a, 176 a, 241 a, b, 560 b, 618 a, 710 a*
coriander *609 a, 835 a*
— seed *44 a*
corn *9 a, 369 a*
— coloured *369 a*
— field *679 a*
corner *5 b, 108 a, 132 a, 140 b, 522 b*
— of eye *104 b, 132 a*
— of mouth *138 b*
corpse *112 b, 120 b, 121 a, 562 b*
correct *380 b*
correction *381 a*
corrupt *405 a*
corruption *148 b*
costly *796 a*
couch *225 a, 270 a, 271 a, 584 a*
counsel nn *616 a*
—, give *616 b*
—, take *615 b, 616 b*
counsellor *616 a*

count *526 a ff*
counter *527 b*
country *131 b*
— (opp. town) *377 a*
countryman *377 a*
couple nn *66 b*
courage, take *403 b*
course nn *275 b, 276 a, 472 a, b, 564 a, 841 a*
— of service *6 a*
court *13 a, 817 b*
cousin *343 a, 585 a*
cover *48 a, 132 a, 658 b, 769 b, 809 a*
— up *710 a*
covered with a growth (such as hair, vegetation) *303 b*
—, well *273 b (Add)*
covering nn *27 b, 140 a, 310 a, 330 b, 656 a, b, 659 a, b, 809 b*
covetous *396 b*
cow *45 a, 64 a, 636 b*
coward *710 a, 721 b (Add)*
cowherd *589 b*
cowl *101 b, 106 a*
crack *276 b, 630 b*
craft *81 a ff*
craftiness *319 b*
craftsman *82 a, 384 a, 674 a*
crane nn *61 b*
crate *777 a*
crawl *535 b*
crease nn *99 a, 522 b*
create *345 a, b, 413 a, 812 b*
creation *345 b, 413 b*
creator *345 b, 413 b*
creature *345 b*
creep *376 b, 558 b*
crepitus ventris *765 a*
cress *560 a*
crested lark *139 b*
crew *238 b*
cricket *110 b*
crippled person *807 b*
criticism *15 b*
criticize *715 b*
crocodile *63 a, 187 b*
crocodile's tongue (plant) *144 b*
crook-backed *25 b, 753 b*
crooked, be *127 b, 818 a, 836 a*
— person *824 a*
crookedness *108 a, 127 b, 818 a*
crop nn *582 a*
cross nn **546** *a*
—, sign of *735 a*
cross over *496 b*
cross-roads *739 b*
crossing nn *82 b, 344 b*
crow nn *2 b*
crowd *202 a, b*
crown *105 a, 516 b*
— nn *104 b, 105 a, 138 a, 829 a*
— of head *374 a*
— -bearer *105 a*

crowning nn *105 a*
crucible *40 a*
crucifixion *89 a*
cruel *508 b, 509 a, 778 a*
crush *145 a, 151 a, 419 a, 505 a, 513 b, 630 b, 662 b*
crushed, be *151 a, 505 a*
crusts *101 a*
crutch *489 b*
crux ansata *13 a*
cry *533 a, 705 a, b*
— nn *119 b, 192 b, 556 a, 619 a, 806 a*
— against *141 b*
— out *533 b, 556 a, b, 806 a*
— to *192 a*
crying, much *257 b*
crypt *696 a*
cubicle *208 a*
cubit *210 b*
—, half *211 a*
—, Lion's (lunar station) *211 a*
cucumber *41 a, 580 b*
cud *363 b*
cuirass *69 a, 144 a, 268 a*
cultivator *473 a*
cumin *56 b, 423 a*
—, black *110 a, 572 a*
— seller *423 b*
cunning *319 b*
cup *14 b, 138 a, 499 a, 676 a, 685 a, 759 b*
— -bearer *499 a*
— -maker *14 b, 140 b*
cure *151 b, 764 a*
curl nn *147 b, 556 b*
curl up *807 a*
curled, curling *104 a, 117 b*
curly *477 a*
curse *387 a, 739 b*
— nn *387 b, 739 b*
curser *387 b*
curtain *148 a, 269 b*
curvature *366 b*
curved, be *103 a*
cushion *573 b, 590 a*
custom *133 a, 346 a, 423 a*
cut *511 a, 562 b, 590 b ff, 599 a, ? 761 a, 769 a, 841 a, 842 b*
— down *115 b, 119 b, 276 a*
— off *331 a, b, 511 a, 591 a, 593 b*
— open ? *785 a*
— out *266 a*
— short, be *592 b*
cutter *592 a, 593 b, ? 841 b*
cutting nn *511 a, 593 b, 843 a*
cycle *126 b*
cylinder (weaver's) *623 b*
cyperus *15 a*
— esculentus *31 a*
cypher *170 b*
cypress *226 a*
cyprinus niloticus (fish) *148 b*

son-in-law *564 a*
song *709 b, 756 a*
soon *104 b*
soot *117 a, 535 b*
soothsayer *374 a*
sorbus (tree) *106 a*
sore nn *357 a, 374 b, 375 a*
sorrel *800 b*
sort nn *172 b, 173 a, 833 a*
sound *533 a*
— nn *335 a, 619 a, 704 b, 705 a*
sound, be *511 b*
soundless *335 a*
sour *561 a, 682 b*
south *299 b ff*
— wind *440 a*
south-east *300 a*
— -west *300 a*
southern *300 a*
southward *300 a*
sow *360 b, 752 a*
sow nn *63 a*
sower *752 b*
sowing nn *361 b, 752 b, 771 b*
space *501 b*
— (of time) *14 a*
spade *425 a*
spadeful *841 b*
span *305 b*
spare *317 a, b, 351 b*
sparing, without *317 b*
sparingness *317 b*
spark *404 b*
sparrow *110 b, 763 a, 798 b*
spasm *720 a*
spathe of palm *746 b*
speak *191 b, 474 b, 613 a ff, 754 a*
— against *442 b, 755 a*
speaker *614 b, 755 b*
spear *184 a, 235 b, 760 a*
speckled *368 b, 371 a*
spectator *234 b*
speculate *420 b*
speech *18 a, 614 b, 755 b*
speechless *614 b*
speed nn *86 b*
spend *752 b, 763 a*
— time *500 a*
spice *688 b*
spider *367 a*
spider's web *367 a, 671 b*
spike *235 b, 354 a, 431 b, 536 b,*
563 a
spin *82 a, 713 a*
spinach *342 a*
spindle *177 b, 806 a*
spine *795 a*
spinner *359 a*
spirit *28 a*
spit *453 a*
spittle *286 b, 453 a, 796 b*
splash (that which is splashed) *249 b*
splayed *625 a*

spleen *236 a, 331 b*
splinter *281 a*
— of reed *144 b*
split *100 b, 130 b, 276 a, b, 281 a,*
630 b, ? 809 b
splitter *281 a*
spoil *558 a*
— nn *558 a, 670 b*
spoiler *558 a*
spoiling nn *558 a*
sport *321 a*
— nn *780 b*
—, make *589 a*
spot *4 a, 396 b*
— (on eye) *368 b*
spotted *329 a, 396 b*
spread *269 b ff, 353 b ff, 439 a,*
605 b, 612 a
— to dry *815 b*
— abroad *35 a*
— forth *503 b*
— wings *703 b*
spreading nn *354 a*
sprig *423 b, 615 a*
spring (of water) *198 a, b, 670 b,*
691 a
sprinkle *249 a, b, 672 a, 839 a*
sprinkled, be *437 a*
sprinkling nn *249 b, 839 a*
sprout *69 a, 303 b*
— nn *129 a, 475 b, 514 a*
spun *359 a*
spy *781 b*
square (builder's) *140 b*
squeeze out *697 b*
squill *213 b*
stab *139 b, 656 b*
stable, training *786 a*
staff *489 b, 554 a, 702 a, 828 a*
— bearer *554 b*
stag ? *828 a*
stagger *810 a*
stain nn *26 b, 411 a*
stained, be *800 b*
stainless *26 b, 411 a*
stair *432 a*
staircase *431 b*
stake nn *218 b, 562 a, 565 a*
stale *329 a, 601 a*
stalk *142 a, 149 a, 306 b*
stammering *144 b*
stamp with foot *273 b, 274 a, 425 a*
— (seal) *398 a*
— nn *765 b*
stand *536 b ff*
— beside *446 a*
— firm *403 a*
— out against *537 a*
—, make to *455 a ff*
standing nn *538 b*
— -place *339 a, 508 a*
star *368 a, b*
— -spangled *368 b*

stare *68 a, 69 a, 84 a*
— about *184 a*
start from *827 a*
state nn *287 a*
stater (coin) *366 a*
statue *589 b*
stave *508 b*
stay *473 b, 536 b*
— behind *636 b*
— by, with *224 b, 446 a*
steadied, mind *716 a*
steal *105 b, 741 a, 793 b*
steam *149 b*
steel *143 b*
— -smith *143 b*
steep place *330 a*
steer *677 b*
steering-oar *689 a*
stem of palm-tree *40 b*
step *303 a*
— nn *266 a, 432 a*
— of ladder *277 a*
—, take *476 b*
stibium *364 b*
stick, be sticky *150 a*
sticks, dry *811 a*
stiff *433 b, 540 a*
— (of hair) *269 b*
— -necked *163 a, 237 b, 242 a, 243 b*
stiffen *388 b, 403 a, 433 b*
stile (for writing) *383 b*
still, be *702 b, 704 a*
— advb *255 b*
sting *76 a*
stink *112 b, 143 a, 184 a, 573 b*
—, make to *112 b*
— nn *112 b*
stir *454 a*
stitch *422 b, 431 a, 558 b, 834 b*
stockade of reeds *138 a*
stocks **546 a**
stoke *404 a, b*
— -hole *404 b*
stoker *387 a, 404 b*
stolen thing *105 b*
stomach *608 a*
stone **2 b**, *524 a, b*
— (of fruit) *120 a, 249 b*
— quarry *524 b*
— thrower *524 b*
stony *524 b*
— heartedness *714 b*
stop *135 a, 377 b, 378 a, 803 b*
— (a hole) *422 b*
— up, (of wells) *583 a*
store house *24 b, 373 b*
storey (of house) *510 b, 643 a*
storing, place of *324 a*
storm *660 b*
straight, be *371 a*
—, make *606 a, 623 b*
straighten *371 b, 743 b*
straightener *372 b*

strain 269 b, 367 a, 378 b
— nn 767 b
strainer 184 a
straits 150 b, 656 a, 740 b, 742 b
strand 113 a, 241 b
— (of cord) 290 a, 560 a
strange 552 a, 565 b
strangeness 566 a
stranger 565 b, 566 a
strangled 540 b
strap 31 a, 181 b, 184 b, 243 a
stray 124 a, 355 a, 778 a
stream 82 b
street 555 a, 696 b, 697 a
strength 226 a, b, 238 a, 284 b,
   403 b, 463 b, 777 a, 783 b, 785 a,
   815 b ff
strengthen 403 a, 463 a, 631 b,
   ? 810 a
strengthener 238 a
stretch 269 b, 282 a, 371 a ff, 340 b,
   360 a, 439 a, 767 a
— out 121 b, 433 b
— toward 270 a
— upon 353 b
stretching nn 340 b, 767 b
strife 418 a, 618 b
strike 106 b, 186 a, 203 a, 311 a ff,
   374 b, 418 b, 447 b, 504 b, 733 a,
   773 b, ? 795 b, 798 b
— (musical instrument) 109 a
— upon 106 b, 130 b, 203 a, 417 a
striker 237 a, 421 a
striking nn 522 a
string 100 a, 113 a
stringency 767 b
strip 46 b, 101 a
— off 100 b
— nn 101 a, 331 b, 397 a, 618 a
stripe 353 b, 697 a
strive 618 b
stroke nn 312 a, 374 b, 583 b
stroll 345 a
strong 8 a, 237 a, b, 403 a, b, 783 a ff,
   813 b, 816 b
—, make 462 b ff
struck, be 311 a, 732 b
stubble 306 b
stubborn 433 b
stubbornness 78 b
studded 406 b, 536 a
study 781 b
stultify 806 b
stumble 283 a, 332 b, 333 a, 611 a,
   786 a, 787 a
stumbling nn 333 a
— block, be 786 b
stump 600 b
— of branch of date-palm 130 b
stupefaction 356 a, 417 a
stupefied, be 356 a, 416 b
styrax 228 a
subdue 334 b

subject, be 306 a
— to 428 b
submerge 69 b
submerged, be 523 a, 768 a
submission 822 a
submit 94 b
— to 327 a, 478 b
subscribe to 382 b
subtle, subtlety 565 a
suburb 452 a
succeed 155 a, 282 a
success, successful 189 b
succumb to 792 b
such 689 b, 833 a
— & such 201 b
suck 58 b, 344 b, 345 a
— in 386 a
—, give 185 a, 435 b
sucking nn 345 a
— pig 299 a
suckle 54 a, 58 b, 435 b
sudden, on a 590 a
suddenly 576 b, 721 b
sue 71 b, 220 b
suffer 164 a, 575 a, 712 a, b
sufferer 164 a, 712 b
suffering nn 164 a, 712 b
suffice 111 a, 309 a ff, 651 a
sufficient, be 648 b
sufficiency 309 b
sufficiently 310 a
suggest 200 b
suit 218 a
sulphur 69 a
summer 564 b
summon 192 b, 419 b, 458 b, 533 b
summoner 459 a
sun 287 b, 630 a
— -tree 287 b
sunk, be 411 a
sunny (place, room) 330 a
sunrise 287 b
sunset 287 b, 725 b
sunshine 287 b
superb 604 a
superfluity 736 b
superfluous 735 a
superintendent (of monastery) 66 b
superior (person) 698 b
superiority 365 b, 366 a
supplement 209 b
suppliant 402 b
supplication 648 b
supply 307 b, 385 b
support 8 a, 10 a, 446 a, 521 a,
   621 a, 709 a, 794 a, ? 810 a
— nn 322 b, 380 b
suppose 95 a
suppository 379 b
surely interj. 64 a, 74 b
surety 62 b, 425 a, b
surfeit 317 a
surmise 420 b

surmount 259 b, 260 a
surpass 496 b, 759 b
surpassing 495 b, 496 b
surround 124 b, 127 b ff, 528 a,
   770 a, 810 a
surrounding nn 126 a, 528 b
suspend 88 b
swaddling bands 235 b
— clothes 433 a
swallow 386 a, 478 b, 523 a
swallow (bird) 40 a
swathe 769 b, 809 a
sway 356 a, 810 a
swaying gait 345 a
swear 529 a ff
—, make to 430 a
swearing nn 12 b
sweat 286 b, 625 a
sweep 386 a
sweeping nn 386 b
sweet 111 b, 231 b, 673 a
—, make 673 b
sweetness 112 a, 231 b, 673 b
swell 240 a, 263 a, 610 a, 843 b
swelling nn 69 b, 240 b, 610 b,
   843 b
swift, be 17 b
swim 222 a, 672 a
swimmer 222 a, 669 a
swine 299 a
— -herd 173 b, 299 a
swollen, 42 b, 480 a
sword 41 a, 379 a, 829 b
sycamore 242 b
—, fruit of 54 b, 145 a
synodontis schall 117 b

table 329 a
take 159 a, 520 a, 575 a, 620 a,
   747 b, 826 a
— away 196 b, 521 a
— heed 94 b
— off 79 b, 262 b
— up 827 a
taker 751 b, 827 a
taking nn 751 b, 827 a
tail 358 b, 359 a, 669 a
tailed, dock- 359 a
tailless 359 a
tailor 431 b, 661 a, 732 a
tale 267 b, 610 b, 611 a (*Add*), 614 b
— -teller 611 a
talent (weight or coin) 824 b
talk 615 a
— against 648 b
— of 267 b
—, ridiculous 321 b
tall 148 a, 149 b, 333 a, 549 a
tamarisk 226 a, 257 a
tame 133 a
tan 31 a
tank 183 a, 336 b, 339 b
tanner 582 b

tar *143 b, 379 a*
— -*water 379 a*
taste 423 a
tasting nn *423 a*
tax 564 b
teach 73 b, 320 a, 434 b, 444 a
teacher 320 a, 383 b, 384 a
teaching nn *319 b, 435 a*
tear 280 a, 281 a
— *asunder 331 b*
— *in pieces 139 a*
— *out 286 a*
tear nn *294 b*
tell 267 a, b, 413 b, 414 a, 442 a, b,
775 a
teller 414 a
tempering nn *535 b*
tempest 176 a, 672 a, 753 b, 832 b
temple 153 a, 298 b
temples (tempora) 342 a, 547 b
ten 70 a, 176 b, 187 b
— *thousand 399 a*
tenant 619 b
tend 347 b
— *cattle 173 a*
— *toward 326 b, 393 a*
tension 767 b
tent 656 a
tenth 187 b
terminate 32 b
terms, come to 33 a, 262 a
—, *make 232 b*
terrible 245 a
terrified, be 562 b
terrify 461 a, 667 a, 721 b
terror 562 b
tertian fever 567 a
test 775 b
testicle 4 a, 336 b, 726 b, 771 b,
791 a, ? 795 a
testify 177 a
testimony 177 a
thankless 681 a
thanks 158 b
—, *give 681 b*
thanksgiving 682 a
that demonstr *196 b, 260 b*
that (so that) 573 a, 764 a
— *not (lest) 167 b*
theft 105 b, 741 b, 794 a
then 74 a, b, 232 a, 291 a, 802 a
thence 196 b
there 154 b, 174 b, 196 b, 392 a
therein 196 b
therefore 802 a
thick 403 a, 479 b
—, *make 583 a*
thicket 595 a
thickness 480 a, 722 b
thief 539 a, 741 b, 794 a
thievishly 105 b
thigh 7 a, 38 b, 114 b, 273 b,
? 795 a, 813 a

thin 261 a, 676 a
thing 223 a, b, 653 a ff, 692 b
think 162 a, 199 a ff
third 566 b
thirst 76 a, b
thirteen 567 a
thirty 161 a
this 259 a
— *& that 468 b*
thistle 16 a
thither 174 b, 197 a
thong 184 b
thorn 114 b, 354 a, b
— -*tree 573 a*
thoroughly 315 b
those there 91 b
thought 162 a, b, 200 a
—, *take 149 a*
thoughtlessly 17 b
thoughtlessness 200 a
thousand 549 b
thread nn *113 a, 560 b, 710 a*
threat 534 b
threaten 88 b, 421 a
three 566 b, 567 a
thresh 504 b, 583 b, 643 a, b, 782 a
thresher 643 b
threshing 643 b, 782 a
— -*floor 28 a, 629 a, 776 b, 782 a*
threshold 266 a, 432 a
throat 189 a, 523 a, 603 a
throb 106 b
throttle 540 b
through 428 a, 429 a, 759 a
throw 247 a ff, 360 b ff, 403 b, 404 a,
420 b, 666 b
— *down 312 a, b, 380 a, 657 a*
— *off 242 a*
— *upon 311 b*
thrower 249 a, 404 a
throwing nn *249 a*
thrust in 432 a
— *off 426 b*
thumb 81 a
thunder 259 a, 705 b
Thursday ? 501 b (Add)
thus 304 b, 639 a, 645 a
thyme 56 b
tick (insect) 318 b
tie 180 a, 532 b
tiger 764 a
tight-fitting 742 b
tighten 631 b
tilapia 294 a, 611 a
till prep *542 a, 636 a*
— *when ? 468 b*
tillage 81 b
time 219 a, 234 b ff, 367 b, 368 a,
391 b, 499 b, 500 a
— *of, in, at 644 b, 645 a*
— *(vices) 349 b ff*
—, *space of 14 a*
timeless 368 a

timid, become, be 805 a
tin 69 a
tip nn *718 a*
— *of nose 102 a (Add)*
— *of tail 833a*
title 13 a, b, 14 a (Add), 14 b, 86 b,
88 a, 113 a, 134 b, 197 a, 303 b,
343 a, 369 b, 374 a, 387 a, 562 b,
623 b, 630 b, 672 a, 697 b, 704 a,
? 739 b, ? 740 a, 787 b
to 50 a ff, 153 b, 154 a, 216 a, b,
427 b, 541 b ff, 634 b, 649 a,
757 b
— *& fro 547 a, b*
to-day 731 a
toe 81 a, 397 b
—, *little 331 b*
— -*nail 302 b*
together 59 a, 154 a
— *(at one time) 350 a*
toil 710 b ff
token 678 b
tolerate 621 a
tomb 212 b, 611 a
to-morrow 302 a, b
tongs 65 a
tongue 144 b
tonsil 55 a
tool ? 104 b, 113 b, 255 a, 363 b,
401 a, 824 a
tooth 249 b, 254 a, 557 b
—-*ache 709 b*
toothless 557 b
top 132 a, 140 b, 259 b, 790 a
torment 720 a
torrent 198 a, 355 b
tortoise 598 b
total 761 b
touch 108 b, 282 a, 455 a, 749 b,
786 b, 797 a, 818 b
—, *sense of* nn *819 a*
touching nn *797 a*
—, *act of 819 a*
tow nn *145 a, 358 b, 844 a*
—, *workers in 213 b*
toward 51 a, 303 b, 390 a, 476 a,
541 b ff, 634 b, 645 b, 649 a, 684 b
towel, hand ? 25 b
tower 214 b, 480 a
town 30 b
townsman 295 a
trace 303 a
— *line 562 a*
track 188 b
trade 81 b, 395 b, 763 a
trader 590 b
trading 81 b, 395 b, 590 b
traffic 590 b
traganum nudatum 835 a
trample 674 b, 682 b
trampling nn *675 a*
trance, be in 525 a
tranquillity 339 a (Add), 598 a

GREEK INDEX

More than one occurrence on a page is indicated by an asterisk.

(Add) indicates Additions and Corrections.

283 *a**, 411 *b**, 412 *a*, 511 *b*, 567 *a*, *b**
θεράπων 30 *a*, 665 *a*
θερίζειν 538 *b**, 539 *a**
θερινός 100 *a*, 564 *b*
θερισμός 391 *b*, 539 *a**
θεριστής 539 *a*
θέριστρον 310 *a*, 539 *a*
θερμαίνειν 459 *b*, 677 *a**
θερμασία 459 *b*
θέρμη 677 *a*, *b*
θερμός 197 *b*, 490 *a*, 530 *a*, 677 *a**, 714 *b*
θερμότης 677 *b*
θέρος 564 *b*
θέσις 339 *a*
θεσμός 337 *a*, 346 *a*, 451 *a*, 616 *a*
θεωρεῖν 233 *b**, 234 *a*, 486 *b*, 837 *a*
θεωρία 839 *a*
θεώριον 153 *b*
θήκη 132 *a*, 397 *a*, 733 *b*
θηλάζειν 54 *a**, 176 *b*, 344 *b*, 345 *a*, 347 *b*, 435 *b*, 478 *a*, 752 *a**
θηλή 176 *b*
θηλυμανής 137 *a* (Add)
θῆλυς 61 *a*, 76 *a*, 385 *a*
θημωνιά (θιμ.) 651 *a*, 776 *b*, 792 *b*
θήρα 277 *a*, 281 *a*, 562 *b*, 572 *a*, 830 *b**
θηρεύειν 455 *a*, 826 *a*, *b**, 830 *a*, *b**
θήρευμα 826 *a*, 830 *b*, 831 *a*
θηρευτής 830 *b*, 831 *a*
θηριάλωτος 3 *b*, 405 *a*, 469 *a*, 479 *a*, 625 *b**
θηρίκλειον 14 *b*, 250 *a*
θηριομαχεῖν 203 *a*
θησαυρίζειν 373 *a**, *b*, 448 *a*, 734 *a*
θησαύρισμα 373 *b*
θησαυρός 24 *b**
θίασος 590 *a*
θίβις 397 *a*
θιγγάνειν 749 *b*, 797 *a*
θίς 105 *b*, 115 *a*
θλαδίας 145 *a*, 324 *b*
θλᾶν 150 *b*, 151 *a*, 276 *b*, 405 *a*, 459 *b*, 505 *a*, 513 *a*, 630 *b**
θλίβειν 151 *a*, 163 *a*, *b*, 503 *a*, 712 *a*, 740 *a*, 743 *b**, 819 *b*, 835 *a*
θλιμμός 744 *a*
θλῖψις 151 *a*, 744 *a*
θνησιμαῖος 159 *a*, *b*, 160 *a*, 223 *a*
θνήσκειν 159 *a*, *b*, 562 *b*
θνητός 159 *a*, 160 *a*
θορυβεῖν 597 *b**, 598 *a*, 656 *a*
θόρυβος 366 *b*, 598 *a**
θράσος 237 *b*, 238 *a*, 802 *a*
θρασυκάρδιος 237 *b*

θρασύς 78 *b**, 237 *b**
θραύειν 478 *a*, 505 *a**, 630 *b**, 833 *b**
θραῦσις 312 *a*, 505 *a*, 630 *b*
θραῦσμα 505 *a*
θραυσμός 630 *b*
θρέμμα 348 *a*
θρηνεῖν 141 *b*, 245 *a**, 294 *a*, *b**, 437 *b**, 655 *a*, *b*, 756 *a*
θρήνημα 245 *a*
θρῆνος 245 *a*, 294 *b*, 437 *b*, 655 *a**
θρησκεία 567 *b*
θρησκεύειν 504 *a*, 567 *b*
θριαμβεύειν 358 *a*, 462 *b*, 487 *a*, 525 *a*
θρίαμβος 525 *a*
θρίδαξ 55 *a*, 145 *b*
θρῖναξ 193 *b*(Add)
θρίξ 113 *b*, 623 *a**, *b*, 761 *a*
θροεῖν 236 *b*, 597 *b*, 598 *a*
θρόμβος 54 *a*
θροῦς 705 *a*
θρυλεῖν (θρυλλ.) 615 *a*, 616 *a*
θρύλημα 613 *b*, 615 *a**
θρύον (θροῖον) 108 *a*, 318 *a*(Add)
θυγάτηρ 5 *a* (error), 385 *a*, 414 *b*, 584 *b*, 585 *a**
θύειν 112 *a*, 409 *a*, 591 *a**, *b*, 603 *b*, 688 *b*, 689 *a*
θύελλα 440 *a*
θυία 214 *a*
θυίσκη 747 *b*, 787 *b*
θῦμα 273 *a*, 591 *a*, 603 *b*
θυμιάζειν 394 *b*
θυμίαμα 363 *a*, 688 *b*
θυμιᾶν 80 *a*, 409 *b*, 591 *a*, 603 *b**, 688 *b**, 689 *a*
θυμιατήριον 603 *b*
θυμομαχεῖν 823 *a*
θυμός 161 *a*, 252 *a*, 823 *a*, *b**
θυμοῦν 161 *a**, 210 *a*, 252 *b**, 823 *a**
θυμώδης 161 *a*, 823 *b*
θύρα 260 *a*, 266 *b*, 289 *a**, 321 *b*, 427 *b*
θυρεός 298 *b*, 324 *a*, 768 *a*
θυρίς 440 *a*, 510 *b*, 608 *b**
θύρσα 299 *a*
θύρωμα 321 *b*, 512 *b*
θυρωρός 176 *b**
θυσία 603 *b**
θυσιάζειν 603 *b*, 618 *a*, 698 *b*
θυσίασμα 363 *a*, 388 *b*, 603 *b*
θυσιαστήριον 601 *b*, 603 *b*
θύσκη 38 *b*
θωπεία 821 *b*
θωπεύειν 118 *a*

θωράκιον 69 *a*
θώραξ 19 *a*, 187 *b*, 662 *a*, 668 *a*, 824 *a*

ἴαμα 282 *b*, 412 *a*, 512 *a*
ἰᾶσθαι 135 *b*, 136 *a**, 151 *b**, 193 *b*, 282 *b*, 283 *a*, 411 *b**, 412 *a**, 449 *a**, 511 *b*, 512 *a*
ἴασις 194 *b*, 412 *a*, 512 *a*
ἰατής 412 *a*
ἰατρεία 342 *b*
ἰατρεῖον 342 *b*, 678 *a*
ἰατρεύειν 282 *b*
ἰατρικός 342 *b*
ἰατρός 119 *b*, 342 *b*
ἴβις 656 *a*
ἰγνύα 273 *b*
ἰδέα 341 *a*
ἰδεῖν 85 *b**, 206 *b*, 233 *b**, 234 *a*, 475 *a*, 819 *b*, 837 *a**, *b**, 838 *a* (v. ὁρᾶν)
ἰδιάζειν 389 *b*, 646 *b*
ἰδιόγραφος 382 *a*
ἰδιοπραγμοσύνη 716 *b*
ἴδιος 168 *b*, 199 *a**, 230 *a*, 242 *a*, 314 *b*, 426 *a*, 470 *b*, 494 *b**, 687 *b*, 692 *b*
ἰδιότης 526 *a*
ἰδιώτης 473 *b*
ἰδού 85 *a*, *b**, 86 *a**, 155 *a*, 696 *a*
ἱδρύειν 338 *b*, 460 *a*
ἱδρώς 625 *a*, 711 *b*
ἰέναι 579 *a*
ἱέραξ 25 *a**, 48 *b*, 598 *b*
ἱερατ(ε)ία 388 *b*, 567 *b*
ἱερατεύειν 388 *a*, *b*, 567 *a*, *b*
ἱερεύς 488 *a**, 691 *b*
ἱερόδουλος 298 *b*
ἱερόν 212 *b*, 298 *b*
ἱεροπρεπής 701 *b*
ἱεροσυλεῖν 298 *b*
ἱερόσυλος 105 *b*, 298 *b*
ἱερουργεῖν 488 *b*
ἱερουργία 603 *b*
ἱεροφάντης 691 *b*
ἱερωσύνη 488 *b*
ἱκανός 111 *a*, 179 *a**, 202 *b*, 250 *a*, 309 *a*, *b**, 391 *b*, 425 *b*, 451 *a*, 530 *b*, 531 *a*, 621 *b*, 648 *b*, 651 *a*, 690 *a*, 785 *a*
ἱκανοῦν 111 *a*, 179 *b*, 309 *a*, *b**, 651 *a*, *b*, 737 *a*
ἱκετηρία 118 *a*
ἱκετεύειν 117 *b*, 352 *a*, *b*, 353 *a*, 402 *a*
ἱκέτης 352 *b*
ἰκμάς 54 *b*, 821 *b*
ἴκτερος 16 *b*, 571 *a**, 677 *a*
ἰκτίν 228 *b*, 429 *b*

λαξεύειν 133 a*, 276 b, 557 a
λαξευτήριον 213 b, 363 b
λαός 202 a, 559 b
λάρναξ 212 b
λάρυγξ 603 a
λασᾶνι 148 a
λατομεῖν 133 a*, 276 b, 331 a, 555 a, b, 593 b, 599 a, 612 a (Add), 841 a, b*
λατομητός 133 a
λατόμος 102 b, 133 a
λάτος 401 b
λατρεία 567 b, 603 b
λατρεύειν 567 a, b*
λατρευτός 567 b
λάτρις 665 a
λάφυρα 558 a
λάχανον 493 b
λέαινα 136 b*, 160 b*
λεαίνειν 334 a, 531 b, 605 b
λέβης 312 b
λέγειν 25 b, 50 b, 191 b, 192 a, 285 b, 442 a, 475 a, 506 a, 534 a, 613 a*, b, 694 b, 754 a, b*, 755 a*, b*, 775 a
λεῖμμα 617 b
λειμών 233 b, 475 b, 568 b
λεῖος 334 a, 386 b, 607 a, 821 b*
λείπειν 322 a, 473 b, 539 b, 592 b*, 593 a*, 829 b*
λειτουργεῖν 278 b, 568 a*, 576 a, b*
λειτουργία 279 a*, 451 a, 567 b, 568 a*
λειτουργός 279 a*, 385 b, 568 a*
λείχειν 150 b, 151 a
λεκάνιον 3 b
λεληθότως 146 b
λεμεῖσα 143 b
λέντιον 144 a*
λέξις 18 a
λεπίζειν 100 b
λεπίς 45 b, 101 a, 261 a, 574 a, 659 b
λέπισμα 101 a, 396 b
λέπρα 100 b, 324 b, 386 b
λεπρᾶν 100 b, 324 b
λεπρός 100 b, 101 a, 324 b*, 386 b, 469 a
λεπροῦσθαι 324 b
λεπτολάχανον 493 b
λεπτόν 397 a
λεπτός 17 b, 93 a, 223 a*, 261 a, 419 a, 453 a, 563 b*, 565 a*, 612 b, 676 a, 805 a*
λεπτύνειν 93 a, 261 a, 453 a*, 565 a, 605 b, 612 a, 630 b, 720 a, 805 a
λέπυρον 101 a

λεσῶνις 148 a
λευκαίνειν 100 b, 267 a, 393 a, 400 a, 476 b*, 531 b
λευκανθίζειν 476 b
λευκάς 45 a, 713 b
λευκός 6 b, 267 a, 476 b*, 723 a
λευκότης 476 b
λεύκωμα 102 b, 197 b, 724 a
λεύκωσις 6 b
λευχείμων 267 a
λεχώ(ς) 185 b, 691 b
λέων 160 b*
λεωπετρία 334 a
λήθη 519 a*, b*
ληκύθιον 99 b, 692 b
λήμη 150 a
ληνοπατεῖν 674 b
ληνός 77 b, 704 b, 833 a
ληρεῖν 715 b
λῆρος 280 a, 321 a, 519 b, 610 b
λῃστής 344 b*, 539 a
λῆψις 395 b
λίαν 180 a*, 190 a, 201 b
λιβανωτός 603 b
λιγ(ο)ύριον 2 b, 258 b
λιθάζειν 106 b, 247 b, 360 b, 404 a, 524 b*
λίθινος 524 a
λιθοβολεῖν 360 b
λιθοβολίζειν 524 b*
λίθος 81 b, 328 b, 524 a*, b*
λιθόστρωτον 407 a
λιθουργικός 81 b, 524 a
λιθουργός 133 a
λιθώδης 153 b, 524 b, 778 a
λικμᾶν 263 b*, 354 a, 400 a, 605 b*, 606 a*, 732 b, 782 b
λικμήτωρ 606 a, 635 a, 643 b
λικμός 177 b, 605 b, 635 b
λιμαγχονεῖν 95 b, 663 b
λιμήν 174 a, 183 a
λίμνη 229 b
λιμοκτονεῖν 201 a
λιμός 39 b, 643 a, 663 b*
λιμώσσειν 663 b
λινοκαλάμη 211 a
λίνον 88 a*, 178 a, 211 a, 330 a, 660 a
λινόσπερμον 211 a
λινοῦς 19 a (κίδαρις λινῆ) 88 a*, 660 a
λιπαίνειν 45 a, 112 a*, 461 b*, 673 b
λιπαρός 129 b
λιτανεύειν 352 a*
λίτρα 88 a
λιχήν 213 b*

λίψ 56 a*
λοβός 105 b, 423 b, 718 a
λόγγη 138 a
λογία 353 b, 513 b, 527 a
λογίζειν 96 a, 162 a*, b, 199 a, b*, 200 a, 206 b, 307 a, 355 a, 420 b*, 526 a*, b*, 527 a*, 615 b*
λογικός 715 a
λόγιον 613 b
λογισμός 162 a, 200 a, 207 a, 616 a
λογομαχεῖν 165 b, 418 a
λογομαχία 165 b
λόγος 54 b, 152 a, 288 b, 307 a, b*, 384 a, 526 a, 527 a, b*, 613 b, 614 a*, b*, 616 a, 646 b, 653 a, 654 a, 749 a
λόγχη 829 b*
λοιδορεῖν 387 b*, 739 b*
λοιδόρησις 739 b
λοιδορία 135 b, 375 b, 387 b, 739 b
λοίδορος 376 a, 387 b, 739 b
λοιμεύεσθαι 797 b
λοιμός 159 b, 378 b
λοιπός 60 a, 91 a, b, 350 b, 351 b*, 617 a*, b*, 635 a, 802 a, b
λοξός 836 a
λούειν 75 b, 703 b, 763 b*
λουτήρ 547 b
λουτρόν 369 b, 763 b
λούφιον 137 b
λοφιά 132 a
λοχεύειν 185 a
λύειν 32 a*, b*, 33 a*, b, 97 a, 118 a, 449 a, 474 a*, 515 b, 782 b
λυθρώδης 432 b
λύκος 485 b
λυμαίνειν 405 a, 457 a, 609 b, 798 a
λυπεῖν 83 b, 163 a, b, 164 a*, b*, 165 b, 377 a, 715 a, 823 a*
λύπη 164 b, 520 a
λυπηρός 655 a
λυριστής 756 a
λύσις 32 b
λυσιτέλεια 239 b
λυσιτελεῖν 240 a, 365 b
λυσιτελής 239 b, 729 a
λύτρον 256 b, 362 b*
λυτροῦν 362 a*, b*, 449 a, 551 b
λύτρωσις 362 b*
λυτρωτής 362 b
λυττᾶν 358 a
λυχνία 658 b
λυχνίς 488 b
λύχνος 480 b, 658 a
λωβᾶσθαι 148 b
λώβη 405 b, 618 b, 807 b
λῶδιξ 146 a

μῖσος 187 a
μνᾶ 7 b
μνεία 200 a, b*
μνῆμα 200 b, 212 b
μνημεῖον 28 a, 212 b*
μνήμη 200 a, b
μνημονεύειν 199 b, 200 b
μνημόσυνον 200 a, b, 201 a
μνησικακεῖν 185 b, 199 b, 200 a
μνησικακία 185 b, 201 a
μνηστεύειν 427 a, 527 a, 688 b*
μνηστήρ 688 b
μογγός 178 b
μογιλάλος 145 a, 178 a
μόδιος 176 a, 213 a, 548 a
μοεῖ 208 a
μοιχαλίς 222 b*
μοιχᾶσθαι 223 a*
μοιχεία 223 a
μοιχεύειν 223 a*
μοιχός 222 b*
μόλιβος 462 a
μόλις 822 a
μολόχινος 53 b
μόλυβδος 462 a
μολυβδοῦσθαι 788 b
μολυβδώδης 20 b
μολυβίς 462 a
μολύνειν 410 b*, 529 a, 788 b, 797 b, 798 a*
μόλυνσις 378 b
μολυσμός 411 a
μομφή 15 a
μοναστήριον 21 b*, 448 b, 580 a, 692 a*
μονή 21 b, 174 a, 177 b, 448 b, 580 a, 692 a*
μονήμερος 730 a
μόνιμος 171 b
μονόγαμος 679 b
μονογενής 199 a, 470 b, 494 a, 585 a, b*
μονόκερως 422 a, 494 a
μονομαχεῖν 199 a, 203 a
μόνορχις 726 b
μόνος 190 b, 199 a*, 290 b, 470 b*, 494 a, 553 a, 803 a, b
μονοῦσθαι 617 a
μονόφθαλμος 494 a
μόροχθος 184 a
μορφή 21 a, 341 a, 646 b, 701 b
μορφοῦν 751 b
μόρφωσις 701 b
μοσχάριον 93 a, 129 a, 186 a, 563 b, 652 b
μόσχευμα 465 a
μόσχος 45 a, 48 a, 185 b, 186 a, 584 b

μοτοῦν 282 b
μοῦλα 165 b
μοῦσθος 149 a, 183 b
μουσικός 477 a, 709 b, 756 a
μουσμόνιον 723 a
μουστάκας 162 b
μοχθεῖν 163 a, 711 a*, b, 712 a, b*
μόχθος 163 b*, 164 b, 711 a, b
μυγαλῆ 6 a
μυεῖν 434 b, 435 a, 775 b
μυελός 6 b
μυελοῦσθαι 6 b(Add), 129 b, 531 b
μυθολόγος 611 a, 780 a
μῦθος 153 b, 610 b*, 614 b*
μυῖα 23 b*, 666 b
μυκᾶσθαι 150 a, 682 b
μυκτήρ 544 a*
μυκτηρίζειν 110 b*, 522 b*
μυκτηρισμός 110 b, 522 b
μύλη 249 b, 250 a
μυλικός 328 b
μύλινος 524 a
μύλος 62 b, 229 b, 328 b, 524 a
μυλωθρίς 229 b
μυλωνικός 524 a
μυξανάρδος 68 b
μυξωτήρ 330 a
μυρεψικός 11 b, 688 b
μυρεψός 273 a*, 388 b
μυριάς 10 b, 399 a*
μυρίζειν 461 b
μυρίκη 226 a
μυρίοι 741 b
μυρίος 399 a
μύρισμα 388 b, 688 b*
μυρμηκιᾶν 16 b, 842 b
μυρμηκιασμός 842 b
μύρμηξ 765 a, 842 b
μυροθήκιον 54 b
μύρον 363 a*, 388 b, 688 b
μύρος 743 a
μυρσίνη 297 a
μυρώδης 240 b
μῦς 263 a
μυσαρός 378 b, 529 a, 561 b
μυσταγωγός 622 b
μύσταξ 353 a
μύστης 251 a
μύστις 616 b
μυχός 66 a, 153 b
μώιον 208 a
μωκᾶσθαι 602 b
μωκός 321 b
μώλωψ 55 a, 105 a, 261 b, 312 a, 374 b, 375 a
μωμᾶσθαι 105 a, 134 b, 375 b, 410 b, 411 a, 464 b

μωμητός 797 b
μῶμος 375 a, 410 b, 411 a*, 590 a, 760 a, 797 b
μωραίνειν 28 b, 83 b, 148 b, 388 a*
μωρεύειν 388 a
μωρία 388 a
μωρολογία 388 a, 614 b
μωρός 388 a*, 714 b

νάβλα 37 a, 40 a
ναί 64 b*, 316 a*, b*, 419 a*, 549 b, 636 b, 637 a
ναός 286 b, 447 b
νάπη 105 b, 115 a, 207 b, 355 b, 568 b, 790 a
ναρδόσταχυς 388 b
ναρκᾶν 164 a, 237 a, 354 b, 519 a, 537 b
ναυαγεῖν 29 b, 48 b(Add), 193 a, 632 b, 710 a*
ναυάγιον 193 b, 523 a, b, 710 a, b*
ναύκληρος 238 b, 250 a
ναῦλον 675 b*
ναυπηγός 44 a
ναῦς 754 a
ναύτης 238 b, 738 a*
ναυτικός 238 b
νάφθα 211 a
νεανίας 584 b, 586 a
νεᾶνις 585 a*, 586 a
νεανίσκος 92 b, 584 b*, 586 a
νέβελ 243 b*
νεβρός 77 a
νεῖκος 619 a
νεῖν 359 a*
νεκρός 120 b*, 159 b, 160 a*, 295 b, 724 a
νεκροῦν 159 a, 201 a, 540 a, 723 b, 816 a
νέκρωσις 159 b, 160 a
νέμειν 173 a*, 242 a, 255 a
νέος 5 a, 43 a, 54 a, 92 b, 93 a*, b, 94 a, 141 b, 322 a, 385 a, 584 b*, 585 a*, 586 a*, 833 a
νεοσσός 228 b
νεότης 5 a, 43 a, 141 b (Add), 585 a
νεόφυτος 43 a, b, 465 b, 752 b
νεύειν 84 b, 210 b, 340 a, 785 b*, 838 b
νεῦμα 31 b, 109 a, 785 b
νευροκοπεῖν 32 a, 100 b
νεῦρον 100 a, 189 a*
νευροῦν 403 a
νεφέλη 104 a, 825 b
νέφος 104 a, 825 b
νεφρός 813 a
νέωμα 81 a

περισσός 190 *a**, 201 *b*, 202 *a*, 268 *a*, 365 *b*, 617 *a*, *b*, 735 *a*, *b**, 736 *a**, *b**, 737 *a**

περίστασις 832 *b*

περιστέλλειν 120 *a*, 407 *b*, 520 *a*, 521 *b*, 606 *b**, 658 *b*, 809 *a*

περιστερά 828 *b**

περιστερεών 334 *a*

περιστέριον 828 *b*

περιστολή 121 *a*

περιστόμιον 718 *a*

περιστρέφειν 124 *a*, 125 *a*

περισύρειν 326 *b*

περισχίζειν 280 *b*

περιτειχίζειν 530 *b*

περίτειχος 128 *a*

περιτέμνειν 322 *a*

περιτιθέναι 94 *b*, 124 *b*, 128 *a*, 150 *b*, 180 *b**, 181 *a*, 288 *a*, 392 *a*, 394 *b*, 406 *b*, 407 *b*, 409 *a*, 809 *b*

περιτομή 119 *b*, 322 *a**, 769 *a*

περιτραχήλιον 594 *a*

περιτρέπειν 589 *a*

περιτρέχειν 124 *b*, 275 *a*, 840 *b*, 841 *a*

περιφέρεια 547 *b*

περιφέρειν 125 *a*, 496 *b*, 515 *a*, 547 *a*, *b**, 621 *a*, *b*, 748 *a**

περιφλέγειν 796 *b*

περιφορά 547 *b*, 622 *b*

περιφράσσειν 128 *a*, 536 *a*, 770 *a*

περιχαίρειν 308 *b*

περιχαρακοῦν 323 *a*, 810 *b*

περιχαρής 308 *b*

περιχεῖν 283 *b*, 836 *b*

περίχρυσος 81 *b*

περιχρυσοῦν 141 *a*, 221 *b**

περίχωρος 452 *a*

περίψημα 551 *a*

περκάζειν 54 *b*, 267 *b*, 281 *b*

πέρυσι 348 *b*

πέσσειν 273 *a*, 404 *b**, 796 *b*

πετανννύναι 665 *b**, 666 *a*, *b**

πέταυρον 266 *b*

πετεινός 341 *a*, 665 *b*, 666 *b*, 671 *b**, 672 *a*, 798 *b*

πέτεσθαι 274 *a*, 665 *b**, 666 *a**, *b*

πέτρα 322 *b**, 441 *a*, 524 *a*

πετροβόλος 524 *a*, *b*

πετροσέλινον 188 *a*

πετρώδης 153 *b*

πέψις 404 *b*

πήγανον 47 *b*

πηγή 198 *b**, 595 *a*, 691 *a*

πηγνύναι 33 *a*, 139 *b*, 247 *b*, 337 *b*, 338 *a*, 403 *a**, 406 *b**, 411 *a**,

432 *a*, 433 *b*, 462 *b*, 463 *a*, *b*, 464 *b**, 540 *a**, 783 *a*, 788 *b*, 814 *a*, 821 *a*

πηγός 788 *b*

πηδάλιον 645 *b**, 689 *a*

πηδᾶν 594 *b*, 626 *a*

πηλίκος 156 *a*, 488 *b*, 833 *a**

πήλινος 131 *a*, 255 *a*

πηλός 131 *a*, 149 *a*, 255 *a**

πήρα 768 *a*

πηρίον 42 *a*

πῆχυς 210 *b*, 211 *a*, 676 *a*

πιαίνειν 111 *b*, 112 *a**, 129 *b*, 490 *a*, *b*

πιέζειν (πιάζειν) 9 *b*, 455 *a*, 467 *b*, 535 *b*, 662 *b*, 826 *a*

πίθος 397 *a*

πικραίνειν 161 *a*, 164 *a*, 252 *b**, 376 *b**, 478 *a*, 823 *a*

πικρία 196 *a*, 253 *a*, *b*, 376 *b**

πικρίς 376 *b*

πικρός 166 *a*, 180 *a*, 376 *b**, 508 *b*, 823 *a*

πιμπλάναι 208 *b*, 209 *a**, 316 *b**, 317 *a**, 399 *b*, 762 *b*

πιμπράναι 286 *a*, 293 *b*, 492 *a*, 612 *b*

πίναξ 41 *b**

πίνειν 318 *a**, *b*

πιότης 112 *a*, 232 *a*, 317 *a*

πιπράσκειν 316 *a*, 394 *b**, 753 *a*

πίπτειν 71 *a*, 283 *a**, *b**, 311 *a**, 312 *a**, 357 *b*, 358 *a*, 405 *a*, 578 *a*, 637 *a**, *b**, 638 *a**, *b*, 700 *a*, *b*, 733 *a**, 734 *a**

πίσσα 143 *b**

πιστεύειν 246 *a**, *b**, 421 *b**, 422 *a**, 438 *b*, 500 *b*

πιστικός 157 *a*, 246 *a*, 365 *a*

πίστις 246 *b*

πιστός 157 *a*, 246 *a*, *b**

πιστοῦν 246 *a*

πιτυρίς 63 *a*

πίτυρον 63 *a**

πίτυς 226 *a*

πίων 112 *a*, 129 *b*, 240 *b*, 347 *b*, 784 *b*

πλαγιάζειν 292 *b*, 417 *a*

πλάγιος 291 *b*, 313 *b*, 352 *a*, 372 *b*, 427 *b*, 606 *a*

πλάζειν 355 *a*

πλανᾶν 124 *a*, 207 *a*, 295 *a*, 355 *a**, *b**

πλάνη 355 *b*

πλάνησις 355 *b*, 356 *a*

πλανήτης 275 *a*

πλανῆτις 355 *b*

πλάσμα 175 *a*, 413 *b*

πλάσσειν 175 *a**, 345 *b*, 413 *a*, 779 *b*, 812 *b*

πλάστιγξ 201 *b*

πλατεῖα 555 *a*, 697 *a*

πλάτος 285 *b*, 452 *a*, 492 *b*, 503 *b**, 504 *a*

πλατύνειν 270 *b*, 482 *b*, 483 *a*, 492 *b**, 503 *b**, 504 *a**

πλατύπους 285 *b*

πλατύς 285 *b*, 492 *b**, 503 *b**, 504 *a*

πλατυσμός 492 *b*, 503 *b*, 504 *a*

πλατύφυλλος 625 *a*

πλέγμα 668 *b*

πλέθρον 574 *b*

Πλειάς 821 *a*

πλεῖν 388 *b*, 389 *a**, 718 *b**, 835 *a*

πλεῖστος 190 *a*, 735 *a*, *b*

πλείων 14 *b*, 19 *a*, 22 *b*, 190 *a*, 202 *b**, 218 *b*, 251 *a*, 365 *b*, 495 *b*, 496 *b*, 531 *a*, 735 *a*, *b**, 736 *a**, *b*, 737 *a**, *b*

πλέκειν 222 *b*, 558 *b*, 572 *b*, 654 *a*, 668 *b*

πλεονάζειν 22 *b*, 236 *a*, 452 *b*, 737 *a**

πλεονάκις 202 *b*, 350 *b*

πλεόνασμα 317 *a*

πλεονασμός 735 *a*, 736 *b*

πλεονεκτεῖν 627 *a**, 737 *b*, 822 *a*

πλεονέκτημα 604 *a*

πλεονέκτης 396 *b*, 627 *b*, 822 *b*

πλεονεξία 156 *b*, 396 *b**, 590 *b*, 627 *b*, 777 *b*, 822 *b**

πλευρά 45 *a*, 313 *b*, 351 *b**, 352 *a**

πλευρόν 351 *b**

πληγή 261 *b*, 312 *a**, 374 *b*, 375 *a*, 583 *b*, 773 *b**

πλῆθος 22 *b**, 202 *a**, 527 *b*, 736 *a*, 741 *b*

πληθύνειν 1 *b*, 22 *b*, 84 *a*, 201 *b*, 219 *b*, 452 *b**, 779 *a*

πλήκτης 237 *a*, 421 *a*

πλημμέλεια (-λια) 222 *a*, 611 *b**, 664 *b*, 715 *b*

πλημμελεῖν 222 *b*, 478 *b*, 611 *a*, 715 *b**

πλημμέλημα 479 *a*

πλήμμυρα 56 *a**

πλήν 34 *a*, 35 *a**, *b*, 190 *b*, 232 *b*, 290 *b**, 314 *b*, 593 *a*

πλήρης 202 *a*, 208 *b**, 209 *a*, *b**, 288 *a*, 316 *b*, 532 *a*, 762 *a*, *b*, 775 *b*, 791 *b*, 792 *a*

πληροῦν 198 *a*, 208 *b**, 209 *a**, *b**, 210 *a**, 289 *a*, 399 *b*, 691 *a*, 761 *b**, 762 *a*, *b**

πληροφορεῖν 438 *a*, *b**

πληροφορία 210 *a*, 226 *a*, 438 *b*

πλήρωμα 126 *a*, 210 *a*, 761 *b*, 762 *b*

στηριγμός 380 b
στηρίζειν 32 a, b(Add), 337 b, 462 b, 463 a*, b*, 464 a, 621 a, 628 b, 784 b, 819 b
στιβαρός (-ῶς) 238 a
στιβίζεσθαι 364 b
στίγμα 170 b, 562 a
στιγμή 371 a, 562 a
στίζειν 765 a*
στίλβειν 44 a, 77 a*, 160 a, 267 a*, 406 a, 439 a, 444 a, 781 a
στίλβωσις 77 a, 439 a
στίμι (στίβι &c.) 364 b*, 365 a
στιππύινος 88 a*, 145 a
στιππύον (στίππιον) 211 a*, 241 a, 358 b, 844 a
στιχάριον (-ριν) 597 a, b
στίχος 564 a
στοιβάζειν 709 a*
στοιβή 709 a, 776 b
στοιχεῖν 189 b, 190 a*, 204 b, 537 a
στοιχίζειν 337 a
στολή 659 b, 660 a
στολίζειν 809 b
στολισμός 769 b, 809 b
στόμα 288 a*, b, 353 a, 423 b*
στόμαχος 608 a
στομοῦν 143 b
στόμωμα 143 b
στοργή 156 b
στοχάζεσθαι 372 b, 420 b*
στοχαστής 420 b
στραγγαλιά 127 b*, 786 b
στραγγαλ(ι)ώδης 127 b, 748 a
στραγγαλοῦσθαι 100 b, 280 a
στραγγίζειν 411 b, 770 a
στρατεία 190 b, 202 a
στρατεύειν 83 b, 190 b, 394 a, 661 b*, 662 a
στρατηγός 143 b, 251 a, 390 a
στρατιά 165 b, 190 b*
στρατιώτης 190 b, 662 a
στρατιωτικός 190 b
στρατολογεῖν 661 b, 662 a
στρατοπεδεύειν 373 a, 447 b, 508 a, 661 b
στρατόπεδον 190 b
στρέβλη 214 a
στρεβλός 107 b, 818 a, 836 a
στρεβλοῦν 818 a
στρεπτός 147 b, 176 a, 276 b, 386 b, 572 b
στρέφειν 124 a, 125 a*, b, 126 a, 128 a*, b, 264 a, 265 b*, 496 b, 514 b*, 515 a*, 711 a
στρηνιάζειν 780 b
στρῆνος 780 b*

στρίφνος 63 a, 285 b
στροβεῖν 598 a
στρόβιλος 92 b
στρουθίον 798 b
στρουθός 798 b
στροφή 127 a, 129 a, 515 a
στρόφιγξ 115 a, 207 a
στροφωτός 436 a
στρυφαλίς 353 a
στρύχνος 285 b
στρῶμα 271 a*, 659 b
στρωμνή 271 a*, 659 b, 815 a*
στρωννύναι 270 a*, 792 a
στυγητός 187 a, b
στυγνάζειν 25 a, 519 b*, 520 a*
στυγνός 519 b
στυππεῖον 145 a
στύππιον (cf. στιππύον) 145 a*, 254 a, 390 a
στυπτηρία 254 a
στυράκινος 828 b
στύφειν 138 b
στύψις 56 a
σύ 22 a, 25 b*, 51 a, b, 52 a, 230 a, 291 a, 294 b, 517 b
συγγένεια 185 b, 304 b
συγγενής 585 a
συγγνώμη 97 b, 527 b
συγγραφή 383 a
συγκαθῆσθαι 553 b
συγκαθίζειν 224 b, 270 b, 460 a, 680 a, b
συγκαθυφαίνειν 381 a, 408 a
συγκαίειν 293 b*, 417 a
συγκαλεῖν 192 a, 373 a, 447 b
συγκάλυμμα 271 a, 659 a
συγκαλύπτειν 341 a, 551 b*, 658 b*, 659 a*
συγκάμπτειν 107 b*, 121 b, 322 b, 522 a
συγκατάβασις 72 a, 73 a*
συγκατάθεσις 574 a
συγκατακόπτειν 498 b
συγκαταμιγνύναι 214 b, 454 a
συγκατατιθέναι 338 a, 621 b
συγκαταψηφίζεσθαι 526 b
συγκεῖσθαι 119 a
συγκεντεῖν 406 b
συγκεραννύναι 438 a, b
συγκινεῖν 453 b
συγκλᾶν 107 b, 118 a, 130 b, 630 b, 702 a
συγκλασμός 131 a, 643 a
συγκλείειν 204 a, 407 b, 447 b, 528 b*, 532 a, 596 a*, b*, 743 a*
συγκλεισμός 165 b, 439 b, 528 b*; 531 b, 532 a

σύγκλητος 251 a
συγκλίνειν 760 b
συγκλύζειν 523 a
συγκοινωνός 553 a, b
συγκολλᾶν 464 b
συγκομίζειν 520 a, 521 a, 750 b
συγκόπτειν 311 b, 591 a, 674 b, 841 a, 842 b, 843 a
σύγκρασις 214 b, 438 a
σύγκριμα 510 a, 607 a
συγκρίνειν 420 a, b, 454 a, 574 a, 606 b, 693 b, 725 a, 728 a, b
σύγκρισις 32 b, 510 a, 526 b
συγκροτεῖν 106 b, 366 a, 618 b
συγκρούειν 732 b
συγκύπτειν 47 b*, 107 b, 283 b, 458 a, 522 a, 756 b
συγκυρεῖν 452 b*, 527 a
συγκυρία 190 a, 590 a, 776 b, 777 a
συγχαίρειν 308 b
συγχέειν 271 b, 453 b, 454 a, 782 b, 837 a, 843 a
συγχρᾶσθαι 214 a, 454 a, 797 a
συγχύνειν 597 b, 598 a
σύγχυσις 272 b, 656 a, 783 a
συγχωρεῖν 97 a, 640 a
συζευγνύναι 243 a, 415 a*, 574 a, 725 a*
συζητεῖν 124 b, 125 b, 418 a*, 569 a, 646 b
συζητητής 728 b
συζυγία 574 a, 726 b
συκάμινον 54 b
συκάμινος 242 b
συκῆ 112 b, 360 b
συκίδιον 581 a
συκομορέα 112 b
σῦκον 112 b, 360 b
συκοφαντεῖν 134 b, 822 a
συκοφάντης 135 a, 247 a, 599 a
συκοφαντία 134 b*, 135 a, 247 a, 810 a
συκοφαντίζειν 598 a
συκῶν 89 b, 112 b
συλαγωγεῖν 105 b, 558 a
συλᾶν 105 b, 794 a
συλλαλεῖν 755 a
συλλαμβάνειν 8 a, 9 b, 10 a, 31 a*, 123 a, 427 a, 455 a, 460 a, 518 a*, 706 b, 748 a, 826 a, b
συλλέγειν 129 b, 294 a, 325 a, b, 328 a, 356 b, 372 b, 373 a*, 447 b, 536 a, 806 b, 824 a
σύλληψις 31 a*, 456 a, 518 a
συλλογή 326 b
συλλογίζειν 162 a, 527 b*
συλλοιδορεῖν 739 b

τακτικός 451 b
τακτός 449 b, 450 a
ταλαιπωρεῖν 806 a
ταλαίπωρος 53 a
ταλανίζειν 53 a, 526 a
ταλαντιαῖος 824 b
τάλαντον 824 b
τάλας 53 a
ταμιεύειν 373 b
τανύειν 767 a
τάξις 337 a, 449 b
ταπεινός 458 a, 805 b, 819 b
ταπεινοῦν 131 b, 457 b, 458 a*,
    459 b, 655 b
ταπεινοφρονεῖν 457 b
ταπεινοφροσύνη 458 a, 715 b
ταπείνωσις 458 a*, 805 b
ταράσσειν 108 b*, 280 b, 366 b, 453 b,
    454 a*, 455 a, 597 b*, 598 a*, b
ταραχή 366 b, 598 a*, b
τάραχος 598 a
ταραχώδης 598 b
ταριχεύειν 166 a
ταρίχιον 127 a
ταρσός 421 a, 824 b
τάρταρος 8 b, 227 a, 556 a
ταρταροῦν 734 a
τάσσειν 94 b, 96 a, b, 219 a, 337 b,
    338 b*, 449 b, 450 a*, b*, 451 b,
    456 b, 462 b, 464 b, 537 b, 579 b,
    688 a
ταυρέα 100 b
ταυροειδής 186 a
ταῦρος 45 a, 186 a, 815 b
ταφή 120 b, 121 a*, 416 b, 724 a
τάφος 121 a, 212 b
τάφρος 162 b
τάχα 15 b, 16 a, 202 a, 291 a, 652 a
ταχινός 86 a, 825 a
τάχος 104 b, 484 b*, 825 b*
ταχυδρόμος 276 a
ταχύνειν 86 a, 104 b, 597 b, 825 a
ταχύς 86 a, b, 104 b*, 406 b, 685 a,
    811 a, 825 a*, b*
τε encl. 255 b*
τείνειν 340 b, 605 b, 767 a*
τειχήρης 122 a, 128 a, 323 a
τειχίζειν 128 a, 323 a, 407 b, 530 a
τεῖχος 323 a
τεκμήριον 170 b
τεκνίον 631 a
τεκνογονία 779 b
τέκνον 101 b, 584 a, b*, 631 a
τεκνοποιεῖν 779 a, b
τεκνοτρόφος 347 b
τεκνοῦν 779 b
τεκταίνειν 199 b, 330 a, 654 a

τεκτονικός 81 b
τέκτων 82 a, 295 a, 546 b*
τελεῖν 111 a, 473 b, 474 a, 761 a, b*,
    762 a*, b
τέλειος 250 a, 511 b, 761 b, 762 a, b*
τελε(ι)οῦν 194 b, 209 b, 399 b,
    691 a, 762 a, b*
τελείωσις 761 b, 762 b
τελειωτής 762 a
τελεσφορεῖν 762 a
τελετή 543 a, 567 b
τελευταῖος 635 a
τελευτᾶν 159 a, 762 a
τελευτή 159 b, 635 a
τελίσκειν 631 b
τέλος 16 b, 36 a*, 314 b, 424 a, b*,
    635 a, b, 636 a*, 761 b, 762 a*, b
τελώνιον 153 b
τέμενος 298 b
τέμνειν 115 b, 276 b, 280 b, 492 a,
    511 a, 515 b, 562 b, 591 a*, b,
    769 a, 834 b
τέρας 170 b*, 211 b, 388 a, 581 a*,
    701 b
τερατοσκόπος 171 a
τερέμινθος 568 b
τέρετρον 276 b, 379 b
τέρμα 635 a
τέρπειν 308 b, 485 b, 490 a, b
τερπνός 228 b, 231 b, 673 a
τερπνότης 194 b, 486 a, 490 b
τέρψις 486 a
τεσσαρακοστή 676 b
τέσσαρες 491 a', 625 a*
τεταρταῖος 625 a
τέταρτος 483 a, b*, 625 a
τετράβολος 186 a
τετράγωνος 132 a
τετράδερμον 582 a
τετράδιον 574 b
τετραίνειν 276 b, 492 a, 834 b*
τετράπλοκος 100 b
τετράποδος 564 a
τετράπους 273 b, 400 b, 625 a
τετράς 368 a, 625 a
τετράστιχος 381 a
τετραυφαντός 381 a
τέφρα 117 a, 827 b
τεφροῦν 117 a
τεχνᾶσθαι 84 a
τέχνη 81 a*
τεχνίτης 82 a*, 84 a, 229 a, 345 b
τέως 290 b
τήγανον 139 b, 451 a
τήκειν 32 b*, 33 a*, 138 b, 163 b,
    175 b, 276 a, 377 a, 474 a, 493 b,
    495 a, 535 a, 731 b

τηλαύγημα 170 b
τηλαυγής 267 a, 486 a
τηλαύγησις 160 a, 480 a
τηλικοῦτος 156 a, 833 a*
τῆλις 409 b
τηνικαῦτα 350 a
τηρεῖν 301 a, b, 532 a, 707 b*,
    708 a, 716 a, 803 a, 830 b*
τήρησις 595 b, 708 a
τηρητής 708 a
τιάρα 106 a
τίγρις 764 a
τί(ν)ειν 399 a
τιθέναι 79 a, 94 b*, 96 a*, b*, 97 b,
    98 a, b, 107 b, 195 b, 224 b, 247 b,
    333 b, 337 a, b, 338 b*, 408 b,
    413 a, 416 b, 448 b, 456 b, 460 a*,
    464 b, 465 a, 506 a, 527 a, 531 b,
    700 a, 716 b, 733 a, 734 a, 750 b
τιθηνεῖν 347 b, 582 a, 669 a
τιθηνός 174 a, 348 a, 669 a*
τίκτειν 184 b, 185 a*, b, 186 b,
    518 a, 779 a, b*
τίλλειν 331 a, 406 a, 410 a, 521 a,
    626 b, 627 a
τιμᾶν 62 a, 155 a, 192 b, 390 b*,
    391 a, 415 b, 575 b, 583 a
τιμή 18 a, 369 b*, 390 b, 391 a,
    678 a, 747 b
τίμημα 179 b
τίμιος 157 a, 390 b*, 391 a, 415 b,
    736 a, b
τιμωρεῖν 459 b
τιμωρία 164 b, 459 b
τίνειν v. τίειν
τίρων 784 b
τις encl. 144 a, 146 a*, b*, 147 a,
    294 b, 469 a, b, 482 a*, b, 653 a*,
    667 b*, 689 b*, 690 a*
τίς 22 a*, 25 a, b*, 34 b, 51 a,
    172 b*, 223 b, 225 a*, b, 232 a,
    235 b, 418 a, 467 b*, 468 a*, b*,
    488 b, 501 a, 538 b, 653 b, 654 a,
    729 a*
τιτρώσκειν 112 a, 401 a, 406 b*,
    748 a, b, 750 a, 765 a, 791 b,
    797 a, 834 b*
τμητός 331 a, 591 a, 592 a
τοιγαροῦν 232 a, 802 b
τοίνυν 232 a*, 485 a*, 802 a, b*
τοιοῦτος 172 b, 173 a, 304 b, 305 a,
    341 a, 451 a, 482 a*, 639 a,
    645 a, 653 a, b, 667 b, 690 a,
    833 a
τοῖχος 753 b*
τοκετός 185 a, 186 b
τόκος 185 a, 186 a*, 779 a

ὕειν 732 a
ὕειος 63 a, b, 299 a
ὑετός 259 a, 535 a, 732 a*
υἱοθεσία 585 b
υἱός 5 a, 584 a, b*, 585 a, b*, 631 a, 739 a
ὑλακτεῖν 509 a
ὕλη 38 b, 60 a, 367 a
ὑλοτόμος 115 b
ὑμήν 223 a
ὑμνεῖν 335 b*, 336 a, 359 b, 709 b*, 755 b, 756 a
ὕμνησις 336 b, 819 b
ὕμνος 335 b, 709 b, 756 a
ὑμνῳδία 709 b
ὑπάγειν 29 a, 30 a*, 203 b, 204 a, 217 b, 218 a*, 220 a, 544 b, 665 b*
ὑπακοή 364 a, b*
ὑπακούειν 364 a*, b, 474 b*, 502 b*, 510 a, 821 b
ὑπαλλαγή 689 b
ὑπαναλίσκειν 175 b
ὕπανδρος 481 a, 636 b*, 679 b
ὑπαντᾶν 72 a, 303 b, 416 b, 649 a
ὑπάντησις 303 b, 416 b, 649 a, 758 a
ὕπαρξις 223 b, 296 a, 692 b
ὑπάρχειν 191 a, 223 b, 230 b, 304 a, 577 b, 578 a, 579 a*, 692 b
ὑπεναντίος 393 b, 476 a, 799 b
ὑπέρ 34 a, 35 b, 51 b, 61 a, 63 b, 174 b, 218 b, 251 b, 260 a, 393 b, 394 b, 495 b, 550 b, 633 a, 634 b, 699 a*, 700 b*, 722 a, 735 b, 736 b*, 756 b*, 757 a*, b*, 758 b, 789 a
ὑπεραινετός 335 b
ὑπεραίρειν 789 a
ὑπέρακμος 251 b
ὑπεράνω 259 b*, 260 a, 313 b, 550 a, b, 698 a, 757 a, 758 b, 789 a, b, 790 a
ὑπεράνωθεν 259 b, 550 b
ὑπερασπίζειν 238 a*, 393 b
ὑπερασπισμός 238 a
ὑπερασπιστής 238 a*
ὑπερβαίνειν 33 a, 37 a, 260 a, 343 b, 496 a, b, 518 b, 550 b, 641 a
ὑπερβάλλειν 236 a, 496 a, b, 735 a, 736 b, 737 a*
ὑπερβαλλόντως 548 a
ὑπερβολή 22 b, 251 b, 735 a, 736 a*, b, 737 a
ὑπερείδειν 456 b, 462 b
ὑπερεκπερισσοῦ 737 a
ὑπερεκχεῖν 263 a, 284 a
ὑπερεκχύνεσθαι 514 a

ὑπερεντυγχάνειν 336 b
ὑπερέχειν 496 b, 788 b, 789 a
ὑπερηφανεῖν 28 b, 252 b
ὑπερηφανεύεσθαι 445 b, 789 a
ὑπερηφανία 604 a, 647 b, 789 b, 790 a*
ὑπερήφανος 33 b, 163 a, 604 b, 647 b, 789 b*
ὑπέρθεσις 326 a
ὑπέρθυρον 289 b, 443 b, 647 a
ὑπεριδεῖν (ὑπερορᾶν) 647 b
ὑπερισχύειν 42 a, 736 b, 817 a
ὑπερκαθῆσθαι 679 b
ὑπερκεῖσθαι 737 a
ὑπερλίαν 496 a
ὑπερμαχεῖν 203 a
ὑπερμήκης 549 a, 788 b
ὑπέρογκος 705 b, 706 a, b, 735 a, 788 b
ὑπεροπτεύειν 789 a
ὑπερορᾶν 339 b, 518 b*, 647 a, 837 b
ὑπερόρασις 519 b
ὕπερος 384 b
ὑπεροχή 251 b, 790 a
ὑπεροψία 647 b
ὑπερπερισσῶς 737 b
ὑπερπέτεσθαι 259 b
ὑπερυψοῦν 737 b, 789 a*
ὑπερφέρειν 737 a
ὑπερφρονεῖν 199 a
ὑπερφωνεῖν 509 b
ὑπερχεῖν (-χέειν) 263 a*, b*, 283 b, 497 a, 514 a
ὑπερῳμία 243 b, 549 a, 735 b, 736 b
ὑπερῷον 259 b*, 550 a, 643 a, 699 b, 788 b, 789 a
ὑπεύθυνος 51 a, 306 a, 826 b
ὑπέχειν 427 a, 594 a, 621 a, 748 a, 826 b
ὑπήκοος 364 b*
ὑπηρεσία 567 b, 653 a
ὑπηρέσιον 704 b
ὑπηρετεῖν 567 b*
ὑπηρέτης 568 a*
ὑπισχνεῖσθαι 58 a
ὕπνος 224 b, 302 b, 356 a, 519 a, 691 a
ὑπνοῦν 224 a*, 519 a*, 691 a, 703 a
ὑπνώδης 318 b
ὑπό 59 b, 60 b*, 303 b, 329 a, 427 b, 428 a, b, 429 a*, b*, 444 b, 452 a, 632 b*, 633 a, 634 a*, 644 a, 684 a, 686 a, b, 756 b, 758 a, 761 b
ὑποβαίνειν 842 a
ὑποβάλλειν 248 b, 528 a
ὑποβλέπειν 73 b, 107 b, 837 b

ὑποβλέφαρον 48 a, 634 a
ὑποβρύχιος 193 b, 710 b, 768 a
ὑπογλωττίς 60 b
ὑπογραμμός 341 a, b
ὑπογράφειν 128 a, 382 a
ὑπογραφεύς 383 b
ὑπογραφή 392 b
ὑπόδειγμα 80 b, 341 a, b, 342 a
ὑποδεικνύναι 171 a, 414 a, 434 b, 435 a, 444 a*, 487 a, 754 b
ὑποδεῖν 303 a, 393 a, 532 b*
ὑποδέχεσθαι 575 a
ὑπόδημα 286 a, 302 b, 443 b*, 532 b
ὑπόδικος 465 b, 694 b
ὑποδύειν 303 a
ὑποδύτης 597 a, 659 b, 686 b
ὑποζύγιον 75 b, 243 a, 400 b
ὑποζωννύναι 180 b
ὑπόθεσις 341 a
ὑποθήκη 62 b
ὑποκαίειν 387 a*
ὑποκάτω 60 b*, 303 b, 632 b*, 700 b
ὑποκάτωθεν 303 b
ὑποκαύστρα 404 b
ὑποκεῖσθαι 49 a, 826 b
ὑποκλίνειν 822 a
ὑπόκουφος 502 a
ὑπόκρισις 552 a
ὑποκριτής 552 a*
ὑποκύπτειν 114 b
ὑπολαμβάνειν 8 a, 84 b, 199 b*, 502 b, 575 a
ὑπόλ(ε)ιμμα 351 b, 601 a
ὑπολείπειν 97 b, 351 a*, 617 a*, b*
ὑπολήνιον 77 b, 704 b
ὑπόληψις 200 a
ὑπόλοιπος 351 b
ὑπολύειν 32 a, 474 a
ὑπόλυσις 32 b
ὑπομένειν 8 a (Add), 172 a, 306 a, 337 a, 403 b, 478 b, 537 a*, 575 a, 617 a*, 620 b, 621 a, 655 a, 704 a, 803 a, b*, 804 b, 837 b, 838 a*, b
ὑπομιμνήσκειν 200 b*, 401 a
ὑπόμνησις 200 b
ὑπομονή 8 b
ὑπομόνητος 620 a
ὑπονοεῖν 199 b
ὑπονύσσειν 406 b
ὑποπέσσιον 107 b, 117 b
ὑποπιέζειν 535 b
ὑποπνεῖν 238 b
ὑποπόδιον 153 b, 339 a, 507 b
ὑποπροίκειος 688 b
ὑποπτεύειν 199 b, 345 a
ὑπόπτωσις 283 b
ὑποπυρρίζειν 432 b

φλέγμα 286 b
φλεγμαίνειν 210 a, 407 b, 459 b, 677 a, b
φλιά 266 a, 443 b, 512 b
φλογίζειν 417 a, 530 a, 612 a
φλόγινος 116 a, 612 a
φλογώδης 137 b
φλοιός 101 a
φλόξ 116 a, 133 b, 293 b, 612 a*
φλυαρεῖν 604 b
φλυαρία 614 b, 737 b
φλυαρός 135 a, 604 a
φλυκτίς 102 b
φοβεῖν 431 b, 562 a, 640 b*, 693 a, 721 a*, b*
φοβερίζειν 721 b
φοβερισμός 721 a
φοβερός 208 b, 250 a, 693 a, 720 b, 721 a*, b*
φόβηθρον (-τρον) 720 b, 721 b
φόβος 417 a, 667 a, 693 a, 704 b, 720 b, 721 a*, b*
φοιβᾶν 590 a
φοινικοῦς 48 a
φοῖνιξ 40 a, 40 a, b*, 45 a, 48 a, 599 a, 608 b
φοιτᾶν 204 b
φόλλις 120 a
φονεύειν 201 a, 723 b*, 724 a*
φονεύς 724 a
φονευτής 724 a
φόνος 723 b
φορά 21 a, 67 b
φοράς 723 a*
φορβεά 595 b
φορεῖν 27 a
φορολόγητος 564 b, 722 b
φορολόγος 564 b
φόρος 564 b*, 722 a, b*
φορτίζειν 532 a
φορτίον 21 a, 532 b*
φραγμός 129 a, 323 a, 413 a, 753 b, 754 a, 770 a, 810 a
φράζειν 32 a
φράσσειν 412 b*, 596 a, b, 743 a, 770 a, 810 a
φρέαρ 227 a, 547 b, 595 a
φρεναπατᾶν 664 b
φρεναπάτης 406 a, 664 b
φρενοβλάβεια 280 a
φρίκη 245 a, 562 b
φρικτός 366 b, 721 a
φρικτώδης 562 b
φρίσσειν (-ττειν) 245 a, 366 a, 366 b*, 562 b, 597 b, 640 b
φρονεῖν 123 a, 162 a, 199 b, 200 a*, 307 b, 319 a, 339 b, 820 b, 837 b

φρόνημα 200 a*, 562 b
φρόνησις 78 a, 123 a, 162 b, 319 a, b, 715 a
φρόνιμος 319 a*, 715 a
φροντίζειν 162 a, 307 a*, b*, 740 a
φροντίς 307 a, b*
φρουρά 532 a
φρουρεῖν 707 b
φρουρός 301 b
φρύαγμα 790 a
φρύγανον 138 a, 233 a, 811 a
φρύγειν 21 a, 271 b, 503 a, 843 a
φρύγιον 524 a, 800 a
φυγαδεύειν 274 b
φυγαδευτήριον 275 b
φυγάς 275 a, 465 b, 794 a
φυγή 275 b
φύειν 228 a*, 267 a, 303 b, 304 a*, 475 b, 606 a, 779 a
φυή 514 a
φυκίς 623 b
φύλαγμα 688 a, 708 a
φυλακή 171 b, 301 b, 324 a, 491 a, 532 a*, 574 b, 595 b*, 708 a*, 819 a
φυλακίζειν 521 b, 531 b, 532 a, 734 a
φύλαξ 300 b, 301 b, 452 a, 491 a, 708 a*, 738 a*, 803 a
φυλάσσειν 301 a, b, 317 a, 399 b, 677 b, 697 b, 702 b, 707 b*, 708 a*, 716 a*, 726 a, 819 b
φυλή 469 b
φυλλολόγος 129 b, 805 a
φύλλον 298 b, 402 a, 804 b*, 805 a
φυλλορροεῖν 769 a, 805 a
φύραμα 503 a
φυρᾶν 503 a*
φύρασις 503 a
φύρειν 410 b*, 495 a, 703 b
φυρμός 454 b, 462 a
φυσᾶν 150 a, 239 a, 769 b
φυσητήρ 238 b, 239 b, 651 a, 718 b
φυσιοῦν 604 a, 788 b, 789 a, 790 a
φύσις 157 b, 172 b, 651 b
φυσίωσις 790 a
φύσσα 358 a
φυτεία 465 a, 752 b
φυτεύειν 360 b, 432 a, 465 a*, 466 a, 752 a*, 791 a
φύτευμα 465 a, 752 b
φυτόν 303 b, 465 a, 568 b, 752 b
φωλεός 28 b
φωνεῖν 191 b*, 192 a*, 334 b, 533 b*
φωνή 144 b, 334 b*, 335 a*, 533 b, 556 b*, 705 a*, b*
φωρᾶν 812 b
φῶς 77 a, 133 b, 287 b(Add), 387 a, 480 a, b*

φωστήρ 84 a, 480 b
φωσφόρος 368 b
φωτεινός 480 b
φωτίζειν 74 a, 480 b*, 481 a*
φωτισμός 480 a

χαίνειν 482 b*
χαίρειν 159 a, 308 b*, 321 a
χάλαζα 4 a, 105 b
χαλᾶν 97 b, 98 a, 241 b, 376 b, 443 a, 523 a, 667 a, 700 a
χαλαστόν 81 b, 89 a, 572 b
χαλεπός 163 a, 237 b, 706 a, 731 b*, 736 a, 821 a
χαλινός 560 a
χαλινοῦν 596 a
χάλκανθον 12 a
χάλκειος 41 a, 678 a
χαλκεύειν 498 b
χαλκεύς 44 b, 104 a
χαλκίον 44 a
χαλκολίβανον 44 a
χαλκοπλάστης 678 b
χαλκός 44 a, 81 b, 678 a*
χαλκοῦς 678 a, b*
χάλκωμα 43 b*
χαμαί 131 a
χαμαιλέων 23 a
χαμαίμηλον 240 b
χαμευνία 60 b, 225 a
χάος 272 b
χαρά 309 a*
χάραγμα 383 a, 398 a*, 562 a*, 599 a
χαρακοβολία 298 b
χαρακοῦν 130 b, 407 b, 455 a
χαρακτήρ 341 a, 562 a, 647 a
χάραξ 130 b, 203 b, 323 a, 561 b, 562 a, 770 a, 810 a
χαράσσειν 224 a, 382 b
χαρίεις 681 a
χαριεντίζεσθαι 490 a
χαρίζειν 97 a, 681 a, b*
χάρις 575 a, 600 b, 681 a*, b*, 682 a*, 729 a
χάρισμα 681 a, b
χαριτοῦν 681 a, b, 682 a
χαρμονή 309 a
χαρμοσύνη 309 a
χαροποιός 183 b
χάρτης 770 b, 771 a
χαρτίον 770 b*
χάσμα 501 b, 556 a
χασμᾶν 262 a, 333 a
χάσμη 25 a, 333 a
χαῦνος 33 a, 95 a, 782 b
χαυνότης 33 b

ψευδής 246 a, 246 b, 247 a*, 806 b
ψευδολόγος 755 b
ψευδομαρτυρεῖν 246 b
ψευδομαρτυρία 246 b
ψευδομάρτυς 177 b, 246 b
ψευδοπροφήτης 246 b
ψεῦδος 247 a*, 806 b*
ψευδώνυμος 246 b
ψεῦσμα 247 a, 806 b
ψεύστης 247 a, 296 a, 755 b, 806 b*
ψηλαφᾶν 743 a, 818 b, 819 a*
ψηλάφησις 819 a
ψηλαφητός 819 a
ψηφίζειν 527 b
ψηφολογεῖν 407 a
ψῆφος 4 a, 37 b, 527 b, 616 a
ψιάθιον 412 b, 415 b
ψίαθος 81 a, 108 a, 271 a, 408 a, 415 b
ψιθυρίζειν 121 a, b*
ψιθυρισμός 121 a, b
ψιθυριστής 121 b
ψίθυρος 121 b
ψιλός 434 a, 435 b, 602 b, 842 a
ψιλοῦν 521 a, 621 a
ψιμύθιον 254 a
ψιχίον 149 a, 357 b
ψόα 423 a, 813 a
ψόγος 375 b, 376 a
ψοφεῖν 273 b, 705 a
ψόφος 705 a
ψυγμός 153 b, 270 b, 815 b*
ψύλλος 260 b, 266 a

ψύχειν 16 a, 100 a, 270 b, 530 a, 540 a, 744 b, 815 b
ψυχή 28 a, 440 a, 714 a, 716 a, 717 a, 800 a
ψῦχος 16 b, 540 a, 795 b
ψυχρολογεῖν 842 a
ψυχρός 100 a, 197 b*, 530 a, 610 a, 742 b, 842 a
ψυχρότης 530 a
ψωμίζειν 416 a*, 478 a
ψωμίον 66 b, 142 b, 254 a
ψωμός 139 a, 140 b, 142 b, 254 a
ψώρα 830 a
ψωραγριᾶν 830 a
ψώχειν 386 b*

ὤ (ὦ) 170 b, 517 b, 518 a
ᾦα 321 b
ὧδε 154 b, 155 a, 174 a, b*, 189 a, 216 a, 313 a, 390 a, 392 a
ᾠδή 477 a, 709 b
ὠδίν 223 a*
ὠδίνειν 164 b, 223 a*, 518 a
ᾠδός 709 b
ὠθεῖν 42 a, 312 b, 386 b, 427 a, 466 a, b, 477 b, 733 b, 810 a, 835 a
ὠμία 113 a
ὠμόλινον 844 a
ὦμος 189 a, 243 a, 582 a, 777 a, 805 a
ὠμός 238 a, 493 a, 509 a

ὠμότης 238 a
ὠμοτοκεῖν 185 a, 642 b
ὠνεῖσθαι 575 b*, 678 b
ᾠόν 374 a*
ὥρα 14 a, 94 a, 219 a, 234 b*, 235 a*, b, 391 b*, 483 b, 484 b*, 499 b, 721 b, 777 b, 778 a*
ὡραῖος 228 b*, 229 a, 304 b, 315 a*, b
ὡραιότης 315 a, b
ὡραιοῦσθαι 228 b, 315 a, 365 a
ὡραισμός 315 a, 332 a
ὥριμος 391 b*, 484 b
ὠρύεσθαι 119 b, 150 a, 682 b*
ὠρύωμα 150 a, 682 b
ὡς 1 b*, 63 b*, 64 a, 232 a, 287 a, 305 a*, 341 a, b, 600 b, 639 a*, b*, 640 a, 684 b, 685 a
ὡσανεί 747 a
ὡσαύτως 639 a, b, 645 a, 651 b
ὡσεί 1 a, b, 63 b, 154 a, 234 b, 305 a, 341 a, 639 a, b
ὥσπερ 63 b*, 305 a*, 341 a, 639 a*, b*
ὠτίον 212 b*, 423 b
ὠτότμητος 212 b, 841 a
ὠφέλεια 239 b, 240 a, 729 a
ὠφελεῖν 122 b, 193 b, 240 a, 490 b, 729 a*, b*
ὠφέλημα 729 a
ὠφέλιμος 239 b*, 240 a, 729 a*
ὤχρα 494 a

ARABIC INDEX

In strictly alphabetical order.   (Add) indicates Additions and Corrections.

OTHER TITLES IN THIS HARDBACK REPRINT PROGRAMME FROM
SANDPIPER BOOKS LTD (LONDON) AND POWELLS BOOKS (CHICAGO)

ISBN 0–19–	Author	Title
8143567	ALFÖLDI A.	The Conversion of Constantine and Pagan Rome
6286409	ANDERSON George K.	The Literature of the Anglo-Saxons
8219601	ARNOLD Benjamin	German Knighthood
8208618	ARNOLD T.W.	The Caliphate
8228813	BARTLETT & MacKAY	Medieval Frontier Societies
8219733	BARTLETT Robert	Trial by Fire and Water
8111010	BETHURUM Dorothy	Homilies of Wulfstan
8142765	BOLLING G. M.	External Evidence for Interpolation in Homer
814332X	BOLTON J.D.P.	Aristeas of Proconnesus
9240132	BOYLAN Patrick	Thoth, the Hermes of Egypt
8114222	BROOKS Kenneth R.	Andreas and the Fates of the Apostles
8203543	BULL Marcus	Knightly Piety & Lay Response to the First Crusade
8216785	BUTLER Alfred J.	Arab Conquest of Egypt
8148046	CAMERON Alan	Circus Factions
8148054	CAMERON Alan	Porphyrius the Charioteer
8148348	CAMPBELL J.B.	The Emperor and the Roman Army 31 BC to 235
826643X	CHADWICK Henry	Priscillian of Avila
826447X	CHADWICK Henry	Boethius
8222025	COLGRAVE B. & MYNORS R.A.B.	Bede's Ecclesiastical History of the English People
8131658	COOK J.M.	The Troad
8219393	COWDREY H.E.J.	The Age of Abbot Desiderius
8644043	CRUM W.E.	Coptic Dictionary
8148992	DAVIES M.	Sophocles: Trachiniae
825301X	DOWNER L.	Leges Henrici Primi
814346X	DRONKE Peter	Medieval Latin and the Rise of European Love-Lyric
8142749	DUNBABIN T.J.	The Western Greeks
8154372	FAULKNER R.O.	The Ancient Egyptian Pyramid Texts
8221541	FLANAGAN Marie Therese	Irish Society, Anglo-Norman Settlers, Angevin Kingship
8143109	FRAENKEL Edward	Horace
8201540	GOLDBERG P.J.P.	Women, Work and Life Cycle in a Medieval Economy
8140215	GOTTSCHALK H.B.	Heraclides of Pontus
8266162	HANSON R.P.C.	Saint Patrick
8224354	HARRISS G.L.	King, Parliament and Public Finance in Medieval England to 1369
8581114	HEATH Sir Thomas	Aristarchus of Samos
8140444	HOLLIS A.S.	Callimachus: Hecale
8212968	HOLLISTER C. Warren	Anglo-Saxon Military Institutions
8226470	HOULDING J.A.	Fit for Service
2115480	HENRY Blanche	British Botanical and Horticultural Literature before 1800
8219523	HOUSLEY Norman	The Italian Crusades
8223129	HURNARD Naomi	The King's Pardon for Homicide – before AD 1307
8140401	HUTCHINSON G.O.	Hellenistic Poetry
9240140	JOACHIM H.H.	Aristotle: On Coming-to-be and Passing-away
9240094	JONES A.H.M	Cities of the Eastern Roman Provinces
8142560	JONES A.H.M	The Greek City
8218354	JONES Michael	Ducal Brittany 1364–1399
8271484	KNOX & PELCZYNSKI	Hegel's Political Writings
8212755	LAWRENCE C.H.	St Edmund of Abingdon
8225253	LE PATOUREL John	The Norman Empire
8212720	LENNARD Reginald	Rural England 1086–1135
8212321	LEVISON W.	England and the Continent in the 8th century
8148224	LIEBESCHUETZ J.H.W.G.	Continuity and Change in Roman Religion
8143486	LINDSAY W.M.	Early Latin Verse
8141378	LOBEL Edgar & PAGE Sir Denys	Poetarum Lesbiorum Fragmenta
9240159	LOEW E.A.	The Beneventan Script
8241445	LUKASIEWICZ, Jan	Aristotle's Syllogistic
8152442	MAAS P. & TRYPANIS C.A.	Sancti Romani Melodi Cantica
8142684	MARSDEN E.W.	Greek and Roman Artillery—Historical
8142692	MARSDEN E.W.	Greek and Roman Artillery—Technical
8148178	MATTHEWS John	Western Aristocracies and Imperial Court AD 364–425
9240205	MAVROGORDATO John	Digenes Akrites
8223447	McFARLANE K.B.	Lancastrian Kings and Lollard Knights
8226578	McFARLANE K.B.	The Nobility of Later Medieval England
814296X	MEIGGS Russell	The Athenian Empire
8148100	MEIGGS Russell	Roman Ostia
8148402	MEIGGS Russell	Trees and Timber in the Ancient Mediterranean World
8141718	MERKELBACH R. & WEST M.L.	Fragmenta Hesiodea
8143362	MILLAR F.G.B.	Casssius Dio
8142641	MILLER J. Innes	The Spice Trade of the Roman Empire

8147813	MOORHEAD John	Theoderic in Italy
8264259	MOORMAN John	A History of the Franciscan Order
8181469	MORISON Stanley	Politics and Script
9240582	MUSURILLO H.	Acts of the Pagan Martyrs & Christian Martyrs (2 vols)
9240213	MYRES J.L.	Herodotus The Father of History
8219512	OBOLENSKY Dimitri	Six Byzantine Portraits
8270259	O'DONNELL J.J.	Augustine: Confessions (3 vols)
8116020	OWEN A.L.	The Famous Druids
8131445	PALMER, L.R.	The Interpretation of Mycenaean Greek Texts
8143427	PFEIFFER R.	History of Classical Scholarship (vol 1)
8143648	PFEIFFER Rudolf	History of Classical Scholarship 1300–1850
8111649	PHEIFER J.D.	Old English Glosses in the Epinal-Erfurt Glossary
8142277	PICKARD–CAMBRIDGE A.W.	Dithyramb Tragedy and Comedy
8269765	PLATER & WHITE	Grammar of the Vulgate
8213891	PLUMMER Charles	Lives of Irish Saints (2 vols)
820695X	POWICKE Michael	Military Obligation in Medieval England
8269684	POWICKE Sir Maurice	Stephen Langton
821460X	POWICKE Sir Maurice	The Christian Life in the Middle Ages
8225369	PRAWER Joshua	Crusader Institutions
8225571	PRAWER Joshua	The History of The Jews in the Latin Kingdom of Jerusalem
8143249	RABY F.J.E.	A History of Christian Latin Poetry
8143257	RABY F.J.E.	A History of Secular Latin Poetry in the Middle Ages (2 vols)
8214316	RASHDALL & POWICKE	The Universities of Europe in the Middle Ages (3 vols)
8154488	REYMOND E.A.E & BARNS J.W.B.	Four Martyrdoms from the Pierpont Morgan Coptic Codices
8148380	RICKMAN Geoffrey	The Corn Supply of Ancient Rome
8141556	ROSS Sir David	Aristotle: De Anima
8141076	ROSS Sir David	Aristotle: Metaphysics (2 vols)
8141092	ROSS Sir David	Aristotle: Physics
8142307	ROSTOVTZEFF M.	Social and Economic History of the Hellenistic World, 3 vols.
8142315	ROSTOVTZEFF M.	Social and Economic History of the Roman Empire, 2 vols.
8264178	RUNCIMAN Sir Steven	The Eastern Schism
814833X	SALMON J.B.	Wealthy Corinth
8171587	SALZMAN L.F.	Building in England Down to 1540
8218362	SAYERS Jane E.	Papal Judges Delegate in the Province of Canterbury 1198–1254
8221657	SCHEIN Sylvia	Fideles Crucis
8148135	SHERWIN WHITE A.N.	The Roman Citizenship
9240167	SINGER Charles	Galen: On Anatomical Procedures
8113927	SISAM, Kenneth	Studies in the History of Old English Literature
8642040	SOUTER Alexander	A Glossary of Later Latin to 600 AD
8270011	SOUTER Alexander	Earliest Latin Commentaries on the Epistles of St Paul
8222254	SOUTHERN R.W.	Eadmer: Life of St. Anselm
8251408	SQUIBB G.	The High Court of Chivalry
8212011	STEVENSON & WHITELOCK	Asser's Life of King Alfred
8212011	SWEET Henry	A Second Anglo-Saxon Reader—Archaic and Dialectical
8148259	SYME Sir Ronald	History in Ovid
8143273	SYME Sir Ronald	Tacitus (2 vols)
8200951	THOMPSON Sally	Women Religious
924023X	WALBANK F.W.	Historical Commentary on Polybius (3 vols)
8201745	WALKER Simon	The Lancastrian Affinity 1361–1399
8161115	WELLESZ Egon	A History of Byzantine Music and Hymnography
8140185	WEST M.L.	Greek Metre
8141696	WEST M.L.	Hesiod: Theogony
8148542	WEST M.L.	The Orphic Poems
8140053	WEST M.L.	Hesiod: Works & Days
8152663	WEST M.L.	Iambi et Elegi Graeci
9240221	WHEELWRIGHT Philip	Heraclitus
822799X	WHITBY M. & M.	The History of Theophylact Simocatta
8206186	WILLIAMSON, E.W.	Letters of Osbert of Clare
8208103	WILSON F.P.	Plague in Shakespeare's London
8247672	WOODHOUSE C.M.	Gemistos Plethon
8114877	WOOLF Rosemary	The English Religious Lyric in the Middle Ages
8119224	WRIGHT Joseph	Grammar of the Gothic Language